Tolley's Yellow Tax Handbook 2020–21

61st Edition

Part 1b

Primary legislation relating to direct taxes, including—
income tax
corporation tax
capital gains tax
FA 2004 to TIOPA 2010

Consultant Editor

Anne Redston MA (Oxon) LLB FCA CTA(Fellow), Barrister

LexisNexis® UK & Worldwide

United Kingdom	RELX (UK) Limited trading as LexisNexis®, 1–3 Strand, London WC2N 5JR and 9–10 St Andrew Square, Edinburgh EH2 2AF
LNUK Global Partners	LexisNexis® encompasses authoritative legal publishing brands dating back to the 19th century including: Butterworths® in the United Kingdom, Canada and the Asia-Pacific region; Les Editions du Juris Classeur in France; and Matthew Bender® worldwide. Details of LexisNexis® locations worldwide can be found at www.lexisnexis.com

First published in 1962.

© 2020 RELX (UK) Ltd.

Published by LexisNexis®

ISBN: 9781474314183 (for set); 9781474314206 (for Part 1b)
A CIP Catalogue record for this book is available from the British Library.

Printed and bound by CPI Group (UK) Limited, Croydon, CR0 4YY

Visit Tolley at www.tolley.co.uk or email the editorial department on: yellowandorange@lexisnexis.co.uk

Preface

Last years Preface emphasised the effect of the Brexit uncertainties on the legislation in the Yellow Book. This year my focus is, of course, on coronavirus, which is having far-reaching effects on businesses and individuals.

In the spring, the Chancellor announced the Self-employment Income Support Scheme, business support grants and the Coronavirus Job Retention Scheme, all of which radically changed the financial and fiscal landscape. There have also been consequential amendments to other parts of the tax and legal system, including Statutory Sick Pay, home as office expenses and court and tribunal procedures. This edition of the Yellow Book provides the detail of the relevant provisions, whether in Finance Act 2020, the Coronavirus Act or in statutory instruments.

The Act contains several controversial provisions: the extension of IR35 to the private sector, the new loan charge, and a digital services tax. It also reverses some earlier reforms: restrictions to the pensions annual allowance which were introduced in 2016 and have now been eased, while HMRCs preferential creditor status in insolvencies, abolished in 2002, will be partially restored from December 2020.

Working from home is now the new normal, with meetings and conferences conducted online. There is, however, no substitute for the having the hard copy Yellow Book in your hands, so you can see the entire structure of an Act or statutory instrument, and can easily compare one legal provision with another.

As well as new material, this edition of the Yellow Book includes previous legislation, regulations and Statements of Practice, all of which have been organised, updated and cross-referenced to take account of amendments and additions since the previous edition.

Please let us know if you have any thoughts for further improvement: we are always happy to hear your views.

Anne Redston

Barrister, Temple Tax Chambers

Visiting Professor, Kings College London

Publishers' Note

Finance Act 2020—key dates

Budget Day	11 March 2020
Finance Bill published	19 March 2020
Royal Assent	22 July 2020

Tax legislation

Tolleys Yellow and Orange Tax Handbooks are indispensable to the practitioner who needs to refer to the tax legislation as currently in force.

Each year the legislation is augmented and amended by one or more Finance Acts and lesser amendments are made from time to time by a variety of other statutes. An increasing amount of the detailed regulation of taxes is contained in statutory instruments – orders or regulations – which are also amended frequently. The Handbooks are normally published annually. They contain the text of the relevant statutes and statutory instruments as amended together with current texts of extra-statutory concessions, statements of practice, published official interpretations and decisions, selected press releases and internal guidance where available.

The Yellow Tax Handbook covers income tax, corporation tax, capital gains tax, along with annual tax on enveloped dwellings, diverted profits tax, digital services tax, apprenticeship levy and other direct taxes (in Parts 1a, 1b, 1c and 2), and inheritance tax, National Insurance contributions, tax credits and petroleum revenue tax (in Part 3). The companion volume, Tolley's Orange Tax Handbook, covers value added tax (Part 1), and stamp taxes (including land and buildings transaction tax in Scotland and land transaction tax in Wales), insurance premium tax, soft drinks industry levy, landfill tax (including Scottish landfill tax and landfill disposals tax in Wales), aggregates levy and climate change levy (Part 2).

This edition of the Yellow Tax Handbook contains texts as they applied at 3 August 2020, although later amendments have been taken into account where possible.

Organisation

The text of the Handbook is arranged in the following orderParts 1a, 1b, 1c: UK statutes relating to income tax, corporation tax, and capital gains tax and other direct taxes up to and including Finance Act 2020; Part 2: statutory instruments relating to direct taxes, European legislation, concessions, statements of practice, official inter-pretations and decisions, selected press releases, HMRC Codes of Practice and Factsheets and miscellaneous non-statutory material; Part 3: inheritance tax, National Insurance contributions, tax credits, and petroleum revenue tax. Destination tables for consolidation statutes are now available in the digital versions of the Yellow Book.

Within each category, items are printed in chronological order. To enable individual items to be located quickly, an item reference is printed in bold type in the outside top corner of each page.

Amendments and modifications

Amendments to existing legislation which take effect for the current year are made in the text of the amended legislation. An **Amendment** note under the amended text indicates the authority for the amendment and, where appropriate, the timing of its commencement. All relevant provisions of the current Finance Act are reproduced in full but otherwise the text of provisions which merely amend other Acts is generally omitted and replaced by a note indicating the legislation amended.

Sometimes the effect of a provision is modified by a later Act or statutory instrument but the scope of the modification is limited in some way so that the original provision remains generally unaffected. In this case, the original provision is printed without modification but a **Cross reference** to the later Act or statutory instrument is provided, see below.

Prospective amendments

The Handbook sets out the text of the legislation as it applies for the current tax year. Amendments which are stated to come into effect on a specified future date, or with effect from a date to be appointed, are therefore strictly outside the scope of the current edition and are not made in the text of the Act affected. However, a **Prospective amendment** note is provided to indicate the existence of the amendment and to include the full text of the amendment for reference.

Repealed legislation

Generally, repealed legislation is omitted. However, where it may be necessary to refer to the repealed text in dealing with tax liabilities for the current year, the text is retained and is printed in italics. Previous versions of the legislation are included in the Yellow Tax Handbook archives on TolleyLibrary: bit.ly/YellowArchive (subscription sensitive).

Tax law rewrite statutes

The digital versions of the Yellow Tax Handbook include tables of origin/derivation.

Cross references

The notes under each section or Schedule paragraph include references to commentary in *Simons Taxes*.

HMRC Manuals

Extensive references are included to the views and practice of HMRC which are detailed in the Manuals published online at www.gov.uk/government/collections/hmrc-manuals. Please note that, in addition to the current version of the HMRC Manuals, Tolley-Library also contains an archive covering the last six years: www.tolley.co.uk/products/tolley-library

August 2020

Meaning of "the Taxes Acts"

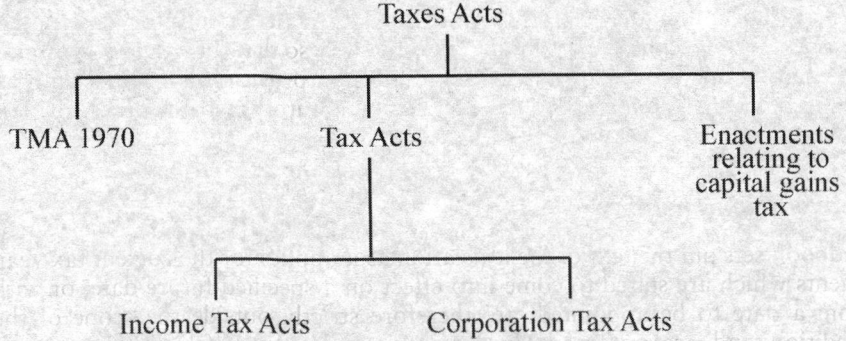

(1)   Defined in TMA 1970 s 118(1).
(2)   Defined in TA 1988 s 831(2).
(3)   Defined in TA 1988 s 831(1)(*b*).
(4)   Defined in TA 1988 s 831(1)(*a*).

See also Interpretation Act 1978 Sch 1:

"The Tax Acts" means the Income Tax Acts and the Corporation Tax Acts.

"The Income Tax Acts" means all enactments relating to income tax, including any provisions of the Corporation Tax Acts which relate to income tax.

"The Corporation Tax Acts" means the enactments relating to the taxation of the income and chargeable gains of companies and of company distributions (including provisions relating to income tax).

Contents

PARTS 1A, 1B, 1C

Preface

Publishers' note and key dates

Meaning of "the Taxes Acts"

Abbreviations

STATUTES

Acts before 1970

Taxes Management Act 1970

Other Acts 1970–1987

Income and Corporation Taxes Act 1988

Other Acts 1988–1991

Taxation of Chargeable Gains Act 1992

Other Acts 1992–2000

Capital Allowances Act 2001

Other Acts 2001–2002

Income Tax (Earnings and Pensions) Act 2003

Finance Act 2003

Finance Act 2004

Other Acts 2004

Income Tax (Trading and Other Income) Act 2005

Other Acts 2005–2006

Income Tax Act 2007

Other Acts 2007–2008

Corporation Tax Act 2009

Finance Act 2009

Corporation Tax Act 2010

Taxation (International and Other Provisions) Act 2010

Finance Act 2010

Constitutional Reform and Governance Act 2010

Finance (No 2) Act 2010

Finance (No 3) Act 2010

Equitable Life (Payments) Act 2010

Budget Responsibility and National Audit Act 2011

Finance Act 2011

Finance Act 2012

Small Charitable Donations Act 2012

Trusts (Capital and Income) Act 2013

Finance Act 2013

Tribunals (Scotland Act) 2014

Finance Act 2014

Revenue Scotland and Tax Powers Act 2014

Wales Act 2014

Taxation of Pensions Act 2014

Finance Act 2015

Corporation Tax (Northern Ireland) Act 2015

Finance (No 2) Act 2015

Scotland Act 2016

Scottish Fiscal Commission Act 2016

Tax Collection and Management (Wales) Act 2016

Bankruptcy (Scotland) Act 2016

Finance Act 2016

Small Charitable Donations and Childcare Payments Act 2017

Savings (Government Contributions) Act 2017

Finance Act 2017

Criminal Finances Act 2017

Digital Economy Act 2017

Finance (No 2) Act 2017

Finance Act 2018

Sanctions and Anti-Money Laundering Act 2018

European Union (Withdrawal) Act 2018

Finance Act 2019

European Union (Withdrawal Agreement) Act 2020

Coronavirus Act 2020

Coronavirus (Scotland) (No 2) Act 2020

Finance Act 2020

Index and "Words & Phrases"

PART 2

Statutory instruments

EU Treaty (TFEU) and European legislation

Extra-statutory concessions

Statements of practice

Revenue interpretations

Revenue decisions

Press releases etc

HMRC codes of practice and factsheets

Miscellaneous non-statutory material

PART 3
INHERITANCE TAX

Statutes

Probate and Legacy Duties Act 1808

Administration of Estates Act 1925

Finance (No 2) Act 1931

Finance Act 1940

Crown Proceedings Act 1947

Finance Act 1975

Inheritance (Provision for Family and Dependants) Act 1975

Finance Act 1976

Interpretation Act 1978

National Heritage Act 1980

Supreme Court Act 1981

Finance Act 1984

Inheritance Tax Act 1984

Finance Act 1985

Finance Act 1986

Finance Act 1987

Finance (No 2) Act 1987

Finance Act 1989

Finance Act 1990

Finance Act 1991

Finance (No 2) Act 1992

Finance Act 1993

Finance Act 1994

Finance Act 1995

Finance Act 1996

Finance Act 1997

Finance Act 1998

Human Rights Act 1998

Finance Act 1999

Finance Act 2000

Finance Act 2001

Finance Act 2002

Finance Act 2003

Finance Act 2004

Finance Act 2006

Finance Act 2007

Finance Act 2008

Finance Act 2009

Finance Act 2010

Finance (No 3) Act 2010

Finance Act 2011

Finance Act 2012

Finance Act 2013

Finance Act 2014

Finance Act 2015

Finance Act 2016

Finance (No 2) Act 2017

Finance Act 2018

Finance Act 2019

Finance Act 2020

Statutory instruments

Extra-statutory concessions

Statements of practice

HMRC Interpretations

Press releases etc

Index and Words & Phrases

NATIONAL INSURANCE CONTRIBUTIONS

Statutes

Social Security Pensions Act 1975

Social Security (Miscellaneous Provisions) Act 1977

Interpretation Act 1978 (see Part 1 of this publication)

Social Security Act 1980

Bankruptcy (Scotland) Act 1985

Insolvency Act 1986

Social Security Act 1986

Social Security Act 1989

Finance Act 1989

Destination Table: Social Security Acts 1992

Social Security Contributions and Benefits Act 1992

Social Security Administration Act 1992

Social Security (Consequential Provisions) Act 1992

Pension Schemes Act 1993

Social Security (Contributions) Act 1994

Finance Act 1996

Employment Rights Act 1996

Finance Act 1997

Social Security Act 1998

Social Security Contributions (Transfer of Functions, etc) Act 1999

Social Security Contributions (Share Options) Act 2001

National Insurance Contributions Act 2002

Employment Act 2002

National Insurance Contributions and Statutory Payments Act 2004

Pensions Act 2004

Constitutional Reform Act 2005

Commissioners for Revenue and Customs Act 2005

Pensions Act 2007

Finance Act 2012

National Insurance Contributions Act 2014

Finance Act 2014

National Insurance Contributions Act 2015

National Insurance Contributions (Rate Ceilings) Act 2015

Finance Act 2016

Finance Act 2017

Finance (No 2) Act 2017

Statutory instruments

European legislation
Press releases etc
Index and words & phrases

TAX CREDITS

Statutes
Tax Credits Act 2002
Civil Partnership Act 2004
Welfare Reform Act 2012
Childcare Payments Act 2014
Statutory instruments
Miscellaneous
Index and words & phrases

PETROLEUM REVENUE TAX

Statutes
Finance Act 1973
Oil Taxation Act 1975
Finance (No 2) Act 1979
Petroleum Revenue Tax Act 1980
Finance Act 1980
Finance Act 1981
Finance Act 1982
Finance Act 1983
Oil Taxation Act 1983
Finance Act 1984
Finance Act 1985
Finance Act 1986
Finance Act 1987
Finance (No 2) Act 1987
Income and Corporation Taxes Act 1988
Finance Act 1988
Finance Act 1989
Finance Act 1990
Finance Act 1991
Taxation of Chargeable Gains Act 1992
Finance (No 2) Act 1992
Finance Act 1993
Finance Act 1994
Finance Act 1995
Finance Act 1996
Finance Act 1997
Finance Act 1998
Finance Act 1999
Finance Act 2000
Finance Act 2001
Finance Act 2002

Finance Act 2004

Finance Act 2006

Finance Act 2007

Finance Act 2008

Finance Act 2009

Finance Act 2010

Finance (No 3) Act 2010

Finance Act 2011

Finance Act 2012

Finance Act 2013

Finance Act 2014

Finance Act 2015

Finance Act 2016

Finance (No 2) Act 2017

Finance Act 2018

Finance Act 2019

Statutory instruments

Extra-statutory concessions

Statements of practice

Press releases

Index and Words & Phrases

List of abbreviations

AEA 1925	Administration of Estates Act 1925
ACT	Advance Corporation Tax
APRT	Advanced petroleum revenue tax
art	article(s)
ATED	annual tax on enveloped dwellings
BES	Business Expansion Scheme
CAA	Capital Allowances Act
CCAB	Consultative Committee of Accountancy Bodies
C&E	Customs & Excise
CGT	Capital gains tax
CGTA 1979	Capital Gains Tax Act 1979
Ch	Chapter of statute
CIOT	Chartered Institute of Taxation
col	column(s)
Comrs	Commissioners
CPA 1947	Crown Proceedings Act 1947
CRCA 2005	Commissioners for Revenue and Customs Act 2005
CRT	Composite rate tax
CSPSSA 2000	Child Support, Pensions and Social Security Act 2000
CT	Corporation tax
CTA 2009/2010	Corporation Tax Act 2009/2010
CTD	Certificates of tax deposit
CTT	Capital transfer tax
CTTA 1984	Capital Transfer Tax Act 1984
Dir	EC Directive
DLT	Development land tax
DLTA 1976	Development Land Tax Act 1976
DPT	Diverted Profits Tax
DSS	Department of Social Security
DST	Digital Services Tax
DTI	Department of Trade and Industry
DTR	Double taxation relief
EC	European Community/Communities

edn	edition
EEC	European Economic Community
EEIG	European Economic Interest Grouping
EIS	Enterprise Investment Scheme
ESC	Extra-statutory concession
ESOT	Employee share ownership trust
et seq	(et sequens) and the following
EU	European Union
EU(W)A 2018	European Union (Withdrawal) Act 2018
FA	Finance Act
FII	Franked investment income
FIMBRA	Financial Intermediaries, Managers and Brokers Regulatory Association
F(No 2)A	Finance (No 2) Act
FSA	Friendly Societies Act
FYA	first-year allowance
GAAR	General Anti-abuse Rule
HA 1988	Housing Act 1988
HL	House of Lords
HM	Her Majesty
HMRC	Her Majesty's Revenue & Customs
HMSO	Her Majesty's Stationery Office
IA	Interpretation Act
IA 1986	Insolvency Act 1986
ICAEW	Institute of Chartered Accountants in England & Wales
IHT	Inheritance tax
IHTA 1984	Inheritance Tax Act 1984
IR	Inland Revenue
IR Comrs	Commissioners of Inland Revenue
IRRA 1890	Inland Revenue Regulation Act 1890
IT	Income tax
ITA 2007	Income Tax Act 2007
ITEPA 2003	Income Tax (Earnings and Pensions) Act 2003
ITTOIA 2005	Income Tax (trading and Other Income) Act 2005
LAUTRO	Life Assurance and Unit Trust Regulatory Organisation
LIFFE	London International Financial Futures and Options Exchange
MIRAS	Mortgage interest relief at source

MTD	Making Tax Digital
NB	(nota bene) note well
NHA 1980	National Heritage Act 1980
NI	National insurance
NIC	National insurance contributions
NRCGT	Non-resident capital gains tax
OJ	Official Journal of the European Union
OPBAS	Office for Professional Body Anti-Money Laundering Supervision
OTA	Oil Taxation Act
para	paragraph(s)
PAYE	Pay as you earn
PCTA 1968	Provisional Collection of Taxes Act 1968
PR	Press release
PRP	Profit-related pay
PRT	Petroleum revenue tax
PSO	Pension Schemes Office
Pt	Part(s)
QCB	Qualifying corporate bond
r	rule(s)
RD	Revenue decision
reg	regulations
R&D	research & development
RI	Revenue Interpretation
s(s)	section(s)
SAYE	Save as you earn
Sch	Schedule
SSA	Social Security Act
SSAA 1992	Social Security Administration Act 1992
SS(C)A	Social Security (Contributions) Act
SSCBA 1992	Social Security Contributions and Benefits Act 1992
SSCPA 1992	Social Security (Consequential Provisions) Act 1992
SS(No 2)A	Social Security (No 2) Act
SSHBA	Social Security and Housing Benefits Act
SS(MP)A	Social Security (Miscellaneous Provisions) Act
SSPA 1975	Social Security Pensions Act 1975
SSPA 1991	Statutory Sick Pay Act 1991
SI	Statutory Instrument

SP	Statement of Practice
SSAP	Statement of Standard Accounting Practice
STC	Simon's Tax Cases
sub-para	sub-paragraph(s)
sub-s	sub-section(s)
SWTI	Simon's Weekly Tax Intelligence
TA	Income and Corporation Taxes Act
TaA 2000	Transport Act 2000
TCGA 1992	Taxation of Chargeable Gains Act 1992
TCA 1999	Tax Credits Act 1999
TIOPA 2010	Taxation (International and other Provisions) Act 2010
TMA 1970	Taxes Management Act 1970
TPA 2014	Taxation of Pensions Act 2014
TSBA	Trustee Savings Banks Act
UCITS	Undertakings for Collective Investment in Transferable Securities
UK	United Kingdom
VAT	Value added tax
VATA 1994	Value Added Tax Act 1994
VCT	Venture capital trust
vol	volume(s)
WDA	writing down allowance
WRA	Welfare Reform Act

Part 1b:

Acts 2004–2010

List of statutes

Part 1a

Partnership Act 1890
Finance (No 2) Act 1931
Finance Act 1940
Crown Proceedings Act 1947
Provisional Collection of Taxes Act 1968
Finance Act 1969
Taxes Management Act 1970
Finance Act 1972
Finance Act 1973
Finance Act 1974
Interpretation Act 1978
Finance Act 1984
Police and Criminal Evidence Act 1984
Films Act 1985
Finance Act 1986
Insolvency Act 1986
Finance (No 2) Act 1987
Income and Corporation Taxes Act 1988
Finance Act 1988
Housing Act 1988
Finance Act 1989
Finance Act 1990
Finance Act 1991
Taxation of Chargeable Gains Act 1992
Finance (No 2) Act 1992
Finance Act 1993
Finance Act 1994
Criminal Justice and Public Order Act 1994
Finance Act 1995
Finance Act 1996
Finance Act 1997
Finance (No 2) Act 1997
Data Protection Act 1998
Finance Act 1998
Human Rights Act 1998
Scotland Act 1998
Finance Act 1999
Limited Liability Partnerships Act 2000
Finance Act 2000
Trustee Act 2000
Freedom of Information Act 2000
Transport Act 2000
Capital Allowances Act 2001
Finance Act 2001
Criminal Justice and Police Act 2001
Anti-Terrorism, Crime and Security Act 2001
Finance Act 2002
Proceeds of Crime Act 2002
Police Reform Act 2002
Enterprise Act 2002
Income Tax (Earnings and Pensions) Act 2003
Finance Act 2003

Child Trust Funds Act 2004

Part 1b

Finance Act 2004
Income Tax (Trading and Other Income) Act 2005
Finance Act 2005
Commissioners for Revenue and Customs Act 2005
Railways Act 2005
Serious Organised Crime and Police Act 2005
Finance (No 2) Act 2005
Finance Act 2006
Income Tax Act 2007
Finance Act 2007
Tribunals, Courts and Enforcement Act 2007
Serious Crime Act 2007
Finance Act 2008
Crossrail Act 2008
Counter-terrorism Act 2008
Corporation Tax Act 2009
Finance Act 2009
Taxation (International and Other Provisions) Act 2010

Part 1c

Corporation Tax Act 2010
Finance Act 2010
Constitutional Reform and Governance Act 2010
Finance (No 2) Act 2010
Finance (No 3) Act 2010
Equitable Life (Payments) Act 2010
Budget Responsibility and National Audit Act 2011
Finance Act 2011
Charities Act 2011
Scotland Act 2012
Finance Act 2012
Small Charitable Donations Act 2012
Trusts (Income and Capital) Act 2013
Finance Act 2013
Tribunals (Scotland Act) 2014
Finance Act 2014
Revenue Scotland and Tax Powers Act 2014
Wales Act 2014
Taxation of Pensions Act 2014
Finance Act 2015
Corporation Tax (Northern Ireland) Act 2015
Finance (No 2) Act 2015
Scotland Act 2016
Scottish Fiscal Commission Act 2016
Tax Collection and Management (Wales) Act 2016
Bankruptcy (Scotland) Act 2016 (Scottish Parliament)
Finance Act 2016
Small Charitable Donations and Childcare Payments Act 2017
Savings (Government Contributions) Act 2017
Finance Act 2017
Criminal Finances Act 2017
Digital Economy Act 2017
Finance (No 2) Act 2017

Finance Act 2018
Sanctions and Anti-Money Laundering Act 2018
European Union (Withdrawal) Act 2018
Finance Act 2019
European Union (Withdrawal Agreement) Act 2020
Coronavirus Act 2020
Coronavirus (Scotland) (No 2) Act 2020
Finance Act 2020

List of statutes

Insolvency Act 2018
Sanctions and Anti-Money Laundering Act 2018
European Union (Withdrawal) Act 2018
Finance Act 2019
European Union (Withdrawal Agreement) Act 2020
Coronavirus Act 2020
Coronavirus (Scotland) (No. 2) Act 2020
Finance Act 2020

FINANCE ACT 2004

(2004 Chapter 12)

ARRANGEMENT OF SECTIONS

Part 3 Income Tax, Corporation Tax and Capital Gains Tax
Chapter 1 Income Tax and Corporation Tax Charge and Rate Bands
Corporation tax
25   Charge and main rate for financial year 2005
27   Corporation tax starting rate and fraction for financial year 2004
Chapter 2 Corporation Tax: General
Penalties: temporary relaxation
33   Provision not at arm's length: temporary relaxation of liability to penalty
Transfer pricing and thin capitalisation: commencement
37   Commencement and transitional provisions
Expenses of companies with investment business and insurance companies
42   Commencement of sections 38 to 41
43   Companies with investment business: transitional provisions
Power to make consequential amendments
46   Power to make consequential amendments
Insurance companies: miscellaneous
47   Insurance companies etc
Accounting practice
52   Amendment of enactments that operate by reference to accounting practice
53   Treatment of expenditure on research and development
Miscellaneous
55   Duty of company to give notice of coming within charge to corporation tax
55A   Section 55: exception to duty to give notice
Chapter 3 Construction Industry Scheme
Introduction
57   Introduction
58   Sub-contractors
59   Contractors
Deductions on account of tax from contract payments to sub-contractors
60   Contract payments
61   Deductions on account of tax from contract payments
62   Treatment of sums deducted
Registration of sub-contractors
63   Registration for gross payment or for payment under deduction
64   Requirements for registration for gross payment
65   Change in control of company registered for gross payment
66   Cancellation of registration for gross payment
67   Registration for gross payment: appeals
68   Registration for payment under deduction: cancellation and appeals
Verification, returns, security etc and penalties
69   Verification etc of registration status of sub-contractors
70   Periodic returns by contractors etc
70A   Security for payments to HMRC
71   Collection and recovery of sums to be deducted
72   Penalties
Supplementary
73   Regulations under this Chapter: supplementary
73A   Designated international organisations: exemption from section 59
74   Meaning of "construction operations"
75   Meaning of "the Inland Revenue" etc and delegation of Board's functions
76   Consequential amendments
77   Commencement and transitional provision
Chapter 4 Personal Taxation
Taxable benefits
78   Childcare and childcare vouchers
80   Vans
81   Emergency vehicles
82   European travel expenses of MPs and other representatives
Gifts with a reservation
84   Charge to income tax by reference to enjoyment of property previously owned
Employment-related securities and options
85   Relief where national insurance contributions met by employee
86   Shares in employee-controlled companies and unconnected companies
87   Restricted securities with artificially depressed value

88   Shares under approved plans and schemes
89   Shares acquired on public offer
90   Associated persons etc

Miscellaneous

92   Minor amendments of or connected with ITEPA 2003

Chapter 5 Enterprise Incentives

93   Enterprise investment scheme
94   Venture capital trusts
95   Corporate venturing scheme
96   Enterprise management incentives: subsidiaries

Chapter 6 Exemption From Income Tax for Certain Interest and Royalty Payments

Supplementary

105   Consequential amendments

Chapter 8 Chargeable Gains

116   Restriction of gifts relief etc
117   Private residence relief
118   Authorised unit trusts: treatment of umbrella schemes

Chapter 10 Avoidance: Miscellaneous

134   Finance leasebacks
136   Manufactured dividends

Chapter 11 Miscellaneous

Reliefs for business

144   Lloyd's names: conversion to limited liability underwriting

Offshore matters

145   Offshore funds
146   Meaning of "offshore installation"

Part 4 Pension Schemes etc

Chapter 1 Introduction

Introductory

149   Overview of Part 4

Main concepts

150   Meaning of "pension scheme"
151   Meaning of "member"
152   Meaning of "arrangement"

Chapter 2 Registration of Pension Schemes

Registration

153   Registration of pension schemes
153A   Power to require information or documents in relation to applications for registration
153B   Power to inspect documents in relation to applications for registration
153C   Penalties for failure to comply with information notices etc
153D   Penalties for inaccurate information in applications
153E   Penalties for inaccurate information or documents provided under information notice
153F   Penalties for false declarations
154   Persons by whom registered pension scheme may be established
156   Appeal against decision not to register
156A   Cases where application for registration not decided within 6 months

De-registration

157   De-registration
158   Grounds for de-registration
159   Appeal against decision to de-register
159A   Power to require information or documents for purpose of considering if scheme administrator is fit and proper
159B   Power to inspect documents for purpose of considering if scheme administrator is fit and proper
159C   Penalties for failure to comply with information notices etc
159D   Penalties for inaccurate information or documents provided under information notice

Chapter 3 Payments by Registered Pension Schemes

Introductory

160   Payments by registered pension schemes
161   Meaning of "payment" etc
162   Meaning of "loan"
163   Meaning of "borrowing" etc

Authorised member payments

164   Authorised member payments
165   Pension rules
166   Lump sum rule
167   Pension death benefit rules
168   Lump sum death benefit rule
169   Recognised transfers

170 Appeal against decision to exclude recognised overseas pension scheme
171 Scheme administration member payments
Unauthorised member payments
172 Assignment
172A Surrender
172B Increase in rights of connected persons on death
172C Allocation of unallocated employer contributions
172D Limit on increase in benefits
173 Benefits
174 Value shifting
174A Taxable property held by investment-regulated pension schemes
Authorised employer payments
175 Authorised employer payments
176 Public service scheme payment
177 Authorised surplus payment
178 Compensation payments
179 Authorised employer loan
180 Scheme administration employer payments
Unauthorised employer payments
181 Value shifting
Borrowing
182 Unauthorised borrowing: money purchase arrangements
183 Effect of unauthorised borrowing: money purchase arrangements
184 Unauthorised borrowing: other arrangements
185 Effect of unauthorised borrowing: other arrangements
Income and gains from taxable property
185A Income from taxable property
185B Annual profits and deemed profits
185C Deemed market value
185D Apportionment to pension scheme
185E Credit for tax paid
185F Gains from taxable property
185G Disposal by person holding directly
185H Disposal of interest in vehicle
185I Credit for tax paid
Repayments of lump sums
185J Effect of repayment of certain pre-6 April 2015 lump sums
Chapter 4 Registered Pension Schemes: Tax Reliefs and Exemptions
Scheme investments
186 Income
187 Chargeable gains
Members' contributions
188 Relief for contributions
189 Relevant UK individual
190 Annual limit for relief
191 Methods of giving relief
192 Relief at source
192A Relief at source: additional relief
192B Relief at source: excessive relief given
193 Relief under net pay arrangements
194 Relief on making of claim
195 Transfer of certain shares to be treated as payment of contribution
195A Life assurance premium contributions
Employers' contributions
196 Relief for employers in respect of contributions paid
196A Power to restrict relief
196B Employer asset-backed contributions: denial of relief (1)
196C Employer asset-backed contributions: "acceptable structured finance arrangement" (1)
196D Employer asset-backed contributions: denial of relief (2)
196E Employer asset-backed contributions: "acceptable structured finance arrangement" (2)
196F Employer asset-backed contributions: denial of relief (3)
196G Employer asset-backed contributions: "acceptable structured finance arrangement" (3)
196H Employer asset-backed contributions: "relevant change in relation to the partnership" and "person involved in the relevant change"
196I Employer asset-backed contributions: change in lender's original position under acceptable structured finance arrangement etc
196J Employer asset-backed contributions: further events which cause section 196I to apply
196K Employer asset-backed contributions: "advances" under acceptable structured finance arrangements

196L   Employer asset-backed contributions: supplementary
197   Spreading of relief
198   Spreading of relief: cessation of business
199   Deemed contributions
199A   Indirect contributions
200   No other relief for employers in connection with contributions
Inland Revenue contributions
202   Minimum contributions under pensions legislation
Inheritance tax exemptions
Chapter 5 Registered Pension Schemes: Tax Charges
Charges on authorised payments
204   Authorised pensions and lump sums
205   Short service refund lump sum charge
206   Special lump sum death benefits charge
207   Authorised surplus payments charge
Unauthorised payments charge
208   Unauthorised payments charge
209   Unauthorised payments surcharge
210   Surchargeable unauthorised member payments
211   Valuation of crystallised rights for purposes of section 210
212   Valuation of uncrystallised rights for purposes of section 210
213   Surchargeable unauthorised employer payments
Lifetime allowance charge
214   Lifetime allowance charge
215   Amount of charge
216   Benefit crystallisation events and amounts crystallised
217   Persons liable to charge
218   Individual's lifetime allowance and standard lifetime allowance
219   Availability of individual's lifetime allowance
220   Pension credits from previously crystallised rights
221   Non-residence: general
222   Non-residence: money purchase arrangements
223   Non-residence: other arrangements
224   Transfers from recognised overseas pension scheme: general
225   Overseas scheme transfers: money purchase arrangements
226   Overseas scheme transfers: other arrangements
Annual allowance charge
227   Annual allowance charge
227ZA   The chargeable amount
227B   The alternative chargeable amount
227C   Meaning of "money-purchase input sub-total"
227D   Pension input amounts in respect of certain hybrid arrangements
227F   Pension input periods in which rights are first flexibly accessed
227G   When pension rights are first flexibly accessed
228   Annual allowance
228ZA   Tapered reduction of annual allowance: high-income individual
228ZB   Anti-avoidance in connection with section 228ZA
228A   Carry forward of unused annual allowance
228B   Carry forward: certain periods treated as pension input periods
228C   Annual allowance for, and carry-forward from, 2015–16
229   Total pension input amount
230   Cash balance arrangements
231   Cash balance arrangements: uprating of opening value
232   Cash balance arrangements: adjustments of closing value
233   Other money purchase arrangements
234   Defined benefits arrangements
235   Defined benefits arrangements: uprating of opening value
236   Defined benefits arrangements: adjustments of closing value
236A   Post-entitlement enhancements
237   Hybrid arrangements
237ZA   Pension input amounts for input periods ending in 2015–16
237A   Liability of individual
237B   Liability of scheme administrator
237C   Exceptions
237D   Discharge of scheme administrator's liability
237E   Consequential benefit adjustments to be reasonable etc
237F   Power to modify rules
238   Pension input period: arrangement commencing before 9 July 2015
238ZA   Pension input periods from 9 July 2015 for existing arrangement

238ZB   Pension input periods for arrangement commencing after 8 July 2015
238A   Power to make orders about charge
Scheme sanction charge
239   Scheme sanction charge
240   Amount of charge
241   Scheme chargeable payment
De-registration charge
242   De-registration charge
Chapter 5A Registered pension schemes established outside the United Kingdom
242A   Meaning of "non-UK registered scheme"
242B   Meaning of "UK-relieved funds"
242C   Application of this Part to non-UK registered schemes
242D   Non-UK registered schemes: annual allowance charge
242E   Investment-regulated non-UK registered schemes
Chapter 6 Schemes that are not Registered Pension Schemes
Non-UK schemes
243   Overseas pension schemes: migrant member relief
244   Non-UK schemes: application of certain charges
Non-UK schemes: the overseas transfer charge
244A   Overseas transfer charge
244B   Exclusion: member and receiving scheme in same country
244C   Exclusion: member and receiving scheme in EEA states
244D   Exclusion: receiving scheme is an occupational pension scheme
244E   Exclusion: receiving scheme set up by international organisation
244F   Exclusion: receiving scheme is an overseas public service scheme
244G   Exclusions: avoidance of double charge, and transitional protections
244H   Power to provide for further exclusions
244I   Circumstances in which exclusions do not apply
244J   Persons liable to charge
244K   Amount of charge
244L   Accounting for overseas transfer charge by scheme managers
244M   Repayments of charge on subsequent excluding events
244N   Discharge of liability of scheme administrator or manager
Employer-financed retirement benefit schemes
245   Restriction of deduction for contributions by employer
246   Restriction of deduction for non-contributory provision
246A   Case where no relief for provision by an employer
247   Abolition of income tax charge in respect of employer payments
248   Employer's cost of insuring against non-payment of benefit
249   Taxation of non-pension benefits
Chapter 7 Compliance
Information
250   Registered pension scheme return
251   Information: general requirements
Accounting and assessment
254   Accounting for tax by scheme administrators
255   Assessments under this Part
255A   Electronic payment
255B   Payments to be cleared payments
Registration regulations
256   Enhanced lifetime allowance regulations
Penalties
257   Registered pension scheme return
258   Information required by regulations
261   Enhanced lifetime allowance regulations: documents and information
262   Enhanced lifetime allowance regulations: failures to comply
263   Lifetime allowance enhanced protection: benefit accrual
264   False statements etc
265   Winding-up to facilitate payment of lump sums
266   Transfers to insured schemes
Relief from liability in respect of returned unauthorised member payments
266A   Member's liability
266B   Scheme's liability
Discharge of tax liability: good faith
267   Lifetime allowance charge
268   Unauthorised payments surcharge and scheme sanction charge
269   Appeal against decision on discharge of liability
Scheme administrator
270   Meaning of "scheme administrator"

271 Liability of scheme administrator
272 Trustees etc liable as scheme administrator
272A Liabilities of independent trustee
272B Liabilities of scheme administrator appointed by independent trustee etc
272C Former scheme administrator etc to retain liability
273 Members liable as scheme administrator
273ZA Income and gains from taxable property
273A Insurance company liable as scheme administrator
273B Power of trustees or managers to make certain payments
274 Supplementary
274A Power to split schemes
Chapter 8 Supplementary
National Employment Savings Trust and Master Trust schemes
274B National Employment Savings Trust and Master Trust schemes
Interpretation
275 Insurance company
276 Relevant valuation factor
277 Valuation assumptions
278 Market value
279 Other definitions
280 Abbreviations and general index
Other supplementary provisions
281 Minor and consequential amendments
282 Orders and regulations
283 Transitionals and savings
284 Commencement
Part 7 Disclosure of Tax Avoidance Schemes
306 Meaning of "notifiable arrangements" and "notifiable proposal"
306A Doubt as to notifiability
307 Meaning of "promoter"
308 Duties of promoter
308A Supplemental information
309 Duty of person dealing with promoter outside United Kingdom
310 Duty of parties to notifiable arrangements not involving promoter
310A Duty to provide further information requested by HMRC
310B Failure to provide information under section 310A: application to the Tribunal
310C Duty of promoters to provide updated information
311 Arrangements to be given reference number
312 Duty of promoter to notify client of number
312A Duty of client to notify parties of number
312B Duty of client to provide information to promoter
313 Duty of parties to notifiable arrangements to notify Board of number, etc
313ZA Duty to provide details of clients
313ZB Enquiry following disclosure of client details
313ZC Duty of employer to notify HMRC of details of employees etc
313A Pre-disclosure enquiry
313B Reasons for non-disclosure: supporting information
313C Provision of information to HMRC by introducers
314 Legal professional privilege
314A Order to disclose
315 Penalties
316 Information to be provided in form and manner specified by HMRC
316A Duty to provide additional information
316B Confidentiality
316C Publication by HMRC
316D Section 316C: subsequent judicial rulings
317 Regulations under Part 7
318 Interpretation of Part 7
319 Part 7: commencement and savings
Part 8 Miscellaneous Matters
320 Exclusion of extended limitation period in England, Wales and Northern Ireland
321 Exclusion of extended prescriptive period in Scotland
322 Mutual assistance: customs union with the Principality of Andorra
323 Ending of shipbuilders' relief
324 Government borrowing: preparations for possible adoption of Euro
325 Premium bonds
Part 9 Supplementary Provisions
326 Repeals
327 Interpretation

328   Short title

Schedules:

Schedule 5—Provision not at arm's length: related amendments

Schedule 7—Insurance companies etc

Schedule 10—Amendment of enactments that operate by reference to accounting practice

Schedule 11—Conditions for registration for gross payment

Schedule 12—Construction industry scheme: consequential amendments

Schedule 13—Childcare and childcare vouchers

Schedule 14—Vans

Schedule 15—Charge to income tax on benefits received by former owner of property

Schedule 16—Relief where national insurance contributions met by employee

Schedule 17—Minor amendments of or connected with the Income Tax (Earnings and Pensions) Act 2003

Schedule 18—Enterprise investment scheme

Schedule 19—Venture capital trusts

Schedule 20—Corporate venturing scheme

Schedule 21—Chargeable gains: restriction of gifts relief etc

Schedule 22—Chargeable gains: private residence relief

Schedule 23—Finance leasebacks: transitional provision

Schedule 25—Lloyd's names: conversion to limited liability underwriting

Schedule 26—Offshore funds

Schedule 27—Meaning of "offshore installation"

Schedule 28—Registered pension schemes: authorised pensions—supplementary

Schedule 29—Registered pension schemes: authorised lump sums—supplementary

Schedule 29A—Taxable property held by investment-regulated pension schemes

Schedule 30—Registered pension schemes: employer loans

Schedule 31—Taxation of benefits under registered pension schemes

Schedule 32—Registered pension schemes: benefit crystallisation events—supplementary

Schedule 33—Overseas pension schemes: migrant member relief

Schedule 34—Non-UK schemes: application of certain charges

Schedule 35—Pension schemes etc: minor and consequential amendments

PART 3

INCOME TAX, CORPORATION TAX AND CAPITAL GAINS TAX

CHAPTER 1

INCOME TAX AND CORPORATION TAX CHARGE AND RATE BANDS

Corporation tax

25 Charge and main rate for financial year 2005

Corporation tax shall be charged for the financial year 2005 at the rate of 30%.

27 Corporation tax starting rate and fraction for financial year 2004

For the financial year 2004—

(a) the corporation tax starting rate shall be 0%, and

(b) the fraction mentioned in section 13AA of the Taxes Act 1988 (marginal relief for small companies) shall be 19/400ths.

CHAPTER 2

CORPORATION TAX: GENERAL

Penalties: temporary relaxation

33 Provision not at arm's length: temporary relaxation of liability to penalty

(1) This section has effect in relation to—

(a) the years of assessment 2004–05 and 2005–06, and

(b) accounting periods beginning on or after 1st January 2004 and ending on or before 31st March 2006,

and in the following provisions of this section "relevant period" means any of those years of assessment or accounting periods.

(2) In this section "records relating to an arm's length provision" means such records as might have been requisite for the purpose of making and delivering a correct and complete return, so far as relating to the determination of the provision asserted to be the arm's length provision for the purposes of Schedule 28AA to the Taxes Act 1988 in a case where that Schedule applies.

(3) In relation to any relevant period, the following provisions (which provide for penalties for failure to keep and preserve records for purposes of returns)—

(a) section 12B(5) of the Taxes Management Act 1970 (c 9), and

(b) paragraph 23 of Schedule 18 to the Finance Act 1998 (c 36), do not apply if the records which the person in question fails to keep or preserve are records relating to an arm's length provision.

(4) (*amends* FA 1998 Sch 18 para 23(2)).

(5) Where a person delivers an incorrect return for any relevant period, he shall not be regarded as doing so negligently for the purposes of—

    (*a*)   section 95 of the Taxes Management Act 1970, or

    (*b*)   paragraph 20 of Schedule 18 to the Finance Act 1998,

by reason only of his failure, or the failure of any other person, to keep or preserve records relating to an arm's length provision.

(6) For the purposes of section 95A of the Taxes Management Act 1970, where a partner delivers an incorrect partnership return for any relevant period—

    (*a*)   he shall not be regarded as doing so negligently, and

    (*b*)   his doing so shall not be regarded as attributable to negligent conduct on the part of any relevant partner,

by reason only of his failure, or the failure of any other person, to keep or preserve records relating to an arm's length provision.

(7) For the purposes of section 99 of the Taxes Management Act 1970 (penalty for assisting in preparation of incorrect documents) a person shall not be taken to know that a return is incorrect by reason only of his failure, or the failure of any other person, to keep or preserve records relating to an arm's length provision.

Thin capitalisation

34 Payments of excessive interest etc

(1) (*repeals* TA 1988 s 209(2)(*da*), (8A)–(8F))

(2), (3) (*inserted* TA 1988 Sch 28AA paras 1A, 1B; *repealed by* TIOPA 2010 s 503, Sch 10 Pt 2)

(4) (*amended* FA 1996 Sch 6 para 11A; *repealed by* CTA 2009 s 1326, Sch 3 Pt 1)

Transfer pricing and thin capitalisation: commencement

37 Commencement and transitional provisions

(1) In this section "the amending provisions" means—

    (*a*)   sections 30 to 32 (transfer pricing);

    (*b*)   sections 34 to 36 (thin capitalisation);

    (*c*)   Schedule 5 (provision not at arm's length: related amendments).

(2) The amendments made by those provisions have effect in relation to chargeable periods beginning on or after 1st April 2004 (whenever the actual provision, within the meaning of Schedule 28AA to the Taxes Act 1988, is or was made or imposed).

(3) Where an accounting period of a company begins before, and ends on or after, 1st April 2004, it shall be assumed for the purposes of the amending provisions, the amendments which they make and subsection (2) that that accounting period ("the straddling period") consists of two separate accounting periods—

    (*a*)   the first beginning with the straddling period and ending with 31st March 2004, and

    (*b*)   the second beginning with 1st April 2004 and ending with the straddling period,

and the company's profits and losses shall be computed accordingly for tax purposes.

(4) Where a period of account of any person within the charge to income tax begins before, and ends on or after, 6th April 2004, it shall be assumed for the purposes of the amending provisions, the amendments which they make and subsection (2) that that period ("the straddling period of account") consists of two separate periods of account—

    (*a*)   the first beginning with the straddling period of account and ending with 5th April 2004, and

    (*b*)   the second beginning with 6th April 2004 and ending with the straddling period of account,

and the person's profits and losses shall be computed accordingly for the purposes of income tax.

Expenses of companies with investment business and insurance companies

42 Commencement of sections 38 to 41

(1) The amendments made by sections 38 to 41 and Schedule 6 have effect for accounting periods beginning on or after 1st April 2004.

(2) This is subject to the transitional provisions in sections 43 and 44 and that Schedule.

43 Companies with investment business: transitional provisions

(1) Any amount which, apart from this subsection, would have fallen to be treated under the old section 75(3) as if it had been disbursed as expenses of management for the first new accounting period of a company shall instead be treated as if it were expenses of management deductible for that period by virtue of the new section 75(9).

(2) To the extent that any amount was deductible under subsection (1) of section 75 for an old accounting period, the amount shall not again be deductible under that subsection for a new accounting period.

(3) Subsection (2) is without prejudice to the old section 75(3) and the new section 75(9) (carry forward of unrelieved excess to later accounting period).

(4) To the extent that an amount—

    (*a*) was not deductible under section 75(1) by an investment company for any old accounting period, but

    (*b*) would have been deductible under the new section 75(1) for an old accounting period if the amendments made by sections 38 and 39 and Schedule 6 or any order under section 46 (so far as having effect in relation to the first new accounting period) had been in force in relation to that period,

the amount shall be deductible under section 75(1) for the first new accounting period of the company.

(5) Where there is an accounting period that begins before, and ends on or after, 1st April 2004 ("the commencement date"), it shall be assumed, for the purpose of determining the amounts that are deductible for that period under section 75(1) of the Taxes Act 1988, that that accounting period (the "straddling period") consists of two separate accounting periods—

    (*a*) the first beginning with the straddling period and ending with the day preceding the commencement date, and

    (*b*) the second beginning with the commencement date and ending with the straddling period,

but this is subject to subsection (6).

(6) In the case of an investment company, subsection (5) does not have effect for the purpose of determining the amounts that are deductible for the straddling period under section 75(1) by virtue of—

    (*a*) subsection (3) of the old section 75, or

    (*b*) any provision of the Corporation Tax Acts, apart from section 75 and this section.

(7) Where, for the purposes of section 768B or 768C of the Taxes Act 1988, there is a change in the ownership of a company during the straddling period, then for the purposes of the section in question (and Schedule 28A to that Act), before making any such division as is required by section 768B(4) or 768C(3) of that Act,—

    (*a*) the straddling period shall be divided into two parts in accordance with subsection (5), and

    (*b*) those parts shall be treated in accordance with that subsection as two separate accounting periods, but

    (*c*) subsection (6) shall be disregarded,

and section 768B or 768C of, and Schedule 28A to, the Taxes Act 1988 shall have effect accordingly.

(8) In this section—

    "the commencement date" shall be construed in accordance with subsection (5);

    "investment company" has the same meaning as in Part 4 of the Taxes Act 1988 (see section 130 of that Act);

    "new accounting period" means an accounting period beginning on or after the commencement date;

    "old accounting period" means an accounting period beginning before the commencement date;

    "the new section 75" means section 75 as it has effect in relation to a new accounting period;

    "the old section 75" means section 75 as it has effect (apart from subsection (5) above) in relation to an old accounting period;

    "section 75" means section 75 of the Taxes Act 1988.

Commentary—*Simon's Taxes* **D7.305, D7.301**.
HMRC Manuals—Company Taxation Manual CTM08010 (transitional rules for management expenses).

Amounts reversing expenses of management deducted

Power to make consequential amendments

46 Power to make consequential amendments

(1) The Treasury may by order make such amendments, repeals or revocations in any enactment (including an enactment amended by this Act) as appear to them to be appropriate in consequence of sections 38 to 40 and 45 and Schedule 6.

(2) The power conferred by subsection (1) to make an order includes power—

    (*a*) to make different provision for different cases, and

    (*b*) to make incidental, consequential, supplemental or transitional provision and savings.

(3) Any order made under this section on or before 31st December 2004 may make provision having effect in relation to accounting periods ending before the date on which the order is made (but not before 1st April 2004).

(4) In this section—

    "enactment" includes an enactment comprised in subordinate legislation;

    "subordinate legislation" has the same meaning as in the Interpretation Act 1978 (c 30) (see section 21 of that Act).

Insurance companies: miscellaneous

47 Insurance companies etc

Schedule 7 to this Act (which makes provision about insurance companies and companies which have ceased to be insurance companies after a transfer of business) shall have effect.

Loan relationships and derivative contracts

49 Derivative contracts: miscellaneous amendments

Schedule 9 to this Act (which makes amendments relating to derivative contracts) shall have effect.

Accounting practice

52 Amendment of enactments that operate by reference to accounting practice

(1) Schedule 10 makes amendments of provisions of the Tax Acts that operate by reference to accounting practice.

(2) In that Schedule—

Part 1 makes amendments relating to loan relationships;

Part 2 makes amendments relating to derivative contracts;

Part 3 makes amendments relating to intangible fixed assets;

Part 4 makes amendments relating to foreign currency accounting.

(3) The amendments have effect in relation to—

(a) periods of account beginning on or after 1st January 2005, . . . [1]

(b) . . . [1]

Amendments—[1] Sub-s (3)(b) and preceding word "and" repealed by FA 2005 ss 80, 104, Sch 4 para 50, Sch 11 Pt 2(7) and deemed always to have had effect.

53 Treatment of expenditure on research and development

(1) Expenditure by a company on research and development, if not of a capital nature, is not prevented from being regarded for tax purposes as deductible in computing profits by reason of the fact that for accounting purposes it is brought into account by the company in determining the value of an intangible asset.

(2) Subsection (1) applies, in particular, for the purposes of—

section 82A of the Taxes Act 1988 (deduction of expenditure on research and development),

Schedule 20 to the Finance Act 2000 (R&D tax relief),

Schedule 12 to the Finance Act 2002 (tax relief for expenditure on research and development), and

Schedule 13 to that Act (tax relief for expenditure on vaccine research etc).

(3) Where expenditure is brought into account by a company for tax purposes in accordance with subsection (1), no deduction may be made in computing for tax purposes the profits of the company in respect of the writing down of so much of the value of an intangible asset as is attributable to that expenditure.

(4) Expenditure shall not be regarded by virtue of subsection (1) as deductible in computing a company's profits for an accounting period to the extent that—

(a) a deduction has been made in respect of it in computing the company's profits for a previous accounting period, or

(b) the company has benefited from a tax relief in respect of it for a previous accounting period under any of the provisions specified in subsection (2).

(5) In this section—

"intangible asset" has the meaning it has for accounting purposes; and

"research and development" has the meaning given by section 837A of the Taxes Act 1988.

(6) This section shall come into force in accordance with provision made by the Treasury by order made by statutory instrument.

Commentary—*Simon's Taxes* **D1.401, D1.403**.

HMRC Manuals—Corporate Intangibles Research And Development Manual CIRD81450 (allowable as a deduction in computing the profit).

CIRD98400 (when R&D expenditure can be deducted).

CIRD98500 (IAS changes).

Orders—Finance Act 2004, Section 53 (Commencement) Order, SI 2004/3268 (the above section comes into force on 1 January 2005 and has effect in relation to accounting periods beginning on or after that day).

Miscellaneous

55 Duty of company to give notice of coming within charge to corporation tax

(1) A company must give notice to the Board—

(a) of the beginning of its first accounting period, and

(b) of the beginning of any subsequent accounting period that does not immediately follow the end of a previous accounting period.

(2) The notice required by this section—

(a) must be in writing;

(b) must state when the accounting period began;

(c) must contain such other information as may be prescribed;

(d) may be given to any officer of the Board; and

(e) must be given not later than three months after the beginning of the accounting period.

(3) "Prescribed" in subsection (2)(c) means prescribed by regulations made by the Board.

(4) A company that has a reasonable excuse for failing to give notice as required by this section—

(a) is not to be regarded as having failed to comply with this section until the excuse ceases, and

(b) after the excuse ceases is not to be regarded as having failed to comply with this section if the required notice is given without unreasonable delay after the excuse ceases.

(5) In this section—

(a) "accounting period" means an accounting period for the purposes of corporation tax;

(b) "company" means a body corporate and does not include an unincorporated association or a partnership; and

(c) "the Board" means the Commissioners of Inland Revenue.

(6) (*amends* TMA 1970 s 98).

(7) This section applies in relation to accounting periods beginning on or after the day on which this Act is passed.

Commentary—*Simon's Taxes* **D1.1302, D1.105, A6.202, A4.543**.

HMRC Manuals—COTAX Manual COM40030 (information a company must provide to HM Revenue & Customs).

Regulations—Corporation Tax (Notice of Coming within Charge—Information) Regulations, SI 2004/2502.

[55A Section 55: exception to duty to give notice

(1) A company is not required to give notice under section 55 of the beginning of an accounting period if it reasonably expects that—

(a) all the income on which it will be chargeable to corporation tax for the period will consist of payments on which it bears income tax by deduction, . . . [2]

(b) it will have no chargeable gains for the period[, and

(c) in consequence of the deduction of the income tax mentioned in paragraph (a) at the fourth step in paragraph 8 of Schedule 18 to the Finance Act 1998 (calculation of tax payable), the amount of tax payable for the period will be nil.][2]

(2) Subsection (3) applies if—

(a) by reason of subsection (1) a company is not required to give notice under section 55 of the beginning of an accounting period ("the unreported period"), and

(b) a subsequent accounting period immediately follows the end of the unreported period.

(3) The subsequent accounting period is to be treated for the purposes of section 55 as if it does not immediately follow the end of a previous accounting period.

(4) If by reason of subsection (1) ceasing to apply a company becomes subject to the duty to give notice under section 55 of the beginning of an accounting period the notice must be given not later than three months after the date on which it becomes subject to that duty.][1]

Amendments—[1]   Section 55A inserted by FA 2019 s 17, Sch 5 para 7 with effect from 6 April 2020, subject to transitional provisions in FA 2019 Sch 5 Pt 3 (paras 36–50).

[2]   In Sub-s (1), in para (a) word "and" repealed, and para (c) and preceding word "and" inserted, by FA 2020 s 32, Sch 6 para 7 with effect from 6 April 2020. These amendments have effect as if incorporated into FA 2019 Sch 5 and so are subject to transitional provisions in FA 2019 Sch 5 Pt 3 (paras 36–50).

CHAPTER 3

CONSTRUCTION INDUSTRY SCHEME

Introduction

57 Introduction

(1) This Chapter provides for certain payments (see section 60) under construction contracts to be made under deduction of sums on account of tax (see sections 61 and 62).

(2) In this Chapter "construction contract" means a contract relating to construction operations (see section 74) which is not a contract of employment but where—

(a) one party to the contract is a sub-contractor (see section 58); and

(b) another party to the contract ("the contractor") either—

(i) is a sub-contractor under another such contract relating to all or any of the construction operations, or

(ii) is a person to whom section 59 applies.

(3) In sections 60 and 61 "the contractor" has the meaning given by this section.

(4) In this Chapter—

(a) references to registration for gross payment are to registration under section 63(2),

(b) references to registration for payment under deduction are to registration under section 63(3), and

(c) references to registration under section 63 are to registration for gross payment or registration for payment under deduction.

(5) To the extent that any provision of this Chapter would not, apart from this subsection, form part of the Tax Acts, it shall be taken to form part of those Acts.

Commentary—*Simon's Taxes* **E5.540, E5.542**.

HMRC Manuals—Construction Industry Scheme Reform Manual CISR12020 (contractors: definition of contractor). CISR16020 (outline of the main elements of the scheme).

58 Sub-contractors

For the purposes of this Chapter a party to a contract relating to construction operations is a sub-contractor if, under the contract—

    (a) he is under a duty to the contractor to carry out the operations, or to furnish his own labour (in the case of a company, the labour of employees or officers of the company) or the labour of others in the carrying out of the operations or to arrange for the labour of others to be furnished in the carrying out of the operations; or

    (b) he is answerable to the contractor for the carrying out of the operations by others, whether under a contract or under other arrangements made or to be made by him.

Commentary—*Simon's Taxes* **E5.543**.

HMRC Manuals—Construction Industry Scheme Reform Manual CISR14020 (scope of CIS: subcontractor). CISR16030 (definition of sub-contractor).

59 Contractors

(1) This section applies to the following bodies or persons—

    (a) any person carrying on a business which includes construction operations;

    (b) any public office or department of the Crown (including any Northern Ireland department and any part of the Scottish Administration);

    (c) the Corporate Officer of the House of Lords, the Corporate Officer of the House of Commons[, the Scottish Parliamentary Corporate Body and the National Assembly for Wales Commission][3];

    (d) any local authority;

    (e) any development corporation or new town commission;

    (f) the [Homes and Communities Agency][4];

    [(fa) the Greater London Authority in the exercise of its functions relating to housing or regeneration or its new towns and urban development functions;][8];

    (g) the Secretary of State if the contract is made by him under section 89 of the Housing Associations Act 1985 (c 69);

    (h) the [Regulator of Social Housing][7], a housing association, a housing trust, Scottish Homes, and the Northern Ireland Housing Executive;

    (i) any NHS trust;

    (j) any HSS trust;

    (k) any such body or person, being a body or person (in addition to those falling within paragraphs (b) to (j)) which has been established for the purpose of carrying out functions conferred on it by or under any enactment, as may be designated as a body or person to which this section applies in regulations made by the Board of Inland Revenue;

    (l) a person carrying on a business at any time if—

        (i) his average annual expenditure on construction operations in the period of three years ending with the end of the last period of account before that time exceeds £1,000,000, or

        (ii) where he was not carrying on the business at the beginning of that period of three years, one-third of his total expenditure on construction operations for the part of that period during which he has been carrying on the business exceeds £1,000,000.

(2) But this section only applies to a body or person falling within subsection (1)(b) to [(fa)][8] or (h) to (k) if—

    (a) in any period of three years, that body or person has had an average annual expenditure on construction operations of more than £1,000,000, and

    (b) since the condition in paragraph (a) was last satisfied, there have not been three successive years in each of which the body or person has had expenditure on construction operations of less than £1,000,000.

In this subsection "year" means a year ending with 31st March.

(3) Where section 57(2)(b) begins to apply to a person in any period of account by virtue of his falling within subsection (1)(l), it shall continue to apply to him until he satisfies the Board of Inland Revenue that his expenditure on construction operations has been less than £1,000,000 in each of three successive years beginning in or after that period of account.

(4) Where the whole or part of a trade is transferred by a company ("the transferor") to another company ("the transferee") and [Chapter 1 of Part 22 of the Corporation Tax Act 2010][6] has effect in relation to the transfer, then in determining for the purposes of this section the amount of expenditure incurred by the transferee—

(a) the whole or, as the case may be, a proportionate part of any expenditure incurred by the transferor at a time before the transfer is to be treated as if it had been incurred at that time by the transferee; and

(b) where only a part of the trade is transferred, the expenditure is to be apportioned in such manner as appears to the Board of Inland Revenue, or on appeal to the [tribunal][5], to be just and reasonable.

(5) In this section—

"development corporation" has the same meaning as in—

(a) the New Towns Act 1981 (c 64), or

(b) the New Towns (Scotland) Act 1968 (c 16);

"enactment" includes an enactment comprised in an Act of the Scottish Parliament and a provision comprised in Northern Ireland legislation;

"housing association" has the same meaning as in—

(a) the Housing Associations Act 1985 (c 69), or

(b) Part 2 of the Housing (Northern Ireland) Order 1992 (SI 1992/1725 (NI 15));

"housing trust" has the same meaning as in the Housing Associations Act 1985;

"HSS trust" means a Health and Social Services trust established under the Health and Personal Social Services (Northern Ireland) Order 1991 (SI 1991/194 (NI 1));

"new town commission" has the same meaning as in the New Towns Act (Northern Ireland) 1965 (c 13 (NI));

"NHS trust" means a National Health Service trust—

(a) established under [section 25 of the National Health Service Act 2006 or section 18 of the National Health Service (Wales) Act 2006][2], or

(b) constituted under section 12A of the National Health Service (Scotland) Act 1978 (c 29).

(6) In this section references to a body or person include references to an office or department.

(7) The Board of Inland Revenue may make regulations amending this section for the purpose of removing references to bodies which have ceased to exist.

[(8) This section is subject to section 73A (designated international organisations: exemption from section 59).][1]

Commentary—*Simon's Taxes* **E5.542.**

HMRC Manuals—Construction Industry Scheme Reform Manual CISR12020 (contractors: definition of contractor). CISR16040 (definition of contractor).

Amendments—[1]   Sub-s (8) inserted by ITA 2007 s 1027, Sch 1 paras 456, 459 with effect for income tax purposes from 6 April 2007, and corporation tax purposes for accounting periods ending after 5 April 2007.

[2]   In sub-s (5) in definition "NHS trust" words substituted by the National Health Service (Consequential Provisions) Act 2006 s 2, Sch 1 paras 255, 256 with effect from 1 March 2007.

[3]   In sub-s (1)(c) words substituted by the Government of Wales Act 2006 (Consequential Modifications and Transitional Provisions) Order, SI 2007/1388 art 3, Sch 1 paras 106, 107(b)) with effect from 25 May 2007, being the date on which the initial period ended (following the appointment of the First Minister) (SI 2007/1388, art 1(2) and the Government of Wales Act 2006, ss 46, 161(5)).

[4]   In sub-s (1)(f), words substituted for words "Commission for the New Towns", by the Housing and Regeneration Act 2008 s 56, Sch 8 para 82 with effect from 1 December 2008 (by virtue of SI 2008/3068 arts 1(2), 2(1)(w), (3)).

[5]   In sub-s (4)(b) word substituted for the word "Commissioners" by the Transfer of Tribunal Functions and Revenue and Customs Appeals Order, SI 2009/56 art 3, Sch 1 para 420 with effect from 1 April 2009.

[6]   In sub-s (4) words "section 343 of the Taxes Act 1988" substituted by CTA 2010 s 1177, Sch 1 paras 423, 426. CTA 2010 has effect for corporation tax purposes for accounting periods ending on or after 1 April 2010, and for income and capital gains tax purposes for the tax year 2010–11 and subsequent tax years.

[7]   In sub-s (1)(h), words substituted for words "Housing Corporation", by the Housing and Regeneration Act 2008 s 227, Sch 9 para 33 with effect from 1 April 2010 (see SI 2010/862 art 2).

[8]   Sub-s (1)(fa) inserted, and in sub-s (2), reference substituted by the Localism Act 2011 s 195, Sch 19 para 42 with effect from 1 April 2012 by virtue of SI 2012/628 art 6(i).

Prospective amendments—In sub-s (5), in para (a) of the definition of "NHS Trust", words "section 25 of the National Health Service Act 2006 or" to be repealed by the Health and Social Care Act 2012 s 179, Sch 14 para 95 with effect from a date to be appointed.

Deductions on account of tax from contract payments to sub-contractors

60 Contract payments

(1) In this Chapter "contract payment" means any payment which is made under a construction contract and is so made by the contractor (see section 57(3)) to—

(a) the sub-contractor,

(b) a person nominated by the sub-contractor or the contractor, or

(c) a person nominated by a person who is a sub-contractor under another such contract relating to all or any of the construction operations.

(2) But a payment made under a construction contract is not a contract payment if any of the following exceptions applies in relation to it.

(3) This exception applies if the payment is treated as earnings from an employment by virtue of Chapter 7 of Part 2 of the Income Tax (Earnings and Pensions) Act 2003 (c 1) (agency workers).

(4) This exception applies if the person to whom the payment is made or, in the case of a payment made to a nominee, each of the following persons—

    (*a*) the nominee,

    (*b*) the person who nominated him, and

    (*c*) the person for whose labour (or, where that person is a company, for whose employees' or officers' labour) the payment is made,

is registered for gross payment when the payment is made. But this is subject to subsections (5) and (6).

(5) Where a person is registered for gross payment as a partner in a firm (see section 64), subsection (4) applies only in relation to payments made under contracts under which—

    (*a*) the firm is a sub-contractor, or

    (*b*) where a person has nominated the firm to receive payments, the person who has nominated the firm is a sub-contractor.

(6) Where a person is registered for gross payment otherwise than as a partner in a firm but he is or becomes a partner in a firm, subsection (4) does not apply in relation to payments made under contracts under which—

    (*a*) the firm is a sub-contractor, or

    (*b*) where a person has nominated the firm to receive payments, the person who has nominated the firm is a sub-contractor.

(7) This exception applies if such conditions as may be prescribed in regulations made by the Board of Inland Revenue for the purposes of this subsection are satisfied; and those conditions may relate to any one or more of the following—

    (*a*) the payment,

    (*b*) the person making it, and

    (*c*) the person receiving it.

(8) For the purposes of this Chapter a payment (including a payment by way of loan) that has the effect of discharging an obligation under a contract relating to construction operations is to be taken to be made under the contract; and if—

    (*a*) the obligation is to make a payment to a person ("A") within paragraph (*a*) to (*c*) of subsection (1), but

    (*b*) the payment discharging that obligation is made to a person ("B") not within those paragraphs,

the payment is for those purposes to be taken to be made to A.

Commentary—*Simon's Taxes* E5.545, E5.545A.

HMRC Manuals—Construction Industry Scheme Reform Manual CISR16050 (definition of contract payment).

Prospective amendments—Sub-ss (3A)–(3C) to be inserted by FA 2020 s 7, Sch 1 para 20 with effect in relation to payments made under a construction contract on or after 6 April 2021 (subject to transitional provisions in FA 2020 Sch 1 paras 30–34). Sub-ss (3A)–(3C) to read as follows—

"(3A) This exception applies in so far as—

    (*a*) the payment can reasonably be taken to be for the services of an individual, and

    (*b*) the provision of those services gives rise to an engagement to which Chapter 10 of Part 2 of ITEPA 2003 applies (workers' services provided through intermediaries to public authorities or medium or large clients).

    (3B) But the exception in subsection (3A) does not apply if, in the case of the engagement mentioned in paragraph (*b*) of that subsection, the client for the purposes of section 61M(1) of ITEPA 2003—

    (*a*) is not a public authority, and

    (*b*) either—

        (i) does not qualify as medium or large for the tax year in which the payment concerned is made, or

        (ii) does not have a UK connection for the tax year in which the payment concerned is made.

    (3C) Sections 60I (when a person has a UK connection for a tax year), 61K(3) (when a person qualifies as medium or large for a tax year) and 61L (meaning of public authority) of ITEPA 2003 apply for the purposes of subsection (3B).".

61 Deductions on account of tax from contract payments

(1) On making a contract payment the contractor (see section 57(3)) must deduct from it a sum equal to the relevant percentage of so much of the payment as is not shown to represent the direct cost to any other person of materials used or to be used in carrying out the construction operations to which the contract under which the payment is to be made relates.

(2) In subsection (1) "the relevant percentage" means such percentage as the Treasury may by order determine.

(3) That percentage must not exceed—

    (*a*) if the person for whose labour (or for whose employees' or officers' labour) the payment in question is made is registered for payment under deduction, the percentage which is the basic rate for the year of assessment in which the payment is made, or

(b) if that person is not so registered, the percentage which is the higher rate for that year of assessment.

Commentary—*Simon's Taxes* **E5.546**.

HMRC Manuals—Construction Industry Scheme Reform Manual CISR16060 (deductions to be made from contract payments).

Regulations—FA 2004, s 61(2), (Relevant Percentage) Order, SI 2007/46 (the relevant percentage is 20% if the person is registered for payment under deduction, or 30% if they are not registered).

62 Treatment of sums deducted

(1) A sum deducted under section 61 from a payment made by a contractor—

    (a) must be paid to the Board of Inland Revenue, and

    (b) is to be treated for the purposes of income tax or, as the case may be, corporation tax as not diminishing the amount of the payment.

(2) If the sub-contractor is not a company a sum deducted under section 61 and paid to the Board is to be treated as being income tax paid in respect of the sub-contractor's relevant profits.

If the sum is more than sufficient to discharge his liability to income tax in respect of those profits, so much of the excess as is required to discharge any liability of his for Class 4 contributions is to be treated as being Class 4 contributions paid in respect of those profits.

(3) If the sub-contractor is a company—

    (a) a sum deducted under section 61 and paid to the Board is to be treated, in accordance with regulations, as paid on account of any relevant liabilities of the sub-contractor;

    (b) regulations must provide for the sum to be applied in discharging relevant liabilities of the year of assessment in which the deduction is made;

    (c) if the amount is more than sufficient to discharge the sub-contractor's relevant liabilities, the excess may be treated, in accordance with the regulations, as being corporation tax paid in respect of the sub-contractor's relevant profits; and

    (d) regulations must provide for the repayment to the sub-contractor of any amount not required for the purposes mentioned in paragraphs (b) and (c).

(4) For the purposes of subsection (3) the "relevant liabilities" of a sub-contractor are any liabilities of the sub-contractor, whether arising before or after the deduction is made, to make a payment to the Inland Revenue in pursuance of an obligation as an employer or contractor.

(5) In this section—

    (a) "the sub-contractor" means the person for whose labour (or for whose employees' or officers' labour) the payment is made;

    (b) references to the sub-contractor's "relevant profits" are to the profits from the trade, profession or vocation carried on by him in the course of which the payment was received;

    (c) "Class 4 contributions" means Class 4 contributions within the meaning of the Social Security Contributions and Benefits Act 1992 (c 4) or the Social Security Contributions and Benefits (Northern Ireland) Act 1992 (c 7).

(6) References in this section to regulations are to regulations made by the Board of Inland Revenue.

(7) Regulations under this section may contain such supplementary, incidental or consequential provision as appears to the Board to be appropriate.

Commentary—*Simon's Taxes* **E5.547**.

HMRC Manuals—Construction Industry Scheme Reform Manual CISR16070 (treatment of deductions made from contract payments).

Regulations—Income Tax (Construction Industry Scheme) (Amendment) Regulations, SI 2012/820.

Income Tax (Construction Industry Scheme) (Amendment) Regulations, SI 2013/620.

Income Tax (Construction Industry Scheme) (Amendment) Regulations, SI 2015/429.

Statutory Parental Bereavement Pay (Miscellaneous Amendments) Regulations, SI 2020/240.

Registration of sub-contractors

63 Registration for gross payment or for payment under deduction

(1) If the Board of Inland Revenue are satisfied, on the application of an individual or a company, that the applicant has provided—

    (a) such documents, records and information as may be required by or in accordance with regulations made by the Board, and

    (b) such additional documents, records and information as may be required by the Inland Revenue in connection with the application,

the Board must register the individual or company under this section.

(2) If the Board are satisfied that the requirements of subsection (2), (3) or (4) of section 64 are met, the Board must register—

    (a) the individual or company, or

    (b) in a case falling within subsection (3) of that section, the individual or company as a partner in the firm in question,

for gross payment.

(3) In any other case, the Board must register the individual or company for payment under deduction.

Commentary—*Simon's Taxes* **E5.550**.

HMRC Manuals—Construction Industry Scheme Reform Manual CISR16080 (registration process).

64 Requirements for registration for gross payment

(1) This section sets out the requirements (in addition to that in subsection (1) of section 63) for an applicant to be registered for gross payment.

(2) Where the application is for the registration for gross payment of an individual (otherwise than as a partner in a firm), he must satisfy the conditions in Part 1 of Schedule 11 to this Act.

(3) Where the application is for the registration for gross payment of an individual or a company as a partner in a firm—

    (a) the applicant must satisfy the conditions in Part 1 of Schedule 11 to this Act (if an individual) or Part 3 of that Schedule (if a company), and

    (b) in either case, the firm itself must satisfy the conditions in Part 2 of that Schedule.

(4) Where the application is for the registration for gross payment of a company (otherwise than as a partner in a firm)—

    (a) the company must satisfy the conditions in Part 3 of Schedule 11 to this Act, and

    (b) if the Board of Inland Revenue have given a direction under subsection (5), each of the persons to whom any of the conditions in Part 1 of that Schedule applies in accordance with the direction must satisfy the conditions which so apply to him.

(5) Where the applicant is a company, the Board may direct that the conditions in Part 1 of Schedule 11 to this Act or such of them as are specified in the direction shall apply to—

    (a) the directors of the company,

    (b) if the company is a close company, the persons who are the beneficial owners of shares in the company, or

    (c) such of those directors or persons as are so specified,

as if each of them were an applicant for registration for gross payment.

(6) See also section 65(1) (power of Board to make direction under subsection (5) on change in control of company applying for registration etc).

(7) In subsection (5) "director" has the meaning given by section 67 of the Income Tax (Earnings and Pensions) Act 2003 (c 1).

Commentary—*Simon's Taxes* E5.551.
HMRC Manuals—Construction Industry Scheme Reform Manual CISR16090 (gross payment registration requirements). CISR46050 (shadow directors).
CISR46110 (making a S64(5) direction).

65 Change in control of company registered for gross payment

(1) Where it appears to the Board of Inland Revenue that there has been a change in the control of a company—

    (a) registered for gross payment, or

    (b) applying to be so registered,

the Board may make a direction under section 64(5).

(2) The Board may make regulations requiring the furnishing of information with respect to changes in the control of a company—

    (a) registered for gross payment, or

    (b) applying to be so registered.

[(3) In this section references to a change in the control of a company are references to such a change determined in accordance with section 995 of the Income Tax Act 2007.][1]

Commentary—*Simon's Taxes* E5.551.
HMRC Manuals—Construction Industry Scheme Reform Manual CISR16100 (board's powers where the control of a company changes).
Amendments—[1]   Sub-s (3) substituted by ITA 2007 s 1027, Sch 1 paras 456, 460 with effect for income tax purposes from 6 April 2007, and corporation tax purposes for accounting periods ending after 5 April 2007.

66 Cancellation of registration for gross payment

(1) The Board of Inland Revenue may at any time make a determination cancelling a person's registration for gross payment if it appears to them that—

    (a) if an application to register the person for gross payment were to be made at that time, the Board would refuse so to register him,

    (b) he has made an incorrect return or provided incorrect information (whether as a contractor or as a sub-contractor) under any provision of this Chapter or of regulations made under it, or

    (c) he has failed to comply (whether as a contractor or as a sub-contractor) with any such provision.

(2) Where the Board make a determination under subsection (1), the person's registration for gross payment is cancelled with effect from the end of a prescribed period after the making of the determination (but see section 67(5)).

(3) The Board of Inland Revenue may at any time make a determination cancelling a person's registration for gross payment if they have reasonable grounds to suspect that the person—

    (a) became registered for gross payment on the basis of information which was false,

(b) has fraudulently made an incorrect return or provided incorrect information (whether as a contractor or as a sub-contractor) under any provision of this Chapter or of regulations made under it, or

(c) has knowingly failed to comply (whether as a contractor or as a sub-contractor) with any such provision.

(4) Where the Board make a determination under subsection (3), the person's registration for gross payment is cancelled with immediate effect.

(5) On making a determination under this section cancelling a person's registration for gross payment, the Board must without delay give the person notice stating the reasons for the cancellation.

(6) Where a person's registration for gross payment is cancelled by virtue of a determination under subsection (1), the person must be registered for payment under deduction.

(7) Where a person's registration for gross payment is cancelled by virtue of a determination under subsection (3), the person may, if the Board thinks fit, be registered for payment under deduction.

(8) A person whose registration for gross payment is cancelled under this section may not, within the period of one year after the cancellation takes effect (see subsections (2) and (4) and section 67(5)), apply for registration for gross payment.

(9) In this section "a prescribed period" means a period prescribed by regulations made by the Board.

Commentary—*Simon's Taxes* **E5.552**.

HMRC Manuals—Construction Industry Scheme Reform Manual CISR16110 (circumstances in which registration may be cancelled).

67 Registration for gross payment: appeals

(1) A person aggrieved by—

(a) the refusal of an application for registration for gross payment, or

(b) the cancellation of his registration for gross payment,

may by notice appeal . . . [1].

(2) The notice must be given to the Board of Inland Revenue within 30 days after the refusal or cancellation.

(3) The notice must state the person's reasons for believing that—

(a) the application should not have been refused, or

(b) his registration for gross payment should not have been cancelled.

(4) The jurisdiction of the [tribunal][1] on such an appeal [that is notified to the tribunal][1] shall include jurisdiction to review any relevant decision taken by the Board of Inland Revenue in the exercise of their functions under section 63, 64, 65 or 66.

(5) Where a person appeals against the cancellation of his registration for gross payment by virtue of a determination under section 66(1), the cancellation of his registration does not take effect until whichever is the latest of the following—

(a) the abandonment of the appeal,

(b) the determination of the appeal by the [tribunal][1], or

(c) the determination of the appeal by the [Upper Tribunal or a court][1].

(6) . . . [1]

Commentary—*Simon's Taxes* **E5.553**.

HMRC Manuals—Construction Industry Scheme Reform Manual CISR16120 (appeals process where registration has been cancelled).

Amendments—[1] In sub-s (1) words repealed; in sub-s (4) word substituted and words inserted; in sub-ss (5)(b), (c) words substituted; sub-s (6) repealed by the Transfer of Tribunal Functions and Revenue and Customs Appeals Order, SI 2009/56 art 3, Sch 1 para 421 with effect from 1 April 2009.

68 Registration for payment under deduction: cancellation and appeals

The Board of Inland Revenue may make regulations providing for—

(a) the cancellation, in such circumstances as may be prescribed by the regulations, of a person's registration for payment under deduction;

(b) appeals against a refusal to register a person for payment under deduction or the cancellation of such registration.

Commentary—*Simon's Taxes* **E5.554**.

HMRC Manuals—Construction Industry Scheme Reform Manual CISR16130 (powers of the board to make regulations).

Verification, returns [, security][1] etc and penalties

69 Verification etc of registration status of sub-contractors

(1) The Board of Inland Revenue may make regulations requiring persons who make payments under contracts relating to construction operations, except in prescribed circumstances, to verify with the Board whether a person to whom they are proposing to make—

(a) a contract payment, or

(b) a payment which would be a contract payment but for section 60(4), is registered for gross payment or for payment under deduction.

(2) The provision that may be made by regulations under subsection (1) includes provision—

(*a*) for preventing a person from verifying unless such conditions as may be prescribed have been satisfied;

(*b*) as to the period for which the verification remains valid.

(3) The Board of Inland Revenue may make regulations requiring the Board to notify persons of a prescribed description who make payments under contracts relating to construction operations that—

(*a*) a person registered for gross payment has become registered for payment under deduction or has ceased to be registered under section 63, or

(*b*) a person registered for payment under deduction has become registered for gross payment or has ceased to be registered under section 63.

(4) The provision that may be made by regulations under subsection (1) or (3) includes provision for a person to be entitled to assume, except in prescribed circumstances, that—

(*a*) a person verified or notified as being registered for gross payment, or

(*b*) a person verified or notified as being registered for payment under deduction,

has not subsequently ceased to be so registered.

(5) In this section "prescribed" means prescribed by regulations under this section.

Regulations—Income Tax (Construction Industry Scheme) (Amendment) Regulations, SI 2016/348.
Amendments—[1]   In heading word inserted by FA 2019 s 82(1)(*a*) with effect from 12 February 2019.

70 Periodic returns by contractors etc

(1) The Board of Inland Revenue may make regulations requiring persons who make payments under construction contracts—

(*a*) to make to the Board, at such times and in respect of such periods as may be prescribed, returns relating to such payments;

(*b*) to keep such records as may be prescribed relating to such payments;

(*c*) to provide such information as may be prescribed, at such times as may be prescribed, to persons to whom such payments are made or to such of those persons as are of a prescribed description.

(2) The provision that may be made by regulations under subsection (1)(*a*) includes provision requiring, except in such circumstances as may be prescribed,—

(*a*) the person making a return to declare in the return that none of the contracts to which the return relates is a contract of employment;

(*b*) the person making a return to declare in the return that, in the case of each person to whom a payment to which the return relates is made, he has complied with the requirements of any regulations made under section 69(1) (verification of registration status);

(*c*) returns to contain such other information and to be in such form as may be prescribed;

(*d*) a return to be made where no payments have been made in the period to which the return relates.

(3) The Board of Inland Revenue may make regulations with respect to—

(*a*) the production, copying and removal of, and the making of extracts from, any records kept by virtue of any such requirement as is referred to in subsection (1)(*b*), and

(*b*) rights of access to, or copies of, any such records which are removed.

(4) Regulations under this section may make provision—

(*a*) for or in connection with enabling a person who makes payments under construction contracts to appoint another person (a "scheme representative") to act on his behalf in connection with any requirements imposed on him by regulations under this section, and

(*b*) as to the rights, obligations or liabilities of scheme representatives.

(5) In this section "prescribed" means prescribed by regulations under this section.

Commentary—*Simon's Taxes* E5.561.
HMRC Manuals—Construction Industry Scheme Reform Manual CISR16150 (periodic returns of payments).
Regulations—Income Tax (Construction Industry Scheme) (Amendment) Regulations, SI 2015/429.
Income Tax (Construction Industry Scheme) (Amendment) Regulations, SI 2016/348.

[70A Security for payments to HMRC

(1) The Commissioners for Her Majesty's Revenue and Customs may by regulations make provision for and in connection with requiring the giving, by prescribed persons and in prescribed circumstances, of security for the payment of amounts that a person is or may be liable to pay to the Commissioners under this Chapter.

(2) Regulations under this section must provide that security may be required only where an officer of Revenue and Customs considers it necessary for the protection of the revenue.

(3) Regulations under this section must provide for a right of appeal against—

(*a*) decisions to require security to be given;

(*b*) decisions as to the amount, terms or duration of any security required.

(4) A person commits an offence if—

(*a*) the person fails to comply with a requirement to give security that is imposed by regulations under this section, and

(*b*) the failure continues for such period as is prescribed.

(5) A person who commits an offence under subsection (4) is liable on summary conviction—

    (*a*)   in England and Wales, to a fine;

    (*b*)   in Scotland or Northern Ireland, to a fine not exceeding level 5 on the standard scale.

(6) In this section—

    "prescribed" means prescribed in regulations under this section;

    "security" includes further security.][1]

Regulations—Income Tax (Construction Industry Scheme) (Amendment) and the Corporation Tax (Security for Payments) Regulations, SI 2019/384.

Amendments—[1]   Section 70A inserted by FA 2019 s 82(1)(*b*) with effect from 12 February 2019.

71 Collection and recovery of sums to be deducted

(1) The Board of Inland Revenue must make regulations with respect to the collection and recovery, whether by assessment or otherwise, of sums required to be deducted from any payments under section 61.

(2) The regulations may include any matters with respect to which PAYE regulations may be made.

(3) Interest required to be paid by the regulations—

    (*a*)   is to be paid without any deduction of income tax . . . .

    (*b*)   . . . .[1],[2]

Commentary—*Simon's Taxes* **E5.547C**.

HMRC Manuals—Construction Industry Scheme Reform Manual CISR16160 (collection and recovery of deductions).

Regulations—Income Tax (Construction Industry Scheme) (Amendment) Regulations, SI 2012/820.

Statutory Parental Bereavement Pay (Miscellaneous Amendments) Regulations, SI 2020/240.

Amendments—[1]   Words in sub-s (3)(*b*) substituted by ITTOIA 2005 s 882(1), Sch 1 paras 629, 630 with effect from 6 April 2005. ITTOIA 2005 has effect—

    (a)   for income tax purposes, for 2005–06 and subsequent tax years, and

    (b)   for corporation tax purposes, for accounting periods ending after 5 April 2005: ITTOIA 2005 s 883(1).

[2]   Sub-s (3)(*b*) and preceding word "and" repealed by CTA 2009 ss 1322, 1326, Sch 1 paras 569, 570, Sch 3 Part 1. CTA 2009 applies for accounting periods ending on or after 1 April 2009 (for corporation tax purposes) and for tax years 2009–10 onwards (for income and capital gains tax purposes).

72 Penalties

If a person, for the purpose of becoming registered for gross payment or for payment under deduction,—

    (*a*)   makes any statement, or furnishes any document, which he knows to be false in a material particular, or

    (*b*)   recklessly makes any statement, or furnishes any document, which is false in a material particular,

he shall be liable to a penalty not exceeding £3,000.

Supplementary

73 Regulations under this Chapter: supplementary

(1) The Board of Inland Revenue may by regulations make such other provision for giving effect to this Chapter as they consider necessary or expedient.

(2) The provision that may be made by regulations under subsection (1) includes provision for or in connection with modifying the application of this Chapter in circumstances where—

    (*a*)   a person acts as the agent of a contractor or sub-contractor;

    (*b*)   a person's right to payments under a construction contract is assigned or otherwise transferred to another person.

(3) Regulations under this Chapter may make different provision for different cases.

(4) Any power under this Chapter to make regulations authorising or requiring a document (whether or not of a particular description), or any records or information, to be given or requested by or to be sent or produced to the Board of Inland Revenue includes power—

    (*a*)   to authorise the Board to nominate a person who is not an officer of the Board to be the person who on behalf of the Board—

        (i)   gives or requests the document, records or information; or

        (ii)   is the recipient of the document, records or information; and

    (*b*)   to require the document, records or information, in cases prescribed by or determined under the regulations, to be sent or produced to the address (determined in accordance with the regulations) of the person nominated by the Board to receive it on their behalf.

Commentary—*Simon's Taxes* **E5.540**.

HMRC Manuals—Construction Industry Scheme Reform Manual CISR16180 (board's supplementary powers to make regulations in connection with documents and records).

Regulations—Income Tax (Construction Industry Scheme) (Amendment) Regulations, SI 2012/820.

Income Tax (Pay As You Earn) and the Income Tax (Construction Industry Scheme) (Amendment) Regulations, SI 2014/472.

Income Tax (Construction Industry Scheme) (Amendment) Regulations, SI 2016/348.

[73A Designated international organisations: exemption from section 59

(1) The Treasury may by order designate for the purposes of this section any international organisation of which the United Kingdom is a member.

(2) Section 59 does not apply to an organisation which is so designated.][1]

Commentary—*Simon's Taxes* **D1.240**.
Amendments—[1]   This section inserted by ITA 2007 s 1027, Sch 1 paras 456, 461 with effect for income tax purposes from
6 April 2007, and corporation tax purposes for accounting periods ending after 5 April 2007.

74 Meaning of "construction operations"

(1) In this Chapter "construction operations" means operations of a description specified in subsection (2), not being operations of a description specified in subsection (3); and references to construction operations—

    (a) except where the context otherwise requires, include references to the work of individuals participating in the carrying out of such operations; and

    (b) do not include references to operations carried out or to be carried out otherwise than in the United Kingdom (or the territorial sea of the United Kingdom).

(2) The following operations are, subject to subsection (3), construction operations for the purposes of this Chapter—

    (a) construction, alteration, repair, extension, demolition or dismantling of buildings or structures (whether permanent or not), including offshore installations;

    (b) construction, alteration, repair, extension or demolition of any works forming, or to form, part of the land, including (in particular) walls, roadworks, power-lines, electronic communications apparatus, aircraft runways, docks and harbours, railways, inland waterways, pipe-lines, reservoirs, water-mains, wells, sewers, industrial plant and installations for purposes of land drainage, coast protection or defence;

    (c) installation in any building or structure of systems of heating, lighting, air-conditioning, ventilation, power supply, drainage, sanitation, water supply or fire protection;

    (d) internal cleaning of buildings and structures, so far as carried out in the course of their construction, alteration, repair, extension or restoration;

    (e) painting or decorating the internal or external surfaces of any building or structure;

    (f) operations which form an integral part of, or are preparatory to, or are for rendering complete, such operations as are previously described in this subsection, including site clearance, earth-moving, excavation, tunnelling and boring, laying of foundations, erection of scaffolding, site restoration, landscaping and the provision of roadways and other access works.

(3) The following operations are not construction operations for the purposes of this Chapter—

    (a) drilling for, or extraction of, oil or natural gas;

    (b) extraction (whether by underground or surface working) of minerals and tunnelling or boring, or construction of underground works, for this purpose;

    (c) manufacture of building or engineering components or equipment, materials, plant or machinery, or delivery of any of these things to site;

    (d) manufacture of components for systems of heating, lighting, air-conditioning, ventilation, power supply, drainage, sanitation, water supply or fire protection, or delivery of any of these things to site;

    (e) the professional work of architects or surveyors, or of consultants in building, engineering, interior or exterior decoration or in the laying-out of landscape;

    (f) the making, installation and repair of artistic works, being sculptures, murals and other works which are wholly artistic in nature;

    (g) signwriting and erecting, installing and repairing signboards and advertisements;

    (h) the installation of seating, blinds and shutters;

    (i) the installation of security systems, including burglar alarms, closed circuit television and public address systems.

(4) The Treasury may by order made by statutory instrument amend either or both of subsections (2) and (3) by—

    (a) adding,

    (b) varying, or

    (c) removing,

any description of operations.

(5) No statutory instrument containing an order under subsection (4) shall be made unless a draft of the instrument has been laid before and approved by a resolution of the House of Commons.

Commentary—*Simon's Taxes* **E5.541**.
HMRC Manuals—Construction Industry Scheme Reform Manual CISR16190 (what is and what is not a construction operation).

75 Meaning of "the Inland Revenue" etc and delegation of Board's functions

(1) In this Chapter "the Inland Revenue" means any officer of the Board of Inland Revenue.

(2) In this Chapter "the Board of Inland Revenue" means the Commissioners of Inland Revenue (as to which, see in particular the Inland Revenue Regulation Act 1890 (c 21)).

(3) The Board of Inland Revenue may make regulations providing for any of the following to be done on behalf of the Board—

    (a) the registration of persons under section 63;

    (b) the giving of directions under section 64(5); and

    (c) the cancellation under section 66 of a person's registration for gross payment.

Regulations—Income Tax (Construction Industry Scheme) (Amendment) Regulations, SI 2012/820.
Income Tax (Construction Industry Scheme) (Amendment) Regulations, SI 2013/620.

76 Consequential amendments

Schedule 12 to this Act (which makes consequential amendments) has effect.

77 Commencement and transitional provision

(1) This Chapter has effect in relation to payments made on or after the appointed day under contracts relating to construction operations.

(2) Where a certificate issued to a person under section 561 of the Taxes Act 1988 is in force immediately before the appointed day, the person is to be treated as if, on the appointed day, the Board of Inland Revenue had registered him for gross payment.

(3) Where a registration card issued to a person in accordance with regulations made under section 566(2A) of the Taxes Act 1988 is in force immediately before the appointed day, the person is to be treated as if, on the appointed day, the Board of Inland Revenue had registered him for payment under deduction.

(4) Subsection (5) applies in relation to the first payment ("the relevant payment") made after the appointed day by a person ("C") to a sub-contractor ("SC") under a contract relating to construction operations if—

    (*a*) before the appointed day, C had made one or more payments to SC under the contract or another such contract,

    (*b*) the last of those payments ("the last payment") was made in the year of assessment in which the relevant payment was made or in either of the two years of assessment before that,

    (*c*) at the time of the last payment—

        (i) a certificate issued to SC under section 561 of the Taxes Act 1988 was in force, or

        (ii) a registration card issued to SC in accordance with regulations made under section 566(2A) of that Act was in force, and

    (*d*) on making the relevant payment, C has no reason to believe that SC—

        (i) did not become registered for gross payment or (as the case may be) for payment under deduction by virtue of subsection (2) or (3), and

        (ii) is not still so registered.

(5) Where this subsection applies, regulations under section 69(1) shall not require C, before making the relevant payment, to verify whether SC is registered for gross payment or for payment under deduction.

(6) Where subsection (5) applies, C shall be entitled to assume, on making any further payments to SC under a contract relating to construction operations, that SC has not subsequently ceased to be so registered, unless notified to the contrary in accordance with regulations made under section 69(3).

(7) In this section "the appointed day" means such day as the Treasury may by order appoint.

(8) The Treasury may by order make such further supplemental and transitional provision and savings as they think fit in connection with the coming into effect of this Chapter.

Commentary—*Simon's Taxes* **E5.540**.

HMRC Manuals—Construction Industry Scheme Reform Manual CISR16220 (commencement of the new scheme and certain transitional arrangements).

Orders—Finance Act 2004, Section 77(1) and (7), (Appointed Day) Order, SI 2006/3240 (the appointed day for the purposes of s 77(1) is 6 April 2007).

CHAPTER 4

PERSONAL TAXATION

Taxable benefits

78 Childcare and childcare vouchers

(1) Schedule 13 to this Act contains amendments of the Income Tax (Earnings and Pensions) Act 2003 (c 1) relating to childcare and childcare vouchers.

(2) The amendments have effect for the year 2005–06 and subsequent years of assessment.

80 Vans

(1) Schedule 14 to this Act contains amendments of the Income Tax (Earnings and Pensions) Act 2003 relating to vans.

(2) The amendments have effect for the year 2005–06 and subsequent years of assessment.

Commentary—*Simon's Taxes* **E4.630**.

81 Emergency vehicles

(1) (*inserts* ITEPA 2003 s 248A)

(2) (*amends* ITEPA s 236(2)(*c*))

(3) This section has effect for the year 2004–05 and subsequent years of assessment.

Commentary—*Simon's Taxes* **E4.723A**.

HMRC Manuals—Employment Income Manual EIM23605 (emergency vehicles exemption from 2004/05: conditions 4-5).

82 European travel expenses of MPs and other representatives

(1) The Income Tax (Earnings and Pensions) Act 2003 (c 1) is amended as follows.

(2)–(4) (*amend* ITEPA 2003 s 294)

(5) This section has effect in relation to sums paid in respect of costs or expenses incurred on or after 6th April 2004.

Gifts with a reservation

84 Charge to income tax by reference to enjoyment of property previously owned

(1) Schedule 15 (which contains provisions imposing a charge to income tax by reference to benefits received in certain circumstances by a former owner of property) has effect.

(2) That Schedule has effect for the year 2005–06 and subsequent years of assessment.

Commentary—*Simon's Taxes* I3.401.

Employment-related securities and options

85 Relief where national insurance contributions met by employee

(1) Schedule 16 to this Act provides—

    (a) for income tax relief in certain cases where national insurance contributions are met by an employee, and

    (b) for consequential amendments.

(2) This section (and that Schedule) come into force in accordance with provision made by the Treasury by order made by statutory instrument.

Commentary—*Simon's Taxes* E4.508F.

Orders—Finance Act 2004, Section 85 (Commencement) Order, SI 2004/1945 (the commencement date is 1 September 2004).

86 Shares in employee-controlled companies and unconnected companies

(1) Each of the provisions of Part 7 of the Income Tax (Earnings and Pensions) Act 2003 (c 1) (employment income: securities) specified in subsection (2) (exception from charges for certain company shares) is amended in accordance with subsections (3) to (5).

(2) The provisions are—

    (a) section 429 (restricted securities),

    (b) section 443 (convertible securities),

    (c) section 446R (securities acquired for less than market value), and

    (d) section 449 (post-acquisition benefits from securities).

(3)–(5) (*amend* ITEPA 2003 ss 429, 443, 446R, 449; sub-s (4) *repealed by* F(No 2)A 2005 s 70, Sch 11 Pt 2(1))

(6), (7) (*insert* ITEPA 2003 ss 446IA, 446NA)

(8) This section applies on and after 7th May 2004.

Commentary—*Simon's Taxes* E4.507E, E4.507L, E4.507V.

87 Restricted securities with artificially depressed value

(1) Section 446E of the Income Tax (Earnings and Pensions) Act 2003 (c 1) (employee securities with artificially depressed market value: charge on restricted securities) is amended as follows.

(2)–(3) (*amend* ITEPA 2003 s 446E)

(4) This section applies on and after 7th May 2004.

(5) But if the employment-related securities were acquired before that date, section 446E of the Income Tax (Earnings and Pensions) Act 2003 (c 1) does not apply by virtue of the amendment made by subsection (2) of this section unless their market value would be artificially low immediately before the disposal or cancellation if the date on which the relevant period began were the later of—

    (a) that on which it did begin, and

    (b) 7th May 2004.

Commentary—*Simon's Taxes* E4.507O.

88 Shares under approved plans and schemes

(1) The Income Tax (Earnings and Pensions) Act 2003 is amended as follows.

(2) (*repeals* ITEPA 2003 s 421G)

(3)–(7) (*insert* ITEPA 2003 ss 431A, 489(4), 505(4A), 506(4A), 519(1)(c), 524(1)(c))

(8) Section 701 (PAYE: meaning of "asset") is amended as follows.

(9), (10) (*amend* ITEPA 2003 s 701)

(11) This section has effect on and after 18th June 2004 and (so far as it does not relate to the award or acquisition of shares) applies in relation to shares awarded or acquired before that date as well as in relation to those awarded or acquired on or after that date.

(12) Where section 431A(1) of the Income Tax (Earnings and Pensions) Act 2003 (c 1) (as inserted by subsection (3)) has effect (by virtue of subsection (11)) in relation to shares acquired before 18th June 2004, it applies in relation to them so as to treat an election under section 431(1) of that Act as made in relation to them on that date.

(13) For the purposes of the application of Chapter 3B of Part 7 of that Act (securities with artificially enhanced market value) by reason of subsections (2) and (11) in relation to shares acquired before 18th June 2004, section 446O of that Act (meaning of "relevant period") has effect as if they were acquired on that date.

Commentary—*Simon's Taxes* **E4.507FA**.

HMRC Manuals—Employment Related Securities Manual ERSM60200 (shares under approved plans & schemes).

89 Shares acquired on public offer

(1) Section 421F of the Income Tax (Earnings and Pensions) Act 2003 (c 1) (exclusion from Chapters 2 to 4 of Part 7 of shares acquired under terms of offer to the public) is amended as follows.
(2) In subsection (1), for "Chapters 2 to 4" substitute "Chapters 2, 3 and 3C".
(3) (*inserts* ITEPA s 421F(1A))
(4) This section has effect on and after 18th June 2004 and applies in relation to shares acquired before that date as well as in relation to those acquired on or after that date.
(5) For the purposes of the application of Chapter 3B of Part 7 of the Income Tax (Earnings and Pensions) Act 2003 (securities with artificially enhanced market value) by reason of subsections (2) and (4) in relation to shares acquired before that date, section 446O of that Act (meaning of "relevant period") has effect as if they were acquired on that date.

Commentary—*Simon's Taxes* **E4.508B**.

HMRC Manuals—Employment Related Securities Manual ERSM20370 (employment-related securities and options: exclusions: public offers).

90 Associated persons etc

(1) Part 7 of the Income Tax (Earnings and Pensions) Act 2003 (employment income: securities) is amended as follows.
(2)–(4) (*amend* ITEPA 2003 ss 421C(2), 472(2), 477(3)(c))
(5) This section has effect on and after 18th June 2004 and applies in relation to securities, interests and options that were employment-related securities or employment-related securities options on that date (as well as those acquired on or after that date).

Commentary—*Simon's Taxes* **E4.508K**.

HMRC Manuals—Employment Related Securities Manual ERSM20250 (employment-related securities and options: associated person and 'the box').

Miscellaneous

92 Minor amendments of or connected with ITEPA 2003

Schedule 17 to this Act contains minor amendments of or connected with the Income Tax (Earnings and Pensions) Act 2003 (c 1).

CHAPTER 5
ENTERPRISE INCENTIVES

93 Enterprise investment scheme

Schedule 18 (which makes amendments to the enterprise investment scheme) has effect.

Commentary—*Simon's Taxes* **E3.102, E3.136, E3.185**.

94 Venture capital trusts

(1), (2) . . . [1]
(3) Schedule 19 (which makes amendments relating to venture capital trusts) has effect.

Commentary—*Simon's Taxes* **E3.201, E3.220**.

Amendments—[1] Sub-ss (1), (2) repealed by ITA 2007 s 1031, Sch 3 Pt 1 with effect for income tax purposes from 6 April 2007, and corporation tax purposes for accounting periods ending after 5 April 2007.

95 Corporate venturing scheme

Schedule 20 (which makes amendments relating to the corporate venturing scheme) has effect.

Commentary—*Simon's Taxes* **D8.320, D8.332**.

96 Enterprise management incentives: subsidiaries

(1) Schedule 5 to the Income Tax (Earnings and Pensions) Act 2003 (enterprise management incentives) is amended as follows.
(2)–(5) (*amend* ITEPA 2003 Sch 5 paras 8, 10, 11, *insert* paras 11A, 11B)
(6) The amendments made by this section have effect in relation to any right to acquire shares granted on or after 17th March 2004.

CHAPTER 6

EXEMPTION FROM INCOME TAX FOR CERTAIN INTEREST AND ROYALTY PAYMENTS

Supplementary

105 Consequential amendments

(1) Section 98 of the Taxes Management Act 1970 (c 9) (special returns etc) is amended as follows.

(2) (*amends* TMA 1970 s 98)

(3) (*inserts* TMA 1970 s 98(4D))

(4), (5) (*inserted* TA 1988 ss 18(6), 349(7); *repealed by* ITTOIA 2005 s 884, Sch 3)

CHAPTER 7

SAVINGS INCOME: DOUBLE TAXATION ARISING FROM WITHHOLDING TAX

CHAPTER 8
CHARGEABLE GAINS

116 Restriction of gifts relief etc

Schedule 21 (which makes provision for relief under section 165 or 260 of the Taxation of Chargeable Gains Act 1992 (c 12) not to be available on certain transfers to settlor-interested settlements etc or on transfers of shares etc to companies, and makes minor amendments in sections 79 and 281 of that Act) has effect.

Commentary—*Simon's Taxes* **C3.501, C3.502, I3.612, I3.613**.

HMRC Manuals—Capital Gains Tax And Inheritance Tax LLM8230 (capital gains: names: relief for gifts of business assets).

117 Private residence relief

Schedule 22 (which makes provision about private residence relief) has effect.

Commentary—*Simon's Taxes* **C3.1701, C3.1708**.

118 Authorised unit trusts: treatment of umbrella schemes

(1) The Taxation of Chargeable Gains Act 1992 is amended as follows.

(2), (3) (*amend* TCGA 1992 s 99(2), *insert* s 99A)

(4) (*amends* TCGA 1992 ss 288(1), (8))

(5) The amendments made by this section have effect in relation to years of assessment and accounting periods beginning on or after 1st April 2004.

Commentary—*Simon's Taxes* **C2.719, C1.209, C2.803**.

HMRC Manuals—Capital Gains Manual CG57701 (umbrella schemes).

CHAPTER 9

AVOIDANCE INVOLVING LOSS RELIEF OR PARTNERSHIP

CHAPTER 10
AVOIDANCE: MISCELLANEOUS

134 Finance leasebacks

(1) (*inserts* CAA 2001 ss 228A–J)

(2) In sections 228A to 228J of the Capital Allowances Act 2001 (c 2) (as inserted by subsection (1) above), a reference to a provision of that Act includes a reference to an equivalent provision of the Capital Allowances Act 1990 (c 1) (with any necessary modification).

(3) This section applies to income tax and corporation tax chargeable in relation to periods that end on or after 17 March 2004.

(4) Schedule 23 contains transitional provision.

Commentary—*Simon's Taxes* **B3.340K, B3.340L**.

HMRC Manuals—Capital Allowances Manual CA28910 (PMA: anti-avoidance: finance leaseback: background, commencement and definitions).

136 Manufactured dividends

Schedule 24 to this Act (which makes provision in relation to cases where payments are or have been made, or treated as made, which are representative of dividends on shares of companies resident in the United Kingdom) has effect.

Commentary—*Simon's Taxes* **D9.701**.

HMRC Manuals—Corporate Finance Manual CFM74350 (manufactured dividends on UK shares).

CHAPTER 11

MISCELLANEOUS

Reliefs for business

144 Lloyd's names: conversion to limited liability underwriting

Schedule 25 to this Act (which makes provision for certain reliefs to be available where a member of Lloyd's converts to limited liability underwriting) has effect.

Commentary—*Simon's Taxes* **E5.621, E5.625, E5.625A**.

Offshore matters

145 Offshore funds

(1) The provisions of the Taxes Act 1988 relating to offshore funds are amended in accordance with Schedule 26 to this Act.

(2) Except as otherwise provided—

    (*a*) the amendments have effect for account periods (within the meaning of Chapter 5 of Part 17 of that Act) ending on or after the day on which this Act is passed, and

    (*b*) regulations made under a power conferred by virtue of any of the amendments may be made so as to have effect in relation to any such account period.

146 Meaning of "offshore installation"

Schedule 27 to this Act (which makes amendments relating to the meaning of "offshore installation") has effect.

Commentary—*Simon's Taxes* **B3.353**.

PART 4

PENSION SCHEMES ETC

CHAPTER 1

INTRODUCTION

Introductory

149 Overview of Part 4

(1) This Part contains tax provision about pension schemes and other similar schemes.

(2) This Chapter defines some basic concepts.

(3) As for the rest of this Part—

    Chapter 2 is about the registration and de-registration of pension schemes,

    Chapter 3 is about the payments that may be made by registered pension schemes and related matters,

    Chapter 4 deals with tax reliefs and exemptions in connection with registered pension schemes,

    Chapter 5 imposes tax charges in connection with registered pension schemes,

    Chapter 6 is about some schemes that are not registered pension schemes,

    Chapter 7 makes provision about compliance, and

    Chapter 8 contains interpretation and other supplementary provisions.

Main concepts

150 Meaning of "pension scheme"

(1) In this Part "pension scheme" means a scheme or other arrangements, comprised in one or more instruments or agreements, having or capable of having effect so as to provide benefits to or in respect of persons—

    (*a*) on retirement,

    (*b*) on death,

    (*c*) on having reached a particular age,

    (*d*) on the onset of serious ill-health or incapacity, or

    (*e*) in similar circumstances.

(2) A pension scheme is a registered pension scheme for the purposes of this Part at any time if it is at that time registered under Chapter 2.

(3) In this Part "public service pension scheme" means a pension scheme—

    (*a*) established by or under any enactment,

    (*b*) approved by a relevant governmental or Parliamentary person or body, or

    (*c*) specified in an order made by the Treasury.

(4) In subsection (3) "a relevant governmental or Parliamentary person or body" means—

    (*a*) a Minister of the Crown or a government department,

    (*b*) the Scottish Parliament, the Scottish Parliamentary Corporate Body or a member of the Scottish Executive,

(c) the National Assembly for Wales, or

(d) the Northern Ireland Assembly, the Northern Ireland Assembly Commission, a Northern Ireland Minister, the head of a Northern Ireland department or a Northern Ireland department.

(5) In this Part "occupational pension scheme" means a pension scheme established by an employer or employers and having or capable of having effect so as to provide benefits to or in respect of any or all of the employees of—

(a) that employer or those employers, or

(b) any other employer,

(whether or not it also has or is capable of having effect so as to provide benefits to or in respect of other persons).

[(5A) This Part applies in relation to certain pension schemes that are not occupational pension schemes as it applies in relation to occupational pension schemes (see section 274B and paragraph 1(4A) of Schedule 36).][2]

(6) In this Part "sponsoring employer", in relation to an occupational pension scheme, means the employer, or any of the employers, to or in respect of any or all of whose employees the pension scheme has, or is capable of having, effect so as to provide benefits.

(7) In this Part "overseas pension scheme" means a pension scheme (other than a registered pension scheme) which—

(a) is established in a country or territory outside the United Kingdom, and

(b) satisfies any requirements prescribed for the purposes of this subsection by regulations made by the Board of Inland Revenue.

(8) In this Part "recognised overseas pension scheme" means an overseas pension scheme [which satisfies any requirements prescribed for the purposes of this subsection by regulations made by the Commissioners for Her Majesty's Revenue and Customs.][1]

Commentary—*Simon's Taxes* E4.126, I5.633.

HMRC Manuals—Savings And Investment Manual SAIM6210 (pension funds pooling schemes).

Regulations—Pension Schemes (Categories of Country and Requirements for Overseas Pension Schemes and Recognised Overseas Pension Schemes) Regulations, SI 2006/206.

Registered Pension Schemes and Overseas Pension Schemes (Miscellaneous Amendments) Regulations, SI 2012/884.

Overseas Pension Schemes (Miscellaneous Amendments) Regulations, SI 2015/673.

Pension Schemes (Categories of Country and Requirements for Overseas Pension Schemes and Recognised Overseas Pension Schemes) (Amendments) Regulations, SI 2017/398.

Finance Act 2004 (Specified Pension Schemes) Order, SI 2019/1425.

Amendments—[1] In sub-s (8), words substituted by FA 2013 s 53(1) with effect from 17 July 2013.

[2] Sub-s (5A) inserted by FA 2018 s 13, Sch 3 para 1(1), (2) with effect from 15 March 2018.

151 Meaning of "member"

(1) In this Part "member" in relation to a pension scheme, means any active member, pensioner member, deferred member or pension credit member of the pension scheme.

(2) For the purposes of this Part a person is an active member of a pension scheme if there are presently arrangements made under the pension scheme for the accrual of benefits to or in respect of the person.

(3) For the purposes of this Part a person is a pensioner member of a pension scheme if the person is entitled to the present payment of benefits under the pension scheme and is not an active member.

(4) A person is a deferred member of a pension scheme if the person has accrued rights under the pension scheme and is neither an active member nor a pensioner member.

(5) A person is a pension credit member of a pension scheme if the person has rights under the pension scheme which are attributable (directly or indirectly) to pension credits[; and, if a person dies having become entitled to pension credits but without having rights attributable to them, the person is to be treated as having acquired, immediately before death, the rights by virtue of which the liability in respect of the pension credits is subsequently discharged][1].

Commentary—*Simon's Taxes* E7.221.

HMRC Manuals—Pensions Tax Manual PTM025400 (member).

Amendments—[1] Words in sub-s (5) inserted by FA 2006 s 161, Sch 23 paras 1, 2. This amendment is deemed to have come into force on 6 April 2006.

152 Meaning of "arrangement"

(1) In this Part "arrangement", in relation to a member of a pension scheme, means an arrangement relating to the member under the pension scheme.

(2) For the purposes of this Part an arrangement is a "money purchase arrangement" at any time if, at that time, all the benefits that may be provided to or in respect of the member under the arrangement are cash balance benefits or other money purchase benefits.

(3) For the purposes of this Part a money purchase arrangement is a "cash balance arrangement" at any time if, at that time, all the benefits that may be provided to or in respect of the member under the arrangement are cash balance benefits.

(4) In this Part "money purchase benefits", in relation to a member of a pension scheme, means benefits the rate or amount of which is calculated by reference to an amount available for the provision of benefits to or in respect of the member (whether the amount so available is calculated by reference to payments made under the pension scheme by the member or any other person in respect of the member or any other factor).

(5) In this Part "cash balance benefits" means benefits the rate or amount of which is calculated by reference to an amount available for the provision of benefits to or in respect of the member calculated otherwise than wholly by reference to payments made under the arrangement by the member or by any other person in respect of the member (or transfers or other credits).

(6) For the purposes of this Part an arrangement is a "defined benefits arrangement" at any time if, at that time, all the benefits that may be provided to or in respect of the member under the arrangement are defined benefits.

(7) In this Part "defined benefits", in relation to a member of a pension scheme, means benefits which are not money purchase benefits (but which are calculated by reference to earnings or service of the member or any other factor other than an amount available for their provision).

(8) For the purposes of this Part an arrangement is a "hybrid arrangement" at any time if, at that time, all of the benefits that may be provided to or in respect of the member under the arrangement are, depending on the circumstances, to be of one of any two or three of the following varieties—

    (*a*) cash balance benefits,

    (*b*) other money purchase benefits, and

    (*c*) defined benefits.

(9) Where not all of the benefits that may be provided under an arrangement to or in respect of the member are of the same one of those varieties of benefits, the arrangement is to be treated for the purposes of this Part as being two or three separate arrangements one of which relates to each of the two or three varieties of benefits that may be so provided.

Commentary—*Simon's Taxes* **E7.110**.
HMRC Manuals—Pensions Tax Manual PTM023100 (what is meant by an arrangement).
PTM023200 (arrangement: types of arrangement).
PTM023300 (money purchase and defined benefits arrangements).
PTM023600 (hybrid arrangements).

CHAPTER 2

REGISTRATION OF PENSION SCHEMES
Registration

153 Registration of pension schemes

(1) An application may be made to the Inland Revenue for a pension scheme to be registered.

(2) The application—

    (*a*) must contain any information which is reasonably required by the Inland Revenue in any form specified by the Board of Inland Revenue, and

    (*b*) must be accompanied by a declaration that the application is made by the scheme administrator (see section 270) and any other declarations by the scheme administrator which are reasonably required by the Inland Revenue.

(3) The declarations which the Inland Revenue may require to accompany an application for the registration of a pension scheme include, in particular, a declaration that the instruments or agreements by which it is constituted do not entitle any person to unauthorised payments (see section 160(5)).

(4) [Following][2] receipt of an application for a pension scheme to be registered the Inland Revenue must decide whether or not to register the pension scheme.

(5) The Inland Revenue's decision must be to register the pension scheme unless it appears that—

    [(*a*) any information falling within subsection (5A) is inaccurate in a material respect,

    (*b*) any document falling within subsection (5B) contains a material inaccuracy,

    (*c*) any declaration accompanying the application is false,

    (*d*) the scheme administrator has failed to comply with an information notice under section 153A given in connection with the application (including any declaration accompanying it),

    (*e*) the scheme administrator has deliberately obstructed an officer of Revenue and Customs in the course of an inspection under section 153B carried out in connection with the application (including any declaration accompanying it) where the inspection has been approved by the tribunal,

    (*f*) the pension scheme has not been established, or is not being maintained, wholly or mainly for the purpose of making payments falling within section 164(1)(*a*) or (*b*) (authorised payments of pensions and lump sums), or

    (*g*) the person who is, or any of the persons who are, the scheme administrator is not a fit and proper person to be, as the case may be—

        (i) the scheme administrator, or

        (ii) one of the persons who are the scheme administrator][2][, or

(h) the pension scheme is an occupational pension scheme, and a sponsoring employer in relation to the scheme is a body corporate that has been dormant during a continuous period of one month that falls within the period of one year ending with the day on which the decision is made, or

(i) the pension scheme is an unauthorised Master Trust scheme.][3]

[(5A) The information falling within this subsection is any information—

(a) contained in the application, or

(b) otherwise provided to an officer of Revenue and Customs by the scheme administrator (whether under section 153A or otherwise) in connection with the application (including any declaration accompanying it).

(5B) The documents falling within this subsection are any documents produced to an officer of Revenue and Customs by the scheme administrator (whether under section 153A or otherwise) in connection with the application (including any declaration accompanying it).

(5C) The reference in subsection (5)(d) to the scheme administrator having failed to comply with an information notice under section 153A includes a case where the scheme administrator has concealed, destroyed or otherwise disposed of, or has arranged for the concealment, destruction or disposal of, a document in breach of paragraph 42 or 43 of Schedule 36 to the Finance Act 2008 as applied by section 153A(3).][2]

(6) The Inland Revenue must notify the scheme administrator of the decision on the application.

(7) Unless the Inland Revenue's decision is not to register the pension scheme, the notification must state the day on and after which the pension scheme will be a registered pension scheme.

(8) An annuity contract [made with an insurance company[1]]—

(a) by means of which benefits under a registered pension scheme have been secured, but

(b) which does not provide for the immediate payment of benefits,

is to be treated as having become a registered pension scheme on the day on which it is made.

[(8A) Where an order has been made under section 19(4) or 21(2)(a) of the Pensions Act 2004 or Article 15(4) or 17(2)(a) of the Pensions (Northern Ireland) Order 2005 (restitution by order of court or Pensions Regulator) that property or money be transferred, or a sum be paid, towards an annuity contract made with an insurance company, the annuity contract is to be treated as having become a registered pension scheme on the day on which it is made.][1]

(9) Schedule 36 contains (in Part 1) provisions treating certain pension schemes in existence immediately before 6th April 2006 as registered pension schemes (and related provisions).

Commentary—*Simon's Taxes* E7.208.

HMRC Manuals—Pensions Tax Manual PTM031200 (conditions for registering a pension scheme).

PTM032100 (how to make the application to register a pension scheme).

PTM053940 (deferred annuity contracts).

Modifications—In relation to an application made before 1 September 2014, sub-s (5) (as amended by FA 2014 Sch 7 para 2(3)) has effect with the omission of para (g) (FA 2014 Sch 7 para 5(2)).

Amendments—[1]   Sub-s (8A) and words in sub-s (8) inserted by FA 2005 s 101, Sch 10 paras 2, 3, 64(1) with effect from 6 April 2006.

[2]   In sub-s (4), word substituted for word "On" , in sub-s (5) paras (a)–(g) substituted for previous paras (a), (b), and sub-ss (5A)–(5C) inserted, by FA 2014 s 46, Sch 7 paras 1, 2 with effect in relation to applications made on or after 20 March 2014.

[3]   Sub-s (5)(h), (i) inserted by FA 2018 s 13, Sch 3 para 1(1), (3) with effect as follows—

–   para (h) and preceding word "or" inserted with effect from 6 April 2018 (FA 2018 Sch 3 para 2(2)(a));

–   para (i) and preceding word "or" inserted with effect from the later of (a) the date on which the Pension Schemes Act 2017 s 3 comes into force, or (b) 15 March 2018 (FA 2018 Sch 3 para 2(1)(a)).

For the purposes of sub-s (5)(h), (i) it is immaterial when the application in question was made (FA 2018 Sch 3 para 2(5)).

[153A Power to require information or documents in relation to applications for registration

(1) This section applies where an application for a pension scheme to be registered is made.

(2) An officer of Revenue and Customs may by notice (an "information notice") require the scheme administrator or any other person—

(a) to provide the officer with any information, or

(b) to produce a document to the officer,

if the officer reasonably requires the information or document in connection with the application (including any declaration accompanying it).

(3) Paragraphs 6(2), 7, 8, 15, 16, 18 to 20, 23 to 27, 42 and 43 of Schedule 36 to the Finance Act 2008 (information notices etc) apply in relation to information notices under this section as they apply in relation to information notices under that Schedule.

(4) Where an information notice under this section is given to a person other than the scheme administrator, an officer of Revenue and Customs must give a copy of the notice to the scheme administrator.

(5) A person, other than the scheme administrator, who is given an information notice under this section may appeal against the notice or any requirement in the notice.

(6) Paragraph 32 of Schedule 36 to the Finance Act 2008 (procedures for appeals against information notices) applies for the purposes of an appeal under subsection (5) as it applies for the purposes of an appeal under Part 5 of that Schedule.]¹

Commentary—*Simon's Taxes* E7.208.
HMRC Manuals—Pensions Tax Manual PTM032200 (information notices).
Amendments—¹ Sections 153A–153F inserted by FA 2014 s 46, Sch 7 paras 1, 3 with effect in relation to applications made on or after 20 March 2014.

[153B Power to inspect documents in relation to applications for registration
(1) This section applies where an application for a pension scheme to be registered is made.
(2) An officer of Revenue and Customs may—
    (*a*) enter any business premises of the scheme administrator or any other person, and
    (*b*) inspect documents that are on the premises,
if the officer reasonably requires to inspect the documents in connection with the application (including any declaration accompanying it).
(3) In subsection (2)(*a*) "business premises" has the meaning given by paragraph 10(3) of Schedule 36 to the Finance Act 2008 (power to inspect business premises etc).
(4) Paragraphs 10(2), 12, 15 and 16 of Schedule 36 to the Finance Act 2008 apply in relation to the power of inspection conferred by this section as they apply in relation to the power of inspection conferred by paragraph 10 of that Schedule.
(5) An officer of Revenue and Customs may not inspect a document under this section if or to the extent that, by virtue of a provision of Part 4 of Schedule 36 to the Finance Act 2008 (restrictions on powers) applied by section 153A(3), an information notice under section 153A given at the time of the inspection to the occupier of the premises could not require the occupier to produce the document.
(6) An officer of Revenue and Customs may ask the tribunal to approve an inspection under this section.
(7) Paragraph 13(1A), (2) and (3) of Schedule 36 to the Finance Act 2008 (approval of tribunal for inspections) applies in relation to an application under subsection (6) as it applies in relation to an application under paragraph 13 of that Schedule in relation to an inspection under paragraph 10 of that Schedule.]¹

Commentary—*Simon's Taxes* E7.208.
HMRC Manuals—Pensions Tax Manual PTM032200 (power to inspect documents - inspection visits).
Amendments—¹ Sections 153A–153F inserted by FA 2014 s 46, Sch 7 paras 1, 3 with effect in relation to applications made on or after 20 March 2014.

[153C Penalties for failure to comply with information notices etc
(1) This section applies where a person other than the scheme administrator—
    (*a*) fails to comply with an information notice under section 153A, or
    (*b*) deliberately obstructs an officer of Revenue and Customs in the course of an inspection under section 153B that has been approved by the tribunal.
(2) The reference in subsection (1)(*a*) to a person who fails to comply with an information notice includes a person who conceals, destroys or otherwise disposes of, or arranges for the concealment, destruction or disposal of, a document in breach of paragraph 42 or 43 of Schedule 36 to the Finance Act 2008 as applied by section 153A(3).
(3) Paragraphs 39(2), 40 and 44 to 49 of Schedule 36 to the Finance Act 2008 (penalties for failure to comply with information notice etc) apply in relation to the failure or obstruction as they apply in relation to a failure or obstruction mentioned in paragraph 39(1) of that Schedule.]¹

Commentary—*Simon's Taxes* **E7.208**.
HMRC Manuals—Pensions Tax Manual PTM032200 (penalties for failing to comply with an information notice or inspection visit).
Amendments—¹ Sections 153A–153F inserted by FA 2014 s 46, Sch 7 paras 1, 3 with effect in relation to applications made on or after 20 March 2014.

[153D Penalties for inaccurate information in applications
(1) This section applies where—
    (*a*) an application under section 153 contains information which is inaccurate,
    (*b*) the inaccuracy is material, and
    (*c*) condition A, B or C is met.
(2) Condition A is that the inaccuracy is careless or deliberate.
(3) An inaccuracy is careless if it is due to a failure by the scheme administrator to take reasonable care.
(4) Condition B is that the scheme administrator knows of the inaccuracy at the time the application is made but does not inform an officer of Revenue and Customs at that time.
(5) Condition C is that the scheme administrator—
    (*a*) discovers the inaccuracy some time later, and
    (*b*) fails to take reasonable steps to inform an officer of Revenue and Customs.

(6) The scheme administrator is liable to a penalty not exceeding the maximum penalty for which the scheme administrator could have been liable under paragraph 40A of Schedule 36 to the Finance Act 2008 (penalties for inaccurate information and documents) had that paragraph applied in relation to the inaccuracy.

(7) Where the information contains more than one material inaccuracy, a penalty is payable for each inaccuracy.

(8) Paragraphs 46 to 49 of Schedule 36 to the Finance Act 2008 (assessment of penalties etc) apply in relation to a penalty under this section as they apply in relation to a penalty under paragraph 40A of that Schedule.][1]

Commentary—*Simon's Taxes* E7.208.

HMRC Manuals—Pensions Tax Manual PTM032100 (inaccurate information or false statements are made in the application).

Amendments—[1]   Sections 153A–153F inserted by FA 2014 s 46, Sch 7 paras 1, 3 with effect in relation to applications made on or after 20 March 2014.

[153E Penalties for inaccurate information or documents provided under information notice

(1) This section applies where—
    (*a*) in complying with an information notice under section 153A, a person provides inaccurate information or produces a document that contains an inaccuracy, and
    (*b*) the inaccuracy is material.

(2) Paragraphs 40A and 46 to 49 of Schedule 36 to the Finance Act 2008 (penalties for inaccurate information and documents) apply in relation to the inaccuracy as they apply in relation to an inaccuracy connected with an information notice under that Schedule.][1]

Commentary—*Simon's Taxes* E7.208.

HMRC Manuals—Pensions Tax Manual PTM032200 (penalties for providing inaccurate information in response to an information notice).

Amendments—[1]   Sections 153A–153F inserted by FA 2014 s 46, Sch 7 paras 1, 3 with effect in relation to applications made on or after 20 March 2014.

[153F Penalties for false declarations

(1) This section applies where—
    (*a*) a declaration accompanying an application under section 153 is false, and
    (*b*) at least one of conditions A to C in section 153D is met (reading references to an inaccuracy as references to a falsehood and references to the scheme administrator as references to the person who made the declaration).

(2) The person who made the declaration is liable to a penalty not exceeding the maximum penalty for which the person could have been liable under paragraph 40A of Schedule 36 to the Finance Act 2008 (penalties for inaccurate information and documents) had that paragraph applied in relation to the falsehood.

(3) Where the declaration contains more than one falsehood, a penalty is payable in relation to each falsehood.

(4) Paragraphs 46 to 49 of Schedule 36 to the Finance Act 2008 (assessment of penalties etc) apply in relation to a penalty under this section as they apply in relation to a penalty under paragraph 40A of that Schedule.][1]

Commentary—*Simon's Taxes* E7.208.

HMRC Manuals—Pensions Tax Manual PTM032100 (inaccurate information or false statements are made in the application).

Amendments—[1]   Sections 153A–153F inserted by FA 2014 s 46, Sch 7 paras 1, 3 with effect in relation to applications made on or after 20 March 2014.

154 Persons by whom registered pension scheme may be established

[(1) An application to register a pension scheme may be made only if the pension scheme—
    (*a*) is an occupational pension scheme, or
    (*b*) has been established by a person with permission under FISMA 2000 to establish in the United Kingdom a personal pension scheme or a stakeholder pension scheme.][1]

(2) But subsection (1) does not apply to a public service pension scheme.

[(2A) Subsection (1) is to be construed in accordance with section 22 of FISMA 2000, any relevant order under that section and Schedule 2 to that Act.][1]

(3) . . . [1]

(4) The Treasury may by order amend this section . . . [1].

Commentary—*Simon's Taxes* E7.208.

HMRC Manuals—Pensions Tax Manual PTM031200 (who may set up a registered pension scheme).

Amendments—[1]   Sub-s (1) substituted, sub-s (2A) inserted, and sub-s (3) and words in sub-s (4) repealed, by FA 2007 ss 70, 114, Sch 20 paras 1, 2, 24(1), Sch 27 para 3(2). These amendments are deemed to have come into force on 6 April 2007.

156 Appeal against decision not to register

(1) This section applies where, on an application for a pension scheme to be registered, the Inland Revenue's decision is not to register the pension scheme.

(2) The scheme administrator may appeal against the decision.

(3), (4) . . . [1]

(5) An appeal under this section against a decision must be brought within the period of 30 days beginning with the day on which the scheme administrator was notified of the decision.

(6) [On an appeal under this section that is notified to the tribunal, the tribunal][1] must consider whether the pension scheme ought to have been registered by the Inland Revenue.

(7) If [the tribunal decides][1] that the pension scheme ought not to have been registered by the Inland Revenue, [the tribunal must][1] dismiss the appeal.

(8) If [the tribunal decides][1] that the pension scheme ought to have been registered by the Inland Revenue, the pension scheme is to be treated as having been registered on such date as the [tribunal determines][1] (but subject to any further appeal . . .[1]).

Commentary—*Simon's Taxes* E7.208.

HMRC Manuals—Pensions Tax Manual PTM032400 (HMRC decides not to register the scheme). PTM032300 (HMRC register the scheme).

Amendments—[1] Sub-ss (3), (4) and words in sub-s (8) repealed, in sub-ss (6)–(8) words substituted by the Transfer of Tribunal Functions and Revenue and Customs Appeals Order, SI 2009/56 art 3, Sch 1 para 423 with effect from 1 April 2009.

[156A Cases where application for registration not decided within 6 months

(1) This section applies where—

 (a) an application for a pension scheme to be registered is made, but

 (b) the scheme administrator is not notified under section 153(6) within the period of 6 months after the day on which the application is made.

(2) The scheme administrator may appeal to the tribunal as if, at the end of that period of 6 months, the scheme administrator had been notified under section 153(6) of a decision not to register the scheme; and section 156(5) to (8) applies accordingly.][1]

Commentary—*Simon's Taxes* E7.208.

HMRC Manuals—Pensions Tax Manual PTM032200 (outline of HMRC's role in the registration process).

Amendments—[1] Section 156A inserted by FA 2014 s 46, Sch 7 paras 1, 4 with effect in relation to applications made on or after 20 March 2014 .

De-registration

157 De-registration

(1) The Inland Revenue may withdraw the registration of a pension scheme.

(2) If the Inland Revenue withdraws the registration of a pension scheme the Inland Revenue must notify the scheme administrator.

(3) If there is no-one who is the scheme administrator, the Inland Revenue must instead notify any person or persons—

 (a) who has or have responsibility for the discharge of any obligation relating to the pension scheme under section 271(4) (continuation of liability where no scheme administrator), section 272 (trustees etc) or section 273 (members), and

 (b) whom it is reasonably practicable for the Inland Revenue to identify.

(4) The notification must state the date on and after which the pension scheme will not be a registered pension scheme.

Commentary—*Simon's Taxes* E7.209.

HMRC Manuals—Pensions Tax Manual PTM033100 (notification of de-registration).

158 Grounds for de-registration

(1) The registration of a pension scheme may be withdrawn under section 157 only if it appears to the Inland Revenue—

 [(za) that the pension scheme has not been established, or is not being maintained, wholly or mainly for the purpose of making payments falling within section 164(1)(a) or (b) (authorised payments of pensions and lump sums),][2]

 [(zb) that the person who is, or any of the persons who are, the scheme administrator is not a fit and proper person to be, as the case may be—

  (i) the scheme administrator, or

  (ii) one of the persons who are the scheme administrator,][3]

 (a) that the amount of the scheme chargeable payments (see section 241) made by the pension scheme during any period of 12 months exceeds the de-registration threshold,

 (b) that the scheme administrator fails to pay a substantial amount of tax (or interest on tax) due from the scheme administrator by virtue of this Part,

 (c) that the scheme administrator fails to provide information required to be provided to the Inland Revenue by virtue of this Part [or Part 1 of Schedule 36 to the Finance Act 2008][1] and the failure is significant,

 (d) that any information contained in the application to register the pension scheme or otherwise provided to the Inland Revenue is [inaccurate][2] in a material particular,

 [(da) that the scheme administrator fails to produce any document required to be produced to an officer of Revenue and Customs by virtue of this Part or Part 1 of Schedule 36 to the Finance Act 2008, (*db*) that any document produced to an officer of Revenue and Customs by the scheme administrator contains a material inaccuracy in relation to which at least one of conditions A to C in subsections (7) to (10) is met,][2]

[(*e*) that any declaration accompanying the application to register the pension scheme, or otherwise made to an officer of Revenue and Customs in connection with the pension scheme, is false in a material particular,

(*ea*) that the scheme administrator has deliberately obstructed an officer of Revenue and Customs in the course of an inspection under [section 159B or][3] Part 2 of Schedule 36 to the Finance Act 2008 that has been approved by the tribunal, or][2]

(*f*) that there is no scheme administrator[, or

(*g*) that the pension scheme is an occupational pension scheme, and a sponsoring employer in relation to the scheme is a body corporate that has been dormant during a continuous period of one month that falls within the period of one year ending with the day on which the decision to withdraw registration is made, or

(*h*) that the scheme is an unauthorised Master Trust scheme.][4]

(2) The amount of the scheme chargeable payments made by a pension scheme during any period of 12 months exceeds the de-registration threshold if the scheme chargeable payments percentage is 25% or more.

(3) The scheme chargeable payments percentage is—

(*a*) if only one scheme chargeable payment is made during the period of 12 months, the percentage of the pension fund used up on the occasion of that scheme chargeable payment, and

(*b*) if two or more scheme chargeable payments are made during the period of 12 months, the aggregate of the percentages of the pension fund used up on the occasion of each of those scheme chargeable payments.

(4) The percentage of the pension fund used up on the occasion of a scheme chargeable payment is—

$$\frac{SCP}{AA} \times 100$$

where—

SCP is the amount of the scheme chargeable payment, and

AA is an amount equal to the aggregate of the amount of the sums and the market value of the assets held for the purposes of the pension scheme at the time when the scheme chargeable payment is made.

(5) A failure by a scheme administrator to provide information required to be provided to the Inland Revenue by or under this Part [or Part 1 of Schedule 36 to the Finance Act 2008][1] is significant if—

(*a*) the amount of information which the scheme administrator fails to provide is substantial, or

(*b*) the failure to provide the information is likely to result in serious prejudice to the assessment or collection of tax.

[(6) Subsections (7) to (10) apply for the purposes of subsection (1)(*db*).

(7) Condition A is that the inaccuracy is careless or deliberate.

(8) An inaccuracy is careless if it is due to a failure by the scheme administrator to take reasonable care.

(9) Condition B is that the scheme administrator knows of the inaccuracy at the time the document is produced to an officer of Revenue and Customs but does not inform such an officer at that time.

(10) Condition C is that the scheme administrator—

(*a*) discovers the inaccuracy some time later, and

(*b*) fails to take reasonable steps to inform an officer of Revenue and Customs.][2]

Commentary—*Simon's Taxes* E7.209.
HMRC Manuals—Pensions Tax Manual PTM033100 (when HMRC may de-register a scheme).
Amendments—[1]   Words in sub-ss (1)(*c*), (5) inserted by the Pension Schemes (Miscellaneous Amendments) Order, SI 2013/1114 art 2 with effect in relation to any information notices given under FA 2008 Sch 36 Part 1 on or after 1 June 2013.
[2]   In sub-s (1), paras (*za*), (*da*), (*db*), inserted, in para (*d*) word substituted for word "incorrect", paras (*e*), (*ea*) substituted for previous para (*e*), and sub-ss (6)–(10) inserted, by FA 2014, s 46 Sch 7 paras 1, 6(1), (2), (4) with effect in relation to pension schemes whenever registered (including schemes registered by virtue of FA 2004 Sch 36 para 1 (deemed registration of existing schemes)). These amendments are treated as having come into force on 20 March 2014.
[3]   In sub-s (1), para (*zb*), and words in para (*ea*), inserted, by FA 2014 s 46, Sch 7 paras 1, 6(1), (3) with effect in relation to pension schemes whenever registered (including schemes registered by virtue of FA 2004 Sch 36 para 1 (deemed registration of existing schemes)). The amendments came into force on 1 September 2014.
[4]   Sub-s (1)(*g*), (*h*) inserted by FA 2018 s 13, Sch 3 para 1(1), (4) with effect as follows—
   –   para (*g*) and preceding word "or" are inserted with effect from 6 April 2018 (FA 2018 Sch 3 para 2(2)(*b*));
   –   para (*h*) and preceding word "or" are inserted with effect from the later of (a) the date on which the Pension Schemes Act 2017 s 3 comes into force, or (b) 15 March 2018 (FA 2018 Sch 3 para 2(1)(*b*)).

159 Appeal against decision to de-register
(1) This section applies where the Inland Revenue decides to withdraw the registration of a pension scheme under section 157.
(2) The scheme administrator, or any person notified under that section of the withdrawal of registration, may appeal against the decision.
(3), (4) . . . [1]
(5) An appeal under this section against a decision must be brought within the period of 30 days beginning with the day on which the appellant was notified of the decision.
(6) [On an appeal that is notified to the tribunal, the tribunal][1] must consider whether the registration of the pension scheme ought to have been withdrawn.
(7) If [the tribunal decides][1] that the registration of the pension scheme ought to have been withdrawn, [the tribunal must][1] dismiss the appeal.
(8) If [the tribunal decides][1] that the registration of the pension scheme ought not to have been withdrawn, the pension scheme is to be treated as having remained a registered pension scheme (but subject to any further appeal . . . [1]).

Commentary—*Simon's Taxes* **E7.209**.
HMRC Manuals—Pensions Tax Manual PTM033100 (appeal against de-registration).
Amendments—[1] Sub-ss (3), (4) and words in sub-s (8) repealed, in sub-ss (6), (7) words substituted by the Transfer of Tribunal Functions and Revenue and Customs Appeals Order, SI 2009/56 art 3, Sch 1 para 424 with effect from 1 April 2009.

[159A Power to require information or documents for purpose of considering if scheme administrator is fit and proper
(1) An officer of Revenue and Customs may by notice (an "information notice") require the scheme administrator of a registered pension scheme or any other person—
    (*a*) to provide the officer with any information, or
    (*b*) to produce a document to the officer,
if the officer reasonably requires the information or document for the purpose of considering whether the person who is, or any of the persons who are, the scheme administrator is a fit and proper person to be the scheme administrator or one of those persons (as the case may be).
(2) Paragraphs 6(2), 7, 8, 15, 16, 18 to 20, 23 to 27, 42 and 43 of Schedule 36 to the Finance Act 2008 (information notices etc) apply in relation to information notices under this section as they apply in relation to information notices under that Schedule.
(3) Where an information notice under this section is given to a person other than the scheme administrator, an officer of Revenue and Customs must give a copy of the notice to the scheme administrator.
(4) A person who is given an information notice under this section may appeal against the notice or any requirement in the notice.
(5) Paragraph 32 of Schedule 36 to the Finance Act 2008 (procedures for appeals against information notices) applies for the purposes of an appeal under subsection (4) as it applies for the purposes of an appeal under Part 5 of that Schedule.][1]

Commentary—*Simon's Taxes* **E7.209**.
HMRC Manuals—Pensions Tax Manual PTM153000 (information notices).
Amendments—[1] Sections 159A–159D inserted by FA 2014 s 46, Sch 7 paras 1, 7 with effect in relation to pension schemes whenever registered (including schemes registered by virtue of FA 2004 Sch 36 para 1 (deemed registration of existing schemes)). The amendments came into force on 1 September 2014.

[159B Power to inspect documents for purpose of considering if scheme administrator is fit and proper
(1) An officer of Revenue and Customs may—
    (*a*) enter any business premises of the scheme administrator of a registered pension scheme or of any other person, and
    (*b*) inspect documents that are on the premises,
if the officer reasonably requires to inspect the documents for the purpose of considering whether the person who is, or any of the persons who are, the scheme administrator is a fit and proper person to be the scheme administrator or one of those persons (as the case may be).
(2) In subsection (1)(*a*) "business premises" has the meaning given by paragraph 10(3) of Schedule 36 to the Finance Act 2008 (power to inspect business premises etc).
(3) Paragraphs 10(2), 12, 15 and 16 of Schedule 36 to the Finance Act 2008 apply in relation to the power of inspection conferred by this section as they apply in relation to the power of inspection conferred by paragraph 10 of that Schedule.
(4) An officer of Revenue and Customs may not inspect a document under this section if or to the extent that, by virtue of a provision of Part 4 of Schedule 36 to the Finance Act 2008 (restrictions on powers) applied by section 159A(2), an information notice under section 159A given at the time of the inspection to the occupier of the premises could not require the occupier to produce the document.
(5) An officer of Revenue and Customs may ask the tribunal to approve an inspection under this section.

(6) Paragraph 13(1A), (2) and (3) of Schedule 36 to the Finance Act 2008 (approval of tribunal for inspections) applies in relation to an application under subsection (5) as it applies in relation to an application under paragraph 13 of that Schedule in relation to an inspection under paragraph 10 of that Schedule.][1]

Commentary—*Simon's Taxes* **E7.209**.
HMRC Manuals—Pensions Tax Manual PTM153000 (power to inspect documents).
Amendments—[1]   Sections 159A–159D inserted by FA 2014 s 46, Sch 7 paras 1, 7 with effect in relation to pension schemes whenever registered (including schemes registered by virtue of FA 2004 Sch 36 para 1 (deemed registration of existing schemes)). The amendments came into force on 1 September 2014.

[159C Penalties for failure to comply with information notices etc

(1) This section applies where a person—
   (a) fails to comply with an information notice under section 159A, or
   (b) deliberately obstructs an officer of Revenue and Customs in the course of an inspection under section 159B that has been approved by the tribunal.
(2) The reference in subsection (1)(a) to a person who fails to comply with an information notice includes a person who conceals, destroys or otherwise disposes of, or arranges for the concealment, destruction or disposal of, a document in breach of paragraph 42 or 43 of Schedule 36 to the Finance Act 2008 as applied by section 159A(2).
(3) Paragraphs 39(2), 40 and 44 to 49 of Schedule 36 to the Finance Act 2008 (penalties for failure to comply with information notice etc) apply in relation to the failure or obstruction as they apply in relation to a failure or obstruction mentioned in paragraph 39(1) of that Schedule.][1]

Commentary—*Simon's Taxes* **E7.209**.
HMRC Manuals—Pensions Tax Manual PTM153000 (power to inspect documents).
Amendments—[1]   Sections 159A–159D inserted by FA 2014 s 46, Sch 7 paras 1, 7 with effect in relation to pension schemes whenever registered (including schemes registered by virtue of FA 2004 Sch 36 para 1 (deemed registration of existing schemes)). The amendments came into force on 1 September 2014.

[159D Penalties for inaccurate information or documents provided under information notice

(1) This section applies where—
   (a) in complying with an information notice under section 159A, a person provides inaccurate information or produces a document that contains an inaccuracy, and
   (b) the inaccuracy is material.
(2) Paragraphs 40A and 46 to 49 of Schedule 36 to the Finance Act 2008 (penalties for inaccurate information and documents) apply in relation to the inaccuracy as they apply in relation to an inaccuracy connected with an information notice under that Schedule.][1]

Commentary—*Simon's Taxes* **E7.209**.
HMRC Manuals—Pensions Tax Manual PTM153000 (power to inspect documents).
Amendments—[1]   Sections 159A–159D inserted by FA 2014 s 46, Sch 7 paras 1, 7 with effect in relation to pension schemes whenever registered (including schemes registered by virtue of FA 2004 Sch 36 para 1 (deemed registration of existing schemes)). The amendments came into force on 1 September 2014.

CHAPTER 3

PAYMENTS BY REGISTERED PENSION SCHEMES
Introductory

160 Payments by registered pension schemes

(1) The only payments which a registered pension scheme is authorised to make to or in respect of a [person who is or has been a][2] member of the pension scheme are those specified in section 164.
(2) In this Part "unauthorised member payment" means—
   (a) a payment by a registered pension scheme to or in respect of a [person who is or has been a][2] member of the pension scheme which is not authorised by section 164, and
   (b) anything which is to be treated as an unauthorised payment to or in respect of a [person who is or has been a][2] member of the pension scheme under [this Part][2].
(3) The only payments which a registered pension scheme that is an occupational pension scheme is authorised to make to or in respect of a [person who is or has been a][2] sponsoring employer are those specified in section 175.
(4) In this Part "unauthorised employer payment" means—
   (a) a payment by a registered pension scheme that is an occupational pension scheme, to or in respect of a [person who is or has been a][2] sponsoring employer, which is not authorised by section 175, and
   (b) anything which is to be treated as an unauthorised payment to a [person who is or has been a][2] sponsoring employer under section 181.
[(4A) If an unauthorised member payment or unauthorised employer payment made to or in respect of a person would have been greater but for a reduction made in respect of the whole, or any proportion, of the amount which the scheme administrator considers may be the amount of the liability to the scheme sanction charge in respect of it, it is to be regarded for the purposes of this Part as increased by the amount of the reduction.][3]

[(4B) But if the amount, or that proportion of the amount, of that liability is in fact less than the amount of the reduction, a subsequent payment of an amount not exceeding the difference between that amount and the amount of the reduction made—

    (*a*) to or in respect of the same person, and

    (*b*) before the end of the period of two years beginning with the date on which the unauthorised member payment or unauthorised employer payment was made,

is not to be regarded for the purposes of this Part as an unauthorised member payment or unauthorised employer payment.][3]

(5) In this Part "unauthorised payment" means—

    (*a*) an unauthorised member payment, or

    (*b*) an unauthorised employer payment.

(6) As well as section 157 (de-registration), the following provisions—

    (*a*) section 208 (unauthorised payments charge),

    (*b*) section 209 (unauthorised payments surcharge),

    (*c*) section 239 (scheme sanction charge), and

    (*d*) section 242 (de-registration charge),

specify consequences of making unauthorised payments.

(7) Sections 182 to 185 contain provision about amounts that a registered pension scheme is not authorised to borrow.

[(7A) Sections 185A to 185I contain provision about the receipt of income and gains from taxable property.][1]

(8) As well as section 157, sections 239 and 242 specify consequences of unauthorised borrowing [and the receipt of income and gains from taxable property][1].

(9) Schedule 36 contains (in Parts 3 and 4) transitional provision about unauthorised payments.

Commentary—*Simon's Taxes* **E7.245**.

HMRC Manuals—Pensions Tax Manual PTM132000 (what is an unauthorised payment?).

PTM024500 (unauthorised payments).

Amendments—[1] Sub-s (7A), and words in sub-s (8), inserted by FA 2006 s 158, Sch 21 paras 2, 3. These amendments are deemed to have come into force on 6 April 2006.

[2] Words in sub-ss (1)–(4) inserted, and words in sub-s (2)(*b*) substituted, by FA 2006 s 161, Sch 23 paras 1, 3. These amendments are deemed to have come into force on 6 April 2006.

[3] Sub-ss (4A), (4B) inserted by FA 2007 ss 70, 114, Sch 20 paras 1, 5, 24(2).with effect in relation to payments made on or after 6 April 2007.

161 Meaning of "payment" etc

(1) This section applies for the interpretation of this Chapter.

(2) "Payment" includes a transfer of assets and any other transfer of money's worth.

(3) Subsection (4) applies to a payment made or benefit provided under or in connection with an investment (including an insurance contract or annuity) acquired using sums or assets held for the purposes of a registered pension scheme.

(4) The payment or benefit is to be treated as made or provided from sums or assets held for the purposes of the pension scheme, even if the pension scheme has been wound up since the investment was acquired.

(5) A payment made by a registered pension scheme to [or in respect of][1] a person who—

    (*a*) is connected with a [person who is or has been a][2] member or sponsoring employer (or was connected with [such a person at the date of the person's][2] death), and

    (*b*) is not a [person who is or has been a][2] member or sponsoring employer,

is to be treated as made in respect of the [person who is or has been a][2] member or sponsoring employer.

(6) Any asset held by a person connected with a [person who is or has been a][2] member or sponsoring employer (or who was connected with [such a person at the date of the person's][2] death) is to be treated as held for the benefit of the [person who is or has been a][2] member or sponsoring employer.

(7) Any increase in the value of an asset held by, or reduction in the liability of, a person connected with a [person who is or has been a][2] member or sponsoring employer (or who was connected with [such a person at the date of the person's][2] death) is to be treated as an increase or reduction for the benefit of the [person who is or has been a][2] member or sponsoring employer.

[(8) For the purposes of this section whether a person is connected with another person is determined in accordance with section 993 of ITA 2007.][3]

Commentary—*Simon's Taxes* **E7.221**.

HMRC Manuals—Pensions Tax Manual PTM026000 (overview of payments).

PTM027000 (meaning of connected person).

Modifications—Taxation of Pension Schemes (Transitional Provisions) Order, SI 2006/572 art 2(1)–(3) (modification of this section in respect in its application to any pension scheme, which by virtue of FA 2004 Sch 38 para 1(1) is to be treated as becoming a registered pension scheme on 6 April 2006; would have been so treated had it not been wound up before that date; or would have been so treated if the scheme administrator had not notified HMRC under FA 2004 Sch 36 para 2 that the pension scheme was not to become a registered pension scheme on that date).

Taxation of Pension Schemes (Transitional Provisions) Order, SI 2006/572 art 2(4), (5) (modification of sub-s (4) above in its application to any pension scheme which by virtue of FA 2004 Sch 36 para 1(1) would have been treated as becoming a registered pension scheme on 6 April 2006 had it not been wound up before that date).

Amendments—[1]   Words in sub-s (5) inserted by FA 2005 s 101, Sch 10 paras 5, 64(1) with effect from 6 April 2006.

[2]   Words in sub-ss (5)–(7) inserted and substituted by FA 2006 s 161, Sch 23 paras 1, 4. These amendments are deemed to have come into force on 6 April 2006.

[3]   Sub-s (8) substituted by ITA 2007 s 1027, Sch 1 paras 456, 467 with effect for income tax purposes from 6 April 2007, and corporation tax purposes for accounting periods ending after 5 April 2007.

162 Meaning of "loan"

(1) This section applies for the interpretation of this Chapter.

(2) "Loan" does not include the purchase of or subscription to debentures, debenture stock, loan stock, bonds, certificates of deposit or other instruments creating or acknowledging indebtedness which are—

  (a) listed or dealt in on a recognised stock exchange (within the meaning of [section 1005 of ITA 2007][3]), or

  (b) offered to the public.

(3) A guarantee of a loan made to or in respect of a [person who is or has been a][2] member or sponsoring employer of a registered pension scheme[, or to or in respect of a person who is connected with a [person who is or has been a][2] member or sponsoring employer of a registered pension scheme but is not [such a person][2],][1] is to be treated as a loan to or in respect of the [person who is or has been a][2] member or sponsoring employer of an amount equal to the amount guaranteed.

(4) If a [person who is or has been a][2] member or sponsoring employer of a registered pension scheme [or a person who is connected with a [person who is or has been a][2] member or sponsoring employer of a registered pension scheme but is not [[such a person][2]][1]—

  (a) is liable to pay a debt, the right to payment of which constitutes an asset held for the purposes of the pension scheme, but

  (b) is not required to pay it by the relevant date,

the debt is to be treated as a loan made by the pension scheme to the [person who is or has been a][2] member or sponsoring employer on that date.

(5) The relevant date is the date by which a person at arm's length from the pension scheme might be expected to be required to pay the debt.

[(6) For the purposes of this section whether a person is connected with another person is determined in accordance with section 993 of ITA 2007.][3]

Commentary—*Simon's Taxes* E7.241.

HMRC Manuals—Pensions Tax Manual PTM123100 (meaning of loan).

Amendments—[1]   Sub-s (6) and words in sub-ss (3), (4) inserted by FA 2005 s 101, Sch 10 paras 5, 64(1) with effect from 6 April 2006.

[2]   Words in sub-ss (3), (4) inserted and substituted by FA 2006 s 161, Sch 23 paras 1, 5. These amendments are deemed to have come into force on 6 April 2006.

[3]   Words in sub-s (2)(a) substituted, and sub-s (6) substituted, by ITA 2007 s 1027, Sch 1 paras 456, 468 with effect for income tax purposes from 6 April 2007, and corporation tax purposes for accounting periods ending after 5 April 2007.

163 Meaning of "borrowing" etc

(1) This section applies for the interpretation of this Chapter.

(2) Borrowing is borrowing by a registered pension scheme if the amount borrowed is to be repaid from sums or assets held for the purposes of the pension scheme.

(3) A liability is a liability of a registered pension scheme if the liability is to be met from sums or assets held for the purposes of the pension scheme.

(4) Borrowing by a registered pension scheme is in respect of an arrangement if it is properly attributable to the arrangement in accordance with the provisions of the pension scheme and any just and reasonable apportionment.

Commentary—*Simon's Taxes* E7.241.

Authorised member payments

164 Authorised member payments

[(1)] [2]The only payments a registered pension scheme is authorised to make to or in respect of a [person who is or has been a][1] member of the pension scheme are—

  (a) pensions permitted by the pension rules or the pension death benefit rules [to be paid to or in respect of a member][1] (see sections 165 and 167),

  (b) lump sums permitted by the lump sum rule or the lump sum death benefit rule [to be paid to or in respect of a member][1] (see sections 166 and 168),

  (c) recognised transfers (see section 169),

  (d) scheme administration member payments (see section 171),

  (e) payments pursuant to a pension sharing order or provision, and

  (f) payments of a description prescribed by regulations made by the Board of Inland Revenue.

[(2) Regulations under subsection (1)(f) may—

(*a*) provide that for the purposes of Part 9 of ITEPA 2003 all or part of a prescribed payment is to be treated as pension under a registered pension scheme, or as a lump sum of a prescribed description,

(*b*) provide that all or part of a prescribed payment is subject to the short service refund lump sum charge ... [5] or the special lump sum death benefits charge,

(*c*) provide that a prescribed event in relation to a prescribed payment is to be treated for the purposes of the lifetime allowance charge as a benefit crystallisation event, and make provision as to the amount crystallised by that event,

(*d*) . . . [3]

and "prescribed" means prescribed in regulations under subsection (1)(f).][2]

[(3) The Commissioners for Her Majesty's Revenue and Customs may by regulations make provision—

(*a*) having the effect that the making of a prescribed authorised payment does not (directly or indirectly) result in an individual first flexibly accessing pension rights for the purposes of sections 227B to 227F,

(*b*) having the effect that the making of a prescribed authorised payment is not a relevant withdrawal for the purposes of section 579CA of ITEPA 2003, and

(*c*) having the effect that the making of a prescribed payment by a pension scheme that is not a registered pension scheme, where the payment would be an authorised payment if the scheme were a registered pension scheme, is not a relevant withdrawal for the purposes of section 576A of ITEPA 2003.

(4) In subsection (3)—

"authorised payment" means a payment specified in subsection (1), and

"prescribed" means prescribed in regulations under subsection (3).[4]][5]

Commentary—*Simon's Taxes* **E7.225, E7.245**.

HMRC Manuals—Pensions Tax Manual PTM142000 (authorised member payments).

Regulations—Registered Pension Schemes (Authorised Payments) (Transfers to the Pension Protection Fund) Regulations, SI 2006/134.

Registered Pension Schemes (Authorised Member Payments) Regulations, SI 2006/137.

Registered Pension Schemes (Authorised Payments) Regulations, SI 2006/209.

Registered Pension Schemes (Authorised Member Payments) (No 2) Regulations, SI 2006/571.

Registered Pension Schemes (Authorised Payments—Arrears of Pension) Regulations, SI 2006/614.

Registered Pension Schemes (Authorised Payments) Regulations, SI 2007/3532.

Registered Pension Schemes (Authorised Payments) Regulations, SI 2009/1171.

Registered Pension Schemes (Authorised Payments) (Amendment) Regulations SI 2012/522.

Registered Pension Schemes (Authorised Payments) (Amendment) (No 2) Regulations 2012/1881.

Registered Pension Schemes (Authorised Payments) (Amendment) Regulations, SI 2013/1818.

Registered Pension Schemes (Authorised Payments) (Amendment) Regulations, SI 2017/397.

Amendments—[1]   Words inserted by FA 2006 s 161, Sch 23 paras 1, 6. These amendments are deemed to have come into force on 6 April 2006.

[2]   Sub-s (1) numbered as such and sub-s (2) inserted, by FA 2008 s 92, Sch 29 para 1 with effect from 21 July 2008.

[3]   Sub-s (2)(*d*) repealed by FA 2009 s 75(2)(*a*) with effect from 21 July 2009.

[4]   Sub-ss (3), (4) inserted by the Taxation of Pensions Act 2014 s 1, Sch 1 para 85 with effect from 17 December 2014.

[5]   In sub-s (2)(*b*), words ", the serious ill-health lump sum charge" repealed by FA 2016 s 22, Sch 5 para 3(1)(*a*) with effect in relation to lump sums paid after 15 September 2016.

165 Pension rules

(1) These are the rules relating to the payment of pensions by a registered pension scheme to a member of the pension scheme ("the pension rules").

Pension rule 1

No payment of pension may be made before the day on which the member reaches normal minimum pension age, unless the ill-health condition was met immediately before the member became entitled to a pension under the pension scheme.

Pension rule 2

If the member dies before the end of the period of ten years beginning with the day on which the member became entitled to a scheme pension [or an annuity][2], [and if in the case of an annuity that day was before 6 April 2015,][7] payment of the scheme pension [or annuity][2] may continue to be made (to any person) until the end of that period.

[If the member becomes entitled to an annuity on or after 6 April 2015 and the annuity is payable until the later of the member's death and the end of a term certain, payment of the annuity may continue to be made (to any person) until the end of that term.][7]

[Except as provided by the preceding provisions of this rule, no][7] payment of the member's pension may be made after the member's death.

Pension rule 3

No payment of pension other than a scheme pension may be made in respect of a defined benefits arrangement.

Pension rule 4

[No payment of pension[3] other than—

   (*a*) a scheme pension,
   (*b*) a lifetime annuity, or
   (*c*) [drawdown pension,][3]

may be made in respect of a money purchase arrangement; but a scheme pension may only be paid if the member had an opportunity to select a lifetime annuity instead.

[Pension rule 5
The total amount of drawdown pension paid in each drawdown pension year [from, or under a short-term annuity purchased using sums or assets out of, the member's drawdown pension fund][6] in respect of a money purchase arrangement must not exceed [150%][5] of the basis amount for the drawdown pension year.
But this limit does not apply in relation to an arrangement to which subsection (3A) applies.[8]][3]
. . .[3]

(2) In this Part "pension", in relation to a registered pension scheme, includes—
   (*a*) an annuity, and
   (*b*) income withdrawal.
(3) For the purposes of this Part, a person becomes entitled to a pension under a registered pension scheme—
   (*a*) in the case of income withdrawal under the pension scheme, whenever sums or assets held for the purposes of an arrangement under the pension scheme are designated as available for the payment of [drawdown pension][4], and
   (*b*) in any other case, when the person first acquires an actual (rather than a prospective) right to receive the pension
[and, for this purpose, the abatement of a scheme pension under a public service pension scheme is not to be taken to affect the right to receive it.][1]
[(3A) This subsection applies to an arrangement if—
   (*a*) the member meets the flexible drawdown conditions,
   (*b*) the member makes a valid declaration to the scheme administrator to that effect, and
   (*c*) the declaration is accepted by the scheme administrator.
(3B) The member meets the flexible drawdown conditions if—
   (*a*) the member satisfied the minimum income requirement on the relevant day,
   (*b*) no relevant contributions are paid under any money purchase arrangement (other than a cash balance arrangement) relating to the member under a registered pension scheme in the tax year in which the declaration is made, and
   (*c*) at the time of the declaration the member is not an active member of any registered pension scheme under which there is a defined benefits or cash balance arrangement relating to the member.][3]
(4) Part 1 of Schedule 28 gives the meaning of expressions used in the pension rules.

Commentary—*Simon's Taxes* E7.227, E7.230.
HMRC Manuals—National Insurance Manual NIM02767 (pension rules 1 and 3).
NIM02768 (pension rules 4 and 6).
Pensions Tax Manual PTM062310 (pensions: overview).
PTM061100 (pensions).
Amendments—[1]   Words in sub-s (3) inserted by FA 2005 s 101, Sch 10 paras 5, 64(1) with effect from 6 April 2006.
[2]   Words in sub-s (1) substituted by FA 2007 s 69, Sch 19 paras 1, 2(1), (2), 29(1) with effect in relation to deaths of members of registered pension schemes occurring on or after 6 April 2007.
[3]   In sub-s (1) in pension rule 4, words substituted for words "If the member has not reached the age of 75, no payment of pension" and para (*c*) substituted, pension rule 5 substituted, pension rules 6 and 7 repealed, and sub-ss (3A), (3B) inserted, by FA 2011 s 65, Sch 16 para 1 with effect for the tax year 2011–12 and subsequent tax years, subject to transitional provisions in FA 2011 Sch 16 Pt 3.
[4]   Words in sub-s (3)(*a*) substituted for words "unsecured pension" by FA 2011 s 65, Sch 16 paras 62, 64 with effect for the tax year 2011–12 and subsequent tax years, subject to transitional provisions in FA 2011 Sch 16 Pt 3.
[5]   In sub-s (1), in pension rule 5, figure substituted for previous figure "120%" by FA 2014 s 39(1) with effect in relation to drawdown pension years beginning on or after 27 March 2014.
[6]   In sub-s (1), in pension rule 5, words inserted by the Taxation of Pensions Act 2014 s 1, Sch 1 para 1 with effect from 17 December 2014.
[7]   In sub-s (1), in pension rule 2, words inserted, and in final sentence words substituted for words "But no other", by the Taxation of Pensions Act 2014 s 1, Sch 1 para 41 with effect from 17 December 2014.
[8]   In sub-s (1), in pension rule 5, second sentence repealed, and sub-ss (3A), (3B) repealed, by the Taxation of Pensions Act 2014 s 1, Sch 1 para 32(1)(*a*), (*b*) with effect from 6 April 2015.

166 Lump sum rule
(1) This is the rule relating to the payment of lump sums by a registered pension scheme to a member of the pension scheme ("the lump sum rule").
   Lump sum rule
No lump sum may be paid other than—
   (*a*) a pension commencement lump sum,
   (*b*) a serious ill-health lump sum,

[(*ba*) an uncrystallised funds pension lump sum,][4]
(*c*) a short service refund lump sum,
(*d*) a refund of excess contributions lump sum,
(*e*) a trivial commutation lump sum,
(*f*) a winding-up lump sum, . . . [2]
(*g*) a lifetime allowance excess lump sum[, or
(*h*) a transitional 2013/14 lump sum.][2]

(2) For the purposes of this Part, a person becomes entitled to a lump sum under a registered pension scheme—

[(*za*) in the case of a pension commencement lump sum to which paragraph 1B of Schedule 29 applies (certain sums paid before 6 April 2015), immediately before the person becomes entitled to the actual pension (see paragraph 1B(2)(*h*) of that Schedule),][2]
(*a*) in the case [of any other][2] pension commencement lump sum, immediately before the person becomes entitled to the pension in connection with which it is paid [(or, if the person dies before becoming entitled to the pension in connection with which it was anticipated it would be paid, immediately before death)][1],
[(*aa*) in the case of an uncrystallised funds pension lump sum, immediately before it is paid,][4] and
(*b*) in any other case, when the person acquires an actual (rather than a prospective) right to receive the lump sum.

(3) Part 1 of Schedule 29 gives the meaning of expressions used in the lump sum rule.
(4) Schedule 36 contains (in Part 3) transitional provisions about lump sums.
[(5) The Commissioners for Her Majesty's Revenue and Customs may by regulations amend Part 1 of Schedule 29, or Part 3 of Schedule 36, in connection with cases involving a lump sum within subsection (6).
(6) A lump sum is within this subsection if—
(*a*) the sum is paid on or after 19 September 2013 and before 6 April 2015, or
(*b*) the sum is paid before 19 September 2013, a contract for a lifetime annuity is entered into to provide the pension in connection with which the sum is paid, and on or after 19 March 2014 the contract is cancelled.
(7) The provision that may be made under subsection (5) includes provision altering the effect of amendments made by the Finance Act 2014.][3]

Commentary—*Simon's Taxes* **E7.231, E7.232**.
HMRC Manuals—Pensions Tax Manual PTM088200 (performing the lifetime allowance test on a benefit crystallisation event (BCE)).
PTM088670 (benefit crystallisation events: each of the benefit crystallisation events (bces) in detail: bce 6 relevant lumpsums).
Modifications—Pension Protection Fund (Tax) Regulations, SI 2006/575 reg 11(1), (2) (modification of sub-s (2) above in respect of the payment of lump sums by the Pensions Protection Fund to an individual).
Taxation of Pension Schemes (Transitional Provisions) Order, SI 2006/572 art 23B (modification of sub-s (2)(*a*) above in respect of trivial commutation lump sums).
Taxation of Pension Schemes (Transitional Provisions) Order, SI 2006/572 arts 23ZC, 23ZE(modification of sub-s (2)(*a*) in respect of an individual who has received a pension commencement lump sum but who dies before becoming entitled to the pension in connection with the lump sum).
Amendments—[1] Words in sub-s (2)(*a*) inserted by FA 2007 s 70, Sch 20 paras 1, 9, 24(3). These amendments are deemed always to have had effect.
[2] In sub-s (1) in the lump sum rule, word in para (*f*) repealed and para (*h*) and preceding word inserted; sub-s (1)(*za*) inserted; and in sub-s (2)(*a*), words substituted, by FA 2014 s 43, Sch 5 paras 2(2), 5(1). These amendments are to be treated as having come into force on 19 March 2014 (FA 2014 Sch 5 para 15).
[3] Sub-ss (5)–(7) inserted by FA 2014 s 43, Sch 5 para 13 with effect from 17 July 2014.
[4] Sub-ss (1)(*ba*), (2)(*aa*) inserted by the Taxation of Pensions Act 2014 s 1, Sch 1 paras 53–55 with effect from 17 December 2014.

167 Pension death benefit rules

(1) These are the rules relating to the payment of pension death benefits by a registered pension scheme in respect of a member of the pension scheme ("the pension death benefit rules").
Pension death benefit rule 1
No payment of pension death benefit may be made otherwise than to a dependant[, or nominee or successor,][6] of the member.
Pension death benefit rule 2
No payment of pension death benefit other than a dependants' scheme pension may be made in respect of a defined benefits arrangement.
Pension death benefit rule 3
[No payment of pension death benefit][3] other than—
(*a*) a dependants' scheme pension,
(*b*) a dependants' annuity, or
(*c*) [dependants' drawdown pension,][3]

may be made to [a dependant][3] in respect of a money purchase arrangement; but a dependants' scheme pension may only be paid if the member or dependant had an opportunity to select a dependants' annuity instead.

> [*Pension death benefit rule 3A*

>> No payment of pension death benefit, other than [a nominees' annuity in respect of a money purchase arrangement or][7] nominees' drawdown pension in respect of a money purchase arrangement, may be made to a nominee of the member.

> *Pension death benefit rule 3B*

>> No payment of pension death benefit, other than [a successors' annuity in respect of a money purchase arrangement or][7] successors' drawdown pension in respect of a money purchase arrangement, may be made to a successor of the member.][6]

[*Pension death benefit rule 4*

The total amount of dependants' drawdown pension paid to a dependant in each drawdown pension year [from, or under a dependants' short-term annuity purchased using sums or assets out of, the dependant's drawdown pension fund][5] in respect of a money purchase arrangement must not exceed[1] [150%][4] of the basis amount for the drawdown pension year.

But this limit does not apply in relation to an arrangement, subject to which subsection (2A) applies.]

. . .[3]

. . .[3]

[(1A) For the purposes of this Part, a person becomes entitled to dependants' income withdrawal, nominees' income withdrawal or successors' income withdrawal under a registered pension scheme whenever sums or assets held for the purposes of an arrangement under the pension scheme are designated as available for the payment of (as the case may be) dependants' drawdown pension, nominees' drawdown pension or successors' drawdown pension.][6]

(2) [In this Part "pension][2] death benefit" means a pension payable on the death of the member (other than a member's pension payable after the member's death under pension rule 2: see section 165)[, or a pension payable in respect of the member on the subsequent death of a dependant, nominee or successor of the member][6].

[(2A) This subsection applies to an arrangement if—

    (*a*) the dependant meets the flexible drawdown conditions,

    (*b*) the dependant makes a valid declaration to the scheme administrator to that effect, and

    (*c*) the declaration is accepted by the scheme administrator.

(2B) The dependant meets the flexible drawdown conditions if—

    (*a*) the dependant satisfied the minimum income requirement on the relevant day,

    (*b*) no relevant contributions are paid under any money purchase arrangement (other than a cash balance arrangement) relating to the dependant under a registered pension scheme in the tax year in which the declaration is made, and

    (*c*) at the time of the declaration the dependant is not an active member of any registered pension scheme under which there is a defined benefits or cash balance arrangement relating to the dependant.][3]

(3) Part 2 of Schedule 28 gives the meaning of expressions used in the pension death benefit rules.

Commentary—*Simon's Taxes* **E7.237, E7.238**.

HMRC Manuals—Pensions Tax Manual PTM072110 (conditions).

PTM072330 (death benefits: types of pension: dependant's drawdown pension: dependants' flexible drawdown pension (up to 5 april 2015).

PTM072200 (beneficiary's annuity).

Modifications—Pensions Schemes (Application of UK Provisions to Relevant Non-UK Schemes) Regulations, SI 2006/207 reg 7 (modification of this section in respect of relevant non-UK schemes).

Taxation of Pension Schemes (Transitional Provisions) Order, SI 2006/572 arts 3, 4 (modification of this section in its application to any pension which—

    (a)   was paid by way of income withdrawal, income drawdown or annuity purchase deferral from a retirement benefits scheme, or a personal pension scheme approved under TA 1988 Pt 14 immediately before 6 April 2006; and

    (b)   on 6 April 2006 becomes an unsecured pension or a dependant's unsecured pension by virtue of a scheme which is treated as becoming a registered pension scheme on that date).

FA 2011 Sch 16 para 98 (modification of this section in relation to limit on amount of pension payable in year).

FA 2011 Sch 16 para 100 (modification of this section in relation to previous alternatively secured pension year).

Amendments—[1]   Figure in sub-s (1) substituted by FA 2007 s 69, Sch 19 paras 1, 4, 29(2) with effect for alternatively secured pension years beginning on or after 6 April 2007.

[2]   Words in sub-s (2) substituted by FA 2007 s 70, Sch 20 paras 22(1), 24(3). This amendment is deemed always to have had effect.

[3]   In sub-s (1) words substituted for words "If a dependant has not reached the age of 75, no payment of pension death benefit to the dependant", and "the dependant", in pension death benefit rule 3, para (c) substituted, pension death benefit rule 4 substituted, pension death benefit rules 5 and 6 repealed, and sub-ss (2A), (2B) inserted, by FA 2011 s 65, Sch 16 para 11 with effect for the tax year 2011–12 and subsequent tax years, subject to transitional provisions in FA 2011 Sch 16 Pt 3.

[4]   In sub-s (1), in pension death benefit rule 4, figure substituted for previous figure "120%" by FA 2014 s 39(2) with effect in relation to drawdown pension years beginning on or after 27 March 2014.

[5]   In sub-s (1), in pension death benefit rule 4, words inserted by the Taxation of Pensions Act 2014 s 1, Sch 1 paras 5, 6 with effect from 17 December 2014.

[6]   In sub-s (1), words in pension death benefit rule 1 inserted, Pension death benefit rules 3A, 3B inserted, sub-s (1A) inserted, and words in sub-s (2) inserted by the Taxation of Pensions Act 2014 s 3, Sch 2 paras 1, 2 with effect from 17 December 2014.

[7]   In sub-s (1), words in pension death benefit rules 3A, 3B inserted by FA 2015 s 34, Sch 4 paras 1, 2 with effect from 26 March 2015.

168 Lump sum death benefit rule

(1) This is the rule relating to the payment of lump sum death benefits by a registered pension scheme in respect of a member of the pension scheme ("the lump sum death benefit rule").

Lump sum death benefit rule

No lump sum death benefit may be paid other than—

    (*a*)   a defined benefits lump sum death benefit,

    (*b*)   a pension protection lump sum death benefit,

    (*c*)   an uncrystallised funds lump sum death benefit,

    (*d*)   an annuity protection lump sum death benefit,

    [(*e*)   a drawdown pension fund lump sum death benefit,][2]

    [(*ea*)   a flexi-access drawdown fund lump sum death benefit,][3]

    (*f*)   a charity lump sum death benefit,

    (*g*)   . . .[1]

    (*h*)   a trivial commutation lump sum death benefit, or

    (*i*)   a winding-up lump sum death benefit.

(2) In this Part "lump sum death benefit" means a lump sum payable on the death of the member[, or a lump sum payable in respect of the member on the subsequent death of a dependant, nominee or successor of the member.][4]

(3) Part 2 of Schedule 29 gives the meaning of expressions used in the lump sum death benefit rule.

(4) Schedule 36 contains (in Part 3) transitional provision about lump sum death benefits.

Commentary—*Simon's Taxes* **E7.239**.

HMRC Manuals—Pensions Tax Manual PTM062400 (a lifetime annuity contract and annuity protection). PTM074000 (life cover lump sum). PTM071000 (essential principles).

Modifications—Taxation of Pension Schemes (Transitional Provisions) Order, SI 2006/572 arts 6, 8(1), (2) (modification of this section in the case of a member of a registered pension scheme who satisfies certain conditions).

Amendments—[1]   Sub-s (1)(*g*) repealed by FA 2007 ss 69, 114, Sch 19 paras 1, 5, 29(3), Sch 27 Pt 3(1) with effect in relation to lump sum death benefits paid in respect of members of schemes whose deaths occur on or after 6 April 2007.

[2]   Sub-s (1)(*e*) substituted by FA 2011 s 65, Sch 16 paras 62, 65 with effect for the tax year 2011–12 and subsequent tax years, subject to transitional provisions in FA 2011 Sch 16 Pt 3. The amendments made by FA 2011 Sch 16 paras 33–39, 41, 42(2)(*b*), (*c*), (4), (5), 65, 67, 68, 75(*a*), 76, 77(5), 79(4), 82(6) have effect in relation to deaths occurring on or after 6 April 2011 (FA 2011 Sch 16 para 103).

[3]   Sub-s (1)(*ea*), inserted by the Taxation of Pensions Act 2014 s 1, Sch 1 paras 5, 7 with effect from 17 December 2014.

[4]   In sub-s (2), words inserted by F(No 2)A 2015 s 22(9). This amendment is to be treated as having come into force on 15 July 2015.

169 Recognised transfers

(1) A "recognised transfer" is a transfer of sums or assets held for the purposes of, or representing accrued rights under, a registered pension scheme so as to become held for the purposes of, or to represent rights under—

    (*a*)   another registered pension scheme, or

    (*b*)   a qualifying recognised overseas pension scheme,

in connection with a member of that pension scheme.

[(1A) A transfer of sums or assets held for the purposes of, or representing accrued rights under, a registered pension scheme to an insurance company is to be treated as a recognised transfer if the sums or assets had been applied by the pension scheme towards the provision of a scheme pension or a dependants' scheme pension (but subject to regulations under subsections (1B) and (1C)).

(1B) The Board of Inland Revenue may by regulations provide that, where any of the sums or assets transferred represent rights in respect of a scheme pension to which a member of a registered pension scheme has become entitled ("the original scheme pension")—

    (*a*)   the transfer is not a recognised transfer unless those sums and assets are, after the transfer, applied towards the provision of a scheme pension (a "new scheme pension"), and

    (*b*)   if they are so applied, the new scheme pension is to be treated, to such extent as is prescribed by the regulations and for such of the purposes of this Part as are so prescribed, as if it were the original scheme pension.

(1C) The Board of Inland Revenue may by regulations provide that, where any of the sums or assets transferred represent rights in respect of a dependants' scheme pension to which a dependant of a member of a registered pension scheme has become entitled in respect of the member ("the original dependants' scheme pension")—

    (*a*)   the transfer is not a recognised transfer unless those sums and assets are, after the transfer, applied towards the provision of a dependants' scheme pension (a "new dependants' scheme pension"), and

(b) if they are so applied, the new dependants' scheme pension is to be treated, to such extent as is prescribed by the regulations and for such of the purposes of this Part as are so prescribed, as if it were the original dependants' scheme pension.

(1D) The Board of Inland Revenue may by regulations provide that, where any of the sums or assets transferred represent—

(a) a [member's drawdown pension fund or dependant's drawdown pension fund][2], . . . [2] [or

(aa) a member's flexi-access drawdown fund or dependant's flexi-access drawdown fund,][5] [or

(ab) a nominee's flexi-access drawdown fund, or

(ac) a successor's flexi-access drawdown fund,][7]

(b) . . . [2]

under an arrangement ("the old arrangement"), the transfer is not a recognised transfer unless all of those sums and assets become held under an arrangement under which no other sums or assets are held ("the new arrangement").

(1E) If regulations so provide they may make in relation to cases in which the sums and assets become so held provision as to the treatment for the purposes of any provision of this Part of—

(a) the sums and assets transferred, and

(b) the new arrangement,

including provision for treating the sums and assets transferred as remaining, to such extent as is prescribed by the regulations and for such of the purposes of this Part as are so prescribed, sums and assets held under the old arrangement.][1]

(2) For the purposes of this Part a recognised overseas pension scheme is a qualifying recognised overseas pension scheme if—

(a) the scheme manager has given to the Inland Revenue notification that it is a recognised overseas pension scheme and has provided any such evidence that it is a recognised overseas pension scheme as the Inland Revenue may require,

(b) the scheme manager has undertaken to the Inland Revenue to inform the Inland Revenue if it ceases to be a recognised overseas pension scheme,

[(ba) the scheme manager has confirmed to an officer of Revenue and Customs that the scheme manager understands the scheme manager's potential liability to overseas transfer charge and has undertaken to such an officer to operate the charge including by meeting the scheme manager's liabilities to the charge,][8]

(c) the scheme manager has undertaken to the Inland Revenue to comply with [any requirements imposed under subsection (4)][3], and

(d) the recognised overseas pension scheme is not excluded from being a qualifying recognised overseas pension scheme by subsection (5).

[(2A) Regulations may make provision as to—

(a) information that is to be included in, or is to accompany, a notification under subsection (2)(a);

(b) the way and form in which such a notification, or any required information or evidence, is to be given or provided.][8]

(3) In this Part "scheme manager", in relation to a pension scheme, means the person or persons administering, or responsible for the management of, the pension scheme.

[(4) Regulations may require the scheme manager of a QROPS or former QROPS to—

(a) give the Commissioners information of a prescribed description,

(b) give the Commissioners such evidence as they may require of a prescribed matter,

[(ba) give information of a prescribed description to the scheme manager of a QROPS or former QROPS,

(bb) give information of a prescribed description to the scheme administrator of a registered pension scheme,

(bc) give information of a prescribed description to a member, or former member, of the QROPS or former QROPS,][6] and

(c) give a prescribed authority, in prescribed circumstances, information of a prescribed description.

[(4ZA) Regulations may require a member, or former member, of a QROPS or former QROPS to give information of a prescribed description to the scheme manager of a QROPS or former QROPS.][8]

(4A) Regulations under subsection (4) [or (4ZA)][8] may make provision as to—

(a) the way and form in which information or evidence is to be given, and

(b) the times or intervals at which information or evidence is to be given.

(4B) The regulations may apply any provision of Part 7 of Schedule 36 to FA 2008 (penalties), with or without modifications, in relation to requirements imposed under the regulations on a former QROPS.][3]

[(4C) Provision under subsection (2A)(b) or (4A)(a) may, in particular, provide for use of a way or form specified by the Commissioners.][8]

(5) A recognised overseas pension scheme is excluded from being a qualifying recognised overseas pension scheme by this subsection if [the Commissioners have][3] decided that—
[(*a*) any of the following conditions is met in relation to the scheme—
  (i) there has been a failure to comply with a relevant requirement and the failure is significant,
  (ii) any information given pursuant to a relevant requirement is [inaccurate][4] in a material respect,
  (iii) any declaration given pursuant to a relevant requirement is false in a material respect,
  (iv) there is no scheme manager,][3] and
(*b*) by reason of [that condition being met][3] it is not appropriate that transfers of sums or assets held for the purposes of, or representing accrued rights under, registered pension schemes so as to become held for the purposes of, or to represent rights under, the recognised overseas pension scheme should be recognised transfers,

and has notified the person or persons appearing to be the scheme manager of that decision (but subject to subsection (7) and section 170).
[(6) A failure to comply with a requirement is significant if—
(*a*) it is a failure to give information or evidence that is (or may be) of significance, or
(*b*) there are reasonable grounds for believing that the failure prejudices (or might prejudice) the assessment or collection of tax by the Commissioners.][3]
(7) The Inland Revenue—
(*a*) may at any time after a recognised overseas pension scheme becomes excluded from being a qualifying recognised overseas pension scheme decide that the pension scheme is to cease to be so excluded, and
(*b*) must notify the scheme manager of the decision.
[(7A) Regulations may, in a case where—
(*a*) any of the sums and assets transferred by a relevant overseas transfer represent rights in respect of a pension to which a person has become entitled under the transferring scheme ("the original pension"), and
(*b*) those sums and assets are, after the transfer, applied towards the provision of a pension under the other scheme ("the new pension"),
provide that the new pension is to be treated, to such extent as is prescribed and for such of the purposes of this Part as are prescribed, as if it were the original pension.
(7B) For the purposes of subsection (7A), a "relevant overseas transfer" is a transfer of sums or assets held for the purposes of, or representing accrued rights under, a relevant overseas scheme ("the transferring scheme") so as to become held for the purposes of, or to represent rights under—
(*a*) another relevant overseas scheme, or
(*b*) a registered pension scheme,
in connection with a member of that pension scheme.
(7C) In subsection (7B) "relevant overseas scheme" means—
(*a*) a QROPS, or
(*b*) a relevant non-UK scheme (see paragraph 1(5) of Schedule 34).
(7D) Regulations under subsection (7A) may—
(*a*) apply generally or only in specified cases, and
(*b*) make different provision for different cases.][8]
[(8) In subsections (4) to (6)[, (7A) to (7D)][8] and this subsection—
  "the Commissioners" means the Commissioners for Her Majesty's Revenue and Customs;
  "prescribed" means prescribed by regulations;
  "QROPS" means a qualifying recognised overseas pension scheme, and "former QROPS" means a scheme that has at any time been a QROPS;
  "regulations" means regulations made by the Commissioners;
  "relevant requirement" means—
    (*a*) a requirement imposed by regulations under subsection (4), or
    (*b*) a requirement imposed by virtue of Part 1 of Schedule 36 to FA 2008 (powers to obtain information and documents)[, or
    (*c*) a requirement to pay overseas transfer charge, or interest on overseas transfer charge, imposed by regulations under section 244L(2) or by an assessment under such regulations.][8]][3]

Commentary—*Simon's Taxes* **E7.240, E7.248A**.
HMRC Manuals—Pensions Tax Manual PTM104000 (transfer of drawdown pensions).
PTM112100 (ROPS to QROPS).
PTM112500 (exclusion and other losses of QROPS status).
Regulations—Pension Schemes (Information Requirements — Qualifying Overseas Pension Schemes, Qualifying Recognised Overseas Pensions Schemes and Corresponding Relief) Regulations, SI 2006/208.
Registered Pension Schemes (Transfer of Sums and Assets) Regulations, SI 2006/499.
Registered Pension Schemes and Overseas Pension Schemes (Miscellaneous Amendments) Regulations, SI 2012/884.

Registered Pension Schemes (Transfer of Sums and Assets) (Amendment) Regulations, SI 2014/1449
Overseas Pension Schemes (Miscellaneous Amendments) Regulations, SI 2015/673.
Registered Pension Schemes and Overseas Pension Schemes (Miscellaneous Amendments) Regulations, 2018/5.
Relevant Overseas Schemes (Transfer of Sums and Assets) Regulations, SI 2018/372.
Pension Schemes (Information Requirements — Qualifying Overseas Pension Schemes, Qualifying Recognised Overseas Pension Schemes and Corresponding Relief) (Amendment) Regulations, SI 2019/773.

Amendments—[1]   Sub-ss (1A)–(1E) inserted by FA 2005 s 101, Sch 10 paras 36, 64(1) with effect from 6 April 2006.

[2]   Words in sub-s (1D)(*a*) substituted for words "person's unsecured pension fund or dependant's unsecured pension fund", and sub-s (1D)(*b*) and preceding word "or" repealed, by FA 2011 s 65, Sch 16 paras 62, 66 with effect for the tax year 2011–12 and subsequent tax years, subject to transitional provisions in FA 2011 Sch 16 Pt 3.

[3]   Amendments are made by FA 2013 s 53(2)–(7) with effect from 17 July 2013

[4]   In sub-s (5)(*a*)(ii), word substituted for word "incorrect" by FA 2014 s 46, Sch 7 paras 1, 23(*a*) with effect from 17 July 2014.

[5]   Sub-s (1D)(*aa*) and preceding word inserted by the Taxation of Pensions Act 2014 s 1, Sch 1 paras 5, 8 with effect from 17 December 2014.

[6]   Sub-s (4)(*ba*), (*bc*) inserted by the Taxation of Pensions Act 2014 s 1, Sch 1 para 92 with effect from 17 December 2014.

[7]   Sub-s (1D)(*ab*), (*ac*) inserted by the Taxation of Pensions Act 2014 s 3, Sch 2 para 4 with effect from 17 December 2014.

[8]   Sub-ss (2)(*ba*), (2A), (4ZA), (4C), (7A)–(7D) inserted, and words in sub-ss (4A), (8) inserted, by FA 2017 s 10, Sch 4 paras 12, 13 with effect from 9 March 2017.

   Note that sub-s (2)(*ba*) has effect—

     (a)   on and after 9 March 2017 in the case of a recognised overseas pension scheme where: (i) the notification mentioned in sub-s (2)(*a*) is given on or after 9 March 2017; or (ii) although that notification is given before 9 March 2017, the letter from the HMRC Commissioners advising the scheme of the reference number allocated to the scheme is dated on or after 9 March 2017; and

     (b)   on and after 14 April 2017 in the case of a recognised overseas pension scheme where that letter is dated before 9 March 2017. See FA 2017 Sch 4 para 25(2).

170 Appeal against decision to exclude recognised overseas pension scheme

(1) This section applies where a recognised overseas pension scheme is excluded from being a qualifying recognised overseas pension scheme by a decision of the Inland Revenue under section 169(5).

(2) The scheme manager may appeal against the decision.

(3), (4) . . .[1].

(5) An appeal under this section against a decision must be brought within the period of 30 days beginning with the day on which the notification of the decision was given.

(6) [On an appeal that is notified to the tribunal, the tribunal][1] must consider whether the recognised overseas pension scheme ought to have been excluded from being a qualifying recognised overseas pension scheme.

(7) If [the tribunal decides][1] that the recognised overseas pension scheme ought to have been excluded from being a qualifying recognised overseas pension scheme, [the tribunal must][1] dismiss the appeal.

(8) If [the tribunal decides][1] that the recognised overseas pension scheme ought not to have been excluded from being a qualifying recognised overseas pension scheme, the recognised overseas pension scheme is to be treated as having remained a qualifying recognised overseas pension scheme (but subject to any further appeal . . .[1]).

Amendments—[1]   Sub-ss (3), (4) and words in sub-s (8) repealed, in sub-ss (6)–(8) words substituted by the Transfer of Tribunal Functions and Revenue and Customs Appeals Order, SI 2009/56 art 3, Sch 1 para 425 with effect from 1 April 2009.

171 Scheme administration member payments

(1) A "scheme administration member payment" is a payment by a registered pension scheme to or in respect of a [person who is or has been a][1] member of the pension scheme which is made for the purposes of the administration or management of the pension scheme.

(2) But if a payment falling within subsection (1) exceeds the amount which might be expected to be paid to a person who was at arm's length, the excess is not a scheme administration member payment.

(3) Scheme administration member payments include in particular—

   (*a*) the payment of wages, salaries or fees to persons engaged in administering the pension scheme, and

   (*b*) payments made for the purchase of assets to be held for the purposes of the pension scheme.

(4) A loan to or in respect of a [person who is or has been a][1] member of the pension scheme is not a scheme administration member payment.

(5) Regulations made by the Board of Inland Revenue may provide that payments of a description specified in the regulations are, or are not, scheme administration member payments.

Commentary—*Simon's Taxes* E7.245.

HMRC Manuals—Pensions Tax Manual PTM143100 (what can be a scheme administration member payment).

Amendments—[1]   Words in sub-ss (1), (4) inserted by FA 2006 s 161, Sch 23 paras 1, 7. These amendments are deemed to have come into force on 6 April 2006.

Unauthorised member payments

172 Assignment

(1) Subsection (2) applies if a member of a registered pension scheme (or the member's personal representatives) assigns or agrees to assign—

    [(*a*) any benefit, other than an excluded pension, to which the member (or any dependant[, nominee or successor][3] of the member) has an actual or prospective entitlement under the pension scheme, or

    (*b*) any right in respect of any sums or assets held for the purposes of any arrangement under the pension scheme.][1].

(2) Unless the assignment or agreement is pursuant to a pension sharing order or provision, the pension scheme is to be treated as making an unauthorised payment to the member (or to the member's personal representatives in respect of the member).

(3) Subsection (4) applies if a person (or a person's personal representatives) assigns or agrees to assign—

    [(*a*) any benefit, other than an excluded pension, to which the person has [a][2] prospective entitlement under the pension scheme in respect of a member of the pension scheme, or

    (*b*) any right in respect of any sums or assets held for the purposes of any arrangement relating to [a member of the pension scheme][2] under the pension scheme.][1].

(4) Unless the assignment or agreement is pursuant to a pension sharing order or provision, the pension scheme is to be treated as making an unauthorised payment to the person (or the person's personal representatives) in respect of the member.

(5) The amount of the unauthorised payment is the greater of—

    (*a*) the consideration received in respect of the assignment or agreement, and

    (*b*) the consideration which might be expected to be received in respect of the assignment or agreement if the parties to the transaction were at arm's length [and any power to reduce the entitlement to the benefit or right did not exist][1].

(6) Where a pension scheme is treated by this section as having made an unauthorised payment in relation to an assignment (or an agreement to assign), payments by the pension scheme of the benefit [or right][1] assigned (or agreed to be assigned) are not unauthorised payments.

[(6A) References in this section to a benefit to which the member or a person has an entitlement under the pension scheme includes rights to payments under—

    (*a*) a scheme pension or dependants' scheme pension provided by the scheme administrator or as a result of the application of sums or assets held for the purposes of the pension scheme, or

    (*b*) a lifetime annuity or dependants' annuity[, or nominees' annuity or successors' annuity,][4] purchased by the application of sums or assets held for the purposes of the pension scheme.][2]

[(7) An excluded pension is so much of any pension which under pension rule 2 may continue to be paid after the member's death as may be so paid.][1]

(8) "Assignment" includes assignation and related expressions are to be read accordingly.

Commentary—*Simon's Taxes* **E7.236, E7.247**.
HMRC Manuals—Pensions Tax Manual PTM133200 (assignment).
Amendments—[1]   Words in sub-ss (1), (3) and sub-s (7) substituted, and words in sub-ss (5)(*b*), (6) inserted by FA 2005 s 101, Sch 10 paras 37, 64(1) with effect from 6 April 2006.
[2]   Words in sub-s (3)(*a*), (*b*) substituted, and sub-s (6A) inserted, by FA 2008 s 91, Sch 28 paras 1, 2 with effect in relation to assignments or agreements to assign made on or after 10 October 2007.
[3]   Words in sub-s (1)(*a*) inserted by the Taxation of Pensions Act 2014 s 3, Sch 2 para 5 with effect from 17 December 2014.
[4]   Words in sub-s (6A)(*b*) inserted by FA 2015 s 34, Sch 4 paras 1, 8 with effect from 26 March 2015.

[172A Surrender

(1) Subsection (2) applies if a member of a registered pension scheme surrenders or agrees to surrender—

    (*a*) any benefit, other than an excluded pension, to which the member (or any dependant[, nominee or successor][7] of the member) has a prospective entitlement under an arrangement under the pension scheme,

    [(*aa*) any rights to payments under a lifetime annuity or dependants' annuity[, or nominees' annuity or successors' annuity,][8] purchased by the application of sums or assets held for the purposes of the pension scheme,][4] or

    (*b*) any right in respect of any sums or assets held for the purposes of any arrangement under the pension scheme.

(2) The pension scheme is to be treated as making an unauthorised payment to the member.

(3) Subsection (4) applies if a person surrenders or agrees to surrender—

    (*a*) any benefit, other than an excluded pension, to which the person has a prospective entitlement under an arrangement under the pension scheme [in respect of][4] a member of a pension scheme, or

    (*b*) any right in respect of any sums or assets held for the purposes of any arrangement relating to a member of the pension scheme under the pension scheme.

(4) The pension scheme is to be treated as making an unauthorised payment to the person in respect of the member.

(5) Subsections (2) and (4) do not apply to—

    (*a*) a surrender pursuant to a pension sharing order or provision,

    (*b*) a surrender (or agreement to surrender) by the member in return for the conferring on a dependant[, or nominee,]⁷ of an entitlement to benefits after the member's death,

    [(*ba*) a surrender (or agreement to surrender) by a dependant, nominee or successor of the member ("the beneficiary") in return for the conferring, on a successor of the member, of an entitlement to benefits after the beneficiary's death,]⁷

    (*c*) a transfer of (or agreement to transfer) benefits or rights so as to become benefits or rights under another arrangement under the pension scheme relating to the member[, dependant, nominee or successor]⁷,

    [(*ca*) a surrender of (or agreement to surrender) rights to payments under an annuity in any case covered by regulations under paragraph 3(2B) or 17(3) of Schedule 28;]⁴

    (*d*) , . . . ⁶

    [(*da*) a surrender made as part of a retirement-benefit activities compliance exercise,]³

    [(*db*) a surrender of a prospective entitlement to pension death benefits within section 167(1) or lump sum death benefits within section 168(1) (or both) made in order to comply with [Part 5 of the Equality Act 2010, so far as relating to age, or the"]⁵ Employment Equality (Age) Regulations (Northern Ireland) 2006 (or any regulations amending or replacing [those Regulations]⁵),]³

    (*e*) a surrender (or agreement to surrender) which constitutes an assignment (or agreement to assign) within section 172, or

    (*f*) any surrender (or agreement to surrender) of a description prescribed by regulations made by the Board of Inland Revenue.

[(5A) Subsection (5)(*b*) applies only if the entitlement is held (or is to be held) by the dependant[, or nominee,]⁷ under an arrangement under the pension scheme relating to the member or dependant [or nominee]⁷.]⁶

[(5B) Subsection (5)(*ba*) applies only if the entitlement is held (or is to be held) by the successor under an arrangement under the pension scheme relating to the beneficiary or successor.]⁷

(6) Regulations under subsection (5)(*f*) may include provision having effect in relation to times before they are made.

(7) Subsections (2) and (4) do not apply to the surrender of a benefit to which the member (or a dependant [or nominee or successor]⁷ of the member) has a prospective entitlement, or to which the person has a prospective entitlement in respect of a member, under an arrangement that is a defined benefits arrangement or cash balance arrangement unless—

    (*a*) in consequence of the surrender, the actual or prospective entitlement of another member (or dependant[, or nominee or successor,]⁷ of another member) of the pension scheme, or of another person in respect of another member, to benefits under the scheme is increased, and

    (*b*) the two members are or have been connected persons.

(8) The amount of the unauthorised payment is the consideration that might be expected to be received if what is surrendered were assigned by a transaction between parties at arm's length and any power to reduce the entitlement to the benefit or right did not exist.

(9) In this section "surrender", in relation to any benefit or right of a member (or dependant of a member) of a pension scheme or other person, includes any schemes, arrangements or understandings of any kind (whether or not legally enforceable) the main purpose, or one of the main purposes, of which is to reduce the member's (or dependant's), or person's, entitlement to the benefit or right.

[(9A) References in this section to a benefit to which the member or a person has an entitlement under the pension scheme includes rights to payments under—

    (*a*) a scheme pension or dependants' scheme pension provided by the scheme administrator or as a result of the application of sums or assets held for the purposes of the pension scheme, or

    (*b*) a lifetime annuity or dependants' annuity[, or nominees' annuity or successors' annuity,]⁸ purchased by the application of sums or assets held for the purposes of the pension scheme.]⁴

(10) [For the purposes of this section an]³ excluded pension is so much of any pension which under pension rule 2 may continue to be paid after the member's death as may be so paid.

[(10A) For the purposes of this section a surrender relating to an arrangement under the pension scheme ("the old arrangement") is made as part of a retirement-benefit activities compliance exercise if—

    (*a*) it is made in connection with the making of an arrangement under another pension scheme relating to the member ("the new arrangement"),

    (*b*) the old arrangement and the new arrangement relate to the same employment,

    (*c*) both the rights surrendered and the rights conferred under the new arrangement consist of or include a prospective entitlement to pension death benefits within section 167(1) or lump sum death benefits within section 168(1) (or both), (*d*) the surrender and the making of the new arrangement constitute or form part of a transaction the purpose of which is to secure that the activities of the pension scheme are limited to retirement-benefit activities within the meaning of section 255 of the Pensions Act 2004 or Article 232 of the Pensions (Northern Ireland) Order 2005, and

(*e*) the rights surrendered and the rights conferred under the new arrangement are not significantly different.][3]

[(11) For the purposes of this section whether a person is connected with another person is determined in accordance with section 993 of ITA 2007.][2][1]

Commentary—*Simon's Taxes* E7.236.

HMRC Manuals—Pensions Tax Manual PTM133300 (surrender of rights or benefits).

Regulations—Registered Pension Schemes (Surrender of Relevant Excess) Regulations, SI 2006/211.

Amendments—[1]   Sections 172A–172D inserted by FA 2005 s 101, Sch 10 paras 38, 64(1) with effect from 6 April 2006.

[2]   Sub-s (11) substituted by ITA 2007 s 1027, Sch 1 paras 456, 469 with effect for income tax purposes from 6 April 2007, and corporation tax purposes for accounting periods ending after 5 April 2007.

[3]   Sub-ss (5)(*da*), (*db*), (10A) inserted, and words in sub-s (10) substituted, by FA 2007 s 70, Sch 20 paras 1, 6, 24(3). These amendments are deemed always to have had effect.

[4]   Words in sub-s (3)(*a*) substituted and sub-ss (1)(*aa*), (5)(*ca*), (9A) inserted, by FA 2008 s 91, Sch 28 paras 1, 3 with effect in relation to surrenders and agreements to surrender made on or after 10 October 2007.

[5]   In sub-s(5)(*db*) words substituted by the Equality Act 2010 s 211(1), Sch 26, Pt 1, paras 57, 58(*a*) with effect from 1 October 2010 by virtue of SI 2010/2279, arts 2, 12, Sch 1, para 5.

[6]   Sub-s (5)(*d*) repealed, and sub-s (5A) inserted, by FA 2014 s 46, Sch 7 paras 1, 10. These amendments have effect in relation to surrenders (or agreements to surrender) made on or after 20 March 2014.

[7]   In sub-s (1)(*a*) words inserted, in sub-s (5) words inserted and words substituted for words "or dependant", in sub-ss (5A), (7) words inserted, and sub-s (5B) inserted, by the Taxation of Pensions Act 2014 s 3, Sch 2 paras 6–10 with effect from 17 December 2014.

[8]   In sub-s (1)(*aa*), (9A)(*b*) words inserted by FA 2015 s 34, Sch 4 paras 1, 9 with effect from 26 March 2015.

172B Increase in rights of connected person on death

(1) This section applies if—

(*a*) at any time after the death of a relevant member of a registered pension scheme, there is an increase in the pension rights of another member of the pension scheme which is attributable to the death, and

(*b*) the dead member and other member were connected persons immediately before the death.

(2) A member of a registered pension scheme is a relevant member if, immediately before his death, any of his rights under the pension scheme are—

(*a*) rights to benefit to which the member (or any dependant [or nominee or successor][10] of the member) has a prospective entitlement under an arrangement under the pension scheme,

[(*aa*) rights to payments under a scheme pension or dependants' scheme pension provided by the scheme administrator or as a result of the application of sums or assets held for the purposes of the pension scheme or under a lifetime annuity or dependants' annuity[, or nominees' annuity or successors' annuity,][11] purchased by the application of sums or assets held for the purposes of the pension scheme,][7] . . . [9]

[(*ab*) rights representing the nominee's flexi-access drawdown fund or successor's flexi-access drawdown fund in respect of an arrangement under the pension scheme,][10]

(*b*) rights representing the [member's drawdown pension fund or dependant's drawdown pension fund[4]][8] in respect of an arrangement under the pension scheme[, or

(*c*) rights representing the member's flexi-access drawdown fund or dependant's flexi-access drawdown fund in respect of an arrangement under the pension scheme.][9]

(3) There is at any time an increase in the pension rights of the other member of the pension scheme which is attributable to the death if—

(*a*) the consideration which might be expected to be received in respect of an assignment (or assignation) of the benefits to which he [has an actual or prospective entitlement][7] under the pension scheme at that time, exceeds

(*b*) the consideration which might be expected to be received in respect of such an assignment (or assignation) immediately before that time,

in consequence of the death (ignoring for the purposes of paragraphs (a) and (b) any power to reduce the entitlement to the benefits).

(4) The pension scheme is to be treated as making an unauthorised payment to the other member (or to the other member's personal representatives) of an amount equal to the excess (but subject to subsection [(5)][5]).

(5) The amount which would (apart from this subsection) constitute the unauthorised payment is to be reduced by so much of the excess as arises—

(*a*) . . . [3]

(*b*) from the other member becoming entitled to pension death benefits or lump sum death benefits in respect of the dead member, or

(*c*) in any manner prescribed by regulations made by the Board of Inland Revenue.

(6) Regulations under subsection (5)(c) may include provision having effect in relation to times before they are made.

(7) This section does not apply if—

  (a) . . .[7]

  (b) the benefits to which each of [at least 20 members of the pension scheme][7] [has an actual or prospective entitlement][7] under the pension scheme are increased at the same rate in consequence of the death.

[(7A) This section does not apply if—

  (a) the increase mentioned in subsection (1)(a) is an increase in the rate of a dependants' annuity[, nominees' annuity, successors' annuity][11] or dependants' scheme pension or in rights representing a [nominee's flexi-access drawdown fund, successor's flexi-access drawdown fund,][10] [dependant's drawdown pension fund][8] [or dependant's flexi-access drawdown fund][9], and

  (b) the increase is attributable to rights of the dead member to payments under a dependants' annuity[, nominees' annuity, successors' annuity][11] or dependants' scheme pension or rights representing a [nominee's flexi-access drawdown fund, successor's flexi-access drawdown fund,][10] [dependants' drawdown pension fund][8] [or dependant's flexi-access drawdown fund][9].

(7B) References in this section to a benefit to which the member or a person has an entitlement under the pension scheme includes rights to payments under—

  (a) a scheme pension or dependants' scheme pension provided by the scheme administrator or as a result of the application of sums or assets held for the purposes of the pension scheme, or

  (b) a lifetime annuity or dependants' annuity[, or nominees' annuity or successors' annuity,][11] purchased by the application of sums or assets held for the purposes of the pension scheme.][7]

(8) This section does not apply if the increase in the pension rights of the other member is brought about by an assignment (or agreement to assign) within section 172.

(8A) [6] . . . [8]

[(9) For the purposes of this section whether a person is connected with another person is determined in accordance with section 993 of ITA 2007.][2]][1]

Commentary—*Simon's Taxes* **E7.237, E7.247.**

HMRC Manuals—Pensions Tax Manual PTM133400 (when an increase in rights of a connected person on death is an unauthorised payment).

Amendments—[1] Sections 172A–172D inserted by FA 2005 s 101, Sch 10 paras 38, 64(1) with effect from 6 April 2006.

[2] Sub-s (9) substituted by ITA 2007 s 1027, Sch 1 paras 456, 470 with effect for income tax purposes from 6 April 2007, and corporation tax purposes for accounting periods ending after 5 April 2007.

[3] Sub-s (5)(a) repealed by FA 2007 ss 69, 114, Sch 19 paras 1, 6, 29(3), Sch 27 Pt 3(1) with effect in relation to lump sum death benefits paid in respect of members of schemes whose deaths occur on or after 6 April 2007.

[4] Words in sub-s (2)(b) substituted by FA 2007 s 69, Sch 19 paras 1, 12(1), (2), 29(5) with effect in relation to members of registered pension schemes becoming entitled to alternatively secured rights on or after 6 April 2007 in respect of members whose deaths occur on or after that date.

[5] Figure in sub-s (4) substituted by FA 2007 s 69, Sch 19 paras 1, 12(1), (3), (4) with effect from 19 July 2007.

[6] Sub-s (8A) inserted by FA 2007 s 69, Sch 19 paras 1, 12(1), (5) and deemed to have come into force on 6 April 2006.

[7] Words in sub-s (3)(a), (7)(b) substituted, sub-ss (2)(aa), (7A), (7B) inserted and sub-s (7)(a) repealed, by FA 2008 s 91, Sch 28 paras 1, 4 with effect in relation to deaths occurring on or after 6 April 2008.

[8] Words in sub-s (2)(b) substituted for words "member's unsecured pension fund or dependant's unsecured pension fund", words in sub-s (7A)(a) substituted for words "dependants' unsecured pension fund or dependants' alternatively secured pension fund", words in sub-s (7A)(b) substituted for words "dependants' unsecured pension fund", and sub-s (8A) repealed, by FA 2011 s 65, Sch 16 paras 62, 67 with effect for the tax year 2011–12 and subsequent tax years, subject to transitional provisions in FA 2011 Sch 16 Pt 3. The amendments made by FA 2011 Sch 16 paras 33–39, 41, 42(2)(b), (c), (4), (5), 65, 67, 68, 75(a), 76, 77(5), 79(4), 82(6) have effect in relation to deaths occurring on or after 6 April 2011 (FA 2011 Sch 16 para 103).

[9] In sub-s (2), word "or" at end of para (aa) repealed, and para (c) and preceding word inserted, and in sub-s (7A) words inserted in both places, by the Taxation of Pensions Act 2014 s 1, Sch 1 paras 5, 9, 10 with effect from 17 December 2014.

[10] In sub-ss (2), (7A), words inserted by the Taxation of Pensions Act 2014 s 3, Sch 2 paras 1, 11, 12 with effect from 17 December 2014.

[11] In sub-ss (2)(aa), (7A), (7B)(b) words inserted by FA 2015 s 34, Sch 4 paras 1, 10 with effect from 26 March 2015.

[172C Allocation of unallocated employer contributions

(1) This section applies if—

  (a) contributions are paid under a registered pension scheme by an employer otherwise than in respect of any individual,

  (b) in any tax year any of the contributions become held for the purposes of the provision of benefits to or in respect of a member of the pension scheme under any relevant arrangement or arrangements ("the allocated contributions"),

  (c) the amount of the allocated contributions exceeds the permitted maximum, and

  (d) the member and the employer, or the member and any person connected with the employer at any time during the tax year, are connected persons at any time during the tax year.

(2) An arrangement is a relevant arrangement if it is—

  (a) a money purchase arrangement that is not a cash balance arrangement, or

  (b) a hybrid arrangement under which the benefits that may be provided to or in respect of the member are, or include, money purchase benefits other than cash balance benefits.

(3) "The permitted maximum" is—

    (*a*) the maximum amount of relief to which the member is entitled under section 188 (relief for contributions) in respect of relievable pension contributions paid during the tax year (see section 190), less

    (*b*) the amount of any contributions paid by employers under any registered pension scheme in respect of the member in the tax year.

(4) But if the member is a also a member of one or more other registered pension schemes, the permitted maximum in relation to each of the registered pension schemes of which he is a member is—

$$\frac{PM}{N}$$

where—

    PM is the amount arrived at under subsection (3), and

    N is the number of registered pension schemes of which he is a member.

(5) The pension scheme is to be treated as making an unauthorised payment to the member (or to the member's personal representatives).

(6) The amount of the unauthorised payment is the amount by which the amount of the allocated contributions exceeds the permitted maximum.

[(7) For the purposes of this section whether a person is connected with another person is determined in accordance with section 993 of ITA 2007.][2]][1]

Commentary—*Simon's Taxes* **E7.222**.
HMRC Manuals—Pensions Tax Manual PTM133500 (allocation of unallocated employer contributions).
Amendments—[1]   Sections 172A–172D inserted by FA 2005 s 101, Sch 10 paras 38, 64(1) with effect from 6 April 2006.
[2]   Sub-s (7) substituted by ITA 2007 s 1027, Sch 1 paras 456, 471 with effect for income tax purposes from 6 April 2007, and corporation tax purposes for accounting periods ending after 5 April 2007.

[172D Limit on increase in benefits

(1) This section applies where, at any time during any pension input period in respect of a relevant arrangement relating to a member of an occupational pension scheme that is a registered pension scheme, the member and—

    (*a*) a sponsoring employer, or

    (*b*) a person connected with a sponsoring employer.

are connected persons.

(2) If—

    (*a*) the pension input amount for the pension input period in respect of the relevant arrangement, exceeds

    (*b*) the notional unconnected person input amount for the pension input period in respect of the relevant arrangement,

the pension scheme is to be treated as making an unauthorised payment to the member (or to the member's personal representatives) of an amount equal to the excess.

(3) A relevant arrangement is an arrangement under the pension scheme that is—

    (*a*) a defined benefits arrangement,

    (*b*) a cash balance arrangement, or

    (*c*) a hybrid arrangement under which the benefits that may be provided to or in respect of the member are, or include, defined benefits or cash balance benefits.

(4) The pension input amount for a pension input period in respect of the relevant arrangement is to be determined in accordance with—

    (*a*) sections 230 to 232 if the relevant arrangement is a cash balance arrangement,

    (*b*) sections 234 to [236A][3] if it is a defined benefits arrangement, and

    (*c*) section 237 if it is a hybrid arrangement,

treating references in those sections to the individual as to the member and treating section 237 as if the references to input amount B were omitted.

(5) The notional unconnected person input amount for the pension input period in respect of the relevant arrangement is what the pension input amount, as so determined, would have been if the member were connected with—

    (*a*) a sponsoring employer, or

    (*b*) a person connected with a sponsoring employer,

at no time during the pension input period.

[(6) For the purposes of this section whether a person is connected with another person is determined in accordance with section 993 of ITA 2007.][2]][1]

Commentary—*Simon's Taxes* **E7.212**.
HMRC Manuals—Pensions Tax Manual PTM133600 (limit on pension input amount).
Amendments—[1]   Sections 172A–172D inserted by FA 2005 s 101, Sch 10 paras 38, 64(1) with effect from 6 April 2006.

2   Sub-s (6) substituted by ITA 2007 s 1027, Sch 1 paras 456, 472 with effect for income tax purposes from 6 April 2007, and
     corporation tax purposes for accounting periods ending after 5 April 2007.
3   Figure in sub-s (4)(*b*) substituted for figure "236" by FA 2011 s 66, Sch 17 paras 1, 2 with effect for the tax year 2011–12
     and subsequent tax years, and in relation to pension input periods ending in the tax year 2011–12 but beginning earlier (or in
     2011–12). For transitional provisions see FA 2011 Sch 17 paras 28–34.

173 Benefits

(1) A registered pension scheme is to be treated as having made an unauthorised payment to a [person who is or has been a][2] member of the pension scheme if an asset held for the purposes of the pension scheme is used to provide a benefit (other than a payment) to—

    (*a*) the [person][2], or

    (*b*) a member of the [person's][2] family or household.

(2) If the benefit is received by reason of an employment which is not [lower-paid employment as a minister of religion][3], subsection (1) does not apply.

(3) If the benefit is received by reason of [an employment which is lower-paid employment as a minister of religion][3], subsection (1) only applies if—

    (*a*) it is a benefit to which Chapter 6 or 10 of the benefits code (cars and vans, and benefits not dealt with elsewhere in benefits code) would apply if the employment were not [lower-paid employment as a minister of religion][3],

    (*b*) the pension scheme is an occupational pension scheme, and

    (*c*) the [person][2], or a member of the [person's][2] family or household, is a director of, and has a material interest in, a sponsoring employer.

(4) A registered pension scheme is to be treated as having made an unauthorised payment in respect of a [person who is or has been a][2] member of the pension scheme if, after the [person's][2] death, an asset held for the purposes of the pension scheme is used to provide a benefit (other than a payment) to a person who, at the date of the [person's][2] death, was a member of the [person's][2] family or household.

(5) The person who receives the benefit is to be treated as having received the unauthorised payment.

(6) If the benefit is received by reason of an employment which is not [lower-paid employment as a minister of religion][3], subsections (4) and (5) do not apply.

(7) If the benefit is received by reason of [an employment which is lower-paid employment as a minister of religion][3], subsections (4) and (5) only apply if—

    (*a*) paragraphs (*a*) and (*b*) of subsection (3) apply, and

    (*b*) at the date of the [person's][2] death the [person][2], or a member of the [person's][2] family or household, was a director of, and had a material interest in, a sponsoring employer.

[(7A) This section does not apply if—

    (*a*) the pension scheme is an investment-regulated pension scheme, and

    (*b*) the asset consists of taxable property.][1]

(8) The amount of an unauthorised payment treated as having been made by this section—

    (*a*) in relation to such benefits, and in such circumstances, as may be prescribed by regulations made by the Board of Inland Revenue, is an amount determined in accordance with the regulations, and

    (*b*) otherwise, is the amount which would be the cash equivalent of the benefit under the benefits code if the benefit were received by reason of an employment and the benefits code applied to it.

(9) For the purposes of subsection (8)—

    (*a*) references in the benefits code to the employee are to be treated as references to the [person who is or has been a][2] member, and

    (*b*) references in the benefits code to the employer are to be treated as references to the pension scheme.

(10) In this section—

    "the benefits code" has the meaning given by section 63(1) of ITEPA 2003,

    "director" has the meaning given by section 67 of that Act,

    ["lower-paid employment as a minister of religion" has the meaning given by section 290D of that Act,][3] and

    "material interest" has the meaning given by section 68 of that Act.

(11) Section 721 of ITEPA 2003 applies for the purposes of determining the members of a person's family or household.

Commentary—*Simon's Taxes* **E7.241, E7.247.**

HMRC Manuals—Pensions Tax Manual PTM133930 (living accommodation). PTM133910 (overview).

Regulations—Registered Pension Schemes (Co-ownership of Living Accommodation) Regulations, SI 2006/133.

Amendments—[1]   Sub-s (7A) inserted by FA 2006 s 158, Sch 21 paras 2, 4. This amendment is deemed to have come into force
     on 6 April 2006.
2   Words in sub-ss (1), (4), (9)(*a*) inserted; and words in sub-ss (3), (4), (7)(*b*) substituted; by FA 2006 s 161, Sch 23 paras 1,
     8. These amendments are deemed to have come into force on 6 April 2006.
3   In sub-ss (2), (3), (3) (*a*), (6), (7), words substituted, and in sub-s (10), definition substituted by FA 2015 s 13, Sch 1 para 25
     with effect for the tax year 2016–17 and subsequent tax years.

174 Value shifting

(1) A registered pension scheme is to be treated as having made an unauthorised payment to a [person who is or has been a]¹ member of the pension scheme if, in connection with any of the events mentioned in subsection (3) or a change in the value of a currency—

  (a) the value of an asset held for the purposes of the pension scheme is reduced or a liability of the pension scheme is increased, and

  (b) the value of an asset held by or for the benefit of the [person]¹ is increased, a liability of the [person]¹ is reduced, or a liability of another person is reduced for the benefit of the [person]¹.

(2) But if the event or the change in the value of the currency occurs after the [person's]¹ death—

  (a) the pension scheme is to be treated as having made an unauthorised payment in respect of the [person]¹ (rather than to the [person]¹), and

  (b) the person who holds the asset or is subject to the liability in relation to which subsection (1)(b) is satisfied is to be treated as having received the unauthorised payment.

(3) The events are—

  (a) the creation, alteration, release or extinction of any power, right, option or liability relating to assets held for the purposes of the pension scheme (whether or not provided for in the terms on which the asset is acquired or held),

  (b) the creation, alteration, release or extinction of any power, right or option relating to a liability of the pension scheme (whether or not provided for in the terms on which the liability is incurred),

  (c) the exercise of, or failure to exercise, any power, right or option in relation to assets held for the purposes of the pension scheme or a liability of the pension scheme, or

  (d) the exercise of, or failure to exercise, any power, right or option which constitutes an asset held for the purposes of the pension scheme,

in a way which differs from that which might be expected if the parties to the transaction were at arm's length.

(4) The amount of the unauthorised payment is the amount by which the reduction in value of the asset held for the purposes of the pension scheme, or the increase in the liability of the pension scheme, exceeds that which might be expected if the parties to the transaction were at arm's length.

(5) Regulations made by the Board of Inland Revenue may make provision as to how the excess is to be calculated in relation to events of a description specified in the regulations (including provision as to the times at which the asset or liability is to be valued).

Commentary—*Simon's Taxes* **E7.247.**
HMRC Manuals—Pensions Tax Manual PTM133700 (general).
Amendments—¹   Words in sub-s (1) inserted; and words in sub-ss (1), (2) substituted; by FA 2006 s 161, Sch 23 paras 1, 9. These amendments are deemed to have come into force on 6 April 2006.

[174A Taxable property held by investment-regulated pension schemes

(1) An investment-regulated pension scheme is to be treated as making an unauthorised payment to a member of the pension scheme if—

  (a) the pension scheme acquires an interest in taxable property, and

  (b) the interest is held by the pension scheme for the purposes of an arrangement under the pension scheme relating to the member.

(2) An investment-regulated pension scheme is to be treated as making an unauthorised payment to a member of the pension scheme if—

  (a) an interest in taxable property is held by the pension scheme for the purposes of an arrangement under the pension scheme relating to the member, and

  (b) the property is improved.

(3) An investment-regulated pension scheme is to be treated as making an unauthorised payment to a member of the pension scheme if—

  (a) an interest in property which is not residential property is held by the pension scheme for the purposes of an arrangement under the pension scheme relating to the member, and

  (b) the property is converted or adapted to become residential property.

(4) Schedule 29A makes provision supplementing this section; and in that Schedule—

  (a) Part 1 defines "investment-regulated pension scheme",

  (b) Part 2 defines "taxable property" (and "residential property"),

  (c) Part 3 explains what it means to acquire, and to hold, an interest in taxable property, and

  (d) Part 4 contains provision for calculating the amounts of unauthorised payments treated as made by this section and explains when the unauthorised payments are treated as made.]¹

Amendments—¹   This section inserted by FA 2006 s 158, Sch 21 paras 2, 5. This amendment is deemed to have come into force on 6 April 2006.

Authorised employer payments

175 Authorised employer payments

The only payments which a registered pension scheme that is an occupational pension scheme is authorised to make to or in respect of a [person who is or has been a][1] sponsoring employer are—

(a) public service scheme payments (see section 176),

(b) authorised surplus payments (see section 177),

(c) compensation payments (see section 178),

(d) authorised employer loans (see section 179),

(e) scheme administration employer payments (see section 180), and

(f) payments of a description prescribed by regulations made by the Board of Inland Revenue.

Commentary—*Simon's Taxes* E7.245.
HMRC Manuals—Pensions Tax Manual PTM145100 (authorised employer payments).
Amendments—[1] Words inserted by FA 2006 s 161, Sch 23 paras 1, 10. This amendment is deemed to have come into force on 6 April 2006.

176 Public service scheme payment

A payment is a public service scheme payment if—

(a) it is made by a public service pension scheme, and

(b) it is not of a description prescribed by regulations made by the Board of Inland Revenue.

177 Authorised surplus payment

For the purposes of this Part a payment is an authorised surplus payment if it is of a description prescribed by regulations made by the Board of Inland Revenue.

Commentary—*Simon's Taxes* E7.247.
HMRC Manuals—Pensions Tax Manual PTM145200 (authorised surplus payment).
PTM145300 (general conditions).
Regulations—Registered Pension Schemes (Authorised Surplus Payments) Regulations, SI 2006/574.

178 Compensation payments

A payment is a compensation payment if it is made in respect of a member's liability to a sponsoring employer in respect of a criminal, fraudulent or negligent act or omission by the member.

179 Authorised employer loan

(1) A loan made to or in respect of a [person who is or has been a][1] sponsoring employer is an authorised employer loan if—

(a) the amount loaned does not exceed an amount equal to 50% of the aggregate of the amount of the sums, and the market value of the assets, held for the purposes of the pension scheme immediately before the loan is made,

(b) the loan is secured by a charge which is of adequate value, and

(c) the repayment terms comply with subsection (2).

(2) The repayment terms comply with this subsection if—

(a) the rate of interest payable on the loan is not less than the rate prescribed by regulations made by the Board of Inland Revenue,

(b) the loan repayment date is before the end of the period of five years beginning with the date on which the loan is made, or has been postponed to a date after the end of that period under subsection (3), and

(c) the amount payable in each period beginning with the date on which the loan is made, and ending with the last day of a loan year, is not less than the required amount.

(3) If on a standard loan repayment date any amount (including interest) is owing, the loan repayment date may be postponed to a date before the end of the period of five years beginning with the standard loan repayment date.

(4) The loan repayment date may be postponed under subsection (3) only once.

(5) If the amount of a loan to or in respect of a [person who is or has been a][1] sponsoring employer is increased, the amount of the increase is to be treated as a loan made on the date of the increase.

(6) Schedule 30 gives the meaning of expressions used in this section and explains how to calculate the amount of the unauthorised payment when a loan to or in respect of a [person who is or has been a][1] sponsoring employer does not comply with subsection (1).

(7) In this section and that Schedule "charge" includes a right in security or an agreement to create a right in security; and any reference to assets subject to a charge or assets charged includes a reference to the property over which such a right is granted.

(8) Schedule 36 contains (in Part 4) transitional provision about loans to sponsoring employers.

Commentary—*Simon's Taxes* E7.241.
HMRC Manuals—Pensions Tax Manual PTM123200 (loans to sponsoring employers).
Regulations—Registered Pension Schemes (Prescribed Interest Rates for Authorised Employer Loans) Regulations, SI 2005/3449.
Amendments—[1] Words in sub-ss (1), (5), (6) inserted by FA 2006 s 161, Sch 23 paras 1, 11. These amendments are deemed to have come into force on 6 April 2006.

180 Scheme administration employer payments

(1) A "scheme administration employer payment" is a payment made—
- (*a*) by a registered pension scheme that is an occupational pension scheme, and
- (*b*) to or in respect of a [person who is or has been a][1] sponsoring employer,

for the purposes of the administration or management of the pension scheme.

(2) But if a payment falling within subsection (1) exceeds the amount which might be expected to be paid to a person who was at arm's length, the excess is not a scheme administration employer payment.

(3) Scheme administration employer payments include in particular—
- (*a*) the payment of wages, salaries or fees to persons engaged in administering the pension scheme, and
- (*b*) payments made for the purchase of assets to be held for the purposes of the pension scheme.

(4) A loan to or in respect of a [person who is or has been a][1] sponsoring employer is not a scheme administration employer payment.

(5) Payments made to acquire shares in a sponsoring employer are not scheme administration employer payments if, when the payment is made—
- (*a*) the market value of shares in the sponsoring employer held for the purposes of the pension scheme is equal to or greater than 5% of the aggregate of the amount of the sums, and the market value of the assets, held for the purposes of the pension scheme, or
- (*b*) the total market value of shares in sponsoring employers held for the purposes of the pension scheme is equal to or greater than 20% of the aggregate of the amount of the sums, and the market value of the assets, held for the purposes of the pension scheme.

(6) Regulations made by the Board of Inland Revenue may provide that payments of a description specified in the regulations are, or are not, scheme administration employer payments.

Commentary—*Simon's Taxes* **E7.210, E7.245**.
HMRC Manuals—Pensions Tax Manual PTM122000 (limits on shares in sponsoring employer companies).
PTM144000 (scheme administration employer payments - explained).
Modifications—Finance Act 2004, Section 180(5) (Modification) Regulations, SI 2012/1258 (in its application to a pension scheme established under the Pensions Act 2008 s 67 (duty on Secretary of State to establish a pension scheme), this section has effect as if sub-s (5)(*b*) were omitted, in relation to any payments made on or after 6 April 2012).
Amendments—[1] Words in sub-ss (1), (4) inserted by FA 2006 s 161, Sch 23 paras 1, 12. These amendments are deemed to have come into force on 6 April 2006.

Unauthorised employer payments

181 Value shifting

(1) A registered pension scheme that is an occupational pension scheme is to be treated as having made an unauthorised payment to a [person who is or has been a][1] sponsoring employer if, in connection with any of the events mentioned in subsection (2) or a change in the value of a currency—
- (*a*) the value of an asset held for the purposes of the pension scheme is reduced or a liability of the pension scheme is increased, and
- (*b*) the value of an asset held by or for the benefit of the [person][1] is increased, a liability of the [person][1] is reduced, or a liability of another person is reduced for the benefit of the [person][1].

(2) The events are—
- (*a*) the creation, alteration, release or extinction of any power, right, option or liability relating to assets held for the purposes of the pension scheme (whether or not provided for in the terms on which the asset is acquired or held),
- (*b*) the creation, alteration, release or extinction of any power, right or option relating to a liability of the pension scheme (whether or not provided for in the terms on which the liability is incurred),
- (*c*) the exercise of, or failure to exercise, any power, right or option in relation to assets held for the purposes of the pension scheme or a liability of the pension scheme, or
- (*d*) the exercise of, or failure to exercise, any power, right or option which constitutes an asset held for the purposes of the pension scheme,

in a way which differs from that which might be expected if the parties to the transaction were at arm's length.

(3) The amount of the unauthorised payment is the amount by which the reduction in value of the asset held for the purposes of the pension scheme, or the increase in the liability of the pension scheme, exceeds that which might be expected if the parties to the transaction were at arm's length.

(4) Regulations made by the Board of Inland Revenue may make provision as to how the excess is to be calculated in relation to events of a description specified in the regulations (including provision as to the times at which the asset or liability is to be valued).

Commentary—*Simon's Taxes* **E7.247**.
HMRC Manuals—Pensions Tax Manual PTM026000 (payments to a sponsoring employer of an occupational pension scheme).

Amendments—[1] Words in sub-s (1) inserted and substituted by FA 2006 s 161, Sch 23 paras 1, 13. These amendments are deemed to have come into force on 6 April 2006.

Borrowing

182 Unauthorised borrowing: money purchase arrangements

(1) A registered pension scheme is not authorised to borrow an amount in respect of a money purchase arrangement unless the arrangement borrowing condition is met.

(2) The arrangement borrowing condition is met if—

$$(APB + PB) < \frac{VA}{2}$$

where—

 APB is the aggregate of the amounts previously borrowed in respect of the arrangement (excluding any amounts which have been repaid),

 PB is the amount proposed to be borrowed in respect of the arrangement, and

 VA is the value of the arrangement.

(3) The value of the arrangement is the aggregate of—

 (*a*) the amount of such of the sums and the market value of such of the assets as represent the [member's drawdown pension fund][1] in respect of the arrangement (if any),

 [(*aa*) the amount of such of the sums and the market value of such of the assets as represent the member's flexi-access drawdown fund in respect of the arrangement (if any),][2]

 (*b*) the amount of such of the sums and the market value of such of the assets as represent [dependants' drawdown pension funds][1] [or dependants' flexi-access drawdown funds][2] in respect of the arrangement (if any),

 [(*ba*) the amount of such of the sums and the market value of such of the assets as represent nominees' flexi-access drawdown funds in respect of the arrangement (if any),

 (*bb*) the amount of such of the sums and the market value of such of the assets as represent successors' flexi-access drawdown funds in respect of the arrangement (if any),][3]

 (*c*) the aggregate of the value of each scheme pension or dependants' scheme pension payable in respect of the arrangement, and

 (*d*) the value of the uncrystallised rights under the arrangement.

(4) The value of a scheme pension or dependants' scheme pension payable in respect of the arrangement is—

$$RVF \times ARP$$

where—

 RVF is the relevant valuation factor (see section 276), and ARP is the annual rate at which the pension is payable.

(5) Rights are uncrystallised if no-one has become entitled to the present payment of benefits in respect of the rights; and a person is to be treated as entitled to the present payment of benefits in respect of the sums and assets representing the person's [drawdown pension fund][1] [or the person's flexi-access drawdown fund][2].

(6) If the arrangement is a cash balance arrangement, the value of the uncrystallised rights under the arrangement is the amount which would, on the valuation assumptions (see section 277), be available for the provision of benefits in respect of those rights if a person became entitled to benefits in respect of those rights.

(7) If the arrangement is a money purchase arrangement other than a cash balance arrangement, the value of the uncrystallised rights under the arrangement is the aggregate of the amount of such of the sums, and the market value of such of the assets, held for the purposes of the arrangement as represent those rights.

(8) If the arrangement is a hybrid arrangement under which either cash balance benefits or other money purchase benefits (but not defined benefits) may be provided, the value of the uncrystallised rights under the arrangement is the greater of—

 (*a*) their value calculated under subsection (6) (on the assumption that cash balance benefits are provided), and

 (*b*) their value calculated under subsection (7) (on the assumption that other money purchase benefits are provided).

Commentary—*Simon's Taxes* **E7.241.**

HMRC Manuals—Pensions Tax Manual PTM124000 (money purchase schemes - borrowing).

Amendments—[1] Words in sub-s (3)(*a*) substituted for words "member's unsecured pension fund or alternatively secured pension fund", words in sub-s (3)(*b*) substituted for words "dependants' unsecured pension funds or alternatively secured pension funds", and words in sub-s (5) substituted for words "unsecured pension fund or alternatively secured pension fund", by FA 2011 s 65, Sch 16 paras 62, 70 with effect for the tax year 2011–12 and subsequent tax years, subject to transitional provisions in FA 2011 Sch 16 Pt 3.

[2] In sub-s (3), para (*aa*) inserted, and in para (*b*) words inserted, and in sub-s (5) words inserted, by the Taxation of Pensions Act 2014 s 1, Sch 1 paras 5, 11, 12 with effect from 17 December 2014.

[3] Sub-s (3)(*ba*), (*bb*) inserted by the Taxation of Pensions Act 2014 s 3, Sch 2 paras 1, 13 with effect from 17 December 2014.

183 Effect of unauthorised borrowing: money purchase arrangements

(1) Subsection (2) applies if a registered pension scheme borrows in respect of a money purchase arrangement an amount which it is not authorised to borrow under section 182.

(2) The pension scheme is to be treated as having made a scheme chargeable payment—

(*a*) if subsection (3) applies, of an amount calculated in accordance with subsection (4), and

(*b*) otherwise, of the amount borrowed.

(3) This subsection applies if, immediately before the amount is borrowed—

$$APB < \frac{VA}{2}$$

(4) If subsection (3) applies, the amount of the scheme chargeable payment is—

$$APB + AB - \frac{VA}{2}$$

(5) In subsections (3) and (4)—

APB is the aggregate of the amounts previously borrowed in respect of the arrangement (excluding any amounts which have been repaid),

AB is the amount borrowed, and

VA is the value of the arrangement, calculated in accordance with section 182(3), immediately before the amount is borrowed.

Commentary—*Simon's Taxes* E7.241.

HMRC Manuals—Pensions Tax Manual PTM124000 (effect of unauthorised borrowing - money purchase schemes and other arrangements).

184 Unauthorised borrowing: other arrangements

(1) A registered pension scheme is not authorised to borrow an amount in respect of any arrangement which is not a money purchase arrangement unless the scheme borrowing condition is met.

(2) The scheme borrowing condition is met if—

$$(APB + PB) < \frac{AARA}{2}$$

where—

APB is the aggregate of the amounts previously borrowed by the pension scheme in respect of arrangements which are not money purchase arrangements (excluding any amounts which have been repaid),

PB is the amount proposed to be borrowed by the pension scheme, and

AARA is the aggregate amount of the relevant sums and assets.

(3) The aggregate amount of the relevant sums and assets is the aggregate of—

(*a*) the amount of the sums held for the purposes of such of the arrangements under the pension scheme as are not money purchase arrangements, and

(*b*) the market value of the assets held for the purposes of such of the arrangements under the pension scheme as are not money purchase arrangements.

Commentary—*Simon's Taxes* E7.241.

HMRC Manuals—Pensions Tax Manual PTM124000 (other arrangements: borrowing by schemes other than money purchase schemes).

185 Effect of unauthorised borrowing: other arrangements

(1) Subsection (2) applies if a registered pension scheme borrows, in respect of an arrangement which is not a money purchase arrangement, an amount which it is not authorised to borrow under section 184.

(2) The pension scheme is to be treated as having made a scheme chargeable payment—

(*a*) if subsection (3) applies, of an amount calculated in accordance with subsection (4), and

(*b*) otherwise, of the amount borrowed.

(3) This subsection applies if, immediately before the amount is borrowed—

$$APB < \frac{AARA}{2}$$

(4) If subsection (3) applies, the amount of the scheme chargeable payment is—

$$APB + AB - \frac{AARA}{2}$$

(5) In subsections (3) and (4)—

APB is the aggregate of the amounts previously borrowed by the pension scheme in respect of arrangements which are not money purchase arrangements (excluding any amounts which have been repaid),

AB is the amount borrowed, and

AARA is the aggregate amount of the relevant sums and assets, calculated in accordance with section 184(3), immediately before the amount is borrowed.

Commentary—*Simon's Taxes* **E7.241**.

HMRC Manuals—Pensions Tax Manual PTM124000 (effect of unauthorised borrowing - money purchase schemes and other arrangements).

[Income and gains from taxable property

185A Income from taxable property

(1) An investment-regulated pension scheme is to be treated as having made a scheme chargeable payment if the pension scheme holds an interest in taxable property in a tax year.

(2) The amount of the scheme chargeable payment depends on whether a person who holds the interest in the property directly receives profits arising from the interest in the tax year.

(3) If a person who holds the interest in the property directly receives such profits in the tax year, the amount of the scheme chargeable payment is the greater of—

    (*a*) an amount equal to the amount of the annual profits from the interest in the property (see section 185B(1)), and

    (*b*) the amount of the deemed profits from the interest in the property for the year (see sections 185B(2) and 185C).

(4) If no person who holds the interest in the property directly receives such profits in the tax year, the amount of the scheme chargeable payment is the amount of the deemed profits from the interest in the property for the year (see sections 185B(2) and 185C).

(5) But where section 185D applies, the amount of the scheme chargeable payment is the amount found under subsection (3) or (4) as apportioned to the pension scheme in accordance with that section.

(6) Section 185E makes provision for credits against income tax charged under section 239 (scheme sanction charge) in respect of a scheme chargeable payment treated as made by virtue of this section.][1]

Amendments—[1] Sections 185A–185I inserted by FA 2006 s 158, Sch 21 paras 2, 6. This amendment is deemed to have come into force on 6 April 2006.

[185B Annual profits and deemed profits

(1) For the purposes of section 185A(3) the amount of the annual profits from the interest in the property is the total amount of profits received from the interest in the tax year—

    (*a*) by each person who holds the interest directly, and

    (*b*) at a time when the property is scheme-held taxable property.

(2) For the purposes of section 185A(3) and (4) the amount of the deemed profits from the interest in the property for the tax year is—

$$\frac{DMV}{10} \times \frac{DTP}{DY}$$

where—

DMV is the deemed market value of the interest in the property for the year (see section 185C), DTP is the number of days in the year for which the property is scheme-held taxable property, and

DY is the number of days in the year.

(3) In this Part "scheme-held taxable property" means property—

    (*a*) which is taxable property, and

    (*b*) an interest in which is held by the pension scheme.][1]

Amendments—[1] Sections 185A–185I inserted by FA 2006 s 158, Sch 21 paras 2, 6. This amendment is deemed to have come into force on 6 April 2006.

[185C Deemed market value

(1) For the purposes of section 185B(2), where no person who holds the interest in the property directly during the tax year does so by virtue of a lease of residential property, the deemed market value of the interest for the year is—

$$(MV + UP) \times (1 + RPI)$$

where—

MV is the opening market value (see subsection (2)),

UP is the total of any unauthorised payments treated as made by the pension scheme under section 174A in relation to the property in the tax year, other than any such payment treated as made by virtue of the property becoming scheme-held taxable property in the year, and

RPI is the figure expressed as a decimal which represents the percentage increase in the retail prices index between the first day in the tax year on which the property is scheme-held taxable property and the last such day (or, if there is no such increase, is nil).

(2) In subsection (1) "the opening market value" means—

    (a) if the property is not scheme-held taxable property immediately before the beginning of the tax year, the market value of the interest in the property immediately after the time during the year when the property first becomes scheme-held taxable property, and

    (b) otherwise, the deemed market value of the interest for the previous tax year.

(3) For the purposes of section 185B(2), where a person who holds the interest in the property directly during the tax year does so by virtue of a lease of residential property, the deemed market value of the interest for the year is the relevant rental value of the property calculated in accordance with paragraph 34 of Schedule 29A on the following assumptions—

    (a) that the lease was granted when the property first became scheme-held taxable property;

    (b) that the term of the lease is 50 years;

    (c) that a fully commercial rent is payable for the first five years of that term;

    (d) that afterwards the rent is reviewed on an upwards-only basis.][1]

Amendments—[1] Sections 185A–185I inserted by FA 2006 s 158, Sch 21 paras 2, 6. This amendment is deemed to have come into force on 6 April 2006.

[185D Apportionment to pension scheme

(1) This section applies where the pension scheme holds the interest in the property indirectly for the whole of the period in the tax year for which the property is scheme-held taxable property.

(2) The amount that would otherwise be the amount of the scheme chargeable payment is to be apportioned to the pension scheme by applying paragraphs 41 to 43 of Schedule 29A to it as if it were the total taxable amount in relation to an unauthorised payment treated as made—

    (a) by the pension scheme,

    (b) in connection with the acquisition of the interest in the property, and

    (c) at the end of the last day in the tax year on which the property is scheme-held taxable property.

(3) But where—

    (a) the amount found in relation to the pension scheme on the day mentioned in paragraph (c) of subsection (2), differs from

    (b) the amount that would be found in relation to the pension scheme under that subsection on another day in the tax year on which the property is scheme-held taxable property,

the amount to be apportioned to the pension scheme under this section is the average of the amounts produced by applying subsection (2) in relation to the pension scheme on each day in the tax year on which the property is scheme-held taxable property.][1]

Amendments—[1] Sections 185A–185I inserted by FA 2006 s 158, Sch 21 paras 2, 6. This amendment is deemed to have come into force on 6 April 2006.

[185E Credit for tax paid

(1) This section applies where—

    (a) the pension scheme holds the interest in the property indirectly in the tax year,

    (b) a person who holds the interest directly receives profits arising from the interest at a time in the tax year when the property is scheme-held taxable property,

    (c) tax is payable on those profits by that person (assuming them to be the highest part of the person's income for the tax year in which they are received), and

    (d) that tax has been paid.

(2) The amount determined under subsection (3) is to be allowed as a credit against any income tax charged under section 239 in respect of the scheme chargeable payment treated as made by virtue of the pension scheme holding the interest in the property in the tax year.

(3) That amount is a proportion of the tax payable and paid determined by reference to the proportion of the amount that would otherwise be the amount of the scheme chargeable payment that is apportioned to the pension scheme under section 185D.

(4) Where—

    (a) by virtue of this section an amount is allowed as a credit against income tax charged under section 239, and

    (b) the amount of tax payable and paid by reference to which the amount of the credit was calculated is subsequently varied, the amount of the credit is to be varied accordingly, and any necessary adjustments are to be made to give effect to the variation (whether by making assessments or otherwise).][1]

Amendments—[1]   Sections 185A–185I inserted by FA 2006 s 158, Sch 21 paras 2, 6. This amendment is deemed to have come into force on 6 April 2006.

[185F Gains from taxable property

(1) An investment-regulated pension scheme is to be treated as having made a scheme chargeable payment where—

    (a) in a tax year the pension scheme holds an interest in property which is taxable property or which has been taxable property at any time whilst the interest has been held by the pension scheme (a "taxable interest"),

    (b) a gain is treated as accruing to the pension scheme in respect of the taxable interest in the tax year, and

    (c) the total amount of gains treated as accruing to the pension scheme in respect of taxable interests in the tax year exceeds

the total amount of losses treated as accruing to the pension scheme in respect of taxable interests in the tax year.

(2) The amount of the scheme chargeable payment is an amount equal to the difference between—

    (a) the total amount of gains treated as accruing to the pension scheme in respect of taxable interests in the tax year, and

    (b) the total amount of losses treated as accruing to the pension scheme in respect of taxable interests in the tax year,

(but this is subject to section 185G(10)).

(3) A gain or loss is treated as accruing to a pension scheme in respect of a taxable interest in a tax year if—

    (a) by virtue of section 185G a chargeable gain or allowable loss is treated for the purposes of this section as accruing in the tax year to the person who holds the taxable interest directly, or

    (b) in the tax year the pension scheme or another vehicle ceases to hold all or part of an interest in a vehicle through which the pension scheme holds the taxable interest indirectly (see section 185H).][1]

Amendments—[1]   Sections 185A–185I inserted by FA 2006 s 158, Sch 21 paras 2, 6. This amendment is deemed to have come into force on 6 April 2006.

[185G Disposal by person holding directly

(1) For the purposes of this section the person ("the transferor") who holds the taxable interest directly is to be treated as holding an asset (a "taxable asset") consisting of the interest.

(2) For the purpose of determining—

    (a) whether the transferor disposes of the taxable asset,

    (b) when such a disposal takes place, and

    (c) whether a chargeable gain or allowable loss is treated for the purposes of section 185F as accruing to the transferor on a disposal of the taxable asset in a tax year and, if so, the amount of the chargeable gain or allowable loss,

TCGA 1992 is to be treated as applying to the transferor and the taxable asset, but subject as follows.

(3) TCGA 1992 is to be treated as applying as if—

    (a) throughout the tax year the transferor were resident . . . [3] and domiciled in the United Kingdom,

    (b) no allowable losses accrued to the transferor in any previous tax year,

    (c)   . . .[2]

    (d) notice under section 16(2A) (losses) of that Act were given by the transferor in relation to the year in respect of any loss treated as accruing to the transferor in the year from a disposal of the taxable asset,

    (e) section 45(1) (wasting assets) of that Act did not apply to a disposal of the taxable asset,

    (f) for the purposes of section 53 (indexation allowance) of that Act the transferor were not chargeable to corporation tax in respect of any chargeable gain accruing to the transferor from a disposal of the taxable asset,

    (g) section 171(1) (transfers within a group) of that Act did not apply to a disposal of the taxable asset (so that no election could be made in relation to such a disposal under section 171A (notional transfers within a group) of that Act), and

    (h) sections 222 to 224 (relief on disposal of private residence) of that Act did not apply to a gain on a disposal of the taxable asset by virtue of section 225 (private residence occupied under terms of settlement) of that Act.

(4) Where the taxable asset became taxable property whilst held directly by the pension scheme, TCGA 1992 is to be treated as applying to a disposal of the asset as if—

    (a) the asset had been acquired by the transferor at the time it became taxable property, and (*b*)　the amount deductible under section 38(1)(*a*) (consideration for acquisition of asset) of that Act in respect of the disposal were the amount of the unauthorised payment treated as made by the pension scheme at that time.

(5)　Subsections (6) to (8) apply where the pension scheme holds the taxable asset indirectly.

(6)　TCGA 1992 is to be treated as applying to a disposal of the asset as if the amount deductible under section 38(1) of that Act in respect of the disposal were—

(*a*)　the total amount of unauthorised payments treated as made by the pension scheme in respect of the taxable asset up to the time of the disposal, less

(*b*)　the amount found under paragraph (*a*) to the extent that it has already been taken into account in calculating the gains or losses accruing to the pension scheme in respect of the taxable asset by virtue of this section or section 185H.

(7)　The amount that would otherwise be the amount of the consideration for which the disposal is made (or treated as made) is to be scaled down by applying paragraphs 41 to 43 of Schedule 29A to it as if it were the total taxable amount in relation to an unauthorised payment treated as made—

(*a*)　by the pension scheme,

(*b*)　in connection with the acquisition of the interest in the property which constitutes the taxable asset, and

(*c*)　at the time of the disposal.

(8)　Subsection (6) is subject to section 42 of TCGA 1992 (part disposals); but in the application of that section in relation to the taxable asset the amount of the consideration for the disposal is to be taken to be that amount apart from subsection (7).

(9)　Where the taxable asset was not taxable property for the whole period beginning with—

(*a*)　the time when the pension scheme acquired the asset, or

(*b*)　if later, the time when the asset first became taxable property,

and ending with the disposal, the amount that would otherwise be the amount of any chargeable gain or allowable loss treated as accruing on a disposal of the asset is to be reduced by reference to the proportion of the period for which the asset was not taxable property.

(10)　Where—

(*a*)　the taxable asset is a wasting asset consisting of tangible moveable property, and

(*b*)　by virtue of section 185F, a loss is treated as accruing to the pension scheme from a disposal of the asset in a tax year,

the loss is only to be allowed as a deduction from any gains treated as accruing to the pension scheme by virtue of that section from other disposals in the year of taxable assets which are wasting assets consisting of tangible moveable property.][1]

Amendments—[1]　Sections 185A–185I inserted by FA 2006 s 158, Sch 21 paras 2, 6. This amendment is deemed to have come into force on 6 April 2006.

[2]　Sub-s (3)(*c*) repealed by FA 2008 s 8, Sch 2 para 53 with effect in relation to chargeable gains accruing or treated as accruing in the tax year 2008–09 or any subsequent tax year.

[3]　Words in sub-s (3)(*a*) repealed by FA 2013 s 219, Sch 46 paras 119, 120 with effect in relation to the tax year 2013–14 and any subsequent tax year.

[185H Disposal of interest in vehicle

(1)　This section applies for the purposes of section 185F where the pension scheme or another vehicle ceases to hold all or part of an interest in a vehicle through which the pension scheme holds the taxable interest indirectly.

(2)　The pension scheme is to be treated as disposing of the interest in the vehicle through which the pension scheme holds the taxable interest indirectly.

(3)　The amount of the gain or loss treated as accruing to the pension scheme on the disposal of the interest in the vehicle is the difference between—

(*a*)　the deemed consideration received for the disposal of the interest, and

(*b*)　the deemed consideration given for the interest.

(4)　The deemed consideration received for the disposal of the interest in the vehicle is the difference between—

(*a*)　the market value of the taxable interest at the time of the disposal, apportioned to the pension scheme in accordance with subsection (5) immediately before that time, and

(*b*)　the market value of the taxable interest at the time of the disposal, apportioned to the pension scheme in accordance with subsection (5) immediately after that time.

(5)　An amount mentioned in subsection (4) is to be apportioned to the pension scheme by applying paragraphs 41 to 43 of Schedule 29A to it as if it were the total taxable amount in relation to an unauthorised payment treated as made—

(*a*)　by the pension scheme,

(*b*)　in connection with the acquisition of the taxable interest, and

(*c*)　at the time at which the amount is to be apportioned to the pension scheme in accordance with that subsection.

(6)　The deemed consideration given for the interest in the vehicle is—

(*a*) the total amount of unauthorised payments treated as made by the pension scheme in respect of the taxable interest up to the time of the disposal, less

(*b*) the amount found under paragraph (*a*) to the extent that it has already been taken into account in calculating the gains or losses accruing to the pension scheme in respect of the taxable interest by virtue of section 185G or this section.][1]

Amendments—[1] Sections 185A–185I inserted by FA 2006 s 158, Sch 21 paras 2, 6. This amendment is deemed to have come into force on 6 April 2006.

[185I Credit for tax paid

(1) This section applies where by virtue of section 185F a pension scheme is to be treated as making a scheme chargeable payment which is to any extent attributable—

(*a*) to a chargeable gain treated by virtue of section 185G as accruing to another person on a disposal of a taxable asset, or

(*b*) to a gain treated by virtue of section 185H as accruing to the pension scheme as a result of another person disposing of an interest in a vehicle through which the pension scheme holds a taxable interest indirectly.

(2) Where—

(*a*) tax is payable in respect of the disposal by the person who makes the disposal, and

(*b*) that tax has been paid,

the amount determined under subsection (3) or (4) (as appropriate) is to be allowed as a credit against any income tax charged under section 239 in respect of the scheme chargeable payment.

(3) In a case within paragraph (*a*) of subsection (1), that amount is a proportion of the amount of tax paid and payable determined by reference to the proportion of the amount of consideration for the disposal that is apportioned under section 185G(7).

(4) In a case within paragraph (*b*) of subsection (1), that amount is the amount of tax paid and payable apportioned to the pension scheme by applying paragraphs 41 to 43 of Schedule 29A to it as if it were the total taxable amount in relation to an unauthorised payment treated as made—

(*a*) by the pension scheme,

(*b*) in connection with an acquisition of the taxable interest by the person disposing of the interest in the vehicle, and

(*c*) at the time of the disposal.

(5) Where—

(*a*) by virtue of this section an amount is allowed as a credit against income tax charged under section 239, and

(*b*) the amount of tax payable and paid by reference to which the amount of the credit was calculated is subsequently varied,

the amount of the credit is to be varied accordingly, and any necessary adjustments are to be made to give effect to the variation (whether by making assessments or otherwise).][1]

Amendments—[1] Sections 185A–185I inserted by FA 2006 s 158, Sch 21 paras 2, 6. This amendment is deemed to have come into force on 6 April 2006.

[Repayments of lump sums

185J Effect of repayment of certain pre-6 April 2015 lump sums

(1) For the purposes of this Part—

(*a*) a lump sum to which this section applies is treated as never having been paid, and

(*b*) the payment by which it is repaid is treated as not being a payment.

(2) This section applies to a lump sum if—

(*a*) the sum is paid by a registered pension scheme to a member of the scheme in respect of a money purchase arrangement,

(*b*) the sum is paid to the member in connection with a pension under the scheme to which it is expected that the member will become entitled ("the expected pension"),

(*c*) the expected pension is income withdrawal, a lifetime annuity or a scheme pension,

(*d*) the sum is paid before the member becomes entitled to the expected pension,

(*e*) either—

(i) the sum is paid on or after 19 September 2013 but before 6 April 2015, or

(ii) the sum is paid before 19 September 2013, a contract for a lifetime annuity is entered into to provide the expected pension, and on or after 19 March 2014 the contract is cancelled,

(*f*) before the member becomes entitled to the expected pension, the member repays the sum to the pension scheme that paid it, and

(*g*) the repayment is made before 6 October 2015.

(3) For the purposes of subsection (2), if the circumstances are as described in subsection (2)(*e*)(ii), the member is treated as not having become entitled to the expected pension as a result of the cancelled contract having been entered into.][1]

Commentary—*Simon's Taxes* **E7.232.**

Amendments—[1]   Section 185J and preceding crosshead inserted by FA 2014 s 43, Sch 5 para 3. This amendment is to be treated as having come into force on 19 March 2014 (FA 2014 Sch 5 para 15).

CHAPTER 4

REGISTERED PENSION SCHEMES: TAX RELIEFS AND EXEMPTIONS

Scheme investments

186 Income

(1) No liability to income tax arises in respect of—

    (*a*) income derived from investments or deposits held for the purposes of a registered pension scheme, or

    (*b*) underwriting commissions applied for the purposes of a registered pension scheme [which are not relevant foreign income and which would otherwise be chargeable to income tax under Chapter 8 of Part 5 of ITTOIA 2005 (income not otherwise charged).][1]

(2) The exemption provided by subsection (1) does not apply to income derived from investments or deposits held as a member of a property investment LLP; and for this purpose "income" includes relevant stock lending fees, in relation to any investments, to which subsection (1) would apply by virtue of section 129B of ICTA (inclusion of relevant stock lending fees in income).

[(2A) The exemption provided by subsection (1) does not prevent the income from being charged to tax by virtue of section 185A.][2]

(3) In this Part "investments", in relation to a registered pension scheme, includes futures contracts and options contracts; and income derived from transactions relating to futures contracts or options contracts is to be treated as derived from the contracts.

(4) For that purpose a contract is not prevented from being a futures contract or an options contract by the fact that a party is or may be entitled to receive or liable to make, or entitled to receive and liable to make, only a payment of a sum (as opposed to a transfer of assets) in full settlement of all obligations.

Commentary—*Simon's Taxes* **E7.241.**

HMRC Manuals—Pensions Tax Manual Pensions Tax Manual PTM024400 (investments). PTM121000 (tax reliefs for registered pension scheme investments). Offshore Funds Manual OFM16650 (investors in non-reporting funds: exceptions to the charge top tax: registered pension schemes).

Modifications—Pension Protection Fund (Tax) Regulations, SI 2006/575 reg 17 (modification of this section in relation to each of the Pension Act Funds).

Amendments—[1]   Words in sub-s (1)(*b*) substituted by ITTOIA 2005 s 882(1), Sch 1 paras 629, 644. This amendment comes into force at the same time as this section: ITTOIA 2005 Sch 2 para 161.

[2]   Sub-s (2A) inserted by FA 2006 s 158, Sch 21 paras 2, 7. This amendment is deemed to have come into force on 6 April 2006.

187 Chargeable gains

(1) Section 271 of TCGA 1992 (exemptions) is amended as follows.

(2) (*amends* TCGA 1992 s 271(1)(*b*))

(3) (*repeals* TCGA 1992 s 271(1)(*d*), (*g*), (*h*), (*j*))

(4) (*inserts* TCGA 1992 s 271(1A))

(5) (*repeals* TCGA 1992 s 271(2))

(6), (7) (*insert* TCGA 1992 s 271(10), (12))

Commentary—*Simon's Taxes* **C1.216, C2.803, E7.241.**

HMRC Manuals—Pensions Tax Manual PTM114000 (relief for employers' contributions).

Members' contributions

188 Relief for contributions

(1) An individual who is an active member of a registered pension scheme is entitled to relief under this section in respect of relievable pension contributions paid during a tax year if the individual is a relevant UK individual for that year.

(2) In this Part "relievable pension contributions", in relation to an individual and a pension scheme, means contributions by or on behalf of the individual under the pension scheme other than contributions to which subsection (3) [or (3A)][4] applies.

(3) This subsection applies to—

    (*a*) any contributions paid after the individual has reached the age of 75,

    [(*aa*) any contributions which are life assurance premium contributions (see section 195A),][1]

    (*b*) any contributions paid by an employer of the individual (as to which see sections 196 to 201),

    (*c*) . . . [5]

[(3A) This subsection applies to a contribution if the contribution results from the transfer of property or money, or the payment of a sum, towards the pension scheme pursuant to a relevant order in a case where—

    (*a*) section 266A (members' liability in respect of unauthorised member payments) applies, and (*b*) relief is claimed under that section in respect of the liability mentioned in subsection (1)(*a*) of that section.

(3B) In the case of a contribution which is greater than UMP (see section 266A(5)), subsection (3A) does not apply to the contribution so far as it is greater than UMP.

(3C) In subsection (3A) "relevant order" means an order under any of the following—

    (*a*) section 16(1), 19(4) or 21(2)(*a*) of the Pensions Act 2004 (orders for money etc to be restored to pension schemes), or

    (*b*) Article 12(1), 15(4) or 17(2)(*a*) of the Pensions (Northern Ireland) Order 2005 (corresponding provision for Northern Ireland).][4]

(4) For the purposes of this Part a pension credit which increases the rights of the individual under the pension scheme is only to be treated as a contribution on behalf of the individual if it derives from a pension scheme that is not a registered pension scheme.

(5) For the purposes of this Part—

    (*a*) any other transfer of any sum held for the purposes of, or representing accrued rights under, a pension scheme so as to become held for the purposes of, or to represent rights under, another pension scheme, . . .[2]

    (*b*) . . .[2]

is not to be treated as a contribution.

(6) . . .[3]

(7) References in the Income Tax Acts to relief in respect of life assurance premiums do not include relief under this section.

(8) The following sections make further provision about relief under this section—

    section 189 (relevant UK individual),

    section 190 (annual limit for relief),

    sections 191 to 194 (methods of giving relief), and

    section 195 (transfer of certain shares to be treated as payment of contribution).

Commentary—*Simon's Taxes* E4.139, E7.221, E7.247, E8.317.

HMRC Manuals—Pensions Tax Manual PTM042100 (payments not regarded as contributions).

PTM111600 (tax relief for individuals).

PTM111200 (international: migrant member relief).

Amendments—[1] Sub-s (3)(*aa*) inserted by FA 2007 s 68, Sch 18 paras 1, 2 with effect in accordance with FA 2007 Sch 18 paras 4–8.

[2] Sub-s (5)(*b*) and preceding word repealed by FA 2007 ss 69, 114, Sch 19 paras 1, 7, 29(3), Sch 27 Pt 3(1) with effect in relation to lump sum death benefits paid in respect of members of schemes whose deaths occur on or after 6 April 2007.

[3] Sub-s (6) repealed by FA 2013 s 52(1), (3) with effect from 6 April 2013.

[4] Words in sub-s (2), and sub-ss (3A)–(3C), inserted, by FA 2014 s 43, Sch 5 paras 1, 13 with effect in relation to orders made on or after 1 September 2014.

[5] Sub-s (3)(*c*) and preceding word "and" repealed by FA 2013 s 52(1), (2) with effect from 6 April 2015.

189 Relevant UK individual

(1) For the purposes of this Part an individual is a relevant UK individual for a tax year if—

    (*a*) the individual has relevant UK earnings chargeable to income tax for that year,

    (*b*) the individual is resident in the United Kingdom at some time during that year,

    (*c*) the individual was resident in the United Kingdom both at some time during the five tax years immediately before that year and when the individual became a member of the pension scheme, or

    (*d*) the individual, or the individual's spouse [or civil partner][2], has for the tax year general earnings from overseas Crown employment subject to UK tax.

(2) In this Part "relevant UK earnings" means—

    (*a*) employment income,

    (*b*) income which is chargeable under [Part 2 of ITTOIA 2005][1] and is immediately derived from the carrying on or exercise of a trade, profession or vocation (whether individually or as a partner acting personally in a partnership), . . .[3]

    [(*ba*) income which is chargeable under Part 3 of ITTOIA 2005 and is immediately derived from the carrying on of a UK furnished holiday lettings business (whether individually or as a partner acting personally in a partnership), . . .[5]]

    [(*bb*) income which is chargeable under Part 3 of ITTOIA 2005 and is immediately derived from the carrying on of an EEA furnished holiday lettings business (whether individually or as a partner acting personally in a partnership), and][5]

    [(*c*) income to which subsection (2A) applies.][3]

[(2A) This subsection applies to income if—

    (*a*) it is patent income, and

    (*b*) the individual, alone or jointly, devised the invention for which the patent in question was granted.][3]

[(2B) The income covered by subsection (2)(*b*) includes—

    (*a*) an amount treated as a profit under section 863J(2) of ITTOIA 2005, and

    (*b*) income treated as received under section 863J(4) of that Act.][6]

(3) For the purposes of this section and section 190 relevant UK earnings are to be treated as not being chargeable to income tax if, in accordance with arrangements having effect [under section 2(1) of the Taxation (International and Other Provisions) Act 2010][4] (double taxation agreements), they are not taxable in the United Kingdom.

(4) "General earnings from overseas Crown employment subject to UK tax" has the meaning given by section 28 of ITEPA 2003.

[(5) "UK furnished holiday lettings business" means a UK property business so far as consisting of the commercial letting of furnished holiday accommodation (within the meaning of Chapter 6 of Part 3 of ITTOIA 2005).][3]

[(6) If there is a letting of accommodation only part of which is holiday accommodation, just and reasonable apportionments are to be made for the purpose of determining what is comprised in a UK furnished holiday lettings business.][3]

[(6A) "EEA furnished holiday lettings business" means an overseas property business so far as consisting of the commercial letting of furnished holiday accommodation (within the meaning of Chapter 6 of Part 3 of ITTOIA 2005) in one or more EEA states.

(6B) If there is a letting of accommodation only part of which is holiday accommodation, just and reasonable apportionments are to be made for the purpose of determining what is comprised in an EEA furnished holiday lettings business.][5]

[(7) "Patent income" means—

    (a) royalties or other sums paid in respect of the use of a patent charged to tax under section 579 of ITTOIA 2005,

    (b) amounts on which tax is payable under section 587 or 593 of ITTOIA 2005, or

    (c) amounts on which tax is payable under—

        (i) section 472(5) of the Capital Allowances Act, or

        (ii) paragraph 100 of Schedule 3 to that Act.][3]

Commentary—*Simon's Taxes* B2.808, B5.333, B6.401, E7.221, E7.222, E7.223.

HMRC Manuals—Pensions Tax Manual PTM044100 (conditions).

Amendments—[1]   In sub-s (2), words in para (*b*) substituted, and para (*c*) substituted, by ITTOIA 2005 s 882(1), Sch 1 paras 629, 645. This amendment comes into force at the same time as this section: ITTOIA 2005 Sch 2 para 161.

[2]   Words in sub-s (1)(*d*) inserted by the Tax and Civil Partnership Regulations, SI 2005/3229, regs 175, 176 with effect from 6 April 2006 (reg 1(7)).

[3]   In sub-s (2), word repealed, para (*ba*) inserted, and para (*c*) substituted; sub-ss (2A), (5)–(7) inserted; by ITA 2007 ss 1027, 1031, Sch 1 paras 456, 473, Sch 3 Pt 1 with effect for income tax purposes from 6 April 2007, and corporation tax purposes for accounting periods ending after 5 April 2007.

[4]   In sub-s (3), words substituted for words "by virtue of section 788 of ICTA" by TIOPA 2010 s 501, Sch 8 paras 61, 63. TIOPA 2010 has effect for corporation tax purposes for accounting periods ending on or after 1 April 2010, for income and capital gains tax purposes for the tax year 2010–11 and subsequent tax years, and for petroleum revenue tax purposes for chargeable periods beginning on or after 1 July 2010.

[5]   In sub-s (2)(*ba*), word "and" repealed, and sub-ss (2)(*bb*), (6A), (6B) inserted, by FA 2011 s 52, Sch 14 para 1 with effect in relation to the tax year 2011–12 and subsequent tax years.

[6]   Sub-s (2B) inserted by FA 2014 s 74, Sch 17 para 18 with effect for the tax year 2014–15 and subsequent tax years.

190 Annual limit for relief

(1) The maximum amount of relief to which an individual is entitled under section 188 (relief for contributions) for a tax year is (subject as follows) the amount of the individual's relevant UK earnings which are chargeable to income tax for the tax year.

(2) If the amount of the individual's relevant UK earnings which are chargeable to income tax for the tax year is less than the basic amount, the maximum amount of relief to which the individual is entitled under section 188 for the tax year is increased by the difference between—

    (a) the amount of the individual's relevant UK earnings which are so chargeable, and

    (b) the basic amount,

(so that, if the individual has no relevant UK earnings which are so chargeable, the maximum amount of such relief is the basic amount).

(3) Subsection (2) is subject to section 191(7) (limit on methods of giving relief to which individual is entitled by virtue of subsection (2)).

(4) "The basic amount" is £3,600 or such greater amount as the Treasury may by order specify.

(5) . . . [1]

Commentary—*Simon's Taxes* E7.222.

HMRC Manuals—Pensions Tax Manual PTM044100 (annual limits).

Amendments—[1]   Sub-s (5) repealed by FA 2013 s 52(1), (4) with effect from 6 April 2013.

191 Methods of giving relief

(1) Relief to which an individual is entitled under section 188 (relief for contributions) in respect of contributions is to be given as provided by this section.

(2) Subject as follows, the relief is to be given in accordance with section 192 (relief at source).

(3) Subject to subsection (7), relief in respect of contributions under a pension scheme made by a member of the pension scheme may (instead of being given in accordance with section 192) be given in accordance with section 193 (relief under net pay arrangements) if—

(a) the pension scheme is an occupational pension scheme,

(b) the member is an employee of a sponsoring employer, and

(c) relief in respect of contributions made under the pension scheme by all of the other members of the pension scheme who are employees of the sponsoring employer is given in accordance with that section.

(4) Subject to subsection (7), relief in respect of contributions under a pension scheme made by a member of the pension scheme may (instead of being given in accordance with section 192) be given in accordance with section 193 if—

(a) the pension scheme is a public service pension scheme or marine pilots' benefits fund, and

(b) the member is an employee.

(5) Subject to subsection (7), subsection (6) applies where—

(a) contributions are made under a public service pension scheme or marine pilots' benefit fund by a member who is not an employee, or

(b) contributions are made otherwise than by a member of the pension scheme under a net pay pension scheme.

(6) Relief in respect of the contributions—

(a) may (but need not) be given in accordance with section 192, but

(b) where not so given, is to be given in accordance with section 194 (relief on making of claim).

(7) Relief to which an individual is entitled by virtue of section 190(2)—

(a) may only be given in accordance with section 192, and

(b) is not required to be given in respect of contributions under a net pay pension scheme.

(8) In this section "marine pilots' benefits fund" means—

(a) a fund established under section 15(1)(i) of the Pilotage Act 1983 (c 21), or

(b) any scheme supplementing or replacing such a fund.

(9) In this Part "net pay pension scheme" means a pension scheme in the case of which some or all of the members of the pension scheme are entitled to be given relief in accordance with section 193 in respect of the payment of contributions by them under the pension scheme.

(10) Schedule 36 contains (in Part 4) transitional provision about relief in respect of contributions to pre-commencement retirement annuity contracts.

192 Relief at source

(1) Where an individual is entitled to be given relief in accordance with this section in respect of the payment of a contribution under a pension scheme, the individual or other person by whom the contribution is paid is entitled, on making the payment, to deduct and retain out of it a sum equal to income tax on the contribution [at the relevant rate]³.

[(1A) For the purposes of this section and sections 192A and 192B "the relevant rate" is—

(a) if the Commissioners for Her Majesty's Revenue and Customs so notify the scheme administrator, the Scottish basic rate for the tax year in which the payment is made;

[(aa) if the Commissioners for Her Majesty's Revenue and Customs so notify the scheme administrator, the Welsh basic rate for the tax year in which the payment is made;]⁶ and

(b) the basic rate for that tax year in all other cases.]³

(2) If a sum is deducted from the payment of the contribution—

(a) the scheme administrator must allow the deduction on receipt of the residue,

(b) the individual or other person is acquitted and discharged of so much money as is represented by the deduction as if the sum had actually been paid, and

(c) the sum deducted is to be treated as income tax paid by the scheme administrator.

(3) When the payment of the contribution is received—

(a) the scheme administrator is entitled to recover from the Board of Inland Revenue the amount which is treated as income tax paid by the scheme administrator in relation to the contribution, and

(b) any amount so recovered is to be treated for the purposes of the Tax Acts in the same manner as the payment of the contribution.

[(4) If (apart from this section) income tax at the higher rate[[or]⁴ the additional rate or . . . .⁴]³ is chargeable in respect of any part of the individual's total income for the tax year, on the making of a claim the basic rate limit and the higher rate limit for the tax year in the individual's case are increased by the amount of the contribution.]²

[(4A) Where—

(a) the individual is a Scottish taxpayer for the tax year,

(b) (apart from this section) income tax is chargeable in respect of any part of that individual's total income for the tax year at a Scottish rate, and

(c) that rate is higher than the Scottish basic rate for that year,

on the making of a claim, the Scottish basic rate limit, and any other Scottish rate limit for the tax year in the individual's case [that is above the Scottish basic rate limit]⁵, are increased by the amount of the contribution.]⁴

[(4B) Where—

(a) the individual is a Welsh taxpayer for the tax year, and (*b*) (apart from this section) income tax is chargeable in respect of any part of that individual's total income for the tax year at the Welsh higher rate or Welsh additional rate,

on the making of a claim, the basic rate limit and the higher rate limit for the tax year in the individual's case, are increased by the amount of the contribution.][6]

(5) . . .[1].

(6) Subsections (1) and (2) have effect subject to such conditions as the Board of Inland Revenue may prescribe by regulations.

(7) The Board of Inland Revenue may by regulations make provision for carrying subsections (1) to (3) into effect, in particular by making provision—

(*a*) about how a sum is to be recovered under subsection (3)(*a*) (including the manner in which a claim for the recovery of a sum is to be made),

(*b*) for the giving of such information, in such form, as may be prescribed by or under the regulations,

(*c*) for the inspection of documents by persons authorised by the Board of Inland Revenue, and

(*d*) specifying the consequences of failure to comply with conditions prescribed by virtue of subsection (6).

(8) Regulations under this section may, in particular—

(*a*) modify the operation of any provision of the Tax Acts, or

(*b*) provide for the application of any provision of the Tax Acts (with or without modification).

(9) Where, after relief is given to an individual in accordance with this section for a tax year, an assessment, alteration of an assessment or other adjustment of the individual's liability to tax is made, any appropriate consequential adjustments are to be made in relief given to the individual in accordance with this section.

(10) Where relief is given to an individual in accordance with this section for a tax year in respect of a contribution, relief is not to be given—

(*a*) in respect of the contribution under any other provision of the Income Tax Acts, or

(*b*) (in the case of a contribution under an annuity contract) in respect of any other premium or consideration for an annuity under the same contract.

[(11) Subsection (10) does not apply to prevent the giving of relief in respect of the contribution in accordance with subsection 192A.][3]

Commentary—*Simon's Taxes* **E7.222**.

HMRC Manuals—Pensions Tax Manual PTM044220 (relief at source).

Regulations—Registered Pension Schemes (Relief at Source) Regulations, SI 2005/3448.

Registered Pension Schemes (Relief at Source) (Amendment) Regulations, SI 2018/150.

Amendments—[1]   Sub-s (5) repealed by ITA 2007 ss 1027, 1031, Sch 1 paras 456, 474, Sch 3 Pt 1 with effect for income tax purposes from 6 April 2007, and corporation tax purposes for accounting periods ending after 5 April 2007.

[2]   Sub-s (4) substituted by FA 2009 s 6, Sch 2 paras 10, 11 with effect for the tax year 2010–11 and subsequent tax years. The powers conferred by the amendments made by FA 2009 Sch 2 may be exercised at any time on or after 21 July 2009 but not so as to make provision having effect before the tax year 2010–11 (FA 2009 Sch 2 para 25(1)).

[3]   In sub-ss (1), (4), words substituted, and sub-ss (1A), (11) inserted by the Scottish Rate of Income Tax (Consequential Amendments) Order, SI 2015/1810 arts 2, 3, with effect in relation to the tax year 2016–17 (the tax year appointed by the Treasury under the Scotland Act 2012 s 25(5) by virtue of SI 2015/2000) and subsequent tax years.

[4]   In sub-s (4), words substituted and words repealed, and sub-s (4A) inserted, by the Scotland Act 2016 (Income Tax Consequential Amendments) Regulations, SI 2017/468 regs 2, 3 with effect in relation to 2017–18 (the tax year appointed under the Scotland Act 2016 section 13(15)(*b*)) and subsequent tax years.

[5]   In sub-s (4A), words inserted by the Scottish Rates of Income Tax (Consequential Amendments) Order, SI 2018/459 art 3 with effect for the tax year commencing on 6 April 2018 and subsequent tax years.

[6]   Sub-ss (1A)(*aa*), (4B) inserted by the Devolved Income Tax Rates (Consequential Amendments) Order, SI 2019/201 arts 3, 4 with effect in relation to the tax year commencing on 6 April 2019 and subsequent tax years.

[192A Relief at source: additional relief

(1) An individual to whom relief is given in accordance with section 192 in respect of a contribution is entitled to a tax reduction for the tax year in which the payment of the contribution is made if the conditions in subsection (2)[, (3A)][2] or (4) are met.

(2) The conditions are that—

(*a*) the relevant rate [is not the Scottish basic rate][2] for the tax year in which the payment of the contribution is made,

(*b*) the individual is a Scottish taxpayer for that tax year, and

(*c*) the Scottish basic rate for that tax year is higher than [the relevant rate][2].

(3) If the conditions in subsection (2) are met, the amount of the tax reduction is an amount equal to the difference between the amount of relief which would have been given if the relevant rate were the Scottish basic rate for the tax year in which the payment is made and the amount of relief given under section 192.

[(3A) The conditions are that—

(*a*) the relevant rate is not the Welsh basic rate for the tax year in which the payment of the contribution is made,

(*b*) the individual is a Welsh taxpayer for that tax year, and

(*c*) the Welsh basic rate for that tax year is higher than the relevant rate.

(3B) If the conditions in subsection (3A) are met, the amount of the tax reduction is an amount equal to the difference between the amount of relief which would have been given if the relevant rate were the Welsh basic rate for the tax year in which the payment is made and the amount of relief given under section 192.][2]

[(4) The conditions are that—

    (a) the relevant rate is not the basic rate for the tax year in which the payment of the contribution is made,

    (b) the individual is neither a Scottish taxpayer nor a Welsh taxpayer for that tax year, and

    (c) the basic rate for that tax year is higher than the relevant rate.][2]

(5) If the conditions in subsection (4) are met, the amount of the tax reduction is an amount equal to the difference between the amount of relief which would have been given if the relevant rate were the basic rate for the tax year in which the payment is made and the amount of relief given under section 192.

(6) A tax reduction under this section is given effect at Step 6 of the calculation in section 23 of ITA 2007.][1]

Commentary—*Simon's Taxes* **E7.222, E1.102**.

HMRC Manuals—Pensions Tax Manual PTM044220 (the relevant rate of tax).

Amendments—[1]   Sections 192A, 192B inserted by the Scottish Rate of Income Tax (Consequential Amendments) Order, SI 2015/1810 arts 2, 4 with effect in relation to the tax year 2016–17 (the tax year appointed by the Treasury under the Scotland Act 2012 s 25(5) by virtue of SI 2015/2000) and subsequent tax years.

[2]   In sub-s (1) words inserted, in sub-s (2)(a) words substituted for words "is the basic rate", in sub-s (2)(c) words substituted for words "the basic rate", sub-ss (3A), (3B) inserted, and sub-s (4) substituted, by the Devolved Income Tax Rates (Consequential Amendments) Order, SI 2019/201 arts 3, 5 with effect in relation to the tax year commencing on 6 April 2019 and subsequent tax years.

[192B Relief at source: excessive relief given

(1) If relief is given to an individual in accordance with section 192 in respect of a contribution and the conditions in subsection (2)[, (3A)][2] or (4) [are met][2], an amount of excessive relief given is treated as an amount of tax for which the individual is liable for the tax year in which the payment of the contribution is made.

(2) The conditions are that—

    (a) the relevant rate [is not the Scottish basic rate][2] for the tax year in which the payment of the contribution is made,

    (b) the individual is a Scottish taxpayer for that tax year, and

    (c) the Scottish basic rate for that tax year is lower than [the relevant rate][2].

(3) If the conditions in subsection (2) [are met][2], the amount of excessive relief given is an amount equal to the difference between the amount of relief given and the amount of relief which would have been given if the relevant rate were the Scottish basic rate for the tax year in which the payment is made.

[(3A) The conditions are that—

    (a) the relevant rate is not the Welsh basic rate for the tax year in which the payment of the contribution is made,

    (b) the individual is a Welsh taxpayer for that tax year, and

    (c) the Welsh basic rate for that tax year is lower than the relevant rate.

(3B) If the conditions in subsection (3A) are met, the amount of excessive relief given is an amount equal to the difference between the amount of relief given and the amount of relief which would have been given if the relevant rate were the Welsh basic rate for the tax year in which the payment is made.][2]

[(4) The conditions are that—

    (a) the relevant rate is not the basic rate for the tax year in which the payment of the contribution is made, and

    (b) the individual is neither a Scottish taxpayer nor a Welsh taxpayer for that tax year, and

    (c) the basic rate for that tax year is lower than the relevant rate.][2]

(5) If the conditions in subsection (4) [are met][2], the amount of excessive relief given is an amount equal to the difference between the amount of relief given and the amount of relief which would have been given if the relevant rate were the basic rate for the tax year in which the payment is made.

(6) An amount of excessive relief treated as an amount of tax under this section is added at Step 7 of the calculation in section 23 of ITA 2007.][1]

Commentary—*Simon's Taxes* **E7.222**.

HMRC Manuals—Pensions Tax Manual PTM044220 (the relevant rate of tax).

Amendments—[1]   Sections 192A, 192B inserted by the Scottish Rate of Income Tax (Consequential Amendments) Order, SI 2015/1810 arts 2, 4 with effect in relation to the tax year 2016–17 (the tax year appointed by the Treasury under the Scotland Act 2012 s 25(5) by virtue of SI 2015/2000) and subsequent tax years.

[2]   In sub-s (1) words inserted, in sub-ss (1), (3), (5) words substituted for word "apply", in sub-s (2)(a) words substituted for words "is the basic rate", in sub-s (2)(c) words substituted for words "that rate", sub-ss (3A), (3B) inserted, and sub-s (4) substituted, by the Devolved Income Tax Rates (Consequential Amendments) Order, SI 2019/201 arts 3, 6 with effect in relation to the tax year commencing on 6 April 2019 and subsequent tax years.

193 Relief under net pay arrangements

(1) This section applies where an individual is entitled to be given relief in accordance with this section in respect of the payment of a contribution under a pension scheme.

(2) The amount of the contribution is to be allowed to be deducted by the sponsoring employer from the employment income from the individual's employment with the employer for the tax year in which the payment is made.

(3) A deduction may be made only once in respect of the same contribution.

(4) A claim for excess relief may be made if—

    (*a*) the amount of the contributions paid by an individual under one or more relevant net pay pension schemes in a tax year exceeds the employment income from the individual's employment or employments with the sponsoring employer or employers for the tax year, or

    (*b*) it is not possible for the sponsoring employer or employers for any other reason to deduct the whole amount of the contribution from the individual's employment income.

(5) A net pay pension scheme is a relevant net pay pension scheme if the members of the pension scheme entitled to be given relief in accordance with this section in respect of the payment of contributions by them under the pension scheme include the individual.

(6) On the making of the claim for excess relief the amount of the excess may be deducted [in calculating the net income][1] of the individual for the tax year [(see Step 2 of the calculation in section 23 of ITA 2007)][1].

(7) Where, after relief is given to an individual in accordance with this section for a tax year, an assessment, alteration of an assessment or other adjustment of the individual's liability to tax is made, any appropriate consequential adjustments are to be made in relief given to the individual in accordance with this section.

(8) Where relief is given to an individual in accordance with this section for a tax year in respect of a contribution, relief is not to be given in respect of it under any other provision of the Income Tax Acts.

Commentary—*Simon's Taxes* **E1.113, E7.222**.
HMRC Manuals—Pensions Tax Manual PTM044240 (methods: claims).
Amendments—[1]   Words in sub-s (6) substituted and inserted by ITA 2007 ss 1027, Sch 1 paras 456, 475 with effect for income
    tax purposes from 6 April 2007, and corporation tax purposes for accounting periods ending after 5 April 2007.

194 Relief on making of claim

(1) Where an individual is entitled to be given relief in accordance with this section in respect of the payment of a contribution, on the making of a claim the amount of the contribution may be deducted [in calculating the net income][1] of the individual for the tax year in which the payment is made [(see Step 2 of the calculation in section 23 of ITA 2007)][1].

(2) Where, after relief is given to an individual in accordance with this section for a tax year, an assessment, alteration of an assessment or other adjustment of the individual's liability to tax is made, any appropriate consequential adjustments are to be made in relief given to the individual in accordance with this section.

(3) Where relief is given to an individual in accordance with this section for a tax year in respect of a contribution, relief is not to be given—

    (*a*) in respect of the contribution under any other provision of the Income Tax Acts, or

    (*b*) (in the case of a contribution under an annuity contract) in respect of any other premium or consideration for an annuity under the same contract.

Commentary—*Simon's Taxes* **E7.222**.
Cross-references—See FA 2016 Sch 18 para 20(4) (claims under sub-s (1) excluded from restriction of relief provisions under
    serial tax avoidance regime).
Amendments—[1]   Words in sub-s (1) substituted and inserted by ITA 2007 ss 1027, Sch 1 paras 456, 476 with effect for income
    tax purposes from 6 April 2007, and corporation tax purposes for accounting periods ending after 5 April 2007.

195 Transfer of certain shares to be treated as payment of contribution

(1) For the purposes of sections 188 to 194 (relief for contributions) references to contributions paid by an individual include contributions made in the form of the transfer by the individual of eligible shares in a company within the permitted period.

(2) For the purposes of those sections the amount of a contribution made by way of a transfer of shares is the market value of the shares at the date of the transfer.

(3) "Eligible shares", in relation to a contribution made by an individual, means shares—

    (*a*) which the individual has exercised a right to acquire in accordance with the provisions of an SAYE option scheme, or

    (*b*) which have been appropriated to the individual in accordance with the provisions of a share incentive plan.

(4) "The permitted period"—

    (*a*) in relation to shares which the individual has exercised a right to acquire in accordance with the provisions of an SAYE option scheme, is the period of 90 days following the exercise of that right, and

(b) in relation to shares which have been appropriated to the individual in accordance with the provisions of a share incentive plan, is the period of 90 days following the date when the individual directed the trustees of the share incentive plan to transfer the ownership of the shares to the individual.

(5) In this section—

"SAYE option scheme" has the same meaning as in the SAYE code (see section 516 of ITEPA 2003 (. . . [2] SAYE option schemes)), and

"share incentive plan" has the same meaning as in the SIP code (see section 488 of ITEPA 2003 (. . . [1] share incentive plans)).

Commentary—*Simon's Taxes* **E7.222, E7.241**.

HMRC Manuals—Pensions Tax Manual PTM042100 (transfers of certain shares from Save As You Earn (SAYE) option schemes or share incentive plans).

Amendments—[1]   In sub-s (5), in definition of "share incentive plan", word "approved" repealed by FA 2014 s 51, Sch 8 para 52 with effect from 6 April 2014. The effect of the FA 2014 changes on SIPs established before 6 April 2014 is set out in FA 2014 Sch 8 paras 91 to 96.

[2]   In sub-s (5), in definition of "SAYE option scheme", word "approved" repealed by FA 2014 s 51, Sch 8 para 139 with effect from 6 April 2014. The effect of the FA 2014 changes on SAYE option schemes established before 6 April 2014 is set out in FA 2014 Sch 8 paras 148 to 157.

[195A Life assurance premium contributions

(1) Contributions paid by or on behalf of an individual under a registered pension scheme are life assurance premium contributions for the purposes of section 188(3)(*aa*) if—

(a) rights under a non-group life policy (see subsection (2)) are (or later become) held for the purposes of the pension scheme, and

(b) the contributions are treated by this section as paid in respect of premiums under the non-group life policy (see subsections (3) to (5)).

(2) For the purposes of this section a "non-group life policy" is a policy of insurance under which the only benefits which may become payable are benefits payable in consequence, or in anticipation, of—

(a) the death of the individual or one of a group of individuals which includes the individual, or

(b) the deaths of more than one of a group of individuals—

(i) which includes the individual, and

(ii) the other members of which are connected with the individual.

(3) Contributions paid by or on behalf of the individual under the pension scheme are treated as paid in respect of premiums under the non-group life policy if—

(a) the payment of the contributions constitutes the payment of premiums under the policy, or

(b) the person by whom the contributions are paid intends the contributions (or an amount equivalent to them) to be applied towards paying premiums under the policy.

(4) Where the amount of the premiums under the policy in a tax year exceeds the amount of any contributions treated as paid in respect of the premiums by subsection (3), other contributions paid by or on behalf of the individual under the pension scheme in the tax year are treated as paid in respect of premiums under the policy to the extent that their amount does not exceed the difference between the amount of the premiums and the amount of any contributions treated as paid in respect of the premiums by subsection (3).

(5) But where—

(a) the benefits under the policy relate to the death of one or more of a group of individuals, and

(b) contributions are also paid under the pension scheme in the tax year by or on behalf of another member or other members of the group,

the amount of the contributions paid by or on behalf of the individual which are treated as paid in respect of premiums under the policy by subsection (4) does not exceed what is just and reasonable having regard to the operation of section 188(3)(aa) in relation to the contributions paid by or on behalf of another member or other members of the group.

(6) The Commissioners for Her Majesty's Revenue and Customs may by regulations amend subsections (2) to (5).

(7) Regulations under subsection (6) which limit—

(a) the policies of insurance which are non-group life assurance policies for the purposes of this section, or

(b) the contributions which are treated by this section as paid in respect of premiums under such policies,

may be made so as to have effect in relation to times before they are made.

(8) For the purposes of this section an individual ("A") is connected with another individual ("B") if—

(a) A is B's spouse or civil partner,

(b) A is a relative of B,

(c) A is the spouse or civil partner of a relative of B,

(d) A is a relative of B's spouse or civil partner, or

(*e*) A is the spouse or civil partner of a relative of B's spouse or civil partner;

and for the purposes of this subsection "relative" means brother, sister, ancestor or lineal descendant.][1]

Commentary—*Simon's Taxes* **E7.222**.

HMRC Manuals—Pensions Tax Manual PTM044100 (life assurance premium contributions).

Amendments—[1]   This section inserted by FA 2007 s 68, Sch 18 paras 1, 3 with effect in accordance with FA 2007 Sch 18 paras 4–8.

Employers' contributions

196 Relief for employers in respect of contributions paid

(1) This section makes provision about an employer's entitlement to relief in respect of contributions paid by the employer under a registered pension scheme in respect of any individual.

(2) For the purposes of [Part 2 of ITTOIA 2005][1] [or Part 3 of CTA 2009 (trading income)[2]]—

    (*a*) the contributions are to be treated as not being payments of a capital nature to the extent that they otherwise would be, and

    (*b*) if they are allowed to be deducted in computing the amount of the profits of the employer, they are deductible in computing the amount of the profits for the period of account in which they are paid.

(3) For the purposes of [Chapter 2 of Part 16 of CTA 2009][2] (expenses of management: companies with investment business), the contributions—

    (*a*) are to be treated as being expenses of management to the extent that they otherwise would not be, and

    (*b*) are referable to the accounting period in which they are paid.

(4) For the purposes of [section 76 of FA 2012][3] (expenses of insurance companies), the contributions—

    (*a*) are to be [treated as meeting the conditions in section 77(2)(*a*) and (*c*) of that Act to the extent that they would otherwise not meet them][3], and

    (*b*) are referable to the accounting period in which they are paid.

(5) . . .[4]

(6) This section is subject to sections 197 and 198 (spreading of relief) (and to transitional provision contained in Part 4 of Schedule 36).

Commentary—*Simon's Taxes* **D7.309, E7.224**.

HMRC Manuals—Pensions Tax Manual PTM043200 (conditions).

PTM114000 (relief for employers' contributions).

Business Income Manual BIM46005 (overview).

BIM46025 (capital expenditure: purchase of a business).

Amendments—[1]   Words in sub-s (2) inserted by ITTOIA 2005 s 882(1), Sch 1 paras 629, 646. This amendment comes into force at the same time as this section: ITTOIA 2005 Sch 2 para 161.

[2]   In sub-s (2) words substituted for words "(trading income) or Case I or II of Schedule D", and in sub-s (3) words substituted for words "section 75 of ICTA", by CTA 2009 s 1322, Sch 1 paras 569, 573. CTA 2009 applies for accounting periods ending on or after 1 April 2009 (for corporation tax purposes) and for tax years 2009–10 onwards (for income and capital gains tax purposes).

[3]   In sub-s (4) words substituted for words "section 76 of ICTA", and in para (*a*) words substituted for words "brought into account at Step 1 in subsection (7) of that section to the extent that they otherwise would not be", by FA 2012 s 146, Sch 16 paras 112, 113 with effect in relation to accounting periods of companies beginning on or after 1 January 2013 (subject to transitional provisions in FA 2012 Sch 17). For accounting periods straddling 1 January 2013, see FA 2012 s 149.

[4]   Sub-s (5) repealed by FA 2013 s 52(1), (5) with effect from 6 April 2013.

[196A Power to restrict relief

(1) The Board of Inland Revenue may make regulations for restricting the extent to which contributions paid by an employer under a registered pension scheme in respect of an individual are subject to relief in circumstances in which subsection (2) or (3) applies (or both do).

(2) This subsection applies where any of the benefits which will or may be payable to or in respect of the individual under the registered pension scheme will be payable only if relevant benefits expected to be so paid under an employer-financed retirement benefits scheme are not so paid.

(3) This subsection applies where, because relevant benefits are or may be payable to or in respect of the individual under an employer-financed retirement benefits scheme, the aggregate of the amount of any sums and the market value of any assets—

    (*a*) held for the purposes of, or

    (*b*) representing accrued rights under,

the registered pension scheme which may be transferred by way of a recognised transfer in respect of the individual will or may be less than it otherwise would be.

(4) The reference in subsection (1) to contributions paid by an employer being subject to relief is to—

    (*a*) their being deductible in computing the amount of the profits of the employer for the purposes of Part 2 of ITTOIA 2005 [or Part 3 of CTA 2009 (trading income)][2],

    (*b*) their being expenses of management of the employer for the purposes of [section 1219 of CTA 2009][2] (expenses of management: companies with investment business), or (*c*) their being [ordinary BLAGAB management expenses of the employer for an accounting period for the purposes of section 76 of FA 2012][3],

(depending on which is appropriate in relation to the employer).

(5) In this section—

"employer-financed retirement benefits scheme", and
"relevant benefits",

have the same meaning as in Chapter 2 of Part 6 of ITEPA 2003 (see sections 393A and 393B of that Act).][1]

Commentary—*Simon's Taxes* **E7.224, E7.240**.

HMRC Manuals—Pensions Tax Manual PTM043200 (when tax relief may be restricted).

Regulations—Registered Pension Schemes (Restriction of Employers' Relief) Regulations, SI 2005/3458.

Amendments—[1]   Section inserted by FA 2005 s 101, Sch 10 paras 39, 64(1) with effect from 6 April 2006.

[2]   In sub-s (4)(*a*) words substituted for words "(trading income) or Case I or II of Schedule D", and in sub-s (4)(*b*) words substituted for words "section 75 of ICTA", by CTA 2009 s 1322, Sch 1 paras 569, 574. CTA 2009 applies for accounting periods ending on or after 1 April 2009 (for corporation tax purposes) and for tax years 2009–10 onwards (for income and capital gains tax purposes).

[3]   In sub-s (4)(*c*), words substituted for words "brought into account at Step 1 in section 76(7) of ICTA (expenses of insurance companies) in respect of the employer" by FA 2012 s 146 and Sch 16, paras 112, 114 with effect in relation to accounting periods of companies beginning on or after 1 January 2013 (subject to transitional provisions in FA 2012 Sch 17). For accounting periods straddling 1 January 2013, see FA 2012 s 149.

[196B Employer asset-backed contributions: denial of relief (1)

(1) An employer ("E") is not to be given relief in respect of a contribution ("E's contribution") paid by E under a registered pension scheme if conditions A, B and C are met.

(2) Condition A is that—

(a) under an arrangement ("the asset-backed arrangement")—

(i) a person ("the borrower") receives money or another asset ("the advance") from another person ("the lender"),

(ii) the borrower, or a person connected with the borrower, makes a disposal of an asset ("the security") to or for the benefit of the lender or a person connected with the lender, and

(iii) the lender, or a person connected with the lender, is entitled to payments in respect of the security,

(b) the borrower is E or a person connected with E, and

(c) the advance is (wholly or partly) paid or provided by the lender out of E's contribution (directly or indirectly),

and the case is not one in relation to which either condition A in section 196D or condition A in section 196F is met.

(3) For the purposes of subsection (2)(a)(iii) it does not matter if an entitlement of the lender, or a person connected with the lender, is subject to any condition.

(4) Condition B is that the asset-backed arrangement is not an acceptable structured finance arrangement (see section 196C).

(5) Condition C is that it is reasonable to suppose that the amount of one or more of the payments mentioned in subsection (2)(a)(iii) has been, or is to be, determined (wholly or partly) on the basis that, in essence, the whole or a part of the advance represents a loan which is (wholly or partly) to be repaid by way of one or more of those payments.

(6) For the purposes of subsection (5) it does not matter—

(a) that the repayment of the loan might be subject to any condition, or

(b) that the accounts of any person do not record a financial liability in respect of the whole or a part of the advance or that the whole or a part of the advance is not otherwise treated as representing a loan for the purposes of the accounts of any person,

but, subject to that, all relevant circumstances are to be taken into account in order to get to the essence of the matter.

(7) For the purposes of this section—

(a) the borrower and the lender are not connected with one another if that would otherwise be the case,

(b) if the borrower is not E, references to a person connected with the borrower include a person connected with E who would not otherwise be connected with the borrower, and

(c) "loan" includes any advance of money.][1]

Commentary—*Simon's Taxes* **E7.224**.

HMRC Manuals—Pensions Tax Manual PTM043320 (simple asset-backed contribution arrangement).

Amendments—[1]   Sections 196B–196L inserted by FA 2012 s 48, Sch 13 para 15, with effect in relation to contributions paid by employers on or after 22 February 2012, subject to transitional provisions in FA 2012 Sch 13 paras 18–31.

FA 2012 Sch 13 para 1 also inserted ss 196B–196J with effect in relation to contributions paid by employers on or after 29 November 2011 but before 22 February 2012 (see detailed commencement provisions in FA 2012 Sch 13 para 3(2)–(6)), subject to transitional provisions in FA 2012 Sch 13 paras 4–14.

[196C Employer asset-backed contributions: "acceptable structured finance arrangement" (1)

(1) For the purposes of section 196B the asset-backed arrangement is an "acceptable structured finance arrangement" if conditions M to Q are met.

(2) Condition M is that—

    (a) in accordance with generally accepted accounting practice, the borrower's accounts for the period in which the advance is received record a financial liability ("the recorded financial liability") in respect of the advance, and

    (b) the asset-backed arrangement is a type 1 finance arrangement for the purposes of Chapter 5B of Part 13 of ITA 2007 or Chapter 2 of Part 16 of CTA 2010 (finance arrangements).

(3) Condition N is that—

    (a) the lender is a responsible authority,

    (b) the advance is money which is paid by the lender directly to the borrower wholly and directly out of E's contribution, and

    (c) the advance and the recorded financial liability (as originally recorded) are both of an amount equal to the amount of E's contribution.

(4) Condition O is that, as at the time the advance is paid, the position of the lender is as follows—

    (a) it is the lender (and not any person connected with the lender) who is entitled to the payments mentioned in section 196B(2)(a)(iii),

    (b) those payments are to arise at times which have been fixed and fall at intervals of no more than one year (but allowing for payments otherwise due to arise on a non-working day to arise on the next working day),

    (c) the lender is to receive each payment no later than 3 months after the day on which the payment arises (but allowing for payments otherwise due to be received on a non-working day to be received on the next working day),

    (d) on receipt by the lender, each payment is directly to become part of the sums held for the purposes of the registered pension scheme,

    (e) the payments are all to be of the same amount,

    (f) the total amount of the payments is not to be less than the amount of E's contribution, and

    (g) all the payments are to be received by the lender within a period ("the payment period") ending no later than the end of the period of 25 years beginning with the day on which E's contribution is paid.

(5) For the purposes of subsection (4)(b) the first payment is to arise no later than one year after the day on which the advance is paid.

(6) For the purposes of subsection (4)(e) the following are to be ignored—

    (a) negligible differences in the amounts of payments;

    (b) differences in the amounts of payments which would be caused by a term of the asset-backed arrangement that requires the amounts of all outstanding payments to be increased periodically by a percentage which cannot be higher than the highest of the following—

        (i) the percentage increase in the consumer prices index for the reference period, being a period determined, in relation to each periodic increase, under the term of the asset-backed arrangement in question;

        (ii) the percentage increase in the retail prices index for the reference period;

        (iii) the percentage for the reference period which corresponds to 5% per annum.

(7) For the purposes of subsection (4), in determining the lender's position, regard must be had (in particular) to any arrangements connected (directly or indirectly) to the asset-backed arrangement.

(8) Condition P is that, as at the time the advance is paid, in accordance with generally accepted accounting practice the recorded financial liability is to be reduced to nil by the end of the payment period by (and only by) the payments mentioned in section 196B(2)(a)(iii).

(9) Condition Q is that, as at the time the advance is paid, no commitment to which subsection (10) applies has been given.

(10) This subsection applies to a commitment (whether or not legally enforceable and whether or not subject to any conditions) if—

    (a) it is given (directly or indirectly) to a relevant person,

    (b) it is a commitment to secure that a person receives money or another asset, and

    (c) it is linked (directly or indirectly) to the receipt by the lender of a payment mentioned in section 196B(2)(a)(iii).

(11) In subsection (10)(a) "relevant person" means—

    (a) E;

    (b) a person connected with E;

    (c) a person acting (directly or indirectly) at the direction or request, or with the agreement, of E or a person connected with E;

    (d) a person chosen (directly or indirectly) by E or a person connected with E;

    (e) a person within a class of person chosen (directly or indirectly) by E or a person connected with E;

    (f) a partnership;

but does not include a responsible authority.

(12) In this section "responsible authority" means—

    (a) the persons who from time to time are the trustees of the registered pension scheme, or

    (b) the persons who from time to time are the persons controlling the management of the registered pension scheme,

in their capacity as such.]¹

Commentary—*Simon's Taxes* **E7.224**.

HMRC Manuals—Pensions Tax Manual PTM043320 (meaning of acceptable structured finance arrangement).

Amendments—¹   Sections 196B–196L inserted by FA 2012 s 48, Sch 13 para 15, with effect in relation to contributions paid by employers on or after 22 February 2012, subject to transitional provisions in FA 2012 Sch 13 paras 18–31.

    FA 2012 Sch 13 para 1 also inserted ss 196B–196J with effect in relation to contributions paid by employers on or after 29 November 2011 but before 22 February 2012 (see detailed commencement provisions in FA 2012 Sch 13 para 3(2)–(6)), subject to transitional provisions in FA 2012 Sch 13 paras 4–14.

[196D Employer asset-backed contributions: denial of relief (2)

(1) An employer ("E") is not to be given relief in respect of a contribution ("E's contribution") paid by E under a registered pension scheme if conditions A and B are met.

(2) Condition A is that—

    (a) under an arrangement ("the asset-backed arrangement") a person ("the transferor") makes a disposal of an asset ("the security") to a partnership,

    (b) the transferor is E or a person connected with E,

    (c) the transferor, or a person connected with the transferor, is a member of the partnership immediately after the disposal (whether or not a member immediately before it),

    (d) under the asset-backed arrangement the partnership receives money or another asset ("the advance") from a person ("the lender") other than the transferor,

    (e) the advance is (wholly or partly) paid or provided by the lender out of E's contribution (directly or indirectly),

    (f) there is a relevant change in relation to the partnership (see section 196H), and

    (g) under the asset-backed arrangement the share in the partnership's profits of the person involved in the relevant change (see section 196H) is determined by reference (wholly or partly) to payments in respect of the security.

(3) If the transferor is not E, for the purposes of this section references to a person connected with the transferor include a person connected with E who would not otherwise be connected with the transferor.

(4) For the purposes of subsection (2)(g) it does not matter if any determination of the share in the partnership's profits of the person involved in the relevant change as mentioned is subject to any condition.

(5) Condition B is that the asset-backed arrangement is not an acceptable structured finance arrangement (see section 196E).]¹

Commentary—*Simon's Taxes* **E7.224**.

HMRC Manuals—Pensions Tax Manual PTM043320 (complex asset-backed contribution arrangement involving a new partnership).

Amendments—¹   Sections 196B–196L inserted by FA 2012 s 48, Sch 13 para 15, with effect in relation to contributions paid by employers on or after 22 February 2012, subject to transitional provisions in FA 2012 Sch 13 paras 18–31.

    FA 2012 Sch 13 para 1 also inserted ss 196B–196J with effect in relation to contributions paid by employers on or after 29 November 2011 but before 22 February 2012 (see detailed commencement provisions in FA 2012 Sch 13 para 3(2)–(6)), subject to transitional provisions in FA 2012 Sch 13 paras 4–14.

[196E Employer asset-backed contributions: "acceptable structured finance arrangement" (2)

(1) For the purposes of section 196D the asset-backed arrangement is an "acceptable structured finance arrangement" if conditions M to Q are met.

(2) Condition M is that—

    (a) in accordance with generally accepted accounting practice, the partnership's accounts for the period in which the advance is received record a financial liability ("the recorded financial liability") in respect of the advance, and

    (b) the asset-backed arrangement is a type 2 finance arrangement for the purposes of Chapter 5B of Part 13 of ITA 2007 or Chapter 2 of Part 16 of CTA 2010 (finance arrangements).

(3) Condition N is that—

    (a) the lender is a responsible authority,

    (b) the advance is money which is paid by the lender directly to the partnership wholly and directly out of E's contribution, and

    (c) the advance and the recorded financial liability (as originally recorded) are both of an amount equal to the amount of E's contribution.

(4) Condition O is that, as at the time the advance is paid, the position of the lender is as follows—

    (a) it is the lender (and not any person connected with the lender) who is or is to be the person involved in the relevant change in relation to the partnership,

    (b) the lender's share in the partnership's profits is to be determined wholly by reference to the payments mentioned in section 196D(2)(g),

    (c) determinations of the lender's share in the partnership's profits are to be made at times which have been fixed and fall at intervals of no more than one year (but allowing for determinations otherwise due to be made on a non-working day to be made on the next working day),

    (d) no later than 3 months after the day on which a determination of the lender's share in the partnership's profits is made, the lender is to make a drawing from the partnership on account of its determined share (but allowing for drawings otherwise due to be made on a non-working day to be made on the next working day),

    (e) on its making, each drawing is directly to become part of the sums held for the purposes of the registered pension scheme,

    (f) the drawings are all to be of the same amount,

    (g) the total amount of the drawings is not to be less than the amount of E's contribution, and

    (h) all of the lender's share in the partnership's profits is to be drawn by the lender from the partnership within a period ("the drawing period") ending no later than the end of the period of 25 years beginning with the day on which E's contribution is paid.

(5) For the purposes of subsection (4)(c) the first determination is to be made no later than one year after the day on which the advance is paid.

(6) For the purposes of subsection (4)(f) the following are to be ignored—

    (a) negligible differences in the amounts of drawings;

    (b) differences in the amounts of drawings which would be caused by a term of the asset-backed arrangement that requires the amounts of all outstanding drawings to be increased periodically by a percentage which cannot be higher than the highest of the following—

        (i) the percentage increase in the consumer prices index for the reference period, being a period determined, in relation to each periodic increase, under the term of the asset-backed arrangement in question;

        (ii) the percentage increase in the retail prices index for the reference period;

        (iii) the percentage for the reference period which corresponds to 5% per annum.

(7) In determining the lender's position for the purposes of subsection (4), regard must be had (in particular) to any arrangements connected (directly or indirectly) to the asset-backed arrangement.

(8) Condition P is that, as at the time the advance is paid, in accordance with generally accepted accounting practice the recorded financial liability is to be reduced to nil by the end of the drawing period by (and only by) the payments mentioned in section 196D(2)(g).

(9) Condition Q is that, as at the time the advance is paid, no commitment to which subsection (10) applies has been given.

(10) This subsection applies to a commitment (whether or not legally enforceable and whether or not subject to any conditions) if—

    (a) it is given (directly or indirectly) to a relevant person,

    (b) it is a commitment to secure that a person receives money or another asset, and

    (c) it is linked (directly or indirectly) to any determination of the lender's share in the partnership's profits or any drawing from the partnership on account of that share.

(11) In subsection (10)(a) "relevant person" means—

    (a) E;

    (b) a person connected with E;

    (c) a person acting (directly or indirectly) at the direction or request, or with the agreement, of E or a person connected with E;

    (d) a person chosen (directly or indirectly) by E or a person connected with E;

    (e) a person within a class of person chosen (directly or indirectly) by E or a person connected with E;

    (f) a partnership; but does not include a responsible authority.

(12) In this section—

    (a) "responsible authority" means—

        (i) the persons who from time to time are the trustees of the registered pension scheme, or

        (ii) the persons who from time to time are the persons controlling the management of the registered pension scheme,

in their capacity as such, and

    (b) references to the making of drawings from the partnership include references to the receiving of distributions from the partnership.][1]

Commentary—*Simon's Taxes* E7.224.

HMRC Manuals—Pensions Tax Manual PTM043320 (meaning of acceptable structured finance arrangement).

Amendments—[1] Sections 196B–196L inserted by FA 2012 s 48, Sch 13 para 15, with effect in relation to contributions paid by employers on or after 22 February 2012, subject to transitional provisions in FA 2012 Sch 13 paras 18–31.

    FA 2012 Sch 13 para 1 also inserted ss 196B–196J with effect in relation to contributions paid by employers on or after 29 November 2011 but before 22 February 2012 (see detailed commencement provisions in FA 2012 Sch 13 para 3(2)–(6)), subject to transitional provisions in FA 2012 Sch 13 paras 4–14.

[196F Employer asset-backed contributions: denial of relief (3)

(1) An employer ("E") is not to be given relief in respect of a contribution ("E's contribution") paid by E under a registered pension scheme if conditions A and B are met.

(2) Condition A is that—

    (a) a partnership holds an asset ("the security") at any time before an arrangement ("the asset-backed arrangement") is made,

    (b) under the asset-backed arrangement the partnership receives money or another asset ("the advance") from another person ("the lender"),

    (c) the advance is (wholly or partly) paid or provided by the lender out of E's contribution (directly or indirectly),

    (d) there is a relevant change in relation to the partnership (see section 196H), and

    (e) under the asset-backed arrangement the share in the partnership's profits of the person involved in the relevant change (see section 196H) is determined by reference (wholly or partly) to payments in respect of the security.

(3) For the purposes of subsection (2)(e) it does not matter if any determination of the share in the partnership's profits of the person involved in the relevant change as mentioned is subject to any condition.

(4) Condition B is that the asset-backed arrangement is not an acceptable structured finance arrangement (see section 196G).]¹

Commentary—*Simon's Taxes* E7.224.

HMRC Manuals—Pensions Tax Manual PTM043320 (complex asset-backed contribution arrangement using an existing partnership).

PTM043330 (anti-avoidance rule).

Amendments—¹ Sections 196B–196L inserted by FA 2012 s 48, Sch 13 para 15, with effect in relation to contributions paid by employers on or after 22 February 2012, subject to transitional provisions in FA 2012 Sch 13 paras 18–31.

    FA 2012 Sch 13 para 1 also inserted ss 196B–196J with effect in relation to contributions paid by employers on or after 29 November 2011 but before 22 February 2012 (see detailed commencement provisions in FA 2012 Sch 13 para 3(2)–(6)), subject to transitional provisions in FA 2012 Sch 13 paras 4–14.

[196G Employer asset-backed contributions: "acceptable structured finance arrangement" (3)

(1) For the purposes of section 196F the asset-backed arrangement is an "acceptable structured finance arrangement" if conditions M to Q are met.

(2) Condition M is that—

    (a) in accordance with generally accepted accounting practice, the partnership's accounts for the period in which the advance is received record a financial liability ("the recorded financial liability") in respect of the advance, and

    (b) the asset-backed arrangement is a type 3 finance arrangement for the purposes of Chapter 5B of Part 13 of ITA 2007 or Chapter 2 of Part 16 of CTA 2010 (finance arrangements).

(3) Condition N is that—

    (a) the lender is a responsible authority,

    (b) the advance is money which is paid by the lender directly to the partnership wholly and directly out of E's contribution, and

    (c) the advance and the recorded financial liability (as originally recorded) are both of an amount equal to the amount of E's contribution.

(4) Condition O is that, as at the time the advance is paid, the position of the lender is as follows—

    (a) it is the lender (and not any person connected with the lender) who is or is to be the person involved in the relevant change in relation to the partnership,

    (b) the lender's share in the partnership's profits is to be determined wholly by reference to the payments mentioned in section 196F(2)(e),

    (c) determinations of the lender's share in the partnership's profits are to be made at times which have been fixed and fall at intervals of no more than one year (but allowing for determinations otherwise due to be made on a non-working day to be made on the next working day),

    (d) no later than 3 months after the day on which a determination of the lender's share in the partnership's profits is made, the lender is to make a drawing from the partnership on account of its determined share (but allowing for drawings otherwise due to be made on a non-working day to be made on the next working day),

    (e) on its making, each drawing is directly to become part of the sums held for the purposes of the registered pension scheme,

    (f) the drawings are all to be of the same amount,

    (g) the total amount of the drawings is not to be less than the amount of E's contribution, and

    (h) all of the lender's share in the partnership's profits is to be drawn by the lender from the partnership within a period ("the drawing period") ending no later than the end of the period of 25 years beginning with the day on which E's contribution is paid.

(5) For the purposes of subsection (4)(c) the first determination is to be made no later than one year after the day on which the advance is paid.

(6) For the purposes of subsection (4)(f) the following are to be ignored—

    (a) negligible differences in the amounts of drawings;

    (b) differences in the amounts of drawings which would be caused by a term of the asset-backed arrangement that requires the amounts of all outstanding drawings to be increased periodically by a percentage which cannot be higher than the highest of the following—

        (i) the percentage increase in the consumer prices index for the reference period, being a period determined, in relation to each periodic increase, under the term of the asset-backed arrangement in question;

        (ii) the percentage increase in the retail prices index for the reference period;

        (iii) the percentage for the reference period which corresponds to 5% per annum.

(7) In determining the lender's position for the purposes of subsection (4), regard must be had (in particular) to any arrangements connected (directly or indirectly) to the asset-backed arrangement.

(8) Condition P is that, as at the time the advance is paid, in accordance with generally accepted accounting practice the recorded financial liability is to be reduced to nil by the end of the drawing period by (and only by) the payments mentioned in section 196F(2)(e).

(9) Condition Q is that, as at the time the advance is paid, no commitment to which subsection (10) applies has been given.

(10) This subsection applies to a commitment (whether or not legally enforceable and whether or not subject to any conditions) if—

    (a) it is given (directly or indirectly) to a relevant person,

    (b) it is a commitment to secure that a person receives money or another asset, and

    (c) it is linked (directly or indirectly) to any determination of the lender's share in the partnership's profits or any drawing from the partnership on account of that share.

(11) In subsection (10)(a) "relevant person" means—

    (a) E;

    (b) a person connected with E;

    (c) a person acting (directly or indirectly) at the direction or request, or with the agreement, of E or a person connected with E;

    (d) a person chosen (directly or indirectly) by E or a person connected with E;

    (e) a person within a class of person chosen (directly or indirectly) by E or a person connected with E;

    (f) a partnership; but does not include a responsible authority.

(12) In this section—

    (a) "responsible authority" means—

        (i) the persons who from time to time are the trustees of the registered pension scheme, or

        (ii) the persons who from time to time are the persons controlling the management of the registered pension

        scheme, in their capacity as such, and

    (b) references to the making of drawings from the partnership include references to the receiving of distributions from the partnership.][1]

Commentary—*Simon's Taxes* **E7.224.**

HMRC Manuals—Pensions Tax Manual PTM043330 (reduction of financial liability).

Modifications—FA 2012 Sch 13 para 3(4) (modification of this section in relation to cases where the relevant time falls before 21 March 2012).

[1] Sections 196B–196L inserted by FA 2012 s 48, Sch 13 para 15, with effect in relation to contributions paid by employers on or after 22 February 2012, subject to transitional provisions in FA 2012 Sch 13 paras 18–31.

    FA 2012 Sch 13 para 1 also inserted ss 196B–196J with effect in relation to contributions paid by employers on or after 29 November 2011 but before 22 February 2012 (see detailed commencement provisions in FA 2012 Sch 13 para 3(2)–(6)), subject to transitional provisions in FA 2012 Sch 13 paras 4–14.

[196H Employer asset-backed contributions: "relevant change in relation to the partnership" and "person involved in the relevant change"

(1) For the purposes of sections 196D and 196F there is a relevant change in relation to the partnership if condition X or Y is met.

(2) Condition X is that, in connection with the asset-backed arrangement, the lender or a person connected with the lender becomes a member of the partnership at any time.

(3) Condition Y is that—

    (a) in connection with the asset-backed arrangement, there is at any time a change in a member's share in the partnership's profits, and

    (b) the member is the lender or a person connected with the lender or a person who in connection with the asset-backed arrangement becomes at any time connected with the lender.

(4) For the purposes of subsections (2) and (3) an event occurs in connection with the asset-backed arrangement if it occurs directly or indirectly in consequence of it or otherwise in connection with it.

(5) For the purposes of sections 196D to 196G references to the person involved in the relevant change in relation to the partnership are—

    (a) if it is condition X that is met, to the lender or the person connected with the lender (as the case may be), and

(b) if it is condition Y that is met, to the member of the partnership in whose share in the partnership's profits there is a change.]¹

Commentary—*Simon's Taxes* **E7.224**.

HMRC Manuals—Pensions Tax Manual PTM043320 (complex asset-backed contribution arrangements: meaning of "relevant change" in relation to a partnership).

PTM043330 (specified events occurring on or after 21 March 2012).

Amendments—¹ Sections 196B–196L inserted by FA 2012 s 48, Sch 13 para 15, with effect in relation to contributions paid by employers on or after 22 February 2012, subject to transitional provisions in FA 2012 Sch 13 paras 18–31.

FA 2012 Sch 13 para 1 also inserted ss 196B–196J with effect in relation to contributions paid by employers on or after 29 November 2011 but before 22 February 2012 (see detailed commencement provisions in FA 2012 Sch 13 para 3(2)–(6)), subject to transitional provisions in FA 2012 Sch 13 paras 4–14.

[196I Employer asset-backed contributions: change in lender's original position under acceptable structured finance arrangement etc

(1) This section applies if—

    (a) an employer ("E") pays a contribution ("E's contribution") under a registered pension scheme,

    (b) conditions A and C in section 196B are met or condition A in section 196D or 196F is met,

    (c) the asset-backed arrangement is an acceptable structured finance arrangement for the purposes of section 196B, 196D or 196F (as the case may be) and, accordingly, condition B in that section is not met, and

    (d) at any time ("the relevant time") after the advance is paid—

        (i) the lender's position changes from the lender's original position in any respect (whether as a result of a term of the asset-backed arrangement or another arrangement or otherwise),

        (ii) an event occurs or does not occur and the occurrence or non-occurrence of the event does not accord with the lender's original position in any respect,

        (iii) in accordance with generally accepted accounting practice, the recorded financial liability is reduced to nil other than by a payment mentioned in section 196B(2)(a)(iii), 196D(2)(g) or section 196F(2)(e) (as the case may be),

        (iv) a commitment to which section 196C(10), 196E(10) or 196G(10) (as the case may be) applies is given, or

        (v) an event falling within section 196J occurs.

(2) This section also applies if—

    (a) the requirements of subsection (1)(a) to (c) are met, and

    (b) at any time ("the relevant time") after the advance is paid, in accordance with generally accepted accounting practice, the recorded financial liability is reduced in part other than by a payment mentioned in section 196B(2)(a)(iii), 196D(2)(g) or section 196F(2)(e) (as the case may be).

(3) Subject to subsection (4), the relevant amount is treated as follows as relevant—

    (a) for corporation tax purposes, the relevant amount is treated as if it were a profit which E has in respect of E's loan relationships chargeable to corporation tax under section 299 of CTA 2009 for E's accounting period in which the relevant time falls, or

    (b) for income tax purposes, the relevant amount is treated as if it were an amount of income of E chargeable to income tax under Chapter 8 of Part 5 of ITTOIA 2005 for the tax year in which the relevant time falls.

(4) The amount treated as profit or income by subsection (3)(a) or (b), together with any amounts so treated on any previous applications of this section in relation to the asset-backed arrangement, is not to exceed the total amount of relief given in respect of E's contribution.

(5) If this section applies by virtue of subsection (1), from the relevant time Chapter 5B of Part 13 of ITA 2007 or Chapter 2 of Part 16 of CTA 2010 (as relevant) is no longer to apply in relation to the asset-backed arrangement.

(6) But no person is, by virtue of subsection (5), to be placed in a position which is more advantageous than the position in which the person would have been had this section never applied; and, in order to give effect to this principle, such assessments to tax or adjustments to any assessment to tax as are just and reasonable are to be made.

(7) Subsection (1)(d)(i) and (ii) does not cover—

    (a) cases in which the lender's change in position, or the occurrence or non-occurrence of the event, is the direct result of a mere administrative error, so long as the consequences of the error are remedied promptly, or

    (b) mere changes in the persons who are the trustees of the registered pension scheme or in the persons who control the management of the registered pension scheme.

(8) For the purposes of subsection (1)(d)(ii) it does not matter if the occurrence or non-occurrence of the event is authorised by a term of the asset-backed arrangement or results from the occurrence or non-occurrence of another event which is so authorised.

(9) If this section applies by virtue of subsection (1)(d)(v), in subsection (3) references to the relevant time are to be read as references to the time immediately before the relevant time.

(10) In this section—

"the advance" and "the asset-backed arrangement" have the same meaning as in section 196B, 196D or 196F (as the case may be),

"the lender's original position" means the lender's position as at the time the advance is paid set out in the paragraphs of section 196C(4), 196E(4) or 196G(4) (as the case may be),

"the recorded financial liability" has the same meaning as in section 196C, 196E or 196G (as the case may be), and

"the relevant amount" means—

    (a) if this section applies by virtue of subsection (1), the outstanding amount of the recorded financial liability immediately before the relevant time determined in accordance with generally accepted accounting practice, or

    (b) if this section applies by virtue of subsection (2), the amount of the reduction of the recorded financial liability.][1]

Commentary—*Simon's Taxes* **E7.224**.

HMRC Manuals—Pensions Tax Manual PTM043320 (acceptable structured finance arrangements: changes from the lender's original position).

Modifications—FA 2012 Sch 13 para 17(2) (modification of this section so that sub-s (6) does not apply in relation to cases where the relevant time falls before 21 March 2012).

Amendments—[1]   Sections 196B–196L inserted by FA 2012 s 48, Sch 13 para 15, with effect in relation to contributions paid by employers on or after 22 February 2012, subject to transitional provisions in FA 2012 Sch 13 paras 18–31.

FA 2012 Sch 13 para 1 also inserted ss 196B–196J with effect in relation to contributions paid by employers on or after 29 November 2011 but before 22 February 2012 (see detailed commencement provisions in FA 2012 Sch 13 para 3(2)–(6)), subject to transitional provisions in FA 2012 Sch 13 paras 4–14.

[196J Employer asset-backed contributions: further events which cause section 196I to apply

(1) The events falling within this section are those listed in subsection (2).

(2) The events are—

    (a) if E is a company within the charge to corporation tax when E's contribution is paid, E ceases to be within that charge;

    (b) if E is a limited liability partnership in relation to which section 863(1) of ITTOIA 2005 or section 1273(1) of CTA 2009 applies when E's contribution is paid, that provision ceases to apply in relation to E;

    (c) if E is a firm for the purposes of ITTOIA 2005 (see section 847) or CTA 2009 (see section 1257) (other than a limited liability partnership) when E's contribution is paid, the partnership ceases to carry on the trade, profession or business in question;

    (d) in any case—

       (i) if E is a company, E enters administration or the winding up of E starts;

       (ii) if E is a partnership, the partnership is dissolved;

       (iii) if E is an individual, E dies.

(3) Sections 10(3) and 12(7) of CTA 2009 apply for the purposes of subsection (2)(d)(i).][1]

Commentary—*Simon's Taxes* **E7.224**.

HMRC Manuals—Pensions Tax Manual PTM043320 (acceptable structured finance arrangements: changes from the employer's original position).

Amendments—[1]   Sections 196B–196L inserted by FA 2012 s 48, Sch 13 para 15, with effect in relation to contributions paid by employers on or after 22 February 2012, subject to transitional provisions in FA 2012 Sch 13 paras 18–31. Note that an event falls within this section only if it occurs after the beginning of 21 March 2012 (see FA 2012 Sch 13 para 17(3)).

FA 2012 Sch 13 para 1 also inserted ss 196B–196J with effect in relation to contributions paid by employers on or after 29 November 2011 but before 22 February 2012 (see detailed commencement provisions in FA 2012 Sch 13 para 3(2)–(6)), subject to transitional provisions in FA 2012 Sch 13 paras 4–14.

[196K Employer asset-backed contributions: "advances" under acceptable structured finance arrangements

(1) This section applies if—

    (a) an employer pays a contribution under a registered pension scheme,

    (b) condition A in section 196B, 196D or 196F is met,

    (c) the asset-backed arrangement is an acceptable structured finance arrangement for the purposes of section 196B, 196D or 196F (as the case may be) and, accordingly, condition B in that section is not met, and

    (d) the advance gives rise to a loan within the meaning of Chapter 3 (see section 162).

(2) Section 180(4) does not prevent the advance from being a scheme administration employer payment (if it would otherwise do so).

(3) In this section "the advance" and "the asset-backed arrangement" have the same meaning as in section 196B, 196D or 196F (as the case may be).][1]

Commentary—*Simon's Taxes* **E7.224**.

Amendments—[1]   Sections 196B–196L inserted by FA 2012 s 48, Sch 13 para 15, with effect in relation to contributions paid by employers on or after 22 February 2012, subject to transitional provisions in FA 2012 Sch 13 paras 18–31.

[196L Employer asset-backed contributions: supplementary

(1) This section applies for the purposes of sections 196B to 196K.

(2) References to relief being given in respect of a contribution paid by an employer under a registered pension scheme are references to relief being given by way of—

    (a) the contribution being deducted in computing the amount of the employer's profits for the purposes of Part 2 of ITTOIA 2005 or Part 3 of CTA 2009 (trading income),

    (b) the contribution being treated as an expense of management of the employer for the purposes of Chapter 2 of Part 16 of CTA 2009 (expenses of management: companies with investment business), or

    [(c) the contribution being ordinary BLAGAB management expenses of the employer for an accounting period for the purposes of section 76 of FA 2012.][2]

(3) Whether a person is connected with another person is determined in accordance with section 1122 of CTA 2010.

(4) Sections 774, 775 and 776(2) and (4) of CTA 2010 apply as they apply for the purposes of Chapter 2 of Part 16 of that Act.

(5) A reference to a disposal of an asset includes—

    (a) anything constituting a disposal of an asset for the purposes of TCGA 1992, and

    (b) so far as not covered by paragraph (a), the taking of any step by virtue of which a person receives an asset.

(6) Section 776(2) of CTA 2010 applies for the purposes of subsection (5)(b).

(7) "Non-working day" means—

    (a) a Saturday or Sunday,

    (b) a Christmas Eve, Christmas Day or Good Friday, or

    (c) a day which is a bank holiday under the Banking and Financial Dealings Act 1971 in any part of the United Kingdom,

and "working day" is to be read accordingly.][1]

Commentary—*Simon's Taxes* **E7.224**.

Amendments—[1] Sections 196B–196L inserted by FA 2012 s 48, Sch 13 para 15, with effect in relation to contributions paid by employers on or after 22 February 2012, subject to transitional provisions in FA 2012 Sch 13 paras 18–31.

[2] In sub-s (2), para (c) substituted by FA 2012 s 146, Sch 16 paras 112, 115 with effect in relation to accounting periods of companies beginning on or after 1 January 2013 (subject to transitional provisions in FA 2012 Sch 17). For accounting periods straddling 1 January 2013, see FA 2012 s 149.

197 Spreading of relief

(1) This section applies where—

    (*a*) contributions are paid by an employer under a registered pension scheme in two consecutive chargeable periods ("the previous chargeable period" and "the current chargeable period"), and

    (*b*) the amount of the contributions paid in the current chargeable period otherwise than for an excepted purpose ("CCCP") exceeds 210% of the amount of the contributions paid in the previous chargeable period ("CPCP").

(2) Relief under [the relieving provisions][2] is to be given in respect of so much of CCCP as exceeds 110% of CPCP ("the amount of the relevant excess contributions") in accordance with subsections (4) and (5).

(3) But subsection (2)—

    (*a*) does not apply if the amount of the relevant excess contributions is less than £500,000, and

    (*b*) has effect subject to section 198 (cessation of business).

(4) A fraction of the whole of the amount of the relevant excess contributions is to be treated for the purposes of [the relieving provisions][2] as if it had been paid in the chargeable period, or in each of the two or three chargeable periods, immediately after the current chargeable period (leaving only the remainder to be treated as paid in the current chargeable period).

(5) The following table specifies (by reference to the amount of the relevant excess contributions)—

    (*a*) the fraction of the whole of the amount of the relevant excess contributions which is to be treated as paid in the chargeable period, or in each of the two or three chargeable periods, immediately after the current chargeable period, and

    (*b*) the chargeable period or periods in which it is to be treated as paid.

AMOUNT OF THE RELEVANT EXCESS CONTRIBUTIONS	FRACTION AND CHARGEABLE PERIOD OR PERIODS
£500,000 or more but less than £1,000,000	One-half of the whole of the amount of the relevant excess contributions is to be treated as paid in the chargeable period immediately after the current chargeable period

AMOUNT OF THE RELEVANT EXCESS CONTRIBUTIONS	FRACTION AND CHARGEABLE PERIOD OR PERIODS
£1,000,000 or more but less than £2,000,000	One-third of the whole of the amount of the relevant excess contributions is to be treated as paid in each of the two chargeable periods immediately after the current chargeable period
£2,000,000 or more	One-quarter of the whole of the amount of the relevant excess contributions is to be treated as paid in each of the three chargeable periods immediately after the current chargeable period

(6) Subsection (7) specifies for the purposes of subsection (1) when contributions paid by the employer in the current chargeable period are paid for an excepted purpose.

(7) They are paid for an excepted purpose if paid with a view to funding—

    (a) an increase in the amount of pensions paid to pensioner members of the pension scheme to reflect increases in the cost of living, or

    (b) benefits which may accrue under the pension scheme to or in respect of individuals who become members of the pension scheme in the current chargeable period as a result of future service as employees of the employer.

(8) Where the previous chargeable period and the current chargeable period are not of equal length, this section has effect as if CPCP were the amount it would otherwise be as adjusted by being multiplied by the appropriate factor.

(9) The appropriate factor is—

$$\frac{DCCP}{DPCP}$$

where—

    DCCP is the number of days in the current chargeable period, and

    DPCP is the number of days in the previous chargeable period.

[(9A) In this section "the relieving provisions" means the provisions mentioned in subsections (2) to (4) of section 196 (relief for employers in respect of contributions paid), as they have effect under that section.][2]

(10) In this section "chargeable period" means—

    (a) in a case where the contributions are deducted in computing profits to be charged under [Part 2 of ITTOIA 2005][1] [or Part 3 of CTA 2009 (trading income),][3] a period of account, and

    (b) in a case where relief in respect of the contributions is given under [[section 76 of FA 2012][4] (expenses of insurance companies) or Chapter 2 of Part 16 of CTA 2009 (expenses of management: companies with investment business), an accounting period][3].

Commentary—*Simon's Taxes* **E7.224.**

HMRC Manuals—Pensions Tax Manual PTM043400 (spreading).

Amendments—[1] Words in sub-s (10)(a) inserted by ITTOIA 2005 s 882(1), Sch 1 paras 629, 647. This amendment comes into force at the same time as this section: ITTOIA 2005 Sch 2 para 161.

[2] In sub-s (2), words substituted for words "section 196 (relief for employers in respect of contributions paid)", and in sub-s (4), word substituted for words "section 196", and sub-s (9A) inserted, by FA 2008 s 92, Sch 29 para 14 with effect from 21 July 2008.

[3] In sub-s (10)(a) words substituted for words "(trading income) or Case I or II of Schedule D,", and in sub-s (10)(b) words substituted for words "section 75 or 76 of ICTA (expenses of management: companies with investment business and expenses of insurance companies), an accounting period", by CTA 2009 s 1322, Sch 1 paras 569, 575. CTA 2009 applies for accounting periods ending on or after 1 April 2009 (for corporation tax purposes) and for tax years 2009–10 onwards (for income and capital gains tax purposes).

[4] In sub-s (10)(b), words substituted for words "section 76 of ICTA" by FA 2012 s 146, Sch 16 paras 112, 116 with effect in relation to accounting periods of companies beginning on or after 1 January 2013 (subject to transitional provisions in FA 2012 Sch 17). For accounting periods straddling 1 January 2013, see FA 2012 s 149.

198 Spreading of relief: cessation of business

(1) This section applies if—

    (a) the employer ceases to carry on business in the current chargeable period or a later chargeable period in which section 197(4) would require a fraction of the amount of the relevant excess contributions to be treated as paid, and

    (b) were section 197(4) to apply, relief in relation to the whole of the amount of the relevant excess contributions would not be given pre-cessation.

(2) Relief is given pre-cessation if it is given for the chargeable period in which the employer ceases to carry on business or any earlier chargeable period.

(3) The portion of the amount of the relevant excess contributions in relation to which relief would not have been given pre-cessation ("the unrelieved portion") is be treated as paid (at the option of the employer) either—

    (a) in the chargeable period in which the employer ceases to carry on business, or (*b*) as provided by subsection (4).

(4) This subsection provides that the amount determined under subsection (5) is to be treated as paid on each day in the period—

    (*a*) beginning with the current chargeable period, and

    (*b*) ending with the day on which the employer ceases to carry on business, ("the relevant period").

(5) The amount referred to in subsection (4) is—

$$\frac{UP}{DRP}$$

where—

    UP is the amount of the unrelieved portion, and

    DRP is the number of days in the relevant period.

(6) Expressions used in this section and section 197 have the same meaning in this section as in that section.

Commentary—*Simon's Taxes* **E7.224.**

HMRC Manuals—Pensions Tax Manual PTM043400 (spreading of tax relief when an employer ceases business).

199 Deemed contributions

(1) This section applies where a sum is paid to the trustees or managers of a registered pension scheme by an employer in or towards the discharge of any liability of the employer under—

    (*a*) section 75 of the Pensions Act 1995 (c 26) (deficiencies in the assets of a pension scheme), or

    (*b*) Article 75 of the Pensions (Northern Ireland) Order 1995 (SI 1995/3213 (NI 22)) (corresponding provision for Northern Ireland).

(2) The making of the payment is to be treated for the purposes of [the relieving provisions (within the meaning of section 197) and sections 197 and 198][1] as if it were the payment of a contribution by the employer under the pension scheme.

(3) Subsections (4) and (5) apply if the employer's trade, profession, vocation or business is discontinued before the making of the payment.

(4) The payment is to be relieved—

    (*a*) to the same extent as it would have been but for the discontinuance, and

    (*b*) as if it had been made on the last day on which the trade, profession, vocation or business was carried on.

[(5) And, for the purposes of section 76 of FA 2012, it is to be treated as meeting the conditions in section 77(2)(*a*) and (*c*) of that Act to the extent that it would otherwise not meet them.][2]

Commentary—*Simon's Taxes* **E7.224.**

HMRC Manuals—Pensions Tax Manual PTM043200 (payment of a deficiency on a scheme wind up).

Amendments—[1]   Words in sub-s (2) substituted for previous paras (*a*)–(*c*), by FA 2008 s 92 Sch 29 para 14 with effect from 21 July 2008.

[2]   Sub-s (5) substituted by FA 2012 s 146, Sch 16 paras 112, 117 with effect in relation to accounting periods of companies beginning on or after 1 January 2013 (subject to transitional provisions in FA 2012 Sch 17). For accounting periods straddling 1 January 2012, see FA 2012 s 149.

[199A Indirect contributions

(1) This section applies where an employer ("E")—

    (*a*) pays contributions under a registered pension scheme ("the original scheme") in a chargeable period, and

    (*b*) would (apart from subsection (4)) be entitled in the next chargeable period to an amount of relief in respect of a payment within subsection (2),

and the avoidance condition is met.

(2) A payment is within this subsection if all or part of the payment is intended to facilitate the payment of pension contributions under the original scheme or a substitute scheme by a person other than E.

(3) The avoidance condition is that—

    (*a*) section 197 would apply if, in the chargeable period mentioned in subsection (1)(*b*), E paid pension contributions under the original scheme of the amount of the relevant relief, and

    (*b*) the purpose, or one of the purposes, of facilitating the payment of pension contributions by a person other than E is to enable pension contributions to be paid without that section applying.

(4) For the purposes of the spreading provisions, the amount of the relevant relief is to be treated as the amount of a pension contribution paid by E under the original scheme in the chargeable period mentioned in subsection (1)(*b*).

(5) The "relevant relief" is the relief to which the employer would (apart from subsection (4)) be entitled in that chargeable period in respect of—

    (*a*) the payment within subsection (2), or

(*b*) where only part of the payment is intended to facilitate the payment of pension contributions as mentioned in that subsection, that part of the payment.

(6) A "substitute scheme" is any registered pension scheme—

(*a*) to which there is a relevant transfer in the period of 2 years ending with the day on which the payment within subsection (2) is made, or

(*b*) to which it is envisaged that a relevant transfer will or may be made after that day.

(7) A relevant transfer is a recognised transfer from the original scheme of more than 30% of the aggregate of—

(*a*) in a case within subsection (6)(*a*), the amount of the sums and the market value of the assets held for the purposes of, or representing accrued rights under, the original scheme immediately before the transfer, and

(*b*) in a case within subsection (6)(*b*), the amount of those sums and the market value of those assets on the day on which the payment is made.

(8) If there is a transfer from a substitute scheme to another registered pension scheme which would have been a relevant transfer had it been a transfer from the original scheme at the time the relevant transfer was made, that other scheme is also a substitute scheme.

(9) In subsection (1)(*b*) the reference to relief in respect of a payment within subsection (2) includes relief for a liability in respect of the making of the payment by a person other than E.

(10) In this section references to E being entitled to an amount of relief are to an amount—

(*a*) being deductible in computing the amount of the profits of E for the purposes of Part 2 of ITTOIA 2005 [or Part 3 of CTA 2009 (trading income)]^2,

(*b*) being expenses of management of E for the purposes of [Chapter 2 of Part 16 of CTA 2009]^2 (expenses of management: companies with investment business), or

(*c*) being [ordinary BLAGAB management expenses of E for an accounting period for the purposes of section 76 of FA 2012]^3.

(11) In this section—

"the spreading provisions" means sections 197 and 198 and this section, and

"chargeable period" has the meaning given by section 197.]^1

Commentary—*Simon's Taxes* **E7.224.**
HMRC Manuals—Pensions Tax Manual PTM043400 (spreading of relief on indirect contributions).
Amendments—^{1} Section 199A inserted by FA 2008 s 90(1) with effect in relation to payments within FA 2004 s 199A(2) made on or after 10 October 2007, except for such payments made pursuant to a contract entered into before 9 October 2007.
^{2} In sub-s (10)(*a*) words substituted for words "(trading income) or Case I or II of Schedule D", and in sub-s (10)(*b*) words substituted for words "section 75 of ICTA", by CTA 2009 s 1322, Sch 1 paras 569, 576. CTA 2009 applies for accounting periods ending on or after 1 April 2009 (for corporation tax purposes) and for tax years 2009–10 onwards (for income and capital gains tax purposes).
^{3} In sub-s (10)(*c*), words substituted for words "brought into account at Step 1 in section 76(7) of ICTA (expenses of insurance companies) in respect of E" by FA 2012 s 146, Sch 16 paras 112, 118 with effect in relation to accounting periods of companies beginning on or after 1 January 2013 (subject to transitional provisions in FA 2012 Sch 17). For accounting periods straddling 1 January 2013, see FA 2012 s 149.

200 No other relief for employers in connection with contributions

No sums other than contributions paid by an employer under a registered pension scheme—

(*a*) are deductible in computing the amount of the profits of the employer for the purposes of [Part 2 of ITTOIA 2005]^1 [or Part 3 of CTA 2009 (trading income)]^2,

(*b*) are expenses of management for the purposes of [Chapter 2 of Part 16 of CTA 2009]^2 (expenses of management: companies with investment business), or

[(*c*) are to count as ordinary BLAGAB management expenses of the employer for an accounting period for the purposes of section 76 of FA 2012,]^3

in connection with the cost of providing benefits under the pension scheme.

Commentary—*Simon's Taxes* **E7.224.**
Amendments—^{1} Words in para (*a*) inserted by ITTOIA 2005 s 882(1), Sch 1 paras 629, 649. This amendment comes into force at the same time as this section: ITTOIA 2005 Sch 2 para 161.
^{2} In para (*a*) words substituted for words "(trading income) or Case I or II of Schedule D", and in para (*b*) words substituted for words "section 75 of ICTA", by CTA 2009 s 1322, Sch 1 paras 569, 577. CTA 2009 applies for accounting periods ending on or after 1 April 2009 (for corporation tax purposes) and for tax years 2009–10 onwards (for income and capital gains tax purposes).
^{3} Para (*c*) substituted by FA 2012 s 146, Sch 16 paras 112, 119 with effect in relation to accounting periods of companies beginning on or after 1 January 2013 (subject to transitional provisions in FA 2012 Sch 17). For accounting periods straddling 1 January 2013, see FA 2012 s 149.

201 Relief for employees

(1) (*amends* ITEPA 2003 s 307(1))

(2) (*substitutes* ITEPA 2003 s 308)

Inland Revenue contributions

202 Minimum contributions under pensions legislation

(1)–(4) . . . ^{1}

(5) The Board of Inland Revenue may by regulations—

    (*a*) prescribe circumstances in which this section does not apply, or

    (*b*) make provision supplementing this section.

(6) . . . [1]

Regulations—Registered Pension Schemes (Minimum Contributions) Regulations, SI 2005/3450.

Amendments—[1]   Section 202 repealed by FA 2013 s 52(1), (6) with effect from 6 April 2016, but see Prospective Amendment note below.

Prospective amendments—Section 202(5) to be repealed by FA 2013 s 52(1), (6) with effect from a date to be appointed (FA 2013 s 52(12)).

Inheritance tax exemptions

203 Inheritance tax exemptions

(1) The Inheritance Tax Act 1984 (c 51) is amended as follows.

(2) In section 12 (dispositions that are not transfers of value)—

    (*a*) (*amends* IHTA 1984 s 12(2))

    (*b*) (*repeals* IHTA 1984 s 12(3), (4))

(3) (*amends* IHTA 1984 s 58(1))

(4) In section 151 (treatment of pension rights etc)—

    (*a*) (*repeals* IHTA 1984 s 151(1), (1A))

    (*b*), (*c*) (*amend* IHTA 1984 s 151(2), (4), (5))

(5), (6) (*amend* IHTA 1984 ss 152, 272)

CHAPTER 5

REGISTERED PENSION SCHEMES: TAX CHARGES

Charges on authorised payments

204 Authorised pensions and lump sums

(1) Schedule 31 contains provision about the taxation of pensions and lump sums which are authorised to be paid by this Part.

(2) Schedule 36 contains (in Part 4) transitional provision about the taxation of annuities under existing retirement annuity contracts and other relevant transitional provision.

205 Short service refund lump sum charge

(1) A charge to income tax, to be known as the short service refund lump sum charge, arises where a short service refund lump sum is paid by a registered pension scheme.

(2) The person liable to the short service refund lump sum charge is the scheme administrator.

(3) The scheme administrator is liable to the short service refund lump sum charge whether or not—

    (*a*) the scheme administrator, and

    (*b*) the person to whom the short service refund lump sum is paid,

are resident . . . [2] or domiciled in the United Kingdom.

(4) The rate of the charge is—

    (*a*) 20% in respect of so much of the lump sum as does not exceed [£20,000][1], and

    (*b*) [50%][1] in respect of so much (if any) of it as exceeds that limit.

(5) The Treasury may by order amend subsection (4) so as to—

    (*a*) increase or decrease either or both of the rates for the time being specified in that subsection, or

    (*b*) increase the limit for the time being specified in paragraph (*a*) of that subsection.

(6) Tax under this section is to be charged on the amount of the lump sum paid or, if the rules of the pension scheme permit the scheme administrator to deduct the tax before payment, on the amount of the lump sum before deduction of tax.

(7) A short service refund lump sum is not to be treated as income for any purpose of the Tax Acts.

Commentary—*Simon's Taxes* E7.234.

HMRC Manuals—Pensions Tax Manual PTM045000 (conditions that must be met for a short service refund lump sum to be paid).

Orders—Taxation of Pensions Schemes (Rates, etc) Order 2010, SI 2010/536.

Modifications—Registered Pension Schemes (Splitting of Schemes) Regulations, SI 2006/569 reg 3 (modification of this provision in relation to sub-scheme administrators).

Amendments—[1]   In sub-s (4)(*a*), (*b*) figure substituted by the Taxation of Pensions Schemes (Rates, etc) Order 2010 SI 2010/536, art 3 with effect for the year 2010–11 and subsequent tax years.

[2]   Words in sub-s (3) repealed by FA 2013 s 219, Sch 46 paras 119, 121 with effect in relation to the tax year 2013–14 and any subsequent tax year.

206 Special lump sum death benefits charge

(1) A charge to income tax, to be known as the special lump sum death benefits charge, arises where—

    (*a*) a pension protection lump sum death benefit,

    (*b*) an annuity protection lump sum death benefit, . . . [4]

    [(*c*) a drawdown pension fund lump sum death benefit,][1] [or

    (*d*) a flexi-access drawdown fund lump sum death benefit,][4] is paid[, to a non-qualifying person,]⁶ by a registered pension scheme [in respect of a member who had reached the age of 75 at the date of the member's death]³.

[(1ZA) In subsection (1) the reference to a member (and to the member's death) are to be read—

    (*a*) in relation to—

        (i) a drawdown pension fund lump sum death benefit under paragraph 17(2) of Schedule 29, or

        (ii) a flexi-access drawdown fund lump sum death benefit under paragraph 17A(2) of Schedule 29,

      as a reference to a dependant (and to the dependant's death),

    (*b*) in relation to a flexi-access drawdown fund lump sum death benefit under paragraph 17A(3) of Schedule 29, as a reference to a nominee (and to the nominee's death), and

    (*c*) in relation to a flexi-access drawdown fund lump sum death benefit under paragraph 17A(4) of Schedule 29, as a reference to a successor (and to the successor's death).]⁵

[(1A) The special lump sum death benefits charge also arises where—

    (*a*) a defined benefits lump sum death benefit, or

    (*b*) an uncrystallised funds lump sum death benefit,

is paid[, to a non-qualifying person,]⁶ by a registered pension scheme in respect of a member who had reached the age of 75 at the date of the member's death.]¹

[(1B) The special lump sum death benefits charge also arises where—

    (*a*) a lump sum death benefit is paid[, to a non-qualifying person,]⁶ by a registered pension scheme in respect of a member of the scheme who had not reached the age of 75 at the date of the member's death,

    (*b*) the lump sum death benefit is—

        (i) a drawdown pension fund lump sum death benefit under paragraph 17(1) of Schedule 29,

        (ii) a flexi-access drawdown fund lump sum death benefit under paragraph 17A(1) of Schedule 29,

        [(iia) a defined benefits lump sum death benefit,]⁶ or

        (iii) an uncrystallised funds lump sum death benefit, and

    (*c*) the lump sum death benefit is not paid before the end of the period of two years beginning with the earlier of the day on which the scheme administrator of the scheme first knew of the member's death and the day on which the scheme administrator could first reasonably have been expected to have known of it.

(1C) The special lump sum death benefits charge also arises where—

    (*a*) a lump sum death benefit is paid[, to a non-qualifying person,]⁶ by a registered pension scheme on the death of a dependant, nominee or successor of a deceased member of the scheme,

    (*b*) the dependant, nominee or successor ("the beneficiary") had not reached the age of 75 at the date of the beneficiary's death,

    (*c*) the lump sum death benefit is—

        (i) a drawdown pension fund lump sum death benefit under paragraph 17(2) of Schedule 29, or

        (ii) a flexi-access drawdown fund lump sum death benefit under paragraph 17A(2), (3) or (4) of Schedule 29, and

    (*d*) the lump sum death benefit is not paid before the end of the period of two years beginning with the earlier of the day on which the scheme administrator of the scheme first knew of the beneficiary's death and the day on which the scheme administrator could first reasonably have been expected to have known of it.]⁵

(2) The person liable to the special lump sum death benefits charge is the scheme administrator.

(3) The scheme administrator is liable to the special lump sum death benefits charge whether or not—

    (*a*) the scheme administrator, and

    (*b*) the person to whom the lump sum death benefit is paid,

are resident . . . ² or domiciled in the United Kingdom.

(4) The rate of the charge is [45%]³ in respect of the lump sum death benefit.

(5) The Treasury may by order increase or decrease the rate for the time being specified in subsection (4).

(6) Tax under this section is to be charged on the amount of the lump sum paid or, if the rules of the pension scheme permit the scheme administrator to deduct the tax before payment, on the amount of the lump sum before deduction of tax.

[(7) A lump sum death benefit in respect of which income tax is charged under this section is not to be treated as income for any purpose of the Tax Acts [(but see subsection (8))]⁶.]⁵

[(8) Where—

    (*a*) a lump sum death benefit in respect of which tax is charged under this section is one paid to a non-qualifying person in the person's capacity as a trustee, and (*b*) a payment of any part of the lump sum is made out of a settlement to a beneficiary who is an individual,

the amount received by the beneficiary, together with so much of the tax charged under this section on the lump sum as is attributable to the amount received by the beneficiary, is income of the beneficiary for income tax purposes but the beneficiary may claim to deduct that much of that tax from the income tax charged on the beneficiary's total income for the tax year in which the payment is made to the beneficiary.

(9) For the purposes of this section, a person is a "non-qualifying person" in relation to payment of a lump sum if—

    (*a*) the person is not an individual, or

    (*b*) the person is an individual and the payment is made to the person in the person's capacity as—

        (i) a trustee or personal representative,

        (ii) a director of a company,

        (iii) a partner in a firm, or

        (iv) a member of a limited liability partnership,

except that a person is not a "non-qualifying person" in relation to payment of a lump sum if the payment is made to the person in the person's capacity as a bare trustee.

(10) In subsection (9)—

    "bare trustee" means a person acting as trustee for—

        (*a*) an individual absolutely entitled as against the trustee,

        (*b*) two or more individuals who are so entitled,

        (*c*) an individual who would be so entitled but for being a minor or otherwise lacking legal capacity, or

        (*d*) two or more individuals who would be so entitled but for all or any of them being a minor or otherwise lacking legal capacity,

    "director" is read in accordance with section 452 of CTA 2010, and

    references to a firm are to be read in the same way as references to a firm in Part 9 of ITTOIA 2005 (which contains special provision about partnerships).][6]

Commentary—*Simon's Taxes* E7.239.

HMRC Manuals—Pensions Tax Manuals PTM092300 (protecting pre-april 2006 pension rights: primary protection).
PTM073600 (flexi-access drawdown fund lump sum death benefit).
PTM073500 (drawdown pension fund lump sum death benefit).
PTM073400 (annuity protection lump sum death benefit).
PTM073200 (uncrystallised funds lump sum death benefit).
PTM073100 (defined benefits lump sum death benefit).
PTM073010 (tax on authorised lump sum death benefits).
PTM073300 (pension protection lump sum death benefit).

Modifications—Registered Pension Schemes (Splitting of Schemes) Regulations, SI 2006/569 reg 3 (modification of this provision in relation to sub-scheme administrators).

Amendments—[1] Sub-s (1)(*c*) substituted, and sub-s (1A) inserted, by FA 2011 s 65, Sch 16 para 41 with effect for the tax year 2011–12 and subsequent tax years, subject to transitional provisions in FA 2011 Sch 16 Pt 3. The amendments made by FA 2011 Sch 16 paras 33–39, 41, 42(2)(b), (c), (4), (5), 65, 67, 68, 75(a), 76, 77(5), 79(4), 82(6) have effect in relation to deaths occurring on or after 6 April 2011 (FA 2011 Sch 16 para 103).
[2] Words in sub-s (3) repealed by FA 2013 s 219, Sch 46 paras 119, 123 with effect in relation to the tax year 2013–14 and any subsequent tax year.
[3] Words in sub-s (1) substituted, and in sub-s (4) figure substituted for previous figure "55%", by the Taxation of Pensions Act 2014 s 2(1)–(3) with effect in relation to lump sums paid on or after 6 April 2015.
[4] In sub-s (1), word "or" at end of para (*b*) repealed and para (*d*) and preceding word inserted, by the Taxation of Pensions Act 2014 s 1, Sch 1 paras 5, 13 with effect from 17 December 2014.
[5] Sub-ss (1ZA), (1B), (1C) inserted, and sub-s (7) substituted, by the Taxation of Pensions Act 2014 s 3, Sch 2 para 17(1)–(4) with effect for lump sums paid on or after 6 April 2015.
[6] In sub-ss (1), (1A), (1B)(*a*), (1C)(*a*), (7), words inserted, and sub-ss (1B)(*b*)(iia), (8)–(10) inserted by F(No 2)A 2015 s 21(1)–(5) with effect in relation to lump sums paid on or after 6 April 2016.

207 Authorised surplus payments charge

(1) A charge to income tax, to be known as the authorised surplus payments charge, arises where an authorised surplus payment is made to a sponsoring employer by an occupational pension scheme that is a registered pension scheme.

(2) The person liable to the authorised surplus payments charge is the scheme administrator.

(3) The scheme administrator is liable to the authorised surplus payments charge whether or not—

    (*a*) the scheme administrator, and

    (*b*) the sponsoring employer,

are resident . . . [1] or domiciled in the United Kingdom.

(4) The rate of the charge is 35% in respect of the authorised surplus payment.

(5) The Treasury may by order increase or decrease the rate for the time being specified in subsection (4).

(6) Subsection (1) does not apply to any authorised surplus payment—

    (*a*) to the extent that (if this section had not been enacted) the sponsoring employer would have been exempt, or entitled to claim exemption, from income tax or corporation tax in respect of it, or

    (*b*) if the sponsoring employer is a charity.

[(6A) Subsection (1) does not apply to an authorised surplus payment to the extent that the payment is funded (directly or indirectly) by a surrender of (or an agreement to surrender) benefits or rights which results in the registered pension scheme being treated as making an unauthorised payment under section 172A.

(6B) Terms used in subsection (6A) which are defined in section 172A have the same meaning as they have in that section.][2]

(7) An authorised surplus payment in respect of which income tax is charged under this section is not to be treated as income for any purpose of the Tax Acts.

(8) Schedule 36 contains (in Part 4) transitional provisions about the authorised surplus payments charge.

Commentary—*Simon's Taxes* **E7.247**.

HMRC Manuals—Pensions Tax Manual PTM145200 (authorised surplus payments).

Modifications—Registered Pension Schemes (Splitting of Schemes) Regulations, SI 2006/569 reg 3 (modification of this provision in relation to sub-scheme administrators).

Amendments—[1]   Words in sub-s (3) repealed by FA 2013 s 219, Sch 46 paras 119, 124 with effect in relation to the tax year 2013–14 and any subsequent tax year.

[2]   Sub-ss (6A), (6B) inserted by FA 2014 s 46, Sch 7 paras 1, 11 with effect in relation to surrenders (or agreements to surrender) made on or after 20 March 2014.

Unauthorised payments charge

208 Unauthorised payments charge

(1) A charge to income tax, to be known as the unauthorised payments charge, arises where an unauthorised payment is made by a registered pension scheme.

(2) The person liable to the charge—

    (*a*) in the case of an unauthorised member payment [made to or in respect of a person before the person's death, is the person,][1]

    (*b*) in the case of an unauthorised member payment made [in respect of a person after the person's][1] death, is the recipient, and

    (*c*) in the case of an unauthorised employer payment, is the [person][1] to or in respect of whom the payment is made.

(3) If more than one person is liable to the unauthorised payments charge in respect of an unauthorised payment, those persons are jointly and severally liable to the charge in respect of the payment.

(4) A person is liable to the unauthorised payments charge whether or not—

    (*a*) that person,

    (*b*) any other person who is liable to the unauthorised payments charge, and

    (*c*) the scheme administrator,

are resident . . . [3] or domiciled in the United Kingdom.

(5) The rate of the charge is 40% in respect of the unauthorised payment.

[(6) The Treasury may by order amend subsection (5) so as to vary the rate of the unauthorised payments charge.

(6A) An order under subsection (6) may make provision for there to be different rates in different circumstances.][2]

(7) An unauthorised payment may also be subject to—

    (*a*) the unauthorised payments surcharge under section 209, and

    (*b*) the scheme sanction charge under section 239.

(8) An unauthorised payment is not to be treated as income for any purpose of the Tax Acts.

Commentary—*Simon's Taxes* **E7.247, E7.240**.

HMRC Manuals—Pensions Tax Manual PTM134100 (unauthorised Payments charge and surcharge : essential principles).

PTM131000 (unauthorised Payments : essential principles).

PTM134400 (surchargeable unauthorised member payments).

PTM134200 (who is liable to the charges on unauthorised payments).

PTM121000 (the unauthorised payments charge).

Amendments—[1]   Words in sub-s (2) substituted by FA 2006 s 161, Sch 23 paras 1, 14. These amendments are deemed to have come into force on 6 April 2006.

[2]   Sub-ss (6), (6A) substituted for sub-s (6) by FA 2009 s 6, Sch 2 paras 10, 12 with effect for the tax year 2010–11 and subsequent tax years. The powers conferred by the amendments made by FA 2009 Sch 2 may be exercised at any time on or after 21 July 2009 but not so as to make provision having effect before the tax year 2010–11 (FA 2009 Sch 2 para 25(1))

[3]   Words in sub-s (4) repealed by FA 2013 s 219, Sch 46 paras 119, 125 with effect in relation to the tax year 2013–14 and any subsequent tax year.

209 Unauthorised payments surcharge

(1) A charge to income tax, to be known as the unauthorised payments surcharge, arises where a surchargeable unauthorised payment is made by a registered pension scheme.

(2) "Surchargeable unauthorised payments" means—

    (*a*) surchargeable unauthorised member payments (see section 210), and

    (*b*) surchargeable unauthorised employer payments (see section 213).

(3) The person liable to the charge—

    (*a*) in the case of a surchargeable unauthorised member payment [made to or in respect of a person before the person's death, is the person,][2]

    (*b*) in the case of a surchargeable unauthorised member payment made [in respect of a person after the person's][2] death, is the recipient, and

    (*c*) in the case of a surchargeable unauthorised employer payment, is the [person][2] to or in respect of whom the payment was made.

(4) If more than one person is liable to the unauthorised payments surcharge in respect of a surchargeable unauthorised payment, those persons are jointly and severally liable to the surcharge in respect of the payment.

(5) A person is liable to the unauthorised payments surcharge whether or not—

    (*a*) that person,

    (*b*) any other person who is liable to the unauthorised payments surcharge, . . . [1]

    (*c*) the scheme administrator [and][1],

    [(*d*) the sub-scheme administrator,][1]

are resident . . . [4] or domiciled in the United Kingdom.

(6) The rate of the charge is 15% in respect of the surchargeable unauthorised payment.

[(7) The Treasury may by order amend subsection (6) so as to vary the rate of the unauthorised payments surcharge.

(8) An order under subsection (7) may make provision for there to be different rates in different circumstances.][3]

Commentary—*Simon's Taxes* E7.247.

HMRC Manuals—Pensions Tax Manual PTM134100 (unauthorised Payments charge and surcharge : essential principles). PTM121000 (an unauthorised payment surcharge).

Amendments—[1] In sub-s (5), word in para (*b*) repealed, word in para (*c*) inserted, and para (*d*) inserted, by the Registered Pension Schemes (Splitting of Schemes) Regulations, SI 2006/569 reg 4 with effect from 6 April 2006.

[2] Words in sub-s (3) substituted by FA 2006 s 161, Sch 23 paras 1, 15. These amendments are deemed to have come into force on 6 April 2006.

[3] Sub-ss (7), (8) substituted for sub-s (7), by FA 2009 s 6, Sch 2 paras 10, 13 with effect for the tax year 2010–11 and subsequent tax years. The powers conferred by the amendments made by FA 2009 Sch 2 may be exercised at any time on or after 21 July 2009 but not so as to make provision having effect before the tax year 2010–11 (FA 2009 Sch 2 para 25(1)).

[4] Words in sub-s (5) repealed by FA 2013 s 219, Sch 46 paras 119, 126 with effect in relation to the tax year 2013–14 and any subsequent tax year.

210 Surchargeable unauthorised member payments

(1) This section identifies which unauthorised member payments made by a registered pension scheme [to or in respect of a person who is or has been a member of][1] the pension scheme are surchargeable.

(2) If the surcharge threshold is reached before the end of the period of 12 months beginning with a reference date, each unauthorised member payment made [to or in respect of the person][1] in the surcharge period is surchargeable.

(3) The surcharge period is the period—

    (*a*) beginning with the reference date, and

    (*b*) ending with the day on which the surcharge threshold is reached.

(4) The first reference date is the date on which the pension scheme first makes an unauthorised member payment [to or in respect of the person][1].

(5) Each subsequent reference date is the date, after the end of the previous reference period, on which the pension scheme next makes an unauthorised member payment [to or in respect of the person][1].

(6) The previous reference period is the period of 12 months beginning with the previous reference date or, if the surcharge threshold is reached in that period, is the surcharge period ending with the date on which it was reached.

(7) The surcharge threshold is reached if the unauthorised payments percentage reaches 25%.

(8) The unauthorised payments percentage is the aggregate of the percentages of the pension fund used up by each unauthorised member payment made by the pension scheme [to or in respect of the person][1] on or after the reference date.

(9) The percentage of the pension fund used up on the occasion of an unauthorised member payment is—

$$\frac{UMP}{VR} \times 100$$

where—

UMP is the amount of the unauthorised member payment, and

VR is an amount equal to the [aggregate of the value of the member's rights under arrangements relating to the member under the pension scheme when the unauthorised payment is made (or, if the unauthorised member payment is made after the member has died or has otherwise ceased to be a member of the pension scheme, at the date when the member died or otherwise ceased to be a member).][1]

(10) The value of the member's rights under [an arrangement on any][1] date is the aggregate of—

(*a*) the value of the member's crystallised rights under the arrangement on that date, calculated in accordance with section 211, and

(*b*) the value of the member's uncrystallised rights under the arrangement on that date, calculated in accordance with section 212.

Commentary—*Simon's Taxes* E7.247.

HMRC Manuals—Pensions Tax Manual PTM134400 (surchargeable unauthorised member payments).

Amendments—[1] Words in sub-ss (1), (2), (4), (5), (8)–(10) substituted by FA 2006 s 161, Sch 23 paras 1, 16. These amendments are deemed to have come into force on 6 April 2006.

211 Valuation of crystallised rights for purposes of section 210

(1) The value of the member's crystallised rights under [an arrangement][1] on any date is the aggregate of—

(*a*) the value of each scheme pension or lifetime annuity to which the member has an actual (rather than a prospective) entitlement under the arrangement on that date, . . .[3]

(*b*) the aggregate of the amount of the sums, and the market value of the assets, representing the [member's drawdown pension fund][2] in respect of the arrangement on that date (if any)[, and

(*c*) the aggregate of the amount of the sums, and the market value of the assets, representing the member's flexi-access drawdown fund in respect of the arrangement on that date (if any).][3]

(2) The value of a scheme pension or lifetime annuity is—

$$RVF \times ARP$$

where—

RVF is the relevant valuation factor (see section 276), and

ARP is an amount equal to the annual rate of the pension or annuity on the date.

Amendments—[1] Words in sub-s (1) substituted by FA 2006 s 161, Sch 23 paras 1, 17. This amendment is deemed to have come into force on 6 April 2006.

[2] Words in sub-s (1)(*b*) substituted for words "member's unsecured pension fund or alternatively secured pension fund" by FA 2011 s 65, Sch 16 paras 62, 71 with effect for the tax year 2011–12 and subsequent tax years, subject to transitional provisions in FA 2011 Sch 16 Pt 3.

[3] In sub-s (1), word "and" at end of para (*a*) repealed and para (*c*) and preceding word inserted, by the Taxation of Pensions Act 2014 s 1, Sch 1 paras 5, 14 with effect from 17 December 2014.

212 Valuation of uncrystallised rights for purposes of section 210

(1) Rights are uncrystallised if the member is not entitled to the present payment of benefits in respect of the rights.

(2) The member is to be treated as entitled to the present payment of benefits in respect of the sums and assets representing the [member's drawdown pension fund][2] [or the member's flexi-access drawdown fund][3].

(3) The value of the member's uncrystallised rights under [an arrangement][1] on any date is to be calculated—

(*a*) in accordance with subsection (4) if the arrangement is a cash balance arrangement,

(*b*) in accordance with subsection (5) if the arrangement is a money purchase arrangement other than a cash balance arrangement,

(*c*) in accordance with subsection (6) if the arrangement is a defined benefits arrangement, and

(*d*) in accordance with subsection (7) if the arrangement is a hybrid arrangement.

(4) If this subsection applies, the value of the member's uncrystallised rights under the arrangement on the date is the amount which would, on the valuation assumptions (see section 277), be available for the provision of benefits in respect of those rights if the member became entitled to benefits in respect of those rights on the date.

(5) If this subsection applies, the value of the member's uncrystallised rights under the arrangement on the date is the aggregate of—

(*a*) the amount of such of the sums held for the purposes of the arrangement on the date as represent those rights, and (*b*) the market value of such of the assets held for the purposes of the arrangement on the date as represent those rights.

(6) If this subsection applies, the value of the member's uncrystallised rights under the arrangement on the date is—

$$(RVF \times ARP) + LS$$

where—

RVF is the relevant valuation factor (see section 276),

ARP is the annual rate of pension to which the member would, on the valuation assumptions, be entitled under the arrangement on the date if, on the date, the member acquired an actual (rather than a prospective) right to receive a pension in respect of the rights, and

LS is the amount of any lump sum to which the member would, on the valuation assumptions, be entitled under the arrangement on the date (otherwise than by way of commutation of pension) if, on the date, the member acquired an actual (rather than a prospective) right to payment of a lump sum in respect of the rights.

(7) If this subsection applies, the value of the member's uncrystallised rights under the arrangement on the date is—

(*a*) if each of subsections (4), (5) and (6) is relevant, the greatest of the values of the rights calculated in accordance with each of those subsections, or

(*b*) if only two of those subsections are relevant, the greater of the values of the rights calculated in accordance with each of the two subsections.

(8) Subsection (4) is relevant if, in any circumstances, cash balance benefits may be provided to or in respect of the member under the arrangement.

(9) Subsection (5) is relevant if, in any circumstances, money purchase benefits other than cash balance benefits may be provided to or in respect of the member under the arrangement.

(10) Subsection (6) is relevant if, in any circumstances, defined benefits may be provided to or in respect of the member under the arrangement.

Commentary—*Simon's Taxes* **E7.233**.

HMRC Manuals—Pensions Tax Manual PTM134500 (surchargeable unauthorised member payments - valuing members rights in calculation the unauthorised payments percentage).

PTM094310 (valuing pension savings for individual protection 2016).

Modifications—Taxation of Pension Schemes (Transitional Provisions) Order, SI 2006/572 arts 9, 10 (modification of this section in its application to any individual who has given notice of intention to rely on FA 2004 Sch 36 para 7 where certain conditions are met).

Amendments—[1] Words in sub-s (3) substituted by FA 2006 s 161, Sch 23 paras 1, 18. This amendment is deemed to have come into force on 6 April 2006.

[2] Words in sub-s (2) substituted for words "member's unsecured pension fund or alternatively secured pension fund" by FA 2011 s 65, Sch 16 paras 62, 72 with effect for the tax year 2011–2012 and subsequent tax years, subject to transitional provisions in FA 2011 Sch 16 Pt 3.

[3] Words in sub-s (2) inserted by the Taxation of Pensions Act 2014 s 1, Sch 1 paras 5, 15 with effect from 17 December 2014.

213 Surchargeable unauthorised employer payments

(1) This section identifies which unauthorised employer payments made by a registered pension scheme to or in respect of a [person who is or has been a][1] sponsoring employer are surchargeable.

(2) If the surcharge threshold is reached before the end of the period of 12 months beginning with a reference date, each unauthorised employer payment made to or in respect of the [person][1] in the surcharge period is surchargeable.

(3) The surcharge period is the period—

(*a*) beginning with the reference date, and

(*b*) ending with the day on which the surcharge threshold is reached.

(4) The first reference date is the date on which the pension scheme first makes an unauthorised employer payment to or in respect of the [person][1].

(5) Each subsequent reference date is the date, after the end of the previous reference period, on which the pension scheme next makes an unauthorised employer payment to or in respect of the [person][1].

(6) The previous reference period is the period of 12 months beginning with the previous reference date or, if the surcharge threshold is reached in that period, is the surcharge period ending with the date on which it was reached.

(7) The surcharge threshold is reached if the unauthorised payments percentage reaches 25%.

(8) The unauthorised payments percentage is the aggregate of the percentages of the pension fund used up by each unauthorised employer payment made by the pension scheme to or in respect of the [person][1] on or after the reference date.

(9) The percentage of the pension fund used up on the occasion of an unauthorised employer payment is—

$$\frac{\text{UEP}}{\text{AA}} \times 100$$

where—
  UEP is the amount of the unauthorised employer payment, and
  AA is an amount equal to the aggregate of the amount of the sums and the market value of the assets held for the purposes of the pension scheme at the time when the unauthorised employer payment is made.

Commentary—*Simon's Taxes* **E7.247**.

HMRC Manuals—Pensions Tax Manual PTM134600 (surchargeable unauthorised employer payments).

Amendments—[1]   Words in sub-s (1) inserted, and words in sub-ss (2), (4), (5) and (8) substituted, by FA 2006 s 161, Sch 23 paras 1, 19. This amendment is deemed to have come into force on 6 April 2006.

Lifetime allowance charge

Commentary—*Simon's Taxes* **E7.247**.

214 Lifetime allowance charge

(1) A charge to income tax, to be known as the lifetime allowance charge, arises where—
  (a) a benefit crystallisation event occurs in relation to an individual who is a member of one or more registered pension schemes, and
  (b) either the first lifetime allowance charge condition or the second lifetime allowance charge condition is met.

(2) The first lifetime allowance charge condition is that—
  (a) the whole or any part of the individual's lifetime allowance is available on the benefit crystallisation event, but
  (b) the amount crystallised by the benefit crystallisation event exceeds the amount of the individual's lifetime allowance which is available on the benefit crystallisation event.

(3) The second lifetime allowance charge condition is that none of the individual's lifetime allowance is available on the benefit crystallisation event.

(4) The following sections make further provision about the lifetime allowance charge—
  section 215 (amount of charge),
  section 216 and Schedule 32 (benefit crystallisation events and amounts crystallised),
  section 217 (persons liable to charge),
  section 218 (individual's lifetime allowance and standard lifetime allowance),
  section 219 (availability of individual's lifetime allowance), and
  sections 220 to 226 (lifetime allowance enhancement factors).

(5) In sections 215 to 219—
  (a) references to "the individual", in relation to the lifetime allowance charge, are to the individual in relation to whom the benefit crystallisation event giving rise to the charge occurs, and
  (b) references to "the pension scheme", in relation to the lifetime allowance charge, are to the pension scheme to which the benefit crystallisation event giving rise to the charge, or the amount crystallised by it, relates.

(6) Schedule 36 contains (in Part 2) transitional provision about the lifetime allowance charge.

Commentary—*Simon's Taxes* **E7.202–E7.207, E7.217**.

HMRC Manuals—Pensions Tax Manual PTM081000 (essential principles of the lifetime allowance).

215 Amount of charge

(1) The lifetime allowance charge is a charge in respect of the chargeable amount.

(2) The lifetime allowance charge is a charge—
  (a) at the rate of 55% in respect of so much (if any) of the chargeable amount as constitutes the lump-sum amount, and
  (b) at the rate of 25% in respect of so much (if any) of the chargeable amount as constitutes the retained amount.

[(2A) The Treasury may by order amend subsection (2) so as to vary the rates of the lifetime allowance charge.

(2B) An order under subsection (2A) may make provision for there to be different rates in different circumstances.][3]

(3) The "chargeable amount" is the aggregate of—
  (a) the basic amount, and
  (b) any amount which is treated as forming part of the lump-sum amount under subsection (6) or of the retained amount under subsection (8).

(4) The "basic amount"—
  (a) if the first lifetime allowance [charge][2] condition is met, is the amount by which the amount crystallised by the benefit crystallisation event exceeds the amount of the individual's lifetime allowance available on it, and

(*b*) if the second lifetime allowance charge condition is met, is the amount crystallised by the benefit crystallisation event.

(5) The "lump-sum amount" is the aggregate of—

(*a*) so much of the basic amount as is paid as a lump sum to the individual or a lump sum death benefit in respect of the individual, and

(*b*) any amount which is treated as forming part of the lump-sum amount under subsection (6).

(6) If and to the extent that the tax payable under this section on any of the lump-sum amount is covered by a scheme-funded tax payment, it is to be treated as itself forming part of the lump-sum amount.

(7) The "retained amount" is the aggregate of—

(*a*) so much of the basic amount as is not paid as a lump sum to the individual or a lump sum death benefit in respect of the individual, and

(*b*) any amount which is treated as forming part of the retained amount under subsection (8).

(8) If and to the extent that the tax payable under this section on any of the retained amount is covered by a scheme-funded tax payment, it is to be treated as itself forming part of the retained amount.

(9) An amount of tax payable under this section is "covered by a scheme-funded tax payment" if—

(*a*) the tax is paid by the scheme administrator, . . . [1]

(*b*) . . . [1]

(10) . . . [1]

(11) The chargeable amount is not to be treated as income for any purpose of the Tax Acts.

Commentary—*Simon's Taxes* **E7.217, E7.220**.

HMRC Manuals—Pensions Tax Manual PTM085000 (chargeable amount where the lifetime allowance is used up).

Modifications—Registered Pension Schemes (Splitting of Schemes) Regulations, SI 2006/569 reg 3 (modification of this provision in relation to sub-scheme administrators).

Amendments—[1] Sub-s (9) and preceding word "and", and sub-s 10 repealed by FA 2005 ss 101, 104, Sch 10 paras 41, 64(1), Sch 11 Pt 4 with effect from 6 April 2006.

[2] Words in sub-s (4)(*a*) inserted by FA 2008 s 92, Sch 29 para 15 with effect from 21 July 2008.

[3] Sub-ss (2A), (2B) inserted by FA 2009 s 6, Sch 2 paras 10, 14 with effect for the tax year 2010–11 and subsequent tax years. The powers conferred by the amendments made by FA 2009 Sch 2 may be exercised at any time on or after 21 July 2009 but not so as to make provision having effect before the tax year 2010–11 (FA 2009 Sch 2 para 25(1)).

216 Benefit crystallisation events and amounts crystallised

(1) This table sets out—

(*a*) the events which are benefit crystallisation events in relation to the individual, and

(*b*) the amount which is crystallised by each of those events.

BENEFIT CRYSTALLISATION EVENTS	AMOUNT CRYSTALLISED
1. The designation of sums or assets held for the purposes of a money purchase arrangement under any of the relevant pension schemes as available for the payment of [drawdown pension][7] to the individual	The aggregate of the amount of the sums and the market value of the assets designated
2. The individual becoming entitled to a scheme pension under any of the relevant pension schemes	$RVF \times P$
3. The individual, having become so entitled, becoming entitled to payment of the scheme pension, otherwise than in excepted circumstances, at an increased annual rate which[— (a) exceeds the threshold annual rate, and, (b)][5] exceeds by more than the permitted margin the rate at which it was payable on the day on which the individual became entitled to it	$RVF \times XP$
4. The individual becoming entitled to a lifetime annuity purchased under a money purchase arrangement under any of the relevant pension schemes	The aggregate of the amount of such of the sums, and the market value of such of the assets, representing the individual's rights under the arrangement as are applied to purchase the lifetime annuity [and any related dependants' annuity][1] [and any related nominees' annuity][10]
5. The individual reaching the age of 75 when prospectively entitled to a scheme pension or a lump sum (or both) under a defined benefits arrangement under any of the relevant pension schemes	$(RVF \times DP) + DSLS$

BENEFIT CRYSTALLISATION EVENTS	AMOUNT CRYSTALLISED
[5A. The individual reaching the age of 75 having designated sums or assets held for the purposes of a money purchase arrangement under any of the relevant pension schemes as available for the payment of [drawdown pension][7] to the individual	The aggregate of the amount of the sums and the market value of the assets representing the [individual's drawdown pension fund][7] under the arrangement [(if any), plus the aggregate of the amount of the sums and the market value of the assets representing the individual's flexi-access drawdown fund under the arrangement (if any),][8] less the aggregate of amounts crystallised by benefit crystallisation event 1 in relation to the arrangement and the individual][3]
[5B The individual reaching the age of 75 when there is a money purchase arrangement relating to the individual under any of the relevant pension schemes	The amount of any remaining unused funds][6]
[5C. The designation, on or after 6 April 2015 but before the end of the relevant two-year period, of relevant unused uncrystallised funds as available for the payment, to a dependant or nominee of the individual, of (as the case may be) dependants' flexi-access drawdown pension or nominees' flexi-access drawdown pension	The aggregate of the amount of the sums and the market value of the assets designated][9]
[5D. A person becoming entitled, on or after 6 April 2015 but before the end of the relevant two-year period, to a dependants' annuity or nominees' annuity in respect of the individual if— (a) the annuity is purchased using (whether or not exclusively) relevant unused uncrystallised funds, and (b) the individual died on or after 3 December 2014	The aggregate of— (a) the amount of such of the sums, and (b) the market value of such of the assets, applied to purchase the annuity as are relevant unused uncrystallised funds][10]
6. The individual becoming entitled to a relevant lump sum under any of the relevant pension schemes	The amount of the lump sum [paid to the individual][2]
7. A person being paid a relevant lump sum death benefit in respect of the individual under any of the relevant pension schemes	The amount of the lump sum death benefit
8. The transfer of sums or assets held for the purposes of, or representing accrued rights under, any of the relevant pension schemes so as to become held for the purposes of or to represent rights under a qualifying recognised overseas pension scheme in connection with the individual's membership of that pension scheme	The aggregate of the amount of any sums transferred and the market value of any assets transferred
[9. If regulations under section 164(1)(*f*) so provide, the happening of an event prescribed in the regulations in relation to a payment prescribed in the regulations	An amount determined in accordance with the regulations][4]

(2) Schedule 32 gives the meaning of expressions used in the table in subsection (1).

Commentary—*Simon's Taxes* E7.216, E7.217.

HMRC Manuals—Pensions Tax Manual PTM100010 (transfers: essential principles). PTM045000 (short service refund lump sum and the lifetime allowance).

Amendments—[1]   In sub-s (1), words in table inserted by FA 2005 s 101, Sch 10 paras 31, 64(1) with effect from 6 April 2006.

[2]   In sub-s (1), words in table inserted by FA 2005 s 101, Sch 10 paras 42, 64(1) with effect from 6 April 2006.

[3]   Event 5A inserted by FA 2006 s 161, Sch 23 paras 1, 30. This amendment is deemed to have come into force on 6 April 2006.

[4]   Event 9 inserted by FA 2008 s 92, Sch 29 para 1 with effect from 21 July 2008.

[5]   Words in Event 3 inserted by FA 2008 s 92, Sch 29 paras 4, 5. This amendment is treated as having come into force on 6 April 2006, subject to FA 2008 Sch 29 para 12(2).

[6]   Event 5B inserted by FA 2011 s 65, Sch 16 para 43 with effect for the tax year 2011–12 and subsequent tax years, subject to transitional provisions in FA 2011 Sch 16 Pt 3. The amendments made by FA 2011 Sch 16 paras 43, 44, 73, 80, 82(2) have effect in relation to benefit crystallisation events occurring on or after 6 April 2011 (FA 2011 Sch 16 para 104(1)).

[7]   Words in Events 1 and 5A substituted for words "unsecured pension", and words in Event 5A substituted for words "individual's unsecured pension fund", by FA 2011 s 65, Sch 16 paras 62, 73 with effect for the tax year 2011–12 and subsequent tax years, subject to transitional provisions in FA 2011 Sch 16 Pt 3. The amendments made by FA 2011 Sch 16 paras 43, 44, 73, 80, 82(2) have effect in relation to benefit crystallisation events occurring on or after 6 April 2011 (FA 2011 Sch 16 para 104(1)).

[8]   In sub-s (1), in column 2 of the entry in the table for benefit crystallisation event 5A, words inserted by the Taxation of Pensions Act 2014 s 1, Sch 1 paras 5, 16 with effect from 17 December 2014.

[9]   In sub-s (1), entry for benefit crystallisation event 5C inserted by the Taxation of Pensions Act 2014 s 3, Sch 2 para 21 with effect from 17 December 2014.

[10]   In sub-s (1), in column 2 of the entry in the table for benefit crystallisation event 4, words inserted, and entry for benefit crystallisation event 5D inserted, by FA 2015 s 34, Sch 4 paras 1, 4 with effect from 26 March 2015.

217 Persons liable to charge

(1) The persons liable to the lifetime allowance charge are—
    (a) the individual, and
    (b) the scheme administrator of the pension scheme, and their liability is joint and several.
[(1A) Subsection (1) is subject to subsections (2) and (2A).][2]
(2) [Where][2] the liability arises by reason of the payment of a relevant lump sum death benefit it is a liability of the person to whom the lump sum death benefit is paid.
[(2A) Where the liability arises by reason of a designation mentioned in the description of benefit crystallisation event 5C, [or by reason of a person becoming entitled to an annuity as mentioned in the description of benefit crystallisation event 5D,][3] it is a liability of the dependant or nominee (as the case may be).][2]
[(3) Subsection (4) applies if—
    (a) two or more relevant post-death benefit crystallisation events occur in respect of an individual, and
    (b) tax is not chargeable on the whole of the total of the amounts crystallised by them.
(4) The person liable under subsection (2) or (2A) to the lifetime allowance charge charged by reason of the occurrence of any one of the relevant post-death benefit crystallisation events is liable to such portion of the total amount of the tax payable by reason of the relevant post-death benefit crystallisation events having occurred as appears to an officer of Revenue and Customs to be just and reasonable.
(4A) For the purposes of subsections (3) and (4), a benefit crystallisation event is a "relevant post-death benefit crystallisation event" if it is benefit crystallisation event 5C[, 5D][3] or 7.][2]
(5) A person is liable to the lifetime allowance charge whether or not—
    (a) that person,
    (b) any other person who is liable to the lifetime allowance charge, and
    (c) the scheme administrator (if not so liable),
are resident . . . [1] or domiciled in the United Kingdom.

Commentary—*Simon's Taxes* **E7.217, E7.220**.
HMRC Manuals—Pensions Tax Manual PTM086000 (liability for the lifetime allowance charge in the member's lifetime).
Amendments—[1]   Words in sub-s (5) repealed by FA 2013 s 219, Sch 46 paras 119, 127 with effect in relation to the tax year 2013–14 and any subsequent tax year.
[2]   Sub-ss (1A), (2A) inserted, in sub-s (2) word substituted for words "But where", and sub-ss (3)–(4A) substituted for previous sub-ss (3), (4), by the Taxation of Pensions Act 2014 s 3, Sch 2 para 22. The insertion of sub-ss (1A), (2A) and substitution of words in sub-s (2) have effect from 17 December 2014. The substitution of previous sub-ss (3), (4) has effect from 6 April 2015.
[3]   In sub-ss (2A), (4A) words inserted by FA 2015 s 34, Sch 4 paras 1, 5 with effect from 26 March 2015.

218 Individual's lifetime allowance and standard lifetime allowance

(1) Subject as follows, the individual's lifetime allowance is the standard lifetime allowance.
[(2) The standard lifetime allowance for the tax years 2016–17 and 2017–18 is £1,000,000.][2]
(2A) The standard lifetime allowance for any later tax year ("the subsequent tax year") is the same as the standard lifetime allowance for the tax year immediately preceding the subsequent tax year, unless subsection (2C) provides for it to be higher.
(2B) Subsection (2C) applies if—
    (a) the consumer prices index for the month of September in any tax year ("the prior tax year") is higher than it was for the previous September, and
    (b) the prior tax year is the tax year 2017–18 or a later tax year.
(2C) The standard lifetime allowance for the tax year following the prior tax year is the standard lifetime allowance for the prior tax year—
    (a) increased by the percentage increase in the index, and
    (b) if the result is not a multiple of £100, rounded up to the nearest amount which is such a multiple.
(2D) The Treasury must before the tax year 2018–19, and before each subsequent tax year, make regulations specifying the amount given by subsections (2A) to (2C) as the standard lifetime allowance for the tax year concerned.][4]
(4) Where one or more lifetime allowance enhancement factors operate in relation to a benefit crystallisation event occurring in relation to the individual, the individual's lifetime allowance at the time of the benefit crystallisation event is—

$$SLA + (SLA \times LAEF)$$

where—
    SLA is the standard lifetime allowance at the time of the benefit crystallisation event, and

LAEF is the lifetime allowance enhancement factor which operates with respect to the benefit crystallisation event and the individual or (where more than one so operates) the aggregate of them.

(5) The following make provision for the operation of lifetime allowance enhancement factors—

section 220 (pension credits from previously crystallised rights), sections 221 to 223 (individuals who are not always relevant UK individuals),

sections 224 to 226 (transfers from recognised overseas pension schemes), paragraphs 7 to 11 of Schedule 36 (primary protection), and

paragraph 18 of that Schedule (pre-commencement pension credits).

[(5A) Where the operation of a lifetime allowance enhancement factor is provided for by any of sections 220, 222, 223 and 224 and the time mentioned in the definition of SLA in the section concerned was before 6 April 2012, subsection (4) has effect as if the amount to be multiplied by LAEF were £1,800,000 (the standard lifetime allowance for the tax year 2011–12) if that is greater than SLA.

(5B) Where the operation of a lifetime allowance enhancement factor is provided for by paragraph 7 of Schedule 36, subsection (4) has effect as if SLA were £1,800,000 (the standard lifetime allowance for the tax year 2011–12) if that is greater than SLA.

[(5BA) Where the operation of a lifetime allowance enhancement factor is provided for by any of sections 220, 222, 223 and 224 and the time mentioned in the definition of SLA in the section concerned fell within the period consisting of the tax year 2012–13 and the tax year 2013–14, subsection (4) has effect as if the amount to be multiplied by LAEF were £1,500,000 if that is greater than SLA.

(5BB) Where more than one lifetime allowance enhancement factor operates, subsection (5BA) does not apply if subsection (5A) or (5B) applies.][3]

[(5BC) Where the operation of a lifetime allowance enhancement factor is provided for by any of sections 220, 222, 223 and 224 and the time mentioned in the definition of SLA in the section concerned fell within the period consisting of the tax year 2014–15 and the tax year 2015–16, subsection (4) has effect as if the amount to be multiplied by LAEF were £1,250,000 if that is greater than SLA.

(5BD) Where more than one lifetime allowance enhancement factor operates, subsection (5BC) does not apply if any of subsections (5A), (5B) and (5BA) applies.][4]

(5C) Where benefit crystallisation event 7 occurs on or after 6 April 2012 by reason of the payment of a relevant lump sum death benefit in respect of the death of the individual before that date, the standard lifetime allowance at the time of the benefit crystallisation event is £1,800,000 (the standard lifetime allowance for the tax year 2011–12).][1]

[(5D) Where benefit crystallisation event 7 occurs on or after 6 April 2014 by reason of the payment of a relevant lump sum death benefit in respect of the death of the individual during the period consisting of the tax year 2012–13 and the tax year 2013–14, the standard lifetime allowance at the time of the benefit crystallisation event is £1,500,000.][3]

[(5E) Where benefit crystallisation event 7 occurs on or after 6 April 2016 by reason of the payment of a relevant lump sum death benefit in respect of the death of the individual during the period consisting of the tax year 2014–15 and the tax year 2015-16,

the standard lifetime allowance at the time of the benefit crystallisation event is £1,250,000.][4]

[(5F) Where—

(a) benefit crystallisation event 5C occurs by reason of the designation on or after 6 April 2015 of sums or assets held for the purposes of an arrangement relating to the individual, and

(b) the individual died before 6 April 2012,

the standard lifetime allowance at the time of the benefit crystallisation event is £1,800,000.

(5G) Where—

(a) benefit crystallisation event 5C occurs by reason of the designation on or after 6 April 2015 of sums or assets held for the purposes of an arrangement relating to the individual, and

(b) the individual died in the period consisting of the tax year 2012–13 and the tax year 2013–14,

the standard lifetime allowance at the time of the benefit crystallisation event is £1,500,000.

(5H) Where—

(a) benefit crystallisation event 5C occurs by reason of the designation on or after 6 April 2016 of sums or assets held for the purposes of an arrangement relating to the individual, and

(b) the individual died in the period consisting of the tax year 2014–15 and the tax year 2015-6,

the standard lifetime allowance at the time of the benefit crystallisation event is £1,250,000.

(5I) Where—

(a) benefit crystallisation event 5D occurs by reason of a person becoming entitled on or after 6 April 2016 to an annuity in respect of the individual, and

(b) the individual died in the period beginning with 3 December 2014 and ending with 5 April 2016,

the standard lifetime allowance at the time of the benefit crystallisation event is £1,250,000.][5]

(6) Paragraph 19 of that Schedule makes provision for the reduction of what would otherwise be the individual's lifetime allowance in certain cases where the individual is permitted to take pension before normal minimum pension age.

(7) In this Part references (however expressed) to a person's lifetime allowance at any time are to what would be the person's lifetime allowance, calculated in accordance with this section, if a benefit crystallisation event occurred in relation to the person at that time.

Note—The standard lifetime allowance is as follows, for the following tax years—

-    2020–21: £1,073,100
-    2019–20: £1,055,000
-    2018–19: £1,030,000
-    2016–17 to 2017–18: £1,000,000
-    2014–15 to 2015–16: £1,250,000
-    2010–11 to 2013–14: £1,800,000
-    2009–10: £1,750,000
-    2008–09: £1,650,000
-    2007–08: £1,600,000

Commentary—*Simon's Taxes* **E7.216, E7.218, E7.219**.

HMRC Manuals—Pensions Tax Manual PTM095600 (how to apply lifetime allowance enhancement factors at a BCE). PTM095100 (lifetime allowance enhancement factors: overview). PTM095500 (applying lifetime allowance enhancement factors).

Regulations and Orders—Registered Pension Schemes (Standard Lifetime and Annual Allowances) Order, SI 2007/494.

Finance Act 2004 (Standard Lifetime Allowance) Regulations, SI 2018/206.

Finance Act 2004 (Standard Lifetime Allowance) Regulations, SI 2019/29.

Finance Act 2004 (Standard Lifetime Allowance) Regulations, SI 2020/342.

Amendments—[1]   Sub-ss (2), (3) substituted, and sub-ss (5A)–(5C) inserted, by FA 2011 s 67, Sch 18 paras 1, 2 with effect for the tax year 2012–13 and subsequent tax years, subject to transitional provisions in FA 2011 Sch 18 para 14.

[2]   Sub-s (2) substituted, and in sub-s (3) words substituted, by FA 2013 s 48(1)–(3) with effect for the tax year 2014–15 and subsequent tax years.

[3]   Sub-ss (5BA), (5BB), (5D) inserted by FA 2013 s 48(5), Sch 22 paras 5, 6 with effect for the tax year 2014–15 and subsequent tax years.

[4]   Sub-ss (2)–(2D) substituted for previous sub-ss (2), (3), and sub-ss (5BC), (5BD), (5E) inserted, by FA 2016 s 19(1)–(4) with effect for the tax year 2016–17 and subsequent tax years.

[5]   Sub-ss (5F)–(5I) inserted by FA 2016 s 19(1), (5). This amendment has effect as follows—

     (a)   so far as it consists of the insertion of new sub-ss (5F) and (5G)—

         (i)   the amendment is to be treated as having come into force on 6 April 2015, and

         (ii)   has effect in relation to benefit crystallisation events occurring on or after that date, and

     (b)   so far as it consists of the insertion of new sub-ss (5H) and (5I)—

         (i)   the amendment is to be treated as having come into force on 6 April 2016, and

         (ii)   has effect in relation to benefit crystallisation events occurring on or after that date.

219 Availability of individual's lifetime allowance

(1) This section is about the availability of the individual's lifetime allowance on the occurrence of a benefit crystallisation event in relation to the individual ("the current benefit crystallisation event").

(2) If no benefit crystallisation event has occurred in relation to the individual before the current benefit crystallisation event, the whole of the individual's lifetime allowance is available on the current benefit crystallisation event.

(3) If one or more benefit crystallisation events have occurred in relation to the individual before the current benefit crystallisation event—

     (a)   in a case in which the previously-used amount is equal to or greater than the amount of the individual's lifetime allowance, none of the individual's lifetime allowance is available on the current benefit crystallisation event, and

     (b)   in any other case, so much of the individual's lifetime allowance as is left after deducting the previously-used amount is available on the current benefit crystallisation event.

(4) The previously-used amount is—

     (a)   where one benefit crystallisation event has occurred in relation to the individual before the current benefit crystallisation event, the amount [which is the relevant untaxed amount in relation to][1] the previous benefit crystallisation event as adjusted under subsection (5), or

     (b)   where two or more benefit crystallisation events have occurred in relation to the individual before the current benefit crystallisation event, the aggregate of the amounts [which are the relevant untaxed amounts in relation to][1] each previous benefit crystallisation event as adjusted under subsection (5).

[(4A) "The relevant untaxed amount", in relation to a previous benefit crystallisation event, is—

     (a)   where no tax was charged in relation to the benefit crystallisation event, the amount in respect of which tax would have been so charged if none of the individual's lifetime allowance had been available, and

     (b)   where tax was charged in relation to the benefit crystallisation event, so much of the amount in respect of which tax would have been so charged if none of the individual's lifetime allowance had been available as exceeds the amount in respect of which tax was so charged.][1]

(5) The adjustment of the [relevant untaxed amount in relation to][1] a previous benefit crystallisation event referred to in subsection (4)(*a*) and (*b*) is the multiplication of that amount by—

$$\frac{CSLA}{PSLA}$$

where—

CSLA is the standard lifetime allowance at the time of the current benefit crystallisation event, and

PSLA is the standard lifetime allowance at the time of the previous benefit crystallisation event.

[(5A) If paragraph 7 of Schedule 36 (primary protection) makes provision for a lifetime allowance enhancement factor in relation to the individual, subsection (5) has effect [where the previous benefit crystallisation event occurred before 6 April 2014][4] as if CSLA were £1,500,000 if that is greater than CSLA.][3]

(6) Where more than one benefit crystallisation event occurs in relation to an individual on the same day, it is for the individual to decide the order in which they are to be treated as occurring for the purposes of this section; but this subsection is subject to section 166(2) (entitlement to pension commencement lump sum to arise immediately before entitlement to associated pension).

(7) Where more than one [relevant post-death][5] benefit crystallisation event occurs . . . in respect of an [individual, the relevant post-death][5] benefit crystallisation events are to be treated for the purposes of this section as occurring immediately before the individual's death [but immediately after any benefit crystallisation event occurring immediately before the individual's death by virtue of section 166(2)][2].

[(7A) For the purposes of subsection (7), a benefit crystallisation event is a "relevant post-death benefit crystallisation event" if it is benefit crystallisation event 5C[, 5D][6] or 7.][5]

(8) Paragraph 20 of Schedule 36 makes provision affecting this section in relation to pre-commencement pensions.

(9) In this Part references (however expressed) to the portion of a person's lifetime allowance that is available at any time are to the portion of the person's lifetime allowance that would be available, calculated in accordance with this section, if a benefit crystallisation event occurred in relation to the person at that time.

Commentary—*Simon's Taxes* **E7.216, E7.217, E7.218**.

HMRC Manuals—Pensions Tax Manual PTM088680 (the benefit crystallisation events in detail: BCE 7 relevant lump sum death benefits).

PTM088100 (pensions in payment on 5 April 2006).

PTM088200 (where benefit crystallisation events (BCEs) occur simultaneously).

PTM092300 (protection from lifetime allowance charge - taking benefits at different times).

Amendments—[1]   Words in sub-ss (4), (5) substituted, and sub-s (4A) inserted, by FA 2006 s 161, Sch 23 paras 1, 31. These amendments are deemed to have come into force on 6 April 2006.

[2]   Words in sub-s (7) inserted by FA 2007 s 70, Sch 20 paras 1, 10, 24(3). These amendments are deemed always to have had effect.

[3]   Sub-s (5A) inserted by FA 2013 s 48(5), Sch 22 paras 5, 7 with effect for cases in which the time of the current benefit crystallisation event falls on or after 6 April 2014.

[4]   Words in sub-s (5A) inserted by FA 2014 s 44, Sch 6 para 10. This amendment is treated as having come into force on 6 April 2014.

[5]   In sub-s (7), words inserted, words "by reason of the payment of lump sum death benefits" repealed and words substituted for words "individual the", and sub-s (7A) inserted, by the Taxation of Pensions Act 2014 s 3, Sch 2 para 23 with effect from 6 April 2015.

[6]   In sub-s (7A), words inserted by FA 2015 s 34, Sch 4 paras 1, 6 with effect from 26 March 2015.

220 Pension credits from previously crystallised rights

(1) This section makes provision for the operation of a lifetime allowance enhancement factor with respect to a benefit crystallisation event occurring in relation to an individual where—

(*a*) the individual has (at any time after 5th April 2006 but before the benefit crystallisation event) acquired rights under a registered pension scheme by reason of having become entitled to a pension credit,

(*b*) the pension credit derived from the same or another registered pension scheme, and

(*c*) the rights under that registered pension scheme which became subject to the corresponding pension debit consisted of or included rights to a post-commencement pension in payment.

(2) "Post-commencement pension in payment" means a pension to which a person became (actually) entitled on or after 6th April 2006.

(3) The lifetime allowance enhancement factor is the pension credit factor.

(4) The pension credit factor is—

$$\frac{APC}{SLA}$$

where—

    APC is [the post-commencement pension in payment portion of][1] the amount which is the appropriate amount for the purposes of section 29(1) of WRPA 1999 or Article 26(1) of WRP(NI)O 1999 in relation to the pension credit, and

    SLA is the standard lifetime allowance at the time when the rights were acquired.

[(4A) The post-commencement pension in payment portion of the appropriate amount referred to in the definition of APC—

    (a) in a case where the appropriate amount is arrived at under section 29(2) or (3)(b) of WRPA 1999 or Article 26(2) or (3)(b) of WRP(NI)O 1999, is so much of that amount as is attributable to rights to a post-commencement pension in payment, and

    (b) in a case where the appropriate amount is arrived at under section 29(3)(a) of WRPA 1999 or Article 26(3)(a) of WRP(NI)O 1999, is so much of that amount as is just and reasonable.][1]

(5) This section only applies if notice of intention to rely on it is given to the Inland Revenue in accordance with regulations made by the Board of Inland Revenue.

Commentary—*Simon's Taxes* **E7.218**.
HMRC Manuals—Pensions Tax Manual PTM095200 (lifetime allowance enhancement factors: pension credit factor).
Regulations—Registered Pension Schemes (Enhanced Lifetime Allowance) Regulations, SI 2006/131.
Registered Pension Schemes (Provision of Information) Regulations, SI 2006/567.
Amendments—[1] Words in sub-s (4) and sub-s (4A) inserted by FA 2005 ss 101, 104, Sch 10 paras 45, 64(1) with effect from 6 April 2006.

221 Non-residence: general

(1) This section makes provision for the operation of a lifetime allowance enhancement factor with respect to a benefit crystallisation event occurring in relation to an individual where, during any part of the period that is the active membership period in relation to an arrangement relating to the individual under a registered pension scheme, the individual is a relevant overseas individual.

(2) Section 222 provides the lifetime allowance enhancement factor in the case of an arrangement that is a money purchase arrangement; and section 223 provides the lifetime allowance enhancement factor in the case of any other arrangement.

(3) For the purposes of this Part an individual is a relevant overseas individual at any time if, at that time, the individual either is not a relevant UK individual or—

    (a) is a relevant UK individual only by virtue of paragraph (c) of section 189(1) (individuals resident in UK at some time in previous five tax years), and

    (b) is not employed by a person resident in the United Kingdom.

(4) In this section and sections 222 and 223 "the active membership period", in relation to a benefit crystallisation event occurring in relation to an arrangement relating to the individual, is the period—

    (a) beginning with the date on which the benefits first began to accrue to or in respect of the individual under the arrangement or, if later, 6th April 2006, and

    (b) ending immediately before the benefit crystallisation event.

(5) But if benefits ceased to accrue to or in respect of the individual under the arrangement before the benefit crystallisation event, the active membership period is to be treated as having ended then.

(6) This section only applies if notice of intention to rely on it is given to the Inland Revenue in accordance with regulations made by the Board of Inland Revenue.

Commentary—*Simon's Taxes* **E7.218**.
HMRC Manuals—Pensions Tax Manual PTM095310 (non-residence factor: basic principles).
Regulations—Registered Pension Schemes (Enhanced Lifetime Allowance) Regulations, SI 2006/131.
Registered Pension Schemes (Provision of Information) Regulations, SI 2006/567.

222 Non-residence: money purchase arrangements

(1) This section applies in the case of an arrangement that is a money purchase arrangement.

(2) The lifetime allowance enhancement factor is—

    (a) if the arrangement is a cash balance arrangement, the cash balance arrangement non-residence factor (see subsections (3) to (5)), and

    (b) if the arrangement is any other sort of money purchase arrangement, the other money purchase arrangement non-residence factor (see subsections (6) and (7)).

(3) The cash balance arrangement non-residence factor is—

    (a) the factor arrived at by the application of subsection (4) in relation to the part of the active membership period during which the individual was a relevant overseas individual, or

    (b) if there have been two or more parts of that period during which the individual was a relevant overseas individual, the aggregate of the factors arrived at by the application of subsection (4) in relation to each of those parts of that period.

(4) The factor arrived at by the application of this subsection in relation to any part of the active membership period is—

$$\frac{CV - OV}{SLA}$$

where—
   CV is the closing value of the individual's rights under the arrangement,
   OV is the opening value of the individual's rights under the arrangement, and
   SLA is the standard lifetime allowance at the time when that part of that period ended.
(5) For the purposes of subsection (4)—
   (a) the closing value of the individual's rights under the arrangement is the amount which would,
       on the valuation assumptions (see section 277), be available for the provision of benefits to or
       in respect of the individual under the arrangement if the individual became entitled to the
       benefits at the end of that part of that period, and
   (b) the opening value of the individual's rights under the arrangement is the amount which
       would, on the valuation assumptions, be available for the provision of benefits to or in respect
       of the individual under the arrangement if the individual became entitled to the benefits at the
       beginning of that part of that period.
(6) The other money purchase arrangement non-residence factor is—
   (a) the factor arrived at by the application of subsection (7) in relation to the part of the active
       membership period during which the individual was a relevant overseas individual, or
   (b) if there have been two or more parts of that period during which the individual was a relevant
       overseas individual, the aggregate of the factors arrived at by the application of subsection (7)
       in relation to each of those parts of that period.
(7) The factor arrived at by the application of this subsection in relation to any part of the active
membership period is—

$$\frac{ROIC}{SLA}$$

where—
   ROIC is the amount of the contributions made under the arrangement by or in respect of the
   individual in any part of the active membership period during which the individual is a relevant
   overseas individual, and
   SLA is the standard lifetime allowance at the time when that part of that period ended.

Commentary—*Simon's Taxes* **E7.218**.
HMRC Manuals—Pensions Tax Manual PTM095330 (the non-residence factor for other money purchase arrangements).
PTM095320 (how to calculate the non-residence factor for a cash balance arrangement).
Modifications—Taxation of Pension Schemes (Transitional Provisions) Order, SI 2006/572 arts 12, 13 (modification of this
   section in its application to any individual who has satisfied certain conditions).

223 Non-residence: other arrangements
(1) This section applies in the case of an arrangement that is not a money purchase arrangement.
(2) The lifetime allowance enhancement factor is—
   (a) if the arrangement is a defined benefits arrangement, the defined benefits arrangement non-
       residence factor (see subsections (3) and (4)), and
   (b) if the arrangement is a hybrid arrangement, the hybrid arrangement non-residence factor (see
       subsections (5) to (7)).
(3) The defined benefits arrangement non-residence factor is—
   (a) the factor arrived at by the application of subsection (4) in relation to the part of the active
       membership period during which the individual was a relevant overseas individual, or
   (b) if there have been two or more parts of that period during which the individual was a relevant
       overseas individual, the aggregate of the factors arrived at by the application of subsection (4)
       in relation to each of those parts of that period.
(4) The factor arrived at by the application of this subsection in relation to any part of the active
membership period is—

$$\frac{(RVF \times PE + LSE) - (RVF \times PB + LSB)}{SLA}$$

where—
   RVF is the relevant valuation factor (see section 276),
   PE is the amount of the annual rate of the pension which would, on the valuation assumptions
   (see section 277), be payable to the individual under the arrangement if the individual became
   entitled to payment of it at the end of that part of that period,
   LSE is the amount of the lump sum to which the individual would, on the valuation
   assumptions, be entitled under the arrangement (otherwise than by commutation of pension) if
   the individual became entitled to payment of it at the end of that part of that period,
   PB is the amount of the annual rate of the pension which would, on the valuation assumptions,
   be payable to the individual under the arrangement if the individual became entitled to payment
   of it at the beginning of that part of that period,

LSB is the amount of the lump sum to which the individual would, on the valuation assumptions, be entitled under the arrangement (otherwise than by commutation of pension) if the individual became entitled to payment of it at the beginning of that part of that period, and SLA is the standard lifetime allowance at the time when that part of that period ended.

(5) The hybrid arrangement non-residence factor is the greater or greatest of such of—

    (a) what would be the cash balance arrangement non-residence factor (under section 222) if the arrangement were a cash balance arrangement,

    (b) what would be the other money purchase arrangement non-residence factor (under that section) if the arrangement were any other sort of money purchase arrangement, and

    (c) what would be the defined benefits arrangement non-residence factor (under subsections (3) and (4)) if the arrangement were a defined benefits arrangement,

as are relevant factors in relation to the arrangement.

(6) A factor is a relevant factor in relation to a hybrid arrangement if, in any circumstances, the benefits that may be provided to or in respect of the individual under the arrangement may be benefits linked to that factor.

(7) For that purpose—

    (a) cash balance benefits are linked to the cash balance arrangement non-residence factor,

    (b) other money purchase benefits are linked to the other money purchase arrangement non-residence factor, and

    (c) defined benefits are linked to the defined benefits arrangement non-residence factor.

Commentary—*Simon's Taxes* E7.218.

HMRC Manuals—Pension Tax Manual PTM095340 (how to calculate the non-residence factor for a defined benefits arrangement).

PTM0953350 (how to calculate the non-residence factor for a hybrid arrangement).

Modifications—Taxation of Pension Schemes (Transitional Provisions) Order, SI 2006/572 arts 12, 14 (modification of this section in its application to any individual who has satisfied certain conditions).

224 Transfers from recognised overseas pension scheme: general

(1) This section makes provision for the operation of a lifetime allowance enhancement factor with respect to a benefit crystallisation event occurring in relation to an individual where (at any time after 5th April 2006 but before the benefit crystallisation event) there has been a recognised overseas scheme transfer.

(2) There is a "recognised overseas scheme transfer" if any sums or assets—

    (a) held for the purposes of an arrangement under a recognised overseas pension scheme, or

    (b) representing accrued rights under such an arrangement,

are transferred so as to become held for the purposes of, or to represent rights under, an arrangement under a registered pension scheme relating to the individual.

(3) The arrangement specified in subsection (2)(a) or (b) is referred to in this section and sections 225 and 226 as the "recognised overseas scheme arrangement".

(4) The lifetime allowance enhancement factor is the recognised overseas scheme transfer factor.

(5) The recognised overseas scheme transfer factor is—

$$\frac{AAT - RRA}{SLA}$$

where—

    AAT is the aggregate of the amount of any sums transferred, and the market value of any assets transferred, on the recognised overseas scheme transfer,

    RRA is the relevant relievable amount, and

    SLA is the standard lifetime allowance at the time when the recognised overseas scheme transfer took place.

(6) Section 225 specifies the relevant relievable amount in the case of a recognised overseas scheme arrangement that was a money purchase arrangement; and section 226 specifies the relevant relievable amount in the case of an recognised overseas scheme arrangement that was any other sort of arrangement.

(7) In this section and sections 225 and 226 "overseas arrangement active membership period" is the period—

    (a) beginning with the date on which the benefits first began to accrue to or in respect of the individual under the recognised overseas scheme arrangement or, if later, 6th April 2006, and

    (b) ending immediately before the recognised overseas scheme transfer.

(8) But if benefits ceased to accrue to or in respect of the individual under the recognised overseas scheme arrangement before the recognised overseas scheme transfer, the overseas arrangement active membership period is to be treated as having ended then.

(9) This section only applies if notice of intention to rely on it is given to the Inland Revenue in accordance with regulations made by the Board of Inland Revenue.

Commentary—*Simon's Taxes* E7.218.

HMRC Manuals—Pensions Tax Manual PTM095410 (the recognised overseas scheme transfer factor).
Regulations—Registered Pension Schemes (Enhanced Lifetime Allowance) Regulations, SI 2006/131.
Registered Pension Schemes (Provision of Information) Regulations, SI 2006/567.

225 Overseas scheme transfers: money purchase arrangements

(1) This section applies in the case of a recognised overseas scheme arrangement that was a money purchase arrangement.

(2) The relevant relievable amount is—

    (*a*) if the recognised overseas scheme arrangement was a cash balance arrangement, the cash balance relevant relievable amount (see subsections (3) to (5)), and

    (*b*) if the recognised overseas scheme arrangement was any other sort of money purchase arrangement, the other money purchase relevant relievable amount (see subsections (6) and (7)).

(3) The cash balance relevant relievable amount is—

    (*a*) the amount arrived at by the application of subsection (4) in relation to the part of the overseas arrangement active membership period during which the individual was not a relevant overseas individual, or

    (*b*) if there have been two or more parts of that period during which the individual was not a relevant overseas individual, the aggregate of the amounts arrived at by the application of subsection (4) in relation to each of those parts of that period.

(4) The amount arrived at by the application of this subsection in relation to any part of the overseas arrangement active membership period is—

$$CV - OV$$

where—

    CV is the closing value of the individual's rights under the arrangement, and

    OV is the opening value of the individual's rights under the arrangement.

(5) For the purposes of subsection (4)—

    (*a*) the closing value of the individual's rights under the recognised overseas scheme arrangement is the amount which would, on the valuation assumptions (see section 277), be available for the provision of benefits to or in respect of the individual under the arrangement if the individual became entitled to the benefits at the end of that part of that period, and

    (*b*) the opening value of the individual's rights under the arrangement is the amount which would, on the valuation assumptions, be available for the provision of benefits to or in respect of the individual under the arrangement if the individual became entitled to the benefits at the beginning of that part of that period.

(6) The other money purchase relevant relievable amount is—

    (*a*) the amount arrived at by the application of subsection (7) in relation to the part of the overseas arrangement active membership period during which the individual was not a relevant overseas individual, or

    (*b*) if there have been two or more parts of that period during which the individual was not a relevant overseas individual, the aggregate of the amounts arrived at by the application of subsection (7) in relation to each of those parts of that period.

(7) The amount arrived at by the application of this subsection in relation to any part of the overseas arrangement active membership period is the amount of the contributions made under the arrangement by or in respect of the individual in any part of the overseas arrangement active membership period during which the individual was not a relevant overseas individual.

Commentary—*Simon's Taxes* E7.218.
HMRC Manuals—Pensions Tax Manual PTM095430 (the relevant relievable amount for an other money purchase arrangement).
PTM095420 (how to calculate the relevant relievable amount for a cash balance arrangement).

226 Overseas scheme transfers: other arrangements

(1) This section applies in the case of a recognised overseas scheme arrangement that was not a money purchase arrangement.

(2) The relevant relievable amount is—

    (*a*) if the recognised overseas scheme arrangement was a defined benefits arrangement, the defined benefits relevant relievable amount (see subsections (3) and (4)), and

    (*b*) if the recognised overseas scheme arrangement was a hybrid arrangement, the hybrid relevant relievable amount (see subsections (5) to (7)).

(3) The defined benefits relevant relievable amount is—

    (*a*) the amount arrived at by the application of subsection (4) in relation to the part of the overseas arrangement active membership period during which the individual was not a relevant overseas individual, or

    (*b*) if there have been two or more parts of that period during which the individual was not a relevant overseas individual, the aggregate of the amounts arrived at by the application of subsection (4) in relation to each of those parts of that period.

(4) The amount arrived at by the application of this subsection in relation to any part of the overseas arrangement active membership period is—

$$(RVF \times PE + LSE) - (RVF \times PB + LSB)$$

where—

RVF is the relevant valuation factor (see section 276),

PE is the annual rate of the pension which would, on the valuation assumptions (see section 277), be payable to the individual under the recognised overseas scheme arrangement if the individual became entitled to payment of it at the end of that part of that period,

LSE is the amount of the lump sum to which the individual would, on the valuation assumptions, be entitled under the arrangement (otherwise than by commutation of pension) if the individual became entitled to payment of it at the end of that part of that period,

PB is the annual rate of the pension which would, on the valuation assumptions, be payable to the individual under the arrangement if the individual became entitled to payment of it at the beginning of that part of that period, and

LSB is the amount of the lump sum to which the individual would, on the valuation assumptions, be entitled under the arrangement (otherwise than by commutation of pension) if the individual became entitled to payment of it at the beginning of that part of that period.

(5) The hybrid relevant relievable amount is the greater or greatest of such of—

(a) what would be the cash balance relevant relievable amount (under section 225) if the recognised overseas scheme arrangement had been a cash balance arrangement,

(b) what would be the other money purchase relevant relievable amount (under that section) if that arrangement had been any other sort of money purchase arrangement, and

(c) what would be the defined benefits relevant relievable amount (under subsections (3) and (4)) if that arrangement had been a defined benefits arrangement,

as are relevant to that arrangement.

(6) An amount is relevant to a hybrid arrangement if, in any circumstances, the benefits that may be provided to or in respect of the individual under the arrangement may be benefits linked to that amount.

(7) For that purpose—

(a) cash balance benefits are linked to the cash balance relevant relievable amount,

(b) other money purchase benefits are linked to the other money purchase relevant relievable amount, and

(c) defined benefits are linked to the defined benefits relevant relievable amount.

Commentary—*Simon's Taxes* E7.218.

HMRC Manuals—Pensions Tax Manual PTM095440 (the relevant relievable amount for a defined benefits arrangement). PTM095450 (the relevant relievable amount for a hybrid arrangement).

Annual allowance charge

227 Annual allowance charge

(1) A charge to income tax, to be known as the annual allowance charge, arises [where an individual who is a member of one or more registered pension schemes has a [non-zero][6] chargeable amount for a tax year.][4]

[(1A) The chargeable amount . . . [6] is to be determined in accordance with section 227ZA.][4]

(2) . . . [3]

(3) . . . [3]

(4) The annual allowance charge is a charge at the [appropriate rate][3] in respect of [the chargeable amount.][4]

[But see section 227A (individuals who meet flexible drawdown conditions).][2, 5]

[(4A) The appropriate rate is—

(a) the basic rate . . . [7] in relation to so much (if any) of the [chargeable amount][4] as, when added to the individual's reduced net income for the tax year, does not exceed the basic rate limit for the tax year,

(b) the higher rate . . . [7] in relation to so much (if any) of the [chargeable amount][4] as, when so added, exceeds the basic rate limit for the tax year but does not exceed the higher rate limit for the tax year, and

(c) the additional . . . [7] rate in relation to so much (if any) of the excess as, when so added, exceeds the higher rate limit for the tax year.

[But subsection (4AA) applies in the case of a Scottish taxpayer [and subsection (4AB) applies in the case of a Welsh taxpayer][8].][7]

[(4AA) The appropriate rate for a Scottish taxpayer is—

(a) where the only Scottish rate is the Scottish basic rate (the "SBR"), that rate, or

(b) where there is more than one Scottish rate—

    (i) the SBR in relation to so much (if any) of the chargeable amount as, when added to the individual's reduced net income for the tax year, does not exceed the Scottish basic rate limit ("SBRL") for the tax year,

    (ii) the next highest rate after the SBR in relation to so much (if any) of the chargeable amount as, when so added, exceeds the SBRL for the tax year but does not exceed the rate limit for that rate for the tax year, and

    (iii) where applicable, any other higher Scottish rate in relation to so much (if any) of the chargeable amount as, when so added, does not exceed the rate limit for that rate for the tax year.][7]

[(4AB) The appropriate rate for a Welsh taxpayer is—

    (*a*) the Welsh basic rate in relation to so much (if any) of the chargeable amount as, when added to the individual's reduced net income for the tax year, does not exceed the basic rate limit for the tax year,

    (*b*) the Welsh higher rate in relation to so much (if any) of the chargeable amount as, when so added, exceeds the basic rate limit for the tax year but does not exceed the higher rate limit for the tax year, and

    (*c*) the Welsh additional rate in relation to so much (if any) of the chargeable amount as, when so added, exceeds the higher rate limit for the tax year.][8]

(4B) The individual's reduced net income for the tax year is the amount after taking Step 3 in section 23 of ITA 2007 in the case of the individual for the tax year.

[(4C) Where—

    (*a*) the basic rate limit,

    (*b*) the higher rate limit,

    (*c*) the Scottish basic rate limit, or

    (*d*) any other Scottish rate limit,

is (in accordance with section 192 of this Act or section 414 of ITA 2007) increased in the case of the individual, the references to the limit in subsections (4A)[, (4AA) and (4AB)][8] are to the limit as so increased.][7][3]

(5) [The chargeable amount][4] is not to be treated as income for any purpose of the Tax Acts.

(5A) [1] . . . [3]

(5B) [1] . . . [3]

(6) The following sections make further provision about the annual allowance charge—

    [sections 227ZA and 227B (chargeable amount),

    sections 227C to 227G (supplemental provision for calculations under section 227B),][4]

    section 228 (annual allowance),

    section [229(1)][4] (total pension input amount to be aggregate of pension input amounts for pension input periods ending in tax year),

    [section 229(2) to (4) (how to arrive at the pension input amount in respect of an arrangement),][4]

    sections 230 to 237 (pension input amounts),

    [sections 237A to 237F (persons liable to charge),][3] and

    section 238 (pension input period).

(7) Schedule 36 contains (in Part 4) transitional provision about the annual allowance charge.

Commentary—*Simon's Taxes* **E7.215, E8.1114**.

HMRC Manuals—Pensions Tax Manual PTM113310 (non UK schemes: the annual allowance charge and non-UK schemes: the annual allowance charge and non-UK schemes: essential principles - tax liability).
PTM056300 (when an annual allowance charge is due).

Modifications—Pensions Schemes (Application of UK Provisions to Relevant Non-UK Schemes) Regulations, SI 2006/207 reg 8 (modification of this section in respect of relevant non-UK schemes).

Registered Pension Schemes (Splitting of Schemes) Regulations, SI 2006/569 reg 3 (modification of this provision in relation to sub-scheme administrators).

Amendments—[1]   Sub-ss (5A), (5B) inserted by FA 2009 s 6, Sch 2 paras 10, 15 with effect for the tax year 2010–11 and subsequent tax years. The powers conferred by the amendments made by FA 2009 Sch 2 may be exercised at any time on or after 21 July 2009 but not so as to make provision having effect before the tax year 2010–11 (FA 2009 Sch 2 para 25(1)).

[2]   Words in sub-s (4) inserted by FA 2011 s 65, Sch 16 para 45(1) with effect for the tax year 2011–12 and subsequent tax years, subject to transitional provisions in FA 2011 Sch 16 Pt 3.

[3]   Sub-ss (2), (3), (5A), (5B) repealed, words in sub-s (4) substituted for words "rate of 40%", sub-ss (4A)–(4C) inserted, and words in sub-s (6) inserted, by FA 2011 s 66, Sch 17 paras 1, 3 with effect for the tax year 2011–12 and subsequent tax years, and in relation to pension input periods ending in the tax year 2011–12 but beginning earlier (or in 2011–12). For transitional provisions see FA 2011 Sch 17 paras 28–34.

[4]   In sub-ss (1), (4), (4A), sub-s (5), words substituted, and in sub-s (6) words inserted and in the entry for section 229, reference substituted, by the Taxation of Pensions Act 2014 s 1, Sch 1 para 63 with effect for the tax year 2015–16 and subsequent tax years.

[5]   In sub-s (4), second sentence repealed by the Taxation of Pensions Act 2014 s 1, Sch 1 para 66(2)(*a*) with effect for the tax year 2015–16 and subsequent tax years.

[6]   In sub-s (1), words inserted, and in sub-s (1A), words "(if any)" repealed, by F(No 2)A 2015 s 23, Sch 4 para 11(1), (2) with effect for the tax year 2015–16 and subsequent tax years.

[7]   In sub-s (4A)(a)–(c), words repealed, and words at the end of sub-s (4A) inserted, sub-s (4AA) inserted, and sub-s (4C) substituted, by the Scotland Act 2016 (Income Tax Consequential Amendments) Regulations, SI 2017/468 regs 2, 4 with effect in relation to 2017–18 (the tax year appointed under the Scotland Act 2016 section 13(15)(b)) and subsequent tax years.

[8]   In sub-s (4A) words inserted, sub-s (4AB) inserted, and in sub-s (4C) words substituted for words "and (4AA)", by the Devolved Income Tax Rates (Consequential Amendments) Order, SI 2019/201 arts 3, 7 with effect in relation to the tax year commencing on 6 April 2019 and subsequent tax years.

[227ZA The chargeable amount

(1) The chargeable amount is the alternative chargeable amount (see section 227B) if—
    (a) the year is—
        (i) the tax year in which the individual first flexibly accesses pension rights (see section 227G), or
        (ii) a tax year later than that tax year,
    (b) the money-purchase input sub-total (see section 227C) exceeds [£4,000][3], and
    (c) the alternative chargeable amount exceeds the default chargeable amount.
(2) Otherwise, the chargeable amount is the default chargeable amount.
(3) The default chargeable amount is the amount (if any) by which—
    (a) the total pension input amount calculated in accordance with section 229(1), exceeds
    (b) the annual allowance for the year in the case of the individual (see sections 228(1) and 228A).][1]
[(4) If there is no such excess, the default chargeable amount is zero.][2]

Commentary—*Simon's Taxes* **E7.213**.
Amendments—[1]   Section 227ZA inserted by the Taxation of Pensions Act 2014 s 1, Sch 1 para 64 with effect for the tax year 2015–16 and subsequent tax years.
[2]   Sub-s (4) inserted by F(No 2)A 2015 s 23, Sch 4 para 11(1), (3) with effect for the tax year 2015–16 and subsequent tax years.
[3]   In sub-s (1)(b), figure substituted by F(No 2)A 2017 s 7(1), (2) with effect for the tax year 2017–18 and subsequent tax years. Previous figure was £10,000.

[227B The alternative chargeable amount

(1) The alternative chargeable amount is the total of—
    (a) the amount (if any) by which the defined-benefit input sub-total exceeds the alternative annual allowance, and
    (b) the amount by which the money-purchase input sub-total exceeds [£4,000][3].
(2) The alternative annual allowance is—
$$AA-[£4,000]^3$$
where AA is the annual allowance for the year in the case of the individual (see sections 228(1) and 228A).
(3) The defined-benefit input sub-total is the total of—
    (a) the pension input amounts in respect of each defined benefits arrangement relating to the individual under a registered pension scheme of which the individual is a member (see section 229(2)(c)),
    (b) the pension input amounts in respect of each hybrid arrangement—
        (i) relating to the individual under a registered pension scheme of which the individual is a member, and
        (ii) in respect of which the pension input amount is input amount C mentioned in section 237, and
    (c) any amounts required to be included by section . . . [2] 227F(4) or (6) (pension input periods that end in the year [and contain][2] the day on which rights are first flexibly accessed . . . [2]).
(4) Subsection (3)(b) is subject to section 227D (pension input amounts for certain hybrid arrangements).
(5) If, in the case of a hybrid arrangement, input amount C mentioned in section 237—
    (a) is a relevant input amount for the purposes of section 237, and
    (b) is equal to—
        (i) input amount A or B mentioned in section 237 if that is the only other relevant input amount for the purposes of section 237, or
        (ii) the greater of input amounts A and B mentioned in section 237 if both are relevant input amounts for the purposes of section 237,
the pension input amount in respect of the arrangement is, for the purposes of subsection (3)(b) and sections 227C(1)(b) and 227D(1)(c), treated as being input amount A or B or, as the case may be, the greater of input amounts A and B (and, in either case, not input amount C).][1]

Commentary—*Simon's Taxes* **E7.213**.
HMRC Manuals—Pensions Tax Manual PTM056560 (annual allowance: hybrid arrangements: any hybrid arrangements).
Amendments—[1]   Sections 227B–227G inserted by the Taxation of Pensions Act 2014 s 1, Sch 1 para 65 with effect for the tax year 2015–16 and subsequent tax years.
[2]   In sub-s (3)(c), words "227E(3) or" and "or that end in the year and contain that day" repealed, and words substituted for words "but before", by F(No 2)A 2015 s 23, Sch 4 paras 1, 4(2)(a) with effect for the post-alignment tax year and subsequent tax years. The "post-alignment tax year" is one beginning with 9 July 2015 and ending with 5 April 2016: see FA 2004 s 228C(2)(b).

[3] In sub-ss (1)(*b*), (2), figure substituted by F(No 2)A 2017 s 7(1), (3) with effect for the tax year 2017–18 and subsequent tax years. Previous figure was £10,000.

[227C Meaning of "money-purchase input sub-total"

(1) The money-purchase input sub-total is the total of—

    (*a*) the pension input amounts in respect of each money purchase arrangement relating to the individual under a registered pension scheme of which the individual is a member (see section 229(2)(*a*) and (*b*)), and

    (*b*) the pension input amounts in respect of each hybrid arrangement—

        (i) relating to the individual under a registered pension scheme of which the individual is a member, and

        (ii) in respect of which the pension input amount is input amount A or B mentioned in section 237.

(2) Subsection (1) is to be read with—

    (*a*)   . . .[2]

    (*b*) section 227F(2), (3) and (5) (pension input periods that end in the tax year and contain [the day on which rights are first flexibly accessed][2]).

(3) Subsection (1)(*b*) is to be read with—

    (*a*) section 227B(5) (hybrid arrangements where input amount C is highest-equal input amount), and

    (*b*) section 227D (pension input amounts for certain hybrid arrangements).][1]

Commentary—*Simon's Taxes* E7.213.

Amendments—[1]   Sections 227B–227G inserted by the Taxation of Pensions Act 2014 s 1, Sch 1 para 65 with effect for the tax year 2015–16 and subsequent tax years.

[2]   Sub-s 2(*a*) and following word "and" repealed, and in sub-s (2)(*b*), words substituted for words "that day", by F(No 2)A 2015 s 23, Sch 4 paras 1, 4(2)(*b*), (*c*) with effect for the post-alignment tax year and subsequent tax years. The "post-alignment tax year" is one beginning with 9 July 2015 and ending with 5 April 2016: see FA 2004 s 228C(2)(*b*).

[227D Pension input amounts in respect of certain hybrid arrangements

(1) In this section "relevant hybrid arrangement" means a hybrid arrangement—

    (*a*) relating to the individual under a registered pension scheme of which the individual is a member,

    (*b*) made on or after 14 October 2014 or having become a hybrid arrangement (whether or not for the first time) on or after that day, and

    (*c*) in respect of which the pension input amount is input amount C mentioned in section 237.

(2) As respects each relevant hybrid arrangement in the maximising set of relevant hybrid arrangements—

    (*a*) the pension input amount in respect of the arrangement is for the purposes of sections 227B(3)(*b*) and 227C(1)(*b*) treated as being not input amount C mentioned in section 237 but, instead, the greater of such of input amounts A and B mentioned in section 237 as are, for the purposes of section 237, relevant input amounts in the case of the arrangement, and

    (*b*) accordingly, the arrangement—

        (i) is not to be included among the arrangements mentioned in section 227B(3)(*b*) whose pension input amounts are totalled under section 227B(3), but

        (ii) is to be included among the arrangements mentioned in section 227C(1)(*b*) whose pension input amounts are totalled under section 227C(1).

(3) For the purposes of subsection (2)—

    (*a*) the maximising set contains no relevant hybrid arrangements,

    (*b*) a particular relevant hybrid arrangement makes up that set, or

    (*c*) two or more particular relevant hybrid arrangements make up that set,

if the alternative chargeable amount with the maximising set so made up is not less than it would be with the maximising set made up in any other way.

(4) In particular, the maximising set may be identified by taking the following steps—

    Step 1

        Identify all of the relevant hybrid arrangements.

    Step 2

        Identify all of the different combinations of the arrangements identified at Step 1 (including the combination consisting of all of those arrangements, and the combination consisting of none of them, as well as every possible combination of each possible size in between).

    Step 3

        For each combination identified at Step 2 calculate what the money-purchase input sub-total would be if each relevant hybrid arrangement in the combination were treated in accordance with the rules in paragraphs (*a*) and (*b*) of subsection (2).

    Step 4

If the result of each calculation at Step 3 is less than or equal to [£4,000][3] the chargeable amount is the default chargeable amount.

Step 5

If the amount calculated at Step 3 for a combination is greater than [£4,000][3] then calculate in accordance with section 227B what the alternative chargeable amount would be if—

(a) each relevant hybrid arrangement in the combination were treated in accordance with the rules in paragraphs (a) and (b) of subsection (2), and

(b) for each relevant hybrid arrangement not in the combination, input amount C mentioned in section 237 were included in the total under section 227B(3).

Step 6

Identify the highest (or higher) of the amounts calculated at Step 5. The maximising set is made up of each relevant hybrid arrangement in the combination concerned.

(5) Subsection (1)(c) is to be read with section 227B(5) (hybrid arrangements where input amount C is highest-equal input amount).

(6) . . . [2]][1]

Commentary—*Simon's Taxes* E7.213.

HMRC Manuals—Pensions Tax Manual PTM056570 (annual allowance: hybrid arrangements: relevant hybrid arrangements). PTM056580 (annual allowance: hybrid arrangements: relevant hybrid arrangements: example: one relevant hybrid arrangement). PTM056590 (annual allowance: hybrid arrangements: relevant hybrid arrangement: example: multiple relevant hybrid arrangements).

Amendments—[1] Sections 227B–227G inserted by the Taxation of Pensions Act 2014 s 1, Sch 1 para 65 with effect for the tax year 2015–16 and subsequent tax years.

[2] Sub-s (6) repealed by F(No 2)A 2015 s 23, Sch 4 paras 1, 4(2)(d) with effect for the post-alignment tax year and subsequent tax years. The "post-alignment tax year" is one beginning with 9 July 2015 and ending with 5 April 2016: see FA 2004 s 228C(2)(b).

[3] In sub-s (4), Steps 4 and 5, figure substituted by F(No 2)A 2017 s 7(1), (4) with effect for the tax year 2017–18 and subsequent tax years. Previous figure was £10,000.

[227F Pension input periods in which rights are first flexibly accessed

(1) Subject to subsection (7), subsections (2) to (6) apply if, for an arrangement mentioned in section 227C(1), the pension input period ending in the tax year contains the day on which the individual first flexibly accesses pension rights (whether or not that day is in the tax year).

(2) If the arrangement is a cash balance arrangement, the pension input amount in respect of that arrangement is for the purposes of section 227C(1)(a) treated as being—

$$\frac{F}{PIP} \times APIA$$

where—

APIA is the (actual) pension input amount in respect of the arrangement (see section 229(2)(a)),

F is the number of days in the period—

(a) beginning with the day after that on which the individual first flexibly accesses pension rights, and

(b) ending at the end of the pension input period mentioned in subsection (1), and

PIP is the number of days in that pension input period.

(3) If the arrangement is a money purchase arrangement other than a cash balance arrangement, the pension input amount in respect of that arrangement is for the purposes of section 227C(1)(a) treated as being the amount in respect of the arrangement that would be arrived at under section 233 for a pension input period—

(a) beginning with the day after that on which the individual first flexibly accesses pension rights, and

(b) ending at the end of the pension input period mentioned in subsection (1).

(4) If the arrangement is a money purchase arrangement, the amount (if any) by which—

(a) the (actual) pension input amount in respect of the arrangement (see section 229(2)(a) or (b)), exceeds

(b) the amount treated by subsection (2) or (3) as being the pension input amount in respect of the arrangement,

is required to be included in the defined-benefit input sub-total calculated under section 227B(3).

(5) If the arrangement is a hybrid arrangement—

(a) input amount A mentioned in section 237 is for the purposes of sections 227C(1)(b) and 227D(2) treated as being—

$$\frac{F}{PIP} \times AAIAA$$

where—

> AAIAA is the (actual) amount of input amount A for the arrangement,
>
> F is the number of days in the period—
>> (a) beginning with the day after that on which the individual first flexibly accesses pension rights, and
>> (b) ending at the end of the pension input period mentioned in subsection (1), and
>
> PIP is the number of days in that pension input period, and

(b) input amount B mentioned in section 237 is for the purposes of sections 227C(1)(b) and 227D(2) treated as being the amount for the arrangement that would be arrived at under section 233 for a pension input period—
  (i) beginning on the day after that on which the individual first flexibly accesses pension rights, and
  (ii) ending at the end of the pension input period mentioned in subsection (1).

(6) If the arrangement is a hybrid arrangement, the amount (if any) by which—
  (a) the (actual) pension input amount in respect of the arrangement (see section 229(2)(d)), exceeds
  (b) the amount which, in accordance with subsection (5) and section 227D, is for the purposes of section 227C(1)(b) the pension input amount in respect of the arrangement,

is required to be included in the defined-benefit input sub-total calculated under section 227B(3).

(7) Subsections (2) to (6) do not apply if section 165(3A) applied in the individual's case to the arrangement, or any other arrangement, at any time before 6 April 2015.][1]

Commentary—*Simon's Taxes* **E7.213**.
Amendments—[1] Sections 227B–227G inserted by the Taxation of Pensions Act 2014 s 1, Sch 1 para 65 with effect for the tax year 2015–16 and subsequent tax years.

[227G When pension rights are first flexibly accessed

(1) References in sections 227B to 227F to when the individual first flexibly accesses pension rights are to the time, or the earlier or earliest of the times, given for that by the following subsections.

(2) If—
  (a) the individual has a member's flexi-access drawdown fund in respect of an arrangement, and
  (b) the fund came into being—
    (i) as a result of sums or assets being designated on or after 6 April 2015 as available for the payment of drawdown pension, or
    (ii) as a result of the operation of paragraph 8D(2) of Schedule 28,

the individual first flexibly accesses pension rights immediately before the first qualifying payment is made from the fund (see subsection (10)).

(3) If section 165(3A) applied in the individual's case to an arrangement at any time before 6 April 2015, the individual first flexibly accesses pension rights at the start of 6 April 2015.

(4) If—
  (a) the individual has a member's drawdown pension fund in respect of an arrangement, and
  (b) the sums and assets that make up the fund become newly-designated funds by the operation of paragraph 8B of Schedule 28,

the individual first flexibly accesses pension rights immediately before the first qualifying payment (see subsection (10)) is made from the individual's member's flexi-access drawdown fund in respect of the arrangement (whether that is the payment that triggers the operation of paragraph 8B of Schedule 28 or a subsequent payment).

(5) If—
  (a) the individual has a member's drawdown pension fund in respect of an arrangement, and
  (b) the sums and assets that make up the fund become newly-designated funds by the operation of paragraph 8C of Schedule 28,

the individual first flexibly accesses pension rights immediately before the first qualifying payment is made from the individual's member's flexi-access drawdown fund in respect of the arrangement (see subsection (10)).

(6) The individual first flexibly accesses pension rights immediately before the payment of the first uncrystallised funds pension lump sum paid to the individual.

(7) If the individual is entitled to payment of a lifetime annuity under a flexible annuity contract (see subsection (8)), the individual first flexibly accesses pension rights immediately before the first payment of the annuity is made.

(8) In subsection (7) "flexible annuity contract" means a contract for a lifetime annuity where—
  (a) the annuity is within paragraph 3(1A) of Schedule 28, and
  (b) the terms of the contract are such that there will or could be decreases in the amount of the annuity other than decreases from time to time allowed by regulations under paragraph 3(1)(d) of Schedule 28 (and any such regulations are to be treated as having effect for this purpose).

(9) If—

(a) the individual is entitled to payment of a scheme pension under a money purchase arrangement under a registered pension scheme,

(b) the individual became entitled to the scheme pension—

(i) on or after 6 April 2015, and

(ii) at a time when fewer than 11 other individuals were entitled to the present payment of a scheme pension, or dependants' scheme pension, under the registered pension scheme, and

(c) the scheme pension is not payable under an annuity contract treated under section 153(8) or (8A) as having become a registered pension scheme,

the individual first flexibly accesses pension rights immediately before the first payment of the scheme pension is made.

(10) In subsections (2), (4) and (5), a reference to a qualifying payment from a fund is a reference to—

(a) payment of income withdrawal from the fund, or

(b) payment of a short-term annuity purchased using sums or assets out of the fund,

but does not include payment at a time when the whole of the fund represents rights attributable to a disqualifying pension credit.

(11) In subsection (10) "disqualifying pension credit" is to be read in accordance with paragraph 2(3) and (4) of Schedule 29.]¹

Commentary—*Simon's Taxes* E7.238, E7.213.

HMRC Manuals—Pensions Tax Manual PTM056520 (annual allowance: trigger events).

Amendments—¹ Sections 227B–227G inserted by the Taxation of Pensions Act 2014 s 1, Sch 1 para 65 with effect for the tax year 2015–16 and subsequent tax years.

[228 Annual allowance

[(1) The annual allowance for the tax year 2014–15 and, subject to subsection (2), each subsequent tax year is £40,000.]²

(2) The Treasury may by order provide that the annual allowance for any tax year subsequent to the tax year [2014–15]² is such amount as is specified in the order.]¹

Commentary—*Simon's Taxes* E7.211–E7.215.

HMRC Manuals—Pensions Tax Manual PTM051100 (essential principles).

Amendments—¹ This section substituted by FA 2011 s 66, Sch 17 paras 1, 4 with effect for the tax year 2011–12 and subsequent tax years, and in relation to pension input periods ending in the tax year 2011–12 but beginning earlier (or in 2011–12). For transitional provisions see FA 2011 Sch 17 paras 28–34.

² Sub-s (1) substituted, and in sub-s (2), tax year substituted, by FA 2013 s 49 with effect for the tax year 2014–15 and subsequent tax years.

[228ZA Tapered reduction of annual allowance: high-income individual

[(1) If the individual is a high-income individual for the tax year, the amount of the annual allowance for the tax year in the case of the individual is the amount specified for the tax year by or under section 228 reduced (but not below £4,000) by—

(AI – £240,000) x 1/2

where AI is the individual's adjusted income for the tax year.]²

(2) If the amount of the reduction under subsection (1) would otherwise not be a multiple of £1, it is to be rounded down to the nearest amount which is a multiple of £1.

(3) The individual is a "high-income individual" for the tax year if—

(a) the individual's adjusted income for the tax year is more than [£240,000]², and

(b) the individual's threshold income for the tax year is more than the amount given by [£240,000 minus the amount specified for the tax year by or under section 228]².

(4) The individual's "adjusted income" for the tax year is—

(a) the individual's net income for the year (see Step 2 of the calculation in section 23 of ITA 2007), plus

(b) the amount of any relief under section 193(4) or 194(1) deducted at that Step, plus

(c) the amount of any deductions made from employment income of the individual for the year—

(i) under section 193(2), or

(ii) under Chapter 2 of Part 5 of ITEPA 2003 in accordance with paragraph 51(2) of Schedule 36, plus

(d) an amount equal to—

(i) the total pension input amount calculated in accordance with section 229(1), less

(ii) the amount of any contributions paid by or on behalf of the individual during the year under registered pension schemes of which the individual is a member, less

(e) the amount of any lump sum which accrues in the year and in relation to which section 579A of ITEPA 2003 is applied by section 636A(4ZA) of ITEPA 2003.

(5) The individual's "threshold income" for the tax year is—

(a) the individual's net income for the year (see Step 2 of the calculation in section 23 of ITA 2007), plus

(b) any amount by which what would otherwise be general earnings or specific employment income of the individual for the year has been reduced by relevant salary sacrifice arrangements or relevant flexible remuneration arrangements, less

(c) the amount (before any deduction under section 192(1)) of any contribution paid in the year in respect of which the individual is entitled to be given relief under section 192 (relief at source), less

(d) the amount of any lump sum which accrues in the year and in relation to which section 579A of ITEPA 2003 is applied by section 636A(4ZA) of ITEPA 2003.

(6) In subsection (5)—

"relevant salary sacrifice arrangements" means arrangements—

   (a) under which the individual gives up the right to receive general earnings or specific employment income in return for the making of relevant pension provision, and

   (b) which are made on or after 9 July 2015 (and whether before or after the start of the employment concerned), and

"relevant flexible remuneration arrangements" means arrangements—

   (a) under which the individual and an employer of the individual agree that relevant pension provision is to be made rather than the individual receive some description of employment income, and

     (b) which are made on or after 9 July 2015 (and whether before or after the start of the employment concerned).

(7) In subsection (6) "relevant pension provision" means the payment of contributions (or additional contributions) to a pension scheme in respect of the individual or otherwise (by an employer of the individual or any other person) to secure an increase in the amount of the benefits to which the individual or any person who is a dependant of, or is connected with, the individual is actually or prospectively entitled under a pension scheme.

(8) In subsection (7) "increase" includes increase from nil.

(9) Section 993 of ITA 2007 (meaning of "connected" persons) applies for the purposes of subsection (7).][1]

Commentary—*Simon's Taxes* **E7.213**.

HMRC Manuals—Pensions Tax Manual PTM057100 (annual allowance).

Amendments—[1] Sections 228ZA, 228ZB inserted by F(No 2)A 2015 s 23, Sch 4 para 10 with effect for the tax year 2016–17 and subsequent tax years.

[2] Sub-s (1) substituted, figure in sub-s (3)(a) substituted for figure "£150,000", and words in sub-s (3)(b) substituted for words "£150,000 minus A", by FA 2020 s 22 with effect for the tax year 2020–21 and subsequent tax years.

[228ZB Anti-avoidance in connection with section 228ZA

(1) Subsection (5) applies if there are arrangements in respect of which conditions A to C are met.

(2) Condition A is that it is reasonable to assume that the main purpose, or one of the main purposes, of the arrangements is to reduce the amount of the reduction under section 228ZA(1) in the individual's case—

   (a) for the tax year, or

   (b) for two or more tax years which include the tax year.

(3) Condition B is that the arrangements involve either or both of the following—

   (a) reducing the individual's adjusted income for the tax year, and

   (b) reducing the individual's threshold income for the tax year.

(4) Condition C is that the arrangements involve the reduction within subsection (3), or any of the reductions within subsection (3), being redressed by an increase in the individual's adjusted income, or threshold income, for a different tax year.

(5) The reduction under section 228ZA(1) in the individual's case for the tax year is to be treated as being what it would be apart from the arrangements.

(6) In subsection (2) "reduce" includes reduce to nil.

(7) The increase mentioned in subsection (4) may be an increase in what would be the individual's adjusted income, or threshold income, for the tax year 2015–16 if section 228ZA—

   (a) had effect for that year, and

   (b) did so as if the total pension input amount mentioned in section 228ZA(4)(d)(i) were the sum of the total pension input amounts for the pre-alignment and post-alignment tax years (see section 228C(2)).

(8) In this section "arrangements" includes any agreement, understanding, scheme, transaction or series of transactions (whether or not legally enforceable).][1]

Commentary—*Simon's Taxes* **E7.213**.

HMRC Manuals—Pensions Tax Manual PTM057100 (annual allowance - anti-avoidance rule for tapered annual allowance).

Amendments—[1] Sections 228ZA, 228ZB inserted by F(No 2)A 2015 s 23, Sch 4 para 10 with effect for the tax year 2016–17 and subsequent tax years.

[228A Carry forward of unused annual allowance

(1) This section applies if the individual has unused annual allowance available for the tax year ("the current tax year").

(2) The annual allowance for the current tax year in the case of the individual is to be treated as increased by the amount of the unused annual allowance available for the current tax year.

(3) The individual has unused annual allowance available for the current tax year if—

  (a) the amount of the annual allowance (before any increase under this section) for the immediately preceding tax year exceeded the total pension input amount in the case of the individual for that tax year, or

  (b) the amount of the annual allowance (before any such increase) for either or both of the two tax years immediately preceding that immediately preceding tax year exceeded the total pension input amount in the case of the individual for the tax year concerned and the excess (or, where there is an excess for both of those tax years, the excess for both tax years) has not been used up,

or both.

(4) Subsection (3)—

  (a) does not apply in relation to a tax year preceding the current tax year unless the individual was a member of a registered pension scheme at some time during that tax year, but

  (b) subject to that, applies in relation to such a tax year even if the total pension input amount in the case of the individual for that tax year was nil (in which case the excess within paragraph (a) or (b) of that subsection is the whole amount of the annual allowance before any increase under this section).

(5) The amount of the unused annual allowance available for the current tax year is the aggregate of—

  (a) any excess within subsection (3)(a), and

  (b) so much of any excess within subsection (3)(b) as has not been used up.

(6) An amount of an excess within subsection (3)(b) for a tax year has been "used up" if—

  (a) for a tax year falling between that tax year and the current tax year (an "intervening tax year"), the total pension input amount in the case of the individual exceeded the annual allowance (apart from any increase under this section), and

  (b) the amount of the excess had effect by virtue of this section to reduce (or eliminate) the annual allowance charge for the intervening tax year in the case of the individual.

(7) In calculating for the purposes of subsection (6) the amount of which of the excesses for different tax years had effect to reduce or eliminate the annual allowance charge for an intervening tax year, an amount of the excess for an earlier tax year is to be taken to have done so before that for a later tax year.

[(8) If, for a tax year preceding the current tax year, the chargeable amount in the individual's case was the alternative chargeable amount—

  (a) a reference in subsection (3)(a) or (b), (4)(b) or (6)(a) to the annual allowance for that preceding tax year is a reference to the alternative annual allowance for that preceding tax year (see section 227B(2)), and

  (b) a reference in subsection (3)(a) or (b), (4)(b) or (6)(a) to the total pension input amount in the case of the individual for that preceding tax year is a reference to the defined-benefit input sub-total in the case of the individual for that preceding tax year (see section 227B(3) to (5)).

(9) Subsection (3) does not apply in relation to a tax year—

  (a) preceding the current tax year, and

  (b) ending not later than 5 April 2015,

if, at any time in that preceding tax year, section 165(3A) or 167(2A) applied to an arrangement relating to the individual.]²]¹

Commentary—*Simon's Taxes* E7.213, E1.1409.

HMRC Manuals—Pensions Tax Manual PTM051100 (essential principles).

Amendments—¹ This section inserted by FA 2011 s 66, Sch 17 paras 1, 5 with effect for the tax year 2011–12 and subsequent tax years, and in relation to pension input periods ending in the tax year 2011–12 but beginning earlier (or in 2011–12). For transitional provisions see FA 2011 Sch 17 paras 28–34.

² Subsections (8), (9) inserted by the Taxation of Pensions Act 2014 s 1, Sch 1 para 67 with effect where the current tax year is the tax year 2015–16 or a subsequent tax year.

[228B Carry forward: certain periods treated as pension input periods

(1) This section applies where the first pension input period for a relevant arrangement relating to an individual ends in the tax year 2011–12, 2012–13 or 2013–14.

(2) A period is a "carry forward period" for the purposes of this section if it—

  (a) is one of the 3 consecutive periods of 12 months immediately before the commencement date of the first pension input period, and

  (b) is a period in which the arrangement was in existence at any time.

(3) Any amount that would, if a carry forward period were a pension input period of the arrangement, have been unused annual allowance available to the individual for the tax year 2011–12, 2012–13 or 2013–14 is to be treated as unused annual allowance available to the individual for that tax year.

(4) In this section "relevant arrangement" means—

(*a*) a cash balance arrangement,

(*b*) a defined benefits arrangement, or

(*c*) a hybrid arrangement the only benefits under which may be cash balance benefits or defined benefits.][1]

Commentary—*Simon's Taxes* **E7.214**.

HMRC Manuals—Pensions Tax Manual PTM055200 (calculating unused annual allowance).

Amendments—[1]   This section inserted by the Finance Act 2004 (Registered Pension Schemes and Annual Allowance Charge) (Amendment) Order, SI 2015/80 arts 10, 11 with effect from 28 January 2015.

[228C   Annual allowance for, and carry-forward from, 2015–16

(1) The provisions relating to the annual allowance charge (whether provisions contained in or made under this or any other Act) have effect subject to the following rules.

2015–16 split into two tax years for annual allowance purposes

(2) For the purposes of those provisions but subject to subsection (3), the tax year 2015–16 is to be treated as consisting of two tax years as follows—

(*a*) one beginning with 6 April 2015 and ending with 8 July 2015 ("the pre-alignment tax year"), and

(*b*) one beginning with 9 July 2015 and ending with 5 April 2016 ("the post-alignment tax year").

(3) Despite subsection (2)—

(*a*) separate annual allowance charges for each of the pre-alignment and post-alignment tax years cannot arise, but a single annual allowance charge for the tax year 2015-16 arises if the individual has a chargeable amount for either or each of the pre-alignment and post-alignment tax years, and

(*b*) that single annual allowance charge is calculated as if—

  (i) in section 227(4) the reference to the chargeable amount were a reference to the sum of the chargeable amounts for the pre-alignment and post-alignment tax years, and

  (ii) in section 227(4A) to (4C) each reference to the tax year were to the tax year 2015–16.

Double allowances allocated to earlier part of 2015–16

(4) For the pre-alignment tax year—

(*a*) the amount specified in section 228(1) (annual allowance for tax year) is treated as being £80,000, and

(*b*) in each of sections 227ZA(1)(*b*) and 227B(1)(*b*) and (2), the reference to £10,000 is treated as a reference to £20,000.

Allowances for later part of 2015–16 limited to carried-forward allowances

(5) Where the individual was a member of a registered pension scheme at some time in the pre-alignment tax year then, for the post-alignment tax year—

(*a*) the amount specified in section 228(1) is treated as being nil,

(*b*) section 227B(2) (amount of alternative annual allowance) has effect as if "AA" were substituted for "AA – £10,000",

(*c*) if the chargeable amount in the individual's case for the pre-alignment tax year is the alternative chargeable amount, the reference to £10,000 in each of sections 227ZA(1)(*b*) and 227B(1)(*b*) is treated as being a reference to nil, and

(*d*) if the chargeable amount in the individual's case for the pre-alignment tax year is the default chargeable amount, the reference to £10,000 in each of sections 227ZA(1)(*b*) and 227B(1)(*b*) is treated as being a reference—

  (i) to nil where the money-purchase input sub-total in the individual's case for the pre-alignment tax year is £20,000 or more, or

  (ii) to the amount equal to £20,000 minus that sub-total where that sub-total is more than £10,000 but less than £20,000.

Limit on carry-forward of unused allowances from earlier part of 2015–16

(6) Where the current tax year for the purposes of section 228A (carry-forward of annual allowance) is the post-alignment tax year—

(*a*) if—

  (i) the chargeable amount in the individual's case for the pre-alignment tax year is the default chargeable amount, and

  (ii) the excess mentioned in section 228A(5)(*a*) would otherwise be more than £40,000,

  that excess is treated as being £40,000, and

(*b*) if—

  (i) the chargeable amount in the individual's case for the pre-alignment tax year is the alternative chargeable amount, and

  (ii) the excess mentioned in section 228A(5)(*a*) would otherwise be more than £30,000,

  that excess is treated as being £30,000.

Further provisions about carry-forward of unused allowances

(7) Where the current tax year for the purposes of section 228A is the post-alignment tax year or the tax year 2016–17, 2017–18 or 2018–19, section 228A applies in relation to that current tax year as if in section 228A(3)(*b*)—

    (*a*) for "either or both of the two" there were substituted "any one or more of the three", and

    (*b*) for "(or, where there is an excess for both of those tax years, the excess for both tax years)" there were substituted "(or, where there is an excess for two or all three of those tax years, the excess for both or all those tax years)".

(8) Where the current tax year for the purposes of section 228A is the tax year 2016–17, 2017–18 or 2018–19—

    (*a*) if—

        (i) the chargeable amount in the individual's case for the pre-alignment tax year is the default chargeable amount, and

        (ii) the excess within section 228A(3)(*b*) in the case of the pre-alignment tax year would otherwise be more than £40,000,

    that excess is treated as being £40,000 (and accordingly the amount aggregated under section 228A(5) in respect of that excess is so much of the £40,000 as has not been used up),

    (*b*) if—

        (i) the chargeable amount in the individual's case for the pre-alignment tax year is the alternative chargeable amount, and

        (ii) the excess within section 228A(3)(*b*) in the case of the pre-alignment year would otherwise be more than £30,000,

    that excess is treated as being £30,000 (and accordingly the amount aggregated under section 228A(5) in respect of that excess is so much of the £30,000 as has not been used up), and

    (*c*) in calculating for the purposes of section 228A(6) the amount of which of the excesses for different tax years had effect to reduce or eliminate the annual allowance charge for the post-alignment tax year, the amount of the excess for the pre-alignment tax year is to be taken to have done so before that for any other tax year and, subject to that, the amount of the excess for an earlier tax year is to be taken to have done so before that for a later year.

Supplementary provision

(9) For the pre-alignment tax year, section 229(3) applies as if the reference to the end of the tax year were a reference to the end of the post-alignment tax year.][1]

Commentary—*Simon's Taxes* E7.212, E7.213, E7.215 .
HMRC Manuals—Pensions Tax Manual PTM058020 (transitional rules for tax year 2015-16: amount of annual allowance).
PTM058030 (transitional rules for tax year 2015-16: amount of money purchase annual allowance).
PTM058040 (transitional rules for tax year 2015-16: pension input periods).
PTM058010 (tax year 2015-16 split into two 'mini' tax years).
Amendments—[1]   This section inserted by F(No 2)A 2015 s 23, Sch 4 para 6 with effect from 18 November 2015.

229 Total pension input amount

(1) The total pension input amount is arrived at by aggregating the pension input amounts in respect of each arrangement relating to the individual under a registered pension scheme of which the individual is a member.

(2) The pension input amount in respect of an arrangement—

    (*a*) is the amount arrived at under sections 230 to 232 if it is a cash balance arrangement,

    (*b*) is the amount arrived at under section 233 if it is any other sort of money purchase arrangement,

    (*c*) is the amount arrived at under sections 234 to [236A][1] if it is a defined benefits arrangement, and

    (*d*) is the amount arrived at under section 237 if it is a hybrid arrangement.

(3) But there is no pension input amount in respect of an arrangement if, before the end of the tax year, the individual—

    [(*a*) satisfies the severe ill-health condition, or][1]

    (*b*) has died.

[(4) For the purposes of subsection (3)(*a*) the individual satisfies the severe ill-health condition if the individual—

    (*a*) becomes entitled to all the benefits to which the individual is entitled under the arrangement in consequence of the scheme administrator having received evidence from a registered medical practitioner that the individual is suffering from ill-health which makes the individual unlikely to be able (otherwise than to an insignificant extent) to undertake gainful work (in any capacity) before reaching pensionable age,

    (*b*) becomes entitled to a serious ill-health lump sum under the arrangement, or

    (*c*) is a member of the armed forces of the Crown who becomes entitled under the arrangement to a benefit on which no liability to income tax arises by virtue of section 641(1) of ITEPA 2003.][1]

[(5) Subsection (2) is subject to section 237ZA (calculation of pension input amounts for input periods ending in 2015–16).][2]

Commentary—*Simon's Taxes* E7.212.
HMRC Manuals—Pensions Tax Manual PTM053100 (valuing for different types of arrangement).
PTM051200 (when the annual allowance charge does not apply).
Amendments—[1]　Figure in sub-s (2)(c) substituted for figure "236", sub-s (3)(a) substituted, and sub-s (4) inserted, by FA 2011
　　s 66, Sch 17 paras 1, 6 with effect for the tax year 2011–12 and subsequent tax years, and in relation to pension input periods
　　ending in the tax year 2011–12 but beginning earlier (or in 2011–12). For transitional provisions see FA 2011 Sch 17
　　paras 28–34.
[2]　Sub-s (5) inserted by F(No 2)A 2015 s 23, Sch 4 paras 7, 8 with effect from 18 November 2015.

230 Cash balance arrangements

(1) The pension input amount in respect of a cash balance arrangement is the amount of any increase in the value of the individual's rights under the arrangement during the pension input period of the arrangement that ends in the tax year.
(2) There is an increase in the value of the individual's rights under the arrangement during the pension input period if—
　(a) the opening value of the individual's rights under the arrangement, is exceeded by
　(b) the closing value of the individual's rights under the arrangement.
(3) The amount of the increase in the value of the individual's rights under the arrangement during the pension input period is the amount of that excess.
[(4) The opening value of the individual's rights under the arrangement—
　(a) where the pension input period is the first pension input period of the arrangement, is the amount which would, on the valuation assumptions (see section 277), be available for the provision of benefits to or in respect of the individual under the arrangement if the individual became entitled to the benefits immediately before that pension input period (or is nil if no such amount would be available), or
　(b) in any other case, is the amount which would, on the valuation assumptions, be available for the provision of benefits to or in respect of the individual under the arrangement if the individual became entitled to the benefits at the end of the immediately preceding pension input period.][2]
(5) The closing value of the individual's rights under the arrangement is the amount which would, on the valuation assumptions, be available for the provision of benefits to or in respect of the individual under the arrangement if the individual became entitled to the benefits at the end of the pension input period.
[(5A) If, during the pension input period, minimum payments are made under—
　(a) section 8 of the Pension Schemes Act 1993, or
　(b) section 4 of the Pension Schemes (Northern Ireland) Act 1993,
in relation to the individual in connection with the arrangement, their amount is to be subtracted from what would otherwise be the pension input amount in the case of the individual in respect of the arrangement.
[(5B) The pension input amount in respect of the cash balance arrangement is nil where subsection (5BA) or (5BB) applies and the value of the relevant rights of the individual under the arrangement does not increase during the pension input period by more than—
　(a) the relevant percentage, plus
　(b) the relevant statutory increase percentage.
(5BA) This subsection applies where the individual—
　(a) is, throughout the pension input period, a deferred member of the pension scheme that the arrangement is under,
　(b) is such a deferred member for part of the pension input period and a pensioner member for the rest of it, or
　(c) would meet the condition in paragraph (a) or (b) if the arrangement were the only arrangement under the pension scheme relating to that individual.
(5BB) This subsection applies where—
　(a) during the pension input period all the sums or assets held for the purposes of, or representing accrued rights under, the arrangement are transferred so as to become held for the purposes of, or to represent rights under—
　　(i) a registered pension scheme, or
　　(ii) a qualifying recognised overseas pension scheme,

　　in connection with the individual,
　(b) the individual is a deferred member of the pension scheme that the arrangement is under from the beginning of the pension input period until the transfer (or would be if the arrangement were the only arrangement under the pension scheme relating to that individual), and
　(c) rights do not accrue under the arrangement to or in respect of the individual during so much of the pension input period as falls after the transfer.

(5BC) In determining for the purposes of this section whether or not a member of a pension scheme is a deferred member (see particularly the definition of "active member" in section 151(2)), arrangements made under the pension scheme for benefits to accrue, as a consequence of (and immediately after) a relevant inward transfer (as defined in section 232(6)) to or in respect of that member, are to be disregarded—

- (*a*) if condition B in section 232(6A) is met in relation to the accrual of benefits under the arrangements, or
- (*b*) so far as the accrual of benefits under the arrangements is to be an increase in the rights of the individual which falls to be subtracted by virtue of section 232(6A)(b).][2]

(5C) In this section—

"guaranteed minimum pension" has the meaning given by—

- (*a*) section 8(2) of the Pension Schemes Act 1993, or
- (*b*) section 4(2) of the Pension Schemes (Northern Ireland) Act 1993;

"predecessor arrangement", in relation to an arrangement, means another arrangement (under the same or another registered pension scheme) from which some or all of the sums or assets held for the purposes of the arrangement directly or indirectly derive;

"predecessor registered pension scheme", in relation to a pension scheme, means another registered pension scheme from which some or all of the sums or assets held for the purposes of the arrangement under the pension scheme directly or indirectly derive;

["the relevant percentage"means—

- (*a*) where throughout the pension input period the arrangement (or a predecessor arrangement) includes provision for the value of the relevant rights of the individual to increase at an annual rate which is an RPI-related rate specified in the rules of the pension scheme (or a predecessor registered pension scheme) on 6th April 2012, that rate,
- (*b*) where throughout the pension input period the arrangement (or a predecessor arrangement) includes provision for the value of the relevant rights of the individual to increase at an annual rate, other than an RPI-related rate, specified in the rules of the pension scheme (or a predecessor registered pension scheme) on 14th October 2010, that rate, and
- (*c*) in a case not falling within paragraph (a) or (b), the percentage by which the consumer prices index for a month falling within the pension input period and nominated by the scheme administrator is higher than it was for the same month in the previous period of 12 months (or nil per cent if it is not higher);][2]

"the relevant rights of the individual" means rights of the individual under the arrangement, other than any rights to a guaranteed minimum pension;

["the relevant statutory increase percentage" in relation to a pension input period means the percentage increase in the value of the individual's rights under the arrangement during the pension input period so far as it is attributable solely to one or more of the following—

- (*a*) an increase in accordance with section 15 of the Pension Schemes Act 1993 or section 11 of the Pension Schemes (Northern Ireland) Act 1993 (increase of guaranteed minimum where commencement of guaranteed minimum pension postponed);
- (*b*) a revaluation in accordance with section 16 of the Pension Schemes Act 1993 or section 12 of the Pension Schemes (Northern Ireland) Act 1993 (early leavers: revaluation of earning factors);
- (*c*) a revaluation in accordance with Chapter 2 of Part 4 of the Pension Schemes Act 1993 or the Pension Schemes (Northern Ireland) Act 1993 (early leavers: revaluation of accrued benefits);
- (*d*) a revaluation in accordance with Chapter 3 of Part 4 of the Pension Schemes Act 1993 or the Pension Schemes (Northern Ireland) Act 1993 (early leavers: protection of increases in guaranteed minimum pensions);
- (*e*) the application of section 67 of the Equality Act 2010 (sex equality rule for occupational pension schemes);

"RPI-related rate" (in the definition of "the relevant percentage") means—

- (*a*) a rate produced solely by movement in the retail prices index, or
- (*b*) a rate which (however expressed) is the lower of such a rate and a percentage figure;][2]

"specified", in relation to an annual rate, means specified as a percentage figure or as a percentage produced by movement in an index (or a combination of the two) but does not include a percentage produced by the exercise of a discretion by any person.][1]

(6) Section 231 (uprating of opening value) and section 232 (adjustments of closing value) supplement this section.

Commentary—*Simon's Taxes* **E7.212**.

HMRC Manuals—Pensions Tax Manual PTM053400 (cash balance arrangements).

PTM051200 (when the annual allowance charge does not apply).

Modifications—Registered Pension Schemes (Restriction of Employers' Relief) Regulations, SI 2005/3458 regs 3–5 (determination of the individual's pension input amount for a period of account in respect of a cash balance arrangement: modification of this section).

Registered Pension Schemes (Restriction of Employers' Relief) Regulations, SI 2005/3458 regs 3, 4, 8 (determination of the individual's pension input amount for a period of account in respect of a hybrid arrangement: modification of this section).

Finance Act 2004 (Registered Pension Schemes and Annual Allowance Charge) (Amendment) Order, SI 2015/80 art 12(b) (modification of sub-s (5B), as substituted, in respect of times before 28 January 2015 (SI 2015/80 art 3(1))).

Amendments—[1]   Words in sub-s (4) substituted for words "beginning of the pension input period", and sub-ss (5A)–(5C) inserted, by FA 2011 s 66, Sch 17 paras 1, 7 with effect for the tax year 2011–12 and subsequent tax years, and in relation to pension input periods ending in the tax year 2011–12 but beginning earlier (or in 2011–12). For transitional provisions see FA 2011 Sch 17 paras 28–34.

[2]   Sub-s (4) substituted, sub-ss (5B)–(5BC) substituted for former sub-s (5B), and in sub-s (5C), definition of "the relevant percentage" substituted and definitions of "the relevant statutory increase percentage" and "RPI-related rate" inserted by the Finance Act 2004 (Registered Pension Schemes and Annual Allowance Charge) (Amendment) Order, SI 2015/80 arts 10, 12 with effect in relation to pension input periods ending in the tax year 2011–12 and subsequent years.

231 Cash balance arrangements: uprating of opening value

(1) This section applies for adjusting the opening value of the individual's rights as calculated under section 230(4).

(2) The opening value is to be increased by the appropriate percentage.

[(3) The appropriate percentage is the percentage (if any) by which the consumer prices index for the September before the start of the tax year is higher than it was for the previous September.][1]

Commentary—*Simon's Taxes* E7.212.

HMRC Manuals—Pensions Tax Manual PTM053400 (cash balance arrangements).

Modifications—Pensions Schemes (Application of UK Provisions to Relevant Non-UK Schemes) Regulations, SI 2006/207 reg 9 (modification of this section in respect of relevant non-UK schemes).

Amendments—[1]   Sub-s (3) substituted by FA 2011 s 66, Sch 17 paras 1, 8 with effect for the tax year 2011–12 and subsequent tax years, and in relation to pension input periods ending in the tax year 2011–12 but beginning earlier (or in 2011–12). For transitional provisions see FA 2011 Sch 17 paras 28–34.

232 Cash balance arrangements: adjustments of closing value

(1) This section applies for adjusting the closing value of the individual's rights under the arrangement as calculated under section 230(5).

(2) If, during the pension input period, the rights of the individual under the arrangement have been reduced by having become subject to a pension debit, the amount of [the reduction][1] is to be added.

(3) If, during the pension input period, the rights of the individual under the arrangement have been increased by the individual having become entitled to a pension credit deriving from the same or another registered pension scheme, the amount of [the increase][1] is to be subtracted.

(4) [[In subsection (4A) "relevant outward transfer" means"][2] a transfer relating to the individual of any sums or assets][1] held for the purposes of, or representing accrued rights under, the arrangement so as to become held for the purposes of, or to represent rights under, any . . . [1] pension scheme that is—

   (a) a registered pension scheme, or

   (b) a qualifying recognised overseas pension scheme,

    . . . [2]

[(4A) If there is a relevant outward transfer during the pension input period, then—

   (a) if condition A is met, the amount of the reduction specified in paragraph (b) of that condition is to be added;

   (b) if condition A is not met but the rights of the individual under the arrangement have been reduced by reason of the relevant outward transfer, the amount of that reduction is to be added.

   Condition A is that—

   (a) the relevant outward transfer ("the transfer") takes place within a block transfer,

   (b) the rights of the individual under the arrangement have been reduced, and the rights of the individual under the pension scheme mentioned in subsection (4) have been increased, as a consequence (whether direct or indirect) of the transfer, and

   (c) the amount of that reduction is equal (or virtually equal) to the amount of that increase.][2]

(5)   . . . [1]

(6) [[In subsection (6A) "relevant inward transfer" means][3] a transfer relating to the individual][1] of any sums or assets held for the purposes of, or representing accrued rights under, any pension scheme so as to become held for the purposes of, or to represent rights under, the arrangement[3].

[(6A) If there is a relevant inward transfer during the pension input period, then—

   (a) if condition B is met, the amount of the increase specified in paragraph (b) of that condition is to be subtracted;

   (b) if condition B is not met but the rights of the individual under arrangement have been increased by reason of the relevant inward transfer, the amount of that increase is to be subtracted.

   Condition B is that—

   (a) the relevant inward transfer ("the transfer") takes place within a block transfer, (*b*) the rights of the individual under the arrangement have been increased, and the rights of the individual under the pension scheme mentioned in subsection (6) have been reduced, as a consequence (whether direct or indirect) of the transfer, and

(*c*) the amount of that increase is equal (or virtually equal) to the amount of that reduction.

(6B) For the purposes of Condition A in subsection (4A) and Condition B in subsection (6A)—

(*a*) normal actuarial practice must be used when determining and comparing the amount of the reduction, and the amount of the increase, in rights,

(*b*) the amount of a reduction or increase in rights under the arrangement is the difference between the amount of those rights under the arrangement immediately before the transfer and immediately after the transfer, and

(*c*) the amount of an increase or reduction in rights under a pension scheme is the difference between the amount of those rights under the pension scheme immediately before the transfer and immediately after the transfer.

(6C) In subsections (4A) and (6A)—

"block transfer" means a transfer which involves the transfer in a single transaction of all the sums or assets held for the purposes of, or representing accrued rights under, the arrangements under a pension scheme which relate to the individual and at least one other member of that pension scheme so as to become held for the purposes of, or to represent rights under, any pension scheme.][3]

[(6D) For the purposes of subsections (4A) and (6A), the rights of the individual under the arrangement have been reduced or increased, as the case may be, "by reason of" a transfer of sums or assets only where that reduction or increase is solely attributable to the value of those sums or assets.][4]

(7) . . .[1]

[(8) If, during the pension input period, the rights of the individual under the arrangement have been reduced by any surrender made, or similar action taken, pursuant to an option available to the individual under the arrangement, the amount of the reduction is to be added.

(8A) If, during the pension input period—

(*a*) benefit crystallisation event 1, 2 or 4 occurs in relation to the individual and the arrangement,

(*b*) benefit crystallisation event 3 occurs in relation to the individual and the arrangement otherwise than by reason of a provision contained in, or made under, any enactment,

(*c*) benefit crystallisation event 6 occurs or, but for paragraph 15A of Schedule 32, would occur in relation to the individual and the arrangement by virtue of the individual becoming entitled to a pension commencement lump sum or a lifetime allowance excess lump sum, or

(*d*) there is an allocation of rights of the individual under the arrangement (not falling within paragraph (*a*)),

the relevant amount is to be added.

(8B) In subsection (8A) "the relevant amount" is—

(*a*) . . .[5]

(*b*) . . .[5]

(*c*) in the case of benefit crystallisation event 6, the amount of the lump sum, and

(*d*) in any other case, the amount of the reduction in the amount of the rights available for the provision of benefits to or in respect of the individual occurring by reason of the benefit crystallisation event or allocation.

(8C) If, during the pension input period, an adjustment to the individual's rights under the arrangement is made in consequence of the scheme administrator satisfying a liability under section 237B in respect of the individual, if and to the extent that the adjustment is reflected in the closing amount the amount of the adjustment is to be added to the closing amount.

(8D) But no amount is to be added under subsection (8C) by reason of an adjustment made in consequence of the scheme administrator satisfying a liability under section 237B [in a case where—.

(*a*) the individual becomes actually entitled to all of the individual's benefits under the pension scheme or benefit crystallisation event 5, 5A or 5B occurs in relation to the individual and the pension scheme, and

(*b*) the adjustment takes place after the individual becomes so entitled or the benefit crystallisation event occurs.]°][1]

(9) . . .[1]

Commentary—*Simon's Taxes* E7.212.
HMRC Manuals—Pensions Tax Manual PTM053400 (cash balance arrangements).
PTM053710 (defined benefits and cash balance arrangements: examples of adjustments to closing values).
Modifications—Registered Pension Schemes (Restriction of Employers' Relief) Regulations, SI 2005/3458 regs 3–5 (determination of the individual's pension input amount for a period of account in respect of a cash balance arrangement: modification of this section).
Registered Pension Schemes (Restriction of Employers' Relief) Regulations, SI 2005/3458 regs 3, 4, 8 (determination of the individual's pension input amount for a period of account in respect of a hybrid arrangement: modification of this section).

Amendments—[1]   The following amendments made by FA 2011 s 66, Sch 17 paras 1, 9 with effect for the tax year 2011–12 and subsequent tax years, and in relation to pension input periods ending in the tax year 2011–12 but beginning earlier (or in 2011–12). For transitional provisions see FA 2011 Sch 17 paras 28–34.

[2]   In sub-s (4), words substituted for words "If, during the pension input period, the rights of the individual under the arrangement have been reduced by reason of", and words "the amount of the reduction is to be added" revoked, and sub-s (4A) inserted by the Finance Act 2004 (Registered Pension Schemes and Annual Allowance Charge) (Amendment) Order, SI 2015/80 arts 10, 13(*a*), (*b*) with effect in relation to pension input periods ending in the tax year 2011–12 and subsequent years. These amendments do not have effect in relation to any transfer of sums or assets that occurs before 28 January 2015 if any person's liability to tax would be higher as a result of—

     (a)   the application of those amendments in relation to that transfer; and

     (b)   any application in relation to that transfer of the amendments made by article 13(*c*) and (*d*),

than it would have been if none of those amendments had effect (SI 2015/80 art 3(3)).

[3]   In sub-s (6), words substituted and words revoked, and sub-ss (6A)–(6C) inserted by the Finance Act 2004 (Registered Pension Schemes and Annual Allowance Charge) (Amendment) Order, SI 2015/80 arts 10, 13(*c*), (*d*) with effect in relation to pension input periods ending in the tax year 2011–12 and subsequent years.

[4]   Sub-s (6D) inserted by the Finance Act 2004 (Registered Pension Schemes and Annual Allowance Charge) (Amendment) Order, SI 2015/80 arts 10, 13(*e*) with effect from 28 January 2015. This amendment does not have effect in relation to transfers of sums or assets that occur before that date (SI 2015/80 art 3(4)).

[5]   Sub-s (8B)(*a*), (*b*) revoked by the Finance Act 2004 (Registered Pension Schemes and Annual Allowance Charge) (Amendment) Order, SI 2015/80 arts 10, 13(*f*) with effect in relation to benefit crystallisation events that occur on or after 28 January 2015.

[6]   Words in sub-s (8D) substituted for words "in a case where subsection (6) of that section applied" by the Finance Act 2004 (Registered Pension Schemes and Annual Allowance Charge) (Amendment) Order, SI 2015/80 arts 10, 13(*g*) with effect in relation to cases where the liability mentioned in section 232(8D) arose on or after 28 January 2015 and results from a notice under section 237B given on or after that date.

233 Other money purchase arrangements

(1) The pension input amount in respect of a money purchase arrangement other than a cash balance arrangement is the total of—

     (*a*)   any relievable pension contributions paid by or on behalf of the individual under the arrangement, and

     (*b*)   contributions paid in respect of the individual under the arrangement by an employer of the individual,

during the pension input period of the arrangement that ends in the tax year.

(2)   . . .[1]

(3) When at any time contributions paid under a pension scheme by an employer otherwise than in respect of any individual become held for the purposes of the provision under an arrangement under the pension scheme of benefits to or in respect of an individual, they are to be treated as being contributions paid at that time in respect of the individual under the arrangement.

[(4) References to "contributions" in subsection (1) do not include any amount which is a refund of excess contributions lump sum (see paragraph 6 of Schedule 29).][2]

Commentary—Simon's Taxes **E7.212.**

HMRC Manuals—Pensions Tax Manual PTM053200 (other money purchase arrangements).

PTM058060 (transitional rules for tax year 2015-16: pension input amounts: other money purchase arrangements).

Modifications—Registered Pension Schemes (Restriction of Employers' Relief) Regulations, SI 2005/3458 regs 3, 4, 6 (determination of the individual's pension input amount for a period of account in respect of a money purchase arrangement other than a cash balance arrangement: modification of this section).

Registered Pension Schemes (Restriction of Employers' Relief) Regulations, SI 2005/3458 regs 3, 4, 8 (determination of the individual's pension input amount for a period of account in respect of a hybrid arrangement: modification of this section).

Amendments—[1]   Sub-s (2) repealed by the Finance Act 2013 s 52(1), (7) with effect from 6 April 2013.

[2]   Sub-s (4) inserted by the Finance Act 2004 (Registered Pension Schemes and Annual Allowance Charge) (Amendment) Order, SI 2015/80 arts 10, 14 with effect in relation to payments of a refund of excess contributions lump sum made in pension input periods ending in tax year 2014–15 and subsequent tax years.

234 Defined benefits arrangements

(1) The pension input amount in respect of a defined benefits arrangement is the amount of any increase in the value of the individual's rights under the arrangement during the pension input period of the arrangement that ends in the tax year.

(2) There is an increase in the value of the individual's rights under the arrangement during the pension input period if—

     (*a*)   the opening value of the individual's rights under the arrangement, is exceeded by

     (*b*)   the closing value of the individual's rights under the arrangement.

(3) The amount of the increase in the value of the individual's rights under the arrangement during the pension input period is the amount of that excess.

(4) The opening value of the individual's rights under the arrangement is—

[

$$(16 \times PB) + LSB$$

][1]

[where—

PB is—

   (*a*) if the pension input period is the first pension input period of the arrangement, the annual rate of the pension which would, on the valuation assumptions (see section 277), be payable to the individual under the arrangement if the individual became entitled to payment of it immediately before that pension input period (or is nil if no such annual rate would be so payable), or

   (*b*) in any other case, the annual rate of the pension which would, on the valuation assumptions, be payable to the individual under the arrangement if the individual became entitled to payment of it at the end of the immediately preceding pension input period, and

   LSB is—

   (*a*) if the pension input period is the first pension input period of the arrangement, the amount of the lump sum to which the individual would, on the valuation assumptions, be entitled under the arrangement (otherwise than by commutation of pension) if the individual became entitled to the payment of it immediately before that pension input period (or is nil if there is no such lump sum to which the individual would be so entitled), or

   (*b*) in any other case, the amount of the lump sum to which the individual would, on the valuation assumptions, be entitled under the arrangement (otherwise than by commutation of pension) if the individual became entitled to the payment of it at the end of the immediately preceding pension input period.]^2

(5) The closing value of the individual's rights under the arrangement is—

[

$$(16 \times PE) + LSE$$

]^1

where—

   PE is the annual rate of the pension which would, on the valuation assumptions, be payable to the individual under the arrangement if the individual became entitled to payment of it at the end of the pension input period, and

   LSE is the amount of the lump sum to which the individual would, on the valuation assumptions, be entitled under the arrangement (otherwise than by commutation of pension) if the individual became entitled to the payment of it at that time.

[(5A) If, during the pension input period, minimum payments are made under—

   (*a*) section 8 of the Pension Schemes Act 1993, or

   (*b*) section 4 of the Pension Schemes (Northern Ireland) Act 1993, in relation to the individual in connection with the arrangement, their amount is to be subtracted from what would otherwise be the pension input amount in the case of the individual in respect of the arrangement.

[(5B) The pension input amount in respect of the arrangement is nil where—

   (*a*) subsection (5BA) or (5BB) applies and the value of the relevant rights of the individual under the arrangement does not increase during the pension input period by more than—

     (i) the relevant percentage, plus

     (ii) the relevant statutory increase percentage, or

   (*b*) subsection (5BC) applies.

(5BA) This subsection applies where the individual—

   (*a*) is, throughout the pension input period, a deferred member of the pension scheme that the arrangement is under,

   (*b*) is such a deferred member for part of the pension input period and a pensioner member for the rest of it, or

   (*c*) would meet the condition in paragraph (*a*) or (*b*) if the arrangement were the only arrangement under the pension scheme relating to the individual.

(5BB) This subsection applies where—

   (*a*) during the pension input period there is a transfer of all the sums or assets held for the purposes of, or representing accrued rights under, the arrangement so as to become held for the purposes of, or to represent rights under—

     (i) a registered pension scheme, or

     (ii) a qualifying recognised overseas pension scheme,

   in connection with the individual,

   (*b*) the individual is a deferred member of the pension scheme that the arrangement is under from the beginning of the pension input period until the transfer (or would be if the arrangement were the only arrangement under the pension scheme relating to that individual), and

   (*c*) rights do not accrue under the arrangement to or in respect of the individual during so much of the pension input period as falls after the transfer.

(5BC) This subsection applies where—

   (*a*) the arrangement ("the annuity arrangement") is a defined benefits arrangement under an annuity contract which is treated as a registered pension scheme under section 153(8), (*b*) throughout the pension input period the annuity arrangement (or a predecessor arrangement) includes provision for the relevant rights of the individual to increase at an annual rate ("the annuity rate") which—

    (i) was specified in the contract (or in the rules of a predecessor registered pension scheme) on 14 October 2010, or

    (ii) is the CPI percentage or the RPI percentage, and

(*c*) the value of the relevant rights of the individual does not increase during the pension input period at an annual rate greater than the annuity rate plus the relevant statutory increase percentage.

(5BD) In determining for the purposes of this section whether or not a member of a pension scheme is a deferred member (see particularly the definition of "active member" in section 151(2)), arrangements made under the pension scheme for benefits to accrue, as a consequence of (and immediately after) a relevant inward transfer (as defined in section 236(5)) to or in respect of that member, are to be disregarded—

(*a*) if condition B in section 236(5A) is met in relation to the accrual of benefits under the arrangements, or

(*b*) so far as the accrual of benefits under the arrangements is to be a subtractable increase in the annual rate of the pension, or the amount of the lump sum, to which the individual would be entitled under the defined benefits arrangement.

(5BE) In subsection (5BD) "subtractable increase" means an increase which falls to be subtracted from PE or LSE by virtue of section 236(5A)(b).][2]

(5C) In this section—

[CPI percentage" means the percentage mentioned in paragraph (c) of the definition of "the relevant percentage" (see below);][2]

"guaranteed minimum pension" has the meaning given by—

    (*a*) section 8(2) of the Pension Schemes Act 1993, or

    (*b*) section 4(2) of the Pension Schemes (Northern Ireland) Act 1993;

"predecessor arrangement", in relation to an arrangement, means another arrangement (under the same or another registered pension scheme) from which some or all of the sums or assets held for the purposes of the arrangement directly or indirectly derive;

"predecessor registered pension scheme", in relation to a pension scheme, means another registered pension scheme from which some or all of the sums or assets held for the purposes of the arrangement under the pension scheme directly or indirectly derive;

["the relevant percentage" means—

    (*a*) where throughout the pension input period the arrangement (or a predecessor arrangement) includes provision for the value of the relevant rights of the individual to increase at an annual rate, which is an RPI-related rate, specified in the rules of the pension scheme (or a predecessor registered pension scheme) on 6 April 2012, that rate,

    (*b*) where throughout the pension input period the arrangement (or a predecessor arrangement) includes provision for the value of the relevant rights of the individual to increase at an annual rate, other than an RPI-related rate, specified in the rules of the pension scheme (or a predecessor registered pension scheme) on 14 October 2010, that rate, and

    (*c*) in a case not falling within paragraph (*a*) or (*b*), the percentage by which the consumer prices index for a month falling within the pension input period and nominated by the scheme administrator is higher than it was for the same month in the previous period of 12 months (or nil per cent if it is not higher);][2]

"the relevant rights of the individual" means rights of the individual under the arrangement, other than any rights to a guaranteed minimum pension;

["the relevant statutory increase percentage" in relation to a pension input period means the percentage increase in the value of the individual's rights under the arrangement during the pension input period so far as it is attributable solely to one or more of the following—

    (*a*) an increase in accordance with section 15 of the Pension Schemes Act 1993 or section 11 of the Pension Schemes (Northern Ireland) Act 1993 (increase of guaranteed minimum where commencement of guaranteed minimum pension postponed);

    (*b*) a revaluation in accordance with section 16 of the Pension Schemes Act 1993 or section 12 of the Pension Schemes (Northern Ireland) Act 1993 (early leavers: revaluation of earning factors);

    (*c*) a revaluation in accordance with Chapter 2 of Part 4 of the Pension Schemes Act 1993 or the Pension Schemes (Northern Ireland) Act 1993 (early leavers: revaluation of accrued benefits);

    (*d*) a revaluation in accordance with Chapter 3 of Part 4 of the Pension Schemes Act 1993 or the Pension Schemes (Northern Ireland) Act 1993 (early leavers: protection of increases in guaranteed minimum pensions);

    (*e*) the application of section 67 of the Equality Act 2010 (sex equality rule for occupational pension schemes);

"RPI percentage" means the percentage by which the retail prices index for a month falling within the pension input period and nominated by the scheme administrator is higher than it was for the same month in the previous period of 12 months (or nil per cent if it is not higher);

"RPI-related rate" (in the definition of "the relevant percentage") means—

    (*a*) a rate produced solely by movement in the retail prices index, or

    (*b*) a rate which (however expressed) is the lower of such a rate and a percentage figure;][2]

"specified", in relation to an annual rate, means specified as a percentage figure or as a percentage produced by movement in an index (or a combination of the two) but does not include a percentage produced by the exercise of a discretion by any person.][1]

(6) Section 235 (uprating of opening value)[, section 236 (adjustments of closing value) and section 236A (post-entitlement enhancements)][1] supplement this section.

Commentary—*Simon's Taxes* **E7.212, E7.214**.

HMRC Manuals—Pensions Tax Manual PTM053301 (general).

Amendments—[1]   Amendments made by FA 2011 s 66, Sch 17 paras 1, 10 with effect for the tax year 2011–12 and subsequent tax years, and in relation to pension input periods ending in the tax year 2011–12 but beginning earlier (or in 2011–12). For transitional provisions see FA 2011 Sch 17 paras 28–34.

[2]   In sub-s (4), words substituted, sub-ss (5B)–(5BE) substituted for former sub-s (5B), and in sub-s (5C), definitions of "guaranteed minimum pension", "the relevant statutory increase percentage", "RPI percentage" and "RPI-related rate" inserted, and definition of "the relevant percentage" substituted by the Finance Act 2004 (Registered Pension Schemes and Annual Allowance Charge) (Amendment) Order, SI 2015/80 arts 10, 15 with effect in relation to pension input periods ending in tax year 2011–12 and subsequent years.

235 Defined benefits arrangements: uprating of opening value

(1) This section applies for adjusting the opening value of the individual's rights as calculated under section 234(4) . . . [1]

(2) The opening value is to be increased by the appropriate percentage.

[(3) The appropriate percentage is the percentage (if any) by which the consumer prices index for the September before the start of the tax year is higher than it was for the previous September.][1]

Commentary—*Simon's Taxes* **E7.212**.

HMRC Manuals—Pensions Tax Manual PTM053301 (general - how to find the opening value).

Regulations—Registered Pension Schemes (Uprating Percentages for Defined Benefits Arrangements and Enhanced Protection Limits) Regulations, SI 2006/130.

Amendments—[1]   In sub-s (1) words "in a case where rights do not accrue to the individual under the arrangement during the pension input period" repealed, and sub-s (3) substituted, by FA 2011 s 66, Sch 17 paras 1, 11 with effect for the tax year 2011–12 and subsequent tax years, and in relation to pension input periods ending in the tax year 2011–12 but beginning earlier (or in 2011–12). For transitional provisions see FA 2011 Sch 17 paras 28–34.

236 Defined benefits arrangements: adjustments of closing value

(1) This section applies for adjusting [PE and LSE][1] under section 234(5).

(2) If, during the pension input period, the [annual rate of the pension, or the amount of the lump sum, to which the individual would be entitled under the arrangement has][1] been reduced by having become subject to a pension debit, the amount of [the reduction][1] is to be added [to PE or LSE][1].

(3) If, during the pension input period, [annual rate of the pension, or the amount of the lump sum, to which the individual would be entitled under the arrangement has][1] been increased by the individual having become entitled to a pension credit deriving from the same or another registered pension scheme, the amount of [the increase][1] is to be subtracted [from PE or LSE][1].

[(4) [In subsection (4A) "relevant outward transfer means][2] a transfer relating to the individual of any sums or assets held for the purposes of, or representing accrued rights under, the arrangement so as to become held for the purposes of, or to represent rights under, any pension scheme that is—

    (*a*) a registered pension scheme, or

    (*b*) a qualifying recognised overseas pension scheme,

. . . [2]

[(4A) If there is a relevant outward transfer during the pension input period, then—

    (*a*) if condition A is met, and there has been a reduction in the annual rate of the pension or a reduction in the amount of the lump sum to which the individual would be entitled under the arrangement, as a consequence (whether direct or indirect) of the relevant outward transfer, the amount of that reduction is to be added to PE or LSE, so far as that amount is reflected in the reduction in the value of benefits mentioned in paragraph (b) of condition A;

    (*b*) if condition A is not met but the annual rate of the pension, or the amount of the lump sum, to which the individual would be entitled under the arrangement has been reduced by reason of the relevant outward transfer, the amount of that reduction is to be added to PE or LSE.

   Condition A is that—

   (*a*) the relevant outward transfer ("the transfer") takes place within a block transfer,

(a) the time-apportioned percentage for the post-alignment tax year is treated as being nil, and

(b) the time-apportioned percentage for the pre-alignment tax year is treated as being 100.

(18) If the nil result is for so much of the combined period as precedes 9 July 2015—

(a) the time-apportioned percentage for the pre-alignment tax year is treated as being nil, and

(b) the time-apportioned percentage for the post-alignment tax year is treated as being 100.][1]

Commentary—*Simon's Taxes* E7.212.

Amendments—[1]   This section inserted by F(No 2)A 2015 s 23, Sch 4 paras 7, 9 with effect from 18 November 2015.

[237A Liability of individual

(1) The individual is liable to the annual allowance charge.

(2) The individual is liable to the annual allowance charge whether or not—

(a) the individual, and

(b) the scheme administrator of the pension scheme or pension schemes concerned,

are resident . . . [2] or domiciled in the United Kingdom.[1]

Commentary—*Simon's Taxes* E7.215.

HMRC Manuals—Pensions Tax Manual PTM056300 (who pays the annual allowance charge?).

Amendments—[1]   Sections 237A–237F inserted by FA 2011 s 66, Sch 17 paras 1, 15 with effect for the tax year 2011–12 and subsequent tax years, and in relation to pension input periods ending in the tax year 2011–12 but beginning earlier (or in 2011–12). For transitional provisions see FA 2011 Sch 17 paras 28–34.

[2]   Words in sub-s (2) repealed by FA 2013 s 219, Sch 46 paras 119, 128 with effect in relation to the tax year 2013–14 and any subsequent tax year.

[237B Liability of scheme administrator

(1) This section applies if—

(a) the amount of the individual's liability to the annual allowance charge for a tax year exceeds £2,000, and

(b) the pension scheme input amount in the case of the individual in relation to a registered pension scheme for the tax year exceeds the amount of the annual allowance specified in section 228(1) for the tax year.

(2) The pension scheme input amount in the case of the individual in relation to a pension scheme for a tax year is the aggregate of the pension input amounts for the tax year in respect of arrangements relating to the individual under the pension scheme.

[(2A) If the chargeable amount for the tax year in the individual's case is the alternative chargeable amount, each of the following is treated as being a reference to the amount that the annual allowance charge for the tax year would be in the individual's case if the chargeable amount were the default chargeable amount—

(a) the reference in subsection (1)(a) to the amount of the individual's liability to the annual allowance charge for the tax year, and

(b) the reference in subsection (3) to the annual allowance charge arising in the case of the individual.][3]

(3) The individual may give a notice to the scheme administrator of the pension scheme specifying that the individual and the scheme administrator are to be jointly and severally liable in respect of so much of the annual allowance charge arising in the case of the individual as—

(a) does not exceed the amount of the annual allowance charge which would be chargeable on the excess mentioned in subsection (1)(b) if it were charged at the relevant rate, and

(b) is specified in the notice,

("the joint liability amount").

(4) In subsection (3)(a) "the relevant rate" means—

(a) in relation to so much of the excess as does not exceed the amount (if any) on which tax is chargeable in the case of the individual for the tax year at the additional . . . [6] rate by virtue of paragraph (c) of subsection (4A) of section 227, the additional rate . . . [6],

(b) in relation to so much of the excess as is not within paragraph (a) and does not exceed the amount (if any) on which tax is so chargeable at the higher rate . . . [6] by virtue of paragraph (b) of that subsection, the higher rate . . . [6], and

(c) in relation to any remaining part of the excess, the basic rate . . . [6].

[But subsection (4A) applies in the case of a Scottish taxpayer [and subsection (4B) applies in the case of a Welsh taxpayer][8].][6]

[(4A) In the case of a Scottish taxpayer, the "relevant rate" in subsection (3)(a) means—

(a) where the only Scottish rate is the Scottish basic rate, that rate;

(b) where there is more than one Scottish rate—

(i) the highest Scottish rate in relation to so much of the excess as does not exceed the amount (if any) on which tax is chargeable in the case of the individual at that rate by virtue of section 227(4AA)(b)(ii) or (iii),

(ii) the next highest Scottish rate in relation to so much of the excess as is not within sub-paragraph (i) and does not exceed the amount (if any) on which tax is so chargeable by virtue of section 227(4AA)(b)(i), (ii) or (iii),

      (iii) if there is one, the next highest Scottish rate in relation to so much of the excess as is not
within sub-paragraph (i) or (ii) and does not exceed the amount (if any) on which tax is
so chargeable by virtue of section 227(4AA)(*b*)(i), (ii) or (iii),

    and so on.][6]

[(4B) In the case of a Welsh taxpayer, the "relevant rate" in subsection (3)(*a*) means—

    (*a*) in relation to so much of the excess as does not exceed the amount (if any) on which tax is
chargeable in the case of the individual for the tax year at the Welsh additional rate by virtue
of paragraph (*c*) of subsection (4AB) of section 227, the Welsh additional rate,

    (*b*) in relation to so much of the excess as is not within paragraph (*a*) and does not exceed the
amount (if any) on which tax is so chargeable at the Welsh higher rate by virtue of paragraph
(*b*) of that subsection, the Welsh higher rate, and

    (*c*) in relation to the remaining part of the excess, the Welsh basic rate.][7]

(5) The notice—

    (*a*) must be given not later than 31 July in the year following that in which the tax year ends (but
subject to subsection (6)),

    (*b*) must be made in such manner and form, and contain such particulars, as may be prescribed
by regulations made by the Commissioners for Her Majesty's Revenue and Customs, and

    (*c*) may be amended by giving the scheme administrator notice in accordance with provision
made by regulations made by the Commissioners for Her Majesty's Revenue and Customs
but may not be revoked.

(6) [A notice may not be given after][4] the individual becomes actually entitled to all of the
individual's benefits under the pension scheme . . . [4] or benefit crystallisation event 5, 5A or 5B
occurs . . . [4] in relation to the individual and the pension scheme, . . . [4].

(7) On receipt by the scheme administrator of the notice the scheme administrator and the individual
become jointly and severally liable to pay the joint liability amount, but subject to sections 237C and
237D and to any amendment made to the notice in accordance with regulations under subsection
(5)(*c*).

(8) The scheme administrator is liable under subsection (7) whether or not—

    (*a*) the individual, and

    (*b*) the scheme administrator,

are resident . . . [2] or domiciled in the United Kingdom.

(9) Where (but for this subsection) a notice could be given to a scheme administrator of a pension
scheme but, before it is given, there is a transfer of all of the sums or assets—

    (*a*) held for the purposes of, or

    (*b*) representing accrued rights under,

[arrangements relating to the individual under the pension scheme][5] so as to become held for the
purposes of, or to represent rights under, another registered pension scheme, the notice may not be
given to that scheme administrator but may instead be given to the scheme administrator of that other
pension scheme.

(10) The Treasury may by regulations make provision modifying the operation of this section in
other cases in which there is a transfer of any of the sums or assets—

    (*a*) held for the purposes of, or

    (*b*) representing accrued rights under,

the pension scheme so as to become held for the purposes of, or to represent rights under, another
registered pension scheme.

(11) The Treasury may by order amend paragraph (*a*) of subsection (1) so as to increase the sum for
the time being specified in that paragraph.[1]

Commentary—*Simon's Taxes* E7.215.
HMRC Manuals—Pensions Tax Manual PTM056430 (deadlines).
PTM056300 (the conditioned for scheme to apply).
Amendments—[1]   Sections 237A–237F inserted by FA 2011 s 66, Sch 17 paras 1, 15 with effect for the tax year 2011–12 and
    subsequent tax years, and in relation to pension input periods ending in the tax year 2011–12 but beginning earlier (or in
    2011–12). For transitional provisions see FA 2011 Sch 17 paras 28–34.
[2]   Words in sub-s (8) repealed by FA 2013 s 219, Sch 46 paras 119, 129 with effect in relation to the tax year 2013–14 and any
    subsequent tax year.
[3]   Subsection (2A) inserted by the Taxation of Pensions Act 2014 s 1, Sch 1 para 68 with effect from 17 December 2014.
[4]   In sub-s (6), words substituted and revoked by the Finance Act 2004 (Registered Pension Schemes and Annual Allowance
    Charge) (Amendment) Order, SI 2015/80 arts 10, 17(*a*) with effect in relation to–
       (a)   the individual becoming actually entitled to benefits; and
       (b)   benefit crystallisation events occurring,
    after the end of the period of 6 months beginning with 28 January 2015.
[5]   In sub-s (9), words substituted for words "the pension scheme" by the Finance Act 2004 (Registered Pension Schemes and
    Annual Allowance Charge) (Amendment) Order, SI 2015/80 arts 10, 17(*b*) with effect in relation to transfers of sums or assets
    that occur on or after 28 January 2015.

[6]   In sub-s (4)(*a*), (*b*), (*c*), words inserted by the Scottish Rate of Income Tax (Consequential Amendments) Order, SI 2015/1810 art 7(1), (3) with effect in relation to the tax year 2016–17 (the tax year appointed by the Treasury under the Scotland Act 2012 s 25(5) by virtue of SI 2015/2000) and subsequent tax years.

[7]   In sub-s (4) words inserted, and sub-s (4B) inserted, by the Devolved Income Tax Rates (Consequential Amendments) Order, SI 2019/201 arts 3, 8 with effect in relation to the tax year commencing on 6 April 2019 and subsequent tax years.

[237C Exceptions

(1) The scheme administrator of a pension scheme does not become liable under section 237B if the time when the scheme administrator would become liable is during an assessment period in relation to the pension scheme; and if an assessment period in relation to a pension scheme begins at a time when the scheme administrator is already so liable (but has not satisfied the liability), the liability ceases when the assessment period begins.

References to an assessment period are to be construed in accordance with sections 132 and 159 of the Pensions Act 2004 and articles 116 and 143 of the Pensions (Northern Ireland) Order 2005 (S.I. 2005/255 (N.I. 1)).

(2) The scheme administrator of a pension scheme is not liable under section 237B in respect of any amount if there is no power to make a consequential adjustment to the entitlement of the individual concerned to benefits under the pension scheme in respect of the amount because of section 237E(2) (inalienability of guaranteed minimum pension etc).

(3) The Treasury may by regulations prescribe other circumstances in which a scheme administrator of a pension scheme does not become, or ceases to be, liable under section 237B.[1]

Commentary—*Simon's Taxes* **E7.215**.
HMRC Manuals—Pensions Tax Manual PTM056300 (when the scheme administrator will not be liable).
Amendments—[1]   Sections 237A–237F inserted by FA 2011 s 66, Sch 17 paras 1, 15 with effect for the tax year 2011–12 and subsequent tax years, and in relation to pension input periods ending in the tax year 2011–12 but beginning earlier (or in 2011–12). For transitional provisions see FA 2011 Sch 17 paras 28–34.

[237D Discharge of scheme administrator's liability

(1) If the scheme administrator of a pension scheme is liable under section 237B, the scheme administrator may apply to an officer of Revenue and Customs for the discharge of the scheme administrator's liability on either of the following grounds.

(2) The grounds are—

(*a*) that paying the amount to which the scheme administrator is liable would be to the substantial detriment of the interests of the members of the pension scheme, and

(*b*) that in all the circumstances of the case it would not be just and reasonable for the scheme administrator to be liable to that amount.

(3) On receiving an application under subsection (1), an officer of Revenue and Customs must decide whether to discharge the scheme administrator's liability.

(4) An officer of Revenue and Customs must notify the scheme administrator of the decision on the application.

(5) The discharge of the scheme administrator's liability does not affect the liability of any other person in respect of the same amount.

(6) The Treasury may by regulations amend this section so as to alter the grounds on which an application under subsection (1) may be made.

(7) Regulations made by the Commissioners for Her Majesty's Revenue and Customs may make provision supplementing this section; and the regulations may in particular make provision as to the time limits for the making of an application.[1]

Commentary—*Simon's Taxes* **E7.215**.
HMRC Manuals—Pensions Tax Manual PTM158000 (other scheme administrator rights - right to apply for a discharge from joint and several liability to the annual allowance charge).
Amendments—[1]   Sections 237A–237F inserted by FA 2011 s 66, Sch 17 paras 1, 15 with effect for the tax year 2011–12 and subsequent tax years, and in relation to pension input periods ending in the tax year 2011–12 but beginning earlier (or in 2011–12). For transitional provisions see FA 2011 Sch 17 paras 28–34.

[237E Consequential benefit adjustments to be reasonable etc

(1) Where the scheme administrator of a pension scheme satisfies a liability under section 237B in respect of the individual, consequential adjustment must be made to the entitlement of the individual to benefits under the pension scheme on a basis that is just and reasonable having regard to normal actuarial practice.

(2) Any power to make such consequential adjustment is subject to section 159 of the Pension Schemes Act 1993 or section 155 of the Pension Schemes (Northern Ireland) Act 1993 (inalienability of guaranteed minimum pension etc).[1]

Commentary—*Simon's Taxes* **E7.215**.
HMRC Manuals—Pensions Tax Manual PTM056460 (adjustment to member's benefits).
PTM056300 (consequential adjustment to the member's pension benefits).
Amendments—[1]   Sections 237A–237F inserted by FA 2011 s 66, Sch 17 paras 1, 15 with effect for the tax year 2011–12 and subsequent tax years, and in relation to pension input periods ending in the tax year 2011–12 but beginning earlier (or in 2011–12). For transitional provisions see FA 2011 Sch 17 paras 28–34.

[237F Power to modify rules

The Commissioners for Her Majesty's Revenue and Customs may by regulations make any modification of the rules of registered pension schemes that appear appropriate to facilitate the operation of sections 237A to 237E.]¹

Commentary—*Simon's Taxes* E7.215.

Amendments—¹   Sections 237A–237F inserted by FA 2011 s 66, Sch 17 paras 1, 15 with effect for the tax year 2011–12 and subsequent tax years, and in relation to pension input periods ending in the tax year 2011–12 but beginning earlier (or in 2011–12). For transitional provisions see FA 2011 Sch 17 paras 28–34.

238 Pension input period[: arrangement commencing before 9 July 2015]³

(1) In the case of an arrangement under a registered pension scheme [where the relevant commencement date is before 9 July 2015, but subject to section 238ZA,]³ the following are pension input periods—

- (a) the period beginning with the relevant commencement date and ending with[—
  - (i) a nominated date falling before the anniversary of the relevant commencement date, or
  - (ii) if there is not such a nominated date, the first 5 April after the relevant commencement date (or, if the relevant commencement date is itself 5 April, that date), and]¹
- (b) each subsequent period beginning immediately after the end of a period which is a pension input period (under paragraph (a) or this paragraph) and ending with the appropriate date.

(2) "The relevant commencement date" means—

- (a) in the case of a cash balance arrangement or a defined benefits arrangement, or a hybrid arrangement the only benefits under which may be cash balance benefits or defined benefits, the date on which rights under the arrangement begin to accrue to or in respect of the individual,
- (b) in the case of a money purchase arrangement other than a cash balance arrangement, the first date on which a contribution within section 233(1) is made, and
- (c) in the case of a hybrid arrangement not within paragraph (a), whichever is the earlier of the date mentioned in that paragraph and the date mentioned in paragraph (b).

(3) "Nominated date" means—

- (a) in the case of a money purchase arrangement other than a cash balance arrangement, such date as the individual or scheme administrator nominates, and
- (b) in the case of any other arrangement, such date as the scheme administrator nominates.

(4) A nomination for the purposes of subsection (3)—

- (a) if by the individual, is to be made by notice to the scheme administrator, and
- (b) if by the scheme administrator, is to be made by notice to the individual.

[(4A) A date nominated for the purposes of subsection (3) must not be a date before that on which the nomination is made.]²

(5) If more than one date is nominated for the purposes of subsection (3)—

- (a) in relation to the period beginning with the relevant commencement date, or
- (b) in relation to a tax year following that in which the pension input period beginning with that date ends,

the date nominated first is the nominated date.

(6) "The appropriate date" means¹ . . . —

- (a) a nominated date falling in the tax year immediately after that in which the last pension input period ended, [or]¹
- (b) [if there is not such a nominated date,]¹ the anniversary of the date on which that period ended.

(7) Once the individual has become entitled to all the benefits which may be provided to the individual under an arrangement, the last pension input period in the case of the arrangement is [that in which]² that was first so.

Commentary—*Simon's Taxes* E7.212.

HMRC Manuals—Pensions Tax Manual PTM052100 (pension input periods).

Pensions Tax Manual PTM058040 (pension input periods for the post-alignment tax year).

Modifications—Registered Pension Schemes (Splitting of Schemes) Regulations, SI 2006/569 reg 3 (modification of this provision in relation to sub-scheme administrators).

Amendments—¹   In sub-s (1)(a), words substituted for words "the earlier of a nominated date and the anniversary of the relevant commencement date, and", in sub-s (6) words "the earlier of" repealed, word "or" substituted for word "and" and words inserted, by FA 2011 s 66, Sch 17 paras 1, 16(1), (2), (4) with effect for the tax year 2011–12 and subsequent tax years. For transitional provisions see FA 2011 Sch 17 paras 28–34.

²   Sub-s (4A) inserted and words in sub-s (7) substituted for words "to be treated as having ended when", by FA 2011 s 66, Sch 17 paras 1, 16(1), (3), (5) with effect for the tax year 2011–12 and subsequent tax years, and in relation to pension input periods ending in the tax year 2011–12 but beginning earlier (or in 2011–12). For transitional provisions see FA 2011 Sch 17 paras 28–34.

³   In heading and sub-s (1), words inserted by F(No 2)A 2015 s 23, Sch 4 paras 1, 2 with effect from 18 November 2015.

[238ZA Pension input periods from 9 July 2015 for existing arrangement
(1) If the relevant commencement date in the case of an arrangement under a registered pension scheme is before 9 July 2015, section 238(1) and (3) to (6) apply in relation to the arrangement subject to the following.
(2) If a pension input period for the arrangement—
    (*a*) begins with 8 July 2015 or an earlier day, and
    (*b*) but for this subsection would end with 9 July 2015 or a later day,
it ends with 8 July 2015.
(3) If a pension input period for the arrangement ends with 8 July 2015 (whether or not because of subsection (2)), the subsequent pension input periods for the arrangement are—
    (*a*) the period beginning with 9 July 2015 and ending with 5 April 2016, and
    (*b*) the tax year 2016–17 and each subsequent tax year.
(4) No nominations for the purposes of section 238(3) may be made on or after 9 July 2015.
(5) "The relevant commencement date" has the meaning given by section 238(2).]¹
Commentary—*Simon's Taxes* **E7.212**.
HMRC Manuals—Pensions Tax Manual PTM052100 (meaning of pension input periods).
Amendments—¹   Sections 238ZA, 238ZB inserted by F(No 2)A 2015 s 23, Sch 4 paras 1, 3 with effect from 18 November 2015.

[238ZB Pension input periods for arrangement commencing after 8 July 2015
(1) In the case of an arrangement under a registered pension scheme where the relevant commencement date is 9 July 2015 or later, the following are pension input periods—
    (*a*) the period beginning with the relevant commencement date and ending with the first 5 April after the relevant commencement date (or, if the relevant commencement date is itself 5 April, that date), and
    (*b*) each tax year beginning after the end of that period.
(2) "The relevant commencement date" has the meaning given by section 238(2).
(3) Once the individual has become entitled to all the benefits which may be provided to the individual under the arrangement, the last pension input period in the case of the arrangement is that in which that was first so.]¹
Commentary—*Simon's Taxes* **E7.212**.
HMRC Manuals—Pensions Tax Manual PTM052100 (meaning of pension input periods).
Amendments—¹   Sections 238ZA, 238ZB inserted by F(No 2)A 2015 s 23, Sch 4 paras 1, 3 with effect from 18 November 2015.

[238A Power to make orders about charge
(1) The Treasury may by order make provision about the annual allowance charge.
(2) The provision may include modifications of any of sections 227 to 238.
(3) The provision may include provision consequential on, or supplementary or incidental to, the provision made by those sections and transitional provisions (including provision making modifications of enactments).
(4) "Modifications" includes amendments.]¹
Orders—Finance Act 2004 (Registered Pension Schemes and Annual Allowance Charge) (Amendment) Order, SI 2015/80.
Amendments—¹   This section inserted by FA 2011 s 66, Sch 17 paras 1, 17 with effect for the tax year 2011–12 and subsequent tax years, and in relation to pension input periods ending in the tax year 2011–12 but beginning earlier (or in 2011–12). For transitional provisions see FA 2011 Sch 17 paras 28–34.

Scheme sanction charge

239 Scheme sanction charge
(1) A charge to income tax, to be known as the scheme sanction charge, arises where in any tax year one or more scheme chargeable payments are made by a registered pension scheme.
(2) The person liable to the scheme sanction charge is the scheme administrator.
(3) But[—
    (*a*)] ³in the case of a payment treated by virtue of section 161(3) and (4) (payments under investments acquired with scheme assets) as having been made by a pension scheme which has been wound up, the person liable to the scheme sanction charge is the person who was, or each of the persons who were, the scheme administrator immediately before the pension scheme was wound up[, and
    (*b*) in the case of a payment of a lump sum to a member where the conditions in paragraphs 1(1)(*b*) and (*d*) and 1B(2)(*a*) to (*g*) of Schedule 29 are met, the person liable to the scheme sanction charge so far as relating to any part of the lump sum within the permitted maximum is the scheme administrator of the registered pension scheme to which the transfer mentioned in paragraph 1B(2)(*g*) of Schedule 29 is made.]³
[(3A) For the purposes of subsection (3)(*b*) "the permitted maximum", in the case of a lump sum paid to an individual, is the amount that in accordance with paragraph 2 of Schedule 29 would be the permitted maximum for that lump sum if the individual became entitled at the time the lump sum is paid to the pension at that time expected to be the pension in connection with which the lump sum is paid.]³

(4) A person liable to the scheme sanction charge is liable whether or not—
  (*a*) that person, and
  (*b*) any other person who is liable to the scheme sanction charge,
are resident . . . [2] or domiciled in the United Kingdom.
(5) The following sections make further provision about the scheme sanction charge—
    section 240 (amount of charge), and
    section 241 (scheme chargeable payment).
[(6) This section is subject to provision made by regulations under section 273ZA (income and gains from taxable property).][1]

Commentary—*Simon's Taxes* E7.247.
HMRC Manuals—Pensions Tax Manual PTM121000 (a scheme sanction charge).
PTM135100 (the scheme sanction charge - scheme chargeable payments).
PTM135300 (liability to the scheme sanction charge).
Modifications—Registered Pension Schemes (Splitting of Schemes) Regulations, SI 2006/569 reg 3 (modification of this provision in relation to sub-scheme administrators).
Amendments—[1]   Sub-s (6) inserted by FA 2006 s 158, Sch 21 paras 2, 8. This amendment is deemed to have come into force on 6 April 2006.
[2]   Words in sub-s (4) repealed by FA 2013 s 219, Sch 46 paras 119, 130 with effect in relation to the tax year 2013–14 and any subsequent tax year.
[3]   In sub-s (3), para (*a*) designated as such, and para (*b*) and preceding word inserted, and sub-s (3A) inserted, by FA 2014 s 43, Sch 5 para 12(1), (2). These amendments are to be treated as having come into force on 19 March 2014 (FA 2014 Sch 5 para 15).

240 Amount of charge
(1) The scheme sanction charge for any tax year is a charge at the rate of 40% in respect of the scheme chargeable payment, or the aggregate of the scheme chargeable payments, made by the pension scheme in the tax year.
(2) But if—
  (*a*) the scheme chargeable payment is an unauthorised payment, or any of the scheme chargeable payments are unauthorised payments, and
  (*b*) tax charged in relation to that payment, or any of those payments, under section 208 (unauthorised payments charge) has been paid,
a deduction is to be made from the amount of tax that would otherwise be chargeable for the tax year by virtue of subsection (1).
(3) The amount of the deduction is the lesser of—
  (*a*) 25% of the amount of the scheme chargeable payment, or of the aggregate amount of such of the scheme chargeable payments as are tax-paid, and
  (*b*) the amount of the tax which has been paid under section 208 in relation to the scheme chargeable payment, or in relation to such of the scheme chargeable payments as are tax-paid.
[(3A) The Treasury—
  (*a*) may by order amend subsection (1) so as to vary the rate of the scheme sanction charge, and
  (*b*) may by order amend subsection (3)(*a*) so as to vary the percentage mentioned there.
(3B) An order under subsection (3A) may make provision for there to be different rates or percentages in different circumstances.]
(4) A scheme chargeable payment is "tax-paid" if the whole or any part of the tax chargeable in relation to it under section 208 has been paid.

Commentary—*Simon's Taxes* E7.247.
HMRC Manuals—Pensions Tax Manual PTM135100 (amount of the scheme sanction charge).
Amendments—Sub-ss (3A), (3B) inserted by FA 2009 s 6, Sch 2 paras 10, 16 with effect for the tax year 2010–11 and subsequent tax years. The powers conferred by the amendments made by FA 2009 Sch 2 may be exercised at any time on or after 21 July 2009 but not so as to make provision having effect before the tax year 2010–11 (FA 2009 Sch 2 para 25(1)).

241 Scheme chargeable payment
(1) In this Part "scheme chargeable payment", in relation to a registered pension scheme, means—
  (*a*) an unauthorised payment by the pension scheme, other than one which is exempt from being scheme chargeable, and
  (*aa*) . . . [2]
  (*b*) a scheme chargeable payment which the pension scheme is to be treated as having made by section 183 or 185 (unauthorised borrowing)[, and][1]
  [(*c*) a scheme chargeable payment which the pension scheme is to be treated as having made by section 185A (income from taxable property) or 185F (gains from taxable property)][1].
(2) An unauthorised payment is exempt from being scheme chargeable if—
  (*a*) it is treated as having been made by section 173 (use of scheme assets to provide benefits) and the asset used to provide the benefit in question is not a wasting asset,
  (*b*) it is a compensation payment (see section 178),
  (*c*) it is made to comply with an order of a court or of a person or body with power to order the making of the payment,

(*d*) it is made on the ground that a court or any such person or body is likely to order the making of the payment (or would be were it asked to do so), or

(*e*) it is of a description prescribed by regulations made by the Board of Inland Revenue.

(3) "Wasting asset" has the same meaning as in section 44 of TCGA 1992.

(4) Schedule 36 contains (in Part 3) transitional provision about scheme chargeable payments.

Commentary—*Simon's Taxes* E7.241, E7.247.

HMRC Manuals—Pensions Tax Manual PTM135200 (scheme chargeable payments and exceptions).

Regulations—Registered Pension Schemes (Unauthorised Payments by Existing Schemes) Regulations, SI 2006/365.

Amendments—[1]   Sub-s (1)(*c*) and preceding word ", and" inserted by FA 2006 s 158, Sch 21 paras 2, 9. This amendment is deemed to have come into force on 6 April 2006.

[2]   Sub-s (1)(*aa*) repealed by FA 2011 s 65, Sch 16 paras 62, 74 with effect for the tax year 2011–12 and subsequent tax years, subject to transitional provisions in FA 2011 Sch 16 Pt 3.

De-registration charge

242 De-registration charge

(1) A charge to income tax, to be known as the de-registration charge, arises where the registration of a registered pension scheme is withdrawn.

(2) The liability to the de-registration charge is a liability of the person who was, or each of the persons who were, the scheme administrator immediately before the registration was withdrawn.

(3) That person, or each of those persons, is liable to the de-registration charge whether or not—

(*a*) that person, and

(*b*) any other person who is liable to the de-registration charge,

are resident . . . [2] or domiciled in the United Kingdom.

(4) The de-registration charge is a charge at the rate of 40% in respect of the aggregate of—

(*a*) the amount of any sums held for the purposes of the pension scheme immediately before it ceased to be a registered pension scheme, and

(*b*) the market value at that time of any assets held for the purposes of the pension scheme.

[(5) The Treasury may by order amend subsection (4) so as to vary the rate of the de-registration charge.

(6) An order under subsection (5) may make provision for there to be different rates in different circumstances.][1]

Commentary—*Simon's Taxes* E7.209, E7.247, E7.241.

HMRC Manuals—Pensions Tax Manual PTM033300 (the de-registration charge).

Amendments—[1]   Sub-ss (5), (6) inserted by FA 2009 s 6, Sch 2 paras 10, 17 with effect for the tax year 2010–11 and subsequent tax years. The powers conferred by the amendments made by FA 2009 Sch 2 may be exercised at any time on or after 21 July 2009 but not so as to make provision having effect before the tax year 2010–11 (FA 2009 Sch 2 para 25(1)).

[2]   Words in sub-s (3) repealed by FA 2013 s 219, Sch 46 paras 119, 131 with effect in relation to the tax year 2013–14 and any subsequent tax year.

[CHAPTER 5A

REGISTERED PENSION SCHEMES ESTABLISHED OUTSIDE THE UNITED KINGDOM

242A Meaning of "non-UK registered scheme"

In this Chapter "non-UK registered scheme" means a registered pension scheme established in a country or territory outside the United Kingdom.][1]

Amendments—[1]   Sections 242A, 242B inserted by FA 2017 s 10, Sch 4 paras 12, 14 with effect in relation to transfers made on or after 9 March 2017.

[242B Meaning of "UK-relieved funds"

(1) For the purposes of this Chapter, the "UK-relieved funds" of a non-UK registered scheme are sums or assets held for the purposes of, or representing accrued rights under, the scheme—

(*a*) that (directly or indirectly) represent sums or assets that at any time were held for the purposes of, or represented accrued rights under, a registered pension scheme established in the United Kingdom,

(*b*) that (directly or indirectly) represent sums or assets that at any time formed the UK tax-relieved fund under a relevant non-UK scheme of a relieved member of that scheme, or

(*c*) that—

(i) are held for the purposes of, or represent accrued rights under, an arrangement under the scheme relating to a member of the scheme who on any day has been an accruing member of the scheme, and

(ii) in accordance with regulations made by the Commissioners for Her Majesty's Revenue and Customs, are to be taken to have benefited from relief from tax.

(2) In this Chapter "relevant contribution" has the meaning given by regulation 14ZB(8) of the Information Regulations.

(3) Paragraphs (7) and (8) of regulation 14ZB of the Information Regulations (meaning of "accruing member") apply for the purposes of this section as for those of that regulation.

(4) "The Information Regulations" means the Registered Pension Schemes (Provision of Information) Regulations 2006 (SI 2006/567).][1]

Commentary—*Simon's Taxes* E7.201A.
Amendments—[1]   Sections 242A, 242B inserted by FA 2017 s 10, Sch 4 paras 12, 14 with effect in relation to transfers made on or after 9 March 2017.

[242C Application of this Part to non-UK registered schemes
(1) This Part (so far as would not otherwise be the case) is to be read—
  (*a*) as applying in relation to UK-relieved funds of a non-UK registered scheme as it applies in relation to sums or assets held for the purposes of, or representing accrued rights under, a registered pension scheme established in the United Kingdom,
  (*b*) as applying in relation to a non-UK registered scheme, so far as the scheme relates to the scheme's UK-relieved funds, as it applies in relation to a registered pension scheme established in the United Kingdom,
  (*c*) as applying in relation to members of a non-UK registered scheme, so far as their rights under the scheme are represented by UK-relieved funds of the scheme, as it applies in relation to members of a registered pension scheme established in the United Kingdom, and
  (*d*) as applying to relevant contributions to a non-UK registered scheme as it applies in relation to contributions to a registered pension scheme established in the United Kingdom.
(2) Subsection (1) has effect subject to, and in accordance with, the following provisions of this Chapter.
(3) The Commissioners for Her Majesty's Revenue and Customs may by regulations make—
  (*a*) provision elucidating the application of, or supplementing, subsection (1) or other provisions of this Chapter, or
  (*b*) where relief from tax is involved, other provision for or in connection with the application of this Part where the interpretative presumption against extra-territorial application means that it would otherwise not apply.
(4) Regulations under subsection (3) may (in particular)—
  (*a*) amend provisions of or made under—
    (i) this Part, or
    (ii) any other enactment related to taxation in connection with pensions, and
  (*b*) make consequential amendments of provisions of, or made under, any enactment.
(5) See section 242B for the meaning of "UK-relieved funds" and "relevant contribution".][1]

Commentary—*Simon's Taxes* E7.201A.
Amendments—[1]   Sections 242C–242E inserted by FA 2017 s 9, Sch 3 para 1 with effect for the tax year 2017–18 and subsequent tax years.

[242D Non-UK registered schemes: annual allowance charge
(1) This section is about the application of the provisions of this Part relating to the annual allowance charge.
(2) Pension input amounts in respect of arrangements relating to an individual under a non-UK registered scheme are to be taken into account in applying the provisions for a tax year in relation to the individual only if, in accordance with regulations made by the Commissioners for Her Majesty's Revenue and Customs, relieved inputs are to be taken to have been made in respect of the individual under the scheme in the year.][1]

Commentary—*Simon's Taxes* E7.201A.
Amendments—[1]   Sections 242C–242E inserted by FA 2017 s 9, Sch 3 para 1 with effect for the tax year 2017–18 and subsequent tax years.

[242E Investment-regulated non-UK registered schemes
For the purposes of the application of the taxable property provisions in relation to a non-UK registered scheme, property is taxable property in relation to the scheme if it would be taxable property in relation to the scheme were the scheme a registered pension scheme established in the United Kingdom.][1]

Commentary—*Simon's Taxes* E7.201A.
Amendments—[1]   Sections 242C–242E inserted by FA 2017 s 9, Sch 3 para 1 with effect for the tax year 2017–18 and subsequent tax years.

CHAPTER 6

SCHEMES THAT ARE NOT REGISTERED PENSION SCHEMES

Commentary—*Simon's Taxes* E7.247.

Non-UK schemes

243 Overseas pension schemes: migrant member relief
Schedule 33 contains provision about migrant member relief in respect of contributions under overseas pension schemes.

244 Non-UK schemes: application of certain charges

Schedule 34 contains provision applying certain charges under this Part in relation to non-UK schemes.

[Non-UK schemes: the overseas transfer charge

244A Overseas transfer charge

(1) A charge to income tax, to be known as the overseas transfer charge, arises where—

 (a) a recognised transfer is made to a QROPS, or

 (b) an onward transfer is made during the relevant period for the original transfer,

and the transfer is not excluded from the charge by or under any of sections 244B to 244H.

(2) Sections 244B to 244H are subject to section 244I (circumstances in which exclusions do not apply).

(3) In this group of sections, an "onward transfer" is a transfer of sums or assets held for the purposes of, or representing accrued rights under, an arrangement under a QROPS or former QROPS in relation to a member so as to become held for the purposes of, or to represent rights under, an arrangement under another QROPS in relation to that person as a member of that other QROPS.

(4) In this group of sections "relevant period" means—

 (a) in the case of a recognised transfer made on 6 April in any year, the 5 years beginning with the date of the transfer,

 (b) in the case of any other recognised transfer, the period consisting of the combination of—

  (i) the period beginning with the date of the transfer and ending immediately before the next 6 April, and

  (ii) the 5 years beginning at the end of that initial period,

 (c) in the case of an onward transfer, the period—

  (i) beginning with the date of the transfer, and

  (ii) ending at the end of the relevant period for the original transfer (see paragraphs (a) and (b) or, as the case may be, paragraphs (d) and (e)),

 (d) in the case of a relevant transfer that—

  (i) is made on 6 April in any year, and

  (ii) is the original transfer for an onward transfer,

 the 5 years beginning with the date of the relevant transfer, and

 (e) in the case of a relevant transfer that—

  (i) is made otherwise than on 6 April in any year, and

  (ii) is the original transfer for an onward transfer,

 the period consisting of the combination of: the period beginning with the date of the relevant transfer and ending immediately before the next 6 April; and the 5 years beginning at the end of that initial period.

(5) In this group of sections "the original transfer", in relation to an onward transfer, means (subject to subsection (6))—

 (a) the recognised transfer in respect of which the following conditions are met—

  (i) it is from a registered pension scheme to a QROPS,

  (ii) the sums and assets transferred by the onward transfer directly or indirectly derive from those transferred by it, and

  (iii) it is more recent than any other recognised transfer in respect of which the conditions in sub-paragraphs (i) and (ii) are met, or

 (b) where there is no such recognised transfer, the relevant transfer (see paragraph 1(6) of Schedule 34) in respect of which the following conditions are met—

  (i) it is from a relevant non-UK scheme (see paragraph 1(5) of Schedule 34),

  (ii) it is a transfer of the whole or part of the UK tax-relieved fund (see paragraph 3 of Schedule 34) of a member of the scheme,

  (iii) it is to a QROPS, and

  (iv) the sums and assets transferred by the onward transfer directly or indirectly derive from those transferred by it.

(6) Where apart from this subsection there would be different original transfers for different parts of an onward transfer, each such part of the onward transfer is to be treated as a separate onward transfer for the purposes of this group of sections.

(7) In this section and sections 244B to 244N—

 "QROPS" means a qualifying recognised overseas pension scheme, and "former QROPS" means a scheme that has at any time been a QROPS;

 "ring-fenced transfer fund", in relation to a QROPS or former QROPS, has the meaning given by paragraph 1 of Schedule 34;

 "this group of sections" means this section and sections 244B to 244N.][1]

Commentary—*Simon's Taxes* E7.248A, E4.1322, E7.247.

Amendments—[1] Sections 244A–244N inserted by FA 2017 s 10, Sch 4 para 11 with effect in relation to transfers made on or after 9 March 2017.

[244B Exclusion: member and receiving scheme in same country

(1) A recognised transfer to a QROPS is excluded from the overseas transfer charge if during the relevant period—

    (*a*) the member is resident in the country or territory in which the QROPS is established, and

    (*b*) there is no onward transfer—

        (i) for which the recognised transfer is the original transfer, and

        (ii) which is not excluded from the charge.

(2) If the member is resident in that country or territory at the time of the transfer mentioned in subsection (1), it is to be assumed for the purposes of subsection (1) that the member will be resident in that country or territory during the relevant period; but if, at a time before the end of the relevant period, the transfer ceases to be excluded by subsection (1) otherwise than by reason of the member's death—

    (*a*) that assumption is from that time no longer to be made, and

    (*b*) the charge on the transfer is treated as charged at that time.

(3) An onward transfer to a QROPS ("transfer A") is excluded from the overseas transfer charge if during so much of the relevant period as is after the time of transfer A—

    (*a*) the member is resident in the country or territory in which the QROPS is established, and

    (*b*) there is no subsequent onward transfer that—

        (i) is of sums and assets which, in whole or part, directly or indirectly derive from those transferred by transfer A, and

        (ii) is not excluded from the charge.

(4) If the member is resident in that country or territory at the time of transfer A, it is to be assumed for the purposes of subsection (3) that the member will be resident in that country or territory during so much of the relevant period as is after the time of transfer A; but if, at a time before the end of the relevant period, the transfer ceases to be excluded by subsection (3) otherwise than by reason of the member's death—

    (*a*) that assumption is from that time no longer to be made, and

    (*b*) the charge on transfer A is treated as charged at that time.][1]

Commentary—*Simon's Taxes* **E7.248A, E4.1322.**

Amendments—[1] Sections 244A–244N inserted by FA 2017 s 10, Sch 4 para 11 with effect in relation to transfers made on or after 9 March 2017.

[244C Exclusion: member and receiving scheme in EEA states

(1) This section applies to a transfer to a QROPS established in an EEA state.

(2) If the transfer is a recognised transfer, the transfer is excluded from the overseas transfer charge if during the relevant period—

    (*a*) the member is resident in an EEA state (whether or not the same EEA state throughout that period), and

    (*b*) there is no onward transfer—

        (i) for which the recognised transfer is the original transfer, and

        (ii) which is not excluded from the charge.

(3) If the member is resident in an EEA state at the time of the recognised transfer mentioned in subsection (2), it is to be assumed for the purposes of this section that the member will be resident in an EEA state during the relevant period; but if, at a time before the end of the relevant period, the transfer ceases to be excluded by subsection (2) otherwise than by reason of the member's death—

    (*a*) that assumption is from that time no longer to be made, and

    (*b*) the charge on the transfer is treated as charged at that time.

(4) If the transfer is an onward transfer ("transfer B"), the transfer is excluded from the overseas transfer charge if during so much of the relevant period as is after the time of the onward transfer—

    (*a*) the member is resident in an EEA state (whether or not the same EEA state at all those times), and

    (*b*) there is no subsequent onward transfer that—

        (i) is of sums and assets which, in whole or part, directly or indirectly derive from those transferred by transfer B, and

        (ii) is not excluded from the charge.

(5) If the member is resident in an EEA state at the time of transfer B, it is to be assumed for the purposes of subsection (4) that the member will be resident in an EEA state during so much of the relevant period as is after the time of transfer B; but if, at a time before the end of the relevant period, the transfer ceases to be excluded by subsection (4) otherwise than by reason of the member's death—

    (*a*) that assumption is from that time no longer to be made, and

    (*b*) the charge on transfer B is treated as charged at that time.][1]

Commentary—*Simon's Taxes* **E7.248A, E4.1322.**

Amendments—[1]   Sections 244A–244N inserted by FA 2017 s 10, Sch 4 para 11 with effect in relation to transfers made on or after 9 March 2017.

Prospective amendments—In the heading words "receiving scheme in EEA state, and member resident in UK or EEA state" to be substituted for words "member and receiving scheme in EEA states", in sub-ss (2)–(5) words "a relevant territory" to be substituted for words "an EEA state", in each place where the expression occurs, in sub-ss (2), (4) words "same relevant territory" to be substituted for words "same EEA state", and sub-s (6) to be inserted, by the Taxes (Amendments) (EU Exit) Regulations, SI 2019/689 reg 12(1), (2) with effect from Implementation Period completion day (see EU(WA)A 2020 Sch 5 para 1(1)). Sub-s (6) to read as follows—

"(6) In this section "relevant territory" means the United Kingdom or an EEA state.".

[244D Exclusion: receiving scheme is an occupational pension scheme

A transfer to a QROPS is excluded from the overseas transfer charge if—

    (*a*) the QROPS is an occupational pension scheme, and

    (*b*) when the transfer is made, the member is an employee of a sponsoring employer of the QROPS.][1]

Commentary—*Simon's Taxes* **E4.1322, E7.248A.**
Amendments—[1]   Sections 244A–244N inserted by FA 2017 s 10, Sch 4 para 11 with effect in relation to transfers made on or after 9 March 2017.

[244E Exclusion: receiving scheme set up by international organisation

(1) A transfer to a QROPS is excluded from the overseas transfer charge if—

    (*a*) the QROPS is established by an international organisation and has effect so as to provide benefits for, or in respect of, past service as an employee of the organisation, and

    (*b*) when the transfer is made, the member is an employee of the organisation.

(2) In this section "international organisation" means an organisation to which section 1 of the International Organisations Act 1968 applies by virtue of an Order in Council under subsection (1) of that section.][1]

Commentary—*Simon's Taxes* **E4.1322, E7.248A.**
Amendments—[1]   Sections 244A–244N inserted by FA 2017 s 10, Sch 4 para 11 with effect in relation to transfers made on or after 9 March 2017.

[244F Exclusion: receiving scheme is an overseas public service scheme

(1) A transfer to a QROPS is excluded from the overseas transfer charge if—

    (*a*) the QROPS is an overseas public service pension scheme, and

    (*b*) when the transfer is made, the member is an employee of an employer that participates in the scheme.

(2) A QROPS is an "overseas public service pension scheme" for the purposes of this section if—

    (*a*) either—

        (i) it is established by or under the law of the country or territory in which it is established, or

        (ii) it is approved by the government of that country or territory, and

    (*b*) it is established solely for the purpose of providing benefits to individuals for or in respect of services rendered to—

        (i) that country or territory, or

        (ii) any political subdivision or local authority of that country or territory.

(3) For the purposes of this section, an employer participates in a QROPS that is an overseas public service pension scheme if the scheme has effect so as to provide benefits to or in respect of any or all of the employees of the employer in respect of their employment by the employer.][1]

Commentary—*Simon's Taxes* **E4.1322, E7.248A.**
Amendments—[1]   Sections 244A–244N inserted by FA 2017 s 10, Sch 4 para 11 with effect in relation to transfers made on or after 9 March 2017.

[244G Exclusions: avoidance of double charge, and transitional protections

(1) A recognised transfer to a QROPS is excluded from the overseas transfer charge if it is made in execution of a request made before 9 March 2017.

(2) An onward transfer ("the current onward transfer") is excluded from the overseas transfer charge if—

    (*a*) the charge has been paid on the original transfer and the amount paid is not repayable, or

    (*b*) the charge has been paid on an onward transfer ("the earlier onward transfer") in respect of which the conditions in subsection (4) are met and the amount paid is not repayable, or

    (*c*) the original transfer was made before 9 March 2017, or

    (*d*) the original transfer was made on or after 9 March 2017 in execution of a request made before 9 March 2017.

(3) An onward transfer is excluded from the overseas transfer charge so far as the transfer is made otherwise than out of the member's ring-fenced transfer funds under the scheme from which the onward transfer is made.

(4) The conditions mentioned in subsection (2)(*b*) are—

    (*a*) that the earlier onward transfer was made before the current onward transfer,

    (*b*) that the earlier onward transfer was made after the original transfer, and (*c*) that all the sums and assets transferred by the current onward transfer directly or indirectly derive from those transferred by the earlier onward transfer.]¹

Commentary—*Simon's Taxes* **E4.1322, E7.248A**.
Amendments—¹ Sections 244A–244N inserted by FA 2017 s 10, Sch 4 para 11 with effect in relation to transfers made on or after 9 March 2017.

[244H Power to provide for further exclusions

The Commissioners for Her Majesty's Revenue and Customs may by regulations make provision for a recognised transfer to a QROPS, or an onward transfer, to be excluded from the overseas transfer charge if the transfer is of a description specified in the regulations.]¹

Commentary—*Simon's Taxes* **E7.248A**.
Amendments—¹ Sections 244A–244N inserted by FA 2017 s 10, Sch 4 para 11 with effect in relation to transfers made on or after 9 March 2017.

[244I Circumstances in which exclusions do not apply

(1) Subsection (2) applies if a recognised transfer to a QROPS, or an onward transfer, would (but for this section) be excluded from the overseas transfer charge by any of sections 244B to 244F.

(2) The transfer is not excluded from the charge if the member has, in connection with the transfer, failed to comply with the relevant information regulation.

(3) In subsection (2) "the relevant information regulation" means whichever of the following is applicable—

(*a*) regulation 11BA of the Registered Pension Schemes (Provision of Information) Regulations 2006 (SI 2006/567), or any regulation having effect in place of any of that regulation, as (in either case) from time to time amended, and

(*b*) regulation 3AE of the Pension Schemes (Information Requirements for Qualifying Overseas Pension Schemes, Qualifying Recognised Overseas Pension Schemes and Corresponding Relief) Regulations 2006 (SI 2006/208), or any regulation having effect in place of any of that regulation, as (in either case) from time to time amended.]¹

Commentary—*Simon's Taxes* **E4.1322, E7.248A**.
Amendments—¹ Sections 244A–244N inserted by FA 2017 s 10, Sch 4 para 11 with effect in relation to transfers made on or after 9 March 2017.

[244J Persons liable to charge

(1) In the case of a recognised transfer to a QROPS, the persons liable to the overseas transfer charge are—

(*a*) the scheme administrator of the registered pension scheme from which the transfer is made, and

(*b*) the member,

and their liability is joint and several.

(2) In the case of an onward transfer, the persons liable to the overseas transfer charge are—

(*a*) the scheme manager of the QROPS, or former QROPS, from which the transfer is made, and

(*b*) the member,

and their liability is joint and several.

(3) Subsections (1) and (2) are subject to subsection (4), and subsections (2) and (4) are subject to subsection (5).

(4) If a transfer is one required by section 244B or 244C to be initially assumed to be excluded by that section but an event occurring before the end of the relevant period means that the transfer is not so excluded, the persons liable to the overseas transfer charge in the case of the transfer are—

(*a*) the scheme manager of any QROPS, or former QROPS, under which the member has, at the time of the event, ring-fenced transfer funds in which any of the sums and assets referred to in section 244K(6) in the case of the transfer are represented, and

(*b*) the member,

and their liability is joint and several.

(5) The scheme manager of a former QROPS is liable to the overseas transfer charge in the case of a transfer ("the transfer concerned") only if the former QROPS—

(*a*) was a QROPS when a relevant inward transfer was made, and

(*b*) where a relevant inward transfer was made before 9 March 2017, was a QROPS at the start of 9 March 2017;

and here "relevant inward transfer" means a recognised or onwards transfer to the former QROPS (at a time when it was a QROPS) of sums and assets which, to any extent, are represented by sums or assets transferred by the transfer concerned.

(6) A person is liable to the overseas transfer charge whether or not—

(*a*) that person, and

(*b*) any other person who is liable to the charge,

are resident or domiciled in the United Kingdom.]¹

Commentary—*Simon's Taxes* **E7.248A**.

Amendments—[1]   Sections 244A–244N inserted by FA 2017 s 10, Sch 4 para 11 with effect in relation to transfers made on or after 9 March 2017.

[244K Amount of charge

(1) Where the overseas transfer charge arises in the case of a transfer, the charge is 25% of the transferred value.

(2) If the transfer is from a registered pension scheme established in the United Kingdom, the transferred value is the total of—

(*a*) the amount of any sums transferred, and

(*b*) the value of any assets transferred,

but this is subject to subsections (5) to (9).

(3) If the transfer is from a registered pension scheme established in a country or territory outside the United Kingdom, the transferred value is the total of—

(*a*) the amount of any sums transferred that are attributable to UK-relieved funds of the scheme, and

(*b*) the value of any assets transferred that are attributable to UK-relieved funds of the scheme,

but this is subject to subsections (5) to (9).

(4) If the transfer is from a QROPS or former QROPS, the transferred value is the total of—

(*a*) the amount of any sums transferred that are attributable to the member's ring-fenced transfer funds under the scheme, and

(*b*) the value of any assets transferred that are attributable to the member's ring-fenced transfer funds under the scheme,

but this is subject to subsections (5) to (9).

(5) If the lifetime allowance charge arises in the case of the transfer and is to be deducted from the transfer, paragraphs (*a*) and (*b*) of subsections (2) to (4) are to be read as referring to what is to be transferred after deduction of the lifetime allowance charge.

(6) If the transfer is one initially assumed to be excluded by section 244B or 244C but an event occurring before the end of the relevant period means that the transfer is not so excluded, the sums and assets mentioned in whichever of subsections (2) to (4) is applicable include only those that at the time of the event are represented in any of the member's ring-fenced transfer funds under any QROPS or former QROPS.

(7) If the operator pays the charge on the transfer and does so—

(*a*) otherwise than by deduction from the transfer, and

(*b*) out of sums and assets held for the purposes of, or representing accrued rights under, the scheme from which the transfer is made,

the transferred value is the amount given by subsections (2) to (6) grossed up by reference to the rate specified in subsection (1).

(8) If the operator pays the charge on the transfer and does so by deduction from the transfer, the transferred value is the amount given by subsections (2) to (6) before the deduction.

(9) If the member pays the charge on the transfer, the transferred value is the amount given by subsections (2) to (6) without any deduction for the charge.

(10) The provisions of this Part relating to the lifetime allowance charge apply (whether or not in relation to the transfer) as if the overseas transfer charge did not arise in the case of the transfer.

(11) In this section—

"the operator" means—

(*a*) the scheme administrator of the scheme from which the transfer is to be made if that scheme is a registered pension scheme, or

(*b*) the scheme manager of the scheme from which the transfer is to be made if that scheme is a QROPS or former QROPS;

"UK-relieved funds", in relation to a registered pension scheme established in a country or territory outside the United Kingdom, has the meaning given by section 242B.][1]

Commentary—*Simon's Taxes* E4.1322, E7.248A.

Amendments—[1]   Sections 244A–244N inserted by FA 2017 s 10, Sch 4 para 11 with effect in relation to transfers made on or after 9 March 2017.

[244L Accounting for overseas transfer charge by scheme managers

(1) In this section "charge" means overseas transfer charge for which the scheme manager of a QROPS or former QROPS is liable.

(2) The Commissioners for Her Majesty's Revenue and Customs may by regulations make provision for or in connection with—

(*a*) the payment of charge, including due dates for payment,

(*b*) the charging of interest on charge not paid on or before its due date,

(*c*) notification by the scheme manager of errors in information provided by the scheme manager to the Commissioners in connection with charge or the scheme manager's liability for overseas transfer charge,

(*d*) repayments to scheme managers under section 244M of amounts paid by way of charge, and

(e) the making of assessments, repayments or adjustments in cases where the correct amount of charge has not been paid by the due date for payment of the charge.

(3) The regulations may, in particular—

(a) modify the operation of any provision of the Tax Acts, or

(b) provide for the application of any provision of the Tax Acts (with or without modification).][1]

Commentary—*Simon's Taxes* E4.1322, E7.248A.

Amendments—[1] Sections 244A–244N inserted by FA 2017 s 10, Sch 4 para 11 with effect in relation to transfers made on or after 9 March 2017.

[244M Repayments of charge on subsequent excluding events

(1) This section applies if—

(a) overseas transfer charge arose on a transfer at the time the transfer was made, and

(b) at a time during the relevant period for the transfer, circumstances arise such that, had those circumstances existed at the time the transfer was made, the transfer would at the time it was made have been excluded from the charge by sections 244B to 244F or under section 244H.

(2) Any amount paid in respect of charge on the transfer is to be repaid by the Commissioners for Her Majesty's Revenue and Customs so far as not already repaid.

(3) Subsection (2) does not give rise to entitlement to repayment of, or cancellation of liabilities to, interest or penalties in respect of late payment of charge on the transfer.

(4) Repayment under this section to the scheme administrator of a registered pension scheme, or the scheme manager of a QROPS or former QROPS, is conditional on prior compliance with any requirements to give information to the Commissioners, about the circumstances in which the right to the repayment arises, that are imposed on the prospective recipient under section 169 or 251 (but repayment is not conditional on compliance with any time limits so imposed for compliance with any such requirements).

(5) Repayment under this section is not a relievable pension contribution.

(6) Repayment under this section to the member is conditional on making a claim, and such a claim must be made no later than one year after the end of the relevant period for the transfer concerned.

(7) The Commissioners for Her Majesty's Revenue and Customs may by regulations make provision for or in connection with claims or repayments under this section, including provision—

(a) requiring claims,

(b) about who may claim,

(c) imposing conditions for making claims, including conditions about time limits,

(d) as to additional circumstances in which repayments may be made,

(e) modifying the operation of any provision of the Tax Acts, or

(f) applying any provision of the Tax Acts (with or without modifications).][1]

Commentary—*Simon's Taxes* E7.248A.

Regulations—Pension Schemes (Information Requirements – Repayment of Overseas Transfer Charge) Regulations, SI 2019/774.

Amendments—[1] Sections 244A–244N inserted by FA 2017 s 10, Sch 4 para 11 with effect in relation to transfers made on or after 9 March 2017.

[244N Discharge of liability of scheme administrator or manager

(1) In this section "operator" means—

(a) the scheme administrator of a registered pension scheme, or

(b) the scheme manager of a QROPS or former QROPS.

(2) If an operator is liable under section 244J, the operator may apply to an officer of Revenue and Customs for the discharge of the operator's liability on the following ground.

(3) The ground is that—

(a) the operator reasonably believed that there was no liability to the overseas transfer charge on the transfer concerned, and

(b) in all the circumstances of the case, it would not be just and reasonable for the operator to be liable to the charge on the transfer.

(4) On receiving an application under subsection (2), an officer of Revenue and Customs must decide whether to discharge the operator's liability.

(5) An officer of Revenue and Customs must notify the operator of the decision on the application.

(6) The discharge of the operator's liability does not affect the liability of any other person to overseas transfer charge on the transfer concerned.

(7) The Commissioners for Her Majesty's Revenue and Customs may by regulations make provision supplementing this section, including provision for time limits for making an application under this section.][1]

Commentary—*Simon's Taxes* E7.248A.

Amendments—[1] Sections 244A–244N inserted by FA 2017 s 10, Sch 4 para 11 with effect in relation to transfers made on or after 9 March 2017.

Employer-financed retirement benefit schemes

245 Restriction of deduction for contributions by employer

(1) Schedule 24 to the Finance Act 2003 (c 14) (restriction of deductions for employee benefit contributions) is amended as follows.

(2) *(amended FA 2003 Sch 24 para 1(2)(b); repealed by FA 2007 s 114, Sch 27 Pt 2(5))*

(3) *(inserts FA 2003 Sch 24 para 2(1)(c))*

(4) *(amends FA 2003 Sch 24 para 2(5))*

(5) *(substitutes FA 2003 Sch 24 para 8(b), (c))*

(6) *(amends FA 2003 Sch 24 para 9(1))*

(7), (8) *(amend FA 2003 Sch 24 para 9(1))*

Commentary—*Simon's Taxes* E7.224.

Modifications—Taxation of Pension Schemes (Transitional Provisions) Order, SI 2006/572 arts 15, 16 (employers or employees with pre-commencement entitlement to corresponding relief: modification of this section in relation to such cases).

246 Restriction of deduction for non-contributory provision

(1) This section applies in relation to an employer's expenses of providing benefits to or in respect of present or former employees under an employer-financed retirement benefits scheme in a case where—

    (a) the expenses do not consist of the making of contributions under the scheme, but

    (b) in accordance with generally accepted accounting practice they are shown in the employer's accounts.

(2) Unless the benefits are ones in respect of which a person is, on receipt, chargeable to income tax, the expenses—

    (a) are not deductible in computing the amount of the profits of the employer for the purposes of [Part 2 of ITTOIA 2005][1] [or Part 3 of CTA 2009 (trading income)][2],

    (b) are not expenses of management of the employer for the purposes of [Chapter 2 of Part 16 of CTA 2009][2] (expenses of management: companies with investment business), and

    [(c) are not to count as ordinary BLAGAB management expenses of the employer for an accounting period for the purposes of section 76 of FA 2012.][3]

(3) But where the benefits are ones in respect of which a person is, on receipt, chargeable to income tax—

    (a) if the expenses are allowed to be deducted in computing the amount of the profits of the employer to be charged under [Part 2 of ITTOIA 2005][1] [or Part 3 of CTA 2009 (trading income),][2] they are deductible in computing the amount of the profits for the period of account in which they are paid, and

    (b) for the purposes of the operation of [in relation to the employer of [section 76 of FA 2012][3] or Chapter 2 of Part 16 of CTA 2009,][2] the expenses are referable to the accounting period in which they are paid.

(4) In this section "employer-financed retirement benefits scheme" has the same meaning as in Chapter 2 of Part 6 of ITEPA 2003 (see section 393A of that Act).

Commentary—*Simon's Taxes* E7.247, E7.252.

Amendments—[1] Words in sub-ss (2)(a), (3)(a) inserted by ITTOIA 2005 s 882(1), Sch 1 paras 629, 650. This amendment comes into force at the same time as this section: ITTOIA 2005 Sch 2 para 161.

[2] In sub-s (2)(a) words substituted for words "(trading income) or Case I or II of Schedule D", in sub-s (2)(b) words substituted for words "section 75 of ICTA", in sub-s (3)(a) words substituted for words "(trading income) or Case I or II of Schedule D," and in sub-s (3)(b) words substituted for words "of section 75 or 76 of ICTA in relation to the employer," by CTA 2009 s 1322, Sch 1 paras 569, 578. CTA 2009 applies for accounting periods ending on or after 1 April 2009 (for corporation tax purposes) and for tax years 2009–10 onwards (for income and capital gains tax purposes).

[3] In sub-s (2), para (c) substituted and in sub-s (3)(b) words substituted for words "section 76 of ICTA" by FA 2012 s 146, Sch 16 paras 112, 120 with effect in relation to accounting periods of companies beginning on or after 1 January 2013 (subject to transitional provisions in FA 2012 Sch 17). For accounting periods straddling 1 January 2013, see FA 2012 s 149.

[246A Case where no relief for provision by an employer

(1) An employer's expenses of providing relevant benefits to or in respect of a present or former employee ("the employee") under an employer-financed retirement benefits scheme (whether or not by the making of contributions under the scheme) are not subject to relief if subsection (2) applies.

(2) This subsection applies where—

    (a) the provision of the relevant benefits results in a reduction in the benefits payable to or in respect of the employee under a registered pension scheme, or

    (b) a reduction in the benefits payable to or in respect of the employee under a registered pension scheme results in the provision of the relevant benefits.

(3) But if the extent to which contributions paid by the employer under the registered pension scheme in respect of the employee are subject to relief has been restricted in accordance with regulations under section 196A, the employer's expenses of providing the relevant benefits are not prevented from being subject to relief to the extent that is just and reasonable.

(4) The references in this section to expenses of an employer being subject to relief are to—

(a) their being deductible in computing the amount of the profits of the employer for the purposes of Part 2 of ITTOIA 2005 [or Part 3 of CTA 2009 (trading income)][2],

(b) their being expenses of management of the employer for the purposes of [Chapter 2 of Part 16 of CTA 2009][2] (expenses of management: companies with investment business), or

(c) their being [ordinary BLAGAB management expenses of the employer for an accounting period for the purposes of section 76 of FA 2012][3],

(depending on which is appropriate in relation to the employer).

(5) In this section—

"employer-financed retirement benefits scheme", and

"relevant benefits",

have the same meaning as in Chapter 2 of Part 6 of ITEPA 2003 (see sections 393A and 393B of that Act).][1]

Commentary—*Simon's Taxes* E7.247, E7.253.

Amendments—[1]   Section inserted by FA 2005 s 101, Sch 10 paras 40, 64(1) with effect from 6 April 2006.

[2]   In sub-s (4)(a) words substituted for words "(trading income) or Case I or II of Schedule D", and in sub-s (4)(b) words substituted for words "section 75 of ICTA", by CTA 2009 s 1322, Sch 1 paras 569, 579. CTA 2009 applies for accounting periods ending on or after 1 April 2009 (for corporation tax purposes) and for tax years 2009–10 onwards (for income and capital gains tax purposes).

[3]   In sub-s(4)(c), words substituted for words "brought into account at Step 1 in section 76(7) of ICTA (expenses of insurance companies) in respect of the employer" by FA 2012 s 146, Sch 16 paras 112, 121 with effect in relation to accounting periods of companies beginning on or after 1 January 2013 (subject to transitional provisions in FA 2012 Sch 17). For accounting periods straddling 1 January 2013, see FA 2012 s 149.

247 Abolition of income tax charge in respect of employer payments

In Part 6 of ITEPA 2003, omit Chapter 1 (payments by employer for the provision of benefits for an employee under certain schemes to count as employment income of employee).

Commentary—*Simon's Taxes* E7.247, E7.252.

248 Employer's cost of insuring against non-payment of benefit

(1) Section 307 of ITEPA 2003 (no liability to income tax in respect of chargeable benefit on provision made by employer for a retirement or death benefit) is amended as follows.

(2) (*inserts* ITEPA 2003 s 307(1A), (1B))

(3) In subsection (2), for "subsection (1)" substitute "this section".

Commentary—*Simon's Taxes* E7.247.

249 Taxation of non-pension benefits

(1) Chapter 2 of Part 6 of ITEPA 2003 (taxation of non-pension benefits from certain pension schemes) is amended as follows.

(2) In the heading of the Chapter, for "NON-APPROVED PENSION" substitute "EMPLOYER-FINANCED RETIREMENT BENEFITS".

(3) (*substitutes* ITEPA 2003 ss 393–393B)

(4) Section 394 (charge on benefit) is amended as follows.

(5) (*inserts* ITEPA 2003 s 394(1A))

(6), (7) (*amend* ITEPA 2003 s 394(2), (3))

(8) (*inserts* ITEPA 2003 s 395)

(9), (10) (*amend* ITEPA 2003 s 399(1), (2))

(11) (*substitutes* ITEPA 2003 ss 399A, 400)

(12) (*amends* ITEPA 2003 Sch 1 Part 2)

CHAPTER 7

COMPLIANCE

Information

250 Registered pension scheme return

(1) The Inland Revenue may, in relation to any tax year, by notice require the scheme administrator of a registered pension scheme—

(a) to make and deliver to the Inland Revenue a return containing any information reasonably required by the notice, and

(b) to deliver with the return any accounts, statements or other documents relating to information contained in the return which may reasonably be required by the notice.

(2) The information that may be required to be included in the return is any information relating to—

(a) contributions made under the pension scheme,

(b) transfers of sums or assets held for the purposes of, or representing accrued rights under, another pension scheme so as to become held for the purposes of, or to represent rights under, the pension scheme,

(c) income and gains derived from investments or deposits held for the purposes of the pension scheme, (*d*) other receipts of the pension scheme,

(*e*) the sums and other assets held for the purposes of the pension scheme,

(*f*) the liabilities of the pension scheme,

(*g*) the provision of benefits by the pension scheme,

(*h*) transfers of sums or assets held for the purposes of, or representing accrued rights under, the pension scheme so as to become held for the purposes of, or to represent rights under, another pension scheme,

(*i*) other expenditure of the pension scheme,

(*j*) the membership of the pension scheme, or

(*k*) any other matter relating to the administration of the pension scheme.

(3) The information that may be required to be included in the return may be limited to information concerning any particular arrangement or arrangements under the pension scheme.

(4) The notice must specify the period to be covered by the return.

(5) The period may be—

(*a*) the whole or any specified part of the tax year, or

(*b*) if audited accounts of the pension scheme have been prepared for any period or periods ending in the tax year, the period or periods covered by the accounts.

(6) "Audited accounts" means accounts audited by a person of a description specified in regulations made by the Board of Inland Revenue.

(7) A return relating to the whole or part of, or to a period or periods ending in, a tax year must be delivered—

(*a*) where the notice requiring the return is given after the 31st October in the next tax year, before the end of the period of three months beginning with the day on which the notice is given, and

(*b*) otherwise, not later than the 31st January in the next tax year (but subject as follows).

(8) If, in a case within paragraph (*b*) of subsection (7), the winding-up of the pension scheme has been completed before 31st October in the next tax year, the return must be delivered before the end of the period of three months beginning with the day on which the winding-up is completed.

(9) But subsection (8) does not apply if the end of that period is before the end of the period of three months beginning with the day on which the notice is given; and in that case the return must be delivered before the end of that period.

Commentary—*Simon's Taxes* **E7.243**.

HMRC Manuals—Pensions Tax Manual PTM163000 (the pension scheme return),

Regulations—Registered Pension Schemes (Audited Accounts) (Specified Persons) Regulations, SI 2005/3456.

Registered Pension Schemes (Audited Accounts) (Specified Persons) Regulations, SI 2015/1518.

251 Information: general requirements

(1) The Board of Inland Revenue may by regulations make provision requiring persons of a prescribed description—

(*a*) to provide to the Inland Revenue, in a form specified by the Board of Inland Revenue, information of a prescribed description relating to any of the matters mentioned in subsection (2), and

(*b*) to preserve for a prescribed period any documents relating to such information.

(2) Those matters are—

(*a*) any matter relating to a registered pension scheme,

(*b*) any matter relating to a pension scheme which has ceased to be a registered pension scheme,

(*c*) any matter relating to a pension scheme in relation to which an application for registration has been made,

(*d*) any matter relating to an annuity purchased with sums or assets held for the purposes of a registered pension scheme,

(*e*) the coming into operation of an employer-financed retirement benefits scheme, and

(*f*) the provision of relevant benefits under an employer-financed retirement benefits scheme.

(3) In subsection (2)—

"employer-financed retirement benefits scheme", and "relevant benefits",

have the same meaning as in Chapter 2 of Part 6 of ITEPA 2003 (see sections 393A and 393B of that Act).

(4) The Board of Inland Revenue may by regulations make provision—

(*a*) requiring scheme administrators of registered pension schemes or other persons of a prescribed description to provide information of a prescribed description to persons of such of the descriptions mentioned in subsection (5) as are prescribed [or to the scheme administrators of other registered pension schemes][1], . . .[3]

(*b*) requiring persons of such of the descriptions specified in subsection (5) as are prescribed to provide information of a prescribed description to the scheme administrators of registered pension schemes, [(*ba*) requiring, in a case where a payment ("the onwards payment") is made directly or indirectly out of a sum on whose payment tax has been charged under section 206, the person making the onwards payment to provide information of a prescribed description to the person to whom the onwards payment is made,]⁴

[(*c*) requiring scheme administrators of registered pension schemes to provide information of a prescribed description to scheme managers of qualifying recognised overseas pension schemes, or

(*d*) requiring members or former members of a relevant non-UK pension scheme to provide information to the scheme administrators, or scheme managers, of registered pension schemes or other relevant non-UK pension schemes.]³

(5) Those persons are—

    (*a*) members of a registered pension scheme,

    [(*aa*) employers of members of a registered pension scheme,]²

    (*b*) persons who have ceased to be members of a registered pension scheme,

    (*c*) persons to whom benefits under a registered pension scheme are being, or have been, provided,

    (*d*) the personal representatives of any person within paragraphs (*a*) to (*c*), and

    (*e*) insurance companies who pay annuities purchased with sums or assets held for the purposes of registered pension schemes.

(6) "Prescribed", in relation to regulations, means prescribed by the regulations[; and "relevant non-UK scheme" has the meaning given by paragraph 1 of Schedule 34]³.

Commentary—*Simon's Taxes* **E7.239, E7.243, E7.244.**

HMRC Manuals—Pensions Tax Manual PTM063600 (reporting scheme wind-up to HMRC). PTM063210 (reporting payment of a pension commencement lump sum to HMRC).
Employment Income Manual EIM15200 (employer-financed retirement benefit schemes, reporting responsibilities).

Regulations—Employer-Financed Retirement Benefits Schemes (Provision of Information) Regulations, SI 2005/3453.
Registered Pension Schemes (Enhanced Lifetime Allowance) Regulations, SI 2006/131.
Registered Pension Schemes (Provision of Information) Regulations, SI 2006/567.
Registered Pension Schemes and Overseas Pension Schemes (Miscellaneous Amendments) Regulations, SI 2012/884.
Registered Pension Schemes and Relieved Non-UK Pension Schemes (Lifetime Allowance Transitional Protection) (Notification) Regulations, SI 2013/1741.
Registered Pension Schemes (Provision of Information) (Amendment) Regulations, SI 2013/1742.
Registered Pension Schemes and Relieved Non-UK Pension Schemes (Lifetime Allowance Transitional Protection) (Individual Protection 2014 Notification) Regulations, SI 2014/1842.
Registered Pension Schemes (Provision of Information) (Amendment) Regulations, SI 2014/1843.
Registered Pension Schemes (Provision of Information) (Amendment) Regulations, SI 2015/606.
Overseas Pension Schemes (Miscellaneous Amendments) Regulations, SI 2015/673.
Registered Pension Schemes (Provision of Information) (Amendment No 2) Regulations, SI 2015/1455.
Registered Pension Schemes (Provision of Information) (Amendment) Regulations, SI 2016/308.
Registered Pension Schemes (Provision of Information) (Amendment) Regulations, SI 2017/11.
Registered Pension Schemes and Overseas Pension Schemes (Miscellaneous Amendments) Regulations, 2018/5.

Amendments—¹ Words in sub-s (4)(*a*) inserted by FA 2005 s 101, Sch 10 paras 47, 64(1) with effect from 6 April 2006.
² Sub-s (5)(*aa*) inserted by FA 2010 s 49 with effect from 8 April 2010.
³ In sub-s (4), word "and" at end of para (*a*) repealed, paras (*c*), (*d*) inserted, and in sub-s (6) words inserted, by the Taxation of Pensions Act 2014 s 1, Sch 1 para 93 with effect from 17 December 2014.
⁴ Sub-s (4)(*ba*) inserted by F(No 2)A 2015 s 21(6) with effect in relation to lump sums paid on or after 6 April 2016.

Accounting and assessment

254 Accounting for tax by scheme administrators

(1) A scheme administrator of a registered pension scheme must make returns to the Inland Revenue of the income tax to which the scheme administrator is liable under this Part.

(2) A return is to be made for each period of three months ending with 31st March, 30th June, 30th September or 31st December if tax has been charged on the scheme administrator by virtue of this Part in that period.

(3) A return for any period must be made before the end of the period of 45 days beginning with the day immediately following the end of that period.

(4) A return must—

    (*a*) show the income tax to which the scheme administrator is liable, and

    (*b*) include such particulars of the events or other circumstances giving rise to the liability (including particulars as to the persons to whom the events or other circumstances relate) as are required to be included in returns under this section by regulations made by the Board of Inland Revenue.

(5) The income tax required to be shown in a return is due at the time by which the return is to be made and is payable without the making of an assessment.

(6) The Board of Inland Revenue may by regulations make provision for and in connection with—

    (*a*) the charging of interest on tax due under this section which is not paid on or before the due date, (*b*) the making of amended returns by scheme administrators in the event of error in a return under this section,

    [(*ba*) repayments under section 244M to scheme administrators,][2]

    (*c*) the making of assessments, repayments or adjustments in cases where the correct tax due under this section has not been paid on or before the due date, and

    (*d*) otherwise for supplementing this section.

(7) The regulations may, in particular—

    (*a*) modify the operation of any provision of the Tax Acts, or

    (*b*) provide for the application of any provision of the Tax Acts (with or without modifications).

[(7A) Where a scheme administrator is liable under section 237B in respect of the annual allowance charge for a tax year, for the purposes of subsection (2) the tax is to be taken to be charged on the scheme administrator in the period ending with 31 December in the year following that in which that tax year ended (or such earlier period as the scheme administrator may elect in a return for that earlier period).

(7B) But if the notice which gave rise to the liability is amended in accordance with regulations under section 237B(5)(*c*), any additional tax to which the scheme administrator becomes liable is to be taken for the purposes of subsection (2) to be charged in the later of the period in which it is taken to be charged by virtue of subsection (7A) and the period in which the scheme administrator receives notice of the amendment.][1]

(8) References in this section to the income tax to which a scheme administrator is liable under this Part do not include any to which the scheme administrator is liable under section 239 (scheme sanction charge).

(9) Where the registration of a registered pension scheme has been withdrawn, this section has effect as if references to the scheme administrator were to the person who was, or each of the persons who were, the scheme administrator immediately before the registration was withdrawn.

Commentary—*Simon's Taxes* **A4.560, E7.243**.
HMRC Manuals—Pensions Tax Manual PTM162100 (essential principles).
PTM162300 (payment of tax reported on the accounting for tax return).
PTM08600 (how the scheme administrator accounts for the lifetime allowance charge).
PTM145200 (accounting for and paying the authorised surplus payments charge).
Regulations—Registered Pension Schemes (Accounting and Assessment) Regulations, SI 2005/3454.
Registered Pension Schemes (Reduction in Pension Rates, Accounting and Assessment) (Amendment) Regulations, SI 2013/1111.
Modifications—Registered Pension Schemes (Splitting of Schemes) Regulations, SI 2006/569 reg 3 (modification of this provision in relation to sub-scheme administrators).

Amendments—[1] Sub-ss (7A), (7B) inserted by FA 2011 s 66, Sch 17 paras 1, 18 with effect for the tax year 2011–12 and subsequent tax years, and in relation to pension input periods ending in the tax year 2011–12 but beginning earlier (or in 2011–12). For transitional provisions see FA 2011 Sch 17 paras 28–34.

[2] Sub-s (6)(*ba*) inserted by FA 2017 s 10, Sch 4 paras 12, 15 with effect in relation to transfers made on or after 9 March 2017. Note that overseas transfer charge on transfers made in the period beginning with 9 March 2017 and ending with 30 June 2017 is, for the purposes of this section, to be treated as charged in the three months ending with 30 September 2017 if it would otherwise be considered for those purposes as charged in an earlier period (FA 2017 Sch 4 para 25(5)).

255 Assessments under this Part

(1) The Board of Inland Revenue may by regulations make provision for and in connection with the making of assessments in respect of—

    (*a*) the unauthorised payments charge,

    (*b*) the unauthorised payments surcharge,

    (*c*) liability to the lifetime allowance charge under section 217(2) (person to whom lump sum death benefit paid),

    [(*ca*) liability to the annual allowance charge by virtue of section 237B,][1]

    (*d*) the scheme sanction charge,

    [(*da*) liability of the scheme administrator of a registered pension scheme, or the scheme manager of a qualifying recognised overseas pension scheme or of a former such scheme, to the overseas transfer charge,][3]

    (*e*) liability under section 272 (trustees etc liable as scheme administrator),

    [(*ea*) liability under section 272C (former scheme administrator to retain liability in cases involving independent trustees etc),][2]

    (*f*) liability under section 273 (member liable as scheme administrator), and

    (*g*) liability under section 394 of ITEPA 2003 (benefit under employer-financed retirement benefits scheme: charge on responsible person).

(2) The provision that may be made by the regulations includes (in particular) provision for the charging of interest on tax due under such assessments which remains unpaid.

(3) The regulations may, in particular—

    (*a*) modify the operation of any provision of the Tax Acts, or

    (*b*) provide for the application of any provision of the Tax Acts (with or without modification).

Commentary—*Simon's Taxes* **E7.246**.
HMRC Manuals—Pensions Tax Manual PTM135300 (reporting the scheme sanction charge).

Regulations—Registered Pension Schemes (Accounting and Assessment) Regulations, SI 2005/3454.
Registered Pension Schemes (Accounting and Assessment) (Amendment) Regulations, SI 2014/1928.
Amendments—[1]   Sub-s (1)(*ca*) inserted by FA 2011 s 66, Sch 17 paras 1, 19 with effect for the tax year 2011–12 and
subsequent tax years, and in relation to pension input periods ending in the tax year 2011–12 but beginning earlier (or in
2011–12). For transitional provisions see FA 2011 Sch 17 paras 28–34.
[2]   Sub-s (1)(*ea*) inserted by FA 2014 s 43, Sch 5 paras 1, 17 with effect from 17 July 2014.
[3]   Sub-s (1)(*da*) inserted by FA 2017 s 10, Sch 4 paras 12, 16 with effect from 9 March 2017.

[Payment

255A Electronic payment

(1) The Board of Inland Revenue may give directions requiring specified persons to use electronic means for the making of specified payments required to be made under or by virtue of this Part.
(2) Directions under this section may make provision—

(*a*) as to conditions that must be complied with in connection with the use of electronic means for the making of any payment,
(*b*) for treating a payment as not having been made unless conditions imposed by the directions are satisfied, and
(*c*) for determining the time when a payment in accordance with directions under this section is to be taken to be made.

(3) Directions under this section may also make provision (which may include provision for the application of conclusive or other presumptions) as to the manner of proving for any purpose—

(*a*) whether any use of electronic means for making a payment is to be taken as having resulted in the payment being made,
(*b*) the time of the making of any payment for the making of which electronic means have been used, and
(*c*) any other matter for which provision may be made by directions under this section.

(4) Directions under this section—

(*a*) may be specific or general, and
(*b*) may provide that the conditions of any authorisation or requirement imposed by the directions are to be taken to be satisfied only where the Inland Revenue is satisfied as to specified matters.

(5) Directions under this section may—

(*a*) suspend for any period during which the use of electronic means for the making of payments is impossible or impractical, any requirements imposed by the directions relating to the use of such means,
(*b*) substitute alternative requirements for the suspended ones, and
(*c*) make any provision that is necessary in consequence of the imposition of the substituted requirements.

(6) Directions under this section may—

(*a*) make different provision for different cases,
(*b*) make such incidental, supplementary, consequential and transitional provision in connection with any provision contained in such directions as the Board of Inland Revenue thinks fit.

(7) In this section—

"the Inland Revenue" includes any person who for the purposes of the electronic means of payment is acting under the authority of the Board of Inland Revenue, and
"specified" means specified in a direction under this section.][1]

Commentary—*Simon's Taxes* E7.243.
Amendments—[1]   Sections 255A, 255B inserted by FA 2005 s 101, Sch 10 paras 48, 64(1) with effect from 6 April 2006.

[255B Payments to be cleared payments

(1) A payment made to the Board of Inland Revenue or the Inland Revenue under or by virtue of this Part (otherwise than in cash) is to be treated as not having been made until the earliest date on or before which all the transactions that need to be completed before the whole amount of the payment becomes available to the Board are capable of being completed.
(2) In this section "the Inland Revenue" includes any person who is acting under the authority of the Board of Inland Revenue.][1]

Commentary—*Simon's Taxes* E7.243.
HMRC Manuals—Debt Management and Banking Manual DMBM570260 (accounting for tax charges).
Amendments—[1]   Sections 255A, 255B inserted by FA 2005 s 101, Sch 10 paras 48, 64(1) with effect from 6 April 2006.

Registration regulations

256 Enhanced lifetime allowance regulations

(1) This section applies to regulations made by the Board of Inland Revenue under—

(*a*) section 220(5) (lifetime allowance enhancement: registration of pension credits),
(*b*) section 221(6) (lifetime allowance enhancement: individuals who are not always relevant UK individuals),
(*c*) section 224(9) (lifetime allowance enhancement: transfers from recognised overseas pension scheme),

    (*d*)   paragraph 7(1)(*b*) [or 11A(1)(*c*)][1] of Schedule 36 (lifetime allowance enhancement: primary protection),

    (*e*)   paragraph 12(1) [or 15A(1)(*b*)][1] of that Schedule (lifetime allowance: enhanced protection), and

    (*f*)   paragraph 18(6) of that Schedule (lifetime allowance enhancement: pre-commencement pension credits).

(2) The regulations to which this section applies are referred to in this Part as "enhanced lifetime allowance regulations".

(3) Enhanced lifetime allowance regulations may include any provision that appears appropriate for securing that the correct tax is charged—

    (*a*)   by way of the lifetime allowance charge in respect of amounts crystallised by benefit crystallisation events, and

    (*b*)   in respect of the payment of lump sums by registered pension schemes.

(4) Enhanced lifetime allowance regulations may, for that purpose, in particular contain provision—

    (*a*)   requiring any person to produce or make available documents, produce certificates or provide information, and

    (*b*)   for the review from time to time of any matter registered in accordance with the regulations.

Regulations—Registered Pension Schemes (Enhanced Lifetime Allowance) Regulations, SI 2006/131.
Registered Pension Schemes (Provision of Information) Regulations, SI 2006/567.
Amendments—[1]   Words in sub-s (1)(*d*), (*e*) inserted by FA 2006 s 161, Sch 23 paras 37, 42. These amendments are deemed to have come into force on 6 April 2006.

Penalties

257 Registered pension scheme return

(1) If the scheme administrator of a registered pension scheme fails to comply with a notice under section 250 (registered pension scheme return), the scheme administrator is liable to a penalty of £100.

(2) If the failure continues after a penalty is imposed under subsection (1), the scheme administrator is liable to a further penalty not exceeding £60 for each day on which the failure continues after the day on which that penalty was imposed (but excluding any day for which a penalty under this subsection has already been imposed).

(3) No penalty may be imposed under subsection (1) or (2) in respect of a failure after it has been remedied.

(4) If the scheme administrator of a registered pension scheme fraudulently or negligently—

    (*a*)   makes an [inaccurate][1] return required by a notice under section 250, or

    (*b*)   delivers any [inaccurate][1] accounts, statements or other documents with such a return,

the scheme administrator is liable to a penalty not exceeding £3,000.

Commentary—*Simon's Taxes* E7.250.
HMRC Manuals—Pensions Tax Manual PTM163000 (what happens if the pension scheme return isn't filed on time or is inaccurate).
Modifications—Registered Pension Schemes (Splitting of Schemes) Regulations, SI 2006/569 reg 3 (modification of this provision in relation to sub-scheme administrators).
Amendments—[1]   In sub-s (4)(*a*), (*b*) word substituted for word "incorrect" by FA 2014 s 46, Sch 7 paras 1, 23(*b*) with effect from 17 July 2014.

258 Information required by regulations

(1) (*amends* TMA 1970 s 98)

(2) A person who fails to comply with regulations under section 251(1)(*b*) (preservation of documents) is liable to a penalty not exceeding £3,000.

Commentary—*Simon's Taxes* E7.250.
HMRC Manuals—Pensions Tax Manual PTM160200 (retention of records).
PTM160200 (retention of records).
PTM159000 (failure to preserve documents).
Modifications—Registered Pension Schemes (Splitting of Schemes) Regulations, SI 2006/569 reg 3 (modification of this provision in relation to sub-scheme administrators).

261 Enhanced lifetime allowance regulations: documents and information

(1) This section applies where an individual fraudulently or negligently—

    (*a*)   produces or makes available an [inaccurate][1] document, or produces an [inaccurate][1] certificate, in connection with any matter registered in accordance with enhanced lifetime allowance regulations, or

    (*b*)   provides false information in connection with any such matter,

and the condition in subsection (2) is met.

(2) The condition is that—

    (*a*)   the amount of the individual's lifetime allowance at the time which is relevant for the purposes of this paragraph, or

    (*b*)   the amount of the pension commencement lump sums to which the individual may be entitled at the time which is relevant for the purposes of this paragraph, would be greater than it actually is were the document or certificate correct or the information true.

(3) The individual is liable to a penalty not exceeding 25% of the relevant excess.

(4) In a case within paragraph (*a*) of subsection (2), the relevant excess is the difference between what would be the amount of the individual's lifetime allowance at the time which is relevant for the purposes of that paragraph (were the document or certificate correct or the information true) and whichever is the higher of—

    (*a*) the actual amount of the individual's lifetime allowance at that time, and

    (*b*) the standard lifetime allowance at that time.

(5) The time which is relevant for the purposes of paragraph (*a*) of subsection (2)—

    (*a*) where a benefit crystallisation event has occurred in relation to the individual since the document was produced or made available, the certificate produced or the information provided (but before a penalty under this section is imposed), is the time when the benefit crystallisation event occurred, and

    (*b*) otherwise, is the time when the document was produced or made available, the certificate produced or the information provided.

(6) In a case within paragraph (*b*) of subsection (2), the relevant excess is the difference between—

    (*a*) what would be the amount of the pension commencement lump sums to which the individual may be entitled at the time which is relevant for the purposes of that paragraph (were the document or certificate correct or the information true), and

    (*b*) the actual amount at that time of the pension commencement lump sums to which the individual may be entitled.

(7) The time which is relevant for the purposes of paragraph (*b*) of subsection (2) is the time when the document was produced or made available, the certificate produced or the information provided.

Commentary—*Simon's Taxes* E7.250.

HMRC Manuals—Pensions Tax Manual PTM160800 (provision of inaccurate documents in relation to a requirement under the enhanced lifetime allowance regulations).

PTM164200 (the member must provide information about any lifetime allowance protection they have).

Amendments—[1] In sub-s (1)(*a*) word substituted for word "incorrect", in both places, by FA 2014 s 46, Sch 7 paras 1, 23(*c*) with effect from 17 July 2014.

262 Enhanced lifetime allowance regulations: failures to comply

An individual who fails—

    (*a*) to produce or make available any document required to be produced by enhanced lifetime allowance regulations,

    (*b*) to produce any certificate required to be produced by enhanced lifetime allowance regulations, or

    (*c*) to provide any information required to be provided by enhanced lifetime allowance regulations,

is liable to a penalty not exceeding £3,000.

Commentary—*Simon's Taxes* E7.250.

HMRC Manuals—Pensions Tax Manual PTM160800 (failure to comply with the enhanced lifetime allowance regulations).

263 Lifetime allowance enhanced protection: benefit accrual

(1) This section applies where—

    (*a*) paragraph 12 of Schedule 36 (lifetime allowance charge: enhanced protection) applies in relation to an individual, and

    (*b*) relevant benefit accrual occurs in relation to the individual (as to which see paragraph 13 of that Schedule).

(2) If the individual fails to notify the Inland Revenue of the relevant benefit accrual within the period of 90 days beginning with the day on which it occurs, the individual is liable to a penalty not exceeding £3,000.

Commentary—*Simon's Taxes* E7.203, E7.250.

HMRC Manuals—Pensions Tax Manual PTM160400 (requirement to tell HMRC about relevant benefit accrual).

PTM160800 (failure to notify loss of enhanced protection due to relevant benefit accrual).

264 False statements etc

(1) A person who fraudulently or negligently makes a false statement or representation is liable to a penalty not exceeding £3,000 if, in consequence of the statement or representation—

    (*a*) that person or any other person obtains relief from, or repayment of, tax chargeable under this Part, or

    (*b*) a registered pension scheme makes a payment which is an unauthorised payment.

(2) A person who assists in or induces the preparation of any document which the person knows—

    (*a*) is [inaccurate][1], and

    (*b*) will, or is likely to, cause a registered pension scheme to make an unauthorised payment,

is liable to a penalty not exceeding £3,000.

Commentary—*Simon's Taxes* E7.250.

HMRC Manuals—Pensions Tax Manual PTM159000 (provision of false statements or documents).

PTM160800 (provision of false statements or documents).

Amendments—[1]   In sub-s (2)(*a*) word substituted for word "incorrect" by FA 2014 s 46, Sch 7 paras 1, 23(*d*) with effect from 17 July 2014.

265 Winding-up to facilitate payment of lump sums

(1) This section applies where the winding-up of a registered pension scheme has begun and the Inland Revenue considers the pension scheme is being wound up wholly or mainly for the purpose specified in subsection (2).

(2) That purpose is facilitating the payment of winding-up lump sums or winding-up lump sum death benefits (or both) under the pension scheme.

(3) The scheme administrator is liable to a penalty not exceeding the relevant amount.

(4) The relevant amount is £3,000 in respect of—

    (*a*) each member to whom a winding-up lump sum is paid under the pension scheme, and

    (*b*) each member in respect of whom a winding-up lump sum death benefit is paid under the pension scheme.

Commentary—*Simon's Taxes* **E7.250**.

HMRC Manuals—Pensions Tax Manual PTM159000 (winding up to facilitate payment of lump sums).
PTM063600 (winding up a scheme to facilitate paymnet of winding-up lumpsum).

Modifications—Registered Pension Schemes (Splitting of Schemes) Regulations, SI 2006/569 reg 3 (modification of this provision in relation to sub-scheme administrators).

266 Transfers to insured schemes

(1) This section applies where sums held for the purposes of, or representing accrued rights under, a registered pension scheme ("the transferor scheme") are transferred so as to become held for the purposes of, or to represent rights under, a registered pension scheme that is an insured scheme ("the transferee scheme").

(2) The scheme administrator of the transferor scheme is liable to a penalty not exceeding £3,000 unless the sums are transferred either to the scheme administrator of the transferee scheme or to a relevant insurance company.

(3) In this section—

    "insured scheme" means a pension scheme all the income and other assets of which are invested in policies of insurance, and

    "relevant insurance company" means an insurance company that issued any of the policies of insurance.

Commentary—*Simon's Taxes* **E7.250**.

HMRC Manuals—Pensions Tax Manual PTM100010 (transfers must be made between pension schemes).
PTM159000 (transfer to insured schemes).

Modifications—Registered Pension Schemes (Splitting of Schemes) Regulations, SI 2006/569 reg 3 (modification of this provision in relation to sub-scheme administrators).

[Relief from liability in respect of returned unauthorised member payments

266A Member's liability

(1) This section applies where—

    (*a*) a liability to the unauthorised payments charge, or to both the unauthorised payments charge and the unauthorised payments surcharge, has arisen in respect of an unauthorised member payment, and

    (*b*) property or money is transferred, or a sum paid, towards a registered pension scheme pursuant to [a relevant order][3] as a result of the unauthorised member payment.

(2) The member of the registered pension scheme to or in respect of whom the unauthorised member payment was made (or, if it was paid after his death, the recipient) may claim relief from—

    (*a*) the relevant proportion of the unauthorised payments charge, and

    (*b*) if a liability to the unauthorised payments surcharge has arisen and subsection (4) is satisfied, the relevant proportion of the unauthorised payments surcharge.

(3) The claim must be made within the period of one year beginning with the day on which the property or money is transferred, or the sum paid.

(4) This subsection is satisfied if no part of the unauthorised member payment and no asset or sum representing it—

    (*a*) has been received by (or on behalf of) the member or a person connected with the member, or

    (*b*) has been held for more than 180 days by a person or succession of persons, other than the member or a person connected with the member, involved in any transaction by which the unauthorised member payment was made.

(5) The relevant proportion of the unauthorised payments charge or the unauthorised payments surcharge is—

$$\frac{ASO}{UMP}$$

where—

ASO is the amount subject to the [relevant][3] order, that is the aggregate of the market value of any property and the amount of any money transferred, or the amount of the sum paid, towards a registered pension scheme pursuant to the [relevant order][3] in respect of the unauthorised member payment, and

UMP is the amount of the unauthorised member payment.

(6) But if ASO is greater than UMP, the relevant proportion of the unauthorised payments charge or the unauthorised payments surcharge is the whole of it.

[(6A) In this section "relevant order" means an order under any of the following—

    (a) section 16(1), 19(4) or 21(2)(a) of the Pensions Act 2004 (orders for money etc to be restored to pension schemes), or

    (b) Article 12(1), 15(4) or 17(2)(a) of the Pensions (Northern Ireland) Order 2005 (corresponding provision for Northern Ireland).][3]

[(7) For the purposes of this section whether a person is connected with another person is determined in accordance with section 993 of ITA 2007.][2]][1]

Commentary—*Simon's Taxes* **E7.247**.

HMRC Manuals—Pensions Tax Manual PTM134200 (relief from members liability when orders made by court or the pensions regulator).

Amendments—[1]   Section inserted by FA 2005 s 101, Sch 10 paras 4, 64(1) with effect from 6 April 2006.

[2]   Sub-s (7) substituted by ITA 2007 ss 1027, Sch 1 paras 456, 477 with effect for income tax purposes from 6 April 2007, and corporation tax purposes for accounting periods ending after 5 April 2007.

[3]   In sub-s (1)(b) words substituted for words "an order under section 19(4) or 21(2)(a) of the Pensions Act 2004 or Article 15(4) or 17(2)(a) of the Pensions (Northern Ireland) Order 2005 (restitution by order of court or Pensions Regulator)", in sub-s (5) word inserted and words substituted for words "order under section 19(4) or 21(2)(a) of the Pensions Act 2004 or Article 15(4) or 17(2)(a) of the Pensions (Northern Ireland) Order 2005", and (sub-s (6A) inserted, by FA 2014 s 46, Sch 7 paras 1, 14 with effect in relation to orders made on or after 1 September 2014.

[266B Scheme's liability

(1) This section applies where—

    (a) the scheme administrator of a registered pension scheme has become liable to the scheme sanction charge in respect of an unauthorised member payment, and

    (b) property or money is transferred, or a sum paid, towards a registered pension scheme pursuant to [a relevant order][2] as a result of the unauthorised member payment.

(2) The scheme administrator may, within the period of one year beginning with the day on which the property or money is transferred, or the sum paid, claim relief from the relevant proportion of the scheme sanction charge.

(3) The relevant proportion of the scheme sanction charge is—

$$\frac{ASO}{UMP}$$

where—

ASO is the amount subject to the [relevant][2] order, that is the aggregate of the market value of any property and the amount of any money transferred, or the amount of the sum paid, towards a registered pension scheme pursuant to the [relevant order][2] in respect of the unauthorised member payment, and

UMP is the amount of the unauthorised member payment.

(4) But if ASO is greater than UMP, the relevant proportion of the scheme sanction charge is the whole of it.

[(5) In this section "relevant order" means an order under any of the following—

    (a) section 16(1), 19(4) or 21(2)(a) of the Pensions Act 2004 (orders for money etc to be restored to pension schemes), or

    (b) Article 12(1), 15(4) or 17(2)(a) of the Pensions (Northern Ireland) Order 2005 (corresponding provision for Northern Ireland).][2]][1]

Commentary—*Simon's Taxes* **E7.247**.

HMRC Manuals—Pensions Tax Manual PTM158000 (right to claim relief from the scheme sanction charge).

Pensions Tax Manual PTM135300 (relief from liability to the scheme sanction charge).

Modifications—Registered Pension Schemes (Splitting of Schemes) Regulations, SI 2006/569 reg 3 (modification of this provision in relation to sub-scheme administrators).

Amendments—[1]   Section inserted by FA 2005 s 101, Sch 10 paras 4, 64(1) with effect from 6 April 2006.

[2]   In sub-s (1)(b) words substituted for words "an order under section 19(4) or 21(2)(a) of the Pensions Act 2004 or Article 15(4) or 17(2)(a) of the Pensions (Northern Ireland) Order 2005 (restitution by order of court or Pensions Regulator)", in sub-s (3) word inserted and words substituted for words "order under section 19(4) or 21(2)(a) of the Pensions Act 2004 or Article 15(4) or 17(2)(a) of the Pensions (Northern Ireland) Order 2005", and sub-s (5) inserted, by FA 2014 s 46, Sch 7 paras 1, 15 with effect in relation to orders made on or after 1 September 2014.

Discharge of tax liability: good faith

267 Lifetime allowance charge

(1) This section applies where the scheme administrator of a registered pension scheme is liable to the lifetime allowance charge in respect of a benefit crystallisation event.

(2) The scheme administrator may apply to the Inland Revenue for the discharge of the scheme administrator's liability to the lifetime allowance charge in respect of the benefit crystallisation event on the ground mentioned in subsection (3).

(3) The ground is that—

 (a) the scheme administrator reasonably believed that there was no liability to the lifetime allowance charge in respect of the benefit crystallisation event, and

 (b) in all the circumstances of the case, it would not be just and reasonable for the scheme administrator to be liable to the lifetime allowance charge in respect of the benefit crystallisation event.

(4) On receiving an application under subsection (2), the Inland Revenue must decide whether to discharge the scheme administrator's liability to the lifetime allowance charge in respect of the benefit crystallisation event.

(5) The scheme administrator may apply to the Inland Revenue for the discharge of part of the scheme administrator's liability to the lifetime allowance charge in respect of the benefit crystallisation event on the ground mentioned in subsection (6).

(6) The ground is that—

 (a) the scheme administrator reasonably believed that the amount of the lifetime allowance charge in respect of the benefit crystallisation event was less than the actual amount, and

 (b) in all the circumstances of the case, it would not be just and reasonable for the scheme administrator to be liable to an amount ("the excess amount") equal to the difference between the amount which the scheme administrator believed to be the amount of the charge and the actual amount.

(7) On receiving an application under subsection (5), the Inland Revenue must decide whether to discharge the scheme administrator's liability to the lifetime allowance charge in respect of the excess amount (or part of the excess amount).

(8) The discharge of the scheme administrator's liability to the lifetime allowance charge (or to the excess amount or part of the excess amount) does not affect the liability of any other person to the lifetime allowance charge.

(9) The Inland Revenue must notify the scheme administrator of the decision on an application under this section.

(10) Regulations made by the Board of Inland Revenue may make provision supplementing this section; and the regulations may in particular make provision as to the time limits for the making of an application.

Commentary—*Simon's Taxes* **E7.247**.

HMRC Manuals—Pensions Tax Manual PTM158000 (right to apply for a lifetime allowance charge to be discharged). PTM086000 (discharge of scheme administrator's liability).
PTM088400 (summary of the process for testing Bces against the lifetime allowance during the member's lifetime).

Regulations—Registered Pension Schemes (Discharge of Liabilities under Sections 267 and 268 of the Finance Act 2004) Regulations, SI 2005/3452.

Modifications—Registered Pension Schemes (Splitting of Schemes) Regulations, SI 2006/569 reg 3 (modification of this provision in relation to sub-scheme administrators).

268 Unauthorised payments surcharge and scheme sanction charge

(1) This section applies where—

 (a) a person is liable to the unauthorised payments surcharge in respect of an unauthorised payment, or

 (b) the scheme administrator of a registered pension scheme is liable to the scheme sanction charge in respect of a scheme chargeable payment.

(2) The person liable to the unauthorised payments surcharge may apply to the Inland Revenue for the discharge of the person's liability to the unauthorised payments surcharge in respect of the unauthorised payment on the ground mentioned in subsection (3).

(3) The ground is that in all the circumstances of the case, it would not be just and reasonable for the person to be liable to the unauthorised payments surcharge in respect of the payment.

(4) On receiving an application by a person under subsection (2) the Inland Revenue must decide whether to discharge the person's liability to the unauthorised payments surcharge in respect of the payment.

(5) The scheme administrator may apply to the Inland Revenue for the discharge of the scheme administrator's liability to the scheme sanction charge in respect of a scheme chargeable payment on the ground mentioned in subsection (6) or (7).

(6) In the case of a scheme chargeable payment which is treated as being an unauthorised member payment by section 172[, 172A, 172B, . . . ² 172C or 172D . . . ²]¹, the ground is that, in all the circumstances of the case, it would not be just and reasonable for the scheme administrator to be liable to the scheme sanction charge.

(7) In any other case, the ground is that—

    (a) the scheme administrator reasonably believed that the unauthorised payment was not a scheme chargeable payment, and

    (b) in all the circumstances of the case, it would not be just and reasonable for the scheme administrator to be liable to the scheme sanction charge in respect of the unauthorised payment.

[(7A) Subsection (7) applies with the omission of its paragraph (a) if the scheme chargeable payment is a payment of a lump sum where the conditions in paragraph 1B(2)(a) to (g) of Schedule 29 are met.]³

(8) On receiving an application under subsection (5), the Inland Revenue must decide whether to discharge the scheme administrator's liability to the scheme sanction charge in respect of the unauthorised payment.

(9) The Inland Revenue must notify the applicant of the decision on an application under this section.

(10) Regulations made by the Board of Inland Revenue may make provision supplementing this section; and the regulations may in particular make provision as to the time limits for the making of an application.

Commentary—*Simon's Taxes* **E7.247**.
HMRC Manuals—Pensions Tax Manual PTM135400 (discharge from the scheme sanction charge).
PTM112400 (good faith release from scheme sanction charge).
Regulations—Registered Pension Schemes (Discharge of Liabilities under Sections 267 and 268 of the Finance Act 2004) Regulations, SI 2005/3452.
Modifications—Registered Pension Schemes (Splitting of Schemes) Regulations, SI 2006/569 reg 3 (modification of this provision in relation to sub-scheme administrators).
Amendments—¹ Words in sub-s (6) substituted by FA 2007 s 69, Sch 19 paras 1, 17, 29(7) and deemed to have come into force on 6 April 2007.
² In sub-s (6) words "172BA," and "or arises under section 181A" repealed by FA 2011 s 65, Sch 16 paras 62, 75 with effect for the tax year 2011–12 and subsequent tax years, subject to transitional provisions in FA 2011 Sch 16 Pt 3. The amendments made by FA 2011 Sch 16 paras 33–39, 41, 42(2)(b), (c), (4), (5), 65, 67, 68, 75(a), 76, 77(5), 79(4), 82(6) have effect in relation to deaths occurring on or after 6 April 2011 (this includes the repeal of the words "172BA,") (FA 2011 Sch 16 para 103).
³ Sub-s (7A) inserted by FA 2014 s 43, Sch 5 para 12(3). This amendment is to be treated as having come into force on 19 March 2014 (FA 2014 Sch 5 para 15).

269 Appeal against decision on discharge of liability

(1) This section applies where the Inland Revenue—

    (a) decides to refuse an application under [section 237D (discharge of scheme administrator's liability to annual allowance charge),]² [section 244N (discharge of liability to overseas transfer charge),]³ section 267(2) (discharge of liability to lifetime allowance charge) or section 268 (discharge of liability to unauthorised payments surcharge or scheme sanction charge), or

    (b) on an application under section 267(5), decides to refuse the application or to discharge the applicant's liability to the lifetime allowance charge in respect of part only of the excess amount.

(2) The applicant may appeal against the decision.

(3), (4) . . . ¹

(5) An appeal under this section against a decision must be brought within the period of 30 days beginning with the day on which the applicant was given notification of the decision.

(6) [On an appeal under subsection (1)(a) that is notified to the tribunal, the tribunal]¹ must consider whether the applicant's liability to the lifetime allowance charge, unauthorised payments surcharge or scheme sanction charge ought to have been discharged.

(7) If [the tribunal considers]¹ that the applicant's liability ought not to have been discharged, [the tribunal must]¹ dismiss the appeal.

(8) If [the tribunal considers]¹ that the applicant's liability ought to have been discharged, [the tribunal must]¹ grant the application.

(9) [On an appeal under subsection (1)(b) that is notified to the tribunal, the tribunal]¹ must consider whether the applicant's liability to the lifetime allowance charge ought to have been discharged in respect of the excess amount or a greater part of the excess amount.

(10) If [the tribunal considers]¹ that the applicant's liability ought not to have been discharged in respect of the excess amount or a greater part of the excess amount, [the tribunal]¹ must dismiss the appeal.

(11) If [the tribunal considers]¹ that the applicant's liability ought to have been discharged in respect of the excess amount or a greater part of the excess amount, [the tribunal must]¹ discharge the applicant's liability in respect of the excess amount or that part of the excess amount.

Commentary—*Simon's Taxes* **E7.247**.
HMRC Manuals—Pensions Tax Manual PTM134700 (application for discharge).
PTM135400 (appeal against refusal of application to discharge liability to the scheme sanction charge).
Amendments—[1]   Sub-ss (3), (4) repealed, sub-(10) and words in sub-ss (6)–(9), (11) substituted by the Transfer of Tribunal Functions and Revenue and Customs Appeals Order, SI 2009/56 art 3, Sch 1 para 427 with effect from 1 April 2009.
[2]   Words inserted in sub-s (1)(*a*) by FA 2011 s 66, Sch 17 paras 1, 20 with effect for the tax year 2011–12 and subsequent tax years, and in relation to pension input periods ending in the tax year 2011–12 but beginning earlier (or in 2011–12). For transitional provisions see FA 2011 Sch 17 paras 28–34.
[3]   Words inserted in sub-s (1)(*a*) by FA 2017 s 10, Sch 4 paras 12, 17 with effect in relation to transfers made on or after 9 March 2017.

Scheme administrator

270 Meaning of "scheme administrator"

(1) References in this Part to the scheme administrator, in relation to a pension scheme, are to the person who is, or persons who are, appointed in accordance with the rules of the pension scheme to be responsible for the discharge of the functions conferred or imposed on the scheme administrator of the pension scheme by and under this Part.

(2) But a person cannot be the person who is, or one of the persons who are, the scheme administrator of a pension scheme unless the person—

    (*a*) is resident in the United Kingdom or another state which is a member State or a non-member EEA State, . . . [1]

    (*b*) has made the required declaration to the Inland Revenue[, and[1]

    (*c*) has made to an officer of Revenue and Customs any other declarations which are reasonably required by Her Majesty's Revenue and Customs.][1]

(3) "The required declaration" is a declaration that the person—

    (*a*) understands that the person will be responsible for discharging the functions conferred or imposed on the scheme administrator of the pension scheme by and under this Part, and

    (*b*) intends to discharge those functions at all times, whether resident in the United Kingdom or another state which is a member State or a non-member EEA State.

(4) "Non-member EEA State" means a State which is a contracting party to the Agreement on the European Economic Area signed at Oporto on 2nd May 1992 (as adjusted by the Protocol signed at Brussels on 17th March 1993) but which is not a member State.

Commentary—*Simon's Taxes* **E7.242**.
HMRC Manuals—Pensions Tax Manual PTM025100 (scheme administrator).
PTM151000 (who can be a scheme administrator?).
PTM154000 (appointing a new scheme administrator).
Modifications—Registered Pension Schemes (Splitting of Schemes) Regulations, SI 2006/569 reg 3 (modification of this section in relation to sub-scheme administrators).
Amendments—[1]   In sub-s (2) the word "and" at the end of para (*a*) repealed, and para (*c*) and preceding word "and" inserted, by FA 2014 s 46, Sch 7 paras 1, 9 with effect in relation to appointments on or after 1 September 2014.

271 Liability of scheme administrator

(1) Any liability of a person who is, or of any of the persons who are, the scheme administrator of a registered pension scheme ceases to be a liability of that person on the person ceasing to be, or to be one of the persons who is, the scheme administrator of the pension scheme.

This subsection does not apply to a liability to pay a penalty and is subject to subsection (4).

(2) Where a person becomes, or becomes one of the persons who is, the scheme administrator of a registered pension scheme, the person assumes any existing liabilities of the scheme administrator of the pension scheme, other than any liability to pay a penalty.

(3) Subsection (4) applies where, on the person who is or the persons who are the scheme administrator of a registered pension scheme ceasing to be the scheme administrator, there is no scheme administrator of the pension scheme.

(4) Any liability of the person or persons as scheme administrator remains a liability of that person or those persons as if still the scheme administrator (unless dead or having ceased to exist) until another person becomes, or other persons become, the scheme administrator of the pension scheme.

(5) But a person who retains, or persons who retain, any liability by virtue of subsection (4) may apply to the Inland Revenue to be released from the liability.

(6) On receipt of the application the Inland Revenue must decide whether or not to release the applicant or applicants from the liability and must notify the applicant, or each of the applicants, of the decision.

(7) If the decision is not to release the applicant or applicants from the liability the applicant or applicants may appeal against the decision.

(8) . . . [1]

(9) The appeal must be brought within the period of 30 days beginning with the day on which the applicant was notified of the decision.

(10) . . . [1]

(11) [On an appeal that is notified to the tribunal, the tribunal][1] must consider whether the applicant or applicants ought to have been released from the liability.

(12) If [the tribunal decides][1] that the applicant or applicants ought not to have been released from the liability, [the tribunal must][1] dismiss the appeal.

(13) If [the tribunal decides][1] that the applicant or applicants ought to have been released from the liability, the applicant is, or applicants are, to be treated as having been released from the liability (but subject to any further appeal . . . [1]).

Commentary—*Simon's Taxes* E7.242.

HMRC Manuals—Pensions Tax Manual PTM154000 (ceasing to act as a scheme administrator).

PTM158000 (right to apply for a release from liabilities on ceasing to be the scheme administrator).

Modifications—Registered Pension Schemes (Splitting of Schemes) Regulations, SI 2006/569 reg 3 (modification of this provision in relation to sub-scheme administrators).

Amendments—[1] Sub-ss (8), (10) repealed, words in sub-ss (11)–(13) substituted by the Transfer of Tribunal Functions and Revenue and Customs Appeals Order, SI 2009/56 art 3, Sch 1 para 428 with effect from 1 April 2009.

272 Trustees etc liable as scheme administrator

(1) This section applies in relation to a registered pension scheme if—

    (a) there is no scheme administrator of the pension scheme and no-one who remains subject to the liabilities of the scheme administrator by virtue of section 271(4) (continuation of liability where no scheme administrator),

    (b) the person who is, or all the persons who are, the scheme administrator of the pension scheme or remain so subject cannot be traced, or

    (c) the person who is, or all the persons who are, the scheme administrator of the pension scheme or remain so subject are in serious default.

(2) Any person who assumes liability by reason of this section applying in relation to the pension scheme—

    (a) is liable to pay any tax (and any interest on tax) due from the scheme administrator of the pension scheme by virtue of this Part, and

    (b) is responsible for the discharge of all other obligations imposed on the scheme administrator of the pension scheme by or under this Part.

(3) In subsection (2)—

    (a) the references in paragraph (a) to tax, and interest on tax, include any that has become due before this section applied in relation to the pension scheme and remains unpaid, and

    (b) the reference in paragraph (b) to obligations includes any that have become due before this section applied in relation to the pension scheme and remain unsatisfied, other than any liability to pay a penalty which has become due before this section so applied.

(4) The following heads specify the persons who assume liability by reason of this section applying in relation to the pension scheme [or by reason of section 272C(7) applying in relation to a liability][1]; but if—

    (a) a person assumes, or persons assume, liability by virtue of being specified under one head, and

    (b) that person, or any of those persons, can be traced and is not in default, no-one assumes liability by virtue of being specified under a later head.

Head 1

If there are one or more trustees of the pension scheme who are resident in the United Kingdom, that trustee or each of those trustees.

Head 2

If there are one or more persons who control the management of the pension scheme, that person or each of those persons.

Head 3

If alive or still in existence, the person, or any of the persons, who established the pension scheme and any person by whom that person, or any of those persons, has been directly or indirectly succeeded in relation to the provision of benefits under the pension scheme.

Head 4

If the pension scheme is an occupational pension scheme, any sponsoring employer.

Head 5

If there are one or more trustees of the pension scheme who are not resident in the United Kingdom, that trustee or each of those trustees.

(5) Where a person assumes liability by reason of this section applying in relation to the pension scheme, the Inland Revenue must, as soon as is reasonably practicable, notify the person of that fact; but failure to do so does not affect the person's liability.

(6) For the purposes of this section a person is in default if the person—

    (a) has failed to pay all or any of the tax (or interest on tax) due from the person by virtue of this Part, or

    (b) has failed to discharge any other obligation imposed on the person by or under this Part,

and a person in default is in serious default if the Inland Revenue considers the failure to be of a serious nature.

Commentary—*Simon's Taxes* E7.242.

HMRC Manuals—Pensions Tax Manual PTM155000 (trustees, scheme managers etc. liable as scheme administrator).
Modifications—Registered Pension Schemes (Splitting of Schemes) Regulations, SI 2006/569 reg 3 (modification of this section in relation to sub-scheme administrators).
Amendments—[1]   Words in sub-s (4) inserted by FA 2014 s 46, Sch 7 paras 1, 18 with effect from 17 July 2014.

[272A   Liabilities of independent trustee

(1) This section applies in relation to a person ("P") who is an independent trustee of a registered pension scheme.

(2) For the purposes of this section and section 272B an "independent trustee" is a trustee of a pension scheme—

    (*a*)   who is appointed by, or otherwise pursuant to, an order made—

        (i)   by the Pensions Regulator under section 7 of the Pensions Act 1995 or Article 7 of the Pensions (Northern Ireland) Order 1995 (appointment of trustees by the Pensions Regulator), or

        (ii)   by a court on an application made by the Pensions Regulator, and

    (*b*)   who is not a trustee of the pension scheme at any time before—

        (i)   the day on which the trustee's appointment as mentioned in paragraph (*a*) takes effect, or

        (ii)   if the trustee is appointed as mentioned in paragraph (*a*) on more than one occasion, the day on which the first appointment takes effect.

(3) In this section "the relevant day" means—

    (*a*)   the day on which P's appointment as trustee of the pension scheme as mentioned in subsection (2)(*a*) takes effect, or

    (*b*)   if P is appointed as trustee of the pension scheme as mentioned in subsection (2)(*a*) on more than one occasion, the day on which P's first appointment takes effect.

(4) If P is, or is one of the persons who are, the scheme administrator, P does not assume any liability falling within subsection (7) which P would otherwise assume (including by reason of section 272C(3) or (4)).

(5) Subsection (4) does not apply if P is, or is one of the persons who are, the scheme administrator at any time before the relevant day.

(6) In relation to any liability falling within subsection (7), in section 272(4) references to trustees or to persons who control the management of the pension scheme do not include P.

(7) The liabilities falling within this subsection are—

    (*a*)   liabilities for the following in respect of payments made (or treated as having been made) by the pension scheme on or before the relevant day—

        (i)   the short service refund lump sum charge;

        (ii)   *the serious ill-health lump sum charge;*[2]

        (iii)   the special lump sum death benefits charge;

        (iv)   the authorised surplus payments charge;

        (v)   the scheme sanction charge in respect of scheme chargeable payments falling within section 241(1)(*a*) or (*b*);

    (*b*)   liabilities for the lifetime allowance charge in respect of benefit crystallisation events occurring on or before the relevant day;

    (*c*)   liabilities for the scheme sanction charge in respect of scheme chargeable payments treated under section 185A or 185F as having been made by the pension scheme in tax years earlier than the one in which the relevant day falls;

    (*d*)   any liability for the scheme sanction charge in respect of the relevant fraction of any scheme chargeable payment treated under section 185A as having been made by the pension scheme in the tax year in which the relevant day falls;

    (*e*)   where the pension scheme is treated under section 185F as having made a scheme chargeable payment in the tax year in which the relevant day falls and there is a relevant net gain, any liability for the scheme sanction charge in respect of the relevant amount;

    (*f*)   any liability to pay interest in respect of a liability mentioned in paragraphs (*a*) to (*e*) arising at any time.

(8) For the purposes of subsection (7)(*d*) "the relevant fraction" is—

    A / B

    where—

             A is the number of days in the tax year up to (and including) the relevant day, and

             B is the number of days in the tax year.

(9) For the purposes of subsection (7)(*e*)—

    (*a*)   there is a "relevant net gain" if—

        (i)   the total amount of any gains treated under section 185F as accruing in the tax year on or before the relevant day, exceeds

        (ii)   the total amount of any losses treated under section 185F as so accruing, and

    (*b*)   "the relevant amount" is—

        (i)   the scheme chargeable payment, or

      (ii) if that payment is greater than the excess of gains over losses mentioned in paragraph (*a*), the amount of that excess.

(10) Subsection (11) applies if—

    (*a*) apart from that subsection, losses in relation to which section 185G(10) applies would be included in the total amount mentioned in subsection (9)(*a*)(ii), and

    (*b*) the losses exceed the gains—

      (i) which are included in the total amount mentioned in subsection (9)(*a*)(i), and

      (ii) from which the losses can be deducted in accordance with section 185G(10).

(11) The losses are not to be included in the total amount mentioned in subsection (9)(*a*)(ii) so far as they exceed the gains.][1]

Amendments—[1] Sections 272A–272C inserted by FA 2014 s 46, Sch 7 paras 1, 19 with effect for cases where the relevant day falls on or after 1 September 2014.

[2] Sub-s (7)(*a*)(ii) repealed by FA 2016 s 22, Sch 5 para 3(1)(*b*) with effect in relation to lump sums paid after 15 September 2016

[272B Liabilities of scheme administrator appointed by independent trustee etc

(1) This section applies in relation to a person ("Q") who is, or is one of the persons who are, the scheme administrator of a registered pension scheme where Q's appointment as such takes effect at a time when the pension scheme has one or more independent trustees.

(2) Q does not assume any liability falling within section 272A(7) which Q would otherwise assume.

(3) In relation to any liability falling within section 272A(7), in section 272(4) references to persons who control the management of the pension scheme do not include Q.

(4) Subsections (2) and (3) do not apply if Q is, or is one of the persons who are, the scheme administrator at any time before the relevant day.

(5) In this section, and in section 272A as it applies for the purposes of this section, "the relevant day" means the first day on which the pension scheme has an independent trustee (whether or not there are days between that day and the day on which Q's appointment takes effect on which the pension scheme has no independent trustees).][1]

Amendments—[1] Sections 272A–272C inserted by FA 2014 s 46, Sch 7 paras 1, 19 with effect for cases where the relevant day falls on or after 1 September 2014.

[272C Former scheme administrator etc to retain liability

(1) This section applies in relation to a liability which, by reason of section 272A(4), is not assumed by P (in which case "the relevant day" is to be read in accordance with section 272A(3)).

(2) This section also applies in relation to a liability which, by reason of section 272B(2), is not assumed by Q (in which case "the relevant day" is to be read in accordance with section 272B(5)).

(3) The liability is to be retained or assumed by the person who is, or the persons who are, the scheme administrator immediately before the relevant day (unless dead or having ceased to exist).

(4) If there is no scheme administrator immediately before the relevant day, the liability is to be retained or assumed by the person who was, or the persons who were, the scheme administrator when there last was a scheme administrator before the relevant day (unless dead or having ceased to exist).

(5) Nothing in section 271 prevents a person from having (and continuing to have) the liability by reason of subsection (3) or (4).

(6) Subsection (7) applies if—

    (*a*) no-one has the liability by reason of subsection (3) or (4),

    (*b*) no-one who has the liability by reason of subsection (3) or (4) can be traced, or

    (*c*) the person who has, or all the persons who have, the liability by reason of subsection (3) or (4) are in serious default (as determined in accordance with section 272(6)).

(7) The liability is to be assumed by the person or persons determined in accordance with section 272(4).

(8) Section 272(5) applies in relation to a person who assumes the liability by reason of subsection (7) as it applies in relation to a person who assumes a liability by reason of section 272.

(9) Nothing in this section prevents any person from being subject to the liability apart from this section (in addition to any person who is subject to the liability by reason of this section), and in particular the liability continues to be a liability of the scheme administrator for the purposes of section 271(2).

(10) If a person assumes the liability under section 271(2) at a time after P or Q's appointment as, or as one of the persons who are, the scheme administrator has ceased, the person who has, or the persons who have, the liability by reason of subsection (3) or (4) is, or are, released from the liability.

(11) A person who has, or persons who have, the liability by reason of subsection (3) or (4) may apply to an officer of Revenue and Customs to be released from the liability.

(12) Section 271(6) to (13) applies in relation to an application under subsection (11) as it applies in relation to an application under section 271(5).][1]

Amendments—[1] Sections 272A–272C inserted by FA 2014 s 46, Sch 7 paras 1, 19 with effect for cases where the relevant day falls on or after 1 September 2014.

273 Members liable as scheme administrator

(1) This section applies in relation to a registered pension scheme if—

    (*a*) a person has, or persons have, assumed liability by reason of section 272 (trustees etc) applying in relation to the pension scheme,

    (*b*) the person has, or the persons have, become liable to pay tax (or interest on tax) which became due by virtue of section 239 (scheme sanction charge) or section 242 (de-registration charge) before section 272 applied in relation to the pension scheme,

    (*c*) that person, or each of those persons, has failed (in whole or in part) to satisfy the liability, and

    (*d*) that person, or each of those persons, has either died or ceased to exist or is a person in whose case the Inland Revenue considers the person's failure to satisfy the liability to be of a serious nature.

[(1A) This section also applies in relation to a registered pension scheme if—

    (*a*) a person has, or persons have, by reason of section 272C(7) assumed a liability to pay tax (or interest on tax) by virtue of section 239 (scheme sanction charge) in respect of the whole or a part of a scheme chargeable payment falling within section 241(1)(*b*) or (*c*) made (or treated as having been made) by the pension scheme,

    (*b*) that person, or each of those persons, has failed (in whole or in part) to satisfy the liability, and

    (*c*) that person, or each of those persons, has either died or ceased to exist or is a person in whose case an officer of Revenue and Customs considers the person's failure to satisfy the liability to be of a serious nature.][4]

(2) Any person who was a member of the pension scheme at any time during the relevant three-year period is liable to pay the appropriate share of the unpaid amount if—

    (*a*) any of the conditions in subsection (5) is met, and

    (*b*) the Inland Revenue notifies the person of the person's liability to do so.

(3) "The relevant three-year period" is the period of three years ending with the date on which the liability to pay the tax arose.

(4) The "appropriate share of the unpaid amount", in the case of a person, is—

$$\frac{AAP}{AA} \times UT$$

where—

    AA is an amount equal to aggregate of the amount of the sums and the market value of the assets held for the purposes of the pension scheme at the time when the liability to pay the tax arose,

    AAP is an amount equal to so much of AA as is held for the purposes of such of the arrangements under the pension scheme as relate to the person or a person connected with the person, and

    UT is so much of the tax (and any interest on it) as remains unpaid.

(5) The conditions referred to in subsection (2)(*a*) are—

    (*a*) that the pension scheme . . . [2] was not an occupational pension scheme,

    (*b*) that at any time during the relevant three-year period the pension scheme received a transfer value in which there were represented relevant personal pension contributions made by or in respect of the person,

    (*c*) that the pension scheme was an occupational pension scheme and at any time during the relevant three-year period the person was a controlling director of a company that was a sponsoring employer, and

    (*d*) that at any time during the relevant three-year period the pension scheme received a transfer value in which there were represented relevant controlling director contributions made by or in respect of the person.

(6) A notification under subsection (2)(*b*) may be included in an assessment in respect of a liability under this section; and such an assessment made in relation to an amount is not out of time if made within the period of three years beginning with the date on which the person assessed first became liable to pay the amount.

(7) "Relevant personal pension contributions" means contributions under a pension scheme (whether or not the pension scheme from which the transfer value was received) which . . . [2] was not an occupational pension scheme.

(8) "Relevant controlling director contributions" means contributions under an occupational pension scheme (whether or not the pension scheme from which the transfer value was received) made by reference to service (or remuneration in respect of service) as a controlling director of a company that was a sponsoring employer.

(9) A person is a "controlling director" of a company if the person is a director of the company and is within [section 452(2)(b) of the Corporation Tax Act 2010][3] (director able to control 20% of ordinary share capital) in relation to the company.

(10) References to receipt of a transfer value by the pension scheme are to the transfer, so as to become held for the purposes of or to represent rights under the pension scheme, of any sums or assets held for the purposes of or representing accrued rights under any other pension scheme.

[(11) For the purposes of this section whether a person is connected with another person is determined in accordance with section 993 of ITA 2007.][1]

Commentary—*Simon's Taxes* E7.242.

HMRC Manuals—Pensions Tax Manual PTM155000 (members liable as scheme administrator).

Modifications—Registered Pension Schemes (Splitting of Schemes) Regulations, SI 2006/569 reg 3 (modification of this section in relation to sub-scheme administrators).

Amendments—[1]　　Sub-s (11) substituted by ITA 2007 ss 1027, Sch 1 paras 456, 478 with effect for income tax purposes from 6 April 2007, and corporation tax purposes for accounting periods ending after 5 April 2007.

[2]　　Words in sub-ss (5)(a), (7) repealed by FA 2007 ss 70, 114, Sch 20 paras 1, 4, 24(1), Sch 27 para 3(2). These amendments are deemed to have come into force on 6 April 2007.

[3]　　In sub-s (9) words "section 417(5)(b) of ICTA" substituted by CTA 2010 s 1177, Sch 1 paras 423, 428. CTA 2010 has effect for corporation tax purposes for accounting periods ending on or after 1 April 2010, and for income and capital gains tax purposes for the tax year 2010–11 and subsequent tax years.

[4]　　Sub-s (1A) inserted by FA 2014 s 46, Sch 7 paras 1, 20 with effect from 17 July 2014.

[273ZA Income and gains from taxable property
(1) The Treasury may make regulations in relation to cases where—
　(a) an investment-regulated pension scheme holds an interest in taxable property,
　(b) the pension scheme is non-UK resident, and
　(c) the property is not located in the United Kingdom.

(2) The regulations may make provision for a member of the pension scheme for the purposes of whose arrangement the interest is held to be liable to the scheme sanction charge so far as relating to a scheme chargeable payment treated as made by the pension scheme—
　(a) under section 185A (income from taxable property) by virtue of the pension scheme holding the interest in the property, or
　(b) under section 185F (gains from taxable property) by virtue of a gain treated as accruing to the pension scheme in respect of the interest in the property.

(3) The regulations may make provision—
　(a) for the member to be liable to all of the scheme sanction charge arising by virtue of the scheme chargeable payment or to the charge to such extent as the regulations may provide,
　(b) for the charge to be apportioned between members of the pension scheme where the interest in the property is held for the purposes of more than one arrangement under the pension scheme, and
　(c) for the scheme administrator not to be liable to the scheme sanction charge or not to be liable to the charge to such extent as the regulations may provide.

(4) The regulations may make provision for cases where—
　(a) a member of a pension scheme would otherwise be liable to the scheme sanction charge arising by virtue of a scheme chargeable payment treated as made by the pension scheme under section 185F in a tax year,
　(b) the member does not meet such conditions as to residence in the tax year as the regulations may prescribe,
　(c) the member meets those conditions in a subsequent tax year, and
　(d) such other conditions as the regulations may prescribe are met.

(5) The regulations may make provision for the member—
　(a) not to be liable to the scheme sanction charge in the tax year in which the scheme chargeable payment is treated as made, but
　(b) to be liable in a subsequent tax year to such extent as the regulations may provide to the scheme sanction charge arising by virtue of the payment.

(6) The regulations may—
　(a) amend this Part (apart from this section),
　(b) include provision having effect in relation to times before they are made,
　(c) contain transitional provisions and savings, and
　(d) make different provision for different cases.

(7) For the purposes of this section a pension scheme is non-UK resident if it is established in a country or territory outside the United Kingdom.][1]

Regulations—Income Tax (Removal of Ordinary Residence) Regulations, SI 2013/605.

Temporary Non-Residence (Miscellaneous Amendments) Regulations, SI 2013/1810.

Amendments—[1]　　This section inserted by FA 2006 s 158, Sch 21 paras 2, 10. This amendment is deemed to have come into force on 6 April 2006.

[273A Insurance company liable as scheme administrator

(1) The Board of Inland Revenue may make regulations in relation to cases where an insurance company makes a payment of—

    (*a*) a pension protection lump sum death benefit,

    (*b*) an annuity protection lump sum death benefit, . . . [3]

    [(*c*) a drawdown pension fund lump sum death benefit,][2] [or

    (*d*) a flexi-access drawdown fund lump sum death benefit,][3]

which (by virtue of section 161(3) and (4)) is treated for the purposes of Chapter 3 as made by a registered pension scheme.

(2) The regulations may provide that the insurance company—

    (*a*) is to be treated as the scheme administrator for the purposes of the operation of section 206 in relation to the lump sum death benefit, and

    (*b*) is responsible for the discharge of all obligations imposed on the scheme administrator by or under this Part so far as related to the liability imposed by that section to pay tax in respect of it.

(3) Where an insurance company is liable to pay any tax or interest, or is responsible for the discharge of any other obligation, by virtue of regulations under this section, no other person is liable to pay that tax, or responsible for the discharge of that obligation, under sections 270 to 273.][1]

Regulations—Pension Benefits (Insurance Company Liable as Scheme Administrator) Regulations, SI 2006/136.
Amendments—[1]   Section inserted by FA 2005 s 101, Sch 10 paras 49(1), 64(1) with effect from 6 April 2006.
[2]   Sub-s (1)(*c*) substituted by FA 2011 s 65, Sch 16 paras 62, 76 with effect for the tax year 2011–12 and subsequent tax years, subject to transitional provisions in FA 2011 Sch 16 Pt 3. The amendments made by FA 2011 Sch 16 paras 33–39, 41, 42(2)(*b*), (*c*), (4), (5), 65, 67, 68, 75(*a*), 76, 77(5), 79(4), 82(6) have effect in relation to deaths occurring on or after 6 April 2011 (FA 2011 Sch 16 para 103).
[3]   In sub-s (1), word "or" at end of para (*b*) repealed, and para (*d*) and preceding word inserted, by the Taxation of Pensions Act 2014 s 1, Sch 1 paras 5, 17 with effect from 17 December 2014.

[273B Power of trustees or managers to make certain payments

(1) Subsection (2) applies to a payment by a registered pension scheme to or in respect of a person who is or has been a member of the scheme if it is paid in respect of a money purchase arrangement and is—

    (*a*) a payment of drawdown pension,

    (*b*) paid to purchase a short-term annuity,

    (*c*) a payment of dependants' drawdown pension,

    (*d*) paid to purchase a dependants' short-term annuity,

    (*e*) a payment of nominees' drawdown pension,

    (*f*) paid to purchase a nominees' short-term annuity,

    [(*fa*) paid to purchase a nominees' annuity,]

    (*fb*) paid to purchase a successors' annuity,][2]

    (*g*) a payment of successors' drawdown pension,

    (*h*) paid to purchase a successors' short-term annuity,

    (*i*) an uncrystallised funds pension lump sum,

    (*j*) a flexi-access drawdown fund lump sum death benefit,

    (*k*) a pension commencement lump sum where the person becomes entitled to it in connection with becoming entitled to income withdrawal (or where the person dies after becoming entitled to it but before becoming entitled to the income withdrawal in connection with which it was expected that the person would become entitled to the lump sum), or

    (*l*) a trivial commutation lump sum death benefit where condition B in paragraph 20(1B) of Schedule 29 is met.

(2) The trustees or managers of the scheme may make the payment despite any provision of the rules of the scheme (however framed) prohibiting the making of the payment.][1]

Commentary—*Simon's Taxes* E7.230, E7.237.
Amendments—[1]   Section 273B inserted by the Taxation of Pensions Act 2014 s 1, Sch 1 para 79 with effect from 17 December 2014.
[2]   In sub-s (1), paras (*fa*), (*fb*) inserted by FA 2015 s 34, Sch 4 paras 1, 11 with effect from 26 March 2015.

274 Supplementary

(1) The fact that any person is liable to pay any tax or interest, or is responsible for the discharge of any other obligation, under section 272 (trustees etc)[, section 272C(7)][2] or section 273 (members) does not relieve any other person of any liability to pay the tax or interest, or any obligation to discharge the obligation, arising—

    (*a*) by reason of that other person being, or being one of the persons who is, the scheme administrator of the pension scheme, or

    (*b*) under section 271(4) (continuation of liability where no scheme administrator)[, section 272C(3) or (4)][2] [or regulations under section 273A][1].

(2) Where a liability imposed on the scheme administrator of a registered pension scheme falls to be satisfied by two or more persons (whether or not they constitute the scheme administrator), they are jointly and severally liable.

(3) No liability to pay tax or interest, or other obligation, of any person in relation to a registered pension scheme arising—

(a) by reason of the person being, or being one of the persons who is, the scheme administrator of the pension scheme concerned, or

(b) under section 271(4), 272[, 272C]² or 273,

is affected by the termination of the pension scheme or by its ceasing to be a registered pension scheme.

Commentary—*Simon's Taxes* **E7.242**.

Modifications—Registered Pension Schemes (Splitting of Schemes) Regulations, SI 2006/569 reg 3 (modification of this section in relation to sub-scheme administrators).

Amendments—¹ Words in sub-s (3)(b) inserted by FA 2005 s 101, Sch 10 paras 49(2), 64(1) with effect from 6 April 2006.
² In sub-ss (1), (3)(b) words inserted by FA 2014 s 46, Sch 7 paras 1, 21 with effect from 17 July 2014.

[274A Power to split schemes

(1) The Board of Inland Revenue may make regulations for and in connection with treating registered pension schemes to which this section applies as if they were a number of separate registered pension schemes for such of the purposes of this Part and of provision made under it as are prescribed by the regulations.

(2) This section applies to pension schemes prescribed, or of a description prescribed, by the regulations.

(3) The provision that may be made by the regulations may, in particular, include—

(a) provision as to who is to be treated as the scheme administrator in relation to each of the separate pension schemes, and

(b) any such other modifications of the provision made by and under this Part as appears appropriate in consequence of, or otherwise in connection with, provision made under subsection (1) (including provision so made by virtue of paragraph (a) of this subsection).

(4) The regulations may make different provision for different cases.]¹

Regulations—Registered Pension Schemes (Splitting of Schemes) Regulations, SI 2006/569.
Registered Pension Schemes (Splitting of Schemes) (Amendment) Regulations, SI 2015/667.

Amendments—¹ Section inserted by FA 2005 s 101, Sch 10 paras 50, 64(1) with effect from 6 April 2006.

CHAPTER 8

SUPPLEMENTARY

[National Employment Savings Trust and Master Trust schemes

274B National Employment Savings Trust and Master Trust schemes

(1) This Part applies in relation to a pension scheme that—

(a) is established under section 67 of the Pensions Act 2008, and

(b) is not an occupational pension scheme,

as it applies in relation to an occupational pension scheme.

(2) This Part applies in relation to a pension scheme that—

(a) is a Master Trust scheme, and

(b) is not an occupational pension scheme,

as it applies in relation to an occupational pension scheme.]¹

Commentary—*Simon's Taxes* **E7.208, E7.209**.

Amendments—¹ Section 274B inserted by FA 2018 s 13, Sch 3 para 1(1), (5) with effect from 15 March 2018. Sub-s (2) is treated as always having had effect in relation to a pension scheme that is a Master Trust scheme, that is not an occupational pension scheme, and was registered under FA 2004 Pt 4 Ch 2 before 15 March 2018 (FA 2018 Sch 3 para 4).

Interpretation

275 Insurance company

(1) In this Part "insurance company" means—

(a) a person who has permission under Part 4 of FISMA 2000 to effect or carry out contracts of long-term insurance, or

(b) an EEA firm of the kind mentioned in paragraph 5(d) of Schedule 3 to FISMA 2000 (certain direct insurance undertakings) which has permission under paragraph 15 of that Schedule (as a result of qualifying for authorisation under paragraph 12 of that Schedule) to effect or carry out contracts of long-term insurance.

(2) "Contracts of long-term insurance" means contracts which fall within Part 2 of Schedule 1 to the Financial Services and Markets Act 2000 (Regulated Activities) Order 2001 (SI 2001/544).

Modifications—Pensions Schemes (Application of UK Provisions to Relevant Non-UK Schemes) Regulations, SI 2006/207 reg 11 (modification of this section in respect of relevant non-UK schemes).

Prospective amendments—Sub-s (1)(*b*), and the word ", or" at the end of sub-s (1)(*a*), to be repealed, by the Taxes (Amendments) (EU Exit) Regulations, SI 2019/689 reg 12(1), (5) with effect from Implementation Period completion day (see EU(WA)A 2020 Sch 5 para 1(1)). The amendments do not apply where a person qualifies for authorisation under FSMA 2000 Sch 3 by virtue of SI 2001/3084 (see SI 2019/689 reg 41(*d*)).

276 Relevant valuation factor

(1) For the purposes of this Part the relevant valuation factor in relation to any registered pension scheme, or any arrangement under a registered pension scheme, is 20.

(2) But the Inland Revenue and the scheme administrator of any registered pension scheme may agree that the relevant valuation factor in relation to the pension scheme, or any arrangement under the pension scheme, is to be a number greater than 20.

Commentary—*Simon's Taxes* **E7.217, E7.256.**

HMRC Manuals—Pensions Tax Manual PTM088620 (entitlement to a scheme pension).

PTM158000 (agreement of relevant valuation factor).

Modifications—Pensions Schemes (Application of UK Provisions to Relevant Non-UK Schemes) Regulations, SI 2006/207 reg 12 (modification of this section in respect of relevant non-UK schemes).

277 Valuation assumptions

For the purposes of this Part the valuation assumptions in relation to a person, benefits and a date are—

    (*a*) if the person has not reached such age (if any) as must have been reached to avoid any reduction in the benefits on account of age, that the person reached that age on the date, and

    (*b*) that the person's right to receive the benefits had not been occasioned by physical or mental impairment.

Commentary—*Simon's Taxes* **E7.256.**

HMRC Manuals—Pensions Tax Manual PTM088620 (pensionable earnings).

PTM093510 (Valuation assumptions for benefit accrual under a cash balance or defined benefits arrangement).

PTM095420 (how to calculate the relevant relievable amount for a cash balance arrangement).

PTM095440 (how to calculate the relevant relievable amount for a defined benefits arrangement).

278 Market value

(1) For the purposes of this Part the market value of an asset held for the purposes of a pension scheme is to be determined in accordance with section 272 of TCGA 1992.

(2) Where an asset held for the purposes of a pension scheme is a right or interest in respect of any money lent (directly or indirectly) to any relevant associated person, the value of the asset is to be treated as being the amount owing (including any unpaid interest) on the money lent.

(3) The following are "relevant associated persons"—

    (*a*) any employer who has at any time (whether or not before the making of the loan) made contributions under the pension scheme,

    (*b*) any company connected (at the time of the making of the loan or subsequently) with any such employer,

    (*c*) any person who has at any time (whether or not before the making of the loan) been a member of the pension scheme, and

    (*d*) any person connected (at the time of the making of the loan or subsequently) with any such person.

[(3A) For the purposes of this Part the market value of taxable property, or of an interest in taxable property, is to be determined in accordance with section 272 of TCGA 1992.][1]

[(3B) Subsection (3A) is subject to any provision made by regulations under paragraph 36(2) of Schedule 29A.][1]

[(4) For the purposes of this section whether a person is connected with another person is determined in accordance with section 993 of ITA 2007.][2]

Amendments—[1] Sub-ss (3A), (3B) inserted by FA 2006 s 158, Sch 21 paras 2, 11. This amendment is deemed to have come into force on 6 April 2006.

[2] Sub-s (4) substituted by ITA 2007 ss 1027, Sch 1 paras 456, 479 with effect for income tax purposes from 6 April 2007, and corporation tax purposes for accounting periods ending after 5 April 2007.

279 Other definitions

(1) In this Part—

    ["abatement", in relation to a scheme pension [to which a person has become entitled][2] under a public service pension scheme, means the reduction of the pension (including its reduction to nil) in accordance with the rules of the pension scheme by reason of [the person's employment][2] in public service,][1]

    "the Board of Inland Revenue" means the Commissioners of Inland Revenue,

    . . .[3]

    ["consumer prices index" means—

        (*a*) the general index for consumer prices published by the Statistics Board, or

        (*b*) if that index is not published for a relevant month, any substituted index or index figures published by the Statistics Board,][4] "employee" and "employer" have the same meaning as in the employment income Parts of ITEPA 2003 (see sections 4 and 5 of that Act) but include (respectively) a former employee and a former employer (and "employment" is to be read accordingly),

"the Inland Revenue" means any officer of the Board of Inland Revenue,

"normal minimum pension age" means—

    (a) before 6th April 2010, 50, and

    (b) on and after that date, 55,

"pension credit" and "pension debit" have the same meaning as in Chapter 1 of Part 4 of WRPA (see section 46(1) of that Act) or Chapter 1 of Part 5 of WRP(NI)O 1999 (see Article 43(1) of that Order), [and][3]

"pension sharing order or provision" means any order or provision mentioned in section 28(1) of WRPA 1999 or Article 25(1) of WRP(NI)O 1999,

. . .[3]

["pensionable age" has the meaning given by the rules in paragraph 1 of Schedule 4 to the Pensions Act 1995 or paragraph 1 of Schedule 2 to the Pensions (Northern Ireland) Order 1995,][4]

["Scottish basic rate limit" means a rate limit set by the Scottish Parliament under section 80C(2A) of the Scotland Act 1998 for the purposes of determining the extent to which a Scottish taxpayer's income is charged at the Scottish basic rate where a Scottish rate resolution under that Act has set more than one rate for the tax year.][5]

[(1A) In this Part, so far as it forms part of the Corporation Tax Acts, expressions which are defined for the purposes of the Income Tax Acts are to be given the same meaning as they have in the Income Tax Acts.][3]

[(1B) In this Part "Master Trust scheme" means a pension scheme—

    (a) that is a Master Trust scheme within the meaning of the Pension Schemes Act 2017 (see sections 1 and 2 of that Act) or corresponding provision in force in Northern Ireland, and

    (b) whose operation would be unlawful under Part 1 of that Act (Master Trusts), or corresponding provision in force in Northern Ireland, were the scheme not authorised under that Part or that corresponding provision.

(1C) For the purposes of determining whether the condition in subsection (1B)(b) is met, the following are to be ignored—

    (a) any regulations under section 40 of the Pension Schemes Act 2017 (regulations modifying application of Part 1 of that Act);

    (b) any provision in force in Northern Ireland corresponding to regulations that could be made under that section.

(1D) For the purposes of this Part a Master Trust scheme is "unauthorised" if—

    (a) it is not authorised under Part 1 of the Pension Schemes Act 2017 or corresponding provision in force in Northern Ireland, and

    (b) its operation would be unlawful under that Part or that corresponding provision without such authorisation.

(1E) Section 1169 of the Companies Act 2006 (dormant companies) applies for the purposes of this Part.][6]

(2) In this Part references to payments made, or benefits provided, by a pension scheme are to payments made or benefits provided from sums or assets held for the purposes of the pension scheme.

(3) For the purposes of this Part the sums and assets held for the purposes of an arrangement under a pension scheme are so much of the sums and assets held for the purposes of the pension scheme under which the arrangement is made as are properly attributable, in accordance with the provisions of the pension scheme and any just and reasonable apportionment, to the arrangement.

Commentary—*Simon's Taxes* **E7.218, E7.227.**

HMRC Manuals—Pensions Tax Manual PTM028000 (normal minimum pension age).

PTM146600 ("contributions" to a pension scheme that are not contributions).

PTM062400 (pensions: lifetime annuity).

Modifications—Pensions Schemes (Application of UK Provisions to Relevant Non-UK Schemes) Regulations, SI 2006/207 reg 13 (modification of this section in respect of relevant non-UK schemes).

Amendments—[1] In sub-s (1), definition of "abatement" inserted by FA 2005 s 101, Sch 10 paras 9, 64(1) with effect from 6 April 2006.

[2] In sub-s (1), words in the definition of "abatement" inserted and substituted by FA 2006 s 161, Sch 23 paras 1, 33. These amendments are deemed to have come into force on 6 April 2006.

[3] In sub-s (1), definition of "charity" repealed; word inserted after the definitions of "pension credit" and "pension debit"; and definitions repealed; and sub-s (1A) inserted; by ITA 2007 ss 1027, 1031, Sch 1 paras 456, 480, Sch 3 Pt 1 with effect for income tax purposes from 6 April 2007, and corporation tax purposes for accounting periods ending after 5 April 2007.

[4] In sub-s (1), definitions of "consumer prices index" and "pensionable age" inserted by FA 2011 s 66, Sch 17 paras 1, 21 with effect for the tax year 2011–12 and subsequent tax years, and in relation to pension input periods ending in the tax year 2011–12 but beginning earlier (or in 2011–12). For transitional provisions see FA 2011 Sch 17 paras 28–34.

⁵ In sub-s (1), definition of "Scottish basic rate limit" inserted by the Scotland Act 2016 (Income Tax Consequential Amendments) Regulations, SI 2017/468 regs 2, 6 with effect in relation to 2017–18 (the tax year appointed under the Scotland Act 2016 section 13(15)(*b*)) and subsequent tax years.

⁶ Sub-ss (1B)–(1E) inserted by FA 2018 s 13, Sch 3 para 1(1), (6) with effect as follows—

- sub-ss (1B), (1C) inserted with effect from 15 March 2018. However, note that, before the coming into force of the Pension Schemes Act 2017 s 3, this section has effect as if sub-ss (1B)(*b*), (1C) were omitted (FA 2018 Sch 3 para 3).
- sub-s (1D) inserted with effect from the later of (a) the date on which the Pension Schemes Act 2017 s 3 comes into force, or (b) 15 March 2018 (FA 2018 Sch 3 para 2(1)(*c*)).
- sub-s (1E) inserted with effect from 6 April 2018 (FA 2018 Sch 3 para 2(2)(*c*));

280 Abbreviations and general index

(1) In this Part—

"NIA 1965" means the National Insurance Act 1965 (c 51),

"NIA(NI) 1966" means the National Insurance Act (Northern Ireland) 1966 (c 6 (NI)),

"TMA 1970" means the Taxes Management Act 1970 (c 9),

"ICTA 1970" means the Income and Corporation Taxes Act 1970 (c 10),

"ICTA" means the Income and Corporation Taxes Act 1988 (c 1),

"SSCBA 1992" means the Social Security Contributions and Benefits Act 1992 (c 4),

"SSCB(NI)A 1992" means the Social Security Contributions and Benefits (Northern Ireland) Act 1992 (c 7),

"TCGA 1992" means the Taxation of Chargeable Gains Act 1992 (c 12),

"WRPA 1999" means the Welfare Reform and Pensions Act 1999 (c 30),

"WRP(NI)O 1999" means the Welfare Reform and Pensions (Northern Ireland) Order 1999 (SI 1999/3147 (NI 11)),

"FISMA 2000" means the Financial Services and Markets Act 2000 (c 8), . . . ¹

"ITEPA 2003" means the Income Tax (Earnings and Pensions) Act 2003 (c 1) [. . . ⁷

"ITTOIA 2005" means the Income Tax (Trading and Other Income Act) 2005]¹[, . . . ¹¹

"ITA 2007" means the Income Tax Act 2007]⁷ [, . . . ¹⁶

["FA 2008" means the Finance Act 2008,]¹⁸

"CTA 2009" means the Corporation Tax Act 2009]¹¹[, and

"CTA 2010" means the Corporation Tax Act 2010.]¹⁶

["FA 2012" means the Finance Act 2012.]¹⁷

(2) In this Part the following expressions are defined or otherwise explained by the provisions indicated—

[abatement	section 279(1)]²
accounting period	section 834(1) of ICTA
[acquiring an interest in property (for the purposes of the taxable property provisions)	paragraphs 12 and 27 to 29 of Schedule 29A]⁵
active member (of a pension scheme)	section 151(2)
active membership period (in sections 221 to 223)	section 221(4) and (5)
[additional rate	section 6(2) of ITA 2007 (as applied by section 989 of that Act)]¹²
amount crystallised	section 216
annual allowance	section 228
annual allowance charge	section 227(1)
annuity protection lump sum death benefit	paragraph 16 of Schedule 29
arrangement	section 152(1)
authorised surplus payment	section 177
available (in relation to a person's lifetime allowance)	section 219
basic rate	[section 6(2) of ITA 2007 (as applied by section 989 of that Act)]⁸
basic rate limit	[section [10]¹³ of ITA 2007 (as applied by section 989 of that Act)]⁸
benefits (provided by pension scheme)	section 279(2)
benefit crystallisation event	section 216
the Board of Inland Revenue	section 279(1)
borrowing (in Chapter 3)	section 163
[building (for the purposes of the taxable property provisions)	paragraph 7(2) of Schedule 29A]⁵
cash balance arrangement	section 152(3)
cash balance benefits	section 152(5)

chargeable gain	[section 989 of ITA 2007][8]
charity	[section 989 of ITA 2007][8]
company	[section 992 of ITA 2007][8]
compensation payment	section 178
[consumer prices index	section 279(1)][15]
contribution	sections 188(4) to (6) and 195
defined benefits	section 152(7)
defined benefits arrangement	section 152(6)
defined benefits lump sum death benefit	paragraph 13 of Schedule 29
. . .	. . .[14]
[dependant (of a member of a registered pension scheme)	paragraph 15 of Schedule 28][22]
[dependants' annuity	paragraph 17 of Schedule 28][3]
[dependant's drawdown pension fund	paragraph 22 of Schedule 28][14]
[dependant's flexi-access drawdown fund	paragraph 22A of Schedule 28][20]
dependants' scheme pension	paragraph 16 of Schedule 28
[dependants' short term annuity	paragraph 20 of Schedule 28][3]
. . .	. . .[14]
[dormant (in relation to a body corporate)	section 279(1E)][30]
[drawdown pension fund lump sum death benefit	paragraph 17 of Schedule 29][14]
employee and employer (and employment)	section 279(1)
employment income	section 7(2) of ITEPA 2003
enhanced lifetime allowance	section 256(2)
regulations	
entitled (in relation to a lump sum)	section 166(2)
entitled (in relation to a pension)	section 165(3)
[flexi-access drawdown fund lump sum death benefit	paragraph 17A of Schedule 29][20]
higher rate	[section 6(2) of ITA 2007 (as applied by section 989 of that Act)][8]
[higher rate limit	section 10 of ITA 2007][12]
[holding an interest in a person (for the purposes of the taxable property provisions)	paragraph 16(2) to (4) of Schedule 29A][5]
[holding an interest in property (for the purposes of the taxable property provisions)	paragraph 13 of Schedule 29A][5]
[holding directly an interest in a vehicle (for the purposes of the taxable property provisions)	paragraph 20(3) of Schedule 29A][5]
[holding directly an interest in property (for the purposes of the taxable property provisions)	paragraphs 14 and 15 of Schedule 29A][5]
[holding indirectly an interest in a vehicle (for the purposes of the taxable property provisions)	paragraph 20(4) of Schedule 29A][5]
[holding indirectly an interest in property (for the purposes of the taxable property provisions)	paragraph 16(1) of Schedule 29A][5]
hybrid arrangement	section 152(8)
ill-health condition	paragraph 1 of Schedule 28
the individual (in sections 215 to 219)	section 214(5)
the Inland Revenue	section 279(1)
insurance company	section 275
[investment-regulated pension scheme (for the purposes of the taxable property provisions)	paragraphs 1 to 3 of Schedule 29A][5]
investments (in relation to a pension scheme)	section 186(3) and (4)
liability (in Chapter 3)	section 163
lifetime allowance (in relation to a person)	section 218
lifetime allowance charge	section 214(1)
lifetime allowance enhancement factors	section 218(5)
lifetime allowance excess lump sum	paragraph 11 of Schedule 29
lifetime annuity	paragraph 3 of Schedule 28
loan (in Chapter 3)	section 162
lump sum death benefit	section 168(2)

market value	section 278
[Master Trust scheme	section 279(1B) and (1C)][30]
member (of a pension scheme)	section 151(1)
. . .	. . .[14]
[member's drawdown pension fund	paragraph 8 of Schedule 28][14]
[member's flexi-access drawdown fund	paragraph 8A of Schedule 28][20]
. . .	. . .[14]
money purchase arrangement	section 152(2)
money purchase benefits	section 152(4)
[net income	section 23 of ITA 2007 (as applied by section 989 of that Act)][8]
net pay pension scheme	section 191(9)
[nominee (of a member of a registered pension scheme)	paragraph 27A of Schedule 28][22]
[nominees' annuity	paragraph 27AA of Schedule 28][24]
[nominees' drawdown pension	paragraph 27B of Schedule 28][22]
[nominee's flexi-access drawdown fund	paragraph 27E of Schedule 28][22]
[nominees' income withdrawal	paragraph 27D of Schedule 28][22]
[nominees' short-term annuity	paragraph 27C of Schedule 28][22]
normal minimum pension age	section 279(1)
occupational pension scheme	section 150(5)
overseas arrangement active membership period (in sections 224 to 226)	section 224(7) and (8)
overseas pension scheme	section 150(7)
payment (in Chapter 3)	section 161
payments (made by pension scheme)	section 279(2)
pension	section 165(2)
pension commencement lump sum	paragraph 1 of Schedule 29
pension credit and pension debit	section 279(1)
[pension death benefit	section 167(2)][10]
pension input amount	section 229
pension input period	[sections 238 to 238ZB][25]
pension protection lump sum death benefit	paragraph 14 of Schedule 29
pension scheme	section 150(1)
the pension scheme (in sections 215 to 219)	section 214(5)
pension sharing order or provision	section 279(1)
[pensionable age	section 279(1)][15]
pensioner member (of a pension scheme)	section 151(3)
period of account	[section 989 of ITA 2007][8]
personal representatives	[section 989 of ITA 2007][8]
property investment LLP	[section 1004 of ITA 2007][8]
public service pension scheme	section 150(3)
qualifying recognised overseas pension scheme	section 169(2)
recognised overseas pension scheme	section 150(8)
recognised overseas scheme arrangement (in sections 224 to 226)	section 224(2) and (3)
registered pension scheme	section 150(2)
[related dependants' annuity	paragraph 3(4A) of Schedule 29][4]
[related dependants' scheme pension	paragraph 3(7C) of Schedule 29][6]
[related nominees' annuity	paragraph 3(4B) of Schedule 29][24]
relevant overseas individual	section 221(3)
relevant UK earnings	section 189(2)
relevant UK individual	section 189
relevant valuation factor	section 276
relievable pension contributions	section 188(2) and (3)
[residential property (for the purposes of the taxable property provisions)	paragraphs 7(1), 8 and 9 of Schedule 29A][5]

retail prices index	[section 989 of ITA 2007][8]
scheme administrator	section 270 (but see also sections 271 to 274)
scheme chargeable payment	section 241
[scheme-held taxable property	section 185B(3)][5]
scheme manager	section 169(3)
scheme pension	paragraph 2 of Schedule 28
scheme sanction charge	section 239(1)
. . . [29]	. . . [29]
. . . [29]	. . . [29]
. . . [29]	. . . [29]
Scottish taxpayer	section 989 of ITA 2007][26].
serious ill-health lump sum	paragraph 4 of Schedule 29
...[28]	[28]
short service refund lump sum	paragraph 5 of Schedule 29
short service refund lump sum charge	section 205(1)
[short term annuity	paragraph 6 of Schedule 28][3]
special lump sum death benefits charge	section 206 . . . [23]
sponsoring employer	section 150(6)
standard lifetime allowance	section 218(2) [to (2C)][27]
[successor (of a member of a registered pension scheme)	paragraph 27F of Schedule 28][22]
[successors' annuity	paragraph 27FA of Schedule 28][24]
[successors' drawdown pension	paragraph 27G of Schedule 28][22]
[successor's flexi-access drawdown fund	paragraph 27K of Schedule 28][22]
[successors' income withdrawal	paragraph 27J of Schedule 28][22]
[successors' short-term annuity	paragraph 27H of Schedule 28][22]
sums and assets held for the purposes of an arrangement	section 279(3)
[sums and assets held for the purposes of an arrangement (for the purposes of the taxable property provisions)	paragraph 5 of Schedule 29A][5]
[taxable property (for the purposes of the taxable property provisions)	paragraphs 6, 10 and 11 of Schedule 29A][5]
[the taxable property provisions	paragraph 1(3) of Schedule 29A][5]
tax year	[section 4(2) of ITA 2007 (as applied by section 989 of that Act)][8]
the tax year 2006–07 etc	[section 4(4) of ITA 2007 (as applied by section 989 of that Act)][8]
total income	[section 23 of ITA 2007 (as applied by section 989 of that Act)][8]
total pension input amount	section 229
[transitional 2013/14 lump sum	paragraph 11A of Schedule 29][19]
. . . [9]	. . . [9]
trivial commutation lump sum	paragraph 7 of Schedule 29
unauthorised employer payment	section 160(4)
[unauthorised (in relation to a Master Trust scheme)	section 279(1D)][30]
unauthorised member payment	section 160(2)
unauthorised payment	section 160(5)
unauthorised payments charge	section 208(1)
unauthorised payments surcharge	section 209(1)
uncrystallised funds lump sum death benefit	paragraph 15 of Schedule 29
[uncrystallised funds pension lump sum	paragraph 4A of Schedule 29][21]
. . .	. . . [14]
valuation assumptions (in relation to a person)	section 277
[vehicle (in the taxable property provisions)	paragraph 20(2) of Schedule 29A][5]
winding-up lump sum	paragraph 10 of Schedule 29
winding-up lump sum death benefit	paragraph 21 of Schedule 29

Amendments—[1]   In sub-s (1), word preceding definition of "ITEPA 2003" repealed, and definition of "ITTOIA 2005" and word preceding inserted, by ITTOIA 2005 ss 882(1), 884, Sch 1 paras 629, 652, Sch 3 with effect from 6 April 2005. ITTOIA 2005 has effect—

  (a)   for income tax purposes, for 2005–06 and subsequent tax years, and

  (b)   for corporation tax purposes, for accounting periods ending after 5 April 2005: ITTOIA 2005 s 883(1).

[2]   In sub-s (2), entry inserted by FA 2005 s 101, Sch 10 paras 10, 64(1) with effect from 6 April 2006.

[3]   In sub-s (2), entries inserted by FA 2005 s 101, Sch 10 paras 17, 64(1) with effect from 6 April 2006.

[4]   In sub-s (2), entry inserted by FA 2005 s 101, Sch 10 paras 33, 64(1) with effect from 6 April 2006.

[5]   In sub-s (2), entries inserted by FA 2006 s 158, Sch 21 paras 2, 12. These amendments are deemed to have come into force on 6 April 2006.

[6]   In sub-s (2), entry inserted by FA 2006 s 161, Sch 23 paras 1, 26. This amendment is deemed to have come into force on 6 April 2006.

[7]   In sub-s (1), word repealed, and entry inserted, by ITA 2007 ss 1027, 1031, Sch 1 paras 456, 481(1), (2), Sch 3 Pt 1 with effect for income tax purposes from 6 April 2007, and corporation tax purposes for accounting periods ending after 5 April 2007.

[8]   In sub-s (2), words substituted and inserted, and entry inserted, by ITA 2007 s 1027, Sch 1 paras 456, 481(1), (3) with effect for income tax purposes from 6 April 2007, and corporation tax purposes for accounting periods ending after 5 April 2007.

[9]   In sub-s (2), entry repealed by FA 2007 ss 69, 114, Sch 19 paras 1, 8, 29(3), Sch 27 Pt 3(1) with effect in relation to lump sum death benefits paid in respect of members of schemes whose deaths occur on or after 6 April 2007.

[10]   In sub-s (2), entry inserted by FA 2007 s 70, Sch 20 paras 22(2), 24(3). This amendment is deemed always to have had effect.

[11]   In sub-s (1), word "and" following entry for "ITTOIA 2005" repealed, and entry for "CTA 2009" inserted, by CTA 2009 ss 1322, 1326, Sch 1 paras 569, 580, Sch 3 Part 1. CTA 2009 applies for accounting periods ending on or after 1 April 2009 (for corporation tax purposes) and for tax years 2009–10 onwards (for income and capital gains tax purposes).

[12]   In sub-s (2) entries inserted by FA 2010 s 68(1), (2), (4) with effect for the tax year 2010–11 and subsequent tax years.

[13]   In sub-s (2), in definition of "basic rate limit" figure substituted by FA 2010 s 68(1), (3) with effect for the tax year 2008–09 and subsequent tax years.

[14]   In sub-s (2) entries inserted and repealed by FA 2011 s 65, Sch 16 paras 62, 77 with effect for the tax year 2011–12 and subsequent tax years, subject to transitional provisions in FA 2011 Sch 16 Pt 3. The insertion of the entry relating to "serious ill-health lump sum charge" has effect in relation to lump sums paid on or after 6 April 2011 (FA 2011 Sch 16 para 102). The repeal of the entry relating to "unsecured pension fund lump sum death benefit" and the insertion of the entry for "drawdown pension fund lump sum death benefit" have effect in relation to deaths occurring on or after 6 April 2011 (FA 2011 Sch 16 para 103).

[15]   In sub-s (2), definitions of "consumer prices index" and "pensionable age" inserted by FA 2011 s 66, Sch 17 paras 1, 22 with effect for the tax year 2011–12 and subsequent tax years, and in relation to pension input periods ending in the tax year 2011–12 but beginning earlier (or in 2011–12). For transitional provisions see FA 2011 Sch 17 paras 28–34.

[16]   In sub-s (1), word "and" at the end of definition of "ITA 2007" repealed, and definition of "CTA 2010" inserted, by FA 2012 s 48, Sch 13 para 16, with effect in relation to contributions made by employers on or after 22 February 2012. Note that identical amendments were made by FA 2012 Sch 13 para 2 with effect in relation to contributions paid by employers on or after 29 November 2011 but before 22 February 2012.

[17]   Definition inserted by FA 2012 s 146, Sch 16 paras 112, 122 with effect in relation to accounting periods of companies beginning on or after 1 January 2013 (subject in transitional provisions in FA 2012 Sch 17). For accounting periods straddling 1 January 2013, see FA 2012 s 149.

[18]   Definition of "FA 2008" inserted by FA 2013 s 53(8) with effect from 17 July 2013.

[19]   In sub-s (2), definition inserted by FA 2014 s 43, Sch 5 para 5(4). This amendment is to be treated as having come into force on 19 March 2014 (FA 2014 Sch 5 para 15).

[20]   In sub-s (2), definitions inserted by the Taxation of Pensions Act 2014 s 1, Sch 1 paras 5, 18 with effect from 17 December 2014.

[21]   Definition inserted by the Taxation of Pensions Act 2014 s 1, Sch 1 paras 53, 56 with effect from 17 December 2014.

[22]   Definitions inserted by the Taxation of Pensions Act 2014 s 3, Sch 2 paras 1, 14 with effect from 17 December 2014.

[23]   In definition of "special lump sum death benefits charge", reference substituted for "206(1)" by the Taxation of Pensions Act 2014 s 3, Sch 2 para 18 with effect from 6 April 2015.

[24]   In sub-s (2), definitions inserted by FA 2015 s 34, Sch 4 paras 1, 12 with effect from 26 March 2015.

[25]   In sub-s (2), in definition of "pension input period", words substituted for words "section 238" by F(No 2)A 2015 s 23, Sch 4 paras 1, 5 with effect from 18 November 2015.

[26]   In sub-s (2), definitions inserted by the Scottish Rate of Income Tax (Consequential Amendments) Order, SI 2015/1810 art 7(1), (3) with effect in relation to the tax year 2016–17 (the tax year appointed by the Treasury under the Scotland Act 2012 s 25(5) by virtue of SI 2015/2000) and subsequent tax years.

[27]   In sub-s (2), in definition of "standard lifetime allowance" words substituted for words "and (3)" by FA 2016 s 19(6) with effect from 15 September 2016. Note that FA 2004 s 218(2)–(2D) were inserted by FA 2016 s 19(1), (2) with effect for the tax year 2016-17 and subsequent tax years.

[28]   In sub-s (2), entry for "serious ill-health lump sum charge" repealed by FA 2016 s 22, Sch 5 para 3(1)(c) with effect in relation to lump sums paid after 15 September 2016.

[29]   In sub-s (2), entries for "Scottish additional rate", "Scottish basic rate" and "Scottish higher rate" repealed by the Scotland Act 2016 (Income Tax Consequential Amendments) Regulations, SI 2017/468 regs 2, 7 with effect in relation to 2017–18 (the tax year appointed under the Scotland Act 2016 section 13(15)(b)) and subsequent tax years.

[30]   In sub-s (2), definitions inserted by FA 2018 s 13, Sch 3 para 1(1), (7) with effect as follows—

  –   definition of "dormant (in relation to a body corporate)" inserted with effect from 6 April 2018 (FA 2018 Sch 3 para 2(2)(d));

  –   definition of "Master Trust scheme" inserted with effect from 15 March 2018; and

  –   definition of "unauthorised (in relation to a Master Trust scheme)" inserted with effect from the later of (a) the date on which the Pension Schemes Act 2017 s 3 comes into force, or (b) 15 March 2018 (FA 2018 Sch 3 para 2(1)(d)).

Other supplementary provisions

281 Minor and consequential amendments

(1) Schedule 35 contains minor and consequential amendments of enactments in consequence of, or otherwise in connection with, this Part.

(2) The Treasury may by order make such other amendments (including repeals and revocations) as may appear appropriate in consequence of, or otherwise in connection with, this Part—

    (*a*) in any enactment contained in an Act passed before 6th April 2006 or in the Session in which that date falls, and

    (*b*) in any instrument made before that date or in the Session in which that date falls.

[(2A) The Treasury may by order make in any relevant enactment such amendments (including repeals and revocations) as may appear appropriate in consequence of, or otherwise in connection with, any amendment (or repeal or revocation) made in this Part by any enactment contained in an Act passed after this Act (an "amending Act").][1]

[(2B) For this purpose a relevant enactment is—

    (*a*) an enactment contained in an Act passed, or

    (*b*) an instrument made,

before the passing of the amending Act or in the Session in which the amending Act is passed.][1]

(3) An order under subsection (2) [or (2A)][1] may include any transitional provisions or savings appearing to the Treasury to be appropriate.

[*(4) An order under subsection (2) or (2A) may include provision having effect in relation to times before it is made if it does not increase any person's liability to tax.*][1], [2]

Orders—Pension Schemes (Miscellaneous Amendments) Order, SI 2013/1114.

Amendments—[1] Sub-ss (2A), (2B), (4) inserted, and words in sub-s (3) inserted, by FA 2006 s 161, Sch 23 paras 1, 34. These amendments are deemed to have come into force on 6 April 2006.

[2] Sub-s (4) repealed by FA 2009 s 75(2)(*b*) with effect from 21 July 2009.

282 Orders and regulations

[(A1) Any order or regulations made by the Treasury or the Commissioners for Her Majesty's Revenue and Customs under this Part may include provision having effect in relation to times before the order is, or regulations are, made if that provision does not increase any person's liability to tax.

(A2) Subsection (A1) does not limit any specific power to make provision by an order or regulations in relation to times before the order is, or regulations are, made.][1]

(1) Any power of the Treasury or the [Commissioners for Her Majesty's Revenue and Customs][4] to make any order or regulations under this Part is exercisable by statutory instrument.

[(1A) No order may be made under section 208(6), 209(7), 215(2A), [237B(11)][3], 240(3A) or 242(5)[, no order may be made under section 228(2) which specifies an amount for any tax year less than the annual allowance for the immediately preceding tax year and no order may be made under section 238A which increases any person's liability to tax][3] unless a draft of the statutory instrument containing it has been laid before, and approved by a resolution of, the House of Commons.][2]

(2) Any statutory instrument containing any order or regulations made by the Treasury or the [Commissioners for Her Majesty's Revenue and Customs][4] under this Part[, if made without a draft having been approved by a resolution of the House of Commons,][2] is subject to annulment in pursuance of a resolution of the House of Commons.

[(3) Subsection (2) does not apply to an instrument containing only regulations under section 218(2D).][5]

Commentary—*Simon's Taxes* A1.106.

Orders—Pension Schemes (Miscellaneous Amendments) Order, SI 2013/1114.

Finance Act 2004 (Registered Pension Schemes and Annual Allowance Charge) (Amendment) Order, SI 2015/80.

Regulations—Registered Pension Schemes (Relevant Income) Regulations, SI 2011/1783.

Registered Pension Schemes (Relevant Annuities) (Amendment) Regulations, SI 2012/2940.

Registered Pension Schemes (Provision of Information) (Amendment) Regulations, SI 2013/1742.

Registered Pension Schemes (Authorised Payments) (Amendment) Regulations, SI 2013/1818.

Registered Pension Schemes (Transfer of Sums and Assets) (Amendment) Regulations, SI 2014/1449.

Registered Pension Schemes (Provision of Information) (Amendment) Regulations, SI 2014/1843.

Registered Pension Schemes (Audited Accounts) (Specified Persons) Regulations, SI 2015/1518.

Registered Pension Schemes (Provision of Information) (Amendment) Regulations, SI 2017/11.

Registered Pension Schemes and Overseas Pension Schemes (Miscellaneous Amendments) Regulations, 2018/5.

Pension Schemes (Application of UK Provisions to Relevant Non-UK Schemes) (Amendment) Regulations, SI 2018/373.

Note—This section was to have been amended by FA 2010 s 23, Sch 2 para 3 with effect for the tax year 2011–12 and subsequent tax years. However, FA 2010 s 23, Sch 2 were repealed by SI 2010/2938 art 2 with effect from 10 December 2010.

Modifications—See FA 2011 Sch 16 para 108 (modification of sub-s (A1) in relation to orders or regs relating to FA 2011 Sch 16 para 108)).

Amendments—[1] Sub-ss (A1), (A2) inserted by FA 2009 s 75(1) with effect from 21 July 2009.

[2] Sub-s (1A) inserted, and in sub-s (2) words inserted by FA 2009 s 6, Sch 2 paras 10, 18 with effect for the tax year 2010–11 and subsequent tax years. The powers conferred by the amendments made by FA 2009 Sch 2 may be exercised at any time on or after 21 July 2009 but not so as to make provision having effect before the tax year 2010–11 (FA 2009 Sch 2 para 25(1)).

[3] In sub-s (1A),figure substituted for figure "227(5A)" and words inserted, by FA 2011 s 66, Sch 17 paras 1, 23 with effect for the tax year 2011–12 and subsequent tax years, and in relation to pension input periods ending in the tax year 2011–12 but beginning earlier (or in 2011–12). For transitional provisions see FA 2011 Sch 17 paras 28–34.

[4] In sub-ss (1), (2), words substituted for words "Board of Inland Revenue" by FA 2014 s 43, Sch 5 para 14 with effect from 17 July 2014.

[5] Sub-s (3) inserted by FA 2016 s 19(7) with effect from 15 September 2016. Note that FA 2004 s 218(2D) was inserted by FA 2016 s 19(1), (2) with effect for the tax year 2016-17 and subsequent tax years.

283 Transitionals and savings

(1) Schedule 36 contains miscellaneous transitional provisions and savings.

(2) The Treasury may by order make any other transitional provision which may appear appropriate in consequence of, or otherwise in connection with, this Part or the repeals made by this Act in consequence of this Part.

(3) An order under subsection (2) may, in particular, include savings from the effect of any amendment made by this Part or any repeal made by this Act in consequence of this Part.

[(3A) The Treasury may by order make any transitional provision which may appear appropriate in consequence of, or otherwise in connection with, any amendment (or repeal or revocation) made in this Part by any enactment contained in an Act passed after this Act (an "amending Act").

[(3B) An order under subsection (3A) may, in particular, include savings from the effect of any amendment (or repeal or revocation) made by the amending Act.

(3C) . . . [2]][1]

(4) Nothing in Schedule 36 limits the power conferred by subsection (2) [or (3A)][1].

(5) Nothing in that Schedule or in any provision made by virtue of subsection (2) [or (3A)][1] prejudices the operation of sections 16 and 17 of the Interpretation Act 1978 (c 30) (effect of repeals).

Regulations—Taxation of Pension Schemes (Transitional Provisions) Order, SI 2006/572.
Pension Schemes (Transfers, Reorganisations and Winding Up) (Transitional Provisions) Order, SI 2006/573.
Amendments—[1] Sub-ss (3A)–(3C) inserted, and words in sub-ss (4), (5) inserted, by FA 2006 s 161, Sch 23 paras 1, 35. These amendments are deemed to have come into force on 6 April 2006.
[2] Sub-s (3C) repealed by FA 2009 s 75(2)(c) with effect from 21 July 2009.

284 Commencement

(1) Chapters 3 to 7 and section 281 (with Schedule 35) do not come into force until 6th April 2006.

(2) But any power to make an order or regulations under any of those provisions may be exercised at any time after this Act is passed.

PART 5

OIL

285 Certain receipts not to be tariff receipts

(1)–(4) *See PRT in Part 3 of this Publication.*

(5) Schedule 37 to this Act has effect; and in that Schedule—

Part 1 makes amendments to the Oil Taxation Act 1983 (c 56) relating to allowable expenditure and disposal receipts;

Part 2 makes transitional provision;

Part 3 makes amendments to the Taxes Act 1988;

Part 4 makes amendments to other enactments.

(6) In Part 1 of Schedule 37 to this Act—

(a) the amendments made by paragraph 5 (which relate to disposal receipts) have effect in relation to disposals in chargeable periods ending on or after 30th June 2004, and

(b) the other amendments made by that Part have effect in relation to expenditure incurred on or after 1st January 2004.

(7) . . . [1], [2]

(8) The amendments made by Part 4 of that Schedule have effect in relation to chargeable periods (within the meaning of section 98 of the Finance Act 1999 ending on or after 30th June 2004.

Amendment—[1] Sub-s (7) repealed by CTA 2010 s 1181 Sch 3 Pt 2 with effect for corporation tax purposes for accounting periods ending on or after 1 April 2010.
[2] Sub-s (7) repealed by TIOPA 2010 s 503, Sch 10 Pt 2. TIOPA 2010 has effect for corporation tax purposes for accounting periods ending on or after 1 April 2010, for income and capital gains tax purposes for the tax year 2010–11 and subsequent tax years, and for petroleum revenue tax purposes for chargeable periods beginning on or after 1 July 2010.

286 Petroleum extraction activities: exploration expenditure supplement

(1) Chapter 5 of Part 12 of the Taxes Act 1988 (petroleum extraction activities) is amended as follows.

(2) (*inserts* TA 1988 s 496A)

(3) (*inserts* TA 1988 Sch 19B)

PART 7

DISCLOSURE OF TAX AVOIDANCE SCHEMES

306 Meaning of "notifiable arrangements" and "notifiable proposal"

(1) In this Part "notifiable arrangements" means any arrangements which—

(a) fall within any description prescribed by the Treasury by regulations,

(b) enable, or might be expected to enable, any person to obtain an advantage in relation to any tax that is so prescribed in relation to arrangements of that description, and

(c) are such that the main benefit, or one of the main benefits, that might be expected to arise from the arrangements is the obtaining of that advantage.

(2) In this Part "notifiable proposal" means a proposal for arrangements which, if entered into, would be notifiable arrangements (whether the proposal relates to a particular person or to any person who may seek to take advantage of it).

Commentary—*Simon's Taxes* A7.202, A7.203, A7.205, A7.206.

Regulations—Tax Avoidance Schemes (Prescribed Descriptions of Arrangements) Regulations, SI 2004/1863, Tax Avoidance Schemes (Prescribed Descriptions of Arrangements) Regulations, SI 2006/1543.

Annual Tax on Enveloped Dwellings Avoidance Schemes (Prescribed Descriptions of Arrangements) Regulations, SI 2013/2571.

Tax Avoidance Schemes (Prescribed Descriptions of Arrangements) (Amendment) Regulations, SI 2013/2595.

Annual Tax on Enveloped Dwellings Avoidance Schemes (Prescribed Descriptions of Arrangements) (Amendment) Regulations, SI 2015/464.

Tax Avoidance Schemes (Prescribed Descriptions of Arrangements) (Amendment) Regulations, SI 2016/99.

[306A Doubt as to notifiability

(1) HMRC may apply to the [tribunal][2] for an order that—

(a) a proposal is to be treated as notifiable, or

(b) arrangements are to be treated as notifiable.

(2) An application must specify—

(a) the proposal or arrangements in respect of which the order is sought, and

(b) the promoter.

(3) On an application the [tribunal][2] may make the order only if satisfied that HMRC—

(a) have taken all reasonable steps to establish whether the proposal or arrangements are notifiable, and

(b) have reasonable grounds for suspecting that the proposal or arrangements may be notifiable.

(4) Reasonable steps under subsection (3)(a) may (but need not) include taking action under section 313A or 313B.

(5) Grounds for suspicion under subsection (3)(b) may include—

(a) the fact that the relevant arrangements fall within a description prescribed under section 306(1)(a);

(b) an attempt by the promoter to avoid or delay providing information or documents about the proposal or arrangements under or by virtue of section 313A or 313B;

(c) the promoter's failure to comply with a requirement under or by virtue of section 313A or 313B in relation to another proposal or other arrangements.

(6) Where an order is made under this section in respect of a proposal or arrangements, the prescribed period for the purposes of section 308(1) or (3) in so far as it applies by virtue of the order—

(a) shall begin after a date prescribed for the purpose, and

(b) may be of a different length than the prescribed period for the purpose of other applications of section 308(1) or (3).

(7) An order under this section in relation to a proposal or arrangements is without prejudice to the possible application of section 308, other than by virtue of this section, to the proposal or arrangements.][1]

Commentary—*Simon's Taxes* A7.243.

Cross references—Tax Avoidance Schemes (Information) Regulations, SI 2012/1836 reg 16 (higher rate of penalty following a failure to comply with an order under s 306A or 314A).

Regulations—Tax Avoidance Schemes (Penalty) Regulations, SI 2007/3104 reg 3 (where a penalty is imposed under TMA 1970 s 98C(1), following an order under FA 2004 s 306A, the amount specified in s 98C(1)(b) is increased to £5,000).

Tax Avoidance Schemes (Information) Regulations, SI 2012/1836.

Inheritance Tax Avoidance Schemes (Prescribed Descriptions of Arrangements) Regulations, SI 2017/1172.

Amendments—[1]   This section inserted by FA 2007 s 108(1), (2), (10) with effect from 19 July 2007.

[2]   In sub-ss (1), (3) word substituted for the words "Special Commissioners" by the Transfer of Tribunal Functions and Revenue and Customs Appeals Order, SI 2009/56 art 3, Sch 1 para 429 with effect from 1 April 2009.

307 Meaning of "promoter"

(1) For the purposes of this Part a person is a promoter—

(a) in relation to a notifiable proposal, if, in the course of a relevant [business, the person ("P")—

(i) is to any extent responsible for the design of the proposed arrangements,

(ii) makes a firm approach to another person ("C") in relation to the notifiable proposal with a view to P making the notifiable proposal available for implementation by C or any other person, or

(iii) makes][3] the notifiable proposal available for implementation by other persons, and

(b) in relation to notifiable arrangements, if he is by virtue of paragraph (a)(ii) [or (iii)][3] a promoter in relation to a notifiable proposal which is implemented by those arrangements or if, in the course of a relevant business, he is to any extent responsible for—

    (i) the design of the arrangements, or

    (ii) the organisation or management of the arrangements.

[(1A) For the purposes of this Part a person is an introducer in relation to a notifiable proposal if the person makes a marketing contact with another person in relation to the notifiable proposal.]³

(2) In this section "relevant business" means any trade, profession or business which—

    (a) involves the provision to other persons of services relating to taxation, or

    (b) is carried on by a bank, as defined by [section 1120 of the Corporation Tax Act 2010]², or by a securities house, as defined by [section 1009(3)]² of that Act.

(3) For the purposes of this section anything done by a company is to be taken to be done in the course of a relevant business if it is done for the purposes of a relevant business falling within subsection (2)(b) carried on by another company which is a member of the same group.

(4) Section 170 of the Taxation of Chargeable Gains Act 1992 has effect for determining for the purposes of subsection (3) whether two companies are members of the same group, but as if in that section—

    (a) for each of the references to a 75 per cent subsidiary there were substituted a reference to a 51 per cent subsidiary, and

    (b) subsection (3)(b) and subsections (6) to (8) were omitted.

[(4A) For the purposes of this Part a person makes a firm approach to another person in relation to a notifiable proposal if the person makes a marketing contact with the other person in relation to the notifiable proposal at a time when the proposed arrangements have been substantially designed.

(4B) For the purposes of this Part a person makes a marketing contact with another person in relation to a notifiable proposal if—

    (a) the person communicates information about the notifiable proposal to the other person,

    (b) the communication is made with a view to that other person, or any other person, entering into transactions forming part of the proposed arrangements, and

    (c) the information communicated includes an explanation of the advantage in relation to any tax that might be expected to be obtained from the proposed arrangements.

(4C) For the purposes of subsection (4A) proposed arrangements have been substantially designed at any time if by that time the nature of the transactions to form part of them has been sufficiently developed for it to be reasonable to believe that a person who wished to obtain the advantage mentioned in subsection (4B)(c) might enter into—

    (a) transactions of the nature developed, or

    (b) transactions not substantially different from transactions of that nature.]³

(5) A person is not to be treated as a promoter [or introducer]³ for the purposes of this Part by reason of anything done in prescribed circumstances.

[(6) In the application of this Part to a proposal or arrangements which are not notifiable, a reference to a promoter [or introducer]³ is a reference to a person who would be a promoter [or introducer]³ under subsections (1) to (5) if the proposal or arrangements were notifiable.]¹

Commentary—*Simon's Taxes* **A7.210.**

Regulations—Tax Avoidance Schemes (Promoters and Prescribed Circumstances) Regulations, SI 2004/1865.
Tax Avoidance Schemes (Information) Regulations, SI 2012/1836.
Tax Avoidance Schemes (Promoters and Prescribed Circumstances) (Amendment) Regulations, SI 2015/945.

Amendments—¹ Sub-s (6) inserted by FA 2007 s 108(1), (3), (10) with effect from 19 July 2007.
² In sub-s (2)(b) words "section 840A of the Taxes Act 1988" and "section 209A(4)" substituted by CTA 2010 s 1177, Sch 1 paras 423, 429. CTA 2010 has effect for corporation tax purposes for accounting periods ending on or after 1 April 2010, and for income and capital gains tax purposes for the tax year 2010–11 and subsequent tax years.
³ In sub-s (1)(a) words substituted, in sub-ss (1)(b), (5), (6) words inserted, and sub-ss (1A), (4A)–(4C) inserted, by FA 2010 s 56, Sch 17 paras 1, 2 with effect from 1 January 2011 (by virtue of SI 2010/3019 art 2).

308 Duties of promoter

(1) [A person who is a promoter in relation to a notifiable proposal]¹ must, within the prescribed period after the relevant date, provide the Board with prescribed information relating to [the]¹ notifiable proposal.

(2) In subsection (1) "the relevant date" means the [earliest]² of the following—

    [(za) the date on which the promoter first makes a firm approach to another person in relation to a notifiable proposal,]²

    (a) the date on which the promoter makes [the]¹ notifiable proposal available for implementation by any other person, or

    (b) the date on which the promoter first becomes aware of any transaction forming part of notifiable arrangements implementing the notifiable proposal.

(3) [A person who is a promoter in relation to notifiable arrangements]¹ must, within the prescribed period after the date on which he first becomes aware of any transaction forming part of [the notifiable]¹ arrangements, provide the Board with prescribed information relating to those arrangements, unless those arrangements implement a proposal in respect of which notice has been given under subsection (1).

[(4) Subsection (4A) applies where a person complies with subsection (1) in relation to a notifiable proposal for arrangements and another person is—

(*a*) also a promoter in relation to the notifiable proposal or is a promoter in relation to a notifiable proposal for arrangements which are substantially the same as the proposed arrangements (whether they relate to the same or different parties), or

(*b*) a promoter in relation to notifiable arrangements implementing the notifiable proposal or notifiable arrangements which are substantially the same as notifiable arrangements implementing the notifiable proposal (whether they relate to the same or different parties).

(4A) Any duty of the other person under subsection (1) or (3) in relation to the notifiable proposal or notifiable arrangements is discharged if—

(*a*) the person who complied with subsection (1) has notified the identity and address of the other person to HMRC or the other person holds the reference number allocated to the proposed notifiable arrangements under section 311, and

(*b*) the other person holds the information provided to HMRC in compliance with subsection (1).

(4B) Subsection (4C) applies where a person complies with subsection (3) in relation to notifiable arrangements and another person is—

(*a*) a promoter in relation to a notifiable proposal for arrangements which are substantially the same as the notifiable arrangements (whether they relate to the same or different parties), or

(*b*) also a promoter in relation to the notifiable arrangements or notifiable arrangements which are substantially the same (whether they relate to the same or different parties).

(4C) Any duty of the other person under subsection (1) or (3) in relation to the notifiable proposal or notifiable arrangements is discharged if—

(*a*) the person who complied with subsection (3) has notified the identity and address of the other person to HMRC or the other person holds the reference number allocated to the notifiable arrangements under section 311, and

(*b*) the other person holds the information provided to HMRC in compliance with subsection (3).][1]

(5) Where a person is a promoter in relation to two or more notifiable proposals or sets of notifiable arrangements which are substantially the same (whether they relate to the same parties or different parties), he need not provide information under subsection (1) or (3) if he has already provided information under either of those subsections in relation to any of the other proposals or arrangements.

[(6) The Treasury may by regulations provide for this section to apply with modifications in relation to proposals or arrangements that—

(*a*) enable, or might be expected to enable, a person to obtain an advantage in relation to stamp duty land tax, and

(*b*) are of a description specified in the regulations.][3]

Commentary—*Simon's Taxes* **A7.230, A7.231, A7.233.**
Regulations—Tax Avoidance Schemes (Information) Regulations, SI 2012/1836.
Stamp Duty Land Tax (Avoidance Schemes) (Specified Proposals or Arrangements) Regulations, SI 2012/2396.
Tax Avoidance Schemes (Information) (Amendment, etc) Regulations, SI 2013/2592.
Amendments—[1]   In sub-ss (1), (2)(*a*), (3) words substituted, and sub-ss (4)–(4C) substituted for previous sub-s (4), by FA 2008 s 116, Sch 38 paras 1, 2 with effect from 1 November 2008 (by virtue of SI 2008/1935 art 2, except in relation to stamp duty land tax, in relation to which the effective date is to be appointed).
[2]   In sub-s (2) word substituted for word "earlier", and sub-s (2)(*za*) inserted by FA 2010 s 56, Sch 17 paras 1, 3 with effect from 1 January 2011 (by virtue of SI 2010/3019 art 2).
[3]   Sub-s (6) inserted by FA 2012 s 215 with effect from 17 July 2012.

[308A Supplemental information

(1) This section applies where—

(*a*) a promoter (P) has provided information in purported compliance with section 308(1) or (3), but

(*b*) HMRC believe that P has not provided all the prescribed information.

(2) HMRC may apply to the [tribunal][2] for an order requiring P to provide specified information about, or documents relating to, the notifiable proposal or arrangements.

(3) The [tribunal][2] may make an order under subsection (2) in respect of information or documents only if satisfied that HMRC have reasonable grounds for suspecting that the information or documents—

(*a*) form part of the prescribed information, or

(*b*) will support or explain the prescribed information.

(4) A requirement by virtue of subsection (2) shall be treated as part of P's duty under section 308(1) or (3).

(5) In so far as P's duty under section 308(1) or (3) arises out of a requirement by virtue of subsection (2) above, the prescribed period shall begin after a date prescribed for the purpose.

(6) In so far as P's duty under section 308(1) or (3) arises out of a requirement by virtue of subsection (2) above, the prescribed period—

(*a*) may be of a different length than the prescribed period for the purpose of other applications of section 308(1) or (3), and

(*b*) may be extended by HMRC by direction.][1]

Commentary—*Simon's Taxes* **A7.244**.
Regulations—Tax Avoidance Schemes (Information) Regulations, SI 2012/1836.
Amendments—[1] This section inserted by FA 2007 s 108(1), (4), (10) with effect from 19 July 2007.
[2] In sub-ss (2), (3) word substituted for the words "Special Commissioners" by the Transfer of Tribunal Functions and Revenue and Customs Appeals Order, SI 2009/56 art 3, Sch 1 para 429 with effect from 1 April 2009.

309 Duty of person dealing with promoter outside United Kingdom

(1) Any person ("the client") who enters into any transaction forming part of any notifiable arrangements in relation to which—

(a) a promoter is resident outside the United Kingdom, and

(b) no promoter is resident in the United Kingdom,

must, within the prescribed period after doing so, provide the Board with prescribed information relating to the notifiable arrangements.

(2) Compliance with section 308(1) by any promoter in relation to the notifiable arrangements discharges the duty of the client under subsection (1).

Commentary—*Simon's Taxes* **A7.211, A7.231**.
HMRC Manuals—Employment Related Securities Manual ERSM210010 (disclosure of tax avoidance schemes).
Regulations—Tax Avoidance Schemes (Information) Regulations, SI 2012/1836.

310 Duty of parties to notifiable arrangements not involving promoter

Any person who enters into any transaction forming part of notifiable arrangements as respects which neither he nor any other person in the United Kingdom is liable to comply with section 308 (duties of promoter) or section 309 (duty of person dealing with promoter outside the United Kingdom) must at the prescribed time provide the Board with prescribed information relating to the notifiable arrangements.

Commentary—*Simon's Taxes* **A7.230, A7.231, A7.233, A7.212**.
HMRC Manuals—Employment Related Securities Manual ERSM210010 (disclosure of tax avoidance schemes).
Regulations—Tax Avoidance Schemes (Information) Regulations, SI 2012/1836.

[310A Duty to provide further information requested by HMRC

(1) This section applies where—

(a) a person has provided the prescribed information about notifiable proposals or arrangements in compliance with section 308, 309 or 310, or

(b) a person has provided information in purported compliance with section 309 or 310 but HMRC believe that the person has not provided all the prescribed information.

(2) HMRC may require the person to provide—

(a) further specified information about the notifiable proposals or arrangements (in addition to the prescribed information under section 308, 309 or 310);

(b) documents relating to the notifiable proposals or arrangements.

(3) Where HMRC impose a requirement on a person under this section, the person must comply with the requirement within—

(a) the period of 10 working days beginning with the day on which HMRC imposed the requirement, or

(b) such longer period as HMRC may direct.][1]

Commentary—*Simon's Taxes* **A7.246**.
Amendments—[1] Sections 310A, 310B inserted by FA 2014 s 284(1), (2) with effect from 17 July 2014. Note that this section applies to a person who provides the prescribed information about notifiable proposals or arrangements in compliance or purported compliance with FA 2004 ss 308, 309 or 310 on or after 17 July 2014 (FA 2014 s 284(11)).

[310B Failure to provide information under section 310A: application to the Tribunal

(1) This section applies where HMRC—

(a) have required a person to provide information or documents under section 310A, but

(b) believe that the person has failed to provide the information or documents required.

(2) HMRC may apply to the tribunal for an order requiring the person to provide the information or documents required.

(3) The tribunal may make an order under subsection (2) only if satisfied that HMRC have reasonable grounds for suspecting that the information or documents will assist HMRC in considering the notifiable proposals or arrangements.

(4) Where the tribunal makes an order under subsection (2), the person must comply with it within—

(a) the period of 10 working days beginning with the day on which the tribunal made the order, or

(b) such longer period as HMRC may direct.][1]

Commentary—*Simon's Taxes* **A7.246**.
Amendments—[1] Sections 310A, 310B inserted by FA 2014 s 284(1), (2) with effect from 17 July 2014.

[310C Duty of promoters to provide updated information

(1) This section applies where—

(*a*) information has been provided under section 308 about any notifiable arrangements, or proposed notifiable arrangements, to which a reference number is allocated under section 311, and

(*b*) after the provision of the information, there is a change in relation to the arrangements of a kind mentioned in subsection (2).

(2) The changes referred to in subsection (1)(*b*) are—

(*a*) a change in the name by which the notifiable arrangements, or proposed notifiable arrangements, are known;

(*b*) a change in the name or address of any person who is a promoter in relation to the notifiable arrangements or, in the case of proposed notifiable arrangements, the notifiable proposal.

(3) A person who is a promoter in relation to the notifiable arrangements or, in the case of proposed notifiable arrangements, the notifiable proposal must inform HMRC of the change mentioned in subsection (1)(*b*) within 30 days after it is made.

(4) Subsections (5) and (6) apply for the purposes of subsection (3) where there is more than one person who is a promoter in relation to the notifiable arrangements or proposal.

(5) If the change in question is a change in the name or address of a person who is a promoter in relation to the notifiable arrangements or proposal, it is the duty of that person to comply with subsection (3).

(6) If a person provides information in compliance with subsection (3), the duty imposed by that subsection on any other person, so far as relating to the provision of that information, is discharged.]¹

Commentary—*Simon's Taxes* **A7.233, A7.202**.

Amendments—¹ Section 310C inserted by FA 2015 s 117, Sch 17 para 1 with effect in relation to notifiable arrangements, or proposed notifiable arrangements, only if a reference number under FA 2004 s 311 is allocated to the arrangements on or after 26 March 2015. This section does not apply in relation to notifiable arrangements, or proposed notifiable arrangements, where prescribed information relating to the arrangements was provided to HMRC before that day in compliance with FA 2004 s 308 (FA 2015 Sch 17 para 19).

311 Arrangements to be given reference number

(1) Where a person complies [or purports to comply]¹ with section 308(1) or (3), 309(1) or 310 in relation to any notifiable proposal or notifiable arrangements, the Board¹ . . . —

(*a*) [may within [90 days]²]¹ allocate a reference number to the notifiable arrangements or, in the case of a notifiable proposal, to the proposed notifiable arrangements, and

(*b*) if it does so, [must notify that number to the person and (where the person is one who has complied or purported to comply with section 308(1) or (3)) to any other person—

(i) who is a promoter in relation to the notifiable proposal (or arrangements implementing the notifiable proposal) or the notifiable arrangements (or proposal implemented by the notifiable arrangements), and

(ii) whose identity and address has been notified to HMRC by the person.]¹

(2) The allocation of a reference number to any notifiable arrangements (or proposed notifiable arrangements) is not to be regarded as constituting any indication by the Board that the arrangements could as a matter of law result in the obtaining by any person of a tax advantage.

(3) In this Part "reference number", in relation to any notifiable arrangements, means the reference number allocated under this section.

Commentary—*Simon's Taxes* **A7.233, A7.202**.

Amendments—¹ In sub-s (1), words inserted, substituted and repealed by FA 2008 s 116, Sch 38 paras 1, 2 with effect from 1 November 2008 (by virtue of SI 2008/1935 art 2, except in relation to stamp duty land tax, in relation to which the effective date is to be appointed).

² In sub-s (1)(*a*), figure substituted for "30" by FA 2015 s 117, Sch 17 para 4 with effect from 26 March 2015.

[312 Duty of promoter to notify client of number

(1) This section applies where a person who is a promoter in relation to notifiable arrangements is providing (or has provided) services to any person ("the client") in connection with the notifiable arrangements.

(2) The promoter must, within 30 days after the relevant date, provide the client with prescribed information relating to any reference number (or, if more than one, any one reference number) that has been notified to the promoter (whether by HMRC or any other person) in relation to—

(*a*) the notifiable arrangements, or

(*b*) any arrangements substantially the same as the notifiable arrangements (whether involving the same or different parties).

(3) In subsection (2) "the relevant date" means the later of—

(*a*) the date on which the promoter becomes aware of any transaction which forms part of the notifiable arrangements, and

(*b*) the date on which the reference number is notified to the promoter.

(4) But where the conditions in subsection (5) are met the duty imposed on the promoter under subsection (2) to provide the client with information in relation to notifiable arrangements is discharged.

(5) Those conditions are—

(*a*) that the promoter is also a promoter in relation to a notifiable proposal and provides services to the client in connection with them both,

(*b*) the notifiable proposal and the notifiable arrangements are substantially the same, and

(*c*) the promoter has provided to the client, in a form and manner specified by HMRC, prescribed information relating to the reference number that has been notified to the promoter in relation to the proposed notifiable arrangements.

(6) HMRC may give notice that, in relation to notifiable arrangements specified in the notice, promoters are not under the duty under subsection (2) after the date specified in the notice.][1]

Commentary—*Simon's Taxes* **A7.233, A7.202, A7.234.**

Regulations—Tax Avoidance Schemes (Information) Regulations, SI 2012/1836.

Tax Avoidance Schemes (Information) (Amendment) Regulations, SI 2015/948.

Amendments—[1]   Sections 312, 312A substituted for previous s 312, by FA 2008 s 116, Sch 38 paras 1, 4 with effect as follows—

   –   except in relation to stamp duty land tax, from 1 November 2008 (by virtue of SI 2008/1935 art 2); and

   –   in relation to stamp duty land tax, from 1 April 2010 (by virtue of SI 2010/409, art 2).

[312A Duty of client to notify parties of number

(1) This section applies where a person (a "client") to whom a person who is a promoter in relation to notifiable arrangements or a notifiable proposal is providing (or has provided) services in connection with the notifiable arrangements or notifiable proposal receives prescribed information relating to the reference number allocated to the notifiable arrangements or proposed notifiable arrangements.

(2) The client must, within the prescribed period, provide prescribed information relating to the reference number to any other person—

(*a*) who the client might reasonably be expected to know is or is likely to be a party to the arrangements or proposed arrangements, and

(*b*) who might reasonably be expected to gain a tax advantage in relation to any relevant tax by reason of the arrangements or proposed arrangements.

[(2A) Where the client—

(*a*) is an employer, and

(*b*) by reason of the arrangements or proposed arrangements, receives or might reasonably be expected to receive an advantage, in relation to any relevant tax, in relation to the employment of one or more of the client's employees,

the client must, within the prescribed period, provide to each of the client's relevant employees prescribed information relating to the reference number.][2]

[(3) For the purposes of this section—

(*a*) a tax is a "relevant tax", in relation to arrangements or arrangements proposed in a proposal of any description, if it is prescribed in relation to arrangements or proposals of that description by regulations under section 306;

(*b*) "relevant employee" means an employee in relation to whose employment the client receives or might reasonably be expected to receive the advantage mentioned in subsection (2A);

(*c*) "employee" includes a former employee;

(*d*) a reference to employment includes holding an office (and references to "employee" and "employer" are to be construed accordingly).][2]

(4) HMRC may give notice that, in relation to notifiable arrangements or a notifiable proposal specified in the notice, persons are not under [one or both of the duties under this section][2] after the date specified in the notice.

(5) The duty under subsection (2) [or (2A)][2] does not apply in prescribed circumstances.][1]

Commentary—*Simon's Taxes* **A7.233.**

Regulations—Tax Avoidance Schemes (Information) Regulations, SI 2012/1836.

Tax Avoidance Schemes (Information) (Amendment) Regulations, SI 2015/947.

Amendments—[1]   Sections 312, 312A substituted for previous s 312, by FA 2008 s 116, Sch 38 paras 1, 4 with effect as follows—

   –   except in relation to stamp duty land tax, from 1 November 2008 (by virtue of SI 2008/1935 art 2); and

   –   in relation to stamp duty land tax, from 1 April 2010 (by virtue of SI 2010/409, art 2).

[2]   Sub-s (2A) and words in sub-s (5) inserted, and sub-s (3) and words in sub-s (4) substituted, by FA 2015 s 117, Sch 17 para 5 with effect from 26 March 2015. Any notice given by HMRC under FA 2004 s 312A(4) before 26 March 2015 is treated on and after that day as given also in relation to the duty under FA 2004 s 312A(2A) (FA 2015 Sch 17 para 20).

[312B Duty of client to provide information to promoter

(1) This section applies where a person who is a promoter in relation to notifiable arrangements has provided a person ("the client") with the information prescribed under section 312(2) (duty of promoter to notify client of reference number).

(2) The client must, within the prescribed period, provide the promoter with prescribed information relating to the client.

(3) The duty under subsection (2) is subject to any exceptions that may be prescribed.][1]

Commentary—*Simon's Taxes* **A7.233.**

Regulations—Tax Avoidance Schemes (Information) (Amendment, etc) Regulations, SI 2013/2592.

Amendments—[1]   Section 312B inserted by FA 2013 s 223(1), (2) with effect from 17 July 2013.

313 Duty of parties to notifiable arrangements to notify Board of number, etc

(1) Any person who is a party to any notifiable arrangements must provide the Board with prescribed information relating to—

- (a) any reference number notified to him . . . [1], and
- (b) the time when he obtains or expects to obtain by virtue of the arrangements an advantage in relation to any relevant tax.

(2) For the purposes of subsection (1) a tax is a "relevant tax" in relation to any notifiable arrangements if it is prescribed in relation to arrangements of that description by regulations under section 306.

(3) Regulations [made by HMRC][1] may—

- (a) in prescribed cases, require the [information prescribed under subsection (1)][1] to be included in any return or account which the person is required by or under any enactment to deliver to the Board, and
- (b) in prescribed cases, require the [information prescribed under subsection (1) and such other information as is prescribed][1] to be provided separately to the Board at the prescribed time or times.

(4) A person is not liable to a penalty under—

- [(a) any provision relating to incorrect or uncorrected returns made under section 98 of the Finance Act 1986 (administration of stamp duty reserve tax),
- (b) Schedule 24 to the Finance Act 2007 (penalties for errors), or
- (c) any other prescribed provision,][2]

by reason of any failure to include in any return or account any reference number or other information required by virtue of subsection (3)(a) (but see section 98C of the Taxes Management Act 1970 for the penalty for failure to comply with this section).

[(5) HMRC may give notice that, in relation to notifiable arrangements specified in the notice, persons are not under the duty under subsection (1) after the date specified in the notice.][1]

[(6) The duty under subsection (1) does not apply in prescribed circumstances.][3]

Commentary—*Simon's Taxes* A7.233, A4.573.

Regulations—Tax Avoidance Schemes (Information) Regulations, SI 2012/1836.
Tax Avoidance Schemes (Information) (Amendment, etc) Regulations, SI 2013/2592.
Tax Avoidance Schemes (Information) (Amendment) Regulations, SI 2015/947.
Tax Avoidance Schemes (Miscellaneous Amendments) Regulations, SI 2017/1171.
Amendments—[1]   In sub-s (1)(a), words repealed; in sub-s (3), words substituted; in paras (a) and (b), words substituted; and
    sub-s (5) inserted, by FA 2008 s 116, Sch 38 paras 1, 5 with effect from 1 November 2008 (by virtue of SI 2008/1935 art 2,
    except in relation to stamp duty land tax, in relation to which the effective date is to be appointed).
[2]   Sub-s (4)(a)–(c) substituted for previous sub-s (4)(a)–(g), by the Finance Act 2008, Schedule 40 (Appointed Day, Transitional
    Provisions and Consequential Amendments) Order, SI 2009/571 art 8, Sch 1 para 26(1), (2) with effect from 1 April 2009.
[3]   Sub-s (6) inserted by FA 2015 s 117, Sch 17 para 6 with effect from 26 March 2015.

[313ZA Duty to provide details of clients

(1) This section applies where a person who is a promoter in relation to notifiable arrangements is providing (or has provided) services to any person ("the client") in connection with the notifiable arrangements and either—

- (a) the promoter is subject to the reference number information requirement, or
- (b) the promoter has failed to comply with section 308(1) or (3) in relation to the notifiable arrangements (or the notifiable proposal for them) but would be subject to the reference number information requirement if a reference number had been allocated to the notifiable arrangements.

(2) For the purposes of this section "the reference number information requirement" is the requirement under section 312(2) to provide to the client prescribed information relating to the reference number allocated to the notifiable arrangements.

(3) The promoter must, within the prescribed period after the end of the relevant period, provide HMRC with prescribed information in relation to the client.

(4) In subsection (3) "the relevant period" means such period during which the promoter is or would be subject to the reference number information requirement as is prescribed.

(5) The promoter need not comply with subsection (3) in relation to any notifiable arrangements at any time after HMRC have given notice under section 312(6) in relation to the notifiable arrangements.]

Commentary—*Simon's Taxes* A7.234.

Regulations—Tax Avoidance Schemes (Information) Regulations, SI 2012/1836.
Tax Avoidance Schemes (Information) (Amendment, etc) Regulations, SI 2013/2592.
Amendments—Section inserted by FA 2010 s 56, Sch 17 paras 1, 6 with effect from 1 January 2011 (by virtue of SI 2010/3019
    art 2).

[313ZB Enquiry following disclosure of client details

(1) This section applies where—

(a) a person who is a promoter in relation to notifiable arrangements has provided HMRC with information in relation to a person ("the client") under section 313ZA(3) (duty to provide client details), and

(b) HMRC suspect that a person other than the client is or is likely to be a party to the arrangements.

(2) HMRC may by written notice require the promoter to provide prescribed information in relation to any person other than the client who the promoter might reasonably be expected to know is or is likely to be a party to the arrangements.

(3) The promoter must comply with a requirement under or by virtue of subsection (2) within—

(a) the prescribed period, or

(b) such longer period as HMRC may direct.][1]

Commentary—*Simon's Taxes* **A7.234**.
Cross references See FA 2014 s 238 (compliance with this section under conditions of conduct notice issued to promoter).
Regulations—Tax Avoidance Schemes (Information) (Amendment, etc) Regulations, SI 2013/2592.
Amendments—[1]   Section 313ZB inserted by FA 2013 s 223(1), (3) with effect from 17 July 2013.

[313ZC Duty of employer to notify HMRC of details of employees etc

(1) This section applies if conditions A, B and C are met.

(2) Condition A is that a person who is a promoter in relation to notifiable arrangements or a notifiable proposal is providing (or has provided) services in connection with the notifiable arrangements or notifiable proposal to a person ("the client").

(3) Condition B is that the client receives information under section 312(2) or as mentioned in section 312(5).

(4) Condition C is that the client is an employer in circumstances where, as a result of the notifiable arrangement or proposed notifiable arrangement—

(a) one or more of the client's employees receive, or might reasonably be expected to receive, in relation to their employment, an advantage in relation to any relevant tax, or

(b) the client receives or might reasonably be expected to receive such an advantage in relation to the employment of one or more of the client's employees.

(5) Where an employee is within subsection (4)(a), or is an employee mentioned in subsection (4)(b), the client must provide HMRC with prescribed information relating to the employee at the prescribed time or times.

(6) The client need not comply with subsection (5) in relation to any notifiable arrangements at any time after HMRC have given notice under section 312(6) or 313(5) in relation to the notifiable arrangements.

(7) The duty under subsection (5) does not apply in prescribed circumstances.

(8) Section 312A(3) applies for the purposes of this section as it applies for the purposes of that section.][1]

Commentary—*Simon's Taxes* **A7.233**.
Regulations—Tax Avoidance Schemes (Information) (Amendment) Regulations, SI 2015/947.
Amendments—[1]   Section 313ZC inserted by FA 2015 s 117, Sch 17 para 9 with effect from 26 March 2015.

[313A Pre-disclosure enquiry

(1) Where HMRC suspect that a person (P) is the promoter [or introducer of a proposal, or the promoter of arrangements,][2] which may be notifiable, they may by written notice require P to state—

(a) whether in P's opinion the proposal or arrangements are notifiable by P, and

(b) if not, the reasons for P's opinion.

(2) A notice must specify the proposal or arrangements to which it relates.

(3) For the purpose of subsection (1)(b)—

(a) it is not sufficient to refer to the fact that a lawyer or other professional has given an opinion,

(b) the reasons must show, by reference to this Part and regulations under it, why P thinks the proposal or arrangements are not notifiable by P, and

(c) in particular, if P asserts that the arrangements do not fall within any description prescribed under section 306(1)(a), the reasons must provide sufficient information to enable HMRC to confirm the assertion.

(4) P must comply with a requirement under or by virtue of subsection (1) within—

(a) the prescribed period, or

(b) such longer period as HMRC may direct.][1]

Commentary—*Simon's Taxes* **A7.241**.
Regulations—Tax Avoidance Schemes (Information) Regulations, SI 2012/1836.
Amendments—[1]   This section inserted by FA 2007 s 108(1), (5), (10) with effect from 19 July 2007.
[2]   In sub-s (1) words substituted for words "of a proposal or arrangements" by FA 2010 s 56, Sch 17 paras 1, 4 with effect from 1 January 2011 (by virtue of SI 2010/3019 art 2).

[313B Reasons for non-disclosure: supporting information

(1) Where HMRC receive from a person (P) a statement of reasons why a proposal or arrangements are not notifiable by P, HMRC may apply to the [tribunal][2] for an order requiring P to provide specified information or documents in support of the reasons.

(2) P must comply with a requirement under or by virtue of subsection (1) within—
    (a) the prescribed period, or
    (b) such longer period as HMRC may direct.
(3) The power under subsection (1)—
    (a) may be exercised more than once, and
    (b) applies whether or not the statement of reasons was received under section 313A(1)(b).][1]

Commentary—*Simon's Taxes* A7.241.
Regulations—Tax Avoidance Schemes (Information) Regulations, SI 2012/1836.
Amendments—[1]   This section inserted by FA 2007 s 108(1), (5), (10) with effect from 19 July 2007.
[2]   In sub-s (1) word substituted for the words "Special Commissioners" by the Transfer of Tribunal Functions and Revenue and Customs Appeals Order, SI 2009/56 art 3, Sch 1 para 431 with effect from 1 April 2009.

[313C [Provision of information to HMRC by introducers]
[(1) This section applies where HMRC suspect—
    (a) that a person ("P") is an introducer in relation to a proposal, and
    (b) that the proposal may be notifiable.
(1A) HMRC may by written notice require P to provide HMRC with one or both of the following—
    (a) prescribed information in relation to each person who has provided P with any information relating to the proposal;
    (b) prescribed information in relation to each person with whom P has made a marketing contact in relation to the proposal.][2]
(2) A notice must specify the proposal to which it relates.
(3) P must comply with a requirement under [subsection (1A)][2] within—
    (a) the prescribed period, or
    (b) such longer period as HMRC may direct.][1]

Commentary—*Simon's Taxes* A7.245.
Regulations—Tax Avoidance Schemes (Information) Regulations, SI 2012/1836.
Tax Avoidance Schemes (Information) (Amendment) Regulations, SI 2015/947.
Amendments—[1]   Section inserted by FA 2010 s 56, Sch 17 paras 1, 9 with effect from 1 January 2011 (by virtue of SI 2010/3019 art 2).
[2]   Sub-ss (1), (1A) substituted for previous sub-s (1), heading substituted, and words in sub-s (3) substituted, by FA 2015 s 117, Sch 17 para 12 with effect from 26 March 2015.

314 Legal professional privilege
(1) Nothing in this Part requires any person to disclose to the Board any privileged information.
(2) In this Part "privileged information" means information with respect to which a claim to legal professional privilege, or, in Scotland, to confidentiality of communications, could be maintained in legal proceedings.

Commentary—*Simon's Taxes* A4.129, A1.118, A7.225, A7.228, A7.210 .

[314A Order to disclose
(1) HMRC may apply to the [tribunal][2] for an order that—
    (a) a proposal is notifiable, or
    (b) arrangements are notifiable.
(2) An application must specify—
    (a) the proposal or arrangements in respect of which the order is sought, and
    (b) the promoter.
(3) On an application the [tribunal][2] may make the order only if satisfied that section 306(1)(a) to (c) applies to the relevant arrangements.][1]

Commentary—*Simon's Taxes* A7.242.
Regulations—Tax Avoidance Schemes (Penalty) Regulations, SI 2007/3104 reg 4 (where a penalty is imposed under TMA 1970 s 98C(1), following an order under FA 2004 s 314A, the amount specified in s 98C(1)(b) is increased to £5,000).
Amendments—[1]   This section inserted by FA 2007 s 108(1), (6), (10) with effect from 19 July 2007.
[2]   In sub-ss (1), (3) word substituted for the words "Special Commissioners" by the Transfer of Tribunal Functions and Revenue and Customs Appeals Order, SI 2009/56 art 3, Sch 1 para 432 with effect from 1 April 2009.

315 Penalties
(1) (*inserts* TMA 1970 s 98C)
(2) (*amends* TMA 1970 s 100(2))
(3) (*inserts* TMA 1970 s 110C(1A))

Commentary—*Simon's Taxes* A7.261.

[316 Information to be provided in form and manner specified by HMRC
(1) HMRC may specify the form and manner in which information required to be provided by any of the information provisions must be provided if the provision is to be complied with.
(2) The "information provisions" are sections 308(1) and (3), 309(1), 310, [310A,][3] [310C,][4] 312(2), 312A(2) [and (2A)][4] [, 313(1) and (3)[, 313ZA(3) and 313ZC(5)][4][2].][1]

Commentary—*Simon's Taxes* A7.230, A7.232, A7.262.
Amendments—[1]   This section substituted by FA 2008 s 116, Sch 38 paras 1, 6 with effect from 1 November 2008 (by virtue of SI 2008/1935 art 2, except in relation to stamp duty land tax, in relation to which the effective date is to be appointed).

2 Words substituted for words "and 313(1) and (3)" by FA 2010 s 56, Sch 17 paras 1, 7 with effect from 1 January 2011 (by virtue of SI 2010/3019 art 2).
3 In sub-s (2), words inserted by FA 2014 s 284(1), (3) with effect from 17 July 2014.
4 In sub-s (2), words inserted and substituted by FA 2015 s 117, Sch 17 paras 2, 7, 10 with effect from 26 March 2015.

[316A Duty to provide additional information

(1) This section applies where a person is required to provide information under section 312(2) or 312A(2) or (2A).

(2) HMRC may specify additional information which must be provided by that person to the recipients under section 312(2) or 312A(2) or (2A) at the same time as the information referred to in subsection (1).

(3) HMRC may specify the form and manner in which the additional information is to be provided.

(4) For the purposes of this section "additional information" means information supplied by HMRC which relates to notifiable proposals or notifiable arrangements in general.][1]

Commentary—*Simon's Taxes* **A7.233**.
Amendments—[1] Section 316A inserted by FA 2015 s 117, Sch 17 para 14 with effect from 26 March 2015.

[316B Confidentiality

No duty of confidentiality or other restriction on disclosure (however imposed) prevents the voluntary disclosure by any person to HMRC of information or documents which the person has reasonable grounds for suspecting will assist HMRC in determining whether there has been a breach of any requirement imposed by or under this Part.][1]

Commentary—*Simon's Taxes* **A7.202**.
Amendments—[1] Section 316B inserted by FA 2015 s 117, Sch 17 para 16 with effect from 26 March 2015.

[316C Publication by HMRC

(1) HMRC may publish information about—

  (a) any notifiable arrangements, or proposed notifiable arrangements, to which a reference number is allocated under section 311;

  (b) any person who is a promoter in relation to the notifiable arrangements or, in the case of proposed notifiable arrangements, the notifiable proposal.

(2) The information that may be published is (subject to subsection (4))—

  (a) any information relating to arrangements within subsection (1)(a), or a person within subsection (1)(b), that is prescribed information for the purposes of section 308, 309 or 310;

  (b) any ruling of a court or tribunal relating to any such arrangements or person (in that person's capacity as a promoter in relation to a notifiable proposal or arrangements);

  (c) the number of persons in any period who enter into transactions forming part of notifiable arrangements within subsection (1)(a);

  (d) whether arrangements within subsection (1)(a) are APN relevant (see subsection (7));

  (e) any other information that HMRC considers it appropriate to publish for the purpose of identifying arrangements within subsection (1)(a) or a person within subsection (1)(b).

(3) The information may be published in any manner that HMRC considers appropriate.

(4) No information may be published under this section that identifies a person who enters into a transaction forming part of notifiable arrangements within subsection (1)(a).

(5) But where a person who is a promoter within subsection (1)(b) is also a person mentioned in subsection (4), nothing in subsection (4) is to be taken as preventing the publication under this section of information so far as relating to the person's activities as a promoter.

(6) Before publishing any information under this section that identifies a person as a promoter within subsection (1)(b), HMRC must—

  (a) inform the person that they are considering doing so, and

  (b) give the person reasonable opportunity to make representations about whether it should be published.

(7) Arrangements are "APN relevant" for the purposes of subsection (2)(d) if HMRC has indicated in a publication that it may exercise (or has exercised) its power under section 219 of the Finance Act 2014 (accelerated payment notices) by virtue of the arrangements being DOTAS arrangements within the meaning of that section.][1]

Commentary—*Simon's Taxes* **A7.202**.
Amendments—[1] Section 316C inserted by FA 2015 s 117, Sch 17 para 17 with effect in relation to notifiable arrangements, or proposed notifiable arrangements, only if a reference number under FA 2004 s 311 is allocated to the arrangements on or after 26 March 2015. This section does not apply in relation to notifiable arrangements, or proposed notifiable arrangements, where prescribed information relating to the arrangements was provided to HMRC before that day in compliance with FA 2004 ss 308, 309 or 310 (FA 2015 Sch 17 para 21(1), (2)). Sub-s (2)(b) applies in relation to a ruling of a court or tribunal only if the ruling is given on or after 26 March 2015 (FA 2015 Sch 17 para 21(3)).

[316D Section 316C: subsequent judicial rulings

(1) This section applies if—

  (a) information about notifiable arrangements, or proposed notifiable arrangements, is published under section 316C,

(b) at any time after the information is published, a ruling of a court or tribunal is made in relation to tax arrangements, and

(c) HMRC is of the opinion that the ruling is relevant to the arrangements mentioned in paragraph (a).

(2) A ruling is "relevant" to the arrangements if—

(a) the principles laid down, or reasoning given, in the ruling would, if applied to the arrangements, allow the purported advantage arising from the arrangements in relation to tax, and

(b) the ruling is final.

(3) HMRC must publish information about the ruling.

(4) The information must be published in the same manner as HMRC published the information mentioned in subsection (1)(a) (and may also be published in any other manner that HMRC considers appropriate).

(5) A ruling is "final" if it is—

(a) a ruling of the Supreme Court, or

(b) a ruling of any other court or tribunal in circumstances where—

   (i) no appeal may be made against the ruling,

   (ii) if an appeal may be made against the ruling with permission, the time limit for applications has expired and either no application has been made or permission has been refused,

   (iii) if such permission to appeal against the ruling has been granted or is not required, no appeal has been made within the time limit for appeals, or

   (iv) if an appeal was made, it was abandoned or otherwise disposed of before it was determined by the court or tribunal to which it was addressed.

(6) Where a ruling is final by virtue of sub-paragraph (ii), (iii) or (iv) of subsection (5)(b), the ruling is to be treated as made at the time when the sub-paragraph in question is first satisfied.

(7) In this section "tax arrangements" means arrangements in respect of which it would be reasonable to conclude (having regard to all the circumstances) that the obtaining of an advantage in relation to tax was the main purpose, or one of the main purposes.]¹

Commentary—*Simon's Taxes* A7.202.

Amendments—¹   Section 316D inserted by FA 2015 s 117, Sch 17 para 17 with effect from 26 March 2015.

317 Regulations under Part 7

(1) Any power of the Treasury or the Board to make regulations under this Part is exercisable by statutory instrument.

(2) Regulations made by the Treasury or the Board under this Part may [make different provision for different cases and may]¹ contain transitional provisions and savings.

(3) A statutory instrument containing regulations made by the Treasury or the Board under any provision of this Part is subject to annulment in pursuance of a resolution of the House of Commons.

Regulations—Tax Avoidance Schemes (Information) Regulations, SI 2012/1836.

Stamp Duty Land Tax (Avoidance Schemes) (Specified Proposals or Arrangements) Regulations, SI 2012/2396.

Annual Tax on Enveloped Dwellings Avoidance Schemes (Prescribed Descriptions of Arrangements) Regulations, SI 2013/2571.

Tax Avoidance Schemes (Information) (Amendment, etc) Regulations, SI 2013/2592.

Tax Avoidance Schemes (Prescribed Descriptions of Arrangements) (Amendment) Regulations, SI 2013/2595.

Annual Tax on Enveloped Dwellings Avoidance Schemes (Prescribed Descriptions of Arrangements) (Amendment) Regulations, SI 2015/464.

Tax Avoidance Schemes (Information) (Amendment) Regulations, SI 2015/947.

Tax Avoidance Schemes (Prescribed Descriptions of Arrangements) (Amendment) Regulations, SI 2016/99.

Tax Avoidance Schemes (Miscellaneous Amendments) Regulations, SI 2017/1171.

Inheritance Tax Avoidance Schemes (Prescribed Descriptions of Arrangements) Regulations, SI 2017/1172.

Amendments—¹   In sub-s (2), words inserted by FA 2010 s 56, Sch 17 paras 1, 8 with effect from 1 January 2011 (by virtue of SI 2010/3019 art 2).

318 Interpretation of Part 7

(1) In this Part—

"advantage", in relation to any tax, means—

   (a) relief or increased relief from, or repayment or increased repayment of, that tax, or the avoidance or reduction of a charge to that tax or an assessment to that tax or the avoidance of a possible assessment to that tax,

   (b) the deferral of any payment of tax or the advancement of any repayment of tax, or

   (c) the avoidance of any obligation to deduct or account for any tax;

"arrangements" includes any scheme, transaction or series of transactions;

["company" has the meaning given by section 1121 of the Corporation Tax Act 2010;]³

"corporation tax" includes any amount which, by virtue of any of the provisions mentioned in paragraph 1 of Schedule 18 to the Finance Act 1998 (c 36) (company tax returns, assessments and related matters) is assessable and chargeable as if it were corporation tax;

["HMRC" means the Commissioners for Her Majesty's Revenue and Customs;]¹

["introducer", in relation to a notifiable proposal, has the meaning given by section 307;
"make a firm approach" has the meaning given by section 307(4A);
"make a marketing contact" has the meaning given by section 307(4B);][4]
"notifiable arrangements" has the meaning given by section 306(1);
"notifiable proposal" has the meaning given by section 306(2);
"prescribed", except in section 306, means prescribed by regulations made by the Board;
"promoter", in relation to notifiable arrangements or a notifiable proposal, has the meaning given by section 307;
"reference number", in relation to notifiable arrangements, has the meaning given by section 311(3);

   . . .[2]

"tax" means—

   (a) income tax,

   (b) capital gains tax,

   (c) corporation tax,

   (d) petroleum revenue tax,

   [(da) apprenticeship levy,][7]

   (e) inheritance tax,

   (f) stamp duty land tax, . . .[5]

   (g) stamp duty reserve tax[, or

   (h) annual tax on enveloped dwellings.][5]

["trade" includes every venture in the nature of trade.][3]

["tribunal" means the First-tier tribunal, or where determined by or under Tribunal Procedure Rules, the Upper Tribunal.][2]

["working day" means a day which is not a Saturday or a Sunday, Christmas Day, Good Friday or a bank holiday under the Banking and Financial Dealings Act 1971 in any part of the United Kingdom.][6]

(2) . . .[3]

Commentary—*Simon's Taxes* **A7.203, A7.205, A7.210**.

Amendments—[1]   In sub-s (1), definitions of "HMRC" and "the Special Commissioners" inserted by FA 2007 s 108(1), (8), (10) with effect from 19 July 2007.

[2]   Definition of "Special Commissioners" repealed and definition of "tribunal" inserted by the Transfer of Tribunal Functions and Revenue and Customs Appeals Order, SI 2009/56 art 3, Sch 1 para 434 with effect from 1 April 2009.

[3]   In sub-s (1), definitions of "company" and "trade" inserted, and sub-s (2) repealed, by TIOPA 2010 ss 501, 503, Sch 8 paras 301, 302, Sch 10 Pt 12. TIOPA 2010 has effect for corporation tax purposes for accounting periods ending on or after 1 April 2010, for income and capital gains tax purposes for the tax year 2010–11 and subsequent tax years, and for petroleum revenue tax purposes for chargeable periods beginning on or after 1 July 2010.

[4]   In sub-s (1), definitions of "introducer", "make a firm approach" and "make a marketing contact" inserted, by FA 2010 s 56, Sch 17 paras 1, 5 with effect from 1 January 2011 (by virtue of SI 2010/3019 art 2).

[5]   In sub-s (1), in definition of "tax", in para (f) word "or" repealed, and para (h) and preceding word "or" inserted, by FA 2013 s 168, Sch 35 para 2 with effect from 17 July 2013.

[6]   In sub-s (1), definition of "working day" inserted by FA 2014 s 284(1), (4) with effect from 17 July 2014.

[7]   In sub-s (1), in definition of "tax", para (da) inserted by FA 2016 s 104(1) with effect from 15 September 2016.

319 Part 7: commencement and savings

(1) The following provisions of this Part come into force on the passing of this Act—

   sections 306 to 315, so far as is necessary for enabling the making of any regulations for which they provide, and

   sections 317 and 318 and this section.

(2) Except as provided by subsection (1), the provisions of this Part come into force on 1st August 2004.

(3) Section 308 does not apply to a promoter in the case of—

   (a) any notifiable proposal as respects which the relevant date, as defined by subsection (2) of that section, fell before 18th March 2004,

   (b) any notifiable arrangements which implement such a proposal, or

   (c) any notifiable arrangements which include any transaction entered into before 18th March 2004.

(4) Sections 309 and 310 do not apply in relation to notifiable arrangements which include any transaction entered into before 23rd April 2004.

(5) Section 313 does not apply in relation to any notifiable arrangements in respect of which, by virtue of subsection (3) or (4), none of the duties imposed by sections 308 to 310 arises.

PART 8
MISCELLANEOUS MATTERS

320 Exclusion of extended limitation period in England, Wales and Northern Ireland

(1) Section 32(1)(c) of the Limitation Act 1980 (c 58) or, in Northern Ireland, Article 71(1)(c) of the Limitation (Northern Ireland) Order 1989 (SI 1989/1339 (NI 11)) (extended period for bringing an action in case of mistake) does not apply in relation to a mistake of law relating to a taxation matter under the care and management of the Commissioners of Inland Revenue.

This subsection has effect in relation to actions brought on or after 8th September 2003.

(2) For the purposes of—

> (a) section 35(5)(a) of the Limitation Act 1980 or, in Northern Ireland, Article 73(4)(a) of the Limitation (Northern Ireland) Order 1989 (circumstances in which time-barred claim may be brought in course of existing action), and
>
> (b) rules of court or county court rules having effect for the purposes of those provisions,

as they apply to claims in respect of mistakes of the kind mentioned in subsection (1), a new claim shall not be regarded as arising out of the same facts, or substantially the same facts, if it is brought in respect of a different payment, transaction, period or other matter.

This subsection has effect in relation to claims made on or after 20th November 2003.

(3) If before the passing of this Act—

> (a) an action is brought in relation to which a defence of limitation would have been available if subsection (1) had been in force, or
>
> (b) a claim is made on or after 20th November 2003 that by virtue of section 35(1)(b) of the Limitation Act 1980 (c 58) or, in Northern Ireland, Article 73(1)(b) of the Limitation (Northern Ireland) Order 1989 is treated as an action brought before 8th September 2003 and that claim would not have been allowed if subsections (1) and (2) above had been in force,

the action (or so much of it as relates to a cause of action in respect of which a defence of limitation would have been available or, as the case may be, a claim would not have been allowed) shall be deemed to be discontinued on the passing of this Act and any payment made by the Commissioners in or towards meeting their liability in the action (or so much of the action as so relates) may be recovered by them (with interest from the date of the payment).

(4) Nothing in this section affects a claim made before 20th November 2003 that by virtue of section 35(1)(b) of the Limitation Act 1980 or, in Northern Ireland, Article 73(1)(b) of the Limitation (Northern Ireland) Order 1989 is treated as an action brought before 8th September 2003.

(5) For the purposes of this section a claim is treated as made before 20th November 2003 if—

> (a) the Commissioners have before that date consented in writing to the making of the claim; or
>
> (b) immediately before that date—
>
> > (i) the consent of the Commissioners has been sought and has not been refused, or
> >
> > (ii) an application to the court for permission to make the claim has been made and has not been refused.

(6) The provisions of this section apply to any action or claim for relief from the consequences of a mistake of law, whether expressed to be brought on the ground of mistake or on some other ground (such as unlawful demand or *ultra vires* act).

(7) This section shall be construed as one with the Limitation Act 1980 or, in Northern Ireland, the Limitation (Northern Ireland) Order 1989.

Commentary—*Simon's Taxes* A1.706, A2.206.

321 Exclusion of extended prescriptive period in Scotland

(1) Section 6(4)(a)(ii) of the Prescription and Limitation (Scotland) Act 1973 (c 52) (extinction of obligations by prescriptive period: exclusion of period during which creditor induced by error to refrain from making claim) does not apply in relation to an obligation based on redress of unjustified enrichment arising from an error of law relating to a taxation matter under the care and management of the Commissioners of Inland Revenue.

(2) Subsection (1) has effect in relation to an obligation in respect of which no relevant claim has been made before 8th September 2003.

(3) In the case of a relevant claim made on or after that date and before the passing of this Act relating to an obligation that would have been extinguished if subsections (1) and (2) had been in force—

> (a) proceedings on the claim (or so much of the proceedings as relates to such an obligation) shall be deemed to be discontinued on the passing of this Act, and
>
> (b) any payment made by the Commissioners in or towards meeting their liability on the claim (or so much of it as so relates) may be recovered by them (with interest from the date of the payment).

(4) The provisions of this section apply in relation to any relevant claim for redress of unjustified enrichment arising from an error of law, whether expressed to be made on the ground of error or on some other ground.

(5) In this section "relevant claim" has the same meaning as in section 6 of the Prescription and Limitation (Scotland) Act 1973.

Commentary—*Simon's Taxes* **A1.706**.

322 Mutual assistance: customs union with the Principality of Andorra

(1) The UK mutual assistance provisions have effect for the purposes of giving effect to the EC-Andorra Mutual Assistance Recovery Decision as they have effect for the purposes of giving effect to the Mutual Assistance Recovery Directive.

(2) In this section—

"the EC-Andorra Mutual Assistance Recovery Decision" means Chapter 2 of Title 1 of, and Annex 1 to, Decision No 1/2003 of the EC-Andorra Joint Committee of 3 September 2003 (on the laws, regulations and administrative provisions necessary for the proper functioning of the Customs Union between the European Community and the Principality of Andorra);

"the Mutual Assistance Recovery Directive" has the same meaning as [MARD has][1] in the UK mutual assistance provisions;

["the UK mutual assistance provisions" means the provisions of section 87 of the Finance Act 2011 (mutual assistance for recovery of taxes etc) and Schedule 25 to that Act.][1]

[(3) In the UK mutual assistance provisions as they have effect in accordance with subsection (1)—

(a) references (except for the one in paragraph 1 of Schedule 25) to MARD are to be read as references to the EC-Andorra Mutual Assistance Recovery Decision,

(b) references to another member State are to be read as references to the Principality of Andorra,

(c) references to an applicant authority of another member State are to be read as references to the competent authority of the Principality of Andorra,

(d) references to a MARD-related instrument are to be disregarded, and

(e) paragraph 10 of Schedule 25 (power to make further provision) is to be treated as omitted.][1]

(4) The powers in [section 87(2) of the Finance Act 2011 and paragraph 9 of Schedule 25][1] to that Act may be exercised so as to make provision for the purposes of giving effect to the EC-Andorra Mutual Assistance Recovery Decision (or amendments of the Decision) which is different to that made for the purposes of giving effect to the Mutual Assistance Recovery Directive (or amendments of the Directive).

Commentary—*Simon's Taxes* **A2.104**.

Cross references—See FA 2011 Sch 25 (mutual assistance for recovery of taxes).

Amendments—[1] In sub-s (2), in definition of "the Mutual Assistance Recovery Directive", words inserted, definition of "the UK mutual assistance provisions" substituted, sub-s (3) substituted, and in sub-s (4), words substituted for words "section 134(6) of the Finance Act 2002 and paragraph 3 of Schedule 39", by FA 2011 s 87, Sch 25 para 18(1)–(5) with effect from 1 January 2012. Note that any regulations made by virtue of FA 2004 s 322(4) and in force immediately before 1 January 2012 are to have effect on and after that date as if made by virtue of that subsection as amended by FA 2011 Sch 25 para 18(5).

323 Ending of shipbuilders' relief

(1) Relief under section 2 of the Finance Act 1966 (c 18) (relief for shipbuilders in respect of certain taxes and duties) is not available, and shall be regarded as never having been available, in any case where the contract mentioned in subsection (2) of that section is—

(a) a contract made on or after 1st January 2001 relating to a self-propelled sea-going commercial vessel, within the meaning of the 1998 Regulation, or

(b) in a case not falling within paragraph (a), a contract made on or after 13th January 2004.

(2) In this section "the 1998 Regulation" means Council Regulation (EC) No 1540/98 of 29 June 1998 establishing new rules on aid to shipbuilding (under which operating aid for shipbuilding ended on 31st December 2000).

324 Government borrowing: preparations for possible adoption of Euro

(1) The Treasury may incur expenditure with a view to securing that they would be able to exercise their functions under sections 12 to 20A of (and Schedule 5A to) the National Loans Act 1968 (c 13) (national debt and government accounting) if the United Kingdom were to adopt the single currency in accordance with [the Treaty on the Functioning of the European Union][1].

(2) The Director of Savings may incur expenditure with a view to securing that he would be able to exercise his functions if the United Kingdom were to adopt the single currency in accordance with [[the Treaty on the Functioning of the European Union][1].

Amendments—[1] In sub-ss (1), (2) words substituted for words "the Treaty establishing the European Communities" by the Treaty of Lisbon (Changes in Terminology or Numbering) Order, SI 2012/1809 art 3 Schedule Pt 1 with effect from 1 August 2012. Note that this amendment does not affect the application of s 324 to things done before 1st December 2009 (the date on which the Treaty of Lisbon came into force): SI 2012/1809 art 2.

325 Premium bonds

Regulations under section 11 of the National Debt Act 1972 (c 65) (power of Treasury to make regulations as to raising of money under auspices of Director of Savings) may repeal any provision contained in section 54 of, or Schedule 18 to, the Finance Act 1968 (c 44) (terms of issue of premium savings bonds).

PART 9
SUPPLEMENTARY PROVISIONS

326 Repeals

(1) The enactments mentioned in Schedule 42 to this Act (which include provisions that are spent or of no practical utility) are repealed to the extent specified.

(2) The repeals specified in that Schedule have effect subject to the commencement provisions and savings contained or referred to in the notes set out in that Schedule.

327 Interpretation

In this Act "the Taxes Act 1988" means the Income and Corporation Taxes Act 1988 (c 1).

328 Short title

This Act may be cited as the Finance Act 2004.

SCHEDULES

SCHEDULE 5

PROVISION NOT AT ARM'S LENGTH: RELATED AMENDMENTS

Section 30

Commentary—*Simon's Taxes* **B4.121**.

TAXES MANAGEMENT ACT 1970

Notice of enquiry

1— (1) Section 9A of the Taxes Management Act 1970 (c 9) is amended as follows.
(2) (*substitutes* TMA 1970 s 9A(4))

INCOME AND CORPORATION TAXES ACT 1988

Petroleum extraction activities: ring fence trade: charges on income

3—(1) Section 494 of the Taxes Act 1988 (charges on income) is amended as follows.
(2), (3) (*amend* TA 1988 s 494)[1]

Amendment—[1]   Sub-para 3(2)(*a*) repealed by CTA 2010 s 1181, Sch 3 Pt 1. CTA 2010 has effect for corporation tax purposes
    for accounting periods ending on or after 1 April 2010, and for income and capital gains tax purposes for the tax year 2010–11
    and subsequent tax years.

Assumptions for calculating chargeable profits etc: transfer pricing

4   (*repeals* TA 1988 Sch 24 para 20)

FINANCE ACT 1998

Introductory

9   The Finance Act 1998 (c 36) is amended as follows.

Scope of enquiry

10—(1) In Schedule 18 (company tax returns, assessments and related matters) paragraph 25 is
amended as follows.
(2) (*amends* FA 1998 Sch 18 para 25)

FINANCE ACT 2000

SCHEDULE 7

INSURANCE COMPANIES ETC

Section 47

Chargeable gains

6—(1) (*amends* TCGA 1992 s 210A(10))
(2) Sub-paragraph (1) has effect in relation to accounting periods beginning on or after 17th March
2004.

Meaning of "referable"

9—(1) (*amended* TA 1988 ss 438(1), 439B(6); *repealed by* FA 2007 Sch 27 Pt 2(7))
(2) (*amended* FA 1989 ss 88, 89; *repealed* by FA 2012 s 146 Sch 16 para 247(*k*)(iv))
(3) (*amends* TCGA 1992 ss 210A(13), 211ZA(10), 213(1A))

SCHEDULE 10

AMENDMENT OF ENACTMENTS THAT OPERATE BY REFERENCE TO ACCOUNTING PRACTICE

Section 52

Commentary—*Simon's Taxes* **B2.101; D1.710, D1.831, D1.611, D4.202**.

PART 1

LOAN RELATIONSHIPS

Main computational provisions

5   (*repeals* FA 1996 ss 88(2)(*b*), (3)(*b*))

7   (*repeals* FA 1996 s 90)

9   (*repealed* FA 1996 s 92); *repealed by* CTA 2009 s 1326, Sch 3 Pt 1, CTA 2009 ss 1322, 1326, Sch 1 paras 569, 570, Sch 3 Part 1)

10   (*repeals* FA 1996 s 92A)

11—(1) (*repeals* FA 1996 ss 93, 93A and 93B)

(2) Where at the relevant time a company holds an asset to which section 93 applies—

    (*a*) section 93B (deemed disposal and re-acquisition) shall have effect as if the asset had ceased at that time to be an asset to which section 93 applied (but without ceasing to represent a creditor relationship of the company), and

    (*b*) any amount falling to be brought into account under the Taxation of Chargeable Gains Act 1992 (c 12) shall be brought into account in accordance with section 93(4) accordingly.

(3) The relevant time for this purpose is immediately before the end of the last period of account before that in relation to which sub-paragraph (1) has effect (see section 52(3) of this Act).

15   (*repeals* FA 1996 s 96(3))

Special computational provisions

18   Schedule 9 to the Finance Act 1996 (c 8) (loan relationships: special computational provisions) is amended as follows.

29   (*repeals* FA 1996 Sch 9 sub-paragraph 10A(5))

46   (*amends* Transport Act 2000 Sch 26 para 7(3))

PART 4
FOREIGN CURRENCY ACCOUNTING

[Transitional provision

79   Where a company carries forward to its first period of account beginning on or after 1st January 2005 an amount by way of—

    (*a*) management expenses brought forward under section 75 of the Taxes Act 1988,

    (*b*) losses brought forward under section 392B or 393 of that Act, or

    (*c*) non-trading deficits on loan relationships brought forward under section 83 of the Finance Act 1996,

that amount shall be translated into sterling using the London closing exchange rate for the last day of the previous period of account.]¹

Amendments—¹   Paragraph inserted by FA 2005 s 80, Sch 4 para 51 with effect for periods of account beginning on or after 1 January 2005

SCHEDULE 11
CONDITIONS FOR REGISTRATION FOR GROSS PAYMENT

Section 64

Commentary—*Simon's Taxes* **E5.501**.

PART 1
CONDITIONS TO BE SATISFIED BY INDIVIDUALS

General

1—(1) In the case of an application for an individual to be registered for gross payment, the following conditions must be satisfied by the individual.

(2) But where the application is for the registration of the individual as a partner in a firm, this Part of this Schedule has effect with the omission of paragraphs 2 and 3.

Commentary—*Simon's Taxes* **E5.551**.

The business test

2   The applicant must satisfy the Inland Revenue, by such evidence as may be prescribed in regulations made by the Board of Inland Revenue, that he is carrying on a business in the United Kingdom which—

    (*a*) consists of or includes the carrying out of construction operations or the furnishing or arranging for the furnishing of labour in carrying out construction operations, and

    (*b*) is, to a substantial extent, carried on by means of an account with a bank.

Commentary—*Simon's Taxes* **E5.551**.

The turnover test

3—(1) The applicant must satisfy the Inland Revenue, by such evidence as may be prescribed in regulations made by the Board of Inland Revenue, that the carrying on of the business mentioned in paragraph 2 is likely to involve the receipt in the year following the making of the application of an aggregate amount by way of relevant payments which is not less than the amount specified in regulations made by the Board as the minimum turnover for the purposes of this sub-paragraph.

(2) In sub-paragraph (1) "relevant payments" means payments under contracts relating to, or to the work of individuals participating in the carrying out of, any operations which—

(*a*) are of a description specified in subsection (2) of section 74; but

(*b*) are not of a description specified in subsection (3) of that section, other than so much of the payments as represents the direct cost to the person receiving the payments of materials used or to be used in carrying out the operations in question.

(3) The Board may make regulations for the purpose of enabling a person who does not satisfy the condition in sub-paragraph (1) to be treated as satisfying that condition in such circumstances as may be prescribed.

Commentary—*Simon's Taxes* **E5.551**.

The compliance test

4—(1) The applicant must, subject to sub-paragraphs (3) and (4), have complied with—

[(*a*) any obligation imposed on him in the qualifying period (see paragraph 14)—

 (i) to pay the amount liable to be deducted under section 61 of this Act from payments made during that period,

 (ii) to submit returns as required by regulations made under section 70 of this Act,

 (iii) to pay the tax liable to be deducted under the PAYE Regulations (SI 2003/2682), and

 (iv) to submit a self-assessment return, and][2]

(*b*) all requests made in the qualifying period to supply to the Inland Revenue accounts of, or other information about, any business of his.

(2) An applicant who at any time in the qualifying period had control of a company is to be taken not to satisfy the condition in sub-paragraph (1) unless the company has satisfied that condition in relation to the period or periods within the qualifying period during which he had control of it; and for this purpose "control" is to be construed in accordance with [sections 450 and 451 of the Corporation Tax Act 2010][1].

(3) An applicant or company that has failed to comply with such an obligation or request as—

(*a*) is referred to in sub-paragraph (1), and

(*b*) is of a kind prescribed by regulations made by the Board of Inland Revenue,

is, in such circumstances as may be prescribed by the regulations, to be treated as satisfying the condition in that sub-paragraph as regards that obligation or request.

(4) An applicant or company that has failed to comply with such an obligation or request as is referred to in sub-paragraph (1) is to be treated as satisfying the condition in that sub-paragraph as regards that obligation or request if the Board of Inland Revenue are of the opinion that—

(*a*) the applicant or company had a reasonable excuse for the failure to comply, and

(*b*) if the excuse ceased, he or it complied with the obligation or request without unreasonable delay after the excuse had ceased.

(5) Where the applicant states, for the purpose of showing that he has complied with all obligations imposed on him as mentioned in sub-paragraph (1), that he was not subject to any of one or more obligations in respect of any period within the qualifying period—

(*a*) he must satisfy the Board of Inland Revenue of that fact by such evidence as may be prescribed in regulations made by the Board; and

(*b*) if for that purpose he states that he has been outside the United Kingdom for the whole or any part of the qualifying period, he must also satisfy them, by such evidence as may be so prescribed, that he has complied with any obligations imposed under the tax laws of any country in which he was living during that period which are comparable to the obligations mentioned in sub-paragraph (1).

(6) The applicant must, if any contribution has at any time during the qualifying period become due from him under—

(*a*) Part 1 of the Social Security Contributions and Benefits Act 1992 (c 4), or

(*b*) Part 1 of the Social Security Contributions and Benefits (Northern Ireland) Act 1992 (c 7), have paid the contribution when it became due.

(7) There must be reason to expect that the applicant will, in respect of periods after the qualifying period, comply with—

(*a*) such obligations as are referred to in sub-paragraphs (1) to (6), and (*b*) such requests as are referred to in sub-paragraph (1).

(8) Subject to sub-paragraphs (3) and (4), a person is not to be taken for the purposes of this paragraph to have complied with any such obligation or request as is referred to in sub-paragraphs (1) to (5) if there has been a contravention of a requirement as to—

    (*a*) the time at which, or

    (*b*) the period within which,

the obligation or request was to be complied with.

Commentary—*Simon's Taxes* **E5.551**.

Regulations—Income Tax (Construction Industry Scheme) (Amendment) Regulations, SI 2012/820.
Income Tax (Construction Industry Scheme) (Amendment) Regulations, SI 2013/620.
Income Tax (Construction Industry Scheme) (Amendment) Regulations, SI 2016/348.

Amendments—[1]   In sub-para (2) words "section 416(2) to (6) of the Taxes Act 1988" substituted by CTA 2010 s 1177, Sch 1 paras 423, 430. CTA 2010 has effect for corporation tax purposes for accounting periods ending on or after 1 April 2010, and for income and capital gains tax purposes for the tax year 2010–11 and subsequent tax years.

[2]   Sub-para (1)(*a*) substituted by the Income Tax (Construction Industry Scheme) (Amendment of Schedule 11 to the Finance Act 2004) Order, SI 2016/404 art 2(*a*) with effect from 6 April 2016.

PART 2
CONDITIONS TO BE SATISFIED BY FIRMS

General

5 In the case of an application for an individual or a company to be registered for gross payment as a partner in a firm, the following conditions must be satisfied by the firm.

Commentary—*Simon's Taxes* **E5.551**.

The business test

6 The applicant must satisfy the Inland Revenue, by such evidence as may be prescribed in regulations made by the Board of Inland Revenue, that the firm's business—

    (*a*) is carried on in the United Kingdom, and

    (*b*) satisfies the conditions mentioned in paragraph 2(*a*) and (*b*).

Commentary—*Simon's Taxes* **E5.551**.

The turnover test

7—(1) The partners must satisfy the Inland Revenue, by such evidence as may be prescribed in regulations made by the Board of Inland Revenue, that the carrying on of the firm's business is likely to involve the receipt in the year following the making of the application of an aggregate amount by way of relevant payments which is not less than whichever is the smaller of—

    (*a*) the multiple turnover threshold; and

    (*b*) the amount specified for the purposes of this paragraph in regulations made by the Board;

and in this sub-paragraph "relevant payments" has the meaning given by paragraph 3(2).

(2) In sub-paragraph (1) "the multiple turnover threshold" means the sum of—

    (*a*) the amount obtained by multiplying the number of partners in the firm who are individuals by the amount specified in regulations as the minimum turnover for the purposes of paragraph 3(1); and

    (*b*) in respect of each partner in the firm which is a company (other than one to which paragraph 11(1)(*b*) would apply), the amount equal to what would have been the minimum turnover for the purposes of paragraph 11(1) if the application had been for registration of that company for gross payment.

(3) The Board may make regulations—

    (*a*) for determining the number of partners in the firm to be taken into account for the purposes of sub-paragraph (2) (for example, where the number of partners has fluctuated over a period);

    (*b*) for the purpose of enabling a firm which does not satisfy the condition in sub-paragraph (1) to be treated as satisfying that condition in such circumstances as may be prescribed.

Commentary—*Simon's Taxes* **E5.551**.

Regulations—Income Tax (Construction Industry Scheme) (Amendment) Regulations, SI 2016/348.

The compliance test

8—(1) Subject to sub-paragraphs (2) and (3), each of the persons who are partners at the time of the application must have complied, so far as any such charge to income tax or corporation tax is concerned as falls to be computed by reference to the profits or gains of the firm's business, with—

    [(*a*) any obligation imposed on that partner in the qualifying period (see paragraph 14)—

    (i) to pay the amount liable to be deducted under section 61 of this Act from payments made during that period,

    (ii) to submit returns as required by regulations made under section 70 of this Act,

    (iii) to pay the tax liable to be deducted under the PAYE Regulations (SI 2003/2682), and

    (iv) to submit a self-assessment return, and][2]

  (b) all requests made in the qualifying period to him as such a partner to supply to the Inland Revenue accounts of, or other information about, the firm's business or his share of the profits or gains of that business.

(2) Where a person has failed to comply with such an obligation or request as—

  (a) is referred to in sub-paragraph (1), and

  (b) is of a kind prescribed by regulations made by the Board of Inland Revenue,

the firm is, in such circumstances as may be prescribed by the regulations, to be treated, in relation to that partner, as satisfying the condition in that sub-paragraph as regards that obligation or request.

(3) Where a person has failed to comply with such an obligation or request as is referred to in sub-paragraph (1), the firm is to be treated, in relation to that partner, as satisfying the condition in that sub-paragraph as regards that obligation or request if the Board of Inland Revenue are of the opinion that—

  (a) the person had a reasonable excuse for the failure to comply, and

  (b) if the excuse ceased, he complied with the obligation or request without unreasonable delay after the excuse had ceased.

(4) There must be reason to expect that each of the persons who are from time to time partners in the firm will, in respect of periods after the qualifying period, comply with such obligations and requests as are referred to in sub-paragraph (1).

(5) Subject to sub-paragraphs (2) and (3), a person is not to be taken for the purposes of this paragraph to have complied with any such obligation or request as is referred to in sub-paragraph (1) if there has been a contravention of a requirement as to—

  (a) the time at which, or

  (b) the period within which,

the obligation or request was to be complied with.

[(6) This paragraph is subject to paragraph 8A (exception from compliance test: firms).][1]

Commentary—*Simon's Taxes* E5.551.
Regulations—Income Tax (Construction Industry Scheme) (Amendment) Regulations, SI 2012/820.
Income Tax (Construction Industry Scheme) (Amendment) Regulations, SI 2013/620.
Income Tax (Construction Industry Scheme) (Amendment) Regulations, SI 2016/348.
Amendments—[1] Sub-para (6) inserted by the Income Tax (Construction Industry Scheme) (Amendment of Schedule 11 to the Finance Act 2004) Order, SI 2015/789 art 2(a) with effect from 6 April 2015.
[2] Sub-para (1)(a) substituted by the Income Tax (Construction Industry Scheme) (Amendment of Schedule 11 to the Finance Act 2004) Order, SI 2016/404 art 2(b) with effect from 6 April 2016.

[Exception from compliance test: firms

8A—(1) The conditions in paragraph 8 (the compliance test: firms) do not need to be satisfied by the firm if, at the time of the application—

  (a) one or more of the partners is already registered for gross payment as a partner in another firm or otherwise than as a partner in a firm, and

  (b) that partner has, or those partners together have, a right to a share of at least half the assets, or at least half the income, of the firm.

(2) In sub-paragraph (1)(a) the reference to registration for gross payment does not include registration for gross payment by virtue of this paragraph or paragraph 12A (exception from compliance test: companies).][1]

Commentary—*Simon's Taxes* E5.551.
Amendments—[1] Para 8A inserted by the Income Tax (Construction Industry Scheme) (Amendment of Schedule 11 to the Finance Act 2004) Order, SI 2015/789 art 2(b) with effect from 6 April 2015.

PART 3
CONDITIONS TO BE SATISFIED BY COMPANIES
General

9 In the case of an application for a company to be registered for gross payment (whether as a partner in a firm or otherwise), the following conditions must be satisfied by the company.

Commentary—*Simon's Taxes* E5.551.

The business test

10 The company must satisfy the Inland Revenue, by such evidence as may be prescribed in regulations made by the Board of Inland Revenue, that—

   (*a*) it is carrying on (whether or not in partnership) a business in the United Kingdom, and

   (*b*) that business satisfies the conditions mentioned in paragraph 2(*a*) and (*b*).

Commentary—*Simon's Taxes* E5.551.

The turnover test

11—(1) The company must either—

   (*a*) satisfy the Inland Revenue, by such evidence as may be prescribed in regulations made by the Board of Inland Revenue, that the carrying on of its business is likely to involve the receipt in the year following the making of the application of an aggregate amount by way of relevant payments which is not less than the amount which is the minimum turnover for the purposes of this sub-paragraph; or

   (*b*) satisfy the Inland Revenue that the only persons with shares in the company are companies which are limited by shares and themselves are registered for gross payment;

and in this sub-paragraph "relevant payments" has the meaning given by paragraph 3(2).

(2) The minimum turnover for the purposes of sub-paragraph (1) is whichever is the smaller of—

   (*a*) the amount obtained by multiplying the amount specified in regulations as the minimum turnover for the purposes of paragraph 3(1) by the number of persons who are relevant persons in relation to the company; and

   (*b*) the amount specified for the purposes of this paragraph in regulations made by the Board of Inland Revenue.

(3) For the purposes of sub-paragraph (2) a person is a relevant person in relation to the company—

   (*a*) where the company is a close company, if he is a director of the company (within the meaning given by section 67 of the Income Tax (Earnings and Pensions) Act 2003 (c 1)) or a beneficial owner of shares in the company; and

   (*b*) in any other case, if he is such a director of the company.

(4) The Board may make regulations—

   (*a*) for determining the number of relevant persons to be taken into account for the purposes of sub-paragraph (2) (for example, where the number of such persons has fluctuated over a period);

   (*b*) for the purpose of enabling a company which does not satisfy the condition in sub-paragraph (1) to be treated as satisfying that condition in such circumstances as may be prescribed.

Commentary—*Simon's Taxes* E5.551.

Regulations—Income Tax (Construction Industry Scheme) (Amendment) Regulations, SI 2016/348.

The compliance test

12—(1) The company must, subject to sub-paragraphs (2) and (3), have complied with—

   [(*a*) any obligation imposed on it in the qualifying period (see paragraph 14)—

     (i) to pay the amount liable to be deducted under section 61 of this Act from payments made during that period,

     (ii) to submit returns as required by regulations made under section 70 of this Act,

     (iii) to pay the tax liable to be deducted under the PAYE Regulations (SI 2003/2682), and

     (iv) to submit a self-assessment return, and][2]

   (*b*) all requests made in the qualifying period to supply to the Inland Revenue accounts of, or other information about, its business.

(2) A company that has failed to comply with such an obligation or request as—

   (*a*) is referred to in sub-paragraph (1), and

   (*b*) is of a kind prescribed by regulations made by the Board of Inland Revenue,

is, in such circumstances as may be prescribed by the regulations, to be treated as satisfying the condition in that sub-paragraph as regards that obligation or request.

(3) A company that has failed to comply with such an obligation or request as is referred to in sub-paragraph (1) is to be treated as satisfying the condition in that sub-paragraph as regards that obligation or request if the Board of Inland Revenue are of the opinion that—

   (*a*) the company had a reasonable excuse for the failure to comply, and

   (*b*) if the excuse ceased, it complied with the obligation or request without unreasonable delay after the excuse had ceased.

(4) The company must, if any contribution has at any time during the qualifying period become due from the company under—

   (*a*) Part 1 of the Social Security Contributions and Benefits Act 1992 (c 4), or

   (*b*) Part 1 of the Social Security Contributions and Benefits (Northern Ireland) Act 1992 (c 7),

have paid the contribution when it became due.

(5) The company must have complied with any obligations imposed on it by the following provisions of the Companies Act 1985 (c 6) in so far as those obligations fell to be complied with within the qualifying period—

(*a*)   sections 226, 241 and 242 (contents, laying and delivery of annual accounts);

(*b*)   section 288(2) (return of directors and secretary and notification of changes therein);

(*c*)   sections 363 to 365 (annual returns);

(*d*)   section 691 (registration of constitutional documents and list of directors and secretary of oversea company);

(*e*)   section 692 (notification of changes in constitution or directors or secretary of oversea company);

(*f*)   section 693 (oversea company to state its name and country of incorporation);

(*g*)   section 699 (obligations of companies incorporated in Channel Islands or Isle of Man);

(*h*)   Chapter 2 of Part 23 (accounts of oversea company).

(6) The company must have complied with any obligations imposed on it by the following provisions of the Companies (Northern Ireland) Order 1986 (SI 1986/1032 (NI 6)) in so far as those obligations fell to be complied with within the qualifying period—

(*a*)   Articles 234, 249 and 250 (contents, laying and delivery of annual accounts);

(*b*)   Article 296(2) (return of directors and secretary and notification of changes therein);

(*c*)   Articles 371 to 373 (annual returns);

(*d*)   Article 641 (registration of constitutional documents and list of directors and secretary of Part XXIII company);

(*e*)   Article 642 (notification of changes in constitution or directors or secretary of Part XXIII company);

(*f*)   Article 643 (Part XXIII company to state its name and country of incorporation);

(*g*)   Article 649 (accounts of Part XXIII company).

(7) There must be reason to expect that the company will, in respect of periods after the qualifying period, comply with—

(*a*)   all such obligations as are referred to in paragraphs 10 and 11 and sub-paragraphs (1) to (6), and

(*b*)   such requests as are referred to in sub-paragraph (1).

(8) Subject to sub-paragraphs (2) and (3), a company is not to be taken for the purposes of this paragraph to have complied with any such obligation or request as is referred to in sub-paragraphs (1) to (6) if there has been a contravention of a requirement as to—

(*a*)   the time at which, or

(*b*)   the period within which,

the obligation or request was to be complied with.

[(9) This paragraph is subject to paragraph 12A (exception from compliance test: companies).][1]

Commentary—*Simon's Taxes* **E5.551**.

Regulations—Income Tax (Construction Industry Scheme) (Amendment) Regulations, SI 2012/820.

Income Tax (Construction Industry Scheme) (Amendment) Regulations, SI 2013/620.

Income Tax (Construction Industry Scheme) (Amendment) Regulations, SI 2016/348.

Amendments—[1]   Sub-para (9) inserted by the Income Tax (Construction Industry Scheme) (Amendment of Schedule 11 to the Finance Act 2004) Order, SI 2015/789 art 3(*a*) with effect from 6 April 2015.

[2]   Sub-para (1)(*a*) substituted by the Income Tax (Construction Industry Scheme) (Amendment of Schedule 11 to the Finance Act 2004) Order, SI 2016/404 art 2(*c*) with effect from 6 April 2016.

[Exception from the compliance test: companies

12A—(1) The conditions in paragraph 12 (compliance test: companies) do not need to be satisfied by the company if, at the time of the application—

(*a*)   one or more of its members is registered for gross payment (whether as a partner in a firm or otherwise), and

(*b*)   that member possesses or is entitled to acquire or those members together possess or are entitled to acquire—

(i)   at least 50% of the share capital or issued share capital of the company,

(ii)   at least 50% of the voting power in the company,

(iii)   so much of the issued share capital of the company as would, on the assumption that the whole of the income of the company were distributed among its members, entitle the member or members mentioned in paragraph (*a*) to receive at least 50% of the amount so distributed, or

(iv)   such rights as would entitle the member or members mentioned in paragraph (*a*), in the event of the winding up of the company or in any other circumstances, to receive at least 50% of the assets of the company which would then be available for distribution among its members.

(2) In sub-paragraph (1)(*a*) the reference to registration for gross payment does not include registration for gross payment by virtue of this paragraph or paragraph 8A (exception from compliance test: firms).

(3) For the purposes of this paragraph a person is treated as entitled to acquire anything which the person—

(*a*) is entitled to acquire at a future date, or

(*b*) will at a future date be entitled to acquire.

(4) Any rights that a member or any other person has as a loan creditor are to be disregarded for the purposes of the assumption in sub-paragraph (1)(*b*)(iii); and for this purpose "loan creditor" has the same meaning as in Part 10 of the Corporation Tax Act 2010 (close companies).]¹

Commentary—*Simon's Taxes* E5.551.

Amendments—¹ Para 12A inserted by the Income Tax (Construction Industry Scheme) (Amendment of Schedule 11 to the Finance Act 2004) Order, SI 2015/789 art 3(*b*) with effect from 6 April 2015.

PART 4
SUPPLEMENTARY PROVISIONS

Power to amend conditions for registration for gross payment

13—(1) The Treasury may by order made by statutory instrument amend this Schedule by—

(*a*) adding,

(*b*) varying, or

(*c*) removing,

a condition for registration for gross payment.

(2) No statutory instrument containing an order under this paragraph shall be made unless a draft of the instrument has been laid before and approved by a resolution of the House of Commons.

Commentary—*Simon's Taxes* E5.551.

Orders—Income Tax (Construction Industry Scheme) (Amendment of Schedule 11 to the Finance Act 2004) Order, SI 2015/789. Income Tax (Construction Industry Scheme) (Amendment of Schedule 11 to the Finance Act 2004) Order, SI 2016/404.

"Qualifying period"

14 In this Schedule "the qualifying period" means the period of 12 months ending with the date of the application in question.

Commentary—*Simon's Taxes* E5.551.

[**14A**—(1) For any part of the qualifying period falling on 1 October 2009 or later, paragraph 12(5) must be understood as referring instead to—

(*a*) the Companies Act 2006 (c 46) sections 394, 395, 437 and 441 (accounts);

(*b*) sections 167(1), 167(2), 276(1) and 276(2) of that Act (changes in director or secretary);

(*c*) Part 24 of that Act (annual returns);

(*d*) regulations under Part 34 of that Act (overseas companies) which are about—

(i) registration of particulars,

(ii) accounts, reports or returns,

(iii) trading disclosures.

(2) For such part of the qualifying period, paragraph 12(6) must be disregarded and paragraphs 12(7)(a) and 12(8) understood as referring to sub-paragraphs (1) to (5) instead of (1) to (6).]¹

Amendments—¹ This para inserted by the Companies Act 2006 (Consequential Amendments) (Taxes and National Insurance) Order, SI 2009/1890 art 6 with effect from 1 October 2009.

Regulations under this Schedule

15 Any power under this Schedule to make regulations prescribing the evidence required for establishing what is likely to happen at any time includes power to provide for such matters to be presumed (whether conclusively or unless the contrary is shown in the manner provided for in the regulations) from evidence of what has previously happened.

Commentary—*Simon's Taxes* E5.551.

16 Regulations under paragraph 3(1), 7(1) or 11(1) prescribing the evidence required for establishing the amount by way of relevant payments likely to be received by a person may make different provision according to whether—

(*a*) the person is applying for registration for gross payment, or

(*b*) the Board of Inland Revenue are considering whether to make a determination under section 66(1)(*a*) cancelling the person's registration for gross payment.

Commentary—*Simon's Taxes* E5.551.

SCHEDULE 12

CONSTRUCTION INDUSTRY SCHEME: CONSEQUENTIAL AMENDMENTS

Section 76

Commentary—*Simon's Taxes* **E5.501**.

Records to be kept for purposes of returns

1—(1) Section 12B of the Taxes Management Act 1970 (c 9) is amended as follows.
(2) (*amends* TMA 1970 s 12B)

General rule as to when corporation tax is due and payable

2—(1) Section 59D of the Taxes Management Act 1970 is amended as follows.
(2) (*amends* TMA 1970 s 59D)

Claim for repayment in advance of liability being established

3—(1) Section 59DA of the Taxes Management Act 1970 is amended as follows.
(2) (*amends* TMA 1970 s 59DA)

Priority of claim for tax

4—(1) Section 62 of the Taxes Management Act 1970 is amended as follows.
(2) (*amends* TMA 1970 s 62)

Recovery of tax in Scotland

5—(1) Section 63 of the Taxes Management Act 1970 (c 9) is amended as follows.
(2) (*amends* TMA 1970 s 63)

Priority of claim for tax in Scotland

6—(1) Section 64 of the Taxes Management Act 1970 is amended as follows.
(2) (*amends* TMA 1970 s 64)

Special returns etc

7—(1) Section 98 of the Taxes Management Act 1970 is amended as follows.
(2)–(5) (*amend* TMA 1970 s 98)

Special penalties in the case of certain returns

8—(1) Section 98A of the Taxes Management Act 1970 is amended as follows.
(2)–(4) (*amend* TMA 1970 s 98A)

Sub-contractors in the construction industry

9—(1) The Taxes Act 1988 is amended as follows.
(2) (*repeals* TA 1988 Ch 4)

Supplementary provisions relating to contributions: Great Britain

13—(1) Schedule 1 to the Social Security Contributions and Benefits Act 1992 (c 4) is amended as follows.
(2) (*amends* Social Security Contributions and Benefits Act 1992 Sch 1 para 7)

Supplementary provisions relating to contributions: Northern Ireland

14—(1) Schedule 1 to the Social Security Contributions and Benefits (Northern Ireland) Act 1992 (c 7) is amended as follows.
(2) (*amends* Social Security Contributions and Benefits (Northern Ireland) Act 1992 Sch 1 para 7)

Transitional provisions concerning construction workers supplied by agencies

15—(1) Section 56 of the Finance Act 1998 (c 36) is amended as follows.
(2) (*amends* FA 1998 s 56(8))

Company tax returns, assessments and related matters

16—(1) Schedule 18 to the Finance Act 1998 is amended as follows.
(2) (*amends* FA 1998 Sch 18 para 22)

Calculation of deemed employment payment

17—(1) Section 54 of the Income Tax (Earnings and Pensions) Act 2003 (c 1) is amended as follows.

(2) (*amends* ITEPA 2003 s 54(2))

SCHEDULE 13

CHILDCARE AND CHILDCARE VOUCHERS

Section 78

Commentary—*Simon's Taxes* **E4.432**.

Childcare

1 (*substitutes* ITEPA 2003 s 318, *inserts* ITEPA 2003 ss 318A–D)

Childcare vouchers

2—(1) Chapter 4 of Part 3 of the Income Tax (Earnings and Pensions) Act 2003 (c 1) (taxable benefits: vouchers and credit-tokens) is amended as follows.

(2)–(4) (*insert* ITEPA 2003 ss 84(2A), 87(3A), 95(3A))

3 (*inserts* ITEPA 2003 s 270A)

SCHEDULE 14

VANS

Section 80

1 The Income Tax (Earnings and Pensions) Act 2003 (c 1) is amended as follows.

2—(1) Section 114 (cars, vans and related benefits) is amended as follows.

(2) (*amends* ITEPA 2003 s 114)

3 (*amends* ITEPA 2003 s 116(2))

4 (*amends* ITEPA 2003 s 119)

5 (*substitutes* ITEPA 2003 ss 155–164)

6 (*inserts* ITEPA 2003 s 169A)

7—(1) Section 170 (orders etc) is amended as follows.

(2) (*inserts* ITEPA 2003 s 170(1A))

(3), (4) (*amend* ITEPA ss 170(2), (5))

8 (*amends* ITEPA s 237)

Commentary—*Simon's Taxes* **E7.237**.

SCHEDULE 15

CHARGE TO INCOME TAX ON BENEFITS RECEIVED BY FORMER OWNER
OF PROPERTY

Section 84

Commentary—*Simon's Taxes* **Division I3.7**.

Introductory

1 In this Schedule—

"IHTA 1984" means the Inheritance Tax Act 1984 (c 51);

"the 1986 Act" means the Finance Act 1986 (c 41);

"chattel" means any tangible movable property (or, in Scotland, corporeal movable property) other than money;

"excluded transaction" has the meaning given by paragraph 10;

"intangible property" means any property other than chattels or interests in land;

"interest in land" has the same meaning as in Chapter 4 of Part 6 of IHTA 1984;

["ITTOIA 2005" means the Income Tax (Trading and Other Income Act) 2005;][1]

"land" has the same meaning as in IHTA 1984;

"prescribed" means prescribed by regulations;

"property" has the same meaning as in IHTA 1984;

"regulations" means regulations made by the Treasury under this Schedule;

"settlement" and "settled property" have the same meanings as in IHTA 1984.

Commentary—*Simon's Taxes* **I3.710, I3.711, I3.715, I3.716, I3.730**.
Regulations—Charge to Income Tax by Reference to Enjoyment of Property Previously Owned Regulations, SI 2005/724.
Amendments—[1]   Definition of "ITTOIA 2005" inserted by ITTOIA 2005 s 882(1), Sch 1 paras 629, 653(1), (2) with effect from 6 April 2005. ITTOIA 2005 has effect: (a) for income tax purposes, for 2005–06 and subsequent tax years, and (b) for corporation tax purposes, for accounting periods ending after 5 April 2005: ITTOIA 2005 s 883(1).

[2—(1) For the purposes of this Schedule whether a person is connected with another person is determined in accordance with section 993 of the Income Tax Act 2007.
(2) But for those purposes sections 993 and 994 of that Act are to be read as if in those sections—
    (*a*) "relative" included uncle, aunt, nephew and niece, and
    (*b*) "settlement", "settlor" and "trustee" had the same meanings as in IHTA 1984.]**[1]**

Amendments—[1]   This paragraph substituted by ITA 2007 s 1027, Sch 1 paras 456, 482(1), (2) with effect for income tax purposes from 6 April 2007, and corporation tax purposes for accounting periods ending after 5 April 2007.

Land

3—(1) This paragraph applies where—
    (*a*) an individual ("the chargeable person") occupies any land ("the relevant land"), whether alone or together with other persons, and
    (*b*) the disposal condition or the contribution condition is met as respects the land.
(2) The disposal condition is that—
    (*a*) at any time after 17th March 1986 the chargeable person owned an interest—
        (i)   in the relevant land, or
        (ii) in other property the proceeds of the disposal of which were (directly or indirectly) applied by another person towards the acquisition of an interest in the relevant land, and
    (*b*) the chargeable person has disposed of all, or part of, his interest in the relevant land or the other property, otherwise than by an excluded transaction.
(3) The contribution condition is that at any time after 17th March 1986 the chargeable person has directly or indirectly provided, otherwise than by an excluded transaction, any of the consideration given by another person for the acquisition of—
    (*a*) an interest in the relevant land, or
    (*b*) an interest in any other property the proceeds of the disposal of which were (directly or indirectly) applied by another person towards the acquisition of an interest in the relevant land.
(4) For the purposes of this paragraph a disposition which creates a new interest in land out of an existing interest in land is to be taken to be a disposal of part of the existing interest.
(5) Where this paragraph applies to a person in respect of the whole or part of a year of assessment, an amount equal to the chargeable amount determined under paragraph 4 is to be treated as income of his chargeable to income tax.

Commentary—*Simon's Taxes* **I3.703, I3.704, I3.711, I3.714–I3.718, I3.721**.

4—(1) For any taxable period the chargeable amount in relation to the relevant land is the appropriate rental value (as determined under sub-paragraph (2)), less the amount of any payments which, in pursuance of any legal obligation, are made by the chargeable person during the period to the owner of the relevant land in respect of the occupation of the land by the chargeable person.
(2) The appropriate rental value is—

$$R \times \frac{DV}{V}$$

where—
    R is the rental value of the relevant land for the taxable period,
    DV is—
        (*a*) in a case falling within paragraph 3(2)(*a*)(i), the value as at the valuation date of the interest in the relevant land that was disposed of as mentioned in paragraph 3(2)(*b*) by the chargeable person or, where the disposal was a non-exempt sale, the appropriate proportion of that value,
        (*b*) in a case falling within paragraph 3(2)(*a*)(ii), such part of the value of the relevant land at the valuation date as can reasonably be attributed to the property originally disposed of by the chargeable person or, where the original disposal was a non-exempt sale, to the appropriate proportion of that property, and
        (*c*) in a case falling within paragraph 3(3), such part of the value of the relevant land at the valuation date as can reasonably be attributed to the consideration provided by the chargeable person, and

V is the value of the relevant land at the valuation date.

(3) The "rental value" of the land for the taxable period is the rent which would have been payable for the period if the property had been let to the chargeable person at an annual rent equal to the annual value.

(4) The disposal by the chargeable person of an interest in land is a "non-exempt sale" if (although not an excluded transaction) it was a sale of his whole interest in the property for a consideration paid in money in sterling or any other currency; and, in relation to a non-exempt sale, "the appropriate proportion" is—

$$\frac{MV - P}{MV}$$

where—

MV is the value of the interest in land at the time of the sale;

P is the amount paid.

(5) Regulations may—

    (*a*) in relation to any valuation date, provide for a valuation of the relevant land or any interest in the relevant land by reference to an earlier valuation date to apply subject to any prescribed adjustments, and

    (*b*) in relation to any year of assessment, provide for a determination of the rental value of the land by reference to any earlier year of assessment to apply subject to any prescribed adjustments.

(6) In this paragraph—

    "the taxable period" means the year of assessment, or part of a year of assessment, during which paragraph 3 applies to the chargeable person;

    "the valuation date", in relation to a taxable period, means such date as may be prescribed.

Commentary—*Simon's Taxes* I3.721.

5—(1) For the purposes of paragraph 4 the annual value of the relevant land is the rent which might reasonably be expected to be obtained on a letting from year to year if—

    (*a*) the tenant undertook to pay all taxes, rates and charges usually paid by a tenant, and

    (*b*) the landlord undertook to bear the costs of the repairs and insurance and the other expenses (if any) necessary for maintaining the property in a state to command that rent.

(2) For the purposes of sub-paragraph (1) that rent—

    (*a*) is to be taken to be the amount that might reasonably be expected to be so obtained in respect of a letting of the land, and

    (*b*) is to be calculated on the basis that the only amounts that may be deducted in respect of services provided by the landlord are amounts in respect of the cost to the landlord of providing any relevant services.

(3) In this paragraph "relevant service" means a service other than the repair, insurance or maintenance of the premises.

Commentary—*Simon's Taxes* I3.721.

Chattels

6—(1) This paragraph applies where—

    (*a*) an individual ("the chargeable person") is in possession of, or has the use of, a chattel, whether alone or together with other persons, and

    (*b*) the disposal condition or the contribution condition is met as respects the chattel.

(2) The disposal condition is that—

    (*a*) at any time after 17th March 1986 the chargeable person had (whether alone or jointly with others) owned—

        (i) the chattel, or

        (ii) any other property the proceeds of the disposal of which were (directly or indirectly) applied by another person towards the acquisition of the chattel, and

    (*b*) the chargeable person disposed of all or part of his interest in the chattel or other property otherwise than by an excluded transaction.

(3) The contribution condition is that at any time after 17th March 1986 the chargeable person had directly or indirectly provided, otherwise than by an excluded transaction, any of the consideration given by another person for the acquisition of—

    (*a*) the chattel, or

    (*b*) any other property the proceeds of the disposal of which were (directly or indirectly) applied by another person towards the acquisition of the chattel.

(4) For the purposes of this paragraph, a disposition which creates a new interest in a chattel out of an existing interest in a chattel is to be taken to be a disposal of part of the existing interest.

(5) Where this paragraph applies to a person in respect of the whole or part of a year of assessment, an amount equal to the chargeable amount determined under paragraph 7 is to be treated as income of his chargeable to income tax.

7—(1) For any taxable period the chargeable amount in relation to any chattel is the appropriate amount (as determined under sub-paragraph (2)), less the amount of any payments which, in pursuance of any legal obligation, are made by the chargeable person during the period to the owner of the chattel in respect of the possession or use of the chattel by the chargeable person.

(2) The appropriate amount is—

$$N \times \frac{DV}{V}$$

where—

N is the amount of the interest that would be payable for the taxable period if interest were payable at the prescribed rate on an amount equal to the value of the chattel as the valuation date,

DV is—

    (a) in a case falling within paragraph 6(2)(a)(i), the value as at the valuation date of the interest in the chattel that was disposed of as mentioned in paragraph 6(2)(b) by the chargeable person or, where the disposal was a non-exempt sale, the appropriate proportion of that value,

    (b) in a case falling within paragraph 6(2)(a)(ii), such part of the value of the chattel at the valuation date as can reasonably be attributed to the property originally disposed of by the chargeable person or, where the original disposal was a non-exempt sale, to the appropriate proportion of that property, and

    (c) in a case falling within paragraph 6(3), such part of the value of the chattel at the valuation date as can reasonably be attributed to the consideration provided by the chargeable person, and

    V is the value of the chattel at the valuation date.

(3) The disposal by the chargeable person of an interest in a chattel is a "non-exempt sale" if (although not an excluded transaction) it was a sale of his whole interest in the chattel for a consideration paid in money in sterling or any other currency; and, in relation to a non-exempt sale, "the appropriate proportion" is—

$$\frac{MV - P}{MV}$$

where—

MV is the value of the interest in the chattel at the time of the sale;

P is the amount paid.

(4) Regulations may, in relation to any valuation date, provide for a valuation of the chattel or any interest in the chattel by reference to an earlier valuation date to apply subject to any prescribed adjustments.

(5) In this paragraph—

"the taxable period" means the year of assessment, or part of a year of assessment, during which paragraph 6 applies to the chargeable person;

"the valuation date", in relation to a taxable period, means such date as may be prescribed.

Commentary—*Simon's Taxes* I3.717, I3.722.

Intangible property comprised in settlement where settlor retains an interest

8—(1) This paragraph applies where—

    (a) the terms of a settlement, as they affect any property comprised in the settlement, are such that any income arising from the property would be treated by virtue of [section 624 of ITTOIA 2005][1] (income arising under settlement where settlor retains an interest) as income of a person ("the chargeable person") who is for the purposes of [Chapter 5 of Part 5][1] of that Act the settlor,

    (b) any such income would be so treated even if [section 625(1) of ITTOIA 2005 (settlor's retained interest)][1] did not include any reference to the spouse [or civil partner][2] of the settlor, and (*c*) that property includes any property as respects which the condition in sub-paragraph (2) is met ("the relevant property").

(2) The condition mentioned in sub-paragraph (1)(*c*) is that the property is intangible property which is or represents property which the chargeable person settled, or added to the settlement, after 17th March 1986.

(3) Where this paragraph applies in respect of the whole or part of a year of assessment, an amount equal to the chargeable amount determined under paragraph 9 is to be treated as income of the chargeable person chargeable to income tax.

[(4) For the purpose of deciding whether the condition in sub-paragraph (1)(*a*) is met, ignore section 628A of ITTOIA 2005 (which provides for section 624 of that Act not to apply to certain foreign income arising under a settlement).][3]

Commentary—*Simon's Taxes* I3.703, I3.730.
Amendments—[1]   Words in sub-para (1) substituted by ITTOIA 2005 s 882(1), Sch 1 paras 629, 653(1), (3) with effect from 6 April 2005. ITTOIA 2005 has effect: (a) for income tax purposes, for 2005–06 and subsequent tax years, and (b) for corporation tax purposes, for accounting periods ending after 5 April 2005: ITTOIA 2005 s 883(1).
[2]   Words in sub-para (1)(*b*) inserted by Tax and Civil Partnership Regulations, SI 2005/3229, regs 175, 179(*a*), with effect from 5 December 2005 (reg 1(1)).
[3]   Sub-para (4) inserted by F(No 2)A 2017 s 29(2), Sch 8 para 19 with effect for the tax year 2017–18 and subsequent tax years.

9—(1) For any taxable period the chargeable amount in relation to the relevant property is N minus T where—

N is the amount of the interest that would be payable for the taxable period if interest were payable at the prescribed rate on an amount equal to the value of the relevant property at the valuation date, and

T is the amount of any income tax or capital gains tax payable by the chargeable person in respect of the taxable period by virtue of any of the following provisions—

(*a*) [section 461 of ITTOIA 2005][1],
(*b*) [section 624 of that Act][1],
[(*c*) sections 720 to 730 of the Income Tax Act 2007,][2],
(*d*) section 77 of the Taxation of Chargeable Gains Act 1992 (c 12), and
(*e*) section 86 of that Act,

so far as the tax is attributable to the relevant property.

(2) Regulations may, in relation to any valuation date, provide for a valuation of the relevant property by reference to an earlier valuation date to apply subject to any prescribed adjustments.

(3) In this paragraph—

"the taxable period" means the year of assessment, or part of a year of assessment, during which paragraph 8 applies to the chargeable person;

"the valuation date", in relation to a year of assessment, means such date as may be prescribed.

Commentary—*Simon's Taxes* I3.731.
Amendments—[1]   Words in sub-para (1) substituted by ITTOIA 2005 s 882(1), Sch 1 paras 629, 653(1), (4) with effect from 6 April 2005. ITTOIA 2005 has effect: (a) for income tax purposes, for 2005–06 and subsequent tax years, and (b) for corporation tax purposes, for accounting periods ending after 5 April 2005: ITTOIA 2005 s 883(1).
[2]   Sub-para (1)(*c*) substituted by ITA 2007 s 1027, Sch 1 paras 456, 482(1), (3) with effect for income tax purposes from 6 April 2007, and corporation tax purposes for accounting periods ending after 5 April 2007.

Excluded transactions

10—(1) For the purposes of paragraphs 3(2) and 6(2) (the disposal condition), the disposal of any property is an "excluded transaction" in relation to any person ("the chargeable person") if—

(*a*) it was a disposal of his whole interest in the property, except for any right expressly reserved by him over the property, either—
　(i) by a transaction made at arm's length with a person not connected with him, or
　(ii) by a transaction such as might be expected to be made at arm's length between persons not connected with each other,
(*b*) the property was transferred to his spouse [or civil partner][1] (or where the transfer has been ordered by a court, to his former spouse [or civil partner][1]),
(*c*) it was a disposal by way of gift (or, where the transfer is for the benefit of his former spouse [or civil partner][1], in accordance with a court order), by virtue of which the property became settled property in which his spouse [or civil partner][1] or former spouse [or civil partner][1] is beneficially entitled to an interest in possession,
(*d*) the disposal was a disposition falling within section 11 of IHTA 1984 (dispositions for maintenance of family), or
(*e*) the disposal is an outright gift to an individual and is for the purposes of IHTA 1984 a transfer of value that is wholly exempt by virtue of section 19 (annual exemption) or section 20 (small gifts).

(2) For the purposes of paragraphs 3(3) and 6(3) (the contribution condition) the provision by a person ("the chargeable person") of consideration for another's acquisition of any property is an "excluded transaction" in relation to the chargeable person if—

    (a) the other person was his spouse [or civil partner][1] (or, where the transfer has been ordered by the court, his former spouse [or civil partner][1]),

    (b) on its acquisition the property became settled property in which his spouse [or civil partner][1] or former spouse [or civil partner][1] is beneficially entitled to an interest in possession,

    (c) the provision of the consideration constituted an outright gift of money (in sterling or any other currency) by the chargeable person to the other person and was made at least seven years before the earliest date on which the chargeable person met the condition in paragraph 3(1)(a) or, as the case may be, 6(1)(a),

    (d) the provision of the consideration is a disposition falling within section 11 of IHTA 1984 (dispositions for maintenance of family), or

    (e) the provision of the consideration is an outright gift to an individual and is for the purposes of IHTA 1984 a transfer of value that is wholly exempt by virtue of section 19 (annual exemption) or section 20 (small gifts).

(3) A disposal is not an excluded transaction by virtue of sub-paragraph (1)(c) or (2)(b), if the interest in possession of the spouse [or civil partner][1] or former spouse [or civil partner][1] has come to an end otherwise than on the death of the spouse [or civil partner][1] or former spouse [or civil partner][1].

Commentary—*Simon's Taxes* 13.703, 13.711, 13.715, 13.723, 13.753.
Amendments—[1] Words in sub-paras (1), (2), (3) inserted by Tax and Civil Partnership Regulations, SI 2005/3229, regs 175, 179(b), with effect from 5 December 2005 (reg 1(1)).

Exemptions from charge

11—(1) Paragraph 3 (land), paragraph 6 (chattels) and paragraph 8 (intangible property) do not apply to a person at a time when his estate for the purposes of IHTA 1984 includes—

    (a) the relevant property, or

    (b) other property—

        (i) which derives its value from the relevant property, and

        (ii) whose value, so far as attributable to the relevant property, is not substantially less than the value of the relevant property.

(2) Where the estate for the purposes of IHTA 1984 of a person to whom paragraph 3, 6 or 8 applies includes property—

    (a) which derives its value from the relevant property, and

    (b) whose value, so far as attributable to the relevant property, is substantially less than the value of the relevant property,

the appropriate rental value in paragraph 4, the appropriate amount in paragraph 7 or the chargeable amount in paragraph 9 (as the case may be) is to be reduced by such proportion as is reasonable to take account of the inclusion of the property in his estate.

(3) Paragraphs 3, 6 and 8 do not apply to a person at a time when—

    (a) the relevant property, or

    (b) any other property—

        (i) which derives its value from the relevant property, and

        (ii) whose value, so far as attributable to the relevant property, is not substantially less than the value of the relevant property,

falls within sub-paragraph (5) in relation to him.

(4) Where any property which falls within sub-paragraph (5) in relation to a person includes property—

    (a) which derives its value from the relevant property, and

    (b) whose value, so far as attributable to the relevant property, is substantially less than the value of the relevant property,

the appropriate rental value in paragraph 4, the appropriate amount in paragraph 7 or the chargeable amount in paragraph 9 (as the case may be) is to be reduced by such proportion as is reasonable to take account of that fact.

(5) Property falls within this sub-paragraph in relation to a person at a time when it—

    (a) would fall to be treated by virtue of any provision of Part 5 of the 1986 Act (inheritance tax) as property which in relation to him is property subject to a reservation,

    (b) would fall to be so treated but for any of paragraphs (d) to (i) of subsection (5) of section 102 of the 1986 Act (certain cases where disposal by way of gift is an exempt transfer for purposes of inheritance tax),

(c) would fall to be so treated but for subsection (4) of section 102B of the 1986 Act (gifts with reservation: share of interest in land), or would have fallen to be so treated but for that subsection if the disposal by way of gift of an undivided share of an interest in land had been made on or after 9th March 1999, or

(d) would fall to be so treated but for section 102C(3) of, and paragraph 6 of Schedule 20 to, the 1986 Act (exclusion of benefit).

(6) Where at any time the value of a person's estate for the purposes of IHTA 1984 is reduced by an excluded liability affecting any property, that property is not to be treated for the purposes of sub-paragraph (1) or (2) as comprised in his estate except to the extent that the value of the property exceeds the amount of the excluded liability.

(7) For the purposes of sub-paragraph (6) a liability is an excluded liability if—

(a) the creation of the liability, and

(b) any transaction by virtue of which the person's estate came to include the relevant property or property which derives its value from the relevant property or by virtue of which the value of property in his estate came to be derived from the relevant property,

were associated operations, as defined by section 268 of IHTA 1984.

(8) In determining whether any property falls within sub-paragraph (5)(b), (c) or (d) in a case where the contribution condition in paragraph 3(3) or 6(3) is met, paragraph 2(2)(b) of Schedule 20 (exclusion of gifts of money) is to be disregarded.

(9) In [this paragraph][1] "the relevant property" means—

(a) in relation to paragraphs 3 and 6—

(i) where the disposal condition in paragraph 3(2) or 6(2) is met, the property disposed of,

(ii) where the contribution condition in paragraph 3(3) or 6(3) is met, the property representing the consideration directly or indirectly provided,

(b) in relation to paragraph 8, the relevant property within the meaning of that paragraph.

(10) Property is not to be treated as falling within sub-paragraph (5)(b) at any time in a case falling within section 102(5)(h) of the 1986 Act unless the property remains subject to trusts which comply with the requirements of paragraph 3(1) of Schedule 4 to IHTA 1984.

[(11) Sub-paragraph (12) applies where at any time—

(a) the relevant property has ceased to be comprised in a person's estate for the purposes of IHTA 1984, or

(b) he has directly or indirectly provided any consideration for the acquisition of the relevant property,

and at any subsequent time the relevant property or any derived property is comprised in his estate for the purposes of IHTA 1984 as a result of section 49(1) of that Act (treatment of interests in possession).][1]

[(12) Where this sub-paragraph applies, the relevant property and any derived property—

(a) are not to be treated for the purposes of sub-paragraphs (1) and (2) as comprised in his estate at that subsequent time, and

(b) are not to be treated as falling within sub-paragraph (5) in relation to him at that subsequent time.][1]

[(13) For the purposes of sub-paragraphs (11) and (12) references, in relation to the relevant property, to any derived property are to other property—

(a) which derives its value from the relevant property, and

(b) whose value, so far as attributable to the relevant property, is not substantially less than the value of the relevant property.][1]

Commentary—*Simon's Taxes* I3.735–I3.738, I3.751.
Amendments—[1] Words in sub-para (9) substituted, and sub-paras (11)–(13) inserted, by FA 2006 s 80(1), (2), (5)–(7) with effect: (a) for the part of the year 2005–06 beginning with 5 December 2005, and (b) for 2006–07 and subsequent years of assessment.

Chargeable person resident or domiciled outside the United Kingdom

12—(1) This Schedule does not apply in relation to any person for any year of assessment during which he is not resident in the United Kingdom.

(2) Where in any year of assessment a person is resident in the United Kingdom but is domiciled outside the United Kingdom, this Schedule does not apply to him unless the property falling within paragraph 3(1)(a), 6(1)(a) or 8(1)(c) is situated in the United Kingdom.

(3) In the application of this Schedule to a person who was at any time domiciled outside the United Kingdom, no regard is to be had to any property which is for the purposes of IHTA 1984 excluded property in relation to him by virtue of section 48(3)(a) of that Act.

(4) For the purposes of this paragraph, a person is to be treated as domiciled in the United Kingdom at any time only if he would be so treated for the purposes of IHTA 1984.

Commentary—*Simon's Taxes* I3.740.

Exemption in cases where aggregate notional annual values do not exceed £5,000

13—(1) This paragraph applies where, in relation to any person who would (apart from this paragraph) be chargeable under this Schedule for any year of assessment, the aggregate of the amounts specified in sub-paragraph (2) in respect of that year does not exceed £5,000.

(2) Those amounts are—

(*a*) in relation to any land to which paragraph 3 applies in respect of him, the appropriate rental value as determined under paragraph 4(2),

(*b*) in relation to any chattel to which paragraph 6 applies in respect of him, the appropriate amount as determined under paragraph 7(2), and

(*c*) in relation to any intangible property to which paragraph 8 applies in respect of him, the chargeable amount determined under paragraph 9.

(3) Where this paragraph applies, the person is not chargeable for that year of assessment under any of the following provisions—

(*a*) paragraph 3(5) (land),

(*b*) paragraph 6(5) (chattels), or

(*c*) paragraph 8(3) (intangible property).

Commentary—*Simon's Taxes* I3.739, I3.744.

Power of Treasury to confer further exemptions by regulations

14   Regulations may confer further exemptions from the charges to income tax imposed by paragraphs 3, 6 and 8.

Commentary—*Simon's Taxes* I3.735, I3.745.

Valuation

15   Except as otherwise provided by this Schedule, the value of any property shall for the purposes of this Schedule be the price which the property might reasonably be expected to fetch if sold in the open market at that time; but that price shall not be assumed to be reduced on the ground that the whole property is to be placed on the market at one and the same time.

Commentary—*Simon's Taxes* I3.724, I3.743.

Changes in distribution of deceased's estate

16   Any disposition made by a person ("the chargeable person") in relation to an interest in the estate of a deceased person is to be disregarded for the purposes of this Schedule if by virtue of section 17 of IHTA 1984 (changes in distribution of deceased's estate, etc) the disposition is not treated for the purposes of inheritance tax as a transfer of value by the chargeable person.

Commentary—*Simon's Taxes* I3.741.

Guarantees

17   Where a person ("A") acts as guarantor in respect of a loan made to another person ("B") by a third party in connection with B's acquisition of any property, the mere giving of the guarantee is not to be regarded as the provision by A of consideration for B's acquisition of the property.

Commentary—*Simon's Taxes* I3.742.

Persons chargeable under different provisions by reference to same property

18—(1) Where, in any year of assessment, a person ("the chargeable person") is (apart from this paragraph) chargeable to income tax both—

(*a*) under paragraph 3 (land) or paragraph 6 (chattels) by reason of his occupation of any land or his possession or use of any chattel, and

(*b*) under paragraph 8 (intangible property) by reference to any intangible property which derives its value (whether in whole or part) from the land or the chattel,

he is to be charged to income tax under whichever provision produces the higher chargeable amount in relation to him.

(2) Where sub-paragraph (1) applies, only the amount under the paragraph under which he is chargeable is to be taken into account in relation to the chargeable person for the purposes of paragraph 13(2).

Commentary—*Simon's Taxes* I3.744.

Relationship with Part 3 of Income Tax (Earnings and Pensions) Act 2003

19   Where, in any year of assessment, a person is (apart from this paragraph) chargeable, in respect of his occupation of any land or his possession or use of any chattel, to income tax both—

(*a*) under this Schedule, and

(*b*) under Part 3 of the Income Tax (Earnings and Pensions) Act 2003 (c 1),

the provisions of that Part shall have priority and he shall not be chargeable to income tax under this Schedule, except to the extent that the amount chargeable under this Schedule exceeds the amount to be treated as earnings under that Part.

Commentary—*Simon's Taxes* I3.744.

Regulations

20—(1) Regulations under this Schedule may—

(*a*) make different provision for different cases, and

(*b*) include transitional provisions and savings.

(2) Any power conferred by this Schedule to prescribe a rate of interest includes power—

(*a*) to prescribe different rates in relation to property of different descriptions, and

(*b*) to prescribe a rate by reference to a rate specified in the regulations.

Commentary—*Simon's Taxes* I3.745.

Election for application of inheritance tax provisions

21—(1) This paragraph applies where—

(*a*) a person ("the chargeable person") would (apart from this paragraph) be chargeable under paragraph 3 (land) or paragraph 6 (chattels) for any year of assessment ("the initial year") by reference to his enjoyment of any property ("the relevant property"), and

(*b*) he has not been chargeable under the paragraph in question in respect of any previous year of assessment by reference to his enjoyment of the relevant property, or of any other property for which the relevant property has been substituted.

(2) The chargeable person may elect in accordance with paragraph 23 that—

(*a*) the preceding provisions of this Schedule shall not apply to him during the initial year and subsequent years of assessment by reference to his enjoyment of the relevant property or of any property which may be substituted for the relevant property, but

(*b*) so long as the chargeable person continues to enjoy the relevant property or any property which is substituted for the relevant property—

(i) the chargeable proportion of the property is to be treated for the purposes of Part 5 of the 1986 Act (in relation to the chargeable person) as property subject to a reservation[, but only so far as the chargeable person is not beneficially entitled to an interest in possession in the property][1],

[(ii) section 102(3) and (4) of that Act shall apply, but only so far as the chargeable person is not beneficially entitled to an interest in possession in the property, and][1]

[(iii) if the chargeable person is beneficially entitled to an interest in possession in the property, sections 53(3) and (4) and 54 of IHTA 1984 (which deal with cases of property reverting to the settlor etc) shall not apply in relation to the chargeable proportion of the property.][1]

(3) In this paragraph, "the chargeable proportion", in relation to any property, means—

$$\frac{DV}{V}$$

where DV and V are to be read in accordance with paragraph 4(2) or 7(2), as the case requires, but as if—

(*a*) any reference in paragraph 4(2) or 7(2) to the valuation date were a reference—

(i) in the case of property falling within subsection (3) of section 102 of the Finance Act 1986, to the date of the death of the chargeable person, and

(ii) in the case of property falling within subsection (4) of that section, to the date on which the property ceases to be treated as property subject to a reservation, and

[(iii) in the case of property in which the chargeable person is beneficially entitled to an interest in possession, to the date of his death or (if his interest comes to an end on an earlier date) that earlier date, and][1]

(*b*) the transactions to be taken into account in calculating DV included transactions after the time when the election takes effect as well as transactions before that time.

(4) For the purposes of this paragraph a person "enjoys" property if—

(*a*) in the case of an interest in land, he occupies the land, and

(*b*) in the case of an interest in a chattel, he is in possession of, or has the use of, the chattel.

Commentary—*Simon's Taxes* I3.746.

Regulations—Income Tax (Benefits Received by Former Owner of Property) (Election for Inheritance Tax Treatment) Regulations 2007, SI 2007/3000 (Form IHT 500).

Amendments—[1]   Words in sub-para (2)(*b*)(i) inserted; sub-para (2)(*b*)(ii), (iii) substituted for sub-para (2)(*b*)(ii) and preceding word; and sub-para (3)(*a*)(iii) inserted; by FA 2006 s 80(1), (3), (5)–(7) with effect: (a) for the part of the year 2005-06 beginning with 5 December 2005, and (b) for 2006-07 and subsequent years of assessment.

22—(1) This paragraph applies where—

    (*a*)   a person ("the chargeable person") would (apart from this paragraph) be chargeable under paragraph 8 (intangible property) for any year of assessment ("the initial year") by reference to any property ("the relevant property"), and

    (*b*)   he has not been chargeable under that paragraph in respect of any previous year of assessment by reference to the relevant property or any property which the relevant property represents or is derived from.

(2) The chargeable person may elect in accordance with paragraph 23 that—

    (*a*)   the preceding provisions of this Schedule shall not apply to him during the initial year and subsequent years of assessment by reference to the relevant property or any property which represents or is derived from the relevant property, but

    (*b*)   so long as the conditions in sub-paragraph (3) are satisfied—

        (i)   the relevant property and any property which represents or is derived from the relevant property shall be treated for the purposes of Part 5 of the 1986 Act (in relation to the chargeable person) as property subject to a reservation[, but only so far as the chargeable person is not beneficially entitled to an interest in possession in the property concerned][2],

        [(ii) section 102(3) and (4) of that Act shall apply, but only so far as the chargeable person is not beneficially entitled to an interest in possession in the property concerned, and][2]

        [(iii)   if the chargeable person is beneficially entitled to an interest in possession in the property concerned, sections 53(3) and (4) and 54 of IHTA 1984 (which deal with cases of property reverting to the settlor etc) shall not apply in relation to that property.][2]

(3) The conditions referred to in sub-paragraph (2)(*b*) are—

    (*a*)   that the relevant property or the property which represents or is derived from the relevant property remains comprised in the settlement, and

    (*b*)   that any income arising under the settlement would be treated by virtue of [section 624 of ITTOIA 2005][1] as income of the chargeable person.

Commentary—*Simon's Taxes* I3.746.

Regulations—Income Tax (Benefits Received by Former Owner of Property) (Election for Inheritance Tax Treatment) Regulations 2007, SI 2007/3000 (Form IHT 500).

Amendments—[1]   Words in sub-para (3)(*b*) substituted by ITTOIA 2005 s 882(1), Sch 1 paras 629, 653(1), (5) with effect from 6 April 2005. ITTOIA 2005 has effect: (a) for income tax purposes, for 2005–06 and subsequent tax years, and (b) for corporation tax purposes, for accounting periods ending after 5 April 2005: ITTOIA 2005 s 883(1).

[2]   Words in sub-para (2)(*b*)(i) inserted; sub-para (2)(*b*)(ii), (iii) substituted for sub-para (2)(*b*)(ii) and preceding word; by FA 2006 s 80(1), (4)–(7) with effect: (a) for the part of the year 2005-06 beginning with 5 December 2005, and (b) for 2006-07 and subsequent years of assessment.

23—(1) In this paragraph—

    "election" means an election under paragraph 21 or 22;

    "the relevant filing date" means 31st January in the year of assessment that immediately follows the initial year within the meaning of paragraph 21 or (as the case requires) paragraph 22.

(2) The election must be made in the prescribed manner.

[(3) The election must be made on or before—

    (*a*)   the relevant filing date, or

    (*b*)   such later date as an officer of Revenue and Customs may, in a particular case, allow.][1]

(5) The election may be withdrawn or amended, during the life of the chargeable person, at any time on or before the relevant filing date.

(6) Subject to sub-paragraph (5), the election takes effect for the purposes of inheritance tax from the beginning of the initial year within the meaning of paragraph 21 or (as the case requires) paragraph 22 or, if later, the date on which the chargeable person would (but for the election) have first become chargeable under this Schedule by reference to the property to which the election relates.

Commentary—*Simon's Taxes* I3.746.

Regulations—Income Tax (Benefits Received by Former Owner of Property) (Election for Inheritance Tax Treatment) Regulations 2007, SI 2007/3000 (Form IHT 500).

Amendments—[1]   Sub-para (3) substituted for original sub-paras (3), (4) by FA 2007 s 66. This amendment is deemed to have come into force on 21 March 2007.

SCHEDULE 16

RELIEF WHERE NATIONAL INSURANCE CONTRIBUTIONS MET BY EMPLOYEE

Section 85

Commentary—*Simon's Taxes* E4.507, E4.507G.

Income tax relief: restricted securities

1—(1) Chapter 2 of Part 7 of the Income Tax (Earnings and Pensions) Act 2003 (c 1) (employment income: restricted securities) is amended as follows.
(2) (*substitutes* ITEPA 2003 s 426(1))
(2) For this purpose—
   (*a*) "chargeable event" has the meaning given by section 427,
   (*b*) "the taxable amount" is the amount determined under section 428, and
   (*c*) "the relevant tax year" is the tax year in which the chargeable event occurs.
(3) Relief may be available under section 428A (relief for secondary Class 1 contributions met by employee) against an amount counting as employment income under this section.
(3) (*inserts* ITEPA 2003 s 428A)

Income tax relief: convertible securities

2—(1) Chapter 3 of Part 7 of the Income Tax (Earnings and Pensions) Act 2003 (c 1) (employment income: convertible securities) is amended as follows.
(2) (*substitutes* ITEPA 2003 ss 438(1)–(4))
(3) (*inserts* ITEPA 2003 s 442A)

Income tax relief: securities options

3—(1) Chapter 5 of Part 7 of the Income Tax (Earnings and Pensions) Act 2003 (c 1) (employment income: securities options) is amended as follows.
(2) (*substitutes* ITEPA 2003 ss 476 (1)–(4))
(3) (*repeals* ITEPA 2003 s 480(7))
(4) (*amends* ITEPA 2003 s 481, *inserts* ITEPA 2003 ss 4A, 4B)
(5) (*amends* ITEPA 2003 s 482, *inserts* ITEPA 2003 ss 482(6), (7))

Consequential amendments: PAYE

4—(1) Part 11 of the Income Tax (Earnings and Pensions) Act 2003 (Pay As You Earn) is amended as follows.
(2) (*inserts* ITEPA 2003 s 698(2A))
(3) (*inserts* ITEPA 2003 s 700(4A))

Consequential amendments: capital gains tax

6—(1) Section 119A of the Taxation of Chargeable Gains Act 1992 (c 12) (increase in expenditure by reference to tax charged in relation to employment-related securities) is amended as follows.
(2), (3) (*substitute* TCGA 1992 s 119A(5), *repeal* TCGA 1992 s 119A(8)).
(4) Nothing in this paragraph affects the operation of section 119A(5) of the Taxation of Chargeable Gains Act 1992, as inserted by paragraph 50(1) of Schedule 22 to the Finance Act 2003, in relation to amounts deducted under section 481 or 482 of the Income Tax (Earnings and Pensions) Act 2003 before the amendment of those sections by this Schedule.

Other consequential amendments

7—(1) (*amends* ITEPA 2003 s 484(7))
(2) (*amends* ITEPA 2003 s 721(1))
(3) (*amends* ITEPA 2003 Sch 1 Part 2 (index of defined expressions))

SCHEDULE 17

MINOR AMENDMENTS OF OR CONNECTED WITH THE INCOME TAX (EARNINGS AND PENSIONS) ACT 2003

Section 92

Commentary—*Simon's Taxes* **E4.101A**.

Free or subsidised meals

1—(1) (*substitutes* ITEPA 2003 s 317(1))
(2) This amendment has effect for the year 2004–05 and subsequent tax years.

Time limit for assessment: income received after year for which it is assessable

3—(1) (*substitutes* TMA 1970 s 35)
(2) This amendment has effect in relation to income assessable for the year 2004–05 and subsequent years of assessment.

Donations to charity by individuals: application to Crown employment

5—(1) (*amends* FA 1990 s 25(2))

(2) This amendment (which supersedes the amendment made by paragraph 166(3) of Schedule 6 to the Income Tax (Earnings and Pensions) Act 2003) has effect for the year 2003–04 and subsequent years of assessment.

Payments on account of income tax

6—(1) Section 108 of the Finance Act 1995 (c 4) shall be deemed not to have been repealed by Part 1 of Schedule 8 to the Income Tax (Earnings and Pensions) Act 2003 (c 1) and the inclusion of that section among the enactments so repealed shall be deemed not to have affected the amendments made by that section in section 59A of the Taxes Management Act 1970 (c 9) (payments on account of income tax).

(2) Nothing in this paragraph affects anything done—

    (*a*) on or after 6th April 2003 (when the Income Tax (Earnings and Pensions) Act 2003 came into force), and

    (*b*) before the passing of this Act,

in reliance on the view that the amendments referred to in sub-paragraph (1) had ceased to have effect.

Minor corrections of the Income Tax (Earnings and Pensions) Act 2003

9—(1) The Income Tax (Earnings and Pensions) Act 2003 (c 1) is amended as follows.

(2)–(5) (*amend* ITEPA 2003 ss 286, 554(1), 577, 677)

Other minor corrections

10—(1) (*amended* TMA 1970 s 59A(8); *repealed by* ITTOIA 2005 s 884, Sch 3)

(2) (*amended* ICTA 1988 s 336; *repealed by* ITA 2007 s 1031, Sch 3 Pt 1)

(3) (*amends* FA 1988 s 38(9))

(4) (*amends* FA 1989 s 76)

Amendment—Sub-para (4) repealed by FA 2004 s 326, Sch 42 Pt 3 with effect from 6 April 2006, but subject to transitional provisions and savings in FA 2004 Sch 36.

SCHEDULE 18
ENTERPRISE INVESTMENT SCHEME

Section 93

Commentary—*Simon's Taxes* **E3.102; E3.185.**

PART 2
DEFERRAL RELIEF

12–20 (*amend* TCGA 1992 Sch 5B paras 1(2), (4), 1A, 10, 13, 14, 14A, 16, 19; *partially repealed by* FA 2009 s 27, Sch 8 para 10)

PART 3
COMMENCEMENT

21 Except where otherwise provided, the amendments made by this Schedule have effect in relation to shares issued on or after 17th March 2004.

SCHEDULE 19
VENTURE CAPITAL TRUSTS

Section 94

PART 2
ABOLITION OF DEFERRAL RELIEF

Main amendments

4, 5 (*repeal* TCGA 1992 s 151A(3), Sch 5C)

Consequential amendment

6—(1) The Taxation of Chargeable Gains Act 1992 is amended as follows.

(2) (*amends* TCGA 1992 Sch 5B, para 2(4))

Commencement

7—(1) The amendments made by this Part have effect in relation to shares issued on or after 6th April 2004 which are shares by reference to which an individual is given relief under Part 1 of Schedule 15B to the Taxes Act 1988.

(2) But nothing in this Act affects the continuing operation of Schedule 5C to the Taxation of Chargeable Gains Act 1992 (c 12) for the purposes of section 151B(8)(*b*)(ii) of that Act.

SCHEDULE 20

CORPORATE VENTURING SCHEME

Section 95

Commentary—*Simon's Taxes* **D8.320, D8.332**.

1 Schedule 15 to the Finance Act 2000 (c 17) (the corporate venturing scheme) is amended as follows.

2 (*amends* FA 2000 Sch 15 para 3)

3 (*amends* FA 2000 Sch 15 para 15)

4 (*amends* FA 2000 Sch 15 para 20)

5—(1) Paragraph 21 (meaning of "qualifying subsidiary") is amended as follows.
(2)–(4) (*amend* FA 2000 Sch 15 para 21)

6 (*inserts* FA 2000 Sch 15 para 21A)

7–12(*amended* FA 2000 Sch 15 paras 23–25, 35, 36, 40; para 7(*d*) *repealed by* FA 2007 s 114, Sch 27 Pt 2(16))

13 (*inserts* FA 2000 Sch 15 para 102(8))

14 (*amends* FA 2000 Sch 15 para 103)

15 The amendments made by this Schedule have effect in relation to shares issued on or after 17th March 2004.

SCHEDULE 21

CHARGEABLE GAINS: RESTRICTION OF GIFTS RELIEF ETC

Section 116

Commentary—*Simon's Taxes* **C3.501, C3.502; I3.613**.

Relief for gifts of business assets

3—(1) Section 165 of the Taxation of Chargeable Gains Act 1992 is amended as follows.
(2)–(5) (*amend* TCGA 1992 s 165; *repealed*) in part by FA 2008 s 8, Sch 2 para 55(*g*))

Gifts relief not to be available on certain transfers to settlor-interested settlements etc

4—(*inserts* TCGA 1992 ss 169B–169G)

Gifts on which inheritance tax is chargeable etc

5—(1) Section 260 of the Taxation of Chargeable Gains Act 1992 (c 12) is amended as follows.
(2)–(5) (*amend* TCGA 1992 s 260)

Payment by instalments of tax on gifts

6—(1) Section 281 of the Taxation of Chargeable Gains Act 1992 is amended as follows.
(2), (3) (*amend* TCGA 1992 s 281, *insert* TCGA 1992 s 281(8))

Recovery of tax from donee

7—(1) Section 282 of the Taxation of Chargeable Gains Act 1992 (c 12) is amended as follows.
(2) (*inserts* TCGA 1992 s 282(5))

Relief for gifts of business assets

9—(1) Schedule 7 to the Taxation of Chargeable Gains Act 1992 is amended as follows.
(2) (*amends* TCGA 1992 Sch 7 para 2(1))

Commencement

10—(1) The amendment in paragraph 1(2) of this Schedule has effect in relation to any notice given—
  (a) after the passing of this Act, and
  (b) in respect of the year 2003–04 or any subsequent year of assessment.
(2) The amendment in paragraph 2(2) of this Schedule has effect in relation to the provision of property on or after 10th December 2003.
(3) The amendments in paragraphs 2(3) and 6(2) of this Schedule have effect in relation to any notice given in respect of the year 2004–05 or any subsequent year of assessment.
(4) The amendments in paragraphs 3(2), 4, 5(2), 6(3), 7(2) . . . [1] and 9(2) of this Schedule have effect in relation to disposals on or after 10th December 2003 (whenever any earlier disposal as mentioned in section 169B(3)(b) or 169C(3)(b) was made).
(5) The amendment in paragraph 3(3) of this Schedule has effect in relation to disposals on or after 21st October 2003.
(6) . . . [1]
(7) The amendment in paragraph 3(5) of this Schedule has effect in relation to disposals on or after 10th December 2003.
The amendments in paragraph 5(3) and (4) of this Schedule have effect in relation to gains 6th April 2004 or after 6th April 2004.
The amendment in paragraph 5(5) of this Schedule has effect in relation to disposals on or after

Amendments—[1] Words in subparagraph omitted by FA 2008 s 8, Sch 2 para 55(g) with effect in relation to chargeable gains accruing or treated as accruing in the tax year or any subsequent tax year.

SCHEDULE 22
CHARGEABLE GAINS: PRIVATE RESIDENCE RELIEF
Section 117

Commentary—*Simon's Taxes* **C3.1701, C3.1708**.

Relief on disposal of private residence

1—(1) Section 222 of the Taxation of Chargeable Gains Act 1992 (c 12) is amended as follows.
(2) (*amends TCGA s 222(5)*)

Amount of relief

2—(1) Section 223 of the Taxation of Chargeable Gains Act 1992 is amended as follows.
(2) (*amends TCGA s 223(4)*)
(3) (*inserts TCGA s 222(8)*)

Amount of relief: further provisions

3—(1) Section 224 of the Taxation of Chargeable Gains Act 1992 (c 12) is amended as follows.
(2) (*amends TCGA s 224(1)*)

Private residence occupied under terms of settlement

4—(1) Section 225 of the Taxation of Chargeable Gains Act 1992 is amended as follows.
(2)–(5) (*amend TCGA s 225*)

Private residence held by personal representatives

5 (*inserts TCGA s 225A*)

Private residence relief: cases where relief obtained under section 260

6 (*inserts TCGA ss 226A, 226B*)

Commencement

7—(1) The amendments in paragraphs 1(2) and 4(4)(a) of this Schedule have effect in relation to any notice given on or after 10th December 2003.
(2) The amendments in paragraphs 2(2), 3(2), 4(2), (3), (4)(b) and (5) and 5 of this Schedule have effect in relation to disposals made on or after 10th December 2003.
(3) Subject to paragraph 8 of this Schedule, the amendments in paragraphs 2(3) and 6 of this Schedule have effect in relation to gains or parts of gains accruing on later disposals (within the meaning of the section 226A inserted by paragraph 6 of this Schedule) made on or after 10th December 2003 (whenever any relevant earlier disposal was made).

(4) In sub-paragraph (3) above "relevant earlier disposal", in relation to a later disposal (within the meaning of the section 226A inserted by paragraph 6 of this Schedule), means an earlier disposal in respect of which a claim mentioned in subsection (1)(c) of that section is made.

Transitional provision

8—(1) This paragraph has effect where section 226A of the Taxation of Chargeable Gains Act 1992 (c 12) (as inserted by paragraph 6 of this Schedule) ("section 226A") applies in circumstances in which—

  (a) the relevant earlier disposal, or

  (b) if there were two or more such disposals, each of them,

was made before 10th December 2003.

(2) Section 226A shall have effect subject to the following modifications.

(3) In subsection (2), omit "not" and at the end insert "subject to the modifications set out in subsections (2A) to (2C) below".

(4) After subsection (2) insert—

  "(2A)   Section 223 (1) shall not apply.

  (2B)   For the purposes of section 223(2)(a) and (3)—

      (a)   the dwelling-house or the part of the dwelling-house in question is to be taken not
              to have been the individual's only or main residence during the post-commencement
              period or any part of that period, and

      (b)   the words "but inclusive of the last 36 months of the ... ... months as
              event" shall not have effect in respect of ... ...
              falls within the post-commencement period" means the period beginning on

  (2C)   In subsection (2B) above "post ... ...mmencement period" means the period beginning on
  10th December 2003 and en... ...g on the date of the later disposal.".

(5) In subsection (3), omit "never" and at the end insert "subject to the modifications set out in subsections (2A) to (2C) above".

(6) In this paragraph "relevant earlier disposal". in relation to a later disposal, means an earlier disposal in respect of which a claim mentioned in subsection (1)(c) of section 226A is made.

(7) This paragraph is to be construed as one with section 226A.

(8) Subsections (5) and (6) of section 223 of the Taxation of Chargeable Gains Act 1992 apply in relation to the subsection (2B)(b) treated as inserted by sub-paragraph (4) above as they apply in relation to subsections (1) and (2)(a) of that section.

SCHEDULE 23

FINANCE LEASEBACKS: TRANSITIONAL PROVISION

Section 134

Commentary—*Simon's Taxes* **B3.368, B3.369**.

Introduction

1—(1) Sections 228B to 228E of the Capital Allowances Act 2001 (c 2) (as inserted by section 134) are subject to paragraphs 2 to 9 of this Schedule in their application in relation to existing leasebacks.

(2) Paragraph 10 of this Schedule makes provision in relation to the taxation of chargeable gains where an existing leaseback terminates.

Section 228B

2—(1) This paragraph applies if the pre-commencement rentals are greater than the total of the actual rental deductions for periods of account up to, but excluding, the transitional period of account.

(2) Section 228B shall not apply in relation to—

  (a) the transitional period of account if the lessee's excess rentals are greater than the notional
      rental deduction for that period, or

  (b) a subsequent period of account if the unrelieved portion of the lessee's excess rentals is
      greater than the notional rental deduction for that period.

(3) Section 228B is subject to sub-paragraph (4) in its application to—

  (a) the transitional period of account if the lessee's excess rentals are not greater than the
      notional rental deduction for that period, or

  (b) a subsequent period of account if the unrelieved portion of the lessee's excess rentals is not
      greater than the notional rental deduction for that period.

(4) The permitted maximum for that period of account is the total of—

  (a) the lessee's excess rentals (in the case of the transitional period of account) or the unrelieved
      portion of the lessee's excess rentals (in the case of a subsequent period of account), and

(*b*) the amount given by this calculation—

$$\text{Basic Amount} \times \frac{(\text{Notional Rental Deduction} - \text{Deductible Excess})}{\text{Notional Rental Deduction}}$$

where—

"Basic Amount" means the amount calculated in accordance with section 228B(2),

"Notional Rental Deduction" means the notional rental deduction for the period of account in question, and

"Deductible Excess" means the amount included in the permitted maximum by virtue of sub-paragraph (4)(*a*).

(5) But where, in relation to the transitional period of account, the amount given by sub-paragraph (4) is less than the appropriate fraction of the notional rental deduction for that period, the permitted maximum shall be that fraction of that deduction.

(6) In this paragraph—

(*a*) "the lessee's excess rentals" means—

(i) the pre-commencement rentals, minus

(ii) the total of the actual rental deductions referred to in sub-paragraph (1), and

(*b*) "the unrelieved portion of the lessee's excess rentals", in relation to a period of account, means—

(i) the lessee's excess rentals, minus

(ii) the total of the actual rental deductions for periods of account from and including the transitional period up to, but excluding, the period in question.

(7) In this paragraph—

"actual rental deduction", in relation to a period of account, means the amount that may be deducted in respect of amounts payable under the existing leaseback in calculating the lessee's income or profits for that period of account for the purpose of income tax or corporation tax;

"notional rental deduction", in relation to a period of account, means the amount that could, if section 228B did not apply, be deducted in respect of amounts payable under the existing leaseback in calculating the lessee's income or profits for that period of account for the purpose of income tax or corporation tax.

(8) Nothing in sub-paragraphs (3) to (5) prevents the inclusion of an amount in the permitted maximum by virtue of section 228B(3) and (4).

(9) This paragraph does not apply in relation to any period of account later than a period of account for which the permitted maximum has been determined in accordance with sub-paragraph (3) to (5).

Commentary—*Simon's Taxes* **B3.372**.

3—(1) This paragraph applies where—

(*a*) the existing leaseback terminates, and

(*b*) in the period of account immediately following that in which it terminates, paragraph 2(2)(*b*) or 2(3)(*b*) would apply were it not for the termination.

(2) The permitted maximum for the period of account in which the leaseback terminates shall also include an amount equal to the amount that the unrelieved portion of the lessee's excess rentals would have been in the period of account immediately following.

Section 228C

4   Section 228C shall not apply where the existing leaseback terminates before 17 March 2004.

5—(1) Section 228C applies subject to this paragraph where—

(*a*) the existing leaseback terminates otherwise than by expiry of its term, and

(*b*) the amount calculated in accordance with section 228C(3) exceeds the relevant cap.

(2) In determining the amount by which income or profits are to be increased under section 228C(2), the amount calculated in accordance with section 228C(3) shall be disregarded to the extent that it exceeds the relevant cap.

(3) The relevant cap is—

$$(\text{Original Consideration} - \text{Relevant Rentals}) \times \frac{\text{Net Consideration}}{\text{Original Consideration}}$$

where—

"Original Consideration" has the same meaning as in section 228B;

"Relevant Rentals" means—

    (a) the pre-commencement rentals, minus

    (b) the total of—

        (i) finance charges shown in the accounts for periods that end before 17 March 2004, and

        (ii) the appropriate proportion of finance charges shown in the accounts for the transitional period of account;

"Net Consideration" has the same meaning as in section 228C.

Commentary—*Simon's Taxes* B3.372A.

6—(1) This paragraph applies if—

    (a) the existing leaseback terminates otherwise than by expiry of its term,

    (b) upon the termination of the leaseback, or during the period of one month beginning with the date of termination, the lessee becomes the owner of the plant of machinery by acquiring it—

        (i) from the lessor, or

        (ii) where no person other than the lessor or a person connected with the lessee has owned the plant or machinery at any time since the termination of the leaseback, from a person connected with the lessee,

    (c) the person who first acquires the plant or machinery from the lessor does so as a result of incurring capital expenditure equal (at least) to the market value of the plant or machinery at the termination of the leaseback, and

    (d) the amount of the lessee acquisition expenditure that counts as qualifying expenditure is restricted under section 226.

(2) If the section 226 restriction is greater than the amount calculated in accordance with section 228C(3)—

    (a) section 228C(2) to (4) shall not apply, but

    (b) if there is a taxable disposal, section 228C(2) to (4) shall apply subject to sub-paragraph (5).

(3) If the section 226 restriction is not greater than the amount calculated in accordance with section 228C(3)—

    (a) the amount by which profits or income are increased in accordance with section 228C(2) shall be reduced by the section 226 restriction, and

    (b) if there is a taxable disposal, section 228C(2) to (4) shall apply again subject to sub-paragraph (5).

(4) For the purposes of sub-paragraphs (2) and (3) there is a taxable disposal if, during the period of six years beginning with the date of termination of the leaseback—

    (a) the whole of the plant or machinery is the subject of a disposal event (within the meaning of Part 2), or

    (b) part of the plant or machinery is the subject of such a disposal event.

(5) Where section 228C(2) to (4) applies subject to this sub-paragraph—

    (a) a reference to the termination shall be treated as a reference to the cessation of ownership of the plant or machinery, and

    (b) the amount by which profits or income are increased in accordance with section 228C(2) shall be—

        (i) in a case falling within sub-paragraph (2)(b), the relevant fraction of the amount calculated in accordance with section 228C(3), or

        (ii) in a case falling within sub-paragraph (3)(b), the relevant fraction of the section 226 restriction.

(6) In sub-paragraph (5)(b)(i) and (ii) "relevant fraction" means—

$$\frac{\text{(Disposal Proceeds} - \text{Restricted Qualifying Expendture)}}{\text{(Lessee Acquisition Expenditure} - \text{Restricted Qualifying Expenditure)}}$$

where "Disposal Proceeds" means the consideration due to the lessee under the taxable disposal or, if higher, the market value of the plant or machinery at the time of the taxable disposal; but—

    (a) where that amount is greater than the lessee acquisition expenditure, the Disposal Proceeds shall be the amount of the lessee acquisition expenditure, or

    (b) where that amount is less than the restricted qualifying expenditure, the Disposal Proceeds shall be the amount of the restricted qualifying expenditure.

(7) Where there is a taxable disposal by virtue of sub-paragraph (4)(b), this paragraph applies in relation to that disposal with the following modifications—

    (a) references in sub-paragraphs (5)(a) and (6) to the plant or machinery shall be taken to be references to the part of the plant or machinery comprised in the taxable disposal;

(b) the amount by which profits or income are to be increased by virtue of sub-paragraph (5)(b) shall be the partial disposal fraction of the amount given by sub-paragraph (5)(b)(i) or (ii);

(c) the partial disposal fraction of the restricted qualifying expenditure and of the lessee acquisition expenditure shall be used for the purposes of sub-paragraph (6) instead of those amounts of expenditure.

(8) For the purposes of sub-paragraph (7) the partial disposal fraction is—

$$\frac{\text{Apportioned Lessee Acquisition Expenditure}}{\text{Lessee Acquisition Expenditure}}$$

where "Apportioned Lessee Acquisition Expenditure" means so much of the lessee acquisition expenditure as was attributable to the acquisition of the part of the plant or machinery comprised in the taxable disposal.

(9) In this paragraph—

"lessee acquisition expenditure" means the capital expenditure incurred by the lessee in acquiring the plant or machinery as described in sub-paragraph (1)(b),

"restricted qualifying expenditure" means the qualifying expenditure under section 226, and

"section 226 restriction" means—

(a) the lessee acquisition expenditure, minus

(b) the restricted qualifying expenditure.

Commentary—*Simon's Taxes* **B3.372A**.

Section 228D

7—(1) This paragraph applies if the pre-commencement rentals are greater than the total of the actual taxed rentals for periods of account up to, but excluding, the transitional period of account.

(2) Section 228D shall not apply in relation to—

(a) the transitional period of account if the lessor's excess rentals are greater than the notional taxed rental for that period, or

(b) a subsequent period of account if the untaxed portion of the lessor's excess rentals is greater than the notional taxed rental for that period.

(3) Section 228D is subject to sub-paragraph (4) in its application to—

(a) the transitional period of account if the lessor's excess rentals are not greater than the notional taxed rental for that period, or

(b) a subsequent period of account if the untaxed portion of the lessor's excess rentals is not greater than the notional taxed rental for that period.

(4) The permitted threshold for that period of account is the total of—

(a) the lessor's excess rentals (in the case of the transitional period of account) or the untaxed portion of the lessor's excess rentals (in the case of a subsequent period of account), and

(b) the amount given by this calculation—

$$\text{Basic Amount} \times \frac{(\text{Notional Taxed Rental} - \text{Deductible Excess})}{\text{Notional Taxed Rental}}$$

where—

"Basic Amount" means the amount calculated in accordance with section 228D(4);

"Notional Taxed Rental" means the notional taxed rental for the period of account in question, and

"Deductible Excess" means the amount included in the permitted threshold by virtue of sub-paragraph (4)(a).

(5) But where, in relation to the transitional period of account, the amount given by sub-paragraph (4) is less than the appropriate fraction of the notional taxed rental for that period, the permitted threshold shall be that fraction of that rental.

(6) In this paragraph—

(a) "the lessor's excess rentals" means—

(i) the pre-commencement rentals, minus

(ii) the total of the actual taxed rentals referred to in sub-paragraph (1), and

(b) "the untaxed portion of the lessor's excess rentals", in relation to a period of account, means—

(i) the lessor's excess rentals, minus

(ii) the total of the actual taxed rentals for periods of account from and including the transitional period up to, but excluding, the period in question.

(7) In this paragraph—

"actual taxed rental", in relation to a period of account, means the amount that should be taken into consideration in respect of amounts receivable under the existing leaseback in calculating the

lessor's income or profits for that period of account for the purpose of income tax or corporation tax;

"notional taxed rental", in relation to a period of account, means the amount that would, if section 228D did not apply, be taken into consideration in respect of amounts receivable under the existing leaseback in calculating the lessor's income or profits for that period of account for the purpose of income tax or corporation tax.

(8) Nothing in sub-paragraphs (3) to (5) prevents the inclusion of an amount in the permitted threshold by virtue of section 228D(2).

(9) This paragraph does not apply in relation to any period of account later than a period of account for which the permitted threshold has been determined in accordance with sub-paragraphs (3) to (5).

Commentary—*Simon's Taxes* **B3.373.**

8—(1) This paragraph applies where—

    (*a*) the existing leaseback terminates, and

    (*b*) in the period of account immediately following that in which it terminates, paragraph 7(2)(*b*) or 7(3)(*b*) would apply were it not for the termination.

(2) The permitted threshold for the period of account in which the leaseback terminates shall also include an amount equal to the amount that the untaxed portion of the lessor's excess rentals would have been in the period of account immediately following.

Commentary—*Simon's Taxes* **B3.373.**

Section 228E

9   Section 228E shall not apply where the existing leaseback terminates before 17 March 2004.

Commentary—*Simon's Taxes* **B3.373A.**

Chargeable gains

10—(1) Sub-paragraph (2) applies where—

    (*a*) an existing leaseback is the leaseback in a lease and finance leaseback,

    (*b*) the leaseback terminates,

    (*c*) on or after the termination there is a disposal, by the user, of the whole or part of the plant and machinery subject to the leaseback, and

    (*d*) a chargeable gain that accrues on that disposal ("the relevant chargeable gain") falls to be taken into account for the purposes of a chargeable gains computation.

(2) The following fraction of the relevant chargeable gain shall instead be taken into account for the purposes of the chargeable gains computation—

$$\frac{\text{(Net Rentals – Termination Charge)}}{\text{Lease Premium}}$$

where—

"Net Rentals" means—

    (*a*) the total of the amounts deducted in calculating the user's income or profits, for the purpose of income tax or corporation tax, in respect of amounts payable under the leaseback, minus

    (*b*) the total of the amounts shown in the user's accounts in respect of finance charges relating to the leaseback;

"Termination Charge" means the amount by which the user's income or profits are to be increased by virtue of section 228C(2) of the CAA 2001 because of the termination;

"Lease Premium" means the consideration relating to the leaseback referred to in section 228F(6)(*b*) of the CAA 2001.

(3) References in this paragraph to termination of the leaseback shall be construed in accordance with section 228H(1) of the CAA 2001.

(4) In this paragraph—

"CAA 2001" means the Capital Allowances Act 2001;

"chargeable gains computation" means the computation, for the purposes of the TCGA 1992, of the total amount of chargeable gains that accrue to the user in any chargeable period that ends on or after 17 March 2004;

"disposal" shall be construed in accordance with the TCGA 1992;

"lease and finance leaseback" has the same meaning as in section 228F of the CAA 2001;

"TCGA 1992" means the Taxation of Chargeable Gains Act 1992;

"user" means the person who is the lessee under the leaseback.

Commentary—*Simon's Taxes* **B3.374**.

Interpretation

11—(1) In this Schedule—

"existing leaseback" means a leaseback the term of which began before 17 March 2004;

"pre-commencement rentals", in relation to an existing leaseback, means—

(*a*) any amounts payable by the lessee to the lessor under the leaseback before 17 March 2004,

(*b*) any amounts so payable on or after 17 March 2004 in respect of a period that ends before 17 March 2004, or

(*c*) where any amounts are so payable on or after 17 March 2004 in respect of a period which begins before that date and ends on or after that date, the appropriate fraction of each of those amounts;

"transitional period of account" means a period of account that includes 17 March 2004.

(2) In this Schedule the "appropriate fraction", in respect of an amount that relates to a particular period, means this fraction—

$$\frac{\text{Pre-commencement Period}}{\text{Whole Period}}$$

where—

"Pre-commencement Period" means the number of days in the part of the period that falls before 17 March 2004, and

"Whole Period" means the number of days in the whole of the period.

SCHEDULE 25

LLOYD'S NAMES: CONVERSION TO LIMITED LIABILITY UNDERWRITING

Section 144

Commentary—*Simon's Taxes* **E5.625, E5.621, E5.629**.

1   The Finance Act 1993 (c 34) is amended as follows.

2, 3(*insert* FA 1993 s 179B, Sch 20A)

SCHEDULE 26

OFFSHORE FUNDS

Section 145

Commentary—*Simon's Taxes* **B8.626, B8.630**.

Modifications—Offshore Funds Regulations, SI 2004/2572 reg 6 (modification of this Schedule where an existing umbrella fund has not made an election under either or both of FA 2004 Sch 26 para 1(3) or 2(3), in respect of new parts of the fund which are treated as separate offshore funds for the purposes of TA 1988 Pt 17 Chapter 5).

SI 2004/2572 reg 7 (modification of this Schedule where an existing main fund has not made an election under either or both of FA 2004 Sch 26 para 1(3) or 2(3), in respect of new classes of interest which are treated as separate offshore funds for the purposes of TA 1988 Pt 17 Chapter 5).

Computation of UK equivalent profits: creditor relationships

1—(*1*) (*amended* TA 1988 Sch 27 para 5(3); *repealed by* the Offshore Funds (Tax) Regulations, SI 2009/3001 reg 13(2), Sch 2)

(2) (*repeals* FA 1996 Sch 10 para 3)

(3) In relation to a fund established on or before the day on which this Act is passed, this paragraph only has effect if an election that it should have effect has been made by or on behalf of the fund.

(4) Any such election—

(*a*) must be made by notice to an officer of the Board, in such form and within such time as the Board may determine, and

(*b*) is irrevocable.

(5) For the purpose of determining the United Kingdom equivalent profits of an offshore fund for the first account period of the fund in relation to which this paragraph has effect—

(a) any profits, gains or losses arising from a creditor relationship that were taken into account in determining the United Kingdom equivalent profits of the fund for the preceding account period shall be disregarded, and

(b) any profits, gains or losses arising from a creditor relationship that—

    (i) arose in, or in respect of, the preceding account period, but

    (ii) were not taken into account in determining the United Kingdom equivalent profits of the fund for that period,

shall be taken into account.

(6) In this paragraph—

"creditor relationship" has the same meaning as in [Part 5 of the Corporation Tax Act 2009][1]; and

"United Kingdom equivalent profits" has the meaning given in paragraph 5 of Schedule 27 to the Taxes Act 1988.

Modifications—Offshore Funds Regulations, SI 2004/2572 reg 6 (modification of this paragraph where an existing umbrella fund has not made an election under either or both of FA 2004 Sch 26 para 1(3) or 2(3), in respect of new parts of the fund which are treated as separate offshore funds for the purposes of TA 1988 Pt 17 Chapter 5).

SI 2004/2572 reg 7 (modification of this paragraph where an existing main fund has not made an election under either or both of FA 2004 Sch 26 para 1(3) or 2(3), in respect of new classes of interest which are treated as separate offshore funds for the purposes of TA 1988 Pt 17 Chapter 5).

Amendments—[1] In sub-para (6) words substituted for words "Chapter 2 of Part 4 of the Finance Act 1996" by CTA 2009 s 1322, Sch 1 paras 569, 581(1), (2). CTA 2009 applies for accounting periods ending on or after 1 April 2009 (for corporation tax purposes) and for tax years 2009–10 onwards (for income and capital gains tax purposes).

Computation of UK equivalent profits: derivative contracts

2—(1) (*amended* TA 1988 Sch 27 para 5(3); *repealed by* the Offshore Funds (Tax) Regulations, SI 2009/3001 reg 13(2), Sch 2)

(2) (*repeals* FA 2002 Sch 26 para 35)

(3) In relation to a fund established on or before the day on which this Act is passed, this paragraph only has effect if an election that it should have effect has been made by or on behalf of the fund.

(4) Any such election—

(a) must be made by notice to an officer of the Board, in such form and within such time as the Board may determine, and

(b) is irrevocable.

(5) For the purpose of determining the United Kingdom equivalent profits of an offshore fund for the first account period of the fund in relation to which this paragraph has effect—

(a) any profits or losses arising from a derivative contract that were taken into account in determining the United Kingdom equivalent profits of the fund for the preceding account period shall be disregarded, and

(b) any profits or losses arising from a derivative contract that—

    (i) arose in, or in respect of, the preceding account period, but

    (ii) were not taken into account in determining the United Kingdom equivalent profits of the fund for that period,

shall be taken into account.

(6) In this paragraph—

"derivative contract" has the same meaning as in [Part 7 of the Corporation Tax Act 2009][1];

"United Kingdom equivalent profits" has the meaning given in paragraph 5 of Schedule 27 to the Taxes Act 1988.

Modifications—Offshore Funds Regulations, SI 2004/2572 reg 6 (modification of this paragraph where an existing umbrella fund has not made an election under either or both of FA 2004 Sch 26 para 1(3) or 2(3), in respect of new parts of the fund which are treated as separate offshore funds for the purposes of TA 1988 Pt 17 Chapter 5).

SI 2004/2572 reg 7 (modification of this paragraph where an existing main fund has not made an election under either or both of FA 2004 Sch 26 para 1(3) or 2(3), in respect of new classes of interest which are treated as separate offshore funds for the purposes of TA 1988 Pt 17 Chapter 5).

Amendments—[1] In sub-para (6) words substituted for words "Schedule 26 to the Finance Act 2002" by CTA 2009 s 1322, Sch 1 paras 569, 581(1), (3). CTA 2009 applies for accounting periods ending on or after 1 April 2009 (for corporation tax purposes) and for tax years 2009–10 onwards (for income and capital gains tax purposes).

Treatment of umbrella funds and funds comprising more than one class of interest

3 (*inserts* TA 1988 ss 756A–756C)

11 (*amends* TCGA 1992 s 212(6A))

Transitional provision

17—(1) This paragraph applies for the purposes of determining whether an offshore fund that is—

(*a*) a part of an umbrella fund (which is treated as an offshore fund under section 756B of the Taxes Act 1988), or

(*b*) a class of interest in a part of an umbrella fund (which is treated as an offshore fund under section 756C of that Act),

may be certified as a distributing fund under Chapter 5 of Part 17 of that Act in respect of an account period ending on or after the day on which this Act is passed and on or before 31st December 2005.

(2) Where this paragraph applies—

(*a*) subsection (3) of section 760 of the Taxes Act 1988 shall not have effect, and

(*b*) the fund shall not be certified as a distributing fund in respect of a period if at any time in that period—

(i) more than 5 per cent by value of the assets of that offshore fund consists of interests in other offshore funds, and

(ii) more than 5 per cent by value of the assets of the umbrella fund consists of interests in other offshore funds.

(3) Where this paragraph applies, references to subsection (3) of section 760 of the Taxes Act 1988 shall have effect as references to sub-paragraph (2)(*b*) above.

(4) Words used in Chapter 5 of Part 17 of the Taxes Act 1988 have the same meaning in this paragraph as they have in that Chapter.

SCHEDULE 27

MEANING OF "OFFSHORE INSTALLATION"

Section 146

Commentary—*Simon's Taxes* **B3.353; E4.123**.

PART 2

MINOR AND CONSEQUENTIAL AMENDMENTS

The Taxes Act 1988

4—(1)–(5) . . . [2]

(6) Nothing in this paragraph affects the operation of any of the following provisions in relation to shares issued before that date—

(*a*) . . . [2]

(*b*) [section 573][1] of that Act (relief for losses on unlisted shares in trading companies);

(*c*) . . . [2]

Amendments—[1] Words substituted by ITA 2007 s 1027, Sch 1 paras 456, 483 with effect for income tax purposes from 6 April 2007, and corporation tax purposes for accounting periods ending after 5 April 2007.

[2] This paragraph, save for sub-para (6)(*b*), repealed by ITA 2007 s 1031, Sch 3 Pt 2 with effect in relation to shares issued after 5 April 2007.

Finance Act 2000 (c 17)

6—(1) Schedule 15 to the Finance Act 2000 (the corporate venturing scheme) is amended as set out in sub-paragraphs (2) to (4).

(2)–(4) (*amend FA 2000 Sch 15 paras 23, 28*)

(5) This paragraph has effect in relation to shares issued on or after 6th April 2004.

(6) Nothing in this paragraph affects the operation of Schedule 15 to the Finance Act 2000 in relation to shares issued before that date.

7—(1) (*repeals FA 2000 Sch 22 para 20(5)*)

(2) This paragraph has effect for accounting periods ending on or after 1st April 2004.

Capital Allowances Act 2001 (c 2)

8 (*repeals CAA 2001 ss 94(2)(b), (3)*)

9—(1) Section 153 of the Capital Allowances Act 2001 (ships that are not qualifying ships) is amended as follows.

(2), (3) (*substitute CAA 2001 s 153(2), repeal CAA 2001 s 153(3)*)

10 (*amends CAA 2001 Sch 1 Part 2*)

11—(1) Paragraphs 8 to 10 have effect—

(*a*) for income tax purposes, as respects allowances and charges falling to be made for chargeable periods ending on or after 6th April 2004;

(*b*) for corporation tax purposes, as respects allowances and charges falling to be made for chargeable periods ending on or after 1st April 2004.

(2) In this paragraph "chargeable period" has the meaning given by section 6 of the Capital Allowances Act 2001.

Income Tax (Earnings and Pensions) Act 2003 (c 1)

12, 13   (*amend* ITEPA 2003 ss 40(5), 305(6))

14   (*substitutes* ITEPA s 385)

15   (*amends* ITEPA 2003 Sch 1 Part 2)

16   Paragraphs 12 to 15 have effect for the year 2004–05 and subsequent years of assessment.

17—(1) Schedule 5 to the Income Tax (Earnings and Pensions) Act 2003 (enterprise management incentives) is amended as follows.
(2)–(5) (*amend* ITEPA 2003 Sch 5 paras 18, 59)
(6) This paragraph has effect in relation to a right to acquire shares in a company granted on or after 6th April 2004.
(7) Nothing in this paragraph affects the operation of Schedule 5 to the Income Tax (Earnings and Pensions) Act 2003 in relation to a right to acquire shares in a company granted before that date.

SCHEDULE 28
REGISTERED PENSION SCHEMES: AUTHORISED PENSIONS—SUPPLEMENTARY

Sections 165 and 167

Modifications—Taxation of Pension Schemes (Transitional Provisions) Order, SI 2006/572 arts 3, 5 (modification of this Schedule in its application to any pension which—

(a)   was paid by way of income withdrawal, income drawdown or annuity purchase deferral from a retirement benefits scheme, or a personal pension scheme approved under TA 1988 Pt 14 immediately before 6 April 2006; and

(b)   on 6 April 2006 becomes an unsecured pension or a dependant's unsecured pension by virtue of a scheme which is treated as becoming a registered pension scheme on that date).

Commentary—*Simon's Taxes* **E7.102**.

PART 1
PENSION RULES

DEFINED BENEFITS AND MONEY PURCHASE ARRANGEMENTS

Ill-health condition

1   For the purposes of this Part the ill-health condition is met if—
  (*a*) the scheme administrator has received evidence from a registered medical practitioner that the member is (and will continue to be) incapable of carrying on the member's occupation because of physical or mental impairment, and
  (*b*) the member has in fact ceased to carry on the member's occupation.

Commentary—*Simon's Taxes* **E7.224**.
Modifications—Pensions Schemes (Application of UK Provisions to Relevant Non-UK Schemes) Regulations, SI 2006/207 reg 14 (modification of this paragraph in respect of relevant non-UK schemes).
Registered Pension Schemes (Splitting of Schemes) Regulations, SI 2006/569 reg 3 (modification of this provision in relation to sub-scheme administrators).

Scheme pension

2—(1) . . . [1]
(2) [A][1] pension payable to the member is a scheme pension for the purposes of this Part if—
  (*a*) it is payable by the scheme administrator or by an insurance company selected by the scheme administrator, and
  (*b*) it satisfies the condition in sub-paragraph (3).
(3) The condition is that (subject to sub-paragraph (4))—
  (*a*) the pension is payable (at least annually) until the member's death or until the later of the member's death and the end of a term certain not exceeding ten years, and
  (*b*) the rate of pension payable [at any time during any][1] relevant 12 month period is not less than the rate payable [at the relevant time][1].
[(3A) "The relevant time" is—
  (*a*) in the case of the first relevant 12 month period, the day on which the member becomes entitled to the pension, and
  (*b*) in the case of any other relevant 12 month period, immediately before the beginning of that period][1]
(4) None of the following prevent the pension satisfying the condition in sub-paragraph (3)—

[(*a*) the reduction of the pension if the member became entitled to it by reason of the ill-health condition being met,][4]

(*b*) a reduction in the rate of the pension which applies to all the scheme pensions being paid to or in respect of members of the pension scheme, ... [1]
. . . [6]

[(*d*) the reduction of the pension in consequence of a pension sharing order or provision,

(*e*) forfeiture of entitlement to the pension in circumstances prescribed by regulations made by the Board of Inland Revenue,

(*f*) the reduction of the pension in consequence of an order of a court,

(*g*) if the pension is under a public service pension scheme, its reduction by abatement, or

(*h*) the reduction of the pension in any other circumstances prescribed by regulations made by the Board of Inland Revenue.][1]

[(4A) In sub-paragraph (4) references to the reduction of a pension include its ceasing to be payable (whether temporarily or permanently).][1]

[(4B)–(5A) . . . [6]

(6) A pension is payable until the end of a term certain even if it may, after the death of the member during the term, end on the pensioner—

(*a*) marrying,

[(*aa*) entering into a civil partnership,][3]

(*b*) reaching the age of 18, or

(*c*) ceasing to be in full-time education.

[(6A) The Board of Inland Revenue may by regulations provide that if—

(*a*) a scheme pension payable by an insurance company selected by the scheme administrator of a registered pension scheme ("the original scheme pension") ceases to be payable, and

(*b*) in consequence of the transfer of sums or assets (or both) from the insurance company to another insurance company in connection with the original scheme pension ceasing to be payable, another scheme pension becomes payable by the other insurance company ("the new scheme pension"),

the new scheme pension is to be treated, to such extent as is prescribed by the regulations and for such of the purposes of this Part as are so prescribed, as if it were the original scheme pension.][1]

(7) A relevant 12 month period is any 12 month period which—

(*a*) begins on or after the first anniversary of the day on which the member becomes entitled to the pension, and

(*b*) ends before the day on which the pension ceases to be payable.

[(8) Regulations under sub-paragraph [(4)(*e*) or (*h*) . . . [6]][2] may include provision having effect in relation to times before they are made.][1]

Commentary—*Simon's Taxes* **E7.224**.

Regulations—Pension Schemes (Reduction in Pension Rates) Regulations, SI 2006/138.

Registered Pension Schemes (Transfer of Sums and Assets) Regulations, SI 2006/499.

Registered Pension Schemes (Bridging Pensions) Regulations 2007, SI 2007/826 (the prescribed percentage under sub-para (5)(*c*)).

Registered Pension Schemes (Reduction in Pension Rates, Accounting and Assessment) (Amendment) Regulations, SI 2013/1111.

Registered Pension Schemes (Bridging Pensions) and Appointed Day Regulations, SI 2016/1005.

Relevant Overseas Schemes (Transfer of Sums and Assets) Regulations, SI 2018/372.

Modifications—Pensions Schemes (Application of UK Provisions to Relevant Non-UK Schemes) Regulations, SI 2006/207 reg 14 (modification of this paragraph in respect of relevant non-UK schemes).

Taxation of Pension Schemes (Transitional Provisions) Order, SI 2006/572 art 5A (modification of para (4) to insert new sub-para (*da*) where conditions in SI 2006/572 art 5A(1) are satisfied).

Amendments—[1] Sub-para (1) repealed, words in sub-paras (2), (3)(*b*) substituted, sub-paras (3A), (4A), (6A), (8) inserted, word in sub-para (4)(*b*) repealed and sub-paras (4)(*d*)–(*h*) inserted by FA 2005 ss 101, 104, Sch 10 paras 11, 64(1) and Sch 11 Pt 4 with effect from 6 April 2006.

[2] Sub-para (4)(*c*) substituted; sub-paras (5), (5A) substituted for sub-para (5); and words in sub-para (8) substituted; by FA 2006 s 161, Sch 23 paras 1, 20. These amendments are deemed to have come into force on 6 April 2006.

[3] Sub-para (6)(*aa*) inserted by the Tax and Civil Partnerships Regulations, SI 2007/493 reg 2(1), (2) with effect from 22 February 2007.

[4] Sub-para (4)(*a*) substituted by FA 2007 s 70, Sch 20 paras 1, 7(1), (2), 24(3). This amendment is deemed always to have had effect.

[5] In sub-para (4)(*c*), words substituted, and words inserted , and sub-para (4B) inserted, by FA 2013 s 51(1), (2) with effect for the tax year 2013–14 and subsequent tax years.

[6] Sub-paras (4)(*c*), (4B), (5), (5A) repealed, and in sub-para (8), words "or (5)" repealed, by FA 2016 s 20(1)–(4) with effect from 8 November 2016 (by virtue of SI 2016/1005).

[2A—(1) Where this paragraph applies in relation to a pension payable to the member, the pension scheme is to be treated as making an unauthorised payment to the member of the appropriate amount.

(2) This paragraph applies to a pension if it fails to satisfy the condition in sub-paragraph (3) of paragraph 2—

(*a*) by reason of not complying with paragraph (*a*) of that subparagraph, or (*b*) by reason of not complying with paragraph (*b*) of that sub-paragraph because a substantial reduction occurs in the rate of the pension,

or if it is a pension [which is reduced in accordance with paragraph (a) of sub-paragraph (4) of paragraph 2, or the rate of which is reduced in accordance with paragraph (b) of that sub-paragraph, and]² the reduction is part of avoidance arrangements.

(3) For the purposes of sub-paragraph (2)(*b*) a substantial reduction occurs in the rate of a pension if the rate at which the pension is payable at any time during any relevant 12 month period (within the meaning of paragraph 2(7)) is less than 80% of the rate payable when the member became entitled to the pension.

(4) For the purposes of sub-paragraph (2) "avoidance arrangements" includes schemes, arrangements and understandings of any kind (whether or not legally enforceable) the main purpose, or one of the main purposes, of which is to increase the member's entitlement to a lump sum on which there is no liability to income tax.

(5) "The appropriate amount", in relation to the pension, is the amount of any lump sum on which there is no liability to tax to which the member became entitled in connection with the pension.

(6) Once this paragraph has applied in relation to the pension, it does not apply in relation to it again.

(7) The application of this paragraph in relation to the pension does not prevent any payments of the pension themselves being unauthorised member payments.]¹

Amendments—¹   Paragraph inserted by FA 2005 s 101, Sch 10 paras 12, 64(1) with effect from 6 April 2006.
²   Words in sub-para (2) substituted by FA 2007 s 70, Sch 20 paras 1, 7(1), (3), 24(4) with effect in relation to reductions occurring on or after 6 April 2007.

MONEY PURCHASE ARRANGEMENTS

Lifetime annuity

3—(1) For the purposes of this Part an annuity payable to the member is a lifetime annuity if—

(*a*) it is payable by an insurance company,

(*b*) the member had an opportunity to select the insurance company,

[(*ba*) the member becomes entitled to it before 6 April 2015,]⁶

(*c*) it is payable until the member's death or until the later of the member's death and the end of a term certain not exceeding ten years, and

[(*d*) its amount either cannot decrease or falls to be determined in any manner prescribed by regulations made by the Board of Inland Revenue.]¹

[(1A) For the purposes of this Part, but subject to any provision made under sub-paragraph (2C)(za), an annuity payable to the member is also a lifetime annuity if—

(*a*) it is payable by an insurance company,

(*b*) the member becomes entitled to it on or after 6 April 2015, and

(*c*) it is payable until the member's death or until the later of the member's death and the end of a term certain.]⁵

(2) An annuity is payable until the end of a term certain even if it may, after the death of the member during the term, end on the annuitant—

(*a*) marrying,

[(*aa*) entering into a civil partnership,]²

(*b*) reaching the age of 18, or

(*c*) ceasing to be in full-time education.

[(2A) An annuity does not fail to satisfy sub-paragraph (1)(d) by reason of the operation of a pension sharing order or provision.

(2B) The Board of Inland Revenue may by regulations make provision in relation to cases in which a lifetime annuity payable by an insurance company ("the original lifetime annuity") ceases to be payable and in consequence of that—

(*a*) sums or assets (or both) are transferred from the insurance company to another insurance company and are applied towards the provision of either another lifetime annuity (a "new lifetime annuity") or a scheme pension, short-term annuity, dependants' scheme pension, dependants' annuity[, nominees' annuity]⁷ or dependants' short-term annuity by the other insurance company, or

(*b*) sums or assets are transferred to the relevant registered pension scheme.

(2C) The regulations may provide that—

[(*za*) in a case where—

(i) a new annuity becomes payable,

(ii) the member becomes entitled to it on or after 6 April 2015,

(iii) it would be a lifetime annuity if any provision made under this paragraph were ignored,

(iv) the terms of the contract for it are such that there will or could be decreases in its amount other than allowed decreases (see sub-paragraph (2E)), and

(v) any other conditions prescribed by the regulations are met,

the new annuity is not a lifetime annuity for the purposes of this Part,][6]

(a) in a case where a new lifetime annuity becomes payable, the new lifetime annuity is to be treated, to such extent as is prescribed by the regulations and for such of the purposes of this Part as are so prescribed, as if it were the original lifetime annuity, and

(b) in [a case other than one where a new lifetime annuity becomes payable][6], the relevant registered pension scheme is to be treated as making an unauthorised payment to the member of an amount equal to the aggregate of the amount of the sums, and the market value of the assets, transferred.

[(2CA) . . .][3, 4]

(2D) For the purposes of sub-paragraphs (2B) and (2C) a registered pension scheme is the relevant registered pension scheme if the original lifetime annuity was acquired using sums or assets held for the purposes of the pension scheme.][1]

[(2E) In sub-paragraph (2C)(za)(iv) "allowed decreases" means decreases from time to time allowed by regulations under sub-paragraph (1)(d); and any such regulations are to be treated as having effect for this purpose.][6]

(3)–(6) . . . [1]

Regulations—Registered Pension Schemes (Transfer of Sums and Assets) Regulations, SI 2006/499.
Registered Pension Schemes (Prescribed Manner of Determining Amount of Annuities) Regulations, SI 2006/568.
Registered Pension Schemes (Transfer of Sums and Assets) (Amendment) Regulations, SI 2015/633.
Modifications—Pensions Schemes (Application of UK Provisions to Relevant Non-UK Schemes) Regulations, SI 2006/207 reg 14 (modification of this paragraph in respect of relevant non-UK schemes).
Amendments—[1] Sub-para (1)(d) substituted, sub-paras (2A)–(2D) inserted, and sub-paras (3)–(6) repealed by FA 2005 ss 101, 104, Sch 10 paras 13, 64(1) and Sch 11 Pt 4 with effect from 6 April 2006.
[2] Sub-para (2)(aa) inserted by the Tax and Civil Partnerships Regulations, SI 2007/493 reg 2(1), (2) with effect from 22 February 2007.
[3] Sub-para (2CA) inserted by FA 2008 s 92, Sch 29 para 2 with effect from 21 July 2008.
[4] Sub-para (2CA) repealed by FA 2009 s 75(2)(d) with effect from 21 July 2009.
[5] Sub-para (1A) inserted by the Taxation of Pensions Act 2014 s 1, Sch 1 paras 36, 37 with effect from 17 December 2014.
[6] Sub-paras (1)(ba), (2C)(za), (2E) inserted, and in sub-para (2C)(b) words substituted for words "any other case", by the Taxation of Pensions Act 2014 s 1, Sch 1 paras 42–44 with effect from 17 December 2014.
[7] Words inserted in sub-para (2B)(a) by FA 2015 s 34, Sch 4 paras 1, 13(1), (2) with effect from 26 March 2015.

[Drawdown pension][1]

4 ["Drawdown pension"][1] means—

(a) a short-term annuity, or

(b) income withdrawal.

Amendments—[1] Heading substituted, and words substituted for words "Unsecured pension", by FA 2011 s 65, Sch 16 paras 2, 3 with effect for the tax year 2011–12 and subsequent tax years, subject to transitional provisions in FA 2011 Sch 16 Pt 3.

Short-term annuity

6—(1) [For the purposes of this Part, an][1] annuity payable to the member is a short-term annuity if—

(a) it is purchased by the application of sums or assets representing the whole or any part of the [member's drawdown pension fund][2] in respect of an arrangement,

(b) it is payable by an insurance company,

(c) the member had an opportunity to select the insurance company,

[(ca) the member becomes entitled to it before 6 April 2015,][4]

(d) it is payable for a term which does not exceed five years . . . [2] and

[(e) its amount either cannot decrease or falls to be determined in any manner prescribed by regulations made by the Board of Inland Revenue.][1]

[(1ZA) For the purposes of this Part, but subject to any provision made under sub-paragraph (1C)(za), an annuity payable to the member is also a short-term annuity if—

(a) it is purchased by the application of sums or assets representing the whole or any part of the member's drawdown pension fund, or of the member's flexi-access drawdown fund, in respect of an arrangement,

(b) it is payable by an insurance company,

(c) the member becomes entitled to it on or after 6 April 2015, and

(d) it is payable for a term which does not exceed five years.][3]

[(1A) An annuity does not fail to satisfy sub-paragraph (1)(e) by reason of the operation of a pension sharing order or provision.

(1B) The Board of Inland Revenue may by regulations make provision in relation to cases in which a short-term annuity payable by an insurance company ("the original short-term annuity") ceases to be payable and in consequence of that—

(*a*) sums or assets (or both) are transferred from the insurance company to another insurance company and are applied towards the provision of either another short-term annuity (a "new short-term annuity") or a scheme pension, lifetime annuity, dependants' scheme pension, dependants' annuity[, nominees' annuity][5] or dependants' short-term annuity by the other insurance company, or

(*b*) sums or assets are transferred to the relevant registered pension scheme.

(1C) The regulations may provide that—

[(*za*) in a case where—

(i) a new annuity becomes payable,

(ii) the member becomes entitled to it on or after 6 April 2015,

(iii) it would be a short-term annuity if any provision made under this paragraph were ignored,

(iv) the terms of the contract for it are such that there will or could be decreases in its amount other than allowed decreases (see sub-paragraph (1E)), and

(v) any other conditions prescribed by the regulations are met,

the new annuity is not a short-term annuity for the purposes of this Part,][4]

(*a*) in a case where a new short-term annuity becomes payable, the new short-term annuity is to be treated, to such extent as is prescribed by the regulations and for such of the purposes of this Part as are so prescribed, as if it were the original short-term annuity, and

(*b*) in [a case other than one where a new short-term annuity becomes payable][4], the relevant registered pension scheme is to be treated as making an unauthorised payment to the member of an amount equal to the aggregate of the amount of the sums, and the market value of the assets, transferred.

(1D) For the purposes of sub-paragraphs (1B) and (1C) a registered pension scheme is the relevant registered pension scheme if the original short-term annuity was acquired using sums or assets held for the purposes of the pension scheme.][1]

[(1E) In sub-paragraph (1C)(*za*)(iv) "allowed decreases" means decreases from time to time allowed by regulations under sub-paragraph (1)(*e*); and any such regulations are to be treated as having effect for this purpose.][4]

(2) . . .[1]

Commentary—*Simon's Taxes* **E7.224**.

Regulations—Registered Pension Schemes (Transfer of Sums and Assets) Regulations, SI 2006/499.

Registered Pension Schemes (Prescribed Manner of Determining Amount of Annuities) Regulations, SI 2006/568.

Registered Pension Schemes (Transfer of Sums and Assets) (Amendment) Regulations, SI 2015/633.

Modifications—Pensions Schemes (Application of UK Provisions to Relevant Non-UK Schemes) Regulations, SI 2006/207 reg 14 (modification of this paragraph in respect of relevant non-UK schemes).

F(No 2)A 2010 Sch 3 para 3 (sub-para (1) has effect in relation to an annuity that is purchased on or after 22 June 2010 and is payable to a person who reaches the age of 75 on or after 22 June 2010, as if the reference in sub-para (1)(*d*) to the age of 75 were a reference to the age of 77).

FA 2011 Sch 16 para 87 (application of this para on and after 6 April 2011 in relation to an annuity purchased before that date by the application of sums or assets representing the member's unsecured pension fund).

Amendments—[1]   Words in sub-paras (1) and (1)(*e*) substituted, and sub-paras (1A)–(1D) inserted, and sub-para (2) repealed by FA 2005 ss 101, 104, Sch 10 paras 14, 64(1), Sch 11 Pt 4 with effect from 6 April 2006.

[2]   In sub-para (1)(*a*) words substituted for words "member's unsecured pension fund", and in sub-para (1)(*d*), words "and ends before the member reaches the age of 75" repealed, by FA 2011 s 65, Sch 16 paras 2, 4 with effect for the tax year 2011–12 and subsequent tax years, subject to transitional provisions in FA 2011 Sch 16 Pt 3.

[3]   Sub-para (1ZA) inserted by the Taxation of Pensions Act 2014 s 1, Sch 1 paras 36, 38 with effect from 17 December 2014.

[4]   Sub-paras (1)(*ca*), (1C)(*za*), (1E) inserted, and in sub-para (1C)(*b*), words substituted for words "any other case", by the Taxation of Pensions Act 2014 s 1, Sch 1 paras 42, 45, 46 with effect from 17 December 2014.

[5]   Words inserted in sub-para (1B)(*a*) FA 2015 s 34, Sch 4 paras 1, 13(1), (3) with effect from 26 March 2015.

Income withdrawal

[7   "Income withdrawal" means an amount (other than an annuity) which the member is entitled to be paid from the member's drawdown pension fund in respect of an arrangement [or from the member's flexi-access drawdown fund in respect of an arrangement][2].][1]

Amendments—[1]   This para substituted by FA 2011 s 65, Sch 16 paras 2, 5 with effect for the tax year 2011–12 and subsequent tax years, subject to transitional provisions in FA 2011 Sch 16 Pt 3.

[2]   Words inserted by the Taxation of Pensions Act 2014 s 1, Sch 1 paras 5, 19 with effect from 17 December 2014.

[Member's drawdown pension fund][2]

8—(1) For the purposes of this Part the [member's drawdown pension fund][2] in respect of an arrangement consists of such of the sums or assets held for the purposes of the arrangement [as are member-designated funds.][1]

[(1A) For the purposes of this Part sums or assets held for the purposes of an arrangement are member-designated funds if[3] . . . —

(a) [they have, at any time before 6 April 2015, been designated]³ under the arrangement as available for the payment of [drawdown pension]²,

[(aa) they have, at any time on or after 6 April 2015, been designated under the arrangement as available for the payment of drawdown pension, and—

   (i) sums or assets held for the purposes of the arrangement have, at any time before 6 April 2015, been designated under the arrangement as so available, and

   (ii) section 165(3A) did not apply to the arrangement immediately before 6 April 2015,]³ or

(b) [they]³ arise, or (directly or indirectly) derive, from [member-designated funds under paragraph (a) or (aa) or from sums or assets]³ which so arise or derive,

and have not been applied towards the provision of a scheme pension.]¹

(2) . . . ²

(3) . . . ²

[(4) If any sums or assets representing the member's [drawdown pension fund]² in respect of an arrangement under the pension scheme would (apart from this sub-paragraph) come to be taken to represent another [drawdown pension fund]² of his under the pension scheme, or a dependant's [drawdown pension fund]² of his under the pension scheme, they are to be treated as not doing so.]¹

Modifications—Taxation of Pension Schemes (Transitional Provisions) Order, SI 2006/572 art 29 (modification of this paragraph in the case of an individual who meets certain conditions).

Amendments—¹ Words in sub-paras (1), (3) substituted and sub-paras (1A), (4) inserted by FA 2005 s 101, Sch 10 paras 18, 64(1) with effect from 6 April 2006.

² Words in sub-para (1) substituted for words "member's unsecured pension fund", words in sub-para (1A)(a) substituted for words "unsecured pension", words in sub-para (4) substituted for words "unsecured pension fund" (in each place), sub-paras (2), (3) repealed, and heading substituted for previous heading "Member's unsecured pension fund", by FA 2011 s 65, Sch 16 para 6 with effect for the tax year 2011–12 and subsequent tax years, subject to transitional provisions in FA 2011 Sch 16 Pt 3.

³ In sub-para (1A), in opening words word "they" repealed, in para (a) words substituted for words "have been designated at any time", para (aa) inserted, and in para (b) word inserted and words substituted for words "sums or assets which have been so designated or", by the Taxation of Pensions Act 2014 s 1, Sch 1 para 2 with effect from 17 December 2014.

[Member's flexi-access drawdown fund

8A—(1) For the purposes of this Part the member's flexi-access drawdown fund in respect of an arrangement consists of such of the sums or assets held for the purposes of the arrangement as are newly-designated funds.

(2) For the purposes of this Part sums or assets held for the purposes of an arrangement are newly-designated funds if—

(a) they—

   (i) have, at any time on or after 6 April 2015, been designated under the arrangement as available for the payment of drawdown pension, and

   (ii) are not member-designated funds, or

(b) they were member-designated funds immediately before 6 April 2015 and section 165(3A) applied to the arrangement at that time, or

(c) they have become newly-designated funds by the operation of paragraph 8B, 8C or 8D, or

(d) they arise, or (directly or indirectly) derive, from newly-designated funds under paragraph (a), (b) or (c) or from sums or assets which so arise or derive.

(3) Any sums or assets that become newly-designated funds under sub-paragraph (2)(b) cease to be member-designated funds as from the start of 6 April 2015.]¹

Amendments—¹ Para 8A inserted by the Taxation of Pensions Act 2014 s 1, Sch 1 para 3(1) with effect from 17 December 2014.

[Conversion of certain drawdown pension funds into flexi-access drawdown funds

8B—(1) Sub-paragraph (2) applies if—

(a) a member's drawdown pension fund in respect of an arrangement came into being before 6 April 2015,

(b) section 165(3A) did not apply to the arrangement immediately before 6 April 2015, and

(c) at a time on or after 6 April 2015, a payment—

   (i) of income withdrawal from the fund, or

   (ii) of a short-term annuity purchased using sums or assets out of the fund,

   is made that (apart from sub-paragraph (2)) would breach the cap.

(2) The sums and assets that make up the fund immediately before the payment is made become newly-designated funds immediately before the payment is made (so that the payment is made out of the member's flexi-access drawdown fund in respect of the arrangement and therefore is not part of the total capped by pension rule 5).

(3) For the purposes of sub-paragraph (1)(*c*), a payment of drawdown pension in respect of an arrangement is one that would breach the cap if, when its amount is added to the amounts of any drawdown pension in respect of the arrangement—

    (*a*) paid—

        (i) before it is made, but

        (ii) in the same drawdown pension year in respect of the arrangement, or

    (*b*) paid at the time it is made,

the total is greater than the cap set by pension rule 5 for that drawdown pension year.][1]

Amendments—[1]   Para 8B inserted by the Taxation of Pensions Act 2014 s 1, Sch 1 para 3(1) with effect from 17 December 2014.

[**8C**—(1) Sub-paragraph (2) applies if—

    (*a*) a member's drawdown pension fund in respect of an arrangement came into being before 6 April 2015,

    (*b*) section 165(3A) did not apply to the arrangement immediately before 6 April 2015, and

    (*c*) the member notifies the scheme administrator that the member wishes the fund to become the member's flexi-access drawdown fund in respect of the arrangement.

(2) At—

    (*a*) the time the scheme administrator accepts the notification, or

    (*b*) the start of 6 April 2015 if that is later,

the sums and assets that then make up that fund become newly-designated funds, if they have not previously done so by the operation of paragraph 8B.][1]

Amendments—[1]   Para 8C inserted by the Taxation of Pensions Act 2014 s 1, Sch 1 para 3(1) with effect from 17 December 2014.

[**8D**—(1) Sub-paragraphs (2) and (3) apply if—

    (*a*) there is a recognised transfer from one registered pension scheme ("the old scheme") to another registered pension scheme ("the new scheme") of member-designated funds held for the purposes of an arrangement under the old scheme, and

    (*b*) the sums or assets transferred are, under the arrangement under the new scheme for whose purposes they are first held after the transfer, designated as available for the payment of drawdown pension.

(2) If the member, when or before making the designation, notifies the scheme administrator of the new scheme that the member wishes the sums or assets to be newly-designated funds, the sums or assets become newly-designated funds and do so—

    (*a*) when the designation is made, or

    (*b*) if later, immediately after the transfer,

except that, if both the designation and transfer are made before 6 April 2015, the sums or assets become newly-designated funds at the start of 6 April 2015.

(3) If sub-paragraph (2) does not provide for the sums or assets to become newly-designated funds, the sums or assets become member-designated funds and do so—

    (*a*) when the designation is made, or

    (*b*) if later, immediately after the transfer.][1]

Amendments—[1]   Para 8D inserted by the Taxation of Pensions Act 2014 s 1, Sch 1 para 3(1). This amendment has effect in relation to: (a) cases where both the designation and transfer are made after the end of two months beginning with 17 December 2014 (ie after 16 February 2015); and (b) cases not within (a) where the transfer is made before 6 April 2015 and the designation is made on or after 6 April 2015, or the designation is made before 6 April 2015 and the transfer is made on or after 6 April 2015.

[Drawdown pension year and basis amount for drawdown pension year][1]

9—(1) ["Drawdown pension year"][1] means—

    (*a*) the period of 12 months beginning with the day on which the member first becomes entitled to [drawdown pension][1] in respect of the arrangement, and

    (*b*) each succeeding period of 12 months.

[This is subject to paragraph 10B.][1]

[(2) The drawdown pension year in which the member dies is the last drawdown pension year and ends immediately before the member's death.][1]

Amendments—[1]   In sub-para (1) words substituted for words ""Unsecured pension year"" and words inserted, in sub-para (1)(*a*) words substituted for words "unsecured pension", sub-para (2) substituted, and heading substitued, by FA 2011 s 65, Sch 16 para 7 with effect for the tax year 2011–12 and subsequent tax years, subject to transitional provisions in FA 2011 Sch 16 Pt 3.

10—[(A1) This paragraph applies in relation to drawdown pension years beginning on or before the member's 75th birthday.

(1) Subject as follows, the period of three drawdown pension years beginning with the first drawdown pension year, and each succeeding period of three drawdown pension years, is a "reference period".

(1ZA) But the reference period in which the member reaches the age of 75 ends with the drawdown pension year in which the member reaches that age.][3]

[(1A) Sub-paragraph (1B) applies if, at any time during a reference period ("the current reference period"), the member notifies the scheme administrator that the member wishes a new reference period to begin on the next day that is an anniversary of the reference date in relation to the current reference period.][2]

[(1B) The scheme administrator may determine—

    (a) that the current reference period is to end immediately before that day (so that sub-paragraph (1) no longer applies), and

    (b) that (subject to [sub-paragraph (1ZA) and][3] any further operation of this sub-paragraph) the period of [three drawdown pension years][3] beginning with that day, and each succeeding period of [three drawdown pension years][3], is to be a reference period.][2]

[(1C) The first day of each reference period is, in relation to that period, "the reference date".][2]

(2) For the first [drawdown pension year][3] falling within a reference period, the basis amount is the annual amount of the relevant annuity which could have been purchased by the application of the sums and assets representing the [member's drawdown pension fund][3] on the nominated date (but subject to sub-paragraph (5)).

(3) "The nominated date"—

    (a) in relation to the first reference period, is the reference date, and

    (b) in relation to any subsequent reference period, is such day, within the period of 60 days ending with the reference date, as is nominated by the scheme administrator (or, if no day is nominated by the scheme administrator, is the reference date).

(4) For each other [drawdown pension year][3] falling within a reference period, the basis amount is the annual amount of the relevant annuity which could have been purchased by the application of the sums and assets representing the [member's drawdown pension fund][3]

    (a) if there has been no recent annuity[, recent additional fund designation or recent pension sharing event][1], on the nominated date, and

    (b) otherwise, immediately after the last annuity purchase or[, additional fund designation or pension sharing event][1],

(but subject to sub-paragraph (5)).

(5) On the occasion of each additional fund designation during [a drawdown pension year][3], the basis amount for [that drawdown pension year][3] is to be recalculated in accordance with sub-paragraph (6).

(6) The basis amount for the [drawdown pension year][3] is the annual amount of the relevant annuity which could have been purchased by the application of the sums and assets representing the [member's drawdown pension fund][3] immediately after the additional fund designation.

[(6A) But sub-paragraph (5) does not apply where the operation of that sub-paragraph in relation to an additional fund designation during a drawdown pension year would reduce the basis amount for that drawdown pension year.][3]

(7) "Annuity purchase" means the purchase of a scheme pension or a lifetime annuity by the application of sums or assets representing the whole or part of the [member's drawdown pension fund][3].

(8) "Additional fund designation" means the designation under the arrangement of further sums or assets held for the purposes of the arrangement as available for the payment of [drawdown pension][3].

[(8A) "Pension sharing event" means the coming into operation of a pension sharing order or provision relating to the sums and assets representing the [member's drawdown pension fund][3].][1]

(9) An annuity purchase[, additional fund designation or pension sharing event][1] is "recent" if it took place during the period—

    (a) beginning with the reference date, and

    (b) ending with the last day of the immediately preceding [drawdown pension year][3].

(10) Paragraph 14 defines "relevant annuity".

[(11) *Nothing in this paragraph applies in respect of an arrangement to which section 165(3A) applies.]*[3, 4]

Commentary—*Simon's Taxes* E7.224.

Amendments—[1] Words in sub-paras (4)(a), (b), (9) substituted and sub-para (8A) inserted by FA 2005 s 101, Sch 10 paras 19, 64(1) with effect from 6 April 2006.

[2] Sub-paras (1)–(1C) substituted for sub-para (1) by FA 2007 s 70, Sch 20 paras 1, 8(1), (2), 24(5) with effect in relation to notifications given on or after 6 December 2006.

[3] Sub-paras (A1)–(1ZA) substituted for previous sub-para (1), in sub-para (1B)(b) words inserted and words substituted for words "five unsecured pension years" in both places, in sub-paras (2), (4) words substituted for words "unsecured pension year" and "member's unsecured pension fund", in sub-para (5) words substituted for words "an unsecured pension year" and "that unsecured pension year", in sub-para (6) words substituted for words "unsecured pension year" and "mem-

ber's unsecured pension fund", para (6A) inserted, in sub-para (7) words substituted for words "member's unsecured pension fund", in sub-para (8) words substituted for words "unsecured pension", in sub-para (8A) words substituted for words "member's unsecured pension fund", in sub-para (9)(*b*) words substituted for words "unsecured pension year", and sub-para (11) inserted, by FA 2011 s 65, Sch 16 para 8 with effect for the tax year 2011–12 and subsequent tax years, subject to transitional provisions in FA 2011 Sch 16 Pt 3.

4   Sub-para (11) repealed by the Taxation of Pensions Act 2014 s 1, Sch 1 para 32(1)(*e*)(i) with effect from 6 April 2015.

[10A—(1) This paragraph applies in relation to drawdown pension years beginning after the member's 75th birthday.

(2) For the first drawdown pension year beginning after the member reached the age of 75, and each succeeding drawdown pension year, the basis amount is the annual amount of the relevant annuity which could have been purchased by the application of the sums and assets representing the member's drawdown pension fund on the nominated date.

But this is subject to sub-paragraph (6).

(3) In a case where the member first becomes entitled to drawdown pension in respect of the arrangement after reaching the age of 75, "the nominated date", in relation to the first drawdown pension year in respect of the arrangement, is the first day of that year.

(4) In any other case, "the nominated date", in relation to the first drawdown pension year beginning after the member reached the age of 75, is—

    (*a*) if the member and the scheme administrator so agree, the day immediately before the member's 75th birthday, or

    (*b*) if they do not so agree, such day within the period of 60 days ending with the first day of the drawdown pension year as is nominated by the scheme administrator (or, if no day is nominated by the scheme administrator, the first day of that year).

(5) "The nominated date", in relation to each other drawdown pension year, is such day within the period of 60 days ending with the first day of the drawdown pension year as is nominated by the scheme administrator (or, if no day is nominated by the scheme administrator, is the first day of that year).

(6) On the occasion of each additional fund designation during a drawdown pension year, the basis amount of that drawdown pension year is to be recalculated in accordance with sub-paragraph (7).

(7) The basis amount for the drawdown pension year is the annual amount of the relevant annuity which could have been purchased by the application of the sums and assets representing the member's drawdown pension fund immediately after the additional fund designation.

(8) But sub-paragraph (6) does not apply where the operation of that sub-paragraph in relation to an additional fund designation during a drawdown pension year would reduce the basis amount for that drawdown pension year.

(9) "Additional fund designation" has the meaning given by paragraph 10(8).

(10) Paragraph 14 defines "relevant annuity".

(11) Nothing in this paragraph applies in respect of an arrangement to which section 165(3A) applies.²]¹

Amendments—¹   Paras 10A, 10B inserted by FA 2011 s 65, Sch 16 para 9 with effect for the tax year 2011–12 and subsequent tax years, subject to transitional provisions in FA 2011 Sch 16 Pt 3. The amendments made by FA 2011 Sch 16 para 9 have effect in relation to drawdown pension years beginning on or after 6 April 2011 (FA 2011 Sch 16 para 91(3)).

2   Sub-para (11) repealed by the Taxation of Pensions Act 2014 s 1, Sch 1 para 32(1)(*e*)(ii) with effect from 6 April 2015.

[10B—(1) This paragraph applies if the member has reached the age of 75.

(2) Sub-paragraph (3) applies if, at any time during a drawdown pension year in respect of an arrangement ("the current drawdown pension year"), the member notifies the scheme administrator that the member wishes the drawdown pension year following the current drawdown pension year to begin on the day on which the next drawdown pension year in respect of another arrangement relating to the member under the pension scheme (including any arrangement relating to that person as a dependant) will begin.

(3) The scheme administrator may determine—

    (*a*) that the current drawdown pension year is to end immediately before that day, and

    (*b*) that the period of 12 months beginning with that day, and each succeeding period of 12 months, is a drawdown pension year in respect of the arrangement.

(4) The scheme administrator may not make a determination under this paragraph more than once in relation to the same arrangement.]¹

Amendments—¹   Paras 10A, 10B inserted by FA 2011 s 65, Sch 16 para 9 with effect for the tax year 2011–12 and subsequent tax years, subject to transitional provisions in FA 2011 Sch 16 Pt 3.

Relevant annuity

14—(1) A "relevant annuity" is an annuity of a description prescribed by regulations made by the Board of Inland Revenue.

(2) The annual amount of a relevant annuity is to be ascertained in accordance with regulations made by the Board of Inland Revenue.

(3) The regulations may in particular provide for the annual amount to be ascertained by reference to—

    (*a*) comparative annuity tables published by the [Financial Conduct Authority or the Prudential Regulation Authority][1], or

    (*b*) material published by any other person.

Regulations—Registered Pension Schemes (Relevant Annuities) Regulations, SI 2006/129.

Registered Pension Schemes (Relevant Annuities) (Amendment) Regulations, SI 2012/2940.

Amendments—[1] In sub-para (3)(*a*), words substituted by FSA 2012 s 114(1), Sch 18 para 100 with effect from 1 April 2013 by virtue of SI 2013/423 art 3, Schedule.

PART 2
PENSION DEATH BENEFIT RULES

DEFINED BENEFITS AND MONEY PURCHASE ARRANGEMENTS

Meaning of "dependant"

15—(1) A person who was married to[, or a civil partner of,][2] the member at the date of the member's death is a dependant of the member.

[(1A) If the rules of the pension scheme so provide, a person who was married to[, or a civil partner of,][2] the member when the member first became entitled to a pension under the pension scheme is a dependant of the member.][1]

(2) A child of the member is a dependant of the member if the child—

    (*a*) has not reached the age of 23, or

    (*b*) has reached that age and, in the opinion of the scheme administrator, was at the date of the member's death dependent on the member because of physical or mental impairment.

[(2A) A child of the member is a dependant of the member if the child—

    (*a*) has reached the age of 23, and

    (*b*) is not within sub-paragraph (2)(*b*).

(2B) But this paragraph, so far as it has effect for the purpose of determining the meaning of "dependant"—

    (*a*) in paragraphs 16 to 17 and 27A, and

    (*b*) in paragraph 18 of Schedule 29,

has effect with the omission of sub-paragraph (2A).][3]

(3) A person who was not married to[, or a civil partner of,][2] the member at the date of the member's death and is not a child of the member is a dependant of the member if, in the opinion of the scheme administrator, at the date of the member's death—

    (*a*) the person was financially dependent on the member,

    (*b*) the person's financial relationship with the member was one of mutual dependence, or

    (*c*) the person was dependent on the member because of physical or mental impairment.

Commentary—*Simon's Taxes* **E7.224**.

HMRC Manuals—Registered Pension Schemes Manual RPSM10104040 (a person who had been legally adopted by the member at the date of the member's death is a child of the member, as parental responsibility for the child has been granted to the member).

Modifications—Pensions Schemes (Application of UK Provisions to Relevant Non-UK Schemes) Regulations, SI 2006/207 reg 14 (modification of this paragraph in respect of relevant non-UK schemes).

Registered Pension Schemes (Splitting of Schemes) Regulations, SI 2006/569 reg 3 (modification of this provision in relation to sub-scheme administrators).

Amendments—[1] Sub-para (1A) inserted by FA 2005 s 101, Sch 10 paras 26, 64(1) with effect from 6 April 2006.

[2] Words in sub-paras (1), (1A), (3) inserted by Tax and Civil Partnership Regulations, SI 2005/3229, regs 175, 180, with effect from 6 April 2006 (reg 1(7)).

[3] Sub-paras (2A), (2B) inserted by FA 2016 s 22, Sch 5 para 6(1), (2) with effect from 16 September 2016. Those sub-paras apply as follows—

    (a)   for the purpose of determining whether a payment of an annuity is a payment of a dependants' short-term annuity only if the annuity is purchased after 15 September 2016;

    (b)   for the purpose of determining whether a payment to a person is a payment of dependants' income withdrawal if, but only if, the person reaches the age of 23 after 15 September 2016.

Dependants' scheme pension

16—(1) . . . [1]

(2) [A][1] pension payable to a dependant is a dependants' scheme pension [for the purposes of this Part][2] if—

    (*a*) it is payable by the scheme administrator or by an insurance company selected by the scheme administrator, . . . [1]

    (*b*) . . . [1]

[(2A) The Board of Inland Revenue may by regulations make provision in relation to cases in which a dependants' scheme pension payable to a dependant of a member of a registered pension scheme by an insurance company ("the original dependants' scheme pension") ceases to be payable and in consequence of that—

    (a) sums or assets (or both) are transferred from the insurance company to another insurance company and are applied towards the provision of either another dependants' scheme pension (a "new dependants' scheme pension") or a scheme pension, lifetime annuity, short-term annuity, dependants' annuity or dependants' short-term annuity by the other insurance company, or

    (b) sums or assets are transferred to the relevant registered pension scheme.

(2B) The regulations may provide that—

    (a) in a case where a new dependants' scheme pension becomes payable, the new dependants' scheme pension is to be treated, to such extent as is prescribed by the regulations and for such of the purposes of this Part as are so prescribed, as if it were the original dependants' scheme pension, and

    (b) in any other case, the relevant registered pension scheme is to be treated as making an unauthorised payment in respect of the member of an amount equal to the aggregate of the amount of the sums, and the market value of the assets, transferred.

(2C) For the purposes of sub-paragraphs (2A) and (2B) a registered pension scheme is the relevant registered pension scheme if the original dependants' scheme pension was acquired using sums or assets held for the purposes of the pension scheme.]¹

(3)–(6) . . . ¹

Commentary—*Simon's Taxes* E7.224.
Regulations—Registered Pension Schemes (Transfer of Sums and Assets) Regulations, SI 2006/499.
Modifications—Pensions Schemes (Application of UK Provisions to Relevant Non-UK Schemes) Regulations, SI 2006/207 reg 14 (modification of this paragraph in respect of relevant non-UK schemes).
Amendments—¹   Sub-paras (1), (2)(b) (and preceding word "and"), (3)–(6) repealed, words in sub-para (2) substituted, sub-para (2A)–(2C) inserted by FA 2005 ss 101, 104, Sch 10 paras 27, 64(1), Sch 11 Pt 4 with effect from 6 April 2006.
²   Words in sub-s (2) inserted by FA 2008 s 91, Sch 28 paras 1, 5 with effect from 21 July 2008.

[**16A**—(1) Paragraphs 16B and 16C apply where—

    (a) the member dies after 5th April 2006,

    (b) he has reached the age of 75 before his death, and

    (c) at the time of his death he is actually or prospectively entitled to one or more scheme pensions under the pension scheme.

[(1A) Sub-paragraph (1) is subject to paragraphs 16AA and 16AB.]²

(2) References in this paragraph and paragraph 16B to a scheme pension include a pension payable before 6th April 2006 which would be a scheme pension if payable after that date.]¹

Commentary—*Simon's Taxes* E7.224.
Modifications—Taxation of Pension Schemes (Transitional Provisions) Order, SI 2006/572 art 24 (modification of this paragraph where the member in respect of whom the dependant's scheme pension is payable was actually entitled to one or more relevant existing pensions on 5 April 2006).
Amendments—¹   Paragraph inserted by FA 2005 s 101, Sch 10 paras 28, 64(1) with effect from 6 April 2006.
²   Sub-para (1A) inserted by FA 2016 s 21(1), (2). This amendment is treated as having come into force on 6 April 2016. So far as it relates to FA 2004 Sch 28 para 16B, this amendment has effect where the last day of "the post-death year" (see para 16B(1)) is 6 April 2016 or any later day. So far as it relates to FA 2004 Sch 28 para 16C, this amendment has effect where the last day of "the 12 months in question" (see para 16C(1)), is 6 April 2016 or any later day.

[**16AA**   Paragraphs 16B and 16C do not apply if—

    (a) each benefit crystallisation event that has occurred in relation to the member by reference to arrangements relating to the member under the scheme is benefit crystallisation event 5B (having unused funds under a money purchase arrangement at age 75), or

    (b) paragraph 12 of Schedule 36 (enhanced protection by reference to pre-6 April 2006 rights) applies in the case of the member immediately before the member's death.]¹

Amendments—¹   Paras 16AA–16AE inserted by FA 2016 s 21(1), (3). This amendment is treated as having come into force on 6 April 2016. So far as it relates to FA 2004 Sch 28 para 16B, this amendment has effect where the last day of "the post-death year" (see para 16B(1)) is 6 April 2016 or any later day. So far as it relates to FA 2004 Sch 28 para 16C, this amendment has effect where the last day of "the 12 months in question" (see para 16C(1)), is 6 April 2016 or any later day.

[**16AB**   (1) Paragraph 16B does not apply if, at all times in the post-death year (as defined in that paragraph), the payable annual rate is less than the limit.

(2) Paragraph 16C does not apply in relation to a period of 12 months within paragraph (a) or (b) of paragraph 16C(1) if, at all times in that period of 12 months, the payable annual rate is less than the limit.

(3) "The payable annual rate", at any time, is arrived at as follows—

(*a*) identify each dependants' scheme pension payable in respect of the member under the scheme to which a dependant of the member is actually entitled at that time, and

(*b*) identify the annual rate at which each pension identified at paragraph (*a*) is payable at that time, and

(*c*) if only one pension is identified at paragraph (*a*), the payable annual rate is the annual rate identified at paragraph (*b*), and

(*d*) if two or more pensions are identified at paragraph (*a*), the payable annual rate is the total of the annual rates identified at paragraph (*b*).

(4) "The limit", at any time, is—

(*a*) the general limit at that time (see paragraph 16AC), or,

(*b*) if higher, the personal limit at that time (see paragraph 16AD).]¹

Amendments—¹ Paras 16AA–16AE inserted by FA 2016 s 21(1), (3). This amendment is treated as having come into force on 6 April 2016. So far as it relates to FA 2004 Sch 28 para 16B, this amendment has effect where the last day of "the post-death year" (see para 16B(1)) is 6 April 2016 or any later day. So far as it relates to FA 2004 Sch 28 para 16C, this amendment has effect where the last day of "the 12 months in question" (see para 16C(1)), is 6 April 2016 or any later day.

[16AC (1) This paragraph applies for the purposes of paragraph 16AB(4).

(2) "The general limit" at a time in the tax year 2016-17 is £25,000.

(3) "The general limit" at a time in a later tax year ("year T")—

(*a*) is given by—

$$G + (G \times U\%)$$

where G is the general limit at times in the tax year ("year P") that precedes year T, or

(*b*) if the amount given by paragraph (*a*) is not a multiple of £100, is that amount rounded up to the nearest amount that is such a multiple.

(4) See paragraph 16AE for the meaning of U%.]¹

Amendments—¹ Paras 16AA–16AE inserted by FA 2016 s 21(1), (3). This amendment is treated as having come into force on 6 April 2016. So far as it relates to FA 2004 Sch 28 para 16B, this amendment has effect where the last day of "the post-death year" (see para 16B(1)) is 6 April 2016 or any later day. So far as it relates to FA 2004 Sch 28 para 16C, this amendment has effect where the last day of "the 12 months in question" (see para 16C(1)), is 6 April 2016 or any later day.

[16AD (1) This paragraph applies for the purposes of paragraph 16AB(4).

(2) "The personal limit" at a time in the tax year in which the member dies is arrived at as follows—

(*a*) identify each scheme pension under the scheme to which the member is actually or prospectively entitled immediately before the member's death, and

(*b*) as regards each pension identified at paragraph (*a*)—

(i) if it is one to which the member is actually entitled immediately before the member's death, identify the annual rate at which it is payable immediately before the member's death, or

(ii) if it is one to which the member is prospectively entitled immediately before the member's death, identify the annual rate at which it would have been payable immediately before the member's death had the member been actually entitled to it immediately before the member's death, and

(*c*) if only one pension is identified at paragraph (*a*), the personal limit is the annual rate identified at paragraph (*b*), and

(*d*) if two or more pensions are identified at paragraph (*a*), the personal limit is the total of the annual rates identified at paragraph (*b*).

(3) "The personal limit" at a time in a tax year ("year S") later than the tax year in which the member dies—

(*a*) is given by—

$$L + (L \times U\%)$$

where L is the personal limit at times in the tax year ("year P") that precedes year S, or

(*b*) if the amount given by paragraph (*a*) is not a multiple of £100, is that amount rounded up to the nearest amount that is such a multiple.

(4) See paragraph 16AE for the meaning of U%.

(5) If the scheme is a public service pension scheme, ignore any abatement when identifying at sub-paragraph (2)(*b*) the annual rate of any scheme pension under the scheme.]¹

Amendments—¹ Paras 16AA–16AE inserted by FA 2016 s 21(1), (3). This amendment is treated as having come into force on 6 April 2016. So far as it relates to FA 2004 Sch 28 para 16B, this amendment has effect where the last day of "the post-death year" (see para 16B(1)) is 6 April 2016 or any later day. So far as it relates to FA 2004 Sch 28 para 16C, this amendment has effect where the last day of "the 12 months in question" (see para 16C(1)), is 6 April 2016 or any later day.

[16AE (1) In paragraphs 16AC(3) and 16AD(3), U% means the highest of—

(a) 5%,

(b) CPI% (see sub-paragraph (2)), and

(c) RPI% (see sub-paragraph (3)).

(2) If the consumer prices index for September in year P is higher than the consumer prices index for September in the tax year preceding year P, CPI% is the percentage increase in the index (but is otherwise 0%).

(3) If the retail prices index for September in year P is higher than the retail prices index for September in the tax year preceding year P, RPI% is the percentage increase in the index (but is otherwise 0%).

(4) In this paragraph "year P" has the same meaning as in paragraph 16AC or (as the case may be) paragraph 16AD.][1]

Amendments—[1]   Paras 16AA–16AE inserted by FA 2016 s 21(1), (3). This amendment is treated as having come into force on 6 April 2016. So far as it relates to FA 2004 Sch 28 para 16B, this amendment has effect where the last day of "the post-death year" (see para 16B(1)) is 6 April 2016 or any later day. So far as it relates to FA 2004 Sch 28 para 16C, this amendment has effect where the last day of "the 12 months in question" (see para 16C(1)), is 6 April 2016 or any later day.

[16B—(1) Where a pension is payable under the pension scheme to a dependant of the member in the period of 12 months beginning with the date of the member's death ("the post-death year"), so much of the pension as exceeds the initial member pension limit is not a dependants' scheme pension.

(2) But if—

(a) more than one pension is so payable to one of the dependants of the member in the post-death year, or

(b) pensions are so payable to more than one dependant of the member in the post-death year, (or both), so much of any of the pensions as exceeds the appropriate portion of the initial member pension limit is not a dependants' scheme pension.

(3) The "initial member pension limit" is (subject to sub-paragraph (4)) the sum of—

(a) the aggregate of the amounts of the scheme pensions to which the member is actually entitled under the pension scheme immediately before his death payable to the member in the period of 12 months ending with the date of his death ("the pre-death year"),

(b) the aggregate of the amounts of the scheme pensions to which the member is prospectively entitled under the pension scheme at that time which would have been so payable if he had been actually entitled to the pensions throughout the pre-death year, and

(c) 5% of the aggregate of the [uprated amounts (see sub-paragraph (6))][2] of the lump sums on which there is no liability to income tax to which the member has become entitled in connection with scheme pensions under the pension scheme before his death.

(4) But if the member became (actually) entitled to a scheme pension under the pension scheme during the pre-death year, sub-paragraph (3)(a) has effect as if the amount of that scheme pension which was payable to the member under the pension scheme in the pre-death year were the amount which would have been payable to him in the period of 12 months beginning with the date on which he became entitled to it had he not died.

(5) The "appropriate portion" of the initial member pension limit, in relation to any pension payable under the pension scheme to a dependant of the member in the post-death year, is—

$$\frac{P}{AP}$$

where—

P is the amount of that pension payable in the post-death year, and

AP is the aggregate of the amounts of each of the pensions payable under the pension scheme to dependants of the member in the post-death year.][1]

[(6) The "uprated amount" of a lump sum is the amount of the lump sum increased by the higher of C% and R%, where–

(a) if the consumer prices index for the month in which the member dies is higher than it was for the month in which the member became entitled to the lump sum, C% is the percentage increase in the index (but is otherwise 0%), and

(b) if the retail prices index for the month in which the member dies is higher than it was for the month in which the member became entitled to the lump sum, R% is the percentage increase in the index (but is otherwise 0%).][2]

Commentary—*Simon's Taxes* E7.224.

HMRC Manuals—Registered Pension Schemes Manual RPSM10104160 (an outline of why prospective entitlements are included in the initial member limit).

Amendments—[1]   Paragraph inserted by FA 2005 s 101, Sch 10 paras 28, 64(1) with effect from 6 April 2006.

[2]   In sub-para (3)(c) words substituted for word "amount", and sub-s (6) inserted, by FA 2016 s 21(1), (4). These amendments are treated as having come into force on 6 April 2016. So far as they relate to FA 2004 Sch 28 para 16B, these amendments

have effect where the last day of "the post-death year" (see para 16B(1)) is 6 April 2016 or any later day. So far as they relate to FA 2004 Sch 28 para 16C, these amendments have effect where the last day of "the 12 months in question" (see para 16C(1)), is 6 April 2016 or any later day.

[16C—(1) Where a pension is payable under the pension scheme to a dependant of the member, otherwise than in excepted circumstances, in—

(*a*) the period of 12 months beginning with the end of the post-death year, or

(*b*) any succeeding period of 12 months,

("the 12 months in question"), so much of the pension as exceeds the current member pension limit is not a dependants' scheme pension.

(2) But if—

(*a*) more than one pension is so payable to one of the dependants in the 12 months in question, or

(*b*) pensions are so payable to more than one dependant of the member in the 12 months in question,

(or both), so much of any of the pensions as exceeds the appropriate portion of the current member pension limit is not a dependants' scheme pension.

(3) "Excepted circumstances" means—

(*a*) that at the beginning of the . . . ² 12 months in question there are at least 50 pensioner members of the pension scheme, and

(*b*) that the condition in [sub-paragraph]² (4) is met.

[(4) The condition is that if the annual rate of a pension payable under the pension scheme to a dependant of the member is increased at any time in the period of 12 months in question—

(*a*) the dependant is at that time one of a group of at least 20 pensioner members of the pension scheme, and

(*b*) all the pensions being paid under the pension scheme to pensioner members of that group are at that time increased at the same rate.]²

(6) The "current member pension limit", in relation to the 12 [months]² in question, is the initial member pension limit increased by [the permitted margin.]²

(7) The "permitted margin" is the amount by which the initial member pension limit would be greater if it had been increased by whichever of calculation A and calculation B gives the greater amount.

(8) Calculation A involves increasing the initial member pension limit by the relevant annual percentage rate for the whole of the period—

(*a*) beginning with the first month beginning after the [member's death]² ("the opening month"), and

(*b*) ending with the first month [ending after the start]² of the 12 months in question ("the closing month").

(9) The relevant annual percentage rate is—

(*a*) if the relevant valuation factor in relation to the pension scheme is a number greater than 20, the annual rate agreed by the Inland Revenue and the scheme administrator, and

(*b*) otherwise, 5% per annum.

(10) Calculation B involves increasing the initial member pension limit by the relevant indexation percentage.

(11) If the retail prices index for the closing month is higher than it was for the [month in which the member died]², the relevant indexation percentage is the percentage increase in the retail prices index.

(12) If it is not, the relevant indexation percentage is 0%.

(13), (14) . . . ²

(15) The "appropriate portion" of the current member pension limit, in relation to any pension payable under the pension scheme to a dependant of the member in the 12 months in question, is—

$$\frac{P}{AP}$$

where—

P is the amount of that pension payable in the 12 months in question, and

AP is the aggregate of the amounts of each of the pensions payable under the pension scheme to one or more dependants of the member in the 12 months in question.]¹

Commentary—*Simon's Taxes* E7.224.

Amendments—¹ Paragraph inserted by FA 2005 s 101, Sch 10 paras 28, 64(1) with effect from 6 April 2006.

² Words in sub-para (3)(*a*) repealed, words in sub-paras (3)(*b*), (6), (8)(*a*), (11) substituted, words in sub-para (8)(*b*) inserted, sub-para (4) substituted for previous sub-paras (4), (5), and sub-paras (13), (14) repealed, by FA 2016 s 2ɪ(1), (5). These amendments are treated as having come into force on 6 April 2016. So far as they relate to FA 2004 Sch 28 para 16B, these

amendments have effect where the last day of "the post-death year" (see para 16B(1)) is 6 April 2016 or any later day. So far as they relate to FA 2004 Sch 28 para 16C, these amendments have effect where the last day of "the 12 months in question" (see para 16C(1)), is 6 April 2016 or any later day.

MONEY PURCHASE ARRANGEMENTS

Dependants' annuity

17—(1) [For the purposes of this Part, an][1] annuity payable to a dependant is a dependants' annuity if—

[(*za*) either—

  (i) it is purchased together with a lifetime annuity payable to the member and the member becomes entitled to that lifetime annuity before 6 April 2015, or

  (ii) it is purchased after the member's death and the dependant becomes entitled to it before 6 April 2015,][7]

(*a*) it is payable by an insurance company,

(*b*) the member or dependant had an opportunity to select the insurance company,

[(*c*) its amount either cannot decrease or falls to be determined in any manner prescribed by regulations made by the Board of Inland Revenue,][1]

(*d*) where the dependant is not the member's child, it is payable until the dependant's death or until the earlier of the dependant's marrying[, entering into a civil partnership][3] or dying, and

(*e*) where the dependant is the member's child, it is payable until the earlier of the dependant's ceasing to be a dependant or dying, or until the earliest of the dependant's marrying[, entering into a civil partnership][3], ceasing to be a dependant or dying.

[(1ZA) For the purposes of this Part, but subject to any provision made under sub-paragraph (4)(za), an annuity payable to a dependant is also a dependants' annuity if—

(*a*) either—

  (i) it is purchased together with a lifetime annuity payable to the member and the member becomes entitled to that lifetime annuity on or after 6 April 2015, or

  (ii) it is purchased after the member's death and the dependant becomes entitled to it on or after 6 April 2015,

(*b*) it is payable by an insurance company,

(*c*) where the dependant is not the member's child, it is payable until the dependant's death or until the earliest of the dependant's marrying, entering into a civil partnership or dying, and

(*d*) where the dependant is the member's child, it is payable until the earlier of the dependant's ceasing to be a dependant or dying, or until the earliest of the dependant's marrying, entering into a civil partnership, ceasing to be a dependant or dying.][6]

[(1A) For the purposes of [sub-paragraphs (1)(*za*) and (1ZA)(*a*)][7] a dependants' annuity is purchased together with a lifetime annuity if the dependant's annuity is related to the lifetime annuity.][2]

[(2) An annuity does not fail to satisfy sub-paragraph (1)(*c*) by reason of the operation of a pension sharing order or provision.

(3) The Board of Inland Revenue may by regulations make provision in relation to cases in which a dependants' annuity payable to a person ("the original dependants' annuity") ceases to be payable and in consequence of that—

(*a*) sums or assets (or both) are transferred from the insurance company to another insurance company and are applied towards the provision of either another dependants' annuity (a "new dependants' annuity") or a scheme pension, lifetime annuity, short-term annuity, dependants' scheme pension or dependants' short-term annuity by the other insurance company, or

(*b*) sums or assets are transferred to the relevant registered pension scheme.

(4) The regulations may provide that—

[(*za*) in a case where—

  (i) a new annuity becomes payable,

  (ii) the dependant becomes entitled to it on or after 6 April 2015,

  (iii) it would be a dependants' annuity if any provision made under this paragraph were ignored,

  (iv) the terms of the contract for it are such that there will or could be decreases in its amount other than allowed decreases (see sub-paragraph (6)), and

  (v) any other conditions prescribed by the regulations are met,

the new annuity is not a dependants' annuity for the purposes of this Part,][7]

(*a*) in a case where a new dependants' annuity becomes payable, the new dependants' annuity is to be treated, to such extent as is prescribed by the regulations and for such of the purposes of this Part as are so prescribed, as if it were the original dependants' annuity, and (*b*) in [a case other than one where a new dependants' annuity becomes payable][7], the relevant registered pension scheme is to be treated as making an unauthorised payment in respect of the member of an amount equal to the aggregate of the amount of the sums, and the market value of the assets, transferred.

[(4A) . . .][4], [5]

(5) For the purposes of sub-paragraphs (3) and (4) a registered pension scheme is the relevant registered pension scheme if the original dependants' annuity was acquired using sums or assets held for the purposes of the pension scheme.][1]

[(6) In sub-paragraph (4)(*za*)(iv) "allowed decreases" means decreases from time to time allowed by regulations under sub-paragraph (1)(*c*); and any such regulations are to be treated as having effect for this purpose.][7]

Regulations—Registered Pension Schemes (Prescribed Manner of Determining Amount of Annuities) Regulations, SI 2006/568. Registered Pension Schemes (Transfer of Sums and Assets) (Amendment) Regulations, SI 2015/633.

Modifications—Pensions Schemes (Application of UK Provisions to Relevant Non-UK Schemes) Regulations, SI 2006/207 reg 14 (modification of this paragraph in respect of relevant non-UK schemes).

Amendments—[1]   Words in sub-para (1), sub-paras (1)(*c*), (2)–(5) substituted by FA 2005 s 101, Sch 10 paras 15, 64(1) with effect from 6 April 2006.

[2]   Sub-para (1A) inserted by FA 2005 s 101, Sch 10 paras 29, 64(1) with effect from 6 April 2006.

[3]   Words in sub-paras (1)(*d*), (*e*) inserted by the Tax and Civil Partnerships Regulations, SI 2007/493 reg 2(1), (3) with effect from 22 February 2007.

[4]   Sub-para (4A) inserted by FA 2008 s 92, Sch 29 para 2 with effect from 21 July 2008.

[5]   Sub-para (4A) repealed by FA 2009 s 75(2)(*d*) with effect from 21 July 2009.

[6]   Sub-para (1ZA) inserted by the Taxation of Pensions Act 2014 s 1, Sch 1 paras 36, 39 with effect from 17 December 2014.

[7]   Sub-para (1)(*za*) substituted, in sub-para (1A) words substituted, in sub-para (4) para (*za*) inserted and in para (*b*) words substituted, and sub-para (6) inserted, by the Taxation of Pensions Act 2014 s 1, Sch 1 paras 42, 47–49 with effect from 17 December 2014.

[Dependants' drawdown pension][1]

18   ["Dependants' drawdown pension"][1] means—

    (*a*) a dependants' short-term annuity, or

    (*b*) dependants' income withdrawal.

Sch 16 para ... Heading substituted, and words substituted for words '"Dependants' unsecured pension"' by FA 2011 s 65, Sch 16 Pt 3.   ... tax year 2011–12 and subsequent tax years, subject to transitional provisions in FA 2011

Dependants' short-term annuity

20—(1) [For the purposes of this Part, an][1] annuity payable to a dependant is a dependants' short-term annuity if—

    (*a*) it is purchased by the application of sums or assets representing the whole or any part of the [dependant's drawdown pension fund][2] in respect of an arrangement,

    (*b*) it is payable by an insurance company,

    (*c*) the dependant had an opportunity to select the insurance company,

    [(*ca*) the dependant becomes entitled to it before 6 April 2015,][4]

    (*d*) it is payable for a term which does not exceed five years and ends before the dependant . . . [2] dies, and

    [(*e*) its amount either cannot decrease or falls to be determined in any manner prescribed by regulations made by the Board of Inland Revenue.][1]

[(1ZA) For the purposes of this Part, but subject to any provision made under sub-paragraph (1C)(za), an annuity payable to a dependant is also a dependants' short-term annuity if—

    (*a*) it is purchased by the application of sums or assets representing the whole or any part of the dependant's drawdown pension fund, or of the dependant's flexi-access drawdown fund, in respect of an arrangement,

    (*b*) it is payable by an insurance company,

    (*c*) the dependant becomes entitled to it on or after 6 April 2015, and

    (*d*) it is payable for a term which does not exceed five years and ends before the dependant dies.][3]

[(1A) An annuity does not fail to satisfy sub-paragraph (1)(*e*) by reason of the operation of a pension sharing order or provision.

(1B) The Board of Inland Revenue may by regulations make provision in relation to cases in which a dependants' short-term annuity payable to a person ("the original dependants' short-term annuity") ceases to be payable and in consequence of that—

    (*a*) sums or assets (or both) are transferred from the insurance company to another insurance company and are applied towards the provision of either another dependants' short-term annuity (a "new dependants' short-term annuity") or a scheme pension, lifetime annuity, short-term annuity, dependants' scheme pension or dependants' annuity by the other insurance company, or

(b) sums or assets are transferred to the relevant registered pension scheme.

(1C) The regulations may provide that—

    [(*za*) in a case where—

        (i) a new annuity becomes payable,

        (ii) the dependant becomes entitled to it on or after 6 April 2015,

        (iii) it would be a dependants' short-term annuity if any provision made under this paragraph were ignored,

        (iv) the terms of the contract for it are such that there will or could be decreases in its amount other than allowed decreases (see sub-paragraph (1E)), and

        (v) any other conditions prescribed by the regulations are met,

    the new annuity is not a dependants' short-term annuity for the purposes of this Part,][4]

    (a) in a case where a new dependants' short-term annuity becomes payable, the new dependants' short-term annuity is to be treated, to such extent as is prescribed by the regulations and for such of the purposes of this Part as are so prescribed, as if it were the original dependants' short-term annuity, and

    (b) in [a case other than one where a new dependants' short-term annuity becomes payable][4], the relevant registered pension scheme is to be treated as making an unauthorised payment in respect of the member of an amount equal to the aggregate of the amount of the sums, and the market value of the assets, transferred.

(1D) For the purposes of sub-paragraphs (1B) and (1C) a registered pension scheme is the relevant registered pension scheme if the original dependants' short-term annuity was acquired using sums or assets held for the purposes of the pension scheme.][1]

[(1E) In sub-paragraph (1C)(*za*)(iv) "allowed decreases" means decreases from time to time allowed by regulations under sub-paragraph (1)(*e*); and any such regulations are to be treated as having effect for this purpose.][4]

(2) . . . [1]

Regulations—Registered Pension Schemes (Prescribed Manner of Determining Amount of Annuities) Regulations, SI 2006/56⁹ Registered Pension Schemes (Transfer of Sums and Assets) (Amendment) Regulations, SI 2015/633.   ....ons, SI 2006/207

Modifications—Pensions Schemes (Application of UK Provisions to Relevant Non-UK S .... reg 14 (modification of this paragraph in respect of relev.... UK schemes).

F(No 2)A 2010 Sch 3 para 3 (sub-para (1) has effect in relation to an annuity that is purchased on or after 22 June 2010 and is payable to a person who reaches the age of 75 on or after 22 June 2010, as if the reference in sub-para (1)(*d*) to the age of 75 were a reference to the age of 77).

FA 2011 Sch 16 paras 94, 95 (modification of this para in relation to dependants' entitlement to unsecured or alternatively secured pension on 5 April 2011).

Amendments—¹   Words in sub-para (1) and sub-para (1)(*e*) substituted, sub-paras (1A)–(1D) inserted and sub-para (2) repealed by FA 2005 ss 101, 104, Sch 10 paras 16, 64(1), Sch 11 Pt 4 with effect from 6 April 2006.

²   Words in sub-para (1)(*a*) substituted for words "dependant's unsecured pension fund" and words "reaches the age of 75 or" in sub-para (1)(*d*) repealed, by FA 2011 s 65, Sch 16 para 14 with effect for the tax year 2011–12 and subsequent tax years, subject to transitional provisions in FA 2011 Sch 16 Pt 3.

³   Sub-para (1ZA) inserted by the Taxation of Pensions Act 2014 s 1, Sch 1 paras 36, 40 with effect from 17 December 2014.

⁴   Sub-paras (1)(*ca*), (1C)(*za*), (1E) inserted, and words in sub-para (1C)(*b*) substituted for words "any other case", by the Taxation of Pensions Act 2014 s 1, Sch 1 paras 42, 50, 51 with effect from 17 December 2014.

Dependants' income withdrawal

[21 "Dependants' income withdrawal" means an amount (other than an annuity) which the dependant is entitled to be paid from the dependant's drawdown pension fund in respect of an arrangement [or from the dependant's flexi-access drawdown fund in respect of an arrangement"²].][1]

Amendments—¹   This para substituted by FA 2011 s 65, Sch 16 para 15 with effect for the tax year 2011–12 and subsequent tax years, subject ... Words inserted by the Taxation of Pensions Act 2014 s 1, Sch 1 paras 5, 20 with effect from 17 December 2014.

[Dependant's drawdown pension fund]²

22—(1) For the purposes of this Part a [dependant's drawdown pension fund]² in respect of an arrangement consists of such of the sums and assets held for the purposes of the arrangement—

    [(*a*) as are dependant-designated funds, and

    (*b*) have not been applied towards the provision of a dependants' scheme pension.][1]

[(2) For the purposes of this Part sums or assets held for the purposes of an arrangement are dependant-designated funds if³ . . . —

    (*a*) [they have, at any time before 6 April 2015, been designated]³ under the arrangement as available for the payment of [dependant's drawdown pension]²... ⁴,

[(*aa*) they have, at any time on or after 6 April 2015, been designated under the arrangement as available for the payment of dependants' drawdown pension ...[4], and—
    (i) sums or assets held for the purposes of the arrangement have, at any time before 6 April 2015, been designated under the arrangement as so available, and
    (ii) section 167(2A) did not apply to the arrangement immediately before 6 April 2015,][3] or
(*b*) [they][3] arise, or (directly or indirectly) derive, from [dependant-designated funds under paragraph (*a*) or (*aa*) or from sums or assets][3] which so arise or derive.

(3) If any sums or assets representing a [person's][4] [dependant's drawdown pension fund][2] in respect of an arrangement under the pension scheme would (apart from this sub-paragraph)—
    (*a*) come to be taken to represent another [dependant's drawdown pension fund][2] of his under the pension scheme, or [a drawdown pension fund][2] of his under the pension scheme, or
    (*b*) are applied towards the provision of a scheme pension or a lifetime annuity,
they are to be treated as not doing so.][1]

Modifications—Taxation of Pension Schemes (Transitional Provisions) Order, SI 2006/572 art 30 (modification of this paragraph in the case of an individual who meets certain conditions).
FA 2011 Sch 16 para 96 (modification of this para in relation to dependants' unsecured or alternatively secured pension fund existing on 5 April 2011).
Amendments—[1]   Sub-para (1)(*a*), (*b*) substituted and sub-paras (2), (3) inserted by FA 2005 s 101, Sch 10 paras 21, 64(1) with effect from 6 April 2006.
[2]   In sub-paras (1), (3), words substituted for words "dependant's unsecured pension fund", in sub-para (2)(*a*) words substituted for words "dependant's unsecured pension", in sub-para (3)(*a*), words substituted for words "an unsecured pension fund", and heading substituted for previous heading "Dependant's unsecured pension fund", by FA 2011 s 65, Sch 16 para 16 with effect for the tax year 2011–12 and subsequent tax years, subject to transitional provisions in FA 2011 Sch 16 Pt 3.
[3]   In sub-para (2), in opening words word "they" repealed, in para (*a*) words substituted for words "have been designated at any time", para (*aa*) inserted, and in para (*b*) word inserted and words substituted for words "sums or assets which have been so designated or", by the Taxation of Pensions Act 2014 s 1, Sch 1 paras 5, 21 with effect from 17 December 2014.
[4]   In sub-para (2)(*a*), (*aa*) words "to the dependant" repealed, and in sub-para (3) words inserted, by FA 2016 s 22, Sch 5 para 6(1), (3) with effect from 16 September 2016.

[Dependant's flexi-access drawdown fund

22A—(1) For the purposes of this Part a dependant's flexi-access drawdown fund in respect of an arrangement consists of such of the sums or assets held for the purposes of the arrangement as are newly-designated dependant funds.
(2) For the purposes of this Part sums or assets held for the purposes of an arrangement are newly-designated dependant funds if—
    (*a*) they—
        (i) have, at any time on or after 6 April 2015, been designated under the arrangement as available for the payment of dependants' drawdown pension, and
        (ii) are not dependant-designated funds, or
    (*b*) they were dependant-designated funds immediately before 6 April 2015 and section 167(2A) applied to the arrangement at that time, or
    (*c*) they have become newly-designated dependant funds by the operation of paragraph 22B, 22C or 22D, or
    (*d*) they arise, or (directly or indirectly) derive, from newly-designated dependant funds under paragraph (*a*), (*b*) or (*c*) or from sums or assets which so arise or derive.
(3) Any sums or assets that become newly-designated dependant funds under sub-paragraph (2)(*b*) cease to be dependant-designated funds as from the start of 6 April 2015.][1]

Amendments—[1]   Para 22A inserted by the Taxation of Pensions Act 2014 s 1, Sch 1 para 4(1) with effect from 17 December 2014.

[Conversion of certain dependants' drawdown funds into flexi-access drawdown funds

22B—(1) Sub-paragraph (2) applies if—
    (*a*) a dependant's drawdown pension fund in respect of an arrangement came into being before 6 April 2015,
    (*b*) section 167(2A) did not apply to the arrangement immediately before 6 April 2015, and
    (*c*) at a time on or after 6 April 2015, a payment—
        (i) of dependants' income withdrawal from the fund, or
        (ii) of a dependants' short-term annuity purchased using sums or assets out of the fund,
        is made that (apart from sub-paragraph (2)) would breach the cap.
(2) The sums and assets that make up the fund immediately before the payment is made become newly-designated dependant funds immediately before the payment is made (so that the payment is made out of the dependant's flexi-access drawdown fund in respect of the arrangement and therefore is not part of the total capped by pension death benefit rule 4).

(3) For the purposes of sub-paragraph (1)(*c*), a payment of dependants' drawdown pension in respect of an arrangement is one that would breach the cap if, when its amount is added to the amounts of any dependants' drawdown pension in respect of the arrangement—

    (*a*) paid—

        (i) before it is made, but

        (ii) in the same drawdown pension year in respect of the arrangement, or

    (*b*) paid at the time it is made,

the total is greater than the cap set by pension death benefit rule 4 for that drawdown pension year.]¹

Amendments—¹   Para 22B inserted by the Taxation of Pensions Act 2014 s 1, Sch 1 para 4(1) with effect from 17 December 2014.

[22C—(1) Sub-paragraph (2) applies if—

    (*a*) a dependant's drawdown pension fund in respect of an arrangement came into being before 6 April 2015,

    (*b*) section 167(2A) did not apply to the arrangement immediately before 6 April 2015, and

    (*c*) the dependant notifies the scheme administrator that the dependant wishes the fund to become the dependant's flexi-access drawdown fund in respect of the arrangement.

(2) At—

    (*a*) the time the scheme administrator accepts the notification, or

    (*b*) the start of 6 April 2015 if that is later,

the sums and assets that then make up that fund become newly-designated dependant funds, if they have not previously done so by the operation of paragraph 22B.]¹

Amendments—¹   Para 22C inserted by the Taxation of Pensions Act 2014 s 1, Sch 1 para 4(1) with effect from 17 December 2014.

[22D—(1) Sub-paragraphs (2) and (3) apply if—

    (*a*) there is a recognised transfer from one registered pension scheme ("the old scheme") to another registered pension scheme ("the new scheme") of dependant-designated funds held for the purposes of an arrangement under the old scheme, and

    (*b*) the sums or assets transferred are, under the arrangement under the new scheme for whose purposes they are first held after the transfer, designated as available for the payment of drawdown pension.

(2) If the dependant, when or before the designation is made, notifies the scheme administrator of the new scheme that the dependant wishes the sums or assets to be newly-designated dependant funds, the sums or assets become newly-designated dependant funds and do so—

    (*a*) when the designation is made, or

    (*b*) if later, immediately after the transfer,

except that, if both the designation and transfer are made before 6 April 2015, the sums or assets become newly-designated dependant funds at the start of 6 April 2015.

(3) If sub-paragraph (2) does not provide for the sums or assets to become newly-designated dependant funds, the sums or assets become dependant-designated funds and do so—

    (*a*) when the designation is made, or

    (*b*) if later, immediately after the transfer.]¹

Amendments—¹   Para 22D inserted by the Taxation of Pensions Act 2014 s 1, Sch 1 para 4(1). This amendment has effect in relation to—

    (a)   cases where both the designation and transfer are made after the end of two months beginning with 17 December 2014 (ie after 16 February 2015); and

    (b)   cases not within (a) where the transfer is made before 6 April 2015 and the designation is made on or after 6 April 2015, or the designation is made before 6 April 2015 and the transfer is made on or after 6 April 2015.

*[Drawdown pension year and basis amount for drawdown pension year]*¹

23—(1) ["Drawdown pension year"]¹ means—

    (*a*) the period of 12 months beginning with the day on which the dependant first becomes entitled to [dependants' drawdown pension]¹ in respect of the arrangement, and

    (*b*) each succeeding period of 12 months.

[This is subject to paragraph 24B.]¹

[(2) The drawdown pension year in which the dependant dies is the last drawdown pension year and ends immediately before the dependant's death.]¹

Modifications—Taxation of Pension Schemes (Transitional Provisions) Order, SI 2006/572 art 30 (modification of this paragraph in the case of an individual who meets certain conditions).

FA 2011 Sch 16 para 97 (modification of this para in relation to dependants' unsecured or alternatively secured pension on 5 April 2011).

  (b) the value of the benefits to be paid to or in respect of the individual under the arrangement has been reduced and the value of the benefits to be paid to or in respect of the individual under the pension scheme mentioned in subsection (4) has been increased, as a consequence (whether direct or indirect) of the transfer,

  (c) the amount of that reduction is equal (or virtually equal) to the amount of that increase, and

  (d) the transfer is not part of an arrangement the main purpose (or one of the main purposes) of which is the avoidance of tax.][2]

(5) [In subsection (5A) "relevant inward transfer means][3] a transfer relating to the individual of any sums or assets held for the purposes of, or representing accrued rights under, any pension scheme so as to become held for the purposes of, or to represent rights under, the arrangement . . . .[3].][1]

[(5A) If there is a relevant inward transfer during the pension input period, then—

  (a) if condition B is met, and there has been an increase in the annual rate of the pension or an increase in the amount of the lump sum to which the individual would be entitled under the arrangement, as a consequence (whether direct or indirect) of the relevant inward transfer, the amount of that increase is to be subtracted from PE or LSE, so far as that amount is reflected in the increase in the value of benefits mentioned in paragraph (b) of condition B;

  (b) if condition B is not met but the annual rate of the pension, or the amount of the lump sum, to which the individual would be entitled under the arrangement has been increased by reason of the relevant inward transfer, the amount of that increase is to be subtracted from PE or LSE.

  Condition B is that—

  (a) the relevant inward transfer ("the transfer") took place within a block transfer,

  (b) the value of the benefits to be paid to or in respect of the individual under the arrangement has been increased, and the value of the benefits to be paid to or in respect of the individual under the pension scheme mentioned in subsection (5) has been reduced, as a consequence (whether direct or indirect) of the transfer,

  (c) the amount of that increase in value is equal (or virtually equal) to the amount of that reduction, and

  (d) the transfer is not part of an arrangement the main purpose (or one of the main purposes) of which is the avoidance of tax.

(5B) For the purposes of Condition A in subsection (4A) and Condition B in subsection (5A)—

  (a) normal actuarial practice must be used when determining and comparing the amount of a reduction, and the amount of an increase, in the value of benefits to be paid to or in respect of the individual,

  (b) the amount of a reduction or increase in the value of benefits to be paid to or in respect of the individual under the arrangement is the difference between the value of those benefits under that arrangement immediately before the transfer and immediately after the transfer, and

  (c) the amount of an increase or reduction in the value of benefits to be paid to or in respect of an individual under a pension scheme is the difference between the value of those benefits under that pension scheme immediately before and immediately after the transfer.

(5C) In subsections (4A) and (5A)—

  "block transfer" means a transfer which involves the transfer in a single transaction of all the sums or assets held for the purposes of, or representing accrued rights under, the arrangements under a pension scheme which relate to the individual and at least one other member of that pension scheme so as to become held for the purposes of, or to represent rights under, any pension scheme.][3]

[(5D) For the purposes of subsections (4A) and (5A), the annual rate of the pension, or the amount of the lump sum, to which the individual would be entitled under the arrangement has been reduced or increased, as the case may be, "by reason of" a transfer of sums or assets only where that reduction or increase is solely attributable to the value of those sums or assets.][4]

[(8) If, during the pension input period, the annual rate of the pension, or the amount of the lump sum, to which the individual would be entitled under the arrangement has been reduced by any surrender made in return for any other entitlement, any allocation made, or any similar action taken, pursuant to an option available to the individual under the arrangement, the amount of the reduction (to the extent that it is not reflected in an amount added under subsection (8A)) is to be added to PE or LSE.

(8A) If, during the pension input period—

  (a) benefit crystallisation event 2 occurs in relation to the individual and the arrangement,

  (b) benefit crystallisation event 3 occurs in relation to the individual and the arrangement otherwise than by reason of a provision contained in, or made under, any enactment, or

  (c) benefit crystallisation event 6 occurs in relation to the individual and the arrangement by virtue of the individual becoming entitled to a pension commencement lump sum or a lifetime allowance excess lump sum,

the relevant amount is to be added to PE or LSE.

(8B) In subsection (8A) "the relevant amount" is—

(*a*) in the case of benefit crystallisation event 2, the annual rate of the pension to which the individual became entitled,

(*b*) in the case of benefit crystallisation event 3, the increase in the annual rate of the pension, and

(*c*) in the case of benefit crystallisation event 6, the amount of the lump sum.

(8C) If, during the pension input period, an adjustment to the annual rate of the pension, or the amount of the lump sum, to which the individual would be entitled under the arrangement has been made in consequence of the scheme administrator satisfying a liability under section 237B in respect of the individual, if and to the extent that the adjustment is reflected in PE or LSE the amount of the adjustment is to be added to PE or LSE.

(8D) But no amount is to be added under subsection (8C) by reason of an adjustment made in consequence of the scheme administrator satisfying a liability under section 237B [in a case where—]¹

(*a*) the individual becomes actually entitled to all of the individual's benefits under the pension scheme or benefit crystallisation event 5, 5A or 5B occurs in relation to the individual and the pension scheme, and

(*b*) the adjustment takes place after the individual becomes so entitled or the benefit crystallisation event occurs.]⁵

(9) . . .¹

Commentary—*Simon's Taxes* E7.212.

HMRC Manuals—Pensions Tax Manual PTM053700 (adjustments to closing values: contents).

Amendments—¹   Amendments made by FA 2011 s 66, Sch 17 paras 1, 12 with effect for the tax year 2011–12 and subsequent tax years, and in relation to pension input periods ending in the tax year 2011–12 but beginning earlier (or in 2011–12). For transitional provisions see FA 2011 Sch 17 paras 28–34.

² In sub-s (4), words substituted for words "In a case which" and words "in the tax year (in both places" and ", the notice must be given" revoked, and sub-s (4A) inserted by the Finance Act 2004 (Registered Pension Schemes and Annual Allowance Charge) (Amendment) Order, SI 2015/80 arts 10, 16(*a*), (*b*) with effect in relation to pension input periods ending in tax year 2011–12 and subsequent years. These amendments do not have effect in relation to any transfer of sums or assets that occurs before 28 January 2015 if any person's liability to tax would be higher as a result of—

    (a)   the application of those amendments in relation to that transfer; and

    (b)   any application in relation to that transfer of the amendments made by article 16(*c*) and (*d*),

than it would have been if none of those amendments had effect (SI 2015/80 art 3(5))

³ In sub-s (5), words substituted and revoked, and sub-ss (5A)–(5C) inserted by the Finance Act 2004 (Registered Pension Schemes and Annual Allowance Charge) (Amendment) Order, SI 2015/80 arts 10, 16(*c*), (*d*) with effect in relation to pension input periods ending in tax year 2011–12 and subsequent years.

⁴ Sub-s (5D) inserted by the Finance Act 2004 (Registered Pension Schemes and Annual Allowance Charge) (Amendment) Order, SI 2015/80 arts 10, 16(*e*) with effect from 28 January 2015, but not have effect in relation to transfers of sums or assets that occur before that date.

⁵ In sub-s (8D), words substituted for word "in a case where subsection (6) of that section applied" by the Finance Act 2004 (Registered Pension Schemes and Annual Allowance Charge) (Amendment) Order, SI 2015/80 arts 10, 16(*f*) with effect in relation to cases where the liability mentioned in section 236(8D) arose on or after 28 January 2015 and results from a notice under section 237B given on or after that date.

[236A Post-entitlement enhancements

(1) This section applies in relation to the arrangement if, during the pension input period ("the affected pension input period"), the individual enters into a scheme for the making of an avoidance-inspired post-entitlement enhancement.

(2) A "post-entitlement enhancement" is an increase in the annual rate of a scheme pension under the arrangement, at a time after the member has become entitled to the scheme pension.

(3) A post-entitlement enhancement is "avoidance-inspired" if the main purpose, or one of the main purposes, of the individual in entering into the scheme was to avoid or reduce a liability to the annual allowance charge.

(4) This Part has effect in relation to the arrangement and the individual, as respects the affected pension input period and all subsequent pension input periods, as if—

(*a*) section 234 were modified in accordance with subsection (5), and

(*b*) sections 235 and 236 were omitted.

(5) The modifications of section 234 are that—

(*a*) in subsection (4), for the words after "the arrangement is" there are substituted "such amount as, applying normal actuarial practice, is the expected cost of giving effect to the individual's rights under the arrangement at the end of the immediately preceding pension input period (or is nil if the pension input period is the first pension input period of the arrangement).",

(*b*) in subsection (5), for the words after "the arrangement is" there are substituted "such amount as, applying normal actuarial practice, is the expected cost of giving effect to the individual's rights under the arrangement at the end of the pension input period.", and

(*c*) subsection (6) is omitted.

(6) In this section "scheme" includes any arrangements, agreement, understanding, transaction or series of transactions (whether or not legally enforceable).]¹

Commentary—*Simon's Taxes* E7.212.

HMRC Manuals—Pensions Tax Manual PTM053390 (anti-avoidance rule for post-entitlement enhancements).
Amendments—[1]   This section inserted by FA 2011 s 66, Sch 17 paras 1, 13 with effect for the tax year 2011–12 and subsequent
    tax years, and in relation to pension input periods ending in the tax year 2011–12 but beginning earlier (or in 2011–12). For
    transitional provisions see FA 2011 Sch 17 paras 28–34.

237 Hybrid arrangements

(1) The pension input amount in respect of a hybrid arrangement is the greater or greatest of such of
input amounts A, B and C as are relevant input amounts.
(2) An input amount is a relevant input amount in the case of a hybrid arrangement if, in any
circumstances, the benefits that may be provided to or in respect of the individual under the
arrangement may be benefits of the variety mentioned in the definition of that input amount.
(3) Input amount A is what would be the pension input amount under sections 230 to 232 if the
benefits provided to or in respect of the individual under the arrangement were cash balance benefits.
(4) Input amount B is what would be the pension input amount under section 233 if the benefits
provided to or in respect of the individual under the arrangement were other money purchase
benefits.
(5) Input amount C is what would be the pension input amount under sections 234 to [236A][1] if the
benefits provided to or in respect of the individual under the arrangement were defined benefits.

Commentary—*Simon's Taxes* **E7.212**.
HMRC Manuals—Pensions Tax Manual PTM053500 (hybrid arrangements).
PTM13340 (pension input amounts for hybrid arrangements).
Modifications—Registered Pension Schemes (Restriction of Employers' Relief) Regulations, SI 2005/3458 regs 3, 4, 8
    (determination of the individual's pension input amount for a period of account in respect of a hybrid arrangement: modification
    of this section).
Amendments—[1]   In sub-s (5) figure substituted for figure "236" by FA 2011 s 66, Sch 17 paras 1, 14 with effect for the tax
    year 2011–12 and subsequent tax years, and in relation to pension input periods ending in the tax year 2011–12 but beginning
    earlier (or in 2011–12). For transitional provisions see FA 2011 Sch 17 paras 28–34.

[237ZA Pension input amounts for input periods ending in 2015–16

(1) This section applies where the tax year is the pre-alignment tax year or the post-alignment tax
year (see section 228C(2)).
Modified rules for cash balance, or defined benefits, arrangement
(2) The rules for calculating the pension input amount in respect of a cash balance arrangement, or
a defined benefits arrangement, are modified as follows (and the rules for calculating the pension
input amount in respect of a hybrid arrangement have effect accordingly).
Single input amount to be calculated for combined period
(3) The pension input amount in respect of the arrangement is the time-apportioned percentage of
any increase in the value of the individual's rights under the arrangement during the period ("the
combined period") that consists of the combination of all pension input periods of the arrangement
that end—
    (a) on or after 6 April 2015 but on or before 8 July 2015, or
    (b) on 5 April 2016.
(4) To calculate the increase (if any) in the value of the individual's rights under the arrangement
during the combined period, apply (as the case may be) sections 230 to 232 (except section 230(1)),
or sections 234 to 236A (except section 234(1)), as if—
    (a) references to the pension input period were references to the combined period,
    (b) the combined period were a pension input period of the arrangement,
    (c) 2.5% were the appropriate percentage specified in section 231(3) or 235(3), and
    (d) 2.5% were the percentage mentioned in paragraph (c) of the definition of "relevant
         percentage" given by section 230(5C) or 234(5C),
but paragraph (d) does not have effect for the purposes of the definition of "CPI percentage" given by
section 234(5C).
Apportioning input amount for combined period to tax years
(5) "The time-apportioned percentage" for the post-alignment tax year is—

$$\frac{272}{D} \times 100$$

and "the time-apportioned percentage" for the pre-alignment tax year is—

$$\frac{D - 272}{D} \times 100$$

where D is the number of days in the combined period.
Calculation and apportionment rules modified in certain cases
(6) Subsections (3) to (5) have effect subject to the following provisions of this section.
Exceptions in certain cases where individual is deferred member of scheme

(7) Subsections (3) to (5) do not apply, and subsections (8) and (9) apply instead, if—

    (*a*) because of section 238ZA(2), a pension input period for the arrangement ends with 8 July 2015,

    (*b*) another pension input period for the arrangement ends with a day ("the unchanged last day") after 5 April 2015 but before 8 July 2015, and

    (*c*) section 230(5B) or 234(5B), when applied separately to each of—

        (i) the pension input period for the arrangement ending with 8 July 2015, and

        (ii) the pension input period for the arrangement ending with 5 April 2016,

    gives the result that the pension input amount in respect of the arrangement for each of those periods is nil.

(8) The pension input amount in respect of the arrangement for the post-alignment tax year is nil.

(9) The pension input amount in respect of the arrangement for the pre-alignment tax year is the amount which would be the pension input amount in respect of the arrangement for the pre-alignment tax year if—

    (*a*) the pension input period ending with the unchanged last day were the only pension input period for the arrangement ending in the pre-alignment tax year, and

    (*b*) subsections (3) to (5) were ignored.

Modifications in some other cases where individual is deferred member of scheme

(10) Subsections (11) to (13) apply if—

    (*a*) because of section 238ZA(2), a pension input period for the arrangement ends with 8 July 2015,

    (*b*) apart from section 238ZA(2), that pension input period ("the cut-short period") would have ended with a day ("the original last day") after 8 July 2015 but before 5 April 2016,

    (*c*) at or after the beginning of the cut-short period but not later than the original last day, or in an earlier pension input period for the arrangement, the individual becomes a deferred member of the pension scheme that the arrangement is under, and

    (*d*) were the period—

        (i) beginning with the day after the original last day, and

        (ii) ending with 5 April 2016,

    a pension input period for the arrangement, the pension input amount in respect of the arrangement for that period would be nil by virtue of section 230(5B) or 234(5B).

(11) Subsections (3) to (5) have effect as if the original last day, and not 5 April 2016, were the last day of the combined period (so that, in particular, D in subsection (5) is the number of days in the combined period as so shortened).

(12) If the individual becomes a deferred member of the pension scheme in a pension input period for the arrangement earlier than the cut-short period—

    (*a*) the time-apportioned percentage for the post-alignment tax year is treated as being nil, and

    (*b*) the time-apportioned percentage for the pre-alignment tax year is treated as being 100.

(13) If the individual becomes a deferred member of the pension scheme at or after the beginning of the cut-short period but not later than the original last day, subsection (5) has effect as if for "272", in each place, there were substituted the number of days in the period beginning with 9 July 2015 and ending with the original last day.

Modification where first input period ends with 5 April 2016

(14) If the first pension input period for the arrangement ends with 5 April 2016—

    (*a*) the time-apportioned percentage for the post-alignment tax year is treated as being 100, and

    (*b*) the time-apportioned percentage for the pre-alignment tax year is treated as being nil.

Modification where last input period ends before 9 July 2015

(15) If the last pension input period for the arrangement ends after 5 April 2015 but before 9 July 2015—

    (*a*) the time-apportioned percentage for the post-alignment tax year is treated as being nil, and

    (*b*) the time-apportioned percentage for the pre-alignment tax year is treated as being 100.

Alternative modifications where individual is deferred member of scheme

(16) Subsections (17) and (18) apply if—

    (*a*) subsections (8) and (9) do not apply,

    (*b*) subsections (11) to (13) do not apply,

    (*c*) subsection (14) does not apply, and

    (*d*) section 230(5B) or 234(5B), when applied separately to each of—

        (i) so much of the combined period as consists of the post-alignment tax year, and

        (ii) the remainder of the combined period (for this purpose treating that remainder as a single pension input period if not otherwise the case),

    gives the result that the pension input amount in respect of the arrangement for one (but not the other) of those parts of the combined period is nil.

(17) If the nil result is for so much of the combined period as consists of the post-alignment tax year—

FA 2011 Sch 16 para 100 (modification of this para in relation to previous alternatively secured pension year).

[1] Words in sub-para (1) substituted for words ""Unsecured pension year"", words in sub-para(1)(*a*) substituted for words "dependants' unsecured pension" and words inserted, heading substituted for previous heading "Unsecured pension year and basis amount for unsecured pension year" and sub-para (2) substituted. by FA 2011 s 65, Sch 16 para 17 with effect for the tax year 2011–12 and subsequent tax years, subject to transitional provisions in FA 2011 Sch 16 Pt 3.

24—

[(A1) This paragraph applies in relation to drawdown pension years beginning on or before the dependant's 75th birthday.

(1) Subject as follows, the period of three drawdown pension years beginning with the first drawdown pension year, and each succeeding period of three drawdown pension years, is a "reference period".

(1ZA) But the reference period in which the dependant reaches the age of 75 ends with the drawdown pension year in which the dependant reaches that age.][3]

[(1A) Sub-paragraph (1B) applies if, at any time during a reference period ("the current reference period"), the dependant notifies the scheme administrator that the dependant wishes a new reference period to begin on the next day that is an anniversary of the reference date in relation to the current reference period.][2]

[(1B) The scheme administrator may determine—

(*a*) that the current reference period is to end immediately before that day (so that sub-paragraph (1) no longer applies), and

(*b*) that (subject to [sub-paragraph (1ZA) and][3] any further operation of this sub-paragraph) the period of [three drawdown pension years][3] beginning with that day, and each succeeding period of [three drawdown pension years][3], is to be a reference period.][2]

[(1C) The first day of each reference period is, in relation to that period, "the reference date".][2]

(2) For the first [drawdown pension year][3] falling within a reference period, the basis amount is the annual amount of the relevant annuity which could have been purchased by the application of the sums and assets representing the [dependant's drawdown pension fund][3] on the nominated date (but subject to sub-paragraph (5)).

(3) "The nominated date"—

(*a*) in relation to the first reference period, is the reference date, and

(*b*) in relation to any subsequent reference period, is such day, within the period of 60 days ending with the reference date, as is nominated by the scheme administrator (or if no day is nominated by the scheme administrator, is the reference date).

(4) For each other [drawdown pension year][3] falling within a reference period, the basis amount is the annual amount of the relevant annuity which could have been purchased by the application of the sums and assets representing the [dependant's drawdown pension fund[3]]—

(*a*) if there has been no recent annuity[, recent additional fund designation or recent pension sharing event][1], on the nominated date, and

(*b*) otherwise, immediately after the last annuity purchase[, additional fund designation or recent pension sharing event][1],

(but subject to sub-paragraph (5)).

(5) On the occasion of each additional fund designation during [a drawdown pension year][3], the basis amount for [that drawdown pension year][3] is to be recalculated in accordance with sub-paragraph (6).

(6) The basis amount for the [drawdown pension year][3] is the annual amount of the relevant annuity which could have been purchased by the application of the sums and assets representing the [dependant's drawdown pension fund][3] immediately after the additional fund designation.

[(6A) But sub-paragraph (5) does not apply where the operation of that sub-paragraph in relation to an additional fund designation during a drawdown pension year would reduce the basis amount for that drawdown pension year.][3]

(7) "Annuity purchase" means the purchase of a dependants' scheme pension or dependants' annuity by the application of sums or assets representing the whole or part of the [dependant's drawdown pension fund][3].

(8) "Additional fund designation" means the designation under the arrangement of further [sums or assets][3] held for the purposes of the arrangement as available for the payment of [dependant's drawdown pension][3] to the dependant.

[(8A) "Pension sharing event" means the coming into operation of a pension sharing order or provision relating to the sums and assets representing the [dependant's drawdown pension fund][3].][1]

(9) An annuity purchase[, additional fund designation or pension sharing event][1] is "recent" if it took place during the period—

    (*a*) beginning with the reference date, and

    (*b*) ending with the last day of the immediately preceding [drawdown pension year][3].

(10) Paragraph 14 defines "relevant annuity".

[(11) Nothing in this paragraph applies in respect of an arrangement to which section 167(2A) applies.][3], [4]

Modifications—Pensions Schemes (Application of UK Provisions to Relevant Non-UK Schemes) Regulations, SI 2006/207 reg 14 (modification of this paragraph in respect of relevant non-UK schemes).

Taxation of Pension Schemes (Transitional Provisions) Order, SI 2006/572 arts 3, 5 (modification of this Schedule in its application to any pension which—

    (a)   was paid by way of income withdrawal, income drawdown or annuity purchase deferral from a retirement benefits scheme, or a personal pension scheme approved under TA 1988 Pt 14 immediately before 6 April 2006; and

    (b)   on 6 April 2006 becomes an unsecured pension or a dependant's unsecured pension by virtue of a scheme which is treated as becoming a registered pension scheme on that date).

FA 2011 Sch 16 para 98 (modification of this para in relation to limit on amount of pension payable in year).

Amendments—[1]   Words in sub-paras (4)(*a*), (*b*), (9) substituted and sub-para (4A) inserted by FA 2005 s 101, Sch 10 paras 22, 64(1) with effect from 6 April 2006.

[2]   Sub-paras (1)–(1C) substituted for sub-para (1) by FA 2007 s 70, Sch 20 paras 1, 8(1), (3), 24(5) with effect in relation to notifications given on or after 6 December 2006.

[3]   Sub-paras (A1)–(1ZA) substituted for previous sub-para (1), in sub-para (1B)(*b*) words inserted and words substituted for words "five unsecured pension years" in both places, in sub-paras (2), (4) words substituted for words "unsecured pension year" and "dependant's unsecured pension fund", in sub-para (5) words substituted for words "an unsecured pension year" and "that unsecured pension year", in sub-para (6) words substituted for words "unsecured pension year and "dependant's unsecured pension fund", in sub-para (7) words substituted for words "dependant's unsecured pension fund", in sub-para (8) words substituted for words "sums and assets" and "unsecured dependants' pension", in sub-para (8A) words substituted for words "dependant's unsecured pension fund", in sub-para (9)(*b*) words substituted for words "unsecured pension year", and sub-paras (6A), (11) inserted, by FA 2011 s 65, Sch 16 para 18 with effect for the tax year 2011–12 and subsequent tax years, subject to transitional provisions in FA 2011 Sch 16 Pt 3.

[4]   Sub-para (11) repealed by the Taxation of Pensions Act 2014 s 1, Sch 1 para 32(1)(*e*)(iv) with effect from 6 April 2015.

[24A—(1) This paragraph applies in relation to drawdown pension years beginning after the dependant's 75th birthday.

(2) For each drawdown pension year beginning after the dependant reached the age of 75, the basis amount is the annual amount of the relevant annuity which could have been purchased by the application of the sums and assets representing the dependant's drawdown pension fund on the nominated date. But this is subject to sub-paragraph (4).

(3) "The nominated date" is such day within the period of 60 days ending with the first day of the drawdown pension year as is nominated by the scheme administrator (or, if no day is nominated by the scheme administrator, is the first day of that year).

(4) On the occasion of each additional fund designation during a drawdown pension year, the basis amount of that drawdown pension year is to be recalculated in accordance with sub-paragraph (5).

(5) The basis amount for the drawdown pension year is the annual amount of the relevant annuity which could have been purchased by the application of the sums and assets representing the dependant's drawdown pension fund immediately after the additional fund designation.

(6) But sub-paragraph (4) does not apply where the operation of that sub-paragraph in relation to an additional fund designation during a drawdown pension year would reduce the basis amount for that drawdown pension year.

(7) "Additional fund designation" has the meaning given by paragraph 24(8).

(8) Paragraph 14 defines "relevant annuity".

(9) Nothing in this paragraph applies in respect of an arrangement to which section 167(2A) applies.[2]*]*[1]

Amendments—[1]   Paras 24A, 24B inserted by FA 2011 s 65, Sch 16 para 19 with effect for the tax year 2011–12 and subsequent tax years, subject to transitional provisions in FA 2011 Sch 16 Pt 3. The amendments made by FA 2011 Sch 16 para 19 have effect in relation to drawdown pension years beginning on or after 6 April 2011 (FA 2011 Sch 16 para 99(3)).

[2]   Sub-para (9) repealed by the Taxation of Pensions Act 2014 s 1, Sch 1 para 32(1)(*e*)(v) with effect from 6 April 2015.

[24B—(1) This paragraph applies if the dependant has reached the age of 75.

(2) Sub-paragraph (3) applies if, at any time during a drawdown pension year in respect of an arrangement ("the current drawdown pension year"), the dependant notifies the scheme administrator that the dependant wishes the drawdown pension year following the current drawdown pension year to begin on the day on which the next drawdown pension year in respect of another arrangement relating to the dependant under the pension scheme (including any arrangement relating to that person as a member of the scheme) will begin.

(3) The scheme administrator may determine—

    (*a*) that the current drawdown pension year is to end immediately before that day, and

    (*b*) that the period of 12 months beginning with that day, and each succeeding period of 12 months, is a drawdown pension year in respect of the arrangement.

(4) The scheme administrator may not make a determination under this paragraph more than once in relation to the same arrangement.]**[1]

Amendments—[1]   Paras 24A, 24B inserted by FA 2011 s 65, Sch 16 para 19 with effect for the tax year 2011–12 and subsequent tax years, subject to transitional provisions in FA 2011 Sch 16 Pt 3.

[Meaning of "nominee"

27A—(1) "Nominee of the member" means an individual—

(a)   nominated by the member, or

(b)   nominated by the scheme administrator,

who is not a dependant of the member, but see sub-paragraph (2).

(2) In relation to any particular benefits under an arrangement, no individual nominated by the scheme administrator counts as a nominee of the member at any time when there is—

(a)   a dependant of the member, or

(b)   an individual, or charity, nominated by the member in relation to the benefits.

(3) The reference in sub-paragraph (2)(b) to being nominated in relation to particular benefits under an arrangement includes—

(a)   a reference to being nominated in relation to the scheme,

(b)   a reference to being nominated in relation to arrangements that include the arrangement,

(c)   a reference to being nominated in relation to the arrangement, and

(d)   a reference to being nominated in relation to benefits that include the particular benefits.][1]

Amendments—[1]   Paras 27A–27K inserted by the Taxation of Pensions Act 2014 s 3, Sch 2 paras 1, 3 with effect from 17 December 2014. Paras 27A–27K have effect even in relation to cases where the member concerned, or any dependant concerned, dies before 6 April 2015 (TPA 2014 Sch 2 para 3(2)).

[Nominees' annuity

27AA—(1) For the purposes of this Part an annuity payable to a nominee is a nominees' annuity if—

(a)   either—

(i)   it is purchased together with a lifetime annuity payable to the member and the member becomes entitled to that lifetime annuity on or after 6 April 2015, or

(ii)   it is purchased after the member's death, the member dies on or after 3 December 2014 and the nominee becomes entitled to the annuity on or after 6 April 2015,

(b)   it is payable by an insurance company, and

(c)   it is payable until the nominee's death or until the earliest of the nominee's marrying, entering into a civil partnership or dying.

(2) For the purposes of sub-paragraph (1)(a) a nominees' annuity is purchased together with a lifetime annuity if the nominees' annuity is related to the lifetime annuity.

(3) The Commissioners for Her Majesty's Revenue and Customs may by regulations make provision in relation to cases in which a nominees' annuity payable to a person ("the original nominees' annuity") ceases to be payable and in consequence of that—

(a)   sums or assets (or both) are transferred from the insurance company to another insurance company and are applied—

(i)   towards the provision of another nominees' annuity (a "new nominees' annuity") by the other insurance company, or

(ii)   otherwise, or

(b)   sums or assets are transferred to the relevant registered pension scheme.

(4) The regulations may provide that—

(a)   in a case where a new nominees' annuity becomes payable, the new nominees' annuity is to be treated, to such extent as is prescribed by the regulations and for such of the purposes of this Part as are so prescribed, as if it were the original nominees' annuity, and

(b)   in any other case, the relevant registered pension scheme is to be treated as making an unauthorised payment in respect of the member of an amount equal to the aggregate of the sums, and the market value of the assets, transferred.

(5) For the purposes of sub-paragraphs (3) and (4) a registered pension scheme is the relevant registered pension scheme if the original nominees' annuity was acquired using sums or assets held for the purposes of the pension scheme.][1]

Regulations—Registered Pension Schemes (Transfer of Sums and Assets) (Amendment No 2) Regulations, SI 2015/1454.

Amendments—[1]   Para 27AA inserted by FA 2015 s 34, Sch 4 paras 1, 3(1), (2) with effect from 26 March 2015. Regulations made before 25 December 2015 under the para 27AA may, for cases where the transfer concerned takes place on or after 6 April 2015, include provision having effect in relation to times before the regulations are made (FA 2015 Sch 4 para 3(4)).

[Nominees' drawdown pension

27B—"Nominees' drawdown pension" means—

(a)   a nominees' short-term annuity, or

(*b*) nominees' income withdrawal.][1]

Amendments—[1]   Paras 27A–27K inserted by the Taxation of Pensions Act 2014 s 3, Sch 2 paras 1, 3 with effect from 17 December 2014. Paras 27A–27K have effect even in relation to cases where the member concerned, or any dependant concerned, dies before 6 April 2015 (TPA 2014 Sch 2 para 3(2)).

[Nominees' short-term annuity

27C—(1) For the purposes of this Part an annuity payable to a nominee is a nominees' short-term annuity if—

    (*a*) it is purchased by the application of sums or assets representing the whole or any part of the nominee's flexi-access drawdown fund in respect of an arrangement,

    (*b*) it is payable by an insurance company,

    (*c*) the nominee becomes entitled to it on or after 6 April 2015, and

    (*d*) it is payable for a term which does not exceed five years and ends before the nominee dies.

(2) The Commissioners for Her Majesty's Revenue and Customs may by regulations make provision in relation to cases in which a nominees' short-term annuity payable to a person ("the original nominees' short-term annuity") ceases to be payable and in consequence of that—

    (*a*) sums or assets (or both) are transferred from the insurance company to another insurance company and are applied—

        (i) towards the provision of another nominees' short-term annuity (a "new nominees' short-term annuity") by the other insurance company, or

        (ii) otherwise, or

    (*b*) sums or assets are transferred to the relevant registered pension scheme.

(3) The regulations may provide that—

    (*a*) in a case where a new nominees' short-term annuity becomes payable, the new nominees' short-term annuity is to be treated, to such extent as is prescribed by the regulations and for such of the purposes of this Part as are so prescribed, as if it were the original nominees' short-term annuity, and

    (*b*) in any other case, the relevant registered pension scheme is to be treated as making an unauthorised payment in respect of the member of an amount equal to the aggregate of the sums, and the market value of the assets, transferred.

(4) For the purposes of sub-paragraphs (2) and (3) a registered pension scheme is the relevant registered pension scheme if the original nominees' short-term annuity was acquired using sums or assets held for the purposes of the pension scheme.][1]

Regulations—Registered Pension Schemes (Transfer of Sums and Assets) (Amendment) Regulations, SI 2015/633.

Amendments—[1]   Paras 27A–27K inserted by the Taxation of Pensions Act 2014 s 3, Sch 2 paras 1, 3 with effect from 17 December 2014. Paras 27A–27K have effect even in relation to cases where the member concerned, or any dependant concerned, dies before 6 April 2015 (TPA 2014 Sch 2 para 3(2)).

[Nominees' income withdrawal

27D   "Nominees' income withdrawal" means an amount (other than an annuity) which the nominee is entitled to be paid from the nominee's flexi-access drawdown fund in respect of an arrangement.][1]

Amendments—[1]   Paras 27A–27K inserted by the Taxation of Pensions Act 2014 s 3, Sch 2 paras 1, 3 with effect from 17 December 2014. Paras 27A–27K have effect even in relation to cases where the member concerned, or any dependant concerned, dies before 6 April 2015 (TPA 2014 Sch 2 para 3(2)).

[Nominee's flexi-access drawdown fund

27E—(1) For the purposes of this Part a nominee's flexi-access drawdown fund in respect of an arrangement consists of such of the sums or assets held for the purposes of the arrangement as are newly-designated nominee funds.

(2) For the purposes of this Part sums or assets held for the purposes of an arrangement are newly-designated nominee funds if—

    (*a*) they—

        (i) have, at any time on or after 6 April 2015, been designated under the arrangement as available for the payment of nominees' drawdown pension, and

        (ii) were, immediately before being so designated, unused drawdown funds or unused uncrystallised funds, or

    (*b*) they arise, or (directly or indirectly) derive, from newly-designated nominee funds under paragraph (*a*) or from sums or assets which so arise or derive.

(3) Sums or assets held for the purposes of an arrangement after the member's death are unused drawdown funds if—

    (*a*) immediately before the member's death, they were held for the purposes of the arrangement and represented (whether alone or with other sums or assets) the member's flexi-access drawdown fund, or drawdown pension fund, in respect of the arrangement, or

   (b) they arise, or (directly or indirectly) derive, from unused drawdown funds under paragraph
      (a) or from sums or assets which so arise or [derive,][2]
[and since the member's death they have not been designated as available for the payment of
dependants' drawdown pension, not been designated as available for the payment of nominees'
drawdown pension, not been applied towards the provision of a dependants' annuity, not been applied
towards the provision of a nominees' annuity and not been applied towards the provision of a
dependants' scheme pension.][2]
(4) In the case of a cash balance arrangement, sums or assets held for the purposes of the
arrangement after the member's death are unused uncrystallised funds if—
   (a) they represent the whole or any part of the sum that would have been available immediately
      before the member's death for the provision of benefits to or in respect of the member if
      entitlement had arisen immediately before the member's death to all benefits under the
      arrangement to which entitlement had not previously arisen, and
   (b) since the member's death they have not been designated as available for the payment of
      dependants' drawdown pension, not been designated as available for the payment of
      nominees' drawdown pension, not been applied towards the provision of a dependants'
      annuity[, not been applied towards the provision of a nominees' annuity][3] and not been
      applied towards the provision of a dependants' scheme pension.
(5) In the case of any other money purchase arrangement, sums or assets held for the purposes of the
arrangement after the member's death are unused uncrystallised funds if—
   (a) immediately before the member's death they were held for the purposes of the arrangement
      and at that time—
      (i) were not member-designated funds,
      (ii) were not newly-designated funds,
      (iii) had not been applied towards the provision of a scheme pension, and
      (iv) had not been applied towards the provision of a dependants' scheme pension, or
      paragraph (a) or from sums or assets which so arise or derive,
and since the member's death they have not been designated as available for the payment of
dependants' drawdown pension, not been designated as available for the payment of nominees'
drawdown pension, not been applied toward the provision of a dependants' annuity[, not been applied
toward the provision of a nominees' annuity][3] and not been applied toward the provision of a
dependants' scheme pension.][1]

Amendments—[1]   Paras 27A–27K inserted by the Taxation of Pensions Act 2014 s 3, Sch 2 paras 1, 3 with effect from
17 December 2014. Paras 27A–27K have effect even in relation to cases where the member concerned, or any dependant
concerned, dies before 6 April 2015 (TPA 2014 Sch 2 para 3(2)).
[2]   In sub-para (3)(b), word "derive," substituted for word "derive.", and words inserted after para (b), by FA 2015 s 34, Sch 4
paras 1, 13(1), (4) with effect from 26 March 2015.
[3]   In sub-paras (4)(b), (5), words inserted by FA 2015 s 34, Sch 4 paras 1, 13(1), (5) with effect from 26 March 2015.

Meaning of "successor"

27F—(1) "Successor of the member" means an individual—
   (a) nominated by a dependant of the member,
   (b) nominated by a nominee of the member,
   (c) nominated by a successor of the member, or
   (d) nominated by the scheme administrator,
but see sub-paragraph (2).
(2) In relation to any particular benefits under an arrangement relating to a dependant, nominee or
successor of the member ("the beneficiary") in that capacity, no individual nominated by the scheme
administrator counts as a successor of the member at any time after the beneficiary's death when
there is an individual, or charity, nominated by the beneficiary in relation to the benefits.
(3) A reference in sub-paragraph (2) to being nominated in relation to particular benefits under an
arrangement includes—
   (a) a reference to being nominated in relation to the scheme,
   (b) a reference to being nominated in relation to arrangements that include the arrangement,
   (c) a reference to being nominated in relation to the arrangement, and
   (d) a reference to being nominated in relation to benefits that include the particular benefits.
(4) Where a successor of the member is an individual who is also a dependant of the member, the
individual in the capacity of a successor of the member is to be treated as not also being a dependant
of the member.][1]

Amendments—[1]   Paras 27A–27K inserted by the Taxation of Pensions Act 2014 s 3, Sch 2 paras 1, 3 with effect from
17 December 2014. Paras 27A–27K have effect even in relation to cases where the member concerned, or any dependant
concerned, dies before 6 April 2015 (TPA 2014 Sch 2 para 3(2)).

[Successors' annuity

27FA—(1) For the purposes of this Part an annuity payable to a successor is a successors' annuity if—

(a) the successor becomes entitled to it on or after 6 April 2015,

(b) it is payable by an insurance company,

(c) it is payable until the successor's death or until the earliest of the successor's marrying, entering into a civil partnership or dying,

(d) it is purchased after the death of a dependant, nominee or successor of the member ("the beneficiary"),

(e) it is purchased using undrawn funds, and

(f) the beneficiary dies on or after 3 December 2014.

(2) For the purposes of sub-paragraph (1)(e), sums or assets held for the purposes of an arrangement after the beneficiary's death are undrawn funds if—

(a) immediately before the beneficiary's death, they were held for the purposes of the arrangement and, as the case may be, represented (alone or with other sums or assets) the beneficiary's—

(i) dependant's flexi-access drawdown fund,

(ii) dependant's drawdown pension fund,

(iii) nominee's flexi-access drawdown fund, or

(iv) successor's flexi-access drawdown fund,

in respect of the arrangement, or

(b) they arise, or (directly or indirectly) derive, from undrawn funds under paragraph (a) or from sums or assets which so arise or derive.

(3) The Commissioners for Her Majesty's Revenue and Customs may by regulations make provision in relation to cases in which a successors' annuity payable to a person ("the original successors' annuity") ceases to be payable and in consequence of that—

(a) sums or assets (or both) are transferred from the insurance company to another insurance company and are applied—

(i) towards the provision of another successors' annuity (a "new successors' annuity") by the other insurance company, or

(ii) otherwise, or

(b) sums or assets are transferred to the relevant registered pension scheme.

(4) The regulations may provide that—

(a) in a case where a new successors' annuity becomes payable, the new successors' annuity is to be treated, to such extent as is prescribed by the regulations and for such of the purposes of this Part as are so prescribed, as if it were the original successors' annuity, and

(b) in any other case, the relevant registered pension scheme is to be treated as making an unauthorised payment in respect of the member of an amount equal to the aggregate of the sums, and the market value of the assets, transferred.

(5) For the purposes of sub-paragraphs (3) and (4) a registered pension scheme is the relevant registered pension scheme if the original successors' annuity was acquired using sums or assets held for the purposes of the pension scheme.][1]

Regulations—Registered Pension Schemes (Transfer of Sums and Assets) (Amendment No 2) Regulations, SI 2015/1454.

Amendments—[1] Para 27FA inserted by FA 2015 s 34, Sch 4 paras 1, 3(1), (3) with effect from 26 March 2015. Regulations made before 25 December 2015 under para 27FA may, for cases where the transfer concerned takes place on or after 6 April 2015, include provision having effect in relation to times before the regulations are made (FA 2015 Sch 4 para 3(4)).

[Successors' drawdown pension

27G "Successors' drawdown pension" means—

(a) a successors' short-term annuity, or

(b) successors' income withdrawal.][1]

Amendments—[1] Paras 27A–27K inserted by the Taxation of Pensions Act 2014 s 3, Sch 2 paras 1, 3 with effect from 17 December 2014. Paras 27A–27K have effect even in relation to cases where the member concerned, or any dependant concerned, dies before 6 April 2015 (TPA 2014 Sch 2 para 3(2)).

[Successors' short-term annuity

27H—(1) For the purposes of this Part an annuity payable to a successor is a successors' short-term annuity if—

(a) it is purchased by the application of sums or assets representing the whole or any part of the successor's flexi-access drawdown fund in respect of an arrangement,

(b) it is payable by an insurance company,

(*c*) the successor becomes entitled to it on or after 6 April 2015, and

(*d*) it is payable for a term which does not exceed five years and ends before the successor dies.

(2) The Commissioners for Her Majesty's Revenue and Customs may by regulations make provision in relation to cases in which a successors' short-term annuity payable to a person ("the original successors' short-term annuity") ceases to be payable and in consequence of that—

(*a*) sums or assets (or both) are transferred from the insurance company to another insurance company and are applied—

(i) towards the provision of another successors' short-term annuity (a "new successors' short-term annuity") by the other insurance company, or

(ii) otherwise, or

(*b*) sums or assets are transferred to the relevant registered pension scheme.

(3) The regulations may provide that—

(*a*) in a case where a new successors' short-term annuity becomes payable, the new successors' short-term annuity is to be treated, to such extent as is prescribed by the regulations and for such of the purposes of this Part as are so prescribed, as if it were the original successors' short-term annuity, and

(*b*) in any other case, the relevant registered pension scheme is to be treated as making an unauthorised payment in respect of the member of an amount equal to the aggregate of the sums, and the market value of the assets, transferred.

(4) For the purposes of sub-paragraphs (2) and (3) a registered pension scheme is the relevant registered pension scheme if the original successors' short-term annuity was acquired using sums or assets held for the purposes of the pension scheme.][1]

Regulations—Registered Pension Schemes (Transfer of Sums and Assets) (Amendment) Regulations, SI 2015/633.
Amendments—[1]   Paras 27A–27K inserted by the Taxation of Pensions Act 2014 s 3, Sch 2 paras 1, 3 with effect from 17 December 2014. Paras 27A–27K have effect even in relation to cases where the member concerned, or any dependant concerned. dies before 6 April 2015 (TPA 2014 Sch 2 para 3(2)).

[*Successors' income withdrawal*

27J   "Successors' income withdrawal" means an amount (other than an annuity) which the successor is entitled to be paid from the successor's flexi-access drawdown fund in respect of an arrangement.][1]

Amendments—[1]   Paras 27A–27K inserted by the Taxation of Pensions Act 2014 s 3, Sch 2 paras 1, 3 with effect from 17 December 2014. Paras 27A–27K have effect even in relation to cases where the member concerned, or any dependant concerned, dies before 6 April 2015 (TPA 2014 Sch 2 para 3(2)).

[*Successor's flexi-access drawdown fund*

27K—(1) For the purposes of this Part a successor's flexi-access drawdown fund in respect of an arrangement consists of such of the sums or assets held for the purposes of the arrangement as are newly-designated successor funds.

(2) For the purposes of this Part sums or assets held for the purposes of an arrangement are newly-designated successor funds if—

(*a*) they—

(i) have, at any time on or after 6 April 2015, been designated under the arrangement as available for the payment of successors' drawdown pension, and

(ii) were, immediately before being so designated, unused drawdown funds of the same deceased dependant, nominee or successor of the member, or

(*b*) they arise, or (directly or indirectly) derive, from newly-designated successor funds under paragraph (*a*) or from sums or assets which so arise or derive.

(3) Sums or assets held for the purposes of an arrangement after the death of a dependant, nominee or successor ("the beneficiary") are unused drawdown funds of the beneficiary's if—

(*a*) immediately before the beneficiary's death, they were held for the purposes of the arrangement and represented (whether alone or with other sums or assets) the beneficiary's—

(i) dependant's flexi-access drawdown fund,

(ii) dependant's drawdown pension fund,

(iii) nominee's flexi-access drawdown fund, or

(iv) successor's flexi-access drawdown fund,

in respect of the arrangement, or

(*b*) they arise, or (directly or indirectly) derive, from unused drawdown funds of the beneficiary's under paragraph (*a*) or from sums or assets which so arise or [derive,][2]

[and since the beneficiary's death they have not been designated as available for the payment of successors' drawdown pension and not been applied towards the provision of a successors' annuity.][2][1]

Amendments—[1]   Paras 27A–27K inserted by the Taxation of Pensions Act 2014 s 3, Sch 2 paras 1, 3 with effect from 17 December 2014. Paras 27A–27K have effect even in relation to cases where the member concerned, or any dependant concerned, dies before 6 April 2015 (TPA 2014 Sch 2 para 3(2)).

[2]   In sub-para (3)(b), word "derive," substituted for word "derive.", and words inserted after sub-para (3)(b), by FA 2015 s 34, Sch 4 paras 1, 13(1), (6) with effect from 26 March 2015.

SCHEDULE 29
REGISTERED PENSION SCHEMES: AUTHORISED LUMP SUMS—SUPPLEMENTARY

Sections 166 and 168

Commentary—*Simon's Taxes* **E7.224**.

PART 1
LUMP SUM RULE

Pension commencement lump sum

1—(1) For the purposes of this Part a lump sum is a pension commencement lump sum if—
  (a) . . .[3]
  [(aa) the member becomes entitled to it in connection with becoming entitled to a relevant pension (or dies after becoming entitled to it but before becoming entitled to the relevant pension in connection with which it was anticipated that the member would become entitled to it)][2]
  (b) it is paid when all or part of the member's lifetime allowance is available [(but see sub-paragraph (3A))][3],
  (c) it is paid within the period [beginning six months before, and ending one year after,][2] the day on which the member becomes entitled to it,
  (d) it is paid when the member has reached normal minimum pension age (or the ill-health condition is satisfied),
  (e) . . .[2] and
  (f) it is not an excluded lump sum (see sub-paragraph (4)).
(2) But if a lump sum falling within sub-paragraph (1) exceeds the permitted maximum, the excess is not a pension commencement lump sum.
(3) A pension is a relevant pension if—
  (a) it is income withdrawal, a lifetime annuity or a scheme pension, and
  (b) the member becomes entitled to it [. . . [4] under the pension scheme][1] under which the member becomes entitled to the lump sum.
[(3A) In a case where—
  (a) the member becomes entitled to a lump sum before reaching the age of 75, but
  (b) it is not paid to the member until after the member has reached that age,
the reference in sub-paragraph (1)(b) to the lump sum being paid is to be read as a reference to the member becoming entitled to it.][3]
(4) A lump sum is an excluded lump sum if—
  (a) the pension in connection with which the member becomes entitled to it is a scheme pension the rate of which is to reduce (or which is to cease to be payable) in accordance with paragraph 2(4)(c) of Schedule 28 . . . [5], and
  (b) the sole or main purpose of making provision for the pension to be such a pension was to increase the member's entitlement to a lump sum on which there is no liability to income tax.
(5) Paragraph 2 defines the permitted maximum.
[(6) The Board of Inland Revenue may by regulations provide that, where incorrect income tax has been paid by the scheme administrator in relation to the member by way of the lifetime allowance charge in circumstances prescribed by the regulations, a lump sum subsequently paid to the member in circumstances so prescribed is to be treated as a pension commencement lump sum [even though the condition in sub-paragraph (1)(c) is not met]3.][1]

Commentary—*Simon's Taxes* **E7.224**.
Cross-references—See F(No 2)A 2010 Sch 3 para 8 (treatment of remaining uncrystallised funds at the end of the period referred to in sub-para (1)(c)).
Regulations—Registered Pension Schemes (Meaning of Pension Commencement Lump Sum) Regulations, SI 2006/135.
Modifications—Pensions Schemes (Application of UK Provisions to Relevant Non-UK Schemes) Regulations, SI 2006/207 reg 15 (modification of this paragraph in respect of relevant non-UK schemes).
Taxation of Pension Schemes (Transitional Provisions) Order, SI 2006/572 art 18 (modification of this paragraph, if (and for so long as) FA 2004 Sch 36 paras 27 or 29 applies in relation to an individual, with effect in relation to that individual).
Taxation of Pension Schemes (Transitional Provisions) Order, SI 2006/572 art 28 (modification of this paragraph in the case of an individual who meets certain conditions).
Taxation of Pension Schemes (Transitional Provisions) Order, SI 2006/572 art 23C (modification of sub-para (1)(aa) above in respect of trivial commutation lump sums).

Taxation of Pension Schemes (Transitional Provisions) Order, SI 2006/572 art 45 (modification of this para in relation to the increase in the national minimum pension age from 50 to 55 from 6 April 2010).

F(No 2)A 2010 Sch 3 para 7 (in relation to lump sums to which persons become entitled at age 75, this para has effect as if in sub-para (3)(b) the words "otherwise than by virtue of the operation of paragraph 8(2) of Schedule 28" were repealed).

Amendments—[1]   Words in sub-para (3)(b) substituted and sub-para (6) inserted by FA 2005 s 101, Sch 10 paras 34, 64(1) with effect from 6 April 2006.

[2]   Sub-para (1)(aa) substituted for sub-para (1), words in sub-para (1)(c) substituted, and sub-para (1)(e) repealed, by FA 2007 ss 70, 114, Sch 20 paras 1, 11(1)–(3), 24(3), Sch 27 Pt 3(2). These amendments are deemed always to have had effect.

[3]   Sub-para (1)(a) repealed, words in sub-para (1)(b) inserted, sub-para (3A) inserted, and words in sub-para (6) substituted for words "even though either or both of the conditions in sub-paragraph (1)(a) and (c) are not met", by FA 2011 s 65, Sch 16 paras 23, 24 with effect for the tax year 2011–12 and subsequent tax years, subject to transitional provisions in FA 2011 Sch 16 Pt 3. The amendments made by FA 2011 Sch 16 paras 24–26, 31 and 79(2), (3) have effect in relation to any lump sum to which a person becomes entitled for the purposes of FA 2004 Part 4 on or after 6 April 2011 (FA 2011 Sch 16 para 101).

[4]   In sub-para (3)(b) words ", otherwise than by virtue of the operation of paragraph 8(2) of Schedule 28," repealed by FA 2011 s 65, Sch 16 paras 62, 79(1), (2) with effect for the tax year 2011–12 and subsequent tax years, subject to transitional provisions in FA 2011 Sch 16 Pt 3.

[5]   In sub-para (4)(a), words repealed by FA 2013 s 51(1), (3) with effect for the tax year 2013–14 and subsequent tax years.

[1A—(1) Paragraph 1(1)(c) is to be omitted when deciding whether a lump sum to which this paragraph applies is a pension commencement lump sum.

(2) This paragraph applies to a lump sum if—

    (a) the sum is paid in respect of a money purchase arrangement,

    (b) the sum is paid before the member becomes entitled to the sum,

    (c) either—

        (i)   the sum is paid on or after 19 September 2013 but before 6 April 2015, or

        (ii) the sum is paid before 19 September 2013, a contract for a lifetime annuity is entered into to provide the pension in connection with which the sum is paid, and on or after 19 March 2014 the contract is cancelled, and

    (d) the member becomes entitled to the sum before 6 October 2015.

(3) Where—

    (a) a lump sum to which this paragraph applies is a pension commencement lump sum but would not be a pension commencement lump sum if sub-paragraph (1) were omitted, and

    (b) the lump sum is paid to the member in connection with a pension under the scheme to which it is expected that the member will become entitled ("the expected pension"),

no lump sum paid to the member out of the expected-pension fund is a pension commencement lump sum; and here "the expected-pension fund" means the sums and assets that from time to time represent the sums and assets that, when the lump sum mentioned in paragraph (a) was paid, were held for the purpose of providing the expected pension.

(4) For the purposes of sub-paragraph (2), if the circumstances are as described in sub-paragraph (2)(c)(ii), the member is treated as not having become entitled to the arranged pension as a result of the cancelled contract having been entered into; and here "the arranged pension" means the pension that would have been provided by that contract had it not been cancelled.][1]

Amendments—[1]   Para 1A inserted by FA 2014 s 43, Sch 5 para 1. This amendment is to be treated as having come into force on 19 March 2014 (FA 2014 Sch 5 para 15).

[1B—(1) When deciding whether a lump sum to which this paragraph applies is a pension commencement lump sum—

    (a) paragraph 1(1)(aa) and (c) and (3) are to be omitted,

    (b) paragraph 1(4) is to be treated as referring to the actual pension (see sub-paragraph (2)(h) of this paragraph), and

    (c) paragraph 2(2) is to be treated as referring to the arrangement under which the member was expected to become entitled to the expected pension (see sub-paragraph (2)(b) of this paragraph).

(2) This paragraph applies to a lump sum if—

    (a) the sum is paid in respect of a money purchase arrangement,

    (b) the sum is paid to the member in connection with a pension under a registered pension scheme to which it is expected that the member will become entitled ("the expected pension"),

    (c) the expected pension is income withdrawal, a lifetime annuity or a scheme pension,

    (d) the sum is paid before the member becomes entitled to the expected pension,

    (e) either—

        (i)   the sum is paid on or after 19 September 2013 but before 6 April 2015, or

        (ii) the sum is paid before 19 September 2013, a contract for a lifetime annuity is entered into to provide the expected pension, and on or after 19 March 2014 the contract is cancelled,

    (f) the sum is not repaid at any time before 6 October 2015,

(g) before the member becomes entitled to the expected pension, there is a recognised transfer of the sums and assets that immediately before the transfer represent the sums and assets that when the sum was paid were held for the purpose of providing the expected pension,

(h) the member becomes entitled before 6 October 2015 to a pension under the scheme to which the recognised transfer is made ("the actual pension"),

(i) the actual pension is income withdrawal, a lifetime annuity or a scheme pension, or some combination of them, and

(j) all of the sums and assets that represent the sums and assets transferred by the recognised transfer are used to provide the actual pension.

(3) If a lump sum to which this paragraph applies is a pension commencement lump sum, any lump sum paid—

(a) to the member,

(b) by the scheme to which the recognised transfer mentioned in sub-paragraph (2)(g) is made or by any other registered pension scheme (including the scheme from which the transfer was made), and

(c) in connection with the member's becoming entitled to the actual pension,

is not a pension commencement lump sum.

(4) For the purposes of sub-paragraph (2), if the circumstances are as described in sub-paragraph (2)(e)(ii), the member is treated as not having become entitled to the expected pension as a result of the cancelled contract having been entered into.][1]

Amendments—[1]   Para 1B inserted by FA 2014 s 43, Sch 5 para 2(1). This amendment is to be treated as having come into force on 19 March 2014 (FA 2014 Sch 5 para 15).

2—(1) If sub-paragraph (2) applies, the permitted maximum is nil.

(2) This sub-paragraph applies if all the member's rights under the arrangement under which the member becomes entitled to the relevant pension are attributable to a disqualifying pension credit.

(3) A pension credit is disqualifying if, when the member becomes entitled to it, the person subject to the corresponding pension debit has an actual (rather than a prospective) right to payment of a pension under the relevant arrangement.

(4) The relevant arrangement is the arrangement to which the pension sharing order or provision, by virtue of which the member becomes entitled to the pension credit, relates.

(5) If sub-paragraph (2) does not apply, the permitted maximum is the lower of—

(a) the available portion of the member's lump sum allowance, and

(b) the applicable amount, calculated in accordance with paragraph 3.

[(5A) But if the member dies before becoming entitled to the relevant pension in connection with which it was anticipated that the member would become entitled to the lump sum, the permitted maximum is the available portion of the member's lump sum allowance.][2]

(6) The available portion of the member's lump sum allowance is—

$$\frac{CSLA - AAC}{4}$$

where—

CSLA is the current standard lifetime allowance, and

AAC is the aggregate of the [relevant amount in the case of][1] each benefit crystallisation event which has occurred in relation to the member before the member becomes entitled to the lump sum, as adjusted under sub-paragraph (7) (and if no such benefit crystallisation event has occurred, is nil).

[(6A) Subject to sub-paragraph (6B), the relevant amount in the case of a benefit crystallisation event is the amount crystallised by it.][1]

[(6B) If the benefit crystallisation event is becoming entitled to a scheme pension under a money purchase arrangement, the relevant amount in the case of the benefit crystallisation event is the aggregate of—

(a) the amount of such of the sums held for the purposes of the pension scheme, and

(b) the market value of such of the assets held for the purposes of the pension scheme,

as are applied in (or in connection with) the purchase or provision of the scheme pension and any related dependants' scheme pension.][1]

(7) The adjustment of [the relevant amount in the case of][1] a previous benefit crystallisation event referred to in the definition of AAC is the multiplication of the amount by—

$$\frac{CSLA}{PSLA}$$

where—

CSLA is the current standard lifetime allowance, and

PSLA is the standard lifetime allowance at the time of the previous benefit crystallisation event.

[(7A) For the purposes of determining the available portion of the member's lump sum allowance—

(*a*) the fact that benefit crystallisation event 5 or benefit crystallisation event 5B has occurred in relation to the member is to be disregarded, and

(*b*) anything which, but for paragraph 2 or 15A of Schedule 32, would have been a benefit crystallisation event is to be treated as if it were such an event.][3]

(8) If the amount given by sub-paragraph (6) is negative, no portion of the member's lump sum allowance is available.

[(9) Sub-paragraph (10) applies if the member is a protected individual (but not if this paragraph applies with the modifications set out in paragraph 27 or 28 of Schedule 36).

(10) Sub-paragraphs (6) and (7) have effect[—

(*a*) where the member becomes entitled to the lump sum on or after 6 April 2014, as if PSLA in the case of any previous benefit crystallisation event which occurs on or after 6 April 2014 were £1,500,000 if that is greater than PSLA in that case, and

(*b*)][5] as if CSLA were £1,500,000 if that is greater than CSLA.

(11) The member is a "protected individual" if—

(*a*) paragraph 7 of Schedule 36 (primary protection) makes provision for a lifetime allowance enhancement factor in relation to the member, or

(*b*) at the time the member becomes entitled to the lump sum, paragraph 12 of that Schedule (enhanced protection) applies in relation to the member.][4]

Modifications—FA 2004 Sch 36 para 27 (modification of this paragraph if (and for so long as) FA 2004 Sch 36 para 12 applies in relation to the individual).

FA 2004 Sch 36 para 28 (modification of this paragraph if (and for so long as) FA 2004 Sch 36 para 12 does not apply in relation to the individual).

FA 2004 Sch 36 para 34 (entitlement to lump sums exceeding 25 per cent of uncrystallised rights: modification of this paragraph).

Pensions Schemes (Application of UK Provisions to Relevant Non-UK Schemes) Regulations, SI 2006/207 reg 15 (modification of this paragraph in respect of relevant non-UK schemes).

Taxation of Pension Schemes (Transitional Provisions) Order, SI 2006/572 art 19 (modification of this paragraph in the case of an individual who falls within FA 2004 Sch 36 para 20(1)).

Amendments—[1]   Words in sub-paras (6), (7) substituted, and sub-paras (6A), (6B) inserted, by FA 2006 s 161, Sch 23 paras 1, 23. These amendments are deemed to have come into force on 6 April 2006.

[2]   Sub-para (5A) inserted by FA 2007 s 70, Sch 20 paras 1, 11(1), (4), 24(3). These amendments are deemed always to have had effect.

[3]   Sub-para (7A) inserted by FA 2011 s 65, Sch 16 paras 23, 25 with effect for the tax year 2011–12 and subsequent tax years, subject to transitional provisions in FA 2011 Sch 16 Pt 3. The amendments made by FA 2011 Sch 16 paras 24–26, 31 and 79(2), (3) have effect in relation to any lump sum to which a person becomes entitled for the purposes of FA 2004 Part 4 on or after 6 April 2011 (FA 2011 Sch 16 para 101).

[4]   Sub-paras (9)–(11) inserted by FA 2013 s 48(5), Sch 22 paras 5, 8(1), (2) with effect for cases in which the member becomes entitled to the lump sum on or after 6 April 2014.

[5]   In sub-para (10) words inserted by FA 2016 Sch 4 para 28(1). This amendment is treated as having come into force on 6 April 2014.

3—(1) Where the member becomes entitled to income withdrawal, the applicable amount is one third of the aggregate of—

(*a*) the amount of the sums designated as available for the payment of [drawdown pension][6] on that occasion, and

(*b*) the market value of the assets so designated,

but subject to sub-paragraph (2).

(2) Any of the sums and assets so designated which represent rights attributable to a disqualifying pension credit are to be disregarded.

(3) Where the member becomes entitled to a lifetime annuity, the applicable amount is one third of the annuity purchase price.

(4) "The annuity purchase price" is the aggregate of—

(*a*) the amount of such of the sums held for the purposes of the pension scheme, and

(*b*) the market value of such of the assets held for the purposes of the pension scheme,

as are applied in (or in connection with) the purchase [of the lifetime annuity and any related dependants' annuity [and any related nominees' annuity[9]]][2], but subject to sub-paragraph (5).

[(4A) For the purposes of this Part a dependants' annuity is related to a lifetime annuity payable to a member of a registered pension scheme—

(*a*) if they are purchased either in the form of a joint life annuity or separately in circumstances in which the day on which the one is purchased is no earlier than seven days before, and no later than seven days after, the day on which the other is purchased, and

(*b*) the dependant's annuity will be payable to a dependant of the member.][2]

[(4B) For the purposes of this Part a nominees' annuity is related to a lifetime annuity payable to a member of a registered pension scheme—

    (*a*) if they are purchased either in the form of a joint life annuity or separately in circumstances in which the day on which the one is purchased is no earlier than seven days before, and no later than seven days after, the day on which the other is purchased, and

    (*b*) the nominees' annuity will be payable to a nominee of the member.][9]

[(5) There is to be deducted from that aggregate—

    (*a*) if the sums or assets applied in (or in connection with) the purchase of the annuity or any related dependants' annuity [or any related nominees' annuity][9] consist of or include sums or assets representing the whole or part of the [member's drawdown pension fund][6] [or of the member's flexi-access drawdown fund][8], the aggregate of the amount of those sums and the market value of those assets, and

    (*b*) in any case, so much (if any) of the sums or assets applied in (or in connection with) the purchase of the annuity or any related dependants' annuity [or any related nominees' annuity][9] as represents rights which are attributable to a disqualifying pension credit.][3]

(6) Where the member becomes entitled to a scheme pension [under a defined benefits arrangement][4], the applicable amount is—

$$\frac{LS + AC}{4}$$

but subject to sub-paragraph (8).

(7) In sub-paragraph (6)—

    LS is the amount of the lump sum, and

    [AC is—

      (*a*) in a case where the member becomes entitled to the pension before reaching the age of 75, the amount crystallised by reason of the member becoming entitled to the pension, disregarding paragraph 3 of Schedule 32, and

      (*b*) in a case where the member becomes entitled to the pension after reaching that age, the amount that would have been so crystallised (disregarding that paragraph) but for paragraph 2 of that Schedule.][5]

[(7A) Where the member becomes entitled to a scheme pension under a money purchase arrangement, the applicable amount is one third of the scheme pension purchase price.][4]

[(7B) "The scheme pension purchase price" is the aggregate of—

    (*a*) the amount of such of the sums held for the purposes of the pension scheme, and

    (*b*) the market value of such of the assets held for the purposes of the pension scheme,

as are applied in (or in connection with) the purchase or provision of the scheme pension and any related dependants' scheme pension, but subject to sub-paragraph (8).][4]

[(7C) For the purposes of this Part a dependants' scheme pension is related to a scheme pension payable to a member of a registered pension scheme if—

    (*a*) the day on which one is purchased or sums or assets are applied for its provision is no earlier than seven days before, and no later than seven days after, the day on which the other is purchased or sums or assets are applied for its provision, and

    (*b*) the dependants' scheme pension will be payable to a dependant of the member.][4]

(8) There is to be deducted from the aggregate of the amount of the lump sum and the amount crystallised [or from the scheme pension purchase price[4]]—

    (*a*) if the scheme pension is funded (in whole or in part) by the [application][1] of sums or assets representing the whole or part of the [member's drawdown pension fund][6] [or of the member's flexi-access drawdown fund][8], the aggregate of the amount of those sums and the market value of those assets, and

    (*b*) in any case, so much (if any) of the aggregate of the lump sum and the amount crystallised [or of the scheme pension purchase price][4] as represents rights which are attributable to a disqualifying pension credit.

[(8A) Sub-paragraphs (1) to (8) have effect subject to the following—

    (*a*) if—

      (i) paragraph 1A or 1B applies to the lump sum,

      (ii) the lump sum is paid more than 6 months before the day on which the member becomes entitled to it,

      (iii) a contract for a lifetime annuity is entered into to provide the pension in connection with which the lump sum is paid, and

      (iv) on or after 19 March 2014 the contract is cancelled, the applicable amount is one third of the annuity purchase price that would have been given by sub-paragraphs (4) to (5) in the case of that annuity had the contract not been cancelled, and

(b) if—

    (i) paragraph 1A or 1B applies to the lump sum,

    (ii) the lump sum is paid more than 6 months before the day on which the member becomes entitled to it, and

    (iii) paragraph (a) does not apply,

the applicable amount is one third of the sums, plus one third of the then market value of the assets, held at the time the lump sum is paid for the purpose of providing the pension at that time expected to be the pension in connection with which the lump sum is paid.

(8B) For the purposes of sub-paragraph (8A)(a)(ii), the member is treated as not having become entitled to a pension as a result of the cancelled contract having been entered into.][7]

[(9) Sub-paragraph (10) applies if—

    (a) sums or assets held for the purposes of, or representing accrued rights under, a money purchase arrangement relating to the member under a registered pension scheme ("member money purchase funds") are subject to a relevant surrender or a relevant transfer,

    (b) the sole or main purpose of the relevant surrender or relevant transfer is to increase the applicable amount on the member becoming entitled to a scheme pension, and

    (c) the member becomes entitled to a scheme pension under a relevant defined benefits arrangement.][4]

[(10) The pension scheme under which the relevant defined benefits arrangement is an arrangement is to be treated as making an unauthorised payment to the member of any amount by which—

    (a) the applicable amount in relation to the scheme pension under sub-paragraph (6), exceeds

    (b) the amount which would be that applicable amount under sub-paragraph (7A) if the arrangement were a money purchase arrangement.][4]

[(11) For the purposes of sub-paragraph (9)—

    (a) member money purchase funds are subject to a relevant surrender if they are surrendered and, in consequence of the surrender, there is a corresponding increase in the sums or assets held for the purposes of, or representing rights under, a defined benefits arrangement relating to the member under the pension scheme (or such an arrangement is established), and

    (b) member money purchase funds are subject to a relevant transfer if they are transferred so as to become held for the purposes of, or to represent rights under, a defined benefits arrangement relating to the member under any other registered pension scheme.][4]

[(12) In sub-paragraphs (9) and (10) "relevant defined benefits arrangement" means—

    (a) the defined benefits arrangement mentioned in paragraph (a) or (b) of sub-paragraph (11), or

    (b) any other defined benefits arrangement relating to the member (under the pension scheme or any other registered pension scheme) in the case of which any of the sums or assets held for the purposes of, or representing accrued rights under, the arrangement directly or indirectly represent sums or assets previously held for the purposes of, or representing accrued rights under, the defined benefits arrangement so mentioned.][4]

Modifications—FA 2004 Sch 36 para 29 (modification of this paragraph if (and for so long as) FA 2004 Sch 36 para 12 applies in relation to the individual).

Amendments—[1]   Word in sub-para (8) substituted by FA 2005 s 101, Sch 10 paras 24, 64(1) with effect from 6 April 2006.

[2]   Words in sub-para (4) substituted and sub-para (4A) inserted by FA 2005 s 101, Sch 10 paras 30, 64(1) with effect from 6 April 2006.

[3]   Sub-para (5) substituted and word in sub-para (7) inserted by FA 2005 s 101, Sch 10 paras 35, 64(1) with effect from 6 April 2006.

[4]   Words in sub-paras (6), (8) inserted, and sub-paras (7A)–(7C), (9)–(12) inserted, by FA 2006 s 161, Sch 23 paras 1, 22. These amendments are deemed to have come into force on 6 April 2006.

[5]   Definition of "AC" in sub-para (7) substituted by FA 2011 s 65, Sch 16 paras 23, 26 with effect for the tax year 2011–12 and subsequent tax years, subject to transitional provisions in FA 2011 Sch 16 Pt 3. The amendments made by FA 2011 Sch 16 paras 24–26, 31 and 79(2), (3) have effect in relation to any lump sum to which a person becomes entitled for the purposes of FA 2004 Part 4 on or after 6 April 2011 (FA 2011 Sch 16 para 101).

[6]   Words in sub-para (1)(a) substituted for words "unsecured pension", and words in sub-paras (5)(a), (8)(a) substituted for words "member's unsecured pension fund", by FA 2011 s 65, Sch 16 paras 62, 79(1), (3) with effect for the tax year 2011–12 and subsequent tax years, subject to transitional provisions in FA 2011 Sch 16 Pt 3. The amendments made by FA 2011 Sch 16 paras 24–26, 31 and 79(2), (3) have effect in relation to any lump sum to which a person becomes entitled for the purposes of FA 2004 Part 4 on or after 6 April 2011 (FA 2011 Sch 16 para 101).

[7]   Sub-paras (8A), (8B) inserted by FA 2014 s 43, Sch 5 para 4. This amendment is to be treated as having come into force on 19 March 2014 (FA 2014 Sch 5 para 15).

[8]   In sub-paras (5)(a), (8)(a), words inserted by the Taxation of Pensions Act 2014 s 1, Sch 1 paras 5, 22 with effect from 17 December 2014.

[9]   In sub-paras (4), (5), words inserted, and sub-para (4B) inserted, by FA 2015 s 34, Sch 4 paras 1, 14 with effect from 26 March 2015.

[3A—(1) Where this paragraph applies in relation to a pension commencement lump sum paid to the member, the pension scheme is to be treated as making to the member an unauthorised payment of the appropriate amount.

(2) Subject to [sub-paragraphs (3) to (4A)][2], this paragraph applies in relation to a pension commencement lump sum if—

    (a) because of the lump sum, the amount of the contributions paid by or on behalf of, or in respect of, the member to the pension scheme, or to any other registered pension scheme, is significantly greater than it otherwise would be, and

    (b) the member envisaged at the relevant time that that would be so.

(3) This paragraph does not apply in relation to any lump sum paid to the member on any day if the amount of the lump sum, when added to any other pension commencement lump sum paid to the member within the period of 12 months ending with that day, does not exceed [£7,500][3].

(4) This paragraph does not apply if the amount by which the contributions paid as mentioned in sub-paragraph (2)(a) is greater than it otherwise would be because of the lump sum does not exceed 30% of the amount of the lump sum.

[(4A) This paragraph does not apply if—

    (a) the member has reached the age of 75 when the contributions are paid as mentioned in sub-paragraph (2)(a), and

    (b) the contributions are not paid by an employer of the member.][2]

[(5) "The appropriate amount" is—

    (a) where the member becomes entitled to the lump sum before reaching the age of 75, so much of the amount crystallised by the benefit crystallisation event constituted by its payment (or the amount that would have been so crystallised but for paragraph 15A of Schedule 32) as does not exceed the amount of the member's lifetime allowance which is available on it;

    (b) where the member becomes entitled to the lump sum after reaching that age, the amount of the lump sum.][2]

(6) "The relevant time" is—

    (a) if paragraph (a) of sub-paragraph (2) is satisfied before the lump sum is paid, the time when that paragraph is first satisfied, and

    (b) otherwise, the time when the lump sum is paid.][1]

Commentary—*Simon's Taxes* **E7.224**.

Amendments—[1] This paragraph inserted by FA 2006 s 159. This amendment is deemed to have come into force on 6 April 2006.

[2] Words in sub-para (2) substituted for words "sub-paragraphs (3) and (4)", sub-para (4A) inserted, and sub-para (5) substituted, by FA 2011 s 65, Sch 16 paras 23, 27 with effect for the tax year 2011–12 and subsequent tax years, subject to transitional provisions in FA 2011 Sch 16 Pt 3. The amendments made by FA 2011 Sch 16 paras 27–30, 40, 42(2)(a), (3), 63, 77(4), 81(2), (4), 82(3)–(5) and 83 have effect in relation to lump sums paid on or after 6 April 2011 (FA 2011 Sch 16 para 102).

[3] In sub-para (3), figure substituted for words "1% of the standard lifetime allowance on that day" by the Taxation of Pensions Act 2014 s 1, Sch 1 para 70 with effect in relation to pension commencement lump sums paid on or after 6 April 2015.

Serious ill-health lump sum

4—(1) For the purposes of this Part a lump sum is a serious ill-health lump sum if—

    (a) before it is paid the scheme administrator has received evidence from a registered medical practitioner that the member is expected to live for less than one year,

    (b) it is paid when all or part of the member's lifetime allowance is available, [and][2]

    [(ca) either—

        (i) it is paid in respect of an uncrystallised arrangement, and it extinguishes the member's entitlement to benefits under the arrangement, or

        (ii) it is paid in respect of uncrystallised rights of the member under an arrangement other than an uncrystallised arrangement, and it extinguishes the member's uncrystallised rights under the arrangement.][2]

    (e) . . .[1]

(2) An uncrystallised arrangement is an arrangement in respect of which there has been no previous benefit crystallisation event.

[(2A) In subsection (1)(ca)(ii) "uncrystallised rights", in relation to the member, means rights of the member that are uncrystallised rights as defined by section 212(1) and (2).][2]

[(3) For the purposes of sub-paragraph (2)—

    (a) the fact that benefit crystallisation event 5 or benefit crystallisation event 5B has occurred in relation to the member is to be disregarded, and

    (b) anything which, but for paragraph 2 of Schedule 32, would have been a benefit crystallisation event is to be treated as if it were such an event.][1]

Commentary—*Simon's Taxes* **E7.224**.

Modifications—Pensions Schemes (Application of UK Provisions to Relevant Non-UK Schemes) Regulations, SI 2006/207 reg 15 (modification of this paragraph in respect of relevant non-UK schemes).

Registered Pension Schemes (Splitting of Schemes) Regulations, SI 2006/569 reg 3 (modification of this provision in relation to sub-scheme administrators).

Taxation of Pension Schemes (Transitional Provisions) Order, SI 2006/572 art 33 (modification of this paragraph in the case of an individual who meets certain conditions).

Amendments—[1]   Word in sub-para (1)(*c*) and the whole of sub-para (3) inserted, and sub-para (1)(*e*) and preceding word "and" repealed, by FA 2011 s 65, Sch 16 paras 23, 28 with effect for the tax year 2011–12 and subsequent tax years, subject to transitional provisions in FA 2011 Sch 16 Pt 3. The amendments made by FA 2011 Sch 16 paras 27–30, 40, 42(2)(*a*), (3), 63, 77(4), 81(2), (4), 82(3)–(5) and 83 have effect in relation to lump sums paid on or after 6 April 2011 (FA 2011 Sch 16 para 102).

[2]   Word in sub-para (1)(*b*) inserted, sub-para (1)(*ca*) substituted for previous sub-para (1)(*c*), (*d*), and sub-para (2A) inserted, by FA 2016 s 22, Sch 5 para 1(1), (3)–(5) with effect in relation to lump sums paid after 15 September 2016.

[Uncrystallised funds pension lump sum

4A—(1) For the purposes of this Part a lump sum is an uncrystallised funds pension lump sum if—

(*a*) it is paid on or after 6 April 2015 in respect of a money purchase arrangement,

(*b*) it is paid when all or part of the member's lifetime allowance is available,

(*c*) it is paid when the member has reached normal minimum pension age (or the ill-health condition is met),

(*d*) it is not a pension commencement lump sum,

(*e*) it is not a lump sum that, for the purposes of Part 9 of ITEPA 2003 (pension income), is treated by regulations under section 164(1)(*f*) and (2) as a trivial commutation lump sum paid to the member,

(*f*) immediately before the member becomes entitled to it, the sums or assets that are to be used to provide it—

(i) represent rights of the member under the scheme that are uncrystallised rights as defined by section 212(1) and (2), but

(ii) do not to any extent represent rights attributable to a disqualifying pension credit, and

(*g*) none of sub-paragraphs (3) to (5) applies to the member.

(2) But if a lump sum falling within sub-paragraph (1)—

(*a*) is paid when the member has not reached the age of 75, and

(*b*) exceeds the member's available lifetime allowance,

the excess is not an uncrystallised funds pension lump sum.

(3) This sub-paragraph applies to the member if—

(*a*) paragraph 12 of Schedule 36 applies to the member (enhanced protection from 6 April 2006) immediately before the sum is paid, and

(*b*) the lump sum condition (see paragraphs 24(2) and (3), 25 and 26 of Schedule 36) is met in relation to the member.

(4) This sub-paragraph applies to the member if—

(*a*) paragraph 7 of Schedule 36 makes provision for the operation of a lifetime allowance enhancement factor in relation to the member immediately before the sum is paid, and

(*b*) the lump sum condition (see paragraphs 24(2) and (3), 25 and 26 of Schedule 36) is met in relation to the member.

(5) This sub-paragraph applies to the member if—

(*a*) any of the provisions listed in sub-paragraph (6) makes provision for the operation of a lifetime allowance enhancement factor in relation to the member immediately before the sum is paid, and

(*b*) immediately before the sum is paid, the available portion of the member's lump sum allowance for the purposes of paragraph 2 of Schedule 29 is nil or less than 25% of the sum.

(6) The listed provisions are—

(*a*) paragraph 7 of Schedule 36 (primary protection);

(*b*) section 220 (pension credits from previously crystallised rights);

(*c*) section 221 (non-residence arrangements);

(*d*) section 224 (transfers from recognised overseas pensions schemes);

(*e*) paragraph 18 of Schedule 36 (pre-commencement pension credits).

(7) In sub-paragraph (1)(*f*) "disqualifying pension credit" is to be read in accordance with paragraph 2(3) and (4).][1]

Amendments—[1]   Paragraph 4A inserted by the Taxation of Pensions Act 2014 s 1, Sch 1 para 57 with effect from 17 December 2014.

Short service refund lump sum

5—(1) For the purposes of this Part a lump sum is a short service refund lump sum if—

(*a*) the pension scheme is an occupational pension scheme,

(*b*) the member's pensionable service was terminated before normal pension age but the member is not entitled to short service benefit by virtue of section 71 of the Pension Schemes Act 1993 (c 48) (basic principle as to short service benefit),

(*c*) there has been no previous benefit crystallisation event in relation to the member and the pension scheme, (*d*) it extinguishes the member's entitlement to benefits under the pension scheme [(except to the extent that it is prohibited from being extinguished by the payment of a lump sum by reason of the operation of provision made by or under any enactment)][1], and

(*e*) it is paid when the member has not reached the age of 75.

(2) But if a lump sum falling within sub-paragraph (1) exceeds an amount equal to the aggregate of the member's contributions under the pension scheme, the excess is not a short service refund lump sum.

[(2A) In sub-paragraph (2) the reference to the member's contributions includes—

(*a*) any amount paid under section 7 of the Social Security Act 1986 (incentive payments to schemes becoming contracted-out between 1986 and 1993),

(*b*) any amount paid by the Commissioners for Her Majesty's Revenue and Customs under section 42A(3) of the Pension Schemes Act 1993 or section 38A(3) of the Pension Schemes (Northern Ireland) Act 1993 (rebates), and

(*c*) any amount recovered by the member's employer under regulations falling within sub-paragraph (2B) in respect of minimum payments made to the scheme in relation to any period before 6 April 2012.

(2B) Those regulations are regulations which were made under—

(*a*) section 8(3) of the Pension Schemes Act 1993 (recovery of minimum payments), or

(*b*) section 4(3) of the Pension Schemes (Northern Ireland) Act 1993 (corresponding provision for Northern Ireland).][2]

(3) "Pensionable service", "normal pension age" and "short service benefit" have the same meaning as in the Pension Schemes Act 1993 (see section 181(1) of that Act).

Commentary—*Simon's Taxes* **E7.224**.

Modifications—Pensions Schemes (Application of UK Provisions to Relevant Non-UK Schemes) Regulations, SI 2006/207 reg 15 (modification of this paragraph in respect of relevant non-UK schemes).

Pension Protection Fund (Tax) Regulations, SI 2006/575 reg 11(1), (3) (modification of sub-para (1) above in respect of the payment of lump sums by the Pensions Protection Fund to an individual).

Amendments—[1]   Words in sub-para (1)(*d*) inserted by FA 2006 s 161, Sch 23 paras 1, 27. This amendment is deemed to have come into force on 6 April 2006.

[2]   Sub-paras (2A), (2B) inserted by FA 2013 s 52(1), (8) with effect from 6 April 2013.

Refund of excess contributions lump sum

6—(1) A lump sum is a refund of excess contributions lump sum if—

(*a*) it is paid in respect of a tax year in which the excess contributions condition is met in respect of the member, and

(*b*) it is paid before the end of the period of six years beginning with the last day of the tax year in respect of which it is paid.

(2) But if a lump sum falling within sub-paragraph (1) exceeds the member's available excess contributions allowance for the tax year in respect of which it is paid, the excess is not a refund of excess contributions lump sum.

(3) The excess contributions condition is met in respect of a member and a tax year if the amount of relievable pension contributions (see section 188(2) and (3)) paid in respect of the member in the tax year exceeds the maximum amount of relief to which the member is entitled for the tax year under section 190 (annual limit for relief).

(4) If no refund of excess contributions lump sum has been paid to the member in respect of a tax year (by any registered pension scheme), the available excess contributions allowance for that tax year is [(subject to sub-paragraph (7))[1]]—

$$RPC - MAR$$

(5) If one or more refund of excess contributions lump sums have been paid to the member in respect of a tax year, the available excess contributions allowance for that tax year is [(subject to sub-paragraph (7))[1]]—

$$RPC - MAR - ALS$$

or, if the amount resulting from that calculation is negative, is nil.

(6) In this paragraph—

RPC is the amount of the relievable pension contributions paid in respect of the member in the tax year,

MAR is the maximum amount of relief to which the member is entitled for the tax year under section 190, and

ALS is the aggregate of the refund of excess contributions lump sums previously paid to the member in respect of the tax year.

[(7) If any relief given in accordance with section 192(1) in relation to any contribution included in RPC is in excess of the maximum amount of relief to which the member is entitled under section 190, RPC is to be taken to be reduced by the amount of that excess.][1]

Amendments—[1] Words in sub-paras (4), (5) inserted, and sub-para (7) inserted, by FA 2006 s 161, Sch 23 paras 1, 28. These amendments are deemed to have come into force on 6 April 2006.

Trivial commutation lump sum

7—(1) For the purposes of this Part a lump sum is a trivial commutation lump sum if—

   (*a*) it is paid when no trivial commutation lump sum has previously been paid to the member (by any registered pension scheme) or, if such a lump sum has previously been paid, before the end of the commutation period,

   [(*aa*) it is paid in respect of a defined benefits arrangement,][3] [or in respect of a scheme pension payable by the scheme administrator to which the member has become entitled under a money purchase arrangement (an "in-payment money-purchase in-house scheme pension"), or partly in respect of the former and partly in respect of the latter,][4]

   (*b*) on the nominated date, the value of the member's pension rights does not exceed the commutation limit,

   (*c*) it is paid when all or part of the member's lifetime allowance is available,

   (*d*) it extinguishes [any entitlement to defined benefits[, and any entitlement to payments of in-payment money-purchase in-house scheme pensions,][4] that the member has][3] under the pension scheme, and

   (*e*) it is paid when the member has reached [normal minimum pension age (or the ill-health condition is met)][3] . . . [1].

(2) The commutation period is the period beginning with the day on which a trivial commutation lump sum is first paid to the member and ending 12 months after that day.

(3) The nominated date is the day within the period of three months ending with the first day of the commutation period nominated by the member (or, if no date is nominated, is the first day of the commutation period).

(4) The commutation limit is [£30,000][2].

[(4A) The Treasury may by order substitute for the amount for the time being specified in sub-paragraph (4) such larger amount as is specified in the order.][2]

(5) The value of the member's pension rights on the nominated date is the aggregate of—

   (*a*) the value of the member's relevant crystallised pension rights on that date (calculated in accordance with paragraph 8), and

   (*b*) the value of the member's uncrystallised rights on that date (calculated in accordance with paragraph 9).

Commentary—*Simon's Taxes* **E7.224**.

Modifications—Pensions Schemes (Application of UK Provisions to Relevant Non-UK Schemes) Regulations, SI 2006/207 reg 15 (modification of this paragraph in respect of relevant non-UK schemes).

Taxation of Pension Schemes (Transitional Provisions) Order, SI 2006/572 art 23C(1), (3) (modification of sub-para (1) above in respect of trivial commutation lump sums).

Taxation of Pension Schemes (Transitional Provisions) Order, SI 2006/572 art 23C(1), (4) (modification of this Schedule to insert new para 7A in respect of trivial commutation lump sums).

Amendments—[1] In sub-para (1)(*e*), words "but has not reached the age of 75" repealed by FA 2011 s 65, Sch 16 paras 23, 29 with effect for the tax year 2011–12 and subsequent tax years, subject to transitional provisions in FA 2011 Sch 16 Pt 3. The amendments made by FA 2011 Sch 16 paras 27–30, 40, 42(2)(*a*), (3), 63, 77(4), 81(2), (4), 82(3)–(5) and 83 have effect in relation to lump sums paid on or after 6 April 2011 (FA 2011 Sch 16 para 102).

[2] In sub-para (4), figure substituted for previous figure "£18,000" by FA 2014 s 42(1) with effect for commutation periods beginning on or after 27 March 2014 irrespective of whether the nominated date is before, on or after 27 March 2014.

[3] In sub-para (1), para (*aa*) inserted, in para (*d*) words substituted for words "the member's entitlement to benefits", and in para (*e*) words substituted for words "the age of 60", by the Taxation of Pensions Act 2014 s 1, Sch 1 para 71 with effect for commutation periods beginning on or after 6 April 2015 irrespective of whether the nominated date is before, on or after 6 April 2015.

[4] In sub-para (1)(*aa*), (*d*) words inserted by FA 2016 s 22, Sch 5 para 7 with effect in relation to lump sums paid after 15 September 2016.

8—(1) The value of the member's relevant crystallised pension rights on the nominated date is the aggregate of—

   (*a*) the value of the member's relevant crystallised pension rights on 5th April 2006, calculated in accordance with paragraph 10 of Schedule 36 (as if the member were the individual mentioned there) . . . [1], and

   (*b*) the aggregate of the amounts crystallised on benefit crystallisation events in the period beginning with 6th April 2006 and ending with the nominated date . . . [1].

(2), (3) . . . [1]

Amendments—[1] In sub-para (1)(*a*), (*b*) words repealed, and sub-paras (2), (3) repealed, by FA 2014 s 42(2) with effect for commutation periods beginning on or after 27 March 2014 irrespective of whether the nominated date is before, on or after 27 March 2014.

9—(1) The value of the member's uncrystallised rights on the nominated date is the aggregate value of the member's uncrystallised rights on that date under each arrangement relating to the member under a registered pension scheme.

(2) The value on the nominated date of the member's uncrystallised rights under such an arrangement is to be calculated in accordance with section 212 (valuation of uncrystallised rights for purposes of section 210).

Modification—Taxation of Pension Schemes (Transitional Provisions) Order, SI 2006/572 art 23C(1), (5) (modification of this Schedule to insert new para 9A in respect of trivial commutation lump sums).

Winding-up lump sum

10—(1) For the purposes of this Part a lump sum is a winding-up lump sum if—

    (a) the pension scheme is an occupational pension scheme,

    (b) the pension scheme is being wound-up,

    (c) [any person by whom the member is employed at the time when the lump sum is paid, and who has made contributions under the pension scheme in respect of the member within the period of five years ending with the day on which it is paid,][1] meets the conditions in sub-paragraph (3),

    (d) it is paid when all or part of the member's lifetime allowance is available, [and][2]

    (e) *it extinguishes the member's entitlement to benefits under the pension scheme,* . . . [2]

    (f) . . . [2]

(2) But if a lump sum falling within sub-paragraph (1) exceeds [£18,000,][3] the excess is not a winding-up lump sum.

[(2A) The Treasury may by order substitute for the amount for the time being specified in sub-paragraph (2) such larger amount as is specified in the order.][3]

(3) The conditions [referred to in paragraph (c) of sub-paragraph (1) are that the person mentioned in that paragraph[1]]—

    (a) . . . [1]

    (b) is not making contributions under any other registered pension scheme in respect of the member, and

    (c) undertakes to the Inland Revenue not to make such contributions during the period of one year beginning with the day on which the lump sum is paid.

Modifications—FA 2004 Sch 36 para 35(2) (modification of this paragraph in relation to former approved superannuation funds). Pensions Schemes (Application of UK Provisions to Relevant Non-UK Schemes) Regulations, SI 2006/207 reg 15 (modification of this paragraph in respect of relevant non-UK schemes).

Amendments—[1] Words in sub-paras (1)(c), (3) substituted, and sub-para (3)(a) repealed, by FA 2007 ss 70, 114, Sch 20 paras 1, 12, 24(6), Sch 27 Pt 3(2) with effect in relation to lump sums paid on or after 6 April 2006.

[2] Word in sub-para (1)(d) inserted, and sub-para (1)(f) and preceding word "and" repealed, by FA 2011 s 65, Sch 16 paras 23, 30 with effect for the tax year 2011–12 and subsequent tax years, subject to transitional provisions in FA 2011 Sch 16 Pt 3. The amendments made by FA 2011 Sch 16 paras 27–30, 40, 42(2)(a), (3), 63, 77(4), 81(2), (4), 82(3)–(5) and 83 have effect in relation to lump sums paid on or after 6 April 2011 (FA 2011 Sch 16 para 102).

[3] In sub-para (2), figure substituted for words "1% of the standard lifetime allowance when the lump sum is paid,", and sub-para (2A) inserted, by FA 2011 s 67, Sch 18 paras 3, 5 with effect for the year 2012–13 and subsequent tax years, subject to transitional provisions in FA 2011 Sch 18 para 14.

Lifetime allowance excess lump sum

11 For the purposes of this Part a lump sum is a lifetime allowance excess lump sum if—

    (a) it is paid when none of the member's lifetime allowance is available,

    (b) it is not a short service refund lump sum or a refund of excess contributions lump sum,

    (c) it does not reduce the rate of payment of any pension to which the member has become (actually) entitled, or extinguish the member's entitlement to payment of any such pension,

    (d) it is paid when the member has reached normal minimum pension age (or the ill-health condition is met), and

    (e) it is paid when the member has not reached the age of 75.

Modifications—Pensions Schemes (Application of UK Provisions to Relevant Non-UK Schemes) Regulations, SI 2006/207 reg 15 (modification of this paragraph in respect of relevant non-UK schemes).
FA 2004 Sch 36 para 35(3) (modification of this paragraph in relation to former approved superannuation funds).

[Transitional 2013/14 lump sum, and its related trivial commutation lump sum

11A—(1) A lump sum is a transitional 2013/14 lump sum for the purposes of this Part if—

    (a) the sum ("the earlier sum") is paid to the member in connection with a pension under a registered pension scheme to which it is expected that the member will become entitled ("the expected pension"),

    (b) the earlier sum is paid before the member becomes entitled to the expected pension,

    (c) either—

    (i)   the earlier sum is paid on or after 19 September 2013 but before 27 March 2014, or

    (ii) the earlier sum is paid before 19 September 2013, a contract for a lifetime annuity is entered into to provide the expected pension, and on or after 19 March 2014 the contract is cancelled,

  (*d*) all of the sums and assets for the time being representing the sums and assets that when the earlier sum was paid were held for the purpose of providing the expected pension are, before the member becomes entitled to the expected pension, used in paying a further lump sum to the member ("the further sum"),

  (*e*) the further sum is paid on or after 6 July 2014 but before 6 April 2015, and

  (*f*) the further sum is a trivial commutation lump sum (see sub-paragraph (2)).

(2) Sub-paragraph (4) applies when deciding under paragraph 7 whether the further sum is a trivial commutation lump sum in a case where the earlier sum is paid before the nominated date (see paragraph 7(3) for the meaning of "the nominated date").

(3) If the earlier sum is a transitional 2013/14 lump sum, and the earlier sum and the further sum are not the only lump sums paid under registered pension schemes to the member, sub-paragraph (4) applies when deciding under paragraph 7 whether any other lump sum paid under a registered pension scheme to the member is a trivial commutation lump sum.

(4) If this sub-paragraph applies, the payment of the earlier sum is to be treated for the purposes of paragraph 8(1)(*b*) as a benefit crystallisation event—

  (*a*) which occurs when the earlier sum is paid, and

  (*b*) on which the amount crystallised is the amount of the earlier sum.

(5) If the earlier sum is a transitional 2013/14 lump sum, and only the sums and assets mentioned in sub-paragraph (1)(*d*) are used in paying the further sum, section 636B of ITEPA 2003 applies in relation to the further sum with the omission of its subsection (3).

(6) If the earlier sum is a transitional 2013/14 lump sum, and the sums and assets mentioned in sub-paragraph (1)(*d*) are used together with other sums and assets in paying the further sum—

  (*a*) section 636B of ITEPA 2003 applies in relation to the further sum as if instead of the further sum there were two separate trivial commutation lump sums as follows—

    (i)   one ("the first part of the further sum") consisting of so much of the further sum as is attributable to the sums and assets mentioned in sub-paragraph (1)(*d*), and

    (ii) another consisting of the remainder of the further sum,

  (*b*) the first part of the further sum is to be treated for the purposes of section 636B of ITEPA 2003 as having been paid immediately before the remainder of the further sum,

  (*c*) section 636B of ITEPA 2003 applies in relation to the first part of the further sum with the omission of its subsection (3), and

  (*d*) for the purposes of applying section 636B(3) of ITEPA 2003 in relation to the remainder of the further sum, the rights to which the first part of the further sum relates are to be treated as rights that are not uncrystallised rights immediately before the remainder of the further sum is paid.

(7) For the purposes of sub-paragraph (1), if the circumstances are as described in sub-paragraph (1)(*c*)(ii), the member is treated as not having become entitled to the expected pension as a result of the cancelled contract having been entered into.][1]

Amendments—[1] Para 11A inserted by FA 2014 s 43, Sch 5 para 5(2). This amendment is to be treated as having come into force on 19 March 2014 (FA 2014 Sch 5 para 15).

Interpretation of Part 1

12—(1) Expressions used in this Part of this Schedule and in Schedule 28 have the same meaning in this Part of this Schedule as in Schedule 28.

[(1A) For the purposes of determining whether all or part of the member's lifetime allowance is available—

  (*a*) the fact that benefit crystallisation event 5 or benefit crystallisation event 5B has occurred in relation to the member is to be disregarded, and

  (*b*) anything which, but for paragraph 2 or 15A of Schedule 32, would have been a benefit crystallisation event is to be treated as if it were such an event.][1]

(2) Where all or part of the member's lifetime allowance is available immediately before a lump sum is paid, sub-paragraph (3) applies to the lump sum if—

  (*a*) its amount exceeds the member's available lifetime allowance, and

  (*b*) but for that fact, it would satisfy all the requirements of paragraph 1(1), 4(1), [4A(1),][2] 7(1) or 10(1).

(3) For the purposes of this Schedule, the whole of the lump sum (and not only so much of it as does not exceed the member's available lifetime allowance) is to be treated as paid when all or part of the member's lifetime allowance is available.

(4) But sub-paragraph (3) does not apply—

(a) in the case of a lump sum that would satisfy all the requirements of paragraph 1(1), to so much of it as would be prevented from being a pension commencement lump sum by paragraph 1(2),

[(aa) in the case of a lump sum that would satisfy all the requirements of paragraph 4A(1) and is paid when the member has not reached the age of 75, to so much of it as would be prevented from being an uncrystallised funds pension lump sum by paragraph 4A(2),]² and

(b) in the case of a lump sum that would satisfy all the requirements of paragraph 10(1), to so much of it as would be prevented from being a winding-up lump sum by paragraph 10(2).

(5) Where by virtue of paragraph 1(2), [4A(2),]² 5(2), 6(2) or 10(2) an excess is not an authorised lump sum of one description, that does not prevent the excess being an authorised lump sum of another description.

(6) "Authorised lump sum" means a lump sum authorised to be paid by the lump sum rule.

Amendments—¹ Sub-para (1A) inserted by FA 2011 s 65, Sch 16 paras 23, 31 with effect for the tax year 2011–12 and subsequent tax years, subject to transitional provisions in FA 2011 Sch 16 Pt 3. The amendments made by FA 2011 Sch 16 paras 24–26, 31 and 79(2), (3) have effect in relation to any lump sum to which a person becomes entitled for the purposes of FA 2004 Part 4 on or after 6 April 2011 (FA 2011 Sch 16 para 101).

² In sub-paras (2)(b), (5) words inserted, sub-para (4)(aa) inserted, by the Taxation of Pensions Act 2014 s 1, Sch 1 paras 58–60 with effect from 17 December 2014.

PART 2
LUMP SUM DEATH BENEFIT RULE

DEFINED BENEFITS ARRANGEMENTS
Defined benefits lump sum death benefit

13 [(1)] For the purposes of this Part a lump sum death benefit is a defined benefits lump sum death benefit if—

    (a) . . . ¹

    (b) it is paid in respect of a defined benefits arrangement,

    (c) . . . ¹ and

    (d) it is not a pension protection lump sum death benefit, trivial commutation lump sum death benefit or winding-up lump sum death benefit.]¹

. . . ²

(2) . . . ²

Amendments—¹ Sub-para (1) numbered as such, sub-para (1)(a), (c) repealed, and words in sub-para (1) inserted, and sub-para (2) inserted, by FA 2011 s 65, Sch 16 paras 32, 33 with effect for the tax year 2011–12 and subsequent tax years, subject to transitional provisions in FA 2011 Sch 16 Pt 3. The amendments made by FA 2011 Sch 16 paras 33–39, 41, 42(2)(b), (c), (4), (5), 65, 67, 68, 75(a), 76, 77(5), 79(4), 82(6) have effect in relation to deaths occurring on or after 6 April 2011 (FA 2011 Sch 16 para 103).

² In sub-para (1), sentence repealed, and sub-para (2) repealed, by F(No 2)A 2015 s 21(8) with effect in relation to lump sums paid on or after 6 April 2016.

Pension protection lump sum death benefit

14—(1) For the purposes of this Part a lump sum death benefit is a pension protection lump sum death benefit if—

    (a) . . . ¹

    (b) it is paid in respect of a defined benefits arrangement,

    (c) it is paid in respect of a scheme pension to which the member was entitled at the date of the member's death, and

    (d) the member has specified that it is to be treated as a pension protection lump sum death benefit (instead of a defined benefits lump sum death benefit).

(2) But if the amount of a lump sum falling within sub-paragraph (1) exceeds the pension protection limit, the excess is not a pension protection lump sum death benefit.

(3) The pension protection limit is—

$$AC - AP - TPLS$$

where—

    [AC is—

        (a) in a case where the member became entitled to the pension before reaching the age of 75, the amount crystallised by reason of the member becoming entitled to the pension, and

        (b) in a case where the member became entitled to the pension after having reached that age, the amount that would have been so crystallised but for paragraph 2 of Schedule 32,]¹

    AP is the amount of the pension paid in respect of the period between the member becoming entitled to the pension and the member's death, and

TPLS is the total amount of pension protection lump sum death benefit previously paid in respect of the pension under this paragraph.

Modifications—FA 2004 Sch 36 para 36 (modification of this paragraph if the member dies, having reached the age of 75 and before the end of the guarantee period).

Taxation of Pension Schemes (Transitional Provisions) Order, SI 2006/572 art 33 (modification of this paragraph in the case of an individual who meets certain conditions).

Amendments—[1] Sub-para (1)(*a*) repealed, and in sub-para (3) words substituted for words "AC is the amount crystallised by reason of the member becoming entitled to the pension (see section 216)", by FA 2011 s 65, Sch 16 paras 32, 34 with effect for the tax year 2011–12 and subsequent tax years, subject to transitional provisions in FA 2011 Sch 16 Pt 3. The amendments made by FA 2011 Sch 16 paras 33–39, 41, 42(2)(b), (c), (4), (5), 65, 67, 68, 75(a), 76, 77(5), 79(4), 82(6) have effect in relation to deaths occurring on or after 6 April 2011 (FA 2011 Sch 16 para 103).

MONEY PURCHASE ARRANGEMENTS

Uncrystallised funds lump sum death benefit

15—(1) For the purposes of this Part a lump sum death benefit is an uncrystallised funds lump sum death benefit if—

(*a*) . . . [1]

(*b*) it is paid in respect of a money purchase arrangement,

(*c*) . . . [1]

(*d*) it is paid in respect of relevant uncrystallised funds[, and

(*e*) it is not a charity lump sum death benefit.][1]

. . . [3]

(1A) . . . [3]

(2) "Relevant uncrystallised funds" means such of the sums and assets held for the purposes of the arrangement at the member's death as—

(*a*) had not been applied for purchasing a scheme pension, a lifetime annuity, [a nominees' annuity,][4] a dependants' scheme pension or a dependants' annuity, and

(*b*) had not been designated under the arrangement as available for the payment of [drawdown pension][2].

[(2A) Where—

(*a*) the arrangement is a cash balance arrangement,

(*b*) under the arrangement, a dependant of the member is entitled to be paid after the member's death an amount by way of a lump sum,

(*c*) the dependant's entitlement to a lump sum of that amount under the arrangement comes into being at a time no later than the member's death,

(*d*) such of the sums and assets held for the purposes of the arrangement immediately after the member's death as are held for the purpose of meeting the liability to pay the lump sum are insufficient for that purpose (including where that is because none are held for that purpose), and

(*e*) a person who was an employer in relation to the member pays a contribution to the scheme—

(i) for or towards making good that insufficiency, and

(ii) of no more than is needed for making good the insufficiency,

the sums and assets held for the purposes of the arrangement that represent the contribution are to be treated as "relevant uncrystallised funds" for the purposes of this paragraph.][5]

(3) But if an amount falling within sub-paragraph (1) exceeds the permitted maximum, the excess is not an uncrystallised funds lump sum death benefit.

(4) The permitted maximum is the aggregate of—

(*a*) the amount of the sums, and

(*b*) the market value of the assets,

which constitute the relevant uncrystallised funds immediately before the payment is made.

Commentary—*Simon's Taxes* E7.224.

Amendments—[1] Sub-para (1)(*a*), (*c*) repealed, and sub-para (1)(*e*) and preceding word "and" inserted, by FA 2011 s 65, Sch 16 paras 32, 35 with effect for the tax year 2011–12 and subsequent tax years, subject to transitional provisions in FA 2011 Sch 16 Pt 3. The amendments made by FA 2011 Sch 16 paras 33–39, 41, 42(2)(b), (c), (4), (5), 65, 67, 68, 75(a), 76, 77(5), 79(4), 82(6) have effect in relation to deaths occurring on or after 6 April 2011 (FA 2011 Sch 16 para 103).

[2] Words in sub-para (2)(*b*) substituted for words "unsecured pension" by FA 2011 s 65, Sch 16 paras 62, 79(1), (4) with effect for the tax year 2011–12 and subsequent tax years, subject to transitional provisions in FA 2011 Sch 16 Pt 3. The amendments made by FA 2011 Sch 16 paras 33–39, 41, 42(2)(b), (c), (4), (5), 65, 67, 68, 75(a), 76, 77(5), 79(4), 82(6) have effect in relation to deaths occurring on or after 6 April 2011 (FA 2011 Sch 16 para 103).

[3] In sub-para (1) words repealed, and sub-para (1A) repealed, by the Taxation of Pensions Act 2014 s 3, Sch 2 para 19(1) with effect for lump sums paid on or after 6 April 2015.

[4] Words in sub-para (2)(*a*) inserted by FA 2015 s 34, Sch 4 paras 1, 15 with effect from 26 March 2015.

[5] Sub-para (2A) inserted by FA 2016 s 22, Sch 5 para 10 with effect in relation to contributions paid after 15 September 2016.

Annuity protection lump sum death benefit

16—(1) For the purposes of this Part a lump sum death benefit is an annuity protection lump sum death benefit if—

    (a) . . . [1]

    (b) it is paid in respect of a money purchase arrangement, and

    (c) it is paid in respect of a scheme pension or lifetime annuity to which the member was entitled at the date of the member's death.

(2) But if the amount of a lump sum falling within sub-paragraph (1) exceeds the annuity protection limit, the excess is not an annuity protection lump sum death benefit.

(3) The annuity protection limit is—

$$AC - AP - TPLS$$

where—

    [AC is—

        (a) in a case where the member became entitled to the pension or annuity before reaching the age of 75, the amount crystallised by reason of the member becoming entitled to the pension or annuity, disregarding paragraphs 3 and 4 of Schedule 32, and

        (b) in a case where the member became entitled to the pension or annuity after having reached that age, the amount that would have been so crystallised (disregarding those paragraphs) but for paragraph 2 of that Schedule,][1]

    AP is the amount of the pension paid in respect of the period between the member becoming entitled to the pension or annuity and the member's death, and

    TPLS is the total amount of annuity protection lump sum death benefit previously paid in respect of the pension or annuity under this paragraph.

Modifications—FA 2004 Sch 36 para 36 (modification of this paragraph if the member dies, having reached the age of 75 and before the end of the guarantee period).

Taxation of Pension Schemes (Transitional Provisions) Order, SI 2006/572 art 33 (modification of this paragraph in the case of an individual who meets certain conditions).

Amendments—[1] Sub-para (1)(a) repealed and definition of "AC" in sub-para (3) substituted by FA 2011 s 65, Sch 16 paras 32, 36 with effect for the tax year 2011–12 and subsequent tax years, subject to transitional provisions in FA 2011 Sch 16 Pt 3. The amendments made by FA 2011 Sch 16 paras 33–39, 41, 42(2)(b), (c), (4), (5), 65, 67, 68, 75(a), 76, 77(5), 79(4), 82(6) have effect in relation to deaths occurring on or after 6 April 2011 (FA 2011 Sch 16 para 103).

[Drawdown pension fund lump sum death benefit][1]

17—[(1) For the purposes of this Part a lump sum death benefit is a drawdown pension fund lump sum death benefit if—

    (a) it is paid in respect of income withdrawal to which the member was entitled [to be paid from the member's drawdown pension fund in respect of][2] an arrangement at the date of the member's death, and

    (b) it is not a charity lump sum death benefit.][1]

(2) A lump sum death benefit is also [a drawdown pension fund lump sum death benefit][1] if—

    (a) it is paid on the death of a dependant of the member,

    (b) . . . [1]

    (c) it is paid in respect of dependants' income withdrawal to which the dependant was entitled at the date of the dependant's death [to be paid from the dependant's drawdown pension fund][2] in respect of an arrangement relating to the member[, and

    (d) it is not a charity lump sum death benefit.][1]

(3) But if the amount of a lump sum falling within sub-paragraph (1) or (2) exceeds the permitted maximum, the excess is not [a drawdown pension fund lump sum death benefit][1].

(4) The permitted maximum is the aggregate of—

    (a) the amount of the sums, and

    (b) the market value of the assets,

representing the member's or dependant's [drawdown pension fund][1] in respect of the arrangement immediately before the payment is made.

Modifications—FA 2004 Sch 36 para 36 (modification of this paragraph if the member dies, having reached the age of 75 and before the end of the guarantee period).

Amendments—[1] Heading substituted for previous heading "Unsecured pension fund lump sum death benefit", sub-para (1) substituted, words in sub-paras (2), (3) substituted for words "an unsecured pension fund lump sum death benefit", words in sub-para (4) substituted for words "unsecured pension fund", sub-para (2)(b) repealed and sub-para (2)(d) and preceding word "and" inserted, by FA 2011 s 65, Sch 16 paras 32, 37 with effect for the tax year 2011–12 and subsequent tax years, subject to transitional provisions in FA 2011 Sch 16 Pt 3. The amendments made by FA 2011 Sch 16 paras 33–39, 41, 42(2)(b), (c), (4), (5), 65, 67, 68, 75(a), 76, 77(5), 79(4), 82(6) have effect in relation to deaths occurring on or after 6 April 2011 (FA 2011 Sch 16 para 103).

2 In sub-para (1)(*a*) words substituted for word "under", and in sub-para (2)(*c*) words inserted, by the Taxation of Pensions Act 2014 s 1, Sch 1 paras 5, 23 with effect from 17 December 2014.

[*Flexi-access drawdown fund lump sum death benefit*

17A—(1) For the purposes of this Part a lump sum death benefit is a flexi-access drawdown fund lump sum death benefit if—

> (*a*) it is paid in respect of income withdrawal to which the member was entitled to be paid from the member's flexi-access drawdown fund in respect of an arrangement at the date of the member's death, and
>
> (*b*) it is not a charity lump sum death benefit.

(2) A lump sum death benefit is also a flexi-access drawdown fund lump sum death benefit if—

> (*a*) it is paid on the death of a dependant of the member,
>
> (*b*) it is paid in respect of dependants' income withdrawal to which the dependant was at the date of the dependant's death entitled to be paid from the dependant's flexi-access drawdown fund in respect of an arrangement relating to the member, and
>
> (*c*) it is not a charity lump sum death benefit.

(3) A lump sum death benefit is also a flexi-access drawdown fund lump sum death benefit if—

> (*a*) it is paid on the death of a nominee of the member,
>
> (*b*) it is paid in respect of nominees' income withdrawal to which the nominee was at the date of the nominee's death entitled to be paid from the nominee's flexi-access drawdown fund in respect of an arrangement relating to the member, and
>
> (*c*) it is not a charity lump sum death benefit.

(4) A lump sum death benefit is also a flexi-access drawdown fund lump sum death benefit if—

> (*a*) it is paid on the death of a successor of the member,
>
> (*b*) it is paid in respect of successors' income withdrawal to which the successor was at the date of the successor's death entitled to be paid from the successor's flexi-access drawdown fund in respect of an arrangement relating to the member, and
>
> (*c*) it is not a charity lump sum death benefit.

(5) But if the amount of a lump sum falling within sub-paragraph (1), (2), (3) or (4) exceeds the permitted maximum, the excess is not a flexi-access drawdown fund lump sum death benefit.

(6) The permitted maximum is the aggregate of—

> (*a*) the amount of the sums, and
>
> (*b*) the market value of the assets,

representing the member's, dependant's, nominee's or successor's flexi-access drawdown fund in respect of the arrangement immediately before the payment is made.][1]

Amendments—[1] Para 17A inserted by the Taxation of Pensions Act 2014 s 1, Sch 1 paras 5, 24 with effect from 17 December 2014.

Charity lump sum death benefit

18—(1) A lump sum death benefit is a charity lump sum death benefit if—

> (*a*) . . .[2]
>
> (*b*) there are no dependants of the member,
>
> (*c*) it is paid [in respect of the member's drawdown pension fund][2] in respect of an arrangement[, or in respect of the member's flexi-access drawdown fund in respect of an arrangement,][3] at the date of the member's death, and
>
> (*d*) it is paid to a charity nominated by the member . . .[2]
>
> [(1A) A lump sum death benefit is also a charity lump sum death benefit if—
>
>> (*a*) . . .[5]
>>
>> (*b*) there are no dependants of the member,
>>
>> (*c*) it is paid in respect of relevant uncrystallised funds in respect of a money purchase arrangement at the date of the member's death, and
>>
>> (*d*) it is paid to a charity nominated by the member.
>
> (1B) "Relevant uncrystallised funds" has the meaning given by paragraph 15(2).][2]

(2) A lump sum death benefit is also a charity lump sum death benefit if—

> (*a*) it is paid on the death of a dependant of the member,
>
> (*b*) . . .[2]
>
> (*c*) there are no other dependants of the member,

(*d*) it is paid in respect of [the dependant's drawdown pension fund]²[, or the dependant's flexi-access drawdown fund,]³ at the date of the dependant's death in respect of an arrangement relating to the member, and

(*e*) it is paid to a charity nominated by the member [or, if the member made no nomination, by the dependant]¹ . . . ²

[(2A) A lump sum death benefit is also a charity lump sum death benefit if—

   (*a*) it is paid on the death of an individual who is—

      (i) a nominee of the member, or

      (ii) a successor of the member,

   (*b*) there are no dependants of the member,

   (*c*) it is paid in respect of the individual's nominee's flexi-access drawdown fund or successor's flexi-access drawdown fund at the date of the individual's death in respect of an arrangement relating to the individual in the capacity of a nominee or successor of the member, and

   (*d*) it is paid to a charity nominated by the member or, if the member made no nomination, by the individual.]⁴

(3) But if the amount of a lump sum falling within sub-paragraph (1)[, (2) or (2A)]⁴ exceeds the permitted maximum, the amount of the excess is not a charity lump sum death benefit.

(4) The permitted maximum is the aggregate of—

   (*a*) the amount of the sums, and

   (*b*) the market value of the assets,

[representing what is the member's or dependant's drawdown pension fund]²[, or flexi-access drawdown fund,]³ in respect of the arrangement[, or the nominee's or successor's flexi-access drawdown fund in respect of the arrangement,]⁴ immediately before the payment is made.

Commentary—*Simon's Taxes* **E7.224**.

HMRC Manuals—Registered Pension Schemes Manual RPSM10105390–10105410 (conditions for payment of a charity lump sum benefit).

Amendments—¹ In sub-para (2)(*e*), words substituted by FA 2007 s 69, Sch 19 paras 1, 16(1), (5) with effect from 6 April 2007.

²   Sub-paras (1)(*a*), (2)(*b*) repealed, in sub-para (1)(*d*) words "(or, if the member made no nomination, selected by the scheme administrator)" repealed, in sub-para (2)(*e*) words "(or, if neither the member nor the dependant made a nomination, selected by the scheme administrator)" repealed, words in sub-para (1)(*c*) substituted for words "in respect of the member's alternatively secured pension fund (or what would be the member's alternatively secured pension fund but for paragraph 11(6) and (7) of Schedule 28)", words in sub-para (2)(*d*) substituted for words "the dependant's alternatively secured pension fund", words in sub-para (4) substituted for words "representing what is (or but for paragraph 11(6) and (7) of Schedule 28 would be) the member's or dependant's alternatively secured pension fund", and sub-paras (1A), (1B) inserted, by FA 2011 s 65, Sch 16 paras 32, 38 with effect for the tax year 2011–12 and subsequent tax years, subject to transitional provisions in FA 2011 Sch 16 Pt 3. The amendments made by FA 2011 Sch 16 paras 33–39, 41, 42(2)(b), (c), (4), (5), 65, 67, 68, 75(a), 76, 77(5), 79(4), 82(6) have effect in relation to deaths occurring on or after 6 April 2011 (FA 2011 Sch 16 para 103).

³   In sub-paras (1)(*c*), (2)(*d*), (4) words inserted by the Taxation of Pensions Act 2014 s 1, Sch 1 paras 5, 25 with effect from 17 December 2014.

⁴   Sub-para (2A) inserted, in sub-para (3) words substituted for words "or (2)", and in sub-para (4) words inserted, by the Taxation of Pensions Act 2014 s 3, Sch 2 para 15 with effect from 17 December 2014.

⁵   Sub-para (1A)(*a*) repealed by FA 2016 s 22, Sch 5 para 5 with effect in relation to lump sums paid after 15 September 2016.

DEFINED BENEFITS AND MONEY PURCHASE ARRANGEMENTS

Trivial commutation lump sum death benefit

20—(1) A lump sum death benefit is a trivial commutation lump sum death benefit [if condition A or B is met.]²

[(1A) Condition A is that the lump sum—

   (*a*) is paid to a dependant entitled under the pension scheme to pension death benefit in respect of the member, and

   (*b*) extinguishes the dependant's entitlement under the pension scheme to pension death benefit and lump sum death benefit in respect of the member.

(1B) Condition B is that—

   (*a*) the lump sum is paid after the member's death to an individual entitled to be paid a pension under the scheme—

      (i) which the member was entitled to be paid immediately before the member's death, and

      (ii) which is payable to the individual under pension rule 2 (see section 165),

   (*b*) if the pension is an annuity or scheme pension payable by an insurance company, the lump sum extinguishes all entitlements in respect of the member under the contract concerned, and

(c) if the pension is a scheme pension payable by the scheme administrator, the lump sum extinguishes all entitlements to receive a scheme pension in respect of the member from the scheme administrator under pension rule 2.][2]

(2) But if the amount of a lump sum falling within sub-paragraph (1) exceeds [£30,000,][2] the excess is not a trivial commutation lump sum death benefit.

[(3) The Treasury may by order substitute for the amount for the time being specified in sub-paragraph (2) such larger amount as is specified in the order.][1]

Commentary—*Simon's Taxes* **E7.224.**

HMRC Manuals—Registered Pension Schemes Manual RPSM10105260 (a trivial commutation lump sum death benefit may be paid from any form of arrangement).

Amendments—[1]   In sub-para (2), sub-para (3) inserted by FA 2011 s 67, Sch 18 paras 3, 6 with effect for the year 2012–13 and subsequent tax years, subject to transitional provisions in FA 2011 Sch 18 para 14.

[2]   In sub-para (1), words substituted, sub-paras (1A), (1B) inserted, and in sub-para (2), figure substituted for previous figure "£18,000", by the Taxation of Pensions Act 2014 s 1, Sch 1 para 74(1)–(4) with effect in relation to lump sum death benefits paid on or after 6 April 2015.

[Life cover lump sum

21A   For the purposes of this Part a lump sum death benefit is a life cover lump sum if—

(a) the member had reached the age of 75 before he died;

(b) payment of the sum would not have prejudiced approval of the scheme for the purposes of Chapter 1 of Part 14 of ICTA if it had been made on 5th April 2006.]

Modifications—Taxation of Pension Schemes (Transitional Provisions) Order, SI 2006/572 arts 6, 8(1), (3) (insertion of the above paragraph in the case of a member of a registered pension scheme who satisfies certain conditions).

INTERPRETATION

Interpretation of Part 2

22—(1) Expressions used in this Part of this Schedule and in Schedule 28 have the same meaning in this Part of this Schedule as in Schedule 28.

(2) Where by virtue of paragraph 14(2), 20(2) or 21(2) an excess is not an authorised lump sum death benefit of one description, that does not prevent the excess being an authorised lump sum death benefit of another description.

(3) "Authorised lump sum death benefit" means a lump sum death benefit authorised to be paid by the lump sum death benefit rule.

[SCHEDULE 29A

TAXABLE PROPERTY HELD BY INVESTMENT-REGULATED PENSION SCHEMES

Section 174A][1]

Amendments—[1]   This Schedule inserted by FA 2006 s 158, Sch 21 paras 2, 13. This amendment is deemed to have come into force on 6 April 2006.

[PART 1

INVESTMENT-REGULATED PENSION SCHEMES][1]

Amendments—[1]   This Schedule inserted by FA 2006 s 158, Sch 21 paras 2, 13. This amendment is deemed to have come into force on 6 April 2006.

[Schemes other than occupational pension schemes

1—(1) For the purposes of the taxable property provisions a registered pension scheme which is not an occupational pension scheme is an investment-regulated pension scheme if one or more of its members meets the condition in sub-paragraph (2).

(2) The condition is that either—

(a) the member, or

(b) a person related to the member,

is or has been able (directly or indirectly) to direct, influence or advise on the manner of investment of any of the sums and assets held for the purposes of an arrangement under the pension scheme relating to the member.

(3) In this Part "the taxable property provisions" means—

(a) section 173(7A) (exception from benefit charge where taxable property held by investment-regulated pension scheme),

(b) section 174A and this Schedule,

(c) sections 185A to 185I (income and gains from taxable property),

(d) section 273ZA (member liability for scheme sanction charge where pension scheme non-UK resident), and

(e) paragraphs 37A to 37I of Schedule 36 (transitional provisions).][1]

Amendments—[1]   This Schedule inserted by FA 2006 s 158, Sch 21 paras 2, 13. This amendment is deemed to have come into force on 6 April 2006.

[Occupational pension schemes

2—(1) For the purposes of the taxable property provisions a registered pension scheme which is an occupational pension scheme is an investment-regulated pension scheme if—

    (*a*) there are 50 or fewer members of the pension scheme, and one or more of those members meets the condition in sub-paragraph (2), . . . [2]

    (*b*) . . . [2]

(2) The condition is that either—

    (*a*) the member, or

    (*b*) a person related to the member,

is or has been able (directly or indirectly) to direct, influence or advise on the manner of investment of any of the sums and assets held for the purposes of the pension scheme.]¹

Amendments—[1]   This Schedule inserted by FA 2006 s 158, Sch 21 paras 2, 13. This amendment is deemed to have come into force on 6 April 2006.
[2]   Para (2)(1)(*b*) and preceding word "or" repealed by FA 2008 s 92 Sch 29 para 3. This amendment is treated as having come into force on 6 April 2006.

[Separate self-controlled section

3—(1) This paragraph applies in the case of an arrangement under a registered pension scheme if—

    (*a*) the pension scheme is an occupational pension scheme,

    (*b*) the pension scheme is not an investment-regulated pension scheme by virtue of paragraph 2, and

    (*c*) one or more members of the pension scheme meet the condition in sub-paragraph (2).

(2) The condition is that either—

    (*a*) the member, or

    (*b*) a person related to the member,

is or has been able (directly or indirectly) to direct, influence or advise on the manner of investment of any sums or assets which are linked to an arrangement relating to the member.

(3) For the purposes of sub-paragraph (2) sums or assets are linked to an arrangement relating to a member if—

    (*a*) they are held for the purposes of an arrangement under the pension scheme relating to the member, but

    (*b*) they are not held for the purposes of the arrangement merely by virtue of a just and reasonable apportionment of the sums and assets held for the purposes of the pension scheme.

(4) Where this paragraph applies the arrangement is to be treated for the purposes of this Part as if it were an investment-regulated pension scheme.

(5) The Treasury may by regulations—

    (*a*) amend sub-paragraph (3), and

    (*b*) provide for any of the provisions of this Part to apply to the arrangement with modifications.]¹

Amendments—[1]   This Schedule inserted by FA 2006 s 158, Sch 21 paras 2, 13. This amendment is deemed to have come into force on 6 April 2006.

[Related persons

4—(1) For the purposes of this Part of this Schedule a person is related to a member of a pension scheme if—

    (*a*) the person and the member are connected persons, or

    (*b*) the person acts on behalf of the member or a person connected with the member.

[(2) For the purposes of sub-paragraph (1) whether a person is connected with another person is determined in accordance with section 993 of ITA 2007.]²]¹

Amendments—[1]   This Schedule inserted by FA 2006 s 158, Sch 21 paras 2, 13. This amendment is deemed to have come into force on 6 April 2006.
[2]   Sub-para (2) substituted by ITA 2007 s 1027, Sch 1 paras 456, 484 with effect for income tax purposes from 6 April 2007, and corporation tax purposes for accounting periods ending after 5 April 2007.

[Arrangements

5   Where sums or assets held for the purposes of an investment-regulated pension scheme—

    (*a*) are held otherwise than for the purposes of the administration or management of the pension scheme, and

    (*b*) would not, apart from this paragraph, be treated as held for the purposes of any arrangement relating to a member under the pension scheme, for the purposes of the taxable property provisions the sums or assets are to be treated as held for the purposes of the arrangements under the pension scheme by reference to the respective rights under the scheme of the members to which the arrangements relate.][1]

Amendments—[1]   This Schedule inserted by FA 2006 s 158, Sch 21 paras 2, 13. This amendment is deemed to have come into force on 6 April 2006.

[PART 2
TAXABLE PROPERTY][1]

Amendments—[1]   This Schedule inserted by FA 2006 s 158, Sch 21 paras 2, 13. This amendment is deemed to have come into force on 6 April 2006.

[Taxable property

6   For the purposes of the taxable property provisions property is taxable property if—
   (*a*) it is residential property (see paragraphs 7 to 10), or
   (*b*) it is tangible moveable property (but subject to paragraph 11).][1]

Amendments—[1]   This Schedule inserted by FA 2006 s 158, Sch 21 paras 2, 13. This amendment is deemed to have come into force on 6 April 2006.

[Residential property

7—(1) Subject as follows, for the purposes of the taxable property provisions "residential property" means—
   (*a*) a building that is used or suitable for use as a dwelling,
   (*b*) any land consisting of, or forming part of, the garden or grounds of such a building (including a building on any such land) which is used or intended for use for a purpose connected with the enjoyment of the building,
   (*c*) hotel or similar accommodation (but see paragraph 14(2)), or
   (*d*) a beach hut,
in the United Kingdom or elsewhere.
(2) For the purposes of the taxable property provisions "building" includes—
   (*a*) a structure, and
   (*b*) part of a building or structure.][1]

Amendments—[1]   This Schedule inserted by FA 2006 s 158, Sch 21 paras 2, 13. This amendment is deemed to have come into force on 6 April 2006.

[**8—**(1) For the purposes of the taxable property provisions a building used for any of the following purposes is not residential property—
   (*a*) a home or other institution providing residential accommodation for children;
   (*b*) a hall of residence for students;
   (*c*) a home or other institution providing residential accommodation with personal care for persons in need of personal care by reason of old age, disability, past or present dependence on alcohol or drugs or past or present mental disorder;
   (*d*) a hospital or hospice;
   (*e*) a prison or similar establishment.
(2) Where—
   (*a*) a building is used for a purpose specified in sub-paragraph (1),
   (*b*) a building which is not in use was, immediately before it ceased to be in use, used for such a purpose, or
   (*c*) a building which has never been in use is more suitable for use for such a purpose than for use for any other purpose,
no account is to be taken for the purposes of the taxable property provisions of its suitability for use as a dwelling.][1]

Amendments—[1]   This Schedule inserted by FA 2006 s 158, Sch 21 paras 2, 13. This amendment is deemed to have come into force on 6 April 2006.

[**9—**(1) The Treasury may by order amend this Part of this Schedule to specify descriptions of buildings which are, or are not, to be treated as residential property.
(2) . . . . [2]][1]

Amendments—[1]   This Schedule inserted by FA 2006 s 158, Sch 21 paras 2, 13. This amendment is deemed to have come into force on 6 April 2006.
[2]   Sub-para (2) repealed by FA 2009 s 75(2)(*e*) with effect from 21 July 2009.

[**10—**(1) Residential property is not taxable property in relation to a pension scheme if Condition A or B is met.
(2) Condition A is met if the property is (or, if unoccupied, is to be) occupied by an employee who—

(*a*) is neither a member of the pension scheme nor connected with such a member,

(*b*) is not connected with the employer, and

(*c*) is required as a condition of employment to occupy the property.

(3) Condition B is met if the property is (or, if unoccupied, is to be)—

(*a*) occupied by a person who is neither a member of the pension scheme nor connected with such a member, and

(*b*) used in connection with business premises held as an investment of the pension scheme.

(4) [Section 1122 of the Corporation Tax Act 2010][2] [1] (connected persons) applies for the purposes of this paragraph.][1]

Amendments—[1]   This Schedule inserted by FA 2006 s 158, Sch 21 paras 2, 13. This amendment is deemed to have come into force on 6 April 2006.

[2]   In sub-para (4) words "Section 839 of ICTA" substituted by CTA 2010 s 1177, Sch 1 paras 423, 431(1),(5). CTA 2010 has effect for corporation tax purposes for accounting periods ending on or after 1 April 2010, and for income and capital gains tax purposes for the tax year 2010–11 and subsequent tax years.

[Tangible moveable property

11—(1) The Treasury may by order provide that, for the purposes of the taxable property provisions, any specified description of tangible moveable property is treated as not being taxable property.

(2) An order under this paragraph may include provision having effect in relation to times before it is made.][1]

Amendments—[1]   This Schedule inserted by FA 2006 s 158, Sch 21 paras 2, 13. This amendment is deemed to have come into force on 6 April 2006.

[PART 3
ACQUISITION AND HOLDING OF TAXABLE PROPERTY][1]

Amendments—[1]   This Schedule inserted by FA 2006 s 158, Sch 21 paras 2, 13. This amendment is deemed to have come into force on 6 April 2006.

[Acquisition

12—(1) For the purposes of the taxable property provisions an investment-regulated pension scheme acquires an interest in property if it comes to hold the interest.

(2) Sub-paragraph (1) applies however the pension scheme comes to hold the interest, whether that is—

(*a*) by act of the parties to a transaction,

(*b*) by order of a court or other authority,

(*c*) by or under any statutory provision, or

(*d*) by operation of law.

(3) For instances of deemed acquisition, see paragraphs 27 to 29.][1]

Amendments—[1]   This Schedule inserted by FA 2006 s 158, Sch 21 paras 2, 13. This amendment is deemed to have come into force on 6 April 2006.

[Holding

13—(1) For the purposes of the taxable property provisions an investment-regulated pension scheme holds an interest in property if the scheme holds the interest directly or indirectly.

(2) In the taxable property provisions references to a person holding an interest in property include, in the case of—

(*a*) an investment-regulated pension scheme,

(*b*) an arrangement under a pension scheme, or

(*c*) a trust which is not a pension scheme,

references to the interest in the property being held for the purposes of the pension scheme, the arrangement or the trust.][1]

Amendments—[1]   This Schedule inserted by FA 2006 s 158, Sch 21 paras 2, 13. This amendment is deemed to have come into force on 6 April 2006.

[Direct holding

14—(1) For the purposes of the taxable property provisions a person holds an interest in property directly if the person (whether jointly, in common or alone)—

(*a*) holds the property or any estate, interest, right or power in or over the property,

(*b*) has the right to use, or participate in arrangements relating to the use of, that property or a description of property to which that property belongs, or

(*c*) has the benefit of any obligation, restriction or condition affecting the value of any estate, interest, right or power in or over the property, under the law of any country or territory.

(2) But a person does not hold an interest in residential property consisting of hotel accommodation directly unless—

    (a) the person holds part only of the hotel accommodation or any estate, interest, right or power in or over such a part and, as a result, any person has a right to use or occupy that or any other part of the hotel accommodation, or

    (b) the person has a right to use, or participate in arrangements relating to the use of, part only of the hotel accommodation or a description of property to which that part belongs.

(3) For the purposes of the taxable property provisions a person holds an interest in property directly if the person is entitled (whether jointly, in common or alone) to receive payments determined by reference to the value of or the income from the property.

(4) Sub-paragraph (3) is subject to paragraph 15.][1]

Amendments—[1]   This Schedule inserted by FA 2006 s 158, Sch 21 paras 2, 13. This amendment is deemed to have come into force on 6 April 2006.

[Exception to direct holding

15—(1) A person does not hold an interest in taxable property directly by virtue of paragraph 14(3) where Conditions A to C are met.

(2) Condition A is that—

    (a) the person is entitled to receive the payments by virtue of a policy of life insurance, a contract for a life annuity or a capital redemption policy, and

    (b) the policy or contract is issued by an insurance company.

(3) Condition B is that the property—

    (a) does not constitute a linked asset, or

    (b) has been appropriated by the insurance company to an internal linked fund.

(4) Condition C is that—

    (a) where the person is an occupational pension scheme, the policy or contract, either by itself or taken together with one or more associated policies, does not entitle the pension scheme, either alone or together with one or more associated persons, to receive payments representing 10% or more of the market value of or the income from the property,

    (b) where the person is a pension scheme other than an occupational pension scheme, the policy or contract, either by itself or taken together with one or more associated policies, does not entitle an arrangement under the pension scheme, either alone or together with one or more associated persons, to receive such payments, or

    (c) otherwise, the policy or contract does not entitle the person to receive such payments.

(5) But for the purposes of applying paragraph 14(3) for determining whether a pension scheme holds an interest in taxable property directly or indirectly, this paragraph does not apply if the purpose or one of the purposes for which the person holds rights under the policy or contract is to enable a member of the pension scheme or a person connected with such a member to occupy or use the property.

(6) For the purposes of sub-paragraph (4) "associated policy" means a policy or contract which entitles an associated person to receive payments determined by reference to the value of or the income from the property.

(7) For the definition of "associated person" see paragraph 30.

(8) For the purposes of this paragraph—

    "capital redemption policy" means a contract made in the course of a capital redemption business, as defined in section 458(3) of ICTA;

    "internal linked fund" has the meaning given by—

        (a) the Interim Prudential Sourcebook for Insurers made by the [Prudential Regulation Authority][2] under FISMA 2000, or

        (b) rules made by the [Prudential Regulation Authority][2] under that Act and having effect for the time being in place of the Sourcebook; and

    "linked asset" means an asset of the insurance company which is identified in its records as an asset by reference to the value of which benefits provided for under a policy or contract are to be determined.

(9) For the purposes of this paragraph an annuity is a life annuity if it is—

    (a) granted for consideration in money or money's worth in the ordinary course of a business of granting annuities on human life, and

    (b) payable for a term ending at a time ascertainable only by reference to the end of a human life,

and for this purpose it does not matter that the annuity may in some circumstances end before or after the life.][1]

Modifications—Pensions Schemes (Application of UK Provisions to Relevant Non-UK Schemes) (Amendment) Regulations, SI 2006/207 reg 4C (modification of this paragraph in relation to relevant non-UK schemes).

Amendments—[1]   This Schedule inserted by FA 2006 s 158, Sch 21 paras 2, 13. This amendment is deemed to have come into force on 6 April 2006.

[2]   In sub-para (8), in definition of "internal linked fund", words substituted by the Financial Services Act 2012 (Consequential Amendments) Order, SI 2013/838 art 2, Schedule para 7 with effect from 1 April 2013.

[Indirect holding

16—(1) For the purposes of the taxable property provisions a person holds an interest in property indirectly if the person does not hold the interest directly but (whether jointly, in common or alone)—

     (*a*)   holds an interest in a person who holds the interest in the property directly, or

     (*b*)   holds an interest in a person who holds the interest in the property indirectly by virtue of paragraph (*a*) or this paragraph.

(2) For the purposes of the taxable property provisions a person holds an interest in another person if—

     (*a*)   the person holds an interest, right or power in or over that other person, or

     (*b*)   the person lends money to that other person to fund the acquisition by that other person of an interest in taxable property.

(3) But sub-paragraph (2)(*b*) does not apply where—

     (*a*)   the loan is an authorised employer loan made by a pension scheme to or in respect of a sponsoring employer (see section 179),

     (*b*)   the interest in the property is acquired so that the property may be used for the purposes of a trade, profession or vocation carried on by the sponsoring employer or for the purposes of the sponsoring employer's administration or management, and

     (*c*)   after the acquisition, the property is not occupied or used by a member of the pension scheme or a person connected with such a member.

(4) In the taxable property provisions references to a person holding an interest in another person include, in the case of—

     (*a*)   an investment-regulated pension scheme,

     (*b*)   an arrangement under a pension scheme, or

     (*c*)   a trust which is not a pension scheme,

references to the interest in the other person being held for the purposes of the pension scheme, the arrangement or the trust.

(5) Paragraphs 17 to 19 explain what it means for a person to hold an interest in another person by virtue of sub-paragraph (2)(*a*) in a case where that other person is a company, collective investment scheme or trust.

(6) The Treasury may by regulations—

     (*a*)   amend paragraphs 17 to 19, or

     (*b*)   amend this Part of this Schedule for the purposes of explaining what it means for a person to hold an interest, right or power in or over another person in other cases.

(7) This paragraph is subject to paragraphs 20 to 26.][1]

Amendments—[1]   This Schedule inserted by FA 2006 s 158, Sch 21 paras 2, 13. This amendment is deemed to have come into force on 6 April 2006.

[**17**—(1) For the purposes of paragraph 16 a person holds an interest in a company if—

     (*a*)   the person has, or is entitled to acquire, share capital or voting rights in the company,

     (*b*)   the person has, or is entitled to acquire, a right to receive or participate in distributions of the company,

     (*c*)   the person is entitled to secure that income or assets (whether present or future) of the company will be applied directly or indirectly for the person's benefit, or

     (*d*)   the person, either alone or together with other persons, has control of the company.

(2) In sub-paragraph (1) references to a person being entitled to do anything apply where a person—

     (*a*)   is currently entitled to do it at a future date, or

     (*b*)   will at a future date be entitled to do it.

(3) In sub-paragraph (1) "control" has the meaning given by [sections 450 and 451 of the Corporation Tax Act 2010][2].][1]

Amendments—[1]   This Schedule inserted by FA 2006 s 158, Sch 21 paras 2, 13. This amendment is deemed to have come into force on 6 April 2006.

[2]   In sub-para (3), words substituted by CTA 2010 s 1177, Sch 1 paras 423, 431(1),(2). CTA 2010 has effect for corporation tax purposes for accounting periods ending on or after 1 April 2010, and for income and capital gains tax purposes for the tax year 2010–11 and subsequent tax years.

[**18**—(1) For the purposes of paragraph 16 a person holds an interest in a collective investment scheme if the person is a participant in the scheme.

(2) In this Schedule—

     (*a*)   "collective investment scheme" has the meaning given by section 235 of FISMA 2000, and

(b) "participant", in relation to such a scheme, has the meaning given by subsection (2) of that section.][1]

Amendments—[1]   This Schedule inserted by FA 2006 s 158, Sch 21 paras 2, 13. This amendment is deemed to have come into force on 6 April 2006.

[19—(1) For the purposes of paragraph 16 a pension scheme holds an interest in a trust if Condition A or B is met.

(2) Condition A is that—

   (a) the pension scheme has a relevant interest in the trust,

   (b) the pension scheme, a member of the pension scheme or a person connected with such a member has made a payment to the trust on or after the acquisition of the interest, and

   (c) the payment is not one to which sub-paragraph (7) applies.

(3) Condition B is that—

   (a) a member of the pension scheme or a person connected with such a member has a relevant interest in the trust,

   (b) the pension scheme has made a payment to the trust on or after the acquisition of the interest, and

   (c) the payment is not one to which sub-paragraph (7) applies.

(4) For the purposes of applying paragraph 16 for determining whether a pension scheme holds an interest in property indirectly, a person other than the pension scheme holds an interest in a trust if—

   (a) the person has a relevant interest in the trust,

   (b) the person has made a payment to the trust on or after the acquisition of the interest, and

   (c) the payment is not one to which sub-paragraph (7) applies.

(5) For the purposes of this paragraph a person has a relevant interest in a trust if—

   (a) any property which may at any time be comprised in the trust or any derived property is, or will or may become, payable to or applicable for the benefit of the person in any circumstances, or

   (b) the person enjoys a benefit deriving directly or indirectly from any property which is comprised in the trust or any derived property.

(6) In sub-paragraph (5) "derived property", in relation to any property, means income from that property or any other property directly or indirectly representing proceeds of, or income from, that property.

(7) This sub-paragraph applies to a payment if—

   (a) it is made as part of an arm's length transaction by which property or a benefit is to be provided in return for the payment, and

   (b) it is made otherwise than for the purposes of enabling a member of the pension scheme or a person connected with such a member to occupy or use any property.

(8) [Section 1122 of the Corporation Tax Act 2010][2] (connected persons) applies for the purposes of this paragraph.

(9) This paragraph does not apply in relation to a unit trust scheme within the meaning of section 237(1) of FISMA 2000 (but see paragraph 18).][1]

Amendments—[1]   This Schedule inserted by FA 2006 s 158, Sch 21 paras 2, 13. This amendment is deemed to have come into force on 6 April 2006.
[2]   In sub-para (8), words substituted by CTA 2010 s 1177, Sch 1 paras 423, 431(1),(5). CTA 2010 has effect for corporation tax purposes for accounting periods ending on or after 1 April 2010, and for income and capital gains tax purposes for the tax year 2010–11 and subsequent tax years.

[Exceptions to indirect holding

20—(1) A pension scheme does not hold an interest in property indirectly through a vehicle through which the pension scheme would otherwise hold the interest in the property indirectly where one of the following paragraphs applies in relation to the vehicle, and, in particular—

   (a) paragraph 21 makes provision in relation to holding through vehicles which carry on trading activities,

   (b) [paragraphs 22, 24 and 25 make][2] provision in relation to holding through Real Estate Investment Trusts,

   (c) paragraphs 23 to 25 make provision in relation to holding through other kinds of vehicles, and

   (d) paragraph 26 makes provision in relation to holding through a vehicle which holds the interest in the property directly by virtue of paragraph 14(3) (receipt of payments determined by reference to value of or income from property).

(2) In the taxable property provisions "vehicle", in relation to a pension scheme which holds an interest in taxable property indirectly, means a person through whom the pension scheme holds the interest in the property.

(3) For the purposes of the taxable property provisions a person holds an interest in a vehicle directly if the person holds an interest of the kind mentioned in paragraph 16(2) in the vehicle.

(4) For the purposes of the taxable property provisions a person holds an interest in a vehicle indirectly if the person does not hold the interest directly but—

    (a) holds an interest in a person who holds an interest in the vehicle directly, or

    (b) holds an interest in a person who holds the interest in the vehicle indirectly by virtue of paragraph (a) or this paragraph.][1]

Amendments—[1]   This Schedule inserted by FA 2006 s 158, Sch 21 paras 2, 13. This amendment is deemed to have come into force on 6 April 2006.

[2]   Words in sub-para (1)(b) substituted by FA 2007 s 70, Sch 20 paras 1, 14(1), (2), 24(8). This amendment is deemed to have come into force on 1 January 2007.

[**21**—(1) This paragraph applies to a vehicle in which a pension scheme directly or indirectly holds an interest where—

    (a) the vehicle's main activity is the carrying on of a trade, profession or vocation,

    (b) the pension scheme does not, whether alone or together with one or more associated persons, have control of the vehicle, and

    (c) neither a member of the pension scheme nor a person connected with such a member is a controlling director of the vehicle or any other vehicle which holds an interest in the vehicle directly or indirectly.

(2) But this paragraph does not apply if the purpose or one of the purposes for which the pension scheme holds the interest in the vehicle is to enable a member of the pension scheme or a person connected with such a member to occupy or use the property.

(3) In sub-paragraph (1)—

    (a) "control" has the same meaning as in [sections 450 and 451 of the Corporation Tax Act 2010][2] (reading references in [those sections][2] to a company as references to the vehicle and references to associates as including associated persons), and

    (b) "controlling director", in relation to a vehicle, means a director to whom [section 452(2)(b)][2] of that Act applies (reading the reference to associates in [section 452(3) of that Act][2] as including associated persons).

(4) For the purposes of this paragraph a pension scheme or an arrangement under a pension scheme has control of a vehicle if the pension scheme or the arrangement holds such interest as would, if the pension scheme or the arrangement were a person, mean that the person had control of the vehicle.

(5) [Section 1122 of the Corporation Tax Act 2010][2] (connected persons) applies for the purposes of this paragraph.

(6) For the definition of "associated person" see paragraph 30.][1]

Amendments—[1]   This Schedule inserted by FA 2006 s 158, Sch 21 paras 2, 13. This amendment is deemed to have come into force on 6 April 2006.

[2]   In sub-paras (3)(a), (b), (5), words substituted by CTA 2010 s 1177, Sch 1 paras 423, 431(1),(3), (5). CTA 2010 has effect for corporation tax purposes for accounting periods ending on or after 1 April 2010, and for income and capital gains tax purposes for the tax year 2010–11 and subsequent tax years.

[**22**—(1) This paragraph applies to a vehicle in which a pension scheme directly or indirectly holds an interest where the vehicle [is a company which is, or is a member of, a UK REIT within the meaning of Part 12 of the Corporation Tax Act 2010 (Real Estate Investment Trusts)][3]

[and paragraph 24 applies to the pension scheme's interest in the vehicle][2].

(2) . . . [2]

(3) [Section 1122 of the Corporation Tax Act 2010][3] (connected persons) applies for the purposes of sub-paragraph (2).][1]

Amendments—[1]   This Schedule inserted by FA 2006 s 158, Sch 21 paras 2, 13. This amendment is deemed to have come into force on 6 April 2006.

[2]   Words in sub-para (1) inserted, and sub-para (2) repealed, by FA 2007 ss 70, 114, Sch 20 paras 1, 14(1), (3), 24(8), Sch 27 Pt 3(2). These amendments are deemed to have come into force on 1 January 2007.

[3]   In sub-para (1), (3), words substituted by CTA 2010 s 1177, Sch 1 paras 423, 431(1),(4), (5). CTA 2010 has effect for corporation tax purposes for accounting periods ending on or after 1 April 2010, and for income and capital gains tax purposes for the tax year 2010–11 and subsequent tax years.

[**23**—(1) This paragraph applies to a vehicle in which a pension scheme directly or indirectly holds an interest where—

    (a) Conditions A to C are met in relation to the vehicle, and

    (b) paragraph 24 applies to the pension scheme's interest in the vehicle.

(2) Condition A is that—

    (a) the total value of the assets held directly by the vehicle is at least £1 million, or

    (b) the vehicle holds directly at least three assets which consist of an interest in residential property,

and no asset held directly by the vehicle which consists of an interest in taxable property has a value which exceeds 40% of the total value of the assets held directly by the vehicle.

(3) Condition B is that, if the vehicle is a company—

    (a) it is resident in the United Kingdom and is not a close company, or

    (b) it is not resident in the United Kingdom and would not be a close company if it were resident in the United Kingdom.

(4) Condition C is that the vehicle does not have as its main purpose, or one of its main purposes, the direct or indirect holding of an animal or animals used for sporting purposes.

(5) For the purposes of sub-paragraph (2)—

    (a) assets must be valued in accordance with generally accepted accounting practice,

    (b) no account is to be taken of liabilities secured against or otherwise relating to assets (whether generally or specifically), and

    (c) where generally accepted accounting practice offers a choice of valuation between cost basis and fair value, fair value must be used.

(6) The Treasury may by order—

    (a) increase the amount for the time being specified in paragraph (a) of sub-paragraph (2), or

    (b) increase the percentage for the time being specified in that sub-paragraph.][1]

Amendments—[1]   This Schedule inserted by FA 2006 s 158, Sch 21 paras 2, 13. This amendment is deemed to have come into force on 6 April 2006.

[**24**—(1) For the purposes of [paragraphs 22 and 23][2] this paragraph applies to the interest held directly or indirectly by a pension scheme in a vehicle where—

    (a) Condition A is met, and

    (b) Condition B or C is met.

(2) Condition A is that the pension scheme does not hold the interest in the vehicle for the purpose of enabling a member of the pension scheme or a person connected with such a member to occupy or use the property.

(3) Condition B is that—

    (a) the pension scheme is an occupational pension scheme, and

    (b) the pension scheme does not, either alone or together with one or more associated persons, directly or indirectly hold an interest in the vehicle to which sub-paragraph (5) applies.

(4) Condition C is that—

    (a) the pension scheme is not an occupational pension scheme, and

    (b) no arrangement under the pension scheme, either alone or together with one or more associated persons, directly or indirectly holds an interest in the vehicle to which sub-paragraph (5) applies.

(5) This sub-paragraph applies to the following interests—

    (a) 10% or more of the share capital or issued share capital of the vehicle;

    (b) 10% or more of the voting rights in the vehicle;

    (c) a right to receive 10% or more of the income of the vehicle;

    (d) such interest in the vehicle as gives an entitlement to 10% or more of the amounts distributed on a distribution in relation to the vehicle;

    (e) such interest in the vehicle as gives an entitlement to 10% or more of the assets of the vehicle on a winding-up or in any other circumstances;

    (f) such interest in the vehicle as gives rise to income or gains from a specific property.

(6) [Section 1122 of the Corporation Tax Act 2010][3] (connected persons) applies for the purposes of this paragraph.

(7) For the definition of "associated person" see paragraph 30.][1]

Amendments—[1]   This Schedule inserted by FA 2006 s 158, Sch 21 paras 2, 13. This amendment is deemed to have come into force on 6 April 2006.

[2]   Words in sub-para (1) substituted by FA 2007 s 70, Sch 20 paras 1, 14(1), (4), 24(8). These amendments are deemed to have come into force on 1 January 2007.

[3]   In sub-para (6) words substituted by CTA 2010 s 1177, Sch 1 paras 423, 431(1),(5). CTA 2010 has effect for corporation tax purposes for accounting periods ending on or after 1 April 2010, and for income and capital gains tax purposes for the tax year 2010–11 and subsequent tax years.

[**25**—(1) This paragraph contains provisions supplementary to paragraph 24.

(2) Where—

    (a) paragraph [22 or 23][2] does not apply in relation to a vehicle in which the pension scheme directly or indirectly holds an interest merely because Condition C in paragraph 24(4) is not met in relation to an arrangement under the pension scheme, and

    (b) accordingly, the pension scheme holds an interest in property indirectly through the vehicle,

the interest in the property is to be treated as held through the vehicle for the purposes of another arrangement under the pension scheme only if that arrangement, either alone or together with one or more associated persons, directly or indirectly holds an interest in the vehicle to which paragraph 24(5) applies.

(3) Sub-paragraph (4) applies for determining the percentage of an interest held by a person in a vehicle at a time when the person holds that interest indirectly.

(4) That percentage is equal to the percentage of the total taxable amount that would be apportioned to the person under paragraphs 41 to 43—

    (*a*) where the person is not the pension scheme, if the person were the pension scheme, and

    (*b*) in any case, if the person were treated as making an unauthorised payment by virtue of the vehicle coming to hold the interest in the property directly at that time.

(5) For the definition of "associated person" see paragraph 30.][1]

Amendments—[1]   This Schedule inserted by FA 2006 s 158, Sch 21 paras 2, 13. This amendment is deemed to have come into force on 6 April 2006.

[2]   Words in sub-para (2) substituted by FA 2007 s 70, Sch 20 paras 1, 14(1), (5), 24(8). These amendments are deemed to have come into force on 1 January 2007.

[26—(1) This paragraph applies to a vehicle in which a pension scheme directly or indirectly holds an interest where—

    (*a*) the vehicle holds the interest in the property directly by virtue of paragraph 14(3) merely because it does not meet Condition C in paragraph 15(4), and

    (*b*) sub-paragraph (2) applies in relation to the pension scheme.

(2) This sub-paragraph applies in relation to the pension scheme if—

    (*a*) where the pension scheme is an occupational pension scheme, the pension scheme is not, either alone or together with one or more associated persons, deemed to be entitled to 10% or more of the market value of or the income from the property, or

    (*b*) where the pension scheme is not an occupational pension scheme, no arrangement under the pension scheme, either alone or together with one or more associated persons, is deemed to be so entitled.

(3) For the purposes of this paragraph the percentage of the market value of or the income from the property to which a person is deemed to be entitled at any time is—

$$IG \times TTA$$

where—

    IG is the percentage of the market value of or the income from the property to which the vehicle that holds the interest in the property directly is entitled at that time, and

    TTA is the percentage of the total taxable amount that would be apportioned to the person at that time on the assumptions mentioned in sub-paragraph (4).

(4) Those assumptions are—

    (*a*) if the person is not the pension scheme, that the person is the pension scheme, and

    (*b*) in any case, that the person is treated as making an unauthorised payment by virtue of the vehicle coming to hold the interest in the property directly at that time.

(5) For the definition of "associated person" see paragraph 30.][1]

Amendments—[1]   This Schedule inserted by FA 2006 s 158, Sch 21 paras 2, 13. This amendment is deemed to have come into force on 6 April 2006.

[Deemed acquisition

27 Where—

    (*a*) an investment-regulated pension scheme holds an interest in property which is not taxable property, and

    (*b*) that property becomes taxable property otherwise than by reason of its conversion or adaptation as residential property,

the pension scheme is treated for the purposes of the taxable property provisions as acquiring an interest in the property.][1]

Amendments—[1]   This Schedule inserted by FA 2006 s 158, Sch 21 paras 2, 13. This amendment is deemed to have come into force on 6 April 2006.

[28—(1) Subject to paragraph 29, this paragraph applies where—

    (*a*) an investment-regulated pension scheme holds an interest in taxable property indirectly, and

    (*b*) there is an increase in the extent of the interest held directly in a vehicle by the pension scheme or another vehicle.

(2) The pension scheme is to be treated for the purposes of this Schedule as—

    (*a*) having disposed of the interest in the property immediately before the increase in the extent of the interest in the vehicle, and

    (*b*) having re-acquired the interest immediately afterwards.

(3) The extent of the interest held directly in a vehicle by a person is to be determined for the purposes of this paragraph and paragraph 29 in accordance with paragraphs 42 and 43.][1]

Amendments—[1]   This Schedule inserted by FA 2006 s 158, Sch 21 paras 2, 13. This amendment is deemed to have come into force on 6 April 2006.

[29—(1) Where there is an increase in the extent of the interest held directly in the vehicle otherwise than by reason of the acquisition of a further interest in the vehicle, paragraph 28 does not apply unless the condition in sub-paragraph (2) is met.

(2) The condition is that the event by which the extent of the interest held directly in the vehicle increases forms part of a scheme or arrangement the main purpose or one of the main purposes of which is—

    (*a*) to enable the amount of the unauthorised payment treated as arising on the original acquisition of the interest in the property by the pension scheme to be lower than it otherwise would have been, or

    (*b*) to prevent an unauthorised payment from being treated as made on that original acquisition.

(3) Unless that condition is met, the increase in the extent of the interest is also to be disregarded for the purposes of paragraphs 24 to 26.][1]

Modifications—Pensions Schemes (Application of UK Provisions to Relevant Non-UK Schemes) (Amendment) Regulations, SI 2006/207 reg 4D (modification of this paragraph in relation to relevant non-UK schemes).

Amendments—[1]   This Schedule inserted by FA 2006 s 158, Sch 21 paras 2, 13. This amendment is deemed to have come into force on 6 April 2006.

[*Associated persons*

30—(1) For the purposes of this Part of this Schedule "associated person", in relation to a pension scheme, means—

    (*a*) any member of the pension scheme,

    (*b*) any person connected with such a member,

    (*c*) any arrangement (under that or another pension scheme) relating to a member of the pension scheme,

    (*d*) any arrangement (under that or another pension scheme) relating to a person connected with such a member, and

    (*e*) any associated pension scheme.

(2) For the purposes of sub-paragraph (1) a pension scheme is associated with another pension scheme if members representing at least 10% by value of one pension scheme are members of the other pension scheme or connected with such members.

(3) The percentage by value represented by a member of a pension scheme is—

$$\frac{AM}{AA} \times 100$$

where—

    AM is an amount equal to the aggregate of the amount of the sums and the market value of the assets held for the purposes of an arrangement under the pension scheme relating to the member, and

    AA is an amount equal to the aggregate of the amount of the sums and the market value of the assets held for the purposes of the pension scheme.

(4) For the purposes of this Part of this Schedule "associated person", in relation to an arrangement under a pension scheme, means—

    (*a*) the member of the pension scheme to which that arrangement relates,

    (*b*) any person connected with such a member,

    (*c*) any arrangement (under that or another pension scheme) relating to a member of the pension scheme to which that arrangement relates, and

    (*d*) any arrangement (under that or another pension scheme) relating to a person connected with such a member.][1]

Amendments—[1]   This Schedule inserted by FA 2006 s 158, Sch 21 paras 2, 13. This amendment is deemed to have come into force on 6 April 2006.

[PART 4
AMOUNT AND TIMING OF UNAUTHORISED PAYMENT][1]

Amendments—[1]   This Schedule inserted by FA 2006 s 158, Sch 21 paras 2, 13. This amendment is deemed to have come into force on 6 April 2006.

[*Introduction*

31—(1) This Part of this Schedule has effect for determining—

    (*a*) the amount of an unauthorised payment treated as made to a member of an investment-regulated pension scheme by virtue of section 174A, and (*b*) the time when such a payment is treated as made.

(2) The amount is determined by—

  (*a*) finding the total taxable amount in relation to the unauthorised payment (see paragraphs 32 to 40),

  (*b*) apportioning that amount to the pension scheme (see paragraphs 41 to 43),

  (*c*) in a case to which paragraph 28 applies (acquisition etc of further interest in vehicle), making an adjustment under paragraph 44 to the amount mentioned in paragraph (*b*), and

  (*d*) apportioning that amount to the member to whom the payment is treated as made in accordance with paragraph 45.][1]

Modifications—Pensions Schemes (Application of UK Provisions to Relevant Non-UK Schemes) (Amendment) Regulations, SI 2006/207 reg 4D (modification of this paragraph in relation to relevant non-UK schemes).

Amendments—[1] This Schedule inserted by FA 2006 s 158, Sch 21 paras 2, 13. This amendment is deemed to have come into force on 6 April 2006.

[Acquisition: basic rules

32—(1) This paragraph applies to a case within subsection (1) of section 174A (acquisition of an interest in taxable property).

(2) The unauthorised payment is treated as made when the interest in the property is acquired by the pension scheme.

(3) If the interest in the property is acquired because the pension scheme or another person comes to hold the interest directly, the total taxable amount in relation to the unauthorised payment is—

  (*a*) the amount of consideration, in money or money's worth, given directly or indirectly for the interest, plus

  (*b*) the amount of any fees and other costs incurred in connection with the acquisition.

(4) Sub-paragraph (3) is subject to paragraphs 33 to 35.

(5) If the interest in the property is acquired because the pension scheme or another person comes to hold an interest in a person who already holds the interest in the property directly or indirectly, the total taxable amount in relation to the unauthorised payment is—

  (*a*) the market value, at the date the interest in the person is acquired, of the interest in the property held by the person who holds it directly, or

  (*b*) if the interest in the property is a lease at a rent, the amount of consideration that would be treated as given by the person for the lease by virtue of paragraph 34 if it were assigned to the person at that time.

(6) If the interest in the property is treated as acquired by the pension scheme by virtue of paragraph 27 or 28, the total taxable amount in relation to the unauthorised payment is—

  (*a*) the market value, at the date the interest is treated as acquired, of the interest in the property held by the person who holds it directly, or

  (*b*) if the interest in the property is a lease at a rent, the amount of consideration that would be treated as given by the person for the lease by virtue of paragraph 34 if it were assigned to the person at that time.

(7) This paragraph is subject to paragraph 36.][1]

Amendments—[1] This Schedule inserted by FA 2006 s 158, Sch 21 paras 2, 13. This amendment is deemed to have come into force on 6 April 2006.

[Acquisition: further provisions

33—(1) This paragraph applies where—

  (*a*) an investment-regulated pension scheme acquires an interest in taxable property because it acquires a chargeable interest in the property within the meaning of section 48(1) of the Finance Act 2003,

  (*b*) the interest is acquired because the pension scheme or another person comes to hold the interest directly, and

  (*c*) the whole or part of the consideration for the interest is consideration other than rent.

(2) The provisions of the Finance Act 2003 listed in sub-paragraph (3) apply for determining the amount of the consideration (or the part that is not rent) as they apply for determining the amount of chargeable consideration for a land transaction for the purposes of Part 4 of that Act.

(3) Those provisions are—

  (*a*) paragraphs 2 to 8 and 9 to 16 of Schedule 4 (chargeable consideration);

  (*b*) section 51 (contingent, uncertain or unascertained consideration);

  (*c*) section 52 (annuities etc: chargeable consideration limited to twelve years' payments).

(4) The Treasury may by regulations provide—

  (*a*) for those provisions to apply with modifications to cases to which this paragraph applies, and

  (*b*) for any other provisions of Part 4 of the Finance Act 2003 to apply (with or without modifications) to such cases.][1]

Amendments—[1]   This Schedule inserted by FA 2006 s 158, Sch 21 paras 2, 13. This amendment is deemed to have come into force on 6 April 2006.

[34—(1) This paragraph applies where—

    (*a*) an investment-regulated pension scheme acquires an interest in taxable property because it acquires a chargeable interest in the property within the meaning of section 48(1) of the Finance Act 2003,

    (*b*) the interest is acquired because the pension scheme or another person comes to hold the interest directly, and

    (*c*) the whole or part of the consideration for the acquisition is rent.

(2) The amount of the consideration (or the part that is rent) is to be taken to be the relevant rental value of the property; and paragraphs 2(4)(*a*), 3 and 8 of Schedule 5 (rent) to the Finance Act 2003 apply for determining that value.

(3) The following provisions of the Finance Act 2003 apply for the purposes of sub-paragraph (2) for determining the amount of rent payable as they apply for determining the amount of rent payable under a lease to which that Act applies—

    (*a*) paragraphs 2, 5 to 7A, 9 and 16 of Schedule 17A (further provisions relating to leases);

    (*b*) (subject to the provisions mentioned in paragraph (*a*)) the provisions mentioned in paragraph 33(3).

(4) The Treasury may by regulations provide—

    (*a*) for the provisions mentioned in sub-paragraph (2) or (3) to apply with modifications to cases to which this paragraph applies, and

    (*b*) for any other provisions of Part 4 of the Finance Act 2003 to apply (with or without modifications) to such cases.

(5) For the purposes of this paragraph where on an assignment of a lease the assignee assumes the obligation to pay rent, the assumption counts as consideration for the assignment.][1]

Amendments—[1]   This Schedule inserted by FA 2006 s 158, Sch 21 paras 2, 13. This amendment is deemed to have come into force on 6 April 2006.

[35—(1) This paragraph applies where—

    (*a*) an investment-regulated pension scheme acquires an interest in taxable property because the pension scheme or another person comes to hold the interest directly,

    (*b*) the interest is acquired for less than its market value, and

    (*c*) immediately before the acquisition the interest was held by a registered pension scheme which was not an investment-regulated pension scheme.

(2) This paragraph also applies where—

    (*a*) an investment-regulated pension scheme acquires an interest in taxable property because the pension scheme or another person comes to hold the interest directly,

    (*b*) the interest is acquired for less than its market value, and

    (*c*) tax relief is available under section 188 or 196 in respect of the transfer of the interest.

(3) The amount of the consideration for the interest is treated as—

    (*a*) the market value, at the date the interest is acquired, of the interest in the property held by the person who holds it directly, or

    (*b*) if the interest in the property is a lease at a rent, the amount of consideration that would be treated as given by the person for the lease by virtue of paragraph 34 if it were assigned to the person at that time.][1]

Amendments—[1]   This Schedule inserted by FA 2006 s 158, Sch 21 paras 2, 13. This amendment is deemed to have come into force on 6 April 2006.

[36—(1) The Treasury may by regulations make provision with respect to—

    (*a*) what is to count as consideration for the acquisition of an interest in taxable property, and

    (*b*) the determination of the amount of such consideration.

(2) The Treasury may by regulations make provision with respect to the determination of the market value of an interest held in taxable property.

(3) Regulations under this paragraph may, in particular, make provision for cases where an investment-regulated pension scheme acquires—

    (*a*) an interest in taxable property outside the United Kingdom,

    (*b*) a licence to use or occupy taxable property, or

    (*c*) an interest in taxable property which is tangible moveable property.

(4) Regulations under this paragraph may—

    (*a*) amend this Part of this Schedule, and

    (*b*) include provision having effect in relation to times before they are made.][1]

Amendments—[1]   This Schedule inserted by FA 2006 s 158, Sch 21 paras 2, 13. This amendment is deemed to have come into force on 6 April 2006.

[Post-acquisition unauthorised payments

37—(1) The Treasury may by regulations make provision for an investment-regulated pension scheme which has acquired an interest in taxable property to be treated as making one or more further unauthorised payments where—

    (a) the amount of consideration for the acquisition was determined on the basis of a reasonable estimate, and the actual amount of the consideration turns out to be higher than the estimated amount,

    (b) in the case of an interest which is a lease, there is a variation in the rent payable under the lease, or

    (c) in such a case, the amount of consideration for the acquisition was determined on an assumption about the length of the term of the lease, and the lease continues after the end of the term.

(2) Regulations under this paragraph may—

    (a) amend section 174A or this Schedule (apart from this paragraph), and

    (b) include provision having effect in relation to times before they are made.

(3) References in the taxable property provisions to unauthorised payments treated as made under section 174A include references to payments treated as made under regulations under this paragraph.][1]

Amendments—[1]   This Schedule inserted by FA 2006 s 158, Sch 21 paras 2, 13. This amendment is deemed to have come into force on 6 April 2006.

[Improvement of taxable property

38—(1) This paragraph applies to a case within subsection (2) of section 174A (improvement of taxable property).

(2) An unauthorised payment is treated as made when a payment is made in connection with the improvement works.

(3) The total taxable amount in relation to the unauthorised payment is the amount of the payment mentioned in sub-paragraph (2).][1]

Amendments—[1]   This Schedule inserted by FA 2006 s 158, Sch 21 paras 2, 13. This amendment is deemed to have come into force on 6 April 2006.

[Conversion or adaptation as residential property

39—(1) This paragraph applies to a case within subsection (3) of section 174A (conversion or adaptation as residential property).

(2) The unauthorised payment is treated as made on the occurrence of whichever of the following first occurs after the property has become residential property—

    (a) the substantial completion of the works to convert or adapt the property;

    (b) the interest in the property ceasing to be held by the pension scheme.

(3) But if the property becomes residential property after the end of the period of three years beginning with the date on which the first payment was made in connection with the works to convert or adapt the property, the unauthorised payment is treated as made when the property becomes residential property.

(4) If the works began before the end of the period of twelve months beginning with the acquisition of the interest in the property by the pension scheme, the total taxable amount in relation to the unauthorised payment is—

    (a) the amount of consideration for the interest, determined in accordance with paragraphs 32 to 36, plus

    (b) the development costs (see sub-paragraph (7)).

(5) If the works began after the end of that period, the total taxable amount in relation to the unauthorised payment is—

    (a) the relevant market value (see sub-paragraph (6)), plus

    (b) the development costs (see sub-paragraph (7)).

(6) In this paragraph "the relevant market value" means—

    (a) the market value, at the date the works began, of the interest in the property held by the person who holds it directly, or

    (b) if the interest in the property is a lease at a rent, the amount of consideration that would be treated as given by the person for the lease by virtue of paragraph 34 if it were assigned to the person at that time.

(7) In this paragraph "the development costs" means the total cost of the works to convert or adapt the property at the time when the unauthorised payment is treated as made.

(8) Where, at the time the unauthorised payment is treated as made—

    (a) an amount will be payable for the works only if some uncertain future event occurs, or (*b*) an amount will cease to be payable for the works if some uncertain future event occurs,

the development costs are to be determined on the assumption that the amount will be payable or, as the case may be, will not cease to be payable.

(9) Where, at that time, an amount payable for the works—

(*a*) depends on uncertain future events, or

(*b*) cannot otherwise be ascertained,

that amount is to be determined for the purposes of sub-paragraph (7) on the basis of a reasonable estimate.]¹

Amendments—¹   This Schedule inserted by FA 2006 s 158, Sch 21 paras 2, 13. This amendment is deemed to have come into force on 6 April 2006.

[**40**—(1) This paragraph applies to a case within subsection (3) of section 174A (conversion or adaptation as residential property).

(2) This paragraph applies if —

(*a*) sub-paragraph (8) of paragraph 39 has effect when an unauthorised payment is treated as made under that paragraph,

(*b*) an amount estimated under that sub-paragraph later becomes ascertained, and

(*c*) the ascertained amount is more than the estimated amount.

(3) An unauthorised payment is treated as made when the amount becomes ascertained.

(4) The total taxable amount in relation to the unauthorised payment is the difference between the ascertained amount and the estimated amount.

(5) References in the taxable property provisions to unauthorised payments treated as made under section 174A include references to payments treated as made under this paragraph.]¹

Amendments—¹   This Schedule inserted by FA 2006 s 158, Sch 21 paras 2, 13. This amendment is deemed to have come into force on 6 April 2006.

[Apportionment to pension scheme

41—(1) This paragraph applies for determining—

(*a*) whether the amount of an unauthorised payment treated as made by an investment-regulated pension scheme under section 174A consists of the whole of the total taxable amount in relation to the payment, and

(*b*) if not, how much of the total taxable amount comprises the amount of the unauthorised payment.

(2) The pension scheme is treated as making an unauthorised payment equal to the whole of the total taxable amount where Condition A, B or C is met.

(3) Condition A is that the pension scheme directly holds the interest in the taxable property which gives rise to the unauthorised payment.

(4) Condition B is that—

(*a*) the pension scheme holds the interest in the property indirectly through one vehicle, and

(*b*) that vehicle is wholly owned by the pension scheme.

(5) Condition C is that—

(*a*) the pension scheme holds the interest in the property indirectly through more than one vehicle (a "chain" of vehicles), and

(*b*) each vehicle in the chain is wholly owned by another vehicle in the chain or by the pension scheme.

(6) Where—

(*a*) the pension scheme holds the interest in the property indirectly through one vehicle, and

(*b*) the vehicle is not wholly owned by the pension scheme,

the amount of the unauthorised payment is a proportion of the total taxable amount determined by reference to the extent of the pension scheme's interest in the vehicle.

(7) Where—

(*a*) the pension scheme holds the interest in the property indirectly through one or more chains of vehicles, and

(*b*) one or more vehicles in such a chain is not wholly owned by another vehicle in the chain or by the pension scheme,

the amount of the unauthorised payment is the amount or the total of all the amounts found under sub-paragraph (8) for each chain through which the pension scheme owns the interest in the property.

(8) The amount is a proportion of the total taxable amount determined by reference to the extent of the interest held directly by the pension scheme or another vehicle in the chain in each vehicle in the chain—

(*a*) starting with the vehicle which holds the interest in the property directly, and

(*b*) ending with the vehicle in which the pension scheme directly holds an interest.

(9) For the purposes of this paragraph a vehicle is wholly owned by a person if no other person directly holds an interest in the vehicle.

(10) This paragraph is subject to paragraph 44.]¹

Amendments—¹   This Schedule inserted by FA 2006 s 158, Sch 21 paras 2, 13. This amendment is deemed to have come into force on 6 April 2006.

[**42**—(1) References in this Schedule to the extent of an interest held directly by a person in a vehicle are references to the proportion of the interests of everyone who directly holds an interest in the vehicle which on a just and reasonable apportionment is represented by that interest.

(2) Sub-paragraph (1) is subject to paragraph 43, which explains how to determine the extent of a person's interest in a vehicle for the purposes of the taxable property provisions where the vehicle is a company.

(3) The Treasury may by regulations—

    (*a*) amend paragraph 43, or

    (*b*) amend this Part of this Schedule for the purposes of explaining how to determine the extent of a person's interest in a vehicle in other cases.

(4) Regulations under sub-paragraph (3) may include provision having effect in relation to times before they are made.]¹

Amendments—¹   This Schedule inserted by FA 2006 s 158, Sch 21 paras 2, 13. This amendment is deemed to have come into force on 6 April 2006.

[**43**—(1) For the purposes of this Schedule, and except in a case to which sub-paragraph (3) applies, the extent of a person's interest in a company is determined by reference to whichever of the following gives the person the greatest interest in the company—

    (*a*) the percentage of the share capital or issued share capital of the company owned by the person;

    (*b*) the percentage of the voting rights in the company owned by the person;

    (*c*) the percentage of all the income of the company to which the person has a right;

    (*d*) the percentage of the amounts distributed on a distribution in relation to the company to which the person has a right;

    (*e*) the percentage of the assets of the company to which the person has a right on a winding-up or in any other circumstances;

    (*f*) where the person has a right to a percentage of a particular asset or description of assets of the company, or of the income or gains from such an asset or description (either generally or in particular circumstances), that percentage or the highest of all the percentages found under this paragraph.

(2) For the purposes of sub-paragraph (1) a person is treated as owning or having a right to anything which the person will only acquire—

    (*a*) at some future date,

    (*b*) if the person exercises a right to acquire it, or

    (*c*) if some other uncertain future event occurs or does not occur.

(3) Where—

    (*a*) a person has an interest in a company as a result of lending the company money to fund the acquisition of an interest in taxable property, and

    (*b*) this sub-paragraph gives the person a greater interest in the company than any interest given by sub-paragraph (1),

for the purposes of this Schedule the extent of the person's interest in the company is determined by the proportion that the value of the loan bears to the total value of the assets held directly by the company.

(4) For the purposes of sub-paragraph (3)—

    (*a*) assets must be valued in accordance with generally accepted accounting practice,

    (*b*) no account is to be taken of liabilities secured against or otherwise relating to assets (whether generally or specifically), and

    (*c*) where generally accepted accounting practice offers a choice of valuation between cost basis and fair value, fair value must be used.]¹

Amendments—¹   This Schedule inserted by FA 2006 s 158, Sch 21 paras 2, 13. This amendment is deemed to have come into force on 6 April 2006.

[Deemed acquisition: adjustment

44—(1) This paragraph applies where an investment-regulated pension scheme is treated as acquiring an interest in taxable property by virtue of paragraph 28 (increase in extent of interest in vehicle).

(2) The amount of the unauthorised payment treated as made by the pension scheme is—

UP – UPB

where—

> UP is the amount that would have been the amount of the unauthorised payment apart from this paragraph; and
>
> UPB is the amount that would have been the amount of any unauthorised payment treated as made by the pension scheme if it had acquired the interest in the property immediately before the increase in the extent of the interest in the vehicle (assuming the total taxable amount in relation to the unauthorised payment to be that given under paragraph 32(5)).][1]

Amendments—[1]   This Schedule inserted by FA 2006 s 158, Sch 21 paras 2, 13. This amendment is deemed to have come into force on 6 April 2006.

[Apportionment to member

45—(1) This paragraph has effect for determining—

> (a) whether the whole of an unauthorised payment treated as made by a pension scheme is to be treated as made to a member of the scheme, and
>
> (b) if not, how much of the unauthorised payment is to be treated as made to the member.

(2) If the interest in the taxable property which gives rise to the unauthorised payment is held by the pension scheme for the purposes of—

> (a) the arrangement under the pension scheme relating to the member, and
>
> (b) at least one other arrangement under the pension scheme,

the unauthorised payment is to be apportioned on a just and reasonable basis between all of the arrangements for the purposes of which the interest in the property is held.

(3) Otherwise, the whole of the unauthorised payment is to be treated as made to the member.][1]

Amendment—[1]   This Schedule inserted by FA 2006 s 158, Sch 21 paras 2, 13. This amendment is deemed to have come into force on 6 April 2006.

SCHEDULE 30
REGISTERED PENSION SCHEMES: EMPLOYER LOANS
Section 179

Commentary—*Simon's Taxes* **E7.102**.

DEFINITIONS
Charge of adequate value

1—(1) A charge is of adequate value if it meets conditions A, B and C.

(2) Condition A is that, at the time the charge is given, the market value of the assets subject to the charge—

> (a) in the case of the first charge to secure the loan, is at least equal to the amount owing (including interest), and
>
> (b) in any other case, is at least equal to the lower of that amount and the market value of the assets subject to the previous charge.

(3) Condition B is that if, at any time after the charge is given, the market value of the assets charged is less than would be required under condition A if the charge were given at that time, the reduction in value is not attributable to any step taken by the pension scheme, the sponsoring employer or a person connected with the sponsoring employer.

(4) Condition C is that the charge takes priority over any other charge over the assets.

Commentary—*Simon's Taxes* **E7.237**.

Loan repayment date

2—(1) "Loan repayment date" means the date by which the total amount owing (including interest) must be paid.

(2) A standard loan repayment date is a loan repayment date before the end of the period of five years beginning with the date on which the loan is made.

Loan year

3—(1) "Loan year" means—

> (a) the period of 12 months beginning with the date on which the loan is made, and
>
> (b) each succeeding period of 12 months.

(2) But in the period of 12 months in which the loan repayment date falls, the loan year ends on the loan repayment date (and that loan year is the last loan year).

Required amount

4   "The required amount", in relation to a period beginning with the date on which the loan is made and ending with the last day of a loan year, is—

$$\frac{L + TIP}{TLY} \times NLY$$

where—

L is the amount of the loan,

TIP is the total interest payable on the loan,

TLY is the total number of loan years, and

NLY is the number of loan years in the period.

AMOUNT OF UNAUTHORISED PAYMENT

Loan does not comply with section 179(1) when made

5—(1) If a loan does not comply with section 179(1) (authorised employer loan) when it is made, there is an unauthorised payment of an amount equal to the largest of such of amounts 1, 2, A, B, and C as arise in relation to the loan.

(2) Paragraphs 12 to 16 explain amounts 1, 2, A, B and C.

Commentary—*Simon's Taxes* **E7.237**.

Loan ceases to be secured by charge of adequate value

6   If at any time after a loan is made the loan ceases to be secured by a charge of adequate value, there is an unauthorised payment equal to amount 2 (see paragraph 13).

Commentary—*Simon's Taxes* **E7.237**.

Further reduction in value of charge which is not of adequate value

7—(1) If at any time after a loan is made—

   (*a*) the loan is secured by a charge which is not of adequate value, and

   (*b*) an event mentioned in sub-paragraph (2) occurs,

there is an unauthorised payment.

(2) The events are—

   (*a*) the loan ceasing to be secured by a charge,

   (*b*) a charge being given which does not comply with conditions A or C,

   (*c*) a reduction in the value of the assets charged which does not comply with condition B, and

   (*d*) the charge ceasing to comply with condition C.

(3) The amount of the unauthorised payment is—

$$AAE - ABE$$

where—

AAE is amount 2 (see paragraph 13) calculated after the event, and

ABE is amount 2 (see paragraph 13) calculated before the event.

(4) Paragraph 1 defines conditions A, B and C.

Commentary—*Simon's Taxes* **E7.237**.

Loan ceases to comply with repayment terms

8—(1) If at any time after a loan is made—

   (*a*) there is an alteration in the repayment terms, and

   (*b*) as a result the repayment terms cease to comply with one or more paragraphs of section 179(2) (authorised repayment terms),

there is an unauthorised payment of an amount equal to the larger of such of amounts A, B, and C (see paragraphs 14 to 16) as arise when that paragraph or those paragraphs are not complied with.

Commentary—*Simon's Taxes* **E7.237**.

Increase in extent to which loan does not comply with repayment terms

9—(1) If at any time after a loan is made—

   (*a*) there is an alteration in the repayment terms, and

(*b*) as a result the deterioration condition is met in relation to one or more paragraphs of section 179(2) (authorised repayment terms) which were not complied with before the alteration,

there is an unauthorised payment of an amount calculated in accordance with sub-paragraphs (3) and (4).

(2) The deterioration condition is met in relation to a paragraph if—

$$AAA > ABA$$

(3) For each paragraph in relation to which the deterioration condition is met, calculate—

$$AAA - ABA$$

(4) There is an unauthorised payment of an amount equal to the largest of the amounts calculated under sub-paragraph (3).

(5) In this paragraph—

AAA, in relation to a paragraph of section 179(2) which was not complied with before the alteration in the repayment terms, is the amount arising when that paragraph is not complied with, calculated after the alteration in the repayment terms, and

ABA, in relation to such a paragraph, is the amount arising when that paragraph is not complied with, calculated before the alteration in the repayment terms.

Commentary—*Simon's Taxes* E7.237.

Prevention of double charging

10—(1) This paragraph applies if on any date there is an unauthorised payment under more than one of paragraphs 6 to 9.

(2) There is a single unauthorised payment.

(3) The amount of the unauthorised payment is an amount equal to the amount of the greater or greatest of the unauthorised payments under those paragraphs.

Commentary—*Simon's Taxes* E7.237.

Total unauthorised payments not to exceed amount of loan

11 If the aggregate amount of the unauthorised payments in relation to a loan under paragraphs 5 to 10 exceeds the amount of the loan when it was made, the excess is to be treated as not being an unauthorised payment.

Commentary—*Simon's Taxes* E7.237.

Amount 1

12—(1) Amount 1 arises if paragraph (*a*) of section 179(1) (amount of loan must not exceed 50% of pension scheme assets) is not complied with.

(2) Amount 1 is—

$$\frac{\left(\dfrac{AL}{VA} \times 100\right) - 100}{100} \times VA$$

where—

AL is the amount of the loan, and

VA is an amount equal to 50% of the aggregate of the amount of the sums, and the market value of the assets, held for the purposes of the pension scheme before the loan is made.

Commentary—*Simon's Taxes* E7.237.

Amount 2

13—(1) Amount 2 arises if paragraph (*b*) of section 179(1) (loan must be secured by charge of adequate value) is not complied with.

(2) Amount 2 is—

$$AO - VA$$

where—

AO is the amount owing (including interest) at the relevant time, and

VA is the market value at that time of the assets charged but if the loan is not secured by a charge, or is secured by a charge which does not meet condition C (as defined in paragraph 1), is nil.

Commentary—*Simon's Taxes* **E7.237**.

Amount A

14—(1) Amount A arises if paragraph (*a*) of section 179(2) (interest rate to be not less than prescribed amount) is not complied with.

(2) Amount A is—

$$\frac{100 - \left(\dfrac{IR}{PIR} \times 100\right)}{100} \times AO$$

where—

    IR is the rate of interest payable at the relevant time,

    PIR is the rate of interest prescribed by regulations under that paragraph, and

    AO is the amount owing (not including interest) at the relevant time.

Commentary—*Simon's Taxes* **E7.237**.

Amount B

15—(1) Amount B arises if paragraph (*b*) of section 179(2) (loan repayment date to be within five years unless postponed) is not complied with.

(2) Amount B is—

$$\frac{\left(\dfrac{DLRP}{DFY} \times 100\right) - 100}{100} \times AO$$

where—

    DLRP is the number of days in the period which begins with the date on which the loan is made and ends with the loan repayment date,

    DFY is the number of days in the period which begins with the date on which the loan is made and ends five years after that date, and

    AO is the amount owing (including interest) at the relevant time.

(3) But if the amount produced by the fraction in sub-paragraph (2) is greater than 1, amount B is the amount owing (including interest) at the relevant time.

(4) If the loan repayment date has been postponed under section 179(3), sub-paragraph (2) applies as if references to the date on which the loan is made were to the standard loan repayment date on which the loan repayment date was postponed.

Commentary—*Simon's Taxes* **E7.237**.

Amount C

16—(1) Amount C arises if paragraph (*c*) of section 179(2) (amount payable for a period to be not less than required amount) is not complied with and is calculated as follows.

(2) In relation to each period beginning with the date on which the loan is made and ending with the last day of a loan year, calculate—

$$RA - AP$$

where—

    RA is the required amount in relation to that period, and

    AP is the amount payable during that period.

(3) If an amount calculated under sub-paragraph (2) is negative, treat that amount as nil.

(4) Amount C is the largest of the amounts calculated under sub-paragraph (2).

Commentary—*Simon's Taxes* **E7.237**.

SCHEDULE 31

TAXATION OF BENEFITS UNDER REGISTERED PENSION SCHEMES

Section 204

Commentary—*Simon's Taxes* **E7.102**.

1   Part 9 of ITEPA 2003 (pension income) is amended as follows.

2   (*amends* ITEPA 2003 s 565)

3—(1) Section 566(4) (nature of charge to tax on pension income) is amended as follows.
(2)–(4) (*amend* ITEPA 2003 s 566(4))

4   (*amends* ITEPA 2003 s 567(4)(*a*))

5   (*amends* ITEPA 2003 s 568)

6   (*inserts* ITEPA 2003 Ch 5A (ss 579A–579D))

7   (*repeals* ITEPA 2003 Chs 6–9)

8—(1) Section 610 (annuities under sponsored superannuation schemes) is amended as follows.
(2)–(5) (*amend* ITEPA 2003 s 610(1), (3), (4) and section heading)

9   (*amends* ITEPA 2003 s 611(3))

10   (*repeals* ITEPA 2003 Ch 13)

11   (*inserts* ITEPA 2003 Ch 15A (ss 636A–636C))

12   (*repeals* ITEPA 2003 Ch 16)

13   (*amends* ITEPA 2003 s 644(2))

14—(1) Section 683 of ITEPA 2003 (PAYE income) is amended as follows.
(2), (3) (*amend* ITEPA 2003 s 683(3))
(4) (*repeals* ITEPA 2003 s 683(4))

15   (*inserts* entry into ITEPA 2003 Sch 1 Pt 2)

SCHEDULE 32

REGISTERED PENSION SCHEMES: BENEFIT CRYSTALLISATION EVENTS— SUPPLEMENTARY

Section 216

Commentary—*Simon's Taxes* **E7.102, E7.216**.

General: meaning of "the relevant pension schemes"

1   For the purposes of the benefit crystallisation events "the relevant pension schemes" means the registered pension schemes of which the individual is a member (or, in the case of benefit crystallisation event [5C [or 5D][2] or][1] 7, was a member immediately before death).

Amendments—[1]   Words inserted by the Taxation of Pensions Act 2014 s 3, Sch 2 para 24(1), (2) with effect from 17 December 2014.
[2]   Words inserted by FA 2015 s 34, Sch 4 para 1, 7(*a*) with effect from 26 March 2015.

Post-75 events not generally benefit crystallisation events

2   The only sort of event that constitutes a benefit crystallisation event in relation to the individual after the individual has reached the age of 75 is an event that constitutes benefit crystallisation event 3.

[Avoiding double counting of refunded amounts of overseas transfer charge

2A—(1) This paragraph applies where an amount of overseas transfer charge is repaid (whether or not under section 244M) to the scheme administrator of one of the relevant pension schemes.
(2) The amount crystallised by the first benefit crystallisation event that occurs in respect of the individual and a benefited scheme after receipt of the repayment is to be reduced (but not below nil) by the amount of the repayment.
(3) If the amount of the repayment exceeds the reduction under subparagraph (2), the excess is to be set sequentially until exhausted against the amounts crystallised by subsequent benefit crystallisation events occurring in respect of the individual and a benefited scheme.
(4) In sub-paragraphs (2) and (3) "benefited scheme" means—
   (*a*) the scheme to which the repayment is made, and

(b) any other pension scheme if as a result of a recognised transfer, or a chain of two or more recognised transfers, sums or assets representing the repayment are held for the purposes of, or represent rights under, that other scheme.][1]

Commentary—*Simon's Taxes* **E7.217**.
Amendments—[1]   Para 2A inserted by FA 2017 s 10, Sch 4 paras 12, 18 with effect in relation to transfers made on or after 9 March 2017.

Benefit crystallisation events 1, 2 and 4: prevention of overlap

3—(1) This paragraph applies for the purposes of benefit crystallisation event 2 if the scheme pension is funded (in whole or in part) by the [application][1] of sums or assets representing the whole or part of the individual's [drawdown pension fund][2].

(2) The amount crystallised by the event is to be reduced by the amount (or an appropriate proportion of the amount) previously crystallised on the designation of the sums or assets as available for the payment of [drawdown pension][2].

Amendments—[1]   Word in sub-para (1) substituted by FA 2005 s 101, Sch 10 paras 25(2), 64(1) with effect from 6 April 2006.
[2]   Words in sub-para (1) substituted for words "unsecured pension fund", and words in sub-para (2) substituted for words "unsecured pension", by FA 2011 s 65, Sch 16 paras 62, 80(1), (2) with effect for the tax year 2011–12 and subsequent tax years, subject to transitional provisions in FA 2011 Sch 16 Pt 3. The amendments made by FA 2011 Sch 16 paras 43, 44, 73, 80, 82(2) have effect in relation to benefit crystallisation events occurring on or after 6 April 2011 (FA 2011 Sch 16 para 104(1)).

4—(1) This paragraph applies for the purposes of benefit crystallisation event 4 [if—
(a) the lifetime annuity or a related dependants' annuity or a related nominees' annuity is, or
(b) the lifetime annuity and a related dependants' annuity are, or
(c) the lifetime annuity and a related nominees' annuity are, or
(d) a related dependants' annuity and a related nominees' annuity are, or
(e) the lifetime annuity and a related dependants' annuity and a related nominees' annuity are, purchased][3] (in whole or in part) with sums or assets representing the whole or part of the individual's [drawdown pension fund][1] [or flexi-access drawdown fund][2].

(2) The amount crystallised by the event is to be reduced by the amount (or an appropriate proportion of the amount) previously crystallised on the designation of the sums or assets as available for the payment of [drawdown pension][1].

Amendments—[1]   Words in sub-para (1) substituted for words "unsecured pension fund", and words in sub-para (2) substituted for words "unsecured pension", by FA 2011 s 65, Sch 16 paras 62, 80(1), (3) with effect for the tax year 2011–12 and subsequent tax years, subject to transitional provisions in FA 2011 Sch 16 Pt 3. The amendments made by FA 2011 Sch 16 paras 43, 44, 73, 80, 82(2) have effect in relation to benefit crystallisation events occurring on or after 6 April 2011 (FA 2011 Sch 16 para 104(1)).
[2]   Words in sub-para (1) inserted by the Taxation of Pensions Act 2014 s 1, Sch 1 paras 5, 26 with effect from 17 December 2014.
[3]   In sub-para (1), words substituted for words "if the lifetime annuity or a related dependants' annuity is, or both the lifetime annuity and a related dependants' annuity are, purchased", by FA 2015 s 34, Sch 4 paras 1, 7(b) with effect from 26 March 2015.

Benefit crystallisation events 1 and 5: hybrid arrangements

5—(1) This paragraph applies where—
(a) immediately before the individual reaches the age of 75, there is under any of the relevant pension schemes a hybrid arrangement relating to the individual, and
(b) the benefits that may be provided to or in respect of the individual under the arrangement may, depending on the circumstances, be money purchase benefits or defined benefits.

(2) Benefit crystallisation event 1 applies as if, at that time, the circumstances are such that the benefits to be provided are money purchase benefits . . . .[1].

(3) Benefit crystallisation event 5 applies as if, at that time, the circumstances are such that the benefits to be provided are defined benefits.

(4) The amount crystallised is the greater of the amounts crystallised by the two benefit crystallisation events.

Amendments—[1]   Words "(with the effect that, under paragraph 8(2) of Schedule 28, any relevant uncrystallised funds are to be treated as having been designated under the arrangement as available for the provision of unsecured pension to the individual)" in sub-para (2) repealed by FA 2011 s 65, Sch 16 paras 62, 80(1), (4) with effect for the tax year 2011–12 and subsequent tax years, subject to transitional provisions in FA 2011 Sch 16 Pt 3. The amendments made by FA 2011 Sch 16 paras 43, 44, 73, 80, 82(2) have effect in relation to benefit crystallisation events occurring on or after 6 April 2011 (FA 2011 Sch 16 para 104(1)).

Benefit crystallisation events 2, 3 and 5: meaning of "RVF"

6   For the purposes of benefit crystallisation events 2, 3 and 5 "RVF" is the relevant valuation factor (see section 276).

Benefit crystallisation events 2 and 4: early lifetime annuities

7—(1) This paragraph has effect if—

(a) the individual becomes entitled before reaching normal minimum pension age to the payment of a lifetime annuity purchased under a money purchase arrangement under any of the relevant pension schemes, and

(b) the ill-health condition is not satisfied immediately before the individual becomes so entitled.

(2) Benefit crystallisation event 2 applies as if—

(a) the lifetime annuity were a scheme pension under the pension scheme, and

(b) the individual becomes entitled to it only on reaching normal minimum pension age.

(3) Benefit crystallisation event 4 does not apply in relation to the lifetime annuity.

[(4) Sub-paragraph (5) has effect for the purposes of benefit crystallisation event 2 as it applies in relation to the individual's becoming entitled to the lifetime annuity.

(5) If the total of—

(a) the sums applied to purchase the lifetime annuity and any related dependants' annuity, and

(b) the market value, at the time they are applied, of the assets applied to make the purchase,

is greater than the amount that would apart from this sub-paragraph be the amount crystallised by the event, that total is the amount crystallised by the event.][1]

Amendments—[1]   Sub-paras (4), (5) inserted by the Taxation of Pensions Act 2014 s 1, Sch 1 para 76(1) with effect in relation to a lifetime annuity if, applying the rule in FA 2004 s 165(3)(b), the annuity is one to which an individual becomes entitled on or after 6 April 2015.

Benefit crystallisation event 2: early pensions

8   For the purposes of benefit crystallisation event 2 if—

(a) the individual becomes entitled to the pension before reaching normal minimum pension age, and

(b) the ill-health condition is not satisfied immediately before the individual becomes entitled to the pension,

the individual is to be treated as becoming entitled to it only on reaching normal minimum pension age.

Benefit crystallisation event 2: meaning of "P"

9—(1) For the purposes of benefit crystallisation event 2 "P" is the amount of the pension which will be payable to the individual in the period of 12 months beginning with the day on which the individual becomes entitled to it (assuming that it remains payable throughout that period at the rate at which it is payable on that day).

[(1A) If the pension is under a public service pension scheme, any abatement of the pension is to be left out of account in determining the amount of the pension which will be payable for the purposes of sub-paragraph (1).][1]

(2) If the amount of the pension which will be payable [is][2] reduced so as to reflect the amount of any tax under section 215 to be paid by the scheme administrator, that reduction is to be left out of account in determining the amount of the pension . . . [2] for the purposes of sub-paragraph (1).

[(3) And if the reduction is such that, in accordance with normal actuarial practice, it would be taken fully to reflect the amount of the tax, the tax is not to be treated as tax paid by the scheme administrator for the purposes of section 215(9).][2]

Modifications—Registered Pension Schemes (Splitting of Schemes) Regulations, SI 2006/569 reg 3 (modification of this provision in relation to sub-scheme administrators).

Amendments—[1]   Sub-para (1A) inserted by FA 2005 s 101, Sch 10 paras 8(2), 64(1) with effect from 6 April 2006.

[2]   Words in sub-para (2) substituted and repealed, and sub-para (3) inserted by FA 2005 ss 101, 104, Sch 10 paras 43(2)–(4), 64(1), Sch 11 Pt 4 with effect from 6 April 2006.

[Benefit crystallisation event 3: disregarding abatement

9A   For the purposes of benefit crystallisation event 3, any abatement of the scheme pension is to be left out of account in determining for the purposes of column 1 —

(a) the increased annual rate of the pension, and

(b) the rate at which it was payable on the day on which the individual became entitled to it.][1]

Amendments—[1]   Paragraph inserted by FA 2005 s 101, Sch 10 paras 8(3), 64(1) with effect from 6 April 2006.

Benefit crystallisation event 3: excepted circumstances

10—[(1)] [1] For the purposes of benefit crystallisation event 3 "excepted circumstances" means—

(a) that at the time when the annual rate of the individual's pension is increased there are at least 50 pensioner members of the pension scheme, and [(*b*)　that the individual is one of a class of at least 20 pensioner members of the pension scheme, and all the scheme pensions being paid under the pension scheme to pensioner members of that class are at that time increased at the same rate.]¹

[(2)　A class may consist of all the pensioner members of the pension scheme.

(3)　Sub-paragraph (4) applies where—

(*a*)　the annual rate of the individual's pension is increased in excepted circumstances ("the excepted increase"),

(*b*)　before the end of the period of 12 months beginning with the date of the excepted increase, the annual rate of the individual's pension is increased in circumstances which would (apart from that sub-paragraph) be excepted circumstances ("the subsequent increase"), and

(*c*)　the class by virtue of which sub-paragraph (1)(*b*) is satisfied on the subsequent increase ("the new class") is not the class by virtue of which it was satisfied on the excepted increase.

(4)　If the purpose, or one of the main purposes, of the individual's being included in the new class is to increase the annual rate of the individual's pension without benefit crystallisation event 3 occurring, the subsequent increase is not in excepted circumstances.]¹

Amendments—¹　Sub-para (1) numbered as such, sub-para (1)(*b*) substituted, and sub-paras (2)–(4) inserted, by FA 2008 s 92, Sch 29 para 7. This amendment is treated as having come into force on 6 April 2006, subject to FA 2008 Sch 29 para 12(2)

[Benefit crystallisation event 3: threshold annual rate

10A—(1)　This paragraph applies for the purposes of benefit crystallisation event 3.

(2)　The threshold annual rate is the annual rate of the pension on the date of which the increase date is the first anniversary, increased by the greatest of—

(*a*)　the relevant percentage rate,

(*b*)　the relevant indexation percentage, and

(*c*)　£250,

and rounded up in accordance with sub-paragraph (8).

(3)　But if the person became entitled to the pension after the date of which the increase date is the first anniversary, the threshold annual rate is the annual rate of the pension on the date on which the person became entitled to the pension, increased and rounded up as mentioned in sub-paragraph (2).

(4)　The increase date is the date on which the individual becomes entitled to payment of the pension at the increased annual rate.

(5)　The relevant percentage rate is—

(*a*)　in a case where the pension is paid under a pension scheme, or an arrangement under a pension scheme, in relation to which the relevant valuation factor is a number greater than 20, the rate agreed by the Commissioners for Her Majesty's Revenue and Customs and the scheme administrator, and

(*b*)　otherwise, 5%.

(6)　The relevant indexation percentage means—

(*a*)　if the retail prices index for the reference month is higher than the retail prices index for the same calendar month in the previous year, the percentage increase in the retail prices index, and

(*b*)　if it is not, 0%.

(7)　The scheme administrator may select as the reference month any month in the period of 12 months ending with the month in which the increase date falls.

(8)　An amount is rounded up in accordance with this sub-paragraph if it is rounded up to the next greatest amount which—

(*a*)　where the pension is payable monthly, gives an amount of whole pounds when divided by 12, or

(*b*)　where the pension is payable weekly, gives an amount of whole pounds when divided by 52.

(9)　If the pension is under a public service pension scheme, any abatement of the pension is to be left out of account in determining for the purposes of this paragraph the annual rate of the pension on the date of which the increase date is the first anniversary (or, where sub-paragraph (3) applies, the date on which the person became entitled to the pension).

(10)　An individual who becomes entitled to payment of a scheme pension at an increased annual rate on 29 February in any year is to be treated for the purposes of this paragraph as having become so entitled on 28 February in that year.

(11)　The Treasury may by order substitute for the amount for the time being specified in sub-paragraph (2)(*c*) a different amount (including an amount to be calculated as a percentage of the standard lifetime allowance).]¹

Amendments—¹　Para 10A inserted by FA 2008 s 92, Sch 29, para 8. This amendment is treated as having come into force on 6 April 2006, subject to FA 2008 Sch 29 para 12(2)

Benefit crystallisation event 3: permitted margin

11—(1) This paragraph applies for the purposes of benefit crystallisation event 3 if the individual became entitled to the pension on or after 6th April 2006.

(2) The permitted margin is the amount by which the annual amount of the pension at the rate at which it was payable on the day on which the individual became entitled to it would be greater if it had been increased by whichever of calculation A and calculation B gives the greater amount.

(3) Calculation A involves increasing that annual amount at the relevant annual percentage rate for the whole of the period—

    (*a*) beginning with the month in which the individual became entitled to the pension, and

    (*b*) ending with the month in which the individual becomes entitled to payment of the pension at the increased rate.

(4) The relevant annual percentage rate is—

    (*a*) in a case where the pension is paid under a pension scheme, or an arrangement under a pension scheme, in relation to which the relevant valuation factor is a number greater than 20, the annual rate agreed by the Inland Revenue and the scheme administrator, and

    (*b*) otherwise, 5% per annum.

(5) Calculation B involves increasing that annual amount by the relevant indexation percentage.

(6) If the retail prices index for the [reference month][2] is higher than it was for the [base month][2], the relevant indexation percentage is the percentage increase in the retail prices index.

(7) If it is not, the relevant indexation percentage is 0%.

[(7A) The scheme administrator may select as the reference month any month in the period of 12 months ending with the month in which the individual becomes entitled to payment of the pension at the increased rate.

(7B) The base month is the month which is the same number of months before the month in which the individual became entitled to the pension, as the reference month is before the month in which the individual becomes entitled to payment of the pension at the increased rate.][2]

[(8) If the pension is under a public service pension scheme, any abatement of the pension is to be left out of account in determining for the purposes of this paragraph the annual amount of the pension at the rate at which it was payable on the day on which the individual became entitled to it.][1]

Modifications—Pensions Schemes (Application of UK Provisions to Relevant Non-UK Schemes) Regulations, SI 2006/207 reg 16 (modification of this paragraph in respect of relevant non-UK schemes).

Amendments—[1] Sub-para (8) inserted by FA 2005 s 101, Sch 10 paras 8(4), 64(1) with effect from 6 April 2006.

[2] Words in sub-para (6) substituted and sub-paras (7A), (7B) inserted, by FA 2008 s 92, Sch 29 para 9(3) with effect from 6 April 2008.

12—(1) This paragraph applies for the purposes of benefit crystallisation event 3 if the individual became entitled to the pension before 6th April 2006.

(2) The permitted margin is the greater of—

    (*a*) what would be the permitted margin at that time if the individual had become entitled to the pension on or after that date (see paragraph 11), and

    (*b*) the amount by which the annual amount of the pension at the rate at which it was payable on the day on which the individual became entitled to it would be greater if it had been increased for the whole of the period specified in sub-paragraph (3) of that paragraph at the rate of P% per annum.

(3) "P%" is the percentage by which, in accordance with the rules of the pension scheme immediately before 6th April 2006, the annual rate of the pension is to be increased each year.

[(4) If the pension is under a public service pension scheme, any abatement of the pension is to be left out of account in determining for the purposes of this paragraph the annual amount of the pension at the rate at which it was payable on the day on which the individual became entitled to it.][1]

Amendments—[1] Sub-para (4) inserted by FA 2005 s 101, Sch 10 paras 8(5), 64(1) with effect from 6 April 2006.

Benefit crystallisation event 3: meaning of "XP"

13—(1) For the purposes of benefit crystallisation event 3 XP is (subject to sub-paragraph (2)) the amount by which—

    (*a*) the increased annual rate of the pension, exceeds

    (*b*) the rate at which it was payable on the day on which the individual became entitled to it, as increased by the permitted margin.

[(2) But if one or more benefit crystallisation events has or have previously occurred by reason of the individual having become entitled to payment of the pension at an increased rate, XP does not include the amount of XP on that event or the aggregate of the amounts of XP on those events.

(2A) For the purposes of sub-paragraph (2), the amount of XP on a previous benefit crystallisation event is to be increased by whichever of calculation A and calculation B gives the greater amount.

(2B) Calculation A involves increasing the amount of XP on the previous event at the relevant annual percentage rate for the whole of the period—

(a) beginning with the month in which the previous event occurred, and

(b) ending with the month in which the individual becomes entitled to payment of the pension at the increased rate.

(2C) The relevant annual percentage rate has the same meaning as in paragraph 11(4).

(2D) Calculation B involves increasing the amount of XP on the previous event by the relevant indexation percentage.

(2E) The relevant indexation percentage is—

(a) if the retail prices index for the reference month is higher than the retail prices index for the base month, the percentage increase in the retail prices index, and

(b) if it is not, 0%.

(2F) The scheme administrator may select as the reference month any month in the period of 12 months ending with the month in which the individual becomes entitled to payment of the pension at the increased rate.

(2G) The base month is the month which is the same number of months before the month in which the previous event occurred, as the reference month is before the month in which the individual becomes entitled to payment of the pension at the increased rate.][3]

[(3) If the pension is under a public service pension scheme, any abatement of the pension is to be left out of account in determining for the purposes of sub-paragraph (1)—

(a) the increased annual rate of the pension, and

(b) the rate at which it was payable on the day on which the individual became entitled to it.][1]

[(4) If the rate at which the pension is payable is reduced so as to reflect the amount of any tax under section 215 to be paid by the scheme administrator, that reduction is to be left out of account in determining the rate at which the pension is payable for the purposes of sub-paragraph (1)(a).

(5) And if the reduction is such that, in accordance with normal actuarial practice, it would be taken fully to reflect the amount of the tax, the tax is not to be treated as tax paid by the scheme administrator for the purposes of section 215(9).][2]

Modifications—Registered Pension Schemes (Splitting of Schemes) Regulations, SI 2006/569 reg 3 (modification of this provision in relation to sub-scheme administrators).

Amendments—[1] Sub-para (3) inserted by FA 2005 s 101, Sch 10 paras 8(6), 64(1) with effect from 6 April 2006.
[2] Sub-paras (4), (5) inserted by FA 2005 ss 101, 104, Sch 10 paras 43(5), 64(1) with effect from 6 April 2006.
[3] Sub-paras (2)–(2G) substituted for sub-para (2) by FA 2008 s 92, Sch 29 para 10 with effect for the purposes of any benefit crystallisation event 3 occurring on or after 10 October 2007 (including the calculation, for the purposes of such an event, of the amount of XP on any benefit crystallisation event occurring before that date).

Benefit crystallisation event 5: meaning of "DP" and "DSLS"

14—(1) For the purposes of benefit crystallisation event 5 "DP" is the annual rate of the scheme pension to which the individual would be entitled if, on the date on which the individual reaches 75, the individual acquired an actual (rather than a prospective) right to receive it.

[(1A) If the rate at which the scheme pension would be payable would be reduced so as to reflect the amount of any tax under section 215 to be paid by the scheme administrator, that reduction is to be left out of account in determining the rate at which the pension would be payable for the purposes of sub-paragraph (1).

(1B) And if the reduction is such that, in accordance with normal actuarial practice, it would be taken fully to reflect the amount of the tax, the tax is not to be treated as tax paid by the scheme administrator for the purposes of section 215(9).][1]

(2) For the purposes of benefit crystallisation event 5 "DSLS" is [so much][1] of any lump sum to which the individual would be entitled (otherwise than by way of commutation of pension) [as would be paid to the individual][1] if, on that date, the individual acquired an actual (rather than a prospective) right to receive it.

Modifications—Registered Pension Schemes (Splitting of Schemes) Regulations, SI 2006/569 reg 3 (modification of this provision in relation to sub-scheme administrators).

Amendments—[1] Sub-paras (1A), (1B) inserted, and words in sub-para (2) substituted and inserted by FA 2005 ss 101, 104, Sch 10 paras 43(6)–(8), 64(1) with effect from 6 April 2006.

[Benefit crystallisation event 5B: meaning of "remaining unused funds"

14A For the purposes of benefit crystallisation event 5B "remaining unused funds" means—

(a) in relation to a cash balance arrangement, a sum equal to what would, on the valuation assumption in section 277(a), be available for the provision of benefits to or in respect of the member if the member became entitled to them on reaching the age of 75, and

(b) in relation to any other arrangement, such of the sums and assets held for the purposes of the arrangement as are not member-designated funds and have not been applied towards the provision of a scheme pension or a dependants' scheme pension.][1]

Amendments—[1]   This para and preceding crosshead inserted by FA 2011 s 65, Sch 16 para 44(1), (2) with effect for the tax year 2011–12 and subsequent tax years, subject to transitional provisions in FA 2011 Sch 16 Pt 3. The amendments made by FA 2011 Sch 16 paras 43, 44, 73, 80, 82(2) have effect in relation to benefit crystallisation events occurring on or after 6 April 2011 (FA 2011 Sch 16 para 104(1)).

[Benefit crystallisation [events 5C and 5D]: meaning of "relevant two-year period"

14B   For the purposes of benefit crystallisation [events 5C and 5D][2] "the relevant two-year period", in relation to relevant unused uncrystallised funds held for the purposes of a money purchase arrangement relating to the individual under any of the relevant pension schemes, means the period of two years beginning with the earlier of the day on which the scheme administrator of the scheme first knew of the individual's death and the day on which the scheme administrator could first reasonably have been expected to have known of it.][1]

Amendments—[1]   Paras 14B, 14C inserted by the Taxation of Pensions Act 2014 s 3, Sch 2 para 24(1), (3) with effect from 17 December 2014.
[2]   In italic heading and in para 14B, words substituted for words "event 5C" by FA 2015 s 34, Sch 4 paras 1, 7(c) with effect from 26 March 2015.

[Benefit crystallisation [events 5C and 5D]: meaning of "relevant unused uncrystallised funds"

14C—(1) For the purposes of benefit crystallisation [events 5C and 5D][2], sums or assets held after the death of the individual for the purposes of a money purchase arrangement relating to the individual under any of the relevant pension schemes are relevant unused uncrystallised funds if—
    (*a*)   they are unused uncrystallised funds, and
    (*b*)   the individual had not reached the age of 75 at the date of the individual's death.
(2) Paragraph 27E(4) and (5) of Schedule 28 (meaning of "unused uncrystallised funds") apply for the purposes of sub-paragraph (1)(*a*), but as if references to the member were references to the individual.][1]

Amendments—[1]   Paras 14B, 14C inserted by the Taxation of Pensions Act 2014 s 3, Sch 2 para 24(1), (3) with effect from 17 December 2014.
[2]   In italic heading and in sub-para (1), words substituted for words "event 5C" by FA 2015 s 34, Sch 4 paras 1, 7(d) with effect from 26 March 2015.

Benefit crystallisation event 6: meaning of "relevant lump sum"

15   For the purposes of benefit crystallisation event 6 a lump sum is a relevant lump sum if it is—
    (*a*)   a pension commencement lump sum,
    (*b*)   a serious ill-health lump sum,
    [(*ba*)   an uncrystallised funds pension lump sum,][1] or
    (*c*)   a lifetime allowance excess lump sum.

Amendments—[1]   Sub-para (ba) inserted by the Taxation of Pensions Act 2014 s 1, Sch 1 para 61 with effect from 17 December 2014.

[Benefit crystallisation event 6: prevention of overlap with other events

15A   Benefit crystallisation event 6 does not apply in relation to a pension commencement lump sum paid in respect of a money purchase arrangement if—
    (*a*)   the individual becomes entitled to it before reaching the age of 75, but
    (*b*)   it is not paid to the individual until after the individual has reached that age.][1]

Amendments—[1]   This para and preceding crosshead inserted by FA 2011 s 65, Sch 16 para 44(1), (3) with effect for the tax year 2011–12 and subsequent tax years, subject to transitional provisions in FA 2011 Sch 16 Pt 3. The amendments made by FA 2011 Sch 16 paras 43, 44, 73, 80, 82(2) have effect in relation to benefit crystallisation events occurring on or after 6 April 2011 (FA 2011 Sch 16 para 104(1)).

Benefit crystallisation event 7: meaning of "relevant lump sum death benefit"

16   For the purposes of benefit crystallisation event 7 a lump sum death benefit is a relevant lump sum death benefit if it is—
    (*a*)   a defined benefits lump sum death benefit[, other than one—
       (i)   paid by a registered pension scheme in respect of a member of the scheme who had not reached the age of 75 at the date of the member's death, but
       (ii)   not paid before the end of the relevant two-year period][2], or
    (*b*)   an uncrystallised funds lump sum death benefit[, other than one—
       (i)   paid by a registered pension scheme in respect of a member of the scheme who had not reached the age of 75 at the date of the member's death, but
       (ii)   not paid before the end of the relevant two-year period][1].

[In [paragraphs (*a*)(ii) and][2] (*b*)(ii) "the relevant two-year period", in relation to a member of a registered pension scheme, means the period of two years beginning with the earlier of the day on which the scheme administrator of the scheme first knew of the member's death and the day on which the scheme administrator could first reasonably have been expected to have known of it.]

Amendments—[1]   Words inserted by the Taxation of Pensions Act 2014 s 3, Sch 2 para 19(2) with effect for lump sums paid on or after 6 April 2015.

[2]   In para (*a*), words inserted, and in para (*b*), words substituted by F(No 2)A 2015 s 21(7) with effect in relation to lump sums paid on or after 6 April 2016.

Benefit crystallisation event 8: prevention of overlap with other events

17—(1) This paragraph applies for the purposes of benefit crystallisation event 8.

(2) Where any of the sums or assets transferred represent the whole or part of the individual's [drawdown pension fund][1] [or flexi-access drawdown fund][2], the amount crystallised by the event is to be reduced by the amount (or the appropriate proportion of the amount) previously crystallised on the designation of the sums or assets as available for the payment of [drawdown pension][1].

(3) Where after the transfer a scheme pension to which the individual has become entitled before the transfer is to be payable out of sums or assets transferred, the amount crystallised by the event is to be reduced by the amount (or the appropriate proportion of the amount) previously crystallised in relation to the scheme pension.

Amendments—[1]   Words in sub-para (2) substituted for words "unsecured pension fund" and "unsecured pension" by FA 2011 s 65, Sch 16 paras 62, 80(1), (5) with effect for the tax year 2011–12 and subsequent tax years, subject to transitional provisions in FA 2011 Sch 16 Pt 3. The amendments made by FA 2011 Sch 16 paras 43, 44, 73, 80, 82(2) have effect in relation to benefit crystallisation events occurring on or after 6 April 2011 (FA 2011 Sch 16 para 104(1)).

[2]   Words in sub-para (2) inserted by the Taxation of Pensions Act 2014 s 1, Sch 1 paras 5, 27 with effect from 17 December 2014.

SCHEDULE 33
OVERSEAS PENSION SCHEMES: MIGRANT MEMBER RELIEF
Section 243

Commentary—*Simon's Taxes* **E7.102**.

Relief for members' etc contributions

1—(1) An individual who is a relevant migrant member of a qualifying overseas pension scheme is entitled to relief under section 188 (relief for contributions by or on behalf of members of registered pension schemes) in respect of relievable pension contributions paid during a tax year if the individual—

    (*a*)   has relevant UK earnings chargeable to income tax for that year,

    (*b*)   is resident in the United Kingdom when the contributions are paid, and

    (*c*)   has notified the scheme manager of an intention to claim relief under that section.

(2) Section 190 (annual limit for relief under section 188) applies in relation to the aggregate of the amount of relief to which an individual is entitled under section 188 by virtue of sub-paragraph (1) and any to which the individual is so entitled apart from that sub-paragraph.

(3) Relief to which an individual is entitled under section 188 by virtue of sub-paragraph (1) is to be given in accordance with section 194 (relief on making of claim) (so that nothing in sections 191 to 193 applies in relation to such relief).

(4) Section 195 (transfer of certain shares to be treated as payment of contribution) has effect as if the references to sections 188 to 194 included sections 188 to 190 and 194 as they apply by virtue of this paragraph.

(5) No deduction may be allowed under Chapter 2 of Part 5 of ITEPA 2003 in accordance with section 355 of that Act (deductions for corresponding payments by non-domiciled employees with foreign employers) in respect of contributions under a pension scheme (but subject to Part 4 of Schedule 36).

Commentary—*Simon's Taxes* **E7.222, E7.223**.

HMRC Manuals—Registered Pension Schemes Manual RPSM13101050 (in general an individual will be treated as UK tax resident from their date of arrival until their date of departure).

RPSM13101070–13101080 (definition of an overseas pension scheme and the conditions a scheme needs to meet to be an overseas pension scheme).

Relief for employers' contributions

2—(1) Subsections (2) to (5) of section 196 (relief for contributions by employer) apply in relation to relevant migrant member contributions paid by an employer as in relation to contributions paid by an employer under a registered pension scheme in respect of an individual.

(2) Section 200 (no other relief for employers in connection with contributions) applies as if the reference to contributions under a registered pension scheme included relevant migrant member contributions.

(3) "Relevant migrant member contributions" means contributions paid under a qualifying overseas pension scheme in respect of an individual who is a relevant migrant member of the pension scheme in relation to the contributions.

Commentary—*Simon's Taxes* **E7.222, E7.223**.

3   (*inserts* ITEPA 2003 s 308A)

Commentary—*Simon's Taxes* **E7.222, E7.223**.

Meaning of "relevant migrant member"

4—[(1)] [2] For the purposes of this Schedule an individual who is a member of an overseas pension scheme is a relevant migrant member of the pension scheme, in relation to any contributions, if the individual—

(a) was not resident in the United Kingdom when first a member of the pension scheme,

(b) was a member of the pension scheme at the beginning of the period of residence in the United Kingdom which includes the time when the contributions are paid,

(c) [either][1] was, immediately before the beginning of that period of residence, entitled to tax relief in respect of contributions paid under the pension scheme under the law of the country or territory in which the individual was then resident [or meets such other condition as may be prescribed by regulations made by the Board of Inland Revenue][1], and

(d) has been notified by the scheme manager that information concerning events that are benefit crystallisation events in relation to the individual and the pension scheme will be given to the Inland Revenue.

[(2) The Commissioners for Her Majesty's Revenue and Customs may by regulations provide that, in circumstances prescribed by the regulations, paragraphs (a), (b) and (c) of sub-paragraph (1) have effect as if the references in those paragraphs to the pension scheme were to either the pension scheme or such other pension scheme as is prescribed by the regulations.][2]

[(3) Regulations under sub-paragraph (2) may include provision having effect in relation to times before they are made.][2]

Commentary—*Simon's Taxes* **E7.222, E7.223**.

Regulations—Pension Schemes (Relevant Migrant Members) Regulations, SI 2006/212; Registered Pension Schemes (Extension of Migrant Member Relief) Regulations, SI 2006/1957.

Amendments—[1]   Words in para (c) inserted by FA 2005 s 101, Sch 10 paras 46, 64(1) with effect from 6 April 2006.
[2]   Sub-para (1) numbered as such, and sub-paras (2), (3) inserted, by FA 2006 s 161, Sch 23 paras 1, 32. These amendments are deemed to have come into force on 6 April 2006.

Meaning of "qualifying" overseas pension scheme

5—(1) For the purposes of this Schedule an overseas pension scheme is a qualifying overseas pension scheme if—

(a) the scheme manager has given to the Inland Revenue notification that it is an overseas pension scheme and has provided any such evidence that it is an overseas pension scheme as the Inland Revenue may require,

(b) the scheme manager has undertaken to the Inland Revenue to inform the Inland Revenue if it ceases to be an overseas pension scheme,

(c) the scheme manager has undertaken to the Inland Revenue to comply with any prescribed benefit crystallisation information requirements imposed on the scheme manager, and

(d) the overseas pension scheme is not excluded from being a qualifying overseas pension scheme by sub-paragraph (3).

(2) In sub-paragraph (1)(c) "prescribed benefit crystallisation information requirements" means requirements imposed by or under regulations made by the Board of Inland Revenue to provide to the Inland Revenue any information relating to events that are benefit crystallisation events in relation to members of the pension scheme who have at any time been relevant migrant members of the pension scheme.

[(2A) In sub-paragraph (2) "information relating to events that are benefit crystallisation events", in relation to any individuals, includes (in particular) information relating to occasions that are, or could (depending on their relative timing) be, the occasions on which the individuals first flexibly access pension rights for the purposes of sections 227B to 227F.][1]

(3) An overseas pension scheme is excluded from being a qualifying overseas pension scheme if the Inland Revenue has decided that—

(a) there has been a failure to comply with any prescribed benefit crystallisation information requirements imposed on the scheme manager and the failure is significant, and

(b) by reason of the failure it is not appropriate that relief from tax should be given in respect of contributions under the pension scheme, and has notified the person or persons appearing to be the scheme manager of that decision (but subject to sub-paragraph (5) and paragraph 6).

(4) A failure to comply with prescribed benefit crystallisation information requirements is significant if—

    (*a*) the amount of information which has not been provided is substantial, or

    (*b*) the failure to provide the information is likely to result in serious prejudice to the assessment or collection of tax.

(5) The Inland Revenue—

    (*a*) may at any time after an overseas pension scheme becomes excluded from being a qualifying overseas pension scheme decide that the pension scheme is to cease to be so excluded, and

    (*b*) must notify the scheme manager of the decision.

Commentary—*Simon's Taxes* **E7.222, E7.223**.

HMRC Manuals—Registered Pension Schemes Manual RPSM13101090 (background to the conditions that may lead to a scheme being excluded from being a qualifying overseas pension scheme).

Regulations—Pension Schemes (Information Requirements — Qualifying Overseas Pension Schemes, Qualifying Recognised Overseas Pensions Schemes and Corresponding Relief) Regulations, SI 2006/208.

Registered Pension Schemes and Overseas Pension Schemes (Miscellaneous Amendments) Regulations, SI 2012/884.

Amendments—[1] Sub-para (2A) inserted by the Taxation of Pensions Act 2014 s 1, Sch 1 para 94 with effect from 17 December 2014.

6—(1) This paragraph applies where an overseas pension scheme is excluded from being a qualifying overseas pension scheme by a decision of the Inland Revenue under paragraph 5(3).

(2) The scheme manager may appeal against the decision.

(3), (4) . . . [1]

(5) An appeal under this paragraph against a decision must be brought within the period of 30 days beginning with the day on which the notification of the decision was given.

(6) [If an appeal under this paragraph is notified to the tribunal, the tribunal][1] must consider whether the overseas pension scheme ought to have been excluded from being a qualifying overseas pension scheme.

(7) If [the tribunal decides][1] that the overseas pension scheme ought to have been excluded from being a qualifying overseas pension scheme, [the tribunal must][1] dismiss the appeal.

(8) If they decide that the overseas pension scheme ought not to have been excluded from being a qualifying overseas pension scheme, the pension scheme is to be treated as having remained a qualifying overseas pension scheme (but subject to any further appeal . . . [1]).

Commentary—*Simon's Taxes* **E7.222, E7.223**.

Amendments—[1] Sub-ss (3), (4) and words in sub-s (8) repealed, words in sub-ss (6)–(8) substituted by the Transfer of Tribunal Functions and Revenue and Customs Appeals Order, SI 2009/56 art 3, Sch 1 para 435 with effect from 1 April 2009.

SCHEDULE 34

NON-UK SCHEMES: APPLICATION OF CERTAIN CHARGES

Section 244

Commentary—*Simon's Taxes* **E7.102, E7.202–E7.207**.

Member payment charges

1—(1) For the purposes of the member payment charges the member payment provisions apply in relation to payments made (or treated by this Part as made) to or in respect of—

    (*a*) a relieved member of a relevant non-UK scheme, or

    (*b*) a transfer member of such a scheme,

as in relation to payments made (or treated by this Part as made) to or in respect of a member of a registered pension scheme.

(2) Sub-paragraph (1) has effect subject to the provision made by and under paragraphs 2 to 7.

(3) "The member payment charges" are—

    (*a*) the unauthorised payments charge [(except as imposed by virtue of section 174A (taxable property held by investment-regulated pension schemes))][1],

    (*b*) the unauthorised payments surcharge,

    (*c*) the short service refund lump sum charge,

    (*ca*) *the serious ill-health lump sum charge,*[3]

    (*d*) the special lump sum death benefits charge,

    [(*da*) the charges under section 636A(1A) and (1B) of ITEPA 2003 (uncrystallised funds pension lump sums),][4]

    [(*db*) the charge under section 636A(4ZA) of ITEPA 2003 (certain payments of lump sum death benefits),][5] and

    (*e*) the charges under sections 636B and 636C of ITEPA 2003 (trivial commutation and winding-up lump sums and lump sum death benefits) (inserted by Schedule 31).

(4) "The member payment provisions" are[—

(a)]⁴ the provisions of this Part [(apart from the taxable property provisions)]¹ relating to payments made (or treated by this Part as made) to or in respect of a member of a registered pension scheme[, and

(b) section 636A(1A) to (1C) [and (4ZA) and section 636AA]⁵ of ITEPA 2003.]⁴

(5) A scheme is a relevant non-UK scheme if—

(a) relief from tax has been given in respect of contributions paid under the scheme by virtue of Schedule 33 (overseas pension schemes: migrant member relief),

(b) relief from tax has been so given at any time after 5th April 2006 under double tax arrangements,

(c) a member of the scheme has been, or members of the scheme have been, exempt from liability to tax by virtue of section 307 of ITEPA 2003 (exemption for provision made by employer for retirement or death benefit) in respect of provision made under the scheme at any time after 5th April 2006 when the scheme was an overseas pension scheme, or

(d) there has been a relevant transfer at any time after 5th April 2006 when the scheme was a qualifying recognised overseas pension scheme.

(6) "A relevant transfer" means a (direct or indirect) transfer of sums or assets held for the purposes of, or representing accrued rights under, an arrangement made under—

(a) a registered pension scheme, or

(b) another scheme which is a relevant non-UK scheme,

in relation to a member so as to become held for the purposes of, or to represent rights under, an arrangement under the scheme relating to the member; . . . .²

[(6A) There are three types of relevant transfer—

(a) an original relevant transfer,

(b) a subsequent relevant transfer, and

(c) any other (including, in particular, all relevant transfers before 9 March 2017).

(6B) "An original relevant transfer" is—

(a) a relevant transfer within sub-paragraph (6)(a) made on or after 9 March 2017,

(b) a relevant transfer within sub-paragraph (6)(b), made on or after 9 March 2017, of the whole or part of the UK tax-relieved fund of a relieved member of a qualifying recognised overseas pension scheme, or

(c) a relevant transfer within sub-paragraph (6)(b), made on or after 6 April 2017, of the whole or part of the UK tax-relieved fund of a relieved member of a relevant non-UK scheme that is not a qualifying recognised overseas pension scheme.

(6C) The sums or assets transferred as a result of an original relevant transfer constitute a ring-fenced transfer fund, and the key date for that fund is the date of the transfer.

(6D) Where in the case of a ring-fenced transfer fund ("the source fund") there is a relevant transfer of the whole or part of the fund—

(a) the sums or assets transferred as a result of the transfer constitute a ring-fenced transfer fund,

(b) that fund has the same key date as the source fund, and

(c) the transfer is "a subsequent relevant transfer", and is not an original relevant transfer.

(6E) Sub-paragraph (6D) applies whether the source fund is a ring-fenced transfer fund as a result of sub-paragraph (6C) or as a result of sub-paragraph (6D).

(6F) The Commissioners for Her Majesty's Revenue and Customs may by regulations provide that sums or assets identified in accordance with the regulations are not included in a ring-fenced transfer fund as a result of sub-paragraph (6C) or (6D)(a).]⁶

(7) A member of a relevant non-UK scheme is a relieved member of the scheme if—

(a) any of the contributions in respect of which relief has been given as mentioned in sub-paragraph (5)(a) or (b) were contributions paid by or on behalf of, or in respect of, the member, or

(b) the member is the member, or one of the members, who has been exempt from liability to tax as mentioned in sub-paragraph (5)(c).

(8) A member of a relevant non-UK scheme is a transfer member of the scheme if a relevant transfer related to the member.

Commentary—*Simon's Taxes* **E7.202–E7.207**.

HMRC Manuals—Registered Pension Schemes Manual RPSM13102110 (an unauthorised payments charge could apply if benefits were paid to a member of a relevant non-UK scheme before the normal minimum pension age subject to transitional provisions concerning a member's protected pension age).

RPSM13102120 (definition of "treated as made").

Regulations—Pension Schemes (Application of UK Provisions to Relevant Non-UK Schemes) (Amendment) Regulations, SI 2018/373.

Amendments—¹   Words in sub-paras (3)(a), (4) inserted by FA 2006 s 158, Sch 21 paras 2, 14(1), (2). These amendments are deemed to have come into force on 6 April 2006.

²   Words in sub-para (6) repealed by FA 2007 ss 69, 114, Sch 19 paras 1, 18(1), (2), 29(3), Sch 27 Pt 3(1) with effect in relation to lump sum death benefits paid in respect of members of schemes whose deaths occur on or after 6 April 2007.

³   Sub-para (3)(*ca*) repealed by FA 2016 s 22, Sch 5 para 3(1)(*d*)(i) with effect in relation to lump sums paid after 15 September 2016

⁴   Sub-para (3)(*da*) inserted, and words in sub-para (4) inserted, by the Taxation of Pensions Act 2014 s 1, Sch 1 para 95(1)–(3) with effect from 17 December 2014.

⁵   Sub-para (3)(*db*) inserted, and in sub-para (4)(*b*), words inserted, by F(No 2)A 2015 s 22(10) with effect in relation to lump sums paid on or after 6 April 2016.

⁶   Sub-paras (6A)–(6F) inserted by FA 2017 s 10, Sch 4 paras 1, 2 with effect from 9 March 2017.

2   [(1)] ¹ The member payment provisions do not apply in relation to a payment made (or treated by this Part as made) to or in respect of a relieved member or transfer member of a relevant non-UK scheme [so far as it is referable to 5-year rule funds]¹ unless the member—

(*a*)   is resident in the United Kingdom when the payment is made (or treated as made), or

(*b*)   although not resident in the United Kingdom at that time, has been resident in the United Kingdom earlier in the tax year in which the payment is made (or treated as made) or in any of the five tax years immediately preceding that tax year.

[(2) The member payment provisions do not apply in relation to a payment made (or treated by this Part as made) to or in respect of a relieved member of a relevant non-UK scheme so far as it is referable to 10-year rule funds unless the member—

(*a*)   is resident in the United Kingdom when the payment is made (or treated as made), or

(*b*)   although not resident in the United Kingdom at that time, has been resident in the United Kingdom earlier in the tax year in which the payment is made (or treated as made) or in any of the 10 tax years immediately preceding that year.

(3) The member payment provisions do not apply in relation to a payment made (or treated by this Part as made) to or in respect of a transfer member of a relevant non-UK scheme, so far as it is referable to any particular ring-fenced transfer fund of the member's under the scheme which has a key date of 6 April 2017 or later, unless—

(*a*)   the member is resident in the United Kingdom when the payment is made (or treated as made), or

(*b*)   although the member is not resident in the United Kingdom at that time—

(i)   the member has been resident in the United Kingdom earlier in the tax year containing that time, or

(ii)   the member has been resident in the United Kingdom in any of the 10 tax years immediately preceding the tax year containing that time, or

(iii)   that time is no later than the end of 5 years beginning with the key date for the particular fund.

(4) In this paragraph—

"5-year rule funds", in relation to a payment to or in respect of a relieved member of a relevant non-UK scheme, means so much of the member's UK tax-relieved fund under the scheme as represents tax-relieved contributions, or tax-exempt provision, made under the scheme before 6 April 2017;

"5-year rule funds", in relation to a payment to or in respect of a transfer member of a relevant non-UK scheme, means—

(*a*)   the member's relevant transfer fund under the scheme, and

(*b*)   any of the member's ring-fenced transfer funds under the scheme that has a key date earlier than 6 April 2017;

"10-year rule funds", in relation to a payment to or in respect of a relieved member of a relevant non-UK scheme, means so much of the member's UK tax-relieved fund under the scheme as represents tax-relieved contributions, or tax-exempt provision, made under the scheme on or after 6 April 2017.

(5) See also—

paragraph 1(6C), (6D) and (6F) (meaning of "ring-fenced transfer fund"),

paragraph 3 (meaning of "UK tax-relieved fund", "tax-relieved contributions" and "tax-exempt provision" etc), and

paragraph 4 (meaning of "relevant transfer fund" etc)."]¹

Commentary—*Simon's Taxes* E7.202–E7.207.

Amendments—¹   Sub-para (1) numbered as such and words in that sub-para inserted, and sub-paras (2)–(5) inserted, by FA 2017 s 10, Sch 4 paras 1, 3 with effect in relation to payments made (or treated as made) on or after 6 April 2017.

3—(1) The member payment provisions do not apply in relation to a payment made (or treated by this Part as made) to or in respect of a relieved member of a relevant non-UK scheme unless the payment is referable to the member's UK tax-relieved fund under the scheme.

(2) A member's UK tax-relieved fund under a relevant non-UK scheme is so much of—

    (*a*) the sums or assets held for the purposes of, or representing accrued rights under, the scheme as, in accordance with regulations made by the Board of Inland Revenue, represents

    (*b*) any tax-relieved contributions made under the scheme by or on behalf of, or in respect of, the member and any tax-exempt provision made under the scheme in relation to the member.

(3) "Tax-relieved contributions" means contributions in respect of which relief from tax—

    (*a*) has been given by virtue of Schedule 33 (overseas pension schemes: migrant member relief), or

    (*b*) has been given at any time after 5th April 2006 under double tax arrangements.

(4) "Tax-exempt provision" means provision in respect of which exemption from tax has been given by virtue of section 307 of ITEPA 2003 (exemption for provision made by employer for retirement or death benefit) at any time after 5th April 2006 when the scheme was an overseas pension scheme.

(5) Regulations under sub-paragraph (2) may (in particular) provide that the sums or assets which represent any tax-relieved contributions or tax-exempt provision are to be determined otherwise than by reference to the actual amount of the contributions or the amount or value of the provision (for instance by reference to the increase in the value of the member's rights under the scheme during a period for which relief or exemption in respect of such contributions or provision was given).

[(5A) The Commissioners for Her Majesty's Revenue and Customs may by regulations provide that, in circumstances specified in the regulations, something specified in the regulations is to be treated as done by, to, in respect of or in the case of a relieved member of a relevant non-UK scheme.][2]

(6) Regulations made by the Board of Inland Revenue may make provision for determining whether or not payments made (or treated as made) by[, or other things done by or to or under or in respect of or in the case of,][2] a relevant non-UK scheme are to be treated as referable to a member's UK tax-relieved fund under the scheme (and so whether or not they reduce the fund).

[(7) The provision which may be made under sub-paragraph (6) includes (in particular) provision in consequence of Part 7A of ITEPA 2003.][1]

[(8) Where regulations under sub-paragraph (6) make provision for a payment or something else to be treated as referable to a member's UK tax-relieved fund under a scheme, regulations under that sub-paragraph may make provision for the payment or thing, or any part or aspect of the payment or thing, also to be treated as referable to a particular part of that fund.][2]

Commentary—*Simon's Taxes* **E7.223**.
HMRC Manuals—RPSM13102200 (worked examples of attributing payments to particular funds under a relevant non-UK scheme).
Regulations—Pensions Schemes (Application of UK Provisions to Relevant Non-UK Schemes) Regulations, SI 2006/207.
Pension Schemes (Application of UK Provisions to Relevant Non-UK Schemes) (Amendment) Regulations, SI 2018/373.
Amendments—[1]   Sub-para (7) inserted by FA 2011 s 26 and Sch 2 para 51 with effect on or after 6 April 2011.
[2]   Sub-paras (5A), (8) inserted, and in sub-para (6), words inserted, by FA 2017 s 10, Sch 4 paras 1, 4 with effect from 9 March 2017.

4—(1) The member payment provisions do not apply in relation to a payment made (or treated by this Part as made) to or in respect of a transfer member of a relevant non-UK scheme unless it is referable to the member's relevant transfer fund[, or ring-fenced transfer funds,][2] under the scheme.

(2) A member's relevant transfer fund under a relevant non-UK scheme is[, subject to sub-paragraph (3A),][2] so much of—

    (*a*) the sums or assets held for the purposes of, or representing accrued rights under, the scheme as, in accordance with regulations made by the Board of Inland Revenue, represents

    (*b*) relevant transferred sums or assets.

(3) "Relevant transferred sums or assets" means sums or assets held for the purposes of, or representing accrued rights under, an arrangement under—

    (*a*) a registered pension scheme, or

    (*b*) another scheme which is a relevant non-UK scheme,

which at any time after 5th April 2006 when the scheme was an overseas pension scheme have been transferred (directly or indirectly) so as to become held for the purposes of, or to represent rights under, an arrangement under the scheme relating to the member; . . . .[1]

[(3A) The member's relevant transfer fund under the scheme does not include sums or assets that are in any of the member's ring-fenced transfer funds under the scheme.][2]

(4) Regulations made by the Board of Inland Revenue may make provision for determining whether payments or transfers made (or treated as made) by[, or other things done by or to or under or in respect of or in the case of,][2] a relevant non-UK scheme are to be treated as referable to a member's relevant transfer fund under the scheme (and so whether or not they reduce the fund).

[(5) The Commissioners for Her Majesty's Revenue and Customs may by regulations provide that, in circumstances specified in the regulations, something specified in the regulations is to be treated as done by, to, in respect of or in the case of a transfer member of a relevant non-UK scheme.

(6) Regulations made by the Commissioners for Her Majesty's Revenue and Customs may make provision for determining whether payments or transfers made (or treated as made) by, or other things done by or to or under or in respect of or in the case of, a relevant non-UK scheme are to be treated as referable to a member's ring-fenced transfer funds under the scheme (and so whether or not they reduce the funds or any of them).

(7) Where regulations under sub-paragraph (6) make provision for a payment or transfer or something else to be treated as referable to a member's ring-fenced transfer funds under a scheme, regulations under that sub-paragraph may make provision for the payment or transfer or other thing, or any part or aspect of the payment or transfer or thing, also to be treated as referable to a particular one of those funds.][2]

Regulations—Pensions Schemes (Application of UK Provisions to Relevant Non-UK Schemes) Regulations, SI 2006/207.
Pension Schemes (Application of UK Provisions to Relevant Non-UK Schemes) (Amendment) Regulations, SI 2018/373.
Amendments—[1] Words in sub-para (3) repealed by FA 2007 ss 69, 114, Sch 19 paras 1, 18(1), (3), 29(3), Sch 27 Pt 3(1) with effect in relation to lump sum death benefits paid in respect of members of schemes whose deaths occur on or after 6 April 2007.
[2] In sub-paras (1), (2), (4) words inserted, and sub-paras (3A), (5)–(7) inserted, by FA 2017 s 10, Sch 4 paras 1, 5 with effect from 9 March 2017.

5 [Sections 205 to 206][1] (short service refund lump sum charge ...[2] and special lump sum death benefits charge) apply with respect to a lump sum or lump sum death benefit paid to or in respect of—

(a) a relieved member of a relevant non-UK scheme, or

(b) a transfer member of such a scheme,

so as to make the person to whom the lump sum or lump sum death benefit is paid (rather than the scheme administrator) liable to any charge imposed by either of those sections.

Modifications—Registered Pension Schemes (Splitting of Schemes) Regulations, SI 2006/569 reg 3 (modification of this provision in relation to sub-scheme administrators).
Amendments—[1] Words substituted for words "Sections 205 and 206", by FA 2011 s 65, Sch 16 paras 62, 81(1), (4) with effect for the tax year 2011–12 and subsequent tax years, subject to transitional provisions in FA 2011 Sch 16 Pt 3. The amendments made by FA 2011 Sch 16 paras 27–30, 40, 42(2)(a), (3), 63, 77(4), 81(2), (4), 82(3)–(5) and 83 have effect in relation to lump sums paid on or after 6 April 2011 (FA 2011 Sch 16 para 102).
[2] Words ", serious ill-health lump sum charge" repealed by FA 2016 s 22, Sch 5 para 3(1)(d)(ii) with effect in relation to lump sums paid after 15 September 2016.

[**5A**—(1) Sub-paragraph (2) applies if—

(a) a payment is made (or treated by this Part as made) to or in respect of a relieved member or transfer member of a relevant non-UK scheme, and

(b) there is an amount of tax under a member payment charge that would be payable in respect of the payment, or part of the payment, but for the operation of double taxation arrangements.

(2) The payment or (as the case may be) that part of it—

(a) is "pension" for the purposes of Chapter 4 of Part 9 of ITEPA 2003 (foreign pensions), and

(b) is to be treated as included in the list, in section 576A of ITEPA 2003, of payments that are "relevant withdrawals" for the purposes of that section.][1]

Amendments—[1] Para 5A inserted by the Taxation of Pensions Act 2014 s 1, Sch 1 para 95(1), (4) with effect from 17 December 2014.

6—(1) The amount of any liability to tax imposed on any individual in relation to a payment by virtue of the operation of the member payment charges in consequence of paragraph 1[, or by virtue of the operation of Chapter 4 of Part 9 of ITEPA 2003 in consequence of paragraph 5A,][1] is to be reduced by the amount of any tax paid in respect of the payment under the law of any country or territory outside the United Kingdom.

(2) Where, after any tax which an individual is liable to pay in respect of a payment in consequence of paragraph 1 [or 5A][1] has been paid, tax is paid in respect of the payment under the law of any country or territory outside the United Kingdom, an appropriate adjustment is to be made in the individual's liability to tax (by way of discharge or repayment of tax).

Amendments—[1] Words inserted by the Taxation of Pensions Act 2014 s 1, Sch 1 para 95(1), (5) with effect from 17 December 2014.

7—(1) The member payment provisions apply with respect to a payment made (or treated by this Part as made) to or in respect of—

(a) a relieved member of a relevant non-UK scheme, or

(b) a transfer member of such a scheme,

subject to any omissions, additions and other modifications contained in regulations made by the Board of Inland Revenue.

(2) Regulations under sub-paragraph (1) may—

(a) include provision having effect in relation to times before they are made, (*b*) confer discretion on the Board of Inland Revenue or the Inland Revenue (subject to a right of appeal against any decision taken in exercise of the discretion),

[(*ba*) contain transitional provisions and savings,][1]

(*c*) make different provision in relation to payments treated (in accordance with regulations under paragraph 3(6) or 4(4)) as being referable to a member's UK tax-relieved fund, or to a member's relevant transfer fund [or ring-fenced transfer funds][2], under a relevant non-UK scheme, and

(*d*) otherwise make different provision for different cases.

Regulations—Pensions Schemes (Application of UK Provisions to Relevant Non-UK Schemes) Regulations, SI 2006/207.
Pensions Schemes (Application of UK Provisions to Relevant Non-UK Schemes) (Amendment) Regulations, SI 2012/1795.
Pension Schemes (Application of UK Provisions to Relevant Non-UK Schemes) (Amendment) Regulations, SI 2018/373.
Amendments—[1] Sub-para (2)(*ba*) inserted by the Taxation of Pensions Act 2014 s 1, Sch 1 para 95(1), (6) with effect from 17 December 2014.
[2] In sub-para (2)(*c*), words inserted by FA 2017 s 10, Sch 4 paras 1, 6 with effect from 9 March 2017.

[Unauthorised payment charge: taxable property

7A—(1) The Commissioners for Her Majesty's Revenue and Customs may by regulations make provision for a transfer member of a relevant non-UK scheme to be liable to the unauthorised payment charge in the same or similar circumstances to those in which—

(*a*) a member of a registered pension scheme is liable to that charge by virtue of section 174A and Schedule 29A (taxable property held by investment-regulated pension scheme),

(*b*) the scheme administrator of such a scheme is liable to the scheme sanction charge by virtue of section 185A (income from taxable property) or 185F (gains from taxable property), or

(*c*) a member of such a scheme is liable to the scheme sanction charge by virtue of those provisions in consequence of provision made by regulations under section 273ZA.

(2) The regulations may—

(*a*) make provision for the application of any or all of the taxable property provisions in relation to a transfer member of a relevant non-UK scheme subject to any omissions, additions and other modifications contained in the regulations,

(*b*) include provision having effect in relation to times before they are made,

(*c*) contain transitional provisions and savings, and

(*d*) make different provision for different cases.][1]

Regulations—Pension Schemes (Application of UK Provisions to Relevant Non-UK Schemes) (Amendment) Regulations, SI 2018/373.
Amendments—[1] This paragraph inserted by FA 2006 s 158, Sch 21 paras 2, 14(1), (3). This amendment is deemed to have come into force on 6 April 2006.

Annual allowance charge

8—(1) The provisions of this Part relating to the annual allowance charge ("the annual allowance provisions") apply in relation to an individual who is a currently-relieved member of a currently-relieved non-UK pension scheme [and its scheme manager][1] as if the currently-relieved non-UK pension scheme were a registered pension scheme.

(2) Sub-paragraph (1) has effect subject to the provision made by and under paragraphs 9 to 12.

(3) A pension scheme is a currently-relieved non-UK pension scheme in relation to a tax year if—

(*a*) relief from tax is given in respect of contributions paid during the tax year under the pension scheme by virtue of Schedule 33 (overseas pension schemes: migrant member relief) or double tax arrangements, or

(*b*) a member of the pension scheme is, or members of the pension scheme are, exempt from liability to tax by virtue of section 307 of ITEPA 2003 (exemption for provision made by employer for retirement or death benefit) in respect of provision made under the pension scheme at any time during the tax year when the pension scheme is an overseas pension scheme.

(4) An individual is a currently-relieved member of a currently-relieved non-UK pension scheme in relation to a tax year if—

(*a*) any of the contributions in respect of which relief is given as mentioned in sub-paragraph (3)(*a*) are contributions paid by or on behalf of, or in respect of, the individual, or

(*b*) the individual is the member, or one of the members, who is exempt from liability to tax as mentioned in sub-paragraph (3)(*b*).

Commentary—*Simon's Taxes* **E7.202–E7.207**.
Amendments—[1] Words in sub-para (1) inserted by FA 2011 s 66, Sch 17 para 24(1), (2) with effect for the tax year 2011–12 and subsequent tax years, and in relation to pension input periods ending in the tax year 2011–12 but beginning earlier (or in 2011–12). For transitional provisions see FA 2011 Sch 17 paras 28–34.

9 The annual allowance provisions apply by virtue of paragraph 8 in relation to an individual who is a currently-relieved member of a currently-relieved non-UK pension scheme as if references to the pension input period of an arrangement under the pension scheme that ends in a tax year were to the tax year.

Commentary—*Simon's Taxes* **E7.202–E7.207**.

[9ZA—(1) For the purposes of determining the annual allowance charge in the case of an individual for a relevant tax year, a pension scheme is to be treated for the purposes of section 227G as a registered pension scheme if—

(*a*) in relation to that tax year, or

(*b*) in relation to any earlier tax year (whether or not a relevant tax year),

the scheme is a currently-relieved non-UK pension scheme and the individual is a currently-relieved member of the scheme.

(2) For the purposes of this paragraph, a tax year is a "relevant tax year" in relation to an individual if—

(*a*) it is—

(i) the first tax year in relation to which the individual is a currently-relieved member of any currently-relieved non-UK pension scheme, or

(ii) if later, the tax year 2015-16, or

(*b*) it is a tax year subsequent to the tax year identified under paragraph (*a*).][1]

Amendments—[1] Paras 9ZA, 9ZB inserted by the Taxation of Pensions Act 2014 s 1, Sch 1 para 95(1), (7) with effect from 17 December 2014.

[9ZB—(1) Sub-paragraph (2) has effect if at any particular time—

(*a*) an individual is a transfer member of a relevant non-UK scheme,

(*b*) the scheme is, or at any previous time has been, a qualifying recognised overseas pension scheme, and

(*c*) the particular time is not in a tax year in relation to which the scheme is a currently-relieved non-UK pension scheme of which the individual is a currently-relieved member.

(2) Section 227G applies in the individual's case as if the scheme, so far as relating to the individual's relevant transfer fund [or ring-fenced transfer funds][2] under the scheme, were a registered pension scheme at the particular time.

(3) The reference in sub-paragraph (2) to the individual's relevant transfer fund under the relevant non-UK scheme is to be read in accordance with paragraph 4.

[(4) The reference in sub-paragraph (2) to the individual's ring-fenced transfer funds under the relevant non-UK scheme is to be read in accordance with paragraph 1.][2]][1]

Amendments—[1] Paras 9ZA, 9ZB inserted by the Taxation of Pensions Act 2014 s 1, Sch 1 para 95(1), (7) with effect from 17 December 2014.
[2] In sub-para (2), words inserted, and sub-para (4) inserted, by FA 2017 s 10, Sch 4 paras 1, 7 with effect from 9 March 2017.

[9A—(1) This paragraph applies where an individual—

(*a*) is a currently-relieved member of a currently-relieved non-UK pension scheme in relation to a tax year, but

(*b*) was a member, but not a currently-relieved member, of the currently-relieved non-UK pension scheme in relation to any one or more of the 3 immediately preceding tax years (a "relevant tax year").

(2) Section 228A has effect in relation to the individual for the tax year as it would if the individual had been a currently-relieved member of the pension scheme for the relevant tax year (or each of the relevant tax years) and paragraphs 10 and 11 of this Schedule were omitted.

Commentary—*Simon's Taxes* **E7.202–E7.207**.
Amendments—Paras 9A, 9B inserted by FA 2011 s 66, Sch 17 para 24(1), (3) with effect for the tax year 2011–12 and subsequent tax years, and in relation to pension input periods ending in the tax year 2011–12 but beginning earlier (or in 2011–12). For transitional provisions see FA 2011 Sch 17 paras 28–34.

[9B—(1) This paragraph applies where an individual—

(*a*) is a member of a registered pension scheme in relation to a tax year, and

(*b*) was a currently-relieved member of a currently-relieved non-UK pension scheme in relation to any one or more of the 3 immediately preceding tax years (a "relevant tax year").

(2) Section 228A has effect in relation to the individual for the tax year as it would if the currently-relieved non-UK pension scheme had been a registered pension scheme for the relevant tax year (or each of the relevant tax years).][1]

Commentary—*Simon's Taxes* **E7.202–E7.207**.
Amendments—[1] Paras 9A, 9B inserted by FA 2011 s 66, Sch 17 para 24(1), (3) with effect for the tax year 2011–12 and subsequent tax years, and in relation to pension input periods ending in the tax year 2011–12 but beginning earlier (or in 2011–12). For transitional provisions see FA 2011 Sch 17 paras 28–34.

10—(1) Sections 230(1) and 234(1) (cash balance and defined benefits arrangements) apply by virtue of paragraph 8 in relation to an individual who is a currently-relieved member of a currently-relieved non-UK pension scheme in relation to a tax year as if the increase in the value of the individual's rights under an arrangement under the pension scheme relating to the individual during the tax year were the greater of—

(a) the appropriate fraction of what it otherwise would be, and

(b) the amount of any contributions paid under the arrangement during the tax year by or on behalf of the individual (otherwise than by an employer) in respect of which relief from tax is given by virtue of Schedule 33 (overseas pension schemes: migrant member relief) or double tax arrangements;

and section 237 (hybrid arrangements) applies accordingly.

[(2) The appropriate fraction is—

$$\frac{TE + TSI}{EI}$$

where—

EI is the total amount of employment income of the individual from any relevant employment or employments for the tax year, excluding any such income which is exempt income (within the meaning of section 8 of ITEPA 2003),

TE is so much of EI as constitutes taxable earnings from any such employment (within the meaning of section 10(2) of that Act), and

TSI is so much of EI as constitutes taxable specific income from any such employment (within the meaning of section 10(3) to (5) of that Act).][1]

(3) An employment is a relevant employment if it is an employment with an employer who is a sponsoring employer in relation to the currently-relieved non-UK pension scheme.

Commentary—*Simon's Taxes* E7.202–E7.207.
HMRC Manuals—Registered Pension Schemes Manual RPSM13102360 (worked example of a pension input amount for a defined benefits arrangement).
Amendments—[1]   Sub-para (2) substituted by FA 2014 s 45(1), (2) with effect for the tax year 2014–15 and subsequent tax years.

11—(1) Section 233(1) (other money purchase arrangements) applies by virtue of paragraph 8 in relation to an individual who is a currently-relieved member of a currently-relieved non-UK pension scheme in relation to a tax year as if—

(a) the reference in paragraph (a) to relievable pension contributions paid by or on behalf of the individual under an arrangement under the pension scheme relating to the individual were to those in respect of which relief from tax is given by virtue of Schedule 33 (overseas pension schemes: migrant member relief) or double tax arrangements, and

(b) the reference in paragraph (b) to contributions paid in respect of the individual under such an arrangement by an employer of the individual were to the appropriate fraction of contributions so paid;

and section 237 applies accordingly.

[(2) The appropriate fraction is—

$$\frac{TE + TSI}{EI}$$

where—

EI is the total amount of employment income of the individual from any employment or employments with the employer for the tax year, excluding any such income which is exempt income (within the meaning of section 8 of ITEPA 2003),

TE is so much of EI as constitutes taxable earnings from any such employment (within the meaning of section 10(2) of that Act), and

TSI is so much of EI as constitutes taxable specific income from any such employment (within the meaning of section 10(3) to (5) of that Act).][1]

[(3) Where a calculation under section 233(1) as applied by paragraph 8 is being carried out for the purposes of section 227F(3) in respect of a period that ends at the end of a tax year (see paragraph 9 and section 227F(1)), the appropriate fraction for the purposes of sub-paragraph (1)(b) is the appropriate fraction given by sub-paragraph (2) for that tax year (even where the period in respect of which the calculation is being carried out is part only of that tax year).][2]

Commentary—*Simon's Taxes* E7.202–E7.207.

HMRC Manuals—Registered Pension Schemes Manual RPSM13102370–13102380 (includes worked examples of pension input amounts for other money purchase arrangements and hybrid arrangement situations).
Amendments—[1]   Sub-para (2) substituted by FA 2014 s 45(1), (3) with effect for the tax year 2014–15 and subsequent tax years.
[2]   Sub-para (3) inserted by the Taxation of Pensions Act 2014 s 1, Sch 1 para 95(1), (8) with effect from 17 December 2014.

12—(1) The annual allowance provisions apply by virtue of paragraph 8 in relation to an individual who is a currently-relieved member of a currently-relieved non-UK pension scheme [and its scheme manager][1] subject to any omissions, additions and other modifications contained in regulations made by the Board of Inland Revenue.
(2) Regulations under sub-paragraph (1) may—

    (a) include provision having effect in relation to times before they are made,

    (b) confer discretion on the Board of Inland Revenue or the Inland Revenue (subject to a right of appeal against any decision taken in exercise of the discretion),

    [(ba) contain transitional provisions and savings,][2] and

    (c) make different provision for different cases.

Commentary—*Simon's Taxes* **E7.202–E7.207**.
Regulations—Pensions Schemes (Application of UK Provisions to Relevant Non-UK Schemes) Regulations, SI 2006/207.
Amendments—[1]   Words in sub-s (1) inserted by FA 2011 s 66, Sch 17 para 24(1), (4) with effect for the tax year 2011–12 and subsequent tax years, and in relation to pension input periods ending in the tax year 2011–12 but beginning earlier (or in 2011–12). For transitional provisions see FA 2011 Sch 17 paras 28–34.
[2]   Sub-para (2)(ba) inserted by the Taxation of Pensions Act 2014 s 1, Sch 1 para 95(1), (9) with effect from 17 December 2014.

Lifetime allowance charge

13—(1) The provisions of this Part relating to the lifetime allowance charge ("the lifetime allowance provisions") apply in relation to an individual who is a relieved member of a relieved non-UK pension scheme as if the relieved non-UK pension scheme were a registered pension scheme.
(2) Sub-paragraph (1) has effect subject to the provision made by and under paragraphs 14 to 19.
(3) A pension scheme is a relieved non-UK pension scheme if—

    (a) relief from tax has been given in respect of contributions paid under the pension scheme by virtue of Schedule 33 (overseas pension schemes: migrant member relief),

    (b) relief from tax has been so given at any time after 5th April 2006 under double tax arrangements, or

    (c) a member of the pension scheme has been, or members of the pension scheme have been, exempt from liability to tax by virtue of section 307 of ITEPA 2003 (exemption for provision made by employer for retirement or death benefit) in respect of provision made under the pension scheme at any time after 5th April 2006 when the pension scheme was an overseas pension scheme.

(4) An individual is a relieved member of a relieved non-UK pension scheme if—

    (a) any of the contributions in respect of which relief has been given as mentioned in sub-paragraph (3)(a) or (b) were contributions paid by or on behalf of, or in respect of, the individual, or

    (b) the individual is the member, or one of the members, who has been exempt from liability to tax as mentioned in sub-paragraph (3)(c).

Commentary—*Simon's Taxes* **E7.202–E7.207**.

14—(1) This paragraph applies in relation to the amount crystallised on the occurrence of an event that is a benefit crystallisation event by virtue of this Schedule in relation to an individual who is a relieved member of a relieved non-UK pension scheme.
(2) What would otherwise be the amount crystallised by the event is reduced by so much (if any) of it as exceeds the amount of the untested portion of the relevant relieved amount immediately before the benefit crystallisation event (so that if that amount is nil, there is no amount crystallised).
(3) For the purposes of this paragraph and paragraph 15 the relevant relieved amount is the aggregate of—

    (a) the amounts which for each tax year before that in which the benefit crystallisation event occurs would have been arrived at in relation to arrangements under the relieved non-UK pension scheme relating to the individual as pension input amounts under sections 230 to 237 (annual allowance) as they apply by virtue of this Schedule, and

    (b) the amount which would be so arrived at if the period beginning with the tax year in which the benefit crystallisation event occurs and ending immediately before the benefit crystallisation event were a tax year,

assuming that section 229(3) did not apply.
(4) For the purposes of this paragraph and paragraph 15 the untested portion of the relevant relieved amount is so much of the relevant relieved amount as exceeds the aggregate of the amount which (in accordance with sub-paragraph (2)) is the amount crystallised by each previous event that was a

benefit crystallisation event by virtue of this Schedule in relation to the individual and the relieved non-UK pension scheme (so that if there has been no such previous event the untested portion of the relevant relieved amount is the whole of that amount).

Commentary—*Simon's Taxes* **E7.202–E7.207**.

HMRC Manuals—Registered Pension Schemes Manual RPSM13102550–13102560 (worked examples of relevant relieved amount).

15—(1) An individual who is a relieved member of a relieved non-UK pension scheme may at any time elect by giving notice to the Inland Revenue in a form specified by the Board of Inland Revenue that a benefit crystallisation event is to be treated as occurring on the date specified in the notice in relation to the individual and the relieved non-UK pension scheme.

(2) The amount crystallised on the occurrence of an event that is a benefit crystallisation event by virtue of sub-paragraph (1) is the untested portion of the relevant relieved amount.

Commentary—*Simon's Taxes* **E7.202–E7.207**.

16—(1) This paragraph applies on the occurrence of a transfer of sums or assets held for the purposes of, or representing accrued rights under, a relieved non-UK pension scheme which (apart from sub-paragraph (2)) would by virtue of paragraph 13 be a benefit crystallisation event in relation to an individual who is a relieved member of the relieved non-UK pension scheme.

(2) The event is not a benefit crystallisation event if the transfer is a block transfer.

(3) A transfer is a block transfer if it involves the transfer in a single transaction of all the sums and assets held for the purposes of, or representing accrued rights under, the arrangements under the relieved non-UK pension scheme which relate to—

  (*a*) the individual, and

  (*b*) at least one other member of the relieved non-UK pension scheme (whether or not that member is a relieved member).

Commentary—*Simon's Taxes* **E7.202–E7.207**.

17   Section 217 (persons liable to charge) applies with respect to a liability to the lifetime allowance charge arising by reason of the occurrence of an event that is a benefit crystallisation event by virtue of this Schedule in relation to an individual who is a relieved member of a relieved non-UK pension scheme with the omission of references to the scheme administrator.

Commentary—*Simon's Taxes* **E7.202–E7.207**.

Modifications—Registered Pension Schemes (Splitting of Schemes) Regulations, SI 2006/569 reg 3 (modification of this provision in relation to sub-scheme administrators).

18—(1) This paragraph applies where sums and assets held for the purposes of, or representing accrued rights under, a relieved non-UK pension scheme are transferred so as to become held for the purposes of, or to represent rights under, another pension scheme ("the transferee pension scheme") in circumstances in which, by virtue of paragraph 16, the transfer does not constitute a benefit crystallisation event.

(2) Paragraphs 13 to 17 and sub-paragraph (1) have effect after the transfer as if—

  (*a*) references to a relieved non-UK pension scheme included the transferee pension scheme (if not a relieved non-UK pension scheme),

  (*b*) references to an individual who is a relieved member of a relieved non-UK pension scheme included the individual to whom the transfer related (if not a relieved member of a relieved non-UK pension scheme), and

  (*c*) the relevant relieved amount consisted of, or (if there is a relevant relieved amount in relation to the individual and the transferee pension scheme apart from this paragraph) included, the amount which would have been the amount crystallised had the transfer constituted a benefit crystallisation event.

Commentary—*Simon's Taxes* **E7.202–E7.207**.

19—(1) The provisions of this Part of this Act relating to the lifetime allowance charge apply in relation to an individual who is a relieved member of a relieved non-UK pension scheme subject to any omissions, additions and other modifications contained in regulations made by the Board of Inland Revenue.

(2) Regulations under sub-paragraph (1) may—

  (*a*) include provision having effect in relation to times before they are made,

  (*b*) confer discretion on the Board of Inland Revenue or the Inland Revenue (subject to a right of appeal against any decision taken in exercise of the discretion),

  [(*ba*) contain transitional provisions and savings,][1] and

  (*c*) make different provision for different cases.

Commentary—*Simon's Taxes* **E7.202–E7.207**.

Regulations—Pensions Schemes (Application of UK Provisions to Relevant Non-UK Schemes) Regulations, SI 2006/207.

Amendments—[1]   Sub-para (2)(*ba*) inserted by the Taxation of Pensions Act 2014 s 1, Sch 1 para 95(1), (9) with effect from 17 December 2014.

Revenue and Customs discretion

19A　　. . .

Modifications—Pensions Schemes (Application of UK Provisions to Relevant Non-UK Schemes) Regulations, SI 2006/207 reg 17 (insertion of this paragraph in respect of relevant non-UK schemes).

Meaning of "double tax arrangements"

20　In this Schedule "double tax arrangements" means arrangements having effect [under section 2(1) of the Taxation (International and Other Provisions) Act 2010][1] (relief by agreement with other territories).

Amendments—[1]　Words substituted for words "by virtue of section 788 of ICTA" by TIOPA 2010 s 501, Sch 8 paras 61, 64. TIOPA 2010 has effect for corporation tax purposes for accounting periods ending on or after 1 April 2010, for income and capital gains tax purposes for the tax year 2010–11 and subsequent tax years, and for petroleum revenue tax purposes for chargeable periods beginning on or after 1 July 2010.

SCHEDULE 35

PENSION SCHEMES ETC: MINOR AND CONSEQUENTIAL AMENDMENTS

Section 281

Commentary—*Simon's Taxes* **E7.102**.

Taxes Management Act 1970 (c 9)

1　(*amends* TMA 1970 s 9(1A))

Income and Corporation Taxes Act 1988 (c 1)

2　The Income and Corporation Taxes Act 1988 (c 1) is amended as follows.

3　(*amends* TA 1988 s 21A(2))

4　(*amends* TA 1988 s 56(3)(*b*))

6　(*amends* TA 1988 s 129B(2))

9　(*amends* TA 1988 s 266(1))

Prospective amendments—This para to be repealed by FA 2012 s 227, Sch 39 para 28(1) with effect from a date to be appointed.

10—(1) Section 266A (life assurance premiums paid by employer) is amended as follows.
(2) (*amends* TA 1988 s 266A(1))
(3) (*substitutes* TA 1988 s 266A(3)–(9); *amended by* the Tax and Civil Partnership Regulations, SI 2005/3229, regs 175, 181, with effect from 6 April 2006 (reg 1(7))

Prospective amendments—This para to be repealed by FA 2012 s 227, Sch 39 para 28(1) with effect from a date to be appointed.

21　(*substitutes* TA 1988 s 464(5)(*b*))

22—(1) Section 466 (interpretation of Chapter 2 of Part 12) is amended as follows.
(2) (*amends* TA 1988 s 466(2))
(3) (*inserted* TA 1988 s 466((2A), (2B); *repealed by* FA 2007 Sch 27 Pt 2(7))

26　(*amends* TA 1988 s 613(4))

33　In section 824(9) (repayment supplements), after "settlement" insert ", scheme administrators of registered pension schemes [sub-scheme administrators of sub-schemes which form part of a split scheme pursuant to the Registered Pensions (Splitting of Schemes) Regulations 2006[1]]".

Amendments—[1]　Words inserted by the Registered Pension Schemes (Splitting of Schemes) Regulations, SI 2006/569 reg 5(6), (7) with effect from 6 April 2006.

Taxation of Chargeable Gains Act 1992 (c 12)

38　The Taxation of Chargeable Gains Act 1992 is amended as follows.

39　(*amends* TCGA 1992 s 13(10B)(*b*))

40　(*substitutes* TCGA 1992 s 239A)

41　(*amends* TCGA 1992 s 288(1))

42—(1) Paragraph 2 of Schedule 1 (application of exempt amount and reporting limits in cases involving settled property) is amended as follows.
(2) (*amends* TCGA 1992 Sch 1 para 2(7)(*b*)(ii))
(3) (*repeals* TCGA 1992 Sch 1 para 2(8))

Finance Act 1996 (c 8)

43 The Finance Act 1996 is amended as follows.

44 (*inserts* FA 1996 s 148(6A))

Capital Allowances Act 2001 (c 2)

47 The Capital Allowances Act 2001 is amended as follows.

48 (*substitutes* CAA 2001 s 4(2A)(*d*))

Income Tax (Earnings and Pensions) Act 2003 (c 1)

54 The Income Tax (Earnings and Pensions) Act 2003 is amended as follows.

55 (*amends* ITEPA 2003 s 23(3))

56 (*amends* ITEPA 2003 s 54(1))

57 (*amends* ITEPA 2003 s 56(8))

58 (*amends* ITEPA 2003 s 218(4))

59 (*amends* ITEPA 2003 s 315(5))

60 (*amends* ITEPA 2003 s 327)

61 (*substitutes* ITEPA 2003 s 381(*c*), (*d*))

62—(1) Section 407 (payments and benefits on termination of employment: exception for payments and benefits under tax-exempt pension schemes) is amended as follows.
(2) (*substitutes* ITEPA 2003 s 407(2)(*a*), (*aa*))
(3) (*repeals* ITEPA 2003 s 407(3)).

63—(1) Section 408 (payments and benefits on termination of employment: exception for contributions to tax-exempt pension schemes) is amended as follows.
(2) (*amends* ITEPA 2003 s 408(1))
(3) (*repeals* ITEPA 2003 s 408(2))
(4) (*amends* ITEPA 2003 s 408)

64 (*amends* ITEPA 2003 s 563)

65 (*amends* ITEPA 2003 Sch 1, Pt 1 and Pt 2; sub-para (2) *repealed* by FA 2009 s 126(6)(*a*))

SCHEDULE 36

PENSION SCHEMES ETC: TRANSITIONAL PROVISIONS AND SAVINGS

Section 283

Commentary—*Simon's Taxes* **E7.102**.

PART 1

PRE-COMMENCEMENT PENSION SCHEMES

Deemed registration of existing schemes

1—(1) Any pension scheme which, immediately before 6th April 2006, is—
    (*a*) a retirement benefits scheme approved for the purposes of Chapter 1 of Part 14 of ICTA,
    (*b*) a former approved superannuation fund (see sub-paragraph (3)),
    (*c*) a relevant statutory scheme, as defined in section 611A of ICTA, or a pension scheme treated by the Inland Revenue on that date as if it were such a relevant statutory scheme,
    (*d*) an annuity contract by means of which benefits provided under a pension scheme within paragraph (*a*), (*b*) or (*c*) have been secured but which does not provide for the immediate payment of benefits,
    (*e*) a scheme or fund mentioned in section 613(4)(*b*) to (*d*) of ICTA (Parliamentary pension schemes or funds),
    (*f*) an annuity contract or trust scheme approved under section 620 or 621 of ICTA or a substituted contract within the meaning of section 622(3) of ICTA, or
    (*g*) a personal pension scheme approved under Chapter 4 of Part 14 of ICTA,
is to be treated as becoming a registered pension scheme on that date.

(2) Where immediately before 6th April 2006 a retirement benefits scheme is, in accordance with section 611 of ICTA, treated as two or more separate schemes, the reference in sub-paragraph (1)(*a*) to an approved retirement benefits scheme is to such of the separate schemes as are approved (and not to the whole retirement benefits scheme).

(3) For the purposes of sub-paragraph (1)(*b*) any fund which immediately before 6th April 1980 was an approved superannuation fund for the purposes of section 208 of ICTA 1970 is a former approved superannuation fund unless since 5th April 1980—

  (*a*) the fund has been approved for the purposes of Chapter 1 of Part 14 of ICTA (retirement benefits schemes), or

  (*b*) any sum has been paid under the fund by way of contribution.

(4) Sub-paragraph (1)(*a*) or (*g*) applies in relation to a pension scheme approved (for the purposes of Chapter 1, or under Chapter 4, of Part 14 of ICTA) on or after 6th April 2006 if the approval has effect for a period ending with 5th April 2006.

[(4A) This Part of this Act applies in relation to a pension scheme that—

  (*a*) is a registered pension scheme by virtue of sub-paragraph (1)(*a*), and

  (*b*) is neither a public service pension scheme nor an occupational pension scheme,

as it applies in relation to an occupational pension scheme.][1]

(5) This paragraph is subject to paragraph 2 (opt-out).

Commentary—*Simon's Taxes* **E7.208**.

Modifications—Taxation of Pension Schemes (Transitional Provisions) Order, SI 2006/572 art 27 (modification of this paragraph in the case of an individual who, immediately before 6 April 2006, had rights under a contract which had been approved under TA 1988 s 621(1)(*b*)).

Amendments—[1] Sub-s (4A) inserted by FA 2018 s 13, Sch 3 para 1(1), (8) and is treated as always having had effect (FA 2018 Sch 3 para 2(4)).

Opting out of deemed registration

2—(1) Paragraph 1(1) does not apply to a pension scheme if the relevant administrator has, at any time before 6th April 2006, notified the Inland Revenue that the pension scheme is not to become a registered pension scheme on that date.

(2) If, by virtue of sub-paragraph (1) of this paragraph, sub-paragraph (1) of paragraph 1 does not apply to a pension scheme within any of paragraphs (*a*) to (*d*), (*f*) and (*g*) of that sub-paragraph, income tax is to be charged at the rate of 40% on the relevant amount.

(3) The relevant amount is an amount equal to the aggregate of—

  (*a*) the amount of the sums held for the purposes of the pension scheme immediately before 6th April 2006, and

  (*b*) the market value (at that time) of the assets held for the purposes of the pension scheme at that time.

(4) The liability to income tax is a liability of the person who is the relevant administrator on 5th April 2006 or, if more than one person is the relevant administrator on that date, is a joint and several liability of those persons.

(5) Where tax is charged in accordance with sub-paragraph (2), for the purposes of TCGA 1992 the assets which immediately before 6th April 2006 are held for the purposes of the pension scheme—

  (*a*) are to be treated as having been acquired at that time for a consideration equal to the amount on which tax is charged by virtue of sub-paragraph (2) by the person who would be chargeable in respect of a chargeable gain accruing on a disposal of the assets on that date, and

  (*b*) are not to be treated as having been disposed of by any person at that time.

(6) "Relevant administrator" means—

  (*a*) in the case of a pension scheme within paragraph 1(1)(*a*), (*b*) or (*c*), the person who is, or the persons who are, the administrator of the pension scheme under section 611AA of ICTA,

  (*b*) in the case of a pension scheme within paragraph 1(1)(*d*) or (*f*), the trustee or trustees of the pension scheme, or the insurance company which is a party to the contract in which the pension scheme is comprised,

  (*c*) in the case of a pension scheme within paragraph 1(1)(*e*), the trustees of the scheme or fund, and

  (*d*) in the case of a pension scheme within paragraph 1(1)(*g*), the person who is referred to in section 638(1) of ICTA.

(7) If paragraph 1(1) does not apply to a pension scheme by virtue of sub-paragraph (1), sections 431B(2) and 466(2B) of ICTA (meaning of pension business: pension scheme ceasing to be a registered pension scheme) apply as if the pension scheme had ceased to be a registered pension scheme at the beginning of 6th April 2006.

Commentary—*Simon's Taxes* **E7.208**.

Power to modify rules of existing schemes

3—(1) The Board of Inland Revenue may by regulations make any modifications of the rules of pension schemes to which paragraph 1(1) applies if the modifications appear appropriate in consequence of, or in connection with, the provision made by this Part (or the repeals made by this Act in consequence of the provision made by this Part).

(2) Any modifications of the rules of a pension scheme made by the regulations have effect until the earlier of—

(a) the first date after 5th April 2006 on which amendments of the rules of the pension scheme [which state that the modifications no longer apply in relation to it take effect, or

(b) the end of the tax year 2010–11 or such later time as the Board of Inland Revenue may by regulations prescribe.]¹

(3) The modifications that may be made by the regulations include, in particular—

(a) modifications for relieving pension schemes of obligations to make payments which, on and after 6th April 2006, would be unauthorised payments, and

(b) modifications of provisions (however expressed) referring to any limit contained in, or relevant in relation to approval under or for the purposes of, any provision of Part 14 of ICTA (pension schemes etc) as it has effect at any time before 6th April 2006.

Commentary—*Simon's Taxes* **E7.201.**
Regulations—Registered Pension Schemes (Surrender of Relevant Excess) Regulations, SI 2006/211.
Registered Pension Schemes (Modification of the Rules of Existing Schemes) Regulations, SI 2006/364.
Amendments—¹   Words in sub-para (2) substituted by FA 2005 s 101, Sch 10 paras 51, 64(1) with effect from 6 April 2006.

Scheme administrator

4—(1) Where under paragraph 1(1) a pension scheme is treated as becoming a registered pension scheme on 6th April 2006, (despite anything in section 270) the following person is, or the following persons are, to be treated as becoming the scheme administrator of the pension scheme on that date.

(2) If the pension scheme is within paragraph 1(1)(a), (b) or (c) immediately before that date, the person who is, or the persons who are, the administrator of the pension scheme under section 611AA of ICTA immediately before that date is or are to be treated as becoming the scheme administrator.

(3) If the pension scheme is within paragraph 1(1)(d) or (f) immediately before that date, the trustee or trustees of the pension scheme, or the insurance company which is a party to the contract in which the pension scheme is comprised, is or are to be treated as becoming the scheme administrator.

(4) If the pension scheme is within paragraph 1(1)(e) immediately before that date, the trustees of the scheme or fund are to be treated as becoming the scheme administrator.

(5) If the pension scheme is within paragraph 1(1)(g) immediately before that date, the person who is referred to in section 638(1) of ICTA in relation to the pension scheme immediately before that date is to be treated as becoming the scheme administrator.

Modifications—Registered Pension Schemes (Splitting of Schemes) Regulations, SI 2006/569 reg 3 (modification of this provision in relation to sub-scheme administrators).
Taxation of Pension Schemes (Transitional Provisions) Order, SI 2006/572 art 27 (modification of this paragraph in the case of an individual who, immediately before 6 April 2006, had rights under a contract which had been approved under TA 1988 s 621(1)(b)).

Post-commencement withdrawal of approval

5—(1) The repeal by this Act of—

(a) section 591B(1) of ICTA (withdrawal of approval of retirement benefits scheme),

(b) section 620(7) of ICTA (withdrawal of approval of retirement annuity contract), and

(c) section 650(1) of ICTA (withdrawal of approval of approved personal pension arrangements),

does not prevent the withdrawal of an approval under any of those provisions at any time after 5th April 2006 (from any earlier date until 6th April 2006).

(2) A withdrawal of approval made under any of those provisions by virtue of sub-paragraph (1) has the same consequences as a withdrawal of approval made under the provision concerned before 6th April 2006, so that (in particular)—

(a) sections 591C and 591D of ICTA (tax on cessation of approval of retirement benefits scheme), or

(b) sections 650A and 651 of ICTA (charge on cessation of approval of personal pension arrangements and appeal against such withdrawal of such approval),

apply where they would have applied had the approval been withdrawn before that date.

Pre-commencement liabilities of scheme administrator

6   Any liabilities or obligations of—

(a) the administrator of a retirement benefits scheme (within the meaning of Chapter 1 of Part 14 of ICTA), or (*b*) the scheme administrator of a personal pension scheme (within the meaning of Chapter 4 of Part 14 of ICTA),

incurred in relation to the scheme before 6th April 2006 or by virtue of paragraph 4 are (on and after that date) to be treated as liabilities or obligations of the scheme administrator of the scheme.

Modifications—Registered Pension Schemes (Splitting of Schemes) Regulations, SI 2006/569 reg 3 (modification of this provision in relation to sub-scheme administrators).

PART 2
PRE-COMMENCEMENT RIGHTS: LIFETIME ALLOWANCE CHARGE

Commentary—*Simon's Taxes* **E7.240**.

"Primary protection"

7—(1) This paragraph makes provision for the operation of a lifetime allowance enhancement factor in relation to all benefit crystallisation events occurring in relation to an individual where—

(*a*) the amount of the relevant pre-commencement pension rights of the individual exceeds £1,500,000 (the standard lifetime allowance for the tax year 2006–07), and

(*b*) notice of intention to rely on this paragraph is given to the Inland Revenue in accordance with regulations made by the Board of Inland Revenue.

(2) The lifetime allowance enhancement factor is the primary protection factor.

(3) The primary protection factor is—

$$\frac{RR - SLA}{SLA}$$

where—

RR is the amount of the relevant pre-commencement pension rights of the individual, and

SLA is £1,500,000 (the standard lifetime allowance for the tax year 2006–07).

(4) Sub-paragraph (3) is subject to paragraph 11 (pension debit on or after 6th April 2006).

(5) The amount of the relevant pre-commencement pension rights of the individual is the aggregate of—

(*a*) the value of the individual's relevant uncrystallised pension rights on 5th April 2006 (calculated in accordance with paragraphs 8 and 9), and

(*b*) the value of the individual's relevant crystallised pension rights on that date (calculated in accordance with paragraph 10).

Commentary—*Simon's Taxes* **E7.240**.
Regulations—Registered Pension Schemes (Enhanced Lifetime Allowance) Regulations, SI 2006/131.
Registered Pension Schemes (Provision of Information) Regulations, SI 2006/567.

8—(1) The value of the individual's relevant uncrystallised pension rights on 5th April 2006 is the aggregate value of the individual's uncrystallised rights on that date under each relevant pension arrangement relating to the individual.

(2) An arrangement is a "relevant pension arrangement" if it is an arrangement under a pension scheme within paragraph 1(1).

(3) For the purposes of this paragraph the individual's rights are "uncrystallised" if the individual has not, on 5th April 2006, become entitled to the present payment of benefits in respect of the rights.

(4) And the individual is to be treated as entitled to the present payment of benefits in respect of any accrued rights in relation to which the individual has (under section 634A(1) of ICTA) made an election to defer the purchase of an annuity.

(5) For the purposes of this paragraph the value of the individual's uncrystallised rights on 5th April 2006 under an arrangement is to be calculated in accordance with section 212 (valuation of uncrystallised rights for purposes of section 210) on the assumption that the individual became entitled to the present payment of benefits in respect of the rights on that date.

(6) Section 212 has effect for the purposes of sub-paragraph (5) as if the reference to such age (if any) as must have been reached to avoid any reduction in benefits on account of age in paragraph (*a*) of section 277 were to the relevant age; and for this purpose "the relevant age" is—

(*a*) if on 10th December 2003 the terms of the arrangement made provision for a reduction in the amount of benefits payable in respect of rights under the arrangement on account of the holder of the rights being below a particular age, that age, and

(*b*) otherwise, 60.

Commentary—*Simon's Taxes* **E7.240**.
Modifications—Taxation of Pension Schemes (Transitional Provisions) Order, SI 2006/572 arts 9, 11 (modification of this paragraph in its application to any individual who has given notice of intention to rely on FA 2004 Sch 36 para 7 where certain conditions are met).

9—(1) This paragraph applies if any of the individual's uncrystallised rights on 5th April 2006 are rights under one or more arrangements under a pension scheme or schemes within paragraph 1(1)(*a*) to (*d*).

(2) The value of the individual's uncrystallised rights on 5th April 2006 under the arrangement, or the aggregate of the values of the individual's uncrystallised rights on 5th April 2006 under such of the arrangements as relate to a particular employment, is . . . [1]

    (*a*) the value, or the aggregate of the values, calculated under paragraph 8, [or (if lower)][1]

    (*b*) the amount arrived at in accordance with sub-paragraph (3).

(3) The amount arrived at in accordance with this sub-paragraph is—

$$20 \times MPP$$

where MPP is the maximum permitted pension [as increased, in a case where sub-paragraph (5A) applies, in accordance with sub-paragraph (5B)][2].

(4) "The maximum permitted pension" means—

    [(*a*) in the case of an arrangement under a pension scheme which immediately before 6th April 2006 was within section [611A(1)(*a*)][3] of ICTA, the maximum annual pension that could be paid to the individual under the pension scheme on 5th April 2006, and

    (*b*) in any other case,][1] the maximum annual pension that could be paid to the individual on 5th April 2006 under the arrangement or arrangements if it or they were made under a pension scheme within paragraph 1(1)(*a*) without giving the Board of Inland Revenue grounds for withdrawing approval of the pension scheme under section 591B of ICTA.

(5) For the purposes of sub-paragraph (4) it is to be assumed—

    (*a*) [in the case of any arrangement, that][1] if the individual was in the employment to which the arrangement or arrangements relates or relate on 5th April [2006][1] the individual left the employment on that date, and

    [(*aa*) in the case of an arrangement within sub-paragraph (4)(*a*), that the valuation assumptions apply (see section 277),][1]

    (*b*) [in the case of any other arrangement, that][1] if the individual had not reached the lowest age at which a pension may be paid under a pension scheme within paragraph 1(1)(*a*) to a person in good health without giving the Board of Inland Revenue grounds for withdrawing the approval of the pension [scheme][1] that fact would not give the Board such grounds.

[(5A) This sub-paragraph applies where, in the case of an arrangement under a pension scheme which immediately before 6th April 2006 was within section 611A(1)(*a*) of ICTA—

    (*a*) a lump sum could be paid to the individual on 5th April 2006 under the pension scheme otherwise than by commutation of pension, and

    (*b*) that lump sum could not be exchanged (in whole or in part) for an increased pension.][2]

[(5B) Where sub-paragraph (5A) applies, the amount arrived at under sub-paragraph (3) is the aggregate of what it otherwise would be and so much of the amount of the lump sum as could not be so exchanged.][2]

(6) For the purposes of this paragraph an arrangement relating to an individual relates to an employment if—

    (*a*) the earnings by reference to which benefits under the arrangement are calculated are earnings from the employment, or

    (*b*) the person who is the employer in relation to the employment pays contributions under the arrangement in respect of the individual.

Commentary—*Simon's Taxes* E7.216, E7.240.

Amendments—[1] Words in sub-para (2) repealed and substituted, words in sub-para (4) inserted, words in sub-para (5)(*a*), (*b*) inserted and substituted, and sub-para (5)(*aa*) inserted by FA 2005 ss 101, 104, Sch 10 paras 52(2)–(5), 64(1), Sch 11 Pt 4 with effect from 6 April 2006.

[2] Words in sub-para (3) inserted, and sub-paras (5A), (5B) inserted, by FA 2006 s 161, Sch 23 paras 1, 36. These amendments are deemed to have come into force on 6 April 2006.

[3] Reference in sub-para (4)(*a*) substituted by FA 2006 s 161, Sch 23 paras 1, 44, 45. This amendment is deemed to have come into force on 6 April 2006.

10—(1) The value of the individual's relevant crystallised pension rights on 5th April 2006 is—

$$25 \times ARP$$

where ARP is an amount equal to the annual rate at which any relevant existing pension is payable to the individual on 5th April 2006 or, if more than one relevant existing pension is payable to the individual on that date, to the aggregate of the annual rates at which each of the relevant existing pensions is so payable.

(2) "Relevant existing pension" means—

(*a*) a pension under a retirement benefits scheme approved for the purposes of Chapter 1 of Part 14 of ICTA,

(*b*) a pension under a former approved superannuation fund (defined as for the purposes of paragraph 1(1)(*b*)),

(*c*) a pension under a relevant statutory scheme, as defined in section 611A of ICTA, or a pension scheme treated by the Inland Revenue as if it were such a relevant statutory scheme,

(*d*) an annuity (or pension in the form of income drawdown) under an annuity contract by means of which benefits provided under a pension scheme within paragraph (*a*), (*b*) or (*c*) have been secured,

(*e*) a pension under a scheme or fund mentioned in section 613(4)(*b*) to (*d*) of ICTA (Parliamentary pension schemes or funds),

(*f*) an annuity under an annuity contract or trust scheme approved under section 620 or 621 of ICTA or a substituted contract within the meaning of section 622(3) of ICTA,

(*g*) an annuity acquired using funds held for the purposes of a personal pension scheme approved under Chapter 4 of Part 14 of ICTA, or

(*h*) a right to make income withdrawals under section 634A of ICTA.

(3) But a pension, annuity or right is not a relevant existing pension if entitlement to it was attributable to the death of any person.

(4) In the case of a pension within sub-paragraph (2) taking the form of income drawdown, the annual rate at which the pension is payable on 5th April 2006 is the amount which, on that date, is the maximum annual amount that may be drawn down by the individual as income in accordance with the pension scheme or contract concerned.

(5) In the case of a right which is a relevant existing pension by virtue of sub-paragraph (2)(*h*), the annual rate at which the pension is payable on 5th April 2006 is the maximum amount of income withdrawals that may be made by the individual in the period of 12 months referred to in section 634A(4) of ICTA during which 5th April 2006 falls.

Commentary—*Simon's Taxes* **E7.240**.

11—(1) This paragraph applies where—

(*a*) paragraph 7 makes provision for the operation of a lifetime allowance enhancement factor in relation to an individual, and

(*b*) on or after 6th April 2006, the rights of the individual under a relevant pension arrangement (see paragraph 8(2)) relating to the individual are reduced by becoming subject to a pension debit.

(2) The primary protection factor (see paragraph 7(3)) is to be recalculated.

(3) The recalculation involves reducing RR (see paragraph 7(3)) by the amount by which the individual's rights are reduced and arriving at a revised primary protection factor.

(4) The revised primary protection factor operates in relation to any benefit crystallisation event occurring in relation to the individual after the time when the individual's rights are reduced by becoming subject to the pension debit.

Commentary—*Simon's Taxes* **E7.240**.

[11A—(1) This paragraph applies where—

(*a*) paragraph 7 makes provision for the operation of a lifetime allowance enhancement factor in relation to an individual immediately before the individual's death (and any calculation required by paragraph 11 does not mean that there is then no longer a primary protection factor),

(*b*) a person is paid a defined benefits lump sum death benefit or an uncrystallised funds lump sum death benefit in respect of the individual, and

(*c*) notice of intention to rely on this paragraph is given to an officer of Revenue and Customs by that person in accordance with regulations made by the Commissioners for Her Majesty's Revenue and Customs.

(2) If the value of the individual's pre-commencement rights to death benefits (see paragraphs 11B to 11D) exceeds RR (as adjusted under paragraph 11, where that paragraph applies), the primary protection factor is to be recalculated.

(3) The re-calculation involves taking RR to be the value of the individual's pre-commencement rights to death benefits and arriving at a revised primary protection factor.

(4) The revised primary protection factor operates in relation to—

(*a*) the benefit crystallisation event consisting of the payment of the lump sum death benefit, and

(*b*) any other benefit crystallisation event consisting of the payment of a lump sum death benefit in respect of the individual.]¹

Amendments—¹ Paragraphs 11A–11D inserted by FA 2006 s 161, Sch 23 paras 1, 37, 38. These amendments are deemed to have come into force on 6 April 2006.

[11B—(1) This paragraph and paragraphs 11C and 11D specify the value of the individual's pre-commencement rights to death benefits.

(2) Subject to paragraphs 11C and 11D, the value of the individual's pre-commencement rights to death benefits is the aggregate of the maximum amounts that could have been paid—

    (*a*) in respect of the individual as uncrystallised rights lump sum death benefits, and

    (*b*) under relevant pension arrangements relating to the individual,

if the individual had died on 5th April 2006.

(3) Lump sum death benefits are "uncrystallised rights lump sum death benefits" if they are attributable to rights in respect of which the individual had not, on 5th April 2006, become entitled to the present payment of benefits.

(4) An arrangement is a "relevant pension arrangement" if it is an arrangement under a pension scheme within paragraph 1(1).][1]

Amendments—[1]   Paragraphs 11A–11D inserted by FA 2006 s 161, Sch 23 paras 1, 37, 38. These amendments are deemed to have come into force on 6 April 2006.

[11C—(1) In arriving at the aggregate mentioned in paragraph 11B(2) the following amounts are to be left out of account—

    (*a*) in the case of any lump sum death benefit which could have been paid under a pension scheme in the case of which approval could have been withdrawn under section 591B, 620(7) or 650 of ICTA, any amount in excess of the permitted limit (see sub-paragraph (2)), and

    (*b*) in the case of any lump sum death benefit which could have been paid under an arrangement in the case of which rights to such a benefit are commuted into prospective rights to receive dependants' pensions, any dependants' pension proportion amount (see sub-paragraphs (3) and (4)).

(2) An "amount in excess of the permitted limit" is so much (if any) of the maximum amount of any lump sum death benefit as could not have been paid without having given grounds for withdrawing approval of the pension scheme under section 591B, 620(7) or 650 of ICTA.

(3) A "dependants' pension proportion amount" is so much (if any) of the maximum amount of any lump sum death benefit which could have been paid under the arrangement as is the dependants' pension proportion of the lump sum death benefit.

(4) The dependants' pension proportion is—

$$\frac{UTA - TA}{UTA}$$

where—

    TA is the amount which, at the time when a defined benefits lump sum death benefit or uncrystallised funds lump sum death benefit is first paid in respect of the individual, is the aggregate of the maximum amounts of any defined benefits lump sum death benefits or uncrystallised funds lump sum death benefits which could be paid under the arrangement in respect of the individual, and

    UTA is what TA would be if no prospective rights to the payment of any of those lump sum death benefits had been commuted into prospective rights to receive dependants' pensions.][1]

Amendments—[1]   Paragraphs 11A–11D inserted by FA 2006 s 161, Sch 23 paras 1, 37, 38. These amendments are deemed to have come into force on 6 April 2006.

[11D—(1) Sub-paragraph (2) applies where any of the lump sum death benefits mentioned in sub-paragraph (2) of paragraph 11B would have been payable under a policy of life insurance held for the purposes of a pension scheme and on 5th April 2006 the pension scheme either—

    (*a*) was not an occupational pension scheme, or

    (*b*) was an occupational pension scheme with fewer than 20 members.

(2) The lump sum death benefit is only to be taken into account in arriving at the aggregate mentioned in that sub-paragraph if—

    (*a*) a sum was paid under the policy when the individual actually died, and

    (*b*) the terms of the policy had not been varied significantly during the period beginning with 5th April 2006 and ending with the death;

and any exercise of rights conferred by the policy is to be regarded for this purpose as a variation.

[(2A) A variation of the terms of a policy of life insurance made in order to comply with [Part 5 of the Equality Act 2010, so far as relating to age, or the][4] Employment Equality (Age) Regulations (Northern Ireland) 2006 (or any regulations amending or replacing them) is to be ignored for the purposes of sub-paragraph (2).][3]

[(2B) Where a policy of life insurance held on 5th April 2006 for the purposes of an occupational pension scheme is surrendered and a new one is taken out—

    (*a*) as part of a retirement-benefit activities compliance exercise, or (*b*) to comply with the Employment Equality (Age) Regulations 2006 or Employment Equality (Age) Regulations (Northern Ireland) 2006 (or any regulations amending or replacing [those Regulations][4],

the new policy is to be treated for the purposes of sub-paragraph (2) as if it were the same as the old.][3]

[(2C) For this purpose a policy of life insurance is surrendered and a new one is taken out as part of a retirement-benefit activities compliance exercise if—

(*a*) the surrender of the old policy and taking out of the new policy constitute or form part of a transaction the purpose of which is to secure that the activities of the pension scheme are limited to retirement-benefit activities within the meaning of section 255 of the Pensions Act 2004 or Article 232 of the Pensions (Northern Ireland) Order 2005, and

(*b*) the rights under the old policy and the new policy are not significantly different.][3]

(3) Sub-paragraph (4) applies where any of the lump sum death benefits mentioned in sub-paragraph (2) of paragraph 11B would have been payable under an occupational pension scheme.

(4) The lump sum death benefit is only to be taken into account in arriving at the aggregate mentioned in that sub-paragraph if—

(*a*) the individual was employed by a person on 5th April 2006 and continued to be employed by that person or a person connected with that person until the time when the individual died,

(*b*) that person was a sponsoring employer in relation to the pension scheme on 5th April 2006, and

(*c*) the individual had not become entitled to the present payment of benefits in respect of rights under the pension scheme before the time when the individual died.

[(5) For the purposes of this paragraph whether a person is connected with another person is determined in accordance with section 993 of ITA 2007.][2]][1]

Amendments—[1]   Paragraphs 11A–11D inserted by FA 2006 s 161, Sch 23 paras 1, 37, 38. These amendments are deemed to have come into force on 6 April 2006.

[2]   Sub-para (5) substituted by ITA 2007 s 1027, Sch 1 paras 456, 485 with effect for income tax purposes from 6 April 2007, and corporation tax purposes for accounting periods ending after 5 April 2007.

[3]   Sub-paras (2A)–(2C) inserted by FA 2007 s 70, Sch 20 paras 1, 15, 24(3). This amendment is deemed always to have had effect.

[4]   In sub-ss (2A), (2B)(*b*) words substituted by the Equality Act 2010 s 211(1), Sch 26, Pt 1, paras 57, 59 with effect from 1 October 2010 by virtue of SI 2010/2279, arts 2, 12, Sch 1, para 5.

"Enhanced protection"

12—(1) This paragraph applies on and after 6th April 2006 in the case of an individual who has one or more relevant existing arrangements if notice of intention to rely on it is given to the Inland Revenue in accordance with regulations made by the Board of Inland Revenue.

(2) But this paragraph ceases to apply if—

(*a*) relevant benefit accrual occurs under the arrangement, or any of the arrangements (see paragraph 13),

[(*aa*) there is an impermissible transfer into the arrangement or any of the arrangements (see paragraph 17A),][1]

(*b*) a transfer of sums or assets held for the purposes of, or representing accrued rights under, the arrangement or any of the arrangements is made that is not a permitted transfer, or

(*c*) an arrangement relating to the individual is made under a registered pension scheme otherwise than [in permitted circumstances][2].

[(2A) An arrangement is made in permitted circumstances if it is made—

(*a*) for the purposes of a permitted transfer,

(*b*) as part of a retirement-benefit activities compliance exercise, or

(*c*) as part of an age-equality compliance exercise.][2]

[(2B) For the purposes of sub-paragraph (2A)(*b*) an arrangement ("the new arrangement") relating to an individual is made as part of a retirement-benefit activities compliance exercise if—

(*a*) it is made in connection with the cancellation of rights under another arrangement relating to the individual ("the old arrangement"),

(*b*) the old arrangement and the new arrangement relate to the same employment,

(*c*) there is a prospective entitlement to pension death benefits within section 167(1) or lump sum death benefits within section 168(1) (or both) under both the old arrangement and the new arrangement,

(*d*) the making of the new arrangement and the cancellation of the old arrangement constitute or form part of a transaction the purpose of which is to secure that the activities of the pension scheme under which the arrangement is made are limited to retirement-benefit activities within the meaning of section 255 of the Pensions Act 2004 or Article 232 of the Pensions (Northern Ireland) Order 2005, and (*e*) the rights cancelled under the old arrangement and the rights conferred under the new arrangement are not significantly different.][2]

[(2C) For the purposes of sub-paragraph (2A)(*c*) an arrangement ("the new arrangement") is made as part of an age-equality compliance exercise if—

    (*a*) it is made in connection with the cancellation of rights under another arrangement relating to the individual ("the old arrangement"),

    (*b*) the old arrangement and the new arrangement relate to the same employment,

    (*c*) there is a prospective entitlement to pension death benefits within section 167(1) or lump sum death benefits within section 168(1) (or both) under both the old arrangement and the new arrangement, and

    (*d*) the new arrangement is made, and the old arrangement cancelled, in order to comply with [Part 5 of the Equality Act 2010, so far as relating to age, or the][4] Employment Equality (Age) Regulations (Northern Ireland) 2006 (or any regulations amending or replacing [those Regulations][4]).][2]

(3) Where this paragraph applies in the case of an individual—

    [(*a*) there is no liability to the lifetime allowance charge in respect of the individual, and

    (*b*) the payment of a lifetime allowance excess lump sum to the individual is not permitted by the lump sum rule (see section 166).][1].

(4) An individual has a relevant existing arrangement if—

    (*a*) before 6th April 2006 an arrangement relating to the individual has been made under a pension scheme within paragraph 1(1), and

    (*b*) the pension scheme becomes a registered pension scheme on that date.

(5) Notice of intention to rely on this paragraph in relation to the individual may not be given in a case where—

    (*a*) the value of the uncrystallised rights of the individual on 5th April 2006 under an arrangement, or

    (*b*) the aggregate of the values of the uncrystallised rights of the individual on 5th April 2006 under arrangements,

is arrived at in accordance with paragraph [9(3)][1] unless such rights as, in accordance with regulations made by the Board of Inland Revenue, are to be treated as representing the relevant excess have been surrendered.

(6) In sub-paragraph (5) "the relevant excess" means the amount by which the value of—

    (*a*) the individual's uncrystallised rights, or

    (*b*) the aggregate of the values of the individual's uncrystallised rights, as arrived at in accordance with paragraph 8 exceeds what it would be if arrived at under paragraph [9(3)][1].

(7) For the purposes of this paragraph and paragraphs 13 and 15, a transfer of sums or assets held for the purposes of, or representing accrued rights under, an arrangement is a permitted transfer if—

    (*a*) . . .[2]

    (*b*) the sums or assets . . .[2] are transferred so that sub-paragraph (8) applies in relation to them, and

    (*c*) the aggregate of the amount of [the][2] sums and the market value of [the][2] assets is, applying normal actuarial practice, equivalent before and after the transfer.

(8) This sub-paragraph applies in relation to sums or assets held for the purposes of, or representing accrued rights under, the arrangement if—

    (*a*) they are transferred so as to become held for the purposes of a money purchase arrangement that is not a cash balance arrangement . . .[2] under a registered pension scheme or recognised overseas pension scheme, . . .[2]

    (*b*) where the transfer occurs in connection with the winding up of the pension scheme under which the arrangement is made and the arrangement is a cash balance arrangement or a defined benefits arrangement, they are transferred so as to become held for the purposes of, or to represent rights under, a cash balance arrangement or defined benefits arrangement relating to the same employment as the arrangement and made under a registered pension scheme or recognised overseas pension scheme.

    [(*c*) where the arrangement is a cash balance arrangement or a defined benefits arrangement relating to a present or former employment, they are transferred in connection with a relevant business transfer so as to become held for the purposes of, or to represent rights under, a cash balance arrangement or defined benefits arrangement made under a registered pension scheme or recognised overseas pension scheme, or][2]

    [(*d*) where the arrangement ("the old arrangement") is a cash balance arrangement or a defined benefits arrangement, they are transferred as part of a retirement-benefit activities compliance exercise so as to become held for the purposes of, or to represent rights under, a cash balance arrangement or defined benefits arrangement ("the new arrangement") relating to the same employment as the old arrangement and made under a registered pension scheme or recognised overseas pension scheme.][2]

[(8A) For the purposes of sub-paragraph (8)(c) "relevant business transfer" means a transfer of an undertaking or a business (or part of an undertaking or a business) from one person to another—

  (a) which involves the transfer of at least 20 employees, and

  (b) in the case of which, if the transferor and the transferee are bodies corporate, they would not be treated as members of the same group for the purposes of [Part 5 of the Corporation Tax Act 2010][3].][2]

[(8B) For the purposes of sub-paragraph (8)(d) sums or assets held for the purposes of, or representing accrued rights under, the old arrangement are transferred as part of a retirement-benefit activities compliance exercise if—

  (a) there is a prospective entitlement to pension death benefits within section 167(1) or lump sum death benefits within section 168(1) (or both) under both the old arrangement and the new arrangement, and

  (b) the transfer constitutes or forms part of a transaction the purpose of which is to secure that the activities of the pension scheme under which the old arrangement was made are limited to retirement-benefit activities within the meaning of section 255 of the Pensions Act 2004 or Article 232 of the Pensions (Northern Ireland) Order 2005.][2]

(9) Where there is a permitted transfer—

  (a) if the transfer is a permitted transfer by virtue of sub-paragraph (8)(a), this paragraph (and paragraphs 13[, 14 and 17A(1) and (2)][1]) apply in relation to the arrangement . . . [2] to which the transfer is made, . . . [2]

  (b) if the transfer is a permitted transfer by virtue of sub-paragraph (8)(b) [or (d)][2], this paragraph (and paragraphs 13[, 15 [to 17][2] and 17A(3)][1]) apply as if the arrangement to which the transfer is made were the same as that from which it is made [and

  (c) if the transfer is a permitted transfer by virtue of sub-paragraph (8)(c), this paragraph (and paragraphs 13, 15 to 17 and 17A(3)) apply as if the arrangement to which the transfer is made were the same as that from which it is made and (if the employment is transferred) as if the employment with the transferee were the employment with the transferor.][2]

[(10) The Treasury may by order amend sub-paragraph (8) (and make other amendments consequential on any amendment of that sub-paragraph).][2]

Commentary—*Simon's Taxes* **E7.240**.
HMRC Manuals—Registered Pension Schemes Manual RPSM11101520 (fixed protection and joining a new scheme).
Regulations—Registered Pension Schemes (Enhanced Lifetime Allowance) Regulations, SI 2006/131.
Registered Pension Schemes (Surrender of Relevant Excess) Regulations, SI 2006/211.
Registered Pension Schemes (Provision of Information) Regulations, SI 2006/567.
Modifications—Taxation of Pension Schemes (Transitional Provisions) Order, SI 2006/572 art 35 (modification of this paragraph in the case of an individual who meets certain conditions).
Amendments—[1] Sub-para (2)(aa) inserted, words in sub-para (3) substituted, figure in sub-paras (5), (6) substituted, and words in sub-paras (9)(a), (b) substituted by FA 2005 s 101, Sch 10 paras 53(2)–(5), 64(1) with effect from 6 April 2006.
[2] Words in sub-para (2)(c) substituted; sub-paras (2A)–(2C), (8)(c), (d), (8A), (8B), (9)(c), (10) inserted; sub-para (7)(a) and words in sub-paras (7)(b), (8), (9) repealed; and words in sub-para (9) inserted, by FA 2007 ss 70, 114, Sch 20 paras 1, 16, 17, 24(3), Sch 27 Pt 3(2). These amendments are deemed always to have had effect.
[3] In sub-para (8A)(b) words "Chapter 4 of Part 10 of ICTA" substituted by CTA 2010 s 1177, Sch 1 paras 423, 432(1),(2). CTA 2010 has effect for corporation tax purposes for accounting periods ending on or after 1 April 2010, and for income and capital gains tax purposes for the tax year 2010–11 and subsequent tax years.
[4] In sub-s (2C)(d) words substituted by the Equality Act 2010 s 211(1), Sch 26, Pt 1, paras 57, 59(b) with effect from 1 October 2010 by virtue of SI 2010/2279, arts 2, 12, Sch 1, para 5.

13 Relevant benefit accrual occurs in relation to an individual under an arrangement—

  (a) in the case of a money purchase arrangement that is not a cash balance arrangement, if a relevant contribution is paid under the arrangement [or, where the arrangement has been a hybrid arrangement, if a relevant contribution was so paid at any time after 5th April 2006,][1] (see paragraph 14), and

  (b) in the case of a cash balance arrangement or defined benefits arrangement, if, when a benefit crystallisation event or transfer that is a permitted transfer by virtue of paragraph 12(8)(a) (a "relevant event") occurs in relation to the individual and the arrangement, the relevant crystallised amount exceeds the appropriate limit (see paragraph 15).

Commentary—*Simon's Taxes* E7.240.
Amendments—[1] Words in para (a) inserted by FA 2005 s 101, Sch 10 paras 53(7), 64(1) with effect from 6 April 2006.

14—(1) For the purposes of paragraph 13(a) a relevant contribution is paid under the arrangement if—

  (a) a relievable pension contribution is paid by or on behalf of the individual under the arrangement,

(b) a contribution is paid in respect of the individual under the arrangement by an employer of the individual, or

(c) a contribution paid [otherwise than by or on behalf of the individual or by an employer of the individual][1] in respect of the individual subsequently becomes held for the purposes of the provision under the arrangement of benefits to or in respect of the individual.

(2) . . .[5]

[(3) A contribution is not a relevant contribution for the purposes of paragraph 13(a) if—

(a) it may only be applied for or towards the payment of premiums under a policy of insurance on the life of the individual,

(b) the policy is issued, or issued in respect of insurances made, before 6th April 2006,

(c) there is no right to surrender any rights under the policy,

(d) the terms of the policy are not varied significantly during the period beginning with 6th April 2006 and ending with the individual's actual death so as to increase the benefits payable under the policy or extend the period during which benefits are so payable, and

(e) no benefits are paid, or other payments made, under (or on the surrender of rights under) the policy except by reason of the individual's death;

and any exercise of rights conferred by the policy is to be regarded for this purpose as a variation.][2]

[(3A) A variation of the terms of a policy made in order to comply with [Part 5 of the Equality Act 2010, so far as relating to age, or the][4] Employment Equality (Age) Regulations (Northern Ireland) 2006 (or any regulations amending or replacing them) is to be ignored for the purposes of sub-paragraph (3).][3]

[(3B) Where a policy of insurance on the life of the individual issued, or issued in respect of insurances made, before 6th April 2006 is surrendered and a new one is taken out—

(a) as part of a retirement-benefit activities compliance exercise, or

(b) as part of an age-equality compliance exercise.

the new policy is to be treated for the purposes of sub-paragraph (3) as if it were the same as the old.][3]

[(3C) For the purposes of sub-paragraph (3B)(a) a policy is surrendered, and a new policy of life insurance is taken out, as part of a retirement-benefit activities compliance exercise if—

(a) the surrender of the old policy and the taking out of the new policy constitute or form part of a transaction the purpose of which is to secure that the activities of the pension scheme under which the arrangement is made are limited to retirement-benefit activities within the meaning of section 255 of the Pensions Act 2004 or Article 232 of the Pensions (Northern Ireland) Order 2005, and

(b) the rights under the old policy and the new policy are not significantly different.][3]

[(3D) For the purposes of sub-paragraph (3B)(b) a policy is surrendered, and a new policy of life insurance is taken out, as part of an age-equality compliance exercise if—

(a) the old policy is surrendered, and the new policy is taken out, in order to comply with [Part 5 of the Equality Act 2010, so far as relating to age, or the][4] Employment Equality (Age) Regulations (Northern Ireland) 2006 (or any regulations amending or replacing [those Regulations][4]), and

(b) any significant difference between the rights under the old policy and the rights under the new policy is attributable to the need to comply with those Regulations (or any regulations amending or replacing them).][3]

[(4) A contribution is not a relevant contribution for the purposes of paragraph 13(a) if it is paid—

(a) by a sponsoring employer,

(b) under a relevant hybrid arrangement, and

(c) solely in respect of the provision in respect of the individual of lump sum death benefits which are defined benefits or cash balance benefits.][2]

[(5) A "relevant hybrid arrangement" is a hybrid arrangement under an occupational pension scheme—

(a) which subsequently becomes a money purchase arrangement that is not a cash balance arrangement, and

(b) under which lump sum death benefits would have been payable in respect of the individual if the individual had died on 5th April 2006.][2]

Commentary—*Simon's Taxes* **E7.240**.
HMRC Manuals—RPSM11101530 (fixed protection: benefit accrual).
Amendments—[1] Words in sub-para (1)(c) inserted, and words in sub-para (2) substituted and inserted by FA 2005 s 101, Sch 10 paras 53(8)–(10), 64(1) with effect from 6 April 2006.
[2] Sub-paras (3)–(5) inserted by FA 2006 s 161, Sch 23 paras 1, 37, 39. These amendments are deemed to have come into force on 6 April 2006.
[3] Sub-paras (3A)–(3D) inserted by FA 2007 s 70, Sch 20 paras 1, 16, 18, 24(3). These amendments are deemed always to have had effect.

4   In sub-ss (3A), (3D)(*a*) words substituted by the Equality Act 2010 s 211(1), Sch 26, Pt 1, paras 57, 59 with effect from 1 October 2010 by virtue of SI 2010/2279, arts 2, 12, Sch 1, para 5.
5   Sub-para (2) repealed by FA 2013 s 52(1), (9) with effect from 6 April 2013.

15—(1) For the purposes of paragraph 13(*b*) "the relevant crystallised amount" is—

  (*a*) if the relevant event is the first relevant event occurring in relation to the individual and to the arrangement or any other cash balance arrangement or defined benefits arrangement related to the arrangement ("the first relevant event"), the amount crystallised by that event, and

  (*b*) otherwise, the aggregate of the amount crystallised by the relevant event and the amount crystallised by the relevant event, or by each of the relevant events, which has or have previously occurred in relation to the individual and to the arrangement or any other cash balance arrangement or defined benefits arrangement related to the arrangement.

(2) If the relevant event is a permitted transfer which is not a benefit crystallisation event, sub-paragraph (1) applies as if the amount crystallised by the event were the aggregate of—

  (*a*) the amount of any sums held for the purposes of, or representing accrued rights under, the arrangement [which are transferred]², and

  (*b*) the market value of any assets held for the purposes of, or representing accrued rights under, the arrangement [which are transferred]².

(3) For the purposes of this paragraph (and [paragraphs 15A and 16]¹) another arrangement is related to the arrangement if—

  (*a*) the other arrangement relates to the individual, and

  (*b*) both the arrangement and the other arrangement relate to the same employment;

and whether an arrangement relates to an employment is to be determined in accordance with paragraph 9(6).

(4) For the purposes of paragraph 13(*b*) "the appropriate limit", in relation to a relevant event, [is (subject to paragraph 15A) the greater]¹ of—

  (*a*) the value of the individual's rights on 5th April 2006 under the arrangement, or (where there is or are one or more other cash balance arrangements or defined benefits arrangements related to the arrangement) the aggregate of the value of the individual's rights under the arrangement and the other arrangement or arrangements, arrived at in accordance with paragraphs 8 and 9, as increased by the relevant indexation percentage (see sub-paragraph (5)), and

  (*b*) what would be the value of those rights, so arrived at, on the assumptions specified in sub-paragraph (6).

(5) For the purposes of sub-paragraph (4)(*a*) [and paragraph 15A(2)(*a*)]¹ "the relevant indexation percentage", in relation to a relevant event, means whichever is the greatest of—

  (*a*) the percentage by which an amount would be increased if it were increased for the period beginning with 6th April 2006 and ending with the date on which the relevant event occurs at an annual rate of 5%,

  (*b*) the percentage by which an amount would be increased if it were increased for that period at an annual percentage rate referred to in regulations made by the Board of Inland Revenue, and

  (*c*) the percentage by which the retail prices index for the month in which the relevant event occurs is higher than that for April 2006.

(6) The assumptions referred to in sub-paragraph (4)(*b*) [and paragraph 15A(2)(*b*)]¹ are—

  (*a*) that the individual's age on 5th April 2006 were what it is at the time of the first relevant event (so that neither paragraph 8(6) nor section 277(*a*) applies in arriving at what would be the value of the rights under paragraph 8), and

  (*b*) that the amount of the earnings which would have fallen to be taken into account under the arrangement for calculating the amount of benefits payable to or in respect of the individual (if the individual became entitled to the present payment of benefits in respect of the rights under the arrangement on that date) were the lesser of the two amounts specified in sub-paragraph (7).

(7) The amounts referred to in sub-paragraph (6)(*b*) are—

  (*a*) the current amount of the relevant pensionable earnings immediately before the first relevant event, and

  (*b*) the post-commencement earnings limit (see paragraphs [16 and 17]²).

(8) But sub-paragraph (6)(*b*) applies in relation to an arrangement under a pension scheme within paragraph 1(1)(*c*) or (*e*) as if for "the lesser of the two amounts specified in sub-paragraph (7)" there were substituted "the amount specified in sub-paragraph (7)(*a*)".

(9) In this paragraph "the relevant pensionable earnings" means the description of earnings (or the portion of the description of earnings) of the individual by reference to which the amount of benefits payable to or in respect of the individual would have fallen to be calculated if the individual became entitled to the present payment of benefits in respect of the rights under the arrangement on 5th April 2006.

(10) For the purposes of sub-paragraph (7)(*a*) "the current amount" of the relevant pensionable earnings immediately before the first relevant event is the amount of the relevant pensionable earnings which, at that time, would fall to be taken into account in calculating the amount of benefits payable to or in respect of the individual under the arrangement if the individual became entitled to the present payment of benefits at that time (but subject to sub-paragraph (11)).

(11) If at that time the individual is absent from work in connection with pregnancy, maternity, paternity or adoption, the current amount of the relevant pensionable earnings at that time includes what would be likely to be included in that amount if the individual were not so absent.

Commentary—*Simon's Taxes* **E7.240**.

Regulations—Registered Pension Schemes (Uprating Percentages for Defined Benefits Arrangements and Enhanced Protection Limits) Regulations, SI 2006/130.

Modifications—Taxation of Pension Schemes (Transitional Provisions) Order, SI 2006/572 art 36 (modification of this paragraph in the case of an individual who meets certain conditions).

Amendments—[1] Words in sub-paras (3), (4) substituted, and words in sub-paras (5), (6) inserted, by FA 2006 s 161, Sch 23 paras 1, 37, 40. These amendments are deemed to have come into force on 6 April 2006.

[2] Words in sub-para (2) inserted, and words in sub-para (7) substituted, by FA 2007 s 70, Sch 20 paras 1, 16, 19, 24(3). These amendments are deemed always to have had effect.

[15A—(1) This paragraph applies where—

    (*a*) a person is paid a defined benefits lump sum death benefit or an uncrystallised funds lump sum death benefit in respect of the individual under the arrangement, and

    (*b*) notice of intention to rely on this paragraph is given to an officer of Revenue and Customs by that person in accordance with regulations made by the Commissioners for Her Majesty's Revenue and Customs.

(2) For the purposes of paragraph 13(*b*), if the amount yielded by sub-paragraph (3) is greater than what would otherwise be the appropriate limit in relation to a relevant event which consists of—

    (*a*) the payment of the lump sum death benefit, or

    (*b*) the payment of any other lump sum death benefit in respect of the individual under the arrangement or another cash balance arrangement or defined benefits arrangement related to the arrangement,

that greater amount is the appropriate limit in relation to such a relevant event.

(3) The amount yielded by this sub-paragraph is the greater of—

    (*a*) the value of the individual's pre-commencement rights to death benefits, as increased by the relevant indexation percentage (see sub-paragraph (5) of paragraph 15), or

    (*b*) what would be the value of the individual's pre-commencement rights to death benefits on the assumptions specified in sub-paragraph (6) of that paragraph (but subject to the modifications in sub-paragraph (7) of this paragraph).

(4) The value of the individual's pre-commencement rights to death benefits is the aggregate of the maximum amounts that could have been paid in respect of the individual as uncrystallised rights lump sum death benefits under—

    (*a*) the arrangement, or

    (*b*) any other cash balance arrangement or defined benefits arrangement related to the arrangement,

if the individual had died on 5th April 2006.

(5) Lump sum death benefits are "uncrystallised rights lump sum death benefits" if they are attributable to rights in respect of which the individual had not, on 5th April 2006, become entitled to the present payment of benefits.

(6) Paragraphs 11C and 11D apply in arriving at the aggregate mentioned in sub-paragraph (4) as in arriving at that mentioned in paragraph 11B(2) but as if—

    (*a*) each of the references to paragraph 11B(2) were to sub-paragraph (4) of this paragraph, and

    (*b*) in paragraph 11D(1), for "of a pension scheme" there were substituted "of any arrangement within paragraph 15A(4) under a pension scheme".

(7) In their operation for the purposes of this paragraph sub-paragraphs (6) to (11) of paragraph 15 have effect as if—

    (*a*) for the references in sub-paragraphs (6)(*a*) and (7)(*a*) and (10) to the time of the first relevant event there were substituted a reference to the time immediately before the individual's death, and

    (*b*) the words in parentheses in sub-paragraph (6)(*a*) were omitted.][1]

Amendments—[1] This paragraph inserted by FA 2006 s 161, Sch 23 paras 1, 37, 41. This amendment is deemed to have come into force on 6 April 2006.

16—(1) This paragraph specifies the post-commencement earnings limit if the individual was on 5th April 2006 a person in relation to [whom—

    (*a*) section 590C of ICTA or paragraph 20 of Schedule 6 to FA 1989 (earnings cap) had effect, or

(b) provision similar to section 590C of ICTA had effect by virtue of conditions imposed under section 591 of that Act (discretionary approval),

in]¹ relation to any pension scheme under which the arrangement or any other arrangement related to the arrangement was made.

(2) The post-commencement earnings limit is the lesser of amount A and amount B.

(3) Amount A is 7·5% of the [underpinned lifetime allowance when the first relevant event occurs; and "the underpinned lifetime allowance" is the greater of the current standard lifetime allowance and £1,800,000 (the standard lifetime allowance for the tax year 2011–12).]²

(4) Amount B is the amount of the individual's employment income from the employment to which the arrangement relates for the best period of 12 months during the appropriate three year period.

(5) The appropriate three year period is the period of three years ending with [the earliest of—

    (a) the first relevant event,

    (b) the individual leaving the employment to which the arrangement relates, and

    (c) the individual's death.]¹

[(5A) Where the appropriate three year period ends otherwise than with the first relevant event, Amount B is what it would be apart from this sub-paragraph increased by whichever is the greatest of—

    (a) the percentage by which an amount would be increased if it were increased for the period beginning with the date on which it ends and ending with the date on which the relevant event occurs at an annual rate of 5%,

    (b) the percentage by which an amount would be increased if it were increased for that period at an annual percentage rate referred to in regulations made by the Board of Inland Revenue, or

    (c) the percentage by which the retail prices index for the month in which the first relevant event occurs is higher than that for the month in which the appropriate period ends.]¹

(6) A period of 12 months during the appropriate three year period is the best period of 12 months during the appropriate three year period if the amount of the individual's employment income from the employment to which the arrangement relates is greater for that period of 12 months than for any other period of 12 months during the appropriate three year period.

(7) For the purposes of this paragraph and paragraph 17 the amount of the individual's employment income includes, in relation to any time when the individual is absent from work in connection with pregnancy, maternity, paternity or adoption, what would be likely to be included in that amount if the individual were not so absent.

Commentary—*Simon's Taxes* **E7.240**.

Regulations—Registered Pension Schemes (Uprating Percentages for Defined Benefits Arrangements and Enhanced Protection Limits) Regulations, SI 2006/130.

Amendments—¹   Words in sub-paras (1), (5) substituted and sub-para (5A) inserted by FA 2005 s 101, Sch 10 paras 53(11)–(14), 64(1) with effect from 6 April 2006.

²   In sub-para (3) words substituted for words "standard lifetime allowance when the first relevant event occurs." by FA 2011 s 67, Sch 18 paras 8, 9 with effect for the year 2012–13 and subsequent tax years, subject to transitional provisions in FA 2011 Sch 18 para 14.

17—(1) This paragraph specifies the post-commencement earnings limit in any other case.

(2) The post-commencement earnings limit is—

    (a) if amount B is not greater than amount A, amount B, and

    (b) otherwise, amount C.

(3) Amount A and amount B have the same meanings as in paragraph 16.

(4) Amount C is the greater of—

    (a) amount A, and

    (b) amount D.

(5) Amount D is—

$$\frac{ETY}{3}$$

where ETY is the amount of the individual's employment income from the employment to which the arrangement relates for the appropriate three year period (within the meaning of paragraph 16).

[(6) Where the appropriate three year period ends otherwise than with the first relevant event, Amount D is what it would be apart from this sub-paragraph increased by whichever is the greatest of—

    (a) the percentage by which an amount would be increased if it were increased for the period beginning with the date on which it ends and ending with the date on which the relevant event occurs at an annual rate of 5%,

    (b) the percentage by which an amount would be increased if it were increased for that period at an annual percentage rate referred to in regulations made by the Board of Inland Revenue, or (*c*) the percentage by which the retail prices index for the month in which the first relevant event occurs is higher than that for the month in which the appropriate period ends.]¹

Commentary—*Simon's Taxes* **E7.240**.

Regulations—Registered Pension Schemes (Uprating Percentages for Defined Benefits Arrangements and Enhanced Protection Limits) Regulations, SI 2006/130.

Amendments—¹ Sub-para (6) inserted by FA 2005 s 101, Sch 10 paras 53(15), 64(1) with effect from 6 April 2006.

[**17A**—(1) There is an impermissible transfer into a relevant existing arrangement relating to an individual under a pension scheme in a case where the relevant existing arrangement is a money purchase arrangement that is not a cash balance arrangement if—

(*a*) sums or assets held for the purposes of, or representing rights under, an arrangement relating otherwise than to the individual are transferred so as to become held for the purposes of the relevant existing arrangement, otherwise than pursuant to a pension sharing order or provision, [or]²

(*b*) sums or assets which are neither held for the purposes of, nor represent rights under, a pension scheme are so transferred, . . . ²

(*c*) . . . ²

(2) Sub-paragraph (1) applies where the relevant existing arrangement has been a hybrid arrangement as if the references to sums or assets being transferred . . . ² were to transfer or payment at any time after 5th April 2006.

(3) There is an impermissible transfer into a relevant existing arrangement relating to an individual under a pension scheme in a case where the relevant existing arrangement is a cash balance arrangement or a defined benefits arrangement, if it becomes a money purchase arrangement that is not a cash balance arrangement.]¹

Amendments—¹ Paragraph inserted by FA 2005 s 101, Sch 10 paras 53(16), 64(1) with effect from 6 April 2006.
² Words in sub-para (1) inserted and repealed, and sub-para (1)(*c*) and words in sub-para (2) repealed, by FA 2007 ss 69, 114, Sch 19 paras 1, 10, 29(3), Sch 27 Pt 3(1) with effect in relation to lump sum death benefits paid in respect of members of schemes whose deaths occur on or after 6 April 2007.

Pre-commencement pension credits

18—(1) This paragraph makes provision for the operation of a lifetime allowance enhancement factor in relation to all benefit crystallisation events occurring in relation to an individual where before 6th April 2006 the individual has acquired rights under a pension scheme within paragraph 1(1) by virtue of having become entitled to a pension credit.

(2) The lifetime allowance enhancement factor is the pre-commencement pension credit factor.

(3) The pre-commencement pension credit factor is—

$$\frac{IAPC}{SLA}$$

where—

IAPC is the amount which is the appropriate amount for the purposes of section 29(1) of WRPA 1999 or Article 26(1) of WRP(NI)O 1999 in relation to the pension credit, as increased by the percentage specified in sub-paragraph (4), and

SLA is £1,500,000 (the standard lifetime allowance for the tax year 2006–07).

(4) The percentage is the percentage by which the retail prices index for April 2006 is greater than that for the month in which the rights were acquired.

(5) This paragraph does not apply in the case of an individual if paragraph 7 (primary protection) applies in relation to the individual.

(6) This paragraph only applies if notice of intention to rely on this paragraph is given to the Inland Revenue in accordance with regulations made by the Board of Inland Revenue.

Commentary—*Simon's Taxes* **E7.216, E7.240**.

Regulations—Registered Pension Schemes (Enhanced Lifetime Allowance) Regulations, SI 2006/131.
Registered Pension Schemes (Provision of Information) Regulations, SI 2006/567.

Individuals permitted to take pension before normal minimum pension age

19—(1) This paragraph applies where a benefit crystallisation event occurs in relation to an individual who is a member of a registered pension scheme—

(*a*) in protected circumstances, and

(*b*) before the individual reaches normal minimum pension age.

(2) What would otherwise be the individual's lifetime allowance is to be reduced by the relevant percentage.

(3) A benefit crystallisation event occurs in protected circumstances if—

   (*a*)   paragraph 22 or 23 (right to take pension before normal minimum pension age) applies to the individual and the pension scheme,

   (*b*)   the individual's protected pension age (see paragraph 22(8) or 23(8)) is less than 50, and

   (*c*)   the pension scheme is not prescribed by regulations made by the Board of Inland Revenue.

(4) The relevant percentage is—

$$Y \times 2 \cdot 5$$

where Y is the number of complete years falling between the date on which the benefit crystallisation event occurs and the date on which the individual will reach normal minimum pension age.

(5) Sub-paragraph (6) applies where, after the occurrence in relation to the individual of a benefit crystallisation event in relation to which this paragraph has had effect, another benefit crystallisation event occurs in relation to the individual . . . [1].

(6) If the amount crystallised on the previous benefit crystallisation event exceeded the available amount of the individual's lifetime allowance at the time of that benefit crystallisation event, section 219 (availability of individual's lifetime allowance) applies as if the amount crystallised were the available amount of the individual's lifetime allowance at that time.

Commentary—*Simon's Taxes* E7.224, E7.240, E7.242.

Regulations—Registered Pension Schemes (Prescribed Schemes and Occupations) Regulations, SI 2005/3451.

Amendments—[1]   Words in sub-para (5) repealed by FA 2005 ss 101, 104, Sch 10 paras 54(2), 64(1), Sch 11 Pt 4 with effect from 6 April 2006.

Pre-commencement pensions

20—(1) This paragraph makes provision about an individual who, on 5th April 2006, has an actual (rather than a prospective) right to the payment of one or more relevant existing pensions.

(2) Section 219 (availability of individual's lifetime allowance) applies as if, immediately before the first benefit crystallisation event occurring in relation to the individual—

   (*a*)   a benefit crystallisation event had occurred in relation to the individual, and

   (*b*)   the amount crystallised was the value of the individual's pre-commencement pension rights immediately before the benefit crystallisation event.

(3) The value of the individual's pre-commencement pension rights at any time is—

$$25 \times ARP$$

where (subject to sub-paragraph (4)) ARP is an amount equal to—

   (*a*)   the annual rate at which the relevant existing pension is payable to the individual at that time, or

   (*b*)   if more than one relevant existing pension is payable to the individual at that time, the aggregate of the annual rates at which each of the relevant existing pensions is so payable.

[(4) In the case of drawdown pension, ARP is—

   (*a*)   [80% of][3] the maximum amount that may be paid in the drawdown pension year in which the time falls in accordance with pension rule 5 (see section 165), or

   (*b*)   in the case of an arrangement to which subsection (3A) of section 165 [applied at any time before 6 April 2015][2], [80% of][3] the maximum amount that could have been paid in accordance with that rule in the drawdown pension year in which that subsection first applied to the arrangement if it had not so applied[, or

   (*c*)   in the case of an arrangement to which section 165(3A) never applied but only if the time falls after the member's drawdown pension fund in respect of the arrangement is converted into the member's flexi-access drawdown fund in respect of the arrangement by the operation of any of paragraphs 8B to 8D of Schedule 28, 80% of the maximum amount that could have been paid in accordance with pension rule 5 in the drawdown pension year in which the conversion occurs had no conversion happened in that year by the operation of any of paragraphs 8B to 8D of Schedule 28.][2]][1]

(5) In this paragraph "relevant existing pension" has the same meaning as in paragraph 10(2); and paragraph 10(4) and (5) operates for the purposes of this paragraph for determining the annual rate at which a relevant existing pension is payable at any time (treating the references there to 5th April 2006 as to that time).

Commentary—*Simon's Taxes* E7.240.

HMRC Manuals—Registered Pension Schemes Manual RPSM11104950–11104960 (valuing benefits on benefit crystallisation events: worked examples calculating the capital value of a pre-commencement pension in different circumstances).

RPSM11104980 (valuing benefits on benefit crystallisation events: worked example of increase to a scheme pension in payment).

Modifications—Taxation of Pension Schemes (Transitional Provisions) Order, SI 2006/572 art 20 (modification of this paragraph in the case of an individual who dies on or after 6 April 2006, and meets certain conditions).

Amendments—[1]   Sub-para (4) substituted by FA 2011 s 65, Sch 16 paras 62, 82(1), (2) with effect for the tax year 2011–12 and subsequent tax years, subject to transitional provisions in FA 2011 Sch 16 Pt 3. The amendments made by FA 2011 Sch 16 paras 43, 44, 73, 80, 92(2) have effect in relation to benefit crystallisation events occurring on or after 6 April 2011 (FA 2011 Sch 16 para 104(1)).

[2]   In sub-para (4), in para (*b*) words substituted for word "applies", and para (*c*) and preceding word inserted, by the Taxation of Pensions Act 2014 s 1, Sch 1 paras 5, 28 with effect from 6 April 2015.

[3]   Words in sub-para (4)(*a*), (*b*) inserted by the Taxation of Pensions Act 2014 s 1, Sch 1 para 77. The amendment made to sub-para (4)(*a*) has effect where the benefit crystallisation event mentioned in the opening words of sub-para (2) occurs on or after 6 April 2015. The amendment made to sub-para (4)(*b*) has effect where the benefit crystallisation event mentioned in the opening words of sub-para (2) occurs on or after 6 April 2015, and FA 2004 s 165(3A) first applied to the arrangement concerned in a drawdown pension year that began on or after 27 March 2014.

PART 3
PRE-COMMENCEMENT BENEFIT RIGHTS

Commentary—*Simon's Taxes* **E7.240**.

Rights to take [benefit]¹ before normal minimum pension age

Amendments—[1]   Word in heading substituted by FA 2005 s 101, Sch 10 paras 54(3), 64(1) with effect from 6 April 2006.

21—(1) If paragraph 22 or 23 applies in relation to a registered pension scheme and a member of the pension scheme, this Part of this Act (except for section 218(6) and paragraph 19) has effect in relation to the member and the pension scheme as if references to normal minimum pension age were to the member's protected pension age.

(2) Paragraphs 22(8) and 23(8) define the member's protected pension age.

22—(1) This paragraph applies in relation to a registered pension scheme and a member of the pension scheme if—

    (*a*) the pension scheme is a protected pension scheme, and

    (*b*) the retirement condition is met in relation to the member and the pension scheme.

(2) A pension scheme is a protected pension scheme if condition A or condition B is met.

(3) Condition A is met if—

    (*a*) the pension scheme was within any of paragraphs (*a*) to (*e*) of paragraph 1(1), and

    (*b*) the entitlement condition is met in relation to the member and the pension scheme.

(4) The entitlement condition is met in relation to the member and the pension scheme if—

    (*a*) on 5th April 2006 the member had an actual or prospective right under the pension scheme to [any benefit]¹ from an age of less than 55,

    (*b*) the rules of the pension scheme on 10th December 2003 included provision conferring such a right on some or all of the persons who were then members of the pension scheme, and

    (*c*) such a right either was then conferred on the member or would have been had the member been a member of the scheme on that date.

(5) Condition B is met if the member is a member of the pension scheme [("a transferee pension scheme") as a result of—

    (*a*) a block transfer from the pension scheme ("the original pension scheme") in relation to which condition A is met to the transferee pension scheme, or

    (*b*) a block transfer to the transferee pension scheme from a pension scheme that was a transferee pension scheme in relation to the original pension scheme by virtue of the previous application of paragraph (a) or the previous application (on one or more occasions) of this paragraph.]²

(6) A transfer is a block transfer if—

    (*a*) it involves the transfer in a single transaction of all the sums and assets held for the purposes of, or representing accrued rights under, the arrangements under the pension scheme from which the transfer is made which relate to the member and at least one other member of that pension scheme, and

    [(*b*) either the member was not a member of the pension scheme to which the transfer is made before the transfer or he has been a member of that pension scheme for no longer than such period as is prescribed by regulations made by the Board of Inland Revenue]².

[(6A) A transfer is also a block transfer if—

    (*a*) it involves the transfer in a single transaction of all the sums and assets held for the purposes of, or representing accrued rights under, the arrangements under the pension scheme from which the transfer is made which relate to the member,

    (*b*) the transfer takes place—

        (i) on or after 19 March 2014, and

        (ii) before 6 April 2015, and

    (*c*) the date mentioned in sub-paragraph (7)(*a*) is before 6 October 2015.]⁵

(7) The retirement condition is met in relation to the member and the pension scheme if—

    (*a*) the member becomes entitled to all the [benefits]¹ payable to the member under arrangements under the pension scheme (to which the member did not have an actual entitlement on or before 5th April 2006) on the same date, and

    [(*b*) in a case where on 5th April 2006 the member had an actual or prospective right under the pension scheme to any benefit from an age of less than 50, Condition 1 is met or, in any other case, Condition 2 or 3 is met.]³

[(7A) Condition 1 is met if—

    (*a*) the member is not, after becoming entitled to the benefits mentioned in sub-paragraph (7)(*a*), employed by a person who is a sponsoring employer in relation to the pension scheme and with whom the member is connected, and

    (*b*) the member's becoming entitled to those benefits is not part of an arrangement the main purpose (or one of the main purposes) of which is the avoidance of tax or national insurance contributions.]³

[(7B) Condition 2 is met if—

    (*a*) the member is not, after becoming entitled to the benefits mentioned in sub-paragraph (7)(*a*), employed by a person specified in sub-paragraph (7C), and

    (*b*) the member's becoming entitled to those benefits is not part of an arrangement the main purpose (or one of the main purposes) of which is the avoidance of tax or national insurance contributions.]³

[(7C) The persons referred to in sub-paragraph (7B)(*a*) are—

    (*a*) any person who was a sponsoring employer in relation to the pension scheme at any time during the period of six months ending with the day on which the member became entitled to the benefits mentioned in sub-paragraph (7)(*a*) and by whom the member was employed at any time during that period,

    (*b*) any person who is connected with any such person, or

    (*c*) any person who is a sponsoring employer in relation to the pension scheme and with whom the member is connected.]³

[(7D) If the member has become entitled to the benefits payable under arrangements under the pension scheme by reason of service in the armed forces of the Crown, any employment on compulsory recall is to be disregarded for the purposes of sub-paragraph (7B)(*a*).]³

[(7E) Condition 3 is met if—

    (*a*) paragraph (*a*) of sub-paragraph (7B) is not satisfied but one of the re-employment conditions is met, and

    (*b*) paragraph (*b*) of that sub-paragraph is satisfied.]³

[(7F) The re-employment conditions are—

    (*a*) that the member is not employed as mentioned in sub-paragraph (7B)(*a*) during the period of six months beginning with the day on which the member becomes entitled to the benefits mentioned in sub-paragraph (7)(*a*), and

    (*b*) that the member is not employed as mentioned in sub-paragraph (7B)(*a*) during the period of one month beginning with that day, but is so employed during the period of five months beginning at the end of that period, and either the pension abatement condition or the materially different employment condition is met]³[, and

    (*c*) that the member is or was employed as mentioned in sub-paragraph (7B)(*a*) where—

      (i) the employment began at any time during the coronavirus period, and

      (ii) the only or main reason that the member was taken into employment was to help the employer to respond to the public health, social, economic or other effects of coronavirus.]⁶

[(7G) The pension abatement condition is met if—

    (*a*) the pension scheme is a public service pension scheme, and

    (*b*) the member's benefits under the scheme consist of or include a scheme pension which is liable to reduction by abatement while the member is employed as mentioned in sub-paragraph (7B)(*a*) and is under the age of 55.]³

[(7H) The materially different employment condition is met—

    (*a*) in a case where the member is employed as mentioned in sub-paragraph (7B)(*a*) in more than one employment during the period of five months mentioned in sub-paragraph (7F)(*b*), if each of those employments, and

    (*b*) otherwise, if the employment in which the member is so employed during that period,

is materially different in nature from the employment in which the member was employed immediately before becoming entitled to the benefits mentioned in sub-paragraph (7)(a).]³

[(7I) For the purposes of sub-paragraph (7D) "employment on compulsory recall" means permanent service—

    (*a*) under Part 4 of the Reserve Forces Act 1996,

    (*b*) under Part 5 of that Act,

(*c*) under a call-out or recall order made under that Act,

(*d*) having been called out or recalled under the Reserve Forces Act 1980, or

(*e*) because of any other call-out or recall obligation of an officer.][3]

[(7J) [Section 1122 of the Corporation Tax Act 2010][4] (connected persons) applies for the purposes of this paragraph.][3]

[(7K) In sub-paragraph (7F)(*c*)—

"coronavirus" has the same meaning as in the Coronavirus Act 2020 (see section 1(1) of that Act);

"the coronavirus period" means the period beginning with 1 March 2020 and ending with 1 November 2020.

(7L) The Treasury may by regulations amend the definition of "the coronavirus period" in sub-paragraph (7K) so as to replace the later of the dates specified in it with another date falling before 6 April 2021.

(7M) The power in sub-paragraph (7L) may be exercised on more than one occasion.][6]

(8) The member's protected pension age is the age from which the member had an actual or prospective right to [any benefit][1] under the protected pension scheme on 5th April 2006 (or, where condition B is met, under the original pension scheme on that date).

(9) But this paragraph does not have effect so as to give the member a protected pension age of more than 50 at any time before 6th April 2010.

Regulations—Registered Pension Schemes (Block Transfers) (Permitted Membership Period) Regulations, SI 2006/498.

Modifications—Taxation of Pension Schemes (Transitional Provisions) Order, SI 2006/572 arts 42, 43 (modification of para (7)(*a*) in respect of a member who has a protected pension age in connection with multiple pensions).

Amendments—[1] Words in sub-para (4)(*a*), (7)(*a*), . . . (8) substituted by FA 2005 s 101, Sch 10 paras 54(4)–(7), 64(1) with effect from 6 April 2006.

[2] Words in sub-para (5) and sub-para (6)(*b*) substituted by FA 2005 s 101, Sch 10 paras 55(2)–(4), 64(1) with effect from 6 April 2006.

[3] Sub-para (7)(*b*) substituted, and sub-paras (7A)–(7J) inserted by FA 2006 s 161, Sch 23 paras 1, 43. These amendments are deemed to have come into force on 6 April 2006.

[4] In sub-para (7J) words "Section 839 of ICTA" substituted by CTA 2010 s 1177, Sch 1 paras 423, 432(1),(3). CTA 2010 has effect for corporation tax purposes for accounting periods ending on or after 1 April 2010, and for income and capital gains tax purposes for the tax year 2010–11 and subsequent tax years.

[5] Sub-para (6A) inserted by FA 2014 s 43, Sch 5 para 7(1). This amendment is to be treated as having come into force on 19 March 2014 (FA 2014 Sch 5 para 15).

[6] Sub-para (7F)(*c*) and preceding word inserted, and sub-paras (7K)–(7M) inserted, by FA 2020 s 108. These amendments are treated as having come into force on 1 March 2020.

23—(1) This paragraph applies in relation to a registered pension scheme and a member of the pension scheme if—

(*a*) the pension scheme is a protected pension scheme, and

(*b*) the retirement condition is met in relation to the member and the pension scheme.

(2) A pension scheme is a protected pension scheme if condition A or condition B is met.

(3) Condition A is met if—

(*a*) the pension scheme was within paragraph (*f*) or (*g*) of paragraph 1(1), and

(*b*) the entitlement condition is met in relation to the member and the pension scheme.

(4) The entitlement condition is met in relation to the member and the pension scheme if—

(*a*) on 5th April 2006 the member had an actual or prospective right under the pension scheme to a pension from an age of less than 50, and

(*b*) the member's occupation was on that date (or had been) one prescribed by regulations made by the Board of Inland Revenue.

(5) Condition B is met if the member is a member of the pension scheme [("a transferee pension scheme") as a result of—

(*a*) a block transfer from the pension scheme ("the original pension scheme") in relation to which condition A is met to the transferee pension scheme, or

(*b*) a block transfer to the transferee pension scheme from a pension scheme that was a transferee pension scheme in relation to the original pension scheme by virtue of the previous application of paragraph (*a*) or the previous application (on one or more occasions) of this paragraph.][1]

(6) "Block transfer" has the same meaning as in paragraph 22(6) [and (6A), but for this purpose paragraph 22(6A)(*c*) is to be read as if its reference to paragraph 22(7)(*a*) were a reference to sub-paragraph (7) of this paragraph][2].

(7) The retirement condition is met in relation to the member and the pension scheme if the member becomes entitled to all the pensions payable to the member under arrangements under the pension scheme (to which the member did not have an actual entitlement on or before 5th April 2006) on the same date.

(8) The member's protected pension age is the age from which the member had an actual or prospective right to a pension under the protected pension scheme on 5th April 2006 (or, where condition B is met, under the original pension scheme on that date).

Regulations—Registered Pension Schemes (Prescribed Schemes and Occupations) Regulations, SI 2005/3451.

Modifications—Taxation of Pension Schemes (Transitional Provisions) Order, SI 2006/572 arts 42, 43 (modification of para (7)(a) in respect of a member who has a protected pension age in connection with multiple pensions).

Amendments—[1] Words in sub-para (5) substituted by FA 2005 s 101, Sch 10 paras 55(5), 64(1) with effect from 6 April 2006.
[2] Words inserted in sub-para (6) by FA 2014 s 43, Sch 5 para 7(2). This amendment is to be treated as having come into force on 19 March 2014 (FA 2014 Sch 5 para 15).

[23ZA—(1) Sub-paragraph (2) applies if—

    (a) there is a recognised transfer from one registered pension scheme ("the old scheme") to another registered pension scheme ("the new scheme"), and

    (b) as a result of paragraph 21 or the previous operation of sub-paragraph (2), immediately before the transfer this Part (except for section 218(6) and paragraph 19) applied in relation to all of the transferred sums or assets as if references to normal minimum pension age were to the member's protected pension age as defined by paragraph 22(8) or, as the case may be, paragraph 23(8).

(2) This Part (except for section 218(6) and paragraph 19) applies in relation to—

    (a) the transferred sums or assets while held for the purposes of an arrangement under the new scheme, and

    (b) any sums or assets held for the purposes of such an arrangement that arise, or (directly or indirectly) derive, from—

        (i) any of the transferred sums or assets, or

        (ii) sums or assets which so arise or derive,

as if references to normal minimum pension age were to the member's protected pension age as defined by paragraph 22(8) or, as the case may be, paragraph 23(8).

(3) Paragraphs 22(7)(a) and 23(7) have effect as if the benefits or pensions to which they refer do not include any that are in respect of sums or assets within sub-paragraph (2)(a) or (b) of this paragraph.][1]

Amendments—[1] Para 23ZA inserted by the Taxation of Pensions Act 2014 s 1, Sch 1 para 78 with effect in relation to recognised transfers made on or after 6 April 2015.

[23A—(1) Where—

    (a) paragraph 19 applies to a benefit crystallisation event occurring in relation to an individual, and

    (b) the benefit crystallisation event consists in the individual becoming entitled to a pension or a pension commencement lump sum,

paragraph 2(6) of Schedule 29 has effect as if CSLA were the current standard lifetime allowance reduced by the relevant percentage (within the meaning of paragraph 19).

(2) Sub-paragraph (3) applies where, after the occurrence in relation to an individual of a benefit crystallisation event in relation to which paragraph 19 has had effect, another benefit crystallisation event occurs in relation to the individual.

(3) If the amount crystallised on the previous benefit crystallisation event exceeded the available amount of the individual's lifetime allowance at the time of that benefit crystallisation event, paragraph 2(6) of Schedule 29 has effect as if, for the purposes of AAC, the amount crystallised were the available amount of the individual's lifetime allowance at that time.][1]

Amendments—[1] Paragraph inserted by FA 2005 s 101, Sch 10 paras 56, 64(1) with effect from 6 April 2006.

Lump sum rights exceeding £375,000: primary and enhanced protection

24—(1) If the lump sum condition and the registration condition are met in relation to an individual—

    (a) paragraphs 27 to 29 (which modify Schedule 29 in relation to pension commencement lump sums), and

    (b) paragraph 30 (which makes provision about scheme chargeable payments),

apply in relation to the individual.

(2) The lump sum condition is met if on 5th April 2006 the amount of an individual's total lump sum rights exceeds £375,000 (25% of the standard lifetime allowance for the tax year 2006–07).

(3) Paragraph 25 defines the amount of an individual's total lump sum rights on that date.

(4) The registration condition is met if either or both of the notice requirements is met.

(5) The first notice requirement is met if notice of intention to rely on paragraph 7 (primary protection) is given to the Inland Revenue in accordance with regulations under that paragraph in relation to the individual.

(6) The second notice requirement is met if notice of intention to rely on paragraph 12 (enhanced protection) is given to the Inland Revenue in accordance with regulations under that paragraph in relation to the individual.

25—(1) The amount of an individual's total lump sum rights on 5th April 2006 is—

$$\frac{\text{VCPR}}{4} + \text{VULSR}$$

where—

VCPR is the value of the individual's relevant crystallised pension rights on 5th April 2006, calculated in accordance with paragraph 10, and

VULSR is the value of the individual's relevant uncrystallised lump sum rights on that date.

(2) The value of the individual's relevant uncrystallised lump sum rights on 5th April 2006 is the aggregate value of the individual's uncrystallised lump sum rights on that date under each relevant pension arrangement relating to the individual.

(3) An uncrystallised lump sum right is a right to a lump sum which on 5th April 2006 is prospective (rather than actual).

(4) An arrangement is a "relevant pension arrangement" if it is an arrangement under a pension scheme within paragraph 1(1).

(5) The value of the individual's uncrystallised lump sum rights under an arrangement on 5th April 2006—

    (a) in the case of an arrangement under a pension scheme falling within paragraph 1(1)(*f*), is 25% of the value of the funds held for the purposes of the arrangement on that date, and

    (b) in the case of any other arrangement, is an amount calculated in accordance with sub-paragraph (6).

(6) The amount is the amount of any lump sum to which the individual would have been entitled under the arrangement on 5th April 2006 on the assumption that the individual became entitled to the present payment of a lump sum under the arrangement on that date.

(7) In calculating an amount in accordance with sub-paragraph (6) the valuation assumptions apply but as if the reference to such age (if any) as must have been reached to avoid any reduction in benefits on account of age in paragraph (*a*) of section 277 were to the relevant age; and for this purpose "the relevant age" is—

    (a) if on 10th December 2003 the terms of the arrangement made provision for a reduction in the amount of benefits payable in respect of rights under the arrangement on account of the holder of the rights being below a particular age, that age, and

    (b) otherwise, 60.

26—(1) This paragraph applies if any of the individual's uncrystallised lump sum rights on 5th April 2006 are rights under one or more arrangements under a pension scheme or schemes within paragraph 1(1)(*a*) to (*d*).

(2) The value of the individual's uncrystallised lump sum rights on 5th April 2006 under the arrangement, or the aggregate of the values of the individual's uncrystallised lump sum rights on 5th April 2006 under such of the arrangements as relate to a particular employment, is[1] . . .—

    (a) the value, or the aggregate of the values, calculated under paragraph 25, [or (if lower)][1]

    (b) the maximum permitted lump sum.

(3) "The maximum permitted lump sum" means—

    [(a) in the case of an arrangement under a pension scheme which immediately before 6th April 2006 was within section [611A(1)(*a*)][2] of ICTA, the maximum lump sum that could be paid to the individual under the pension scheme on 5th April 2006, and

    (b) in any other case,][1] the maximum lump sum that could be paid to the individual on 5th April 2006 under the arrangement or arrangements if it or they were made under a pension scheme within paragraph 1(1)(*a*) without giving the Board of Inland Revenue grounds for withdrawing approval of the pension scheme under section 591B of ICTA.

(4) For the purposes of sub-paragraph (3) it is to be assumed—

    (a) [in the case of any arrangement, that][1] if the individual was in the employment to which the arrangement or arrangements relates or relate on 5th April [2006][1] the individual left the employment on that date, and

    [(aa) in the case of an arrangement within sub-paragraph (3)(*a*), that the valuation assumptions apply (see section 277),][1]

    (b) [in the case of any other arrangement, that][1] if the individual had not reached the lowest age at which a lump sum may be paid under a pension scheme within paragraph 1(1)(*a*) to a person in good health without giving the Board of Inland Revenue grounds for withdrawing the approval of the pension [scheme][1] that fact would not give the Board such grounds.

(5) Whether an arrangement relating to an individual relates to an employment is to be determined in accordance with paragraph 9(6).

Amendments—[1]   Words in sub-para (2) repealed and substituted, words in sub-para (3) inserted, words in sub-para (4)(*a*), (*b*) inserted and substituted, and sub-para (4)(*aa*) inserted by FA 2005 ss 101, 104, Sch 10 paras 52(6)–(9), 64(1), Sch 11 Pt 4 with effect from 6 April 2006.

[2]   Reference in sub-para (3)(*a*) substituted by FA 2006 s 161, Sch 23 paras 1, 44, 45. This amendment is deemed to have come into force on 6 April 2006.

27—(1) If (and for so long as) paragraph 12 (enhanced protection) applies in relation to the individual, paragraph 2 of Schedule 29 applies in relation to the individual with the following modifications.

(2) If the value of the individual's relevant uncrystallised lump sum rights on 5th April 2006 (calculated in accordance with paragraphs 25 and 26) was nil, the permitted maximum under paragraph 2 is nil.

(3) Otherwise, paragraph 2 applies as if for sub-paragraphs (5) to (8) there were substituted—

"(5)   If sub-paragraph (2) does not apply, the permitted maximum is the applicable amount, calculated in accordance with paragraph 3."

28—(1) If paragraph 12 (enhanced protection) does not apply in relation to the individual, paragraph 2 of Schedule 29 applies in relation to the individual with the following modifications.

(2) If the value of the individual's relevant uncrystallised lump sum rights on 5th April 2006 (calculated in accordance with paragraphs 25 and 26) was nil, the permitted maximum under paragraph 2 is nil.

(3) Otherwise, paragraph 2 applies as if for [sub-paragraphs (5) to (7A)][1] there were substituted—

"(5)   If sub-paragraph (2) does not apply, the permitted maximum is the available portion of the member's lump sum allowance.

(6)   The available portion of the member's lump sum allowance is—

$$VULSR - APCLS$$

where—

VULSR is the value of the individual's relevant uncrystallised lump sum rights on 5th April 2006 (calculated in accordance with paragraphs 25 and 26 of Schedule 36), as adjusted under sub-paragraph (6A), and

APCLS is the aggregate of the amounts of each pension commencement lump sum to which the individual has previously become entitled, as adjusted under sub-paragraph (7) (or, if the individual has not previously become entitled to a pension commencement lump sum, is nil).

(6A)   The adjustment referred to in the definition of VULSR is the multiplication of the value of the individual's relevant uncrystallised lump sum rights on 5th April 2006 by—

$$\frac{[ULA]}{FSLA}$$

where—

[ULA is the underpinned lifetime allowance, and][2]

FSLA is £1,500,000 (the standard lifetime allowance for the tax year 2006–07).

(7)   The adjustment of the amount of a pension commencement lump sum to which the individual has previously become entitled referred to in the definition of APCLS is the multiplication of the amount by—

$$\frac{[ULA]}{PSLA}$$

where—

[ULA is the underpinned lifetime allowance, and][2]

PSLA is the standard lifetime allowance at the time the individual became entitled to the lump sum [if that occurred before 6 April 2012 but, if that occurred on or after 6 April 2012, PSLA is the greater of £1,800,000 and the standard lifetime allowance at the time the individual became entitled to the lump sum][3].

[(7A)   "The underpinned lifetime allowance" is the greater of the current standard lifetime allowance and £1,800,000 (the standard lifetime allowance for the tax year 2011–12)."][2]

Amendments—[1]   In sub-para (3) words substituted for words "sub-paragraphs (5) to (7)" by FA 2011 s 65, Sch 16 paras 62, 82(1), (3) with effect for the tax year 2011–12 and subsequent tax years, subject to transitional provisions in FA 2011 Sch

16 Pt 3. The amendments made by FA 2011 Sch 16 paras 27–30, 40, 42(2)(*a*), (3), 63, 77(4), 81(2), (4), 82(3)–(5) and 83 have effect in relation to lump sums paid on or after 6 April 2011 (FA 2011 Sch 16 para 102).

2　　In sub-para (3), in paras (6A), (7) of the substituted text, "ULA" substituted for "CSLA" and definition substituted for previous definition of "ULA"; and para (7A) inserted by FA 2011 s 67, Sch 18 paras 8, 10 with effect for the year 2012–13 and subsequent tax years, subject to transitional provisions in FA 2011 Sch 18 para 14.

3　　In sub-para (3), in para (7) of the substituted text, in the definition of "PSLA", words inserted by FA 2016 Sch 4 para 28(2). This amendment is treated as having come into force on 6 April 2012.

29—(1) If (and for so long as) paragraph 12 (enhanced protection) applies in relation to the individual, paragraph 3 of Schedule 29 (applicable amount) applies with the following modifications.

(2) Paragraph 3 applies as if for sub-paragraphs (1) to (3) there were substituted—

"(1)　Where the member becomes entitled to income withdrawal, the applicable amount is—

$$\frac{VULSR}{VUR} \times (LS + AD)$$

where—

VULSR is the value of the individual's relevant uncrystallised lump sum rights on 5th April 2006, calculated in accordance with paragraphs 25 and 26 of Schedule 36,

VUR is the value of the individual's uncrystallised pension rights on 5th April 2006, calculated in accordance with paragraphs 8 and 9 of that Schedule,

LS is the lump sum paid, and

AD is the aggregate of the amount of the sums, and the market value of the assets, designated as available for the payment of [drawdown pension][2] on that occasion.

(2)　For the purposes of sub-paragraph (1) there is to be deducted from the aggregate of the lump sum and the amount of the sums and the market value of the assets designated as available for the payment of [drawdown pension][2] so much (if any) of that amount as represents rights which are attributable to a disqualifying pension credit.

(3)　Where the member becomes entitled to a lifetime annuity, the applicable amount is—

$$\frac{VULSR}{VUR} \times (LS + APP)$$

where—

VULSR, VUR and LS have the same meaning as in sub-paragraph (1), and

APP is the annuity purchase price."

(3) Paragraph 3 applies as if for sub-paragraphs (5) to [(7A)][1] there were substituted—

"(5)　There is to be deducted from the aggregate of the amount of the lump sum and the annuity purchase price—

(*a*)　　if the annuity is purchased (in whole or in part) by the application of sums or assets representing the whole or part of the [member's drawdown pension fund][2] [or flexi-access drawdown fund][4], the aggregate of the amount of those sums and the market value of those assets, and

(*b*)　　in any case, so much (if any) of the aggregate of the lump sum and the annuity purchase price as represents rights which are attributable to a disqualifying pension credit.

(6)　Where the member becomes entitled to a scheme pension [under a defined benefits arrangement][1], the applicable amount is—

$$\frac{VULSR}{VUR} \times (LS + AC)$$

but subject to sub-paragraph (8).

(7)　In sub-paragraph (6)—

VULSR, VUR and LS have the same meaning as in sub-paragraph (1), and

[AC is—

(*a*)　　in a case where the member becomes entitled to the pension before reaching the age of 75, the amount crystallised by reason of the member becoming entitled to the pension, and (*b*)   in a case where the member becomes entitled to the pension after reaching that age, the amount that would have been so crystallised but for paragraph 2 of Schedule 32.][2]

[(7A)   Where the member becomes entitled to a scheme pension under a money purchase arrangement, the applicable amount is (subject to sub-paragraph (8))—

$$\frac{VULSR}{VUR} \times (LS + SPPP)$$

where—

    VULSR, VUR and LS have the same meaning as in sub-paragraph (1), and

    SPPP is the scheme pension purchase price.]"[1]

[(4) Paragraph 3 applies as if in sub-paragraph (8A)(*a*) for "is one third of" there were substituted "is—

$$\frac{VULSR}{VUR} \times (LS + CAPP)$$

where VULSR, VUR and LS have the same meaning as in subparagraph (1), and CAPP is".

(5) Paragraph 3 applies as if in sub-paragraph (8A)(*b*) for "is one third of the sums, plus one third of" there were substituted "is—

$$\frac{VULSR}{VUR} \times (LS + EP)$$

where VULSR, VUR and LS have the same meaning as in subparagraph (1), and EP is the total of the sums, and".][3]

Amendments—[1]   In sub-para (3), reference substituted, and words inserted, by FA 2006 s 161, Sch 23 paras 1, 24. These amendments are deemed to have come into force on 6 April 2006.
[2]   In sub-para (2), in the text treated as substituted for FA 2004 Sch 29 para 9(1)–(3), words substituted for words "unsecured pension" in both places, in sub-para (3) in the text treated as substituted for FA 2004 Sch 29 para 9(5)–(7A) words substituted for words "member's unsecured pension fund", and definition of "AC" substituted, by FA 2011 s 65, Sch 16 paras 62, 82(1), (4) with effect for the tax year 2011–12 and subsequent tax years, subject to transitional provisions in FA 2011 Sch 16 Pt 3. The amendments made by FA 2011 Sch 16 paras 27–30, 40, 42(2)(*a*), (3), 63, 77(4), 81(2), (4), 82(3)–(5) and 83 have effect in relation to lump sums paid on or after 6 April 2011 (FA 2011 Sch 16 para 102).
[3]   Sub-paras (4), (5) inserted by FA 2014 s 43, Sch 5 para 8. This amendment is to be treated as having come into force on 19 March 2014 (FA 2014 Sch 5 para 15).
[4]   In sub-para (3), in the text treated as substituted for FA 2004 Sch 29 para 3(5)(*a*), words inserted by the Taxation of Pensions Act 2014 s 1, Sch 1 paras 5, 29 with effect from 17 December 2014.

30—(1) Any part of a lump sum falling within paragraph 1(1) of Schedule 29 which—

    (*a*)   under paragraph 1(2) of that Schedule is not a pension commencement lump sum (because the lump sum exceeds the permitted maximum), and

    (*b*)   is an unauthorised payment,

is to be treated as exempt from being scheme chargeable (under section 241(2)) if the condition in sub-paragraph (2) is met.

(2) The condition is that it would not have been an unauthorised payment if—

    (*a*)   paragraphs 27 and 29 (in the case of an individual in relation to whom paragraph 12 applies), or

    (*b*)   paragraph 28 (in the case of an individual in relation to whom paragraph 12 does not apply), had not applied.

Entitlement to lump sums exceeding 25% of uncrystallised rights

31—(1) If the pension condition is met in relation to an individual and a registered pension scheme which is a protected pension scheme, the provisions of Schedule 29 relating to pension commencement lump sums apply in relation to the individual and the pension scheme with the modifications specified in paragraph 34 (but subject to sub-paragraph (2)).

(2) Those provisions do not apply with those modifications if the lump sum condition and registration condition in paragraph 24 are met.

(3) The pension condition is that the individual becomes entitled to all the pensions payable to the individual under arrangements under the pension scheme (to which the individual did not have an actual entitlement on or before 5th April 2006) on the same date.

(4) A registered pension scheme is a protected pension scheme if condition A or condition B is met.

(5) Condition A is met if—

(a) the pension scheme was within any of paragraphs (a) to (e) of paragraph 1(1), and

(b) on 5th April 2006 the lump sum percentage of the individual's uncrystallised rights under the pension scheme exceeded 25%.

(6) The lump sum percentage of an individual's uncrystallised pension rights under a pension scheme on 5th April 2006 is—

$$\frac{\text{VULSR}}{\text{VUR}} \times 100$$

where—

VULSR is the value of the individual's uncrystallised lump sum rights under the pension scheme on 5th April 2006, calculated in accordance with paragraph 32, and

VUR is the value of the individual's uncrystallised rights under the pension scheme on 5th April 2006, calculated in accordance with paragraph 33.

(7) Condition B is met if the individual is a member of the pension scheme [("a transferee pension scheme") as a result of—

(a) a block transfer from the pension scheme ("the original pension scheme") in relation to which condition A is met to the transferee pension scheme, or

(b) a block transfer to the transferee pension scheme from a pension scheme that was a transferee pension scheme in relation to the original pension scheme by virtue of the previous application of paragraph (a) or the previous application (on one or more occasions) of this paragraph.][1]

(8) "Block transfer" has the same meaning as in paragraph 22(6) [and (6A)][2], but treating the references there to the member as references to the individual[, and reading paragraph 22(6A)(c) as if its reference to paragraph 22(7)(a) were a reference to sub-paragraph (3) of this paragraph][2].

(9) Where a pension scheme is a protected pension scheme because condition B is met, Schedule 29 as modified by paragraph 34 applies as if the protected pension scheme were the same pension scheme as the original pension scheme.

Commentary—*Simon's Taxes* E7.224, E7.226–E7.236, E7.240, E7.242.

Modifications—Taxation of Pension Schemes (Transitional Provisions) Order, SI 2006/572 arts 21, 22 (transfers and entitlement to lump sums exceeding 25 per cent of uncrystallised rights: modification of above paragraph).

Taxation of Pension Schemes (Transitional Provisions) Order, SI 2006/572 art 26 (modification of this paragraph in the case of an individual who meets certain conditions).

Taxation of Pension Schemes (Transitional Provisions) Order, SI 2006/572 art 23D(1), (2) (modification of sub-para (3) in respect of trivial commutation lump sums).

Taxation of Pension Schemes (Transitional Provisions) Order, SI 2006/572 arts 23ZA(2), 23ZC(3), 23ZD(2), 23ZE(3) (modification of para (3) in respect of an individual who has received a pension commencement lump sum but who dies before becoming entitled to the pension in connection with the lump sum).

Amendments—[1] Words in sub-para (7) substituted by FA 2005 s 101, Sch 10 paras 55(6), 64(1) with effect from 6 April 2006.
[2] Words in sub-para (8) inserted by FA 2014 s 43, Sch 5 para 9. This amendment is to be treated as having come into force on 19 March 2014 (FA 2014 Sch 5 para 15).

32—(1) Subject to sub-paragraph (2), the value of the individual's uncrystallised lump sum rights under the pension scheme on 5th April 2006 is the aggregate of the value of the individual's uncrystallised lump sum rights under each arrangement in respect of the individual under the pension scheme, calculated in accordance with paragraph 25(5), on that date.

(2) If the pension scheme is a relevant pension scheme, the value of the individual's uncrystallised lump sum rights on 5th April 2006 under an arrangement—

(a) which relates to a particular employment, and

(b) in relation to which the excess lump sum condition is met (see sub-paragraph (5) or (6)),

is the amount arrived at in accordance with sub-paragraph (7) or (8).

(3) A pension scheme is a relevant pension scheme if it falls within paragraph 1(1)(a) to (d).

(4) Whether an arrangement relating to the individual relates to a particular employment is to be determined in accordance with paragraph 9(6).

(5) If no other arrangement relating to the individual under a relevant pension scheme relates to the employment to which the arrangement relates, the excess lump sum condition is met in relation to the arrangement if—

(a) the value of the individual's uncrystallised lump sum rights under the arrangement calculated in accordance with paragraph 25(5), exceeds

(b) the amount arrived at in relation to the arrangement in accordance with paragraph 26.

(6) If one or more other arrangements relating to the individual under a relevant pension scheme or relevant pension schemes relates or relate to the employment to which the arrangement relates, the excess lump sum condition is met in relation to the arrangement if—

(*a*) the aggregate of the values of the individual's uncrystallised lump sum rights under the arrangement and the other arrangement or arrangements, calculated in accordance with paragraph 25(5), exceeds

(*b*) the amount arrived at in relation to those arrangements in accordance with paragraph 26;

and the amount by which the aggregate of those values exceeds that amount is the "lump sum excess".

(7) Where the excess lump sum condition is met by virtue of sub-paragraph (5), the value of the individual's uncrystallised lump sum rights under the arrangement is the amount arrived at in accordance with paragraph 26.

(8) Where the excess lump sum condition is met by virtue of sub-paragraph (6), the value of the individual's uncrystallised lump sum rights under the arrangement is the value of those rights calculated in accordance with paragraph 25(5), less the appropriate proportion of the lump sum excess.

(9) The appropriate proportion of the lump sum excess is—

$$\frac{V}{AV}$$

where—

V is the value of the individual's uncrystallised lump sum rights under the arrangement, calculated in accordance with paragraph 25(5), and

AV is the aggregate of the values of the individual's uncrystallised lump sum rights under the arrangement and the other arrangement or arrangements, calculated in accordance with paragraph 25(5).

Commentary—*Simon's Taxes* E7.224, E7.226–E7.236, E7.240, E7.242.

33—(1) Subject to sub-paragraph (2), the value of the individual's uncrystallised rights under the pension scheme on 5th April 2006 is the aggregate of the value of the individual's uncrystallised rights under each arrangement in respect of the individual under the pension scheme, calculated in accordance with paragraph 8(5).

(2) If the pension scheme is a relevant pension scheme, the value of the individual's uncrystallised rights on 5th April 2006 under an arrangement—

(*a*) which relates to a particular employment, and

(*b*) in relation to which the excess rights condition is met (see sub-paragraph (5) or (6)),

is the amount arrived at in accordance with sub-paragraph (7) or (8).

(3) A pension scheme is a relevant pension scheme if it falls within paragraph 1(1)(*a*) to (*d*).

(4) Whether an arrangement relating to the individual relates to a particular employment is to be determined in accordance with paragraph 9(6).

(5) If no other arrangement relating to the individual under a relevant pension scheme relates to the employment to which the arrangement relates, the excess rights condition is met in relation to the arrangement if—

(*a*) the value of the individual's uncrystallised rights under the arrangement calculated in accordance with paragraph 8(5), exceeds

(*b*) the amount arrived at in relation to the arrangement in accordance with paragraph 9(3).

(6) If one or more other arrangements relating to the individual under a relevant pension scheme or relevant pension schemes relates or relate to the employment to which the arrangement relates, the excess rights condition is met in relation to the arrangement if—

(*a*) the aggregate of the values of the individual's uncrystallised rights under the arrangement and the other arrangement or arrangements, calculated in accordance with paragraph 8(5), exceeds

(*b*) the amount arrived at in relation to those arrangements in accordance with paragraph 9(3);

and the amount by which the aggregate of those values exceeds that amount is the "rights excess".

(7) Where the excess rights condition is met by virtue of sub-paragraph (5), the value of the individual's uncrystallised rights under the arrangement is the amount arrived at in accordance with paragraph 9(3).

(8) Where the excess rights condition is met by virtue of sub-paragraph (6), the value of the individual's uncrystallised rights under the arrangement is the value of those rights calculated in accordance with paragraph 8(5), less the appropriate proportion of the rights excess.

(9) The appropriate proportion of the rights excess is—

$$\frac{V}{AV}$$

where—

V is the value of the individual's uncrystallised rights under the arrangement, calculated in accordance with paragraph 8(5), and

AV is the aggregate of the values of the individual's uncrystallised rights under the arrangement and the other arrangement or arrangements, calculated in accordance with paragraph 8(5).

Commentary—*Simon's Taxes* E7.224, E7.226–E7.236, E7.240, E7.242.

34—(1) Schedule 29 applies with the following modifications.

(2) Paragraph 2 applies as if the reference in sub-paragraph (2) to the arrangement under which the member becomes entitled to the relevant pension were to the pension scheme and for sub-paragraphs (5) to (8) there were substituted—

"(5) If paragraph 2(2) does not apply . . . [3], the permitted maximum is—

$$\left(\text{VULSR} \times \frac{[ULA]}{\text{FSLA}} \right) + ALSA$$

[5]

(6) . . . [3]

(7) In this paragraph—

VULSR is the value of the individual's uncrystallised lump sum rights under the pension scheme on 5th April 2006, calculated in accordance with paragraph 32 of Schedule 36,

[ULA is the underpinned lifetime allowance, and][5]

FSLA is £1,500,000 (the standard lifetime allowance for the tax year 2006–07), and

ALSA is the [greater of the additional lump sum amount and nil][1].

(7A) The additional lump sum amount is—

$$\frac{LS + AC - \left(VUR \times \dfrac{CSLA}{FSLA} \right)}{4}$$

where—

LS is the lump sum paid (but this is subject to sub-paragraph (7B)),

[AC is—

(a)   in a case where the member becomes entitled to the pension in connection with which the lump sum is paid before reaching the age of 75, the amount crystallised by reason of the member becoming entitled to the pension, and

(b)   in a case where the member becomes entitled to that pension after reaching that age, the amount that would have been so crystallised but for paragraph 2 of Schedule 32,

(but this is subject to sub-paragraphs [(7AA) to (7B)][7]),][4] . . . [6]

VUR is the value of the individual's uncrystallised rights under the pension scheme on 5th April 2006, calculated in accordance with paragraph 33 of Schedule 36[, and

CSLA is the current standard lifetime allowance.][6]

[(7AZA) "The underpinned lifetime allowance" is the greater of the current standard lifetime allowance and £1,800,000 (the standard lifetime allowance for the tax year 2011–12).][5]

[(7AA) Where the pension in connection with which the lump sum is paid is a scheme pension under a money purchase arrangement, AC is the scheme pension purchase price, as it would be defined by paragraph 3 if the words "but subject to sub-paragraph (8)" in sub-paragraph (7A) and sub-paragraph (8) were omitted.][2]

[(7AB) Where paragraph 1A applies to the lump sum, AC is the total of—

(a)   the sums held, at the time the lump sum is paid, for the purpose of providing the pension at that time expected to be the pension in connection with which the lump sum is paid, and

(b)   the market value at that time of the assets held at that time for that purpose.

(7AC) Where paragraph 1B applies to the lump sum, AC is the total of—

(a)   the sums held, at the time the lump sum is paid, for the purpose of providing the expected pension (see paragraph 1B(2)(b)), and

(b)   the market value at that time of the assets held at that time for that purpose.][7]

(7B) Any part of [what would otherwise be LS or AC][2] which represents rights attributable to a disqualifying pension credit is to be disregarded.

(7C) . . . "[3]

(3) Omit paragraph 3 (applicable amount for pension commencement lump sums) [(but without prejudice to its operation for the purposes of paragraph 2(7AA) of Schedule 29 as inserted by sub-paragraph (2))][2].

Commentary—*Simon's Taxes* E7.224, E7.226–E7.236, E7.240, E7.242.

Modifications—Taxation of Pension Schemes (Transitional Provisions) Order, SI 2006/572 arts 21, 23 (transfers and entitlement to lump sums exceeding 25 per cent of uncrystallised rights: modification of above paragraph).

Taxation of Pension Schemes (Transitional Provisions) Order, SI 2006/572 art 23D(1), (3) (modification of sub-para (7A) above in respect of trivial commutation lump sums).

Taxation of Pension Schemes (Transitional Provisions) Order, SI 2006/572 arts 23ZA(3), 23ZC(3), 23ZE(4) (modification of para (2) in respect of an individual who has received a pension commencement lump sum but who dies before becoming entitled to the pension in connection with the lump sum).

Amendments—[1]   In sub-para (2), words in the substituted sub-para (7) substituted by FA 2005 s 101, Sch 10 paras 57, 64(1) with effect from 6 April 2006.

[2]   Words in sub-paras (2) inserted and substituted, and words in sub-para (3) inserted, by FA 2006 s 161, Sch 23 paras 1, 25. These amendments are deemed to have come into force on 6 April 2006.

[3]   In sub-para (2), in substituted provisions of Sch 29 para 2, words in sub-para (5) and whole of sub-paras (6), (7C) repealed, by FA 2008 s 92 Sch 29 para 13. These amendments are treated as having come into force on 6 April 2006.

[4]   In sub-para (2), in the text treated as substituted for FA 2004 Sch 29 para 2(5)–(8) definition of "AC" substituted, by FA 2011 s 65, Sch 16 paras 62, 82(1), (5) with effect for the tax year 2011–12 and subsequent tax years, subject to transitional provisions in FA 2011 Sch 16 Pt 3. The amendments made by FA 2011 Sch 16 paras 27–30, 40, 42(2)(a), (3), 63, 77(4), 81(2), (4), 82(3)–(5) and 83 have effect in relation to lump sums paid on or after 6 April 2011 (FA 2011 Sch 16 para 102).

[5]   In sub-para 2, in text treated as substituted, in sub-para (5) in the formula, "ULA"substituted for "CSLA", in sub-para (7), definition of "CSLA" substituted, and sub-para (7AZA) inserted by FA 2011 s 67, Sch 18 paras 8, 11 with effect for the year 2012–13 and subsequent tax years, subject to transitional provisions in FA 2011 Sch 18 para 14,

[6]   In sub-para (2), in the sub-s (7A) treated as substituted, in definition of "AC" word "and" repealed, and definition of "CSLA" and preceding word "and" inserted, by the Pension Schemes (Miscellaneous Amendments) Order, SI 2013/1114 art 3 with effect for the tax year 2012–13 and subsequent tax years.

[7]   In sub-para (2), in text treated as substituted, in sub-para (7A), in definition of "AC", words substituted, and sub-paras (7AB), (7AC) inserted, by FA 2014 s 43, Sch 5 para 10. These amendments are to be treated as having come into force on 19 March 2014 (FA 2014 Sch 5 para 15).

Winding-up lump sums paid by former approved superannuation funds

35—(1) For the tax year 2006–07, Schedule 29 (authorised lump sums) applies in relation to former approved superannuation funds with the modifications specified in sub-paragraphs (2) and (3).

(2) Paragraph 10 (winding-up lump sums) applies as if the following were omitted—

    (a)   sub-paragraph (1)(c) and (d),

    (b)   sub-paragraph (2), and

    (c)   sub-paragraph (3).

(3) Paragraph 11 (lifetime allowance excess lump sums) applies as if at the end of paragraph (b) there were inserted "or a winding-up lump sum".

(4) Section 636B of ITEPA 2003 (taxation of trivial commutation and winding-up lump sums) applies in relation to a winding-up lump sum paid by a former approved superannuation fund in the tax year 2006–07 as if—

    (a)   in subsection (2), after "equal to" there were inserted "75% of", and

    (b)   subsection (3) were omitted.

(5) "Former approved superannuation fund" has the meaning given by paragraph 1(3).

Commentary—*Simon's Taxes* E7.226–E7.236, E7.240, E7.242.

Right to payment of lump sum death benefit

36—(1) This paragraph applies to a member of a registered pension scheme if on 5th April 2006—

    (a)   the pension scheme is within any of paragraphs (a) to (e) of paragraph 1(1),

    (b)   the member has an actual (rather than a prospective) right to a pension under an arrangement under the pension scheme, and

    (c)   under the arrangement a lump sum death benefit is payable if the member dies within the guarantee period.

(2) The guarantee period is the period of five years beginning with the day on which the member became entitled to the pension or, if later, the day on which the pension was first paid.

(3) If the member dies after having reached the age of 75 and before the end of the guarantee period—

    (a)   paragraph 14 of Schedule 29 (pension protection lump sum death benefit), [and][1]

    (b)   paragraph 16 of that Schedule (annuity protection lump sum death benefit), . . . [1]

    (c)   . . . [1]

apply in relation to the member and the arrangement with the following modifications.

(4) . . . [1]

(5) Paragraph 14(1) applies as if paragraph (d) were omitted.

(6) Paragraph 14(2) applies as if the reference to the pension protection limit were to the transitional protection limit.

(7) Paragraph 16(2) applies as if the reference to the annuity protection limit were to the transitional protection limit.

(8) . . .[1]

(9) Section 206(1) (special lump sum death benefits charge) does not apply to any pension protection lump sum death benefit [or annuity protection lump sum death benefit][1] paid by virtue of [sub-paragraphs (3) to (7)][1].

(10) If the member dies before having reached the age of 75 and before the end of the guarantee period—

    (a) section 206(1) does not apply to so much of any pension protection lump sum death benefit [or annuity protection lump sum death benefit][1] paid under the arrangement as does not exceed the transitional protection limit, and

    (b) if the arrangement is a defined benefits arrangement, paragraph 14(1)(d) of Schedule 29 is to be treated as satisfied in relation to so much of the lump sum death benefit paid under the arrangement as does not exceed the transitional protection limit.

(11) The transitional protection limit is—

$$P - TPLS$$

where—

    P is the amount of pension to which (had the member lived) the member would have been entitled under the arrangement in respect of the period beginning with the day of the member's death and ending with the last day of the guarantee period, and

    TPLS is the amount of any pension protection lump sum death benefit [or annuity protection lump sum death benefit][1] previously paid in respect of the pension.

Amendments—[1]   In sub-para (3)(a) word "and" inserted, sub-para (3)(c) and the preceding word "and" repealed, sub-paras (4), (8) repealed, in sub-para (9) words substituted for words ", annuity protection lump sum death benefit or unsecured pension fund lump sum death benefit" and "sub-paragraphs (3) to (8)", in sub-para (10)(a) words substituted for words ", annuity protection lump sum death benefit or unsecured pension fund lump sum death benefit", and in sub-para (11) words substituted for words ", annuity protection lump sum death benefit or unsecured pension fund lump sum death benefit", by FA 2011 s 65, Sch 16 paras 62, 82(1), (6) with effect for the tax year 2011–12 and subsequent tax years, subject to transitional provisions in FA 2011 Sch 16 Pt 3. The amendments made by FA 2011 Sch 16 paras 33–39, 41, 42(2)(b), (c), (4), (5), 65, 67, 68, 75(a), 76, 77(5), 79(4), 82(6) have effect in relation to deaths occurring on or after 6 April 2011 (FA 2011 Sch 16 para 103).

PART 4
OTHER PROVISIONS
Pre-commencement ill-health insurance contracts

37—(1) Payments under protected ill-health insurance contracts are not unauthorised member payments.

(2) Ill-health insurance contracts are contracts providing insurance against a risk relating to non-payment by a member of a pension scheme of contributions under the pension scheme.

(3) An ill-health insurance contract is protected if it was made before 6th April 2006 under—

    (a) a personal pension scheme approved under Chapter 4 of Part 14 of ICTA before 6th April 2001, or

    (b) an annuity contract or trust scheme approved under section 620 or 621 of ICTA or a substituted contract within the meaning of section 622(3) of ICTA.

Commentary—*Simon's Taxes* **E7.224**.

[Pre-commencement holdings of taxable property

37A—(1) This paragraph applies in relation to an investment-regulated pension scheme if—

    (a) on 6th April 2006 the pension scheme holds an interest in taxable property which it acquired before that date, and

    (b) immediately before that date the pension scheme was not prohibited from holding the interest in the property,

and, in a case where immediately before that date the interest in the property was held directly by a person other than the pension scheme, if the pension scheme was not prohibited from holding the interest it held in that person at that time.

(2) This paragraph also applies in relation to an investment-regulated pension scheme if—

    (a) before 6th April 2006 a contract to acquire an interest in property was entered into by the pension scheme or a person in whom the pension scheme directly or indirectly held an interest when the contract was entered into,

    (b) the pension scheme does not acquire the interest in the property before that date, (*c*) the property is taxable property on that date, and

(*d*) immediately before that date the pension scheme would not have been prohibited from holding the interest in the property,

and, in a case where the contract to acquire the interest in the property was entered into by a person in whom the pension scheme directly or indirectly held an interest, if the pension scheme was not prohibited from holding the interest it held in that person immediately before that date.

(3) The taxable property provisions (apart from this paragraph and paragraphs 37B to 37E) do not apply in relation to the pension scheme and the interest in the property.

(4) For the purposes of this Schedule a pension scheme is to be treated as having been prohibited from holding an interest in property, or in a person, immediately before 6th April 2006 if approval could have been withdrawn under section 591B, 620(7) or 650 of ICTA on the basis of the holding of the interest at that time.

(5) This paragraph is subject to paragraphs 37B to 37E.]¹

Commentary—*Simon's Taxes* **E7.237**.

Amendments—¹ Paragraphs 37A–37I inserted by FA 2006 s 158, Sch 21 paras 2, 15. This amendment is deemed to have come into force on 6 April 2006.

[37B—(1) Paragraph 37A ceases to apply to an investment-regulated pension scheme and an interest in taxable property on the relevant date if Condition A, B or C is met.

(2) Condition A is that there is a change in the occupation or use of the property such that, if the change had occurred immediately before 6th April 2006, the pension scheme would have been prohibited from holding the interest in the property at that time.

(3) Condition B is that—

(*a*) the taxable property is residential property on 6th April 2006, and

(*b*) improvement works on the property are begun on or after that date.

(4) Condition C is that there is a change in the pension scheme's interest in—

(*a*) any person who holds the interest in the property directly, or

(*b*) any person who has entered into a contract to acquire the interest in the property,

such that, if the change had occurred immediately before 6th April 2006, the pension scheme would have been prohibited from holding the interest in the person at that time.

(5) For the purposes of this paragraph the relevant date is—

(*a*) where Condition A is met, the date on which the change in the occupation or use of the taxable property takes place,

(*b*) where Condition B is met, the date on which the improvement works are substantially completed, or

(*c*) where Condition C is met, the date on which the change in the pension scheme's interest in the person takes place,

but where the pension scheme has not acquired the interest in the property by what would otherwise be the relevant date, the relevant date is the date on which it acquires the interest.

(6) Where Condition A, B or C is met the pension scheme is to be treated for the purposes of the taxable property provisions as acquiring the interest in the property on the relevant date.

(7) For the purposes of Schedule 29A the total taxable amount in relation to any unauthorised payment which the pension scheme is treated as having made by reason of the acquisition is—

(*a*) the market value on the relevant date of the interest in the property held by the person who holds it directly, or

(*b*) if the interest in the property is a lease at a rent, the amount of consideration that would be treated as given by the person for the lease by virtue of paragraph 34 of Schedule 29A if it were assigned to the person on that date.

(8) Where—

(*a*) the pension scheme holds the interest in the property directly, and

(*b*) the interest is not a lease at a rent,

for the purposes of section 185G (gains from taxable property: disposal by person holding directly) the pension scheme is to be treated as having acquired the interest for a consideration equal to its market value on 6th April 2006.

(9) For the purposes of sub-paragraph (3)(*b*) improvement works are to be taken to have been begun before 6th April 2006 only if—

(*a*) a binding contract for the works was entered into before that date, or

(*b*) a substantial amount of the works has been carried out before that date.

(10) For the purposes of this Schedule "improvement works" means, in relation to a property, works which—

(*a*) materially improve the property, and

(*b*) are not carried out wholly for the purposes of complying with a statutory requirement or a requirement imposed by a government department, a statutory body or a person holding a statutory office.

(11) For the purposes of sub-paragraph (10)(*a*) a property is materially improved by works only if—

    (*a*) its market value on the date the works are substantially completed ("MVW") exceeds what would have been its market value on that date if the works had not been carried out ("MV"), and

    (*b*) the amount by which MVW exceeds MV is greater than 20% of MV.

(12) For the purposes of sub-paragraph (10)(*b*)—

    "statutory body" means a body set up by or under an enactment (including an enactment comprised in, or an instrument made under, an Act of the Scottish Parliament);

    "statutory office" means a body set up by or under such an enactment; and

    "statutory requirement" means a requirement imposed by provision made by or under such an enactment.

(13) This paragraph is subject to paragraph 37D.][1]

Commentary—*Simon's Taxes* **E7.237**.
Amendments—[1] Paragraphs 37A–37I inserted by FA 2006 s 158, Sch 21 paras 2, 15. This amendment is deemed to have come into force on 6 April 2006.

[37C—(1) This paragraph applies where—

    (*a*) on 6th April 2006 an investment-regulated pension scheme holds an interest in taxable property which it acquired before that date, and

    (*b*) immediately before that date the pension scheme was prohibited from holding the interest.

(2) This paragraph also applies where—

    (*a*) on 6th April 2006 an investment-regulated pension scheme holds an interest in taxable property indirectly which it acquired before that date, and

    (*b*) immediately before that date the pension scheme was prohibited from holding the interest it held in the person that held the interest in the property directly at that time.

(3) The pension scheme is to be treated for the purposes of the taxable property provisions as acquiring the interest in the property on 6th April 2006.

(4) For the purposes of Schedule 29A the total taxable amount in relation to any unauthorised payment which the pension scheme is treated as having made by reason of the acquisition is—

    (*a*) the market value on 6th April 2006 of the interest in the property held by the person who holds it directly, or

    (*b*) if the interest in the property is a lease at a rent, the amount of consideration that would be treated as given by the person for the lease by virtue of paragraph 34 of Schedule 29A if it were assigned to the person on that date.

(5) Where—

    (*a*) the pension scheme holds the interest in the property directly, and

    (*b*) the interest is not a lease at a rent,

for the purposes of section 185G (gains from taxable property: disposal by person holding directly) the pension scheme is to be treated as having acquired the interest for a consideration equal to its market value on 6th April 2006.][1]

Commentary—*Simon's Taxes* **E7.237**.
Amendments—[1] Paragraphs 37A–37I inserted by FA 2006 s 158, Sch 21 paras 2, 15. This amendment is deemed to have come into force on 6 April 2006.

[37D—(1) This paragraph applies where—

    (*a*) sub-paragraph (1) or (2) of paragraph 37A applies in relation to a pension scheme and an interest in property,

    (*b*) immediately before 6th April 2006 the pension scheme was a self-invested personal pension scheme or a small self-administered scheme,

    (*c*) on that date the pension scheme holds the interest in the property indirectly or (if sub-paragraph (2) of paragraph 37A applies in relation to the pension scheme and the interest in the property) the pension scheme will hold the interest indirectly once it has been acquired pursuant to the contract,

    (*d*) the property is residential property on that date, and

    (*e*) improvement works on the property were begun after 5th December 2005.

(2) This paragraph also applies where—

    (*a*) sub-paragraph (1) or (2) of paragraph 37A applies in relation to a pension scheme and an interest in property,

    (*b*) immediately before 6th April 2006 the pension scheme was a small self-administered scheme,

    (*c*) on that date the pension scheme holds the interest in the property directly,

    (*d*) the pension scheme acquired the interest before 5th August 1991,

    (*e*) the property is residential property on 6th April 2006, and

    (*f*) improvement works on the property were begun after 5th December 2005.

(3) If the works are completed on or after 6th April 2006, paragraph 37B applies in relation to the pension scheme and the interest in the property as if the works were begun on or after that date.

(4) If the works are completed before that date—

    (*a*) paragraph 37A does not apply in relation to the pension scheme and the interest in the property, and

    (*b*) unless the pension scheme has still to acquire the interest in the property on that date, sub-paragraphs (3) to (5) of paragraph 37C apply in relation to the pension scheme and the interest.

(5) For the purposes of this paragraph improvement works are to be taken to have been begun before 6th December 2005 only if—

    (*a*) a binding contract for the works was entered into before that date, or

    (*b*) a substantial amount of the works has been carried out before that date.][1]

Commentary—*Simon's Taxes* **E7.237.**
Amendments—[1] Paragraphs 37A–37I inserted by FA 2006 s 158, Sch 21 paras 2, 15. This amendment is deemed to have come into force on 6 April 2006.

[37E—(1) This paragraph applies where—

    (*a*) paragraph 37A would otherwise apply in relation to a pension scheme and an interest in property,

    (*b*) immediately before 6th April 2006 the pension scheme was a retirement benefits scheme approved under section 590 of ICTA, and

    (*c*) the pension scheme was approved under that section after 5th December 2005.

(2) Paragraph 37A does not apply in relation to the pension scheme and the interest in the property.

(3) Unless the pension scheme has still to acquire the interest in the property on 6th April 2006, sub-paragraphs (3) to (5) of paragraph 37C apply in relation to the pension scheme and the interest.][1]

Commentary—*Simon's Taxes* **E7.237.**
Amendments—[1] Paragraphs 37A–37I inserted by FA 2006 s 158, Sch 21 paras 2, 15. This amendment is deemed to have come into force on 6 April 2006.

[Post-commencement acquisitions of taxable property

37F—(1) This paragraph applies where on or after 6th April 2006 an investment-regulated pension scheme acquires an interest in taxable property consisting of tangible moveable property because a person in whom the pension scheme directly or indirectly holds an interest comes to hold the interest in the property directly.

(2) The taxable property provisions (apart from this paragraph and paragraph 37G) do not apply in relation to the pension scheme and the interest in the property if the conditions in sub-paragraph (3) are met.

(3) Those conditions are that—

    (*a*) on 6th April 2006 the pension scheme held the interest in the person by virtue of acquiring it before that date,

    (*b*) immediately before that date the pension scheme was not prohibited from holding the interest in the person,

    (*c*) at no time during the period beginning with that date and ending immediately before the acquisition of the interest in the property has the pension scheme's interest in the person been such that, if it had held that interest in the person immediately before 6th April 2006, it would have been prohibited from holding that interest at that time, and

    (*d*) the person acquires the interest in the property so that the property may be used for the purposes of a trade, profession or vocation carried on by the person or for the purposes of its administration or management.

(4) This paragraph is subject to paragraph 37G.][1]

Commentary—*Simon's Taxes* **E7.237.**
Amendments—[1] Paragraphs 37A–37I inserted by FA 2006 s 158, Sch 21 paras 2, 15. This amendment is deemed to have come into force on 6 April 2006.

[37G—(1) Where Condition A or B is met in relation to the pension scheme and an interest in property to which paragraph 37F has applied, the pension scheme is to be treated for the purposes of the taxable property provisions as acquiring the interest in the property on the date on which the Condition is met.

(2) Condition A is that there is a change in the pension scheme's interest in the person who holds the interest in the property directly such that, if the change had occurred immediately before 6th April 2006, the pension scheme would have been prohibited from holding the interest in the person at that time.

(3) Condition B is that the property ceases to be used for the purposes of—

    (*a*) a trade, profession or vocation carried on by the person, or

    (*b*) its administration or management.

(4) For the purposes of Schedule 29A the total taxable amount in relation to any unauthorised payment which the pension scheme is treated as having made by reason of the acquisition is the market value on the relevant date of the interest in the property held by the person.][1]

Commentary—*Simon's Taxes* E7.237.
Amendments—[1] Paragraphs 37A–37I inserted by FA 2006 s 158, Sch 21 paras 2, 15. This amendment is deemed to have come into force on 6 April 2006.

[37H—(1) This paragraph applies where on or after 6th April 2006 an investment-regulated pension scheme acquires an interest in taxable property consisting of residential property because a person in whom the pension scheme directly or indirectly holds an interest comes to hold the interest in the property directly.
(2) The taxable property provisions (apart from this paragraph and paragraph 37I) do not apply in relation to the pension scheme and the interest in the property if the conditions in sub-paragraph (3) are met.
(3) Those conditions are that—
   (*a*) on 6th April 2006 the pension scheme held the interest in the person by virtue of acquiring it before that date,
   (*b*) immediately before that date the pension scheme was not prohibited from holding the interest in the person,
   (*c*) immediately before that date the person had a business involving the holding and letting of residential property and held directly five or more assets consisting of interests in residential property for the purposes of that business,
   (*d*) at no time during the period beginning with that date and ending immediately before the acquisition of the interest in the property has the pension scheme's interest in the person been such that, if it had held that interest in the person immediately before 6th April 2006, it would have been prohibited from holding that interest at that time,
   (*e*) the person acquires the interest in the property for the purposes of its property rental business, and
   (*f*) after the acquisition of the interest in the property, the property is not occupied or used by a member of the pension scheme or a person connected with such a member.
(4) This paragraph is subject to paragraph 37I.
(5) [Section 1122 of the Corporation Tax Act 2010][2] (connected persons) applies for the purposes of this paragraph.][1]

Commentary—*Simon's Taxes* E7.237.
Amendments—[1] Paragraphs 37A–37I inserted by FA 2006 s 158, Sch 21 paras 2, 15. This amendment is deemed to have come into force on 6 April 2006.
[2] In sub-para (5) words "Section 839 of ICTA" substituted by CTA 2010 s 1177, Sch 1 paras 423, 432(1),(4). CTA 2010 has effect for corporation tax purposes for accounting periods ending on or after 1 April 2010, and for income and capital gains tax purposes for the tax year 2010–11 and subsequent tax years.

[37I—(1) Where Condition A, B or C is met in relation to the pension scheme and an interest in property to which paragraph 37H has applied, the pension scheme is to be treated for the purposes of the taxable property provisions as acquiring, on the date on which the Condition is met, each interest in property—
   (*a*) which it holds on that date, and
   (*b*) to which paragraph 37H has applied before that date.
(2) Condition A is that there is a change in the pension scheme's interest in the person who holds the interest in the property directly such that, if the change had occurred immediately before 6th April 2006, the pension scheme would have been prohibited from holding the interest in the person at that time.
(3) Condition B is that the property ceases to be used for the purposes of the person's property rental business.
(4) Condition C is that the property is occupied or used by a member of the pension scheme or a person connected with such a member.
(5) For the purposes of Schedule 29A the total taxable amount in relation to any unauthorised payment which the pension scheme is treated as having made by reason of an acquisition of an interest in property treated as made by virtue of this paragraph is—
   (*a*) the market value on the relevant date of the interest in the property held by the person who holds it directly, or
   (*b*) if the interest in the property is a lease at a rent, the amount of consideration that would be treated as given by the person for the lease by virtue of paragraph 34 of Schedule 29A if it were assigned to the person on that date.][1]

Commentary—*Simon's Taxes* E7.237.
Amendments—[1] Paragraphs 37A–37I inserted by FA 2006 s 158, Sch 21 paras 2, 15. This amendment is deemed to have come into force on 6 April 2006.

Pre-commencement loans to sponsoring employers

38—(1) This paragraph applies to a loan if—

    (*a*) the loan was made before 6th April 2006 by an occupational pension scheme which becomes a registered pension scheme on that date,

    (*b*) had this Part had been in force and had the pension scheme been a registered pension scheme at the time when the loan was made, it would have been a loan to a sponsoring employer, and

    (*c*) the date by which the total amount owing (including interest) must be paid is on or after 6th April 2006.

(2) If on or after 6th April 2006 there is no alteration in the repayment terms, section 179 (authorised employer loan) does not apply in relation to the loan.

(3) If on or after 6th April 2006 there is an alteration in the repayment terms, section 179 applies as if, on the date of the alteration, the pension scheme made a loan to the sponsoring employer of an amount equal to the amount owing (including interest) on that date.

(4) The postponement of the date by which the total amount owing (including interest) must be paid is not an alteration in the repayment terms if—

    (*a*) an amount is outstanding on the date by which the total amount owing should have been paid,

    (*b*) the postponement is for a period not exceeding five years, and

    (*c*) there has been no previous postponement on or after 6th April 2006.

Retirement annuity contracts: carry-back of pre-commencement contributions

39   The repeal by this Act of section 619(4) of ICTA (election on or before 31st January following tax year in which retirement annuity contract premium is paid to treat premium as paid in earlier tax year) does not prevent the making of an election under that provision (in relation to a premium paid in the tax year 2005–06) at any time on or before 31st January 2007.

Commentary—*Simon's Taxes* E7.223, E7.224, E7.242.

Members' contributions to pre-commencement retirement annuity contracts

40—(1) Relief in respect of contributions made by a member under pre-commencement retirement annuity arrangements is not required to be given in accordance with section 192 (relief at source).

(2) If relief in respect of contributions made by a member under pre-commencement retirement annuity arrangements is not given in accordance with section 192, relief in respect of the contributions is to be given in accordance with section 194 (relief on making of claim).

(3) "Pre-commencement retirement annuity arrangements" means—

    (*a*) an annuity contract or trust scheme approved under section 620 or 621 of ICTA, or

    (*b*) a substituted contract within the meaning of section 622(3) of ICTA.

Modifications—Taxation of Pension Schemes (Transitional Provisions) Order, SI 2006/572 art 27 (modification of this paragraph in the case of an individual who, immediately before 6 April 2006, had rights under a contract which had been approved under TA 1988 s 621(1)(*b*)).

Employers' contributions relieved before 6th April 2006

41   To the extent that any contribution paid by an employer under a registered pension scheme was—

    (*a*) allowed to be deducted for the purposes of [Part 2 of ITTOIA 2005 (trading income) or][1] Case I or II of Schedule D,

    (*b*) deductible under section 75 of ICTA (expenses of management: companies with investment business), or

    (*c*) brought into account at Step 1 in section 76(7) of ICTA (expenses of insurance companies), for a period beginning before 6th April 2006, it is not allowed to be so deducted, so deductible, or available to be so brought into account for that or any other period in accordance with section 196 (relief for employers in respect of contributions paid).

Amendments—[1]   Words in sub-para (*a*) inserted by ITTOIA 2005 s 882(1), Sch 1 paras 629, 656(1), (2) with effect from 6 April 2005. ITTOIA 2005 has effect—

    (a)   for income tax purposes, for 2005–06 and subsequent tax years, and

    (b)   for corporation tax purposes, for accounting periods ending after 5 April 2005: ITTOIA 2005 s 883(1).

Spreading of employer's contributions

42   The power of the Board of Inland Revenue under section 592(6) of ICTA to direct that a sum paid under an exempt approved scheme otherwise than by way of ordinary annual contribution be treated as an expense to be spread over such period of years as the Board think fit continues to apply in relation to sums paid before 6th April 2006.

Taxation of pensions accruing (but not taxed) pre-commencement and paid or received post-commencement

44—(1) If an amount which accrued but was not paid before 6th April 2006 would have constituted taxable pension income under Chapter 7 of Part 9 of ITEPA 2003 (former approved superannuation fund annuities) had it been paid before that date, it is to be treated for the purposes of Chapter 5A of Part 9 of ITEPA 2003 (as inserted by Schedule 31) as if it accrues when it is paid.

(2) If an amount which accrued but was not received before 6th April 2006 would have constituted taxable pension income under section 596 of ITEPA 2003 (personal pension annuities) had it been received before that date, it is to be treated for the purposes of Chapter 5A of Part 9 of ITEPA 2003 (as inserted by Schedule 31) as if it accrues when it is received.

Pensions taxed pre-commencement but accruing post-commencement

45—(1) If an amount which was paid but had not accrued before 6th April 2006 constituted taxable pension income under Chapter 7 of Part 9 of ITEPA 2003 (former approved superannuation fund annuities), it does not also constitute taxable pension income under Chapter 5A of Part 9 of ITEPA 2003 (as inserted by Schedule 31) when it accrues.

(2) If an amount which was received but had not accrued before 6th April 2006 constituted taxable pension income under section 596 of ITEPA 2003 (personal pension annuities), it does not also constitute taxable pension income under Chapter 5A of Part 9 of ITEPA 2003 (as inserted by Schedule 31) when it accrues.

[Taxation of certain annuities for dependants purchased pre-commencement

45A—(1) The charge to tax under Part 9 of ITEPA 2003 (taxation of pension income) does not apply to an annuity payable to a person ("the dependant") if—

(a) the annuity is payable on the death of a member of a pension scheme,

(b) the annuity is paid in respect of the deceased member,

(c) the member had not reached the age of 75 at the date of the member's death,

(d) the member died on or after 3 December 2014,

(e) no payment of the annuity is made before 6 April 2015,

(f) the annuity has fulfilled the transitional conditions at all times on or after 6 April 2006,

(g) the annuity was purchased together with an annuity payable to the member, and

(h) that annuity payable to the member fulfilled the transitional conditions at all times in the period beginning with 6 April 2006 and ending with the member's death.

(2) For the purposes of sub-paragraph (1)(g), an annuity is purchased together with another if they are purchased—

(a) in the form of a joint life annuity, or

(b) separately in circumstances in which the day on which the one is purchased is no earlier than seven days before, and no later than seven days after, the day on which the other is purchased.

(3) In sub-paragraph (1) "the transitional conditions" means the conditions specified in the subsection (3A) set out in article 2(3) of the Taxation of Pension Schemes (Transitional Provisions) Order 2006 (SI 2006/572).][1]

Amendments—[1]   Para 45A inserted by FA 2015 s 34, Sch 4 para 19 with effect from 26 March 2015.

Authorised surplus payments charge: pre-19th March 1986 winding-up

47 Section 207 (authorised surplus payments charge) does not apply to any payment made in pursuance of the winding-up of a pension scheme if the winding-up commenced before 19th March 1986.

Annual allowance charge: post-commencement contributions to discharge pre-commencement unfunded promises

48—(1) This paragraph applies where, during the period beginning with 6th April 2006 and ending with 7th July 2006, an employer of an individual makes a relevant consolidation contribution in respect of the individual under an arrangement under a registered pension scheme relating to the individual.

(2) The pension input amount in respect of the arrangement during the pension input period of the arrangement ending in the tax year 2006–07 is to be reduced by the amount of the contribution.

(3) "Relevant consolidation contribution" means a contribution made by way of discharge of any liability incurred by the employer before 6th April 2006 to pay any pension or lump sum to or in respect of the individual.

Commentary—*Simon's Taxes* **E7.247.**

Saving of sections 605 and 651A of ICTA

50 The repeal by this Act of sections 605 and 651A of ICTA (information powers) does not affect the operation of those sections, or regulations under them, in relation to times before 6th April 2006.

Individuals with pre-commencement entitlement to corresponding relief

51—(1) This paragraph applies where the Board of Inland Revenue allow contributions made by an individual under a pension scheme as deductions under Chapter 2 of Part 5 of ITEPA 2003 for the tax year 2005–06 in accordance with section 355 of that Act (deductions for corresponding payments by non-domiciled employees with foreign employers).

(2) Where the individual makes contributions under the pension scheme for any subsequent tax year, the Board of Inland Revenue may allow the contributions as deductions under Chapter 2 of Part 5 of that Act if, as well as the Board of Inland Revenue being satisfied that the conditions in section 355 of that Act are met, the scheme manager complies with any prescribed benefit crystallisation information requirements imposed on the scheme manager.

(3) Schedule 34 (non-UK schemes: application of certain charges) applies in relation to the pension scheme and the individual as if allowing the contributions as deductions under Chapter 2 of Part 5 of ITEPA 2003 by virtue of sub-paragraph (2) were the giving of relief by virtue of Schedule 33 (overseas pension schemes: migrant member relief).

(4) "Prescribed benefit crystallisation information requirements" means requirements imposed by or under regulations made by the Board of Inland Revenue to provide to the Inland Revenue any information relating to events that are benefit crystallisation events in relation to the individual.

(5) The references in sub-paragraphs (2) and (3) to the pension scheme include a pension scheme [("a transferee pension scheme") if there has been—

    (a) a block transfer from the pension scheme within sub-paragraph (1) ("the original pension scheme") to the transferee pension scheme, or

    (b) a block transfer to the transferee pension scheme from a pension scheme that was a transferee pension scheme in relation to the original pension scheme by virtue of the previous application of paragraph (a) or the previous application (on one or more occasions) of this paragraph.][1]

(6) "Block transfer" has the same meaning as in paragraph 22(6), but treating the references there to the member as references to the individual.

Regulations—Pension Schemes (Information Requirements — Qualifying Overseas Pension Schemes, Qualifying Recognised Overseas Pensions Schemes and Corresponding Relief) Regulations, SI 2006/208.

Amendments—[1] Words in sub-para (5) substituted by FA 2005 s 101, Sch 10 paras 55(7), 64(1) with effect from 6 April 2006.

Continuing operation of section 392 of ITEPA 2003

52 Section 392 of ITEPA 2003 (non-approved schemes: relief where no benefits are paid or payable) continues to have effect in relation to a sum charged to tax by virtue of section 386 of ITEPA 2003 or section 595 of ICTA (charges on payments to schemes) before 6th April 2006.

Benefits taxable under Chapter 2 of Part 6 of ITEPA 2003: contributions taxed pre-commencement

53—(1) Paragraph 54 or 55 has effect where—

    (a) section 394 of ITEPA 2003 (charge on benefits from non-approved schemes) operates (or would otherwise operate) by reason of the provision of a lump sum under an employer-financed retirement benefits scheme on or after 6th April 2006, and

    (b) before that date an employer has paid any sum or sums, with a view to the provision of benefits under the scheme, in respect of which an employee is taxed.

(2) For the purposes of sub-paragraph (1)(a) section 394 of ITEPA 2003 operates if—

    (a) an amount counts as employment income of an individual under that section, or

    (b) the person who is, or persons who are, the responsible person in relation to the scheme is or are chargeable [to income tax under subsection (2) of][1] that section.

(3) For the purposes of sub-paragraph (1)(b) an employee is taxed in respect of a sum or sums if—

    (a) the employee is assessed to tax by virtue of section 595(1) of ICTA (charges on payments) in respect of the sum or sums, or

    (b) the sum or sums counts or count as employment income of the employee under section 386(1) of ITEPA 2003 (charges on payments).

(4) It is to be assumed, unless the contrary is shown, that neither paragraph 54 nor paragraph 55 has effect.

Amendments—[1] Words in sub-para (2)(b) substituted by ITTOIA 2005 s 882(1), Sch 1 paras 629, 656(1), (3) with effect from 6 April 2005. ITTOIA 2005 has effect—

    (a)   for income tax purposes, for 2005–06 and subsequent tax years, and

    (b)   for corporation tax purposes, for accounting periods ending after 5 April 2005: ITTOIA 2005 s 883(1).

54—(1) This paragraph has effect if—

(a) all of the income and gains accruing to the scheme are brought into charge to tax and the lump sum is provided to the employee, a relative of the employee, the personal representatives of the employee, an ex-spouse [or former civil partner][1] of the employee or any other individual designated by the employee, or

(b) the scheme was entered into before [1st December 1993][2] and has not been varied on or after that date with a view to the provision of benefits under the scheme.

(2) In a case where the employer has not paid any sum or sums with a view to the provision of benefits under the scheme since before 6th April 2006, section 394 of ITEPA 2003 (charge on benefits from non-approved schemes) does not apply in relation to the lump sum.

(3) In a case where the employer has paid any sum or sums with a view to the provision of benefits under the scheme on or after 6th April 2006—

(a) section 394 of ITEPA 2003 does not apply in relation to so much of the lump sum as does not exceed the appropriate fraction of the amount of the market value of the assets of the scheme on 5th April 2006 as increased under sub-paragraph (4), and

(b) only any sum or sums paid by the employee after that date with a view to the provision of benefits under the scheme is or are to be taken into account under section 395 of ITEPA 2003 (general rules).

(4) For the purposes of sub-paragraph (3)(a)—

(a) "the appropriate fraction" of the amount of the market value of the assets of the scheme on 5th April 2006 is the same fraction as the fraction of the assets of the scheme to which the employee would have been entitled had the scheme been wound up on that date, and

(b) the amount of the market value of the assets of the scheme on that date is to be increased by the percentage by which the retail prices index for the month in which the lump sum is provided is greater than that for April 2006.

(5) In this paragraph—

"ex-spouse", in relation to an employee, means the other party to a marriage with the employee that has been dissolved or annulled, and

["former civil partner", in relation to an employee, means the other party to a civil partnership with the employee that has been dissolved or annulled,][1]

"relative", in relation to an employee, means—

(a) the [spouse or civil partner][1] of the employee,

(b) the widow or widower [or surviving civil partner][1] of the employee,

(c) a child of the employee, or

(d) a dependant of the employee.

Commentary—*Simon's Taxes* E7.247.
Amendments—[1] Words in sub-paras (1)(a), (5)(b), definition of "former civil partner" in sub-para (5) inserted, and words in sub-para (5)(a) substituted by Tax and Civil Partnership Regulations, SI 2005/3229, regs 175, 182, with effect from 5 December 2005 (reg 1(1)).
[2] Words in sub-para (1)(b) substituted by FA 2006 s 161, Sch 23 paras 1, 44, 46. This amendment is deemed to have come into force on 6 April 2006.

55—(1) This paragraph has effect if paragraph 54 does not.
(2) Section 394 of ITEPA 2003 (charge on benefits from non-approved schemes) does not apply in relation to so much of the lump sum as does not exceed the sum, or the aggregate of the sums, referred to in paragraph 53(1)(b).
(3) And the reference in section 395 of that Act (general rules) to the amount of the lump sum is to the amount of the remainder of the lump sum.
Commentary—*Simon's Taxes* E7.247.

Inheritance tax

56—(1) This paragraph applies in relation to a fund or scheme—

(a) which is not a registered pension scheme[, a qualifying non-UK pension scheme][1] or a superannuation fund to which section 615(3) of ICTA applies, but

(b) to which section 151 of the Inheritance Tax Act 1984 (c 51) (treatment of pension rights) applied immediately before 6th April 2006.

(2) If no contributions are made under the fund or scheme on or after that date—

(a) section 151 of the Inheritance Tax Act 1984 continues to apply to the fund or scheme on and after that date for all purposes of that Act, and

(b) property which is part of or held for the purposes of the fund or scheme does not constitute relevant property for the purposes of Chapter 3 of Part 3 of that Act (settlements without interest in possession).

(3) In any other case, paragraphs 57 and 58 apply to the fund or scheme on and after that date.

[(4) In this paragraph "qualifying non-UK pension scheme" has the same meaning as in the Inheritance Tax Act 1984 (see section 271A of that Act).][1]

Commentary—*Simon's Taxes* **E7.247**.
Amendments—[1]   Words in sub-para (1) substituted, and sub-para (4) inserted. by FA 2008 s 92, Sch 29 para 18(1), (7). This amendment is treated as having come into force on 6 April 2006.

57—(1) The [percentage][1] of the assets of the fund or scheme which at any time is the protected proportion of those assets does not at that time constitute relevant property for the purposes of Chapter 3 of Part 3 of the Inheritance Tax Act 1984 (settlements without interest in possession).
(2) "The protected [percentage[1]]" of the assets of the fund or scheme at a time is—

$$\frac{ACV}{V} \times 100$$

where—
     V is the market value of the assets of the fund or scheme at that time, and
     ACV is the adjusted commencement value, that is an amount equal to the market value of the assets of the fund or scheme on 5th April 2006, but subject to the adjustments provided by sub-paragraph (3).
(3) The adjustments are—
     (*a*) an increase by the percentage by which the retail prices index for the month of September immediately preceding the time in question is greater than that for April 2006, and
     (*b*) a reduction by the amount of any relevant payments made under the fund or scheme on or after 6th April 2006 and before that time.
(4) "Relevant payments" are payments other than—
     (*a*) payments of costs or expenses, or
     (*b*) payments which are (or will be) income of any person for any of the purposes of income tax.

Amendments—[1]   In sub-paras (1), (2), word substituted by FA 2005 s 101, Sch 10 paras 58(2), 64(1) with effect from 6 April 2006.

58—(1) Section 151 of the Inheritance Tax Act 1984 (c 51) (treatment of pension rights) continues to apply to so much of the assets of the fund or scheme at any time as does not exceed the amount that is the protected amount at that time.
(2) But sub-paragraph (1) does not affect the operation of subsection (1)(*d*) of section 58 of that Act (because paragraph 57 makes provision about the extent to which the assets of the fund or scheme constitute relevant property within the meaning given by that section).
(3) If inheritance tax has not previously been chargeable (otherwise than only because of this paragraph) by reference to the value of the assets of the fund or scheme on or after 6th April 2006, the protected amount is an amount equal to the amount of the market value of the assets of the fund or scheme on 5th April 2006, but subject to the adjustments provided by sub-paragraph (4).
(4) The adjustments are—
     (*a*) an increase by the percentage by which the retail prices index for the month of September immediately preceding the time in question is greater than that for April 2006, and
     (*b*) a reduction by the amount of any relevant payments made under the fund or scheme on or after 6th April 2006 and before that time.
(5) If inheritance tax would (apart from this paragraph) have previously been chargeable by reference to the value of the assets of the fund or scheme on one or more occasions on or after 6th April 2006, the protected amount is what it was immediately before the occasion, or (where there has been more than one) the last occasion, on which inheritance tax would have been so chargeable ("the relevant tax occasion"), but—
     (*a*) reduced by the value of the property on which inheritance tax would have been chargeable on the relevant tax occasion, and
     (*b*) subject to the adjustments provided by sub-paragraph (6).
(6) The adjustments are—
     (*a*) an increase by the percentage by which the retail prices index for the month of September immediately preceding the time in question is greater than that for the month in which the relevant tax occasion fell, and
     (*b*) a reduction by the amount of any [relevant][1] payments made under the fund or scheme since the relevant tax occasion.
(7) "Relevant payments" are payments other than—
     (*a*) payments of costs or expenses, or
     (*b*) payments which are (or will be) income of any person for any of the purposes of income tax.

Amendments—[1]   In sub-para (6)(*b*), word inserted by FA 2005 s 101, Sch 10 paras 58(3), 64(1) with effect from 6 April 2006.

ENERGY ACT 2004

(2004 Chapter 20)

ARRANGEMENT OF SECTIONS

Part 1: The Civil Nuclear Industry
Chapter 1: Nuclear Decommissioning
Financial provisions
21   Financial responsibilities of NDA
22   Expenditure and receipts of NDA
23   Borrowing by the NDA
24   Limit on NDA borrowing
25   Government guarantees for NDA borrowing
26   Accounts of NDA
27   Tax exemption for NDA activities
28   Taxation of NDA activities chargeable under miscellaneous provisions
29   Disregard for tax purposes of cancellation etc of provisions
30   Disregard for tax purposes of provisions recognised by NDA
Chapter 2: Transfers Relating to Nuclear Undertakings
Transfer by scheme of property etc
38   Nuclear transfer schemes
39   Transfers of publicly owned assets
40   Transfers with the consent of the transferor
41   Recovery of property from private ownership
42   Transfer of Nuclear Liabilities Investment Portfolio
Extinguishment of undertakings and tax losses
43   Undertakings given by the Secretary of State
44   Extinguishment of BNFL losses for tax purposes
Provisions relating to transfers
45   Further provision applying to transferee companies
46   Pensions
47   Taxation
48   Supplementary powers of the Secretary of State, the NDA and the UKAEA
Part 2: Sustainability and Renewable Energy Sources
Chapter 2: Offshore Production of Energy
Renewable Energy Zones
86   Prosecutions
Part 4: Miscellaneous and Supplemental
198   Short title, commencement and extent
Schedules:
Schedule 4—Supplemental Taxation Provisions for Exempt Activities
Schedule 9—Taxation Provisions Relating to Nuclear Transfer Schemes

An Act to make provision for the decommissioning and cleaning up of installations and sites used for, or contaminated by, nuclear activities; to make provision relating to the civil nuclear industry; to make provision about radioactive waste; to make provision for the development, regulation and encouragement of the use of renewable energy sources; to make further provision in connection with the regulation of the gas and electricity industries; to make provision for the imposition of charges in connection with the carrying out of the Secretary of State's functions relating to energy matters; to make provision for giving effect to international agreements relating to pipelines and offshore installations; and for connected purposes.

[22nd July 2004]

PART 1
THE CIVIL NUCLEAR INDUSTRY

CHAPTER 1
NUCLEAR DECOMMISSIONING
Financial provisions

21 Financial responsibilities of NDA

(1) The NDA's responsibility for securing—

    (*a*) the decommissioning or operation of an installation or facility to which this section applies, or

    (*b*) the cleaning-up of a site to which this section applies, or of a related site,

includes the financial responsibility for the decommissioning or operation of the installation or facility, or for the cleaning-up.

(2) This section applies to an installation, site or facility which becomes a designated installation, site or facility at a time when the person with control of it is—

    (*a*) a Crown appointee;

    (*b*) the UKAEA;

    (*c*) a wholly-owned subsidiary of the UKAEA;

    (*d*) any other publicly owned company which was so owned on 4th July 2002; or

    (*e*) a wholly-owned subsidiary of such a company.

(3) Where—

    (*a*) the NDA has financial responsibility for decommissioning, operating or cleaning up an installation, site or facility, and

    (*b*) a person other than the NDA is the person with control of it,

that other person is not to be, or to be capable of becoming, liable to meet any of the costs of doing the things that are required to be secured by the NDA in the discharge of its responsibilities in relation to that installation, site or facility.

(4) Accordingly, where the NDA has the financial responsibility in the case of an installation, site or facility—

    (*a*) it must not impose charges on the person with control of the installation, site or facility in respect of anything mentioned in subsection (3);

    (*b*) it must meet the costs of the doing by that person of anything that he is authorised or required to do by virtue of section 17;

    (*c*) it must also meet the costs of the performance by him of his duty to comply with directions under section 18; and

    (*d*) that person is not to be required for any purpose to make, or to continue to make, financial provision for meeting costs which fall, by virtue of its financial responsibility, to be met by the NDA.

(5) Nothing in so much of this section as—

    (*a*) restricts the extent to which a person is, or may become, liable to meet any costs in relation to a site, installation or facility, or

    (*b*) requires any costs in relation to an installation, site or facility to be reimbursed or otherwise met by the NDA,

is to be construed as restricting the extent to which the person with control of the installation, site or facility may be or become subject, in relation to a person other than the NDA, to the liability or obligation in respect of which the costs arise.

(6) It shall be the duty of the NDA for the purpose of discharging its financial responsibilities to make all such arrangements as it thinks fit for securing that the person with control of the installation, site or facility is able to meet, as they become due, all his liabilities to persons other than the NDA in respect of matters for which the NDA has financial responsibility or that those liabilities are otherwise discharged.

(7) It shall also be the duty of the NDA to make all such arrangements as it thinks fit for securing that amounts paid under this section to that person include such sums (if any) as the NDA considers it appropriate to pay by way of incentives to that person to discharge his duty to comply with directions under section 18 in the manner that the NDA thinks most effective.

(8) The NDA is to be taken to have discharged its responsibility for meeting costs under this section if it is satisfied that those costs—

    (*a*) have been met by another person directly or indirectly out of money provided by Parliament; or

    (*b*) are to be so met.

(9) The preceding provisions of this section have effect in relation to an installation, site or facility subject to the terms of—

    (*a*) any agreement between the NDA and the person with control of the installation, site or facility; or

    (*b*) any agreement between the NDA and a body corporate of which that person is a subsidiary.

(10) The NDA's financial responsibilities under this section are in addition to its financial responsibilities apart from this section.

(11) In this section "related site" has the same meaning as in section 18.

22 Expenditure and receipts of NDA

(1) The Secretary of State may make grants to the NDA.

(2) Grants made under this section are to be on such terms as the Secretary of State may determine.

(3) The NDA must pay to the Secretary of State all sums received by it otherwise than under subsection (1).

(4) The Secretary of State must pay sums received by him under subsection (3) into the Consolidated Fund.

(5) In determining—

    (*a*) whether to make a grant under this section to the NDA, and

    (*b*) the amount of such a grant,

the Secretary of State must have regard, in particular, to the extent to which he considers that the NDA should exercise its power to make grants or loans of the kind mentioned in section 10(2)(c) in order to mitigate the effects of the cessation (whether before or after designation) of the operation of a designated installation.

23 Borrowing by the NDA

(1) The NDA has no power to borrow money except in accordance with this section.

(2) The NDA may borrow from the Secretary of State, and the Secretary of State may lend to the NDA, sums in sterling that it requires for or in connection with the carrying out of its functions.

(3) Where a loan is made to the NDA by the Secretary of State—

  (a) the loan must be repaid to him at such times and by such methods as he may determine; and

  (b) interest on the loan must be paid to him at such rates and at such times as he may determine;

and nothing in section 22(3) requires the repayment of sums received by way of such a loan otherwise than in accordance with a determination under this subsection.

(4) The NDA may also borrow temporarily (by overdraft or otherwise) from persons other than the Secretary of State sums in sterling that it requires for or in connection with the carrying out of its functions.

(5) The consent of the Secretary of State is required for borrowing under subsection (4).

(6) The approval of the Treasury is required—

  (a) for a loan to the NDA by the Secretary of State;

  (b) for a determination by the Secretary of State under subsection (3); and

  (c) for a consent by the Secretary of State to any borrowing under subsection (4).

(7) The powers conferred by this section are subject to section 24.

24 Limit on NDA borrowing

(1) The NDA may not borrow if the effect would be—

  (a) to take the aggregate amount mentioned in subsection (2) over its borrowing limit; or

  (b) to increase the amount by which the aggregate amount so outstanding exceeds that limit.

(2) That amount is the aggregate of—

  (a) amounts outstanding from the NDA in respect of the principal of sums borrowed by the NDA; and

  (b) the amount of every outstanding liability of the NDA that is a liability to which it is subject by virtue of a nuclear transfer scheme and is a liability in respect of the principal of a sum borrowed by another person before the transfer took effect.

(3) The NDA's borrowing limit is £2,000 million.

(4) The Secretary of State may by order increase the NDA's borrowing limit.

(5) An order under subsection (4) shall not be made unless a draft of the order has been—

  (a) laid before Parliament; and

  (b) approved by a resolution of the House of Commons.

(6) The reference in this section to a nuclear transfer scheme includes a reference to a modification agreement (within the meaning of Schedule 5) in relation to such a scheme.

25 Government guarantees for NDA borrowing

(1) The Secretary of State may guarantee—

  (a) the repayment of the principal of any sum borrowed by the NDA from a person other than the Secretary of State;

  (b) the payment of interest on such a sum; and

  (c) the discharge of any other financial obligation of the NDA in connection with the borrowing of such a sum.

(2) The Secretary of State may give a guarantee under this section in such manner, and on such terms, as he thinks fit.

(3) As soon as practicable after giving a guarantee under this section, the Secretary of State must lay a statement of the guarantee before Parliament.

(4) If sums are paid out by the Secretary of State under a guarantee given under this section, the NDA must pay him—

  (a) such amounts in or towards the repayment to him of those sums as he may direct; and

  (b) interest, at such rates as he may direct, on amounts outstanding under this subsection.

(5) Payments to the Secretary of State under subsection (4) must be made at such times, and in such manner, as he may from time to time direct.

(6) Where a sum has been paid out by the Secretary of State under a guarantee given under this section, he must lay a statement relating to that sum before Parliament—

  (a) as soon as practicable after the end of the financial year in which that sum is paid out; and

  (b) as soon as practicable after the end of each subsequent relevant financial year.

(7) In relation to a sum paid out under a guarantee, a financial year is a relevant financial year for the purposes of subsection (6) unless—

  (a) before the beginning of that year, the whole of that sum has been repaid to the Secretary of State under subsection (4); and

(b) the NDA is not at any time during that year subject to a liability to pay interest on amounts that became due under that subsection in respect of that sum.

(8) The approval of the Treasury is required—

(a) for the giving of a guarantee under this section; and

(b) for the giving by the Secretary of State of a direction under subsection (4) or (5).

(9) The Secretary of State must pay sums received by him by virtue of subsection (4) into the Consolidated Fund.

26 Accounts of NDA

(1) The NDA must—

(a) keep proper accounts and proper accounting records; and

(b) in respect of each of its accounting years, prepare a statement of its accounts.

(2) A statement of accounts prepared under this section must give a true and fair view of—

(a) the income and expenditure of the NDA for the accounting year in question; and

(b) its state of affairs.

(3) Such a statement of accounts must comply with every requirement which has been notified by the Secretary of State to the NDA.

(4) Those requirements may include, in particular, requirements relating to—

(a) the information to be contained in the statement;

(b) the manner in which that information is to be presented; or

(c) the methods and principles according to which the statement is to be prepared.

(5) The approval of the Treasury is required for the imposition of a requirement under subsection (3).

(6) The accounts of the NDA relating to each of its accounting years, including the statement of accounts prepared for the year under this section, must be audited by the Comptroller and Auditor General.

(7) The Comptroller and Auditor General must send a copy of his report on what is audited to the NDA.

(8) The NDA must send to the Secretary of State and to the Scottish Ministers, in respect of each of its accounting years—

(a) a copy of the accounts for that year that are required to be audited under this section; and

(b) a copy of the Comptroller and Auditor General's report on those accounts.

(9) The NDA must comply with any directions given to it by the Secretary of State about the times by which it must have complied with its obligations under subsections (1)(b), (6) and (8).

(10) The Secretary of State must lay a copy of whatever is sent to him under subsection (8) before Parliament.

(11) The Scottish Ministers must lay a copy of whatever is sent to them under subsection (8) before the Scottish Parliament.

(12) In this section—

"accounting records" includes all books, papers and other records of the NDA relating to—

(a) the accounts which it is required to keep; or

(b) matters dealt with in those accounts;

"accounting year", in relation to the NDA, means—

(a) the NDA's first accounting year; or

(b) a financial year after the end of the NDA's first accounting year;

"the NDA's first accounting year" means—

(a) where the NDA is established at the beginning of a financial year, that financial year; and

(b) in any other case, the period which begins with the day on which the NDA is established and ends—

(i) if no direction is given under sub-paragraph (ii), with 31st March in the financial year current on that day; and

(ii) if the Secretary of State so directs, with 31st March at the end of the following financial year.

27 Tax exemption for NDA activities

(1) For the purposes of corporation tax—

(a) trading income arising or accruing to the NDA or an NDA company from the carrying on of exempt activities shall be disregarded in computing the total profits of the NDA or that company; and

(b) trading losses incurred by the NDA or an NDA company in the carrying on of exempt activities shall be disregarded in determining the amounts that may be[—

(i) relieved under section 37, 45, 45A, 45B or 45F of the Corporation Tax Act 2010 (relief for trading losses),

(ii) surrendered under Part 5 of that Act (group relief), or

(iii) surrendered under Part 5A of that Act (group relief for carried-forward losses).][3]

(2) Schedule 4 (which makes further provision for the purposes of the exemption granted by this section) has effect.

(3) Activities are exempt for the purposes of this section and Schedule 4 if they—

(a) are activities carried on in connection with anything mentioned in section 3(1); and

(b) are specified for the purposes of this section in regulations made by the Treasury.

(4) In this section and Schedule 4 "NDA company" means—

(a) a company the whole of the ordinary share capital in which is owned directly or indirectly by the NDA; or

(b) a company that is a relevant site licensee.

(5) A company is a relevant site licensee for the purposes of subsection (4) if—

(a) it is not a company falling within paragraph (a) of that subsection;

(b) it holds a nuclear site licence for a site the whole or part of which is either a designated site or a site in or on which there is a designated installation or designated facility;

(c) in a case where there is in force a management contract relating to the whole or a part of the site to which that licence relates, or to an installation or facility in or on that site, the parties to the contract include either—

(i) the company in question; or

(ii) a company which owns directly or indirectly at least 90 per cent of the ordinary share capital of that company; and

(d) such further conditions that are required by regulations made by the Treasury to be satisfied have been satisfied.

(6) The concurrence of the Secretary of State is required for the making of any regulations under this section by the Treasury.

(7) A statutory instrument containing regulations under this section shall be subject to annulment in pursuance of a resolution of the House of Commons.

(8) In this section—

"management contract" means a contract between the NDA and another person under which the other person is required to do or secure anything that the NDA is required to secure for the purpose of discharging its responsibilities;

"owned directly or indirectly" has the same meaning as in [Chapter 3 of Part 24 of the Corporation Tax Act 2010][2] (subsidiaries), and "owns directly or indirectly" is to be construed accordingly;

"trading income", in relation to the NDA or an NDA company, means (subject to subsection (9)) income which falls or (apart from this section) would fall to be included—

(a) in respect of a trade [carried on wholly or partly in the United Kingdom][1], and

(b) as chargeable to tax under [Chapter 2 of Part 3 of the Corporation Tax Act 2009][1],

in the total profits for the purposes of corporation tax of the NDA or that company;

"trading losses", in relation to the NDA or an NDA company, means losses incurred in a trade [carried on wholly or partly in the United Kingdom][1] in respect of which the NDA or that company is or (apart from this section) would be within the charge to corporation tax under [Chapter 2 of Part 3 of the Corporation Tax Act 2009][1].

(9) For the purposes of this section income consisting in—

(a) anything giving rise to a credit that would fall to be brought into account for the purposes of [Part 5 of the Corporation Tax Act 2009][1] (loan relationships), or

(b) a credit falling to be brought into account [in accordance with Part 7 of the Corporation Tax Act 2009 (derivative contracts)][1],

is to be treated as trading income accruing to the NDA or an NDA company from the carrying on of exempt activities to the extent only that it would fall (apart from this section) to be taken into account as trading income from a trade consisting in the carrying on of such activities by the NDA or that company.

(10) This section and Schedule 4 are to be construed as one with the Corporation Tax Acts.

Regulations—Energy Act 2004 (Nuclear Decommissioning) (Exempt Activities and Further Conditions) Regulations, SI 2005/644.

Amendment—[1] In sub-s (8), in definition of "trading income", in para (a) words inserted, and in para (b) words substituted for words "Case I of Schedule D", in definition of "trading losses", in para (a) words inserted, and in para (b) words substituted for words "Case I of Schedule D", in sub-s (9)(a) words substituted for words "Chapter 2 of Part 4 of the Finance Act 1996 (c 8)", and in sub-s (9)(b) words substituted for words "under Schedule 26 to the Finance Act 2002 (c 23) (derivative contracts)", by CTA 2009 s 1322, Sch 1 paras 582, 583. CTA 2009 applies for accounting periods ending on or after 1 April 2009 (for corporation tax purposes) and for tax years 2009–10 onwards (for income and capital gains tax purposes).

[2] In sub-s (8), in definition of "owned directly or indirectly", words substituted for words "section 838 of the Income and Corporation Taxes Act 1988 (c 1)" by CTA 2010 s 1177, Sch 1 paras 433, 434. CTA 2010 has effect for corporation tax purposes for accounting periods ending on or after 1 April 2010, and for income and capital gains tax purposes for the tax year 2010–11 and subsequent tax years.

[3] In sub-s (1)(b), words substituted by F(No 2)A 2017 s 18, Sch 4 para 127 with effect in relation to accounting periods beginning on or after 1 April 2017, subject to transitional provisions in Sch 4 para 194. For accounting periods beginning before 1 April 2017 and ending on or after that date ("straddling periods") see F(No 2)A 2017 Sch 4 paras 190–192.

28 Taxation of NDA activities chargeable under [miscellaneous provisions]¹

(1) For the purposes of the Corporation Tax Acts so much of any activity of the NDA as—

    (*a*) is an activity the profits and gains from which would (apart from this section) be chargeable to tax [under or by virtue of any provision to which [section 1173 of the Corporation Tax Act 2010]² (miscellaneous charges) applies]¹, and

    (*b*) is not excluded from the operation of this section by subsection (2),

shall be treated as an activity carried on by it as part of a trade in respect of which it is within the charge to tax under [Chapter 2 of Part 3 of the Corporation Tax Act 2009]¹.

(2) Any activity is excluded from the operation of this section if—

    (*a*) it is carried on by the NDA otherwise than in connection with something mentioned in section 3(1)(*a*), (*d*) or (*e*) of this Act; and

    (*b*) the profits and gains from it would, in the NDA's case, be chargeable to tax [under or by virtue of a provision to which [section 1173 of the Corporation Tax Act 2010]² applies, other than section 979 of the Corporation Tax Act 2009 (income not otherwise charged).]¹

(3) All activities treated under this section as carried on by the NDA as part of a trade—

    (*a*) shall be treated as carried on as part of the same trade; and

    (*b*) may be treated as carried on as part of another trade carried on by the NDA.

(4) Subsection (3) is subject to any other provision made by or under the Corporation Tax Acts that requires an activity to be treated as carried on as part of a separate trade (with or without any other activity).

(5) This section is to be construed as one with the Corporation Tax Acts.

Amendment—¹   In sub-s (1)(*a*) words substituted for words "under Case VI of Schedule D", in words after sub-s (1)(*b*) words substituted for words "Case I of Schedule D", in sub-s (2)(*b*) words substituted for words "under Case VI of Schedule D by virtue of an enactment other than just section 18 of the Income and Corporation Taxes Act 1988 (c 1)", and in the title words substituted for words "Case VI of Schedule D", by CTA 2009 s 1322, Sch 1 paras 582, 584. CTA 2009 applies for accounting periods ending on or after 1 April 2009 (for corporation tax purposes) and for tax years 2009–10 onwards (for income and capital gains tax purposes).

²   In sub-ss (1)(*a*), (2)(*b*) words "section 834A of the Income and Corporation Taxes Act 1988" substituted by CTA 2010 s 1177, Sch 1 paras 433, 435. CTA 2010 has effect for corporation tax purposes for accounting periods ending on or after 1 April 2010, and for income and capital gains tax purposes for the tax year 2010–11 and subsequent tax years.

29 Disregard for tax purposes of cancellation etc of provisions

(1) This section applies where—

    (*a*) a relevant provision is recognised in the accounts of a [BNFL company]¹ in accordance with generally accepted accounting practice;

    [(*b*) that provision—

        (i) relates to decommissioning or cleaning-up which the NDA acquires or has acquired responsibility for securing by virtue of a direction under section 3, but

        (ii) is not provision recognised in order to reflect the terms or effect of a management contract between the company and the NDA;

    and]¹

    [(*c*) the responsibility referred to in paragraph (*b*)(i)—

        (i) includes the financial responsibility under section 21, or

        (ii) would do so but for the fact that the amount of the financial responsibility is for the time being subject to a limit imposed by a capping agreement.]¹

(2) In computing the profits, gains or losses of the company for the purposes of corporation tax, no amount shall be brought into account in respect of a credit or debit to which subsection (3) applies.

[(3) This subsection applies to a credit or debit if it arises from—

    (*a*) the recognition in the accounts of the company for a relevant period beginning on or after 1st April 2005 of—

        (i) the relevant provision, or

        (ii) an asset that, in accordance with generally accepted accounting practice, is recognised in connection with the relevant provision in order to reflect the acquisition of financial responsibility referred to in subsection (1) (a "matching asset");

    (*b*) an adjustment made in the accounts of the company for such a period of—

        (i) the relevant provision, or

        (ii) a matching asset;

    or

    (*c*) the removal from the accounts of the company for such a period of—

        (i) the relevant provision,

        (ii) a matching asset, or

        (iii) an asset or liability recognised in order to reflect the terms or effect of a contract falling within subsection (3A).]¹

[(3A) A contract falls within this subsection if—

(a) it is a contract made before 1st April 2005 and having effect between two or more BNFL companies under which a party to the contract assumed responsibility for securing decommissioning or cleaning-up; and

(b) the rights and obligations under the contract are extinguished by reason of a transfer made under a nuclear transfer scheme.][1]

. . .[1]

(5) In this section—

["BNFL company" means—

(a) BNFL,

(b) a company that immediately before 1st April 2005 was a wholly-owned subsidiary of BNFL, or

(c) a wholly-owned subsidiary of a company falling within paragraph (b);][1]

["capping agreement" means an agreement under subsection (9) of section 21, entered into on 1st April 2005, the sole or main effect of which is to impose a limit on the NDA's financial responsibility under that section;][1]

["management contract" has the same meaning as in section 27;][1]

["relevant period", in relation to a company, means an accounting period during the whole of which the company is publicly owned;][1]

"relevant provision" means [any amount retained as reasonably necessary for the purposes of providing for any liability or loss which is either likely to be incurred, or certain to be incurred but uncertain as to amount or as to the date on which it will arise][2].

[(5A) Where a company ceases to be publicly owned otherwise than at the end of an accounting period—

(a) the accounting period during which it ceases to be publicly owned is treated for the purposes of corporation tax as ending when it so ceases; and

(b) its profits and losses are to be computed accordingly for those purposes.][1]

(6) This section is to be construed as one with the Corporation Tax Acts.

Amendments—[1]   Words in sub-s (1)(a) substituted for words "relevant company"; sub-s (1)(b), (c) substituted; sub-ss (3), (3A) substituted for sub-ss (3), (4); in sub-s (5) definition of "BNFL company" substituted; definitions of "capping agreement" and "management contract" inserted; definition of "relevant company" substituted; sub-s (5A) inserted; by FA 2006 s 99 with effect in relation to accounting periods of a BNFL company ending on or after 22 March 2006.

[2]   In sub-s (5), words in definition of "relevant provision" substituted by the Companies Act 2006 (Consequential Amendments etc) Order, SI 2008/948 art 3(1), Sch 1 para 227 with effect from 6 April 2008.

30 Disregard for tax purposes of provisions recognised by NDA

(1) This section applies where—

(a) by virtue of a direction under section 3 the NDA acquires the responsibility for securing the cleaning-up of a site falling within subsection (2), or the decommissioning of an installation or facility in or on such a site;

[(b) that responsibility—

(i) includes the financial responsibility under section 21, or

(ii) would do so but for the fact that the amount of the financial responsibility is for the time being subject to a limit imposed by a capping agreement;][1]

(c) . . .[1] the NDA recognises in its accounts, in accordance with generally accepted accounting practice, a relevant provision that relates to that responsibility[; and

(d) the provision is recognised—

(i) in order to reflect the coming into force of the direction mentioned in paragraph (a), or

(ii) in consequence of the variation or removal of a limit on the NDA's financial responsibility under section 21 imposed by a capping agreement.][1]

(2) A site falls within this subsection if—

(a) at the time the direction mentioned in subsection (1)(a) comes into force there is a nuclear site licence in force in relation to the site; and

(b) the holder of that licence at that time is a BNFL company that is publicly owned.

[(3) In computing the profits, gains or losses of the NDA for the purposes of corporation tax, no amount shall be brought into account in connection with—

(a) the recognition made in the accounts of the NDA of—

(i) the relevant provision, or

(ii) an asset that, in accordance with generally accepted accounting practice, is recognised in order to reflect a limit on the NDA's financial responsibility under section 21 imposed by a capping agreement;

(b) any adjustment made in those accounts (including the removal from the accounts of an asset falling within paragraph (a)(ii)) in consequence of a variation or removal of the limit mentioned in paragraph (a)(ii).][1]

(4) But subsection (3) shall not affect the amount (if any) to be brought into account in computing the profits, gains or losses of the NDA in connection with [an adjustment not falling within paragraph (b) of that subsection][1].

(5) In this section—

"BNFL company" means BNFL or a wholly-owned subsidiary of BNFL;

["capping agreement" has the same meaning as in section 29;][1]

"relevant provision" means [any amount retained as reasonably necessary for the purposes of providing for any liability or loss which is either likely to be incurred, or certain to be incurred but uncertain as to amount or as to the date on which it will arise][2].

(6) This section is to be construed as one with the Corporation Tax Acts.

Amendments—[1]   Sub-s (1)(b) substituted; in sub-s (1)(c) words repealed; sub-s (1)(d) inserted; sub-s (3) substituted; words in sub-s (4) substituted; and in sub-s (5), definition of "capping agreement" inserted; by FA 2006 ss 100, 178, Sch 26 Pt 3(18) with effect in relation to accounting periods of a Nuclear Decommissioning Authority ending on or after 22 March 2006.
[2]   In sub-s (5), words in definition of "relevant provision" substituted by the Companies Act 2006 (Consequential Amendments etc) Order, SI 2008/948 art 3(1), Sch 1 para 227 with effect from 6 April 2008.

CHAPTER 2

TRANSFERS RELATING TO NUCLEAR UNDERTAKINGS

Transfer by scheme of property etc

38 Nuclear transfer schemes

(1) The Secretary of State may make a scheme providing for one or more transfers authorised by this Chapter (a "nuclear transfer scheme").

(2) Nothing in this Chapter authorises the transfer in accordance with a nuclear transfer scheme of a nuclear site licence.

(3) Before making—

    (a) a nuclear transfer scheme which transfers property, rights or liabilities to or from the NDA or a subsidiary of the NDA, or

    (b) a nuclear transfer scheme not falling within paragraph (a) which he is proposing to make for purposes connected with the carrying out of the NDA's functions,

the Secretary of State must consult the NDA.

(4) Before making a nuclear transfer scheme which transfers property, rights or liabilities to any person—

    (a) from BNFL, or

    (b) from a wholly-owned subsidiary of BNFL,

the Secretary of State must consult BNFL.

(5) Before making a nuclear transfer scheme that transfers property, rights or liabilities to any person—

    (a) from the UKAEA, or

    (b) from a wholly-owned subsidiary of the UKAEA,

the Secretary of State must consult the UKAEA.

(6) The consent of the Treasury is required for the making of a nuclear transfer scheme.

(7) A nuclear transfer scheme shall come into force at such time as the Secretary of State may appoint, whether in the scheme or subsequently.

(8) Schedule 5 (which makes further provision about nuclear transfer schemes) has effect.

39 Transfers of publicly owned assets

(1) A nuclear transfer scheme may provide for a transfer to—

    (a) a publicly owned company,

    (b) the NDA, or

    (c) a consenting person,

of property, rights and liabilities falling within subsection (2) that are set out in the scheme.

(2) The property, rights and liabilities that may be transferred are—

    (a) securities of BNFL;

    (b) securities of a company falling within subsection (3);

    (c) property, rights and liabilities of BNFL or the UKAEA;

    (d) property, rights and liabilities of a company falling within subsection (3);

    (e) property, rights and liabilities of a wholly-owned subsidiary of BNFL, of the UKAEA or of a company falling within that subsection.

(3) A company falls within this subsection if—

    (a) it is a nuclear company that is publicly owned; or

    (b) it is a company designated for the purposes of this section by an order made by the Secretary of State.

(4) The Secretary of State may designate a company for the purposes of this section only if it is a publicly owned company to which—

    (a) securities of BNFL,

    (b) property, rights or liabilities of BNFL, or

    (c) property, rights or liabilities of a wholly-owned subsidiary of BNFL, were transferred (whether in accordance with a nuclear transfer scheme or otherwise) at a time when both the company and BNFL were publicly owned.

(5) The Secretary of State must lay a copy of every order under subsection (3) before Parliament.

(6) Nothing in this section authorises—

    (*a*) a transfer of securities of BNFL, or

    (*b*) a transfer of property, rights or liabilities of BNFL or of a wholly-owned subsidiary of BNFL,

at a time when BNFL is no longer publicly owned.

(7) Nothing in this section authorises—

    (*a*) a transfer of securities of a company designated for the purposes of this section, or

    (*b*) a transfer of property, rights or liabilities of such a company or of a wholly-owned subsidiary of such a company,

at a time when the company is no longer publicly owned.

(8) Schedule 6 (which makes provision about the structure etc of publicly owned companies to which transfers are made that are authorised by this section) has effect.

(9) For the purposes of this section a person is a consenting person, in relation to a nuclear transfer scheme, if he has consented to the provisions of the scheme so far as they relate to him.

40 Transfers with the consent of the transferor

(1) A nuclear transfer scheme may provide for a transfer to—

    (*a*) a publicly owned company, or

    (*b*) the NDA,

of property, rights and liabilities falling within subsection (3) that are set out in the scheme.

(2) But property, rights and liabilities may be transferred by virtue of this section only if the person who is entitled or subject to them has consented to their transfer in accordance with a nuclear transfer scheme.

(3) The property, rights and liabilities that may be transferred are—

    (*a*) securities of a nuclear company that is not publicly owned;

    (*b*) property and rights of such a company in or in relation to a nuclear site or an installation in or on such a site; or

    (*c*) property, rights and liabilities to which such a company is entitled or subject—

        (i) in respect of such a site or installation;

        (ii) in connection with or by reference to activities carried on in or on such a site or installation; or

        (iii) for purposes connected with that site or installation or with any such activities.

(4) In subsection (3) references to the property, rights and liabilities of a company, or to which a company is entitled or subject, include references to the property, rights and liabilities of any of its wholly-owned subsidiaries.

41 Recovery of property from private ownership

(1) This section applies in the case of a nuclear company ("the transferred company") all the shares in which were transferred for the purposes of a management contract to the contractor or to a subsidiary of the contractor where—

    (*a*) the contractor is in breach of that contract; or

    (*b*) that contract has come to an end, whether by the expiry of the period for which it was in force or otherwise.

(2) A nuclear transfer scheme may provide for the transfer to—

    (*a*) a publicly owned company,

    (*b*) the NDA, or

    (*c*) a consenting contractor,

of the property, rights and liabilities falling within subsection (3) that are set out in the scheme.

(3) The property, rights and liabilities that may be transferred are—

    (*a*) securities of the transferred company (whether transferred as mentioned in subsection (1) or issued afterwards);

    (*b*) property, rights and liabilities to which the transferred company was entitled or subject immediately before the transfer so mentioned;

    (*c*) property, rights and liabilities transferred for the purposes of the management contract, to the contractor, to a subsidiary of the contractor or to the transferred company or a wholly-owned subsidiary of the transferred company;

    (*d*) property, rights and liabilities to which the transferred company or a wholly-owned subsidiary of the transferred company first became entitled or subject while that contract was in force.

(4) Subsection (3) does not apply to property, rights or liabilities to the extent that they have been excluded from that subsection by—

    (*a*) provision contained in an agreement between the NDA and the person entitled to or subject to them; or

    (*b*) provision contained in a nuclear transfer scheme by virtue of which the property, rights and liabilities or the shares mentioned in subsection (1) were vested in any person.

(5) A transfer is authorised by this section notwithstanding that what is transferred has ceased, before the transfer, to be the property or a right or liability—

    (*a*) of a person to whom anything was transferred for the purposes of the management contract mentioned in subsection (1);

    (*b*) of the transferred company or of a wholly-owned subsidiary of that company; or

    (*c*) in the case of securities issued after the transfer mentioned in that subsection, of the person to whom they were issued.

(6) Nothing in this section authorises the transfer of property, rights or liabilities from a company at a time when it is publicly owned.

(7) For the purposes of this section a person is a consenting contractor, in relation to a nuclear transfer scheme, if—

    (*a*) he is a contractor under a management contract other than the one that has been broken or come to an end; and

    (*b*) he has consented to the provisions of the scheme so far as they relate to him.

(8) In this section—

"contractor", in relation to a management contract, means a party to the contract who is not the NDA;

"management contract" means a contract between the NDA and another person under which the other person is required to do or secure anything that the NDA is required to secure for the purpose of discharging its responsibilities; and

"transferred", in relation to shares, property, rights or liabilities, means transferred in accordance with a nuclear transfer scheme.

42 Transfer of Nuclear Liabilities Investment Portfolio

(1) A nuclear transfer scheme may provide for the transfer from BNFL to the Secretary of State of—

    (*a*) the Nuclear Liabilities Investment Portfolio; or

    (*b*) so much of that Portfolio as may be specified in the scheme.

(2) Nothing in this section authorises a transfer at a time when BNFL is no longer publicly owned.

(3) Where cash is transferred to the Secretary of State by a transfer authorised by this section, he must pay it into the Consolidated Fund.

(4) Where the Secretary of State receives—

    (*a*) sums by way of income on property or rights transferred to him by a transfer authorised by this section, or

    (*b*) sums in respect of the disposal of any such property or rights,

he must pay those sums into the Consolidated Fund.

(5) The Secretary of State must comply with every direction given to him by the Treasury with respect to—

    (*a*) the disposal of property or rights transferred to him by a transfer authorised by this section; or

    (*b*) the exercise of any other right attached to, or arising in respect of, such property;

and (in a case where there is no applicable direction) the Secretary of State must not dispose of or exercise any property or rights with respect to which he may be given a direction except with the consent of the Treasury.

(6) In this section "the Nuclear Liabilities Investment Portfolio" means property and rights to which BNFL is entitled and which appear to the Secretary of State, from BNFL's published accounts, to represent assets held by BNFL for the purpose of being able to meet costs or liabilities for which the NDA has a financial responsibility under Chapter 1 of this Part.

Extinguishment of undertakings and tax losses

43 Undertakings given by the Secretary of State

(1) This section applies where—

    (*a*) the Secretary of State has given an undertaking to a publicly owned company to make payments to that company or a subsidiary of that company; and

    (*b*) it appears to him that (apart from section 21(8)) the financial responsibilities of the NDA under Chapter 1 of this Part would make it unnecessary for those amounts to be paid.

(2) The Secretary of State may extinguish the undertaking, and every liability of his that has arisen under the undertaking, with effect from such date as he may notify to the other parties to it.

(3) Nothing in this section authorises the extinguishment of an undertaking at a time when the company to whom payments would fall to be made under the undertaking is not publicly owned.

(4) The extinguishment of an undertaking under this section shall neither require nor enable any sum to be brought into account in any person's case for the purposes of corporation tax.

(5) In this section "undertaking" includes any agreement in which an undertaking to make payments is contained.

44 Extinguishment of BNFL losses for tax purposes

(1) In relation to accounting periods beginning on or after the trigger date, all the relevant losses of every BNFL company arising before that date shall be treated for the purposes of corporation tax as extinguished.

(2) The following are relevant losses of a BNFL company for the purposes of this section—

    (*a*) losses incurred by the company in a trade;

    (*b*) losses incurred by the company in a transaction a profit or gain from which would have been chargeable to tax [under or by virtue of any provision to which [section 1173 of the Corporation Tax Act 2010]² (miscellaneous charges) applies]¹;

    (*c*) excesses to be carried forward in the company's case under [section 1223 of the Corporation Tax Act 2009 (carrying forward expenses of management and other amounts)]¹;

    [(*d*) losses incurred by the company in carrying on a UK property business (within the meaning given by Chapter 2 of Part 4 of the Corporation Tax Act 2009);]²

    (*e*) losses to be carried forward in the company's case under [section 66 of the Corporation Tax Act 2010]²;

    [(*f*) any Type 4 carry-forward losses of the company falling within section 95(1) of the Corporation Tax Act 2010;]²

    (*g*) allowable losses (within the meaning of section 8 of the Taxation of Chargeable Gains Act 1992 (c 12)) that have accrued to the company;

    (*h*) deficits of the kind mentioned in [section 456(1) of the Corporation Tax Act 2009]¹ to the extent that they are to be carried forward in the company's case under [section 457(1) of that Act]¹;

    (*i*) excesses of the kind mentioned in section 260 of the Capital Allowances Act 2001 (c 2) in relation to the company;

    (*j*) losses of the kind mentioned in paragraph 35(1) of Schedule 29 to the Finance Act 2002 (c 23) incurred by the company;

    (*k*) unrelieved surplus advance corporation tax of the company (within the meaning of section 32 of the Finance Act 1998 (c 36)).

(3) This section applies to the relevant losses of a BNFL company only if it is publicly owned on the day before the trigger date.

(4) In this section—

    "BNFL company" means—

        (*a*) BNFL;

        (*b*) a company that is a 75 per cent subsidiary of BNFL at a time during the qualifying period; or

        (*c*) a company (other than BNFL) that is a 75 per cent subsidiary of a BNFL parent company at a time during the qualifying period;

    "BNFL parent company" means a company of which BNFL is a 75 per cent subsidiary;

    "qualifying period" means the period beginning with 16th March 2004 and ending with the trigger date;

    "trigger date" means whichever is the earlier of the following—

        (*a*) the date of the first occasion on which section 21 operates so as to confer financial responsibilities on the NDA in relation to an installation, site or facility the person with control of which is a BNFL company that is publicly owned; and

        (*b*) the date of the first occasion on which a transfer takes effect which is a transfer to the NDA or a subsidiary of the NDA in accordance with a nuclear transfer scheme authorised by section 39 of property, rights or liabilities of a BNFL company.

(5) This section is to be construed as one with the Corporation Tax Acts.

Amendments—¹ In sub-s (2)(*b*) words substituted for words "under Case VI of Schedule D", in sub-s (2)(*c*) words substituted for words "section 75(9) of the Income and Corporation Taxes Act 1988", and in sub-s (2)(*h*) words substituted for words "subsection (1) of section 83 of the Finance Act 1996 (c 8)" and "subsection (3A) of that section" respectively, by CTA 2009 s 1322, Sch 1 paras 582, 585. CTA 2009 applies for accounting periods ending on or after 1 April 2009 (for corporation tax purposes) and for tax years 2009–10 onwards (for income and capital gains tax purposes).

² In sub-s (2)(*b*) words "section 834A of the Income and Corporation Taxes Act 1988" substituted; sub-s (2)(*d*), (*f*)substituted; in sub-s (2)(*e*) words "section 392B(1) of that Act" substituted by CTA 2010 s 1177, Sch 1 paras 433, 436. CTA 2010 has effect for corporation tax purposes for accounting periods ending on or after 1 April 2010, and for income and capital gains tax purposes for the tax year 2010–11 and subsequent tax years.

Provisions relating to transfers

45 Further provision applying to transferee companies

(1) Schedule 7 (which makes provision about the finances and accounts of publicly controlled companies to which property, rights and liabilities are transferred) has effect.

(2) In Part 3 of Schedule 1 to the House of Commons Disqualification Act 1975 (c 24) (other disqualifying offices), insert (at the appropriate place)—

"Director of a publicly controlled company (within the meaning of Chapter 2 of Part 1 of the Energy Act 2004) to which transfers have been made in accordance with provisions of nuclear transfer schemes authorised by that Chapter.";

and the corresponding amendment shall also be made in Part 3 of Schedule 1 to the Northern Ireland Assembly Disqualification Act 1975 (c 25).

46 Pensions

Schedule 8 (which makes provision about pensions in connection with transfers affecting nuclear undertakings) has effect.

47 Taxation

Schedule 9 (which makes taxation provision in relation to nuclear transfer schemes) has effect.

48 Supplementary powers of the Secretary of State, the NDA and the UKAEA

(1) The Secretary of State shall have power to enter into agreements for the purpose of accepting or imposing such contractual obligations as he thinks fit with respect to—

    (a) nuclear transfer schemes and proposals for such schemes;

    (b) anything connected with such a scheme or proposal; or

    (c) the exercise of powers conferred on the Secretary of State or any other person by or under this Chapter.

(2) The NDA and the UKAEA shall each have power to enter into agreements for the purpose of accepting or imposing such contractual obligations as it or they think fit with respect to—

    (a) nuclear transfer schemes and proposals for such schemes;

    (b) anything connected with such a scheme or proposal; or

    (c) the exercise of powers conferred on it or them, or any other person, by or under this Chapter.

(3) The NDA and the UKAEA shall also each have power to do anything else which, in its or their opinion, is appropriate for facilitating—

    (a) a transfer which is or is proposed to be effected in accordance with a nuclear transfer scheme; or

    (b) any other transfer of property, rights or liabilities of the NDA or (as the case may be) the UKAEA which is or is proposed to be effected for purposes connected with the carrying out by any person of any functions conferred on that person by or under this Part.

(4) Agreements entered into in exercise of the powers conferred by subsection (1) or (2) may, in particular, include provision for the making of payments (whether by way of consideration or otherwise)—

    (a) to the Secretary of State, or

    (b) to the NDA or the UKAEA,

in respect of anything transferred or created in accordance with a nuclear transfer scheme.

(5) The consent of the Treasury is required for the Secretary of State or the UKAEA to enter into an agreement in exercise of those powers.

(6) The consent of the Secretary of State is also required for the UKAEA to enter into an agreement in exercise of those powers.

(7) Before making any disposal of securities of a company in a case in which—

    (a) the disposal is made in accordance with arrangements entered into by the UKAEA for purposes connected with the carrying out of its functions by the NDA,

    (b) those arrangements are not arrangements to which the Secretary of State has consented under subsection (6), and

    (c) in the opinion of the UKAEA, the disposal is one which they would not have power to make but for section 1(2) of the Atomic Energy (Miscellaneous Provisions) Act 1981 (c 48) (disposal otherwise inconsistent with UKAEA functions),

the UKAEA must consult the Secretary of State.

(8) Subsection (4) of section 1 of the Atomic Energy (Miscellaneous Provisions) Act 1981 (which limits the cases in which the UKAEA may make share disposals that are inconsistent with its functions) shall not apply—

    (a) to anything done by the UKAEA in exercise of powers conferred on them by or under this Chapter; or

    (b) to any disposal of securities in accordance with arrangements entered into by the UKAEA for purposes connected with the carrying out of its functions by the NDA.

(9) Sums received by the Secretary of State in pursuance of an agreement under this section must be paid into the Consolidated Fund.

(10) The powers conferred on the Secretary of State, the NDA and the UKAEA by this section—

    (a) are in addition to their powers apart from this section; and

    (b) are to be disregarded in determining the extent of those powers.

PART 2
SUSTAINABILITY AND RENEWABLE ENERGY SOURCES

CHAPTER 2
OFFSHORE PRODUCTION OF ENERGY
Renewable Energy Zones

86 Prosecutions

(1) Subject to subsection (2), this section applies to an offence alleged to have been committed on, under or above—

    (*a*) a renewable energy installation situated in waters to which section 85 applies; or

    (*b*) waters to which section 85 applies that, at the time of the alleged offence, were within a safety zone.

(2) This section does not apply to an offence created by or under—

    (*a*) the Health and Safety at Work etc Act 1974 (c 37);

    (*b*) the Customs and Excise Acts 1979, or any enactment that has to be construed as one with those Acts or any of them;

    (*c*) the Civil Aviation Act 1982 (c 16) or any enactment that has to be construed as one with that Act;

    (*d*) section 23 of the Petroleum Act 1987 (c 12);

    (*e*) the Pilotage Act 1987 (c 21);

    (*f*) section 4, 29, 35, 36, 37 or 59 of the 1989 Act, or paragraph 3 of Schedule 7 to that Act;

    (*g*) the Value Added Tax Act 1994 (c 23) or any enactment that has to be construed as one with that Act;

    (*h*) the Merchant Shipping Act 1995 (c 21);

    (*i*) section 97 of this Act or Chapter 3 of this Part.

(3) No proceedings for an offence to which this section applies shall be instituted—

    (*a*) in England and Wales, except by or with the consent of the Director of Public Prosecutions; or

    (*b*) in Northern Ireland, except by or with the consent of the Director of Public Prosecutions for Northern Ireland.

(4) Subsection (3) does not require the consent of the Director of Public Prosecutions, or of the Director of Public Prosecutions for Northern Ireland, where the proceedings in question are proceedings for which the consent of the Attorney General, or of the Advocate General for Northern Ireland, is required apart from this section.

(5) In relation to times before the coming into force of section 27(1) of the Justice (Northern Ireland) Act 2002 (c 26), the reference in subsection (4) to the Advocate General for Northern Ireland is to be read as a reference to the Attorney General for Northern Ireland.

(6) Section 3 of the Territorial Waters Jurisdiction Act 1878 (c 73) (consents to prosecution of offences committed on the open sea by persons who are not British citizens) does not apply to proceedings for an offence to which this section applies.

PART 4
MISCELLANEOUS AND SUPPLEMENTAL

198 Short title, commencement and extent

(1) This Act may be cited as the Energy Act 2004.

(2) This Act (apart from this section) shall come into force on such day as the Secretary of State may by order appoint; and different days may be appointed for different purposes.

(3) Subject to subsection (4) of this section, this Act extends to Northern Ireland.

(4) The following provisions of this Act do not extend to Northern Ireland—

    (*a*) Chapter 3 of Part 1 (with the exception of section 59 and paragraphs 1, 5, 6, 8, 10(1) and (2) and 11 of Schedule 14);

    (*b*) so much of Part 2 as amends the 1989 Act;

    (*c*) sections 82, 90, 91 and 100; and

    (*d*) Part 3 (with the exception of section 151(5)).

SCHEDULES

SCHEDULE 4

SUPPLEMENTAL TAXATION PROVISIONS FOR EXEMPT ACTIVITIES

Section 27

Exempt activities to be separate trade

1 Exempt activities carried on—

(*a*) by the NDA, or

(*b*) by a company while it is an NDA company,

are to be treated for corporation tax purposes as a separate trade distinct from all other activities carried on by the NDA or (as the case may be) that company.

Accounting periods of companies carrying on exempt activities

2—(1) An accounting period of the NDA or of an NDA company ends (if it would not otherwise do so)—

(*a*) where it begins to carry on exempt activities, immediately before it begins to carry them on; and

(*b*) where it ceases to carry on such activities, immediately after it so ceases.

(2) An accounting period of a company which—

(*a*) becomes an NDA company, and

(*b*) is carrying on exempt activities immediately after becoming such a company,

ends (if it would not otherwise do so) when it becomes an NDA company.

(3) An accounting period of a company which—

(*a*) ceases to be an NDA company, and

(*b*) is carrying on exempt activities immediately before ceasing to be such a company,

ends (if it would not otherwise do so) when it ceases to be an NDA company.

Charges on income in connection with exempt activities

3   [No qualifying charitable donations made[1]]—

(*a*) by the NDA, or

(*b*) by an NDA company,

in connection with the carrying on of exempt activities are to be deductible from its total profits under [Part 6 of the Corporation Tax Act 2010][1].

Amendments—[1]   Words "No charges on income incurred" and " section 338 of the Income and Corporation Taxes Act 1988 (c 1) (deduction of charges on income)" substituted by CTA 2010 s 1177, Sch 1 paras 433, 437. CTA 2010 has effect for corporation tax purposes for accounting periods ending on or after 1 April 2010, and for income and capital gains tax purposes for the tax year 2010–11 and subsequent tax years.

Finance leasing of plant and machinery

4—(1) This paragraph applies where there is a finance lease in the case of which—

(*a*) the lessor is the NDA or an NDA company;

(*b*) the lessee is the NDA or an NDA company;

(*c*) the lessee is carrying on exempt activities; and

(*d*) the machinery or plant to which the lease relates is used by the lessee for the purposes of those activities.

(2) No allowance under Part 2 of the Capital Allowances Act 2001 (c 2) (plant and machinery allowances) shall be available to the lessor in respect of qualifying expenditure on the provision of the plant or machinery for leasing under the lease.

(3) Expressions used in this paragraph and in Chapter 17 of Part 2 of the Capital Allowances Act 2001 (anti-avoidance provisions relating to plant and machinery allowances) have the same meanings in this paragraph as in that Chapter.

SCHEDULE 9

TAXATION PROVISIONS RELATING TO NUCLEAR TRANSFER SCHEMES

Section 47

PART 1

TRANSFERS TO THE NDA OR A SUBSIDIARY OF THE NDA

Trading losses: transfer of company carrying on exempt activities

1—(1) This paragraph applies for the purposes of corporation tax where—

(*a*) in consequence of a section 39 scheme, a company which is not an NDA company becomes an NDA company falling within section 27(4)(*a*); and

(*b*) the company carried on exempt activities before the coming into force of the scheme.

(2) Trading losses attributable to the exempt activities carried on by the company before the coming into force of the scheme shall be treated, in relation to accounting periods beginning at or after that time, as extinguished.

(3) For the purpose of determining the extent to which trading losses incurred by a company are attributable to exempt activities, such apportionments of receipts, expenses, assets and liabilities shall be made as may be just.

Trading losses: transfer of undertaking carrying on exempt activities

2—(1) This paragraph applies for the purposes of corporation tax where—
   (a) a company ("the transferor company") which is not an NDA company is carrying on a trade which consists in or includes exempt activities; and
   (b) in consequence of a section 39 scheme—
      (i) the transferor company ceases to carry on that trade or a part of it which consists in or includes such activities; and
      (ii) the NDA or an NDA company begins to carry on that trade or that part of it.

(2) Trading losses attributable to so much of the trade or part of a trade as consists in exempt activities carried on by the transferor company before the time when the NDA or the NDA company begins to carry on the trade or that part of it shall be treated, in relation to accounting periods ending after that time, as extinguished.

(3) [Sections 944 and 951 to 953 of the Corporation Tax Act 2010 (transfers of trade without a change of ownership)][1] shall apply in relation to an unextinguished loss sustained by the transferor company in carrying on the trade or the part of it in question as if—
   (a) the case were a case falling within [Chapter 1 of Part 22 of that Act][1];
   (b) the transferor company were the predecessor; and
   (c) the NDA or the NDA company in question were the successor.

Amendments—[1]   In sub-para (3) words "Subsections (3), (4A), (7) to (9) and (11) of section 343 of the Taxes Act (company reconstruction without change of ownership)" substituted and in sub-para (3)(a) words "subsection (1) of that section" substituted by CTA 2010 s 1177, Sch 1 paras 433, 438(1),(2). CTA 2010 has effect for corporation tax purposes for accounting periods ending on or after 1 April 2010, and for income and capital gains tax purposes for the tax year 2010–11 and subsequent tax years.

Chargeable gains: assets to be treated as disposed without a gain or a loss

3—(1) This paragraph applies for the purposes of the 1992 Act where there is a transfer of an asset to the NDA or a subsidiary of the NDA in accordance with a section 39 scheme.

(2) The asset shall be treated as disposed of to the NDA or (as the case may be) to its subsidiary for a consideration of such amount as would secure that, on the disposal, neither a gain nor a loss accrues to the transferor.

(3) This paragraph has effect subject to paragraph 4.

(4) This paragraph does not apply in relation to a transfer to the NDA or to a subsidiary of the NDA in accordance with a nuclear transfer scheme of securities of a company, in consequence of which that company ceases to be a relevant site licensee.

(5) In this paragraph "relevant site licensee" has the same meaning as in subsection (4) of section 27 (see subsection (5)).

Chargeable gains: assets treated as acquired at nil cost

4—(1) This paragraph applies for the purposes of the 1992 Act where the NDA or a subsidiary of the NDA disposes of an asset which—
   (a) was acquired by the NDA or that subsidiary in accordance with a section 39 scheme or a section 40 scheme; and
   (b) is not an asset which, immediately before its transfer to the NDA or that subsidiary, was comprised in the Nuclear Liabilities Investment Portfolio.

(2) No amount shall be allowable as a deduction under section 38(1)(a) or (b) of the 1992 Act (acquisition and enhancement costs) in the computation of the gain accruing on the disposal.

(3) Accordingly, in a case where the disposal is one which under any enactment is treated as a disposal on which neither a gain nor a loss accrues to the NDA or its subsidiary, the consideration for the disposal shall be treated as equal to the amount allowable as a deduction from that consideration under section 38(1)(c) of the 1992 Act (incidental costs of disposal).

(4) This paragraph does not apply in the case of a disposal which under paragraph 29 is to be treated as a disposal on which neither a gain nor a loss accrues to the NDA or a subsidiary of the NDA.

Chargeable gains: degrouping charges

5—(1) This paragraph applies if a company ("the degrouped company")—
   (a) acquired an asset from another company at a time when both were members of the same group of companies ("the old group"); and
   (b) ceases, by virtue of a transfer to the NDA or a subsidiary of the NDA in accordance with a section 39 scheme, to be a member of the old group.

(2) Section 179 of the 1992 Act (company ceasing to be member of group) is not to treat the degrouped company as having by virtue of the transfer sold and immediately reacquired the asset.
(3) Where sub-paragraph (2) has applied to an asset, section 179 of the 1992 Act is to have effect on and after the first subsequent occasion on which the degrouped company ceases to be a member of a group of companies ("the new group") as if—

(a) the degrouped company, and

(b) the company from which it acquired the asset,

had been members of the new group at the time of acquisition.
(4) Expressions used in this paragraph and in section 179 of the 1992 Act have the same meanings in this paragraph as in that section.

Chargeable gains: disposal of debts

6—(1) This paragraph applies if—

(a) a debt owed to any person is transferred to the NDA or a subsidiary of the NDA in accordance with a section 39 scheme; and

(b) the transferor would (apart from this paragraph) be the original creditor in relation to that debt for the purposes of section 251 of the 1992 Act (disposal of debts).

(2) The 1992 Act is to have effect as if the NDA or (as the case may be) its subsidiary (and not the transferor) were the original creditor for those purposes.

Capital allowances: transfer of whole trade

7—(1) This paragraph applies where—

(a) a company ("the transferor company") which is not a subsidiary of the NDA is carrying on a trade; and

(b) in consequence of a section 39 scheme, the transferor company ceases to carry on that trade and the NDA or a subsidiary of the NDA begins to carry it on.

(2) For the purposes of the allowances and charges provided for by the 2001 Act, the trade is not to be treated as permanently discontinued, nor a new trade as set up; but sub-paragraphs (3) and (4) of this paragraph are to apply.
(3) There are to be made to or on the NDA or (as the case may be) its subsidiary, in accordance with the 2001 Act, all such allowances and charges as would, if the transferor company had continued to carry on the trade, have fallen to be made to or on that company.
(4) The amounts of those allowances and charges are to be computed as if—

(a) the NDA or its subsidiary had been carrying on the trade since the transferor company began to do so; and

(b) everything done to or by the transferor company had been done to or by the NDA or that subsidiary;

but so that transfers in accordance with the section 39 scheme, so far as they relate to assets in use for the purposes of the trade, shall not be treated as giving rise to an allowance or charge.

Capital allowances: transfer of part of a trade

8—(1) Where—

(a) a company ("the transferor company") which is not a subsidiary of the NDA is carrying on a trade, and

(b) in consequence of a section 39 scheme, the transferor company ceases to carry on that trade and the NDA or a subsidiary of the NDA begins to carry on activities of the trade as part of a trade carried on by the NDA or that subsidiary,

then that part of the trade carried on by the NDA or its subsidiary shall be treated for the purposes of paragraph 7 as a separate trade.
(2) Where—

(a) a company ("the transferor company") which is not a subsidiary of the NDA is carrying on a trade, and

(b) in consequence of a section 39 scheme, the transferor company ceases to carry on a part of that trade and the NDA or a subsidiary of the NDA begins to carry on activities of that part of that trade,

then the transferor company shall be treated for the purposes of paragraph 7 and sub-paragraph (1) of this paragraph as having carried on that part of its trade as a separate trade.
(3) Where activities fall to be treated for the purposes of this paragraph as a separate trade, such apportionments of receipts, expenses, assets and liabilities shall be made for the purposes of the 2001 Act as may be just.

Capital allowances: transfer of plant or machinery

9—(1) This paragraph applies where—
   (a) there is a transfer of property to the NDA or a subsidiary of the NDA in accordance with a section 39 scheme;
   (b) the property is plant or machinery; and
   (c) paragraph 7 does not apply in relation to the transfer of the plant or machinery.
(2) For the purposes of Part 2 of the 2001 Act (capital allowances for plant and machinery), the NDA or its subsidiary is to be treated—
   (a) as having incurred capital expenditure on the provision of the plant or machinery at the time of the transfer; and
   (b) as having owned the plant or machinery as a result of having incurred that expenditure.
(3) The amount of that expenditure is to be treated as being the book value of the plant or machinery.
(4) For the purposes of the application of section 61 of that Act in relation to the transferor the disposal value of the plant or machinery is to be treated as being the book value of the plant or machinery.
(5) The references in this paragraph to the book value of the plant or machinery are references to the amount which, in accordance with generally accepted accounting practice (within the meaning of the Tax Acts)—
   (a) was recognised as its value in the accounts of the transferor at the time of the transfer; or
   (b) should have been so recognised at that time.
(6) Expressions used in this paragraph and in Part 2 of the 2001 Act have the same meanings in this paragraph as in that Part.

Capital allowances: transfer not to be transaction between connected persons

10 For the purposes of Part 2 of the 2001 Act references in that Part to a transaction (however described) between connected persons (within the meaning of [section 1122 of the Corporation Tax Act 2010][1]) are not to include references to a transfer of anything in accordance with a section 39 scheme to the NDA or a subsidiary of the NDA.

Amendments—[1] Words "section 839 of the Taxes Act" substituted by CTA 2010 s 1177, Sch 1 paras 433, 438(1),(3). CTA 2010 has effect for corporation tax purposes for accounting periods ending on or after 1 April 2010, and for income and capital gains tax purposes for the tax year 2010–11 and subsequent tax years.

Continuity in relation to loan relationships

11—(1) This paragraph applies if, in consequence of a section 39 scheme, the NDA or a subsidiary of the NDA replaces a person as a party to a loan relationship.
(2) [Part 5 of the Corporation Tax Act 2009][1] is to have effect in relation to the time when the transfer takes effect and any later time as if—
   (a) the NDA or its subsidiary had been a party to the loan relationship at the time when the transferor became a party to it and at all times since that time; and
   (b) the loan relationship to which the NDA or its subsidiary is a party after the time when the transfer takes effect is the same loan relationship as that to which, by virtue of paragraph (a), it is treated as having been a party before that time.
(3) Expressions used in this paragraph and in [Part 5 of the Corporation Tax Act 2009][1] have the same meanings in this paragraph as in [that Part][1].

Amendments—[1] In sub-para (2) words substituted for words "Chapter 2 of Part 4 of the Finance Act 1996 (c 8)", and in sub-para (3) words substituted for words "Chapter 2 of Part 4 of the Finance Act 1996" and "that Chapter" respectively, by CTA 2009 s 1322, Sch 1 paras 582, 586(1), (2). CTA 2009 applies for accounting periods ending on or after 1 April 2009 (for corporation tax purposes) and for tax years 2009–10 onwards (for income and capital gains tax purposes).

Continuity in relation to derivative contracts

12—(1) This paragraph applies if, in consequence of a section 39 scheme, the NDA or a subsidiary of the NDA replaces a person as a party to a derivative contract.
(2) [Part 7 of the Corporation Tax Act 2009][1] is to have effect in relation to the time when the transfer takes effect and any later time as if—
   (a) the NDA or its subsidiary had been a party to the derivative contract at the time when the transferor became a party to it and at all times since that time; and
   (b) the derivative contract to which the NDA or its subsidiary is a party after the time when the transfer takes effect is the same derivative contract as that to which, by virtue of paragraph (a), it is treated as having been a party before that time.
(3) Expressions used in this paragraph and in [Part 7 of the Corporation Tax Act 2009][1] have the same meanings in this paragraph as in [that Part][1].

Amendments—[1] In sub-para (2) words substituted for words "Schedule 26 to the Finance Act 2002 (c 23)", and in sub-para (3) words substituted for words "Schedule 26 to the Finance Act 2002" and "that Schedule", by CTA 2009 s 1322, Sch 1 paras 582, 586(1), (3). CTA 2009 applies for accounting periods ending on or after 1 April 2009 (for corporation tax purposes) and for tax years 2009–10 onwards (for income and capital gains tax purposes).

Continuity in relation to transfer of intangible assets

13—(1) Where—

    (*a*) property is transferred in accordance with a section 39 scheme to the NDA or a subsidiary of the NDA, and

    (*b*) the property transferred includes a chargeable intangible asset of the transferor,

the transfer of that asset is to be treated for the purposes of Schedule 29 to the Finance Act 2002 as a tax neutral transfer.

(2) Where, in the case of a transfer in accordance with a section 39 scheme of any property to the NDA or a subsidiary of the NDA—

    (*a*) the property transferred includes an asset which is not a chargeable intangible asset of the transferor, but

    (*b*) that asset falls to be treated after the transfer as a chargeable intangible asset of the NDA or its subsidiary,

that asset shall be treated as acquired by the NDA or its subsidiary for an amount equal to the amount of the consideration determined for the purposes of paragraph 3(2) of this Schedule.

(3) Expressions used in this paragraph and in Schedule 29 to the Finance Act 2002 have the same meanings in this paragraph as in that Schedule.

Chargeable intangible assets: degrouping charges

14—(1) This paragraph applies if a company ("the degrouped company")—

    (*a*) acquired an intangible fixed asset from another company at a time when both were members of the same group of companies ("the old group"); and

    (*b*) ceases by virtue of a transfer to the NDA or a subsidiary of the NDA in accordance with a section 39 scheme to be a member of the old group.

(2) Paragraph 58 of Schedule 29 to the Finance Act 2002 (company ceasing to be member of group) is not to treat the degrouped company as having, by virtue of the transfer, sold and immediately reacquired the asset.

(3) Where sub-paragraph (2) has applied to an asset, paragraph 58 of Schedule 29 to the Finance Act 2002 (c 23) is to have effect on and after the first subsequent occasion on which the degrouped company ceases to be a member of a group of companies ("the new group") as if—

    (*a*) the degrouped company, and

    (*b*) the company from which it acquired the asset,

had been members of the new group at the time of acquisition.

(4) Expressions used in this paragraph and in paragraph 58 of Schedule 29 to the Finance Act 2002 have the same meanings in this paragraph as in that paragraph.

Computation of profits and losses in respect of transfer of trade

15—(1) This paragraph applies where, in consequence of a section 39 scheme—

    (*a*) a BNFL company ceases to carry on a trade or a part of a trade; and

    (*b*) an NDA group member begins to carry on the trade or that part of it.

(2) For the purpose of computing, in relation to the time when the scheme comes into force and subsequent times, the relevant trading profits or losses of the BNFL company and the NDA group member—

    (*a*) the trade or part is to be treated as having been a separate trade at the time of its commencement and as having been carried on by the NDA group member at all times since its commencement as a separate trade; and

    (*b*) the trade carried on by the NDA group member after the time when the section 39 scheme comes into force is to be treated as the same trade as that which it is treated, by virtue of paragraph (*a*), as having carried on as a separate trade before that time.

(3) This paragraph is subject to paragraph 11.

(4) In this paragraph—

    "BNFL company" means BNFL or a subsidiary of BNFL;

    "NDA group member" means the NDA or a subsidiary of the NDA;

    "relevant trading profits and losses" means profits or losses [under Part 3 of the Corporation Tax Act 2009 in respect of the trade or part of a trade in question for periods in which the trade was carried on wholly or partly in the United Kingdom][1].

Amendments—[1]   In sub-para (4) words substituted for words "under Case I of Schedule D in respect of the trade or part of a trade in question" by CTA 2009 s 1322, Sch 1 paras 582, 586(1), (4). CTA 2009 applies for accounting periods ending on or after 1 April 2009 (for corporation tax purposes) and for tax years 2009–10 onwards (for income and capital gains tax purposes).

PART 2
TRANSFERS RELATING TO BNFL OR THE UKAEA ETC
Application of Part 2 of Schedule

16—(1) This Part of this Schedule applies to a transfer if—

(a) it is a transfer in accordance with a section 39 scheme of securities of a BNFL company or of property, rights or liabilities of a BNFL company; and

(b) the transferee is a publicly owned company which is not a subsidiary of the NDA.

(2) This Part of this Schedule also applies to a transfer if it is a transfer in accordance with a section 39 scheme to a transferee falling within sub-paragraph (3) of—

(a) property, rights or liabilities of the UKAEA;

(b) securities of a wholly-owned subsidiary of the UKAEA; or

(c) property, rights or liabilities of such a subsidiary.

(3) The transferee falls within this sub-paragraph if it is—

(a) a publicly owned company which is not a subsidiary of the NDA; or

(b) the UKAEA.

(4) In this paragraph "BNFL company" means BNFL or a wholly-owned subsidiary of BNFL.

Application of rules for reorganisations under same ownership

[**17** Where Chapter 1 of Part 22 of the Corporation Tax Act 2010 (transfers of trade without a change of ownership) applies in relation to a transfer to which this Part of this Schedule applies, that Chapter has effect in relation to the transfer with the omission of section 945.][1]

Amendments—[1] This para substituted by CTA 2010 s 1177, Sch 1 paras 433, 438(1),(4). CTA 2010 has effect for corporation tax purposes for accounting periods ending on or after 1 April 2010, and for income and capital gains tax purposes for the tax year 2010–11 and subsequent tax years.

Chargeable gains: assets to be treated as disposed without a gain or a loss

18—(1) This paragraph applies for the purposes of the 1992 Act where an asset is transferred by a transfer to which this Part of this Schedule applies.

(2) The asset shall be treated as disposed of to the transferee for a consideration of such amount as would secure that, on the disposal, neither a gain nor a loss accrues to the transferor.

Chargeable gains: degrouping charges

19—(1) This paragraph applies if a company ("the degrouped company")—

(a) acquired an asset from another company at a time when both were members of the same group of companies ("the old group"); and

(b) ceases by virtue of a transfer to which this Part of this Schedule applies to be a member of the old group.

(2) Section 179 of the 1992 Act (company ceasing to be member of group) is not to treat the degrouped company as having by virtue of the transfer sold and immediately reacquired the asset.

(3) Where sub-paragraph (2) has applied to an asset, section 179 of the 1992 Act is to have effect on and after the first subsequent occasion on which the degrouped company ceases to be a member of a group of companies ("the new group") as if—

(a) the degrouped company, and

(b) the company from which it acquired the asset,

had been members of the new group at the time of acquisition.

(4) Expressions used in this paragraph and in section 179 of the 1992 Act have the same meanings in this paragraph as in that section.

Chargeable gains: disposal of debts

20—(1) This paragraph applies if—

(a) a debt owed to any person is transferred by a transfer to which this Part of this Schedule applies; and

(b) the transferor would (apart from this paragraph) be the original creditor in relation to that debt for the purposes of section 251 of the 1992 Act (disposal of debts).

(2) The 1992 Act is to have effect as if the transferee (and not the transferor) were the original creditor for those purposes.

Capital allowances: transfer of plant or machinery

21—(1) This paragraph applies where—

(a) property transferred by a transfer to which this Part of this Schedule applies includes plant or machinery; and

(b) [Chapter 1 of Part 22 of the Corporation Tax Act 2010][1] does not apply in relation to the transfer of the plant or machinery.

(2) For the purposes of Part 2 of the 2001 Act (capital allowances for plant and machinery), the transferee is to be treated—

(a) as having incurred capital expenditure on the provision of the plant or machinery at the time of the transfer; and

(b) as having owned the plant or machinery as a result of having incurred that expenditure.

(3) The amount of that expenditure is to be treated as being the book value of the plant or machinery.

(4) For the purposes of the application of section 61 of that Act in relation to the transferor the disposal value of the plant or machinery is to be treated as being the book value of the plant or machinery.

(5) The references in this paragraph to the book value of the plant or machinery are references to the amount which, in accordance with generally accepted accounting practice (within the meaning of the Tax Acts)—

(a) was recognised as its value in the accounts of the transferor at the time of the transfer; or

(b) should have been so recognised at that time.

(6) Expressions used in this paragraph and in Part 2 of the 2001 Act have the same meanings in this paragraph as in that Part.

Amendments—[1]   In sub-para (1)(b) words "section 343 of the Taxes Act" substituted by CTA 2010 s 1177, Sch 1 paras 433, 438(1),(5). CTA 2010 has effect for corporation tax purposes for accounting periods ending on or after 1 April 2010, and for income and capital gains tax purposes for the tax year 2010–11 and subsequent tax years.

Capital allowances: transfer not to be transaction between connected persons

22   For the purposes of Part 2 of the 2001 Act references in that Part to a transaction (however described) between connected persons (within the meaning of [section 1122 of the Corporation Tax Act 2010][1]) are not to include references to a transfer to which this Part of this Schedule applies.

Amendments—[1]   Words "section 839 of the Taxes Act" substituted by CTA 2010 s 1177, Sch 1 paras 433, 438(1),(6). CTA 2010 has effect for corporation tax purposes for accounting periods ending on or after 1 April 2010, and for income and capital gains tax purposes for the tax year 2010–11 and subsequent tax years.

Continuity in relation to loan relationships

23—(1) This paragraph applies if, in consequence of a transfer to which this Part of this Schedule applies, the transferee replaces a person as a party to a loan relationship.

(2) [Part 5 of the Corporation Tax Act 2009][1] is to have effect in relation to the time when the transfer takes effect and any later time as if—

(a) the transferee had been a party to the loan relationship at the time when the transferor became a party to it and at all times since that time; and

(b) the loan relationship to which the transferee is a party after the time when the transfer takes effect is the same loan relationship as that to which, by virtue of paragraph (a), it is treated as having been a party before that time.

(3) Expressions used in this paragraph and in [Part 5 of the Corporation Tax Act 2009][1] have the same meanings in this paragraph as in [that Part][1].

Amendments—[1]   In sub-para (2) words substituted for words "Chapter 2 of Part 4 of the Finance Act 1996 (c 8)", and in sub-para (3) words substituted for words "Chapter 2 of Part 4 of the Finance Act 1996 (c 8)" and "that Chapter", by CTA 2009 s 1322, Sch 1 paras 582, 586(1), (5). CTA 2009 applies for accounting periods ending on or after 1 April 2009 (for corporation tax purposes) and for tax years 2009–10 onwards (for income and capital gains tax purposes).

Continuity in relation to derivative contracts

24—(1) This paragraph applies if, in consequence of a transfer to which this Part of this Schedule applies, the transferee replaces a person as a party to a derivative contract.

(2) [Part 7 of the Corporation Tax Act 2009][1] is to have effect in relation to the time when the transfer takes effect and any later time as if—

(a) the transferee had been a party to the derivative contract at the time when the transferor became a party to it and at all times since that time; and

(b) the derivative contract to which the transferee is a party after the time when the transfer takes effect is the same derivative contract as that to which, by virtue of paragraph (a), it is treated as having been a party before that time.

(3) Expressions used in this paragraph and in [Part 7 of the Corporation Tax Act 2009][1] have the same meanings in this paragraph as in [that Part][1].

Amendments—[1]   In sub-para (2) words substituted for words "Schedule 26 to the Finance Act 2002 (c 23)", and in sub-para (3) words substituted for words "Schedule 26 to the Finance Act 2002" and "that Schedule", by CTA 2009 s 1322, Sch 1 paras 582, 586(1), (6), (7). CTA 2009 applies for accounting periods ending on or after 1 April 2009 (for corporation tax purposes) and for tax years 2009–10 onwards (for income and capital gains tax purposes).

Continuity in relation to transfer of intangible assets

25—(1) Where—

(a) property is transferred by a transfer to which this Part of this Schedule applies, and

(b) the property transferred includes a chargeable intangible asset of the transferor,

the transfer of that asset is to be treated for the purposes of Schedule 29 to the Finance Act 2002 as a tax neutral transfer.

(2) Where, in the case of a transfer of property by a transfer to which this Part of this Schedule applies—

(a) the property transferred includes an asset which is not a chargeable intangible asset of the transferor, but

(b) that asset falls to be treated after the transfer as a chargeable intangible asset of the transferee,

that asset shall be treated as acquired by the transferee for an amount equal to the amount of the consideration determined for the purposes of paragraph 18(2) of this Schedule.

(3) Expressions used in this paragraph and in Schedule 29 to the Finance Act 2002 have the same meanings in this paragraph as in that Schedule.

Chargeable intangible assets: degrouping charges

26—(1) This paragraph applies if a company ("the degrouped company")—

(a) acquired an intangible fixed asset from another company at a time when both were members of the same group of companies ("the old group"); and

(b) ceases by virtue of a transfer to which this Part of this Schedule applies to be a member of the old group.

(2) Paragraph 58 of Schedule 29 to the Finance Act 2002 (c 23) (company ceasing to be member of group) is not to treat the degrouped company as having, by virtue of the transfer, sold and immediately reacquired the asset.

(3) Where sub-paragraph (2) has applied to an asset, paragraph 58 of Schedule 29 to the Finance Act 2002 is to have effect on and after the first subsequent occasion on which the degrouped company ceases to be a member of a group of companies ("the new group") as if—

(a) the degrouped company, and

(b) the company from which it acquired the asset,

had been members of the new group at the time of acquisition.

(4) Expressions used in this paragraph and in paragraph 58 of Schedule 29 to the Finance Act 2002 have the same meanings in this paragraph as in that paragraph.

Computation of profits and losses: transfer of trade

27—(1) This paragraph applies where, in consequence of a section 39 scheme—

(a) a BNFL company ceases to carry on a trade or a part of a trade; and

(b) a publicly owned company that is not a subsidiary of the NDA (the "transferee company") begins to carry on the trade or that part.

(2) For the purpose of computing, in relation to the time when the scheme comes into force and subsequent times, the relevant trading profits or losses of the BNFL company and the transferee company—

(a) the trade or part is to be treated as having been a separate trade at the time of its commencement and as having been carried on by the transferee company at all times since its commencement as a separate trade; and

(b) the trade carried on by the transferee company after the time when the section 39 scheme comes into force is to be treated as the same trade as that which it is treated, by virtue of paragraph (a), as having carried on as a separate trade before that time.

(3) This paragraph is subject to paragraph 23.

(4) In this paragraph—

"BNFL company" means BNFL or a wholly-owned subsidiary of BNFL; and

"relevant trading profits and losses" means profits or losses [under Part 3 of the Corporation Tax Act 2009 in respect of the trade or part of a trade in question for periods in which the trade was carried on wholly or partly in the United Kingdom][1].

Amendments—[1] In sub-para (4) words substituted for words "under Case I of Schedule D in respect of the trade or part of a trade in question" by CTA 2009 s 1322, Sch 1 paras 582, 586(1), (8). CTA 2009 applies for accounting periods ending on or after 1 April 2009 (for corporation tax purposes) and for tax years 2009–10 onwards (for income and capital gains tax purposes).

PART 3
TRANSFERS RELATING TO RELEVANT SITE LICENSEES

28—(1) This paragraph applies where, in consequence of a nuclear transfer scheme, a subsidiary of the NDA becomes a relevant site licensee.

(2) For the purposes of the application of the enactments mentioned in sub-paragraph (3) to the assets of the company which has become a relevant site licensee, that company shall be treated as continuing, for so long as it is a relevant site licensee, to be a member of the group of companies of which it was a member immediately before the scheme took effect.

(3) Those enactments are—

    (*a*) the 1992 Act;

    (*b*) Schedule 29 to the Finance Act 2002 (c 23);

    (*c*) paragraphs 5, 14, 19 and 26 of this Schedule.

(4) The reference in sub-paragraph (2) to the group of companies of which a company was a member is to be construed—

    (*a*) in relation to the 1992 Act in accordance with the provisions of section 170 of that Act; and

    (*b*) in relation to Schedule 29 to the Finance Act 2002, in accordance with Part 8 of that Schedule.

29—(1) This paragraph applies where—

    (*a*) as a consequence of a transfer in accordance with a nuclear transfer scheme of securities of a subsidiary of the NDA, that subsidiary becomes a relevant site licensee;

    (*b*) as a consequence of a transfer to the NDA or to a subsidiary of the NDA in accordance with such a scheme of securities of a company, that company ceases to be a relevant site licensee; or

    (*c*) there is a transfer in accordance with such a scheme of securities of a company that is a relevant site licensee from one person to another person for purposes connected with securing that the condition in section 27(5)(*c*) continues to be satisfied in relation to the company.

(2) For the purposes of the 1992 Act, the securities shall be treated as disposed of to the transferee for a consideration of such amount as would secure that, on the disposal, neither a gain nor a loss accrues to the transferor.

30 In this Part of this Schedule "relevant site licensee" has the same meaning as in subsection (4) of section 27 (see subsection (5)).

PART 4
TRANSFER OF NUCLEAR LIABILITIES INVESTMENT PORTFOLIO

Application of Part 4 of Schedule

31 This Part of this Schedule applies to a transfer to the Secretary of State in accordance with a nuclear transfer scheme containing provision authorised by section 42 of this Act.

Chargeable gains: assets to be treated as disposed without a gain or a loss

32—(1) This paragraph applies for the purposes of the 1992 Act where an asset is transferred by a transfer to which this Part of this Schedule applies.

(2) The asset shall be treated as disposed of to the Secretary of State for a consideration of such amount as would secure that, on the disposal, neither a gain nor a loss accrues to BNFL.

Neutral effect of transfer for loan relationships and derivative contracts

33 No credit or debit shall be required or allowed, in respect of a transfer to which this Part of this Schedule applies, to be brought into account in BNFL's case—

    (*a*) for the purposes of [Part 5 of the Corporation Tax Act 2009][1] (loan relationships); or

    (*b*) for the purposes of [Part 7 of the Corporation Tax Act 2009][1].

Amendments—[1] In paragraph (*a*) words substituted for words "Chapter 2 of Part 4 of the Finance Act 1996 (c 8)", and in paragraph (*b*) words substituted for words "Schedule 26 to the Finance Act 2002 (c 23)", by CTA 2009 s 1322, Sch 1 paras 582, 586(1), (9). CTA 2009 applies for accounting periods ending on or after 1 April 2009 (for corporation tax purposes) and for tax years 2009–10 onwards (for income and capital gains tax purposes).

PART 5
STAMP DUTY ETC

34—(1) Stamp duty is not to be chargeable—

    (*a*) on a nuclear transfer scheme, or

(b) on an instrument certified by the Secretary of State to the Commissioners of Inland Revenue as made for the purposes of such a scheme, or as made for purposes connected with such a scheme,

except to the extent that the scheme or instrument includes provision in relation to private transfers.

(2) But where, by virtue of sub-paragraph (1), stamp duty is not chargeable at all, or is chargeable only to a reduced extent, on a nuclear transfer scheme or instrument, the scheme or instrument is to be treated as duly stamped only if—

(a) in accordance with section 12 of the Stamp Act 1891 (c 39) it has been stamped with a stamp denoting either that it is not chargeable to duty or that it has been duly stamped; or

(b) it is stamped with the duty to which it would be chargeable apart from sub-paragraph (1).

(3) An agreement which is made for the purposes of a nuclear transfer scheme or purposes connected with such a scheme is not to give rise to stamp duty reserve tax except to the extent that the agreement relates to private transfers.

(4) In this paragraph—

"instrument" has the same meaning as in the Stamp Act 1891;

"private transfer" means—

(a) a transfer of any property, right or liability to a person other than the Secretary of State, the NDA or a publicly owned company; or

(b) the creation of an interest or right in favour of a person other than the Secretary of State, the NDA or a publicly owned company.

PART 6
SUPPLEMENTAL PROVISIONS OF SCHEDULE

Groups of companies

(a) sections 170 to ~~~ in the following enactments shall apply to the NDA—

(b) Part 8 of Schedule 29 to the ~~~ Act:

~~~ 92 (c 23).

Interpretation of Schedule

37—(1) In this Schedule—

"the 1992 Act" means the Taxation of Chargeable Gains Act 1992 (c 12);

"the 2001 Act" means the Capital Allowances Act 2001 (c 2);

"exempt activities" has the same meaning as in section 27 of this Act;

"NDA company" has the same meaning as in section 27 of this Act;

"the Nuclear Liabilities Investment Portfolio" means property and rights to which BNFL is entitled and which appear to the Board, from BNFL's published accounts, to represent assets held by BNFL for the purpose of being able to meet costs or liabilities for which the NDA has a financial responsibility under Chapter 1 of Part 1 of this Act;

"section 39 scheme" means a nuclear transfer scheme authorised by section 39 of this Act;

"section 40 scheme" means a nuclear transfer scheme authorised by section 40 of this Act;

"transferee", in relation to a transfer in accordance with a nuclear transfer scheme, means the person to whom the transfer is made;

"transferor", in relation to a transfer in accordance with a nuclear transfer scheme, means the person from whom the transfer is made;

"the Taxes Act" means the Income and Corporation Taxes Act 1988 (c 1).

(2) Before determining for the purposes of this Schedule whether an asset was comprised at a particular time in the Nuclear Liabilities Investment Portfolio, the Board must consult the Secretary of State.

(3) So far as it relates to corporation tax this Schedule is to be construed as one with the Corporation Tax Acts.

(4) So far as it relates to capital allowances this Schedule is to be construed as one with the 2001 Act.

PENSIONS ACT 2004

(2004 Chapter 35)

ARRANGEMENT OF SECTIONS

Part 1: The Pensions Regulator
86   Disclosure for facilitating exercise of functions by other supervisory authorities
88   Tax information
Part 2: The Board of the Pension Protection Fund
Chapter 5 Gathering Information
Disclosure of information
202   Tax information
Part 4: Financial Planning for Retirement
Retirement planning
236   Use and supply of information: private pensions policy and retirement planning
Part 5: Occupational and Personal Pension Schemes: Miscellaneous Provisions
Categories of pension scheme
239   Categories of pension scheme
Payment of surplus to employer
251   Payment of surplus to employer: transitional power to amend scheme
Part 9: Miscellaneous and Supplementary
Dissolution of existing bodies
300   Dissolution of OPRA
302   Dissolution of the Pensions Compensation Board
Miscellaneous and Supplementary
319   Minor and consequential amendments
Schedules:
Schedule 3—Restricted Information Held by the Regulator: Certain Permitted Disclosures to Facilitate Exercise of Functions
Schedule 8—Restricted Information held by the Board: Certain Permitted Disclosures to Facilitate Exercise of Functions
Schedule 10—Use and Supply of Information: Private Pensions Policy and Retirement Planning
Schedule 12—Minor and Consequential Amendments

An Act to make provision relating to pensions and financial planning for retirement and provision relating to entitlement to bereavement payments, and for connected purposes.

[18th November 2004]

PART 1

THE PENSIONS REGULATOR

Disclosure of information

86 Disclosure for facilitating exercise of functions by other supervisory authorities

(1) Section 82 does not preclude the disclosure by the Regulator of restricted information to any person specified in the first column of Schedule 3 if the Regulator considers that the disclosure would enable or assist that person to exercise the functions specified in relation to him in the second column of that Schedule.

(2) The Secretary of State may after consultation with the Regulator—

  (a) by order amend Schedule 3 by—

    (i) adding any person exercising regulatory functions and specifying functions in relation to that person,

    (ii) removing any person for the time being specified in the Schedule, or

    (iii) altering the functions for the time being specified in the Schedule in relation to any person, or

  (b) by order restrict the circumstances in which, or impose conditions subject to which, disclosure may be made to any person for the time being specified in the Schedule.

Orders—Pensions Act 2004 (Commencement No 2, Transitional Provisions and Amendment) Order, SI 2005/275 (the day appointed for the coming into force of this section is 6 April 2005).

Pensions Act 2004 (Disclosure of Restricted Information by the Pensions Regulator—Amendment) Order, SI 2012/691.

NHS Counter Fraud Authority (Investigatory Powers and Other Miscellaneous Amendments) Order, SI 2017/960.

[88 Tax information etc

(1) This section applies to information held by the Revenue and Customs if it is held by them in connection with a function of the Revenue and Customs that relates to any of these matters—

  (a) tax or duty;

  (b) national insurance contributions;

  (c) the national minimum wage.

(2) An officer of Revenue and Customs may disclose to the Regulator information to which this section applies, if the disclosure is made for the purpose of enabling or assisting the Regulator to discharge its functions.

(3) Where information to which this section applies is disclosed to the Regulator by virtue of subsection (2) above or section 19 of the Anti-terrorism, Crime and Security Act 2001 (disclosure of information held by revenue departments), it must, subject to subsections (4) and (5), be treated for the purposes of section 82 as restricted information.

(4) Information to which this section applies which is disclosed to the Regulator as mentioned in subsection (3) may not be disclosed by the Regulator or any person who receives the information directly or indirectly from the Regulator except—

- (a) to, or in accordance with authority given by, the Commissioners for Her Majesty's Revenue and Customs,
- (b) with a view to the institution of, or otherwise for the purposes of, any criminal proceedings,
- (c) with a view to the institution of any other proceedings by the Regulator, or for the purposes of any such proceedings instituted by the Regulator,
- (d) in accordance with section 84, otherwise than for the purposes of any proceedings, or
- (e) in the form of a summary or collection of information so framed as not to enable information relating to any particular person to be ascertained from it.

(5) Accordingly sections 82(3), 83, 85 to 87 and 235, and paragraph 4 of Schedule 10, do not apply to such information, and section 84 applies subject to subsection (4)(*d*).

(6) In subsection (4)(*c*) and (*d*), "proceedings" includes the issue of notices or any other enforcement action taken by the Regulator under Chapter 2 of Part 1 of the Pensions Act 2008 or any other enactment.

(7) In this section "the Revenue and Customs" and a "function of the Revenue and Customs" have the same meaning as in section 18 of the Commissioners for Revenue and Customs Act 2005 (confidentiality).][1]

Amendments—[1] This section substituted by the Pensions Act 2008 s 62 with effect from 26 January 2009 (by virtue of SI 2009/82 art 2(1)(*a*))

PART 2
THE BOARD OF THE PENSION PROTECTION FUND

CHAPTER 5

GATHERING INFORMATION

Disclosure of information

202 Tax information

(1) This section applies to information held by any person in the exercise of tax functions about any matter which is relevant, for the purposes of those functions, to tax or duty in the case of an identifiable person (in this section referred to as "tax information").

(2) No obligation as to secrecy imposed by section 182 of the Finance Act 1989 (c 26) or otherwise shall prevent the disclosure of tax information to the Board for the purpose of enabling or assisting the Board to discharge its functions.

(3) Where tax information is disclosed to the Board by virtue of subsection (2) above or section 19 of the Anti-terrorism, Crime and Security Act 2001 (disclosure of information held by revenue departments), it must, subject to subsection (4), be treated for the purposes of section 197 as restricted information.

(4) Sections 197(3), 198 to 201, 203 and 235 do not apply to tax information which is disclosed to the Board as mentioned in subsection (3), and such information may not be disclosed by the Board or any person who receives the information directly or indirectly from the Board except—

- (a) to, or in accordance with authority given by, the Commissioners of Inland Revenue or the Commissioners of Customs and Excise, or
- (b) with a view to the institution of, or otherwise for the purposes of, any criminal proceedings.

(5) In this section "tax functions" has the same meaning as in section 182 of the Finance Act 1989 (c 26).

Orders—Pensions Act 2004 (Commencement No 2, Transitional Provisions and Amendment) Order, SI 2005/275 (the day appointed for the coming into force of this section is 6 April 2005).

PART 4
FINANCIAL PLANNING FOR RETIREMENT

Retirement planning

236 Use and supply of information: private pensions policy and retirement planning

Schedule 10 (which makes provision about the use and supply of information for purposes relating to private pensions policy and retirement planning) has effect.

PART 5
OCCUPATIONAL AND PERSONAL PENSION SCHEMES: MISCELLANEOUS PROVISIONS

Categories of pension scheme

239 Categories of pension scheme

(1) Section 1 of the Pension Schemes Act 1993 (c 48) (categories of pension scheme) is amended as follows.

(2) The provisions of the section shall become subsection (1) of the section.

(3) In that subsection, for the definitions of "occupational pension scheme" and "personal pension scheme" substitute—

" "occupational pension scheme" means a pension scheme—

    (*a*)   that—

        (i) for the purpose of providing benefits to, or in respect of, people with service in employments of a description, or

        (ii) for that purpose and also for the purpose of providing benefits to, or in respect of, other people,

is established by, or by persons who include, a person to whom subsection (2) applies when the scheme is established or (as the case may be) to whom that subsection would have applied when the scheme was established had that subsection then been in force, and

    (*b*)   that has its main administration in the United Kingdom or outside the member States,

or a pension scheme that is prescribed or is of a prescribed description;

"personal pension scheme" means a pension scheme that—

    (*a*)   is not an occupational pension scheme, and

    (*b*)   is established by a person within any of the paragraphs of section 154(1) of the Finance Act 2004;".

(4) After that subsection insert—

"(2) This subsection applies—

    (*a*)   where people in employments of the description concerned are employed by someone, to a person who employs such people,

    (*b*)   to a person in an employment of that description, and

    (*c*)   to a person representing interests of a description framed so as to include—

        (i) interests of persons who employ people in employments of the description mentioned in paragraph (a), or

        (ii) interests of people in employments of that description.

(3) For the purposes of subsection (2), if a person is in an employment of the description concerned by reason of holding an office (including an elective office) and is entitled to remuneration for holding it, the person responsible for paying the remuneration shall be taken to employ the office-holder.

(4) In the definition in subsection (1) of "occupational pension scheme", the reference to a description includes a description framed by reference to an employment being of any of two or more kinds.

(5) In subsection (1) "pension scheme" (except in the phrases "occupational pension scheme", "personal pension scheme" and "public service pension scheme") means a scheme or other arrangements, comprised in one or more instruments or agreements, having or capable of having effect so as to provide benefits to or in respect of people—

    (*a*)   on retirement,

    (*b*)   on having reached a particular age, or

    (*c*)   on termination of service in an employment.

(6) The power of the Treasury under section 154(4) of the Finance Act 2004 (power to amend sections 154 and 155) includes power consequentially to amend—

    (*a*)   paragraph (*a*) of the definition in subsection (1) of "personal pension scheme", and

    (*b*)   any provision in force in Northern Ireland corresponding to that paragraph."

Payment of surplus to employer

251 Payment of surplus to employer: transitional power to amend scheme

(1) This section applies to a scheme

  [(*a*) which is one to which section 37 of the Pensions Act 1995 applies, and

  (*b*)]¹ which immediately before the commencement of section 250 was one to which section 37 of the Pensions Act 1995 (c 26) applied (see subsection (1) of that section, as it then had effect).

(2) No payment to the employer may be made out of funds held for the purposes of the scheme except by virtue of a resolution of the trustees under this section.

[(2A) But subsection (2) does not apply in the case of any of the payments listed in paragraphs (c) to (f) of section 175 of the Finance Act 2004 (authorised employer payments other than public service scheme payments or authorised surplus payments).]¹

This applies even if the payment is one proposed to be made in fulfilment of an agreement or arrangement entered into before the commencement of this section.

(3) Where the scheme was so expressed as (apart from section 37, as it [applied immediately before the commencement of section 250]¹) to confer power to make payments to the employer out of funds held for the purposes of the scheme otherwise than in pursuance of proposals approved under paragraph 6(1) of Schedule 22 to the Income and Corporation Taxes Act 1988 (c 1), the trustees may resolve that the power—

    (a) shall become exercisable according to its terms, or

    (b) shall become so exercisable, but only in such circumstances and subject to such conditions as may be specified in the resolution.

(4) Where the scheme was so expressed as to confer power to make payments to the employer out of funds held for the purposes of the scheme only in pursuance of proposals approved under paragraph 6(1) of Schedule 22 to the Income and Corporation Taxes Act 1988, the trustees may resolve that the power shall instead be exercisable in such circumstances and subject to such conditions as may be specified in the resolution.

(5) In either case the trustees must be satisfied that it is in the interests of the members of the scheme that the power is exercised in the manner proposed.

(6) The power conferred by subsection (3) or (4)—

    (a) may not be exercised unless notice of the proposal to exercise it has been given, in accordance with prescribed requirements, to the employer and to the members of the scheme,

    [(aa) may be exercised even if the payments to which it relates are, to any extent, payments to which subsection (2) does not apply,]¹

    (b) may [be exercised, after the commencement of section 25 of the Pensions Act 2011, only once (whether or not also exercised before 6 April 2011)]¹, and

    (c) ceases to be exercisable [on 6 April 2016]¹.

[(6A) A resolution passed under this section after the commencement of section 25 of the Pensions Act 2011 may amend or revoke a resolution passed under this section before 6 April 2011.]¹

(7) The exercise of any power to make payments to the employer by virtue of a resolution under this section is subject to section 37 of the Pensions Act 1995 (c 26) as substituted by section 250.

Amendments—¹ Amendments made by the Pensions Act 2011 s 25 with effect from 3 January 2012. Note that these amendments do not affect the continued operation of any resolution under the Pensions Act s 251(3) or (4) passed before 6 April 2011.

PART 9
MISCELLANEOUS AND SUPPLEMENTARY
Dissolution of existing bodies

300 Dissolution of OPRA

(1) The Occupational Pensions Regulatory Authority ("OPRA") is hereby dissolved.

(2) An order under section 322 which appoints the day on which subsection (1) comes into force may provide—

    (a) for all property, rights and liabilities to which OPRA is entitled or subject immediately before that day to become the property, rights and liabilities of the Regulator or the Secretary of State, and

    (b) for any function of OPRA falling to be exercised on or after that day, or which fell to be exercised before that day but has not been exercised, to be exercised by the Regulator, the Secretary of State or the Department for Social Development in Northern Ireland.

(3) Subject to subsection (4), information obtained by the Regulator by virtue of subsection (2) is to be treated for the purposes of sections 82 to 87 (disclosure of information) as having been obtained by the Regulator in the exercise of its functions from the person from whom OPRA obtained it.

(4) Information obtained by the Regulator by virtue of subsection (2) which was supplied to OPRA for the purposes of its functions by an authority exercising functions corresponding to the functions of OPRA in a country or territory outside the United Kingdom (the "overseas authority") is to be treated for the purposes mentioned in subsection (3) as having been supplied to the Regulator for the purposes of its functions by the overseas authority.

(5) Where tax information disclosed to OPRA is obtained by the Regulator by virtue of subsection (2), subsection (3) does not apply and subsections (3) and (4) of section 88 apply as if that information had been disclosed to the Regulator by virtue of subsection (2) of that section.

For this purpose "tax information" has the same meaning as in that section.

Orders—Pensions Act 2004 (Commencement No 2, Transitional Provisions and Amendment) Order, SI 2005/275 (the day appointed for the coming into force of sub-ss (3)–(5) is 6 April 2005).

Pensions Act 2004 (Commencement No 2, Transitional Provisions and Amendment) Order, SI 2005/275 (the day appointed for the coming into force of sub-s (2) above for the purpose only of conferring power to make regulations or orders, as the case may be, is 10 February 2005, and for all other purposes, is 8 March 2005).

Pensions Act 2004 (Commencement No 3, Transitional Provisions and Amendment) Order, SI 2005/695 (the day appointed for the coming into force of sub-s (1) above is 6 April 2005).

302 Dissolution of the Pensions Compensation Board

(1) The Pensions Compensation Board is hereby dissolved.

(2) An order under section 322 appointing the day on which subsection (1) is to come into force may provide—

> (a) for all property, rights and liabilities to which the Pensions Compensation Board is entitled or subject immediately before that day to become property, rights and liabilities of the Board, and

> (b) for any function of the Pensions Compensation Board falling to be exercised on or after that day, or which fell to be exercised before that day but has not been exercised, to be exercised by the Board.

(3) Information obtained by the Board by virtue of subsection (2) is to be treated for the purposes of sections 197 to 201 and 203 (disclosure of information) as having been obtained by the Board in the exercise of its functions from the person from whom the Pensions Compensation Board obtained it.

(4) Where tax information disclosed to the Pensions Compensation Board is obtained by the Board by virtue of subsection (2), subsection (3) does not apply, and subsections (3) and (4) of section 202 apply as if that information had been disclosed to the Board by virtue of subsection (2) of that section.

For this purpose "tax information" has the same meaning as in that section.

(5) Where the Pensions Compensation Board's disclosure under section 114(3) of the Pensions Act 1995 (c 26) of information to which subsection (3) applies was subject to any express restriction, the Board's powers of disclosure under sections 198 to 201 and 203, in relation to that information, are subject to the same restriction.

Orders—Pensions Act 2004 (Commencement No 5) Order, SI 2005/1436 (the day appointed for the coming into force of sub-s (2) above is 27 May 2005).

Pensions Act 2004 (Commencement No 6, Transitional Provisions and Savings) Order, SI 2005/1720 (the day appointed for the coming into force of sub-s (1) above is 1 September 2005).

Miscellaneous and supplementary

319 Minor and consequential amendments

(1) Schedule 12 (which makes minor and consequential amendments) has effect.

(2) The Secretary of State may by order make provision consequential on this Act amending, repealing or revoking (with or without savings) any provision of—

> (a) an Act passed before or in the same session as this Act, or

> (b) an instrument made under an Act before the passing of this Act.

SCHEDULES

SCHEDULE 3

RESTRICTED INFORMATION HELD BY THE REGULATOR: CERTAIN PERMITTED
DISCLOSURES TO FACILITATE EXERCISE OF FUNCTIONS

Section 86

Persons	Functions
The Secretary of State.	Functions under—
	(a) Part 14 of the Companies Act 1985 (c 6),
	(b) the Insolvency Act 1986 (c 45),
	(c) Part 3 of the Companies Act 1989 (c 40),
	(d) Part 1 of the Export and Investment Guarantees Act 1991 (c 67) (apart from sections 5 and 6),
	(e) Part 3 of the Pension Schemes Act 1993 (c 48),
	(f) Part 5 of the Police Act 1997 (c 50),
	(g) the Financial Services and Markets Act 2000 (c 8), or[5]
	[(ga) Section 17 of the Companies (Audit, Investigations and Community Enterprise) Act 2004 (levy to pay expenses of bodies concerned with accounting standards, actuarial standards etc), or][5]
	(h) this Act,

Persons	Functions
	and functions of co-operating with overseas government authorities and bodies in relation to criminal matters.
The Bank of England.	Any of its functions[, apart from its functions as the Prudential Regulation Authority][13].
[The Financial Conduct Authority	Any of its functions.][9]
The Prudential Regulation Authority	Any of its functions.][9]
[The Charity Commission.	Functions under the Charities Act 2006 or the Charities Act 2011.][7]
The Pensions Regulator Tribunal.	Any of its functions.
[The First-tier Tribunal]	Functions relating to decisions of the Regulator
The Upper Tribunal	Functions relating to decisions of the Regulator][6]
The Pensions Ombudsman.	Functions under—
	(*a*) the Pension Schemes Act 1993 (c 48), or
	(*b*) the Pension Schemes (Northern Ireland) Act 1993 (c 49).
The Ombudsman for the Board of the Pension Protection Fund.	Any of his functions.
The Comptroller and Auditor General.	Any of his functions.
The Auditor General for Wales.	Any of his functions.
The Auditor General for Scotland.	Any of his functions.
The Comptroller and Auditor General for Northern Ireland.	Any of his functions.
The Commissioners of Inland Revenue or their officers.	Functions under—
	(*a*) the Income and Corporation Taxes Act 1988 (c 1),
	(*b*) the Taxation of Chargeable Gains Act 1992 (c 12),
	(*c*) Part 3 of the Pension Schemes Act 1993,
	(*d*) Part 3 of the Pension Schemes (Northern Ireland) Act 1993, . . .[1]
	(*e*) the Income Tax (Earnings and Pensions) Act 2003 (c 1) [. . .][2]
	(*f*) the Income Tax (Trading and Other Income) Act 2005 (so far as relating to functions previously exercised under the Income and Corporation Taxes Act 1988)][1],[3]
	[(*g*) Part 4 of the Finance Act 2004 (c 12)][2] [or][3]
	[(*h*) the Income Tax Act 2007 (so far as relating to functions previously exercised under the Income and Corporation Taxes Act 1988).][3]
The Commissioners of Customs and Excise.	Functions under any enactment.
The Official Receiver or, in Northern Ireland, the Official Receiver for Northern Ireland.	Functions under the enactments relating to insolvency.
An inspector appointed by the Secretary of State.	Functions under Part 14 of the Companies Act 1985 (c 6).
A person authorised to exercise powers under—	Functions under those sections or that Article.
(*a*) section 447 of the Companies Act 1985,	
(*b*) Article 440 of the Companies (Northern Ireland) Order 1986 (SI 1986/1032 (NI 6)), or	
(*c*) section 84 of the Companies Act 1989 (c 40).	
A person appointed under—	Functions in relation to that investigation.
(*a*) section 167 of the Financial Services and Markets Act 2000 (c 8),	
(*b*) subsection (3) or (5) of section 168 of that Act, or	
(*c*) section 284 of that Act,	
to conduct an investigation.	

Persons	Functions
A body designated under section 326(1) of that Act.	Functions in its capacity as a body designated under that section.
[A recognised investment exchange, recognised clearing house, [recognised CSD, EEA CSD, third country CSD,][14] EEA central counterparty or third country central counterparty (as defined by section 285 of that Act).	[Functions in its capacity as an exchange, clearing house[, central securities depository][14] or central counterparty.][11]
A body corporate established in accordance with section 212(1) of that Act.	Functions under the Financial Services Compensation Scheme, established in accordance with section 213 of that Act.
The Panel on Takeovers and Mergers.	Functions under the City Code on Takeovers and Mergers and the Rules Governing Substantial Acquisitions of Shares for the time being issued by the Panel.
The General Insurance Standards Council.	Functions of regulating sales and advisory and service standards in relation to insurance.
A recognised professional body (within the meaning of section 391 of the Insolvency Act 1986 (c 45)).	Functions in its capacity as such a body under that Act.
A person on whom functions are conferred by or under Part 2, 3 or 4 of the Proceeds of Crime Act 2002 (c 29).	The functions so conferred.
[A special health authority established under section 28 of the National Health Service Act 2006 directed to carry out counter fraud functions of the Secretary of State within the meaning of section 195 of that Act][15]	Any of its functions.
The Department of Enterprise, Trade and Investment in Northern Ireland.	Functions under—
	(*a*) Part 15 of the Companies (Northern Ireland) Order 1986 (SI 1986/1032 (NI 6)),
	(*b*) the Insolvency (Northern Ireland) Order 1989 (SI 1989/2405 (NI 19)), or
	(*c*) Part 2 of the Companies (No 2) (Northern Ireland) Order 1990 (SI 1990/1504 (NI 10)).
The Department for Social Development in Northern Ireland.	Functions under Part 3 of the Pension Schemes (Northern Ireland) Act 1993 (c 49).
An Inspector appointed by the Department of Enterprise, Trade and Investment in Northern Ireland.	Functions under Part 15 of the Companies (Northern Ireland) Order 1986.
A recognised professional body within the meaning of Article 350 of the Insolvency (Northern Ireland) Order 1989.	Functions in its capacity as such a body under that Order.
[Any body carrying on activities concerned with any of the matters set out in section 16(2) of the Companies (Audit, Investigations and Community Enterprise) Act 2004 (c 27) or Article 16(2) of the Companies (Audit, Investigations and Community Enterprise) (Northern Ireland) Order 2005 (SI 2005/1967 (NI 17)) (a "relevant body"), any subsidiary (within the meaning given by section 736 of the Companies Act 1985 (c 6) or Article 4 of the Companies (Northern Ireland) Order 1986 (SI 1986/1032 (NI 6)) of a relevant body and any body established under the constitution of a relevant body or such a subsidiary. Its functions relating to carrying on activities concerned with any of the following matters—	(*a*) issuing standards to be applied in actuarial work,
	(*b*) issuing standards in respect of matters to be contained in reports or other communications required to be produced or made by actuaries or in accordance with standards within paragraph (*a*),
	(*c*) investigating departures from standards within paragraph (*a*) or (*b*),
	(*d*) taking steps to secure compliance with standards within paragraph (*a*) or (*b*),
	(*e*) carrying out investigations into public interest cases arising in connection with the performance of actuarial functions by members of the [Institute and Faculty of Actuaries ("Institute and Faculty"), or persons who are not such members but are subject to the rules of that body in performing actuarial functions ("members"),][8]
	(*f*) holding disciplinary hearings relating to members following the conclusion of investigations within paragraph (*e*),
	(*g*) deciding whether (and, if so, what) disciplinary action should be taken against members to whom hearings within paragraph (*f*) related,
	(*h*) supervising the exercise by the [Institute and Faculty][8] of:

Persons	Functions
	(i) investigatory or disciplinary functions exercised by the Institute or Faculty in relation to the performance by their members of actuarial functions,
	(ii) the setting by the [Institute and Faculty]^8 of standards in relation to the performance by their members of actuarial functions, and
	(iii) the determining by the [Institute and Faculty]^8 of requirements in relation to the education and training of their members,
	(i) overseeing or directing any of the matters mentioned in paragraphs (*a*) to (*h*),
	and functions relating to the funding of activities concerned with any of the matters mentioned in paragraphs (*a*) to (*i*).
	Any functions in connection with any levy payable to it under section 17 of the Companies (Audit, Investigations and Community Enterprise) Act 2004]^4
[A member of the panel appointed under paragraph 4 of Schedule 17 to the Financial Services and Markets Act 2000 (c 8) by the body corporate [mentioned in]^9 paragraph 2 of that Schedule. Functions under—	(*a*) Part 3 (the compulsory jurisdiction), (*b*) Part 3A (the consumer credit jurisdiction), and (*c*) Part 4 (the voluntary jurisdiction) of that Schedule to that Act]^4
[The Gambling Commission Functions under—	(*a*) the Gaming Act 1968 (c 65), (*b*) the Lotteries and Amusements Act 1976 (c 32), and (*c*) the Gambling Act 2005 (c 19)]^4
. . .]^4	. . .]^4
[Disclosure and Barring Service	Functions under Part 5 of the Police Act 1997.]^{10}
[Director of Labour Market Enforcement or a member of staff provided to the Director under section 1(4) of the Immigration Act 2016	Any of the Director's functions]^{12}

Orders—Pensions Act 2004 (Commencement No 2, Transitional Provisions and Amendment) Order, SI 2005/275 (the day appointed for the coming into force of this Schedule is 6 April 2005).

Amendments—^{1} Word repealed and entry inserted by ITTOIA 2005 s 882(1), Sch 1 paras 657, 658 with effect from 6 April 2005. ITTOIA 2005 has effect: (a) for income tax purposes, for 2005–06 and subsequent tax years, and (b) for corporation tax purposes, for accounting periods ending after 5 April 2005: ITTOIA 2005 s 883(1).

^{2} Word repealed, and word and entry inserted, by the Taxation of Pension Schemes (Consequential Amendments) Order, SI 2006/745 art 18(1), (2) with effect from 6 April 2006.

^{3} Word repealed and entry inserted by ITA 2007 ss 1027, 1031, Sch 1 paras 486, 487, Sch 3 Pt 1 with effect for income tax purposes from 6 April 2007, and corporation tax purposes for accounting periods ending after 5 April 2007.

^{4} Entry relating to "Gaming Board for Great Britain" repealed, entries beginning "Any body carrying on activities" and "A member of the panel", and entry relating to "The Gambling Commission", inserted, by the Pensions Act 2004 (Disclosure of Restricted Information) (Amendment of Specified Persons) Order, SI 2006/2937, art 2 with effect from 7 December 2006.

^{5} In definition of "Secretary of State", word "or" in para (g) repealed, and para (ga) inserted, by the Companies Act 2006 s 1275(7) with effect from 1 October 2009 (by virtue of SI 2008/2860 art 3(y)).

^{6} Entries relating to "The First-tier Tribunal" and "The Upper Tribunal" inserted by the Transfer of Tribunal Functions Order, SI 2010/22 art 5(1), Sch 2 paras 74, 87 with effect from 6 April 2010.

^{7} Entry relating to "The Charity Commission" substituted by the Charities Act 2011 s 354, Sch 7 para 101 with effect from 13 March 2012.

^{8} In second column of entry relating to "Any body carrying on activities concerned with any of the matters set out in section 16(2) of the Companies (Audit, Investigations and Community Enterprise) Act 2004" etc, words in paras (e), (h) substituted by the Pensions Act 2004 (Disclosure of Restricted Information by the Pensions Regulator—Amendment) Order, SI 2012/691, art 2 with effect from 6 April 2004.

^{9} Entry relating to "Financial Services Authority" substituted, and in entry relating to "A member of the panel appointed under paragraph 4 of Schedule 17 to the Financial Services and Markets Act 2000", words substituted by FSA 2012 s 114(1), Sch 18 para 104(1), (3) with effect from 1 April 2013 by virtue of SI 2013/423 art 3, Schedule.

^{10} Entry relating to "Disclosure and Barring Service" inserted by the Protection of Freedoms Act 2012 (Disclosure and Barring Service Transfer of Functions) Order, SI 2012/3006 art 84 with effect from 1 December 2012. Note that this Order does not extend to Scotland (SI 2012/3006 art 1(1)).

^{11} Entry relating to "A recognised investment exchange or a recognised clearing house" substituted by the Financial Services and Markets Act 2000 (Over the Counter Derivatives, Central Counterparties and Trade Repositories) Regulations, SI 2013/504 reg 23 with effect from 1 April 2013.

^{12} Entry relating to "Director of Labour Market Enforcement" inserted by the Immigration Act 2016 s s 31, Sch 3 para 25 with effect from 12 July 2016 (by virtue of SI 2016/603 reg 3(d), (u)).

^{13} In second column of entry relating to "The Bank of England", words inserted by the Bank of England and Financial Services (Consequential Amendments) Regulations, SI 2017/80 reg 2, Schedule para 15(a) with effect from 1 March 2017.

[14] In the entry relating to "A recognised investment exchange" words inserted by the Central Securities Depositories Regulations, SI 2017/701 reg 10, Schedule para 10(1), (2) with effect from 28 November 2017.

[15] In entry beginning "A special health authority established under section 28", in column 1 words substituted for words "The Counter Fraud and Security Management Service established under the Counter Fraud and Security Management Service (Establishment and Constitution) Order 2002 (S.I. 2002/3039)" by the NHS Counter Fraud Authority (Investigatory Powers and Other Miscellaneous Amendments) Order, SI 2017/960 art 2 with effect from 1 November 2017.

Prospective amendments—In the entry relating to "a recognised investment exchange" in the first column words ", EEA CSD" and ", EEA central counterparty" to be repealed by the Occupational and Personal Pension Schemes (Amendment etc) (EU Exit) Regulations, SI 2019/192 reg 5(1), (11) with effect from Implementation Period completion day (see EU(WA)A 2020 Sch 5 para 1(1)).

SCHEDULE 8

RESTRICTED INFORMATION HELD BY THE BOARD: CERTAIN PERMITTED DISCLOSURES TO FACILITATE EXERCISE OF FUNCTIONS

Section 200

Persons	*Functions*
The Secretary of State.	Functions under— (*a*) Part 14 of the Companies Act 1985 (c 6), (*b*) the Insolvency Act 1986 (c 45), (*c*) Part 3 of the Companies Act 1989 (c 40), (*d*) Part 1 of the Export and Investment Guarantees Act 1991 (c 67) (apart from sections 5 and 6), (*e*) Part 3 of the Pension Schemes Act 1993 (c 48), (*f*) Part 5 of the Police Act 1997 (c 50), (*g*) the Financial Services and Markets Act 2000 (c 8), or (*h*) this Act, and functions of co-operating with overseas government authorities and bodies in relation to criminal matters.
The Bank of England.	Any of its functions[, apart from its functions as the Prudential Regulation Authority][8].
[The Financial Conduct Authority.	Any of its functions.
The Prudential Regulation Authority	Any of its functions.][6]
The Charity Commissioners.	Functions under the Charities Act 1993 (c 10).
The Pensions Regulator Tribunal.	Any of its functions.
[The First-tier Tribunal	Functions relating to decisions of the Regulator
The Upper Tribunal	Functions relating to decisions of the Regulator][5]
The Pensions Ombudsman.	Functions under— (*a*) the Pension Schemes Act 1993, or (*b*) the Pension Schemes (Northern Ireland) Act 1993 (c 49).
The Ombudsman for the Board of the Pension Protection Fund.	Any of his functions.
The Comptroller and Auditor General.	Any of his functions.
The Auditor General for Wales.	Any of his functions.
The Auditor General for Scotland.	Any of his functions.
The Comptroller and Auditor General for Northern Ireland.	Any of his functions.
The Commissioners of Inland Revenue or their officers.	Functions under— (*a*) the Income and Corporation Taxes Act 1988 (c 1), (*b*) the Taxation of Chargeable Gains Act 1992 (c 12), (*c*) Part 3 of the Pension Schemes Act 1993 (c 48), (*d*) Part 3 of the Pension Schemes (Northern Ireland) Act 1993 (c 49), . . . [1] (*e*) the Income Tax (Earnings and Pensions) Act 2003 (c 1) [. . . [2]

Persons	Functions
	(*f*) the Income Tax (Trading and Other Income) Act 2005 (so far as relating to functions previously exercised under the Income and Corporation Taxes Act 1988)][1] [or
	(*g*) the Income Tax Act 2007 (so far as relating to functions previously exercised under the Income and Corporation Taxes Act 1988).][2]
The Commissioners of Customs and Excise.	Functions under any enactment.
The Official Receiver or, in Northern Ireland, the Official Receiver for Northern Ireland.	Functions under the enactments relating to insolvency.
An inspector appointed by the Secretary of State.	Functions under Part 14 of the Companies Act 1985 (c 6).
A person authorised to exercise powers under— (*a*) section 447 of the Companies Act 1985, (*b*) . . .[4], or (*c*) section 84 of the Companies Act 1989 (c 40).	Functions under those sections . . .[4].
A person appointed under— (*a*) section 167 of the Financial Services and Markets Act 2000 (c 8), (*b*) subsection (3) or (5) of section 168 of that Act, or (*c*) section 284 of that Act, to conduct an investigation.	Functions in relation to that investigation.
A body designated under section 326(1) of that Act.	Functions in its capacity as a body designated under that section.
[A recognised investment exchange, recognised clearing house, [recognised CSD, EEA CSD, third country CSD,][9] EEA central counterparty or third country central counterparty (as defined by section 285 of that Act).	Functions in its capacity as an exchange, clearing house [, central securities depository][9] or central counterparty.][7]
A body corporate established in accordance with section 212(1) of that Act.	Functions under the Financial Services Compensation Scheme, established in accordance with section 213 of that Act.
The Panel on Takeovers and Mergers.	Functions under the City Code on Takeovers and Mergers and the Rules Governing Substantial Acquisitions of Shares for the time being issued by the Panel.
The General Insurance Standards Council.	Functions of regulating sales and advisory and service standards in relation to insurance.
A recognised professional body (within the meaning of section 391 of the Insolvency Act 1986 (c 45)).	Functions in its capacity as such a body under that Act.
A person on whom functions are conferred by or under Part 2, 3 or 4 of the Proceeds of Crime Act 2002 (c 29).	The functions so conferred.
[A special health authority established under section 28 of the National Health Service Act 2006 directed to carry out counter fraud functions of the Secretary of State within the meaning of section 195 of that Act][10]	Any of its functions.
The Department of Enterprise, Trade and Investment in Northern Ireland.	Functions under— (*a*) . . .[4], (*b*) the Insolvency (Northern Ireland) Order 1989 (SI 1989/2405 (NI 19)), . . .[4] (*c*) . . .[4]
The Department for Social Development in Northern Ireland.	Functions under Part 3 of the Pension Schemes (Northern Ireland) Act 1993 (c 49).
. . .[4]	. . .[4]
A recognised professional body within the meaning of Article 350 of the Insolvency (Northern Ireland) Order 1989.	Functions in its capacity as such a body under that Order.

Persons	Functions
[A member of the panel appointed under paragraph 4 of Schedule 17 to the Financial Services and Markets Act 2000 (c 8) by the body corporate [mentioned in][6] paragraph 2 of that Schedule. Functions under—	(*a*) Part 3 (the compulsory jurisdiction), (*b*) Part 3A (the consumer credit jurisdiction), and (*c*) Part 4 (the voluntary jurisdiction) of that Schedule to that Act.][3]
[The Gambling Commission. Functions under—	(*a*) the Gaming Act 1968 (c 65), (*b*) the Lotteries and Amusements Act 1976 (c 32), and (*c*) the Gambling Act 2005 (c 19).][3]
. . . [3]	. . . [3]

Amendments—[1]   Word repealed and entry inserted by ITTOIA 2005 s 882(1), Sch 1 paras 657, 659 with effect from 6 April 2005. ITTOIA 2005 has effect: (a) for income tax purposes, for 2005–06 and subsequent tax years, and (b) for corporation tax purposes, for accounting periods ending after 5 April 2005: ITTOIA 2005 s 883(1).

[2]   Word repealed and entry inserted by ITA 2007 ss 1027, 1031, Sch 1 paras 486, 488, Sch 3 Pt 1 with effect for income tax purposes from 6 April 2007, and corporation tax purposes for accounting periods ending after 5 April 2007.

[3]   Entry relating to "The Gaming Board for Great Britain" repealed, entry beginning "A member of the panel" and entry relating to "The Gambling Commission" inserted, by the Pensions Act 2004 (Disclosure of Restricted Information) (Amendment of Specified Persons) Order, SI 2006/2937, art 3 with effect from 7 December 2006.

[4]   Words repealed by the Companies Act 2006 (Consequential Amendments, Transitional Provisions and Savings) Order, SI 2009/1941 art 2(1), Sch 1 para 243(1), (13) with effect from 1 October 2009.

[5]   Entries relating to "The First-tier Tribunal" and "The Upper Tribunal" inserted by the Transfer of Tribunal Functions Order, SI 2010/22 art 5(1), Sch 2 paras 74, 89 with effect from 6 April 2010.

[6]   Entry relating to "Financial Services Authority" substituted, and in entry relating to "A member of the panel appointed under paragraph 4 of Schedule 17 to the Financial Services and Markets Act 2000", words substituted by FSA 2012 s 114(1), Sch 18 para 104(1), (3) with effect from 1 April 2013 by virtue of SI 2013/423 art 3, Schedule.

[7]   Entry relating to "A recognised investment exchange or a recognised clearing house" substituted by the Financial Services and Markets Act 2000 (Over the Counter Derivatives, Central Counterparties and Trade Repositories) Regulations, SI 2013/504 reg 23 with effect from 1 April 2013.

[8]   In second column of entry relating to "The Bank of England", words inserted by the Bank of England and Financial Services (Consequential Amendments) Regulations, SI 2017/80 reg 2, Schedule para 15(*b*) with effect from 1 March 2017.

[9]   In the entry relating to "a recognised investment exchange" words inserted by the Central Securities Depositories Regulations, SI 2017/1064 reg 10, Schedule para 10(1), (3) with effect from 28 November 2017.

[10]   In column 1 words substituted for words "The Counter Fraud and Security Management Service established under the Counter Fraud and Security Management Service (Establishment and Constitution) Order 2002 (S.I. 2002/3039)" by the NHS Counter Fraud Authority (Investigatory Powers and Other Miscellaneous Amendments) Order, SI 2017/960 art 2 with effect from 1 November 2017.

Prospective amendments—In the entry relating to "a recognised investment exchange" in the first column words ", EEA CSD" and ", EEA central counterparty" to be repealed by the Occupational and Personal Pension Schemes (Amendment etc) (EU Exit) Regulations, SI 2019/192 reg 5(1), (11) with effect from Implementation Period completion day (see EU(WA)A 2020 Sch 5 para 1(1)).

SCHEDULE 10

USE AND SUPPLY OF INFORMATION: PRIVATE PENSIONS POLICY AND RETIREMENT PLANNING

Section 236

Use of information held by Secretary of State etc

1—(1) Section 3 of the Social Security Act 1998 (c 14) (use of information) is amended as follows.

(2), (4) (*amend* SSA 1998 s 3(1), (2)(*a*))

(3), (5) (*insert* SSA 1998 ss 3(1A), (5))

(4) (*amends* SSA 1998 s 3(2)(*a*))

Supply of information held by tax authorities

2—(1) This paragraph applies to information which is held—

(*a*) by the Commissioners of Inland Revenue;

(*b*) by a person providing services to the Commissioners of Inland Revenue, in connection with the provision of those services;

(*c*) by the Commissioners of Customs and Excise;

(*d*) by a person providing services to the Commissioners of Customs and Excise, in connection with the provision of those services.

(2) Information to which this paragraph applies may be supplied—

(*a*) to the Secretary of State or the Northern Ireland Department, or

(*b*) to a person providing services to the Secretary of State or the Northern Ireland Department,

for use for the purposes of functions relating to private pensions policy or retirement planning.

(3) In this paragraph—

"private pensions policy" means policy relating to occupational pension schemes or personal pension schemes;

"retirement planning" means promoting financial planning for retirement;

"the Northern Ireland Department" means the Department for Social Development in Northern Ireland.

Supply of housing benefit and council tax benefit information

3—(1) Section 122D of the Social Security Administration Act 1992 (c 5) (supply of information by authorities administering housing benefit or council tax benefit) is amended as follows.

(2) (*amends SSAA 1992 s 122D(1)*)

(3), (4) (*insert SSAA 1992 s 122D(2A), (6)*)

Amendments—[1] Para 3 repealed in so far as it relates to the abolition of council tax benefit, by the Welfare Reform Act 2012 Sch 14 Pt 1 with effect from 1 April 2013 (by virtue of SI 2013/358 art 8(c), Sch 4). Note that certain transitional provisions apply in relation to the abolition of council tax benefit (see SI 2013/358 art 9).

[Supply of information held by the Regulator

4—(1) This paragraph applies to information which is held—

  (*a*) by the Regulator;

  (*b*) by a person providing services to the Regulator, in connection with the provision of those services.

(2) Information to which this paragraph applies may be supplied—

  (*a*) to the Secretary of State or the Northern Ireland Department, or

  (*b*) to a person providing services to the Secretary of State or the Northern Ireland Department,

for use for the purposes of functions relating to private pensions policy or retirement planning.

(3) In this paragraph—

"private pensions policy" means policy relating to schemes which are occupational pension schemes or personal pension schemes within the meaning of Part 1 of the Pensions Act 2008; "retirement planning" and "the Northern Ireland Department" have the same meaning as in paragraph 2.][1]

Amendments—[1] Para 4 inserted by the Pensions Act 2008 s 63(1) with effect from 26 January 2009 (by virtue of SI 2009/82 art 2(1)(*a*)).

SCHEDULE 12
MINOR AND CONSEQUENTIAL AMENDMENTS

Section 319

Pension Schemes Act 1993 (c 48)

9 The Pension Schemes Act 1993 is amended as follows.

26—(1) Section 158A (other disclosures by the Secretary of State) is amended as follows.

(2), (3) (*amend PSA 1993 s 158A(1)*)

(4) (*inserts PSA 1993 s 158A)1AA)*

INCOME TAX (TRADING AND OTHER INCOME) ACT 2005

(2005 Chapter 5)

ARRANGEMENT OF SECTIONS

Part 1   Overview
1   Overview of Act
2   Overview of priority rules
Part 2   Trading Income
Chapter 1   Introduction
3   Overview of Part 2
4   Provisions which must be given priority over Part 2
Chapter 2   Income Taxed As Trade Profits
Charge to tax on trade profits
5   Charge to tax on trade profits
6   Territorial scope of charge to tax
6A   Arrangements for avoiding tax
6B   Trade of dealing in or developing UK land
7   Income charged
8   Person liable
Trades and trade profits
9   Farming and market gardening
10   Commercial occupation of land other than woodlands
11   Commercial occupation of woodlands
12   Profits of mines, quarries and other concerns
13   Visiting performers
14   Visiting performers: supplementary
15   Divers and diving supervisors
16   Oil extraction and related activities
16A   Voluntary office-holders: compensation for lost profits
16B   Payments to company directors
16C   Professionals in practice: incidental income from an office or employment
Starting and ceasing to trade
17   Effect of becoming or ceasing to be a UK resident
18   Effect of company starting or ceasing to be within charge to income tax
Trading income and property income
19   Tied premises
20   Caravan sites where trade carried on
21   Surplus business accommodation
22   Payments for wayleaves
Trading allowance
22A   Trading allowance
Rent-a-room and qualifying care relief
23   Rent-a-room and qualifying care relief
Trading income provided through third parties
23A   Application of section 23E: conditions
23B   Meaning of "relevant benefit"
23C   Meaning of "qualifying third party payment"
23D   Other definitions
23E   Tax treatment of relevant benefits
23F   Relevant benefits: persons other than T
23G   Anti-avoidance
23H   Double taxation
Chapter 3   Trade Profits: Basic Rules
24   Professions and vocations
25   Generally accepted accounting practice
25A   Cash basis for small businesses
26   Losses calculated on same basis as profits
27   Receipts and expenses
28   Items treated under CAA 2001 as receipts and expenses
28A   Money's worth
29   Interest
30   Animals kept for trade purposes
31   Relationship between rules prohibiting and allowing deductions
Chapter 3A   Trade profits: cash basis
Eligibility
31A   Conditions to be met for profits to be calculated on cash basis
31B   Relevant maximum
31C   Excluded persons

Elections under section 25A
31D   Effect of election under section 25A
Calculation of profits on cash basis
31E   Calculation of profits on cash basis
Overview of rest of Part 2
31F   Overview of rest of Part 2 as it applies to cash basis
Chapter 4   Trade Profits: Rules Restricting Deductions
Introduction
32   Professions and vocations
Cash basis accounting
32A   Application of Chapter to the cash basis
Cash basis: capital expenditure
33   Capital expenditure
33A   Cash basis: capital expenditure
Wholly and exclusively and losses rules
34   Expenses not wholly and exclusively for trade and unconnected losses
Bad and doubtful debts
35   Bad and doubtful debts
Unpaid remuneration
36   Unpaid remuneration
37   Unpaid remuneration: supplementary
Employee benefit contributions
38   Restriction of deductions
39   Making of "employee benefit contributions"
40   Provision of qualifying benefits
41   Timing and amount of certain qualifying benefits
42   Provision or payment out of employee benefit contributions
43   Profits calculated before end of 9 month period
44   Interpretation of sections 38 to 44
Business entertainment and gifts
45   Business entertainment and gifts: general rule
46   Business entertainment: exceptions
47   Business gifts: exceptions
Car... cycle hire
48   Car hire
49   Car hire: supplementary
50A   Short term hiring in and long-term hiring out
50B   Connected persons: application of section 48
Interest payments
51A   Cash basis: interest payments on loans
52   Exclusion of double relief for interest
Social security contributions
53   Social security contributions
Penalties, interest and VAT surcharges
54   Penalties, interest and VAT surcharges
Crime-related payments
55   Crime-related payments
Integral features
55A   Expenditure on integral features
Rental rebates
55B   Rental rebates
Chapter 5   Trade Profits: Rules Allowing Deductions
Introduction
56   Professions and vocations
Cash basis accounting
56A   Application of Chapter to the cash basis
Pre-trading expenses
57   Pre-trading expenses
Subsistence expenses
57A   Expenses incurred by traders on food and drink
Cash basis: interest payments
57B   Cash basis: interest payments on loans
Incidental costs of obtaining finance
58   Incidental costs of obtaining finance
59   Convertible loans and loan stock etc
Tenants under taxed leases
60   Tenants under taxed leases: introduction
61   Tenants occupying land for purposes of trade treated as incurring expenses
62   Limit on deductions if tenant entitled to mineral extraction allowance

63   Tenants dealing with land as property employed for purposes of trade

64   Restrictions on section 61 expenses: lease premium receipts

65   Restrictions on section 61 expenses: lease of part of premises

66   Corporation tax receipts treated as taxed receipts under ICTA

67   Restrictions on section 61 expenses: corporation tax receipts under ICTA

Payments for restrictive undertakings

69   Payments for restrictive undertakings

Seconded employees

70   Employees seconded to charities and educational establishments

71   Educational establishments

Contributions to agents' expenses

72   Payroll deduction schemes: contributions to agents' expenses

Counselling and retraining expenses

73   Counselling and other outplacement services

74   Retraining courses

75   Retraining courses: recovery of tax

Redundancy payments etc

76   Redundancy payments and approved contractual payments

77   Payments in respect of employment wholly in employer's trade

78   Payments in respect of employment in more than one capacity

79   Additional payments

79A   Additional payments: change in the persons carrying on the trade

80   Payments made by the Government

Personal security expenses

81   Personal security expenses

Contributions to local enterprise organisations or urban regeneration companies

82   Contributions to local enterprise organisations or urban regeneration companies

83   Meaning of "local enterprise organisation"

84   Approval of local enterprise agencies

85   Supplementary provisions with respect to approvals

86   Meaning of "urban regeneration company"

Contributions to flood and coastal erosion risk management projects

86A   Contributions to flood and coastal erosion risk management projects

86B   Interpretation of section 86A

Scientific research

87   Expenses of research and development

88   Payments to research associations, universities etc

Expenses connected with patents, designs and trade marks

89   Expenses connected with patents

90   Expenses connected with designs or trade marks

Export Credits Guarantee Department

91   Payments to Export Credits Guarantee Department

Expenses connected with foreign trades

92   Expenses connected with foreign trades

93   Allocation of expenses

94   Family expenses

SAYE option schemes, CSOP schemes

94A   Costs of setting up SAYE option scheme or CSOP scheme

Limited liability partnerships: salaried members

94AA   Deductions in relation to salaried members

Chapter 5A   Trade profits: deductions allowable at a fixed rate

Introduction

94B   Professions and vocations

94C   Provisions not applicable to certain firms

Expenditure on vehicles

94D   Expenditure on vehicles

94E   Excluded vehicles

94F   The appropriate mileage amount

94G   Definitions of types of vehicle

Use of home for business purposes

94H   Use of home for business purposes

Premises used both as home and business premises

94I   Premises used both as a home and as business premises

Chapter 6   Trade Profits: Receipts

Introduction

95   Professions and vocations

Cash basis accounting

95A   Application of Chapter to the cash basis

Capital receipts

96　　Capital receipts
96A　　Capital receipts under, or after leaving, cash basis
96B　　Section 96A: supplementary provision
Debts released
97　　Debts incurred and later released
Cash basis: value of stock and work in progress on cessation
97A　　Cash basis: value of trading stock on cessation of trade
97B　　Cash basis: value of work in progress on cessation of profession or vocation
Amounts received following earlier cessation
98　　Acquisition of trade: receipts from transferor's trade
Reverse premiums
99　　Reverse premiums
100　　Excluded cases
101　　Tax treatment of reverse premiums
102　　Arrangements not at arm's length
103　　Connected persons and property arrangements
Assets of mutual concerns
104　　Distribution of assets of mutual concerns
Industrial development grants
105　　Industrial development grants
Proceeds of insurance etc
106　　Sums recovered under insurance policies etc
Chapter 6A　　Trade profits: amounts not reflecting commercial transactions
106A　　Professions and vocations
106B　　Application of Chapter
106C　　Amounts not reflecting commercial transactions
106D　　Capital receipts
106E　　Gifts to charities etc
Chapter 7　　Trade Profits: Gifts to Charities Etc
107　　Professions and vocations
108　　Gifts of trading stock to charities etc
109　　Receipt by donor or connected person of benefit attributable to certain gifts
110　　Meaning of "designated educational establishment"
Chapter 8　　Trade Profits: Herd Basis Rules
Introduction
111　　Election for application of herd basis rules
111A　　Herd basis rules not to apply where cash basis used
112　　Meaning of "animal", "herd", "production herd" etc
113　　Other interpretative provisions
The herd basis rules
114　　Initial cost of herd and value of herd
115　　Addition of animals to herd
116　　Replacement of animals in herd
117　　Amount of receipt if old animal slaughtered under disease control order
118　　Sale of animals from herd
119　　Sale of whole or substantial part of herd
120　　Acquisition of new herd begun within 5 years of sale
121　　Section 120: sale for reasons outside farmer's control
122　　Replacement of part sold begun within 5 years of sale
123　　Section 122: sale for reasons outside farmer's control
Elections
124　　Herd basis elections
125　　Five year gap in which no production herd kept
126　　Slaughter under disease control order
Preventing abuse of the herd basis rules
127　　Preventing abuse of the herd basis rules
Supplementary
129　　Further assessment etc if herd basis rules apply
Chapter 9　　Trade Profits: Sound Recordings
Introduction
130　　Expenditure to which this Chapter applies
130A　　Chapter not to apply where cash basis used
132　　Meaning of "original master version" and "certified master version"
133　　Meaning of "relevant period"
Expenditure treated as revenue in nature
134　　Expenditure treated as revenue in nature
Rules for allocating expenditure
135　　Allocation of production or acquisition expenditure to relevant periods
Chapter 10　　Trade Profits: Certain Telecommunication Rights

144A   Chapter not to apply where cash basis used
145   Professions and vocations
146   Meaning of "relevant telecommunication right"
147   Expenditure and receipts treated as revenue in nature
148   Credits or debits arising from revaluation
Chapter 10A   Leases of plant or machinery: special rules for long funding leases
Application of Chapter
148ZA   Chapter not to apply where cash basis used
Lessors under long funding finance leases
148A   Lessor under long funding finance lease: rental earnings
148B   Lessor under long funding finance lease: exceptional items
148C   Lessor under long funding finance lease making termination payment
Lessors under long funding operating lease
148D   Lessor under long funding operating lease: periodic deduction
148DA   "Starting value": general
148DB   "Starting value" where plant or machinery originally unqualifying
148E   Long funding operating lease: lessor's additional expenditure
148EA   Determination of remaining residual value resulting from lessor's first additional
         expenditure
148EB   Determination of remaining residual value resulting from lessor's further additional
         expenditure
148F   Lessor under long funding operating lease: termination of lease
Lessors under long funding finance or operating leases: avoidance etc
148FA   Cases where ss 148A to 148F do not apply: plant or machinery held as trading stock
148FB   Cases where ss 148A to 148F do not apply: lessor also lessee under non-long funding
         lease
148FC   Cases where ss 148A to 148F do not apply: other avoidance
148FD   Cases where ss 148A to 148F do not apply: films
Lessees under long funding finance leases
148G   Lessee under long funding finance lease: limit on deductions
148GA   Lessee under long funding finance leases: right-of-use leases
148H   Lessee under long funding finance lease: termination
Lessees under long funding operating leases
148I   Lessee under long funding operating lease
Interpretation of Chapter
148J   Interpretation of Chapter 10A
Chapter 11   Trade Profits: Other Specific Trades
Cash basis accounting
148K   Application to Chapter to the cash basis
Dealers in securities etc
149   Taxation of amounts taken to reserves
150   Conversion etc of securities held as circulating capital
151   Exchanges of gilts for gilt strips
152   Consolidation of gilt strips
153   Meaning of "gilt-edged security" and "strip"
154   Regulations for determining market value of securities or strips
154A   Certain non-UK residents with interest on 3½% War Loan 1952 Or After
Persons authorised for purposes of FISMA 2000
155   Levies and repayments under FISMA 2000
Dealers in land etc
156   Purchase or sale of woodlands
Mineral exploration and access
161   Mineral exploration and access
Intermediaries treated as making employment payments
163   Deduction for deemed employment payment
164   Special rules for partnerships
Managed service companies
164A   Deduction for deemed employment payments
Worker's services provided to public sector through intermediary
164B   Intermediaries providing worker's services to public sector
Waste disposal
165   Deduction for site preparation expenditure
166   Allocation of site preparation expenditure
167   Site preparation expenditure: supplementary
168   Site restoration payments
Cemeteries and crematoria; interests in land
169   Cemeteries and crematoria: introduction
170   Deduction for capital expenditure
171   Allocation of ancillary capital expenditure

172   Exclusion of expenditure met by subsidies

Crematoria: niches, memorials and inscription

172ZA   Niches, memorials and inscriptions: introduction

172ZB   Allowable deductions: niches

172ZC   Allowable deductions: memorials

172ZD   Allowable deductions: inscriptions

172ZE   Costs of the building

Chapter 11A   Trade Profits: Changes in Trading Stock

Introduction

172A   Meaning of "trading stock"

172AA   Chapter not to apply where cash basis used

Transfers of trading stock between trade and trader

172B   Trading stock appropriated by trader

172C   Trading stock supplied by trader

Other disposals not made in the course of trade

172D   Disposals not made in the course of trade

172E   Acquisitions not made in the course of trade

Relationship with transfer pricing rules

172F   Transfer pricing rules to take precedence

Chapter 12   Trade Profits: Valuation of Stock and Work in Progress on Cessation of Trade

Valuation of trading stock

173   Valuation of trading stock on cessation

174   Meaning of "trading stock"

175   Basis of valuation of trading stock

176   Sale basis of valuation: sale to unconnected person

177   Sale basis of valuation: sale to connected person

178   Sale basis of valuation: election by connected persons

179   Connected persons

180   Cost to buyer of stock valued on sale basis of valuation

181   Meaning of "sale" and related expressions

Valuation of work in progress

182   Valuation of work in progress on cessation

183   Meaning of "work in progress"

184   Basis of valuation of work in progress

185   Election for valuation at cost

Supplementary

186   Determination of questions

Chapter 13   Deductions From Profits: Unremittable Amounts

187   Professions and vocations

188   Application of Chapter

188A   Chapter not to apply where cash basis used

189   Relief for unremittable amounts

190   Restrictions on relief

191   Withdrawal of relief

Chapter 14   Disposal and Acquisition of Know-how

191A   Chapter not to apply where cash basis used

192   Meaning of "know-how" etc

193   Disposal of know-how if trade continues to be carried on

194   Disposal of know-how as part of disposal of all or part of a trade

195   Seller controlled by buyer etc

Chapter 15   Basis Periods

Introduction

196   Professions and vocations

Accounting date

197   Meaning of "accounting date"

The normal rules

198   General rule

199   First tax year

200   Second tax year

201   Tax year in which there is no accounting date

202   Final tax year

Apportionment of profits

203   Apportionment etc of profits to basis periods

Overlap profits and losses

204   Meaning of "overlap period" and "overlap profit"

204A   Overlap profit and trading allowance under Chapter 1 of Part 6A

205   Deduction for overlap profit in final tax year

206   Restriction on bringing losses into account twice

207   Treatment of business start-up payments received in an overlap period

Rules where first accounting date shortly before end of tax year
208   When the late accounting date rules apply
209   Rule if there is an accounting date
210   Rules if there is no accounting date
Slight variations in accounting date
211   Treating middle date as accounting date
212   Consequence of treating middle date as accounting date
213   Circumstances in which middle date not treated as accounting date
Special rules if accounting date changes
214   When a change of accounting date occurs
215   Change of accounting date in third tax year
216   Change of accounting date in later tax year
217   Conditions for basis period to end with new accounting date
218   Commercial reasons for change of accounting date
219   The year after an ineffective change of accounting date
220   Deduction for overlap profit on change of accounting date
Chapter 16   Averaging Profits of Farmers and Creative Artists
221   Claim for averaging of fluctuating profits
221A   Claim not available where cash basis used
222   Circumstances in which claim for two-year averaging may be made
222A   Circumstances in which claim for five-year averaging may be made
223   Adjustment of profits
224   Effect of adjustment
225   Effect of later adjustment of profits
Chapter 16ZA   Compensation for compulsory slaughter of animals
225ZA   Application of Chapter 16ZA
225ZAA   Chapter not to apply where cash basis used
225ZB   Right to make claim
225ZC   Book value
225ZD   Effect of claim for spreading profits
225ZE   Adjustment: cessation of trading
225ZF   Time limits etc for spreading claim
225ZG   Interpretation
Chapter 16A   Oil Activities
Application of Chapter
225ZH   Chapter not to apply where cash basis used
Basic definitions
225A   Meaning of "oil extraction activities"
225B   Meaning of "oil rights"
225C   Meaning of "ring fence income"
225D   Meaning of "ring fence trade"
225E   Other definitions
Oil valuation
225F   Valuation where market value taken into account under section 2 of OTA 1975
225G   Valuation where disposal not sale at arm's length
225H   Valuation where excess of nominated proceeds
225I   Valuation where relevant appropriation but no disposal
225J   Valuation where appropriation to refining etc
Regional development grants
225K   Reduction of expenditure by reference to regional development grant
225L   Adjustment as a result of regional development grant
Tariff receipts etc
225M   Tariff receipts etc
Abandonment guarantees
225N   Expenditure on abandonment guarantees
Abandonment expenditure
225R   Introduction to section 225S
225S   Relief for expenditure incurred by a participator in meeting defaulter's abandonment
        expenditure
Interest on repayment of APRT
225U   Interest on repayment of APRT
Receipts arising from decommissioning
225V   Receipts arising from decommissioning
Chapter 17   Adjustment Income
Introduction
226   Professions and vocations
Adjustment on change of basis
227   Application of Chapter
227A   Application of Chapter where cash basis used

227B   Cash basis treatment: full relief under Chapter 1 of Part 6A (trading allowance)
227C   Application of Chapter where section 227B applies
228   Adjustment income and adjustment expense
229   Income charged
230   Person liable
231   Calculation of the adjustment
Treatment of adjustment income and adjustment expense
232   Treatment of adjustment income
233   Treatment of adjustment expense
Expenses previously brought into account
234   No adjustment for certain expenses previously brought into account
Realising or writing off assets
235   Cases where adjustment not required until assets realised or written off
Mark to market
236   Change from realisation basis to mark to market
237   Election for spreading if section 236 applies
Spreading of adjustment income on leaving cash basis
239A   Spreading on leaving cash basis
239B   Election to accelerate charge under section 239A
Supplementary
240   Liability of personal representatives if person liable dies
Chapter 17A   Cash basis: adjustments for capital allowances
Introduction
240A   Professions and vocations
Adjustments on entering cash basis
240B   "Entering the cash basis"
240C   Unrelieved qualifying expenditure: Parts 2, 7 and 8 of CAA 2001
240CA   Unrelieved qualifying expenditure: Part 5 of CAA 2001
240D   Assets not fully paid for
Successions where predecessor and successor are connected persons
240E   Effect of election where predecessor and successor are connected persons
Chapter 18   Post-cessation Receipts
Introduction
241   Professions and vocations
Charge to tax on post-cessation receipts
242   Charge to tax on post-cessation receipts
243   Extent of charge to tax
244   Income charged
245   Person liable
Meaning of "post-cessation receipts"
246   Basic meaning of "post-cessation receipt"
247   Other rules about what counts as post-cessation receipts
Sums treated as post-cessation receipts
248   Debts paid after cessation
249   Debts released after cessation
250   Receipts relating to post-cessation expenditure
251   Transfer of rights if transferee does not carry on trade
Sums that are not post-cessation receipts
252   Transfer of trading stock or work in progress
253   Lump sums paid to personal representatives for copyright etc
Deductions
254   Allowable deductions
255   Further rules about allowable deductions
Reliefs
256   Treatment of post-cessation receipts
257   Election to carry back
Chapter 19   Supplementary
258   Changes in trustees and personal representatives
259   Meaning of "statutory insolvency arrangement"
Part 3   Property Income
Chapter 1   Introduction
260   Overview of Part 3
261   Provisions which must be given priority over Part 3
262   Priority between Chapters within Part 3
Chapter 2   Property Businesses
Introduction
263   Introduction
Basic meaning of UK and overseas property business
264   UK property business

265   Overseas property business

Generating income from land

266   Meaning of "generating income from land"

267   Activities not for generating income from land

Chapter 3   Profits of Property Businesses: Basic Rules

Charge to tax on profits of a property business

268   Charge to tax on profits of a property business

269   Territorial scope of charge to tax

270   Income charged

271   Person liable

Basis of calculation of profits

271A   Basis of calculation of profits: GAAP required

271B   Calculation of profits in accordance with GAAP

271C   Basis of calculation of profits: cash basis required

271D   Calculation of profits on the cash basis

Calculation of profits: application of trading income rules

271E   Profits of a property business: application of trading income rules

272   Application of trading income rules: GAAP

272ZA   Application of trading income rules: cash basis

Calculation of profits: other general rules

272A   Restricting deductions for finance costs related to residential property

272B   Meaning of "costs of a dwelling-related loan"

273   Amounts not brought into account as part of a property business

274   Relationship between rules prohibiting and allowing deductions

Tax reductions for non-deductible costs of a dwelling-related loan

274A   Reduction for individuals: entitlement

274AA   Reduction for individuals: calculation

274B   Reduction for accumulated or discretionary trust income: entitlement

274C   Reduction for accumulated or discretionary trust income: calculation

Apportionment of profits

275   Apportionment etc of profits to tax year

Chapter 4   Profits of Property Businesses: Lease Premiums Etc

Introduction

276   Introduction

276A   Application of Chapter to property businesses using cash basis

Amounts treated as receipts: leases

277   Lease premiums

278   Amount treated as lease premium where work required

279   Sums payable instead of rent

280   Sums payable for surrender of lease

281   Sums payable for variation or waiver of terms of lease

281A   Sums to which sections 277 to 281 do not apply

282   Assignments for profit of lease granted at undervalue

283   Provisions supplementary to section 282

Other amounts treated as receipts

284   Sales with right to reconveyance

285   Sale and leaseback transactions

286   Provisions supplementary to sections 284 and 285

Additional calculation rule for reducing certain receipts

287   Circumstances in which additional calculation rule applies

288   The additional calculation rule

289   The additional calculation rule: special cases

290   Meaning of "unused amount" and "unreduced amount"

Deductions in relation to certain receipts

291   Deductions for expenses under section 292

292   Tenants under taxed leases treated as incurring expenses

293   Restrictions on section 292 expenses: the additional calculation rule

294   Restrictions on section 292 expenses: lease of part of premises

Limit on effect of additional calculation rule and deductions

295   Limit on reductions and deductions

Relationship with ICTA

296   Corporation tax receipts treated as taxed receipts

297   Taking account of reductions in corporation tax receipts

298   Taking account of deductions for rent as a result of section 37(4) or 87(2) of ICTA

Certain administrative provisions

299   Payment of tax by instalments

300   Statement of accuracy for purposes of section 282

301   Claim for repayment of tax payable by virtue of section 284

302   Claim for repayment of tax payable by virtue of section 285

Determinations affecting liability of more than one person
302A   Appeals against proposed determinations
302B   Section 302A: supplementary
302C   Determination by tribunal
Effective duration of lease
303   Rules for determining effective duration of lease
304   Applying the rules in section 303
Other interpretative provisions
306   Provisions about premiums
307   Interpretation
Cash basis: application of Chapter
307A   Cash basis: application of Chapter
Property businesses using cash basis
307B   Cash basis: capital expenditure
307C   Cash basis: deduction for costs of loans
307D   Cash basis: modification of deduction for costs of loans
Property businesses that use, or have used, cash basis
307E   Capital receipts under, or after leaving, cash basis
307F   Deemed capital receipts under, or after leaving, cash basis
Property allowance
307G   Property allowance
Chapter 5   Profits of Property Businesses: Other Rules About Receipts and Deductions
Furnished accommodation: receipts and deductions
308   Furnished lettings
Furnished accommodation: rent-a-room relief
309   Rent-a-room relief
Treatment of receipts on acquisition of business
310   Acquisition of business: receipts from transferor's UK property business
Reverse premiums as receipts
311   Reverse premiums
Deduction for replacement of domestic items
311A   Replacement domestic items relief
Deductions for expenditure on energy-saving items
312   Deduction for expenditure on energy-saving items
313   Restrictions on relief
314   Regulations
Deductions for expenditure on sea walls
315   Deduction for expenditure on sea walls
316   Transfer of interest in premises
317   Ending of lease of premises
318   Transfer involving company within the charge to corporation tax
Apportionments on sale of land
320   Nature of item apportioned on sale of estate or interest in land
Mutual business
321   Mutual business
Chapter 6   Commercial Letting of Furnished Holiday Accommodation
Introduction
322   Introduction
Definition
323   Meaning of "commercial letting of furnished holiday accommodation"
324   Meaning of "relevant period" in sections 325 and 326
325   Meaning of "qualifying holiday accommodation"
326   Under-used holiday accommodation: averaging elections
326A   Under-used holiday accommodation: letting condition not met
Separate profit calculations
327   Capital allowances and loss relief: UK property business
328   Relevant UK earnings for pension purposes: UK property business
328A   Capital allowances and loss relief: overseas property business
328B   Relevant UK earnings for pension purposes: overseas property business
Chapter 7   Adjustment Income
Adjustment on change of basis
329   Application of Chapter
329A   Application of Chapter where cash basis used
330   Adjustment income and adjustment expense
331   Income charged
332   Person liable
Treatment of adjustment income and adjustment expense
333   Treatment of adjustment income
334   Treatment of adjustment expense

Spreading of adjustment income on leaving cash basis
334A   Spreading on leaving cash basis and related election
Chapter 7A   Cash basis: adjustments for capital allowances
334B   "Entering the cash basis"
334C   Unrelieved qualifying expenditure
334D   Assets not fully paid for
334E   Effect of election where predecessor and successor are connected persons
Chapter 8   Rent Receivable in Connection with a UK Section 12(4) Concern
Charge to tax on rent receivable in connection with a UK section 12(4) concern
335   Charge to tax on rent receivable in connection with a UK section 12(4) concern
336   Meaning of "rent receivable in connection with a UK section 12(4) concern"
337   Income charged
338   Person liable
Management expenses of owner of mineral rights
339   Deduction for management expenses of owner of mineral rights
Chapter 9   Rent Receivable for UK Electric-line Wayleaves
Charge to tax on rent receivable for UK electric-line wayleaves
344   Charge to tax on rent receivable for a UK electric-line wayleave
345   Meaning of "rent receivable for a UK electric-line wayleave"
346   Extent of charge to tax
347   Income charged
348   Person liable
Chapter 10   Post-cessation Receipts
Charge to tax on post-cessation receipts
349   Charge to tax on post-cessation receipts
350   Extent of charge to tax
351   Income charged
352   Person liable
Meaning of "post-cessation receipts"
353   Basic meaning of "post-cessation receipt"
354   Other rules about what counts as a "post-cessation receipt"
355   Transfer of rights if transferee does not carry on UK property business
Supplementary
356   Application to businesses within the charge to corporation tax
Chapter 12   Supplementary
361   Changes in trustees and personal representatives
Amounts treated as dividends
386   Open-ended investment company dividend distributions
387   Date when dividends paid under section 386
388   Interpretation of sections 386 and 387
389   Authorised unit trust dividend distributions
390   Date when dividends paid under section 389
391   Interpretation of sections 389 and 390
Shares in Schedule 2 share incentive plans ("SIPs")
392   SIP shares: introduction
393   Later charge where cash dividends retained in SIPs are paid over
394   Distribution when dividend shares cease to be subject to SIP
395   Reduction in tax due in cases within section 394
396   Interpretation of sections 392 to 395
Other amounts treated as distributions
396A   Arrangements offering a choice of capital or income return
396B   Distributions in a winding up
Payment and deduction of tax
399   Tax treated as paid on distributions received by non-UK resident persons
401   Relief: distribution repaying shares or security issued in earlier distribution
401B   Power to obtain information
Anti-avoidance
401C   Temporary non-residents
Chapter 4   Dividends From Non-UK Resident Companies
Charge to tax on dividends from non-UK resident companies
402   Charge to tax on dividends from non-UK resident companies
403   Income charged
404   Person liable
404A   Distributions in a winding up
Shares in Schedule 2 share incentive plans ("SIPs")
405   SIP shares: introduction
406   Later charge where cash dividends retained in SIPs are paid over
407   Dividend payment when dividend shares cease to be subject to SIP
408   Reduction in tax due in cases within section 407

Anti-avoidance
408A   Temporary non-residents
Chapter 5   Stock Dividends From UK Resident Companies
409   Charge to tax on stock dividend income
410   When stock dividend income arises
410A   Conversion etc of bonus share capital
411   Income charged
412   Cash equivalent of share capital
413   Person liable
413A   Temporary non-residents
414A   Interpretation of Chapter
Chapter 6   Release of Loan to Participator in Close Company
415   Charge to tax under Chapter 6
416   Income charged
417   Person liable
418   Relief where borrowers liable as settlors
419   Loans and advances to persons who die
420   Loans and advances to trustees of settlements that have ended
420A   Temporary non-residents
421A   Power to obtain information
Chapter 7   Purchased Life Annuity Payments
422   Charge to tax on purchased life annuity payments
423   Meaning of "purchased life annuity"
424   Income charged
425   Person liable
426   Annuity payments received after deduction of tax
Chapter 8   Profits From Deeply Discounted Securities
Charge to tax under Chapter 8
427   Charge to tax on profits from deeply discounted securities
428   Income charged
429   Person liable
Deeply discounted securities
430   Meaning of "deeply discounted security"
431   Excluded occasions of redemption
432   Securities which are not deeply discounted securities
433   Meaning of "excluded indexed security"
434   Securities issued in separate tranches: preliminary
435   Securities issued in separate tranches: basic rule
436   Deeply discounted securities issued in separate tranches: nominal value rule
Disposals
437   Transactions which are disposals
438   Timing of transfers and acquisitions
Calculating profits
439   Calculating the profit from disposals
440   Market value disposals
441   Market value acquisitions
442   Securities issued in accordance with qualifying earn-out right
Special rules for strips of government securities
443   Application of this Chapter to strips of government securities
444   Meaning of "strip" in Chapter 8
445   Strips of government securities: acquisitions and disposals
446   Strips of government securities: relief for losses
447   Restriction of profits on strips by reference to original acquisition cost
448   Restriction of losses on strips by reference to original acquisition cost
449   Strips of government securities: manipulation of acquisition, transfer or redemption
    payments
450   Market value of strips etc
487   Disregard of certain assignments
488   Disregard of some events after alterations of life insurance policy terms
489   Conditions applicable to alterations of life insurance policy terms
490   Last payment under guaranteed income bonds etc treated as total surrender
Calculating gains: general
491   Calculating gains: general rules
492   The total benefit value of a policy or contract
493   The value of a policy or contract
494   The total allowable deductions for a policy or contract
495   Disregard of certain amounts in calculating gains under section 491
496   Modification of section 494: qualifying endowment policies held as security for
    company debts

497　　Disregard of trivial inducement benefits

Part surrenders and assignments: periodic calculations and excess events

498　　Requirement for periodic calculations in part surrender or assignment cases
499　　Meaning of "insurance year" and "final insurance year"
500　　Events treated as part surrenders
501　　Part surrenders: loans
502　　Exception from section 501 for loans to buy life annuities
503　　Exception from section 501 for certain loans under qualifying policies
504　　Part surrenders: payments under guaranteed income bonds etc.
505　　Assignments etc involving co-ownership
506　　Assignments occurring when there is a co-ownership transaction
507　　Method for making periodic calculations under section 498
507A　 Recalculating gains under section 507
508　　The value of rights partially surrendered or assigned
509　　Chargeable events in certain cases where periodic calculations show gains

Transaction-related calculations and part surrender or assignment events

510　　Requirement for transaction-related calculations in certain part surrender and assignment cases
511　　Method for making transaction-related calculations under section 510
512　　Available premium left for relevant transaction
512A　 Recalculating gains under section 511
513　　Special rules for part surrenders and assignments in final insurance year
514　　Chargeable events where transaction-related calculations show gains

Personal portfolio bonds

515　　Requirement for annual calculations in relation to personal portfolio bonds
516　　Meaning of "personal portfolio bond"
517　　Policies and contracts which are not personal portfolio bonds
518　　The index categories
519　　The index selection conditions
520　　The property categories
521　　The property selection conditions
522　　Method for making annual calculations under section 515
523　　The total amount of personal portfolio bond excesses
524　　The total amount of part surrender gains
525　　Chargeable events where annual calculations show gains
526　　Power to make regulations about personal portfolio bonds

Reductions from gains

527　　Reduction for sums taken into account otherwise than under Chapter 9
528　　Reduction in amount charged on basis of non-UK residence where individual liable for tax.
528A　 Reduction in amount charged on basis of non-UK residence of deceased person

Income tax treated as paid and reliefs

530　　Income tax treated as paid etc.
531　　Exceptions to section 530
532　　Relief for policies and contracts with European Economic Area insurers
533　　Meaning of "comparable EEA tax charge"
534　　Regulations providing for relief in other cases where foreign tax chargeable
535　　Top slicing relief
536　　Top slicing relieved liability: one chargeable event
537　　Top slicing relieved liability: two or more chargeable events
538　　Recovery of tax from trustees

Deficiencies

539　　Relief for deficiencies
540　　When deficiencies arise: events following calculation events
541　　Calculation of deficiencies

Rebated or reinvested commission

541A　 Effect of rebated or reinvested commission in certain cases
541B　 Section 541A: further definitions

Supplementary

542　　Replacement of qualifying policies
543　　Issue time of qualifying policy replacing foreign policy
544　　Application of Chapter to policies and contracts in which companies interested
545　　Minor definitions
546　　Table of provisions subject to special rules for older policies and contracts

Part 5　　Miscellaneous Income

Chapter 1　　Introduction

574　　Overview of Part 5
575　　Provisions which must be given priority over Part 5
576　　Priority between Chapters within Part 5

577 Territorial scope of Part 5 charges
577A Territorial scope of Part 5 charges: receipts from intellectual property
Chapter 2 Receipts From Intellectual Property
Introduction
578 Contents of Chapter
Charge to tax on non-trading income from intellectual property
579 Charge to tax on royalties and other income from intellectual property
580 Income charged under section 579
581 Person liable for tax under section 579
582 Deductions in calculating certain income charged under section 579
Disposals of know-how
583 Charge to tax on income from disposals of know-how
584 Exceptions to charge under section 583
585 Income charged under section 583
586 Person liable for tax under section 583
Sales of patent rights
587 Charge to tax on income from sales of patent rights
588 Income charged under section 587
589 Person liable for tax under section 587
590 UK resident sellers: spreading rules
591 Non-UK resident sellers: election for spreading
592 Further provision about elections for spreading: instalments
593 Death of seller
594 Winding up of a body corporate
595 Deduction of tax from payments to non-UK residents
596 Adjustments where tax has been deducted
597 Licences connected with patents
598 Rights to acquire future patent rights
599 Sums paid for Crown use etc treated as paid under licence
Relief from income tax on patent income
600 Relief for expenses: patent income
601 How relief is given under section 600
Payments received after deduction of tax
602 Payments received after deduction of tax
Supplementary
603 Contributions to expenditure
604 Contributions not made by public bodies nor eligible for tax relief
605 Exchanges
606 Apportionment where property sold together
607 Questions about apportionments affecting two or more persons
608 Meaning of "capital sums" etc.
Chapter 2A Offshore receipts in respect of intangible property
Charge to tax on offshore receipts in respect of intangible property
608A Charge to tax on UK-derived amounts
608B Income charged under section 608A
608C Person liable for tax under section 608A
608D Meaning of residence
608E Meaning of "full treaty territory"
608F Meaning of "UK-derived amount" and "UK sales"
608G Section 608F: apportionment of amounts
608H Meaning of "intangible property"
648 Income arising under a settlement
Chapter 6 Beneficiaries' Income From Estates in Administration
Charge to tax on estate income
649 Charge to tax on estate income
650 Absolute, limited and discretionary interests
651 Meaning of "UK estate" and "foreign estate"
Types of estate income
652 Estate income: absolute interests in residue
653 Meaning of "the administration period" and "the final tax year"
654 Estate income: limited interests in residue
655 Estate income: discretionary interests in residue
Income charged and person liable
656 Income charged: UK estates
657 Income charged: foreign estates
658 Special rules for foreign income
659 Person liable
Basic amount of estate income: general calculation rules
660 Basic amount of estate income: absolute interests

661 Basic amount of estate income: limited interests
662 Basic amount of estate income: discretionary interests
663 The applicable rate for grossing up basic amounts of estate income
664 The aggregate income of the estate
Further provisions for calculating estate income relating to absolute interests
665 Assumed income entitlement
666 The residuary income of the estate
667 Shares of residuary income of estate
668 Reduction in share of residuary income of estate
669 Reduction in residuary income: inheritance tax on accrued income
670 Applicable rate for determining assumed income entitlement (UK estates)
Special rules for successive interests
671 Successive absolute interests
672 Successive interests: assumed income entitlement of holder of absolute interest following limited interest
673 Successive interests: payments in respect of limited interests followed by absolute interests
674 Successive interests: holders of limited interests
675 Basic amount of estate income: successive limited interests
676 Apportionments
Relief where foreign estates have borne UK income tax
677 Relief where UK income tax borne by foreign estate: absolute interests
678 Relief where UK income tax borne by foreign estate: limited and discretionary interests
General
679 Income from which basic amounts are treated as paid
680 Income treated as bearing income tax
680A Income treated as dividend income
681 Transfers of assets etc treated as payments
682 Assessments, adjustments and claims after the administration period
682A Statements relating to estate income
Chapter 7 Annual Payments Not Otherwise Charged
683 Charge to tax on annual payments not otherwise charged
684 Income charged
685 Person liable
685A Settlor-interested settlements
686 Payments received after deduction of tax
Chapter 8 Income Not Otherwise Charged
687 Charge to tax on income not otherwise charged
688 Income charged
689 Person liable
689A Temporary non-residents
Part 6 Exempt Income
Chapter 1 Introduction
690 Overview of Part 6
Chapter 2 National Savings Income
692 Income from savings certificates
693 Income from Ulster Savings Certificates
Chapter 3 Income From Individual Investment Plans
694 Income from individual investment plans
694A Deceased investors
695 Investment plans
695A Investment plans for children
696 Plan managers
697 Special requirements for certain foreign managers
698 Requirements for discharge of foreign institution's duties
699 Non-entitlement to exemption
701 General and supplementary powers
Chapter 4 SAYE Interest
702 Interest under certified SAYE savings arrangements
703 Meaning of "certified SAYE savings arrangement"
704 Types of arrangements and providers
705 Certification of arrangements
706 Withdrawal and variation of certifications and connected requirements
707 Authorisation of providers
708 Withdrawal and variation of authorisations
Chapter 5 Venture Capital Trust Dividends
709 Venture capital trust dividends
710 Treatment of shares where annual acquisition limit exceeded
711 Identification of shares after disposals

712   Identification of shares after reorganisations etc.

Chapter 6   Income From FOTRA Securities

713   Introduction: securities free of tax to residents abroad ("FOTRA securities")

714   Exemption of profits from FOTRA securities

715   Interest from FOTRA securities held on trust

716   Restriction on deductions etc. relating to FOTRA securities

Chapter 7   Purchased Life Annuity Payments

Partial exemption for purchased life annuity payments

717   Exemption for part of purchased life annuity payments

718   Excluded annuities

719   Extent of exemption under section 717

720   Exempt proportion: term dependent solely on duration of life

721   Exempt sum: term dependent solely on duration of life

722   Consideration for the grant of annuities

724   Regulations

Immediate needs annuities

725   Annual payments under immediate needs annuities

726   Meaning of "care provider"

Chapter 8   Other Annual Payments

Certain annual payments by individuals

727   Certain annual payments by individuals

728   Commercial payments

729   Payments for non-taxable consideration

730   Foreign maintenance payments

Periodical payments of personal injury damages etc.

731   Periodical payments of personal injury damages

732   Compensation awards

733   Persons entitled to exemptions for personal injury payments etc

734   Payments from trusts for injured persons

Health and employment insurance payments

735   Health and employment insurance payments

736   Health and employment risks and benefits

737   Period for which payments may be made

738   Risk of significant loss

739   Conditions to be met by policies also providing other benefits

740   Conditions to be met where policies are linked

741   Aggregation of policies where employment ends for health reasons

742   Meaning of "the insured"

743   Policies for the benefit of others who contribute to premiums

Payments to adopters

744   Payments to adopters, etc: England and Wales

745   Payments to adopters, etc: Scotland

746   Payments to adopters, etc: Northern Ireland

747   Power to amend sections 744 to 746

832   Relevant foreign income charged on remittance basis

832A   Section 832: temporary non-residents

832B   Section 832: deductions from remitted income

Chapter 3   Relevant Foreign Income Charged On Arising Basis: Deductions and Reliefs

838   Expenses attributable to collection or payment of relevant foreign income

839   Annual payments payable out of relevant foreign income

840   Relief for backdated pensions charged on the arising basis

840A   Claims under section 840

Chapter 4   Unremittable Income

841   Unremittable income: introduction

842   Claim for relief for unremittable income

843   Withdrawal of relief

844   Income charged on withdrawal of relief after source ceases

845   Valuing unremittable income

Part 9   Partnerships

Introduction

846   Overview of Part 9

847   General provisions

848   Assessment of partnerships

848A   Bare trusts

Calculation of partners' shares

849   Calculation of firm's profits or losses

850   Allocation of firm's profits or losses between partners

850A   Profit-making period in which some partners have losses

850B   Loss-making period in which some partners have profits

850C   Excess profit allocation to non-individual partners
850D   Excess profit allocation: cases involving individuals who are not partners
850E   Payments by B out of the excess part of B's profit share
851   Calculations etc. where firm has other income or losses
Firms with trading income
852   Carrying on by partner of notional trade
852A   Notional trades: indirect partners
853   Basis periods for partners' notional trades
Firms with trading and other source income
854   Carrying on by partner of notional business
855   Basis periods for partners' notional businesses
855A   Notional business: indirect partners
856   Overlap profits from partners' notional businesses
Firms with a foreign element
857   Partners to whom the remittance basis applies
858   Resident partners and double taxation agreements
Miscellaneous
859   Special provisions about farming and property income
860   Adjustment income
861   Sale of patent rights: effect of partnership changes
862   Sale of patent rights: effect of later cessation of trade
863   Limited liability partnerships
863A   Limited liability partnerships: salaried members
863B   Condition A
863C   Condition B
863D   Condition C
863E   M's contribution to the limited liability partnership: the basic calculation
863F   M's contribution to the limited liability partnership: deemed contributions
863G   Anti-avoidance
Alternative investment fund managers
863H   Election for special provision for alternative investment fund managers to apply
863I   Allocation of profit to the AIFM firm
863J   Vesting of remuneration represented by the allocated profit
863K   Vesting statements
863L   The AIFMD remuneration guidelines
Part 10   General Provisions
Chapter 1   Introduction
864   Overview of Part 10
Chapter 2   General Calculation Rules etc
Unpaid remuneration
865   Unpaid remuneration: non-trades and non-property businesses
Employee benefit contributions
866   Employee benefit contributions: non-trades and non-property businesses
Business entertainment and gifts
867   Business entertainment and gifts: non-trades and non-property businesses
Social security contributions
868   Social security contributions: non-trades etc
Penalties, interest and VAT surcharges
869   Penalties, interest and VAT surcharges: non-trades etc
Crime-related payments
870   Crime-related payments: non-trades and non-property businesses
Apportionment of profits
871   Apportionment etc of miscellaneous profits to tax year
Calculation of losses
872   Losses calculated on same basis as miscellaneous income
Chapter 3   Supplementary and General Provisions
Orders and regulations
873   Orders and regulations made by Treasury or Commissioners
Interpretation
874   Activities in UK sector of continental shelf
875   Meaning of "caravan"
878   Other definitions
879   Interpretation: Scotland
880   Interpretation: Northern Ireland
General and final
882   Consequential amendments
883   Commencement and transitional provisions etc
884   Repeals and revocations
885   Abbreviations and general index in Schedule 4

886   Short title

Schedules:

Schedule 1—Consequential amendments

Schedule 2—Transitionals and savings etc

Schedule 3—Repeals and revocations

Schedule 4—Abbreviations and defined expressions

PART 1

OVERVIEW

1 Overview of Act

(1) This Act imposes charges to income tax under—

    [(*za*)   provision about a trading allowance and property allowance (see Part 6A),][3]

    (*a*)   Part 2 (trading income),

    (*b*)   Part 3 (property income),

    (*c*)   Part 4 (savings and investment income), and

    (*d*)   Part 5 (certain miscellaneous income).

(2)   . . . [1]

(3) Exemptions from those charges are dealt with in Part 6 (exempt income) but any Part 6 exemptions which are most obviously relevant to particular types of income are also mentioned in the provisions about those types of income.

(4) What is or is not mentioned in those provisions does not limit the effect of Part 6.

(5) This Act also contains—

    (*a*)   provision about rent-a-room relief and [qualifying care][2] relief (see Part 7),

    (*b*)   special rules for foreign income (see Part 8),

    (*c*)   special rules for partnerships (see Part 9), and

    (*d*)   certain calculation rules and general provisions (see Part 10).

(6) For abbreviations and defined expressions used in this Act, see section 885 and Schedule 4.

Amendments—[1]   Sub-s (2) repealed by ITA 2007 ss 1027, 1031, Sch 1 paras 492, 493, Sch 3 Pt 1 with effect for income tax purposes from 6 April 2007, and corporation tax purposes for accounting periods ending after 5 April 2007.

[2]   In sub-s (5) words substituted for words "foster-care" by F(No 3)A 2010 s 1, Sch 1 paras 30, 31 with effect for the tax year 2010–11 and subsequent tax years, subject to transitional provisions in F(No 3)A 2010 Sch 1 paras 36(2)–(5), 37.

[3]   Sub-s (5)(*za*) inserted by F(No 2)A 2017 s 17, Sch 3 paras 2, 3 with effect for the tax year 2017–18 and subsequent tax years.

2 Overview of priority rules

(1) This Act contains some rules establishing an order of priority in respect of certain amounts which would otherwise—

    (*a*)   fall within a charge to income tax under two or more Chapters or Parts of this Act, or

    (*b*)   fall within a charge to income tax under a Chapter or Part of this Act and ITEPA 2003.

(2) See, in particular—

    section 4 (provisions which must be given priority over Part 2),

    section 261 (provisions which must be given priority over Part 3),

    section 262 (priority between Chapters within Part 3),

    section 366 (provisions which must be given priority over Part 4),

    section 367 (priority between Chapters within Part 4),

    section 575 (provisions which must be given priority over Part 5), and

    section 576 (priority between Chapters within Part 5).

(3) But the rules in those sections need to be read with other rules of law (whether in this Act or otherwise) about the scope of particular provisions or the order of priority to be given to them.

(4) Section 171(2) of FA 1993 (profits of Lloyd's underwriters charged only under Chapter 2 of Part 2 of this Act) [and sections 16A (voluntary officeholders: compensation for lost profits), 16B (payments to company directors) and 16C (professionals in practice: incidental income from an office or employment) of this Act are each an example][1] of another rule of law.

Amendments—[1]   In sub-s (4), words substituted by the Enactment of Extra-Statutory Concessions Order, SI 2018/282 art 3(1), (2) with effect from 6 April 2018.

PART 2

TRADING INCOME

CHAPTER 1

INTRODUCTION

3 Overview of Part 2

(1) This Part imposes charges to income tax under—

    (*a*)   Chapter 2 (the profits of a trade, profession or vocation which meet the territorial conditions mentioned in section 6),

    (*b*)   Chapter 17 (amounts treated as adjustment income under section 228), and

    (*c*)   Chapter 18 (post-cessation receipts that are chargeable under this Part).

(2) Part 6 deals with exemptions from the charges under this Part.

(3) See, in particular, the exemptions under sections 777 (VAT repayment supplements) and 778 (incentives to use electronic communications).

(4) The charges under this Part apply to non-UK residents as well as UK residents but this is subject to sections [6(1A), (2)][1] and (3) and 243(3) and (4) (charges on non-UK residents only on UK income).

(5) The rest of this Part contains rules relevant to the charges to tax under this Part.

(6) This section needs to be read with the relevant priority rules (see sections 2 and 4).

Commentary—*Simon's Taxes* **B1.201.**

HMRC Manuals—Business Income Manual BIM14005 (sources of income charged to tax).

Amendment—[1]   In sub-s (4), reference substituted for reference "6(2)" by FA 2016 s 78(3) with effect in relation to disposals on or after 5 July 2016 (FA 2016 s 82(1)), subject to transitional provisions relating to disposals to associated persons on or after 16 March 2016 and before 5 July 2016 (FA 2016 s 82(4)–(15)).

F(No 2)A 2017 s 39 provides that this amendment has effect (so far as it would not otherwise have effect) in relation to amounts that are recognised in GAAP accounts drawn up for any period of account beginning on or after 8 March 2017 or, in the case of a straddling period, amounts that would be recognised in GAAP accounts drawn up for a period of account beginning on 8 March 2017 and ending when the straddling period ends. "Straddling period" means a period of account beginning before 8 March 2017 and ending on or after that date.

4 Provisions which must be given priority over Part 2

(1) Any receipt or other credit item, so far as it falls within—

    (*a*)   Chapter 2 of this Part (receipts of trade, profession or vocation), and

    (*b*)   Chapter 3 of Part 3 so far as it relates to a UK property business, is dealt with under Part 3.

(2) Any receipt or other credit item, so far as it falls within—

    (*a*)   this Part, and

    (*b*)   Part 2, 9 or 10 of ITEPA 2003 (employment income, pension income or social security income),

is dealt with under the relevant Part of ITEPA 2003.

Commentary—*Simon's Taxes* **B1.201.**

CHAPTER 2

INCOME TAXED AS TRADE PROFITS

Charge to tax on trade profits

5 Charge to tax on trade profits

Income tax is charged on the profits of a trade, profession or vocation.

Commentary—*Simon's Taxes* **B1.202.**

HMRC Manuals Business Income Manual BIM37020 (determining tax adjusted profits). BIM40100 (treatment of compensation receipts).

6 Territorial scope of charge to tax

(1) Profits of a trade arising to a UK resident are chargeable to tax under this Chapter wherever the trade is carried on.

[(1A) Profits of a trade of dealing in or developing UK land arising to a non-UK resident are chargeable to tax under this Chapter wherever the trade is carried on.][2]

(2) Profits of a trade [other than a trade of dealing in or developing UK land][2] arising to a non-UK resident are chargeable to tax under this Chapter only if they arise—

    (*a*)   from a trade carried on wholly in the United Kingdom, or

    (*b*)   in the case of a trade carried on partly in the United Kingdom and partly elsewhere, from the part of the trade carried on in the United Kingdom.

[(2A) If the tax year is a split year as respects a UK resident individual, this section has effect as if, for the overseas part of that year, the individual were non-UK resident.][1]

(3) This section applies to professions and vocations as it applies to trades.

Commentary—*Simon's Taxes* **B1.207.**

HMRC Manuals Business Income Manual BIM15010 (scope of trade profits).

Amendments—[1]   Sub-s (2A) inserted by FA 2013 s 218, Sch 45 paras 74, 75 with effect in calculating an individual's liability to income tax or capital gains tax for the tax year 2013–14 or any subsequent tax year, subject to transitional provisions and savings in FA 2013 Sch 45 paras 154–158.

[2]   Sub-s (1A) inserted, and in sub-s (2), words inserted, by FA 2016 s 78(1) with effect in relation to disposals on or after 5 July 2016 (FA 2016 s 82(1)), subject to transitional provisions relating to disposals to associated persons on or after 16 March 2016 and before 5 July 2016 (FA 2016 s 82(4)–(15)).

F(No 2)A 2017 s 39 provides that these amendments have effect (so far as they would not otherwise have effect) in relation to amounts that are recognised in GAAP accounts drawn up for any period of account beginning on or after 8 March 2017 or, in the case of a straddling period, amounts that would be recognised in GAAP accounts drawn up for a period of account beginning on 8 March 2017 and ending when the straddling period ends. "Straddling period" means a period of account beginning before 8 March 2017 and ending on or after that date.

[6A Arrangements for avoiding tax

(1) Subsection (3) applies if a person has entered into an arrangement the main purpose or one of the main purposes of which is to obtain a relevant tax advantage for the person.

(2) In subsection (1) the reference to obtaining a relevant tax advantage includes obtaining a relevant tax advantage by virtue of any provisions of double taxation arrangements, but only in a case where the relevant tax advantage is contrary to the object and purpose of the provisions of the double taxation arrangements (and subsection (3) has effect accordingly, regardless of anything in section 6(1) of TIOPA 2010).

(3) The relevant tax advantage is to be counteracted by means of adjustments.

(4) For this purpose adjustments may be made (whether by an officer of Revenue and Customs or by the person) by way of an assessment, the modification of an assessment, amendment or disallowance of a claim, or otherwise.

(5) In this section "relevant tax advantage" means a tax advantage in relation to income tax to which the person is chargeable (or would without the tax advantage be chargeable) by virtue of section 6(1A).

(6) In this section "tax advantage" includes—

    (*a*) a relief or increased relief from tax,

    (*b*) repayment or increased repayment of tax,

    (*c*) avoidance or reduction of a charge to tax or an assessment to tax,

    (*d*) avoidance of a possible assessment to tax,

    (*e*) deferral of a payment of tax or advancement of a repayment of tax, and

    (*f*) avoidance of an obligation to deduct or account for tax.

(7) In this section—

    "arrangement" (except in the phrase "double taxation arrangements") includes any agreement, understanding, scheme, transaction or series of transactions, whether or not legally enforceable;

    "double taxation arrangements" means arrangements which have effect under section 2(1) of TIOPA 2010 (double taxation relief by agreement with territories outside the United Kingdom).][1]

Amendments—[1]   Sections 6A, 6B inserted by FA 2016 s 78(2) with effect in relation to disposals on or after 5 July 2016 (FA 2016 s 82(1)), subject to transitional provisions relating to disposals to associated persons on or after 16 March 2016 and before 5 July 2016 (FA 2016 s 82(4)–(15)).

F(No 2)A 2017 s 39 provides that this amendment has effect (so far as it would not otherwise have effect) in relation to amounts that are recognised in GAAP accounts drawn up for any period of account beginning on or after 8 March 2017 or, in the case of a straddling period, amounts that would be recognised in GAAP accounts drawn up for a period of account beginning on 8 March 2017 and ending when the straddling period ends. "Straddling period" means a period of account beginning before 8 March 2017 and ending on or after that date.

[6B Trade of dealing in or developing UK land

(1) A non-UK resident person's "trade of dealing in or developing UK land" consists of —

    (*a*) any activities falling within subsection (2) which the person carries on, and

    (*b*) any activities from which profits arise which are treated under Part 9A of ITA 2007 as profits of the person's trade of dealing in or developing UK land.

(2) The activities within this subsection are—

    (*a*) dealing in UK land;

    (*b*) developing UK land for the purpose of disposing of it.

(3) In this section "land" includes—

    (*a*) buildings and structures,

    (*b*) any estate, interest or right in or over land, and

    (*c*) land under the sea or otherwise covered by water.

(4) In this section—

    "disposal" is to be interpreted in accordance with section 517R of ITA 2007;

    "UK land" means land in the United Kingdom.][1]

Amendments—[1]   Sections 6A, 6B inserted by FA 2016 s 78(2) with effect in relation to disposals on or after 5 July 2016 (FA 2016 s 82(1)), subject to transitional provisions relating to disposals to associated persons on or after 16 March 2016 and before 5 July 2016 (FA 2016 s 82(4)–(15)).

F(No 2)A 2017 s 39 provides that this amendment has effect (so far as it would not otherwise have effect) in relation to amounts that are recognised in GAAP accounts drawn up for any period of account beginning on or after 8 March 2017 or, in the case of a straddling period, amounts that would be recognised in GAAP accounts drawn up for a period of account beginning on 8 March 2017 and ending when the straddling period ends. "Straddling period" means a period of account beginning before 8 March 2017 and ending on or after that date.

7 Income charged

(1) Tax is charged under this Chapter on the full amount of the profits of the tax year.

(2) For this purpose the profits of a tax year are the profits of the basis period for the tax year [(including amounts treated as profits of the tax year under section 23E(1))][1].

(3) For the rules identifying the basis period for a tax year, see Chapter 15.

(4) This section is subject to Part 8 (foreign income: special rules).

(5) And, for the purposes of section 830 (meaning of "relevant foreign income"), the profits of a trade, profession or vocation arise from a source outside the United Kingdom only if the trade, profession or vocation is carried on wholly outside the United Kingdom.

Commentary—Simon's Taxes **B1.203.**
HMRC Manuals Business Income Manual BIM15040 (chargeable profits in a basis period).
Amendments—[1]   In sub-s (2), words inserted by F(No 2)A 2017 s 35(1), (3) with effect in relation to relevant benefits arising on or after 6 April 2017.

8 Person liable

The person liable for any tax charged under this Chapter is the person receiving or entitled to the profits.

Commentary—Simon's Taxes **B1.204.**
HMRC Manuals Business Income Manual BIM15015 (trade profits: categories of persons chargeable).

Trades and trade profits

9 Farming and market gardening

(1) Farming or market gardening in the United Kingdom is treated for income tax purposes as the carrying on of a trade or part of a trade (whether or not the land is managed on a commercial basis and with a view to the realisation of profits).
(2) All farming in the United Kingdom carried on by a person, other than farming carried on as part of another trade, is treated for income tax purposes as one trade.
(3) In the case of farming carried on by a firm, this rule is explained by section 859(1).

Commentary—Simon's Taxes **B5.101, B5.105, B5.101.**
HMRC Manuals Business Income Manual BIM15060 (supplementary charging provisions).
BIM55051 (definition of farming).
BIM55000 (overview and contents for detailed farming guidance).
BIM62601 (definition of market gardening).

10 Commercial occupation of land other than woodlands

(1) The commercial occupation of land in the United Kingdom is treated for income tax purposes as the carrying on of a trade or part of a trade.
(2) For this purpose the occupation of land is commercial if the land is managed—
    (*a*) on a commercial basis, and
    (*b*) with a view to the realisation of profits.
(3) This section does not apply—
    (*a*) to farming or market gardening (which is dealt with by section 9),
    (*b*) if the land is being prepared for forestry purposes, or
    (*c*) if the land comprises woodlands (which is dealt with by section 11).

Commentary—Simon's Taxes **B1.504.**
HMRC Manuals Business Income Manual BIM58601 (profits for historic houses and gardens).
BIM15065 (supplementary guidance on charging provisions for occupation of land).

11 Commercial occupation of woodlands

(1) The commercial occupation of woodlands in the United Kingdom is not a trade or part of a trade for any income tax purpose.
(2) For this purpose the occupation of woodlands is commercial if the woodlands are managed—
    (*a*) on a commercial basis, and
    (*b*) with a view to the realisation of profits.
(3) See also sections 267 and 768 (which, when read with this section, secure that profits or losses from the commercial occupation of woodlands in the United Kingdom are ignored for income tax purposes).

Commentary—Simon's Taxes **B1.505.**
HMRC Manuals Business Income Manual BIM67701 (woodlands: profits outside the scope of income tax and corporation tax).

12 Profits of mines, quarries and other concerns

(1) Profits or losses arising out of land in the case of a concern to which this section applies are calculated as if the concern were a trade.
(2) Any profits arising out of the land are charged to income tax as if the concern were a trade carried on in the United Kingdom.
    But this does not impose a charge to tax on a non-UK resident in the case of a concern outside the United Kingdom.
(3) Any losses arising out of the land are treated for the purposes of [Part 4 of ITA 2007][1] (loss relief) as losses of a trade carried on in the United Kingdom.
(4) The concerns to which this section applies are—
    (*a*) mines and quarries (including gravel pits, sand pits and brickfields),
    (*b*) ironworks, gasworks, salt springs or works, alum mines or works, waterworks and streams of water,
    (*c*) canals, inland navigation, docks and drains or levels,
    (*d*) rights of fishing,

(e) rights of markets and fairs, tolls, bridges and ferries,

(f) railways and other kinds of way, and

(g) a concern of the same kind as one specified in paragraph (b), (c), (d) or (e).

(5) This section does not apply to a concern if section 10 (commercial occupation of land other than woodlands) applies to the occupation of the land out of which the profits or losses arise.

Commentary—*Simon's Taxes* **B1.510.**

HMRC ManualsBusiness Income Manual BIM15070 (supplementary charging provisions for mines and quarries).

BIM60201 (guidance on trading income from mines and quarries).

BIM62001 (measuring profits of mining and quarrying).

Amendments—[1]   Words in sub-s (3) substituted by ITA 2007 s 1027, Sch 1 paras 492, 494 with effect for income tax purposes from 6 April 2007, and corporation tax purposes for accounting periods ending after 5 April 2007.

13 Visiting performers

(1) This section applies if an entertainer, sportsman or sportswoman of a prescribed description (a "performer")—

(a) is non-UK resident in a tax year, and

(b) performs a relevant activity in the United Kingdom in the tax year.

(2) If a payment or transfer connected with the relevant activity is made, the performer is treated for income tax purposes as performing the relevant activity in the course of a trade, profession or vocation carried on in the United Kingdom.

(3) It does not matter whether the payment or transfer is made to the performer or anyone else.

(4) Subsection (2) does not apply—

(a) so far as the performer would otherwise be performing the relevant activity in the course of a trade, profession or vocation carried on in the United Kingdom, or

(b) if the relevant activity is performed in the course of an employment or office.

(5) If a payment or transfer connected with the relevant activity is made to—

(a) a person other than the performer, and

(b) that person is of a prescribed description,

the payment or transfer is treated for income tax purposes as made instead to the performer in the course of a trade, profession or vocation carried on in the United Kingdom.

(6) Subsection (5) does not apply in such circumstances as may be prescribed.

(7) If—

(a) income tax is chargeable on profits arising from payments or transfers (made to any person), and

(b) the payments or transfers are connected with the relevant activity,

the tax is charged as if the payments or transfers were received in the course of a separate trade, profession or vocation (distinct from any other trade, profession or vocation carried on by the performer).

(8) In this section and section 14—

. . . [1]

"prescribed" means prescribed by regulations,

"regulations" means regulations made by the Treasury,

"relevant activity" means an activity of a prescribed description, and

. . . [1]

and a payment or transfer is connected with a relevant activity if it has a connection of the prescribed kind with that activity.

[(9) In this section and section 14—

(a) references to a payment include references to a payment by way of loan of money, and

(b) references to a transfer do not include references to a transfer of money but, subject to that, include references to—

(i) a temporary transfer (as by way of loan), and

(ii) a transfer of a right (whether or not a right to receive money).][1]

[(10) This section does not apply to payments or transfers of a kind prescribed in regulations under section 966(6) of ITA 2007.][1]

Commentary—*Simon's Taxes* **E5.804, E5.805.**

HMRC ManualsBusiness Income Manual BIM50600 (contents and overview for UK resident athletes, sportsmen and women).

BIM50150 (contents and overview for UK resident actors and entertainers).

Amendments—[1]   Definitions in sub-s (8) repealed, and sub-ss (9), (10) inserted, by ITA 2007 ss 1027, 1031, Sch 1 paras 492, 495, Sch 3 Pt 1 with effect for income tax purposes from 6 April 2007, and corporation tax purposes for accounting periods ending after 5 April 2007.

14 Visiting performers: supplementary

(1) Regulations may provide—

(a) for the deduction, in calculating any profits of the performer arising from the payment or transfer, of expenses incurred by other persons in relation to the payment or transfer, (*b*) that any liability to income tax (whether of the performer or anyone else) which would, apart from section 13(5), arise in relation to the payment or transfer is not to arise (or is to arise so far as prescribed).

(2) Regulations may provide—

    (*a*) for the apportionment of profits between different trades, professions or vocations of the performer,

    (*b*) for the apportionment between different tax years of the profits arising from relevant activities of the performer,

    (*c*) for losses made in any trade, profession or vocation of the performer to be deducted from or set off against the profits of another trade, profession or vocation of the performer,

    (*d*) that prescribed provisions of the Income Tax Acts about losses, or about expenses, are not to apply (or are to apply with prescribed modifications) in prescribed circumstances relating to the performer.

(3) References in this section to a trade, profession or vocation of the performer include references to the separate one referred to in section 13(7) as well as to any other carried on by the performer.

(4) Regulations may—

    (*a*) make provision generally for giving effect to section 13, and

    (*b*) make different provision for different cases or descriptions of cases.

Commentary—*Simon's Taxes* E5.805.

15 Divers and diving supervisors

(1) This section applies if—

    (*a*) a person performs the duties of employment as a diver or diving supervisor in the United Kingdom or in any area designated by Order in Council under section 1(7) of the Continental Shelf Act 1964 (c 29),

    (*b*) the duties consist wholly or mainly of seabed diving activities, and

    (*c*) any employment income from the employment would otherwise be chargeable to tax under Part 2 of ITEPA 2003.

(2) The performance of the duties of employment is instead treated for income tax purposes as the carrying on of a trade in the United Kingdom.

(3) For the purposes of this section the following are seabed diving activities—

    (*a*) taking part as a diver in diving operations concerned with the exploration or exploitation of the seabed, its subsoil and their natural resources, and

    (*b*) acting as a diving supervisor in relation to any such diving operations.

Commentary—*Simon's Taxes* E5.701.

HMRC Manuals Business Income Manual BIM53951 (treatment of income from diving in designated areas).

16 Oil extraction and related activities

(1) If a person carries on any oil-related activities as part of a trade, those activities are treated for income tax purposes as a separate trade, distinct from all other activities carried on by the person as part of the trade.

(2) For this purpose the following are oil-related activities—

    (*a*) oil extraction activities, and

    (*b*) any activities consisting of the acquisition, enjoyment or exploitation of oil rights.

(3) "Oil extraction activities" and "oil rights" have the meaning given by [sections 225A and 225B][1].

Commentary—*Simon's Taxes* D7.901.

Amendments—[1] In sub-s (3), words substituted by TIOPA 2010 s 501, Sch 8 paras 189, 190. TIOPA 2010 has effect for corporation tax purposes for accounting periods ending on or after 1 April 2010, for income and capital gains tax purposes for the tax year 2010–11 and subsequent tax years, and for petroleum revenue tax purposes for chargeable periods beginning on or after 1 July 2010.

[16A Voluntary office-holders: compensation for lost profits

(1) This section applies if a payment is made by a relevant authority to a person where—

    (*a*) the person holds a voluntary office with the authority,

    (*b*) the person carries out the duties of the office in a period in which he or she also carries on a trade, profession or vocation,

    (*c*) the payment is made solely to compensate the person for lost profits for the period (and accordingly does not exceed the amount of those profits), and

    (*d*) the payment would otherwise be dealt with under Part 2 of ITEPA 2003 by virtue of section 4(2)(*b*).

(2) The payment is dealt with under this Part.

(3) In subsection (1)(*c*) "lost profits" means the difference between—

    (*a*) the amount of profits that the person would have received from the trade, profession or vocation for the period if he or she had not carried out the duties of the office, and

    (*b*) the amount of profits that the person did receive from the trade, profession or vocation for the period.

(4) For the purposes of subsection (1)—

    "relevant authority" has the meaning given by section 299A of ITEPA 2003;

references to a person holding a voluntary office are to be construed in accordance with section 299A(2) and (3) of that Act.][1]

Amendments—[1]   Section 16A inserted by the Enactment of Extra-Statutory Concessions Order, SI 2018/282 art 3(1), (3) with effect from 6 April 2018.

[16B Payments to company directors

(1) This section applies where—

  (a) a company ("the paying company") makes a payment to, or for the benefit of, a director of the paying company in respect of the director's employment as a director of the paying company,

  (b) the payment would otherwise be employment income of the director chargeable to tax under Part 2 of ITEPA 2003,

  (c) the director was or is a member of a firm, or was appointed by a company ("the appointing company") other than the paying company, and

  (d) condition A or B is met.

(2) The payment is to be treated for income tax purposes as a receipt of—

  (a) a trade carried on by the firm, or

  (b) a trade carried on by the appointing company.

(3) Condition A applies where the director is a member of a firm, and is that—

  (a) the director carries on a profession,

  (b) being a director of a company is a normal incident of that profession and of membership of the firm,

  (c) the director is required by the terms of the partnership agreement to account to the firm for the payment, and

  (d) the amount of the payment is insubstantial, compared with the total amount brought into account as receipts when calculating the firm's profits.

(4) Condition B applies where the director is appointed by a company, and is that—

  (a) the profits of the appointing company are within the charge to income tax,

  (b) by virtue of an agreement with the appointing company, the director is required to account for the payment to that company, and

  (c) either subsection (5) or subsection (6) applies to the appointing company.

(5) This subsection applies if the appointing company had the right to appoint the director by virtue of its shareholding in, or an agreement with, the paying company.

(6) This subsection applies if the appointing company is not one over which—

  (a) the director has control, or

  (b) any person connected with the director has control, or

  (c) the director and any persons connected with him together have control.

(7) For the purposes of subsection (6), the following persons are connected with the director: the spouse, civil partner, parent, child, son-in-law or daughter-in-law of the director.][1]

Amendments—[1]   Sections 16B, 16C inserted by the Enactment of Extra-Statutory Concessions Order, SI 2018/282 art 5 with effect from 6 April 2018.

[16C Professionals in practice: incidental income from an office or employment

(1) This section applies where—

  (a) a payment is received by an individual who carries on a profession (alone or in partnership),

  (b) the payment is made to the individual in his or her capacity as an employee or office-holder, but is not made in respect of employment as a director of a company,

  (c) the payment would otherwise be employment income of the individual chargeable to tax under Part 2 of ITEPA 2003,

  (d) the conditions in subsection (3) are met, and

  (e) where the individual carries on the profession in partnership, the condition in subsection (4) is also met.

(2) The payment is to be treated for income tax purposes as a receipt of a trade carried on by the individual or, where the individual carries on the profession in partnership, by the firm.

(3) The conditions referred to in subsection (1)(d) are that—

  (a) the time spent by the individual in performing the duties of the office or employment is insubstantial compared with the time spent by the individual in carrying on the profession,

  (b) the office or employment is related to the profession carried on by the individual,

  (c) the amount of the payment is insubstantial compared with—

    (i) the total amount brought into account as receipts when calculating the individual's trade profits; or

    (ii) where the individual carries on a profession in partnership, so much of the total amount brought into account as receipts when calculating the firm's profits as is attributable to the individual.

(4) The condition referred to in subsection (1)(e) is that the individual is required by the terms of the partnership agreement to account to the firm for the payment and does so.][1]

Amendments—[1]   Sections 16B, 16C inserted by the Enactment of Extra-Statutory Concessions Order, SI 2018/282 art 5 with effect from 6 April 2018.

Starting and ceasing to trade

17 Effect of becoming or ceasing to be a UK resident

[(1) This section applies if—
  (a) an individual carries on a trade otherwise than in partnership, and
  (b) there is a change of residence.
(1A) For the purposes of this section there is a "change of residence" if—
  (a) the individual becomes or ceases to be UK resident, or
  (b) a tax year is, as respects the individual, a split year.
(1B) The change of residence occurs—
  (a) in a case falling within subsection (1A)(a), at the start of the tax year for which the individual becomes or ceases to be UK resident, and
  (b) in a case falling within subsection (1A)(b), at the start of whichever of the UK part or the overseas part of the tax year is the later part.][2]
(2) [If this section applies and the individual does not actually cease permanently to carry on the trade immediately before the change of residence occurs,][2] the individual is treated for income tax purposes—
  (a) as permanently ceasing to carry on the trade at the time of the change of residence, and
  (b) so far as the individual continues to carry on the trade, as starting to carry on a new trade immediately afterwards.
(3) But subsection (2) does not prevent a loss made before the change of residence from being [deducted under section 83 of ITA 2007 from][1] profits arising after the change.
(4) This section applies to professions and vocations as it applies to trades.
(5) In the case of a trade carried on by a firm, see sections 852(6) and (7) and 854(5).

Commentary—*Simon's Taxes* **B1.206.**
HMRC Manuals Business Income Tax Manual BIM80610 (change in residence status and effect on chargeable income).
Amendments—[1]   Words in sub-s (3) substituted by ITA 2007 s 1027, Sch 1 paras 492, 496 with effect for income tax purposes from 6 April 2007, and corporation tax purposes for accounting periods ending after 5 April 2007.
[2]   Sub-ss (1)–(1B) substituted for former sub-s (1) and words in sub-s (2) inserted by FA 2013 s 218, Sch 45 paras 74, 76 with effect in calculating an individual's liability to income tax or capital gains tax for the tax year 2013–14 or any subsequent tax year, subject to transitional provisions and savings in FA 2013 Sch 45 paras 154–158.

18 Effect of company starting or ceasing to be within charge to income tax

(1) This section applies if a company starts or ceases to be within the charge to income tax under this Chapter in respect of a trade.
(2) The company is treated for the purposes of this Part—
  (a) as starting to carry on the trade when it starts to be within the charge, or
  (b) as permanently ceasing to carry on the trade when it ceases to be within the charge.

Commentary—*Simon's Taxes* **B1.206.**

Trading income and property income

19 Tied premises

(1) This section applies if—
  (a) in the course of carrying on a trade a person ("the trader") supplies, or is concerned in the supply of, goods sold or used on premises occupied by another person,
  (b) the trader has an estate or interest in the premises,
  (c) the estate or interest is dealt with as property employed for the purposes of the trade, and
  (d) receipts and expenses in connection with the premises would otherwise be brought into account in calculating the profits of a property business of the trader.
(2) Both the receipts and expenses are instead brought into account in calculating the profits of the trade.
(3) Any apportionment of receipts or expenses that is necessary because—
  (a) the receipts or expenses do not relate only to the premises, or
  (b) the above conditions are met only in relation to part of the premises,
is to be made on a just and reasonable basis.

Commentary—*Simon's Taxes* **B5.611, B2.216.**
HMRC Manuals Business Income Manual BIM51430 (tied premises: rent receivable and paid).
BIM51420 (tied premises: admissible deductions).
BIM51425 (tied premises: inadmissible deductions).

20 Caravan sites where trade carried on

(1) This section applies if—
  (a) a person ("the trader") carries on material activities connected with the operation of a caravan site,
  (b) the activities are, or are part of, a trade, and

(*c*) receipts from, and expenses of, lettings of caravans or pitches for caravans on the site would otherwise be brought into account in calculating the profits of a property business of the trader.

(2) The trader may instead bring both the receipts and expenses into account in calculating the profits of the trade.

(3) But if the conditions in subsection (1)(*a*) and (*b*) are met for only part of a tax year, subsection (2) applies only to the receipts and expenses that would otherwise be brought into account in calculating the profits of the property business for that part of the tax year.

(4) In this section—

"caravan site" means—

(*a*) land on which a caravan is stationed for the purposes of human habitation, and

(*b*) land which is used in conjunction with land on which a caravan is so stationed, and

"letting" includes a licence to occupy.

Commentary—*Simon's Taxes* **B2.217.**

21 Surplus business accommodation

(1) This section applies if—

(*a*) a person ("the trader") carrying on a trade obtains receipts from a letting of business accommodation that is temporarily surplus to requirements (see subsections (3) and (4)),

(*b*) the accommodation is not held as trading stock,

(*c*) the receipts are in respect of part of a building of which another part is used to carry on the trade,

(*d*) the receipts are relatively small, and

(*e*) the receipts, and the expenses of the letting, would otherwise be brought into account in calculating the profits of a property business of the trader.

(2) The trader may instead bring both the receipts and expenses into account in calculating the profits of the trade.

(3) Accommodation is temporarily surplus to requirements only if—

(*a*) it has been used within the last 3 years to carry on the trade or acquired within the last 3 years,

(*b*) the trader intends to use it to carry on the trade at a later date, and

(*c*) the letting is for a term of not more than 3 years.

(4) If accommodation is temporarily surplus to requirements at the beginning of a period of account, it continues to be temporarily surplus to requirements until the end of that period.

(5) If under this section any of the receipts from and expenses of a letting are brought into account in calculating the profits of the trade, all subsequent receipts from and expenses of the letting must be dealt with in the same way (but only so long as this section continues to apply).

(6) In this section "letting" includes a licence to occupy.

(7) This section applies to professions and vocations as it applies to trades.

Commentary—*Simon's Taxes* **B2.218.**

HMRC Manuals Business Income Manual BIM41015 (letting surplus business accommodation and rent as a trading receipt).

22 Payments for wayleaves

(1) This section applies if—

(*a*) a person ("the trader") carries on a trade on some or all of the land to which a wayleave relates,

(*b*) rent is receivable, or expenses are incurred, by the trader in respect of the wayleave, and

(*c*) apart from any rent or expenses in respect of a wayleave, no other receipts or expenses in respect of any of the land are brought into account in calculating the profits of any property business of the trader.

(2) If—

(*a*) the trader would otherwise be liable to tax under Chapter 9 of Part 3 in respect of the rent for the wayleave (rent receivable for UK electric-line wayleaves), or

(*b*) expenses [incurred by the trader in respect of the wayleave would otherwise be brought into account in calculating profits]¹ charged under that Chapter,

the trader may instead bring both the rent and expenses into account in calculating the profits of the trade.

(3) If—

(*a*) rent for the wayleave would otherwise be brought into account in calculating the profits of a property business of the trader, or

(*b*) expenses incurred by the trader in respect of the wayleave would otherwise be so brought into account,

the trader may instead bring both the rent and expenses into account in calculating the profits of the trade.

(4) In this section "rent" includes—

(*a*) a receipt mentioned in section 266(3), and

(b) any other receipt in the nature of rent.

(5) In this section "wayleave" means an easement, servitude or right in or over land which is enjoyed in connection with—

(a) an electric, telegraph or telephone wire or cable,

(b) a pipe for the conveyance of any thing, or

(c) any apparatus used in connection with such a pipe.

(6) The reference to the enjoyment of an easement, servitude or right in connection with an electric, telegraph or telephone wire or cable includes (in particular) its enjoyment in connection with—

(a) a pole or pylon supporting such a wire or cable, or

(b) apparatus used in connection with such a wire or cable.

(7) This section applies to professions and vocations as it applies to trades.

Commentary—*Simon's Taxes* **B2.219.**

HMRC Manuals Business Income Manual BIM67600 (guidance on wayleaves).

Amendments—[1] In sub-s (2)(b) words substituted by CTA 2009 s 1322, Sch 1 paras 587, 588. CTA 2009 applies for accounting periods ending on or after 1 April 2009 (for corporation tax purposes) and for tax years 2009–10 onwards (for income and capital gains tax purposes).

[Trading allowance

22A Trading allowance

(1) The rules for calculating the profits of a trade, profession or vocation carried on by an individual are subject to Chapter 1 of Part 6A (trading allowance).

(2) That Chapter gives relief on relevant income and, where relief is given, disallows most deductions under this Part (see, in particular, sections 783AC, 783AF and 783AI).][1]

Commentary—*Simon's Taxes* **B2.301.**

Amendments—[1] Section 22A and preceding cross-head inserted by F(No 2)A 2017 s 17, Sch 3 paras 2, 4 with effect for the tax year 2017–18 and subsequent tax years.

Rent-a-room and [qualifying care] relief

23 Rent-a-room and [qualifying care][1] relief

(1) The rules for calculating the profits of a trade carried on by an individual are subject to Chapter 1 of Part 7 (rent-a-room relief).

(2) That Chapter provides relief on income from the use of furnished accommodation in the individual's only or main residence (see, in particular, sections 792 and 796).

(3) The rules for calculating the profits of a trade, profession or vocation carried on by an individual are subject to Chapter 2 of Part 7 ([qualifying care][1] relief).

(4) That Chapter provides relief on income from the provision by the individual of [qualifying care][1] (see, in particular, sections 813, 816, 822 and 823).

Commentary—*Simon's Taxes* **B2.220.**

Amendments—[1] In heading, preceding cross-head, and sub-s (3), words substituted for words "foster-care", and in sub-s (4) words substituted for words "foster care" by F(No 3)A 2010 s 1, Sch 1 paras 30, 32 with effect for the tax year 2010–11 and subsequent tax years, subject to transitional provisions in F(No 3)A 2010 Sch 1 paras 36(2)–(5), 37.

[Trading income provided through third parties

23A Application of section 23E: conditions

(1) Section 23E (tax treatment of relevant benefits) applies if Conditions A to E are met.

(2) Condition A is that a person ("T") is or has been carrying on a trade (the "relevant trade") alone or in partnership.

(3) Condition B is that—

(a) there is an arrangement ("the arrangement") in connection with the relevant trade to which T is a party or which otherwise (wholly or partly) covers or relates to T, and

(b) it is reasonable to suppose that, in essence—

(i) the arrangement, or

(ii) the arrangement so far as it covers or relates to T,

is (wholly or partly) a means of providing, or is otherwise concerned with the provision of, relevant benefits.

(4) Condition C is that—

(a) a relevant benefit arises to T, or a person who is or has been connected with T, in pursuance of the arrangement, or

(b) a relevant benefit arises to any other person in pursuance of the arrangement and any of the enjoyment conditions (see section 23F) is met in relation to the relevant benefit.

(5) Condition D is that it is reasonable to suppose that the relevant benefit (directly or indirectly) represents, or has arisen or derives from, or is otherwise connected with, the whole or part of a qualifying third party payment.

(6) Condition E is that it is reasonable to suppose that a tax advantage would be obtained by T, or a person who is or has been connected with T, as a result of the arrangement.

(7) For the purposes of subsection (3) in particular, all relevant circumstances are to be taken into account in order to get to the essence of the matter.

(8) In this section and sections 23B to 23H, "this group of sections" means this section and those sections.

(9) The provisions of this group of sections apply to professions and vocations as they apply to trades.

(10) See Schedule 12 to F(No.2)A 2017 for provision about the application of this group of sections in relation to loans and quasi-loans that are outstanding on 5 April 2019.][1]

Commentary—*Simon's Taxes* **B1.203**.
Amendments—[1]   Sections 23A–23H and preceding cross-head inserted by F(No 2)A 2017 s 35(1), (2) with effect in relation to relevant benefits arising on or after 6 April 2017.

[23B Meaning of "relevant benefit"

(1) The following provisions apply for the purposes of this group of sections.

(2) "Relevant benefit" means any payment (including a payment by way of a loan), a transfer of money's worth, or any other benefit.

(3) The assumption of a liability of T by another person is to be treated as the provision of a relevant benefit to T.

(4) The assumption, by a person other than T, of a liability of a person ("C") who is or has been connected with T, is to be treated as the provision of a relevant benefit to C.

(5) "Loan" includes—
    (a) any form of credit;
    (b) a payment that is purported to be made by way of a loan.][1]

Commentary—*Simon's Taxes* **B1.203**.
Amendments—[1]   Sections 23A–23H and preceding cross-head inserted by F(No 2)A 2017 s 35(1), (2) with effect in relation to relevant benefits arising on or after 6 April 2017.

[23C Meaning of "qualifying third party payment"

(1) The following provisions apply for the purposes of this group of sections.

(2) A payment is a "third party payment" if it is made (by T or another person) to—
    (a) T acting as trustee, or
    (b) any person other than T.

(3) A third party payment is a "qualifying third party payment" if the deduction condition or the trade connection condition is met in relation to the payment.

(4) The "deduction condition" is met in relation to a payment if—
    (a) a deduction for the payment is made in calculating the profits of the relevant trade, or
    (b) where the relevant trade is or has been carried on in partnership, a deduction for the payment is made in calculating the amount on which T is liable to income tax in respect of the profits of the trade.

(5) The "trade connection condition" is met in relation to a payment if it is reasonable to suppose that in essence—
    (a) the payment is by way of consideration for goods or services provided in the course of the relevant trade, or
    (b) there is some other connection (direct or indirect) between the payment and the provision of goods or services in the course of the relevant trade.

(6) For the purposes of subsection (5) in particular, all relevant circumstances are to be taken into account in order to get to the essence of the matter.][1]

Commentary—*Simon's Taxes* **B1.203**.
Amendments—[1]   Sections 23A–23H and preceding cross-head inserted by F(No 2)A 2017 s 35(1), (2) with effect in relation to relevant benefits arising on or after 6 April 2017.

[23D Other definitions

(1) The following provisions apply for the purposes of this group of sections.

(2) "Arrangement" includes any agreement, understanding, scheme, settlement, trust, transaction or series of transactions (whether or not legally enforceable).

(3) A "tax advantage" includes—
    (a) relief or increased relief from tax,
    (b) repayment or increased repayment of tax,
    (c) avoidance or reduction of a charge to tax or an assessment to tax,
    (d) avoidance of a possible assessment to tax,
    (e) deferral of a payment of tax or advancement of a repayment of tax, and
    (f) avoidance of an obligation to deduct or account for tax.

(4) Section 993 of ITA 2007 (meaning of "connected" persons) applies for the purposes of this group of sections as if subsection (4) of that section 993 were omitted.][1]

Commentary—*Simon's Taxes* **B1.203**.
Amendments—[1]   Sections 23A–23H and preceding cross-head inserted by F(No 2)A 2017 s 35(1), (2) with effect in relation to relevant benefits arising on or after 6 April 2017.

[23E Tax treatment of relevant benefits

(1) Where this section applies (see section 23A), the relevant benefit amount is to be treated for income tax purposes as profits of the relevant trade for—

    (*a*) the tax year in which the relevant benefit arises, or

    (*b*) if T has ceased to carry on the relevant trade in a tax year (the "earlier tax year") before the tax year referred to in paragraph (*a*), the earlier tax year.

(2) For the purposes of this section, "the relevant benefit amount" means—

    (*a*) if the relevant benefit is a payment otherwise than by way of a loan, an amount equal to the amount of the payment,

    (*b*) if the relevant benefit is a payment by way of loan, an amount equal to the principal amount lent, or

    (*c*) in any other case, an amount equal to the value of the relevant benefit.

(3) For the purposes of subsection(2)(*c*), the value of a relevant benefit is—

    (*a*) its market value at the time it arises, or

    (*b*) if higher, the cost of providing it.

(4) In subsection (3) "market value" has the same meaning as it has for the purposes of TCGA 1992 by virtue of Part 8 of that Act.][1]

Commentary—*Simon's Taxes* **B1.203**.

Amendments—[1] Sections 23A–23H and preceding cross-head inserted by F(No 2)A 2017 s 35(1), (2) with effect in relation to relevant benefits arising on or after 6 April 2017.

[23F Relevant benefits: persons other than T

(1) For the purposes of section 23A(4), the enjoyment conditions are—

    (*a*) that the relevant benefit, or part of it, is in fact so dealt with by any person as to be calculated at some time to enure for the benefit of T;

    (*b*) that the arising of the relevant benefit operates to increase the value to T of any assets—

        (i) which T holds, or

        (ii) which are held for the benefit of T;

    (*c*) that T receives, or is entitled to receive, at any time any benefit provided or to be provided out of, or deriving or to be derived from, the relevant benefit (or part of it);

    (*d*) where the relevant benefit is the payment of a sum of money (including a payment by way of loan), that T may become entitled to the beneficial enjoyment of the sum or part of the sum if one or more powers are exercised or successively exercised (and for these purposes it does not matter who may exercise the powers or whether they are exercisable with or without the consent of another person);

    (*e*) where the relevant benefit is the payment of a sum of money (including a payment by way of loan), that T is able in any manner to control directly or indirectly the application of the sum or part of the sum.

(2) Where an enjoyment condition is met in relation to part only of a relevant benefit, that part is to be treated as a separate benefit for the purposes of section 23A(4).

(3) In subsection (1) references to T include references to a person who is or has been connected with T.

(4) In determining whether any of the enjoyment conditions is met in relation to a relevant benefit, regard must be had to the substantial result and effect of all the relevant circumstances.][1]

Commentary—*Simon's Taxes* **B1.203**.

Amendments—[1] Sections 23A–23H and preceding cross-head inserted by F(No 2)A 2017 s 35(1), (2) with effect in relation to relevant benefits arising on or after 6 April 2017.

[23G Anti-avoidance

(1) In determining whether section 23E applies in relation to a relevant benefit, no regard is to be had to any arrangements the main purpose, or one of the main purposes, of which is to secure that section 23E does not apply in relation to the whole, or any part, of—

    (*a*) the relevant benefit, or

    (*b*) the relevant benefit and one or more other relevant benefits (whether or not all arising to the same person).

(2) Where arrangements are disregarded under subsection (1), and a relevant benefit (or part of it)—

    (*a*) would, if the arrangements were not disregarded, arise before 6 April 2017, but

    (*b*) would, when the arrangements are disregarded, arise on or after that date,

the relevant benefit (or part) is to be regarded for the purposes of this group of sections as arising on the date on which it would arise apart from the arrangements.][1]

Commentary—*Simon's Taxes* **B1.203**.

Amendments—[1] Sections 23A–23H and preceding cross-head inserted by F(No 2)A 2017 s 35(1), (2) with effect in relation to relevant benefits arising on or after 6 April 2017.

[23H Double taxation

(1) This section applies where—

    (*a*) income tax is charged on an individual by virtue of the application of section 23E in relation to a relevant benefit amount, and

(b) at any time, a tax (whether income tax or another tax) is charged on the individual or another person otherwise than by virtue of the application of section 23E in relation to the relevant benefit concerned.

(2) In order to avoid a double charge to tax, the individual may make a claim for one or more consequential adjustments to be made in respect of the tax charged as mentioned in subsection (1)(b).

(3) On a claim under this section an officer of Revenue and Customs must make such of the consequential adjustments claimed (if any) as are just and reasonable.

(4) The value of any consequential adjustments must not exceed the lesser of—

(a) the income tax charged on the individual as mentioned in subsection (1)(a), and

(b) the tax charged as mentioned in subsection (1)(b).

(5) Consequential adjustments may be made—

(a) in respect of any period,

(b) by way of an assessment, the modification of an assessment, the amendment of a claim, or otherwise, and

(c) despite any time limit imposed by or under any enactment.][1]

Commentary—*Simon's Taxes* **B1.203**.

Amendments—[1] Sections 23A–23H and preceding cross-head inserted by F(No 2)A 2017 s 35(1), (2) with effect in relation to relevant benefits arising on or after 6 April 2017.

CHAPTER 3

TRADE PROFITS: BASIC RULES

24 Professions and vocations

Apart from section 30 (animals kept for trade purposes), the provisions of this Chapter apply to professions and vocations as they apply to trades.

Commentary—*Simon's Taxes* **B2.101**.

25 Generally accepted accounting practice

(1) The profits of a trade must be calculated in accordance with generally accepted accounting practice, subject to any adjustment required or authorised by law in calculating profits for income tax purposes.

(2) This does not—

(a) require a person to comply with the requirements of [the Companies Act 2006 or subordinate legislation made under that Act][1] except as to the basis of calculation, or

(b) impose any requirements as to audit or disclosure.

(3) This section is subject to [section 25A (cash basis for small businesses)][2].

(4) This section does not affect provisions of the Income Tax Acts relating to the calculation of the profits of Lloyd's underwriters.

Commentary—*Simon's Taxes* **B2.102, B4.201**.

HMRC Manuals Business Income Manual BIM37020 (wholly and exclusively: guidance on determining tax adjusted profits).
BIM15040 (ascertaining trade profits based on GAAP and cash basis).
BIM30510 (generally accepted accounting practice: basic computational rule).
BIM31005 (accounting principles: introduction).

Amendments—[1] Words in sub-s (2)(a) substituted by the Companies Act 2006 (Consequential Amendments) (Taxes and National Insurance) Order, SI 2008/954 arts 35, 36 with effect from 6 April 2008.

[2] In sub-s (3) words substituted for words "section 160 (barristers and advocates in early years of practice)", by FA 2013 s 17, Sch 4 paras 2, 3 with effect for the tax year 2013–14 and subsequent tax years, subject to the provisions of FA 2013 Sch 4 para 57 in relation to barristers and advocates.

[25A Cash basis for small businesses

(1) A person who is or has been carrying on a trade may elect for the profits of the trade to be calculated on the cash basis (instead of in accordance with generally accepted accounting practice).

(2) References in this Part to calculating the profits of a trade on the cash basis are references to doing so in accordance with this section.

(3) Chapter 3A contains provision about—

(a) when a person may make an election under this section, and

(b) the effect of such an election.

(4) Where an election under this section has effect in relation to a trade, sections 27, 28 and 30 do not apply in relation to the calculation of the profits of the trade.][1]

Commentary—*Simon's Taxes* **B2.101B**.

HMRC Manuals Business Income Manual BIM70005 (ascertaining trade profits on cash basis).

Amendments—[1] This section inserted by FA 2013 s 17, Sch 4 paras 2, 4 with effect for the tax year 2013–14 and subsequent tax years, subject to the provisions of FA 2013 Sch 4 para 57 in relation to barristers and advocates.

26 Losses calculated on same basis as profits

(1) The same rules apply for income tax purposes in calculating losses of a trade as apply in calculating profits.

(2) This is subject to any express provision to the contrary.

Commentary—*Simon's Taxes* **B2.107.**

27 Receipts and expenses

(1) In the Income Tax Acts, in the context of the calculation of the profits of a trade, references to receipts and expenses are to any items brought into account as credits or debits in calculating the profits.

(2) There is no implication that an amount has been actually received or paid.

(3) This section is subject to any express provision to the contrary.

Commentary—*Simon's Taxes* **B2.108.**

HMRC Manuals Business Income Manual BIM30515 (statutory rules: receipts and expenses).
BIM40050 (trade receipts).
BIM37000 (trade expenses: wholly and exclusively).

28 Items treated under CAA 2001 as receipts and expenses

The rules for calculating the profits of a trade need to be read with—

(*a*) the provisions of CAA 2001 which treat charges as receipts of a trade, and

(*b*) the provisions of CAA 2001 which treat allowances as expenses of a trade.

Commentary—*Simon's Taxes* **B2.108.**
HMRC Manuals Capital Allowances Manual CA11110 (how capital allowances are made?).

[28A Money's worth

(1) Subsection (2) applies—

(*a*) for the purpose of bringing into account an amount arising in respect of a transaction involving money's worth entered into in the course of a trade, and

(*b*) if an amount at least equal to the amount that would be brought into account under that subsection is not otherwise brought into account as a receipt in calculating the profits of a trade under a provision of this Part other than a provision mentioned in subsection (3).

(2) For the purpose of calculating the profits of the trade, an amount equal to the value of the money's worth is brought into account as a receipt if, had the transaction involved money, an amount would have been brought into account as a receipt in respect of it.

(3) But where another provision of this Part makes express provision for the bringing into account of an amount in respect of money's worth as a receipt in calculating the profits of a trade (however expressed), that other provision applies instead of subsection (2).][1]

Amendments—[1] Section 28A inserted by FA 2016 s 71(1), (2) with effect in relation to transactions entered into on or after 16 March 2016.

29 Interest

For the purpose of calculating the profits of a trade, interest is an item of a revenue nature, whatever the nature of the loan.

Commentary—*Simon's Taxes* **B2.109.**

30 Animals kept for trade purposes

(1) Animals or other living creatures kept for the purposes of a trade are treated as trading stock if they are not kept wholly or mainly—

(*a*) for the work they do in connection with the carrying on of the trade,

(*b*) for public exhibition, or

(*c*) for racing or other competitive purposes.

(2) But they are not treated as trading stock if they are part of a herd in relation to which a herd basis election has effect (see Chapter 8).

(3) This section applies to shares in animals or other living creatures as it applies to the creatures themselves.

(4) This section does not apply to professions or vocations.

Commentary—*Simon's Taxes* **B2.110.**
HMRC Manuals Business Income Manual BIM55401 (general principles: valuation of farming stock).

31 Relationship between rules prohibiting and allowing deductions

(1) Any relevant permissive rule in this Part—

(*a*) has priority over any relevant prohibitive rule in this Part, but

(*b*) is subject to [section 36 (unpaid remuneration), section 38 (employee benefit contributions), section 48 (car . . . [2] hire) and section][1] 55 (crime-related payments).

[(1A) But, if the relevant permissive rule would allow a deduction in calculating the profits of a trade in respect of an amount which arises directly or indirectly in consequence of, or otherwise in connection with, relevant tax avoidance arrangements, that rule—

(*a*) does not have priority under subsection (1)(*a*), and

(*b*) is subject to any relevant prohibitive rule in this Part (and to the provisions mentioned in subsection (1)(*b*)).][5]

(2) In this section "any relevant permissive rule in this Part" means any provision of—

(*a*) Chapter 5 (apart from sections 60 to 67),

[(*aa*) Chapter 5A,][4]

(*b*) Chapter 11, . . . [3]

(c) Chapter 13, [or

(d) Chapter 17A,][3]

which allows a deduction in calculating the profits of a trade

(3) In this section "any relevant prohibitive rule in this Part", in relation to any deduction, means any provision of this Part (apart from sections [36, 38,][1] 48 and 55) which might otherwise be read as—

(a) prohibiting the deduction, or

(b) restricting the amount of the deduction.

[(4) In this section "relevant tax avoidance arrangements" means arrangements—

(a) to which the person carrying on the trade is a party, and

(b) the main purpose, or one of the main purposes, of which is the obtaining of a tax advantage (within the meaning of section 1139 of CTA 2010).

"Arrangements" includes any agreement, understanding, scheme, transaction or series of transactions (whether or not legally enforceable).][5]

Commentary—*Simon's Taxes* **B2.302.**

HMRC Manuals Business Income Manual BIM42080 (deductions: interaction between prohibitive and permissive rules). BIM42060 (deductions: prohibitive rules).

Amendments—[1]   Words in sub-s (1) substituted, and words in sub-s (3) inserted, by FA 2007 s 67(1)–(3), (7) with effect from the tax year 2007–08.

[2]   In sub-s (1)(b) words "or motor cycle" repealed by FA 2009 s 30 Sch 11 para 35 with effect as provided for by FA 2009 Sch 11 paras 65, 66 and subject to savings in FA 2009 Sch 11 para 68. The new system of capital allowances for cars has effect generally from 6 April 2009 (for income tax) and 1 April 2009 (for corporation tax), subject to FA 2009 Sch 11 para 67 (election for new regime not to apply in certain cases).

[3]   In sub-s (2), word "or" at end of para (b) repealed, and para (d) and preceding word "or" inserted, by FA 2013 s 17, Sch 4 para 49 with effect for the tax year 2013–14 and subsequent tax years, subject to the provisions of FA 2013 Sch 4 para 57 in relation to barristers and advocates.

[4]   Sub-s (2)(aa) inserted by FA 2013 s 18, Sch 5 para 3 with effect for the tax year 2013–14 and subsequent tax years.

[5]   Sub-ss (1A), (4) inserted by FA 2013 s 78(1) with effect in relation to deductions in respect of amounts which arise directly or indirectly in consequence of, or otherwise in connection with—

–   arrangements which are entered into on or after 21 December 2012; or

–   any transaction forming part of arrangements which is entered into on or after that date.

This amendment does not have effect where the arrangements are, or any such transaction is, entered into pursuant to an unconditional obligation in a contract made before that date (FA 2013 s 78(6)). "An unconditional obligation" means an obligation which may not be varied or extinguished by the exercise of a right (whether under the contract or otherwise) (FA 2013 s 78(7)).

[CHAPTER 3A

TRADE PROFITS: CASH BASIS]

Amendments—This Chapter inserted by FA 2013 s 17, Sch 4 paras 1, 5 with effect for the tax year 2013–14 and subsequent tax years, subject to the provisions of FA 2013 Sch 4 para 57 in relation to barristers and advocates.

[Eligibility

31A Conditions to be met for profits to be calculated on cash basis

(1) A person may make an election under section 25A for a tax year if conditions A to C are met.

(2) Condition A is that the aggregate of the cash basis receipts of each trade, profession or vocation carried on by the person during that tax year does not exceed any relevant maximum applicable for that tax year (see section 31B).

(3) Condition B is that, in a case where the person is either an individual who controls a firm or a firm controlled by an individual—

(a) the aggregate of the cash basis receipts of each trade, profession or vocation carried on by the individual or the firm during that tax year does not exceed any relevant maximum applicable for that tax year, and

(b) the firm or the individual (as the case may be) has also made an election under section 25A for that tax year.

(4) Condition C is that the person is not an excluded person in relation to the tax year (see section 31C).

(5) For the purposes of this section, the "cash basis receipts" of a trade, profession or vocation, in relation to a tax year, are any receipts that—

(a) are received during the basis period for the tax year,

and (b) would be brought into account in calculating the profits of the trade, profession or vocation for that tax year on the cash basis.][1]

Commentary—*Simon's Taxes* **B2.101B.**

HMRC Manuals Business Income Manual BIM70010 (cash basis: eligibility). BIM70011 (cash basis: eligibility for partnerships).

Amendments—[1]   This Chapter inserted by FA 2013 s 17, Sch 4 paras 1, 5 with effect for the tax year 2013–14 and subsequent tax years, subject to the provisions of FA 2013 Sch 4 para 57 in relation to barristers and advocates.

[31B Relevant maximum

(1) For the purposes of section 31A there is a "relevant maximum" applicable for a tax year in relation to a trade, profession or vocation carried on by a person if any of conditions A to C is met.

(2) Condition A is that an election under section 25A did not have effect in relation to the trade, profession or vocation for the previous tax year.

(3) Condition B is that the aggregate of the cash basis receipts of each trade, profession or vocation carried on by the person during the previous tax year is greater than [the higher of £300,000 or]² an amount equal to twice the VAT threshold for that previous tax year.

(4) Condition C is that, in a case where the person is either an individual who controls a firm or a firm controlled by an individual, the aggregate of the cash basis receipts of each trade, profession or vocation carried on by the individual or the firm during the previous tax year is greater than [the higher of £300,000 or]² an amount equal to twice the VAT threshold for that previous tax year.

(5) If there is a relevant maximum applicable for a tax year, the amount of the relevant maximum is—

(a) [the higher of £150,000 or]² the VAT threshold, or

(b) in the case where the person is an individual who is a universal credit claimant in the tax year, [the higher of £300,000 or]² an amount equal to twice the VAT threshold.

(6) For the purposes of this section, where the basis period for a tax year is less than 12 months, [amounts specified in subsections (3), (4) and (5) and the VAT threshold are]² proportionately reduced.

(7) In this section—

"universal credit claimant", in relation to a tax year, means a person who is entitled to universal credit under the relevant legislation for an assessment period (within the meaning of the relevant legislation) that falls within the basis period for the tax year,

"the relevant legislation" means—

(a) Part 1 of the Welfare Reform Act 2012, or

(b) any provision made for Northern Ireland which corresponds to that Part of that Act, and

"the VAT threshold", in relation to a tax year, means the amount specified at the end of that tax year in paragraph 1(1)(a) of Schedule 1 to VATA 1994.

(8) The Treasury may by order amend this section.

(9) A statutory instrument containing an order under subsection (8) that restricts the circumstances in which an election may be made under section 25A may not be made unless a draft of the instrument containing the order has been laid before, and approved by a resolution of, the House of Commons.]¹

Commentary—*Simon's Taxes* B2.101B.

HMRC Manuals—Business Income Manual BIM70010 (cash basis profits: relevant maximum).

Orders—Income Tax (Relevant Maximum for Calculating Trade Profits on the Cash Basis) Order, SI 2017/293.

Amendments—¹ This Chapter inserted by FA 2013 s 17, Sch 4 paras 1, 5 with effect for the tax year 2013–14 and subsequent tax years, subject to the provisions of FA 2013 Sch 4 para 57 in relation to barristers and advocates.

² In sub-ss (3), (4), (5)(a), (5)(b), words inserted, and in sub-s (6), words substituted, by the Income Tax (Relevant Maximum for Calculating Trade Profits on the Cash Basis) Order, SI 2017/293 art 2 with effect the tax year 2017–18 and subsequent tax years.

[31C Excluded persons

(1) A person is an excluded person in relation to a tax year if the person meets any of conditions A to H.

(2) Condition A is that—

(a) the person is a firm, and

(b) one or more of the persons who have been partners in the firm at any time during the basis period for the tax year was not an individual at that time.

(3) Condition B is that the person was a limited liability partnership at any time during the basis period for the tax year.

(4) Condition C is that the person is an individual who has been a Lloyd's underwriter at any time during the basis period for the tax year.

(5) Condition D is that the person has made an election under Chapter 8 (trade profits: herd basis rules) that has effect in relation to the tax year.

(6) Condition E is that the person has made a claim under [Chapter 16]² (claim for averaging of fluctuating profits) in relation to the tax year.

(7) Condition F is that, at any time within the period of 7 years ending immediately before the basis period for the tax year, the person obtained an allowance under Part 3A of CAA 2001 (business premises renovation allowances).

(8) Condition G is that the person has carried on a mineral extraction trade at any time during the basis period for the tax year. In this subsection "mineral extraction trade" has the same meaning as in Part 5 of CAA 2001 (see section 394(2) of that Act).

(9) Condition H is that—

(a) at any time before the beginning of the basis period for the tax year the person obtained an allowance under Part 6 of CAA 2001 (research and development allowances) in respect of qualifying expenditure incurred by the person, and (*b*) the person owns an asset representing the expenditure.

In this subsection "qualifying expenditure" has the same meaning as in Part 6 of CAA 2001.

(10) The Treasury may by order amend this section.

(11) A statutory instrument containing an order under subsection (10) that restricts the circumstances in which an election may be made under section 25A may not be made unless a draft of the instrument containing the order has been laid before, and approved by a resolution of, the House of Commons.][1]

Commentary—*Simon's Taxes* B2.101B.

Amendments—[1]   This Chapter inserted by FA 2013 s 17, Sch 4 paras 1, 5 with effect for the tax year 2013–14 and subsequent tax years, subject to the provisions of FA 2013 Sch 4 para 57 in relation to barristers and advocates.

[2]   Words in sub-s (6) substituted by FA 2016 s 25(8) with effect for the tax year 2016-17 and subsequent tax years.

[Elections under section 25A

31D Effect of election under section 25A

(1) An election made by a person under section 25A has effect—

(*a*) for the tax year for which it is made, and

(*b*) for every subsequent tax year.

This is subject to subsections (2) and (3).

(2) An election made by a person under section 25A ceases to have effect if any of conditions A to C in section 31A is not met for a subsequent tax year.

(3) An election made by a person under section 25A ceases to have effect if—

(*a*) there is a change of circumstances relating to any trade, profession or vocation carried on by the person which makes it more appropriate for its profits for a subsequent tax year to be calculated in accordance with generally accepted accounting practice, and

(*b*) the person elects to calculate those profits in that way.

(4) Neither subsection (2) nor subsection (3) prevents the person making an election under section 25A for any subsequent tax year.

(5) An election that—

(*a*) is made by a person under section 25A, and

(*b*) has effect for a tax year,

has effect in relation to every trade, profession or vocation carried on by the person during the tax year.

(6) For provision prohibiting a person who has made an election under section 25A from claiming any capital allowances (other than in respect of expenditure incurred on the provision of a car), see section 1(4) of CAA 2001.][1]

Commentary—*Simon's Taxes* B2.101B.

HMRC Manuals—Business Income Manual BIM70055 (leaving the cash basis).

Amendments—[1]   This Chapter inserted by FA 2013 s 17, Sch 4 paras 1, 5 with effect for the tax year 2013–14 and subsequent tax years, subject to the provisions of FA 2013 Sch 4 para 57 in relation to barristers and advocates.

[Calculation of profits on cash basis

31E Calculation of profits on cash basis

(1) This section applies to professions and vocations as it applies to trades.

(2) To determine the profits of a trade for a tax year on the cash basis—

Step 1

Calculate the total amount of receipts of the trade received during the basis period for the tax year.

Step 2

Deduct from that amount the total amount of expenses of the trade paid during the basis period for the tax year.

(3) Subsection (2) is subject to any adjustment required or authorised by law in calculating profits for income tax purposes.][1]

Commentary—*Simon's Taxes* B2.101B.

HMRC Manuals—Business Income Manual BIM70005 (steps: calculation of profits on cash basis).

Amendments—[1]   This Chapter inserted by FA 2013 s 17, Sch 4 paras 1, 5 with effect for the tax year 2013–14 and subsequent tax years, subject to the provisions of FA 2013 Sch 4 para 57 in relation to barristers and advocates.

[Overview of rest of Part 2

31F Overview of rest of Part 2 as it applies to cash basis

(1) For provision about the application of Chapters 4 to 6 (rules about deductions and receipts) in relation to the cash basis, see sections 32A, 56A and 95A.

(2) For provision about the application of Chapter 11 (trade profits: other specific trades) in relation to the cash basis, see section 148K.

(3) The following Chapters apply only where profits are calculated on the cash basis—

Chapter 6A (trade profits: amounts not reflecting commercial transactions),

Chapter 17A (cash basis: adjustments for capital allowances).

(4) The following Chapters do not apply in relation to the cash basis—

Chapter 8 (trade profits: herd basis rules),
Chapter 9 (trade profits: sound recordings),
Chapter 10 (trade profits: certain telecommunication rights),
Chapter 10A (leases of plant or machinery: special rules for long funding leases),
Chapter 11A (trade profits: changes in trading stock),
Chapter 13 (deductions from profits: unremittable amounts),
Chapter 14 (disposal and acquisition of know-how),
Chapter 16 (averaging profits of farmers and creative artists),
Chapter 16ZA (compensation for compulsory slaughter of animal),
Chapter 16A (oil activities).][1]

Commentary—*Simon's Taxes* **B2.101B.**
Amendments—[1] This Chapter inserted by FA 2013 s 17, Sch 4 paras 1, 5 with effect for the tax year 2013–14 and subsequent tax years, subject to the provisions of FA 2013 Sch 4 para 57 in relation to barristers and advocates.

CHAPTER 4

TRADE PROFITS: RULES RESTRICTING DEDUCTIONS

Introduction

32 Professions and vocations

The provisions of this Chapter apply to professions and vocations as they apply to trades.

Commentary—*Simon's Taxes* **B2.303.**
HMRC Manuals—Business Income Manual BIM14010 (meaning and scope of profession and vocation).

[32A Application of Chapter to the cash basis

(1) The following sections do not apply in calculating the profits of a trade on the cash basis—

    section 33 (capital expenditure),
    section 35 (bad and doubtful debts),
    sections 36 and 37 (unpaid remuneration),
    section 43 (employee benefit contributions: profits calculated before end of 9 month period),
    sections 48 to 50B (car hire).

(2) For rules restricting deductions that apply only where profits are calculated on the cash basis, see the following—

    section 33A (cash basis: capital expenditure),
    section 51A (cash basis: interest payments on loans).][1]

Commentary—*Simon's Taxes* **B2.302.**
HMRC Manuals—Business Income Manual BIM70005 (overview of cash basis).
Amendments—[1] This section inserted by FA 2013 s 17, Sch 4 paras 6, 7 with effect for the tax year 2013–14 and subsequent tax years, subject to the provisions of FA 2013 Sch 4 para 57 in relation to barristers and advocates.

Capital expenditure

33 Capital expenditure

In calculating the profits of a trade, no deduction is allowed for items of a capital nature.

Commentary—*Simon's Taxes* **B2.306, B2.412.**
HMRC Manuals—Business Income Manual BIM35002 (treatment of capital expenditures).
BIM35660 (case law to distinguish between capital and revenue expenditure).
BIM35000 (contents of capital and revenue expenditure).

[33A Cash basis: capital expenditure

(1) This section applies in relation to the calculation of the profits of a trade on the cash basis.

(2) No deduction is allowed for an item of a capital nature incurred on, or in connection with, the acquisition or disposal of a business or part of a business.

(3) No deduction is allowed for an item of a capital nature incurred on, or in connection with, education or training.

(4) No deduction is allowed for an item of a capital nature incurred on, or in connection with, the provision, alteration or disposal of—

    (*a*) any asset that is not a depreciating asset (see subsections (6) and (7)),
    (*b*) any asset not acquired or created for use on a continuing basis in the trade,
    (*c*) a car (see subsection (14)),
    (*d*) land,
    (*e*) a non-qualifying intangible asset (see subsections (8) to (11)), or
    (*f*) a financial asset (see subsection (12)).

(5) But subsection (4)(*d*) does not prevent a deduction being made for expenditure that—

    (*a*) is incurred on the provision of a depreciating asset which, in being provided, is installed or otherwise fixed to land so as to become, in law, part of the land, but
    (*b*) is not incurred on, or in connection with, the provision of—
        (i) a building,
        (ii) a wall, floor, ceiling, door, gate, shutter or window or stairs,

(iii) a waste disposal system,

(iv) a sewerage or drainage system, or

(v) a shaft or other structure in which a lift, hoist, escalator or moving walkway may be installed.

(6) An asset is a "depreciating" asset if, on the date the item of a capital nature is incurred, it is reasonable to expect that before the end of 20 years beginning with that date—

(*a*) the useful life of the asset will end, or

(*b*) the asset will decline in value by 90% or more.

(7) The useful life of an asset ends when it could no longer be of use to any person for any purpose as an asset of a business.

(8) "Intangible asset" means anything that is capable of being an intangible asset within the meaning of FRS 105 and, in particular, includes—

(*a*) an internally-generated intangible asset, and

(*b*) intellectual property.

(9) An intangible asset is "non-qualifying" unless, by virtue of having a fixed maximum duration, it must cease to exist before the end of 20 years beginning with the date on which the item of a capital nature is incurred.

(10) An intangible asset is "non-qualifying" if it consists of a right, whether conditional or not, to obtain an intangible asset without a fixed maximum duration by virtue of which that asset must, assuming the right is exercised at the last possible time, cease to exist before the end of 20 years beginning with the date on which the item of a capital nature is incurred.

(11) Where—

(*a*) the trader has an intangible asset, and

(*b*) the trader grants a licence or any other right in respect of that asset to another person,

any intangible asset that consists of a licence or other right granted to the trader in respect of the intangible asset mentioned in paragraph (*a*) is "non-qualifying".

(12) A "financial asset" means any right under or in connection with—

(*a*) a financial instrument, or

(*b*) an arrangement that is capable of producing a return that is economically equivalent to a return produced under any financial instrument.

(13) A reference to acquisition, provision, alteration or disposal includes potential acquisition, provision, alteration or (as the case may be) disposal.

(14) In this section—

"arrangement" includes any agreement, understanding, scheme, transaction or series of transactions (whether or not legally enforceable);

"building" includes any fixed structure;

"car" has the same meaning as in Part 2 of CAA 2001 (see section 268A of that Act);

"financial instrument" has the same meaning as in FRS 105;

"FRS 105" means Financial Reporting Standard 105 (the Financial Reporting Standard applicable to the Micro-entities Regime), issued by the Financial Reporting Council in July 2015;

"intellectual property" means—

(*a*) any patent, trade mark, registered design, copyright or design right, plant breeders' rights or rights under section 7 of the Plant Varieties Act 1997,

(*b*) any right under the law of a country or territory outside the United Kingdom corresponding or similar to a right within paragraph (*a*),

(*c*) any information or technique not protected by a right within paragraph (*a*) or (*b*) but having industrial, commercial or other economic value, or

(*d*) any licence or other right in respect of anything within paragraph (*a*), (*b*) or (*c*);

"provision" includes creation, construction or acquisition;

"the trader" means the person carrying on the trade.][1]

Commentary—*Simon's Taxes* **B2.304.**

HMRC Manuals—Business Income Manual BIM70035 (treatment of capital expenditure in cash basis).

Amendments—[1]   Section 33A substituted by F(No 2)A 2017 s 16, Sch 2 paras 1, 2 with effect for the tax year 2017–18 and subsequent tax years, subject to transitional provisions in F(No 2)A 2017 Sch 2 para 64.

Wholly and exclusively and losses rules

34 Expenses not wholly and exclusively for trade and unconnected losses

(1) In calculating the profits of a trade, no deduction is allowed for—

(*a*) expenses not incurred wholly and exclusively for the purposes of the trade, or

(*b*) losses not connected with or arising out of the trade.

(2) If an expense is incurred for more than one purpose, this section does not prohibit a deduction for any identifiable part or identifiable proportion of the expense which is incurred wholly and exclusively for the purposes of the trade.

Commentary—*Simon's Taxes* **B2.315, B2.316.**

HMRC Manuals—Business Income Manual BIM37000 (contents: wholly and exclusively).
BIM24460 (wholly and exclusively: case law).
BIM37725 (non trade losses: treatment and case law).

Bad and doubtful debts

35 Bad and doubtful debts

(1) In calculating the profits of a trade, no deduction is allowed for a debt owed to the person carrying on the trade, except so far as—

   (*a*) the debt is bad,

   (*b*) the debt is estimated to be bad, or

   (*c*) the debt is released wholly and exclusively for the purposes of the trade as part of a statutory insolvency arrangement.

(2) If the debtor is bankrupt or insolvent, the whole of the debt is estimated to be bad for the purposes of subsection (1)(*b*), except so far as any amount may reasonably be expected to be received on the debt.

Commentary—*Simon's Taxes* **B2.410.**
HMRC Manuals—Business Income Manual BIM42701 (overview of bad and doubtful debts).

Unpaid remuneration

36 Unpaid remuneration

(1) This section applies if, in calculating the profits of a trade of a period of account—

   (*a*) an amount is charged in the accounts for the period in respect of employees' remuneration, and

   (*b*) a deduction for the remuneration would otherwise be allowable for the period.

(2) No deduction is allowed for the remuneration for the period of account unless it is paid before the end of the period of 9 months immediately following the end of the period of account.

(3) If the remuneration is paid after the end of that 9 month period, a deduction for it is allowed for the period of account in which it is paid.

Commentary—*Simon's Taxes* **B2.422.**
HMRC Manuals—Business Income Manual BIM47130 (timing of deduction: unpaid remuneration).

37 Unpaid remuneration: supplementary

(1) For the purposes of section 36 an amount charged in the accounts in respect of employees' remuneration includes an amount for which provision is made in the accounts with a view to its becoming employees' remuneration.

(2) For the purposes of section 36 it does not matter whether an amount is charged for—

   (*a*) particular employments, or

   (*b*) employments generally.

(3) If the profits of the trade are calculated before the end of the 9 month period mentioned in section 36(2)—

   (*a*) it must be assumed, in making the calculation, that any remuneration which is unpaid when the calculation is made will not be paid before the end of that period, but

   (*b*) if the remuneration is subsequently paid before the end of that period, nothing in this subsection prevents the calculation being revised and any tax return being amended accordingly.

(4) For the purposes of this section and section 36 remuneration is paid when it—

   (*a*) is treated as received by an employee for the purposes of ITEPA 2003 by section 18, 19, 31 or 32 of that Act (receipt of money and non-money earnings), or

   (*b*) would be so treated if it were not exempt income.

(5) In this section and section 36—

   "employee" includes an office-holder and "employment" therefore includes an office, and

   "remuneration" means an amount which is or is treated as earnings for the purposes of ITEPA 2003.

Commentary—*Simon's Taxes* **B2.422.**
HMRC Manuals—Business Income Manual BIM47140 (specific deductions: staffing costs: timing of deductions: returns submitted within the nine month period).

Employee benefit contributions

38 Restriction of deductions

[(1) This section applies if, in calculating for income tax purposes the profits of a trade of a person ("the employer") for a period, a deduction would otherwise be allowable for the period in respect of employee benefit contributions made or to be made (but see subsection (4)).][1]

[(1A) No deduction is allowed under this section in respect of employee benefit contributions for a period of account which starts more than 5 years after the end of the period of account in which the contributions are made.][3]

(2) No deduction is allowed for the contributions for the period except so far as—

   (*a*) qualifying benefits are provided, or qualifying expenses are paid, out of the contributions during the period or within 9 months from the end of it, or

ITTOIA 2005

(b) if the making of the contributions is itself the provision of qualifying benefits, the contributions are made during the period or within 9 months from the end of it.

[(2A) In calculating for income tax purposes the profits of a trade on the cash basis, this section has effect as if—

    (a) in subsection (1), the words "or to be made" were omitted, and

    (b) in subsection (2), the words "or within 9 months from the end of it" were omitted (in both places).]²

[(2AA) Subsection (2) is subject to subsections (1A) and (2AB).

(2AB) Where subsection (3C) applies, no deduction is allowed for an amount in respect of the contributions for the period except so far as the amount is a qualifying amount (see subsection (3D)).]³

(3) An amount disallowed under subsection (2) is allowed as a deduction for a subsequent period so far as—

    (a) qualifying benefits are provided out of the contributions before the end of the subsequent period, or

    (b) if the making of the contributions is itself the provision of qualifying benefits, the contributions are made before the end of the subsequent period.

[(3A) Subsection (3) is subject to subsections (1A) and (3B).

(3B) Where subsection (3C) applies, an amount disallowed under subsection (2) is allowed as a deduction for a subsequent period only so far as it is a qualifying amount.

(3C) This subsection applies where the provision of qualifying benefits out of, or by way of, the contributions gives rise both to an employment income tax charge and to an NIC charge.

(3D) An amount in respect of employee benefit contributions is a "qualifying amount" if the relevant tax charges are paid before the end of the relevant period (and are not repaid).

(3E) For the purposes of subsection (3D)—

    (a) the "relevant tax charges", in relation to an amount, are the employment income tax charge and the NIC charge arising in respect of benefits which are provided out of, or by way of, that amount, and

    (b) the "relevant period" is the period of 12 months immediately following the end of the period of account for which the deduction for the employee benefit contributions would (apart from this section) be allowable.

(3F) For the purposes of subsections (3C) and (3E), "employment income tax charge" and "NIC charge" have the meaning given by section 40(7).]³

[(3G) Subsection (3H) applies where—

    (a) a deduction would, apart from this section, be allowable for an amount (the "remuneration amount") in respect of employees' remuneration, and

    (b) in consequence of the payment of the employees' remuneration, employee benefit contributions are made, or are to be made, in respect of the remuneration amount.

(3H) In calculating for income tax purposes the profits of a trade, the deduction referred to in subsection (3G)(a) is to be treated as a deduction in respect of employee benefit contributions made or to be made (and is to be treated as not being a deduction in respect of employees' remuneration).]⁴

(4) This section does not apply to any deduction that is allowable for—

    (a) anything given as consideration for goods or services provided in the course of a trade or profession,

    (b) contributions under a registered pension scheme or under a superannuation fund to which section 615(3) of ICTA applies,

    (c) contributions under a qualifying overseas pension scheme in respect of an individual who is a relevant migrant member of the pension scheme in relation to the contributions, or

    (d) contributions under an accident benefit scheme.

For the purposes of paragraph (c) "qualifying overseas pension scheme" and "relevant migrant member" have the same meaning as in Schedule 33 to FA 2004 (see paragraphs 4 to 6 of that Schedule).

(5) See also—

    section 39 (making of "employee benefit contributions"),

    section 40 (provision of qualifying benefits),

    section 41 (timing and amount of certain qualifying benefits),

    section 42 (provision or payment out of employee benefit contributions),

    section 43 (profits calculated before end of 9 month period), and

    section 44 (interpretation of sections 38 to 44).

Commentary—*Simon's Taxes* B2.422.

HMRC Manuals—Business Income Manual BIM44570 (specific deductions: deductions for employer's contributions: timing of deductions).

BIM44573 (specific deductions: timing of deductions for contributions: contents).

BIM44580 (specific deductions: timing of deductions for contributions: overview).

BIM44590 (specific deductions: timing of deductions for contributions: structure of the legislation).

BIM44605 (specific deductions: timing of deductions for contributions: computing adjustments).

Amendments—[1]   Sub-s (1) substituted by FA 2007 s 34(7), (8), (13) with effect for employee benefit contributions made on or after 21 March 2007.
[2]   Sub-s (2A) inserted by FA 2013 s 17, Sch 4 paras 6, 9 with effect for the tax year 2013–14 and subsequent tax years, subject to the provisions of FA 2013 Sch 4 para 57 in relation to barristers and advocates.
[3]   Sub-ss (1A), (2AA), (2AB), (3A)–(3F) inserted by F(No 2)A 2017 s 36(1)–(4) with effect in relation to employee benefit contributions made, or to be made, on or after 6 April 2017.
[4]   Sub-ss (3G), (3H) inserted by F(No 2)A 2017 s 36(1), (5) with effect in relation to remuneration paid on or after 6 April 2017.

39 Making of "employee benefit contributions"

[(1) For the purposes of section 38, an "employee benefit contribution" is made if, as a result of any act or omission—
(*a*) property is held, or may be used, under an employee benefit scheme, or
(*b*) there is an increase in the total value of property that is so held or may be so used (or a reduction in any liabilities under an employee benefit scheme).][1]
(2) For this purpose "employee benefit scheme" means a trust, scheme or other arrangement for the benefit of persons who are, or include, present or former employees of the employer [or persons linked with present or former employees of the employer][2].
[(3) Section 554Z1 of ITEPA 2003 applies for the purposes of subsection (2) but as if references to A were to a present or former employee of the employer.
(4) So far as it is not covered by subsection (2), "employee benefit scheme" also means—
    [(*a*) an arrangement (the "relevant arrangement") which is—
        (i)   an arrangement within subsection (1)(*b*) of section 554A of ITEPA 2003 to which subsection (1)(*c*) of that section applies, or
        (ii) an arrangement within subsection (1)(*b*) of section 554AA of ITEPA 2003 to which subsection (1)(*c*) of that section applies,][3] or
    (*b*) any other arrangement connected (directly or indirectly) with the relevant arrangement.][2]

Commentary—*Simon's Taxes* **B2.422.**
HMRC Manuals—Business Income Manual BIM44585 (determination of employee benefit contributions).
Amendments—[1]   Sub-s (1) substituted by FA 2007 s 34(7), (9), (13) with effect for employee benefit contributions made on or after 21 March 2007.
[2]   Words in sub-s (2) and sub-ss (3), (4) inserted, by FA 2011 s 26, Sch 2 paras 35, 36 with effect in relation to acts or omissions occurring on or after 6 April 2011 (FA 2011 Sch 2 para 61).
[3]   Sub-s (4)(*a*) substituted by FA 2018 s 11, Sch 1 para 6 with effect in relation to employee benefit contributions (as defined in that section) made, or to be made, on or after 6 April 2018.

40 Provision of qualifying benefits

(1) For the purposes of section 38 qualifying benefits are provided if there is—
    (*a*) a payment of money, or
    (*b*) a transfer of assets,
which meets condition A, B, C or D.
(2) Condition A is that the payment or transfer gives rise both to an employment income tax charge and to an NIC charge.
(3) Condition B is that the payment or transfer would give rise to both charges if—
    (*a*) the duties of the employment in respect of which the payment or transfer was made were performed in the United Kingdom, and
    (*b*) the person in respect of whose employment the payment or transfer was made met at all relevant times the conditions as to residence or presence in Great Britain or Northern Ireland prescribed under section 1(6) of the Contributions and Benefits Act.
(4) Condition C is that the payment or transfer is made in connection with the termination of the recipient's employment with the employer.
(5) Condition D is that the payment or transfer is made under an employer-financed retirement benefits scheme [and the payment or transfer—
    (*a*) gives rise to an employment income tax charge under Chapter 2 of Part 6 of ITEPA 2003 or under Part 9 of that Act, or
    (*b*) is an excluded benefit as defined in section 393B(3) of that Act.][1]
(6) None of the conditions is met if the payment or transfer is by way of loan.
[(6A) For the purposes of section 38 qualifying benefits are also provided if—
    (*a*) a relevant step within the meaning of Part 7A of ITEPA 2003 is taken, and
    (*b*) Chapter 2 of that Part applies by reason of the step.][1]
(7) In this section—
    "the Contributions and Benefits Act" means—
        (*a*) the Social Security Contributions and Benefits Act 1992 (c 4), or
        (*b*) the Social Security Contributions and Benefits (Northern Ireland) Act 1992 (c 7),
    "employment income tax charge" means a charge to tax under ITEPA 2003 (whether on the recipient or on someone else), and
    "NIC charge" means a liability to pay national insurance contributions under section 6 (Class 1 contributions), section 10 (Class 1A contributions) or section 10A (Class 1B contributions) of the Contributions and Benefits Act.

Commentary—*Simon's Taxes* **B2.422.**
HMRC Manuals—Business Income Manual BIM44595 (conditions to be satisfied for qualifying benefit deductions).
Amendments—[1]   Words in sub-s (5) inserted by FA 2011 s 26, Sch 2 paras 35, 37(1), (2) with effect in relation to payments
   or transfers made on or after 6 April 2011; and sub-s (6A) inserted by FA 2011 s 26, Sch 2 paras 35, 37(1), (3) with effect
   in relation to relevant steps taken on or after 6 April 2011, subject to transitional provisions in FA 2011 Sch 2 paras 53–59.

41 Timing and amount of certain qualifying benefits

[(1) If the provision of a qualifying benefit takes the form of a payment of money, the benefit, so far as Chapter 4 of Part 2 of ITEPA 2003 applies to the money, is provided for the purposes of section 38 when the money is treated as received for the purposes of that Chapter (applying the rules in section 18 of that Act (receipt of money earnings)).][2]

[(1A) Except so far as subsection (1) applies to the provision of the qualifying benefit, if the provision of a qualifying benefit is a chargeable relevant step, for the purposes of section 38—

(a) the benefit is provided when A's employment with B starts if the chargeable relevant step is taken before then, or

(b) otherwise, the benefit is provided when the chargeable relevant step is taken.][2]

(2) If the provision of a qualifying benefit takes the form of a transfer of an asset [which meets condition A, B, C or D in section 40][2], the amount provided for the purposes of section 38 is the total of—

(a) the amount (if any) spent on the asset by [a scheme manager][1], ...[2]

(b) in a case where the asset was transferred to [a scheme manager][1] by the employer, the amount of the deduction that would be allowable as mentioned in subsection (1) of that section in respect of the transfer[, and

(c) if the transfer is a chargeable relevant step, the cost of the relevant step so far as not covered by paragraph (a) or (b)][2].

(3) But if the amount given by subsection (2) is more than the amount that—

(a) is charged to tax under ITEPA 2003 in respect of the transfer, or

(b) would be so charged if condition B in section 40 were met,

the deduction allowable under section 38(2) or (3) is limited to that lower amount.

[(4) If the provision of a qualifying benefit is a chargeable relevant step which does not involve a sum of money (see section 554Z(10) of ITEPA 2003) and is not covered by subsection (2), the amount provided for the purposes of section 38 is the cost of the relevant step (subject to subsection (5)).

(5) If the provision of a qualifying benefit is a chargeable relevant step which is not covered by subsection (2) (whether or not it involves a sum of money), the amount provided for the purposes of section 38 is not to exceed the amount that—

(a) is charged to tax under ITEPA 2003 in relation to the relevant step (whether under Part 7A of that Act or otherwise), or

(b) would be charged had not A been non-UK resident in any tax year.

(6) In this section—

(a) "chargeable relevant step" means a relevant step within the meaning of Part 7A of ITEPA 2003 by reason of which Chapter 2 of that Part applies (and references to A and B are to be read accordingly), and

(b) references to the cost of a chargeable relevant step are to be read in accordance with section 554Z3(6) of that Act.][2]

Commentary—*Simon's Taxes* **B2.422.**
HMRC Manuals—Business Income Manual BIM44620 (timing of deductions for employee benefit contributions: transfers of
   asset to employees).
BIM44636 (timing of deductions for employee benefit contributions: disguised remuneration).
Amendments—[1]   Words in sub-s (2) substituted by FA 2007 s 34(7), (10), (13) with effect for employee benefit contributions
   made on or after 21 March 2007.
[2]   Sub-s (1) substituted by FA 2011 s 26, Sch 2 paras 35, 38(1), (2) with effect in relation to money treated as received on or
   after 6 April 2011; and sub-ss (1A), (4), (5), (6) inserted, and in sub-s (2) words inserted, word "and" at end of para (a)
   repealed and para (c) and preceding word "and" inserted, by FA 2011 s 26, Sch 2 paras 35, 38(1), (3)–(5) with effect in relation
   to relevant steps taken on or after 6 April 2011, subject to transitional provisions in FA 2011 Sch 2 paras 53–59.

42 Provision or payment out of employee benefit contributions

(1) For the purposes of section 38(2)(a)—

(a) any qualifying benefits provided, or

(b) any qualifying expenses paid,

by [a scheme manager][1] after the receipt by [the scheme manager][1] of employee benefit contributions are treated as being provided or paid out of the contributions.

(2) This operates up to the total amount of the contributions reduced by the amount of any benefits or expenses previously provided or paid as mentioned in section 38(2)(a).

(3) For the purposes of section 38(3)(a) any qualifying benefits provided by [a scheme manager][1] after the receipt by [the scheme manager][1] of employee benefit contributions are treated as being provided out of the contributions.

(4) This operates up to the total amount of the contributions reduced by the amount of any benefits or expenses previously provided or paid as mentioned in section 38(2)(*a*) or (3)(*a*).

(5) For the purposes of this section no account is taken of any other amount received or paid by the [scheme manager][1].

Commentary—*Simon's Taxes* **B2.422.**

HMRC Manuals—Business Income Manual BIM44615 (provisions and payments out of employee benefit contributions).

Amendments—[1]   Words in sub-ss (1), (3) and (5) substituted by FA 2007 s 34(7), (11), (13) with effect for employee benefit contributions made on or after 21 March 2007.

43 Profits calculated before end of 9 month period

(1) This section applies if the profits of the trade are calculated before the end of the 9 month period mentioned in section 38(2).

(2) It must be assumed, in making the calculation, that any benefits, expenses or contributions which are not provided, paid or made when the calculation is made will not be provided, paid or made before the end of that period.

(3) But if the benefits, expenses or contributions are subsequently provided, paid or made before the end of that period, nothing in this section prevents the calculation being revised and any tax return being amended accordingly.

Commentary—*Simon's Taxes* **B2.422.**

44 Interpretation of sections 38 to 44

(1) In this section and sections 38 to 43—

"accident benefit scheme" means an employee benefit scheme under which benefits may be provided only by reason of a person's disablement, or death, caused by an accident occurring during the person's service as an employee of the employer,

"employee benefit contribution" is to be read in accordance with section 39(1),

"employee benefit scheme" has the meaning given by section [39(2) to (4)][2],

"the employer" is to be read in accordance with section 38(1),

"employer-financed retirement benefits scheme" has the same meaning as

in Chapter 2 of Part 6 of ITEPA 2003 (see section 393A of that Act) [but ignoring section 393B(2)(*a*) and (*c*) of that Act][2],

"qualifying benefits" is to be read in accordance with section 40,

"qualifying expenses" includes any expenses of the third party (other than the provision of benefits to employees of the employer)—

(*a*) which are incurred in operating the employee benefit scheme, and

(*b*) which, if incurred by the employer, would be deductible in calculating for income tax purposes the employer's profits for any period, and

["scheme manager" means a person who administers an employee benefit scheme (acting in that capacity).[1]]

(2) A reference in this section and sections 38 to 43 to a person's employee includes the holder of an office under that person, and "employment" is to be read accordingly.

Commentary—*Simon's Taxes* **B2.422.**

HMRC Manuals—Business Income Manual BIM44525 (Specific deductions employee benefit trusts: accident benefit schemes).

Amendments—[1]   In sub-s (1), definition of "scheme manager" substituted for definition of "the third party" by FA 2007 s 34(7), (12), (13) with effect for employee benefit contributions made on or after 21 March 2007.

[2]   In sub-s (1) in definition of "employee benefit scheme", words substituted by FA 2011 s 26, Sch 2 paras 35, 39(*a*) with effect in relation to acts or omissions occurring on or after 6 April 2011 (FA 2011 Sch 2 para 61); and in definition of "employer-financed retirements benefits scheme" words inserted by FA 2011 s 26, Sch 2 paras 35, 39(*b*) with effect in relation to payments or transfers made on or after 6 April 2011 (FA 2011 Sch 2 para 62).

Business entertainment and gifts

45 Business entertainment and gifts: general rule

(1) The general rule is that no deduction is allowed in calculating the profits of a trade for expenses incurred in providing entertainment or gifts in connection with the trade.

(2) A deduction for expenses which are incurred—

(*a*) in paying sums to or on behalf of an employee of the person carrying on the trade ("the trader"), or

(*b*) in putting sums at the disposal of an employee of the trader,

is prohibited by the general rule if (and only if) the sums are paid, or put at the employee's disposal, exclusively for meeting expenses incurred or to be incurred by the employee in providing the entertainment or gift.

(3) The general rule is subject to exceptions—

for entertainment (see section 46), and

for gifts (see section 47).

(4) For the purposes of this section and those two sections—

(*a*) "employee", in relation to a company, includes a director of the company and a person engaged in the management of the company, (*b*) "entertainment" includes hospitality of any kind, and

(*c*) the expenses incurred in providing entertainment or a gift include expenses incurred in providing anything incidental to the provision of entertainment or a gift.

Commentary—*Simon's Taxes* **B2.432.**
HMRC Manuals—Business Income Manual BIM45000 (business entertainment: Introduction and contents).
BIM37400 (case law: incidental benefits).

46 Business entertainment: exceptions

(1) The prohibition in section 45 on deducting expenses incurred in providing entertainment does not apply in either of cases A and B.

(2) Case A is where—

(*a*) the entertainment is of a kind which it is the trader's trade to provide, and

(*b*) the entertainment is provided in the ordinary course of the trade either for payment or free of charge in order to advertise to the public generally.

(3) Case B is where the entertainment is provided for employees of the trader unless—

(*a*) the entertainment is also provided for others, and

(*b*) the provision of the entertainment for the employees is incidental to its provision for the others.

Commentary—*Simon's Taxes* **B2.432.**
HMRC Manuals—Business Income Manual BIM45030 (business entertainment: exceptions).
BIM45031 (exceptions to the normal course of trade for payment).
BIM45033 (exceptions to business entertainment: staff entertainment).
BIM45032 (exceptions: normal course of trade for purpose of advertising to the public).
BIM45075 (specific deductions for prizes given at competitions).

47 Business gifts: exceptions

(1) The prohibition in section 45 on deducting expenses incurred in providing gifts does not apply in any of cases A, B, C and D.

(2) Case A is where—

(*a*) the gift is of an item which it is the trader's trade to provide, and

(*b*) the item is given away in the ordinary course of the trade in order to advertise to the public generally.

(3) Case B is where the gift incorporates a conspicuous advertisement for the trader unless—

(*a*) the gift is food, drink, tobacco or a token or voucher exchangeable for goods, or

(*b*) the cost of the gift to the trader, together with any other gifts (except food, drink, tobacco or a token or voucher exchangeable for goods) given to the same person in the same basis period, exceeds £50.

The Treasury may by order amend the sum for the time being specified in paragraph (b) so as to increase it.

(4) Case C is where gifts are provided for employees of the trader unless—

(*a*) gifts are also provided for others, and

(*b*) the provision of the gifts for the employees is incidental to the provision of gifts for the others.

(5) Case D is where the gift is given to—

(*a*) a charity,

(*b*) the Historic Buildings and Monuments Commission for England, or

(*c*) the Trustees of the National Heritage Memorial Fund.

Commentary—*Simon's Taxes* **B2.432.**
HMRC Manuals—Business Income Manual BIM45070 (entertainment: gifts carrying a conspicuous advertisement).
BIM45071 (specific deductions: free samples).
BIM45072 (specific deductions: gifts to charities).

Car . . . cycle hire

48 Car . . . [2] hire

(1) This section applies if, in calculating the profits of a trade, a deduction is allowed for expenses incurred on the hiring of a car [which is not—

(*a*) a car that is first registered before 1 March 2001,

(*b*) a car that has low CO2 emissions,

(*c*) a car that is electrically propelled, or

(*d*) a qualifying hire car.][2]

(2) The amount of the deduction which would otherwise be allowable is reduced by [15%][2].

(3) Subsection (4) applies if [a deduction is reduced as a result of subsection (2), or a corresponding provision,][1] and subsequently—

(*a*) there is a rebate (however described) of the hire charges, or

(*b*) a debt in respect of any of the hire charges is released otherwise than as part of a statutory insolvency arrangement.

(4) The amount that, as a result of the rebate or release—

(*a*) is brought into account as a receipt of the trade . . . [1], or (*b*) is treated as a post-cessation receipt under section 249 (debts released after cessation),

is reduced by [15%][2].

[(4A) In this section "corresponding provision" means—

    (*a*) section 56(2) of CTA 2009 (car . . . [2] hire: trade profits and property income), [or][3]

    (*b*) section 1251(2) of CTA 2009 (car . . . [2] hire: expenses of management), [including as applied by section 82(4) of FA 2012.][3]

    (*c*) ...[3], [1]

(5) . . . [2]

Commentary—*Simon's Taxes* **B2.413.**

HMRC Manuals—Business Income Manual BIM47740 (car hire restrictions for periods beginning on or after 6 April 2009). BIM47745 (car hire restrictions based on Co2 emissions).

Amendments—[1]   In sub-s (3) words substituted, in sub-s (4)(*a*) words repealed, and sub-s (4A) inserted, by CTA 2009 s 1322, Sch 1 paras 587, 589. CTA 2009 applies for accounting periods ending on or after 1 April 2009 (for corporation tax purposes) and for tax years 2009–10 onwards (for income and capital gains tax purposes).

[2]   In heading, sub-s (4A)(*a*), (*b*), words "or motor cycle" repealed; in sub-ss (1), (2), words substituted; in sub-s (4) words substituted for words "multiplying it by the fraction in subsection (2)"; and sub-s (5) repealed, by FA 2009 s 30, Sch 11 para 36 with effect as provided for by FA 2009 Sch 11 paras 65, 66 and subject to savings in FA 2009 Sch 11 para 68. The new system of capital allowances for cars has effect generally from 6 April 2009 (for income tax) and 1 April 2009 (for corporation tax), subject to FA 2009 Sch 11 para 67 (election for new regime not to apply in certain cases).

[3]   In sub-s (4A), at end of para (*a*), word inserted, in para (*b*), words inserted, and para (*c*) and preceding word "or" repealed, by FA 2012 s 146, Sch 16 paras 125, 126 with effect in relation to accounting periods of companies beginning on or after 1 January 2013 (subject to transitional provisions in FA 2012 Sch 17). For accounting periods straddling 1 January 2013, see FA 2012 s 149.

49 Car . . . [2] hire: supplementary

(1) In section 48 "car . . . [2]" means a mechanically propelled road vehicle other than[2] . . . —

    [(*za*) a motor cycle (within the meaning of section 185(1) of the Road Traffic Act 1988),][2]

    (*a*) [a vehicle][2] of a construction primarily suited for the conveyance of goods or burden of any description, or

    (*b*) [a vehicle][2] of a type not commonly used as a private vehicle and unsuitable for such use.

[(1A) In section 48—

    "a car that has low CO2 emissions" has the same meaning as in section 104AA of CAA 2001 (special rate expenditure: main rate car);

    "electrically propelled" has the meaning given in section 268B of that Act.][2]

(2) In section 48 "a qualifying hire car[2] . . . " means a car . . . [2] which—

    (*a*) is hired under a hire-purchase agreement . . . [3] under which there is no option to purchase,

    (*b*) is hired under a hire-purchase agreement under which there is an option to purchase exercisable on the payment of a sum equal to not more than 1% of the retail price of the car [or motor cycle][1] when new, or

    (*c*) . . . [2]

    [(*d*) is leased under a long-funding lease (within the meaning of section 70G of CAA 2001).][2]

[(3) For this purpose "hire-purchase agreement" has the meaning given by section 998A of ITA 2007.][3]

(4) . . .

(5) . . .

(6) In this section . . . [2] "new" means unused and not second-hand.

Commentary—*Simon's Taxes* **B2.413.**

HMRC Manuals—Business Income Manual BIM47730 (car hire: overview).

Amendments—[1]   In sub-s (2)(*b*) words inserted by CTA 2009 s 1322, Sch 1 paras 587, 590. CTA 2009 applies for accounting periods ending on or after 1 April 2009 (for corporation tax purposes) and for tax years 2009–10 onwards (for income and capital gains tax purposes).

[2]   Amendments made by FA 2009 s 30, Sch 11 para 37 with effect as provided for by FA 2009 Sch 11 paras 65, 66 and subject to savings in FA 2009 Sch 11 para 68. The new system of capital allowances for cars has effect generally from 6 April 2009 (for income tax) and 1 April 2009 (for corporation tax), subject to FA 2009 Sch 11 para 67 (election for new regime not to apply in certain cases)

[3]   In sub-s (2)(*a*), words repealed, and sub-s (3) substituted for previous sub-ss (3)–(5), by TIOPA 2010 ss 501, 503, Sch 8 paras 253, 254, Sch 10 Pt 9. TIOPA 2010 has effect for corporation tax purposes for accounting periods ending on or after 1 April 2010, for income and capital gains tax purposes for the tax year 2010–11 and subsequent tax years, and for petroleum revenue tax purposes for chargeable periods beginning on or after 1 July 2010.

[50A Short-term hiring in and long-term hiring out

(1) Section 48 does not apply to expenses incurred by a person ("the taxpayer") on the hiring of a car if condition A or B is met.

(2) Condition A is that—

    (*a*) the expenses are incurred in respect of the making available of the car to the taxpayer for a period ("the hire period") of not more than 45 consecutive days, and

    (*b*) if the car is made available to the taxpayer (whether by the same person or different persons) for one or more periods linked to the hire period, the hire period and the linked period or periods, taken together, consist of not more than 45 days.

(3) Condition B is that the expenses are incurred in respect of a period ("the sub-hire period") throughout which the taxpayer makes the car available to another person ("the customer") and—
- (a) the sub-hire period consists of more than 45 consecutive days, or
- (b) if the taxpayer makes the car available to the customer throughout one or more periods linked to the sub-hire period, the sub-hire period and the linked period or periods, taken together, consist of more than 45 days,

but see subsection (4).

(4) Condition B is not met if—
- (a) the customer is an employee of the taxpayer or of a person connected with the taxpayer, or
- (b) during all or part of the sub-hire period (or any period linked to the sub-hire period), the customer makes any car available to an employee of the taxpayer under arrangements with the taxpayer or with a person connected with the taxpayer.

(5) Neither condition A nor condition B is met if the car is hired under arrangements the purpose, or one of the main purposes, of which is—
- (a) to disapply or reduce the effect of section 48, or
- (b) other avoidance of tax.

(6) For the purposes of condition B, the expenses incurred by the taxpayer on the hiring of the car must be apportioned between—
- (a) the sub-hire period, and
- (b) the remainder of the period during which the car is made available to the taxpayer,

according to the respective lengths of those periods.

(7) A period of consecutive days ("the main period") is linked to—
- (a) a period of consecutive days that ends not more than 14 days before the main period begins,
- (b) a period of consecutive days that begins not more than 14 days after the main period ends, and
- (c) a period of consecutive days linked to a period in paragraph (a) or (b).

(8) For the purposes of this section, where arrangements for the hiring of a car include arrangements for the provision of a replacement car in the event that the first car is not available, the first car and any replacement car are to be treated as if they were the same car.

(9) In this section (and section 50B) "arrangements" includes any arrangements, scheme or understanding of any kind, whether or not legally enforceable and whether involving a single transaction or two or more transactions.][1]

Commentary—*Simon's Taxes* **B2.413.**

HMRC Manuals—Business Income Manual BIM47750 (specific deductions for cars: short term hiring in and long term hiring out).

BIM47755 (specific deductions for hiring cars: linked period).

BIM47760 (specific deductions for hiring cars: apportionment).

Amendments—[1]   Sections 50A, 50B inserted by FA 2009 s 30, Sch 11 para 39 with effect as provided for by FA 2009 Sch 11 paras 65, 66 and subject to savings in FA 2009 Sch 11 para 68. The new system of capital allowances for cars has effect generally from 6 April 2009 (for income tax) and 1 April 2009 (for corporation tax), subject to FA 2009 Sch 11 para 67 (election for new regime not to apply in certain cases).

[50B Connected persons: application of section 48

(1) This section applies where connected persons incur expenses on the hiring of the same car for the same period and—
- (a) section 48 would (but for this section) apply to the expenses of two or more of those persons, or
- (b) section 48 and section 56 of CTA 2009 would (but for this section and section 58B of that Act) each apply to the expenses of at least one of those persons.

(2) This section only applies where one or more of the persons mentioned in subsection (1)(a) or (b) incurs the expenses under commercial arrangements (and such a person is referred to below as a "commercial lessee").

(3) In relation to the expenses mentioned in subsection (1) to which section 48 would (but for this section) apply, section 48 only applies to the following—
- (a) where there is one commercial lessee, any such expenses incurred by that lessee, and
- (b) where there is more than one, any such expenses incurred by the first commercial lessee in the chain of arrangements for the hiring of the car for the period.

(4) In this section—
- (a) references to expenses incurred by a commercial lessee include expenses incurred in that or any other capacity, and
- (b) "commercial arrangements" means arrangements the terms of which are such as would reasonably have been expected if the parties to the arrangements had been dealing at arm's length.][1]

Commentary—*Simon's Taxes* **B2.413.**

HMRC Manuals—Business Income Manual BIM47740 (specific deductions for hiring cars: connected persons).

Amendment—[1]   Sections 50A, 50B inserted by FA 2009 s 30, Sch 11 para 39 with effect as provided for by FA 2009 Sch 11 paras 65, 66 and subject to savings in FA 2009 Sch 11 para 68. The new system of capital allowances for cars has effect generally from 6 April 2009 (for income tax) and 1 April 2009 (for corporation tax), subject to FA 2009 Sch 11 para 67 (election for new regime not to apply in certain cases).

Interest payments

[51A Cash basis: interest payments on loans
(1) In calculating the profits of a trade on the cash basis, no deduction is allowed for the interest paid on a loan.

(2) This is subject to section 57B.][1]

Commentary—*Simon's Taxes* **B2.436.**

HMRC Manuals—Business Income Manual BIM70040 (cash basis: interest payments on loans).

Amendments—[1]   This section inserted by FA 2013 s 17, Sch 4 paras 6, 10 with effect for the tax year 2013–14 and subsequent tax years, subject to the provisions of FA 2013 Sch 4 para 57 in relation to barristers and advocates.

52 Exclusion of double relief for interest
(1) In calculating the profits of a trade, no deduction is allowed—

    (*a*)   for any tax year for the interest paid on a debt or liability in respect of which relief is given under [section 383 of ITA 2007][1] (see subsection (5) below), or

    (*b*)   for any relevant tax year for other interest on the same debt or liability.

(2) A tax year is a relevant one if the interest in respect of which the relief is given could, but for the relief, have been brought into account in calculating the profits of a trade of the tax year.

(3) For the purposes of subsection (1)(*b*) all interest which—

    (*a*)   is capable of being brought into account in calculating the profits of a trade, and

    (*b*)   is payable by any person on money advanced to the person on current account,

is treated as interest on the same debt.

(4) It does not matter if the money is advanced—

    (*a*)   on one or more accounts, or

    (*b*)   by the same or separate banks or other persons.

(5) For the purposes of this section relief under [section 383 of ITA 2007][1] is to be treated as given only when the claim for the relief can no longer be varied (whether on appeal or otherwise).

(6) For a rule excluding relief under [section 383 of ITA 2007][1] if interest on a debt or liability is brought into account in calculating the profits of a trade, see [section 387(2) and (3) of that Act][1].

Commentary—*Simon's Taxes* **E1.823.**

HMRC Manuals—Business Income Manual BIM45765 (specific deductions: exclusion of double relief for interest).

Amendments—[1]   Words in sub-ss (1), (5), (6) substituted by ITA 2007 s 1027, Sch 1 paras 492, 498 with effect for income tax purposes from 6 April 2007, and corporation tax purposes for accounting periods ending after 5 April 2007.

Social security contributions

53 Social security contributions
(1) In calculating the profits of a trade, no deduction is allowed for any contribution paid by any person under—

    (*a*)   Part 1 of the Social Security Contributions and Benefits Act 1992 (c 4), or

    (*b*)   Part 1 of the Social Security Contributions and Benefits (Northern Ireland) Act 1992 (c 7).

(2) But this prohibition does not apply to an employer's contribution.

(3) For this purpose "an employer's contribution" means—

    (*a*)   a secondary Class 1 contribution,

    (*b*)   a Class 1A contribution, or

    (*c*)   a Class 1B contribution,

within the meaning of Part 1 of the Social Security Contributions and Benefits Act 1992 or of the Social Security Contributions and Benefits (Northern Ireland) Act 1992.

Commentary—*Simon's Taxes* **B2.425, E8.279B.**

HMRC Manuals—Business Income Manual BIM42523 (specific deductions: administration: national insurance contributions).

Penalties, interest and VAT surcharges

54 Penalties, interest and VAT surcharges
(1) In calculating the profits of a trade, no deduction is allowed for any penalty or interest mentioned in the first column of the following table.

(2) This is the table—

Penalty or interest	*Description of tax, levy or duty*
Interest under any provision of Part 9 of TMA 1970	Income tax, capital gains tax and corporation tax
[Interest under section 101 of FA 2009 in connection with sums required to be deducted under section 61 of FA 2004 (construction industry)][4]	

Penalty or interest	*Description of tax, levy or duty*
Penalty under any of sections 60 to 70 of VATA 1994	Value added tax
Interest under section 74 [or 85A][2] of VATA 1994	
Penalty under any of sections 8 to 11 of FA 1994	Excise duties
Penalty under any of paragraphs 12 to 19 of Schedule 7 to FA 1994	Insurance premium tax
[Interest under section 60(8) of FA 1994 or paragraph 21 of Schedule 7 to FA 1994][2]	
Penalty under any provision of Part 5 of Schedule 5 to FA 1996	Landfill tax
[Interest under section 56(5) of, or paragraph 26 or 27 of Schedule 5 to, FA 1996][2]	
Penalty under any provision of Schedule 6 to FA 2000	Climate change levy
Interest under any of paragraphs 70, 81 to 85[, 109 and 123(6)][2] of that Schedule	
Penalty under any provision of Part 2 of FA 2001	Aggregates levy
Interest under [section 42(6) of, or][2] any of paragraphs 5 to 9 of Schedule 5 to, paragraph 6 of Schedule 8 to and paragraph 5 of Schedule 10 [to, FA 2001][2]	
Penalty under section 25 or 26 of FA 2003	Customs, export and import duties
Penalty under any provision of Part 4 of FA 2003	Stamp duty land tax
Interest under any provision of that Part	
[Penalty under Schedule 24 to FA 2007	Various taxes and excise duties][1]
[Penalty under Schedule 41 to FA 2008	Various taxes and excise duties][3]
[Penalty under Schedule 16 to F(No. 2)A 2017	Various taxes][5]

(3) In calculating the profits of a trade, no deduction is allowed for any surcharge under section 59 of VATA 1994.

Commentary—*Simon's Taxes* **B2.472, D7.307.**

HMRC Manuals—Business Income Manual BIM42520 (specific deductions: administration: interest, penalties and surcharges on UK taxes).

Amendments—[1]   Table entry inserted by the Finance Act 2008, Schedule 40 (Appointed Day, Transitional Provisions and Consequential Amendments) Order, SI 2009/571 art 8, Sch 1 paras 27, 28 with effect from 1 April 2009.

[2]   Words in table entries inserted, table entries and words in table entry substituted by the Transfer of Tribunal Functions and Revenue and Customs Appeals Order, SI 2009/56 art 3, Sch 1 para 438 with effect from 1 April 2009.

[3]   Table entry inserted by the Finance Act 2008 (Penalties for Errors and Failure to Notify etc) (Consequential Amendments) Order 2010, SI 2010/509 art 2, Sch paras 7, 8 with effect from 1 April 2010.

[4]   Table entry substituted by the Finance Act 2009, Sections 101 and 102 (Interest on Late Payments and Repayments) (Consequential Amendments) Order, SI 2014/1283 art 2, Schedule para 5 with effect in relation to payments in respect of Class 1 NIC and construction industry scheme payments made on or after 20th May 2014 for the tax year 2014–15 or for a subsequent tax year.

[5]   Table entry inserted by F(No 2)A 2017 s 65, Sch 16 para 59 with effect in relation to arrangements entered into on or after 16 November 2017. In determining in relation to any particular arrangements whether a person is a person who enabled the arrangements, any action of the person carried out before 16 November 2017 is to be disregarded (F(No 2)A 2017 Sch 16 para 62).

Prospective amendments—In sub-s (2), in the entry relating to a penalty under section 25 or 26 of FA 2003, words "Customs duties" to be substituted for words "Customs, export and import duties" by the Taxation (Cross-border Trade) Act 2018 s 29, Sch 7 para 153, 154 with effect from a date to be appointed.

Crime-related payments

55 Crime-related payments

(1) In calculating the profits of a trade, no deduction is allowed for expenses incurred—

    (*a*)   in making a payment if the making of the payment constitutes a criminal offence, or

    (*b*)   in making a payment outside the United Kingdom if the making of a corresponding payment in any part of the United Kingdom would constitute a criminal offence in that part.

(2) In calculating the profits of a trade, no deduction is allowed for expenses incurred in making a payment induced by a demand which constitutes—

    (*a*)   the offence of blackmail under section 21 of the Theft Act 1968 (c 60) (England and Wales),

    (*b*)   the offence of extortion (Scotland), or

    (*c*)   the offence of blackmail under section 20 of the Theft Act (Northern Ireland) 1969 (c 16 (NI)) (Northern Ireland).

Commentary—*Simon's Taxes* **B2.420** .

HMRC Manuals—Business Income Manual BIM43101 (crime-related expenditure: introduction).

BIM43115 (crime-related expenditure: scope).

BIM43130 (crime-related expenditure: handling of cases).

BIM43160 (crime-related expenditure: blackmail and extortion).

[Integral features

55A Expenditure on integral features[2]

[(1)] Section (3) of CAA 2001 provides that no deduction is allowed in respect of certain expenditure on an integral feature of a building or structure (within the meaning of that section).

[(2) But section 33A(3) of CAA 2001 does not apply in calculating the profits of a trade on the cash basis.][1]

Commentary—*Simon's Taxes* **B3.345.**

HMRC Manuals—Business Income Manual BIM46945 (specific deductions: repairs and renewals: assets on which capital allowances given).

Capital Allowances Manual CA22340 (meaning of "replacement").

Amendments—[1]   Sub-s (1) numbered as such, and sub-s (2) inserted, by FA 2013 s 17, Sch 4 paras 6, 11 with effect for the tax year 2013–14 and subsequent tax years, subject to the provisions of FA 2013 Sch 4 para 57 in relation to barristers and advocates.

[2]   Section 55A inserted by FA 2008 s 73(4) with effect: (a) for corporation tax purposes, in relation to expenditure incurred on or after 1 April 2008, and (b) for income tax purposes, in relation to expenditure incurred on or after 6 April 2008.

[Rental rebates

55B Rental rebates

(1) Where plant or machinery ("the asset") is leased and a rental rebate is payable by the lessor, the amount of the deduction allowable in respect of the rebate is limited to—

  (*a*) the amount of the lessor's income from the lease, or

  (*b*) in the case of a finance lease, that amount excluding the finance charge.

(2) "Rental rebate" means any sum payable to the lessee that is calculated by reference to the termination value of the asset.

(3) For this purpose—

  (*a*) the termination value of an asset is the value of the asset at or about the time when the lease terminates,

  (*b*) calculation by reference to the termination value includes calculation by reference to any one or more of—

    (i)   the proceeds of sale, if the asset is sold,

    (ii) any insurance proceeds, compensation or similar sums in respect of the asset,

    (iii) an estimate of the market value of the asset, and

  (*c*) calculation by reference to the termination value also includes—

    (i)   determination in a way which, or by reference to factors or criteria which, might reasonably be expected to produce a broadly similar result to calculation by reference to the termination value, or

    (ii) any other form of calculation indirectly by reference to the termination value.

(4) For the purposes of this section—

  (*a*) the income of the lessor from the lease is the total of all the amounts receivable in connection with the lease that have been brought into account in calculating the lessor's income for income tax purposes, excluding—

    (i)   disposal receipts brought into account under Part 2 of CAA 2001 (see section 60(1) of that Act), and

    (ii) so much of any amount as represents charges for services or qualifying UK or foreign tax (within the meaning of section 70YE of that Act) to be paid by the lessor, and

  (*b*) the finance charge, in relation to a finance lease, is—

    (i)   if the lease is one that, under generally accepted accounting practice, falls (or would fall) to be treated as a loan, so much of the rentals under the lease as fall (or would fall) to be treated as interest, or

    (ii) in any other case, the amount that, in accordance with generally accepted accounting practice, falls (or would fall) to be treated as the gross return on investment.

(5) Where the asset is acquired by the lessor in a transaction in relation to which an election is made under section 266 of CAA 2001 (election where predecessor and successor are connected persons), this section applies as if the successor had been the lessor at all material times and everything done to or by the predecessor had been done to or by the successor.

(6) Where the whole or part of a rental rebate is disallowed under this section as a deduction in computing profits—

  (*a*) the amount disallowed, or

  (*b*) if less, the amount by which the rental rebate exceeds the amount of capital expenditure incurred by the lessor,

may be treated for the purposes of capital gains tax as an allowable loss accruing to the lessor on the termination of the lease.

That allowable loss is deductible only from chargeable gains accruing to the lessor on the disposal of the asset.

(7) This section does not apply to a long funding finance lease (see section 148C).][1]

Commentary—*Simon's Taxes* **B5.404.**
HMRC Manuals—Business Leasing Manual BLM64000 (plant and machinery leasing anti-avoidance: sales of lease rental
   streams capital allowances and rental rebates: contents).
Amendments—[1]   This section and preceding crosshead inserted by FA 2010 s 27, Sch 5 para 2(1) with effect in relation to rental
   rebates payable on or after 9 December 2009.

CHAPTER 5

TRADE PROFITS: RULES ALLOWING DEDUCTIONS

Introduction

56 Professions and vocations

Apart from sections 87 to 90 (scientific research and expenses connected with patents, designs and
trade marks) [and section 97A (cash basis: value of trading stock on cessation of trade)][1], the
provisions of this Chapter apply to professions and vocations as they apply to trades.

Commentary—*Simon's Taxes* **B1.202.**
Amendments—[1]   Words inserted by FA 2013 s 17, Sch 4 para 50 with effect for the tax year 2013–14 and subsequent tax years,
   subject to the provisions of FA 2013 Sch 4 para 57 in relation to barristers and advocates.

[Cash basis accounting

56A Application of Chapter to the cash basis

(1) The following sections do not apply in calculating the profits of a trade on the cash basis—
   sections 60 to 67 (tenants under taxed leases),
      . . .[2]

(2) For rules allowing deductions that apply only where profits are calculated on the cash basis, see
the following—
   section 57B (cash basis: interest payments on loans).

(3) In calculating the profits of a trade on the cash basis, any reference in this Chapter to the
incurring of expenses is to be read as a reference to the paying of expenses.][1]

Commentary—*Simon's Taxes* **B2.101B.**
Amendments—[1]   This section inserted by FA 2013 s 17, Sch 4 paras 12, 13 with effect for the tax year 2013–14 and subsequent
   tax years, subject to the provisions of FA 2013 Sch 4 para 57 in relation to barristers and advocates.
[2]   In sub-s (1), entry relating to section 68 repealed by FA 2016 s 72(2)(a) with effect in relation to expenditure incurred on or
   after 1 April 2016 for corporation tax purposes and 6 April 2016 for income tax purposes.

Pre-trading expenses

57 Pre-trading expenses

(1) This section applies if a person incurs expenses for the purposes of a trade before (but not more
than 7 years before) the date on which the person starts to carry on the trade ("the start date").

(2) If, in calculating the profits of the trade—
   (*a*) no deduction would otherwise be allowed for the expenses, but
   (*b*) a deduction would be allowed for them if they were incurred on the start date,
the expenses are treated as if they were incurred on the start date (and therefore a deduction is
allowed for them).

Commentary—*Simon's Taxes* **B2.460, D7.905**
HMRC Manuals—Business Income Manual BIM46351 (pre-trading expenditure: scope).
BIM46355 (pre-trading expenditure: relief).

[Subsistence expenses

57A Expenses incurred by traders on food and drink

(1) In calculating the profits of a trade, a deduction is allowed for any reasonable expenses incurred
on food or drink for consumption by the trader at a place to which the trader travels in the course of
carrying on the trade, or while travelling to a place in the course of carrying on the trade, if
conditions A and B are met.

(2) Condition A is met if—
   (*a*) a deduction is allowed for the expenses incurred by the trader in travelling to the place, or
   (*b*) where the expenses of travelling to the place are not incurred by the trader, a deduction would
      be allowed for them if they were.

(3) Condition B is met if—
   (*a*) at the time the expenses are incurred on the food or drink, the trade is by its nature itinerant,
      or
   (*b*) the trader does not travel to the place more than occasionally in the course of carrying on the
      trade and either—
      (i) the travel in connection with which the expenses are incurred on the food or drink is
         undertaken otherwise than as part of the trader's normal pattern of travel in the course of
         carrying on the trade, or
      (ii) the trader does not have such a normal pattern of travel.][1]

Commentary—*Simon's Taxes* **B2.318, B2.476.**
HMRC Manuals—Business Income Manual BIM37670 (accommodation and subsistence: itinerant trades).
BIM47705 (expenditure on meals and accommodation).
Amendments—[1]   This section inserted by the Enactment of Extra-Statutory Concessions Order, SI 2009/730 art 3 with effect
for the tax year 2009–10 and subsequent tax years.

[Cash basis: interest payments

57B   Cash basis: interest payments on loans

(1) This section applies if a person carrying on a trade in a period pays any interest on a loan during
the period and—

     (*a*)   a deduction for the interest would not otherwise be allowable in calculating the profits of the
trade because of section 51A, or

     (*b*)   in the absence of section 51A, a deduction for the interest would not otherwise be allowable
in calculating the profits of the trade because (and only because) it was not an expense
incurred wholly and exclusively for the purposes of the trade.

(2) In calculating the profits of the trade on the cash basis, a deduction is allowed for the interest.

(3) But the maximum amount that may be deducted by virtue of this section or section 58 (incidental
costs of obtaining finance) in calculating the profits of a trade for any period is £500.

(4) The Treasury may by order amend the figure for the time being specified in subsection (3).

(5) A statutory instrument containing an order under this section that amends that figure so as to
substitute a lower figure may not be made unless a draft of the instrument has been laid before, and
approved by a resolution of, the House of Commons.][1]

Commentary—*Simon's Taxes* **B2.436.**
HMRC Manuals—Business Income Manual BIM70040 (interest payments and incidental costs of obtaining finance).
Amendments—[1]   This section inserted by FA 2013 s 17, Sch 4 paras 12, 14 with effect for the tax year 2013–14 and subsequent
tax years, subject to the provisions of FA 2013 Sch 4 para 57 in relation to barristers and advocates.

Incidental costs of obtaining finance

58   Incidental costs of obtaining finance

(1) In calculating the profits of a trade, a deduction is allowed for incidental costs of obtaining
finance by means of—

     (*a*)   a loan, or
     (*b*)   the issue of loan stock,

if the interest on the loan or stock is deductible in calculating the profits of the trade.

(2) "Incidental costs of obtaining finance" means expenses—

     (*a*)   which are incurred on fees, commissions, advertising, printing and other incidental matters,
and

     (*b*)   which are incurred wholly and exclusively for the purpose of obtaining the finance, providing
security for it or repaying it.

(3) Expenses incurred wholly and exclusively for the purpose of—

     (*a*)   obtaining finance, or
     (*b*)   providing security for it,

are incidental costs of obtaining the finance even if it is not in fact obtained.

(4) But the following are not incidental costs of obtaining finance—

     (*a*)   sums paid because of losses resulting from movements in the rate of exchange between
different currencies,

     (*b*)   sums paid for the purpose of protecting against such losses,

     (*c*)   the cost of repaying a loan or loan stock so far as attributable to its being repayable at a
premium or having been obtained or issued at a discount, and

     (*d*)   stamp duty.

(5) This section needs to be read with[—

     (*a*)   section 57B(3) (which imposes a limit on the total amount that may be deducted by virtue of
this section or section 57B), and

     (*b*)   ][1]section 59 (which provides for restrictions in relation to convertible loans and loan stock
etc).

Commentary—*Simon's Taxes* **B2.437.**
HMRC Manuals—Business Income Manual BIM45800 (incidental costs of loan finance).
BIM45801 (incidental costs of loan finance: scope of the legislation).
BIM45815 (incidental costs of loan finance: expenses allowable).
BIM45820 (incidental costs of loan finance: exclusions from relief).
BIM45825 (incidental costs of loan finance: commitment fees).
Amendments—[1]   In sub-s (5) words inserted by FA 2013 s 17, Sch 4 paras 12, 15 with effect for the tax year 2013–14 and
subsequent tax years, subject to the provisions of FA 2013 Sch 4 para 57 in relation to barristers and advocates.

59   Convertible loans and loan stock etc

(1) No deduction is allowed under section 58 in respect of a loan or loan stock if—

     (*a*)   it carries the right of conversion into, or to the acquisition of, shares or other securities, and

(b) the right is exercisable before the end of the period of 3 years from the date when the loan was obtained or the stock issued ("the 3 year period").

(2) "Other securities" does not include a loan or loan stock—

(a) the interest on which is deductible in calculating the profits of the person's trade, and

(b) which does not carry such a right as is mentioned in subsection (1).

(3) But the restriction imposed by subsection (1) does not apply if the right is not, or is not wholly, exercised before the end of the 3 year period.

(4) In such a case any incidental costs of obtaining finance incurred before the end of the 3 year period are treated as incurred immediately after the end of it.

(5) If the right is exercised within the 3 year period as to part of the loan or loan stock, only the following incidental costs of obtaining finance are treated as incurred.

(6) The costs are those corresponding to the proportion of the loan or loan stock in respect of which the right is not exercised within that period.

Commentary—*Simon's Taxes* **B2.437.**
HMRC Manuals—Business Income Manual BIM45810 (convertible loan or loan stock).
BIM45801 (incidental costs of loan finance: scope of the legislation).

Tenants under taxed leases

60 Tenants under taxed leases: introduction

(1) Sections 61 to 67 apply if land used in connection with a trade is subject to a taxed lease.

(2) Section 61 (tenants occupying land for purposes of trade treated as incurring expenses) applies in calculating the profits of a trade carried on by the tenant under the taxed lease for the purpose of making deductions for the expenses of the trade.

(3) But any deduction for an expense under section 61 is subject to the application of any provision of Chapter 4 of this Part.

(4) In this section and sections 61 to 67 the following expressions have the same meaning as in Chapter 4 of Part 3 (profits of property businesses: lease premiums etc)—

"receipt period" (see section 288(6)),

"taxed lease" (see section 287(4)),

"taxed receipt" (see section 287(4)), and

"unreduced amount" (see section 290(2)).

(5) Section 290(3) and (4) (unreduced amount of taxed receipt under section 277 as a result of section 278) applies for the purposes of sections 61 to 65.

(6) In sections 64 to 67 references to a reduction under section 288 [below or section 228 of CTA 2009][1] by reference to a taxed receipt have the same meaning as in Chapter 4 of Part 3 (see section 290(6)).

(7) In the application of sections 64 to 67 to Scotland—

(a) references to a lease being granted out of a taxed lease are to the grant of a sublease of land subject to the taxed lease, and

(b) references to the lease so granted are to be read as references to the sublease.

Commentary—*Simon's Taxes* **B2.447.**
HMRC Manuals—Business Income Manual BIM46251 (lease premiums: introduction).
BIM46280 (specific deductions: premiums: prevention of double allowance).
Amendments—[1] In sub-s (6) words inserted by CTA 2009 s 1322, Sch 1 paras 587, 591. CTA 2009 applies for accounting periods ending on or after 1 April 2009 (for corporation tax purposes) and for tax years 2009–10 onwards (for income and capital gains tax purposes).

61 Tenants occupying land for purposes of trade treated as incurring expenses

(1) The tenant under the taxed lease is treated as incurring an expense of a revenue nature in respect of the land subject to the taxed lease for each qualifying day.

(2) If there is more than one taxed receipt, this section applies separately in relation to each of them.

(3) A day is a "qualifying day", in relation to a taxed receipt, if it is a day—

(a) that falls within the receipt period of the taxed receipt, and

(b) on which the tenant occupies the whole or part of the land subject to the taxed lease for the purposes of carrying on a trade.

(4) If on the qualifying day the tenant occupies the whole of the land subject to the taxed lease for the purposes of the trade, the amount of the expense for the qualifying day by reference to the taxed receipt is given by the formula—

$$\frac{A}{TRP}$$

where—

A is the unreduced amount of the taxed receipt, and

TRP is the number of days in the receipt period of the taxed receipt.

(5) If on the qualifying day the tenant occupies part of the land subject to the taxed lease for the purposes of the trade, the amount of the expense for the qualifying day by reference to the taxed receipt is given by the formula—

$$\frac{F \times A}{TRP}$$

where—

F is the fraction of the land that is so occupied calculated on a just and reasonable basis, and
A and TRP have the same meaning as in subsection (4).

[(5A) No expense is to be determined under this section by reference to the taxed receipt if section 292(4B) or (4C) applies.][1]

(6) This section is subject to section 62 (limit on deductions if tenant entitled to mineral extraction allowance).

Commentary—*Simon's Taxes* **B2.447.**
HMRC Manuals—Business Income Manual BIM46255 (calculation of revenue expense).
BIM46265 (assignment of lease).
Amendments—[1]   Sub-s (5A) inserted by FA 2013 s 75, Sch 28 paras 1, 2 with effect in relation to leases granted on or after 6 April 2013.

62 Limit on deductions if tenant entitled to mineral extraction allowance

(1) This section applies if the tenant under the taxed lease has become entitled, in respect of expenditure on the acquisition of an interest in the land subject to the taxed lease, to an allowance for a tax year under Part 5 of CAA 2001 (mineral extraction allowances) in respect of expenditure falling within section 403 of that Act (qualifying expenditure on acquiring a mineral asset).

(2) If the allowance is in respect of the whole of the expenditure, no deduction is allowed for expenses under section 61 for a qualifying day falling within that or a later tax year.

(3) If the allowance is in respect of only part of the expenditure ("the allowable part") the amount of the deduction for expenses under section 61 for a qualifying day falling within that or a later tax year is calculated by multiplying the amount that, apart from this section, would be the amount of the deduction for the qualifying day by—

$$\frac{WE - AP}{WE}$$

where—

WE is the whole of the expenditure, and
AP is the allowable part of the expenditure.

Commentary—*Simon's Taxes* **B2.447.**

63 Tenants dealing with land as property employed for purposes of trade

(1) This section applies if the tenant under the taxed lease—
  (a) does not occupy the land subject to the taxed lease, or a part of it, but
  (b) deals with the tenant's interest in the land, or the part of it, as property employed for the purposes of carrying on a trade.

(2) Section 61 applies as if the land or the part of it were occupied by the tenant for the purposes of the trade.

(3) But the tenant is not treated as incurring an expense in respect of the land for a qualifying day as a result of this section so far as the tenant is treated as incurring an expense under section 292 (tenants under taxed leases treated as incurring expenses) in respect of the land for the day in calculating the profits of the tenant's property business.

(4) This section is subject to sections 64 and 65 (restrictions on section 61 expenses where the additional calculation rule is relevant).

Commentary—*Simon's Taxes* **B2.447.**
HMRC Manuals—Business Income Manual BIM46270 (tied premises: example).

64 Restrictions on section 61 expenses: lease premium receipts

[(1) This section applies if a lease has been granted out of the taxed lease and—
  (a) in calculating the amount of a receipt of a property business under Chapter 4 of Part 3 (profits of property businesses: lease premiums etc) in respect of the lease, there is a reduction under section 288 (the additional calculation rule) by reference to the taxed receipt, or
  (b) in calculating the amount of a receipt of a property business under Chapter 4 of Part 4 of CTA 2009 (profits of a property business: lease premiums etc) in respect of the lease, there is a reduction under section 228 of that Act (the additional calculation rule) by reference to the taxed receipt.

In this section and sections 65 and 67 the receipt that is so reduced is referred to as a "lease premium receipt".][1]

(2) Subsections (3) to (5) provide for the application of section 61 as a result of section 63 for a qualifying day that falls within the receipt period of the lease premium receipt.

(3) The tenant under the taxed lease is treated as incurring an expense under section 61 as a result of section 63 for the qualifying day by reference to the taxed receipt only if the daily amount of the taxed receipt exceeds the daily reduction of the lease premium receipt.

(4) If the condition in subsection (3) is met, the amount of that expense for the qualifying day by reference to the taxed receipt is equal to that excess.

(5) If the qualifying day falls within the receipt period of more than one lease premium receipt, the reference in subsection (3) to the daily reduction of the lease premium receipt is to be read as a reference to the total of the daily reductions of each of the lease premium receipts whose receipt period includes the qualifying day.

(6) In this section—

the "daily amount" of the taxed receipt is given by the formula—

$$\frac{A}{TRP}$$

where—

A is the unreduced amount of the taxed receipt, and

TRP is the number of days in the receipt period of the taxed receipt, and

the "daily reduction" of a lease premium receipt is given by the formula—

$$\frac{AR}{RRP}$$

where—

AR is the reduction under section 288 [below or section 228 of CTA 2009][1] by reference to the taxed receipt, and

RRP is the number of days in the receipt period of the lease premium receipt.

(7) Section 65 explains how this section operates if the lease does not extend to the whole of the premises subject to the taxed lease.

Commentary—*Simon's Taxes* **B2.447.**

Amendments—[1]   Sub-s (1) substituted, and in sub-s (6) words inserted, by CTA 2009 s 1322, Sch 1 paras 587, 592. CTA 2009 applies for accounting periods ending on or after 1 April 2009 (for corporation tax purposes) and for tax years 2009–10 onwards (for income and capital gains tax purposes).

65 Restrictions on section 61 expenses: lease of part of premises

(1) This section applies if—

(*a*) [section 64 applies][1], and

(*b*) the lease granted out of the taxed lease does not extend to the whole of the premises subject to the taxed lease.

(2) Subsections (3) to (5) apply for a qualifying day that falls within the receipt period of the lease premium receipt.

(3) Sections 61, 63 and 64 apply separately in relation to the part of the premises subject to the lease and to the remainder of the premises.

(4) If—

(*a*) more than one lease that does not extend to the whole of the premises subject to the taxed lease has been granted out of the taxed lease, and

(*b*) the qualifying day falls within the receipt period of two or more lease premium receipts that relate to different leases,

sections 61, 63 and 64 apply separately in relation to each part of the premises subject to a lease to which such a lease premium receipt relates and to the remainder of the premises.

(5) Where sections 61, 63 and 64 apply in relation to a part of the premises, A becomes the amount calculated by multiplying the unreduced amount of the taxed receipt by the fraction of the premises constituted by the part.

(6) This fraction is calculated on a just and reasonable basis.

Commentary—*Simon's Taxes* **B2.447.**

Amendments—[1]   In sub-s (1)(*a*) words substituted by CTA 2009 s 1322, Sch 1 paras 587, 593. CTA 2009 applies for accounting periods ending on or after 1 April 2009 (for corporation tax purposes) and for tax years 2009–10 onwards (for income and capital gains tax purposes).

66 Corporation tax receipts treated as taxed receipts [under ICTA][1]

Section 296 (corporation tax receipts treated as taxed receipts) applies for the purposes of sections 60 to 67.

Commentary—*Simon's Taxes* **B2.447.**

Amendments—[1]   In heading words inserted by CTA 2009 s 1322, Sch 1 paras 587, 594. CTA 2009 applies for accounting periods ending on or after 1 April 2009 (for corporation tax purposes) and for tax years 2009–10 onwards (for income and capital gains tax purposes).

67 Restrictions on section 61 expenses: corporation tax receipts [under ICTA][1]

(1) This section provides for the application of section 61 as a result of section 63 if—

   (*a*) a lease has been granted out of the taxed lease,

   (*b*) in calculating the amount of a corporation tax receipt in respect of the lease, there is a reduction under section 37(2) or (3) of ICTA by reference to the amount chargeable on the superior interest for the purposes of that section, and

   (*c*) the amount chargeable on the superior interest is the taxed receipt for the purposes of section 61.

(2) Sections 61 and 63 to 65 apply as follows—

   (*a*) the corporation tax receipt is treated as if it were a lease premium receipt for the purposes of sections 64 and 65,

   (*b*) references in those sections to the reduction under section 288 by reference to the taxed receipt are, in relation to the corporation tax receipt, to the reduction under section 37(2) or (3) of ICTA by reference to the amount chargeable on the superior interest, and

   (*c*) for the purposes of those sections the receipt period of the corporation tax receipt is—

      (i) in the case of a corporation tax receipt as a result of section 34 of ICTA, the period treated in calculating the amount of the receipt as being the duration of the lease, and

      (ii) in the case of a corporation tax receipt as a result of section 35 of ICTA, the period treated in calculating the amount of the receipt as being the duration of the lease remaining at the date of the assignment.

(3) There is a corporation tax receipt in respect of a lease if—

   (*a*) there is a receipt of a Schedule A business or an overseas property business (within the meaning of section 70A(4) of ICTA) as a result of section 34 or 35 of ICTA (treatment of premiums etc as rent and assignments for profit of lease granted at an undervalue) in respect of the lease for an accounting period ending after 5th April 2005 [but before 1st April 2009][1], or

   (*b*) there would be such a receipt, but for the operation of section 37(2) or (3) of ICTA (reductions in certain receipts under section 34 or 35 of ICTA).

(4) References to a reduction under section 37(2) or (3) of ICTA in a corporation tax receipt by reference to the amount chargeable on the superior interest are to the difference between—

   (*a*) the amount of the corporation tax receipt before the operation of section 37(2) or (3) of ICTA, and

   (*b*) the amount of the corporation tax receipt after the operation of that subsection,

so far as attributable to the amount chargeable on the superior interest for the purposes of section 37 of ICTA.

Commentary—*Simon's Taxes* **B2.447.**

Amendments—[1]   In heading, and in sub-s (3)(*a*), words inserted, by CTA 2009 s 1322, Sch 1 paras 587, 595. CTA 2009 applies for accounting periods ending on or after 1 April 2009 (for corporation tax purposes) and for tax years 2009–10 onwards (for income and capital gains tax purposes).

Payments for restrictive undertakings

69 Payments for restrictive undertakings

(1) In calculating the profits of a trade, a deduction is allowed for a payment—

   (*a*) which is treated as earnings of an employee by virtue of section 225 of ITEPA 2003 (payments for restrictive undertakings), and

   (*b*) which is made, or treated as made for the purposes of section 226 of that Act (valuable consideration given for restrictive undertakings), by the person carrying on the trade.

(2) The deduction is allowed for the period of account in which the payment—

   (*a*) is made, or

   (*b*) is treated as made for the purposes of section 226 of ITEPA 2003.

Commentary—*Simon's Taxes* **B2.469.**

HMRC Manuals—Business Income Manual BIM47005 (restrictive covenants with employees).

Seconded employees

70 Employees seconded to charities and educational establishments

(1) This section applies if a person carrying on a trade ("the employer") makes the services of a person employed for the purposes of the trade available to—

   (*a*) a charity, or

   (*b*) an educational establishment,

on a basis that is stated and intended to be temporary.

(2) In calculating the profits of the trade, a deduction is allowed for expenses of the employer that are attributable to the employee's employment during the period of the secondment.

(3) In this section—

"educational establishment" means—

(a) in England and Wales, any of the bodies mentioned in section 71(1),
(b) in Scotland, any of the bodies mentioned in section 71(2),
(c) in Northern Ireland, any of the bodies mentioned in section 71(3), and
(d) any other educational body which is for the time being approved for the purposes of this section by the Secretary of State or, in Northern Ireland, the Department of Education, and
"the period of the secondment" means the period for which the employee's services are made available to the charity or educational establishment.

Commentary—*Simon's Taxes* **B2.430.**
HMRC Manuals—Business Income Manual BIM47115 (employees seconded to charities).
BIM47120 (employees seconded to educational establishments).

71 Educational establishments

(1) A body in England and Wales is an educational establishment for the purposes of section 70 if it is—

[(a) a local authority (but only to the extent that the services of the employee are made available to the authority for the purposes of, or in connection with, the education functions of the authority),]²
(b) an educational institution maintained or otherwise supported[, in the exercise of their education functions, by a local authority]²,
(c) an independent school within the meaning of the Education Act 1996 (c 56) registered under section 161 of the Education Act 2002 (c 32), . . . ³
[(ca) an alternative provision Academy that is not an independent school within the meaning of the Education Act 1996,]⁴
(d) an institution within the further education sector, or the higher education sector, within the meaning of the Further and Higher Education Act 1992 (c 13)[, or
(e) a 16 to 19 Academy.]³

(2) A body in Scotland is an educational establishment for the purposes of section 70 if it is—

(a) an education authority within the meaning of the Education (Scotland) Act 1980 (c 44),
(b) an educational establishment within the meaning of the Education (Scotland) Act 1980 managed by an education authority within the meaning of that Act,
(c) a public or grant-aided school within the meaning of the Education (Scotland) Act 1980,
(d) an independent school within the meaning of the Education (Scotland) Act 1980,
(e) a central institution within the meaning of the Education (Scotland) Act 1980,
(f) an institution within the higher education sector within the meaning of section 56(2) of the Further and Higher Education (Scotland) Act 1992 (c 37), or
(g) a college of further education within the meaning of section 36(1) of the Further and Higher Education (Scotland) Act 1992.

(3) A body in Northern Ireland is an educational establishment for the purposes of section 70 if it is—

(a) an [education and library board]¹ within the meaning of the Education and Libraries (Northern Ireland) Order 1986 (SI 1986/594 (NI 3)),
(b) a college of education[, a grant-aided school or an]¹ independent school within the meaning of the Education and Libraries (Northern Ireland) Order 1986, or
(c) an institution of further education within the meaning of the Further Education (Northern Ireland) Order 1997 (SI 1997/1772 (NI 15)).

[(4) In subsection (1) "local authority" and "education functions" have the same meaning as in the Education Act 1996 (see section 579(1) of that Act).]²

Commentary—*Simon's Taxes* **B2.430.**
HMRC Manuals—Business Income Manual BIM47120 (employees seconded to educational establishments).
Amendments—¹ In sub-s (3)(a), (3)(b) words substituted by CTA 2009 s 1322, Sch 1 paras 587, 596. CTA 2009 applies for accounting periods ending on or after 1 April 2009 (for corporation tax purposes) and for tax years 2009–10 onwards (for income and capital gains tax purposes).
² Sub-s (1)(a) substituted, in sub-s(1)(b) words substituted and sub-s (4) inserted by the Local Education Authorities and Children's Services Authorities (Integration of Functions) Order, SI 2010/1158 art 5(1), Sch 2 para 56 with effect from 5 May 2010.
³ In sub-s (1) word at the end of para (c) repealed and para (e) and preceding word inserted by the Education Act 2011 s 54, Sch 13 para 14 with effect from 1 April 2012 (by virtue of SI 2012/924 art 2). Note that these amendments do not extend to Scotland: see the Education Act 2011 s 81(1).
⁴ Sub-s (1)(ca) inserted by the Alternative Provision Academies (Consequential Amendments to Acts) (England) Order, SI 2012/976 art 2, Schedule para 15 with effect from 1 April 2012.

Contributions to agents' expenses

72 Payroll deduction schemes: contributions to agents' expenses

(1) This section applies if—

(a) a person carrying on a trade ("the employer") is liable to make payments to an individual,
(b) income tax falls to be deducted from those payments as a result of PAYE regulations, and

   (*c*) the employer withholds sums from those payments in accordance with an approved scheme and pays the sums to an approved agent.

(2) In calculating the profits of the employer's trade, a deduction is allowed for expenses incurred by the employer in making a payment to the agent for expenses which—

   (*a*) have been incurred, or

   (*b*) are to be incurred,

by the agent in connection with the agent's functions under the scheme.

[(2A) In calculating the profits of the employer's trade on the cash basis, subsection (2) has effect as if paragraph (*b*) were omitted.][1]

(3) In this section "approved agent" and "approved scheme" have the same meaning as in section 714 of ITEPA 2003.

Commentary—*Simon's Taxes* **B2.441, E4.1116.**

HMRC Manuals—Business Income Manual BIM45195 (gifts in kind and payroll giving).

Amendments—[1]   Sub-s (2A) inserted by FA 2013 s 17, Sch 4 paras 12, 16 with effect for the tax year 2013–14 and subsequent tax years, subject to the provisions of FA 2013 Sch 4 para 57 in relation to barristers and advocates.

Counselling and retraining expenses

73 Counselling and other outplacement services

(1) In calculating the profits of a trade, a deduction is allowed for counselling expenses if—

   (*a*) the person carrying on the trade ("the employer") incurs the expenses,

   (*b*) the expenses are incurred in relation to a person ("the employee") who holds or has held an office or employment under the employer for the purposes of the trade, and

   (*c*) the relevant conditions are met.

(2) In this section "counselling expenses" means expenses incurred—

   (*a*) in the provision of services to the employee in connection with the cessation of the office or employment,

   (*b*) in the payment or reimbursement of fees for such provision, or

   (*c*) in the payment or reimbursement of travelling expenses in connection with such provision.

(3) In this section "the relevant conditions" means—

   (*a*) conditions A to D for the purposes of section 310 of ITEPA 2003 (employment income exemptions: counselling and other outplacement services), and

   (*b*) in the case of travel expenses, condition E for those purposes.

Commentary—*Simon's Taxes* **B2.428.**

HMRC Manuals—Business Income Manual BIM47217 (staff counselling expenses).

74 Retraining courses

(1) In calculating the profits of a trade, a deduction is allowed for retraining course expenses if—

   (*a*) the person carrying on the trade ("the employer") incurs the expenses,

   (*b*) they are incurred in relation to a person ("the employee") who holds or has held an office or employment under the employer for the purposes of the trade, and

   (*c*) the relevant conditions are met.

(2) In this section—

"retraining course expenses" means expenses incurred in the payment or reimbursement of retraining course expenses within the meaning given by section 311(2) of ITEPA 2003, and "the relevant conditions" means—

   (*a*) the conditions in subsections (3) and (4) of section 311 of ITEPA 2003 (employment income exemptions: retraining courses), and

   (*b*) in the case of travel expenses, the conditions in subsection (5) of that section.

Commentary—*Simon's Taxes* **B2.428.**

HMRC Manuals—Business Income Manual BIM47080 (staff training and development).

Employment Income Manual EIM05005 (explanation and further references of section 311 ITEPA 2003)

75 Retraining courses: recovery of tax

(1) This section applies if—

   (*a*) an employer's liability to tax for a tax year is determined on the assumption that a deduction for expenditure is allowed under section 74, and

   (*b*) the deduction would not otherwise have been allowed.

(2) If, subsequently—

   (*a*) the condition in section 311(4)(*a*) of ITEPA 2003 is not met because of the employee's failure to begin the course within the period of one year after ceasing to be employed, or

   (*b*) the condition in section 311(4)(*b*) of ITEPA 2003 is not met because of the employee's continued employment or re-employment,

an assessment of an amount or further amount of tax due as a result of the condition not being met may be made under section 29(1) of TMA 1970.

(3) Such an assessment must be made before the end of the period of 6 years immediately following the end of the tax year in which the failure to meet the condition occurred.

(4) If subsection (2) applies, the employer must give [an officer of Revenue and Customs] a notice containing particulars of—

    (*a*) the employee's failure to begin the course,

    (*b*) the employee's continued employment, or

    (*c*) the employee's re-employment,

within 60 days of coming to know of it.

(5) . . . [1]

(6) A notice under subsection (5) may specify a time (not less than 60 days) within which the required information must be provided.

Commentary—*Simon's Taxes* **B2.428.**

HMRC Manuals—Employment Income Manual EIM05030 (explanation to withdrawal of exemption for section 312 ITEPA 2003)

Amendments—[1]   Sub-s (5) repealed by Finance Act 2009 Schedule 47 (Consequential Amendments) Order, SI 2009/2035, Art 2, Schedule paras 41, 22 with effect from 13 August 2009.

Redundancy payments etc

76 Redundancy payments and approved contractual payments

(1) Sections 77 to 79 apply if—

    (*a*) a person ("the employer") makes a redundancy payment or an approved contractual payment to another person ("the employee"), and

    (*b*) the payment is in respect of the employee's employment wholly in the employer's trade or partly in the employer's trade and partly in one or more other capacities.

(2) For the purposes of this section and sections 77 to 80 "redundancy payment" means a redundancy payment payable under—

    (*a*) Part 11 of the Employment Rights Act 1996 (c 18), or

    (*b*) Part 12 of the Employment Rights (Northern Ireland) Order 1996 (SI 1996/1919 (NI 16)).

(3) For the purposes of this section and those sections—

"contractual payment" means a payment which, under an agreement, an employer is liable to make to an employee on the termination of the employee's contract of employment, and

a contractual payment is "approved" if, in respect of that agreement, an order is in force under—

    (*a*) section 157 of the Employment Rights Act 1996, or

    (*b*) Article 192 of the Employment Rights (Northern Ireland) Order 1996.

Commentary—*Simon's Taxes* **B2.426.**

HMRC Manuals—Business Income Manual BIM47200 (redundancy payments: general principles). BIM47205 (statutory redundancy and contractual payments).

77 Payments in respect of employment wholly in employer's trade

(1) This section applies if—

    (*a*) the payment is in respect of the employee's employment wholly in the employer's trade, and

    (*b*) no deduction would otherwise be allowable for the payment.

(2) In calculating the profits of the trade, a deduction is allowed under this section for the payment.

(3) The deduction under this section for an approved contractual payment must not exceed the amount which would have been due to the employee if a redundancy payment had been payable.

(4) If the payment is made after the employer has permanently ceased to carry on the trade, it is treated as made on the last day on which the employer carried on the trade.

(5) If there is a change in the persons carrying on the trade, subsection (4) does not apply so long as a person carrying on the trade immediately before the change continues to carry it on after the change.

(6) The deduction under this section is allowed for the period of account in which the payment is made (or treated under subsection (4) as made).

Commentary—*Simon's Taxes* **B2.426.**

HMRC Manuals—Business Income Manual BIM47215 (redundancy payments: timing of deductions). BIM47205 (statutory redundancy payments: the deduction).

78 Payments in respect of employment in more than one capacity

(1) This section applies if the payment is in respect of the employee's employment with the employer—

    (*a*) partly in the employer's trade, and

    (*b*) partly in one or more other capacities.

(2) The amount of the redundancy payment, or the amount which would have been due if a redundancy payment had been payable, is to be apportioned on a just and reasonable basis between—

    (*a*) the employment in the trade, and

    (*b*) the employment in the other capacities.

(3) The part of the payment apportioned to the employment in the trade is treated as a payment in respect of the employee's employment wholly in the trade for the purposes of section 77.

Commentary—*Simon's Taxes* **B2.426.**

HMRC Manuals—Business Income Manuals BIM47205 (statutory redundancy payments: the deduction).

79 Additional payments

(1) This section applies if the employer permanently ceases to carry on a trade or part of a trade and makes a payment to the employee in addition to—

    (*a*) the redundancy payment, or

    (*b*) if an approved contractual payment is made, the amount that would have been due if a redundancy payment had been payable.

(2) . . . [1]

(3) If, in calculating the profits of the trade—

    (*a*) no deduction would otherwise be allowable for the additional payment, but

    (*b*) a deduction would be allowable for it if the employer had not permanently ceased to carry on the trade or the part of the trade,

a deduction is allowed under this section for the additional payment.

(4) The deduction under this section is limited to 3 times the amount of—

    (*a*) the redundancy payment, or

    (*b*) if an approved contractual payment is made, the amount that would have been due if a redundancy payment had been payable.

(5) If the payment is made after the employer has permanently ceased to carry on the trade or the part of the trade, it is treated as made on the last day on which the employer carried on the trade or the part of the trade.

(6) The deduction under this section is allowed for the period of account in which the payment is made (or treated under subsection (5) as made).

Commentary—*Simon's Taxes* **B2.426, B2.306.**

HMRC Manuals—Business Income Manual BIM47210 (additional payments to redundant employees). BIM47215 (redundancy payments: timing of deductions).

Amendments—[1]   Sub-s (2) repealed by CTA 2009 ss 1322, 1326, Sch 1 paras 587, 597, Sch 3 Part 1. CTA 2009 applies for accounting periods ending on or after 1 April 2009 (for corporation tax purposes) and for tax years 2009–10 onwards (for income and capital gains tax purposes).

[79A   Additional payments: change in the persons carrying on the trade

(1) This section deals with the application of section 79 in circumstances where there is a change in the persons carrying on the trade.

(2) The employer is treated for the purposes of section 79 as permanently ceasing to carry on the trade unless a person carrying on the trade immediately before the change continues to carry it on after the change.][1]

Commentary—*Simon's Taxes* **B2.306.**

HMRC Manuals—Business Income Manual BIM47210 (additional payments to redundant employees).

Amendments—[1]   This section inserted by CTA 2009 s 1322, Sch 1 paras 587, 598. CTA 2009 applies for accounting periods ending on or after 1 April 2009 (for corporation tax purposes) and for tax years 2009–10 onwards (for income and capital gains tax purposes).

80 Payments made by the Government

(1) This section applies if, in respect of a redundancy payment or an approved contractual payment payable by an employer—

    (*a*) the Secretary of State makes a payment under section 167 of the Employment Rights Act 1996 (c 18), or

    (*b*) the Department for Employment and Learning makes a payment under Article 202 of the Employment Rights (Northern Ireland) Order 1996 (SI 1996/1919 (NI 16)).

(2) So far as the employer reimburses the Secretary of State or Department for the payment, sections 77 to [79A][1] apply as if the payment were—

    (*a*) a redundancy payment, or

    (*b*) an approved contractual payment,

made by the employer.

Commentary—*Simon's Taxes* **B2.426.**

HMRC Manuals—Business Income Manual BIM47205 (payments direct to employees by a government department).

Amendments—[1]   In sub-s (2) reference substituted for reference "79" by CTA 2009 s 1322, Sch 1 paras 587, 599. CTA 2009 applies for accounting periods ending on or after 1 April 2009 (for corporation tax purposes) and for tax years 2009–10 onwards (for income and capital gains tax purposes).

Personal security expenses

81 Personal security expenses

(1) This section applies if—

    (*a*) an individual ("the trader") carries on a trade (alone or in a partnership of individuals),

    (*b*) there is a special threat to the personal physical security of the trader which arises wholly or mainly because of the particular trade,

    (*c*) a service or asset which improves personal security is used by or provided for the trader to meet the threat, (*d*) the person incurring expenses in connection with that use or provision does so with the sole object of meeting the threat, and

(*e*) a deduction for the expenses would not otherwise be allowable in calculating the profits of the trade because (and only because) they were not incurred wholly and exclusively for the purposes of the trade.

(2) In calculating the profits of the trade, a deduction is allowed for the expenses—

(*a*) in the case of a service, if the benefit resulting to the trader consists wholly or mainly of an improvement of the trader's personal physical security, and

(*b*) in the case of an asset, if the person incurring the expenses intends the asset to be used to improve personal physical security (whether solely or partly).

(3) If the person incurring the expenses intends the asset to be used solely to improve personal physical security, any use of the asset which is incidental to improving personal physical security is ignored.

(4) If the person incurring the expenses intends the asset to be used partly to improve personal physical security, a deduction is allowed only for the proportion of the expenses which is attributable to the intended use to improve personal physical security.

(5) The fact that a service or asset improves the personal physical security of a member of the trader's family or household (as well as that of the trader) does not prevent a deduction from being allowed.

(6) In determining whether or not this section applies in relation to an asset, it does not matter if—

(*a*) the asset becomes fixed to land, or

(*b*) the trader is or becomes entitled to the property in the asset or (if the asset is a fixture) to any estate or interest in the land concerned.

(7) In this section—

"asset" includes equipment and a structure (such as a wall), but does not include a car, ship or aircraft or a dwelling or grounds appurtenant to a dwelling, and

"service" does not include a dwelling or grounds appurtenant to a dwelling.

Commentary—*Simon's Taxes* **B2.471.**

Contributions to local enterprise organisations or urban regeneration companies

82 Contributions to local enterprise organisations or urban regeneration companies

(1) This section applies if a person carrying on a trade ("the contributor") incurs expenses in making a contribution (whether in cash or in kind)—

(*a*) to a local enterprise organisation (see section 83), or

(*b*) to an urban regeneration company (see section 86),

and a deduction would not otherwise be allowable for the expenses in calculating the profits of the trade.

(2) In calculating the profits of the trade, a deduction is allowed under this section for the expenses.

(3) But if, in connection with the making of the contribution, the contributor or a connected person—

(*a*) receives a disqualifying benefit of any kind, or

(*b*) is entitled to receive such a benefit,

the amount of the deduction is restricted to the amount of the expenses less the value of the benefit.

(4) For this purpose it does not matter whether a person receives, or is entitled to receive, the benefit—

(*a*) from the organisation or company concerned, or

(*b*) from anyone else.

(5) Subsection (6) applies if—

(*a*) a deduction has been made under this section, and

(*b*) the contributor or a connected person receives a disqualifying benefit that is in any way attributable to the contribution.

(6) An amount equal to the value of the benefit (so far as not brought into account in determining the amount of the deduction)—

(*a*) is brought into account in calculating the profits of the trade, as a receipt arising on the date on which the benefit is received, or

(*b*) if the contributor has permanently ceased to carry on the trade before that date, is treated as a post-cessation receipt (see Chapter 18).

(7) In this section "disqualifying benefit" means a benefit the expenses of obtaining which, if incurred by the contributor directly in a transaction at arm's length, would not be allowable as a deduction in calculating the profits of the trade.

83 Meaning of "local enterprise organisation"

(1) For the purposes of section 82 "local enterprise organisation" means—

(*a*) a local enterprise agency,

(*b*) a training and enterprise council,

(*c*) a Scottish local enterprise company, or

(*d*) a business link organisation.

(2) "Local enterprise agency" means a body for the time being approved as a local enterprise agency for the purposes of section 82 by the relevant national authority, that is to say by—

    (a) the Secretary of State (in relation to England or Northern Ireland),

    (b) the Scottish Ministers (in relation to Scotland), or

    (c) the National Assembly for Wales (in relation to Wales).

For further provision about approvals by the relevant national authority, see sections 84 and 85.

(3) "Training and enterprise council" means a body with which the Secretary of State has an agreement under which the body is to carry out the functions of a training and enterprise council.

(4) "Scottish local enterprise company" means a company with which—

    (a) Scottish Enterprise, or

    (b) Highlands and Islands Enterprise,

has an agreement under which the company is to carry out the functions of a local enterprise company.

(5) "Business link organisation" means a person authorised by or on behalf of the Secretary of State to use a trade mark designated by the Secretary of State for the purposes of this subsection.

84 Approval of local enterprise agencies

(1) The relevant national authority may approve a body as a local enterprise agency for the purposes of section 82 only if conditions A and B are met.

(2) But if those conditions are met, the body may be approved—

    (a) whatever its status or structure, and

    (b) even if it is not described as a local enterprise agency.

(3) Condition A is that the relevant national authority is satisfied—

    (a) that the body's sole aim is the promotion or encouragement of local enterprise, or

    (b) that one of the body's main aims is the promotion or encouragement of local enterprise and that it has or is about to have a separate fund for the sole purpose of pursuing that aim.

(4) For this purpose "local enterprise" means industrial and commercial activity or enterprise in a particular area in the United Kingdom, with particular reference to encouraging the formation and development of small businesses.

(5) Condition B is that the body is precluded from paying or transferring any of its income or profit directly or indirectly—

    (a) to any of its members, or

    (b) to any person charged with the control and direction of its affairs.

(6) The payment of—

    (a) reasonable remuneration for goods, labour or power supplied or for services provided,

    (b) reasonable interest on money lent, or

    (c) reasonable rent for premises,

does not count as a payment or transfer of income or profit for the purposes of subsection (5).

85 Supplementary provisions with respect to approvals

(1) This section applies for the purposes of section 84.

(2) The relevant national authority may give a body approval that is conditional on its compliance with such requirements as to—

    (a) accounts,

    (b) provision of information, and

    (c) other matters,

as the relevant national authority considers appropriate

(3) If the relevant national authority approves a body on the basis that it has or is about to have a separate fund (see section 84(3)(b))—

    (a) the approval must specify the fund, and

    (b) section 82 applies only to a contribution to the body made wholly to or for the purposes of the fund.

(4) The relevant national authority must withdraw the approval of a body as a local enterprise agency if—

    (a) condition A or B in section 84 is no longer met, or

    (b) the body is failing to comply with a requirement imposed as a condition of its approval.

(5) The relevant national authority must give notice of withdrawal to the body concerned, specifying the date from which the withdrawal takes effect (which may be earlier than the date on which the notice is given).

86 Meaning of "urban regeneration company"

(1) For the purposes of section 82 "urban regeneration company" means any body of persons which the Treasury by order designates as an urban regeneration company for the purposes of that section.

(2) A body may be so designated only if—

    (a) its sole or main function is to co-ordinate the regeneration of a specific urban area in the United Kingdom,

(b) it is expected to seek to perform that function by creating a plan for the development of that area and trying to secure that the plan is carried into effect, and

(c) in co-ordinating the regeneration of that area, it is expected to work together with some or all local or other public authorities which exercise functions in relation to the whole or part of that area.

(3) An order under this section may be framed so as to take effect on a date earlier than the making of the order, but not earlier than three months before the date on which the order is made.

Commentary—*Simon's Taxes* B2.450.

HMRC Manuals—Business Income Manual BIM47610 (urban regeneration company (URC)).

[Contributions to flood and coastal erosion risk management projects

86A Contributions to flood and coastal erosion risk management projects

(1) This section applies if—

(a) a person carrying on a trade ("the contributor") incurs expenses in making a qualifying contribution to a qualifying flood or coastal erosion risk management project, and

(b) a deduction would not otherwise be allowable for the expenses in calculating the profits of the trade.

(2) In determining whether the condition in subsection (1)(b) is satisfied, a deduction giving effect to a capital allowance is to be disregarded.

(3) In calculating the profits of the trade, a deduction is allowed under this section for the expenses.

(4) But if, in connection with the making of the contribution, the contributor or a connected person—

(a) receives a disqualifying benefit, or

(b) is entitled to receive such a benefit,

no deduction is allowed.

(5) For the purposes of subsection (4) it does not matter whether a person receives, or is entitled to receive, the benefit—

(a) from the carrying out of the project, or

(b) from any person.

(6) Subsection (7) applies if—

(a) a deduction has been made under this section in relation to the contribution, and

(b) the contributor or a connected person receives—

    (i) a refund of any part of the contribution, if the contribution is a sum of money, or

    (ii) compensation for any part of the contribution, if the contribution is the provision of services,

in money or money's worth.

(7) The amount of, or an amount equal to the value of, the refund or compensation (so far as not otherwise brought into account in calculating the profits of the trade or treated as a post-cessation receipt)—

(a) is brought into account in calculating the profits of the trade, as a receipt arising on the date on which the refund or compensation is received, or

(b) if the contributor has permanently ceased to carry on the trade before that date, is treated as a post-cessation receipt (see Chapter 18).

(8) In this section "disqualifying benefit" means a benefit consisting of money or other property, but it does not include—

(a) a refund of the contribution, if the contribution is a sum of money;

(b) compensation for the contribution, if the contribution is the provision of services;

(c) a structure that—

    (i) is or is to be used for the purposes of flood or coastal erosion risk management, and

    (ii) is put in place in carrying out the project;

(d) an addition to a structure where—

    (i) the structure is or is to be used for the purposes of flood or coastal erosion risk management, and

    (ii) the addition is made in carrying out the project;

(e) land, plant or machinery that is or is to be used, in the realization of the project, for the purposes of flood or coastal erosion risk management;

(f) a right over land that is or is to be used, in the realization of the project, for the purposes of flood or coastal erosion risk management.

(9) In subsection (8) "structure" includes road, path, pipe, earthwork, plant and machinery.][1]

Commentary—*Simon's Taxes* B2.411.

Amendments—[1] Sections 86A, 86B inserted by FA 2015 s 35, Sch 5 para 1 with effect in relation to contributions paid or provided on or after 1 January 2015.

[86B Interpretation of section 86A

(1) This section applies for the purposes of section 86A.

(2) A flood or coastal erosion risk management project is a qualifying project if—

(*a*) an English risk management authority has applied to the Environment Agency for a grant under section 16 of the Flood and Water Management Act 2010 in order to fund the project, or

(*b*) the Environment Agency has determined that it will carry out the project,

and the Environment Agency has allocated funding by way of grant-in-aid to the project.

(3) A contribution to a flood or coastal erosion risk management project is a qualifying contribution if the contribution is made—

(*a*) for the purposes of the project, and

(*b*) under an agreement between—

(i) the person making the contribution, and

(ii) the applicant authority or (as the case may be) the Environment Agency,

or between those two persons and other persons.

(4) References to a flood risk management project or a coastal erosion risk management project are to be interpreted in accordance with sections 1 to 3 of the Flood and Water Management Act 2010.

(5) In section 86A and this section—

"contribution", in relation to a period of account, means—

(*a*) a sum of money paid in that period of account, or

(*b*) any services provided in that period of account;

"English risk management authority" has the meaning given by section 6(14) of the Flood and Water Management Act 2010.]¹

Commentary—*Simon's Taxes* **B2.411.**

Amendments—¹   Sections 86A, 86B inserted by FA 2015 s 35, Sch 5 para 1 with effect in relation to contributions paid or provided on or after 1 January 2015.

Scientific research

87 Expenses of research and development

(1) If a person carrying on a trade incurs expenses of a revenue nature on research and development—

(*a*) related to the trade, and

(*b*) directly undertaken by or on behalf of the person,

a deduction is allowed for the expenses in calculating the profits of the trade.

(2) For this purpose expenses incurred on research and development—

(*a*) do not include expenses incurred in the acquisition of rights in, or arising out of, research and development, but

(*b*) subject to that, include all expenses incurred in carrying out, or providing facilities for carrying out, research and development.

(3) The reference in this section to research and development related to a trade includes—

(*a*) research and development which may lead to or facilitate an extension of the trade, and

(*b*) research and development of a medical nature which has a special relation to the welfare of workers employed in the trade.

(4) The same expenses may not be brought into account under this section in relation to more than one trade.

(5) In this section "research and development" has the meaning given by [section 1006 of ITA 2007]¹ and includes oil and gas exploration and appraisal.

(6) This section does not apply to professions or vocations.

Commentary—*Simon's Taxes* **B2.467.**

Amendments—¹   Words in sub-s (5) substituted by ITA 2007 s 1027, Sch 1 paras 492, 499 with effect for income tax purposes from 6 April 2007, and corporation tax purposes for accounting periods ending after 5 April 2007.

88 Payments to research associations, universities etc

(1) If a person carrying on a trade—

(*a*) pays any sum to an approved scientific research association which has as its object scientific research related to the class of trade to which the trade belongs, or

(*b*) pays any sum to be used for such scientific research to an approved university, college research institute or other similar institution,

a deduction is allowed for the sum in calculating the profits of the trade.

(2) The deduction is allowed for the period of account in which the payment is made.

(3) "Scientific research" means any activities in the fields of natural or applied science for the extension of knowledge.

(4) For the purposes of this section—

(*a*) a scientific research association, or

(*b*) a university, college research institute or other similar institution,

is approved if it is for the time being approved for the purposes of this section by the Secretary of State.

(5) The references in this section to scientific research related to a class of trade include—

(*a*) scientific research which may lead to or facilitate an extension of trades of the class, and

(*b*) scientific research of a medical nature which has a special relation to the welfare of workers employed in trades of the class.

(6) If a question arises as to—

(*a*) whether, or

(*b*) [to][1] what extent,

any activities constitute or constituted scientific research, [an officer of Revenue and Customs] must refer the question for decision to the Secretary of State, whose decision is final.

(7) The same expenses may not be brought into account under this section in relation to more than one trade.

(8) This section does not apply to professions or vocations.

Commentary—*Simon's Taxes* **B2.467**.

Amendments—[1]   Word in sub-s (6)(*b*) inserted by CTA 2009 s 1322, Sch 1 paras 587, 600. CTA 2009 applies for accounting periods ending on or after 1 April 2009 (for corporation tax purposes) and for tax years 2009–10 onwards (for income and capital gains tax purposes).

Expenses connected with patents, designs and trade marks

89 Expenses connected with patents

(1) In calculating the profits of a trade, a deduction is allowed for expenses incurred—

(*a*) in obtaining for the purposes of the trade the grant of a patent or the extension of a patent's term, or

(*b*) in connection with a rejected or abandoned application for a patent made for the purposes of the trade.

(2) This section does not apply to professions or vocations.

Commentary—*Simon's Taxes* **B2.456, B3.609, B5.331**.

HMRC Manuals—Business Income Manual BIM45951 (costs of obtaining or extending patent rights).

BIM45955 (expenditure on acquisition of knowhow).

90 Expenses connected with designs or trade marks

(1) In calculating the profits of a trade, a deduction is allowed for expenses incurred in obtaining for the purposes of the trade—

(*a*) the registration of a design or trade mark,

(*b*) the extension of a period for which the right in a registered design subsists, or

(*c*) the renewal of registration of a trade mark.

(2) This section does not apply to professions or vocations.

Commentary—*Simon's Taxes* **B2.456, B5.324, B5.350**.

HMRC Manuals—Business Income Manual BIM45960 (costs of registering or extending the life of, trade marks and designs).

Export Credits Guarantee Department

91 Payments to Export Credits Guarantee Department

In calculating the profits of a trade, a deduction is allowed for a sum payable by the person carrying on the trade to the Export Credits Guarantee Department—

(*a*) under an agreement entered into as a result of arrangements made under section 2 of the Export and Investment Guarantees Act 1991 (c 67) (insurance in connection with overseas investment), or

(*b*) with a view to entering into such an agreement.

Commentary—*Simon's Taxes* **B2.435, B2.445**.

HMRC Manuals—Business Income Manual BIM45580 (export credits guarantee scheme).

Expenses connected with foreign trades

92 Expenses connected with foreign trades

(1) This section applies if—

(*a*) an individual ("the trader") carries on a foreign trade (alone or in partnership),

(*b*) the trader is absent from the United Kingdom wholly and exclusively for the purpose of carrying on the foreign trade or the foreign trade and one or more other trades (whether or not foreign trades),

(*c*) qualifying expenses are incurred in connection with the foreign trade, and

(*d*) a deduction for the expenses would not otherwise be allowable in calculating the profits of the foreign trade because (and only because) they were not incurred wholly and exclusively for the purposes of the foreign trade.

(2) In calculating any profits of the foreign trade which are not charged in accordance with section 832 (relevant foreign income charged on the remittance basis), a deduction is allowed for the expenses.

(3) Any of the following expenses are qualifying expenses incurred in connection with the foreign trade—

(*a*) expenses incurred by the trader in travelling between a place in the United Kingdom and a place where the foreign trade is carried on, (*b*) expenses incurred by the trader on board and lodging at a place where the foreign trade is carried on,

(*c*) if the trader's absence from the United Kingdom is for a continuous period of 60 days or more, family expenses (as defined in section 94), and

(*d*) if the trader also carries on another trade outside the United Kingdom (whether or not a foreign trade), expenses incurred by the trader in travelling between a place where the foreign trade is carried on and a place outside the United Kingdom where the other trade is carried on.

(4) In this section and section 93 "foreign trade" means a trade carried on wholly outside the United Kingdom.

Commentary—*Simon's Taxes* **B2.440.**
HMRC Manuals—Business Income Manual BIM47712 (living expenses abroad foreign trades).

93 Allocation of expenses

(1) Expenses within section 92(3)(*a*), (*b*) or (*c*) are allocated to the foreign trade.

(2) If—

(*a*) the expenses are within section 92(3)(*a*) or (*b*), and

(*b*) the trader carries on more than one foreign trade at the place in question outside the United Kingdom,

those expenses are allocated between the foreign trades on a just and reasonable basis.

(3) If—

(*a*) the expenses are within section 92(3)(*c*), and

(*b*) the trader's absence is for the purpose of carrying on more than one foreign trade,

those expenses are allocated between the foreign trades on a just and reasonable basis.

(4) Expenses within section 92(3)(*d*) are allocated—

(*a*) to the trade carried on at the trader's place of destination, if that trade is a foreign trade, and

(*b*) in any other case, to the foreign trade carried on at the trader's place of departure.

(5) If the trader carries on more than one foreign trade at—

(*a*) the place of destination (in a case falling within subsection (4)(*a*)), or

(*b*) the place of departure (in a case falling within subsection (4)(*b*)),

the expenses are allocated between the foreign trades on a just and reasonable basis.

Commentary—*Simon's Taxes* **B2.440.**
HMRC Manuals—Business Income Manual BIM47712 (living expenses abroad foreign trades).

94 Family expenses

(1) In section 92(3)(*c*) "family expenses" means expenses of a journey made by the trader's spouse [or civil partner][1] or child if the journey—

(*a*) is between a place in the United Kingdom and a place outside the United Kingdom where any of the trades is carried on, and

(*b*) is made in order to accompany the trader at the beginning of the period of absence or to visit the trader during that period or to return after a journey made for either purpose.

(2) But no more than two outward and two return journeys made by the same person in a tax year fall within subsection (1).

(3) In this section "child" includes a stepchild but does not include a person who is aged 18 or over at the start of the outward journey.

Commentary—*Simon's Taxes* **B2.440.**
Derivation—TA 1988 s 80(6), (9).
HMRC Manuals—Business Income Manual BIM47712 (living expenses abroad foreign trades).
Amendments—[1] Words in sub-s (1) inserted by Tax and Civil Partnership Regulations, SI 2005/3229, regs 183, 184, with effect from 5 December 2005 (reg 1(1)).

[SAYE option schemes, CSOP schemes

94A Costs of setting up SAYE option scheme or CSOP scheme

(1) This section applies if—

(*a*) a company incurs expenses in setting up a scheme within subsection (2) . . .[3], . . .[3]

(*b*) . . .[3]

(2) The schemes within this subsection are—

(*a*) [Schedule 3][3] SAYE option schemes within the meaning of the SAYE code (see section 516(4) of ITEPA 2003), and

(*b*) [Schedule 4][3] CSOP schemes within the meaning of the CSOP code (see section 521(4) of ITEPA 2003).

. . .[3]

(3) A deduction for the expenses is to be made in calculating the profits of a trade carried on by the company.

(4) If the [relevant date falls][3] more than 9 months after the end of the period of account in which the expenses are incurred, for the purposes of subsection (3) the deduction is to be made for the period of account in which the [relevant date falls][3].][1]

ITTOIA 2005

[(4A) In subsection (4) "the relevant date"—
- (*a*) in relation to a Schedule 3 SAYE option scheme, has the meaning given in paragraph 40A(6) of Schedule 3 to ITEPA 2003, and
- (*b*) in relation to a Schedule 4 CSOP scheme, has the meaning given in paragraph 28A(6) of Schedule 4 to ITEPA 2003.][3]

[(5) But subsection (4) does not apply in calculating the profits of a trade on the cash basis.][2]

Commentary—*Simon's Taxes* **D1.330.**

Derivation—TA 1988 s 84A.

HMRC Manuals—Business Income Manual BIM44020 (costs of setting up schemes).

Amendments—[1] This section inserted by TIOPA 2010 s 371, Sch 7 paras 27, 28. TIOPA 2010 has effect for corporation tax purposes for accounting periods ending on or after 1 April 2010, for income and capital gains tax purposes for the tax year 2010–11 and subsequent tax years, and for petroleum revenue tax purposes for chargeable periods beginning on or after 1 July 2010.

[2] Sub-s (5) inserted by FA 2013 s 17, Sch 4 paras 12, 17 with effect for the tax year 2013–14 and subsequent tax years, subject to the provisions of FA 2013 Sch 4 para 57 in relation to barristers and advocates.

[3] In sub-s (1)(*a*), words repealed, sub-s (1)(*b*) and preceding word repealed, in sub-s (2), words inserted and repealed, in sub-s (4), words substituted, and sub-s (4A) inserted, by FA 2014 s 51, Sch 8 para 140 with effect from 6 April 2014. The effect of the FA 2014 changes on SAYE option schemes established before 6 April 2014 is set out in FA 2014 Sch 8 paras 148–157.

If the scheme was an approved SAYE option scheme before that date, the amendments made by FA 2014 Sch 8 Part 2 do not affect the deductions which may be made in relation to the scheme under this section if they would otherwise do so (FA 2014 Sch 8 para 156).

If the scheme was an approved CSOP scheme before 6 April 2014, the amendments made by FA 2014 Sch 8 Part 3 and paras 140, 142 of that Schedule, do not affect the deductions which may be made in relation to the scheme under this section if they would otherwise do so (FA 2014 Sch 8 para 214).

[Limited liability partnerships: salaried members

94AA Deductions in relation to salaried members

(1) This section applies in relation to a limited liability partnership if section 863A(2) (limited liability partnerships: salaried members) applies in the case of a member of the partnership ("M").

(2) In calculating for a period of account under section 849 (calculation of firm's profits and losses) the profits of a trade carried on by the limited liability partnership, a deduction is allowed for expenses paid by the partnership in respect of M's employment under section 863A(2) if no deduction would otherwise be allowed for the payment.

(3) This section is subject to section 33 (capital expenditure), section 34 (expenses not wholly and exclusively for trade etc), section 45 (business entertainment and gifts) and section 53 (social security contributions).][1]

Commentary—*Simon's Taxes* **B7.310A.**

Amendments—[1] Section 94AA and preceding crosshead inserted by FA 2014 s 74, Sch 17 para 3(1), (2). This amendment is treated as having come into force on 6 April 2014.

[CHAPTER 5A

TRADE PROFITS: DEDUCTIONS ALLOWABLE AT A FIXED RATE]

Amendments—This Chapter (ss 94B–94I) inserted by FA 2013 s 18, Sch 5 paras 1, 2 with effect for the tax year 2013–14 and subsequent tax years.

[Introduction

94B Professions and vocations

The provisions of this Chapter apply to professions and vocations as they apply to trades.][1]

Commentary—*Simon's Taxes* **B1.202.**

Amendments—[1] This Chapter (ss 94B–94I) inserted by FA 2013 s 18, Sch 5 paras 1, 2 with effect for the tax year 2013–14 and subsequent tax years.

[94C Provisions not applicable to certain firms

The provisions of this Chapter do not apply in calculating the profits of a trade carried on by a firm for a period if one or more of the persons who have been partners in the firm at any time during the period was not an individual at that time.][1]

HMRC Manuals—Business Income Manual BIM75001 (Introduction to Chapter 5A simplified expenses).

Amendments—[1] This Chapter (ss 94B–94I) inserted by FA 2013 s 18, Sch 5 paras 1, 2 with effect for the tax year 2013–14 and subsequent tax years.

[Expenditure on vehicles

94D Expenditure on vehicles

(1) This section applies if, in calculating the profits of a trade of a person for a period—
- (*a*) a deduction would otherwise be allowable for the period in respect of qualifying expenditure incurred in relation to a relevant vehicle (see subsection (2)), or
- (*b*) a deduction would be so allowable in respect of such expenditure but for the fact it is capital expenditure.

(2) In this section "relevant vehicle" means a car, motor cycle or goods vehicle that—

    (*a*) is used for the purposes of the trade, and

    (*b*) is not an excluded vehicle (see section 94E).

(3) The person may make a deduction under this section for the period in respect of the qualifying expenditure.

(4) If a deduction for a period is made under this section—

    (*a*) no other deduction is allowed (for that or any other period) in respect of the qualifying expenditure, and

    (*b*) this section applies in relation to the relevant vehicle for every subsequent period for which the vehicle is used for the purposes of the trade.

(5) The amount of the deduction is the appropriate mileage amount in relation to the relevant vehicle for the period (see section 94F).

(6) In this section "qualifying expenditure", in relation to a vehicle, means any expenditure incurred in respect of the acquisition, ownership, hire, leasing or use of the vehicle, other than incidental expenses incurred in connection with a particular journey.

(7) For provision preventing capital allowances from being claimed in respect of qualifying expenditure incurred in relation to a relevant vehicle, see section 38ZA of CAA 2001.][1]

Commentary—*Simon's Taxes* **B2.439A.**

HMRC Manuals—Business Income Manual BIM75005 (forms of relief).

Amendments—[1]   This Chapter (ss 94B–94I) inserted by FA 2013 s 18, Sch 5 paras 1, 2 with effect for the tax year 2013–14 and subsequent tax years.

[94E Excluded vehicles

(1) A car, motor cycle or goods vehicle that is used for the purposes of a trade is an "excluded vehicle" for the purposes of section 94D if condition A or B is met in relation to the vehicle.

(2) Condition A is that the person who is or has been carrying on the trade has at any time claimed any capital allowances under Part 2 of CAA 2001 in respect of any expenditure incurred on the provision of the vehicle.

(3) Condition B is that—

    (*a*) the vehicle is a goods vehicle or a motor cycle, and

    (*b*) any of the expenditure incurred on acquiring the vehicle has been deducted in calculating the profits of [any relevant trade or business][2] for a period on the cash basis (see [sections 25A and 271D][2]).

[(4) In this section "any relevant trade or business" means any trade or property business carried on by the person carrying on the trade mentioned in subsection (1).][2][1]

Commentary—*Simon's Taxes* **B2.439A.**

HMRC Manuals—Business Income Manual BIM75005 (forms of relief).

Modifications—FA 2018 s 36(9) (application of this section in respect of capital allowances claimed by a landlord in the tax years 2013–14 to 2016–17).

Amendments—[1]   This Chapter (ss 94B–94I) inserted by FA 2013 s 18, Sch 5 paras 1, 2 with effect for the tax year 2013–14 and subsequent tax years.

[2]   In sub-s (3)(*b*), words substituted, and sub-s (4) inserted, by FA 2018 s 36(1)–(3) with effect for the tax year 2018–19 and subsequent tax years.

[94F The appropriate mileage amount

(1) In calculating the profits of a trade for a period, the appropriate mileage amount in relation to a relevant vehicle for the period is—

M x R

where—

    M is the number of miles of business journeys made by a person (other than as a passenger) using that vehicle in the period, and

    R is the rate applicable to that kind of vehicle.

(2) The rates applicable are as follows—

TABLE

Kind of vehicle	Rate per mile
Car or goods vehicle	45p for the first 10,000 miles
	25p after that
Motor cycle	24p

(3) In a case where the total number of miles of relevant business journeys made in the period is greater than 10,000, the rate of 45p per mile is available only in relation to 10,000 of those miles.

(4) "Relevant business journey" means any business journey made in the period by a car or goods vehicle—

    (*a*) that is used for the purposes of the trade, and

    (*b*) in relation to which section 94D applies for the period.

(5) In this section—

"business journey", in relation to a vehicle used for the purposes of a trade, means any journey, or any identifiable part or proportion of a journey, that is made wholly and exclusively for the purposes of the trade, and

"relevant vehicle" has the same meaning as in section 94D.

(6) The Treasury may by regulations amend subsection (2) so as to alter the rates or rate bands.

Regulations under this subsection may also make consequential amendments to subsection (3).][1]

Commentary—*Simon's Taxes* **B2.439A.**
HMRC Manuals—Business Income Manual BIM75005 (forms of relief).
Amendments—[1]   This Chapter (ss 94B–94I) inserted by FA 2013 s 18, Sch 5 paras 1, 2 with effect for the tax year 2013–14 and subsequent tax years.

[94G Definitions of types of vehicle

(1) This section applies for the purposes of sections 94D to 94F (and this section).

(2) "Car" means a mechanically propelled road vehicle which is not—
  (a) a goods vehicle,
  (b) a motor cycle,
  (c) an invalid carriage, or
  (d) a vehicle of a type not commonly used as a private vehicle and unsuitable to be so used.

(3) "Goods vehicle" means a mechanically propelled road vehicle which—
  (a) is of a construction primarily suited for the conveyance of goods or burden of any description, and
  (b) is not a motor cycle.

(4) "Motor cycle" has the meaning given by section 185(1) of the Road Traffic Act 1988.

(5) For the purposes of this section "invalid carriage" has the meaning given by section 185(1) of the Road Traffic Act 1988.][1]

Commentary—*Simon's Taxes* **B2.439A.**
Amendments—[1]   This Chapter (ss 94B–94I) inserted by FA 2013 s 18, Sch 5 paras 1, 2 with effect for the tax year 2013–14 and subsequent tax years.

[Use of home for business purposes

94H Use of home for business purposes

(1) This section applies if, in calculating the profits of a trade of a person for a period, a deduction ("the standard deduction") would otherwise be allowable for the period [in respect of—
  (a) the use of the person's home for the purposes of the trade, or
  (b) where the person is a firm, the use of a partner's home for those purposes.][2]

(2) The person may, instead of making the standard deduction, make a deduction for the period under this section.

(3) The amount of the deduction allowable for the period is the sum of the applicable amounts for each month, or part of a month, falling within the period.

(4) The applicable amount for a month, or part of a month, is given by the following Table—

TABLE

Number of hours worked	Applicable amount
25 or more	£10.00
51 or more	£18.00
101 or more	£26.00

where the "number of hours worked" in a month (or part of a month) is the number of hours spent wholly and exclusively on [qualifying work][2].

[(4A) "Qualifying work" means—
  (a) work done by the person, or any employee of the person, in the person's home wholly and exclusively for the purposes of the trade, or
  (b) where the person is a firm, work done by a partner, or any employee of the firm, in the partner's home wholly and exclusively for those purposes.

(4B) Where more than one person does qualifying work in the same home at the same time, any hour spent wholly and exclusively on that work is to be taken into account only once for the purposes of subsection (4).][2]

(5) If the person[, or, where the person is a firm, a partner of the firm,][2] has more than one home, this section has effect as if those homes were a single home.

[(5A) Where a firm makes a deduction for a period under this section in respect of the use of a partner's home for the purposes of a trade, the only deduction which the firm may make for the period in respect of the use of any other partner's home for those purposes is a deduction under this section.][2]

(6) The Treasury may by regulations amend subsection (4) so as to alter the rates or rate bands.][1]

Commentary—*Simon's Taxes* **B2.439A.**

HMRC Manuals—Business Income Manual BIM75010 (use of home for business purposes).
Amendments—[1] This Chapter (ss 94B–94I) inserted by FA 2013 s 18, Sch 5 paras 1, 2 with effect for the tax year 2013–14 and subsequent tax years.
[2] Sub-ss (4A), (4B), (5A) inserted, words in sub-ss (1), (4) substituted, and words in sub-s (5) inserted, by FA 2016 s 24(1)–(7) with effect for the tax year 2016-17 and subsequent tax years.

[Premises used both as home and business premises

94I Premises used both as a home and as business premises

(1) This section applies if—

(a) a person carries on a trade at any premises,

(b) the premises are used mainly for the purposes of carrying on the trade, but are also [used as a home by—

(i) the person carrying on the trade, or

(ii) where that person is a firm, a partner of the firm,][2]

(c) the person incurs expenses in relation to the premises,

(d) the expenses are incurred mainly (but not wholly and exclusively) for the purposes of the trade, and

(e) in calculating the profits of the trade for a period, a deduction ("the standard deduction") would otherwise be allowable for the period in respect of a part or proportion of the expenses in accordance with section 34(2).

(2) The person may, instead of making the standard deduction, make a deduction for the period under this section.

(3) The amount of the deduction allowable for the period is the amount of the expenses less the non-business use amount.

(4) The non-business use amount is the sum of the applicable amounts for each month, or part of a month, falling within the period.

(5) The applicable amount for a month, or part of a month, is given by the following Table—

TABLE

Number of relevant occupants	Applicable amount
1	£350
2	£500
3 or more	£650

(6) For the purposes of subsection (5) "relevant occupant", in relation to a month (or part of a month), means an individual who, at any time during that month (or that part of a month)—

[(6A) Where a person makes a deduction for a period under this section in respect of expenses incurred in relation to premises falling within subsection (1)(b), the only deduction which the person may make for the period in respect of expenses incurred in relation to any other premises falling within subsection (1)(b) is a deduction under this section.][2]

(a) occupies the premises as a home, or

(b) stays at the premises otherwise than in the course of the trade.

(7) The Treasury may by regulations amend subsection (5) so as to alter the rates or rate bands.][1]

Commentary—*Simon's Taxes* B2.439A.
HMRC Manuals—Business Income Manual BIM75015 (private use of business premises).
Amendments—[1] This Chapter (ss 94B–94I) inserted by FA 2013 s 18, Sch 5 paras 1, 2 with effect for the tax year 2013–14 and subsequent tax years.
[2] Words in sub-s (1)(b) substituted, and sub-s (6A) inserted, by FA 2016 s 24(1), (8)–(10) with effect for the tax year 2016-17 and subsequent tax years.

CHAPTER 6

TRADE PROFITS: RECEIPTS
Introduction

95 Professions and vocations

Apart from section 105 (industrial development grants), the provisions of this Chapter apply to professions and vocations as they apply to trades.

Commentary—*Simon's Taxes* B2.201, B1.202.

[Cash basis accounting

95A Application of Chapter to the cash basis

[(1)] [2]For rules about receipts that apply only for the purpose of calculating profits on the cash basis, see the following—

. . .[2]

section 97A (cash basis: value of trading stock on cessation of trade),

section 97B (cash basis: value of work in progress on cessation of profession or vocation).][1]

[(2) Section 96A makes provision about capital receipts in certain cases where the profits of a trade are calculated on the cash basis or have previously been calculated on the cash basis (and see also section 96B).][2]

Commentary—*Simon's Taxes* **B2.201.**
Amendments—[1] This section inserted by FA 2013 s 17, Sch 4 paras 18, 19 with effect for the tax year 2013–14 and subsequent
    tax years, subject to the provisions of FA 2013 Sch 4 para 57 in relation to barristers and advocates.
[2] Sub-s (1) numbered as such, in sub-s (1), entry for section 96A repealed, and sub-s (2) inserted, by F(No 2)A 2017 s 16, Sch
    2 paras 1, 3 with effect for the tax year 2017–18 and subsequent tax years, subject to transitional provisions in F(No 2)A 2017
    Sch 2 para 64.

Capital receipts

96 Capital receipts

(1) Items of a capital nature must not be brought into account as receipts in calculating the profits of a trade.
(2) But this does not apply to items which, as a result of any provision of this Part, are brought into account as receipts in calculating the profits of the trade.

Commentary—*Simon's Taxes* **B2.202.**
HMRC Manuals—Business Income Manual BIM35002 (exclusion of capital items: introduction).
BIM40060 (capital receipts: particular types of transactions).

[96A [Capital receipts under, or after leaving, cash basis]

[(1) This section applies in relation to a trade carried on by a person in two cases—
    (*a*) Case 1 (see subsections (2) to (3A)), and
    (*b*) Case 2 (see subsections (3B) to (3E)).
(2) Case 1 is a case in which conditions A and B are met.
(3) Condition A is that the person receives disposal proceeds or a capital refund in relation to an asset at a time when an election under section 25A (cash basis for trades) has effect in relation to the trade.
For the meaning of "disposal proceeds" and "capital refund" see subsections (3F) and (3G).
(3A) Condition B is that—
    (*a*) an amount of capital expenditure (see subsection (3H)) relating to the asset has been brought into account in calculating the profits of the trade on the cash basis, or
    (*b*) an amount of capital expenditure relating to the asset which—
        (i) has been incurred (or treated as incurred) by the person before the tax year for which the person last entered the cash basis, and
        (ii) is cash basis deductible in relation to that tax year (see section 96B(4)),

    has been brought into account in calculating the profits of the trade for a tax year for which no election under section 25A had effect in relation to the trade.

    The reference in this paragraph to expenditure brought into account includes a reference to expenditure brought into account under CAA 2001 (see section 96B(5)) [except to the extent that it is expenditure in respect of which a capital allowance is made under Part 2A of that Act][3].

(3B) Case 2 is a case in which—
    (*a*) condition C is met, and
    (*b*) condition D or E is met.
(3C) Condition C is that disposal proceeds or a capital refund arise to the person in relation to an asset at a time—
    (*a*) when no election under section 25A has effect in relation to the trade, and
    (*b*) which is after a time when such an election had had effect in relation to the trade.
(3D) Condition D is that an amount of capital expenditure relating to the asset—
    (*a*) has been paid at a time when an election under section 25A had effect in relation to the trade,
    (*b*) has been brought into account in calculating the profits of the trade on the cash basis, and
    (*c*) on the assumption that an election under section 25A had not had effect at the time the expenditure was paid, would not have been qualifying expenditure.
(3E) Condition E is that an amount of capital expenditure relating to the asset has been brought into account in calculating the profits of the trade for a tax year—
    (*a*) for which no election under section 25A had effect in relation to the trade, and
    (*b*) which is before the tax year for which the person last entered the cash basis.
The reference in this subsection to expenditure brought into account does not include a reference to expenditure brought into account under CAA 2001 (see section 96B(5)).
(3F) "Disposal proceeds" means—
    (*a*) any proceeds arising from the disposal of an asset or any part of it,
    (*b*) any proceeds arising from the grant of any right in respect of, or any interest in, the asset, or
    (*c*) any amount of damages, proceeds of insurance or other compensation received in respect of the asset.

See also subsections (4) and (5) for circumstances in which a person is to be regarded as disposing of an asset.

(3G) "Capital refund" means an amount that is (in substance) a refund of capital expenditure relating to an asset.

(3H) "Capital expenditure" means expenditure of a capital nature incurred, or treated as incurred, on or in connection with—

    (*a*) the provision, alteration or disposal of an asset, or

    (*b*) the potential provision, alteration or disposal of an asset.

(3I) The disposal proceeds or capital refund mentioned in condition A or (as the case may be) condition C are to be brought into account as a receipt in calculating the profits of the trade.

(3J) In a case where only part of the total capital expenditure incurred, or treated as incurred, by the person in relation to the asset has been brought into account in calculating the profits of the trade (whether or not on the cash basis), the amount brought into account under subsection (3I) is proportionately reduced.

The reference in this subsection to expenditure brought into account includes a reference to expenditure brought into account under CAA 2001 (see section 96B(5)).

(3K) Subsection (3I) does not apply if the whole of the amount which would otherwise be brought into account under that subsection—

    (*a*) has already been brought into account as a receipt in calculating the profits of the trade under this section,

    (*b*) is brought into account as a receipt in calculating the profits of the trade under any other provision of this Part (except section 240D(3) (assets not fully paid for)), or

    (*c*) is brought into account under any Part of CAA 2001 as a disposal value.

(3L) If part of the amount which would otherwise be brought into account under subsection (3I) has already been or is brought into account as mentioned in subsection (3K), subsection (3I) applies in relation to the remainder of that amount.]²

(4) If—

    (*a*) at any time the person ceases to use the asset or any part of it for the purposes of the trade, but

    (*b*) the person does not dispose of the asset (or that part) at that time,

the person is to be regarded for the purposes of this section as disposing of the asset (or that part) at that time for an amount equal to the market value amount.

(5) If at any time there is a material increase in the person's non-business use of the asset or any part of it, the person is to be regarded for the purposes of this section as disposing of the asset (or that part) at that time for an amount equal to the relevant proportion of the market value amount.

(6) For the purposes of subsection (5)—

    (*a*) there is an increase in a person's non-business use of an asset (or part of an asset) if—

        (i) the proportion of the person's use of the asset (or that part) that is for the purposes of the trade decreases, and

        (ii) the proportion of the person's use of the asset (or that part) that is for other purposes (the "non-business use") increases;

    (*b*) "the relevant proportion" is the difference between—

        (i) the proportion of the person's use of the asset (or part of the asset) that is non-business use, and

        (ii) the proportion of the person's use of the asset (or that part) that was non-business use before the increase mentioned in subsection (5).

(7) . . . ²

Commentary—*Simon's Taxes* **B2.202.**

HMRC Manuals—Business Income Manual BIM70020 (cash basis: treatment of capital receipts).

Amendments—¹   This section inserted by FA 2013 s 17, Sch 4 paras 18, 20 with effect for the tax year 2013–14 and subsequent tax years, subject to the provisions of FA 2013 Sch 4 para 57 in relation to barristers and advocates.

²   Heading substituted for previous heading "Cash basis: capital receipts", sub-ss (1)–(3L) substituted for sub-ss (1)–(3), and sub-s (7) repealed, by F(No 2)A 2017 s 16, Sch 2 paras 1, 4 with effect for the tax year 2017–18 and subsequent tax years, subject to transitional provisions in F(No 2)A 2017 Sch 2 para 64.

³   In sub-s (3A), words inserted by the Capital Allowances (Structures and Buildings Allowances) Regulations, SI 2019/1087 reg 5(1), (2) with effect from 5 July 2019. Note that the structures and buildings allowance in CAA 2001 Part 2A applies from 29 October 2018 (see CAA 2001 s 270AA).

[96B Section 96A: supplementary provision

(1) This section has effect for the purposes of section 96A.

(2) Any question as to whether or to what extent expenditure is brought into account in calculating the profits of a trade is to be determined on such basis as is just and reasonable in all the circumstances.

(3) A person carrying on a trade "enters the cash basis" for a tax year if—

    (*a*) an election under section 25A has effect in relation to the trade for the tax year, and

    (*b*) no such election had effect in relation to the trade for the previous tax year.

(4) Expenditure is "cash basis deductible" in relation to a tax year if, on the assumption that the expenditure was paid in that tax year, a deduction would be allowed in respect of the expenditure in calculating the profits of the trade on the cash basis for that tax year.

(5) Expenditure is "brought into account under CAA 2001" in calculating the profits of a trade if and to the extent that—

    (a) a capital allowance made under Part 2, [2A,]² 5, 6, 7 or 8 of that Act in respect of the expenditure is treated as an expense in calculating those profits (see, for example, section 247 of that Act), or

    (b) qualifying expenditure (within the meaning of Part 2, 7 or 8 of CAA 2001) is allocated to a pool for the trade and is set-off against different disposal receipts.

(6) An amount of qualifying expenditure is "set-off against different disposal receipts" if—

    (a) the amount would have been unrelieved qualifying expenditure carried forward in the pool for the trade, but

    (b) the amount is not so carried forward because (and only because) one or more disposal values in respect of one or more assets, other than the asset in respect of which the qualifying expenditure was incurred (or treated as incurred), have at any time been brought into account in that pool.

(7) For the purposes of subsection (6), an amount of qualifying expenditure incurred (or treated as incurred) by a person is not to be regarded as not carried forward because the person enters the cash basis.

(8) In this section and in section 96A—

    "disposal value" means—

        (a) in section 96A(3K)(c)—

            (i) a disposal value for the purposes of Part 2, 4A, 5, 6, 7 8 or 10 of CAA 2001 (for example, in relation to Part 2 of that Act, see (in particular) section 61 of that Act), or

            (ii) proceeds from a balancing event for the purposes of Part 3 or 3A of that Act (see sections 316 and 360O of that Act), and

        (b) in subsection (6), a disposal value for the purposes of—

            (i) Part 2 of that Act (see, in particular, section 61 of that Act),

            (ii) Part 7 of that Act (see section 462 of that Act), or

            (iii) Part 8 of that Act (see sections 476 and 477 of that Act);

    "market value amount" means the amount that would be regarded as normal and reasonable—

        (a) in the market conditions then prevailing, and

        (b) between persons dealing with each other at arm's length in the open market;

    "pool" means—

        (a) the main pool or a class pool to which qualifying expenditure is allocated under Part 2 of CAA 2001 (see section 54 of that Act),

        (b) a pool to which qualifying expenditure is allocated under Part 7 of that Act (see section 456 of that Act), or

        (c) a pool to which qualifying expenditure is allocated under Part 8 of that Act (see section 470 of that Act);

    "provision" includes creation, construction or acquisition;

    "qualifying expenditure" means—

        (a) qualifying expenditure within the meaning of Part 2 of CAA 2001 (see section 11(4) of that Act for the general rule),

        (b) qualifying expenditure within the meaning of Part 5 of that Act (see section 395 of that Act),

        (c) qualifying expenditure within the meaning of Part 6 of that Act (see section 439 of that Act),

        (d) qualifying expenditure within the meaning of Part 7 of that Act (see section 454 of that Act), or

        (e) qualifying trade expenditure within the meaning of Part 8 of that Act (see section 468 of that Act);

    "unrelieved qualifying expenditure" means unrelieved qualifying expenditure for the purposes of—

        (a) Part 2 of CAA 2001 (see section 59(1) and (2) of that Act),

        (b) Part 7 of that Act (see section 461 of that Act), or

        (c) Part 8 of that Act (see section 475 of that Act).]¹

Commentary—*Simon's Taxes* B2.202.

Amendments—¹ Section 96B inserted by F(No 2)A 2017 s 16, Sch 2 paras 1, 5 with effect for the tax year 2017–18 and subsequent tax years, subject to transitional provisions in F(No 2)A 2017 Sch 2 para 64.

  ² In sub-s (5)(*a*), words inserted by the Capital Allowances (Structures and Buildings Allowances) Regulations, SI 2019/1087 reg 5(1), (3) with effect from 5 July 2019. Note that the structures and buildings allowance in CAA 2001 Part 2A applies from 29 October 2018 (see CAA 2001 s 270AA).

Debts released

97 Debts incurred and later released

(1) This section applies if—

 (*a*) in calculating the profits of a trade, a deduction is allowed for the expense giving rise to a debt owed by the person carrying on the trade,

 (*b*) all or part of the debt is released, and

 (*c*) the release is not part of a statutory insolvency arrangement.

(2) The amount released—

 (*a*) is brought into account as a receipt in calculating the profits of the trade, and

 (*b*) is treated as arising on the date of the release.

Commentary—*Simon's Taxes* B2.206.

Derivation—TA 1988 s 94(1), (2).

HMRC Manuals—Business Income Manual BIM40265 (tax treatment when debt formally released).

[Cash basis: value of stock and work in progress on cessation

97A Cash basis: value of trading stock on cessation of trade

(1) This section applies if—

 (*a*) a person permanently ceases to carry on a trade in a tax year, and

 (*b*) an election under section 25A (cash basis for small businesses) has effect in relation to the trade for the tax year.

(2) The value of any trading stock belonging to the trade at the time of the cessation is brought into account as a receipt in calculating the profits of the trade for the tax year.

(3) The value is to be determined on a basis that is just and reasonable in all the circumstances.

(4) If there is a change in the persons carrying on a trade, subsection (2) does not apply in relation to the trade so long as a person carrying on the trade immediately before the change continues to carry it on after the change.

(5) In this section "trading stock" has the same meaning as in Chapter 12 (see section 174).

(6) This section does not apply to professions or vocations.]¹

Commentary—*Simon's Taxes* B2.617 .

HMRC Manuals—Business Income Manual BIM70025 (value of trading stock and work in progress on cessation of trade, profession or vocation).

Amendments—¹ This section inserted by FA 2013 s 17, Sch 4 paras 18, 21 with effect for the tax year 2013–14 and subsequent tax years, subject to the provisions of FA 2013 Sch 4 para 57 in relation to barristers and advocates.

[97B Cash basis: value of work in progress on cessation of profession or vocation

(1) This section applies if—

 (*a*) a person permanently ceases to carry on a profession or vocation in a tax year, and

 (*b*) an election under section 25A (cash basis for small businesses) has effect in relation to the profession or vocation for the tax year.

(2) The value of any work in progress at the time of the cessation is brought into account as a receipt in calculating the profits of the profession or vocation for the tax year.

(3) The value is to be determined on a basis that is just and reasonable in all the circumstances.

(4) If there is a change in the persons carrying on a profession, subsection (2) does not apply in relation to the profession so long as a person carrying on the profession immediately before the change continues to carry it on after the change.

(5) In this section "work in progress" has the same meaning as in Chapter 12 (see section 183).]¹

Commentary—*Simon's Taxes* B2.618.

HMRC Manuals—Business Income Manual BIM70025 (value of trading stock and work in progress on cessation of trade, profession or vocation).

Amendments—¹ This section inserted by FA 2013 s 17, Sch 4 paras 18, 21 with effect for the tax year 2013–14 and subsequent tax years, subject to the provisions of FA 2013 Sch 4 para 57 in relation to barristers and advocates.

Amounts received following earlier cessation

98 Acquisition of trade: receipts from transferor's trade

(1) This section applies if—

 (*a*) a person ("the transferor") permanently ceased to carry on a trade at any time,

 (*b*) at that time the transferor transferred to another person ("the transferee") the right to receive sums arising from the carrying on of the trade, and

 (*c*) the transferee subsequently carries on the transferor's trade.

(2) Sums—

 (*a*) which the transferee receives as a result of the transfer, and

 (*b*) which are not brought into account in calculating the profits of the transferor's trade for income or corporation tax purposes for any period before the cessation, are brought into account in calculating the profits of the transferee's trade in the period of account in which they are received.

(3) Any sums mentioned in subsection (1)(*b*) which are received after the transferor has permanently ceased to carry on the trade are not post-cessation receipts (see Chapter 18).

Commentary—*Simon's Taxes* **B2.207.**
Derivation—TA 1988 s 106(1), (2).
HMRC Manuals—Business Income Manual BIM90070 (transfer of rights if the transferee carries on the trade).

Reverse premiums

99 Reverse premiums

(1) For the purposes of sections 101 and 102 a payment or other benefit is a reverse premium—
    (*a*) if conditions A to C are met, and
    (*b*) it is not excluded by section 100.

(2) Condition A is that a person ("the recipient") receives the payment or other benefit by way of inducement in connection with a transaction being entered into by—
    (*a*) the recipient, or
    (*b*) a person connected with the recipient.

(3) Condition B is that the transaction (the "property transaction") is one under which—
    (*a*) the recipient, or
    (*b*) the person connected with the recipient,
becomes entitled to an estate, interest or right in or over land.

(4) Condition C is that the payment or other benefit is paid or provided by—
    (*a*) the person ("the grantor") by whom the estate, interest or right is granted or was granted at an earlier time,
    (*b*) a person connected with the grantor, or
    (*c*) a nominee of, or a person acting on the directions of, the grantor or a person connected with the grantor.

Commentary—*Simon's Taxes* **B2.215E, C2.1233, E5.545A.**
Derivation—FA 1999 Sch 6 para 1(1), (2).
HMRC Manuals—Business Income Manual BIM41051 (meaning and terms used in connection with reverse premiums).

100 Excluded cases

(1) A payment or other benefit is not a reverse premium so far as it is brought into account under section 532 of CAA 2001 (the general rule excluding contributions) to reduce the recipient's expenditure qualifying for capital allowances.

(2) A payment or other benefit received in connection with a property transaction is not a reverse premium if—
    (*a*) the person entering into the transaction is an individual, and
    (*b*) the transaction relates to premises occupied or to be occupied by the individual as the individual's only or main residence.

(3) A payment or other benefit is not a reverse premium so far as it is consideration for the transfer of an estate or interest in land which constitutes the sale in a sale and lease-back arrangement.

(4) A "sale and lease-back arrangement" means any such arrangement as is described in [section 681AA(1) or (2), 681AB(1) or (2) or 681BA of ITA 2007 or]² [section 835(1) or (2) or 836(1) or (2) of CTA 2010]¹.

Commentary—*Simon's Taxes* **B2.215E, C2.1233, E5.545A.**
HMRC Manuals—Business Income Manual BIM41140 (specific exclusions of reverse premiums).
Amendments—¹ In sub-s (4) words substituted by CTA 2010 s 1177, Sch 1 paras 444, 445. CTA 2010 has effect for corporation tax purposes for accounting periods ending on or after 1 April 2010, and for income and capital gains tax purposes for the tax year 2010–11 and subsequent tax years.
² In sub-s (4) words inserted by TIOPA 2010 s 501, Sch 8 paras 253, 255. TIOPA 2010 has effect for corporation tax purposes for accounting periods ending on or after 1 April 2010, for income and capital gains tax purposes for the tax year 2010–11 and subsequent tax years, and for petroleum revenue tax purposes for chargeable periods beginning on or after 1 July 2010.

101 Tax treatment of reverse premiums

(1) A reverse premium is treated for income tax purposes as a receipt of a revenue nature.

(2) If the recipient enters into the property transaction for the purposes of a trade carried on (or to be carried on) by the recipient, the reverse premium is brought into account in calculating the profits of the trade.

(3) If subsection (2) does not apply, the reverse premium is charged to income tax in accordance with section 311 (reverse premium taxed as property business receipt).

Commentary—*Simon's Taxes* **B2.215E, B6.205, C2.1233.**
HMRC Manuals—Business Income Manual BIM41055 (reverse premiums: the legislation).

102 Arrangements not at arm's length

(1) This section applies if—
    (*a*) two or more of the parties to the property arrangements are connected persons, and

(*b*) the terms of those arrangements are not such as would reasonably have been expected if those persons had been dealing at arm's length.

(2) The terms of the property arrangements meet the condition in subsection (1)(*b*) if they differ to a significant extent from the terms which, at the time the arrangements were entered into, would be regarded as normal and reasonable—

    (*a*) in the market conditions then prevailing, and

    (*b*) between persons dealing with each other at arm's length in the open market.

(3) The whole amount or value of the reverse premium brought into account under section 101 is brought into account in the first relevant period of account.

(4) "The first relevant period of account" means the period of account in which the property transaction is entered into.

(5) But if the recipient enters into the property transaction for the purposes of a trade—

    (*a*) which is not then carried on by the recipient, but

    (*b*) which the recipient subsequently starts to carry on,

"the first relevant period of account" means the first period of account in which the recipient carries on the trade.

Commentary—*Simon's Taxes* **B2.208.**

HMRC Manuals—Business Income Manual BIM41130 (reverse premium: timing of the receipt). BIM41135 (reverse premium: timing of the receipt).

103 Connected persons and property arrangements

For the purposes of this section and sections 99 to 102—

    (*a*) persons are treated as connected with each other if they are connected (for which see section 878(5)) at any time during the period when the property arrangements are entered into, and

    (*b*) "the property arrangements" means the property transaction and any arrangements entered into in connection with it (whether before it, at the same time as it or after it).

Commentary—*Simon's Taxes* **B2.208.**

Derivation—FA 1999 Sch 6 para 8(1), (2).

HMRC Manuals—Business Income Manual BIM41130 (connected persons and property arrangements).

Assets of mutual concerns

104 Distribution of assets of mutual concerns

(1) This section applies if—

    (*a*) a deduction has been allowed in calculating the profits of a trade for a payment to a mutual concern for the purposes of its mutual business,

    (*b*) the concern is being or has been wound up or dissolved,

    (*c*) a person ("the recipient") who is carrying on the trade, or was doing so at the time of the payment, receives money or money's worth representing the concern's assets, and

    (*d*) the assets in question represent profits of the mutual business conducted by the concern.

(2) If the recipient is carrying on the trade at the time the money or money's worth is received, the amount or value of the money or money's worth is brought into account as a receipt in calculating the profits of the trade.

(3) If the recipient—

    (*a*) is not carrying on the trade at the time the money or money's worth is received, but

    (*b*) was doing so at the time of the payment to the mutual concern,

the amount or value of the money or money's worth is treated as a post-cessation receipt (see Chapter 18).

(4) For the purposes of this section money or money's worth represents assets of a mutual concern if it—

    (*a*) forms part of the assets of the concern,

    (*b*) forms part of the consideration for the transfer of the assets of the concern as part of a scheme of amalgamation or reconstruction which involves its winding up, or

    (*c*) consists of the consideration for a transfer or surrender of a right to receive anything falling within paragraph (*a*) or (*b*) and does not give rise to a charge to income tax on the person receiving it otherwise than as a result of this section.

(5) If a transfer or surrender of a right to receive anything which—

    (*a*) forms part of the assets of a mutual concern, or

    (*b*) forms part of the consideration for the transfer of the assets of a mutual concern,

is not at arm's length, the person making the transfer or surrender is treated as receiving consideration equal to the value of the right.

(6) In this section references to a mutual concern are to a body corporate which has at any time carried on a trade which consists of or includes the conduct of mutual business (whether or not confined to the members of the body corporate).

(7) For the purposes of this section a trade does not consist of or include the conduct of mutual business if all the profits of the trade are chargeable to income or corporation tax.

Commentary—*Simon's Taxes* **B2.209, B1.436, B1.437, B1.439.**
HMRC Manuals—Business Income Manual BIM24555 (distributions: basic approach).
BIM24615 ICTA88/S491 (what is taxed?).

Industrial development grants

105 Industrial development grants

(1) This section applies if a person carrying on a trade receives a payment by way of a grant under—
  (a) section 7 or 8 of the Industrial Development Act 1982 (c 52), or
  (b) Article 7, 9 or 30 of the Industrial Development (Northern Ireland) Order 1982 (SI 1982/1083 (NI 15)).
(2) The payment is brought into account as a receipt in calculating the profits of the trade unless—
  (a) the grant is designated as made towards the cost of specified capital expenditure [(but see subsection (2A))][1],
  (b) the grant is designated as compensation for the loss of capital assets, or
  (c) the grant is for all or part of a corporation tax liability (including one that has already been met).
[(2A) Subsection (2)(a) is to be disregarded in calculating the profits of a trade on the cash basis.][1]
(3) This section does not apply to professions or vocations.

Commentary—*Simon's Taxes* **B2.210.**
Derivation—TA 1988 s 93.
HMRC Manuals—Business Income Manual BIM40465 (grants and subsidies: industrial development grants).
Amendments—[1] Words in sub-s (2)(a), and whole of sub-s (2A), inserted, by FA 2013 s 17, Sch 4 paras 18, 22 with effect for the tax year 2013–14 and subsequent tax years, subject to the provisions of FA 2013 Sch 4 para 57 in relation to barristers and advocates.

Proceeds of insurance etc

106 Sums recovered under insurance policies etc

(1) This section applies if—
  (a) a deduction is allowed for a loss or expense in calculating the profits of a trade,
  (b) a person carrying on the trade recovers a sum under an insurance policy or a contract of indemnity in respect of the loss or expense, and
  (c) the sum is not of a revenue nature.
(2) The sum is brought into account as a receipt in calculating the profits of the trade (but only up to the amount of the deduction).

Commentary—*Simon's Taxes* **B2.211, B2.445.**
HMRC Manuals—Business Income Manual BIM40755 (insurance recoveries: capital recoveries).

[CHAPTER 6A

TRADE PROFITS: AMOUNTS NOT REFLECTING COMMERCIAL TRANSACTIONS]

Amendments—This Chapter (ss 106A–106E) inserted by FA 2013 s 17, Sch 4 para 23 with effect for the tax year 2013–14 and subsequent tax years, subject to the provisions of FA 2013 Sch 4 para 57 in relation to barristers and advocates.

[106A Professions and vocations

The provisions of this Chapter apply to professions and vocations as they apply to trades.][1]

Commentary—*Simon's Taxes* **B1.202.**
Amendments—[1] This Chapter (ss 106A–106E) inserted by FA 2013 s 17, Sch 4 para 23 with effect for the tax year 2013–14 and subsequent tax years, subject to the provisions of FA 2013 Sch 4 para 57 in relation to barristers and advocates.

[106B Application of Chapter

This Chapter applies in calculating the profits of a person's trade for a period on the cash basis.][1]

Commentary—*Simon's Taxes* **B2.101B.**
Amendments—[1] This Chapter (ss 106A–106E) inserted by FA 2013 s 17, Sch 4 para 23 with effect for the tax year 2013–14 and subsequent tax years, subject to the provisions of FA 2013 Sch 4 para 57 in relation to barristers and advocates.

[106C Amounts not reflecting commercial transactions

(1) This section applies if—
  (a) the person does anything in relation to the trade ("the relevant act"),
  (b) there is a difference between—
    (i) the amount (if any) that, as a result of the relevant act, would (apart from this section) be brought into account in calculating the profits of the trade for the period, and
    (ii) the amount (if any) that would have been so brought into account had the relevant act consisted of a transaction between the person and another person dealing with each other at arm's length in the open market ("the arm's length amount"), and
  (c) the profits of the trade for the period are less than they would have been if the arm's length amount had been so brought into account.
(2) The amount to be brought into account in calculating the profits of the trade for the period is an amount that is just and reasonable in all the circumstances.][1]

Commentary—*Simon's Taxes* **B2.215A.**

HMRC Manuals—Business Income Manual BIM70015 (cash basis: receipts: overview).
Amendments—[1]   This Chapter (ss 106A–106E) inserted by FA 2013 s 17, Sch 4 para 23 with effect for the tax year 2013–14 and subsequent tax years, subject to the provisions of FA 2013 Sch 4 para 57 in relation to barristers and advocates.

[106D   Capital receipts
Section 106C does not apply in relation to the relevant act if subsection (4) or (5) of section 96A [(capital receipts under, or after leaving, cash basis)][2] applies in relation to that act.][1]
Commentary—*Simon's Taxes* **B2.215A**.
Amendments—[1]   This Chapter (ss 106A–106E) inserted by FA 2013 s 17, Sch 4 para 23 with effect for the tax year 2013–14 and subsequent tax years, subject to the provisions of FA 2013 Sch 4 para 57 in relation to barristers and advocates.
[2]   Words substituted for words "(cash basis: capital receipts)" by F(No 2)A 2017 s 16, Sch 2 paras 1, 6 with effect for the tax year 2017–18 and subsequent tax years, subject to transitional provisions in F(No 2)A 2017 Sch 2 para 64.

[106E   Gifts to charities etc
Section 106C does not apply in relation to the relevant act if any of the provisions of Chapter 7 (trade profits: gifts to charities etc) applies in relation to that act.][1]
Commentary—*Simon's Taxes* **B2.215A**.
Amendments—[1]   This Chapter (ss 106A–106E) inserted by FA 2013 s 17, Sch 4 para 23 with effect for the tax year 2013–14 and subsequent tax years, subject to the provisions of FA 2013 Sch 4 para 57 in relation to barristers and advocates.

CHAPTER 7

TRADE PROFITS: GIFTS TO CHARITIES ETC

107   Professions and vocations
The provisions of this Chapter apply to professions and vocations as they apply to trades.
Commentary—*Simon's Taxes* **B2.442, B1.202**.
Derivation—TA 1988 s 83A(1), s 84(1).

108   Gifts of trading stock to charities etc
(1) This section applies if a person carrying on a trade ("the donor") gives an article for the purposes of—
    (*a*)   a charity, a registered club or a body listed in subsection (4), or
    (*b*)   a designated educational establishment (see section 110),
and the article is one manufactured, or of a class or description sold, by the donor in the course of the trade.
(2) In calculating the profits of the trade, no amount is required to be brought into account as a receipt in consequence of the disposal of the article.
(3) In this section "registered club" has the meaning given by [section 658 of CTA 2010 (community][2] amateur sports clubs).
(4) The bodies referred to in subsection (1)(*a*) are—
    (*a*)   the Trustees of the National Heritage Memorial Fund,
    (*b*)   the Historic Buildings and Monuments Commission for England,
    (*c*), (*d*)   . . .[1] and
    (*e*)   . . .[4]
(5) This section [—
    (*a*)   ][3] needs to be read with section 109 (receipt by donor or connected person of benefit attributable to certain gifts)[, and
    (*b*)   is subject to section 809ZM of ITA 2007 (removal of income tax relief in respect of tainted charity donations etc).][3]
Commentary—*Simon's Taxes* **B2.442**.
HMRC Manuals—Business Income Manual BIM45155 (relief for gifts of trading stock to charities and other bodies).
BIM45160 (tainted charity donations: relief for gifts of trading stocks to charities and other bodies).
Amendments—[1]   Sub-s (4)(*c*), (*d*) repealed by ITA 2007 ss 1027, 1031, Sch 1 paras 492, 500, Sch 3 Pt 1 with effect for income tax purposes from 6 April 2007, and corporation tax purposes for accounting periods ending after 5 April 2007.
[2]   In sub-s (3) words substituted by CTA 2010 s 1177, Sch 1 paras 444, 446. CTA 2010 has effect for corporation tax purposes for accounting periods ending on or after 1 April 2010, and for income and capital gains tax purposes for the tax year 2010–11 and subsequent tax years.
[3]   Words in sub-s (5) inserted by FA 2011 s 27 and Sch 3 para 6 with effect in relation to relievable charity donations made on or after 1 April 2011.
[4]   Sub-s (4)(*e*) repealed by the Public Bodies (Abolition of the National Endowment for Science, Technology and the Arts) Order, SI 2012/964 art 3(1), Schedule with effect from 1 April 2012.

109   Receipt by donor or connected person of benefit attributable to certain gifts
(1) This section applies if a person carrying on a trade ("the donor") makes a gift in relation to which—
    (*a*)   section 108 applies, or
    (*b*)   section 63(2) of CAA 2001 applies (gifts to charities etc of plant or machinery used in the trade),

and the donor, or a person connected with the donor, receives a benefit which is in any way attributable to the making of the gift.

(2) An amount equal to the value of the benefit—

(*a*) is brought into account in calculating the profits of the trade, as a receipt of the trade arising on the date on which the benefit is received, or

(*b*) if the donor has permanently ceased to carry on the trade before that date, is treated as a post-cessation receipt (see Chapter 18).

Commentary—*Simon's Taxes* **B2.442.**

HMRC Manuals—Business Income Manual BIM45165 (relief for gifts of plant and machinery to charities and other bodies). BIM45155 (gifts in kind and payroll giving: relief for gifts of trading stock to charities and other bodies).

110 Meaning of "designated educational establishment"

(1) For the purposes of section 108 "designated educational establishment" means an educational establishment designated, or within a category designated, in regulations made—

(*a*) for England and Scotland, by the Secretary of State,

(*b*) for Wales, by the National Assembly for Wales, and

(*c*) for Northern Ireland, by the Department of Education.

(2) The regulations may make different provision for different areas.

(3) If any question arises as to whether an educational establishment is within a category designated in the regulations, [an officer of Revenue and Customs] must refer the question for decision—

(*a*) in the case of an establishment in England or Scotland, to the Secretary of State,

(*b*) in the case of an establishment in Wales, to the National Assembly for Wales, and

(*c*) in the case of an establishment in Northern Ireland, to the Department of Education.

(4) The power of the Secretary of State or the National Assembly for Wales to make regulations under this section is exercisable by statutory instrument.

(5) A statutory instrument containing any regulations made by the Secretary of State under this section is subject to annulment in pursuance of a resolution of the House of Commons.

(6) Regulations made under this section by the Department of Education—

(*a*) are a statutory rule for the purposes of the Statutory Rules (Northern Ireland) Order 1979 (SI 1979/1573 (NI 12)), and

(*b*) are subject to negative resolution within the meaning of section 41(6) of the Interpretation Act (Northern Ireland) 1954 (c 33 (NI)).

Commentary—*Simon's Taxes* **B2.442.**

HMRC Manuals—Business Income Manual BIM45170 (designated educational establishments: tax relief).

CHAPTER 8

TRADE PROFITS: HERD BASIS RULES

Commentary—*Simon's Taxes* **Division B5.1.**

Introduction

111 Election for application of herd basis rules

(1) A person who keeps or has kept a production herd for the purposes of a trade may make an election under this Chapter (a "herd basis election").

(2) In calculating the profits of the trade, animals which are part of a production herd in relation to which a herd basis election has effect—

(*a*) are not treated as trading stock (see section 30), but

(*b*) are treated instead in accordance with sections 114 to 123 ("the herd basis rules").

(3) This Chapter is expressed in terms of farmers but applies to any person who keeps or has kept a production herd for the purposes of a trade, whether or not the trade is farming.

(4) References in this Chapter to keeping a production herd are to keeping it for the purposes of the trade.

Commentary—*Simon's Taxes* **B5.150, B5.152, B7.301.**

HMRC Manuals—Business Income Manual BIM55501 (overview of the herd basis). BIM55565 (who can elect?). BIM55505 (herd basis rules).

[111A Herd basis rules not to apply where cash basis used

Nothing in this Chapter applies in calculating the profits of a trade on the cash basis.][1]

Commentary—*Simon's Taxes* **B5.152 , B7.301.**

Amendments—[1]   This section inserted by FA 2013 s 17, Sch 4 para 24 with effect for the tax year 2013–14 and subsequent tax years, subject to the provisions of FA 2013 Sch 4 para 57 in relation to barristers and advocates.

112 Meaning of "animal", "herd", "production herd" etc

(1) In this Chapter—

(*a*) "animal" means any animal or other living creature,

(*b*) "herd" includes a flock and any other collection of animals (however named), and (*c*) "production herd" means, in relation to a farmer, a herd of animals of the same species (irrespective of breed) kept by the farmer wholly or mainly for the products obtainable from the living animal which the animals produce for the farmer to sell.

(2) For this purpose "the products obtainable from the living animal" means—

(*a*) the young of the animal, or

(*b*) any other product obtainable from the animal without slaughtering it.

(3) For the purposes of this Chapter the general rule is that immature animals kept in a production herd are not part of the herd.

(4) There is an exception to this rule if—

(*a*) the nature of the land on which the herd is kept means that animals which die or cease to be part of the herd can be replaced only by animals bred and reared on the land,

(*b*) the immature animals in question are bred in the herd and are maintained in the herd for the purpose of replacing other animals, and

(*c*) it is necessary to maintain the immature animals for that purpose.

(5) In that case the immature animals are part of the herd for the purposes of this Chapter, but only so far as they are required to prevent a fall in the numbers of the herd.

(6) References in this Chapter to an animal being added to a herd include references to an immature animal that is not part of the herd reaching maturity.

(7) This Chapter applies—

(*a*) in relation to animals kept singly as it applies in relation to herds, and

(*b*) in relation to shares in animals as it applies in relation to animals themselves.

Commentary—*Simon's Taxes* **B5.151.**

HMRC Manuals—Business Income Manual BIM55570 (meaning of production herds and animals which are excluded from herd basis).

BIM55575 (immature animals: treatment).

113 Other interpretative provisions

(1) This section applies for the purposes of this Chapter.

(2) A production herd kept by a farmer is of the same class as another production herd only if—

(*a*) the animals kept in both herds are of the same species (irrespective of breed), and

(*b*) the products produced for the farmer to sell (for which the herds are wholly or mainly kept) are of the same kinds in both herds.

(3) References to the sale of an animal include references to its death or destruction.

(4) References to the sale proceeds of an animal include references to—

(*a*) money received from an insurer because of the animal's death or destruction,

(*b*) compensation money received because of the animal's death or destruction, and

(*c*) the sale proceeds of the animal's carcass or any part of its carcass.

(5) Female animals become mature—

(*a*) in the case of laying birds, when they first lay, and

(*b*) in any other case, when they produce their first young.

(6) 20% or more of a herd is a substantial part of the herd, but a lesser percentage than 20% is capable of being a substantial part of the herd depending on the circumstances of the case concerned.

Commentary—*Simon's Taxes* **B5.151, B5.152, B5.142, B5.153.**

HMRC Manuals—Business Income Manual BIM55525 (what constitutes substantial reduction?).

BIM55575 (mature animals).

BIM55635 (shares in animals).

The herd basis rules

114 Initial cost of herd and value of herd

(1) In calculating the profits of the trade, no deduction is allowed for the initial cost of the herd.

(2) In calculating the profits of the trade, the value of the herd is not brought into account.

Commentary—*Simon's Taxes* **B5.153.**

HMRC Manuals—Business Income Manual BIM55530 (initial and additions cost to herd and example).

115 Addition of animals to herd

(1) This section applies for the purpose of calculating the profits of the trade if an animal is added to the herd, unless it replaces another animal in the herd.

(2) No deduction is allowed for the cost of the animal.

(3) If, immediately before it was added to the herd, the animal was part of the farmer's trading stock, the balancing amount is brought into account as a receipt.

(4) "The balancing amount" means—

(*a*) in the case of an animal bred by the farmer, the cost of breeding the animal and rearing it to maturity, and

(*b*) in any other case, the sum of the initial cost of acquiring the animal and the cost (if any) incurred by the farmer in rearing the animal to maturity.

Commentary—*Simon's Taxes* **B5.153.**

Derivation—TA 1988 Sch 5 para 3(2), (3).

HMRC Manuals—Business Income Manual BIM55530 (initial and additions cost to herd and example).

116 Replacement of animals in herd

(1) This section applies for the purpose of calculating the profits of the trade if—

    (*a*) an animal ("the old animal") is sold from the herd or otherwise ceases to be part of the herd, and

    (*b*) it is replaced in the herd by another animal ("the new animal").

(2) The sale proceeds (if any) of the old animal are brought into account as a receipt.

(3) But this needs to be read with—

    (*a*) section 117 (amount of receipt if old animal slaughtered under disease control order),

    (*b*) section 120 (acquisition of new herd begun within 5 years of sale), and

    (*c*) section 122 (replacement of part sold begun within 5 years of sale).

(4) Except so far as otherwise allowable, a deduction is allowed under this section for the cost of the new animal.

(5) But if the new animal is of better quality than the old animal, the amount of the deduction must not exceed the amount that it would have been necessary to spend to replace the old animal with an animal of the same quality.

Commentary—*Simon's Taxes* **B5.153.**
Derivation—TA 1988 Sch 5 para 3(4), (5).
HMRC Manuals—Business Income Manual BIM55535 (replacement of animals and examples).

117 Amount of receipt if old animal slaughtered under disease control order

(1) This section applies for the purposes of section 116.

(2) If—

    (*a*) the old animal was slaughtered under a disease control order, and

    (*b*) the new animal is of worse quality than the old animal,

the amount brought into account as a receipt under section 116 must not exceed the equivalent amount for the new animal.

(3) For this purpose "a disease control order" means an order made under the law relating to the diseases of animals by—

    (*a*) central government,

    (*b*) a devolved authority,

    (*c*) a local authority, or

    (*d*) another public authority.

(4) If, immediately before it was added to the herd, the new animal was part of the farmer's trading stock, "the equivalent amount for the new animal" means—

    (*a*) in the case of an animal bred by the farmer, the cost of breeding the animal and rearing it to maturity, and

    (*b*) in any other case, the sum of the initial cost of acquiring the animal and the cost (if any) incurred by the farmer in rearing the animal to maturity.

(5) Otherwise "the equivalent amount for the new animal" means the cost of the new animal.

Commentary—*Simon's Taxes* **B5.111.**
Derivation—TA 1988 Sch 5 para 3(6).

118 Sale of animals from herd

(1) This section applies for the purpose of calculating the profits of the trade if an animal is sold from the herd unless—

    (*a*) it is replaced in the herd by another animal (see section 116), or

    (*b*) it is sold as part of the sale of the whole or a substantial part of the herd that takes place all at once or over a period not longer than 12 months (see section 119).

(2) A profit arising from the sale is brought into account as a receipt.

(3) A deduction is allowed for a loss arising from the sale.

(4) The amount of the profit or loss is the difference between the sale proceeds of the animal and the deductible amount for the animal.

(5) "The deductible amount for the animal" means—

    (*a*) in the case of an animal bred by the farmer, the cost of breeding the animal and rearing it to maturity,

    (*b*) in the case of an animal acquired by the farmer for valuable consideration, the sum of the initial cost to the farmer of acquiring the animal and the cost (if any) incurred by the farmer in rearing the animal to maturity, and

    (*c*) in the case of an animal acquired by the farmer but not for valuable consideration, the sum of the market value of the animal when acquired and the cost (if any) incurred by the farmer in rearing the animal to maturity.

Commentary—*Simon's Taxes* **B5.153.**
Derivation—TA 1988 Sch 5 para 3(10).
HMRC Manuals—Business Income Manual BIM55550 (minor disposals from the herd without replacement).

119 Sale of whole or substantial part of herd

(1) This section applies for the purpose of calculating the profits of the trade if, either all at once or over a period not longer than 12 months, the herd or a substantial part of the herd is sold unless—

    (*a*) section 120 applies (acquisition of new herd begun within 5 years of sale), or

    (*b*) section 122 applies (replacement of part sold begun within 5 years of sale),

but paragraph (a) is subject to subsection (5) of section 120 (so far as that section provides for a case in which this section is to apply).

(2) A profit arising from the sale is not brought into account as a receipt.

(3) No deduction is allowed for a loss arising from the sale.

Commentary—*Simon's Taxes* **B5.153.**

HMRC Manuals—Business Income Manual BIM55540 (disposal of whole or substantial part of herd).

120 Acquisition of new herd begun within 5 years of sale

(1) This section applies for the purpose of calculating the profits of the trade if—

    (*a*) either all at once or over a period not longer than 12 months, the herd ("the old herd") is sold, and

    (*b*) the farmer acquires or starts to acquire another production herd of the same class ("the new herd") within 5 years of the sale.

(2) Section 116 (replacement of animals in herd) applies as if a number of animals equal to—

    (*a*) the number of animals in the old herd, or

    (*b*) if smaller, the number of animals in the new herd,

had been sold from the old herd and replaced in that herd (but see section 121 (sale for reasons outside farmer's control)).

(3) For the purposes of section 116, the sale proceeds of an animal that is treated as a result of subsection (2) above as if it had been—

    (*a*) sold from the old herd, and

    (*b*) replaced in that herd by another animal ("the new animal"),

are not brought into account as a receipt until the new animal is acquired.

(4) If—

    (*a*) the number of animals in the new herd is smaller than the number of animals in the old herd, and

    (*b*) the difference is not substantial,

section 118 (sale of animals from herd) applies as if a number of animals equal to the difference had been sold from the old herd.

(5) If the number of animals in the new herd is smaller than the number of animals in the old herd and the difference is substantial—

    (*a*) section 119 (sale of whole or substantial part of herd where replacement not begun within 5 years), or

    (*b*) section 122 (sale of substantial part of herd where replacement begun within 5 years),

applies as if a number of animals equal to the difference had been sold from the old herd.

(6) If the number of animals in the new herd is larger than the number of animals in the old herd, section 115 (addition of animals to herd) applies as if a number of animals equal to the difference had been added to the old herd.

(7) For the purposes of this section—

    (*a*) if the difference between the number of animals in the new herd and the number of animals in the old herd is equal to 20% or more of the number of animals in the old herd, the difference is substantial, but

    (*b*) a lesser percentage than 20% is capable of being a substantial difference depending on the circumstances of the case concerned.

Commentary—*Simon's Taxes* **B5.153.**

HMRC Manuals—Business Income Manual BIM55545 (acquisition of new animals following a major disposal).

121 Section 120: sale for reasons outside farmer's control

(1) This section applies for the purposes of section 116, as applied by section 120(2).

(2) If—

    (*a*) the farmer was compelled to sell the old herd for reasons wholly outside the farmer's control, and

    (*b*) an animal ("the new animal") that is treated as a result of section 120(2) as if it replaced an animal sold ("the old animal") is of worse quality than the old animal,

the amount brought into account as a receipt under section 116 must not exceed the equivalent amount for the new animal.

(3) If, immediately before it was added to the herd, the new animal was part of the farmer's trading stock, "the equivalent amount for the new animal" means—

    (*a*) in the case of an animal bred by the farmer, the cost of breeding the animal and rearing it to maturity, and

(b) in any other case, the sum of the initial cost of acquiring the animal and the cost (if any) incurred by the farmer in rearing the animal to maturity.

(4) Otherwise "the equivalent amount for the new animal" means the cost of the new animal.

Commentary—*Simon's Taxes* B5.153.
Derivation—TA 1988 Sch 5 para 3(9).

122 Replacement of part sold begun within 5 years of sale

(1) This section applies for the purpose of calculating the profits of the trade if—
    (a) either all at once or over a period not longer than 12 months, a substantial part of the herd is sold, and
    (b) the farmer acquires or starts to acquire animals to replace the part sold within 5 years of the sale.

(2) Section 116 (replacement of animals in herd) applies so far as the animals included in the part sold are replaced (but see section 123 (sale for reasons outside farmer's control)).

(3) The sale proceeds of an animal included in the part sold are not brought into account as a receipt until the animal that replaces it in the herd is acquired.

(4) If some of the animals included in the part sold are not replaced—
    (a) a profit arising from their sale is not brought into account as a receipt, and
    (b) no deduction is allowed for a loss arising from their sale.

Commentary—*Simon's Taxes* B5.153.
Derivation—TA 1988 Sch 5 para 3(8), (9).

123 Section 122: sale for reasons outside farmer's control

(1) This section applies for the purposes of section 116, as applied by section 122(2).

(2) If—
    (a) the farmer was compelled to sell the part of the herd for reasons wholly outside the farmer's control, and
    (b) an animal ("the new animal") that replaces an animal sold ("the old animal") is of worse quality than the old animal,

the amount brought into account as a receipt under section 116 must not exceed the equivalent amount for the new animal.

(3) If, immediately before it was added to the herd, the new animal was part of the farmer's trading stock, "the equivalent amount for the new animal" means—
    (a) in the case of an animal bred by the farmer, the cost of breeding the animal and rearing it to maturity, and
    (b) in any other case, the sum of the initial cost of acquiring the animal and the cost (if any) incurred by the farmer in rearing the animal to maturity.

(4) Otherwise "the equivalent amount for the new animal" means the cost of the new animal.

Commentary—*Simon's Taxes* B5.153.
Derivation—TA 1988 Sch 5 para 3(9).

Elections

124 Herd basis elections

(1) A herd basis election must specify the class of production herd to which it relates.

(2) A herd basis election must be made—
    (a) on or before the first anniversary of the normal self-assessment filing date for the tax year in which the first relevant period of account ends, or
    (b) if that is the tax year in which the farmer starts to carry on the trade and the farmer is not a firm, on or before the second anniversary of the normal self-assessment filing date for that tax year.

(3) "The first relevant period of account" means the first period of account in which the farmer making the election keeps a production herd of the class to which the election relates (but see subsection (8)).

(4) A herd basis election cannot relate to more than one class of production herd, but separate elections may be made for different classes.

(5) A herd basis election is irrevocable.

(6) A herd basis election has effect in relation to all production herds of the class to which it relates, including any which the farmer—
    (a) has ceased to keep before making the election, or
    (b) first keeps after making the election.

(7) A herd basis election has effect for every period of account in which the farmer—
    (a) carries on the trade, and
    (b) keeps a production herd of the class to which the election relates.

(8) If the farmer is a firm and there is a change in the persons who are partners in the firm—
    (a) any herd basis election made by the old firm ceases to have effect, and

(b) in relation to the new firm, "the first relevant period of account" means the first period of account in which the new firm keeps a production herd of the class to which the election relates.

Commentary—*Simon's Taxes* **B5.152, B5.154, B7.301, E1.265.**
HMRC Manuals—Business Income Manual BIM55585 (elections for the herd basis).
BIM55590 (class of herd).
BIM55600 (time limit for making election).
BIM55610 (new partnerships and changes in partnerships).
BIM55630 (continuing effect of an election).

125 Five year gap in which no production herd kept

(1) This section applies if a farmer—
    (a) keeps a production herd of a particular class, and
    (b) ceases altogether to keep herds of that class for a period of at least 5 years.
(2) If the farmer keeps a production herd of that class after the end of that period—
    (a) the period of account in which the farmer starts to keep the herd is treated as the first period of account in which the farmer keeps a production herd of that class, and
    (b) any herd basis election previously made by the farmer in relation to production herds of that class ceases to have effect.

Commentary—*Simon's Taxes* **B5.152.**

126 Slaughter under disease control order

(1) This section applies if—
    (a) the whole or a substantial part of a production herd kept by a farmer is slaughtered under a disease control order, and
    (b) the circumstances of the slaughter are such that compensation is payable in respect of the animals slaughtered.
(2) The farmer may make a herd basis election in respect of the class of production herd involved in the slaughter as if the period of account—
    (a) in which the compensation falls to be brought into account in calculating the profits of the trade, or
    (b) in which it would (but for the election) fall to be so brought into account,
were the first period of account in which the farmer keeps a production herd of that class.
(3) An election made as a result of this section has effect for that period of account and every subsequent period of account in which the farmer—
    (a) carries on the trade, and
    (b) keeps a production herd of the class to which the election relates.
(4) In this section "disease control order" means an order made under the law relating to the diseases of animals by—
    (a) central government,
    (b) a devolved authority,
    (c) a local authority, or
    (d) another public authority.

Commentary—*Simon's Taxes* **B5.142, E1.265.**
HMRC Manuals—Business Income Manual BIM55180 (compensation received for compulsory slaughter of animals).
BIM55605 (compulsory slaughter: new right of election).

Preventing abuse of the herd basis rules

127 Preventing abuse of the herd basis rules

(1) This section applies if—
    (a) a person carrying on a trade (the "transferor") transfers the whole or part of a production herd to another person (the "transferee"),
    (b) the transfer is not by way of sale or is by way of sale but for a price other than that which the animals sold would have fetched if sold in the open market, and
    (c) the control condition or herd basis benefit condition is met.
(2) The control condition is met if—
    (a) the transferor is a body of persons over which the transferee has control,
    (b) the transferee is a body of persons over which the transferor has control, or
    (c) both the transferor and transferee are bodies of persons and another person has control over both of them.
(3) For this purpose "body of persons" includes a firm.
(4) The herd basis benefit condition is met if—
    (a) the transferor or transferee (or both) might (but for this section) have been expected to obtain a herd basis benefit as a result of the transfer or the transactions of which the transfer is one, and
    (b) the herd basis benefit is the sole or main benefit, or one of the main benefits, that the person in question might have been expected to obtain.

(5) For this purpose a "herd basis benefit" is a benefit resulting from—
  (*a*) the obtaining of a right to make a herd basis election,
  (*b*) the herd basis rules applying or not applying, or
  (*c*) the herd basis rules having a greater or lesser effect.
(6) For the purpose of calculating the profits of—
  (*a*) the trade carried on by the transferor, and
  (*b*) any trade carried on by the transferee,
the animals transferred are treated as having been sold at the price which they would have fetched if sold in the open market.

Commentary—_Simon's Taxes_ **B5.154, B2.617.**
Derivation—TA 1988 Sch 5 para 5(1), (2).
HMRC Manuals—Business Income Manual BIM55560 (tax avoidance: transfers not at market price).

129 Further assessment etc if herd basis rules apply
(1) If the herd basis rules apply in calculating the profits of a tax year after an assessment for that tax year has become final and conclusive, any assessment or repayment of tax that is necessary to give effect to the rules must be made.
(2) But repayment of tax is due only if a claim for it is made.

Commentary—_Simon's Taxes_ **B5.152.**
Derivation—TA 1988 Sch 5 para 11.
HMRC Manuals—Business Income Manual BIM55625 (adjustment of assessments).
BIM55515 (which rule to apply).

CHAPTER 9

TRADE PROFITS: . . . [1] SOUND RECORDINGS

Amendments—[1] Words "films and" repealed by FA 2006 s 178, Sch 26 Pt 3(4) with effect in accordance with FA 2006 ss 46, 47.

Introduction

130 Expenditure to which this Chapter applies
(1) This Chapter makes provision about—
  (*a*) expenditure incurred on the production or acquisition of the original master version of a
      . . . [1] sound recording, . . . [1]
  (*b*) . . . [1]
(2) In this Chapter references to production expenditure are to expenditure incurred on the production of the original master version of a . . . [1] sound recording.
(3) In this Chapter references to acquisition expenditure are to expenditure incurred on the acquisition of the original master version of a . . . [1] sound recording.
(4) In this Chapter references to the original master version of a . . . [1] sound recording include any rights in the original master version of a . . . [1] sound recording that are held or acquired with it.
(5) In this Chapter references to production or acquisition expenditure do not include—
  (*a*) interest (as to which, see section 29), or
  (*b*) the incidental costs of obtaining finance (as to which, see sections 58 and 59).
(6) . . . [1]
(7) In this Chapter "any prohibitive rule" means any provision of the Income Tax Acts which—
  (*a*) prohibits a deduction from being made, or
  (*b*) restricts the extent to which it is allowed,
in calculating the profits of a trade.

Commentary—_Simon's Taxes_ **B5.501, B7.215.**
HMRC Manuals—Business Income Manual BIM56206 (meaning of expenditure on the production or acquisition).
BIM56205 (revenue nature of income and expenditure)
Amendments—[1] Words "film or" repealed; and sub-s (1)(*b*) and preceding word "and", and sub-s (6) repealed; by FA 2006 s 178, Sch 26 Pt 3(4) with effect in accordance with FA 2006 ss 46, 47.

[130A Chapter not to apply where cash basis used
Nothing in this Chapter applies in calculating the profits of a trade on the cash basis.][1]

Commentary—_Simon's Taxes_ **B5.501.**
Amendments—[1] This section inserted by FA 2013 s 17, Sch 4 para 25 with effect for the tax year 2013–14 and subsequent tax years, subject to the provisions of FA 2013 Sch 4 para 57 in relation to barristers and advocates.

132 Meaning of "original master version" and "certified master version"
(1) In this Chapter "original master version" means—
  (*a*) . . . [1]
  (*b*) in relation to a sound recording, the original master audio tape or disc.
(2), (3) . . . [1]

Commentary—_Simon's Taxes_ **B5.501.**
HMRC Manuals—Business Income Manual BIM56205 (meaning of original master version).

Modification—Corporation Tax (Taxation of Films) (Transitional Provisions) Regulations, SI 2007/1050 (modification of this section in relation to films that commenced principal photography before 1 January 2007 but are not completed before that date).

Amendments—[1] Sub-s (1)(*a*) and word "and" following it repealed, and sub-ss (2), (3) repealed; by FA 2006 s 178, Sch 26 Pt 3(4) with effect in accordance with FA 2006 ss 46, 47.

133 Meaning of "relevant period"

In this Chapter "relevant period", in relation to a trade, means—

    (*a*) a period of account of the trade, or

    (*b*) if no accounts of the trade are drawn up for a period, the basis period for a tax year.

Commentary—*Simon's Taxes* **B5.502**.

Derivation—F(No 2)A 1992 s 40B(3), s 40D(5), s 43(1); CAA 2001 Sch 2 para 82.

HMRC Manuals—Business Income Manual BIM56210 (meaning of relevant period and allocation of expenditure to relevant periods).

Expenditure treated as revenue in nature

134 Expenditure treated as revenue in nature

(1) If a person carrying on a trade incurs production or acquisition expenditure, the expenditure is treated for income tax purposes as expenditure of a revenue nature.

(2) If expenditure is treated under this section as revenue in nature, sums received by the person carrying on the trade from the disposal of the original master version—

    (*a*) are treated for income tax purposes as receipts of a revenue nature, and

    (*b*) are brought into account in calculating the profits of the trade of the relevant period in which they are received.

(3) For this purpose sums received from the disposal of the original master version include—

    (*a*) sums received from the disposal of any interest or right in or over the original master version (including an interest or right created by the disposal), and

    (*b*) insurance, compensation or similar money derived from the original master version.

(4) . . . [1]

Commentary—*Simon's Taxes* **B5.501**.

HMRC Manuals—Business Income Manual BIM56205 (revenue nature of income and expenditure). BIM56206 (meaning of expenditure on the production or acquisition).

Amendments—[1] Sub-s (4) repealed by FA 2006 s 178, Sch 26 Pt 3(4) with effect in accordance with FA 2006 ss 46, 47.

[Rules for allocating expenditure][1]

Amendments—[1] Heading substituted by FA 2006 s 178, Sch 26 Pt 3(4) with effect in accordance with FA 2006 ss 46, 47.

135 [Allocation of production or acquisition expenditure to relevant periods][2]

(1) This section applies for the purpose of calculating the profits of a trade of a relevant period if—

    (*a*) the trade consists of or includes the exploitation of the original master versions of . . . [1] sound recordings,

    (*b*) the original master versions do not constitute trading stock of the trade (within the meaning of section 174),

    (*c*) the person carrying on the trade incurs production or acquisition expenditure in, or before, the relevant period, and

    (*d*) . . . [1]

(2) A deduction is allowed for the amount of the production or acquisition expenditure allocated to the relevant period, but this is subject to the application of any prohibitive rule.

(3) The person carrying on the trade must allocate to the relevant period so much of the expenditure as is just and reasonable (but see subsection (5)).

(4) In making this allocation regard must be had to the following—

    (*a*) the amount of the expenditure which remains unallocated at the beginning of the period,

    (*b*) the amount of the expenditure incurred in the period,

    (*c*) the proportion which the estimated value of the original master version realised in the period (by way of income or otherwise) bears to the sum of the value so realised and the estimated remaining value at the end of the period, and

    (*d*) the need to bring the whole of the expenditure into account over the time during which the value of the original master version is expected to be realised.

(5) The person carrying on the trade may also allocate to the relevant period a further amount, so long as the total amount allocated to the period does not exceed the value of the original master version realised in the period (by way of income or otherwise).

(6) Expenditure may not be allocated to the relevant period under this section if it is allocated—

    (*a*) under this section to any other relevant period,

    (*b*)–(*d*) . . . [1]

(7) . . . [1]

Commentary—*Simon's Taxes* **B5.502**.

HMRC Manuals—Business Income Manual BIM56210 (allocation of expenditure to relevant periods). BIM56215 (income matching method). BIM56230 (cost recovery method).

ITTOIA 2005

BIM56243 (sale of the master version).
BIM56255 (excluded expenditure).
Amendments—[1]   Words "films or" in sub-s (1)(*a*) repealed; and sub-ss (1)(*d*), (6)(*b*)–(*d*), (7) repealed; by FA 2006 s 178, Sch
  26 Pt 3(4) with effect in accordance with FA 2006 ss 46, 47.
[2]   Heading substituted by FA 2006 s 178, Sch 26 Pt 3(4) with effect in accordance with FA 2006 ss 46, 47.

CHAPTER 10

TRADE PROFITS: CERTAIN TELECOMMUNICATION RIGHTS

[144A Chapter not to apply where cash basis used
Nothing in this Chapter applies in calculating the profits of a trade on the cash basis.][1]
Commentary—*Simon's Taxes* B2.473.
Amendments—[1]   This section inserted by FA 2013 s 17, Sch 4 para 26 with effect for the tax year 2013–14 and subsequent
  tax years, subject to the provisions of FA 2013 Sch 4 para 57 in relation to barristers and advocates.

145 Professions and vocations
The provisions of this Chapter apply to professions and vocations as they apply to trades.
Commentary—*Simon's Taxes* B2.473, B1.202.

146 Meaning of "relevant telecommunication right"
In this Chapter a "relevant telecommunication right" means—
   (*a*) a licence [granted under section 8 of the Wireless Telegraphy Act 2006 in accordance with
       regulations made under section 14 of that Act (bidding for licences)][1]
   (*b*) an indefeasible right to use a telecommunications cable system, or
   (*c*) a right derived (directly or indirectly) from such a licence or indefeasible right.
Commentary—*Simon's Taxes* B2.473.
Derivation—FA 2000 Sch 23 para 1.
HMRC Manuals—Corporate Intangibles Research and Development Manual CIRD70150 (telecommunications licences and
  rights: introduction).
CIRD70340 (IRUs: definition).
Amendments—[1]   Words in para (*a*) substituted by the Wireless Telegraphy Act 2006 s 123, Sch 7 para 37 with effect from
  8 February 2007.

147 Expenditure and receipts treated as revenue in nature
(1) This section applies if, in accordance with generally accepted accounting practice, an amount in
respect of—
   (*a*) expenditure on the acquisition of a relevant telecommunication right, or
   (*b*) a receipt from the disposal of a relevant telecommunication right,
is recognised in the accounts of a trade as an item in the calculation of profit or loss.
(2) The amount is treated for income tax purposes as an item of a revenue nature.
(3) "The acquisition of a relevant telecommunication right" includes—
   (*a*) the extension of rights attached to a relevant telecommunication right, and
   (*b*) if a relevant telecommunication right is subject to a derivative right, the cancellation or
       restriction of rights attached to the derivative right.
(4) "The disposal of a relevant telecommunication right" includes—
   (*a*) the cancellation or restriction of rights attached to a relevant telecommunication right, and
   (*b*) the granting of a derivative right or the extension of rights attached to a derivative right.
Commentary—*Simon's Taxes* B2.473.
HMRC Manuals—Corporate Intangibles Research and Development Manual CIRD70405 (revenue nature of expenditure on
  acquisition).
CIRD70410 (telecommunication licences and rights: receipts from disposals).

148 Credits or debits arising from revaluation
(1) This section applies if, in accordance with generally accepted accounting practice, an amount in
respect of the revaluation of a relevant telecommunication right is recognised in the accounts of a
trade (whether or not as an item in the calculation of profit or loss).
(2) The amount is treated for income tax purposes as an item of a revenue nature.
(3) In calculating the profits of the trade, the amount is brought into account for the period of account
in which it is recognised.
Commentary—*Simon's Taxes* B2.473.
HMRC Manuals—Corporate Intangibles Research and Development Manual CIRD70150 (telecommunications rights and
  licences and rights: revaluations).

[CHAPTER 10A

LEASES OF PLANT OR MACHINERY: SPECIAL RULES FOR LONG FUNDING LEASES][1]

Amendment—[1]   Chapter inserted by FA 2006 s 81, Sch 8 paras 12, 13, subject to commencement and transitional provisions
  in FA 2006 Sch 8 paras 15–27.

[Application of Chapter

[148ZA Chapter not to apply where cash basis used

Nothing in this Chapter applies in calculating the profits of a trade on the cash basis.][1]

Commentary—*Simon's Taxes* **B5.405, B5.406.**

HMRC Manuals—Business Income Manual BIM70050 (cash basis: rules not applied in calculating profits).

Amendments—[1] This section inserted by FA 2013 s 17, Sch 4 para 27 with effect for the tax year 2013–14 and subsequent tax years, subject to the provisions of FA 2013 Sch 4 para 57 in relation to barristers and advocates.

[Lessors under long funding finance leases

148A Lessor under long funding finance lease: rental earnings

(1) This section applies for the purpose of calculating the profits of a person carrying on a trade for a period of account in which he is the lessor of any plant or machinery under a long funding finance lease.

(2) The amount to be brought into account as the lessor's taxable income from the lease for the period of account is the amount of the rental earnings in respect of the lease for the period of account.

(3) The "rental earnings" for any period is the amount which, in accordance with generally accepted accounting practice, falls (or would fall) to be treated as the gross return on investment for that period in respect of the long funding lease where it meets the finance lease test.

(4) If the lease is one which, under generally accepted accounting practice, falls (or would fall) to be treated as a loan in the accounts in question, so much of the rentals under the lease as fall (or would fall) to be treated as interest are to be treated for the purposes of this section as rental earnings.][1]

Commentary—*Simon's Taxes* **B5.406, B5.415A.**

HMRC Manuals—Business Leasing Manual, BLM40105 (taxation of long funding leases: rental earnings).

BIM40110 (example of rental earnings other than finance charges).

Amendment—[1] Sections 148A–148J inserted by FA 2006 s 81, Sch 8 paras 12, 13, subject to commencement and transitional provisions in FA 2006 Sch 8 paras 15–27.

[148B Lessor under long funding finance lease: exceptional items

(1) This section applies for the purpose of calculating the profits of a person carrying on a trade for a period of account if he is or has been the lessor under a long funding finance lease.

(2) This section has effect where a profit or loss (whether of an income or capital nature)—

    (*a*) arises to the person in connection with the lease, and

    (*b*) in accordance with generally accepted accounting practice falls to be recognised for accounting purposes in a period of account, but

    (*c*) would not, apart from this section, be brought into account in calculating the profits of the person.

(3) The profit or loss is to be treated—

    (*a*) in the case of a profit, as income of the person that is attributable to the lease,

    (*b*) in the case of a loss, as a revenue expense incurred by the person in connection with the lease.

(4) Any reference in this section to an amount falling to be recognised for accounting purposes in a period of account is a reference to an amount falling to be recognised for accounting purposes—

    (*a*) in the person's profit and loss account or income statement,

    (*b*) in the person's statement of recognised gains and losses or statement of changes in equity, or

    (*c*) in any other statement of items brought into account in computing the person's profits or losses for that period.][1]

Commentary—*Simon's Taxes* **B5.406.**

HMRC Manuals—Business Leasing Manual, BLM40115 (taxation of long funding leases: exceptional items).

BLM40125 (example of exceptional item).

Amendment—[1] Sections 148A–148J inserted by FA 2006 s 81, Sch 8 paras 12, 13, subject to commencement and transitional provisions in FA 2006 Sch 8 paras 15–27.

[148C Lessor under long funding finance lease making termination payment

(1) This section applies for the purpose of calculating the profits of a person carrying on a trade for a period of account if he is or has been the lessor under a long funding finance lease.

(2) Where—

    (*a*) the lease terminates, and

    (*b*) a sum calculated by reference to the termination value is paid to the lessee,

no deduction in respect of the sum paid to the lessee is allowed in calculating the profits of the person.

(3) This section does not prevent a deduction in respect of a sum to the extent that the sum is brought into account in determining the person's rental earnings.][1]

Commentary—*Simon's Taxes* **B5.406.**

HMRC Manuals—Business Leasing Manual, BLM40130 (taxation of long funding leases: termination of a finance lease).

Amendment—[1] Sections 148A–148J inserted by FA 2006 s 81, Sch 8 paras 12, 13, subject to commencement and transitional provisions in FA 2006 Sch 8 paras 15–27.

[Lessors under long funding operating leases

148D Lessor under long funding operating lease: periodic deduction
(1) This section applies if a person carrying on a trade is the lessor of any plant or machinery under a long funding operating lease for the whole or part of a period of account.
(2) A deduction is allowed in calculating the profits of the person for the period of account for income tax purposes.
(3) The amount of the deduction is so much of the expected gross reduction in value over the term of the lease as is attributable to the period of account.
(4) The expected gross reduction in value over the term of the lease is—
  (*a*) the starting value of the plant or machinery, less
  (*b*) the amount which at the commencement of the term of the lease is expected to be its residual value (or, if section 148DB applies, would have been expected to be that value had that value been estimated at that time).
(5) The expected gross reduction in value over the term of the lease that is attributable to the period of account is found by apportioning that reduction on a time basis according to the proportion of the term of the lease that falls in the period of account.
(6) For the meaning of "starting value", see—
  (*a*) section 148DA ("starting value": general), and
  (*b*) section 148DB ("starting value" where plant or machinery originally unqualifying).
(7) For the meaning of "residual value", see section 148J(2).][1]
Commentary—*Simon's Taxes* B5.407, B5.409.
HMRC Manuals—Business Leasing Manual BLM24320 (defining long funding leases: depreciation policy of operating leases, with examples).
BLM41005 (taxation of long funding leases: basic rules for taxing lessors under long funding operating leases).
BLM41010 (relevant value).
BLM41015 (example of periodic deduction).
Amendments—[1] Section 148D substituted by CTA 2010 s 1177, Sch 1 paras 444, 447. CTA 2010 has effect for corporation tax purposes for accounting periods ending on or after 1 April 2010, and for income and capital gains tax purposes for the tax year 2010–11 and subsequent tax years.

[148DA "Starting value": general
(1) This section is about the meaning of "starting value" in section 148D in relation to a long funding operating lease ("the section 148D lease").
(2) But this section does not apply if the conditions in section 148DB(2) ("starting value" where plant or machinery originally unqualifying) are met.
(3) If the only use of the plant or machinery by the lessor has been the leasing of it under the section 148D lease as a qualifying activity, the starting value is the amount of the expenditure incurred by the lessor on the provision of the plant or machinery ("cost").
(4) If subsection (3) does not apply, the starting value depends on the last previous use of the plant or machinery by the lessor.
(5) If that use was the leasing of it under another long funding operating lease as a qualifying activity, the starting value is the market value of the plant or machinery at the commencement of the term of the section 148D lease ("market value").
(6) If that use was the leasing of it under a long funding finance lease as a qualifying activity, the starting value is the value at which the plant or machinery is recognised in the books or other finance records of the lessor at the commencement of the term of the section 148D lease.
(7) If that use was for the purposes of a qualifying activity other than leasing under a long funding lease, the starting value is the lower of cost and market value.
(8) For the meaning of "qualifying activity", see section 148J(2).][1]
Commentary—*Simon's Taxes* B5.407, B5.409.
HMRC Manuals—Business Leasing Manual BLM41010 (long funding operating leases: starting value).
Amendments—[1] Sections 148DA–148DB inserted by CTA 2010 s 1177, Sch 1 paras 444, 448. CTA 2010 has effect for corporation tax purposes for accounting periods ending on or after 1 April 2010, and for income and capital gains tax purposes for the tax year 2010–11 and subsequent tax years.

[148DB "Starting value" where plant or machinery originally unqualifying
(1) This section applies if the conditions in subsection (2) are met in relation to a long funding operating lease to which section 148D applies.
(2) The conditions are that—
  (*a*) the lessor owns the plant or machinery as a result of having incurred expenditure on its provision for purposes other than those of a qualifying activity,
  (*b*) the plant or machinery is brought into use by the lessor for the purposes of a qualifying activity on or after 1 April 2006, and
  (*c*) that qualifying activity is the leasing of the plant or machinery under the lease.
(3) For the purposes of section 148D the starting value is the lower of—
  (*a*) first use market value, and
  (*b*) first use amortised market value.

(4) "First use market value" means the market value of the plant or machinery at the time when it is first brought into use for the purposes of the qualifying activity.

(5) "First use amortised value" means the value that the plant or machinery would have at the time when it is first brought into use for the purposes of the qualifying activity on the assumptions in subsection (6).

(6) The assumptions are that—

(a) the cost of acquiring the plant or machinery had been written off on a straight line basis over its remaining useful economic life, and

(b) any further capital expenditure incurred had been written off on a straight line basis over so much of its remaining economic life as remains at the time when the expenditure is incurred.

(7) For the meaning of "qualifying activity", "remaining useful economic life" and writing off on a straight line basis, see section 148J(2), section 148J(4) (and section 70YI of CAA 2001 as applied by that section) and section 148J(3) respectively.][1]

Commentary—*Simon's Taxes* **B5.409.**

HMRC Manuals—Business Leasing Manual BLM41010 (starting value: plant or machinery originally non-qualifying).

Amendments—[1]   Sections 148DA–148DB inserted by CTA 2010 s 1177, Sch 1 paras 444, 448. CTA 2010 has effect for corporation tax purposes for accounting periods ending on or after 1 April 2010, and for income and capital gains tax purposes for the tax year 2010–11 and subsequent tax years.

[148E   Long funding operating lease: lessor's additional expenditure

(1) This section applies if in any period of account—

(a) a person carrying on a trade is the lessor of any plant or machinery under a long funding operating lease,

(b) the person incurs capital expenditure in relation to the plant or machinery (the "additional expenditure"), and

(c) the additional expenditure is not reflected in the market value of the plant or machinery at the commencement time (see subsection (7)).

(2) An additional deduction is allowed in calculating the profits of the person for income tax purposes for each period of account—

(a) which ends after the incurring of the additional expenditure, and

(b) in which the person is the lessor of the plant or machinery under the lease.

(3) The amount of the deduction is so much of the expected reduction in value of the additional expenditure ("the expected reduction") as is attributable to the period of account.

(4) The expected reduction is the amount of the additional expenditure, less the remaining residual value of the plant or machinery resulting from that expenditure.

(5) For how to determine that remaining residual value, see—

(a) section 148EA (determination of remaining residual value resulting from lessor's first additional expenditure), and

(b) section 148EB (determination of remaining residual value resulting from lessor's further additional expenditure).

(6) The amount of the expected reduction attributable to the period of account is found by apportioning that reduction on a time basis according to the proportion of the term of the lease that falls in the period of account.

(7) In this section "the commencement time" means—

(a) except where section 148DB applies, the commencement of the term of the lease, and

(b) if that section applies, the time when the plant or machinery is first brought into use by the lessor for the purposes of the qualifying activity.][1]

Commentary—*Simon's Taxes* **B5.407.**

HMRC Manuals—Business Leasing Manual, BLM41020 (example of additional capital expenditure).

Amendments—[1]   Section 148E substituted by CTA 2010 s 1177, Sch 1 paras 444, 449. CTA 2010 has effect for corporation tax purposes for accounting periods ending on or after 1 April 2010, and for income and capital gains tax purposes for the tax year 2010–11 and subsequent tax years.

[148EA   Determination of remaining residual value resulting from lessor's first additional expenditure

(1) This section sets out how the remaining residual value of the plant or machinery resulting from the additional expenditure ("RRV") is determined for the purposes of section 148E(4) if section 148E has not applied in relation to any previous additional expenditure incurred by the person in relation to the leased plant or machinery.

(2) RRV depends on whether—

(a) the amount ("ARV") which is expected to be the residual value of the plant or machinery at the time when the additional expenditure is incurred, exceeds

(b) the amount ("CRV") which at the commencement of the term of the lease is expected to be its residual value (or, if section 148DB applies, would have been expected to be that value had that value been estimated at that time).

(3) If ARV exceeds CRV, RRV is the part of the excess that is a result of the additional expenditure.

(4) Otherwise, RRV is nil.

(5) For the meaning of "residual value", see section 148J(2).][1]

Commentary—*Simon's Taxes* **B5.407**.
HMRC Manuals—Business Leasing Manual BLM41020 (long funding lease: determination of remaining residual value resulting from lessor's first additional expenditure).
Amendments—[1] Sections 148EA–148EB inserted by CTA 2010 s 1177, Sch 1 paras 444, 450. CTA 2010 has effect for corporation tax purposes for accounting periods ending on or after 1 April 2010, and for income and capital gains tax purposes for the tax year 2010–11 and subsequent tax years.

[148EB Determination of remaining residual value resulting from lessor's further additional expenditure

(1) This section sets out how the remaining residual value of the plant or machinery resulting from the additional expenditure ("RRV") is determined for the purposes of section 148E(4) if section 148E has applied in relation to previous additional expenditure incurred by the person in relation to the leased plant or machinery.

(2) RRV depends on whether—
    (*a*) the amount which is expected to be the residual value of the plant or machinery at the time when the further additional expenditure is incurred ("FARV"), exceeds
    (*b*) the sum of the amounts in subsection (3).

(3) Those amounts are—
    (*a*) the amount which at the commencement of the term of the lease is expected to be the residual value of the plant or machinery (or, if section 148DB applies, would have been expected to be that value had that value been estimated at that time), and
    (*b*) any amounts that were subtracted under section 148E(4) as the remaining residual value of the plant or machinery resulting from the previous additional expenditure.

(4) If FARV exceeds the sum of the amounts in subsection (3), RRV is the portion of the excess that is a result of the further additional expenditure.

(5) Otherwise, RRV is nil.

(6) For the meaning of "residual value", see section 148J(2).][1]

Commentary—*Simon's Taxes* **B5.407**.
HMRC Manuals—Business Leasing Manual BLM41020 (long funding lease: determination of remaining residual value resulting from lessor's further additional expenditure).
Amendments—[1] Sections 148EA–148EB inserted by CTA 2010 s 1177, Sch 1 paras 444, 450. CTA 2010 has effect for corporation tax purposes for accounting periods ending on or after 1 April 2010, and for income and capital gains tax purposes for the tax year 2010–11 and subsequent tax years.

[148F Lessor under long funding operating lease: termination of lease

(1) This section applies in calculating for income tax purposes the profits of a person carrying on a trade if the person is the lessor immediately before the termination of a long funding operating lease.

(2) If the termination amount exceeds the sum of the amounts in subsection (3), an amount equal to the excess is treated as income of the person attributable to the lease arising in the period of account in which it terminates.

(3) The amounts referred to in subsection (2) are—
    (*a*) the total amounts paid to the lessee that are calculated by reference to the termination value,
    (*b*) the excess relevant value for section 148D (see subsection (6)), and
    (*c*) the excess expenditure for section 148E (see subsection (7)).

(4) If the sum of the amounts in subsection (3) exceeds the termination amount, the excess is treated as a revenue expense incurred by the person in connection with the lease in the period of account in which it terminates.

(5) No deduction is allowed in respect of any sums within subsection (3)(*a*).

(6) "The excess relevant value for section 148D" is the amount (if any) by which—
    (*a*) the starting value of the plant or machinery for the purposes of section 148D(4) (lessor under long funding operating lease: periodic deduction), exceeds
    (*b*) the total of the deductions allowable under section 148D for periods of account for the whole or part of which the person was the lessor.

(7) "The excess expenditure for section 148E" is the amount (if any) by which—
    (*a*) the total of any amounts of capital expenditure incurred by the person which constitute additional expenditure in the case of the lease for the purposes of section 148E (long funding operating lease: lessor's additional expenditure), exceeds
    (*b*) the total of any deductions allowable under section 148E for periods of account for the whole or part of which the person was the lessor.

(8) For the meaning of "termination amount" and "termination value", see sections 70YG and 70YH of CAA 2001 (as applied by section 148J(4)).][1]

Commentary—*Simon's Taxes* **B5.407**.
HMRC Manuals—Business Leasing Manual, BLM24325 (defining long funding leases: profits and losses on termination of an operating lease).
BLM24330 (valuation policy of operating leases).
BLM41035 (taxation of long funding leases: termination of long funding operating leases).
BLM41040 (example of lease terminating as expected).

BLM41045 (example of lease terminating early).
BLM41050 (the termination amount).
Amendments—[1] Section 148F substituted by CTA 2010 s 1177, Sch 1 paras 444, 451. CTA 2010 has effect for corporation tax purposes for accounting periods ending on or after 1 April 2010, and for income and capital gains tax purposes for the tax year 2010–11 and subsequent tax years.

[Lessors under long funding finance or operating leases: avoidance etc

148FA Cases where ss 148A to 148F do not apply: plant or machinery held as trading stock
(1) Sections 148A to 148F do not apply in the case of a person carrying on a trade who is or has been the lessor of any plant or machinery under a long funding lease if the following condition is met.
(2) The condition is that any part of the expenditure incurred by the person on the acquisition of the plant or machinery for leasing under the lease—
 (*a*) is (apart from those sections) allowable as a deduction in calculating the profits or losses of the trade, and
 (*b*) is so allowable as a result of the plant or machinery forming part of the trading stock of the trade.
(3) For the purposes of this section the cases in which expenditure incurred by a person carrying on a trade on the acquisition of any plant or machinery for leasing under a lease is allowable as such a deduction include any case where—
 (*a*) the person becomes entitled to the deduction at any time after the expenditure is incurred, and
 (*b*) the deduction arises as a result of the plant or machinery forming part of the trading stock of the trade at that time.
(4) If—
 (*a*) at any time any of sections 148A to 148F has applied for determining the amounts to be taken into account in calculating the profits or losses of the trade, and
 (*b*) the condition in subsection (2) is met at any subsequent time,
those amounts, and any other amounts which (as a result of this section) are to be so taken into account, are subject to such adjustments as are just and reasonable.
(5) All such assessments and adjustments of assessments are to be made as are necessary to give effect to subsection (4).][1]
Commentary—*Simon's Taxes* **B5.409A.**
HMRC Manuals—Business Leasing Manual BLM63040 (long funding lease / non long funding lease interaction: plant and machinery leasing anti-avoidance: plant or machinery held as trading stock).
Amendments—[1] Section 148FA inserted by FA 2008 s 55, Sch 20 para 10(2) with effect where: (a) expenditure is incurred on or after 9 October 2007, or (b) a person carrying on a trade becomes entitled to a deduction in calculating the profits or losses of the trade as a result of any plant or machinery forming part of the trading stock of the trade on or after that date.

[148FB Cases where ss 148A to 148F do not apply: lessor also lessee under non-long funding lease
(1) This section applies if—
 (*a*) a person is the lessee of any plant or machinery under a lease ("lease A") that is not a long funding lease,
 (*b*) the person enters into a lease ("lease B") of any of that plant or machinery (as lessor), and
 (*c*) lease B is a long funding lease.
(2) Sections 148A to 148F do not apply in relation to lease B.
(3) If by virtue of section 70H of CAA 2001 (tax return by lessee treating lease as long funding lease) lease A becomes a long funding lease (and does not cease to be such a lease), treat this section as never having applied in relation to lease B.][1]
Commentary—*Simon's Taxes* **B5.409A.**
Amendments—[1] Section 148FB inserted by FA 2008 s 55, Sch 20 para 10(3) with effect where the lease mentioned in ITTOIA 2005 s 148FB(1)(*b*) is entered into on or after 13 December 2007.

[148FC Cases where ss 148A to 148F do not apply: other avoidance
(1) Sections 148A to 148F do not apply in the case of a person carrying on a trade who is or has been the lessor of any plant or machinery under a long funding lease if conditions A to C are met.
(2) Condition A is that the long funding lease forms part of any arrangement entered into by the person which includes one or more other transactions (whether the arrangement is entered into before or after or at the inception of the lease).
(3) Condition B is that the main purpose, or one of the main purposes, of the arrangement is to secure that, over the relevant period, there would be a substantial difference between—
 (*a*) the total amount of the amounts under the arrangement which are, in accordance with generally accepted accounting practice, recognised in determining the profit or loss of the trade for any period or taken into account in calculating the amounts which are so recognised, and
 (*b*) the total amount of the amounts under the arrangement which are taken into account in calculating the profits or losses of the trade.
(4) For the purposes of condition B "the relevant period" means the period which begins with the inception of the lease and ends with the end of the term of the lease.

(5) Condition C is that the difference would be attributable (wholly or partly) to the application of any of sections 148A to 148F in relation to the person by reference to the plant or machinery under the lease.

(6) The reference in this section to an amount being recognised in determining the profit or loss of a trade for a period is to an amount being recognised for accounting purposes—

    (*a*) in the profit and loss account or income statement relating to the trade,

    (*b*) in the statement of recognised gains and losses or statement of changes in equity relating to the trade, or

    (*c*) in any other statement of items brought into account in calculating the profits and losses of the trade for that period.

(7) For the purposes of this section it does not matter whether the parties to any transaction which forms part of the arrangement differ from the parties to any of the other transactions.

(8) For the purposes of this section the cases in which two or more transactions are to be taken as forming part of an arrangement include any case in which it would be reasonable to assume that one or more of them—

    (*a*) would not have been entered into independently of the other or others, or

    (*b*) if entered into independently of the other or others, would not have taken the same form or been on the same terms.

(9) If—

    (*a*) at any time any of sections 148A to 148F has applied for determining the amounts to be taken into account in calculating the profits or losses of the trade, and

    (*b*) conditions A to C are met at any subsequent time,

those amounts, and any other amounts which (as a result of this section) are to be so taken into account, are subject to such adjustments as are just and reasonable.

(10) All such assessments and adjustments of assessments are to be made as are necessary to give effect to subsection (9).][1]

Commentary—*Simon's Taxes* **B5.409A.**

HMRC Manuals—Business Leasing Manual BLM41066 (long funding lease: anti-avoidance provisions).

Amendments—[1]   Section 148FB inserted by FA 2008 s 55, Sch 20 para 10(4) with effect in relation to arrangements entered into on or after 9 October 2007.

[148FD Cases where ss 148A to 148F do not apply: films

(1) If a person is or has been a lessor under a long funding lease of a film, sections 148A to 148F do not apply in respect of the lease.

(2) "Film" has the same meaning as in Part 15 of the Corporation Tax Act 2009 (see section 1181 of that Act).][1]

Commentary—*Simon's Taxes* **B5.409A.**

HMRC Manuals—Business Leasing Manual BLM41070 (anti-avoidance provisions: lessor under a long funding lease of a film).

Amendments—[1]   Section 148FD inserted by FA 2009 s 65, Sch 33 para 2 with effect where the inception of the long funding lease is on or after 13 November 2008 ("the relevant date").

[Lessees under long funding finance leases

148G Lessee under long funding finance lease: limit on deductions

(1) This section applies for the purpose of calculating the profits of a person carrying on a trade, profession or vocation for a period of account in which the person is the lessee of any plant or machinery under a long funding finance lease.

(2) In calculating the person's profits for the period of account,—

    (*a*) the amount deducted in respect of amounts payable under the lease,

must not exceed

    (*b*) the amounts which, in accordance with generally accepted accounting practice, fall (or would fall) to be shown in the person's accounts as finance charges[, or interest expenses,][2] in respect of the lease.

(3) If the lease is one which, under generally accepted accounting practice, falls (or would fall) to be treated as a loan, subsection (2) applies as if the lease were one which, under generally accepted accounting practice, fell to be treated as a finance lease.][1]

Commentary—*Simon's Taxes* **B5.408.**

HMRC Manuals—Business Leasing Manual BLM42030 (taxation of long funding leases: limit on lease rental deductions for long funding finance lessee).

Amendment—[1]   Sections 148A–148J inserted by FA 2006 s 81, Sch 8 paras 12, 13, subject to commencement and transitional provisions in FA 2006 Sch 8 paras 15–27.

[2]   Words in sub-s (2) inserted by FA 2019 s 36, Sch 14 para 2(1), (2) with effect in relation to periods of account beginning on or after 1 January 2019.

[148GA Lessee under long funding finance leases: right-of-use leases

(1) This section applies if—

    (*a*) for the whole or part of any period of account, a person carrying on a trade, profession or vocation is the lessee of any plant or machinery under a right-of-use lease that is a long funding finance lease, (*b*) there is a change in the amounts payable under the lease, and

(*c*) as a result of the change and in accordance with generally accepted accounting practice—

    (i) a remeasurement of the lease liability is shown in the person's accounts for the period of account, or

    (ii) a deduction is shown in those accounts other than as an interest expense under the lease or an amount of depreciation, or an impairment, in respect of the right-of-use asset arising from the lease.

(2) In calculating the profits of the person's trade, vocation or profession for the period of account, the amount deducted in respect of amounts payable under the lease (after taking account of any limitation as a result of section 148G) is to be increased or decreased so as to take account of the remeasurement or deduction mentioned in subsection (1)(*c*).

(3) No adjustment is to be made under subsection (2) if the remeasurement or deduction results in the person being treated by section 70D of CAA 2001 (long funding finance lease: additional expenditure: allowances for lessee) as having incurred further capital expenditure on the provision of the plant or machinery.][1]

Commentary—*Simon's Taxes* **B5.408**.

Amendments—[1] Section 148GA inserted by FA 2019 s 36, Sch 14 para 2(1), (3) with effect in relation to periods of account beginning on or after 1 January 2019.

[148H Lessee under long funding finance lease: termination

(1) This section applies where—

(*a*) a person carrying on a trade, profession or vocation is or has been the lessee under a long funding finance lease, and

(*b*) in connection with the termination of the lease, a payment calculated by reference to the termination value falls to be made to the person.

(2) The payment is not to be brought into account in calculating the profits of the person for any period of account.

(3) Subsection (2) does not affect the amount of any disposal value that falls to be brought into account by the person under CAA 2001.][1]

Commentary—*Simon's Taxes* **B5.408**.

HMRC Manuals—Business Leasing Manual BLM42035 (taxation of long funding leases: termination for lessee of long funding finance lease, with example).

Amendment—[1] Sections 148A–148J inserted by FA 2006 s 81, Sch 8 paras 12, 13, subject to commencement and transitional provisions in FA 2006 Sch 8 paras 15–27.

[Lessees under long funding operating leases

148I Lessee under long funding operating lease

(1) This section applies for the purpose of calculating the profits of a person carrying on a trade, profession or vocation for a period of account in which the person is the lessee of any plant or machinery under a long funding operating lease.

(2) The deductions that may be allowed in calculating the profits of the person for the period of account are to be reduced in accordance with the following provisions of this section.

(3) The amount of the reduction for any period of account is to be determined as follows.

(4) First, find the "relevant value" for the purposes of subsection (6)(*a*), which is—

(*a*) the market value of the plant or machinery at the commencement of the term of the lease, unless paragraph (*b*) applies;

(*b*) if the lessee—

    (i) owns the plant or machinery as a result of having incurred expenditure on its provision for purposes other than those of a qualifying activity, but

    (ii) brings the plant or machinery into use for the purposes of a qualifying activity on or after 1st April 2006,

the lower of first use market value and first use amortised market value.

(5) In subsection (4)—

"first use amortised market value" means the value that the plant or machinery would have—

    (*a*) at the time when it is first brought into use for the purposes of the qualifying activity, but

    (*b*) on the assumption that the market value of the plant or machinery at the commencement of the term of the lease had been written off on a straight line basis over the remaining useful economic life of the plant or machinery;

"first use market value" means the market value of the plant or machinery at the time when it is first brought into use for the purposes of the qualifying activity.

(6) From—

    (*a*) the relevant value determined in accordance with subsection (4),

subtract

    (*b*) the amount which, at the commencement of the term of the lease, is (or, in a case falling within subsection (4)(*b*), would have been) expected to be the market value of the plant or machinery at the end of the term of the lease, to find the expected gross reduction over the term of the lease.

(7) Apportion the amount of that expected gross reduction to each period of account in which any part of the term of the lease falls.

(8) The apportionment must be on a time basis according to the proportion of the term of the lease that falls in each period of account.

(9) The amount of the reduction for any period of account is the amount so apportioned to that period.][1]

Commentary—*Simon's Taxes* **B5.409, B3.340Y.**

HMRC Manuals—Business Leasing Manual BLM42040 (taxation of long funding leases: limit on deductions for long funding operating lessee, with example).

Amendment—[1]   Sections 148A–148J inserted by FA 2006 s 81, Sch 8 paras 12, 13, subject to commencement and transitional provisions in FA 2006 Sch 8 paras 15–27.

[Interpretation of this Chapter

148J Interpretation of Chapter 10A

(1) This section has effect for the interpretation of this Chapter.

(2) In this Chapter—

   "qualifying activity" has the same meaning as in Part 2 of CAA 2001;

   "residual value", in relation to any plant or machinery leased under a long funding operating lease, means—

   (a) the estimated market value of the plant or machinery on a disposal at the end of the term of the lease, less

   (b) the estimated costs of that disposal.

(3) Any reference in this Chapter to a sum being written off on a straight line basis over a period of time (the "writing-off period") is a reference to—

   (a) the sum being apportioned between each of the periods of account in which any part of the writing-off period falls,

   (b) that apportionment being made on a time basis, according to the proportion of the writing-off period that falls in each of the periods of account, and

   (c) the sum being written off accordingly.

(4) Chapter 6A of Part 2 of CAA 2001 (interpretation of that Part so far as relating to long funding leases) also applies for the purposes of this Chapter.][1]

Commentary—*Simon's Taxes* **B5.407, B5.405, B5.406.**

Amendment—[1]   Sections 148A–148J inserted by FA 2006 s 81, Sch 8 paras 12, 13, subject to commencement and transitional provisions in FA 2006 Sch 8 paras 15–27.

CHAPTER 11

TRADE PROFITS: OTHER SPECIFIC TRADES

[Cash basis accounting

148K Application of Chapter to the cash basis

The following sections do not apply in calculating the profits of a trade, profession or vocation on the cash basis—

   sections 149 to 154A (dealers in securities etc),

   section 157 (relief in respect of mineral royalties),

   section 158 (lease premiums etc: reduction of receipts),

   section 159 (ministers of religion),

   section 161 (mineral exploration and access),

   section 162 (payments by persons liable to pool betting duty),

   sections 163 and 164 (intermediaries treated as making employment payments),

   section 164A (managed service companies),

   sections 165 to 168 (waste disposal),

   sections 169 to 172ZE (cemeteries and crematoria).][1]

Commentary—*Simon's Taxes* **B5.601, B2.101B.**

HMRC Manuals—Business Income Manual BIM70010 (cash basis: eligibility).

Amendments—[1]   This section inserted by FA 2013 s 17, Sch 4 para 28 with effect for the tax year 2013–14 and subsequent tax years, subject to the provisions of FA 2013 Sch 4 para 57 in relation to barristers and advocates.

Dealers in securities etc

149 Taxation of amounts taken to reserves

(1) This section applies for the purpose of calculating the profits of a person's trade if a profit on the sale of securities would be brought into account in calculating the profits of the trade.

(2) Profits and losses from the securities that in accordance with generally accepted accounting practice are—

   (a) calculated by reference to the fair value of the securities, and (*b*) recognised in the person's statement of recognised gains and losses or statement of changes in equity,

are brought into account in calculating the profits of the trade.

(3) But subsection (2) does not apply—

    (*a*) to an amount so far as deriving from or otherwise relating to an amount brought into account under that subsection in an earlier period of account, or

    (*b*) to an amount recognised for accounting purposes by way of correction of a fundamental error.

(4) In this section "securities" includes—

    (*a*) shares,

    (*b*) rights of unit holders in unit trust schemes to which TCGA 1992 applies as a result of section 99 of TCGA 1992,

    [(*ba*) rights of participants [in schemes or funds to which TCGA 1992 applies as a result of section 103D of TCGA 1992,]²

    (*c*) in the case of a company with no share capital, interests in the company possessed by members of the company,

but does not include a loan relationship (within the meaning of Chapter 2 of Part 4 of FA 1996).

Commentary—*Simon's Taxes* **B5.628, B2.607.**

HMRC Manuals—Corporate Finance Manual CFM51040 (derivative contracts: bringing amounts into account: basic computational rule).

Amendments—¹   Sub-s (4)(*ba*) inserted by FA 2009 s 44, Sch 22 para 11(3)(*a*) with effect in relation to the acquisition, holding and disposal of rights in a relevant offshore fund on or after the commencement day, subject to transitional provisions and modifications in FA 2009 paras 13–18. The "commencement day" means: (a) in relation to the acquisition, holding and disposal of rights by a person subject to the charge to capital gains tax, 1 December 2009, and (b) in relation to the acquisition, holding and disposal of rights by a person subject to the charge to corporation tax, such day as the Treasury may by order appoint.

²   In sub-s (4)(*ba*), words substituted for words "in certain offshore funds to which TCGA 1992 applies as a result of section 103A of TCGA 1992, and", by the Collective Investment Schemes and Offshore Funds (Amendment of the Taxation of Chargeable Gains Act 1992) Regulations, SI 2017/1204 regs 2, 11(*a*) with effect in relation to disposals on or after 1 January 2018.

150 Conversion etc of securities held as circulating capital

(1) This section applies for the purpose of calculating the profits of a trade if—

    (*a*) a transaction falling within subsection (2) occurs in relation to securities ("the original holding"), and

    (*b*) a profit on the sale of the securities would be brought into account in calculating the profits of the trade.

(2) A transaction falls within this subsection if—

    (*a*) it results in a new holding being treated as the same as the original holding as a result of sections 126 to 136 of TCGA 1992 (CGT roll-over relief in cases of conversion etc), or

    (*b*) it is treated, as a result of section 134 of TCGA 1992 (compensation stock), as an exchange for a new holding which does not involve a disposal of the original holding,

and it does not fall within section 151(1) or 152(1) below (exchanges of gilts for gilt strips and consolidation of gilt strips).

(3) This section does not apply to securities in respect of which unrealised profits or losses, calculated by reference to the fair value of the securities at the end of the period of account, are taken into account in the period of account in which the transaction occurs.

(4) The transaction is treated as not involving a disposal of the original holding and the new holding is treated as the same asset as the original holding.

(5) But if, under the transaction, the person carrying on the trade—

    (*a*) receives consideration in addition to the new holding, or

    (*b*) becomes entitled to receive such consideration,

subsection (4) applies as if the references to the original holding were to the proportion of the original holding given by the following fraction.

(6) The fraction is—

$$\frac{NH}{NH + C}$$

where—

    NH is the market value of the new holding at the time of the transaction, and

    C is the market value of the consideration at the time of the transaction or (if the consideration is cash) the amount of the consideration.

(7) In determining whether subsection (2)(*a*) applies as a result of section 135 or 136 of TCGA 1992, the reference to capital gains tax in section 137(1) of TCGA 1992 is to be read as a reference to income tax.

(8) In this section "securities" includes—

  (*a*) shares,

  (*b*) loan stocks or similar securities (whether secured or unsecured) of a government, a local or other public authority (in the United Kingdom or elsewhere) or a company,

  (*c*) rights of unit holders in unit trust schemes to which TCGA 1992 applies as a result of section 99 of TCGA 1992,

  [(*ca*) rights of participants [in schemes or funds to which TCGA 1992 applies as a result of section 103D of TCGA 1992,]²

  (*d*) in the case of a company with no share capital, interests in the company possessed by members of the company,

  (*e*) quoted options to subscribe for shares which are treated as shares as a result of section 147 of TCGA 1992, and

  (*f*) earn-out rights which are assumed to be securities as a result of section 138A(3) of TCGA 1992.

Commentary—*Simon's Taxes* **B5.628, B2.607.**
Amendments—¹   Sub-s (8)(*ca*) inserted by FA 2009 s 44, Sch 22 para 11(3)(*b*) with effect in relation to the acquisition, holding and disposal of rights in a relevant offshore fund on or after the commencement day, subject to transitional provisions and modifications in FA 2009 paras 13–18. The commencement day" means—

  (a)   in relation to the acquisition, holding and disposal of rights by a person subject to the charge to capital gains tax, 1 December 2009, and

  (b)   in relation to the acquisition, holding and disposal of rights by a person subject to the charge to corporation tax, such day as the Treasury may by order appoint.

²   In sub-s (8)(*ca*) words substituted for words "in certain offshore funds to which TCGA 1992 applies as a result of section 103A of TCGA 1992", by the Collective Investment Schemes and Offshore Funds (Amendment of the Taxation of Chargeable Gains Act 1992) Regulations, SI 2017/1204 regs 2, 11(*b*) with effect in relation to disposals on or after 1 January 2018.

151 Exchanges of gilts for gilt strips

(1) This section applies for the purpose of calculating the profits of a trade if—

  (*a*) the person carrying it on ("the trader") exchanges a gilt-edged security for strips of the security, and

  (*b*) a profit on the sale of the security would be brought into account in calculating the profits of the trade.

(2) The security is treated as having been redeemed at the time of the exchange by the payment to the trader of its market value.

(3) The trader is treated as having acquired each strip for the proportion of the market value of the security given by the following fraction.

(4) The fraction is—

$$\frac{SV}{TV}$$

where—

  SV is the market value of one strip, and

  TV is the total of the market values of all the strips received in exchange for the security.

(5) In this section references to market value are to market value at the time of the exchange.

(6) This section applies to professions and vocations as it applies to trades.

(7) See also—

  section 153 (meaning of "gilt-edged security" and "strip"), and

  section 154 (regulations for determining market value of securities or strips).

Commentary—*Simon's Taxes* **B5.628.**
Derivation—TA 1988 s 730C; FA 1996 Sch 40 para 7.
HMRC Manuals—Savings and Investment Manual SAIM4250 (special types of transfer: gilt strips).

152 Consolidation of gilt strips

(1) This section applies for the purpose of calculating the profits of a trade if—

  (*a*) strips of a gilt-edged security are consolidated into a single security by being exchanged by the person carrying on the trade ("the trader") for the single security, and

  (*b*) a profit on the sale of any of the strips would be brought into account in calculating the profits of the trade.

(2) Each strip is treated as having been redeemed at the time of the exchange by payment to the trader of its market value.

(3) The trader is treated as having acquired the gilt-edged security for an amount equal to the total of the market values of the strips given in exchange.

(4) In this section references to market value are to market value at the time of the exchange.

(5) This section applies to professions and vocations as it applies to trades.

(6) See also—

  section 153 (meaning of "gilt-edged security" and "strip"), and section 154 (regulations for determining market value of securities or strips).

Commentary—*Simon's Taxes* **B5.628.**
Derivation—TA 1988 s 730C; FA 1996 Sch 40 para 7.
HMRC Manuals—Savings and Investment Manual SAIM3130 (taxation of government strips).

153 Meaning of "gilt-edged security" and "strip"

(1) In this Act "gilt-edged security" means a security which—

(a) is a gilt-edged security for the purposes of TCGA 1992 (see Schedule 9 to that Act), or

(b) will be such a security on the making of an order under paragraph 1 of Schedule 9 to TCGA 1992, if the making of the order is anticipated in the prospectus under which the security is issued.

(2) For the purposes of sections 151 and 152 "strip", in relation to a gilt-edged security, means a security issued under the National Loans Act 1968 (c 13) which meets conditions A to C.

(3) Condition A is that the security is issued for the purpose of representing the right to or of securing—

(a) a payment corresponding to a payment of interest or principal remaining to be made under the gilt-edged security, or

(b) two or more payments each corresponding to a payment to be so made.

(4) Condition B is that the security is issued in conjunction with the issue of one or more other securities which, together with that security—

(a) represent the right to, or

(b) secure,

payments corresponding to every payment remaining to be made under the gilt-edged security.

(5) Condition C is that the security is not itself a security which—

(a) represents the right to, or

(b) secures,

payments corresponding to a part of every payment remaining to be made under the gilt-edged security.

Commentary—*Simon's Taxes* **B5.628, A1.158.**
HMRC Manuals—Corporate Finance Manual CFM37110 (gilt-edged securities: overview).

154 Regulations for determining market value of securities or strips

(1) The Treasury may by regulations make provision for the purposes of sections 151 and 152 as to the manner of determining the market value at any time of a gilt-edged security (including any strip).

(2) The regulations may—

(a) make different provision for different cases, and

(b) contain such incidental, supplemental, consequential and transitional provision as the Treasury consider appropriate.

(3) The power in this section does not affect the power under section 202(5) of FA 1996 (gilt stripping).

Commentary—*Simon's Taxes* **B5.628.**
Derivation—TA 1988 s 730C(6), (7); FA 1996 Sch 40 para 7.
HMRC Manuals—Savings and Investment Manual SAIM3140 (meaning of market value).

[154A Certain non-UK residents with interest on 3¹/₂% War Loan 1952 Or After

(1) This section applies if—

(a) in any tax year a person who is not . . . [2] resident in the United Kingdom carries on a trade there—

(i) consisting of banking or insurance, or

(ii) consisting wholly or partly of dealing in securities, and

(b) in calculating the profits of the trade for the tax year any amount is disregarded as a result of section 714 (exemption of profits from FOTRA securities) because of a condition subject to which any 3¹/₂% War Loan 1952 Or After was issued.

(2) Interest on money borrowed for the purposes of the trade is to be deducted in calculating the profits of the trade of that tax year only so far as it exceeds the ineligible amount.

(3) The ineligible amount is found as follows—

Step 1

Add together all sums borrowed for the purposes of the trade and still owing in the basis period for the tax year.

Step 2

If the person carrying on the trade is a company, deduct any sums carrying interest which is not deducted in calculating the profits of the trade (otherwise than because of subsection (2)).

Step 3

If the amount found at Step 2 exceeds the total cost of the 3¹/₂% War Loan 1952 Or After held for the purposes of the trade in the basis period, deduct the excess from that amount.

Step 4
Calculate the average rate of interest in the basis period on money borrowed for the purposes of the trade.
Step 5
Calculate the amount of interest payable on the amount found at Step 3 at the rate found at Step 4 for the basis period.
The result is the ineligible amount.
(4) If the person's holding of $3\frac{1}{2}\%$ War Loan 1952 Or After has fluctuated during the basis period, the total cost for the purposes of Step 3 is taken to be—

C × (AH / TH)

where—

C is the cost of acquisition of the initial holding (if any) and any holdings acquired during the basis period,

AH is the average holding in that period, and

TH is the total of the initial holding (if any) and any holdings acquired during the basis period.

(5) In subsection (4) "initial holding" means the holding held by the person at the beginning of the basis period.][1]

Commentary—*Simon's Taxes* **B5.628.**
Derivation—TA 1988 s 475.
HMRC Manuals—Corporate Finance Manual CFM37170 (31/2% war loan 1952).
Amendments—[1]   This section inserted by TIOPA 2010 s 371, Sch 7 paras 42, 43. TIOPA 2010 has effect for corporation tax purposes for accounting periods ending on or after 1 April 2010, for income and capital gains tax purposes for the tax year 2010–11 and subsequent tax years, and for petroleum revenue tax purposes for chargeable periods beginning on or after 1 July 2010.
[2]   Word "ordinarily" in sub-s (1)(*a*) repealed by FA 2013 s 219, Sch 46 paras 43, 44 with effect for the purposes of a person's liability to income tax for the tax year 2013–14 or any subsequent tax year, subject to savings in FA 2013 Sch 46 para 73.

Persons authorised for purposes of FISMA 2000

155 Levies and repayments under FISMA 2000
(1) This section applies for the purpose of calculating the profits of a trade . . .[1]
[(2) A deduction is allowed for any sum—
    (*a*) spent by the person carrying on the trade in paying a levy, or
    (*b*) paid by that person as a result of an award of costs under costs rules,
so far as it is not otherwise allowable.][1]
(3) A payment made to the person [carrying on the trade][1] as a result of a repayment provision is brought into account as a receipt.
[(3A) For the purposes of this section "costs rules" means—
    (*a*) rules made under section 230 of FISMA 2000, or
    (*b*) provision relating to costs contained in standard terms fixed under paragraph 18 of Schedule 17 to FISMA 2000.][1]
(4) For the purposes of this section "levy" means—
    (*a*) a payment required under rules made under section 136(2) of FISMA 2000,
    (*b*) a levy imposed under the Financial Services Compensation Scheme,
    (*c*) a payment required under rules made under section 234 of FISMA 2000,
    (*d*) a payment required under the rules referred to in paragraph 14(1) of Schedule 17 to FISMA 2000 ("scheme rules") in accordance with paragraph 15(1) of that Schedule, or
    (*e*) a payment required in accordance with the standard terms fixed under paragraph 18 of that Schedule [(other than a sum paid as a result of an award of costs under costs rules)][1].
(5) For the purposes of this section "repayment provision" means—
    (*a*) any provision made by virtue of section 136(7) or 214(1)(*e*) of FISMA 2000, or
    (*b*) any provision made by scheme rules for fees to be refunded in specified circumstances.

Commentary—*Simon's Taxes* **B5.632.**
Amendments—[1]   In sub-s (1) words repealed, sub-s (2) substituted, in sub-s (3) words inserted, sub-s (3A) inserted, and in sub-s (4)(*e*) words substituted, by CTA 2009 ss 1322, 1326, Sch 1 paras 587, 601, Sch 3 Part 1. CTA 2009 applies for accounting periods ending on or after 1 April 2009 (for corporation tax purposes) and for tax years 2009–10 onwards (for income and capital gains tax purposes).

Dealers in land etc

156 Purchase or sale of woodlands
(1) This section applies for the purpose of calculating the profits of a trade of dealing in land.
(2) If the person carrying on the trade buys woodlands in the United Kingdom in the course of the trade, the part of the cost of the woodlands which is attributable to trees or saleable underwood growing on the land is ignored.
(3) If—
    (*a*) the woodlands are subsequently sold in the course of the trade, and
    (*b*) any of the trees or underwood are still growing on the land at the time of the sale,

the part of the price that is equal to the amount ignored under subsection (2) for the trees or underwood is ignored.

Commentary—*Simon's Taxes* **B5.627, B2.606.**
HMRC Manuals—Business Income Manual BIM51665 (woodlands: purchase and sale).

158 Lease premiums etc: reduction of receipts

(1) This section applies for the purpose of calculating the profits of a trade of dealing in land if a receipt of the trade falls within one of the following categories—

    (*a*) lease premiums within section 277,
    (*b*) sums within section 279 (sums payable instead of rent),
    (*c*) sums within section 280 (sums payable for surrender of a lease),
    (*d*) sums within section 281 (sums payable for variation or waiver of [terms][1] of lease),
    (*e*) consideration for the assignment of a lease within section 282 (lease granted at an undervalue), and
    (*f*) amounts received on the sale of an estate or interest in land within section 284 (sales with right to re-conveyance) or section 285 (sale and leaseback transactions).

(2) The receipt is reduced by the relevant amount.

(3) The relevant amount is the amount which is treated as a receipt of a property business as a result of any of sections 277 to 285.

(4) But if—

    (*a*) the person carrying on the trade makes a claim under section 301 or 302, and
    (*b*) as a result of the claim a repayment of tax is made to that person,

the relevant amount is the amount which, for the purpose of determining the amount of the repayment of tax, is treated as brought into account as a receipt in calculating the profits of the property business.

(5) If subsection (4) applies, any adjustment of liability to tax may be made—

    (*a*) by assessment or otherwise, and
    (*b*) at any time at which it could be made if it related only to tax for the tax year in which the claim under section 301 or 302 is made.

Commentary—*Simon's Taxes* **B5.627, B5.220.**
Derivation—TA 1988 s 99(2), (3).
HMRC Manuals—Business Income Manual BIM51525 (premiums).
Amendments—[1]   In sub-s (1)(*d*) words substituted by CTA 2009 s 1322, Sch 1 paras 587, 602. CTA 2009 applies for accounting periods ending on or after 1 April 2009 (for corporation tax purposes) and for tax years 2009–10 onwards (for income and capital gains tax purposes).

Ministers of religion

159 Ministers of religion

(1) This section applies for the purpose of calculating the profits of the profession or vocation of a minister of a religious denomination.

(2) If the minister pays rent in respect of a dwelling-house and any part of the dwelling-house is used mainly and substantially for the purposes of the minister's duty, a deduction is allowed for—

    (*a*) one-quarter of the rent, or
    (*b*) if less, the part of the rent that, on a just and reasonable apportionment, is attributable to that part of the dwelling-house.

(3) If—

    (*a*) an interest in premises belongs to a charity or an ecclesiastical corporation,
    (*b*) because of that interest, the minister has a residence in the premises from which to perform the minister's duty, and
    (*c*) the minister incurs expenses on the maintenance, repair, insurance or management of the premises,

a deduction is allowed under this subsection for part of those expenses.

(4) The amount of the deduction under subsection (3) is—

$$\frac{A}{4} - B$$

where—

    A is the amount of the expenses, and
    B is the amount of the expenses for which a deduction is otherwise allowable.

Commentary—*Simon's Taxes* **B5.665.**
HMRC Manuals—Employment Income Manual EIM60044 (ministers of religion: allowable expenses: property expenses).

Mineral exploration and access

161 Mineral exploration and access

(1) This section applies for the purpose of calculating the profits of a trade if—

(*a*) the person carrying on the trade incurs expenditure on mineral exploration and access in an area or group of sands, and

(*b*) the presence of mineral deposits in commercial quantities has already been established in that area or group of sands.

(2) A deduction is allowed for the expenditure only if a deduction would have been allowed for it if the presence of mineral deposits in commercial quantities had not already been established in that area or group of sands.

(3) In this section "mineral exploration and access" has the same meaning as in Part 5 of CAA 2001 (see section 396(1) of that Act).

Commentary—*Simon's Taxes* B5.650, B5.653.
Derivation—TA 1988 s 91C.
HMRC Manuals—Capital Allowance CA50230 (meaning of mineral exploration and access).

Intermediaries treated as making employment payments

163 Deduction for deemed employment payment

(1) This section applies for the purpose of calculating the profits of a trade, profession or vocation carried on by an intermediary who is treated as making a deemed employment payment in connection with the trade, profession or vocation.

(2) A deduction is allowed for—

(*a*) the amount of the deemed employment payment, and

(*b*) the amount of any employer's national insurance contributions paid by the intermediary in respect of it.

(3) The deduction is allowed for the period of account in which the deemed employment payment is treated as made.

(4) No deduction in respect of—

(*a*) the deemed employment payment, or

(*b*) any employer's national insurance contributions paid by the intermediary in respect of it,

may be made except in accordance with this section.

(5) In this section "deemed employment payment" and "intermediary" have the same meaning as in Chapter 8 of Part 2 of ITEPA 2003.

Commentary—*Simon's Taxes* B5.645, E4.1021.
HMRC Manuals—Business Income Manual BIM47225 (specific deductions: staffing costs: deemed employment payments). Employment Status Manual ESM35555 (deduction for deemed employment payment).

164 Special rules for partnerships

(1) This section applies for the purpose of calculating the profits of a trade, profession or vocation carried on by a firm that is treated as making a deemed employment payment in connection with the trade, profession or vocation.

(2) The amount of the deduction allowed under section 163 is limited to the amount that reduces the profits of the firm for the tax year to nil.

(3) The expenses of the firm in connection with the relevant engagements for any period of account are limited to the total of—

(*a*) 5% of the amount taken into account in step 1 of the calculation in section 54(1) of ITEPA 2003 (calculation of deemed employment payment), and

(*b*) the amount deductible in step 3 of that calculation.

(4) In this section "deemed employment payment" and "the relevant engagements" have the same meaning as in Chapter 8 of Part 2 of ITEPA 2003.

Commentary—*Simon's Taxes* B5.645, E4.1021.
HMRC Manuals—Employment Status Manual ESM3201 (how to work out the taxable profits of the intermediary: special rules for partnerships).

[Managed service companies

164A Deduction for deemed employment payments

(1) This section applies for the purpose of calculating the profits of a trade, profession or vocation carried on by a managed service company ("the MSC") which is treated as making a deemed employment payment in connection with the trade, profession or vocation.

(2) A deduction is allowed for—

(*a*) the amount of the deemed employment payment, and

(*b*) the amount of any employer's national insurance contributions paid by the MSC in respect of it.

(3) The deduction is allowed for the period of account in which the deemed employment payment is treated as made.

(4) The amount of the deduction allowed under subsection (2) is limited to the amount that reduces the profits of the firm for the tax year to nil.

(5) No deduction in respect of—

(*a*) the deemed employment payment, or

(*b*) any employer's national insurance contributions paid by the MSC in respect of it, may be made except in accordance with this section.

(6) In this section "deemed employment payment", "employer's national insurance contributions" and "managed service company" have the same meaning as in Chapter 9 of Part 2 of ITEPA 2003.][1]

Commentary—*Simon's Taxes* E4.914.
Amendments—[1] Section and preceding heading inserted by FA 2007 s 25, Sch 3 para 9 with effect from 6 April 2007.

[Worker's services provided to public sector through intermediary

164B Intermediaries providing worker's services to public sector

(1) This section applies for the purposes of calculating the trading profits of a person where—

    (*a*) the person is the intermediary in a chain identified under section 61N of ITEPA 2003 (see section 61N(1)(b)),

    (*b*) a deemed direct payment is treated as made under subsection (3) of that section, and

    (*c*) the person receives a payment which can reasonably be taken to be in respect of the same services as those in respect of which the underlying chain payment is made.

(2) The payment mentioned in subsection (1)(*c*) is not required to be brought into account in calculating the profits of the trade.

(3) In this section "underlying chain payment" means the payment whose amount is used at Step 1 of section 61Q(1) of ITEPA 2003 as the starting point for calculating the amount of the deemed direct payment mentioned in subsection (1)(*b*).][1]

Commentary—*Simon's Taxes* B5.645, E4.1045.
Amendments—[1] Section 164B inserted by FA 2017 s 6, Sch 1 para 13 with effect from 27 April 2017. The payments to which this amendment applies include payments made before 27 April 2017 (the date of Royal Assent to FA 2017).

Waste disposal

165 Deduction for site preparation expenditure

(1) This section applies for the purpose of calculating the profits of a trade of a period of account in which waste materials are deposited on a waste disposal site if—

    (*a*) the person carrying on the trade ("the trader"), or a predecessor, has incurred site preparation expenditure in relation to the site in the course of carrying on the trade, and

    (*b*) at the time the trader first deposits waste materials on the site, the trader holds a waste disposal licence which is then in force.

(2) A deduction is allowed for the amount of the site preparation expenditure allocated to the period of account under section 166.

(3) For the purposes of this section "predecessor", in relation to the trader, means a person who—

    (*a*) has ceased to carry on the trade carried on by the trader or ceased to carry on a trade so far as relating to the site, and

    (*b*) has transferred the whole of the site to the trader,

and it does not matter for this purpose whether or not the estate or interest in the site transferred to the trader is the same as that held by that person.

(4) For the purposes of this section and section 166, if site preparation expenditure has been incurred by a predecessor—

    (*a*) the trade carried on by the trader is treated as the same as the trade carried on by the predecessor, and

    (*b*) deductions are to be allowed to the trader (and not to the predecessor) as if everything done to or by the predecessor were done to or by the trader.

(5) For—

    (*a*) the meaning of "site preparation expenditure", "waste disposal licence" and "waste disposal site", and

    (*b*) a rule about pre-trading expenditure,

see section 167.

Commentary—*Simon's Taxes* B5.672, B2.478.
HMRC Manuals—Business Income Manual BIM67400 (waste disposal: contents).
BIM67465 (conditions).
BIM67520 (entitlement of successor to allowances).

166 Allocation of site preparation expenditure

(1) The amount of site preparation expenditure allocated to a period of account for the purposes of section 165(2) is the amount given by the formula—

$$RE \times \frac{WD}{SV + WD}$$

where—

    RE means residual expenditure (see subsection (2)),

    WD means the volume of waste materials deposited on the waste disposal site during the period, and

SV means the volume of the waste disposal site not used up for the deposit of waste materials at the end of the period.

(2) "Residual expenditure" means the total of all site preparation expenditure incurred by the trader in relation to the waste disposal site at any time before the end of the period, less—

(a) any of that expenditure for which an allowance has been, or may be, made for income or corporation tax purposes under the enactments relating to capital allowances,

(b) any of that expenditure for which a deduction has been allowed in calculating for income or corporation tax purposes the profits of an earlier period of account, and

(c) if the trader started to carry on the trade before 6th April 1989, the excluded amount of any unrelieved old expenditure (see subsections (3) and (4)).

(3) The excluded amount of unrelieved old expenditure is calculated by multiplying the unrelieved old expenditure (see subsection (4)) by the fraction—

$$\frac{WD}{SV + WD}$$

where—

WD means the volume of waste materials deposited on the site before 6th April 1989, and

SV means the volume of the site not used up for the deposit of waste materials immediately before that date.

(4) "Unrelieved old expenditure" means site preparation expenditure which—

(a) was incurred by the trader in relation to the waste disposal site before 6th April 1989, and

(b) does not fall within subsection (2)(a) or (b).

Commentary—*Simon's Taxes* B2.478.
Derivation—TA 1988 s 91B; FA 1990 s 78.
HMRC Manuals—Business Income Manual BIM67480 (calculation of relief).

167 Site preparation expenditure: supplementary

(1) For the purposes of this section and sections 165 and 166—

"site preparation expenditure", in relation to a waste disposal site, means expenditure incurred on preparing the site for the deposit of waste materials,

"waste disposal licence" means—

(a) a disposal licence under Part 1 of the Control of Pollution Act 1974 (c 40) or Part 2 of the Pollution Control and Local Government (Northern Ireland) Order 1978 (SI 1978/1049 (NI 19)),

(b) a waste management licence under Part 2 of the Environmental Protection Act 1990 (c 43) or any corresponding provision for the time being in force in Northern Ireland,

(c) a permit under regulations under section 2 of the Pollution Prevention and Control Act 1999 (c 24) or [a permit or authorisation under any corresponding provision for the time being in force in Northern Ireland or Scotland][2],

(d) . . . [1]

(e) a nuclear site licence under the Nuclear Installations Act 1965 (c 57), and

"waste disposal site" means a site used, or to be used, for the disposal of waste materials by their deposit on the site.

(2) For the purposes of sections 165 and 166, expenditure incurred for the purposes of a trade by a person about to carry on the trade is treated as if it were incurred—

(a) on the date on which the person starts to carry on the trade, and

(b) in the course of carrying it on.

Commentary—*Simon's Taxes* B5.672, B2.478.
HMRC Manuals—Business Income Manual BIM67455 (site preparation expenditure : meaning).
Amendments—[1] In sub-s (1), in definition of "waste disposal licence" para (d) repealed, in relation to England and Wales, by the Environmental Permitting (England and Wales) Regulations SI 2010/675, regs 107, 109(1), Sch 26 para 18, Sch 28 with effect from 6 April 2010.
[2] In sub-s (1), in definition of "waste disposal licence", words in para (c) substituted by the Regulatory Reform (Scotland) Act 2014 (Consequential Modifications) Order, SI 2015/374 art 7 with effect from 26 February 2015.

168 Site restoration payments

(1) This section applies for the purpose of calculating the profits of a trade if the person carrying on the trade makes a site restoration payment in the course of carrying it on.

(2) [Subject to subsection (3A),][1] a deduction is allowed for the unrelieved amount of the payment.

[(3) The deduction is allowed—

(a) (if the payment is made, whether directly or indirectly, to a connected person) for the period of account in which that part of the restoration work to which the payment relates is completed, or

(b) (in any other case) for the period of account in which the payment is made.

(3A) But no deduction is allowed if the payment arises from arrangements—

(a) to which the person carrying on the trade is a party, and (*b*) the main purpose, or one of the main purposes, of which is to obtain a deduction under this section.][1]

(4) The unrelieved amount of a site restoration payment is the amount of the payment, less—

    (*a*) any amount of the payment that represents expenditure for which an allowance has been, or may be, made under the enactments relating to capital allowances, and

    (*b*) any amount of the payment that represents expenditure for which a deduction has been allowed in calculating the profits of the trade of an earlier period of account.

(5) A "site restoration payment" means a payment made in connection with the restoration of a site (or part of a site) in order to comply with—

    (*a*) a condition of a waste disposal licence (as defined in section 167(1)),

    (*b*) a condition imposed on the grant of planning permission to use the site for the collection, treatment, conversion and final depositing of waste materials or for the carrying out of any of those activities, or

    (*c*) a relevant planning obligation.

(6) For this purpose "a relevant planning obligation" means—

    (*a*) an obligation arising under an agreement made under section 106 of the Town and Country Planning Act 1990 (c 8) (as originally enacted) or any corresponding provision for the time being in force in Northern Ireland,

    (*b*) an obligation arising under an agreement made under section 75 of the Town and Country Planning (Scotland) Act 1997 (c 8),

    (*c*) a planning obligation entered into under section 106 of the Town and Country Planning Act 1990 (as substituted by section 12 of the Planning and Compensation Act 1991 (c 34)) or any corresponding provision for the time being in force in Northern Ireland, or

    (*d*) a planning obligation entered into under section 299A of the Town and Country Planning Act 1990 or any corresponding provision for the time being in force in Northern Ireland.

[(7) "Arrangements" includes any agreement, understanding, scheme, transaction or series of transactions (whether or not legally enforceable).][1]

Commentary—*Simon's Taxes* **B5.672, B2.478.**

HMRC Manuals—Business Income Manual BIM67400 (site restoration : content sheet).

Amendments—[1]   Words at the beginning of sub-s (2) and the whole of sub-s (7) inserted, and sub-ss (3), (3A) substituted for previous sub-s (3), by FA 2012 s 53(1)–(3) with effect in relation to any site restoration payment made on or after 21 March 2012, other than a payment made pursuant to an unconditional obligation in a contract made before 21 March 2012. An unconditional obligation is an obligation which may not be varied or extinguished by the exercise of a right (whether or not under the contract): FA 2012 s 53(8).

[Cemeteries and crematoria; interests in land]

169 Cemeteries and crematoria: introduction[1]

(1) This section and sections 170 to 172 apply for the purpose of calculating the profits of a period of account ("the relevant period") of a trade which consists of or includes—

    (*a*) the carrying on of a cemetery, or

    (*b*) the carrying on of a crematorium and, in connection with doing so, the maintenance of memorial garden plots,

and the following provisions of this section apply for the interpretation of this section and those sections.

(2) References to the sale of land in a cemetery include the sale of a right of interment in land in a cemetery.

(3) References to the sale of land in a memorial garden include the appropriation of part of a memorial garden in return for a dedication fee or similar payment.

(4) "Ancillary capital expenditure" means capital expenditure incurred for the purposes of the trade by the person carrying on the trade ("the trader"), or a predecessor, on—

    (*a*) any building or structure (other than a dwelling-house) which is in the cemetery or memorial garden and is likely to have little or no value when the cemetery or memorial garden is full,

    (*b*) the purchase of an interest in, or the preparation of, any land taken up by such a building or structure, or

    (*c*) the purchase of an interest in, or the preparation of, any other land in the cemetery or memorial garden which is not suitable or adaptable for use for interments or memorial garden plots and which is likely to have little or no value when the cemetery or memorial garden is full.

(5) "Predecessor", in relation to the trader, means a person who carried on the trade at any time before the trader started to do so.

(6) "Preparation", in relation to land, means levelling or draining the land or making it suitable in some other way for use as a cemetery or memorial garden.

Commentary—*Simon's Taxes* **B5.620.**

Derivation—TA 1988 s 91.

HMRC Manuals—Business Income Manual BIM52500 (cemeteries and crematoria: contents)

ITTOIA 2005

Amendments—Heading substituted for previous heading "Cemeteries and crematoria", by the Enactment of Extra-Statutory Concessions Order, SI 2012/266 art 4(1), (2) with effect in relation to niches and memorials sold, and inscriptions made, after 1 March 2012.

170 Deduction for capital expenditure

(1) This section applies if, in the relevant period, an interest in land in the cemetery or memorial garden is sold with a view to the land being used—

    (a) for the purpose of interments, or

    (b) for memorial garden plots.

(2) A deduction is allowed for—

    (a) capital expenditure incurred by the trader, or a predecessor, on the purchase of an interest in the land or on the preparation of the land, and

    (b) ancillary capital expenditure allocated to the relevant period under section 171 (allocation of ancillary capital expenditure).

(3) But no expenditure is to be brought into account—

    (a) under both paragraphs (a) and (b) of subsection (2), . . . [2]

    (b) under both subsection (2)(a) above and [section 147(2)(b) of CTA 2009][1] (relief for corporation tax purposes) or under both subsection (2)(b) above and [section 147(2)(a) of CTA 2009][1], [or

    (c) under both subsection (2)(b) above and section 172ZB(4), 172ZC(4) or 172ZD(3).][2]

whether for the same or different periods of account.

(4) Any purchase price paid on a sale in connection with a change in the persons carrying on the trade is ignored in calculating the amount of the deduction.

(5) No deduction is allowed for any expenditure which is excluded by section 172 (exclusion of expenditure met by subsidies).

Commentary—*Simon's Taxes* B5.620, C2.217.

HMRC Manuals—Business Income Manual BIM52501(cemeteries and crematoria: tax treatment of capital receipts and expenditure).

Amendments—[1] In sub-s (3)(b) words substituted by CTA 2009 s 1322, Sch 1 paras 587, 603. CTA 2009 applies for accounting periods ending on or after 1 April 2009 (for corporation tax purposes) and for tax years 2009–10 onwards (for income and capital gains tax purposes).

[2] In sub-s (3), word at end of para (a) repealed, and para (c) and preceding word inserted, by the Enactment of Extra-Statutory Concessions Order, SI 2012/266 art 4(1), (3) with effect in relation to niches and memorials sold, and inscriptions made, after 1 March 2012.

171 Allocation of ancillary capital expenditure

(1) The amount of ancillary capital expenditure allocated to the relevant period for the purposes of section 170(2)(b) is the amount given by the formula—

$$RE \times \frac{PSR}{PAR + PSR}$$

where—

    RE means residual expenditure (see subsection (2)),

    PSR means the number of grave-spaces or memorial garden plots in the cemetery or memorial garden sold in the relevant period, and

    PAR means the number of grave-spaces or memorial garden plots in the cemetery or memorial garden which are or could be made available for sale at the end of the relevant period.

(2) "Residual expenditure" means the total of all ancillary capital expenditure incurred at any time before the end of the relevant period, less—

    (a) ancillary capital expenditure incurred on buildings or structures which were destroyed before the beginning of the first sale period,

    (b) the excluded amount of any remaining old expenditure (see subsection (3)),

    (c) if, after the beginning of the first sale period and before the end of the relevant period, an asset representing ancillary capital expenditure was sold or destroyed, the net sale proceeds or the compensation, and

    (d) any amount deducted under section 170(2)(b) above, or under [section 147(2)(b) of CTA 2009][1], for a period of account ending before the relevant period.

(3) The excluded amount of remaining old expenditure is calculated by multiplying the remaining old expenditure by the fraction—

$$\frac{PSB}{PAB + PSB}$$

where—

    PSB means the number of grave-spaces or memorial garden plots in the cemetery or memorial garden sold before the beginning of the basis period for the tax year 1954–55, and

PAB means the number of grave-spaces or memorial garden plots in the cemetery or memorial garden which were or could have been made available for sale immediately before the beginning of the basis period for that tax year.

(4) In this section—

"compensation", in relation to the destruction of an asset, means—

(*a*) insurance money or other compensation received by the trader, or a predecessor, in respect of the destruction, and

(*b*) money received for the remains of the asset by the trader or predecessor,

"the first sale period" means—

(*a*) the period of account in which an interest in land in the cemetery or memorial garden was first sold for the purposes of the trade with a view to the land being used for the purpose of interments or for memorial garden plots, or

(*b*) if later, the basis period for the tax year 1954–55, and "remaining old expenditure" means ancillary capital expenditure

which—

(*a*) was incurred before the beginning of the basis period for the tax year 1954–55, and

(*b*) does not fall within subsection (2)(*a*).

Commentary—*Simon's Taxes* **B5.620**.
Derivation—TA 1988 s 91.
HMRC Manuals—Business Income Manual BIM52501 (deduction for ancillary expenditure).
Amendments—[1] In sub-s (2)(*d*) words substituted by CTA 2009 s 1322, Sch 1 paras 587, 604. CTA 2009 applies for accounting periods ending on or after 1 April 2009 (for corporation tax purposes) and for tax years 2009–10 onwards (for income and capital gains tax purposes).

172 Exclusion of expenditure met by subsidies

(1) Expenditure is excluded for the purposes of section 170 so far as it has been, or is to be, met (directly or indirectly) by—

(*a*) the Crown,

(*b*) a government or local or other public authority (whether in the United Kingdom or elsewhere), or

(*c*) any person other than the person incurring the expenditure.

(2) This is subject to the following exceptions.

(3) Expenditure is not excluded for the purposes of section 170 if it is met (directly or indirectly) by a grant—

(*a*) made under Northern Ireland legislation, and

(*b*) declared by the Treasury by an order under section 534 of CAA 2001 to correspond to a grant under Part 2 of the Industrial Development Act 1982 (c 52).

(4) Expenditure is not excluded for the purposes of section 170 if it is met (directly or indirectly) by—

(*a*) insurance money, or

(*b*) other compensation money,

payable in respect of an asset which has been destroyed, demolished or put out of use.

(5) Expenditure is not excluded for the purposes of section 170 if—

(*a*) it has been, or is to be, met (directly or indirectly) by a person other than the Crown or a government or local or other public authority, and

(*b*) no deduction is allowed for the expenditure in calculating for income or corporation tax purposes the profits of a trade carried on by that person.

Commentary—*Simon's Taxes* **B5.620**.
Derivation—TA 1988 s 91(9); CAA 2001 s 532, s 578, Sch 2 para 19.
HMRC Manuals—Business Income Manual BIM52501(capital expenditure: exclusion).

[Crematoria: niches, memorials and inscription]

[172ZA Niches, memorials and inscriptions: introduction

(1) Sections 172ZB to 172ZE apply in calculating the profits of a trade which consists of or includes—

(*a*) the carrying on of a crematorium, and

(*b*) in connection with carrying on the crematorium—

(i) the sale of niches or memorials, or

(ii) the making of inscriptions.

(2) In those sections—

(*a*) "the trade" is the trade mentioned in subsection (1),

(*b*) "the trader" is the person carrying on the trade, and

(*c*) a "predecessor" is a person who carried on the trade at any time before the trader started doing so.][1]

HMRC Manuals—Business Income Manual BIM52520 (cemeteries and crematoria: sale of niches).

Amendments—[1]   Sections 172ZA–172ZE inserted by the Enactment of Extra-Statutory Concessions Order, SI 2012/266 art 4(1), (4) with effect in relation to niches and memorials sold, and inscriptions made, after 1 March 2012.

[172ZB Allowable deductions: niches

(1) This section sets out the deductions that are allowed in respect of a niche if proceeds from the sale of the niche are brought into account as a receipt in calculating the profits of the trade.

(2) A deduction is allowed for two-thirds of the costs incurred (by the trader or a predecessor) in the formation of the niche.

(3) Formation of the lining and of any tablet associated with the niche is taken to be part of the formation of the niche.

(4) If the niche is in a building that is used wholly or mainly for the purpose of providing niches, a further deduction is allowed for two-thirds of the associated building costs.

(5) In relation to a niche in a building—

    (a) "the associated building costs" is the relevant proportion of the costs of the building, and

    (b) "the relevant proportion" is the proportion that the area occupied by the niche bears to the area of the building as a whole or, if the proportion cannot reasonably be calculated on that basis, such proportion as may be calculated on a just and reasonable basis.][1]

Commentary—*Simon's Taxes* **B5.620.**

HMRC Manuals—Business Income Manual BIM52520 (cemeteries and crematoria: allowable deductions).

Amendments—[1]   Sections 172ZA–172ZE inserted by the Enactment of Extra-Statutory Concessions Order, SI 2012/266 art 4(1), (4) with effect in relation to niches and memorials sold, and inscriptions made, after 1 March 2012.

[172ZC Allowable deductions: memorials

(1) This section sets out the deductions that are allowed in respect of a memorial if proceeds from the sale of the memorial are brought into account as a receipt in calculating the profits of the trade.

(2) A deduction is allowed for the costs incurred (by the trader or a predecessor) in producing the memorial.

(3) If the memorial includes an inscription, making that inscription is taken to be part of producing the memorial.

(4) If the memorial is attached to a building that is used wholly or mainly for the purpose of accommodating memorials or the memorial comprises an entire building, a further deduction is allowed for two-thirds of the associated building costs.

(5) In relation to a memorial attached to or comprising a building, "the associated building costs" means—

    (a) the amount found by dividing the costs of the building by the total number of memorials that the building is capable of accommodating, or

    (b) if the memorial comprises an entire building, the costs of that building.][1]

Commentary—*Simon's Taxes* **B5.620.**

HMRC Manuals—Business Income Manual BIM52525 (memorials: allowable deductions).

Amendments—[1]   Sections 172ZA–172ZE inserted by the Enactment of Extra-Statutory Concessions Order, SI 2012/266 art 4(1), (4) with effect in relation to niches and memorials sold, and inscriptions made, after 1 March 2012.

[172ZD Allowable deductions: inscriptions

(1) This section sets out the deductions that are allowed in respect of an inscription if proceeds from making the inscription are brought into account in calculating the profits of the trade.

(2) A deduction is allowed for the costs incurred (by the trader or a predecessor) in making the inscription.

(3) If the inscription is made on an existing framework designed to hold more than one inscription, a further deduction is allowed for two-thirds of the associated framework costs.

(4) In relation to an inscription made on an existing framework, "the associated framework costs"—

    (a) is the amount found by dividing the costs of the framework by the total number of inscriptions that the framework is designed to hold, and

    (b) includes, if the framework is attached to a building that is used wholly or mainly for the purpose of accommodating memorials, the amount found by dividing the costs of the building by the total number of memorials that the building is capable of accommodating.

(5) This section does not apply to an inscription if it is made as part of producing a memorial (see section 172ZC).][1]

Commentary—*Simon's Taxes* **B5.620.**

HMRC Manuals—Business Income Manual BIM52525 (inscriptions: allowable deductions).

Amendments—[1]   Sections 172ZA–172ZE inserted by the Enactment of Extra-Statutory Concessions Order, SI 2012/266 art 4(1), (4) with effect in relation to niches and memorials sold, and inscriptions made, after 1 March 2012.

[172ZE Costs of the building

(1) For the purposes of sections 172ZB to 172ZD, the costs of a building are to be determined in accordance with this section.

(2) If the building was acquired for the purposes of the trade, the costs of the building are the lower of—

    (a) the market value of the building when it was acquired, and

    (b) the costs incurred in acquiring the building.

(3) If the building was constructed for the purposes of the trade, the costs of the building are the costs incurred in constructing the building.

(4) In either case—

    (a) the acquisition cost (or market value) of the land on which the building is situated is to be ignored, and

    (b) for these purposes, costs (or values) are to be apportioned between the land and the building on a just and reasonable basis.

(5) Any construction costs incurred with respect to the building after it was acquired or constructed for the purposes of the trade must be brought into account as costs of the building.

(6) But costs incurred in maintaining the building must not be brought into account.

(7) Costs must not be included as costs of the building if a deduction is or is to be brought into account for them under section 170(2) (deduction for capital expenditure).

(8) A reference in this section to costs incurred is to costs incurred either by the trader or a predecessor.

(9) In sections 172ZB to 172ZD and this section, "building" includes any other type of structure.][1]

Commentary—*Simon's Taxes* **B5.620.**

HMRC Manuals—Business Income Manual BIM52530 (cemeteries and crematoria: costs of the building).

Amendments—[1] Sections 172ZA–172ZE inserted by the Enactment of Extra-Statutory Concessions Order, SI 2012/266 art 4(1), (4) with effect in relation to niches and memorials sold, and inscriptions made, after 1 March 2012.

[CHAPTER 11A

TRADE PROFITS: CHANGES IN TRADING STOCK
Introduction

172A Meaning of "trading stock"

(1) In this Chapter "trading stock", in relation to a trade, means anything (whether land or other property)—

    (a) which is sold in the ordinary course of trade, or

    (b) which would be so sold if it were mature or its manufacture, preparation or construction were complete.

(2) It does not include—

    (a) materials used in the manufacture, preparation or construction of any such thing,

    (b) any services performed in the ordinary course of the trade, or

    (c) any article produced, or any material used, in the performance of any such services.][1]

Commentary—*Simon's Taxes* **B2.205.**

HMRC Manuals—Business Income Manual BIM33035 (trading stock: statutory definition).

Amendments—[1] Sections 172A–172F inserted by FA 2008 s 37, Sch 15 paras 1, 2 with effect in relation to changes in trading stock occurring on or after 12 March 2008 (see FA 2008 s 37(3) for meaning of "change in trading stock").

[172AA Chapter not to apply where cash basis used

Nothing in this Chapter applies in calculating the profits of a trade on the cash basis.][1]

Commentary—*Simon's Taxes* **B2.205.**

Amendments—[1] This section inserted by FA 2013 s 17, Sch 4 para 29 with effect for the tax year 2013–14 and subsequent tax years, subject to the provisions of FA 2013 Sch 4 para 57 in relation to barristers and advocates.

[Transfers of trading stock between trade and trader

172B Trading stock appropriated by trader

(1) This section applies if trading stock of a person's trade is appropriated by the person for any other purpose.

(2) In calculating the profits of the trade—

    (a) the amount which the stock appropriated would have realised if sold in the open market at the time of the appropriation is brought into account as a receipt, and

    (b) the value of anything in fact received for it is left out of account.

(3) The receipt is treated as arising on the date of the appropriation.][1]

Commentary—*Simon's Taxes* **B2.205.**

HMRC Manuals—Business Income Manual BIM51625 (determining profits of trading stock).

Amendments—[1] Sections 172A–172F inserted by FA 2008 s 37, Sch 15 paras 1, 2 with effect in relation to changes in trading stock occurring on or after 12 March 2008 (see FA 2008 s 37(3) for meaning of "change in trading stock").

[172C Trading stock supplied by trader

(1) This section applies if something that—

    (a) belongs to a person carrying on a trade, but

    (b) is not trading stock of the trade,

becomes trading stock of the trade.

(2) In calculating the profits of the trade—

    (a) the cost of the stock is taken to be the amount which it would have realised if sold in the open market at the time it became trading stock of the trade, and

    (b) the value of anything in fact given for it is left out of account.

(3) The cost is treated as being incurred on the date it became trading stock of the trade.][1]

Commentary—*Simon's Taxes* B2.205.
Amendments—[1]   Sections 172A–172F inserted by FA 2008 s 37, Sch 15 paras 1, 2 with effect in relation to changes in trading stock occurring on or after 12 March 2008 (see FA 2008 s 37(3) for meaning of "change in trading stock").

[Other disposals not made in the course of trade

172D Disposals not made in the course of trade
(1) This section applies if—
  (a) trading stock of a trade is disposed of otherwise than in the course of a trade, and
  (b) section 172B does not apply.
(2) In calculating the profits of the trade—
  (a) the amount which the stock disposed of would have realised if sold in the open market at the time of the disposal is brought into account as the receipt, and
  (b) any consideration obtained for it is left out of account.
(3) The receipt is treated as arising on the date of the disposal.
(4) This section is subject to section 172F.][1]

Commentary—*Simon's Taxes* B2.205.
Amendments—[1]   Sections 172A–172F inserted by FA 2008 s 37, Sch 15 paras 1, 2 with effect in relation to changes in trading stock occurring on or after 12 March 2008 (see FA 2008 s 37(3) for meaning of "change in trading stock").

[172E Acquisitions not made in the course of trade
(1) This section applies if—
  (a) trading stock of a trade has been acquired otherwise than in the course of trade, and
  (b) section 172C does not apply.
(2) In calculating the profits of the trade—
  (a) the cost of the stock is taken to be the amount which it would have realised if sold in the open market at the time of the acquisition, and
  (b) the value of anything in fact given for it is left out of account.
(3) The cost is treated as being incurred on the date of the acquisition.
(4) This section is subject to section 172F.][1]

Commentary—*Simon's Taxes* B2.205, B5.111.
Amendments—[1]   Sections 172A–172F inserted by FA 2008 s 37, Sch 15 paras 1, 2 with effect in relation to changes in trading stock occurring on or after 12 March 2008 (see FA 2008 s 37(3) for meaning of "change in trading stock").

[Relationship with transfer pricing rules

172F Transfer pricing rules to take precedence
(1) Section 172D or 172E does not apply if the relevant consideration—
  (a) falls to be adjusted for tax purposes under [Part 4 of TIOPA 2010][2], or
  (b) falls within [that Part][2] without falling to be so adjusted.
[(1A) Subsection (1B) applies in relation to a disposal or acquisition if—
  (a) by virtue of subsection (1), section 172D or 172E does not apply, and
  (b) the market value amount is greater than the Part 4 TIOPA amount.
(1B) An amount equal to the market value amount less the Part 4 TIOPA amount is to be brought into account in calculating the profits of the trade (in addition to the Part 4 TIOPA amount).
(1C) In subsections (1A) and (1B)—
  "market value amount" means the amount referred to in section 172D(2)(a) or 172E(2)(a);
  "Part 4 TIOPA amount" means the amount which, following the application of Part 4 of TIOPA 2010 to the relevant consideration, is brought into account in respect of the relevant consideration in calculating the profits of the trade.][3]
(2) For the purposes of subsection (1)(b), the relevant consideration falls within [Part 4 of TIOPA 2010 without falling to be adjusted under that Part][2] if—
  [(a) the condition in section 147(1)(a) of TIOPA 2010 is met, and
  (aa) the participation condition is met (see subsection (2B)), but
  (b) either—
    (i) one of the conditions in section 147(1)(c) and (d) of TIOPA 2010 is not met, or
    (ii) one of the exceptions mentioned in subsection (2A) applies.][2]
[(2A) The exceptions are those in—
  (a) section 447(5) of CTA 2009 (exchange gains or losses from loan relationships),
  (b) section 694(8) of CTA 2009 (exchange gains or losses from derivative contracts),
  (c) section 213 of TIOPA 2010 (saving for provisions relating to capital allowances), and
  (d) section 214 of TIOPA 2010 (saving for provisions relating to chargeable gains).
(2B) Section 148 of TIOPA 2010 (when the participation condition is met) applies for the purposes of subsection (2)(aa) as it applies for the purposes of section 147(1)(b) of TIOPA 2010.][2]
(3) In this section "relevant consideration" means—
  (a) in relation to section 172D, the consideration for the disposal of the stock, and
  (b) in relation to section 172E, the consideration for the acquisition of the trading stock.][1]

Commentary—*Simon's Taxes* B2.205.

Amendments—[1]   Sections 172A–172F inserted by FA 2008 s 37, Sch 15 paras 1, 2 with effect in relation to changes in trading stock occurring on or after 12 March 2008 (see FA 2008 s 37(3) for meaning of "change in trading stock").

[2]   In sub-ss (1)(a), (1)(b), (2) words substituted, sub-s (2)(a), (b) substituted; and sub-ss (2A), (2B) inserted, by TIOPA 2010 s 501, Sch 8 paras 120, 121. TIOPA 2010 has effect for corporation tax purposes for accounting periods ending on or after 1 April 2010, for income and capital gains tax purposes for the tax year 2010–11 and subsequent tax years, and for petroleum revenue tax purposes for chargeable periods beginning on or after 1 July 2010—

[3]   Sub-ss (1A)–(1C) inserted by F(No 2)A 2015 s 40(2) with effect in relation to a disposal or acquisition made on or after 8 July 2015, unless it is made pursuant to an obligation, under a contract, that was unconditional before that date. An obligation is "unconditional" if it may not be varied or extinguished by the exercise of a right (whether under the contract or otherwise) (F(No 2)A 2015 s 40(4)).

CHAPTER 12

TRADE PROFITS: VALUATION OF STOCK AND WORK IN PROGRESS [ON CESSATION OF TRADE][1]

Amendments—[1]   Words in heading inserted by FA 2008 s 37, Sch 15 paras 1, 3 with effect in relation to changes in trading stock occurring on or after 12 March 2008 (see FA 2008 s 37(3) for meaning of "change in trading stock").

Valuation of trading stock

173 Valuation of trading stock on cessation

(1) If a person permanently ceases to carry on a trade, in calculating the profits of the trade—

    (a) trading stock belonging to the trade at the time of the cessation must be valued, and

    (b) the value must be determined in accordance with sections 175 to 178 (bases of valuation).

(2) But no valuation of the stock is required under this Chapter if [section 147(3) or (5) of TIOPA 2010][1] (provision not at arm's length) has effect in relation to any provision which—

    (a) is made or imposed in relation to the stock, and

    (b) has effect in connection with the cessation.

[(2A) Subsection (2B) applies if—

    (a) by virtue of subsection (2), no valuation of the stock under this Chapter is required, and

    (b) the market value of the stock is greater than the Part 4 TIOPA amount.

(2B) An amount equal to the market value of the stock less the Part 4 TIOPA amount is to be brought into account in calculating the profits of the trade (in addition to the Part 4 TIOPA amount).

(2C) In subsections (2A) and (2B)—

    "market value", in relation to stock, is the value the stock would have been determined to have if it had been valued in accordance with sections 175 to 178, and

    "Part 4 TIOPA amount" is the amount which, following the application of Part 4 of TIOPA 2010 in relation to the provision referred to in subsection (2), is brought into account in respect of that provision in calculating the profits of the trade.][2]

(3) If there is a change in the persons carrying on a trade, no valuation of the stock is required under this Chapter so long as a person carrying on the trade immediately before the change continues to carry it on after the change.

(4) If an individual carries on a trade alone, no valuation of the stock is required under this Chapter if the cessation is because of the individual's death.

Commentary—*Simon's Taxes* **B2.617, B5.136, C3.802.**

HMRC Manuals—Business Income Manual BIM33470 (stock: valuation on discontinuance of business: general principles). BIM33520 (stock: valuation on discontinuance of business: death of individual).

Amendments—[1]   In sub-s (2), words substituted by TIOPA 2010 s 501, Sch 8 paras 120, 122. TIOPA 2010 has effect for corporation tax purposes for accounting periods ending on or after 1 April 2010, for income and capital gains tax purposes for the tax year 2010–11 and subsequent tax years, and for petroleum revenue tax purposes for chargeable periods beginning on or after 1 July 2010.

[2]   Sub-ss (2A)–(2C) inserted by F(No 2)A 2015 s 41(2) with effect in relation to a cessation of trade on or after 8 July 2015.

174 Meaning of "trading stock"

(1) In this Chapter "trading stock" means—

    (a) any property (whether land or other property) which is sold in the ordinary course of the trade or would be so sold if it were mature or its manufacture, preparation or construction were complete, or

    (b) materials used in the manufacture, preparation or construction of any property mentioned in paragraph (a).

(2) In this Chapter "trading stock" includes also any services performed in the ordinary course of the trade—

    (a) the performance of which is wholly or partly completed at the time of the cessation, and

    (b) for which it would be reasonable to expect that a charge would be made if there were no cessation and, in the case of partly completed services, their performance were fully completed,

and any article produced, and any material used, in the performance of any such services.

(3) In this Chapter references to the sale or transfer of trading stock include the sale or transfer of any benefits and rights which accrue, or might reasonably be expected to accrue, from the performance of any such services.

Commentary—*Simon's Taxes* **B2.617, B2.602.**
HMRC Manuals—Business Income Manual BIM33495 (stock: valuation on discontinuance of business: meanings).
BIM33510 (valuation on discontinuance of business: stock that is an exception from the general rules).

175 Basis of valuation of trading stock

(1) The value of trading stock belonging to the trade at the time of the cessation is determined as follows.

(2) If the stock is sold to a person who—

    (a) carries on, or intends to carry on, a trade[, profession or vocation][1] in the United Kingdom, and

    (b) is entitled to deduct the cost of the stock as an expense in calculating the profits of that trade[, profession or vocation][1] for income or corporation tax purposes,

the value is determined in accordance with section 176 (sale to unconnected person), 177 (sale to connected person) or 178 (election by connected persons).

(3) But if section 127 (preventing abuse of the herd basis rules) applies—

    (a) the value is not determined in accordance with any of those sections, and

    (b) the value is instead taken to be that given by section 127 (the price which the animals transferred would have fetched if sold in the open market at the time of the sale).

(4) In any other case, the value is taken to be the amount which the stock would have realised if sold in the open market at the time of the cessation.

Commentary—*Simon's Taxes* **B2.617.**
HMRC Manuals—Business Income Manual BIM33495 (stock: valuation on discontinuance of business: meanings).
BIM33510 (valuation of stock that is an exception from the general rules).
BIM33525 (valuation of stock not transferred to another trader).
Amendments—[1] In sub-s (2)(a), (b) words inserted by CTA 2009 s 1322, Sch 1 paras 587, 605. CTA 2009 applies for accounting periods ending on or after 1 April 2009 (for corporation tax purposes) and for tax years 2009–10 onwards (for income and capital gains tax purposes).

176 Sale basis of valuation: sale to unconnected person

(1) The value of trading stock is determined in accordance with this section if—

    (a) it is sold to a person who carries on, or intends to carry on, a trade[, profession or vocation][1] in the United Kingdom and is entitled to deduct the cost of the stock as an expense in calculating the profits of that trade[, profession or vocation][1] for income or corporation tax purposes, and

    (b) the buyer is not connected with the seller.

(2) The value is taken to be the amount in fact realised on the sale.

(3) If the stock is sold together with other assets, so much of the amount realised on the sale as, on a just and reasonable apportionment, is properly attributable to each asset is treated as the amount realised on the sale of that asset.

Commentary—*Simon's Taxes* **B2.617, B5.141.**
HMRC Manuals—Business Income Manual BIM33480 (valuation of stock transferred to a UK trader).
BIM33485 (transfer to unconnected trader: amount realised on sale).
BIM33735 (valuation of stock: example).
Amendments—[1] In sub-s (1)(a) words inserted by CTA 2009 s 1322, Sch 1 paras 587, 606. CTA 2009 applies for accounting periods ending on or after 1 April 2009 (for corporation tax purposes) and for tax years 2009–10 onwards (for income and capital gains tax purposes).

177 Sale basis of valuation: sale to connected person

(1) The value of trading stock is determined in accordance with this section if—

    (a) it is sold to a person who carries on, or intends to carry on, a trade[, profession or vocation][1] in the United Kingdom and is entitled to deduct the cost of the stock as an expense in calculating the profits of that trade[, profession or vocation][1] for income or corporation tax purposes,

    (b) the buyer is connected with the seller, and

    (c) no election is made under section 178 (election by connected persons).

(2) The value is taken to be the amount which would have been realised if the sale had been between independent persons dealing at arm's length.

Commentary—*Simon's Taxes* **B2.617, B5.141, D6.805.**
HMRC Manuals—Business Income Manual BIM33480 (valuation of stock transferred to a UK trader).
BIM33495 (stock: valuation on discontinuance of business: meanings).
Amendments—[1] In sub-s (1)(a) words inserted by CTA 2009 s 1322, Sch 1 paras 587, 607. CTA 2009 applies for accounting periods ending on or after 1 April 2009 (for corporation tax purposes) and for tax years 2009–10 onwards (for income and capital gains tax purposes).

178 Sale basis of valuation: election by connected persons

(1) The value of trading stock is determined in accordance with this section if—

(*a*) it is sold to a person who carries on, or intends to carry on, a trade[, profession or vocation][1] in the United Kingdom and is entitled to deduct the cost of the stock as an expense in calculating the profits of that trade[, profession or vocation][1] for income or corporation tax purposes,

(*b*) the buyer is connected with the seller, and

(*c*) an election is made under this section.

(2) The parties to the sale may make an election under this section if the value of the stock determined under section 177 exceeds both—

(*a*) its acquisition value, and

(*b*) the amount in fact realised on the sale.

(3) If an election is made, the value is taken to be—

(*a*) its acquisition value, or,

(*b*) if greater, the amount in fact realised on the sale.

(4) An election under this section must be made by both parties on or before the first anniversary of the normal self-assessment filing date for the tax year in which the cessation occurred.

(5) The "acquisition value" of trading stock means the amount which would have been deductible as representing its acquisition value, in calculating the profits of the trade, on the following assumptions—

(*a*) that the stock had been sold in the course of the trade, immediately before the cessation, for a price equal to the value of the stock determined under section 177, and

(*b*) that the period for which those profits were to be calculated began immediately before the sale.

(6) If the stock is sold together with other assets, so much of the amount realised on the sale as, on a just and reasonable apportionment, is properly attributable to each asset is treated as the amount realised on the sale of that asset.

Commentary—*Simon's Taxes* **B2.617, B5.141.**

HMRC Manuals—Business Income Manual BIM33480 (valuation of stock transferred: election by connected persons). BIM33495 (acquisition value: definition).

Amendments—[1]   In sub-s (1)(*a*) words inserted by CTA 2009 s 1322, Sch 1 paras 587, 608. CTA 2009 applies for accounting periods ending on or after 1 April 2009 (for corporation tax purposes) and for tax years 2009–10 onwards (for income and capital gains tax purposes).

179 Connected persons

For the purposes of sections 175 to 178 two persons are connected with each other if any of the following tests is met—

(*a*) they are connected with each other within the meaning of [section 993 of ITA 2007][1],

(*b*) one of them is a firm and the other has a right to a share of the assets or income of the firm,

(*c*) one of them is a body corporate and the other has control over that body,

(*d*) both of them are firms and some other person has a right to a share of the assets or income of both of them, or

(*e*) both of them are bodies corporate, or one of them is a firm and the other is a body corporate, and in either case some other person has control over both of them.

Commentary—*Simon's Taxes* **B2.617.**

Derivation—TA 1988 s 100(1F); FA 1995 s 140(1).

HMRC Manuals—Business Income Manual BIM33480 (valuation of stock transferred to a UK trader). BIM33495 (meaning of connected persons).

Amendments—[1]   Words in para (*a*) substituted by ITA 2007 s 1027, Sch 1 paras 492, 501 with effect for income tax purposes from 6 April 2007, and corporation tax purposes for accounting periods ending after 5 April 2007.

180 Cost to buyer of stock valued on sale basis of valuation

(1) This section applies for the purpose of calculating the profits of the trade[, profession or vocation][1] carried on by the buyer of trading stock.

(2) If the value of the stock is determined in accordance with—

(*a*) section 175(3) or sections 176 to 178 (sale basis of valuation), or

(*b*) [section 164(3) or sections 165 to 167 of CTA 2009][1] (corresponding corporation tax rules), the cost of the stock to the buyer is taken to be the value as so determined.

Commentary—*Simon's Taxes* **B2.615, B2.617.**

HMRC Manuals—Business Income Manual BIM33480 (valuation of stock transferred to a UK trader). BIM33515 (Stock: valuation on discontinuance of business: purchaser cost value).

Amendments—[1]   In sub-s (1) words inserted, and in sub-s (2)(*b*) words substituted by CTA 2009 s 1322, Sch 1 paras 587, 609. CTA 2009 applies for accounting periods ending on or after 1 April 2009 (for corporation tax purposes) and for tax years 2009–10 onwards (for income and capital gains tax purposes).

181 Meaning of "sale" and related expressions

(1) In sections 175 to 178 (except in section 178(5)) references to a sale include a transfer for valuable consideration.

(2) In relation to a transfer which is not a sale—

"amount realised on the sale" means the value of the consideration given for the transfer,

"buyer" means the person to whom the transfer is made, and

"seller" means the person who makes the transfer.

Valuation of work in progress

182 Valuation of work in progress on cessation

(1) If—

   (a) a person permanently ceases to carry on a profession or vocation, and

   (b) the work in progress is valued in calculating the profits of the profession or vocation,

the value must be determined in accordance with section 184 (basis of valuation of work in progress) or 185 (election for valuation at cost).

(2) If there is a change in the persons carrying on a profession, subsection (1) does not apply so long as a person carrying on the profession immediately before the change continues to carry it on after the change.

(3) If an individual carries on a profession alone or a vocation, subsection (1) does not apply if the cessation is because of the individual's death.

Commentary—*Simon's Taxes* **B2.608**.
HMRC Manuals—Business Income Manual BIM80690 (computing the amount to assess: work in progress).

183 Meaning of "work in progress"

(1) In this Chapter "work in progress" means services performed in the ordinary course of the profession or vocation—

   (a) the performance of which is wholly or partly completed at the time of the cessation, and

   (b) for which it would be reasonable to expect that a charge would be made if there were no cessation and, in the case of partly completed services, their performance were fully completed,

and includes any article produced, and any material used, in the performance of any such services.

(2) In this Chapter references to the transfer of work in progress include the transfer of any benefits and rights which accrue, or might reasonably be expected to accrue, from the performance of any such services.

Commentary—*Simon's Taxes* **B2.608**.
Derivation—TA 1988 s 101(3).
HMRC Manuals—Business Income Manual BIM33020 (stock: meaning of work in progress).

184 Basis of valuation of work in progress

(1) If the work in progress is transferred for money or other valuable consideration to a person who—

   (a) carries on, or intends to carry on, a [trade,][1] profession or vocation in the United Kingdom, and

   (b) is entitled to deduct the cost of the work as an expense in calculating the profits of that [trade,][1] profession or vocation for income or corporation tax purposes,

the value of the work is taken to be the amount paid or other consideration given for the transfer.

(2) In any other case, the value of the work is taken to be the amount which would have been paid for a transfer of the work at the time of the cessation as between independent parties dealing at arm's length.

(3) These rules are subject to any election under section 185 (election for valuation at cost).

HMRC Manuals—Business Income Manual BIM33540 (stock: valuation on discontinuance of business: professional work in progress).
BIM80690 (computing the amount to assess: work in progress).
Amendments—[1]   In sub-s (1)(a), (b) words inserted in both instances by CTA 2009 s 1322, Sch 1 paras 587, 610. CTA 2009 applies for accounting periods ending on or after 1 April 2009 (for corporation tax purposes) and for tax years 2009–10 onwards (for income and capital gains tax purposes).

185 Election for valuation at cost

(1) The person who was carrying on the profession or vocation immediately before the cessation may elect that—

   (a) the value of work in progress brought into account in calculating the profits of the period immediately before the cessation is to be the actual cost of the work, and

   (b) the amount by which any sums received for the transfer of the work exceed the actual cost of the work is to be treated as a post-cessation receipt (see Chapter 18).

(2) An election under this section must be made on or before the first anniversary of the normal self-assessment filing date for the tax year in which the cessation occurred.

Commentary—*Simon's Taxes* **B2.806**.
HMRC Manuals—Business Income Manual BIM33540 (stock: valuation on discontinuance of business: professional work in progress).
BIM80690 (computing the amount to assess: work in progress).

Supplementary

186 Determination of questions . . . [1]

(1) Any question arising under—

    (*a*) section 175(3) or sections 176 to 178 (sale basis of valuation of trading stock), or

    (*b*) section 184(1) (valuation of work in progress transferred for valuable consideration),

must be determined . . . [1] in the same way as an appeal.

(2)–(4) . . . [1]

HMRC Manuals—Business Income Manual BIM33550 (stock: valuation on discontinuance of business: resolving disputes).

Amendments—[1]   In heading, sub-s (1), words repealed; sub-ss (2)–(4) repealed by the Transfer of Tribunal Functions and Revenue and Customs Appeals Order, SI 2009/56 art 3, Sch 1 para 439 with effect from 1 April 2009.

CHAPTER 13

DEDUCTIONS FROM PROFITS: UNREMITTABLE AMOUNTS

187 Professions and vocations

The provisions of this Chapter apply to professions and vocations as they apply to trades.

188 Application of Chapter

(1) This Chapter applies if—

    (*a*) an amount received by, or owed to, a person carrying on a trade ("the trader") is brought into account as a receipt in calculating the profits of the trade,

    (*b*) the amount is paid or owed in a territory outside the United Kingdom, and

    (*c*) some or all of the amount is unremittable.

(2) An amount received is unremittable if it cannot be transferred to the United Kingdom merely because of foreign exchange restrictions.

(3) An amount owed is unremittable if it cannot be paid in the United Kingdom and—

    (*a*) it temporarily cannot be paid in the territory in which it is owed merely because of foreign exchange restrictions, or

    (*b*) it can be paid in that territory but, if it were paid there, the amount paid would not be transferable to the United Kingdom merely because of foreign exchange restrictions.

(4) "Foreign exchange restrictions" are restrictions imposed by any of the following—

    (*a*) the laws of the territory where the amount is paid or owed,

    (*b*) executive action of its government, and

    (*c*) the impossibility of obtaining there currency that could be transferred to the United Kingdom.

HMRC Manuals—Business Income Manual BIM42750 (bad and doubtful debts: currency restrictions).

[188A Chapter not to apply where cash basis used

Nothing in this Chapter applies in calculating the profits of a trade on the cash basis.][1]

Amendments—[1]   This section inserted by FA 2013 s 17, Sch 4 para 30 with effect for the tax year 2013–14 and subsequent tax years, subject to the provisions of FA 2013 Sch 4 para 57 in relation to barristers and advocates.

189 Relief for unremittable amounts

(1) If—

    (*a*) the trader has profits from the trade in a period of account, and

    (*b*) an unremittable amount has been brought into account as a receipt for that period,

a deduction of the amount is allowed from those profits (but see subsection (5)).

(2) If the trader has profits from the trade in a period of account and the total of—

    (*a*) any unremittable amounts brought into account as receipts for that period, and

    (*b*) any amount carried forward under this subsection or subsection (3) from the previous period of account,

exceeds the amount of those profits, the excess may be carried forward to the next period of account.

(3) If the trader does not have profits from the trade in a period of account and an unremittable amount has been brought into account as a receipt for that period, the total of—

    (*a*) any unremittable amounts brought into account as receipts for that period, and

    (*b*) any amount carried forward under this subsection or subsection (2) from the previous period of account,

may be carried forward to the next period of account.

(4) If an amount is carried forward under this section to a period of account in which the trader has profits from the trade, a deduction of the amount is allowed from those profits (but see subsection (5)).

(5) The total amount deducted under this section from the profits from a trade in a period of account must not exceed the amount of the profits.

Commentary—*Simon's Taxes* **B2.702**.

HMRC Manuals—Business Income Manual BIM42750 (meaning of unremittable amounts and reliefs given).

190 Restrictions on relief

(1) No deduction is allowed under section 189 in relation to an amount so far as—

(a) it is used to finance expenditure or investment outside the United Kingdom, or

(b) it is applied outside the United Kingdom in another way.

(2) No deduction is allowed under section 189 in relation to an amount owed so far as a deduction is allowed in respect of it under section 35 (bad and doubtful debts).

(3) No deduction is allowed under section 189 in relation to an amount owed so far as a payment under a contract of insurance has been received in relation to it.

(4) No deduction is allowed under section 189 in relation to an amount brought into account in calculating profits if relief under section 842 (unremittable income) may be claimed in relation to that amount.

Commentary—*Simon's Taxes* **B2.703.**

HMRC Manuals—Business Income Manual BIM42750 (restrictions for reliefs on unremittable amounts).

191 Withdrawal of relief

(1) This section applies if—

(a) some or all of an unremittable amount has been deducted from profits under section 189, and

(b) any of the following events occurs.

(2) The events are that—

(a) the amount or part of it ceases to be unremittable,

(b) the amount or part of it is used to finance expenditure or investment outside the United Kingdom,

(c) the amount or part of it is applied outside the United Kingdom in another way,

(d) the amount or part of it is exchanged for, or discharged by, an amount that is not unremittable,

(e) a deduction is allowed in respect of the amount or part of it under section 35 (bad and doubtful debts), and

(f) if the amount is an amount owed, a payment under a contract of insurance is received in relation to the amount or part of it.

(3) The amount or the part of it in question is brought into account as a receipt in calculating the profits of the trade for the period of account in which the event occurs, but only so far as—

(a) it has been deducted from profits under section 189, and

(b) it has not already been brought into account as a receipt in calculating the profits of the trade as a result of this section.

(4) If the event is the receipt of a payment under a contract of insurance, the amount brought into account as a receipt must not exceed the amount of the payment.

Commentary—*Simon's Taxes* **B2.703.**

CHAPTER 14

DISPOSAL AND ACQUISITION OF KNOW-HOW

[191A Chapter not to apply where cash basis used

Nothing in this Chapter applies in calculating the profits of a trade on the cash basis.][1]

Amendments—[1]   This section inserted by FA 2013 s 17, Sch 4 para 31 with effect for the tax year 2013–14 and subsequent tax years, subject to the provisions of FA 2013 Sch 4 para 57 in relation to barristers and advocates.

192 Meaning of "know-how" etc

(1) In this Chapter "know-how" means any industrial information or techniques likely to assist in—

(a) manufacturing or processing goods or materials,

(b) working a source of mineral deposits (including searching for, discovering or testing mineral deposits or obtaining access to them), or

(c) carrying out any agricultural, forestry or fishing operations.

(2) For this purpose—

"mineral deposits" includes any natural deposits capable of being lifted or extracted from the earth and for this purpose geothermal energy is treated as a natural deposit, and

"source of mineral deposits" includes a mine, an oil well and a source of geothermal energy.

(3) For the purposes of this Chapter any consideration received for giving, or wholly or partly fulfilling, an undertaking which—

(a) is given in connection with a disposal of know-how, and

(b) restricts, or is designed to restrict, any person's activities in any way, is treated as consideration received for the disposal of the know-how.

(4) It does not matter whether or not the undertaking is legally enforceable.

(5) For the purposes of this Chapter references to a sale of know-how include an exchange of know-how and any provision of this Chapter referring to a sale has effect with the necessary modifications.

(6) Those modifications include, in particular, reading references to the proceeds of sale and to the price as including the consideration for the exchange.

HMRC Manuals—Business Income Manual BIM45955 (expenditure on acquisition of knowhow).

Capital Allowances Manual CA70010 (Definition of know-how).

193 Disposal of know-how if trade continues to be carried on

(1) This section applies if—

    (a) a person carrying on a trade receives consideration for the disposal of know-how which has been used in the trade,

    (b) the person continues to carry on the trade after the disposal, and

    (c) neither section 194 (disposal of know-how as part of disposal of all or part of a trade) nor section 195 (seller controlled by buyer etc) applies.

(2) The amount or value of the consideration is treated for all purposes as a trading receipt, except so far as it is brought into account under section 462 of CAA 2001 (disposal values).

(3) If the know-how is sold together with other property, the net proceeds of the sale of the know-how are treated as being so much of the net proceeds of the sale of all the property as, on a just and reasonable apportionment, is attributable to the know-how.

(4) For this purpose all property sold as a result of one bargain is treated as sold together even though—

    (a) separate prices are, or purport to be, agreed for separate items of that property, or

    (b) there are, or purport to be, separate sales of separate items of that property.

(5) Any question about the way in which a sum is to be apportioned under this section must be determined in accordance with section 563(2) to (6) of CAA 2001 (procedure for determining certain questions affecting two or more persons) if it materially affects two or more taxpayers.

(6) For this purpose a question materially affects two or more taxpayers if at the time when the question falls to be determined it appears that the determination is material to the liability to tax (for whatever period) of two or more persons.

Commentary—*Simon's Taxes* **B5.345.**
HMRC Manuals—Capital Allowances Manual CA70050 (treat as property for capital allowances and ITTOIA purposes).
CA72400 (trading receipt treatment).
CA72500 (treatment of receipts).

194 Disposal of know-how as part of disposal of all or part of a trade

(1) This section applies if—

    (a) a person carrying on a trade receives consideration for the disposal of know-how which has been used in the trade, and

    (b) the know-how is disposed of as part of the disposal of all or part of the trade.

(2) If the person disposing of the know-how is within the charge to income tax, the consideration is treated for income tax purposes as a capital receipt for goodwill.

(3) If the person acquiring the know-how—

    (a) is within the charge to income tax, and

    (b) provided the consideration,

the consideration is treated for income tax purposes as a capital payment for goodwill.

(4) But the consideration is not treated for income tax purposes as a capital payment for goodwill if, before the acquisition, the trade was carried on wholly outside the United Kingdom.

(5) If the person disposing of the know-how is within the charge to income tax—

    (a) that person, and

    (b) the person acquiring the know-how (whether or not within the charge to income tax),

may jointly elect for this section not to apply (but see section 195).

(6) The election must be made within two years of the disposal.

(7) If—

    (a) an election is made under [section 178 of CTA 2009][1] (corresponding corporation tax provision), and

    (b) the person making the acquisition mentioned in [that section][1] is within the charge to income tax,

the persons making the election under [that section][1] are treated as also making an election under this section (even though the person disposing of the know-how is not within the charge to income tax).

Commentary—*Simon's Taxes* **B5.346.**
Derivation—TA 1988 s 531(2), (3).
HMRC Manuals—Capital Allowances Manual CA72300 (goodwill treatment).
Amendments—[1]   In sub-s (7) words substituted by CTA 2009 s 1322, Sch 1 paras 587, 611. CTA 2009 applies for accounting periods ending on or after 1 April 2009 (for corporation tax purposes) and for tax years 2009–10 onwards (for income and capital gains tax purposes).

195 Seller controlled by buyer etc

(1) This section applies if a disposal of know-how is by way of sale and—

    (a) the seller is a body of persons over which the buyer has control,

    (b) the buyer is a body of persons over which the seller has control, or

    (c) both the seller and the buyer are bodies of persons and another person has control over both of them.

(2) In such a case—

    (a) section 193 does not apply, and

(*b*) no election may be made under section 194.

(3) For the purposes of this section "body of persons" includes a firm.

Commentary—*Simon's Taxes* **B5.346.**

CHAPTER 15

BASIS PERIODS

Introduction

196 Professions and vocations

The provisions of this Chapter apply to professions and vocations as they apply to trades.

Accounting date

197 Meaning of "accounting date"

(1) In this Chapter "accounting date", in relation to a tax year, means—

    (*a*) the date in the tax year to which accounts are drawn up, or

    (*b*) if there are two or more such dates, the latest of them.

(2) This is subject to—

    (*a*) section 211(2) (middle date treated as accounting date), and

    (*b*) section 214(3) (date treated as accounting date if date changed in tax year in which there is no accounting date).

Commentary—*Simon's Taxes* **B4.101.**

The normal rules

198 General rule

(1) The general rule is that the basis period for a tax year is the period of 12 months ending with the accounting date in that tax year.

(2) This applies unless a different basis period is given by one of the following sections—

    section 199 (first tax year),

    section 200 (second tax year),

    section 201 (tax year in which there is no accounting date),

    section 202 (final tax year),

    section 209 or 210 (first accounting date shortly before end of tax year),

    section 212 (tax year in which middle date treated as accounting date),

    section 215 (change of accounting date in third tax year), and

    section 216 (change of accounting date in later tax year).

Commentary—*Simon's Taxes* **B4.101.**

HMRC Manuals—Business Income Manual BIM81010 (computation of liability: basis periods general rules).

199 First tax year

(1) The basis period for the tax year in which a person starts to carry on a trade—

    (*a*) begins with the date on which the person starts to carry on the trade, and

    (*b*) ends with 5th April in the tax year.

(2) But if a person starts and permanently ceases to carry on a trade in the same tax year, the basis period for the tax year is that given by section 202(2).

Commentary—*Simon's Taxes* **B4.102.**

Derivation—TA 1988 s 61(1); FA 1994 s 201.

HMRC Manuals—Business Income Manual BIM81015 (computation of liability: basis periods first tax year).

200 Second tax year

(1) The basis period for the second tax year in which a person carries on a trade is determined as follows.

(2) If in that tax year—

    (*a*) the accounting date falls less than 12 months after the date on which the person starts to carry on the trade, and

    (*b*) the person does not permanently cease to carry on the trade,

the basis period is the period of 12 months beginning with the date on which the person starts to carry on the trade.

(3) If in that tax year—

    (*a*) the accounting date falls 12 months or more after the date on which the person starts to carry on the trade, and

    (*b*) the person does not permanently cease to carry on the trade,

the basis period is that given by the general rule in section 198.

(4) If in that tax year—

    (*a*) there is no accounting date, and

    (*b*) the person does not permanently cease to carry on the trade, the basis period is the same as the tax year.

(5) If in that tax year the person permanently ceases to carry on the trade, the basis period is that given by section 202(1).

Commentary—*Simon's Taxes* **B4.103.**
HMRC Manuals—Business Income Manual BIM81015 (computation of liability: basis periods second tax year).

201 Tax year in which there is no accounting date

(1) If a person carries on a trade in a tax year and—
   (*a*) there is no accounting date in the tax year, and
   (*b*) the person does not start or permanently cease to carry on the trade in the tax year,

the basis period for the tax year is the period of 12 months beginning immediately after the end of the basis period for the previous tax year.

(2) But this is subject to—
   (*a*) section 200 (second tax year), and
   (*b*) sections 215 and 216 (change of accounting date in third tax year or later tax year).

Commentary—*Simon's Taxes* **B4.104.**
Derivation—TA 1988 s 60(3); FA 1994 s 200.
HMRC Manuals—Business Income Manual BIM81015 (example of basis period where there is no accounting date).

202 Final tax year

(1) The basis period for the tax year in which a person permanently ceases to carry on a trade—
   (*a*) begins immediately after the end of the basis period for the previous tax year, and
   (*b*) ends with the date on which the person permanently ceases to carry on the trade.

(2) But if a person starts and permanently ceases to carry on a trade in the same tax year, the basis period—
   (*a*) begins with the date on which the person starts to carry on the trade, and
   (*b*) ends with the date on which the person permanently ceases to carry on the trade.

Commentary—*Simon's Taxes* **B4.105.**
HMRC Manuals—Business Income Manual BIM80565 (computing the amount to assess: cessation: general principles). BIM81025 (examples of basis periods year of cessation).

Apportionment of profits

203 Apportionment etc of profits to basis periods

(1) This section applies if the basis period for a tax year does not coincide with a period of account.

(2) Any of the following steps may be taken if they are necessary in order to arrive at the profits or losses of the basis period—
   (*a*) apportioning the profits or losses of a period of account to the parts of that period falling in different basis periods, and
   (*b*) adding the profits or losses of a period of account (or part of a period) to profits or losses of other periods of account (or parts).

(3) The steps must be taken by reference to the number of days in the periods concerned.

(4) But the person carrying on the trade may use a different way of measuring the length of the periods concerned if—
   (*a*) it is reasonable to do so, and
   (*b*) the way of measuring the length of periods is used consistently for the purposes of the trade.

Commentary—*Simon's Taxes* **B4.106.**
HMRC Manuals—Business Income Manual BIM81065 (examples of apportioning profits to basis periods).

Overlap profits and losses

204 Meaning of "overlap period" and "overlap profit"

In this Chapter—
   "overlap period" means a period which falls within two basis periods, and
   "overlap profit" means profit which arises in an overlap period.

Commentary—*Simon's Taxes* **B4.107.**
Derivation—TA 1988 s 63A(5); FA 1994 s 205.

[204A Overlap profit and trading allowance under Chapter 1 of Part 6A

(1) This section makes provision about the amount of profit treated as arising in an overlap period which falls within the basis period of a trade for two tax years ("tax year A" and "tax year B") where relief is given under Chapter 1 of Part 6A (trading allowance) in respect of the trade for at least one of those tax years.

(2) The profit which arises in the overlap period is treated as nil if—
   (*a*) the profits or losses of the trade for tax year A or tax year B (or both) are treated as nil under section 783AF (full relief: trade profits), or
   (*b*) in relation to tax year A or tax year B (or both)—
      (i) section 783AI applies in calculating the profits or losses of the trade (partial relief: alternative calculation of trade profits), and
      (ii) the deductible amount subtracted at step 2 of section 783AI(2) in relation to the trade is greater than or equal to the non-adjusted overlap profit.

ITTOIA 2005

(3) Subsection (6) applies if conditions 1 and 2 are met.

(4) Condition 1 is that, in relation to either tax year A or tax year B—

  (*a*) section 783AI applies in calculating the profits or losses of the trade, and

  (*b*) the deductible amount subtracted at step 2 of section 783AI(2) in relation to the trade is less than the non-adjusted overlap profit.

(5) Condition 2 is that neither section 783AF nor section 783AI applies in relation to the trade—

  (*a*) where condition 1 is met in relation to tax year A, for tax year B, or

  (*b*) where condition 1 is met in relation to tax year B, for tax year A.

(6) The profit which arises in the overlap period is treated as equal to the non-adjusted overlap profit less the deductible amount mentioned in subsection (4)(*b*).

(7) Subsection (8) applies if, in relation to each of tax year A and tax year B—

  (*a*) section 783AI applies in calculating the profits or losses of the trade, and

  (*b*) the deductible amount subtracted at step 2 of section 783AI(2) in relation to the trade is less than the non-adjusted overlap profit.

(8) The profit which arises in the overlap period is treated as equal to the non-adjusted overlap profit less the higher of the following—

  (*a*) the deductible amount subtracted at step 2 of section 783AI(2) in calculating the profits or losses of the trade for tax year A, and

  (*b*) the deductible amount subtracted at step 2 of section 783AI(2) in calculating the profits or losses of the trade for tax year B.

(9) In this section "non-adjusted overlap profit" means the amount of profit that would arise in the overlap period apart from—

  (*a*) Chapter 1 of Part 6A, and

  (*b*) this section.]¹

Commentary—*Simon's Taxes* **B4.107**.
Amendments—¹   Section 204A inserted by F(No 2)A 2017 s 17, Sch 3 paras 2, 5 with effect for the tax year 2017–18 and subsequent tax years.

205 Deduction for overlap profit in final tax year

(1) If a person permanently ceases to carry on a trade in a tax year, a deduction is allowed for overlap profit in calculating the profits of the trade of the tax year.

(2) The amount of the deduction is calculated as follows.

  Step 1 Add together the overlap profits arising in all overlap periods.

  Step 2 Subtract from that any deductions for overlap profit made under section 220 (deduction for overlap profit on change of accounting date).

  The balance is the amount of the deduction allowed under this section.

Commentary—*Simon's Taxes* **B4.107**.
Derivation—TA 1988 s 63A(3); FA 1994 s 205.
HMRC Manuals—Business Income Manual BIM81080 (overlap relief introduction). BIM81095 (overlap relief given on cessation).

206 Restriction on bringing losses into account twice

If a loss arises in, or is apportioned under section 203 to, two overlapping basis periods, the amount of the loss—

  (*a*) is brought into account in calculating the profits of the first basis period, and

  (*b*) is not brought into account in calculating the profits of the second basis period.

Commentary—*Simon's Taxes* **B4.107**.
Derivation—TA 1988 s 63A(4); FA 1994 s 205.
HMRC Manuals—Business Income Manual BIM81070 (apportioning losses to basis periods).

207 Treatment of business start-up payments received in an overlap period

(1) This section applies if—

  (*a*) a person carrying on a trade receives a business start-up payment (see subsection (3)) in a period which falls within two basis periods, and

  (*b*) the payment is not a lump sum payment.

(2) The payment—

  (*a*) is brought into account in calculating the profits of the trade of the first basis period, and

  (*b*) is not brought into account in calculating the profits of the trade of the second basis period.

(3) A "business start-up payment" means a payment under a Business Start-Up scheme which is of the kind originally known as enterprise allowance and is made—

  (*a*) in England and Wales, by a training and enterprise council pursuant to arrangements under section 2(2)(*d*) of the Employment and Training Act 1973 (c 50),

  (*b*) in Scotland, by a local enterprise company under section 2(4)(*c*) of the Enterprise and New Towns (Scotland) Act 1990 (c 35) in relation to arrangements under section 2(3) of that Act, or

  (*c*) in Northern Ireland, by or on behalf of the Department for Employment and Learning under section 1(1A)(*d*) of the Employment and Training Act (Northern Ireland) 1950 (c 29 (NI)).

Commentary—*Simon's Taxes* **B4.107**.

Rules where first accounting date shortly before end of tax year

208 When the late accounting date rules apply

(1) Sections 209 and 210 contain rules for the purpose of—

  (a) avoiding the need to apportion profits, and

  (b) preventing overlap profit from arising,

in relation to the tax year in which a person ("the trader") starts to carry on a trade and the following tax year.

(2) Sections 209 and 210 apply in relation to a tax year if—

  (a) the first accounting date is 31st March or 1st, 2nd, 3rd or 4th April, and

  (b) that date falls in the tax year in which the trader starts to carry on the trade or in either of the following two tax years,

but the trader may elect for those sections not to apply in relation to a tax year.

(3) In this section and section 210 "the first accounting date" means—

  (a) the first accounting date after the trader starts to carry on the trade, or

  (b) the date that is intended to be that accounting date if, at the time the trader delivers a return for a tax year, there has been no accounting date.

(4) An election under this section must be made on or before the first anniversary of the normal self-assessment filing date for the tax year to which it relates.

Commentary—*Simon's Taxes* **B4.108.**

HMRC Manuals—Business Income Manual BIM81020 (basis periods where first accounting date just before end of tax year: if there is an accounting date).

209 Rule if there is an accounting date

(1) This section applies if there is an accounting date in a tax year and that date is 31st March or 1st, 2nd, 3rd or 4th April.

(2) If—

  (a) the basis period for the tax year would otherwise end after the accounting date, and

  (b) the part of the basis period that would otherwise fall after the accounting date is included in the basis period for the following tax year,

the basis period for the tax year ends on the accounting date.

Commentary—*Simon's Taxes* **B4.108.**

HMRC Manuals—Business Income Manual BIM81020 (basis periods where first accounting date just before end of tax year: if there is an accounting date).

210 Rules if there is no accounting date

(1) This section applies if there is no accounting date in a tax year ("the relevant tax year").

(2) If the trader—

  (a) starts to carry on the trade in the relevant tax year, and

  (b) does so before 1st April,

the basis period ends on the date in the relevant tax year that corresponds to the first accounting date.

(3) If the trader started to carry on the trade in the previous tax year and there was no accounting date in the previous tax year, the basis period for the relevant tax year—

  (a) begins immediately after the end of the basis period for the previous tax year, and

  (b) ends on the date in the relevant tax year that corresponds to the first accounting date.

(4) If the trader—

  (a) starts to carry on the trade in the relevant tax year, and

  (b) does so after 31st March,

the profits or losses of the trade of the relevant tax year are treated as nil.

(5) In that case, the actual profits or losses of the trade of the relevant tax year are treated as arising in the basis period for the following tax year, so far as they do not already do so.

Commentary—*Simon's Taxes* **B4.108.**

HMRC Manuals—Business Income Manual BIM81020 (basis periods where first accounting date just before end of tax year: if there is no accounting date).

Slight variations in accounting date

211 Treating middle date as accounting date

(1) This section applies for the purpose of preventing the rules in sections 215 to 220 from applying if—

  (a) accounts of a trade are drawn up to a particular day (rather than to a particular date), and

  (b) that day is capable of falling on one of only 7 consecutive dates (or, if that day is in February, on one of only 8 consecutive dates).

(2) The person carrying on the trade may elect in relation to a tax year for the fourth of those dates ("the middle date") to be treated as the accounting date in the tax year.

(3) The election has effect for the purposes of this Chapter, but not for any other purposes.

(4) An election under this section—

  (a) must specify the day to which the accounts are drawn up and the middle date, and

(b) must be made on or before the first anniversary of the normal self-assessment filing date for the tax year to which it relates.

HMRC Manuals—Business Income Manual BIM81030 (basis periods accounts made up to slightly varying dates).

212 Consequence of treating middle date as accounting date

(1) If—
- (a) a date ("the middle date") is treated under section 211 as the accounting date in a tax year ("the current tax year"),
- (b) the basis period for the current tax year would otherwise be that given by the general rule in section 198, and
- (c) subsection (2) or (3) applies,

the basis period for the current tax year begins immediately after the end of the basis period for the previous tax year and ends with the middle date.

(2) This subsection applies if—
- (a) the accounting date in the previous tax year was not determined under section 211, and
- (b) that accounting date was one of the 7 (or 8) dates on which the day in the current tax year to which accounts are drawn up is capable of falling.

(3) This subsection applies if—
- (a) the accounting date in the previous tax year was determined under section 211, and
- (b) the accounting date in the current tax year is the same as the accounting date in the previous tax year.

Commentary—*Simon's Taxes* B4.109.

HMRC Manuals—Business Income Manual BIM81030 (computation of liability: basis periods accounts made up to slightly varying dates).

213 Circumstances in which middle date not treated as accounting date

(1) If—
- (a) a date ("the middle date") is treated under section 211 as the accounting date in a tax year ("the earlier tax year"),
- (b) the basis period for the earlier tax year ends on the middle date, and
- (c) the basis period for the following tax year ("the later tax year") is that given by one of the provisions listed in subsection (2),

the basis period for the later tax year is determined as if the basis period for the earlier tax year had ended on the date to which accounts were actually drawn up in the earlier tax year.

(2) The provisions are—
- (a) section 201(1) (tax year in which there is no accounting date),
- (b) section 202(1) (tax year in which person permanently ceases to carry on a trade),
- (c) section 215(2) (change of accounting date in third tax year), and
- (d) section 216(3) (change of accounting date in later tax year).

Commentary—*Simon's Taxes* B4.109.

HMRC Manuals—Business Income Manual BIM81030 (computation of liability: basis periods accounts made up to slightly varying dates).

Special rules if accounting date changes

214 When a change of accounting date occurs

(1) If there is a change from one accounting date ("the old accounting date") to another accounting date ("the new accounting date"), the change of accounting date occurs—
- (a) in the first tax year in which accounts are drawn up to the new accounting date, or
- (b) if earlier, in the first tax year in which accounts are not drawn up to the old accounting date.

(2) A change from a date determined under section 211 to an actual accounting date is taken to be a change from one accounting date to another, even if the two dates are the same.

(3) If, because of subsection (1)(b), a change of accounting date occurs in a tax year in which there is no actual accounting date, the date corresponding to the new accounting date is treated as the accounting date in that tax year for the purpose of determining—
- (a) the basis period for that tax year, and
- (b) if section 219 applies, the basis period for the following tax year.

Commentary—*Simon's Taxes* B4.110.

Derivation—TA 1988 s 62; FA 1994 s 202.

HMRC Manuals—Business Income Manual BIM81035 (basis periods change of accounting date).

BIM82270 (partner notional trade: change of partnership accounting date).

215 Change of accounting date in third tax year

(1) This section applies if—
- (a) a change of accounting date occurs in the third tax year in which a person carries on a trade,
- (b) the person does not permanently cease to carry on the trade in that tax year, and
- (c) the accounting date in that tax year falls more than 12 months after the end of the basis period for the second tax year in which the person carries on the trade.

(2) The basis period—

(*a*) begins immediately after the end of the basis period for the second tax year in which the person carries on the trade, and

(*b*) ends with the accounting date in the third tax year in which the person carries on the trade.

Commentary—*Simon's Taxes* **B4.110.**

HMRC Manuals—Business Income Manual BIM81040 (basis periods change of accounting date in the opening years of trade).

216 Change of accounting date in later tax year

(1) This section applies if—

    (*a*) a change of accounting date occurs in a tax year in which a person carries on a trade,

    (*b*) the tax year is later than the third tax year in which the person carries on the trade, and

    (*c*) the person does not permanently cease to carry on the trade in the tax year.

(2) If—

    (*a*) the conditions in section 217 are met (conditions for basis period to end with new accounting date), and

    (*b*) the new accounting date falls less than 12 months after the end of the basis period for the previous tax year,

the basis period is that given by the general rule in section 198.

(3) If—

    (*a*) the conditions in section 217 are met, and

    (*b*) the new accounting date falls more than 12 months after the end of the basis period for the previous tax year,

the basis period begins immediately after the end of the basis period for the previous tax year and ends with the accounting date.

(4) If the conditions in section 217 are not met, the basis period for the tax year is the period of 12 months ending with the old accounting date.

Commentary—*Simon's Taxes* **B4.110.**

HMRC Manuals—Business Income Manual BIM81045 (basis periods change of accounting date in year 4 onwards).

217 Conditions for basis period to end with new accounting date

(1) The conditions in this section are met if—

    (*a*) the person carrying on the trade gives appropriate notice of the change of accounting date to [an officer of Revenue and Customs] (see subsection (2)),

    (*b*) the 18 month test is met (see subsection (3)), and

    (*c*) either condition A or B is met (see subsections (4) to (6)).

(2) Appropriate notice of the change of accounting date is given to [an officer of Revenue and Customs] if (and only if) the notice is given—

    (*a*) in a return under the provision of TMA 1970 that applies to the person carrying on a trade (see section 8, 8A or 12AA of that Act), and

    (*b*) on or before the day on which the return is required to be made and delivered under that provision.

(3) The 18 month test is met if the period of account ending—

    (*a*) with the new accounting date in the tax year in which the change of accounting date occurs, or

    (*b*) if there is no new accounting date in that tax year, with the new accounting date in the first tax year in which accounts are drawn up to the new accounting date,

is not longer than 18 months.

(4) Condition A is that, in the 5 tax years immediately before the tax year in which the change of accounting date occurs, there has been no change of accounting date that counts for the purposes of this condition.

(5) A change of accounting date counts for the purposes of condition A if it results in the basis period for the tax year in which the change occurs ending with the accounting date in that tax year.

(6) Condition B is that—

    (*a*) the change of accounting date is made for commercial reasons (see section 218), and

    (*b*) the notice under subsection (2) sets out the reasons for the change.

Commentary—*Simon's Taxes* **B4.110.**

HMRC Manuals—Business Income Manual BIM81045 (basis periods change of accounting date in year 4 onwards).

Prospective amendments—In sub-s (2)(*a*), words ", or of regulations under that Act," to be inserted after words "TMA 1970", and words ", or regulations under paragraph 10 of Schedule A1 to," to be inserted after words "or 12AA of", and in sub-s (2)(*b*), words "section or paragraph" to be substituted for word "provision", by F(No 2)A 2017 s 61(1), Sch 14 para 35 with effect from a day to be appointed.

218 Commercial reasons for change of accounting date

(1) If [an officer of Revenue and Customs] [does][1] not give notice under this section to the person carrying on the trade, a change of accounting date is treated for the purposes of condition B in section 217 as made for commercial reasons.

ITTOIA 2005

(2) If [an officer of Revenue and Customs] [does][1] give notice under this section to the person carrying on the trade, a change of accounting date is treated for the purposes of condition B in section 217 as made for reasons which are not commercial.

(3) The notice must—

  (a) state that [the officer is not][1] satisfied that the change of accounting date is made for commercial reasons, and

  (b) be given within the period of 60 days beginning with the date on which the notice under section 217(2) is received.

(4) A person to whom notice is given under this section may appeal against it within the period of 30 days beginning with the date on which it is given.

(5) On an appeal [that is notified to the tribunal[2]]—

  (a) if the [tribunal is][2] satisfied that the change is made for commercial reasons, [the tribunal][2] may set aside the notice, and

  (b) if [the tribunal is][2] not satisfied that the change is made for commercial reasons, [the tribunal may][2] confirm the notice.

(6) For the purposes of this section obtaining a tax advantage is not a commercial reason.

(7) Part 5 of TMA 1970 (appeals against assessments to tax), apart from section 50, applies in relation to an appeal under this section as it applies in relation to an appeal against an assessment to tax.

Commentary—*Simon's Taxes* **B4.110.**
Derivation—TA 1988 s 62A; FA 1994 s 203.
HMRC Manuals—Business Income Manual BIM81050 (basis periods commercial reasons for change of accounting date).
Amendments—[1]   Words substituted by CRCA 2005 s 50, Sch 4 paras 131, 133(2) with effect from 18 April 2005 (by virtue of SI 2005/1126).
[2]   In sub-s (5) words inserted; in sub-(5)(a) words substituted; in sub-s (5)(b) words substituted by the Transfer of Tribunal Functions and Revenue and Customs Appeals Order, SI 2009/56 art 3, Sch 1 para 440 with effect from 1 April 2009.

219 The year after an ineffective change of accounting date

(1) This section applies to a tax year in which a person carries on a trade if—

  (a) the tax year falls immediately after a tax year in which a change of accounting date occurs, and

  (b) the basis period for the tax year in which the change occurs ends with the old accounting date.

(2) If the accounting date in the tax year is the new accounting date, a change of accounting date is treated as occurring in that tax year for the purposes of sections 216 to 220 (including this section).

(3) If the accounting date in the tax year reverts to the old accounting date, that change of accounting date is ignored for the purposes of—

  (a) section 214, and

  (b) sections 216 to 220 (including this section).

Commentary—*Simon's Taxes* **B4.110.**
Derivation—TA 1988 s 62; FA 1994 s 202.
HMRC Manuals—Business Income Manual BIM81055 (basis periods year after ineffective change of accounting date).

220 Deduction for overlap profit on change of accounting date

(1) This section applies for the purpose of calculating the profits of a trade of a tax year if—

  (a) a change of accounting date occurs in the tax year, and

  (b) the basis period for the tax year is longer than 12 months.

(2) A deduction must be made for overlap profit.

(3) The amount of the deduction is calculated as follows.

  Step 1 Add together the overlap profit arising in all overlap periods ending before the end of the tax year.

  Step 2 Subtract from that any deductions made under this section for previous tax years.
    The balance is "the remaining overlap profit".

  Step 3 Add together the number of days in all overlap periods ending before the end of the tax year.
    Subtract from that the total number of days given by Step 5 on any previous occasions on which a deduction was made under this section.
    The balance is "the number of days on which the remaining overlap profit arises".

  Step 4 Divide the remaining overlap profit by the number of days on which the remaining overlap profit arises.
    The result of this step is "one day's worth of remaining overlap profit".

  Step 5 Subtract the number of days in the tax year from the number of days in the basis period.
    The balance is "the number of days' worth of overlap profit that may be deducted on this occasion".

  Step 6 Multiply one day's worth of remaining overlap profit (see Step 4) by the number of days' worth of overlap profit that may be deducted on this occasion (see Step 5).
    The result of this step is the amount of the deduction.

(4) The above steps are expressed in terms of numbers of days in periods, but the person carrying on the trade may use a different way of measuring the length of the periods concerned if—

(*a*) it is reasonable to do so, and

(*b*) the way of measuring the length of periods is used consistently for the purposes of the trade.

(5) If the accounting date in the tax year is 31st March or 1st, 2nd, 3rd or 4th April, the person carrying on the trade may treat the basis period for the tax year as ending on 5th April for the purpose of calculating the amount of the deduction.

(6) If a period used in calculating the amount of the deduction contains a 29th February and—

(*a*) the accounting date in the tax year is 5th April, or

(*b*) the basis period for the tax year is treated under subsection (5) as ending on 5th April,

the person carrying on the trade may ignore the 29th February for the purpose of calculating the amount of the deduction.

Commentary—*Simon's Taxes* **B4.110.**
HMRC Manuals—Business Income Manual BIM81090 (overlap relief given on change of accounting date).

CHAPTER 16

AVERAGING PROFITS OF FARMERS AND CREATIVE ARTISTS

221 Claim for averaging of fluctuating profits

(1) This Chapter enables an individual (a "taxpayer") to make a claim (an "averaging claim") if—

(*a*) the taxpayer is, or has been, carrying on a qualifying trade, profession or vocation (alone or in partnership), and

(*b*) the taxpayer's profits from it ("the relevant profits") fluctuate from one tax year to the next.

(2) [For the purposes of section 222 (two-year averaging)][2] a trade, profession or vocation is a "qualifying trade, profession or vocation" if—

(*a*) it is farming or market gardening in the United Kingdom,

(*b*) it is the intensive rearing in the United Kingdom of livestock or fish on a commercial basis for the production of food for human consumption, or

(*c*) the taxpayer's profits from it are derived wholly or mainly from creative works.

[(2A) For the purposes of section 222A (five-year averaging), a trade, profession or vocation is a "qualifying trade, profession or vocation" if it falls within subsection (2)(*a*) or (*b*).][2]

(3) For [the purpose of subsection (2)][2] "creative works" means—

(*a*) literary, dramatic, musical or artistic works, or

(*b*) designs,

created by the taxpayer personally or, if the qualifying trade, profession or vocation is carried on in partnership, by one or more of the partners personally.

(4) For the purposes of this Chapter references to the relevant profits of a tax year are to profits before making any deduction for a loss made in any tax year.

(5) If the taxpayer makes a loss in the qualifying trade, profession or vocation in a tax year, the relevant profits of the tax year for the purposes of this Chapter are nil.

[(6) For the purposes of this Chapter references to the relevant profits of a tax year are to profits after any adjustment made under Chapter 16ZA (compensation for compulsory slaughter of animals).][1]

Commentary—*Simon's Taxes* **B5.326.**
HMRC Manuals—Business Income Manual BIM84050 (averaging: who can claim).
BIM84120 (profits for the purpose of averaging).
BIM84185 (averaging claim: partnerships).
Amendments—[1]   Sub-s (6) inserted by the Enactment of Extra-statutory Concessions Order, SI 2012/266 arts 7, 9 with effect for the purposes of making claims in respect of the total compensation profit for periods of account beginning on or after 1 March 2012.
[2]   In sub-s (2) words inserted, sub-s (2A) inserted, and words in sub-s (3) substituted, by FA 2016 s 25(1), (2) with effect for the tax year 2016-17 and subsequent tax years.

[221A Claim not available where cash basis used

Nothing in this Chapter applies in calculating the profits of a trade on the cash basis.][1]

HMRC Manuals—Business Income Manual BIM84050 (averaging: who can claim).
Amendments—[1]   This section inserted by FA 2013 s 17, Sch 4 para 32 with effect for the tax year 2013–14 and subsequent tax years, subject to the provisions of FA 2013 Sch 4 para 57 in relation to barristers and advocates.

222 Circumstances in which claim [for two-year averaging] may be made

(1) An averaging claim may be made [under this section][1] in relation to two consecutive tax years in which a taxpayer is or has been carrying on the qualifying trade, profession or vocation if—

(*a*) the relevant profits of one of the tax years are less than 75% of the relevant profits of the other tax year, or

(*b*) the relevant profits of one (but not both) of the tax years are nil.

[(2) The earlier of the two years to which an averaging claim under this section relates may be a tax year in relation to which an averaging claim under this section or section 222A has already been made.][1]

(3) An averaging claim may not be made [under this section][1] in relation to a tax year if an averaging claim has already been made [under this section or section 222A][1] in relation to a later tax year in respect of the trade, profession or vocation.

(4) An averaging claim may not be made [under this section][1] in relation to the tax year in which—
    (a) the taxpayer starts, or permanently ceases, to carry on the trade, profession or vocation, or
    (b) in the case of a trade, profession or vocation within section 221(2)(c), it begins or ceases to be a qualifying trade, profession or vocation.

(5) An averaging claim [under this section][1] must be made on or before the first anniversary of the normal self-assessment filing date for the second of the tax years to which the claim relates.

(6) But see section 225(4) (extended time limit if profits adjusted for some other reason).

Commentary—*Simon's Taxes* **B5.172**.
HMRC Manuals—Business Income Manual BIM84115 (which years may be averaged).
BIM84155 (time limit for averaging claim).
Amendments—[1]   In heading and in sub-ss (1), (3), (4), (5) words inserted, and sub-s (2) substituted, by FA 2016 s 25(1), (4) with effect for the tax year 2016-17 and subsequent tax years.

[222A Circumstances in which claim for five-year averaging may be made

(1) An averaging claim may be made under this section in relation to five consecutive tax years in which a taxpayer is or has been carrying on the qualifying trade, profession or vocation if the volatility condition in subsection (2) is met.

(2) The volatility condition is that—
    (a) one of the following is less than 75% of the other—
        (i)   the average of the relevant profits of the first four tax years to which the claim relates;
        (ii) the relevant profits of the last of the tax years to which the claim relates; or
    (b) the relevant profits of one or more (but not all) of the five tax years to which the claim relates are nil.

(3) Any of the first four tax years to which an averaging claim under this section relates may be a tax year in relation to which an averaging claim under this section or section 222 has already been made.

(4) An averaging claim ("the subsequent claim") may not be made under this section if an averaging claim in respect of the trade, profession or vocation has already been made under this section or section 222 in relation to a tax year which is later than the last of the tax years to which the subsequent claim relates.

(5) An averaging claim may not be made under this section in relation to the tax year in which the taxpayer starts, or permanently ceases, to carry on the trade, profession or vocation.

(6) An averaging claim under this section must be made on or before the first anniversary of the normal self-assessment filing date for the last of the tax years to which the claim relates.

(7) But see section 225(4) (extended time limit if profits adjusted for some other reason).][1]

Amendments—[1]   Section 222A inserted by FA 2016 s 25(1), (3) with effect for the tax year 2016-17 and subsequent tax years.

223 Adjustment of profits

(1) If a taxpayer makes an averaging claim, the amount taken to be the taxpayer's profits of each of the tax years for which the claim is made is adjusted in accordance with this section.

(2) But this is subject to paragraph 3 of Schedule 1B to TMA 1970 (claim given effect in the [last of the two or five tax years][1]).

[(3) The amount of the adjusted profits of each of the tax years to which the claim relates is the average of the relevant profits of those tax years.][1]

(4) . . .[1]

Commentary—*Simon's Taxes* **B5.328**.
HMRC Manuals—Business Income Manual BIM84135 (averaging: marginal relief).
Amendments—[1]   Words in sub-s (2) substituted, whole of sub-s (3) substituted, and sub-s (4) repealed, by FA 2016 s 25(1), (5) with effect for the tax year 2016-17 and subsequent tax years.

224 Effect of adjustment

(1) The adjusted profits are taken to be the relevant profits of the tax years to which the claim relates for all income tax purposes, including the further application of this Chapter.

(2) This is subject to—
    (a) subsection (3) of this section and section 225(2), and
    (b) paragraph 3 of Schedule 1B to TMA 1970.

(3) If the relevant profits of one of the tax years are nil, this Chapter does not prevent the taxpayer from obtaining relief under the Income Tax Acts for a loss made by the taxpayer in the tax year in question or any other tax year.

(4) A claim by the taxpayer for relief under any other provision of the Income Tax Acts for [any][1] of the tax years to which an averaging claim relates ("the other claim")—
    (a) is not out of time if made on or before the last date on which the averaging claim could have been made, and
    (b) if already made, may be amended or revoked on or before that date.

(5) For this purpose—
    (a) references to a claim include an election or notice, and

(b)   if the other claim is made in a return, the reference to amending or revoking the other claim is to amending the return by amending or omitting the other claim.

(6) For provision determining in which tax year a claim, amendment or revocation made as a result of subsection (4) has effect, see paragraph 4 of Schedule 1B to TMA 1970 (claim, amendment or revocation given effect in the [last of the two or five tax years][1]).

Commentary—*Simon's Taxes* **B5.328**.

HMRC Manuals—Business Income Manual BIM84145 (averaging: giving effect to a claim).
BIM84130 (full averaging).
BIM84170 (averaging claim: adjustments to reliefs).
BIM84160 (averaging: claims to other reliefs).

Amendments—[1]   In sub-ss (4), (6), words substituted by FA 2016 s 25(1), (6) with effect for the tax year 2016-17 and subsequent tax years.

225 Effect of later adjustment of profits

(1) This section applies if, after the taxpayer has made an averaging claim, the relevant profits in [any one or more][1] of the tax years to which the claim relates are adjusted for another reason.

(2) The averaging claim is ignored.

(3) But this does not prevent a further averaging claim from being made in relation to the taxpayer's profits as adjusted for the other reason.

(4) A further averaging claim is not out of time as long as it is made on or before the first anniversary of the normal self-assessment filing date for the tax year in which the adjustment for the other reason is made.

Commentary—*Simon's Taxes* **B5.328**.

HMRC Manuals—Business Income Manual BIM84150 (averaging: amendments to profits: averaging claim in place).

Amendments—[1]   Words in sub-s (1) substituted by FA 2016 s 25(1), (7) with effect for the tax year 2016-17 and subsequent tax years.

[CHAPTER 16ZA

COMPENSATION FOR COMPULSORY SLAUGHTER OF ANIMAL]

[225ZA Application of Chapter 16ZA

(1) This Chapter applies if—
> (a)   an animal treated as trading stock of a farming trade is slaughtered under a disease control order,
> (b)   the animal is not part of a production herd of a class in respect of which a herd basis election may be made under section 126, and
> (c)   the farmer receives or will receive compensation for the animal.

(2) Such an animal is referred to in this Chapter as a "relevant animal".

(3) "Disease control order" has the same meaning as in section 126.][1]

HMRC Manuals—Business Income Manual BIM55180: (Covers S225ZA to S225ZG) (compensation received for compulsory slaughter of animals).
BIM55185: (spreading relief following compulsory slaughter).
BIM55190: (method of allowing spreading relief).

Amendments—[1]   Chapter 16ZA (ss 225ZA–225ZG) inserted by the Enactment of Extra-statutory Concessions Order, SI 2012/266 arts 6, 9 with effect for the purposes of making claims in respect of the total compensation profit for periods of account beginning on or after 1 March 2012.

[225ZAA Chapter not to apply where cash basis used

Nothing in this Chapter applies in calculating the profits of a trade on the cash basis.][1]

Amendments—[1]   This section inserted by FA 2013 s 17, Sch 4 para 33 with effect for the tax year 2013–14 and subsequent tax years, subject to the provisions of FA 2013 Sch 4 para 57 in relation to barristers and advocates.

[225ZB Right to make claim

(1) The farmer may make a claim under this section.

(2) A claim may only be made in respect of the total compensation profit for a period of account.

(3) The total compensation profit for a period of account is the sum of the profits which the farmer makes for all the relevant animals slaughtered in that period.

(4) For the purposes of this Chapter the profit which the farmer makes for a relevant animal is—
> (a)   the amount by which the compensation for the animal exceeds its book value, or
> (b)   if the trade is carried on in partnership, the farmer's share of that amount, determined in accordance with Part 9.

(5) Nothing in this section prevents a claim being made before the amount of the compensation has been finally determined.][1]

Commentary—*Simon's Taxes* **B5.111**.

HMRC Manuals—Business Income Manual BIM55185 (animal slaughter: total compensation profit).

Amendments—[1]   Chapter 16ZA (ss 225ZA–225ZG) inserted by the Enactment of Extra-statutory Concessions Order, SI 2012/266 arts 6, 9 with effect for the purposes of making claims in respect of the total compensation profit for periods of account beginning on or after 1 March 2012.

[225ZC Book value

(1) For the purposes of this Chapter the book value of an animal is the value shown in the accounts as the value of the animal at the start of the period of account in which it was slaughtered.

(2) If, for an animal, no value is shown in the accounts as that value, the book value is as follows—

    (*a*) in the case of an animal which was born in the period of account in which it was slaughtered and did not become part of the trading stock in any other way, the book value is 75% of the compensation payable for it,

    (*b*) in the case of an animal in relation to which section 172C (trading stock supplied by trader) or 172E (acquisitions not made in the course of trade) applies, the book value is the cost treated as incurred under section 172C(2) or 172E(2) as the case may be, and

    (*c*) in any other case, the book value is the cost of acquiring the animal for the purposes of the trade.][1]

Commentary—*Simon's Taxes* **B5.111.**

Amendments—[1]   Chapter 16ZA (ss 225ZA–225ZG) inserted by the Enactment of Extra-statutory Concessions Order, SI 2012/266 arts 6, 9 with effect for the purposes of making claims in respect of the total compensation profit for periods of account beginning on or after 1 March 2012.

[225ZD Effect of claim for spreading profits

(1) If the farmer makes a claim under section 225ZB in respect of the total compensation profit for a period of account ("period X"), the profits of the trade carried on by the farmer are to be adjusted for income tax purposes as follows—

Step 1

Treat the compensation payable for all of the relevant animals slaughtered in period X as a receipt of that period (regardless of when the compensation is finally determined or paid).

Step 2

If the farmer makes a profit in the trade in Year 1, deduct from the profits of Year 1 an amount equal to—

    (*a*) the total compensation profit for period X, or

    (*b*) if the total compensation profit exceeds the profits of Year 1, such portion of the total compensation profit as will reduce the profits to nil.

"Year 1" is—

    (*a*) the tax year whose basis period includes the whole or a part of period X, or

    (*b*) if there is more than one, the earliest of those tax years.

Step 3

If—

    (*a*) there is more than one tax year whose basis period includes the whole or a part of period X,

    (*b*) either—

        (i) the farmer did not make a profit in the trade in Year 1, or

        (ii) by virtue of step 2, a portion only of the total compensation profit for period X is deducted from the profits of Year 1, and

    (*c*) the farmer makes a profit in the trade in the next tax year ("Year 2"),

deduct from the profits of Year 2 the applicable amount.

In a case where the farmer did not make a profit in Year 1, "the applicable amount" is—

    (*a*) the total compensation profit for period X, or

    (*b*) if the total compensation profit exceeds the profits of Year 2, such portion of the total compensation profit as will reduce the profits to nil.

In a case where a portion only of the total compensation profit for period X is deducted from the profits of Year 1, "the applicable amount" is—

    (*a*) an amount equal to the difference between the total compensation profit for period X and the portion so deducted, or

    (*b*) if that amount exceeds the profits of Year 2, such portion of that amount as will reduce the profits to nil.

No further deduction is to be made in respect of the total compensation profit for period X from the profits of any later tax year whose basis period includes a part of that period.

Step 4

Include in the profits of each of the 3 consecutive tax years following Year 1 an amount equal to one third of the total amount deducted by virtue of steps 2 and 3.

    (2) Nothing in this section affects the calculation of overlap profit (within the meaning of Chapter 15 of this Part).][1]

Commentary—*Simon's Taxes* **B5.111.**

Amendments—[1]   Chapter 16ZA (ss 225ZA–225ZG) inserted by the Enactment of Extra-statutory Concessions Order, SI 2012/266 arts 6, 9 with effect for the purposes of making claims in respect of the total compensation profit for periods of account beginning on or after 1 March 2012.

[225ZE Adjustment: cessation of trading

If the farmer permanently ceases to carry on the farming trade before the end of the second of the 3 consecutive tax years following Year 1, step 4 in section 225ZD(1) is to be replaced by the following two steps—

Step 4

Divide the total amount deducted by virtue of steps 2 and 3 by the number of tax years ("the remaining tax years") in which, or in any part of which, the farmer carried on the farming trade, starting with Year 1.

Step 5

Include in the profits of each of the remaining tax years the amount resulting from the division in step 4.][1]

Commentary—*Simon's Taxes* **B5.111.**
Amendments—[1] Chapter 16ZA (ss 225ZA–225ZG) inserted by the Enactment of Extra-statutory Concessions Order, SI 2012/266 arts 6, 9 with effect for the purposes of making claims in respect of the total compensation profit for periods of account beginning on or after 1 March 2012.

[225ZF Time limits etc for spreading claim

(1) A claim under section 225ZB must be made on or before the first anniversary of the normal self-assessment filing date for Year 1.

(2) If the profits of a tax year are to be adjusted or further adjusted in accordance with this Chapter after an assessment for that tax year has become final and conclusive, any assessment or repayment or discharge of tax that is necessary to give effect to this Chapter must be made.

(3) But repayment or discharge of tax is due only if a claim for it is made.][1]

Commentary—*Simon's Taxes* **B5.111.**
Amendments—[1] Chapter 16ZA (ss 225ZA–225ZG) inserted by the Enactment of Extra-statutory Concessions Order, SI 2012/266 arts 6, 9 with effect for the purposes of making claims in respect of the total compensation profit for periods of account beginning on or after 1 March 2012.

[225ZG Interpretation

In this Chapter—

"animal" means any animal or other living creature;

"farming trade" means a trade of farming;

"the farmer", in relation to a farming trade, means the individual who (alone or in partnership) carries on that trade;

"total compensation profit" has the meaning given by section 225ZB.][1]

Amendments—[1] Chapter 16ZA (ss 225ZA–225ZG) inserted by the Enactment of Extra-statutory Concessions Order, SI 2012/266 arts 6, 9 with effect for the purposes of making claims in respect of the total compensation profit for periods of account beginning on or after 1 March 2012.

[CHAPTER 16A

OIL ACTIVITIES][1]

Amendments—[1] Chapter 16A (ss 225A–225U) inserted by TIOPA 2010 s 364, Sch 1 paras 1, 2. TIOPA 2010 has effect for corporation tax purposes for accounting periods ending on or after 1 April 2010, for income and capital gains tax purposes for the tax year 2010–11 and subsequent tax years, and for petroleum revenue tax purposes for chargeable periods beginning on or after 1 July 2010.

[Application of Chapter

225ZH Chapter not to apply where cash basis used

Nothing in this Chapter applies in calculating the profits of a trade on the cash basis.][1]

Amendments—[1] This section inserted by FA 2013 s 17, Sch 4 para 34 with effect for the tax year 2013–14 and subsequent tax years, subject to the provisions of FA 2013 Sch 4 para 57 in relation to barristers and advocates.

[Basic definitions

225A Meaning of "oil extraction activities"

(1) In this Chapter "oil extraction activities" means activities within any of subsections (2) to (5) (but see also section 225M(6)).

(2) Activities of a person in searching for oil in the United Kingdom or a designated area or causing such searching to be carried out for that person.

(3) Activities of a person in extracting, or causing to be extracted for that person, oil at any place in the United Kingdom or a designated area under rights which—

(*a*) authorise the extraction, and

(*b*) are held by that person.

(4) Activities of a person in transporting, or causing to be transported for that person, oil extracted at any such place not on dry land under rights which—

(*a*) authorise the extraction, and

(*b*) are held by that person,

if the transportation meets condition A or B (see subsections (6) and (7)).

(5) Activities of a person in effecting, or causing to be effected for that person, the initial treatment or initial storage of oil won from any oil field under rights which—

(a) authorise its extraction, and

(b) are held by that person.

(6) Condition A is that the transportation is to the place where the oil is first landed in the United Kingdom.

(7) Condition B is that the transportation—

(a) is to the place in the United Kingdom, or

(b) in the case of oil first landed in another country, is to the place in that or any other country (other than the United Kingdom),

at which the seller in a sale at arm's length could reasonably be expected to deliver it (or, if there is more than one such place, the one nearest to the place of extraction).

(8) The definition of "initial storage" in section 12(1) of OTA 1975 applies for the purposes of this section.

(9) But in its application for those purposes in relation to the person mentioned in subsection (5) and to oil won from any one oil field, that definition is to have effect as if the reference to the maximum daily production rate of oil for the field mentioned in that definition were to a share of that maximum daily production rate proportionate to that person's share of the oil won from that field.

(10) In this section "initial treatment" has the same meaning as in Part 1 of OTA 1975 (see section 12(1) of that Act).][1]

Commentary—*Simon's Taxes* **D7.901.**

HMRC Manuals—Oil Taxation OT21003 (definition of oil extraction activities).

Amendments—[1] Sections 225A–225U inserted by TIOPA 2010 s 364, Sch 1 paras 1, 2. TIOPA 2010 has effect for corporation tax purposes for accounting periods ending on or after 1 April 2010, for income and capital gains tax purposes for the tax year 2010–11 and subsequent tax years, and for petroleum revenue tax purposes for chargeable periods beginning on or after 1 July 2010.

[225B Meaning of "oil rights"

In this Chapter "oil rights" means—

(a) rights to oil to be extracted at any place in the United Kingdom or a designated area, or

(b) rights to interests in or to the benefit of such oil.][1]

Commentary—*Simon's Taxes* **D7.901.**

HMRC Manuals—Oil Taxation OT21004 (definition of oil rights).

Amendments—[1] Sections 225A–225U inserted by TIOPA 2010 s 364, Sch 1 paras 1, 2. TIOPA 2010 has effect for corporation tax purposes for accounting periods ending on or after 1 April 2010, for income and capital gains tax purposes for the tax year 2010–11 and subsequent tax years, and for petroleum revenue tax purposes for chargeable periods beginning on or after 1 July 2010.

[225C Meaning of "ring fence income"

In this Chapter "ring fence income" means income arising from oil extraction activities or oil rights.][1]

Commentary—*Simon's Taxes* **D7.901.**

HMRC Manuals—Oil Taxation OT21017 (definition of ring fence income).

Amendments—[1] Sections 225A–225U inserted by TIOPA 2010 s 364, Sch 1 paras 1, 2. TIOPA 2010 has effect for corporation tax purposes for accounting periods ending on or after 1 April 2010, for income and capital gains tax purposes for the tax year 2010–11 and subsequent tax years, and for petroleum revenue tax purposes for chargeable periods beginning on or after 1 July 2010.

[225D Meaning of "ring fence trade"

In this Chapter "ring fence trade" means activities which—

(a) are within the definition of "oil-related activities" in section 16(2) (oil extraction and related activities), and

(b) constitute a separate trade (whether because of section 16(1) or otherwise).][1]

Commentary—*Simon's Taxes* **D7.901.**

HMRC Manuals—Oil Taxation OT21002 (oil extraction as a separate trade).

Amendments—[1] Sections 225A–225U inserted by TIOPA 2010 s 364, Sch 1 paras 1, 2. TIOPA 2010 has effect for corporation tax purposes for accounting periods ending on or after 1 April 2010, for income and capital gains tax purposes for the tax year 2010–11 and subsequent tax years, and for petroleum revenue tax purposes for chargeable periods beginning on or after 1 July 2010.

[225E Other definitions

In this Chapter—

"chargeable period" has the same meaning as in Part 1 of OTA 1975 (see section 1(3) of that Act),

"designated area" means an area designated by Order in Council under section 1(7) of the Continental Shelf Act 1964,

"oil" means any substance won or capable of being won under the authority of a licence granted under Part 1 of the Petroleum Act 1998 or the Petroleum (Production) Act (Northern Ireland) 1964 (c 28 (NI)), other than methane gas won in the course of operations for making and keeping mines safe, "oil field" has the same meaning as in Part 1 of OTA 1975 (see section 12(1) of that Act),

"OTA 1975" means the Oil Taxation Act 1975, and

"participator" has the same meaning as in Part 1 of OTA 1975 (see section 12(1) of that Act).][1]

Commentary—*Simon's Taxes* **D7.901.**
HMRC Manuals—Oil Taxation OT04005 (definition of chargeable period).
OT13940 (definition of designated area).
OT21005 (definition of oil).
OT03100 (definition of oil field).
OT03100 (definition of participator).
Amendments—[1] Sections 225A–225U inserted by TIOPA 2010 s 364, Sch 1 paras 1, 2. TIOPA 2010 has effect for corporation tax purposes for accounting periods ending on or after 1 April 2010, for income and capital gains tax purposes for the tax year 2010–11 and subsequent tax years, and for petroleum revenue tax purposes for chargeable periods beginning on or after 1 July 2010.

[Oil valuation

225F Valuation where market value taken into account under section 2 of OTA 1975

(1) This section applies if a person disposes of oil in circumstances such that the market value of the oil—

(a) falls to be taken into account under section 2 of OTA 1975, otherwise than by virtue of paragraph 6 of Schedule 3 to that Act, in calculating for petroleum revenue tax purposes the assessable profit or allowable loss accruing to that person in a chargeable period from an oil field, or

(b) would so fall but for section 10 of that Act.

(2) For income tax purposes, the disposal of the oil, and its acquisition by the person to whom it was disposed of, are to be treated as having been for a consideration equal to the market value of the oil—

(a) as so taken into account under section 2 of that Act, or

(b) as would have been so taken into account under that section but for section 10 of that Act.][1]

HMRC Manuals—Oil Taxation OT03150 (computation of petroleum revenue tax charge).
Amendments—[1] Sections 225A–225U inserted by TIOPA 2010 s 364, Sch 1 paras 1, 2. TIOPA 2010 has effect for corporation tax purposes for accounting periods ending on or after 1 April 2010, for income and capital gains tax purposes for the tax year 2010–11 and subsequent tax years, and for petroleum revenue tax purposes for chargeable periods beginning on or after 1 July 2010.

[225G Valuation where disposal not sale at arm's length

(1) This section applies if conditions A, B and C are met.

(2) Condition A is that a person disposes of oil acquired by the person—

(a) in the course of oil extraction activities carried on by the person, or

(b) as a result of oil rights held by the person.

(3) Condition B is that the disposal is not a sale at arm's length (as defined in paragraph 1 of Schedule 3 to OTA 1975).

(4) Condition C is that section 225F does not apply in relation to the disposal.

(5) For income tax purposes, the disposal of the oil, and its acquisition by the person to whom it was disposed of, are to be treated as having been for a consideration equal to the market value of the oil.

(6) Paragraphs 2 and 3A of Schedule 3 to OTA 1975 (definition of market value of oil including light gases) apply for the purposes of this section as they apply for the purposes of Part 1 of that Act, but with the following modifications.

(7) Those modifications are that—

(a) any reference in paragraph 2 to the notional delivery day for the actual oil is to be read as a reference to the day on which the oil is disposed of as mentioned in this section, and

(b) paragraph 2(4) is to be treated as omitted.][1]

Commentary—*Simon's Taxes* **D7.906.**
HMRC Manuals—Oil Taxation OT21029 (non-arm's length disposals).
Amendments—[1] Sections 225A–225U inserted by TIOPA 2010 s 364, Sch 1 paras 1, 2. TIOPA 2010 has effect for corporation tax purposes for accounting periods ending on or after 1 April 2010, for income and capital gains tax purposes for the tax year 2010–11 and subsequent tax years, and for petroleum revenue tax purposes for chargeable periods beginning on or after 1 July 2010.

[225H Valuation where excess of nominated proceeds

(1) This section applies if an excess of nominated proceeds for a chargeable period—

(a) is taken into account in calculating a person's profits under section 2(5)(e) of OTA 1975, or

(b) would have been so taken into account if the person were chargeable to tax under OTA 1975 in respect of an oil field.

(2) For income tax purposes, the amount of the excess is to be added to the consideration which the person is treated as having received in respect of oil disposed of by that person in the period.][1]

Commentary—*Simon's Taxes* **D7.906.**
HMRC Manuals—Oil Taxation OT05240 (determining of excess of nominated proceeds).

ITTOIA 2005

Amendments—[1]   Sections 225A–225U inserted by TIOPA 2010 s 364, Sch 1 paras 1, 2. TIOPA 2010 has effect for corporation tax purposes for accounting periods ending on or after 1 April 2010, for income and capital gains tax purposes for the tax year 2010–11 and subsequent tax years, and for petroleum revenue tax purposes for chargeable periods beginning on or after 1 July 2010.

[225I Valuation where relevant appropriation but no disposal

(1) This section applies if conditions A and B are met.

(2) Condition A is that a person makes a relevant appropriation of oil without disposing of it.

(3) Condition B is that the person does so in circumstances such that the market value of the oil—

    (a) falls to be taken into account under section 2 of OTA 1975 in calculating for petroleum revenue tax purposes the assessable profit or allowable loss accruing to that person in a chargeable period from an oil field, or

    (b) would so fall but for section 10 of that Act.

(4) For income tax purposes, the person is to be treated as having, at the time of the appropriation—

    (a) sold the oil in the course of the separate trade consisting of activities falling within the definition of "oil-related activities" in section 16(2) (oil extraction and related activities), and

    (b) purchased it in the course of the separate trade consisting of activities not so falling.

(5) For income tax purposes, that sale and purchase is to be treated as having been at a price equal to the market value of the oil—

    (a) as so taken into account under section 2 of OTA 1975, or

    (b) as would have been so taken into account under that section but for section 10 of that Act.

(6) In this section "relevant appropriation" has the meaning given by section 12(1) of OTA 1975.][1]

Commentary—*Simon's Taxes* D7.906.

Amendments—[1]   Sections 225A–225U inserted by TIOPA 2010 s 364, Sch 1 paras 1, 2. TIOPA 2010 has effect for corporation tax purposes for accounting periods ending on or after 1 April 2010, for income and capital gains tax purposes for the tax year 2010–11 and subsequent tax years, and for petroleum revenue tax purposes for chargeable periods beginning on or after 1 July 2010.

[225J Valuation where appropriation to refining etc

(1) This section applies if conditions A, B and C are met.

(2) Condition A is that a person appropriates oil acquired by the person—

    (a) in the course of oil extraction activities carried on by the person, or

    (b) as a result of oil rights held by the person.

(3) Condition B is that the oil is appropriated to refining or to any use except the production purposes of an oil field (as defined in section 12(1) of OTA 1975).

(4) Condition C is that section 225I does not apply in relation to the appropriation.

(5) For income tax purposes—

    (a) the person is to be treated as having, at the time of the appropriation, sold and purchased the oil as mentioned in section 225I(4)(a) and (b), and

    (b) that sale and purchase is to be treated as having been at a price equal to the market value of the oil.

(6) Paragraphs 2 and 3A of Schedule 3 to OTA 1975 (definition of market value of oil including light gases) apply for the purposes of this section as they apply for the purposes of Part 1 of that Act, but with the following modifications.

(7) Those modifications are that—

    (a) any reference in paragraph 2 to the notional delivery day for the actual oil is to be read as a reference to the day on which the oil is appropriated as mentioned in this section,

    (b) any reference in paragraphs 2 and 2A to oil being relevantly appropriated is to be read as a reference to its being appropriated as mentioned in this section, and

    (c) paragraph 2(4) is to be treated as omitted.][1]

Amendments—[1]   Sections 225A–225U inserted by TIOPA 2010 s 364, Sch 1 paras 1, 2. TIOPA 2010 has effect for corporation tax purposes for accounting periods ending on or after 1 April 2010, for income and capital gains tax purposes for the tax year 2010–11 and subsequent tax years, and for petroleum revenue tax purposes for chargeable periods beginning on or after 1 July 2010.

[Regional development grants

225K Reduction of expenditure by reference to regional development grant

(1) This section applies if conditions A and B are met.

(2) Condition A is that a person has incurred expenditure (by way of purchase, rent or otherwise) on the acquisition of an asset in a transaction to which paragraph 2 of Schedule 4 to OTA 1975 applies (transactions between connected persons or otherwise than at arm's length).

(3) Condition B is that the expenditure incurred by the other person mentioned in that paragraph in acquiring, bringing into existence or enhancing the value of the asset as mentioned in that paragraph—

    (a) has been or is to be met by a regional development grant, and

    (b) falls (in whole or in part) to be taken into account under Part 2 or 6 of CAA 2001 (capital allowances relating to plant and machinery or research and development).

(4) Subsection (5) applies for the purposes of the charge to income tax on the income arising from the activities of the person mentioned in subsection (2) which are treated by section 16(1) (oil extraction and related activities) as a separate trade for those purposes.

(5) The expenditure mentioned in subsection (2) is to be reduced by the amount of the regional development grant mentioned in subsection (3).

(6) In this section "regional development grant" means a grant falling within section 534(1) of CAA 2001 (Northern Ireland regional development grant).][1]

HMRC Manuals—Capital Allowance CA14200 (exceptions to general rule).
Amendments—[1] Sections 225A–225U inserted by TIOPA 2010 s 364, Sch 1 paras 1, 2. TIOPA 2010 has effect for corporation tax purposes for accounting periods ending on or after 1 April 2010, for income and capital gains tax purposes for the tax year 2010–11 and subsequent tax years, and for petroleum revenue tax purposes for chargeable periods beginning on or after 1 July 2010. Note that, in relation to periods of account (within the meaning in CAA 2001 s 6) beginning before 6 April 2011, sub-s (3)(b) has effect as if ", 3" were inserted after "Part 2", and ", industrial buildings" were inserted after "machinery" (TIOPA 2010 Sch 9 para 35).

[225L Adjustment as a result of regional development grant

(1) This section applies if conditions A, B and C are met.

(2) Condition A is that expenditure incurred by a person in relation to an asset in a tax year ("the initial period") has been or is to be met by a regional development grant.

(3) Condition B is that, despite the provisions of section 534(2) and (3) of CAA 2001 (Northern Ireland regional development grants) and section 225K of this Act, in determining that person's liability to income tax for the initial period, the whole or some part of that expenditure falls to be taken into account under Part 2 or 6 of CAA 2001.

(4) Condition C is that—

    (*a*) expenditure on the asset becomes allowable under section 3 or 4 of OTA 1975 in a tax year (an "adjustment period") subsequent to the initial period, or

    (*b*) the proportion of any such expenditure which is allowable in an adjustment period is different as compared with the initial period.

(5) There is to be redetermined for the purposes of subsections (7) and (8) the amount of the expenditure mentioned in subsection (2) which would have been taken into account as mentioned in subsection (3) if the circumstances mentioned in subsection (4) had existed in the initial period.

(6) According to whether the amount as so redetermined is greater or less than the amount actually taken into account as mentioned in subsection (3), the difference is referred to in subsections (7) and (8) as the increase or the reduction in the allowance.

(7) If there is an increase in the allowance, an amount of capital expenditure equal to the increase is to be treated, for the purposes of Part 2 or 6 of CAA 2001, as having been incurred by the person concerned in the adjustment period on an extension of, or addition to, the asset mentioned in subsection (2).

(8) If there is a reduction in the allowance, the person concerned is to be treated, for the purpose of determining that person's liability to income tax, as having received in the adjustment period, as income of the trade in connection with which the expenditure mentioned in subsection (2) was incurred, a sum equal to the amount of the reduction in the allowance.

(9) In this section "regional development grant" has the meaning given by section 225K(6).][1]

Commentary—*Simon's Taxes* **D1.614.**
HMRC Manuals—Oil Taxation OT09025 (allowable expenditure on the assets)
Amendments—[1] Sections 225A–225U inserted by TIOPA 2010 s 364, Sch 1 paras 1, 2. TIOPA 2010 has effect for corporation tax purposes for accounting periods ending on or after 1 April 2010, for income and capital gains tax purposes for the tax year 2010–11 and subsequent tax years, and for petroleum revenue tax purposes for chargeable periods beginning on or after 1 July 2010. Note that, in relation to periods of account (within the meaning in CAA 2001 s 6) beginning before 6 April 2011, sub-ss (3), (7) have effect as if ", 3" were inserted after "Part 2" (TIOPA 2010 Sch 9 para 35).

[Tariff receipts etc

225M Tariff receipts etc

(1) Subsection (5) applies to a sum which meets conditions A, B and C.

(2) Condition A is that the sum constitutes a tariff receipt or tax-exempt tariffing receipt of a person who is a participator in an oil field.

(3) Condition B is that the sum constitutes consideration in the nature of income rather than capital.

(4) Condition C is that the sum would not, but for subsection (5), be treated as mentioned in that subsection.

(5) The sum is to be treated as a receipt of the separate trade mentioned in section 16(1) (oil extraction and related activities).

(6) So far as they would not otherwise be so treated, the activities—

    (*a*) of a participator in an oil field, or

    (*b*) of a person connected with the participator,

in making available an asset in a way which gives rise to tariff receipts or tax-exempt tariffing receipts of the participator are to be treated for the purposes of this Chapter as oil extraction activities.

ITTOIA 2005

(7) In determining for the purposes of subsection (2) whether a sum constitutes a tariff receipt or tax-exempt tariffing receipt of a person who is a participator, no account may be taken of any sum which—

(*a*) is in fact received or receivable by a person connected with the participator, and

(*b*) constitutes a tariff receipt or tax-exempt tariffing receipt of the participator.

But in relation to the person by whom such a sum is actually received, subsection (2) has effect as if the person were a participator and as if condition A were met.

(8) References in this section to a person connected with a participator include a person with whom the person is associated, within the meaning of paragraph 11 of Schedule 2 to the Oil Taxation Act 1983, but section 878(5) of this Act (application of definition of "connected" persons) does not apply for the purposes of this section.

(9) In this section—

"tax-exempt tariffing receipt" has the meaning given by section 6A(2) of the Oil Taxation Act 1983, and

"tariff receipt" has the same meaning as in that Act.][1]

Commentary—*Simon's Taxes* **D7.902.**
HMRC Manuals—Oil Taxation OT15820 (tax-exempt tariffing receipts: definition).
Amendments—[1]   Sections 225A–225U inserted by TIOPA 2010 s 364, Sch 1 paras 1, 2. TIOPA 2010 has effect for corporation tax purposes for accounting periods ending on or after 1 April 2010, for income and capital gains tax purposes for the tax year 2010–11 and subsequent tax years, and for petroleum revenue tax purposes for chargeable periods beginning on or after 1 July 2010.

[Abandonment guarantees

225N [Expenditure on abandonment guarantees][4]

(1) Subsection (2) applies if, as a result of section 3(1)(*hh*) of OTA 1975 (obtaining abandonment guarantee), expenditure incurred by a participator in an oil field is allowable (in whole or in part) for petroleum revenue tax purposes under section 3 of that Act.

[(1A) Subsection (2) also applies if expenditure incurred by a participator in an oil field would be so allowable as a result of section 3(1)(hh) of that Act but for the fact that the oil field is a non-taxable oil field within the meaning of Part 3 of FA 1993 (see section 185 of that Act).][2]

(2) So far as [the expenditure mentioned in subsection (1) or (1A) is or would be so allowable][2], it is to be allowed as a deduction in calculating the participator's ring fence income.

(3)   . . .[3]

(4)   . . .[3]

(5)   . . .[4]

(6) In this Chapter—

"abandonment guarantee" has the same meaning as it has for the purposes of [section 3 of OTA 1975][4] (see section 104 of [FA 1991][4]), and

"the guarantor" and "the relevant participator" have the same meaning as in section 104 of that Act.][1]

Commentary—*Simon's Taxes* **D7.926.**
HMRC Manuals—Oil Taxation OT10400 (reimbursement expenditure, FA91/S106).
OT10300 (abandonment guarantees, OTA75/S3(1)(hh)).
Amendments—[1]   Sections 225A–225U inserted by TIOPA 2010 s 364, Sch 1 paras 1, 2. TIOPA 2010 has effect for corporation tax purposes for accounting periods ending on or after 1 April 2010, for income and capital gains tax purposes for the tax year 2010–11 and subsequent tax years, and for petroleum revenue tax purposes for chargeable periods beginning on or after 1 July 2010.
[2]   Sub-s (1A) inserted, and in sub-s (2), words substituted for words "that expenditure is so allowable", by FA 2013 s 89(1), Sch 31 para 1(1), (2) with effect in relation to expenditure incurred on or after 17 July 2013.
[3]   Sub-ss (3), (4) repealed by FA 2013 s 89(1), Sch 31 para 6(1), (2) with effect in relation to expenditure incurred on or after 17 July 2013.
[4]   Sub-s (5) repealed, in sub-s (6) in definition of "abandonment guarantee", words substituted for words "section 105 of FA 1991" and "that Act", and section heading substituted, by FA 2013 s 89(1), Sch 31 paras 13, 14 with effect in relation to expenditure incurred on or after 17 July 2013.

[Abandonment expenditure

225R [Introduction to section 225S][3]

(1) [Section 225S applies][3] if—

(*a*) paragraph 2A of Schedule 5 to OTA 1975 applies   . . . .[2], and

(*b*) the default payment falls (in whole or part) to be attributed to the contributing participator under paragraph 2A(2) of that Schedule[, or would fall to be so attributed if a claim under paragraph 2A(2) of that Schedule were made][2].

[(1A) The condition in subsection (1)(*b*) is to be treated as met for the purposes of this section if it would be met but for the fact that the contributing participator is (or was) a participator in an oil field that is a non-taxable oil field within the meaning of Part 3 of FA 1993 (see section 185 of that Act).][2]

(2) In section 225S "the additional abandonment expenditure" means the amount which is [or would be][2] attributed to the contributing participator as mentioned in subsection (1)(*b*) (whether representing the whole or only part of the default payment).

(3) In this Chapter "default payment", "the defaulter" and "contributing participator" have the same meaning as in paragraph 2A of Schedule 5 to OTA 1975.][1]

HMRC Manuals—Oil Taxation OT03100 (contributing participator: definition).
Amendments—[1] Sections 225A–225U inserted by TIOPA 2010 s 364, Sch 1 paras 1, 2. TIOPA 2010 has effect for corporation tax purposes for accounting periods ending on or after 1 April 2010, for income and capital gains tax purposes for the tax year 2010–11 and subsequent tax years, and for petroleum revenue tax purposes for chargeable periods beginning on or after 1 July 2010.
[2] In sub-s (1), in para (*a*) words "; or would apply if a claim under paragraph 2A(2) of that Schedule were made" repealed, and in para (*b*) words inserted, sub-s (1A) inserted, and in sub-s (2) words inserted, FA 2013 s 89(1), Sch 31 para 1(1), (3) with effect in relation to expenditure incurred on or after 17 July 2013.
[3] In sub-s (1), words substituted for words "Sections 225S and 225T apply", and section heading substituted, by FA 2013 s 89(1), Sch 31 paras 13, 16 with effect in relation to expenditure incurred on or after 17 July 2013.

[225S Relief for expenditure incurred by a participator in meeting defaulter's abandonment expenditure

(1) Relief by way of capital allowance, or a deduction in calculating ring fence income, is to be available to the contributing participator in respect of the additional abandonment expenditure if any such relief or deduction would have been available to the defaulter if—

    (*a*) the defaulter had incurred the additional abandonment expenditure, and

    (*b*) at the time that that expenditure was incurred the defaulter continued to carry on a ring fence trade.

(2) The basis of qualification for or entitlement to any relief or deduction which is available to the contributing participator under this section is to be determined on the assumption that the conditions in subsection (1)(*a*) and (*b*) are met.

(3) But, subject to subsection (2), any such relief or deduction is to be available in the same way as if the additional abandonment expenditure had been incurred by the contributing participator for the purposes of the ring fence trade carried on by the contributing participator.][1]

Commentary—*Simon's Taxes* **D7.927.**
HMRC Manuals—Oil Taxation OT28430 (relief for expenditure incurred by a participator in meeting a defaulter abandonment expenditure).
Amendments—[1] Sections 225A–225U inserted by TIOPA 2010 s 364, Sch 1 paras 1, 2. TIOPA 2010 has effect for corporation tax purposes for accounting periods ending on or after 1 April 2010, for income and capital gains tax purposes for the tax year 2010–11 and subsequent tax years, and for petroleum revenue tax purposes for chargeable periods beginning on or after 1 July 2010.

[225U Interest on repayment of APRT

(1) Subsection (2) applies if interest is paid to a participator under paragraph 10(4) of Schedule 19 to FA 1982 (interest on advance petroleum revenue tax which becomes repayable).

(2) The interest paid is to be disregarded in calculating the participator's income for income tax purposes.][1]

HMRC Manuals—OT05700 (advanced petroleum revenue tax: interest repayment).
Amendments—[1] Sections 225A–225U inserted by TIOPA 2010 s 364, Sch 1 paras 1, 2. TIOPA 2010 has effect for corporation tax purposes for accounting periods ending on or after 1 April 2010, for income and capital gains tax purposes for the tax year 2010–11 and subsequent tax years, and for petroleum revenue tax purposes for chargeable periods beginning on or after 1 July 2010.

[Receipts arising from decommissioning

225V Receipts arising from decommissioning

(1) This section applies if—

    (*a*) a person that is or has been carrying on a ring fence trade ("the defaulter") has defaulted on a liability under—

        (i) a relevant agreement, or

        (ii) an abandonment programme,

    to make a payment towards decommissioning expenditure,

    (*b*) another person that is or has been carrying on a ring fence trade ("the contributing person") pays an amount ("the relevant contribution") in or towards meeting the whole or part of the default, and

    (*c*) the amount of the relevant contribution is less than the sum of the amounts within subsection (2).

(2) The amounts within this subsection are—

    (*a*) any payments made (directly or indirectly) to the contributing person by the guarantor under an abandonment guarantee as a result of the defaulter defaulting on the liability,

    (*b*) any reimbursement payments, and

    (*c*) any relief from tax which the contributing person obtains in respect of the relevant contribution.

(3) The difference between—

    (*a*) the sum of the amounts within subsection (2), and

    (*b*) the relevant contribution,

("the relevant difference") is to be treated as a receipt (in the nature of income) of the contributing person's ring fence trade for the relevant tax year (see subsection (4)).

(4) "The relevant tax year" means the tax year that includes the day on which the Secretary of State certifies that the relevant abandonment programme has been satisfactorily completed ("the certification date").

This is subject to subsection (5).

(5) If the contributing person's ring fence trade is permanently discontinued before the certification date, "the relevant tax year" is the last tax year in which that trade is carried on.

(6) The relevant difference is to be determined—

    (a)　in a case where subsection (5) applies, at the end of the tax year in which the certification date falls, and

    (b)　in any other case, at the end of the relevant tax year.

(7) In a case where subsection (5) applies, any income tax chargeable for the relevant tax year by virtue of this section is due and payable for the tax year in which the certification date falls.

(8) Any additional assessment to income tax required in order to take account of a receipt arising under this section may be made at any time not later than 4 years after the end of the tax year in which the certification date falls.

(9) In this section—

    "abandonment programme" means an abandonment programme approved under Part 4 of the Petroleum Act 1998 (including such a programme as revised),

    "decommissioning expenditure" has the meaning given by section 330C of CTA 2010,

    "reimbursement payment" means any payment made to the contributing person by the defaulter in reimbursing the contributing person in respect of, or otherwise making good to the contributing person, the whole or any part of the relevant contribution,

    "the relevant abandonment programme" means the abandonment programme in respect of which the decommissioning expenditure mentioned in subsection (1)(a) was incurred, and

    "relevant agreement" has the meaning given by section 104(5)(a) of FA 1991.][1]

HMRC Manuals—Oil Taxation OT10300 (abandonment guarantees, OTA75/S3(1)(hh)).
OT10808 (decommissioning certainty: the effect of claims on oil allowances).
Amendments—[1]　Section 225V and preceding cross-head inserted by FA 2013 s 89(2), Sch 31 para 22 with effect in relation to expenditure incurred on or after 17 July 2013.

CHAPTER 17

ADJUSTMENT INCOME

Introduction

226 Professions and vocations

The provisions of this Chapter apply to professions and vocations as they apply to trades.

Commentary—*Simon's Taxes* **B2.114**.

Adjustment on change of basis

227 Application of Chapter

(1) This Chapter applies if—

    (a)　a person carrying on a trade changes, from one period of account to the next, the basis on which profits of the trade are calculated for income tax purposes,

    (b)　the old basis accorded with the law or practice applicable in relation to the period of account before the change, and

    (c)　the new basis accords with the law and practice applicable in relation to the period of account after the change,

but does not apply to income which is charged in accordance with section 832 (relevant foreign income charged on the remittance basis).

(2) The practice applicable in any case means the accepted practice in cases of that description as to how profits of a trade should be calculated for income tax purposes.

(3) A person changes the basis on which profits of a trade are calculated for income tax purposes if the person makes—

    (a)　a [change of accounting policy][1] (see subsection (4)), or

    (b)　a change in the tax adjustments applied (see subsections (5) and (6)).

[(4) A "change of accounting policy" includes, in particular—

    (a)　a change from using UK generally accepted accounting practice to using generally accepted accounting practice with respect to accounts prepared in accordance with international accounting standards, and

    (b)　a change from using generally accepted accounting practice with respect to accounts prepared in accordance with international accounting standards to using UK generally accepted accounting practice.][1]

(5) A "tax adjustment" means any adjustment required or authorised by law in calculating profits of a trade for income tax purposes.

(6) A "change in the tax adjustments applied"—

(a) does not include a change made in order to comply with amending legislation not applicable to the previous period of account, but

(b) includes a change resulting from a change of view as to what is required or authorised by law or as to whether any adjustment is so required or authorised.

Commentary—*Simon's Taxes* **B2.114**.

HMRC Manuals—Business Income Manual BIM34050 (change of basis of computing taxable profits: accounting policy changes: has there been a change?).

BIM34070 (change of basis of computing taxable profits: change in tax adjustment).

BIM34135 (change of basis of computing taxable profits: adjustment income and expenses: meanings).

Amendments—[1]   Words in sub-s (3)(a) and the whole of sub-s (4) substituted by FA 2012 s 54(1) with effect in relation to a change of basis if the new basis is adopted for a period of account which begins: (a) on or after 1 January 2012; or (b) before 1 January 2012 and the adoption is in consequence of the issue, revocation, amendment or recognition of, or withdrawal of recognition from, an accounting standard by an accounting body on or after 1 January 2012.

[227A Application of Chapter where cash basis used

(1) This Chapter applies if—

(a) an election under section 25A (cash basis for small businesses) has effect in relation to a trade for a tax year but no such election has effect in relation to the trade for the following tax year, or

(b) no such election has effect in relation to a trade for a tax year but such an election has effect in relation to the trade for the following tax year.

(2) But this Chapter does not apply to income which is charged in accordance with section 832.

[(3) This section is subject to section 227C (application of Chapter where section 227B applies).][2]][1]

HMRC Manuals—Business Income Manual BIM70055 (cash basis for small businesses).

Amendments—[1]   This section inserted by FA 2013 s 17, Sch 4 paras 35, 36 with effect for the tax year 2013–14 and subsequent tax years, subject to the provisions of FA 2013 Sch 4 para 57 in relation to barristers and advocates.

[2]   Sub-s (3) inserted by F(No 2)A 2017 s 17, Sch 3 paras 2, 6 with effect for the tax year 2017–18 and subsequent tax years.

[227B Cash basis treatment: full relief under Chapter 1 of Part 6A (trading allowance)

(1) Subsection (2) applies if—

(a) an individual carries on a trade in a tax year, and

(b) the profits or losses of the trade for the tax year are treated as nil under section 783AF (trade profits: full relief under Chapter 1 of Part 6A) by virtue of the fact that the conditions in section 783AE(2) are met.

(2) For the purposes of determining if this Chapter applies, an election under section 25A is to be treated as having effect in relation to the trade for the tax year.][1]

Commentary—*Simon's Taxes* **B4.202**.

Amendments—[1]   Sections 227B, 227C inserted by F(No 2)A 2017 s 17, Sch 3 paras 2, 7 with effect for the tax year 2017–18 and subsequent tax years.

[227C Application of Chapter where section 227B applies

(1) This section applies if, as a result of the operation of section 227B, the basis on which profits of a trade are calculated is treated as changed as mentioned in section 227A(1).

(2) This Chapter applies as if—

(a) in sections 232(1) and 233(1), for "the first period of account for which the new basis is adopted" there were substituted "the first tax year for which the profits or losses of the trade are not treated as nil under section 783AF", and

(b) sections 235, 236, 237, 239A and 239B were omitted.

(3) If there is no tax year after the change of basis for which the profits or losses of the trade are not treated as nil under section 783AF, this Chapter does not apply.][1]

Commentary—*Simon's Taxes* **B4.204**.

Amendments—[1]   Sections 227B, 227C inserted by F(No 2)A 2017 s 17, Sch 3 paras 2, 7 with effect for the tax year 2017–18 and subsequent tax years.

228 Adjustment income and adjustment expense

(1) An amount by way of adjustment must be calculated in accordance with section 231.

(2) If the amount produced by the calculation is positive, it is treated as income and charged to income tax under this Chapter.

It is referred to in this Chapter as "adjustment income".

(3) If the amount produced by the calculation is negative, a deduction is allowed for it in calculating the profits of the trade.

It is referred to in this Chapter as an "adjustment expense".

(4) This section is subject to section 234 (no adjustment for certain expenses previously brought into account).

Commentary—*Simon's Taxes* **B4.201**.

HMRC Manuals—Business Income Manual BIM34095 (change of basis of computing taxable profits: adjustment income and expenses: charge to tax).

229 Income charged

(1) Tax is charged under this Chapter on the full amount of any adjustment income arising in the tax year.

(2) This is subject to—

    (a) .[sections 237 to 239B][1] (which provide for spreading of adjustment income), and

    (b) Part 8 (foreign income: special rules).

HMRC Manuals—Business Income Manual BIM15040 (what is chargeable?).

BIM34095 (tax charged on adjustment income).

Amendments—[1] In sub-s (2)(a) words substituted for words "sections 237 to 239" by FA 2013 s 17, Sch 4 para 52(1), (2) with effect for the tax year 2013–14 and subsequent tax years, subject to the provisions of FA 2013 Sch 4 para 57 in relation to barristers and advocates.

230 Person liable

The person liable for any tax charged under this Chapter is the person receiving or entitled to the adjustment income.

HMRC Manuals—Business Income Manual BIM34095 (the person liable for any tax charged).

231 Calculation of the adjustment

The amount of the adjustment is calculated as follows.

Step 1 Add together any amounts representing the extent to which, comparing the two bases, profits were understated (or losses overstated) on the old basis. The amounts are—

	Amounts
1	Receipts which on the new basis would have been brought into account in calculating the profits of a period of account before the change, so far as they were not so brought into account.
2	Expenses which on the new basis fall to be brought into account in calculating the profits of a period of account after the change, so far as they were brought into account in calculating the profits of a period of account before the change.
3	Deductions in respect of opening trading stock or opening work in progress in the first period of account on the new basis, so far as they— (a) are not matched by credits in respect of closing trading stock or closing work in progress in the last period of account before the change, or (b) are calculated on a different basis that if used to calculate those credits would have given a higher figure.
4	Amounts recognised for accounting purposes in respect of depreciation in the last period of account before the change, so far as they were not the subject of an adjustment for income tax purposes, where such an adjustment would be required on the new basis.

Step 2 Then deduct any amounts representing the extent to which, comparing the two bases, profits were overstated (or losses understated) on the old basis.
The amounts are—

	Amounts
1	Receipts which were brought into account in a period of account before the change, so far as they would not have been so brought into account if the profits had been calculated on the new basis.
2	Expenses which were not brought into account in calculating the profits of a period of account before the change, so far as they— (a) would have been brought into account for a period of account before the change if the profits had been calculated on the new basis, and (b) would have been brought into account for a period of account after the change if the profits had continued to be calculated on the old basis.
3	Credits in respect of closing trading stock or closing work in progress in the last period of account before the change, so far as they— (a) are not matched by deductions in respect of opening trading stock or opening work in progress in the first period of account on the new basis, or (b) are calculated on a different basis that if used to calculate those deductions would have given a lower figure.

An amount so deducted may not be deducted again in calculating the profits of a period of account.

Commentary—*Simon's Taxes* **B2.115**.

Derivation—FA 2002 s 64(1), Sch 22 para 2.

HMRC Manuals—Business Income Manual BIM34130 (change of basis of computing taxable profits: adjustment income and expenses: calculation of adjustment).

Treatment of adjustment income and adjustment expense

232 Treatment of adjustment income

(1) Adjustment income is treated as arising on the last day of the first period of account for which the new basis is adopted.

(2) But this is subject to sections 235 (cases where adjustment not required until assets realised or written off) and 236 (change from realisation basis to mark to market).

(3) Adjustment income is treated for the purposes of [Part 4 of ITA 2007][1] (loss relief) as profits of the trade for the tax year in which tax is charged on it.

(4) In the case of an individual whose income from [the trade is relevant UK earnings within section 189(2)(*b*) of FA 2004, adjustment income is similarly relevant UK earnings.][1]

Commentary—*Simon's Taxes* **B2.115**.

HMRC Manuals—Business Income Manual BIM34095 (adjustment income charge to tax)..

Amendments—[1] Words in sub-ss (3), (4) substituted by ITA 2007 s 1027, Sch 1 paras 492, 502 with effect for income tax purposes from 6 April 2007, and corporation tax purposes for accounting periods ending after 5 April 2007.

233 Treatment of adjustment expense

(1) An adjustment expense is treated as an expense of the trade arising on the last day of the first period of account for which the new basis is adopted.

(2) But this is subject to sections 235 (cases where adjustment not required until assets realised or written off) and 236 (change from realisation basis to mark to market).

Commentary—*Simon's Taxes* **B2.115**.
Derivation—FA 2002 s 64(1), Sch 22 para 5(2).

Expenses previously brought into account

234 No adjustment for certain expenses previously brought into account

(1) This section applies if, as a result of a change of basis, expenses brought into account before the change on the old basis would on the new basis be brought into account over more than one period of account after the change.

(2) In such a case—

    (*a*) no adjustment is made under this Chapter, and

    (*b*) in calculating the profits of the trade no deduction is allowed for the expenses for any period of account after the change.

Commentary—*Simon's Taxes* **B2.115**.
Derivation—FA 2002 s 64(1), Sch 22 para 6(1), (2).
HMRC Manuals—Business Income Manual BIM34105 (change of basis of computing taxable profits: adjustment income and expenses: expenses already allowed).

Realising or writing off assets

235 Cases where adjustment not required until assets realised or written off

(1) This section applies if there is a change of basis resulting from a tax adjustment affecting the calculation of any of the following amounts.

(2) The amounts are—

    (*a*) any amount brought into account in respect of closing trading stock or closing work in progress in the last period of account before the change of basis,

    (*b*) any amount brought into account in respect of opening trading stock or opening work in progress in the first period of account on the new basis, and

    (*c*) any amount brought into account in respect of depreciation.

(3) Adjustment income or (as the case may be) an adjustment expense is treated as arising only when the asset to which it relates is realised or written off.

Commentary—*Simon's Taxes* **B2.115**.
Derivation—FA 2002 s 64(1), Sch 22 para 7(1), (2).
HMRC Manuals—Business Income Manual BIM34110 (change of basis of computing taxable profits: adjustment income and expenses: stock and depreciation).

Mark to market

236 Change from realisation basis to mark to market

(1) This section applies if there is a change of basis from—

    (*a*) not recognising a profit or loss on an asset until the asset is realised, to

    (*b*) bringing assets into account in each period of account at a fair value.

(2) So far as—

    (*a*) a receipt within item 1 of step 1 in section 231 represents the fair value of an asset that is trading stock, or

    (*b*) an expense within item 2 of that step relates to such an asset, adjustment income or (as the case may be) an adjustment expense is treated as not arising until the period of account in which the value of the asset is realised.

(3) In the case of adjustment income, this is subject to any election under section 237 (election for spreading).

(4) In this section "trading stock" has the same meaning as in section 174.

Commentary—*Simon's Taxes* **B2.115**.

Derivation—FA 2002 s 64(1), Sch 22 para 8(1), (2).

HMRC Manuals—Business Income Manual BIM34115 (change from realisation basis to mark to market (fair value) accounting).

237 Election for spreading if section 236 applies

(1) If section 236 applies, the person who is liable to tax on any adjustment income may elect for the adjustment income to be spread over 6 periods of account.

(2) The election must be made on or before the first anniversary of the normal self-assessment filing date for the tax year in which the change of basis occurs.

(3) If an election is made, an amount equal to one-sixth of the amount of the adjustment income—

　　(*a*)　is treated as arising, and

　　(*b*)　is charged to tax,

in each of the 6 periods of account beginning with the first period to which the new basis applies.

(4) But if, before the whole of the adjustment income has been charged to tax, the person permanently ceases to carry on the trade, the whole of the amount so far as not previously brought into charge to tax—

　　(*a*)　is treated as arising, and

　　(*b*)　is charged to tax,

immediately before the cessation.

Commentary—*Simon's Taxes* **B2.115**.

Derivation—FA 2002 s 64(1), Sch 22 para 9.

HMRC Manuals—Business Income Manual BIM34120 (change from realisation basis to mark to market (fair value) accounting: spreading election).

[Spreading of adjustment income on leaving cash basis

239A Spreading on leaving cash basis

(1) This section applies if—

　　(*a*)　an election under section 25A (cash basis for small businesses) has effect in relation to a trade for a tax year, and

　　(*b*)　no such election has effect in relation to the trade for the following tax year.

(2) Any adjustment income is spread over 6 tax years as follows.

(3) In each of the 6 tax years beginning with that in which the whole amount of the adjustment income would otherwise be chargeable to tax, an amount equal to one-sixth of the amount of the adjustment income is treated as arising and is charged to tax.

(4) This section is subject to any election under section 239B (election to accelerate charge).][1]

Commentary—*Simon's Taxes* **B4.205A**.

HMRC Manuals—Business Income Manual BIM70071 (cash basis: transitional adjustments: leaving the cash basis: calculation).

Amendments—[1]　Sections 239A, 239B inserted by FA 2013 s 17, Sch 4 paras 35, 37 with effect for the tax year 2013–14 and subsequent tax years, subject to the provisions of FA 2013 Sch 4 para 57 in relation to barristers and advocates.

[239B Election to accelerate charge under section 239A

(1) A person who under section 239A is liable to tax for a tax year on an amount of adjustment income may elect for an additional amount to be treated as arising in the tax year.

(2) The election must be made on or before the first anniversary of the normal self-assessment filing date for the tax year.

(3) The election must specify the amount to be treated as income arising in the tax year (which may be any amount of the adjustment income not previously charged to tax).

(4) If an election is made, section 239A applies in relation to any subsequent tax year as if the amount of adjustment income (as reduced by any previous application of this section) were reduced by the amount given by the following formula—

A x (6 / T)

where—

　　A is the additional amount treated as arising in the tax year for which the election is made, and

　　T is the number of tax years remaining after that tax year in the period of 6 tax years referred to in section 239A.][1]

Commentary—*Simon's Taxes* **B4.205A**.

Amendments—[1]　Sections 239A, 239B inserted by FA 2013 s 17, Sch 4 paras 35, 37 with effect for the tax year 2013–14 and subsequent tax years, subject to the provisions of FA 2013 Sch 4 para 57 in relation to barristers and advocates.

Supplementary

240 Liability of personal representatives if person liable dies

(1) This section applies in the case of the death of a person who would otherwise have been liable to tax under this Chapter on adjustment income.

(2) The tax under this Chapter for which the person would otherwise have been liable—
  (a) is to be assessed and charged on the personal representatives, and
  (b) is to be a debt due from and payable out of the deceased's estate.

(3) The personal representatives may make any election under this Chapter that the deceased might have made.

Commentary—*Simon's Taxes* **B2.115**.
Derivation—FA 2002 s 64(1), Sch 22 para 14.

[CHAPTER 17A

CASH BASIS: ADJUSTMENTS FOR CAPITAL ALLOWANCE]

Amendments—This Chapter (ss 240A–240E) inserted by FA 2013 s 17, Sch 4 para 38 with effect for the tax year 2013–14 and subsequent tax years, subject to the provisions of FA 2013 Sch 4 para 57 in relation to barristers and advocates.

[Introduction

240A Professions and vocations

The provisions of this Chapter apply to professions and vocations as they apply to trades.][1]

Amendments—[1] This Chapter (ss 240A–240E) inserted by FA 2013 s 17, Sch 4 para 38 with effect for the tax year 2013–14 and subsequent tax years, subject to the provisions of FA 2013 Sch 4 para 57 in relation to barristers and advocates.

[Adjustments on entering cash basis

240B "Entering the cash basis"

For the purposes of this Chapter a person carrying on a trade enters the cash basis for a tax year if—
  (a) an election under section 25A has effect in relation to the trade for the tax year, and
  (b) immediately before the beginning of the basis period for the tax year, such an election does not have effect in relation to the trade.][1]

Commentary—*Simon's Taxes* **B2.710**.
HMRC Manuals—Business Income Manual BIM70060 (entering the cash basis: overview).
Amendments—[1] This Chapter (ss 240A–240E) inserted by FA 2013 s 17, Sch 4 para 38 with effect for the tax year 2013–14 and subsequent tax years, subject to the provisions of FA 2013 Sch 4 para 57 in relation to barristers and advocates.

[240C [Unrelieved qualifying expenditure: Parts 2, 7 and 8 of CAA 2001]

(1) This section applies if—
  (a) a person carrying on a trade enters the cash basis for a tax year ("the current tax year"), and
  (b) at the end of the basis period for the previous tax year, the person has unrelieved qualifying expenditure [relating to the trade][2] to carry forward from the chargeable period ending with that basis period.

(2) But this section does not apply if section 240D (assets not fully paid for) applies.

(3) In calculating the profits of the trade for the current tax year, a deduction is allowed for [any cash basis deductible amount of the expenditure][2].

[(4) A "cash basis deductible amount" of the expenditure means any amount of the expenditure for which a deduction would be allowed in calculating the profits of the trade on the cash basis on the assumption that the expenditure was paid in the current tax year.][2]

(5) [Any cash basis deductible amount][2] of the expenditure is to be determined on such basis as is just and reasonable in all the circumstances.

[(5A) For the purposes of subsection (1)(b), in determining the unrelieved qualifying expenditure the person has to carry forward, disregard sections 59(4), 461A(1) and 475A(1) of CAA 2001 (which provide that an amount is not to be carried forward as unrelieved qualifying expenditure when a person enters the cash basis).][2]

[(6) In this section "unrelieved qualifying expenditure" means unrelieved qualifying expenditure for the purposes of—
  (a) Part 2 of CAA 2001 (see section 59(1) and (2) of that Act),
  (b) Part 7 of that Act (see section 461 of that Act), or
  (c) Part 8 of that Act (see section 475 of that Act).][2][1]

Commentary—*Simon's Taxes* **B2.711**.
Amendments—[1] This Chapter (ss 240A–240E) inserted by FA 2013 s 17, Sch 4 para 38 with effect for the tax year 2013–14 and subsequent tax years, subject to the provisions of FA 2013 Sch 4 para 57 in relation to barristers and advocates.
[2] Heading substituted for previous heading "Unrelieved qualifying expenditure"; in sub-s (1)(b), words inserted; in sub-s (3), words substituted for words "the relevant portion of the expenditure"; sub-ss (4), (6) substituted; in sub-s (5), words substituted for words "The relevant portion"; and sub-s (5A) inserted, by F(No 2)A 2017 s 16, Sch 2 paras 1, 7 with effect for the tax year 2017–18 and subsequent tax years, subject to transitional provisions in F(No 2)A 2017 Sch 2 para 64.

[240CA Unrelieved qualifying expenditure: Part 5 of CAA 2001

(1) This section applies if a person carrying on a mineral extraction trade enters the cash basis for a tax year ("the current tax year").

(2) But this section does not apply if section 240D applies.

(3) In calculating the profits of the trade for the current tax year, a deduction is allowed for any amount of expenditure—

(a) which would, apart from section 419A(1) of CAA 2001, have been unrelieved qualifying expenditure for the current tax year, and

(b) for which a deduction would be allowed in calculating the profits of the trade on the cash basis on the assumption that the expenditure was paid in the current tax year.

(4) In this section—

"mineral extraction trade" has the meaning given in section 394 of CAA 2001;

"unrelieved qualifying expenditure" means unrelieved qualifying expenditure for the purposes of Part 5 of CAA 2001 (see section 419 of that Act).][1]

Commentary—*Simon's Taxes* **B2.711**.

Amendments—[1]   Section 240CA inserted by F(No 2)A 2017 s 16, Sch 2 paras 1, 8 with effect for the tax year 2017–18 and subsequent tax years, subject to transitional provisions in F(No 2)A 2017 Sch 2 para 64.

[240D Assets not fully paid for

(1) This section applies if—

(a) a person carrying on a trade enters the cash basis for a tax year,

(b) at any time before the beginning of the basis period for that tax year the person has [incurred relevant expenditure, and][2]

(c) not all of the relevant expenditure has actually been paid by the person.

[(1A) "Relevant expenditure" means expenditure—

(a) for which a deduction would be allowed in calculating the profits of the trade on the cash basis on the assumption that the expenditure was paid in the tax year, and

(b) in respect of which the person has obtained capital allowances under Part 2, 5, 6, 7 or 8 of CAA 2001.][2]

(2) If the amount of the relevant expenditure that the person has actually paid exceeds the amount of capital allowances given in respect of the relevant expenditure, the difference is to be deducted in calculating the profits of the trade for the tax year.

(3) If the amount of the relevant expenditure that the person has actually paid is less than the amount of capital allowances given in respect of the relevant expenditure, the difference is to be treated as a receipt in calculating the profits of the trade for the tax year.

(4) [Any question as to whether or to what extent expenditure is relevant expenditure, or as to whether or to what extent any capital allowance obtained is in respect of relevant expenditure,][2] is to be determined on such basis as is just and reasonable in all the circumstances.

(5) If the amount of capital allowances given [under Part 2 of CAA 2001][2] in respect of the relevant expenditure has been reduced under section 205 or 207 of CAA 2001 (reduction where asset provided or used only partly for qualifying activity), the amount of the relevant expenditure that the person has actually paid is to be proportionately reduced for the purposes of this section.

(6) . . . [2]

Commentary—*Simon's Taxes* **B2.711**.

HMRC Manuals—Business Income Manual BIM81065 (examples of apportioning profits to basis periods).

Amendments—[1]   This Chapter (ss 240A–240E) inserted by FA 2013 s 17, Sch 4 para 38 with effect for the tax year 2013–14 and subsequent tax years, subject to the provisions of FA 2013 Sch 4 para 57 in relation to barristers and advocates.

[2]   In sub-s (1)(b), words substituted for words "obtained capital allowances in respect of expenditure on the provision of plant or machinery ("the relevant expenditure"), and"; sub-s (1A) inserted; in sub-s (4), words substituted for words "The amount of any capital allowance obtained in respect of expenditure on the provision of any plant or machinery"; in sub-s (5) words inserted; and sub-s (6) repealed, by F(No 2)A 2017 s 16, Sch 2 paras 1, 9 with effect for the tax year 2017–18 and subsequent tax years, subject to transitional provisions in F(No 2)A 2017 Sch 2 para 64.

[Successions where predecessor and successor are connected persons

240E Effect of election where predecessor and successor are connected persons

(1) This section applies if—

(a) a person carrying on a trade enters the cash basis for a tax year,

(b) the person is the successor for the purposes of section 266 of CAA 2001, and

(c) as a result of an election under section 267 of that Act, relevant plant or machinery is treated as sold by the predecessor to the successor at any time during the basis period for the tax year.

(2) The provisions of this Chapter have effect in relation to the successor as if everything done to or by the predecessor had been done to or by the successor.

(3) Any expenditure actually incurred by the successor on acquiring the relevant plant or machinery is to be ignored for the purposes of calculating the profits of the trade for the tax year.

(4) In this section "the predecessor" and "relevant plant or machinery" have the same meaning as in section 267 of CAA 2001.][1]

Commentary—*Simon's Taxes* **B2.712**.

HMRC Manuals—Capital Allowance CA29040 (election where predecessor and successor are connected).

Amendments—[1]   This Chapter (ss 240A–240E) inserted by FA 2013 s 17, Sch 4 para 38 with effect for the tax year 2013–14 and subsequent tax years, subject to the provisions of FA 2013 Sch 4 para 57 in relation to barristers and advocates.

CHAPTER 18

POST-CESSATION RECEIPTS

Introduction

241 Professions and vocations

The provisions of this Chapter apply to professions and vocations as they apply to trades.

Charge to tax on post-cessation receipts

242 Charge to tax on post-cessation receipts

Income tax is charged on post-cessation receipts arising from a trade.

Commentary—*Simon's Taxes* **B2.803**.

Derivation—TA 1988 s 103, s 104; FA 1998 Sch 5 para 4.

HMRC Manuals—Business Income Manual BIM90010 (post cessation receipts and expenses: charge to tax).

243 Extent of charge to tax

(1) A post-cessation receipt is chargeable to tax under this Chapter only so far as it is not otherwise chargeable to income or corporation tax.

(2) Accordingly, a post-cessation receipt arising from a trade is not chargeable to tax under this Chapter so far as it is brought into account in calculating the profits of the trade for any period.

(3) A post-cessation receipt is not chargeable to tax under this Chapter if—

    (*a*) it is received by or on behalf of a non-UK resident who is beneficially entitled to it, and

    (*b*) it represents income arising outside the United Kingdom.

(4) A post-cessation receipt is not chargeable to tax under this Chapter if it arises from a trade carried on wholly outside the United Kingdom[, other than a person's trade of dealing in or developing UK land][2].

(5) A post-cessation receipt is not chargeable to tax under this Chapter in the case of a partner in a firm if—

    (*a*) it represents income arising outside the United Kingdom from a trade carried on by the firm, and

    (*b*) the partner's share of the firm's income arising out of the United Kingdom is treated as relevant foreign income by section 857(3) (partners to whom the remittance basis applies).

[(6) If the tax year is a split year as respects a UK resident individual, this section has effect as if, for the overseas part of that year, the individual were non-UK resident.][1]

Commentary—*Simon's Taxes* **B2.803**.

HMRC Manuals—Business Income Manual BIM90015 (post cessation receipts and expenses: territorial scope of the provisions).

Amendments[1]   Sub-s (6) inserted by FA 2013 s 218, Sch 45 paras 74, 77 with effect in calculating an individual's liability to income tax or capital gains tax for the tax year 2013–14 or any subsequent tax year, subject to transitional provisions and savings in FA 2013 Sch 45 paras 154–158.

[2]   In sub-s (4), words inserted by FA 2016 s 78(4) with effect in relation to disposals on or after 5 July 2016 (FA 2016 s 82(1)), subject to transitional provisions relating to disposals to associated persons on or after 16 March 2016 and before 5 July 2016 (FA 2016 s 82(4)–(15)).

   F(No 2)A 2017 s 39 provides that this amendment has effect (so far as it would not otherwise have effect) in relation to amounts that are recognised in GAAP accounts drawn up for any period of account beginning on or after 8 March 2017 or, in the case of a straddling period, amounts that would be recognised in GAAP accounts drawn up for a period of account beginning on 8 March 2017 and ending when the straddling period ends. "Straddling period" means a period of account beginning before 8 March 2017 and ending on or after that date.

244 Income charged

(1) Tax is charged under this Chapter on the full amount of the receipts received in the tax year.

(2) This is subject to—

    (*a*) sections 254 and 255 (allowable deductions), and

    (*b*) section 257 (election to carry back).

Commentary—*Simon's Taxes* **B2.803**.

Derivation—TA 1988 s 69.

HMRC Manuals—Business Income Manual BIM90010 (post cessation receipts and expenses: charge to tax).

245 Person liable

The person liable for any tax charged under this Chapter is the person receiving or entitled to the receipts.

Commentary—*Simon's Taxes* **B2.803**.

Derivation—TA 1988 s 59(1).

HMRC Manuals—Business Income Manual BIM90020 (post cessation receipts and expenses: person liable to tax).

Meaning of "post-cessation receipts"

246 Basic meaning of "post-cessation receipt"

(1) In this Part "post-cessation receipt" means a sum—

    (*a*) which is received after a person permanently ceases to carry on a trade, and

    (*b*) which arises from the carrying on of the trade before the cessation.

(2) For this purpose the reference to a person permanently ceasing to carry on a trade includes [a reference to a company ceasing to be within the charge to corporation tax in respect of a trade.][1]

[(2A) If, immediately before a person permanently ceases to carry on a trade, an election under section 25A (cash basis for small businesses) has effect in relation to the trade, a sum is to be treated as a post-cessation receipt only if it would have been brought into account in calculating the profits of the trade on the cash basis had it been received at that time.][2]

(3) Subsection (4) applies if—

    (*a*) a firm carries on a trade,

    (*b*) a person ceases to be a partner in the firm, and

    (*c*) the departure results in the partner permanently ceasing to carry on the notional trade (see section 852).

(4) The partner is treated for the purposes of this Chapter as permanently ceasing to carry on the trade.

Commentary—*Simon's Taxes* **B2.804**.

HMRC Manuals—Business Income Manual BIM90030 (meaning).

Amendments—[1]   In sub-s (2) words substituted by CTA 2009 s 1322, Sch 1 paras 587, 612. CTA 2009 applies for accounting periods ending on or after 1 April 2009 (for corporation tax purposes) and for tax years 2009–10 onwards (for income and capital gains tax purposes).

[2]   Sub-s (2A) inserted by FA 2013 s 17, Sch 4 para 39(1), (2) with effect for the tax year 2013–14 and subsequent tax years, subject to the provisions of FA 2013 Sch 4 para 57 in relation to barristers and advocates.

247 Other rules about what counts as post-cessation receipts

(1) The following provisions treat certain amounts as post-cessation receipts for the purposes of this Part—

    section 82(6) (contributions to local enterprise organisations or urban regeneration companies),

    section 104(3) (distribution of assets of mutual concerns),

    section 109(2) (receipt by donor or connected person of benefit attributable to certain gifts),

    section 185(1) (election for valuation at cost),

    section 248 (debts paid after cessation),

    section 249 (debts released after cessation), as qualified, where appropriate, by section 48(4) (car . . . [1] hire),

    section 250 (receipts relating to post-cessation expenditure),

    section 251 (transfer of rights if transferee does not carry on trade), and

    section 844 (income charged on withdrawal of relief after source ceases: unremittable income).

(2) Section 98 (acquisition of trade: receipts from transferor's trade) and section 251 (transfer of rights if transferee does not carry on trade) treat certain amounts as not being post-cessation receipts for the purposes of this Part.

Commentary—*Simon's Taxes* **B2.804**.

HMRC Manuals—Business Income Manual BIM90030 (types of incomes which are treated as post-cessation receipts).

Amendments—[1]   In sub-s (1), in entry relating to "section 249" words "or motor cycle" repealed by FA 2009 s 30, Sch 11 paras 34, 40 with effect in relation to deductions for expenses incurred on the hiring of a car or motor cycle under an agreement under which the hire period begins on or after 1 April 2009 (for corporation tax purposes) or 6 April 2009 (for income tax purposes), subject to transitional provisions in FA 2009 Sch 11 para 67.

Sums treated as post-cessation receipts

248 Debts paid after cessation

(1) Subsection (2) applies if, in calculating the profits of a trade for income or corporation tax purposes, a deduction is made in respect of a debt under—

    (*a*) section 35 (bad and doubtful debts), or

    (*b*) section 74(1)(*j*) of ICTA (corresponding corporation tax provision),

and a person permanently ceases to carry on the trade.

(2) A sum received after the cessation is treated as a post-cessation receipt so far as the deduction is made.

(3) Subsection (4) applies if relief is given under [section 96 of ITA 2007][1] (relief for post-cessation expenditure) [as a result of subsection (1)(*b*) of that section][1] in respect of a debt owed to a person who has permanently ceased to carry on a trade.

(4) A sum received by the person in payment of the debt is treated as a post-cessation receipt so far as relief is given in respect of the sum.

Commentary—*Simon's Taxes* **B2.804, B2.805**.

Derivation—TA 1988 s 103(5), s 109A(4), (4A).

HMRC Manuals—Business Income Manual BIM42745 (specific deductions: bad and doubtful debts: business ceased). BIM90035 (treatment of a sum received by the person in payment of the debt).

Amendments—[1]   Words in sub-s (3) substituted and inserted by ITA 2007 s 1027, Sch 1 paras 492, 503 with effect for income tax purposes from 6 April 2007, and corporation tax purposes for accounting periods ending after 5 April 2007.

249 Debts released after cessation

(1) This section applies if—

    (*a*) in calculating the profits of a trade for any period for income or corporation tax purposes, a deduction is allowed for the expense giving rise to a debt owed by the person who carried on the trade,

    (*b*) the person has permanently ceased to carry on the trade at or after the end of that period,

    (*c*) after the cessation, all or part of the debt is released, and

    (*d*) the release is not part of a statutory insolvency arrangement.

(2) The amount released is treated as a post-cessation receipt.

(3) For the purposes of this section the reference to a person permanently ceasing to carry on a trade includes [a reference to a company ceasing to be within the charge to corporation tax in respect of a trade.][1]

Commentary—*Simon's Taxes* **B2.804, B2.805**.

HMRC Manuals—Business Income Manual BIM90040 (debts released after cessation).

BIM42740 (liability for trade debt released by creditor).

Amendments—[1] In sub-s (3) words substituted by CTA 2009 s 1322, Sch 1 paras 587, 613. CTA 2009 applies for accounting periods ending on or after 1 April 2009 (for corporation tax purposes) and for tax years 2009–10 onwards (for income and capital gains tax purposes).

250 Receipts relating to post-cessation expenditure

(1) This section applies if a person who has permanently ceased to carry on a trade makes a payment in circumstances where relief is available under [section 96 of ITA 2007][1] (relief for post-cessation expenditure).

(2) The following sums are treated as post-cessation receipts—

    (*a*) in the case of a payment within [section 97(2) or (3) of ITA 2007][1] (payment to remedy defective work etc or to defray expenses of a claim), the proceeds of insurance, or other sum received, for the purpose of enabling the payment to be made or by means of which it is reimbursed,

    (*b*) in the case of a payment within [section 97(4) of ITA 2007][1] (payment to insure against claims for defective work etc), a refund of the premium, or other sum received, in connection with the insurance, and

    (*c*) in the case of a payment within [section 97(5) of ITA 2007][1] (payment for the purpose of collecting a debt), any sum received towards the cost of collecting the debt.

(3) If a sum mentioned in subsection (2) is received in a tax year earlier than the tax year in which the related payment is made, it is treated as having been received in the later tax year (and not the earlier tax year).

(4) Any adjustment required to give effect to subsection (3) is to be made by way of—

    (*a*) amendment of an assessment, or

    (*b*) discharge or repayment of tax.

Commentary—*Simon's Taxes* **B2.805**.

Derivation—TA 1988 s 109A(3).

HMRC Manuals—Business Income Manual BIM90045 (types of relief received relating to post cessation expenses).

Amendments—[1] Words in sub-ss (1), (2) substituted by ITA 2007 s 1027, Sch 1 paras 492, 504 with effect for income tax purposes from 6 April 2007, and corporation tax purposes for accounting periods ending after 5 April 2007.

251 Transfer of rights if transferee does not carry on trade

(1) This section applies if—

    (*a*) a person ("the transferor") permanently ceases to carry on a trade,

    (*b*) the transferor transfers to another person ("the transferee") for value the right to receive sums arising from the carrying on of the trade, and

    (*c*) the transferee does not subsequently carry on the trade.

(2) The transferor is treated as receiving a post-cessation receipt.

(3) The amount of the receipt is—

    (*a*) the amount or value of the consideration for the transfer, if the transfer is at arm's length, or

    (*b*) the value of the rights transferred as between parties at arm's length, if the transfer is not at arm's length.

(4) Any sums mentioned in subsection (1)(*b*) which are received after the cessation of the trade are not post-cessation receipts.

(5) This section is subject to—

    (*a*) section 252 (transfer of trading stock or work in progress), and

    (*b*) section 253 (lump sums paid to personal representatives for copyright etc).

Commentary—*Simon's Taxes* **B2.805**.

Derivation—TA 1988 s 106(1).

HMRC Manuals—Business Income Manual BIM42745 (rights to debts transferred).

BIM90050 (effects of transfer of rights).

Sums that are not post-cessation receipts

252 Transfer of trading stock or work in progress

(1) When a person permanently ceases to carry on a trade, a sum realised by—

    (*a*) the transfer of trading stock, or

(*b*) the transfer of work in progress,

is not a post-cessation receipt if a valuation of the stock or work is brought into account in accordance with Chapter 12 (valuation of stock and work in progress).

(2) This does not prevent a sum from being treated as a post-cessation receipt as a result of an election under section 185 (election for valuation of work in progress at cost).

(3) In this section—

(*a*) "trading stock" has the meaning given by section 174, and

(*b*) "work in progress" and "transfer of work in progress" have the meaning given by section 183.

Commentary—*Simon's Taxes* **B2.805, B2.806.**

HMRC Manuals—Business Income Manual BIM90055 (transfer of trading stock: not a post cessation receipt).
BIM90060 (transfer of work in progress: not a post cessation receipt).

253 Lump sums paid to personal representatives for copyright etc

(1) A lump sum which is paid to the personal representatives of the author of a literary, dramatic, musical or artistic work as consideration for the assignment by them of—

(*a*) the copyright in the work, or

(*b*) the public lending right in the work,

is not a post-cessation receipt.

(2) A lump sum which is paid to the personal representatives of the designer of a design in which design right subsists as consideration for the assignment by them of that right is not a post-cessation receipt.

(3) For the purposes of this section it does not matter whether the whole or a part of the right is assigned.

Commentary—*Simon's Taxes* **B2.806, B5.314.**

HMRC Manuals—Business Income Manual BIM90065 (payments received by personal representatives for the sale of literary or design rights are specifically excluded from the scope of the charge to tax).

Deductions

254 Allowable deductions

(1) In calculating the amount on which tax is charged under this Chapter, deductions are allowed in accordance with—

(*a*) this section, and

(*b*) section 255,

from the amount which would otherwise be chargeable to tax under this Chapter.

(2) A deduction is allowed for a loss, expense or debit which, if the person carrying on the trade had not permanently ceased to do so—

(*a*) would have been deducted in calculating the profits of the trade for income or corporation tax purposes, or

(*b*) would have been deducted from or set off against the profits of the trade for income or corporation tax purposes,

but no deduction is allowed if the loss, expense or debit arises directly or indirectly from the cessation itself.

[(2A) If, immediately before the person permanently ceases to carry on the trade, an election under section 25A (cash basis for small businesses) has effect in relation to the trade, assume for the purposes of subsection (2) that such an election has effect in relation to the trade.][2]

[(2B) If—

(*a*) the loss or expense is incurred, or the debit arises, in relation to a vehicle, and

(*b*) immediately before the person permanently ceases to carry on the trade, section 94D (deduction allowable at fixed rate for expenditure on vehicles) applies in relation to the vehicle,

assume for the purposes of subsection (2) that that section applies in relation to the vehicle.][3]

(3) No deduction for an amount is allowed under this section if the amount has been allowed—

(*a*) under any other provision of the Tax Acts, or

(*b*) as a result of [section 261D of TCGA 1992][1] (capital gains tax relief for post-cessation expenditure).

Commentary—*Simon's Taxes* **B2.807.**

HMRC Manuals—Business Income Manual BIM90080 (post-cessation expenses are usually something that would have been deducted in arriving at the profits of the trade had it not ceased).

Modifications—ITTOIA 2005 s 353 (as amended by F(No 2)A 2017 s 16, Sch 2 para 30: in connection with determination of "cash basis tax year", this section to apply as if sub-s (2A) read as follows—

"(2A) If the time immediately before the person permanently ceases to carry on the UK property business falls in a cash basis tax year, assume for the purposes of subsection (2) that the profits of the business are calculated on the cash basis.".

Amendments—[1]   Words in sub-s (3)(*b*) substituted by ITA 2007 s 1027, Sch 1 paras 492, 505 with effect for income tax purposes from 6 April 2007, and corporation tax purposes for accounting periods ending after 5 April 2007.

²   Sub-s (2A) inserted by FA 2013 s 17, Sch 4 para 39(1), (3) with effect for the tax year 2013–14 and subsequent tax years, subject to the provisions of FA 2013 Sch 4 para 57 in relation to barristers and advocates.

³   Sub-s (2B) inserted by FA 2013 s 18, Sch 5 para 4 with effect for the tax year 2013–14 and subsequent tax years.

255 Further rules about allowable deductions

(1) An amount may not be deducted more than once under section 254.

(2) A deduction under that section of a loss must be made from post-cessation receipts charged for an earlier tax year in preference to those charged for a later tax year.

(3) But this does not authorise the deduction of a loss from post-cessation receipts charged for a tax year before the tax year in which the loss is made.

(4) No deduction may be made under section 254 from any amount that is treated as a post-cessation receipt under—

    (*a*) section 248(4) (debts paid after cessation), or

    (*b*) section 250 (receipts relating to post-cessation expenditure).

Commentary—*Simon's Taxes* **B2.807**.

HMRC Manuals—Business Income Manual BIM90090 (post cessation expense: relief).
BIM90095 (relief for post cessation expenses against post cessation receipts).

Reliefs

256 Treatment of post-cessation receipts

(1) This section applies if—

    (*a*) an individual has permanently ceased to carry on a trade, and

    (*b*) the income arising to the individual from the trade was . . . ¹ relevant UK earnings within section 189(2)(*b*) of FA 2004.

(2) Any post-cessation receipts arising to the individual from the trade are similarly . . . ¹ relevant UK earnings.

Commentary—*Simon's Taxes* **B2.808**.

HMRC Manuals—Business Income Manual BIM90025 (amount arising is relevant UK earnings).

Amendments—¹   Words in sub-ss (1)(*b*), (2) repealed by ITA 2007 ss 1027, 1031, Sch 1 paras 492, 506, Sch 3 Pt 1 with effect for income tax purposes from 6 April 2007, and corporation tax purposes for accounting periods ending after 5 April 2007.

257 Election to carry back

(1) This section applies if a post-cessation receipt is received by a person (or a person's personal representatives) in a tax year beginning no later than 6 years after the person permanently ceased to carry on the trade.

(2) The person (or the person's personal representatives) may elect that the tax chargeable in respect of the receipt is to be charged as if the receipt had been received on the date of the cessation.

(3) But this is subject to paragraph 5 of Schedule 1B to TMA 1970 (election given effect in the tax year in which the receipt is actually received).

(4) The election must be made on or before the first anniversary of the normal self-assessment filing date for the tax year.

Commentary—*Simon's Taxes* **B2.808, E1.263**.

HMRC Manuals—Business Income Manual BIM90075 (post cessation receipts: carry back).

CHAPTER 19

SUPPLEMENTARY

258 Changes in trustees and personal representatives

(1) This section applies if there is a change—

    (*a*) in the trustees of a trust, or

    (*b*) in the personal representatives of a person,

at a time when they are carrying on a trade, profession or vocation.

(2) For income tax purposes, the change does not result in—

    (*a*) any of the trustees or personal representatives before the change permanently ceasing to carry on the trade, profession or vocation, or

    (*b*) any of the trustees or personal representatives after the change starting to carry on the trade, profession or vocation.

[259 Meaning of "statutory insolvency arrangement"

(1) In this Part "statutory insolvency arrangement" means—

    (*a*) a voluntary arrangement that has taken effect under or as a result of the Insolvency Act 1986, [the Insolvency (Northern Ireland) Order 1989 or schedule 4 to the Bankruptcy (Scotland) Act 2016]³,

    [(*b*) a compromise or arrangement that has taken effect under Part 26 [or 26A]⁴ of the Companies Act 2006]²

ITTOIA 2005

(c) any arrangement or compromise of a kind corresponding to any of those mentioned in paragraph (a) or (b) that has taken effect under or by virtue of the law of a country or territory outside the United Kingdom.][1]

HMRC Manuals—Business Income Manual BIM42701 (statutory insolvency arrangement: meaning).

Amendments—[1] This section substituted by F(No 2)A 2005 s 37, Sch 6 para 3 with effect for the tax year 2005–06 and subsequent tax years in relation to periods of account beginning on or after 1 January 2005.

[2] Sub-s (1)(b) substituted by the Companies Act 2006 (Consequential Amendments) (Taxes and National Insurance) Order, SI 2008/954 arts 35, 37 with effect from 6 April 2008.

[3] In sub-s (1)(a), words substituted by the Bankruptcy (Scotland) Act 2016 (Consequential Provisions and Modifications) Order, SI 2017/1034 art 7(1), Sch 1 para 27 with effect from 30 November 2016.

[4] In sub-s (1)(b), words inserted by the Corporate Insolvency and Governance Act 2020 s 7, Sch 9 para 28 with effect from 26 June 2020.

PART 3
PROPERTY INCOME

CHAPTER 1

INTRODUCTION

260 Overview of Part 3

(1) This Part imposes charges to income tax under—

(a) Chapter 3 (the profits of a UK property business or an overseas property business),

(b) Chapter 7 (amounts treated as adjustment income under section 330),

(c) Chapter 8 (rent receivable in connection with a UK section 12(4) concern),

(d) Chapter 9 (rent receivable for UK electric-line wayleaves), [and][1]

(e) Chapter 10 (post-cessation receipts arising from a UK property business), . . . [1]

(f) . . . [1]

(2) Part 6 deals with exemptions from the charges under this Part.

(3) See, in particular, the exemptions under sections 769 (housing grants), 777 (VAT repayment supplements) and 778 (incentives to use electronic communications).

(4) The charges under Chapters 3, 7, 8, 9 and 10 apply to non-UK residents as well as UK residents but this is subject to section 269 (charges on non-UK residents only on UK source income).

(5) This section needs to be read with the relevant priority rules (see sections 2 and 261).

Commentary—*Simon's Taxes* B6.102.

Amendments—[1] Word at end of sub-s (1)(d) inserted, and sub-s (1)(f) and preceding word repealed, by FA 2008 s 25, Sch 7 paras 46, 47 with effect for the tax year 2008–09 and subsequent tax years.

261 Provisions which must be given priority over Part 3

Any receipt or other credit item, so far as it falls within—

(a) Chapter 3 of this Part so far as it relates to an overseas property business or Chapter 8 or 9 of this Part (rent receivable in connection with a UK section 12(4) concern or for UK electric-line wayleaves), and

(b) Chapter 2 of Part 2 (receipts of a trade, profession or vocation),

is dealt with under Part 2.

Commentary—*Simon's Taxes* B6.103.

262 Priority between Chapters within Part 3

(1) Any receipt, so far as it falls within—

(a) Chapter 3 so far as it relates to a UK property business, and

(b) Chapter 8 (rent receivable in connection with a UK section 12(4) concern), is dealt with under Chapter 8.

(2) Any receipt, so far as it falls within—

(a) Chapter 3 so far as it relates to a UK property business, and

(b) Chapter 9 (rent receivable for UK electric-line wayleaves),

is dealt with under Chapter 9.

(3) Any receipt, so far as it falls within Chapter 8 (rent receivable in connection with a UK section 12(4) concern) and Chapter 9 (rent receivable for UK electric-line wayleaves), is dealt with under Chapter 9.

Commentary—*Simon's Taxes* B6.103.

CHAPTER 2

PROPERTY BUSINESSES

Introduction

263 Introduction

(1) This Chapter explains for the purposes of this Act what is meant by—

(a) a person's UK property business (see section 264), and

(*b*) a person's overseas property business (see section 265).

(2) Both those sections need to be read with—

    (*a*) section 266 (which explains what is meant by generating income from land), and

    (*b*) section 267 (which provides that certain activities do not count as activities for generating income from land).

(3) In the case of the property business of a firm, the basic rules in sections 264 and 265 are explained in section 859(2) and (3).

(4) References in this Act to an overseas property business are to an overseas property business so far as any profits of the business are chargeable to tax under Chapter 3 (as to which see, in particular, section 269).

(5) Accordingly, nothing in Chapter 4 or 5 is to be read as treating an amount as a receipt of an overseas property business if the profits concerned would not be chargeable to tax under Chapter 3.

(6) In this Act "property business" means a UK property business or an overseas property business.

Commentary—*Simon's Taxes* **B6.201.**

Basic meaning of UK and overseas property business

264 UK property business

A person's UK property business consists of—

    (*a*) every business which the person carries on for generating income from land in the United Kingdom, and

    (*b*) every transaction which the person enters into for that purpose otherwise than in the course of such a business.

Commentary—*Simon's Taxes* **B6.201.**
Derivation—TA 1988 s 15(1) (Sch A para 1); FA 1998 Sch 5 para 1.
HMRC Manuals—Property Income Manual PIM1020 (UK property business: meaning).

265 Overseas property business

A person's overseas property business consists of—

    (*a*) every business which the person carries on for generating income from land outside the United Kingdom, and

    (*b*) every transaction which the person enters into for that purpose otherwise than in the course of such a business.

Commentary—*Simon's Taxes* **B6.201.**
Derivation—TA 1988 s 65A; FA 1998 Sch 5 para 24.
HMRC Manuals—Property Income Manual PIM4703 (overseas property business: meaning).

Generating income from land

266 Meaning of "generating income from land"

(1) In this Chapter "generating income from land" means exploiting an estate, interest or right in or over land as a source of rents or other receipts.

(2) "Rents" includes payments by a tenant for work to maintain or repair leased premises which the lease does not require the tenant to carry out.

(3) "Other receipts" includes—

    (*a*) payments in respect of a licence to occupy or otherwise use land,

    (*b*) payments in respect of the exercise of any other right over land, and

    (*c*) rentcharges and other annual payments reserved in respect of, or charged on or issuing out of, land.

(4) For the purposes of this section a right to use a caravan or houseboat at only one location is treated as a right deriving from an estate or interest in land.

Commentary—*Simon's Taxes* **B6.201.**
HMRC Manuals—Property Income Manual PIM2020 (tenants' contributions to maintenance costs).
PIM2220 (properties not let at a commercial rent).
PIM1051 (income within a rental business).

267 Activities not for generating income from land

For the purposes of this Chapter the following activities are not carried on for generating income from land—

    (*a*) farming or market gardening in the United Kingdom (but see section 9 (UK farming or market gardening treated as trade)),

    (*b*) any other occupation of land (but see section 10 (certain commercial occupation of UK land treated as trade)), and

    (*c*) activities for the purposes of a concern to which section 12 applies (profits of mines, quarries etc).

Commentary—*Simon's Taxes* **B6.201.**
Derivation—TA 1988 s 15(1) (Sch A para 2(1), (2)), s 65A(2); FA 1998 Sch 5 paras 1, 24.
HMRC Manuals—Property Income Manual PIM112 (income excluded from a rental business).

CHAPTER 3

PROFITS OF PROPERTY BUSINESSES: BASIC RULES

Charge to tax on profits of a property business

268 Charge to tax on profits of a property business

Income tax is charged on the profits of a property business.

Commentary—*Simon's Taxes* B6.202, E1.302.
Derivation—TA 1988 s 15(1) (Sch A para 1(1)), s 18; FA 1998 Sch 5 para 1.
HMRC Manuals—Property Income Manual PIM1001 (overview).
Property Income Manual PIM4703 (charge to tax).

269 Territorial scope of charge to tax

(1) Profits of a UK property business are chargeable to tax under this Chapter whether the business is carried on by a UK resident or a non-UK resident.

(2) Profits of an overseas property business are chargeable to tax under this Chapter only if the business is carried on by a UK resident.

(3), (4) . . . [1]

Commentary—*Simon's Taxes* B6.202, B6.214.
HMRC Manuals—Property Income Manual PIM4703 (UK property business/ overseas property: charged to tax).
Amendments—[1] Sub-ss (3), (4) repealed by FA 2008 s 25, Sch 7 paras 46, 48 with effect for the tax year 2008–09 and subsequent tax years.

270 Income charged

(1) Tax is charged under this Chapter on the full amount of the profits arising in the tax year.

(2) Subsection (1) is subject to Part 8 (foreign income: special rules).

[(3) If, as respects an individual carrying on an overseas property business, the tax year is a split year—

    (*a*) tax is charged under this Chapter on so much of the profits referred to in subsection (1) as arise in the UK part of the tax year, and

    (*b*) the portion of the profits arising in the overseas part of the tax year is, accordingly, not chargeable to tax under this Chapter.

(4) In determining how much of the profits arise in the UK part of the tax year—

    (*a*) determine first how much of the non-CAA profits arise in the UK part by apportioning the non-CAA profits between the UK part and the overseas part on a just and reasonable basis, and

    (*b*) then adjust the portion of the non-CAA profits arising in the UK part by deducting any CAA allowances for the year and adding any CAA charges for the year.

(5) In subsection (4)—

    "CAA allowances" means allowances treated under section 250 or 250A of CAA 2001 (capital allowances for overseas property businesses) as an expense of the business;

    "CAA charges" means charges treated under either of those sections as a receipt of the business;

    "non-CAA profits" means profits before account is taken of any CAA allowances or CAA charges.][1]

HMRC Manuals—Property Income Manual PIM1010 (time apportionment).
PIM3050 (example).
Amendments—[1] Sub-ss (3)–(5) inserted by FA 2013 s 218, Sch 45 para 81 with effect, in calculating an individual's liability to income tax or capital gains tax, for the tax year 2013–14 or any subsequent tax year, subject to transitional provisions and savings in FA 2013 Sch 45 paras 154–158.

271 Person liable

The person liable for any tax charged under this Chapter is the person receiving or entitled to the profits.

Commentary—*Simon's Taxes* B6.202.
Derivation—TA 1988 s 21(1), s 59(1).
HMRC Manuals—Property Income Manual PIM1020 (who is charged to tax).

[Basis of calculation of profits

271A Basis of calculation of profits: GAAP required

(1) The profits of a property business for a tax year must be calculated in accordance with GAAP if condition A, B, C, D or E is met.

(2) Condition A is that the business is carried on at any time in the tax year by—

    (*a*) a company,

    (*b*) a limited liability partnership,

    (*c*) a corporate firm, or

    (*d*) the trustees of a trust.

(3) For the purposes of subsection (2) a firm is a "corporate firm" if a partner in the firm is not an individual.

(4) Condition B is that the cash basis receipts for the tax year exceed £150,000.

(5) In subsection (4) "the cash basis receipts for the tax year" means the total of the amounts that would be brought into account as receipts in calculating the profits of the property business for the tax year on the cash basis (see section 271D).

(6) If the property business is carried on for only part of the tax year, the sum given in subsection (4) is proportionately reduced.

(7) Condition C is that—

   (*a*) the property business is carried on by an individual ("P"),

   (*b*) a share of joint property income is brought into account in calculating the profits of the business for the tax year,

   (*c*) a share of that joint property income is brought into account in calculating the profits for the tax year of a property business carried on by another individual ("Q's property business"), and

   (*d*) the profits of Q's property business for the tax year are calculated in accordance with GAAP.

(8) In subsection (7) "joint property income" means income to which P and Q are treated for income tax purposes as beneficially entitled in equal shares by virtue of section 836 of ITA 2007.

(9) Condition D is that—

   (*a*) an allowance under Part 3A of CAA 2001 (business premises renovation allowances) is made at any time in calculating the profits of the property business, and

   (*b*) if the profits of the business were to be calculated in accordance with GAAP for the tax year, there would be a day in the tax year on which the occurrence of a balancing event (within the meaning of that Part) would give rise to a balancing adjustment for the tax year (see section 360M of that Act).

(10) Condition E is that an election under this subsection made by the person who is or has been carrying on the property business has effect in relation to the business for the tax year.

(11) An election under subsection (10) must be made on or before the first anniversary of the normal self-assessment filing date for the tax year for which the election is made.

(12) The Treasury may by regulations—

   (*a*) amend subsection (2);

   (*b*) amend subsection (4) so as to substitute another sum for the sum for the time being specified in that subsection.

(13) A statutory instrument containing regulations under subsection (12) may not be made unless a draft of the instrument has been laid before, and approved by a resolution of, the House of Commons.

(14) Subsection (13) does not apply if the regulations omit one or more paragraphs of subsection (2) and make no other provision.][1]

Commentary—*Simon's Taxes* **B6.202**.

Amendments—[1]   Sections 271A–271D inserted by F(No 2)A 2017 s 16, Sch 2 paras 12, 13 with effect for the tax year 2017–18 and subsequent tax years, subject to transitional provisions in F(No 2)A 2017 Sch 2 para 64.

[271B Calculation of profits in accordance with GAAP

(1) In this Part, references to calculating the profits of a property business in accordance with GAAP are to calculating the profits in accordance with generally accepted accounting practice, subject to any adjustment required or authorised by law in calculating profits for income tax purposes.

(2) A requirement under this Part to calculate profits in accordance with GAAP does not—

   (*a*) require a person to comply with the requirements of the Companies Act 2006 or subordinate legislation made under that Act except as to the basis of calculation, or

   (*b*) impose any requirements as to audit or disclosure.

(3) See section 272 (application of trading income rules: GAAP) which applies only where profits are calculated in accordance with GAAP.][1]

Amendments—[1]   Sections 271A–271D inserted by F(No 2)A 2017 s 16, Sch 2 paras 12, 13 with effect for the tax year 2017–18 and subsequent tax years, subject to transitional provisions in F(No 2)A 2017 Sch 2 para 64.

[271C Basis of calculation of profits: cash basis required

The profits of a property business for a tax year must be calculated on the cash basis if none of conditions A, B, C, D or E in section 271A is met.][1]

Amendments—[1]   Sections 271A–271D inserted by F(No 2)A 2017 s 16, Sch 2 paras 12, 13 with effect for the tax year 2017–18 and subsequent tax years, subject to transitional provisions in F(No 2)A 2017 Sch 2 para 64.

[271D Calculation of profits on the cash basis

(1) In this Part, references to calculating the profits of a property business on the cash basis are to calculating the profits in accordance with subsections (2) and (3).

(2) In calculating the profits, receipts of the business are brought into account at the time they are received, and expenses of the business are brought into account at the time they are paid.

(3) Subsection (2) is subject to any adjustment required or authorised by law in calculating profits for income tax purposes.

(4) For provision about the application of Chapter 4 (profits of property businesses: lease premiums etc) in relation to profits calculated on the cash basis, see section 276A.

(5) For provision about the application of Chapter 5 (rules about deductions and receipts) in relation to profits calculated on the cash basis, see section 307A.

(6) The following provisions apply only where profits are calculated on the cash basis—

    (*a*) section 272ZA (application of trading income rules: cash basis), and

    (*b*) Chapter 7A (cash basis: adjustments for capital allowances).][1]

Commentary—*Simon's Taxes* **B6.202C.**

Amendments—[1] Sections 271A–271D inserted by F(No 2)A 2017 s 16, Sch 2 paras 12, 13 with effect for the tax year 2017–18 and subsequent tax years, subject to transitional provisions in F(No 2)A 2017 Sch 2 para 64.

Calculation of profits[: application of trading income rules][2]

[271E Profits of a property business: application of trading income rules

(1) The profits of a property business are calculated in the same way as the profits of a trade.

(2) But this is subject to—

    (*a*) section 272, which limits the rule in subsection (1) in relation to a property business whose profits are calculated in accordance with GAAP, and

    (*b*) section 272ZA, which limits that rule in relation to a property business whose profits are calculated on the cash basis.][1]

Commentary—*Simon's Taxes* **B6.202B.**

Amendments—[1] Section 271E inserted by F(No 2)A 2017 s 16, Sch 2 paras 12, 15 with effect for the tax year 2017–18 and subsequent tax years, subject to transitional provisions in F(No 2)A 2017 Sch 2 para 64.

[2] In cross-head preceding s 271E, words inserted by F(No 2)A 2017 s 16, Sch 2 paras 12, 14 with effect for the tax year 2017–18 and subsequent tax years, subject to transitional provisions in F(No 2)A 2017 Sch 2 para 64.

272 [Application of trading income rules: GAAP][10]

(1) . . . [10]

(2) [In relation to a property business whose profits are calculated in accordance with GAAP, the provisions of Part 2 (trading income) which apply as a result of section 271E(1) are limited to the following—][10]

In Chapter 3 (basic rules)—	
. . . [10]	. . . [10]
section 26	losses calculated on same basis as profits
[section 28A	money's worth][8]
section 27	receipts and expenses
section 28	items treated under CAA 2001 as receipts
	and expenses
section 29	Interest
In Chapter 4 (rules restricting deductions)—	
section 33	capital expenditure
section 34	expenses not wholly and exclusively for
	trade and unconnected losses
section 35	bad and doubtful debts
sections 36 and 37	unpaid remuneration
sections 38 to 44	employee benefit contributions
sections 45 to 47	business entertainment and gifts
sections 48 to [50B][4]	car . . . [4] hire
. . . [2]	. . . [2]
section 52	exclusion of double relief for interest
section 53	social security contributions
section 54	penalties, interest and VAT surcharges
section 55	crime-related payments
[section 55A	expenditure on integral features][3]
In Chapter 5 (rules allowing deductions)—	
section 57	pre-trading expenses
sections 58 and 59	incidental costs of obtaining finance
. . . [9]	. . . [9]
section 69	payments for restrictive undertakings
sections 70 and 71	seconded employees
section 72	payroll deduction schemes: contributions
	to agents' expenses

sections 73 to 75	counselling and retraining expenses
sections 76 to 80	redundancy payments etc
section 81	personal security expenses
sections 82 to 86	contributions to local Enterprise organisations
	or urban Regeneration companies
[sections 86A and 86B	contributions to flood and coastal erosion risk management projects][7]
sections 87 and 88	scientific research
sections 89 and 90	expenses connected with patents, designs
	and trade marks
section 91	payments to Export Credits Guarantee
	Department
[section 94A	costs of setting up SAYE option scheme or CSOP scheme][5]
[section 94AA	deductions in relation to salaried members of limited liability partnerships][6]
[In Chapter 5A (deductions allowable at a fixed rate)	
section 94C	exclusion of provisions of Chapter 5A for firms with partner who is not an individual
sections 94D to 94G	expenditure on vehicles][11]
In Chapter 6 (receipts)—	
section 96	capital receipts
section 97	debts incurred and later released
section 104	distribution of assets of mutual concerns
section 105	industrial development grants
section 106	sums recovered under insurance policies
	etc
In Chapter 7 (gifts to charities etc)—	
section 109	receipt by donor or connected person of
	benefit attributable to certain gifts
[In Chapter 10A (long funding leases)—	
Sections 148A to 148J	Leases of plant or machinery: special rules for long funding leases][1]
In Chapter 11 (other specific trades)—	
section 155	levies and repayments under FISMA 2000
In Chapter 13 (deductions from profits)—	
sections 188 to 191	unremittable amounts

(3) In those provisions the expression "this Part" is to be read as a reference to those provisions as applied by subsection (2) and to the other provisions of Part 3.

Commentary—*Simon's Taxes* **B6.202.**

Derivation—TA 1988 s 21A, s 65A(5), (6); FA 1998 Sch 5 paras 4, 24; ITEPA 2003 Sch 6 para 7.

HMRC Manuals—Property Income Manual PIM1103 (the profits of a rental business are calculated in the same way as the profits of a trade).

PIM2005 (application of trading income rules).

PIM2060 (criminal payments, bribes and blackmail etc.).

PIM2064 (entertaining expenses and gifts).

PIM2066 (fees for loan finance etc.).

PIM2080 (salaries and wages of employees).

PIM2505 (commencement).

Amendment—[1] Entry inserted by FA 2006 s 81, Sch 8 paras 12, 14 subject to commencement and transitional provisions in FA 2006 Sch 8 paras 15–27.

[2] Entry repealed by ITA 2007 ss 1027, 1031, Sch 1 paras 492, 507, Sch 3 Pt 1 with effect for income tax purposes from 6 April 2007, and corporation tax purposes for accounting periods ending after 5 April 2007.

[3] Entry inserted by FA 2008 s 73(5) with effect: (a) for corporation tax purposes, in relation to expenditure incurred on or after 1 April 2008, and (b) for income tax purposes, in relation to expenditure incurred on or after 6 April 2008.

[4] In entry relating to sections 48–50, reference substituted for "50" and words "or motor cycle" in column 2 repealed, by FA 2009 s 30, Sch 11 para 41 with effect as provided for by FA 2009 Sch 11 paras 65, 66 and subject to savings in FA 2009 Sch 11 para 68. The new system of capital allowances for cars has effect generally from 6 April 2009 (for income tax) and 1 April 2009 (for corporation tax), subject to FA 2009 Sch 11 para 67 (election for new regime not to apply in certain cases).

[5] Entry inserted by TIOPA 2010 s 371, Sch 7 paras 27, 29. TIOPA 2010 has effect for corporation tax purposes for accounting periods ending on or after 1 April 2010, for income and capital gains tax purposes for the tax year 2010–11 and subsequent tax years, and for petroleum revenue tax purposes for chargeable periods beginning on or after 1 July 2010.

[6] Entry inserted by FA 2014 s 74, Sch 17 para 3(1), (3). This amendment is treated as having come into force on 6 April 2014.

[7]   Entry inserted by FA 2015 s 35, Sch 5 para 2 with effect in relation to contributions paid or provided on or after 1 January 2015.

[8]   Entry inserted by FA 2016 s 71(1), (3) with effect in relation to transactions entered into on or after 16 March 2016.

[9]   Entry relating to section 68 repealed by FA 2016 s 72(2)(b) with effect in relation to expenditure incurred on or after 1 April 2016 for corporation tax purposes and 6 April 2016 for income tax purposes.

[10]   Heading substituted for heading "Profits of a property business: application of trading income rules", sub-s (1) repealed, in sub-s (2),words substituted for words "But the provisions of Part 2 (trading income) which apply as a result of subsection (1) are limited to the following—", and table entry relating to "section 25" repealed, by F(No 2)A 2017 s 16, Sch 2 paras 12, 16 with effect for the tax year 2017–18 and subsequent tax years, subject to transitional provisions in F(No 2)A 2017 Sch 2 para 64.

[11]   Entries inserted by FA 2018 s 36(4) with effect for the tax year 2017–18 and subsequent tax years.

[272ZA Application of trading income rules: cash basis

(1) In relation to a property business whose profits are calculated on the cash basis, the provisions of Part 2 (trading income) which apply as a result of section 271E(1) are limited to the following—

In Chapter 3 (basic rules)—

section 26	losses calculated on same basis as profits
section 28A	money's worth
section 29	interest

In Chapter 4 (rules restricting deductions)—

section 34	expenses not wholly and exclusively for trade and unconnected losses
sections 38 to 42 and 44	employee benefit contributions
sections 45 to 47	business entertainment and gifts
section 52	exclusion of double relief for interest
section 53	social security contributions
section 54	penalties, interest and VAT surcharges
section 55	crime-related payments
section 55A	expenditure on integral features

In Chapter 5 (rules allowing deductions)—

section 57	pre-trading expenses
sections 58 and 59	incidental costs of obtaining finance
section 69	payments for restrictive undertakings
sections 70 and 71	seconded employees
section 72	payroll deduction schemes: contributions to agents' expenses
sections 73 to 75	counselling and retraining expenses
sections 76 to 80	redundancy payments etc
section 81	personal security expenses
sections 82 to 86	contributions to local enterprise organisations or urban regeneration companies
sections 86A and 86B	contributions to flood and coastal erosion risk management projects
sections 87 and 88	scientific research
sections 89 and 90	expenses connected with patents, designs and trade marks
section 91	payments to Export Credits Guarantee Department

[In Chapter 5A (deductions allowable at a fixed rate)

section 94C	exclusion of provisions of Chapter 5A for firms with partner who is not an individual
sections 94D to 94G	expenditure on vehicles][2]

In Chapter 6 (receipts)—

section 96	capital receipts
section 97	debts incurred and later released
section 104	distribution of assets of mutual concerns
section 105(1) and (2)(b) and (c)	industrial development grants
section 106	sums recovered under insurance policies etc

In Chapter 6A (amounts not reflecting commercial transactions)—

section 106C	amounts not reflecting commercial transactions
section 106D	capital receipts
section 106E	gifts to charities etc

In Chapter 7 (gifts to charities etc)—

section 109	receipt by donor or connected person of benefit attributable to certain gifts

(2) In those provisions, the expression "this Part" is to be read as a reference to those provisions as applied by subsection (1) and to the other provisions of Part 3.

(3) In section 106D, the reference to subsection (4) or (5) of section 96A is to be read as a reference to subsection (2), (3) or (5) of section 307F (deemed capital receipts under, or after leaving, cash basis).][1]

Commentary—*Simon's Taxes* **B6.202C**.

Amendments—[1]   Section 272ZA inserted by F(No 2)A 2017 s 16, Sch 2 paras 12, 17 with effect for the tax year 2017–18 and subsequent tax years, subject to transitional provisions in F(No 2)A 2017 Sch 2 para 64.

[2]   Entries inserted by FA 2018 s 36(5) with effect for the tax year 2017–18 and subsequent tax years.

[Calculation of profits: other general rules][3]

[272A Restricting deductions for finance costs related to residential property

(1) Where a deduction is allowed for costs of a dwelling-related loan in calculating the profits of a property business for the tax year 2017–18, the amount allowed to be deducted in respect of those costs in calculating those profits for income tax purposes is 75% of what would be allowed apart from this section.

(2) Where a deduction is allowed for costs of a dwelling-related loan in calculating the profits of a property business for the tax year 2018–19, the amount allowed to be deducted in respect of those costs in calculating those profits for income tax purposes is 50% of what would be allowed apart from this section.

(3) Where a deduction is allowed for costs of a dwelling-related loan in calculating the profits of a property business for the tax year 2019–20, the amount allowed to be deducted in respect of those costs in calculating those profits for income tax purposes is 25% of what would be allowed apart from this section.

(4) In calculating the profits of a property business for income tax purposes for the tax year 2020–21 or any subsequent tax year, no deduction is allowed for costs of a dwelling-related loan.

(5) Subsections (1) to (4) do not apply in relation to calculating the profits of a property business for the purposes of charging a company to income tax on so much of those profits as accrue to it otherwise than in a fiduciary or representative capacity.

(6) For the meaning of "costs of a dwelling-related loan" see section 272B

[(7) See also section 307D (cash basis: modification of deduction for costs of loans).][2]][1]

Commentary—*Simon's Taxes* **B6.202F**.

Amendments—[1]   Sections 272A, 272B inserted by F(No 2)A 2015 s 24(1), (2) with effect from 18 November 2015.

[2]   Sub-s (7) inserted by F(No 2)A 2017 s 16, Sch 2 para 12, 19 with effect for the tax year 2017–18 and subsequent tax years.

[3]   Cross-head preceding s 272A inserted by F(No 2)A 2017 s 16, Sch 2 paras 12, 18 with effect for the tax year 2017–18 and subsequent tax years, subject to transitional provisions in F(No 2)A 2017 Sch 2 para 64.

[272B Meaning of "costs of a dwelling-related loan"

(1) Subsections (2) to (5) apply for the purposes of section 272A.

(2) "Dwelling-related loan", in relation to a property business, means so much of an amount borrowed for purposes of the business as is referable (on a just and reasonable apportionment) to so much of the business as is carried on for the purpose of generating income from—

(*a*) land consisting of a dwelling-house or part of a dwelling-house, or

(*b*) an estate, interest or right in or over land within paragraph (*a*),

but see subsections (3) and (4).

(3) Anything that in the course of a property business is done for creating (by construction or adaptation) a dwelling-house, or part of a dwelling-house, from which income is to be generated is, for the purposes of subsection (2), to be treated as done for the purpose mentioned in that subsection.

(4) An amount borrowed for purposes of a property business is not a dwelling-related loan so far as the amount is referable (on a just and reasonable apportionment) to so much of the property business as consists of the commercial letting of furnished holiday accommodation.

(5) "Costs", in relation to a dwelling-related loan, means—

(*a*) interest on the loan,

(*b*) an amount in connection with the loan that, for the person receiving or entitled to the amount, is a return in relation to the loan which is economically equivalent to interest, or

(*c*) incidental costs of obtaining finance by means of the loan.

(6) Section 58(2) to (4) (meaning of "incidental costs of obtaining finance") apply for the purposes of subsection (5)(*c*).

(7) A reference in this section to a "dwelling-house" includes any land occupied or enjoyed with it as its garden or grounds.][1]

Commentary—*Simon's Taxes* **B6.202F**.

Amendments—[1]   Sections 272A, 272B inserted by F(No 2)A 2015 s 24(1), (2) with effect from 18 November 2015.

273 Amounts not brought into account as part of a property business

(1) The rules for calculating the profits of a property business need to be read with the following provisions of Part 2 (trading income)—

(a) section 19 (tied premises),

(b) section 20 (caravan sites where trade carried on),

(c) section 21 (surplus business accommodation), and

(d) section 22(3) (payments for wayleaves).

(2) Those provisions secure that amounts which would otherwise be brought into account in calculating the profits of the business are, or may be, brought into account instead in calculating the profits of a trade.

Commentary—*Simon's Taxes* **B6.202.**
HMRC Manuals—Property Income Manual PIM1113 (Other property income).

274 Relationship between rules prohibiting and allowing deductions

(1) Any relevant permissive rule in this Part—

(a) has priority over any relevant prohibitive rule in this Part, but

[(b) is subject to—

(i)   section 36 (unpaid remuneration), as applied by section 272,

(ii) section 38 (employee benefit contributions), as applied by sections 272 and 272ZA,

(iii) section 48 (car hire), as applied by section 272,

(iv) section 55 (crime-related payments), as applied by sections 272 and 272ZA,

(v)   section 272A (finance costs), and

(vi) section 307D (cash basis: modification of deduction for costs of loans).][5]

[(1A) But, if the relevant permissive rule would allow a deduction in calculating the profits of a property business in respect of an amount which arises directly or indirectly in consequence of, or otherwise in connection with, relevant tax avoidance arrangements, that rule—

(a) does not have priority under subsection (1)(a), and

(b) is subject to any relevant prohibitive rule in this Part (and to the provisions mentioned in subsection (1)(b)).][3]

(2) In this section "any relevant permissive rule in this Part" means any provision of this Part (apart from sections 291 to 294) which allows a deduction in calculating the profits of a property business.

(3) In this section "any relevant prohibitive rule in this Part", in relation to any deduction, means any provision of this Part (apart from sections [36, 38,][1] 48 and 55, as applied by section 272[, or sections 38 and 55 as applied by section 272ZA][5], and apart also from [sections 272A and 307D][5]) which might otherwise be read as—

(a) prohibiting the deduction, or

(b) restricting the amount of the deduction.

[(3A) In this section "relevant tax avoidance arrangements" means arrangements—

(a) to which the person carrying on the property business is a party, and

(b) the main purpose, or one of the main purposes, of which is the obtaining of a tax advantage (within the meaning of section 1139 of CTA 2010).

"Arrangements" includes any agreement, understanding, scheme, transaction or series of transactions (whether or not legally enforceable).][3]

(4) In this section any reference to any provision of this Part includes any provision applied by section 272 [or 272ZA][5].

Commentary—*Simon's Taxes* **B6.202B, B6.202C.**
Amendments—[1] Words in sub-s (1) substituted, and words in sub-s (3) inserted, by FA 2007 s 67(4)–(7) with effect from the tax year 2007–08.

[2] In sub-s (1)(b) words "or motor cycle" repealed by FA 2009 s 30, Sch 11 para 42 with effect as provided for by FA 2009 Sch 11 paras 65, 66 and subject to savings in FA 2009 Sch 11 para 68. The new system of capital allowances for cars has effect generally from 6 April 2009 (for income tax) and 1 April 2009 (for corporation tax), subject to FA 2009 Sch 11 para 67 (election for new regime not to apply in certain cases).

[3] Sub-ss (1A), (3A) inserted by FA 2013 s 78(2) with effect in relation to deductions in respect of amounts which arise directly or indirectly in consequence of, or otherwise in connection with—

–   arrangements which are entered into on or after 21 December 2012; or

–   any transaction forming part of arrangements which is entered into on or after that date.

This amendment does not have effect where the arrangements are, or any such transaction is, entered into pursuant to an unconditional obligation in a contract made before that date (FA 2013 s 78(6)). "An unconditional obligation" means an obligation which may not be varied or extinguished by the exercise of a right (whether under the contract or otherwise) (FA 2013 s 78(7)).

[4] In sub-ss (1)(b), (3) words inserted by F(No 2)A 2015 s 24(1), (3), (4) with effect from 18 November 2015.

[5] Sub-s (1)(b) substituted, in sub-s (3), words substituted for words "section 272A", and in sub-ss (3), (4), words inserted, by F(No 2)A 2017 s 16, Sch 2 paras 12, 20 with effect for the tax year 2017–18 and subsequent tax years, subject to transitional provisions in F(No 2)A 2017 Sch 2 para 64.

[Tax reductions for non-deductible costs of a dwelling-related loan

274A Reduction for individuals: entitlement

(1) If for a tax year an individual has—

    (*a*) a relievable amount in respect of a property business, or

    (*b*) two or more relievable amounts each in respect of a different property business,

the individual is entitled to relief under this section for that year in respect of that relievable amount or (as the case may be) each of those relievable amounts.

(2) An individual has a relievable amount for a tax year in respect of a property business if for that year the individual has any one or more of the following in respect of that business—

    (*a*) a current-year amount;

    (*b*) a current-year estate amount;

    (*c*) a brought-forward amount.

(3) An individual's relievable amount for a tax year in respect of a property business is the total of—

    (*a*) the individual's current-year amount (if any) for that year in respect of that business,

    (*b*) the individual's current-year estate amounts (if any) for that year in respect of that business, and

    (*c*) the individual's brought-forward amount (if any) for that year in respect of that business.

(4) An individual has a current-year amount for a tax year in respect of a property business if—

    (*a*) an amount ("A") would be deductible in calculating the profits for income tax purposes of that business for that year but for section 272A,

    (*b*) the individual is liable for income tax on N% of those profits, where N is a number—

        (i) greater than 0, and

        (ii) less than or equal to 100, and

    (*c*) that liability is not under Chapter 6 of Part 5 (estate income),

in which event the individual's current-year amount for that tax year in respect of that business is equal to N% of A.

(5) An individual has a current-year estate amount for a tax year ("the current year"), in respect of a property business and a particular deceased person's estate, if—

    (*a*) an amount ("A") would, but for section 272A, be deductible in calculating the profits for income tax purposes of that business for a particular tax year ("the profits year"), whether that year is the current year or an earlier tax year,

    (*b*) the personal representatives of the deceased person are liable for income tax on N% of those profits, where N is a number—

        (i) greater than 0, and

        (ii) less than or equal to 100,

    (*c*) the individual is liable for income tax on estate income treated under Chapter 6 of Part 5 as arising in the current year from an interest in the estate, and

    (*d*) the basic amount of that estate income consists of, or includes, an amount representative of E% of the personal representatives' N% of the profits of the business for the profits year, where E is a number—

        (i) greater than 0, and

        (ii) less than or equal to 100,

in which event the individual's current-year estate amount for the current tax year, in respect of that business and estate and the profits year, is equal to E% of N% of A.

(6) As to whether an individual has a brought-forward amount for a tax year in respect of a property business, see section 274AA(4).

(7) In this section and section 274AA—

    "estate income", and

    "basic amount" in relation to any estate income,

have the same meaning as in Chapter 6 of Part 5 (see sections 649 and 656(4)).][1]

Commentary—*Simon's Taxes* **B6.202F.**

Amendments—[1]   Sections 274A–274C substituted for previous ss 274A, 274B by FA 2016 s 26 with effect from 15 September 2016.

[274AA Reduction for individuals: calculation

(1) This section applies if for a tax year an individual is entitled to relief under section 274A in respect of a relievable amount or in respect of each of two or more relievable amounts, and in the following subsections of this section "relievable amount" means that relievable amount or (as the case may be) any of those relievable amounts.

(2) In respect of a relievable amount, the actual amount on which relief for the year is to be given is (subject to subsection (3)) the amount ("L") that is the lower of—

    (*a*) the relievable amount, and

    (*b*) the total of—

        (i) the profits for income tax purposes of the property business concerned for the year after any deduction under section 118 of ITA 2007 ("the adjusted profits") or, if less, the share (if any) of the adjusted profits on which the individual is liable to income tax otherwise than under Chapter 6 of Part 5, and

        (ii) so much (if any) of the relievable amount as consists of current-year estate amounts.

(3) If S is greater than the individual's adjusted total income for the year ("ATI"), the actual amount on which relief for the year is to be given in respect of a relievable amount is given by—

$$\frac{ATI}{S} \times L$$

where—

S is the total obtained by identifying the amount that is L for each relievable amount and then finding the total of the amounts identified, and

L has the same meaning as in subsection (2).

(4) Where—

(a) a relievable amount,

is greater than—

(b) the actual amount on which relief for the year is to be given in respect of the relievable amount,

the difference is the individual's brought-forward amount for the following tax year in respect of the property business concerned.

(5) The amount of the relief for the year in respect of a relievable amount is given by—

AA × BR

where—

AA is the actual amount on which relief for the year is to be given in respect of the relievable amount, and

BR is the basic rate of income tax for the year,

(6) For the purposes of this section, an individual's adjusted total income for a tax year is identified as follows—

Step 1

Identify the individual's net income for the year (see Step 2 of the calculation in section 23 of ITA 2007).

Step 2

Exclude from that net income—

(a) so much of it as is within section 18(3) or (4) of ITA 2007 (income from savings), and

(b) so much of it as is dividend income.

Step 3

Reduce what is left after Step 2 of this calculation by the amount of any allowances deducted for the year in the individual's case at Step 3 of the calculation in section 23 of ITA 2007. The result is the individual's adjusted total income for the year.][1]

Commentary—*Simon's Taxes* **B6.202F**.

Amendments—[1] Sections 274A–274C substituted for previous ss 274A, 274B by FA 2016 s 26 with effect from 15 September 2016.

[274B Reduction for accumulated or discretionary trust income: entitlement

(1) If for a tax year the trustees of a settlement have—

(a) a relievable amount in respect of a property business, or

(b) two or more relievable amounts each in respect of a different property business,

the trustees of the settlement are entitled to relief under this section for that year in respect of that relievable amount or (as the case may be) each of those relievable amounts.

(2) The trustees of a settlement have a relievable amount for a tax year in respect of a property business if for that year the trustees of the settlement have a current-year amount, or brought-forward amount, in respect of that business (or have both).

(3) In the case of trustees of a settlement, their relievable amount for a tax year in respect of a property business is the total of—

(a) their current-year amount (if any) for that year in respect of that business, and

(b) their brought-forward amount (if any) for that year in respect of that business.

(4) The trustees of a settlement have a current-year amount for a tax year in respect of a property business if—

(a) an amount ("A") would be deductible in calculating the profits for income tax purposes of that business for that year but for section 272A,

(b) the trustees of the settlement are liable for income tax on N% of those profits, where N is a number—

(i) greater than 0, and

(ii) less than or equal to 100, and

(c) in relation to the trustees of the settlement, that N% of those profits is accumulated or discretionary income, in which event the current-year amount of the trustees of the settlement for that tax year in respect of that business is equal to N% of A.

(5) As to whether the trustees of a settlement have a brought-forward amount for a tax year in respect of a property business, see section 274C(3).

(6) In this section and section 274C "accumulated or discretionary income" has the meaning given by section 480 of ITA 2007.][1]

Commentary—*Simon's Taxes* **B6.202F.**

Amendments—[1] Sections 274A–274C substituted for previous ss 274A, 274B by FA 2016 s 26 with effect from 15 September 2016.

[274C Reduction for accumulated or discretionary trust income: calculation

(1) This section applies if for a tax year the trustees of a settlement are entitled to relief under section 274B in respect of a relievable amount or in respect of each of two or more relievable amounts, and in the following subsections of this section "relievable amount" means that relievable amount or (as the case may be) any of those relievable amounts.

(2) The amount of the relief in respect of a relievable amount is given by—

L × BR

where—

BR is the basic rate of income tax for the year, and

L is the lower of—

(a) the relievable amount, and

(b) the profits for income tax purposes of the property business concerned for the year after any deduction under section 118 of ITA 2007 ("the adjusted profits") or, if less, the share of the adjusted profits—

(i) on which the trustees of the settlement are liable for income tax, and

(ii) which, in relation to the trustees of the settlement, is accumulated or discretionary income.

(3) Where L in the case of a relievable amount is less than the relievable amount, the difference between them is the brought-forward amount of the trustees of the settlement for the following tax year in respect of the property business concerned.][1]

Amendments—[1] Sections 274A–274C substituted for previous ss 274A, 274B by FA 2016 s 26 with effect from 15 September 2016.

Apportionment of profits

275 Apportionment etc of profits to tax year

(1) This section applies if a period of account of a property business does not coincide with a tax year.

(2) Any of the following steps may be taken if they are necessary in order to arrive at the profits or losses of the tax year—

(a) apportioning the profits or losses of a period of account to the parts of that period falling in different tax years, and

(b) adding the profits or losses of a period of account (or part of a period) to profits or losses of other periods of account (or parts).

(3) The steps must be taken by reference to the number of days in the periods concerned.

(4) But the person carrying on the business may use a different way of measuring the length of the periods concerned if—

(a) it is reasonable to do so, and

(b) the way of measuring the length of periods is used consistently for the purposes of the business.

Commentary—*Simon's Taxes* **B6.202.**

HMRC Manuals—Property Income Manual PIM1010 (basis of assessment and time apportionment).

CHAPTER 4

PROFITS OF PROPERTY BUSINESSES: LEASE PREMIUMS ETC

Introduction

276 Introduction

(1) This Chapter provides for certain amounts (which would otherwise generally be amounts of a capital nature) to be brought into account as receipts in calculating the profits of a property business.

(2) The amounts relate to short-term leases in the case of—

section 277 (lease premiums),

section 278 (amount treated as lease premium where work required),

section 280 (sums payable for surrender of lease), and

section 282 (assignments for profit of lease granted at undervalue).

(3) The amounts relate to any lease in the case of—
section 279 (sums payable instead of rent), and
　　　section 281 (sums payable for variation or waiver of [terms][1] of lease).
(4) The amounts relate to the sale of any estate or interest in land in the case of—
section 284 (sales with right to reconveyance), and
　　　section 285 (sale and leaseback transactions).
(5) This Chapter also permits certain deductions in calculating the profits of property businesses carried on by tenants under certain leases (see sections 291 and 292[; but see also section 276A][2]).
(6) In this Chapter "short-term lease" means a lease whose effective duration is 50 years or less.

Commentary—*Simon's Taxes* **B6.301.**
Amendments—[1]　In sub-s (3) word substituted by CTA 2009 s 1322, Sch 1 paras 587, 614. CTA 2009 applies for accounting periods ending on or after 1 April 2009 (for corporation tax purposes) and for tax years 2009–10 onwards (for income and capital gains tax purposes).
[2]　In sub-s (5), words inserted by F(No 2)A 2017 s 16, Sch 2 paras 12, 21 with effect for the tax year 2017–18 and subsequent tax years, subject to transitional provisions in F(No 2)A 2017 Sch 2 para 64.

[276A　Application of Chapter to property businesses using cash basis
The following provisions of this Chapter do not apply in calculating the profits of a property business on the cash basis—
　　(*a*)　sections 291 to 294 (tenants under taxed leases: deductions), and
　　(*b*)　sections 296 and 298 (ICTA modifications).][1]

Commentary—*Simon's Taxes* **B6.202C, B6.310.**
Amendments—[1]　Section 276A inserted by F(No 2)A 2017 s 16, Sch 2 paras 12, 22 with effect for the tax year 2017–18 and subsequent tax years, subject to transitional provisions in F(No 2)A 2017 Sch 2 para 64.

Amounts treated as receipts: leases

277　Lease premiums
(1) This section applies if a premium is required to be paid—
　　(*a*)　under a short-term lease, or
　　(*b*)　otherwise under the terms subject to which a short-term lease is granted.
(2) The person to whom the premium is due is treated as—
　　(*a*)　entering into a transaction mentioned in section 264 (if the land to which the lease relates is in the United Kingdom) or section 265 (if that land is outside the United Kingdom), and
　　(*b*)　receiving the amount calculated under subsections (4) and (5) as a result of that transaction.
(3) That amount is brought into account as a receipt in calculating the profits of the property business which consists of or includes that transaction for the tax year in which the lease is granted.
(4) The amount of the receipt is given by the formula—

$$P \times \left(\frac{50 - Y}{50} \right)$$

where—
　　P is the premium, and
　　Y is the number of complete periods of 12 months (other than the first) comprised in the effective duration of the lease.
(5) But, if the rule in section 288 (the additional calculation rule) applies, the amount given by the formula in subsection (4) is reduced by the amount calculated in accordance with section 288.

Commentary—*Simon's Taxes* **B6.301.**
HMRC Manuals—Property Income Manual PIM1205 (how the charge is calculated).
PIM1218 (payments to a person other than the landlord).

278　Amount treated as lease premium where work required
(1) This section applies if the terms subject to which a lease is granted impose on the tenant an obligation to carry out work on the premises.
(2) The lease is treated for the purposes of section 277 (lease premiums) as requiring the payment of a premium to the landlord (in addition to any other premium).
(3) The amount of the premium is the amount by which the value of the landlord's estate or interest immediately after the commencement of the lease exceeds what its value would have been at that time if the terms of the lease did not impose the obligation on the tenant.
(4) An obligation, or part of an obligation, that requires the carrying out of excepted work is ignored for the purposes of this section.
(5) Work is "excepted work" if the payment for carrying it out would, if the landlord and not the tenant were obliged to carry it out, be deductible as an expense in calculating the profits of the landlord's property business.

Commentary—*Simon's Taxes* **B6.302.**
Derivation—TA 1988 s 34(2), (3), s 65A(5); FA 1998 Sch 5 paras 15(3), 24.
HMRC Manuals—Property Income Manual PIM1212 (lease requiring tenant to carry out work on premises).

279 Sums payable instead of rent

(1) This section applies if—

    (a) under the terms subject to which a lease is granted a sum becomes payable by the tenant instead of the whole or a part of the rent for a period, and

    (b) the period is 50 years or less.

(2) The person to whom the sum is due is treated as—

    (a) entering into a transaction mentioned in section 264 (if the land to which the lease relates is in the United Kingdom) or section 265 (if that land is outside the United Kingdom), and

    (b) receiving the amount calculated under subsections (4) and (5) as a result of that transaction.

(3) That amount is brought into account as a receipt in calculating the profits of the property business which consists [of or][1] includes that transaction for the tax year in which the sum becomes payable.

(4) The amount of the receipt is given by the formula—

$$S \times \left(\frac{50 - Y}{50} \right)$$

where—

    S is the sum payable instead of rent, and

    Y is the number of complete periods of 12 months (other than the first) comprised in the period in relation to which the sum is payable.

(5) But, if the rule in section 288 (the additional calculation rule) applies, the amount given by the formula in subsection (4) is reduced by the amount calculated in accordance with section 288.

(6) In determining for the purposes of this Chapter the duration of the period in relation to which the sum is payable, any part of the period that falls after the expiry of the effective duration of the lease is excluded.

Commentary—*Simon's Taxes* **B6.303.**

HMRC Manuals—Property Income Manual PIM1214 (sums payable in lieu of rent or for surrender of a lease).

Amendments—[1]   In sub-s (3) words substituted by CTA 2009 s 1322, Sch 1 paras 587, 615. CTA 2009 applies for accounting periods ending on or after 1 April 2009 (for corporation tax purposes) and for tax years 2009–10 onwards (for income and capital gains tax purposes).

280 Sums payable for surrender of lease

(1) This section applies if, under the terms subject to which a short-term lease is granted, a sum becomes payable by the tenant as consideration for the surrender of the lease.

(2) The person to whom the sum is due is treated as—

    (a) entering into a transaction mentioned in section 264 (if the land to which the lease relates is in the United Kingdom) or section 265 (if that land is outside the United Kingdom), and

    (b) receiving the amount calculated under subsections (4) and (5) as a result of that transaction.

(3) That amount is brought into account as a receipt in calculating the profits of the property business which consists of or includes that transaction for the tax year in which the sum becomes payable.

(4) The amount of the receipt is given by the formula—

$$S \times \left(\frac{50 - Y}{50} \right)$$

where—

    S is the sum payable as consideration for the surrender of the lease, and

    Y is the number of complete periods of 12 months (other than the first) comprised in the effective duration of the lease.

(5) But, if the rule in section 288 (the additional calculation rule) applies, the amount given by the formula in subsection (4) is reduced by the amount calculated in accordance with section 288.

Commentary—*Simon's Taxes* **B6.304.**

HMRC Manuals—Property Income Manual PIM1214 (sums payable in lieu of rent or for surrender of a lease). PIM1218 (payments to a person other than the landlord).

281 Sums payable for variation or waiver of [terms][1] of lease

(1) This section applies if—

    (a) a sum becomes payable by the tenant (otherwise than by way of rent) as consideration for the variation or waiver of a term of a lease,

    (b) the sum is due to the landlord or a person who is connected with the landlord, and

    (c) the period for which the variation or waiver has effect is 50 years or less.

(2) The person to whom the sum is due is treated as—

    (a) entering into a transaction mentioned in section 264 (if the land to which the lease relates is in the United Kingdom) or section 265 (if that land is outside the United Kingdom), and

    (b) receiving the amount calculated under subsections (4) and (5) as a result of that transaction.

(3) That amount is brought into account as a receipt in calculating the profits of the property business which consists of or includes that transaction for the tax year in which the contract providing for the variation or waiver is entered into.

(4) The amount of the receipt is given by the formula—

$$S \times \left(\frac{50 - Y}{50} \right)$$

where—

 S is the sum payable as consideration for the variation or waiver, and

 Y is the number of complete periods of 12 months (other than the first) comprised in the period for which the variation or waiver has effect.

(5) But, if the rule in section 288 (the additional calculation rule) applies, the amount given by the formula in subsection (4) is reduced by the amount calculated in accordance with section 288.

(6) In determining for the purposes of this Chapter the duration of the period for which the variation or waiver has effect, any part of the period that falls after the expiry of the effective duration of the lease is excluded.

Commentary—*Simon's Taxes* **B6.305.**

HMRC Manuals—Property Income Manual PIM1216 (sums received for variation or waiver of the terms of a lease). PIM1218 (payments to a person other than the landlord).

Amendments—[1] In heading word substituted by CTA 2009 s 1322, Sch 1 paras 587, 616. CTA 2009 applies for accounting periods ending on or after 1 April 2009 (for corporation tax purposes) and for tax years 2009–10 onwards (for income and capital gains tax purposes).

[281A Sums to which sections 277 to 281 do not apply

(1) This section applies if a grant of a lease constitutes a disposal of an asset for the purposes of section 809BZA(2)(b) or 809BZF(2)(a) of ITA 2007 (disposals under finance arrangements).

(2) Sections 277 to 281 do not apply in relation to a premium paid in respect of the grant.][1]

Amendments—[1] This section inserted by TIOPA 2010 s 501, Sch 8 paras 269, 270. TIOPA 2010 has effect for corporation tax purposes for accounting periods ending on or after 1 April 2010, for income and capital gains tax purposes for the tax year 2010–11 and subsequent tax years, and for petroleum revenue tax purposes for chargeable periods beginning on or after 1 July 2010.

282 Assignments for profit of lease granted at undervalue

(1) This section applies to an assignment of a short-term lease if—

 (a) the lease was granted at an undervalue, and

 (b) a profit is made on the assignment.

(2) The person who assigns the lease is treated as—

 (a) entering into a transaction mentioned in section 264 (if the land to which the lease relates is in the United Kingdom) or section 265 (if that land is outside the United Kingdom), and

 (b) receiving the amount calculated under subsections (4) and (5) as a result of that transaction.

(3) That amount is brought into account as a receipt in calculating the profits of the property business which consists of or includes that transaction for the tax year in which the consideration for the assignment becomes payable.

(4) The amount of the receipt is given by the formula—

$$P \times \left(\frac{50 - Y}{50} \right)$$

where—

 P is the lesser of—

  (a) the profit on the assignment, and

  (b) the amount by which the undervalue exceeds the total of the profits (if any) made on previous assignments of the lease, and

 Y is the number of complete periods of 12 months (other than the first) comprised in the effective duration of the lease.

(5) But, if the rule in section 288 (the additional calculation rule) applies, the amount given by the formula in subsection (4) is reduced by the amount calculated in accordance with section 288.

(6) Section 283 explains references in this section to the grant of a lease at an undervalue and the making of a profit on an assignment of a lease.

Commentary—*Simon's Taxes* **B6.306.**

HMRC Manuals—Property Income Manual PIM1222 (charge on assignment of lease granted at undervalue).

283 Provisions supplementary to section 282

(1) This section operates for the purposes of section 282.

(2) A lease is granted at an undervalue if the terms subject to which it was granted are such that the landlord who granted it could have required the payment of an additional sum by way of premium, or additional premium, for its grant.

(3) The additional sum is the undervalue.

(4) The test in subsection (2) must be applied—

    (a) having regard to values prevailing at the time the lease was granted, and

    (b) on the assumption that the negotiations for the lease were at arm's length.

(5) A profit is made on an assignment of a lease if the consideration for the assignment exceeds—

    (a) if the lease has not previously been assigned, any premium for which it was granted, or

    (b) in any other case, any consideration for which it was last assigned.

(6) The amount of the excess is the profit.

Commentary—*Simon's Taxes* **B6.306.**

Derivation—TA 1988 s 35, s 65A(5); FA 1998 Sch 5 para 24.

HMRC Manuals—Property Income Manual PIM1222 (charge on assignment of lease granted at undervalue).

Other amounts treated as receipts

284 Sales with right to reconveyance

(1) This section applies if—

    (a) an estate or interest in land is sold subject to terms which provide that it is to be, or may be required to be, reconveyed on a future date to the seller or a person connected with the seller,

    (b) the period beginning with the sale and ending with the earliest date on which under the terms of the sale the estate or interest would fall to be reconveyed is 50 years or less, and

    (c) the price at which the estate or interest is sold exceeds the price at which it is to be reconveyed.

(2) The seller is treated as—

    (a) entering into a transaction mentioned in section 264 (if the land is in the United Kingdom) or section 265 (if the land is outside the United Kingdom), and

    (b) receiving the amount calculated under subsection (4) as a result of that transaction.

(3) That amount is brought into account as a receipt in calculating the profits of the property business which consists of or includes that transaction for the tax year in which the estate or interest is sold.

(4) The amount of the receipt is given by the formula—

$$E \times \left(\frac{50 - Y}{50} \right)$$

where—

    E is the amount by which the price at which the estate or interest is sold exceeds the price at which it is to be reconveyed, and

    Y is the number of complete periods of 12 months (other than the first) comprised in the period beginning with the sale and ending with the earliest date on which under the terms of the sale the estate or interest would fall to be reconveyed.

(5) See section 286 for some provisions which are supplementary to this section.

Commentary—*Simon's Taxes* **B6.307.**

HMRC Manuals—Property Income Manual PIM1224 (charge on sale of property with right to re-conveyance).

285 Sale and leaseback transactions

(1) This section applies if—

    (a) an estate or interest in land is sold subject to terms which provide for the grant of a lease directly or indirectly out of the estate or interest to the seller or a person connected with the seller,

    (b) the period beginning with the sale and ending with the earliest date on which under the terms of the sale the lease would fall to be granted is 50 years or less, and

    (c) the price at which the estate or interest is sold exceeds the total of—

        (i) the amount of any premium for the lease, and

        (ii) the value on the date of the sale of the right to receive a conveyance of the reversion immediately after the lease begins to run.

(2) This section does not apply if the lease is granted and begins to run within one month after the sale.

(3) The seller is treated as—

    (a) entering into a transaction mentioned in section 264 (if the land is in the United Kingdom) or section 265 (if the land is outside the United Kingdom), and

    (b) receiving the amount calculated under subsection (5) as a result of that transaction.

(4) That amount is brought into account as a receipt in calculating the profits of the property business which consists of or includes that transaction for the tax year in which the estate or interest is sold.

(5) The amount of the receipt is given by the formula—

$$E \times \left(\frac{50 - Y}{50} \right)$$

where—

    E is the amount by which the price at which the estate or interest is sold exceeds the total of—

        (*a*) the amount of any premium for the lease, and

        (*b*) the value on the date of the sale of the right to receive a conveyance of the reversion immediately after the lease begins to run, and

    Y is the number of complete periods of 12 months (other than the first) comprised in the period beginning with the sale and ending with the earliest date on which under the terms of the sale the lease would fall to be granted.

(6) See section 286 for some provisions which are supplementary to this section.

Commentary—*Simon's Taxes* **B6.308.**

HMRC Manuals—Property Income Manual PIM1226 (sale of property with right to lease back).

286 Provisions supplementary to sections 284 and 285

(1) This section operates for the purposes of sections 284 (sales with right to reconveyance) and 285 (sale and leaseback transactions).

(2) Subsection (3) explains how to determine for the purposes of section 284 the price at which an estate or interest is to be reconveyed when—

    (*a*) the date on which the estate or interest would fall to be reconveyed is not fixed under the terms of the sale, and

    (*b*) the price at which it is to be reconveyed varies with the date.

(3) The price is taken to be the lowest possible under the terms of the sale.

(4) Subsection (5) explains how to determine for the purposes of section 285 the total of—

    (*a*) the amount of any premium for the lease, and

    (*b*) the value on the date of the sale of the right to receive a conveyance of the reversion immediately after the lease begins to run,

when the date for the grant of the lease is not fixed under the terms of the sale and the total varies with the date.

(5) The total is taken to be the lowest possible under the terms of the sale.

(6) For the purposes of sections 284(3) and 285(4) (receipts of property business for tax year in which estate or interest sold) an estate or interest in land is sold when any of the following occurs—

    (*a*) an unconditional contract for its sale is entered into,

    (*b*) a conditional contract for its sale becomes unconditional, or

    (*c*) an option or right of pre-emption is exercised requiring the seller to enter into an unconditional contract for its sale.

Commentary—*Simon's Taxes* **B6.307, B6.308.**

Derivation—TA 1988 s 36, s 65A(5); FA 1998 Sch 5 paras 17(4), 24.

HMRC Manuals—Property Income Manual PIM1224 (what is the date of sale?).

Additional calculation rule for reducing certain receipts

287 Circumstances in which additional calculation rule applies

(1) The rule in section 288 (the additional calculation rule) applies in relation to the calculation of receipts under—

    section 277 (lease premiums),

    section 279 (sums payable instead of rent),

    section 280 (sums payable for surrender of lease),

    section 281 (sums payable for variation or waiver of [terms][1] of lease), or

    section 282 (assignments for profit of lease granted at undervalue).

(2) It applies if conditions A and B are met.

(3) Condition A is that—

    (*a*) in the case of a receipt under section 277, 279 or 280, the lease is granted out of a taxed lease,

    (*b*) in the case of a receipt under section 281, the lease was granted out of a taxed lease, and

    (*c*) in the case of a receipt under section 282, the assignment is of a taxed lease.

(4) A lease is a "taxed lease" for the purposes of this Chapter if—

    (*a*) there is a receipt under any of sections 277 to 282 in respect of the lease, . . . [1]

    (*b*) there would be such a receipt, but for the operation of the [rule in section 288 (the additional calculation rule)][1] in the calculation of its amount.

    [(*c*) there is a receipt under any of sections 217 to 222 of CTA 2009 (receipts in respect of lease premiums, sums payable instead of rent, for surrender of lease and for variation or waiver of terms of lease and assignments) in respect of the lease, or

    (*d*) there would be such a receipt, but for the operation of the rule in section 228 of that Act (the additional calculation rule) in the calculation of its amount.][1]

In this Chapter [a receipt falling within paragraph (*a*), (*b*), (*c*) or (*d*)][1] is referred to as a "taxed receipt".

(5) Condition B is that the taxed receipt, or if there is more than one, at least one of them, has an unused amount.

(6) See section 290 for an explanation of when a taxed receipt has an "unused amount".

Commentary—*Simon's Taxes* B6.309.

Amendments—[1]   In sub-s (1) word substituted, in sub-s (4)(*a*) word repealed, in sub-s (4)(*b*) words substituted, sub-s (4)(*c*), (*d*) inserted, and in sub-s (4), in second sentence, words substituted by CTA 2009 s 1322, Sch 1 paras 587, 617. CTA 2009 applies for accounting periods ending on or after 1 April 2009 (for corporation tax purposes) and for tax years 2009–10 onwards (for income and capital gains tax purposes).

288 The additional calculation rule

(1) The rule in this section applies if the conditions mentioned in section 287 are met.

(2) The additional calculation rule is that the amount given by the formula in section 277, 279, 280, 281 or 282 must be reduced by the amount calculated in accordance with this section in order to give the amount of the receipt under calculation.

(3) The amount of the reduction is—

    (*a*) if there is one taxed receipt which has an unused amount, the basic relieving amount by reference to that receipt, and

    (*b*) if there is more than one taxed receipt which has an unused amount, the total of the basic relieving amounts by reference to each receipt,

adjusted, if necessary, in the light of section 289(5) (reduction not to exceed amount being reduced).

(4) The basic relieving amount by reference to a taxed receipt is given by the formula—

$$\frac{A \times LRP}{TRP}$$

where—

    A is the unreduced amount of the taxed receipt (which is, generally, the amount given by the formula in section 277, 279, 280, 281 or [282 above, or in section 217, 219, 220, 221 or 222 of CTA 2009,][1] but see section 290(2) to (4) [above][1]),

    LRP is the receipt period of the receipt under calculation, and

    TRP is the receipt period of the taxed receipt.

(5) But the basic relieving amount is different if section 289(2) or (4) applies (certain special cases).

(6) For the purposes of this Chapter, the "receipt period" of a receipt is—

    (*a*) in the case of a receipt under section 277 or 280, the effective duration of the lease,

    (*b*) in the case of a receipt under section 279, the period in relation to which the sum payable instead of rent is payable,

    (*c*) in the case of a receipt under section 281, the period for which the variation or waiver has effect, . . . [1]

    (*d*) in the case of a receipt under section 282, the effective duration of the lease remaining at the date of the assignment[, and

    (*e*) in the case of a receipt under Chapter 4 of Part 4 of CTA 2009 (profits of property businesses: lease premiums etc), its receipt period within the meaning of that Chapter (see section 228(6) of that Act).][1]

Commentary—*Simon's Taxes* B6.309.

Amendments—[1]   In sub-s (4) words substituted and word inserted, in sub-s (6)(*c*) word repealed, and sub-s (6)(*e*) and preceding word inserted, by CTA 2009 ss 1322, 1326, Sch 1 paras 587, 618, Sch 3 Part 1. CTA 2009 applies for accounting periods ending on or after 1 April 2009 (for corporation tax purposes) and for tax years 2009–10 onwards (for income and capital gains tax purposes).

289 The additional calculation rule: special cases

(1) This section explains how section 288 operates in some special cases.

(2) If—

    (*a*) the receipt under calculation is under any of sections 277 to 281, and

    (*b*) the lease does not extend to the whole of the premises subject to the taxed lease,

the basic relieving amount by reference to a taxed receipt is calculated by multiplying the amount given by the formula in subsection (4) of section 288 by the fraction of those premises which is subject to the lease.

(3) This fraction is calculated on a just and reasonable basis.

(4) If the basic relieving amount given by section 288(4) or subsection (2) above by reference to a taxed receipt would otherwise exceed the unused amount of the taxed receipt, the basic relieving amount is the unused amount.

(5) If the amount of the reduction under section 288 would otherwise exceed the amount given, in respect of the receipt under calculation, by the formula in section 277, 279, 280, 281 or 282, the amount of the reduction is equal to the amount given by the formula.

Commentary—*Simon's Taxes* B6.309.

290 Meaning of "unused amount" and "unreduced amount"

(1) For the purposes of this Chapter, a taxed receipt has an "unused amount" if the unreduced amount exceeds the total of the reductions and deductions referred to in subsection (5).

(2) In this Chapter the "unreduced amount" of a taxed receipt is the amount given, in respect of the taxed receipt, by the [formula in—

    (*a*) section 277, 279, 280, 281 or 282 above, or

    (*b*) section 217, 219, 220, 221 or 222 of CTA 2009 (corporation tax provisions corresponding to those listed in paragraph (*a*)).][1]

[(3) Subsection (4) applies—

    (*a*) to a taxed receipt under section 277 (lease premiums) as a result of section 278 (amount treated as lease premium where work required), and

    (*b*) to a taxed receipt under section 217 of CTA 2009 (lease premiums) as a result of section 218 of that Act (amount treated as lease premium where work required).][1]

(4) If the obligation to carry out work included the carrying out of work which gives, or will give, rise to qualifying expenditure under CAA 2001, the unreduced amount of the taxed receipt is calculated as if the obligation had not included the carrying out of that work.

(5) The reductions and deductions mentioned in subsection (1) are—

    (*a*) the reductions under section 288 [above or section 228 of CTA 2009 (the additional calculation rule)][1] by reference to the taxed receipt,

    (*b*) the deductions allowed in calculating the profits of a trade, profession or vocation for expenses under section 61 [above or section 63 of CTA 2009][1] (tenant under taxed lease who uses land in connection with trade treated as incurring expenses) by reference to the taxed receipt, and

    (*c*) the deductions allowed in calculating the profits of a property business for expenses under section 292 [below or section 232 of CTA 2009][1] (tenant under taxed lease who uses premises for purposes of property business treated as incurring expenses) by reference to the taxed receipt.

(6) For the purposes of this Chapter references to a reduction under section 288 [above or section 228 of CTA 2009][1] by reference to a taxed receipt are to a reduction under [the section concerned][1] so far as attributable to the taxed receipt.

Commentary—*Simon's Taxes* B6.309.

Amendments—[1]   In sub-s (2) words substituted, sub-s (3) substituted, in sub-s (5)(*a*)–(*c*), words inserted, and in sub-s (6) words inserted and words substituted, by CTA 2009 s 1322, Sch 1 paras 587, 619. CTA 2009 applies for accounting periods ending on or after 1 April 2009 (for corporation tax purposes) and for tax years 2009–10 onwards (for income and capital gains tax purposes).

Deductions in relation to certain receipts

291 Deductions for expenses under section 292

(1) Section 292 (tenants under taxed leases treated as incurring expenses) applies in calculating the profits of a property business carried on by the tenant under a taxed lease for the purpose of making deductions for the expenses of the property business.

(2) A deduction is allowed for an expense under section 292 for a qualifying day on which the whole or part of the premises subject to the taxed lease is—

    (*a*) occupied by the tenant for the purpose of carrying on the property business, or

    (*b*) sublet.

(3) But any deduction for an expense under section 292 is subject to the application of any provision of Chapter 4 of Part 2 (as applied to property businesses by section 272).

(4) The amount of the deduction for an expense under section 292 for a qualifying day by reference to a taxed receipt may be reduced in order to comply with section 295 (limit on reductions and deductions).

(5) For the meaning of expressions used in this section, see in particular—

section 287(4) ("taxed lease"), and

    section 287(4) ("taxed receipt").

Commentary—*Simon's Taxes* B6.310.

292 Tenants under taxed leases treated as incurring expenses

(1) The tenant under a taxed lease is treated as incurring an expense of a revenue nature in respect of the premises subject to the taxed lease for each qualifying day.

(2) If there is more than one taxed receipt, this section applies separately in relation to each of them.

(3) A day is a "qualifying day", in relation to a taxed receipt, if it falls within the receipt period of the taxed receipt.

(4) The amount of the expense for the qualifying day by reference to the taxed receipt is given by the formula—

$$\frac{A}{TRP}$$

where—

A is the unreduced amount of the taxed receipt, and

TRP is the number of days in the receipt period of the taxed receipt.

[(4A) No expense is to be determined under this section by reference to the taxed receipt if subsection (4B) or (4C) applies.

(4B) This subsection applies if there would have been no taxed receipt but for the application of Rule 1 in section 303 in determining the effective duration of the lease.

(4C) This subsection applies if there would have been no taxed receipt but for the application of Rule 1 in section 243 of CTA 2009 in determining the effective duration of the lease for the purposes of Chapter 4 of Part 4 of that Act.][1]

(5) This section is subject to sections 293 and 294 (restrictions on expenses where the additional calculation rule is relevant).

(6) For the meaning of expressions used in this section, see in particular—

section 288(6) ("receipt period"), and

      section 290(2) to (4) ("unreduced amount").

Commentary—*Simon's Taxes* **B6.310.**

Amendments—[1]   Sub-ss (4A)–(4C) inserted by FA 2013 s 75, Sch 28, paras 1, 3 with effect in relation to leases granted on or after 6 April 2013.

293 Restrictions on section 292 expenses: the additional calculation rule

[(1) This section applies if—

     (*a*) in calculating the amount of a receipt under this Chapter there is a reduction under section 288 (the additional calculation rule) by reference to a taxed receipt, or

     (*b*) in calculating the amount of a receipt under Chapter 4 of Part 4 of CTA 2009 (profits of a property business: lease premiums etc) there is a reduction under section 228 of that Act (the additional calculation rule) by reference to a taxed receipt.

The receipt that is so reduced is referred to in this section as the "lease premium receipt".][1]

(2) Subsections (3) to (5) provide for the application of section 292 for a qualifying day that falls within the receipt period of the lease premium receipt.

(3) The tenant under the taxed lease is treated as incurring an expense under section 292 for the qualifying day by reference to the taxed receipt only if the daily amount of the taxed receipt exceeds the daily reduction of the lease premium receipt.

(4) If the condition in subsection (3) is met, the amount of the expense under section 292 for the qualifying day by reference to the taxed receipt is equal to that excess.

(5) If the qualifying day falls within the receipt periods of more than one lease premium receipt, the reference in subsection (3) to the daily reduction of the lease premium receipt is to be read as a reference to the total of the daily reductions of each of the lease premium receipts whose receipt period includes the qualifying day.

(6) In this section—

the "daily amount" of the taxed receipt is given by the formula—

$$\frac{A}{TRP}$$

where—

A is the unreduced amount of the taxed receipt (see section 290(2) to (4)), and

TRP is the number of days in the receipt period of the taxed receipt, and

the "daily reduction" of a lease premium receipt is given by the formula—

$$\frac{AR}{RRP}$$

where—

AR is the reduction under section 288 [above or section 228 of CTA 2009][1] by reference to the taxed receipt (see section 290(6)), and

RRP is the number of days in the receipt period of the lease premium receipt.

(7) Section 294 explains how this section operates if the lease premium receipt is in respect of a lease that has been granted out of the taxed lease and does not extend to the whole of the premises subject to the taxed lease.

Commentary—*Simon's Taxes* **B6.310.**

Amendments—[1] Sub-s (1) substituted, and in sub-s (6) words inserted, by CTA 2009 s 1322, Sch 1 paras 587, 620. CTA 2009 applies for accounting periods ending on or after 1 April 2009 (for corporation tax purposes) and for tax years 2009–10 onwards (for income and capital gains tax purposes).

294 Restrictions on section 292 expenses: lease of part of premises

(1) This section applies if—

    (*a*) a lease has been granted out of the taxed lease,

    (*b*) the lease does not extend to the whole of the premises subject to the taxed lease, and

    [(*c*) the condition in subsection (1A) is met.

(1A) The condition is that—

    (*a*) in calculating the amount of a receipt under any of sections 277 to 281 (receipts in respect of lease premiums or sums payable instead of rent, for surrender of lease or for variation or waiver of terms of lease) in respect of the lease, there is a reduction under section 288 by reference to a taxed receipt, or

    (*b*) in calculating the amount of a receipt under any of sections 217 to 221 of CTA 2009 (receipts in respect of lease premiums or sums payable instead of rent, for surrender of lease or for variation or waiver of terms of lease) in respect of the lease, there is a reduction under section 228 of that Act (the additional calculation rule) by reference to a taxed receipt.

The receipt that is so reduced is referred to in this section as the "lease premium receipt".][1]

(2) Subsections (3) to (5) apply for a qualifying day that falls within the receipt period of the lease premium receipt.

(3) Sections 292 and 293 apply separately in relation to the part of the premises subject to the lease and to the remainder of the premises.

(4) If—

    (*a*) more than one lease that does not extend to the whole of the premises subject to the taxed lease has been granted out of the taxed lease, and

    (*b*) the qualifying day falls within the receipt period of two or more lease premium receipts that relate to different leases,

sections 292 and 293 apply separately in relation to each part of the premises subject to a lease to which such a receipt relates and to the remainder of the premises.

(5) Where sections 292 and 293 apply in relation to a part of the premises, A becomes the amount calculated by multiplying the unreduced amount of the taxed receipt by the fraction of the premises constituted by the part.

(6) This fraction is calculated on a just and reasonable basis.

Commentary—*Simon's Taxes* **B6.310.**

Amendments—[1] Sub-ss (1)(c), (1A) substituted for previous sub-s (1)(c), by CTA 2009 s 1322, Sch 1 paras 587, 621. CTA 2009 applies for accounting periods ending on or after 1 April 2009 (for corporation tax purposes) and for tax years 2009–10 onwards (for income and capital gains tax purposes).

Limit on effect of additional calculation rule and deductions

295 Limit on reductions and deductions

(1) The total of—

    (*a*) the reductions under section 288 by reference to a taxed receipt, and

    (*b*) the deductions allowed in calculating the profits of a property business for expenses under section 292 (tenant under taxed lease who uses premises for purposes of property business treated as incurring expenses) by reference to the taxed receipt,

must not exceed the amount referred to in subsection (2).

(2) The amount mentioned in subsection (1) is the difference between—

    (*a*) the unreduced amount of the taxed receipt, and

    [(*b*) the total of the amounts mentioned in subsection (3).

(3) Those amounts are—

    (*a*) the reductions under section 228 of CTA 2009 (the additional calculation rule) by reference to the taxed receipt,

    (*b*) the deductions allowed in calculating the profits of a property business for expenses under section 232 of CTA 2009 (tenant under taxed lease which uses premises for purposes of property business treated as incurring expenses) by reference to the taxed receipt, and

    (*c*) the deductions allowed in calculating the profits of a trade, profession or vocation for expenses under section 61 above or section 63 of CTA 2009 (tenant under taxed lease who uses land in connection with trade treated as incurring expenses) by reference to the taxed receipt.][1]

Amendments—[1] Sub-ss (2)(b), (3) substituted for previous sub-s (2)(b) by CTA 2009 s 1322, Sch 1 paras 587, 622. CTA 2009 applies for accounting periods ending on or after 1 April 2009 (for corporation tax purposes) and for tax years 2009–10 onwards (for income and capital gains tax purposes).

Relationship with ICTA

296 Corporation tax receipts treated as taxed receipts

(1) This section applies if in respect of a lease—

(a) there is a receipt of a Schedule A business or an overseas property business (within the meaning of section 70A(4) of ICTA) as a result of section 34 or 35 of ICTA (treatment of premiums etc as rent and assignments for profit of lease granted at an undervalue) for an accounting period ending after 5th April 2005 [but before 1st April 2009][1], or

(b) there would be such a receipt, but for the operation of section 37(2) or (3) of ICTA (reductions in certain receipts under section 34 or 35 of ICTA).

In this Chapter such a receipt is referred to as a "corporation tax receipt".

(2) For the purposes of this Chapter—

    (a) the lease is treated as a taxed lease, and

    (b) the corporation tax receipt is treated as a taxed receipt.

(3) For the purposes of this Chapter, the "receipt period" of a taxed receipt which is a corporation tax receipt is—

    (a) in the case of a corporation tax receipt as a result of section 34 of ICTA, the period treated in calculating the amount of the receipt as being the duration of the lease, and

    (b) in the case of a corporation tax receipt as a result of section 35 of ICTA, the period treated in calculating the amount of the receipt as being the duration of the lease remaining at the date of the assignment.

(4) For the purposes of this Chapter the "unreduced amount" of a taxed receipt which is a corporation tax receipt is the amount of the corporation tax receipt as a result of section 34 or 35 of ICTA, before the operation of section 37(2) or (3) of ICTA.

(5) Subsection (6) applies to a taxed receipt which is a corporation tax receipt arising as a result of section 34(2) of ICTA (obligation on tenant to carry out work under lease).

(6) If the obligation to carry out work includes the carrying out of work which gives, or will give, rise to qualifying expenditure under CAA 2001, the unreduced amount of the taxed receipt is calculated as if the obligation had not included the carrying out of that work.

Amendments—[1] In sub-s (1)(a) words inserted by CTA 2009 s 1322, Sch 1 paras 587, 623. CTA 2009 applies for accounting periods ending on or after 1 April 2009 (for corporation tax purposes) and for tax years 2009–10 onwards (for income and capital gains tax purposes).

297 Taking account of reductions in corporation tax receipts

(1) This section applies if—

    (a) in calculating the amount of a corporation tax receipt, there is a reduction under section 37(2) or (3) of ICTA by reference to the amount chargeable on the superior interest for the purposes of that section, and

    (b) the amount chargeable on the superior interest is the taxed receipt for the purposes of this Chapter.

(2) For the purposes of this Chapter references to a reduction under section 37(2) or (3) of ICTA in a corporation tax receipt by reference to the amount chargeable on the superior interest are to the difference between—

    (a) the amount of the corporation tax receipt before the operation of section 37(2) or (3) of ICTA, and

    (b) the amount of the receipt after the operation of that subsection,

so far as attributable to the amount chargeable on the superior interest for the purposes of section 37 of ICTA.

(3) In sections 290(5)(a) (meaning of "unused amount") and 295(1)(a) (limit on reductions and deductions) references to reductions under section 288 by reference to the taxed receipt include references to reductions under section 37(2) or (3) of ICTA in corporation tax receipts by reference to the amount chargeable on the superior interest.

(4) Sections 292 to 294 apply as follows—

    (a) the corporation tax receipt is treated as if it were a lease premium receipt for the purposes of sections 293 and 294,

    (b) references in those sections to the reduction under section 288 by reference to the taxed receipt are, in relation to the corporation tax receipt, to the reduction under section 37(2) or (3) of ICTA by reference to the amount chargeable on the superior interest, and

    (c) for the purposes of those sections the receipt period of the corporation tax receipt is—

        (i) in the case of a corporation tax receipt as a result of section 34 of ICTA, the period treated in calculating the amount of the receipt as being the duration of the lease, and

        (ii) in the case of a corporation tax receipt as a result of section 35 of ICTA, the period treated in calculating the amount of the receipt as being the duration of the lease remaining at the date of the assignment.

298 Taking account of deductions for rent as a result of section 37(4) or 87(2) of ICTA

(1) Subsection (2) applies if—

(*a*) in calculating the profits of a trade, profession or vocation for an accounting period ending after 5th April 2005 [but before 1st April 2009][1], a company is treated as paying rent under section 87(2) of ICTA by reference to the amount chargeable for the purposes of that section, and

(*b*) the amount chargeable is the taxed receipt for the purposes of this Chapter.

(2) References in sections 290(5)(*b*) and [295(3)(*c*)][1] to the deductions allowed for expenses under section 61 by reference to the taxed receipt include references to the deductions allowed in calculating the profits of the trade, profession or vocation for the rent that the company is treated as paying under section 87(2) of ICTA by reference to the amount chargeable.

(3) Subsection (4) applies if—

(*a*) in calculating the profits of a Schedule A business or an overseas property business (within the meaning of section 70A(4) of ICTA) for an accounting period ending after 5th April 2005 [but before 1st April 2009][1], a company is treated as paying rent as a result of section 37(4) of ICTA by reference to the amount chargeable on the superior interest for the purposes of that section, and

(*b*) the amount chargeable on the superior interest is the taxed receipt for the purposes of this Chapter.

(4) References in sections 290(5)(*c*) and 295(1)(*b*) to the deductions allowed for expenses under section 292 by reference to the taxed receipt include references to the deductions allowed in calculating the profits of the Sch A business or overseas property business (within the meaning of section 70A(4) of ICTA) for the rent that the company is treated as paying as a result of section 37(4) of ICTA by reference to the amount chargeable on the superior interest.

Amendments—[1]   In sub-ss (1)(*a*), (3)(*a*) words inserted, and in sub-s (2) words substituted, by CTA 2009 s 1322, Sch 1 paras 587, 624. CTA 2009 applies for accounting periods ending on or after 1 April 2009 (for corporation tax purposes) and for tax years 2009–10 onwards (for income and capital gains tax purposes).

Certain administrative provisions

299 Payment of tax by instalments

(1) This section applies if—

(*a*) there is a receipt under section 277 (lease premiums) in respect of a premium which is payable by instalments, or

(*b*) there is a receipt under any of sections 279 to 281 (sums payable instead of rent, for surrender of lease or for variation or waiver of [terms][1] of lease) in respect of a sum which is payable by instalments.

(2) The person who is liable to pay tax by reference to the receipt may choose to pay the tax by such instalments as [an officer of Revenue and Customs] may allow.

(3) The period over which the instalments of tax must be paid—

(*a*) must be 8 years or less, and

(*b*) must end before, or at the same time as, the time when the last of the instalments mentioned in subsection (1)(*a*) or (*b*) is payable.

Commentary—*Simon's Taxes* B6.312.

HMRC Manuals—Property Income Manual PIM1220 (payable by instalments).

Amendments—[1]   In sub-ss (1)(*b*) word substituted by CTA 2009 s 1322, Sch 1 paras 587, 625. CTA 2009 applies for accounting periods ending on or after 1 April 2009 (for corporation tax purposes) and for tax years 2009–10 onwards (for income and capital gains tax purposes).

300 Statement of accuracy for purposes of section 282

(1) This section applies if any of the persons mentioned in subsection (3) provides [an officer of Revenue and Customs] with a statement showing—

(*a*) whether or not there is, or may be, a receipt under section 282 (assignments for profit of lease granted at undervalue), and

(*b*) the amount of any receipt.

(2) [An officer of Revenue and Customs] must certify the accuracy of the statement, if satisfied as to its accuracy.

(3) The persons referred to in subsection (1) are—

(*a*) the landlord who granted the lease,

(*b*) a person who assigned it, or

(*c*) a person to whom it was assigned.

HMRC Manuals—Property Income Manual PIM1222 (application for a certificate).

301 Claim for repayment of tax payable by virtue of section 284

(1) This section applies if—

(*a*) there is a receipt under section 284 (sales with right to reconveyance), and

(*b*) the date on which the estate or interest would fall to be reconveyed was not fixed under the terms of the sale.

(2) If the seller makes a claim, the seller must be repaid the amount by which A exceeds B, where—

A is the amount of tax paid by the seller which was payable by virtue of section 284, and

B is the amount of tax that would have been so payable if the date on which the estate or interest was reconveyed had been taken as the date fixed by the terms of the sale.

(3) The claim must be made within [4 years]¹ after the day on which the estate or interest was reconveyed.

Amendments—¹ In sub-s (3), words substituted, by FA 2008 s 118, Sch 39 paras 50, 51 with effect from 1 April 2010 (by virtue of SI 2009/403 art 2(2)), subject to transitional provisions in SI 2009/403 art 10(2) (where art 10 applies the appointed day is 1 April 2012).

302 Claim for repayment of tax payable by virtue of section 285

(1) This section applies if—
    (*a*) there is a receipt under section 285 (sale and leaseback transactions), and
    (*b*) the date for the grant of the lease was not fixed under the terms of the sale.

(2) If the seller makes a claim, the seller must be repaid the amount by which A exceeds B, where—
    A is the amount of tax paid by the seller which was payable by virtue of section 285, and
    B is the amount of tax that would have been so payable if the date on which the lease was granted had been taken as the date fixed by the terms of the sale.

(3) The claim must be made within [4 years]¹ after the day on which the lease was granted.

Commentary—*Simon's Taxes* **B6.308.**
Amendments—¹ In sub-s (3), words substituted by FA 2008 s 118, Sch 39 paras 50, 52 with effect from 1 April 2010 (by virtue of SI 2009/403 art 2(2)), subject to transitional provisions in SI 2009/403 art 10(2) (where art 10 applies the appointed day is 1 April 2012).

[Determinations affecting liability of more than one person

302A Appeals against proposed determinations

(1) Subsection (2) applies if it appears to an officer of Revenue and Customs that—
    (*a*) a determination is needed of an amount that is to be brought into account as a receipt under this Chapter in calculating the liability to tax of a person ("the first taxpayer"), and
    (*b*) the determination may affect the liability to income tax, corporation tax or capital gains tax of other persons.

(2) The officer may give notice (a "provisional notice of determination") to the first taxpayer and the other persons of—
    (*a*) the determination the officer proposes to make, and
    (*b*) their rights under this section and section 302C.

(3) A person to whom a provisional notice of determination is given may object to the proposed determination by giving notice (a "notice of objection") to the officer.

(4) The notice of objection must be given within 30 days of the date on which the provisional notice of determination was given.

(5) If an officer gives provisional notices of determination and no person gives a notice of objection—
    (*a*) a determination must be made by the officer as proposed in the provisional notices, and
    (*b*) the determination is not to be called in question in any proceedings.]¹

Commentary—*Simon's Taxes* **B6.314.**
Amendments—¹ Sections 302A–302C and preceding crosshead inserted by TIOPA 2010 s 371, Sch 7 paras 21, 22. TIOPA 2010 has effect for corporation tax purposes for accounting periods ending on or after 1 April 2010, for income and capital gains tax purposes for the tax year 2010–11 and subsequent tax years, and for petroleum revenue tax purposes for chargeable periods beginning on or after 1 July 2010.

[302B Section 302A: supplementary¹

(1) A provisional notice of determination under section 302A(2) may include a statement of the grounds on which the officer proposes to make the determination.

(2) Subsection (1) applies despite any obligation as to secrecy or other restriction on the disclosure of information.

(3) . . .²
(4) . . .²

Commentary—*Simon's Taxes* **B6.314.**
Amendments—¹ Sections 302A–302C and preceding crosshead inserted by TIOPA 2010 s 371, Sch 7 paras 21, 22. TIOPA 2010 has effect for corporation tax purposes for accounting periods ending on or after 1 April 2010, for income and capital gains tax purposes for the tax year 2010–11 and subsequent tax years, and for petroleum revenue tax purposes for chargeable periods beginning on or after 1 July 2010.
² Sub-ss (3), (4) repealed by FA 2011 s 86(1), Sch 23 para 57(1), (2) with effect from 1 April 2012 in relation to relevant data with a bearing on any period (whether before, on or after 1 April 2012) subject to FA 2011 Sch 23 para 3(2). Sub-ss (3), (4) will continue to have effect in relation to notices given under those subsections before 1 April 2012 as if the repeals had not been made (FA 2011 Sch 23 para 65(2)).

[302C Determination by tribunal

(1) If a notice of objection is given under section 302A(3), the amount mentioned in section 302A(1) must be determined in the same way as an appeal.

(2) All persons to whom provisional notices of determination have been given under section 302A(2) may be a party to—

    (*a*) any proceedings under subsection (1), and

    (*b*) any appeal arising out of those proceedings.

(3) Those persons are bound by the determination made in the proceedings or on appeal, whether or not they have taken part in the proceedings.

(4) Their successors in title are bound in the same way.][1]

Commentary—*Simon's Taxes* **B6.314.**

Amendments—[1] Sections 302A–302C and preceding crosshead inserted by TIOPA 2010 s 371, Sch 7 paras 21, 22. TIOPA 2010 has effect for corporation tax purposes for accounting periods ending on or after 1 April 2010, for income and capital gains tax purposes for the tax year 2010–11 and subsequent tax years, and for petroleum revenue tax purposes for chargeable periods beginning on or after 1 July 2010.

Effective duration of lease

303 Rules for determining effective duration of lease

(1) The following rules apply for determining the effective duration of a lease for the purposes of this Chapter.

[*Rule 1*: If—

    (*a*) the terms of the lease or any other circumstances make it unlikely that the lease will continue beyond a date before the end of the term for which the lease was granted, and

    (*b*) the premium was not substantially greater than it would have been had the term been one ending on that date,

the lease is treated as ending on that date (or the earliest such date).][1]

    Rule 2: If the terms of the lease include provision for the extension of the lease beyond a given date by notice given by the tenant, account may be taken of any circumstances making it likely that the lease will be so extended.

    Rule 3: If the tenant or a person connected with the tenant is, or may become, entitled to a further lease or the grant of a further lease (whenever commencing)—

    (*a*) of the same premises, or

    (*b*) of premises including the whole or part of the same premises, the term of the lease may be treated as continuing until the end of the term of the further lease.

(2) The rules are to be applied in accordance with section 304.

[(2A) In Rule 1 "premium" includes—

    (*a*) an amount treated as a premium under section 278 (amount treated as lease premium where work required),

    (*b*) a sum payable by the tenant under the terms subject to which the lease is granted instead of the whole or a part of the rent for a period,

    (*c*) a sum payable by the tenant under the terms subject to which the lease is granted as consideration for the surrender of the lease, and

    (*d*) a sum payable by the tenant (otherwise than by way of rent) as consideration for the variation or waiver of a term of the lease.][1]

(3) In this section and section 304, in relation to Scotland, "term", where referring to the duration of a lease, means period.

Commentary—*Simon's Taxes* **B6.313.**

HMRC Manuals—Property Income Manual PIM1206 (taking a shorter period than the term of the lease). PIM1207 (taking a longer period than the term of the lease).

Amendments—[1] In sub-s (1) Rule 1 substituted, and sub-s (2A) inserted, by CTA 2009 s 1322, Sch 1 paras 587, 626. CTA 2009 applies for accounting periods ending on or after 1 April 2009 (for corporation tax purposes) and for tax years 2009–10 onwards (for income and capital gains tax purposes). The amendments made by para 626 do not have effect in relation to leases granted before 1 April 2009 (CTA 2009 s 1325, Sch 2 para 44).

304 Applying the rules in section 303

(1) The rules in section 303 apply by reference to the facts known or ascertainable—

    (*a*) at the time of the grant of the lease, or

    (*b*) if the determination is for the purposes of section 281 (sums payable for variation or waiver of [terms][1] of lease), at the time when the contract for the variation or waiver is entered into.

(2) In applying those rules, it is assumed that all parties concerned, whatever their relationship, act as if they were at arm's length.

(3) Subsection (5) applies if—

    (*a*) special benefits were conferred by the lease or in connection with its grant, or

    (*b*) payments were made which one would not expect to be made by parties acting at arm's length unless such benefits had been conferred.

(4) But subsection (5) does not apply if it can be shown that the special benefits were not conferred nor the payments made for the purpose of [securing—

    (*a*) an income tax advantage in the application of this Chapter, or

    (*b*) a corporation tax advantage in the application of Chapter 4 of Part 4 of CTA 2009 (profits of property business: lease premiums etc).][1]

(5) In applying [paragraph (b) of][1] rule 1 in section 303, it is assumed that the special benefits would not have been conferred nor the payments made if the lease had been granted for a term ending on the date mentioned in that rule.

(6) In this section "special benefits" means benefits other than—

    (a) vacant possession and beneficial occupation of the premises, or

    (b) the right to receive rent at a reasonable commercial rate in respect of the premises.

Commentary—*Simon's Taxes* B6.313.

Amendments—[1]   In sub-s (1)(b) word substituted, in sub-s (4) words substituted, and in sub-s (5) words inserted, by CTA 2009 s 1322, Sch 1 paras 587, 627. CTA 2009 applies for accounting periods ending on or after 1 April 2009 (for corporation tax purposes) and for tax years 2009–10 onwards (for income and capital gains tax purposes).

Other interpretative provisions

306 Provisions about premiums

(1) For the purposes of this Chapter, the presumption is that a sum paid on or in connection with the granting of a tenancy has been paid by way of premium.

(2) This does not apply if the sum is rent.

(3) This also does not apply so far as other sufficient consideration for the payment can be shown to have been given.

(4) In this section "sum" includes the value of any consideration.

(5) Where rule 3 in section 303 (rules for determining effective duration of lease) applies, the premium, or an appropriate part of it, payable for or in connection with either lease mentioned in that rule may be treated for the purposes of this Chapter as having been required under the other.

Commentary—*Simon's Taxes* B6.313.

Derivation—TA 1988 s 24.

HMRC Manuals—Property Income Manual PIM1207 (successive leases).

307 Interpretation

(1) In this Chapter "premium" includes any similar sum payable to the immediate or a superior landlord or to a person connected with such a person.

(2) In subsection (1) "sum" includes the value of any consideration.

(3) In the application of this Chapter to Scotland—

    "premium" includes, in particular, a grassum payable to the landlord under the lease in respect of which the grassum is payable or the landlord under any other lease of the property, and

    "reversion" means the interest of the landlord in the property subject to the lease.

(4) In the application of this Chapter to Scotland—

    (a) references to a lease being granted out of a taxed lease are to the grant of a sublease of land subject to the taxed lease, and

    (b) references to the lease so granted are to be read as references to the sublease.

Commentary—*Simon's Taxes* B6.313.

Derivation—TA 1988 s 24.

[Cash basis: application of Chapter

307A Cash basis: application of Chapter

(1) The following provisions of this Chapter apply only where the profits of a property business are calculated on the cash basis—

    (a) section 307B (cash basis: capital expenditure),

    (b) section 307C (cash basis: deduction for costs of loans), and

    (c) section 307D (cash basis: modification of deduction for costs of loans).

(2) Sections 307E and 307F make provision about capital receipts in certain cases where the profits of a property business are calculated on the cash basis or have previously been calculated on the cash basis.][1]

Commentary—*Simon's Taxes* B6.202D.

Amendments—[1]   Sections 307A–307F and cross-heads inserted by F(No 2)A 2017 s 16, Sch 2 paras 12, 23 with effect for the tax year 2017–18 and subsequent tax years, subject to transitional provisions in F(No 2)A 2017 Sch 2 para 64.

[Property businesses using cash basis

307B Cash basis: capital expenditure

(1) This section applies in relation to the calculation of the profits of a property business on the cash basis.

(2) No deduction is allowed for an item of a capital nature incurred on, or in connection with, the acquisition or disposal of a business or part of a business.

(3) No deduction is allowed for an item of a capital nature incurred on, or in connection with, education or training.

(4) No deduction is allowed for an item of a capital nature incurred on, or in connection with, the provision, alteration or disposal of land.

(5) But subsection (4) does not prevent a deduction being made for expenditure that—

(a) is incurred on the provision of a depreciating asset which, in being provided, is installed or otherwise fixed to qualifying land (see subsection (8)) so as to become, in law, part of the land, but

(b) is not incurred on, or in connection with, the provision of—

    (i) a building,

    (ii) a wall, floor, ceiling, door, gate, shutter or window or stairs,

    (iii) a waste disposal system,

    (iv) a sewerage or drainage system, or

    (v) a shaft or other structure in which a lift, hoist, escalator or moving walkway may be installed.

(6) No deduction is allowed for an item of a capital nature incurred on, or in connection with, the provision, alteration or disposal of an asset for use in ordinary residential property (see subsection (8)).

But see section 311A (replacement domestic items relief).

(7) If an asset is provided partly for use in ordinary residential property and partly for other purposes, such apportionment of the expenditure incurred on, or in connection with, the provision, alteration or disposal of the asset is to be made for the purposes of subsection (6) as is just and reasonable.

(8) In relation to the calculation of profits for a tax year—

(a) "ordinary residential property" means a dwelling-house or part of a dwelling-house in relation to which an ordinary property business (see subsection (9)) is carried on in the tax year, and

(b) "qualifying land" means land not falling within paragraph (a).

(9) "Ordinary property business" means—

(a) so much of a UK property business as does not consist of the commercial letting of furnished holiday accommodation (within the meaning of Chapter 6) in the UK, or

(b) so much of an overseas property business as does not consist of the commercial letting of furnished holiday accommodation in one or more EEA states.

(10) No deduction is allowed for an item of a capital nature incurred on, or in connection with, the provision, alteration or disposal of—

(a) any asset that is not a depreciating asset (see subsections (11) and (12)),

(b) any asset not acquired or created for use on a continuing basis in the property business,

(c) a car (see subsection (20)),

(d) a non-qualifying intangible asset (see subsections (13) to (16)), or

(e) a financial asset (see subsection (17)).

(11) An asset is a "depreciating" asset if, on the date the item of a capital nature is incurred, it is reasonable to expect that before the end of 20 years beginning with that date—

(a) the useful life of the asset will end, or

(b) the asset will decline in value by 90% or more.

(12) The useful life of an asset ends when it could no longer be of use to any person for any purpose as an asset of a business.

(13) "Intangible asset" means anything that is capable of being an intangible asset within the meaning of FRS 105 and, in particular, includes—

(a) an internally-generated intangible asset, and

(b) intellectual property.

(14) An intangible asset is "non-qualifying" unless, by virtue of having a fixed maximum duration, it must cease to exist before the end of 20 years beginning with the date on which the item of a capital nature is incurred.

(15) An intangible asset is "non-qualifying" if it consists of a right, whether conditional or not, to obtain an intangible asset without a fixed maximum duration by virtue of which that asset must, assuming the right is exercised at the last possible time, cease to exist before the end of 20 years beginning with the date on which the item of a capital nature is incurred.

(16) Where—

(a) the person carrying on the property business ("P") has an intangible asset, and

(b) P grants a licence or any other right in respect of that asset to another person,

any intangible asset that consists of a licence or other right granted to P in respect of the intangible asset mentioned in paragraph (a) is "non-qualifying".

(17) A "financial asset" means any right under or in connection with—

(a) a financial instrument, or

(b) an arrangement that is capable of producing a return that is economically equivalent to a return produced under any financial instrument.

(18) A reference to acquisition, provision, alteration or disposal includes potential acquisition, provision, alteration or (as the case may be) disposal.

(19) If there is a letting of accommodation only part of which is furnished holiday accommodation, such apportionments as are just and reasonable in all the circumstances are to be made for the purposes of this section.

(20) In this section—

"arrangement" includes any agreement, understanding, scheme, transaction or series of transactions (whether or not legally enforceable);

"building" includes any fixed structure;

"car" has the same meaning as in Part 2 of CAA 2001 (see section 268A of that Act);

"financial instrument" has the same meaning as in FRS 105;

"FRS 105" means Financial Reporting Standard 105 (the Financial Reporting Standard applicable to the Micro-entities Regime), issued by the Financial Reporting Council in July 2015;

"intellectual property" means—

    (*a*) any patent, trade mark, registered design, copyright or design right, plant breeders' rights or rights under section 7 of the Plant Varieties Act 1997,

    (*b*) any right under the law of a country or territory outside the United Kingdom corresponding or similar to a right within paragraph (*a*),

    (*c*) any information or technique not protected by a right within paragraph (*a*) or (*b*) but having industrial, commercial or other economic value, or

    (*d*) any licence or other right in respect of anything within paragraph (*a*), (*b*) or (*c*);

"provision" includes creation, construction or acquisition.][1]

Amendments—[1]   Sections 307A–307F and cross-heads inserted by F(No 2)A 2017 s 16, Sch 2 paras 12, 23 with effect for the tax year 2017–18 and subsequent tax years, subject to transitional provisions in F(No 2)A 2017 Sch 2 para 64.

[307C Cash basis: deduction for costs of loans

(1) Section 307D applies in calculating the profits of a property business for a tax year if conditions A to D are met.

(2) Condition A is that the profits of the business are calculated on the cash basis for the tax year.

(3) Condition B is that a deduction for costs of a loan is allowed in calculating the profits of the business for the tax year or, ignoring section 272A (restricting deductions for finance costs related to residential property) and section 307D (cash basis: modification of deduction for costs of loans), would be so allowed.

In this section such a loan is referred to as a "relevant loan".

(4) Condition C is that an amount of the principal of one or more relevant loans is outstanding at the end time (and a relevant loan in respect of which such an amount is outstanding at the end time is referred to in this section as an "outstanding relevant loan").

(5) Condition D is that—

$$L > V$$

   where—

        L is the total outstanding amount of relevant loans (see subsections (6) and (7)), and

        V is the sum of the values of all relevant properties (see subsections (8) to (10)).

(6) The "total outstanding amount of relevant loans"—

    (*a*) if there is only one outstanding relevant loan, is the outstanding business amount of that loan, and

    (*b*) if there are two or more outstanding relevant loans, is found by calculating the outstanding business amount of each such loan and adding those amounts together.

(7) The "outstanding business amount" of a relevant loan is given by—

$$(X/Y) \times A$$

   where—

        A is the amount of the principal of the loan which is outstanding at the end time,

        X is the amount of the deduction for costs of the loan that would be allowed, apart from sections 272A and 307D, in calculating the profits of the business for the tax year, and

        Y is the amount of the deduction for costs of the loan that would be allowed, apart from the wholly and exclusively rule and sections 272A and 307D, in calculating the profits of the business for the tax year.

(8) A property is a "relevant property" if—

    (*a*) it is involved in the property business at the end time, or

    (*b*) although it is not involved in the business at the end time—

        (i) it was last involved in the business at an earlier time in the tax year, and

        (ii) the person carrying on the business holds the property throughout the period beginning with that earlier time and ending with the end time.

(9) The "value" of a relevant property is the total of—

    (*a*) the market value of the property at the time that it is first involved in the property business, and

    (*b*) such amount of any expenditure of a capital nature incurred by the person carrying on the business in respect of the property as is not brought into account in calculating the profits of the business for the tax year or any previous tax year.

(10) A property is "involved in the property business" if it is a property whose exploitation forms the whole or part of the business.

(11) The "end time" is—

    (*a*) the time immediately before the end of the tax year, or

    (*b*) if in the tax year the person carrying on the business permanently ceases to carry it on, the time immediately before the person permanently ceases to carry on the business.

(12) "Costs", in relation to a loan, means—

    (*a*) interest on the loan,

    (*b*) an amount in connection with the loan that, for the person receiving or entitled to the amount, is a return in relation to the loan which is economically equivalent to interest, or

    (*c*) incidental costs of obtaining finance by means of the loan.

(13) Section 58(2) to (4) (meaning of "incidental costs of obtaining finance") apply for the purposes of subsection (12)(*c*).

(14) In this section—

"market value", in relation to a property, means the price which the property might reasonably be expected to fetch—

    (*a*) in the market conditions then prevailing, and

    (*b*) between persons dealing with each other at arm's length in the open market;

"property" means an estate, interest or right in or over land;

"the wholly and exclusively rule" means the rule in section 34 (expenses not wholly and exclusively for trade and unconnected losses), as applied by section 272ZA (application of trading income rules: cash basis).[1]

Commentary—*Simon's Taxes* **B6.202D**.

Amendments—[1] Sections 307A–307F and cross-heads inserted by F(No 2)A 2017 s 16, Sch 2 paras 12, 23 with effect for the tax year 2017–18 and subsequent tax years, subject to transitional provisions in F(No 2)A 2017 Sch 2 para 64.

307D Cash basis: modification of deduction for costs of loans

(1) Where section 307C provides that this section applies in calculating the profits of a property business for a tax year, the amount which is allowed as a deduction for costs of a loan in calculating the profits for the tax year is the non-adjusted deduction multiplied by the relevant fraction.

This is subject to section 272A (restricting deductions for finance costs related to residential property).

(2) "The non-adjusted deduction" means the deduction for costs of the loan that would be allowed, apart from section 272A and this section, in calculating the profits of the business for the tax year.

(3) "The relevant fraction" means—

V / L

where V and L have the same meaning as in section 307C.

(4) For the meaning of "costs of a loan" see section 307C.[1]

Commentary—*Simon's Taxes* **B6.202D**.

Amendments—[1] Sections 307A–307F and cross-heads inserted by F(No 2)A 2017 s 16, Sch 2 paras 12, 23 with effect for the tax year 2017–18 and subsequent tax years, subject to transitional provisions in F(No 2)A 2017 Sch 2 para 64.

Property businesses that use, or have used, cash basis

307E Capital receipts under, or after leaving, cash basis

(1) This section applies in relation to a property business carried on by a person in two cases—

    (*a*) Case 1 (see subsections (2) to (4)), and

    (*b*) Case 2 (see subsections (5) to (8)).

(2) Case 1 is a case in which conditions A and B are met.

(3) Condition A is that the person receives disposal proceeds or a capital refund in relation to an asset in a tax year for which the profits of the property business are calculated on the cash basis (see section 271D).

For the meaning of "disposal proceeds" and "capital refund" see subsections (9) and (10).

(4) Condition B is that—

    (*a*) an amount of capital expenditure (see subsection (11)) relating to the asset has been brought into account in calculating the profits of the property business on the cash basis, or

    (*b*) an amount of relevant capital expenditure (see subsection (17)) relating to the asset has been brought into account in calculating the profits of the property business in accordance with GAAP (see section 271B)—

        (i) by means of a deduction allowed under section 58 or 59 (incidental costs of obtaining finance) (as applied by section 272) or section 311A (replacement domestic items relief), or

        (ii) under CAA 2001 (see subsection (20)).

(5) Case 2 is a case in which—

    (*a*) condition C is met, and

    (*b*) condition D or E is met.

(6) Condition C is that disposal proceeds or a capital refund arise to the person in relation to an asset in a tax year—

    (*a*) for which the profits of the property business are calculated in accordance with GAAP, and

    (*b*) which is after a tax year for which the profits of the business had been calculated on the cash basis.

(7) Condition D is that an amount of capital expenditure relating to the asset—

    (*a*) has been paid in a tax year for which the profits of the property business were calculated on the cash basis,

    (*b*) has been brought into account in calculating the profits of the business on the cash basis, and

    (*c*) on the assumption that the profits had not been calculated on the cash basis at the time the expenditure was paid, would not have been qualifying expenditure.

(8) Condition E is that—

    (*a*) an amount of capital expenditure relating to the asset has been brought into account in calculating the profits of the property business for a tax year in accordance with GAAP by means of a deduction allowed under section 58 or 59 (as applied by section 272) or section 311A, and

    (*b*) that tax year is before the tax year for which the person last entered the cash basis.

(9) "Disposal proceeds" means—

    (*a*) any proceeds arising from the disposal of an asset or any part of it,

    (*b*) any proceeds arising from the grant of any right in respect of, or any interest in, the asset, or

    (*c*) any amount of damages, proceeds of insurance or other compensation received in respect of the asset.

See also section 307F for circumstances in which a person is to be regarded as disposing of an asset.

(10) "Capital refund" means an amount that is (in substance) a refund of capital expenditure relating to an asset.

(11) "Capital expenditure" means expenditure of a capital nature incurred, or treated as incurred, on or in connection with—

    (*a*) the provision, alteration or disposal of an asset, or

    (*b*) the potential provision, alteration or disposal of an asset.

(12) The disposal proceeds or capital refund mentioned in condition A or (as the case may be) condition C are to be brought into account as a receipt in calculating the profits of the property business.

(13) In a case where only part of the total capital expenditure incurred, or treated as incurred, by the person in relation to the asset has been brought into account in calculating the profits of the property business (whether or not on the cash basis), the amount brought into account under subsection (12) is proportionately reduced.

The reference in this subsection to expenditure brought into account includes a reference to expenditure brought into account under CAA 2001 (see subsection (20)).

(14) Subsection (12) does not apply if the whole of the amount which would otherwise be brought into account under that subsection—

    (*a*) has already been brought into account as a receipt in calculating the profits of the property business under this section,

    (*b*) is brought into account as a receipt in calculating the profits of the business under any other provision of this Part (except section 334D(4) (assets not fully paid for)), or

    (*c*) is brought into account under Part 2 or 3A of CAA 2001 as a disposal value.

The reference to any other provision of this Part in paragraph (*b*) includes a reference to any provision applied by section 272 or 272ZA.

(15) If part of the amount which would otherwise be brought into account under subsection (12) has already been or is brought into account as mentioned in subsection (14), subsection (12) applies in relation to the remainder of that amount.

(16) For the purposes of this section, any question as to whether or to what extent expenditure is brought into account in calculating the profits of a property business is to be determined on such basis as is just and reasonable in all the circumstances.

(17) In subsection (4)(*b*) "relevant capital expenditure" means capital expenditure which—

    (*a*) has been incurred (or treated as incurred) by the person before the tax year for which the person last entered the cash basis, and

    (*b*) is cash basis deductible in relation to that tax year.

(18) For the purposes of this section, a person carrying on a property business "enters the cash basis" for a tax year if the profits of the business are calculated—

    (*a*) on the cash basis for the tax year, and

    (*b*) in accordance with GAAP for the previous tax year.

(19) Expenditure is "cash basis deductible" in relation to a tax year if, on the assumption that the expenditure was paid in that tax year, a deduction would be allowed in respect of the expenditure in calculating the profits of the property business on the cash basis for that tax year.

ITTOIA 2005

(20) For the purposes of this section, expenditure is "brought into account under CAA 2001" in calculating the profits of a property business if and to the extent that—
- (*a*) a capital allowance made under Part 2 of that Act in respect of the expenditure is treated as an expense in calculating those profits (see sections 248 to 250A of that Act), or
- (*b*) qualifying expenditure (within the meaning of Part 2 of CAA 2001) is allocated to a pool for a relevant qualifying activity and is set-off against different disposal receipts.

(21) An amount of qualifying expenditure is "set-off against different disposal receipts" if—
- (*a*) the amount would have been unrelieved qualifying expenditure carried forward in the pool for the relevant qualifying activity, but
- (*b*) the amount is not so carried forward because (and only because) one or more disposal values in respect of one or more assets, other than the asset in respect of which the qualifying expenditure was incurred (or treated as incurred), have at any time been brought into account in that pool.

(22) For the purposes of subsections (20) and (21), an activity is a "relevant qualifying activity" if—
- (*a*) it is a qualifying activity mentioned in section 15(1)(*b*) to (da) of CAA 2001 (property business activities), and
- (*b*) the property business consists of or includes that qualifying activity.

(23) For the purposes of subsection (21), an amount of qualifying expenditure incurred (or treated as incurred) by a person is not to be regarded as not carried forward because the person enters the cash basis.

(24) In this section—
"disposal value" means—
- (*a*) in subsection (14)(*c*)—
    - (i) a disposal value for the purposes of Part 2 of CAA 2001 (see, in particular, section 61 of that Act), or
    - (ii) proceeds from a balancing event for the purposes of Part 3A of that Act (see section 360O of that Act), and
- (*b*) in subsection (21), a disposal value for the purposes of Part 2 of that Act;
"pool" means the main pool or a class pool to which qualifying expenditure is allocated under Part 2 of CAA 2001 (see section 54 of that Act);
"provision" includes creation, construction or acquisition;
"qualifying expenditure" means qualifying expenditure within the meaning of Part 2 of CAA 2001 (see section 11(4) of that Act for the general rule);
"unrelieved qualifying expenditure" means unrelieved qualifying expenditure for the purposes of Part 2 of CAA 2001 (see section 59(1) and (2) of that Act).[1]

Commentary—*Simon's Taxes* **B6.202E.**
Amendments—[1] Sections 307A–307F and cross-heads inserted by F(No 2)A 2017 s 16, Sch 2 paras 12, 23 with effect for the tax year 2017–18 and subsequent tax years, subject to transitional provisions in F(No 2)A 2017 Sch 2 para 64.

307F Deemed capital receipts under, or after leaving, cash basis

(1) This section makes provision supplementary to section 307E.

(2) If—
- (*a*) at any time a person ceases to use an asset or any part of it for the purposes of a property business (other than in the circumstances mentioned in subsection (5)), but
- (*b*) the person does not dispose of the asset (or that part) at that time,

the person is to be regarded for the purposes of section 307E as disposing of the asset (or that part) at that time for an amount equal to the market value amount.

(3) If at any time there is a material increase in the person's non-business use of an asset or any part of it, the person is to be regarded for the purposes of section 307E as disposing of the asset (or that part) at that time for an amount equal to the relevant proportion of the market value amount.

(4) For the purposes of subsection (3)—
- (*a*) there is an increase in a person's non-business use of an asset (or part of an asset) if—
    - (i) the proportion of the person's use of the asset (or that part) that is for the purposes of the property business decreases, and
    - (ii) the proportion of the person's use of the asset (or that part) that is for other purposes (the "non-business use") increases;
- (*b*) "the relevant proportion" is the difference between—
    - (i) the proportion of the person's use of the asset (or part of the asset) that is non-business use, and
    - (ii) the proportion of the person's use of the asset (or that part) that was non-business use before the increase mentioned in subsection (3).

(5) If—
- (*a*) the property business in respect of which capital expenditure relating to an asset has been brought into account as mentioned in section 307E is an overseas property business, and
- (*b*) there is a move overseas,

the person is to be regarded for the purposes of section 307E as disposing of the asset at the time of the move overseas for an amount equal to the market value amount.

(6) For the purposes of subsection (5) there is a "move overseas" if—

    (*a*) the person ceases to be UK resident, or

    (*b*) the tax year is, as respects the person, a split year, and the overseas part of the tax year is the later part.

(7) The move overseas occurs—

    (*a*) in a case falling within subsection (6)(*a*), on the last day of the tax year for which the person is UK resident, or

    (*b*) in a case falling within subsection (6)(*b*), on the last day of the UK part of the tax year.

(8) In this section—

    "capital expenditure" has the same meaning as in section 307E,

    "market value amount" means the amount that would be regarded as normal and reasonable—

        (*a*) in the market conditions then prevailing, and

        (*b*) between persons dealing with each other at arm's length in the open market.][1]

Commentary—*Simon's Taxes* **B6.202E.**

Amendments—[1] Sections 307A–307F and cross-heads inserted by F(No 2)A 2017 s 16, Sch 2 paras 12, 23 with effect for the tax year 2017–18 and subsequent tax years, subject to transitional provisions in F(No 2)A 2017 Sch 2 para 64.

[Property allowance

307G Property allowance

(1) The rules for calculating the profits of an individual's property business are subject to Chapter 2 of Part 6A (property allowance).

(2) That Chapter gives relief on relevant property income and, where relief is given, disallows all deductions under this Part which relate to that income (see, in particular, sections 783BC, 783BF and 783BH).][1]

Amendments—[1] Section 307G and preceding cross-head inserted by F(No 2)A 2017 s 17, Sch 3 paras 2, 8 with effect for the tax year 2017–18 and subsequent tax years.

CHAPTER 5

PROFITS OF PROPERTY BUSINESSES: OTHER RULES ABOUT RECEIPTS AND DEDUCTIONS

Furnished accommodation: receipts and deductions

308 Furnished lettings

(1) In calculating the profits of a property business which consists of or includes a furnished letting—

    (*a*) any sum payable for the use of furniture is brought into account as a receipt, and

    (*b*) a deduction is allowed for expenses [of a revenue nature][1] incurred in connection with the provision of furniture.

(2) But subsection (1) does not apply to receipts or expenses brought into account in calculating the profits of a trade which consists of, or involves, making furniture available for use in premises.

(3) A furnished letting is a lease or other arrangement under which—

    (*a*) a sum is payable in respect of the use of premises, and

    (*b*) the person entitled to the use of the premises is also entitled, in connection with that use, to the use of furniture.

(4) In this section—

    (*a*) "premises" includes a caravan and a houseboat, and

    (*b*) "sum" includes the value of any consideration.

Commentary—*Simon's Taxes* **B6.204.**

HMRC Manuals—Property Income Manual PIM1058 (furnished lettings: payments for use of furniture). PIM3200 (background: furnished lettings).

Amendments—[1] In sub-s (1)(*b*), words inserted by FA 2016 s 73(4) with effect in relation to expenditure incurred on or after 1 April 2016 for corporation tax purposes and 6 April 2016 for income tax purposes.

[Furnished accommodation: rent-a-room relief]

309 Rent-a-room relief

(1) The rules for calculating the profits of an individual's UK property business are subject to Chapter 1 of Part 7 (rent-a-room relief).

(2) That Chapter provides relief on income from the use of furnished accommodation in the individual's only or main residence (see, in particular, sections 793 and 797).

Commentary—*Simon's Taxes* **B6.601.**

HMRC Manuals—Property Income Manual PIM4001 (rent-a-room relief: overview).

Amendments—Heading inserted by the Enactment of Extra-Statutory Concessions Order, SI 2011/1037 art 11 with effect for the tax year 2011–12 and subsequent tax years (SI 2011/1037 art 13(1)).

Treatment of receipts on acquisition of business

310 Acquisition of business: receipts from transferor's UK property business

(1) This section applies if—

    (*a*) a person ("the transferor") permanently ceased to carry on a UK property business at any time,

    (*b*) at that time the transferor transferred to another ("the transferee") the right to receive sums arising from the carrying on of any business ("the transferred business") comprised in the transferor's UK property business, and

    (*c*) the transferee subsequently carries on the transferred business.

(2) Sums—

    (*a*) which the transferee receives as a result of the transfer, and

    (*b*) which are not brought into account in calculating the profits of the transferor's UK property business for any period before the cessation,

are brought into account in calculating the profits of the transferee's UK property business in the period of account in which they are received.

(3) Any sums mentioned in subsection (1)(*b*) which are received after the cessation of the transferor's property business are not post-cessation receipts (see Chapter 10).

(4) This section has effect as if it were contained in Chapter 10.

Commentary—*Simon's Taxes* **B6.209.**

Derivation—TA 1988 s 21B, s 106(1), (2); FA 1998 Sch 5 para 4.

Reverse premiums as receipts

311 Reverse premiums

(1) This section applies if—

    (*a*) a person receives a reverse premium, and

    (*b*) the reverse premium is not brought into account under section 101(2) in calculating the profits of any trade carried on by the person.

(2) The person is treated as—

    (*a*) entering into a transaction mentioned in section 264 (if the land to which the property transaction relates is in the United Kingdom) or section 265 (if that land is outside the United Kingdom), and

    (*b*) receiving the reverse premium as a result of that transaction.

(3) Accordingly, the reverse premium is brought into account as a receipt in calculating the profits of the property business which consists of or includes that transaction.

(4) Subsection (5) applies if—

    (*a*) two or more of the parties to the property arrangements are connected persons, and

    (*b*) the terms of those arrangements are not such as would reasonably have been expected if those persons had been dealing at arm's length.

(5) The whole amount or value of the reverse premium is brought into account in the period of account in which the property transaction is entered into.

(6) Expressions used in this section and sections 99 to 103 have the same meaning in this section as they do in those sections.

Commentary—*Simon's Taxes* **B6.205.**

HMRC Manuals—Business Income Manual BIM41055 (specific receipts: reverse premiums).

BIM41130 (specific receipts: reverse premiums: timing of the receipt and how to recognise it).

BIM41135 (reverse premiums: timing of the receipt: timing in the avoidance case).

BIM41051 (reverse premiums: meaning of 'reverse premium' and terms used in connection with reverse premiums).

[Deduction for replacement of domestic items

311A Replacement domestic items relief

(1) This section applies if conditions A to D are met.

(2) Condition A is that a person ("P") carries on a property business in relation to land which consists of or includes a dwelling-house.

(3) Condition B is that—

    (*a*) a domestic item has been provided for use in the dwelling-house ("the old item"),

    (*b*) P incurs expenditure on a domestic item for use in the dwelling-house ("the new item"),

    (*c*) the new item is provided solely for the use of the lessee,

    (*d*) the new item replaces the old item, and

    (*e*) following that replacement, the old item is no longer available for use in the dwelling-house.

(4) Condition C is that a deduction for the expenditure is not prohibited by the wholly and exclusively rule but would otherwise be prohibited by the capital expenditure rule (see subsection (15)).

(5) Condition D is that no allowance under CAA 2001 may be claimed in respect of the expenditure.

(6) In calculating the profits of the business, a deduction for the expenditure is allowed.

But this is subject to subsections (7) and (8).

(7) No deduction is allowed for expenditure in a tax year if—

(*a*) the business consists of or includes the commercial letting of furnished holiday accommodation (see Chapter 6), and

(*b*) the dwelling-house constitutes some or all of that accommodation for the tax year.

(8) No deduction is allowed for expenditure in a tax year if—

(*a*) the person has rent-a-room receipts in respect of the dwelling-house for the tax year, and

(*b*) section 793 or 797 (rent-a-room relief) applies in relation to those receipts.

(9) The basic amount of the deduction is as follows—

(*a*) where the new item is the same or substantially the same as the old item, the deduction is equal to the expenditure incurred by P on the new item;

(*b*) where the new item is not the same or substantially the same as the old item, the deduction is equal to so much of the expenditure incurred by P on the new item as does not exceed the expenditure which P would have incurred on an item which is the same or substantially the same as the old item.

Subsections (10) to (13) make further provision about the calculation of the deduction in certain cases.

(10) If P incurs incidental expenditure of a capital nature in connection with the disposal of the old item or the purchase of the new item, the deduction is increased by the amount of the incidental expenditure.

(11) If the old item is disposed of in part-exchange for the new item—

(*a*) the expenditure incurred by P on the new item is treated as including an amount equal to the value of the old item, and

(*b*) the deduction is reduced by that amount.

(12) If the old item is disposed of other than in part-exchange for the new item, the deduction is reduced by the amount or value of any consideration in money or money's worth which P or a person connected with P receives, or is entitled to receive, in respect of the disposal.

(13) For the purposes of subsection (12), where the old item is disposed of together with other consideration, the consideration in respect of the disposal mentioned in that subsection is taken not to include the amount of, or an amount equal to the value of, that other consideration.

(14) In this section, "domestic item" means an item for domestic use (such as furniture, furnishings, household appliances and kitchenware), and does not include anything that is a fixture.

"Fixture"—

(*a*) means any plant or machinery that is so installed or otherwise fixed in or to a dwelling-house as to become, in law, part of that dwelling-house, and

(*b*) includes any boiler or water-filled radiator installed in a dwelling-house as part of a space or water heating system.

"Plant or machinery" here has the same meaning as in Part 2 of CAA 2001.

(15) In this section—

["the capital expenditure rule" means—

(*a*) in relation to a property business whose profits are calculated in accordance with GAAP, section 33 (capital expenditure), as applied by section 272, and

(*b*) in relation to a property business whose profits are calculated on the cash basis, section 307B (cash basis: capital expenditure);][2]

"lessee" means the person who is entitled to the use of the dwelling-house under a lease or other arrangement under which a sum is payable in respect of the use of the dwelling-house;

"the wholly and exclusively rule" means . . .[2] section 34 (expenses not wholly and exclusively for trade and unconnected losses), as applied by section 272 [or 272ZA][2].][1]

Amendments—[1]   Section 311A inserted by FA 2016 s 73(1) with effect in relation to expenditure incurred on or after 1 April 2016 for corporation tax purposes and 6 April 2016 for income tax purposes.

[2]   In sub-s (15), definition of "the capital expenditure rule" substituted, and in definition of "the wholly and exclusively rule", words "the rule in" repealed, and words inserted, by F(No 2)A 2017 s 16, Sch 2 paras 12, 24 with effect for the tax year 2017–18 and subsequent tax years, subject to transitional provisions in F(No 2)A 2017 Sch 2 para 64.

Deductions for expenditure on energy-saving items

312 Deduction for expenditure on energy-saving items

(1) This section applies if—

(*a*) a person carries on a property business in relation to land which consists of or includes a dwelling-house,

(*b*) the person incurs expenditure in acquiring and installing [an energy-saving item in the dwelling-house or in a building containing the dwelling-house][1] (see subsections (5) to (7)),

(*c*) the expenditure is incurred before 6th April [2015][2],

(*d*) a deduction for the expenditure is not prohibited by the wholly and exclusively rule but would otherwise be prohibited by the capital prohibition rule (see subsection (8)), and

(*e*) no allowance under CAA 2001 may be claimed in respect of the expenditure.

(2) In calculating the profits of the business, a deduction for the expenditure is allowed.

(3) But any deduction is subject to—

(*a*) section 313 (restrictions on the relief), and

(*b*) any provision made by regulations under section 314.

(4) If, on a just and reasonable apportionment of any expenditure, part of the expenditure would qualify for the relief (but the remainder would not), a deduction is allowed for that part.

(5) "Energy-saving item" means—

    (*a*) cavity wall insulation,

    (*b*) loft insulation, or

    (*c*) such other descriptions of items of an energy-saving nature as are for the time being specified in regulations made by the Treasury.

(6) The Treasury may by regulations provide for an item to be treated as an energy-saving item only if it satisfies such conditions as may be—

    (*a*) specified in, or

    (*b*) determined in accordance with,

the regulations.

(7) The conditions may include conditions imposed by reference to information or documents issued by any body, person or organisation.

(8) In this section—

    "the capital prohibition rule" means the rule in section 33 (capital expenditure), as applied by section 272, and

    "the wholly and exclusively rule" means the rule in section 34 (expenses not wholly and exclusively for trade and unconnected losses), as applied by section 272.

Commentary—*Simon's Taxes* **B6.207.**

HMRC Manuals—Property Income Manual PIM2072 (landlord's energy savings allowance (LESA): background).

Regulations—Energy-Saving Items (Income Tax) Regulations 2007, SI 2007/3278 reg 2 (the following items are specified for the purposes of ITTOIA 2005 s 312(5)(*c*)—

    (a)   hot water system insulation;

    (b)   draught proofing;

    (c)   solid wall insulation; and

    (d)   floor insulation.).

Energy-Saving Items (Income Tax) Regulations 2007, SI 2007/3278 reg 3 (maximum amount of expenditure which may be taken into account in calculating the deduction is £1,500 per dwelling house, subject to further rules in SI 2007/3278 regs 4–7).

Amendments—[1]   Words in sub-s (1)(*b*) substituted by FA 2007 s 18(1), (2), (6) with effect in relation to expenditure incurred on or after 6 April 2007.

[2]   In sub-s (1)(*c*), figure substituted by FA 2007 s 18(1), (3) with effect from 19 July 2007.

313 Restrictions on relief

(1) This section restricts deductions that would otherwise be allowable under section 312.

(2) No deduction is allowed if, when the energy-saving item is installed, the dwelling-house—

    (*a*) is in the course of construction, or

    (*b*) is comprised in land in which the person does not have an interest or is in the course of acquiring an interest or further interest.

(3) No deduction is allowed in respect of expenditure in a tax year if—

    (*a*) the business consists of or includes the commercial letting of furnished holiday accommodation (see Chapter 6), and

    (*b*) the dwelling-house constitutes some or all of that accommodation for the tax year.

(4) No deduction is allowed if—

    (*a*) the person derives rent-a-room receipts from the dwelling-house, and

    (*b*) those receipts are brought into account in calculating the profits of the business in accordance with section 793 or 797 (rent-a-room relief).

(5) No deduction is allowed in respect of expenditure treated by section 57 (as applied by section 272) as incurred on the date on which the person starts to carry on the business unless the expenditure was incurred not more than 6 months before that date.

[(6) No deduction is allowed in respect of expenditure incurred in acquiring and installing the energy-saving item in a building containing the dwelling-house in so far as the expenditure is not for the benefit of the dwelling-house.][1]

Commentary—*Simon's Taxes* **B6.207.**

HMRC Manuals—Property Income Manual PIM2072 (landlord's energy savings allowance (LESA): restrictions on relief).

Amendments—[1]   Sub-s (6) inserted by FA 2007 s 18(4), (6) with effect in relation to expenditure incurred on or after 6 April 2007.

314 Regulations

(1) In relation to any deduction under section 312, the Treasury may make regulations for—

    (*a*) restricting or reducing the amount of expenditure for which the deduction is allowable,

    (*b*) excluding entitlement to the deduction in such cases as may be specified in, or determined in accordance with, the regulations,

    (*c*) determining who is (and is not) entitled to the deduction if different persons have different interests in land that consists of or includes the whole or part of a building containing one or more dwelling-houses, (*d*) making apportionments if the property business is carried on by persons in partnership or an interest in land is beneficially owned by persons jointly or in common.

(2) The apportionments that may be made include apportionments to companies within the charge to corporation tax.

[(3) Regulations under this section may—

(*a*) make different provision for different cases, and

(*b*) contain incidental, supplemental, consequential and transitional provision and savings (including provision as to appeals in relation to apportionments mentioned in subsection (1)(*d*)).][1]

Commentary—*Simon's Taxes* **B6.207.**

HMRC Manuals—Property Income Manual PIM2072 (landlord's energy savings allowance (LESA): apportionment).

Regulations—Energy-Saving Items (Income Tax) Regulations 2007, SI 2007/3278 (descriptions of items of an energy-saving nature specified for the purposes of this section).

Amendments—[1]   Sub-s (3) inserted by FA 2007 s 18(5), (7) and deemed always to have had effect.

Deductions for expenditure on sea walls

315 Deduction for expenditure on sea walls

(1) This section applies if in a tax year a person—

(*a*) is the owner or tenant of any premises, and

(*b*) incurs expenditure in making a sea wall or other embankment necessary for the preservation or protection of the premises against the encroachment or overflowing of the sea or any tidal river.

(2) In calculating the profits of any property business carried on by the person in relation to the premises, a deduction is allowed for the expenditure in each tax year in the deduction period.

(3) The deduction period comprises—

(*a*) the tax year in which the expenditure is incurred, and

(*b*) the next 20 tax years.

(4) The amount of the deduction is 1/21 of the expenditure.

(5) No deduction is allowed for any expenditure in respect of which a capital allowance has been made.

(6) Section 316 deals with the case of an interest in the premises being transferred (and this section applies in that case as if the reference to the person in subsection (2) above included the transferor and the transferee).

[(7) In calculating the profits of a property business on the cash basis, any reference in this section to the incurring of expenditure is to the paying of expenditure.][1]

Commentary—*Simon's Taxes* **B6.208.**

Derivation—TA 1988 s 30(1), (5), s 65A(5); FA 1998 Sch 5 paras 11, 24.

HMRC Manuals—Property Income Manual PIM2082 (deductions for expenditure on sea walls).

Amendments—[1]   Sub-s (7) inserted by F(No 2)A 2017 s 16, Sch 2 paras 12, 25 with effect for the tax year 2017–18 and subsequent tax years, subject to transitional provisions in F(No 2)A 2017 Sch 2 para 64.

316 Transfer of interest in premises

(1) This section applies if, during the deduction period, the whole of the person's interest in the premises or in any part of them is transferred, whether by operation of law or otherwise.

(2) For the tax year in which the transfer takes place—

(*a*) the transferor and the transferee are entitled to a part of any deduction under section 315, and

(*b*) the amount of the deduction is determined by what is just and reasonable.

(3) For subsequent tax years in the deduction period, the entitlement to any deduction under section 315 depends on whether the interest transferred is in the whole of the premises or in part of them.

(4) If the interest transferred is in the whole of the premises, the transferee (but not the transferor) is entitled to any deduction under section 315.

(5) If the interest transferred is in part of the premises—

(*a*) the transferor and the transferee are entitled to a part of any deduction under section 315, and

(*b*) the amount of the deduction is determined by reference to what is properly referable to the part of the premises.

(6) This section is supplemented by sections 317 (ending of lease of premises) and 318 (transfer involving company within the charge to corporation tax).

Commentary—*Simon's Taxes* **B6.208.**

317 Ending of lease of premises

(1) If a person's interest in the premises is a lease that comes to an end before the end of the deduction period, the interest is treated as if transferred to the following persons.

(2) If a new lease of the premises is granted and the new tenant makes a payment in respect of the embankment in question to the old tenant, the transferee is the new tenant.

(3) Otherwise the transferee is the owner of the interest in immediate reversion on the lease (or, in Scotland, the landlord).

Commentary—*Simon's Taxes* **B6.208.**

Derivation—TA 1988 s 30(3), s 65A(5); FA 1998 Sch 5 para 24.
HMRC Manuals—Property Income Manual PIM2082 (allocation of the allowance).

318 Transfer involving company within the charge to corporation tax

(1) This section explains how section 316 works if—
  (a) the transferor is a person within the charge to income tax and the transferee is a company within the charge to corporation tax, or
  (b) the transferor is a company within the charge to corporation tax and the transferee is a person within the charge to income tax.
(2) Section 316 applies only for the purpose of determining—
  (a) whether the person within the charge to income tax is entitled to a deduction (or part of a deduction) under section 315, and
  (b) the amount of any such deduction.
(3) Accordingly, any reference to—
  (a) whether a person is entitled to a deduction (or part of a deduction) under section 315, or
  (b) the amount of any such deduction,
is ignored if the person is a company within the charge to corporation tax.
(4) For any entitlement of a company within the charge to corporation tax to a deduction for any of the expenditure, see [sections 255 to 257 of CTA 2009][1] (corresponding corporation tax provision).

Amendments—[1]   In sub-s (4) words substituted by CTA 2009 s 1322, Sch 1 paras 587, 628. CTA 2009 applies for accounting periods ending on or after 1 April 2009 (for corporation tax purposes) and for tax years 2009–10 onwards (for income and capital gains tax purposes).

Apportionments on sale of land

320 Nature of item apportioned on sale of estate or interest in land

(1) This section applies if—
  (a) a person sells an estate or interest in land,
  (b) on the sale a part of a receipt or outgoing in respect of the estate or interest is apportioned to the seller, and
  (c) the receipt or outgoing is receivable or to be paid by the buyer after the apportionment is made.
(2) In calculating the profits of the seller's property business, the part apportioned is treated as being of the same nature as the receipt or outgoing.

Commentary—*Simon's Taxes* B6.210.
Derivation—TA 1988 s 40(3), s 65A(5); FA 1998 Sch 5 para 24.
HMRC Manuals—Property Income Manual PIM2230 (apportionment on sale or purchase of let property: background). PIM2235 (apportionment on sale or purchase of let property: effect).

Mutual business

321 Mutual business

(1) Nothing in this Part is to be read as applying the rules relating to mutual business to property businesses.
(2) Accordingly, receipts and expenses are to be brought into account in calculating the profits of a person's property business even if a relationship of mutuality exists between that person and another.

Commentary—*Simon's Taxes* B6.211.
Derivation—TA 1988 s 21C, s 65A(5); FA 1998 Sch 5 para 24; FA 1998 Sch 5 para 5.
HMRC Manuals—Business Income Manual BIM24782 (non-application of the mutuality principle).

CHAPTER 6

COMMERCIAL LETTING OF FURNISHED HOLIDAY ACCOMMODATION

Note—Subject to ITTOIA 2005 Sch 2 para 74(4), before 6 April 2006 this Chapter applies with amendments made to ss 322(2), 328(2) by ITTOIA 2005 Sch 2 para 74(2), (3). For the amended versions of those subsections, see the note below each of those sections.

Introduction

322 Introduction

(1) This Chapter explains for the purposes of this Part what is meant by the commercial letting of furnished holiday accommodation (see sections 323 to 326).
(2) It matters whether a UK property business consists of or includes the commercial letting of furnished holiday accommodation for the purposes of—
  [(za) section 272B(4) (exception from restriction on deductibility of finance costs),][3]
  [(zaa) section 307B (cash basis: capital expenditure),][5]
  [(zb) section 311A (replacement domestic items relief: see subsection (7)),][4]
  (a) section 312 (deduction for expenditure on energy-saving items: see section 313(3)),
  (b), (c)   . . . [1]
  (d) certain provisions of TCGA 1992 (see section 241 of that Act),
  (e) CAA 2001 (see, for example, sections 248 and 249 of that Act),

[(*f*) section 189(2)(*ba*) of FA 2004 (meaning of "relevant UK earnings" for pension purposes),][1]
[(*g*) Part 4 of ITA 2007 (loss relief: see section 127 of that Act),
[(*ga*) section 399A(9) of ITA 2007 (exception from restriction on deductibility of interest on loans to invest in partnerships),][3] and][1]
[(*h*) section 836(3) of ITA 2007 (jointly held property: see exception D).][1]
[(2A) It matters whether an overseas property business consists of or includes the commercial letting of furnished holiday accommodation in one or more EEA states for the purposes of—
[(*za*) section 272B(4) (exception from restriction on deductibility of finance costs),][3]
[(*zaa*) section 307B (cash basis: capital expenditure),][5]
[(*zb*) section 311A (replacement domestic items relief: see subsection (7)),][4]
(*a*) section 312 (deduction for expenditure on energy-saving items: see section 313(3)),
(*b*) certain provisions of TCGA 1992 (see section 241A of that Act),
(*c*) CAA 2001 (see, for example, sections 250 and 250A of that Act),
(*d*) section 189(2)(bb) of FA 2004 (meaning of "relevant UK earnings" for pension purposes),
(*e*) Part 4 of ITA 2007 (loss relief: see section 127ZA of that Act),
[(*ea*) section 399A(9) of ITA 2007 (exception from restriction on deductibility of interest on loans to invest in partnerships),][3] and
(*f*) section 836(3) of ITA 2007 (jointly held property: see exception DA).][2]
(3) This Chapter also supplements [the provisions mentioned in subsection (2)][2] by providing in certain circumstances for the profits of the furnished holiday lettings part of a UK property business to be calculated separately (see sections 327 and 328).
[(4) This Chapter also supplements the provisions mentioned in subsection (2A) by providing in certain circumstances for the profits of the EEA furnished holiday lettings part of an overseas property business to be calculated separately (see sections 328A and 328B).][2]

Commentary—*Simon's Taxes* **B6.401.**
HMRC Manuals—Capital Allowances Manual CA20025 (furnished holiday lettings business : meaning).
Property Income Manual PIM4105 (what are furnished holiday lettings?).
Amendments—[1]   Sub-s (2)(*b*), (*c*) repealed, and sub-s (2)(*f*), (*g*), (*h*) substituted for sub-s (2)(*f*) and preceding word, by ITA 2007 ss 1027, 1031, Sch 1 paras 492, 508, Sch 3 Pt 1 with effect for income tax purposes from 6 April 2007, and corporation tax purposes for accounting periods ending after 5 April 2007.
[2]   Sub-ss (2A), (4) inserted, and in sub-s (3) words substituted, by FA 2011 s 52, Sch 14 para 2(1), (2) with effect in relation to the tax year 2011–12 and subsequent tax years.
[3]   Sub-ss (2)(*za*), (*ga*), (2A)(*za*), (*ea*) inserted by F(No 2)A 2015 s 24(1), (6) with effect from 18 November 2015.
[4]   Sub-ss (2)(*zb*), (2A)(*zb*) inserted by FA 2016 s 73(5) with effect in relation to expenditure incurred on or after 1 April 2016 for corporation tax purposes and 6 April 2016 for income tax purposes.
[5]   Sub-ss (2)(*zaa*), (2A)(*zaa*) inserted by F(No 2)A 2017 s 16, Sch 2 paras 12, 26 with effect for the tax year 2017–18 and subsequent tax years, subject to transitional provisions in F(No 2)A 2017 Sch 2 para 64.

Definition

323 Meaning of "commercial letting of furnished holiday accommodation"

(1) A letting is a lease or other arrangement under which a person is entitled to the use of accommodation.
(2) A letting of accommodation is commercial if the accommodation is let—
    (*a*) on a commercial basis, and
    (*b*) with a view to the realisation of profits.
(3) A letting is of furnished holiday accommodation if—
    (*a*) the person entitled to the use of the accommodation is also entitled, in connection with that use, to the use of furniture, and
    (*b*) the accommodation is qualifying holiday accommodation (see sections 325 and 326).
(4) This section applies for the purposes of this Chapter.

Commentary—*Simon's Taxes* **B6.402.**
Derivation—TA 1988 s 504.
HMRC Manuals—Property Income Manual PIM4105 (furnished holiday lettings: introduction).

324 Meaning of "relevant period" in sections 325 and 326

(1) For the purposes of sections 325 and 326 "the relevant period" for accommodation let by a person in a tax year is determined as follows.
(2) If the accommodation was not let by the person as furnished accommodation in the previous tax year, "the relevant period" is 12 months beginning with the first day in the tax year on which it is let by the person as furnished accommodation.
(3) If the accommodation—
    (*a*) was let by the person as furnished accommodation in the previous tax year, but
    (*b*) is not let by the person as furnished accommodation in the following tax year,
"the relevant period" is 12 months ending with the last day in the tax year on which it is let by the person as furnished accommodation.
(4) Otherwise "the relevant period" is the tax year.

Commentary—*Simon's Taxes* **B6.403.**
HMRC Manuals—Property Income Manual PIM4112 (period to which tests are to be applied).

325 Meaning of "qualifying holiday accommodation"

(1) Accommodation which is let by a person during a tax year is "qualifying holiday accommodation" for the tax year if the availability, letting and pattern of occupation conditions are met.

(2) The availability condition is that, during the relevant period, the accommodation is available for commercial letting as holiday accommodation to the public generally for at least [210 days][1].

(3) The letting condition is that, during the relevant period, the accommodation is commercially let as holiday accommodation to members of the public for at least [105 days][1].

(4) For the purposes of the letting condition, a letting of accommodation for a period of longer-term occupation (see subsection (6)) is not a letting of it as holiday accommodation.

(5) The pattern of occupation condition is that, during the relevant period, not more than 155 days fall during periods of longer-term occupation.

(6) For the purposes of this section a "period of longer-term occupation" is a continuous period of more than 31 days during which the accommodation is in the same occupation otherwise than because of circumstances that are not normal.

Commentary—*Simon's Taxes* **B6.403.**
HMRC Manuals—Property Income Manual PIM4113 (furnished holiday lettings: changes to the rules 2011–12 and following).
Amendments—[1]   In sub-ss (2), (3) words substituted by FA 2011 s 52, Sch 14 para 2(1), (3) with effect in relation to the tax year 2012–13 and subsequent tax years. This amendment does not have effect in relation to relevant periods which begin before, and end on or after, 6 April 2012): FA 2011 Sch 14 para 5.

326 Under-used holiday accommodation: averaging elections

(1) This section applies if during a tax year a person lets both—

    (*a*)   qualifying holiday accommodation, and

    (*b*)   accommodation that would be qualifying holiday accommodation if the letting condition (see section 325(3)) were met in relation to it ("under-used accommodation").

(2) The person may make an election for the tax year specifying—

    (*a*)   the qualifying holiday accommodation, and

    (*b*)   any or all of the under-used accommodation.

(3) The under-used accommodation so specified is treated as qualifying holiday accommodation for the tax year if the average of the number of let days for the tax year of all the accommodation specified in the election is at least [105][2].

(4) "The number of let days" for a tax year of any accommodation is the number of days during the relevant period for which it is commercially let by the person as holiday accommodation to members of the public.

(5) Qualifying holiday accommodation may not be specified in more than one election for a tax year.

(6) An election for a tax year must be made on or before the first anniversary of the normal self-assessment filing date for the tax year.

[(7) This section is to apply separately in relation to accommodation in the United Kingdom and accommodation in EEA states other than the United Kingdom.][1]

Commentary—*Simon's Taxes* **B6.404.**
HMRC Manuals—Property Income Manual PIM4113 (furnished holiday lettings: changes to the rules 2011–12 and following).
Amendments—[1]   Sub-s (7) inserted by FA 2011 s 52, Sch 14 para 2(1), (4)(*b*) with effect in relation to the tax year 2011–12 and subsequent tax years.
[2]   Figure in sub-s (3) substituted by FA 2011 s 52, Sch 14 para 2(1), (4)(*a*) with effect in relation to the tax year 2012–13 and subsequent tax years. This amendment does not have effect in relation to relevant periods which begin before, and end on or after, 6 April 2012): FA 2011 Sch 14 para 6.
Prospective amendments—In sub-s (7) words "other than the United Kingdom" to be repealed by the Taxes (Amendments) (EU Exit) Regulations, SI 2019/689 reg 13(1), (2) with effect from Implementation Period completion day (see EU(WA)A 2020 Sch 5 para 1(1)).

[326A Under-used holiday accommodation: letting condition not met

(1) This section applies if—

    (*a*)   during a tax year a person lets qualifying holiday accommodation,

    (*b*)   the accommodation is let by the person—

        (i)   during the next tax year, or

        (ii)   during the next two tax years,

    (*c*)   the accommodation would (apart from this section) not be qualifying holiday accommodation—

        (i)   during the tax year mentioned in paragraph (*b*)(i), or

        (ii)   during both of the tax years mentioned in paragraph (*b*)(ii),

        only because of a failure to meet the letting condition (see section 325(3)), and

    (*d*)   there was a genuine intention to meet the letting condition for the tax year within subsection (1)(*c*)(i) or each of the tax years within subsection (1)(*c*)(ii) (as the case may be).

(2) If the person makes an election in respect of that accommodation for any tax year in respect of which the failure mentioned in subsection (1)(*c*) occurs, the accommodation is to be treated as qualifying holiday accommodation for that tax year.

(3) Subsection (2) does not apply for the purposes of section 326 or subsection (1)(*a*).

(4) If an election is not made for the first of the tax years within subsection (1)(*c*)(ii), an election may not be made for the second.

(5) An election for a tax year must be made on or before the first anniversary of the normal self-assessment filing date for the tax year.

(6) References in subsection (1)(*a*) and (*c*) to qualifying holiday accommodation include accommodation treated as such under section 326.]¹

Commentary—*Simon's Taxes* **B6.404.**

Amendments—¹ This section inserted by FA 2011 s 52, Sch 14 para 2(1), (5) with effect where the tax year mentioned in sub-s (1)(*a*) is 2010–11 or a subsequent tax year.

Separate profit calculations

327 Capital allowances and loss [relief: UK property business]³

(1) If a UK property business consists of both—

    (*a*) the commercial letting of furnished holiday accommodation ("the furnished holiday lettings part"), and

    (*b*) other businesses or transactions ("the other part"),

this section requires separate calculations to be made of the profits of the furnished holiday lettings part and the other part.

(2) The calculations must be made if—

    (*a*) section 248 or 249 of CAA 2001 (giving effect to allowances and charges) applies to the furnished holiday lettings part or the other part, or

    (*b*) any provision of [Part 4 of ITA 2007]¹ (loss relief) applies in relation to a loss made in either of those parts . . .²

    [(*c*) . . .²

(3) If there is a letting of accommodation only part of which is holiday accommodation, such apportionments are to be made for the purposes of this section as are just and reasonable.

Commentary—*Simon's Taxes* **B6.405.**

Amendments—¹ Words in sub-s (2)(*b*) substituted by ITA 2007 s 1027, Sch 1 paras 492, 509 with effect for income tax purposes from 6 April 2007, and corporation tax purposes for accounting periods ending after 5 April 2007.

² Sub-s (2)(*c*) and preceding word repealed by FA 2016 s 74(1)(*b*) with effect for the tax year 2016–17 and subsequent tax years.

³ In heading, words substituted by FA 2011 s 52, Sch 14 para 2(1), (6) with effect in relation to the tax year 2011–12 and subsequent tax years.

328 . . . ¹ Relevant UK earnings for pension [purposes: UK property business]²

(1) If a UK property business consists of both—

    (*a*) the commercial letting of furnished holiday accommodation ("the furnished holiday lettings part"), and

    (*b*) other businesses or transactions,

this section requires a separate calculation to be made of the profits of the furnished holiday lettings part.

(2) The calculation must be made if the profits of the furnished holiday lettings part are [relevant UK earnings within section 189(2)(*ba*) of FA 2004.]¹

(3) If there is a letting of accommodation only part of which is holiday accommodation, such apportionments are to be made for the purposes of this section as are just and reasonable.

HMRC Manuals—Property Income Manual PIM4105 (counts as relevant UK earnings for pension purposes).

Amendments—¹ Words in sub-s (2) substituted, and words in Heading repealed, by ITA 2007 ss 1027, 1031, Sch 1 paras 492, 510, Sch 3 Pt 1 with effect for income tax purposes from 6 April 2007, and corporation tax purposes for accounting periods ending after 5 April 2007.

² In heading words substituted by FA 2011 s 52, Sch 14 para 2(1), (7) with effect in relation to the tax year 2011–12 and subsequent tax years.

[328A Capital allowances and loss relief: overseas property business

(1) If an overseas property business consists of both—

    (*a*) the commercial letting of furnished holiday accommodation in one or more EEA states ("the EEA furnished holiday lettings part"), and

    (*b*) other businesses or transactions ("the other part"),

this section requires separate calculations to be made of the profits of the EEA furnished holiday lettings part and the other part.

(2) The calculations must be made if—

    (*a*) section 250 or 250A of CAA 2001 (giving effect to allowances and charges) applies to the EEA furnished holiday lettings part or the other part, or

    (*b*) any provision of Part 4 of ITA 2007 (loss relief) applies in relation to a loss made in either of those parts.

(3) If there is a letting of accommodation only part of which is holiday accommodation, such apportionments are to be made for the purposes of this section as are just and reasonable.]¹

Amendments—[1] Sections 328A, 328B inserted by FA 2011 s 52, Sch 14 para 2(1), (8) with effect in relation to the tax year 2011–12 and subsequent tax years.

[328B Relevant UK earnings for pension purposes: overseas property business

(1) If an overseas property business consists of both—

 (a) the commercial letting of furnished holiday accommodation in one or more EEA states ("the EEA furnished holiday lettings part"), and

 (b) other businesses or transactions,

this section requires a separate calculation to be made of the profits of the EEA furnished holiday lettings part.

(2) The calculation must be made if the profits of the EEA furnished holiday lettings part are relevant UK earnings within section 189(2)(*bb*) of FA 2004.

(3) If there is a letting of accommodation only part of which is holiday accommodation, such apportionments are to be made for the purposes of this section as are just and reasonable.]^[1]

Amendments—[1] Sections 328A, 328B inserted by FA 2011 s 52, Sch 14 para 2(1), (8) with effect in relation to the tax year 2011–12 and subsequent tax years.

CHAPTER 7

ADJUSTMENT INCOME

Adjustment on change of basis

329 Application of Chapter

(1) This Chapter applies if—

 (a) a person carrying on a UK property business changes, from one period of account to the next, the basis on which profits of the business are calculated for income tax purposes,

 (b) the old basis accorded with the law or practice applicable in relation to the period of account before the change, and

 (c) the new basis accords with the law and practice applicable in relation to the period of account after the change.

(2) The practice applicable in any case means the accepted practice in cases of that description as to how profits of a UK property business should be calculated for income tax purposes.

(3) Subsections (3) to (6) of section 227 (what is meant by a person changing the basis on which profits are calculated) apply for the purposes of this section as they apply for the purposes of that section (but as if any reference to a trade were to a UK property business).

Commentary—Simon's Taxes **B6.212.**

Derivation—TA 1988 s 21B; FA 2002 s 64; FA 1998 Sch 5 para 4.

HMRC Manuals—Business Income Manual BIM34135 (Business Income Manual BIM34135 (adjustment income and expenses: change of basis).).

[329A Application of Chapter where cash basis used

This Chapter applies if—

 (a) the profits of a property business are calculated—

  (i) on the cash basis for a tax year (see section 271D), and

  (ii) in accordance with GAAP (see section 271B) for the following tax year, or

 (b) the profits of a property business are calculated—

  (i) in accordance with GAAP for a tax year, and

  (ii) on the cash basis for the following tax year.]^[1]

Commentary—Simon's Taxes **B6.212.**

Amendments—[1] Section 329A inserted by F(No 2)A 2017 s 16, Sch 2 paras 12, 27 with effect for the tax year 2017–18 and subsequent tax years, subject to transitional provisions in F(No 2)A 2017 Sch 2 para 64.

330 Adjustment income and adjustment expense

(1) An amount by way of adjustment must be calculated in accordance with section 231, which applies in relation to a UK property business as it applies in relation to a trade.

(2) If the amount produced by the calculation is positive, it is treated as income and charged to income tax under this Chapter.

 It is referred to in this Chapter as "adjustment income".

(3) If the amount produced by the calculation is negative, a deduction is allowed for it in calculating the profits of the business.

 It is referred to in this Chapter as an "adjustment expense".

(4) This section is subject to section 234 (no adjustment for certain expenses previously brought into account), which applies in relation to a UK property business as it applies in relation to a trade.

Commentary—Simon's Taxes **B6.212.**

Derivation—TA 1988 s 21B; FA 2002 s 64(1), Sch 22 paras 1, 2, 4–6; FA 1998 Sch 5 para 4.

HMRC Manuals—Business Income Manual BIM34095 (UK property business: change of basis of computing taxable profits: adjustment income and expenses: tax treatment).

BIM34105 (change of basis of computing taxable profits: adjustment income and expenses: expenses already allowed).

331 Income charged

[(1)] ¹Tax is charged under this Chapter on the full amount of any adjustment income arising in the tax year.

[(2) This is subject to section 334A (spreading on leaving cash basis and related election).]¹

Commentary—*Simon's Taxes* **B6.212.**

Derivation—TA 1988 s 69.

HMRC Manuals—Business Income Manual BIM34095 (UK property business: change of basis of computing taxable profits: adjustment income and expenses: income charged to tax).

Amendments—¹ Sub-s (1) numbered as such, and sub-s (2) inserted, by F(No 2)A 2017 s 16, Sch 2 paras 12, 28 with effect for the tax year 2017–18 and subsequent tax years, subject to transitional provisions in F(No 2)A 2017 Sch 2 para 64.

332 Person liable

The person liable for any tax charged under this Chapter is the person receiving or entitled to the adjustment income.

Commentary—*Simon's Taxes* **B6.212.**

Derivation—TA 1988 s 59(1).

HMRC Manuals—Business Income Manual BIM34095 (change of basis of computing taxable profits: adjustment income and expenses: person liable for tax charge).

Treatment of adjustment income and adjustment expense

333 Treatment of adjustment income

(1) Adjustment income is treated as arising on the last day of the first period of account for which the

(2) But if there is a change of basis ~~~~~ from a tax adjustment affecting the calculation of any amount brought into account in respect of depreciation, adjustment income is treated as arising only when the asset to which it relates is realised or written off.

(3) Adjustment income is treated for the purposes of [Part 4 of ITA 2007]¹ (loss relief) as profits of the UK property business for the tax year in which tax is charged on it.

Commentary—*Simon's Taxes* **B6.212.**

Derivation—TA 1988 s 21B; FA 2002 s 64(1), Sch 22 paras 4(2), 7; FA 1998 Sch 5 para 4.

HMRC Manuals—Business Income Manual BIM34095 (change of basis of computing taxable profits: treatment of adjustment income).

BIM34110 (change of basis of computing taxable profits: adjustment income and expenses: stock and depreciation).

Amendments—¹ Words in sub-s (3) substituted by ITA 2007 s 1027, Sch 1 paras 492, 511 with effect for income tax purposes from 6 April 2007, and corporation tax purposes for accounting periods ending after 5 April 2007.

334 Treatment of adjustment expense

(1) An adjustment expense is treated as an expense of the business arising on the last day of the first period of account for which the new basis is adopted.

(2) But if there is a change of basis resulting from a tax adjustment affecting the calculation of any amount brought into account in respect of depreciation, an adjustment expense is treated as arising only when the asset to which it relates is realised or written off.

Commentary—*Simon's Taxes* **B6.212.**

Derivation—TA 1988 s 21B; FA 2002 s 64(1), Sch 22 paras 5, 7; FA 1998 Sch 5 para 4.

HMRC Manuals—Business Income Manual BIM34095 (change of basis of computing taxable profits: adjustment income and expenses: charged to tax).

BIM34110 (change of basis of computing taxable profits: adjustment income and expenses: stock and depreciation).

[Spreading of adjustment income on leaving cash basis

334A Spreading on leaving cash basis and related election

Sections 239A (spreading on leaving cash basis) and 239B (election to accelerate charge under section 239A) apply for the purposes of this Chapter as they apply for the purposes of Chapter 17 of Part 2, but as if—

 (*a*) for section 239A(1) there were substituted—

 "(1) This section applies if the profits of a property business are calculated—

  (*a*) on the cash basis for a tax year (see section 271D), and

  (*b*) in accordance with GAAP (see section 271B) for the following tax year.", and

 (*b*) any reference to section 239A or 239B were to the section concerned as applied by this section.]¹

Amendments—¹ Section 334A and preceding cross-head inserted by F(No 2)A 2017 s 16, Sch 2 paras 12, 28 with effect for the tax year 2017–18 and subsequent tax years, subject to transitional provisions in F(No 2)A 2017 Sch 2 para 64.

[CHAPTER 7A

CASH BASIS: ADJUSTMENTS FOR CAPITAL ALLOWANCES]

Amendments—Chapter 7A (sections 334B–334E) inserted by F(No 2)A 2017 s 16, Sch 2 paras 12, 29 with effect for the tax year 2017–18 and subsequent tax years, subject to transitional provisions in F(No 2)A 2017 Sch 2 para 64.

[334B "Entering the cash basis"

For the purposes of this Chapter, a person carrying on a property business enters the cash basis for a tax year if the profits of the business are calculated—

    (a) on the cash basis for the tax year (see section 271D), and

    (b) in accordance with GAAP (see section 271B) for the previous tax year.][1]

Amendments—[1]   Chapter 7A (sections 334B–334E) inserted by F(No 2)A 2017 s 16, Sch 2 paras 12, 29 with effect for the tax year 2017–18 and subsequent tax years, subject to transitional provisions in F(No 2)A 2017 Sch 2 para 64.

[334C Unrelieved qualifying expenditure

(1) This section applies if—

    (a) a person carrying on a property business enters the cash basis for a tax year ("the current tax year"), and

    (b) the person would, apart from section 59(4A) of CAA 2001, have unrelieved qualifying expenditure relating to a relevant property business activity to carry forward from the chargeable period which is the previous tax year.

(2) But this section does not apply if section 334D applies.

(3) In calculating the profits of the property business for the current tax year, a deduction is allowed for any cash basis deductible amount of the expenditure relating to each relevant property business activity.

(4) A "cash basis deductible amount" of the expenditure means any amount of the expenditure for which a deduction would be allowed in calculating the profits of the property business on the cash basis on the assumption that the expenditure was paid in the current tax year.

(5) Any cash basis deductible amount of the expenditure is to be determined on such basis as is just and reasonable in all the circumstances.

(6) In this section—

    "relevant property business activity" means—

        (a) in relation to a UK property business, an ordinary UK property business and a UK furnished holiday lettings business (within the meaning of Part 2 of CAA 2001 (see sections 16 and 17 of that Act)), and

        (b) in relation to an overseas property business, an ordinary overseas property business and an EEA furnished holiday lettings business (within the meaning of Part 2 of that Act (see sections 17A and 17B of that Act));

    "unrelieved qualifying expenditure" means unrelieved qualifying expenditure for the purposes of Part 2 of CAA 2001 (see section 59(1) and (2) of that Act).][1]

Amendments—[1]   Chapter 7A (sections 334B–334E) inserted by F(No 2)A 2017 s 16, Sch 2 paras 12, 29 with effect for the tax year 2017–18 and subsequent tax years, subject to transitional provisions in F(No 2)A 2017 Sch 2 para 64.

[334D Assets not fully paid for

(1) This section applies if—

    (a) a person carrying on a property business enters the cash basis for a tax year ("the current tax year"),

    (b) at any time before the end of the chargeable period which is the previous tax year the person has incurred relevant expenditure, and

    (c) not all of the relevant expenditure has actually been paid by the person.

(2) "Relevant expenditure" means expenditure on plant or machinery—

    (a) for which a deduction would be allowed in calculating the profits of the property business on the cash basis on the assumption that the expenditure was paid in the current tax year, and

    (b) in respect of which the person has obtained capital allowances.

(3) If the amount of the relevant expenditure that the person has actually paid exceeds the amount of capital allowances given in respect of the relevant expenditure, the difference is to be deducted in calculating the profits of the property business for the current tax year.

(4) If the amount of the relevant expenditure that the person has actually paid is less than the amount of capital allowances given in respect of the relevant expenditure, the difference is to be treated as a receipt in calculating the profits of the property business for the current tax year.

(5) Any question as to whether or to what extent expenditure is relevant expenditure, or as to whether or to what extent any capital allowance obtained is in respect of relevant expenditure, is to be determined on such basis as is just and reasonable in all the circumstances.

(6) If the amount of capital allowances given in respect of the relevant expenditure has been reduced under section 205 or 207 of CAA 2001 (reduction where asset provided or used only partly for qualifying activity), the amount of the relevant expenditure that the person has actually paid is to be proportionately reduced for the purposes of this section.][1]

Amendments—[1]   Chapter 7A (sections 334B–334E) inserted by F(No 2)A 2017 s 16, Sch 2 paras 12, 29 with effect for the tax year 2017–18 and subsequent tax years, subject to transitional provisions in F(No 2)A 2017 Sch 2 para 64.

[334E Effect of election where predecessor and successor are connected persons

(1) This section applies if—

    (a) a person carrying on a property business enters the cash basis for a tax year, (*b*) the person is the successor for the purposes of section 266 of CAA 2001, and

   (*c*) as a result of an election under that section, relevant plant or machinery is treated as sold by the predecessor to the successor at any time during the tax year.

(2) The provisions of this Chapter have effect in relation to the successor as if everything done to or by the predecessor had been done to or by the successor.

(3) Any expenditure actually incurred by the successor on acquiring the relevant plant or machinery is to be ignored for the purposes of calculating the profits of the property business for the tax year.

(4) In this section—

    "the predecessor" has the same meaning as in section 266 of CAA 2001, and

    "relevant plant or machinery" has the same meaning as in section 267 of that Act.][1]

Amendments—[1] Chapter 7A (sections 334B–334E) inserted by F(No 2)A 2017 s 16, Sch 2 paras 12, 29 with effect for the tax year 2017–18 and subsequent tax years, subject to transitional provisions in F(No 2)A 2017 Sch 2 para 64.

CHAPTER 8

RENT RECEIVABLE IN CONNECTION WITH A UK SECTION 12(4) CONCERN

Charge to tax on rent receivable in connection with a UK section 12(4) concern

335 Charge to tax on rent receivable in connection with a UK section 12(4) concern

Income tax is charged on rent receivable in connection with a UK section 12(4) concern.

Commentary—*Simon's Taxes* **B6.501.**

Derivation—TA 1988 s 119(1).

HMRC Manuals—Property Income Manual PIM1117 (rent receivable in connection with mines, quarries and similar concerns: tax treatment).

336 Meaning of "rent receivable in connection with a UK section 12(4) concern"

(1) For the purposes of this Chapter rent is receivable in connection with a UK section 12(4) concern if—

   (*a*) it is receivable in respect of an estate, interest or right in or over land in the United Kingdom, and

   (*b*) the estate, interest or right is used, occupied or enjoyed in connection with a concern listed in section 12(4).

(2) For the purposes of this Chapter rent is also receivable in connection with a UK section 12(4) concern if—

   (*a*) it is receivable in respect of an estate, interest or right in or over land in the United Kingdom,

   (*b*) the lease or other agreement under which it is receivable provides for its recoupment by reducing royalties or payments of a similar nature, and

   (*c*) the reduction applies if the estate, interest or right is used, occupied or enjoyed in connection with a concern listed in section 12(4).

(3) In this Chapter "rent" includes—

   (*a*) a receipt mentioned in section 266(3), and

   (*b*) any other receipt in the nature of rent.

Commentary—*Simon's Taxes* **B6.501.**

Derivation—TA 1988 s 119(1), (3).

HMRC Manuals—Property Income Manual PIM1117 (rent receivable in connection with mines, quarries and similar concerns: meaning).

337 Income charged

(1) Tax is charged under this Chapter on the full amount of the profits arising in the tax year.

(2) This is subject to—

    section 339 (deduction for management expenses of owner of mineral rights), . . .

    . . . .

Commentary—*Simon's Taxes* **B6.501.**

HMRC Manuals—Business Income Manual BIM34095 (change of basis of computing taxable profits: adjustment income and expenses: charged to tax).

Amendments—In sub-s (2) entry relating to section 340 and preceding word "and" repealed by FA 2012 s 227, Sch 39 para 43(2)(*a*)(i) with effect in relation to mineral royalties which a person is entitled to receive on or after 6 April 2013.

338 Person liable

The person liable for any tax charged under this Chapter is the person receiving or entitled to the rent.

Commentary—*Simon's Taxes* **B6.501.**

Derivation—TA 1988 s 59(1).

HMRC Manuals—Business Income Manual BIM34095 (change of basis of computing taxable profits: adjustment income and expenses: person liable).

Management expenses of owner of mineral rights

339 Deduction for management expenses of owner of mineral rights

(1) This section applies if in a tax year—

   (*a*) a person lets a right to work minerals in the United Kingdom, and (*b*) the person pays a sum wholly and exclusively as an expense of management or supervision of the minerals in the tax year.

(2) In calculating the amount of rent receivable in connection with a UK section 12(4) concern, a deduction is allowed for the sum for the tax year.

(3) This is subject to section 340 (relief in respect of mineral royalties).

Commentary—*Simon's Taxes* **B6.501, B5.663.**

HMRC Manuals—Relief Instructions RE1950 (mineral rights: management expenses: title to and extent of relief).

Amendments—Sub-s (3) repealed by FA 2012 s 227, Sch 39 para 43(2)(*a*)(ii) with effect in relation to mineral royalties which a person is entitled to receive on or after 6 April 2013.

CHAPTER 9

RENT RECEIVABLE FOR UK ELECTRIC-LINE WAYLEAVES

Charge to tax on rent receivable for UK electric-line wayleaves

344 Charge to tax on rent receivable for a UK electric-line wayleave

Income tax is charged on rent receivable for a UK electric-line wayleave.

Commentary—*Simon's Taxes* **B6.502.**

Derivation—TA 1988 s 120(1).

HMRC Manuals—Property Income Manual PIM1118 (rent receivable from UK electric-line wayleaves: income charge to tax).

345 Meaning of "rent receivable for a UK electric-line wayleave"

(1) For the purposes of this Chapter rent is receivable for a UK electric-line wayleave if—

(*a*) it is receivable in respect of an easement, servitude or right in or over land in the United Kingdom, and

(*b*) the easement, servitude or right is enjoyed in connection with an electric, telegraph or telephone wire or cable.

(2) The reference to the enjoyment of an easement, servitude or right in connection with an electric, telegraph or telephone wire or cable includes (in particular) its enjoyment in connection with—

(*a*) a pole or pylon supporting such a wire or cable, or

(*b*) apparatus used in connection with such a wire or cable.

(3) In this Chapter "rent" includes—

(*a*) a receipt mentioned in section 266(3), and

(*b*) any other receipt in the nature of rent.

Commentary—*Simon's Taxes* **B6.502.**

Derivation—TA 1988 s 120(1), (5).

HMRC Manuals—Property Income Manual PIM1118 (rent receivable from UK electric-line wayleaves: meaning).

346 Extent of charge to tax

(1) Rent receivable for a UK electric-line wayleave is not chargeable to tax under this Chapter for a tax year if—

(*a*) a person carries on a UK property business in relation to some or all of the land to which the wayleave relates, and

(*b*) receipts (other than rents receivable for UK electric-line wayleaves) in respect of some or all of that land are brought into account in calculating the profits of the business for the tax year.

(2) In such a case, the rent receivable for the UK electric-line wayleave is brought into account in calculating the profits of the person's UK property business.

(3) The rules for determining whether an amount is chargeable to tax under this Chapter also need to be read with section 22(2) (payments for wayleaves if person carries on a trade).

(4) That subsection secures that an amount which would otherwise be chargeable to tax under this Chapter may be brought into account instead in calculating the profits of a trade.

Commentary—*Simon's Taxes* **B6.502.**

HMRC Manuals—Property Income Manual PIM1118 (rent receivable from UK electric-line wayleaves: alternative basis of charge).

347 Income charged

Tax is charged under this Chapter on the full amount of the profits arising in the tax year.

Commentary—*Simon's Taxes* **B6.502.**

Derivation—TA 1988 s 69; FA 1994 s 208.

348 Person liable

The person liable for any tax charged under this Chapter is the person receiving or entitled to the rent.

Commentary—*Simon's Taxes* **B6.502.**

Derivation—TA 1988 s 59(1).

CHAPTER 10

POST-CESSATION RECEIPTS

Charge to tax on post-cessation receipts

349 Charge to tax on post-cessation receipts

Income tax is charged on post-cessation receipts arising from a UK property business.

Commentary—*Simon's Taxes* **B6.213.**
Derivation—TA 1988 s 21B, s 103, s 104; FA 1998 Sch 5 para 4.
HMRC Manuals—Property Income Manual PIM2510 (post-cessation receipts).

350 Extent of charge to tax

(1) A post-cessation receipt is chargeable to tax under this Chapter only so far as the receipt is not otherwise chargeable to income or corporation tax.

(2) Accordingly, a post-cessation receipt arising from a UK property business is not chargeable to tax under this Chapter so far as it is brought into account in calculating the profits of the business for any period.

Commentary—*Simon's Taxes* **B6.213.**
HMRC Manuals—Property Income Manual PIM2510 (post-cessation receipts : extent of charged to tax).

351 Income charged

(1) Tax is charged under this Chapter on the full amount of the receipts received in the tax year.

(2) This is subject to—

    (*a*) sections 254 and 255 (allowable deductions), and

    (*b*) section 257 (election to carry back),

which apply for the purposes of this Chapter as they apply for the purposes of Chapter 18 of Part 2 (but as if any reference to a trade were to a UK property business).

[(3) Further to subsection (2), section 254 applies for the purposes of this Chapter as if for subsection (2A) of that section there were substituted—

    "(2A) If the time immediately before the person permanently ceases to carry on the UK property business falls in a cash basis tax year, assume for the purposes of subsection (2) that the profits of the business are calculated on the cash basis."

(4) For the purposes of sections 254 (as so applied) and 353, a tax year is "a cash basis tax year" in relation to a property business if the profits of the business for the tax year are calculated on the cash basis (see section 271D).][1]

Commentary—*Simon's Taxes* **B6.213.**
HMRC Manuals—Property Income Manual PIM2510 (legislation on post-cessation receipts and expenditure).
Amendments—[1] Sub-ss (3), (4) inserted by F(No 2)A 2017 s 16, Sch 2 paras 12, 30 with effect for the tax year 2017–18 and subsequent tax years, subject to transitional provisions in F(No 2)A 2017 Sch 2 para 64.

352 Person liable

The person liable for any tax charged under this Chapter is the person receiving or entitled to the receipts.

Commentary—*Simon's Taxes* **B6.213.**
Derivation—TA 1988 s 59(1).

Meaning of "post-cessation receipts"

353 Basic meaning of "post-cessation receipt"

(1) In this Chapter "post-cessation receipt" means a sum—

    (*a*) which is received after a person permanently ceases to carry on a UK property business, and

    (*b*) which arises from the carrying on of the business before the cessation.

[(1A) If the time immediately before a person permanently ceases to carry on a UK property business falls in a cash basis tax year (see section 351(4)), a sum is to be treated as a post-cessation receipt only if it would have been brought into account in calculating the profits of the business on the cash basis had it been received at that time.][1]

(2) Subsection (3) applies if—

    (*a*) a firm carries on a UK property business,

    (*b*) a person ceases to be a partner in the firm, and

    (*c*) at least one of the persons with whom the partner carried on the business before ceasing to be a partner continues to carry it on afterwards.

(3) The partner is treated for the purposes of this Chapter as permanently ceasing to carry on the business.

Commentary—*Simon's Taxes* **B6.213.**
Amendments—[1] Sub-s (1A) inserted by F(No 2)A 2017 s 16, Sch 2 paras 12, 31 with effect for the tax year 2017–18 and subsequent tax years, subject to transitional provisions in F(No 2)A 2017 Sch 2 para 64.

354 Other rules about what counts as a "post-cessation receipt"

(1) Section 355 (transfer of rights if transferee does not carry on UK property business) treats certain amounts as being, or not being, post-cessation receipts for the purposes of this Chapter.

(2) The following provisions (which treat certain amounts as post-cessation receipts) apply for the purposes of this Chapter as they apply for the purposes of Chapter 18 of Part 2 (but as if any reference to a trade were to a UK property business)—

    section 82(6) (contributions to local enterprise organisations or urban regeneration companies),

    section 104(3) (distribution of assets of mutual concerns),

    section 109(2) (receipt by donor or connected person of benefit attributable to certain gifts),

    section 248 (debts paid after cessation) [(reading the reference in subsection (3) to section 96 of ITA 2007 as a reference to section 125 of that Act)][1],

    section 249 (debts released after cessation), as qualified, where appropriate, by section 48(4) (car . . . [2] hire), and

    section 250 (receipts relating to post-cessation expenditure) [(reading the reference in subsection (1) to section 96 of ITA 2007 as a reference to section 125 of that Act)][1].

(3) This Chapter also needs to be read with—

    (*a*) section 310(3) (which treats certain amounts as not being post-cessation receipts), and

    (*b*) section 844 (which treats certain income as a post-cessation receipt: unremittable income).

Commentary—*Simon's Taxes* B6.213.
Derivation—sub-s (2): TA 1988 s 21B, s 79(9), s 103, s 109A, s 491; FA 1998 Sch 5 para 4.
HMRC Manuals—Business Income Manual BIM90030 (post-cessation receipts and expenses: other receipts which are treated as post-cessation receipts).
Amendments—[1]   Words in sub-s (2) inserted by ITA 2007 s 1027, Sch 1 paras 492, 512 with effect for income tax purposes from 6 April 2007, and corporation tax purposes for accounting periods ending after 5 April 2007.
[2]   In sub-s (2) words "or motor cycle" repealed by FA 2009 s 30, Sch 11 para 43 with effect as provided for by FA 2009 Sch 11 paras 65, 66 and subject to savings in FA 2009 Sch 11 para 68. The new system of capital allowances for cars has effect generally from 6 April 2009 (for income tax) and 1 April 2009 (for corporation tax), subject to FA 2009 Sch 11 para 67 (election for new regime not to apply in certain cases).

355 Transfer of rights if transferee does not carry on UK property business

(1) This section applies if—

    (*a*) a person ("the transferor") permanently ceases to carry on a UK property business,

    (*b*) the transferor transfers to another person ("the transferee") for value the right to receive sums arising from the carrying on of any business ("the transferred business") comprised in the transferor's UK property business, and

    (*c*) the transferee does not subsequently carry on the transferred business.

(2) The transferor is treated as receiving a post-cessation receipt.

(3) The amount of the receipt is—

    (*a*) the amount or value of the consideration for the transfer, if the transfer is at arm's length, or

    (*b*) the value of the rights transferred as between parties at arm's length, if the transfer is not at arm's length.

(4) Any sums mentioned in subsection (1)(*b*) which are received after the cessation of the property business are not post-cessation receipts.

Commentary—*Simon's Taxes* B6.213.
Derivation—TA 1988 s 21B, s 106(1), (2); FA 1998 Sch 5 para 4.
HMRC Manuals—Business Income Manual BIM90050 (post-cessation receipts and expenses: meaning of post-cessation receipts: transfer of rights if transferee does not carry on the trade).

Supplementary

356 Application to [businesses within the charge to corporation tax][1]

(1) In this Chapter (except in [sections 353(1A) and 355, and in the modification of section 254 in section 351(3)][2]) any reference to a UK property business includes [one within the charge to corporation tax][1].

(2) In this Chapter (except in section 355) any reference to a person permanently ceasing to carry on a UK property business [includes, in the case of a company, the occurrence of an event treated under section 289 of CTA 2009 (company starting or ceasing to be within the charge to corporation tax) as the company permanently ceasing to carry on the business.][1]

(3) In applying any provision of Chapter 18 of Part 2 for the purposes of this Chapter references to the calculation of the profits of a trade for corporation tax purposes are to be read as references to the calculation of the profits of a [UK property business][1] for corporation tax purposes.

Commentary—*Simon's Taxes* B6.213.
Amendments—[1]   In title, sub-ss (1)–(3) words substituted by CTA 2009 s 1322, Sch 1 paras 587, 629. CTA 2009 applies for accounting periods ending on or after 1 April 2009 (for corporation tax purposes) and for tax years 2009–10 onwards (for income and capital gains tax purposes).
[2]   In sub-s (1), words substituted for words "section 355" by F(No 2)A 2017 s 16, Sch 2 para 12, 32 with effect for the tax year 2017–18 and subsequent tax years, subject to transitional provisions in F(No 2)A 2017 Sch 2 para 64.

CHAPTER 12

SUPPLEMENTARY

361 Changes in trustees and personal representatives

(1) This section applies if there is a change—

(a) in the trustees of a trust, or

(b) in the personal representatives of a person,

at a time when they are carrying on a property business.

(2) For income tax purposes, the change does not result in—

(a) any of the trustees or personal representatives before the change permanently ceasing to carry on the business, or

(b) any of the trustees or personal representatives after the change starting to carry on the business.

Commentary—*Simon's Taxes* **B6.215.**

Derivation—TA 1988 s 21B, s 113(7), s 65A(5); FA 1998 Sch 5 paras 4, 24.

362 Effect of company starting or ceasing to be within charge to income tax

(1) This section applies if a company starts or ceases to be within the charge to income tax under Chapter 3 of this Part in respect of a UK property business.

(2) The company is treated for the purposes of this Part—

(a) as starting to carry on the business when it starts to be within the charge, or

(b) as permanently ceasing to carry on the business when it ceases to be within the charge.[1]

Commentary—*Simon's Taxes* **B6.215; B6.213.**

Amendments—[1]   Section 362 repealed by FA 2019 s 17, Sch 5 para 8 with effect from 6 April 2020, subject to transitional provisions in FA 2019 Sch 5 Pt 3 (paras 36–50).

363 Overseas property businesses and overseas land: adaptation of rules

(1) This section applies if a provision of this Part—

(a) applies to an overseas property business or land outside the United Kingdom, but

(b) is expressed by reference to a domestic concept of law.

(2) In relation to that business or land, the provision is to be read so as to produce the result most closely corresponding with that produced by the provision in relation to a UK property business or land in the United Kingdom.

HMRC Manuals—Property Income Manual PIM4703 (overseas property businesses and overseas land: IT cases).

364 Meaning of "lease" and "premises"

(1) In this Part "lease" includes—

(a) an agreement for a lease (so far as the context permits), and

(b) any tenancy,

but does not include a mortgage.

(2) In this Part "premises" includes land.

Commentary—*Simon's Taxes* **B6.216.**

PART 4
SAVINGS AND INVESTMENT INCOME

CHAPTER 1
INTRODUCTION

365 Overview of Part 4

(1) This Part imposes charges to income tax under—

    (*a*) Chapter 2 (interest),

    [(*aa*) Chapter 2A (disguised interest),][1]

    (*b*) Chapter 3 (dividends etc. from UK resident companies etc.),

    (*c*) Chapter 4 (dividends from non-UK resident companies),

    (*d*) Chapter 5 (stock dividends from UK resident companies),

    (*e*) Chapter 6 (release of loan to participator in close company),

    (*f*) Chapter 7 (purchased life annuity payments),

    (*g*) Chapter 8 (profits from deeply discounted securities),

    (*h*) Chapter 9 (gains from contracts for life insurance etc.),

    (*i*) *Chapter 10 (distributions from unauthorised unit trusts),*[2]

    (*j*) Chapter 11 (transactions in deposits),

    (*k*) . . .[1] and

    (*l*) Chapter 13 (sales of foreign dividend coupons).

(2) Part 6 deals with exemptions from the charges under this Part.

(3) See, in particular, any exemptions mentioned in the particular Chapters.

(4) The charges under this Part apply to non-UK residents as well as UK residents but this is subject to section 368(2) (charges on non-UK residents only on UK source income).

(5) This section needs to be read with the relevant priority rules (see sections 2 and 366).

Amendments—[1] In sub-s (1), para (*aa*) inserted and para (*k*) repealed by FA 2013 s 28, Sch 12 paras 1, 2 with effect for the tax year 2013–14 and subsequent tax years.

[2] Sub-s (1)(*l*) repealed by the Unauthorised Unit Trusts (Tax) Regulations, SI 2013/2819 reg 36(1), (2) with effect from 6 April 2014. Note that an unauthorised unit trust is not a non-exempt unauthorised unit trust, and these amendments do not apply in relation to the trust, if at all times in the period beginning with 24 May 2012 and ending with 5 April 2014 it had at least one unit holder which was, and at least one unit holder which was not, an eligible investor (ie a mixed unauthorised unit trust); this ceases to apply in relation to the trust if subsequently it no longer has any unit holders which are eligible investors (SI 2013/2819 reg 32).

366 Provisions which must be given priority over Part 4

(1) Any income, so far as it falls within—

    (*a*) any Chapter of this Part, and

    (*b*) Chapter 2 of Part 2 (receipts of a trade, profession or vocation),

is dealt with under Part 2.

(2) Any income, so far as it falls within—

    (*a*) any Chapter of this Part, and

    (*b*) Chapter 3 of Part 3 so far as the Chapter relates to a UK property business,

is dealt with under Part 3.

(3) Any income, so far as it falls within—

    (*a*) any Chapter of this Part other than Chapter 3 or 6, and

    (*b*) Part 2, 9 or 10 of ITEPA 2003 (employment income, pension income or social security income),

is dealt with under the relevant Part of ITEPA 2003.

(4) Nothing in this section prevents amounts both—

    (*a*) being counted as income for the purposes of Chapter 9 of this Part (gains from contracts for life insurance etc.), and

    (*b*) being taken into account in calculating income, or counting as income, for the purposes of other Parts of this Act,

but see section 527 (reduction for sums taken into account otherwise than under Chapter 9).

Commentary—*Simon's Taxes* **E1.402.**

HMRC Manuals—Savings and Investment Manual SAIM1070 (priority of trading and other income over savings and investment income).

SAIM5060 (UK dividends taxed as trading income).

367 Priority between Chapters within Part 4

(1) Any income, so far as it falls within Chapter 2 (interest) and Chapter 8 (profits from deeply discounted securities), is dealt with under Chapter 8.

(2) Any income, so far as it falls within Chapter 3 (dividends etc. from UK resident companies etc.) and another Chapter, is dealt with under Chapter 3 (but this is subject to subsection (3)).

(3) Any income, so far as it falls within—

(*a*) Chapter 2 (interest) as a result of section 372 (building society dividends)[, 378A (offshore fund distributions)][1] or 379 ([payments by registered societies or certain co-operatives][2]), and

(*b*) Chapter 3 [or Chapter 4 (or both)][1],

is dealt with under Chapter 2.

Commentary—*Simon's Taxes* **E1.402.**

HMRC Manuals—Savings and Investment Manual SAIM1070 (priority of one type of savings and investment income over another).

Amendments—[1]   In sub-s (3)(*a*), (*b*) words inserted by FA 2009 s 39(4) with effect in relation to—

(a)   distributions arising on or after 22 April 2009, and

(b)   manufactured overseas dividends that are representative of a distribution arising on or after that date.

[2]   In sub-s (3), words substituted for words "industrial and provident society payments" by the Co-operative and Community Benefit Societies Act 2014 s 151, Sch 4 paras 92, 93 with effect from 1 August 2014 and subject to transitional provisions and provisions preserving the continuity of the law in Sch 5 of that Act.

368 Territorial scope of Part 4 charges

(1) Income arising to a UK resident is chargeable to tax under this Part whether or not it is from a source in the United Kingdom.

(2) Income arising to a non-UK resident is chargeable to tax under this Part only if it is from a source in the United Kingdom.

[(2A) If income arising to an individual who is UK resident arises in the overseas part of a split year, it is to be treated for the purposes of this section as arising to a non-UK resident.][1]

(3) References in this section to income which is from a source in the United Kingdom include, in the case of any income which does not have a source, references to income which has a comparable connection to the United Kingdom.

(4) This section is subject to any express or implied provision to the contrary in this Part (or elsewhere in the Income Tax Acts).

Commentary—*Simon's Taxes* **E1.403.**

HMRC Manuals—Savings and Investment Manual SAIM1130 (territorial scope: UK and non UK resident).

Amendments—[1]   Sub-s (2A) inserted by FA 2013 s 218, Sch 45 paras 82, 83 with effect in calculating an individual's liability to income tax or capital gains tax for the tax year 2013–14 or any subsequent tax year, subject to transitional provisions and savings in FA 2013 Sch 45 paras 154–158.

[368A Interpretation of special rules for temporary non-residents

(1) This section concerns provisions of this Part that are expressed to apply if an individual is "temporarily non-resident" ("TNR provisions").

(2) Part 4 of Schedule 45 to FA 2013 (statutory residence test: anti-avoidance) explains for the purposes of TNR provisions—

(*a*) when an individual is to be regarded as "temporarily non-resident", and

(*b*) what the following terms mean—

(i)   "the temporary period of non-residence",

(ii) "the year of departure", and

(iii) "the period of return".

(3) A reference in TNR provisions to "the year of return" is to the tax year consisting of or including the period of return.

(4) Nothing in any double taxation relief arrangements is to be read as preventing the individual from being chargeable to income tax by virtue of any TNR provisions (or as preventing a charge to that tax from arising as a result).

(5) In this section and in TNR provisions, "double taxation relief arrangements" means arrangements that have effect under section 2(1) of TIOPA 2010.][1]

Commentary—*Simon's Taxes* **E1.415A.**

HMRC Manuals—Residence, Domicile And Remittance Basis Manual RDRM10225 (residence status).

RDRM32500 (temporary non-residents and relevant foreign income: contents).

Amendments—[1]   Section 368A inserted by FA 2013 s 218, Sch 45 paras 131, 132 with effect if the year of departure (as defined in FA 2013 Sch 45 Pt 4) is the tax year 2013–14 or any subsequent tax year, subject to transitional provisions and savings in FA 2013 Sch 45 paras 154–158.

CHAPTER 2

INTEREST

Charge to tax on interest

369 Charge to tax on interest

(1) Income tax is charged on interest.

(2) The following sections extend what is treated as interest for certain purposes—

section 372 (building society dividends),

section 373 (open-ended investment company interest distributions),

section 376 (authorised unit trust interest distributions),

[section 378A (offshore fund distributions),][4]

section 379 ([payments by registered societies or certain co-operatives][9]),

section 380 (funding bonds), and
[section 380A (FSCS payments representing interest),][3]
section 381 (discounts).

(3) For exemptions, see in particular—

(a) Chapter 2 of Part 6 (national savings income),

(b) Chapter 3 of Part 6 (income from individual investment plans),

(c) Chapter 4 of Part 6 (SAYE interest),

(d) Chapter 6 of Part 6 (income from FOTRA securities),

(e) sections 749 to [756A][1] ([repayment interest,][8] interest arising from repayment supplements,
. . .[7] damages for personal injury, employees' share schemes, repayments of student loans,
[unpaid relevant contributions,][6] the redemption of funding bonds[, certain foreign currency
securities and interest on certain deposits of victims of National-Socialist persecution)][1], and

(f) sections 757 to 767 (interest and royalty payments).

(4) Subsection (1) is also subject to [Chapter 3 of Part 12 of ITA 2007 (exemption for interest on
securities to which Chapter 2 of that Part applies)][2].

[(5) See also Chapter 3A of Part 14 of ITA 2007 (which provides for the receipts of certain types of
company being wound up to be charged to income tax under that Chapter instead of under any other
provision that would otherwise apply).][5]

Commentary—*Simon's Taxes* **E1.404, E1.405.**

HMRC Manuals—Savings and Investment Manual SAIM2020 (guidance for charge to tax on interest).
SAIM2200 (list and meaning of specific inclusions).
SAIM2300 (exemptions: tax-free savings income).

Amendments—[1] In sub-s (3), reference and words substituted by FA 2006 s 64(1) with effect from 19 July 2006. However,
in relation to any time before 6 April 2005 (the commencement of ITTOIA 2005)—

(a) ITTOIA 2005 s 756A (as inserted by FA 2006 s 64(2)) is to be treated as if it were inserted into TA 1988 (and
as if, in ITTOIA 2005 s 756A(5), the words, "of ICTA" were omitted), and

(b) any reference to that section in any enactment is to be read accordingly.

In relation to 2005–06 or any earlier year of assessment, all such adjustments are to be made as are required to give effect to
the exemptions conferred as a result of FA 2006 s 64. However, the adjustments are to be made only if the person entitled
to the exemption makes a claim for the exemption on or before 31 January 2012. The adjustments may be made by discharge
or repayment of tax, the making of an assessment or otherwise: FA 2006 s 64(9)–(12).

[2] Words in sub-s (4) substituted by ITA 2007 s 1027, Sch 1 paras 492, 513 with effect for income tax purposes from 6 April
2007, and corporation tax purposes for accounting periods ending after 5 April 2007.

[3] Words inserted by FA 2009 s 33(2) with effect in relation to payments made on or after 6 October 2008.

[4] Words inserted by FA 2009 s 39(2) with effect in relation to—

(a) distributions arising on or after 22 April 2009, and

(b) manufactured overseas dividends that are representative of a distribution arising on or after that date.

[5] Sub-s (5) inserted by TIOPA 2010 s 371, Sch 7 paras 66, 67. TIOPA 2010 has effect for corporation tax purposes for
accounting periods ending on or after 1 April 2010, for income and capital gains tax purposes for the tax year 2010–11 and
subsequent tax years, and for petroleum revenue tax purposes for chargeable periods beginning on or after 1 July 2010.

[6] Words in sub-s (3)(e) inserted by FA 2011 s 69(1), (2) with effect from 19 July 2011.

[7] In sub-s (3)(e), words "tax reserve certificates," repealed by FA 2012 s 227, Sch 39 para 53(2) with effect in relation to tax
reserve certificates redeemed on or after 6 April 2013.

[8] Words in sub-s (3)(e) inserted by the Finance Act 2009, Sections 101 and 102 (Interest on Late Payments and Repayments),
Appointed Days and Consequential Provisions Order, SI 2014/992 art 8(2) with effect in relation to payments due and payable
in respect of the tax year 2014–15 and subsequent tax years.

[9] In sub-s (2), words substituted for words "industrial and provident society payments" by the Co-operative and Community
Benefit Societies Act 2014 s 151, Sch 4 paras 92, 93 with effect from 1 August 2014 and subject to transitional provisions
and provisions preserving the continuity of the law in Sch 5 of that Act.

370 Income charged

(1) Tax is charged under this Chapter on the full amount of the interest arising in the tax year.

(2) Subsection (1) is subject to Part 8 (foreign income: special rules).

Commentary—*Simon's Taxes* **E1.404.**

HMRC Manuals—Savings and Investment Manual SAIM2400 (taxation of the tax charge).
SAIM2440 (taxation of when interest arises).
SAIM1130 (foreign income: special rules).

[370A Valuation of interest not paid in cash

(1) This section applies to the payment of an amount of interest in the form of—

(a) goods or services, or

(b) a voucher.

(2) Where this section applies by virtue of subsection (1)(a), the amount of the payment is to be
taken to be equal to the market value, at the time the payment is made, of the goods or services.

(3) Where this section applies by virtue of subsection (1)(b), the amount of the payment is to be
taken to be equal to whichever is the higher of—

(a) the face value of the voucher,

(b) the amount of money for which the voucher is capable of being exchanged, or

(c) the market value, at the time the payment is made, of any goods or services for which the
voucher is capable of being exchanged.

(4) In this section references to a voucher are to a voucher, stamp or similar document or token which is capable of being exchanged for money, goods or services.][1]

Commentary—*Simon's Taxes* E1.411A

HMRC Manuals—Savings and Investment Manual SAIM2600 (interest in kind).

Amendments—[1]   This section inserted by FA 2013 s 27, Sch 11 para 6 with effect in relation to any payment of interest which is made on or after 17 July 2013.

371 Person liable

The person liable for any tax charged under this Chapter is the person receiving or entitled to the interest.

Commentary—*Simon's Taxes* E1.404.

HMRC Manuals—Savings and Investment Manual SAIM2400 (person liable to tax).

Other income taxed as interest

372 Building society dividends

(1) Any dividend paid by a building society is treated as interest for the purposes of this Act.

(2) In this section "dividend" [includes any distribution (whether or not described as a dividend)][1].

Commentary—*Simon's Taxes* E1.406.

HMRC Manuals—Savings and Investment Manual SAIM2200 (tax treatment for building society dividends).

Amendments—[1]   Words in sub-s (2) substituted by ITA 2007 s 1027, Sch 1 paras 492, 514 with effect for income tax purposes from 6 April 2007, and corporation tax purposes for accounting periods ending after 5 April 2007.

373 Open-ended investment company interest distributions

(1) This section applies if the distribution accounts of an open-ended investment company show the total amount available for distribution to owners of shares in the company as available for distribution as yearly interest.

(2) Subsection (1) is subject to [subsection (7)][2].

(3) For income tax purposes payments of yearly interest are treated as made to the owners of the shares by the company.

(4) . . . [1]

(5) The amount of the payment treated as made to each owner is so much of the total amount mentioned in subsection (1) as is proportionate to the owner's shares.

(6) . . . [1]

(7) This section does not apply if the open-ended investment company is an approved personal pension scheme.

(8) See section 375 for the interpretation of this section and section 374.

Commentary—*Simon's Taxes* E1.407.

HMRC Manuals—Savings and Investment Manual SAIM2200 (tax treatment of interest distributions). SAIM6030 (interest distributions).

Amendments—[1]   Sub-ss (4), (6) repealed by F(No 2)A 2005 s 17(1)(d), s 70, Sch 11 Pt 2(3) with effect—

    (a)   for the purposes of income tax—

        (i)   for 2006–07 and subsequent years of assessment, and

        (ii)   for distributions made on or after 6 April 2006; and

    (b)   for the purposes of corporation tax—

        (i)   on income, for accounting periods beginning on or after 1 April 2006,

        (ii)   on chargeable gains, in relation to disposals made on or after 1 April 2006, and

        (iii)   for distributions made on or after 1 April 2006 (by virtue of SI 2006/982).

[2]   Words in sub-s (2) substituted by the Authorised Investment Funds (Tax) Regulations, SI 2006/964 reg 91(1), (2). SI 2006/964 (which came into force on 1 April 2006) has effect—

    (a)   for the purposes of income tax—

        (i)   for the tax year 2006–07 and subsequent tax years, and

        (ii)   for distributions made on or after 6 April 2006;

    (b)   for the purposes of corporation tax—

        (i)   on income, for accounting periods beginning on or after 1 April 2006,

        (ii)   on chargeable gains, in relation to disposals made on or after 1 April 2006, and

        (iii)   for distributions made on or after 1 April 2006; and

    (c)   for the purposes of capital gains tax, in relation to disposals made on or after 6 April 2006.

374 Date when interest payments under section 373 made

(1) This section applies for determining the date on which payments of interest under section 373 are treated as made.

(2) The date on which the payments are treated as made depends on whether a date is specified for any distribution for the distribution period in question by or in accordance with—

    (*a*) the company's instrument of incorporation and its prospectus in issue for the time being (including any supplements), or

    (*b*) in the case of an open-ended investment company which is part of an umbrella company, such parts of those documents of the umbrella company as apply to the open-ended investment company.

(3) If such a date is so specified, the payments are treated as made on that date.

(4) If no such date is so specified, the payments are treated as made on the last day of that period.

Commentary—*Simon's Taxes* **E1.407.**
HMRC Manuals—Savings and Investment Manual SAIM6030 (OEIC: date of payments).
Modification—Authorised Investment Funds (Tax) Regulations, SI 2006/964 regs 93, 96(1)–(3) (modification of this section in its application in relation to authorised investment funds, shareholders or unit holders in authorised investment funds, and transactions involving authorised investment funds).

375 Interpretation of sections 373 and 374

(1) In sections 373 and 374 and this section—

"approved personal pension scheme" has the same meaning as in Chapter 4 of Part 14 of ICTA (see section 630(1) of that Act),

"distribution" includes investment on behalf of an owner of shares in respect of the owner's accumulation shares,

"distribution accounts" means the accounts showing how the total amount available for distribution to owners of shares is calculated,

"distribution period" means the period by reference to which that amount is ascertained,

"the OEIC Regulations" means the Open-ended Investment Companies (Tax) Regulations 1997 (SI 1997/1154),

"open-ended investment company" has the same meaning as in Chapter 3 of Part 12 of ICTA (unit trust schemes etc.) (see section 468(10) and (11) of ICTA, as inserted by regulation 10 of the OEIC Regulations),

"owner of shares" has the same meaning as in that Chapter (see section 468(10) and (15) of that Act, as so inserted), and

["umbrella company" has the meaning given by section 615 of CTA 2010.][1]

(2) In subsection (1) "accumulation share" means a share in respect of which income is credited periodically to the capital part of the company's scheme property.

(3) In subsection (2) "scheme property" has the same meaning as in Chapter 3 of Part 12 of ICTA (unit trust schemes etc.) (see section 468(10) and (13) of ICTA, as inserted by regulation 10 of the OEIC Regulations).

Modification—Authorised Investment Funds (Tax) Regulations, SI 2006/964 regs 93, 96(1), (4)–(6) (modification of this section in its application in relation to authorised investment funds, shareholders or unit holders in authorised investment funds, and transactions involving authorised investment funds).
Amendments—[1] In sub-s (1) the definition of " umbrella company" substituted by CTA 2010 s 1177, Sch 1 paras 444, 452 with effect for corporation tax purposes for accounting periods ending on or after 1 April 2010, and for income and capital gains tax purposes for the tax year 2010–11 and subsequent tax years.

376 Authorised unit trust interest distributions

(1) This section applies if the distribution accounts of an authorised unit trust show the total amount available for distribution to unit holders as available for distribution as yearly interest.
(2) Subsection (1) is subject to [subsection (7)][2].
(3) For income tax purposes payments of yearly interest are treated as made to the unit holders.
(4) . . .[1]
(5) The amount of the payment treated as made to each unit holder is so much of the total amount mentioned in subsection (1) as is proportionate to the unit holder's rights.
(6) . . .[1]
(7) This section does not apply if the authorised unit trust is an approved personal pension scheme.
(8) See section 378 for the interpretation of this section and section 377.

Commentary—*Simon's Taxes* **E1.408.**
HMRC Manuals—Savings and Investment Manual SAIM6030 (authorised investment funds : the taxation of the investor).
Modification—Authorised Investment Funds (Tax) Regulations, SI 2006/964 regs 93, 96(1)–(3) (modification of this section in its application in relation to authorised investment funds, shareholders or unit holders in authorised investment funds, and transactions involving authorised investment funds).
Amendments—[1] Sub-ss (4), (6) repealed by F(No 2)A 2005 s 17(1)(d), s 70, Sch 11 Pt 2(3) with effect—
    (a)   for the purposes of income tax—
        (i)   for 2006–07 and subsequent years of assessment, and
        (ii)   for distributions made on or after 6 April 2006; and
    (b)   for the purposes of corporation tax—
        (i)   on income, for accounting periods beginning on or after 1 April 2006,
        (ii)   on chargeable gains, in relation to disposals made on or after 1 April 2006, and
        (iii)   for distributions made on or after 1 April 2006 (by virtue of SI 2006/982).
[2] Words in sub-s (2) substituted by the Authorised Investment Funds (Tax) Regulations, SI 2006/964 reg 91(1), (3). SI 2006/964 (which came into force on 1 April 2006) has effect—
    (a)   for the purposes of income tax—
        (i)   for the tax year 2006–07 and subsequent tax years, and
        (ii)   for distributions made on or after 6 April 2006;
    (b)   for the purposes of corporation tax—
        (i)   on income, for accounting periods beginning on or after 1 April 2006,
        (ii)   on chargeable gains, in relation to disposals made on or after 1 April 2006, and
        (iii)   for distributions made on or after 1 April 2006; and
    (c)   for the purposes of capital gains tax, in relation to disposals made on or after 6 April 2006.

377 Date when interest payments under section 376 made

(1) This section applies for determining the date on which payments of interest under section 376 are treated as made.

(2) The date on which the payments are treated as made depends on whether a date is specified by or in accordance with the trust's terms for any distribution for the distribution period in question.

(3) If such a date is so specified, the payments are treated as made on that date.

(4) If no such date is so specified, the payments are treated as made on the last day of that period.

Commentary—*Simon's Taxes* E1.408.

HMRC Manuals—Savings and Investment Manual SAIM6030 (AUT: date of payments).

378 Interpretation of sections 376 and 377

In sections 376 and 377—

"approved personal pension scheme" has the same meaning as in Chapter 4 of Part 14 of ICTA (see section 630(1) of that Act),

"distribution" includes investment on behalf of a unit holder in respect of the holder's accumulation units,

"distribution accounts" means the accounts showing how the total amount available for distribution to unit holders is ascertained, and

"distribution period" means the period by reference to which that amount is ascertained.

Commentary—*Simon's Taxes* E1.408.

[378A Offshore fund distributions

(1) This section applies where—

(a) a dividend is paid by an offshore fund, and

(b) the offshore fund fails to meet the qualifying investments test at any time in the relevant period.

(2) The dividend is treated as interest for income tax purposes.

(3) For the purposes of this section, an offshore fund fails to meet the qualifying investments test if the market value of the fund's qualifying investments exceeds 60% of the market value of all of the assets of the fund (excluding cash awaiting investment).

(4) "The relevant period" means—

(a) the relevant period of account of the offshore fund, or

(b) if longer, the period of 12 months ending on the last day of that period.

(5) "The relevant period of account" means—

(a) the last period of account ending before the dividend is paid, in a case in which the profits available for distribution at the end of that period (and not used since then by distribution or otherwise) equal or exceed the amount of the dividend (aggregated with any other distribution made by the offshore fund at the same time), and

(b) the period of account in which the dividend is paid, in any other case.

(6) This section applies to a manufactured overseas dividend if, and only if, it is representative of a distribution to which this section would apply.

(7) In this section—

"dividend" includes any distribution that (but for this section) would be treated as a dividend for income tax purposes;

"manufactured overseas dividend" has the same meaning as in Chapter 2 of Part 11 of ITA 2007 (manufactured payments);

"offshore fund" has the same meaning as in [section 354 of TIOPA 2010 (see sections 355 to 363 of that Act)][2];

"qualifying investments" has the meaning given in section 494 of CTA 2009.][1]

Commentary—*Simon's Taxes* E1.408A.

HMRC Manuals—Offshore Fund Manual OFM13100 (investors in nonreporting funds: distributions: the charge to tax: general). OFM13300 (corporate funds - 'bond funds').

Amendments—[1] This section inserted by FA 2009 s 39(3) with effect in relation to—

    (a)   distributions arising on or after 22 April 2009, and

    (b)   manufactured overseas dividends that are representative of a distribution arising on or after that date.

[2]   In sub-s (7), words substituted by TIOPA 2010 s 501, Sch 8 paras 167, 168. TIOPA 2010 has effect for corporation tax purposes for accounting periods ending on or after 1 April 2010, for income and capital gains tax purposes for the tax year 2010–11 and subsequent tax years, and for petroleum revenue tax purposes for chargeable periods beginning on or after 1 July 2010.

379 [Payments by registered societies or certain co-operatives]

(1) Any dividend, bonus or other sum payable to a shareholder in—

(a) a [registered society][1], or

(b) a UK agricultural or fishing co-operative,

is treated as interest for income tax purposes if it is payable by reference to the amount of the shareholder's holding in its share capital.

(2) In subsection (1)—

["registered society" means—

(*a*) a registered society within the meaning of the Co-operative and Community Benefit Societies Act 2014,

(*b*) a society registered or treated as registered under the Industrial and Provident Societies Act (Northern Ireland) 1969,

(*c*) a society registered as a credit union under the Credit Unions (Northern Ireland) Order 1985 (S.I. 1985/1205 (N.I. 12)), or

(*d*) an SCE formed in accordance with Council Regulation (EC) No 1435/2003 on the Statute for a European Cooperative Society,][1] and

"UK agricultural or fishing co-operative" means a co-operative association—

(*a*) which is established in the United Kingdom and UK resident, and

(*b*) whose primary object is assisting its members in—

(i) carrying on agricultural or horticultural businesses on land occupied by them in the United Kingdom, or

(ii) carrying on businesses consisting in the catching or taking of fish or shellfish.

(3) In subsection (2) "co-operative association" means a body with a written constitution from which the Secretary of State considers that it is in substance a co-operative association.

(4) For the purposes of subsection (3), the Secretary of State must have regard to the way in which the body's constitution provides for its income to be applied for its members' benefit and all other relevant provisions.

(5) In Northern Ireland subsections (3) and (4) apply with the substitution for "the Secretary of State" of "the Department of Agriculture and Rural Development".

Commentary—*Simon's Taxes* **E1.409.**

HMRC Manuals—Savings and Investment Manual SAIM2200 (provident society payments).

Business Income Manual BIM24735 (meaning of UK agricultural or fishing co-operative association).

Amendments—[1] Heading substituted for previous heading "Industrial and provident society payments", in sub-s (1)(a), words substituted for words "registered industrial and provident society", and in sub-s (2), definition substituted for definition of "registered industrial and provident society", by the Co-operative and Community Benefit Societies Act 2014 s 151, Sch 4 paras 92, 94 (as amended by FA 2014 Sch 39) with effect from 1 August 2014 and subject to transitional provisions and provisions preserving the continuity of the law in Sch 5 of that Act.

380 Funding bonds

(1) This section applies to the issue of funding bonds to a creditor in respect of a liability to pay interest on a debt incurred by a government, public institution, other public authority or body corporate.

(2) The issue is treated for income tax purposes as if it were the payment of so much of that interest as equals the market value of the bonds at their issue.

(3) In this section "funding bonds" includes any bonds, stocks, shares, securities or certificates of indebtedness [(but does not include any instrument providing for payment in the form of goods or services or a voucher)][1].

Commentary—*Simon's Taxes* **E1.410.**

HMRC Manuals—Savings and Investment Manual SAIM2210 (meaning and tax treatment of funding bonds).

Amendments—[1] In sub-s (3) words inserted by FA 2013 s 27, Sch 11 para 7 with effect in relation to any payment of interest made on or after 17 July 2013.

[380A FSCS payments representing interest

(1) Any payment representing interest which is made under the FSCS is treated as interest for the purposes of this Act.

(2) "Payment representing interest" means a payment calculated in the same way as interest which would have been paid to the recipient but for the circumstances giving rise to the making of payments under the FSCS.

(3) Where a payment representing interest is made net of an amount equal to a sum representing income tax that would have been deducted on the payment of interest, the amount treated as interest by this section is the aggregate of the payment representing interest and that sum.

(4) This section applies to payments made under the FSCS whether or not they are made (in whole or in part) on behalf of the Treasury or any other person.

(5) In this section "the FSCS" means the Financial Services Compensation Scheme (established under Part 15 of the Financial Services and Markets Act 2000).][1]

Commentary—*Simon's Taxes* **E1.410A.**

HMRC Manuals—Savings and Investment Manual SAIM2085(interest payable from the financial services compensation scheme).

SAIM2090 (examples of FSCS compensation calculations),

SAIM2095 (FSCS: types of financial products and payments taxable as interest).

Amendments—[1] This section inserted by FA 2009 s 33 with effect in relation to payments made on or after 6 October 2008.

381 Discounts

(1) All discounts, other than discounts in deeply discounted securities, are treated as interest for the purposes of this Act.

(2) In this section "deeply discounted securities" means securities to which Chapter 8 of this Part applies (profits from deeply discounted securities).

Commentary—*Simon's Taxes* E1.411.
HMRC Manuals—Savings and Investment Manual SAIM2230 (tax treatment of discounted securities).
SAIM2240 (discounts: case law).

[CHAPTER 2A

DISGUISED INTEREST]

Amendments—Chapter 2A (ss 381A–381E) inserted by FA 2013 s 28, Sch 12 paras 1, 3 with effect for the tax year 2013–14 and subsequent tax years. Note that this Chapter does not apply in relation to an arrangement that produces a return for a person, in relation to an amount, which is economically equivalent to interest, if the person became party to the arrangement before 6 April 2013, and none of the provisions repealed by FA 2013 Sch 12 paras 13(2) and 15(2) applied in relation to the arrangement before that date (FA 2013 Sch 12 para 18(2)). FA 2013 Sch 12 para 13(2) repeals ITTOIA 2005 Part 4 Chapter 12 (disposals of futures and options involving guarantee returns) and para 15(2) repeals ITA 2007 ss 596(5), 597–605, 606(1)–(7), (9), (10), 607–614 (which deal with deemed manufactured payments and repos).

[381A Charge to tax on disguised interest

(1) This Chapter applies where a person is party to an arrangement which produces for the person a return in relation to any amount which is economically equivalent to interest.
(2) Income tax is charged on the return if the return is not charged to income tax under or as a result of any other provision of this Act or any other Act.
(3) Subsection (2) does not apply to a return that would be charged to income tax under or as a result of another provision but for an exemption.
(4) For the purposes of this Chapter a return produced for a person by an arrangement in relation to any amount is "economically equivalent to interest" if (and only if)—

  (*a*) it is reasonable to assume that it is a return by reference to the time value of that amount of money,
  (*b*) it is at a rate reasonably comparable to what is (in all the circumstances) a commercial rate of interest, and
  (*c*) at the relevant time there is no practical likelihood that it will cease to be produced in accordance with the arrangement unless the person by whom it falls to be produced is prevented (by reason of insolvency or otherwise) from producing it.

(5) In subsection (4)(*c*) "the relevant time" means the time when the person becomes party to the arrangement or, if later, when the arrangement begins to produce a return for the person.
(6) In this Chapter "arrangement" includes any agreement, understanding, scheme, transaction or series of transactions (whether or not legally enforceable).][1]

Commentary—*Simon's Taxes* E1.405A.
HMRC Manuals—Savings and Investment Manual SAIM2700 (disguised interest: overview and contents).
SAIM2730 (determining factors of disguised interest).
SAIM2740 (determining factors of the practical likelihood of the return).
SAIM2800 (examples of disguised interest).
Amendments—[1]   Chapter 2A (ss 381A–381E) inserted by FA 2013 s 28, Sch 12 paras 1, 3 with effect for the tax year 2013–14 and subsequent tax years, subject to the transitional provisions in FA 2013 Sch 12 para 18(2) (for which, see amendment note at beginning of this Chapter).

[381B Income charged

Tax is charged under this Chapter on the full amount of the return, or any part of the return, arising in the tax year.][1]

Commentary—*Simon's Taxes* E1.405A.
HMRC Manuals—Savings and Investment Manual SAIM2760 (disguised interest: the charge to tax).
Amendments—[1]   Chapter 2A (ss 381A–381E) inserted by FA 2013 s 28, Sch 12 paras 1, 3 with effect for the tax year 2013–14 and subsequent tax years, subject to the transitional provisions in FA 2013 Sch 12 para 18(2) (for which, see amendment note at beginning of this Chapter).

[381C Person liable

The person liable for any tax charged under this Chapter is the person receiving or entitled to the return or the part of the return.][1]

Amendments—[1]   Chapter 2A (ss 381A–381E) inserted by FA 2013 s 28, Sch 12 paras 1, 3 with effect for the tax year 2013–14 and subsequent tax years, subject to the transitional provisions in FA 2013 Sch 12 para 18(2) (for which, see amendment note at beginning of this Chapter).

[381D Avoidance of double taxation

(1) This section applies if at any time a tax other than income tax ("the other tax") is charged in relation to a return on which income tax is charged under this Chapter.
(2) In order to avoid a double charge to tax in respect of the return, a person may make a claim for one or more consequential adjustments to be made in respect of the other tax.
(3) On a claim under this section an officer of Revenue and Customs must make such of the consequential adjustments claimed (if any) as are just and reasonable.
(4) Consequential adjustments may be made—

 (*a*) in respect of any period,

 (*b*) by way of an assessment, the modification of an assessment, the amendment of a claim, or otherwise, and

 (*c*) despite any time limit imposed by or under any enactment.]¹

Amendments—¹ Chapter 2A (ss 381A–381E) inserted by FA 2013 s 28, Sch 12 paras 1, 3 with effect for the tax year 2013–14 and subsequent tax years, subject to the transitional provisions in FA 2013 Sch 12 para 18(2) (for which, see amendment note at beginning of this Chapter).

[381E Exception for returns from certain shares

(1) This Chapter does not apply in relation to an arrangement that produces a return for a person, in relation to an amount, which is economically equivalent to interest where—

 (*a*) the arrangement involves only excluded shares, and

 (*b*) no relevant arrangement has been made (by any person) in relation to those excluded shares.

(2) For the purposes of this section shares are excluded shares if they are admitted to trading on a regulated market and—

 (*a*) they were issued before 6 April 2013, or

 (*b*) if issued on or after that date, at the time of issue no arrangements involving only the shares would produce a return, in relation to an amount, which is economically equivalent to interest.

(3) In subsection (2) "regulated market" has the same meaning as in [Directive 2014/65/EU of the European Parliament and of the Council on markets in financial instruments (see Article 4.1.21)]².

(4) For the purposes of this section an arrangement is relevant, in relation to excluded shares, where—

 (*a*) the arrangement is made on or after 6 April 2013, and

 (*b*) it is reasonable to assume that the main purpose, or one of the main purposes, of the arrangement is to secure that arrangements involving only the shares produce a return, in relation to an amount, which is economically equivalent to interest.]¹

Commentary—*Simon's Taxes* **E1.405A.**

HMRC Manuals—Savings and Investment Manual SAIM2770 (disguised interest: excluded shares).

Amendments—¹ Chapter 2A (ss 381A–381E) inserted by FA 2013 s 28, Sch 12 paras 1, 3 with effect for the tax year 2013–14 and subsequent tax years, subject to the transitional provisions in FA 2013 Sch 12 para 18(2) (for which, see amendment note at beginning of this Chapter).
² In sub-s (3) words substituted for words "Directive 2004/39/EC of the European Parliament and of the Council on markets in financial instruments (see Article 4.1(14)" by Financial Services and Markets Act 2000 (Markets in Financial Instruments) Regulations, SI 2017/701 reg 50(3), Sch 4 para 8 with effect from 3 January 2018: see SI 2017/701 reg 1(6).

Prospective amendments—Sub-s (3) to be substituted by the Taxes (Amendments) (EU Exit) Regulations, SI 2019/689 reg 13(1), (3) with effect from Implementation Period completion day (see EU(WA)A 2020 Sch 5 para 1(1)). Sub-s (3) to read as follows—

 "(3) In subsection (2) "regulated market" means—

 (*a*) a UK regulated market within the meaning given by Article 2.1(13A) of Regulation (EU) No 600/2014 of the European Parliament and of the Council of 15 May 2014 on markets in financial instruments,

 (*b*) an EU regulated market within the meaning given by Article 2.1(13B) of that Regulation, and

 (*c*) a regulated market within the meaning given by Article 2.1(13) of that Regulation which is authorised and functions regularly and in accordance with Part 3 of the Financial Services (Markets in Financial Instruments) Act 2018 of Gibraltar."

Sub-s (3)(*c*), as inserted by SI 2019/689 above, to be substituted by the Taxes (Amendments) (EU Exit) (No 2) Regulations, SI 2019/818 reg 5 with effect from Implementation Period completion day, immediately after the coming into force of SI 2019/689 (which also come into force on Implementation Period completion day (see EU(WA)A 2020 Sch 5 para 1(1)). Para (*c*) to read as follows—

 " a Gibraltar regulated market within the meaning given by Article 26(11)(*b*)(i) of that Regulation.".

CHAPTER 3

DIVIDENDS ETC FROM UK RESIDENT COMPANIES [AND TAX [TREATED AS PAID]² IN RESPECT OF CERTAIN DISTRIBUTIONS]¹

Amendments—¹ Words in heading substituted by FA 2008 s 34, Sch 12 paras 1, 2 with effect for the tax year 2008–09 and subsequent tax years.
² Words in heading substituted by FA 2016 s 5, Sch 1 paras 2, 3 with effect in relation to dividends paid or arising (or treated as paid), and other distributions made (or treated as made), in the tax year 2016–17 or at any later time.

Introduction

382 Contents of Chapter

(1) This Chapter—

 (*a*) imposes a charge to income tax on dividends and other distributions of UK resident companies (see section 383),

 (*b*) treats dividends as paid in some circumstances (see sections 386 to 391), . . . ²

(c) makes special provision where the charge is in respect of shares awarded under [a Schedule 2][1] share incentive plan (see sections 392 to 396)[, and

(d) treats distributions as made in some circumstances (see section 396A).][2]

(2) This Chapter also makes provision about . . . [3] tax being treated as paid and reliefs available in respect of certain distributions which applies whether or not the distributions are otherwise dealt with under this Chapter (see sections [399][3] to 401).

(3) For exemptions from the charge under this Chapter, see in particular—

Chapter 3 of Part 6 (income from individual investment plans),

Chapter 5 of that Part (venture capital trust dividends),

section 770 (amounts applied by SIP trustees acquiring dividend shares or retained for reinvestment), and

section 498 of ITEPA 2003 (no charge on shares ceasing to be subject to SIP in certain circumstances).

(4) In this Chapter "dividends" does not include income treated as arising under section 410 (stock dividends).

Commentary—*Simon's Taxes* **E1.412.**

HMRC Manuals—Savings and Investment Manual SAIM5000 (dividends and other company distributions: overview and contents).

Amendments—[1] In sub-s (1)(c) words substituted for words "an approved" by FA 2014 s 51, Sch 8 paras 53, 54 with effect from 6 April 2014. The effect of the FA 2014 changes on SIPs established before 6 April 2014 is set out in FA 2014 Sch 8 paras 91 to 96.

[2] In sub-s (1), in para(b) word "and" repealed, and para (d) and preceding word ", and" inserted, by FA 2015 s 19(1), (3) with effect in relation to things received on or after 6 April 2015 (even if the choice to receive them was made before that date).

[3] In sub-s (2), words repealed and word substituted by FA 2016 s 5, Sch 1 paras 2, 4 with effect in relation to dividends paid or arising (or treated as paid), and other distributions made (or treated as made), in the tax year 2016-17 or at any later time.

Charge to tax on dividends and other distributions

383 Charge to tax on dividends and other distributions

(1) Income tax is charged on dividends and other distributions of a UK resident company.

(2) For income tax purposes such dividends and other distributions are to be treated as income.

(3) For the purposes of subsection (2), it does not matter that those dividends and other distributions are capital apart from that subsection.

Commentary—*Simon's Taxes* **E1.412.**

HMRC Manuals—Savings and Investment Manual SAIM5020 (the charge to tax on UK dividends). SAIM5070 (distributions from OEICs and AUTSs.

384 Income charged

(1) Tax is charged under this Chapter on the amount or value of the dividends paid and other distributions made in the tax year.

(2) Subsection (1) is subject to—

section 393(2) and (3) (later charge where cash dividends retained in SIPs are paid over), and

section 394(3) (distribution when dividend shares cease to be subject to SIP).

(3) . . . [1]

Amendments—[1] Sub-s (3) repealed by FA 2016 s 5, Sch 1 paras 2, 5 with effect in relation to dividends paid or arising (or treated as paid), and other distributions made (or treated as made), in the tax year 2016-17 or at any later time.

385 Person liable

(1) The person liable for any tax charged under this Chapter is—

a) the person to whom the distribution is made or is treated as made (see Part 6 of ICTA and sections 386(3)[, 389(3) and 396A][1]), or

(b) the person receiving or entitled to the distribution.

(2) Subsection (1) is subject to—

section 393(4) (later charge where cash dividends retained in SIPs are paid over), and

section 394(4) (distribution when dividend shares cease to be subject to SIP).

Commentary—*Simon's Taxes* **E1.412.**

HMRC Manuals—Savings and Investment Manual SAIM5020 (person liable to tax).

Amendments—[1] In sub-s (1)(a), words substituted for words "and 389(3)" by FA 2015 s 19(1), (4) with effect in relation to things received on or after 6 April 2015 (even if the choice to receive them was made before that date).

Amounts treated as dividends

386 Open-ended investment company dividend distributions

(1) This section applies if the distribution accounts of an open-ended investment company show the total amount available for distribution to owners of shares in the company as available for distribution as dividends.

(2) Subsection (1) is subject to subsection (5).

(3) For income tax purposes dividends are treated as paid to the owners of the shares by the company.

(4) The amount of the dividends treated as paid to each owner is so much of the total amount mentioned in subsection (1) as is proportionate to the owner's shares.

(5) This section does not apply if the open-ended investment company is an approved personal pension scheme.

(6) See section 388 for the interpretation of this section and section 387.

Commentary—*Simon's Taxes* **E1.413.**

HMRC Manuals—Savings and Investment Manual SAIM6030 (the taxation of the investor for OEICs: dividend distributions).

SAIM5020 (person liable to tax).

387 Date when dividends paid under section 386

(1) This section applies for determining the date on which dividends are treated as paid under section 386.

(2) The date on which the dividends are treated as paid depends on whether a date is specified for the distribution period in question by or in accordance with—

   (*a*) the company's instrument of incorporation and its prospectus in issue for the time being (including any supplements), or

   (*b*) in the case of an open-ended investment company which is part of an umbrella company, such parts of those documents of the umbrella company as apply to the open-ended investment company.

(3) If such a date is so specified, the dividends are treated as paid on that date.

(4) If no such date is so specified, the dividends are treated as paid on the last day of that period.

Commentary—*Simon's Taxes* **E1.413.**

HMRC Manuals—Savings and Investment Manual SAIM6030 (payments of date under section 386).

SAIM6060 (the trustees: taxation overview).

Modification—Authorised Investment Funds (Tax) Regulations, SI 2006/964 regs 93, 96(1)–(3) (modification of this section in its application in relation to authorised investment funds, shareholders or unit holders in authorised investment funds, and transactions involving authorised investment funds).

388 Interpretation of sections 386 and 387

(1) In sections 386 and 387 and this section—

"approved personal pension scheme" has the same meaning as in Chapter 4 of Part 14 of ICTA (see section 630(1) of that Act),

"distribution" includes investment on behalf of an owner of shares in respect of the owner's accumulation shares,

"distribution accounts" means the accounts showing how the total amount available for distribution to owners of shares is calculated,

"distribution period" means the period by reference to which that amount is ascertained,

"the OEIC Regulations" means the Open-ended Investment Companies (Tax) Regulations 1997 (SI. 1997/1154),

"open-ended investment company" has the same meaning as in Chapter 3 of Part 12 of ICTA (unit trust schemes etc.) (see section 468(10) and (11) of ICTA, as inserted by regulation 10 of the OEIC Regulations),

"owner of shares" has the same meaning as in that Chapter (see section 468(10) and (15) of that Act, as so inserted), and

["umbrella company" has the meaning given by section 615 of CTA 2010.][1]

(2) In subsection (1) "accumulation share" means a share in respect of which income is credited periodically to the capital part of the company's scheme property.

(3) In subsection (2) "scheme property" has the same meaning as in Chapter 3 of Part 12 of ICTA (unit trust schemes etc.) (see section 468(10) and (13) of ICTA, as inserted by regulation 10 of the OEIC Regulations).

Commentary—*Simon's Taxes* **E1.413.**

HMRC Manuals—Savings and Investment Manual SAIM5070 (distributions from OEICs).

Modifications—Authorised Investment Funds (Tax) Regulations, SI 2006/964 regs 93, 96(1), (4)–(6) (modification of this section in its application in relation to authorised investment funds, shareholders or unit holders in authorised investment funds, and transactions involving authorised investment funds).

Amendments—[1]   In sub-s (1) the definition of " umbrella company" substituted by CTA 2010 s 1177, Sch 1 paras 444, 453 with effect for corporation tax purposes for accounting periods ending on or after 1 April 2010, and for income and capital gains tax purposes for the tax year 2010–11 and subsequent tax years.

389 Authorised unit trust dividend distributions

(1) This section applies if the distribution accounts of an authorised unit trust show the total amount available for distribution to unit holders as available for distribution as dividends.

(2) Subsection (1) is subject to subsection (6).

(3) For income tax purposes dividends are treated as paid to the unit holders.

(4) The amount of the dividends treated as paid to each unit holder is so much of the total amount mentioned in subsection (1) as is proportionate to the unit holder's rights.

(5) The dividends are treated as paid on the shares and by the company referred to in [section 617(1) of CTA 2010][1] (which relates to the trustees of an authorised unit trust being treated as a UK resident company in which the unit holders' rights are shares).

(6) This section does not apply if the authorised unit trust is an approved personal pension scheme.

ITTOIA 2005

(7) See section 391 for the interpretation of this section and section 390.

Commentary—*Simon's Taxes* E1.413.

HMRC Manuals—Savings and Investment Manual SAIM5020 (AUTs dividend distributions: person liable).

SAIM5070 (distributions from AUTs).

SAIM6030 (the taxation of the investor for AUTs: dividend distributions).

Amendments[1]   In sub-s (5) words substituted by CTA 2010 s 1177, Sch 1 paras 444, 454. CTA 2010 has effect for corporation tax purposes for accounting periods ending on or after 1 April 2010, and for income and capital gains tax purposes for the tax year 2010–11 and subsequent tax years.

390 Date when dividends paid under section 389

(1) This section applies for determining the date on which dividends are treated as paid under section 389.

(2) The date on which the dividends are treated as paid depends on whether a date is specified by or in accordance with the trust's terms for any distribution for the distribution period in question.

(3) If such a date is so specified, the dividends are treated as paid on that date.

(4) If no such date is so specified, the dividends are treated as paid on the last day of that period.

Commentary—*Simon's Taxes* E1.413.

HMRC Manuals—Savings and Investment Manual SAIM6030 (payments of date under section 389).

Modification—Authorised Investment Funds (Tax) Regulations, SI 2006/964 regs 93, 96(1)–(3) (modification of this section in its application in relation to authorised investment funds, shareholders or unit holders in authorised investment funds, and transactions involving authorised investment funds).

391 Interpretation of sections 389 and 390

In sections 389 and 390—

> "approved personal pension scheme" has the same meaning as in Chapter 4 of Part 14 of ICTA (see section 630(1) of that Act),
>
> "distribution" includes investment on behalf of a unit holder in respect of the holder's accumulation units,
>
> "distribution accounts" means the accounts showing how the total amount available for distribution to unit holders is ascertained, and
>
> "distribution period" means the period by reference to which that amount is ascertained.

Commentary—*Simon's Taxes* E1.413.

Shares in [Schedule 2] share incentive plans ("SIPs")

392 SIP shares: introduction

(1) Sections 393 to 395 contain special rules about the charge under this Chapter in respect of shares awarded to an individual under [a Schedule 2][1] share incentive plan.

(2) Those sections only apply if condition A or B was met at the time the shares in question were so awarded.

(3) Condition A is that—

    (a) the earnings from the eligible employment were general earnings (see section 7(3) of ITEPA 2003) to which any of the charging provisions of Chapter 4 or 5 of Part 2 of ITEPA 2003 applied, or

    (b) if there had been any earnings from it, they would have been such earnings.

(4) In subsection (3)—

    (a) "the eligible employment" means the employment resulting in the individual meeting the employment requirement in relation to the plan, and

    (b) the reference to any of the charging provisions of Chapter 4 or 5 of Part 2 of ITEPA 2003 has the same meaning as it has in the employment income Parts of that Act (see sections 14(3) and 20(3) of that Act).

(5) Condition B is that—

    (a) the shares were awarded before 6th April 2003, and

    (b) the individual was liable for tax under Schedule E in respect of the relevant employment.

(6) In subsection (5) "the relevant employment" means the employment by reference to which the individual met the requirements in paragraph 14 of Schedule 8 to FA 2000 (employee share ownership plans: the employment requirement) in relation to the plan.

(7) See section 396 for the general interpretation of this section and sections 393 to 395.

Commentary—*Simon's Taxes* E1.417.

HMRC Manuals—Savings and Investment Manual SAIM5080 (dividends from share incentive plans).

Amendments—[1]   In cross-heading words substituted for word "approved", and in sub-s (1) words substituted for words "an approved", by FA 2014 s 51, Sch 8 paras 53, 55, 56 with effect from 6 April 2014. The effect of the FA 2014 changes on SIPs established before 6 April 2014 is set out in FA 2014 Sch 8 paras 91 to 96.

393 Later charge where cash dividends retained in SIPs are paid over

(1) This section applies if a cash dividend is paid over to a participant under paragraph 68(4) of Schedule 2 to ITEPA 2003 (cash dividend paid over if not reinvested etc.).

(2) Tax charged under this Chapter is charged for the tax year in which the cash dividend is paid over instead of the tax year in which it was originally paid.

(3) Tax so charged is charged on the amount of the cash dividend paid over.

(4) The person liable for any tax so charged is the participant.

(5) . . . [1]

(6) For the purposes of this Chapter, the question whether a cash dividend paid over to a participant under paragraph 68(4) of Schedule 2 to ITEPA 2003 is a dividend paid by a company that is UK resident is determined by reference to the tax year in which the dividend was originally paid.

Amendments—[1]   Sub-s (5) repealed by FA 2016 s 5, Sch 1 paras 2, 6 with effect in relation to cash dividends paid over in the tax year 2016-17 or at any later time.

394 Distribution when dividend shares cease to be subject to SIP

(1) This section applies if dividend shares cease to be subject to [a Schedule 2][1] share incentive plan before the end of the period of 3 years beginning with the date on which the shares were acquired on the participant's behalf.

(2) For income tax purposes a distribution is treated as made to the participant in the tax year in which the shares cease to be subject to the plan.

(3) The amount of the distribution treated as made is the amount of the cash dividend applied to acquire the shares on the participant's behalf, so far as it represents a cash dividend paid in respect of plan shares in a UK resident company.

[(3A) But if the shares cease to be subject to the plan by virtue of a provision of the kind mentioned in paragraph 65(2) of Schedule 2 to ITEPA 2003 (provision requiring dividend shares to be offered for sale), the amount of the distribution treated as made is the amount equal to the relevant fraction of the market value of the shares at the time they are offered for sale if that amount is less than the amount given by subsection (3).

(3B) For the purposes of subsection (3A) "the relevant fraction" is—

   A / B

   where—

      A is so much of the amount of the cash dividend applied to acquire the shares on the participant's behalf as represents a cash dividend paid in respect of plan shares in a UK resident company, and

      B is the amount of the cash dividend applied to acquire the shares on the participant's behalf.

(3C) Paragraph 92(2) of Schedule 2 to ITEPA 2003 (market value of shares subject to a restriction) applies for the purposes of subsection (3A).][1]

(4) The person liable for any tax charged on the distribution as a result of this section is the participant.

(5) . . . [2]

(6) [For][2] the purposes of this Chapter, the question whether the distribution under subsection (2) is a distribution by a company that is UK resident is determined by reference to the year in which the company paid the dividend applied to acquire the shares on the participant's behalf.

(7) For rules identifying shares ceasing to be subject to [Schedule 2][1] share incentive plans, see section 508 of ITEPA 2003.

Commentary—*Simon's Taxes* **E1.419.**

HMRC Manuals—Savings and Investment Manual SAIM5080 (shares cease to be subject to the SIP).

Amendments—[1]   In sub-s (1) words substituted for words "an approved", sub-ss (3A)–(3C) inserted, and in sub-s (7) words substituted for word "approved", by FA 2014 s 51, Sch 8 paras 53, 57 with effect from 6 April 2014. The effect of the FA 2014 changes on SIPs established before 6 April 2014 is set out in FA 2014 Sch 8 paras 91 to 96.

[2]   Sub-s (5) repealed, and word in sub-s (6) substituted, by FA 2016 s 5, Sch 1 paras 2, 7 with effect in relation to dividends paid or arising (or treated as paid), and other distributions made (or treated as made), in the tax year 2016-17 or at any later time.

395 Reduction in tax due in cases within section 394

(1) This section applies if—

   (*a*) a person is liable to tax as a result of section 394, and

   (*b*) any tax is paid on any capital receipts under section 501 of ITEPA 2003 (charge on capital receipts in respect of plan shares) in respect of the shares that cease to be subject to the [Schedule 2][1] share incentive plan.

(2) The tax due is to be reduced by an amount equal to the total tax so paid.

(3) In subsection (2) "the tax due" means the amount of tax due as a result of section 394 . . . [2].

(4) For rules identifying shares ceasing to be subject to [Schedule 2][1] share incentive plans, see section 508 of ITEPA 2003.

Commentary—*Simon's Taxes* **E1.419.**

HMRC Manuals—Savings and Investment Manual SAIM5080 (reduction in tax due).

Amendments—[1]   In sub-ss (1)(*b*), (4) words substituted for word "approved" by FA 2014 s 51, Sch 8 paras 53, 58 with effect from 6 April 2014. The effect of the FA 2014 changes on SIPs established before 6 April 2014 is set out in FA 2014 Sch 8 paras 91 to 96.

[2]   In sub-s (3), words repealed by FA 2016 s 5, Sch 1 paras 2, 8 with effect in relation to dividends paid or arising (or treated as paid), and other distributions made (or treated as made), in the tax year 2016-17 or at any later time.

396 Interpretation of sections 392 to 395

(1) This section and sections 392 to 395 form part of the SIP code (see section 488 of ITEPA 2003 (. . . .[1] share incentive plans)).

(2) Accordingly, expressions used in this section or those sections and contained in the index in paragraph 100 of Schedule 2 to that Act (. . . .[1] share incentive plans) have the meaning indicated by that index.

(3) In particular—

    (*a*) for the meaning of "award of shares" see paragraph 5(1) of that Schedule,

    (*b*) for the meaning of "ceasing to be subject to plan" see paragraph 97 of that Schedule,

    (*c*) for the meaning of "dividend shares" see paragraph 62(3)(*b*) of that Schedule,

    (*d*) for the meaning of "employment requirement" see paragraph 15(3) of that Schedule,

    (*e*) for the meaning of "participant" see paragraph 5(4) of that Schedule,

    (*f*) for the meaning of "plan shares" see paragraphs 86 to 88 and 99(1) of that Schedule, and

    (*g*) for the meaning of "shares" see paragraphs 87(6) and 99(2) of that Schedule.

Amendments—[1]   In sub-ss (1), (2) words "approved" repealed by FA 2014 s 51, Sch 8 paras 53, 59 with effect from 6 April 2014. The effect of the FA 2014 changes on SIPs established before 6 April 2014 is set out in FA 2014 Sch 8 paras 91 to 96.

[Other amounts treated as distributions]

396A Arrangements offering a choice of capital or income return

(1) Subsection (2) applies if a person ("S") has a choice either—

    (*a*) to receive what would (ignoring this section) be a distribution of a company, or

    (*b*) to receive from that company, or from a third party, anything else ("the alternative receipt") which—

        (i) is of the same or substantially the same value, and

        (ii) (ignoring this section) would not be charged to income tax.

(2) If S chooses the alternative receipt—

    (*a*) for income tax purposes it is treated as a distribution made to S by that company in the tax year in which it is received by S, and

    [(*b*) for the purposes of sections 1100 to 1103 of CTA 2010 (statements and returns of details of distributions) it is treated as a distribution that—

        (i) is so made, and

        (ii) is one to which section 1100 of CTA 2010 applies.][2]

(3) For the purposes of this section—

    (*a*) it does not matter if the choice mentioned in subsection (1) is subject to any conditions being met or to the exercise of any power;

    (*b*) where S is offered one thing subject to a right, however expressed, to choose another instead, S is to be regarded as making a choice if S abandons or fails to exercise such a right.

(4) If at any time a tax other than income tax ("the other tax") is charged in relation to the alternative receipt, in order to avoid a double charge to tax in respect of that receipt, a person may make a claim for one or more consequential adjustments to be made in respect of the other tax.

(5) On a claim under subsection (4) an officer of Revenue and Customs must make such of the consequential adjustments claimed (if any) as are just and reasonable.

(6) Consequential adjustments may be made—

    (*a*) in respect of any period,

    (*b*) by way of an assessment, the modification of an assessment, the amendment of a claim, or otherwise, and

    (*c*) despite any time limit imposed by or under an enactment.][1]

Amendments—[1]   Section 396A inserted by FA 2015 s 19(1), (2) with effect in relation to things received on or after 6 April 2015 (even if the choice to receive them was made before that date).

[2]   Sub-s (2)(*b*) substituted by FA 2016 s 5, Sch 1 paras 2, 9 with effect in relation to things received on or after 6 April 2016 (even if the choice to receive them was made before that date).

[396B Distributions in a winding up

(1) For the purposes of this Chapter, a distribution made to an individual in respect of share capital in the winding up of a UK resident company is a distribution of the company if—

    (*a*) Conditions A to D are met, and

    (*b*) the distribution is not excluded (see subsection (7)).

(2) Condition A is that, immediately before the winding up, the individual has at least a 5% interest in the company.

(3) Condition B is that the company—

    (*a*) is a close company when it is wound up, or

    (*b*) was a close company at any time in the period of two years ending with the start of the winding up.

(4) Condition C is that, at any time within the period of two years beginning with the date on which the distribution is made—

    (*a*) the individual carries on a trade or activity which is the same as, or similar to, that carried on by the company or an effective 51% subsidiary of the company,

    (*b*) the individual is a partner in a partnership which carries on such a trade or activity,

    (*c*) the individual, or a person connected with him or her, is a participator in a company in which he or she has at least a 5% interest and which at that time—

        (i) carries on such a trade or activity, or

        (ii) is connected with a company which carries on such a trade or activity, or

    (*d*) the individual is involved with the carrying on of such a trade or activity by a person connected with the individual.

(5) Condition D is that it is reasonable to assume, having regard to all the circumstances, that—

    (*a*) the main purpose or one of the main purposes of the winding up is the avoidance or reduction of a charge to income tax, or

    (*b*) the winding up forms part of arrangements the main purpose or one of the main purposes of which is the avoidance or reduction of a charge to income tax.

(6) The circumstances referred to in subsection (5) include in particular the fact that Condition C is met.

(7) A distribution to an individual is excluded if or to the extent that—

    (*a*) the amount of the distribution does not exceed the amount that would result in no gain accruing for the purposes of capital gains tax, or

    (*b*) the distribution is a distribution of irredeemable shares.

(8) In this section—

    "arrangements" includes any agreement, understanding, scheme, transaction or series of transactions, whether or not legally enforceable;

    "effective 51% subsidiary" has the meaning given by section 170(7) of TCGA 1992;

    "participator" has the meaning given by section 454 of CTA 2010.

(9) For the purposes of this section, an individual has at least a 5% interest in a company if—

    (*a*) at least 5% of the ordinary share capital of the company is held by the individual, and

    (*b*) at least 5% of the voting rights in the company are exercisable by the individual by virtue of that holding.

(10) For the purposes of subsection (9) if an individual holds any shares in a company jointly or in common with one or more other persons, he or she is to be treated as sole holder of so many of them as is proportionate to the value of his or her share (and as able to exercise voting rights by virtue of that holding).][1]

Amendments—[1]   Section 396B inserted by FA 2016 s 35(1) with effect in relation to distributions made on or after 6 April 2016.

           . . . . *Payment and deduction of tax*

Amendments—Words in heading repealed by FA 2016 s 5, Sch 1 paras 2, 10 with effect in relation to dividends paid or arising (or treated as paid), and other distributions made (or treated as made), in the tax year 2016-17 or at any later time.

399 [Tax treated as paid on distributions received by non-UK resident persons]

[(1) This section applies if—

    (*a*) a person's income for a tax year includes a distribution of a company, and

    (*b*) the person is non-UK resident.][1]

(2) The person is treated as having paid income tax at the dividend ordinary rate on the amount or value of the distribution . . .[1].

(3)–(5A) . . .[1]

(6) The income tax treated as paid under subsection (2) is not repayable.

(7) . . .[1]

Commentary—*Simon's Taxes* E1.415.

HMRC Manuals—Savings and Investment Manual SAIM5120 (qualifying distributions received by persons not entitled to tax credits).

SAIM5070 (the provisions about tax credits or tax).

SAIM6060 (tax rate on tax credits).

Amendments—[1]   Heading substituted; sub-s (1) substituted; in sub-s (2), words repealed; and sub-ss (3)–(5A), (7) repealed; by FA 2016 s 5, Sch 1 paras 2, 11 with effect in relation to dividends paid or arising (or treated as paid), and other distributions made (or treated as made), in the tax year 2016-17 or at any later time.

401 Relief: [distribution repaying shares or security issued in earlier distribution]

[(1) Where a person is liable to income tax on a CD distribution, the person's liability to income tax on a subsequent non-CD distribution is reduced in accordance with this section if the non-CD distribution consists of a repayment of—

    (*a*) the share capital, or

    (*b*) the principal of the security,

which constituted the CD distribution.

(1A) The reduction is—

    (*a*) the amount of income tax to which the person is liable on the CD distribution, or

    (*b*) if lower, the amount of income tax to which the person is liable on the non-CD distribution.

(1B) For the purposes of calculating the amounts mentioned in subsection (1A)(*a*) and (*b*) assume—

    (*a*) that the CD distribution is the lowest part of the person's dividend income in the tax year ("year 1") in which it is made,

    (*b*) that the non-CD distribution, if it is made in year 1, is the part of the person's dividend income in year 1 that is next lowest after the CD distribution, and

    (*c*) that the non-CD distribution, if it is made after year 1, is the lowest part of the person's dividend income in the tax year in which it is made.][3]

[(6A) The reduction under this section is given effect at Step 6 of the calculation in section 23 of ITA 2007.][1]

(7) In this section [—

    "CD distribution" means a distribution which is a distribution for the purposes of the Corporation Tax Acts only because it falls within paragraph C or D in section 1000(1) of CTA 2010 (redeemable share capital or security issued as bonus in respect of shares in, or securities of, the company),

    "non-CD distribution" means a distribution which is not a CD distribution, and][3]

    "security" has the meaning given in [section 1117(1) of CTA 2010][2].

Commentary—*Simon's Taxes* **E1.415.**

HMRC Manuals—Savings and Investment Manual SAIM5130 (relief for qualifying distribution after linked non-qualifying distribution).

Amendments—[1] Sub-s (6A) inserted by ITA 2007 s 1027, Sch 1 paras 492, 518 with effect for income tax purposes from 6 April 2007, and corporation tax purposes for accounting periods ending after 5 April 2007.

[2] In sub-s (7) words substituted by CTA 2010 s 1177, Sch 1 paras 444, 455. CTA 2010 has effect for corporation tax purposes for accounting periods ending on or after 1 April 2010, and for income and capital gains tax purposes for the tax year 2010–11 and subsequent tax years.

[3] In heading, words substituted; sub-ss (1), (1A), (1B) substituted for previous sub-ss (1)–(6); and in sub-s (7), definitions of "CD distribution" and "non-CD distribution" inserted; by FA 2016 s 5, Sch 1 paras 2, 12 with effect where the subsequent distribution is made in the tax year 2016-17 or at any later time, even if the prior distribution is made before 6 April 2016.

[401B Power to obtain information

(1) An officer of Revenue and Customs may, for the purposes of [this Chapter][2], by notice require any person in whose name any shares or loan capital are registered—

    (*a*) to state whether or not that person is the beneficial owner of the shares or loan capital, and

    (*b*) if that person is not the beneficial owner of the shares or loan capital, to provide the name and address of the person on whose behalf the shares or loan capital are registered in that person's name.

(2) Subsections (3) and (4) apply if a company ("the issuing company") appears to an officer of Revenue and Customs to be a close company.

(3) The officer may, for the purposes of [this Chapter][2], by notice require the issuing company to provide the officer with—

    (*a*) particulars of any bearer securities issued by the company,

    (*b*) the names and addresses of the persons to whom the securities were issued, and

    (*c*) details of the amounts issued to each person.

(4) The officer may, for the purposes of [this Chapter][2], by notice require—

    (*a*) any person to whom bearer securities were issued by the company, or

    (*b*) any person to or through whom bearer securities issued by the company were subsequently sold or transferred,

to provide any further information that the officer reasonably requires with a view to enabling the officer to find out the names and addresses of the persons beneficially interested in the securities.

(5) In this section—

    "loan creditor" has the meaning given by section 453 of CTA 2010, and

    "securities" includes—

    (*a*) shares, stocks, bonds, debentures and debenture stock, and

    (*b*) any promissory note or other instrument evidencing indebtedness to a loan creditor of the company.][1]

Amendments—[1] Section 401B inserted by CTA 2010 s 1177, Sch 1 paras 444, 457. CTA 2010 has effect for corporation tax purposes for accounting periods ending on or after 1 April 2010, and for income and capital gains tax purposes for the tax year 2010–11 and subsequent tax years.

[2] In sub-ss (1), (3) and (4), words substituted by FA 2016 s 5, Sch 1 paras 2, 14 with effect from 15 September 2016.

[Anti-avoidance

401C Temporary non-residents

(1) This section applies if—

    (*a*) an individual is temporarily non-resident,

    (*b*) a relevant distribution is made or treated as made to the individual in the temporary period of non-residence,

    (*c*) the tax year in which it is made or treated as made ("the distribution year") is a tax year for which the individual is UK resident, and (*d*) the amount of income tax charged on the distribution under this Chapter is less than it would have been if the existence of double taxation relief arrangements were disregarded.

(2) Subsections (3) and (4) have effect in cases where the distribution year is not the year of return.

(3) The total income (see Step 1 of the calculation in section 23 of ITA 2007) on which the individual is charged to income tax for the year of return is to be increased by an amount equal to the amount on which tax would be charged under this Chapter in respect of the distribution disregarding any double taxation relief arrangements.

(4) But the notional UK tax on that distribution is to be allowed as a credit against the individual's liability to income tax for the year of return under Step 6 of the calculation in section 23.

(5) If the distribution year is the year of return, the tax charged under this Chapter in respect of the relevant distribution is to be charged and assessed without regard to the existence of double taxation relief arrangements.

(6) For the purposes of this section, a dividend or other distribution is a "relevant distribution" if—
   (*a*) it is a dividend or other distribution of a close company, and
   (*b*) it is made or treated as made to the individual because the individual was at a relevant time—
      (i) a material participator in the company, or
      (ii) an associate of a material participator in the company.

(7) But a dividend or other distribution within subsection (6) in the form of a cash dividend is not a "relevant distribution" to the extent that the dividend is paid in respect of post-departure trade profits.

(8) "Post-departure trade profits" are—
   (*a*) trade profits of the close company arising in an accounting period that begins after the start of the temporary period of non-residence, and
   (*b*) so much of any trade profits of the close company arising in an accounting period that straddles the start of that temporary period as is attributable (on a just and reasonable basis) to a time after the start of that temporary period.

(9) The extent to which a dividend is paid in respect of post-departure trade profits is to be determined on a just and reasonable basis.

(10) The "notional UK tax" on the relevant distribution is so much of the income tax paid by the individual for the distribution year as is attributable on a just and reasonable basis to the relevant distribution.

(11) If section 393 applies, references in this section to a distribution being made to the individual are to a cash dividend being paid over to the individual.

(12) In this section—
   "associate" and "participator" have the same meanings as in Part 10 of CTA 2010 (see sections 448 and 454);
   "material participator" means a participator who has a material interest in the company, as defined in section 457 of that Act;
   "relevant time" means—
      (*a*) any time in the year of departure or, if the year of departure is a split year as respects the individual, the UK part of that year, or
      (*b*) any time in one or more of the 3 tax years preceding that year;
   "trade profits of the close company" means the profits of any trade carried on by the close company, as calculated in accordance with Part 3 of CTA 2009 (trading income).][1]

Commentary—*Simon's Taxes* **E1.415A.**
HMRC Manuals—Capital Gains Manual CG26100 (temporary non-residents: content sheet).
Amendments—[1]   Section 401C and preceding heading inserted by FA 2013 s 218, Sch 45 paras 131, 133 with effect if the year of departure (as defined in FA 2013 Sch 45 Pt 4) is the tax year 2013–14 or any subsequent tax year, subject to transitional provisions and savings in FA 2013 Sch 45 paras 154–158.

CHAPTER 4

DIVIDENDS FROM NON-UK RESIDENT COMPANIES

Charge to tax on dividends from non-UK resident companies

402 Charge to tax on dividends from non-UK resident companies

(1) Income tax is charged on dividends of a non-UK resident company.

(2) For exemptions, see in particular section 770 (amounts applied by SIP trustees acquiring dividend shares or retained for reinvestment).

(3) Subsection (1) is also subject to section 498 of ITEPA 2003 (no charge on shares ceasing to be subject to SIP in certain circumstances).

(4) In this Chapter "dividends" does not include dividends of a capital nature.

Commentary—*Simon's Taxes* **E1.416.**
HMRC Manuals—Savings and Investment Manual SAIM5210 (dividends from non-UK resident companies).

403 Income charged

(1) Tax is charged under this Chapter on the . . . [1] amount of the dividends arising in the tax year.

(2) Subsection (1) is subject to—

section 406(2) and (3) (later charge where cash dividends retained in SIPs are paid over), section 407(3) (dividend payment when dividend shares cease to be subject to SIP), and Part 8 (foreign income: special rules).

Commentary—*Simon's Taxes* E1.416.

HMRC Manuals—Savings and Investment Manual SAIM5210 (dividends from non-UK resident companies: income charged to tax).

SAIM5020 (the charge to tax on UK dividends).

Amendments—[1]   Word in sub-s (1) repealed by FA 2008 s 34, Sch 12 paras 17, 18 with effect for the tax year 2008–09 and subsequent tax years.

404 Person liable

(1) The person liable for any tax charged under this Chapter is the person receiving or entitled to the dividends.

(2) Subsection (1) is subject to—

section 406(4) (later charge where cash dividends retained in SIPs are paid over), and

section 407(4) (dividend payment when dividend shares cease to be subject to SIP).

Commentary—*Simon's Taxes* E1.416.

HMRC Manuals—Savings and Investment Manual SAIM2400 (taxation of the tax charge).

SAIM2410 (taxation of person chargeable: examples).

[404A Distributions in a winding up

(1) For the purposes of this Chapter, a distribution made to an individual in respect of share capital in a winding up of a non-UK resident company is a dividend of the company if—

   (a) Conditions A to D are met, and

   (b) the distribution is not excluded (see subsection (7)).

(2) Condition A is that, immediately before the winding up, the individual has at least a 5% interest in the company.

(3) Condition B is that the company—

   (a) is a close company when it is wound up, or

   (b) was a close company at any time in the period of two years ending with the start of the winding up.

(4) Condition C is that, at any time within the period of two years beginning with the date on which the distribution is made—

   (a) the individual carries on a trade or activity which is the same as, or similar to, that carried on by the company or an effective 51% subsidiary of the company,

   (b) the individual is a partner in a partnership which carries on such a trade or activity,

   (c) the individual, or a person connected with him or her, is a participator in a company in which he or she has at least a 5% interest and which at that time—

      (i) carries on such a trade or activity, or

      (ii) is connected with a company which carries on such a trade or activity, or

   (d) the individual is involved with the carrying on of such a trade or activity by a person connected with the individual.

(5) Condition D is that it is reasonable to assume, having regard to all the circumstances, that—

   (a) the main purpose or one of the main purposes of the winding up is the avoidance or reduction of a charge to income tax, or

   (b) the winding up forms part of arrangements the main purpose or one of the main purposes of which is the avoidance or reduction of a charge to income tax.

(6) The circumstances referred to in subsection (5) include in particular the fact that Condition C is met.

(7) A distribution to an individual is excluded if or to the extent that—

   (a) the amount of the distribution does not exceed the amount that would result in no gain accruing for the purposes of capital gains tax, or

   (b) the distribution is a distribution of irredeemable shares.

(8) In this section—

"arrangements" includes any agreement, understanding, scheme, transaction or series of transactions, whether or not legally enforceable;

"close company" includes a company which would be a close company if it were a UK resident company;

"effective 51% subsidiary" has the meaning given by section 170(7) of TCGA 1992;

"participator" has the meaning given by section 454 of CTA 2010.

(9) For the purposes of this section, a person has at least a 5% interest in a company if—

   (a) at least 5% of the ordinary share capital of the company is held by the individual, and

   (b) at least 5% of the voting rights in the company are exercisable by the individual by virtue of that holding.

(10) For the purposes of subsection (9) if an individual holds any shares in a company jointly or in common with one or more other persons, he or she is to be treated as sole holder of so many of them as is proportionate to the value of his or her share (and as able to exercise voting rights by virtue of that holding).][1]

Amendments—[1] Section 404A inserted by FA 2016 s 35(2) with effect in relation to distributions made on or after 6 April 2016.

Shares in [Schedule 2] share incentive plans ("SIPs")

405 SIP shares: introduction

(1) Sections 406 to 408 contain special rules about the charge under this Chapter in respect of shares awarded to an individual under [a Schedule 2][1] share incentive plan.

(2) Those sections only apply if the condition in section 392(3) or (5) was met at the time the shares in question were so awarded (earnings within ITEPA 2003).

(3) This section and sections 406 to 408 form part of the SIP code (see section 488 of ITEPA 2003 (. . . [1] share incentive plans)).

(4) Accordingly, expressions used in this section or those sections and contained in the index in paragraph 100 of Schedule 2 to that Act (. . . [1] share incentive plans) have the meaning indicated by that index.

(5) In particular—

    (*a*) for the meaning of "award of shares" see paragraph 5(1) of that Schedule,

    (*b*) for the meaning of "ceasing to be subject to plan" see paragraph 97 of that Schedule,

    (*c*) for the meaning of "dividend shares" see paragraph 62(3)(*b*) of that Schedule,

    (*d*) for the meaning of "participant" see paragraph 5(4) of that Schedule,

    (*e*) for the meaning of "plan shares" see paragraphs 86 to 88 and 99(1) of that Schedule, and

    (*f*) for the meaning of "shares" see paragraphs 87(6) and 99(2) of that Schedule.

Commentary—*Simon's Taxes* **E1.417.**

HMRC Manuals—Savings and Investment Manual SAIM5080 (dividends from share incentive plans).

Amendments—[1] In cross-heading words substituted for word "approved", in sub-s (1) words substituted for words "an approved", and in sub-ss (3), (4) word "approved" repealed, by FA 2014 s 51, Sch 8 paras 60, 61, 62 with effect from 6 April 2014. The effect of the FA 2014 changes on SIPs established before 6 April 2014 is set out in FA 2014 Sch 8 paras 91 to 96.

406 Later charge where cash dividends retained in SIPs are paid over

(1) This section applies if a cash dividend is paid over to a participant under paragraph 68(4) of Schedule 2 to ITEPA 2003 (cash dividend paid over if not reinvested etc.).

(2) Tax charged under this Chapter is charged for the tax year in which the cash dividend is paid over instead of the tax year in which in which it was originally paid.

(3) Tax so charged is charged on the amount of the cash dividend paid over.

(4) The person liable for any tax so charged is the participant.

(4A) . . . [1]

(5) For the purposes of this Chapter, the question whether a cash dividend so paid over is a dividend paid by a company that is non-UK resident is determined by reference to the tax year in which the dividend was originally paid.

Amendments—[1] Sub-s (4A) repealed by FA 2016 s 5, Sch 1 paras 2, 15 with effect in relation to cash dividends paid over in the tax year 2016-17 or at any later time.

407 Dividend payment when dividend shares cease to be subject to SIP

(1) This section applies if dividend shares cease to be subject to [a Schedule 2][1] share incentive plan before the end of the period of 3 years beginning with the date on which the shares were acquired on the participant's behalf.

(2) For income tax purposes a dividend is treated as paid to the participant in the tax year in which the shares cease to be subject to the plan.

(3) The amount of the dividend treated as paid is the amount of the cash dividend applied to acquire the shares on the participant's behalf, so far as it represents a cash dividend paid in respect of plan shares in a non-UK resident company.

[(3A) But if the shares cease to be subject to the plan by virtue of a provision of the kind mentioned in paragraph 65(2) of Schedule 2 to ITEPA 2003 (provision requiring dividend shares to be offered for sale), the amount of the dividend treated as paid is the amount equal to the relevant fraction of the market value of the shares at the time they are offered for sale if that amount is less than the amount given by subsection (3).

(3B) For the purposes of subsection (3A) "the relevant fraction" is—

    A / B

    where—

            A is so much of the amount of the cash dividend applied to acquire the shares on the participant's behalf as represents a cash dividend paid in respect of plan shares in a non-UK resident company, and

ITTOIA 2005

B is the amount of the cash dividend applied to acquire the shares on the participant's behalf.

(3C) Paragraph 92(2) of Schedule 2 to ITEPA 2003 (market value of shares subject to a restriction) applies for the purposes of subsection (3A).][1]

(4) The person liable for any tax charged as a result of this section is the participant.

(4A) . . . [2]

(5) For rules identifying shares ceasing to be subject to [Schedule 2][1] share incentive plans, see section 508 of ITEPA 2003.

Commentary—*Simon's Taxes* E1.419.

Amendments—[1]   In sub-s (1) words substituted for words "an approved", sub-ss (3A)–(3C) inserted, and in sub-s (5) words substituted for word "approved", by FA 2014 s 51, Sch 8 paras 60, 63 with effect from 6 April 2014. The effect of the FA 2014 changes on SIPs established before 6 April 2014 is set out in FA 2014 Sch 8 paras 91 to 96.

[2]   Sub-s (4A) repealed by FA 2016 s 5, Sch 1 paras 2, 15 with effect in relation to dividends paid or arising (or treated as paid), and other distributions made (or treated as made), in the tax year 2016-17 or at any later time.

408 Reduction in tax due in cases within section 407

(1) This section applies if—

  (*a*) a person is liable for tax as a result of section 407, and

  (*b*) any tax is paid on any capital receipts under section 501 of ITEPA 2003 (charge on capital receipts in respect of plan shares) in respect of the shares that cease to be subject to the [Schedule 2][2] share incentive plan.

(2) The tax due as a result of section 407 is to be reduced by an amount equal to the total tax so paid.

[(2A) In subsection (2) "the tax due" means the amount of tax due as a result of section 407 . . . [3]][1]

(3) For rules identifying shares ceasing to be subject to [Schedule 2][2] share incentive plans, see section 508 of ITEPA 2003.

Amendments—[1]   Sub-s (2A) inserted by FA 2008 s 34, Sch 12 paras 17, 21 with effect for the tax year 2008–09 and subsequent tax years.

[2]   In sub-ss (1)(*b*), (3) words substituted for word "approved" by FA 2014 s 51, Sch 8 paras 60, 64 with effect from 6 April 2014. The effect of the FA 2014 changes on SIPs established before 6 April 2014 is set out in FA 2014 Sch 8 paras 91 to 96.

[3]   In sub-s (2A), words repealed by FA 2016 s 5, Sch 1 paras 2, 16 with effect in relation to dividends paid or arising (or treated as paid), and other distributions made (or treated as made), in the tax year 2016-17 or at any later time.

[Anti-avoidance

408A Temporary non-residents

(1) This section applies if an individual is temporarily non-resident.

(2) Dividends within subsection (3) are to be treated for the purposes of this Chapter as if they were received by the individual, or as if the individual became entitled to them, in the period of return.

(3) A dividend is within this subsection if—

  (*a*) the individual receives or becomes entitled to it in the temporary period of non-residence,

  (*b*) it is a dividend of a company that would be a close company if the company were UK resident,

  (*c*) the individual receives or becomes entitled to it by virtue of being at a relevant time—

    (i) a material participator in the company, or

    (ii) an associate of a material participator in the company, and

  (*d*) ignoring this section, the individual—

    (i) is not liable for tax under this Chapter in respect of the dividend, but

    (ii) would have been so liable if the individual had received the dividend, or become entitled to it, in the period of return.

(4) For the purposes of subsection (3)—

  (*a*) "associate" and "participator" have the same meanings as in Part 10 of CTA 2010 (see sections 448 and 454),

  (*b*) a "material participator" is a participator who has a material interest in the company, as defined in section 457 of that Act,

  (*c*) "relevant time" means—

    (i) any time in the year of departure or, if the year of departure is a split year as respects the individual, the UK part of that year, or

    (ii) any time in one or more of the 3 tax years preceding that year, and

  (*d*) paragraph (*d*)(i) includes a case where the individual could be relieved of liability on the making of a claim under section 6 of TIOPA 2010 (double taxation relief), even if no claim is in fact made.

(5) If section 809B, 809D or 809E of ITA 2007 (remittance basis) applies to the individual for the year of return, any dividend within subsection (3) that was remitted to the United Kingdom in the temporary period of non-residence is to be treated as remitted to the United Kingdom in the period of return.

(6) This section does not apply to a dividend within subsection (3) to the extent that it is paid in respect of post-departure trade profits.

(7) "Post-departure trade profits" are—

   (a) trade profits of the company arising in an accounting period that begins after the start of the temporary period of non-residence, and

   (b) so much of any trade profits of the company arising in an accounting period that straddles the start of that temporary period as is attributable (on a just and reasonable basis) to a time after the start of that temporary period.

(8) The extent to which a dividend is paid in respect of post-departure trade profits is to be determined on a just and reasonable basis.

(9) If section 406 or 407 applies, references in this section to a dividend being received by the individual are to a cash dividend being paid over to the individual or (as the case may be) a dividend being treated as paid to the individual.

(10) In this section—

    "remitted to the United Kingdom" has the meaning given in Chapter A1 of Part 14 of ITA 2007;

    "trade profits of the company" means the profits of any trade carried on by the company, as they would be calculated in accordance with Part 3 of CTA 2009 (trading income) if the company were UK resident.][1]

Commentary—*Simon's Taxes* **E1.415A.**

Amendments—[1]   Section 408A and preceding heading inserted by FA 2013 s 218, Sch 45 paras 131, 134 with effect if the year of departure (as defined in FA 2013 Sch 45 Pt 4) is the tax year 2013–14 or any subsequent tax year, subject to transitional provisions and savings in FA 2013 Sch 45 paras 154–158.

CHAPTER 5

STOCK DIVIDENDS FROM UK RESIDENT COMPANIES

409 Charge to tax on stock dividend income

(1) Income tax is charged on stock dividend income.

(2) In this Chapter "stock dividend income" means the income that is treated as arising under section 410.

Commentary—*Simon's Taxes* **E1.420, E1.421.**

HMRC Manuals—Savings and Investment Manual SAIM5150 (stock dividend income: meaning).

410 When stock dividend income arises

[(1) This section applies to—

   (a) share capital issued by a UK resident company in lieu of a cash dividend, and

   (b) bonus share capital issued by a UK resident company in respect of shares in the company of a qualifying class.

(1A) For the purposes of subsection (1)(b), shares are of a qualifying class if—

   (a) shares of that class carry the right to receive bonus share capital in the company (of the same or a different class), and

   (b) that right is conferred by the terms on which shares of that class were originally issued or by those terms as subsequently extended or otherwise varied.][2]

(2) If an individual is beneficially entitled to that share capital, income is treated as arising to the individual.

(3) If—

   (a) the share capital is issued to trustees in respect of shares they hold in the company (alone or with others), and

   (b) a cash dividend paid to them in respect of the shares would have been to any extent [accumulated or discretionary income (as defined in section 480 of ITA 2007 but excluding income arising under a [charitable trust][3] or an unauthorised unit trust in relation to which [regulation 12 of the Unauthorised Unit Trusts (Tax) Regulations 2013][4] applies)][1],

income is treated as arising to the trustees.

(4) If the share capital is issued to personal representatives during the administration period, income is treated as arising (but see section 413(4)).

(5) In subsection (4) "administration period" has the meaning given by section 653.

(6) Income within this section is treated as arising on the earliest date on which the company is required to issue the share capital in question.

(7) See section 413(5) (apportionment) if two or more persons are entitled to the share capital.

[(8) There are special rules in paragraph 78A of Schedule 2 for share capital issued in respect of shares issued before 6 April 1975.][2]

Commentary—*Simon's Taxes* **D6.243.**

HMRC Manuals—Savings and Investment Manual SAIM5150 (stock dividends: rights to receive bonus share capital).

SAIM5160 (stock dividends: the tax charge).

SAIM5170 (stock dividends: the tax charge: cash equivalent).

Amendments—[1]   Words in sub-s (3) substituted by ITA 2007 s 1027, Sch 1 paras 492, 519 with effect for income tax purposes from 6 April 2007, and corporation tax purposes for accounting periods ending after 5 April 2007.

[2]   Sub-ss (1), (1A) substituted for former sub-s (1), sub-s (8) inserted by CTA 2010 s 1177, Sch 1 paras 444, 458. CTA 2010 has effect for corporation tax purposes for accounting periods ending on or after 1 April 2010, and for income and capital gains tax purposes for the tax year 2010–11 and subsequent tax years.

[3]   In sub-s (3)(b) words substituted by FA 2010 s 30, Sch 6 para 21(1), (2) with effect for the tax year 2012–13 and subsequent tax years (SI 2012/736 art 15).

[4]   In sub-s (3), words substituted for words "section 504 of that Act" by the Unauthorised Unit Trusts (Tax) Regulations, SI 2013/2819 reg 36(1), (7) with effect from 6 April 2014. Note that an unauthorised unit trust is not a non-exempt unauthorised unit trust, and these amendments do not apply in relation to the trust, if at all times in the period beginning with 24 May 2012 and ending with 5 April 2014 it had at least one unit holder which was, and at least one unit holder which was not, an eligible investor (ie a mixed unauthorised unit trust); this ceases to apply in relation to the trust if subsequently it no longer has any unit holders which are eligible investors (SI 2013/2819 reg 32).

[410A Conversion etc of bonus share capital

(1) This section applies if bonus share capital falling within section 410(1)(b) is converted into, or exchanged for, shares in the company of a different class.

(2) Section 410 does not apply to any shares in the company issued—

    (a) in connection with the conversion or exchange, and

    (b) in consideration of the cancellation, extinguishment or acquisition by the company of the bonus share capital.]

Amendments—Section 410A inserted by CTA 2010 s 1177, Sch 1 paras 444, 459. CTA 2010 has effect for corporation tax purposes for accounting periods ending on or after 1 April 2010, and for income and capital gains tax purposes for the tax year 2010–11 and subsequent tax years.

411 Income charged

(1) Tax is charged under this Chapter on the amount of stock dividend income treated for income tax purposes as arising in the tax year.

(2) That amount is the cash equivalent of the share capital on the issue of which the stock dividend income arises (see section 412) . . . [1].

Commentary—*Simon's Taxes* D6.243.

HMRC Manuals—Savings and Investment Manual SAIM5160 (stock dividends: the tax charge).

Amendments—[1] In sub-s (2), words repealed by FA 2016 s 5, Sch 1 paras 2, 17 with effect in relation to stock dividend income treated as arising in the tax year 2016-17 or at any later time.

412 Cash equivalent of share capital

(1) The cash equivalent of share capital [issued as mentioned in section 410(1)(a) is the amount of the cash dividend alternative (see section 414A(2)).][1]

(2) But if the difference between the cash dividend alternative and the share capital's market value equals or exceeds 15% of that market value—

    (a) subsection (1) does not apply, and

    (b) the cash equivalent of the share capital is its market value.

(3) The cash equivalent of share capital [issued as mentioned in section 410(1)(b)][1] is its market value.

(4) For the purposes of this section, market value is determined—

    (a) in the case of listed share capital, on the date of first dealing, and

    (b) in the case of other share capital, on the earliest date on which the company is required to issue it.

(5) In this section—

    "listed" means listed in the Stock Exchange Daily Official List, and

    "market value" has the same meaning as in sections 272(1) and (3) and 273(3) of TCGA 1992.

Commentary—*Simon's Taxes* D6.243.

HMRC Manuals—Savings and Investment Manual SAIM5170 (stock dividends: meaning of cash equivalent).

Amendments—[1] In sub-ss (1), (3) words substituted by CTA 2010 s 1177, Sch 1 paras 444, 460. CTA 2010 has effect for corporation tax purposes for accounting periods ending on or after 1 April 2010, and for income and capital gains tax purposes for the tax year 2010–11 and subsequent tax years.

413 Person liable

(1) The person liable for any tax charged under this Chapter is the person indicated by this section.

(2) If section 410(2) applies, the individual is liable for the tax.

(3) If section 410(3) applies, the trustees are liable for the tax.

(4) If section 410(4) applies, tax is not charged under this Chapter, but see—

    (a) section 664 (under which the income treated as arising to the personal representatives under section 410 is treated as part of the aggregate income of the estate for the purposes of Chapter 6 of Part 5), and

    [(b) section 947 of CTA 2009 (under which similar provision is made for the purposes of Chapter 3 of Part 10 of that Act).][1]

(5) If two or more persons are entitled to the share capital on the issue of which the stock dividend income arises, this Chapter applies as if the company issuing it had issued to each of those persons a proportionate part of the share capital.

(6) In subsection (5) "proportionate part" means a part proportionate to the person's interest on the earliest date on which the company is required to issue the share capital.

Commentary—*Simon's Taxes* **D6.243.**
HMRC Manuals—Savings and Investment Manual SAIM5160 (stock dividends: the person liable for the tax).
Amendments—[1] Sub-s (4)(*b*) substituted by CTA 2009 s 1322, Sch 1 paras 587, 630. CTA 2009 applies for accounting periods ending on or after 1 April 2009 (for corporation tax purposes) and for tax years 2009–10 onwards (for income and capital gains tax purposes).

[413A Temporary non-residents

(1) This section applies if—

    (*a*) an individual is temporarily non-resident,

    (*b*) relevant stock dividend income is treated under this Chapter as arising to the individual in the temporary period of non-residence,

    (*c*) the tax year in which it is treated as arising ("the arising year") is a tax year for which the individual is UK resident, and

    (*d*) the amount of income tax charged on the relevant stock dividend income under this Chapter is less than it would have been if the existence of double taxation relief arrangements were disregarded.

(2) Subsections (3) and (4) have effect in cases where the arising year is not the year of return.

(3) The total income (see Step 1 of the calculation in section 23 of ITA 2007) on which the individual is charged to income tax for the year of return is to be increased by an amount equal to the amount on which tax would be charged under this Chapter in respect of the relevant stock dividend income disregarding any double taxation relief arrangements.

(4) But the notional UK tax on that relevant stock dividend income is to be allowed as a credit against the individual's liability to income tax for the year of return under Step 6 of the calculation in section 23.

(5) If the arising year is the year of return, the tax charged under this Chapter in respect of the relevant stock dividend income is to be charged and assessed without regard to the existence of double taxation relief arrangements.

(6) Stock dividend income is "relevant stock dividend income" if—

    (*a*) the UK resident company that issues the share capital or bonus share capital is a close company, and

    (*b*) the individual is beneficially entitled to that share capital or bonus share capital by virtue of being at a relevant time—

        (i) a material participator in the company, or

        (ii) an associate of a material participator in the company.

(7) But stock dividend income within subsection (6) is not "relevant stock dividend income" to the extent that the share capital or bonus share capital is issued in respect of post-departure trade profits.

(8) "Post-departure trade profits" are—

    (*a*) trade profits of the close company arising in an accounting period that begins after the start of the temporary period of non-residence, and

    (*b*) so much of any trade profits of the close company arising in an accounting period that straddles the start of that temporary period as is attributable (on a just and reasonable basis) to a time after the start of that temporary period.

(9) The extent to which share capital or bonus share capital is issued in respect of post-departure trade profits is to be determined on a just and reasonable basis.

(10) The "notional UK tax" on the relevant stock dividend income is so much of the income tax paid by the individual for the arising year as is attributable on a just and reasonable basis to that income.

(11) In this section—

    "associate" and "participator" have the same meanings as in Part 10 of CTA 2010 (see sections 448 and 454);

    "material participator" means a participator who has a material interest in the company, as defined in section 457 of that Act;

    "relevant time" means—

        (*a*) any time in the year of departure or, if the year of departure is a split year as respects the individual, the UK part of that year, or

        (*b*) any time in one or more of the 3 tax years preceding that year;

    "trade profits of the close company" means the profits of any trade carried on by the close company, as calculated in accordance with Part 3 of CTA 2009 (trading income).][1]

Commentary—*Simon's Taxes* **E1.415A.**
Amendments—[1] Section 413A inserted by FA 2013 s 218, Sch 45 paras 131, 135 with effect if the year of departure (as defined in FA 2013 Sch 45 Pt 4) is the tax year 2013–14 or any subsequent tax year, subject to transitional provisions and savings in FA 2013 Sch 45 paras 154–158.

[414A Interpretation of Chapter

(1) In this Chapter "bonus share capital" means—

    (*a*) share capital issued otherwise than wholly for new consideration, or

    (*b*) the part (if there is such a part) of any share capital so issued that is not properly referable to new consideration.

(2) For the purposes of this Chapter share capital is issued by a company in lieu of a cash dividend if—
  (*a*) it is issued in consequence of the exercise by any person of an option conferred on the person, and
  (*b*) that option is an option to receive, in respect of shares in the company, either a dividend in cash or additional share capital.

(3) For the purposes of subsection (2), an option to receive either a dividend in cash or additional share capital is conferred on a person not only—
  (*a*) if the person is required to choose one or the other, but also
  (*b*) if the person is offered the one subject to a right, however expressed, to choose the other instead.

(4) The reference in subsection (2) to a person's exercise of an option includes a person's abandonment of, or failure to exercise, a right such as is mentioned in subsection (3)(*b*).

(5) In this Chapter "share" includes stock, and any other interest of a member in a company.

(6) If two or more companies enter into arrangements to make distributions to each other's members, all parties concerned (however many) may, for the purposes of this Chapter, be treated as if anything done by any one of those companies had been done by any one of the others.

(7) The following apply in relation to this Chapter as they apply in relation to Part 23 of CTA 2010—
  (*a*) section 1113 ("in respect of shares") of CTA 2010,
  (*b*) section 1115 ("new consideration") of CTA 2010.][1]

Amendments—[1]   Section 414A inserted by CTA 2010 s 1177, Sch 1 paras 444, 461. CTA 2010 has effect for corporation tax purposes for accounting periods ending on or after 1 April 2010, and for income and capital gains tax purposes for the tax year 2010–11 and subsequent tax years.

CHAPTER 6

RELEASE OF LOAN TO PARTICIPATOR IN CLOSE COMPANY

415 Charge to tax under Chapter 6

(1) Income tax is charged if—
  (*a*) a company [is or was chargeable to tax under section 455 of CTA 2010][1] (loans to participators in close companies etc.) in respect of a loan or advance, and
  (*b*) the company releases or writes off the whole or part of the debt in respect of the loan or advance.

(2) Subsection (1) is subject to section 418 (relief where borrowers liable as settlors).

(3) Subsection (4) applies if [, as a result of section 460 of CTA 2010, sections 455 to 459 of that Act have effect][1] as if a loan or advance had been made by a company ("A"), rather than the company ("B") which—
  (*a*) actually made it,
  (*b*) is regarded as having made it under [section 455(4) of that Act][1] (deemed loans where debt incurred or assigned to close company), or
  (*c*) would be so regarded if it were a close company.

(4) If the whole or part of the debt is released or written off by B, for the purposes of subsection (1), A rather than B is treated as releasing it or writing it off.

(5) Expressions used in this Chapter have the same meanings [as they have for the purposes of section 455 of CTA 2010][2].

Amendments—[1]   In sub-s (1)(*a*), (3) words substituted by CTA 2010 s 1177, Sch 1 paras 444, 462. CTA 2010 has effect for corporation tax purposes for accounting periods ending on or after 1 April 2010, and for income and capital gains tax purposes for the tax year 2010–11 and subsequent tax years.
[2]   In sub-s (5), words substituted for words "as if they were in section 419 of ICTA", by the Tax Law Rewrite Acts (Amendment) Order, SI 2013/463 art 8 with effect from 1 April 2013.

416 Income charged

(1) Tax is charged under this Chapter on the . . . [1] amount of the debt released or written off in the tax year.

(2) . . . [1]

(3) For the purposes of calculating the total income of the person liable for the tax, the amount charged is treated as income.

(4) This section is subject to section 418 (relief where borrowers liable as settlors).

Commentary—*Simon's Taxes* **E1.425.**
HMRC Manuals—Savings and Investment Manual SAIM5200 (income charged to tax).
Amendments—[1]   Word in sub-s (1), and sub-s (2) repealed by FA 2016 s 5, Sch 1 paras 2, 18 with effect in relation to amounts released or written off in the tax year 2016-17 or at any later time.

417 Person liable

[(1) The person liable for any tax charged under this Chapter is—
  (*a*) in the case of a loan or advance made to a partnership, any partner who is an individual, and
  (*b*) in any other case, the person to whom the loan or advance was made.

(1A) If more than one person is liable in a case within subsection (1)(*a*), the liability is to be apportioned between them in a just and reasonable manner.][2]

(2) This is subject to—

section 419 (loans and advances to persons who die), and

section 420 (loans and advances to [trustees of settlements][1] that have ended).

Commentary—*Simon's Taxes* E1.425.

HMRC Manuals—Company Taxation Manual CTM61655 (close companies: loans to participators: release or writing off of loan or advance).

Amendments—[1]   Words in sub-s (2) substituted by FA 2006 s 89, Sch 13 para 31(1) with effect from 6 April 2006 in respect of settlements whenever created, and in respect of loans or advances whenever made.

[2]   Sub-ss (1), (1A) substituted for previous sub-s (1) by FA 2013 s 79, Sch 30 para 14 with effect in relation to loans or advances made on or after 20 March 2013.

418 Relief where borrowers liable as settlors

(1) Relief is given under this section if the person to whom the loan or advance was made—

    (*a*) is liable for the tax year for income tax on a sum in respect of it under Chapter 5 of Part 5 as a result of section 633 (capital sums paid to settlor by trustees of settlement), or

    (*b*) has been so liable for any previous tax year.

(2) If the total amount previously charged (see subsection (4)) equals or exceeds the total amount released (see subsection (6)), tax is not charged under this Chapter.

(3) If the total amount released exceeds the total amount previously charged, tax is charged under this Chapter on the excess . . . .[2].

(4) In this section "the total amount previously charged" means the total of—

    (*a*) the sums included in the person's income under section 633 in respect of the loan or advance for the tax year or for previous tax years, and

    (*b*) the amounts charged under this Chapter in respect of the loan or advance for previous tax years.

(5) For the purposes of subsection (4)(*a*), section 640(1) (which requires the grossing up of the sums treated as paid to the settlor by reference to the [trust rate][1]) is ignored.

(6) In this section "the total amount released" means the total amount released or written off in respect of the loan or advance in the tax year and previous tax years.

Commentary—*Simon's Taxes* E1.427.

HMRC Manuals—Savings and Investment Manual SAIM5200 (relief where borrowers liable as settlors).

Amendments—[1]   Words in sub-s (5) substituted by ITA 2007 s 1027, Sch 1 paras 492, 521 with effect for income tax purposes from 6 April 2007, and corporation tax purposes for accounting periods ending after 5 April 2007.

[2]   Words in sub-s (3) repealed by FA 2016 s 5, Sch 1 paras 2, 19 with effect in relation to amounts released or written off in the tax year 2016-17 or at any later time.

419 Loans and advances to persons who die

(1) This section applies if—

    (*a*) a loan or advance is made to a person who dies,

    (*b*) a company [is or was chargeable to tax under section 455 of CTA 2010 (charge to tax in case of loan to participator)][2] in respect of the loan or advance, and

    (*c*) after the death the company releases or writes off the whole or part of the debt in respect of the loan or advance.

(2) Tax is not charged under this Chapter if at the time of the release or writing off the debt is due from the person's personal representatives in that capacity, but see—

    (*a*) section 664 (under which the amount that would be so charged is treated as part of the aggregate income of the estate for the purposes of Chapter 6 of Part 5), and

    [(*b*) section 947 of CTA 2009 (under which similar provision is made for the purposes of Chapter 3 of Part 10 of that Act).][1]

(3) If subsection (2) does not apply, tax is charged under this Chapter on the person from whom the debt is due at the time of release or writing off.

Commentary—*Simon's Taxes* E1.425.

HMRC Manuals—Savings and Investment Manual SAIM5200 (rules on the taxation of beneficiaries where loans and advances to persons die).

Amendments—[1]   Sub-s (2)(*b*) substituted by CTA 2009 s 1322, Sch 1 paras 587, 631. CTA 2009 applies for accounting periods ending on or after 1 April 2009 (for corporation tax purposes) and for tax years 2009–10 onwards (for income and capital gains tax purposes).

[2]   In sub-s (1)(*b*) words substituted by CTA 2010 s 1177, Sch 1 paras 444, 463. CTA 2010 has effect for corporation tax purposes for accounting periods ending on or after 1 April 2010, and for income and capital gains tax purposes for the tax year 2010–11 and subsequent tax years.

420 Loans and advances to [trustees of settlements][1] that have ended

(1) This section applies if—

    (*a*) a loan or advance is made to trustees of a [settlement][1],

    (*b*) a company [is or was chargeable to tax under section 455 of CTA 2010 (charge to tax in case of loan to participator)][2] in respect of the loan or advance, and

(c) after the [settlement][1] has ended the company releases or writes off the whole or part of the debt in respect of the loan or advance.

(2) Tax is charged under this Chapter on the person from whom the debt is due at the time of release or writing off.

Commentary—*Simon's Taxes* **E1.425.**

Amendments—[1]   Words substituted by FA 2006 s 89, Sch 13 para 31(1) with effect from 6 April 2006 in respect of settlements whenever created, and in respect of loans or advances whenever made. (Note that FA 2006 Sch 13 para 31(1) actually provides for slightly different amendments to language that does not appear in this section; it is presumed that these are minor drafting errors and the publishers have made changes as thought appropriate.)

[2]   In sub-s (1)(b) words substituted by CTA 2010 s 1177, Sch 1 paras 444, 464. CTA 2010 has effect for corporation tax purposes for accounting periods ending on or after 1 April 2010, and for income and capital gains tax purposes for the tax year 2010–11 and subsequent tax years.

[420A Temporary non-residents

(1) This section applies if an individual is temporarily non-resident.

(2) Debts within subsection (3) are to be treated for the purposes of this Chapter as if they had been released or written off in the period of return.

(3) A debt is within this subsection if—

    (a) it is the debt, or a part of the debt, in respect of a loan or advance made by a company to the individual,

    (b) it is released or written off in the temporary period of non-residence, and

    (c) ignoring this section, the individual—

        (i) is not liable for tax under this Chapter in respect of the release or write-off, but

        (ii) would have been so liable, had the release or write-off taken place in the period of return.

(4) Subsection (3)(c)(i) includes a case where the individual could be relieved of liability on the making of a claim under section 6 of TIOPA 2010 (double taxation relief), even if no claim is in fact made.][1]

Commentary—*Simon's Taxes* **E1.425.**

HMRC Manuals—Corporate Taxation Manual CTM61657 (release or writing off of loan or advance while temporarily non-resident).

Amendments—[1]   Section 420A inserted by FA 2013 s 218, Sch 45 paras 131, 136 with effect if the year of departure (as defined in FA 2013 Sch 45 Pt 4) is the tax year 2013–14 or any subsequent tax year, subject to transitional provisions and savings in FA 2013 Sch 45 paras 154–158.

[421A Power to obtain information

(1) An officer of Revenue and Customs may, for the purposes of this Chapter, by notice require any person in whose name any shares or loan capital are registered—

    (a) to state whether or not that person is the beneficial owner of the shares or loan capital, and

    (b) if that person is not the beneficial owner of the shares or loan capital, to provide the name and address of the person on whose behalf the shares or loan capital are registered in that person's name.

(2) Subsections (3) and (4) apply if a company ("the issuing company") appears to an officer of Revenue and Customs to be a close company.

(3) The officer may, for the purposes of this Chapter, by notice require the issuing company to provide the officer with—

    (a) particulars of any bearer securities issued by the company,

    (b) the names and addresses of the persons to whom the securities were issued, and

    (c) details of the amounts issued to each person.

(4) The officer may, for the purposes of this Chapter, by notice require—

    (a) any person to whom bearer securities were issued by the company, or

    (b) any person to or through whom bearer securities issued by the company were subsequently sold or transferred,

to provide any further information that the officer reasonably requires with a view to enabling the officer to find out the names and addresses of the persons beneficially interested in the securities.

(5) In this section—

    "loan creditor" has the meaning given by section 453 of CTA 2010, and

    "securities" includes—

        (a) shares, stocks, bonds, debentures and debenture stock, and

        (b) any promissory note or other instrument evidencing indebtedness to a loan creditor of the company.][1]

Amendments—[1]   Section 421A inserted by CTA 2010 s 1177, Sch 1 paras 444, 465. CTA 2010 has effect for corporation tax purposes for accounting periods ending on or after 1 April 2010, and for income and capital gains tax purposes for the tax year 2010–11 and subsequent tax years.

CHAPTER 7

PURCHASED LIFE ANNUITY PAYMENTS

422 Charge to tax on purchased life annuity payments

(1) Income tax is charged on annuity payments made under a purchased life annuity.

(2) For exemptions, see in particular—

    (*a*) section 717 (exemption for part of purchased life annuity payments),

    (*b*) section 725 (annual payments under immediate needs annuities),

    (*c*) section 731 (periodical payments of personal injury damages), and

    (*d*) section 732 (compensation awards).

Commentary—*Simon's Taxes* **E1.428.**

HMRC Manuals—Insurance Policyholder Taxation Manual IPTM5010 (periodical payments in personal injury cases: introduction and overview).

423 Meaning of "purchased life annuity"

(1) In this Chapter "purchased life annuity" means an annuity—

    (*a*) granted for consideration in money or money's worth in the ordinary course of a business of granting annuities on human life, and

    (*b*) payable for a term ending at a time ascertainable only by reference to the end of a human life.

(2) For this purpose it does not matter that the annuity may in some circumstances end before or after the life.

Commentary—*Simon's Taxes* **E1.428.**

HMRC Manuals—Insurance Policyholder Taxation Manual IPTM1135 (fundamental concepts: what is a purchased life annuity?).

IPTM4220 (purchased life annuity: meaning).

IPTM4370 (purchased life annuities: record-keeping requirements and provision of information to HMRC).

424 Income charged

(1) Tax is charged under this Chapter on the full amount of the annuity payments arising in the tax year.

(2) Subsection (1) is subject to Part 8 (foreign income: special rules).

Commentary—*Simon's Taxes* **E1.428.**

HMRC Manuals—Insurance Policyholder Taxation Manual IPTM4300 (income charged to tax).

425 Person liable

The person liable for any tax charged under this Chapter is the person receiving or entitled to the annuity payments.

Commentary—*Simon's Taxes* **E1.428.**

HMRC Manuals—Insurance Policyholder Taxation Manual IPTM4300 (person liable for tax).

426 Annuity payments received after deduction of tax

[In accordance with section 848 of ITA 2007 a sum representing income tax deducted under section 901 of that Act][1] from an annuity payment within this Chapter is treated as income tax paid by the recipient . . . .[1]

Commentary—*Simon's Taxes* **E1.429.**

Amendments—[1] Words substituted and repealed by ITA 2007 ss 1027, 1031, Sch 1 paras 492, 523, Sch 3 Pt 1 with effect for income tax purposes from 6 April 2007, and corporation tax purposes for accounting periods ending after 5 April 2007.

CHAPTER 8

PROFITS FROM DEEPLY DISCOUNTED SECURITIES

Charge to tax under Chapter 8

427 Charge to tax on profits from deeply discounted securities

(1) Income tax is charged on profits on the disposal of deeply discounted securities.

(2) The profits are treated as income for income tax purposes if they would not otherwise be income.

Commentary—*Simon's Taxes* **D9.510.**

HMRC Manuals—Savings and Investment Manual SAIM3010 (deeply discounted securities: profits charged to income tax).

428 Income charged

(1) Tax is charged under this Chapter on the full amount of profits arising in the tax year.

(2) The profits on a disposal are to be taken to arise when the disposal occurs.

(3) If the profits arise on a disposal of securities that are outside the United Kingdom—

    (*a*) they are treated for the purposes of section 830 (meaning of "relevant foreign income") as arising from a source outside the United Kingdom, and

    (*b*) subsection (1) is subject to Part 8 (foreign income: special rules).

(4) Subsection (2) needs to be read with section 438 (timing of transfers and acquisitions).

Commentary—*Simon's Taxes* **D9.502, D9.510.**

HMRC Manuals—Savings and Investment Manual SAIM3070 (taxation: profit on disposal).

429 Person liable

(1) The person liable for any tax charged under this Chapter is the person making the disposal.

(2) See section 437 for who that person is.

Commentary—*Simon's Taxes* **D9.510.**

HMRC Manuals—Savings and Investment Manual SAIM3070 (person liable for tax).

Deeply discounted securities

430 Meaning of "deeply discounted security"

(1) The general rule is that a security is a "deeply discounted security" for the purposes of this Chapter if, as at the time it is issued, the amount payable on maturity or any other possible occasion of redemption ("A") exceeds or may exceed the issue price by more than $A \times 0.5\% \times Y$, where Y is the number of years in the redemption period or 30, whichever is the lower.

(2) If the redemption period is not a number of complete years, for the purposes of subsection (1) the incomplete year is expressed as twelfths, treating each complete month and any remaining part of a month as one-twelfth.

(3) In this section "redemption period" means the period between the date of issue and the date of the occasion of redemption in question.

(4) Interest payable on an occasion of redemption is ignored in determining for the purposes of this section the amount payable on that occasion.

(5) For the purposes of this section, in the case of an issue to which section 442 applies (securities issued in accordance with qualifying earn-out right), the issue price of the security is to be taken as the amount paid to acquire it (see section 442(2)).

(6) The general rule in subsection (1) is subject to—

> section 431 (excluded occasions of redemption),
>
> section 432 (securities which are not deeply discounted securities),
>
> sections 434 to 436 (securities issued in separate tranches),   . . . [1]
>
> section 443(1) (strips of government securities)[, and
>
> section 452A(1) (corporate strips).][1]

Commentary—*Simon's Taxes* **D9.502.**

HMRC Manuals—Savings and Investment Manual SAIM3020 (meaning of deeply discounted security). SAIM2230 (specific inclusions: discounts: taxation).

Amendments—[1]   Word repealed and words inserted by F(No 2)A 2005 s 39, Sch 7 para 25(2), s 70, Sch 11 Part 2(8) with effect as if originally included when ITTOIA 2005 enacted.

431 Excluded occasions of redemption

(1) An occasion of redemption of a security other than maturity is ignored for the purposes of section 430(1) if the third-party option conditions or the commercial protection conditions are met.

(2) The third-party option conditions are that—

> (*a*) the security may be redeemed on the occasion at the option of a person other than its holder,
>
> (*b*) the security is issued to a person who is not connected with the issuer, and
>
> (*c*) the obtaining of a tax advantage by any person is not the main benefit, or one of the main benefits, that might have been expected to accrue from the provision in accordance with which the security may be redeemed on the occasion.

(3) The commercial protection conditions are that—

> (*a*) the security may be redeemed on the occasion as the result of an exercise of an option that is exercisable only on the occurrence of—
>
>> (i)   an event adversely affecting the holder (see subsection (8)), or
>>
>> (ii) a default by any person, and
>
> (*b*) as at the time of the security's issue it appears unlikely that the option will be exercisable on the occasion.

(4) Subsection (1) does not apply to an occasion just because the occasion coincides or may coincide with an occasion meeting the third-party option conditions or the commercial protection conditions.

(5) If—

> (*a*) the only reason that a security is not a deeply discounted security is that an occasion on which it may be redeemed is ignored because the third-party option conditions are met, and
>
> (*b*) at some time after its issue the security is acquired by, or its holder becomes, a person connected with the issuer,

in relation to that time and later this Chapter applies as if the security were a deeply discounted security.

(6) If a person ("P") who is not connected with the issuer acquires—

> (*a*) a security which is only a deeply discounted security because it was issued to a person connected with the issuer and so fails to meet the condition specified in subsection (2)(*b*), or
>
> (*b*) a security within subsection (5),

this Chapter applies in relation to P as if the security ceased to be a deeply discounted security on the acquisition.

(7) For the purposes of the application of this section to a security, the question whether persons are connected is determined without regard to the security or any other security issued under the same prospectus.

(8) In this section "event adversely affecting the holder", in relation to a security, means an event the occurrence of which appears, as at the time of the security's issue, likely to have an adverse effect on the interests of its holder at the time of the event if there were no provision for redemption on its occurrence.

Commentary—*Simon's Taxes* **D9.502.**
HMRC Manuals—Savings and Investment Manual SAIM3030 (occasions when redemption is ignored).

432 Securities which are not deeply discounted securities

(1) The following are not deeply discounted securities—
- (a) shares in a company,
- (b) gilt-edged securities that are not strips,
- (c) life assurance policies, and
- (d) capital redemption policies.

(2) An excluded indexed security (see section 433) is only a deeply discounted security if treated as such under section 431(5) (acquisition by a person connected with the issuer or holder becoming such a person).

(3) In this section "capital redemption policies" has the same meaning as in Chapter 9 of this Part (see section 473(2)).

(4) See also sections 434 to 436 (rules under which securities issued under the same prospectus on separate occasions may be treated as being, or as not being, deeply discounted securities).

Commentary—*Simon's Taxes* **D9.502.**
HMRC Manuals—Savings and Investment Manual SAIM3040 (securities which are not deeply discounted securities).

433 Meaning of "excluded indexed security"

(1) In this Chapter "excluded indexed security" means a security under the terms of which the amount payable on redemption is determined by applying to the amount for which the security was issued the percentage change (if any) over the security's redemption period in—
- (a) the value of chargeable assets of a particular description, or
- (b) an index of the value of such assets.

(2) The fact that the terms under which the security is issued include a provision to the effect that the amount payable on its redemption must be at least a specified percentage of the amount for which it was issued only prevents it from falling within the definition in subsection (1) if that percentage exceeds 10%.

(3) Interest payable on redemption is ignored in determining for the purposes of this section the amount payable on redemption.

(4) In subsection (1) "redemption period" means—
- (a) the period beginning with the date of issue and ending with the date of redemption, or
- (b) a period which is or includes almost all that period and only differs from it for purposes connected with giving effect to a valuation in relation to rights or liabilities under the security.

(5) An asset is a chargeable asset for the purposes of subsection (1) if a gain accruing to a person on its disposal would be a chargeable gain for the purposes of TCGA 1992 on the assumptions specified in subsection (6).

(6) The assumptions are that—
- (a) the asset is an asset of the person,
- (b) the person is not entitled to the exemption conferred by section 100 of TCGA 1992 (exemption for authorised unit trusts etc.),
- (c) disposal of the asset by the person would not be treated for income tax purposes as a disposal in the course of a trade, profession or vocation, and
- (d) section 116(10) of TCGA 1992 is ignored (chargeable gains on subsequent disposals of qualifying corporate bonds acquired in reorganisations, conversions and reconstructions).

(7) For the purposes of this section—
- (a) neither the retail prices index nor any similar general index of prices published by the government of a territory or by an agent of such a government is an index of the value of chargeable assets, and
- (b) "redemption", in relation to a security, does not include its redemption on an occasion which is to be ignored under section 431(1) (excluded occasions of redemption).

Commentary—*Simon's Taxes* **D9.503.**
HMRC Manuals—Savings and Investment Manual SAIM3050 (excluded indexed securities: meaning).
SAIM3055 (excluded indexed securities: chargeable assets).

434 Securities issued in separate tranches: preliminary

(1) Sections 435 and 436 set out rules under which securities issued under the same prospectus on separate occasions may be treated as being, or as not being, deeply discounted securities.

(2) If any of the securities in the original issue under the prospectus is a deeply discounted security—
- (a) the rule in section 435 applies to securities in later issues under it, and

(b) the rule in section 436 does not apply to any securities issued under it.

(3) If none of the securities in the original issue under the prospectus is a deeply discounted security, the rule in section 435 applies to securities in a later issue except where the rule in section 436 applies.

Commentary—*Simon's Taxes* **D9.530.**

HMRC Manuals—Savings and Investment Manual SAIM3060 (securities issued in separate tranches: overview).

435 Securities issued in separate tranches: basic rule

(1) The rule in this section is that if securities in any of the issues made on separate occasions under the same prospectus are not deeply discounted securities, securities in any later issue under it are not deeply discounted securities, unless they are treated as such for one of the reasons specified in subsection (2).

(2) The reasons are—

(a) that the securities were issued to a person connected with the issuer and so fail to meet the condition specified in section 431(2)(b), and

(b) that such a person has acquired or become the holder of the securities and so section 431(5) applies to them.

Commentary—*Simon's Taxes* **D9.530.**

HMRC Manuals—Savings and Investment Manual SAIM3060 (securities issued in separate tranches: basic rule).

436 Deeply discounted securities issued in separate tranches: nominal value rule

(1) This section only applies if some of the securities in one or more later issues under the same prospectus are deeply discounted securities (or are such securities if the rule in section 435 is ignored).

(2) The rule in this section applies for any disposal or acquisition after the time when the condition specified in subsection (3) is first met.

(3) The condition is that the aggregate nominal value as at a particular time of the securities within subsection (1) exceeds the aggregate nominal value as at that time of all the other securities issued under the prospectus at any time.

(4) The rule is that all securities issued under the prospectus (including those issued after the time when the condition specified in subsection (3) is first met) are to be treated as deeply discounted securities and as having been acquired as such (whenever actually issued or acquired).

(5) Subsection (6) applies where the question is whether a security held by a person who is not connected with the issuer is a deeply discounted security as a result of the rule in this section.

(6) For the purpose of determining whether the rule in this section applies, securities that are only within subsection (1) for one of the reasons specified in section 435(2) are treated as not being within it.

Commentary—*Simon's Taxes* **D9.530.**

HMRC Manuals—Savings and Investment Manual SAIM3060 (deeply discounted securities: nominal value rule).

Disposals

437 Transactions which are disposals

(1) References in this Chapter to the disposal of a deeply discounted security are—

(a) to its redemption,

(b) to its transfer by sale, exchange, gift or otherwise, including a transfer treated as made by subsection (3), and

(c) so far as not covered by paragraph (a) or (b), to its conversion under its terms into shares in a company or other securities (including other deeply discounted securities).

(2) The person treated as making a disposal is—

(a) in the case of a disposal within subsection (1)(a), the person entitled as the security's holder to any payment on the disposal,

(b) in the case of a disposal within subsection (1)(b), the transferor, and

(c) in the case of a disposal within subsection (1)(c), the person who would be entitled as the security's holder to any payment on the disposal, if such a payment were made.

(3) A person who dies while entitled to a deeply discounted security is treated as transferring it immediately before death to the personal representatives.

(4) In the case of strips, further provision about occasions counting as disposals is made by section 445(2) and (6)(a).

[(5) In the case of interest-bearing corporate securities, further provision about occasions counting as disposals is made by section 452F(2)(a).

(6) In the case of corporate strips, further provision about occasions counting as disposals is made by section 452F(2)(a) and (3)(a).]¹

Commentary—*Simon's Taxes* **D9.504.**

HMRC Manuals—Savings and Investment Manual SAIM3070 (meaning of disposal).

SAIM3110 (taxation: death of a person).

SAIM3130 (gilt strips: introduction).

SAIM3150 (corporate strips: basic information).

Amendments—[1]   Sub-sections (5), (6) inserted by F(No 2)A 2005 s 39, Sch 7 para 25(3) with effect as if originally included when ITTOIA 2005 enacted.

438 Timing of transfers and acquisitions

(1) This section applies if—

(a) a transfer or acquisition of a deeply discounted security is made under an agreement, and

(b) the transferee or the person making the acquisition becomes entitled to the security at the time the agreement is made.

(2) The transfer or acquisition is treated as occurring at that time.

(3) For this purpose a conditional agreement is taken to be made when the condition is met.

[(4) This section is subject to—

section 445(7) (exchanges for and consolidations of strips);

section 452F(4) (conversion into and consolidations of corporate strips).][1]

Commentary—Simon's Taxes **D9.504.**

HMRC Manuals—Savings and Investment Manual SAIM3070 (timing of transfer).

Amendments—[1]   Sub-s (4) substituted by F(No 2)A 2005 s 39, Sch 7 para 25(4) with effect as if originally included when ITTOIA 2005 enacted.

Calculating profits

439 Calculating the profit from disposals

(1) A person's profit on a disposal is the amount by which the amount payable on the disposal exceeds the amount paid by the person to acquire the security.

(2) No account is to be taken of any incidental expenses incurred in connection with the disposal or acquisition.

(3) Subsection (2) is subject to subsection (4) and section 455 (listed securities held since 26th March 2003: calculating the profit or loss on disposals).

(4) Incidental expenses incurred before 27th March 2003 by the person making the disposal in connection with the acquisition or disposal of the security are deducted from the person's profit.

(5) Where a person re-acquires a security, any previous acquisition of it is ignored in determining on a subsequent disposal—

(a) the amount the person paid to acquire the security, and

(b) incidental expenses within subsection (4).

Commentary—Simon's Taxes **D9.511.**

HMRC Manuals—Savings and Investment Manual SAIM3070 (computation of profits).

440 Market value disposals

(1) On the disposal of a deeply discounted security by a transfer of a kind specified in subsection (2), for the purposes of this Chapter an amount equal to the market value at the time of the disposal is treated as payable.

(2) The transfers are—

(a) a transfer made otherwise than by a bargain at arm's length,

(b) a transfer between connected persons,

(c) a transfer for a consideration which is not wholly in money or money's worth,

(d) a transfer treated as made by section 437(3) (death), and

(e) a transfer by personal representatives to a legatee.

(3) Subsection (1) is subject to subsection (4).

(4) On a conversion of a deeply discounted security into shares or other securities which counts as its disposal under section 437(1), an amount equal to the market value of the shares or other securities at the time of the conversion is treated as the amount payable.

[(5) Subsection (4) is subject to—

section 445(8) (exchanges for and consolidations of strips);

section 452F(5) (conversion into and consolidations of corporate strips).][1]

(6) In this section "legatee" includes any person taking (whether beneficially or as trustee)—

(a) on a testamentary disposition, or

(b) on an intestacy or partial intestacy.

(7) Such a person includes a person taking as a result of an appropriation by personal representatives in or towards the satisfaction of a legacy or other interest or share in the deceased's property.

Commentary—Simon's Taxes **D9.505.**

HMRC Manuals—Savings and Investment Manual SAIM3090 (deemed disposals: market value rules).

SAIM3110 (transfer by personal representative to a legatee).

SAIM3160 (corporate strips: taxation rule).

Amendments—[1]   Sub-s (5) substituted by F(No 2)A 2005 s 39, Sch 7 para 25(5) with effect as if originally included when ITTOIA 2005 enacted.

441 Market value acquisitions

(1) A person who acquires a deeply discounted security on a disposal of a kind specified in subsection (2) is treated for the purposes of this Chapter as acquiring it by the payment of an amount equal to its market value at the time of the disposal.

(2) The disposals are—

(a) a transfer within section 440(2), and

(b) a conversion of a deeply discounted security into other deeply discounted securities which counts as its disposal under section 437(1).

[(3) Subsection (2) is subject to—

section 445(8) (exchanges for and consolidations of strips);

section 452F(5) (conversion into and consolidations of corporate strips).][1]

Commentary—*Simon's Taxes* **D9.505.**

HMRC Manuals—Savings and Investment Manual SAIM3090 (acquisition of deeply discounted security: market value rules).

Amendments—[1] Sub-s (3) substituted by F(No 2)A 2005 s 39, Sch 7 para 25(6) with effect as if originally included when ITTOIA 2005 enacted.

442 Securities issued in accordance with qualifying earn-out right

(1) This section applies if a security is issued to a person in accordance with the terms of a qualifying earn-out right.

(2) The amount paid by the person to acquire the security is to be taken for the purposes of this Chapter to be the total of—

(a) the market value, immediately before the issue, of the right to be issued with the security in accordance with the terms of the qualifying earn-out right, and

(b) any amount payable for the issue in accordance with those terms.

(3) In this section "qualifying earn-out right" means a right that meets conditions A to C, or so much of a right as does so.

(4) Condition A is that the right constitutes the whole or part of the consideration for—

(a) the transfer by the person on whom the right is conferred of shares in or debentures of a company, or

(b) the transfer of the whole or part of—

(i) a business carried on by that person, or by that person and others in partnership, or

(ii) an interest in such a business.

(5) Condition B is that the right is either—

(a) a right to be issued with securities of another company, or

(b) a right which is capable of being discharged in accordance with its terms by the issue of such securities.

(6) Condition C is that the right is such that the value of the consideration mentioned in condition A is unascertainable at the time when the right is conferred.

Commentary—*Simon's Taxes* **D9.512.**

HMRC Manuals—Savings and Investment Manual SAIM3100 (taxation: 'earn-out' rights).

Special rules for strips of government securities

443 Application of this Chapter to strips of government securities

(1) All strips are treated as deeply discounted securities for the purposes of this Chapter, whether or not they would otherwise be so.

(2) This Chapter applies to strips subject to the rules in—

(a) section 445 (strips of government securities: acquisitions and disposals),

(b) section 446 (strips of government securities: relief for losses),

(c) section 447 (restriction of profits on strips by reference to original acquisition cost),

(d) section 448 (restriction of losses on strips by reference to original acquisition cost),

(e) section 449 (strips of government securities: manipulation of acquisition, transfer or redemption payments), [and][1]

(f) section 450 (market value of strips etc.), and

(g) . . .[1]

Commentary—*Simon's Taxes* **D9.520.**

HMRC Manuals—Savings and Investment Manual SAIM2500 (strips of government securities: treatment for tax).

SAIM3130 (strips treated as deeply discounted securities).

Amendments—[1] Word in sub-s (2)(e) inserted, and sub-s (2)(g) repealed, by FA 2007 ss 109, 114, Sch 26 para 11(1), (2), Sch 27 Pt 6(5) with effect from 19 July 2007.

444 Meaning of "strip" in Chapter 8

(1) In this Chapter "strip", in relation to any stock or bond ("the underlying security"), means a security which—

(a) meets conditions A to C,

(b) if it was acquired after 26th March 2003, was issued by or on behalf of the government of any territory, and

(c) if it was acquired on or before that date, was issued under the National Loans Act 1968 (c. 13) in a case where the underlying security was itself a gilt-edged security.

(2) Condition A is that the security is issued for the purpose of representing the right to or of securing—

(a) a payment corresponding to a payment of interest or principal remaining to be made under the underlying security, or

(b) two or more payments each corresponding to a payment to be so made.

(3) Condition B is that the security is issued in conjunction with the issue of one or more other securities which, together with that security—

(a) represent the right to, or

(b) secure,

payments corresponding to every payment remaining to be made under the underlying security.

(4) Condition C is that the security is not itself a security which—

(a) represents the right to, or

(b) secures,

payments corresponding to a part of every payment remaining to be made under the underlying security.

(5) After the balance has been struck for a dividend on any underlying security, a payment to be made in respect of that dividend is treated for the purposes of conditions A to C as not being a payment remaining to be made under the underlying security.

[(6) Nothing in this section affects the meaning of the expression "corporate strip" in this Chapter (see section 452E).][1]

Commentary—*Simon's Taxes* **D9.520.**

HMRC Manuals—Savings and Investment Manual SAIM3130 (strips: meaning).

Amendments—[1] Sub-s (6) inserted by F(No 2)A 2005 s 39, Sch 7 para 25(7) with effect as if originally included when ITTOIA 2005 enacted.

445 Strips of government securities: acquisitions and disposals

(1) A person who receives strips of a security ("the underlying security") in exchange for the underlying security is treated as having acquired each strip by the payment of an amount equal to—

$$A \times \frac{B}{C}$$

where—

A is the market value of the underlying security at the time of the exchange,

B is the market value of the strip at that time, and

C is the total of the market values at that time of all the strips received in the exchange.

(2) For the purposes of this Chapter—

(a) a person who holds a strip of a security on 5th April in any tax year is treated as having transferred the strip on that day, and

(b) an amount equal to its market value on that day is treated as payable on the transfer.

(3) For the purposes of this Chapter that person is also treated as having immediately re-acquired the strip for the same amount.

(4) Subsections (2) and (3) do not apply if there is any other disposal of the strip on that day.

(5) Section 439(4) (deduction of incidental expenses incurred before 27th March 2003) does not apply to transfers and reacquisitions within subsections (2) and (3).

(6) For the purposes of this Chapter—

(a) the consolidation of a strip of a security with other such strips into a single security is a disposal of the strip by the person consolidating it (whether or not it would be apart from this subsection), and

(b) an amount equal to the market value of the strip at the consolidation is treated as payable on the disposal.

(7) Section 438 (timing of transfers and acquisitions) does not apply to an exchange within subsection (1) or a consolidation within subsection (6).

(8) Subsections (1) and (6) apply instead of sections 440(4) (market value on general conversions of deeply discounted securities) and 441 (market value acquisitions).

Derivation—sub-ss (1)–(6): FA 1996 Sch 13 paras 1(2), 14; FA 2003 Sch 39 paras 5(3), 6(1).

sub-ss (7), (8): FA 1996 Sch 13 paras 4(5), 5(3).

Changes in the law—sub-s (3): see ITTOIA 2005 EN Annex 1 Change 87. This change alters the time at which strips of government securities held at 5 April that are deemed to be transferred at market value on that day are re-acquired. The reacquisition is deemed to be immediate, rather than to occur on 6 April.

446 Strips of government securities: relief for losses

(1) Relief from income tax may be claimed under this section for any loss made on the disposal of a strip of a security.

[(2) If a person makes a claim under this section, the relief is given by deducting the loss in calculating the person's net income for the tax year in which the disposal occurs (see Step 2 of the calculation in section 23 of ITA 2007).][1]

(3) For this purpose a person makes a loss on the disposal of a strip if—

(a) the person disposes of the strip, and

(b) the amount the person paid for the strip, ignoring any incidental expenses incurred in connection with the acquisition, exceeds the amount payable on the disposal, ignoring any incidental expenses incurred in connection with the disposal.

(4) The loss is an amount equal to the excess.

(5) A claim under this section must be made on or before the first anniversary of the normal self-assessment filing date for the tax year in which the disposal occurs.

(6) The relief may be claimed by the person making the disposal.

(7) Relief for a loss on a disposal may not be claimed under this section if section 454 (listed securities held since 26th March 2003: relief for losses) applies in respect of the disposal.

(8) This section is subject to—

    (*a*) section 448 (restriction of losses on strips by reference to original acquisition cost),

    (*b*) section 449 (strips of government securities: manipulation of acquisition, sale or redemption payments), and

    (*c*) section 458(2) (strips held by non-UK resident trustees).

Commentary—*Simon's Taxes* **D9.523.**

HMRC Manuals—Savings and Investment Manual SAIM3140 (relief for losses on gilt strips).

Amendments—[1] Sub-s (2) substituted by ITA 2007 s 1027, Sch 1 paras 492, 524 with effect for income tax purposes from 6 April 2007, and corporation tax purposes for accounting periods ending after 5 April 2007.

447 Restriction of profits on strips by reference to original acquisition cost

(1) This section applies if—

    (*a*) a person makes a profit on the disposal of a strip (apart from this section), and

    (*b*) the person's original acquisition cost for the strip (see subsection (4)) exceeds the amount that falls to be brought into account as the amount paid by the person to acquire the strip in determining the amount of the profit.

(2) If the amount that falls to be brought into account as the amount payable on the disposal in determining the amount of the profit exceeds the person's original acquisition cost for the strip, the amount of the profit is restricted to that excess.

(3) Otherwise the person is treated as not making a profit on the disposal.

(4) For the purposes of this section and section 448, a person's original acquisition cost for a strip is the amount that falls to be taken into account as the amount paid by the person to acquire the strip in determining whether the person makes a profit or loss on its disposal if 5th April disposals and acquisitions are ignored.

(5) In subsection (4) "5th April disposals and acquisitions" means—

    (*a*) disposals under section 445(2) (other than the disposal in question), and

    (*b*) acquisitions under section 445(3).

Commentary—*Simon's Taxes* **D9.521.**

HMRC Manuals—Savings and Investment Manual SAIM3140 (restriction of profits on strips by reference to original acquisition cost).

448 Restriction of losses on strips by reference to original acquisition cost

(1) This section applies if—

    (*a*) a person makes a loss on the disposal of a strip (apart from this section), and

    (*b*) the person's original acquisition cost for the strip exceeds the amount that falls to be brought into account as the amount payable on the disposal of the strip in determining the amount of the loss.

(2) If the amount that falls to be brought into account as the amount paid by the person to acquire the strip in determining the amount of the loss exceeds the person's original acquisition cost for the strip, the amount of the loss is reduced.

(3) The amount of the reduction is A–B where—

    A is the person's original acquisition cost for the strip, and

    B is the amount that falls to be brought into account as the amount payable on the disposal of the strip in determining the amount of the loss.

(4) If subsection (2) does not apply, the person is treated as not making a loss on the disposal.

(5) In this section any reference to making a loss on the disposal of a strip has the meaning given in section 446(3) and (4).

Commentary—*Simon's Taxes* **D9.523.**

HMRC Manuals—Savings and Investment Manual SAIM3140 (restriction of losses on strips by reference to original acquisition cost).

449 Strips of government securities: manipulation of acquisition, transfer or redemption payments

(1) This section applies if—

    (*a*) as a result of a scheme or arrangement an amount referred to in subsection (2)(*a*), (*b*) or (*c*) differs from the market value of a strip in a way specified in that subsection, and

    (*b*) the obtaining of a tax advantage by any person is the main benefit, or one of the main benefits, that might have been expected to accrue from, or from any provision of, the scheme or arrangement.

(2) The ways are that—

    (*a*) the amount paid by a person in respect of the acquisition of the strip is or was more than the market value at the time of the acquisition, (*b*) the amount payable to a person on transferring the strip is less than the market value at the time of the transfer, or

(*c*) on redemption of the strip the amount payable to a person, as the person holding the strip, is less than the market value on the day before redemption.

(3) In a case within subsection (2)(*a*), for the purposes of sections 439(1) and 446(3) on transferring the strip the person is treated as if the person had paid to acquire the strip an amount equal to the market value of the strip at the time of the acquisition.

(4) In a case within subsection (2)(*b*), for those purposes the person is treated as if the amount payable to the person on the transfer were an amount equal to the market value of the strip at the time of the transfer.

(5) In a case within subsection (2)(*c*), for those purposes the person is treated as if the amount payable to the person on redemption were an amount equal to the market value of the strip on the day before redemption.

(6) For the purposes of this section, no account is to be taken of any incidental expenses incurred in connection with any disposal or acquisition of a strip.

Commentary—*Simon's Taxes* **D9.524.**

HMRC Manuals—Savings and Investment Manual SAIM3160 (strips: anti-avoidance rules).

[450 Market value of strips etc.

(1) The Treasury may make regulations as to the manner for determining—

(*a*) the market value at any time of a strip for the purposes of this Chapter, and

(*b*) the market value at any time of a security exchanged for strips of that security for the purposes of section 445(1).

(2) The regulations may—

(*a*) make different provision for different cases, and

(*b*) contain incidental, supplemental, consequential and transitional provision and savings.][1]

Commentary—*Simon's Taxes* **D9.522.**

HMRC Manuals—Savings and Investment Manual SAIM3140 (meaning of market value of strips).

Amendments—[1]   This section substituted for previous ss 450, 451 by FA 2007 s 109, Sch 26 para 5 with effect where the date of valuation falls on or after 6 April 2015 (by virtue of SI 2015/635).

452 Power to modify this Chapter for strips

(1) The Treasury may by regulations provide that this Chapter is to apply to a strip with such modifications as they consider appropriate.

(2) This section is without prejudice to the general power to make regulations under section 202 of FA 1996 (gilt stripping).

Commentary—*Simon's Taxes* **D9.520.**

Cross reference—See ITTOIA 2005 Sch 2 para 80 (deemed transfers of strips on 5 April 2004).

[Special rules for corporate strips]

452A Application of this Chapter to corporate strips

(1) All corporate strips are treated as deeply discounted securities for the purposes of this Chapter, whether or not they would otherwise be so.

(2) This Chapter applies to corporate strips subject to the rules in—

(*a*) section 452F (corporate strips: acquisitions and disposals), and

(*b*) section 452G (corporate strips: manipulation of acquisition, transfer or redemption payments).][1]

Amendments—[1]   Sections 452A–452G inserted by F(No 2)A 2005 s 39, Sch 7 para 25(8) with effect as if originally included when ITTOIA 2005 enacted.

[452B Meaning of "interest-bearing corporate security" in Chapter 8

(1) In this Chapter "interest-bearing corporate security" means any interest-bearing security other than—

(*a*) a security issued by the government of a territory, or

(*b*) a share in a company.

(2) In this section "interest-bearing security" includes any loan stock or similar security.

(3) Section 452D(4)(*a*) gives an extended meaning to references to converting an interest-bearing corporate security into corporate strips (and related expressions).][1]

Amendments—[1]   Sections 452A–452G inserted by F(No 2)A 2005 s 39, Sch 7 para 25(8) with effect as if originally included when ITTOIA 2005 enacted.

[452C Conversion of interest-bearing corporate securities into corporate strips

(1) For the purposes of this Chapter a person converts an interest-bearing corporate security into corporate strips of the security if he has an interest-bearing corporate security ("the converted corporate security") but—

(*a*) as a result of any scheme or arrangements, he acquires two or more separate assets in place of the converted corporate security,

(*b*) each of those separate assets satisfies condition A,

(*c*) those separate assets, taken together, satisfy condition B, and

ITTOIA 2005

    (*d*) at least one of those separate assets is not prevented from being a corporate strip by section 452E(2) or (3),

and related expressions shall be construed accordingly.

(2) Condition A is that the asset—

    (*a*) represents the right to, or

    (*b*) secures,

one or more stripped payments.

(3) For the purposes of this section, a "stripped payment" is—

    (*a*) the payment of, or

    (*b*) a payment corresponding to,

the whole or a part of one or more payments (whether of interest or principal) remaining to be made under the converted corporate security.

(4) Condition B is that the assets, taken together,—

    (*a*) represent the right to, or

    (*b*) secure,

every payment (whether of interest or principal) remaining to be made under the converted corporate security (or payments corresponding to every such payment).

(5) Where a person—

    (*a*) has an interest-bearing corporate security, but

    (*b*) sells or transfers the right to one or more payments remaining to be made under it (so that, as a result, there are two or more separate assets which, taken together, satisfy condition B),

this Chapter has effect as if, as a result of a scheme or arrangements, the person had acquired the separate assets in place of the security immediately before the sale or transfer.

(6) After a balance has been struck for a dividend on an interest-bearing corporate security, any payment to be made in respect of that dividend shall, at times falling after that balance has been struck, be treated for the purposes of this paragraph as not being a payment remaining to be made under the security.][1]

Commentary—*Simon's Taxes* **D9.526.**

HMRC Manuals—Savings and Investment Manual SAIM3160 (conversion of interest-bearing corporate securities into corporate strips).

Amendments—[1]   Sections 452A–452G inserted by F(No 2)A 2005 s 39, Sch 7 para 25(8) with effect as if originally included when ITTOIA 2005 enacted.

[452D Conversion into corporate strips: lower level conversions

(1) For the purposes of this Chapter, section 452C also has effect in relation to each of the separate assets mentioned in subsection (1) of that section as if that separate asset were itself an interest-bearing corporate security (if that is not in fact the case).

(2) In subsection (1), the reference to section 452C includes a reference to that section as it has effect by virtue of this section.

(3) In the application of section 452C by virtue of this section, references to payments the right to which a separate asset represents or secures shall be construed in accordance with subsection (6) of that section.

(4) Where section 452C has effect by virtue of subsection (1)—

    (*a*) any reference in this Chapter to converting an interest-bearing corporate security into corporate strips of the security shall be construed accordingly, and

    (*b*) section 452E (meaning of "corporate strip") has effect accordingly.][1]

Amendments—[1]   Sections 452A–452G inserted by F(No 2)A 2005 s 39, Sch 7 para 25(8) with effect as if originally included when ITTOIA 2005 enacted.

[452E Meaning of "corporate strip" in Chapter 8

(1) In this Chapter "corporate strip" means any asset—

    (*a*) which is, or has at any time been, one of the separate assets mentioned in section 452C(1), and

    (*b*) which is not prevented from being a corporate strip by subsection (2) or (3).

(2) An asset is not a corporate strip if it—

    (*a*) represents the right to, or

    (*b*) secures,

payments of, or corresponding to, a part of every payment remaining to be made under an interest-bearing corporate security or a corporate strip.

(3) An asset is a corporate strip in the case of any person only if he acquired it—

    (*a*) on or after 2nd December 2004, and

    (*b*) otherwise than in pursuance of an agreement entered into before that date.][1]

Commentary—*Simon's Taxes* **D9.526.**

HMRC Manuals—Savings and Investment Manual SAIM3160 (corporate strips: meaning and taxation).

Amendments—[1]   Sections 452A–452G inserted by F(No 2)A 2005 s 39, Sch 7 para 25(8) with effect as if originally included when ITTOIA 2005 enacted.

[452F Corporate strips: acquisitions and disposals
(1) A person who converts an interest-bearing corporate security into corporate strips of the security is treated as having acquired each corporate strip by the payment of an amount equal to—

$$A \times \frac{B}{C}$$

where—
     A is acquisition cost of the converted corporate security;
     B is the market value of the corporate strip;
     C is the total of the market values of all the separate assets resulting from the conversion.
(2) If the converted corporate security is a deeply discounted security—
     (a) its conversion into corporate strips is to be treated for the purposes of this Chapter as a transfer of the security, but
     (b) the amount payable on the transfer is taken to be an amount equal to the acquisition cost of the converted corporate security.
(3) For the purposes of this Chapter—
     (a) the consolidation of a corporate strip with other corporate strips into a single security is a disposal of the corporate strip by the person consolidating it (whether or not it would be apart from this subsection), and
     (b) an amount equal to the market value of the corporate strip at the consolidation is treated as payable on the disposal.
(4) Section 438 (timing of transfers and acquisitions) does not apply to a conversion within subsection (1) or a consolidation within subsection (3).
(5) Subsections (1) to (3) apply instead of sections 440(4) (market value on general conversions of deeply discounted securities) and 441 (market value acquisitions).
(6) For the purposes of this section, the acquisition cost of the converted corporate security is the amount paid in respect of his acquisition of the security by the person who has it immediately before the conversion (no account being taken of any costs incurred in connection with that acquisition).
(7) References in this section to the market value of a security given or received in exchange for, or otherwise converted into, another are references to its market value at the time of the exchange or conversion.]¹

Commentary—*Simon's Taxes* **D9.527.**
HMRC Manuals—Savings and Investment Manual SAIM3160 (corporate strips: acquisitions and disposals).
Amendments—¹   Sections 452A–452G inserted by F(No 2)A 2005 s 39, Sch 7 para 25(8) with effect as if originally included when ITTOIA 2005 enacted.

[452G Corporate strips: manipulation of acquisition, transfer or redemption payments
(1) This section applies if—
     (a) as a result of any scheme or arrangement, an amount referred to in subsection (2)(a), (b) or (c) differs from the market value of the corporate strip in a way specified in that subsection, and
     (b) the obtaining of a tax advantage by any person is the main benefit, or one of the main benefits, that might have been expected to accrue from, or from any provision of, the scheme or arrangement.
(2) The ways are that—
     (a) the amount paid by a person in respect of the acquisition of the corporate strip is or was more than the market value of the corporate strip at the time of that acquisition,
     (b) the amount payable to a person on transferring the corporate strip is less than the market value at the time of the transfer, or
     (c) on redemption of the corporate strip the amount payable to a person, as the person holding the corporate strip, is less than the market value on the day before redemption.
(3) In a case within subsection (2)(a), for the purposes of section 439(1) on transferring the corporate strip the person is treated as if the person had paid to acquire the corporate strip an amount equal to the market value of the corporate strip at the time of the acquisition.
(4) In a case falling within subsection (2)(b), for those purposes the person is treated as if the amount payable to the person on the transfer were an amount equal to the market value of the corporate strip at the time of the transfer.
(5) In a case falling within subsection (2)(c), for those purposes the person is treated as if the amount payable to the person on redemption were an amount equal to the market value of the corporate strip on the day before redemption.
(6) The market value of a corporate strip at any time is to be determined for the purposes of this section without regard to any increase or diminution in the value of the corporate strip as a result of the scheme or arrangement mentioned in subsection (1).
(7) For the purposes of this section, no account is to be taken of any incidental expenses incurred in connection with any disposal or acquisition of a corporate strip.]¹

Commentary—*Simon's Taxes* **D9.524.**
HMRC Manuals—Savings and Investment Manual SAIM3150 (corporate strips: anti-avoidance rules).
SAIM3160 (corporate strips: anti-avoidance rules).
Amendments—[1]   Sections 452A–452G inserted by F(No 2)A 2005 s 39, Sch 7 para 25(8) with effect as if originally included
when ITTOIA 2005 enacted.

Special rules for listed securities held since 26th March 2003

453 Application of sections 454 to 456

(1) In the case of a disposal of a deeply discounted security that meets conditions A and B, the rules in sections 454 to 456 apply for—

(a) providing for relief for losses on the disposal, and

(b) calculating the amount of profits chargeable under this Chapter on the disposal or the losses for which such relief may be given.

(2) Condition A is that the person making the disposal has held the security continuously since a time before 27th March 2003.

(3) Condition B is that the security was listed on a recognised stock exchange at any time before 27th March 2003.

Commentary—*Simon's Taxes* **D9.513.**
HMRC Manuals—Savings and Investment Manual SAIM3080 (losses: listed securities held since 26 March 2003).

454 Listed securities held since 26th March 2003: relief for losses

(1) A person may claim relief from income tax under this section for a loss the person has made on disposing of deeply discounted securities.

(2) For this purpose a person makes such a loss only if A exceeds B, where—

A is the amount the person paid for the securities, excluding any incidental expenses incurred in connection with the acquisition, and

B is the amount payable on the disposal, excluding any incidental expenses incurred in connection with the disposal.

(3) For the calculation of the amount of the loss, see section 455(2) to (4) (under which those expenses are taken into account).

[(4) If a claim under this section is made by a person other than a trustee, the relief is given by deducting the loss in calculating the person's net income for the tax year in which the disposal occurs (see Step 2 of the calculation in section 23 of ITA 2007).][1]

(5) If such a claim is made by a trustee, the amount of profits arising in the tax year in which the disposal occurs that is charged under this Chapter is reduced by the amount of the loss.

(6) A claim under this section must be made on or before the first anniversary of the normal self-assessment filing date for the tax year in which the disposal occurs.

(7) This section is subject to section 458(2) (securities held by non-UK resident trustees).

Commentary—*Simon's Taxes* **D9.513.**
HMRC Manuals—Savings and Investment Manual SAIM3080 (losses: listed securities held since 26 March 2003).
Amendments—[1]   Sub-s (4) substituted by ITA 2007 s 1027, Sch 1 paras 492, 525 with effect for income tax purposes from
6 April 2007, and corporation tax purposes for accounting periods ending after 5 April 2007.

455 Listed securities held since 26th March 2003: calculating the profit or loss on disposals

(1) A person's profit on a disposal, as calculated under section 439, is reduced by any incidental expenses incurred [before 6 April 2015][1] by that person in connection with the disposal or the acquisition of the security that have not been deducted under section 439(4).

(2) A person's loss on a disposal for the purposes of section 454 (relief for losses) is the amount by which the deductible costs exceed the amount payable on the disposal.

(3) In this section the "deductible costs" means—

(a) the amount paid by the person to acquire the security, and

(b) the incidental expenses incurred [before 6 April 2015][1] by that person in connection with the disposal or the acquisition.

(4) Where a person re-acquires a security, any previous acquisition of it is ignored in determining the person's incidental expenses within subsection (1) or deductible costs on a subsequent disposal.

(5) For the purposes of this section, no incidental expenses are treated as incurred in connection with transfers and reacquisitions within section 445(2) and (3) (transfer and immediate reacquisition of strips on 5th April).

Commentary—*Simon's Taxes* **D9.513.**
HMRC Manuals—Savings and Investment Manual SAIM3080 (losses: listed securities held since 26 March 2003).
Amendments—[1]   In sub-ss (1), (3)(b), words inserted by FA 2012 s 227, Sch 39 para 48 with effect for the tax year 2015–16
and subsequent tax years.

456 Securities issued to connected persons etc. at excessive price: subsequent transfers to connected persons

(1) No loss is taken to occur for the purposes of section 454 on a transfer of a deeply discounted security to a person connected with the transferor if conditions A and B and either condition C or conditions D and E are met.

(2) Condition A is that the transferor acquired the security on its issue.

(3) Condition B is that the amount paid by the transferor to acquire the security exceeded the market value of the security at the time of its issue.

(4) Condition C is that at that time the transferor was connected with the issuer.

(5) Condition D is that at that time the issuer was a close company.

(6) Condition E is that at that time the transferor controlled that company with other persons to whom securities of the same kind were also issued.

[(7) Chapter 2 of Part 10 of CTA 2010 (meaning of "close company") applies for the purposes of this section but with the omission of section 442(*a*) (exclusion of non-UK resident companies).][1]

(8) In this section "control" has the meaning given by [sections 450 and 451 of CTA 2010][1].

Amendments—[1]   Sub-s (7) substituted and in sub-s (8) words substituted by CTA 2010 s 1177, Sch 1 paras 444, 466 with effect for corporation tax purposes for accounting periods ending on or after 1 April 2010, and for income and capital gains tax purposes for the tax year 2010–11 and subsequent tax years.

Trustees

457 Trustees

(1) This section applies if profits are taken to arise on a disposal of a deeply discounted security by trustees.

(2) For the purposes of Chapter 5 of Part 5 (settlements: amounts treated as income of settlor), the profits are to be taken to be income arising under the settlement from the security.

(3) . . . [2]

(4) . . . [1]

[(5) If the trustees are trustees of a scheme in relation to which section 504 of ITA 2007 applies, subsection (2) does not apply to profits which are shown in the scheme's accounts as income available for payment to unit holders or for investment.][2]

Commentary—*Simon's Taxes* **D9.531.**

HMRC Manuals—Savings and Investment Manual SAIM3120 (taxation of trustees).

Amendments—[1]   Sub-s (4) repealed by FA 2006 ss 89, 178, Sch 13 para 32(1), Sch 26 Pt 3(15) with effect in relation to payments made on or after 6 April 2006 to the trustees of a settlement (whenever created).

[2]   Sub-s (3) repealed, and sub-s (5) substituted, by ITA 2007 ss 1027, 1031, Sch 1 paras 492, 526, Sch 3 Pt 1 with effect for income tax purposes from 6 April 2007, and corporation tax purposes for accounting periods ending after 5 April 2007.

458 Non-UK resident trustees

(1) Tax is not charged under this Chapter if the disposal is made by the trustees of a settlement and they are non-UK resident.

(2) The following provisions do not apply if the disposal falls within subsection (1)—

section 446 (strips of government securities: relief for losses), and

section 454 (listed securities held since 26th March 2003: relief for losses).

(3) In this section "settlement" has the same meaning as in Chapter 5 of Part 5 (see section 620).

Commentary—*Simon's Taxes* **D9.531.**

HMRC Manuals—Savings and Investment Manual SAIM3080 (taxation: non-UK resident trustees). SAIM3120 (taxation: non-UK resident trustees).

Miscellaneous and supplementary

459 Transfer of assets abroad

(1) This section applies if profits are taken to arise on the disposal of a deeply discounted security by a person resident or domiciled outside the United Kingdom ("A").

(2) For the purpose of determining whether [a UK resident individual][2] is liable for income tax in respect of the profits, [Chapter 2 of Part 13 of ITA 2007 (transfer of assets abroad) has][1] effect as if the profits, when arising, constituted income becoming payable to A.

(3) For this purpose it does not matter if A is not liable to income tax under this Chapter because of section 458 (non-UK resident trustees).

Commentary—*Simon's Taxes* **D9.532.**

HMRC Manuals—Savings and Investment Manual SAIM3120 (disposal or transfer of deeply discounted security or assets abroad).

Amendments—[1]   Words in sub-s (2) substituted by ITA 2007 s 1027, Sch 1 paras 492, 527 with effect for income tax purposes from 6 April 2007, and corporation tax purposes for accounting periods ending after 5 April 2007.

[2]   Words in sub-s (2) substituted for words "an individual ordinarily UK resident" by FA 2013 s 219, Sch 46 paras 43, 45 with effect for the purposes of a person's liability to income tax for the tax year 2013–14 or any subsequent tax year, subject to savings in FA 2013 Sch 46 para 73.

460 Minor definitions

(1) In this Chapter "share", in the case of a share in a company, means any share under which an entitlement to receive distributions may arise, but does not include a share in a building society.

(2) In this Chapter "tax advantage" has the meaning given by [section 1139 of CTA 2010][2].

(3) In this Chapter "market value" has the same meaning as in TCGA 1992 (see sections 272 to 274 of that Act), except as provided in section 450 . . . [1] (market value of strips etc.).

Amendments—[1]   Words in sub-s (3) repealed by FA 2007 ss 109, 114, Sch 26 para 11(1), (3), Sch 27 Pt 6(5) with effect from 19 July 2007.

² In sub-s (2) words substituted by CTA 2010 s 1177, Sch 1 paras 444, 467. CTA 2010 has effect for corporation tax purposes for accounting periods ending on or after 1 April 2010, and for income and capital gains tax purposes for the tax year 2010–11 and subsequent tax years.

CHAPTER 9

GAINS FROM CONTRACTS FOR LIFE INSURANCE ETC.

Charge to tax under Chapter 9

461 Charge to tax under Chapter 9

(1) Income tax is charged on gains treated as arising from policies and contracts to which this Chapter applies.

(2) For the policies and contracts to which this Chapter applies, see sections 473 to 483.

(3) See also sections 530 to 538 (provisions relating to tax treated as paid on gains and to reliefs).

(4) For exemptions, see in particular Chapter 3 of Part 6 (income from individual investment plans).

(5) For the application of this Chapter where corresponding provision for corporation tax purposes is also relevant, see section 544 (application of Chapter to policies and contracts in which companies interested).

462 When gains arise from policies and contracts

(1) For the purposes of this Chapter, a gain from a policy or contract arises when a chargeable event occurs in relation to the policy or contract (see section 484).

(2) But certain chargeable events are only treated as occurring because a calculation required to be made as at a particular time shows that the gain has arisen.

(3) See, in particular—

    (*a*) section 509(1) (under which a chargeable event is treated as occurring where a periodic calculation following a part surrender or assignment shows a gain),

    (*b*) section 514(1) (under which a part surrender or assignment is treated as a chargeable event where a calculation related to it shows a gain), and

    (*c*) section 525(2) (under which a chargeable event is treated as occurring where an annual personal portfolio bond calculation shows a gain).

463 Income charged

(1) Tax is charged under this Chapter on the amount of the gains arising in the tax year.

(2) Subsection (1) is subject to section 514(4) (under which certain gains are charged for a later tax year).

(3) See section 469(3) for the apportionment of gains where two or more persons are interested in a policy or contract.

(4) See sections 491 to 497, 507, 508, 511 to 513, 522 to 524 and 527 to 529 for the rules as to how the gains are calculated.

[463A Restricted relief qualifying policies: disapplication of section 485 etc

(1) This section applies for the purpose of determining if an individual is liable for tax charged under this Chapter.

(2) In relation to an event occurring on or after 6 April 2013, section 485 (disregard of certain events in relation to qualifying policies) does not apply in relation to a policy ("policy X") which is a restricted relief qualifying policy (see paragraph A2 of Schedule 15 to ICTA).

(3) If an individual is liable for tax charged under this Chapter as a result of subsection (2), the gain on which the tax is charged in the case of the individual is reduced by the following amount—

$$G \times (TAP / TP)$$

where—

    G is the amount of the gain (apart from this subsection),

    TAP is the total amount of premiums payable under policy X during the policy X period so far as they are allowable premiums as determined in accordance with section 463B, and

    TP is the total amount of premiums payable under policy X during the policy X period.

(4) If section 528 also applies in the case of the individual in relation to the gain, subsection (3) is to be applied to the gain before section 528 and, accordingly, the reduction to be made under section 528 is to be determined by reference to the gain as reduced by subsection (3).

(5) The following subsections apply for the purposes of this section (except subsection (2)) and section 463B.

(6) "The policy X period" means the period for which policy X has run before the chargeable event occurs.

(7) Subsections (8) and (9) apply if policy X is a new policy in relation to another policy.

(8) For the purposes of subsection (6) policy X is to be taken to have run—

    (*a*) from the issue of the other policy, or

    (*b*) if the other policy was also a new policy in relation to an earlier policy, from the issue of the earlier policy, and so on.

(9) References to premiums payable under policy X are to be read as including references to premiums payable under any earlier policy taken into account under subsection (8).

(10) The following are to be left out of account in determining the premiums payable under a policy—

(a) so much of a premium as is charged on the grounds that an exceptional risk of death or disability is involved;

(b) subject to subsection (11), so much of the first premium payable the liability for the payment of which—

(i) is discharged in accordance with paragraph 15(2) of Schedule 15 to ICTA, or

(ii) in the case of a policy in relation to which paragraph 3 of that Schedule applies, is discharged under a provision of the policy falling within paragraph 3(4)(c) of that Schedule.

(11) The maximum amount that may be left out of account under subsection (10)(b) in the case of a policy is—

£3,600 x N

where N is the number of complete years for which ran—

(a) the other policy involved, or

(b) if there is more than one other policy involved, the policy which ran for the most number of complete years.

(12) In determining the premiums payable under a policy any provision for the waiver of premiums by reason of a person's disability is to be ignored.

(13) "New policy" has the meaning given in paragraph 17 of Schedule 15 to ICTA.][1]

Commentary—*Simon's Taxes* **E1.452CA.**
HMRC Manuals—Insurance Policyholder Taxation Manual IPTM2076 (effect of a policy becoming a RRQP).
Amendments—[1]   Sections 463A–463E inserted by FA 2013 s 25, Sch 9 paras 7, 8 with effect from 17 July 2013.

[463B Restricted relief qualifying policies: allowable premiums

(1) This section sets out how to determine the extent to which premiums payable under policy X during the policy X period are allowable premiums for the purposes of section 463A(3).

(2) A premium payable under policy X is allowable if it is payable before the restricted relief date.

(3) In this section "the restricted relief date" means—

(a) 6 April 2013, or

(b) if later, the date on which policy X became a restricted relief qualifying policy.

(4) Premiums payable under policy X in a relevant premium period are allowable so far as they do not exceed in total the premium limit for the period.

(5) In subsection (4) "relevant premium period" means—

(a) any period of one year which—

(i) begins with a relevant date, and

(ii) ends in the policy X period, and

(b) if it is not covered by paragraph (a), the period which—

(i) begins with the last relevant date to fall within the policy X period, and

(ii) ends at the end of the policy X period.

(6) In subsection (5) "relevant date" means—

(a) the restricted relief date, or

(b) any anniversary of the restricted relief date.

(7) For the purposes of subsection (4) "the premium limit" for a relevant premium period is determined in accordance with subsections (8) to (10).

(8) Determine the premiums payable in the relevant premium period under policies related to policy X.

(9) If the total of those premiums is £3,600 or more, the premium limit is nil (and, accordingly, no premiums payable under policy X in the relevant premium period are allowable).

(10) If the total of those premiums is less than £3,600, the premium limit is the difference between that total and £3,600.

(11) Subsection (4) does not apply if, at the time policy X became a restricted relief qualifying policy, any policy related to policy X was itself a restricted relief qualifying policy.

(12) For the purposes of this section a policy is "related" to policy X if it met the following requirements at the time policy X became a restricted relief qualifying policy—

(a) the policy is a qualifying policy under which the individual is a beneficiary (as determined in accordance with paragraph A5 of Schedule 15 to ICTA);

(b) the policy is neither a protected policy nor a pure protection policy.

(13) In subsection (12)(b)—

"protected policy" is to be read in accordance with paragraph A4 of Schedule 15 to ICTA, and "pure protection policy" has the meaning given by paragraph A6(1)(c) of that Schedule.

(14) A policy which is a new policy in relation to a policy "related" to policy X (whether by virtue of subsection (12) or this subsection) is also "related" to policy X if it meets the requirements of subsection (12)(*a*) and (*b*) when issued.

(15) A policy ceases to be "related" to policy X if it ceases to meet those requirements.

(16) If policy X is a restricted relief qualifying policy as provided for by paragraph A2(14) of Schedule 15 to ICTA, references in this section to policy X becoming a restricted relief qualifying policy are to be read as references to the policy determined under subsection (17) becoming a restricted relief qualifying policy.

(17) The policy is—

    (*a*) the policy ("policy Y") in relation to which policy X was the new policy, or

    (*b*) if policy Y was also a restricted relief qualifying policy as provided for by paragraph A2(14) of Schedule 15 to ICTA, the policy in relation to which policy Y was the new policy,

and so on.

(18) The following subsections apply for the purposes of this section if—

    (*a*) a premium ("premium A") is payable under policy X on a day ("day A") which is on or after 21 March 2012 but before 6 April 2013, and

    (*b*) the next premium payable under policy X is payable on a day ("day B") which is—

        (i) on or after 6 April 2013, and

        (ii) more than one month after day A.

(19) Premium A is to be treated as if, instead of being one premium payable on day A, it were a series of premiums payable at monthly intervals with the first premium in the series payable on day A.

(20) The number of premiums in the series is equal to the number of complete months falling within the period beginning with day A and ending with day B.

(21) The amount of each premium in the series is the amount of premium A divided by the number of premiums in the series.][1]

Commentary—*Simon's Taxes* E1.452CA.

HMRC Manuals—Insurance Policyholder Taxation Manual IPTM2070 (qualifying policies: rules from 6 April 2013).

Amendments—[1]   Sections 463A–463E inserted by FA 2013 s 25, Sch 9 paras 7, 8 with effect from 17 July 2013.

[463C Restricted relief qualifying policies: personal representatives and trustees with deceased settlors

(1) This section applies for the purpose of determining if personal representatives are liable for tax charged under this Chapter as provided for by section 466.

(2) This section also applies for the purpose of determining if trustees are liable for tax charged under this Chapter as provided for by section 467 where—

    (*a*) condition B in that section is met, and

    (*b*) the person who created the trusts has died.

(3) In relation to an event occurring on or after 6 April 2013, section 485 (disregard of certain events in relation to qualifying policies) does not apply in relation to a policy if the policy is a restricted relief qualifying policy (see paragraph A2 of Schedule 15 to ICTA).

(4) If any personal representatives or trustees are liable for tax charged under this Chapter as a result of subsection (3), section 463A(3) is to apply in the case of the personal representatives or the trustees—

    (*a*) as if the reference to the individual were to the personal representatives or to the trustees, and

    (*b*) as if the restricted relief qualifying policy were policy X.

(5) For this purpose—

    (*a*) in section 463B(12)(*a*) the reference to the individual is to be read as a reference to the deceased, and

    (*b*) a policy—

        (i) which would otherwise have ceased to be "related" to policy X for the purposes of section 463B on the deceased's death, but

        (ii) which continues to run after the deceased's death,

        is to be treated as "related" to policy X after the deceased's death.

(6) A policy which is a new policy (as defined in paragraph 17 of Schedule 15 to ICTA) in relation to a policy treated as "related" to policy X under subsection (5)(*b*) or this subsection is also to be treated as "related" to policy X if, apart from the deceased's death, it would meet the requirements of section 463B(12)(*a*) and (*b*) on its issue.

(7) A policy treated as "related" to policy X under subsection (5)(*b*) or (6) ceases to be so treated if, apart from the deceased's death, it would cease to meet the requirements of section 463B(12)(*a*) and (*b*).

(8) If section 528A also applies in the case of the personal representatives or the trustees in relation to the gain, section 463A(3) is to be applied to the gain before section 528A and, accordingly, the reduction to be made under section 528A is to be determined by reference to the gain as reduced by section 463A(3).][1]

Amendments—[1]   Sections 463A–463E inserted by FA 2013 s 25, Sch 9 paras 7, 8 with effect from 17 July 2013.

[463D Restricted relief qualifying policies: assignments and events following assignments etc

(1) This section applies if—

    (*a*) paragraph A1 of Schedule 15 to ICTA applies in relation to a policy by virtue of paragraph A1(8) in consequence of an event relating to the policy ("the relevant event"),

    (*b*) after the relevant event, the policy is not a qualifying policy by virtue of paragraph A1(2), and

    (*c*) in relation to an event occurring after the relevant event—

        (i) an individual is liable for tax charged under this Chapter on a gain from the policy, and

        (ii) but for the application of paragraph A1 in relation to the policy, section 463A(3) would have applied in the case of the individual so as to reduce the gain.

(2) Section 463A(3) is to apply in the case of the individual in relation to the gain as if the policy were policy X.

(3) But, for this purpose, section 463B(5) has effect as if the references to the policy X period were to the part of that period falling before the relevant event.

(4) If section 528 also applies in the case of the individual in relation to the gain, section 463A(3) is to be applied to the gain before section 528 and, accordingly, the reduction to be made under section 528 is to be determined by reference to the gain as reduced by section 463A(3).][1]

Commentary—*Simon's Taxes* **E1.452CA.**

Amendments—[1]   Sections 463A–463E inserted by FA 2013 s 25, Sch 9 paras 7, 8 with effect from 17 July 2013.

[463E Transitional protection for policies issued in respect of insurances made on or after 21 March 2012 but before 6 April 2013

(1) This section applies if—

    (*a*) a policy ("policy Z") is issued,

    (*b*) the issue of policy Z is an event falling within paragraph A2(3) of Schedule 15 to ICTA by virtue of paragraph (*e*),

    (*c*) after its issue, policy Z is a qualifying policy but not a restricted relief qualifying policy,

    (*d*) policy Z is varied on or after 6 April 2013 and the variation is an event falling within paragraph A1(3) of Schedule 15,

    (*e*) after the variation, policy Z is not a qualifying policy by virtue of paragraph A1(2) of that Schedule,

    (*f*) in relation to an event occurring after the variation, an individual is liable for tax charged under this Chapter on a gain from policy Z, and

    (*g*) but for the application of paragraph A1 of Schedule 15 in relation to policy Z, the individual would not have been liable because of section 485.

(2) The gain on which the tax is charged in the case of the individual is reduced by the following amount—

$$G \times (TPV / TP)$$

where—

    G is the amount of the gain (apart from this subsection),

    TPV is the total amount of premiums payable under policy Z before the variation, and

    TP is the total amount of premiums payable under policy Z before the chargeable event.

(3) If section 528 also applies in the case of the individual in relation to the gain, subsection (2) is to be applied to the gain before section 528 and, accordingly, the reduction to be made under section 528 is to be determined by reference to the gain as reduced by subsection (2).

(4) Section 463A(10) to (12) applies for the purposes of subsection (2).][1]

Commentary—*Simon's Taxes* **E1.452CB.**

HMRC Manuals—Insurance Policyholder Taxation Manual IPTM2075 (policies issued on or after 21 March 2012 and before 6 April 2013).

Amendments—[1]   Sections 463A–463E inserted by FA 2013 s 25, Sch 9 paras 7, 8 with effect from 17 July 2013.

Person liable etc.

464 Person liable for tax: introduction

(1) The person liable for any tax charged under this Chapter is the person indicated by—

    section 465 (person liable: individuals),

    section 466 (person liable: personal representatives), and

    section 467 (person liable: UK resident trustees),

according to how the rights under the policy or contract are owned or held immediately before the chargeable event in question occurs.

(2) References in those sections to the ownership or holding of those rights are references to their ownership or holding at that time.

(3) If there has been a surrender or assignment of only a part of or share in rights under the policy or contract, the references in this section and those sections to the rights are references to that part or share.

(4) For cases where such surrenders or assignments are taken to occur, see—

    section 500 (events treated as part surrenders), and

section 505 (assignments etc. involving co-ownership).

(5) This section and sections 470 to 472 are subject to section 469(4) (application of this section and those sections where two or more persons are interested in the policy or contract in question).

(6) See also—

section 468 (non-UK resident trustees and foreign institutions),

section 471 (determination of shares etc.), and

section 472 (trusts created by two or more persons).

Commentary—*Simon's Taxes* E1.445.

HMRC Manuals—Insurance Policyholder Taxation Manual IPTM3200 (person liable to charge).

465 Person liable: individuals

(1) An individual is liable for tax under this Chapter if the individual is UK resident [for the tax year][2] in which the gain arises and condition A, B or C is met.

[(1A) But if the tax year is a split year as respects the individual, the individual is not liable for tax under this Chapter in respect of gains arising in the overseas part of that year (subject to section 465B).][1]

(2) Condition A is that the individual beneficially owns the rights under the policy or contract in question.

(3) Condition B is that those rights are held on non-charitable trusts which the individual created.

(4) Condition C is that those rights are held as security for the individual's debt.

(5) For the purposes of calculating the total income of an individual liable for tax under this Chapter, the amount charged is treated as income.

(6) References in this Chapter to trusts which an individual created include references to trusts arising under any of the following provisions (and references to a settlor or to a person creating trusts are to be read accordingly)—

(*a*) section 11 of the Married Women's Property Act 1882 (c. 75),

(*b*) section 2 of the Married Women's Policies of Assurance (Scotland) Act 1880 (c. 26), and

(*c*) section 4 of the Law Reform (Husband and Wife) Act (Northern Ireland) 1964 (c. 23 (NI)).

(7) For the right of an individual to recover certain amounts from the trustees of non-charitable trusts, see section 538 (recovery of tax from trustees).

Commentary—*Simon's Taxes* E1.446.

HMRC Manuals—Insurance Policyholder Taxation Manual IPTM3220 (conditions in which an individual is chargeable).

Amendments—[1]   Sub-s (1A) inserted by FA 2013 s 218, Sch 45 paras 82, 84 with effect in calculating an individual's liability to income tax or capital gains tax for the tax year 2013–14 or any subsequent tax year, subject to transitional provisions and savings in FA 2013 Sch 45 paras 154–158.

[2]   Words in sub-s (1) substituted for words "in the tax year" by FA 2013 s 218, Sch 45 para 150 with effect from 17 July 2013.

[465A Amounts for which individuals liable to be treated as highest part of total income

(1) This section applies if—

(*a*) an individual is liable for tax under this Chapter in respect of an amount, and

(*b*) the individual is treated by section 530 as having paid income tax at the [basic rate][2] on the amount.

(2) The amount is treated as the highest part of the individual's total income.

(3) Subsection (2) has effect for all income tax purposes except the purposes of sections 535 to 537 (gains from contracts for life insurance etc: top slicing relief).

(4) See section 1012 of ITA 2007 (relationship between highest part rules) for the relationship between—

(*a*) the rule in subsection (2), and

(*b*) other rules requiring particular income to be treated as the highest part of a person's total income.][1]

Commentary—*Simon's Taxes* E1.446.

Amendments—[1]   This section inserted by ITA 2007 s 1027, Sch 1 paras 492, 529 with effect for income tax purposes from 6 April 2007, and corporation tax purposes for accounting periods ending after 5 April 2007.

[2]   Words in sub-s (1)(*b*) substituted by FA 2008 s 5, Sch 1 paras 50, 51 with effect for the tax year 2008–09 and subsequent tax years.

[465B Temporary non-residents

(1) This section applies if an individual is temporarily non-resident.

(2) The individual is liable for tax under this Chapter for the year of return in respect of any gain that meets the conditions in subsection (3).

(3) The conditions are—

(*a*) the gain arose in the temporary period of non-residence,

(*b*) it arose from a policy issued in respect of an insurance made, or from a contract made, before the start of that period,

(*c*) the chargeable event giving rise to it was neither a death nor a chargeable event treated as occurring under section 525(2),

(*d*) no-one is liable under section 466 or 467 in respect of the gain, (*e*) no-one is liable by virtue of section 468 for either the year of return or an earlier tax year as a result of the gain, and

    (*f*) the individual would have been liable under section 465 in respect of the gain, applying the assumptions in subsection (4).

(4) The assumptions are—

    (*a*) the individual was UK resident for the tax year in which the gain arose, and

    (*b*) that tax year was not a split year as respects the individual.

(5) If the individual is liable by virtue of subsection (2) in respect of a gain—

    (*a*) the amount of the gain in respect of which he or she is liable is the amount on which tax would have been charged under this Chapter applying the assumptions in subsection (4), but

    (*b*) in determining that amount, section 528 must be applied ignoring those assumptions.

(6) That amount is treated as income of the individual for the year of return.

(7) If the gain arises from a policy or contract treated under section 473A as a single policy or contract, the date, for the purposes of subsection (3)(*b*), on which the insurance or contract is made is the date on which the first insurance is made in respect of which the connected policies were issued or, as the case may be, the date on which the first of the connected contracts is made.

(8) This section does not apply to a gain if—

    (*a*) in relation to the policy or contract from which the gain arises, a terminal event occurs in the temporary period of non-residence or in the period of return,

    (*b*) the chargeable event giving rise to the gain occurred before that terminal event,

    (*c*) the chargeable event giving rise to the gain is one that is treated as occurring under section 509(1) as a result of the application of section 498(1)(*a*),

    (*d*) section 498(1)(*a*) applies other than by virtue of section 500, and

    (*e*) a person (whether or not the individual) is liable for tax under this Chapter (including by virtue of this section) in respect of any gain resulting from the terminal event.

(9) Nothing in any double taxation relief arrangements is to be read as preventing the individual from being liable for tax under this Chapter in respect of any gain in respect of which the individual is liable for tax by virtue of subsection (2) (or as preventing a charge to tax on that gain from arising under this Chapter).

(10) Part 4 of Schedule 45 to FA 2013 (statutory residence test: anti-avoidance) explains—

    (*a*) when an individual is to be regarded as "temporarily non-resident", and

    (*b*) what "the temporary period of non-residence" and "the period of return" mean.

(11) In this section—

    "terminal event" means an event mentioned in section 499(3);

    "year of return" means the tax year that consists of or includes the period of return.][1]

Amendments—[1]   Section 465B inserted by FA 2013 s 218, Sch 45 paras 139, 140 with effect if the year of departure (as defined in FA 2013 Sch 45 Pt 4) is the tax year 2013–14 or any subsequent tax year, subject to transitional provisions and savings in FA 2013 Sch 45 paras 154–158.

466 Person liable: personal representatives

(1) Personal representatives are liable for tax under this Chapter if the rights under the policy or contract are held by them and the condition in subsection (2) is met (and accordingly the gain is treated for income tax purposes as income of the personal representatives in that capacity).

(2) The condition is that if an individual were liable for tax on a gain in respect of the policy or contract, section 530(1) (individual treated as having paid tax at the [basic rate][1]) would be disapplied as a result of—

    (*a*) section 531(1) (exceptions from section 530 for policies and contracts specified in section 531(3)), or

    (*b*) paragraph 109(2) of Schedule 2 (contracts in accounting periods beginning before 1st January 1992).

(3) For cases where the condition in subsection (2) is not met, see section 664 of this Act and [section 947 of CTA 2009][2] (under which the gain is treated as part of the aggregate income of the estate for the purposes of Chapter 6 of Part 5 of this Act and [Chapter 3 of Part 10 of CTA 2009][2] respectively).

Commentary—*Simon's Taxes* E1.447.

HMRC Manuals—Insurance Policyholder Taxation Manual IPTM3240 (cases where personal representatives are liable).

Amendments—[1]   Words in sub-s (2) substituted by FA 2008 s 5, Sch 1 paras 50, 52 with effect for the tax year 2008–09 and subsequent tax years.

[2]   Words in sub-s (3) substituted by CTA 2009 s 1322, Sch 1 paras 587, 632. CTA 2009 applies for accounting periods ending on or after 1 April 2009 (for corporation tax purposes) and for tax years 2009–10 onwards (for income and capital gains tax purposes).

467 Person liable: UK resident trustees

(1) Trustees are liable for tax under this Chapter if immediately before the chargeable event in question occurs they are UK resident and condition A, B, C or D is met.

[(1A) If trustees are liable for tax under this Chapter, the gain is treated for income tax purposes as income of the trustees.][1]

ITTOIA 2005

(2) Condition A is that the rights under the policy or contract are held by the trustees on charitable trusts.

(3) Condition B is that—

    (*a*) those rights are held by the trustees on non-charitable trusts, and

    (*b*) one or more of the absent settlor conditions is met.

(4) The absent settlor conditions are that the person who created the trusts—

    (*a*) is non-UK resident,

    [(*aa*) is UK resident but the gain arises in the overseas part of a tax year that is, as respects the person who created the trusts, a split year,][4]

    (*b*) has died, or

    (*c*) in the case of a company or foreign institution (see section 468(5)), has been dissolved or wound up or has otherwise come to an end.

(5) Condition C is that—

    (*a*) the rights under the policy or contract are held by the trustees on non-charitable trusts,

    (*b*) condition B does not apply, and

    [(*c*) neither section 465 nor section 466 applies.][2]

(6) Condition D is that the rights under the policy or contract are held as security for a debt owed by the trustees.

[(7) If trustees are liable for tax under this Chapter, it is charged at the [basic rate][3] if—

    (*a*) condition A is met, or

    (*b*) condition D is met and the trustees are trustees of a charitable trust.][1]

Commentary—*Simon's Taxes* **E1.448.**

HMRC Manuals—Insurance Policyholder Taxation Manual IPTM3230 (UK resident trustees).

Amendments—[1] Sub-s (1A) inserted, and sub-s (7) substituted, by ITA 2007 s 1027, Sch 1 paras 492, 531 with effect for income tax purposes from 6 April 2007, and corporation tax purposes for accounting periods ending after 5 April 2007.

[2] Sub-s (5)(*c*) substituted by FA 2008 s 36, Sch 14 paras 10, 11 with effect—

    (a) so far as relating to corporation tax for accounting periods beginning on or after 1 April 2008, and

    (b) so far as relating to income tax, for the tax year 2008–09 and subsequent tax years.

[3] Words in sub-s (7) substituted by FA 2008 s 5, Sch 1 paras 50, 53 with effect for the tax year 2008–09 and subsequent tax years.

[4] Sub-s (4)(*aa*) inserted by FA 2013 s 218, Sch 45 paras 82, 85 with effect in calculating an individual's liability to income tax or capital gains tax for the tax year 2013–14 or any subsequent tax year, subject to transitional provisions and savings in FA 2013 Sch 45 paras 154–158.

468 Non-UK resident trustees and foreign institutions

(1) This section applies if a gain is treated as arising under this Chapter and either—

    (*a*) trustees who are non-UK resident would be liable for tax in respect of the gain as a result of section 467 if the trustees were UK resident immediately before the chargeable event in question occurs, or

    (*b*) immediately before that event occurs—

        (i) a foreign institution beneficially owns a share in the rights,

        (ii) the rights are held for the purposes of a foreign institution, or

        (iii) a share in them is held as security for a foreign institution's debt.

[(2) Chapter 2 of Part 13 of ITA 2007 (which prevents avoidance of tax where a UK resident individual benefits from a transfer of assets) applies with the modifications specified in subsection (3) or (4).][3]

(3) In a case within subsection (1)(*a*), [Chapter 2 of Part 13 of ITA 2007 applies][1] as if—

    (*a*) the gain were income becoming payable to the trustees, and

    (*b*) that income arose to the trustees in the tax year in which the gain arises.

(4) In a case within subsection (1)(*b*), [Chapter 2 of Part 13 of ITA 2007 applies][1] as if—

    (*a*) the gain were income becoming payable to the institution, and

    (*b*) that income arose to the institution in the tax year in which the gain arises.

(5) In this Chapter "foreign institution" means a company or other institution resident or domiciled outside the United Kingdom.

(6) If there has been a surrender or assignment of only a part of or share in rights under the policy or contract, the references in this section to those rights are references to that part or share.

[(7) This section does not apply if someone is liable under section 465B in respect of the gain.][2]

Commentary—*Simon's Taxes* **E1.449.**

HMRC Manuals—Insurance Policyholder Taxation Manual IPTM3260 (special rules for non-UK resident trustees and foreign institutions).

Amendments—[1] Words in sub-ss (3), (4) substituted, by ITA 2007 s 1027, Sch 1 paras 492, 532 with effect for income tax purposes from 6 April 2007, and corporation tax purposes for accounting periods ending after 5 April 2007.

[2] Sub-s (7) inserted by FA 2013 s 218, Sch 45 paras 139, 141 with effect if the year of departure (as defined in FA 2013 Sch 45 Pt 4) is the tax year 2013–14 or any subsequent tax year, subject to transitional provisions and savings in FA 2013 Sch 45 paras 154–158.

[3] Sub-s (2) substituted by FA 2013 s 219, Sch 46 paras 43, 46 with effect for the purposes of a person's liability to income tax for the tax year 2013–14 or any subsequent tax year, subject to savings in FA 2013 Sch 46 para 73.

469 Two or more persons interested in policy or contract

(1) This section applies if immediately before a chargeable event two or more persons have material interests in the rights under the policy or contract.

(2) Section 470 sets out the circumstances in which persons have such interests for the purposes of this section (which correspond to the circumstances referred to in sections 465 to 468 . . . [1]).

(3) Section 463 (income charged) applies in the case of any of the persons with such interests as if the amount of the gain arising when the event occurs were such part of it as is proportionate to the share of the rights to which the person's interest relates.

(4) Sections 464 to 468 (persons liable for tax etc.) apply in relation to each of those persons as if that person were the only person with such an interest at that time.

(5) Section 539(1) (relief for deficiencies) applies in relation to each of those persons as if the amount of deficiency arising when that event occurs were such part of it as is proportionate to the share of the rights to which that person's interest relates.

(6) If a person ("A") has two or more material interests in the rights under a policy or contract, this section applies in the same way as where two or more persons have separate such interests, unless A—

    (*a*) is the only person with such interests, and

    (*b*) has all those interests in the same capacity.

(7) If there has been a surrender or assignment of only a part of or share in rights under the policy or contract, the references to those rights in this section and sections 470 to 472 are references to that part or share.

Commentary—*Simon's Taxes* **E1.450.**
HMRC Manuals—Insurance Policyholder Taxation Manual IPTM3270 (multiple interests).
Amendments—[1]   In sub-s (2), words repealed by FA 2008 s 36, Sch 14 paras 1, 12 with effect as follows—
    (a)   so far as relating to corporation tax, for accounting periods beginning on or after 1 April 2008, and
    (b)   so far as relating to income tax, for the tax year 2008–09 and subsequent tax years.

470 Interests in rights under a policy or contract for section 469

(1) This section sets out the circumstances in which a person has a material interest in the rights under a policy or contract for the purposes of section 469.

(2) An individual has such an interest if—

    (*a*) the individual beneficially owns a share in the rights,

    (*b*) a share in them is held on non-charitable trusts which the individual created, or

    (*c*) a share in them is held as security for the individual's debt.

(3) A company has such an interest if—

    (*a*) the company beneficially owns a share in the rights,

    (*b*) a share in them is held on non-charitable trusts which the company created, or

    (*c*) a share in them is held as security for the company's debt.

(4) Personal representatives have such an interest if they hold a share in the rights.

(5) Trustees of a charitable trust have such an interest if a share in the rights—

    (*a*) is held by them, or

    (*b*) is held as security for a debt owed by them.

(6) Trustees of a non-charitable trust have such an interest if—

    (*a*) a share in the rights is held by the trustees and one of the absent settlor conditions specified in section 467(4) is met,

    (*b*) a share in the rights is held by them, none of those conditions is met and no individual, company or personal representatives have an interest in the share, or

    (*c*) a share in them is held as security for a debt owed by the trustees.

(7) A foreign institution has such an interest if—

    (*a*) the institution beneficially owns a share in the rights,

    (*b*) the rights are held for the institution's purposes, or

    (*c*) a share in them is held as security for the institution's debt.

Commentary—*Simon's Taxes* **E1.450.**

471 Determination of shares etc.

(1) For the purposes of this Chapter—

    (*a*) rights under a policy or contract which are beneficially owned by two or more persons jointly, and

    (*b*) an interest in such rights which is so owned,

are treated as if they were beneficially owned by those persons in equal shares.

(2) Subsections (3) and (4) apply if immediately before a chargeable event the rights under the policy or contract are, or a share in those rights is, held as security for one or more debts owed by two or more persons.

(3) Each of those persons is treated for the purposes of this Chapter as the sole debtor for a separate debt.

(4) The appropriate share of the security for the actual debt or debts, so far as it consists of the rights under the policy or contract or a share in them, is treated for the purposes of this Chapter as the security for each separate debt.

(5) In subsection (4) "the appropriate share" means—

    (a) if there is only one actual debt for which the person is liable as between the debtors, a share proportionate to the share of that debt for which the person is so liable, and

    (b) if there are two or more such actual debts, a share proportionate to the share of the total such debts for which the person is so liable.

(6) For the purposes of this section, property held for the purposes of a foreign institution is treated as being beneficially owned by the institution.

(7) An interest in some or all of the rights under a policy or contract which is not a share in all those rights is treated for the purposes of this Chapter as such a share in those rights as may, on a just and reasonable apportionment, be regarded as representing the interest.

472 Trusts created by two or more persons

(1) For the purposes of this Chapter, if immediately before a chargeable event—

    (a) the rights under a policy or contract are held on non-charitable trusts created by two or more persons, or

    (b) a share in those rights is so held,

each of the persons is treated as the sole settlor of a separate share of the rights or share held on trusts.

(2) Each settlor's separate share is proportionate to the share originating from that settlor of the whole of the property subject to the trusts immediately before the event.

(3) If immediately before a chargeable event non-charitable trusts apply to property originating from different persons (for example, where property is added by different persons to an existing settlement)—

    (a) as respects that event the trusts are taken to have been created by them all, and

    (b) accordingly, each of them is treated as a sole settlor under subsection (1).

(4) Property originates from a person for the purposes of subsections (2) and (3) if—

    (a) it is property provided by the person for the purposes of the trusts,

    (b) it is property representing such property, or

    (c) in a case where property represents both property within paragraph (a) and other property, it is so much of that property as, on a just and reasonable apportionment, is to be taken to represent the property within paragraph (a).

(5) References in subsection (4) to property representing other property include property representing accumulated income from other property.

(6) For the purposes of this section, property is treated as provided by a person ("A") if—

    (a) it is provided by A directly or indirectly, or

    (b) it is provided directly or indirectly by another person under reciprocal arrangements with A.

(7) Property is not treated as provided by A if it is provided by A directly or indirectly under reciprocal arrangements with another person.

Commentary—*Simon's Taxes* **E1.450.**

HMRC Manuals—Insurance Policyholder Taxation Manual IPTM3290 (trusts created by more than one person).

Policies and contracts to which Chapter 9 applies

473 Policies and contracts to which Chapter 9 applies: general

(1) This Chapter applies to—

    (a) policies of life insurance,

    (b) contracts for life annuities, and

    (c) capital redemption policies.

(2) In this Chapter—

    "capital redemption policy" means a contract made in the course of a capital redemption business, [within the meaning given by section 56(3) of FA 2012][2], and

    "life annuity" means—

        (a) an annuity that—

            (i) is a purchased life annuity for the purposes of Chapter 7 of this Part (see section 423), and

            (ii) is not specified in section 718 (annuities excluded from the exemption for part of purchased life annuity payments under section 717), *or*

        (b) . . . [1]

(3) Subsection (1) is subject to—

    section 478 (exclusion of mortgage repayment policies),

    section 479 (exclusion of pension policies),

    section 480 (exclusion of excepted group life policies), and

    section 483 (exclusion of credit union group life policies).

Commentary—*Simon's Taxes* **E1.441, E1.442.**

HMRC Manuals—Insurance Policyholder Taxation Manual IPTM3300 (policies and contracts charged: general).
Amendments—[1]   Sub-s (2)(*b*) and preceding word repealed by FA 2008 s 36, Sch 14 para 17 with effect as follows—
    (a)   so far as relating to corporation tax, for accounting periods beginning on or after 1 April 2008, and
    (b)   so far as relating to income tax, for the tax year 2008–09 and subsequent tax years.
[2]   In sub-s (2), in the definition of "capital redemption policy", words substituted for words "within the meaning of Chapter 1 of Part 12 of ICTA", by FA 2012 s 146, Sch 16 paras 125, 127 with effect in relation to accounting periods of companies beginning on or after 1 January 2013 (subject to transitional provisions in FA 2012 Sch 17). For accounting periods straddling 1 January 2013, see FA 2012 s 149.

[473A Connected policies or contracts treated as single policy or contract

(1) Policies or contracts which are connected with each other are treated as a single policy or contract for the purposes of this Chapter.

(2) A policy or contract is "connected" with another policy or contract if—
    (*a*) they meet the condition in subsection (3) in relation to each other, and
    (*b*) the terms on which either of them is issued are significantly more or less favourable than would reasonably be expected if the other were ignored or any policy or contract meeting the condition in that subsection in relation to either of them were ignored.

(3) A policy or contract meets the condition in this subsection in relation to another policy or contract if—
    (*a*) they are at any time simultaneously in force, and
    (*b*) either of them is issued with reference to the other or with a view to enabling the other to be issued on particular terms or facilitating its being issued on those terms.

(4) If—
    (*a*) there is a policy or contract ("A") with which two or more other policies or contracts are connected as a result of subsection (2), but
    (*b*) the other policies or contracts are not connected with each other as a result of that subsection,
  A and the other policies or contracts are (as a result of this subsection) to be regarded as "connected" with each other.][1]

Commentary—*Simon's Taxes* E1.442.
Amendments—[1]   This section inserted by FA 2012 s 11(1) with effect in relation to—
    (a)   any policy issued in respect of an insurance made on or after 21 March 2012; or any contract made on or after that date;
    (b)   any insurance or contract made before 21 March 2012 if on or after that date—
        (i)   the policy or contract is varied with the result that there is an increase in the benefits secured;
        (ii)   there is an assignment of rights, or a share of the rights, conferred by the policy or contract (whether or not for money's worth); or
        (iii)   some or all of the rights conferred by the policy or contract become held as security for a debt.
  In (b)(i) a variation of a policy or contract includes an exercise of rights conferred by a policy or contract; and an increase in benefits secured includes an increase in the benefits secured by another policy or contract with which the policy or contract is connected (within the meaning given by s 473A): see FA 2012 s 10(6).

474 Special rules: qualifying policies

(1) In the application of this Chapter to policies of insurance that are qualifying policies for the purposes of Chapter 1 of Part 7 of ICTA (policies within the conditions in Schedule 15 to that Act that qualify for special tax treatment) special rules apply.

(2) See, in particular—
    section 485 (disregard of certain events in relation to qualifying policies),
    section 503 (exception from section 501 for certain loans under qualifying policies),
    section 542 (replacement of qualifying policies), and
    section 543 (issue time of qualifying policy replacing foreign policy).

(3) Policies within the definition of "foreign policy of life insurance" in section 476(3) that would otherwise be qualifying policies are treated for the purposes of this Chapter as not being qualifying policies in the cases specified in subsections (4) and (5).

(4) Policies within paragraph (*a*) of that definition are so treated once the conditions in paragraph 24(3) of Schedule 15 to ICTA have ceased to be met with respect to them (conditions that are required to be met for certain policies issued by non-UK resident companies to be qualifying policies).

(5) Policies within paragraph (*b*) of that definition immediately before an event do not count as qualifying policies in relation to that event.

475 Special rules: personal portfolio bonds

(1) In the application of this Chapter to personal portfolio bonds, certain special rules apply.

(2) See, in particular—
    section 515 (requirement for annual calculations in relation to personal portfolio bonds), and
    sections 522 to 525 (method for making calculations and chargeable events where calculations show gains).

(3) For the meaning of "personal portfolio bond" see section 516.

Commentary—*Simon's Taxes* E1.454.
HMRC Manuals—Insurance Policyholder Taxation Manual IPTM7710 (scope and outline of the PPB legislation).

476 Special rules: foreign policies

(1) In the application of this Chapter to foreign policies of life insurance and foreign capital redemption policies, certain special rules apply.

(2) See, in particular—

section 474(3) to (5) (certain foreign policies treated as not being qualifying policies), [and][3]
. . .[3]

sections 531 to 534 (under which foreign policies are excepted from section 530 (income tax treated as paid etc.) subject to certain reliefs), . . .[3]
. . .[3]

(3) In this Chapter—

"foreign policy of life insurance" means—

  (a) a policy of life insurance issued by a non-UK resident company, and

  (b) a policy of life insurance which forms part of the overseas life assurance business of an insurance company or friendly society . . .[1],

"foreign capital redemption policy" means—

  (a) a capital redemption policy issued by a non-UK resident company, and

  (b) a capital redemption policy which forms part of the overseas life assurance business of an insurance company . . .[1], and

"overseas life assurance business" has the [meaning given by section 61 of FA 2012][2].

Commentary—*Simon's Taxes* **E1.441.**

HMRC Manuals—Insurance Policyholder Taxation Manual IPTM3330 (meaning foreign policies).

Amendments—[1] Words repealed by FA 2008 s 43, Sch 17 para 27 with effect for income tax purposes from 2007–08, and for corporation tax purposes for periods of account of insurance companies beginning on or after 1 January 2007 (FA 2008 Sch 17 para 27(3): these amendments have effect as if they were made by FA 2007 Sch 7).

[2] In sub-s (3), in definition of "overseas life assurance business", words substituted for words "same meaning as in Part 12 of ICTA (see section 431D of that Act)", by FA 2012 s 146, Sch 16 paras 125, 128 with effect in relation to accounting periods for companies beginning on or after 1 January 2013 (subject to transitional provisions in FA 2012 Sch 17). For accounting periods straddling 1 January 2013, see FA 2012 s 149.

[3] In sub-s (2), word "and" after entry relating to section 474(3) to (5) inserted, entries relating to sections 528 and to 536(6) repealed, and word "and" after entry relating to sections 531 to 534 repealed, by FA 2013 s 24, Sch 8 paras 1, 2 with effect in relation to any policy of life insurance issued in respect of an insurance made on or after 6 April 2013 or any contract constituting a capital redemption policy made on or after that date. Note that, in the case of a policy or contract treated under s 473A of this Act as a single policy or contract, for these purposes the date on which the insurance or contract is made is the date on which, as the case may be, the first insurance is made in respect of which the connected policies are issued, or the first of the connected contracts is made (FA 2013 Sch 8 para 7(4)).

477 Special rules: certain older policies and contracts

(1) In the case of—

  (a) certain contracts made before particular dates, and

  (b) certain policies issued, or issued in respect of insurances made, before particular dates,

this Chapter applies subject to Parts 6 and 7 of Schedule 2 (special provisions for older policies and contracts).

(2) See the table in section 546 for the provisions affected.

478 Exclusion of mortgage repayment policies

(1) This Chapter does not apply to a mortgage repayment policy.

(2) In this section "mortgage repayment policy" means a policy of life insurance with the sole object of providing, on an individual's death or disability, a sum substantially the same as any amount then outstanding under a repayment mortgage—

  (a) of the individual's residence, or

  (b) of any premises occupied by the individual for the purposes of a business.

(3) In this section "repayment mortgage" means a mortgage securing a principal amount which is repayable by instalments payable annually or at shorter regular intervals.

Commentary—*Simon's Taxes* **E1.444.**

HMRC Manuals—Insurance Policyholder Taxation Manual IPTM7055 (mortgage protection policies). IPTM1540 (policies and contracts not chargeable).

479 Exclusion of pension policies

This Chapter does not apply to a policy of insurance which—

  (a) constitutes a registered pension scheme, or

  (b) is issued or held in connection with such a scheme.

Commentary—*Simon's Taxes* **E1.444.**

HMRC Manuals—Insurance Policyholder Taxation Manual IPTM7060 (pension policies). IPTM1540 (policies and contracts not chargeable).

480 Exclusion of excepted group life policies

(1) This Chapter does not apply to an excepted group life policy.

(2) In this Chapter "group life policy" means a policy of life insurance whose terms provide—

  (a) for the payment of benefits on the death of more than one individual, and

  (b) for those benefits to be paid on the death of each of those individuals.

(3) In this section "excepted group life policy" means a group life policy with respect to which the conditions specified in the following sections are met—

    (*a*) section 481 (conditions about benefits), and

    (*b*) section 482 (conditions about persons intended to benefit).

Commentary—*Simon's Taxes* **E1.444.**

HMRC Manuals—Insurance Policyholder Taxation Manual IPTM7020 (definition of a group life policy for tax purposes). IPTM1125 (what is a group life policy?)
IPTM1540 (policies and contracts not chargeable).

481 Excepted group life policies: conditions about benefits

(1) Conditions A to D are the conditions referred to in section 480(3)(*a*) (definition of "excepted group life policy").

(2) Condition A is that under the terms of the policy a sum or other benefit of a capital nature is payable or arises—

    (*a*) on the death in any circumstances of each of the individuals insured under the policy who dies under an age specified in the policy that does not exceed 75, or

    (*b*) on the death, except in the same specified circumstances, of each of those individuals who dies under such an age.

(3) Condition B is that under the terms of the policy—

    (*a*) the same method is to be used for calculating the sums or other benefits of a capital nature payable or arising on each death, and

    (*b*) any limitation on those sums or other benefits is the same in the case of any death.

(4) Condition C is that the policy does not have, and is not capable of having, on any day—

    (*a*) a surrender value that exceeds the proportion of the amount of premiums paid which, on a time apportionment, is referable to the unexpired paid-up period beginning with the day, or

    (*b*) if there is no such period, any surrender value.

(5) In subsection (4) "the unexpired paid-up period", in relation to a period beginning with a day, means the period beginning then and ending with the earliest subsequent day on which a payment of premium falls due under the policy or the term of the policy ends.

(6) Condition D is that no sums or other benefits may be paid or conferred under the policy, except as mentioned in condition A or C.

Commentary—*Simon's Taxes* **E1.444.**

HMRC Manuals—Insurance Policyholder Taxation Manual IPTM7025 (exceptions: group life policies: conditions about when benefits may be paid and how they are calculated).

482 Excepted group life policies: conditions about persons intended to benefit

(1) Conditions A to C are the conditions referred to in section 480(3)(*b*) (definition of "excepted group life policy").

(2) Condition A is that any sums payable or other benefits arising under the policy must (whether directly or indirectly) be paid to or for, or conferred on, or applied at the direction of—

    (*a*) an individual or charity beneficially entitled to them, or

    (*b*) a trustee or other person acting in a fiduciary capacity who will secure that the sums or other benefits are paid to or for, or conferred on, or applied in favour of, an individual or charity beneficially.

(3) Condition B is that no person who is, or is connected with, an individual whose life is insured under the policy may, as a result of a group membership right relating to that individual, receive (directly or indirectly) any death benefit in respect of another individual whose life is so insured.

(4) In subsection (3)—

"death benefit in respect of an individual" means any sums or other benefits payable or arising under the policy on the individual's death or anything representing any such sums or benefits, and

"group membership right", in relation to an individual insured by a group life policy, means any right (including the right of any person to be considered by trustees in their exercise of a discretion) that is referable to that individual being one of the individuals whose lives are insured by the policy.

(5) Condition C is that a tax avoidance purpose is not the main purpose, or one of the main purposes, for which a person is at any time—

    (*a*) the holder, or one of the holders, of the policy, or

    (*b*) the person, or one of the persons, beneficially entitled under the policy.

(6) In subsection (5)—

    ¹

"tax avoidance purpose" means any purpose that consists in securing a tax advantage (whether for the holder of the policy or any other person).

[(7) In this section "tax advantage" has the meaning given by [section 1139 of CTA 2010]².]¹

Commentary—*Simon's Taxes* **E1.444.**

HMRC Manuals—Insurance Policyholder Taxation Manual IPTM7035 (conditions about nature of persons intended to benefit).

ITTOIA 2005

Amendments—[1]   In sub-s (6), definition of "tax advantage" repealed; and sub-s (7) inserted, by ITA 2007 ss 1027, 1031, Sch 1 paras 492, 533, Sch 3 Pt 1 with effect for income tax purposes from 6 April 2007, and corporation tax purposes for accounting periods ending after 5 April 2007.
[2]   In sub-s (7) words substituted by CTA 2010 s 1177, Sch 1 paras 444, 468. CTA 2010 has effect for corporation tax purposes for accounting periods ending on or after 1 April 2010, and for income and capital gains tax purposes for the tax year 2010–11 and subsequent tax years.

483 Exclusion of credit union group life policies

(1) This Chapter does not apply to a credit union group life policy.

(2) In this section "credit union group life policy" means a group life policy with the sole object of providing, on the death or disability of any of the individuals insured under it, a sum substantially the same as any amount then outstanding under a loan made to that individual by a credit union.

(3) In this section "credit union" means a society registered as a credit union under—

[(a)   the Co-operative and Community Benefit Societies Act 2014,][1] or

(b)   the Credit Unions (Northern Ireland) Order 1985 (SI 1985/1205 (NI 12)).

Commentary—*Simon's Taxes* E1.444.

HMRC Manuals—Insurance Policyholder Taxation Manual IPTM1540 (meaning of credit union loan protection policies). IPTM1540 (policies and contracts not chargeable).

Amendments—[1]   Sub-s (3)(a) substituted by the Co-operative and Community Benefit Societies Act 2014 s 151, Sch 4 paras 92, 94(1), (4) with effect from 1 August 2014 and subject to transitional provisions and provisions preserving the continuity of the law in Sch 5 of that Act.

When chargeable events occur: general

484 When chargeable events occur

(1) The following are chargeable events—

   (a)   in the case of any kind of policy or contract—

      (i)   the surrender of all rights under the policy or contract,

      (ii)   the assignment of all those rights for money or money's worth,

      (iii)   the falling due of a sum payable as a result of a right under a policy or contract to participate in profits, if there are no remaining rights under it,

      (iv)   a chargeable event treated as occurring under section 509(1) (chargeable events in certain cases where periodic calculations show gains),

      (v)   a surrender or assignment treated as a chargeable event under section 514(1) (chargeable events where transaction-related calculations show gains), and

      (vi)   a chargeable event treated as occurring under section 525(2) (chargeable events where annual personal portfolio bond calculations show gains),

   (b)   in the case of a policy of life insurance, a death giving rise to benefits under it,

   (c)   in the case of a policy of life insurance or a capital redemption policy, its maturity,

   (d)   in the case of a contract for a life annuity which provides for the payment of a capital sum on death, the death, and

   (e)   in the case of a contract for a life annuity which provides for a capital sum to be taken as a complete alternative to the annuity payments (or any further annuity payments), taking the capital sum.

(2) Subsection (1) is subject to—

   section 485 (disregard of certain events in relation to qualifying policies),

   section 486 (exclusion of maturity of capital redemption policies in certain circumstances),

   section 487 (disregard of certain assignments), and

   section 488 (disregard of certain events following alterations of life insurance policy terms).

(3) See also section 490 (last payment under guaranteed income bonds etc. treated as total surrender).

Commentary—*Simon's Taxes* E1.451.

HMRC Manuals—Insurance Policyholder Taxation Manual IPTM3400 (when events occur: general).

485 Disregard of certain events in relation to qualifying policies

(1) In relation to a qualifying policy, the events that count as chargeable events are restricted as follows.

(2) Death or the maturity of the policy is only a chargeable event if—

   (a)   the policy has been converted into a paid-up policy before the end of whichever of the following periods ends sooner—

      (i)   10 years from the making of the insurance, and

      (ii)   three-quarters of the term for which the policy is to run (assuming it is not ended by death or disability), or

   (b)   there is a company interest in the rights under the policy immediately before the event occurs.

(3) An event specified in section 484(1)(a)(i) to (iv) (surrender or assignment of all rights, final participation in profits and chargeable event where periodic calculation shows gain) is only a chargeable event if—

(*a*) the event occurs or the policy has been converted into a paid-up policy before the end of whichever of the periods specified in subsection (2)(*a*)(*i*) and (ii) ends sooner, or

(*b*) there is a company interest in the rights under the policy immediately before the event occurs.

(4) For the purposes of subsections (2)(*b*) and (3)(*b*) there is a company interest in the rights under a policy if—

(*a*) a company beneficially owns them,

(*b*) they are held on trusts created by a company, or

(*c*) they are held as security for a company's debt.

(5) An event specified in section 484(1)(*a*)(v) (part surrenders and assignments: chargeable events where transaction-related calculations show gains) is only a chargeable event if—

(*a*) the time as at which the calculation showing the gain is required to be made under section 498(2) is before the end of whichever of the periods specified in subsection (2)(*a*)(*i*) and (ii) ends sooner, or

(*b*) the policy has been converted into a paid-up policy before that time.

(6) If the policy has been varied so as to increase the premiums payable under it, subsections (2), (3) and (5) apply as if they referred instead to the following periods—

(*a*) 10 years from the variation taking effect, and

(*b*) three-quarters of the term for which the policy is to run from the variation (assuming it is not ended by death or disability).

(7) If a qualifying policy is substituted for another policy in circumstances where paragraph 25(1) or (3) of Schedule 15 to ICTA applies (replacement of a policy issued by a non-UK resident company by a policy which is not so issued), the surrender of the rights conferred by the other policy is not a chargeable event.

[(8) This section is subject to sections 463A and 463C.][1]

Commentary—*Simon's Taxes* **E1.451A.**

HMRC Manuals—Insurance Policyholder Taxation Manual IPTM3310 (restricted circumstances for qualifying policies to consider as chargeable events).

Amendments—[1]   Sub-s (8) inserted by FA 2013 s 25, Sch 9 paras 7, 9 with effect from 17 July 2013.

487 Disregard of certain assignments

For the purposes of this Chapter, an assignment of rights under a policy or contract or a share in such rights is ignored if it is—

(*a*) by way of security for a debt,

(*b*) on the discharge of a debt secured by the rights or share, or

(*c*) between spouses [or civil partners][1] living together.

Commentary—*Simon's Taxes* **E1.451B.**

HMRC Manuals—Insurance Policyholder Taxation Manual IPTM3430 (disregard of certain assignments).

Amendments—[1]   Words in para (*c*) inserted by Tax and Civil Partnership Regulations, SI 2005/3229, regs 183, 185, with effect from 5 December 2005 (reg 1(1)).

488 Disregard of some events after alterations of life insurance policy terms

(1) This section applies if—

(*a*) the terms of a policy of life insurance are altered,

(*b*) the alteration is not itself a chargeable event, and

(*c*) the conditions specified in section 489 are met.

(2) After the alteration a chargeable event is only treated as occurring in relation to the policy if one would have been treated as occurring had the alteration not occurred.

(3) If the alteration results in the policy being regarded as replaced by another, this section and section 489 apply as if they were a single policy.

Commentary—*Simon's Taxes* **E1.451B.**

HMRC Manuals—Insurance Policyholder Taxation Manual IPTM8050 (insurer ceasing to collect premiums).

489 Conditions applicable to alterations of life insurance policy terms

(1) Conditions A to E are the conditions referred to in section 488.

(2) Condition A is that the policy was issued in respect of an insurance made at least 20 years before the alteration.

(3) Condition B is that the alteration results from a decision by the insurance company that it will not collect further premiums due from any of the holders under a number of policies of the same description if a particular period of time has elapsed since the contracts were made.

(4) Condition C is that no premiums are payable or paid after the date of the alteration.

(5) Condition D is that the benefits to be provided under the policy after the alteration are the same or substantially the same as those before the alteration.

(6) A deduction from the benefits is ignored for the purposes of subsection (5) if it does not exceed the total net premiums which, apart from the alteration, would have been payable under the policy between—

(*a*) the date of the alteration, and

(*b*) the date on which the benefits become payable.

(7) In subsection (6) "net premiums" means the premiums reduced by any tax relief which would have been due on the premiums had they been paid.

(8) Condition E is that the premiums payable under the policy before the alteration—

   (a) have not been reduced to a nominal amount on the exercise of an option, in circumstances where the reduction is connected with a right to surrender in part the rights conferred by the policy after the date of the reduction, and

   (b) are not capable of being so reduced in such circumstances.

Commentary—*Simon's Taxes* **E1.451B.**

HMRC Manuals—Insurance Policyholder Taxation Manual IPTM8050 (insurer ceasing to collect premiums).

490 Last payment under guaranteed income bonds etc. treated as total surrender

(1) This section applies to a payment that would fall within section 500(d) (payments under guaranteed income bonds etc. treated as surrenders of part of the rights under the contract) apart from section 504(5) (which prevents payments comprising the whole of the last benefit to be paid under such contracts from being so treated).

(2) The payment is treated for the purposes of this Chapter as the surrender of all the rights under the contract.

(3) A payment to which this section applies is not regarded as interest or as an annual payment for any income tax purposes.

Commentary—*Simon's Taxes* **E1.453B.**

Calculating gains: general

491 Calculating gains: general rules

(1) This section deals with calculating—

   (a) whether a gain has arisen on a chargeable event within section 484(1)(a)(i) to (iii) or (b) to (e) (surrender or assignment of all rights, final participation in profits, death, maturity, or taking a capital sum as a complete alternative to annuity payments), and

   (b) if so, the amount of the gain.

(2) There is a gain if TB exceeds the sum of TD and PG where—

   TB is the total benefit value of the policy or contract (see section 492),

   TD is the total allowable deductions for the policy or contract (see section 494), and

   PG is the total amount of gains treated as arising on calculation events occurring in relation to the policy or contract before the chargeable event in question [but only in so far as those gains have been, or fall to be, taken into account in calculating the total income of a person as a result of this Chapter or Chapter 2 of Part 13 of ITA 2007][1].

(3) The gain is equal to the excess.

(4) In this Chapter—

   "calculation event" means an excess event, a part surrender or assignment event or a personal portfolio bond event,

   "excess event" means a chargeable event within section 509(1),

   "part surrender or assignment event" means a chargeable event within section 514(1), and

   "personal portfolio bond event" means a chargeable event within section 525(2).

(5) The reference to the policy in the definition of "PG" in subsection (2) includes any related policy.

(6) For the purposes of this Chapter, a policy ("policy A") is a related policy as respects another ("policy B") if—

   (a) policy B is a new policy (as defined in paragraph 17 of Schedule 15 to ICTA (substitutions and variations)) in relation to policy A, or

   (b) policy B is a new policy (as so defined) in relation to another policy ("policy C") and policy C is a new policy (as so defined) in relation to policy A,

and so on.

(7) See section 539 (relief for deficiencies) if there is no gain under subsection (2), but a gain arose on a calculation event occurring in relation to the policy or contract before the chargeable event in question.

(8) For the rules about calculating gains on calculation events, see—

   section 507 (method for making periodic calculations under section 498),

   section 511 (method for making transaction-related calculations under section 510), and

   section 522 (method for making annual calculations under section 515).

Commentary—*Simon's Taxes* **E1.452.**

HMRC Manuals—Insurance Policyholder Taxation Manual IPTM7505 (calculation of gains: general).

Amendments–[1]   Words inserted in sub-s (2) by FA 2012 s 11(2) with effect in relation to—

   (a)   any policy issued in respect of an insurance made on or after 21 March 2012; or any contract made on or after that date;

   (b)   any insurance or contract made before 21 March 2012 if on or after that date—

      (i)   the policy or contract is varied with the result that there is an increase in the benefits secured;

      (ii)   there is an assignment of rights, or a share of the rights, conferred by the policy or contract (whether or not for money's worth); or

      (iii)   some or all of the rights conferred by the policy or contract become held as security for a debt.

492 The total benefit value of a policy or contract

(1) To calculate the total benefit value of a policy or contract for the purposes of section 491, add together—

- (a) its value in accordance with section 493,
- (b) any capital sum paid under the policy or contract before the event,
- (c) the value of any other benefit of a capital nature conferred by the policy or contract before the event,
- (d) the amount of any loan made before the event, the making of which is treated as the surrender of a part of the rights under the policy or contract under section 500(c) (loans by insurers to which section 501 applies),
- (e) in the case of a guaranteed income bond contract, as defined in section 504(7), any amount paid before the event, the payment of which is treated as a surrender of a part of the rights under the contract under section 500(d) of this Act (payments by insurers under such contracts), and
- (f) in the case of an assignment, the amount or value of any share in the rights under the policy or contract that was assigned before the event.

(2) References to the policy in subsection (1)(b) to (e) include any related policy.

(3) This section is subject to—

    section 495 (disregard of certain amounts in calculating gains under section 491), and

    section 497 (disregard of trivial inducement benefits).

Commentary—*Simon's Taxes* **E1.452A**.
HMRC Manuals—Insurance Policyholder Taxation Manual IPTM7520 (total benefit value: value of the policy or contract), IPTM3510 (total benefit).

493 The value of a policy or contract

(1) In the case of a chargeable event within section 484(1)(a) (i) or (iii), (c), (d) or (e) (surrender of all rights, final participation in profits, maturity or, in the case of a contract for a life annuity that provides for taking a capital sum on death, death or taking a capital sum as a complete alternative to annuity payments), the value of the policy or contract is the total of—

- (a) any sum payable because of the event, and
- (b) in the case of a policy of life insurance or a capital redemption policy, any value or amount specified in subsection (2).

(2) The value or amount is—

- (a) if a right to periodical payments arises because of the event, an amount equal to the capital value of those payments at the time the right arises, and
- (b) the amount or value of any other benefits arising because of the event.

(3) Subsection (1) does not apply to a surrender treated as made under section 490 (last payment under guaranteed income bond contracts etc. treated as total surrender).

(4) In that case the value of the rights treated as surrendered is treated as being equal to the amount of the payment treated as the surrender.

(5) In the case of a chargeable event within section 484(1)(a)(ii) (assignment of all rights), the value of the policy or contract is the amount or value of the consideration for the assignment.

(6) But an assignment of a policy of life insurance or a contract for a life annuity between connected persons is treated as made for a consideration equal to the market value of the policy or contract.

(7) In the case of a chargeable event within section 484(1)(b) (death), the value of the policy is its surrender value immediately before the death.

(8) This section is subject to—

    section 495 (disregard of certain amounts in calculating gains under section 491), and

    section 497 (disregard of trivial inducement benefits).

Commentary—*Simon's Taxes* **E1.452A**.
HMRC Manuals—Insurance Policyholder Taxation Manual IPTM3515 (value of a policy or contract).

494 The total allowable deductions for a policy or contract

(1) To calculate the total allowable deductions for a policy or contract for the purposes of section 491—

    Step 1 Add together—

- (a) the total amount of premiums paid under the policy or contract before the event, and
- (b) if the event occurs at the end of the final insurance year (see section 499), the amount of any repayment or partial repayment of a loan treated under section 500(c) as a surrender of a part of the rights under the policy or contract.

    Step 2 In the case of a contract for a life annuity under which any annuity payments have been made, reduce the result of step 1 by so much of those payments as is—

- (a) exempt under section 717 (exemption for part of purchased life annuity payments), or
- (b) determined to be the capital element in those payments under section 658 of ICTA.

(2) In the case of a capital redemption policy which has been assigned for money or money's worth before the event, the reference in paragraph (*a*) of step 1 in subsection (1) to the total amount of premiums paid under the policy or contract before the event is a reference to the total of—

  (*a*) the amount or value of the consideration given for the last such assignment, and
  (*b*) the total amount of premiums paid under the policy or contract after that assignment and before the event.

(3) References to the policy in paragraphs (*a*) and (*b*) of step 1 in subsection (1) and in subsection (2) include any related policy.

(4) Subsection (1) is subject to—

  section 495 (disregard of certain amounts in calculating gains under section 491), and
  section 496 (modification of this section: qualifying endowment policies held as security for company debts).

Commentary—*Simon's Taxes* **E1.452B.**
HMRC Manuals—Insurance Policyholder Taxation Manual IPTM3510 (total deductions of a policy).

495 Disregard of certain amounts in calculating gains under section 491

(1) A retained replacement policy premium is ignored in calculating—

  (*a*) the total benefit value of a policy under section 492(1), or
  (*b*) the total allowable deductions for a policy under section 494(1).

(2) In subsection (1) "retained replacement policy premium" means a sum which—

  (*a*) has been payable under a policy which is one of two or more policies treated as a single policy under section 542(1) (qualifying policies and policies replacing them), and
  (*b*) is such a sum as is mentioned in section 542(4) and meets the condition in that section.

(3) For the purposes of section 492(1)(*b*) and (*c*) (total benefit value: capital sums and benefits paid or conferred before the event in question), any sum paid or benefit conferred under a policy is ignored if it is attributable to a person's disability.

(4) For the purposes of section 492(1)(*f*) (total benefit value: assignments), a share assigned before the event is ignored if—

  (*a*) it was assigned in an insurance year (see section 499) that began on or after 6th April 2001, and
  (*b*) it was not assigned for money or money's worth.

(5) The reference to the policy in subsection (3) includes any related policy.

Commentary—*Simon's Taxes* **E1.452C.**
HMRC Manuals—Insurance Policyholder Taxation Manual IPTM3520 (replacement policies).

496 Modification of section 494: qualifying endowment policies held as security for company debts

(1) This section applies if—

  (*a*) a chargeable event within section 484(1)(*a*)(*i*), (*b*) or (*c*) (surrender of all rights, death or maturity) occurs in relation to a qualifying endowment policy (see subsection (7)),
  (*b*) immediately before the event occurs the rights under the policy are held as security for a debt owed by a company, and
  (*c*) the company debt conditions are met (see subsection (4)).

(2) If—

  (*a*) the amount of the debt exceeds the amounts referred to in paragraph (*a*) of step 1 in section 494(1) (the total amount of premiums paid before the event), and
  (*b*) the company makes a claim within two years after the end of the accounting period in which the chargeable event occurs,

section 494 applies as if that paragraph referred instead to the amount of the debt.

(3) If the amount of the debt varied during the policy period, it is to be taken for the purposes of subsection (2) as the lowest amount at which it stood during that period.

(4) The company debt conditions are that—

  (*a*) throughout the policy period, the rights conferred by the policy have been held as security for a debt owed by the company referred to in subsection (1)(*b*),
  (*b*) the capital sum payable under the policy in the event of death during the term of the policy is not less than the amount of the debt when the insurance was made,
  (*c*) any sum payable under the policy as a result of the event is applied in repayment of the debt (except so far as it exceeds the debt), and
  (*d*) the debt was incurred to pay money applied for the purposes of the company's trade premises.

(5) Money is applied for the purposes of a company's trade premises if it is applied—

  (*a*) in purchasing an estate or interest in land to be occupied by the company for the purposes of a trade carried on by it, or
  (*b*) for the purpose of the construction, extension or improvement (but not the repair or maintenance) of buildings which are or are to be so occupied.

(6) If during the policy period the company incurs a debt by borrowing in order to repay another debt, references to a debt in subsections (3) and (4) include both debts where appropriate.

(7) In this section—

"accounting period" is to be read in accordance with [Chapter 2 of Part 2 of CTA 2009][1],

"the policy period" means the period beginning with the making of the insurance and ending immediately before the chargeable event, and

"qualifying endowment policy" means a policy which is a qualifying policy as a result of paragraph 2 of Schedule 15 to ICTA.

Commentary—*Simon's Taxes* **E1.452B.**

HMRC Manuals—Insurance Policyholder Taxation Manual IPTM3530 (qualifying endowment policies held as security for company debts).

Amendments—[1] In sub-s (7) words substituted by CTA 2009 s 1322, Sch 1 paras 587, 633. CTA 2009 applies for accounting periods ending on or after 1 April 2009 (for corporation tax purposes) and for tax years 2009–10 onwards (for income and capital gains tax purposes).

497 Disregard of trivial inducement benefits

(1) A benefit other than a payment of money is ignored for the purposes of calculating any gain under this Chapter if—

  (*a*) it is provided by an insurance company for any person as an inducement for the person to enter into—

    (i) a policy or contract to which this Chapter applies, or

    (ii) a later transaction in relation to such a policy or contract, and

  (*b*) the condition specified in subsection (2) is met.

(2) The condition is that the total cost to the insurance company of providing the benefit and any other such benefits provided by it at any time in connection with the policy or contract, or any linked policy or contract, does not exceed £30.

(3) The Treasury may by order amend the sum for the time being specified in subsection (2) so as to increase it.

(4) For the purposes of this section, a policy or contract is linked to another policy or contract if—

  (*a*) their terms are substantially identical, and

  (*b*) when one of them is issued or made the issue or making of the other is contemplated.

Commentary—*Simon's Taxes* **E1.452C.**

HMRC Manuals—Insurance Policyholder Taxation Manual IPTM3535 (disregard of trivial inducement benefits).

Part surrenders and assignments: periodic calculations and excess events

498 Requirement for periodic calculations in part surrender or assignment cases

(1) This section applies if—

  (*a*) a part of, or share in, the rights under a policy or contract is surrendered, or

  (*b*) such a part or share is assigned for money or money's worth.

(2) A calculation is to be made in accordance with section 507 in relation to the policy or contract as at the end of the insurance year in which the surrender or assignment occurs (see section 499) to determine—

  (*a*) whether a gain has arisen on the policy or contract, and

  (*b*) if so, the amount of the gain.

(3) For cases where surrenders and assignments of a part of the rights under a policy or contract are treated as occurring where they would not otherwise do so, see sections 500 to 506.

Commentary—*Simon's Taxes* **E1.453.**

HMRC Manuals—Insurance Policyholder Taxation Manual IPTM3540 (rules of periodic calculations).

IPTM3560 (calculation method).

IPTM1510 (part surrenders and part assignments for consideration).

499 Meaning of "insurance year" and "final insurance year"

(1) In this Chapter "insurance year", in relation to a policy or contract, means the 12 months beginning with—

  (*a*) the date on which the insurance or contract is made, or

  (*b*) any anniversary of that date.

(2) Subsection (1) is subject to subsections (3) and (5).

(3) An event referred to in section 484(1)(*a*)(i) or (iii) or (*b*) to (*e*) (surrender of all rights, final participation in profits, death, maturity, or taking a capital sum as a complete alternative to annuity payments) is treated as ending the insurance year in which it occurs.

(4) In this Chapter "final insurance year" means an insurance year that is ended as a result of subsection (3).

(5) But if, as a result of subsection (3), an insurance year would begin and end in the same tax year—

  (*a*) that insurance year and the previous insurance year are treated as one insurance year, and

  (*b*) "final insurance year" needs to be read accordingly.

Commentary—*Simon's Taxes* **E1.453.**

HMRC Manuals—Insurance Policyholder Taxation Manual IPTM3505 (meaning : insurance year).

500 Events treated as part surrenders

The following events are treated for the purposes of this Chapter as a surrender of a part of the rights under the policy or contract in question—

(*a*) the falling due of a sum payable as a result of a right under a policy or contract to participate in profits where further rights remain under it,

(*b*) in the case of a contract for a life annuity which provides for a capital sum to be taken as an alternative in part to the annuity payments, taking the capital sum,

(*c*) the making of a loan to which section 501 applies, and

(*d*) the making of a payment to which section 504 applies (payments by insurers under guaranteed income bonds etc.).

Commentary—*Simon's Taxes* **E1.453A.**

HMRC Manuals—Insurance Policyholder Taxation Manual IPTM3545 (events treated as part surrenders).

501 Part surrenders: loans

(1) This section applies to a loan (and so it falls within section 500(*c*)) if it is made by the insurer under a policy or contract—

(*a*) to an individual falling within subsection (2), [or][1]

(*b*) to trustees falling within subsection (3), . . .[1]

(*c*) . . .[1]

(2) An individual falls within this subsection at any time if, were a gain to arise in respect of the policy or contract at that time, the individual would be liable for tax under this Chapter as a result of section 465 (person liable: individuals).

(3) Trustees fall within this subsection at any time if, were a gain to arise in respect of the policy or contract at that time, they would be liable for tax under this Chapter as a result of section 467 (person liable: UK resident trustees).

(4) . . .[1]

(5) For the purposes of subsection (1), a loan—

(*a*) is treated as made by an insurer if it is made by arrangement with it, and

(*b*) is treated as made to an individual, trustees or a company if it is made at the individual's, trustees' or company's direction.

(6) In this section "insurer", in relation to a policy or contract, means the body issuing the policy or with which the contract is made.

(7) This section is subject to—

(*a*) section 502 (exception for loans to buy life annuities), and

(*b*) section 503 (exception for certain loans under qualifying policies).

Commentary—*Simon's Taxes* **E1.453A.**

Amendments—[1] Words in sub-s(1)(*a*) inserted, sub-s (1)(*c*) and preceding word, and sub-s (4), repealed, by FA 2008 s 36, Sch 14 paras 1, 14 with effect as follows—

(a)   so far as relating to corporation tax, for accounting periods beginning on or after 1 April 2008, and

(b)   so far as relating to income tax, for the tax year 2008–09 and subsequent tax years.

502 Exception from section 501 for loans to buy life annuities

(1) Section 501 does not apply to a loan made under a contract for a life annuity if all the interest on the loan is eligible for tax relief.

(2) If part of the interest is eligible for tax relief, section 501 only applies to the part of the loan carrying ineligible interest.

(3) For the purposes of this section, interest is eligible for tax relief if it is eligible for relief under section 353 of ICTA (general provision for relief for interest) as a result of section 365 of ICTA (loan to buy life annuity).

Commentary—*Simon's Taxes* **E1.453A.**

HMRC Manuals—Insurance Policyholder Taxation Manual IPTM4100 (purchased life annuities: background).

503 Exception from section 501 for certain loans under qualifying policies

(1) Section 501 does not apply to a loan made by the body issuing a qualifying policy if either or both of conditions A and B are met.

(2) Condition A is that interest is payable on the loan at a commercial rate.

(3) Condition B is that the loan was made—

(*a*) before 6th April 2000,

(*b*) to a full-time employee of the body issuing the policy, and

(*c*) to assist the employee in purchasing or improving a dwelling to be used as the employee's only or main residence.

Commentary—*Simon's Taxes* **E1.453A.**

HMRC Manuals—Insurance Policyholder Taxation Manual IPTM3545 (exceptions to loans under qualifying policies).

504 Part surrenders: payments under guaranteed income bonds etc.

(1) This section applies to so much of any payment of an amount by an insurer under a guaranteed income bond contract as meets conditions A to C (and so it falls within section 500(d)).

(2) Condition A is that it is a sum which, but for subsection (6), would be treated for income tax purposes as interest or an annual payment.

(3) Condition B is that it is not a sum paid or falling to be paid because of provisions of the guaranteed income bond contract which, taken alone, would constitute a contract of insurance—

   (*a*) within Part 1 or 2 of Schedule 1 to the Financial Services and Markets Act 2000 (Regulated Activities) Order 2001 (SI 2001/544), but

   (*b*) not within paragraph 1 or 3 of Part 2 of that Schedule (life and annuity contracts including certain linked long-term contracts).

(4) Condition C is that it does not represent late payment interest.

(5) This section does not apply if the payment comprises the whole of the last benefit to be paid under the contract (ignoring late payment interest).

(6) A sum to which this section applies is not regarded as interest or as an annual payment for any income tax purposes.

(7) In this section—

     "guaranteed income bond contract" means a policy of life insurance that is a contract of insurance which—

   (*a*) is within paragraph 1 or 3 of Part 2 of Schedule 1 to the Financial Services and Markets Act 2000 (Regulated Activities) Order 2001, and

   (*b*) is neither an annuity contract nor a contract effected in the course of a company's pension business,

     "late payment interest", in relation to a contract, means interest on an amount payable under the contract which is paid for a period beginning on or after the date of the occurrence as a result of which the amount is payable, and

     "pension business" has the meaning given by [section 58 of FA 2012][1] (or the corresponding enactment in force when the contract was effected).

Commentary—*Simon's Taxes* **E1.453B.**

HMRC Manuals—Insurance Policyholder Taxation Manual IPTM1420 (guaranteed income bonds :definition).

IPTM3550 (guaranteed income bonds : interest payment conditions).

Amendments—[1]   In sub-s (7), in definition of "pension business", words substituted for words "section 431B of ICTA", by FA 2012 s 146, Sch 16 paras 125, 129 with effect in relation to accounting periods of companies beginning on or after 1 January 2013 (subject to transitional provisions in FA 2012 Sch 17). For accounting periods straddling 1 January 2013, see FA 2012 s 149.

505 Assignments etc. involving co-ownership

(1) For the purposes of this Chapter (except this section and section 506)—

   (*a*) a transaction to which this section applies is taken to be one or more assignments of part only of the rights under the policy or contract in respect of which the transaction occurs, and

   (*b*) those assignments are the ones specified in section 506.

(2) If subsection (1) applies to a transaction that is an assignment—

   (*a*) of the whole of the rights under a policy or contract, or

   (*b*) of a part of or a share in those rights,

any reference to the assignment in this Chapter (except this section and section 506) is to be read as a reference to the assignment or assignments that the transaction is taken to be under subsection (1).

(3) This section applies to a transaction in respect of which conditions A and B and either condition C or D or E are met.

(4) Condition A is that—

   (*a*) immediately before the transaction the whole or part of, or a share in, the rights under the policy or contract ("the ownership interest") was in the beneficial ownership of one person or of two or more persons jointly ("the old ownership"), and

   (*b*) as a result of the transaction the ownership interest becomes beneficially owned by one person or by two or more persons jointly or in common ("the new ownership").

(5) Condition B is that at least one person who is a member of the old ownership is also a member of the new ownership.

(6) Condition C is that there is only one member of the old ownership and there are two or more members of the new ownership.

(7) Condition D is that there are two or more members of the old ownership and at least one of them is not a member of the new ownership.

(8) Condition E is that there are two or more members of the old ownership and the share in the ownership interest of at least one of those members (see section 506(5)) exceeds that member's share in the ownership interest as a member of the new ownership (see section 506(6)).

Commentary—*Simon's Taxes* **E1.453C.**

HMRC Manuals—Insurance Policyholder Taxation Manual IPTM3575 (rules of assignments involving co-ownership).

506 Assignments occurring when there is a co-ownership transaction

(1) This section sets out the assignment or assignments that are taken to occur under section 505 when there is a transaction to which that section applies ("a co-ownership transaction").

(2) If there is only one member of the old ownership, that member is to be treated as if the co-ownership transaction had been the assignment by that member of so much of the ownership interest as exceeds that member's share in the ownership interest as a member of the new ownership.

(3) If there are two or more members of the old ownership, each such member who is not a member of the new ownership is to be treated as if the co-ownership transaction had been the assignment by that member of that member's share in the ownership interest.

(4) If there are two or more members of the old ownership, each such member whose share in the ownership interest as a member of the old ownership exceeds that member's share in the ownership interest as a member of the new ownership is to be treated as if the co-ownership transaction had been the assignment by that member of that excess.

(5) If the old ownership consists of two or more persons beneficially entitled jointly, the members of the old ownership are to be treated as if the ownership interest had been in their beneficial ownership in equal shares instead of jointly.

(6) If the new ownership consists of two or more persons beneficially entitled jointly, the members of the old ownership are to be treated as if the result of the co-ownership transaction had been that the ownership interest was in the beneficial ownership of the members of the new ownership in equal shares instead of jointly.

(7) In this section "the ownership interest", "the old ownership" and "the new ownership" are to be read as indicated in section 505(4).

Commentary—*Simon's Taxes* **E1.453C**

HMRC Manuals—Insurance Policyholder Taxation Manual IPTM3575 (assignments involving co-ownership transaction).

507 Method for making periodic calculations under section 498

(1) This section deals with the calculation required to be made in relation to a policy or contract as at the end of an insurance year under section 498(2) (requirement for periodic calculations in part surrender and assignment cases) to determine—

    (a) whether a gain has arisen, and

    (b) if so, the amount of the gain.

(2) There is a gain if the net total value of rights surrendered or assigned exceeds the net total allowable payments (see subsections (4) and (5)).

(3) The gain is equal to the excess.

(4) To calculate the net total value of rights surrendered or assigned—

    Step 1 Find—

        (a) the value, as at the time of its surrender or assignment, of any part of or share in the rights under the policy or contract which has been surrendered at any time or assigned at any time for money or money's worth, and

        (b) the value, as at the time of its assignment, of any part of or share in the rights under the policy or contract which has been assigned otherwise than for money or money's worth in an insurance year beginning on or before 5th April 2001,

    in each case determining the value in accordance with section 508.

    Step 2 Add together those values.

    Step 3 If any previous calculation events (other than personal portfolio bond events) have occurred in relation to the policy or contract—

        (a) add together each such value which has been brought into account under this subsection on those events, and

        (b) subtract the result of paragraph (a) from the result of step 2.

(5) To calculate the net total allowable payments—

    Step 1 Find the allowable element in each allowable payment by multiplying the amount of the payment by—

$$\frac{X}{20}$$

    where X is the number of insurance years in the period beginning with the year in which the payment is made and ending with the insurance year as at the end of which the calculation under this section is required to be made or, if it is less, 20.

    Step 2 Add together the allowable elements for all allowable payments.

    Step 3 Add together all the allowable elements brought into account under this subsection on a previous calculation event.

    Step 4 Subtract the result of step 3 from the result of step 2.

(6) In this section—

"allowable payment" means a premium, other than a retained replacement policy premium, and "retained replacement policy premium" has the meaning given in section 495(2).

Commentary—*Simon's Taxes* **E1.453D**.

HMRC Manuals—Insurance Policyholder Taxation Manual IPTM3560 (periodic calculations method).

[507A   Recalculating gains under section 507

(1) An interested person may apply to an officer of Revenue and Customs for a review of a calculation under section 507 on the ground that the gain arising from it is wholly disproportionate.

(2) For the purposes of this section an interested person in relation to a calculation under section 507 is a person who would be liable for all or any part of the amount of tax that would be chargeable under this Chapter if the gain were not recalculated.

(3) Applications under subsection (1) must be—

    (*a*) made in writing, and

    (*b*) received by an officer of Revenue and Customs within—

        (i) the four tax years following the tax year in which the gain arose, or

        (ii) such longer period as the officer may agree.

(4) In considering whether the gain is wholly disproportionate, the officer may take into account (as well as the amount of the gain) any factor which the officer considers appropriate including, so far as the officer considers it appropriate to do so—

    (*a*) the economic gain on the rights surrendered or assigned,

    (*b*) the amount of the premiums paid under the policy or contract,

    (*c*) the amount of tax that would be chargeable under this Chapter if the gain were not recalculated.

(5) If, following an application under subsection (1), an officer considers that the gain arising from the calculation under section 507 is wholly disproportionate, the officer must recalculate the gain on a just and reasonable basis.

(6) Following a recalculation under subsection (5), references in this Chapter (but excluding this section) to a calculation under section 507 are to be regarded as references to a recalculation under this section.

(7) Following a recalculation under subsection (5), an officer of Revenue and Customs must notify the interested person of the result of the recalculation.

(8) If two or more persons are interested persons in relation to a calculation under section 507—

    (*a*) an application under subsection (1) may be made only by all the interested persons jointly, and

    (*b*) subsection (7) applies as if the reference to the interested person were a reference to each of the interested persons.

(9) Following a recalculation under subsection (5), all necessary adjustments and repayments of income tax are to be made.

(10) No recalculation is to be made under this section if the gain mentioned in subsection (1) arises as a result of one or more transactions which form part of arrangements, the main purpose, or one of the main purposes, of which is to obtain a tax advantage for any person.

(11) In this section—

    "arrangements" includes any agreement, understanding, scheme, transaction or series of transactions (whether or not legally enforceable), and

    "tax advantage" has the meaning given by section 1139 of CTA 2010.][1]

Amendments—[1]   Section 507A inserted by F(No 2)A 2017 s 9(1), (2) with effect from 16 November 2017.

508   The value of rights partially surrendered or assigned

(1) For the purposes of sections 507, 511 and 512, where any part of or share in rights conferred by a policy or contract is surrendered, the value of the part of or share in the rights surrendered is the amount or value of the sum payable or other benefits arising because of the surrender, except where subsection (2) or (3) applies.

(2) In the case of a surrender within section 500(*c*) (loans by insurers to which section 501 applies), the value for those purposes is an amount equal to the loan.

(3) In the case of a surrender within section 500(*d*) (payments by insurers under guaranteed income bonds etc.), the value for those purposes is the amount to which section 504 applies.

(4) For the purposes of sections 507, 511 and 512, where any part of or share in rights conferred by a policy or contract is assigned, the value of the part or share as at the time of the assignment is its surrender value at that time.

(5) For the requirement to ignore certain benefits, see section 497 (disregard of trivial inducement benefits).

Commentary—*Simon's Taxes* **E1.453E.**

HMRC Manuals—Insurance Policyholder Taxation Manual IPTM3565 (value of rights surrendered or assigned).

509   Chargeable events in certain cases where periodic calculations show gains

(1) If the calculation in section 507 shows that a gain has arisen as at the end of the insurance year, the gain is treated as arising on the occurrence of a chargeable event at the end of that year, unless condition A, B or C is met.

(2) Subsection (1) is subject to section 485(3) (which restricts the circumstances in which such events occur in relation to qualifying policies).

(3) Condition A is that during the insurance year there has been an assignment for money or money's worth of part of or a share in the rights conferred by the policy or contract.

(4) Condition B is that during the insurance year there has been both—

    (*a*) a surrender of part of or a share in the rights conferred by the policy or contract, and

    (*b*) a later assignment, otherwise than for money or money's worth, of the whole or part of or a share in the rights conferred by the policy or contract.

(5) Condition C is that the insurance year is the final insurance year.

(6) See section 510 (transaction-related calculations in certain part surrender and assignment cases) if one or both of conditions A and B are met.

Commentary—*Simon's Taxes* **E1.453D, E1.453F.**

HMRC Manuals—Insurance Policyholder Taxation Manual IPTM3580 (transaction-related calculations).

Transaction-related calculations and part surrender or assignment events

510 Requirement for transaction-related calculations in certain part surrender and assignment cases

(1) This section applies if—

    (*a*) the calculation in section 507 shows that a gain has arisen as at the end of the insurance year, but

    (*b*) one or both of the conditions specified in section 509(3) and (4) are met (and so no chargeable event is treated as occurring at the end of the year under section 509).

(2) A calculation is to be made in accordance with section 511 in relation to each relevant transaction during the insurance year to determine—

    (*a*) whether the transaction resulted in a gain arising on the policy or contract, and

    (*b*) if so, the amount of the gain.

(3) In this section and sections 511 to 514 "relevant transaction" means—

    (*a*) a surrender of part of or a share in the rights under the policy or contract, or

    (*b*) an assignment of such a part or share for money or money's worth.

(4) If two or more relevant transactions occurred during the insurance year, a calculation in accordance with section 511 is to be made in relation to each of them successively in the order in which they occurred.

(5) A calculation falling to be made in accordance with section 511 in relation to a relevant transaction occurring in the final insurance year is to be made before any calculation under section 491 for the chargeable event that ends that year.

(6) But, in the case of a relevant transaction so occurring, subsections (2) and (4) are subject to section 513(5) (under which those subsections do not apply to some such relevant transactions).

Commentary—*Simon's Taxes* **E1.453F.**

HMRC Manuals—Insurance Policyholder Taxation Manual IPTM7625 (transaction- related calculations: part surrender or assignment events).

511 Method for making transaction-related calculations under section 510

(1) This section deals with the calculation required to be made under section 510 to determine—

    (*a*) whether a relevant transaction which has occurred during an insurance year resulted in a gain arising on the policy or contract, and

    (*b*) if so, the amount of the gain.

(2) There is a gain if the transaction value for the relevant transaction (see subsection (4)) exceeds the amount of available premium left for the relevant transaction as calculated in accordance with section 512.

(3) The gain is equal to the excess.

(4) The transaction value for the relevant transaction is the value in accordance with section 508, as at the time of its surrender or assignment, of the part of or share in the rights under the policy or contract which has been surrendered or assigned in the transaction.

(5) Subsections (2) and (4) are subject to section 513(4) (under which the transaction value is to be reduced in certain cases where the relevant transaction occurs in the final insurance year).

Commentary—*Simon's Taxes* **E1.453F.**

512 Available premium left for relevant transaction

(1) For the purposes of section 511(2), the amount of available premium left for a relevant transaction is the amount, if any, by which the available net allowable payments (see subsection (3)) exceed the available net total values for the year (see subsection (4)).

(2) But the amount of available premium left for the relevant transaction is nil if—

    (*a*) one or more other relevant transactions have occurred in respect of the relevant contract earlier in the insurance year, and

    (*b*) for the latest of them the calculation in section 511(2) produced a gain.

(3) To calculate the available net allowable payments—

    Step 1 Calculate the net total allowable payments as at the end of the insurance year in accordance with section 507(5).

    Step 2 If—

(*a*) one or more other relevant transactions ("the earlier transactions") have occurred in respect of the policy or contract earlier in the insurance year, and

(*b*) for the latest of them the calculation in section 511(2) produced no gain, subtract the sum of the transaction values for the earlier transactions from the result of step 1.

(4) To calculate the available net total values for the year—

Step 1 Calculate the net total value of rights surrendered or assigned, as at the end of the insurance year, in accordance with section 507(4), ignoring for the purposes of step 3 in that section any relevant transactions in that year that are treated as chargeable events under section 514.

Step 2 Subtract from the result of step 1 the value, as at the time of its surrender or assignment, of any part of or share in the rights under the policy or contract which has been surrendered in the insurance year or assigned in that year for money or money's worth, determining the value in accordance with section 508.

Commentary—*Simon's Taxes* **E1.453F.**

HMRC Manuals—Insurance Policyholder Taxation Manual IPTM3585 (available premium left: meaning).

[512A Recalculating gains under section 511

(1) An interested person may apply to an officer of Revenue and Customs for a review of a calculation under section 511 on the ground that the gain arising from it is wholly disproportionate.

(2) For the purposes of this section an interested person in relation to a calculation under section 511 is a person who would be liable for all or any part of the amount of tax that would be chargeable under this Chapter—

(*a*) if the gain were not recalculated, or

(*b*) if all rights under the policy or contract had been surrendered immediately after the surrender or assignment of rights which gave rise to the calculation.

(3) Applications under subsection (1) must be—

(*a*) made in writing, and

(*b*) received by an officer of Revenue and Customs within—

(i) the four tax years following the tax year in which the gain arose, or

(ii) such longer period as the officer may agree.

(4) In considering whether the gain is wholly disproportionate, the officer may take into account (as well as the amount of the gain) any factor which the officer considers appropriate including, so far as the officer considers it appropriate to do so—

(*a*) the economic gain on the rights surrendered or assigned,

(*b*) the amount of the premiums paid under the policy or contract,

(*c*) the amount of tax that would be chargeable under this Chapter if the gain were not recalculated.

(5) If, following an application under subsection (1), an officer considers that the gain arising from the calculation under section 511 is wholly disproportionate, the officer must recalculate the gain on a just and reasonable basis.

(6) Following a recalculation under subsection (5), references in this Chapter (but excluding this section) to a calculation under section 511 are to be regarded as references to a recalculation under this section.

(7) Following a recalculation under subsection (5), an officer of Revenue and Customs must notify the interested person of the result of the recalculation.

(8) If two or more persons are interested persons in relation to a calculation under section 511—

(*a*) an application under subsection (1) may be made only by all the interested persons jointly, and

(*b*) subsection (7) applies as if the reference to the interested person were a reference to each of the interested persons.

(9) Following a recalculation under subsection (5), all necessary adjustments and repayments of income tax are to be made.

(10) No recalculation is to be made under this section if the gain mentioned in subsection (1) arises as a result of one or more transactions which form part of arrangements, the main purpose, or one of the main purposes, of which is to obtain a tax advantage for any person.

(11) In this section—

"arrangements" includes any agreement, understanding, scheme, transaction or series of transactions (whether or not legally enforceable), and

"tax advantage" has the meaning given by section 1139 of CTA 2010.][1]

Amendments—[1]   Section 512A inserted by F(No 2)A 2017 s 9(1), (3) with effect from 16 November 2017.

513 Special rules for part surrenders and assignments in final insurance year

(1) This section applies if—

(*a*) the calculation in section 511 falls to be made in relation to a relevant transaction occurring in the final insurance year, (*b*) the total transaction value for that transaction exceeds the gains limit (see subsections (2) and (3)), and

(*c*) paragraph (*b*) has not applied to a relevant transaction occurring earlier in the final insurance year in respect of the policy or contract in question.

(2) The total transaction value is the total of—

(*a*) the transaction value for the transaction in question in accordance with section 511(4), and

(*b*) the transaction values for any relevant transactions occurring earlier in the final insurance year in respect of the policy or contract in accordance with that section.

(3) The gains limit is the amount calculated, as at the end of the final insurance year, as the amount of the gain that would have been treated as arising on the occurrence of the chargeable event that ends that year if in relation to that year—

(*a*) section 509(1) did not refer to condition C, and

(*b*) sections 510(2) and (4) and 514(1) did not apply.

(4) The transaction value for the relevant transaction used for the calculation in section 511(2) is reduced by the excess mentioned in subsection (1)(*b*).

(5) No calculations are required to be made under section 510(2) and (4) in relation to any subsequent relevant transaction in respect of the policy or contract.

Commentary—*Simon's Taxes* **E1.453G**.

HMRC Manuals—Insurance Policyholder Taxation Manual IPTM3590 ('final insurance year': special rules).

514 Chargeable events where transaction-related calculations show gains

(1) If the calculation in section 511 shows that a relevant transaction resulted in a gain arising on the policy or contract, the relevant transaction is treated as a chargeable event.

(2) Subsection (1) is subject to section 485(5) (which restricts the circumstances in which such events occur in relation to qualifying policies).

(3) Subsection (4) applies if—

(*a*) a relevant transaction that is a chargeable event occurs in a different tax year from that in which the insurance year ends, and

(*b*) apart from subsection (4), a person would be liable to tax on the gain under this Chapter for the tax year in which the transaction occurs.

(4) The gain is charged to tax under this Chapter for the tax year in which the insurance year ends instead.

[(4A) Subsection (3)(*b*) includes a case where a person would be liable to tax on the gain under section 465B for the tax year in which the transaction occurs (because the transaction occurs in the year of return, as defined in that section).[1]

(5) If the relevant transaction occurs in the final insurance year, the chargeable event within subsection (1) is treated as occurring before the chargeable event that ends that year.

Commentary—*Simon's Taxes* **E1.453F, E1.455**.

HMRC Manuals—Insurance Policyholder Taxation Manual IPTM7195 (transaction-related calculations show gains: general rules).

IPTM3595 (chargeable event).

Amendments—[1]　Sub-s (4A) inserted by FA 2013 s 218, Sch 45 paras 139, 142 with effect if the year of departure (as defined in FA 2013 Sch 45 Pt 4) is the tax year 2013–14 or any subsequent tax year, subject to transitional provisions and savings in FA 2013 Sch 45 paras 154–158.

Personal portfolio bonds

515 Requirement for annual calculations in relation to personal portfolio bonds

(1) This section applies if a policy or contract to which this Chapter applies is a personal portfolio bond at the end of an insurance year.

(2) But this section does not apply if the insurance year is the final insurance year.

(3) A calculation is to be made in accordance with section 522 in relation to the policy or contract as at the end of the insurance year to determine—

(*a*) whether a gain has arisen on the policy or contract in relation to that year, and

(*b*) if so, the amount of the gain.

(4) The calculation is in addition to any other calculation which is required to be made under this Chapter in relation to the policy or contract.

Commentary—*Simon's Taxes* **E1.454**.

HMRC Manuals—Insurance Policyholder Taxation Manual IPTM3650 (personal portfolio bonds: calculation method).

516 Meaning of "personal portfolio bond"

(1) In this Chapter "personal portfolio bond" means a policy of life insurance, contract for a life annuity or capital redemption policy which meets conditions A and B.

This is subject to section 517.

(2) Condition A is that, under the terms of the policy or contract, some or all of the benefits are determined by reference to—

(*a*) fluctuations in, or in an index of, the value of property of any description, or

(*b*) the value of, or the income from, property of any description.

(3) For this purpose it does not matter whether or not the index or property is specified in the policy or contract.

(4) Condition B is that the terms of the policy or contract permit the selection of the index or some or all of the property by—

    (*a*)   the holder of the policy or contract,

    (*b*)   a person connected with the holder,

    (*c*)   the holder and such a connected person acting together,

    (*d*)   a person acting on behalf of the holder,

    (*e*)   a person acting on behalf of a person connected with the holder, or

    (*f*)   a person acting on behalf of the holder and such a connected person acting together.

(5) In subsection (4) "holder", in the case of a policy or contract held by two or more persons, means any of them.

Commentary—*Simon's Taxes* **E1.454A.**

HMRC Manuals—Insurance Policyholder Taxation Manual IPTM3600 (personal portfolio bonds: background).
IPTM3320 (personal portfolio bond : meaning).
IPTM3610 (meaning: bonds made on or after 17 march 1998).

517 Policies and contracts which are not personal portfolio bonds

(1) A policy or contract is not a personal portfolio bond merely because its terms permit the selection of an index as described in section 516(4) if that index—

    (*a*)   falls within one of the categories listed in section 518, and

    (*b*)   meets one of the index selection conditions (see section 519).

(2) A policy or contract is not a personal portfolio bond merely because its terms permit the selection of property as described in section 516(4) if all of the property which may be so selected—

    (*a*)   falls within one or more of the categories listed in section 520, and

    (*b*)   meets one or both of the property selection conditions (see section 521).

Commentary—*Simon's Taxes* **E1.454C.**

HMRC Manuals—Insurance Policyholder Taxation Manual IPTM3630 (meaning: index selection).
IPTM3640 (meaning: property selection).

518 The index categories

(1) This section sets out the categories of index referred to in section 517(1).

(2) Category 1 is the retail prices index.

(3) Category 2 is any general index which—

    (*a*)   is similar to the retail prices index, and

    (*b*)   is published by the government of any foreign state or an agent of such a government.

(4) Category 3 is any published index of prices of shares listed on a recognised stock exchange.

Commentary—*Simon's Taxes* **E1.454C.**

HMRC Manuals—Insurance Policyholder Taxation Manual IPTM3630 (the index categories).

519 The index selection conditions

(1) The index selection conditions are—

    (*a*)   the general selection condition (see subsection (2)), and

    (*b*)   the class selection condition (see subsection (3)).

(2) An index meets the general selection condition if, at the time when it may be selected, the opportunity to select the same index is available to—

    (*a*)   all policy holders of the insurance company, or

    (*b*)   persons acting on behalf of those policy holders.

(3) An index meets the class selection condition if, at the time when it may be selected, the opportunity to select the same index is available to—

    (*a*)   a particular class or classes of policy holders of the insurance company, or

    (*b*)   persons acting on behalf of the members of that class or those classes.

(4) A group of policy holders to whom the opportunity to select an index is available is a "class" for the purposes of subsection (3) if—

    (*a*)   neither membership of the class nor the opportunity are limited to connected persons,

    (*b*)   the question whether a policy holder is a member of the class, or has the opportunity, is determined solely by the insurance company, and

    (*c*)   the opportunity is clearly identified in marketing or other promotional material published by the insurance company to members of the public, or members of the public who are intending investors, as available generally to any person falling within its terms.

(5) In this section—

    "holder" has the meaning given by section 516(5), and

    "policy holder" includes a holder of a life annuity contract.

Commentary—*Simon's Taxes* **E1.454C.**

HMRC Manuals—Insurance Policyholder Taxation Manual IPTM3630 (the index selection conditions).

520 The property categories

(1) The table in subsection (2) sets out the categories of property referred to in section 517(2).

(2) This is the table—

Category	Property
Category 1	property which the insurance company has appropriated to an internal linked fund
Category 2	units in an authorised unit trust
Category 3	shares in an investment trust [or an overseas equivalent][5]
Category 4	shares in an open-ended investment company
Category 5	cash
Category 6	a policy or contract to which this Chapter applies, other than an excluded policy or contract (see subsection (3))
Category 7	an interest in a collective investment scheme constituted by—
	(a) a company which is resident outside the United Kingdom (other than an open-ended investment company),[5]
	(b) a unit trust scheme the trustees of which are non-UK resident, or
	(c) any other arrangement which takes effect by virtue of the law of a territory outside the United Kingdom, and which under that law creates rights in the nature of co-ownership (without restricting that term to its legal meaning in any part of the United Kingdom)
[Category 8	shares in a UK REIT or an overseas equivalent
Category 9	an interest in an authorised contractual scheme][5]

(3) A policy or contract is "excluded" if—

    (a) the policy or contract is itself a personal portfolio bond,

    (b) the value of any benefits under the policy or contract is or has at any time been capable of being determined directly or indirectly by reference to a personal portfolio bond, or

    (c) a personal portfolio bond is related property in relation to the policy or contract.

(4) In this section—

["authorised contractual scheme" means a contractual scheme (within the meaning given by section 235A(1) of FISMA 2000) which is authorised for the purposes of FISMA 2000 by an authorisation order in force under section 261D(1) of that Act,][5]

"cash"—

    (a) includes any sum which is deposited—

        (i) in a building society account (including a share account) or similar account, or

        (ii) in a bank account or similar account, but

    (b) does not include cash which is acquired wholly or partly for the purpose of realising a gain from its disposal,

"collective investment scheme" has the meaning given by section 235 of FISMA 2000, and "interest", in relation to such a scheme, means the beneficial entitlement of a participant in such a scheme,

"internal linked fund" has the meaning given by—

    (a) the Interim Prudential Sourcebook for Insurers made by the [Prudential Regulation Authority][3] under FISMA 2000, or

    (b) rules made by the [Prudential Regulation Authority][3] under FISMA 2000 and having effect for the time being in place of the Sourcebook,

["investment trust" has the meaning given by [section 1158 of CTA 2010][2],][1]

"open-ended investment company" has the meaning given by section 236 of FISMA 2000, and

["overseas equivalent", in relation to an investment trust or a UK REIT, means a company—

    (a) which is resident in a territory outside the United Kingdom in accordance with the law of that territory relating to taxation, and

    (b) which is, under the law of that territory, the equivalent of an investment trust or a UK REIT (respectively),][5]

"related property" has the same meaning as in section 625 (see subsection (5)),

["UK REIT" has the same meaning as in Part 12 of CTA 2010 (see section 518(4)).][5]

[(5) The Treasury may by regulations—

    (a) amend the table in subsection (2) by adding, removing or amending a category of property;

    (b) add, remove or amend a definition relating to any category of property in that table; and

    (c) make consequential amendments.

(6) A statutory instrument containing regulations under this section which have the effect of removing a category of property from the table in subsection (2)—

(a) must be laid before the House of Commons; and

(b) ceases to have effect at the end of the period of 28 days beginning with the day on which it was made, unless it is approved during that period by a resolution of the House of Commons.

(7) In reckoning the period of 28 days, no account is to be taken of any time during which Parliament is dissolved or prorogued, or during which the House of Commons is adjourned for more than four days.][4]

Commentary—*Simon's Taxes* **E1.454D.**

HMRC Manuals—Insurance Policyholder Taxation Manual IPTM3640 (the property categories).

Amendments—[1]   In sub-s (4), definition of "investment trust" inserted by ITA 2007 s 1027, Sch 1 paras 492, 534 with effect for income tax purposes from 6 April 2007, and corporation tax purposes for accounting periods ending after 5 April 2007.

[2]   In sub-s (4) in the definition of "investment trust" words substituted by CTA 2010 s 1177, Sch 1 paras 444, 469. CTA 2010 has effect for corporation tax purposes for accounting periods ending on or after 1 April 2010, and for income and capital gains tax purposes for the tax year 2010–11 and subsequent tax years.

[3]   In sub-s (4)(b), in definition of "internal linked fund", words substituted by the Financial Services (Consequential Amendments) Order, SI 2013/636 art 2, Schedule para 8 with effect from 1 April 2013.

[4]   Sub-ss (5)–(7) inserted by F(No 2)A 2017 s 10 with effect from 16 November 2017.

[5]   The following amendments made by the Personal Portfolio Bonds (Amendment of Property Categories in Section 520 of the Income Tax (Trading and Other Income) Act 2005) Regulations, SI 2017/1182 reg 2 with effect from 1 January 2018—

–   in sub-s (2), in Table—

    –   in entry relating to Category 3, in the second column, wrds inserted;
    –   in entry relating to Category 7, in the second column, para (a) repealed; and
    –   entries relating to Categories 8, 9, inserted; and

–   in sub-s (4), definitions of "authorised contractual scheme", "overseas equivalent" and "UK REIT" inserted.

521 The property selection conditions

(1) The property selection conditions are—

(a) the general selection condition (see subsection (2)), and

(b) the class selection condition (see subsection (3)).

(2) Property meets the general selection condition if, at the time when it may be selected, the opportunity to select property falling within the same category is available to—

(a) all policy holders of the insurance company, or

(b) persons acting on behalf of those policy holders.

(3) Property meets the class selection condition if, at the time when it may be selected, the opportunity to select property falling within the same category is available to—

(a) a particular class or classes of policy holders of the insurance company, or

(b) persons acting on behalf of the members of that class or those classes.

(4) A group of policy holders to whom the opportunity to select property falling within a particular category is available is a "class" for the purposes of subsection (3) if—

(a) neither membership of the class nor the opportunity are limited to connected persons,

(b) the question whether a policy holder is a member of a class, or has the opportunity, is determined solely by the insurance company, and

(c) the opportunity is clearly identified in marketing or other promotional material published by the insurance company to members of the public, or members of the public who are intending investors, as available generally to any person falling within its terms.

(5) In this section—

"holder" has the meaning given by section 516(5), and

"policy holder" includes a holder of a life annuity contract.

Commentary—*Simon's Taxes* **E1.454D.**

HMRC Manuals—Insurance Policyholder Taxation Manual IPTM3640 (the property selection conditions).

522 Method for making annual calculations under section 515

(1) This section deals with the calculation required to be made in relation to a policy or contract as at the end of an insurance year under section 515 to determine—

(a) whether a gain has arisen in relation to that year, and

(b) if so, the amount of the gain.

(2) There is a gain if, as at the end of the insurance year, the sum of PP and TPE exceeds TSG.

(3) In subsection (2)—

PP is the total amount of premiums paid up to the end of the insurance year,

TPE is the total amount of personal portfolio bond excesses (see section 523), and

TSG is the total amount of part surrender gains (see section 524).

(4) The gain is equal to 15% of the excess.

Commentary—*Simon's Taxes* **E1.454E.**

HMRC Manuals—Insurance Policyholder Taxation Manual IPTM3650 (personal portfolio bonds: calculation method).

523 The total amount of personal portfolio bond excesses

(1) To calculate the total amount of personal portfolio bond excesses—

Step 1 Apply the calculation in section 522 in relation to the policy or contract as at the end of each previous insurance year during its existence in succession starting with the first such year.

Step 2 Determine whether in each case the calculation produces a gain and, if so, its amount.

Step 3 Add together all the amounts produced by step 2.

(2) But if there is no previous insurance year during the existence of the policy or contract, the total amount of personal portfolio bond excesses is nil.

Commentary—*Simon's Taxes* **E1.454E**.

HMRC Manuals—Insurance Policyholder Taxation Manual IPTM3660 (total amount of personal portfolio bond excesses: example).

524 The total amount of part surrender gains

(1) To calculate the total amount of part surrender gains—

Step 1 Apply the provisions of this Chapter mentioned in subsection (3) as modified by subsections (4) and (5) in relation to the policy or contract as at the end of each previous insurance year during its existence.

Step 2 Determine whether in each case those provisions produce a gain and, if so, its amount.

Step 3 Add together all of the amounts produced by step 2.

(2) But if there is no previous insurance year during the existence of the policy or contract, the total amount of part surrender gains is nil.

(3) The provisions of this Chapter which apply for the purposes of the calculation in subsection (1) are—

(a) subsections (2) to (6) of section 507 (method for making periodic calculations), and

(b) subsections (1) to (3) and (5) of section 508 (the value of rights partially surrendered).

(4) The provisions of section 507 mentioned in subsection (3) apply for the purposes of this section with the omission of all references in that section—

(a) to the assignment of any part of or share in the rights under the policy or contract, or

(b) to the value of any part of or share in the rights under the policy or contract so assigned.

(5) In the application of step 3 in subsection (4) of section 507 for the purposes of this section, the reference in that step to previous calculation events does not include a reference to an excess event consisting of the assignment of a part of or share in the rights under the policy or contract.

Commentary—*Simon's Taxes* **E1.454E**.

HMRC Manuals—Insurance Policyholder Taxation Manual IPTM3650 (the total amount of part surrender gains: steps).

525 Chargeable events where annual calculations show gains

(1) This section applies if the calculation in section 522 shows that a gain has arisen in relation to an insurance year.

(2) The gain is treated as arising at the end of the insurance year on the occurrence of a chargeable event at that time.

Commentary—*Simon's Taxes* **E1.454E**.

HMRC Manuals—Insurance Policyholder Taxation Manual IPTM3670 (chargeable events: meaning).

526 Power to make regulations about personal portfolio bonds

(1) The Treasury may by regulations make provision about the administration of the charge to tax on personal portfolio bonds.

(2) The regulations may modify—

(a) any provision of this Chapter, or

(b) any provision of Chapter 2 of Part 13 of ICTA.

(3) The regulations may—

(a) make different provision for different cases, different circumstances or different periods, and

(b) make incidental, supplemental, consequential or transitional provision or savings.

(4) In this section "modify" includes amend or repeal.

Commentary—*Simon's Taxes* **A3.204, E1.454**.

Reductions from gains

527 Reduction for sums taken into account otherwise than under Chapter 9

(1) This section applies if the whole or part of any receipt or other credit item is taken into account in calculating both—

(a) the amount of a gain treated as arising under this Chapter, and

(b) an amount on which income tax is charged otherwise than under this Chapter or on which corporation tax is charged.

(2) The amount of the gain on which tax is charged under this Chapter is reduced by so much of the amount of that receipt or other credit item as is taken into account in both those calculations.

Commentary—*Simon's Taxes* **E1.452C**.

HMRC Manuals—Insurance Policyholder Taxation Manual IPTM1560 (tax charged on gain on a policy or contract).

[528 Reduction in amount charged on basis of non-UK residence where individual liable for tax

(1) Subsection (2) applies if—

(a) an individual is liable for tax charged on a gain from a policy of life insurance or a capital redemption policy, and

(b) there are one or more days in the material interest period [that are foreign days][2].

[(1A) [Foreign days" are—
  (a) days falling within any tax year for which the individual is not UK resident, and
  (b) days falling within the overseas part of any tax year that is a split year as respects the individual.]²

(2) In determining the individual's liability for tax, the gain on which the tax is charged in the case of the individual is to be reduced by the appropriate fraction.

(3) The appropriate fraction is—

A / B

where—

> A is the number of days in the material interest period which are [foreign days]², and
> B is the number of days in the material interest period.

(4) In subsection (2) the reference to the gain is to be read in accordance with section 463A(4), 463D(4) or 463E(3) (which relates to restricted relief qualifying policies) if applicable.

(5) In this section "the material interest period" means so much of the policy period as during which the individual meets condition A, B or C in section 465 in relation to the policy (subject to subsection (7)).

(6) Subsections (7) and (8) apply if, before the chargeable event, there is an assignment falling within section 487(c) in relation to the policy where the individual is the assignee.

(7) There is to be added to the material interest period any part of the policy period falling before the assignment—
  (a) during which the assignor meets condition A, B or C in section 465 in relation to the policy, and
  (b) which is not included in the material interest period under subsection (5).

(8) In relation to any period added to the material interest period under subsection (7), in [subsection (1A)(a) and (b)]² the reference to the individual is to be read as a reference to the assignor.

(9) For the purposes of subsections (5) and (7), in section 465(2) to (4) references to the rights under the policy are to be read as including references to a share of those rights.

(10) In this section "the policy period" means the period for which the policy has run before the chargeable event occurs.

(11) If the policy is a policy of life insurance which is a new policy in relation to another policy, for the purposes of subsection (10) the new policy is to be taken to have run—
  (a) from the issue of the other policy, or
  (b) if it also was a new policy in relation to an earlier policy, from the issue of the earlier policy,
and so on; and in subsections (5) to (9) references to the policy are to be read accordingly as including any relevant earlier policy.

(12) In subsection (11) "new policy" has the meaning given in paragraph 17 of Schedule 15 to ICTA.]¹

Commentary—*Simon's Taxes* **E1.452D.**
HMRC Manuals—Insurance Policyholder Taxation Manual IPTM3732 (calculation of the reduction in gain).
Amendments—¹   Sections 528, 528A substituted for previous s 528 by FA 2013 s 24, Sch 8 paras 1, 3 with effect in relation to any policy of life insurance issued in respect of an insurance made on or after 6 April 2013 or any contract constituting a capital redemption policy made on or after that date. For the effect of the substitution on insurances or contracts made before 6 April 2013 and varied etc on or after that date, see FA 2013 Sch 8 para 7(2)–(4).
²   Words in sub-s (1)(b) substituted for words "on which the individual is not UK resident", sub-s (1A) inserted, words in sub-s (3) substituted for words "days falling within subsection (1)(b)", and words in sub-s (8) substituted for words "subsection (1)(b)", by FA 2013 s 218, Sch 45 para 86(1)–(6) with effect in relation to policies and contracts in relation to which s 528 (as substituted by FA 2013 Sch 8 para 3) has effect.

[528A Reduction in amount charged on basis of non-UK residence of deceased person

(1) Subsection (3) applies if—
  (a) personal representatives are liable for tax charged on a gain from a policy of life insurance or a capital redemption policy under section 466, and
  (b) there were one or more days in the material interest period [that were foreign days]².

(2) Subsection (3) also applies if—
  (a) trustees are liable for tax charged on a gain from a policy of life insurance or a capital redemption policy under section 467 where—
    (i) of conditions A to D in that section, only condition B is met, and
    (ii) the absent settlor condition which is met is the one in subsection (4)(b) of that section (deceased settlor),
  (b) there were one or more days in the material interest period [that were foreign days, and]²
  [(c) the deceased died—
    (i) in a tax year for which the deceased was UK resident but not one that was a split year as respects the deceased, or
    (ii) in the UK part of a tax year that was a split year as respects the deceased.]²

[(2A) "Foreign days" are—
  (a) days falling within any tax year for which the deceased was not UK resident, and

(*b*) days falling within the overseas part of any tax year that was a split year as respects the deceased.]²

(3) In determining the liability for tax of the personal representatives or trustees, the gain on which the tax is charged in the case of the personal representatives or trustees is to be reduced by the appropriate fraction.

(4) The appropriate fraction is—

A / B

where—

A is the number of days in the material interest period which [were foreign days, and]²

B is the number of days in the material interest period.

(5) In subsection (3) the reference to the gain is to be read in accordance with section 463C(8) (which relates to restricted relief qualifying policies) if applicable.

(6) In this section "the material interest period" means so much of the policy period falling before the deceased's death as during which the deceased met condition A, B or C in section 465 in relation to the policy (subject to subsection (8)).

(7) Subsections (8) and (9) apply if, before the deceased's death, there was an assignment falling within section 487(*c*) in relation to the policy where the deceased was the assignee.

(8) There is to be added to the material interest period any part of the policy period falling before the assignment—

(*a*) during which the assignor met condition A, B or C in section 465 in relation to the policy, and

(*b*) which is not included in the material interest period under subsection (6).

(9) In relation to any period added to the material interest period under subsection (8), in [subsection (2A)(*a*) and (*b*)]² the reference to the deceased is to be read as a reference to the assignor.

(10) For the purposes of subsections (6) and (8), in section 465(2) to (4) references to the rights under the policy are to be read as including references to a share of those rights.

(11) In this section "the policy period" means the period for which the policy has run before the chargeable event occurs.

(12) If the policy is a policy of life insurance which is a new policy in relation to another policy, for the purposes of subsection (11) the new policy is to be taken to have run—

(*a*) from the issue of the other policy, or

(*b*) if it also was a new policy in relation to an earlier policy, from the issue of the earlier policy, and so on; and in subsections (6) to (10) references to the policy are to be read accordingly as including any relevant earlier policy.

(13) In subsection (12) "new policy" has the meaning given in paragraph 17 of Schedule 15 to ICTA.]¹

Commentary—*Simon's Taxes* E1.452D.

HMRC Manuals—Insurance Policyholder Taxation Manual IPTM3735 (gains arising to personal representatives and trustees).

Amendments—¹ Sections 528, 528A inserted by FA 2013 s 24, Sch 8 paras 1, 3 with effect in relation to any policy of life insurance issued in respect of an insurance made on or after 6 April 2013 or any contract constituting a capital redemption policy made on or after that date. For the effect of the substitution on insurances or contracts made before 6 April 2013 and varied etc on or after that date, see FA 2013 Sch 8 para 7(2)–(4).

² Words in sub-s (1)(*b*), (2)(*b*), (4), (9) substituted, sub-s (2)(*c*) substituted, and sub-s (2A) inserted, by FA 2013 s 218, Sch 45 para 87 with effect in calculating an individual's liability to income tax or capital gains tax for the tax year 2013-14 or any subsequent tax year—

Income tax treated as paid and reliefs

530 Income tax treated as paid etc.

(1) An individual or trustees who are liable for tax on an amount under this Chapter are treated as having paid income tax at the [basic rate]² on that amount.

(2) The income tax treated as paid under subsection (1) is not repayable.

(3) The amount on which an individual is treated under subsection (1) as having paid income tax is reduced if subsection (4) applies.

(4) This subsection applies if the individual's total income is reduced by any deductions which fall to be made [at Step 2 or 3 of the calculation in section 23 of ITA 2007 (calculation of income tax liability)]¹ from the part of the income charged to tax under this Chapter.

(5) The reduction under subsection (3) is equal to the amount of those deductions.

(6) . . . ²

(7) This section is subject to section 531.

Commentary—*Simon's Taxes* E1.455A.

HMRC Manuals—Insurance Policyholder Taxation Manual IPTM3810 (income tax treated as paid under the chargeable event regime).

Amendments—¹ Words in sub-s (4) inserted, by ITA 2007 s 1027, Sch 1 paras 492, 535 with effect for income tax purposes from 6 April 2007, and corporation tax purposes for accounting periods ending after 5 April 2007.

² Words in sub-s (1) substituted and sub-s (6) repealed, by FA 2008 s 5, Sch 1 paras 50, 54 with effect for the tax year 2008–09 and subsequent tax years.

531 Exceptions to section 530

(1) Section 530 does not apply to gains from the kinds of policies and contracts specified in subsection (3), except for the purposes of calculating relief under section 535 (top slicing relief).

(2) Subsection (1) is subject to—

     section 532 (relief for policies and contracts with European Economic Area insurers), and

     section 534 (regulations providing for relief in other cases where foreign tax chargeable).

(3) The policies and contracts are—

     (a) a policy of life insurance issued or a contract for a life annuity made by a friendly society in the course of [exempt BLAGAB or eligible PHI business][2],

     (b) a foreign policy of life insurance that does not meet conditions A and B,

     [(ba) a contract the effecting or carrying out of which constitutes protection business within the meaning of section 62 of FA 2012,

     (bb) a contract which is not within paragraph (ba) but which, as a result of subsection (4) of that section, is treated for the purposes of that section as being made at any time,][1]

     (c) a contract for a life annuity (other than one within paragraph (a)) which has at any time not formed part of any insurance company's or friendly society's basic life assurance and general annuity business the income and gains of which are subject to corporation tax, and

     (d) a foreign capital redemption policy.

(4) In this section and section 532—

     "basic life assurance and general annuity business" has the same meaning as in [Part 2 of FA 2012 (see sections 57 and 67(5))][1], and

     ["exempt BLAGAB or eligible PHI business" has the same meaning as in Part 3 of FA 2012 (see sections 154 and 155).][2]

(5) Condition A is that the policy falls within paragraph (a) of the definition of "foreign policy of life insurance" in section 476(3) (policy issued by a non-UK resident company).

(6) Condition B is that the conditions in paragraph 24(3) of Schedule 15 to ICTA (conditions that are required to be met for certain policies issued by non-UK resident companies to be qualifying policies) are met throughout the period between—

     (a) the date on which the policy was issued, and

     (b) the date on which the gain arises.

Commentary—*Simon's Taxes* **E1.455A.**

HMRC Manuals—Insurance Policyholder Taxation Manual IPTM3810 (exceptions to income tax treated as paid under the chargeable event regime).

IPTM3720 (lower rate tax not treated as paid).

Amendments—[1]   In sub-s (3), paras (ba) and (bb) inserted, and in sub-s (4), in definition of "basic life assurance and general annuity business" words substituted for words "Chapter 1 of Part 12 of ICTA (see section 431F)", by FA 2012 s 146, Sch 16 paras 125, 130 with effect in relation to accounting periods of companies beginning on or after 1 January 2013 (subject to transitional provisions in FA 2012 Sch 17). For accounting periods straddling 1 January 2013, see FA 2012 s 149.

[2]   In sub-s (3)(a), words substituted for words "tax exempt life or endowment business", and in sub-s (4), words substituted for words " "tax exempt life or endowment business" has the meaning given in section 466(2) of ICTA.", by FA 2012 s 176, Sch 18 paras 17, 18 with effect in relation to accounting periods of companies beginning on or after 1 January 2013, subject to transitional provisions in FA 2012 s 179.

532 Relief for policies and contracts with European Economic Area insurers

(1) Section 530 applies to a gain from a foreign policy of life insurance or a foreign capital redemption policy or to a gain from a contract for a life annuity (and accordingly section 531 and paragraph 109(2) of Schedule 2 do not apply) if a claim is made that conditions A to C have been met throughout the policy period.

(2) Condition A is that the company liable to make payments under the policy or contract ("the insurer") has not been UK resident.

(3) Condition B is that a comparable EEA tax charge has applied to the insurer (see section 533).

(4) Condition C is that no excluded reinsurance contract has been made in relation to the policy or contract.

(5) In this section—

     "excluded reinsurance contract", in relation to a policy or contract, means any reinsurance contract—

     (a) wholly or partly covering any of the insurer's obligations to pay any sum or to meet any other liability arising under the policy or contract, and

     (b) relating to risk other than that the individual whose life is insured by the policy or the annuitant will die or suffer any sickness or accident,

     "policy period"—

     (a) in relation to a policy, means the period between—

         (i) the making of the insurance or contract, and

         (ii) the date on which the gain arises,

     but excluding any period when the conditions in paragraph 24(3) of Schedule 15 to ICTA are met (conditions that are required to be met for certain policies issued by non-UK resident companies to be qualifying policies), and

(b) in relation to a contract for a life annuity, means the period between—
  (i) the date the insurer entered into the contract, and
  (ii) the date on which the gain arises,

but excluding any period when the contract fell to be regarded as forming part of a basic life assurance and general annuity business the income and gains of which were subject to corporation tax.

Commentary—*Simon's Taxes* E1.455A.

533 Meaning of "comparable EEA tax charge"

(1) In section 532 "comparable EEA tax charge" in relation to the company liable to make payments under the policy or contract under which the gain has arisen ("the insurer") means a charge that meets conditions A to F.

(2) Condition A is that the charge is imposed on the insurer under the laws of a territory outside the United Kingdom that is within the European Economic Area when the gain arises.

(3) Condition B is that the charge has applied to the insurer—
  (a) as a body deriving its status as a company from those laws,
  (b) as a company with its place of management there, or
  (c) as a company falling under those laws to be regarded for any other reason as resident or domiciled there.

(4) Condition C is that the charge applies at a rate of at least 20% in relation to the amounts subject to tax in the insurer's hands, other than amounts arising or accruing in respect of investments of a description for which a special relief or exemption is generally available.

(5) Condition D is that the charge is made otherwise than by reference to the insurer's profits.

(6) Condition E is that the charge requires sums payable and other liabilities arising under policies or contracts of the same class as the policy or contract in question to be treated as falling to be met out of amounts subject to tax in the insurer's hands.

(7) Condition F is that the charge so requires them by disallowing their deduction in calculating the amount chargeable.

Commentary—*Simon's Taxes* E1.455A.

534 Regulations providing for relief in other cases where foreign tax chargeable

(1) This section applies if—
  (a) apart from this section, as a result of section 531 or paragraph 109(2) of Schedule 2, section 530 would not apply to gains from a policy or contract (except for the purposes of section 535 (top slicing relief)), and
  (b) [the Commissioners for Her Majesty's Revenue and Customs] consider it appropriate to disapply section 531 and paragraph 109(2) of Schedule 2 in relation to such gains by reference to tax chargeable under the laws of a territory outside the United Kingdom in cases other than those where they are disapplied as a result of section 532.

(2) [The Commissioners for Her Majesty's Revenue and Customs] may by regulations provide for section 530 to apply to those gains (and accordingly section 531 and paragraph 109(2) of Schedule 2 not to apply to them) if a claim is made that the conditions specified in the regulations are met in relation to any time.

(3) That time may be a time before the regulations are made or a later time.

Commentary—*Simon's Taxes* E1.455A.

535 Top slicing relief

(1) An individual is entitled to relief under this section for a tax year if—
  (a) the individual's liability for the tax year, as calculated under subsection (3), exceeds
  (b) the individual's relieved liability for the tax year, as calculated under—
    section 536 (top slicing relieved liability: one chargeable event), or
    section 537 (top slicing relieved liability: two or more chargeable events).

(2) The relief is given by a reduction in or repayment of income tax equal to the excess.

[(2A) If the relief is given by a reduction in income tax, it is given effect at Step 6 of the calculation in section 23 of ITA 2007.][1]

(3) An individual's liability for a tax year for the purposes of subsection (1)(a) equals $TL - [BRL]^2$, where—

TL is the amount of the individual's total liability to income tax on income charged to tax under this Chapter for the tax year, calculated on the basis that no relief is available under this section and the highest part assumptions apply, and

$[BRL]^2$ is the amount of income tax at the [basic rate][2] that the individual is treated as having paid under section 530(1) for the tax year.

(4) For the purposes of subsection (3) and sections 536 and 537, the highest part assumptions, in calculating liability to income tax on an amount, are that—
  (a) the amount is the highest part of the individual's total income for the tax year, and
  (b) any provision directing any other amount to be treated as the highest part is ignored.

(5) For the purposes of this section and sections 536 and 537, an individual's total income is treated as not including any amount which—

    (*a*) is charged to tax under Chapter 4 of Part 3 (profits of property businesses: lease premiums etc.) as the profits of a UK property business, or

    (*b*) counts as employment income under section 403 of ITEPA 2003 (payments and benefits on termination of employment etc.).

(6) For the purposes of this section and sections 536 and 537—

    (*a*) any chargeable event under section 525(2) (chargeable events where annual personal portfolio bond calculations show gains),

    (*b*) any gain treated as arising on the occurrence of such an event, and

    (*c*) the amount of any liability to income tax arising on such a gain, are ignored.

[(7) For the purposes of the calculations mentioned in subsection (1) any relief under Chapter 2 or 3 of Part 8 of ITA 2007 (which relate to gift aid and other gifts to charities) is ignored.][1]

[(8) For the purposes of the calculations mentioned in subsection (1)—

    (*a*) section 25(2) of ITA 2007 (deductions of reliefs and allowances in most beneficial way for taxpayer) does not apply, and

    (*b*) reliefs and allowances are available for deduction from an amount that, for the purposes of those calculations, is the highest part of the individual's total income for the tax year only so far as they cannot be deducted from other amounts.][3]

Commentary—*Simon's Taxes* **E1.455B.**
HMRC Manuals—Insurance Policyholder Taxation Manual IPTM3820 (top slicing relief: general).
Amendments—[1]   Sub-ss (2A), (7) inserted by ITA 2007 s 1027, Sch 1 paras 492, 536 with effect for income tax purposes from 6 April 2007, and corporation tax purposes for accounting periods ending after 5 April 2007.
[2]   Words in sub-s (3) substituted by FA 2008 s 5, Sch 1 paras 50, 55 with effect for the tax year 2008–09 and subsequent tax years.
[3]   Sub-s (8) inserted by FA 2020 s 37(1), (2) with effect in relation to the tax year 2019–20 and subsequent tax years. This amendment does not have effect in relation to the tax year 2019–20 or 2020–21 in the case of an individual who is only liable to tax under ITTOIA 2005 Part 4 Chapter 9 for the year in question—
    (a) on a gain from one chargeable event that occurs before 11 March 2020, or
    (b) on gains from chargeable events each of which occurs before that day (FA 2020 s 37(6)).

536 Top slicing relieved liability: one chargeable event

(1) To calculate an individual's relieved liability for the purposes of section 535(1) for a tax year for which the individual is only liable for tax on a gain from one chargeable event—

    Step 1 Find the annual equivalent of the amount of that gain ("the annual equivalent") by dividing that amount by the number of complete years for which the policy or contract has run before the chargeable event ("N").

    See subsections (2) to (8) for further provisions about calculating N.

    Step 2 Find the relieved liability on the annual equivalent by—

        (*a*) calculating the individual's liability (if any) to income tax on the annual equivalent, on the basis that—

            (i) the gain from the chargeable event is limited to the amount of the annual equivalent,

               . . .[4]

            (ii) the highest part assumptions apply, and

            [(iii)in determining the amount of the individual's personal allowance under section 35 of ITA 2007 (but not the amount of any other relief or allowance), it is assumed that the gain from the chargeable event is equal to the amount of the annual equivalent, and][4]

        (*b*) subtracting the amount of income tax at the [basic rate][1] on the annual equivalent which the individual is treated as having paid under section 530(1).

    Step 3 Multiply the relieved liability on the annual equivalent by N.

(2) In the case of a calculation event that is not the first calculation event in relation to the policy or contract, for steps 1 and 3 in subsection (1) N is the number of complete years since the previous such event (but see subsection (6)).

(3) For the purposes of subsection (2), part surrender or assignment events are taken to occur at the end of the insurance year in which the surrender or assignment occurs.

(4) If, in a case where subsection (2) does not apply, the gain is from a policy of life insurance which is a new policy in relation to another policy, for steps 1 and 3 N is calculated from—

    (*a*) the issue of the other policy, or

    (*b*) if it also was a new policy in relation to an earlier policy, the issue of the earlier policy,

and so on.

(5) In subsection (4) "new policy" has the meaning given in paragraph 17 of Schedule 15 to ICTA.

(6) Subsection (2) does not apply if the gain is [reduced under section 528 in the case of the individual.][2]

[(7) If in the case of the individual the gain is reduced under section 528—

    (*a*) divide the number of foreign days in the material interest period (as determined in accordance with that section, including subsections (7) and (8)) by 365, (*b*) if the result is not a whole number, round it down to the nearest whole number, and

(*c*) reduce N, for steps 1 and 3 in subsection (1), by the number found by applying paragraphs (*a*) and (*b*).][3]

(8) If subsections (4) and (7) both apply, subsection (7) applies to N as calculated under subsection (4).

Commentary—*Simon's Taxes* E1.455B.

HMRC Manuals—Insurance Policyholder Taxation Manual IPTM3736 (interaction between restricted relief qualifying policies and top slicing relief).

IPTM3840 (how relief is given : one chargeable event).

Amendments—[1] Words in sub-s (1) step 2 substituted by FA 2008 s 5, Sch 1 paras 50, 56 with effect for the tax year 2008–09 and subsequent tax years.

[2] In sub-s (6) words substituted for words "from a foreign policy of life insurance or a foreign capital redemption policy," by FA 2013 s 24, Sch 8 paras 1, 5 with effect in relation to any policy of life insurance issued in respect of an insurance made on or after 6 April 2013 or any contract constituting a capital redemption policy made on or after that date. Note that, in the case of a policy or contract treated under s 473A of this Act as a single policy or contract, for these purposes the date on which the insurance or contract is made is the date on which, as the case may be, the first insurance is made in respect of which the connected policies are issued, or the first of the connected contracts is made (FA 2013 Sch 8 para 7(4)).

Note that FA 2013 Sch 8 para 5(3) also substituted sub-s (7) with effect from the same date. See "Note" above.

[3] Sub-s (7) substituted by FA 2013 s 218, Sch 45 para 86(1)–(3) with effect in accordance with FA 2013 Sch 8 para 7. See "Note" above.

[4] In sub-s (1), in step 2 para (*a*), word "and" at end of para (i) repealed, and para (iii) inserted, by FA 2020 s 37(1), (3) with effect in relation to the tax year 2019–20 and subsequent tax years. This amendment does not have effect in relation to the tax year 2019–20 or 2020–21 in the case of an individual who is only liable to tax under ITTOIA 2005 Part 4 Chapter 9 for the year in question—

    (a)   on a gain from one chargeable event that occurs before 11 March 2020, or

    (b)   on gains from chargeable events each of which occurs before that day (FA 2020 s 37(6)).

537 Top slicing relieved liability: two or more chargeable events

To calculate an individual's relieved liability for the purposes of section 535(1) for a tax year for which the individual is liable for tax on gains from two or more chargeable events—

Step 1 Calculate the total annual equivalent by adding together the annual equivalents for each of the chargeable events, found as specified in step 1 in section 536(1).

Step 2 Find the total relieved liability on the total annual equivalent by—

(*a*) calculating the individual's liability to income tax (if any) on the total annual equivalent, on the basis that—

    (i) the total gains from the chargeable events are limited to the amount of the total annual equivalent,[2]

    (ii) the highest part assumptions apply, and

    [(iii) in determining the amount of the individual's personal allowance under section 35 of ITA 2007 (but not the amount of any other relief or allowance), it is assumed that the total gains from the chargeable events are equal to the amount of the total annual equivalent, and][2]

(*b*) subtracting the amount of income tax at the [basic rate][1] on the total annual equivalent which the individual is treated as having paid under section 530(1).

Step 3 Multiply the total relieved liability on the total annual equivalent by the total gains charged to tax under this Chapter for the tax year in respect of all the events.

Step 4 Divide the result of step 3 by the total annual equivalent.

Commentary—*Simon's Taxes* E1.455B.

HMRC Manuals—Insurance Policyholder Taxation Manual IPTM3840 (how relief is given when there are two or more chargeable events).

Amendments—[1] Words in Step 2(*b*) substituted by FA 2008 s 5, Sch 1 paras 50, 57 with effect for the tax year 2008–09 and subsequent tax years.

[2] In step 2 para (*a*), word "and" at end of para (i) repealed, and para (iii) inserted, by FA 2020 s 37(1), (4) with effect in relation to the tax year 2019–20 and subsequent tax years. This amendment does not have effect in relation to the tax year 2019–20 or 2020–21 in the case of an individual who is only liable to tax under ITTOIA 2005 Part 4 Chapter 9 for the year in question—

    (a)   on a gain from one chargeable event that occurs before 11 March 2020, or

    (b)   on gains from chargeable events each of which occurs before that day (FA 2020 s 37(6)).

538 Recovery of tax from trustees

(1) This section applies if—

(*a*) immediately before a chargeable event the rights under the policy or contract, or the part of or share in them in question, were held on non-charitable trusts,

(*b*) an individual is liable for tax under this Chapter for the tax year on the gain from the event, and

(*c*) the income tax for which the individual is liable for the tax year, after any relief available in respect of the gain under section 535 (top slicing relief), exceeds that for which the individual would have been liable apart from the event.

(2) The individual is entitled to recover that excess from the trustees, subject to the restriction specified in subsection (3).

(3) The amount recovered must not exceed the total of—
    (*a*) any sums received by the trustees because of the chargeable event, and
    (*b*) the value of any benefits so received.

(4) If the individual's relief under section 535 for the tax year does not relate only to the gain from the event in question, for the purposes of subsection (1)(*c*) a proportionate part of that relief is taken to be relief in respect of that gain.

(5) An individual may require [an officer of Revenue and Customs] to certify an amount recoverable by the individual under this section.

(6) Such a certificate is conclusive evidence of the amount.

(7) Subsection (8) applies where—
    (*a*) an individual has recovered an amount from trustees under this section, and
    (*b*) subsequently the individual's liability to tax under this Chapter has been reduced (or removed) as a result of a recalculation under section 507A or 512A.

(8) The individual must repay to the trustees the amount (if any) by which the recovered amount exceeds the individual's revised entitlement.

(9) In subsection (8) the individual's revised entitlement is the amount to which the individual is entitled under this section calculated by reference to the individual's liability to tax under this Chapter as reduced (or removed) as a result of the recalculation under section 507A or 512A.[1]

Commentary—*Simon's Taxes* **E1.455C.**
HMRC Manuals—Insurance Policyholder Taxation Manual IPTM3220 (recovery of taxes from trustees : individuals).
Amendments—[1] Sub-ss (7)–(9) inserted by F(No 2)A 2017 s 9(1), (4) with effect in relation to amounts recovered before, as well as after, 16 November 2017.

Deficiencies

[539 Relief for deficiencies

(1) An individual is entitled to a tax reduction for a tax year in which a deficiency arises from a policy or contract on a chargeable event if—
    (*a*) the condition in subsection (2) is met,
    (*b*) the individual would (apart from this section) be liable to income tax at [one or more of the higher rate, the Scottish higher rate[, the Welsh higher rate][4] or the dividend upper rate][3] for the tax year, and
    (*c*) the individual makes a claim.

(2) The condition is that, if a gain had arisen instead on the chargeable event—
    (*a*) the individual would have been liable to income tax on the gain for the year, or
    (*b*) the individual would have been so liable apart from the requirement in section 465(1) that the individual must be UK resident in the tax year in which the gain arises.

(3) The tax reduction is given effect at Step 6 of the calculation in section 23 of ITA 2007.

(4) See section 540 for the cases in which a deficiency is treated as arising from a policy or contract on a chargeable event, section 541 for how the deficiency is calculated and section 469(5) for the apportionment of deficiencies in cases where two or more persons are interested in a policy or contract.

(5) The amount of the tax reduction is calculated as follows. [If the individual is a Scottish taxpayer [or a Welsh taxpayer][4], instead of Step 3 carry out Steps 3A and 3B.][3]
Step 1 Attribute to the amount of the deficiency an amount of the individual's income for the tax year which is liable at the dividend upper rate, so far as is possible.
Step 2 . . . .[2]
Step 3 If there is an amount of the deficiency remaining after Step [1][2], attribute to the remaining amount of the deficiency an amount of the individual's . . . [2] income for the tax year which is liable [at any of the higher rate, the default higher rate and the savings higher rate,][4] so far as is possible.
[*Step 3A* If there is an amount of deficiency remaining after Step 1, attribute to the remaining amount of the deficiency an amount of the individual's income for the tax year which [(in the case of a Scottish taxpayer)][4] is liable at the higher of the Scottish higher rate [and the savings higher rate or (in the case of a Welsh taxpayer) is liable at the higher of the Welsh higher rate and the savings higher rate][4], so far as is possible.
Step 3B If there is an amount of deficiency remaining after Step 3A, attribute to the remaining amount of the deficiency an amount of the individual's income for the tax year which [(in the case of a Scottish taxpayer)][4] is liable at the lower of the Scottish higher rate [and the savings higher rate or (in the case of a Welsh taxpayer) is liable at the lower of the Welsh higher rate and the savings higher rate][4], so far as is possible.][3]
Step 4 Calculate the amount of the individual's preliminary income tax liability for the tax year (see subsection (6)).
Step 5 Calculate the amount of the individual's preliminary income tax liability for the tax year again, on these assumptions—
    Assume that any income attributed to the deficiency at Step 1 is liable at the dividend ordinary rate.

. . . [2]

[Assume that any income liable at the higher rate[, or at the default higher rate or the savings higher rate,][4] and attributed to the deficiency at Step 3, Step 3A or Step 3B is liable at the basic rate.][3]

[Assume that any income liable at the Scottish higher rate[, or at the Welsh higher rate][4] and attributed to the deficiency at Step 3A or Step 3B is liable at the Scottish basic rate [or (as the case may be) the Welsh basic rate][4].][3]

Step 6 Deduct the amount found at Step 5 from the amount found at Step 4. The result is the amount of the tax reduction.

(6) The individual's preliminary income tax liability is the amount found by calculating the individual's income tax liability in accordance with section 23 of ITA 2007, ignoring Steps 6 and 7 of that calculation.

[(7) For the purposes of Steps 3A and 3B of the calculation at subsection (3) of this section—
    (a) if the Scottish higher rate and the savings higher rate are equal, the Scottish higher rate is to be treated as the higher of the two rates (and the savings higher rate as the lower), and
    (b) if the Welsh higher rate and the savings higher rate are equal, the Welsh higher rate is to be treated as the higher of the two rates (and the savings higher rate as the lower).][4]][1]

Commentary—*Simon's Taxes* **E1.455D.**

HMRC Manuals—Insurance Policyholder Taxation Manual IPTM3860 (deficiency relief : conditions).

Amendments—[1]   This section substituted by ITA 2007 s 1027, Sch 1 paras 492, 539 with effect for income tax purposes from 6 April 2007, and corporation tax purposes for accounting periods ending after 5 April 2007.

[2]   Words in sub-s (5) substituted and repealed by FA 2008 s 5, Sch 1 paras 50, 58 with effect for the tax year 2008–09 and subsequent tax years.

[3]   In sub-s (1)(b), words substituted, in sub-s (5), words inserted, Steps 3A, 3B inserted, and in Step 5, words substituted and words inserted by the Scottish Rate of Income Tax (Consequential Amendments) Order, SI 2015/1810 arts 8, 9 with effect in relation to the tax year 2016–17 (the tax year appointed by the Treasury under the Scotland Act 2012 s 25(5) by virtue of SI 2015/2000) and subsequent tax years.

[4]   In sub-ss (1)(b) and (5) words inserted, in sub-s (5), in step 3 words substituted for words "at the higher rate,", in steps 3A and 3B words substituted for words "and the higher rate", and sub-s (7) inserted, by the Devolved Income Tax Rates (Consequential Amendments) Order, SI 2019/201 art 10(1), (2) with effect in relation to the tax year commencing on 6 April 2019 and subsequent tax years.

540 When deficiencies arise: events following calculation events

(1) A deficiency is treated as arising from a policy or contract on a chargeable event ("the later event") if conditions A to C are met.

(2) Condition A is that the later event is an event within section 484(1)(a)(i) or (iii) or (b) to (e) (surrender of all rights, final participation in profits, death, maturity, or taking a capital sum as a complete alternative to annuity payments).

(3) Condition B is that a gain from the policy or contract has arisen on a calculation event other than a personal portfolio bond event, occurring in relation to the policy or contract in question before the later event.

(4) Condition C is that on the later event no gain is shown by the calculation in section 491(2) (calculation of gains for such events).

Commentary—*Simon's Taxes* **E1.455D.**

HMRC Manuals—Insurance Policyholder Taxation Manual IPTM3860 (deficiency relief: entitlement and calculation).

541 Calculation of deficiencies

(1) This section sets out how the amount of a deficiency treated as arising under section 540(1) on a chargeable event ("the later event") is calculated.

(2) If, when the calculation in section 491(2) is made for the later event, the total allowable deductions equal or exceed the total benefit value, the amount of the deficiency is equal to the total previous gains.

(3) If, when that calculation is made, the total benefit value exceeds the total allowable deductions, the amount of the deficiency is equal to the total previous gains, less that excess.

(4) In this section "the total previous gains" means the total amount of gains that—
    (a) were treated as arising on calculation events (other than personal portfolio bond events) occurring in relation to the policy or contract in question before the later event, and
    (b) formed part of the total income of the individual mentioned in section 539(1) for a tax year earlier than the tax year mentioned in that section [or formed part of the total income of that individual by virtue of section 465B for the tax year mentioned in section 539(1)][1].

Commentary—*Simon's Taxes* **E1.455D.**

HMRC Manuals—Insurance Policyholder Taxation Manual IPTM3860 (deficiency relief: entitlement and calculation).
IPTM3880 (deficiency relief: examples).

Amendments—[1]   Words in sub-s (4)(b) inserted by FA 2013 s 218, Sch 45 paras 139, 143 with effect if the year of departure (as defined in FA 2013 Sch 45 Pt 4) is the tax year 2013–14 or any subsequent tax year, subject to transitional provisions and savings in FA 2013 Sch 45 paras 154–158.

[Rebated or reinvested commission

541A Effect of rebated or reinvested commission in certain cases

(1) This section applies if—

    (a) a chargeable event within section 484(1)(a)(i) to (iii), (c) or (e) occurs in respect of a policy or contract,

    (b) commission in respect of the policy or contract has at any time been rebated or reinvested, and

    (c) condition A or B is met.

(2) For the purposes of performing the calculation in section 494 (total allowable deductions) for the chargeable event, the total amount of premiums under the policy or contract paid in the period mentioned in section 494(1) or (2)(b) is to be reduced by the total amount of commission attributable to those premiums that has been rebated or reinvested.

(3) Condition A is that the total amount of premiums under the policy or contract paid in a relevant period exceeds £100,000.

(4) Condition B is that—

    (a) at a time when the policy or contract was the taxable person's, the taxable person's policies and contracts exceeded the relevant threshold as respects a relevant period, and

    (b) premiums under the policy or contract were paid in that relevant period.

(5) In subsection (4)(a) "taxable person" means the person whose policy or contract the policy or contract is, immediately before the chargeable event.

(6) For the purposes of subsection (4)(a) a person's policies and contracts "exceed the relevant threshold" as respects a relevant period if the total amount of premiums under them paid in that relevant period exceeds the sum specified in subsection (3).

(7) In this section "relevant period" means—

    (a) the period beginning with the beginning of the tax year in which the chargeable event occurs and ending with the chargeable event, or

    (b) any of the 3 preceding tax years.

(8) The Treasury may by order—

    (a) substitute another sum for the sum for the time being specified in subsection (3);

    (b) amend the definition of "relevant period".][1]

Commentary—*Simon's Taxes* E1.452B.

Amendments—[1]　Section and the preceding heading inserted by FA 2007 s 29(3), (4) with effect for a policy or contract if: (a) it is made on or after 21 March 2007, or (b) on or after that date, any of its terms are varied, or a right under it is exercised, so as to increase the benefits under it.

[541B Section 541A: further definitions

(1) This section supplements section 541A.

(2) "Commission", in relation to a policy or contract, includes any passing of value to or for the benefit of an intermediary, or a person connected with an intermediary, that can reasonably be taken to represent a reward in respect of the policy or contract.

(3) Commission in respect of a policy or contract is "reinvested" if, as a result of a waiver of an entitlement to it, there is an increase in the total value of a relevant person's policies and contracts.

(4) The amount of commission reinvested is the amount of the increase.

(5) Commission in respect of a policy or contract is "rebated" if—

    (a) value passes (directly or indirectly) from an intermediary, or a person connected with an intermediary, to or for the benefit of a relevant person (and the passing of value does not amount to the reinvestment of the commission), and

    (b) the passing of value can reasonably be taken to be in respect of the commission.

(6) The amount of commission rebated is the amount of value passed.

(7) A policy or contract is a person's policy or contract if a gain arising in connection with it would be—

    (a) a gain for which the person, or (if the person is an individual) the person's spouse or civil partner, would be liable to tax under this Chapter, . . .[2]

    (b) . . .[2]

(8) Any necessary apportionment is to be made (on a just and reasonable basis) as regards—

    (a) commission which is attributable to two or more premiums, and

    (b) any part of such commission that has been rebated or reinvested.

(9) Commission which is in respect of one or more policies or contracts (but is not attributable to particular premiums) is to be attributed to such premiums as is just and reasonable.

(10) In subsections (3) and (5), "relevant person" means—

    (a) any of the policyholders (including any of the persons who hold the contract),

    (b) a person who beneficially owns the rights under the policy or contract,

    (c) if those rights are held on trust, any of the trustees, or

    (d) a person connected with a person within any of paragraphs (a) to (c).][1]

Commentary—*Simon's Taxes* E1.452B.

Amendments—[1]   Section inserted by FA 2007 s 29(3), (4) with effect for a policy or contract if: (a) it is made on or after 21 March 2007, or (b) on or after that date, any of its terms are varied, or a right under it is exercised, so as to increase the benefits under it.

[2] Sub-s (7)(*b*) and preceding word repealed by FA 2008 s 36, Sch 14 paras 1, 15 with effect as follows: (a) so far as relating to corporation tax, for accounting periods beginning on or after 1 April 2008, and (b) so far as relating to income tax, for the tax year 2008–09 and subsequent tax years.

Supplementary

542 Replacement of qualifying policies

(1) A qualifying policy ("the replaced policy") and a policy of life insurance ("the replacement policy") which replaces the replaced policy are treated as a single policy for the purposes of sections 484 to 497 if conditions A to D are met.

(2) Condition A is that the replacement policy is also a qualifying policy under the rules in paragraph 17 of Schedule 15 to ICTA.

(3) Condition B is that the replacement results from a change in the life or lives insured.

(4) Condition C is that any sum becoming payable by the insurance company on or in connection with the termination of the replaced policy is retained by it and applied in the discharge of some or all of the liability for any premium becoming due under the replacement policy.

(5) Condition D is that no consideration in money or money's worth (other than the benefits for which provision is made by the replacement policy) is receivable by any person on or in connection with—

(*a*) the termination of the replaced policy, or

(*b*) the coming into existence of the replacement policy.

(6) The single policy is treated for the purposes of sections 484 to 497 as issued in respect of an insurance made at the time of the making of the insurance in respect of which the replaced policy was issued.

(7) So long as the replacement policy continues to be a qualifying policy, the single policy is also treated as a qualifying policy for those purposes.

(8) This section applies equally to a second or subsequent replacement policy.

(9) References in Schedule 2 (transitionals and savings) to—

(*a*) a policy of life insurance,

(*b*) the time of the making of the insurance in respect of which a policy of life insurance is issued, and

(*c*) a qualifying policy,

are to be read in accordance with this section.

Commentary—*Simon's Taxes* **E1.451A.**

HMRC Manuals—Insurance Policyholder Taxation Manual IPTM3520 (replacement policies: conditions to be met).

543 Issue time of qualifying policy replacing foreign policy

(1) This section applies if—

(*a*) there has been a substitution of policies falling within paragraph 25(1) or (3) of Schedule 15 of ICTA (replacement of a policy issued by a non-UK resident company by a policy which is not so issued), and

(*b*) the new policy is a qualifying policy.

(2) The new policy is treated for the purposes of sections 484 to 497 as having been issued in respect of an insurance made on the day on which the insurance was made in respect of which the old policy was issued.

(3) References in Schedule 2 (transitionals and savings) to the time of the making of the insurance in respect of which a policy of life insurance is issued are to be read in accordance with this section.

Commentary—*Simon's Taxes* **E1.443.**

544 Application of Chapter to policies and contracts in which companies interested

(1) This section applies where, for the purposes of determining the application of this Chapter in relation to a policy or contract at any time, it is necessary to have regard to its application at another time.

(2) It makes no difference to the application of this Chapter at that other time whether liability in respect of a gain arising at that time would have arisen or (as the case may be) would arise because of the application of this Chapter or the corporation tax provisions.

(3) In subsection (2) "the corporation tax provisions" means—

(*a*) Chapter 2 of Part 13 of ICTA (which makes provision for corporation tax purposes corresponding to that made by this Chapter),

(*b*) paragraph 20 of Schedule 15 to that Act (replacement of qualifying policies), and

(*c*) section 79 of FA 1997 (payments under certain life insurance policies).

545 Minor definitions

(1) In this Chapter—

. . .[1]

"contract of insurance" has the meaning given by Article 3(1) of the Financial Services and Markets Act 2000 (Regulated Activities) Order 2001 (SI 2001/544),

"friendly society" has the meaning given in the Friendly Societies Act 1992 (c. 40) and includes a society which under section 96(2) of that Act is to be treated as a registered friendly society,

"insurance company" means an undertaking carrying on the business of effecting or carrying out contracts of insurance,

"market value" has the meaning given by sections 272 and 273 of TCGA 1992,

"non-charitable trust" means a trust other than a charitable trust, and

"policy" means a policy of life insurance or a capital redemption policy.

(2) References in this Chapter to a premium include a reference to—

(*a*) lump sum consideration, and

(*b*) property other than cash transferred to the insurance company in satisfaction of a premium.

(3) References in this Chapter to the amount of premiums paid include a reference to—

(*a*) the amount of lump sum consideration paid by way of premium, and

(*b*) the market value at the date of transfer of property other than cash transferred to the insurance company in satisfaction of any premium.

Commentary—*Simon's Taxes* **E1.441.**

Amendments—[1]   In sub-s (1) definition of "charitable trust" repealed by FA 2010 s 30, Sch 6 para 21(1), (3) with effect in relation to insurances and contracts made on or after 6 April 2012.

546 Table of provisions subject to special rules for older policies and contracts

(1) Column 1 of the table in subsection (4) specifies provisions of this Chapter which are subject to Part 6 or 7 of Schedule 2 (transitionals and savings), and column 2 of the table specifies the provisions of that Schedule to which they are subject.

(2) See also paragraphs 85 to 91 of that Schedule.

(3) The provisions of that Schedule referred to in subsections (1) and (2) are to be read as if they were in this Chapter.

(4) This is the table—

Provisions of Chapter 9	*Provisions of Schedule 2*
Section 467	paragraph 112 (pre-17th March 1998 policies and contracts) and paragraph 114 (pre-9th April 2003 policies and contracts)
Section 473	paragraph 96 (exclusion of pre-20th March 1968 policies and contracts) and paragraph 102 (exclusion of certain pre-26th June 1982 policies and contracts)
Section 476(3)	paragraphs 103 and 111 (certain pre-18th November 1983 and pre-17th March 1998 policies not foreign policies of life insurance) and paragraphs 104 and 113 (certain pre-23rd February 1984 and pre-23rd March 1999 policies not foreign capital redemption policies)
Section 480	paragraph 116 (pre-9th April 2003 policies)
Section 484	paragraph 99 (pre-10th December 1974 contracts for a life annuity: disregard of death)
Section 485(2) and (3)	paragraph 107 (pre-14th March 1989 qualifying policies)
Section 494(1)	paragraph 105(a) (pre-14th March 1984 policies: disregard of amounts deducted and repaid after tax relief by deduction from premiums abolished)
Section 500(*c*)	paragraph 97 (disapplication in relation to pre-27th March 1974 policies and contracts) and paragraph 102(9) (exclusion of certain pre-26th June 1982 policies and contracts)
Section 501	paragraph 102(9) (exclusion of certain pre-26th June 1982 policies and contracts), paragraph 108 (pre-14th March 1989 policies and contracts) and paragraph 115 (pre-9th April 2003 policies and contracts: loans to trustees)
Section 507	paragraph 100 (pre-14th March 1975 policies and contracts) and paragraph 105(*b*) (pre-14th March 1984 policies: disregard of amounts deducted and repaid after tax relief by deduction from premiums abolished)
Section 516	paragraph 119 (pre-17th March 1998 policies and contracts)
Section 525	paragraph 124(3) (pre-17th March 1998 policies and contracts) and paragraph 125(3) (pre-17th March 1998 policies and contracts)
Section 529	paragraph 106 (disapplication of section 529(1)(*a*) and (*b*) for certain pre-20th March 1985 policies) and paragraph 110 (disapplication of section 529(1)(*c*) for certain pre-17th March 1998 policies)
Section 530	paragraph 109(2) (disapplication for contracts for life annuities made in accounting periods beginning before 1st January 1992)
Section 531	paragraph 98 (pre-27th March 1974 policies and contracts: disapplication of section 531(3)(*c*)) and paragraph 118 (pre-1st January 2005 contracts for immediate needs annuities: income tax treated as paid)

Provisions of Chapter 9	Provisions of Schedule 2
[Section 539][1]	paragraph 109(4) (contracts made in accounting periods beginning before 1st January 1992)
Section 541(4)	paragraph 117 (pre-3rd March 2004 contract or policy: calculation of deficiencies)
Section 542	paragraph 101 (disapplication in the case of pre-25th March 1982 replacement policies)

Amendments—[1]   Words substituted by ITA 2007 s 1027, Sch 1 paras 492, 540 with effect for income tax purposes from 6 April 2007, and corporation tax purposes for accounting periods ending after 5 April 2007.

CHAPTER 11

TRANSACTIONS IN DEPOSITS

551 Charge to tax on profits from disposal of deposit rights

(1) Income tax is charged on profits and gains from the disposal of deposit rights.

(2) For the purposes of this section, the exercise of a deposit right is a disposal of it . . . [1].

Commentary—*Simon's Taxes* **E1.461.**
HMRC Manuals—Savings and Investment Manual SAIM2500 (sale of interest rights: introduction).
SAIM2510 (the taxation of certificates of deposit).
Amendments—[1]   In sub-s (2) words repealed by FA 2009 s 49, Sch 25 para 9(2)(a) with effect in relation to transfers on or after 22 April 2009.

552 Meaning of "deposit rights"

(1) In this Chapter "deposit rights" means—

  (a) a right to receive, with or without interest, a principal amount stated in, or determined in accordance with, the current terms of issue of an eligible debt security, where in accordance with those terms the issue of uncertificated units of the eligible debt security corresponds to the issue of a certificate of deposit,

  (b) a right to receive the principal amount stated in a certificate of deposit, with or without interest,

  (c) an uncertificated right to receive a principal amount, with or without interest, as a result of a deposit of money,

  (d) a right which—

    (i) is not within paragraph (c),

    (ii) is acquired in a transaction in which no certificate of deposit or security or uncertificated eligible debt security units are issued, and

    (iii) is a right to receive a principal amount payable with interest by a bank or similar institution or a person regularly engaging in similar transactions . . . [2]

  (e) . . . [1]

(2) In this section—

  "certificate of deposit" means a document—

    (a) relating to the deposit of money in any currency,

    (b) recognising an obligation to pay a stated principal amount to bearer or to order, with or without interest, and

    (c) by the delivery of which, with or without endorsement, the right to receive that stated amount, with or without interest, is transferable,

  "eligible debt security" has the meaning given in regulation 3(1) of the Uncertificated Securities Regulations 2001 (SI 2001/3755),

  "security" (except in relation to an eligible debt security) includes any loan stock or similar security, whether secured or unsecured and whether issued by—

    (a) the Government of the United Kingdom or another government,

    (b) any local or other public authority in the United Kingdom or elsewhere, or

    (c) any company,

  "uncertificated", in relation to a unit, has the meaning given in regulation 3(1) of the Uncertificated Securities Regulations 2001,

  "uncertificated eligible debt security units" means uncertificated units of an eligible debt security where the issue of the units corresponds, in accordance with the current terms of issue of the eligible debt security, to the issue of a certificate of deposit,

  "uncertificated right" means a right in respect of which no certificate of deposit has been issued, although the person for the time being entitled to it is entitled to call for the issue of such a certificate, and

  "unit" has the meaning given in regulation 3(1) of the Uncertificated Securities Regulations 2001.

Commentary—*Simon's Taxes* **E1.460.**

HMRC Manuals—Savings and Investment Manual SAIM2520 (disposal of deposit rights: meaning).

Amendments—[1] Sub-s (1)(e) (and the "and" before it) repealed by FA 2009 s 49, Sch 25 para 9(2)(a) with effect in relation to transfers on or after 22 April 2009.

[2] Sub-s (1) substituted by FA 2012 s 11(3) with effect in relation to: (a) any policy issued in respect of an insurance made on or after 21 March 2012; or any contract made on or after that date; (b) any insurance or contract made before 21 March 2012 if on or after that date—

    (i)   the policy or contract is varied with the result that there is an increase in the benefits secured;

    (ii)   there is an assignment of rights, or a share of the rights, conferred by the policy or contract (whether or not for money's worth); or

    (iii)   some or all of the rights conferred by the policy or contract become held as security for a debt.

553 Income charged

Tax is charged under this Chapter on the full amount of profits or gains arising in the tax year.

Commentary—*Simon's Taxes* E1.461.

HMRC Manuals—Savings and Investment Manual SAIM2520 (disposal of deposit rights).

554 Person liable

The person liable for any tax charged under this Chapter is the person receiving or entitled to the profits or gains.

Commentary—*Simon's Taxes* E1.461.

HMRC Manuals—Savings and Investment Manual SAIM2520 (person liable).

PART 5

MISCELLANEOUS INCOME

CHAPTER 1

INTRODUCTION

574 Overview of Part 5

(1) This Part imposes charges to income tax under—

    (a) Chapter 2 (receipts from intellectual property),

    [(aa) Chapter 2A (offshore receipts in respect of intangible property),][1]

    (b) Chapter 3 (films and sound recordings: non-trade businesses),

    (c) Chapter 4 (certain telecommunication rights: non-trading income),

    (d) Chapter 5 (settlements: amounts treated as income of settlor),

    (e) Chapter 6 (beneficiaries' income from estates in administration),

    (f) Chapter 7 (annual payments not otherwise charged), and

    (g) Chapter 8 (income not otherwise charged).

(2) Part 6 deals with exemptions from the charges under this Part [(but see section 608X)][1].

(3) See, in particular, any exemptions mentioned in the Chapters of this Part.

(4) The charges under this Part apply to non-UK residents as well as UK residents but this is subject to section 577(2) (charges on non-UK residents only on UK source income).

(5) This section needs to be read with the relevant priority rules (see sections 2, 575 and 576).

Amendments—[1] Sub-s (1)(aa), and words in sub-s (2), inserted, by FA 2019 s 15, Sch 3 paras 1, 2 with effect for the tax year 2019–20 and subsequent tax years.

575 Provisions which must be given priority over Part 5

(1) Any income, so far as it falls within—

    (a) any Chapter of this Part, and

    (b) Chapter 2 of Part 2 (receipts of a trade, profession or vocation),

is dealt with under Part 2.

(2) Any income, so far as it falls within—

    (a) any Chapter of this Part, and

    (b) Chapter 3 of Part 3 so far as the Chapter relates to a UK property business,

is dealt with under Part 3.

(3) Any income, so far as it falls within—

    (a) any Chapter of this Part, and

    (b) Chapter 2 or 3 of Part 4 (interest and dividends etc. from UK resident companies etc.),

is dealt with under the relevant Chapter of Part 4.

(4) Any income, so far as it falls within—

    (a) any Chapter of this Part, and

    (b) Part 2, 9 or 10 of ITEPA 2003 (employment income, pension income or social security income),

is dealt with under the relevant Part of ITEPA 2003.

Commentary—*Simon's Taxes* E1.502.

576 Priority between Chapters within Part 5

[(1) Any income, so far as it falls within Chapter 2 (receipts from intellectual property) and Chapter 2A (offshore receipts in respect of intangible property), is dealt with under Chapter 2.][1]

ITTOIA 2005

[(2)] [1] Any income, so far as it falls within Chapter 2 (receipts from intellectual property) and Chapter 3 (films and sound recordings: non-trade businesses), is dealt with under Chapter 3.

Commentary—*Simon's Taxes* **E1.502**.

Amendments–[1] Sub-s (1) inserted, and sub-s (2) numbered as such, by FA 2019 s 15, Sch 3 paras 1, 3 with effect for the tax year 2019–20 and subsequent tax years.

577 Territorial scope of Part 5 charges

(1) Income arising to a UK resident is chargeable to tax under this Part whether or not it is from a source in the United Kingdom.

(2) Income arising to a non-UK resident is chargeable to tax under this Part only if it is from a source in the United Kingdom.

[(2A) If income arising to an individual who is UK resident arises in the overseas part of a split year, it is to be treated for the purposes of this section as arising to a non-UK resident.][1]

(3) References in this section to income which is from a source in the United Kingdom include, in the case of any income which does not have a source, references to income which has a comparable connection to the United Kingdom.

(4) This section is subject to any express or implied provision to the contrary in this Part (or elsewhere in the Income Tax Acts).

[(5) See also section 577A (territorial scope of Part 5 charges: receipts from intellectual property).][2]

Commentary—*Simon's Taxes* **E1.503**.

HMRC Manuals—Savings and Investment Manual SAIM1170 (non-residents).

Amendments–[1] Sub-s (2A) inserted by FA 2013 s 218, Sch 45 paras 82, 89 with effect in calculating an individual's liability to income tax or capital gains tax for the tax year 2013–14 or any subsequent tax year, subject to transitional provisions and savings in FA 2013 Sch 45 paras 154–158.

[2] Sub-s (5) inserted by FA 2016 s 42(1) with effect in relation to royalties or other sums paid in respect of intellectual property on or after 28 June 2016.

[**577A Territorial scope of Part 5 charges: receipts from intellectual property**

(1) References in section 577 to income which is from a source in the United Kingdom include income arising where—

    (*a*) a royalty or other sum is paid in respect of intellectual property by a person who is non-UK resident, and

    (*b*) the payment is made in connection with a trade carried on by that person through a permanent establishment in the United Kingdom.

(2) Subsection (3) applies where a royalty or other sum is paid in respect of intellectual property by a person who is non-UK resident in connection with a trade carried on by that person only in part through a permanent establishment in the United Kingdom.

(3) The payment referred to in subsection (2) is to be regarded for the purposes of subsection (1)(*b*) as made in connection with a trade carried on through a permanent establishment in the United Kingdom to such extent as is just and reasonable, having regard to all the circumstances.

(4) In determining for the purposes of section 577 whether income arising is from a source in the United Kingdom, no regard is to be had to arrangements the main purpose of which, or one of the main purposes of which, is to avoid the effect of the rule in subsection (1).

(5) In this section—

    "arrangements" includes any agreement, understanding, scheme, transaction or series of transactions (whether or not legally enforceable);

    "intellectual property" has the same meaning as in section 579;

    "permanent establishment"—

        (*a*) in relation to a company, is to be read (by virtue of section 1007A of ITA 2007) in accordance with Chapter 2 of Part 24 of CTA 2010, and

        (*b*) in relation to any other person, is to be read in accordance with that Chapter but as if references in that Chapter to a company were references to that person.][1]

Amendments–[1] Section 577A inserted by FA 2016 s 42(2) with effect in relation to royalties or other sums paid in respect of intellectual property on or after 28 June 2016, subject to anti-avoidance rules in FA 2016 s 42(4)–(9).

CHAPTER 2

RECEIPTS FROM INTELLECTUAL PROPERTY

Introduction

578 Contents of Chapter

(1) This Chapter imposes charges to income tax under—

    (*a*) section 579 (royalties and other income from intellectual property),

    (*b*) section 583 (income from disposals of know-how), and

    (*c*) section 587 (income from sales of patent rights).

(2) For exemptions from the charge under section 579, see, in particular, sections 727 (certain annual payments by individuals) and 758 (certain interest and royalty payments).

(3) This Chapter also provides for relief from income tax on patent income (see section 600).

Charge to tax on non-trading income from intellectual property

579 Charge to tax on royalties and other income from intellectual property

(1) Income tax is charged on royalties and other income from intellectual property.

(2) In this section "intellectual property" means—

(a) any patent, trade mark, registered design, copyright, design right, performer's right or plant breeder's right,

(b) any rights under the law of any part of the United Kingdom which are similar to rights within paragraph (a),

(c) any rights under the law of any territory outside the United Kingdom which correspond or are similar to rights within paragraph (a), and

(d) any idea, information or technique not protected by a right within paragraph (a), (b) or (c).

Commentary—*Simon's Taxes* **B5.301, B5.311, B5.314, B5.315, B5.316.**
HMRC Manuals—Business Income Manual BIM90010 (amount subject to tax).
BIM50725 (royalties to person other than author).
BIM50740 (post-cessation receipts).
BIM100190 (miscellaneous income: losses).

580 Income charged under section 579

(1) Tax is charged under section 579 on the full amount of the income arising in the tax year.

(2) Subsection (1) is subject to Part 8 (foreign income: special rules).

(3) See section 582 for provision about the calculation of the amount of income charged under section 579.

(4) This section needs to be read with section 527 of ICTA (spreading of patent royalties etc. over several years).

Commentary—*Simon's Taxes* **B5.316.**

581 Person liable for tax under section 579

The person liable for any tax charged under section 579 is the person receiving or entitled to the income.

Commentary—*Simon's Taxes* **B5.316.**

582 Deductions in calculating certain income charged under section 579

(1) This section applies for calculating the amount of income charged under section 579 other than annual payments.

(2) Expenses wholly and exclusively incurred for the purpose of generating the income are deductible.

(3) If an expense is incurred for more than one purpose, a deduction may be made for any identifiable part or identifiable proportion of the expense which is incurred wholly and exclusively for the purpose of generating the income.

(4) Expenses which would not have been allowable as a deduction in calculating the profits of a trade, if they had been incurred for its purposes, are not deductible under this section.

(5) Expenses for which any kind of relief is given under any other provision of the Income Tax Acts are not deductible under this section.

(6) The relief given under section 600 (relief for expenses: patent income) is additional to the relief under this section.

(7) The frequency with which payments are made is ignored in determining whether they are annual payments for the purposes of subsection (1).

Commentary—*Simon's Taxes* **B5.316.**

Disposals of know-how

583 Charge to tax on income from disposals of know-how

(1) Income tax is charged on profits arising where consideration is received by a person—

(a) for the disposal of know-how, or

(b) for giving, or wholly or partly fulfilling, an undertaking which—

(i)   is given in connection with a disposal of know-how, and

(ii) restricts or is designed to restrict any person's activities in any way.

(2) For the purposes of subsection (1)(b), it does not matter whether or not the undertaking is legally enforceable.

(3) Subsection (1) is subject to the exceptions in section 584.

(4) In this Chapter "know-how" means any industrial information or techniques likely to assist in—

(a) manufacturing or processing goods or materials,

(b) working a source of mineral deposits (including searching for, discovering or testing mineral deposits or obtaining access to them), or

(c) carrying out any agricultural, forestry or fishing operations.

(5) In subsection (4)—

(a) "mineral deposits" includes any natural deposits capable of being lifted or extracted from the earth and for this purpose geothermal energy is treated as a natural deposit, and

(b) "source of mineral deposits" includes a mine, an oil well and a source of geothermal energy.

Commentary—*Simon's Taxes* **B5.343, B5.347,**
HMRC Manuals—Capital Allowances Manual CA72500 (treatment of receipts).

584 Exceptions to charge under section 583

(1) Section 583 does not apply in the following cases.
(2) Case A is if the consideration is brought into account under—
   (a) section 579 (charge to tax on royalties etc.), or
   (b) section 462 of CAA 2001 (disposal values).
(3) Case B is if the consideration is dealt with in relation to the person receiving it as a capital receipt for goodwill under section 194(2) (disposal of know-how as part of disposal of all or part of a trade).
(4) Case C is if the disposal of the know-how is by way of a sale and—
   (a) the buyer is a body of persons over which the seller has control,
   (b) the seller is a body of persons over which the buyer has control, or
   (c) the buyer and the seller are both bodies of persons and another person has control over both of them.
(5) In subsection (4) "body of persons" includes a firm.
(6) See also Chapter 14 of Part 2 and section 575 (disposals of know-how used in a trade dealt with by Part 2).

Commentary—*Simon's Taxes* **B5.347.**

585 Income charged under section 583

(1) Tax is charged under section 583 on the full amount of the profits arising in the tax year.
(2) The profits charged under section 583 are—
   (a) the amount of the consideration, less
   (b) any expenditure incurred by the recipient wholly and exclusively in the acquisition or disposal of the know-how.
(3) Such expenditure may not be taken into account more than once, whether under this section or otherwise.
(4) This section needs to be read with section 603 (contributions to expenditure).

Commentary—*Simon's Taxes* **B5.347.**

586 Person liable for tax under section 583

The person liable for any tax charged under section 583 is the person receiving the consideration.

Commentary—*Simon's Taxes* **B5.343.**

Sales of patent rights

587 Charge to tax on income from sales of patent rights

(1) Income tax is charged on profits from sales of the whole or part of any patent rights.
(2) The tax is charged if—
   (a) the seller is a UK resident, or
   (b) the seller is a non-UK resident and the patent is granted under the laws of the United Kingdom.
(3) Where the seller is a non-UK resident company, tax is not charged if the seller is chargeable to corporation tax in respect of the proceeds of the sale.
(4) In this Chapter "patent rights" means the right to do or authorise the doing of anything which, but for the right, would be an infringement of a patent.

Commentary—*Simon's Taxes* **B5.333, B5.334, B5.336.**
HMRC Manuals—Capital Allowances Manual CA75020 (definitions).
CA75200 (sale of patent rights).
Registered Pension Schemes Manual RPSM05101150 (relevant UK earnings).

588 Income charged under section 587

(1) A seller's profits from the sale of the whole or part of patent rights are—
   (a) any capital sum comprised in the proceeds of the sale, less
   (b) the deductible costs.
(2) The deductible costs are—
   (a) the capital cost (if any) of the rights sold, and
   (b) any incidental expenses incurred by the seller in connection with the sale.
(3) If—
   (a) the seller acquired the rights sold, or the rights out of which they were granted, by purchase,
   (b) the seller has previously sold part of the purchased rights, and
   (c) the proceeds of that sale, after deducting any incidental expenses, consisted wholly or partly of a capital sum,
the capital cost is reduced by that capital sum.
(4) References in this Chapter to the capital cost of patent rights are to any capital sum included in any price paid by the seller to purchase—
   (a) the rights, or

(b) the rights out of which they were granted.
(5) This section needs to be read with sections 600 (relief for expenses: patent income) and 603 (contributions to expenditure).

Commentary—*Simon's Taxes* B5.333.
HMRC Manuals—Capital Allowances Manual CA75200 (income charged to tax).

589 Person liable for tax under section 587

The person liable for any tax charged under section 587 is the seller of the patent rights.

Commentary—*Simon's Taxes* B5.333.
HMRC Manuals—Capital Allowances Manual CA75200 (person liable to tax).

590 UK resident sellers: spreading rules

(1) This section applies if the person liable under section 587 is a UK resident.
(2) If the person does not receive the proceeds of sale in instalments, one-sixth of the amount chargeable is taxed in the tax year in which the person receives the proceeds of the sale and in each of the next 5 tax years.
(3) The person may elect to be taxed instead on the whole of the amount chargeable under section 587 in the tax year in which the person receives the proceeds of sale.
(4) If the person receives the proceeds of sale in instalments, one-sixth of the amount chargeable in respect of each instalment is taxed in the tax year in which the person receives the instalment and in each of the next 5 tax years.
(5) The person may elect to be taxed instead on the whole of any instalment in the tax year in which the person receives it.
(6) An election under subsection (3) or (5) must be made on or before the first anniversary of the filing date for that tax year.

Commentary—*Simon's Taxes* ~~last filing~~ date for that tax year.
HMRC Manuals—Capital Allowances Manual CA75200 (sale of patent rights: taxation).
CA75210 (taxation of lump sum).
CA75310 (devising a patented invention).

591 Non-UK resident sellers: election for spreading

(1) If the person liable under section 587—
    (a) is a non-UK resident, and
    (b) does not receive the proceeds of sale in instalments,
the whole amount chargeable is taxed in the tax year in which the person receives the proceeds.
(2) The person may elect to be taxed instead on one-sixth of the amount chargeable in the tax year in which the person receives the proceeds of sale and in each of the next 5 tax years.
(3) An election under subsection (2) must be made on or before the first anniversary of the normal self-assessment filing date for the tax year in which the proceeds of sale are received.
(4) Such repayments and assessments are to be made for each of the tax years affected as are necessary to give effect to the election.
(5) Subsection (4) is subject to the qualifications in section 596 (adjustments where tax has been deducted).

Commentary—*Simon's Taxes* B5.336.
HMRC Manuals—Capital Allowances Manual CA75210 (taxation of lump sum: non-UK resident).

592 Further provision about elections for spreading: instalments

(1) If the person liable under section 587—
    (a) is a non-UK resident, and
    (b) receives the proceeds of sale in instalments,
the amount chargeable in respect of each instalment is taxed in the tax year in which the person receives the instalment.
(2) The person may, for any instalment, elect to be taxed instead on one-sixth of the amount chargeable in respect of the instalment in the tax year in which the person receives it and in each of the next 5 tax years.
(3) An election under subsection (2) must be made on or before the first anniversary of the normal self-assessment filing date for the tax year in which the instalment is received.
(4) Such repayments and assessments are to be made for each of the tax years affected as are necessary to give effect to the election.
(5) Subsection (4) is subject to the qualifications in section 596 (adjustments where tax has been deducted).

Commentary—*Simon's Taxes* B5.333, B5.336.
HMRC Manuals—Capital Allowances Manual CA75210 (non-UK resident: election for spreading on receipt of sale proceeds in instalments).

593 Death of seller

(1) If a seller who is liable to income tax under section 587 dies, any amounts which would have been chargeable in later tax years under—
    (a) section 590(2) or (4) (UK resident sellers: spreading rules), or

(b) section 591(2) or 592(2) (non-UK resident sellers: elections for spreading), are taxed in the tax year in which the seller dies.

(2) The personal representatives may elect that the tax payable by reason of subsection (1) b reduced to the total amount of income tax that the seller and the estate would have been liable to pa if the amounts chargeable by reason of that subsection had been taxed in equal parts in each of th lifetime tax years.

(3) In subsection (2) "the lifetime tax years" means—
(a) the tax year in which the seller received the proceeds or, as the case may be, the instalment and
(b) each of the next tax years up to and including that in which the seller died.

(4) An election under subsection (2) must be made on or before the first anniversary of the normal self-assessment filing date for the tax year in which the death occurs.

Commentary—*Simon's Taxes* B5.338.
HMRC Manuals—Capital Allowances Manual CA75220 (death of seller).

594 Winding up of a body corporate

(1) If a body corporate which is liable to income tax under section 587 commences to be wound up, any amounts falling within subsection (2) are taxed in the year in which the winding up commences.

(2) The amounts are—
(a) any amounts which would have been chargeable in later tax years under section 591(2) or 592(2), and
(b) any amounts (arising to the body in a fiduciary or representative capacity) which would have been chargeable in later tax years under section 590(2) or (4).

Commentary—*Simon's Taxes* B5.339.

595 Deduction of tax from payments to non-UK resident is liable to tax under section 587 on

(1) This section applies if a profits from the sale of the whole or part of any patent rights.

(2) The rules in section 588 allowing the capital cost (if any) of the rights sold to be deducted in calculating the profits from the sale do not affect the amount of income tax which [is to be deducted under section 910 of ITA 2007][1] (by virtue of section 349ZA of ICTA: application of rules for deduction of income tax by the payer) is to be—
(a) deducted under section 349(1) of ICTA, and
(b) assessed under section 350 of that Act (assessment on the payer).

(3) No election made by the seller under section 591(2) or 592(2) (election for spreading) in relation to the proceeds of sale or any instalment affects the amount of income tax which [is to be deducted under section 910 of ITA 2007][1] (by virtue of section 349ZA of ICTA: application of rules for deduction of income tax by the payer) is to be—
(a) deducted from the proceeds of sale or instalment under section 349(1) of ICTA, and
(b) assessed under section 350 of that Act.

Commentary—*Simon's Taxes* B5.336.
HMRC Manuals—Capital Allowances Manual CA75230 (deduction of tax from payments to non-residents).
Amendments—[1] Words in sub-ss (2), (3) inserted by ITA 2007 s 1027, Sch 1 paras 492, 546 with effect for income tax purposes from 6 April 2007, and corporation tax purposes for accounting periods ending after 5 April 2007.

596 Adjustments where tax has been deducted

(1) Where any sum has been deducted from a payment by virtue of section 595(2), any adjustment necessary—
(a) because of section 595(2), or
(b) because of an election under section 591(2) or 592(2),
must be made by way of repayment of tax.

(2) Adjustments necessary to give effect to an election under section 591(2) or 592(2) must be made year by year, treating one-sixth of the sum deducted from the proceeds of sale or instalment as income tax paid for each of the 6 years.

(3) No repayment is to be made of any tax treated under subsection (2) as income tax paid for a particular year unless and until it is ascertained that the income tax ultimately falling to be paid for that year is less than the amount which was paid for that year.

Commentary—*Simon's Taxes* B5.336.

597 Licences connected with patents

(1) The acquisition of a licence in respect of a patent is treated for the purposes of sections 587 to 596 as a purchase of patent rights.

(2) The grant of a licence in respect of a patent is treated for the purposes of sections 587 to 596 as a sale of part of patent rights.

(3) But the grant by a person entitled to patent rights of an exclusive licence is treated for the purposes of sections 587 to 596 as a sale of the whole of those rights.

(4) In subsection (3) "exclusive licence" means a licence to exercise the rights to the exclusion of the grantor and all other persons for the period remaining until the rights come to an end.

Commentary—*Simon's Taxes* B5.333.

HMRC Manuals—Capital Allowances Manual CA75030 (licences connected with patents: meanings).

Corporate Intangibles Research & Development Manual CIRD210120 (exclusive licence: meaning of 'exclusive licence').

598 Rights to acquire future patent rights

(1) If a sum is paid to obtain a right to acquire future patent rights, then for the purposes of sections 587 to 596—

    (a) the payer is treated as purchasing patent rights for that sum, and

    (b) the recipient is treated as selling patent rights for that sum.

(2) If a person—

    (a) pays a sum to obtain a right to acquire future patent rights, and

    (b) subsequently acquires those rights,

the expenditure is to be treated for the purposes of sections 587 to 596 as having been expenditure on the purchase of those rights.

(3) In this section "a right to acquire future patent rights" means a right to acquire in the future patent rights relating to an invention in respect of which the patent has not yet been granted.

Commentary—*Simon's Taxes* B5.333.

599 Sums paid for Crown use etc treated as paid under licence

(1) This section applies if an invention which is the subject of a patent is used by or for the service of—

    (a) the Crown under sections 55 to 59 of the Patents Act 1977 (c. 37), or

    (b) the government of a country outside the United Kingdom under corresponding provisions of the law of that country.

(2) The use is treated for the purposes of sections 587 to 596 as having taken place under a licence.

(3) Sums paid in respect of the use are treated for the purposes of sections 587 to 596 as having been paid under a licence.

Commentary—*Simon's Taxes* B5.333.

HMRC Manuals—Capital Allowances Manual CA75030 (licences: payments received for Crown or foreign government user). CA75410 (payments received for Crown user).

Relief from income tax on patent income

600 Relief for expenses: patent income

(1) Relief may be claimed under this section for—

    (a) inventor's expenses, and

    (b) patent application and maintenance expenses.

(2) In this section "inventor's expenses" means expenses which—

    (a) have been incurred by an individual who, alone or jointly, devised an invention for which a patent has been granted, and

    (b) are attributable to devising it.

(3) In this section "patent application and maintenance expenses" means expenses incurred by a person in connection with—

    (a) the grant or maintenance of a patent,

    (b) the extension of the term of a patent, or

    (c) a rejected or abandoned application for a patent,

but not incurred for the purposes of any trade carried on by the person.

(4) Relief may not be claimed under this section for patent application and maintenance expenses unless they are expenses which would, if incurred for the purposes of a trade, have been allowable as a deduction in calculating the profits of the trade.

(5) Relief may not be claimed under this section for any expenses if relief for them is given under—

    (a) section 582 (calculation of income for the purposes of the charge to tax on royalties etc.), or

    (b) any other provision of the Tax Acts.

(6) This section needs to be read with section 603 (contributions to expenditure).

Commentary—*Simon's Taxes* B5.331.

HMRC Manuals—Corporate Intangibles Research & Development Manual CA75300 (fees). CA75310 (devising a patented invention).

601 How relief is given under section 600

(1) This section sets out how relief for expenses is given where a person makes a claim under section 600.

(2) The amount of the expenses must be deducted from or set off against the person's income from patents for the tax year in which the expenses were incurred.

[(2A) The deduction or set-off is given effect at Step 2 of the calculation in section 23 of ITA 2007.][1]

(3) If the amount to be allowed is greater than the amount of the person's income from patents for that tax year, the excess must be deducted from or set off against the person's income from patents for the next tax year, and so on for subsequent tax years, without the need for a further claim.

(4) In this section "income from patents" means—

(a) royalties or other sums paid in respect of the use of a patent (whether chargeable under this Chapter or otherwise),

(b) amounts on which tax is payable under section 587, 593 or 594, and

(c) amounts on which tax is payable under—

    (i) section 472(5) of CAA 2001 (patent allowances: balancing charges), or

    (ii) paragraph 100 of Schedule 3 to that Act (balancing charges in respect of pre-1st April 1986 expenditure on the purchase of patent rights).

(5) In this section references to a person's income from patents are to the income after any allowance has been deducted from or set off against it under section 479 of CAA 2001 (certain allowances against income from patents).

Commentary—*Simon's Taxes* **B5.331.**

HMRC Manuals—Corporate Intangibles Research & Development Manual CA75300 (relief for expenses against patent income).

CA75310 (patent income: relief for expenses).

CA75020 (income from patents).

Amendments—[1]   Sub-s (2A) inserted by ITA 2007 s 1027, Sch 1 paras 492, 547 with effect for income tax purposes from 6 April 2007, and corporation tax purposes for accounting periods ending after 5 April 2007.

Payments received after deduction of tax

602 Payments received after deduction of tax

[In accordance with section 848 of ITA 2007, a sum representing income tax deducted under either of the following Chapters][1] from a payment of royalties or other income within this Chapter is treated as income tax paid by the recipient—

    [Chapter 6 of Part 15 of ITA 2007 (deduction from annual payments and patent royalties), and Chapter 7 of that Part (deduction from other payments connected with intellectual property).][1]

Commentary—*Simon's Taxes* B5.316.

HMRC Manuals—Corporate Intangibles Research & Development Manual CA75300 (relief for expenses against patent income).

CA75310 (patent income: relief for expenses).

CA75020 (income from patents).

Amendments—[1]   Words substituted by ITA 2007 s 1027, Sch 1 paras 492, 548 with effect for income tax purposes from 6 April 2007, and corporation tax purposes for accounting periods ending after 5 April 2007.

Supplementary

603 Contributions to expenditure

(1) For the purposes of sections 585, 588 and 600, the general rule is that a person ("A") is to be regarded as not having incurred expenditure so far as it has been, or is to be, met (directly or indirectly) by—

    (a) a public body, or

    (b) a person other than A.

(2) In this Chapter "public body" means the Crown or any government, local authority or other public authority (whether in the United Kingdom or elsewhere).

(3) The general rule does not apply to the expenses mentioned in section 588(2)(b) (incidental expenses incurred by a seller of patent rights).

(4) The general rule is subject to the exception in section 604.

Commentary—*Simon's Taxes* **B5.333, B5.347.**

604 Contributions not made by public bodies nor eligible for tax relief

(1) A person ("A") is to be regarded as having incurred expenditure (despite section 603(1)) so far as the requirements in subsections (2) and (3) are met in relation to the expenditure.

(2) The first requirement is that the person meeting A's expenditure ("B") is not a public body.

(3) The second requirement is that—

    (a) no allowance can be made under Chapter 2 of Part 11 of CAA 2001 (contribution allowances) in respect of B's expenditure, and

    (b) the expenditure is not allowed to be deducted in calculating the profits of a trade, profession or vocation carried on by B.

(4) When determining for the purposes of subsection (3)(a) whether such an allowance can be made, assume that B is within the charge to tax.

Commentary—*Simon's Taxes* **B5.331.**

605 Exchanges

(1) In this Chapter references to the sale of property include the exchange of property.

(2) In this section—

    references to property include know-how, and

    references to the sale of property include the disposal of know-how.

(3) For the purposes of subsection (1), any provision of this Chapter referring to a sale has effect with the necessary modifications, including, in particular, those in subsections (4) and (5).

(4) References to the proceeds of sale and to the price include the consideration for the exchange.

(5) References to capital sums included in the proceeds of sale include references to so much of the consideration for the exchange as would have been a capital sum if it had been a money payment.

Commentary—*Simon's Taxes* **B5.333**.

HMRC Manuals—Capital Allowances Manual CA70050 (treat as property for capital allowances). CA71300 (disposal values).

606 Apportionment where property sold together

(1) Any reference in this Chapter to the sale of property includes the sale of that property together with other property.

(2) In this section—

references to property include know-how, and

references to the sale of property include the disposal of know-how.

(3) For the purposes of subsection (1), all property sold as a result of one bargain is to be treated as sold together even though—

(*a*) separate prices are, or purport to be, agreed for separate items of that property, or

(*b*) there are, or purport to be, separate sales of separate items of that property.

(4) If an item of property is sold together with other property, then, for the purposes of the charges under sections 583 and 587—

(*a*) the net proceeds of the sale of that item are treated as being so much of the net proceeds of the sale of all the property as, on a just and reasonable apportionment, is attributable to that item, and

(*b*) the expenditure incurred on the provision or purchase of that item is treated as being so much of the consideration given for all the property as, on a just and reasonable apportionment, is attributable to that item.

Commentary—*Simon's Taxes* **B5.333**.

607 Questions about apportionments affecting two or more persons

(1) Any question about the way in which a sum is to be apportioned under section 606 must be determined in accordance with section 563(2) to (6) of CAA 2001 (procedure for determining certain questions affecting two or more persons) if it materially affects two or more taxpayers.

(2) For the purposes of subsection (1) a question materially affects two or more taxpayers if at the time when the question falls to be determined it appears that the determination is material to the liability to tax (for whatever period) of two or more persons.

Commentary—*Simon's Taxes* **B5.333**.

608 Meaning of "capital sums" etc.

Section 4 of CAA 2001 (meaning of "capital sums" etc.) applies in relation to this Chapter as it applies in relation to that Act.

Commentary—*Simon's Taxes* **B3.103**

[CHAPTER 2A

OFFSHORE RECEIPTS IN RESPECT OF INTANGIBLE PROPERTY

Charge to tax on offshore receipts in respect of intangible property

608A Charge to tax on UK-derived amounts

(1) This section applies if—

(*a*) at any time in a tax year, a person is not UK resident and is not resident in a full treaty territory, and

(*b*) UK-derived amounts arise to the person in the tax year.

(2) Income tax is charged on the UK-derived amounts.

(3) See—

sections 608D to 608H for the meaning of expressions used in this section;

sections 608J to 608N for exemptions from the charge under this section.

(4) References in the Tax Acts to income from a source in the United Kingdom include UK-derived amounts.][1]

Amendments—[1] Sections 608A–608Z inserted by FA 2019 s 15, Sch 3 paras 1, 4 with effect for the tax year 2019–20 and subsequent tax years.

[608B Income charged under section 608A

Tax is charged under section 608A on the full amount of the UK-derived amounts arising in the tax year.][1]

Amendments—[1] Sections 608A–608Z inserted by FA 2019 s 15, Sch 3 paras 1, 4 with effect for the tax year 2019–20 and subsequent tax years.

[608C Person liable for tax under section 608A

The person liable for any tax charged under section 608A is the person receiving or entitled to the UK-derived amounts.][1]

Amendments—[1]   Sections 608A–608Z inserted by FA 2019 s 15, Sch 3 paras 1, 4 with effect for the tax year 2019–20 and subsequent tax years.

[608D Meaning of residence

(1) This section applies for the purposes of this Chapter.

(2) A person is "resident" in a territory if, under the laws of the territory, the person is liable to tax there—

    (*a*) by reason of the person's domicile, residence or place of management, but

    (*b*) not in respect only of—

        [(i) income from sources in that territory or capital situated there, or

        (ii) such income and capital, and amounts remitted to or otherwise received in the territory.][2]

(3) Where—

    (*a*) a person is resident in a territory outside the United Kingdom generally for the purposes of the laws of the territory or for particular purposes under those laws, and

    (*b*) the laws of the territory have no provision for a person to be resident there for tax purposes, the person is "resident" in the territory.][1]

[(4) Despite subsections (2) and (3), a person is treated as not resident in a full treaty territory if—

    (a) the double taxation arrangements made in relation to the territory contain provision expressly excluding persons of a particular description from relief under the arrangements, and

    (b) the person is of that description.

(5) In subsection (4) the reference to provision of the kind mentioned there does not include provision corresponding to the provision made by paragraphs 1 to 7 of article 29 of the OECD Model Tax Convention on Income and on Capital (entitlement to benefits), published on 21 November 2017.][2]

Amendments—[1]   Sections 608A–608Z inserted by FA 2019 s 15, Sch 3 paras 1, 4 with effect for the tax year 2019–20 and subsequent tax years.

[2]   Sub-ss (2)(*b*)(i), (*b*)(ii), (4), (5) inserted by Income Tax (Trading and Other Income) Act 2005 (Amendments to Chapter 2A of Part 5) Regulations, SI 2019/1452 reg 3 with effect for the tax year 2019–20 and subsequent tax years.

[608E Meaning of "full treaty territory"

(1) For the purposes of this Chapter a territory is a "full treaty territory" if—

    (*a*) double taxation arrangements have been made in relation to the territory, and

    (*b*) the arrangements contain a non-discrimination provision.

(2) In subsection (1) "non-discrimination provision", in relation to double taxation arrangements, means a provision to the effect that nationals of a state which is a party to those arrangements (a "contracting state") are not to be subject in the other contracting state to—

    (*a*) any taxation, or

    (*b*) any requirement connected with taxation,

which is other or more burdensome than the taxation and connected requirements to which nationals of that other contracting state in the same circumstances (in particular with respect to residence) are or may be subjected.

(3) In subsection (2) "national", in relation to a contracting state, includes—

    (*a*) an individual possessing the nationality or citizenship of the contracting state, and

    (*b*) a legal person, partnership or association deriving its status as such from the laws in force in that contracting state.][1]

Amendments—[1]   Sections 608A–608Z inserted by FA 2019 s 15, Sch 3 paras 1, 4 with effect for the tax year 2019–20 and subsequent tax years.

[608F Meaning of "UK-derived amount" and "UK sales"

(1) For the purposes of this Chapter an amount is a "UK-derived amount" if—

    (*a*) it is an amount (whether of a revenue or capital nature) in respect of the enjoyment or exercise of rights that constitute any intangible property, and

    (*b*) the enjoyment or exercise of those rights (or of any rights derived, directly or indirectly, from those rights) enables, facilitates or promotes UK sales (directly or indirectly).

(2) It does not matter whether the amount relates to UK sales in the tax year mentioned in section 608A or any other tax year.

(3) In this Chapter "UK sales" means any services, goods or other property—

    (*a*) provided in the United Kingdom, or

    (*b*) provided to persons in the United Kingdom.][1]

[(4) In subsection (3) the reference to anything being provided does not include it being provided for resale.

(5) For the purposes of subsection (4) a thing is provided "for resale" where it is provided to a person who obtains it for the purpose of providing it to another person in the following circumstances—

    (a) there is no change in the thing itself, and

    (b) if what is provided differs in any way from what was obtained, the difference is merely incidental to the provision of the thing.

(6) For the purposes of this Chapter a service consisting of the provision of online advertising constitutes a UK sale so far as the advertising is targeted at persons in the United Kingdom.][2]

Amendments—[1] Sections 608A–608Z inserted by FA 2019 s 15, Sch 3 paras 1, 4 with effect for the tax year 2019–20 and subsequent tax years.

[2] Sub-ss (4)–(6) inserted by Income Tax (Trading and Other Income) Act 2005 (Amendments to Chapter 2A of Part 5) Regulations, SI 2019/1452 reg 4 with effect for the tax year 2019–20 and subsequent tax years.

[608G Section 608F: apportionment of amounts

(1) This section applies where—
- (a) a person receives or is entitled to an amount in respect of the enjoyment or exercise of rights that constitute any intangible property, and that enjoyment or exercise enables, facilitates or promotes UK sales and other sales, or
- (b) a person receives or is entitled to an amount in respect of—
  - (i) the enjoyment or exercise of rights that constitute any intangible property, where that enjoyment or exercise enables, facilitates or promotes UK sales, and
  - (ii) anything else.

(2) The amount is to be regarded for the purposes of this Chapter as constituting a UK-derived amount to such extent as is just and reasonable.

(3) In a case within subsection (1)(a) it is to be presumed, unless the contrary is shown, that the proportion of the amount that is just and reasonable is—

$$X / (X + Y)$$

where X is the value of UK sales and Y is the value of other sales.][1]

Amendments—[1] Sections 608A–608Z inserted by FA 2019 s 15, Sch 3 paras 1, 4 with effect for the tax year 2019–20 and subsequent tax years.

[608GA Section 608F: disregard for third party sales where intangible property makes insignificant contribution

(1) This section applies where—
- (a) a person (A) receives or is entitled to a UK-derived amount,
- (b) the services, goods or other property in question are not provided in the United Kingdom, or to persons there, by A or a person connected with A, and
- (c) the UK sales in question are enabled, facilitated or promoted to an insignificant extent by the enjoyment or exercise of the rights in question.

(2) For the purposes of this Chapter no account is to be taken of A's receipt of, or entitlement to, the UK-derived amount.

(3) For the purposes of subsection (1)(b), anything provided by a reseller (including anything treated as so provided by virtue of this subsection) is to be treated as provided by the person who provided it to the reseller.

(4) For this purpose "reseller" means a person to whom a thing is provided for resale (within the meaning of section 608F(5)).][1]

Amendments—[1] Section 608GA inserted by Income Tax (Trading and Other Income) Act 2005 (Amendments to Chapter 2A of Part 5) Regulations, SI 2019/1452 reg 5 with effect for the tax year 2019–20 and subsequent tax years.

[608H Meaning of "intangible property"

(1) In this Chapter "intangible property" means any property except—
- (a) tangible property,
- (b) an estate, interest or right in or over land,
- (c) a right in respect of anything within paragraph (a) or (b),
- (d) a financial asset,
- (e) a share or other right in relation to the profits, governance or winding up of a company, or
- (f) any property of a prescribed description.

(2) In this section—
"financial asset" has the meaning given by section 806 of CTA 2009;
"prescribed" means prescribed by regulations made by the Treasury.][1]

Amendments—[1] Sections 608A–608Z inserted by FA 2019 s 15, Sch 3 paras 1, 4 with effect for the tax year 2019–20 and subsequent tax years.

[Exemptions]

608J Exemption where limited UK sales

(1) Section 608A does not apply in relation to a person for a tax year if the total value of the person's UK sales in that tax year does not exceed £10,000,000.

(2) Where—
- (a) a person (a), or a person connected with A, receives or is entitled to an amount (whether of a revenue or capital nature), and
- (b) the amount relates (wholly or in part, and directly or indirectly) to the provision of services, goods or other property constituting UK sales,

the UK sales are regarded for the purposes of subsection (1) as A's UK sales.][1]

Amendments—[1]   Sections 608A–608Z inserted by FA 2019 s 15, Sch 3 paras 1, 4 with effect for the tax year 2019–20 and subsequent tax years.

[608JA Exemption where company resident in specified territory

(1) Section 608A does not apply in relation to a company for a tax year if—

    (*a*) the company is resident in a specified territory throughout the tax year,

    (*b*) UK-derived amounts arising to the company in the tax year are chargeable to tax under the laws of the territory,

    (*c*) where those amounts are chargeable only if remitted or otherwise received in the territory, the amounts are remitted or otherwise received there in the tax year,

    (*d*) the amount of tax which is paid in the territory in respect of the UK-derived amounts is not determined under designer tax provisions, and

    (*e*) the company is not, at any time in the tax year, involved in an arrangement the main purpose, or one of the main purposes, of which is to obtain a tax advantage for itself or any other person.

(2) For the purposes of this section—

    (*a*) section 608D (meaning of residence) applies as if subsections (2)(*b*), (4) and (5) were omitted;

    (*b*) "specified territory" means a territory specified in regulations made by the Commissioners.

(3) Regulations under this section may have effect from a date before the day on which they are made, except insofar as they result in a territory ceasing to be specified.][1]

Amendments—[1]   Section 608JA inserted by Income Tax (Trading and Other Income) Act 2005 (Amendments to Chapter 2A of Part 5) Regulations, SI 2019/1452 reg 7 with effect for the tax year 2019–20 and subsequent tax years.

[608K Exemption where business undertaken within territory of residence

(1) Section 608A does not apply in relation to a person ("the relevant person") for a tax year if—

    (*a*) the relevant person is resident in a territory throughout the tax year,

    (*b*) all (or substantially all) relevant activity in relation to relevant intangible property is, and has at all times been, undertaken in that territory,

    (*c*) there is no relevant connection between relevant intangible property and a related person, and

    (*d*) the person makes a claim under this section.

[(1A) For the purposes of this section, section 608D (meaning of residence) applies as if subsections (2)(*b*), (4) and (5) were omitted.][2]

(2) For the purposes of this section intangible property is "relevant" if any UK-derived amount arising to the person in the tax year relates to it.

(3) In subsection (1)(*b*) "relevant activity", in relation to relevant intangible property, means anything done (by any person)—

    (*a*) for the purpose of creating, developing or maintaining any of the relevant intangible property; or

    (*b*) for the purpose of generating, for the relevant person, amounts (whether of a revenue or capital nature) that relate, wholly or in part and directly or indirectly, to the enjoyment or exercise of rights that constitute any of the relevant intangible property.

(4) For the purposes of subsection (1)(*c*) there is a "relevant connection" between relevant intangible property and a related person if any relevant intangible property—

    (*a*) has been transferred (directly or indirectly) from a person related to the relevant person,

    (*b*) derives (directly or indirectly) from anything so transferred, or

    (*c*) derives (directly or indirectly) from intangible property held by a person related to the relevant person.

(5) See section 608T for the meaning of two persons being "related".][1]

Amendments—[1]   Sections 608A–608Z inserted by FA 2019 s 15, Sch 3 paras 1, 4 with effect for the tax year 2019–20 and subsequent tax years.

[2]   Sub-s (1A) inserted by Income Tax (Trading and Other Income) Act 2005 (Amendments to Chapter 2A of Part 5) Regulations, SI 2019/1452 reg 8 with effect for the tax year 2019–20 and subsequent tax years.

[608L Exemption where foreign tax at least half of UK tax

(1) Section 608A does not apply in relation to a person for a tax year if—

    (*a*) the person is resident in a territory outside the United Kingdom in that year,

    (*b*) the amount of tax ("the local tax amount") which is paid in the territory in respect of UK-derived amounts arising in the tax year is at least half of the corresponding UK tax, and

    (*c*) the local tax amount is not determined under designer tax provisions.

(2) See section 608M for provisions about the local tax amount.

(3) "The corresponding UK tax" means the amount of income tax that would be charged under this Chapter in respect of UK-derived amounts arising in the tax year, calculated on the following basis—

    (*a*) section 608A applies in relation to the UK-derived amounts, and

    (*b*) the person is not entitled to any relief or allowance for the tax year.

(4) . . . [2]][1]

[(5) For the purposes of this section, section 608D (meaning of residence) applies as if subsections (2)(*b*), (4) and (5) were omitted.][2]

Amendments—[1]   Sections 608A–608Z inserted by FA 2019 s 15, Sch 3 paras 1, 4 with effect for the tax year 2019–20 and subsequent tax years.
[2]   Sub-s (4) repealed, sub-s (5) inserted by Income Tax (Trading and Other Income) Act 2005 (Amendments to Chapter 2A of Part 5) Regulations, SI 2019/1452 reg 9 with effect for the tax year 2019–20 and subsequent tax years.

[608M Section 608L: the local tax amount

(1) This section applies for the purposes of section 608L.

(2) Where an amount of tax is paid in the territory in respect of—

(a) UK-derived amounts arising in the tax year, and

(b) other amounts,

the amount of tax is to be apportioned between the amounts mentioned in paragraph (a) and paragraph (b) on a just and reasonable basis.

(3) Where—

(a) in the territory any tax falls to be paid in respect of UK-derived amounts arising in the tax year,

(b) under the laws of the territory, a repayment of tax, or a payment in respect of credit for tax, is made to any person, and

(c) that repayment or payment is directly or indirectly in respect of the whole or part of the tax mentioned in paragraph (a),

the local tax amount is to be reduced by the amount of that repayment or payment (but this is subject to subsections (4) and (5)).

(4) Subsection (5) applies if the repayment or payment mentioned in subsection (3)(b) is in respect of—

(a) the tax mentioned in subsection (3)(a), and

(b) other tax.

(5) The amount of the repayment or payment is to be apportioned between the tax mentioned in subsection (3)(a) and the other tax on a just and reasonable basis, and the reduction under subsection (3) is limited to the amount apportioned to the tax mentioned in subsection (3)(a).

(6) Any reduction under subsection (3) is to be undertaken after any apportionment under subsection (2).][1]

Amendments—[1]   Sections 608A–608Z inserted by FA 2019 s 15, Sch 3 paras 1, 4 with effect for the tax year 2019–20 and subsequent tax years.

[608MA Exemption where income of opaque partnership taxable in full treaty territory

(1) This section applies where—

(a) under the laws of a full treaty territory, a partnership is regarded for tax purposes as an entity separate and distinct from the partners,

(b) the partnership is resident in the territory throughout a tax year,

(c) UK-derived amounts arise to the partnership in the tax year, and

(d) the UK-derived amounts are chargeable to tax under the laws of the territory.

(2) In the application of section 608A to a partner for the tax year, no account is to be taken of the UK-derived amounts.

(3) For the purposes of subsection (1)(b), the partnership is "resident" in a territory if (and only if) it is resident there by virtue of section 608D(2) (references there to be a person being read as references to the partnership).][1]

Amendments—[1]   Section 608MA inserted by Income Tax (Trading and Other Income) Act 2005 (Amendments to Chapter 2A of Part 5) Regulations, SI 2019/1452 reg 10 with effect for the tax year 2019–20 and subsequent tax years.

[608MB Exemption for certain bodies corporate that are transparent in full treaty territory

(1) This section applies where—

(a) a body corporate formed under the laws of a full treaty territory ("the relevant territory") is not regarded under those laws, for tax purposes, as an entity separate and distinct from its members,

(b) the body is not resident, at any time in a tax year, in a territory that is not a full treaty territory,

(c) UK-derived amounts arise to the body in the tax year, and

(d) each relevant member is resident in the relevant territory throughout the tax year.

(2) In the application of section 608A to the body for the tax year, no account is to be taken of the UK-derived amounts.

(3) The relevant members are to be determined as follows—

(a) each member of the body is a relevant member (subject to paragraph (b));

(b) if a body corporate that meets the conditions in subsection (4) would otherwise be a relevant member, that body's members are relevant members (and that body is not a relevant member);

(c) paragraph (b) applies in relation to a body that would otherwise be a relevant member by virtue of that paragraph (as well as in relation to a body that would otherwise be a relevant member by virtue of paragraph (a)).

(4) The conditions referred to in subsection (3)(*b*) are—
    (*a*) that the body is formed under the laws of the relevant territory;
    (*b*) that under those laws, the body is not regarded for tax purposes as an entity separate and distinct from its members;
    (*c*) that the body is not resident, at any time in the tax year, in a territory that is not a full treaty territory.][1]

Amendments—[1]   Section 608MB inserted by Income Tax (Trading and Other Income) Act 2005 (Amendments to Chapter 2A of Part 5) Regulations, SI 2019/1452 reg 11 with effect for the tax year 2019–20 and subsequent tax years.

[608MC Exemption for double taxation on amounts within same control group
(1) This section applies where—
    (*a*) two persons (A and B) are in the same control group throughout a tax year,
    (*b*) neither A nor B is, at any time in the tax year, involved in an arrangement the main purpose, or one of the main purposes, of which is to obtain a tax advantage for A, B or any other person,
    (*c*) income tax is charged under section 608A on a UK-derived amount arising to A in the tax year, and A is not entitled to any relief in respect of the UK-derived amount,
    (*d*) the UK-derived amount is a direct or indirect payment from B to A in respect of rights ("relevant rights") that—
        (i) constitute any of B's intangible property, and
        (ii) derive, directly or indirectly, from rights that constitute any of A's intangible property.
(2) In the application of section 608A to B for the tax year, the amount of any UKderived amount arising to B in the tax year in respect of B's relevant rights is to be reduced (but not below nil) by the amount of the UK-derived amount mentioned in subsection (1)(*c*).
(3) For the purposes of this section where a UK-derived amount is in respect of relevant rights and anything else, the amount is to be regarded as being in respect of relevant rights to such extent as is just and reasonable.
(4) For the meaning of "control group" see section 608S.][1]

Amendments—[1]   Section 608MC inserted by Income Tax (Trading and Other Income) Act 2005 (Amendments to Chapter 2A of Part 5) Regulations, SI 2019/1452 reg 12 with effect for the tax year 2019–20 and subsequent tax years.

[608N Exemptions: further provision
(1) The Treasury may by regulations—
    (*a*) amend this Chapter for the purpose of creating additional exemptions;
    (*b*) amend any exemption for the time being in force.
(2) "Exemption" means a total or partial exemption from the charge under thisChapter.
(3) The regulations may confer a power to make subordinate legislation or confer a discretion on any person.
(4) The regulations may make retrospective provision, except insofar as they impose or increase taxation.
(5) A statutory instrument containing regulations under this section may not be made unless a draft of the instrument has been laid before and approved by a resolution of the House of Commons.][1]

Amendments—[1]   Sections 608A–608Z inserted by FA 2019 s 15, Sch 3 paras 1, 4 with effect for the tax year 2019–20 and subsequent tax years.

[Recovery of tax from person in same control group

608O Notice requiring payment from person in same control group as taxpayer
(1) This section applies where—
    (*a*) an amount of income tax has been assessed on a person ("the taxpayer") for a tax year by virtue of this Chapter, and
    (*b*) the whole or any part of that amount, or of any interest on that amount, is unpaid at the end of the period of 6 months after the relevant date.
(2) A designated officer may give a notice to a relevant person requiring that person, within 30 days of the giving of the notice, to pay any unpaid tax and interest.
(3) The notice must state—
    (*a*) the amount of income tax and interest that remains unpaid,
    (*b*) the date when the income tax first became payable, and
    (*c*) the relevant person's right of appeal.
(4) A notice under this section may not be given more than 3 years and 6 months after the relevant date.
(5) In this section "relevant person" means any person who was in the same control group as the taxpayer at any time in the tax year (see section 608S for the meaning of being in the same "control group").
(6) In this section "the relevant date" means—
    (*a*) in relation to an amount of income tax determined under section 28C of TMA 1970, the date on which the determination was issued;

(*b*) in relation to an amount of income tax under a self-assessment in a case where the taxpayer's return under section 8 or 8A of TMA 1970 was delivered after the last day for delivering it in accordance with that section, the date on which the return was delivered;

(*c*) in any other case, the date the amount mentioned in subsection (1)(*a*) became due and payable.

(7) A notice may be given anywhere in the world, to any relevant person (whether or not UK resident).

(8) In this section—

"assessment": any reference to an amount of income tax that has been assessed on a person includes an amount of income tax that has been determined under section 28C of TMA 1970 in relation to the person;

"designated officer" means an officer of Revenue and Customs who has been designated by the Commissioners for the purposes of this Chapter.][1]

Amendments—[1] Sections 608A–608Z inserted by FA 2019 s 15, Sch 3 paras 1, 4 with effect for the tax year 2019–20 and subsequent tax years.

[608P Payment notice: effect

(1) This section applies where a notice under section 608O is given to a person.

(2) For the purposes of the recovery from the person of any unpaid tax and interest (including interest accruing after the date of the notice), the person is treated as if—

(*a*) the amount of income tax assessed as mentioned in section 608O(1)(*a*) had been assessed on the person,

(*b*) that amount became due and payable when the tax mentioned in section 608O(1)(*a*) became due and payable, and

(*c*) any payments made in respect of the amount mentioned in section 608O(1)(*a*) (or in respect of interest on that amount) had been made in respect of the amount treated as assessed by virtue of paragraph (*a*) of this subsection (or in respect of interest on that amount).

(3) Nothing in subsection (2) gives the person a right to appeal against the assessment mentioned in section 608O(1)(*a*) (or against any assessment treated as made by virtue of subsection (2) of this section).

(4) Any appeal by the taxpayer against the assessment mentioned in section 608O(1)(*a*) does not affect the liabilities arising by virtue of the giving of the notice.][1]

Amendments—[1] Sections 608A–608Z inserted by FA 2019 s 15, Sch 3 paras 1, 4 with effect for the tax year 2019–20 and subsequent tax years.

[608Q Payment notice: appeals

(1) This section applies where a notice under section 608O is given to a person.

(2) The person may appeal against the notice, within the period of 30 days beginning with the date on which it is given, on the ground that the person is not a relevant person (as defined by section 608O).

(3) Where an appeal is made, anything required by the notice to be paid is due and payable as if there had been no appeal.

(4) Section 56 of TMA 1970 (payment of tax where further appeal) applies in relation to any further appeal against the notice, but the relevant court or tribunal may, on the application of Her Majesty's Revenue and Customs, direct that section 56(2) does not apply to anything required by the notice to be paid.

(5) A direction may be given if the relevant court or tribunal considers it necessary for the protection of the revenue.

(6) In this section "relevant court or tribunal" has the same meaning as in section 56 of TMA 1970.][1]

Amendments—[1] Sections 608A–608Z inserted by FA 2019 s 15, Sch 3 paras 1, 4 with effect for the tax year 2019–20 and subsequent tax years.

[608R Payment notice: effect of making payment etc

(1) This section applies where a notice under section 608O is given to a person.

(2) A person who pays an amount in pursuance of the notice may recover that amount from the taxpayer.

(3) In calculating the person's income, profits or losses for any tax purposes—

(*a*) a payment in pursuance of the notice is not allowed as a deduction, and

(*b*) the reimbursement of any such payment is not regarded as a receipt.

(4) Any amount paid by the person in pursuance of the notice is to be taken into account in calculating—

(*a*) the amount unpaid, and

(*b*) the amount due by virtue of any other notice under section 608O relating to the amount unpaid.

(5) Similarly, any payment by the taxpayer of any of the amount unpaid is to be taken into account in calculating the amount due by virtue of the notice (or by virtue of any other notice under section 608O relating to the amount unpaid).][1]

Amendments—[1]   Sections 608A–608Z inserted by FA 2019 s 15, Sch 3 paras 1, 4 with effect for the tax year 2019–20 and subsequent tax years.

[Meaning of "control group" and "related person"

608S Control groups

(1) Two persons are in the same control group at any time if—
  (*a*) they are consolidated for accounting purposes for a period which includes that time,
  (*b*) one of them has a 51% investment in the other at that time, or
  (*c*) a third person has a 51% investment in each of them at that time.
(2) Two persons are consolidated for accounting purposes for a period if—
  (*a*) their financial results for the period are required to be comprised in group accounts,
  (*b*) their financial results for the period would be required to be comprised in group accounts but for the application of an exemption, or
  (*c*) their financial results for the period are in fact comprised in group accounts.
(3) In this section "group accounts" means accounts prepared under—
  (*a*) section 399 of the Companies Act 2006, or
  (*b*) any corresponding provision of the law of a territory outside the United Kingdom.
(4) For the meaning of having a 51% investment, see section 608U.][1]

Amendments—[1]   Sections 608A–608Z inserted by FA 2019 s 15, Sch 3 paras 1, 4 with effect for the tax year 2019–20 and subsequent tax years.

[608T Related persons

(1) Two persons are "related" at any time if—
  (*a*) at that time—
    (i)   they are in the same control group,
    (ii) one of them has a 25% investment in the other, or
    (iii) a third person has a 25% investment in both of them, or
  (*b*) at any time in the period of 6 months beginning or ending at that time—
    (i)   one of them directly or indirectly participates in the management, control or capital of the other, or
    (ii) a third person directly or indirectly participates in the management, control or capital of both of them.
(2) See—
    section 608S for the meaning of being in the same "control group";
    section 608U for the meaning of having a 25% investment;
    section 608V for the meaning of direct or indirect participation in the management, control or capital of a person.][1]

Amendments—[1]   Sections 608A–608Z inserted by FA 2019 s 15, Sch 3 paras 1, 4 with effect for the tax year 2019–20 and subsequent tax years.

[608U Meaning of "51% investment" and "25% investment"

(1) A person (P) has a 51% investment in another person (*c*) if any of the following apply—
  (*a*) P possesses or is entitled to acquire more than half of the voting power in C;
  (*b*) in the event of a disposal of the whole of the equity in C, P would receive more than half of the proceeds;
  (*c*) in the event that the income in respect of the equity in C were distributed among the equity holders in C, P would receive more than half of the amount so distributed;
  (*d*) in the event of a winding-up of C or in any other circumstances, P would receive more than half of C's assets which would then be available for distribution among the equity holders in C in respect of the equity in C.
(2) A person (P) has a 25% investment in another person (*c*) where any paragraph of subsection (1) would apply if in that paragraph for "more than half" there were substituted "at least a quarter".
(3) Section 464(2) to (11) and section 465 of TIOPA 2010 apply for the purposes of subsections (1) and (2) of this section.
(4) In the application of section 464(10) of TIOPA for the purposes of subsection (1), the reference to a "25% investment" is to be read as a "51% investment".][1]

Amendments—[1]   Sections 608A–608Z inserted by FA 2019 s 15, Sch 3 paras 1, 4 with effect for the tax year 2019–20 and subsequent tax years.

[608V Meaning of direct or indirect participation in management, control or capital

(1) This section applies for the purposes of section 608T.
(2) A person is directly participating in the management, control or capital of another person at a particular time only if section 157 of TIOPA 2010 so provides.
(3) A person is indirectly participating in the management, control or capital of another person at a particular time only if section 159 or 160 of TIOPA 2010 so provides.][1]

Amendments—[1]   Sections 608A–608Z inserted by FA 2019 s 15, Sch 3 paras 1, 4 with effect for the tax year 2019–20 and subsequent tax years.

[General

608W Anti-avoidance

(1) This section applies if a person has entered into any arrangements the main purpose, or one of the main purposes, of which is to obtain a tax advantage for the person as a result (wholly or partly) of—

(*a*) anything not being subject to the charge under section 608A, or

(*b*) any provisions of double taxation arrangements having effect in a case where the advantage is contrary to the object and purpose of the provisions.

(2) The tax advantage is to be counteracted by the making of such adjustments as are just and reasonable.

(3) The adjustments may be made (whether by an officer of Revenue and Customs or the person) by way of an assessment, the modification of an assessment, amendment or disallowance of a claim, or otherwise.

(4) Where this section applies by virtue of subsection (1)(*b*), the counteraction has effect despite section 6(1) of TIOPA 2010.

(5) In this [Chapter]² "tax advantage" includes—

(*a*) relief or increased relief from tax,

(*b*) repayment or increased repayment of tax,

(*c*) avoidance or reduction of a charge to tax or an assessment to tax,

(*d*) avoidance of a possible assessment to tax,

(*e*) deferral of a payment of tax or advancement of a repayment of tax, and

(*f*) avoidance of an obligation to deduct or account for tax.]¹

Amendments—¹ Sections 608A–608Z inserted by FA 2019 s 15, Sch 3 paras 1, 4 with effect for the tax year 2019–20 and subsequent tax years.

² In sub-s (5) word "section" substituted by Income Tax (Trading and Other Income) Act 2005 (Amendments to Chapter 2A of Part 5) Regulations, SI 2019/1452 reg 13 with effect for the tax year 2019–20 and subsequent tax years.

[608X Interaction with other general provisions

(1) This section applies where section 608A applies in relation to a person for a tax year (or would apply, if the following provisions of this section applied).

(2) Part 6 (exempt income) does not apply in relation to UK-derived amounts arising to the person in the tax year.

(3) For the purposes of calculating the person's liability to income tax for the tax year—

(*a*) Chapter 1 of Part 14 of ITA 2007 (limits on liability to income tax of non-residents) does not apply in relation to UK-derived amounts arising to the person in the tax year;

(*b*) accordingly, the person's liability is the sum of—

(i) the person's liability as regards UK-derived amounts (with that Chapter not applying), and

(ii) the person's liability as regards anything else (with that Chapter applying, to the extent it would otherwise apply).]¹

Amendments—¹ Sections 608A–608Z inserted by FA 2019 s 15, Sch 3 paras 1, 4 with effect for the tax year 2019–20 and subsequent tax years.

[608Y Appeals against assessments

(1) This section applies where a person ("the taxpayer") makes an appeal in relation to an amount of income tax charged on the taxpayer under section 608A.

(2) Section 55(3) to (8A) of TMA 1970 (application for postponement of payment of tax pending appeal) do not apply in relation to the tax charged (and no agreement as to the postponement of payment of any of that tax, or of interest on it, may be made).

(3) In the case of a further appeal, the relevant court or tribunal (as defined by section 56 of TMA 1970) may, on the application of Her Majesty's Revenue and Customs, direct that section 56(2) of TMA 1970 does not apply to the tax charged.

(4) A direction may be given if the relevant court or tribunal considers it necessary for the protection of the revenue.

(5) Nothing in this section applies in relation to a liability arising as a result of the giving of a notice under section 608O.]¹

Amendments—¹ Sections 608A–608Z inserted by FA 2019 s 15, Sch 3 paras 1, 4 with effect for the tax year 2019–20 and subsequent tax years.

Interpretation: general

[608Z Interpretation of Chapter: general

In this Chapter—

"arrangements" includes any agreement, understanding, scheme, transaction or series of transactions (whether or not legally enforceable);

"the Commissioners" means the Commissioners for Her Majesty's Revenue and Customs;

"control group" has the meaning given by section 608S;

ITTOIA 2005

["designer tax provisions" means provisions which appear to the Commissioners to be designed to enable persons to exercise significant control over the amount of tax which they pay in respect of UK-derived amounts;][2]

"double taxation arrangements" means arrangements that have effect under section 2(1) of TIOPA 2010;

"full treaty territory" has the meaning given by section 608E;

"intangible property" has the meaning given by section 608H;

"related": references to two persons being related are to be read in accordance with section 608T;

"resident": references to being resident in a territory are to be read in accordance with section 608D;

["tax": any reference (however expressed) to tax payable or paid under the laws of a territory outside the United Kingdom is a reference to a tax which—

(a) is charged on income, and

(b) corresponds to income tax or corporation tax;

and for this purpose tax may correspond to income tax or corporation tax even though it is payable under the laws of a province, state or other part of a country or is levied by or on behalf of a municipality or other local body;][2]

["tax advantage" has the meaning given by section 608W(5);][2]

"UK-derived amount" has the meaning given by section 608F;

"UK sales" has the meaning given by section 608F.][1]

Amendments—[1] Sections 608A–608Z inserted by FA 2019 s 15, Sch 3 paras 1, 4 with effect for the tax year 2019–20 and subsequent tax years.

[2] Definitions inserted by Income Tax (Trading and Other Income) Act 2005 (Amendments to Chapter 2A of Part 5) Regulations, SI 2019/1452 reg 14 with effect for the tax year 2019–20 and subsequent tax years.

CHAPTER 3

FILMS AND SOUND RECORDINGS: NON-TRADE BUSINESSES

609 Charge to tax on films and sound recordings businesses

(1) Income tax is charged on income from a business involving the exploitation of films or sound recordings where the activities carried on do not amount to a trade.

Such a business is referred to in this Chapter as a "non-trade business".

(2) Expressions which are used in this Chapter and in Chapter 9 of Part 2 (trade profits: films and sound recordings) have the same meaning in this Chapter as they do in that Chapter.

Commentary—*Simon's Taxes* B5.510.
HMRC Manuals—Business Income Manual BIM56025 (rules apply to cases V & VI).

610 Income charged

(1) Tax is charged under this Chapter on the full amount of the income arising in the tax year.

(2) See sections 612 and 613 for provision about the calculation of the amount of income charged under this Chapter.

(3) This section is subject to Part 8 (foreign income: special rules).

Commentary—*Simon's Taxes* B5.510.

611 Person liable

The person liable for any tax charged under this Chapter is the person receiving or entitled to the income.

Commentary—*Simon's Taxes* B5.510

612 Calculation of income

(1) This section applies for calculating the amount of income charged under this Chapter.

(2) Expenses wholly and exclusively incurred for the purpose of generating the income are deductible.

(3) If an expense is incurred for more than one purpose, a deduction may be made for any identifiable part or identifiable proportion of the expense which is incurred wholly and exclusively for the purpose of generating the income.

(4) Expenses which would not have been allowable as a deduction in calculating the profits of a trade, if they had been incurred for its purposes, are not deductible under this section.

(5) Expenses for which any kind of relief is given under any other provision of the Income Tax Acts are not deductible under this section.

(6) Any relief given as a result of section 613 is additional to the relief under this section.

Commentary—*Simon's Taxes* B5.510

613 Application of trading income rules to non-trade businesses

The provisions of Chapter 9 of Part 2 apply in relation to non-trade businesses as they apply in relation to trades but as if—

(*a*) references to a basis period were to a tax year, and

(*b*) references to anything not constituting trading stock of a trade were omitted.

Commentary—*Simon's Taxes* **B5.510**

HMRC Manuals—Business Income Manual BIM56025 (rules apply to cases V & VI).

CHAPTER 4

CERTAIN TELECOMMUNICATION RIGHTS: NON-TRADING INCOME

614 Charge to tax on certain telecommunication rights of a non-trader

(1) Income tax is charged on income derived from a relevant telecommunication right that is not used or held for the purposes of a trade, profession or vocation.

(2) "Relevant telecommunication right" has the same meaning as in Chapter 10 of Part 2 (see section 146).

Commentary—*Simon's Taxes* **B2.473.**

615 Income charged

(1) Tax is charged under this Chapter on the full amount of the income arising in the tax year.

(2) See section 617 for provision about the calculation of the amount of certain income charged under this Chapter.

(3) This section is subject to Part 8 (foreign income: special rules).

616 Person liable

The person liable for any tax charged under this Chapter is the person receiving or entitled to the income.

617 Deductions in calculating certain income charged

(1) This section applies for calculating the amount of income charged under this Chapter other than annual payments.

(2) The following sections apply as they apply for the purpose of calculating the profits of a trade, profession or vocation—

(*a*) section 147 (expenditure and receipts in respect of relevant telecommunication rights treated as revenue in nature), and

(*b*) section 148 (credits or debits arising from revaluation in respect of relevant telecommunication rights).

(3) Expenses wholly and exclusively incurred for the purpose of generating the income are deductible.

(4) If an expense is incurred for more than one purpose, a deduction may be made for any identifiable part or identifiable proportion of the expense which is incurred wholly and exclusively for the purpose of generating the income.

(5) Expenses which would not have been allowable as a deduction in calculating the profits of a trade, if they had been incurred for its purposes, are not deductible under this section.

(6) Expenses for which any kind of relief is given under any other provision of the Income Tax Acts are not deductible under this section.

(7) The frequency with which payments are made is ignored in determining whether they are annual payments for the purposes of this Chapter.

Commentary—*Simon's Taxes* **B2.473.**

618 Payments received after deduction of tax

[In accordance with section 848 of ITA 2007, a sum representing income tax deducted under Chapter 6 of Part 15 of that Act][1] from an annual payment within this Chapter is treated as income tax paid by the recipient . . . [1]

Commentary—*Simon's Taxes* **E1.513.**

Amendments—[1] Words substituted and words repealed by ITA 2007 ss 1027, 1031, Sch 1 paras 492, 549, Sch 3 Pt 1 with effect for income tax purposes from 6 April 2007, and corporation tax purposes for accounting periods ending after 5 April 2007.

CHAPTER 5

SETTLEMENTS: AMOUNTS TREATED AS INCOME OF SETTLOR [OR FAMILY]

Charge to tax under Chapter 5

619 Charge to tax under Chapter 5

(1) Income tax is charged on—

(*a*) income which is treated as income of a settlor as a result of section 624 (income where settlor retains an interest),

(*b*) income which is treated as income of a settlor as a result of section 629 (income paid to [relevant][1] children of settlor),

(*c*) capital sums which are treated as income of a settlor as a result of section 633 (capital sums paid to settlor by trustees of settlement), . . . [4]

(*d*) capital sums which are treated as income of a settlor as a result of section 641 (capital sums paid to settlor by body connected with settlement).

[(*e*) benefits whose amount or value is treated as income of the settlor or a close family member as a result of section 643A (benefits provided out of protected foreign-source income), and

(*f*) amounts treated as income of the settlor or a close family member by section 643J or 643L (gifts provided out of benefits).][4]

[(2) For the purposes of [Chapter 2 of Part 2 of ITA 2007 (rates at which income tax is charged)][3], where income of another person is treated as income of the settlor and is charged to tax under subsection (1)(*a*) or (*b*) above, it shall be charged in accordance with whichever provisions of the [Income Tax Acts][3] would have been applied in charging it if it had arisen directly to the settlor.][2]

Commentary—*Simon's Taxes* **C4.320, C4.350, C4.340.**

HMRC Manuals—Trusts, Settlements and Estates Manual TSEM4573 (taxing income on settlor).

TSEM8615 (trust management expenses: mixed trusts: part settlor interested and part non settlor interested).

Amendments—[1]   Word in sub-s (1)(*b*) substituted by the Tax and Civil Partnership Regulations, SI 2005/3229, regs 183, 186, with effect from 5 December 2005 (reg 1(1)).

[2]   Sub-s (2) substituted for sub-ss (2)–(4) by FA 2006 s 89, Sch 13 para 5 with effect—

     (a)   in relation to income which arises or is treated as arising on or after 6 April 2006, and

     (b)   in relation to income which is paid to a minor child of the settlor, where the child is unmarried and is not in a civil partnership, on or after 6 April 2006 and in relation to which ITTOIA 2005 s 631 applies (irrespective of when the income arose).

[3]   Words in sub-s (2) substituted by ITA 2007 s 1027, Sch 1 paras 492, 550 with effect for income tax purposes from 6 April 2007, and corporation tax purposes for accounting periods ending after 5 April 2007.

[3]   In heading to Chapter 5, words inserted, word in sub-s (1)(*c*) repealed, and subs (1)(*e*), (*f*) inserted, by FA 2018 s 35, Sch 10 paras 3, 4 with effect for the tax year 2018–19 and subsequent tax years.

[619A Income treated as highest part of settlor's total income

(1) This section applies to income which is treated as income of a settlor as a result of section 624 (income where settlor retains an interest) or 629 (income paid to unmarried minor children of settlor).

(2) The income is treated as the highest part of the settlor's total income for the purposes of section 619 (so far as it relates to the income).

(3) See section 1012 of ITA 2007 (relationship between highest part rules) for the relationship between—

     (*a*) the rule in subsection (2), and

     (*b*) other rules requiring particular income to be treated as the highest part of a person's total income.][1]

Commentary—*Simon's Taxes* **C4.320, C4.350.**

Amendments—[1]   This section inserted by ITA 2007 s 1027, Sch 1 paras 492, 551 with effect for income tax purposes from 6 April 2007, and corporation tax purposes for accounting periods ending after 5 April 2007.

620 Meaning of "settlement" and "settlor"

(1) In this Chapter—

"settlement" includes any disposition, trust, covenant, agreement, arrangement or transfer of assets (except that it does not include a charitable loan arrangement), and

"settlor", in relation to a settlement, means any person by whom the settlement was made.

(2) A person is treated for the purposes of this Chapter as having made a settlement if the person has made or entered into the settlement directly or indirectly.

(3) A person is, in particular, treated as having made a settlement if the person—

     (*a*) has provided funds directly or indirectly for the purpose of the settlement,

     (*b*) has undertaken to provide funds directly or indirectly for the purpose of the settlement, or

     (*c*) has made a reciprocal arrangement with another person for the other person to make or enter into the settlement.

(4) This Chapter applies to settlements wherever made.

(5) In this section—

"charitable loan arrangement" means any arrangement so far as it consists of a loan of money made by an individual to a charity either—

     (*a*) for no consideration, or

     (*b*) for a consideration which consists only of interest, and

"charity" includes—

     [(*a*) the Trustees of the National Heritage Memorial Fund, [and][2]

     (*b*) the Historic Buildings and Monuments Commission for England,   . . . [2]

     (*c*)   . . . [2]][1].

Commentary—*Simon's Taxes* **C4.305, C4.321.**

HMRC Manuals—Trusts, Settlements and Estates Manual TSEM4120 (definition of settlor).

TSEM4100 (definition of settlement).

Amendments—[1]   Words in sub-s (5) substituted by ITA 2007 s 1027, Sch 1 paras 492, 552 with effect for income tax purposes from 6 April 2007, and corporation tax purposes for accounting periods ending after 5 April 2007.

[2]   In sub-s (5), in definition of "charity", word in para (*a*) inserted, and para (*c*) and preceding word repealed by the Public Bodies (Abolition of the National Endowment for Science, Technology and the Arts) Order, SI 2012/964 art 3(1), Schedule with effect from 1 April 2012.

Income charged and person liable

621 Income charged

Tax is charged under this Chapter on all [income, capital sums and benefits][1] to which section 619(1) applies.

Commentary—*Simon's Taxes* **C4.320, C4.350.**

Amendments[1]   Words substituted by FA 2018 s 35, Sch 10 paras 3, 5 with effect for the tax year 2018–19 and subsequent tax years.

622 Person liable

The person liable for any tax charged under this Chapter is the settlor[, but this is subject to sections 643A and 643I to 643M.][1]

Commentary—*Simon's Taxes* **C4.320.**

Amendments[1]   Words inserted by FA 2018 s 35, Sch 10 paras 3, 6 with effect for the tax year 2018–19 and subsequent tax years.

Rules for calculating income

[623 Calculation of income

For the purpose of calculating liability to tax under this Chapter (but for no other purpose), [an individual][2] shall be allowed the same deductions and reliefs as if any amount treated under this Chapter as income of [the individual][2] had actually been received by [the individual][2].][1]

Commentary—*Simon's Taxes* **C4.320, C4.340.**

HMRC Manuals—Trusts, Settlements and Estates Manual TSEM4017 (settlements legislation: calculation of income).

Amendments—[1]   Section substituted by FA 2006 s 89, Sch 13 para 31(2) with effect from 6 April 2006 in respect of settlements whenever created, and in respect of loans or advances whenever made.

[2]   Words substituted by FA 2018 s 35, Sch 10 paras 3, 7 with effect for the tax year 2018–19 and subsequent tax years.

Income treated as income of settlor: retained interests

624 Income where settlor retains an interest

(1) Income which arises under a settlement is treated for income tax purposes as the income of the settlor and of the settlor alone if it arises—

    (*a*) during the life of the settlor, and

    (*b*) from property in which the settlor has an interest.

[(1A) If the settlement is a trust, expenses of the trustees are not to be used to reduce the income of the settlor.][2]

(2) For more on a settlor having an interest in property, see section 625.

(3) For exceptions to the rule in subsection (1), see—

    section 626 (exception for outright gifts between spouses [or civil partners][1]),

    section 627 (exceptions for certain types of income), [3]

    section 628 (exception for gifts to charities)[, and

    section 628A (exception for protected foreign-source income).][3]

Commentary—*Simon's Taxes* **C4.325, C4.309, C4.321.**

HMRC Manuals—Trusts, Settlements and Estates Manual TSEM4200 (where settlor has retained an interest).

TSEM4205 (exceptions to the statutory definition of settlement).

Amendments—[1]   Words in sub-s (3) inserted by the Tax and Civil Partnership Regulations, SI 2005/3229, regs 183, 187, with effect from 5 December 2005 (reg 1(1)).

[2]   Sub-s (1A) inserted by ITA 2007 s 1027, Sch 1 paras 492, 553 with effect for income tax purposes from 6 April 2007, and corporation tax purposes for accounting periods ending after 5 April 2007.

[3]   In sub-s (3), in entry for "section 627", word "and" repealed, and entry for "section 628A" and preceding word inserted by F(No 2)A 2017 s 29(2), Sch 8 paras 20, 21 with effect for the tax year 2017–18 and subsequent tax years.

625 Settlor's retained interest

(1) A settlor is treated for the purposes of section 624 as having an interest in property if there are any circumstances in which the property or any related property—

    (*a*) is payable to the settlor or the settlor's spouse [or civil partner][1],

    (*b*) is applicable for the benefit of the settlor or the settlor's spouse [or civil partner][1], or

    (*c*) will, or may, become so payable or applicable.

(2) Subsection (1) does not apply if the only circumstances are one or more of—

    (*a*) the bankruptcy of a person who is, or may become, beneficially entitled to the property or any related property,

    (*b*) the assignment of the property or any related property by such a person,

    (*c*) the charging of (or, in Scotland, the granting of a right in security over) the property or any related property by such a person,

    [(*d*) in the case of a marriage settlement or civil partnership settlement, the death of both parties to the marriage or civil partnership and of all or any of the children of the family of the parties to the marriage or civil partnership, and][1] (*e*) the death of a child of the settlor who had become beneficially entitled to the property or any related property at not more than 25 years old.

[(2A) In subsection (2) "child of the family", in relation to parties to a marriage or civil partnership, means a child of one or both of them.][1]

(3) Subsection (1) does not apply if—

(*a*) there are no circumstances in which the property or any related property can become payable or applicable as mentioned in that subsection during the life of a person other than—

   (i) the bankruptcy of the person, or

   (ii) the assignment or charging of the person's interest in the property or any related property, and

(*b*) the person is alive and under 25 years old.

(4) In subsection (1) "the settlor's spouse [or civil partner[1]]" does not include—

(*a*) a spouse [or civil partner][1] from whom the settlor is separated under an order of a court or a separation agreement,

(*b*) a spouse [or civil partner][1] from whom the settlor is separated where the separation is likely to be permanent,

(*c*) the widow or widower [or surviving civil partner][1] of the settlor, or

(*d*) a person to whom the settlor is not married but may later marry [or a person of whom the settlor is not a civil partner but of whom the settlor may later be a civil partner][1].

(5) In this section "related property", in relation to any property, means income from that property or any other property directly or indirectly representing proceeds of, or of income from, that property or income from it.

Commentary—*Simon's Taxes* **C4.327, C4.328.**
HMRC Manuals—Company Taxation Manual CTM15270 (application of settlements legislation to dividend waivers).
Trusts, Settlements and Estates Manual, TSEM4005 (introduction to the settlements legislation).
TSEM4105 (settlements legislation: interpretation of statutory definition of settlement).
TSEM4200 (where settlor has retained an interest).
Amendments—[1] Words in sub-ss (1), (4), sub-s (2A) inserted, and sub-s (2)(*d*) substituted by Tax and Civil Partnership Regulations, SI 2005/3229, regs 183, 188, with effect from 5 December 2005 (reg 1(1)).

626 Exception for outright gifts between spouses [or civil partners][1]

(1) The rule in section 624(1) does not apply in respect of an outright gift—

(*a*) of property from which income arises,

(*b*) made by one spouse to the other [or one civil partner to the other][1], and

(*c*) meeting conditions A and B.

(2) Condition A is that the gift carries a right to the whole of the income.

(3) Condition B is that the property is not wholly or substantially a right to income.

(4) A gift is not an outright gift for the purposes of this section if—

(*a*) it is subject to conditions, or

(*b*) there are any circumstances in which the property, or any related property—

   (i) is payable to the giver,

   (ii) is applicable for the benefit of the giver, or

   (iii) will, or may become, so payable or applicable.

(5) "Related property" has the same meaning in this section as in section 625.

Commentary—*Simon's Taxes* **C4.309, C4.326, E1.1419, E5.103B.**
HMRC Manuals—Trusts, Settlements and Estates Manual TSEM4205 (exceptions: outrights gift by one spouse or civil partner and examples).
TSEM4215 (partnerships -settlements legislation does not apply).
TSEM4355 (settlements legislation - summary - additional examples where does not apply).
Amendments—[1] Words in sub-s (1)(*b*) and words in heading inserted by Tax and Civil Partnership Regulations, SI 2005/3229, regs 183, 189, with effect from 5 December 2005 (reg 1(1)).

627 Exceptions for certain types of income

(1) The rule in section 624(1) does not apply to income which—

(*a*) arises under a settlement made by one party to a marriage [or civil partnership][1] by way of provision for the other—

   (i) after the dissolution or annulment of the marriage [or civil partnership][1], or

   (ii) while they are separated under an order of a court, or under a separation agreement, or where the separation is likely to be permanent, and

(*b*) is payable to, or applicable for the benefit of, the other party.

(2) The rule in section 624(1) does not apply to income which consists of—

(*a*) annual payments made by an individual for commercial reasons in connection with the individual's trade, profession or vocation,

(*b*) qualifying donations for the purposes of [Chapter 2 of Part 8 of ITA 2007 (gift aid)][2], or

(*c*) a benefit under a relevant pension scheme.

(3) In subsection (2)(*c*) "relevant pension scheme" means—

(*a*) a registered pension scheme,

   (*b*) a pension scheme established by a government outside the United Kingdom for the benefit, or primarily for the benefit, of its employees (or an annuity acquired using funds held for the purposes of such a pension scheme), or

   (*c*) any pension arrangements of any description prescribed by regulations made under section 11(2)(*h*) of the Welfare Reform and Pensions Act 1999 (c 30) or Article 12(2)(*h*) of the Welfare Reform and Pensions (Northern Ireland) Order 1999 (SI 1999/3147 (NI 11)).

[(4) The rule in section 624(1) does not apply in relation to income which—

   (*a*) arises under a settlement, and

   (*b*) originates from any settlor who was not an individual.][3]

Commentary—*Simon's Taxes* **C4.326.**

HMRC Manuals—Trusts, Settlements and Estates Manual TSEM4206 (settlor retains an interest exceptions certain types of income).

TSEM4016 (settlements legislation: effects of the settlements legislation corporate settlors).

Amendments—[1] Words in sub-s (1)(*a*) inserted by the Tax and Civil Partnership Regulations, SI 2005/3229, regs 183, 190, with effect from 5 December 2005 (reg 1(1)).

[2] Words in sub-s (2) substituted by ITA 2007 s 1027, Sch 1 paras 492, 554 with effect for income tax purposes from 6 April 2007, and corporation tax purposes for accounting periods ending after 5 April 2007.

[3] Sub-s (4) inserted by FA 2012 s 12(1), (2) with effect in relation to income arising on or after 21 March 2012.

628 Exception for gifts to charities

(1) The rule in section 624(1) does not apply to any qualifying income which arises under a [UK settlement][2] if—

   (*a*) it is given by the trustees to a charity in the tax year in which it arises, or

   (*b*) it is income to which a charity is entitled under the terms of the trust.

(2) In this section "qualifying income" means—

   (*a*) income which [must][4] be accumulated,

   (*b*) income which is payable at the discretion of the trustees or any other person . . . [4], or

   (*c*) income which (before being distributed) is income of any person other than the trustees.

[(2A) The cases covered by subsection (2)(*b*) include cases where the trustees have, or any other person has, any discretion over one or more of the following matters—

   (*a*) whether, or the extent to which, the income is to be accumulated,

   (*b*) the persons to whom the income is to be paid, and

   (*c*) how much of the income is to be paid to any person.][4]

(3) Subsection (4) applies if in any tax year qualifying income which arises under a [UK settlement][2] from different sources exceeds the total of—

   (*a*) the amount of that income which falls within subsection (1), and

   (*b*) the amount of that income which falls within section 630(1) (comparable exception for income of [relevant][1] children of settlor).

(4) The amount of the qualifying income from different sources which falls within subsection (1) above is rateably apportioned between those sources.

(5) This does not affect the operation of any requirement that the whole, or any specified part, of the income from a particular source is to be given to a charity.

(6) In this section—

   "charity" includes—

     [(*a*) the Trustees of the National Heritage Memorial Fund, [and][5]

     (*b*) the Historic Buildings and Monuments Commission for England,][5]

     (*c*) . . . [5]][4]

   . . . [4]

["UK settlement" means a settlement the trustees of which are resident . . . [6] in the United Kingdom.][3]

Commentary—*Simon's Taxes* **C4.326.**

HMRC Manuals—Trusts, Settlements and Estates Manual TSEM4207 (settlement legislation: settlor retains an interest exceptions gifts to charities).

Amendments—[1] Word in sub-s (3)(*b*) substituted by Tax and Civil Partnership Regulations, SI 2005/3229, regs 183, 191, with effect from 5 December 2005 (reg 1(1)).

[2] Words substituted throughout section, by FA 2006 s 89, Sch 13 para 33(1) with effect from 6 April 2006.

[3] In sub-s (6), definition of "UK settlement" substituted by FA 2006 s 89, Sch 13 para 33(2) with effect from 6 April 2006.

[4] Words in sub-ss (2), (6) repealed, words in sub-s (2) repealed, sub-s (2A) inserted, and in sub-s (6), definition repealed, by ITA 2007 ss 1027, 1031, Sch 1 paras 492, 555, Sch 3 Pt 1 with effect for income tax purposes from 6 April 2007, and corporation tax purposes for accounting periods ending after 5 April 2007.

[5] In sub-s (6), in definition of "charity", word in para (*a*) inserted, and para (*c*) and preceding word repealed by the Public Bodies (Abolition of the National Endowment for Science, Technology and the Arts) Order, SI 2012/964 art 3(1), Schedule with effect from 1 April 2012.

[6] In sub-s (6), in definition of "UK settlement", words "and ordinarily resident" repealed by the Income Tax (Removal of Ordinary Residence) Order, SI 2014/3062 art 2 with effect in relation to the tax year 2015–16 and any subsequent tax year.

[628A Exception for protected foreign-source income

(1) The rule in section 624(1) does not apply to income which arises under a settlement if it is protected foreign-source income for a tax year.

ITTOIA 2005

(4) In subsection (3) a child's "relevant settlement income" means income—

    (*a*) which is paid to or for the benefit of, or otherwise treated as income of, the child, and

    (*b*) which (apart from subsection (3)) would be treated as income of the settlor under subsection (1).

(5) Subsection (1) does not apply so far as provided by section 630 (exception for gifts to charities) [or section 630A (exception for protected foreign-source income)][3].

(6) See—

    section 631 for the treatment for the purposes of subsection (1) of retained or accumulated income, and

    section 632 for the treatment for the purposes of this section and section 631 of certain deemed income connected to offshore income gains.

(7) In this section and sections 631 and 632—

    (*a*) "child" includes a stepchild,

    (*b*) "minor" means a person under the age of 18 years, and "minor child" is to be read accordingly,

    (*c*) references to payments include payments in money's worth[, and][1]

    [(*d*) "relevant child" means a minor child who is unmarried or not in a civil partnership.][1]

[(8) Subsection (1) is subject to section 28A of FA 2005.][2]

Commentary—*Simon's Taxes* **C4.330, C4.331.**

HMRC Manuals—Trusts, Settlements and Estates Manual TSEM4512 (settlements legislation: trusts for minor child of settlor). TSEM4105 (settlements legislation: interpretation of statutory definition of settlement). TSEM4300 (application to non-trust arrangements and trusts) TSEM4310 (settlement for minor child: income less than £100).

Amendments—[1]   Words in sub-s (1), and words in heading and cross-heading substituted, in sub-s (7)(*b*) word repealed, word in sub-s (7)(*c*) and sub-s (7)(*d*) inserted by Tax and Civil Partnership Regulations, SI 2005/3229, regs 183, 192, with effect from 5 December 2005 (reg 1(1)).

[2]   Sub-s (8) inserted by FA 2006 s 89, Sch 13 para 34(1) with effect in relation to payments made on or after 6 April 2004.

[3]   In sub-s (5), words inserted by F(No 2)A 2017 s 29(2), Sch 8 paras 20, 23(1) with effect for the tax year 2017–18 and subsequent tax years.

630 Exception for gifts to charities

(1) The rule in section 629(1) does not apply to any qualifying income which arises under a [UK settlement][1] if—

    (*a*) it is given by the trustees to a charity in the tax year in which it arises, or

    (*b*) it is income to which a charity is entitled under the [terms of the settlement][2].

(2) Subsection (3) applies if in any tax year qualifying income which arises under a [UK settlement][1] from different sources exceeds the total of—

    (*a*) the amount of that income which falls within subsection (1), and

    (*b*) the amount of that income which falls within section 628(1) (comparable exception for income where settlor retains an interest).

(3) The amount of the qualifying income from different sources which falls within subsection (1) above is rateably apportioned between those sources.

(4) This does not affect the operation of any requirement that the whole, or any specified part, of the income from a particular source is to be given to a charity.

(5) In this section "charity", "qualifying income" and "[UK settlement][1]" have the same meaning as in section 628.

Commentary—*Simon's Taxes* **C4.330.**

Amendments—[1]   Words substituted throughout section, by FA 2006 s 89, Sch 13 para 33(1) with effect from 6 April 2006.

[2]   Words in sub-s (1)(*b*) substituted by FA 2006 s 89, Sch 13 para 33(3) with effect from 6 April 2006.

[630A Exception for protected foreign-source income

(1) The rule in section 629(1) does not apply to income which arises under a settlement if it is protected foreign-source income for a tax year.

(2) Sections 628A(2) to (12) and 628B (meaning of "protected foreign-source income") have effect also for this purpose.

(3) Section 648(3) to (5) (relevant foreign income treated as arising under settlement only if and when remitted) do not apply for the purposes of this section.][1]

Commentary—*Simon's Taxes* **C4.330.**

Amendments—[1]   Section 630A inserted by F(No 2)A 2017 s 29(2), Sch 8 paras 20, 23(2) with effect for the tax year 2017–18 and subsequent tax years.

631 Retained and accumulated income

(1) This section applies if—

    (*a*) the trustees of a settlement retain or accumulate income arising under the settlement, and

    (*b*) a payment is subsequently made in connection with the settlement to, or for the benefit of, [a child of the settlor who is unmarried or not in a civil partnership][1].

(2) The payment is treated for the purposes of section 629(1) as a payment of income, but only so far as there is retained or accumulated income available.

(3) For the purposes of subsection (1) a payment is made in connection with a settlement if it is made by virtue of or in consequence of—

    (*a*) the settlement, or

    (*b*) any enactment relating to the settlement.

(4) For the purposes of subsection (2) retained or accumulated income is available at any time when—

$$A > B$$

where—

    A is the total amount of the income which has arisen under the settlement since it was made, and

    B is the total amount of disregarded income.

(5) In subsection (4) "disregarded income" means any income arising under the settlement since it was made which has been—

    (*a*) treated as income of the settlor,

    (*b*) paid (whether as income or capital) to, or for the benefit of, a beneficiary other than [a relevant][1] child of the settlor,

    (*c*) otherwise treated as the income of such a beneficiary,

    (*d*) treated as income of an unmarried minor child of the settlor, and subject to income tax, in any of the tax years 1995–96, 1996–97 and 1997– 98, or

    (*e*) applied in meeting expenses of the trustees which—

        (i) were properly chargeable to income, or

        (ii) would have been so chargeable but for any express [terms of the settlement][2].

(6) For the purposes of subsection (5)(*d*), income arising under the settlement that is treated as income of the child is subject to income tax so far as it does not exceed the taxable amount.

(7) In subsection (6) "the taxable amount", in relation to a tax year, means the amount by which—

$$TI > TAD$$

where—

    TI is the child's total income for income tax purposes, and

    TAD is the total amount of allowances and deductions that may be set against [the child's total income or net income at Step 2 or 3 of the calculation in section 23 of ITA 2007][3].

Commentary—*Simon's Taxes* **C4.331.**

HMRC Manuals—Trusts, Settlements and Estates Manual TSEM4300 (settlement for minor child: accumulation/discretionary trusts).

Amendments—[1]   Words in sub-ss (1)(*b*), (5)(*b*) substituted by Tax and Civil Partnership Regulations, SI 2005/3229, regs 183, 193, with effect from 5 December 2005 (reg 1(1)).

[2]   Words in sub-s (5)(*e*)(ii) substituted by FA 2006 s 89, Sch 13 para 33(4) with effect from 6 April 2006.

[3]   Words in sub-s (7) substituted by ITA 2007 s 1027, Sch 1 paras 492, 556 with effect for income tax purposes from 6 April 2007, and corporation tax purposes for accounting periods ending after 5 April 2007.

632 Offshore income gains

(1) This section applies if—

    (*a*) an offshore income gain accrues in respect of a disposal by a trustee of assets held by the trustee for a minor, and

    (*b*) the minor would be absolutely entitled as against the trustee but for being a minor.

(2) The income which, under [regulation 17 of the Offshore Funds (Tax) Regulations 2009 (SI 2009/3001) (charge to tax)][1], is treated as arising by reference to that gain is treated for the purposes of sections 629 and 631 as paid to the minor.

(3) In this section "offshore income gain" has the same meaning as in [Chapter 5 of Part 2 of those Regulations][1].

Commentary—*Simon's Taxes* **C4.331.**

Amendments—[1]   In sub-ss (2), (3) words substituted by the Offshore Funds (Tax) Regulations, SI 2009/3001 reg 128(1), (3) with effect for the purposes of income tax for the tax year 2009–10 and subsequent tax years and for distributions made on or after 1 December 2009; for the purposes of corporation tax, on income, for accounting periods ending on or after 1 December 2009 and for distributions made on or after that date and, on chargeable gains, in relation to disposals made on or after 1 December 2009; and for the purposes of capital gains tax, in relation to disposals made on or after 1 December 2009.

Capital sums treated as income of settlor: trustees' payments

633 Capital sums paid to settlor by trustees of settlement

(1) Any capital sum paid directly or indirectly in any tax year by the trustees of a settlement to the settlor is treated for income tax purposes as follows.

(2) The sum is treated as the income of the settlor for the tax year so far as the amount of the sum falls within the amount of income available up to the end of the year.

(3) The sum is treated as the income of the settlor for the following year so far as the amount of the sum—

(a) is not treated under subsection (2) as the settlor's income for the tax year in which it is paid, and

(b) falls within the amount of the income available up to the end of the following year.

(4) Subsection (3) also applies for each subsequent year up to a maximum of 10 years subsequent to the tax year in which the sum is paid.

(5) For this purpose the reference in subsection (3)(a) to being treated under subsection (2) as the settlor's income for the tax year in which the capital sum is paid is a reference to being treated under subsection (2) or (3) as the settlor's income for that year and any other year before the subsequent year in question.

(6) For the meaning of certain expressions used in this section, see—

section 634 (meaning of "capital sum" and "sums paid to settlor"),

section 635 (amount of available income),

section 636 (calculation of undistributed income), and

section 637 (qualifications to section 636).

(7) For other provisions, see—

section 638 (capital sums paid by way of loan or repayment of loan),

section 639 (loans to participators in close companies), and

section 640 (grossing-up of deemed income).

Commentary—*Simon's Taxes* **C4.335, C4.336.**

HMRC Manuals—Company Taxation Manual CTM61050 (introduction to capital payments to settlors).

Trusts, Settlements and Estates Manual TSEM4400 (capital sums paid to settlor: introduction).

634 Meaning of "capital sum" and "sums paid to settlor"

(1) In this Chapter "capital sum" means—

(a) any sum paid by way of loan or repayment of a loan, and

(b) any other sum which—

(i) is paid otherwise than as income, and

(ii) is not paid for full consideration in money or money's worth.

(2) But this is subject to subsections (3) to (6).

(3) It does not include any sum which could not have become payable to the settlor except—

(a) in one of the circumstances mentioned in subsection (2) of section 625, or

(b) on the death under the age of 25 of any person of the kind mentioned in subsection (3) of that section.

(4) It does include a sum treated as a capital sum by subsection (5) below.

(5) Any sum which—

(a) is paid by the trustees of a settlement to a third party—

(i) at the settlor's direction, or

(ii) as a result of the assignment by the settlor of the settlor's right to receive the sum, or

(b) is otherwise paid, or applied by, the trustees for the benefit of the settlor,

is treated as a capital sum paid to the settlor by the trustees.

(6) Subsection (5) does not apply to any sum which would, apart from that subsection, be treated as a capital sum paid to the settlor.

(7) References in sections 633 to 638 to sums paid to the settlor include references to sums paid to—

(a) the spouse [or civil partner][1] of the settlor, or

(b) the settlor (or the spouse [or civil partner][1] of the settlor) jointly with another person.

Commentary—*Simon's Taxes* **C4.335, C4.338.**

HMRC Manuals—Company Taxation Manual CTM61100 (loans paid directly or indirectly).

Trusts, Settlements and Estates Manual TSEM4400 (capital sum: meaning).

Amendments—[1] Words in sub-s (7) inserted by the Tax and Civil Partnership Regulations, SI 2005/3229 regs 183, 194, with effect from 5 December 2005.

635 Amount of available income

(1) For the purposes of section 633 the amount of income available up to the end of any tax year is, in relation to any capital sum paid as mentioned in subsection (1) of that section by the trustees of a settlement, calculated as follows.

(2) Add together the amount of [unprotected][2] income arising under the settlement in that year and any previous year which has not been distributed.

(3) Deduct from that figure—

(a) the amount of that income taken into account under section 633 in relation to that sum in any previous year or years,

(b) the amount of that income taken into account under section 633 in relation to any other capital sums paid to the settlor in any year before that sum was paid,

(c) any income arising under the settlement in that year or any previous year which has been treated as income of the settlor under section 624 or 629, and

(d) an amount equal to the sum of tax at the [trust rate][1] on—

(i) the total amount of [unprotected][3] income arising under the settlement in that year and any previous year which has not been distributed, less

(ii) any income of the kind mentioned in paragraph (*c*).

(4) See sections 636 and 637 for how to calculate amounts of undistributed income.

[(5) In [this section and sections 636 and 637][3] "unprotected income" means income which is not protected foreign-source income, and sections 628A(2) to (13) and 628B (meaning of "protected foreign-source income") have effect also for this purpose.][2]

Commentary—*Simon's Taxes* **C4.337.**

HMRC Manuals—Company Taxation Manual CTM61150 (capital payments to settlors: available income).

Amendments—[1]   Words in sub-s (3) substituted by ITA 2007 s 1027, Sch 1 paras 492, 557 with effect for income tax purposes from 6 April 2007, and corporation tax purposes for accounting periods ending after 5 April 2007.

[2]   In sub-s (2), word inserted, and sub-s (5) inserted, by F(No 2)A 2017 s 29(2), Sch 8 paras 20, 24 with effect for the tax year 2017–18 and subsequent tax years.

[3]   In sub-s (3)(*d*)(i), word inserted, and words in sub-s (5) substituted, by FA 2018 s 35, Sch 10 para 8 with effect for the tax year 2018–19 and subsequent tax years.

636 Calculation of undistributed income

(1) For the purposes of section 635, [unprotected][3] income arising under a settlement in any tax year is treated as [unprotected][3] income which has not been distributed so far as it exceeds the total amount of—

    (*a*) the sums to which subsection (2) applies,

    (*b*) the expenses to which subsection (4) applies, and

    (*c*) if the trustees of the settlement are trustees for charitable purposes, the amount to which subsection (6) applies.

(2) This subsection applies to . . .[4] sums paid in the tax year to any persons by the trustees of the settlement [that are payments of unprotected income, or sums treated as representing unprotected income, and that][4]—

    (*a*) are treated in that year (otherwise than under section 633) as the income of those persons for income tax purposes, or

    (*b*) would be [treated as mentioned in paragraph (*a*)][4] if those persons were domiciled [and resident][2] in the United Kingdom and the sums had been paid to them there.

(3) Subsection (2) is subject to section 637(1).

(4) This subsection applies to any expenses of the trustees of the settlement paid in the tax year which, in the absence of any express provision of the settlement, would be properly chargeable to [unprotected][4] income.

(5) Subsection (4)—

    (*a*) does not apply to expenses so far as they are included in the sums mentioned in subsection (2), and

    (*b*) is subject to section 637(2) to (7).

(6) This subsection applies to the amount by which—

$$A > B$$

where—

    A is any [unprotected][4] income arising under the settlement in the tax year in respect of which exemption from tax may be granted under [any provision to which subsection (7) applies][1], and

    B is the total amount of any such sums or expenses as are mentioned in subsections (2) and (4) paid in that year which are properly chargeable to the income.

[(7) This subsection applies to the following provisions of ITA 2007—

    section 521(4) (gifts entitling donor to gift-aid relief),

    section 522(5) (gifts of money from companies),

    section 523(5) (payments from other charities),

    section 524 (profits etc of charitable trades),

    section 529 (profits from fund-raising events),

    section 530 (profits from lotteries),

    section 531 (property income etc),

    section 532 (savings and investment income),

    section 533 (public revenue dividends),

    section 536 (miscellaneous income), and

    section 537 (income from estates in administration).][1]

Commentary—*Simon's Taxes* **C4.337.**

HMRC Manuals—Company Taxation Manual CTM61150 (capital payments to settlors: available income).

Amendments—[1]   Words in sub-s (6) substituted, and sub-s (7) inserted, by ITA 2007 s 1027, Sch 1 paras 492, 558 with effect for income tax purposes from 6 April 2007, and corporation tax purposes for accounting periods ending after 5 April 2007.

[2]   Words in sub-s (2)(*b*) substituted for words ", resident and ordinarily resident" by FA 2013 s 219, Sch 46 paras 43, 48(1) with effect in calculating income arising under a settlement in tax years ending on or after 6 April 2013.

[3]   In sub-s (1), word inserted in both places by F(No 2)A 2017 s 29(2), Sch 8 paras 20, 25 with effect for the tax year 2017–18 and subsequent tax years.

[4]   In sub-s (2), words repealed and substituted, and words in sub-ss (4), (6) inserted, by FA 2018 s 35, Sch 10 para 9 with effect for the tax year 2018–19 and subsequent tax years.

637 Qualifications to section 636

(1) Section 636(2) does not apply—

    (a) to any interest paid by the trustees of the settlement, or

    (b) to any sums paid to—

       (i) a body corporate connected with the settlement, or

       (ii) the trustees of another settlement made by the settlor or by the trustees of the settlement.

(2) Section 636(4) applies to any [relevant][2] interest paid by the trustees of the settlement subject to subsections (3) to (7).

(3) The whole of any [relevant][2] interest paid by the trustees of the settlement is excluded from subsection (4) of section 636 if no sums within subsection (2) of that section were paid to any person other than the settlor or the spouse [or civil partner][1] of the settlor.

(4) If any sum within section 636(2) was so paid, the relevant fraction of any [relevant][2] interest paid by the trustees of the settlement is excluded from section 636(4).

(5) The relevant fraction is—

$$\frac{A - B}{A}$$

where—

    A is the whole of the [unprotected][2] income arising under the settlement in the tax year, less the sums referred to in subsection (4) of section 636 apart from subsections (2), (3) and (6) of this section, and

    B is so much of the sums within subsection (2) of that section as is paid to persons other than the settlor or the spouse [or civil partner][1] of the settlor.

(6) Subsections (2) to (5) do not apply to—

    (a) interest in respect of which relief from tax is allowable under any provision of the Income Tax Acts, or

    (b) interest payable to the settlor or the spouse [or civil partner][1] of the settlor if living with the settlor.

(7) Nothing in subsections (2) to (6) affects the liability to tax of the person receiving or entitled to the interest.

[(7A) In this section "relevant interest" means interest which, in the absence of any express provision of the settlement, would be properly chargeable to unprotected income.][2]

(8) For the purposes of this Chapter, a body corporate is treated as connected with a settlement in any tax year if at any time in that year—

    (a) it is a close company (or only is not a close company because it is non-UK resident) and the participators then include the trustees of the settlement, or

    (b) it is controlled by a company falling within paragraph (a).

Commentary—*Simon's Taxes* **C4.337, C4.339.**

Amendments—[1]   Words in sub-ss (3), (5), (6)(b) inserted by Tax and Civil Partnership Regulations, SI 2005/3229, regs 183, 195, with effect from 5 December 2005 (reg 1(1)).

[2]   Words in sub-ss (2), (3), (4), (5) inserted, and sub-s (7A) inserted, by FA 2018 s 35, Sch 10 paras 3, 10 with effect for the tax year 2018–19 and subsequent tax years.

Trustees' payments: further provisions

638 Capital sums paid by way of loan or repayment of loan

(1) No part of a capital sum which is paid to a settlor by way of loan is treated under section 633 as the settlor's income for any tax year after the tax year in which the whole of the sum is repaid.

(2) Subsection (3) applies if—

    (a) a capital sum is paid to the settlor by way of loan, and

    (b) one or more capital sums have previously been paid to the settlor by way of loan and wholly repaid.

(3) The amount of the capital sum mentioned in subsection (2)(a) is treated for the purposes of section 633 as equal to the amount (if any) by which it exceeds so much of the capital sum or sums previously paid as has already been treated as the settlor's income under that section.

(4) Subsection (5) applies if—

    (a) a capital sum is paid to the settlor by way of complete repayment of a loan, and

    (b) an amount not less than the capital sum is subsequently lent by the settlor to the trustees of the settlement.

(5) No part of the capital sum is treated under section 633 as the settlor's income for any tax year after that in which the further loan is made.

Commentary—*Simon's Taxes* **C4.338.**

HMRC Manuals—Company Taxation Manual CTM1130 (capital payment to settlors: interaction).

639 Loans to participators in close companies

(1) This section applies if any amount has been included in a person's income under Chapter 6 of Part 4 (release of loan to participator in close company) in respect of any loan or advance.

(2) There is a corresponding reduction in the amount (if any) afterwards falling to be so included under section 633 in respect of the loan or advance.

Commentary—*Simon's Taxes* **C4.336.**
HMRC Manuals—Company Taxation Manual CTM61505 (loans to participators: general).

640 Grossing-up of deemed income

(1) The whole or any part of a capital sum which is treated under section 633 as income of the settlor for any tax year is treated as income of an amount equal to the sum or the part of the sum, grossed up by reference to the [trust rate]¹ for that year.

(2) The deductible amount is to be set off against the amount of tax charged on any amount treated under section 633 as income of the settlor for any year.

(3) In subsection (2) the "deductible amount" is an amount equal to—

    (*a*) tax at the [trust rate]¹ for the year on the amount treated under section 633 as the settlor's income,

    (*b*) so much of the amount of tax at that rate as is equal to the tax charged, or

    (*c*) the amount of tax paid by the trustees on the grossed-up amount of so much of the amount of income available up to the end of the year, in relation to the capital sum, as is taken into account under section 633 in relation to that sum in that year (see subsections (4) to (7) below),

whichever is the least.

(4) For the purposes of subsection (3)(*c*)—

    (*a*) any reduction falling to be made under section 635(3)(*d*) is treated as made against income arising under the settlement in an earlier tax year before income arising under the settlement in a later tax year, and

    (*b*) income arising under the settlement in an earlier tax year is treated as taken into account under section 633 before income arising under the settlement in a later tax year.

(5) For the purposes of subsection (3)(*c*)—

    (*a*) the grossed-up amount of any sum is an amount equal to the sum, grossed up by reference to the appropriate rate for each part of the sum, and

    (*b*) the amount of tax paid by the trustees on that grossed-up amount is the difference between the grossed-up amount and the sum in question.

(6) For the purposes of subsection (5)—

    (*a*) the appropriate rate for any part of a sum is 0% if—

        (i) the income that falls to be treated in accordance with subsection (4) as representing that part of the sum is income from a source outside the United Kingdom, and

        (ii) the trustees were non-UK resident for the relevant tax year, and

    (*b*) the appropriate rate for any part of a sum in relation to which paragraph (*a*) does not apply is—

        (i) 34%, if the relevant tax year is the year 2003–04 or any earlier tax year, . . . ²

        (ii) 40%, if the relevant tax year is the year 2004–05 or any subsequent tax year [up to and including the year 2009–2010, . . . ³

        (iii) 50%, if the relevant tax year is the year 2010–2011[, 2011–12 or 2012–13]³]²

        [(iv) 45%, if the relevant year is the year 2013–14 or any subsequent tax year.]³

(7) In subsection (6) "the relevant tax year", in relation to any part of a sum, means the tax year in which the income treated in accordance with subsection (4) as representing that part of the sum arose under the settlement.

Commentary—*Simon's Taxes* **C4.340.**
HMRC Manuals—Company Taxation Manual CTM61150 (capital payment to settlors: grossing up of income).
CTM61130 (capital payment to settlors: the loan amount grossed at the aggregate of the basic and additional rates).
Amendments—¹   Words in sub-ss (1), (3) substituted by ITA 2007 s 1027, Sch 1 paras 492, 559 with effect for income tax purposes from 6 April 2007, and corporation tax purposes for accounting periods ending after 5 April 2007.
²   In sub-s (6)(*b*), word at end of sub-para (i) repealed, words at end of sub-para (ii) and whole of sub-para (iii) inserted, by FA 2009 s 6, Sch 2 paras 19, 20 with effect for the tax year 2010–11 and subsequent tax years. The powers conferred by the amendments made by FA 2009 Sch 2 may be exercised at any time on or after 21 July 2009 but not so as to make provision having effect before the tax year 2010–11 (FA 2009 Sch 2 para 25(1)).
³   In sub-s (6)(*b*), word "and" at end of sub-para (ii) repealed, in sub-para (iii), words substituted for words "or any subsequent tax year.", and sub-para (iv) inserted, by FA 2012 s 1(5) with effect for the tax year 2013–14 and subsequent tax years.

Capital sums treated as income of settlor: connected bodies

641 Capital sums paid to settlor by body connected with settlement

(1) This section applies if—

    (*a*) a capital sum is paid to the settlor in a tax year by any body corporate connected with the settlement in that year, and

ITTOIA 2005

(b) an associated payment has been, or is, made directly or indirectly to the body by the trustees of the settlement.

(2) The capital sum is, in accordance with this section, treated for the purposes of section 633 as having been paid to the settlor by the trustees of the settlement.

(3) A capital sum to which subsection (2) applies is treated as having been paid to the settlor in the tax year in which it is paid so far as the amount of the sum falls within the total of the associated payment or payments made up to the end of the year.

(4) A capital sum to which subsection (2) applies is treated as having been paid to the settlor in the following year so far as the amount of the sum—

(a) is not treated as paid to the settlor in the year mentioned in subsection (3), and

(b) falls within the total of the associated payment or payments made up to the end of the following year (less what was taken into account under subsection (3) in relation to the sum in the previous year).

(5) Subsection (4) also applies for each subsequent year.

(6) In its application to a subsequent year—

(a) the references to the following year are to the subsequent year,

(b) the reference to the year mentioned in subsection (3) is to that year and any other year before the subsequent year, and

(c) the reference to what was taken into account under subsection (3) in relation to the sum in the previous year is to what was taken into account under this section in relation to the sum in the previous years.

(7) See also—

section 642 (exception for certain loans or repayments of loans), and

section 643 (interpretation of sections 641 and 642).

Commentary—*Simon's Taxes* **C4.338, C4.339.**
HMRC Manuals—Company Taxation Manual CTM61060 (interposition between settlor and trustee).
CTM61090 (exception for certain loans or repayments of loans).
Trusts, Settlements and Estates Manual TSEM4405 (outline of capital sums paid to settlor).
TSEM4410 (instructions on capital sums paid to settlor).
Savings and Investment Manual SAIM1070 (priority of trading and other income over savings and investment income).
SAIM5060 (UK dividends taxed as trading income).

642 Exception for certain loans or repayments of loans

(1) Section 641 does not apply to any sum paid to the settlor by way of loan or repayment of a loan if conditions A and B are met.

(2) Condition A is that the whole of the loan is repaid within 12 months of the date on which it was made.

(3) Condition B is that the period for which amounts are outstanding in respect of relevant loans in any period of 5 years is not more than 12 months.

(4) In subsection (3) "relevant loans" means loans made—

(a) to the settlor by the body corporate connected with the settlement or by any other body corporate so connected, or

(b) by the settlor to the body corporate connected with the settlement or to any other body corporate so connected.

Commentary—*Simon's Taxes* **C4.339.**
HMRC Manuals—Company Taxation Manual CTM61090 (capital payments to settlors: temporary loans).

643 Interpretation of sections 641 and 642

(1) Any question in section 641 or 642 whether a capital sum has been paid—

(a) to the settlor by a body corporate, or

(b) to a body corporate by the trustees,

is determined in the same way as any question under section 633 whether a capital sum has been paid to the settlor by the trustees.

(2) For the circumstances in which a body corporate is treated for the purposes of this Chapter as connected with a settlement, see section 637(8).

(3) In section 641 and this section "associated payment", in relation to any capital sum paid to the settlor by a body corporate, means—

(a) any capital sum paid to the body by the trustees of the settlement, and

(b) any other sum paid, or asset transferred, to the body by the trustees which is not paid or transferred for full consideration in money or money's worth,

being any sum paid, or asset transferred, in the 5 years ending or beginning with the date on which the capital sum is paid to the settlor.

(4) For the purposes of sections 641 and 642 and this section any capital sum paid by a body corporate, and any associated payment made to a body corporate, at a time when it is (within the meaning of [section 449 of CTA 2010][1]) associated with another body corporate may be treated as paid by, or made to, the other body corporate.

Commentary—*Simon's Taxes* **C4.339.**

HMRC Manuals—Company Taxation Manual CTM61120 (capital payments to settlors: associated payments).
Amendments—[1] In sub-s (4) words substituted by CTA 2010 s 1177, Sch 1 paras 444, 470. CTA 2010 has effect for corporation tax purposes for accounting periods ending on or after 1 April 2010, and for income and capital gains tax purposes for the tax year 2010–11 and subsequent tax years.

[Benefits matched with protected foreign-source income

643A Deemed income because of benefits for settlor or close family member

(1) If an individual has an untaxed benefits total for a settlement for a tax year (see section 643B), an amount equal to so much of that total as does not exceed the settlement's available protected income up to the end of the year (see section 643C) is—

   (*a*) where the individual is UK resident for the year, treated for income tax purposes as income of the individual for the year, subject to subsections (2) to (5), and

   (*b*) where the individual is non-UK resident for the year, treated for the purposes of subsection (2) and sections 643I to 643L (but no other purpose) as income of the individual for the year, subject to subsection (5).

(2) Subsections (3) and (4) apply if—

   (*a*) an amount ("the deemed income") is treated by subsection (1), before the application of subsections (3) and (4), as income of an individual for a tax year,

   (*b*) the individual is not the settlor,

   (*c*) either—

      (i) the individual is non-UK resident for the year, or

      (ii) the individual is UK resident for the year and one of sections 809B, 809D and 809E of ITA 2007 (remittance basis) applies to the individual for the year,

   (*d*) the settlor is UK resident for the year,

   (*e*) there is no time in the year when the settlor is domiciled in the United Kingdom, and

   (*f*) there is no time in the year when the settlor is regarded for the purposes of section 809B(1)(*b*) of ITA 2007 as domiciled in the United Kingdom as a result of section 835BA of ITA 2007 having effect because of Condition A in that section being met.

(3) If the case is one—

   (*a*) where the condition in subsection (2)(*c*)(i) is met, or

   (*b*) where the condition in subsection (2)(*c*)(ii) is met and none of the deemed income is remitted to the United Kingdom in the year,

the deemed income is to be treated for income tax purposes as income of the settlor for the year and, in a case within paragraph (*b*), not as income of the individual for the year.

(4) If the case is one—

   (*a*) where the condition in subsection (2)(*c*)(ii) is met, and

   (*b*) part only of the deemed income is remitted to the United Kingdom in the year,

the remainder of the deemed income is to be treated for income tax purposes not as income of the individual for the year but as income of the settlor for the year.

(5) If there is a choice about the individuals in whose case income is to be treated as arising by subsection (1) (before the application of subsections (3) and (4))—

   (*a*) income is to be treated as arising to such one or more of them as appears to an officer of Revenue and Customs to be just and reasonable, and

   (*b*) if more than one, in such respective proportions as appears to the officer to be just and reasonable.

(6) Sections 809L to 809Z6 of ITA 2007 (remittance basis: rules about when income is remitted) apply for the purposes of this section.

(7) If—

   (*a*) an enactment other than this section contains a reference (however expressed) to—

      (i) income treated as arising by this section, or

      (ii) an amount treated as income by this section, and

   (*b*) the reference mentions this section without mentioning any particular provision of this section,

the reference is (in accordance with subsection (1)(*b*)) to be read as not including amounts treated as income by subsection (1)(*b*) except so far as they are treated as income of the settlor of a settlement by subsection (3) or (4).][1]

Amendments—[1] Sections 643A–643H inserted by FA 2018 s 35, Sch 10 paras 3, 11 with effect for the tax year 2018–19 and subsequent tax years.

[643B Meaning of "untaxed benefits total" in section 643A

(1) For the purposes of section 643A, whether an individual has an untaxed benefits total for a settlement for a tax year ("the current year"), and (if so) its amount, are determined as follows—

Step 1

If the individual is the settlor, identify each benefit provided by the trustees to the individual at a time—

   (*a*) when the individual is not relevantly domiciled, and

(b) in a tax year that is the current year or an earlier tax year.
If the individual is not the settlor, identify each benefit provided by the trustees to the individual at a time—

(a) when the individual is a close member of the settlor's family (see section 643H), and

(b) in a tax year that is the current year or an earlier tax year.

Step 2
Identify the amount or value of each benefit identified in the individual's case at Step 1, and calculate the total of those amounts and values.

Step 3
Take the total calculated at Step 2 and deduct from it the following—

(a) any part of it on which the individual is liable to income tax otherwise than under section 643A,

(b) any income treated by section 643A, 643J or 643L as arising, to a person for a tax year earlier than the current year, by reference to any of the benefits identified in the individual's case at Step 1,

(c) where the whole or part of a benefit identified in the individual's case at Step 1 is taken into account in charging income tax under Chapter 2 of Part 13 of ITA 2007, the amount or value of so much of the benefit as is taken into account in doing that, and

(d) any amount required to be deducted by section 643D(2) (gains treated as accruing in a year before the current year).

Step 4
If the result of the calculation at Step 3 is an amount greater than nil, that amount is the individual's untaxed benefits total for the settlement for the current year.

(2) For the purposes of Step 1 in subsection (1), an individual is "relevantly domiciled" at any time if at that time—

(a) the individual is domiciled in the United Kingdom, or

(b) the individual is regarded for the purposes of section 809(1)(b) of ITA 2007 as domiciled in the United Kingdom as a result of section 835BA of ITA 2007 having effect because of Condition A in that section being met.

(3) Sections 742C to 742E of ITA 2007 (value of certain benefits) apply for the purpose of calculating the value of a benefit for the purposes of this section as they apply for the purpose of calculating an income tax charge under Chapter 2 of Part 13 of ITA 2007.

(4) In this section and sections 643C to 643M, a reference to a benefit provided by trustees of a settlement is to—

(a) a benefit treated by subsection (6) as provided by the trustees, or

(b) any other benefit if it is provided by the trustees directly, or indirectly, out of—

(i) property comprised in the settlement, or

(ii) income arising under the settlement.

(5) In this section and sections 643C to 643M, a reference to a benefit provided by trustees of a settlement to an individual is to—

(a) a benefit treated by subsection (6) as provided by the trustees to the individual, or

(b) any other benefit if it is provided by the trustees to the individual directly, or indirectly, out of—

(i) property comprised in the settlement, or

(ii) income arising under the settlement.

(6) Where—

(a) income arises under a settlement, and

(b) the income, before being distributed, is the income of a person other than the trustees,

a benefit is for the purposes of subsection (4)(a) treated as provided by the trustees and is for the purposes of subsection (5)(a) treated as provided by the trustees to the person.

(7) A benefit treated as provided by subsection (6) is treated—

(a) as consisting of the income mentioned in that subsection, but after any reduction in accordance with Chapter 8 of Part 9 of ITA 2007 for trustees' expenses, and

(b) as provided at the time that income arises.][1]

Amendments—[1] Sections 643A–643H inserted by FA 2018 s 35, Sch 10 paras 3, 11 with effect for the tax year 2018–19 and subsequent tax years. None of the references to an earlier tax year in Step 1 includes any tax year earlier than the tax year 2018–19 except that, in the phrase "benefits provided by the trustees in the year or in an earlier tax year" in the definition of "TOAA" in ITTOIA 2005 s 643C(2), the reference to an earlier tax year does include tax years earlier than the tax year 2018–19 (FA 2018 Sch 10 para 21(2)).

[643C Meaning of "available protected income" in section 643A

(1) For the purposes of the application of section 643A(1) in the case of an individual and a settlement, the settlement has available protected income up to the end of a tax year if—

PFSI − TOAA > TI

and, if the settlement has available protected income up to the end of a tax year, its amount is given by—

PFSI – TOAA – TI

(2) In this section—

    PFSI is the total of—

      (*a*) any protected foreign-source income—

          (i) arising under the settlement in the year or in any earlier tax year,

          (ii) that would be treated under section 624 as income of the settlor but for section 628A,

          (iii) that can be used directly or indirectly to provide benefits for the individual, and

          (iv) on which the individual is not liable to income tax (ignoring for this purpose any liability under section 643A), and

      (*b*) any protected foreign-source income—

          (i) arising under the settlement in the year or in any earlier tax year,

          (ii) that would be treated under section 629 as income of the settlor but for section 630A, and

          (iii) on which the relevant child concerned (see section 629) is not liable to income tax (ignoring for this purpose any liability under section 643A),

    TOAA is so much of PFSI as is, in respect of benefits provided by the trustees in the year or in an earlier tax year, taken into account in charging income tax under Chapter 2 of Part 13 of ITA 2007 (transfer of assets abroad) for the year or any earlier tax year, and

    TI is the total of—

      (*a*) so much of PFSI as is, by reference to benefits provided by the trustees to the individual, treated by section 643A, 643J or 643L as income for any earlier tax year, and

      (*b*) so much of PFSI as is, by reference to benefits provided by the trustees to other individuals, treated by section 643A, 643J or 643L as income for the year or any earlier tax year.

(3) As regards the definition of PFSI in subsection (2)—

      (*a*) section 648(3) to (5) (relevant foreign income treated as arising under settlement only if and when remitted) do not apply for the purposes of that definition,

      (*b*) that definition has effect as if section 648(3) to (5) do not apply for the purposes of sections 624 and 629, and

      (*c*) in that definition "protected foreign-source income" has the meaning given by sections 628A(2) to (13) and 628B.][1]

Amendments—[1]   Sections 643A–643H inserted by FA 2018 s 35, Sch 10 paras 3, 11 with effect for the tax year 2018–19 and subsequent tax years. None of the references to an earlier tax year in Step 1 of ITTOIA 2005 s 643B(1), or in sub-s (2), includes any tax year earlier than the tax year 2018–19 except that, in the phrase "benefits provided by the trustees in the year or in an earlier tax year" in the definition of "TOAA" in sub-s (2), the reference to an earlier tax year does include tax years earlier than the tax year 2018–19 (FA 2018 Sch 10 para 21(2)).

[643D Reduction in section 643A income: previous capital gains tax charge

(1) Subsection (2) applies if—

      (*a*) in the case of a settlement, benefits provided to an individual as mentioned at Step 1 in section 643B(1) are received in a tax year, and

      (*b*) chargeable gains are treated by section 87, 87K, 87L or 89(2) of, or paragraph 8 of Schedule 4C to, TCGA 1992 as accruing to a person in that or a subsequent tax year by reference (direct or indirect) to the whole or part of any benefits so provided.

(2) In the calculation under section 643B of the individual's untaxed benefits total for the settlement for any tax year after the one in which such chargeable gains are so treated, the amounts to be deducted at Step 3(*d*) of that calculation include the amount of those gains.

(3) References in this section to chargeable gains treated as accruing to an individual include offshore gains treated as arising to the individual (see regulations 20 and 22 to 24 of the Offshore Funds (Tax) Regulations 2009 (S.I. 2009/3001)).][1]

Amendments—[1]   Sections 643A–643H inserted by FA 2018 s 35, Sch 10 paras 3, 11 with effect for the tax year 2018–19 and subsequent tax years. Subsection (3) is to be treated as inserted by the Treasury under the powers to make regulations conferred by TIOPA 2010 s 354 (FA 2018 Sch 10 para 22).

[643E Reimbursement of tax paid by settlor because of section 643A

(1) Where any tax for which the settlor of a settlement is liable as a result of section 643A(3) or (4) is paid, the settlor is entitled to recover the amount of the tax from the individual concerned.

(2) For the purpose of recovering that amount, the settlor is entitled to require an officer of Revenue and Customs to give the settlor a certificate specifying—

      (*a*) the amount of the income concerned, and

      (*b*) the amount of tax paid,

and any such certificate is conclusive evidence of the facts stated in it.][1]

Amendments—[1]   Sections 643A–643H inserted by FA 2018 s 35, Sch 10 paras 3, 11 with effect for the tax year 2018–19 and subsequent tax years.

[643F Income attributed by section 643A to user of remittance basis

(1) This section applies where—

    (*a*) in the case of a settlement, income ("the deemed income") is treated by section 643A as arising to an individual for a tax year, and

    (*b*) section 809B, 809D or 809E of ITA 2007 (remittance basis) applies to the individual for that year.

(2) The deemed income is treated as relevant foreign income of the individual.

(3) In the application of section 832 to the deemed income, subsection (2) of that section has effect with the omission of paragraph (*b*).

(4) For the purposes of Chapter A1 of Part 14 of ITA 2007 (remittance basis) treat a benefit, or any protected income, that relates to any part of the deemed income as deriving from that part of the deemed income.

(5) In subsection (4)—

    "relates" has the meaning given by section 643G.

(6) In this section and section 643G—

    "protected income" means the income that forms PFSI in the calculation of the settlement's available protected income in the case of the relevant individual for the year, and "the relevant individual"—

        (*a*) where the deemed income is treated as income of an individual by section 643A(1)(*a*) both before and after the application of section 643A(3) and (4), means that individual, and

        (*b*) where the deemed income is treated as income of the settlor by section 643A(3) or (4) after having been treated as income of another individual by section 643A(1), means that other individual.][1]

Amendments—[1] Sections 643A–643H inserted by FA 2018 s 35, Sch 10 paras 3, 11 with effect for the tax year 2018–19 and subsequent tax years.

[643G Section 643F(4): benefits and income "relating" to deemed income

(1) In this section—

    (*a*) references to a step are to a step under section 643B(1) as it applies in the case of the settlement, the year and the relevant individual,

    (*b*) "protected income" and "the relevant individual" have the meaning given by section 643F(6), and

    (*c*) "the settlement" and "the year" mean, respectively, the settlement and tax year mentioned in section 643F.

(2) For the purposes of section 643F(4)—

    (*a*) place the benefits identified at Step 1 in the order in which they were received by the relevant individual (starting with the earliest benefit received),

    (*b*) where a deduction is allowed by any of paragraphs (*a*), (*c*) and (*d*) of Step 3 by reference to the whole or part of any of those benefits, reduce the benefit by the amount of the deduction,

    (*c*) place the protected income in the order in which it arose (starting with the earliest income to arise),

    (*d*) where the whole or part of an item of the protected income is, in respect of benefits provided by the trustees in the year or in any earlier tax year, taken into account in charging income tax under Chapter 2 of Part 13 of ITA 2007 (transfer of assets abroad) for the year or any earlier tax year, reduce the item by so much of itself as is so taken into account,

    (*e*) where the whole or part of an item of the protected income is, by reference to benefits provided by the trustees to individuals other than the relevant individual, treated by section 643A or 643J or 643L as income for the year or any earlier tax year, reduce the item by so much of itself as is so treated,

    (*f*) place the income treated by section 643A(1) (before the application of section 643A(3) and (4)) as arising to the relevant individual in respect of the benefits referred to in paragraph (*a*) in the order in which it is treated as arising (starting with the earliest income treated as having arisen), and

    (*g*) treat the income mentioned in paragraph (*f*) as related to—

        (i) the benefits referred to in paragraph (*a*), and

        (ii) the protected income,

    by matching the income mentioned in paragraph (*f*) with those benefits and the protected income (in the orders mentioned in paragraphs (*a*), (*c*) and (*f*)).

(3) For the purposes of subsection (2)(*d*), the whole or part of an item of the protected income is to be treated as taken into account in respect of a benefit so far as the item or part—

    (*a*) is matched under section 735A of ITA 2007 with notional income with which the benefit is matched under that section, or (*b*) would be matched under that section (if it applied also for this purpose) with notional income with which the benefit would be matched under that section (if it applied also for this purpose),

and here "notional income" means income which is treated as arising under section 732 of ITA 2007.]¹

Amendments—¹   Sections 643A–643H inserted by FA 2018 s 35, Sch 10 paras 3, 11 with effect for the tax year 2018–19 and subsequent tax years.

[643H   Meaning of close member of settlor's family in sections 643B to 643M

(1) For the purposes of sections 643B to 643M, a person is a close member of the family of the settlor of a settlement at any time if the settlor is living at that time and—

    (*a*) the person is the settlor's spouse or civil partner at that time, or

    (*b*) the person—

       (i)   is a child of the settlor, or of a person who at that time is the settlor's spouse or civil partner, and

       (ii)   at that time has not reached the age of 18.

[(2) For the purposes of subsection (1), two people living together as if they were a married couple or civil partners are treated as if they were spouses or civil partners of each other.²]¹

Amendments—¹   Sections 643A–643H inserted by FA 2018 s 35, Sch 10 paras 3, 11 with effect for the tax year 2018–19 and subsequent tax years.
²   Sub-s (2) substituted by the Civil Partnership (Opposite-sex Couples) Regulations, SI 2019/1458 reg 27 with effect from 2 December 2019.

[643I   Recipients of onward gifts

(1) Sections 643J to 643L apply if—

    (*a*) in the case of a settlement, an amount—

       (i)   is treated by section 643A(1)(*a*), both before and after the application of section 643A(3) and (4), as income of an individual ("the original beneficiary") for a tax year ("the matching year"), or

       (ii)   having been treated by section 643A(1) before the application of section 643A(3) and (4) as income of an individual ("the original beneficiary") for a tax year ("the matching year"), is treated by section 643A(3) or (4) as income of the settlor for the matching year, or

       (iii) is treated by section 643A(1)(*b*), before the application of section 643A(3) and (4), as income of an individual ("the original beneficiary") for a tax year ("the matching year") but is not treated by section 643A(3), and is not treated by section 643A(4), as income of the settlor for the matching year,

    (*b*) under section 643G (if it applied also for this purpose) the amount would be matched with a benefit provided in the matching year, or an earlier tax year, to the original beneficiary,

    (*c*) at the time the benefit is provided to the original beneficiary—

       (i)   there are arrangements, or there is an intention, as regards the (direct or indirect) passing-on of the whole, or part, of the benefit to another person, and

       (ii)   it is reasonable to expect that, in the event of the whole or part of the benefit being passed on to another person as envisaged by the arrangements or intention, that other person will be UK resident when they receive at least part of what is passed on to them,

    (*d*) the original beneficiary makes, directly or indirectly, a gift ("the onward payment") to a person ("the subsequent recipient")—

       (i)   at the time the benefit is provided to the original beneficiary, or at any later time in the 3 years beginning with the day containing the start time, or

       (ii)   at any time before the benefit is provided to the original beneficiary and, it is reasonable to assume, in anticipation of the benefit being provided,

    (*e*) the gift is of or includes—

       (i)   the whole or part of the benefit,

       (ii)   anything that (wholly or in part, and directly or indirectly) derives from, or represents, the whole or part of the benefit, or

       (iii) any other property, but only if the benefit is provided with a view to enabling or facilitating, or otherwise in connection with, the making of the gift of the property to the subsequent recipient,

    (*f*) in a case within paragraph (*a*)(i), either—

       (i)   the original beneficiary is non-UK resident for the matching year, or

       (ii)   section 809B, 809D or 809E of ITA 2007 (remittance basis) applies to the original beneficiary for the matching year and none of the amount is relevantly remitted in the matching year or in any tax year later than the matching year but not later than the tax year in which the onward payment is made,

(g) in a case within paragraph (a)(ii), section 809B, 809D or 809E of ITA 2007 (remittance basis) applies to the settlor for the matching year and none of the amount is relevantly remitted in the matching year or in any tax year later than the matching year but not later than the tax year in which the onward payment is made, and

(h) the subsequent recipient—
   (i) is the settlor, or
   (ii) is a close member of the settlor's family (see section 643H) at the time the onward payment is made or, where that time is given by subsection (4), at either or both of the time so given and the actual time the onward payment is made.

(2) Where, in a case within subsection (1)(a)(i) and by reference to the amount mentioned in subsection (1)(a), income is treated by section 643J or 643L as arising to a person for a tax year, the original beneficiary is not liable to tax for any later tax year on so much of the amount mentioned in subsection (1)(a) as is equal to that income; and where, in a case within subsection (1)(a)(ii) and by reference to the amount mentioned in subsection (1)(a), income is treated by section 643J as arising to a person for a tax year, the settlor is not liable to tax for any later tax year on so much of the amount mentioned in subsection (1)(a) as is equal to that income.

(3) The amount mentioned in subsection (1)(a) need not be—
   (a) the whole amount that in the case of the settlement is treated by section 643A(1), before the application of section 643A(3) and (4), as income of the original beneficiary for the matching year;
   (b) the whole amount that would be matched with the benefit mentioned in subsection (1)(b).

(4) Where the onward payment is made as mentioned in subsection (1)(d)(ii), the onward payment is to be treated—
   (a) for the purposes of the provisions of this section following subsection (1)(d), and
   (b) for the purposes of sections 643J to 643L,
as made immediately after, and in the tax year in which, the benefit is provided to the original beneficiary.

(5) For the purposes of subsection (1)(d)(i)—
   (a) if the amount mentioned in subsection (1)(a) is not one that is treated as arising by section 643K, "the start time"—
      (i) is the time the benefit mentioned in subsection (1)(b) is provided to the original beneficiary, or
      (ii) where that benefit is one that section 643M(3) treats as provided, is the time the original benefit in that case (see section 643M(1)(a)) is provided, and
   (b) if the amount mentioned in subsection (1)(a) is one that is treated as arising by section 643K in connection with the operation of this section and section 643K on a previous occasion, "the start time" is the time given by this subsection as the start time on that occasion.

(6) Where subsection (1)(d) and (e) are met in any case, it is to be presumed (unless the contrary is shown) that subsection (1)(c) is also met in that case.

(7) In this section (and sections 643J to 643L)—
   "arrangements" includes any agreement, understanding, scheme, transaction or series of transactions (whether or not legally enforceable),
   "the charging year" means the gift year or, if later, the matching year,
   "gift" includes any benefit,
   "the gift year" means the tax year in which the onward payment is made (but see subsection (4)),
   "make", in relation to a gift that is a benefit, means confer, and
   "relevantly remitted" means remitted to the United Kingdom in a tax year for which the original beneficiary is UK resident but, in a case within subsection (1)(a)(ii), means remitted to the United Kingdom in a tax year for which the settlor is UK resident.

(8) Sections 742C to 742E of ITA 2007 (value of certain benefits)—
   (a) apply for the purpose of calculating the value of the onward payment for the purposes of sections 643J to 643L as they apply for the purpose of calculating an income tax charge under Chapter 2 of Part 13 of ITA 2007, and
   (b) apply for that purpose as if their references to a benefit provided were references to a gift made.

(9) Sections 809L to 809Z6 of ITA 2007 (remittance basis: rules about when income is remitted)—
   (a) apply for the purposes of this section and sections 643J to 643L, and
   (b) apply for those purposes in relation to references to remittance of the onward payment as if the onward payment were relevant foreign income of the subsequent recipient.][1]

Amendments—[1] Sections 643I–643L and 643N inserted by FA 2018 s 35, Sch 10 paras 3, 11 with effect only in relation to onward payments made on or after 6 April 2018.

[643J Cases where income treated as arising to recipient of onward gift

(1) Subsection (3) applies if—
   (a) this section applies (see section 643I(1)), and

(b) the subsequent recipient is UK resident for the gift year, and

(c) the subsequent recipient is UK resident for the matching year if that is later than the gift year, and

(d) none of sections 809B, 809D and 809E of ITA 2007 (remittance basis) applies to the subsequent recipient for the charging year.

(2) Subsection (3) also applies if—

  (a) this section applies (see section 643I(1)), and

  (b) the subsequent recipient is UK resident for the gift year, and

  (c) the subsequent recipient is UK resident for the matching year if that is later than the gift year, and

  (d) section 809B, 809D or 809E of ITA 2007 applies to the subsequent recipient for the charging year, and

  (e) the whole, or part only, of the onward payment is remitted to the United Kingdom in the charging year.

(3) For income tax purposes, an amount of income—

  (a) equal to the amount or value of so much of the onward payment as is within any of sub-paragraphs (i) to (iii) of section 643I(1)(e), or

  (b) where this subsection applies because of subsection (2) and part only of that much of the onward payment is remitted to the United Kingdom in the charging year, equal to the amount or value of that part,

is treated as income of the subsequent recipient for the charging year, subject to subsection (4).

(4) The amount given by subsection (3) (before adjustment under this subsection) is to be adjusted as follows—

  (a) deduct any part of the amount on which the subsequent recipient is liable to income tax otherwise than under this section, and

  (b) if following any adjustment under paragraph (a) the amount exceeds the amount mentioned in section 643I(1)(a), deduct the excess.][1]

Amendments—[1]   Sections 643I–643L and 643N inserted by FA 2018 s 35, Sch 10 paras 3, 11 with effect only in relation to onward payments made on or after 6 April 2018.

[643K Cases where deemed income attributed to recipient of onward gift

(1) Subsection (3) applies if this section applies (see section 643I(1)) and—

  (a) the subsequent recipient is non-UK resident for the gift year, or

  (b) the matching year is later than the gift year and the subsequent recipient is UK resident for the gift year but non-UK resident for the matching year.

(2) Subsection (3) also applies if—

  (a) this section applies (see section 643I(1)), and

  (b) the subsequent recipient is UK resident for the gift year, and

  (c) the subsequent recipient is UK resident for the matching year if that is later than the gift year, and

  (d) section 809B, 809D or 809E of ITA 2007 applies to the subsequent recipient for the charging year, and

  (e) none, or part only, of the onward payment is remitted to the United Kingdom in the charging year.

(3) Section 643I(1)(a) has effect—

  (a) as if the subsequent recipient were an individual to whom, in the case of the settlement, income is treated by section 643A(1)(a), both before and after the application of section 643A(3) and (4), as arising for the charging year, and

  (b) as if, subject to subsection (4), the amount of that income—

    (i) were equal to the amount or value of so much of the onward payment as is within any of sub-paragraphs (i) to (iii) of section 643I(1)(e) and is not treated as arising to the settlor as a result of the operation of section 643L, or

    (ii) were, where this subsection applies because of subsection (2) and part only of that much of the onward payment is remitted to the United Kingdom in the charging year, equal to the amount or value of the remainder of that much of the onward payment.

(4) The amount given by subsection (3) (before adjustment under this subsection) is to be adjusted as follows: if that amount exceeds the amount mentioned in section 643I(1)(a) in the case of the original beneficiary, deduct the excess.

(5) Where the amount mentioned in section 643I(1)(a) is treated as arising by this section in connection with the operation of section 643I and this section on a previous occasion, section 643I(1) has effect—

  (a) with the omission of its paragraphs (b) and (c),

  (b) as if the references in its paragraph (d) to the benefit mentioned in its paragraph (b) were, instead, to what was the onward payment on that previous occasion,

  (c) as if the references in its paragraph (d) to when that benefit is provided were, instead, to when that onward payment was made, and (*d*) as if the references in its paragraph (*e*) to that benefit were, instead, to so much of that onward payment as was on that previous occasion within any of sub-paragraphs (i) to (iii) of that paragraph.][1]

Amendments—[1] Sections 643I–643L and 643N inserted by FA 2018 s 35, Sch 10 paras 3, 11 with effect only in relation to onward payments made on or after 6 April 2018.

[643L Cases where settlor liable following onward gift

(1) Subsection (3) applies if—

(*a*) this section applies (see section 643I(1)),

(*b*) the subsequent recipient is a close member of the settlor's family (see section 643H) when the onward payment is made,

(*c*) the subsequent recipient is UK resident for the charging year,

(*d*) section 809B, 809D or 809E of ITA 2007 applies to the subsequent recipient for the charging year,

(*e*) none, or part only, of the onward payment is remitted to the United Kingdom in the charging year,

(*f*) there is a time in the charging year when the settlor is UK resident,

(*g*) there is no time in the charging year when the settlor is domiciled in the United Kingdom, and

(*h*) there is no time in the charging year when the settlor is regarded for the purposes of section 809B(1)(*b*) of ITA 2007 as domiciled in the United Kingdom as a result of section 835BA of ITA 2007 having effect because of Condition A in that section being met.

(2) Subsection (3) also applies if—

(*a*) this section applies (see section 643I(1)),

(*b*) the subsequent recipient is a close member of the settlor's family when the onward payment is made,

(*c*) the subsequent recipient is non-UK resident for the charging year,

(*d*) there is a time in the charging year when the settlor is UK resident,

(*e*) there is no time in the charging year when the settlor is domiciled in the United Kingdom, and

(*f*) there is no time in the charging year when the settlor is regarded for the purposes of section 809B(1)(*b*) of ITA 2007 as domiciled in the United Kingdom as a result of section 835BA of ITA 2007 having effect because of Condition A in that section being met.

(3) For income tax purposes, an amount of income—

(*a*) equal to the amount or value of so much of the onward payment as is within any of sub-paragraphs (i) to (iii) of section 643I(1)(*e*), or

(*b*) where this subsection applies because of subsection (1) in a case where part only of that much of the onward payment is remitted to the United Kingdom in the charging year, equal to the amount or value of the remainder of that much of the onward payment,

is treated as arising to the settlor for the charging year, subject to subsection (4).

(4) The amount given by subsection (3) (before adjustment under this subsection) is to be adjusted as follows—

(*a*) deduct any part of the amount on which the settlor is liable to income tax otherwise than under this section, and

(*b*) if following any adjustment under paragraph (*a*) the amount exceeds the amount mentioned in section 643I(1)(*a*), deduct the excess.

(5) Where any tax for which the settlor is liable as a result of subsections (3) and (4) is paid, the settlor is entitled to recover the amount of the tax from the subsequent recipient.

(6) For the purpose of recovering that amount, the settlor is entitled to require an officer of Revenue and Customs to give the settlor a certificate specifying—

(*a*) the amount of the income concerned, and

(*b*) the amount of tax paid,

and any such certificate is conclusive evidence of the facts stated in it.][1]

Amendments—[1] Sections 643I–643L and 643N inserted by FA 2018 s 35, Sch 10 paras 3, 11 with effect only in relation to onward payments made on or after 6 April 2018.

[643M Onward gift to settlor or close family member by other recipient

(1) Subsection (3) applies if—

(*a*) the trustees of a settlement provide a benefit ("the original benefit") to an individual ("the original recipient"),

(*b*) the original recipient is not the settlor,

(*c*) at the time the original benefit is provided, the original recipient is not a close member of the settlor's family (see section 643H),

(*d*) the original recipient is not taxed on the original benefit (see subsection (7)),

(*e*) at the time the original benefit is provided—

(i)   there are arrangements, or there is an intention, as regards the (direct or indirect) passing-on of the whole, or part, of the original benefit to another person, and

(ii) it is reasonable to expect that, in the event of the whole or part of the original benefit being passed on to another person as envisaged by the arrangements or intention, that other person will be UK resident when they receive at least part of what is passed on to them,

(*f*) the original recipient makes, directly or indirectly, a gift ("the onward payment") to a person ("the subsequent recipient")—

(i)   at the time the original benefit is provided to the original recipient, or at any later time in the 3 years beginning with the day containing that time, or

(ii) at any time before the original benefit is provided to the original recipient and, it is reasonable to assume, in anticipation of the original benefit being provided,

(*g*) the gift is of or includes—

(i)   the whole or part of the original benefit,

(ii) anything that (wholly or in part, and directly or indirectly) derives from, or represents, the whole or part of the original benefit, or

(iii) any other property, but only if the original benefit is provided with a view to enabling or facilitating, or otherwise in connection with, the making of the gift of the property to the subsequent recipient, and

(*h*) the subsequent recipient—

(i)   is the settlor, or

(ii) is a close member of the settlor's family at the time the onward payment is made or, where that time is given by subsection (4), at either or both of the time so given and the actual time the onward payment is made.

(2) Where—

(*a*) there is a series of two or more gifts,

(*b*) the first gift in the series is made, directly or indirectly, by the original recipient—

(i)   at the time the original benefit is provided, or at any later time in the 3 years beginning with the day containing that time, or

(ii) at any time before the original benefit is provided and, it is reasonable to assume, in anticipation of the original benefit being provided,

(*c*) the recipient of a gift in the series is the person who makes, directly or indirectly, the next gift in the series,

(*d*) the recipient of the last gift in the series is the settlor or, at the time that last gift is made, is a close member of the settlor's family,

(*e*) as regards any earlier gift in the series, its recipient—

(i)   is not the settlor, and

(ii) is not, at the time that earlier gift is made, a close member of the settlor's family, and

(*f*) the condition in subsection (1)(*g*) is met in relation to each gift in the series,

the last gift in the series is to be treated for the purposes of subsection (1)(*f*) as if its maker were the original recipient (and not its actual maker).

(3) So much of the onward payment as is within any of sub-paragraphs (i) to (iii) of subsection (1)(*g*) is treated for the purposes of Step 1 in section 643B(1) as a benefit provided by the trustees to the subsequent recipient at the time the onward payment is made.

(4) Where the onward payment is made as mentioned in subsection (1)(*f*)(ii), the onward payment is to be treated, for the purposes of subsections (1)(*h*) and (3), as made immediately after, and in the tax year in which, the original benefit is provided to the original recipient.

(5) Where subsection (1)(*f*) to (*h*) are met in any case, it is to be presumed (unless the contrary is shown) that subsection (1)(*e*) is also met in that case.

(6) Where the benefit mentioned in section 643I(1)(*b*) is one that subsection (3) of this section treats as provided, section 643I(1) has effect with the omission of its paragraph (*c*).

(7) For the purposes of subsection (1)(*d*), the original recipient is taxed on the original benefit if the original recipient is liable to income tax, or capital gains tax, by reference to the amount or value of the original benefit; and where the original recipient is so liable by reference to the amount or value of part only of the original benefit, this section applies as if the two parts of the original benefit were separate benefits.

(8) In this section—

"arrangements" includes any agreement, understanding, scheme, transaction or series of transactions (whether or not legally enforceable),

"gift" includes any benefit, and

"make", in relation to a gift that is a benefit, means confer,

and see also section 643B(4) to (7) (interpretation of references to provision of benefits by trustees).]¹

Amendments—[1]   Section 643M inserted by FA 2018 s 35, Sch 10 paras 3, 11 with effect only in relation to onward payments made on or after 6 April 2018. This section has effect in relation to an onward payment made on or after that date even where the onward payment is referable to a benefit received before that date (FA 2018 Sch 10 para 21(4)).

[643N Person liable under section 643J or 643L and remittance basis applies

(1) This section applies in relation to income if—

    (a) the income is treated as arising to an individual for a tax year—

        (i) by section 643J(3) and (4) where section 643J(3) applies because of section 643J(2), or

        (ii) by section 643L, and

    (b) section 809B, 809D or 809E of ITA 2007 (remittance basis) applies to the individual for that year.

(2) The income is treated as relevant foreign income of the individual.

(3) For the purposes of Chapter A1 of Part 14 of ITA 2007 (remittance basis) treat the onward payment, or (as the case may be) the part of it whose amount or value is equal to the amount of the income, as deriving from the income.

(4) In the application of section 832 in relation to the income, subsection (2) of that section has effect with the omission of its paragraph (b).][1]

Amendments—[1]   Sections 643I–643L and 643N inserted by FA 2018 s 35, Sch 10 paras 3, 11 with effect only in relation to onward payments made on or after 6 April 2018.

Settlements by two or more settlors

644 Application to settlements by two or more settlors

(1) In the case of a settlement where there is more than one settlor, this Chapter has effect in relation to each settlor as if that settlor were the only settlor.

(2) This works as follows.

(3) In this Chapter, in relation to a settlor—

    (a) references to the property comprised in a settlement include only property originating from the settlor, and

    (b) references to income arising under the settlement include only income originating from the settlor.

(4) For the purposes of sections 629, 631 and 632 only the following are taken into account in relation to a child of the settlor—

    (a) income originating from the settlor, and

    (b) in a case in which section 631 applies, payments which under that section (as adapted by subsection (5) below) are treated as payments of income.

(5) In applying section 631 to a settlor—

    (a) the reference to income arising under the settlement includes only income originating from the settlor, and

    (b) the reference to any payment made in connection with the settlement includes only a payment made out of property originating from the settlor or income originating from the settlor.

(6) See section 645 for the meaning of references in this section to property or income originating from a settlor.

Commentary—*Simon's Taxes* **C4.322.**

HMRC Manuals—Trusts, Settlements and Estates Manual TSEM4555 (more than one settlor).

645 Property or income originating from settlor

(1) References in [sections 628A and][2] 644 to property originating from a settlor are references to—

    (a) property which the settlor has provided directly or indirectly for the purposes of the settlement,

    (b) property representing property so provided, and

    (c) so much of any property which represents both property so provided and other property as, on a just and reasonable apportionment, represents the property so provided.

(2) References in [sections 627 and 644][1] to income originating from a settlor are references to—

    (a) income from property originating from the settlor, and

    (b) income provided directly or indirectly by the settlor.

(3) In this section references to property or income which a settlor has provided directly or indirectly—

    (a) include references to property or income which has been provided directly or indirectly by another person under reciprocal arrangements with the settlor, but

    (b) do not include references to property or income which the settlor has provided directly or indirectly under reciprocal arrangements with another person.

(4) In this section references to property which represents other property include references to property which represents accumulated income from the other property.

Commentary—*Simon's Taxes* **C4.322, C4.430.**

Amendments—[1]   Words in sub-s (2) substituted by FA 2012 s 12(1), (3) with effect in relation to income arising on or after 21 March 2012.

[2]   In sub-s (1), words substituted for word "section" by F(No 2)A 2017 s 29(2), Sch 8 paras 20, 26 with effect for the tax year 2017–18 and subsequent tax years.

Other supplementary provisions

646 Adjustments between settlor and trustees etc.

(1) A settlor is entitled to recover from—

    (a) any trustee, or

    (b) any other person to whom the income is payable in connection with the settlement,

the amount of any tax paid by the settlor which became chargeable on the settlor under section 624 or 629.

(2) For this purpose, the settlor may require [an officer of Revenue and Customs] to provide the settlor with a certificate specifying—

    (a) the amount of income in respect of which the settlor has so paid tax, and

    (b) the amount of tax so paid.

(3) A certificate provided under subsection (2) is conclusive evidence of the facts stated in it.

[(4) Subsection (5) applies if a settlor chargeable to tax under section 624 or 629 obtains a repayment by reason of the payment of the tax by—

    (a) any trustee, or

    (b) any other person to whom the income is payable by virtue of or as a result of the settlement.][2]

(5) The settlor must pay an amount equal to the [repayment][2] to—

    (a) the trustee, or

    (b) the other person to whom the income is payable by virtue of or as a result of the settlement.

(6) If there are two or more such persons, the amount must be apportioned among them as the case may require.

[(6A) For the purpose of subsection (5), the settlor may require an officer of Revenue and Customs to provide the settlor with a certificate specifying—

    (a) that the settlor has obtained a repayment as mentioned in subsection (4), and

    (b) the amount of the repayment.

(6B) A certificate provided under subsection (6A) is conclusive evidence of the facts stated in it.][2]

(7) [Subject to subsections (6A) and (6B), any][2] question as to—

    (a) the amount of a payment under subsection (5), or

    (b) an apportionment to be made under subsection (6),

is to be decided by the [tribunal and, notwithstanding the provisions of sections 11 and 13 of the Tribunals, Courts and Enforcement Act 2007, the decision of the tribunal is final][1].

(8) Nothing in sections 624 to 632 is to be read as excluding a charge to tax on the trustees as persons by whom any income is received.

Commentary—*Simon's Taxes* **C4.352.**

HMRC Manuals—Trusts, Settlements and Estates Manual TSEM4505 (certification under S646 ITTOIA).

TSEM4512 (settlements legislation: tax paid by trustees where income is treated as that of the settlor).

TSEM4550 (trustee or beneficiary entitled to share tax repayment).

TSEM4552 (settlements legislation: trustee or beneficiary entitled to share tax repayment certificate section 646 (6A) ITTOIA).

TSEM4553 (settlements legislation: wording of certificate under ITTOIA/S646 (6A)).

TSEM4554 (inheritance tax implications of adjustments).

Amendments—[1] In sub-s (7), words substituted by the Transfer of Tribunal Functions and Revenue and Customs Appeals Order, SI 2009/56 art 3, Sch 1 para 441 with effect from 1 April 2009.

[2] Sub-s (4) substituted, in sub-s (5) word substituted, sub-ss (6A), (6B) inserted, and in sub-s (7) words substituted by F(No 3)A 2010 s 7 with effect in relation to repayments of tax for the tax year 2010–11 or any subsequent tax year.

[646A Trustees' expenses to be rateably apportioned

(1) This section applies if—

    (a) in a tax year qualifying income arises under a UK settlement, and

    (b) the qualifying income consists of charitable income and non-charitable income.

(2) If expenses of the trustees are to be set against the charitable income by virtue of section 484 of ITA 2007, the amount of those expenses which can used for that purpose is limited to the amount allocated to the charitable income.

(3) If—

    (a) Chapter 8 of Part 9 of ITA 2007 applies in relation to the charitable income, and

    (b) expenses of the trustees are to be used to reduce the charitable income for income tax purposes,

the amount of those expenses which can used for that purpose is limited to the amount allocated to the charitable income.

(4) For the purposes of subsections (2) and (3) the amount of the expenses allocated to the charitable income is determined by apportioning them rateably between the charitable income and the non-charitable income.

(5) In this section—

    "charitable income" means income within section 628(1) or 630(1),

    "non-charitable income" means income which is not charitable income, and

    "qualifying income" and "UK settlement" have the same meaning as in section 628.][1]

Commentary—*Simon's Taxes* **C4.330.**

HMRC Manuals—TSEM4550 (trustee or beneficiary entitled to share tax repayment).
Amendments—[1]   This section inserted by ITA 2007 s 1027, Sch 1 paras 492, 560 with effect for income tax purposes from
   6 April 2007, and corporation tax purposes for accounting periods ending after 5 April 2007.

648 Income arising under a settlement

(1) References in this Chapter to income arising under a settlement include—
   (a) any income chargeable to income tax by deduction or otherwise, and
   (b) any income which would have been so chargeable if it had been received in the United
       Kingdom by a person domiciled [and resident][2] there.

[(2) But if, in a tax year, the settlor is not UK resident, references in this Chapter to income arising under a settlement do not include income arising under the settlement in that tax year in respect of which the settlor, if actually entitled to it, would not be chargeable to income tax by deduction or otherwise because of not being UK resident.

(3) And if, for a tax year, section 809B, 809D or 809E of ITA 2007 (remittance basis) applies to the settlor, references in this Chapter to income arising under a settlement include in relation to any relevant foreign income arising under the settlement in that tax year only such of it as is remitted to the United Kingdom (in that tax year or any subsequent tax year) in circumstances such that, if the settlor remitted it, the settlor would be chargeable to income tax.

(4) See Chapter A1 of Part 14 of ITA 2007 for the meaning of "remitted to the United Kingdom" etc

(5) Where subsection (3) applies the remitted income is treated for the purposes of this Chapter as arising under the settlement in the tax year in which it is remitted.][1]

Commentary—*Simon's Taxes* C4.323.

HMRC Manuals—Trusts, Settlements and Estates Manual TSEM10310 (non-residents trusts: settlor chargeability: income tax
   amount of charge).
Amendments—[1]   Sub-ss (2)–(5) substituted by FA 2009 s 51, Sch 27 para 13 with effect from 22 April 2009.
[2]   Words in sub-s (1)(b) substituted for words ", resident and ordinarily resident" by FA 2013 s 219, Sch 46 paras 43, 49 with
   effect for the purposes of a person's liability to income tax for the tax year 2013–14 or any subsequent tax year, subject to
   savings in FA 2013 Sch 46 para 73.

CHAPTER 6

BENEFICIARIES' INCOME FROM ESTATES IN ADMINISTRATION
Charge to tax on estate income

649 Charge to tax on estate income

(1) Income tax is charged on estate income.

(2) In this Chapter—
   "estate income" means the income treated under this Chapter as arising from an absolute,
       limited or discretionary interest in the whole or part of the residue of an estate, and
   "estate" means the estate of a deceased person (whether a UK estate or a foreign estate).

(3) Estate income is treated as income for income tax purposes.

(4) If different parts of an estate are subject to different residuary dispositions, those parts are treated for the purposes of this Chapter as if they were separate estates.

Commentary—*Simon's Taxes* C4.115, C4.117.

HMRC Manuals—Trusts, Settlements and Estates Manual TSEM7452 (deceased persons: beneficiaries of estates introduction).
TSEM7676 (deceased persons: interests in residue: practical and computational aspects: introduction).

650 Absolute, limited and discretionary interests

(1) A person has an absolute interest in the whole or part of the residue of an estate for the purposes of this Chapter if—
   (a) the capital of the residue or that part is properly payable to the person, or
   (b) it would be so payable, if the residue had been ascertained.

(2) A person has a limited interest in the whole or part of the residue of an estate during any period for the purposes of this Chapter if—
   (a) the person does not have an absolute interest in it, and
   (b) the income from it would be properly payable to the person if the residue had been
       ascertained at the beginning of that period.

(3) A person has a discretionary interest in the whole or part of the residue of an estate for the purposes of this Chapter if—
   (a) a discretion may be exercised in the person's favour, and
   (b) on its exercise in the person's favour any of the income of the residue during the whole or
       part of the administration period (see section 653) would be properly payable to the person if
       the residue had been ascertained at the beginning of that period.

(4) For the purposes of this section, an amount is only treated as properly payable to a person if it is properly payable to the person, or to another in the person's right, for the person's benefit, except where subsection (5) applies.

(5) The personal representatives of a deceased person ("A") are to be treated as having an absolute or limited interest in the whole or part of the residue of the estate of another deceased person ("B") if—

(a) they have a right in their capacity as A's personal representatives, and

(b) were the right vested in them for their own benefit, they would have that interest in B's estate.

(6) For the purposes of subsection (4), it does not matter whether the amount is payable directly by the personal representatives or through a trustee or other person.

Commentary—*Simon's Taxes* **C4.117.**

HMRC Manuals—Trusts, Settlements and Estates Manual TSEM7452 (deceased persons: limited interests in residue description).

TSEM7602 (Deceased persons: absolute interests in residue definition).

651 Meaning of "UK estate" and "foreign estate"

(1) In this Chapter—

"UK estate", in relation to a tax year, means an estate which meets conditions A and B, or condition C, for that year, and

"foreign estate", in relation to a tax year, means an estate which is not a UK estate in relation to that year.

(2) Condition A is that all the income of the estate either—

(a) has borne United Kingdom income tax by deduction, or

(b) is income in respect of which the personal representatives are directly assessable to United Kingdom income tax for the tax year.

(3) Condition B is that none of the income of the estate is income for which the personal representatives are not liable to United Kingdom income tax for the tax year because they are not UK resident . . . [1].

(4) For the purposes of conditions A and B sums within section [664(2)(c) or (d) or 680(4) (sums not liable to tax and sums][2] treated as bearing tax) are ignored.

(5) Condition C is that the aggregate income of the estate for the tax year consists only of sums within section [664(2)(c) or (d) or 680(4)][2].

Commentary—*Simon's Taxes* **C4.104.**

HMRC Manuals—Trusts, Settlements and Estates Manual TSEM7680 (meaning of UK estate).

Amendments—[1]   In sub-s (3) words "or not ordinarily UK resident" repealed by FA 2013 s 219, Sch 46 paras 43, 50 with effect for the purposes of a person's liability to income tax for the tax year 2013–14 or any subsequent tax year, subject to savings in FA 2013 Sch 46 para 73.

[2]   In sub-ss (4) and (5), words substituted by FA 2016 s 5, Sch 1 paras 2, 20 with effect: so far as relating to income within ITTOIA 2005 s 664(2)(c), in relation to stock dividend income treated as arising in the tax year 2016-17 or at any later time; and, so far relating to income within ITTOIA 2005 s 664(2)(d), in relation to amounts released or written off in the tax year 2016-17 or at any later time.

Types of estate income

652 Estate income: absolute interests in residue

(1) Income is treated as arising in a tax year from a person's absolute interest in the whole or part of the residue of an estate if—

(a) the person has an assumed income entitlement for the tax year in respect of the interest (see sections 665 to 670), and

(b) condition A or B is met.

(2) Condition A is that a payment is made in respect of the interest in the tax year and before the end of the administration period (see section 653).

(3) Condition B is that the tax year is the final tax year (see section 653).

(4) Income treated as arising as a result of this section is estate income for the purposes of this Chapter.

Commentary—*Simon's Taxes* **C4.121.**

HMRC Manuals—Trusts, Settlements and Estates Manual TSEM7604 (deceased persons: absolute interest in residue tax rules).

653 Meaning of "the administration period" and "the final tax year"

(1) In this Chapter "the administration period", in relation to the estate of a deceased person, means the period beginning with the deceased's death and ending with the completion of the administration of the estate.

(2) In the application of subsection (1) to Scotland, the reference to the completion of the administration is to be taken as a reference to the date at which, after discharge of, or provision for, liabilities falling to be met out of the deceased's estate, the free balance held in trust for the residuary legatees or for the persons with the right to the intestate estate has been ascertained.

(3) In this Chapter "the final tax year" means the tax year in which the administration period ends.

Commentary—*Simon's Taxes* **C4.103, C4.116.**

HMRC Manuals—Trusts, Settlements and Estates Manual TSEM7360 (definition of period of administration).

654 Estate income: limited interests in residue

(1) Income is treated as arising in a tax year from a person's limited interest in the whole or part of the residue of an estate in cases A, B and C.

(2) Case A is where—

(a) the interest has not ceased before the beginning of the tax year, and (*b*) a sum is paid in respect of the interest in that year and before the end of the administration period.

(3) Case B is where—

    (*a*) the tax year is the final tax year,

    (*b*) the interest has not ceased before the beginning of that year, and

    (*c*) a sum remains payable in respect of the interest at the end of the administration period.

(4) Case C is where—

    (*a*) the tax year is a year before the final tax year,

    (*b*) the interest ceases in the tax year, and

    (*c*) a sum is paid in respect of the interest in a later tax year but before the end of the administration period, or remains payable in respect of it at the end of that period.

(5) This section does not apply to limited interests to which section 674 (successive interests: holders of limited interests) applies.

(6) Income treated as arising as a result of this section or section 674 is estate income for the purposes of this Chapter.

Commentary—*Simon's Taxes* **C4.122.**

HMRC Manuals—Trusts, Settlements and Estates Manual TSEM7650 (limited interests in residue statutory conventional basis of taxation).

655 Estate income: discretionary interests in residue

(1) Income is treated as arising in a tax year from a person's discretionary interest in the whole or part of the residue of an estate if a payment is made in the tax year in exercise of the discretion in that person's favour.

(2) Income treated as arising as a result of this section is estate income for the purposes of this Chapter.

Commentary—*Simon's Taxes* **C4.123.**

HMRC Manuals—Trusts, Settlements and Estates Manual TSEM7660 (discretionary interests in residue: definition).

Income charged and person liable

656 Income charged: UK estates

(1) In the case of a UK estate, tax is charged under section 649 on the amount of estate income treated as arising in the tax year.

(2) That amount is the basic amount of that income for the tax year (see subsection (4)) grossed up by reference to the applicable rate for that year (see section 663).

(3) The gross amount is treated as having borne income tax at that rate.

(4) In this Chapter "the basic amount", in relation to estate income, has the meaning given by—

    (*a*) section 660 (basic amount of estate income: absolute interests),

    (*b*) section 661 (basic amount of estate income: limited interests),

    (*c*) section 662 (basic amount of estate income: discretionary interests), and

    (*d*) section 675 (basic amount of estate income: successive limited interests).

Commentary—*Simon's Taxes* **C4.118, C4.121.**

HMRC Manuals—Trusts, Settlements and Estates Manual TSEM7684 (Interests in residue: practical and computational aspects tax rules for UK estates).

657 Income charged: foreign estates

(1) In the case of a foreign estate, tax is charged under section 649 on the full amount of estate income treated as arising in the tax year.

(2) That amount depends on whether the estate income arising in the tax year is paid from sums within section [680(4)][1] (sums treated as bearing income tax).

(3) So far as the estate income is paid from such sums, that amount is the basic amount of that income for the tax year grossed up by reference to the applicable rate for that year (see section 663).

(4) That gross amount is treated as having borne income tax at that rate.

(5) So far as the estate income is not paid from sums within section [680(4)][1], the amount of estate income treated as arising in the tax year is the basic amount of that income for that year.

Commentary—*Simon's Taxes* **C4.119.**

HMRC Manuals—Trusts, Settlements and Estates Manual TSEM7682 (Interests in residue: practical and computational aspects foreign estates).

Amendments—[1] In sub-s (2) and (5), word substituted by FA 2016 s 5, Sch 1 paras 2, 21 with effect: so far as relating to income within ITTOIA 2005 s 664(2)(*c*), in relation to stock dividend income treated as arising in the tax year 2016-17 or at any later time; and, so far relating to income within ITTOIA 2005 s 664(2)(*d*), in relation to amounts released or written off in the tax year 2016-17 or at any later time.

658 Special rules for foreign income

(1) The charge to tax under section 649 on the amount of income arising in a tax year is subject to Part 8 (foreign income: special rules).

(2) For the purposes of section 830(1) (meaning of "relevant foreign income") amounts charged to tax under section 649—

    (*a*) are treated as arising from a source outside the United Kingdom if the estate is a foreign estate, and (*b*) are treated as not arising from such a source if the estate is a UK estate.

Commentary—*Simon's Taxes* **C4.119**.

659 Person liable

(1) If the estate income is from a person's absolute interest or limited interest, that person is liable for any tax charged under section 649 unless subsection (3) or (4) provides that another person is liable.

(2) If the estate income is from a discretionary interest, the person in whose favour the discretion is exercised in making the payment in question is liable for any tax charged under section 649.

(3) If, in a case where the estate income is from an absolute interest—

    (*a*) section 671 (successive absolute interests) applies, or

    (*b*) section 672 (successive interests: assumed income entitlement of holder of absolute interest following limited interest) applies and the income is treated as arising because of that section,

the person by reference to whose assumed income entitlement the estate income is determined is liable for any tax charged under section 649.

(4) If, in a case where the estate income is from a limited interest—

    (*a*) section 673(1) applies and the income is treated as arising because of section 673(2) (payment in respect of a previous limited interest), or

    (*b*) section 674 (successive interests: holders of limited interests) applies,

the person entitled to receive the payment in question is liable for any tax charged under section 649.

Commentary—*Simon's Taxes* **C4.116**.

Basic amount of estate income: general calculation rules

660 Basic amount of estate income: absolute interests

(1) The basic amount of estate income relating to a person's absolute interest in the whole or part of the residue of an estate for a tax year before the final tax year is the lower of—

    (*a*) the total of all sums paid in the tax year in respect of that interest, and

    (*b*) the amount of the person's assumed income entitlement for the tax year in respect of it.

(2) The basic amount for the final tax year is equal to the amount of the person's assumed income entitlement for that year in respect of that interest.

(3) But if the residuary income of the estate for the final tax year is nil because the allowable estate deductions exceed the aggregate income of the estate, the basic amount for that year is reduced—

    (*a*) where the person has an absolute interest in the whole of the residue of the estate, by an amount equal to the excess, and

    (*b*) in any other case, by an amount equal to such part of the excess as is just and reasonable.

(4) See sections 665 to 670 for the meaning of references to assumed income entitlement and residuary income of an estate.

(5) See sections 664 and 666(2) for the meaning of aggregate income of an estate and allowable estate deductions respectively.

(6) This section is subject to sections 671 to 673 (successive interests).

Commentary—*Simon's Taxes* **C4.121**.

661 Basic amount of estate income: limited interests

(1) The basic amount of estate income relating to a person's limited interest in the whole or part of the residue of an estate for a tax year is the total of the sums within section 654(2)(*b*), (3)(*c*) and (4)(*c*) for that year.

(2) This does not apply, and section 675 applies instead, if the limited interest is one to which section 674 (successive interests: holders of limited interests) applies.

Commentary—*Simon's Taxes* **C4.122**.

662 Basic amount of estate income: discretionary interests

The basic amount of estate income relating to a person's discretionary interest in the whole or part of the residue of an estate for a tax year is the total of the payments made in the tax year in exercise of the discretion in favour of the person.

Commentary—*Simon's Taxes* **C4.123**.

HMRC Manuals—Trusts, Settlements and Estates Manual TSEM7452 (beneficiaries of estates: discretionary interest).

663 The applicable rate for grossing up basic amounts of estate income

(1) The applicable rate by reference to which a basic amount of estate income is grossed up for the purposes of sections 656 and 657 depends on the rate at which income tax is borne for the tax year by the aggregate income of the estate.

(2) If the aggregate income of the estate all bears income tax at the same rate, the applicable rate is that rate.

(3) If—

    (*a*) different parts of the aggregate income of the estate bear income tax at different rates, and

    (*b*) the same rate applies to all the income from which section 679 treats the basic amount as having been paid,

the applicable rate is that rate.

(4) If—

(*a*) different parts of the aggregate income of the estate bear income tax at different rates, and

(*b*) different rates apply to different parts of the income from which section 679 treats the basic amount as having been paid,

each of those rates is the applicable rate by reference to which the corresponding part of the basic amount is grossed up.

[(5) The aggregate income of the estate, so far as it consists of income within section 664(2)(*c*) or (*d*), is treated for the purposes of this section as bearing income tax at 0%.]¹

Commentary—*Simon's Taxes* **C4.118**.

HMRC Manuals—Trusts, Settlements and Estates Manual TSEM8245 (trust management expenses: accumulation/discretionary trusts: grossing up of basic amount).

Amendments—¹ Sub-s (5) inserted by FA 2016 s 5, Sch 1 paras 2, 22 with effect: so far as relating to income within ITTOIA 2005 s 664(2)(*c*), in relation to stock dividend income treated as arising in the tax year 2016-17 or at any later time; and, so far relating to income within ITTOIA 2005 s 664(2)(*d*), in relation to amounts released or written off in the tax year 2016-17 or at any later time.

664 The aggregate income of the estate

(1) For the purposes of this Chapter the aggregate income of the estate for a tax year is the total of the income and amounts specified in subsection (2), but excluding the income specified in subsection (5).

(2) The income and amounts are—

(*a*) the income of the deceased's personal representatives in that capacity which is charged to United Kingdom income tax for the tax year,

(*b*) the income of the deceased's personal representatives in that capacity on which such tax would have been charged for the tax year if—

(i) it was income of a UK resident . . . ¹, and

(ii) it was income from a source in the United Kingdom,

(*c*) any amount of income treated as arising to the personal representatives under section 410(4) (stock dividends) that would be charged to income tax under Chapter 5 of Part 4 if income arising to personal representatives were so charged (see section 411),

(*d*) in a case where section 419(2) applies (release of loans to participator in close company: loans and advances to persons who die), the amount that would be charged to income tax under Chapter 6 of Part 4 apart from that section, and

(*e*) any amount that would have been treated as income of the personal representatives in that capacity under section 466 if the condition in section 466(2) had been met (gains from contracts for life insurance).

(3) In calculating the amount of the income within subsection (2)(*a*), any allowable deductions are to be taken into account.

(4) In calculating the amount of the income within subsection (2)(*b*), any deductions which would be allowable if the income had been charged to United Kingdom income tax are to be deducted from the full amount of the income actually arising in the tax year.

(5) The excluded income is—

(*a*) income to which any person is or may become entitled under a specific disposition, and

(*b*) income from property devolving on the personal representatives otherwise than as assets for payment of the deceased's debts.

(6) In subsection (5)(*a*) "specific disposition" means a gift of specific property under a will, including—

(*a*) the disposition of personal chattels by section 46 of the Administration of Estates Act 1925 (c 23) (succession on intestacy), and

(*b*) any disposition which under the law of another country has a similar effect to a gift of specific property by will under the law of England and Wales,

but excluding real property included in a residuary gift made by will by a specific or general description of it or, in Scotland, heritable estate included in such a gift.

Commentary—*Simon's Taxes* **C4.115A**.

Amendments—¹ In sub-s (2)(*b*)(i) words "who was ordinarily UK resident" repealed by FA 2013 s 219, Sch 46 paras 43, 51 with effect for the purposes of a person's liability to income tax for the tax year 2013–14 or any subsequent tax year, subject to savings in FA 2013 Sch 46 para 73.

Further provisions for calculating estate income relating to absolute interests

665 Assumed income entitlement

(1) Whether a person has an assumed income entitlement for a tax year in respect of an absolute interest in the whole or part of the residue of an estate depends on the results of the following steps.

Step 1 Find the amount of the person's share of the residuary income of the estate that is attributable to that interest for that tax year and each previous tax year during which the person had that interest (see sections 666 to 669).

Step 2 If the estate is a UK estate in relation to any tax year for which an amount has been found under step 1, deduct from that amount income tax on that amount at the applicable rate for that year (see section 670).

Step 3 Add together the amounts found under step 1 after making any deductions necessary under step 2.

Step 4 Add together the basic amounts relating to the person's absolute interest in respect of which the person was liable for income tax for all previous tax years (or would have been so liable if the person had been a person liable for income tax for those years).

(2) For the purposes of this Chapter the person has an assumed income entitlement for the tax year if the amount resulting from step 3 exceeds the amount resulting from step 4.

(3) The assumed income entitlement is equal to the excess.

(4) This section is subject to—

section 671 (successive absolute interests), and

section 672 (successive interests: assumed income entitlement of holder of absolute interest following limited interest).

Commentary—*Simon's Taxes* **C4.120, C4.121**.

HMRC Manuals—Trusts, Settlements and Estates Manual TSEM7678 (computational aspects of residuary income).

666 The residuary income of the estate

(1) For the purposes of this Chapter the residuary income of an estate for a tax year is the aggregate income of the estate for that year, less the allowable estate deductions for that year.

This is subject to section 669 (reduction in residuary income: inheritance tax on accrued income).

(2) The allowable estate deductions for a tax year are—

(*a*) all interest paid in that year by the personal representatives in that capacity (but see section 233 of IHTA 1984: exclusion of interest on unpaid inheritance tax),

(*b*) all annual payments for that year which are properly payable out of residue,

(*c*) all payments made in that year in respect of expenses incurred by the personal representatives in that capacity in the management of the assets of the estate, and

(*d*) any excess deductions from the previous tax year.

This is subject to subsections (3) to (5).

(3) No sum is to be treated as an allowable estate deduction if it is allowable in calculating the aggregate income of the estate.

(4) No sum is to be counted twice as an allowable estate deduction.

(5) Payments in respect of expenses are only allowable estate deductions if they are properly chargeable to income (ignoring any specific direction in a will).

(6) In this section "excess deductions from the previous tax year" means so much of the allowable deductions for the previous tax year as exceeded the aggregate income of the estate for that year.

Commentary—*Simon's Taxes* **C4.120**.

HMRC Manuals—Trusts, Settlements and Estates Manual TSEM7690 (interests in residue: practical and computational aspects excess expenses).

667 Shares of residuary income of estate

(1) In the case of a person who has an absolute interest in the whole of the residue of an estate for a whole tax year, the person's share of the residuary income of the estate in respect of that interest for that year is equal to the whole of that income for that year.

(2) In the case of a person who—

(*a*) has an absolute interest in the whole of the residue of an estate for part of the tax year, or

(*b*) an absolute interest in part of the residue of an estate for the whole or part of the tax year,

the person's share of the residuary income of the estate is a proportionate part of that income for that year.

(3) This section is subject to section 668 (reduction in share of residuary income of estate).

Commentary—*Simon's Taxes* **C4.120**.

668 Reduction in share of residuary income of estate

(1) This section applies if a person has an absolute interest in the whole or part of the residue of an estate at the end of the administration period and—

(*a*) the total of the person's shares of the residuary income of the estate in respect of that interest for all tax years (apart from this section), exceeds

(*b*) the total of all sums paid during or payable at the end of the administration period in respect of that interest to any person (grossed up where subsection (5) applies).

(2) In the final tax year the person's share of the residuary income of the estate is to be reduced by that excess.

(3) If that excess is greater than the person's share of that income for the final tax year, that person's share of that income for the previous tax year is to be reduced, and so on.

(4) If subsection (3) applies all necessary adjustments and repayments of income tax are to be made.

(5) For the purposes of calculating the total mentioned in subsection (1)(*b*)—

(*a*) if the estate is a UK estate in relation to a tax year in which a sum is paid, the sum is to be grossed up by reference to the basic rate for that year, and

(*b*) if the estate is a UK estate in relation to the final tax year, a sum payable at the end of the administration period is to be grossed up by reference to the basic rate for that year.

(6) For the application of this section where two or more absolute interests in the whole or the same part of the residue are held successively by different persons, see section 671(5) and (6).

Commentary—*Simon's Taxes* **C4.121**.

669 Reduction in residuary income: inheritance tax on accrued income

(1) This section applies if on the death of a person ("D") income which accrued before D's death ("pre-death income") is taken into account both—

    (*a*) in determining the value of D's estate for the purposes of inheritance tax charged on D's death, and

    (*b*) in calculating the residuary income of D's estate for a tax year.

(2) A reduction is made in the residuary income of D's estate for that tax year in ascertaining the extra liability, if any, of a person with an absolute interest in the whole or part of the residue of D's estate or any other estate to which that residuary income is relevant.

(3) A person's extra liability is the amount by which the person's liability to income tax exceeds the amount it would be if—

    [(*a*) income charged at [an applicable]³ [rate]² were charged at the basic rate, and

    (*b*) income charged at the dividend additional rate or the dividend upper rate were charged at the dividend ordinary rate.]¹

[(3A) For the purposes of subsection (3), each of the following is an "applicable rate"—

    (*a*) the higher rate,

    (*b*) the additional rate,

    (*c*) any Scottish rate that—

        (i) is above the Scottish basic rate, but

        (ii) is not the Scottish intermediate rate,

    (*d*) the Welsh higher rate, and

    (*e*) the Welsh additional rate.]³

(4) The amount of the reduction under subsection (2) is calculated as follows:

Step 1 Calculate the net pre-death income by subtracting from the pre-death income any liabilities which have been taken account both—

    (*a*) in determining the value of D's estate for the purposes of inheritance tax, and

    (*b*) in calculating the residuary income of D's estate for the tax year.

Step 2 Calculate the inheritance tax attributable to net pre-death income by multiplying the inheritance tax to be charged by—

$$\frac{NPDI}{VE}$$

where—

    NPDI is the net pre-death income, and

    VE is the value of D's estate.

Step 3 Gross up the inheritance tax attributable to net pre-death income by reference to the basic rate for the tax year.

(5) The amount of pre-death income taken into account in determining the value of D's estate is taken to be the actual amount of income accruing before D's death, less income tax at the basic rate for the tax year in which D died.

(6) Subsection (5) applies even if the income so accruing was not valued separately or its amount was not known at the date of D's death.

(7) For the purposes of this section, the amounts agreed between the persons liable for inheritance tax and [an officer of Revenue and Customs], or determined in proceedings between them, as the value of the estate and the amount of inheritance tax to be charged are conclusive.

(8) Evidence of those amounts and of any facts relevant to their calculation may be given by the production of a document that appears to be a certificate from [an officer of Revenue and Customs].

Commentary—*Simon's Taxes* **C4.120**.

HMRC Manuals—Trusts, Settlements and Estates Manual TSEM7688 (special relief for higher rate tax payers; relief under ITTOIA/S669).

Amendments—¹   Sub-s (3)(*a*), (*b*) substituted by FA 2016 s 4(13) with effect where the tax year mentioned in sub-s (1)(*b*) is the tax year 2016-17 or a later tax year.

²   In sub-s (3)(*a*), words substituted, and sub-s (3A) inserted, by the Scotland Act 2016 (Income Tax Consequential Amendments) Regulations, SI 2017/468 regs 2, 8(1)–(3) with effect in relation to 2017–18 (the tax year appointed under the Scotland Act 2016 section 13(15)(*b*)) and subsequent tax years.

³   In sub-s (3)(*a*) words substituted for words "the applicable", and sub-s (3A) substituted, by the Devolved Income Tax Rates (Consequential Amendments) Order, SI 2019/201 art 10(1), (3) with effect in relation to the tax year commencing on 6 April 2019 and subsequent tax years.

670 Applicable rate for determining assumed income entitlement (UK estates)

(1) The applicable rate by reference to which income tax on a person's share of the residuary income of the estate for a tax year is calculated for the purposes of step 2 of the calculation in section 665(1) depends on the rate at which income tax is borne by the aggregate income of the estate for the year.

(2) If the aggregate income of the estate all bears income tax at the same rate, the applicable rate is that rate.

(3) If different parts of the aggregate income of the estate bear income tax at different rates, the applicable rate is the rate that applies to the income to which the person's share of the residuary income of the estate relates.

(4) If different rates apply to different parts of that income, each of those rates is the applicable rate that applies to the corresponding part of the income to which the person's share of the residuary income of the estate relates.

[(4A) The aggregate income of the estate, so far as it consists of income within section 664(2)(c) or (d), is treated for the purposes of this section as bearing income tax at 0%.][1]

(5) For the purposes of this section, if there is more than one person with an absolute interest in the residue of the estate, such apportionments of parts of the aggregate income of the estate bearing income tax at different rates are to be made as are just and reasonable for their different interests.

Commentary—*Simon's Taxes* **C4.121.**

Amendments—[1] Sub-s (4A) inserted by FA 2016 s 5, Sch 1 paras 2, 23 with effect: so far as relating to income within ITTOIA 2005 s 664(2)(c), in relation to stock dividend income treated as arising in the tax year 2016-17 or at any later time; and, so far relating to income within ITTOIA 2005 s 664(2)(d), in relation to amounts released or written off in the tax year 2016-17

Special rules for successive interests

671 Successive absolute interests

(1) This section applies if two or more absolute interests in the whole or the same part of the residue of an estate are held successively during the administration period by different persons.

(2) In determining whether a person with a later such interest ("the later holder") has an assumed income entitlement in respect of that interest and, if so, its amount—

   (a) the later holder's share of the residuary income of the estate in respect of that interest for any tax year is to be treated as including the share of any person with a previous such interest ("a previous holder"), and

   (b) the basic amounts relating to the later holder's interest are to be treated as including the basic amounts relating to any previous such interest.

(3) In applying subsection (2), all determinations under that subsection or section 672(2) that fall to be made in relation to a person with an earlier interest are to be made before determinations under those provisions relating to a person with a later interest.

(4) A person who is a previous holder in the final tax year is to be taxed in that year, in relation to the interest as to which that person is a previous holder, as if that year were not the final tax year, and the later holder's assumed income entitlement in that year is to be calculated accordingly [(or, where the previous holder is a company chargeable to corporation tax, having regard to the application of section 954(4) of CTA 2009 to the previous holder)][1].

(5) The calculation under section 668(1)(a) and (b) (amount of reduction in the share of the residuary income of the person with an absolute interest at the end of the administration period) is to be made by reference to all the absolute interests taken together.

(6) If the amount resulting from that calculation is greater than the total amount of the reductions which can be made under section 668(2) and (3), the share of the residuary income of the estate of the last previous holder of the interest for the last tax year in which that last holder had that interest is to be reduced, and so on [(but, in a case where the last previous holder or any earlier previous holder is a company chargeable to corporation tax, having regard to the application of section 954(6) of CTA 2009 to the previous holder)][1].

(7) For the purposes of this section and sections 672 to 676, two interests are held successively even where one is not held immediately before or after the other.

(8) It is assumed for those purposes that each of the persons holding the interests in question is a person liable to income tax.

Commentary—*Simon's Taxes* **C4.124.**

Amendments—[1] In sub-ss (4), (6) words inserted by CTA 2009 s 1322, Sch 1 paras 587, 634. CTA 2009 applies for accounting periods ending on or after 1 April 2009 (for corporation tax purposes) and for tax years 2009–10 onwards (for income and capital gains tax purposes).

672 Successive interests: assumed income entitlement of holder of absolute interest following limited interest

(1) This section applies if—

   (a) two or more interests in the whole or part of the residue of an estate are held successively during the administration period by different persons,

   (b) each later interest arises or is created on the cessation of the previous interest otherwise than by death,

   (c) at least one of the interests is an absolute interest, and

   (d) at least one of the interests preceding that interest is a limited interest.

(2) Rules A and B apply to determine in relation to such an absolute interest—

   (a) whether the person with the interest has an assumed income entitlement in respect of the interest, and

   (b) if so, its amount.

(3) Rule A is that the person's share of the residuary income of the estate in respect of the absolute interest for any tax year is treated as including any amount which would be included in it if—

   (a) the interest had subsisted throughout the period when any such limited interest subsisted, and

   (b) no such limited interest had ever subsisted.

(4) Rule B is that the basic amounts relating to the absolute interest are treated as including the basic amounts relating to any such limited interest.

Commentary—*Simon's Taxes* **C4.124**.

673 Successive interests: payments in respect of limited interests followed by absolute interests

(1) This section applies if—

   (a) two or more interests in the whole or part of the residue of an estate are held successively during the administration period by different persons,

   (b) each later interest arises or is created on the cessation of the previous interest otherwise than by death,

   (c) at least one of the interests is an absolute interest, and

   (d) at least one of the interests preceding that interest is a limited interest.

(2) A sum to which a person ("P") with ~~such~~ limited interest which is *paid* while P has the absolute interest is treated as paid in respect of the absolute interest (and not the limited interest).

(3) Subsection (4) applies if—

   (a) P's absolute interest ceases during the administration period, and

   (b) a sum to which P is entitled in respect of any such limited interest—

      (i) is paid after the absolute interest ceases but before the end of the administration period, or

      (ii) remains payable at the end of it.

(4) This Chapter applies as respects any such sum as if the limited interest had continued to subsist while that absolute interest subsisted and had been held by P.

(5) Subsection (4) is subject to subsection (6).

(6) For the purposes only of section 668 (reduction in share of residuary income of estate), any such sum is treated as paid or payable in respect of the absolute interest.

Commentary—*Simon's Taxes* **C4.124**.

674 Successive interests: holders of limited interests

(1) This section applies if—

   (a) two or more interests in the whole or part of the residue of an estate are held successively during the administration period by different persons,

   (b) the earlier or, if there are more than two, the earliest of the interests is a limited interest, and

   (c) each later interest arises or is created on the cessation of the previous interest otherwise than by death.

(2) Income is treated as arising from a limited interest in the whole or part of the residue of the estate in a tax year in cases A, B and C.

(3) Case A is where—

   (a) one of the successive interests subsists at the beginning of the tax year,

   (b) a sum is paid in respect of one of the interests in that year and before the end of the administration period, and

   (c) a person who has or has had one of the interests which is a limited interest ("a limited holder") is entitled to receive the payment.

(4) Case B is where—

   (a) the tax year is the final tax year,

   (b) one of the successive interests subsists at the beginning of that year,

   (c) a sum remains payable in respect of one of the interests at the end of the administration period, and

   (d) a limited holder is entitled to receive the payment.

(5) Case C is where—

   (a) the tax year is a year before the final tax year,

   (b) the last of the successive interests ceases in the tax year,

   (c) a sum is either—

      (i) paid in respect of one of the interests in a later tax year but before the end of the administration period, or

      (ii) remains payable in respect of it at the end of that period, and

(*d*) a limited holder is entitled to receive the payment.

Commentary—*Simon's Taxes* **C4.124**.

675 Basic amount of estate income: successive limited interests

The basic amount of estate income relating to a limited interest within section 674 for a tax year is the total of the sums within section 674(3)(*b*), (4)(*c*) and (5)(*c*) for that year.

Commentary—*Simon's Taxes* **C4.124**.

HMRC Manuals—Trusts, Settlements and Estates Manual TSEM7656 (basic amount of estate income: examples).

676 Apportionments

(1) Such apportionments as are just and reasonable are to be made for the purposes of this Chapter if—

    (*a*) the part of a residuary estate in which an interest within any of the provisions specified in subsection (2) subsists does not wholly correspond with the part in which another such interest held successively subsists, or

    (*b*) one of those interests is in the whole of the residuary estate and the other is only in part of it.

(2) The provisions are—

    section 671 (successive absolute interests),

    section 672 (successive interests: assumed income entitlement of holder of absolute interest following limited interest),

    section 673 (successive interests: payments in respect of limited interests followed by absolute interests),

    section 674 (successive interests: holders of limited interest), and

    section 675 (basic amount of estate income: successive limited interests).

Commentary—*Simon's Taxes* **C4.124**.

Relief where foreign estates have borne UK income tax

677 Relief where UK income tax borne by foreign estate: absolute interests

(1) This section applies if—

    (*a*) an estate is a foreign estate in relation to a tax year,

    (*b*) United Kingdom income tax has been charged on a person for the tax year on estate income treated as arising from the estate under section 652 (estate income: absolute interests in residue), and

    (*c*) United Kingdom income tax has already been borne by part of the aggregate income of the estate for the tax year.

(2) If the person makes a claim under this section, the income tax charged on the person on that estate income is to be reduced by an amount equal to—

$$T \times \frac{A}{B}$$

where—

    T is the income tax charged on the person,

    A is so much of the aggregate income of the estate as has already borne United Kingdom income tax for the tax year, and

    B is the aggregate income of the estate for the tax year.

[(3) The tax reduction under this section is given effect at Step 6 of the calculation in section 23 of ITA 2007.][1]

Commentary—*Simon's Taxes* **C4.126**.

Amendments—[1]   Sub-s (3) inserted by ITA 2007 s 1027, Sch 1 paras 492, 562 with effect for income tax purposes from 6 April 2007, and corporation tax purposes for accounting periods ending after 5 April 2007.

678 Relief where UK income tax borne by foreign estate: limited and discretionary interests

(1) This section applies if—

    (*a*) an estate is a foreign estate in relation to a tax year,

    (*b*) United Kingdom income tax has been charged on a person for the tax year on estate income from the estate treated as arising under—

      (i) section 654 (estate income: limited interests in residue), or

      (ii) section 655 (estate income: discretionary interests in residue), and

    (*c*) United Kingdom income tax has already been borne by part of the aggregate income of the estate for the tax year.

(2) If the person makes a claim under this section, the income tax charged on the person on that estate income is to be reduced by an amount equal to—

$$T \times \frac{A - C}{B - C}$$

where—

     T is the income tax charged on the person,

     A is so much of the aggregate income of the estate as has already borne United Kingdom income tax for the tax year,

     B is the aggregate income of the estate for the tax year, and

     C is the amount of United Kingdom income tax already borne by the aggregate income of the estate for the tax year.

[(3) The tax reduction under this section is given effect at Step 6 of the calculation in section 23 of ITA 2007.][1]

Commentary—*Simon's Taxes* **C4.126.**
Amendments—[1]   Sub-s (3) inserted by ITA 2007 s 1027, Sch 1 paras 492, 563 with effect for income tax purposes from 6 April 2007, and corporation tax purposes for accounting periods ending after 5 April 2007.

General

679 Income from which basic amounts are treated as paid

(1) The part of the aggregate income of the estate from which a basic amount is treated as paid is determined by applying assumptions A and B in that order.

(2) Assumption A is that if there are different persons with interests in the residue of the estate, payments in respect of their basic amounts are paid out of the different parts of the aggregate income of the estate in such proportions as are just and reasonable for their different interests.

(3) Assumption B is that payments are made from those parts in the following order—

     (*a*) income bearing income tax at the basic rate,

     (*b*)   . . . [1] and

     (*c*) income bearing income tax at the dividend ordinary rate.

(4) If some, but not all, of the aggregate income of the estate is income treated under section 680 as bearing income tax, assumption C is applied before assumptions A and B.

(5) Assumption C is that the basic amount is paid from income that is not within section 680 before it is paid from income within that section.

(6) Assumptions A and B then apply—

     (*a*) first to determine the part of the income not within that section from which the basic amount is paid, and

     (*b*) then to determine the part of the income within that section from which the basic amount is paid.

Commentary—*Simon's Taxes* **C4.118.**
Amendments—[1]   Sub-s (3)(*b*) (apart from word "and") repealed by FA 2008 s 5, Sch 1 paras 50, 60 with effect for the tax year 2008–09 and subsequent tax years.

680 Income treated as bearing income tax

(1) This section has effect for the purposes of—

     section 663 (the applicable rate for grossing up basic amounts of estate income),

     section 670 (applicable rate for determining assumed income entitlement (UK estates)), and

     section 679 (income from which basic amounts are treated as paid).

(2) If the aggregate income of the estate includes a sum within subsection . . . [2] (4), the sum is treated as bearing income tax at the rate specified for it in that subsection.

(3)   . . . [2]

(4) A sum that is part of the aggregate income of the estate because of falling within section 664(2)(e) (gains from life insurance contracts etc) is treated as bearing income tax at the [basic rate][1].

(5) Income tax treated as borne under section 656(3) or 657(4) (gross amount of estate income treated as bearing tax at the applicable rate) is not repayable so far as the basic amount of the estate income in question is paid from sums within this section.

Commentary—*Simon's Taxes* **C4.118.**
HMRC Manuals—Trusts, Settlements and Estates Manual TSEM7686 (sources of income considered to be bearing income tax).
Amendments—[1]   Words in sub-s (4) substituted by FA 2008 s 5, Sch 1 paras 50, 61 with effect for the tax year 2008–09 and subsequent tax years.
[2]   Words in sub-s (2), and sub-s (3), repealed by FA 2016 s 5, Sch 1 paras 2, 24 with effect: so far as relating to income within ITTOIA 2005 s 664(2)(*c*), in relation to stock dividend income treated as arising in the tax year 2016-17 or at any later time; and, so far relating to income within ITTOIA 2005 s 664(2)(*d*), in relation to amounts released or written off in the tax year 2016-17 or at any later time. Note that the repeal of sub-s (3)(*a*) has effect in relation to dividends paid or arising (or treated as paid), and other distributions made (or treated as made), in the tax year 2016-17 or at any later time.

[680A Income treated as . . . [2] dividend income

(1) [Subsection (3) applies][2] to income if it—

     (*a*) is treated under section 656(3) or 657(4) (gross amount of estate income treated as bearing tax at the applicable rate) as bearing tax at . . . [2] the dividend ordinary rate [or as bearing tax at 0% because of section 663(5)][3], and

     (*b*) is not paid through a trustee.

(2)   . . . [2]

(3) [The income]^2 is treated as dividend income.

(4) [Subsection (6) applies]^2 to income if it—

(a) is treated by section 662, read with section 656(3) or 657(4), as bearing tax at . . . .^{2} the dividend ordinary rate [or as bearing tax at 0% because of section 663(5)]^3, and

(b) is paid through a trustee.

(5) . . .^{2}

(6) [The income]^2 is treated as dividend income of the trustee.]^1

Amendments—^{1} This section inserted by ITA 2007 s 1027, Sch 1 paras 492, 566 with effect for income tax purposes from 6 April 2007, and corporation tax purposes for accounting periods ending after 5 April 2007.

^{2} Words in sub-ss (1), (3), (4), (6) substituted; words in sub-ss (1), (4) and heading, and whole of sub-ss (2), (5), repealed; by FA 2008 s 5, Sch 1 paras 50, 62 with effect for the tax year 2008–09 and subsequent tax years.

^{3} Words in sub-ss (1)(a) and (4)(a) inserted by FA 2016 s 5, Sch 1 paras 2, 25 with effect: so far as relating to income within ITTOIA 2005 s 664(2)(c), in relation to stock dividend income treated as arising in the tax year 2016-17 or at any later time; and, so far relating to income within ITTOIA 2005 s 664(2)(d), in relation to amounts released or written off in the tax year 2016-17 or at any later time.

681 Transfers of assets etc. treated as payments

(1) For the purposes of this Chapter—

(a) a transfer of assets, or

(b) the appropriation of assets by personal representatives to themselves,

is treated as the payment of an amount equal to the assets' value at the date of transfer or appropriation.

(2) The set off or release of a debt is treated for the purposes of this Chapter as the payment of an amount equal to it.

(3) If at the end of the administration period—

(a) there is an obligation to transfer assets to any person, or

(b) personal representatives are entitled to appropriate assets to themselves,

an amount equal to the assets' value at that time is treated as payable then for the purposes of this Chapter.

(4) If at the end of the administration period—

(a) there is an obligation to release or set off a debt owed by any person, or

(b) personal representatives are entitled to release or set off a debt in their own favour,

~~. . . . . payable~~ then for the purposes of this Chapter.

Commentary—*Simon's Taxes* **C4.116.**

682 Assessments, adjustments and claims after the administration period

(1) This subsection applies if after the administration period ends it is apparent that a person is liable for income tax on estate income for any tax year who previously appeared not to be so liable or to be liable for tax on a lesser amount.

(2) If subsection (1) applies—

(a) the person may be assessed and taxed for the tax year, and

(b) any relief or additional relief to which the person may be entitled for the tax year is to be allowed if a claim is made.

(3) This subsection applies if after the administration period ends it is apparent that a person who previously appeared to be liable for income tax on estate income for any tax year is not so liable or is liable for tax on a lesser amount.

(4) If subsection (3) applies—

(a) all necessary adjustments and repayments of income tax for the tax year are to be made, and

(b) if the person has been allowed relief which exceeds the relief that could have been given by reference to the amount actually charged for the tax year, income tax is charged on the person for that year under this subsection on the excess.

[(4A) The excess charged under subsection (4)(b) is treated as an amount of income for income tax purposes, except so far as it represents a tax reduction given effect at Step 6 of the calculation in section 23 of ITA 2007.]^1

(5) An assessment or adjustment made for the purposes of this Chapter or a claim made as a result of this Chapter may be made after the end of the period otherwise allowed if it is made on or before the third anniversary of the normal self-assessment filing date for the tax year in which the administration period ends.

Commentary—*Simon's Taxes* **C4.127.**

HMRC Manuals—Trusts, Settlements and Estates Manual TSEM7692 (time limit: adjustments after the administration period).

Amendments—^{1} Sub-s (4A) inserted by ITA 2007 s 1027, Sch 1 paras 492, 567 with effect for income tax purposes from 6 April 2007, and corporation tax purposes for accounting periods ending after 5 April 2007.

[682A Statements relating to estate income

(1) If a person within subsection (2) requests it in writing, a personal representative of a deceased person must provide the person with a statement showing—

(a) the amount treated as estate income arising from the person's interest in the whole or part of the deceased person's estate for which the person is liable to income tax for a tax year, and

(b) the amount of any tax at the applicable rate which any such amount is treated as having borne.

(2) A person is within this subsection if—

(a) the person has or has had an absolute or limited interest in the whole or part of the residue of the estate, or

(b) estate income has arisen to the person from a discretionary interest the person has or has had in the whole or part of the residue of the estate.

(3) A statement under subsection (1) must be in writing.

(4) The duty to comply with a request under this section is enforceable by the person who made it.][1]

Amendments—[1]   Section inserted by TIOPA 2010 s 371, Sch 7 paras 46, 47. TIOPA 2010 has effect for corporation tax purposes for accounting periods ending on or after 1 April 2010, for income and capital gains tax purposes for the tax year 2010–11 and subsequent tax years, and for petroleum revenue tax purposes for chargeable periods beginning on or after 1 July 2010.

CHAPTER 7

ANNUAL PAYMENTS NOT OTHERWISE CHARGED

683 Charge to tax on annual payments not otherwise charged

(1) Income tax is charged under this Chapter on annual payments that are not charged to income tax under or as a result of any other provision of this Act or any other Act.

(2) Subsection (1) does not apply to annual payments that would be charged to income tax under or as a result of another provision but for an exemption.

(3) The frequency with which payments are made is ignored in determining whether they are annual payments for the purposes of this Chapter.

(4) For exemptions, see in particular—

(a) sections 727 to 730 (certain annual payments by individuals),

(b) section 731 (periodical payments of personal injury damages),

(c) section 732 (compensation awards),

(d) section 734 (payments from trusts for injured persons),

(e) sections 735 to 743 (health and employment insurance payments),

(f) sections 744 to 747 (payments to adopters),

(g) *section 748 (payments by persons liable to pool betting duty),*

(h) sections 757 to 767 (interest and royalty payments), and

(i) section 776 (scholarship income).

Commentary—*Simon's Taxes* E1.510.

HMRC Manuals—Savings and Investment Income Manual SAIM8010 (how annual payments are taxed).

Amendments—Sub-s (4)(g) repealed by FA 2012 s 227, Sch 39 para 21(2) with effect in relation to payments made on or after 6 April 2013.

684 Income charged

(1) Tax is charged under this Chapter on the full amount of the annual payments arising in the tax year.

(2) Subsection (1) is subject to Part 8 (foreign income: special rules).

(3) The amount charged under this Chapter in the case of certain payments made by trustees in the exercise of a discretion is subject to [section 494 of ITA 2007][1] (grossing up of discretionary payments from trusts).

Commentary—*Simon's Taxes* E1.513.

HMRC Manuals—Savings and Investment Income Manual SAIM8010 (annual payments: income charged).

SAIM8020 (meaning of annual payment).

Amendments—[1]   Words in sub-s (3) substituted by ITA 2007 s 1027, Sch 1 paras 492, 568 with effect for income tax purposes from 6 April 2007, and corporation tax purposes for accounting periods ending after 5 April 2007.

685 Person liable

The person liable for any tax charged under this Chapter is the person receiving or entitled to the annual payments.

Commentary—*Simon's Taxes* E1.513.

HMRC Manuals—Savings and Investment Income Manual SAIM8010 (annual payments: person liable).

[685A Settlor-interested settlements

(1) This section applies if—

(a) a person receives an annual payment in respect of income from the trustees of a settlement,

(b) the payment is made in the exercise of a discretion (whether of the trustees of the settlement or any other person), and

(c) a settlor is charged to tax under section 619(1) on the income arising to the trustees of the settlement (whether in the current year of assessment or in a previous year of assessment) out of which the annual payment is made.

(2) This section applies only in respect of that proportion of the annual payment which corresponds to the proportion of the total income arising to the trustees of the settlement in respect of which a settlor is chargeable to tax under section 619(1).

(3) If and in so far as this section applies, the recipient of the annual payment shall be treated for the purposes of this Chapter as having paid income tax at the [applicable rate]⁶ in respect of the annual payment.

[(3A) For the purposes of subsection (3), the "applicable rate" means—
    (*a*) in the case of a Scottish taxpayer, the highest Scottish rate,
    (*b*) in the case of a Welsh taxpayer, the Welsh additional rate, or
    (*c*) in any other case, the additional rate.]⁶

(4) But—
    (*a*) tax which the recipient is treated by virtue of this section as having paid is not repayable,
    (*b*) tax which the recipient is treated by virtue of this section as having paid may not be taken into account in relation to a tax liability of the recipient in respect of any other income of his,
    . . . ²
    (*c*) . . . ²

(5) If the recipient of the annual payment is a settlor in relation to the settlement, if and in so far as this section applies the annual payment shall not be treated as his income for the purposes of the Income Tax Acts (and subsection (3) does not apply).

[(5A) If the recipient of the annual payment is treated by subsection (3) as having paid income tax in respect of the annual payment, the amount of the payment is treated as the highest part of the recipient's total income for all income tax purposes except the purposes of sections 535 to 537 (gains from contracts for life insurance etc: top slicing relief).

(5B) See section 1012 of ITA 2007 (relationship between highest part rules) for the relationship between—
    (*a*) the rule in subsection (5A), and
    (*b*) other rules requiring particular income to be treated as the highest part of a person's income.]³

(6) [Sections 494 and 495 of ITA 2007]² shall not apply in relation to an annual payment if and in so far as this section applies.]¹

Commentary—*Simon's Taxes* **C3.512.**
Amendments—¹   Section inserted by FA 2006 s 89, Sch 13 para 6 with effect for payments in respect of income made on or
    after 6 April 2006.
²   Sub-s (4)(*c*) and preceding word repealed, and words in sub-s (6) substituted, by ITA 2007 ss 1027, 1031, Sch 1 paras 492,
    569, Sch 3 Pt 1 with effect for income tax purposes from 6 April 2007, and corporation tax purposes for accounting periods
    ending after 5 April 2007.
³   Sub-ss (5A), (5B) inserted by FA 2008 s 67(1) with effect for the tax year 2006–07 and subsequent tax years.
⁵   In sub-s (3), words inserted by the Scottish Rate of Income Tax (Consequential Amendments) Order, SI 2015/1810 arts 8, 11
    with effect in relation to the tax year 2016–17 (the tax year appointed by the Treasury under the Scotland Act 2012 s 25(5)
    by virtue of SI 2015/2000) and subsequent tax years.
⁶   In sub-s (3) words substituted for words reading "additional rate or, in the case of a Scottish taxpayer, at the highest Scottish rate",
    and sub-s (3A) inserted, by the Devolved Income Tax Rates (Consequential Amendments) Order, SI 2019/201 art 10(1), (4)
    with effect in relation to the tax year commencing on 6 April 2019 and subsequent tax years.

686 Payments received after deduction of tax
(1) [In accordance with section 848 of ITA 2007, a sum representing income tax deducted under Chapter 6 of Part 15 of that Act]¹ from an annual payment within this Chapter is treated as income tax paid by the recipient . . . ¹.

(2) See also [section 494(3) of ITA 2007]¹ (sum treated as deducted from payments made under a discretionary trust treated as income tax paid by the person to whom the payment is made or the settlor).

Commentary—*Simon's Taxes* **E1.513.**
HMRC Manuals—Savings and Investment Income Manual SAIM8010 (The basic rate tax deducted from income).
Amendments—¹   Words in sub-ss (1), (2) substituted, and words in sub-s (1) repealed, by ITA 2007 ss 1027, 1031, Sch 1
    paras 492, 570, Sch 3 Pt 1 with effect for income tax purposes from 6 April 2007, and corporation tax purposes for accounting
    periods ending after 5 April 2007.

CHAPTER 8

INCOME NOT OTHERWISE CHARGED

687 Charge to tax on income not otherwise charged
(1) Income tax is charged under this Chapter on income from any source that is not charged to income tax under or as a result of any other provision of this Act or any other Act.

(2) Subsection (1) does not apply to annual payments [or to income falling within Chapter 2A of Part 4]¹.

(3) Subsection (1) does not apply to income that would be charged to income tax under or as a result of another provision but for an exemption.

(4) The definition of "income" in section 878(1) does not apply for the purposes of this section.

(5) For exemptions from the charge under this Chapter, see in particular—
  section 768 (commercial occupation of woodlands), and
  section 779 (gains on commodity and financial futures).

Commentary—*Simon's Taxes* E1.513, E1.520.
HMRC Manuals—Business Income Manual BIM100000 (miscellaneous income: contents).
Amendments—[1]   In sub-s (2), words inserted by FA 2013 s 28, Sch 12 para 13(1), (3) with effect for the tax year 2013–14 and subsequent tax years.

688 Income charged

(1) Tax is charged under this Chapter on the . . . [1] amount of the income arising in the tax year.
(2) Subsection (1) is subject to—
  [(za) Chapter 1 of Part 6A (which gives relief on relevant income which may consist of or include income chargeable under this Chapter: see, in particular, sections 783AB, 783AC, 783AG and 783AJ),][3]
  (a) Chapter 1 of Part 7 (which provides relief on income from the use of furnished accommodation in an individual's only or main residence: see, in particular, sections 794 and 798),
  (b) Chapter 2 of that Part (which provides relief on income from the provision by an individual of [qualifying care][2]: see, in particular, sections 814 and 817), and
  (c) Part 8 (foreign income: special rules).

Commentary—*Simon's Taxes* E1.520, E1.587, E3.522.
Amendments—[1]   Word in sub-s (1) repealed by FA 2008 s 34, Sch 12 paras 17, 22 with effect for the tax year 2008–09 and subsequent tax years.
[2]   In sub-s (2)(b) words substituted for words "foster care" by F(No 3)A 2010 s 1, Sch 1 paras 30, 33 with effect for the tax year 2010–11 and subsequent tax years, subject to transitional provisions in F(No 3)A 2010 Sch 1 paras 36(2)–(5), 37.
[3]   Sub-s (2)(za) inserted by F(No 2)A 2017 s 17, Sch 3 paras 2, 9 with effect for the tax year 2017–18 and subsequent tax years.

689 Person liable

The person liable for any tax charged under this Chapter is the person receiving or entitled to the income.

Commentary—*Simon's Taxes* C1.102, E1.587.

[689A Temporary non-residents

(1) This section applies if an individual is temporarily non-resident.
(2) Distributions within subsection (3) are to be treated for the purposes of this Chapter as if they had been received by the individual, or as if the individual had become entitled to them, in the period of return.
(3) A distribution is within this subsection if—
  (a) the individual receives or becomes entitled to it in the temporary period of non-residence,
  (b) it is a distribution of a company that is a close company or that would be a close company if the company were UK resident,
  (c) the individual receives or becomes entitled to the distribution by virtue of being at a relevant time—
    (i) a material participator in the company, or
    (ii) an associate of a material participator in the company, and
  (d) ignoring this section, the individual—
    (i) is not liable for tax under this Chapter in respect of the distribution, but
    (ii) would have been so liable if the individual had received the distribution, or become entitled to it, in the period of return.
(4) For the purposes of subsection (3)—
  (a) "associate" and "participator" have the same meanings as in Part 10 of CTA 2010 (see sections 448 and 454),
  (b) a "material participator" is a participator who has a material interest in the company, as defined in section 457 of that Act,
  (c) "relevant time" means—
    (i) any time in the year of departure or, if the year of departure is a split year as respects the individual, the UK part of that year, or
    (ii) any time in one or more of the 3 tax years preceding that year, and
  (d) paragraph (d)(i) includes a case where the individual could be relieved of liability on the making of a claim under section 6 of TIOPA 2010 (double taxation relief), even if no claim is in fact made.
(5) If section 809B, 809D or 809E of ITA 2007 (remittance basis) applies to the individual for the year of return, any distribution within subsection (3) that is relevant foreign income and is remitted to the United Kingdom in the temporary period of non-residence is to be treated as remitted to the United Kingdom in the period of return.
(6) In this section, "remitted to the United Kingdom" has the meaning given in Chapter A1 of Part 14 of ITA 2007.][1]

Commentary—*Simon's Taxes* **C1.102, C1.201, E1.425.**
Amendments—[1]   Section 689A inserted by FA 2013 s 218, Sch 45 paras 131, 137 with effect if the year of departure (as defined in FA 2013 Sch 45 Pt 4) is the tax year 2013–14 or any subsequent tax year, subject to transitional provisions and savings in FA 2013 Sch 45 paras 154–158.

PART 6

EXEMPT INCOME

CHAPTER 1

INTRODUCTION

690 Overview of Part 6

(1) This Part provides for certain exemptions from charges to income tax under this Act.
(2) The exemptions are dealt with in—

    (a) Chapter 2 (national savings income),
    (b) Chapter 3 (income from individual investment plans),
    (c) Chapter 4 (SAYE interest),
    (d) Chapter 5 (venture capital trust dividends),
    (e) Chapter 6 (income from FOTRA securities),
    (f) Chapter 7 (purchased life annuity payments),
    (g) Chapter 8 (other annual payments), and
    (h) Chapter 9 (other income).

(3) Chapter 10 explains that, in general, the effect of the exemptions is that the exempt amounts are ignored for other income tax purposes.
(4) Other exemptions, such as exemptions relating to particular categories of persons, may also be relevant to the charges to income tax under this Act.
(5) And the exemptions dealt with in this Part may themselves be relevant to charges to income tax outside this Act.

Commentary—*Simon's Taxes* **E1.520.**
HMRC Manuals—Savings and Investment Manual SAIM1120 (tax exempt savings).

CHAPTER 2

NATIONAL SAVINGS INCOME

692 Income from savings certificates

(1) No liability to income tax arises in respect of income from authorised savings certificates.
(2) A savings certificate is authorised so far as its acquisition was not prohibited by regulations made by the Treasury limiting a person's holding.
(3) In this section "savings certificates" means—

    (a) savings certificates issued under—

        (i) section 12 of the National Loans Act 1968 (c. 13) (power of Treasury to borrow),
        (ii) section 7 of the National Debt Act 1958 (c. 6) (power of Treasury to issue national savings certificates), or
        (iii) section 59 of FA 1920 (power to borrow on national savings certificates),

    (b) war savings certificates, as defined in section 9(3) of the National Debt Act 1972 (c. 65), or
    (c) savings certificates issued under any enactment forming part of the law of Northern Ireland and corresponding to section 12 of the National Loans Act 1968.

(4) But subsection (3)(c) does not include Ulster Savings Certificates (for which there are special rules in section 693).

Commentary—*Simon's Taxes* **E1.522.**
HMRC Manuals—Corporate Finance Manual CFM70120 (income from savings certificates and Ulster savings certificates).

693 Income from Ulster Savings Certificates

(1) No liability to income tax arises in respect of income from authorised Ulster Savings Certificates if condition A, B or C is met.
(2) Condition A is that—

    (a) the holder purchased them, and
    (b) at the time of the purchase the holder was resident and ordinarily resident in Northern Ireland.

(3) Condition B is that the holder is so resident and ordinarily resident when they are repaid.
(4) Condition C is that—

    (a) they are repaid after the holder's death, and
    (b) at the time of the purchase the holder was so resident and ordinarily resident.

(5) An Ulster Savings Certificate is authorised so far as its acquisition was not prohibited by regulations made by the Department of Finance and Personnel limiting a person's holding.
(6) The exemption under this section requires a claim.
(7) In this Act "Ulster Savings Certificates" means savings certificates issued or treated as issued under section 15 of the Exchequer and Financial Provisions Act (Northern Ireland) 1950 (c. 3 (NI)).

Commentary—*Simon's Taxes* **E1.523.**
HMRC Manuals—Savings and Investment Manual SAIM2300 (exemptions: tax-free savings income).

CHAPTER 3

INCOME FROM INDIVIDUAL INVESTMENT PLANS

694 Income from individual investment plans

(1) The Treasury may by regulations provide that income of an individual from investments under a plan—

    (*a*) is exempt from income tax, or

    (*b*) is exempt from income tax to such extent as is specified in the regulations.

[(1A) In subsection (1) "income of an individual from investments under a plan" includes income from investments which is treated as the individual's income by virtue of section 629 (income paid to relevant children of settlor).][1]

(2) In this Chapter such regulations are referred to as "investment plan regulations".

(3) Investment plan regulations may, in particular, specify—

    (*a*) the description of individuals who may invest, and

    (*b*) maximum investment limits.

(4) They may provide for investment by an individual under more than one plan in the same tax year.

(5) They must set out conditions subject to which plans are to operate.

(6) The following provisions of this Chapter contain more particular provisions about the scope of investment plan regulations.

Commentary—*Simon's Taxes* **E1.524.**
HMRC Manuals—Savings and Investment Manual SAIM2310 (exemptions: individual investment plans).
Regulations—Individual Savings Account (Amendment) Regulations, SI 2012/705.
Individual Savings Account (Amendment) (No 2) Regulations, SI 2012/1871.
Individual Savings Account (Amendment) Regulations, SI 2013/267.
Income Tax (Removal of Ordinary Residence) Regulations, SI 2013/605.
Individual Savings Account (Amendment No 2) Regulations, SI 2013/623.
Individual Savings Account (Amendment No 3) Regulations, SI 2013/1743.
Individual Savings Account (Amendment) Regulations, SI 2014/654.
Individual Savings Account (Amendment No 2) Regulations, SI 2014/1450.
Individual Savings Account (Amendment) Regulations, SI 2015/608.
Individual Savings Account (Amendment No 2) Regulations, SI 2015/869.
Individual Savings Account (Amendment No 3) Regulations, SI 2015/941.
Individual Savings Account (Amendment No 4) Regulations, SI 2015/1370.
Individual Savings Account (Amendment) Regulations, SI 2016/16.
Individual Savings Account (Amendment No 2) Regulations, SI 2016/364.
Individual Savings Account (Amendment No 3) Regulations, SI 2016/977.
Individual Savings Account (Amendment) Regulations, SI 2017/186.
Individual Savings Account (Amendment No 2) Regulations, SI 2017/466.
Individual Savings Account (Amendment No 3) Regulations, SI 2017/1089.
Individual Savings Account (Amendment) Regulations, SI 2018/359.
Individual Savings Account (Amendment) Regulations, SI 2020/30.
Individual Savings Account (Amendment No 2) Regulations, SI 2020/261.
Individual Savings Account (Amendment No 3) (Coronavirus) Regulations, SI 2020/506.
Amendments—[1]   Sub-s (1A) inserted by FA 2011 s 40(1), (2) with effect from 19 July 2011.

[694A Deceased investors

(1) In section 694(1) "income of an individual from investments under a plan" includes—

    (*a*) income (of any person) from administration-period investments under a plan, and

    (*b*) income (of any person) from the estate of a deceased person ("D") where the whole or any part of the income of D's personal representatives is income from administration-period investments under a plan.

(2) For the purposes of sections 694(3)(*a*) and (4) and 695(1) "individual", in relation to investments that are administration-period investments, includes—

    (*a*) the personal representatives of the deceased individual concerned, and

    (*b*) any other person on whose directions plan managers agree to act in relation to the investments.

(3) In sections 699 and 701 "investor" includes a person entitled to an exemption given by investment plan regulations by virtue of subsection (1) of this section.

(4) Investments are "administration-period investments" if—

    (*a*) an individual dies, and

    (*b*) immediately before the individual's death—

        (i) the investments were held under a plan,

        (ii) the individual was entitled to the income from the investments, and

(iii) as a result of investment plan regulations, the individual's income from investments under the plan was exempt from income tax (either wholly or to an extent specified in the regulations).

(5) Investments are also "administration-period investments" if (directly or indirectly) they represent investments that are administration-period investments as a result of subsection (4).

(6) Investment plan regulations may provide that investments are administration-period investments as a result of subsection (4) or (5) only at times specified in, or ascertained in accordance with, the regulations.

(7) Provision under subsection (6) may (in particular) be framed by reference to the completion of the administration of a deceased individual's estate.

(8) In the application of subsection (7) in relation to Scotland, the reference to the completion of the administration is to be read in accordance with section 653(2).][1]

Regulations—Individual Savings Account (Amendment No 3) Regulations, SI 2017/1089.
Individual Savings Account (Amendment) Regulations, SI 2019/382.
Amendments—[1]   Section 694A inserted by FA 2016 s 27(1) with effect from 15 September 2016.

695 Investment plans

(1) Investment plan regulations may specify the kind of investments which may be made under a plan or which may be made by particular descriptions of individuals under a plan.

(2) They may—
    (*a*) provide for a plan in the form of an account, and
    (*b*) authorise the ways in which the subscriptions to an account are to be invested.

(3) They may—
    (*a*) provide that plans are to be such as are approved by [the Commissioners for Her Majesty's Revenue and Customs], and
    (*b*) specify the circumstances in which approval may be granted and withdrawn.

(4) They may—
    (*a*) provide for plans to be treated as being of different kinds, according to criteria set out in the regulations,
    (*b*) provide for the [Commissioners][1] to register a plan as being of a particular kind, and
    (*c*) make different provision about different kinds of plan.

Commentary—*Simon's Taxes* E1.525.
Regulations—Individual Savings Account (Amendment) (No 2) Regulations, SI 2012/1871.
Income Tax (Removal of Ordinary Residence) Regulations, SI 2013/605.
Individual Savings Account (Amendment No 2) Regulations, SI 2013/623.
Individual Savings Account (Amendment No 3) Regulations, SI 2013/1743.
Individual Savings Account (Amendment) Regulations, SI 2014/654.
Individual Savings Account (Amendment No 2) Regulations, SI 2014/1450.
Individual Savings Account (Amendment No 2) Regulations, SI 2015/869.
Individual Savings Account (Amendment No 3) Regulations, SI 2015/941.
Individual Savings Account (Amendment No 4) Regulations, SI 2015/1370.
Individual Savings Account (Amendment) Regulations, SI 2016/16.
Individual Savings Account (Amendment No 2) Regulations, SI 2016/364.
Individual Savings Account (Amendment No 3) Regulations, SI 2016/977.
Individual Savings Account (Amendment) Regulations, SI 2017/186.
Individual Savings Account (Amendment No 2) Regulations, SI 2017/466.
Individual Savings Account (Amendment No 3) Regulations, SI 2017/1089.
Individual Savings Account (Amendment) Regulations, SI 2018/359.
Individual Savings Account (Amendment) Regulations, SI 2020/30.
Individual Savings Account (Amendment No 3) (Coronavirus) Regulations, SI 2020/506.
Amendments—[1]   Word in sub-s (4) substituted by CRCA 2005 s 50, Sch 4 paras 131, 132(3)(*b*) with effect from 18 April 2005 (by virtue of SI 2005/1126).

[695A Investment plans for children

(1) This section applies where investment plan regulations provide that income of a child from investments under a plan (a "child plan") is exempt from income tax (either wholly or to such extent as is specified in the regulations).

(2) In addition to any provision which may be made by virtue of any other provision of this Chapter, investment plan regulations may—
    (*a*) specify descriptions of persons by whom investments may be made for a child,
    (*b*) provide that withdrawals may be made only in the circumstances specified in the regulations, and
    (*c*) provide that, in the case of a child who is under 16, the plan managers may act only on the direction of a person of a description specified in the regulations.

(3) They may also provide—
    (*a*) that any assignment of, or agreement to assign, investments under a child plan, and any charge on or agreement to charge any such investments, is void,

(b) that, on the bankruptcy of a child with investments under a child plan, the entitlement to those investments does not pass to any trustee or other person acting on behalf of the child's creditors, and

(c) that, where a contract is entered into by or on behalf of a child who is 16 or over in connection with a child plan under which investments are held—

    (i) by the child, or

    (ii) by another child in relation to whom the child has parental responsibility,

the contract has effect as if the child had been 18 or over when it was entered into.

(4) Where, by virtue of provision made in investment plan regulations under subsection (2)(a), investments are made for a child under a child plan, for the purposes of this Chapter the child is treated as having made those investments.

(5) In this section—

"assignment" includes assignation, and "assign" is to be construed accordingly;

"bankruptcy", in relation to a child, includes the sequestration of the child's estate;

"charge on or agreement to charge" includes a right in security over or an agreement to create a right in security over;

"child" means an individual under 18;

"parental responsibility" means—

    (a) parental responsibility within the meaning of the Children Act 1989 or the Children (Northern Ireland) Order 1995, or

    (b) parental responsibilities within the meaning of the Children (Scotland) Act 1995;

and any reference to investments being held by a child includes a reference to investments being held by plan managers on behalf of the child by virtue of section 696(1).][1]

Regulations—Individual Savings Account (Amendment) (No 2) Regulations, SI 2012/1871.
Income Tax (Removal of Ordinary Residence) Regulations, SI 2013/605.
Individual Savings Account (Amendment No 3) Regulations, SI 2013/1743.
Individual Savings Account (Amendment) Regulations, SI 2014/654.
Individual Savings Account (Amendment No 2) Regulations, SI 2015/869.
Individual Savings Account (Amendment No 3) Regulations, SI 2015/941.
Individual Savings Account (Amendment No 4) Regulations, SI 2015/1370.
Individual Savings Account (Amendment No 2) Regulations, SI 2016/364.
Individual Savings Account (Amendment) Regulations, SI 2018/359.
Amendments—[1] Section 695A inserted by FA 2011 s 40(1), (3) with effect from 19 July 2011.

696 Plan managers

(1) Investment plan regulations may provide that investments are to be held by persons on behalf of investors.

(2) In this Chapter those persons, including the managers of any such account as is specified in section 695(2), are referred to as "plan managers", and references to "plan managers" in any other enactment are to be read accordingly.

(3) Investment plan regulations may—

    (a) provide that plan managers are to be such as are approved by [the Commissioners for Her Majesty's Revenue and Customs], and

    (b) specify the circumstances in which approval may be granted and withdrawn.

Commentary—*Simon's Taxes* E1.526.
HMRC Manuals—CH Compliance Handbook CH25360 (involved third parties, relevant information, relevant documents and relevant tax).
Regulations—Individual Savings Account (Amendment) (No 2) Regulations, SI 2012/1871.
Individual Savings Account (Amendment No 2) Regulations, SI 2013/623.
Individual Savings Account (Amendment) Regulations, SI 2014/654.
Individual Savings Account (Amendment No 2) Regulations, SI 2015/869.
Individual Savings Account (Amendment No 3) Regulations, SI 2015/941.
Individual Savings Account (Amendment No 4) Regulations, SI 2015/1370.
Individual Savings Account (Amendment) Regulations, SI 2016/16.
Individual Savings Account (Amendment No 2) Regulations, SI 2016/364.
Individual Savings Account (Amendment No 3) Regulations, SI 2016/977.
Individual Savings Account (Amendment No 2) Regulations, SI 2017/466.
Individual Savings Account (Amendment No 3) Regulations, SI 2017/1089.
Individual Savings Account (Amendment) Regulations, SI 2018/359.

697 Special requirements for certain foreign managers

(1) Investment plan regulations may provide that a foreign institution may only be a plan manager if one of the requirements set out in section 698(2), (3) and (4) about the discharge of such of the institution's duties as are specified in the regulations is met.

(2) In this section "foreign institution" means—

    (a) an EEA firm of the kind mentioned in paragraph 5(a), (b) or (c) of Schedule 3 to FISMA 2000 which is an authorised person for the purposes of that Act as a result of qualifying for authorisation under paragraph 12 of that Schedule, (*b*) a firm which is an authorised person for those purposes as a result of qualifying for authorisation under paragraph 2 of Schedule 4 to that Act, or

    (*c*) an insurance company which is non-UK resident.

(3) Different duties may be specified under subsection (1) for different institutions or different descriptions of institution.

(4) In this section—

    "insurance company" means an undertaking carrying on the business of effecting or carrying out contracts of insurance, and

    "contract of insurance" has the meaning given by Article 3(1) of the Financial Services and Markets Act 2000 (Regulated Activities) Order 2001 (SI 2001/544).

Commentary—*Simon's Taxes* **E1.527.**
Regulations—Individual Savings Account (Amendment) (No 2) Regulations, SI 2012/1871.
Individual Savings Account (Amendment No 2) Regulations, SI 2015/869.
Individual Savings Account (Amendment No 2) Regulations, SI 2015/941.
Individual Savings Account (Amendment No 2) Regulations, SI 2016/364.
Prospective amendments—Sub-s (2)(*a*) and (*b*) to be repealed by the Taxes (Amendments) (EU Exit) Regulations, SI 2019/689 reg 13(1), (4) with effect from Implementation Period completion day (see EU(WA)A 2020 Sch 5 para 1(1)). The repeal of sub-s (2)(*a*) does not apply where a person qualifies for authorisation under FSMA 2000 Sch 3 by virtue of SI 2001/3084 (see SI 2019/689 reg 41(*e*)).

698 Requirements for discharge of foreign institution's duties

(1) The requirements about the discharge of an institution's duties which are referred to in section 697(1) (one of which may be imposed in the case of certain foreign managers) are requirements A, B and C.

(2) Requirement A is that—

    (*a*) a person is currently appointed by the institution to be responsible for securing the discharge of the duties,

    (*b*) that person either—

        (i) is an individual who is a UK resident, or

        (ii) is not an individual and has a business establishment in the United Kingdom, and

    (*c*) the institution has notified [the Commissioners for Her Majesty's Revenue and Customs] of that person's identity and appointment.

(3) Requirement B is that there are other current arrangements with the [Commissioners][1] for a person other than the institution to secure the discharge of the duties.

(4) Requirement C is that there are other current arrangements with the [Commissioners][1] designed to secure the discharge of the duties.

(5) Investment plan regulations may provide—

    (*a*) that requirement A or B is only met if the person concerned is of a description specified in the regulations as respects that requirement,

    (*b*) that appointments made for the purposes of requirement A or arrangements made for the purposes of requirement B are treated as terminated in circumstances specified in the regulations as respects that requirement.

(6) Investment plan regulations may provide that a person currently appointed as mentioned in subsection (2) or as to whom there is a current arrangement within subsection (3)—

    (*a*) may act on the institution's behalf for any of the purposes of the provisions relating to the duties,

    (*b*) is to secure the institution's compliance with, and discharge of, the duties, where appropriate by acting on its behalf,

    (*c*) is personally liable for the institution's failure to comply with or discharge any of the duties, as if they were imposed on the person and the institution jointly and severally.

Commentary—*Simon's Taxes* **E1.527.**
Regulations—Individual Savings Account (Amendment) (No 2) Regulations, SI 2012/1871.
Individual Savings Account (Amendment No 2) Regulations, SI 2015/869.
Individual Savings Account (Amendment No 23 Regulations, SI 2015/941.
Amendments—[1]   Word in sub-ss (3), (4) substituted by CRCA 2005 s 50, Sch 4 paras 131, 132(3)(*c*) with effect from 18 April 2005 (by virtue of SI 2005/1126).

699 Non-entitlement to exemption

(1) Investment plan regulations may—

    (*a*) provide that in circumstances specified in the regulations an investor ceases to be entitled to the exemption given by regulations made under section 694(1) and is treated as not having been entitled to it,

    (*b*) adapt or modify the effect of any enactment relating to income tax for that purpose, and

    (*c*) provide that in those circumstances the investor or the plan manager (depending on the terms of the regulations) is to account to [the Commissioners for Her Majesty's Revenue and Customs] for income tax from which exemption has already been given on the basis that the investor was entitled to the exemption.

(2) They may provide that an investor or the plan manager (depending on the terms of the regulations) is to account to the [Commissioners[1]]—

(a) for income tax from which the exemption has been given in circumstances where the investor was not entitled to it, or

(b) for an amount determined in accordance with the regulations to be the amount to be taken as representing that tax.

(3) They may modify the effect of or adapt any enactment relating to income tax for the purposes of securing that investors or plan managers account for the tax and other amounts mentioned in subsections (1) and (2).

(4) They may also modify the provisions of or adapt Chapter 9 of Part 4 of this Act (gains from contracts for life insurance etc.) or Chapter 2 of Part 13 of ICTA (life policies, life annuities and capital redemption policies) for cases where an investor—

(a) ceases to be entitled to the exemption given by regulations made under section 694(1) and is treated as not having been entitled to it, or

(b) has been given the exemption on the basis of an entitlement to it when there was no such entitlement.

(5) They may provide for plan managers (as well as investors) to be liable to account for amounts becoming due from investors as a result of regulations made under subsection (4).

(6) They may provide that, instead of having to account as mentioned in subsection (2) or (5), an investor or a plan manager is liable to a penalty of an amount specified in the regulations if—

(a) an exemption has been given to which there was no entitlement, and

(b) the circumstances are such as are specified in the regulations.

(7) They may provide that liabilities are imposed in cases which—

(a) are not cases in which liabilities may be imposed under subsections (1) to (6) where relief has been given to which there was no entitlement, but

(b) are cases where—

(i) a contravention or failure to comply with investment plan regulations that is specified in the regulations, or

(ii) the existence of such other circumstances as are so specified,
would have the effect of excluding or limiting an entitlement to exemption, apart from the regulations under this subsection.

(8) Regulations under subsection (7)—

(a) may only provide for the imposition of liabilities equivalent to those which may be imposed under subsections (1) to (6), and

(b) must provide for those liabilities to replace the liabilities to tax which would otherwise arise.

[(9) In this section references to an investor include an individual entitled to an exemption given by investment plan regulations by virtue of section 694(1A).][2]

Commentary—*Simon's Taxes* E1.528.
Regulations—Individual Savings Account (Amendment) Regulations, SI 2017/186.
Individual Savings Account (Amendment No 2) Regulations, SI 2017/466.
Individual Savings Account (Amendment No 3) Regulations, SI 2017/1089.
Individual Savings Account (Amendment) Regulations, SI 2020/30.
Amendments—[1]   Word in sub-s (2) substituted by CRCA 2005 s 50, Sch 4 paras 131, 132(3)(d) with effect from 18 April 2005
   (by virtue of SI 2005/1126).
[2]   Sub-s (9) inserted by FA 2011 s 40(1), (4) with effect from 19 July 2011.

701 General and supplementary powers

(1) Investment plan regulations may make provision generally for the purpose of—

(a) the establishment and administration of plans, and

(b) the administration of income tax in relation to them.

(2) They may adapt or modify the effect of any enactment relating to income tax for the purpose of securing that investors are entitled to exemption from income tax in respect of investments.

(3) They may specify how exemption from tax is to be claimed by, and granted to, investors or plan managers on behalf of investors.

[(4) They may include provision having effect in relation to times before they are made if the provision does not impose or increase any liability to tax.

(5) They may make different provision for different cases or circumstances.][1]

[(6) In this section references to an investor include an individual entitled to an exemption given by investment plan regulations by virtue of section 694(1A).][2]

Regulations—Individual Savings Account (Amendment) Regulations, SI 2017/186.
Individual Savings Account (Amendment No 2) Regulations, SI 2017/466.
Individual Savings Account (Amendment No 3) Regulations, SI 2017/1089.
Individual Savings Account (Amendment) Regulations, SI 2018/359.
Individual Savings Account (Amendment) Regulations, SI 2020/30.
Individual Savings Account (Amendment No 3) (Coronavirus) Regulations, SI 2020/506.
Amendments—[1]   Sub-ss (4), (5) inserted by FA 2008 s 40 with effect from 21 July 2008.
[2]   Sub-s (6) inserted by FA 2011 s 40(1), (5) with effect from 19 July 2011.

CHAPTER 4

SAYE INTEREST

702 Interest under certified SAYE savings arrangements

(1) No liability to income tax arises in respect of interest payable under a certified SAYE savings arrangement.

(2) In this section "certified SAYE savings arrangement" has the meaning given in section 703(1).

(3) Subsection (1) is subject to—

    (*a*) section 707(1) (which requires the providers of certain arrangements to be authorised), and

    (*b*) paragraph 7 of Schedule 12 to FA 1988 (application of exemption on change of status of building society).

(4) In this Chapter "interest" includes any bonus.

Commentary—*Simon's Taxes* **E1.531.**

HMRC Manuals—Savings and Investment Manual SAIM2300 (exemptions: tax-free savings income: Save As You Earn (SAYE)).

703 Meaning of "certified SAYE savings arrangement"

(1) In this Chapter "certified SAYE savings arrangement" means a linked savings arrangement which is certified under section 705.

(2) In this Chapter "linked savings arrangement" means an arrangement—

    (*a*) which is of a kind specified in section 704(1), and

    (*b*) under which an individual who is eligible to participate in [a Schedule 3][1] SAYE option scheme enters into a contract to make periodical contributions for a specified period for the purpose of being able to participate in that scheme.

(3) In subsection (2)—

    "to participate" means to obtain and exercise rights under the scheme, and

    ["Schedule 3 SAYE option scheme" has the meaning given in Schedule 3 to ITEPA 2003.][1]

Commentary—*Simon's Taxes* **E1.531.**

HMRC Manuals—Employee Share Scheme Option User Guide ESSUM30105 (introduction: meaning of "certified SAYE savings arrangement").

ESSUM34130 (certified SAYE savings arrangement: meaning).

Amendments—[1] In sub-s (2)(*b*) words substituted for words "an approved", and in sub-s (3) definition of "Schedule 3 SAYE option scheme" substituted for previous definition of "SAYE option scheme", by FA 2014 s 51, Sch 8 para 141 with effect from 6 April 2014. The effect of the FA 2014 changes on SAYE option schemes established before 6 April 2014 is set out in FA 2014 Sch 8 paras 148 to 157.

704 Types of arrangements and providers

(1) A linked savings arrangement may be—

    (*a*) a national savings arrangement, or

    (*b*) an institutional arrangement.

(2) In this Chapter "national savings arrangement" means an arrangement which—

    (*a*) provides for contributions to be paid to raise money under section 12 of the National Loans Act 1968 (c. 13) (power of Treasury to borrow),

    (*b*) is governed by regulations made under section 11 of the National Debt Act 1972 (c. 65) (power of Treasury to make regulations as to raising of money under auspices of Director of Savings), and

    (*c*) provides for the repayment of those contributions, together with interest, in accordance with those regulations.

(3) In this Chapter "institutional arrangement" means—

    (*a*) a bank arrangement,

    (*b*) a building society arrangement, or

    (*c*) a European authorised institution arrangement.

(4) In this Chapter—

    (*a*) "bank arrangement" means an arrangement which provides for contributions to be paid to a person within [section 991(2)(*b*) of ITA 2007][1] (banks), and

    (*b*) "provider", in relation to such an arrangement, means that person.

(5) In this Chapter—

    (*a*) "building society arrangement" means an arrangement which provides for contributions to be paid by way of investment in shares in a building society, and

    (*b*) "provider", in relation to such an arrangement, means that society.

(6) In this Chapter—

    "European authorised institution" means an EEA firm of the kind mentioned in paragraph 5(*b*) of Schedule 3 to FISMA 2000 which has permission under paragraph 15 of that Schedule (as a result of qualifying for authorisation under paragraph 12 of that Schedule) to accept deposits,

    "European authorised institution arrangement" means an arrangement which provides for contributions to be paid to such a firm, and

    "provider", in relation to such an arrangement, means that firm.

Commentary—*Simon's Taxes* E1.532.
HMRC Manuals—Employee Share Scheme Option User Guide ESSUM34170 (the SAYE contract).
Amendments—[1]   Words in sub-s (4)(*a*) substituted by ITA 2007 s 1027, Sch 1 paras 492, 571 with effect for income tax
purposes from 6 April 2007, and corporation tax purposes for accounting periods ending after 5 April 2007.
Prospective amendments—In sub-s (3)(*a*) word "or" to be inserted at the end, in sub-s (3)(*b*) word ", or" to be repealed, and sub-ss (3)(*c*) and (6) to be repealed, by the Taxes (Amendments) (EU Exit) Regulations, SI 2019/689 reg 13(1), (5) with effect from
Implementation Period completion day (see EU(WA)A 2020 Sch 5 para 1(1)). These amendments do not apply where a person
qualifies for authorisation under FSMA 2000 Sch 3 by virtue of SI 2001/3084 (see SI 2019/689 reg 41(*e*)).

705 Certification of arrangements

(1) A linked savings arrangement is certified under this section if it is certified by the [Commissioners][1]
    (*a*) as a linked savings arrangement, and
    (*b*) in the case of an institutional arrangement, as meeting such requirements as the Treasury may specify for the purposes of this Chapter.
(2) The requirements which may be specified under subsection (1)(*b*) are such requirements as the [Commissioners][1] consider appropriate.
(3) They may, in particular, relate to—
    (*a*) the descriptions of individuals who may enter into contracts under an arrangement,
    (*b*) the contributions to be paid by them, and
    (*c*) the sums to be paid or repaid to them.
(4) Different requirements may be specified for—
    (*a*) bank arrangements,
    (*b*) building society arrangements, and
    (*c*) European authorised institution arrangements.
[(5) In this Chapter "the Commissioners" means the Commissioners for Her Majesty's Revenue and Customs.][1]

Amendments—[1]   In sub-ss (1), (2), word substituted and sub-s (5) inserted, by FA 2009 s 50, Sch 26 para 2. These amendments
are treated as having come into force on 29 April 2009.

706 Withdrawal and variation of certifications and connected requirements

(1) The [Commissioners][1] may—
    (*a*) withdraw the requirements specified under section 705(1)(*b*) for any description of arrangements and any certification made by reference to those requirements, or
    (*b*) vary those requirements and withdraw any certification made by reference to them.
(2) The withdrawal, or variation and withdrawal, is only effective if the [Commissioners][1]
    (*a*) specify the date on which it is to take effect, and
    (*b*) give notice of it . . . [1] at least [15 days][1] before that date to the provider authorised under section 707 to enter into contracts under the arrangement concerned.
(3) The withdrawal, or variation and withdrawal, does not affect
    [(*a*) the operation of the arrangement concerned before that date,
    (*b*) contracts made under that arrangement before that date, or
    (*c*) where the notice so provides, contracts which are of a description specified in the notice and are made under that arrangement after that date.][1]

Amendments—[1]   In sub-ss (1), (2), (3) words substituted FA 2009 s 50, Sch 26 paras 3, 6–8. These amendments are treated
as having come into force on 29 April 2009.

707 Authorisation of providers

(1) In the case of an institutional arrangement, section 702(1) (exemption of interest payable under certified SAYE savings arrangements) only applies if, at the time the contract under the arrangement is made, the provider is authorised by the [Commissioners][1] to enter into contracts under it.
(2) If the authorisation is conditional, the conditions must be met at that time.
(3) Authorisation may be given for arrangements generally or a particular arrangement.
(4) More than one authorisation may be given to the same provider.

Commentary—*Simon's Taxes* E1.534.
Amendments—[1]   In sub-s (1), word substituted by FA 2009 s 50, Sch 26 para 4. This amendment is treated as having come
into force on 29 April 2009.

708 Withdrawal and variation of authorisations

(1) The [Commissioners][1] may withdraw the authorisation of a provider or vary it by imposing, varying or removing conditions.
(2) The withdrawal or variation is only effective if the [Commissioners][1]—
    (*a*) specify the date on which it is to take effect, and
    (*b*) except in the case of a variation removing all conditions, give notice of it . . . [1] to the provider at least 28 days before that date.
(3) The withdrawal or variation does not affect contracts made before that date.
(4) The fact that a provider has had its authorisation withdrawn or varied does not affect the later exercise by the [Commissioners of their][1] powers under section 707 or this section as respects the provider.

Commentary—*Simon's Taxes* **E1.533.**
Amendments—[1]   In sub-ss (1), (2), word substituted; in sub-s (2)(*b*), words repealed; and in sub-s (4) words substituted, by FA
2009 s 50, Sch 26 paras 5, 6. These amendments are treated as having come into force on 29 April 2009.

CHAPTER 5

VENTURE CAPITAL TRUST DIVIDENDS

709 Venture capital trust dividends

(1) No liability to income tax arises in respect of a venture capital trust dividend if—
  (*a*) conditions A and B are met, and
  (*b*) where the dividend is paid in respect of shares acquired after 8th March 1999, condition C is met.

(2) In subsection (1) a "venture capital trust dividend" means a dividend paid in respect of ordinary shares in a company which—
  (*a*) is a venture capital trust—
    (i) at the end of the accounting period in which the profits or gains in respect of which it is paid arose or accrued, and
    (ii) when the dividend is paid, and
  (*b*) was such a trust when the person to whom it is paid acquired the shares.

(3) Condition A is that the person beneficially entitled to the dividend—
  (*a*) is an individual of at least 18 years, and
  (*b*) is beneficially entitled to it as the holder of the shares or as the person for whom, or for whose benefit, they are held by a nominee.

(4) Condition B is that—
  (*a*) in the tax year in which the shares were acquired the market value of all the shares acquired by the individual or any nominee of the individual in companies which were venture capital trusts at the time of acquisition did not exceed £200,000, or
  (*b*) in that year that market value exceeded £200,000, but the shares are treated under section 710 as having been acquired within that limit.

(5) For the purposes of subsection (4), the market value of a share is determined as at the time of its acquisition.

(6) Condition C is that the shares were acquired for genuine commercial reasons and not as part of a scheme or arrangement the main purpose of which, or one of the main purposes of which, was the avoidance of tax.

(7) Shares that were not so acquired are ignored for the purposes of subsection (4) and section 710 (whether or not they were acquired after 8th March 1999).

(8) In this section and in sections 710 and 711—
  "market value" has the same meaning as in TCGA 1992 (see sections 272 and 273),
  "nominee", in relation to an individual, includes the trustees of a bare trust of which the individual is the only beneficiary, and
  "ordinary shares" means shares forming part of the company's ordinary share capital.

Commentary—*Simon's Taxes* **E1.535.**
HMRC Manuals—Venture Capital Trust VCM51200 (dividend exemption from income tax).

710 Treatment of shares where annual acquisition limit exceeded

(1) This section sets out the rules for determining which shares whose market value is relevant for the limit in section 709(4) are treated as shares acquired within that limit ("exempt shares") where that limit is exceeded in a tax year.

(2) Shares are treated as exempt shares so far as their acquisition does not cause the limit to be exceeded at the time they are acquired.

(3) Subsection (2) is subject to subsection (4).

(4) If shares of different descriptions acquired on the same day cause the limit to be exceeded on that day, shares of each description are treated as exempt shares so far as their market value does not exceed the appropriate proportion of the available value.

(5) In subsection (4)—
  "the appropriate proportion", in relation to shares of a particular description, means the proportion which their market value bears to the market value of all the shares acquired on that day, and
  "available value" means the maximum value of shares which could be acquired on that day without exceeding the limit.

Commentary—*Simon's Taxes* **E1.536.**
HMRC Manuals—Venture Capital Trust VCM52040 (acquisitions over permitted maximum).

711 Identification of shares after disposals

(1) In determining whether a disposal relates to shares in a company which were acquired when it was a venture capital trust or others, it is assumed that the others are disposed of first.

(2) In determining whether a disposal of shares in a company which were acquired when it was a venture capital trust relates to shares which meet the condition in section 709(4) (annual acquisition limit) or others ("excess shares"), assumptions A and B are to be made.

(3) Assumption A is that shares acquired on an earlier day are disposed of before those acquired on a later day.

(4) Assumption B is that where the shares were acquired on the same day, excess shares are disposed of first.

(5) For the purposes of this section, acquisitions and disposals by an individual's nominee are treated as made by the individual, and acquisitions and disposals between them are ignored.

Commentary—*Simon's Taxes* **E1.537.**

HMRC Manuals—Venture Capital Trust VCM52070 (share identification rules).
VCM52080 (share identification rules: example 1).
VCM52080 (share identification rules: example 2).

712 Identification of shares after reorganisations etc.

(1) This section applies if shares ("the new shares") are treated under Chapter 2 of Part 4 of TCGA 1992 (reorganisations etc.) as the same assets as other shares ("the old shares").

(2) If all the old shares met—

   (a) the condition in section 709(4) (annual acquisition limit), and

   (b) if it applied to the old shares, the condition in section 709(6) (acquisition for genuine commercial reasons),

the new shares are treated as doing so.

(3) If only some of the old shares met those conditions, the corresponding proportion of the new shares are treated as meeting them and the remainder are treated as not doing so.

(4) In the tax year in which the new shares are acquired the value of the new shares is ignored in determining whether other shares acquired in the same tax year meet the condition in section 709(4).

Commentary—*Simon's Taxes* **E1.538.**

HMRC Manuals—Venture Capital Trusts VCM51200 (dividend exemption from income tax: new shares).

CHAPTER 6

INCOME FROM FOTRA SECURITIES

713 Introduction: securities free of tax to residents abroad ("FOTRA securities")

(1) This Chapter provides for exemptions from income tax in respect of FOTRA securities.

(2) In this Chapter "FOTRA security" means—

   (a) a security issued with a condition about exemption from taxation authorised by section 22 of F(No.2)A 1931,

   (b) a gilt-edged security which was issued before 6th April 1998 and without any such condition (other than 31/2% War Loan 1952 Or After), or

   (c) 31/2% War Loan 1952 Or After.

(3) In this Chapter "the exemption condition" has the meaning given by subsections (4) to (6), according to the kind of FOTRA security involved.

(4) In relation to a security within subsection (2)(a), it means the condition authorised by section 22 of F(No 2)A 1931.

(5) In relation to a security within subsection (2)(b), it means a condition with which 7.25% Treasury Stock 2007 was first issued, being a condition treated by section 161(1) of FA 1998 (non-FOTRA securities)—

   (a) as a condition with which the security within subsection (2)(b) was issued, and

   (b) as a condition authorised in relation to its issue by section 22 of F(No 2)A 1931.

(6) In relation to 3^1/2% War Loan 1952 Or After, it means a condition of its issue authorised by section 47 of F(No 2)A 1915.

Commentary—*Simon's Taxes* **E1.539.**

HMRC Manuals—Savings and Investment Manual SAIM1180 (non-residents: FOTRA securities).

714 Exemption of profits from FOTRA securities

(1) No liability to income tax arises in respect of profits from a FOTRA security if conditions A and B are met.

(2) Subsection (1) is subject to subsection (5).

(3) Condition A is that the profits are stated in the exemption condition to be exempt from income tax.

(4) Condition B is that any requirements for obtaining the exemption imposed by the security's conditions of issue are met.

(5) Whatever the exemption condition provides, amounts charged under the provisions specified in subsection (6) are not exempted by subsection (1).

(6) The provisions are—

   Chapter 5 of Part 5 (settlements: amounts treated as income of settlor) so far as it applies to income within section 619(1)(a) or (b), and

[Chapter 2 of Part 13 of ITA 2007][1] (anti-avoidance provisions: transfer of assets abroad).

(7) This section does not affect the need to claim repayment of tax within the time limit applicable for a claim.

Commentary—*Simon's Taxes* **E1.540.**
Amendments—[1]   Words in sub-s (6) substituted by ITA 2007 s 1027, Sch 1 paras 492, 572 with effect for income tax purposes from 6 April 2007, and corporation tax purposes for accounting periods ending after 5 April 2007.

715 Interest from FOTRA securities held on trust

(1) This section applies if—

    (*a*) a FOTRA security is held on trust, and

    (*b*) apart from this section, interest payable on the security would not be exempt from income tax under section 714 because of the security not being in the beneficial ownership of a [non-UK resident person.][1]

(2) For the purposes of determining whether the interest is exempt under section 714 it is to be assumed that the security is in the beneficial ownership of a [non-UK resident person][1] if none of the beneficiaries of the trust [is UK resident for the tax year in which][1] the interest arises.

(3) In subsection (2) "beneficiaries of the trust" includes any person known to the trustees as a person—

    (*a*) who is, or will or may become, entitled under the terms of the trust to receive income under the trust, or

    (*b*) to whom or for whose benefit such income may be paid or applied.

(4) In subsection (3) "income under the trust" includes any property held on the terms of the trust and falling to be treated as capital so far as it is or represents amounts received by the trustees as income.

Commentary—*Simon's Taxes* **E1.541.**
HMRC Manuals—Savings and Investment Manual SAIM3120 (taxation: Non-UK resident trustees).
Amendments—[1]   In sub-ss (1)(*b*), (2) words substituted for words "person not ordinarily UK resident", and in sub-s (2) words substituted for words "is ordinarily UK resident at the time when", by FA 2013 s 219, Sch 46 paras 43, 52 with effect for the purposes of a person's liability to income tax for the tax year 2013–14 or any subsequent tax year. In relation to a FOTRA security issued before 6 April 2013, these amendments apply only if the security was acquired by the trust on or after that date (FA 2013 Sch 46 para 52(4)).

716 Restriction on deductions etc. relating to FOTRA securities

(1) A person who meets conditions A and B may not bring into account for income tax purposes—

    (*a*) any amount relating to changes in the value of a FOTRA security, or

    (*b*) expenses related to holding it or to any transaction concerning it.

(2) Condition A is that the person is the beneficial owner of the security.

(3) Condition B is that the person is a person who would be exempt from tax on the security under this Chapter.

Commentary—*Simon's Taxes* **E1.542.**
HMRC Manuals—Savings and Investment Manual SAIM1180 (non-residents: FOTRA securities).

CHAPTER 7

PURCHASED LIFE ANNUITY PAYMENTS

Partial exemption for purchased life annuity payments

717 Exemption for part of purchased life annuity payments

(1) No liability to income tax arises under Chapter 7 of Part 4 in respect of so much of an annuity payment made under a purchased life annuity as is within this subsection in accordance with section 719 (extent of exemption).

(2) Subsection (1) is subject to section 718.

[(3) The exemption under this section requires a claim.][1]

(4) In this Chapter "purchased life annuity" has the same meaning as in Chapter 7 of Part 4 (see section 423).

Commentary—*Simon's Taxes* **E1.543.**
HMRC Manuals—Insurance Policyholder Taxation Manual IPTM4220 (life annuities and purchased life annuities: exemption).
Amendments—[1]   Sub-s (3) repealed by FA 2007 ss 46(5), (9), 114, Sch 27 Pt 2(13) with effect from 6 April 2008 (by virtue of SI 2008/561 art 2).

718 Excluded annuities

(1) The exemption in section 717(1) does not apply to payments made under the annuities specified in subsection (2).

(2) The annuities are—

    (*a*) an annuity the whole or part of the consideration for which consisted of sums satisfying the conditions for relief under section 266 of ICTA (life assurance premiums),

    (*b*) an annuity purchased following a direction in a will, and

    (*c*) an annuity purchased to provide for an annuity payable as a result of a will or settlement out of income of property disposed of by the will or settlement.

(3) For the purposes of subsection (2)(*c*), it does not matter whether or not capital could also be used to pay the annuity.

Commentary—*Simon's Taxes* E1.430, E1.544, E1.545.

HMRC Manuals—Insurance Policyholder Taxation Manual IPTM7065 (certain life annuities).

719 Extent of exemption under section 717

(1) This section sets out the rules for determining the extent to which an annuity payment is within the exemption in section 717(1).

(2) The rules depend on—

- (*a*) whether or not the amount of the annuity payments under the annuity depends solely on the duration of a human life or lives (see subsections (3) to (5)), and
- (*b*) whether or not the annuity's term depends solely on the duration of a human life or lives (see subsections (6) to (8)).

(3) If the amount of the annuity payments depends solely on the duration of a human life or lives, the same proportion of each payment ("the exempt proportion") is exempt.

(4) But if the amount of the annuity payments also depends on another contingency, each payment is exempt so far as it does not exceed a fixed sum ("the exempt sum").

(5) If an annuity payment within subsection (4) is less than the exempt sum, the shortfall is added to the exempt sum for the next payment (and so on).

(6) The ways to determine the exempt proportion and the exempt sum differ according to whether or not the annuity's term depends solely on the duration of a human life or lives.

(7) If the annuity's term depends solely on the duration of a human life or lives—

- (*a*) the exempt proportion is determined as set out in section 720, and
- (*b*) the exempt sum is determined as set out in section 721.

(8) If the annuity's term also depends on another contingency—

- (*a*) the exempt proportion is the proportion which is just and reasonable, having regard to the contingencies affecting the annuity and to section 720, and
- (*b*) the exempt sum is the amount which is just and reasonable, having regard to the contingencies affecting the annuity and to section 721.

Commentary—*Simon's Taxes* E1.430–E1.430B, E1.545.

HMRC Manuals—Insurance Policyholder Taxation Manual IPTM4310 (effect of life and other contingencies on term of annuity and on amount of annuity payments).

720 Exempt proportion: term dependent solely on duration of life

(1) In the case of an annuity within section 719(7) (term dependent solely on duration of life), the exempt proportion is—

$$AP \times \frac{PP}{AV}$$

where—

> AP is the annuity payment,
> PP is the purchase price of the annuity, and
> AV is the actuarial value of the annuity payments.

(2) The purchase price of the annuity is the total amount or value of the consideration given for the annuity.

(3) The actuarial value of the annuity payments is their value at the date when the first of the payments starts to accrue.

(4) That value is determined—

- (*a*) by reference to tables of mortality prescribed under section 724,
- (*b*) taking the age at that date of a person during whose life the annuity is payable as that person's age in whole years on that date, and
- (*c*) without discounting any payment for the time to elapse before it is payable.

(5) But if it is not possible to determine that actuarial value by reference to the tables mentioned in subsection (4)(*a*), it is such amount as may be certified by the Government Actuary or the Deputy Government Actuary.

Commentary—*Simon's Taxes* E1.430A, E1.430, E1.546.

HMRC Manuals—Insurance Policyholder Taxation Manual IPTM4320 (exempt proportion formula).

721 Exempt sum: term dependent solely on duration of life

(1) In the case of an annuity within section 719(7) (term dependent solely on duration of life), the exempt sum is—

$$PP \times \frac{1}{TY} \times \frac{PM}{12}$$

where—

PP is the purchase price of the annuity,

TY is the expected term of the annuity in years (and any odd fraction of a year), and

PM is the period in months (and any odd fraction of a month) in respect of which the annuity payment is made.

(2) The purchase price of the annuity is the total amount or value of the consideration given for the annuity.

(3) The expected term of the annuity is the period from the date when the first annuity payment starts to accrue to the date when it is expected that the last payment will become payable.

(4) The expected term of the annuity is determined—

    (*a*) as at the date when the first annuity payment starts to accrue,

    (*b*) by reference to tables of mortality prescribed under section 724, and

    (*c*) taking the age at that date of a person during whose life the annuity is payable as that person's age in whole years on that date.

(5) But if it is not possible to determine that term by reference to the tables mentioned in subsection (4)(*b*), it is such period as may be certified by the Government Actuary or the Deputy Government Actuary.

Commentary—*Simon's Taxes* **E1.430B, E1.430C, E1.547.**
HMRC Manuals—Insurance Policyholder Taxation Manual IPTM4330 (exempt sum formula).

722 Consideration for the grant of annuities

(1) This section applies if the amount or value given for an annuity is to be determined for the purposes of sections 720(2) or 721(2) and either—

    (*a*) consideration is not given solely for the annuity, or

    (*b*) it appears that the amount or value of the consideration nominally given for it affected, or was affected by, the consideration given for something else.

(2) For the purposes of subsection (1), consideration given for a right to a return of premiums or of other consideration for an annuity is treated as given solely for the annuity.

(3) If subsection (1)(*a*) applies, the consideration is to be apportioned in such way as is just and reasonable.

(4) If subsection (1)(*b*) applies, the total amount or value of the considerations given is to be apportioned in such way as is just and reasonable.

Commentary—*Simon's Taxes* **E1.430C.**
HMRC Manuals—Insurance Policyholder Taxation Manual IPTM4340 (consideration).

724 Regulations

(1) [The Commissioners for Her Majesty's Revenue and Customs] may by regulations—

    (*a*) prescribe the procedure to be used in giving effect to sections 717 to [722]² and this section where no provision is made in those provisions,

    (*b*) apply any provision of the Income Tax Acts, with or without modifications, for the purposes of those provisions or the regulations,

    (*c*) prescribe tables of mortality for the purposes of sections 720(4) and 721(4).

(2) . . . ²

(3) . . . ¹

Commentary—*Simon's Taxes* **E1.430D.**
Regulations—Income Tax (Purchased Life Annuities) (Amendment) Regulations, SI 2012/2902.
Amendments—¹ Sub-s (3) repealed by ITA 2007 ss 1027, 1031, Sch 1 paras 492, 573, Sch 3 Pt 1 with effect for income tax purposes from 6 April 2007, and corporation tax purposes for accounting periods ending after 5 April 2007.
² Reference in sub-s (1)(*a*) substituted for "723", and sub-s (2) repealed, by FA 2007 ss 46(7), (9), 114, Sch 27 Pt 2(13) with effect from 6 April 2008: SI 2008/561 art 2.

Immediate needs annuities

725 Annual payments under immediate needs annuities

(1) No liability to income tax arises under Chapter 7 of Part 4 in respect of so much of an annual payment made under an immediate needs annuity as is made—

    (*a*) for the benefit of the person protected under that annuity, and

    (*b*) to a care provider or a local authority in respect of the provision of care for that person.

(2) In this section "immediate needs annuity" means a contract for a purchased life annuity—

    (*a*) the purpose or one of the purposes of which is to protect a person against the consequences of the person being unable, at the time the contract is made, to live independently without assistance because of a condition to which subsection (3) applies, and

    (*b*) under which benefits are payable in respect of the provision of care for the person protected.

(3) This subsection applies to—

    (*a*) mental or physical impairment, or

    (*b*) injury, sickness or other infirmity,

which is expected to be permanent.

(4) In this section and section 726 "care" means accommodation, goods or services which it is necessary or desirable to provide to a person because of a condition to which subsection (3) applies.

(5) In this section—

"care provider" has the meaning given in section 726, and

"purchased life annuity" has the same meaning as in Chapter 7 of Part 4 (see section 423).

(6) The Treasury may by order amend—

    (*a*) subsection (2), and

    (*b*) subsection (3), so far as it applies for the purposes of subsection (2).

Commentary—*Simon's Taxes* E1.431, E1.550.

HMRC Manuals—Insurance Policyholder Taxation Manual IPTM6200 (immediate needs annuities: introduction).

IPTM6210 (immediate needs annuity: general rules and scope of the exemption).

IPTM6215 (meaning of immediate needs annuity and care provider).

IPTM6220 (payments made to the insured person or after their death).

IPTM6225 (tax treatment up to 30 September 2004).

726 Meaning of "care provider"

(1) In section 725 "care provider" means a person who—

    (*a*) carries on a trade, profession or vocation which consists of or includes the provision of care, and

    (*b*) meets the care registration requirement.

[(2) A person meets the care registration requirement in relation to care provided in England if the person is registered under Part 2 of the Care Standards Act 2000 or Chapter 2 of Part 1 of the Health and Social Care Act 2008 in respect of the provision of care.][1]

[(2A) A person meets the care registration requirement in relation to care provided in Wales if the person is registered under—

    (*a*) Part 2 of the Care Standards Act 2000, or

    (*b*) Part 1 of the Regulation and Inspection of Social Care (Wales) Act 2016 (anaw 2),

in respect of the provision of the care.][2]

(3) A person meets the care registration requirement in relation to care provided in Scotland if the person provides care as, or as part of, a service which is registered under Part 1 of the Regulation of Care (Scotland) Act 2001 (asp 8).

(4) A person meets the care registration requirement in relation to care provided in Northern Ireland if the person is registered in respect of the provision of care under—

    (*a*) Part 2 or 3 of the Registered Homes (Northern Ireland) Order 1992 (SI 1992/3204 (NI 20)), or

    (*b*) Part 3 of the Health and Personal Social Services (Quality, Improvement and Regulation) (Northern Ireland) Order 2003 (SI 2003/431 (NI 9)).

(5) A person meets the care registration requirement in relation to care provided in a territory outside the United Kingdom if the person meets requirements under the law of that territory relating to the provision of care that are comparable to those mentioned in subsections (2) to (4).

(6) The Treasury may by order amend this section.

Commentary—*Simon's Taxes* E1.431.

HMRC Manuals—Insurance Policyholder Taxation Manual IPTM6215 (meaning of immediate needs annuity and care provider).

Amendments—[1]   Sub-s (2) substituted by the Health and Social Care Act 2008 (Consequential Amendments No 2) Order, SI 2010/813 art 16 with effect from 1 October 2010.

[2]   Sub-s (2A) substituted by the Regulation and Inspection of Social Care (Wales) Act 2016 (Consequential Amendments) Regulations, SI 2018/195 reg 26 with effect from 2 April 2018.

CHAPTER 8

OTHER ANNUAL PAYMENTS

Certain annual payments by individuals

727 Certain annual payments by individuals

(1) No liability to income tax arises under Part 5 in respect of an annual payment if it—

    (*a*) is made by an individual, and

    (*b*) arises in the United Kingdom.

(2) Subsection (1) is subject to—

    section 728 (commercial payments), and

    section 729 (payments for non-taxable consideration).

(3) Subsection (1) also applies to a payment made by an individual's personal representatives if—

    (*a*) the individual would have been liable to make it, and

    (*b*) that subsection would have applied if the individual had made it.

(4) For the purposes of subsection (1) and section 728, "individual" includes a Scottish partnership if at least one partner is an individual.

Commentary—*Simon's Taxes* E1.514, E1.551.

HMRC Manuals—Savings and Investment Manual SAIM9120 (annual payments: individuals).

SAIM8070 (exemptions: annual payments made by individuals).

Corporate Finance Manual CFM74420 (manufactured overseas dividends: mods from overseas debt securities: individuals: payments).

Insurance Policyholder Taxation Manual IPTM6215 (payments made to a registered care provider: individual (care provider)).

728 Commercial payments

A payment by an individual is not exempt from income tax under section 727(1) if it is made for commercial reasons in connection with the individual's trade, profession or vocation.

Commentary—*Simon's Taxes* **E1.514, A4.433.**

HMRC Manuals—Savings and Investment Manual SAIM9120 (annual payments: deduction of tax).

Corporate Finance Manual CFM74420 (mods from overseas debt securities: individuals: payments).

SAIM8070 (exemptions: annual payments made by individuals).

729 Payments for non-taxable consideration

(1) A payment that meets condition A is only exempt from income tax under section 727(1) if condition B or C is met.

(2) Condition A is that—

    (*a*) the payment is made under a liability incurred at any time for consideration in money or money's worth, and

    (*b*) some or all of the consideration is not required to be brought into account in calculating the payer's income for income tax purposes.

(3) Condition B is that the payment is income within section 627(1) (payments on [dissolution][1] or separation) in the recipient's hands.

(4) Condition C is that the payment is made to an individual under a liability incurred at any time in consideration of the individual surrendering, assigning or releasing an interest in settled property to or in favour of a person with a subsequent interest.

(5) In the application of subsection (4) to Scotland, the reference to settled property is to be read as a reference to property held in trust.

Commentary—*Simon's Taxes* **E1.514, E1.551.**

HMRC Manuals—Savings and Investment Manual SAIM8070 (exemptions: payments for non-taxable consideration by an individual).

Amendments—[1]   Word in sub-s (3) substituted by Tax and Civil Partnership Regulations, SI 2005/3229, regs 183, 196, with effect from 5 December 2005 (reg 1(1)).

730 Foreign maintenance payments

(1) No liability to income tax arises under Part 5 in respect of an annual payment if—

    (*a*) it is a maintenance payment,

    (*b*) it arises outside the United Kingdom, and

    (*c*) had it arisen in the United Kingdom it would be exempt from income tax under section 727 (certain annual payments by individuals).

(2) In subsection (1) "maintenance payment" means a periodical payment which meets conditions A and B.

(3) Condition A is that the payment is made under a court order or a written or oral agreement.

(4) Condition B is that the payment is made by a person—

    (*a*) as one of the parties to a marriage [or civil partnership][1] to, or for the benefit of, and for the maintenance of, the other party,

    (*b*) to any person under 21 for that person's own benefit, maintenance or education, or

    (*c*) to any person for the benefit, maintenance or education of a person under 21.

(5) In subsection (4) "marriage" includes a marriage that has been dissolved or annulled[, and "civil partnership" includes a civil partnership that has been dissolved or annulled][1].

(6) Subsection (1) also applies to a payment made by an individual's personal representatives if—

    (*a*) the individual would have been liable to make it, and

    (*b*) that subsection would have applied if the individual had made it.

Commentary—*Simon's Taxes* **E1.552.**

HMRC Manuals—Savings and Investment Manual SAIM8070 (exemption: maintenance payments arises outside UK).

Amendments—[1]   Words in sub-ss (4)(*a*), (5) inserted by Tax and Civil Partnership Regulations, SI 2005/3229, regs 183, 197, with effect from 5 December 2005 (reg 1(1)).

Periodical payments of personal injury damages etc.

731 Periodical payments of personal injury damages

(1) No liability to income tax arises for the persons specified in section 733 in respect of periodical payments to which subsection (2) applies or annuity payments to which subsection (3) applies.

(2) This subsection applies to periodical payments made pursuant to—

    (*a*) an order of the court, so far as it is made in reliance on section 2 of the Damages Act 1996 (c. 48) (periodical payments) (including an order as varied),

    (*b*) an order of a court outside the United Kingdom which is similar to an order made in reliance on that section (including an order as varied),

    (*c*) an agreement, so far as it settles a claim or action for damages in respect of personal injury (including an agreement as varied), (*d*) an agreement, so far as it relates to making payments on account of damages that may be awarded in such a claim or action (including an agreement as varied), or

(*e*) a Motor Insurers' Bureau undertaking in relation to a claim or action in respect of personal injury (including an undertaking as varied).

(3) This subsection applies to annuity payments made under an annuity purchased or provided—

(*a*) by the person by whom payments to which subsection (2) applies would otherwise fall to be made, and

(*b*) in accordance with such an order, agreement or undertaking as is mentioned in subsection (2) or a varying order, agreement or undertaking.

(4) In this section "damages in respect of personal injury" includes damages in respect of a person's death from personal injury.

(5) In this section "personal injury" includes disease and impairment of physical or mental condition.

(6) In this section "a Motor Insurers' Bureau undertaking" means an undertaking given by—

(*a*) the Motor Insurers' Bureau (being the company of that name incorporated on 14th June 1946 under the Companies Act 1929 (c. 23)), or

(*b*) an Article 75 insurer under the Bureau's Articles of Association.

Commentary—*Simon's Taxes* **E1.553.**

HMRC Manuals—Insurance Policyholder Taxation Manual IPTM5010 (periodical payments in personal injury cases: tax treatment and exemption).

IPTM5040 (personal injury: claims or actions in UK in respect of fatal accidents).

IPTM5020 (periodical payments: tax exemption: court orders and other relevant documentation).

IPTM1140 (what is a structured settlement?).

Savings and Investment Manual SAIM8070 (Exemptions: periodical payments of personal injury damages).

Modifications—MFET Limited (Application of Sections 731, 733 and 734 of the Income Tax (Trading and Other Income) Act 2005) Order 2010, SI 2010/673 art 2 (modification of this section in relation to payments made pursuant to a scheme or arrangement administered by MFET Limited to an Eligible Person).

Skipton Fund Limited (Application of Sections 731, 733 and 734 of the Income Tax (Trading and Other Income) Act 2005) Order, SI 2011/1157 art 2 (modification of this section in relation to payments made pursuant to a scheme or arrangement administered by Skipton Fund Limited to a qualifying person).

Scottish Infected Blood Support Scheme (Application of Sections 731, 733 and 734 of the Income Tax (Trading and Other Income) Act 2005) Order, SI 2017/446 art 2 (modification of this section in relation to payments made pursuant to the Scheme of Support and Assistance for those Infected with Hepatitis C, or HIV, or both, as a result of NHS treatment).

Infected Blood Schemes (Application of Sections 731, 733 and 734 of the Income Tax (Trading and Other Income) Act 2005) Order. SI 2017/904 art 2 (modification of this section in relation to payments made pursuant to an Infected Blood Scheme for those infected with Hepatitis C, HIV or both, through contaminated blood or blood products used by the NHS).

732 Compensation awards

(1) No liability to income tax arises for the persons specified in section 733 in respect of annuity payments if they are made under an annuity purchased or provided under an award of compensation made under the Criminal Injuries Compensation Scheme [or the Victims of Overseas Terrorism Compensation Scheme][1].

(2) The Treasury may by order provide for sections 731, 733 and 734 to apply, with such modifications as they consider necessary, to periodical payments by way of compensation for personal injury for which provision is made under a scheme or arrangement other than the Criminal Injuries Compensation Scheme [or the Victims of Overseas Terrorism Compensation Scheme][1].

(3) In this section—

"the Criminal Injuries Compensation Scheme" means—

(*a*) the schemes established by arrangements made under the Criminal Injuries Compensation Act 1995 (c. 53),

(*b*) arrangements made by the Secretary of State for compensation for criminal injuries in operation before the commencement of those schemes, or

(*c*) the scheme established under the Criminal Injuries (Northern Ireland) Order 2002 (SI 2002/796) (NI1), and

"personal injury" includes disease and impairment of physical or mental condition.

Commentary—*Simon's Taxes* **E1.554.**

HMRC Manuals—Insurance Policyholder Taxation Manual IPTM5020 (periodical payments: main condition for tax exemption).

IPTM5080 (annuities purchased under the criminal injuries compensation scheme: tax exemption).

IPTM5060 (persons exempt).

IPTM5040 (meaning of 'personal injury': includes fatal accidents).

Savings and Investment Manual SAIM8070 (exemption: compensation awards).

Orders—MFET Limited (Application of Sections 731, 733 and 734 of the Income Tax (Trading and Other Income) Act 2005) Order 2010, SI 2010/673.

Scottish Infected Blood Support Scheme (Application of Sections 731, 733 and 734 of the Income Tax (Trading and Other Income) Act 2005) Order, SI 2017/446.

Infected Blood Schemes (Application of Sections 731, 733 and 734 of the Income Tax (Trading and Other Income) Act 2005) Order. SI 2017/904.

Amendment—[1]   Words at the end of sub-ss (1), (2) inserted by the Crime and Security Act 2010, s 48(4), Sch 2 para 3 with effect from 8 April 2010: see the Crime and Security Act 2010, s 59(2)(b).

733 Persons entitled to exemptions for personal injury payments etc.

The persons entitled to the exemptions given by sections 731(1) and 732(1) for payments are—

    (a) the person entitled to the damages under the order, agreement, undertaking or to the compensation under the award in question ("A"),

    (b) a person who receives the payment in question on behalf of A, and

    (c) a trustee who receives the payment in question on trust for the benefit of A under a trust under which A is, while alive, the only person who may benefit.

Commentary—*Simon's Taxes* **E1.515.**

HMRC Manuals—Savings and Investment Manual SAIM8070 (periodical payments of personal injury: persons entitled to exemptions).

Modifications—MFET Limited (Application of Sections 731, 733 and 734 of the Income Tax (Trading and Other Income) Act 2005) Order 2010, SI 2010/673 art 2 (modification of this section in relation to payments made pursuant to a scheme or arrangement administered by MFET Limited to an Eligible Person).

Skipton Fund Limited (Application of Sections 731, 733 and 734 of the Income Tax (Trading and Other Income) Act 2005) Order, SI 2011/1157 art 2 (modification of this section in relation to payments made pursuant to a scheme or arrangement administered by Skipton Fund Limited to a qualifying person).

Scottish Infected Blood Support Scheme (Application of Sections 731, 733 and 734 of the Income Tax (Trading and Other Income) Act 2005) Order, SI 2017/446 art 2 (modification of this section in relation to payments made pursuant to the Scheme of Support and Assistance for those Infected with Hepatitis C, or HIV, or both, as a result of NHS treatment).

Infected Blood Schemes (Application of Sections 731, 733 and 734 of the Income Tax (Trading and Other Income) Act 2005) Order, SI 2017/904 art 2 (modification of this section in relation to payments made pursuant to an Infected Blood Scheme for those infected with Hepatitis C, HIV or both, through contaminated blood or blood products used by the NHS).

734 Payments from trusts for injured persons

(1) No liability to income tax arises for the persons specified in subsection (2) in respect of sums paid under a lifetime trust—

    (a) to the person ("A") who is entitled to—

        (i) a payment under an order, agreement or undertaking within section 731(2) or an annuity purchased or provided as mentioned in section 731(3), or

        (ii) compensation under an award within section 732(1), or

    (b) for the benefit of A.

(2) The persons are—

    (a) A, and

    (b) if subsection (1)(b) applies, a person who receives the sum on behalf of A.

(3) For the purposes of subsection (1), sums are paid under a lifetime trust if they are paid—

    (a) by the trustees of a trust under which A is, while alive, the only person who may benefit, and

    (b) out of payments within section 731(2) or (3) or 732(1) which are received by them on trust for A.

Commentary—*Simon's Taxes* **E1.555.**

HMRC Manuals—Insurance Policyholder Taxation Manual IPTM5070 (payments from trusts for injured persons).

Savings and Investment Manual SAIM8070 (periodical payments of personal injury damages from trust).

Modifications—MFET Limited (Application of Sections 731, 733 and 734 of the Income Tax (Trading and Other Income) Act 2005) Order 2010, SI 2010/673 art 2 (modification of this section in relation to payments made pursuant to a scheme or arrangement administered by MFET Limited to an Eligible Person).

Skipton Fund Limited (Application of Sections 731, 733 and 734 of the Income Tax (Trading and Other Income) Act 2005) Order, SI 2011/1157 art 2 (modification of this section in relation to payments made pursuant to a scheme or arrangement administered by Skipton Fund Limited to a qualifying person).

Scottish Infected Blood Support Scheme (Application of Sections 731, 733 and 734 of the Income Tax (Trading and Other Income) Act 2005) Order, SI 2017/446 art 2 (modification of this section in relation to payments made pursuant to the Scheme of Support and Assistance for those Infected with Hepatitis C, or HIV, or both, as a result of NHS treatment).

Infected Blood Schemes (Application of Sections 731, 733 and 734 of the Income Tax (Trading and Other Income) Act 2005) Order, SI 2017/904 art 2 (modification of this section in relation to payments made pursuant to an Infected Blood Scheme for those infected with Hepatitis C, HIV or both, through contaminated blood or blood products used by the NHS).

Health and employment insurance payments

735 Health and employment insurance payments

(1) No liability to income tax arises under this Act in respect of an annual payment under an insurance policy if—

    (a) the payment is a benefit provided under so much of the policy as insures against a health or employment risk (see section 736),

    (b) no part of any premiums under the policy has been deductible in calculating the income of the insured for income tax purposes, and

    (c) the conditions in sections 737 and 738 and, so far as applicable, those in sections 739 and 740 are met in relation to the policy.

(2) Subsection (1)(b) is subject to section 743.

(3) For the meaning of "the insured", see sections 742 and 743(2).

Commentary—*Simon's Taxes* **E1.516, E1.556.**

HMRC Manuals—Insurance Policyholder Taxation Manual IPTM6100 (sickness disability and unemployment insurance: introduction).

(a) any payment or reward falling within section 57(3) of the Adoption Act 1976 (c. 36) (payments authorised by the court) which is made to a person who has adopted or intends to adopt a child,

(b) payments under section 57(3A)(a) of that Act (payments by adoption agencies of legal or medical expenses of persons seeking to adopt),

(c) payments of allowances under regulations under section 57A of that Act (permitted allowances to persons who have adopted or intend to adopt children),

(d) payments of financial support made in the course of providing adoption support services within the meaning of the Adoption and Children Act 2002 (c. 38) (see section 2(6) and (7) of that Act), . . .¹

(e) payments made under regulations under paragraph 3(1) of Schedule 4 to that Act (transitional and transitory provisions: adoption support services).

[(f) payments made under regulations under section 14F of the Children Act 1989 (special guardianship support services) to a person appointed as a child's special guardian,

(g) payments made to a person under section 17 of that Act (provision of services for children in need, their families and others) by reason of that person being a person [named in a child arrangements order as a person with whom a child is to live]¹,

(h) payments made to a person, in respect of a child, under paragraph 15 of Schedule 1 to that Act (local authority contribution to child's maintenance to recipients [with whom a child is living, or is to live, as a result of a child arrangements order]²), and

(i) payments made in accordance with—

    (i) an order under that Schedule (orders for financial relief against parents etc), or

    (ii) a maintenance agreement,

for the benefit of a child, to a person appointed as the child's special guardian or a person [named in a child arrangements order as a person with whom the child is to live]²;]¹

[(j) payments made to a person under sections 37 to 39 of the Social Services and Well-being (Wales) Act 2014 (meeting care and support needs of children) by reason of that person being named in a child arrangements order as a person with whom a child is to live.]³

[(2) But a payment is not within subsection (1)(f), (g), (h) [(i) or (j)]³ if—

    (a) it is made to an excluded relative of the child,

    (b) it is made to a person appointed as the child's special guardian and an excluded relative is also appointed as the child's special guardian, or

    [(c) it is made to a person ("P") named in a child arrangements order as a person with whom the child is to live and an excluded relative who lives in the same household as P is also named in that order as a person with whom the child is to live]²;

(3) In this section—

    "excluded relative", in relation to a child, means—

        (a) a parent of the child, or

        (b) a person who is, or has been, the husband or wife or civil partner of a parent of the child;

    "maintenance agreement" has the meaning given by paragraph 10(1) of Schedule 1 to the Children Act 1989;

    "[child arrangements]² order" has the meaning given by section 8 of that Act.]¹

Commentary—*Simon's Taxes* E1.517, E1.560.

HMRC Manuals—Business Income Manual BIM52815 (capital gains).

Amendments—¹ In heading word inserted, existing provision renumbered as sub-s (1), word immediately preceding sub-s (1)(e) repealed, and sub-ss (1)(f)–(i), (2), (3) inserted, by F(No 3)A 2010 s 2(1), (2) with effect in relation to the tax year 2010–11 and subsequent tax years.

² In sub-ss (1)(g), (h), (i), (3) words substituted, and in sub-s (2)(c) substituted, by the Children and Families Act 2014 s 12, Sch 2 paras 67, 68 with effect from 22 April 2014 (by virtue of SI 2014/889 art 4(f))

³ Sub-s (1)(j) inserted, and in sub-s (2), words substituted by the Social Services and Well-being (Wales) Act 2014 (Consequential Amendments) Regulations, SI 2016/413 regs 222, 223 with effect from 6 April 2016.

745 Payments to adopters[, etc]²: Scotland

[(1)] No liability to income tax arises in respect of the following payments—

    (a) any payment [which is an excepted payment by virtue of paragraph (a) or (c) of subsection (2) of section 73 of the Adoption and Children (Scotland) Act 2007 (asp 4),]¹ which is made to a person who has adopted or intends to adopt a child,

    (b) payments [which are excepted payments by virtue of paragraph (b) of that subsection,"]¹,

    (c) . . .¹ , . . .²

    (d) payments of allowances in accordance with an adoption allowances scheme under [section 71]¹ of that Act.

    [(e) payments made to a person under section 50 of the Children Act 1975, or section 22 of the Children (Scotland) Act 1995, by reason of that person being a person with whom a child is to live by virtue of a residence order, and

    (f) payments of aliment made—

        (i) in accordance with an award of aliment under the Family Law (Scotland) Act 1985, or

     (ii) under an agreement (within the meaning of section 7(5) of that Act),

     for the benefit of a child, to a person in whose favour a residence order with respect to the child is in force.][2]

[(2) A payment is not within subsection (1)(e) or (f) if

     (a) it is made to an excluded relative of the child, or

     (b) it is made to a person in whose favour a residence order is in force with respect to the child and that order is also in favour of an excluded relative.

(3) In this section—

     "excluded relative", in relation to a child, means—

         (a) a parent of the child, or

         (b) a person who is, or has been, the husband or wife or civil partner of a parent of the child;

     "residence order" has the meaning given by section 11(2)(c) of the Children (Scotland) Act 1995.][2]

Commentary—*Simon's Taxes* **E1.517, E1.560.**
HMRC Manuals—Savings and Investment Manual SAIM8070 (exemptions: payments to adopters).
Amendments—[1]   In paras (a), (b), (d) words substituted, and para (c) repealed, by the Adoption and Children (Scotland) Act 2007 s 120(1), Sch 2 para 13 with effect from 28 September 2009 (by virtue of SSI 2009/267, arts 1(2), 2. The same amendments also made by the Adoption and Children (Scotland) Act 2007 (Consequential Modifications) Order, SI 2011/1740 art 3, Sch 2 para 6 and Sch 2 Pt 3 with effect from 15 July 2011.
[2]   In heading word inserted, existing provision renumbered as sub-s (1), word immediately preceding sub-s (1)(d) repealed, and sub-ss (1)(e), (f), (2), (3) inserted, by F(No 3)A 2010 s 2(1), (3) with effect in relation to the tax year 2010–11 and subsequent tax years.

746 Payments to adopters[, etc][1]: Northern Ireland

[(1)] No liability to income tax arises in respect of the following payments—

     (a) any payment or reward falling within Article 59(2)(b) of the Adoption (Northern Ireland) Order 1987 (SI 1987/2203 (NI 22)) (payments authorised by the court) which is made to a person who has adopted or intends to adopt a child,

     (b) any payment under Article 59(2)(c) of that Order (payments by registered adoption societies) which is made to a person who has adopted or intends to adopt a child, . . . [1]

     (c) payments of allowances under regulations under Article 59A of that Order (permitted allowances to persons who have adopted or intend to adopt children).

     [(d) payments made to a person under Article 18 of the Children (Northern Ireland) Order 1995 (SI 1995/755 (NI 2)) (general duty of authority to provide personal social services) by reason of that person being a person in whose favour a residence order with respect to a child is in force,

     (e) payments made to a person, in respect of a child, under paragraph 17 of Schedule 1 to that Order (local authority contribution to child's maintenance to recipients in whose favour residence order is in force), and

     (f) payments made in accordance with—

         (i) an order under that Schedule (orders for financial relief against parents etc), or

         (ii) a maintenance agreement,

     for the benefit of a child, to a person in whose favour a residence order with respect to the child is in force.][1]

[(2) But a payment is not within subsection (1)(d), (e) or (f) if—

     (a) it is made to an excluded relative of the child, or

     (b) it is made to a person in whose favour a residence order is in force with respect to the child and that order is also in favour of an excluded relative.

(3) In this section—

     "excluded relative", in relation to a child, means—

         (a) a parent of the child, or

         (b) a person who is, or has been, the husband or wife or civil partner of a parent of the child;

     "maintenance agreement" has the meaning given by paragraph 12 of Schedule 1 to the Children (Northern Ireland) Order 1995;

     "residence order" has the meaning given by Article 8 of that Order.][1]

Commentary—*Simon's Taxes* **E1.517, E1.560.**
Amendments—[1]   In heading word inserted, existing provision renumbered as sub-s (1), word immediately preceding sub-s (1)(c) repealed, and sub-ss (1)(d)–(f), (2), (3) inserted, by F(No 3)A 2010 s 2(1), (4) with effect in relation to the tax year 2010–11 and subsequent tax years.

747 Power to amend sections 744 to 746

The Treasury may by order amend section 744, 745 or 746 for the purposes of—

     (a) adding a description of payment, or

     (b) removing a description of payment if the power to make a payment of that description has been repealed or revoked or has otherwise ceased to be exercisable.

Commentary—*Simon's Taxes* **E1.560.**

CHAPTER 9

OTHER INCOME

Interest only income

749 [Repayment interest, and interest][1] paid under repayment supplements

No liability to income tax arises in respect of interest paid under—

(a) section 824 of ICTA (repayment supplements: individuals and others), . . . [1]

(b) section 283 of TCGA 1992 (repayment supplements)[, or

(c) section 102 of FA 2009 (repayment interest).][1]

Commentary—*Simon's Taxes* **E1.562.**

HMRC Manuals—Savings and Investment Manual SAIM2320 (exemptions to repayment supplements).

Amendments—[1]   Words in heading substituted, word in para (a) repealed, and para (c) and preceding word inserted, by the Finance Act 2009, Sections 101 and 102 (Interest on Late Payments and Repayments), Appointed Days and Consequential Provisions Order, SI 2014/992 art 8(1) with effect in relation to payments due and payable in respect of the tax year 2014–15 and subsequent tax years.

[749A Interest on tax overpaid

No liability to income tax arises in respect of interest paid under section 826 of ICTA (interest on tax overpaid).][1]

Commentary—*Simon's Taxes* **D5.511.**

Amendments—[1]   This section inserted by CTA 2009 s 1322, Sch 1 paras 587, 635. CTA 2009 applies for accounting periods ending on or after 1 April 2009 (for corporation tax purposes) and for tax years 2009–10 onwards (for income and capital gains tax purposes).

751 Interest on damages for personal injury

(1) No liability to income tax arises in respect of interest on damages for personal injury or death if—

(a) it is included in a sum awarded by a court,

(b) it does not relate to the period between the making and satisfaction of the award, and

(c) in the case of an award by a court in a country outside the United Kingdom, it is exempt from any charge to tax in that place.

(2) No liability to income tax arises in respect of interest if—

(a) it is included in a payment in satisfaction of a cause of action (including a payment into court), and

(b) it would fall within subsection (1) if it were included in a sum awarded by a court in respect of a cause of action.

(3) In subsection (1)—

"damages" in Scotland includes solatium, and

"personal injury" includes disease and impairment of physical or mental condition.

Commentary—*Simon's Taxes* **E1.564.**.

HMRC Manuals—Savings and Investment Manual SAIM2330 (exemptions: personal injury damages).

752 Interest under employees' share schemes

(1) This section applies if—

(a) a scheme is set up to comply with section [682(2)(b) of the Companies Act 2006 (c 46)][1] (financial assistance for the purposes of an employees' share scheme), and

(b) under the scheme the trustees receive interest from a participant in the scheme.

(2) So far as the scheme requires the trustees to pay to the company an equivalent amount as interest, no liability to income tax arises under Chapter 2 of Part 4 for the trustees in respect of the interest they receive.

Commentary—*Simon's Taxes* **E1.565.**

HMRC Manuals—Savings and Investment Manual SAIM2320 (exemptions: employee share schemes).

Amendments—[1]   In sub-s (1)(a), words substituted by the Companies Act 2006 (Consequential Amendments) (Taxes and National Insurance) Order, SI 2009/1890 art 12 with effect from 1 October 2009.

753 Interest on repayment of student loan

(1) No liability to income tax arises in respect of interest if—

(a) it is paid to a person to whom a student loan has been made, and

(b) it relates to an amount repaid to the person after being recovered from the person in respect of the loan.

(2) In this section "student loan" means a loan made under—

section 22 of the Teaching and Higher Education Act 1998 (c. 30),

section 73(f) of the Education (Scotland) Act 1980 (c. 44), or

Article 3 of the Education (Student Support) (Northern Ireland) Order 1998 (SI 1998/1760 (NI 14)).

Commentary—*Simon's Taxes* **E1.566.**

HMRC Manuals—Savings and Investment Manual SAIM2320 (exemptions: student loan).

[753A Interest on unpaid relevant contributions

(1) No liability to income tax arises in respect of interest paid in compliance with a requirement in a compliance notice or an unpaid contributions notice to pay interest in respect of unpaid relevant contributions.

(2) In this section—

"compliance notice" means a notice under section 35 of the Pensions Act;

"the Pensions Act" means the Pensions Act 2008 or the Pensions (No 2) Act (Northern Ireland) 2008;

"unpaid contributions notice" means a notice under section 37 of the Pensions Act;

"unpaid relevant contributions" has the same meaning as in section 38(2)(*a*) of the Pensions Act.][1]

Amendments—[1]   This section inserted by FA 2011 s 69(1), (3) with effect from 19 July 2011.

754 Redemption of funding bonds

(1) The redemption of funding bonds is not treated as the payment of interest on a debt for income tax purposes if their issue was treated under section 380 of this Act or [section 413 of CTA 2009][1] as the payment of interest on the debt.

(2) In this section "funding bonds" includes any bonds, stocks, shares, securities or certificates of indebtedness.

Commentary—*Simon's Taxes* E1.567.

HMRC Manuals—Savings and Investment Manual SAIM2210 (specific inclusions: funding bonds).

Amendments—[1]   In sub-s (1) words substituted by CTA 2009 s 1322, Sch 1 paras 587, 636. CTA 2009 applies for accounting periods ending on or after 1 April 2009 (for corporation tax purposes) and for tax years 2009–10 onwards (for income and capital gains tax purposes).

755 Interest on foreign currency securities etc. owned by non-UK residents

(1) This section applies to interest on—

(*a*) such foreign currency securities issued by a local authority or a statutory corporation as the Treasury direct, and

(*b*) such foreign currency loans made to a statutory corporation as the Treasury direct.

(2) No liability to income tax arises in respect of interest to which this section applies if—

(*a*) in the case of interest on a security, its beneficial owner is a non-UK resident, and

(*b*) in the case of interest on a loan, the person for the time being entitled to repayment or eventual repayment is a non-UK resident.

(3) But interest is not exempt under subsection (2) because a person is a non-UK resident if it is treated as another person's income under—

Chapter 5 of Part 5 (settlements: amounts treated as income of settlor), or

[Chapter 2 of Part 13 of ITA 2007][1] (anti-avoidance provisions: transfer of assets abroad).

(4) In this section—

"company" means a company, as defined in section [1(1)][2] of the Companies Act [2006 (c 46)][2] . . .[2],

"foreign currency", in relation to loans and securities, has the meaning given by section 756, and

"statutory corporation" means—

(*a*) a corporation incorporated by an Act (other than a company), or

(*b*) any other corporation on which functions connected with carrying on an undertaking are conferred by an Act or by an order made under or confirmed by an Act.

Commentary—*Simon's Taxes* E1.568.

HMRC Manuals—Savings and Investment Manual SAIM1180 (non-residents: FOTRA securities).

Amendments—[1]   Words in sub-s (3) substituted by ITA 2007 s 1027, Sch 1 paras 492, 574 with effect for income tax purposes from 6 April 2007, and corporation tax purposes for accounting periods ending after 5 April 2007.

[2]   In sub-para (4), word substituted, and words repealed, by the Companies Act 2006 (Consequential Amendments) (Taxes and National Insurance) Order, SI 2009/1890 art 3(6) with effect from 1 October 2009.

756 Which securities and loans are foreign currency ones for section 755

(1) For the purposes of section 755, a security or loan is a foreign currency one if under its terms the currency to be used for repayment is not sterling.

(2) Subsection (1) is subject to the following qualifications.

(3) A security issued before 6th April 1982 is a foreign currency one if under its terms the currency to be used for repayment is not that of a country specified in Schedule 1 to the Exchange Control Act 1947 (c. 14) at the time of the issue of the security.

(4) A loan made before that date is a foreign currency one if under its terms the currency to be used for repayment is not that of a country specified in that Schedule at the time the loan was made.

(5) If in the case of a security there is an option as to the currency to be used for repayment, the security is only to be treated as a foreign currency one if the option is exercisable only by its holder.

(6) If in the case of a loan there is an option as to the currency to be used for repayment, the loan is only to be treated as a foreign currency one if the option is exercisable only by the person for the time being entitled to repayment or eventual repayment.

Commentary—*Simon's Taxes* E1.568.

[756A Interest on certain deposits of victims of National-Socialist persecution
(1) No liability to income tax arises in respect of interest which is paid—
  (*a*) to or in respect of a victim of National-Socialist persecution,
  (*b*) under a qualifying compensation scheme, and
  (*c*) for a qualifying purpose in respect of a qualifying deposit of the victim.
(2) A scheme is a qualifying compensation scheme if—
  (*a*) it is constituted (whether under the law of any part of the United Kingdom or elsewhere) by an instrument in writing, and
  (*b*) the purpose of the scheme, or one of its purposes, is to make payments of interest to or in respect of victims of National-Socialist persecution for qualifying purposes in respect of qualifying deposits.
(3) Interest is paid for a qualifying purpose in respect of a deposit if—
  (*a*) it is paid for meeting a liability in respect of interest on the deposit, or
  (*b*) it is paid for compensating for the effects of inflation on the deposit.
(4) In relation to a victim of National-Socialist persecution, a deposit is a qualifying deposit if it was made—
  (*a*) by, or on behalf of, the victim, and
  (*b*) on or before 5th June 1945.
(5) In this section "deposit" has the [same meaning as in Chapter 19 of Part 15 of ITA 2007 (see section 983 of that Act)]².]¹

Commentary—*Simon's Taxes* I4.129. A100.
HMRC Manuals—Inheritance Tax Manual IHTM10262 (compensation: national socialist persecution).
Amendments—¹   This section inserted by FA 2006 s 64(2). This amendment has effect (and is deemed always to have had effect): (a) for 1996–97, and (b) subsequent years of assessment.
  However, in relation to any time before 6 April 2005 (the commencement of ITTOIA 2005)—
    (a)   this section (as inserted above) is to be treated as if it were inserted into TA 1988 (and as if, in sub-s (5) above, the words, "of ICTA" were omitted), and
    (b)   any reference to this section in any enactment is to be read accordingly.
  In relation to 2005–06 or any earlier year of assessment, all such adjustments are to be made as are required to give effect to the exemptions conferred as a result of FA 2006 s 64. However, the adjustments are to be made only if the person entitled to the exemption makes a claim for the exemption on or before 31 January 2012. The adjustments may be made by discharge or repayment of tax, the making of an assessment or otherwise: FA 2006 s 64(7), (9)–(12).
²   Words in sub-s (5) substituted by ITA 2007 s 1027, Sch 1 paras 492, 575 with effect for income tax purposes from 6 April 2007, and corporation tax purposes for accounting periods ending after 5 April 2007.

Interest and royalty payments

757 Interest and royalty payments: introduction
(1) Sections 758 to 767 make provision for an exemption from income tax in respect of certain interest and royalty payments.
(2) They give effect to Council Directive 2003/49/EC of 3rd June 2003 on a common system of taxation applicable to interest and royalty payments made between associated companies of different member States[, as amended by Council Directives 2004/66/EC[, 2004/76/EC and 2006/98/EC]³]² ("the Directive").
(3) Specifically—
  (*a*) section 758 sets out the conditions to be met for the exemption to apply,
  (*b*) sections 759 to 761 explain certain terms used in those conditions,
  (*c*) section 762 confers powers on the [Commissioners]¹ to make regulations about exemption notices,
  (*d*) sections 763 and 764 make provision for limiting the exemption in the case of certain special relationships,
  (*e*) section 765 contains anti-avoidance provisions,
  (*f*) section 766 contains interpretation provisions, and
  (*g*) section 767 confers power on the Treasury to amend references in sections 757 to 766 to the Directive.
[(4) See section 914 of ITA 2007 for provision enabling a company to make a royalty payment gross if it reasonably believes that the payment is exempt from income tax as a result of section 758 of this Act.]⁴

Commentary—*Simon's Taxes* E1.569, A4.451.
HMRC Manuals—International Manual INTM400020 (EU interest and royalties directive: legislation implementing the directive).
Amendments—¹   Word in sub-s (3) substituted by CRCA 2005 s 50, Sch 4 paras 131, 132(3)(*f*) with effect from 18 April 2005 (by virtue of SI 2005/1126).
²   Words in sub-s (2) inserted by the Exemption From Income Tax For Certain Interest and Royalty Payments (Amendment to Section 97(1) of the Finance Act 2004 and Section 757(2) of the Income Tax (Trading and Other Income) Act 2005) Order, SI 2005/2899 art 3 with effect from 8 November 2005.
³   Words in sub-s (2) substituted by the Exemption from Income Tax for Certain Interest and Royalty Payments (Amendment of Section 757(2) of the Income Tax (Trading and Other Income) Act 2005) Order, SI 2006/3288 art 2 with effect in relation to payments made on or after 1 January 2007.

⁴   Sub-s (4) inserted by ITA 2007 s 1027, Sch 1 paras 492, 576 with effect for income tax purposes from 6 April 2007, and corporation tax purposes for accounting periods ending after 5 April 2007.

758 Exemption for certain interest and royalty payments

(1) No liability to income tax arises in respect of a payment of interest or a payment of a royalty if, at the time the payment is made, conditions A to D are met.

(2) Condition A is that the person making the payment is—

 (*a*) a UK company, but not such a company's permanent establishment in a territory other than the United Kingdom, or

 (*b*) a UK permanent establishment of an EU company.

See section 759 as to when a permanent establishment is to be treated as the person making the payment.

(3) Condition B is that the person beneficially entitled to the income in respect of which the payment is made is an EU company, but not such a company's UK permanent establishment or non-EU permanent establishment.

See section 760 as to when a permanent establishment is to be treated as the person beneficially entitled to the income in respect of which the payment is made.

(4) Condition C is that the company in condition A and the company in condition B are 25% associates (see section 761).

(5) Condition D is that, if the payment is a payment of interest, [the Commissioners for Her Majesty's Revenue and Customs] [have]¹ issued an exemption notice in accordance with regulations under section 762.

(6) This section is subject to—

 sections 763 and 764 (special relationships), and

 section 765 (anti-avoidance).

Commentary—*Simon's Taxes* **E1.569, A4.451.**
HMRC Manuals—International Manual INTM367040 (exemptions for certain interests and royalty payments: conditions).
Amendments—¹   Word in sub-s (5) substituted by CRCA 2005 s 50, Sch 4 paras 131, 133(6) with effect from 18 April 2005 (by virtue of SI 2005/1126).

759 The person making the payment

(1) This section supplements condition A in section 758.

(2) It applies in a case where a company is resident in one territory and has a permanent establishment in another territory.

(3) The permanent establishment (and not the company) is to be treated as the person making the payment so far as (within the meaning of Article 1(3) of the Directive) the payment represents a tax-deductible expense for the permanent establishment in the territory in which it is situated.

Commentary—*Simon's Taxes* **A4.452, E1.569.**

760 The person beneficially entitled to the payment

(1) This section supplements condition B in section 758.

(2) It applies in a case where an EU company has a UK permanent establishment or a non-EU permanent establishment.

(3) The permanent establishment (and not the company) is to be treated as the person beneficially entitled to the income in respect of which the payment is made so far as subsections (4) and (5) apply to the payment.

(4) This subsection applies to the payment if (within the meaning of Article 1(5) of the Directive) it arises in respect of a debt-claim, right or use of information which is effectively connected with the permanent establishment.

(5) This subsection applies to the payment if (within the meaning of Article 1(5) of the Directive) it represents income in respect of which the permanent establishment is subject in the territory in which it is situated to United Kingdom corporation tax or a tax corresponding to that tax.

Commentary—*Simon's Taxes* **A4.452, E1.569.**

761 Meaning of "25% associates"

For the purposes of condition C in section 758, two companies are 25% associates if—

 (*a*) one holds directly—

   (i)   25% or more of the capital in the other, or

   (ii) 25% or more of the voting rights in the other, or

 (*b*) a third company holds directly—

   (i)   25% or more of the capital in each of them, or

   (ii) 25% or more of the voting rights in each of them.

Commentary—*Simon's Taxes* **A4.450, E1.569.**
HMRC Manuals—International manual INTM40040 (meaning of 25% associates).

762 Interest payments: exemption notices

(1) [The Commissioners for Her Majesty's Revenue and Customs] may make regulations about exemption notices under section 758(5).

(2) The regulations may in particular make provision for or in connection with—

(a) enabling an exemption notice to be issued only on the request of a person of a prescribed description,

(b) requiring a person requesting the issue of an exemption notice to certify that conditions A to C in section 758 are met and that section 765 (anti-avoidance) does not apply,

(c) the information to be provided in the certificate,

(d) the person to whom an exemption notice is to be given,

(e) in a case where section 763 (special relationships) applies or may apply to a payment of interest, requiring an exemption notice to specify—

  (i) the amount of the payment in relation to which the notice has effect, or

  (ii) the method to be used for determining that amount,

(f) imposing a time limit for the issue of an exemption notice,

(g) imposing notification requirements,

(h) the cancellation of exemption notices by the [Commissioners][1],

(i) prescribing circumstances in which exemption notices are to become ineffective,

(j) the making of appeals (for example, against a refusal to grant, or the cancellation of, an exemption notice),

(k) authorising, in cases where—

  (i) an exemption notice has been issued,

  (ii) tax has not been deducted from a payment of interest, and

  (iii) any of the conditions in section 758 were not met in the case of the payment,

the recovery of that tax by assessment or by deduction from subsequent payments.

Commentary—*Simon's Taxes* A4.453, E1.569.

HMRC Manuals—International manual INTM400050 (what an interest payment exemption notice covers).

Amendments—[1] Word in sub-s (2) substituted by CRCA 2005 s 50, Sch 4 paras 131, 132(3)(g) with effect from 18 April 2005 (by virtue of SI 2005/1126).

763 Special relationships

(1) This section applies if—

(a) apart from this section, section 758 would apply in relation to a payment of interest or of a royalty,

(b) at the time the payment is made there is a special relationship (within the meaning of Article 4(2) of the Directive)—

  (i) between the company in condition A of section 758 and the company in condition B of that section, or

  (ii) between one of those companies and another person, and

(c) owing to the special relationship, the amount of the payment exceeds the amount which would have been paid in the absence of the relationship ("the arm's length amount").

(2) Sections 757 to 767, apart from this section and section 764, have effect in relation to only so much of the payment as does not exceed the arm's length amount (which may be nil).

(3) Nothing in this section or section 764 affects any relief which may be allowed under any arrangements having effect under [section 2(1) of TIOPA 2010][1] (double taxation relief by agreement with other territories).

Commentary—*Simon's Taxes* E1.570.

HMRC Manuals—International manual INTM332670 (what special relationship is).
INTM400080 (Special Relationship regulation).

Amendments—[1] In sub-s (3), words substituted by TIOPA 2010 s 501, Sch 8 paras 65, 68. TIOPA 2010 has effect for corporation tax purposes for accounting periods ending on or after 1 April 2010, for income and capital gains tax purposes for the tax year 2010–11 and subsequent tax years, and for petroleum revenue tax purposes for chargeable periods beginning on or after 1 July 2010.

764 Application of [TIOPA 2010][1] provisions about special relationships

(1) The provisions in [TIOPA 2010][1] mentioned in subsections (2) and (3) apply in relation to section 763 as if that section were a [special relationship rule][1] within the meaning of those provisions.

(2) In the case of a payment of interest, those provisions are [section 131(3), (5) and (6) of TIOPA 2010][1] (interest: special relationship).

(3) In the case of a payment of a royalty, those provisions are [sections 132(3) to (5), (7) and (8) and 133 of TIOPA 2010][1] (royalties: special relationship).

(4) In those provisions as applied in relation to section 763, expressions also used in sections 757 to 767 have the same meaning as in those sections.

Commentary—*Simon's Taxes* E1.570.

Amendments—[1] In heading, sub-ss (1), (2), (3) words substituted by TIOPA 2010 s 501, Sch 8 paras 65, 69. TIOPA 2010 has effect for corporation tax purposes for accounting periods ending on or after 1 April 2010, for income and capital gains tax purposes for the tax year 2010–11 and subsequent tax years, and for petroleum revenue tax purposes for chargeable periods beginning on or after 1 July 2010.

765 Anti-avoidance

(1) Section 758 does not apply in relation to a payment of interest if it was the main purpose or one of the main purposes of any person concerned with the creation or assignment of the debt-claim in respect of which the interest is paid to take advantage of that section by means of that creation or assignment.

(2) Section 758 does not apply in relation to a payment of a royalty if it was the main purpose or one of the main purposes of any person concerned with the creation or assignment of the right in respect of which the royalty is paid to take advantage of that section by means of that creation or assignment.

Commentary—*Simon's Taxes* **A4.451, E1.571.**
HMRC Manuals—International manual INTM400110 (anti-avoidance measures).

766 Interest and royalty payments: interpretation

In sections 757 to 767—

"company" has the same meaning as the expression "company of a member State" has for the purposes of the Directive (see Article 3(*a*) of the Directive),

"debt-claim" has the same meaning as in the Directive,

"the Directive" has the meaning given by section 757(2),

"EU company" means a company resident in a member State other than the United Kingdom,

"interest" and "royalties" have the meaning given by Article 2 of the Directive,

"non-EU permanent establishment" means a permanent establishment in a territory other than a member State,

"UK company" means a company resident in the United Kingdom, and

"UK permanent establishment" means a permanent establishment in the United Kingdom.

Commentary—*Simon's Taxes* **A4.450, E1.569.**

767 Power to amend references to the Directive by Order

(1) The Treasury may by order make such provision amending any reference in sections 757 to 766 to, or to a provision of,—

(*a*) the Directive, or

(*b*) any instrument referred to in those sections by virtue of an order made under this section,

as appears to them appropriate for the purpose of giving effect to any Council Directive adopted after 8th April 2004 amending or replacing the Directive.

(2) This includes a power to make provision amending any such reference as it applies to [sections 914 to 916 of ITA 2007][1] (payment of royalties without deduction of tax) as a result of [section 917(2) of that Act][1].

Commentary—*Simon's Taxes* **A4.450, E1.569.**
Amendments—[1]   Words in sub-s (2) substituted by ITA 2007 s 1027, Sch 1 paras 492, 577 with effect for income tax purposes from 6 April 2007, and corporation tax purposes for accounting periods ending after 5 April 2007.

Income from commercial occupation of woodlands

768 Commercial occupation of woodlands

(1) No liability to income tax arises under Chapter 8 of Part 5 (income not otherwise charged) in respect of income arising from the commercial occupation of woodlands in the United Kingdom.

(2) For this purpose the occupation of woodlands is commercial if the woodlands are managed—

(*a*) on a commercial basis, and

(*b*) with a view to the realisation of profits.

Commentary—*Simon's Taxes* **B5.130, B5.130, E1.572.**
HMRC Manuals—Business Income Manual BIM67701 (woodlands: overview).

Housing grants

769 Housing grants

(1) No liability to income tax arises in respect of a payment if it is made—

(*a*) under an enactment relating to the giving of financial assistance for the provision, maintenance or improvement of housing accommodation or other residential accommodation, and

(*b*) by way of grant or other contribution towards expenses.

(2) It does not matter whether—

(*a*) the payment is made to the person who incurs the expenses, or

(*b*) the expenses have been, or are to be, incurred.

(3) Subsection (1) does not apply so far as the payment is made towards an expense which is deductible in calculating income for any income or corporation tax purpose.

Commentary—*Simon's Taxes* **E1.573.**
HMRC Manuals—Savings and Investment Manual SAIM8070 (housing grants: exemptions).

[Schedule 2] share incentive plan distributions

770 Amounts applied by SIP trustees acquiring dividend shares or retained for reinvestment

(1) This section applies if—

(*a*) shares are awarded to a participant under [a Schedule 2][1] share incentive plan, and

(*b*) the condition in section 392(3) or (5) is met at the time the shares in question are so awarded (earnings within ITEPA 2003).

This is subject to subsection (4).

(2) No liability to income tax arises for the participant in respect of—

(*a*) the amount applied by the trustees in acquiring dividend shares on behalf of the participant, or

(*b*) any amount retained under paragraph 68(2) of Schedule 2 to ITEPA 2003 (amount of cash dividend not reinvested).

(3) Subsection (2) does not affect any liability arising as a result of—

(*a*) the retained amount later being paid out (see sections 393 and 406), or

(*b*) the dividend shares ceasing to be subject to the plan (see sections 394 and 407).

(4) This section does not apply if the main purpose or one of the main purposes of the arrangements under which the shares are awarded or acquired is the avoidance of tax or national insurance contributions.

(5) This section forms part of the SIP code (see section 488 of ITEPA 2003: . . . [1] share incentive plans).

(6) Accordingly, expressions used in this section and contained in the index in paragraph 100 of Schedule 2 to that Act (. . . [1] share incentive plans) have the meaning indicated by that index.

(7) In particular—

(*a*) for the meaning of "dividend shares" see paragraph 62(3)(*b*) of that Schedule,

(*b*) for the meaning of "participant" see paragraph 5(4) of that Schedule, and

(*c*) for the meaning of "the trustees" see paragraphs 2(2) and 71(1) of that Schedule.

Commentary—*Simon's Taxes* E1.418, E1.574.

HMRC Manuals—Savings and Investment Manual SAIM5080 (dividends from share incentive plans).

Amendments—[1] In cross-heading, words substituted for word "Approved", in sub-s (1)(*a*) words substituted for words "an approved", and in sub-ss (5), (6) word "approved" repealed, by FA 2014 s 51, Sch 8 paras 65, 66, 67 with effect from 6 April 2014. The effect of the FA 2014 changes on SIPs established before 6 April 2014 is set out in FA 2014 Sch 8 paras 91 to 96.

Foreign income of consular officers and employees

771 Relevant foreign income of consular officers and employees

(1) No liability to income tax arises in respect of relevant foreign income of a consular officer or employee in the United Kingdom for a foreign state if—

(*a*) Her Majesty by Order in Council directs that this section applies to the foreign state for the purpose of giving effect to a reciprocal arrangement with that state, and

(*b*) the officer or employee meets conditions A to C.

(2) Condition A is that the officer or employee is not—

(*a*) a British citizen,

(*b*) a British overseas territories citizen,

(*c*) a British National (Overseas), or

(*d*) a British Overseas citizen.

(3) Condition B is that the officer or employee is not engaged in any trade, profession, vocation or employment in the United Kingdom, otherwise than as a consular officer or employee of the state in question.

[(4) Condition C is that—

(*a*) the officer or employee is a permanent employee of that state, or

(*b*) the officer or employee was non-UK resident for each of the 2 tax years preceding the tax year in which the officer or employee became a consular officer or employee in the United Kingdom of that state.][1]

(5) In this section and section 772—

"consular officer or employee" includes any person employed for the purposes of the official business of a consular officer at—

(*a*) any consulate,

(*b*) any consular establishment, or

(*c*) any other premises used for those purposes, and

"reciprocal arrangement" means a consular convention or other arrangement with a foreign state, making similar provision to that made by this section and sections 302, 646A and 681A of ITEPA 2003 in the case of Her Majesty's consular officers or employees in that state.

Commentary—*Simon's Taxes* A1.109, C1.221, E1.575, E5.401C, E6.464.

HMRC Manuals—Representatives of overseas governments RE2300 (consular relations act 1968).

Amendments—[1] Sub-s (4) substituted by FA 2013 s 219, Sch 46 paras 43, 53 with effect in relation to a person who became a consular officer or employee in the United Kingdom on or after 6 April 2013.

772 Further provisions about Orders under section 771

(1) An Order in Council under section 771 may limit the operation of that section in relation to a state in any way appearing to Her Majesty appropriate having regard to the reciprocal arrangement with the state.

(2) An Order under that section may be made so as to have effect from a date earlier than that on which it is made, but not earlier than the reciprocal arrangement in question comes into force.

(3) An Order under that section may contain such transitional provisions as appear to Her Majesty appropriate.

(4) A statutory instrument containing an Order under that section is subject to annulment in pursuance of a resolution of the House of Commons.

Commentary—*Simon's Taxes* **E1.575.**

Income of non-UK residents from certain securities

773 Income from Inter-American Development Bank securities

(1) No liability to income tax arises for a non-UK resident in respect of income from a security issued by the Inter-American Development Bank if the liability only arises because one or more of circumstances A to C apply.

(2) Circumstance A is that the security is issued in the United Kingdom or in sterling.

(3) Circumstance B is that the income is made payable or paid in the United Kingdom or in sterling.

(4) Circumstance C is that the Bank maintains an office or other place of business in the United Kingdom.

Commentary—*Simon's Taxes* **D4.601, E1.576.**
HMRC Manuals—Stamp taxes on shares manual STSM041040 (government securities and miscellaneous exemptions).

774 Income from securities issued by designated international organisations

(1) No liability to income tax arises for a non-UK resident in respect of income from a security issued by an organisation if—

    (*a*) the organisation has been designated by the Treasury for the purposes of this section, and

    (*b*) the liability only arises because one or more of circumstances A to C apply.

(2) Circumstance A is that the security is issued in the United Kingdom or in sterling.

(3) Circumstance B is that the income is made payable or paid in the United Kingdom or in sterling.

(4) Circumstance C is that the organisation maintains an office or other place of business in the United Kingdom.

(5) The Treasury may by order designate for the purposes of this section—

    (*a*) any of the Communities,

    (*b*) the European Investment Bank,

    (*c*) any international organisation that meets conditions A and B.

(6) Condition A is that one of its members is the United Kingdom or any of the Communities.

(7) Condition B is that the agreement under which that member became a member provides for the same kind of exemption from tax for income from securities issued by the organisation as this section provides.

Commentary—*Simon's Taxes* **D1.239, E1.577.**
HMRC Manuals—Stamp taxes on shares manual STSM041040 (government securities and miscellaneous exemptions).

Other

775 Income towards reducing the national debt

(1) This section applies if property is held on trust in accordance with directions which are valid and effective under section 9 of the Superannuation and other Trust Funds (Validation) Act 1927 (c. 41) (validation of trust funds for the reduction of the national debt).

(2) No liability to income tax arises in respect of any of the following—

    (*a*) income arising from the property,

    (*b*) income arising from the accumulation of that income, and

    (*c*) profits of any description otherwise accruing to the property and liable to be accumulated under the trust.

Commentary—*Simon's Taxes* **C4.203, E1.578.**

[775A Government bonus for savings account or other investment plan

No liability to income tax arises in respect of a payment of, or in respect of, a government bonus under section 1 or 2 of the Savings (Government Contributions) Act 2017.][1]

Amendments—[1]   Section 775A inserted by the Savings (Government Contributions) Act 2017 s 3(1) with effect from 17 January 2017.

776 Scholarship income

(1) No liability to income tax arises in respect of income from a scholarship held by an individual in full-time education at a university, college, school or other educational establishment.

(2) This exemption is subject to section 215 of ITEPA 2003 (under which only the scholarship holder is entitled to the exemption if the scholarship is provided by reason of another person's employment).

[(2A) No liability to income tax arises in respect of income from a payment made under section 23C(5A) of the Children Act 1989 (duty to make payments to former relevant children who pursue higher education) [or under sections 110(6) or 112(2) of the Social Services and Well-being (Wales) Act 2014 (duty to make payments to certain young people who pursue higher education)][2].]

(3) In this section "scholarship" includes a bursary, exhibition or other similar educational endowment.

Commentary—*Simon's Taxes* E1.579, E4.325, E4.618, E4.1191, E5.204.

HMRC Manuals—Savings and Investment Manual SAIM8070 (scholarship income: exemption).

Employment Income Manual EIM06205 (scholarship income: general principles).

EIM06210 (Scholarship Income: Taxable As Trading Or Employment Income?).

EIM06220–06230 (meaning of "scholarship", "full-time instruction", and "at a university, college, school or other educational establishment").

EIM06235 (scholarships and apprenticeship schemes at universities and colleges).

EIM06240–06245 (scholarship income: rates of payment including examples).

EIM06250–06270 (scholarships income: examples of miscellaneous awards).

EIM06275 (scholarship income: treatment of student union officials).

Amendment—[1]   Sub-s (2A) inserted by the Children and Young Persons Act 2008 s 21(4) with effect in relation to England from 22 August 2009 (by virtue of SI 2009/2273, art 2(1)) and with effect in relation to Wales from 18 March 2011 (by virtue of SI 2011/824, art 2(b)).

[2]   In sub-s (2A), words inserted by the Social Services and Well-being (Wales) Act 2014 (Consequential Amendments) Regulations, SI 2016/413 regs 222, 224 with effect from 6 April 2016.

777 VAT repayment supplements

No liability to income tax arises in respect of a sum paid by way of supplement under section 79 of VATA 1994 (VAT repayment supplements).

Commentary—*Simon's Taxes* E1.580.

HMRC Manuals—Business Income Manual BIM31610 (value added tax: penalties and repayment supplement).

Corporate Finance Manual CFM70140 (other tax rules on corporate finance: exemptions from loan relationships: VAT repayment supplement).

Savings And Investment Manual SAIM2320 (exemptions: other statutory exemptions).

778 Incentives to use electronic communications

No liability to income tax arises in respect of anything received by way of incentive under any regulations made in accordance with Schedule 38 to FA 2000 (regulations for providing incentives for electronic communications).

Commentary—*Simon's Taxes* A4.170, E1.581.

779 Gains on commodity and financial futures

(1) No liability to income tax arises as a result of Chapter 8 of Part 5 (income not otherwise charged) in respect of a gain arising to a person in the course of dealing in—

    (a) commodity or financial futures,

    (b) traded options, or

    (c) financial options.

(2) The reference in subsection (1) to a gain arising in the course of dealing in commodity or financial futures includes a gain regarded as so arising under section 143(3) of TCGA 1992 (gains arising from transactions otherwise than in the course of dealing on a recognised futures exchange, involving authorised persons).

(3) In this section—

    "commodity or financial futures" means commodity futures or financial futures that are for the time being dealt in on a recognised futures exchange,

    "financial option" has the meaning given by section 144(8)(c) of TCGA 1992, and

    "traded option" has the meaning given by section 144(8)(b) of that Act.

Commentary—*Simon's Taxes* E1.582.

HMRC Manuals—Savings and Income Manual SAIM7010 (introduction).

Capital Gain CG56004 (futures: income or capital gain).

780 Disabled person's vehicle maintenance grant

(1) No liability to income tax arises in respect of a disabled person's vehicle maintenance grant.

(2) For this purpose a "disabled person's vehicle maintenance grant" means a grant to any person owning a vehicle that is made under—

    [(a) paragraph 10 of Schedule 1 to the National Health Service Act 2006 or paragraph 10 of Schedule 1 to National Health Service (Wales) Act 2006,][1]

    (b) section 46(3) of the National Health Service (Scotland) Act 1978 (c. 29), or

    (c) Article 30 of the Health and Personal Social Services (Northern Ireland) Order 1972 (SI 1972/1265 (NI 14)).

Commentary—*Simon's Taxes* E1.583.

Amendments—[1]   Sub-s (2)(a) substituted by the National Health Service (Consequential Provisions) Act 2006 s 2, Sch 1 paras 275, 276 with effect from 1 March 2007.

781 Payments under New Deal 50plus

(1) No liability to income tax arises in respect of a payment that is made—

(*a*) by way of training grant under the "New Deal 50plus" scheme, and

(*b*) to a person as a participant in that scheme.

(2) For this purpose the "New Deal 50plus" scheme means—

(*a*) the scheme under section 2(2) of the Employment and Training Act 1973 (c. 50) known as "New Deal 50plus", or

(*b*) the corresponding scheme under section 1 of the Employment and Training Act (Northern Ireland) 1950 (c. 29 (NI)).

Commentary—*Simon's Taxes* **E1.584.**

HMRC Manuals—Employment Income Manual EIM01651 (new deal: introduction).

National Insurance Manual NIM21027 (new deal 50 plus payments).

782 Payments under employment zone programme

(1) No liability to income tax arises in respect of a payment that is made to a person as a participant in an employment zone programme.

(2) For this purpose an "employment zone programme" means an employment zone programme established for an area or areas designated under section 60 of the Welfare Reform and Pensions Act 1999 (c. 30).

Commentary—*Simon's Taxes* **E1.585.**

HMRC Manuals—National Insurance Manual NIM02396 (payment received under employment zones programmed: exempt).

[782A Domestic microgeneration

(1) No liability to income tax arises in respect of income arising to an individual from the sale of electricity generated by a microgeneration system if—

(*a*) the system is installed at or near domestic premises occupied by the individual, and

(*b*) the individual intends that the amount of electricity generated by it will not significantly exceed the amount of electricity consumed in those premises.

(2) In subsection (1)—

"domestic premises" means premises used wholly or mainly as a separate private dwelling, and

["microgeneration system" has the same meaning as in section 263AZA of the Taxation of Chargeable Gains Act 1992.]²]¹

Commentary—*Simon's Taxes* **C3.1808, E1.586.**

HMRC Manuals—Business Income Manual BIM40520 (income tax exemption for domestic microgeneration).

Amendments—¹ This section inserted by FA 2007 s 20 with effect from 2007–08.

² In sub-s (2), definition of "microgeneration system" substituted by the Deregulation Act 2015 s 57(3)(*b*) with effect from 26 May 2015.

[782B Renewables obligation certificates for domestic microgeneration

(1) No liability to income tax arises in respect of the receipt by an individual of a renewables obligation certificate if—

(*a*) the individual receives the certificate in connection with the generation of electricity by a microgeneration system,

(*b*) the system is installed at or near domestic premises occupied by the individual, and

(*c*) the individual intends that the amount of electricity generated by it will not significantly exceed the amount of electricity consumed in those premises.

(2) In subsection (1)—

"domestic premises" and "microgeneration system" have the same meaning as in section 782A, and

"renewables obligation certificate" means a certificate issued under section 32B of the Electricity Act 1989 or Article 54 of the Energy (Northern Ireland) Order 2003.]¹

Commentary—*Simon's Taxes* **E1.586.**

HMRC Manuals—Business Income Manual BIM40530 (renewables obligation certificates for domestic microgeneration).

Amendments—¹ This section inserted by FA 2007 s 21(1), (3) with effect from 2007–08.

[782C Volunteers etc: compensation for lost employment income

(1) No liability to income tax arises in respect of a payment by a relevant authority to a person if—

(*a*) the person performs services for the authority for no financial benefit in a period in which he or she is also employed,

(*b*) the payment is made solely to compensate the person for lost employment income for the period (and accordingly does not exceed the amount of that income), and

(*c*) the person does not perform the services as the holder of an office with the authority (as to which, see section 299A of ITEPA 2003).

(2) For the purposes of subsection (1) a person performs services for no financial benefit if, at the time the payment referred to in that subsection is made, the person—

(*a*) is not entitled to any payment or benefit in connection with performing the services,

(*b*) has not received any such payment or benefit, and

(*c*) does not expect to receive any such payment or benefit.

(3) For the purposes of subsection (2)(*a*), (*b*) and (*c*) disregard—

(*a*) a payment in respect of reasonable expenses incurred in performing the services,

(b) a payment compensating the person for loss of social security income arising as a result of performing the services, and

(c) a payment to which subsection (1) applies.

(4) In subsection (1)(b) "lost employment income" means the difference between—

    (a) the amount of employment income, after deduction of tax and national insurance contributions, that the person would have received from the employment for the period if he or she had not performed the services, and

    (b) the amount of employment income, after deduction of tax and national insurance contributions, that the person did receive from the employment for the period.

(5) In this section—

    "employment" has the meaning given by section 4 of ITEPA 2003;

    "relevant authority" has the meaning given by section 299A of ITEPA 2003;

    "services" includes services as a juror;

    "social security income" has the meaning given by section 657 of ITEPA 2003.][1]

Amendments—[1]   Section 782A inserted by the Enactment of Extra-Statutory Concessions Order, SI 2018/282 art 3(1), (4) with effect from 6 April 2018.

CHAPTER 10

GENERAL

783 General disregard of exempt income for income tax purposes

(1) Amounts of income which are exempt from income tax as a result of this Part (whether because the type of income concerned is exempt from every charge to income tax or because it is exempt from every charge that is relevant to those particular amounts) are accordingly to be ignored for all other income tax purposes.

[(2) There are exceptions to this in the following cases.][1]

[(2A) Interest on deposits in ordinary accounts with the National Savings Bank which is exempt under this Part from every charge to income tax is not to be ignored for the purpose of providing information.][1]

[(2B) Interest paid to or in respect of victims of National-Socialist persecution which is so exempt is not to be ignored for the purposes of sections 17 and 18 of TMA 1970 (information provisions relating to interest).][1]

(3) [These express exceptions to subsection (1) are][1] without prejudice to the existence of any other implied or express exception to that subsection (whether in connection with the provision of information or otherwise).

Commentary—*Simon's Taxes* E1.520.

HMRC Manuals—Tax Credits Technical Manual TCTM04510 (payments disregarded in the calculation of investment income).

Amendments—[1]   Sub-ss (2), (2A), (2B) substituted for sub-s (2); and in sub-s (3), words substituted by FA 2006 s 64(3) with effect from 19 July 2006.

However, in relation to any time before 6 April 2005 (the commencement of ITTOIA 2005)—

    (a)   ITTOIA 2005 s 756A (as inserted by FA 2006 s 64(2)) is to be treated as if it were inserted into TA 1988 (and as if, in ITTOIA 2005 s 756A(5), the words, "of ICTA" were omitted), and

    (b)   any reference to ITTOIA 2005 s 756A in any enactment is to be read accordingly.

In relation to 2005–06 or any earlier year of assessment, all such adjustments are to be made as are required to give effect to the exemptions conferred as a result of FA 2006 s 64. However, the adjustments are to be made only if the person entitled to the exemption makes a claim for the exemption on or before 31 January 2012. The adjustments may be made by discharge or repayment of tax, the making of an assessment or otherwise: FA 2006 s 64(7), (9)–(12).

[PART 6A

INCOME CHARGED UNDER THIS ACT: TRADING AND PROPERTY ALLOWANCES]

Amendments–Part 6A (ss 783A–783BQ) inserted by F(No 2)A 2017 s 17, Sch 3 para 1 with effect for the tax year 2017–18 and subsequent tax years.

[CHAPTER 1

TRADING ALLOWANCE

Introduction

78_A   _f under this Chapter

(1) The C___er gives relief to an individual on—

    the ___ of a relevant trade (see section 783AA), and

    ____ income (see section 783AB).

    ___ ___fies for full relief (see section 783AE), the individual's relevant income (see

    ___ char_ed to income tax (see sections 783AF and 783AG).

    ___ ___es for partial relief (see section 783AH), the individual's relevant income

    ___ ___ve methods (see sections 783AI to 783AK).

    ___ __is Chapter which gives relief is subject to sections 783AN to 783AQ, which

    ___s in which relief under this Chapter is not given.][1]

Commentary—*Simon's Taxes* **B2.101AA**.
Amendments–[1]   Part 6A (ss 783A–783BQ) inserted by F(No 2)A 2017 s 17, Sch 3 para 1 with effect for the tax year 2017–18
and subsequent tax years.

[Basic definitions

783AA "Relevant trade" of an individual

(1) For the purposes of this Chapter, a trade carried on by an individual is a "relevant trade" of the individual for a tax year if—

  (*a*) the individual carries on the trade otherwise than in partnership, and

  (*b*) the trade is not a rent-a-room trade in relation to the individual for the tax year.

(2) For the purposes of subsection (1)(*b*) a trade is a "rent-a-room trade" in relation to an individual for a tax year if—

  (*a*) the individual qualifies for rent-a-room relief for the tax year, and

  (*b*) the individual has rent-a-room receipts for the tax year which would, apart from Chapter 1 of Part 7 (rent-a-room relief), be brought into account in calculating the profits of the trade.

See section 783AR for definitions relevant to this subsection.

(3) In this Chapter references to a trade include references to a profession or vocation.][1]

Commentary—*Simon's Taxes* **B2.101AA**.
Amendments–[1]   Part 6A (ss 783A–783BQ) inserted by F(No 2)A 2017 s 17, Sch 3 para 1 with effect for the tax year 2017–18
and subsequent tax years.

[783AB "Miscellaneous income"

(1) For the purposes of this Chapter, an individual's "miscellaneous income" for a tax year is all the income arising to the individual in the tax year which would be chargeable to income tax under Chapter 8 of Part 5 (income not otherwise charged) for the tax year.

(2) But if—

  (*a*) the individual qualifies for rent-a-room relief for the tax year, and

  (*b*) the individual has rent-a-room receipts for the tax year which would, apart from Chapter 1 of Part 7, be chargeable to income tax under Chapter 8 of Part 5,

the rent-a-room receipts are not miscellaneous income.

(3) The reference in subsection (1) to the amount which would be chargeable to income tax under Chapter 8 of Part 5 is to the amount which would be so chargeable—

  (*a*) apart from this Chapter, and

  (*b*) if no deduction were made for expenses or any other matter.][1]

Commentary—*Simon's Taxes* **B2.101AA**.
Amendments–[1]   Part 6A (ss 783A–783BQ) inserted by F(No 2)A 2017 s 17, Sch 3 para 1 with effect for the tax year 2017–18
and subsequent tax years.

[783AC The individual's "relevant income"

(1) For the purposes of this Chapter, an individual's "relevant income" for a tax year is the sum of the following—

  (*a*) the receipts for the tax year of the individual's relevant trades for the tax year, and

  (*b*) the individual's miscellaneous income for the tax year.

(2) In subsection (1)(*a*) the reference to the receipts of a trade for a tax year is to all the amounts which would, apart from this Chapter, be brought into account as a receipt in calculating the profits of the trade for the tax year.][1]

Commentary—*Simon's Taxes* **B2.101AA**.
Amendments–[1]   Part 6A (ss 783A–783BQ) inserted by F(No 2)A 2017 s 17, Sch 3 para 1 with effect for the tax year 2017–18
and subsequent tax years.

[783AD The individual's trading allowance

(1) For the purposes of this Chapter, an individual's trading allowance for a tax year is £1,000.

(2) The Treasury may by regulations amend subsection (1) so as to substitute a higher sum for the sum for the time being specified in that subsection.][1]

Commentary—*Simon's Taxes* **B2.101AA**.
Amendments–[1]   Part 6A (ss 783A–783BQ) inserted by F(No 2)A 2017 s 17, Sch 3 para 1 with effect for the tax year 2017–18
and subsequent tax years.

[Full relief

783AE Full relief: introduction

(1) An individual qualifies for full relief for a tax year if—

  (*a*) the individual has relevant income for the tax year,

  (*b*) the relevant income does not exceed the individual's trading allowance for the tax year, and

  (*c*) no election by the individual under section 783AL has effect for the tax year (election for full relief not to be given).

(2) An individual also qualifies for full relief for a tax year if—

  (*a*) the individual has relevant income for the tax year which consists of or includes receipts of one or more relevant trades,

  (*b*) the relevant income exceeds the individual's trading allowance for the tax year, (*c*) the conditions mentioned in subsection (3) are met,

(*d*) no election by the individual under section 783AL has effect for the tax year, and

(*e*) no election by the individual under section 783AM has effect for the tax year (election for partial relief).

(3) The conditions are that—

(*a*) no election by the individual under section 25A (cash basis for trades) has effect for the tax year,

(*b*) the individual's relevant income would not exceed the individual's trading allowance for the tax year if it were to be assumed that an election by the individual under section 25A had effect for the tax year,

(*c*) the individual is eligible to make an election under section 25A (see section 31A) for the tax year, and

(*d*) if any trade carried on by the individual in the tax year was carried on in the immediately preceding tax year—

(i)   an election by the individual under section 25A had effect for that preceding tax year, or

(ii) the individual was eligible to make such an election for that preceding tax year.]¹

Commentary—*Simon's Taxes* **B2.101AA**.

Amendments—¹   Part 6A (ss 783A–783BQ) inserted by F(No 2)A 2017 s 17, Sch 3 para 1 with effect for the tax year 2017–18 and subsequent tax years.

[783AF Full relief: trade profits

(1) This section applies if—

(*a*) an individual qualifies for full relief for a tax year, and

(*b*) the individual's relevant income for the tax year consists of or includes receipts of one or more relevant trades.

(2) The profits or losses of each such trade for the tax year are treated as nil.]¹

Commentary—*Simon's Taxes* **B2.101AA**.

Amendments—¹   Part 6A (ss 783A–783BQ) inserted by F(No 2)A 2017 s 17, Sch 3 para 1 with effect for the tax year 2017–18 and subsequent tax years.

[783AG Full relief: miscellaneous income

(1) This section applies if—

(*a*) an individual qualifies for full relief for a tax year, and

(*b*) the individual's relevant income for the tax year consists of or includes miscellaneous income.

(2) The amount of—

(*a*) the miscellaneous income arising in the tax year, less

(*b*) any expenses associated with that income,

is treated as nil.]¹

Commentary—*Simon's Taxes* **B2.101AA**.

Amendments—¹   Part 6A (ss 783A–783BQ) inserted by F(No 2)A 2017 s 17, Sch 3 para 1 with effect for the tax year 2017–18 and subsequent tax years.

[Partial relief

783AH Partial relief: alternative calculation of profits: introduction

An individual qualifies for partial relief for a tax year if—

(*a*) the individual has relevant income for the tax year,

(*b*) the relevant income exceeds the individual's trading allowance for the tax year, and

(*c*) an election by the individual under section 783AM has effect for the tax year (election for partial relief).]¹

Commentary—*Simon's Taxes* **B2.101AA**.

Amendments—¹   Part 6A (ss 783A–783BQ) inserted by F(No 2)A 2017 s 17, Sch 3 para 1 with effect for the tax year 2017–18 and subsequent tax years.

[783AI Partial relief: alternative calculation of trade profits

(1) This section applies if—

(*a*) an individual qualifies for partial relief for a tax year, and

(*b*) the individual's relevant income for the tax year consists of or includes receipts of one or more relevant trades.

(2) The profits or losses for the tax year of each of the individual's relevant trades are given by taking the following steps—

Step 1

Calculate the total of all the amounts which would, apart from this Chapter, be brought into account as a receipt in calculating the profits of the trade for the tax year.

Step 2

Subtract the deductible amount.

Step 3

Subtract from the amount given by step 2 any deduction for overlap profit allowed in calculating the profits of the trade for the tax year under section 205 (deduction for overlap profit in final tax year) or section 220 (deduction for overlap profit on change of accounting date).

(3) Subject to section 783AK, the deductible amount is equal to the individual's trading allowance for the tax year.

(4) "Overlap profit" has the same meaning in this section as it has in Chapter 15 of Part 2 (see sections 204 and 204A).]¹

Commentary—*Simon's Taxes* **B2.101AA**.

Amendments—¹ Part 6A (ss 783A–783BQ) inserted by F(No 2)A 2017 s 17, Sch 3 para 1 with effect for the tax year 2017–18 and subsequent tax years.

[783AJ Partial relief: alternative calculation of chargeable miscellaneous income

(1) This section applies if—

(a) an individual qualifies for partial relief for a tax year, and

(b) the individual's relevant income for the tax year consists of or includes miscellaneous income.

(2) The amount of miscellaneous income chargeable to income tax for the tax year is—

(a) the miscellaneous income for the tax year, less

(b) the deductible amount.

(3) Subject to section 783AK, the deductible amount is equal to the individual's trading allowance for the tax year.]¹

Commentary—*Simon's Taxes* **B2.101AA**.

Amendments—¹ Part 6A (ss 783A–783BQ) inserted by F(No 2)A 2017 s 17, Sch 3 para 1 with effect for the tax year 2017–18 and subsequent tax years.

[783AK Deductible amount: splitting of trading allowance

(1) This section applies where the individual's relevant income for the tax year includes—

(a) receipts of a relevant trade, and

(b) receipts of any other relevant trade or miscellaneous income (or both).

(2) The references in section 783AI and (where it applies) section 783AJ to the deductible amount are to amounts which, in total, equal the individual's trading allowance for the tax year.

(3) The question of how to allocate the individual's trading allowance for the tax year for the purposes of subsection (2) is to be decided by the individual, subject to subsections (4) and (5).

(4) The deductible amount in respect of a relevant trade must not be such that the amount given by step 2 of section 783AI(2) is negative.

(5) The deductible amount in respect of miscellaneous income must not be such as to result in the individual making a loss in the transactions giving rise to the miscellaneous income.]¹

Commentary—*Simon's Taxes* **B2.101AA**.

Amendments—¹ Part 6A (ss 783A–783BQ) inserted by F(No 2)A 2017 s 17, Sch 3 para 1 with effect for the tax year 2017–18 and subsequent tax years.

[Elections

783AL Election for full relief not to be given

(1) An individual may elect not to be given full relief for a tax year (see sections 783AF and 783AG).

(2) An election must be made on or before the first anniversary of the normal self-assessment filing date for the tax year for which the election is made.]¹

Commentary—*Simon's Taxes* **B2.101AA**.

Amendments—¹ Part 6A (ss 783A–783BQ) inserted by F(No 2)A 2017 s 17, Sch 3 para 1 with effect for the tax year 2017–18 and subsequent tax years.

[783AM Election for partial relief

(1) An individual may elect for partial relief to be given for a tax year if the individual's relevant income for the tax year exceeds the individual's trading allowance for the tax year (see sections 783AI and 783AJ).

(2) An election must be made on or before the first anniversary of the normal self-assessment filing date for the tax year for which the election is made.]¹

Commentary—*Simon's Taxes* **B2.101AA**.

Amendments—¹ Part 6A (ss 783A–783BQ) inserted by F(No 2)A 2017 s 17, Sch 3 para 1 with effect for the tax year 2017–18 and subsequent tax years.

[Exclusions from relief

783AN Exclusion from relief: expenses deducted against rent-a-room receipts

(1) No relief under this Chapter is given to an individual for a tax year if—

(a) the individual qualifies for rent-a-room relief for the tax year,

(b) the individual has rent-a-room receipts mentioned in subsection (2) for the tax year, and

(c) condition A or B is met.

(2) The rent-a-room receipts mentioned in subsection (1) are—

[783BC The individual's "relevant property income"

For the purposes of this Chapter, an individual's "relevant property income" for a tax year is the relievable receipts for the tax year of the individual's relevant property businesses for the tax year.][1]

Commentary—*Simon's Taxes* B6.202A.

Amendments—[1]   Part 6A (ss 783A–783BQ) inserted by F(No 2)A 2017 s 17, Sch 3 para 1 with effect for the tax year 2017–18 and subsequent tax years.

[783BD The individual's property allowance

(1) For the purposes of this Chapter, an individual's property allowance for a tax year is £1,000.

(2) The Treasury may by regulations amend subsection (1) so as to substitute a higher sum for the sum for the time being specified in that subsection.][1]

Commentary—*Simon's Taxes* B6.202A.

Amendments—[1]   Part 6A (ss 783A–783BQ) inserted by F(No 2)A 2017 s 17, Sch 3 para 1 with effect for the tax year 2017–18 and subsequent tax years.

[Relief if relevant property income does not exceed property allowance

783BE Full relief: introduction

An individual qualifies for full relief for a tax year if—

   (*a*) the individual has relevant property income for the tax year,

   (*b*) the relevant property income does not exceed the individual's property allowance for the tax year, and

   (*c*) no election by the individual under section 783BJ has effect for the tax year (election for full relief not to be given).][1]

Commentary—*Simon's Taxes* B6.202A.

Amendments—[1]   Part 6A (ss 783A–783BQ) inserted by F(No 2)A 2017 s 17, Sch 3 para 1 with effect for the tax year 2017–18 and subsequent tax years.

[783BF Full relief: property profits

(1) If an individual qualifies for full relief for a tax year, this section applies in relation to the calculation of the profits of the individual's relevant property business for the tax year or, where the individual's relevant property income for the tax year consists of the relievable receipts of two relevant property businesses, the profits of each property business for the tax year.

(2) The following are not brought into account—

   (*a*) the relievable receipts of the property business for the tax year, and

   (*b*) any expenses associated with those receipts.][1]

Commentary—*Simon's Taxes* B6.202A.

Amendments—[1]   Part 6A (ss 783A–783BQ) inserted by F(No 2)A 2017 s 17, Sch 3 para 1 with effect for the tax year 2017–18 and subsequent tax years.

[Relief if relevant property income exceeds property allowance

783BG Partial relief: alternative calculation of property profits: introduction

An individual qualifies for partial relief for a tax year if—

   (*a*) the individual has relevant property income for the tax year,

   (*b*) the relevant property income exceeds the individual's property allowance for the tax year, and

   (*c*) an election by the individual under section 783BK has effect for the tax year (election for partial relief).][1]

Commentary—*Simon's Taxes* B6.202A.

Amendments—[1]   Part 6A (ss 783A–783BQ) inserted by F(No 2)A 2017 s 17, Sch 3 para 1 with effect for the tax year 2017–18 and subsequent tax years.

[783BH Partial relief: alternative calculation of property profits

(1) If an individual qualifies for partial relief for a tax year, this section applies in relation to the calculation of the profits of the individual's relevant property business for the tax year or, where the individual's relevant property income for the tax year consists of the relievable receipts of two relevant property businesses, the profits of each property business for the tax year.

(2) The relievable receipts of the property business for the tax year are brought into account.

(3) No relevant expenses are brought into account.

(4) The deductible amount is brought into account.

(5) Subject to section 783BI, the deductible amount is equal to the individual's property allowance for the tax year.

(6) In subsection (3) "relevant expenses" means all the amounts—

   (*a*) which would, apart from this section, be brought into account as a deduction in calculating the profits of the business for the tax year, and

   (*b*) which are associated with the relievable receipts.][1]

Commentary—*Simon's Taxes* B6.202A.

Amendments—[1]   Part 6A (ss 783A–783BQ) inserted by F(No 2)A 2017 s 17, Sch 3 para 1 with effect for the tax year 2017–18 and subsequent tax years.

[783BI Deductible amount: splitting of property allowance

(1) This section applies where the individual's relevant property income for the tax year consists of the relievable receipts of two relevant property businesses.

(2) The references in section 783BH to the deductible amount are to amounts which, in total, equal the individual's property allowance for the tax year.

(3) The question of how to allocate the individual's property allowance for the tax year for the purposes of subsection (2) is to be decided by the individual, subject to subsection (4).

(4) The deductible amount in respect of a relevant property business must not be such as to result in a loss of the business.][1]

Commentary—*Simon's Taxes* B6.202A.

Amendments—[1]   Part 6A (ss 783A–783BQ) inserted by F(No 2)A 2017 s 17, Sch 3 para 1 with effect for the tax year 2017–18 and subsequent tax years.

[Elections

783BJ Election for full relief not to be given

(1) An individual may elect not to be given full relief for a tax year (see section 783BF).

(2) An election must be made on or before the first anniversary of the normal self-assessment filing date for the tax year for which the election is made.][1]

Commentary—*Simon's Taxes* B6.202A.

Amendments—[1]   Part 6A (ss 783A–783BQ) inserted by F(No 2)A 2017 s 17, Sch 3 para 1 with effect for the tax year 2017–18 and subsequent tax years.

[783BK Election for partial relief

(1) An individual may elect for partial relief to be given for a tax year if the individual's relevant property income for the tax year exceeds the individual's property allowance for the tax year (see section 783BH).

(2) An election must be made on or before the first anniversary of the normal self-assessment filing date for the tax year for which the election is made.][1]

Commentary—*Simon's Taxes* B6.202A.

Amendments—[1]   Part 6A (ss 783A–783BQ) inserted by F(No 2)A 2017 s 17, Sch 3 para 1 with effect for the tax year 2017–18 and subsequent tax years.

[Exclusions from relief

783BL Exclusion from relief: tax reduction under section 274A

No relief under this Chapter is given to an individual for a tax year if, in calculating the individual's liability to income tax for the tax year, a tax reduction under section 274A (property business: relief for non-deductible costs of a dwelling-related loan) is applied at Step 6 of the calculation in section 23 of ITA 2007.][1]

Commentary—*Simon's Taxes* B6.202A.

Amendments—[1]   Part 6A (ss 783A–783BQ) inserted by F(No 2)A 2017 s 17, Sch 3 para 1 with effect for the tax year 2017–18 and subsequent tax years.

[783BM Exclusion from relief: expenses deducted against rent-a-room receipts

(1) No relief under this Chapter is given to an individual for a tax year if—

    (*a*) the individual qualifies for rent-a-room relief for the tax year,

    (*b*) the individual has rent-a-room receipts for the tax year which would, apart from Chapter 1 of Part 7 (rent-a-room relief), be brought into account in calculating the profits of a property business, and

    (*c*) condition A or B is met.

(2) Condition A is that—

    (*a*) the individual's total rent-a-room amount for the tax year does not exceed the individual's limit for the tax year (see section 783BQ), and

    (*b*) an election by the individual under section 799 has effect to disapply full rent-a-room relief for the tax year.

(3) Condition B is that—

    (*a*) the individual's total rent-a-room amount for the tax year exceeds the individual's limit for the tax year, and

    (*b*) no election by the individual under section 800 has effect to apply the alternative method of calculating profits for the tax year.][1]

Commentary—*Simon's Taxes* B6.202A.

Amendments—[1]   Part 6A (ss 783A–783BQ) inserted by F(No 2)A 2017 s 17, Sch 3 para 1 with effect for the tax year 2017–18 and subsequent tax years.

[783BN Exclusion from relief: payments by employer

No relief under this Chapter is given to an individual for a tax year if—

    (*a*) the individual has relevant property income for the tax year, and

    (*b*) the income includes a payment made by, or on behalf of, a person at a time when the individual is—

        (i) an employee of the person, or

(ii) the spouse or civil partner of an employee of the person.][1]

Commentary—*Simon's Taxes* B6.202A.
Amendments—[1]   Part 6A (ss 783A–783BQ) inserted by F(No 2)A 2017 s 17, Sch 3 para 1 with effect for the tax year 2017–18 and subsequent tax years.

[783BO Exclusion from relief: payments by firm

No relief under this Chapter is given to an individual for a tax year if—
  (a) the individual has relevant property income for the tax year, and
  (b) the income includes a payment made by, or on behalf of, a firm at a time when the individual is—
      (i) a partner in the firm, or
      (ii) connected with a partner in the firm.][1]

Commentary—*Simon's Taxes* B6.202A.
Amendments—[1]   Part 6A (ss 783A–783BQ) inserted by F(No 2)A 2017 s 17, Sch 3 para 1 with effect for the tax year 2017–18 and subsequent tax years.

[783BP Exclusion from relief: payments by close company

(1) No relief under this Chapter is given to an individual for a tax year if—
  (a) the individual has relevant property income for the tax year, and
  (b) the income includes a payment made by, or on behalf of, a close company at a time when the individual is—
      (i) a participator in the close company, or
      (ii) an associate of a participator in the close company.
(2) In this section "associate" and "participator" have the same meanings as in Part 10 of CTA 2010 (see sections 448 and 454).][1]

Commentary—*Simon's Taxes* B6.202A.
Amendments—[1]   Part 6A (ss 783A–783BQ) inserted by F(No 2)A 2017 s 17, Sch 3 para 1 with effect for the tax year 2017–18 and subsequent tax years.

[Interpretation

783BQ Interpretation of this Chapter

In this Chapter—
  (a) "rent-a-room relief", "rent-a-room receipts" and "total rent-a-room amount" have the same meanings as in Chapter 1 of Part 7 (rent-a-room relief: see sections 784, 786 and 788), and
  (b) references to "the individual's limit" are to be construed in accordance with section 789 (the individual's limit for the purposes of rent-a-room relief).][1]

Commentary—*Simon's Taxes* B6.202A.
Amendments—[1]   Part 6A (ss 783A–783BQ) inserted by F(No 2)A 2017 s 17, Sch 3 para 1 with effect for the tax year 2017–18 and subsequent tax years.

PART 7

INCOME CHARGED UNDER THIS ACT: RENT-A-ROOM AND [QUALIFYING CARE] RE-LIEF

Amendments—Words substituted for words "Foster-care" by F(No 3)A 2010 s 1, Sch 1 paras 30, 34 with effect for the tax year 2010–11 and subsequent tax years, subject to transitional provisions in F(No 3)A 2010 Sch 1 paras 36(2)–(5), 37.

CHAPTER 1

RENT-A-ROOM RELIEF

Introduction

784 Overview of Chapter 1

(1) This Chapter provides relief on income from the use of furnished accommodation in an individual's only or main residence.
  The relief is referred to in this Chapter as "rent-a-room relief".
(2) The form of relief depends on whether the individual's total rent-a-room amount exceeds the individual's limit (see sections 788 to 790).
(3) If it does not, the income is not charged to income tax unless the individual elects otherwise (see sections 791 to 794).
(4) If it does, the individual may elect for alternative methods of calculating the income (see sections 795 to 798).

Commentary—*Simon's Taxes* B6.601.
HMRC Manuals—Property Income Manual PIM4001 (rent-a-room relief: introduction and overview).

785 Person who qualifies for relief

(1) An individual qualifies for rent-a-room relief for a tax year if the individual—
  (a) has rent-a-room receipts for the tax year (see section 786), and
  (b) does not derive any taxable income other than rent-a-room receipts from a relevant trade, letting or agreement.

(2) "Taxable income" means receipts or other income in respect of which the individual is liable to income tax for the tax year.

(3) A relevant trade, letting or agreement is one from which the individual derives rent-a-room receipts for the tax year.

Commentary—*Simon's Taxes* **B6.601, B6.604.**
HMRC Manuals—Property Income Manual PIM4001 (qualifying individuals for relief).

Basic definitions

786 Meaning of "rent-a-room receipts"

(1) For the purposes of this Chapter an individual has rent-a-room receipts for a tax year if—

(a) the receipts are in respect of the use of furnished accommodation in a residence in the United Kingdom or in respect of goods or services supplied in connection with that use,

(b) they accrue to the individual during the income period for those receipts (see subsections (3) and (4)),

(c) for some or all of that period the residence is the individual's only or main residence, and

(d) the receipts would otherwise be brought into account in calculating the profits of a trade or UK property business or chargeable to income tax under Chapter 8 of Part 5 (income not otherwise charged).

(2) Meals, cleaning and laundry are examples of goods or services supplied in connection with the use of furnished accommodation in a residence.

(3) If the receipts would otherwise be brought into account in calculating the profits of a trade, the income period is the basis period for the tax year (see Chapter 15 of Part 2).

(4) Otherwise the income period is the period which—

(a) begins at the beginning of the tax year or, if later, the beginning of the letting in respect of which the receipts arise, and

(b) ends at the end of the tax year or, if earlier, the end of that letting.

[(5) Subsections (6) and (7) apply if—

(a) the receipts would otherwise be brought into account in calculating the profits of a trade, and

(b) an election under section 25A (cash basis for small businesses) has effect in relation to the trade.

(6) Any amounts brought into account under section 96A [(capital receipts under, or after leaving, cash basis)]² as a receipt in calculating the profits of the trade are to be treated as receipts within paragraph (a) of subsection (1) above.

[(6A) Subsections (6B) and (7) apply if—

(a) the receipts would otherwise be brought into account in calculating the profits of a UK property business, and

(b) the profits are calculated on the cash basis (see section 271D).

(6B) Any amounts brought into account under section 307E (capital receipts under, or after leaving, cash basis) as a receipt in calculating the profits of the property business are to be treated as receipts within paragraph (a) of subsection (1) above.]³

(7) The reference in subsection (1)(b) to receipts that accrue to an individual during the income period for those receipts is to be read as a reference to receipts that are received by the individual during that period.]¹

Commentary—*Simon's Taxes* **B6.601, B6.602.**
HMRC Manuals—Property Income Manual PIM4001 (rent-a-room relief: meaning).
Amendments—¹   Sub-ss (5)–(7) inserted by FA 2013 s 17, Sch 4 para 40 with effect for the tax year 2013–14 and subsequent tax years, subject to the provisions of FA 2013 Sch 4 para 57 in relation to barristers and advocates.
²   In sub-s (6), words substituted for words "capital receipts)" by F(No 2)A 2017 s 16, Sch 2 paras 1, 10 with effect for the tax year 2017–18 and subsequent tax years, subject to transitional provisions in F(No 2)A 2017 Sch 2 para 64.
³   Sub-s (6A), (6B) inserted by F(No 2)A 2017 s 16, Sch 2 paras 12, 33 with effect for the tax year 2017–18 and subsequent tax years, subject to transitional provisions in F(No 2)A 2017 Sch 2 para 64.

787 Meaning of "residence"

(1) In this Chapter "residence" means—

(a) a building, or part of a building, occupied or intended to be occupied as a separate residence, or

(b) a caravan or houseboat.

(2) If a building, or part of a building, designed for permanent use as a single residence is temporarily divided into two or more separate residences, it is still treated as a single residence.

Commentary—*Simon's Taxes* **B6.602.**
HMRC Manuals—Property Income Manual PIM4001 (residence: meaning).
PIM4004 (building divided into separate residences: definition of residence).

788 Meaning of "total rent-a-room amount"

(1) For the purposes of this Chapter an individual's "total rent-a-room amount" for a tax year is the total of—

(a) the individual's rent-a-room receipts for the tax year, and

(b) any relevant balancing charges for the tax year (see section 802).

(2) In calculating the total rent-a-room amount, no deduction is allowed for expenses or any other matter.

Commentary—*Simon's Taxes* **B6.603.**
HMRC Manuals—Property Income Manual PIM4020 (receipts below exemption limit).

Individual's limit

789 The individual's limit

(1) For the purposes of this Chapter an individual's limit for a tax year depends on whether the individual meets the exclusive receipts condition for the tax year (see section 790).
(2) If the individual does, the individual's limit for the tax year is the basic amount for the tax year.
(3) If the individual does not, the individual's limit for the tax year is half that amount.
(4) The basic amount for a tax year is [£7,500][1].
(5) The Treasury may by order amend the sum for the time being specified in subsection (4).

Commentary—*Simon's Taxes* **B6.603.**
HMRC Manuals—Property Income Manual PIM4010 (exemption limits).
Amendments[1]   In sub-s (4), figure substituted by the Income Tax (Limit for Rent-a-Room Relief) Order, SI 2015/1539 art 2 with effect for the tax year 2016–17 and subsequent tax years. Figure was previously £4,250.

790 Exclusive receipts condition

(1) An individual meets the exclusive receipts condition for a tax year if, for each rent-a-room residence of the individual, no receipts accrue to any other person during any relevant period in respect of—
    (a) the use of residential accommodation (whether furnished or not) in the residence, or
    (b) goods or services supplied in connection with that use (such as meals, cleaning or laundry),
at a time when the residence is the individual's only or main residence.
(2) Each of the following periods is a relevant period—
    (a) any income period specified in section 786 for any rent-a-room receipts of the individual for the tax year,
    (b) the period of 12 months which begins at the same time as any such income period begins, and
    (c) the period of 12 months which ends at the same time as any such income period ends.
(3) A "rent-a-room residence of the individual" means a residence in respect of which the individual derives rent-a-room receipts for the tax year.

Commentary—*Simon's Taxes* **B6.603.**

Relief if amount does not exceed limit

791 Full rent-a-room relief: introduction

Sections 792 to 794 (which give the full form of rent-a-room relief) apply if—
    (a) an individual qualifies for rent-a-room relief for a tax year,
    (b) the individual's total rent-a-room amount for the tax year does not exceed the individual's limit for the tax year, and
    (c) no election by the individual under section 799 has effect to disapply the full relief for the tax year.

Commentary—*Simon's Taxes* **B6.604.**
HMRC Manuals—Property Income Manual PIM4020 (full rent-a-room relief: introduction to receipts below exemption limit).

792 Full rent-a-room relief: trading income

(1) This section applies if the individual has any rent-a-room receipts for the tax year which would otherwise be brought into account in calculating the profits of a trade.
(2) The profits or losses of the trade for the tax year are treated as nil.

Commentary—*Simon's Taxes* **B6.604.**
HMRC Manuals—Property Income Manual PIM4020 (receipts below exemption limit: trading income).
PIM4001 (rent-a-room relief: trading income: introduction and overview).
PIM4010 (exemption limits: lodger provided with services which amount to a trade: basis period).

793 Full rent-a-room relief: property income

(1) This section applies if the individual has any rent-a-room receipts for the tax year which would otherwise be brought into account in calculating the profits of a UK property business.
(2) In calculating those profits—
    (a) those receipts for the tax year, and
    (b) any expenses associated with them,
are not brought into account.
(3) No relevant balancing charge or relevant allowance (see section 802) is made in calculating those profits for the tax year.

Commentary—*Simon's Taxes* **B6.604.**
HMRC Manuals—Property Income Manual PIM4020 (receipts below exemption limit: property income).
PIM4030 (receipts above exemption limit).

794 Full rent-a-room relief: income chargeable under Chapter 8 of Part 5

(1) This section applies if the individual has any rent-a-room receipts for the tax year which would otherwise be chargeable to income tax under Chapter 8 of Part 5 (income not otherwise charged).

(2) For each agreement from which those receipts arise, the amount of—

  (*a*) those receipts arising in the tax year from the agreement, less

  (*b*) any expenses associated with them,

is treated as nil.

Commentary—*Simon's Taxes* **B6.604.**

HMRC Manuals—Property Income Manual PIM4020 (receipts below exemption limit: what happens if receipts fall below the limit?).

Alternative calculation of profits if amount exceeds limit

795 Alternative calculation of profits: introduction

Sections 796 to 798 (which provide for alternative methods of calculating profits) apply if—

  (*a*) an individual qualifies for rent-a-room relief for a tax year,

  (*b*) the individual's total rent-a-room amount for the tax year exceeds the individual's limit for the tax year, and

  (*c*) an election by the individual under section 800 has effect to apply the alternative method of calculating profits for the tax year.

Commentary—*Simon's Taxes* **B6.605.**

HMRC Manuals—Property Income Manual PIM4030 (receipts above exemption limit: alternative method of calculation of profit: introduction).

796 Alternative calculation of profits: trading income

(1) This section applies if the individual has any rent-a-room receipts for the tax year which are the receipts of a trade.

(2) The profits of the trade for the tax year are—

  (*a*) the sum of the amount of the rent-a-room receipts for the tax year arising from the trade and the amount of any relevant balancing charge, less

  (*b*) the deductible amount.

(3) The deductible amount—

  (*a*) is L if all the individual's rent-a-room receipts for the tax year arise from the trade, and

  (*b*) otherwise, is—

$$L \times \frac{T}{R}$$

but, in either case, subject to a maximum of T.

(4) In subsection (3)—

  L is the individual's limit for the tax year,

  T is the individual's rent-a-room receipts for the tax year arising from the trade, and

  R is all the individual's rent-a-room receipts for the tax year.

(5) In calculating the amount of any rent-a-room receipts for the purposes of this section, no deduction is allowed for expenses or any other matter.

Commentary—*Simon's Taxes* **B6.605.**

HMRC Manuals—Property Income Manual PIM4030 (receipts above exemption limit: trading income).

797 Alternative calculation of profits: property income

(1) This section applies if the individual has any rent-a-room receipts for the tax year ("Part 3 rent-a-room receipts") which are to be brought into account in calculating the profits of a UK property business.

(2) In calculating those profits for the tax year—

  (*a*) the Part 3 rent-a-room receipts for the tax year are brought into account only in calculating the profits of the business for the tax year, and

  (*b*) any expenses associated with those receipts are not brought into account.

(3) In calculating those profits for the tax year—

  (*a*) a deduction is allowed, and

  (*b*) no relevant allowance, but any relevant balancing charge, is made.

(4) The amount of the deduction—

  (*a*) is L if all the individual's rent-a-room receipts for the tax year are Part 3 rent-a-room receipts, and

  (*b*) otherwise, is—

$$L \times \frac{P}{R}$$

but, in either case, subject to a maximum of P.

(5) In subsection (4)—

L is the individual's limit for the tax year,

P is the individual's Part 3 rent-a-room receipts for the tax year, and

R is all the individual's rent-a-room receipts for the tax year.

Commentary—*Simon's Taxes* **B6.605.**

HMRC Manuals—Property Income Manual PIM4030 (receipts above exemption limit: property income).

798 Alternative calculation of profits: income chargeable under Chapter 8 of Part 5

(1) This section applies if the individual has any rent-a-room receipts for the tax year which are chargeable to income tax under Chapter 8 of Part 5 (income not otherwise charged).

(2) The amount charged for the tax year arising from all the agreements from which the receipts are derived is—

(a) the amount of the receipts for the tax year so arising, less

(b) the deductible amount.

(3) The deductible amount is—

$$\frac{L \times I}{R}$$

subject to a maximum of I.

(4) In subsection (3)—

L is the individual's limit for the tax year,

I is the amount of the receipts for the tax year arising from the agreements, and

R is all the individual's rent-a-room receipts for the tax year.

(5) In calculating the amount of any rent-a-room receipts for the purposes of this section, no deduction is allowed for expenses or any other matter.

Commentary—*Simon's Taxes* **B6.605.**

HMRC Manuals—Property Income Manual PIM4030 (receipts above exemption limit: income chargeable).

Elections

799 Election not to apply full relief

(1) An individual may elect for sections 792 to 794 (full relief) not to apply.

(2) The election—

(a) must specify the tax year for which it is made, and

(b) has effect for that year (unless withdrawn by notice given by the individual).

(3) An election or notice of withdrawal must be made or given to [an officer of Revenue and Customs] on or before—

(a) the first anniversary of the normal self-assessment filing date for the tax year for which the election is made, or

(b) such later date as [an officer of Revenue and Customs] may, in a particular case, allow.

Commentary—*Simon's Taxes* **B6.604.**

HMRC Manuals—Property Income Manual PIM4050 (elections and time limits).

800 Election for alternative method of calculating profits

(1) An individual may elect for the alternative method of calculating profits given in sections 796 to 798 to apply if—

(a) the individual qualifies for rent-a-room relief for a tax year, and

(b) the individual's total rent-a-room amount for the tax year exceeds the individual's limit for the tax year.

(2) The election—

(a) must specify the tax year for which it is made, and

(b) has effect for that year and subsequent tax years (unless withdrawn by notice given by the individual).

(3) A notice of withdrawal of an election must specify the tax year for which it is given.

The election ceases to have effect for that tax year and subsequent tax years.

(4) Withdrawal of an election does not prevent a fresh election from being made for a subsequent tax year.

(5) An election or notice of withdrawal must be made or given to [an officer of Revenue and Customs] on or before—

(a) the first anniversary of the normal self-assessment filing date for the tax year specified in the election or notice of withdrawal, or

(b) such later date as [an officer of Revenue and Customs] may, in a particular case, allow.

(6) If—

(a) an election would otherwise have effect for a tax year, but

(b) the individual's total rent-a-room amount for the tax year does not exceed the individual's limit for the tax year, the individual is treated as giving a notice of withdrawal of the election which specifies that tax year as the one for which it is given (and the election, therefore, ceases to have effect for that tax year and subsequent tax years).

Commentary—*Simon's Taxes* B6.605, B6.606.
HMRC Manuals—Property Income Manual PIM4050 (elections and time limits: election for simplified calculation of profit).

801 Time limit on adjustment of assessment

(1) This section applies if it is necessary to make an adjustment by way of assessment to give effect to an election or notice of withdrawal under section 799 or 800.

(2) The assessment is not out of time if it is made on or before the first anniversary of the normal self-assessment filing date for the tax year for which the election was made or notice was given (or treated as given).

Commentary—*Simon's Taxes* B6.604, B6.606.
HMRC Manuals—Property Income Manual PIM4050 (elections and time limits).
PIM4030 (receipts above exemption limit: election).

Interpretation

802 Minor definitions

In this Chapter—

"letting" includes a licence to occupy,
"relevant allowance", for a tax year, means a capital allowance falling to be made for the tax year under Part 2 of CAA 2001 in respect of plant or machinery provided for the purposes of a trade or letting from which rent-a-room receipts are derived, and
"relevant balancing charge", for a tax year, means a balancing charge falling to be made for the tax year under Part 2 of CAA 2001 in respect of plant or machinery provided for the purposes of a trade or letting from which rent-a-room receipts are derived.

Commentary—*Simon's Taxes* B6.601, B6.603, B6.604.

CHAPTER 2

[QUALIFYING CARE RELIEF]

Amendments—Heading substituted for previous heading "Foster-care Relief" by F(No 3)A 2010 s 1, Sch 1 paras 1, 29 with effect for the tax year 2010–11 and subsequent tax years, subject to transitional provisions in F(No 3)A 2010 Sch 1 paras 36(2)–(5), 37.

Introduction

803 Overview of Chapter 2

[(1) This Chapter provides relief on income from the provision by an individual of qualifying care. The relief is referred to in this Chapter as "qualifying care relief".][1]

(2) The form of relief depends on whether the individual's total [qualifying care][1] receipts exceed the individual's limit (see sections 807 to 811).

(3) If they do not, the income is not charged to income tax (see sections 812 to 814).

(4) If they do, the individual may elect for an alternative method of calculating the income (see sections 815 to 819).

(5) If the [qualifying care][1] receipts are the receipts of a trade, special rules apply—

   (*a*) if the period of account of the trade does not end on 5th April (see sections 820 to 823), and
   (*b*) in relation to capital allowances (see sections 824 to 827).

(6) The provisions of this Chapter which are expressed to apply in relation to trades also apply in relation to professions and vocations.

Commentary—*Simon's Taxes* E1.701.
HMRC Manuals—Business Income Manual BIM52753 (qualifying care relief: introduction).
Amendments—[1] Sub-s (1) substituted, and in sub-ss (2), (5), words substituted by F(No 3)A 2010 s 1, Sch 1 paras 1, 2 with effect for the tax year 2010–11 and subsequent tax years, subject to transitional provisions in F(No 3)A 2010 Sch 1 paras 36(2)–(5), 37.

804 Person who qualifies for relief

[(1) An individual qualifies for qualifying care relief for a tax year if the individual—

   (*a*) has qualifying care receipts for the tax year (see section 805), and
   (*b*) does not derive any taxable income, other than qualifying care receipts, from a relevant trade or arrangement.][1]

(2) "Taxable income" means receipts or other income in respect of which the individual is liable to income tax for the tax year.

(3) A relevant trade or arrangement is one from which the individual derives [qualifying care][1] receipts for the tax year.

[(4) Subsection (1) is subject to section 804A.][1]

Commentary—*Simon's Taxes* E1.701.

Amendments—[1]   Sub-s (1) substituted, in sub-s (3) words substituted, and sub-s (4) inserted, by F(No 3)A 2010 s 1, Sch 1 paras 1, 3 with effect for the tax year 2010–11 and subsequent tax years, subject to transitional provisions in F(No 3)A 2010 Sch 1 paras 36(2)–(5), 37.

[804A Shared lives care: further condition for relief

(1) This section applies if an individual ("N") has qualifying care receipts for a tax year in respect of the provision of shared lives care.

(2) N does not qualify for qualifying care relief in respect of those receipts if the placement cap is exceeded for the residence (or any of the residences) used by N to provide the care from which those receipts are derived.

(3) The placement cap is exceeded for a residence if, at any given time during the relevant period, shared lives care is being provided there (whether by N or anyone else) for more than 3 people in total.

(4) The relevant period, in relation to a residence, is the period for which the residence is N's only or main residence during the income period for the receipts (see section 805).

(5) If the placement cap is so exceeded but N also has qualifying care receipts for the tax year in respect of the provision of foster care, this Chapter is to apply to N for the tax year as if—

  (*a*) references to qualifying care were to foster care, and
  (*b*) accordingly, references (other than in this section) to qualifying care receipts did not include receipts in respect of the provision of shared lives care.

(6) In determining the number of people for whom shared lives care is being provided at any given time, brothers and sisters (including half-brothers and half-sisters) count as one person.][1]

Commentary—*Simon's Taxes* **E1.701.**

HMRC Manuals—Business Income Manual BIM52758 (shared lives care: qualifying care relief).

Amendments—[1]   This section inserted by F(No 3)A 2010 s 1, Sch 1 paras 1, 4 with effect for the tax year 2010–11 and subsequent tax years, subject to transitional provisions in F(No 3)A 2010 Sch 1 paras 36(2)–(5), 37.

Basic definitions

805 Meaning of "[qualifying care][1] receipts"

(1) For the purposes of this Chapter an individual has [qualifying care][1] receipts for a tax year if—

  (*a*) the receipts are in respect of the provision of [qualifying care][1],
  (*b*) they accrue to the individual during the income period for those receipts (see subsections (2) and (3)), and
  (*c*) the receipts would otherwise be brought into account in calculating the profits of a trade or chargeable to income tax under Chapter 8 of Part 5 (income not otherwise charged).

(2) If the receipts would otherwise be brought into account in calculating the profits of a trade, the income period is the basis period for the tax year (see Chapter 15 of Part 2).

(3) Otherwise the income period is the tax year.

[(4) Subsections (5) and (6) apply if—

  (*a*) the receipts would otherwise be brought into account in calculating the profits of a trade, and
  (*b*) an election under section 25A (cash basis for small businesses) has effect in relation to the trade.

(5) Any amounts brought into account under section 96A [(capital receipts under, or after leaving, cash basis)][3] as a receipt in calculating the profits of the trade are to be treated as receipts within paragraph (*a*) of subsection (1) above.

(6) The reference in subsection (1)(*b*) to receipts that accrue to an individual during the income period for those receipts is to be read as a reference to receipts that are received by the individual during that period.][2]

Commentary—*Simon's Taxes* **E1.702.**

HMRC Manuals—Business Income Manual BIM52760 (qualifying care receipts).

Amendments—[1]   In heading and sub-ss (1), (1)(*a*) words substituted, by F(No 3)A 2010 s 1, Sch 1 paras 1, 5 with effect for the tax year 2010–11 and subsequent tax years, subject to transitional provisions in F(No 3)A 2010 Sch 1 paras 36(2)–(5), 37.

[2]   Sub-ss (4)–(6) inserted by FA 2013 s 17, Sch 4 paras 41, 42 with effect for the tax year 2013–14 and subsequent tax years, subject to the provisions of FA 2013 Sch 4 para 57 in relation to barristers and advocates.

[3]   In sub-s (5), words substituted for words "(capital receipts)" by F(No 2)A 2017 s 16, Sch 2 paras 1, 11 with effect for the tax year 2017–18 and subsequent tax years, subject to transitional provisions inf F(No 2)A 2017 Sch 2 para 64.

[805A Meaning of providing qualifying care

For the purposes of this Chapter qualifying care is provided if an individual (alone or in partnership) provides—

  (*a*) foster care but not shared lives care,
  (*b*) shared lives care but not foster care, or
  (*c*) both foster care and shared lives care.][1]

Commentary—*Simon's Taxes* **E1.702.**

HMRC Manuals—Business Income Manual BIM52753 (providing qualifying care: meaning).

Amendments—[1]   This section inserted by F(No 3)A 2010 s 1, Sch 1 paras 1, 6 with effect for the tax year 2010–11 and subsequent tax years, subject to transitional provisions in F(No 3)A 2010 Sch 1 paras 36(2)–(5), 37.

806 Meaning of providing foster care

(1) For the purposes of this Chapter foster care is provided if an individual—

   (a) provides accommodation and maintenance for a child, and

   (b) does so as a foster carer.

[(2) An individual is a foster carer if the child is placed with the individual by virtue of a compulsory supervision order or interim compulsory supervision order, or under any of the following enactments, unless the individual is excluded by subsection (5).]^2

(3) The enactments are—

   (a) section [22C]^1 or 59(1)(a) of the Children Act 1989 (c. 41) (provision of accommodation for children by local authorities or voluntary organisations),

   [(aa) section 81 of the Social Services and Well-being (Wales) Act 2014 (provision of accommodation for children by local authorities),]^4

   (b) regulations under section 5 of the Social Work (Scotland) Act 1968 (c. 49),

   (c) . . . ^{2}

   (d) Article 27(2)(a) or 75(1)(a) of the Children (Northern Ireland) Order 1995 (SI 1995/755 (NI 2)) (provision of accommodation for children by authorities or voluntary organisations).

[(4) An individual is also a foster carer if the individual is approved as a foster carer by a local authority or a voluntary organisation in accordance with regulations under section 5 of the Social Work (Scotland) Act 1968, and the child in respect of whom the accommodation is provided—

   (a) is being looked after by a local authority within the meaning of section 17(6) of the Children (Scotland) Act 1995, or

   (b) is subject to an order or warrant made by the children's hearing or sheriff under the Children's Hearings (Scotland) Act 2011,

unless the individual is excluded by subsection (5).]^2

(5) The following are excluded individuals—

   (a) a parent of the child,

   (b) an individual who is not a parent of the child but who has parental responsibility (or, in Scotland, parental responsibilities) in relation to the child,

   [(ba) where the child is in care and there was a child arrangements order in force with respect to the child immediately before the care order was made, a person named in the child arrangements order as a person with whom the child is to live,

   (bb) (in Scotland) where the child is in care and there was a child arrangements order in force with respect to the child immediately before the child was placed in care, a person named in the child arrangements order as a person with whom the child was to live, spend time with or otherwise have contact,]^3

   (c) if the child is in care and there was a residence order in force with respect to the child immediately before the care order was made, an individual in whose favour the residence order was made, . . . ^{1}

   (d) (in Scotland) if the child is in care and there was a residence order or contact order in force with respect to the child immediately before the child was placed in care, an individual in whose favour the residence order or contact order was made; [and

   (e) an individual with whom the child is placed under a placement falling within section 22C(6)(d) of the Children Act 1989,]^1

   [(f) an individual with whom the child is placed under a placement falling within section 81(6)(d) of the Social Services and Well-being (Wales) Act 2014.]^4

[(6) In this section—

   "compulsory supervision order" has the meaning given by section 83 of the Children's Hearings (Scotland) Act 2011; and

   "interim compulsory supervision order" has the meaning given by section 86 of that Act.]^2

Commentary—*Simon's Taxes* E1.702.

HMRC Manuals—Business Income Manual BIM52755 (foster carer: meaning). BIM52754 (Qualifying Care Relief: excluded individuals).

Amendments—^{1} In sub-s (3)(a), reference substituted; in sub-s (5)(c), word repealed; and sub-s (5)(e) and preceding word inserted, by the Children and Young Persons Act 2008, ss 8(2), 42, Sch 1, para 18, Sch 4 with effect in relation to England from 1 April 2011 (by virtue of SI 2010/2981, art 4(a)), and with effect in relation to Wales from 6 April 2016 (by virtue of SI 2016/452, art 2(b)).

^{2} Sub-ss (2), (4) substituted, sub-s (3)(c) repealed, and sub-s (6) inserted, by the Children's Hearings (Scotland) Act 2011 (Consequential and Transitional Provisions and Savings) Order, SI 2013/1465 with effect from 24 June 2013 (being the day the Children's Hearings (Scotland) Act 2011 s 7 came into force: see SSI 2013/195 art 2 and art 1(2)).

^{3} Sub-s (5)(ba) and (bb) inserted by the Children and Families Act 2014 s 12, Sch 2 paras 67, 69 with effect from 22 April 2014 (by virtue of SI 2014/889 art 4(f)).

^{4} Sub-ss (3)(aa), (5)(f) inserted by the Social Services and Well-being (Wales) Act 2014 (Consequential Amendments) Regulations, SI 2016/413 regs 222, 225 with effect from 6 April 2016.

[806A Meaning of providing shared lives care

(1) For the purposes of this Chapter shared lives care is provided by an individual if—

(a) the individual provides accommodation and care for an adult or child ("X") who has been placed with the individual, and

(b) the conditions in subsection (2) are met.

(2) The conditions are—

(a) the accommodation is in the individual's own home,

(b) the accommodation and care are provided on the basis that X will share the individual's home and daily family life during the placement,

(c) the placement is made under a specified social care scheme,

(d) the individual does not provide the accommodation and care as a foster carer, and

(e) the individual is not excluded within the meaning of section 806(5).

(3) Section 806(5) has effect for the purposes of subsection (2)(e) as if references to the child were to X (whatever X's age).

(4) "Specified social care scheme" means a social care scheme of a kind specified or described in an order made by the Treasury.

(5) An order under subsection (4) may make provision having effect in relation to the tax year current on the day on which the order is made.

(6) In this section—

"care" means personal care, including assistance and support;

"home" means an individual's only or main residence;

"social care scheme" means a scheme, service or arrangement for those who, by reason of age, illness, disability or other vulnerability, are in need of care.]¹

Commentary—*Simon's Taxes* E1.702.

HMRC Manuals—Business Income Manual BIM52758 (shared lives care: meaning).

Orders—Qualifying Care Relief (Specified Social Care Schemes) Order, SI 2011/712

Qualifying Care Relief (Specified Social Care Schemes) (Amendment) Order, SI 2018/317.

Amendments—¹ Sections 806A, 806B inserted by F(No 3)A 2010 s 1, Sch 1 paras 1, 7 with effect for the tax year 2010–11 and subsequent tax years, subject to transitional provisions in F(No 3)A 2010 Sch 1 paras 36(2)–(5), 37.

[806B Meaning of "residence"

(1) In this Chapter "residence" means—

(a) a building, or part of a building, occupied or intended to be occupied as a separate residence, or

(b) a caravan or houseboat.

(2) If a building, or part of a building, designed for permanent use as a single residence is temporarily divided into two or more separate residences, it is still treated as a single residence.]¹

Commentary—*Simon's Taxes* E1.702, E1.703.

HMRC Manuals—Property Income Manual PIM4004 (residence: meaning).

Amendments—¹ Sections 806A, 806B inserted by F(No 3)A 2010 s 1, Sch 1 paras 1, 7 with effect for the tax year 2010–11 and subsequent tax years, subject to transitional provisions in F(No 3)A 2010 Sch 1 paras 36(2)–(5), 37.

807 Calculation of "total [qualifying care]¹ receipts"

For the purposes of this Chapter, in calculating an individual's "total [qualifying care]¹ receipts" for a tax year, no deduction is allowed for expenses or any other matter.

Commentary—*Simon's Taxes* E1.702.

HMRC Manuals—Business Income Manual BIM52760 (calculating qualifying care receipts).

Amendments—¹ Words substituted by F(No 3)A 2010 s 1, Sch 1 paras 1, 8 with effect for the tax year 2010–11 and subsequent tax years, subject to transitional provisions in F(No 3)A 2010 Sch 1 paras 36(2)–(5), 37.

Individual's limit

808 The individual's limit

(1) For the purposes of this Chapter an individual's limit for a tax year is the total of—

(a) the fixed amount for the tax year or, if section 809 or 810 applies, the individual's share of that amount, and

(b) each amount per [adult or]¹ child for the individual for the tax year (see section 811).

(2) For the purposes of this Chapter the fixed amount for a tax year is £10,000.

(3) The Treasury may by order amend the sum for the time being specified in subsection (2).

Commentary—*Simon's Taxes* E1.703.

HMRC Manuals—Business Income Manual BIM52765 (individual's limit for the tax year).

Amendments—¹ Words in sub-s (1)(b) inserted by F(No 3)A 2010 s 1, Sch 1 paras 1, 9 with effect for the tax year 2010–11 and subsequent tax years, subject to transitional provisions in F(No 3)A 2010 Sch 1 paras 36(2)–(5), 37.

[809 Share of fixed amount: residence used by more than one carer

"(1) This section applies if in a tax year—

(a) the residence used to provide the qualifying care from which an individual's qualifying care receipts for the tax year are derived is also used by another individual to provide qualifying care, and

(b) the other individual also has qualifying care receipts for the tax year.

(2) Each individual's share of the fixed amount for the tax year is the fixed amount divided by the total number of individuals who—

(*a*)   use the residence in the tax year to provide qualifying care, and
(*b*)   have qualifying care receipts for the tax year.][1]

Commentary—*Simon's Taxes* **E1.703**.
HMRC Manuals—Business Income Manual BIM52765 (An individual's qualifying amount for a tax year).
Amendments—[1]   This section substituted by F(No 3)A 2010 s 1, Sch 1 paras 1, 10 with effect for the tax year 2010–11 and subsequent tax years, subject to transitional provisions in F(No 3)A 2010 Sch 1 paras 36(2)–(5), 37.

810   Share of fixed amount: income period not a year

(1) This section applies if in a tax year an individual's income period for the individual's [qualifying care][1] receipts is a period other than a year.
(2) The individual's share of the fixed amount for the tax year is—

$$\frac{AS \times D}{365}$$

where—

> AS is the fixed amount or (if section 809 applies) the individual's share of the fixed amount, and
> D is the number of days in the individual's income period.

Commentary—*Simon's Taxes* **E1.703**.
HMRC Manuals—Business Income Manual BIM52765 (income period not a year).
Amendments—[1]   In sub-s (1) words substituted by F(No 3)A 2010 s 1, Sch 1 paras 1, 11 with effect for the tax year 2010–11 and subsequent tax years, subject to transitional provisions in F(No 3)A 2010 Sch 1 paras 36(2)–(5), 37.

811   The amount per [adult or][1] child

[(1) An individual's amount per adult or child for a tax year is found by multiplying—
     (*a*)   the number of weeks during the income period for the tax year in which the individual provides qualifying care for the adult or child, by
     (*b*)   the weekly amount for the adult or child.
(1A) The weekly amount for an adult is £250.][1]
(2) The weekly amount for a child is—
     (*a*)   £200 for a week throughout which the child is under 11 years old, and
     (*b*)   £250 for other weeks.
(3) The Treasury may by order amend any amount for the time being specified in [subsection (1A) or (2)][1].
(4) If an individual provides [qualifying care for an adult or child][1] during an income period for only part of a week, the part is treated as a whole week.
(5) If an income period begins or ends during a week, the week is treated as falling within the income period ending during the week.
   But if there is no such income period, the week is treated as falling within the income period beginning during the week.
(6) A week is a period of 7 days beginning with a Monday.

Commentary—*Simon's Taxes* **E1.703**.
HMRC Manuals—Business Income Manual BIM52765 (qualifying amount for each adult or child).
Amendments—[1]   In heading words inserted, sub-ss (1), (1A) substituted for previous sub-s (1), in sub-ss (3), (4) words substituted, by F(No 3)A 2010 s 1, Sch 1 paras 1, 12 with effect for the tax year 2010–11 and subsequent tax years, subject to transitional provisions in F(No 3)A 2010 Sch 1 paras 36(2)–(5), 37.

Relief if amount does not exceed limit

[812   Full qualifying care relief: introduction

Sections 813 and 814 (which give the full form of qualifying care relief) apply if—
     (*a*)   an individual qualifies for qualifying care relief for a tax year,
     (*b*)   the individual's total qualifying care receipts for the tax year do not exceed the individual's limit for the tax year, and
     (*c*)   sections 822 and 823 do not apply (accounting date for trade not 5 April).][1]

Commentary—*Simon's Taxes* **E1.704**.
HMRC Manuals—Business Income Manual BIM52760 (full qualifying care relief: overview of receipts above the limit).
Amendments—[1]   This section substituted by F(No 3)A 2010 s 1, Sch 1 paras 1, 13 with effect for the tax year 2010–11 and subsequent tax years, subject to transitional provisions in F(No 3)A 2010 Sch 1 paras 36(2)–(5), 37.

813   Full [qualifying care relief][1]: trading income

(1) This section applies if the individual's [qualifying care][1] receipts for the tax year would otherwise be brought into account in calculating the profits of a trade.
(2) The profits or losses of the trade for the tax year are treated as nil.

Commentary—*Simon's Taxes* **E1.704**.
HMRC Manuals—Business Income Manual BIM52760 (qualifying care relief included in trading income: treatment).
Amendments—[1]   In heading and sub-s (1), words substituted by F(No 3)A 2010 s 1, Sch 1 paras 1, 14 with effect for the tax year 2010–11 and subsequent tax years, subject to transitional provisions in F(No 3)A 2010 Sch 1 paras 36(2)–(5), 37.

814 Full [qualifying care][1] relief: income chargeable under Chapter 8 of Part 5

(1) This section applies if the individual's [qualifying care][1] receipts for the tax year would otherwise be chargeable to income tax under Chapter 8 of Part 5 (income not otherwise charged).

(2) For each arrangement from which those receipts arise, the amount of—
  (a) those receipts arising in the tax year from the arrangement, less
  (b) any expenses associated with them,

is treated as nil.

Commentary—*Simon's Taxes* E1.704.
HMRC Manuals—Business Income Manual BIM52760 (receipts below exemption limit: income not otherwise charged).
Amendments—[1] In heading and sub-s (1), words substituted by F(No 3)A 2010 s 1, Sch 1 paras 1, 15 with effect for the tax year 2010–11 and subsequent tax years, subject to transitional provisions in F(No 3)A 2010 Sch 1 paras 36(2)–(5), 37.

Alternative calculation of profits if amount exceeds limit

815 Alternative calculation of profits: introduction

Sections 816 and 817 (which provide for an alternative method of calculating profits) apply if—
  (a) an individual qualifies for [qualifying care][1] relief for a tax year,
  (b) the individual's total [qualifying care][1] receipts for the tax year exceed the individual's limit for the tax year,
  (c) sections 822 and 823 do not apply (accounting date for trade not 5th April), and
  (d) an election by the individual has effect to apply the alternative method of calculating profits for the tax year (see sections 818 and 819).

Commentary—*Simon's Taxes* E1.705.
HMRC Manuals—Business Income Manual BIM52760 (receipts above exemption limit: introduction to alternative calculation).

Amendments—[1] In paras (a), (b) words substituted by F(No 3)A 2010 s 1, Sch 1 paras 1, 16 with effect for the tax year 2010–11 and subsequent tax years, subject to transitional provisions in F(No 3)A 2010 Sch 1 paras 36(2)–(5), 37.

816 Alternative calculation of profits: trading income

(1) This section applies if the individual's [qualifying care][1] receipts for the tax year are the receipts of a trade.

(2) The profits of the trade for the tax year are—
  (a) the individual's total [qualifying care][1] receipts for the tax year, less
  (b) the individual's limit for the tax year.

Commentary—*Simon's Taxes* E1.705.
HMRC Manuals—Business Income Manual BIM52760 (receipts above exemption limit: trading income).
Amendments—[1] In sub-ss (1), (2)(a) words substituted by F(No 3)A 2010 s 1, Sch 1 paras 1, 17 with effect for the tax year 2010–11 and subsequent tax years, subject to transitional provisions in F(No 3)A 2010 Sch 1 paras 36(2)–(5), 37.

817 Alternative calculation of profits: income chargeable under Chapter 8 of Part 5

(1) This section applies if the individual has [qualifying care][1] receipts for the tax year which are chargeable to income tax under Chapter 8 of Part 5 (income not otherwise charged).

(2) The amount charged for the tax year arising from all the arrangements from which the receipts are derived is—
  (a) the individual's total [qualifying care][1] receipts for the tax year, less
  (b) the individual's limit for the year.

Commentary—*Simon's Taxes* E1.705.
HMRC Manuals—Business Income Manual BIM52760 (qualifying care receipts above exemption limit: income not otherwise charged).
Amendments—[1] In sub-ss (1), (2)(a) words substituted by F(No 3)A 2010 s 1, Sch 1 paras 1, 18 with effect for the tax year 2010–11 and subsequent tax years, subject to transitional provisions in F(No 3)A 2010 Sch 1 paras 36(2)–(5), 37.

818 Election for alternative method of calculating profits

(1) An individual may elect for the alternative method of calculating profits given in sections 816 and 817 to apply if—
  (a) the individual qualifies for [qualifying care][1] relief for a tax year,
  (b) the individual's total [qualifying care][1] receipts for the tax year exceed the individual's limit for the tax year, and
  (c) sections 822 and 823 do not apply (accounting date for trade not 5th April).

(2) An election under this section—
  (a) must specify the tax year for which it is made, and
  (b) has effect for that year (unless withdrawn by notice given by the individual).

(3) An election or notice of withdrawal under this section must be made or given to [an officer of Revenue and Customs] on or before—
  (a) the first anniversary of the normal self-assessment filing date for the tax year for which the election is made, or
  (b) such later date as [an officer of Revenue and Customs] may, in a particular case, allow.

Commentary—*Simon's Taxes* E1.705.
HMRC Manuals—Business Income Manual BIM52760 (qualifying care receipts above exemption limit: election).

Amendments—[1]   In sub-s (1)(*a*), (*b*) words substituted by F(No 3)A 2010 s 1, Sch 1 paras 1, 19 with effect for the tax year 2010–11 and subsequent tax years, subject to transitional provisions in F(No 3)A 2010 Sch 1 paras 36(2)–(5), 37.

819 Adjustment of assessment

(1) This section applies if—

    (*a*) an individual does not make an election under section 818 for a tax year on or before the date for making the election, and

    (*b*) an adjustment is made after that date to the profits from the individual's provision of [qualifying care][1] on which the individual is liable to tax for the tax year.

(2) The individual may make an election under this section to apply the alternative method of calculating profits given in sections 816 and 817 for the tax year.

(3) The election—

    (*a*) must specify that tax year, and

    (*b*) has effect for that tax year (unless withdrawn by notice given by the individual).

(4) An election or notice of withdrawal under this section must be made or given to [an officer of Revenue and Customs] on or before—

    (*a*) the first anniversary of the normal self-assessment filing date for the tax year in which the adjustment is made, or

    (*b*) such later date as [an officer of Revenue and Customs] may, in a particular case, allow.

Commentary—*Simon's Taxes* E1.705.

HMRC Manuals—Business Income Manual BIM52760 (receipts above exemption limit: further assessment).

Amendments—[1]   In sub-s (1)(*b*) words substituted by F(No 3)A 2010 s 1, Sch 1 paras 1, 20 with effect for the tax year 2010–11 and subsequent tax years, subject to transitional provisions in F(No 3)A 2010 Sch 1 paras 36(2)–(5), 37.

Periods of account not ending on 5th April

820 Periods of account not ending on 5th April

[(1)] Sections 822 and 823 (which deal with the period of account of a trade not ending on 5th April) apply if—

    (*a*) an individual qualifies for [qualifying care][1] relief for a tax year,

    (*b*) the individual's [qualifying care][1] receipts for the tax year are the receipts of a trade, and

    (*c*) the period of account in which those receipts accrue does not end on 5th April in the tax year.

[(2) Where an election under section 25A (cash basis for small businesses) has effect in relation to the trade, any reference in this section or sections 821 to 823 to the period of account in which receipts accrue is to be read as a reference to the period of account in which receipts are received.][2]

Commentary—*Simon's Taxes* E1.706.

HMRC Manuals—Business Income Manual BIM52760 (qualifying care relief: actual tax year to 5 April).

Amendments—[1]   In sub-s (1)(*a*), (*b*) words substituted by F(No 3)A 2010 s 1, Sch 1 paras 1, 21 with effect for the tax year 2010–11 and subsequent tax years, subject to transitional provisions in F(No 3)A 2010 Sch 1 paras 36(2)–(5), 37.

[2]   Sub-s (1) numbered as such, and sub-s (2) inserted, by FA 2013 s 17, Sch 4 paras 41, 43 with effect for the tax year 2013–14 and subsequent tax years, subject to the provisions of FA 2013 Sch 4 para 57 in relation to barristers and advocates.

821 Meaning of "relevant limit"

(1) For the purposes of sections 822 and 823 the "relevant limit" for a period of account in which the individual's [qualifying care][1] receipts accrue is found by adding—

    (*a*) the fixed amount for the tax year in which that period ends or (as the case may be) the individual's share of the fixed amount for that year (found in accordance with sections 808 to 810), and

    (*b*) for each of the tax years in which the period of account falls, each amount per [adult or][1] child for the individual for each part of the period of account falling in that tax year.

(2) For this purpose an individual's amount per [adult or][1] child for a part of the period of account is each amount that would be the individual's amount per [adult or][1] child under section 811 for the tax year in which the part falls if that part were the income period for that year.

Commentary—*Simon's Taxes* E1.706.

HMRC Manuals—Business Income Manual BIM52765 (relevant limit: meaning).

Amendments—[1]   In sub-s (1) words substituted, and in sub-ss (1)(*b*), (2) words inserted, by F(No 3)A 2010 s 1, Sch 1 paras 1, 22 with effect for the tax year 2010–11 and subsequent tax years, subject to transitional provisions in F(No 3)A 2010 Sch 1 paras 36(2)–(5), 37.

822 Full relief

(1) This section applies if the individual's total [qualifying care][1] receipts for the period of account do not exceed the individual's relevant limit for the period.

(2) The profits or losses of the trade for the tax year are treated as nil.

Commentary—*Simon's Taxes* E1.706.

HMRC Manuals—Business Income Manual BIM52760 (when does full qualifying relief apply).

Amendments—[1]   In sub-s (1) words substituted by F(No 3)A 2010 s 1, Sch 1 paras 1, 23 with effect for the tax year 2010–11 and subsequent tax years, subject to transitional provisions in F(No 3)A 2010 Sch 1 paras 36(2)–(5), 37.

823 Alternative method of calculating profits

(1) This section applies if—

    (a) the individual's total [qualifying care][1] receipts for the period of account exceed the individual's relevant limit for the period, and

    (b) the individual makes an election under this section.

(2) The profits of the trade for the tax year are—

    (a) the individual's total [qualifying care][1] receipts for the period of account, less

    (b) the individual's relevant limit for the period.

(3) Sections 818(2) and (3) and 819 (adjustment of assessment) apply for the purposes of an election under this section as they apply for the purposes of an election under those sections.

Commentary—*Simon's Taxes* **E1.706.**

HMRC Manuals—Business Income Manual BIM52760 (alternative method of calculating profits).

Amendments—[1] In sub-ss (1)(a), (2)(a) words substituted by F(No 3)A 2010 s 1, Sch 1 paras 1, 24 with effect for the tax year 2010–11 and subsequent tax years, subject to transitional provisions in F(No 3)A 2010 Sch 1 paras 36(2)–(5), 37.

Capital allowances for foster carers carrying on trade

824 Capital allowances: introduction

(1) In this group of sections (that is, this section and sections 825 to 827) an individual is a "relevant individual" if in a tax year—

    (a) the full [qualifying care][1] relief in section 813 or 822 (trading income), or

    (b) the alternative method of calculating profits under section 816 or 823 (trading income),

applies to the individual for the tax year.

(2) In this group of sections a period is a "relevant chargeable period" of a relevant individual if—

    (a) it is a chargeable period of the individual, and

    (b) it corresponds to the income period for the individual's [qualifying care][1] receipts in the tax year for which the individual is a relevant individual.

[(2A) In this group of sections, in relation to a relevant individual—

    (a) "the care business" means the provision of qualifying care by the individual,

    (b) "care business expenditure" means qualifying expenditure incurred on the provision of plant or machinery wholly or partly for the care business,

    (c) "care business pool" means a pool of care business expenditure (even if the balance for the time being is nil), and

    (d) a reference to "another activity" is to a qualifying activity carried on by the individual other than the care business.

(2B) In this group of sections, plant or machinery is referred to as being "in" a pool if qualifying expenditure incurred on its provision has been allocated at any time to that pool.][2]

(3) Expressions—

    (a) which are used in CAA 2001 and in this group of sections, but

    (b) which are not otherwise defined in this Chapter,

have the same meaning in this group of sections as in CAA 2001.

Commentary—*Simon's Taxes* **E1.707.**

HMRC Manuals—Business Income Manual BIM52775 (capital allowances).

Amendments—[1] In sub-ss (1)(a), (2)(b) words substituted by F(No 3)A 2010 s 1, Sch 1 paras 1, 25 with effect for the tax year 2010–11 and subsequent tax years, subject to transitional provisions in F(No 3)A 2010 Sch 1 paras 36(2)–(5), 37.

[2] Sub-ss (2A), (2B) inserted by F(No 3)A 2010 s 3(1), (2) with effect in relation to chargeable periods ending on or after 16 December 2010.

[825 Unallocated capital expenditure

(1) This section applies if—

    (a) at the beginning of a relevant chargeable period of a relevant individual, there is care business expenditure which has not been allocated to a care business pool,

    (b) the individual is entitled under CAA 2001 to allocate the expenditure, or a part of it, to a care business pool for that period, and

    (c) the previous chargeable period was not a relevant chargeable period.

(2) So much of the expenditure as the individual is entitled to allocate to a care business pool for that period is to be treated for the purposes of CAA 2001 as allocated to the appropriate kind of care business pool for that period (whether or not any of it is actually so allocated).

(3) For the different kinds of pool, see section 54 of CAA 2001.][1]

Commentary—*Simon's Taxes* **E1.707.**

HMRC Manuals—Business Income Manual BIM52775 (capital expenditure which are unallocated).

Amendments—[1] Sections 825–825D substituted for former s 825 by F(No 3)A 2010 s 3(1), (3) with effect in relation to chargeable periods ending on or after 16 December 2010. Note that for anyone who was a relevant individual for the most recent chargeable period ending before that date, ss 825B, 825C have effect (on and after that date) as if references in those sections to s 825A were references to s 825 as it was in force immediately before that date (F(No 3)A 2010 s 3(5)).

[825A Deemed disposal event

(1) Subsection (2) applies to a care business pool for a relevant chargeable period of a relevant individual if the previous chargeable period was not a relevant chargeable period.

(2) CAA 2001 is to apply as if—

   (*a*) a disposal event occurs immediately after the beginning of the relevant chargeable period in respect of plant or machinery in the pool,

   (*b*) disposal receipts fall to be brought into account in the pool for the period because of that event, and

   (*c*) the total of the receipts equals the sum of amount A and amount B (or nil if there are no such amounts).

(3) Amount A is the amount of any expenditure treated as allocated to the pool for the period by virtue of section 825 (whether or not any of it is actually so allocated).

(4) Amount B is the amount of any unrelieved qualifying expenditure carried forward in the pool from the previous chargeable period.]¹

Commentary—*Simon's Taxes* E1.707.

HMRC Manuals—Business Income Manual BIM52775 (deemed disposal: change from profit method to exempt or simplified method).

Amendments—¹ Sections 825–825D substituted for former s 825 by F(No 3)A 2010 s 3(1), (3) with effect in relation to chargeable periods ending on or after 16 December 2010. Note that for anyone who was a relevant individual for the most recent chargeable period ending before that date, ss 825B, 825C have effect (on and after that date) as if references in those sections to s 825A were references to s 825 as it was in force immediately before that date (F(No 3)A 2010 s 3(5)).

[825B Plant or machinery used for care business

(1) This section applies if—

   (*a*) disposal receipts fall to be brought into account in a pool for a relevant chargeable period by virtue of section 825A, and

   (*b*) on the re-start date, the relevant individual still owns any of the plant or machinery which was in that pool and is still using any of it for the purposes of the care business.

(2) The re-start date is the first day of the first subsequent chargeable period which is not a relevant chargeable period.

(3) A reference in this section to the retained plant or machinery is to so much of the plant or machinery in the pool as the relevant individual—

   (*a*) still owns on the re-start date, and

   (*b*) is still using on that date for the purposes of the care business.

(4) The individual is to be treated under CAA 2001—

   (*a*) as having brought the retained plant or machinery into use on the re-start date for the purposes of the care business,

   (*b*) as having incurred capital expenditure on the provision of that plant or machinery for those purposes on that date, and

   (*c*) as owning that plant and machinery as a result of having incurred that expenditure.

(5) The total amount of expenditure which the individual is to be treated as having incurred (for all of the retained plant or machinery) is the smaller of—

   (*a*) the total market value of the retained plant or machinery on the re-start date, and

   (*b*) an amount equal to the disposal receipts brought into account in the pool as described in subsection (1)(*a*).

(6) If the individual is treated under section 13 of CAA 2001 as having incurred notional expenditure before the re-start date as a result of bringing plant or machinery in the pool into use for the purposes of another activity, the amount mentioned in subsection (5)(*b*) must be reduced by the total amount of that expenditure, as determined in accordance with section 825C(2).

(7) But subsection (6) does not apply if the plant or machinery which was brought into use for the purposes of another activity is the retained plant or machinery (for example, where it was brought into use only partly for the purposes of that other activity).

(8) The question whether the provision of the retained plant or machinery is to be treated as wholly or only partly for the purposes of the care business is to be determined according to whether the use referred to in subsection (3)(*b*) is wholly or only partly for those purposes.]¹

Commentary—*Simon's Taxes* E1.707.

Amendments—¹ Sections 825–825D substituted for former s 825 by F(No 3)A 2010 s 3(1), (3) with effect in relation to chargeable periods ending on or after 16 December 2010. Note that for anyone who was a relevant individual for the most recent chargeable period ending before that date, ss 825B, 825C have effect (on and after that date) as if references in those sections to s 825A were references to s 825 as it was in force immediately before that date (F(No 3)A 2010 s 3(5)).

[825C Plant or machinery used for other qualifying activities

(1) This section applies if—

   (*a*) disposal receipts fall to be brought into account in a pool by virtue of section 825A because of a disposal event, and

   (*b*) after that disposal event, the relevant individual brings any of the plant or machinery in that pool into use for the purposes of another activity.

(2) Section 13 of CAA 2001 has effect as if the total amount of the notional expenditure which the individual is treated under that section as having incurred, for all of the plant or machinery in that pool which is brought into use for the purposes of the other activity, were the smaller of—

   (*a*) the total market value of that plant or machinery on the day on which it is brought into use for the purposes of that other activity, and (*b*) an amount equal to the disposal receipts brought into account in the pool as mentioned in subsection (1)(*a*).

(3) Subsection (2) does not apply to plant or machinery brought into use for the purposes of another activity if—

(*a*) the individual is treated by virtue of section 825B as having already brought that plant or machinery into use for the purposes of the care business, or

(*b*) this section has already applied to that plant or machinery since the disposal event.

(4) The amount mentioned in subsection (2)(*b*) must be reduced by the appropriate sum if some plant or machinery in the pool is brought into use for the purposes of another activity after—

(*a*) the individual is treated by virtue of section 825B as having brought other plant or machinery in that pool into use for the purposes of the care business, or

(*b*) this section has applied to other plant or machinery in that pool since the disposal event.

(5) The appropriate sum is—

(*a*) in a case within paragraph (*a*) of subsection (4), the total amount of expenditure which the individual is treated by virtue of section 825B as having incurred on the provision of that other plant or machinery, and

(*b*) in a case within paragraph (*b*) of that subsection, the total amount of the notional expenditure (as determined in accordance with subsection (2)) which the individual is treated under section 13 of CAA 2001 as having incurred on the provision of that other plant or machinery since the disposal event.][1]

Commentary—*Simon's Taxes* E1.707.
Amendments—[1] Sections 825–825D substituted for former s 825 by F(No 3)A 2010 s 3(1), (3) with effect in relation to chargeable periods ending on or after 16 December 2010. Note that for anyone who was a relevant individual for the most recent chargeable period ending before that date, ss 825B, 825C have effect (on and after that date) as if references in those sections to s 825A were references to s 825 as it was in force immediately before that date (F(No 3)A 2010 s 3(5)).

[825D Subsequent disposal events

(1) This section applies to an item of plant or machinery which a relevant individual—

(*a*) is treated by virtue of section 825B as bringing into use, or

(*b*) brings into use in circumstances where section 825C(2) applies.

(2) The date (in either case) on which the item is brought or treated as brought into such use is referred to in this section as the applicable date.

(3) The first disposal event to occur in respect of the item on or after the applicable date is to be regarded for the purposes of section 60(3) of CAA 2001 as the first such event.

(4) That event requires a disposal value to be brought into account regardless of anything to the contrary in section 64(1) of that Act.

(5) But a reference in section 62 of that Act to the amount of qualifying expenditure incurred by the individual on the provision of that item is a reference to the amount of qualifying expenditure originally incurred by the individual on its provision (and not to any proportion of the total amount treated by virtue of section 825B or 825C as having been incurred).][1]

Commentary—*Simon's Taxes* E1.707.
Amendments—[1] Sections 825–825D substituted for former s 825 by F(No 3)A 2010 s 3(1), (3) with effect in relation to chargeable periods ending on or after 16 December 2010.

826 Excluded capital expenditure

Capital expenditure ("excluded capital expenditure") does not constitute qualifying expenditure for the purposes of CAA 2001 if it is—

(*a*) incurred by a relevant individual in a relevant chargeable period, and

(*b*) incurred on the provision of plant or machinery wholly or partly for the provision of [qualifying care][1] by the individual.

Commentary—*Simon's Taxes* E1.707.
HMRC Manuals—Business Income Manual BIM52775 (foster carers: excluded capital expenditure).
Amendments—[1] In para (*b*) words substituted by F(No 3)A 2010 s 1, Sch 1 paras 1, 27 with effect for the tax year 2010–11 and subsequent tax years, subject to transitional provisions in F(No 3)A 2010 Sch 1 paras 36(2)–(5), 37.

827 Excluded capital expenditure: subsequent treatment of asset

If a relevant individual incurs excluded capital expenditure in a relevant chargeable period, section 13 of CAA 2001 applies as if, on the first day of the first subsequent chargeable period which is not a relevant chargeable period—

(*a*) the individual brings into use for the provision of [qualifying care][1] such of the plant or machinery on which the expenditure was incurred as the individual still owns on that day, and

(*b*) the individual owns the plant or machinery as a result of incurring capital expenditure on its provision for other purposes.

Commentary—*Simon's Taxes* E1.707.
Amendments—[1] In para (*a*) words substituted by F(No 3)A 2010 s 1, Sch 1 paras 1, 28 with effect for the tax year 2010–11 and subsequent tax years, subject to transitional provisions in F(No 3)A 2010 Sch 1 paras 36(2)–(5), 37.

Overlap profit

828 Overlap profit

(1) This section applies if the profits or losses of a trade for a tax year are calculated in accordance with section 813, 816, 822 or 823.

(2) Nothing in this Chapter is to be read—

    (*a*) as preventing a deduction for overlap profit under section 205 or 220 in calculating the profits or losses of the trade for the tax year, or

    (*b*) as preventing overlap profit from arising by reference to profits of the trade calculated for the tax year in accordance with section 816 or 823 (alternative calculation of profits).

(3) "Overlap profit" has the same meaning in this section as it has in Chapter 15 of Part 2 (see [sections 204 and 204A][1]).

Commentary—*Simon's Taxes* **E1.708**.

HMRC Manuals—Business Income Manual BIM52760 (overlap relief).

Amendments—[1]   In sub-s (3), words substituted by F(No 2)A 2017 s 17, Sch 3 paras 2, 10 with effect for the tax year 2017–18 and subsequent tax years.

PART 8

FOREIGN INCOME: SPECIAL RULES

CHAPTER 1

INTRODUCTION

829 Overview of Part 8

This Part provides for—

    [(*a*) the charging of relevant foreign income of a person to whom section 809B, 809D or 809E of ITA 2007 applies (remittance basis),][1]

    (*b*) certain deductions in calculating relevant foreign income where that basis does not apply (see Chapter 3), and

    (*c*) relief where a person is prevented from transferring income to the United Kingdom (see Chapter 4).

Amendments—[1]   Para (*a*) substituted by FA 2008 s 25, Sch 7 paras 46, 50 with effect for the tax year 2008–09 and subsequent tax years.

830 Meaning of "relevant foreign income"

(1) In this Act "relevant foreign income" means income [which—

    (*a*) arises from a source outside the United Kingdom, and

    (*b*) is chargeable under any of the provisions specified in subsection (2) (or would be so chargeable if section 832 did not apply to it).]

(2) The provisions are—

    (*a*) Chapter 2 of Part 2 (trade profits),

    (*b*) Chapter 17 of Part 2 (adjustment income),

    (*c*) Chapter 3 of Part 3 (profits of property business),

    (*d*) . . . [1]

    (*e*) Chapter 2 of Part 4 (interest),

    (*f*) Chapter 4 of Part 4 (dividends from non-UK resident companies),

    (*g*) Chapter 7 of Part 4 (purchased life annuity payments),

    (*h*) Chapter 8 of Part 4 (profits from deeply discounted securities),

    (*i*) Chapter 13 of Part 4 (sales of foreign dividend coupons),

    (*j*) section 579 (royalties and other income from intellectual property),

    (*k*) Chapter 3 of Part 5 (films and sound recordings: non-trading businesses),

    (*l*) Chapter 4 of Part 5 (certain telecommunication rights: non-trading income),

    (*m*) section 649 (estate income),

    (*n*) Chapter 7 of Part 5 (annual payments not otherwise charged), and

    (*o*) Chapter 8 of Part 5 (income not otherwise charged).

(3) But "relevant foreign income" does not include income chargeable as a result [of—

    (*a*) section 844 (unremittable income: income charged on withdrawal of relief after source ceases), or

    (*b*) section 517C or 517E of ITA 2007 (profits on certain disposals concerned with land in the United Kingdom treated as trading profits).][4]

(4) For the treatment of other income as relevant foreign income, see—

    (*a*) section 857(3) (a partner's share of a firm's trading income),

    [(*aa*) regulation 19 of the Offshore Funds (Tax) Regulations 2009 (SI 2009/3001),][3]

    (*b*) paragraph 6(3) of Schedule 3 to the Commonwealth Development Corporation Act 1999 (c. 20) (distributions by the Commonwealth Development Corporation),

    (*c*) section 575(3) of ITEPA 2003 (taxable pension income: foreign pensions),

    (*d*) section 613(4) of that Act (taxable pension income: foreign annuities),

ITTOIA 2005

(e) section 631(3) of that Act (pre–1973 pensions paid under the Overseas Pensions Act 1973 (c. 21)),

(f) section 635(4) of that Act (taxable pension income: foreign voluntary annual payments), . . .²

(g) section 679(2) of that Act (taxable social security income: foreign benefits),

[(h) section 670A of ITA 2007 (accrued income profits),]² [and

(i) sections 726, 730 and 735 of that Act (transfer of assets abroad: foreign deemed income).]²

Commentary—*Simon's Taxes* **E1.602.**

HMRC Manuals—Residence, Domicile and Remittance Basis RDRM31140 (Relevant foreign income: meaning).

Amendments—¹   Words in sub-s (1) substituted, and sub-s (2)(d) repealed, by FA 2008, s 25 Sch 7 paras 46, 51 with effect for the tax year 2008–09 and subsequent tax years.

²   Word at end of sub-s (4)(f) repealed, and sub-s (4)(h) inserted, by FA 2008 s 25, Sch 7 para 156 with effect in relation to transfers of securities where the settlement day is on or after 6 April 2008. Sub-s (4)(i) and preceding word inserted by FA 2008 s 25, Sch 7 para 162 with effect for the tax year 2008–09 and subsequent tax years.

³   Sub-s (4)(aa) substituted by the Offshore Funds (Tax) Regulations, SI 2009/3001 reg 128(1), (4) with effect for the purposes of income tax for the tax year 2009–10 and subsequent tax years and for distributions made on or after 1 December 2009; for the purposes of corporation tax, on income, for accounting periods ending on or after 1 December 2009 and for distributions made on or after that date and, on chargeable gains, in relation to disposals made on or after 1 December 2009; and for the purposes of capital gains tax, in relation to disposals made on or after 1 December 2009.

⁴   In sub-s (3), words substituted for words "of section 844 (unremittable income: income charged on withdrawal of relief after source ceases)." by FA 2016 s 79(11) with effect in relation to disposals on or after 5 July 2016 (FA 2016 s 82(1)), subject to transitional provisions relating to disposals to associated persons on or after 16 March 2016 and before 5 July 2016 (FA 2016 s 82(4)–(15)).

F(No 2)A 2017 s 39 provides that this amendment has effect (so far as it would not otherwise have effect) in relation to amounts that are recognised in GAAP accounts drawn up for any period of account beginning on or after 8 March 2017 or, in the case of a straddling period, amounts that would be recognised in GAAP accounts drawn up for a period of account beginning on 8 March 2017 and ending when the straddling period ends. "Straddling period" means a period of account beginning before 8 March 2017 and ending on or after that date.

CHAPTER 2

RELEVANT FOREIGN INCOME CHARGED ON REMITTANCE BASIS

Remittance basis

[832 Relevant foreign income charged on remittance basis

(1) This section applies to an individual's relevant foreign income for a tax year ("the relevant foreign income") if section 809B, 809D or 809E of ITA 2007 (remittance basis) applies to the individual for that year.

[(2) For any tax year for which the individual is UK resident, income tax is charged on the full amount of so much (if any) of the relevant foreign income as is remitted to the United Kingdom—

(a) in that year, or

(b) in the UK part of that year, if that year is a split year as respects the individual.]²

(3) Subsection (2) applies whether or not the source of the income exists when the income is remitted.

(4) See Chapter A1 of Part 14 of ITA 2007 for the meaning of "remitted to the United Kingdom" etc.]¹

Commentary—*Simon's Taxes* **E1.603, C4.436, D9.439, E1.602, E1.1127, E6.324.**

Amendments—¹   Sections 832–832B substituted for s 832 by FA 2008 s 25, Sch 7 paras 46, 53 with effect for the tax year 2008–09 and subsequent tax years.

This section applies in relation to an individual's relevant foreign income for the tax year 2007–08 or any earlier tax year, if the individual made a claim under s 831 or TA 1988 s 65(5) applied to the individual for the relevant tax year, as if ITA 2007 s 809B applied to the individual for that tax year. This section does not apply in relation to any of the relevant foreign income that arose in the Republic of Ireland, and nothing in s 832A applies in relation to anything remitted to the UK in the tax year 2007–08 or any earlier tax year (FA 2008 Sch 7 para 83).

²   Sub-s (2) substituted by FA 2013 s 218, Sch 45 para 90 with effect in calculating an individual's liability to income tax or capital gains tax for the tax year 2013–14 or any subsequent tax year, subject to transitional provisions and savings in FA 2013 Sch 45 paras 154–158.

[832A Section 832: temporary non-residents

(1) This section applies if an individual is temporarily non-resident.

(2) Treat any of the individual's relevant foreign income within subsection (3) that is remitted to the United Kingdom in the temporary period of non-residence as remitted to the United Kingdom in the period of return.

(3) Relevant foreign income is within this subsection if—

(a) it is relevant foreign income for the UK part of the year of departure or an earlier tax year, and

(b) section 832 applies to it.

(4) Any apportionment required for the purposes of subsection (3)(a) is to be done on a just and reasonable basis.

(5) Nothing in any double taxation relief arrangements is to be read as preventing the individual from being chargeable to income tax in respect of any relevant foreign income treated by virtue of this section as remitted to the United Kingdom in the period of return (or as preventing a charge to that tax from arising as a result).

(6) Part 4 of Schedule 45 to FA 2013 (statutory residence test: anti-avoidance) explains—

    (*a*) when an individual is to be regarded as "temporarily non-resident", and

    (*b*) what "the temporary period of non-residence" and "the period of return" mean.

(7) In this section, "double taxation relief arrangements" means arrangements that have effect under section 2(1) of TIOPA 2010.]¹

Commentary—*Simon's Taxes* **E1.603, E6.137A, E6.137B, E6.106.**

HMRC Manuals—Residence, Domicile and Remittance Basis RDRM31440 (relevant foreign income and the temporary non-residents rule).

Amendments—¹   Section 832A substituted by FA 2013 s 218, Sch 45 para 118 with effect if the year of departure (as defined in FA 2013 Sch 45 Pt 4) is the tax year 2013–14 or any subsequent tax year), subject to transitional provisions and savings in FA 2013 Sch 45 paras 154–158.

[832B Section 832: deductions from remitted income

(1) The only case in which deductions are allowed from the income mentioned in section 832(2) is where the income is from a trade, profession or vocation carried on outside the United Kingdom.

(2) In that case the same deductions are allowed as are allowed under the Income Tax Acts where the trade, profession or vocation is carried on in the United Kingdom.]¹

Commentary—*Simon's Taxes* **E1.603.**

HMRC Manuals—Residence, Domicile and Remittance Basis RDRM31150 (relevant foreign income allowable expenses).

Amendments—¹   Sections 832–832B substituted for s 832 by FA 2008 s 25, Sch 7 paras 46, 53 with effect for the tax year 2008–09 and subsequent tax years.

CHAPTER 3

RELEVANT FOREIGN INCOME CHARGED ON ARISING BASIS: DEDUCTIONS AND RELIEFS

838 Expenses attributable to collection or payment of relevant foreign income

(1) In calculating the amount of relevant foreign income to be charged to income tax for a tax year, a deduction is allowed for expenses incurred outside the United Kingdom that are attributable to the collection or payment of the income.

(2) Subsection (1) does not apply to income charged for the tax year in accordance with section 832 (relevant foreign income charged on the remittance basis).

Commentary—*Simon's Taxes* **E1.606.**

HMRC Manuals—Savings and Investment Manual SAIM1130 (deductions from foreign income).

839 Annual payments payable out of relevant foreign income

(1) In calculating the amount of relevant foreign income to be charged to income tax for a tax year, a deduction is to be allowed for an annual payment other than interest if it meets conditions [A, B1 or B2 and C]².

(2) Condition A is that the payment is payable out of the relevant foreign income.

(3) Condition [B1]² is that, had the payment arisen in the United Kingdom, it would have been chargeable to income tax under one of the following provisions² . . . —

    Chapter 10 of Part 4 (distributions from unauthorised unit trusts),³

    section 579 (charge to tax on royalties and other income from intellectual property),

    Chapter 4 of Part 5 (certain telecommunication rights: non-trading income), . . .³

    Chapter 7 of Part 5 (annual payments not otherwise charged)[, or

    regulation 15 of the Unauthorised Unit Trusts (Tax) Regulations 2013.]³

[(3A) Condition B2 is that, had the payment arisen in the United Kingdom it would have been—

    (*a*) required to be brought into account under Part 5 of CTA 2009 (loan relationships) as a non-trading credit, or

    (*b*) chargeable to corporation tax under [Chapter 7 of Part 10 of that Act (annual payments not otherwise charged) or regulation 15 of the Unauthorised Unit Trusts (Tax) Regulations 2013]³.]²

(4) Condition C is that the payment is made to a non-UK resident.

(5) Subsection (1) does not apply if—

    (*a*) the relevant foreign income is received in the United Kingdom, or

    (*b*) it is charged for the tax year in accordance with section 832 (relevant foreign income charged on remittance basis).

(6) . . .¹

Commentary—*Simon's Taxes* **E1.606, E4.127, E5.108.**

Amendments—¹   Sub-s (6) repealed by FA 2008 s 25, Sch 7 paras 66, 67 with effect for the tax year 2008–09 and subsequent tax years.

ITTOIA 2005

²   In sub-ss (1) words substituted, in sub-s (3) word substituted and words repealed, and sub-s (3A) inserted, by CTA 2009
s 1322, Sch 1 paras 587, 637. CTA 2009 applies for accounting periods ending on or after 1 April 2009 (for corporation tax
purposes) and for tax years 2009–10 onwards (for income and capital gains tax purposes).
³   In sub-s (3), entry relating to ITTOIA 2005 Part 4 Chapter 10 repealed, word "or" repealed and words inserted, and in
sub-s (3A)(*b*), words substituted by the Unauthorised Unit Trusts (Tax) Regulations, SI 2013/2819 reg 36(1), (9) with effect
from 6 April 2014. Note that an unauthorised unit trust is not a non-exempt unauthorised unit trust, and these amendments
do not apply in relation to the trust, if at all times in the period beginning with 24 May 2012 and ending with 5 April 2014
it had at least one unit holder which was, and at least one unit holder which was not, an eligible investor (ie a mixed
unauthorised unit trust); this ceases to apply in relation to the trust if subsequently it no longer has any unit holders which are
eligible investors (SI 2013/2819 reg 32).

840 Relief for backdated pensions charged on the arising basis

(1) This section applies if—

    (*a*) as a result of section 575(3), 613(4) or 635(4) of ITEPA 2003 a pension or annuity or an
increase in a pension or annuity is treated as relevant foreign income,

    (*b*) the pension, annuity or increase is paid in respect of a tax year ("the earlier year") before the
tax year in which the pension, annuity or increase arose, and

    (*c*) the income is not charged in accordance with section 832 (relevant foreign income charged
on the remittance basis).

(2) If the person liable for the income tax makes a claim for relief under this section for the tax year
in which the pension, annuity or increase paid in respect of the earlier year arises, that pension,
annuity or increase is treated as income arising in the earlier year from a source that the person
possessed in the earlier year.

(3) But subsection (2) does not affect the calculation of the full amount of the income so arising
under section 575(2), 613(3) or 635(3) of ITEPA 2003 (under which the full amount of that income
is to be calculated on the basis that the pension or annuity is 90% of its actual amount).

(4) . . . ¹

Commentary—*Simon's Taxes* **E1.606.**
Amendments—¹   Sub-s (4) repealed by FA 2008 s 25, Sch 7 paras 66, 68 with effect for the tax year 2008–09 and subsequent
    tax years.

[840A Claims under section 840

(1) A claim under section 840 must be made [not more than 4 years after the end of]² the tax year
for which the relief is claimed.

(2) All adjustments (by way of repayment of tax, assessment or otherwise) are to be made which are
necessary to give effect to section 840.

(3) Those adjustments may be made at any time, despite anything to the contrary in the Income Tax
Acts.

(4) A person's personal representatives may make any claim under section 840 which the person
might have made.

(5) If a person dies—

    (*a*) any tax paid by the person and repayable because of a claim under section 840 is to be repaid
to the personal representatives, and

    (*b*) the person's personal representatives are liable for any additional tax which arises because of
a claim under that section.

(6) If subsection (5)(*b*) applies, the additional tax—

    (*a*) is to be assessed on the personal representatives, and

    (*b*) is a debt due and payable out of the estate.]¹

Commentary—*Simon's Taxes* **E1.606.**
Amendments—¹   Section 840A inserted by FA 2008 s 25, Sch 7 paras 66, 69 with effect for the tax year 2008–09 and
    subsequent tax years.
²   In sub-s (1), words substituted by FA 2008 s 118, Sch 39 paras 50, 53 with effect from 1 April 2010 (by virtue of SI 2009/403
    art 2(2)), subject to transitional provisions in SI 2009/403 art 10(2) (where art 10 applies the appointed day is 1 April 2012).

CHAPTER 4

UNREMITTABLE INCOME

841 Unremittable income: introduction

(1) This Chapter applies if—

    (*a*) a person is liable for income tax on income arising in a territory outside the United Kingdom,
and

    (*b*) the income is unremittable.

(2) For the purposes of this Chapter, income is unremittable if conditions A and B are met.

(3) Condition A is that the income cannot be transferred to the United Kingdom by the person who
is liable for income tax in respect of the income because of—

    (*a*) the laws of the territory where the income arises,

    (*b*) executive action of its government, or

    (*c*) the impossibility of obtaining there currency that could be transferred to the United Kingdom.

(4) Condition B is that the person who is liable for income tax in respect of the income has not realised it outside that territory for an amount in sterling or in another currency which the person is not prevented from transferring to the United Kingdom.

[(5) This Chapter does not apply to accrued income profits which a person is treated as making under Chapter 2 of Part 12 of ITA 2007, but see sections 668 and 669 of that Act (which make similar provision).][1]

Commentary—*Simon's Taxes* **E1.607, E4.1326, E6.414A.**

HMRC Manuals—Savings and Investment Manual SAIM1150 (foreign income: unremittable income).

Amendments—[1]   Sub-s (5) substituted by ITA 2007 s 1027, Sch 1 paras 492, 578 with effect for income tax purposes from 6 April 2007, and corporation tax purposes for accounting periods ending after 5 April 2007.

842 Claim for relief for unremittable income

(1) If a person liable for income tax on unremittable income makes a claim for relief under this section in respect of that income, it is not taken into account for income tax purposes.

(2) Subsection (1) is subject to section 843.

(3) No claim under this section may be made in respect of any income so far as an ECGD payment has been made in relation to it.

(4) In subsection (3) "ECGD payment" means a payment made by the Export Credit Guarantee Department under an agreement entered into as a result of arrangements made under—

- (*a*)   section 2 of the Export and Investment Guarantees Act 1991 (c. 67) (insurance in connection with overseas investment), or
- (*b*)   section 11 of the Export Guarantees and Overseas Investment Act 1978 (c. 18).

(5) A claim under this section must be made on or before the first anniversary of the normal self-assessment filing date for the tax year for which the income would be charged to tax if no claim were made.

Commentary—*Simon's Taxes* **E1.607, E4.1326, E6.414A.**

HMRC Manuals—Savings and Investment Manual SAIM1160 (unremittable income: claims).

843 Withdrawal of relief

(1) This section applies if—

- (*a*)   a claim under section 842 has been made in relation to any income, and
- (*b*)   either—
    - (i)   the income ceases to be unremittable, or
    - (ii)   an ECGD payment is made in relation to it.

(2) In this section "ECGD payment" has the meaning given by section 842(4).

(3) If income ceases to be unremittable, the income is treated as arising on the date on which it ceases to be unremittable.

(4) If an ECGD payment is made in relation to income, the income is treated, to the extent of the payment, as arising on the date on which the ECGD payment is made.

(5) The income treated as arising under subsection (3) or (4), and any tax payable in respect of it under the law of the territory where it arises, are taken into account for income tax purposes at their value at the date on which the income is treated as arising.

(6) Subsections (3) to (5) do not apply so far as the income has already been treated as arising as a result of this section.

(7) If a person who would have become liable for income tax as a result of this section has died—

- (*a*)   the personal representatives are liable for the tax instead, and
- (*b*)   the tax is a debt due from and payable out of the estate.

Commentary—*Simon's Taxes* **E1.608, E4.1326, E6.414A.**

HMRC Manuals—Savings and Investment Manual SAIM1160 (unremittable income: withdrawal relief).

844 Income charged on withdrawal of relief after source ceases

(1) This section applies if—

- (*a*)   income is treated as arising as a result of section 843, and
- (*b*)   at the time it is so treated the person who would have become liable for income tax as a result of that section—
    - (i)   has permanently ceased to carry on the trade, profession, vocation or property business from which the income arises, or
    - (ii)   in the case of income from another source, has ceased to possess that source.

(2) In the case of income from a trade, profession or vocation—

- (*a*)   the income is treated as a post-cessation receipt for the purposes of Chapter 18 of Part 2 (trading income: post-cessation receipts), but
- (*b*)   in the application of that Chapter to that income, section 243 (extent of charge to tax) is omitted.

(3) In the case of income from a property business—

- (*a*)   the income is treated as a post-cessation receipt from a UK property business for the purposes of Chapter 10 of Part 3 (property income: post-cessation receipts), but (*b*) in the application of that Chapter to that income, section 350 (extent of charge to tax) is omitted.

(4) In the case of income from another source, the income is taxed as if the person continued to possess that source.

Commentary—*Simon's Taxes* **E1.608, E6.414A.**

HMRC Manuals—Savings and Investment Manual SAIM1160 (unremittable income: withdrawal relief after source ceases).

845 Valuing unremittable income

(1) If no claim is made under section 842 in relation to unremittable income arising in a territory outside the United Kingdom, the amount of the income to be taken into account for income tax purposes is determined as follows.

(2) If the currency in which the income is denominated has a generally recognised market value in the United Kingdom, the amount is determined by reference to that value.

(3) In any other case, the amount is determined according to the official rate of exchange of the territory where the income arises.

Commentary—*Simon's Taxes* **E1.609.**

HMRC Manuals—Savings and Investment Manual SAIM1160 (unremittable income: valuing).

PART 9

PARTNERSHIPS

Introduction

846 Overview of Part 9

This Part contains some special rules about partnerships.

847 General provisions

(1) In this Act persons carrying on a trade in partnership are referred to collectively as a "firm".

(2) The provisions of this Part [which are expressed to apply to trades also apply, unless otherwise indicated (whether expressly or by implication)[1]]—

   (*a*) to professions, and

   (*b*) in the case of this section and sections 849, 850, 857 and 858 to businesses that are not trades or professions.

(3) In those sections as applied by subsection (2)(*b*)—

   (*a*) references to a trade are references to a business, and

   (*b*) references to the profits of a trade are references to the income arising from a business.

[(4) For the purposes of this Part, a person is an indirect partner in a partnership ("the underlying partnership") if the person is a partner in—

   (*a*) a partnership which is a partner in the underlying partnership, or

   (*b*) any partnership which is an indirect partner in the underlying partnership by virtue of the preceding application of this subsection.][2]

Commentary—*Simon's Taxes* **B7.101, B7.110.**

HMRC Manuals—Partnership Manual PM40600 (extending the meaning of trade to "business" for the purposes of s857). Business Income Manual BIM82320 (partnership computation and assessment: investment business: partner basis period).

Amendments—[1]   In sub-s (2) words substituted by CTA 2009 s 1322, Sch 1 paras 587, 638. CTA 2009 applies for accounting periods ending on or after 1 April 2009 (for corporation tax purposes) and for tax years 2009–10 onwards (for income and capital gains tax purposes).

[2]   Sub-s (4) inserted by FA 2018 s 18, Sch 6 para 5(1), (2) with effect in relation to the tax year 2018–19 and subsequent tax years.

848 Assessment of partnerships

Unless otherwise indicated (whether expressly or by implication), a firm is not to be regarded for income tax purposes as an entity separate and distinct from the partners.

Commentary—*Simon's Taxes* **B7.101, B7.205, E6.135.**

Simon's Tax Cases—*R&C Comrs v Vaines* [2016] UKUT 2 (TCC), [2016] STC 1201.

[848A Bare trusts

(1) This section applies if—

   (*a*) a partner in a firm is partner as trustee for a beneficiary who is absolutely entitled to the partner's share of the profits of the firm, and

   (*b*) the beneficiary is chargeable to tax on those profits.

(2) References in this Part to a partner or member of the firm include references to the beneficiary.][1]

Amendments—[1]   Section 848A inserted by FA 2018 s 18, Sch 6 para 1 with effect in relation to the tax year 2018–19 and subsequent tax years.

Calculation of partners' shares

849 Calculation of firm's profits or losses

(1) If—

   (*a*) a firm carries on a trade, and

   (*b*) any partner in the firm is chargeable to income tax,

the profits or losses of the trade are calculated on the basis set out in subsection (2) or (3), as the case may require.

(2) For any period of account in which the partner is a UK resident individual, the profits or losses of the trade are calculated as if the firm were a UK resident individual.

(3) For any period of account in which the partner is non-UK resident, the profits or losses of the trade are calculated as if the firm were a non-UK resident individual.

[(3A) For any tax year that is a split year as respects the partner, this section has effect as if the partner were non-UK resident in the overseas part of the year."][2]

[(4) In calculating under subsection (2) or (3) the profits of a trade for any period of account no account is taken of any losses for another period of account.][1]

Commentary—*Simon's Taxes* **E1.1004, B7.110, B7.203.**

HMRC Manuals—Business Income Manual BIM82210 (partnerships computation and assessment: profits and losses computed at partnership level).

BIM82235 (partnerships computation and assessment: individual, company and non-resident members).

BIM82275 (partnerships computation and assessment: other income: computation of income).

Amendments—[1]   Sub-s (4) inserted by CTA 2009 s 1322, Sch 1 paras 587, 639. CTA 2009 applies for accounting periods ending on or after 1 April 2009 (for corporation tax purposes) and for tax years 2009–10 onwards (for income and capital gains tax purposes).

[2]   Sub-s (3A) inserted by FA 2013 s 218, Sch 45 paras 74, 78 with effect in calculating an individual's liability to income tax or capital gains tax for the tax year 2013–14 or any subsequent tax year, subject to transitional provisions and savings in FA 2013 Sch 45 paras 154–158.

[850 Allocation of firm's profits or losses between partners

(1) For any period of account a partner's share of a profit or loss of a trade carried on by a firm is determined for income tax purposes in accordance with the firm's profit-sharing arrangements during that period.

This is subject to sections 850A [to 850D][2] [and section 12ABZB of TMA 1970 (partnership return is conclusive)][3].

(2) In this section and sections 850A and 850B "profit-sharing arrangements" means the rights of the partners to share in the profits of the trade and the liabilities of the partners to share in the losses of the trade.][1]

Commentary—*Simon's Taxes* **B7.120, B7.135, E1.1004, E1.1013, D7.104.**

HMRC Manuals—Business Income Manual BIM82240 (partnerships computation and assessment: allocation of profits and losses).

BIM82280 (partnerships computation and assessment: other income: allocation of income).

BIM82320 (partnerships computation and assessment: investment business: allocation of profit and loss).

Partnership Manual PM31500 (calculating the taxable profits: allocating the taxable profits or allowable losses to partners).

Amendments—[1]   Sections 850–850B substituted for previous s 850 by CTA 2009 s 1322, Sch 1 paras 587, 640. CTA 2009 applies for accounting periods ending on or after 1 April 2009 (for corporation tax purposes) and for tax years 2009–10 onwards (for income and capital gains tax purposes).

[2]   In sub-s (1), words substituted for previous words "and 850B" by FA 2014 s 74, Sch 17 para 7(1), (2). This amendment is treated as having come into force on 5 December 2013.

[3]   Words in sub-s (1) nserted by FA 2018 s 18, Sch 6 para 11 with effect in relation to returns relating to the tax year 2018–19 or any subsequent tax year.

[850A Profit-making period in which some partners have losses

(1) For any period of account, if—

    (*a*) the calculation under section 849 in relation to a partner ("A") produces a profit, and

    (*b*) A's share determined under section 850 is a loss,

A's share of the profit of the trade is neither a profit nor a loss.

(2) For any period of account, if—

    (*a*) the calculation under section 849 in relation to A produces a profit,

    (*b*) A's share determined under section 850 is a profit, and

    (*c*) the comparable amount for at least one other partner is a loss,

    A's share of the profit of the trade is the amount produced by the formula in subsection (3).

(3) The formula is—

$$FP \times \frac{PP}{PP + TCP}$$

where—

    FP is the amount of the firm's profit calculated under section 849 in relation to A,

    PP is the amount determined under section 850 to be A's profit, and

    TCP is the total of the comparable amounts attributed to other partners under step 3 in subsection (4) that are profits.

(4) The comparable amount for each partner other than A is determined as follows.

Step 1

Take the firm's profit calculated under section 849 in relation to A.

Step 2

Determine in accordance with the firm's profit-sharing arrangements during the relevant period of account the shares of that profit that are attributable to each of the other partners.

Step 3

Each such share is the comparable amount for the partner to whom it is attributed.

(5) In subsections (2) to (4) "partner" means any partner in the firm, whether or not chargeable to income tax.][1]

Commentary—*Simon's Taxes* **B7.401, B7.502, B7.503, D7.104.**

HMRC Manuals—Business Income Manual BIM82245 (partnerships computation and assessment: allocation must not create or increase a loss).

BIM2250 (partnerships computation and assessment: examples of allocation of profits and losses).

Partnership Manual PM31500 (calculating the taxable profits: allocating the taxable profits or allowable losses to partners).

Amendments—[1]   Sections 850–850B substituted for previous s 850 by CTA 2009 s 1322, Sch 1 paras 587, 640. CTA 2009 applies for accounting periods ending on or after 1 April 2009 (for corporation tax purposes) and for tax years 2009–10 onwards (for income and capital gains tax purposes).

[850B Loss-making period in which some partners have profits

(1) For any period of account, if—

  (*a*) the calculation under section 849 in relation to a partner ("A") produces a loss, and

  (*b*) A's share determined under section 850 is a profit,

  A's share of the loss of the trade is neither a profit nor a loss.

(2) For any period of account, if—

  (*a*) the calculation under section 849 in relation to A produces a loss,

  (*b*) A's share determined under section 850 is a loss, and

  (*c*) the comparable amount for at least one other partner is a profit,

  A's share of the loss of the trade is the amount produced by the formula in subsection (3).

(3) The formula is—

$$FL \times \frac{PL}{PL + TCL}$$

where—

  FL is the amount of the firm's loss calculated under section 849 in relation to A,

  PL is the amount determined under section 850 to be A's loss, and

  TCL is the total of the comparable amounts attributed to other partners under step 3 in subsection (4) that are losses.

(4) The comparable amount for each partner other than A is determined as follows.

Step 1

Take the firm's loss calculated under section 849 in relation to A.

Step 2

Determine in accordance with the firm's profit-sharing arrangements during the relevant period of account the shares of that loss that are attributable to each of the other partners.

Step 3

Each such share is the comparable amount for the partner to whom it is attributed.

(5) In subsections (2) to (4) "partner" means any partner in the firm, whether or not chargeable to income tax.][1]

Commentary—*Simon's Taxes* **B7.401, B7.502, B7.503, D7.104.**

HMRC Manuals—Business Income Manual BIM82245 (partnerships computation and assessment: allocation must not create or increase a loss).

BIM2250 (partnerships computation and assessment: examples of allocation of profits and losses).

Partnership Manual PM31500 (calculating the taxable profits: allocating the taxable profits or allowable losses to partners).

Amendments—[1]   Sections 850–850B substituted for previous s 850 by CTA 2009 s 1322, Sch 1 paras 587, 640. CTA 2009 applies for accounting periods ending on or after 1 April 2009 (for corporation tax purposes) and for tax years 2009–10 onwards (for income and capital gains tax purposes).

[850C Excess profit allocation to non-individual partners

(1) Subsections (4) and (5) apply if—

  (*a*) for a period of account ("the relevant period of account")—

    (i) the calculation under section 849 in relation to an individual partner ("A") (see subsection (6)) produces a profit for the firm, and

    (ii) A's share of that profit determined under section 850 or 850A ("A's profit share") is a profit or is neither a profit nor a loss,

  (*b*) a non-individual partner ("B") (see subsection (6)) has a share of the profit for the firm mentioned in paragraph (*a*)(i) ("B's profit share") which is a profit (see subsection (7)), and

  (*c*) condition X or Y is met.

(2) Condition X is that it is reasonable to suppose that—

(a) amounts representing A's deferred profit (see subsection (8)) are included in B's profit share, and

(b) in consequence, both A's profit share and the relevant tax amount (see subsection (9)) are lower than they would otherwise have been.

(3) Condition Y is that—

(a) B's profit share exceeds the appropriate notional profit (see subsections (10) to (17)),

(b) A has the power to enjoy B's profit share ("A's power to enjoy") (see subsections (18) to (21)), and

(c) it is reasonable to suppose that—

(i) the whole or any part of B's profit share is attributable to A's power to enjoy, and

(ii) both A's profit share and the relevant tax amount (see subsection (9)) are lower than they would have been in the absence of A's power to enjoy.

(4) A's profit share is increased by so much of the amount of B's profit share as, it is reasonable to suppose, is attributable to—

(a) A's deferred profit, or

(b) A's power to enjoy,

as determined on a just and reasonable basis.

But any increase by virtue of paragraph (b) is not to exceed the amount of the excess mentioned in subsection (3)(a) after deducting from that amount any increase by virtue of paragraph (a).

(5) If B is chargeable to income tax, in applying sections 850 to 850B in relation to B for the relevant period of account, such adjustments are to be made as are just and reasonable to take account of the increase in A's profit share under subsection (4).

(This subsection does not apply for the purposes of subsection (7) or section 850D(7).)

(6) A partner in a firm is an "individual partner" if the partner is an individual and "non-individual partner" does not include the firm itself where ~~~~~~~~~~~~~~~~~ a partner ordinarily but "non-individual partner" does not include the firm itself where ~~~~~~~~~~~~~~~~~~~ ~~~~~~~ to AIFM firm).

(7) B's profit share is to be determined by applying section 850 and, if relevant, section 850A in relation to B for the relevant period of account (whether or not B is chargeable to income tax) on the assumption that the calculation under section 849 in relation to B produces the profit for the firm mentioned in subsection (1)(a)(i).

(8) "A's deferred profit"—

(a) is any remuneration or other benefits or returns the provision of which to A has been deferred (whether pending the meeting of any conditions (including conditions which may never be met) or otherwise), and

(b) includes A's share (as determined on a just and reasonable basis) of any remuneration or other benefits or returns the provision of which to A and one or more other persons, taken together, has been deferred (whether pending the meeting of any conditions (including conditions which may never be met) or otherwise).

(9) "The relevant tax amount" is the total amount of tax which, apart from this section, would be chargeable in respect of A and B's income as partners in the firm.

(10) "The appropriate notional profit" is the sum of the appropriate notional return on capital and the appropriate notional consideration for services.

(11) "The appropriate notional return on capital" is—

(a) the return which B would receive for the relevant period of account in respect of B's contribution to the firm were the return to be calculated on the basis mentioned in subsection (12), less

(b) any return actually received for the relevant period of account in respect of B's contribution to the firm which is not included in B's profit share.

(12) The return mentioned in subsection (11)(a) is to be calculated on the basis that it is a return which is—

(a) by reference to the time value of an amount of money equal to B's contribution to the firm, and

(b) at a rate which (in all the circumstances) is a commercial rate of interest.

(13) For the purposes of subsections (11) and (12) B's contribution to the firm is amount A determined under section 108 of ITA 2007 (meaning of "contribution to the LLP").

(14) That section is to be applied—

(a) reading references to the individual as references to B and references to the LLP as references to the firm, and

(b) with the omission of—

(i) subsections (5)(b) and (9), and

(ii) in subsection (6) the words from "but" to the end.

(15) "The appropriate notional consideration for services" is—

(a) the amount which B would receive in consideration for any services provided to the firm by B during the relevant period of account were the consideration to be calculated on the basis mentioned in subsection (16), less

(b) any amount actually received in consideration for any such services which is not included in B's profit share.

(16) The consideration mentioned in subsection (15)(a) is to be calculated on the basis that B is not a partner in the firm and is acting at arm's length from the firm.

(17) Any services, the provision of which involves any partner in the firm in addition to B, are to be ignored for the purposes of subsection (15).

(18) A has the power to enjoy B's profit share if—

(a) A is connected with B by virtue of a provision of section 993 of ITA 2007 (meaning of "connected" persons) other than subsection (4) of that section,

(b) A is a party to arrangements the main purpose, or one of the main purposes, of which is to secure that an amount included in B's profit share—

(i) is charged to corporation tax rather than income tax, or

(ii) is otherwise subject to the provisions of the Corporation Tax Acts rather than the provisions of the Income Tax Acts, or

(c) any of the enjoyment conditions (see subsection (20)) is met in relation to B's profit share or any part of B's profit share.

(19) In subsection (18)(b) "arrangements" includes any agreement, understanding, scheme, transaction or series of transactions (whether or not legally enforceable).

(20) The enjoyment conditions are—

(a) B's profit share, or the part, is in fact so dealt with by any person as to be calculated at some time to enure for the benefit of A, whether in the form of income or not;

(b) the receipt or accrual of B's profit share, or the part, by or to B operates to increase the value to A of any assets held by, or for the benefit of, A;

(c) A receives or is entitled to receive at any time any benefit provided or to be provided (directly or indirectly) out of B's profit share or the part;

(d) A may become entitled to the benefit exercised or successively exercised by any person;
more powers are exercised or successively exercised by any person;

(e) A is able in any manner to control (directly or indirectly) the application of B's profit share or the part.

(21) In subsection (20) references to A include any person connected with A apart from B.

(22) Subsection (23) applies if—

(a) the increase under subsection (4), or any part of it, is allocated by A to the firm itself under section 863I (allocation of profit to AIFM firm), and

(b) B makes a payment to the firm representing any income tax for which the firm is liable by virtue of section 863I in respect of the amount of the increase allocated to it.

(23) For income tax purposes, the payment—

(a) is not to be income of any partner in the firm, and

(b) is not to be taken into account in calculating any profits or losses of B or otherwise deducted from any income of B.]¹

Commentary—*Simon's Taxes* B7.123, B7.124, D7.104.

Amendments—¹ Sections 850C–850E inserted by FA 2014 s 74, Sch 17 para 7(1), (3). These amendments are treated as having come into force generally on 5 December 2013, although s 850C(8)(b), (18)(b), (19) are treated as having come into force on 6 April 2014. Sections 850C, 850D have effect for periods of account beginning on or after 6 April 2014 subject to transitional provisions in respect of accounting periods straddling that date (FA 2014 Sch 17 paras 12, 13).

[850D Excess profit allocation: cases involving individuals who are not partners

(1) Subsections (4) and (5) apply if—

(a) at a time during a period of account ("the relevant period of account") in respect of a firm, an individual ("A") personally performs services for the firm,

(b) if A had been a partner in the firm throughout the relevant period of account, the calculation under section 849 in relation to A for the relevant period of account would have produced a profit for the firm,

(c) a non-individual partner ("B") in the firm (see subsection (6)) has a share of that profit ("B's profit share") which is a profit (see subsection (7)),

(d) it is reasonable to suppose that A would have been a partner in the firm at a time during the relevant period of account or any earlier period of account but for the provision contained in section 850C (see also subsections (8) to (10)), and

(e) condition X or Y is met.

(2) Condition X is that it is reasonable to suppose that amounts representing A's deferred profit (see subsection (11)) are included in B's profit share.

(3) Condition Y is that—

(a) B's profit share exceeds the appropriate notional profit (see subsection (12)),

(b) A has the power to enjoy B's profit share ("A's power to enjoy") (see subsection (13)), and

(c) it is reasonable to suppose that the whole or any part of B's profit share is attributable to A's power to enjoy.

(4) A is to be treated on the following basis—

This is subject to subsection (5).

(5) If the partner carries on the actual trade (whether alone or in partnership) after the underlying partnership permanently ceases to carry on the underlying trade, the partner permanently ceases to carry on the notional trade when the partner permanently ceases to carry on the actual trade."][1]

Amendments—[1]   Section 852A inserted by FA 2018 s 18, Sch 6 para 5(1), (3) with effect in relation to the tax year 2018–19 and subsequent tax years.

853 Basis periods for partners' notional trades

(1) The basis period of a partner's notional trade is determined by applying the rules in Chapter 15 of Part 2 as if—

    (*a*)   the trade were carried on by an individual, and

    (*b*)   its accounts were drawn up to the same dates as the accounts of the actual trade.

   This is subject to subsection (2).

(2) If, on the assumption that the actual trade is carried on by an individual,—

    (*a*)   section 216 (change of accounting date in later tax year) would apply in relation to the actual trade, but

    (*b*)   the basis period for the actual trade would be given by subsection (4) of that section (ineffective change of accounting date), because the conditions in section 217 (conditions for basis period to end with new accounting date) would not be met in relation to that trade,

the accounts of the actual trade are treated for the purposes of subsection (1) as drawn up to the old accounting date.

(3) For the purposes of determining whether, on the assumption that the actual trade is carried on by an individual, the conditions in section 217 would be met in relation to that trade—

    (*a*)   a notice under section 217(2) must be given by one of the partners in the firm nominated by them for the purposes of this subsection, and

    (*b*)   any appeal under section 218(4) against a notice by [an officer of Revenue and Customs] must be made by a partner so nominated.

(4) Section 207 (treatment of business start-up payments received in overlap period) applies as a result of this section in relation to a partner's notional trade so that—

    (*a*)   the requirement in subsection (1)(*a*) of that section becomes a requirement that the partner's share of the firm's profits so far as attributable to a business start-up payment falls within two basis periods, and

    (*b*)   the reference in subsection (2) of that section to the payment is a reference to any part of the partner's share of the firm's profits which is so attributable.

Commentary—*Simon's Taxes B7.125.*

HMRC Manuals—Business Income Manual BIM82265 (partnerships computation and assessment: partner notional trade: basis period rules).

BIM82270 (partnerships computation and assessment: partner notional trade: change of partnership accounting date).

Partnership Manual PM11040 (trading profits: accounting date changes).

Firms with trading and other source income

854 Carrying on by partner of notional business

(1) For each tax year in which a firm—

    (*a*)   carries on a trade, and

    (*b*)   has untaxed income or relievable losses from other sources,

each partner's share of the firm's untaxed income or relievable losses other than trading profits or losses is treated, for the purposes of Chapter 15 of Part 2, as profits or losses of a trade carried on by the partner alone (the "notional business").

(2) A partner starts to carry on a notional business at the later of—

    (*a*)   when becoming a partner in the firm, and

    (*b*)   when the firm starts to carry on a trade.

(3) A notional business continues even if either or both of the following occur—

    (*a*)   separate sources of income that comprise the business start and cease, and

    (*b*)   no income arises during a particular tax year.

   This is subject to subsections (4) and (5).

(4) A partner permanently ceases to carry on a notional business at the earlier of—

    (*a*)   when the partner ceases to be a partner in the firm, and

    (*b*)   when the firm permanently ceases to carry on a trade.

[(5) If there is a change of residence, the partner is treated as permanently ceasing to carry on one notional business when that change of residence occurs and starting to carry on another immediately afterwards.][1]

[(5A) Subsections (1A) and (1B) of section 17 apply for the purposes of subsection (5).][1]

(6) In this section "untaxed income" means any income that is not—

    (*a*)   income from which income tax has been deducted,

    (*b*)   income from or on which income tax is treated as having been deducted or paid, . . . [2]

    (*c*) dividends or other distributions of a company chargeable under Chapter 3 of Part 4,

    [(*d*) income chargeable under Chapter 5 of Part 4 (stock dividends from UK resident companies), or

    (*e*) income chargeable under Chapter 6 of Part 4 (release of loan to participator in closed company).]²

Commentary—*Simon's Taxes B7.101, B7.113, B7.125, B7.129, E6.135.*

HMRC Manuals—Business Income Manual BIM82230 (partnerships computation and assessment: changes of partners: loss relief).

BIM82285 (partnerships computation and assessment: other income: partner basis periods).

BIM82295 (partnerships computation and assessment: other income: partner basis period: untaxed income).

BIM82300 (partnerships computation and assessment: other income: partner basis period: losses).

Amendments—¹   Sub-s (5) substituted and sub-s (5A) inserted by FA 2013 s 218, Sch 45 paras 74, 80 with effect, in calculating an individual's liability to income tax or capital gains tax, for the tax year 2013–14 or any subsequent tax year, subject to transitional provisions and savings in FA 2013 Sch 45 paras 154–158.

²   In sub-s (6), paras (*d*) and (*e*) inserted, and word "or" at end of para (*b*) repealed, by FA 2016 s 5, Sch 1 paras 2, 26 with effect for the tax year 2016-17 and subsequent tax years.

855 Basis periods for partners' notional businesses

(1) The general rule is that the basis period for a partner's notional business is the same as the basis period for a partner's notional trade, but subject to the exceptions in subsections (2) and (3).

(2) If the partner carries on the actual trade alone before the firm starts to carry it on the partner is treated as starting to carry on the notional business when the partnership is set up.

(3) If the partner carries on the actual trade alone after the firm permanently ceases to carry it on the partner is treated as permanently ceasing to carry on the notional business when the firm permanently ceases to carry on the actual trade.

Commentary—*Simon's Taxes B7.129.*

HMRC Manuals—Business Income Manual BIM82295 (partnerships computation and assessment: other income: partner basis period: untaxed income).

BIM82300 (partnerships computation and assessment: other income: partner basis period: losses).

[855A Notional business: indirect partners

(1) This section applies in relation to the notional business of a partner in a firm if—

    (*a*) the firm consists of a partnership which is a partner or indirect partner in another partnership ("the underlying partnership"),

    (*b*) the members of the underlying partnership carry on a trade ("the underlying trade"),

    (*c*) the firm's untaxed income or relievable losses referred to in section 854(1)(*b*) arise by virtue of untaxed income or relievable losses ("the underlying profits or losses") arising to members of the underlying partnership—

        (i)   from sources other than the carrying on of a trade, and

        (ii) otherwise than by virtue of the underlying partnership's membership of a partnership.

(2) Section 854 (carrying on by partner of notional business) has effect as if—

    (*a*) for subsection (2) there were substituted—

"(2) The partner starts to carry on the notional business at the later of—

    (*a*) when the partner becomes an indirect partner in the underlying partnership, and

    (*b*) when the underlying partnership starts to carry on the underlying trade.";

    (*b*) for subsection (4) there were substituted—

"(4) The partner permanently ceases to carry on the notional business at the earlier of—

    (*a*) when the partner ceases to be an indirect partner in the underlying partnership, and

    (*b*) when the underlying partnership permanently ceases to carry on the underlying trade."

(3) Section 855 has effect as if for subsections (2) and (3) there were substituted—

"(2) If the partner carries on the actual trade (whether alone or in partnership) before the firm starts to carry it on, the partner starts to carry on the notional business when the firm starts to carry on the actual trade.

(3) If the partner carries on the actual trade (whether alone or in partnership) after the firm permanently ceases to carry it on, the partner permanently ceases to carry on the notional business when the firm permanently ceases to carry on the actual trade."

(4) In this section "untaxed income" has the same meaning as in section 854.]¹

Amendments—¹   Section 855A inserted by FA 2018 s 18, Sch 6 para 5(1), (4) with effect in relation to the tax year 2018–19 and subsequent tax years.

856 Overlap profits from partners' notional businesses

(1) This section applies if—

    (*a*) the basis period for a partner's notional business for a tax year is given by—

        (i)   section 215 (change of accounting date in third tax year), or

        (ii) section 216(3) (change of accounting date in later tax year),

    (*b*) a deduction is to be made for overlap profit under section 220 in calculating the profits of the notional business of the tax year, and

(c) the amount to be deducted exceeds the amount which would otherwise be the amount of the profits of the notional business of the tax year.

(2) This section also applies if—

    (a) the basis period for a partner's notional business for a tax year is given by section 202 (final tax year),

    (b) a deduction is to be made for overlap profit under section 205 in calculating the profits of the notional business of the tax year, and

    (c) the amount to be deducted exceeds the amount which would otherwise be the amount of the profits of the notional business of the tax year.

(3) The amount of the excess is to be deducted in calculating the partner's income for the tax year.

Firms with a foreign element

857 Partners to whom the remittance basis [applies][1]

(1) This section applies if—

    (a) a firm carries on a trade wholly or partly outside the United Kingdom,

    (b) the control and management of the trade is outside the United Kingdom, and

    [(c) section 809B, 809D or 809E of ITA 2007 (remittance basis) applies to a partner for a tax year.][1]

(2) The partner's share of the profits of the trade arising in the United Kingdom is determined in accordance with sections 849 to 856.

(3) The partner's share of the profits of the trade arising outside the United Kingdom is treated as relevant foreign income . . . [1].

Commentary—*Simon's Taxes B2.803, B7.203, B7.302, B6.125.*

HMRC Manuals—Partnership Manual PM40600 (mixed member partnerships and international aspects: management and control).

Amendments—[1] Sub-s (1)(c) and heading substituted, and words in sub-s (3) repealed, by FA 2008 s 25, Sch 7 paras 66, 70 with effect for the tax year 2008–09 and subsequent tax years.

858 Resident partners and double taxation agreements

(1) This section applies if—

    (a) a UK resident ("the partner") is a member of a firm which—

        (i) resides outside the United Kingdom, or

        (ii) carries on a trade the control and management of which is outside the United Kingdom, and

    (b) by virtue of any arrangements having effect under [section 2(1) of TIOPA 2010][2] ("the arrangements") any of the income of the firm is relieved from income tax in the United Kingdom.

(2) The partner is liable to income tax on the partner's share of the income of the firm despite the arrangements.

(3) . . . [3]

[(4) For the purposes of this section the members of a firm include any person entitled to a share of income of the firm.][1]

Commentary—*Simon's Taxes B7.302, F1.512.*

HMRC Manuals—Partnership Manual PM41400 (mixed member partnerships and international aspects: double taxation).

Amendments—[1] Sub-s (4) inserted by FA 2008 s 58(3) and deemed always to have had effect.

[2] In sub-s (1)(b) words substituted by TIOPA 2010 s 501, Sch 8 paras 65, 70. TIOPA 2010 has effect for corporation tax purposes for accounting periods ending on or after 1 April 2010, for income and capital gains tax purposes for the tax year 2010–11 and subsequent tax years, and for petroleum revenue tax purposes for chargeable periods beginning on or after 1 July 2010.

[3] Sub-s (3) repealed by FA 2016 s 5, Sch 1 paras 2, 27 with effect in relation to dividends paid or arising (or treated as paid), and other distributions made (or treated as made), in the tax year 2016-17 or at any later time.

Miscellaneous

859 Special provisions about farming and property income

(1) The rule in section 9(2) (farming trades) operates in relation to firms so that—

    (a) all farming in the United Kingdom which a firm carries on, other than farming carried on as part of another trade, is treated as one trade, but

    (b) the farming carried on by a firm which is treated as one trade is not included in any farming trade of any partner in the firm.

(2) Section 264 (UK property business) operates in relation to firms so that—

    (a) every business and transaction mentioned in that section carried on, or entered into, by a firm constitutes the firm's UK property business, but

    (b) each business or transaction included in the firm's UK property business is not included in any UK property business of any partner in the firm.

(3) Section 265 (overseas property business) operates in relation to firms so that—

    (a) every business and transaction mentioned in that section carried on, or entered into, by a firm constitutes the firm's overseas property business, but

(b) each business or transaction included in the firm's overseas property business is not included in any overseas property business of any partner in the firm.

Commentary—*Simon's Taxes B1.502, B7.120, B7.129, B7.301.*

860 Adjustment income

(1) A change in the persons carrying on a trade from one period of account to the next does not prevent Chapter 17 of Part 2 (adjustment income) applying in relation to the trade so long as a person carrying on the trade immediately before the change continues to carry on the trade immediately after the change.

[(1A) A change in the persons carrying on a property business from one period of account to the next does not prevent Chapter 7 of Part 3 (adjustment income) applying in relation to the property business so long as a person carrying on the property business immediately before the change continues to carry on the property business immediately after the change.][1]

(2) A change in the persons carrying on a trade does not constitute the permanent cessation of the trade for the purposes of Chapter 17 of Part 2 so long as a person carrying on the trade immediately before the change continues to carry on the trade immediately after the change.

(3) In the case of a trade [or property business][1] carried on by a firm the amount of any adjustment under Chapter 17 of Part 2[, or Chapter 7 of Part 3,][1] is calculated as if the firm were a UK resident individual.

(4) Each partner's share of any amount of adjustment income is determined according to the firm's profit-sharing arrangements for the 12 months ending immediately before the date on which the new basis was adopted.

(5) Any election under Chapter 17 of Part 2[, or under section 239B as applied to property businesses by section 334A,][2] must be made jointly by all the persons who have been members of the firm in that 12 month period.

(6) For the purposes of this section—

   (a) "adjustment income" and "change of basis" have the same meaning as in Chapter 17 of Part 2 [or Chapter 7 of Part 3 (as the case requires)][1],

   (b) "profit-sharing arrangements" means the rights of the partners to share in the profits of the trade [or property business (as the case requires)][1], and

   (c) references to the date on which a new basis was adopted are to the first day of the first period of account for which the new basis was adopted.

(7) Sections 849 to 856 do not apply so far as this section applies.

Commentary—*Simon's Taxes B7.114.*

Amendments—[1]   Sub-s (1A), and words in sub-ss (3), (6), inserted, by CTA 2009 s 1322, Sch 1 paras 587, 641. CTA 2009 applies for accounting periods ending on or after 1 April 2009 (for corporation tax purposes) and for tax years 2009–10 onwards (for income and capital gains tax purposes).
[2]   In sub-s (5), words inserted by F(No 2)A 2017 s 16, Sch 2 paras 12, 34 with effect for the tax year 2017–18 and subsequent tax years, subject to transitional provisions in F(No 2)A 2017 Sch 2 para 64.

[861 Sale of patent rights: effect of partnership changes

(1) This section applies if each of the following conditions is met—

   (a) a person ("the trader") sells the whole or part of any patent rights in carrying on a trade,

   (b) tax is chargeable under section 587 of this Act or section 912 of CTA 2009 on the proceeds of the sale or on any instalment of those proceeds,

   (c) the tax is chargeable in one or more tax years or accounting periods (referred to in this section as "the tax charge periods"),

   (d) there is a change in the persons carrying on the trade at any time between the beginning of the first of those tax charge periods and the end of the last of them, and

   (e) the partnership condition and the continuity condition are met.

(2) The partnership condition is that—

   (a) the trader is a firm at the time of the sale, or

   (b) the trade is carried on in partnership at any time between the beginning of the first of the tax charge periods and the end of the last of them.

(3) The continuity condition is—

   (a) in the case of an amount chargeable under section 587, that a person who carried on the trade immediately before the change continues to carry it on after the change, or

   (b) in the case of an amount chargeable under section 912 of CTA 2009, that a company which carried on the trade in partnership immediately before the change continues to carry it on in partnership after the change.

(4) Any amounts chargeable in respect of the proceeds or instalment that would (apart from this section) be treated in accordance with Chapter 2 of Part 5 of this Act or Chapter 3 of Part 9 of CTA 2009 as profits of the seller of the patent rights chargeable in tax charge periods falling wholly after the change are treated for income tax purposes—

   (a) as proceeds, arising at a constant daily rate during the remainder of the relevant period, of a sale of patent rights by the person or persons carrying on the trade after the change, and (*b*) if the trade is carried on in partnership after the change, as arising to the partners in shares calculated in accordance with the firm's profit-sharing arrangements.

(5) If the change occurs during the course of a tax charge period—

    (*a*) any person who would, but for this section, have been charged to income tax in that period on a sum ("S") in respect of the proceeds or instalment is so charged on a fraction of S proportionate to the length of the part of the period before the change, and

    (*b*) the balance of S not dealt with under paragraph (*a*) is treated for the purposes of this section and section 1271 of CTA 2009 (sale of patent rights: effect of partnership changes) as if it were an amount such as is described in subsection (4).

(6) In this section "the remainder of the relevant period" means—

    (*a*) if one or more tax charge periods begins after the tax charge period in which the change occurs, the period beginning immediately after the change and ending 6 years after the beginning of the first of the tax charge periods, or

    (*b*) otherwise, the period beginning immediately after the change and ending at the end of the tax charge period in which the change occurs.

(7) In this section "profit-sharing arrangements" means the rights of the partners to share in the profits of the trade.][1]

Commentary—*Simon's Taxes B5.340.*

Amendments—[1]   Section 861 substituted by CTA 2009 s 1322, Sch 1 paras 587, 642. CTA 2009 applies for accounting periods ending on or after 1 April 2009 (for corporation tax purposes) and for tax years 2009–10 onwards (for income and capital gains tax purposes).

862 Sale of patent rights: effect of later cessation of trade

[(1) This section applies if—

    (*a*) a person ("the trader") sells the whole or part of any patent rights in carrying on a trade,

    (*b*) by virtue of section 861 amounts are chargeable to income tax under section 587 as profits of one or more persons for the time being carrying on the trade in partnership,

    (*c*) a partner permanently ceases to carry on the trade after that, and

    (*d*) no person who carried on the trade immediately before the cessation continues to carry on the trade immediately after the cessation.

(2) Any amounts mentioned in subsection (1)(*b*) which would have been chargeable in any tax year later than that in which the cessation occurred are charged in the tax year in which the cessation occurred.][1]

(3) . . . [1]

(4) If an additional amount is chargeable under subsection (2), the person liable may elect that the amount of income tax payable should be reduced to the amount that would have been payable on the assumptions mentioned in subsection (5).

(5) The assumptions are—

    (*a*) that subsection (2) does not apply, and

    (*b*) that the total of the amounts that would have been charged in later tax years is charged in equal instalments in each of the tax years—

        (i) beginning with the year in which the trader received the proceeds of the sale or instalment of those proceeds, and

        (ii) ending with the year in which the cessation occurs.

(6) The election must be made on or before the first anniversary of the normal self-assessment filing date for the tax year in which the cessation occurred.

(7) . . . [1]

Commentary—*Simon's Taxes B5.340.*

Amendments—[1]   Sub-ss (1), (2) substituted, and sub-ss (3), (7) repealed, by CTA 2009 ss 1322, 1326, Sch 1 paras 587, 643, Sch 3 Part 1. CTA 2009 applies for accounting periods ending on or after 1 April 2009 (for corporation tax purposes) and for tax years 2009–10 onwards (for income and capital gains tax purposes).

863 Limited liability partnerships

(1) For income tax purposes, if a limited liability partnership carries on a trade, profession or business with a view to profit—

    (*a*) all the activities of the limited liability partnership are treated as carried on in partnership by its members (and not by the limited liability partnership as such),

    (*b*) anything done by, to or in relation to the limited liability partnership for the purposes of, or in connection with, any of its activities is treated as done by, to or in relation to the members as partners, and

    (*c*) the property of the limited liability partnership is treated as held by the members as partnership property.

References in this subsection to the activities of the limited liability partnership are to anything that it does, whether or not in the course of carrying on a trade, profession or business with a view to profit.

(2) For all purposes, except as otherwise provided, in the Income Tax Acts—

   (*a*) references to a firm [or partnership][1] include a limited liability partnership in relation to which subsection (1) applies,

   (*b*) references to members [or partners][1] of a firm [or partnership][1] include members of such a limited liability partnership,

   (*c*) references to a company do not include such a limited liability partnership, and

   (*d*) references to members of a company do not include members of such a limited liability partnership.

(3) Subsection (1) continues to apply in relation to a limited liability partnership which no longer carries on any trade, profession or business with a view to profit—

   (*a*) if the cessation is only temporary, or

   (*b*) during a period of winding up following a permanent cessation, provided—

      (i) the winding up is not for reasons connected in whole or in part with the avoidance of tax, and

      (ii) the period of winding up is not unreasonably prolonged.

   This is subject to subsection (4).

(4) Subsection (1) ceases to apply in relation to a limited liability partnership—

   (*a*) on the appointment of a liquidator or (if earlier) the making of a winding-up order by the court, or

   (*b*) on the occurrence of any event under the law of a territory outside the United Kingdom corresponding to an event specified in paragraph (*a*).

Commentary—*Simon's Taxes* **B7.310, B7.310A.**

HMRC Manuals—Business Income Manual BIM82115 (partnerships: limited liability partnership (LLP): taxation).

Partnership Manual PM50510 (limited liability partnerships: statutory provisions for tax transparency: tax transparency witched on).

Amendments—[1] Words in sub-s (2) inserted by ITA 2007 s 1027, Sch 1 paras 492, 580 with effect for income tax purposes from 6 April 2007, and corporation tax purposes for accounting periods ending after 5 April 2007.

[863A Limited liability partnerships: salaried members

(1) Subsection (2) applies at any time when conditions A to C in sections 863B to 863D are met in the case of an individual ("M") who is a member of a limited liability partnership in relation to which section 863(1) applies.

(2) For the purposes of the Income Tax Acts—

   (*a*) M is to be treated as being employed by the limited liability partnership under a contract of service instead of being a member of the partnership, and

   (*b*) accordingly, M's rights and duties as a member of the limited liability partnership are to be treated as rights and duties under that contract of service.

(3) This section needs to be read with section 863G (anti-avoidance).][1]

Commentary—*Simon's Taxes* **B7.310A.**

Regulations—Social Security Contributions (Limited Liability Partnership) Regulations, SI 2014/3159.

Amendments—[1] Sections 863A–863G inserted by FA 2014 s 74, Sch 17 para 1. These amendments are treated as having come into force on 6 April 2014, with the exception of s 863G(4A) which comes into force on 18 July 2014 (the day after Royal Assent to FA 2014).

[863B Condition A

(1) The question of whether condition A is met is to be determined at the following times—

   (*a*) if relevant arrangements are in place—

      (i) at the beginning of the tax year 2014–15, or

      (ii) if later, when M becomes a member of the limited liability partnership,

at the time mentioned in sub-paragraph (i) or (ii) (as the case may be);

   (*b*) at any subsequent time when relevant arrangements are put in place or modified;

   (*c*) where—

      (i) the question has previously been determined, and

      (ii) the relevant arrangements which were in place at the time of the previous determination do not end, and are not modified, by the end of the period which was the relevant period for the purposes of the previous determination (see step 1 in subsection (3)),

immediately after the end of that period.

(2) "Relevant arrangements" means arrangements under which amounts are to be, or may be, payable by the limited liability partnership in respect of M's performance of services for the partnership in M's capacity as a member of the partnership.

(3) Take the following steps to determine whether condition A is met at a time ("the relevant time").

Step 1

Identify the relevant period by reference to the relevant arrangements which are in place at the relevant time.

"The relevant period" means the period—

   (*a*) beginning with the relevant time, and

(b) ending at the time when, as at the relevant time, it is reasonable to expect that the relevant arrangements will end or be modified.

Step 2

Condition A is met if, at the relevant time, it is reasonable to expect that at least 80% of the total amount payable by the limited liability partnership in respect of M's performance during the relevant period of services for the partnership in M's capacity as a member of the partnership will be disguised salary.

An amount within the total amount is "disguised salary" if it—

(a) is fixed,

(b) is variable, but is varied without reference to the overall amount of the profits or losses of the limited liability partnership, or

(c) is not, in practice, affected by the overall amount of those profits or losses.

(4) If condition A is determined to be met, or not to be met, at a time, the condition is to be treated as met, or as not met, at all subsequent times until the question is required to be re-determined under subsection (1)(b) or (c).

(5) In this section "arrangements" includes any agreement, understanding, scheme, transaction or series of transactions (whether or not legally enforceable).][1]

Commentary—*Simon's Taxes B7.310A, B8.1137.*

Regulations—Social Security Contributions (Limited Liability Partnership) Regulations, SI 2014/3159.

Amendments—[1] Sections 863A–863G inserted by FA 2014 s 74, Sch 17 para 1. These amendments are treated as having come into force on 6 April 2014, with the exception of s 863G(4A) which comes into force on 18 July 2014 (the day after Royal Assent to FA 2014).

[863C Condition B

Condition B is that the mutual rights and duties of the members of the limited liability partnership, and of the partnership and its members, do not give M significant influence over the affairs of the partnership.][1]

Commentary—*Simon's Taxes B7.310A.*

Regulations—Social Security Contributions (Limited Liability Partnership) Regulations, SI 2014/3159.

Amendments—[1] Sections 863A–863G inserted by FA 2014 s 74, Sch 17 para 1. These amendments are treated as having come into force on 6 April 2014, with the exception of s 863G(4A) which comes into force on 18 July 2014 (the day after Royal Assent to FA 2014).

[863D Condition C

(1) Condition C is that, at the time at which it is being determined whether the condition is met ("the relevant time"), M's contribution to the limited liability partnership (see sections 863E and 863F) is less than 25% of the amount given by subsection (2) (subject to subsection (7)).

(2) That amount is the total amount of the disguised salary which, at the relevant time, it is reasonable to expect will be payable by the limited liability partnership in respect of M's performance during the relevant tax year of services for the partnership in M's capacity as a member of the partnership. In this section "the relevant tax year" means the tax year in which the relevant time falls and an amount is "disguised salary" if it falls within any of paragraphs (a) to (c) at step 2 in section 863B(3).

(3) The question of whether condition C is met is to be determined—

(a) at the beginning of the tax year 2014–15 or, if later, the time at which M becomes a member of the limited liability partnership;

(b) after that, at the beginning of each tax year.

(4) If in a tax year—

(a) there is a change in M's contribution to the limited liability partnership, or

(b) there is otherwise a change of circumstances which might affect the question of whether condition C is met,

the question of whether the condition is met is to be re-determined at the time of the change.

This subsection is subject to section 863F(3).

(5) If condition C is determined to be met (including by virtue of subsection (7)), or not to be met, at the relevant time, the condition is to be treated as met, or as not met, at all subsequent times until the question is required to be re-determined under subsection (3)(b) or (4).

(6) Subsection (7) applies if—

(a) the relevant time coincides with an increase in M's contribution to the limited liability partnership, and

(b) apart from subsection (7), that increase would cause condition C not to be met at the relevant time.

(7) Condition C is to be treated as met at the relevant time unless, at that time, it is reasonable to expect that condition C will not be met for the remainder of the relevant tax year (ignoring this subsection).

(8) If there are any excluded days in the relevant tax year (see subsections (9) to (11)), in subsection (1) the reference to M's contribution to the limited liability partnership is to be read as a reference to that contribution multiplied by the following fraction—

ITTOIA 2005

$(D - E) / D$

where—

D is the number of days in the relevant tax year, and

E is the number of excluded days in the relevant tax year.

(9) Any day in the relevant tax year—

    (*a*) which is before the day on which the relevant time falls, and

    (*b*) on which M is not a member of the limited liability partnership,

is an "excluded" day for the purposes of subsection (8).

(10) If, at the relevant time, it is reasonable to expect that M will not be a member of the limited liability partnership for the remainder of the relevant tax year, any day in the relevant tax year—

    (*a*) which is after the day on which the relevant time falls, and

    (*b*) on which it is reasonable to expect that M will not be a member of the limited liability partnership,

is an "excluded" day for the purposes of subsection (8).

(11) If the relevant time coincides with an increase in M's contribution to the limited liability partnership, any day in the relevant tax year—

    (*a*) which is before the day on which the relevant time falls, and

    (*b*) on which condition C is met,

is an "excluded" day for the purposes of subsection (8).

(12) In subsections (6) and (11) references to an increase in M's contribution to the limited liability partnership include (in particular)—

    (*a*) the making of M's first contribution to the capital of the limited liability partnership, and

    (*b*) M being treated as having made a contribution by section 863F(2).][1]

Commentary—*Simon's Taxes* **B7.310A.**

Regulations—Social Security Contributions (Limited Liability Partnership) Regulations, SI 2014/3159.

Amendments—[1] Sections 863A–863G inserted by FA 2014 s 74, Sch 17 para 1. These amendments are treated as having come into force on 6 April 2014, with the exception of s 863G(4A) which comes into force on 18 July 2014 (the day after Royal Assent to FA 2014).

[863E M's contribution to the limited liability partnership: the basic calculation

(1) For the purposes of condition C in section 863D M's contribution to the limited liability partnership at a time is amount A.

(2) Amount A is the total amount which M has contributed to the limited liability partnership as capital less so much of that amount (if any) as is within subsection (6).

(3) In particular, M's share of any profits of the limited liability partnership is to be included in the amount which M has contributed to the partnership as capital so far as that share has been added to the partnership's capital.

(4) In subsection (3) the reference to profits is to profits calculated in accordance with generally accepted accounting practice (before any adjustment required or authorised by law in calculating profits for income tax purposes).

(5) Subsection (3) applies as well for the purpose of construing references to contributions to the capital of the limited liability partnership in sections 863D(12)(*a*) and 863F.

(6) An amount of capital is within this subsection if it is an amount which—

    (*a*) M has previously drawn out or received back,

    (*b*) M is or may be entitled to draw out or receive back at any time when M is a member of the limited liability partnership, or

    (*c*) M is or may be entitled to require another person to reimburse to M.

(7) In subsection (6) any reference to drawing out or receiving back an amount is to doing so directly or indirectly.][1]

Commentary—*Simon's Taxes B7.310A.*

Regulations—Social Security Contributions (Limited Liability Partnership) Regulations, SI 2014/3159.

Amendments—[1] Sections 863A–863G inserted by FA 2014 s 74, Sch 17 para 1. These amendments are treated as having come into force on 6 April 2014, with the exception of s 863G(4A) which comes into force on 18 July 2014 (the day after Royal Assent to FA 2014).

[863F M's contribution to the limited liability partnership: deemed contributions

(1) This section applies if—

    (*a*) by the time mentioned in section 863D(3)(*a*), M has given an undertaking (whether or not legally enforceable) to make a contribution to the capital of the limited liability partnership but has not made the contribution,

    (*b*) the undertaking requires M to make the contribution by the end of—

        (i) the period of 3 months ending with 5 July 2014, or

        (ii) if it ends after that date, the period of 2 months beginning with the date on which M becomes a member of the limited liability partnership, and

    (*c*) when it is made, the contribution will be included in amount A under section 863E.

In the following subsections "the relevant period" means the period mentioned in paragraph (b)(i) or (ii) (as the case may be).

(2) For the purpose of determining whether condition C in section 863D is met—

   (a) at the time mentioned in section 863D(3)(a), or

   (b) at any subsequent time during the relevant period,

M is to be treated as having made the contribution at the time mentioned in section 863D(3)(a) (so far as M has not (actually) made the contribution at the time at which it is being determined whether condition C is met).

(3) If M (actually) makes the contribution (in whole or in part) during the relevant period, the question of whether condition C is met is not to be re-determined under section 863D(4) just because of the making of the contribution (in whole or in part).

(4) If M does not (actually) make the contribution (in whole or in part) by the end of the relevant period, any determination in relation to which subsection (2) applied is to be made again (as at the time at which it was originally made).

(5) In making a determination again—

   (a) if it is the whole of the contribution which M does not make by the end of the relevant period, subsection (2) is to be ignored;

   (b) if M makes part of the contribution by the end of the relevant period, in subsection (2) references to the contribution are to be read as references to that part of it.][1]

Commentary—*Simon's Taxes B7.310A.*

Regulations—Social Security Contributions (Limited Liability Partnership) Regulations, SI 2014/3159.

Amendments—[1]   Sections 863A–863G inserted by FA 2014 s 74, Sch 17 para 1. These amendments are treated as having come into force on 6 April 2014, with the exception of s 863G(4A) which comes into force on 18 July 2014 (the day after Royal Assent to FA 2014).

[863G Anti-avoidance

(1) In determining whether section 863A(2) applies in the case of an individual who is a member of a limited liability partnership, no regard is to be had to any arrangements the main purpose, or one of the main purposes, of which is to secure that section 863A(2) does not apply in the case of—

   (a) the individual, or

   (b) the individual and one or more other individuals.

(2) Subsection (4) applies if—

   (a) an individual ("X") personally performs services for a limited liability partnership at a time when X is not a member of the partnership,

   (b) X performs the services under arrangements involving a member of the limited liability partnership ("Y") who is not an individual,

   (c) the main purpose, or one of the main purposes, of those arrangements is to secure that section 863A(2) does not apply in the case of X or in the case of X and one or more other individuals, and

   (d) in relation to X's performance of the services, an amount falling within subsection (3) arises to Y in respect of Y's membership of the limited liability partnership.

(3) An amount falls within this subsection if—

   (a) were X performing the services under a contract of service by which X were employed by the limited liability partnership, and

   (b) were the amount to arise to X directly from the limited liability partnership,

the amount would be employment income of X in respect of the employment.

(4) If this subsection applies, in relation to X's performance of the services, X is to be treated on the following basis—

   (a) X is a member of the limited liability partnership in whose case section 863A(2) applies,

   (b) the amount arising to Y arises instead to X directly from the limited liability partnership,

   (c) that amount is employment income of X in respect of the employment under section 863A(2) accordingly, and

   (d) neither that amount, nor any amount representing that amount, is to be income of X for income tax purposes on any other basis.

(4A) Section 863A(2) does not apply in the case of a member of a limited liability partnership if, apart from this subsection, it would apply in consequence of arrangements the main purpose, or one of the main purposes, of which is to secure that section 850C does not apply for one or more periods of account in relation to—

   (a) the member, or

   (b) the member and one or more other members of the limited liability partnership.

(5) In this section "arrangements" includes any agreement, understanding, scheme, transaction or series of transactions (whether or not legally enforceable).][1]

Commentary—*Simon's Taxes B7.310A.*

Regulations—Social Security Contributions (Limited Liability Partnership) Regulations, SI 2014/3159.

Amendments—[1]   Sections 863A–863G inserted by FA 2014 s 74, Sch 17 para 1. These amendments are treated as having come into force on 6 April 2014, with the exception of s 863G(4A) which comes into force on 18 July 2014 (the day after Royal Assent to FA 2014).

[Alternative investment fund managers

863H Election for special provision for alternative investment fund managers to apply

(1) Section 863I applies in relation to an AIFM trade of an AIFM firm if the AIFM firm elects for that section to apply.

(2) An election under this section must be made within 6 months after the end of the first period of account for which the election is to have effect.

(3) An "AIFM firm" is a firm—

    (*a*) the regular business of which is managing one or more AIFs, or

    (*b*) which carries out one or more functions of managing one or more AIFs—

        (i) as the delegate of, or

        (ii) as the sub-delegate of a delegate of,

    a person whose regular business is managing one or more AIFs.

(4) An "AIFM trade" is a trade of an AIFM firm which involves the firm's activities mentioned in subsection (3)(*a*) or (*b*).

(5) Subsection (3)(*a*) and (*b*) is to be construed as if it were contained in regulation 4 of the Alternative Investment Fund Managers Regulations 2013 (SI 2013/1773).]¹

Commentary—*Simon's Taxes* B7.304.

Amendments—[1]   Sections 863H–863L and preceding crosshead inserted by FA 2014 s 74, Sch 17 para 15 with effect for the tax year 2014–15 and subsequent tax years. See also FA 2014 Sch 17 para 20 for HMRC powers to apply equivalent provisions (with modifications if required) to other regulated firms.

[863I Allocation of profit to the AIFM firm

(1) This section applies for a period of account of the AIFM trade if—

    (*a*) the calculation under section 849 in relation to a partner ("P") in the AIFM firm produces a profit, and

    (*b*) P's share of that profit determined under section 850, 850A or 850C would, apart from this section, be a profit consisting (wholly or partly) of relevant restricted profit (see subsections (6) to (9)) chargeable to income tax under Chapter 2 of Part 2.

(2) P may allocate all or a part of the relevant restricted profit ("the allocated profit") to the AIFM firm itself.

(3) If P does so—

    (*a*) the allocated profit is to be excluded from P's share of the AIFM firm's profit mentioned in subsection (1)(*b*),

    (*b*) the AIFM firm is to be treated in accordance with subsection (4) as if it were itself a person who is a partner in the AIFM firm (and for this purpose, in the case of a limited liability partnership, it is the body corporate which is to be treated as that person), and

    (*c*) all enactments applying generally to income tax are to apply accordingly with any necessary modifications (subject to subsection (5)).

(4) The AIFM firm is treated on the following basis—

    (*a*) the calculation under section 849 in relation to the AIFM firm for the period of account produces the profit mentioned in subsection (1)(*a*),

    (*b*) the AIFM firm's share of that profit determined under section 850 is the allocated profit (and sections 850A and 850C are to be ignored),

    (*c*) that share is chargeable to tax under Chapter 2 of Part 2 for the tax year in which the period of account ends (with the person liable for the tax charged being the AIFM firm), and

    (*d*) the tax is charged at the additional rate.

(5) The Commissioners for Her Majesty's Revenue and Customs may make regulations modifying any of the following enactments applying to income tax as they apply by virtue of this section in relation to the AIFM firm—

    (*a*) those relating to returns of information and supply of accounts, statements and reports,

    (*b*) those relating to the assessing, collecting and receiving of income tax,

    (*c*) those conferring or regulating a right of appeal, and

    (*d*) those concerning administration, penalties, interest on unpaid tax and priority of tax in cases of insolvency under the law of any part of the United Kingdom.

(6) P's profit determined under section 850, 850A or 850C is "relevant restricted profit" so far as it represents variable remuneration awarded to P—

    (*a*) as deferred remuneration (including deferred remuneration which, if it vests in P, will vest in the form of instruments), or

    (*b*) as upfront remuneration which vests in P in the form of instruments with a retention period of at least 6 months.

(7) In order for any variable remuneration to count for the purposes of subsection (6) it must be awarded to P in accordance with arrangements which are consistent with the AIFMD remuneration guidelines (see section 863L).

(8) In the case of a firm which is an AIFM firm by virtue of section 863H(3)(*b*) only, this section applies only in relation to partners who fall within a category of staff which is classified as identified staff.

(9) Terms used in subsections (6) to (8) have the same meaning as in the AIFMD remuneration guidelines.][1]

Commentary—*Simon's Taxes* **B7.304, D7.104**.

Amendments—[1]   Sections 863H–863L and preceding crosshead inserted by FA 2014 s 74, Sch 17 para 15 with effect for the tax year 2014–15 and subsequent tax years. See also FA 2014 Sch 17 para 20 for HMRC powers to apply equivalent provisions (with modifications if required) to other regulated firms.

[863J Vesting of remuneration represented by the allocated profit

(1) Subsection (2) applies if all or a part of the variable remuneration represented by the allocated profit vests in P at a time when P is carrying on the AIFM trade (whether as a partner in the AIFM firm or otherwise).

(2) The amount given by subsection (5) is treated as a profit of the relevant tax year (see subsection (7)) made by P in the AIFM trade chargeable to income tax under Chapter 2 of Part 2.

(3) Subsection (4) applies if all or a part of the variable remuneration represented by the allocated profit vests in P at a time when P is no longer carrying on the AIFM trade (whether as a partner in the AIFM firm or otherwise).

(4) If this subsection applies—
    (*a*) P is treated as receiving, in the relevant tax year (see subsection (7)), income of the amount given by subsection (5),
    (*b*) income tax is charged under this subsection on that income, and
    (*c*) P is the person liable for that tax.

(5) The amount to be treated as a profit or as income received by P is—
    (*a*) the amount of the allocated profit, or the part of it representing the part of the variable remuneration, net of the income tax for which the AIFM firm is liable by virtue of section 863I in respect of the allocated profit or the part of it, plus
    (*b*) an amount equal to—
        (i) so much of the income tax mentioned in paragraph (*a*) as is paid by the AIFM firm by the time the vesting occurs, or
        (ii) if the vesting occurs in the tax year for which the allocated profit is chargeable to tax under Chapter 2 of Part 2 by virtue of section 863I, so much of the income tax mentioned in paragraph (a) as is paid by the AIFM firm.

(6) Further—
    (*a*) P is treated as paying, when the vesting occurs, an amount of income tax equal to the amount given by subsection (5)(*b*), and
    (*b*) that amount is accordingly to be taken into account in determining the income tax payable by, or repayable to, P.

(7) "The relevant tax year" is—
    (*a*) if the variable remuneration or the part of it is deferred remuneration, the tax year in which the vesting occurs, or
    (*b*) if the variable remuneration or the part of it is upfront remuneration, the tax year for which the allocated profit would have been chargeable to income tax under Chapter 2 of Part 2 as mentioned in section 863I(1)(*b*).

(8) Terms used in this section have the same meaning as in the AIFMD remuneration guidelines (see section 863L).

(9) Section 850E (payment from B to other persons after application of section 850C(4) or 850D(4)) is to be ignored for the purposes of this section.][1]

Commentary—*Simon's Taxes* **B7.304**.

Amendments—[1]   Sections 863H–863L and preceding crosshead inserted by FA 2014 s 74, Sch 17 para 15 with effect for the tax year 2014–15 and subsequent tax years. See also FA 2014 Sch 17 para 20 for HMRC powers to apply equivalent provisions (with modifications if required) to other regulated firms.

[863K Vesting statements

(1) This section applies if all or a part of the variable remuneration represented by the allocated profit vests in P.

(2) If P requests it in writing, the AIFM firm must provide P with a statement showing—
    (*a*) the amount of the allocated profit, or the part of it representing the part of the variable remuneration, gross of the income tax for which the AIFM firm is liable by virtue of section 863I in respect of the allocated profit or the part of it,
    (*b*) the amount of the income tax for which the AIFM firm is liable, and
    (*c*) so much of that amount of income tax as is paid by the AIFM firm by the time the vesting occurs or, if section 863J(5)(b)(ii) applies, as is paid by the AIFM firm.

(3) The duty to comply with a request under this section is enforceable by P.

(4) In the case of a limited liability partnership, the duty is enforceable against the body corporate.][1]

Commentary—*Simon's Taxes* **B7.304**.

Amendments—[1] Sections 863H–863L and preceding crosshead inserted by FA 2014 s 74, Sch 17 para 15 with effect for the tax year 2014–15 and subsequent tax years. See also FA 2014 Sch 17 para 20 for HMRC powers to apply equivalent provisions (with modifications if required) to other regulated firms.

[863L The AIFMD remuneration guidelines

In sections 863I to 863K "the AIFMD remuneration guidelines" means the "Guidelines on Sound Remuneration Policies under the AIFMD" issued by the European Securities and Markets Authority on 3 July 2013 (ESMA/2013/232).][1]

Amendments—[1] Sections 863H–863L and preceding crosshead inserted by FA 2014 s 74, Sch 17 para 15 with effect for the tax year 2014–15 and subsequent tax years. See also FA 2014 Sch 17 para 20 for HMRC powers to apply equivalent provisions (with modifications if required) to other regulated firms.

PART 10
GENERAL PROVISIONS

CHAPTER 1
INTRODUCTION

864 Overview of Part 10

This Part—

    (a) contains general rules which are of wider application than to a particular Part of this Act including certain calculation rules (see Chapter 2), and

    (b) deals with supplementary matters including general definitions (see Chapter 3).

CHAPTER 2
GENERAL CALCULATION RULES ETC.
Unpaid remuneration

865 Unpaid remuneration: non-trades and non-property businesses

(1) This section applies if, in calculating profits or other income of a period of account for income tax purposes—

    (a) an amount is charged in the accounts for the period in respect of employees' remuneration, and

    (b) a deduction for the remuneration would otherwise be allowable for the period.

(2) For this purpose "profits or other income" does not include the profits of—

    (a) a trade, profession or vocation, or

    (b) a property business,

but see subsection (6).

(3) No deduction is allowed for the remuneration for the period of account unless it is paid before the end of the period of 9 months immediately following the end of the period of account.

(4) If the remuneration is paid after the end of that 9 month period, a deduction for it is allowed for the period of account in which it is paid.

(5) Section 37 (supplementary provision) applies for the purposes of this section as it applies for the purposes of section 36 (unpaid remuneration: trades, professions and vocations).

(6) Provision corresponding to that made by this section is made by—

    (a) sections 36 and 37 (in relation to trades, professions and vocations), and

    (b) section 272 (in relation to property businesses).

Employee benefit contributions

866 Employee benefit contributions: non-trades and non-property businesses

(1) This section applies if, in calculating a person's profits or other income of a period for income tax purposes—

    (a) the profits or other income of the period are required to be calculated for those purposes, and

    (b) a deduction would otherwise be allowable for the period for any employee benefit contributions made or to be made by the person ("the employer") (but see subsection (5)).

(2) For this purpose "profits or other income" does not include the profits of—

    (a) a trade, profession or vocation, or

    (b) a property business,

but see subsection (7).

[(2A) No deduction is allowed under this section in respect of employee benefit contributions for a period of account which starts more than 5 years after the end of the period of account in which the contributions are made.][1]

(3) No deduction is allowed for the contributions for the period except so far as—
- (a) qualifying benefits are provided, or qualifying expenses are paid, out of the contributions during the period or within 9 months from the end of it, or
- (b) if the making of the contributions is itself the provision of qualifying benefits, the contributions are made during the period or within 9 months from the end of it.

[(3A) Subsection (3) is subject to subsections (2A) and (3B).

(3B) Where subsection (4C) applies, no deduction is allowed for an amount in respect of the contributions for the period except so far as the amount is a qualifying amount (see subsection (4D)).]¹

(4) An amount disallowed under subsection (3) is allowed as a deduction for a subsequent period so far as—
- (a) qualifying benefits are provided out of the contributions before the end of the subsequent period, or
- (b) if the making of the contributions is itself the provision of qualifying benefits, the contributions are made before the end of the subsequent period.

[(4A) Subsection (4) is subject to subsections (2A) and (4B).

(4B) Where subsection (4C) applies, an amount disallowed under subsection (3) is allowed as a deduction for a subsequent period only so far as it is a qualifying amount.

(4C) This subsection applies where the provision of qualifying benefits out of, or by way of, the contributions gives rise both to an employment income tax charge and to an NIC charge.

(4D) An amount in respect of employee benefit contributions is a "qualifying amount" if the relevant tax charges are paid before the end of the relevant period (and are not repaid).

(4E) For the purposes of subsection (4D)—
- (a) the "relevant tax charges", in relation to an amount, are the employment income tax charge and the NIC charge arising in respect of benefits which are provided out of, or by way of, that amount, and
- (b) the "relevant period" is the period of 12 months immediately following the end of the period of account for which the deduction for the employee benefit contributions would (apart from this section) be allowable.

(4F) For the purposes of subsections (4C) and (4E), "employment income tax charge" and "NIC charge" have the meaning given by section 40(7).]¹

[(4G) Subsection (4H) applies where—
- (a) a deduction would, apart from this section, be allowable for an amount (the "remuneration amount") in respect of employees' remuneration, and
- (b) in consequence of the payment of the employees' remuneration, employee benefit contributions are made, or are to be made, in respect of the remuneration amount.

(4H) In calculating for income tax purposes a person's profits or other income, the deduction referred to in subsection (4G)(a) is to be treated as a deduction in respect of employee benefit contributions made or to be made (and is to be treated as not being a deduction in respect of employees' remuneration).]²

(5) This section does not apply to any deduction that is allowable for—
- (a) anything given as consideration for goods or services provided in the course of a trade or profession,
- (b) contributions under a registered pension scheme or under a superannuation fund to which section 615(3) of ICTA applies,
- (c) contributions under a qualifying overseas pension scheme in respect of an individual who is a relevant migrant member of the pension scheme in relation to the contributions, or
- (d) contributions under an accident benefit scheme.

For the purposes of paragraph (c) "qualifying overseas pension scheme" and "relevant migrant member" have the same meaning as in Schedule 33 to FA 2004 (see paragraphs 4 to 6 of that Schedule).

(6) Sections 39 to 44 (supplementary provisions) apply for the purposes of this section as they apply for the purposes of section 38 (employee benefit contributions: trades, professions and vocations).

(7) Provision corresponding to that made by this section is made by—
- (a) sections 38 to 44 (in relation to trades, professions and vocations), and
- (b) [sections 272 and 272ZA]³ (in relation to property businesses).

Amendments—¹   Sub-ss (2A), (3A), (3B), (4A)–(4F) inserted by F(No 2)A 2017 s 36(6)–(9) with effect in relation to employee benefit contributions made, or to be made, on or after 6 April 2017.
²   Sub-ss (4G), (4H) inserted by F(No 2)A 2017 s 36(6), (10) with effect in relation to remuneration paid on or after 6 April 2017.
³   In sub-s (7)(b), words substituted for words "section 272" by F(No 2)A 2017 s 16, Sch 2 paras 12, 35 with effect for the tax year 2017–18 and subsequent tax years, subject to transitional provisions in F(No 2)A 2017 Sch 2 para 64.

Business entertainment and gifts

867 Business entertainment and gifts: non-trades and non-property businesses

(1) This section applies for the purpose of calculating profits or other income charged to income tax which arise from the carrying on of a business.

(2) For this purpose "business" does not include—

    (*a*) a trade, profession or vocation, or

    (*b*) a property business,

but see subsection (7).

(3) The general rule is that no deduction is allowed in calculating the profits or other income for expenses incurred in providing entertainment or gifts in connection with the business.

(4) A deduction for expenses which are incurred—

    (*a*) in paying sums to or on behalf of an employee of the person carrying on the business, or

    (*b*) in putting sums at the disposal of an employee of that person,

is prohibited by the general rule if (and only if) the sums are paid, or put at the employee's disposal, exclusively for meeting expenses incurred or to be incurred by the employee in providing the entertainment or gift.

(5) The general rule is subject to—

    section 46 (business entertainment: exceptions), and

    section 47 (business gifts: exceptions),

which apply in relation to a business as they apply in relation to a trade (but as if the reference to a basis period were to a tax year).

(6) For the purposes of this section and those two sections as so applied—

    (*a*) "employee", in relation to a company, includes a director of the company and a person engaged in the management of the company,

    (*b*) "entertainment" includes hospitality of any kind, and

    (*c*) the expenses incurred in providing entertainment or a gift include expenses incurred in providing anything incidental to the provision of entertainment or a gift.

(7) Provision corresponding to that made by this section is made by—

    (*a*) sections 45 to 47 (in relation to trades, professions and vocations), and

    (*b*) [sections 272 and 272ZA][1] (in relation to property businesses).

Amendments—[1]   In sub-s (7)(*b*), words substituted for words "section 272" by F(No 2)A 2017 s 16, Sch 2 paras 12, 36 with effect for the tax year 2017–18 and subsequent tax years, subject to transitional provisions in F(No 2)A 2017 Sch 2 para 64.

Social security contributions

868 Social security contributions: non-trades etc.

(1) This section applies for the purpose of calculating profits or other income charged to income tax.

(2) For this purpose "profits or other income" does not include—

    (*a*) the profits of a trade, profession, or vocation,

    (*b*) the profits of a property business, or

    (*c*) employment income,

but see subsection (6).

(3) No deduction is allowed for any contribution paid by any person under—

    (*a*) Part 1 of the Social Security Contributions and Benefits Act 1992 (c. 4), or

    (*b*) Part 1 of the Social Security Contributions and Benefits (Northern Ireland) Act 1992 (c. 7).

(4) But this prohibition does not apply to an employer's contribution.

(5) For this purpose "an employer's contribution" means—

    (*a*) a secondary Class 1 contribution,

    (*b*) a Class 1A contribution, or

    (*c*) a Class 1B contribution,

within the meaning of Part 1 of the Social Security Contributions and Benefits Act 1992 (c. 4) or of the Social Security Contributions and Benefits (Northern Ireland) Act 1992 (c. 7).

(6) Provision corresponding to that made by this section is made by—

    (*a*) section 53 (in relation to trades, professions and vocations),

    (*b*) [sections 272 and 272ZA][1] (in relation to property businesses), and

    (*c*) section 360A of ITEPA 2003 (in relation to employment income).

Commentary—*Simon's Taxes E8.323.*

Amendments—[1]   In sub-s (6)(*b*), words substituted for words "section 272" by F(No 2)A 2017 s 16, Sch 2 paras 12, 37 with effect for the tax year 2017–18 and subsequent tax years, subject to transitional provisions in F(No 2)A 2017 Sch 2 para 64.

Penalties, interest and VAT surcharges

869 Penalties, interest and VAT surcharges: non-trades etc.

(1) This section applies for the purpose of calculating profits or other income charged to income tax.

(2) For this purpose "profits or other income" does not include the profits of—

    (*a*) a trade, profession, or vocation, or

    (*b*) a property business,

but see subsection (6).

(3) No deduction is allowed for any penalty or interest mentioned in the first column of the following table.

(4) This is the table—

Penalty or interest	Description of tax, levy or duty
Interest under any provision of Part 9 of TMA 1970	Income tax, capital gains tax and corporation tax
Interest required to be paid by regulations made under section 71 of FA 2004 (construction industry)	
Penalty under any of sections 60 to 70 of VATA 1994	Value added tax
Interest under section 74 [or 85A]² of VATA 1994	
Penalty under any of sections 8 to 11 of FA 1994	Excise duties
Penalty under any of paragraphs 12 to 19 of Schedule 7 to FA 1994	Insurance premium tax
[Interest under section 60(8) of FA 1994 or paragraph 21 to Schedule 7 to FA 1994]²	
Penalty under any provision of Part 5 of Schedule 5 to FA 1996	Landfill tax
[Interest under section 56(5) of, or paragraph 26 or 27 of Schedule 5 to, FA 1996]²	
Penalty under any provision of Schedule 6 to FA 2000	Climate change levy
Interest under any of paragraphs 70, 81 to 85[, 109 and 123(6)]² of that Schedule	
Penalty under any provision of Part 2 of FA 2001	Aggregates levy
Interest under [section 42(6) of, or]² any of paragraphs 5 to 9 of Schedule 5 to, paragraph 6 of Schedule 8 to and paragraph 5 of Schedule 10 [to, FA 2001]²	
Penalty under section 25 or 26 of FA 2003	Customs, export and import duties
Penalty under any provision of Part 4 of FA 2003	Stamp duty land tax
Interest under any provision of that Part	
[Penalty under Schedule 24 to FA 2007	Various taxes and excise duties]¹
[Penalty under Schedule 41 to FA 2008	Various taxes and excise duties]³

(5) No deduction is allowed for any surcharge under section 59 of VATA 1994.

(6) Provision corresponding to that made by this section is made by—
   (a) section 54 (in relation to trades, professions and vocations), and
   (b) [sections 272 and 272ZA]⁴ (in relation to property businesses).

Amendments—¹ Table entry inserted by the Finance Act 2008, Schedule 40 (Appointed Day, Transitional Provisions and Consequential Amendments) Order, SI 2009/571 art 8, Sch 1 paras 27, 29 with effect from 1 April 2009.
² Words in table entries inserted, table entries and words in table entry substituted by the Transfer of Tribunal Functions and Revenue and Customs Appeals Order, SI 2009/56 art 3, Sch 1 para 442 with effect from 1 April 2009.
³ Table entry inserted by the Finance Act 2008 (Penalties for Errors and Failure to Notify etc) (Consequential Amendments) Order 2010, SI 2010/509 art 2, Sch paras 7, 9 with effect from 1 April 2010.
⁴ In sub-s (6)(b), words substituted for words "section 272" by F(No 2)A 2017 s 16, Sch 2 paras 12, 38 with effect for the tax year 2017–18 and subsequent tax years, subject to transitional provisions in F(No 2)A 2017 Sch 2 para 64.

Prospective amendments—In sub-s (4), in the entry relating to a penalty under section 25 or 26 of the Finance Act 2003, words "Customs duties" to be substituted for words "Customs, export and import duties" by the Taxation (Cross-border Trade) Act 2018 s 29, Sch 7 para 153, 155 with effect from a date to be appointed.

Crime-related payments

870 Crime-related payments: non-trades and non-property businesses

(1) This section—
   (a) applies for the purpose of calculating profits or other income charged to income tax, but
   (b) does not apply for the purpose of calculating the profits of a trade, profession or vocation or of a property business (but see subsection (4)).

(2) No deduction is allowed for expenses incurred—
   (a) in making a payment if the making of the payment constitutes a criminal offence, or
   (b) in making a payment outside the United Kingdom if the making of a corresponding payment in any part of the United Kingdom would constitute a criminal offence in that part.

(3) No deduction is allowed for expenses incurred in making a payment induced by a demand which constitutes—
   (a) the offence of blackmail under section 21 of the Theft Act 1968 (c. 60) (England and Wales),
   (b) the offence of extortion (Scotland), or
   (c) the offence of blackmail under section 20 of the Theft Act (Northern Ireland) 1969 (c. 16 (NI)) (Northern Ireland).

(4) Provision corresponding to that made by this section is made by—
   (a) section 55 (in relation to trades, professions and vocations), and
   (b) [sections 272 and 272ZA]¹ (in relation to property businesses).

Amendments—¹ In sub-s (4)(b), words substituted for words "section 272" by F(No 2)A 2017 s 16, Sch 2 paras 12, 39 with effect for the tax year 2017–18 and subsequent tax years, subject to transitional provisions in F(No 2)A 2017 Sch 2 para 64.

Apportionment of profits

871 Apportionment etc. of miscellaneous profits to tax year

(1) This section applies if—

    (*a*) income is chargeable to income tax under or by virtue of any provision to which [section 1016 of ITA 2007][1] applies, and

    (*b*) any period for which the accounts are drawn up (a "period of account") does not coincide with a tax year.

(2) For this purpose the reference to any provision to which [section 1016 of ITA 2007][1] applies is to be read as if [subsection (3)(*a*)][1] of that section were omitted (exclusion for relevant foreign income charged under this Act).

(3) Any of the following steps may be taken if they are necessary in order to arrive at the profits or losses of the tax year—

    (*a*) apportioning the profits or losses of a period of account to the parts of that period falling in different tax years, and

    (*b*) adding the profits or losses of a period of account (or part of a period) to profits or losses of other periods of account (or parts).

(4) The steps must be taken by reference to the number of days in the periods concerned.

(5) But the person to whom the profits or losses arise may use a different way of measuring the length of the periods concerned if—

    (*a*) it is reasonable to do so, and

    (*b*) the way of measuring the length of periods is used consistently for the purpose of charging to income tax the income in question.

Amendments—[1] Words in sub-ss (1), (2) substituted by ITA 2007 s 1027, Sch 1 paras 492, 581 with effect for income tax purposes from 6 April 2007, and corporation tax purposes for accounting periods ending after 5 April 2007.

Calculation of losses

872 Losses calculated on same basis as miscellaneous income

(1) The same rules apply for income tax purposes in calculating miscellaneous losses as apply in calculating corresponding miscellaneous income.

(2) This is subject to any express provision to the contrary.

(3) In this section—

    (*a*) "miscellaneous income" means profits or other income charged to income tax under or by virtue of a provision to which [section 1016 of ITA 2007][1] applies, and

    (*b*) "miscellaneous losses" means losses arising from a transaction which is of such a nature that, if profits or other income had arisen from it, the income would have been charged to income tax under or by virtue of such a provision.

(4) Provision corresponding to that made by this section is made by—

    (*a*) section 26 (in relation to trades, professions and vocations), and

    (*b*) [sections 272 and 272ZA][2] (in relation to property businesses).

Amendments—[1] Words in sub-s (3) substituted by ITA 2007 s 1027, Sch 1 paras 492, 582 with effect for income tax purposes from 6 April 2007, and corporation tax purposes for accounting periods ending after 5 April 2007.

[2] In sub-s (4)(*b*), words substituted for words "section 272" by F(No 2)A 2017 s 16, Sch 2 paras 12, 40 with effect for the tax year 2017–18 and subsequent tax years, subject to transitional provisions in F(No 2)A 2017 Sch 2 para 64.

CHAPTER 3

SUPPLEMENTARY AND GENERAL PROVISIONS

Orders and regulations

873 Orders and regulations made by Treasury or [Commissioners][1]

(1) Any power of the Treasury or [the Commissioners for Her Majesty's Revenue and Customs] to make any order or regulations under this Act is exercisable by statutory instrument.

(2) Any statutory instrument containing any order or regulations made by the Treasury or [the Commissioners for Her Majesty's Revenue and Customs] under this Act is subject to annulment in pursuance of a resolution of the House of Commons.

(3) Subsection (2) does not apply in relation to any order or regulations made under—

    (*a*) section 86 (meaning of "urban regeneration company"),

    (*b*) . . .[2]

    [(*ba*) section 608N (offshore receipts in respect of intangible property),][4]

    (*c*) section 774 (income from securities issued by designated international organisations), or

    (*d*) section 883(5) (transitional or saving provision).

[(4) Further, subsection (2) does not apply if any other Parliamentary procedure is expressly provided to apply in relation to the order or regulations.][3]

Amendments—[1] Word in Heading substituted by CRCA 2005 s 50, Sch 4 paras 131, 132(3)(*h*) with effect from 18 April 2005 (by virtue of SI 2005/1126).

[2] Sub-s (3)(*b*) repealed by FA 2007 ss 46(8), 114, Sch 27 Pt 2(13) with effect from 19 July 2007.

³ Sub-s (4) inserted by FA 2009 s 40, Sch 19 paras 1, 8 with effect from 22 April 2009 in accordance with FA 2009 Sch 19
   para 14.
⁴ Sub-s (3)(*ba*) inserted by FA 2019 s 15, Sch 3 paras 1, 5 with effect for the tax year 2019–20 and subsequent tax years.

Interpretation

874 Activities in UK sector of continental shelf

(1) Any profits—
   (*a*) from exploration or exploitation activities carried on in the UK sector of the continental shelf,
         or
   (*b*) from exploration or exploitation rights,
are treated for income tax purposes as profits from activities or property in the United Kingdom.

(2) In this section—
      "exploration or exploitation activities" means activities carried on in connection with the
      exploration or exploitation of so much of the seabed and subsoil and their natural resources as
      is situated in the United Kingdom or the UK sector of the continental shelf,
      "exploration or exploitation rights" means rights to assets to be produced by exploration or
      exploitation activities or interests in or to the benefit of such assets, and
      "the UK sector of the continental shelf" means the areas designated by Order in Council under
      section 1(7) of the Continental Shelf Act 1964 (c. 29).

Commentary—*Simon's Taxes B1.208, D4.1101, F1.503.*

875 Meaning of "caravan"

(1) In this Act "caravan" means—
   (*a*) a structure designed or adapted for human habitation which is capable of being moved by
         being towed or being transported on a motor vehicle or trailer, or
   (*b*) a motor vehicle designed or adapted for human habitation,
but does not include railway rolling stock which is on rails forming part of a railway system or any
tent.

(2) A structure composed of two sections—
   (*a*) separately constructed, and
   (*b*) designed to be assembled on a site by means of bolts, clamps or other devices,
is not prevented from being a caravan just because it cannot, when assembled, be lawfully moved on
a highway (or, in Scotland or Northern Ireland, road) by being towed or being transported on a motor
vehicle or trailer.

878 Other definitions

(1) In this Act, unless otherwise indicated (whether expressly or by implication)—
   . . .¹
   . . .²
      "houseboat" means a boat or similar structure designed or adapted for use as a place of human
      habitation, [and]²
      "income" includes amounts treated as income (whether expressly or by implication),
   . . .¹
   . . .²

(2) . . .³

(3) In this Act any reference to a claim or election is to a claim or election in writing or in any form
authorised (in relation to the case in question) by directions under [section 43E(1) of TMA 1970]⁴.

(4) For further information about claims and elections, see TMA 1970 [more generally (but in]⁴
particular, section 42(2), (10) and (11) and Schedule 1A).

(5) [Section 993 of ITA 2007]² (how to tell whether persons are connected) applies for the purposes
of this Act unless otherwise indicated (whether expressly or by implication).

(6) [Section 995 of ITA 2007 (meaning of "control")]² applies for the purposes of this Act unless
otherwise indicated (whether expressly or by implication).

Commentary—*Simon's Taxes B2.208.*
Amendments—¹ Definitions in sub-s (1) repealed by CRCA 2005 ss 50, 52, Sch 4 paras 131, 134(1), Sch 5 with effect from
   18 April 2005 (by virtue of SI 2005/1126).
² In sub-s (1), definition of "charity" repealed, word inserted, and words repealed; and words in sub-ss (5), (6) substituted; by
   ITA 2007 ss 1027, 1031, Sch 1 paras 492, 585, Sch 3 Pt 1 with effect for income tax purposes from 6 April 2007, and
   corporation tax purposes for accounting periods ending after 5 April 2007.
³ Sub-s (2) repealed by FA 2008 s 25, Sch 7 paras 66, 71 with effect for the tax year 2008–09 and subsequent tax years.
⁴ In sub-s (3), (4) words substituted by TIOPA 2010 s 371, Sch 7 paras 89, 90. TIOPA 2010 has effect for corporation tax
   purposes for accounting periods ending on or after 1 April 2010, for income and capital gains tax purposes for the tax year
   2010–11 and subsequent tax years, and for petroleum revenue tax purposes for chargeable periods beginning on or after 1 July
   2010.

879 Interpretation: Scotland

(1) In the application of this Act to Scotland—
   . . .¹

"mortgage" means—

(a) a standard security, or

(b) a heritable security, as defined in the Conveyancing (Scotland) Act 1924 (c. 27), but including a security constituted by ex facie absolute disposition or assignation, . . . [1]

. . . [1]

(2) . . . [1]

(3) In the application of section 755 (interest on foreign currency securities etc. owned by non-UK residents) to Scotland, "Act" includes an Act of the Scottish Parliament.

(4) In the application of sections 769 (housing grants) and 882 (consequential amendments) and Part 1 of Schedule 2 (transitionals and savings: general provisions) to Scotland, "enactment" includes an enactment comprised in, or in an instrument made under, an Act of the Scottish Parliament.

(5) The express provision made by subsection (4) does not affect the construction of "enactment" in the application of section 631 (retained and accumulated income) to Scotland.

Amendments—[1]   In sub-s (1), definitions of "assignment" and "surrender" repealed, and word repealed; and sub-s (2) repealed, by ITA 2007 ss 1027, 1031, Sch 1 paras 492, 586, Sch 3 Pt 1 with effect for income tax purposes from 6 April 2007, and corporation tax purposes for accounting periods ending after 5 April 2007.

880 Interpretation: Northern Ireland

(1) In the application of section 755 (interest on foreign currency securities etc. owned by non-UK residents) to Northern Ireland, "Act" includes any Act, Order in Council or Measure constituting Northern Ireland legislation.

(2) In the application of section 769 (housing grants) and 882 (consequential amendments) and Part 1 of Schedule 2 (transitionals and savings: general provisions) to Northern Ireland, "enactment" includes an enactment comprised in, or in an instrument made under, Northern Ireland legislation.

(3) The express provision made by subsection (2) does not affect the construction of "enactment" in the application of section 631 (retained and accumulated income) to Northern Ireland.

General and final

882 Consequential amendments

(1) Schedule 1 (which contains consequential amendments) has effect.

(2) The Treasury may by order make such modifications of any enactment or provision made under an enactment as the Treasury consider appropriate in consequence of this Act.

(3) In subsection (2) "modifications" includes amendments or repeals.

(4) An order under subsection (2)—

(a) must not change the effect of the law as it was immediately before 6th April 2005, and

(b) may include such transitional or saving provision as the Treasury consider appropriate.

(5) Subsection (4)(a) does not apply so far as an order contains provision made in consequence of a change already made by this Act in the effect of the law.

883 Commencement and transitional provisions etc.

(1) This Act comes into force on 6th April 2005 and has effect—

(a) for income tax purposes, for the tax year 2005–06 and subsequent tax years, and

(b) for corporation tax purposes, for accounting periods ending after 5th April 2005.

(2) Subsection (1) is subject to subsections (3) to (5) (including Schedule 2).

(3) Subsection (1) does not apply to the following provisions of this Act (which therefore come into force on the passing of this Act)—

(a) section 873 (orders and regulations made by Treasury or [Commissioners][1]),

(b) sections 875 to 881 (certain interpretation and general provisions),

(c) section 882(2) to (5) (power to make consequential amendments),

(d) this section other than subsection (4) below,

(e) section 885 and Schedule 4 (abbreviations and general index),

(f) section 886 (short title), and

(g) paragraphs 78 and 148(5) of Schedule 2 (powers relating to open-ended investment companies and periodical payments of personal injury damages etc.) and subsection (4) below so far as it applies for the purposes of those provisions.

(4) Schedule 2 (which contains transitional provisions and savings etc.) has effect.

(5) The Treasury may by order make such transitional or saving provision as the Treasury consider appropriate in connection with the coming into force of this Act.

Commentary—Simon's Taxes B4.101.

Amendments—[1]   Word in sub-s (3) substituted by CRCA 2005 s 50, Sch 4 paras 131, 132(3)(i) with effect from 18 April 2005 (by virtue of SI 2005/1126).

884 Repeals and revocations

Schedule 3 (which contains repeals and revocations of enactments including certain spent enactments) has effect.

885 Abbreviations and general index in Schedule 4

(1) Schedule 4 (which contains abbreviations and defined expressions that apply for the purposes of this Act) has effect.

(2) Part 1 of that Schedule gives the meaning of the abbreviated references to Acts used in this Act.

(3) Part 2 of that Schedule lists the places where expressions used in this Act are defined or otherwise explained—

    (*a*) in this Act for the purposes of this Act or for purposes including this Act,

    (*b*) in this Act for the purposes of a Part or Chapter of this Act, or

    (*c*) in [another Act][1] for the purposes of this Act.

Amendments—[1]   Words in sub-s (3) substituted by ITA 2007 s 1027, Sch 1 paras 492, 587 with effect for income tax purposes from 6 April 2007, and corporation tax purposes for accounting periods ending after 5 April 2007.

886 Short title

This Act may be cited as the Income Tax (Trading and Other Income) Act 2005.

588 Abbreviations and general index in Schedule 4

(1) Schedule 4 (which contains: (a) the abbreviations and defined expressions that apply for the purposes of this Act) has effect.

(2) Part 1 of that Schedule gives the meaning of the abbreviated references to Acts used in this Act.

(b) Part 2 of that Schedule lists the places where expressions used in this Act are defined or otherwise explained.

(c) all this Act for the purposes of this Act... or for purposes including this Act.

(2) in this Act is for the purposes of a Part or Chapter of this Act; or

(e) in that other Act for the purpose of a whole Act.

Amendments.— Words inserted by F(No.2)A 2005; F2 FA 2005; F3 FA 2008; F4 FA 2009; F5 inserted for income tax purposes from 1 April 2009 and inspection for income tax purposes...

794. Short title.

This Act may be cited as the Income Tax (Trading and Other Income) Act 2005.

SCHEDULES

SCHEDULE 1
CONSEQUENTIAL AMENDMENTS

SCHEDULE 2
TRANSITIONALS AND SAVINGS ETC

Section 883

PART 1
GENERAL PROVISIONS

Continuity of the law: general

1   The repeal of provisions and their enactment in a rewritten form by this Act does not affect the continuity of the law.

2   Paragraph 1 does not apply to any change made by this Act in the effect of the law.

3   Any subordinate legislation or other thing which—

    (*a*) has been made or done, or has effect as if made or done, under or for the purposes of a superseded enactment so far as it applied for relevant tax purposes, and

    (*b*) is in force or effective immediately before the commencement of the corresponding rewritten provision,

has effect after that commencement as if made or done under or for the purposes of the rewritten provision.

4—   (1) Any reference (express or implied) in this Act, another enactment or an instrument or document to a rewritten provision is to be read as including, in relation to times, circumstances or purposes in relation to which any corresponding superseded enactment had effect for relevant tax purposes, a reference to the superseded enactment so far as applying for those relevant tax purposes.

(2) In particular, any reference (express or implied) in this Act, another enactment or an instrument or document to—

    (*a*) the profits of a UK property business,

    (*b*) relevant foreign income, or

    (*c*) similar concepts created by this Act,

         is to be read as including, in relation to times, circumstances or purposes in relation to which any corresponding concept in a superseded enactment had effect for income tax purposes, a reference to that concept so far as applying for income tax purposes.

(3) Any reference (express or implied) in this Act, another enactment or an instrument or document to—

    (*a*) things done under or for the purposes of a rewritten provision, or

    (*b*) things falling to be done under or for the purposes of a rewritten provision,

         is to be read as including, in relation to times, circumstances or purposes in relation to which any corresponding superseded enactment had effect for relevant tax purposes, a reference to things done or falling to be done under or for the purposes of the superseded enactment so far as applying for those relevant tax purposes.

5— (1) Any reference (express or implied) in any enactment, instrument or document to a superseded enactment in its application for relevant tax purposes is to be read, so far as is required for those relevant tax purposes, as including, in relation to times, circumstances or purposes in relation to which any corresponding rewritten provision has effect, a reference to the rewritten provision.

(2) In particular, any reference (express or implied) in any enactment, instrument or document to Schedule A, D or F or the Cases of Schedule D in their application for income tax purposes is to be read, so far as is required for income tax purposes, as including, in relation to times, circumstances or purposes in relation to which any corresponding rewritten concept has effect, a reference to the rewritten concept.

(3) Any reference (express or implied) in any enactment, instrument or document to—

    (*a*) things done under or for the purposes of a superseded enactment in its application for relevant tax purposes, or

    (*b*) things falling to be done under or for the purposes of a superseded enactment in its application for relevant tax purposes,

         is to be read, so far as is required for those relevant tax purposes, as including, in relation to times, circumstances or purposes in relation to which any corresponding rewritten provision has effect, a reference to things done or falling to be done under or for the purposes of the rewritten provision.

6—(1) Paragraphs 1 to 5 have effect instead of section 17(2) of the Interpretation Act 1978 (c 30) (but are without prejudice to any other provision of that Act).
(2) Paragraphs 4 and 5 apply only so far as the context permits.

General saving for old transitional provisions and savings

7—(1) The repeal by this Act of a transitional or saving provision relating to the coming into force of a provision rewritten in this Act does not affect the operation of the transitional or saving provision, so far as it is not specifically rewritten in this Act but remains capable of having effect in relation to the corresponding provision of this Act.
(2) The repeal by this Act of an enactment previously repealed subject to savings does not affect the continued operation of those savings.
(3) The repeal by this Act of a saving on the previous repeal of an enactment does not affect the operation of the saving so far as it is not specifically rewritten in this Act but remains capable of having effect.

General saving for section 9(5) of ICTA

8—(1) Sub-paragraph (2) applies if—
    (*a*) as a result of this Act, an enactment which applies to both income tax and corporation tax ("the original enactment") has become an enactment which applies to income tax and an enactment which applies to corporation tax ("the successor enactments"),
    (*b*) immediately before 6th April 2005, section 9(5) of ICTA (taxes treated as one in certain circumstances) had effect in relation to the original enactment, and
    (*c*) no express provision is made by this Act to preserve this effect.
(2) The successor enactments are not to be affected in their operation by the fact that income tax and corporation tax are distinct taxes but they are to apply in relation to income tax and corporation tax as if they were one tax so far as is—
    (*a*) consistent with the Corporation Tax Acts, and
    (*b*) required to preserve the effect of section 9(5) of ICTA,

    and the successor enactments are to be read accordingly.

Partnerships involving companies

9—(1) References in this Act to any person are to be read, in the case of a person acting in partnership with other persons of whom at least one is a company chargeable to corporation tax, as references to all the partners so far as is required for the purposes of preserving the continuity of the law.
(2) References to a company or other person in any provision amended in its application for corporation tax purposes by this Act are to be read, in the case of a company acting in partnership with other persons of whom at least one is not a company, as references to all the partners so far as is required for the purposes of preserving the continuity of the law.

Interpretation

10—(1) In this Part—
    "enactment" includes an enactment comprised in subordinate legislation (within the meaning of the Interpretation Act 1978 (c 30)),
    "relevant tax purposes" means, in relation to a superseded enactment, tax purposes for which the enactment has been rewritten by this Act, and
    "superseded enactment" means an earlier enactment which has been rewritten by this Act for certain tax purposes (whether it applied only for those purposes or for those and other tax purposes).
(2) References in this Part to the repeal of a provision include references to its revocation and to its express or implied disapplication for income tax purposes of this Act.
(3) References in this Part to tax purposes are not limited to income tax purposes.

PART 2
CHANGES IN THE LAW

11—(1) This paragraph applies if, in the case of any person—
    (*a*) a thing is done or an event occurs before 6th April 2005, and
    (*b*) because of a change in the law made by this Act, the tax consequences of that thing or event for the relevant period are different from what they would otherwise have been.

(2) If that person so elects, this Act applies with such modifications as may be necessary to secure that the tax consequences for the relevant period are the same as they would have been if the change in the law had not been made.

(3) In sub-paragraphs (1) and (2) "the relevant period" means—

    (*a*) for income tax purposes, any period of account beginning before and ending on or after 6th April 2005, and

    (*b*) for corporation tax purposes, any accounting period beginning before and ending on or after 6th April 2005.

(4) If this paragraph applies in the case of two or more persons in relation to the same thing or event, an election made under this paragraph by any one of those persons is of no effect unless a corresponding election is made by the other or each of the others.

(5) An election under this paragraph must be made—

    (*a*) for income tax purposes, on or before the first anniversary of the normal self-assessment filing date for the tax year in which the period of account ends, and

    (*b*) for corporation tax purposes, no later than two years after the end of the accounting period.

PART 3
TRADING INCOME
Unpaid remuneration

12—(1) This paragraph applies for the purposes of section 36.

(2) In relation to a period of account ending before 27th November 2002, an amount charged in the accounts in respect of employees' remuneration includes an amount which is held by an intermediary with a view to its becoming employees' remuneration.

(3) In relation to a period of account ending on or after 27th November 2002, an amount charged in the accounts in respect of employees' remuneration includes an amount—

    (*a*) in respect of employee benefit contributions (within the meaning of sections 38 to 44) made before that date, and

    (*b*) which is held by an intermediary,

with a view to its becoming employees' remuneration.

Employee benefit contributions

13   Sections 38 to 44 do not apply to deductions that would otherwise be allowed—

    (*a*) for a period ending before 27th November 2002, or

    (*b*) in respect of employee benefit contributions made before that date.

14—(1) In relation to any time before the coming into force of ITEPA 2003—

    (*a*) section 40(7) applies as if, in the definition of "employment income tax charge", for "tax under ITEPA 2003" there were substituted "income tax under Schedule E",

    (*b*) section 41(1) applies as if for "treated as received" to the end there were substituted "treated as received for the purposes of section 202A(1)(*a*) of ICTA (applying the rules in section 202B(1) to (6) of that Act (receipts basis of assessment for Schedule E)).", and

    (*c*) section 41(3) applies as if for "tax under ITEPA 2003" there were substituted "income tax under Schedule E".

(2) The express provision made by this paragraph does not affect the construction of other provisions of this Act as a result of the operation of paragraph 5 of this Schedule on paragraph 4 of Schedule 7 to ITEPA 2003 (references in enactment to rewritten provisions include corresponding repealed provisions) or on any similar provision (for example paragraph 4 of Schedule 3 to CAA 2001).

15—(1) Subject to sub-paragraph (7), sections 38 to 44 apply before 6th April 2006 with the following amendments.

(2) In section 38(4)—

    (*a*) for paragraphs (*b*) and (*c*) and the word "or" at the end of paragraph (*c*) substitute—

        "(*b*)   contributions under a retirement benefits scheme within the meaning of Chapter 1 of Part 14 of ICTA (see section 611 of that Act),

        (*c*)   contributions under a personal pension scheme approved under Chapter 4 of that Part (see section 630 of that Act), or", and

    (*b*) omit "For the purposes of paragraph (*c*)" to the end.

(3) In section 39—

    (*a*) in subsection (1)(*b*) omit ", or in respect of, present or former", and

    (*b*) in subsection (2) omit "present or former".

(4) In section 40—

    (*a*) in subsection (1) for ", C or D" substitute "or C", and

    (*b*) omit subsection (5).

(5) In section 41(1) omit paragraph (*b*) and the word "and" before it.

(6) In section 44(1) omit the definition of "employer-financed retirement benefits scheme".

(7) The power of the Treasury to make an order under section 281 or 283 of FA 2004 has effect as if Schedule 35 to that Act contained an amendment substituting sections 38 to 44 of this Act for those sections as amended by sub-paragraphs (2) to (6) above.

Crime-related payments

18   Section 55(1)(*b*) does not apply to expenditure which was incurred before 1st April 2002.

Tenants under taxed leases

19—(1) This paragraph relates to the operation of sections 60 to 67 where, in respect of a lease—

  (*a*) there is a receipt of a Schedule A business or an overseas property business (within the meaning of section 65A(4) or 70A(4) of ICTA) as a result of section 34 or 35 of ICTA (treatment of premiums etc as rent and assignments for profit of lease granted at an undervalue) for a tax year before the tax year 2005–06 or an accounting period ending before 6th April 2005, or

  (*b*) there would be such a receipt, but for the operation of section 37(2) or (3) of ICTA (reductions in certain receipts under section 34 or 35 of ICTA).

In this paragraph and paragraph 20 such a receipt is referred to as a "pre-commencement receipt".

(2) For the purposes of sections 60 to 67—

  (*a*) the lease is treated as a taxed lease, and

  (*b*) the pre-commencement receipt is treated as a taxed receipt.

(3) For the purposes of those sections, the "receipt period" of a taxed receipt which is a pre-commencement receipt is—

  (*a*) in the case of a pre-commencement receipt as a result of section 34 of ICTA, the period treated in calculating the amount of the receipt as being the duration of the lease, and

  (*b*) in the case of a pre-commencement receipt as a result of section 35 of ICTA, the period treated in calculating the amount of the receipt as being the duration of the lease remaining at the date of the assignment.

(4) For the purposes of sections 60 to 67 the "unreduced amount" of a taxed receipt which is a pre-commencement receipt is the amount of the pre-commencement receipt as a result of section 34 or 35 of ICTA, before the operation of section 37(2) or (3) of ICTA.

(5) Sub-paragraph (6) applies to a taxed receipt which is a pre-commencement receipt arising as a result of section 34(2) of ICTA (obligation on tenant to carry out work under lease).

(6) If the obligation to carry out work included the carrying out of work which gave or will give rise to expenditure for which an allowance has been, or may be, made under the enactments relating to capital allowances, the unreduced amount of the taxed receipt is calculated as if the obligation had not included the carrying out of that work.

20—(1) This paragraph provides for the application of section 61 as a result of section 63 if—

  (*a*) a lease is a taxed lease as a result of paragraph 19,

  (*b*) another lease is granted out of the taxed lease,

  (*c*) in calculating the amount of a pre-commencement receipt in respect of the other lease, there is a reduction under section 37(2) or (3) of ICTA by reference to the amount chargeable on the superior interest for the purposes of that section, and

  (*d*) as a result of paragraph 19 the amount chargeable on the superior interest is the taxed receipt for the purposes of section 61.

(2) Sections 61 to 65 apply as follows—

  (*a*) the pre-commencement receipt is treated as if it were a lease premium receipt for the purposes of sections 64 and 65,

  (*b*) references in those sections to the reduction under section 288 by reference to the taxed receipt are, in relation to the pre-commencement receipt, to the reduction under section 37(2) or (3) of ICTA by reference to the amount chargeable on the superior interest, and

  (*c*) for the purposes of those sections the receipt period of the pre-commencement receipt is—

    (i) in the case of a pre-commencement receipt as a result of section 34 of ICTA, the period treated in calculating the amount of the receipt as being the duration of the lease, and

    (ii) in the case of a pre-commencement receipt as a result of section 35 of ICTA, the period treated in calculating the amount of the receipt as being the duration of the lease remaining at the date of the assignment.

(3) References to a reduction under section 37(2) or (3) of ICTA in a pre-commencement receipt by reference to the amount chargeable on the superior interest are to the difference between—

  (*a*) the amount of the pre-commencement receipt before the operation of section 37(2) or (3) of ICTA, and

  (*b*) the amount of the receipt after the operation of that subsection, so far as attributable to the amount chargeable on the superior interest for the purposes of section 37 of ICTA.

Seconded employees

21—(1) This paragraph applies if—

  (a) the period of account of a trade begins before 1st April 2003 and ends on or after 6th April 2005, and

  (b) in that period of account the person carrying on the trade made the services of a person employed for the purposes of the trade available to a self-governing school within the meaning of the Self-Governing Schools etc (Scotland) Act 1989 (c 39) on a basis that was stated and intended to be temporary.

(2) For the purposes of section 70 an "educational establishment", in Scotland, includes such a school (despite the fact that, following the abolition of such schools on 1st April 2003, section 86(5)(d) of ICTA is not re-written in this Act).

(3) This paragraph applies to professions and vocations as it applies to trades.

Training courses for employees

22—(1) This paragraph applies if, without the modifications to section 588 of ICTA (training courses for employees) made by this Act—

  (a) section 588(5) of ICTA would operate in relation to an employee by virtue of paragraph (a) of that provision and paragraph 37 of Schedule 7 to ITEPA 2003 (savings in relation to tax years before 2003–04),

  (b) section 588(5) of ICTA would operate in relation to an employer by virtue of paragraph (b) of that provision and paragraph 37 of Schedule 7 to ITEPA 2003, or

  (c) section 588(6) and (7) of ICTA would operate in relation to an employer by virtue of paragraph 37 of Schedule 7 to ITEPA 2003.

(2) Those modifications do not apply in relation to—

  (a) the operation of section 588(5) of ICTA in relation to the employee as mentioned in sub-paragraph (1)(a),

  (b) the operation of section 588(5) of ICTA in relation to the employer as mentioned in sub-paragraph (1)(b), and

  (c) the operation of section 588(6) and (7) of ICTA in relation to the employer as mentioned in sub-paragraph (1)(c).

23—(1) This paragraph applies if—

  (a) at any time during the period beginning with 6th April 2003 and ending with 5th April 2005, a person ("the employer") incurred expenditure in paying or reimbursing retraining course expenses within the meaning of section 311 of ITEPA 2003,

  (b) the employer's liability to income tax for any tax year has been determined (before or after the passing of this Act, and by assessment or otherwise) on the assumption that, by virtue only of section 588(3) of ICTA, the employer is entitled to a deduction on account of the expenditure, and

  (c) before 6th April 2005, no assessment has been made under section 29(1) of TMA 1970 by virtue of section 588(5) of ICTA of an amount due in consequence of the failure by the person in respect of whom the expenditure was incurred to meet a condition of the kind mentioned in section 312(1)(b)(i) or (ii) of ITEPA 2003.

(2) Section 75 (retraining courses: recovery of tax) applies in relation to the employer as if the condition in subsection (1) were met.

(3) In the application of that section to the employer, references to "the employee" are to the person in respect of whom the expenditure was incurred by the employer.

Contributions to urban regeneration companies

24   Section 82 does not apply to any contribution which was made to an urban regeneration company before 1st April 2003.

Local enterprise agencies

25   To the extent that any function of the Scottish Ministers under section 79 of ICTA was, before 6th April 2005, also exercisable by the Secretary of State for the purposes specified in section 2(2) of the European Communities Act 1972 (c 68) that function as rewritten in—

  (a) section 83(2) (meaning of "local enterprise agency"),

  (b) section 84 (approval of local enterprise agencies), or

  (c) section 85 (supplementary provisions with respect to approvals), continues to be also exercisable by the Secretary of State for those purposes.

Expenses connected with patents, designs and trade marks

26—(1) This paragraph applies if—
- (*a*) fees have been incurred, but not paid, for the purposes of a trade in connection with any of the matters mentioned in section 89 or 90,
- (*b*) the fees were incurred in a period of account no part of which falls in the basis period for the tax year 2005–06 or a subsequent tax year, and
- (*c*) the fees have not been taken into account in calculating the profits of the trade of any tax year.

(2) A deduction is allowed for the fees in calculating the profits of the period of account in which they are paid.

Payments to Export Credits Guarantee Department

27—(1) This paragraph applies if—
- (*a*) a sum is payable, but not paid, by the person carrying on a trade to the Export Credits Guarantee Department under an agreement mentioned in section 91(1)(*a*) or with a view to entering into such an agreement,
- (*b*) the sum was incurred in a period of account no part of which falls in the basis period for the tax year 2005–06 or a subsequent tax year, and
- (*c*) the sum has not been taken into account in calculating the profits of the trade of any tax year.

(2) A deduction is allowed for the sum in calculating the profits of the period of account in which it is paid.

(3) This paragraph applies to professions and vocations as it applies to trades.

Reverse premiums

28—(1) Sections 101 and 102 do not apply to a reverse premium—
- (*a*) which was received before 9th March 1999, or
- (*b*) to which the recipient was entitled immediately before that date.

(2) In determining whether a reverse premium was one to which the recipient was entitled immediately before 9th March 1999, no account is to be taken of any arrangements made on or after that date.

Sums recovered under insurance policies etc

29—(1) Section 106 does not apply if—
- (*a*) a person carrying on a trade recovers a sum mentioned in that section, and
- (*b*) the sum has been taken into account in calculating the profits of the trade of a tax year before the tax year 2005–06.

(2) This paragraph applies to professions and vocations as it applies to trades.

Meaning of "designated educational establishment"

30 To the extent that the power of the National Assembly for Wales to make regulations under section 84(5) of ICTA was, before 6th April 2005, also exercisable by the Secretary of State for the purpose of—
- (*a*) implementing any Community obligation of the United Kingdom,
- (*b*) enabling any such obligation to be implemented,
- (*c*) enabling any rights enjoyed or to be enjoyed by the United Kingdom under or by virtue of the Community Treaties to be exercised, or
- (*d*) dealing with matters arising out of or related to any such obligation or rights or the operation of section 2(1) of the European Communities Act 1972 (c 68),

that power as rewritten in section 110 continues to be also exercisable by the Secretary of State for those purposes.

Films and sound recordings

31—(1) This paragraph applies to—
- (*a*) production expenditure in respect of the original master version of a film which (within the meaning of Chapter 9 of Part 2) was completed before 21st March 2000,
- (*b*) production expenditure in respect of the original master version of a film which (within the meaning of that Chapter) is completed on or after that date, if the first day of principal photography was before that date (but see sub-paragraph (4)), and

(*c*) acquisition expenditure in respect of the original master version of a film which was incurred before 6th April 2000.

(2) For this purpose acquisition expenditure in respect of the original master version of a film includes the acquisition of any description of rights in the original master version of a film (whether or not held or acquired with it).

(3) In relation to expenditure to which this paragraph applies—

(*a*) section 130(4) applies with the omission of "that are held or acquired with it",

(*b*) section 131(5) applies with the insertion at the end of "or, if the expenditure is acquisition expenditure and the acquisition takes place after that time, at the time of the acquisition", and

(*c*) section 134(1) applies with the insertion after "acquisition expenditure," of "and the expenditure would otherwise constitute capital expenditure on the provision of plant or machinery for the purposes of Part 2 of CAA 2001,".

(4) This paragraph does not apply to expenditure falling within sub-paragraph (1)(*b*) if the person incurring the expenditure so elects.

(5) Any such election is irrevocable.

32—(1) Sections 134 and 135 do not apply in relation to expenditure incurred by a person carrying on a trade which consists of or includes the exploitation of original master versions of films if—

(*a*) the expenditure is incurred on the production or acquisition of an original master version of a film completed before 10th March 1992 (within the meaning of Chapter 9 of Part 2),

(*b*) the original master version is a certified master version,

(*c*) its value is expected to be realised over a period of not less than two years, and

(*d*) the film is genuinely intended for theatrical release.

(2) Sub-paragraph (1)(*d*) does not apply if—

(*a*) the original master version of the film was certified before 17th April 2002 by the Secretary of State under Schedule 1 to the Films Act 1985 (c 21) as a qualifying film, tape or disc, or

(*b*) an application for such certification was received by the Secretary of State before that date.

33 Section 137 does not apply in relation to expenditure which was incurred before 10th March 1992.

34 [Sections 138 and 138A do][1] not apply in relation to production or acquisition expenditure in respect of the original master version of a film which was completed before 10th March 1992.

Amendments—[1] Reference to ss 138, 138A substituted by FA 2005 s 59, Sch 3 paras 30(4), 31(2) with effect from 2005–06.

35—(1) Any requirement in Chapter 9 of Part 2 for a film to be genuinely intended for theatrical release does not apply to a film completed (within the meaning of that Chapter)—

(*a*) on or after 17th April 2002 if—

(i) an application for certification was received by the Secretary of State before that date, or

(ii) the film is a qualifying drama (see sub-paragraph (2)),

(*b*) before 1st January 2002 if—

(i) the film was certified by the Secretary of State before 17th April 2002, or

(ii) an application for certification was received by the Secretary of State before 17th April 2002, or

(*c*) at any time in the period beginning with 1st January 2002 and ending with 16th April 2002. References in this sub-paragraph to certification are to certification of the original master version of the film under Schedule 1 to the Films Act 1985 (c 21) as a qualifying film, tape or disc.

(2) A film is a qualifying drama if—

(*a*) it is a drama with an average production expenditure per hour of running time of the completed film greater than £500,000,

(*b*) it was commissioned on or before 17th April 2002, and

(*c*) the first day of principal photography was on or before 30th June 2002.

(3) For the purposes of sub-paragraph (2) "drama" does not include—

(*a*) anything in the nature of—

(i) an advertisement or promotional film,

(ii) a discussion programme, news or current affairs programme, quiz show, panel show, variety show or similar entertainment, or

(iii) a training film, or

(*b*) a film of a live event or of a theatrical or artistic performance given otherwise than for the purpose of being filmed,

but it includes a documentary involving the dramatic reconstruction of events if the dramatic content forms 50% or more of the running time.

(4) For the purposes of sub-paragraph (2) the production expenditure on a film means the total production expenditure in respect of the original master version of the film (as defined by section 141).

36   Sections 139 and 140 do not apply if—

     (*a*)   the expenditure was incurred before 2nd July 1997 (as determined by section 142), or

     (*b*)   the film was completed before that date (within the meaning of Chapter 9 of Part 2).

Derivation—F(No 2)A 1997 s 48(2).

37   Sections 139(4) and 141(3) do not apply to any film which was completed before 17th April 2002.

38   The requirement in section 140 for the acquisition to be a relevant acquisition does not apply in relation to expenditure which was incurred before 30th June 2002 (as determined by section 142).

Certain telecommunication rights

39   Chapter 10 of Part 2 does not apply to an indefeasible right to use a telecommunications cable system ("IRU") acquired before 21st March 2000.

40—(1) That Chapter also does not apply to an IRU acquired by a person on or after that date (directly or indirectly) from an associate or an associated company if the associate or associated company acquired the IRU before that date.

(2) In sub-paragraph (1)—

     "associate" has the meaning given by [section 448 of CTA 2010][1], and

     "associated company"—

         (*a*)   in relation to another company, has the meaning given by [section 449 of that Act][1], and

         (*b*)   in relation to any other person, means a company of which that person has control within the meaning of [sections 450 and 451 of that Act][1].

Amendments—[1]   In sub-(2), in the definitiona of "associate", "associated company", words substituted by CTA 2010 s 1177, Sch 1 paras 444, 471(1),(2). CTA 2010 has effect for corporation tax purposes for accounting periods ending on or after 1 April 2010, and for income and capital gains tax purposes for the tax year 2010–11 and subsequent tax years.

Dealers in securities etc: taxation of amounts taken to reserves

41—(1) Section 149 does not apply in relation to periods of account beginning before 1st January 2005.

(2) But, in the case of a company required to prepare accounts—

     (*a*)   under the Companies Act 1985 (c 6), or

     (*b*)   under the Companies (Northern Ireland) Order 1986 (SI 1986/1032 (NI 6)),

     that section does apply in relation to a period of account beginning before that date for which the company is required or permitted to prepare such accounts in accordance with international accounting standards.

Purchase or sale of woodlands

42   Section 156 does not apply if the purchase mentioned in subsection (2) of that section was made under a contract entered into before 1st May 1963.

Ministers of religion

43—(1) This paragraph applies if—

     (*a*)   expenses have been incurred, but not borne, by a minister of a religious denomination on any of the matters mentioned in section 159(3),

     (*b*)   the expenses were incurred in a period of account no part of which falls in the basis period for the tax year 2005–06 or a subsequent tax year, and

     (*c*)   the part of the expenses corresponding to the amount under section 159(4) has not been taken into account in calculating the profits of the profession or vocation of the minister of any tax year.

(2) A deduction is allowed under section 159(3) for that part of the expenses in calculating the profits of the period of account in which the expenses are borne.

Waste disposal

44   If the predecessor ceased to carry on the trade carried on by the trader, or ceased to carry on a trade so far as relating to the site, before 21st March 2000, section 165 applies as if—

     (*a*)   ", or a predecessor," in subsection (1) were omitted, and (*b*) subsections (3) and (4) were omitted.

45 If the trade carried on by the trader was started before 1st April 1993, the definition of "waste disposal licence" in section 167(1) applies for the purposes of sections 165 and 166 as if paragraphs (*d*) and (*e*) of the definition were omitted (radioactive waste and nuclear site authorisations or licences).

46 Section 167(2) does not apply for the purposes of sections 165 and 166 if the trade was started before 1st April 1993.

Valuation of trading stock on cessation

47—(1) This paragraph applies if—

(*a*) a period of account of a trade begins before 6th April 2004 and ends on or after 6th April 2005 ("the straddling period of account"), and

(*b*) as a result of paragraph 48, the profits or losses of the period of account are to be calculated in accordance with Part 2 of this Act.

(2) Subsection (2) of section 173 (valuation of trading stock on cessation) does not apply in relation to the part of the period of account which—

(*a*) begins with the straddling period of account, and

(*b*) ends with 5th April 2004,

and the profits or losses of the trade are to be calculated accordingly.

Apportionment of profits or losses to tax years before tax year 2005–06

48—(1) This paragraph applies if—

(*a*) a period of account of a trade, profession or vocation begins before 6th April 2005 and ends on or after that date,

(*b*) the period of account, or part of the period of account, falls in the basis period for the tax year 2005–06,

(*c*) part of the period of account also falls in the basis period (or periods) for an earlier tax year (or years), and

(*d*) in order to arrive at the profits or losses of the basis period for any earlier tax year it is necessary to apportion the profits or losses of the period of account to any part of the period of account falling in that basis period.

(2) The profits or losses of the period of account—

(*a*) are calculated in accordance with Part 2 of this Act (and therefore, to that extent, that Part has effect for tax years before the tax year 2005–06), and

(*b*) may be apportioned in accordance with section 203 to any part of the period of account falling in a basis period for a tax year before the tax year 2005–06.

Treatment of business start-up payments received in an overlap period

49—(1) There is an exception to the rule that, subject to Part 8, the charge to tax under Chapter 2 of Part 2 on the profits of a trade, profession or vocation of a tax year operates by reference to the profits of the basis period for the tax year (which may include a period falling before 6th April 2005).

(2) The exception is that section 207 does not apply to payments received before 6th April 2005.

Profits or losses of a trade, profession or vocation previously chargeable in accordance with section 65(1) of ICTA

50—(1) This paragraph applies if—

(*a*) a person carries on a trade, profession or vocation wholly outside the United Kingdom, and

(*b*) the trade, profession or vocation was chargeable to income tax in accordance with section 65(1) of ICTA (Case IV and V assessments: general) for a tax year before 2005–06.

(2) If the trade, profession or vocation was so chargeable for the tax year 2004–05, the person is treated for the purpose of determining the basis period for the tax year 2005–06 and subsequent tax years as if the person started to carry on the trade, profession or vocation on 6th April 2005.

(3) . . . [1]

Amendments—[1] Sub-para (3) repealed by ITA 2007 s 1031, Sch 3 Pt 1 with effect for income tax purposes from 6 April 2007, and corporation tax purposes for accounting periods ending after 5 April 2007.

Profits of mines, quarries and other concerns not chargeable by reference to a basis period

51—(1) This paragraph applies if any profits or losses arising out of land in the case of any concern specified in section 55(2) of ICTA—

(*a*) arose in the tax year 2004–05, and

(*b*) were calculated for that tax year otherwise than by reference to a basis period.

(2) For the purpose of determining the basis period for the tax year 2005–06 and subsequent tax years, the concern is treated as if it were a trade which was started to be carried on by a person on 6th April 2005.

(3) Paragraph 48 of this Schedule applies in relation to any case to which this paragraph applies as if references to a basis period for a tax year (an "earlier tax year") before the tax year 2005–06 were references to that earlier tax year.

Overlap profit: pre-April 1994 trades, professions and vocations

52—(1) This paragraph applies in the case of a trade, profession or vocation which was—

    (*a*) set up and commenced by a person before 6th April 1994, and

    (*b*) continued by the person after 5th April 1997,

and the profits of which were chargeable to income tax under Case I or II of Schedule D for the tax year 1997–98.

(2) For the purposes of Chapter 15 of Part 2 "overlap profit" includes the amount of profits or gains of the basis period for the tax year 1997–98 which—

    (*a*) arose after the end of the basis period for the tax year 1996–97 or, in the case of a trade or profession carried on by a firm, the basis period of the firm for that year, and

    (*b*) arose before 6th April 1997.

(3) In calculating the amount of the profits or gains of the basis period for the tax year 1997–98 which arose as mentioned above—

    (*a*) any deduction of a capital allowance, and

    (*b*) any addition of a balancing charge,

are ignored.

(4) But sub-paragraph (3) does not apply in the case of a trade or profession carried on by a firm which included both an individual and a company.

(5) For the purposes of this paragraph the basis period for the tax year 1996–97 is determined in accordance with paragraph 1 of Schedule 20 to FA 1994 despite the repeal by this Act of that paragraph.

(6) This paragraph is subject to Schedule 22 to FA 1995 (prevention of exploitation of the transitional rules facilitating self-assessment).

53—(1) This paragraph applies in the case of income which—

    (*a*) was immediately derived from the carrying on of a trade, profession or vocation set up and commenced by a person before 6th April 1994 and continued by the person after 5th April 1998, and

    (*b*) was chargeable to income tax under Case IV or V of Schedule D for the tax year 1997–98.

(2) But, in the case of income which was chargeable to tax by reference to the amounts of income received in the United Kingdom, this paragraph applies only if the date on which the first amount of income was received in the United Kingdom was before 6th April 1994.

(3) For the purposes of Chapter 15 of Part 2 "overlap profit" includes the amount of profits or gains of the basis period for the tax year 1997–98 which arose before 6th April 1997.

(4) This paragraph is subject to Schedule 22 to FA 1995 (prevention of exploitation of the transitional rules facilitating self-assessment).

54 The repeal by this Act of paragraphs 2, 6 and 10 of Schedule 20 to FA 1994 (changes for facilitating self-assessment: transitional provisions and savings) does not affect the continuing application of the assumptions mentioned in paragraph 11(4) of that Schedule (double taxation relief).

Averaging profits of farmers and creative artists

55—(1) The first tax years which may be the subject of an averaging claim under section 222 are the tax years 2004–05 and 2005–06.

(2) If—

    (*a*) an individual carries on a trade of farming or market gardening in the United Kingdom in partnership, and

    (*b*) but for the repeal by this Act of section 96 of ICTA the individual could have made a claim under that section in relation to the profits of that trade for the tax years 2004–05 and 2005–06,

the individual may make an averaging claim under section 222 of this Act in relation to those profits for those tax years (despite anything in Chapter 16 of Part 2 of this Act to the contrary).

Adjustment on change of basis

56—(1) Chapter 17 of Part 2 applies to a change of basis taking effect for a period of account which ends on or after 6th April 2005.

(2) For this purpose the period of account for which a change of basis takes effect is the first period of account for which the new basis is adopted.

57—(1) Subject to sub-paragraph (3), section 232 applies before 6th April 2006 with the following amendment.

(2) In subsection (4)—

    (*a*) before paragraph (*a*) insert—

        "(*aa*) relevant earnings within section 623(2)(*c*) or 644(2)(*c*) of ICTA, or",

    (*b*) omit paragraph (*b*) and the word "or" before it, and

    (*c*) for "earned income or relevant UK earnings" substitute "relevant earnings or earned income".

(3) The power of the Treasury to make an order under section 281 or 283 of FA 2004 has effect as if Schedule 35 to that Act contained an amendment substituting section 232(4) of this Act for that subsection as amended by sub-paragraph (2) above.

58 If—

    (*a*) an individual has made an election under paragraph 12 of Schedule 22 to FA 2002 (election by barrister or advocate to accelerate adjustment charge),

    (*b*) as a result of the election sub-paragraph (4) of that paragraph applies in relation to the tax year 2004–05, and

    (*c*) the election is in force immediately before 6th April 2005,

the election continues to apply in relation to the tax year 2005–06 and subsequent tax years (despite paragraph 3 of this Schedule).

59 Section 104(4) of ICTA (which, despite its repeal, applies in relation to any change of accounting basis occurring before 6th April 1999) does not apply if the person who would be liable to tax as a result of the change was born before 6th April 1917.

Post-cessation receipts

60—(1) Subject to sub-paragraph (4), section 256 applies before 6th April 2006 with the following amendments.

(2) In subsection (1)(*b*)—

    (*a*) after "from the trade was" insert "relevant earnings within section 623(2)(*c*) or 644(2)(*c*) of ICTA or", and

    (*b*) omit "or relevant UK earnings within section 189(2)(*b*) of FA 2004".

(3) In subsection (2) for "earned income or relevant UK earnings" substitute "relevant earnings or earned income".

(4) The power of the Treasury to make an order under section 281 or 283 of FA 2004 has effect as if Schedule 35 to that Act contained an amendment substituting section 256 of this Act for that section as amended by sub-paragraphs (2) and (3) above.

61 Chapter 18 of Part 2 does not apply in relation to a post-cessation receipt if—

    (*a*) the person who would be liable to tax on the receipt was born before 6th April 1917, and

    (*b*) the cessation of the trade occurred before 6th April 2000.

PART 4
PROPERTY INCOME

Apportionment of profits or losses to tax years before tax year 2005–06

62—(1) This paragraph applies if—

    (*a*) a period of account of a property business begins before 6th April 2005 and ends on or after that date, and

    (*b*) in order to arrive at the profits or losses of a tax year before the tax year 2005–06 it is necessary to apportion the profits or losses of the period of account to any part of that period falling in a tax year before the tax year 2005–06.

(2) The profits or losses of the period of account—

    (*a*) are calculated in accordance with Part 3 of this Act (and therefore, to that extent, that Part has effect for tax years before the tax year 2005–06), and

    (*b*) may be apportioned in accordance with section 275 to any part of the period of account falling in a tax year before the tax year 2005–06.

Lease premiums

63   Section 277 does not apply in relation to a lease granted pursuant to a contract entered into before 4th April 1963.

Lease premiums: sums payable instead of rent

64   Section 279 does not apply in relation to a lease granted—
- (a) before 6th April 1963, or
- (b) pursuant to a contract entered into before 4th April 1963.

Lease premiums: sums payable for surrender of lease

65   Section 280 does not apply in relation to a lease granted—
- (a) before 6th April 1963, or
- (b) pursuant to a contract entered into before 4th April 1963.

Lease premiums: assignments for profit of lease granted at undervalue

66   Section 282 does not apply in relation to a lease granted —
- (a) before 6th April 1963, or
- (b) pursuant to a contract entered into before 4th April 1963.

Lease premiums: pre-commencement receipts treated as taxed receipts

67—(1) This paragraph relates to the operation of sections 287 to 298 where, in respect of a lease—
- (a) there is a receipt of a Schedule A business or an overseas property business (within the meaning of section 65A(4) or 70A(4) of ICTA) as a result of section 34 or 35 of ICTA (treatment of premiums etc as rent and assignments for profit of lease granted at an undervalue) for a tax year before the tax year 2005–06 or an accounting period ending before 6th April 2005, or
- (b) there would be such a receipt, but for the operation of section 37(2) or (3) of ICTA (reductions in certain receipts under section 34 or 35 of ICTA).
  In this paragraph and paragraphs 68 and 69 such a receipt is referred to as a "pre-commencement receipt".

(2) For the purposes of Chapter 4 of Part 3—
- (a) the lease is treated as a taxed lease, and
- (b) the pre-commencement receipt is treated as a taxed receipt.

(3) For the purposes of that Chapter, the "receipt period" of a taxed receipt which is a pre-commencement receipt is—
- (a) in the case of a pre-commencement receipt as a result of section 34 of ICTA, the period treated in calculating the amount of the receipt as being the duration of the lease, and
- (b) in the case of a pre-commencement receipt as a result of section 35 of ICTA, the period treated in calculating the amount of the receipt as being the duration of the lease remaining at the date of the assignment.

(4) For the purposes of that Chapter the "unreduced amount" of a taxed receipt which is a pre-commencement receipt is the amount of the pre-commencement receipt as a result of section 34 or 35 of ICTA, before the operation of section 37(2) or (3) of ICTA.

(5) Sub-paragraph (6) applies to a taxed receipt which is a pre-commencement receipt arising as a result of section 34(2) of ICTA (obligation on tenant to carry out work under lease).

(6) If the obligation to carry out work included the carrying out of work which gave or will give rise to expenditure for which an allowance has been, or may be, made under the enactments relating to capital allowances, the unreduced amount of the taxed receipt is calculated as if the obligation had not included the carrying out of that work.

Lease premiums: taking account of reductions in pre-commencement receipts

68—(1) This paragraph applies if—
- (a) in calculating the amount of a pre-commencement receipt, there is a reduction under section 37(2) or (3) of ICTA by reference to the amount chargeable on the superior interest for the purposes of that section, and
- (b) as a result of paragraph 67 the amount chargeable on the superior interest is the taxed receipt for the purposes of Chapter 4 of Part 3.

(2) References to a reduction under section 37(2) or (3) of ICTA in a pre-commencement receipt by reference to the amount chargeable on the superior interest are to the difference between—
- (a) the amount of the pre-commencement receipt before the operation of section 37(2) or (3) of ICTA, and

(*b*) the amount of the receipt after the operation of that subsection,

so far as attributable to the amount chargeable on the superior interest for the purposes of section 37 of ICTA.

(3) In sections 290(5)(*a*) (meaning of "unused amount") and 295(1)(*a*) (limit on reductions and deductions) references to reductions under section 288 by reference to the taxed receipt include references to reductions under section 37(2) or (3) of ICTA in pre-commencement receipts by reference to the amount chargeable on the superior interest.

(4) Sections 292 to 294 apply as follows—

    (*a*) the pre-commencement receipt is treated as if it were a lease premium receipt for the purposes of sections 293 and 294,

    (*b*) references in those sections to the reduction under section 288 by reference to the taxed receipt are, in relation to the pre-commencement receipt, to the reduction under section 37(2) or (3) of ICTA by reference to the amount chargeable on the superior interest, and

    (*c*) for the purposes of those sections the receipt period of the pre-commencement receipt is—

        (i) in the case of a pre-commencement receipt as a result of section 34 of ICTA, the period treated in calculating the amount of the receipt as being the duration of the lease, and

        (ii) in the case of a pre-commencement receipt as a result of section 35 of ICTA, the period treated in calculating the amount of the receipt as being the duration of the lease remaining at the date of the assignment.

Lease premiums: taking account of deductions for rent as a result of section 37(4) or 87(2) of ICTA

69—(1) Sub-paragraph (2) applies if—

    (*a*) in calculating the profits of a trade, profession or vocation for a tax year before the tax year 2005–06 or an accounting period ending before 6th April 2005, a person is treated as paying rent under section 87(2) of ICTA by reference to the amount chargeable for the purposes of that section, and

    (*b*) as a result of paragraph 67 the amount chargeable is the taxed receipt for the purposes of Chapter 4 of Part 3.

(2) References in sections 290(5)(*b*) and 295(2)(*b*) to the deductions allowed for expenses under section 61 by reference to the taxed receipt include references to the deductions allowed in calculating the profits of the trade, profession or vocation for the rent that the person is treated as paying under section 87(2) of ICTA by reference to the amount chargeable.

(3) Sub-paragraph (4) applies if—

    (*a*) in calculating the profits of a Schedule A business or an overseas property business (within the meaning of section 65A(4) or 70A(4) of ICTA) for a tax year before the tax year 2005–06 or an accounting period ending before 6th April 2005, a person is treated as paying rent as a result of section 37(4) of ICTA by reference to the amount chargeable on the superior interest for the purposes of that section, and

    (*b*) as a result of paragraph 67 the amount chargeable on the superior interest is the taxed receipt for the purposes of Chapter 4 of Part 3.

(4) References in sections 290(5)(*c*) and 295(1)(*b*) to the deductions allowed for expenses under section 292 by reference to the taxed receipt include references to the deductions allowed in calculating the profits of the Schedule A business or overseas property business (within the meaning of section 65A(4) or 70A(4) of ICTA) for the rent that the person is treated as paying as a result of section 37(4) of ICTA by reference to the amount chargeable on the superior interest.

Lease premiums: rules for determining effective duration of lease

70—(1) In relation to a lease granted after 12th June 1969 and before 25th August 1971, for sections 303 and 304 substitute—

"303 Rules for determining effective duration of lease

(1) The following rules apply for determining the effective duration of a lease for the purposes of this Chapter.

Rule 1: Where the terms of a lease include provision for the determination of the lease by notice given by the landlord, the lease is not to be treated as granted for a term longer than one ending at the earliest date on which it could be determined by notice so given.

Rule 2: A lease is not to be treated as having been granted for a term longer than one ending on a date before the end of the term for which the lease was granted, if the terms of the lease or any other circumstances make it unlikely that the lease will continue beyond that date.

Rule 3: Where the terms of the lease include provision for the extension of the lease beyond a given date by notice given by the tenant, account may be taken of any circumstances making it likely that the lease will be so extended.

(2) Rule 2 applies by reference to the facts known or ascertainable at the time of the grant of the lease.

(3) In applying the rules, it is assumed that all parties concerned, whatever their relationship, act as if they were at arm's length.

(4) In this section, in relation to Scotland, "term", where referring to the duration of a lease, means period."

(2) This paragraph does not apply if the determination is for the purposes of section 281 (sums payable for variation or waiver of [terms][1] of lease).

Amendments—[1]   In sub-para (2), word substituted by CTA 2009 s 1322, Sch 1 paras 587, 646(1), (2). CTA 2009 applies for accounting periods ending on or after 1 April 2009 (for corporation tax purposes) and for tax years 2009–10 onwards (for income and capital gains tax purposes).

71—(1) In relation to a lease granted before 13th June 1969, for sections 303 [and 304][2] substitute—

"303 Rules for determining effective duration of lease

(1) The following rules apply for determining the effective duration of a lease for the purposes of this Chapter.

Rule 1: Where the effective duration of a lease is being determined after the date on which the lease has for any reason come to an end, the duration is taken to have extended from its commencement to that date.

Rule 2: Where the terms of the lease include provision for the determination of the lease by notice given either by the landlord or by the tenant, the lease is not to be treated as granted for a term longer than one ending at the earliest date on which it could be determined by notice.

Rule 3: A lease is not to be treated as having been granted for a term longer than one ending on a date before the end of the term for which the lease was granted, if the terms of the lease or any other circumstances make it unlikely that the lease will continue beyond that date.

(2) Rules 2 and 3 are subject to rule 1.

(3) Rules 2 and 3 apply in accordance with circumstances prevailing at the time of the determination.

(4) In this section, in relation to Scotland, "term", where referring to the duration of a lease, means period."

(2) This paragraph does not apply if the determination is for the purposes of section 281 (sums payable for variation or waiver of [terms][1] of lease).

Amendments—[1]   In sub-para (2), word substituted by CTA 2009 s 1322, Sch 1 paras 587, 646(1), (3). CTA 2009 applies for accounting periods ending on or after 1 April 2009 (for corporation tax purposes) and for tax years 2009–10 onwards (for income and capital gains tax purposes).

[2]   In sub-para (1) words substituted for words by Finance Act 2009 Schedule 47 (Consequential Amendments) Order, SI 2009/2035, Art 2 Schedule, paras 41, 45, with effect from 13 August 2009.

Reverse premiums

72—(1) Section 311 does not apply to a reverse premium—

(*a*) which was received before 9th March 1999, or

(*b*) to which the recipient was entitled immediately before that date.

(2) In determining whether a reverse premium was one to which the recipient was entitled immediately before 9th March 1999, no account is to be taken of any arrangements made on or after that date.

Deductions for expenditure on energy-saving items

73   Sections 312 to 314 do not apply to expenditure incurred before 6th April 2004.

Commercial letting of furnished holiday accommodation

74—(1) Subject to sub-paragraph (4), Chapter 6 of Part 3 applies before 6th April 2006 with the following amendments.

(2) In section 322(2)—

(*a*) after paragraph (*b*) insert—

"(*ba*)   section 623(2)(*c*) or 644(2)(*c*) of ICTA (income regarded as relevant earnings for pension purposes: see section 504A of that Act),",

(*b*) at the end of paragraph (*d*) insert "and", and

(*c*) omit paragraph (*f*) and the word "and" before it.

(3) In section 328(2)—

(*a*) before paragraph (*a*) insert—

"(*aa*)   income regarded as relevant earnings for pension purposes under section 623(2)(*c*) or 644(2)(*c*) of ICTA, or", and (*b*) omit paragraph (*b*) and the word "or" before it.

(4) The power of the Treasury to make an order under section 281 or 283 of FA 2004 has effect as if Schedule 35 to that Act contained amendments substituting sections 322(2) and 328(2) of this Act for those subsections as amended by sub-paragraphs (2) and (3) above.

75—(1) Subject to sub-paragraph (3), section 504A of ICTA (as inserted by Schedule 1 to this Act) applies before 6th April 2006 with the following amendment.

(2) In subsection (2)—

(*a*) after paragraph (*a*) insert—

"(*ab*) section 623(2)(*c*) or 644(2)(*c*) (income regarded as relevant earnings for pension purposes), and", and

(*b*) omit paragraph (*c*) and the word "and" before it.

(3) The power of the Treasury to make an order under section 281 or 283 of FA 2004 has effect as if Schedule 35 to that Act contained an amendment substituting section 504A of ICTA (as inserted by Schedule 1 to this Act) for that section as amended by sub-paragraph (2) above.

Adjustment on change of basis

76—(1) Chapter 7 of Part 3 applies to a change of basis taking effect for a period of account which ends on or after 6th April 2005.

(2) For this purpose the period of account for which a change of basis takes effect is the first period of account for which the new basis is adopted.

Meaning of "mineral royalties"

77 The definition of "mineral royalties" in section 341(2) does not include any rent receivable before 6th April 1970.

PART 5
SAVINGS AND INVESTMENT INCOME: GENERAL

Open-ended investment companies: saving for powers to make provision corresponding to provisions applicable to unit trusts

78—(1) Despite the enactment by this Act in the OEIC sections of provisions previously contained in regulations made under section 152 of FA 1995, the Treasury may continue to make regulations under that section for achieving any purpose that could be achieved by such regulations before the coming into force of the OEIC sections.

(2) Accordingly—

(*a*) regulations under that section may make provision for securing, in relation to the matters mentioned in subsection (1)(*a*) to (*c*) of that section, that the provision made by the OEIC sections corresponds, subject to such modifications as the Treasury consider appropriate, to the provision made by the enactments mentioned in subsection (2) of that section in relation to—

(i) unit trusts,

(ii) rights under, and the assets subject to, such trusts, and

(iii) transactions for purposes connected with such trusts, and

(*b*) that section has effect with such modifications as are required for the purposes of this paragraph.

(3) In this paragraph—

"the OEIC sections" means—

(*a*) sections 373 to 375 of this Act (under which certain amounts are treated as interest paid by open-ended investment companies), and

(*b*) sections 386 to 388 of this Act (under which certain amounts are treated as dividends paid by open-ended investment companies), and

"unit trust" has the same meaning as in section 152 of FA 1995 (see subsection (7)).

[Stock dividends issued in respect of shares issued before 6 April 1975

78A (1) This paragraph applies if—

(*a*) share capital is issued by a UK resident company in respect of shares in the company issued before 6 April 1975 ("the old shares"),

(*b*) the old shares confer on the holder a right to convert them into, or exchange them for, shares of a different class, and

(*c*) as a result of the issue of the share capital, income would (apart from this paragraph) be treated as arising under section 410(2), (3) or (4) (stock dividend income).

(2) Section 410 does not apply to the protected part of any bonus share capital issued by the company in connection with an exercise of that right.

(3) For the purposes of sub-paragraph (2), the protected part of the bonus share capital is however much of it (if any) would have been issued if the right had been exercised so as to bring about the conversion or exchange of the shares on the earliest possible date after 5 April 1975.

(4) In this paragraph "share" includes stock, and any other interest of a member in a company

(5) Section 1113 of CTA 2010 (meaning of "in respect of shares") applies in relation to this paragraph as it applies in relation to Part 23 of CTA 2010.][1]

Amendments—[1] Paragraph 78A inserted by CTA 2010 s 1177, Sch 1 paras 444, 471(1),(3). CTA 2010 has effect for corporation tax purposes for accounting periods ending on or after 1 April 2010, and for income and capital gains tax purposes for the tax year 2010–11 and subsequent tax years.

Deeply discounted securities issued in accordance with qualifying earn-out right

79 Despite the repeal by this Act of section 104(4) of FA 2002, sections 430(5) and 442 (securities issued in accordance with qualifying earn-out right) apply whenever the security was issued.

Deeply discounted securities: deemed transfers of strips on 5th April

80—(1) Despite the repeal by this Act of paragraph 14(4) of Schedule 13 to FA 1996, a person who was deemed under that paragraph to have transferred a strip on 5th April 2005 is treated for the purposes of Chapter 8 of Part 4 (profits from deeply discounted securities) as if the person had re-acquired the strip under that paragraph on 6th April 2005 for an amount equal to the amount for which it was deemed to have been transferred.

(2) That Chapter and this Part of this Schedule apply to a deemed transfer and reacquisition under that paragraph (including a reacquisition within sub-paragraph (1)) as if it were a transfer and reacquisition under section 445(2) and (3).

(3) Section 452 (power to modify that Chapter for strips) applies as if this paragraph were in that Chapter.

Deeply discounted securities: restriction of profits and losses on strips

81—(1) Sections 447 and 448 (restriction of profits and losses on strips by reference to original acquisition cost) do not apply to a strip acquired before 15th January 2004.

(2) For the purposes of paragraph (1) any deemed acquisitions under paragraph 14(4) of Schedule 13 to FA 1996 or section 445(3) of this Act are ignored.

Deeply discounted securities: saving for charities' losses

82 The references in section 454(4) and (5) to trustees include any person who, had the loss been a profit—

    (a) would have been eligible for relief from tax for the tax year in which the loss is sustained as a result of [any of sections 521(4), 522(5), 523(5), 524, 529 to 533, 536 and 537 of ITA 2007 (certain exemptions: special rules about charitable trusts)][1], or

    (b) would have been so eligible but for section [541 of that Act (restrictions on exemptions: attributing items of income to the non-exempt amount)][1].

Amendments—[1] Words substituted by ITA 2007 s 1027, Sch 1 paras 492, 588, 589 with effect for income tax purposes from 6 April 2007, and corporation tax purposes for accounting periods ending after 5 April 2007.

Deeply discounted securities: saving for pension trustees' losses

83 The references in section 454(4) and (5) to trustees include any person who, had the loss been a profit, would have been eligible for relief from tax for the tax year in which the loss is sustained as a result of—

    (a) section 592(2) of ICTA (exemption from income tax for income from investments or deposit held for exempt approved pension schemes),

    (b) section 608(2)(a) of ICTA (corresponding exemption for superannuation funds approved before 6th April 1980),

    (c) section 613(4) of ICTA (corresponding exemption for parliamentary pension funds),

    (d) section 614(2), (3), (4) or (5) of ICTA (corresponding exemption for certain overseas pension funds),

    (e) section 620(6) of ICTA (corresponding exemption for retirement annuity funds), or

    (f) section 643(2) of ICTA (corresponding exemption for approved personal pension schemes).

Gains from contracts for life insurance etc: foreign policies of life insurance

85—(1) This paragraph modifies the application of—

(a) section 474(4) (foreign policies of life insurance which are not qualifying policies),

(b) section 531(6) (foreign policies of life insurance to which section 530 applies), and

(c) section 532 (relief for policies and contracts with European Area Insurers),

in relation to a policy of life insurance which meets conditions A and B.

(2) Condition A is that the policy is a foreign policy of life insurance by virtue of paragraph (a) of the definition of that term in section 476(3).

(3) Condition B is that the income of the company which issued the policy was charged to corporation tax under section 445 of ICTA for an accounting period ending on or after the day on which the policy was issued.

(4) The policy is treated as having been a qualifying policy for any part of the chargeable period when—

(a) it would have been treated as a qualifying policy apart from section 474(4), and

(b) the conditions in either sub-paragraph (3) or sub-paragraph (4) of paragraph 24 of Schedule 15 to ICTA (as it then had effect) were met.

(5) The policy meets condition B in section 531(6) if—

(a) the conditions in either sub-paragraph (3) or sub-paragraph (4) of paragraph 24 of Schedule 15 to ICTA (as it then had effect) were met throughout the chargeable period, and

(b) the conditions in sub-paragraph (3) of that paragraph are met throughout the period—

(i) beginning immediately after the end of the chargeable period, and

(ii) ending with the date on which the gains mentioned in section 531(1) arise.

(6) Despite the definition of "policy period" in section 532(5), for the purposes of determining whether conditions A to C in that section have been met in relation to the policy or contract throughout the policy period, that period is to be taken not to include—

(a) any part of the chargeable period when the conditions in either sub-paragraph (3) or sub-paragraph (4) of paragraph 24 of Schedule 15 to ICTA (as it then had effect) were met, and

(b) any subsequent period when the conditions in sub-paragraph (3) of that paragraph are met.

(7) In this paragraph "the chargeable period" means the period—

(a) beginning with the date on which the policy was issued, and

(b) ending with the last day of the last accounting period for which the company which issued the policy was liable to tax under section 445 of ICTA.

Gains from contracts for life insurance etc: exclusion of pension policies

86—(1) Subject to sub-paragraph (4), before 6th April 2006 Chapter 9 of Part 4 applies with the following amendments.

(2) For section 479 (exclusion of pension policies) substitute—

"479 Exclusion of pension policies

(1) This Chapter does not apply to a pension policy.

(2) In this section "pension policy" means—

(a) a policy of life insurance issued in connection with an approved scheme,

(b) a policy of insurance which is, or is evidence of, a contract for the time being approved under section 621 of ICTA (contracts to provide for surviving spouses [and surviving civil partners][1] and dependants), or

(c) a policy of life insurance held in connection with an approved personal pension scheme.

(3) In this section—

"approved scheme" has the meaning given by section 612(1) of ICTA, and

"personal pension scheme" and "approved", in relation to such a scheme, have the meaning given by section 630(1) of ICTA."

(3) In section 486 (exclusion of maturity of capital redemption policies in certain circumstances) for "non-registered occupational pension" substitute "sponsored superannuation".[2]

(4) The power of the Treasury to make an order under section 281 or 283 of FA 2004 has effect as if Schedule 35 to that Act contained amendments—

(a) substituting section 479 of this Act for that section as substituted by sub-paragraph (2), and

(b) substituting "non-registered occupational pension" for "sponsored superannuation" in section 486 of this Act.

Amendments—[1]   Words in sub-para (2), in inserted s 479(2)(b), inserted by Tax and Civil Partnership Regulations, SI 2005/3229, regs 183, 199, with effect from 5 December 2005 (reg 1(1)).

[2]   Sub-para (3) repealed by FA 2008 s 36, Sch 14 para 17 with effect as follows—

(a)   so far as relating to corporation tax, for accounting periods beginning on or after 1 April 2008, and

(b)   so far as relating to income tax, for the tax year 2008–09 and subsequent tax years.

Gains from contracts for life insurance etc: rights partially assigned

87   Section 505 (assignments involving co-ownership) does not have effect in relation to any transaction which—

(a)   took place in relation to a policy or contract in an insurance year beginning on or before 5th April 2001, and

(b)   would otherwise and by reason only of the application of that section fall to be taken into account as an assignment of a part of or a share in the rights conferred by the policy or contract in a calculation under—

(i)   section 507 (periodic calculations in part surrender and assignment cases), or

(ii)   section 511 (transaction-related calculations in part surrender and assignment cases).

88—(1) This paragraph applies if a calculation under section 507 or 511 in relation to a policy or contract requires account to be taken of any part of or share in the rights conferred by the policy or contract which has been assigned for money or money's worth in an insurance year beginning on or before 5th April 2001.

(2) Section 508 (the value of rights partially assigned) applies for the purposes of the valuation of each such part or share as if—

(a)   in subsection (1) after "surrendered" (in both places where it occurs) there were inserted "or assigned",

(b)   in that subsection after "surrender" there were inserted "or assignment", and

(c)   subsection (4) were omitted.

Gains from contracts for life insurance etc: regulations providing for relief where foreign tax chargeable

89   Regulations made under section 534 by virtue of paragraph 4 of this Schedule may apply—

(a)   in relation to gains arising on or after 29th November 1994, and

(b)   in relation to any gain arising before that date the income tax on which has not been the subject of an assessment that became final and conclusive before that date.

Gains from contracts for life insurance etc: pure protection group life policies

90—(1) For the purposes of Chapter 9 of Part 4, any event occurring before 9th April 2003 in relation to a policy of life insurance which, at the time of the event, was a pure protection group life policy is deemed not to be a chargeable event.

(2) For the purposes of this paragraph a policy of life insurance is at any time a pure protection group life policy if at that time it is a group life policy whose terms do not provide for any sums or other benefits to be paid or conferred except on death or disability.

Transactions in deposits

92   Section 551 (charge to income tax on profits from disposal of deposit rights) does not apply if the person disposing of the rights acquired them before 7th March 1973.

93—(1) This paragraph applies if—

(a)   a right falling within the definition of "uncertificated right" in section 552(2) is a right under an arrangement made on or before 16th July 1992, and

(b)   the right to call for the issue of a certificate of deposit (as defined in that section) is a right under that arrangement.

(2) Chapter 11 of Part 4 (transactions in deposits) applies with the omission of section 552(1)(c) and (d)(i).

Disposals of futures and options involving guaranteed returns: certain pre-6th February 1998 transactions

94—(1) A transaction consisting in the running of a future to delivery or the exercise of an option is not treated as a disposal for the purposes of Chapter 12 of Part 4 if it took place before 6th February 1998.

(2) Sub-paragraph (1) is to be read as if it were part of section 564 (deemed disposal where futures run to delivery or options are exercised) (see, in particular, section 565).

PART 6

SAVINGS AND INVESTMENT INCOME: INSURANCE CONTRACTS AND POLICIES MADE BEFORE CERTAIN DATES

Pre-20th March 1968 policies and contracts excluded from Chapter 9 of Part 4

96—(1) Chapter 9 of Part 4 does not apply to—

(*a*) a policy of life insurance issued in respect of an insurance made before 20th March 1968,

(*b*) a contract for a life annuity made before that date, or

(*c*) a capital redemption policy where the contract was made before that date.

(2) For this purpose a policy of life insurance is treated as issued in respect of an insurance made on or after 20th March 1968 if it is varied on or after that date so as to extend its term or increase the benefits secured.

(3) A variation is ignored for the purposes of sub-paragraph (2) if—

(*a*) before the variation the policy complied with paragraph 2 of Schedule 9 to FA 1968 (general requirements for qualifying endowment policies) except for the amount guaranteed on death,

(*b*) the variation's only effect was to make the policy comply with that paragraph,

(*c*) the variation was effected before 1st January 1969, and

(*d*) the variation did not increase the premiums payable under the policy.

Pre-27th March 1974 policies and contracts: disapplication of section 500(c)

97 Section 500(*c*) (events treated as part surrenders: loan by insurer) does not apply to a policy issued in respect of an insurance made before 27th March 1974 or a contract made before that date.

Pre-27th March 1974 contracts: disapplication of section 531(3)(c)

98 Section 531(3)(*c*) (certain contracts for life annuities excluded from section 530) does not apply to a contract made before 27th March 1974.

Pre-10th December 1974 contracts for a life annuity: disapplication of section 484(1)(d)

99 Section 484(1)(*d*) (chargeable events: death in case of contract for a life annuity which provides for payment of a capital sum on death) does not apply if the contract was made before 10th December 1974.

Pre-14th March 1975 policies and contracts: calculation of gains under section 507

100—(1) This paragraph applies to—

(*a*) a policy in respect of an insurance made before 14th March 1975, and

(*b*) a contract made before that date.

(2) Section 507 (method for making periodic calculations under section 498) applies to a policy or contract to which this paragraph applies with the following modifications.

(3) In subsection (4) (calculation of net total value of rights assigned and surrendered)—

(*a*) in paragraph (*a*) of step 1 after "at any time", in both places where it occurs, and

(*b*) in paragraph (*b*) of step 1 after "assigned", insert "during the reference period".

(4) In subsection (5) (calculation of net total allowable payments), for step 1 substitute—

"Step 1

Find the allowable element in each allowable payment made during the reference period by multiplying the amount of the payment by—

$$\frac{X}{20}$$

where X is the number of insurance years in the period beginning with the year in which the payment is made and ending with the reference period or, if it is less, 20."

(5) After that step insert—

"Step 1A

Find any allowable element in any allowable payment made before the reference period by multiplying the amount of the payment by—

$$\frac{20-Y}{20}$$

where Y is the number of insurance years in the period beginning with the year in which the payment is made and ending with the last insurance year before the reference period or, if it is less, 20."

(6) In subsection (6) insert the following definition in the appropriate place—

ITTOIA 2005

" "the reference period" means the period beginning with the first insurance year which falls wholly after 13th March 1975 and ending with the insurance year as at the end of which the calculation under this section is required to be made,".

Pre-25th March 1982 replacement policies: disapplication of section 542

101 Section 542 (replacement of qualifying policies) does not apply if the replacement policy comes into existence before 25th March 1982.

Certain pre-26th June 1982 policies and contracts excluded from Chapter 9 of Part 4

102—(1) Chapter 9 of Part 4 does not apply to a pre-1982 assigned policy or contract unless on a date after 23rd August 1982 it has met condition A, B or C.

(2) In sub-paragraph (1) "pre-1982 assigned policy or contract" means—

(*a*) a policy of life insurance issued in respect of an insurance made before 26th June 1982, or

(*b*) a contract for a life annuity made before that date,

the rights under which were assigned for money or money's worth before that date and are not held by the original beneficial owner.

(3) Condition A is that the rights under the policy or contract are again assigned for money or money's worth.

(4) Condition B is that a payment is made under the policy or contract by way of premium.

(5) Condition C is that a sum is lent—

(*a*) by, or by arrangement with, the body issuing the policy or the body with which the contract was made, and

(*b*) to or at the direction of an individual falling within sub-paragraph (6).

(6) An individual falls within this sub-paragraph at any time if—

(*a*) were a gain to arise in respect of the policy or contract at that time the individual—

(i) would be liable for tax in respect of it as a result of section 465 (person liable: individuals), or

(ii) would be so liable apart from the requirement in section 465(1) that the individual must be UK resident in the tax year in which the gain arises, or

(*b*) at that time the rights under the policy or contract are held on charitable trusts created by the individual.

(7) In the case of a qualifying policy, condition C is not met if—

(*a*) interest is payable on the loan at a commercial rate, or

(*b*) the loan is to a full-time employee of the body to assist the employee in purchasing or improving a dwelling to be used as the employee's only or main residence.

(8) In the case of a policy issued in respect of an insurance made before 27th March 1974 or a contract made before that date, this paragraph applies as if sub-paragraph (1) did not refer to condition C.

(9) A loan which causes condition C to be met is treated for the purposes of sections 500(*c*) and 501 (loans treated as part surrenders) as having been made at a time when Chapter 9 of Part 4 does apply to gains on the policy or contract.

Certain pre-18th November 1983 policies not foreign policies of life insurance

103—(1) A policy of life insurance is not a "foreign policy of life insurance" for the purposes of Chapter 9 of Part 4 (see the definition in section 476(3)) if it is issued in respect of an insurance made before 18th November 1983.

(2) For the purposes of sub-paragraph (1), a policy issued in respect of an insurance made before 18th November 1983 is treated as issued in respect of one made on or after that date if it is varied on or after that date so as—

(*a*) to increase the benefits secured, or

(*b*) to extend the term of the insurance.

(3) A change in the terms of a policy counts as its variation for the purposes of sub-paragraph (2) if it results from the exercise of an option conferred by the policy to have another policy substituted for it or to have any of its terms changed.

Certain pre-23rd February 1984 policies not foreign capital redemption policies

104 A capital redemption policy is not a "foreign capital redemption policy" for the purposes of Chapter 9 of Part 4 (see the definition in section 476(3)) if it is issued in respect of a contract made before 23rd February 1984.

Pre-14th March 1984 policies: disregard of amounts deducted and repaid after tax relief by deduction from premiums abolished

105   In the case of a policy issued in respect of an insurance made before 14th March 1984, any amount treated under section 72(9) of FA 1984 as an additional premium is to be ignored for the purposes of—

> (*a*)   calculating the total allowable deductions for the policy under section 494(1), and
>
> (*b*)   the definition of "allowable payment" in section 507(6).

Certain pre-20th March 1985 policies: application of section 529(1)

106—(1) This paragraph makes provision for the application of section 529(1) (exceptions to section 528) in relation to—

> (*a*)   a foreign policy of life insurance issued in respect of an insurance made on or before 19th March 1985, and
>
> (*b*)   a foreign capital redemption policy issued in respect of a contract made on or before that date.

(2) Section 529(1)(*a*) (which disapplies section 528 if when the chargeable event occurs or at any time during the policy period the policy is or was held by a non-UK resident trustee) does not apply if the policy was held by a non-UK resident trustee on 19th March 1985.

(3) Section 529(1)(*b*) (which disapplies section 528 if when the chargeable event occurs or at any time during the policy period the policy is or was held by non-UK resident trustees) does not apply if on 19th March 1985 the policy was held by a non-UK resident trustee or by two or more trustees any of whom was non-UK resident.

Pre-14th March 1989 qualifying policies: application of section 485(2)(b) and (3)(b)

107—(1) In the case of a policy issued in respect of an insurance made before 14th March 1989, section 485(2) and (3) (by virtue of which certain events are only chargeable events if the condition in paragraph (*a*) or (*b*) is met) have effect with the omission of paragraph (*b*) (company interest in the rights under the policy) and the word "or" preceding that paragraph.

(2) For this purpose a policy is treated as issued in respect of an insurance made on or after 14th March 1989 if it is varied on or after that date so as—

> (*a*)   to increase the benefits secured, or
>
> (*b*)   to extend the term of the insurance.

(3) Any exercise of rights conferred by a policy counts as its variation for the purposes of sub-paragraph (2).

Pre-14th March 1989 policies and contracts: application of section 501

108—(1) In the case of a policy issued in respect of an insurance made before 14th March 1989 or a contract made before that date, section 501 (part surrenders: loans) does not apply if—

> (*a*)   a company beneficially owns the rights under the policy,
>
> (*b*)   they are held on trusts which a company created, or
>
> (*c*)   they are held as security for a company's debt.

(2) For the purposes of this paragraph, a policy is treated as issued in respect of an insurance made on or after 14th March 1989 if it is varied on or after that date so as—

> (*a*)   to increase the benefits secured, or
>
> (*b*)   to extend the term of the insurance.

(3) Any exercise of rights conferred by a policy counts as its variation for the purposes of sub-paragraph (2).

Contracts in accounting periods beginning before 1st January 1992: disapplication of sections 530 and 539(3)

109—(1) This paragraph applies to a contract for a life annuity made—

> (*a*)   after 26th March 1974, but
>
> (*b*)   in an accounting period of the insurance company or friendly society beginning before 1st January 1992.

(2) Section 530 (income tax treated as paid etc) does not apply to gains from such a contract, except for the purposes of calculating relief under section 535 (top slicing relief).

(3) Sub-paragraph (2) is subject to—

> (*a*)   section 532 (relief for policies and contracts with European Economic Area insurers), and
>
> (*b*)   section 534 (regulations providing for relief in other cases where foreign tax chargeable).

(4) [Section 539 (relief for deficiencies) has effect as if for subsections (1) to (6) there were substituted—

"(1) A deficiency from a policy or contract arising on a chargeable event is allowable as a deduction in calculating an individual's net income for a tax year if, had a gain arisen instead on the chargeable event—

    (*a*)   the individual would have been liable to income tax on the gain for that year, or

    (*b*)   the individual would have been so liable apart from the requirement in section 465(1) that the individual must be UK resident in the tax year in which the gain arises.

(2) See section 540 for the cases in which a deficiency is treated as arising from a policy or contract on a chargeable event, section 541 for how the deficiency is calculated and section 469(5) for the apportionment of deficiencies in cases where two or more persons are interested in a policy or contract."]¹

(5) In sub-paragraph (1) "accounting period" is to be read in accordance with [Chapter 2 of Part 2 of CTA 2009]².

Amendments—¹   Words in sub-s (4) substituted by ITA 2007 s 1027, Sch 1 paras 492, 588, 590 with effect for income tax purposes from 6 April 2007, and corporation tax purposes for accounting periods ending after 5 April 2007.

²   In sub-para (5), words substituted by CTA 2009 s 1322, Sch 1 paras 587, 646(1), (4). CTA 2009 applies for accounting periods ending on or after 1 April 2009 (for corporation tax purposes) and for tax years 2009–10 onwards (for income and capital gains tax purposes).

Certain pre-17th March 1998 policies: application of section 529(1)

110—(1) This paragraph makes provision for the application of section 529(1) (exceptions to section 528) in relation to—

    (*a*)   a foreign policy of life insurance issued in respect of an insurance made before 17th March 1998, and

    (*b*)   a foreign capital redemption policy issued in respect of a contract made before that date.

(2) Section 529(1)(*c*) (which disapplies section 528 if when the chargeable event occurs or at any time during the policy period the policy is or was held by a foreign institution) does not apply if the policy was held by a foreign institution on 16th March 1998.

Certain pre-17th March 1998 policies not foreign policies of life insurance

111—(1) A policy of life insurance issued in respect of an insurance made before 17th March 1998 is only a "foreign policy of life insurance" for the purposes of Chapter 9 of Part 4 if—

    (*a*)   it falls within paragraph (*a*) of the definition of that expression in section 476(3), and

    (*b*)   it is not excluded by paragraph 103 (certain pre-18th November 1983 policies not foreign policies of life insurance).

(2) For the purposes of sub-paragraph (1), a policy issued in respect of an insurance made before 17th March 1998 is treated as issued in respect of one made on or after that date if it is varied on or after that date so as—

    (*a*)   to increase the benefits secured, or

    (*b*)   to extend the term of the insurance.

(3) Any exercise of rights conferred by a policy counts as its variation for the purposes of sub-paragraph (2).

Pre-17th March 1998 policy or contract: UK resident trustees

112—(1) In the case of a 1998 Act excluded policy or contract, section 467 (person liable: UK resident trustees) does not apply if—

    (*a*)   the trusts were created before 17th March 1998, and

    (*b*)   the person or at least one of the persons who created them was an individual who died before that date.

(2) For the purposes of sub-paragraph (1)(*b*), section 472(1) is ignored.

(3) In this paragraph "a 1998 Act excluded policy or contract" means—

    (*a*)   a policy of life insurance issued in respect of an insurance made before 17th March 1998,

    (*b*)   a contract for a life annuity made before that date, or

    (*c*)   a capital redemption policy where the contract was made before that date,

but excluding a policy or contract within sub-paragraph (4).

(4) A policy or contract is within this sub-paragraph if it has been varied on or after 17th March 1998 so as—

    (*a*)   to increase the benefits secured, or

    (*b*)   to extend the term of the insurance, annuity or capital redemption policy.

(5) Any exercise of rights conferred by a policy or contract counts as its variation for the purposes of sub-paragraph (4).

Certain pre-23rd March 1999 policies not foreign capital redemption policies

113   A capital redemption policy where the contract was made before 23rd March 1999 is only a "foreign capital redemption policy" for the purposes of Chapter 9 of Part 4 if—

   (*a*) it falls within paragraph (*a*) of the definition of that expression in section 476(3), and

   (*b*) it is not excluded by paragraph 104 (certain pre-23rd February 1984 policies not foreign capital redemption policies).

Pre-9th April 2003 policy or contract: UK resident trustees

114—(1) In the case of a 2003 Act excluded policy or contract, section 467(1) (person liable: UK resident trustees) has effect with the omission of the reference to condition C (the effect of which is to extend the circumstances in which trustees holding rights under a policy or contract on non-charitable trusts may be liable for tax).

(2) In this paragraph "a 2003 Act excluded policy or contract" means—

   (*a*) a policy of life insurance issued in respect of an insurance made before 9th April 2003,

   (*b*) a contract for a life annuity made before that date, or

   (*c*) a capital redemption policy where the contract was made before that date,

   but excluding a policy or contract within sub-paragraph (3).

(3) A policy or contract is within this sub-paragraph if—

   (*a*) it has been varied on or after that date (but before the chargeable event on which the gain arises) so as to increase the benefits secured or extend the term of the insurance, annuity or capital redemption policy, or

   (*b*) there has been an assignment of the rights, or a share in the rights, conferred by the policy or contract to trustees of a non-charitable trust.

(4) Any exercise of rights conferred by a policy or contract counts as its variation for the purposes of sub-paragraph (3)(*a*).

Pre-9th April 2003 policy or contract: loans to trustees

115—(1) This paragraph makes provision for the application of section 501 (part surrenders: loans) in relation to—

   (*a*) a policy of life insurance issued in respect of an insurance made before 9th April 2003,

   (*b*) a contract for a life annuity made before that date, or

   (*c*) a capital redemption policy where the contract was made before that date.

(2) In the case of a loan made before that date that section applies with the omission—

   (*a*) of subsections (1)(*b*) and (3) (by virtue of which the section applies to loans to trustees), and

   (*b*) in subsection (5)(*b*) of the words ", trustees" and ", trustees'".

Pre-9th April 2003 policy: excepted group life policies

116—(1) Sub-paragraph (2) applies to a policy if—

   (*a*) it was issued in respect of an insurance made before 9th April 2003, and

   (*b*) immediately before 6th April 2005, paragraph 4(1) (excepted group life policies: time for compliance with conditions in section 539A of ICTA) of Schedule 34 to FA 2003 applied to it.

(2) The policy is to be taken to have met the conditions referred to in section 480(3) (conditions to be met by an excepted group life policy) throughout the period mentioned in that paragraph.

(3) Sub-paragraphs (3) and (4) apply where immediately before 6th April 2005 paragraph 4(3) of Schedule 34 to FA 2003 applied to treat two policies as a single policy issued in respect of an insurance made at the time of the making of the insurance in respect of which the earlier of those policies was issued.

(4) Those policies are to be treated as a single policy so issued for the purposes of—

   (*a*) Chapter 9 of Part 4,

   (*b*) paragraph 90 of this Schedule, and

   (*c*) this Part of this Schedule (and, in particular, sub-paragraph (2)).

(5) Sub-paragraph (2) applies to that single policy taking the reference to the period mentioned in paragraph 4(1) of Schedule 34 to FA 2003 as a reference to the period so mentioned as a result of the application of paragraph 4(3)(*b*) of that Schedule.

Pre-3rd March 2004 policy or contract: calculation of deficiencies

117—(1) In the case of a 2004 Act excluded policy or contract, section 541(4) (calculation of deficiencies) applies with the omission of paragraph (*b*) and the word "and" immediately preceding it.

(2) In this paragraph "a 2004 Act excluded policy or contract" means—

    (*a*) a policy of life insurance issued in respect of an insurance made before 3rd March 2004,

    (*b*) a contract for a life annuity made before that date, or

    (*c*) a capital redemption policy where the contract was made before that date,

      but excluding a policy or contract within sub-paragraph (3).

(3) A policy or contract is within this sub-paragraph if on or after 3rd March 2004—

    (*a*) it is varied so as to increase the benefits secured,

    (*b*) there is an assignment of the rights, or a share of the rights, conferred by it, or

    (*c*) all or part of those rights become held as security for a debt.

(4) Any exercise of rights conferred by a policy or contract counts as its variation for the purposes of sub-paragraph (3)(*a*).

Pre-1st January 2005 contracts for immediate needs annuities: income tax treated as paid

118—(1) A contract for a life annuity made before 1st January 2005 is not to be treated for the purposes of paragraph (*c*) of section 531(3) (policies and contracts excluded from section 530) as having not formed part of any insurance company's or friendly society's basic life assurance and general annuity business the income and gains of which are subject to corporation tax by reason only of the immediate needs annuities exclusion.

(2) In sub-paragraph (1) "the immediate needs annuities exclusion" [means the application of section 57(2)(*d*) of FA 2012[1]][2]

Amendments—[1]   Words in sub-para (2) substituted by FA 2007 s 38, Sch 7 paras 76, 79 with effect for income tax purposes from 2007–08, and for corporation tax purposes for periods of account of insurance companies beginning on or after 1 January 2007. This is subject to the transitional provisions in FA 2007 Sch 7 Pt 2.

[2]   In sub-para (2) words substituted for words "means the words following paragraph (*b*) in the definition of "life assurance business" in section 431(2) of ICTA.", by FA 2012 s 146, Sch 16 paras 125, 131 with effect in relation to accounting periods of companies beginning on or after 1 January 2013 (subject to transitional provisions in FA 2012 Sch 17). For accounting periods straddling 1 January 2013, see FA 2012 s 149.

PART 7

SAVINGS AND INVESTMENT INCOME: GAINS FROM CONTRACTS FOR LIFE INSURANCE ETC (PERSONAL PORTFOLIO BONDS)

Pre-17th March 1998 contract or policy: conditions to be met for contract or policy not to be a personal portfolio bond

119   For the purposes of Chapter 9 of Part 4, a policy or contract is not a personal portfolio bond if—

    (*a*) it meets the date condition (see paragraph 120),

    (*b*) it meets the non-variation condition (see paragraph 121), and

    (*c*) it meets either the first selection condition (see paragraph 122) or the second selection condition (see paragraph 123).

The date condition

120—(1) A policy meets the date condition if it is a policy issued in respect of an insurance made before 17th March 1998.

(2) A contract meets the date condition if it was made before that date.

The non-variation condition

121—(1) A policy or contract meets the non-variation condition if it has not been varied on or after 16th July 1998 so as—

    (*a*) to increase the benefits secured, or

    (*b*) to extend the term of the policy or contract.

(2) Any exercise of rights conferred by a policy or contract counts as its variation for the purposes of this paragraph.

The first selection condition

122   A policy or contract meets the first selection condition at any time if for the whole of the period beginning with 6th April 1994 and ending with that time it has not been possible to determine the whole or any part of the benefits under the policy or contract by reference to—

    (*a*) an index other than a permitted index (see paragraph 126), or

    (*b*) property other than permitted property (see paragraph 127).

The second selection condition

123—(1) A policy or contract meets the second selection condition at any time if it meets conditions A to C.

(2) Condition A is that for some or all of the period beginning with 6th April 1994 and ending with that time it has been possible to determine the whole or any part of the benefits under the policy or contract by reference to—

    (*a*) an index other than a permitted index, or

    (*b*) property other than permitted property.

(3) Condition B is that at no time during that period have the benefits under the policy or contract actually been determined by reference to such property or such an index.

(4) Condition C is that the terms of the policy or contract were varied before the end of the first insurance year in relation to the policy or contract which began on or after 6th April 1999 so that, since that variation,—

    (*a*) the only index which it has been possible to select as mentioned in section 516(4) is a permitted index, and

    (*b*) the only property which it has been possible to select as mentioned in section 516(4) is permitted property.

(5) Condition C is subject to paragraphs 124 and 125 (which modify it in cases where any holder of the policy or contract was not UK resident on 17th March 1998 and has become UK resident since that date).

Policy holders becoming UK resident after 17th March 1998

124—(1) This paragraph applies to a policy or contract if—

    (*a*) any holder of the policy or contract on 17th March 1998 was not UK resident on that date,

    (*b*) such a holder has become UK resident since that date, and

    (*c*) the holder did not intend, on the date of the holder's arrival in the United Kingdom by virtue of which the holder became UK resident—

        (i) to become permanently UK resident, or

        (ii) to stay in the United Kingdom for at least two years.

(2) The policy or contract meets condition C in the second selection condition if it has been varied as described in that condition before the later of—

    (*a*) the end of the first insurance year in relation to the policy or contract beginning on or after 6th April 1999, and

    (*b*) the end of the first insurance year in relation to the policy or contract beginning after the date since 17th March 1998 on which the holder of the policy or contract first became UK resident.

(3) No gain is treated as arising from the policy or contract under section 525 (chargeable events where annual personal portfolio calculations show gains) in relation to any insurance year which ends—

    (*a*) on or after the date since 17th March 1998 on which the holder of the policy or contract first became UK resident, and

    (*b*) before the insurance year in which the variation was made.

Policy holders becoming permanently UK resident after 17th March 1998

125—(1) This paragraph applies to a policy or contract if—

    (*a*) any holder of the policy or contract on 17th March 1998 was a non-UK resident individual on that date,

    (*b*) such a holder has become UK resident since that date, and

    (*c*) the holder intended, on the date of the holder's arrival in the United Kingdom by virtue of which the holder became UK resident,—

        (i) to become permanently UK resident, or

        (ii) to stay in the United Kingdom for at least two years.

(2) The policy or contract meets condition C in the second selection condition if it has been varied as described in that condition before the later of—

    (*a*) the end of the first insurance year in relation to the policy or contract beginning on or after 6th April 1999, and

    (*b*) the end of the first insurance year in relation to the policy or contract beginning on or after the date mentioned in sub-paragraph (1)(*c*).

(3) No gain is treated as arising from the policy or contract under section 525 in relation to any insurance year which ends—

    (*a*) on or after the date since 17th March 1998 on which the holder of the policy or contract first became UK resident, and

(b) before the insurance year in which the variation was made.

Meaning of "permitted index"

126   In this Part of this Schedule "permitted index" means an index falling within a category listed in section 518.

Meaning of "permitted property"

127—(1) In this Part of this Schedule "permitted property", in relation to a policy or contract, means any of the following—
  (a) property falling within any of the categories listed in the table in section 520(2),
  (b) shares or securities listed on a recognised stock exchange, and
  (c) subject to sub-paragraph (2), shares or securities of a company which are dealt in on the Unlisted Securities Market or the Alternative Investment Market.
(2) Shares or securities of a company which fall within sub-paragraph (1)(c) are not permitted property at any time at which—
  (a) the whole or any part of the benefits under the policy or contract may be determined by reference to shares or securities of the company which represent more than 10% of its issued share capital, or
  (b) the amount invested in shares or securities of the company under the policy or contract exceeds 10% of the total amount of premiums paid up to that time under the policy or contract.

Other definitions

128—(1) In this Part of this Schedule "security" has the same meaning as in section 132(3)(b) of TCGA 1992.
(2) Any references in this Part of this Schedule to shares or securities include a reference to any option, warrant or other right to acquire shares or securities.
(3) In sub-paragraph (3) "warrant" has the same meaning as in paragraph 14 of Schedule 2 to FISMA 2000.

PART 8
MISCELLANEOUS INCOME

Intellectual property: contributions to expenditure not made by public bodies nor eligible for tax relief

129   Section 604 applies with the omission of subsection (3)(b) in relation to contributions made before 27th July 1989.

Certain telecommunication rights

130   Chapter 4 of Part 5 does not apply to an indefeasible right to use a telecommunications cable system ("IRU") acquired before 21st March 2000.

131—(1) That Chapter also does not apply to an IRU acquired by a person on or after that date (directly or indirectly) from an associate or an associated company if the associate or associated company acquired the IRU before that date.
(2) In sub-paragraph (1)—
    "associate" has the meaning given by [section 448 of CTA 2010][1], and
    "associated company"—
      (a) in relation to another company, has the meaning given by [section 449 of that Act][1], and
      (b) in relation to any other person, means a company of which that person has control within the meaning of [sections 450 and 451 of that Act][1].

Amendments—[1]   In sub-para (2) in the definitions of "associate" and "associated company, words substituted by CTA 2010 s 1177, Sch 1 paras 444, 471(1),(4). CTA 2010 has effect for corporation tax purposes for accounting periods ending on or after 1 April 2010, and for income and capital gains tax purposes for the tax year 2010–11 and subsequent tax years.

Income treated as income of settlor: exception for pension income

132—(1) Subject to sub-paragraph (4), section 627 applies before 6th April 2006 with the following amendments.
(2) In subsection (2)(c) for "a relevant pension scheme" substitute "an approved pension arrangement".
(3) For subsection (3) substitute—

"(3) In subsection (2) an "approved pension arrangement" means—

(*a*) an approved scheme or exempt approved scheme,

(*b*) a relevant statutory scheme,

(*c*) a retirement benefits scheme set up by a government outside the United Kingdom for the benefit, or primarily for the benefit, of its employees,

(*d*) a contract or scheme which is approved under Chapter 3 of Part 14 of ICTA (retirement annuities),

(*e*) a personal pension scheme which is approved under Chapter 4 of that Part,

(*f*) an annuity purchased for the purpose of giving effect to rights under a scheme falling within any of paragraphs (*a*) to (*c*) and (*e*), or

(*g*) any pension arrangements of any description prescribed by regulations made under section 11(2)(*h*) of the Welfare Reform and Pensions Act 1999 (c 30) or Article 12(2)(*h*) of the Welfare Reform and Pensions (Northern Ireland) Order 1999 (SI 1999/3147 (NI 11)).

(4) In subsection (3) "approved scheme", "exempt approved scheme", "relevant statutory scheme" and "retirement benefits scheme" have the same meaning as in Chapter 1 of Part 14 of ICTA (retirement benefit schemes)."

(4) The power of the Treasury to make an order under section 281 or 283 of FA 2004 has effect as if Schedule 35 to that Act contained an amendment substituting section 627 of this Act for that section as amended by sub-paragraphs (2) and (3) above.

Amounts treated as income of settlor: income paid to unmarried minor children of settlor

133—(1) In relation to income which—

(*a*) arises under a settlement made or entered into before 9th March 1999, and

(*b*) does not arise directly or indirectly from funds provided on or after that date,

section 629 applies with the omission from subsection (1) of paragraph (b) and the word "or" before that paragraph.

(2) Where subsection (1) of section 629 applies for a tax year only in relation to such income as is mentioned in sub-paragraph (1), that section applies with the substitution for subsections (3) and (4) of—

"(3) Income paid to or for the benefit of a child of a settlor is not treated as provided in subsection (1) for a tax year in which the total amount paid to or for the benefit of that child which but for this subsection would be so treated does not exceed £100."

(3) Where subsection (1) of section 629 applies for a tax year in relation to such income as is mentioned in sub-paragraph (1) above and other income, that section applies with the substitution for subsection (4) of—

"(4) In subsection (3) a child's "relevant settlement income" means income which (apart from that subsection) would be treated as income of the settlor under subsection (1) and which—

(*a*) so far as consisting of such income as is mentioned in paragraph 133 of Schedule 2, is income paid to or for the benefit of the child, and

(*b*) so far as consisting of other income, is income paid to or for the benefit of, or otherwise treated as income of, the child."

(4) Any apportionment required for the purposes of sub-paragraph (1)(*b*) is to be made on a just and reasonable basis.

Amounts treated as income of settlor: capital sums paid to settlor by trustees of settlement

134—(1) In relation to any case which involves any previous tax years before 1995–96, subsection (3) of section 635 applies in accordance with sub-paragraphs (2) and (3) below.

(2) So far as that subsection applies in relation to those previous tax years, for paragraph (*c*) substitute—

"(*c*) so much of any income arising under the settlement in any previous year which has not been distributed as is shown to consist of income which has been treated as income of the settlor by virtue of section 671, 672, 674, 674A or 683 of ICTA,

(*d*) any income arising under the settlement in any previous year which has been treated as the income of the settlor by virtue of section 673 of ICTA,

(*e*) any sums paid by virtue or in consequence of the settlement, to the extent that they are not allowable, by virtue of section 676 of ICTA, as deductions in computing the settlor's income for any previous year,

(*f*) any sums paid by virtue or in consequence of the settlement in any previous year which have been treated as the income of the settlor by virtue of section 664(2)(*b*) of ICTA,

> (g)   any sums included in the income arising under the settlement as amounts which have been or could have been apportioned to a beneficiary as mentioned in section 681(1)(*b*) of ICTA, and".

(3) For paragraph (*d*) of that subsection substitute—

> "(h)   an amount equal to the sum of tax at the rate applicable to trusts on—
>
> > (i)   the total amount of income arising under the settlement in that year and any previous year which has not been distributed, less
> >
> > (ii)   the total amount of the income and sums referred to in paragraph (*c*) (in relation to tax years 1995–96 onwards) and paragraphs (*c*), (*d*), (*e*), (*f*) and (*g*) as substituted by paragraph 134 of Schedule 2 (in relation to tax years before 1995–96)."

(4) In relation to any sum paid before 6th April 1995, subsection (3) of section 634 applies with the substitution of "in one of the events specified in section 673(3) of ICTA" for paragraphs (*a*) and (*b*).

(5) Subsection (5)(*a*) of section 634 does not apply if the direction or assignment was given or made before 6th April 1981.

Amounts treated as income of settlor: capital sums paid to settlor by body connected with settlement

135   In relation to any capital sum paid to the settlor before tax year 1995–96, section 641 applies with the insertion after subsection (6) of—

> "(6A)   Where a capital sum is paid to the settlor in a tax year by a body corporate connected with the settlement in that year it is to be assumed until the contrary is shown that an associated payment of an amount not less than that of the capital sum has been made to that body by the trustees of the settlement."

Beneficiaries' income from estates in administration: basic amounts

136—(1) Sub-paragraph (2) applies if any previous tax year to which regard is to be had for the purposes of section 665 (assumed income entitlement) is a tax year before 2005–06 (an "old tax year").

(2) In relation to the old tax year, the reference in step 4 in subsection (1) of that section to basic amounts relating to the person's absolute interest in respect of which the person is liable to income tax for that year is to be taken as a reference to the amount deemed to have been paid to that person as income for that year in respect of that interest by virtue of section 696 of ICTA.

(3) Sub-paragraph (4) applies if one or more of the absolute interests referred to in section 671(1) (successive absolute interests) was held in one or more old tax years.

(4) The reference in section 671(2)(*b*) to the basic amounts relating to any previous such interest includes a reference to the amounts deemed to have been paid to the previous holder as income for the old tax years in respect of that interest by virtue of section 696 of ICTA.

(5) Sub-paragraph (6) applies if any of the limited interests referred to in section 672(1)(*d*) (successive interests: assumed income entitlement of holder of absolute interest following limited interest) was held in one or more old tax years.

(6) The reference in section 672(4) to the basic amounts relating to any previous such interest includes a reference to the amounts deemed to have been paid to the holders of any such interests as income for the old tax years in respect of those interests by virtue of section 695 of ICTA.

(7) In the case of a UK estate, references in this paragraph to the amounts deemed to have been paid are references to the amounts that would be deemed to have been paid apart from sections 695(4)(*a*) and 696(4) of ICTA (grossing up).

Beneficiaries' income from estates in administration: income treated as bearing income tax

137   A sum treated as part of the aggregate income of an estate by virtue of section 547(1)(*c*) of ICTA (gains from life insurance contracts etc) as the result of an event that occurred before 6th April 2004 is treated for the purposes mentioned in section 680 of this Act as bearing income tax at the basic rate.

PART 9
EXEMPT INCOME

Ulster savings certificates

138   In the case of certificates acquired before 27th July 1981, section 693(5) applies with the substitution for "the Department of Finance and Personnel" of "the Treasury".

SAYE interest

139   Any scheme which was certified as mentioned in section 326(2)(*c*), (3)(*b*) or (4)(*b*) of ICTA before 1st December 1994 is treated as a certified SAYE savings arrangement for the purposes of Chapter 4 of Part 6 of this Act.

140   A European authorised institution arrangement is not an institutional arrangement for the purposes of Chapter 4 of Part 6 if the arrangement was established before 2nd May 1995.

141—(1) Neither—

     (*a*)   the Treasury specification rules, nor

     (*b*)   the Treasury authorisation rules,

apply to any scheme which was certified as mentioned in section 326(3)(b), (4)(b) or (5)(b) of ICTA before 31st July 1995.

(2) In sub-paragraph (1)—

     "the Treasury specification rules" means sections 705(1)(*b*) and (2) to (4) and 706 of this Act, and

     "the Treasury authorisation rules" means sections 707 and 708 of this Act.

Venture capital trust dividends: shares acquired before the tax year 2004–05

142   In the case of dividends paid in respect of shares acquired before the tax year 2004–05, Chapter 5 of Part 6 (venture capital trust dividends) applies as if the references in section 709(4) (annual acquisition limit) to £200,000 were references to £100,000.

Purchased life annuity payments: carry forward of excess capital elements

144—(1) This paragraph applies if, in the case of an annuity to which section 656(2) of ICTA applied immediately before 6th April 2005, the total of the amounts determined in accordance with that section to be capital elements in respect of the annuity payments that arose before that date (and accordingly not to be annual payments for income tax purposes) exceeded the total of those annuity payments.

(2) The amount of the excess is to be added to the fixed sum mentioned in section 719(4) for the first payment that arises after 5th April 2005.

Certain annual payments by individuals

146—(1) Sections 727 (exemption for certain annual payments by individuals) and 730 (exemption for foreign maintenance payments) do not apply to—

     (*a*)   any payment falling due before 16th March 1988, or

     (*b*)   any payment falling due on or after that date but before 6th April 2000 to which this paragraph applies.

(2) Paragraph (*b*) of sub-paragraph (1) applies to a payment made in pursuance of an existing obligation (within the meaning of section 36(3) of FA 1988) unless it meets any of conditions A to E.

(3) Condition A is that the payment is treated as income of the payer under Chapter 5 of Part 5 as a result of section 624 or 629.

(4) Condition B is that the payment fell due from a husband to a wife or a wife to a husband at a time after 5th April 1990 when they were living together.

(5) Condition C is that an election is duly made under section 39 of FA 1988 in respect of the payment.

(6) Condition D is that the payment fell due on or after 6th April 1994 and is made—

     (*a*)   in pursuance of an obligation within section 36(4)(*a*) to (*c*) of FA 1988 that is an obligation under—

         (i)   an order made by a court,

         (ii)   a written or oral agreement, or

         (iii) a deed executed for giving effect to an agreement, and

     (*b*)   for the benefit, maintenance or education of a person (whether or not the person to whom the payment is made) who attained the age of 21 on or before the day on which the payment fell due but after 5th April 1994.

(7) Condition E is that—

     (*a*)   the payment is made in pursuance of an obligation within section 36(4)(*a*) of FA 1988 (existing obligations under certain court orders),

     (*b*)   the payment is made for the benefit, maintenance or education of a person (whether or not the person to whom the payment is made) who attained the age of 21 before 6th April 1994, and

     (*c*)   section 38 of FA 1988 (treatment of certain maintenance payments under existing obligations) does not apply to the payment.

Commentary—*Simon's Taxes* **E1.514.**

Annual payments for non-taxable consideration

147   Section 729 (exemption for payments for non-taxable consideration) applies in the case of an annuity granted before 30th March 1977—

(*a*) with the substitution in subsection (1) of "condition B, C or D" for "condition B or C", and

(*b*) with the substitution of the following subsections for subsection (5)—

"(5)   Condition D is that the payment is a payment under an annuity charged on an interest in settled property and granted by an individual to a company—

(*a*)   whose business then consisted wholly or mainly in the acquisition of interests in settled property, or

(*b*)   which was then carrying on life assurance business in the United Kingdom.

(6)   In the application of subsections (4) and (5) to Scotland, the references in those subsections to settled property are to be read as references to property held in trust."

Commentary—*Simon's Taxes* **E1.514.**

Periodical payments of personal injury damages etc

148—(1) Subject to sub-paragraphs (4) and (5), sections 731, 733 and 734 apply with the modifications in sub-paragraphs (2) and (3).

(2) In section 731 (periodical payments of personal injury damages)—

(*a*) for subsection (2) substitute—

"(2)   This subsection applies to periodical payments made in pursuance of—

(*a*)   a court order making a final or interim award of damages in respect of personal injury,

(*b*)   an agreement settling a claim or action for such damages, or

(*c*)   an agreement for a payment on account of the damages that may be awarded in such an action.",

(*b*) in subsection (3)(*b*) for the words from "agreement" to the end of the paragraph substitute "or agreement as is mentioned in subsection (2) or a subsequent agreement", and

(*c*) omit subsection (6).

(3) In sections 733(*a*) and 734(1)(*a*)(i) for "agreement, undertaking" substitute "or agreement".

(4) The modifications in sub-paragraphs (2) and (3) do not apply if an order has been made under section 110(1) of the Courts Act 2003 (c 39) (commencement) making provision for section 100(2) and (3) of that Act to come into force on a day earlier than 6th April 2005.

(5) The power in section 110(1) of that Act includes power to make provision in accordance with which the modifications in sub-paragraphs (2) and (3) do not apply on or after a day appointed by the order that is later than 5th April 2005.

PART 10
FOSTER-CARE RELIEF

149—(1) This paragraph applies if—

(*a*) a disposal event is treated as occurring in relation to an individual under paragraph 17(2) of Schedule 36 to FA 2003 (foster-care relief: capital allowances),

(*b*) the individual is a relevant individual for the tax year 2004–05,

(*c*) the individual has a chargeable period which corresponds to the income period for the individual's foster-care receipts in that tax year (and therefore the chargeable period is a relevant chargeable period), and

(*d*) the next chargeable period of the individual is not a relevant chargeable period.

(2) Subsection (4) of section 825 applies (despite anything in subsection (1) of that section to the contrary) as if the reference to the first subsequent chargeable period which is not a relevant chargeable period were to the period mentioned in sub-paragraph (1)(*d*).

PART 11
FOREIGN INCOME: SPECIAL RULES

Relief for backdated pensions charged on arising basis

152   The fact that the earlier year referred to in subsections (1)(*b*) and (2) of section 840 (relief for backdated pensions charged on the arising basis) is a tax year before 2005–06 does not prevent—

(*a*) a claim being made under that section, or

(*b*) such adjustments (by way of repayment of tax, assessment or otherwise) as are necessary to give effect to that section being made as respects such a tax year.

Unremittable income that arose before the tax year 2005–06

153—(1) A claim may be made under section 842 (claim for relief on unremittable income) for the tax year 2005–06 or any later tax year, despite the income having arisen in a tax year before 2005–06.

(2) . . . [1]

(3) Sub-paragraph (4) applies if an appeal against an assessment for the tax year 2005–06 or a later tax year involves a question as to the operation of section 584 of ICTA or Chapter 4 of Part 8 of this Act as respects income that arose in a tax year before 2005–06.

(4) . . . [1]

Amendments—[1] Sub-paras (2), (4) repealed by the Transfer of Tribunal Functions and Revenue and Customs Appeals Order, SI 2009/56 art 3, Sch 1 para 444 with effect from 1 April 2009.

PART 12
OTHER PROVISIONS

Unpaid remuneration: non-trades and non-property businesses

154—(1) This paragraph applies for the purposes of section 865.

(2) In relation to a period of account ending before 27th November 2002, an amount charged in the accounts in respect of employees' remuneration includes an amount which is held by an intermediary with a view to its becoming employees' remuneration.

(3) In relation to a period of account ending on or after 27th November 2002, an amount charged in the accounts in respect of employees' remuneration includes an amount—

    (*a*) in respect of employee benefit contributions (within the meaning of sections 38 to 44) made before that date, and

    (*b*) which is held by an intermediary,

    with a view to its becoming employees' remuneration.

Employee benefit contributions: non-trades and non-property businesses

155 Section 866 does not apply to deductions that would otherwise be allowed—

    (*a*) for a period ending before 27th November 2002, or

    (*b*) in respect of employee benefit contributions made before that date.

156—(1) Subject to sub-paragraph (3), section 866 applies before 6th April 2006 with the following amendment.

(2) In subsection (5)—

    (*a*) for paragraphs (*b*) and (*c*) and the word "or" at the end of paragraph (*c*) substitute—

        "(*b*)   contributions under a retirement benefits scheme within the meaning of Chapter 1 of Part 14 of ICTA (see section 611 of that Act),

        (*c*)   contributions under a personal pension scheme approved under Chapter 4 of that Part (see section 630 of that Act), or", and

    (*b*) omit "For the purposes of paragraph (*c*)" to the end.

(3) The power of the Treasury to make an order under section 281 or 283 of FA 2004 has effect as if Schedule 35 to that Act contained an amendment substituting section 866(5) of this Act for that subsection as amended by sub-paragraph (2) above.

Crime-related payments: non-trades and non-property businesses

157 Section 870(2)(*b*) does not apply to expenditure which was incurred before 1st April 2002.

Apportionment of miscellaneous profits or losses to tax years before tax year 2005–06

158—(1) This paragraph applies if—

    (*a*) a relevant period of account begins before 6th April 2005 and ends on or after that date, and

    (*b*) in order to arrive at the profits or losses of a tax year before the tax year 2005–06 it is necessary to apportion the profits or losses of the relevant period of account to any part of that period falling in a tax year before the tax year 2005–06.

(2) A period of account is a "relevant period of account" if—

    (*a*) section 871 applies to the period of account, and

    (*b*) the profits or losses of the part of the period of account falling in the tax year 2005–06 are calculated in accordance with this Act.

(3) The profits or losses of the relevant period of account—

    (*a*) are calculated in accordance with this Act (and therefore, to that extent, this Act has effect for tax years before the tax year 2005–06), and

    (*b*) may be apportioned in accordance with section 871 to any part of the period of account falling in a tax year before the tax year 2005–06.

General deduction rules

159 Neither—

(*a*) the inclusion of rules in section 582 for calculating income chargeable to tax under section 579, nor

(*b*) the inclusion of rules in sections 612 and 617(3) to (6) for calculating income chargeable to tax under Chapter 3 or 4 of Part 5,

prevents the continued operation of similar rules of law in relation to the calculation of other income (including profits) chargeable to tax under other provisions of this Act.

Section 820 of ICTA

160 Section 820 of ICTA (application of Income Tax Acts from year to year) applies to this Act as if this Act were in force on the day before 6th April 2005.

Amendments of Part 4 of FA 2004 (pension schemes etc)

161 The amendments made by paragraphs 644 to 651 and 655 of Schedule 1 come into force at the same time as the enactments which they amend.

SCHEDULE 3

REPEALS AND REVOCATIONS

Section 884

SCHEDULE 4

ABBREVIATIONS AND DEFINED EXPRESSIONS

Section 885

PART 1

ABBREVIATIONS OF ACTS

[FA followed by a year	The Finance Act of that year
F(No 2)A followed by a year	The Finance (No 2) Act of that year][3]
TMA 1970	The Taxes Management Act 1970 (c 9)
IHTA 1984	The Inheritance Tax Act 1984 (c 51)
ICTA	The Income and Corporation Taxes Act 1988 (c 1)
TCGA 1992	The Taxation of Chargeable Gains Act 1992 (c 12)
VATA 1994	The Value Added Tax Act 1994 (c 23)
FISMA 2000	The Financial Services and Markets Act 2000 (c 8)
CAA 2001	The Capital Allowances Act 2001 (c 2)
ITEPA 2003	The Income Tax (Earnings and Pensions) Act 2003 (c 1)
[ITA 2007	The Income Tax Act 2007][1]
[CTA 2009	The Corporation Tax Act 2009][2]
[CTA 2010	The Corporation Tax Act 2010][4]
[TIOPA 2010	The Taxation (International and Other Provisions) Act 2010][5]

Amendments—[1] Entry inserted by ITA 2007 s 1027, Sch 1 paras 492, 588, 591 with effect for income tax purposes from 6 April 2007, and corporation tax purposes for accounting periods ending after 5 April 2007.

[2] Entry inserted by CTA 2009 s 1322, Sch 1 paras 587, 647(1), (2). CTA 2009 applies for accounting periods ending on or after 1 April 2009 (for corporation tax purposes) and for tax years 2009–10 onwards (for income and capital gains tax purposes).

[3] Entries inserted, and entries relating to a Finance Act or a Finance (No 2) Act repealed, by FA 2009 s 126(3), (4) with effect from 21 July 2009.

[4] Entry inserted by CTA 2010 s 1177, Sch 1 paras 444, 472(1), (2). CTA 2010 has effect for corporation tax purposes for accounting periods ending on or after 1 April 2010, and for income and capital gains tax purposes for the tax year 2010–11 and subsequent tax years.

[5] Entry inserted by TIOPA 2010 s 501, Sch 8 paras 324, 325. TIOPA 2010 has effect for corporation tax purposes for accounting periods ending on or after 1 April 2010, for income and capital gains tax purposes for the tax year 2010–11 and subsequent tax years, and for petroleum revenue tax purposes for chargeable periods beginning on or after 1 July 2010.

PART 2

INDEX OF EXPRESSIONS DEFINED IN THIS ACT ETC

[abandonment guarantee (in Chapter 16A of Part 2)	section 225N(6)][11]

absolute interest (for the purposes of Chapter 6 of Part 5)	section 650(1)
accounting date (in Chapter 15 of Part 2)	section 197
accounting period	[section]8 [section 1119 of CTA 2010]9 [and Chapter 2 of Part 2 of CTA 2009]8
acquisition expenditure (in Chapter 9 of Part 2)	section 130(3)
[additional rate	section 6(2) of ITA 2007 (as applied by section 989 of that Act)]10
adjustment expense (in Chapter 17 of Part 2)	section 228(3)
adjustment expense (in Chapter 7 of Part 3)	section 330(3)
adjustment income (in Chapter 17 of Part 2)	section 228(2)
adjustment income (in Chapter 7 of Part 3)	section 330(2)
the administration period (in Chapter 6 of Part 5)	section 653(1)
the aggregate income of the estate (for the purposes of Chapter 6 of Part 5)	section 664(1)
the amount of premiums paid (in Chapter 9 of Part 4)	section 545(3)
animal (in Chapter 8 of Part 2)	section 112(1)
[animal (in Chapter 16ZA of Part 2)	section 225ZG]13
animal being added to a herd (in Chapter 8 of Part 2)	section 112(6)
animals in a herd or part of a herd (for the purposes of Chapter 8 of Part 2)	section 112(3) to (5)
assignment (in the application of the Act to Scotland)	[section 1008(1) of ITA 2007]4
assignment (of part or share in rights under a policy or contract) (in Chapter 9 of Part 4)	section 505(2)
assignment (of whole of rights under a policy or contract) (in Chapter 9 of Part 4)	section 505(2)
assumed income entitlement (for the purposes of Chapter 6 of Part 5)	section 665(2), (3)
authorised unit trust	[section 989 of ITA 2007]4
averaging claim (in Chapter 16 of Part 2)	section 221(1)
bank arrangement (in Chapter 4 of Part 6)	section 704(4)(*a*)
the basic amount (in relation to estate income) (in Chapter 6 of Part 5)	section 656(4)
basic rate	[section 6(2) of ITA 2007 (as applied by section 989 of that Act)]4
basic relieving amount by reference to a taxed receipt (in Chapter 4 of Part 3)	sections 288(4), 289(2), (4)
. . .1	. . .1
body of persons	[section 989 of ITA 2007]4
[bonus share capital (in Chapter 3 of Part 4)	section 414A(1)]9
building society	[section 989 of ITA 2007]4
building society arrangement (in Chapter 4 of Part 6)	section 704(5)(*a*)
calculation event (in Chapter 9 of Part 4)	section 491(4)
capital allowance	[section 989 of ITA 2007]4
capital cost of patent rights (in Chapter 2 of Part 5)	section 588(4)
capital redemption policy (in Chapter 9 of Part 4)	section 473(2)
capital sums (in Chapter 2 of Part 5)	section 608
capital sums included in the proceeds of sale (in relation to the exchange of property) (in Chapter 2 of Part 5)	section 605(5)
caravan	section 875
[the cash basis (in Part 2)	section 25A]16
[the cash basis (in Part 3)	section 271D]20
certified master version (in Chapter 9 of Part 2)	section 132(3)
certified SAYE savings arrangement (in Chapter 4 of Part 6)	section 703(1)
chargeable event (in Chapter 9 of Part 4)	section 484
[chargeable period (in Chapter 16A of Part 2)	section 225E]11
. . .4	. . .4
charitable trust . . .14	[paragraph 1 of Schedule 6 to FA 2010]14

charity	[paragraph 1 of Schedule 6 to FA 2010][14]
. . . [4]	. . . [4]
claim	section 878(3)
close company	[Chapter 2 of Part 10 of CTA 2010][9]
commercial letting of furnished holiday accommodation (for purposes of Chapter 6 of Part 3)	sections 323 to 326
company	[section 992 of ITA 2007][4]
company (for all purposes in the Income Tax Acts)	section 863(2)(*c*)
connected (in the context of "connected person" or one person being "connected" with another)	[section 993 of ITA 2007][4] (see section 878(5) of this Act)
consideration received for disposal of know-how (for purposes of Chapter 14 of Part 2)	section 192(3), (4)
contract of insurance (in Chapter 9 of Part 4)	section 545(1)
[contributing participator (in Chapter 16A of Part 2)	section 225R(3)][11]
control . . . [4]	[section 995 of ITA 2007][4] (see section 878(6) of this Act)
[conversion of an interest-bearing corporate security into corporate strips of the security (for the purposes of Chapter 8 of Part 4)	sections 452C and 452D][2]
[corporate strip (for the purposes of Chapter 8 of Part 4)	section 452E][2]
corporation tax receipt (in Chapter 4 of Part 3)	section 296(1)
coupons (in Chapter 13 of Part 4)	section 571(3)
deeply discounted security (for the purposes of Chapter 8 of Part 4)	sections 430 to 443(1)
[the defaulter (in Chapter 16A of Part 2)	section 225R(3)][11]
[default payment (in Chapter 16A of Part 2)	section 225R(3)][11]
deposit rights (in Chapter 11 of Part 4)	section 552
[designated area (in Chapter 16A of Part 2)	section 225E][11]
discretionary interest (for the purposes of Chapter 6 of Part 5)	section 650(3)
disposal of a deeply discounted security (in Chapter 8 of Part 4)	section 437(1)
distribution	[section 989 of ITA 2007][4]
[the dividend additional rate	section 8(3) of ITA 2007 (as applied by section 989 of that Act)][10]
the dividend ordinary rate	[section 8(1) of ITA 2007 (as applied by section 989 of that Act)][4]
the dividend trust rate	[section 9(2) of ITA 2007 (as applied by section 989 of that Act)][4]
the dividend upper rate	[section 8(2) of ITA 2007 (as applied by section 989 of that Act)][4]
dividends (in Chapter 3 of Part 4)	section 382(4)
dividends (in Chapter 4 of Part 4)	section 402(4)
election	section 878(3)
employment income	section 7(2) of ITEPA 2003
[entering the cash basis (in Chapter 17A of Part 2)	section 240B][16]
estate (in Chapter 6 of Part 5)	section 649(2)
estate income (in Chapter 6 of Part 5)	section 649(2)
estate in land (in relation to any land in Scotland)	[section 1008(1) of ITA 2007][4]
European authorised institution (in Chapter 4 of Part 6)	section 704(6)
European authorised institution arrangement (in Chapter 4 of Part 6)	section 704(6)
excess event (in Chapter 9 of Part 4)	section 491(4)
excluded indexed security (in Chapter 8 of Part 4)	section 433(1)
the exemption condition (in Chapter 6 of Part 6)	section 713(3)
[the farmer (in Chapter 16ZA of Part 2)	section 225ZG][13]
farmers (in Chapter 8 of Part 2)	section 111(3)
farming	[section 996 of ITA 2007][4]

[farming trade (in Chapter 16ZA of Part 2)	section 225ZG][13]
film (in Chapter 9 of Part 2)	section 131
final insurance year (in Chapter 9 of Part 4)	section 499(4), (5)
the final tax year (in Chapter 6 of Part 5)	section 653(3)
firm	sections 847(1) and 863
firm (for all purposes in the Income Tax Acts)	section 863(2)(*a*)
for accounting purposes	[section 997 of ITA 2007][4]
foreign capital redemption policy (in Chapter 9 of Part 4)	section 476(3)
foreign estate (in Chapter 6 of Part 5)	section 651(1)
foreign holdings (in Chapter 13 of Part 4)	section 571(1)
foreign institution (in Chapter 9 of Part 4)	section 468(5)
foreign policy of life insurance (in Chapter 9 of Part 4)	section 476(3)
forestry	[section 996(3) of ITA 2007][4]
. . .	. . . [12]
. . .	[12]
FOTRA security (in Chapter 6 of Part 6)	section 713(2)
friendly society (in Chapter 9 of Part 4)	section 545(1)
. . .	. . . [17]
generally accepted accounting practice	[section 997 of ITA 2007][4]
generating income from land (in Chapter 3 of Part 3)	sections 266 and 267
gilt-edged security	section 153(1)
grossing up	[section 998 of ITA 2007][4]
group life policy (in Chapter 9 of Part 4)	section 480(2)
[the guarantor (in Chapter 16A of Part 2)	section 225N(6)][11]
herd (in Chapter 8 of Part 2)	section 112(1)
herd basis election (in Chapter 8 of Part 2)	section 111(1)
herd basis rules (in Chapter 8 of Part 2)	section 111(2)
higher rate	[section 6(2) of ITA 2007 (as applied by section 989 of that Act)][4]
houseboat	section 878(1)
[in accordance with GAAP (in Part 3)	section 271B][20]
income	section 878(1)
income arising under a settlement (in Chapter 5 of Part 5)	section 648
income arising under the settlement (in relation to a settlor) (in Chapter 5 of Part 5)	section 644(3)(*b*)
income period (in Chapter 2 of Part 7)	section 805(2) and (3)
individual's limit (in Chapter 1 of Part 7)	section 789
individual's limit (in Chapter 2 of Part 7)	section 808
[individual's property allowance (in Chapter 2 of Part 6A)	section 783BD][19]
[individual's trading allowance (in Chapter 1 of Part 6A)	section 783AD][19]
. . . [1]	. . . [1]
institutional arrangement (in Chapter 4 of Part 6)	section 704(3)
insurance company (in Chapter 9 of Part 4)	section 545(1)
insurance year (in Chapter 9 of Part 4)	section 499(1), (3), (5)
. . . [4]	. . . [4]
[interest	section 564M of ITA 2007][11]
interest (in Chapter 4 of Part 6)	section 702(4)
[interest-bearing corporate security (for the purposes of Chapter 8 of Part 4)	section 452B][2]
international accounting standards	[section 997 of ITA 2007][4]
investment plan regulations (in Chapter 3 of Part 6)	section 694(2)
. . . [4]	. . . [4]
keeping a production herd (in Chapter 8 of Part 2)	section 111(4)
know-how (in Chapter 14 of Part 2)	section 192(1), (2)
know-how (in Chapter 2 of Part 5)	section 583(4), (5)

lease (in Part 3)	section 364(1)
letting (in Chapter 1 of Part 7)	section 802
life annuity (in Chapter 9 of Part 4)	section 473(2)
limited interest (for the purposes of Chapter 6 of Part 5)	section 650(2)
linked savings arrangement (in Chapter 4 of Part 6)	section 703(2)
local authority	[section 999 of ITA 2007][4]
. . .[4]	. . .[4]
market gardening	[section 996(5) of ITA 2007][4]
market value (in Chapter 8 of Part 4)	section 460(3)
market value (in Chapter 9 of Part 4)	section 545(1)
mature (in relation to female animals) (for the purposes of Chapter 8 of Part 2)	section 113(5)
members of a company (for all purposes in the Tax Acts)	section 863(2)(d)
members of a firm (for all purposes in the Income Tax Acts)	section 863(2)(b)
mineral lease or agreement (in Chapter 8 of Part 3)	section 341(1)
mineral royalties (in Chapter 8 of Part 3)	sections 341(2), 342, 343
[miscellaneous income (in Chapter 1 of Part 6A)	section 783AB][19]
mortgage (in the application of the Act to Scotland)	section 879(1)
national savings arrangement (in Chapter 4 of Part 6)	section 704(2)
non-charitable trust (in Chapter 9 of Part 4)	section 545(1)
non-trade business (in Chapter 3 of Part 5)	section 609(1)
non-UK resident (and references to a non-UK resident or a non-UK resident person)	[section 989 of ITA 2007][4]
normal self-assessment filing date	[section 989 of ITA 2007][4]
notice	[section 989 of ITA 2007][4]
oil and gas exploration and appraisal	[section 1003 of ITA 2007][4]
[oil (in Chapter 16A of Part 2)	section 225E][11]
[oil extraction activities (in Chapter 16A of Part 2)	section 225A][11]
[oil field (in Chapter 16A of Part 2)	section 225E][11]
[oil rights (in Chapter 16A of Part 2)	section 225B][11]
option (in Chapter 12 of Part 4)	section 558(2)
ordinary share capital	[section 989 of ITA 2007][4]
original master version (in Chapter 9 of Part 2)	section 132(1), (2)
[OTA 1975 (in Chapter 16A of Part 2)	section 225E][11]
overlap period (in Chapter 15 of Part 2)	section 204
overlap profit (in Chapter 15 of Part 2)	[sections 204 and 204A][19]
overseas life assurance business (in Chapter 9 of Part 4)	section 476(3)
[the overseas part	section 989 of ITA 2007][15]
overseas property business	Chapter 2 of Part 3
overseas property income (in Chapter 11 of Part 3)	section 358
part surrender or assignment event (in Chapter 9 of Part 4)	section 491(4)
[participator (in Chapter 16A of Part 2)	section 225E][11]
patent rights (in Chapter 2 of Part 5)	section 587(4)
period of account	[section 989 of ITA 2007][4]
permanent establishment	[[Chapter 2 of Part 24 of CTA 2010][9] (as applied by section 989 of ITA 2007)][4]
. . .[6]	. . .[6]
person creating trusts (for the purposes of Chapter 9 of Part 4)	section 465(6)
personal portfolio bond (in Chapter 9 of Part 4)	sections 516, 517
personal portfolio bond event (in Chapter 9 of Part 4)	section 491(4)
personal representatives	[section 989 of ITA 2007][4]
plan managers (in Chapter 3 of Part 6)	section 696(2)
policy (in Chapter 9 of Part 4)	section 545(1)
post-cessation receipt (in Part 2)	sections 246 and 247
post-cessation receipt (in Chapter 10 of Part 3)	sections 353 and 354

preliminary expenditure (in Chapter 9 of Part 2)	section 130(6)
premises (in Part 3)	section 364(2)
premium (in Chapter 4 of Part 3)	section 307(1), (3)
premium (in Chapter 9 of Part 4)	section 545(2)
the price (in relation to the exchange of knowhow) (in Chapter 14 of Part 2)	section 192(6)
the price (in relation to the exchange of property) (in Chapter 2 of Part 5)	section 605(4)
proceeds of sale (in relation to the exchange of know-how) (in Chapter 14 of Part 2)	section 192(6)
proceeds of sale (in relation to the exchange of property) (in Chapter 2 of Part 5)	section 605(4)
production expenditure (in Chapter 9 of Part 2)	section 130(2)
production herd (in Chapter 8 of Part 2)	section 112(1), (2)
production herd (of the same class) (for the purposes of Chapter 8 of Part 2)	section 113(2)
profits from a trade, profession or vocation (for the purposes of Chapter 16 of Part 2)	section 221(4), (5)
profits or gains	[section 989 of ITA 2007][4]
any prohibitive rule (in Chapter 9 of Part 2)	section 130(7)
property business	section 263(6)
property comprised in a settlement (in relation to a settlor) (in Chapter 5 of Part 5)	section 644(3)(*a*)
property or rights held on trust or on trusts (in the application of the Act to Scotland)	[section 1008(2) of ITA 2007][4]
provider (in relation to a bank arrangement) (in Chapter 4 of Part 6)	section 704(4)(*b*)
provider (in relation to a building society arrangement) (in Chapter 4 of Part 6)	section 704(5)(*b*)
provider (in relation to a European authorised institution arrangement) (in Chapter 4 of Part 6)	section 704(6)
provides foster care (and related expressions) (in Chapter 2 of Part 7)	section 806
[provides qualifying care (in Chapter 2 of Part 7)	section 805A][12]
[provides shared lives care (in Chapter 2 of Part 7)	section 806A][12]
public body (in Chapter 2 of Part 5)	section 603(2)
purchased life annuity (in Chapter 7 of Part 4)	section 423
[qualifying care receipts (in Chapter 2 of Part 7)	section 805][12]
[qualifying care relief (in Chapter 2 of Part 7)	section 803(1)][12]
qualifying distribution	[section 989 of ITA 2007][4]
qualifying policy	[section 989 of ITA 2007][4]
qualifying trade, profession or vocation (in Chapter 16 of Part 2)	section 221(2)
. . .[4]	. . .[4]
receipt period (of a receipt) (for the purposes of Chapter 4 of Part 3)	sections 288(6), 296(3)
receipts and expenses (in the context of the calculation of the profits of a trade, profession or vocation or of a property business) (in the Income Tax Acts)	section 27 (including as applied by section 272)
recognised futures exchange	section 558(3)
recognised stock exchange	[section 1005 of ITA 2007][4]
reduction under section 288 by reference to a taxed receipt (in Chapter 4 of Part 3)	section 290(6)
reduction under section 37(2) or (3) of ICTA by reference to an amount chargeable on the superior interest (in Chapter 4 of Part 3)	section 297(2)
registered pension scheme	[section 150(2) of FA 2004 (as applied by section 989 of ITA 2007)][4]
related (in relation to a policy) (in Chapter 9 of Part 4)	section 491(6)
related transactions (in Chapter 12 of Part 4)	section 566
relevant allowance (in Chapter 1 of Part 7)	section 802
relevant balancing charge (in Chapter 1 of Part 7)	section 802
relevant foreign income	section 830
[relevant income (in Chapter 1 of Part 6A)	section 783AC][19]

[the relevant participator (in Chapter 16A of Part 2)	section 225N(6)][11]
relevant period (in Chapter 9 of Part 2)	section 133
the relevant profits (in Chapter 16 of Part 2)	section 221(1), (4), (5)
[relevant property business (in Chapter 2 of Part 6A)	section 783BA][19]
[relevant property income (in Chapter 2 of Part 6A)	section 783BC][19]
relevant telecommunication right (in Chapter 10 of Part 2)	section 146
[relevant trade (in Chapter 1 of Part 6A)	section 783AA][19]
[relievable receipts (in Chapter 2 of Part 6A)	section 783BB][19]
rent receivable for a UK electric-line wayleave (in Chapter 9 of Part 3)	section 345
rent receivable in connection with a UK section 12(4) concern (in Chapter 8 of Part 3)	section 336
rent (in Chapter 8 of Part 3)	section 336(3)
rent (in Chapter 9 of Part 3)	section 345(3)
rent-a-room receipts (in Chapter 1 of Part 7)	section 786
rent-a-room relief (in Chapter 1 of Part 7)	section 784
residence (in Chapter 1 of Part 7)	section 787
[residence (in Chapter 2 of Part 7)	section 806B][12]
the residuary income of the estate (for the purposes of Chapter 6 of Part 5)	section 666(1)
retail prices index	[section 989 of ITA 2007][4]
return from one or more disposals (in Chapter 12 of Part 4)	section 561(1)
reversion (in the application of Chapter 4 of Part 3 to Scotland)	section 307(3)
[ring fence income (in Chapter 16A of Part 2)	section 225C][11]
[ring fence trade (in Chapter 16A of Part 2)	section 225D][11]
sale of an animal (for the purposes of Chapter 8 of Part 2)	section 113(3)
sale of know-how (for purposes of Chapter 14 of Part 2)	sections 192(5)
sale of property (in Chapter 2 of Part 5)	sections 605(1), 606(1)
sale or transfer of trading stock (in Chapter 12 of Part 2)	section 174(3)
sale proceeds of an animal (for the purposes of Chapter 8 of Part 2)	section 113(4)
[Scottish additional rate	section 6A of ITA 2007 (as applied by section 989 of that Act)
Scottish basic rate	section 6A of ITA 2007 (as applied by section 989 of that Act)
Scottish higher rate	section 6A of ITA 2007 (as applied by section 989 of that Act)
Scottish taxpayer	section 989 of ITA 2007][18]
. . .[5]	. . .[5]
Schedule A business	[section 989 of ITA 2007][4,8]
settlement (in Chapter 5 of Part 5)	section 620
settlor (in Chapter 5 of Part 5)	section 620(1)
settlor (for the purposes of Chapter 9 of Part 4)	section 465(6)
share (in Chapter 8 of Part 4)	section 460(1)
share of residuary income of estate (for the purposes of Chapter 6 of Part 5)	section 667
short-term lease (in Chapter 4 of Part 3)	section 276(6)
[split year	section 989 of ITA 2007][15]
[starting rate for savings	section 7 of ITA 2007 (as applied by section 989 of that Act)][5]
[starting rate limit for savings	section 12 of ITA 2007 (as applied by section 989 of that Act)[5]
statutory insolvency arrangement (in Part 2)	section 259
[stepchild	[section 246 of the Civil Partnership Act 2004 (as applied by section 989 of ITA 2007)][4]][3]

stock dividend income (in Chapter 5 of Part 4)	section 409(2)
strip (in Chapter 8 of Part 4)	section 444
substantial part of a herd (for purposes of Chapter 8 of Part 2)	section 113(6)
surrender (in the application of the Act to Scotland)	[section 1008(1) of ITA 2007][4]
tax advantage (in Chapter 8 of Part 4)	section 460(2)
tax year	[section 4(2) of ITA 2007 (as applied by section 989 of that Act)][4]
the tax year 2005–06 etc	[section 4(4) of ITA 2007 (as applied by section 989 of that Act)][4]
taxed lease (in Chapter 4 of Part 3)	section 287(4)
taxed receipt (in Chapter 4 of Part 3)	section 287(4)
taxpayer (in Chapter 16 of Part 2)	section 221(1)
[total compensation profit (in Chapter 16ZA of Part 2)	section 225ZB][13]
total income	[section 23 of ITA 2007 (as applied by section 989 of that Act)][4]
total [qualifying care][12] receipts (in Chapter 2 of Part 7)	section 807
total rent-a-room amount (in Chapter 1 of Part 7)	section 788
trade	[section 989 of ITA 2007][4]
[trading stock (in relation to a trade) (in Chapter 11A of Part 2)	section 172A][7]
trading stock (in relation to a trade) (in Chapter 12 of Part 2)	section 174
transfer of work in progress (in Chapter 12 of Part 2)	section 183(2)
[trust rate	section 9(1) of ITA 2007 (as applied by section 989 of that Act)][4]
trusts an individual created (for the purposes of Chapter 9 of Part 4)	section 465(6)
UK estate (in Chapter 6 of Part 5)	section 651(1)
[the UK part	section 989 of ITA 2007][15]
UK property business	Chapter 2 of Part 3
UK resident (and references to a UK resident or a UK resident person)	[section 989 of ITA 2007][4]
Ulster Savings Certificates	section 693(7)
unit holder	[section 989 of ITA 2007][4]
unit trust scheme	[section 1007 of ITA 2007][4]
United Kingdom	[section 1013 of ITA 2007][4]
unreduced amount (of a taxed receipt) (in Chapter 4 of Part 3)	sections 290(2) to (4), 296(4) to (6)
unused amount (of a taxed receipt) (for the purposes of Chapter 4 of Part 3)	section 290(1), (5)
venture capital trust	[section 989 of ITA 2007][4]
within the charge to tax	[section 1009 of ITA 2007][4]
woodlands	[section 996(4) of ITA 2007][4]
work in progress (in Chapter 12 of Part 2)	section 183(1)

Commentary—Simon's Taxes **E1.405.**

Amendments—[1] Entries repealed by CRCA 2005 ss 50, 52, Sch 4 paras 131, 134(2), Sch 5 with effect from 18 April 2005 (by virtue of SI 2005/1126).

[2] Entries inserted by F(No 2)A 2005 s 39, Sch 7 para 25(9) with effect as if originally included when ITTOIA 2005 enacted.

[3] Entry inserted by Tax and Civil Partnership Regulations, SI 2005/3229, regs 183, 200, with effect from 5 December 2005 (reg 1(1)).

[4] Amendments made by ITA 2007 ss 1027, 1031, Sch 1 paras 492, 588, 592, Sch 3 Pt 1 with effect for income tax purposes from 6 April 2007, and corporation tax purposes for accounting periods ending after 5 April 2007.

[5] Entries "starting rate for savings", and "starting rate limit for savings", substituted for "starting rate", and entry "savings rate" repealed, by FA 2008 s 5, Sch 1 paras 50, 63 with effect for the tax year 2008–09 and subsequent tax years.

[6] Entry "person to whom the remittance basis applies" repealed by FA 2008 s 25, Sch 7 paras 66, 73 with effect for the tax year 2008–09 and subsequent tax years.

[7] Entry "trading stock (in relation to a trade) (in relation to Chapter 11A of Part 2)" inserted by FA 2008 s 37, Sch 15 paras 1, 4 with effect in relation to changes in trading stock occurring on or after 12 March 2008 (see FA 2008 s 37(3) for meaning of "change in trading stock").

[8] In entry "accounting period", in second column, words substituted inserted, and entry "Schedule A business" repealed, by CTA 2009 ss 1322, 1326, Sch 1 paras 587, 647(1), (3), Sch 3 Part 1. CTA 2009 applies for accounting periods ending on or

after 1 April 2009 (for corporation tax purposes) and for tax years 2009–10 onwards (for income and capital gains tax purposes).

9   Entry for "bonus share capital" inserted, in the entry for " accounting period", in second column, words "section 834(1) of ICTA" substituted, in the entry for "close company", in second column, words "sections 414 and 415 of ICTA" substituted and in the entry for "permanent establishment", in second column, words "section 148 of FA 2003" substituted by CTA 2010 s 1177, Sch 1 paras 444, 472(1),(3). CTA 2010 has effect for corporation tax purposes for accounting periods ending on or after 1 April 2010, and for income and capital gains tax purposes for the tax year 2010–11 and subsequent tax years.

10   Entries for "additional rate", "the dividend additional rate" inserted, by FA 2009 s 6, Sch 2 paras 19, 23 with effect for the tax year 2010–11 and subsequent tax years. The powers conferred by the amendments made by FA 2009 Sch 2 may be exercised at any time on or after 21 July 2009 but not so as to make provision having effect before the tax year 2010–11 (FA 2009 Sch 2 para 25(1)). Those definitions to read as follows—

11   Entries inserted by TIOPA 2010 s 501, Sch 8 paras 189, 191, 211, 212. TIOPA 2010 has effect for corporation tax purposes for accounting periods ending on or after 1 April 2010, for income and capital gains tax purposes for the tax year 2010–11 and subsequent tax years, and for petroleum revenue tax purposes for chargeable periods beginning on or after 1 July 2010.

12   Entries for "foster-care receipts" and "foster-care relief" repealed, entries inserted, and in entry for "total qualifying care receipts", words substituted for words "foster-care", by F(No 3)A 2010 s 1, Sch 1 paras 30, 35 with effect for the tax year 2010–11 and subsequent tax years, subject to transitional provisions in F(No 3)A 2010 Sch 1 paras 36(2)–(5), 37.

13   Definitions inserted by the Enactment of Extra-statutory Concessions Order, SI 2012/266 arts 8, 9 with effect for the purposes of making claims in respect of the total compensation profit for periods of account beginning on or after 1 March 2012.

14   In definition of "charitable trust", words repealed and substituted, and in definition of "charity", words substituted, by FA 2010 s 30, Sch 6 para 21(1), (5) with effect for the tax year 2012–13 and subsequent tax years. In so far as the amendments to the definition of "charitable trust" apply in relation to ITTOIA 2005 Part 4 Chapter 9, those amendments have effect in relation to insurances and contracts made on or after 6 April 2012 (SI 2012/736 art 15).

15   Entries for "the overseas part", "split year" and "the UK part" inserted by FA 2013 s 218, Sch 45 para 106 with effect in calculating an individual's liability to income tax or capital gains tax for the tax year 2013–14 and subsequent tax years, subject to transitional provisions and savings in FA 2013 Sch 45 paras 154–158.

16   Entries for "the cash basis" and "entering the cash basis" inserted by FA 2013 s 17, Sch 4 para 53 with effect for the tax year 2013–14 and subsequent tax years, subject to the provisions of FA 2013 Sch 4 para 57 in relation to barristers and advocates.

17   Entry for "future (in Chapter 12 of Part 4)" repealed by FA 2013 s 28, Sch 12 para 13(1), (6) with effect for the tax year 2013–14 and subsequent tax years.

18   Definitions inserted by the Scottish Rate of Income Tax (Consequential Amendments) Order, SI 2015/1810 arts 9, 12 with effect in relation to the tax year 2016–17 (the tax year appointed by the Treasury under the Scotland Act 2012 s 25(5) by virtue of SI 2015/2000) and subsequent tax years.

19   Definitions inserted, and in definition of "overlap profit", words substituted, by F(No 2)A 2017 s 17, Sch 3 paras 2, 11 with effect for the tax year 2017–18 and subsequent tax years.

20   Definitions inserted by F(No 2)A 2017 s 16, Sch 2 paras 12, 32 with effect for the tax year 2017–18 and subsequent tax years, subject to transitional provisions in F(No 2)A 2017 Sch 2 para 64.

FINANCE ACT 2005

(2005 Chapter 7)

ARRANGEMENT OF SECTIONS

Part 2: Income Tax, Corporation Tax and Capital Gains Tax
Chapter 1 — Income Tax and Corporation Tax Charge and Rate Bands
Corporation tax
10   Charge and main rate for financial year 2006
12   Corporation tax starting rate and fraction for financial year 2005
13   Non-corporate distribution rate for financial year 2005
Chapter 2 — Personal Taxation
Taxable benefits
15   Childcare vouchers: exempt amount
16   Extension of exemptions for childcare, workplace parking, cycles etc
17   Transfer of previously loaned computer or cycle etc
18   Extension of outplacement services etc exemption: part-time employees
Armed forces
19   Armed forces pensions and compensation schemes
Chapter 3 — Employment-related Securities
20   Research institution spin-out companies
21   Research institution spin-out companies: pre-2nd December 2004 cases
22   Capital gains
Chapter 4 — Trusts with Vulnerable Beneficiary
Introductory
23   Introduction
Income tax
25   Qualifying trusts income: special income tax treatment
26   Amount of relief
27   Trustees' liability: TQTI
28   Vulnerable person's liability: VQTI
28A   Disapplication of section 629 of ITTOIA 2005
29   Part years
Capital gains tax
30   Qualifying trusts gains: special capital gains tax treatment
31   UK resident vulnerable persons: amount of relief
32   Non-UK resident vulnerable persons: amount of relief
Chapter 8 — Accounting Practice and Related Matters
80   Accounting practice and related matters
82   Change of accounting practice: deferment of transitional adjustments
83   Application of accounting standards to securitisation companies
Chapter 9 — International Matters
Annual payments and double taxation relief
91   Tax avoidance involving annual payments and double taxation relief
Chapter 10 — Miscellaneous
Capital allowances
92   Capital allowances: renovation of business premises in disadvantaged areas
Tonnage tax
93   Tonnage tax
Part 4: Other Taxes
Lorry road-user charge
100   Lorry road-user charge
Part 5: Pensions etc
101   Pension schemes etc
102   Pension Protection Fund etc
Part 6: Miscellaneous
103   Civil partnerships etc
Part 7: Supplementary Provisions
104   Repeals
105   Interpretation
106   Short title
Schedules:
Schedule 1—Non-UK resident vulnerable persons: interpretation
Schedule 1A—Meaning of "disabled person"
Schedule 4—Accounting practice and related matters
Schedule 6—Capital allowances: renovation of business premises in disadvantaged areas
Schedule 7—Tonnage tax
Schedule 10—Pension schemes etc
Schedule 11—Repeals

PART 2

Corporation tax

10 Charge and main rate for financial year 2006

Corporation tax shall be charged for the financial year 2006 at the rate of 30%.

12 Corporation tax starting rate and fraction for financial year 2005

For the financial year 2005—

    (*a*) the corporation tax starting rate shall be 0%, and

    (*b*) the fraction mentioned in section 13AA of ICTA (marginal relief for small companies) shall be 19/400ths.

13 Non-corporate distribution rate for financial year 2005

The non-corporate distribution rate for the financial year 2005 shall be 19%.

CHAPTER 2
PERSONAL TAXATION

Taxable benefits

15 Childcare vouchers: exempt amount

(1) Section 270A of ITEPA 2003 (limited exemption for qualifying childcare vouchers) is amended as follows.

(2) (*amends* ITEPA 2003 s 270A(6))

(3), (4) (*insert* ITEPA 2003 s 270A(6A), (10A))

(5) This section has effect for the year 2005–06 and subsequent years of assessment.

16 Extension of exemptions for childcare, workplace parking, cycles etc

(1) ITEPA 2003 is amended as follows.

(2) (*amends* ITEPA 2003 s 237(1))

(3) (*amends* ITEPA 2003 s 244(1))

(4) (*amends* ITEPA 2003 s 270A(1))

(5) (*amends* ITEPA 2003 s 318(1))

(6) (*amends* ITEPA 2003 s 318A(1))

(7) This section has effect for the year 2005–06 and subsequent years of assessment.

17 Transfer of previously loaned computer or cycle etc

(1) Section 206 of ITEPA 2003 (cost of the benefit: transfer of used or depreciated asset) is amended as follows.

(2) (*amends* ITEPA 2003 s 206(3)(*a*))

(3) (*inserts* ITEPA 2003 s 206(6))

(4) This section has effect for the year 2005–06 and subsequent years of assessment.

18 Extension of outplacement services etc exemption: part-time employees

(1) ITEPA 2003 is amended as follows.

(2) (*amends* ITEPA 2003 s 310(4))

(3) (*amends* ITEPA 2003 s 311(3)(*b*), (*c*) and *repeals* sub-s (3)(*d*))

(4) (*amends* ITEPA 2003 s 311(4)(*c*))

(5) This section has effect in relation to the year 2005–06 and subsequent years of assessment.

Armed forces

19 Armed forces pensions and compensation schemes

(1) ITEPA 2003 is amended as follows.

(2) (*amends* ITEPA 2003 s 393(1))

(3) (*amends* ITEPA 2003 s 639(1)(*a*))

(4) (*creates* ITEPA 2003 s 639(1) and *inserts* sub-ss (2), (3))

(5) (*inserts* ITEPA 2003 s 640A)

(6) (*inserts* ITEPA 2003 s 641(1)(*h*))

(7) The amendment made by subsection (2) has effect for the year 2005–06.

(8) The amendments made by subsections (3) and (4) are deemed always to have had effect.

(9) The amendments made by subsections (5) and (6) have effect for the year 2005–06 and subsequent years of assessment.

CHAPTER 3
EMPLOYMENT-RELATED SECURITIES

20 Research institution spin-out companies

(1) (*inserts* ITEPA 2003 Part 7 Ch 4A (ss 451–460))

(2) (*amends* ITEPA 2003 s 421B, the heading of and the heading above that section, and s 421D)

(4) (*amends* ITEPA 2003 s 421K(3)(*g*))

(5) The amendments made by this section have effect in relation to shares (or an interest in shares) acquired before an agreement for the transfer of intellectual property is made, or within the period of 183 days beginning with the date on which such an agreement is made, if—

    (*a*) the date of acquisition of the shares (or interest in shares), or

    (*b*) the date on which the agreement was made,

or both, fell on or after 2nd December 2004.

(6) Where section 454 of ITEPA 2003 (as inserted by subsection (1)) has effect (by virtue of subsection (5)) in relation to shares (or an interest in shares) acquired before 2nd December 2004, it applies in relation to them (or it) so as to treat the election under section 431(1) as made on that date.

(7) Where section 454 of ITEPA 2003 (as inserted by subsection (1)) has effect (by virtue of subsection (5)) in relation to shares (or an interest in shares) acquired before 1st October 2005, it has effect with the substitution in subsection (3)(*b*) of that section of "later than 15th October 2005" for "more than 14 days after the acquisition of the shares (or interest in shares)".

Commentary—*Simon's Taxes* E4.508AA–E4.508AC.

21 Research institution spin-out companies: pre-2nd December 2004 cases

(1) Subsections (2) to (7) have effect where—

    (*a*) Chapter 4A of Part 7 of ITEPA 2003 (as inserted by section 20) would apply but for subsection (5) of that section (commencement), and

    (*b*) an election is made under this subsection by the employee and the employer no later than 15th October 2005.

(2) Section 452(1) and (2)(*a*), (*c*) and (*d*) and section 453(1) of ITEPA 2003 apply.

(3) But when the chargeable event occurs in relation to the shares (or interest in shares), the taxable amount counts as employment income of the employee for the tax year in which the chargeable event occurs.

(4) The chargeable event occurs in relation to the shares (or interest in shares) on the earlier of—

    (*a*) the day on which there is a disposal for consideration of the shares, or any interest in them, by an associated person otherwise than to another associated person, and

    (*b*) the day specified in any election made by an employee under this subsection.

(5) The taxable amount for the purposes of subsection (3) is—

$$MV - DA$$

where—

MV is the market value of the shares (or interest in shares) immediately before the occurrence of the chargeable event, and

DA is the total of any deductible amounts.

(6) Each of the following is a deductible amount—

    (*a*) the amount of any consideration given for the acquisition of the shares (or interest in shares),

    (*b*) any amount that constituted earnings from the employee's employment under Chapter 1 of Part 3 of ITEPA 2003 (earnings) in respect of the acquisition of the shares (or interest in shares),

    (*c*) any amount that counted as employment income in relation to the shares (or interest in shares) under Chapter 2 or 4 of Part 7 of that Act as originally enacted otherwise than by virtue of section 457 of that Act (as originally enacted) (charge on receipt of chargeable benefit),

    (*d*) if the shares (or interest in shares) were (or was) acquired on a conversion of other shares (or of another interest in shares), any amount that counted as employment income of the employee under Chapter 3 of that Part (including that Chapter as originally enacted) (convertible securities) by reason of the conversion,

    (*e*) if the acquisition of the shares (or interest in shares) was pursuant to a securities option, any amount that counted as employment income of the employee under section 476 of that Act (or section 476 or 477 as originally enacted) (acquisition of securities pursuant to securities option) by reason of the acquisition, and

    (*f*) in the case of a chargeable event under subsection (4)(*a*), the amount of any expenses incurred by the holder of the shares (or interest in shares) in connection with the disposal.

(7) An election under subsection (1) or (4) is irrevocable and must be made in a form approved by the Board of Inland Revenue.

(8) The Treasury may by regulations modify—

    (*a*) this section,

    (*b*) any provision of Part 4 of TCGA 1992, and

    (*c*) any provision of Part 7 of ITEPA 2003,

in relation to shares (or interests in shares) to which Chapter 4A of that Part would apply but for section 20(5) and which are restricted securities (or restricted interests in securities) or convertible securities (or interests in convertible securities).

(9) The power conferred by subsection (8) is exercisable by statutory instrument.

(10) A statutory instrument containing regulations under subsection (8) is subject to annulment in pursuance of a resolution of the House of Commons.

(11) In this section—

"associated person" has the same meaning as in Chapters 1 to 5 of Part 7 of ITEPA 2003 (see section 421C of that Act),

"Board of Inland Revenue" has the same meaning as in that Act (see section 720(2) of that Act), and

"convertible securities" has the same meaning as in Chapter 3 of Part 7 of that Act (see section 436 of that Act),

and expressions used in this section and in Chapter 4A of Part 7 of that Act have the same meaning in this section as in that Chapter.

Commentary—*Simon's Taxes* E4.508AD.

22 Capital gains

(1) TCGA 1992 is amended as follows.

(2) (*amends* TCGA 1992 s 119A(3))

(3) (*inserts* TCGA 1992 s 149AB)

(4) The amendment made by paragraph (*b*) of subsection (2) has effect only in relation to disposals on or after 6th April 2005; but the other amendments made by that subsection have effect in relation to any disposal (whether before or after the passing of this Act).

(5) The amendment made by subsection (3) has effect in relation to any acquisition (whether before or after the passing of this Act).

Commentary—*Simon's Taxes* C2.811.

CHAPTER 4

TRUSTS WITH VULNERABLE BENEFICIARY

Introductory

23 Introduction

(1) This Chapter contains tax provision in connection with—

(*a*) income arising to [the trustees of a settlement][1] from property held on qualifying trusts for the benefit of a vulnerable person, and

(*b*) chargeable gains accruing to [the trustees of a settlement][1] from the disposal of such property.

(2) Section 24 contains provision as to the making of claims for special tax treatment under this Chapter.

(3) Sections 25 to 29 contain provision relating to income tax.

(4) Sections 30 to [32][2] contain provision relating to capital gains tax.

(5) Sections 34 to 36 apply for the purpose of determining whether trusts on which property is held for the benefit of a vulnerable person are qualifying trusts.

(6) In this Chapter "vulnerable person election" means an election under section 37.

(7) In this Chapter "vulnerable person" means—

(*a*) a disabled person (see section 38), or

(*b*) a relevant minor (see section 39).

Commentary—*Simon's Taxes* C4.255.

Amendment—[1]   Words in sub-s (1)(*a*), (*b*) substituted for word "trustees" in each place by FA 2006 s 89, Sch 13 para 35(1), (2) with effect from 6 April 2006.

[2]   Figure in sub-s (4) substituted by FA 2008 s 8, Sch 2 paras 11, 12 with effect for the tax year 2008–09 and subsequent tax years.

24 Entitlement to make claim for special tax treatment

A claim for special tax treatment under this Chapter for a tax year may be made by [the trustees of a settlement][1] if—

(*a*) in the tax year they hold property on qualifying trusts for the benefit of a vulnerable person, and

(*b*) a vulnerable person election has effect for all or part of the tax year in relation to those trusts and that person.

Commentary—*Simon's Taxes* C4.255.

Amendment—[1]   Words substituted for word "trustees" by FA 2006 s 89, Sch 13 para 35(2) with effect from 6 April 2006. (Note: Sch 13 para 35(2)(*b*) provides instruction to amend FA 2005 s 24(1). The publisher suggests that, as there is no sub-s (1), the amendment applies to the opening sentence of s 24. This is shown in the text.)

Income tax

25 Qualifying trusts income: special income tax treatment

(1) This section has effect in relation to a tax year if—

(*a*) in the tax year income arises (or is treated as arising) to [the trustees of a settlement][1] from property held on qualifying trusts for the benefit of a vulnerable person ("qualifying trusts income"), and

(*b*) a claim for special tax treatment under this Chapter for the tax year is made by the trustees.
(2) Special income tax treatment applies for the tax year in accordance with sections 26 to 29.
(3) But this section does not have effect in relation to the tax year if the property from which the qualifying trusts income arises (or is treated as arising) is property in which a person who is a settlor (within the meaning given by [section 620(1) of ITTOIA 2005[1]) is regarded as having an interest for the purposes of [sections 624 and 625 of that Act.][1] (income arising under settlement where settlor retains an interest).

Commentary—*Simon's Taxes* **C4.256.**
Amendment—[1]   Words in sub-ss (1), (3) substituted by FA 2006 s 89, Sch 13 para 35(2), (3) with effect from 6 April 2006.

26 Amount of relief

[(1)] [1] The trustees' liability to income tax for the tax year is to be reduced by an amount equal to—

$$TQTI - VQTI$$

where—
> TQTI is an amount determined in accordance with section 27 (income tax liability of trustees in respect of qualifying trusts income), and
> VQTI is an amount determined in accordance with section 28 (extra [income][2] tax to which vulnerable person would be liable if qualifying trusts income were income of his).

[(2) The tax reduction is given effect at Step 6 of the calculation in section 23 of ITA 2007.][1]

Commentary—*Simon's Taxes* **C4.256.**
Amendments—[1]   Sub-s (1) numbered as such, and sub-s (2) inserted, by ITA 2007 s 1027, Sch 1 paras 593, 594 with effect for income tax purposes from 6 April 2007, and corporation tax purposes for accounting periods ending after 5 April 2007.
[2]   In sub-s (1), word in definition of "VQTI" inserted by FA 2008 s 8, Sch 2 paras 11, 13 with effect for the tax year 2008–09 and subsequent tax years.

27 Trustees' liability: TQTI

(1) For the purposes of section 26, TQTI is the amount of income tax to which the trustees would (apart from this Chapter) be liable for the tax year in respect of the qualifying trusts income arising (or treated as arising) to them in that year (or to which they would be so liable if their liability were computed in accordance with subsection (2) in a case to which that subsection applies).
(2) In a case where—
> (*a*) income arising (or treated as arising) to the trustees in the tax year ("total income") includes income ("other income") which is not qualifying trusts income, and
> (*b*) the trustees have [allowable expenses][1],

there shall be disregarded, in computing the income tax liability of the trustees for the tax year in respect of the qualifying trusts income arising (or treated as arising) to them in that year, such part of the [allowable][1] expenses as bears the same proportion to all those expenses as other income bears to total income.
[(2A)References in subsection (2) to allowable expenses are to expenses which can be set against the total income in accordance with Chapter 4 of Part 9 of ITA 2007.][1]
(3) This section is subject to section 29 (vulnerable person election having effect for only part of tax year).

Commentary—*Simon's Taxes* **C4.256.**
Amendment—[1]   Words in sub-s (2) substituted, and sub-s (2A) inserted, by ITA 2007 s 1027, Sch 1 paras 593, 595 with effect for income tax purposes from 6 April 2007, and corporation tax purposes for accounting periods ending after 5 April 2007.

28 Vulnerable person's liability: VQTI

(1) For the purposes of section 26, VQTI is an amount equal to—

$$TLV1 - TLV2$$

where—
> TLV2 is an amount determined in accordance with subsection (2) (and subsection (4) where it applies) (total [income][1] tax liability of vulnerable person), and
> TLV1 is an amount determined in accordance with subsection (3) (and subsection (4) where it applies) (what total [income][1] tax liability of vulnerable person would be if his income included qualifying trusts income).

(2) TLV2 is the total amount of income tax . . . [1] to which the vulnerable person would be liable for the tax year if his income tax liability were computed in accordance with subsections (5) and (6).
(3) TLV1 is what TLV2 would be if the qualifying trusts income arising (or treated as arising) to the trustees in the tax year in respect of which the trustees are liable to income tax were income of the vulnerable person for the tax year.
[(4) Where the vulnerable person is non-UK resident for the tax year, his or her income tax liability for the purposes of determining TLV1 and TLV2 is to be computed in accordance with the Income Tax Acts on the assumption that—
> (*a*) he or she is UK resident for the tax year,

(*b*) that year is not, as respects him or her, a split year within the meaning of Part 3 of Schedule 45 to FA 2013, and

(*c*) he or she is domiciled in the United Kingdom throughout that year.][2]

(5) For the purposes of this section, in a case where income which has arisen to the trustees (whenever it arose) is distributed to the vulnerable person in the tax year, that income is to be disregarded in computing income tax to which he would be liable for the tax year for the purposes of determining TLV1 and TLV2.

(6) For the purposes of this section, in computing income tax to which the vulnerable person would be liable for the tax year for the purposes of determining TLV1 and TLV2, there is to be disregarded any relief which is given by way of a reduction in the amount of income tax to which the vulnerable person would be liable apart from that relief.

(7) For the purposes of this section—

(*a*) whether or not a vulnerable person is non-UK resident is to be determined in accordance with section 41(2), . . . [1]

(*b*) . . . [1]

(8) This section is subject to section 29 (vulnerable person election having effect for only part of tax year).

Commentary—*Simon's Taxes* C4.256.
Amendments—[1]   Words in sub-s (1) inserted, words in sub-s (2), and whole of sub-s (7)(*b*) and preceding word "and", repealed, by FA 2008 s 8, Sch 2 paras 11, 14 with effect for the tax year 2008–09 and subsequent tax years.
[2]   Sub-s (4) substituted by FA 2013 s 218, Sch 45 para 151(1), (2) with effect from 17 July 2013.

[28A Disapplication of section 629 of ITTOIA 2005

(1) In a case where this section applies, section 629(1) of ITTOIA 2005 shall not apply in respect of a payment by the trustees of a settlement to a beneficiary under the settlement.

(2) This section applies if in a year of assessment—

(*a*) the trustees make a payment to a vulnerable person,

(*b*) the payment is made out of qualifying trusts income,

(*c*) the vulnerable person is a relevant child (within the meaning given by section 629 of ITTOIA 2005) of a settlor in relation to the settlement, and

(*d*) the trustees have made a successful claim for special income tax treatment under section 25.][1]

Amendment—[1]   Section inserted by FA 2006 s 89, Sch 13 para 36 with effect in relation to payments made on or after 6 April 2004.

29 Part years

(1) Where the vulnerable person election has effect for only part of the tax year ("the elected part of the tax year") sections 26, 27 and 28 apply with the modifications in subsection (2).

(2) Those modifications are—

(*a*) that references to the qualifying trusts income arising (or treated as arising) to the trustees in the tax year are to be treated as references to the qualifying trusts income arising (or treated as arising) to them in the elected part of the tax year, and

(*b*) that the references in section 27(2) to income arising (or treated as arising) to the trustees in the tax year and expenses of the trustees in the tax year are to be treated as (respectively) references to income arising (or treated as arising) to the trustees in the elected part of the tax year and expenses of the trustees in that part of the tax year.

Commentary—*Simon's Taxes* C4.256.

Capital gains tax

30 Qualifying trusts gains: special capital gains tax treatment

(1) This section has effect in relation to a tax year if—

(*a*) in the tax year chargeable gains accrue to the trustees of a settlement from the disposal of settled property which is held on qualifying trusts for the benefit of a vulnerable person ("the qualifying trusts gains"),

(*b*) the trustees would (apart from this Chapter) be chargeable to capital gains tax in respect of those gains,

[(*c*) the trustees are resident in the United Kingdom during any part of the tax year, and][3]

(*d*) a claim for special tax treatment under this Chapter for the tax year is made by the trustees.

(1A) . . . [1]

(2) Special capital gains tax treatment applies for the tax year in accordance with—

(*a*) section 31 (vulnerable person UK resident [for][2] the tax year), or

(*b*) section 32 (vulnerable person non-UK resident [for][2] the tax year).

(3) But this section does not have effect in relation to the tax year if the vulnerable person dies during that year.

(3A) . . . [1]

(4) The reference in subsection (1)(*a*) to chargeable gains accruing to the trustees from the disposal of settled property includes a reference to chargeable gains treated as accruing to them under section 13 of TCGA 1992 (attribution of gains to members of non-resident companies).

(5) . . .[2]

Commentary—*Simon's Taxes* **C4.257.**

Amendment—[1]   Sub-ss (1A), (3A) repealed by FA 2008 s 8, Sch 2 paras 11, 15 with effect for the tax year 2008–09 and subsequent tax years.

[2]   Word in sub-s (2)(*a*), (*b*) substituted, and sub-s (5) repealed, by FA 2013 s 218, Sch 45 para 151(1), (3) with effect from 17 July 2013.

[3]   Sub-s (1)(*c*) substituted by FA 2013 s 219, Sch 46 para 133 with effect in relation to the tax year 2013–14 and any subsequent tax year

31 UK resident vulnerable persons: [amount of relief][1]

(1) Special capital gains tax treatment applies for the tax year in accordance with this section if the vulnerable person is UK resident [for][2] the tax year.

[(2) The trustees' liability to capital gains tax for the tax year is to be reduced by an amount equal to—

$$TQTG - VQTG$$

where—

TQTG is the amount of capital gains tax to which the trustees would (apart from this Chapter) be liable for the tax year in respect of the qualifying trust gains, and

VQTG is the amount arrived at under subsection (3).

(3) That amount is—

$$TLVA - TLVB$$

where—

TLVB is the total amount of capital gains tax to which the vulnerable person is liable for the tax year, and

TLVA is what TLVB would be if the qualifying trust gains accrued to the vulnerable person (instead of to the trustees) and no allowable losses were deducted from the qualifying trust gains.][1]

Commentary—*Simon's Taxes* **C4.257.**

Amendments—[1]   Sub-ss (2), (3), and words in heading, substituted, by FA 2008 s 8, Sch 2 paras 11,16 with effect for the tax year 2008–09 and subsequent tax years.

[2]   Word in sub-s (1) substituted for word "during" by FA 2013 s 218, Sch 45 para 151(1), (4) with effect from 17 July 2013.

32 Non-UK resident vulnerable persons: amount of relief

(1) Special capital gains tax treatment applies for the tax year in accordance with this section if the vulnerable person is non-UK resident [for][2] the tax year.

(2) The trustees' liability to capital gains tax for the tax year is to be reduced by an amount equal to—

$$TQTG - VQTG$$

where—

TQTG is the amount of capital gains tax to which the trustees would (apart from this Chapter) be liable for the tax year in respect of the qualifying trusts gains, and

[VQTG is the amount arrived at under subsection (3).][1]

[(3) That amount is—

$$TLVA - TLVB$$

where—

TLVB is the total amount of capital gains tax to which the vulnerable person would be liable for the tax year if the vulnerable person's taxable amount for the tax year . . .[3] were equal to the vulnerable person's deemed CGT taxable amount for the tax year (if any), and

TLVA is what TLVB would be if the vulnerable person's taxable amount for the tax year . . .[3] were equal to the aggregate of the vulnerable person's deemed CGT taxable amount for the tax year (if any) and the amount of the qualifying trust gains.

[(3A) For the purposes of this section "the vulnerable person's taxable amount for the tax year" means the amount on which that person would be chargeable to capital gains tax for the tax year if no account were taken of section 1K of TCGA 1992.][3]

(4) For the purposes of this section the vulnerable person's deemed CGT taxable amount for the tax year is to be determined in accordance with Schedule 1.][1]

Commentary—*Simon's Taxes* **C4.257.**

Amendments—[1]   Definition of VQTG substituted, and sub-ss (3), (4) inserted, by FA 2008 s 8, Sch 2 paras 11, 17 with effect for the tax year 2008–09 and subsequent tax years.

[2]   Word in sub-s (1) substituted for word "during" by FA 2013 s 218, Sch 45 para 151(1), (5) with effect from 17 July 2013.

³ In sub-s (3) words "for the purposes of section 3 of TCGA 1992" repealed, and sub-s (3A) inserted, by FA 2019 s 13, Sch 1 paras 96, 97 with effect for capital gains tax purposes for the tax year 2019–20 and subsequent tax years, and for corporation tax purposes for accounting periods beginning on or after 6 April 2019. These amendments also have effect for corporation tax purposes in relation to disposals made on or after 6 April 2019 (whether in their application to accounting periods beginning on, and ending on or after, that date or to later accounting periods). See also transitional provisions in FA 2019 Sch 1 paras 121–126.

Qualifying trusts

34 Disabled persons

(1) For the purposes of this Chapter where property is held on trusts for the benefit of a disabled person those trusts are qualifying trusts if they secure that the conditions in subsection (2) are met—

    (a) during the lifetime of the disabled person, or

    (b) until the termination of the trusts (if that occurs before his death).

(2) Those conditions are—

    (a) that if any of the property is applied for the benefit of a beneficiary, it is applied for the benefit of the disabled person, and

    [(b) either—

        (i) that the disabled person is entitled to all the income (if there is any) arising from any of the property, or

        (ii) if any such income is applied for the benefit of a beneficiary, it is applied for the benefit of the disabled person.]¹

[(3) The trusts on which property is held are not to be treated as failing to secure that the conditions in subsection (2) are met by reason only of—

    (a) the trustees' having powers that enable them to apply in any tax year otherwise than for the benefit of the disabled person amounts (whether consisting of income or capital, or both) not exceeding the annual limit,

    (b) the trustees' having the powers conferred by section 32 of the Trustee Act 1925 (powers of advancement),

    (c) the trustees' having those powers but free from, or subject to a less restrictive limitation than, the limitation imposed by proviso (a) of subsection (1) of that section,

    (d) the trustees' having the powers conferred by section 33 of the Trustee Act (Northern Ireland) 1958 (corresponding provision for Northern Ireland),

    (e) the trustees' having those powers but free from, or subject to a less restrictive limitation than, the limitation imposed by subsection (1)(a) of that section, or

    (f) the trustees' having powers to the like effect as the powers mentioned in any of paragraphs (b) to (e).

(3B) For the purposes of this section, the "annual limit" for a tax year is whichever is the lower of the following amounts—

    (a) £3,000, and

    (b) 3% of the amount that is the maximum value of the settled property during the tax year in question.

(3C) The Treasury may by order made by statutory instrument—

    (a) specify circumstances in which subsection (3)(a) is, or is not, to apply in relation to a trust, and

    (b) amend the definition of "the annual limit" in subsection (3B).

(3D) An order under subsection (3C) may—

    (a) make different provision for different cases, and

    (b) contain transitional and saving provision.

(3E) A statutory instrument containing an order under subsection (3C) may not be made unless a draft of the instrument has been laid before, and approved by a resolution of, the House of Commons.]¹

(4) The reference in subsection (1) to the lifetime of the disabled person is, where property is held for his benefit on trusts of the kind described in section 33 of the Trustee Act 1925 (protective trusts), to be construed as a reference to the period during which such property is held on trust for him.

Commentary—*Simon's Taxes* C4.258.

Amendment—¹ Sub-s (2)(b) substituted, and sub-ss (3)–(3E) substituted for previous sub-s (3), by FA 2013 s 216, Sch 44 paras 14, 15 with effect for the tax year 2013–14 and subsequent tax years.

35 Relevant minors

(1) For the purposes of this Chapter where property is held on trusts for the benefit of a relevant minor those trusts are qualifying trusts if they are—

    (a) statutory trusts for the relevant minor under sections 46 and 47(1) of the Administration of Estates Act 1925 (c 23) (succession on intestacy and statutory trusts in favour of relatives of intestate), or

    (b) trusts to which subsection (2) below applies.

(2) This subsection applies to trusts—

    (a) established under the will of a deceased parent of the relevant minor, or

(b) established under the Criminal Injuries Compensation Scheme, [or

(c) established under the Victims of Overseas Terrorism Compensation Scheme,][1]

which secure that the conditions in subsection (3) are met.

(3) Those conditions are—

(a) that the relevant minor will, on attaining the age of 18, become absolutely entitled to the property, any income arising from it and any income that has arisen from property held on the trusts for his benefit and been accumulated before that time,

(b) that, until that time, for so long as the relevant minor is living, if any of the property is applied for the benefit of a beneficiary, it is applied for the benefit of the relevant minor, and

(c) that, until that time, for so long as the relevant minor is living, either—

(i) the relevant minor is entitled to all the income (if there is any) arising from any of the property, or

[(ii) if any such income is applied for the benefit of a beneficiary, it is applied for the benefit of the relevant minor.][2]

[(4) Trusts to which subsection (2) applies are not to be treated as failing to secure that the conditions in subsection (3) are met by reason only of—

(a) the trustees' having powers that enable them to apply in any tax year otherwise than for the benefit of the relevant minor amounts (whether consisting of income or capital, or both) not exceeding the annual limit,

(b) the trustees' having the powers conferred by section 32 of the Trustee Act 1925 (powers of advancement),

(c) the trustees' having those powers but free from, or subject to a less restrictive limitation than, the limitation imposed by proviso (a) of subsection (1) of that section,

(d) the trustees' having the powers conferred by section 33 of the Trustee Act (Northern Ireland) 1958 (corresponding provision for Northern Ireland),

(e) the trustees' having those powers but free from, or subject to a less restrictive limitation than, the limitation imposed by subsection (1)(a) of that section, or

(f) the trustees' having powers to the like effect as the powers mentioned in any of paragraphs (b) to (e).

(4B) For the purposes of this section, the "annual limit" for a tax year is whichever is the lower of the following amounts—

(a) £3,000, and

(b) 3% of the amount that is the maximum value of the settled property during the tax year in question.

(4C) The Treasury may by order made by statutory instrument—

(a) specify circumstances in which subsection (4)(a) is, or is not, to apply in relation to a trust, and

(b) amend the definition of "the annual limit" in subsection (4B).

(4D) An order under subsection (4C) may—

(a) make different provision for different cases, and

(b) contain transitional and saving provision.

(4E) A statutory instrument containing an order under subsection (4C) may not be made unless a draft of the instrument has been laid before, and approved by a resolution of, the House of Commons.][2]

(5) In this section "the Criminal Injuries Compensation Scheme" means—

(a) the schemes established by arrangements made under the Criminal Injuries Compensation Act 1995 (c 53),

(b) arrangements made by the Secretary of State for compensation for criminal injuries in operation before the commencement of those schemes, or

(c) the scheme established under the Criminal Injuries (Northern Ireland) Order 2002 (SI 2002/796 (NI 1)).

Commentary—*Simon's Taxes* C4.258.

Amendment—[1] Sub-s (2)(c) and preceding word "or" inserted by the Crime and Security Act 2010, s 48(4), Sch 2 para 4 with effect from 8 April 2010 (Crime and Security Act 2010 s 59(2)(b)).

[2] Sub-s (3)(c)(ii) substituted, and sub-ss (4)–(4E) substituted for previous sub-s (4), by FA 2013 s 216, Sch 44 paras 14, 16 with effect for the tax year 2013–14 and subsequent tax years.

36 Parts of assets

For the purposes of this Chapter references to property being held on trusts include references to a part of an asset being held on trusts if—

(a) that part of the asset, and

(b) any income arising from it (or treated as arising from it),

can be identified for the purpose of determining whether the trusts on which it is held are qualifying trusts.

Commentary—*Simon's Taxes* C4.258.

Vulnerable persons

37 Vulnerable person election

(1) Where [the trustees of a settlement]² hold property on trusts for the benefit of a person, the trustees and that person may jointly make a vulnerable person election in relation to those trusts and that person if—

    (a) the person in relation to whom the election is made is a vulnerable person, and

    (b) the trusts in relation to which the election is made are qualifying trusts.

(2) A vulnerable person election is an election in such form as the Board of Inland Revenue may require—

    (a) specifying the date from which it is to have effect ("the effective date"),

    (b) made by notice to the Inland Revenue no later than 12 months after 31st January next following the tax year in which the effective date falls, or within such further time, if any, as the Board of Inland Revenue may by notice have allowed, and

    (c) containing the items specified in subsection (3).

(3) Those items are—

    (a) such information as the Board of Inland Revenue may require, including in particular information relating to the trusts, the trustees, the vulnerable person and his entitlement under the trusts and any other person connected with the trusts,

    (b) a statement that the trusts in relation to which the election is made are qualifying trusts,

    (c) a declaration that all the information contained in the election is correct to the best of the knowledge and belief of the trustees and vulnerable person,

    (d) a declaration by the vulnerable person that he authorises the trustees to make any claim under this Chapter for any tax year as they consider appropriate, and

    (e) such other declarations as the Board of Inland Revenue may reasonably require.

(4) A vulnerable person election is irrevocable.

(5) A vulnerable person election has effect from the effective date until one of the following events occurs—

    (a) the person in relation to whom the election is made ceases to be a vulnerable person,

    (b) the trusts in relation to which the election is made cease to be qualifying trusts, and

    (c) the trusts are terminated.

(6) If the trustees become aware that an event mentioned in subsection (5) has occurred—

    (a) they must inform the Inland Revenue that the vulnerable person election has ceased to have effect, and

    (b) they must do so by giving notice containing particulars of the event within the period of 90 days beginning on the date on which they first become aware that the event has occurred.

[(7) Where—

    (a) a vulnerable person election has effect in relation to qualifying trusts,

    (b) the property held on those trusts is treated for the purposes of TCGA 1992 and of the Tax Acts as comprised in a sub-fund settlement, and

    (c) the vulnerable person election was not made by the trustees of the sub-fund settlement,

the vulnerable person election shall have effect, in relation to the trusts mentioned in paragraph (a), in respect of matters arising at or after the time when the sub-fund election is treated as having taken effect, as if it had been made by the trustees of the sub-fund settlement and the vulnerable person.]¹

[(8) In relation to matters arising before the time when the sub-fund election is treated as having taken effect, nothing in subsection (7)—

    (a) relieves the trustees of the settlement which is the principal settlement in relation to the sub-fund settlement of their obligation under subsection (6), or

    (b) prevents a notice from being given to those trustees under section 40(1) or (3).]¹

[(9) In this section—

    (a) "principal settlement" has the meaning given by paragraph 1 of Schedule 4ZA to TCGA 1992,

    (b) "sub-fund election" has the meaning given by paragraph 2 of that Schedule,

    (c) "sub-fund settlement" has the meaning given by paragraph 1 of that Schedule, and

    (d) the time when a sub-fund election is treated as having taken effect shall be the time when it is treated as having taken effect under paragraph 2 of that Schedule.]¹

Commentary—*Simon's Taxes* C4.259.

Amendment—¹ Sub-ss (7)–(9) inserted by FA 2006 s 88, Sch 12 para 48(4), (5) with effect from 6 April 2006 (in relation to vulnerable persons elections whenever made).

²   Words in sub-s (1) substituted for word "trustees" by FA 2006 s 89, Sch 13 para 35(2) with effect from 6 April 2006.

[38 Meaning of "disabled person"

In this Chapter "disabled person" has the meaning given by Schedule 1A.]¹

Commentary—*Simon's Taxes* C4.259.

Amendment—¹ This section substituted by FA 2013 s 216, Sch 44 paras 14, 17 with effect for the tax year 2013–14 and subsequent tax years.

39 Meaning of "relevant minor"

For the purposes of this Chapter a person is a "relevant minor" if—

(a) he has not yet attained the age of 18, and

(b) at least one of his parents has died.

Commentary—*Simon's Taxes* **C4.259.**

Miscellaneous and supplementary

40 Power to make enquiries

(1) Where a vulnerable person election has been made the Inland Revenue may by notice require the trustees or the vulnerable person by whom the election was made to furnish them with such particulars as they may reasonably require for the purposes of determining—

(a) whether the requirements mentioned in subsection (1)(a) and (b) of section 37 were met at the time the election was made, and

(b) whether an event mentioned in subsection (5) of that section has occurred since the effective date.

(2) The notice must specify the time within which the information must be furnished (not being less than 60 days).

(3) If the Board of Inland Revenue determine—

(a) that either or both of the requirements mentioned in subsection (1)(a) and (b) of section 37 were not met at the time the election was made, or

(b) that an event mentioned in subsection (5) of that section has occurred since the effective date of the election,

they may give notice to the trustees and the person in relation to whom the vulnerable person election was made that the election never had effect or ceased to have effect from a date specified in the notice.

(4) A person aggrieved by a determination of the Board of Inland Revenue under subsection (3) may by notice appeal . . . [1].

(5) The notice of appeal must be given to the Board of Inland Revenue within 30 days after the notice of the determination was given under subsection (3).

(6) All such adjustments shall be made, whether by discharge or repayment of tax, the making of assessments or otherwise, as are required to give effect to a determination under subsection (3) (despite any limitation on the time within which any adjustment may be made).

(7) In subsection (6) "tax" means income tax or capital gains tax.

Commentary—*Simon's Taxes* **C4.260.**

Amendments—[1] In sub-s (4), words "to the Special Commissioners" repealed by the Transfer of Tribunal Functions and Revenue and Customs Appeals Order, SI 2009/56 art 3, Sch 1 para 445 with effect from 1 April 2009.

41 Interpretation etc

(1) In this Chapter—

"the Board of Inland Revenue" means the Commissioners of Inland Revenue (as to which, see in particular the Inland Revenue Regulation Act 1890 (c 21)),

"the Inland Revenue" means any officer of the Board of Inland Revenue,

["non-UK resident" means not resident in the United Kingdom in accordance with the statutory residence test in Part 1 of Schedule 45 to FA 2013,][3]

"notice" means notice in writing, and

  . . . [2]

["UK resident" means resident in the United Kingdom in accordance with the statutory residence test in Part 1 of Schedule 45 to FA 2013.][3]

(2) . . . [3]

(3) Sections 30 to [32][1] and Schedule 1 are to be construed as one with TCGA 1992.

(4) To the extent that any provision of this Chapter would not, apart from this subsection, form part of Income Tax Acts, the provisions of the Income Tax Acts are to apply for the purposes of any references in the provision relating to income arising (or treated as arising) to a person or to the income tax liability of a person.

Commentary—*Simon's Taxes* **C4.260.**

Amendments—[1] Figure in sub-s (3) substituted by FA 2008 s 8, Sch 2 paras 11, 19 with effect for the tax year 2008–09 and subsequent tax years.

[2] Definition of "tax year" repealed by FA 2008 s 8, Sch 2 para 102(a) with effect from 21 July 2008.

[3] Definitions in sub-s (1) inserted and sub-s (2) repealed by FA 2013 s 218, Sch 45 para 151(1), (6) with effect from 17 July 2013.

42 Application in relation to Scotland

(1) This Chapter applies in relation to Scotland with the following modifications.

(2) In section 23(5), for "trusts on which property is held for the benefit of a vulnerable person are qualifying trusts" substitute "property held in trust for the benefit of a vulnerable person is held in qualifying trust".

(3) In section 31(3)(*a*), for "on the qualifying trusts" substitute "in qualifying trust (in the same trust as the settled property disposed of)".

(4) In section 34—

    (*a*) in subsection (1), for "those trusts are qualifying trusts if they" substitute "the property is held in qualifying trust if the trust purposes", and

    (*b*) in subsection (4), for "on trusts" substitute "in a trust".

(5) In section 35—

    (*a*) in subsection (1), for "those trusts are qualifying trusts if they are" substitute "the property is held in qualifying trust if the trust is",

    (*b*) . . .[1]

    (*c*) in subsection (2), before "which" insert "the purposes of".

(6) In section 36, for "the trusts on which it is held are qualifying trusts" substitute "it is held in qualifying trust".

(7) In section 37—

    (*a*) in subsection (1), for paragraph (*b*) substitute—

        "(*b*) property held in the trust in relation to which the election is made is held in qualifying trust.",

    (*b*) in subsection (3)(*b*), for "the trusts in relation to which the election is made are qualifying trusts" substitute "property held in the trust in relation to which the election is made is held in qualifying trust", and

    (*c*) in subsection (5), for paragraph (*b*) substitute—

        "(*b*) property held in the trust in relation to which the election is made ceases to be held in qualifying trust,".

(8) Sections 34(3) and 35(4) do not apply to Scotland

(9) Unless otherwise modified by this section, any reference to anything being held on trusts is to be construed as a reference to it being held in trust.

(10) Unless otherwise modified or disapplied by this section, any reference to trusts is to be construed as a reference to a trust or the trust (as appropriate).

Commentary—*Simon's Taxes* C4.260.

Amendment—[1] Sub-s (5)(*b*) repealed by FA 2006 ss 89, 178, Sch 13 para 35(5), Sch 26 Pt 3(15) with effect from 6 April 2006.

43 Penalties under TMA 1970

(1) Section 98 of TMA 1970 (special returns, etc) is amended as follows.

(2), (3) (*amend* the table in TMA 1970 s 98).

(4) For the purposes of that section, any information, statements or declarations given or made jointly by [the trustees of a settlement][1] and a vulnerable person are to be treated as given or made by the trustees.

Commentary—*Simon's Taxes* C4.260.

Amendment—[1] Words in sub-s (4) substituted for word "trustees" by FA 2006 s 89, Sch 13 para 35(6) with effect from 6 April 2006.

45 Commencement

This Chapter has effect for the tax year beginning on 6th April 2004 and subsequent tax years.

Commentary—*Simon's Taxes* C4.255.

CHAPTER 5

ALTERNATIVE FINANCE ARRANGEMENTS

48 Arrangements within section 47: foreign currency and non-residents

(1) . . . [1]

(2) (*inserted* FA 2003 s 148(5A); *repealed by* CTA 2010 s 1181 Sch 3 Pt 1)

(3) (*inserted* FA 1995 s 127(1)(*cc*); *repealed by* TIOPA 2010 ss 501, 503, Sch 8 paras 213, 214, Sch 10 Pts 7, 11)

Amendment—[1] Sub-s (1) repealed by TIOPA 2010 ss 501, 503, Sch 8 paras 213, 214, Sch 10 Pts 7, 11. TIOPA 2010 has effect for corporation tax purposes for accounting periods ending on or after 1 April 2010, for income and capital gains tax purposes for the tax year 2010–11 and subsequent tax years, and for petroleum revenue tax purposes for chargeable periods beginning on or after 1 July 2010.

CHAPTER 8

ACCOUNTING PRACTICE AND RELATED MATTERS

80 Accounting practice and related matters

(1) Schedule 4 (accounting practice and related matters) has effect.

(2) In that Schedule—

    Part 1 makes provision about bad debts and related matters;

    Part 2 makes other provision connected with accounting practice.

(3) Part 1 of the Schedule, so far as it amends provisions that have effect both for income tax and corporation tax, has effect for the purposes of corporation tax only.

(4) Except as otherwise provided, the provisions of the Schedule have effect for periods of account beginning on or after 1st January 2005.

82 Change of accounting practice: deferment of transitional adjustments

(1) This section applies where—

    (*a*) a company enters into a transaction on or after 14th December 2004, otherwise than in the ordinary course of its business,

    (*b*) as a result of the transaction it incurs a loss in respect of a loan relationship or derivative contract in respect of which, apart from this section, a debit would fall to be brought into account for tax purposes in a period of account beginning before 1st January 2005,

    (*c*) the sole or main purpose of the company in entering into the transaction at the time it did was to enable it to bring a debit into account for tax purposes in such a period, and

    (*d*) if the company had continued to hold the asset or liability representing the loan relationship or derivative contract, as it was held immediately before the transaction referred to in paragraph (*a*), in its first period of account beginning on or after 1st January 2005, a debit would have arisen in respect of the loan relationship or derivative contract in that period that was a prescribed debit for the purposes of regulation 3 of the Loan Relationship and Derivative Contracts (Change of Accounting Practice) Regulations 2004 (SI 2004/3271) (debits not to be brought into account until the company's first period beginning on or after 1st January 2006).

(2) Where this section applies no such debit as is mentioned in subsection (1)(*b*) shall be brought into account in the period of account mentioned there, but a debit of the same amount shall instead be brought into account as if it were a prescribed debit for the purposes of the regulation referred to in subsection (1)(*d*) (even though the loss giving rise to the debit was incurred before 1st January 2005).

(3) In determining the sole or main purpose of a company for the purposes of subsection (1)(*c*) regard shall be had to anything done by a connected company that would be relevant for the purposes of that determination if done by the company in question.

For this purpose companies are connected if they are connected persons within the meaning of section 839 of ICTA.

(4) For the purposes of subsection (1)(*d*) it shall be assumed that the loan relationship or derivative contract has the same value at the beginning of the company's first period of account beginning on or after 1st January 2005 as it had at the time of the transaction referred to in subsection (1)(*a*).

(5) This section does not apply where the transaction is entered into in pursuance of legally binding arrangements entered into before 14th December 2004.

(6) In this section, references to a company entering into a transaction include a reference to the company, or the directors of the company, taking a decision about a loan relationship or derivative contract that affects its treatment for accounting purposes (other than a decision to prepare some or all of the company's accounts in accordance with international accounting standards).

Commentary—*Simon's Taxes* D1.8104.

83 Application of accounting standards to securitisation companies

(1) For the purposes of the Corporation Tax Acts as they apply to a securitisation company in relation to a period of account—

    (*a*) beginning on or after 1st January 2005, and

    (*b*) [(subject to subsection (7A)(*a*))][2] ending before [1st January 2008][1],

generally accepted accounting practice shall be taken to be UK generally accepted accounting practice as it applied for a period of account ending on 31st December 2004.

(2) For the purposes of this section a "securitisation company" means a company that is—

    (*a*) a note-issuing company,

    (*b*) an asset-holding company,

    (*c*) an intermediate borrowing company,

    (*d*) a warehouse company, or

    (*e*) a commercial paper funded company,

as defined below.

(3) A "note-issuing company" means a company in relation to which the following conditions are met—

    (*a*) it is party as debtor to a capital market investment,

    (*b*) the securities that represent the capital market investment are issued wholly or mainly to independent persons,

    (*c*) the capital market investment is part of a capital market arrangement, . . . [1]

    (*d*) the total value of the capital market investments made under that capital market arrangement is at least £50 million[; and

(e) if it has any business apart from the activity mentioned in paragraph (a) (and any incidental activities) it consists in one or both of the following—

    (i) acquiring, holding and managing assets forming the whole or part of the security for the capital market arrangement;

    (ii) acting as guarantor in respect of loan relationships, derivative contracts, finance leases or other liabilities of other companies where the whole, or substantially the whole, of the company's rights in respect of the guarantee (including any right of subrogation) form the whole or part of the security for the capital market arrangement.][1]

(4) An "asset-holding company" means a company—

(a) whose business (apart from any incidental activities) consists in acquiring, holding and managing assets forming the whole or part of the security for a capital market arrangement entered into by a note-issuing company, and

(b) whose liabilities representing debtor relationships are owed wholly or mainly to a note-issuing company or intermediate borrowing company.

(5) An "intermediate borrowing company" means a company—

(a) whose only business is to enter into and be a party to creditor relationships with an asset-holding company [(or another intermediate borrowing company)][1], and

(b) whose liabilities representing debtor relationships are owed wholly, or substantially wholly, to a note-issuing company[(or another intermediate borrowing company)][1].

(6) A "warehouse company" means a company whose business consists wholly of acquiring and holding financial assets for the purpose—

(a) of transferring them to a company (whether or not yet in existence) that at the time of the transfer is, or as a result of the transfer will become, an asset-holding or note-issuing company, or

(b) of itself becoming an asset-holding or note-issuing company.

(7) A "commercial paper funded company" means—

(a) a company that was an asset-holding company but whose obligations under debtor relationships to a note-issuing company or intermediate borrowing company—

    (i) have been transferred to, or

    (ii) have been replaced by obligations under debtor relationships to,

one or more companies carrying on a business of banking, or

(b) a company that was an intermediate borrowing company but whose obligations under debtor relationships to a note-issuing company—

    (i) have been transferred to, or

    (ii) have been replaced by obligations under debtor relationships to,

one or more companies carrying on a business of banking.

[(7A) The Treasury may by regulations—

(a) make provision for subsection (1) to apply in relation to periods of account ending on or after 1st January 2008 but before a date specified by the regulations, and

(b) make provision modifying any provision of, or made under, the Corporation Tax Acts in relation to the first period of account of securitisation companies in the case of which subsection (1) does not apply (whether by virtue of that subsection itself or regulations under paragraph (a)).][2]

[(7B) Regulations under subsection (7A)(a) may, in particular—

(a) specify a date only in relation to specified descriptions of company,

(b) specify different dates in relation to different descriptions of company, and

(c) include provision for a company to elect that the regulations are to apply to it or provision for a company to elect that they are not to apply to it.][2]

(8) In this section—

"asset" includes any option, future or contract for differences as defined for the purposes of [Part 7 of CTA 2009 (derivative contracts) (see sections 580, 581 and 582 of that Act)][3];

"capital market investment" and "capital market arrangement" have the same meaning as in section 72B(1) of the Insolvency Act 1986 (c 45) (see paragraphs 1, 2 and 3 of Schedule 2A to that Act);

"company" includes a partnership;

"financial asset" has the meaning it has for accounting purposes; and

"independent persons" means persons who are not connected with the company.

(9) Section 839 of ICTA (connected persons) applies for the purposes of the definition above of "independent persons", except that in applying the definition of "control" in that section a person is not to be treated as a participator in a company by reason only that he is a loan creditor of the company.

Regulations—The Securitisation Companies (Application of Section 83(1) of the Finance Act 2005: Accounting Standards) Regulations, SI 2007/3338 (continued application of sub-s (1) for periods of account ending before 1 January 2017 in relation to companies to which the provision applied in a period of account ending before 1 January 2008, unless companies elect otherwise).

The Securitisation Companies (Application of Section 83(1) of the Finance Act 2005: Accounting Standards) Regulations, SI 2016/1182 (continued application of sub-s (1) for periods of account ending before 1 January 2037 in relation to companies to which the provision applied in a period of account ending before 1 January 2008, unless companies elect otherwise).

Modifications—This section modified, so as not to apply to a securitisation company, by the Taxation of Securitisation Companies Regulations, SI 2006/3296 reg 21.

This section modified in relation to the first period of account of a securitisation company, by the Securitisation Companies (Application of Section 83(1) of the Finance Act 2005: Accounting Standards) Regulations, SI 2007/3338.

Amendments—[1]   In sub-s (1)(b) words substituted for the words "1st January 2007", in sub-s (3)(c) word "and" repealed, para (e) and preceding word inserted, and words in sub-s (5) inserted, by FA 2006 ss 101(1)–(4), (6)–(8), 178, Sch 26 Pt 3(19) and deemed always to have had effect, subject to FA 2006 s 101(7), (8).

[2]   Words in sub-s (1)(b) inserted, and sub-ss (7A), (7B) inserted, by FA 2007 s 59(1)–(3) with effect from 19 July 2007.

[3]   In sub-para (8) words substituted for words "Schedule 26 to FA 2002 (derivative contracts) (see paragraph 12 of that Schedule)" by CTA 2009 s 1322, Sch 1 paras 648, 662. CTA 2009 applies for accounting periods ending on or after 1 April 2009 (for corporation tax purposes) and for tax years 2009–10 onwards (for income and capital gains tax purposes).

CHAPTER 9

INTERNATIONAL MATTERS

Double taxation relief: restrictions

86 Limits on credit: income tax and corporation tax: trading profits

(1) (substituted TA 1988 ss 798–798C; *repealed by* TIOPA 2010 s 503, Sch 10 Pt 1)

(2) (amended TA 1988 s 803(1) and *repeals* TA 1988 s 803(4)–(9); *repealed* in part by TIOPA 2010 s 503, Sch 10 Pt 1)

(3) Subsections (1) and (2) shall have effect—

(a) for the purposes of corporation tax, in relation to a credit for foreign tax which relates to—

(i) a payment of foreign tax on or after 16th March 2005, or

(ii) income received on or after that date in respect of which foreign tax has been deducted at source, and

(b) for the purposes of income tax, in relation to a credit for foreign tax which relates to—

(i) a payment of foreign tax on or after 6th April 2005, or

(ii) income received on or after that date in respect of which foreign tax has been deducted at source.

(4) In subsection (3) a reference to tax deducted at source is a reference to tax deducted or treated as deducted from income, or treated as paid in respect of income.

(5) In respect of dividends paid before 1st January 2006, the effect of section 798 or 798A of ICTA in respect of credit for foreign tax shall be disregarded to the extent that it would otherwise reduce the allowable credit to less than 50% of the foreign tax; but this subsection shall not apply to tax paid as part of a scheme or arrangement designed or entered into for the purposes of causing this subsection to apply.

88 Self-assessment amendments

(1), (2) *(insert* TMA 1970 ss 9A(4)(c), 29(7A)).

(3) *(amended* FA 1998 Sch 18 para 25(1); *repealed by* TIOPA 2010 s 503, Sch 10 Pt 1))

(4) *(inserts* FA 1998 Sch 18 para para 42(2A))

(5) The amendments made by this section have effect in accordance with section 87(3).

Annual payments and double taxation relief

91 Tax avoidance involving annual payments and double taxation relief

(1) ICTA is amended as follows.

(2) *(substituted* TA 1988 s 125(2)(b); *repealed by* CTA 2009 s 1326, Sch 3 Pt 1)

(3) *(amended* heading to TA 1988 s 125; *repealed by* CTA 2009 s 1326, Sch 3 Pt 1))

(4) Section 801 (dividends paid between related companies: relief for UK and third country taxes) is amended as follows.

(5) *(amended* TA 1988 s 801(2); *repealed by* TIOPA 2010 s 503, Sch 10 Pt 1)

(6) *(repeals* TA 1988 s 801(4A)–(4D)).

(7) . . .

(8) The amendments made by subsections (4) to (6) have effect in relation to dividends paid on or after 2nd December 2004.

Amendment—Sub-s (7) repealed by CTA 2009 s 1326, Sch 3 Pt 1. CTA 2009 applies for accounting periods ending on or after 1 April 2009 (for corporation tax purposes) and for tax years 2009–10 onwards (for income and capital gains tax purposes).

CHAPTER 10

MISCELLANEOUS
Capital allowances

92 Capital allowances: renovation of business premises in disadvantaged areas

Schedule 6 (capital allowances in respect of expenditure on the conversion or renovation of qualifying business premises in disadvantaged areas) has effect in relation to expenditure incurred on or after such day as the Treasury may by order appoint.

Commentary—*Simon's Taxes* **B3.1101.**

Orders—Finance Act 2005, Section 92 and Schedule 6, (Appointed Day) Order, SI 2007/949 (appointed day is 11 April 2007).

Tonnage tax

93 Tonnage tax

Schedule 7 (which makes provision amending Schedule 22 to FA 2000) has effect.

PART 4
OTHER TAXES

Lorry road-user charge

100 Lorry road-user charge

(*substitutes* FA 2002 s 137(7) (not reproduced))

PART 5
PENSIONS ETC

101 Pension schemes etc

Schedule 10 contains provision about pension schemes and related matters.

Commentary—*Simon's Taxes* **E7.201.**

102 Pension Protection Fund etc

(1) The Treasury may by regulations make provision for and in connection with the application of the relevant taxes in relation to—

    (*a*) the Pension Protection Fund,

    (*b*) the Fraud Compensation Fund, and

    (*c*) the Board of the Pension Protection Fund,

and in relation to any person in connection with either of those Funds or that Board.

(2) The provision that may be made by the regulations includes provision imposing any of the relevant taxes (as well as provision for exemptions or reliefs).

(3) The relevant taxes are—

    (*a*) income tax,

    (*b*) capital gains tax,

    (*c*) corporation tax,

    (*d*) inheritance tax,

    (*e*) value added tax, and

    (*f*) stamp duty land tax.

(4) The regulations may, in particular, include provision for and in connection with the taxation of payments made in accordance with the pension compensation provisions (within the meaning of Part 2 of the Pensions Act 2004 (c 35): see section 162(2) of that Act).

(5) The exemptions and reliefs that may be given by the regulations include, in particular, exemption from—

    (*a*) charges to corporation tax in respect of any income arising from any assets of the Board (or in either Fund) and other receipts of the Board (or either Fund) and any chargeable gains arising from the disposal of any assets of the Board (or in either Fund),

    (*b*) charges to income tax and corporation tax in respect of the levies referred to in sections 117, 174, 175, 189 and 209 of the Pensions Act 2004, and

    (*c*) any charge to capital gains tax, or corporation tax on chargeable gains, in respect of the receipt of fraud compensation payments (within the meaning of Part 2 of that Act: see section 182(1) of that Act).

(6) The regulations may make provision in relation to any time after 5th April 2005.

(7) The provision made by the regulations may be framed as provision applying with appropriate modifications—

    (*a*) for times before 6th April 2006, provisions having effect in relation to exempt approved schemes (within the meaning of Chapter 1 of Part 14 of ICTA: see section 592(1) of that Act), and

    (*b*) for times on or after that date, provisions having effect in relation to registered pension schemes (within the meaning of [section 150(2) of the Finance Act 2004][1]).

(8) The regulations may include—

    (*a*) provision amending any enactment or instrument, and

(*b*) consequential, supplementary and transitional provisions.

(9) The regulations are to be made by statutory instrument which shall be subject to annulment in pursuance of a resolution of the House of Commons.

(10) In this section—

"the Board of the Pension Protection Fund" means the body corporate established under section 107 of the Pensions Act 2004 (c 35),

"the Fraud Compensation Fund" means the Fund required to be held, managed and applied by that Board under paragraph (*b*) of subsection (1) of section 110 of that Act, and

"the Pension Protection Fund" means the Fund required to be held, managed and applied by that Board under paragraph (*a*) of that subsection.

Regulations—Pension Protection Fund (Tax) (2005–06) Regulations, SI 2005/1907.

Pension Protection Fund (Tax) Regulations, SI 2006/575.

Pension Protection Fund (Tax) (Amendment) Regulations, SI 2013/1117.

Amendments—[1] In sub-s (7)(*b*) words substituted by CTA 2010 s 1177, Sch 1 paras 473, 477. CTA 2010 has effect for corporation tax purposes for accounting periods ending on or after 1 April 2010, and for income and capital gains tax purposes for the tax year 2010–11 and subsequent tax years.

PART 6
MISCELLANEOUS

103 Civil partnerships etc

(1) In the case of any tax or duty, the Treasury may by regulations make provision for the purpose of securing that the events or persons specified in column 1 of the Table are treated in the same way as (or a similar way to) the corresponding events or persons specified in column 2 of the Table.

1. Events or persons	2. Corresponding events or persons
1. The formation of a civil partnership.	A marriage.
2. Persons who are, have been, or may in future be, civil partners of each other.	Persons who are, have been, or may in future be, married to each other.
3. Persons who are not civil partners of each other but who are living together as if they were.	Persons who are not married to each other but who are living together as husband and wife.
4. Persons who are not civil partners of each other.	Persons who are not married to each other.
5. A person who is not a civil partner of any other person.	A person who is not married.

(2) The provision that may be made by regulations under subsection (1) includes provision for or in connection with varying, for the purpose specified in subsection (1), the treatment that would, apart from the regulations, apply—

(*a*) on the occurrence of an event specified in column 2 of the Table, or

(*b*) in the case of persons specified in column 2 of the Table.

(3) The Treasury may by regulations make provision for the purpose of removing any inequality of treatment of persons based on gender or, in the case of a parent, marital status.

(4) Any power to make regulations under this section is exercisable by statutory instrument.

(5) A statutory instrument containing regulations under this section shall not be made unless a draft of the instrument has been laid before, and approved by a resolution of, the House of Commons.

(6) The provision that may be made by regulations under this section includes provision—

(*a*) amending any enactment, or

(*b*) applying any provision of any enactment with or without modifications.

(7) Any power to make regulations under this section includes power—

(*a*) to make different provision for different cases;

(*b*) to make incidental, supplemental, consequential or transitional provision or savings.

(8) The powers conferred by this section are exercisable in relation to enactments (including enactments contained in, or made under, this Act) passed or made at any time before the end of the Session following that in which this Act is passed.

(9) In this section—

"civil partnership" means a civil partnership which exists under or by virtue of the Civil Partnership Act 2004 (c 33) (and "civil partner" is to be read accordingly);

"enactment" includes any provision comprised in—

(*a*) an Act of the Scottish Parliament;

(*b*) Northern Ireland legislation;

(*c*) an instrument made under any enactment.

Commentary—*Simon's Taxes* E1.101.

PART 7
SUPPLEMENTARY PROVISIONS

104 Repeals

(1) The enactments mentioned in Schedule 11 (which include provisions that are spent or of no practical utility) are repealed to the extent specified.

(2) The repeals specified in that Schedule have effect subject to the commencement provisions and savings contained or referred to in the notes set out in that Schedule.

105 Interpretation

In this Act—

"ALDA 1979" means the Alcoholic Liquor Duties Act 1979 (c 4);

"CAA 2001" means the Capital Allowances Act 2001 (c 2);

["CTA 2009" means the Corporation Tax Act 2009;][2]

"FA", followed by a year, means the Finance Act of that year;

"F(No 2)A", followed by a year, means the Finance (No 2) Act of that year;

"HODA 1979" means the Hydrocarbon Oil Duties Act 1979 (c 5);

"ICTA" means the Income and Corporation Taxes Act 1988 (c 1);

"IHTA 1984" means the Inheritance Tax Act 1984 (c 51);

["ITA 2007" means the Income Tax Act 2007;][1]

"ITEPA 2003" means the Income Tax (Earnings and Pensions) Act 2003 (c 1);

"ITTOIA 2005" means the Income Tax (Trading and Other Income) Act 2005 (c 5);

"TCGA 1992" means the Taxation of Chargeable Gains Act 1992 (c 12);

"TMA 1970" means the Taxes Management Act 1970 (c 9);

"VERA 1994" means the Vehicle Excise and Registration Act 1994 (c 22).

Amendment—[1]   Entry inserted by ITA 2007 s 1027, Sch 1 paras 593, 601 with effect for income tax purposes from 6 April 2007, and corporation tax purposes for accounting periods ending after 5 April 2007.

[2]   Definition inserted by CTA 2009 s 1322, Sch 1 paras 648, 663. CTA 2009 applies for accounting periods ending on or after 1 April 2009 (for corporation tax purposes) and for tax years 2009–10 onwards (for income and capital gains tax purposes).

106 Short title

This Act may be cited as the Finance Act 2005.

SCHEDULES

SCHEDULE 1

NON-UK RESIDENT VULNERABLE PERSONS: INTERPRETATION

Sections 28 and 33

Vulnerable person's deemed CGT taxable amount

3—(1) The "vulnerable person's deemed CGT taxable amount" for the tax year means the sum of—

(a) the vulnerable person's taxable amount for the tax year [(as defined by section 32(3A))][1] calculated by reference only to actual gains and actual losses, and

(b) the vulnerable person's taxable amount for the tax year [(as defined by section 32(3A))][1] calculated by reference only to assumed gains and assumed losses.

(2) But in calculating the taxable amount under sub-paragraph (1)(b)—

(a) no deduction is to be made under [section 1(3)(b)][1] of TCGA 1992, . . . [1]

(b) . . . [1]

(3) In determining the vulnerable person's deemed CGT taxable amount for the tax year any claims or elections made in relation to any assumed gains of the vulnerable person are to be disregarded.

(4) In this paragraph—

(a) "actual gains" and "actual losses" have the meanings given in paragraph 5, and

(b) "assumed gains" and "assumed losses" have the meanings given in paragraph 6.

Amendments—[1]   In sub-para (1)(a) words substituted for words "for the purposes of section 3 of TCGA 1992"; in sub-para (1)(b) words substituted for words "for the purposes of that section"; in sub-para (2)(a) words substituted for words "section 2(2)(b)"; and sub-para (2)(b) and preceding word "and" repealed; by FA 2019 s 13, Sch 1 paras 96, 98(1), (2) with effect for capital gains tax purposes for the tax year 2019–20 and subsequent tax years, and for corporation tax purposes for accounting periods beginning on or after 6 April 2019. These amendments also have effect for corporation tax purposes in relation to disposals made on or after 6 April 2019 (whether in their application to accounting periods beginning on, and ending on or after, that date or to later accounting periods). See also transitional provisions in FA 2019 Sch 1 paras 121–126.

Actual gains and actual losses

5—(1) "Actual gains" means any chargeable gains which accrue to the vulnerable person and in respect of which he is chargeable to capital gains tax for the tax year.

(2) "Actual losses" means—

(a) any allowable losses accruing to the vulnerable person in the tax year, and

(b) so far as they have not been allowed as a deduction from chargeable gains accruing to him in any previous tax year, any allowable losses accruing to him in any previous tax year (not earlier than that beginning on 6th April 1965).

Assumed gains and assumed losses

6—(1) "Assumed gains" means any chargeable gains, other than actual gains, which, on the relevant assumptions, would accrue to the vulnerable person and in respect of which, on those assumptions, he would be chargeable to capital gains tax for the tax year.

(2) "Assumed losses" means any allowable losses, other than actual losses, which, on the relevant assumptions, would accrue to the vulnerable person in the tax year.

(3) In this paragraph "relevant assumptions" has the meaning given in paragraph 7.

Relevant assumptions

7—(1) For the purposes of [paragraph 6]¹ the "relevant assumptions" are—

(a) that the vulnerable person is resident and domiciled in the United Kingdom throughout the tax year, and

(b) that he has given a notice under subsection (2A) of section 16 of TCGA 1992 (computation of losses) in respect of each loss accruing to him in the tax year which by virtue of [section 1E(2) of that Act]² would not be an allowable loss (but for the assumption in paragraph (a)).

(2) But the relevant assumption in sub-paragraph (1)(a) does not apply for the purposes of [section 1M]² of TCGA 1992 (temporary non-residents).

Amendments—¹   Words in sub-para (1) substituted by FA 2008 s 8, Sch 2 paras 11, 20(1), (4) with effect for the tax year 2008–09 and subsequent tax years.

²   In sub-para (1)(b) words substituted for words "subsection (3) of that section", and in sub-para (2) words substituted for words "section 10A", by FA 2019 s 13, Sch 1 paras 96, 98(1), (3) with effect for capital gains tax purposes for the tax year 2019–20 and subsequent tax years, and for corporation tax purposes for accounting periods beginning on or after 6 April 2019. These amendments also have effect for corporation tax purposes in relation to disposals made on or after 6 April 2019 (whether in their application to accounting periods beginning on, and ending on or after, that date or to later accounting periods). See also transitional provisions in FA 2019 Sch 1 paras 121–126.

[SCHEDULE 1A
MEANING OF "DISABLED PERSON"]

Section 38

Amendments—This Schedule inserted by FA 2013 s 216, Sch 44 paras 14, 19 with effect from 17 July 2013.

["Disabled person"

1   "Disabled person" means—

(a) a person who by reason of mental disorder within the meaning of the Mental Health Act 1983 is incapable of administering his or her property or managing his or her affairs,

(b) a person in receipt of attendance allowance,

[(c) a person in receipt of a disability living allowance by virtue of entitlement to—

   (i) the care component at the highest or middle rate, or

   (ii) the mobility component at the higher rate,]²

(d) a person in receipt of personal independence payment . . . ²,

(e) a person in receipt of an increased disablement pension

(f) a person in receipt of constant attendance allowance, or

(g) a person in receipt of armed forces independence payment.]¹

Amendments—¹   This Schedule inserted by FA 2013 s 216, Sch 44 paras 14, 19 with effect from 17 July 2013.

²   Sub-para (c) substituted and words in sub-para (d) repealed by FA 2014 s 291(1), (2) with effect for the purposes of IHTA 1984 ss 89, 89A and 89B, in relation to property transferred into settlement, on or after 6 April 2014, and with effect for all other purposes, for the tax year 2014–15 and subsequent tax years.

[Attendance allowance

2   A person is to be treated as a disabled person under paragraph 1(b) if he or she satisfies HMRC that he or she would be entitled to receive attendance allowance but for—

(a) the conditions as to residence and presence prescribed under section 64(1) of SSCBA 1992 or section 64(1) of SSCB(NI)A 1992,

(b) provision made by regulations under section 67(1) or (2) of SSCBA 1992 or section 67(1) or (2) of SSCB(NI)A 1992 (non-satisfaction of conditions for attendance allowance where person is undergoing treatment for renal failure in hospital or is provided with certain accommodation), or (*c*) section 113(1) of SSCBA 1992 or section 113(1) of SSCB(NI)A 1992 or provision made by regulations under section 113(2) of SSCBA 1992 or section 113(2) of SSCB(NI)A 1992 (general provisions as to disqualification and suspension).][1]

Amendments—[1] This Schedule inserted by FA 2013 s 216, Sch 44 paras 14, 19 with effect from 17 July 2013.

[Disability living allowance

[3 A person is to be treated as a disabled person under paragraph 1(*c*) if he or she satisfies HMRC that he or she would be entitled to receive a disability living allowance by virtue of entitlement to the care component at the highest or middle rate[, or to the mobility component at the higher rate,][2] but for—

(*a*) the conditions as to residence and presence prescribed under section 71(6) of SSCBA 1992 or section 71(6) of SSCB(NI)A 1992,

(*b*) provision made by regulations under section 72(8) of SSCBA 1992 or section 72(8) of SSCB(NI)A 1992 (no payment of disability allowance for persons for whom certain accommodation is provided), or

(*c*) section 113(1) of SSCBA 1992 or section 113(1) of SSCB(NI)A 1992 or provision made by regulations under section 113(2) of SSCBA 1992 or section 113(2) of SSCB(NI)A 1992 (general provisions as to disqualification and suspension).][1]

Amendments—[1] This Schedule inserted by FA 2013 s 216, Sch 44 paras 14, 19 with effect from 17 July 2013.
[2] Words inserted by FA 2014 s 291(1), (3) with effect for the purposes of IHTA 1984 ss 89, 89A and 89B, in relation to property transferred into settlement, on or after 6 April 2014, and with effect for all other purposes, for the tax year 2014–15 and subsequent tax years.

[Personal independence payment

4 A person is to be treated as a disabled person under paragraph 1(*d*) if he or she satisfies HMRC that he or she would be entitled to receive personal independence payment . . . [2] but for—

(*a*) the conditions as to residence and presence prescribed under section 77(3) of WRA 2012 or the corresponding provision having effect in Northern Ireland,

(*b*) provision made by regulations under section 85 of WRA 2012 (exclusion of certain care home residents) or the corresponding provision having effect in Northern Ireland,

(*c*) provision made by regulations under section 86 of WRA 2012 (exclusion of certain hospital in-patients) or the corresponding provision having effect in Northern Ireland, or

(*d*) section 87 of WRA 2012 (exclusion of prisoners and detainees) or the corresponding provision having effect in Northern Ireland.][1]

Amendments—[1] This Schedule inserted by FA 2013 s 216, Sch 44 paras 14, 19 with effect from 17 July 2013.
[2] Words repealed by FA 2014 s 291(1), (4) with effect for the purposes of IHTA 1984 ss 89, 89A and 89B, in relation to property transferred into settlement, on or after 6 April 2014, and with effect for all other purposes, for the tax year 2014–15 and subsequent tax years.

[Increased disablement pension

[5 A person is to be treated as a disabled person under paragraph 1(*e*) if he or she satisfies HMRC that he or she would be entitled to receive an increased disablement pension but for—

(*a*) conditions as to residence and presence that have effect in relation to increased disablement pension by virtue of regulations under section 104(3) of SSCBA 1992 or section 104(3) of SSCB(NI)A 1992 (application of attendance allowance provisions),

(*b*) provision made under section 67(1) or (2) of SSCBA 1992 or section 67(1) or (2) of SSCB(NI)A 1992 (non-satisfaction of conditions for attendance allowance where person is undergoing treatment for renal failure in hospital or is provided with certain accommodation) that has effect in relation to increased disablement pension by virtue of such regulations, or

(*c*) section 113(1) of SSCBA 1992 or section 113(1) of SSCB(NI)A 1992 or provision made by regulations under section 113(2) of SSCBA 1992 or section 113(2) of SSCB(NI)A 1992 (general provisions as to disqualification and suspension).][1]

Amendments—[1] This Schedule inserted by FA 2013 s 216, Sch 44 paras 14, 19 with effect from 17 July 2013.

[Constant attendance allowance

6 A person is to be treated as a disabled person under paragraph 1(*f*) if he or she satisfies HMRC that he or she would be entitled to receive constant attendance allowance but for—

(*a*) article 61 (residence outside United Kingdom) or article 64 (maintenance in hospital or institution) of the Personal Injuries (Civilians) Scheme 1983 (S.I. 1983/686), or

(*b*) article 53 (maintenance in hospital or institution) of the Naval, Military and Air Forces etc. (Disablement and Death) Service Pensions Order 2006 (S.I. 2006/606).][1]

Amendments—[1] This Schedule inserted by FA 2013 s 216, Sch 44 paras 14, 19 with effect from 17 July 2013.

[Armed forces independence payment

[7 A person is to be treated as a disabled person under paragraph 1(*g*) if he or she satisfies HMRC that he or she would be entitled to receive armed forces independence payment but for article 42 of the Armed Forces and Reserve Forces (Compensation Scheme) Order 2011 (S.I. 2011/517) (cessation of payment on admission to Royal Hospital, Chelsea).]¹

Amendments—¹ This Schedule inserted by FA 2013 s 216, Sch 44 paras 14, 19 with effect from 17 July 2013.

[Interpretation

8 In this Schedule—

"armed forces independence payment" means armed forces independence payment under a scheme established under section 1 of the Armed Forces (Pensions and Compensation) Act 2004,

"attendance allowance" means an allowance under section section 64 of the SSCBA 1992 or section 64 of the SSCB(NI)A 1992,

"constant attendance allowance" means an allowance under–

    (*a*) article 14 of the Personal Injuries (Civilians) Scheme 1983 (S.I. 1983/686), or

    (*b*) article 8 of the Naval, Military and Air Forces etc. (Disablement and Death) Service Pensions Order 2006 (S.I. 2006/606),

"disability living allowance" means a disability living allowance under section 71 of the SSCBA 1992 or section 71 of the SSCB(NI)A 1992,

"HMRC" means Her Majesty's Revenue and Customs,

increased disablement pension" means an increase of disablement pension under—

    (*a*) section 104 of SSCBA 1992, or

    (*b*) section 104 of SSCB(NI)A 1992,

"personal independence payment" means personal independence payment under—

    (*a*) WRA 2012, or

    (*b*) the corresponding provision having effect in Northern Ireland,

"SSCBA 1992" means the Social Security Contributions and Benefits Act 1992,

"SSCB(NI)A 1992" means the Social Security Contributions and Benefits (Northern Ireland) Act 1992,

"WRA 2012" means the Welfare Reform Act 2012.]¹

Amendments—¹ This Schedule inserted by FA 2013 s 216, Sch 44 paras 14, 19 with effect from 17 July 2013.

SCHEDULE 4
ACCOUNTING PRACTICE AND RELATED MATTERS
Section 80

PART 1
BAD DEBTS AND RELATED MATTERS

ICTA

1 (*repealed* TA 1988 s 74(1)(*j*), (2); *repealed by* CTA 2009 s 1326, Sch 3 Pt 1))

14 (*repeals* FA 1996 Sch 9 para 6B)

PART 2
OTHER PROVISIONS CONNECTED WITH ACCOUNTING PRACTICE

ICTA

21 (*amends* TA 1988 s 43A)

24—(1) (*repeals* TA 1988 s 747A)
(2) This amendment has effect in relation to accounting periods beginning on or after 16th March 2005.

25 (*repeals* TA 1988 s 836A)

FA 1997

32 (*amends* FA 1997 Sch 12 para 30(1))

CAA 2001

33 (*substitutes* CAA 2001 s 219(3)(*b*))

ITEPA 2003

48 (*amends* ITEPA 2003 Sch 5 para 59)

FA 2004

49 (*substitutes* FA 2004 s 50(2), (3))

50 (*repeals* FA 2004 ss 50(6)(*b*), 51(6)(*b*), 52(3)(*b*), 54(2)(*b*))

51 (*inserts* FA 2004 Sch 10 para 79)

SCHEDULE 6

CAPITAL ALLOWANCES: RENOVATION OF BUSINESS PREMISES IN DISADVANTAGED AREAS

Section 92

Commentary—*Simon's Taxes* **B3.1101.**
Orders—Finance Act 2005, Section 92 and Schedule 6, (Appointed Day) Order 2007 (appointed day is 11 April 2007).

PART 1

NEW PART 3A OF THE CAPITAL ALLOWANCES ACT 2001

1 (*inserts* CAA 2001 Part 3A (ss 360A–360Z4))

PART 2

CONSEQUENTIAL AMENDMENTS

2 (*inserts* CAA 2001 s 1(2)(*ba*))

3 (*amends* CAA 2001 s 2(3))

4 (*inserts* CAA 2001 s 3(2A))

5 (*amends* CAA 2001 s 537(1), section heading and cross-heading preceding that section).

6 (*inserts* CA 2001 s 546(*ba*))

7–10(*amend* CAA 2001 ss 567(1), 570(1), 570A(1), 573(1))

11—(1) Part 2 of Schedule 1 to CAA 2001 (list of defined expressions) is amended as follows.
(2) (*amends* table in CAA 2001 Sch 1 Part 2).
(3) (*amends* entry in table in CAA 2001 Sch 1 Part 2).

SCHEDULE 7

TONNAGE TAX

Section 93

PART 1

AMENDMENTS OF SCHEDULE 22 TO FA 2000

Introduction

1 Schedule 22 to FA 2000 shall be amended as follows.

Period for which election is in force

2—(1) Paragraph 13 is amended as follows.
(2) (*inserts* FA 2000 Sch 22 para 13(2A))

Withdrawal notices

3 (*inserts* FA 2000 Sch 22 paras 15A, 15B)

Qualifying ships

4—(1) Paragraph 19 is amended as follows.
(2), (3) (*amend* FA 2000 Sch 22 para 19(1), (3))

(4) (*inserts* FA 2000 Sch 22 para 19(5))

Vessels excluded from being qualifying ships

5—(1) Paragraph 20 is amended as follows.
(2) (*amends* FA 2000 Sch 22 para 20)
(3) (*inserts* FA 2000 Sch 22 para (7))

Qualifying dredgers and tugs

6　(*inserts* FA 2000 Sch 22 para 20A)

Effect of change of use

7—(1) Paragraph 22 is amended as follows.
(2)–(4) (*amend* FA 2000 Sch 22 para 22(1), (2)(*b*), (5))
(5) (*inserts* FA 2000 Sch 22 para 22(6))

Flagging: rule for ships other than dredgers and tugs

8　(*inserts* FA 2000 Sch 22 paras 22A–22C)

Flagging: rules for dredgers and tugs

9　(*inserts* FA 2000 Sch 22 paras 22D, 22E)

Flagging: restrictions where dredger or tug ceases to be qualifying ship under paragraph 22E

10　(*inserts* FA 2000 Sch 22 para 22F)

Requirement to prove compliance with safety etc standards

11　(*inserts* FA 2000 Sch 22 para 43A)

The ring fence: capital allowances: general: introduction

12—(1) Paragraph 68 is amended as follows.
(2) (*substitutes* FA 2000 Sch 22 para 68(2)(*c*))

The ring fence: capital allowances: exit: plant and machinery

13—(1) Paragraph 85 is amended as follows.
(2) (*inserts* FA 2000 Sch 22 para 85(1A)–(1C))
(3) (*amends* FA 2000 Sch 22 para 85(2))

The ring fence: capital allowances: ship leasing: sale and lease-back arrangements

14—(1) Paragraph 92 is amended as follows.
(2) (*amends* FA 2000 Sch 22 para 92(2))
(3) (*inserts* FA 2000 Sch 22 para 92(3A))

Meaning of "offshore activities"

15—(1) Paragraph 104 is amended as follows.
(2) (*inserts* FA 2000 Sch 22 para 104(1A), (1B))

Vessels to which the special rules for offshore activities do not apply

16　(*repeals* FA 2000 Sch 22 para 105)

Index of defined expressions

17—(1) Paragraph 147 is amended as follows.
(2) (*amends* FA 2000 Sch 22 para 147)

PART 2

COMMENCEMENT AND TRANSITIONAL PROVISION

Commencement

18—(1) Subject to paragraphs 19 to 21, paragraphs 4 to 6, 8 to 10 and 15 to 17 (and paragraph 1 so far as relating to those paragraphs) shall be deemed to have come into force on 1st July 2005.

Lifetime annuities and dependants' annuities purchased together

29—(1) Paragraph 17 of Schedule 28 (dependants' annuity) is amended as follows.
(2), (3) (*insert FA 2004 Sch 28 para 17(1)(za), (1A)*)

30—(1) Paragraph 3 of Schedule 29 (pension commencement lump sum: applicable amount) is amended as follows.
(2) (*amends FA 2004 Sch 29 para 3(4)*)
(3) (*inserts FA 2004 Sch 29 para 3(4A)*)

31   (*amends FA 2004 s 216(1)*)

33   (*amends FA 2004 s 280(2)*)

Pension commencement lump sums

34—(1) Paragraph 1 of Schedule 29 (meaning of "pension commencement lump sum") is amended as follows.
(2) (*amends FA 2004 Sch 29 para 1(3)(b)*)
(3) (*inserts FA 2004 Sch 29 para 1(6)*)

35—(1) Paragraph 3 of Schedule 29 (applicable amount limit) is amended as follows.
(2) (*substitutes FA 2004 Sch 29 para 3(5)*)
(3) (*amends FA 2004 Sch 29 para 3(7)*)

Recognised transfers

36   (*inserts FA 2004 s 169(1A)–(1E)*)

Assignment

37—(1) Section 172 (assignment of benefit to which member has actual or prospective entitlement to constitute unauthorised payment) is amended as follows.
(2)–(5) (*amend FA 2004 s 172(1) (3), (5)(b), (6), (7)*)
(6) (*substitutes FA 2004 s 172(7)*)

Surrender and allocation of rights etc

38   (*inserts FA 2004 ss 172A–172D*)

Restriction of employers' relief in respect of contributions

39   (*inserts FA 2004 s 196A*)

40   (*inserts FA 2004 s 246A*)

Lifetime allowance: reduction of rights in respect of tax paid

41, 42   (*amend FA 2004 ss 215(9), (10), 216(1)*)

43—(1) Schedule 32 (benefit crystallisation events: supplementary) is amended as follows.
(2) In paragraph 9 (benefit crystallisation event 2: meaning of "P") is amended as follows.
(3) (*amends FA 2004 Sch 32 para 9(2)*)
(4), (5) (*insert FA 2004 Sch 32 paras 9(3), 13(4), (5)*)
(6) Paragraph 14 (benefit crystallisation event 5: meaning of "DP" and "DSLS") is amended as follows.
(7) (*inserts FA 2004 Sch 32 para 14(1A), (1B)*)
(8) (*amends FA 2004 Sch 32 para 14(2)*)

Lifetime allowance: pension credits

45—(1) Section 220 (lifetime allowance enhancement factor in case of pension credits from previously crystallised rights) is amended as follows.
(2) (*amends FA 2004 s 220(4)*)
(3) (*inserts FA 2004 s 220(4A)*)

Migrant member relief

46   (*amends FA 2004 Sch 33 para 4(c)*)

Information

47   (*amends FA 2004 s 251(4)(a)*)

Electronic payment

48   (*inserts* FA 2004 ss 255A, 255B)

Insurance company liable as scheme administrator

49—(1) (*inserts* FA 2004 s 273A)
(2) (*amends* FA 2004 s 274(3)(*b*))

Power to split schemes

50   (*inserts* FA 2004 s 274A)

Power to modify rules of existing schemes

51   (*amends* FA 2004 Sch 36 para 3(2))

Primary and enhanced protection: valuation of uncrystallised rights

52—(1) Schedule 36 (transitional provisions) is amended as follows.
(2) Paragraph 9 (valuation of uncrystallised rights under pension schemes within paragraph 1(1)(*a*)
to (*d*)) is amended as follows.
(3)–(5) (*amend* FA 2004 Sch 36 para 9(2), (4), (5))
(6) Paragraph 26 (lump sum protection: limit on value of uncrystallised rights under pension
schemes within paragraph 1(1)(*a*) to (*d*)) is amended as follows.
(7)–(9) (*amend* FA 2004 Sch 36 para 26(2)–(4))

Enhanced protection

53—(1) Schedule 36 (transitional provisions) is amended as follows.
(2) Paragraph 12 (enhanced protection) is amended as follows.
(3) (*inserts* FA 2004 Sch 36 para 12(2)(*aa*)).
(4)–(6) (*amend* FA 2004 Sch 36 para 12(3). (5), (6), (9))
(7) (*amends* FA 2004 Sch 36 para 123(*a*))
(8) Paragraph 14 (loss of enhanced protection: relevant benefit accrual) is amended as follows.
(9), (10) (*amend* FA 2004 Sch 36 para 14(1)(*c*), (2))
(11) Paragraph 16 (enhanced protection: post-commencement earnings limit for capped individuals)
is amended as follows.
(12), (13) (*amend* FA 2004 Sch 36 para 16(1), (5))
(14)–(16) (*insert* FA 2004 Sch 36 paras 16(5A), 17(6), 17A)

Transitional provisions: persons who may take benefits before normal minimum pension age

54—(1) Schedule 36 (transitional provisions) is amended as follows.
(2) (*amends* FA 2004 Sch 36 para 19(5))
(3) (*amends* heading before FA 2004 Sch 36 para 21)
(4) Paragraph 22 (right to take pension before normal minimum pension age: protected pension
scheme where original pension scheme within paragraph 1(1)(*a*), (*b*), (*c*), (*d*) or (*e*)) is amended as
follows.
(5)–(7) (*amend* FA 2004 Sch 36 para 22(4)(*a*), (7), (8))

Transitional provisions: block transfers

55—(1) Schedule 36 (transitional provisions) is amended as follows.
(2) Paragraph 22 (right to take pension before normal minimum pension age: protected pension
scheme where original pension scheme within paragraph 1(1)(*a*), (*b*), (*c*), (*d*) or (*e*)) is amended as
follows.
(3) (*amends* FA 2004 Sch 36 para 22(5))
(4) (*substitutes* FA 2004 Sch 36 para 22(6)(*b*))
(5)–(7) (*amend* FA 2004 Sch 36 paras 23(5), 31(7), 51(5))

Transitional provisions: lump sums before normal minimum pension age

56   (*inserts* FA 2004 Sch 36 para 23A)

Transitional provisions: lump sums exceeding 25% of uncrystallised rights

57   (*amends* FA 2004 para 34(2))

Transitional provisions: inheritance tax

58—(1) Schedule 36 (transitional provisions) is amended as follows.
(2), (3) (*amend* FA 2004 Sch 36 paras 57(1), (2), 58(6)(*b*))

Trivial commutation and winding-up lump sums

59   (*amends* ITEPA 2003 s 636B(3))

Application of PAYE to annuities etc

60   (*amends* ITEPA 2003 s 683(3))

61   (*repeals* FA 2004 Sch 36 paras 43, 46)

62   (*amends* TA 1988 ss 348(1A), 349(1A))

House of Commons Members' Fund

63   Section 613(1) and (2) of ICTA (tax relief for contributions to House of Commons Members' Fund) shall be treated as not having been repealed by ITEPA 2003.

Commencement

64—(1) Subject as follows, the preceding provisions of this Schedule come into force on 6th April 2006.
(2) Paragraphs 60 to 62 come into force on 6th April 2007.
(3) Paragraph 63 comes into force on the day on which this Act is passed.

COMMISSIONERS FOR REVENUE AND CUSTOMS ACT 2005

(2005 Chapter 11)

ARRANGEMENT OF SECTIONS

Commissioners and officers
1   The Commissioners
2   Officers of Revenue and Customs
3   Declaration of confidentiality
4   "Her Majesty's Revenue and Customs"
Functions
5   Commissioners' initial functions
6   Officers' initial functions
7   Former Inland Revenue matters
8   Power to transfer functions
8A   The Extractive Industries Transparency Initiative
9   Ancillary powers
10   The Valuation Office
Exercise of functions
11   Treasury directions
12   Commissioners' arrangements
13   Exercise of Commissioners' functions by officers
14   Delegation
15   Agency: Scotland, Northern Ireland and Wales
16   Restrictions, &c
16A   Charter of standards and values
Information
17   Use of information
18   Confidentiality
19   Wrongful disclosure
20   Public interest disclosure
21   Disclosure to prosecuting authority
22   Data protection, &c
23   Freedom of information
Proceedings
24   Evidence
25   Conduct of civil proceedings
25A   Certificates of debt
26   Rewards
Inspection and complaints
27   Inspection
28   Complaints and misconduct: England and Wales
29   Confidentiality, &c
Offences
30   Impersonation
31   Obstruction
32   Assault
33   Power of arrest
Prosecutions
40   Confidentiality
Money and property
43   Expenditure
44   Payment into Consolidated Fund
45   Remuneration, &c
46   Accounts
47   Payment out of Consolidated Fund
48   Transfer of property, &c: general
General
50   Consequential amendments, &c
51   Interpretation
52   Repeals
53   Commencement
54   Transitional: general
55   Transitional: penalties
56   Extent
57   Short title
Schedules
Schedule 1—Former Inland Revenue Matters
Schedule 2—Functions of Commissioners and Officers: Restrictions, &c

Schedule 4—Consequential Amendments, &c

An Act to make provision for the appointment of Commissioners to exercise functions presently vested in the Commissioners of Inland Revenue and the Commissioners of Customs and Excise; for the establishment of a Revenue and Customs Prosecutions Office; and for connected purposes.

[7th April 2005]

Commissioners and officers

1 The Commissioners

(1) Her Majesty may by Letters Patent appoint Commissioners for Her Majesty's Revenue and Customs.

(2) The Welsh title of the Commissioners shall be Comisynwyr Cyllid a Thollau Ei Mawrhydi.

(3) A Commissioner—
- (a) may resign by notice in writing to the Treasury, and
- (b) otherwise, shall hold office in accordance with the terms and conditions of his appointment (which may include provision for dismissal).

(4) In exercising their functions, the Commissioners act on behalf of the Crown.

(5) Service as a Commissioner is service in the civil service of the State.

Commentary—*Simon's Taxes* A3.101A.

2 Officers of Revenue and Customs

(1) The Commissioners may appoint staff, to be known as officers of Revenue and Customs.

(2) A person shall hold and vacate office as an officer of Revenue and Customs in accordance with the terms of his appointment (which may include provision for dismissal).

(3) An officer of Revenue and Customs shall comply with directions of the Commissioners (whether he is exercising a function conferred on officers of Revenue and Customs or exercising a function on behalf of the Commissioners).

(4) Anything (including anything in relation to legal proceedings) begun by or in relation to one officer of Revenue and Customs may be continued by or in relation to another.

(5) Appointments under subsection (1) may be made only with the approval of the Minister for the Civil Service as to terms and conditions of service.

(6) Service in the employment of the Commissioners is service in the civil service of the State.

(7) (*amends* IA 1978 Sch 1).

Commentary—*Simon's Taxes* A1.710, A3.101A , .

HMRC Manuals—Debt Management And Banking Manual DMBM513180 (commissioners for revenue and customs act 2005).

3 Declaration of confidentiality

(1) Each person who is appointed under this Act as a Commissioner or officer of Revenue and Customs shall make a declaration acknowledging his obligation of confidentiality under section 18.

(2) A declaration under subsection (1) shall be made—
- (a) as soon as is reasonably practicable following the person's appointment, and
- (b) in such form, and before such a person, as the Commissioners may direct.

(3) For the purposes of this section, the renewal of a fixed term appointment shall not be treated as an appointment.

Commentary—*Simon's Taxes* A3.101A, , A3.104A, , A6.105.

HMRC Manuals—Compliance Operational Guidance Manual COG11655 (general).

Debt Management And Banking Manual DMBM510210 (confidentiality: introduction).

Enquiry Manual EM0070 (introduction: confidentiality and personal security).

Information Disclosure Guidance Manual IDG40110 (sharing information outside of HMRC: general).

National Minimum Wage Manual NMWM16020 (duty of confidentiality and the declaration of confidentiality).

4 "Her Majesty's Revenue and Customs"

(1) The Commissioners and the officers of Revenue and Customs may together be referred to as Her Majesty's Revenue and Customs.

(2) The Welsh title of the Commissioners and the officers of Revenue and Customs together shall be Cyllid a Thollau Ei Mawrhydi.

(3) (*amends* Interpretation Act 1978 Sch 1).

Functions

5 Commissioners' initial functions

(1) The Commissioners shall be responsible for—
- (a) the collection and management of revenue for which the Commissioners of Inland Revenue were responsible before the commencement of this section,
- (b) the collection and management of revenue for which the Commissioners of Customs and Excise were responsible before the commencement of this section, and
- (c) the payment and management of tax credits for which the Commissioners of Inland Revenue were responsible before the commencement of this section.

(2) The Commissioners shall also have all the other functions which before the commencement of this section vested in—

(*a*) the Commissioners of Inland Revenue (or in a Commissioner), or

(*b*) the Commissioners of Customs and Excise (or in a Commissioner).

(3) This section is subject to section 35.

(4) In this Act "revenue" includes taxes, duties and national insurance contributions.

Commentary—*Simon's Taxes* **A3.101A,, A4.101**.

HMRC Manuals—Admin Law Manual ADML3200 (legal background).

Order—See the Commissioners for Revenue and Customs Act 2005 (Commencement) Order, SI 2005/1126, art 2(2) (this section came into force on 18 April 2005).

6 Officers' initial functions

(1) A function conferred by an enactment (in whatever terms) on any of the persons listed in subsection (2) shall by virtue of this subsection vest in an officer of Revenue and Customs.

(2) Those persons are—

(*a*) an officer as defined by section 1(1) of the Customs and Excise Management Act 1979 (c 2),

(*b*) a person acting under the authority of the Commissioners of Customs and Excise,

(*c*) an officer of the Commissioners of Customs and Excise,

(*d*) a customs officer,

(*e*) an officer of customs,

(*f*) a customs and excise officer,

(*g*) an officer of customs and excise, and

(*h*) a collector of customs and excise.

(3) This section is subject to sections 7 and 35.

HMRC Manuals—Debt Management And Banking Manual DMBM535020 (excise duties: introduction). DMBM655040 (distraint: the department's statutory right to distrain and charge costs).

Order—See the Commissioners for Revenue and Customs Act 2005 (Commencement) Order, SI 2005/1126, art 2(2) (this section came into force on 18 April 2005).

7 Former Inland Revenue matters

(1) This section applies to the matters listed in Schedule 1.

(2) A function conferred by an enactment (in whatever terms) on any of the persons specified in subsection (3) shall by virtue of this subsection vest in an officer of Revenue and Customs—

(*a*) if or in so far as it relates to a matter to which this section applies, and

(*b*) in so far as the officer is exercising a function (whether or not by virtue of paragraph (*a*)) which relates to a matter to which this section applies.

(3) Those persons are—

(*a*) an officer of the Commissioners of Inland Revenue,

(*b*) an officer of the Board of Inland Revenue,

(*c*) an officer of inland revenue,

(*d*) a collector of Inland Revenue,

(*e*) an inspector of taxes,

(*f*) a collector of taxes,

(*g*) a person authorised to act as an inspector of taxes or collector of taxes for specific purposes,

(*h*) an officer having powers in relation to tax,

(*i*) a revenue official,

(*j*) a person employed in relation to Inland Revenue (or "the Inland Revenue"), and

(*k*) an Inland Revenue official.

(4) In so far as an officer of Revenue and Customs is exercising a function which relates to a matter to which this section applies, section 6(1) shall not apply.

(5) This section is subject to section 35.

HMRC Manuals—Information Disclosure Guidance Manual IDG40470 (former Inland Revenue functions).

Order—See the Commissioners for Revenue and Customs Act 2005 (Commencement) Order, SI 2005/1126, art 2(2) (this section and Sch 1 came into force on 18 April 2005).

8 Power to transfer functions

(1) (*inserts* Ministers of the Crown Act 1975 s 5A).

(2) For the purposes of sections 63 and 108 of the Scotland Act 1998 (c 46) (transfer of functions)—

(*a*) the Commissioners shall be treated as a Minister of the Crown, and

(*b*) the officers of Revenue and Customs shall be treated as a Minister of the Crown.

(3) An Order in Council under section 63 or 108 of that Act—

(*a*) may not make provision about a function specified in section 5(1) of this Act, and

(*b*) if it transfers a function to the Commissioners or to officers of Revenue and Customs—

(i) may restrict or prohibit the exercise of specified powers in relation to that function, and

(ii) may provide that the function may be exercised only with the consent of a specified member of the Scottish Executive.

(4) For the purposes of section 22 of and Schedule 3 to the Government of Wales Act 1998 (c 38) (transfer of functions)—

(*a*) the Commissioners shall be treated as a Minister of the Crown, and

(*b*) the officers of Revenue and Customs shall be treated as a Minister of the Crown.

(5) An Order in Council under section 22 of that Act may not make provision about a function specified in section 5(1) of this Act.

Order—See the Commissioners for Revenue and Customs Act 2005 (Commencement) Order, SI 2005/1126, art 2(2) (this section came into force on 18 April 2005).

[8A The Extractive Industries Transparency Initiative

(1) The Commissioners may do anything which they think necessary or expedient in connection with the Extractive Industries Transparency Initiative in so far as it relates to taxes the collection and management of which is the responsibility of the Commissioners.

(2) In this section "the Extractive Industries Transparency Initiative" means the international initiative of that name which has the aim of promoting openness in the management of revenues from natural resources.][1]

Amendments—[1]   Section 8A inserted by the Infrastructure Act 2015 s 40 with effect from 12 April 2015.

9 Ancillary powers

(1) The Commissioners may do anything which they think—

(*a*) necessary or expedient in connection with the exercise of their functions, or

(*b*) incidental or conducive to the exercise of their functions.

(2) This section is subject to section 35.

10 The Valuation Office

(1) An officer of Revenue and Customs may provide a valuation of property—

(*a*) for a purpose relating to the functions of Her Majesty's Revenue and Customs, or

(*b*) at the request of any person who appears to the officer to be a public authority, or

(*c*) at the request of any other person if the officer is satisfied that the valuation is necessary or expedient in connection with—

   (i) the exercise of a function of a public nature, or

   (ii) the management of money or assets received from a person exercising functions of a public nature.

(2) The Commissioners may charge a fee for the provision of a valuation under subsection (1)(*b*) or (*c*).

(3) In this section a reference to providing valuations of property includes a reference to advising about matters appearing to an officer of Revenue and Customs to be connected to the valuation of property.

Exercise of functions

11 Treasury directions

In the exercise of their functions the Commissioners shall comply with any directions of a general nature given to them by the Treasury.

Commentary—*Simon's Taxes* **A3.101A, I11.102**.

12 Commissioners' arrangements

(1) The Commissioners shall make arrangements for—

(*a*) the conduct of their proceedings, and

(*b*) the conduct of the proceedings of any committee established by them.

(2) Arrangements under subsection (1) may, in particular—

(*a*) make provision for a quorum at meetings;

(*b*) provide that a function of the Commissioners—

   (i) may be exercised by two Commissioners, or

   (ii) may be exercised by a specified number of Commissioners (greater than two).

(3) A decision to make arrangements under subsection (1) must be taken with the agreement of more than half of the Commissioners holding office at the time.

Commentary—*Simon's Taxes* **A3.101A, I11.102**.

13 Exercise of Commissioners' functions by officers

(1) An officer of Revenue and Customs may exercise any function of the Commissioners.

(2) But subsection (1)—

(*a*) does not apply to the functions specified in subsection (3), and

(*b*) is subject to directions under section 2(3) and arrangements under section 12.

(3) The non-delegable functions mentioned in subsection (2)(*a*) are—

(*a*) making, by statutory instrument, regulations, rules or an order,

(*b*) . . . .[1]

(*c*) . . . .[1]

(*d*) giving instructions for the disclosure of information under section 20(1)(*a*), except that an officer of Revenue and Customs may give an instruction under section 20(1)(*a*) authorising disclosure of specified information relating to—

   (i) one or more specified persons,

   (ii) one or more specified transactions, or

(iii) specified goods.

HMRC Manuals—International Exchange of Information Manual IEIM101400 (concepts: competent authorities).

Stamp Taxes On Shares Manual STSM154050 (determination of free standing penalties).

Amendments—[1]   Sub-s (3)(b), (c) repealed by FA 2007 ss 84, 114, Sch 22 paras 3, 17(a), Sch 27 Pt 5(1) with effect from 1 December 2007 (by virtue of SI 2007/3166 art 3(a)).

14 Delegation

(1) Arrangements under section 12 may, in particular, enable the Commissioners, or a number of Commissioners acting in accordance with arrangements by virtue of section 12(2)(b), to delegate a function of the Commissioners, other than a function specified in subsection (2) below—

    (a) to a single Commissioner,

    (b) to a committee established by the Commissioners (which may include persons who are neither Commissioners nor staff of the Commissioners nor officers of Revenue and Customs), or

    (c) to any other person.

(2) The non-delegable functions mentioned in subsection (1) are—

    (a) making, by statutory instrument, regulations, rules or an order,

    (b) . . .[1]

    (c) . . .[1]

(3) The Commissioners may not delegate the function under section 20(1)(a) except to a single Commissioner.

(4) The delegation of a function by virtue of subsection (1) by the Commissioners or a number of Commissioners—

    (a) shall not prevent the exercise of the function by the Commissioners or those Commissioners, and

    (b) shall not, subject to express provision to the contrary in directions under section 2(3) or arrangements under section 12, prevent the exercise of the function by an officer of Revenue and Customs.

(5) Where the Commissioners or a number of Commissioners delegate a function to a person by virtue of subsection (1)(c)—

    (a) the Commissioners or those Commissioners shall monitor the exercise of the function by that person, and

    (b) in the exercise of the function the delegate shall comply with any directions of the Commissioners or of those Commissioners.

Amendments—[1]   Sub-s (2)(b), (c) repealed by FA 2007 ss 84, 114, Sch 22 paras 3, 17(b), Sch 27 Pt 5(1) with effect from 1 December 2007 (by virtue of SI 2007/3166 art 3(a)).

15 [Agency: Scotland, Northern Ireland and Wales]

(1) For the purposes of section 93 of the Scotland Act 1998 (c 46) (agency)—

    (a) the Commissioners shall be treated as a Minister of the Crown, and

    (b) the officers of Revenue and Customs shall be treated as a Minister of the Crown.

(2) For the purposes of section 28 of the Northern Ireland Act 1998 (c 47) (agency)—

    (a) the Commissioners shall be treated as a Minister of the Crown, and

    (b) the officers of Revenue and Customs shall be treated as a Minister of the Crown.

[(3) For the purposes of section 83 of the Government of Wales Act 2006 (agency arrangements)—

    (a) the Commissioners are to be treated as a relevant authority, and

    (b) the officers of Revenue and Customs are to be treated as a relevant authority.][1]

Commentary—*Simon's Taxes* A1.542.

Amendments—[1]   Sub-s (3) inserted, and heading substituted, by the Wales Act 2014 s 7(2)–(4) with effect from 17 February 2015.

16 Restrictions, &c

Part 1 of Schedule 2 (which restricts, or makes other provision in connection with, the exercise of certain functions) shall have effect.

Commentary—*Simon's Taxes* A3.101A.

Order—See the Commissioners for Revenue and Customs Act 2005 (Commencement) Order, SI 2005/1126, art 2(2) (this section and Sch 2 Pt 1 came into force on 18 April 2005).

[16A Charter of standards and values

(1) The Commissioners must prepare a Charter.

(2) The Charter must include standards of behaviour and values to which Her Majesty's Revenue and Customs will aspire when dealing with people in the exercise of their functions.

(3) The Commissioners must—

    (a) regularly review the Charter, and

    (b) publish revisions, or revised versions, of it when they consider it appropriate to do so.

(4) The Commissioners must, at least once every year, make a report reviewing the extent to which Her Majesty's Revenue and Customs have demonstrated the standards of behaviour and values included in the Charter.][1]

Commentary—*Simon's Taxes* A3.104.
Amendments—[1]   This section inserted by FA 2009 s 92(1) with effect from 21 July 2009.

Information

17 Use of information

(1) Information acquired by the Revenue and Customs in connection with a function may be used by them in connection with any other function.

(2) Subsection (1) is subject to any provision which restricts or prohibits the use of information and which is contained in—

    (*a*) this Act,

    (*b*) any other enactment, or

    (*c*) an international or other agreement to which the United Kingdom or Her Majesty's Government is party.

(3) In subsection (1) "the Revenue and Customs" means—

    (*a*) the Commissioners,

    (*b*) an officer of Revenue and Customs,

    (*c*) a person acting on behalf of the Commissioners or an officer of Revenue and Customs,

    (*d*) a committee established by the Commissioners,

    (*e*) a member of a committee established by the Commissioners,

    (*f*) the Commissioners of Inland Revenue (or any committee or staff of theirs or anyone acting on their behalf),

    (*g*) the Commissioners of Customs and Excise (or any committee or staff of theirs or anyone acting on their behalf), and

    (*h*) a person specified in section 6(2) or 7(3).

(4) In subsection (1) "function" means a function of any of the persons listed in subsection (3).

(5) In subsection (2) the reference to an enactment does not include—

    (*a*) an Act of the Scottish Parliament or an instrument made under such an Act,

    [(*aa*) an Act of the National Assembly for Wales or an instrument made under such an Act,][1]

    (*b*) an Act of the Northern Ireland Assembly or an instrument made under such an Act.

(6) Part 2 of Schedule 2 (which makes provision about the supply and other use of information in specified circumstances) shall have effect.

Commentary—*Simon's Taxes* A6.105.
HMRC Manuals—Information Disclosure Guidance Manual IDG20000 (sharing information within HMRC).
National Minimum Wage Manual NMWM16060 (exchange of information with other HM Revenue & Customs' teams).
Compliance Handbook Manual CH23740 (information & groups: groups of undertakings).
CH28150 (data gathering: details of powers: purpose and scope of power).
Amendments—[1]   Sub-s (5)(*aa*) inserted by the Wales Act 2014 s 7(2), (5) with effect from 17 February 2015.

18 Confidentiality

(1) Revenue and Customs officials may not disclose information which is held by the Revenue and Customs in connection with a function of the Revenue and Customs.

(2) But subsection (1) does not apply to a disclosure—

    (*a*) which—

        (i) is made for the purposes of a function of the Revenue and Customs, and

        (ii) does not contravene any restriction imposed by the Commissioners,

    (*b*) which is made in accordance with section 20 or 21,

    (*c*) which is made for the purposes of civil proceedings (whether or not within the United Kingdom) relating to a matter in respect of which the Revenue and Customs have functions,

    (*d*) which is made for the purposes of a criminal investigation or criminal proceedings (whether or not within the United Kingdom) relating to a matter in respect of which the Revenue and Customs have functions,

    (*e*) which is made in pursuance of an order of a court,

    (*f*) which is made to Her Majesty's Inspectors of Constabulary, the Scottish inspectors or the Northern Ireland inspectors for the purpose of an inspection by virtue of section 27,

    (*g*) which is made to the [Director General of the Independent Office for Police Conduct][6], or a person acting on [the Director General's][6] behalf, for the purpose of the exercise of a function by virtue of section 28, . . . [1]

    (*h*) which is made with the consent of each person to whom the information relates[, . . .][3]

    (*i*) which is made to [Revenue Scotland][2] in connection with the collection and management of a devolved tax within the meaning of the Scotland Act 1998[,.][1] . . . [4]

    (*j*) which is made to [the Welsh Revenue Authority][5] in connection with the collection and management of a devolved tax within the meaning of the Government of Wales Act 2006[,][3]

    (*k*) which is made in connection with (or with anything done with a view to) the making or implementation of an agreement referred to in section 64A(1) or (2) of the Scotland Act 1998 (assignment of VAT).][4]

[(2A) Information disclosed in reliance on subsection (2)(*k*) may not be further disclosed without the consent of the Commissioners (which may be general or specific).][4]

(3) Subsection (1) is subject to any other enactment permitting disclosure.

(4) In this section—

    (*a*) a reference to Revenue and Customs officials is a reference to any person who is or was—

        (i) a Commissioner,

        (ii) an officer of Revenue and Customs,

        (iii) a person acting on behalf of the Commissioners or an officer of Revenue and Customs, or

        (iv) a member of a committee established by the Commissioners,

    (*b*) a reference to the Revenue and Customs has the same meaning as in section 17,

    (*c*) a reference to a function of the Revenue and Customs is a reference to a function of—

        (i) the Commissioners, or

        (ii) an officer of Revenue and Customs,

    (*d*) a reference to the Scottish inspectors or the Northern Ireland inspectors has the same meaning as in section 27, and

    (*e*) a reference to an enactment does not include—

        (i) an Act of the Scottish Parliament or an instrument made under such an Act,

        [(*ia*) an Act of the National Assembly for Wales or an instrument made under such an Act,][3] or

        (ii) an Act of the Northern Ireland Assembly or an instrument made under such an Act.

Commentary—*Simon's Taxes* **A1.511, A3.104A, A6.105, E3.931.**

HMRC Manuals—Debt Management And Banking Manual DMBM510210 (confidentiality: introduction).
Information Disclosure Guidance Manual IDG40120 (sharing information outside of HMRC: legal obligations).
National Minimum Wage Manual NMWM16020 (duty of confidentiality and the declaration of confidentiality).

Amendments—[1] In sub-s (2), word "or" at end of para (*g*) repealed, and para (*i*) and preceding word "or" inserted by the Scotland Act 2012 s 24(1)–(4) with effect from 1 July 2012.

[2] In sub-s (2)(*i*), words substituted for words "the Scottish Ministers", and sub-s (2A) repealed, by the Revenue Scotland and Tax Powers Act 2014 (Consequential Provisions and Modifications) Order, SI 2014/3294 art 4(1)(*a*) with effect from 1 January 2015.

[3] In sub-s (2), word "or" at end of para (*h*) repealed, and para (*j*) inserted, and sub-s (4)(*e*)(ia) inserted, by the Wales Act 2014 s 7(2), (6)–(9) with effect from 17 February 2015. Note that s 7(8) also purports to amend the wording of sub-s (2A) (inserting words "or (*j*)" after words "(2)(*i*)"), although sub-s (2A) was repealed with effect from 1 January 2015.

[4] In sub-s (2), word "or" at the end of para (*i*) repealed, and para (*k*) and preceding word inserted, and sub-s (2A) inserted, by the Scotland Act 2016 s 16(4)–(6) with effect from 23 May 2016.

[5] In sub-s (2)(*j*), words substituted by the Wales Act 2017 s 69, Sch 6 para 64 with effect from 1 April 2018 (by virtue of SI 2017/1179 reg 3(*n*), (*r*)).

[6] In sub-s (2)(*g*), words substituted for words "Independent Police Complaints Commission", and "its" by the Policing and Crime Act 2017 s 33(9), Sch 9 para 68(1), (2) with effect from 8 January 2018 (by virtue of SI 2017/1249 regs 1(2), 2(1), (2)(*a*), (*d*)). These amendments extend to England and Wales, Scotland and Northern Ireland (Policing and Crime Act 2017 s 182(2)(*e*)).

Prospective amendments—Sub-s (2)(*ia*) to be inserted by the Childcare Funding (Wales) Act 2019 s 9 with effect from a date to be appointed. Sub-s (2)(*ia*) to read as follows—

    "(*ia*) which is made to the Welsh Ministers, or to a person providing services to the Welsh Ministers, by virtue of regulations made under the Childcare Funding (Wales) Act 2019,".

19 Wrongful disclosure

(1) A person commits an offence if he contravenes section[1] 18(1) [or (2A)][4] or 20(9) by disclosing revenue and customs information relating to a person whose identity—

    (*a*) is specified in the disclosure, or

    (*b*) can be deduced from it.

(2) In subsection (1) "revenue and customs information relating to a person" means information about, acquired as a result of, or held in connection with the exercise of a function of the Revenue and Customs (within the meaning given by section 18(4)(*c*)) in respect of the person; but it does not include information about internal administrative arrangements of Her Majesty's Revenue and Customs (whether relating to Commissioners, officers or others).

(3) It is a defence for a person charged with an offence under this section of disclosing information to prove that he reasonably believed—

    (*a*) that the disclosure was lawful, or

    (*b*) that the information had already and lawfully been made available to the public.

(4) A person guilty of an offence under this section shall be liable—

    (*a*) on conviction on indictment, to imprisonment for a term not exceeding two years, to a fine or to both, or

    (*b*) on summary conviction, to imprisonment for a term not exceeding 12 months, to a fine not exceeding the statutory maximum or to both.

(5) A prosecution for an offence under this section may be instituted in England and Wales [only by or with the consent of the Director of Public Prosecutions][2]

(6) A prosecution for an offence under this section may be instituted in Northern Ireland only—

(a) by the Commissioners, or

(b) with the consent of the Director of Public Prosecutions for Northern Ireland.

(7) In the application of this section to Scotland or Northern Ireland the reference in subsection (4)(b) to 12 months shall be taken as a reference to six months.

(8) This section is without prejudice to the pursuit of any remedy or the taking of any action in relation to a contravention of section 18(1) [or (2A)][4] or 20(9) (whether or not this section applies to the contravention).

Commentary—*Simon's Taxes* **A1.542, A3.104A, A6.105, A6.802.**

HMRC Manuals—Compliance Handbook Manual CH207323 (information from professionals about their clients).
Complaints And Remedy Guidance Manual CRG3150 (mistakes: data security issues).
IDG40130 (sharing information outside of HMRC: criminal sanction under section 19 CRCA).
National Minimum Wage Manual NMWM16040 (sanction for unlawful disclosure).

Amendments—[1]   In sub-ss (1), (8) words inserted by the Scotland Act 2012 s 24(1), (2), (5) with effect from 1 July 2012.

[2]   In sub-s (5), words substituted by the Public Bodies (Merger of the Director of Public Prosecutions and the Director of Revenue and Customs Prosecutions) Order, SI 2014/834 art 3(3), Sch 1 paras 5, 6 with effect from 27 March 2014.

[3]   In sub-ss (1), (8) words repealed by the Revenue Scotland and Tax Powers Act 2014 (Consequential Provisions and Modifications) Order, SI 2014/3294 art 4(1)(b) with effect from 1 January 2015.

[4]   In sub-ss (1), (8), words inserted by the Scotland Act 2016 s 16(4), (7) with effect from 23 May 2016.

20 Public interest disclosure

(1) Disclosure is in accordance with this section (as mentioned in section 18(2)(b)) if—

(a) it is made on the instructions of the Commissioners (which may be general or specific),

(b) it is of a kind—

(i)   to which any of subsections (2) to (7) applies, or

(ii) specified in regulations made by the Treasury, and

(c) the Commissioners are satisfied that it is in the public interest.

(2) This subsection applies to a disclosure made—

(a) to a person exercising public functions (whether or not within the United Kingdom),

(b) for the purposes of the prevention or detection of crime, and

(c) in order to comply with an obligation of the United Kingdom, or Her Majesty's Government, under an international or other agreement relating to the movement of persons, goods or services.

(3) This subsection applies to a disclosure if—

(a) it is made to a body which has responsibility for the regulation of a profession,

(b) it relates to misconduct on the part of a member of the profession, and

(c) the misconduct relates to a function of the Revenue and Customs.

(4) This subsection applies to a disclosure if—

(a) it is made to a constable, and

(b) either—

(i)   the constable is exercising functions which relate to the movement of persons or goods into or out of the United Kingdom, or

(ii) the disclosure is made for the purposes of the prevention or detection of crime.

(5) This subsection applies to a disclosure if it is made—

(a) to the National Criminal Intelligence Service, and

(b) for a purpose connected with its functions under section 2(2) of the Police Act 1997 (c 50) (criminal intelligence).

(6) This subsection applies to a disclosure if it is made—

(a) to a person exercising public functions in relation to public safety or public health, and

(b) for the purposes of those functions.

(7) This subsection applies to a disclosure if it—

(a) is made to the [Secretary of State][1] for the purpose of enabling information to be entered in a computerised database, and

(b) relates to—

(i)   a person suspected of an offence,

(ii) a person arrested for an offence,

(iii) the results of an investigation, or

(iv) anything seized.

(8) Regulations under subsection (1)(b)(ii)—

(a) may specify a kind of disclosure only if the Treasury are satisfied that it relates to—

(i)   national security,

(ii) public safety,

(iii) public health, or

(iv) the prevention or detection of crime;

(b) may make provision limiting or restricting the disclosures that may be made in reliance on the regulations; and that provision may, in particular, operate by reference to—

(i)   the nature of information,

(ii) the person or class of person to whom the disclosure is made,

(iii) the person or class of person by whom the disclosure is made,

(iv) any other factor, or

(v) a combination of factors;

(c) shall be made by statutory instrument;

(d) may not be made unless a draft has been laid before and approved by resolution of each House of Parliament.

(9) Information disclosed in reliance on this section may not be further disclosed without the consent of the Commissioners (which may be general or specific); (but the Commissioners shall be taken to have consented to further disclosure by use of the computerised database of information disclosed by virtue of subsection (7)).

Commentary—*Simon's Taxes* **A3.104A, I11.372.**
HMRC Manuals—Compliance Handbook Manual CH860200 (reporting agent misconduct).
Information Disclosure Guidance Manual IDG60100 (introduction).
National Minimum Wage Manual NMWM16100 (no legal gateway: lawful disclosure In the public interest).
NMWM16105 (public interest disclosures for public health or public safety).
Amendments—[1] In sub-s (7)(*a*), words substituted for words "national Policing Improvement Agency" by the Crime and Courts Act 2013 s 15, Sch 8 para 156 with effect from 7 October 2013 by virtue of SI 2013/1682, art 3(*v*).

21 Disclosure to prosecuting authority

(1) Disclosure is in accordance with this section (as mentioned in section 18(2)(*b*)) if made—

(a) to a prosecuting authority, and

(b) for the purpose of enabling the authority—

(i) to consider whether to institute criminal proceedings in respect of a matter considered in the course of an investigation conducted by or on behalf of Her Majesty's Revenue and Customs, . . .

(ii) to give advice in connection with a criminal investigation . . . [2] or criminal proceedings [or

(iii) in the case of [the Director of Public Prosecutions][2], to exercise his functions under, or in relation to, Part 5 or 8 of the Proceeds of Crime Act 2002 (c 29)][1].

(2) In subsection (1) "prosecuting authority" means—

(a) [the Director of Public Prosecutions][2],

(b) in Scotland, the Lord Advocate or a procurator fiscal, and

(c) in Northern Ireland, the Director of Public Prosecutions for Northern Ireland.

[(2A) In subsection (1) "criminal investigation" means any process—

(i) for considering whether an offence has been committed,

(ii) for discovering by whom an offence has been committed, or

(iii) as a result of which an offence is alleged to have been committed.][2]

(3) Information disclosed to a prosecuting authority in accordance with this section may not be further disclosed except—

(a) for a purpose connected with the exercise of the prosecuting authority's functions, or

(b) with the consent of the Commissioners (which may be general or specific).

(4) A person commits an offence if he contravenes subsection (3).

(5) It is a defence for a person charged with an offence under this section to prove that he reasonably believed—

(a) that the disclosure was lawful, or

(b) that the information had already and lawfully been made available to the public.

(6) A person guilty of an offence under this section shall be liable—

(a) on conviction on indictment, to imprisonment for a term not exceeding two years, to a fine or to both, or

(b) on summary conviction, to imprisonment for a term not exceeding 12 months, to a fine not exceeding the statutory maximum or to both.

(7) A prosecution for an offence under this section may be instituted in England and Wales [only by or with the consent of the Director of Public Prosecutions][2]

(8) A prosecution for an offence under this section may be instituted in Northern Ireland only—

(a) by the Commissioners, or

(b) with the consent of the Director of Public Prosecutions for Northern Ireland.

(9) In the application of this section to Scotland or Northern Ireland the reference in subsection (6)(*b*) to 12 months shall be taken as a reference to six months.

Commentary—*Simon's Taxes* **A3.104A, I11.372.**
Amendments—[1] In sub-s (1)(*b*)(i), word "or" repealed, and sub-s (1)(*b*)(iii) and preceding word "or" inserted, by the Serious Crime Act 2007 ss 74(2), 92, Sch 8 para 164, Sch 14 with effect from 1 April 2008: SI 2008/755 art 2(1)(*a*), subject to transitional provisions and savings in art 3.
[2] In sub-s (1)(*b*)(ii), words repealed, in sub-ss (1)(*b*)(iii), (2)(*a*), (7), words substituted, and sub-s (2A) inserted, by the Public Bodies (Merger of the Director of Public Prosecutions and the Director of Revenue and Customs Prosecutions) Order, SI 2014/834 art 3(3), Sch 1 paras 5, 7 with effect from 27 March 2014.

22 Data protection, &c

[(1)] Nothing in sections 17 to 21 authorises the making of a disclosure which—

  (a) contravenes [the data protection legislation][1], or

  (b) is prohibited by [any of Parts 1 to 7 or Chapter 1 of Part 9 of the Investigatory Powers Act 2016][2].

[(2) In this section, "the data protection legislation" has the same meaning as in the Data Protection Act 2018 (see section 3 of that Act).][1]

Amendments—[1] Sub-s (1) numbered as such, in sub-s (1)(a) words substituted for words "the Data Protection Act 1998 (c 29)", and sub-s (2) inserted, by the Data Protection Act 2018 s 211(1)(a), Sch 19 para 110(1)–(4) with effect from 25 May 2018 (by virtue of SI 2018/625, reg 2(1)(g)).

[2] In para (b), words substituted for words "Part 1 of the Regulation of Investigatory Powers Act 2000 (c. 23)" by the Investigatory Powers Act 2016 s 271(1), Sch 10 para 18 with effect from 27 June 2018 (by virtue of see SI 2018/652, reg 12(g)(iii)).

23 Freedom of information

(1) Revenue and customs information relating to a person, the disclosure of which is prohibited by section 18(1), is exempt information by virtue of section 44(1)(a) of the Freedom of Information Act 2000 (c 36) (prohibitions on disclosure) if its disclosure—

  (a) would specify the identity of the person to whom the information relates, or

  (b) would enable the identity of such a person to be deduced.

[(1A) Subsections (2) and (3) of section 18 are to be disregarded in determining for the purposes of subsection (1) of this section whether the disclosure of revenue and customs information relating to a person is prohibited by subsection (1) of that section.][1]

(2) Except as specified in subsection (1), information the disclosure of which is prohibited by section 18(1) is not exempt information for the purposes of section 44(1)(a) of the Freedom of Information Act 2000.

(3) In subsection (1) "revenue and customs information relating to a person" has the same meaning as in section 19.

Amendments—[1] Sub-s (1A) inserted by the Borders, Citizenship and Immigration Act 2009 s 19(4) with effect from 12 November 2009.

Proceedings

24 Evidence

(1) A document that purports to have been issued or signed by or with the authority of the Commissioners—

  (a) shall be treated as having been so issued or signed unless the contrary is proved, and

  (b) shall be admissible in any legal proceedings.

(2) A document that purports to have been issued by the Commissioners and which certifies any of the matters specified in subsection (3) shall (in addition to the matters provided for by subsection (1)(a) and (b)) be treated as accurate unless the contrary is proved.

(3) The matters mentioned in subsection (2) are—

  (a) that a specified person was appointed as a commissioner on a specified date,

  (b) that a specified person was appointed as an officer of Revenue and Customs on a specified date,

  (c) that at a specified time or for a specified purpose (or both) a function was delegated to a specified Commissioner,

  (d) that at a specified time or for a specified purpose (or both) a function was delegated to a specified committee, and

  (e) that at a specified time or for a specified purpose (or both) a function was delegated to another specified person.

(4) A photographic or other copy of a document acquired by the Commissioners shall, if certified by them to be an accurate copy, be admissible in any legal proceedings to the same extent as the document itself.

(5) Section 2 of the Documentary Evidence Act 1868 (c 37) (proof of documents) shall apply to a Revenue and Customs document as it applies in relation to the documents mentioned in that section.

(6) In the application of that section to a Revenue and Customs document the Schedule to that Act shall be treated as if—

  (a) the first column contained a reference to the Commissioners, and

  (b) the second column contained a reference to a Commissioner or a person acting on his authority.

(7) In this section—

  (a) "Revenue and Customs document" means a document issued by or on behalf of the Commissioners, and

  (b) a reference to the Commissioners includes a reference to the Commissioners of Inland Revenue and to the Commissioners of Customs and Excise.

25 Conduct of civil proceedings

(1) An officer of Revenue and Customs or a person authorised by the Commissioners may conduct civil proceedings, in a magistrates' court or in the sheriff court, relating to a function of the Revenue and Customs.

[(1A) An officer of Revenue and Customs or a person authorised by the Commissioners may conduct county court proceedings for the recovery of an amount payable to the Commissioners under or by virtue of an enactment or under a contract settlement.][1]

(2) A solicitor member of the Commissioners' staff may act as a solicitor in connection with civil proceedings relating to a function of the Revenue and Customs.

(3) A legally qualified member of the Commissioners' staff may conduct county court proceedings relating to a matter specified in section 7.

(4) A court shall grant any rights of audience necessary to enable a person to exercise a function under this section.

(5) In this section—

    (*a*) a reference to a function of the Revenue and Customs is a reference to a function of—

        (i) the Commissioners, or

        (ii) an officer of Revenue and Customs,

    (*b*) a reference to civil proceedings is a reference to proceedings other than proceedings in respect of an offence,

    (*c*) a reference to county court proceedings is a reference to civil proceedings [in England and Wales in the county court or in Northern Ireland][2] in a county court,

    (*d*) the reference to a legally qualified member of the Commissioners' staff is a reference to a member of staff who has been admitted as a solicitor, or called to the Bar, whether or not he holds a practising certificate, and

    (*e*) the reference to a solicitor member of the Commissioners' staff—

        (i) except in relation to Scotland, is a reference to a member of staff who has been admitted as a solicitor, whether or not he holds a practising certificate,

        (ii) in relation to Scotland, is a reference to a member of staff who has been admitted as a solicitor and who holds a practising certificate.

[(6) In this section "contract settlement" means an agreement made in connection with any person's liability to make a payment to the Commissioners under or by virtue of an enactment.][1]

Commentary—*Simon's Taxes* **A3.101A**.
HMRC Manuals—Debt Management And Banking Manual DMBM665100 (parties to the action).
DMBM665760 (country defence filed).
DMBM666120 (country right of audience).
Amendments—[1] Sub-ss (1A), (6) inserted by FA 2008 s 137(1) with effect from 21 July 2008.
[2] In sub-s (5)(*c*), words inserted by the Crime and Courts Act 2013 s 17, Sch 9 para 68 with effect from 22 April 2014, by virtue of SI 2014/954 art 2.

[25A Certificates of debt

(1) A certificate of an officer of Revenue and Customs that, to the best of that officer's knowledge and belief, a relevant sum has not been paid is sufficient evidence that the sum mentioned in the certificate is unpaid.

(2) In subsection (1) "relevant sum" means a sum payable to the Commissioners under or by virtue of an enactment or under a contract settlement (within the meaning of section 25).

(3) Any document purporting to be such a certificate shall be treated as if it were such a certificate until the contrary is proved.

(4) Subsection (1) has effect subject to any provision treating the certificate as conclusive evidence.][1]

Commentary—*Simon's Taxes* **A1.702, A1.705**.
HMRC Manuals—Debt Management And Banking Manual DMBM615420 (pre-enforcement: recovery documentation and checks: certificates of debt).
DMBM665855 (country defences in tax credit overpayment cases).
Amendments—[1] This section inserted by FA 2008 s 138(1) with effect from 21 July 2008.

26 Rewards

The Commissioners may pay a reward to a person in return for a service which relates to a function of—

    (*a*) the Commissioners, or

    (*b*) an officer of Revenue and Customs.

Inspection and complaints

27 Inspection

(1) The Treasury may make regulations conferring functions on Her Majesty's Inspectors of Constabulary, the Scottish inspectors or the Northern Ireland inspectors in relation to—

    (*a*) the Commissioners for Her Majesty's Revenue and Customs, and

    (*b*) officers of Revenue and Customs.

(2) Regulations under subsection (1)—

(*a*) may—

   (i) in relation to Her Majesty's Inspectors of Constabulary, apply (with or without modification) or make provision similar to any provision of sections 54 to 56 of the Police Act 1996 (c 16) (inspection);

   (ii) in relation to the Scottish inspectors, apply (with or without modification) or make provision similar to any provision of section 33 or 34 of the Police (Scotland) Act 1967 (c 77) (inspection);

   (iii) in relation to the Northern Ireland inspectors, apply (with or without modification) or make provision similar to any provision of section 41 or 42 of the Police (Northern Ireland) Act 1998 (c 32) (inspection);

(*b*) may enable a Minister of the Crown or the Commissioners to require an inspection to be carried out;

(*c*) shall provide for a report of an inspection to be made and, subject to any exceptions required or permitted by the regulations, published;

(*d*) shall provide for an annual report by Her Majesty's Inspectors of Constabulary;

(*e*) may make provision for payment by the Commissioners to or in respect of Her Majesty's Inspectors of Constabulary, the Scottish inspectors or the Northern Ireland inspectors.

(3) An inspection carried out by virtue of this section may not address a matter of a kind which the Comptroller and Auditor General may examine under section 6 of the National Audit Act 1983 (c 44).

(4) An inspection carried out by virtue of this section shall be carried out jointly by Her Majesty's Inspectors of Constabulary and the Scottish inspectors—

(*a*) if it is carried out wholly in Scotland, or

(*b*) in a case where it is carried out partly in Scotland, to the extent that it is carried out there.

(5) Regulations under subsection (1)—

(*a*) shall be made by statutory instrument, and

(*b*) shall be subject to annulment in pursuance of a resolution of either House of Parliament.

(6) In this section—

(*a*) "the Scottish inspectors" means the inspectors of constabulary appointed under section 33(1) of the Police (Scotland) Act 1967, and

(*b*) "the Northern Ireland inspectors" means the inspectors of constabulary appointed under section 41(1) of the Police (Northern Ireland) Act 1998.

Commentary—*Simon's Taxes* **A6.1101**.

HMRC Manuals—Information Disclosure Guidance Manual IDG52100 (Her Majesty's Inspectorate Of Constabulary).

Regulations—See the Revenue and Customs (Inspections) Regulations, SI 2005/1133.

28 Complaints and misconduct: England and Wales

(1) The Treasury may make regulations conferring functions on the [Director General of the Independent Office for Police Conduct ("the Director General")][1] in relation to—

(*a*) the Commissioners for Her Majesty's Revenue and Customs, and

(*b*) officers of Revenue and Customs.

(2) Regulations under subsection (1)—

(*a*) may apply (with or without modification) or make provision similar to any provision of or made under Part 2 of the Police Reform Act 2002 (c 30) (complaints);

(*b*) may confer on the [Director General][1], or on a person acting on [the Director General's][1] behalf, a power of a kind conferred by this Act or another enactment on an officer of Revenue and Customs;

(*c*) may make provision for payment by the Commissioners to or in respect of the [Director General][1].

(3) The [Director General][1] and the Parliamentary Commissioner for Administration may disclose information to each other for the purposes of the exercise of a function—

(*a*) by virtue of this section, or

(*b*) under the Parliamentary Commissioner Act 1967 (c 13).

(4) The [Director General][1] and the Parliamentary Commissioner for Administration may jointly investigate a matter in relation to which—

(*a*) the [Director General][1] has functions by virtue of this section, and

(*b*) the Parliamentary Commissioner for Administration has functions by virtue of the Parliamentary Commissioner Act 1967.

(5) Regulations under subsection (1)—

(*a*) shall be made by statutory instrument, and

(*b*) shall be subject to annulment in pursuance of a resolution of either House of Parliament.

(6) Regulations under subsection (1) shall relate to the Commissioners or officers of Revenue and Customs only in so far as their functions are exercised in or in relation to England and Wales[, including the sea and other waters within the seaward limits of the territorial sea adjacent to England and Wales][2].

Regulations—Revenue and Customs (Complaints and Misconduct) (Amendment) Regulations, SI 2011/3061.
Amendments—[1]   In sub-s (1), words substituted for words "Independent Police Complaints Commission"; in sub-ss (2)–(4), words substituted for words "Independent Police Complaints Commission" in each place; and in sub-s (2), words substituted for word "its" by the Policing and Crime Act 2017 s 33(9), Sch 9 para 68(1), (3) with effect from 8 January 2018 (by virtue of SI 2017/1249 regs 1(2), 2(1), (2)(*a*), (*d*)). These amendments extend to England and Wales, Scotland and Northern Ireland (Policing and Crime Act 2017 s 182(2)(*e*)).
[2]   In sub-s (6), words inserted at the end by the Policing and Crime Act 2017 s 21(2) with effect from 1 February 2020 (by virtue of SI 2020/5 reg 2(*h*), subject to transitional provisions). This amendment extends to England and Wales, Scotland and Northern Ireland (Policing and Crime Act 2017 s 182(2)(*e*)).

29 Confidentiality, &c

(1) Where Her Majesty's Inspectors of Constabulary, the Scottish inspectors or the Northern Ireland inspectors obtain information in the course of exercising a function by virtue of section 27—

(*a*) they may not disclose it without the consent of the Commissioners, and

(*b*) they may not use it for any purpose other than the exercise of the function by virtue of section 27.

(2) A report of an inspection by virtue of section 27 may not include information relating to a specified person without his consent.

(3) Where the [Director General of the Independent Office for Police Conduct][2] or a person acting on [the Director General's][2] behalf obtains information from the Commissioners or an officer of Revenue and Customs, or from the Parliamentary Commissioner for Administration, in the course of exercising a function by virtue of section 28—

(*a*) the [Director General][2] or person shall comply with any restriction on disclosure imposed by regulations under that section (and those regulations may, in particular, prohibit disclosure generally or only in specified circumstances or only without the consent of the Commissioners), and

(*b*) the [Director General][2] or person may not use the information for any purpose other than the exercise of the function by virtue of that section.

(4) A person commits an offence if he contravenes a provision of this section.

(5) It is a defence for a person charged with an offence under this section of disclosing or using information to prove that he reasonably believed—

(*a*) that the disclosure or use was lawful, or

(*b*) that the information had already and lawfully been made available to the public.

(6) A person guilty of an offence under this section shall be liable—

(*a*) on conviction on indictment, to imprisonment for a term not exceeding two years, to a fine or to both, or

(*b*) on summary conviction, to imprisonment for a term not exceeding 12 months, to a fine not exceeding the statutory maximum or to both.

(7) A prosecution for an offence under this section may be instituted in England and Wales [only by or with the consent of the Director of Public Prosecutions.][1]

(8) A prosecution for an offence under this section may be instituted in Northern Ireland only—

(*a*) by the Commissioners, or

(*b*) with the consent of the Director of Public Prosecutions for Northern Ireland.

(9) In the application of this section to Scotland or Northern Ireland the reference in subsection (6)(*b*) to 12 months shall be taken as a reference to six months.

(10) In this section a reference to the Scottish inspectors or the Northern Ireland inspectors has the same meaning as in section 27.

Amendments—[1]   In sub-s (7), words substituted by the Public Bodies (Merger of the Director of Public Prosecutions and the Director of Revenue and Customs Prosecutions) Order, SI 2014/834 art 3(3), Sch 1 paras 5, 8 with effect from 27 March 2014.
[2]   In sub-s (3), in the words before para (*a*), words substituted for words "Independent Police Complaints Commission" and word "its", and in sub-s (3)(*a*), (*b*), words substituted for word "Commission" by the Policing and Crime Act 2017 s 33(9), Sch 9 para 68(1), (4) with effect from 8 January 2018 (by virtue of SI 2017/1249, regs 1(2), 2(1), (2)(*a*), (*d*)). These amendments extend to England and Wales, Scotland and Northern Ireland (Policing and Crime Act 2017 s 182(2)(*e*)).

Offences

30 Impersonation

(1) A person commits an offence if he pretends to be a Commissioner or an officer of Revenue and Customs with a view to obtaining—

(*a*) admission to premises,

(*b*) information, or

(*c*) any other benefit.

(2) A person guilty of an offence under this section shall be liable on summary conviction to—

(*a*) imprisonment for a period not exceeding 51 weeks,

(*b*) a fine not exceeding level 5 on the standard scale, or

(*c*) both.

(3) In the application of this section to Scotland or Northern Ireland the reference in subsection (2)(*a*) to 51 weeks shall be taken as a reference to six months.

Commentary—*Simon's Taxes* A6.1110.

31 Obstruction

(1) A person commits an offence if without reasonable excuse he obstructs—
  (a) an officer of Revenue and Customs,
  (b) a person acting on behalf of the Commissioners or an officer of Revenue and Customs, or
  (c) a person assisting an officer of Revenue and Customs.
(2) A person guilty of an offence under this section shall be liable on summary conviction to—
  (a) imprisonment for a period not exceeding 51 weeks,
  (b) a fine not exceeding level 3 on the standard scale, or
  (c) both.
(3) In the application of this section to Scotland or Northern Ireland the reference in subsection (2)(a) to 51 weeks shall be taken as a reference to six months.

Commentary—*Simon's Taxes* **A6.1110**.

32 Assault

(1) A person commits an offence if he assaults an officer of Revenue and Customs.
(2) A person guilty of an offence under this section shall be liable on summary conviction to—
  (a) imprisonment for a period not exceeding 51 weeks,
  (b) a fine not exceeding level 5 on the standard scale, or
  (c) both.
(3) In the application of this section to Scotland or Northern Ireland the reference in subsection (2)(a) to 51 weeks shall be taken as a reference to six months.

33 Power of arrest

(1) An authorised officer of Revenue and Customs may arrest a person without warrant if the officer reasonably suspects that the person—
  (a) has committed an offence under section 30, 31 or 32,
  (b) is committing an offence under any of those sections, or
  (c) is about to commit an offence under any of those sections.
(2) In subsection (1) "authorised" means authorised by the Commissioners.
(3) Authorisation for the purposes of this section may be specific or general.
(4) In Scotland or Northern Ireland, a constable may arrest a person without warrant if the constable reasonably suspects that the person—
  (a) has committed an offence under this Act,
  (b) is committing an offence under this Act, or
  (c) is about to commit an offence under this Act.

Prosecutions

40 Confidentiality

(1) [The Crown Prosecution Service][4] may not disclose information which—
  (a) is held by [the Service in connection with any of the Director of Public Prosecution's functions][4], . . . [4]
  (b) relates to a person whose identity is specified in the disclosure or can be deduced from it[, and
  (c) was disclosed to the Director of Public Prosecutions by Her Majesty's Revenue and Customs for use in connection with a Revenue and Customs function of the Director of Public Prosecutions.][4]
(2) But subsection (1)—
  (a) does not apply to a disclosure which—
    (i) is made for the purposes of a function of [the Director of Public Prosecutions][4], and
    (ii) does not contravene any restriction imposed by the Director [of Public Prosecutions][4],
  (b) does not apply to a disclosure made to Her Majesty's Revenue and Customs in connection with a function of the Revenue and Customs (within the meaning of section 25),
  (c) does not apply to a disclosure made for the purposes of a criminal investigation or criminal proceedings (whether or not within the United Kingdom),
  [(ca) does not apply to a disclosure made for the purposes of—
    (i) the exercise of any functions of the prosecutor under Parts 2, 3 and 4 of the Proceeds of Crime Act 2002 (c 29),
    (ii) the exercise of any functions of the [National Crime Agency][3] under that Act,
    (iii) the exercise of any functions of . . . . [4] the Director of the Serious Fraud Office, the Director of Public Prosecutions for Northern Ireland or the Scottish Ministers under, or in relation to, Part 5 or 8 of that Act,
    (iv) the exercise of any functions of an officer of Revenue and Customs[, an accredited financial investigator][2] or a constable under Chapter 3 of Part 5 of that Act, or
    (v) investigations or proceedings outside the United Kingdom which have led or may lead to the making of an external order within the meaning of section 447 of that Act,][1]

(*cb*) . . . [4]

(*d*) does not apply to a disclosure which in the opinion of the Director [of Public Prosecutions][4] is desirable for the purpose of safeguarding national security,

(*e*) does not apply to a disclosure made in pursuance of an order of a court,

[(*ea*) does not apply to a disclosure made with the consent of the Commissioners (which may be general or specific),][4]

(*f*) does not apply to a disclosure made with the consent of each person to whom the information relates, and

(*g*) is subject to any other enactment.

(3) A person commits an offence if he contravenes subsection (1).

(4) Subsection (3) does not apply to the disclosure of information about internal administrative arrangements of [the Crown Prosecution Service][4] (whether relating to a member of [the service][2] or to another person).

(5) It is a defence for a person charged with an offence under this section of disclosing information to prove that he reasonably believed—

(*a*) that the disclosure was lawful, or

(*b*) that the information had already and lawfully been made available to the public.

(6) In this section a reference to [the Crown Prosecution Service][4] includes a reference to—

[(*za*) former members of the Crown Prosecution Service,

(*zb*) persons who hold or have held appointment under section 5 of the Prosecution of Offences Act 1985,][4]

(*a*) former members of [the Revenue and Customs Prosecutions Office][4], and

(*b*) persons who . . . [4] have held appointment under section 38.

[(6A) In this section "Revenue and Customs function of the Director of Public Prosecutions" means—

(*a*) a function of the Director of Public Prosecutions under section 3(2)(*ab*), (*bb*) or (*ee*) of the Prosecution of Offences Act 1985, or

(*b*) a function of the Director of Public Prosecutions under the Proceeds of Crime Act 2002 that relates to a function of the Commissioners for Her Majesty's Revenue and Customs or an officer of Revenue and Customs.][4]

(7) A person guilty of an offence under this section shall be liable—

(*a*) on conviction on indictment, to imprisonment for a term not exceeding two years, to a fine or to both, or

(*b*) on summary conviction, to imprisonment for a term not exceeding 12 months, to a fine not exceeding the statutory maximum or to both.

(8) A prosecution for an offence under this section may be instituted in England and Wales [only by or with the consent of the Director of Public Prosecutions.][4]

(9) A prosecution for an offence under this section may be instituted in Northern Ireland only—

(*a*) by the Commissioners, or

(*b*) with the consent of the Director of Public Prosecutions for Northern Ireland.

(10) In the application of this section to Scotland or Northern Ireland the reference in subsection (7)(*b*) to 12 months shall be taken as a reference to six months.

(10A) . . . [4]

(11) In subsection (2) the reference to an enactment does not include—

(*a*) an Act of the Scottish Parliament or an instrument made under such an Act,

[(*aa*) an Act of the National Assembly for Wales or an instrument made under such an Act,][5] or

(*b*) an Act of the Northern Ireland Assembly or an instrument made under such an Act.

Amendments—[1] Sub-s (2)(*ca*) inserted by the Serious Crime Act 2007 s 74(2), Sch 8 para 167 with effect from 1 April 2008: SI 2008/755 art 2(1)(a), subject to transitional provisions and savings in art 3.

[2] Words in sub-s (2)(*ca*)(iv) inserted by the Serious Crime Act 2007 s 79, Sch 11 para 16 with effect from 6 April 2008: SI 2008/755 art 17(1)(f) subject to transitional provisions and savings in SI 2008/755 art 3.

[3] In sub-s (2)(*ca*)(ii), words substituted for words "Serious Organised Crime Agency" by the Crime and Courts Act 2013 s 15, Sch 8 para 156 with effect from 7 October 2013 by virtue of SI 2013/1682, art 3(*v*).

[4] The following amendments made by the Public Bodies (Merger of the Director of Public Prosecutions and the Director of Revenue and Customs Prosecutions) Order, SI 2014/834 art 3(3), Sch 1 paras 5, 10 with effect from 27 March 2014—

    – in sub-s (1), words substituted and repealed, and para (*c*) and preceding word "and" inserted;

    – in sub-s (2), words substituted, inserted and repealed, and para (*ea*) inserted;

    – in sub-s (4), words substituted;

    – in sub-s (6), words substituted and repealed, and paras (*za*), (*zb*) inserted;

    – sub-s (6A) inserted;

    – in sub-s (8), words substituted; and

    – sub-s (10A) repealed.

[5] Sub-s (11)(*aa*) inserted by the Wales Act 2014 s 7(2), (10) with effect from 17 February 2015.

Money and property

43 Expenditure

Expenditure of the Commissioners in connection with the exercise of their functions shall be paid out of money provided by Parliament.

44 Payment into Consolidated Fund

(1) The Commissioners shall pay money received in the exercise of their functions into the Consolidated Fund—

    (*a*) at such times and in such manner as the Treasury directs,

    (*b*) with the exception of receipts specified in subsection (2), and

    (*c*) after deduction of the disbursements specified in subsection (3).

(2) The exceptions mentioned in subsection (1)(*b*) are—

    (*a*) contributions under Part I of the Social Security Contributions and Benefits Act 1992 (c 4),

    (*b*) contributions under Part I of the Social Security Contributions and Benefits (Northern Ireland) Act 1992 (c 7),

    (*c*) any other sums payable, under or by virtue of an enactment, into the National Insurance Fund or the Northern Ireland National Insurance Fund,

    [(*ca*) sums required by section 30A(15) of the Finance Act 1994 (air passenger duty: Northern Ireland long haul rates of duty) to be paid into the Consolidated Fund of Northern Ireland,][3]

    (*d*) sums required under or by virtue of an enactment to be paid into the National Loans Fund,

    (*e*) sums required to be paid to a Minister of the Crown [or other person][1] by virtue of an enactment relating to financial support for students,

    (*f*) *penalties under section 21 of the National Minimum Wage Act 1998 (c 39) (non-compliance),* and[2]

    (*g*) sums required under or by virtue of an enactment to be paid into the Scottish Consolidated Fund.

(3) The disbursements mentioned in subsection (1)(*c*) are—

    (*a*) payments in connection with drawback, repayments and discounts,

    (*b*) payments under section 77 of the Scotland Act 1998 (c 46) (additional tax),

    (*c*) payments under section 2 of the Isle of Man Act 1979 (c 58) (Isle of Man share of common duties), and

    (*d*) tax credits.

(4) In subsection (3)(*a*) "repayments" includes—

    (*a*) payments in respect of actual or deemed credits relating to any tax or duty, and

    (*b*) payments of interest (or repayment supplement) on—

        (i) repayments, or

        (ii) payments treated as repayments.

Amendments—[1] In sub-s (2)(*e*), words inserted, in relation to England and Wales, by the Sale of Student Loans Act 2008 s 6(5) with effect from 21 July 2008 (by virtue of the Sale of Student Loans Act 2008 s 14).

[2] Sub-s (2)(*f*) repealed by the Employment Act 2008, ss 9(5), 20, Schedule Pt 2 with effect from 6 April 2009 (by virtue of SI 2009/603 arts 2, 3 and subject to savings in relation to the enforcement of the agricultural minimum wage in Scotland and Northern Ireland in s 9(7) thereof).

[3] Sub-s (2)(*ca*) inserted by FA 2012 s 190, Sch 23 para 14 with effect from 17 July 2012.

Prospective amendments—Sub-s (3)(*b*) repealed by the Scotland Act 2012 s 25, Sch 2 para 3(1), (2) with effect from a date to be appointed.

In sub-s (3)(*b*), word "and" to be inserted at the end by WRA 2012 s 33, Sch 3 paras 19, 21 with effect from a date to be appointed.

Sub-s (3)(*d*) and preceding word "and" to be repealed by WRA 2012 s 147, Sch 14 Pt 1 with effect from a date to be appointed.

45 Remuneration, &c

(1) The Commissioners shall be paid, out of money provided by Parliament, such remuneration, expenses and other allowances as may be determined by the Minister for the Civil Service.

(2) The Commissioners may incur expenditure in respect of staff (whether in respect of remuneration, allowances, pensions, gratuities or otherwise).

(3) The Commissioners shall pay to the Minister for the Civil Service, at such times as the Minister may direct, such sums as the Minister may determine in respect of any increase attributable to this Act in the sums payable under the Superannuation Act 1972 (c 11) out of money provided by Parliament.

46 Accounts

(1) The Commissioners shall provide to the Comptroller and Auditor General, in such form as the Treasury shall direct, a daily account of—

    (*a*) the amount of revenue received, and

    (*b*) the disposal of revenue received.

(2) The Commissioners shall provide to the Comptroller and Auditor General, in such form and at such times as the Treasury shall direct, an account of liabilities satisfied by the acceptance of property in satisfaction of tax under—

    (*a*) section 230 of the Inheritance Tax Act 1984 (c 51), or (*b*) any other enactment.

47 Payment out of Consolidated Fund

(1) This section applies if the Treasury think that the funds available to the Commissioners may be insufficient to make, under or by virtue of an enactment—

(*a*) a payment into the National Insurance Fund,

(*b*) a payment into the Northern Ireland National Insurance Fund,

(*c*) a payment of a kind specified in section 44(2)(*c*) to (*g*), or

(*d*) a disbursement of a kind specified in section 44(3).

(2) Where this section applies the Treasury may pay money to the Commissioners out of the Consolidated Fund to enable them to make a payment or disbursement.

(3) This section applies whether or not the reason for a deficiency is or may be that an amount has been paid or retained on the basis of an estimate that has proved or may prove to be inaccurate.

48 Transfer of property, &c: general

(1) Upon commencement the property, rights and liabilities of any of the old commissioners shall by virtue of this section vest in the new commissioners.

(2) Anything done by, on behalf of or in relation to any of the old commissioners which has effect immediately before commencement shall continue to have effect as if done by, on behalf of or in relation to the new commissioners.

(3) Anything (including any legal proceedings) which immediately before commencement is in the process of being done by, on behalf of or in relation to any of the old commissioners may be continued by, on behalf of or in relation to the new commissioners.

(4) Upon commencement the property, rights and liabilities of any of the old officers shall by virtue of this section vest in the officers of Revenue and Customs.

(5) Anything done by, on behalf of or in relation to any of the old officers which has effect immediately before commencement shall continue to have effect as if done by, on behalf of or in relation to an officer of Revenue and Customs.

(6) Anything (including any legal proceedings) which immediately before commencement is in the process of being done by, on behalf of or in relation to any of the old officers may be continued by, on behalf of or in relation to an officer of Revenue and Customs.

(7) So far as is necessary or appropriate in consequence of section 5 or the preceding provisions of this section, on and after commencement—

(*a*) a reference to any of the old commissioners in an agreement (whether written or not), instrument or other document shall be treated as a reference to the new commissioners, and

(*b*) a reference in an agreement (whether written or not), instrument or other document to any of the old officers shall be treated as a reference to an officer of Revenue and Customs.

(8) This section shall operate in relation to property, rights or liabilities—

(*a*) whether or not they would otherwise be capable of being transferred,

(*b*) without any instrument or other formality being required, and

(*c*) irrespective of any requirement for consent that would otherwise apply.

(9) In this section—

"commencement" means the time appointed under section 53 for the commencement of section 5,

"rights and liabilities" includes rights and liabilities relating to employment,

"the old commissioners" means—

(*a*) the Commissioners of Inland Revenue, and

(*b*) the Commissioners of Customs and Excise,

"the old officers" means any of the persons listed in section 6(2) or 7(3), and

"the new commissioners" means the Commissioners for Her Majesty's Revenue and Customs.

(10) This section is subject to section 49.

General

50 Consequential amendments, &c

(1) In so far as is appropriate in consequence of section 5 a reference in an enactment, instrument or other document to the Commissioners of Customs and Excise, to customs and excise or to the Commissioners of Inland Revenue (however expressed) shall be taken as a reference to the Commissioners for Her Majesty's Revenue and Customs.

(2) In so far as is appropriate in consequence of sections 6 and 7 a reference in an enactment, instrument or other document to any of the persons specified in section 6(2) or 7(3) (however expressed) shall be taken as a reference to an officer of Revenue and Customs.

(3) In so far as is appropriate in consequence of this Act a reference in an enactment, instrument or other document to the Valuation Office of the Inland Revenue (however expressed) shall be taken as a reference to the Valuation Office of Her Majesty's Revenue and Customs.

(4) The Treasury may by regulations make such provision as they think appropriate in consequence of section 5, 6 or 7 in respect of a reference in an enactment (however expressed) to—

(a)　the Commissioners of Inland Revenue (or to a Commissioner),

(b)　the Commissioners of Customs and Excise (or to a Commissioner),

(c)　customs,

(d)　customs and excise,

(e)　Inland Revenue, or

(f)　any of the persons specified in section 6(2) or 7(3).

(5)　Regulations under subsection (4) in respect of a reference in an enactment—

(a)　may amend an enactment,

(b)　may make incidental and consequential provision,

(c)　shall be made by statutory instrument, and

(d)　shall not be made unless a draft has first been laid before, and approved by resolution of, each House of Parliament.

(6)　Schedule 4 (consequential amendments, &c) shall have effect (and is without prejudice to the generality of subsections (1) to (4)).

(7)　Subsections (1) to (4) shall, subject to any express provision to the contrary, have effect in relation to enactments passed or made, and instruments and documents issued, whether before or after the passing of this Act.

Commentary—*Simon's Taxes* A3.101A, E2.250, I11.102.

Order—See the Commissioners for Revenue and Customs Act 2005 (Commencement) Order, SI 2005/1126, art 2(2) (this section and Sch 4 came into force on 18 April 2005).

51 Interpretation

(1)　In this Act—

except where otherwise expressly provided, "enactment" includes—

(a)　an Act of the Scottish Parliament,

(b)　an instrument made under an Act of the Scottish Parliament,

[(ba)　an Act of the National Assembly for Wales,

[(bb)　an instrument made under an Act of the National Assembly for Wales,][2]

(c)　Northern Ireland legislation, and

(d)　an instrument made under Northern Ireland legislation,

"officer of Revenue and Customs" means a person appointed under section 2, and

"revenue" has the meaning given by section 5(4).

(2)　In this Act—

(a)　"function" means any power or duty (including a power or duty that is ancillary to another power or duty), and

(b)　a reference to the functions of the Commissioners or of officers of Revenue and Customs is a reference to the functions conferred—

(i)　by or by virtue of this Act, or

(ii)　by or by virtue of any enactment passed or made after the commencement of this Act.

[(2A)　But a reference to the functions of the Commissioners or of officers of Revenue and Customs does not include a function which—

(a)　is conferred on them by or by virtue of an Act of the Scottish Parliament or an instrument made under such an Act, and

(b)　relates to a devolved tax within the meaning of the Scotland Act 1998.][1]

[(2B)　Nor does such a reference include a function which—

(a)　is conferred on the Commissioners or on officers of Revenue and Customs by or by virtue of an Act of the National Assembly for Wales or an instrument made under such an Act, and

(b)　relates to a devolved tax within the meaning of the Government of Wales Act 2006.][2]

(3)　A reference in this Act, in an enactment amended by this Act or, subject to express provision to the contrary, in any future enactment, to responsibility for collection and management of revenue has the same meaning as references to responsibility for care and management of revenue in enactments passed before this Act.

(4)　In this Act a reference to information acquired in connection with a matter includes a reference to information held in connection with that matter.

Amendments—[1]　Sub-s (2A) inserted by the Scotland Act 2012 s 24(1), (2), (6) with effect from 1 July 2012.

[2]　Sub-ss (1)(ba), (bb), (2B) inserted by the Wales Act 2014 s 7(2), (11)–(13) with effect from 17 February 2015.

52 Repeals

(1)　The following shall cease to have effect—

(a)　(*repeals* CEMA 1979 ss 12, 15, 32, 84, 86, 152(c), (d), 169).

(b)　(*repeals* TMA 1970 s 111(2)).

(2)　The enactments specified in Schedule 5 are hereby repealed to the extent specified.

Order—See the Commissioners for Revenue and Customs Act 2005 (Commencement) Order, SI 2005/1126, art 2(2) (this section and Sch 5 came into force on 18 April 2005).

53 Commencement

(1) This Act shall come into force in accordance with provision made by order of the Treasury.

(2) An order under subsection (1)—

    (a) may make provision generally or only in relation to specified provisions or purposes,

    (b) may include transitional, consequential or incidental provision or savings, and

    (c) shall be made by statutory instrument.

Orders—See the Commissioners for Revenue and Customs Act 2005 (Commencement) Order, SI 2005/1126 (the Act came into force on 7 April 2005 at 5.45pm, subject to the provisions specified in SI 2005/1126 art 2(2) which came into force on 18 April 2005).

54 Transitional: general

(1) In the application of section 5—

    (a) a reference to responsibility before commencement of that section includes a reference to responsibility under an enactment passed or made, but not yet in force, before commencement, and

    (b) a reference to a function vesting includes a reference to a function which is to vest under an enactment passed or made, but not yet in force, before commencement of that section.

(2) In the application of section 6 or 7 a reference to a function conferred by an enactment includes a reference to a function conferred by an enactment passed or made, but not yet in force, before commencement of that section.

(3) Where immediately before the commencement of section 6 a person holds appointment as a member of the staff of the Commissioners of Inland Revenue or of the Commissioners of Customs and Excise, his appointment shall have effect on commencement as if made by the Commissioners for Her Majesty's Revenue and Customs under section 2.

(4) The following shall be treated as being included in the list in Schedule 1—

    (a) development land tax,

    (b) disabled person's tax credit,

    (c) estate duty,

    (d) the national defence contribution under Part III of the Finance Act 1937 (c 54),

    (e) the special tax on banking deposits under section 134 of the Finance Act 1981 (c 35), and

    (f) working families tax credit.

(5) The Treasury may by order made by statutory instrument add to the list in subsection (4) an item relating to a matter for which the Commissioners of Inland Revenue or a person listed in section 7(3) had responsibility before the commencement of section 5, if it appears to the Treasury that the law relating to that matter has lapsed or ceased to have effect but that transitional matters may continue to arise in respect of it.

(6) An order under subsection (5)—

    (a) may include consequential, transitional or incidental provision,

    (b) shall be made by statutory instrument, and

    (c) shall be subject to annulment in pursuance of a resolution of either House of Parliament.

(7) A reference in this Act to anything done by, on behalf of or in relation to a specified person or class of person includes a reference to anything treated as if done by, on behalf of or in relation to that person by virtue of transitional provision of an enactment passed or made before this Act.

Order—See the Commissioners for Revenue and Customs Act 2005 (Commencement) Order, SI 2005/1126, art 2(2) (this section came into force on 18 April 2005).

Prospective amendments—Sub-s (4)(f), and preceding word "and" to be repealed by WRA 2012 s 147, Sch 14 Pt 1 with effect from a date to be appointed.

55 Transitional: penalties

(1) In relation to an offence under section 19 committed before the commencement of section 282 of the Criminal Justice Act 2003 (c 44) (short sentences) the reference in section 19(4)(b) to 12 months shall have effect as if it were a reference to six months.

(2) In relation to an offence under section 21 committed before the commencement of section 282 of the Criminal Justice Act (short sentences), the reference in section 21(6)(b) to 12 months shall have effect as if it were a reference to six months.

(3) In relation to an offence under section 29 committed before the commencement of section 282 of the Criminal Justice Act 2003 (c 44) (short sentences) the reference in section 29(6)(b) to 12 months shall have effect as if it were a reference to six months.

(4) In relation to an offence under section 30 committed before the commencement of section 281(4) and (5) of the Criminal Justice Act 2003 (51 week maximum term of sentences) the reference in section 30(2)(a) to 51 weeks shall have effect as if it were a reference to six months.

(5) In relation to an offence under section 31 committed before the commencement of section 281(4) and (5) of the Criminal Justice Act 2003 (51 week maximum term of sentences) the reference in section 31(2)(a) to 51 weeks shall have effect as if it were a reference to one month.

(6) In relation to an offence under section 32 committed before the commencement of section 281(4) and (5) of the Criminal Justice Act 2003 (51 week maximum term of sentences) the reference in section 32(2)(a) to 51 weeks shall have effect as if it were a reference to six months.

(7) In relation to an offence under section 40 committed before the commencement of section 282 of the Criminal Justice Act 2003 (short sentences) the reference in section 40(7)(*b*) to 12 months shall have effect as if it were a reference to six months.

56 Extent

(1) This Act extends to the United Kingdom.

(2) But an amendment, modification or repeal effected by this Act has the same extent as the enactment (or the relevant part of the enactment) to which it relates.

57 Short title

This Act may be cited as the Commissioners for Revenue and Customs Act 2005.

SCHEDULES

SCHEDULE 1

FORMER INLAND REVENUE MATTERS

Section 7

Order—See the Commissioners for Revenue and Customs Act 2005 (Commencement) Order, SI 2005/1126, art 2(2) (this Schedule and s 7 came into force on 18 April 2005).

1   Capital gains tax.

2   Charities.

3   Child benefit.

4   Child tax credit.

Prospective amendments—This para to be repealed by WRA 2012 s 147, Sch 14 Pt 1 with effect from a date to be appointed.

5   Child trust funds.

6   Corporation tax (and amounts assessable or chargeable as if they were corporation tax).

7   Guardian's allowance.

8   Income tax.

9   Inheritance tax.

10   The issue of bank notes.

11   National insurance contributions.

12   The National Insurance Fund.

13   The national minimum wage.

14   Oil and gas royalties.

15   Payment of or in lieu of rates.

16   Payment in lieu of tax reliefs, in so far as the Commissioners of Inland Revenue were responsible before the commencement of section 5.

17   Pension schemes.

18   Petroleum revenue tax.

19   Rating lists.

20   Recovery of taxes due in other member States, in relation to matters corresponding to those for which the Commissioners of Inland Revenue were responsible before the commencement of section 5.

21   Stamp duty.

22   Stamp duty land tax.

23   Stamp duty reserve tax.

24   Statutory adoption pay.

25   Statutory maternity pay.

[26   [Statutory]² paternity pay.]¹

Amendments—[1]   Paragraphs 26, 26A substituted for previous para 26 by the Work and Families Act 2006 s 11(1), Sch 1 para 61 with effect from 6 April 2010 (by virtue of SI 2010/495).
[2]   Word substituted by the Children and Families Act 2014 s 126, Sch 7 para 64(1), (2) with effect from 5 April 2015 (by virtue of SI 2014/1640 art 7(kk));

Prospective amendments—This para to be repealed by WRA 2012 s 147, Sch 14 Pt 1 with effect from a date to be appointed.

26A   . . . [1]

Amendments—[1]   Para 26A (additional statutory paternity pay) repealed by the Children and Families Act 2014 s 126, Sch 7 para 64(1), (3) with effect from 5 April 2015 (by virtue of SI 2014/1640 art 7(kk));

[26C   Statutory parental bereavement pay.][1]

Amendments—[1]   Para 26C inserted by the Parental Bereavement (Leave and Pay) Act 2018 s 1, Schedule para 48 with effect from 18 January 2020 (by virtue of SI 2020/45 reg 2).

27   Statutory sick pay.

28   Student loans.

29   Valuation lists in relation to council tax.

30   Valuation of property.

31   Working tax credit.

Prospective amendments—This para to be repealed by WRA 2012 s 147, Sch 14 Pt 1 with effect from a date to be appointed.

SCHEDULE 2

FUNCTIONS OF COMMISSIONERS AND OFFICERS: RESTRICTIONS, &C

Sections 16 and 17

PART 1

GENERAL

Order—See the Commissioners for Revenue and Customs Act 2005 (Commencement) Order, SI 2005/1126, art 2(2) (Part 1 of this Schedule and s 16 came into force on 18 April 2005).

3   Section 113(3) of that Act (form of documents) shall have effect only in connection with functions relating to matters to which section 7 above applies.

Customs and Excise Management Act 1979 (c 2)

4   Section 8(2) and (3) of the Customs and Excise Management Act 1979 (person acting deemed to be proper officer) shall not apply to a person engaged in connection with a function relating to a matter to which section 7 above applies.

5—(1) Section 11 of that Act (assistance to be rendered by police, &c) shall not apply in connection with a function relating to a matter to which section 7 above applies.
(2) A person may rely for the purposes of section 11 of that Act on a statement (written or oral) of an officer of Revenue and Customs that a function does not relate to a matter to which section 7 above applies.

6   Sections 167 (untrue declarations, &c) and 168 (counterfeiting documents, &c) of that Act shall not apply in relation to a declaration, document or statement in respect of a function relating to a matter to which section 7 above applies.

Finance Act 1985 (c 54)

8   Section 10 of the Finance Act 1985 (computer records &c) shall not apply in connection with a function relating to a matter to which section 7 above applies.

Finance Act 1998 (c 36)

10   (_amends_ FA 1998 s 163(1)).

PART 2
USE OF INFORMATION
Teaching and Higher Education Act 1998 (c 30)

15   The Commissioners may supply information in accordance with section 24 of the Teaching and Higher Education Act 1998 (supply of information in connection with the student loan scheme) only if the information was obtained or is held in the exercise of a function relating to matters to which section 7 above applies.

Prospective amendments—Words "student support" to be substituted for words "the student loan scheme" by the Higher Education and Research Act 2017 s 87(4) with effect from a date to be appointed. This amendment extends to England and Wales only (Higher Education and Research Act 2017 s 123).

Employment Relations Act 1999 (c 26)

16   The Commissioners may supply information in accordance with section 39 of the Employment Relations Act 1999 (supply of information in connection with the national minimum wage and agricultural wages) only if the information was obtained or is held in the exercise of a function relating to matters to which section 7 above applies.

Financial Services and Markets Act 2000 (c 8)

18   The Commissioners may supply information in accordance with section 350 of the Financial Services and Markets Act 2000 (supply of information to assist with an investigation under section 168 of that Act) only if the information was obtained or is held in the exercise of a function relating to matters to which section 7 above applies.

Terrorism Act 2000 (c 11)

19   Information may be supplied in accordance with paragraph 4(2) of Schedule 14 to the Terrorism Act 2000 (exercise of officers' powers) only if the information has not been held solely in the exercise of functions relating to matters to which section 7 above applies.

SCHEDULE 4
CONSEQUENTIAL AMENDMENTS, &C
Section 50

Order—See the Commissioners for Revenue and Customs Act 2005 (Commencement) Order, SI 2005/1126, art 2(2) (this Schedule and s 50 came into force on 18 April 2005).

Harbours, Docks, and Piers Clauses Act 1847 (c 27)

1   (*amends* Harbours, Docks and Piers Clauses Act 1847 s 14).

Public Revenue and Consolidated Fund Charges Act 1854 (c 94)

2   (*amends* Public Revenue and Consolidated Fund Charges Act Sch (*b*)).

Exchequer and Audit Departments Act 1866 (c 39)

3   (*amends* Exchequer and Audit Departments Act 1866 s 10).

Game Laws Amendment (Scotland) Act 1877 (c 28)

4   (*amends* Game Laws Amendment (Scotland) Act 1877 s 11).

Inland Revenue Regulation Act 1890 (c 21)

5   (*repeals* Inland Revenue Regulation Act 1890).

Public Accounts and Charges Act 1891 (c 24)

6   (*repeals* Public Accounts and Charges Act 1891)

Judicial Pensions Act (Northern Ireland) 1951 (c 20 (N.I))

7   (*amends* Judicial Pensions Act (Northern Ireland) 1951 Sch 2Apara 6(3) (as inserted by Judicial Pensions (Northern Ireland) Order, SI 1991/2631, Sch 2)).

County Courts Act (Northern Ireland) 1959 (c 25 (NI))

8   (*amends* County Courts Act (Northern Ireland) 1959 Sch 2A para 6(3) (as inserted by Judicial Pensions (Northern Ireland) Order, SI 1991/2631, Sch 2)).

Resident Magistrates' Pensions Act (Northern Ireland) 1960 (c 2 (NI))

9   (*amends* Resident Magistrates' Pensions Act (Northern Ireland) 1960 Sch 3 para 6(3) (as inserted by Judicial Pensions (Northern Ireland) Order, SI 1991/2631, Sch 2)).

Parliamentary Commissioner Act 1967 (c 13)

10   (*amends* Parliamentary Commissioner Act 1967 Sch 2).

Taxes Management Act 1970 (c 9)

11   The Taxes Management Act 1970 shall be amended as follows.

12   (*substitutes* TMA 1970 s 1).

13   (*repeals* TMA 1970 s 6(3), (4)).

14   (*repeals* TMA 1970 s 111(2)).

15   (*amends* TMA 1970 Sch 1 Part 1).

Finance Act 1972 (c 41)

16   (*repeals* FA 1972 s 127).

Biological Weapons Act 1974 (c 6)

17   (*amends* Biological Weapons Act 1974 s 1B).

Health and Safety at Work etc Act 1974 (c 37)

18—(1) Section 27A of the Health and Safety at Work etc Act 1974 (disclosure by Commissioners of Customs and Excise) shall be amended as follows.
(2)–(4) (*amend* Health and Safety at Work etc Act 1974 s 27A(1), (3) and section heading).

Health and Safety at Work (Northern Ireland) Order 1978 (SI 1978/1039 (NI 9))

19—(1) Article 29A of the Health and Safety at Work (Northern Ireland) Order 1978 (disclosure by Commissioners of Customs and Excise) shall be amended as follows.
(2)–(4) (*amend* Health and Safety at Work (Northern Ireland) Order 1978 art 29A(1), (3) and section heading).

Customs and Excise Management Act 1979 (c 2)

20   The Customs and Excise Management Act 1979 shall be amended as follows.

21   (*repeals* CEMA 1979 ss 6, 7, 8(1), 13, 14, 16, 17, 18, 153, 155(2), 165).

22   (*amends* CEMA 1979 s 1(1)).

23   (*amends* CEMA 1979 s 145(1), (2), (4), (6)).

24   (*amends* CEMA 1979 s 146A(7)).

26   (*amends* CEMA 1979 s 152(*a*)).

27   (*substitutes* CEMA 1979 s 155(1)).

28   (*inserts* CEMA 1979 s 171(4A)).

Judicial Pensions Act 1981 (c 20)

29   (*amends* Judicial Pensions Act 1981 Sch 1A para 6(3)).

31   (*repeals* PACE 1984 s114(4)).

Debtors (Scotland) Act 1987 (c 18)

32   The Debtors (Scotland) Act 1987 shall be amended as follows.

33   (*amends* Debtors (Scotland) Act 1987 s 1(5)(*d*)).

34   (*amends* Debtors (Scotland) Act 1987 s 5(4)(*d*)).

Criminal Justice Act 1987 (c 38)

35—(1) (*amends* CJA 1987 s 3(1), (2)).
(2) (*inserts* CJA 1987 s 3(8)).

Consumer Protection Act 1987 (c 43)

36—(1) Section 37 of the Consumer Protection Act 1987 (disclosure by Commissioners of Customs and Excise) shall be amended as follows.
(2)–(4) (*amend* Consumer Protection Act 1987 s 37(1), (3) and section heading).

Copyright, Designs and Patents Act 1988 (c 48)

38   (*repeals* Copyright, Designs and Patents Act 1988 s 112(5)).

Finance Act 1989 (c 26)

39   (*inserts* FA 1989 s 182(10A)).

Police and Criminal Evidence (Northern Ireland) Order 1989 (SI 1989/1341 (NI 12))

40   (*repeals* Police and Criminal Evidence (Northern Ireland) Order 1989 art 85(3)).

Child Support Act 1991 (c 48)

42   (*amends* Child Support Act 1991 Sch 2).

Social Security Contributions and Benefits Act 1992 (c 4)

43   (*amends* Social Security Contributions and Benefits Act 1992 s 171).

Social Security Administration Act 1992 (c 5)

44   The Social Security Administration Act 1992 shall be amended as follows.

46   (*amends* Social Security Administration Act 1992 s 122AA).

47   (*substitutes* Social Security Administration Act 1992 s 161(1)).

Social Security Contributions and Benefits (Northern Ireland) Act 1992 (c 7)

48   (*amends* Social Security Contributions and Benefits (Northern Ireland) Act 1992 s 167(1)).

Social Security Administration (Northern Ireland) Act 1992 (c 8)

49   (*amends* Social Security Administration (Northern Ireland) Act 1992 s 116ZA).

Prospective amendments—This para to be repealed by the Welfare Reform (Northern Ireland) Order, SI 2015/2006 art 140, Sch 12 Pt 12 with effect from a date to be appointed.

50   (*amends* Social Security Administration (Northern Ireland) Act 1992 s 116AA).

Pension Schemes Act 1993 (c 48)

51   (*amends* Pension Schemes Act 1993 s 158).

Pension Schemes (Northern Ireland) Act 1993 (c 49)

52   (*amends* Pension Schemes (Northern Ireland) Act 1993 s 154).

Finance Act 1994 (c 9)

53   (*repeals* FA 1994 Sch 7 para 32).

Value Added Tax Act 1994 (c 23)

54   The Value Added Tax Act 1994 shall be amended as follows.

55   (*substitutes* VATA 1994 Sch 3B para 21(1)(*b*)).

56   (*substitutes* VATA 1994 Sch 11 para 1).

Trade Marks Act 1994 (c 26)

57   (*repeals* Trade Marks Act 1994 s 90(5)).

58   (*amends* Trade Marks Act 1994 s 91 and section heading).

Drug Trafficking Act 1994 (c 37)

59   (*amends* Drug Trafficking Act 1994 s 60).

Finance Act 1995 (c 4)

60   (*repeals* FA 1995 s 158).

Merchant Shipping Act 1995 (c 21)

61   (*repeals* Merchant Shipping Act 1995 s 303).

Criminal Appeal Act 1995 (c 35)

62   (*substitutes* Criminal Appeal Act 1995 s 22(4)(*e*), (*f*)).

Criminal Law (Consolidation) (Scotland) Act 1995 (c 39)

63—(1) Section 30 of the Criminal Law (Consolidation) (Scotland) Act 1995 (disclosure of information) shall be amended as follows.
(2)–(4) (*amend* Criminal Law (Consolidation) (Scotland) Act 1995 s 30(1), (2), (7)).

Chemical Weapons Act 1996 (c 6)

64   (*amends* Chemical Weapons Act 1996 s 30A).

Finance Act 1996 (c 8)

65   (*repeals* FA 1996 Sch 5 para 41).

Landmines Act 1998 (c 33)

66   (*amends* Landmines Act 1998 s 21).

Finance Act 1998 (c 36)

67   (*repeals* FA 1998 s 145).

68   Schedule 18 to that Act (company tax returns &c) shall have effect—
    (*a*) with the substitution for "the Inland Revenue", in each place, of "an officer of Revenue and Customs",
    (*b*) with the omission of paragraph 95 (meaning of references to Inland Revenue), and
    (*c*) with any other necessary consequential modifications.

Scotland Act 1998 (c 46)

70   The Scotland Act 1998 shall be amended as follows.

Prospective amendments—Paras 70–72 to be repealed by the Scotland Act 2012 s 25, Sch 2 para 3(1), (3) with effect from a date to be appointed.

71   (*amends* Scotland Act 1988 s 77).

Prospective amendments—Paras 70–72 to be repealed by the Scotland Act 2012 s 25, Sch 2 para 3(1), (3) with effect from a date to be appointed.

72   (*repeals* Scotland Act 1998 s 78(8)).

Prospective amendments—Paras 70–72 to be repealed by the Scotland Act 2012 s 25, Sch 2 para 3(1), (3) with effect from a date to be appointed.

Social Security Contributions (Transfer of Functions, etc) Act 1999 (c 2)

73   The Social Security Contributions (Transfer of Functions etc) Act 1999 shall be amended as follows.

74   (*substitutes* Social Security Contributions (Transfer of Functions etc) Act 1999 s 3(1)).

75   (*repeals* Social Security Contributions (Transfer of Functions etc) Act 1999 s 7).

Finance Act 1999 (c 16)

76   (*amends* FA 1999 s 135(2)).

Terrorism Act 2000 (c 11)

78   (*amends* Terrorism Act 2000 s 121).

Finance Act 2000 (c 17)

79   The Finance Act 2000 shall be amended as follows.

80   (*repeals* FA 2000 s 148(2)).

81   (*repeals* FA 2000 Sch 6 para 140).

Capital Allowances Act 2001 (c 2)

82   The Capital Allowances Act 2001 shall be amended as follows.

83—(1) For "the Inland Revenue", wherever that expression appears, substitute "an officer of Revenue and Customs" (except as provided in paragraph 84).
(2) For "the Board of Inland Revenue", wherever that expression appears, substitute "the Commissioners for Her Majesty's Revenue and Customs".

85   (*repeals* CAA 2001 s 576).

86   (*amends* CAA 2001 Sch 1 Part 2).

Anti-terrorism, Crime and Security Act 2001 (c 24)

87   (*amends* Anti-terrorism, Crime and Security Act s 53).

Tax Credits Act 2002 (c 21)

88   (*substitutes* TCA 2002 s 2).

89   (*repeals* TCA 2002 s 40(1)(*a*)).

90   (*substitutes* TCA 2002 s 53).

91   (*repeals* TCA 2002 Sch 5 para 2).

92   To the extent that the Tax Credits Act 1999 (c 10) is saved by the Tax Credits Act 2002 (Commencement No 4, Transitional and Savings) Order 2003 (SI 2003/962), the modifications made by paragraphs 88 to 91 shall have effect in relation to the relevant provisions of that Act as they have effect in relation to the Tax Credits Act 2002 (c 21).

Employment Act 2002 (c 22)

93   (*repeals* Employment Act 2002 s 5).

Finance Act 2002 (c 23)

94   The Finance Act 2002 shall be amended as follows.

95—(1) (*amends* FA 2002 s 135).
(2) (*amended* FA 2002 s 135(1); *repealed by* FA 2007 s 114, Sch 27 Pt 5(4)).

96   (*repeals* FA 2002 Sch 13 para 26).

99   (*amends* Proceeds of Crime Act 2002 s 451).

100   In Schedule 8 to that Act (declarations) for "an offence relating to inland revenue,", in each place, substitute "an offence relating to a former Inland Revenue matter (being a matter listed in Schedule 1 to the Commissioners for Revenue and Customs Act 2005 except for paragraphs 2, 10, 13, 14, 15, 17, 19, 28, 29 and 30),".

Income Tax (Earnings and Pensions) Act 2003 (c 1)

101   The Income Tax (Earnings and Pensions) Act 2003 shall be amended as follows.

102—(1) For the expression "the Inland Revenue", wherever it appears, substitute "an officer of Revenue and Customs" (except as provided in paragraphs 109, 117 and 118).
(2) For the expression "the Board of Inland Revenue", wherever it appears, substitute "the Commissioners for Her Majesty's Revenue and Customs".
(3) In the following provisions for "Board" substitute "Commissioners" and for "Board's" substitute "Commissioners'"—
   (*a*) section 28(6),
   (*b*) –(*d*)(*amended* ITEPA 2003 ss 42, 43; *repealed by* FA 2008 s 25, Sch 7 para 79(*c*)
   (*e*) section 343,
   (*f*) section 355,
   (*g*) section 594,
   (*h*) section 647,
   (*i*) section 691,

    (*j*)   section 703,

    (*k*)   section 704, and

    (*l*)   the title of section 717.

103—(1) In the following provisions for "they" or "them" in each place substitute "the officer"—

    (*a*)   section 58(3),

    (*b*)   section 65(3),

    (*c*)   section 79(2),

    (*d*)   section 96(2),

    (*e*)   section 179(3),

    (*f*)   section 312(5),

    (*g*)   section 344(3),

    (*h*)   section 392(4) and (5),

    (*i*)   section 421J(4),

    (*j*)   paragraph 81(1) and (3) of Schedule 2,

    (*k*)   paragraph 84(2) of Schedule 2,

    (*l*)   paragraph 85(1) of Schedule 2,

    (*m*)   paragraph 93(1) of Schedule 2,

    (*n*)   paragraph 40(1) and (3) of Schedule 3,

    (*o*)   paragraph 42(2A) of Schedule 3,

    (*p*)   paragraph 43 of Schedule 3,

    (*q*)   paragraph 44(1) of Schedule 3,

    (*r*)   paragraph 45(1) of Schedule 3,

    (*s*)   paragraph 28(1) and (3) of Schedule 4,

    (*t*)   paragraph 30(3) of Schedule 4,

    (*u*)   paragraph 31 of Schedule 4,

    (*v*)   paragraph 32(1) of Schedule 4,

    (*w*)   paragraph 33(1) of Schedule 4,

    (*x*)   paragraph 46(2) of Schedule 5,

    (*y*)   paragraph 46(3) of Schedule 5,

    (*z*)   paragraph 47 of Schedule 5, and

    (*aa*)   paragraph 51(1) of Schedule 5.

(2) In the following provisions for "their" in each place substitute "the officer's"—

    (*a*)   section 715(3)(*b*),

    (*b*)   paragraph 85(3) of Schedule 2,

    (*c*)   paragraph 93(1)(*a*) of Schedule 2,

    (*d*)   paragraph 41(2) of Schedule 3,

    (*e*)   paragraph 44(3) of Schedule 3,

    (*f*)   paragraph 45(1) of Schedule 3,

    (*g*)   paragraph 29(2) of Schedule 4,

    (*h*)   paragraph 32(3) of Schedule 4,

    (*i*)   paragraph 33(1) of Schedule 4,

    (*j*)   paragraph 46(2) and (3) of Schedule 5,

    (*k*)   paragraph 47(1)(*b*) and (3)(*b*) of Schedule 5,

    (*l*)   paragraph 49(2) and (3) of Schedule 5, and

    (*m*)   paragraph 51(1) of Schedule 5.

(3) In the following provisions in each place for "their" substitute "the"—

    (*a*)   paragraph 81(3) of Schedule 2,

    (*b*)   paragraph 82(2) of Schedule 2,

    (*c*)   paragraph 85(3) of Schedule 2,

    (*d*)   paragraph 40(3) of Schedule 3,

    (*e*)   paragraph 43 of Schedule 3,

    (*f*)   paragraph 28(3) of Schedule 4,

    (*g*)   paragraph 31 of Schedule 4, and

    (*h*)   paragraph 47(1)(*a*) and (3)(*a*) of Schedule 5.

(4) In the following provisions omit "their"—

    (*a*)   paragraph 84(2) of Schedule 2,

    (*b*)   paragraph 42(2A) of Schedule 3, and

    (*c*)   paragraph 30(3) of Schedule 4.

105   (*amends* ITEPA 2003 s 58(3)).

106   (*amends* ITEPA 2003 s 65(3), (4)).

107   (*amends* ITEPA 2003 s 79(2)).

108   (*amends* ITEPA 2003 s 96(2), (3)).

109   (*amends* ITEPA 2003 s 79(3)).

110   (*amends* ITEPA 2003 s 183(1)(*a*)).

111   (*amends* ITEPA 2003 s 312(5)).

112   (*amends* ITEPA 2003 s (3)).

113   (*amends* ITEPA 2003 s 392(4), (5)).

114   (*amends* ITEPA 2003 s 511(2)(*a*), (*b*)).

115   (*amends* ITEPA 2003 s 514(2)(*a*), (*b*))

116   (*amends* ITEPA 2003 s 647(3)(*b*)).

117   (*amends* ITEPA 2003 s 684).

118   (*amends* ITEPA 2003 s 715(3)(*b*)).

119   (*repeals* ITEPA 2003 s 720).

120   (*amends* ITEPA 2003 Sch 1, Pt 2).

121   In Schedule 2—
  (*a*)   (*amends* ITEPA 2003 Sch 2 para 81(1), (3)).
  (*b*)   (*amends* ITEPA 2003 Sch 2 para 82(1)).
  (*c*)   (*amends* ITEPA 2003 Sch 2 para 85(1)).
  (*d*)   (*amends* ITEPA 2003 Sch 2 para 93(1)(*a*)).
  (*e*)   (*amends* ITEPA 2003 Sch 2 para 100).

122   In Schedule 3—
  (*a*)   (*amends* ITEPA 2003 Sch 3 para 40(1), (3)).
  (*b*)   (*amends* ITEPA 2003 Sch 3 para 41(1)).
  (*c*)   (*amends* ITEPA 2003 Sch 3 para 43).
  (*d*)   (*amends* ITEPA 2003 Sch 3 para 44(1)).
  (*e*)   (*amends* ITEPA 2003 Sch 3 para 45(1)).
  (*f*)   (*amends* ITEPA 2003 Sch 3 para 49).

123   In Schedule 4—
  (*a*)   (*amends* ITEPA 2003 Sch 4 para 28(1), (3)).
  (*b*)   (*amends* ITEPA 2003 Sch 4 para 29(1)).
  (*c*)   (*amends* ITEPA 2003 Sch 4 para 31).
  (*d*)   (*amends* ITEPA 2003 Sch 4 para 32(1)).
  (*e*)   (*amends* ITEPA 2003 Sch 4 para 33(1)(*a*)).
  (*f*)   (*amends* ITEPA 2003 Sch 4 para 37).

124   In Schedule 5—
  (*a*)   (*amends* ITEPA 2003 Sch 5 para 46(2), (3), (6)).
  (*b*)   (*amends* ITEPA 2003 Sch 5 para 47(1)–(3)).
  (*c*)   (*amends* ITEPA 2003 Sch 5 para 48(5)).
  (*d*)   (*amends* ITEPA 2003 Sch 5 para 49(1), (2)).
  (*e*)   (*amends* ITEPA 2003 Sch 5 para 51(1)(*a*)).
  (*f*)   (*amends* ITEPA 2003 Sch 5 para 59).

Dealing in Cultural Objects (Offences) Act 2003 (c 27)

128   (*amends* Dealing in Cultural Objects (Offences) Act 2003 s 4).

Criminal Justice Act 2003 (c 44)

129   (*amends* Criminal Justice Act 2003 s 27).

130   (*inserts* Criminal Justice Act 2003 s 29(5)(*ca*)).

Income Tax (Trading and Other Income) Act 2005 (c 5)

131 The Income Tax (Trading and Other Income) Act 2005 shall be amended as follows.

132—(1) For the expression "the Inland Revenue", wherever it appears, substitute "an officer of Revenue and Customs" (except as provided by paragraph 133(2)(*b*) and (5)).

(2) For the expression "the Board of Inland Revenue", wherever it appears, substitute "the Commissioners for Her Majesty's Revenue and Customs".

(3) In the following provisions, for "Board" substitute "Commissioners" and for "Board's" substitute "Commissioners'"—

 (*a*) the title of section 343,[2]

 (*b*) section 695(4),

 (*c*) section 698(3) and (4),

 (*d*) section 699(2),

 (*e*) *section 700(1)(b)*, (2) and (5),[1]

 (*f*) section 757(3),

 (*g*) section 762(2),

 (*h*) the title of section 873, and

Amendments—[1] Sub-para (3)(*e*) repealed by the Finance Act 2009, Section 96 and Schedule 48 (Appointed Day, Savings and Consequential Amendments) Order, SI 2009/3054 art 3, Schedule para 16(*e*) with effect from 1 April 2010.

[2] Sub-para (3)(*a*) repealed by FA 2012 s 227, Sch 39 para 43(2)(*b*) with effect in relation to mineral royalties which a person is entitled to receive on or after 6 April 2013.

 (*i*) section 883(3).

133—*(1) In section 75(5)*—

 (*a*) for "have" substitute "has", and

 (*b*) in each place for "they" substitute "the officer".[2]

(2) In section 218—

 (*a*) in subsections (1) and (2) for "do" substitute "does", and

 (*b*) in subsection (3)(*a*) for "the Inland Revenue are not" substitute "the officer is not".

(3) In section 305(1) for "have" substitute "has".[2]

(4) In section 647(1)

 (*a*) for "them" substitute "the officer",

 (*b*) for "they" in each place substitute "the officer", and

 (*c*) for "consider" substitute "considers".

(5) . . .[1]

(6) In section 758(5) for "has" substitute "have" '.

Amendments—[1] Sub-para (5) repealed by FA 2007 s 114, Sch 27 Pt 2(13) with effect from 6 April 2008 (by virtue of FA 2007, ss 46(9), 114, Sch 27, Pt 2(13), SI 2008/561 art 2).

[2] Sub-paras (1), (3) repealed by Finance Act 2009 Schedule 47 (Consequential Amendments) Order, SI 2009/2035, Art 2 Schedule, para 60(*k*) with effect from 13 August 2009.

134—(1) In section 878(1), omit the definitions of "the Board of Inland Revenue" and "the Inland Revenue".

(2) In Part 2 of Schedule 4, omit the entries for "the Board of Inland Revenue" and "the Inland Revenue".

RAILWAYS ACT 2005

(2005 Chapter 14)

An Act to amend the law relating to the provision and regulation of railway services; and for connected purposes.

[7 April 2005]

PART 6

GENERAL AND SUPPLEMENTAL

General

53 Taxation

Schedule 10 (which makes taxation provision in relation to transfer schemes under sections 1(2) and 12) has effect.

Supplemental

60 Short title, commencement and extent

(1) This Act may be cited as the Railways Act 2005.

(2) This Act (apart from this section and section 56(1)) shall come into force on such day as the Secretary of State by order appoints; and different days may be appointed for different purposes.

(3) The Secretary of State may by order make such transitional provisions and savings in connection with the bringing into force of—

(*a*) section 21,

(*b*) Part 4 of this Act, or

(*c*) the repeal of sections 37 to 49 of the 1993 Act or of Schedule 5 to that Act (closures), as he thinks fit.

(4) An order containing provision made by virtue of subsection (3) is subject to the negative resolution procedure.

(5) The following provisions of this Act extend to England and Wales only—

(*a*) section 13;

(*b*) section 39; and

(*c*) section 52.

(6) This Act does not extend to Northern Ireland.

SCHEDULES

SCHEDULE 10

TAXATION PROVISIONS RELATING TO TRANSFER SCHEMES

Section 53

PART 1

TRANSFERS TO A NATIONAL AUTHORITY UNDER SECTION 1(2) SCHEMES

Meaning of "relevant transfer" in Part 1 of Schedule

1 In this Part of this Schedule, "relevant transfer" means a transfer in accordance with a scheme made under section 1(2) to a national authority.

Capital allowances: determination of disposal value of plant or machinery

2—(1) This paragraph applies to a relevant transfer of plant or machinery which is a disposal event for the purposes of Part 2 of the 2001 Act (capital allowances for plant and machinery).

(2) For the purposes of the application of section 61 of that Act in relation to the transferor, the disposal value of the plant or machinery is to be treated—

(*a*) if a capital sum is received by the transferor by way of consideration or compensation in respect of the transfer, as an amount equal to that sum; or

(*b*) if no such sum is received, as nil.

(3) For the purposes of this paragraph a sum received by a person connected with the transferor is to be treated as received by the transferor.

(4) Section 88 of the 2001 Act (sales at an undervalue) is to be disregarded.

(5) This paragraph is subject to sections 63(5) and 68 of the 2001 Act.

Capital allowances: determination of disposal value of fixtures

3—(1) This paragraph applies to a relevant transfer if—

(*a*) it is a disposal event for the purposes of Part 2 of the 2001 Act; and (*b*) by virtue of the transfer a person is treated by section 188 of that Act as ceasing to own a fixture.

(2) For the purposes of the application of section 196 of that Act in relation to the transferor, the disposal value of the fixture is to be treated—

(*a*) if a capital sum is received by the transferor by way of consideration or compensation in respect of the transfer, as an amount equal to that portion of that sum which, if the person to whom the disposal is made were entitled to an allowance, would fall to be treated for the purposes of Part 2 of that Act as expenditure incurred by that person on the provision of the fixture; or

(*b*) if no such sum is received, as nil.

(3) For the purposes of this paragraph a sum received by a person connected with the transferor is to be treated as received by the transferor.

(4) This paragraph is subject to section 63(5) of the 2001 Act.

Capital allowances: determination of capital value of industrial buildings etc

4—(1) This paragraph applies for the purposes of Part 3 of the 2001 Act, and the other provisions of that Act which are relevant to that Part, in relation to a relevant transfer of the relevant interest in an industrial building or structure.

(2) The transfer is to be treated as a sale of that relevant interest.

(3) The net proceeds of that sale are to be treated—

(*a*) if a capital sum is received by the transferor by way of consideration or compensation in respect of the transfer, as an amount equal to that sum; or

(*b*) if no such sum is received, as nil.

(4) Sections 567 to 570 of the 2001 Act (sales treated as being for alternative amount) are not to have effect in relation to that sale.

(5) For the purposes of this paragraph a sum received by a person connected with the transferor is to be treated as received by the transferor.

Chargeable gains: assets to be treated as disposed without a gain or a loss

5 For the purposes of the 1992 Act, a relevant transfer of an asset is to be treated as a disposal of that asset to the transferee for a consideration of such amount as would secure that, on the disposal, neither a gain nor a loss accrues to the transferor.

Continuity in relation to transfer of intangible assets

6—(1) For the purposes of Schedule 29 to the Finance Act 2002 (c 23), a relevant transfer of a chargeable intangible asset of the transferor is to be treated as a tax-neutral transfer.

(2) Expressions used in this paragraph and in that Schedule have the same meanings in this paragraph as in that Schedule.

Neutral effect of transfer for loan relationships and derivative contracts

7 No credit or debit shall be required or allowed, in respect of a relevant transfer, to be brought into account in the transferor's case—

(*a*) for the purposes of [Part 5 of the Corporation Tax Act 2009][1] (loan relationships); or

(*b*) for the purposes of [Part 7 of the Corporation Tax Act 2009 (derivative contracts)][1].

Amendments—[1] In sub-para (*a*) words substituted for words "Chapter 2 of Part 4 of the Finance Act 1996 (c 8)", and in sub-para (2)(*b*) words substituted for words "Schedule 26 to the Finance Act 2002 (derivative contracts)", by CTA 2009 s 1322, Sch 1 paras 666, 667(1), (2), Sch 3 Part 1. CTA 2009 applies for accounting periods ending on or after 1 April 2009 (for corporation tax purposes) and for tax years 2009–10 onwards (for income and capital gains tax purposes).

Leased assets

8—(1) This paragraph applies for the purposes of section 781 of the Taxes Act (assets leased to traders and others) where—

(*a*) the interest of the lessor or the lessee under a lease, or any other interest in an asset, is transferred under a relevant transfer; or

(*b*) a lease, or any other interest in a lease, is granted to a national authority in accordance with provision contained by virtue of paragraph 3 or 4 of Schedule 2 in a scheme made under section 1(2).

(2) Section 783(4) of that Act is to be disregarded and the transfer or grant is to be treated as made without any capital sum having been obtained in respect of the interest or lease by the transferor or grantor.

(3) Expressions used in this paragraph and in sections 781 to 785 of that Act have the same meanings in this paragraph as in those sections.

PART 2
OTHER TRANSFERS UNDER SECTION 1(2) SCHEMES

Meaning of "relevant transfer" in Part 2 of Schedule

9   In this Part of this Schedule, "relevant transfer" means a transfer in accordance with a scheme made under section 1(2) to a person other than a national authority.

Computation of profits and losses in respect of transfer of trade

10—(1) This paragraph applies where a person ("the predecessor") is carrying on a trade or a part of a trade and, in consequence of a scheme made under section 1(2)—

  (*a*) the predecessor ceases to carry on that trade or that part of that trade; and

  (*b*) a person who is not a national authority ("the successor") begins to carry on that trade or that part of it.

(2) For the purpose of computing, in relation to the time when the scheme comes into force and subsequent times, the relevant trading profits or losses of the predecessor and the successor—

  (*a*) the trade or part is to be treated as having been a separate trade at the time of its commencement and as having been carried on by the successor at all times since its commencement as a separate trade; and

  (*b*) the trade carried on by the successor after the time when the scheme comes into force is to be treated as the same trade as that which it is treated, by virtue of paragraph (*a*), as having carried on as a separate trade before that time.

(3) Where a trade or a part of a trade falls to be treated under this paragraph as a separate trade, such apportionments of receipts, expenses, assets and liabilities shall be made for the purpose of computing relevant trading profits and losses as may be just and reasonable.

(4) This paragraph is subject to paragraphs 12 and 18.

(5) In this paragraph, "relevant trading profits and losses" means profits or losses [under Part 3 of the Corporation Tax Act 2009 in respect of the trade or part of a trade in question for periods in which the trade was carried on wholly or partly in the United Kingdom.][1].

Amendments—[1]   In sub-para (5) words substituted for words "under Case I of Schedule D in respect of the trade or part of a trade in question." by CTA 2009 s 1322, Sch 1 paras 648, 667(1), (3), Sch 3 Part 1. CTA 2009 applies for accounting periods ending on or after 1 April 2009 (for corporation tax purposes) and for tax years 2009–10 onwards (for income and capital gains tax purposes).

Trading losses: change in ownership

11—(1) This paragraph applies to a relevant transfer of all the issued share capital of a company (the "transferred company").

(2) For the purposes of [the provisions of the Corporation Tax Act 2010 specified in sub-paragraph (3)][1], the transfer is not to be taken to result in a change in the ownership of—

  (*a*) the transferred company; or

  (*b*) a company which is a wholly-owned subsidiary of the transferred company when the transfer takes effect.

[(3) Those provisions are—

  (*a*) Chapter 2 of Part 14 (but not section 674(1)),

  (*b*) section 683,

  (*c*) section 684,

  (*d*) section 700,

  (*e*) section 701,

  (*f*) section 704, and

  (*g*) section 705.][1]

Amendments—[1]   In sub-para (2) words substituted for words "sections 768 and 768D of the Taxes Act", sub-para (3) inserted by CTA 2010 s 1177, Sch 1 para 478(1) ,(2). CTA 2010 has effect for corporation tax purposes for accounting periods ending on or after 1 April 2010, and for income and capital gains tax purposes for the tax year 2010–11 and subsequent tax years.

Capital allowances: transfer of whole trade

12—(1) This paragraph applies where a person ("the predecessor") is carrying on a trade and, in consequence of a scheme made under section 1(2)—

  (*a*) the predecessor ceases to carry on that trade; and

  (*b*) a person who is not a national authority ("the successor") begins to carry on that trade.

(2) For the purposes of the allowances and charges provided for by the 2001 Act, the trade is not to be treated as permanently discontinued, nor a new trade as set up; but sub-paragraphs (3) and (4) of this paragraph are to apply.

(3) There are to be made to or on the successor, in accordance with the 2001 Act, all such allowances and charges as would, if the predecessor had continued to carry on the trade, have fallen to be made to or on the predecessor.

(4) The amounts of those allowances and charges are to be computed as if—

    (*a*) the successor had been carrying on the trade since the predecessor began to do so; and

    (*b*) everything done to or by the predecessor had been done to or by the successor;

but so that transfers in accordance with the scheme, so far as they relate to assets in use for the purposes of the trade, shall not be treated as giving rise to an allowance or charge.

Capital allowances: transfer of part of a trade

13—(1) Where a person ("the predecessor") is carrying on a trade and, in consequence of a scheme made under section 1(2)—

    (*a*) the predecessor ceases to carry on a trade, and

    (*b*) a person who is not a national authority ("the successor") begins to carry on activities of that trade as part of a trade carried on by the successor,

then that part of the trade carried on by the successor shall be treated for the purposes of paragraph 12 as a separate trade.

(2) Where a person ("the predecessor") is carrying on a trade and, in consequence of a scheme made under section 1(2)—

    (*a*) the predecessor ceases to carry on a part of a trade, and

    (*b*) a person who is not a national authority begins to carry on activities of that part of that trade,

then the predecessor shall be treated for the purposes of paragraph 12 and sub-paragraph (1) of this paragraph as having carried on that part of its trade as a separate trade.

(3) Where activities fall to be treated for the purposes of this paragraph as a separate trade, such apportionments of receipts, expenses, assets and liabilities shall be made for the purposes of the 2001 Act as may be just and reasonable.

Capital allowances: transfer of plant or machinery

14—(1) This paragraph applies where—

    (*a*) there is a relevant transfer of plant or machinery;

    (*b*) paragraph 12 does not apply in relation to that transfer;

    (*c*) the plant or machinery would be treated for the purposes of the 2001 Act as disposed of by the transferor to the transferee on the transfer taking effect; and

    (*d*) the scheme in accordance with which the transfer is made contains provision for the disposal value of the plant or machinery to be treated for the purposes of that Act as an amount specified in or determined in accordance with the scheme.

(2) For the purposes of the 2001 Act—

    (*a*) the provision mentioned in sub-paragraph (1)(*d*) is to have effect (instead of section 61(2) to (4), 72(3) to (5), 88, 171, 196 or 423 of that Act) for determining an amount as the disposal value of the plant or machinery or the price at which a fixture is to be treated as sold;

    (*b*) the transferee is to be treated as having incurred capital expenditure of that amount on the provision of the plant or machinery for the purposes for which it is used by the transferee on and after the taking effect of the transfer;

    (*c*) the property is to be treated as belonging to the transferee in consequence of the transferee having incurred that expenditure; and

    (*d*) in the case of a fixture, the expenditure which falls to be treated as incurred by the transferee is to be treated for the purposes of sections 181(1) and 182(1) of that Act to be incurred by the giving of a consideration consisting in a capital sum of that amount.

(3) The provision mentioned in sub-paragraph (1)(*d*) for the determination of an amount may include provision for a determination—

    (*a*) to be made by the Secretary of State in a manner described in the scheme;

    (*b*) to be made by reference to factors so described or to the opinion of a person so described; and

    (*c*) to be capable of being modified (on one or more occasions) in a manner and in circumstances so described.

(4) The consent of the Treasury is required for the making or modification of a determination under the provision mentioned in sub-paragraph (1)(*d*).

(5) The consent of the transferee is required for the modification of a determination under the provision mentioned in sub-paragraph (1)(*d*).

(6) If there is a determination or a modification of a determination under the provision mentioned in sub-paragraph (1)(*d*), all necessary adjustments—

    (*a*) must be made by making assessments or by repayment or discharge of tax; and

    (*b*) must be made despite any limitation on the time within which assessments may be made.

(7) Expressions used in this paragraph and in Part 2 of the 2001 Act have the same meanings in this paragraph as in that Part.

Capital allowances: determination of capital value of industrial buildings etc

15—(1) This paragraph applies for the purposes of Part 3 of the 2001 Act, and the other provisions of that Act which are relevant to that Part, to a relevant transfer of the relevant interest in an industrial building or structure.

(2) Section 573 of that Act is not to have effect in relation to that transfer.

Chargeable gains: assets to be treated as disposed of without a gain or a loss

16 For the purposes of the 1992 Act, a relevant transfer of an asset is to be treated as a disposal of that asset to the transferee for a consideration of such amount as would secure that, on the disposal, neither a gain nor a loss accrues to the transferor.

Continuity in relation to transfer of intangible assets

17—(1) For the purposes of [Part 8 of the Corporation Tax Act 2009[1]]—

 (*a*) a relevant transfer of a chargeable intangible asset of the transferor is to be treated as a tax-neutral transfer; and

 (*b*) an intangible fixed asset which is [a pre-FA 2002 asset][1] of the transferor at the time of the transfer is to be treated, on and after the transfer, as a [pre-FA 2002 asset][1] in the hands of the transferee.

(2) Expressions used in this paragraph and in [that Part][1] have the same meanings in this paragraph as in [that Part][1].

Amendments—[1] In sub-para (1) words substituted for words "Schedule 29 to the Finance Act 2002 (c 23)" and words substituted for words "existing asset" in both places; and in sub-para (2) words substituted for words "that Schedule" in both places; by CTA 2009 ss 1322, Sch 1 para 667(4), Sch 3 Part 1. CTA 2009 applies for accounting periods ending on or after 1 April 2009 (for corporation tax purposes) and for tax years 2009–10 onwards (for income and capital gains tax purposes).

Continuity in relation to loan relationships

18—(1) For the purposes of the application of [Part 5 of the Corporation Tax Act 2009][1] (loan relationships) in relation to a relevant transfer, the transferee and the transferor are to be treated as if, at the time of the transfer, they were members of the same group.

(2) In sub-paragraph (1), the reference to being members of the same group must be construed in accordance with [section 335(6) of][1] that Act.

Amendments—[1] In sub-para (1) words substituted for words "Chapter 2 of Part 4 of the Finance Act 1996 (c 8)"; and in sub-para (2) words substituted for words "paragraph 12(8) of Schedule 9 to"; by CTA 2009 s 1322, Sch 1 paras 648, 667(1), (5). CTA 2009 applies for accounting periods ending on or after 1 April 2009 (for corporation tax purposes) and for tax years 2009–10 onwards (for income and capital gains tax purposes).

Continuity in relation to derivative contracts

19—(1) For the purposes of the application of [Part 7 of the Corporation Tax Act 2009 (derivative contracts)][1] in relation to a relevant transfer, the transferee and the transferor are to be treated as if, at the time of the transfer, they were members of the same group.

(2) In sub-paragraph (1), the reference to being members of the same group must be construed in accordance with [section 624(3) of that Act][1].

Amendments—[1] In sub-para (1) words substituted for words "Schedule 26 to the Finance Act 2002 (derivative contracts)"; and in sub-para (2) words substituted for words "paragraph 28(6) of that Schedule"; by CTA 2009 s 1322, Sch 1 paras 648, 667(1), (6). CTA 2009 applies for accounting periods ending on or after 1 April 2009 (for corporation tax purposes) and for tax years 2009–10 onwards (for income and capital gains tax purposes).

Leased assets

20—(1) This paragraph applies for the purposes of section 781 of the Taxes Act (assets leased to traders and others) where—

 (*a*) the interest of the lessor or the lessee under a lease, or any other interest in an asset, is transferred under a relevant transfer; or

 (*b*) a lease, or any other interest in a lease, is granted to a person who is not a national authority in accordance with provision contained by virtue of paragraph 3 or 4 of Schedule 2 in a scheme made under section 1(2).

(2) Section 783(4) of that Act is to be disregarded and the transfer or grant is to be treated as made without any capital sum having been obtained in respect of the interest or lease by the transferor or grantor.

(3) In the case of the transfer of an interest under a lease, payments made by the transferor under the lease before the transfer takes effect are to be treated as if they had been made under that lease by the transferee.

(4) Expressions used in this paragraph and in sections 781 to 785 of that Act have the same meanings in this paragraph as in those sections.

PART 3
TRANSFERS UNDER SECTION 12 SCHEMES

Meaning of "relevant transfer" in Part 3 of Schedule

21 In this Part of this Schedule, "relevant transfer" means a transfer in accordance with a scheme made under section 12.

Capital allowances: determination of disposal value of plant or machinery

22—(1) This paragraph applies to a relevant transfer of plant or machinery which is a disposal event for the purposes of Part 2 of the 2001 Act (capital allowances for plant and machinery).

(2) For the purposes of the application of section 61 of that Act in relation to the transferor, the disposal value of the plant or machinery is to be treated—

(*a*) if a capital sum is received by the transferor by way of consideration or compensation in respect of the transfer, as an amount equal to that sum; or

(*b*) if no such sum is received, as nil.

(3) For the purposes of this paragraph a sum received by a person connected with the transferor is to be treated as received by the transferor.

(4) Section 88 of the 2001 Act (sales at an undervalue) is to be disregarded.

(5) This paragraph is subject to sections 63(5) and 68 of the 2001 Act.

Capital allowances: determination of disposal value of fixtures

23—(1) This paragraph applies to a relevant transfer if—

(*a*) it is a disposal event for the purposes of Part 2 of the 2001 Act; and

(*b*) by virtue of the transfer a person is treated by section 188 of that Act as ceasing to own a fixture.

(2) For the purposes of the application of section 196 of that Act in relation to the transferor, the disposal value of the fixture is to be treated—

(*a*) if a capital sum is received by the transferor by way of consideration or compensation in respect of the transfer, as an amount equal to that portion of that sum which falls (or, if the person to whom the disposal is made were entitled to an allowance, would fall) to be treated for the purposes of Part 2 of that Act as expenditure incurred by that person on the provision of the fixture; or

(*b*) if no such sum is received, as nil.

(3) For the purposes of this paragraph a sum received by a person connected with the transferor is to be treated as received by the transferor.

(4) This paragraph is subject to section 63(5) of the 2001 Act.

Capital allowances: determination of capital value of industrial buildings etc

24—(1) This paragraph applies for the purposes of Part 3 of the 2001 Act, and the other provisions of that Act which are relevant to that Part, in relation to a relevant transfer of the relevant interest in an industrial building or structure.

(2) The transfer is to be treated as a sale of that relevant interest.

(3) The net proceeds of that sale, in relation to the transferor, are to be treated—

(*a*) if a capital sum is received by the transferor by way of consideration or compensation in respect of the transfer, as an amount equal to that sum; or

(*b*) if no such sum is received, as nil.

(4) Sections 567 to 570 of the 2001 Act (sales treated as being for alternative amount) are not to have effect in relation to that sale.

(5) For the purposes of this paragraph a sum received by a person connected with the transferor is to be treated as received by the transferor.

Chargeable gains: disposals not be treated as made at market value

25—(1) Section 17 of the 1992 Act (disposals and acquisitions treated as made at market value) is not to have effect in relation to—

(*a*) a disposal constituted by a relevant transfer or a disposal in accordance with provision contained by virtue of paragraph 3 or 4 of Schedule 2 to this Act in a scheme made under section 12 of this Act; or

(*b*) the acquisition made by the person to whom the disposal is made.

(2) But sub-paragraph (1) does not apply—

(a) if the person making the disposal is connected with the person making the acquisition; or

(b) in the case of a disposal in accordance with provision contained in a scheme by virtue of paragraph 3 or 4 of Schedule 2, if the disposal is made by or to a person other than the transferor or transferee.

(3) If sub-paragraph (1) applies to the disposal of an asset, the disposal is to be taken (in relation to the person making the acquisition as well as the person making the disposal) to be—

(a) in a case where consideration in money or money's worth is given by the person making the acquisition or on his behalf in respect of the vesting of the asset in him, for a consideration equal to the amount or value of that consideration; or

(b) in a case where no such consideration is given, for a consideration of nil.

Chargeable gains: degrouping charges

26—(1) This paragraph applies if a company ("the degrouped company")—

(a) acquired an asset from another company at a time when both were members of the same group of companies ("the old group"); and

(b) ceases by virtue of a relevant transfer to be a member of the old group.

(2) Section 179 of the 1992 Act (company ceasing to be member of group) is not to treat the degrouped company as having by virtue of the transfer sold and immediately reacquired the asset.

(3) Where sub-paragraph (2) has applied to an asset, section 179 of the 1992 Act is to have effect on and after the first subsequent occasion on which the degrouped company ceases to be a member of a group of companies ("the new group") otherwise than by virtue of a relevant transfer as if—

(a) the degrouped company, and

(b) the company from which it acquired the asset,

had been members of the new group at the time of acquisition.

(4) If, disregarding any preparatory transactions, a company would be regarded for the purposes of section 179 of the 1992 Act (and, accordingly, of this paragraph) as ceasing to be a member of a group of companies by virtue of a relevant transfer, it is to be regarded for those purposes as so doing by virtue of the relevant transfer and not by virtue of any preparatory transactions.

(5) In this paragraph, "preparatory transactions" means anything done under or by virtue of the 1993 Act or this Act for the purpose of initiating, advancing or facilitating the relevant transfer in question.

(6) Expressions used in this paragraph and in section 179 of the 1992 Act have the same meanings in this paragraph as in that section.

Chargeable gains: disposal of debts

27—(1) This paragraph applies to a relevant transfer of a debt owed to the transferor if the transferor would (apart from this paragraph) be the original creditor in relation to that debt for the purposes of section 251 of the 1992 Act (disposal of debts).

(2) The 1992 Act is to have effect as if the transferee (and not the transferor) were the original creditor for those purposes.

Loan relationships

28—(1) [Section 444 of the Corporation Tax Act 2009][1] is not to have effect where, as a result of a relevant transfer, the transferee replaces the transferor as a party to a loan relationship.

(2) Expressions used in this paragraph and in [Part 5 of the Corporation Tax Act 2009][1] have the same meanings in this paragraph as in [that Part][1].

Amendments—[1]   In sub-para (1) words substituted for words "Paragraph 11 of Schedule 9 to the Finance Act 1996 (c 8)";and in sub-para (2) words substituted for words "Chapter 2 of Part 4 of the Finance Act 1996" and "that Chapter"; by CTA 2009 s 1322, Sch 1 paras 648, 667(1), (7). CTA 2009 applies for accounting periods ending on or after 1 April 2009 (for corporation tax purposes) and for tax years 2009–10 onwards (for income and capital gains tax purposes).

PART 4
OTHER PROVISIONS CONCERNING TRANSFERS
Stamp duty

29—(1) Stamp duty is not to be chargeable—

(a) on a scheme made under section 1(2); or

(b) on an instrument certified by the Secretary of State to the Commissioners of Inland Revenue as made for the purposes of such a scheme, or as made for purposes connected with such a scheme.

(2) But where, by virtue of sub-paragraph (1), stamp duty is not chargeable on a scheme or instrument, the scheme or instrument is to be treated as duly stamped only if—

(a) in accordance with section 12 of the Stamp Act 1891 (c 39) it has been stamped with a stamp denoting either that it is not chargeable to duty or that it has been duly stamped; or (*b*) it is stamped with the duty to which it would be chargeable apart from sub-paragraph (1).

(3) In this paragraph, "instrument" has the same meaning as in the Stamp Act 1891.

Stamp duty land tax

30—(1) No transfer in accordance with a scheme made under section 1(2) is to give rise to any liability to stamp duty land tax.

(2) Relief under this paragraph must be claimed in a land transaction return or in an amendment of a land transaction return.

(3) In sub-paragraph (2) "land transaction return" has the meaning given by section 76(1) of the Finance Act 2003 (c 14).

Chargeable gains: value shifting

31   No scheme made under section 1(2) or 12 is to be regarded as a scheme or arrangement for the purposes of section 30 of the 1992 Act.

Group relief

32   Neither the power of the Secretary of State[, the Welsh Ministers][2] to make a scheme under section 1(2) nor the power of the Secretary of State or the Scottish Ministers to make a scheme under section 12 is to be regarded as constituting—

   (*a*)   arrangements falling within [section 154(3) or 155(3) of the Corporation Tax Act 2010][1] (arrangements for transfer of company to another group or consortium); or

   (*b*)   option arrangements for the purposes of [section 173 of][1] that Act.

Amendments—[1]   Words "section 410(1) or (2) of the Taxes Act" and "paragraph 5B of Schedule 18 to" substituted by CTA 2010 s 1177, Sch 1 para 478(1), (3). CTA 2010 has effect for corporation tax purposes for accounting periods ending on or after 1 April 2010, and for income and capital gains tax purposes for the tax year 2010–11 and subsequent tax years.

[2]   Words inserted by the Welsh Ministers (Transfer of Functions) (Railways) Order 2018/631 art 2, Schedule para 34, 68(1), (2) with effect in relation to England and Wales and Scotland only from 13 June 2018.

PART 5
INTERPRETATION OF SCHEDULE

34—(1) In this Schedule—

   "the 1992 Act" means the Taxation of Chargeable Gains Act 1992 (c 12);

   "the 2001 Act" means the Capital Allowances Act 2001 (c 2);

   "national authority" means—

   (*a*)   the Secretary of State;

   (*b*)   the Scottish Ministers;

   (*c*)   [the Welsh Ministers][2]; or

   (*d*)   [the Office of Rail and Road][1];

   "the Taxes Act" means the Income and Corporation Taxes Act 1988 (c 1);

   "transferee", in relation to a transfer in accordance with a scheme made under section 1(2) or 12, means the person to whom the transfer is made;

   "transferor", in relation to a transfer in accordance with a scheme made under section 1(2) or 12, means the person from whom the transfer is made.

(2) So far as it relates to corporation tax this Schedule is to be construed as one with the Corporation Tax Acts.

(3) So far as it relates to capital allowances this Schedule is to be construed as one with the 2001 Act.

Amendments—[1]   In sub-para (1), in definition of "national authority", para (*c*) substituted by the Office of Rail Regulation (Change of Name) Regulations, SI 2015/1682 reg 2(2), Schedule para 3(*v*) with effect from 16 October 2015.

[2]   In sub-para (1)(c) words substituted for words "the National Assembly for Wales" by the Welsh Ministers (Transfer of Functions) (Railways) Order 2018/631 art 2, Schedule para 34, 68(1), (3) with effect in relation to England and Wales and Scotland only from 13 June 2018.

SERIOUS ORGANISED CRIME AND POLICE ACT 2005

(2005 Chapter 15)

ARRANGEMENT OF SECTIONS

Part 2: Investigations, Prosecutions, Proceedings and Proceeds of Crime
Chapter 1 Investigatory Powers of DPP, etc
Introductory
60 Investigatory powers of DPP etc
61 Offences to which this Chapter applies
Disclosure notices
62 Disclosure notices
Chapter 2 Offenders Assisting Investigations and Prosecutions
71 Assistance by offender: immunity from prosecution
Chapter 6 Proceeds of Crime
97 Confiscation orders by magistrates' courts
98 Civil recovery: freezing orders
99 Civil recovery: interim receivers'expenses etc
100 Detention of seized cash: meaning of "48 hours"
101 Appeal in proceedings for forfeiture of cash
102 Money laundering: defence where overseas conduct is legal under local law
103 Money laundering: threshold amounts
104 Money laundering: disclosures to identify persons and property
105 Money laundering: form and manner of disclosures
106 Money laundering: miscellaneous amendments
107 Money laundering offences
108 International co-operation
109 Minor and consequential amendments relating to Chapter 6
Part 6: Final Provisions
177 Interpretation
178 Commencement
179 Short title and extent

PART 2

INVESTIGATIONS, PROSECUTIONS, PROCEEDINGS AND PROCEEDS OF CRIME

CHAPTER 1

INVESTIGATORY POWERS OF DPP, ETC

Introductory

60 Investigatory powers of DPP etc

(1) This Chapter confers powers on—

 (*a*) the Director of Public Prosecutions,

 (*b*) . . .[3]

 (*c*) the Lord Advocate, [and

 (*d*) the Director of Public Prosecutions for Northern Ireland,][2]

in relation to the giving of disclosure notices in connection with the investigation of offences to which this Chapter applies [or in connection with a terrorist investigation][1].

(2) The Director of Public Prosecutions may, to such extent as he may determine, delegate the exercise of his powers under this Chapter to a Crown prosecutor.

(3) . . .[3]

(4) The Lord Advocate may, to such extent as he may determine, delegate the exercise of his powers under this Chapter to a procurator fiscal.

[(4A) The Director of Public Prosecutions for Northern Ireland may, to such extent as he may determine, delegate the exercise of his powers under this Chapter to a Public Prosecutor.][2]

(5) In this Chapter "the Investigating Authority" means—

 (*a*) the Director of Public Prosecutions,

 (*b*) . . .[3]

 (*c*) the Lord Advocate[, or

 (*d*) the Director of Public Prosecutions for Northern Ireland][2].

(6) But, in circumstances where the powers of any of those persons are exercisable by any other person by virtue of subsection (2), . . .[3] [(4) or (4A)][2], references to "the Investigating Authority" accordingly include any such other person.

[(7) In this Chapter "terrorist investigation" means an investigation of—

 (*a*) the commission, preparation or instigation of acts of terrorism,

 (*b*) any act or omission which appears to have been for the purposes of terrorism and which consists in or involves the commission, preparation or instigation of an offence, or

(c)   the commission, preparation or instigation of an offence under the Terrorism Act 2000 (c 11) or under Part 1 of the Terrorism Act 2006 other than an offence under section 1 or 2 of that Act.][1]

Amendments—[1]   Words in sub-s (1) inserted, and sub-s (7) inserted, by the Terrorism Act 2006 s 33(1), (2) with effect from 13 April 2006.

[2]   Sub-s (1)(d) and preceding word "and", sub-s (4A), sub-s (5)(d) and preceding word "or", inserted, and in sub-s (6) words substituted, by the Northern Ireland (Miscellaneous Provisions) Act 2006 s 26(2), Sch 3 paras 1, 2 with effect from 1 December 2006 (by virtue of SI 2006/2966 art 3).

[3]   Sub-ss (1)(b), (3), (5)(b) repealed, and in sub-s (6) word repealed, by the Public Bodies (Merger of the Director of Public Prosecutions and the Director of Revenue and Customs Prosecutions) Order, SI 2014/834 art 3(3) Sch 2 paras 40, 41 with effect from 27 March 2014.

61 Offences to which this Chapter applies

(1) This Chapter applies to the following offences—

(a)   any offence listed in Schedule 2 to the Proceeds of Crime Act 2002 (c 29) (lifestyle offences: England and Wales);

(b)   any offence listed in Schedule 4 to that Act (lifestyle offences: Scotland);[1]

[(ba)   any offence listed in Schedule 5 to that Act (lifestyle offences: Northern Ireland);][2]

(c)   any offence under sections 15 to 18 of the Terrorism Act 2000 (c 11) (offences relating to fund-raising, money laundering etc);

(d)   any offence under section 170 of the Customs and Excise Management Act 1979 (c 2) (fraudulent evasion of duty) or section 72 of the Value Added Tax Act 1994 (c 23) (offences relating to VAT) which is a qualifying offence;

(e)   any offence under section 17 of the Theft Act 1968 (c 60) [or section 17 of the Theft Act (Northern Ireland) 1969][2] (false accounting), or any offence at common law of cheating in relation to the public revenue, which is a qualifying offence;

(f)   any offence under section 1 of the Criminal Attempts Act 1981 (c 47) [or Article 3 of the Criminal Attempts and Conspiracy (Northern Ireland) Order 1983][2], or in Scotland at common law, of attempting to commit any offence in paragraph (c) or any offence in paragraph (d) or (e) which is a qualifying offence;

(g)   any offence under section 1 of the Criminal Law Act 1977 (c 45) [or Article 9 of the Criminal Attempts and Conspiracy (Northern Ireland) Order 1983][2], or in Scotland at common law, of conspiracy to commit any offence in paragraph (c) or any offence in paragraph (d) or (e) which is a qualifying offence;

[(h)   any offence under the Bribery Act 2010.][3]

[(i)   any offence under section 45 or 46 of the Criminal Finances Act 2017 (failure to prevent the facilitation of UK tax evasion offences or foreign tax evasion offences).][4]

[(j)   any offence under regulations under section 1 of the Sanctions and Anti-Money Laundering Act 2018 (sanctions regulations) which is specified by those regulations by virtue of section 17(8) of that Act.][5]

(2) For the purposes of subsection (1) an offence in paragraph (d) or (e) of that subsection is a qualifying offence if the Investigating Authority certifies that in his opinion—

(a)   in the case of an offence in paragraph (d) or an offence of cheating the public revenue, the offence involved or would have involved a loss, or potential loss, to the public revenue of an amount not less than £5,000;

(b)   in the case of an offence under section 17 of the Theft Act 1968 (c 60) [or section 17 of the Theft Act (Northern Ireland) 1969][2], the offence involved or would have involved a loss or gain, or potential loss or gain, of an amount not less than £5,000.

(3) A document purporting to be a certificate under subsection (2) is to be received in evidence and treated as such a certificate unless the contrary is proved.

(4) The Secretary of State may by order—

(a)   amend subsection (1), in its application to England and Wales [or Northern Ireland][2], so as to remove an offence from it or add an offence to it;

(b)   amend subsection (2), in its application to England and Wales [or Northern Ireland][2], so as to—

(i)   take account of any amendment made by virtue of paragraph (a) above, or

(ii)   vary the sums for the time being specified in subsection (2)(a) and (b).

(5) The Scottish Ministers may by order—

(a)   amend subsection (1), in its application to Scotland, so as to remove an offence from it or add an offence to it;

(b)   amend subsection (2), in its application to Scotland, so as to—

(i)   take account of any amendment made by virtue of paragraph (a) above, or

(ii)   vary the sums for the time being specified in subsection (2)(a) and (b).

Amendments—[1]   Sub-s (1)(h) inserted by the Serious Organised Crime and Police Act 2005 (Amendment of Section 61(1)) Order, SI 2006/1629 with effect from 20 June 2006.

[2]   Sub-s (1)(ba), words in sub-ss (1)(e), (f), (g), (2)(b), (4), inserted, by the Northern Ireland (Miscellaneous Provisions) Act 2006 s 26(2), Sch 3 paras 1, 3 with effect from 1 December 2006 (by virtue of SI 2006/2966 art 3).

³   Sub-s (1)(*h*) substituted by the Bribery Act 2010 s 17(2), Sch 1 paras 7, 8 with effect from 1 July 2011 (SI 2011/1418 art 2.
⁴   Sub-s (1)(*l*) inserted by the Criminal Finances Act 2017 s 51(1) with effect from 30 September 2017 (SI 2017/739 reg 3).
⁵   Sub-s (1)(*j*) inserted by the Sanctions and Anti-Money Laundering Act 2018 s 59(4), (5), Sch 3 para 4 with effect from
2 November 2018 (by virtue of SI 2018/1213 reg 2(*f*)).

Disclosure notices

62 Disclosure notices

(1) If it appears to the Investigating Authority—

    (*a*)   that there are reasonable grounds for suspecting that an offence to which this Chapter applies has been committed,

    (*b*)   that any person has information (whether or not contained in a document) which relates to a matter relevant to the investigation of that offence, and

    (*c*)   that there are reasonable grounds for believing that information which may be provided by that person in compliance with a disclosure notice is likely to be of substantial value (whether or not by itself) to that investigation,

he may give, or authorise an appropriate person to give, a disclosure notice to that person.

[(1A) If it appears to the Investigating Authority—

    (*a*)   that any person has information (whether or not contained in a document) which relates to a matter relevant to a terrorist investigation, and

    (*b*)   that there are reasonable grounds for believing that information which may be provided by that person in compliance with a disclosure notice is likely to be of substantial value (whether or not by itself) to that investigation,

he may give, or authorise an appropriate person to give, a disclosure notice to that person.]¹

(2) In this Chapter "appropriate person" means—

    (*a*)   a constable,

    [(*b*)   a National Crime Agency officer who is for the time being designated under section 9 or 10 of the Crime and Courts Act 2013, or]³

    (*c*)   an officer of Revenue and Customs.

[But in the application of this Chapter to Northern Ireland, this subsection has effect as if paragraph (*b*) were omitted.]²

(3) In this Chapter "disclosure notice" means a notice in writing requiring the person to whom it is given to do all or any of the following things in accordance with the specified requirements, namely—

    (*a*)   answer questions with respect to any matter relevant to the investigation;

    (*b*)   provide information with respect to any such matter as is specified in the notice;

    (*c*)   produce such documents, or documents of such descriptions, relevant to the investigation as are specified in the notice.

(4) In subsection (3) "the specified requirements" means such requirements specified in the disclosure notice as relate to—

    (*a*)   the time at or by which,

    (*b*)   the place at which, or

    (*c*)   the manner in which,

the person to whom the notice is given is to do any of the things mentioned in paragraphs (a) to (c) of that subsection; and those requirements may include a requirement to do any of those things at once.

(5) A disclosure notice must be signed or counter-signed by the Investigating Authority.

(6) This section has effect subject to section 64 (restrictions on requiring information etc).

Amendments—¹   Sub-s (1A) inserted by the Terrorism Act 2006 s 33(3) with effect from 13 April 2006.
²   In sub-s (2), words inserted by the Northern Ireland (Miscellaneous Provisions) Act 2006 s 26(2), Sch 3 paras 1, 4 with effect from 1 December 2006 (by virtue of SI 2006/2966 art 3).
³   Sub-s (2)(*b*) substituted by the Crime and Courts Act 2013 s 15, Sch 8 paras 157, 159 with effect from 7 October 2013 by virtue of SI 2013/1682 art 3(*v*).

CHAPTER 2

OFFENDERS ASSISTING INVESTIGATIONS AND PROSECUTIONS

71 Assistance by offender: immunity from prosecution

(1) If a specified prosecutor thinks that for the purposes of the investigation or prosecution of [an indictable offence or an offence triable either way]¹ it is appropriate to offer any person immunity from prosecution [for any offence]¹ he may give the person a written notice under this subsection (an "immunity notice").

(2) If a person is given an immunity notice, no proceedings for an offence of a description specified in the notice may be brought against that person in England and Wales or Northern Ireland except in circumstances specified in the notice.

(3) An immunity notice ceases to have effect in relation to the person to whom it is given if the person fails to comply with any conditions specified in the notice.

(4) Each of the following is a specified prosecutor—
  (*a*) the Director of Public Prosecutions;
  (*b*) . . . ³
  (*c*) the Director of the Serious Fraud Office;
  (*d*) the Director of Public Prosecutions for Northern Ireland;
  ([*da*) the Financial Conduct Authority;
  (*daa*) the Prudential Regulation Authority;
  (*dab*) he Bank of England, where the indictable offence or offence triable either way which is being investigated or prosecuted is an offence under the Financial Services and Markets Act 2000;]²
  (*db*) the [Secretary of State for Business, Energy and Industrial Strategy]⁴, acting personally;]¹
  (*e*) a prosecutor designated for the purposes of this section by a prosecutor mentioned in paragraphs (*a*) to [(*db*)]¹.
(5) The Director of Public Prosecutions or a person designated by him under subsection (4)(*e*) may not give an immunity notice in relation to proceedings in Northern Ireland.
(6) The Director of Public Prosecutions for Northern Ireland or a person designated by him under subsection (4)(*e*) may not give an immunity notice in relation to proceedings in England and Wales.
[(6A) In exercising the power to designate a prosecutor under subsection (4)(e), the [Financial Conduct Authority, the Prudential Regulation Authority, the Bank of England]² and the [Secretary of State for Business, Energy and Industrial Strategy]⁴ may each designate only—
  (*a*) one prosecutor (a "chief prosecutor") to act at any one time, and
  (*b*) an alternative prosecutor (a "deputy prosecutor") to act as a specified prosecutor—
    (i) when the chief prosecutor is unavailable, or
    (ii) during any period when no chief prosecutor is designated.
[(6B) Paragraph 8(1) of Schedule 1ZA . . . ⁵ to the Financial Services and Markets Act 2000 (arrangements for discharging functions) [and paragraph 17(1) of Schedule 6A to the Bank of England Act 1998 (delegation of functions)]⁵ do not apply to the exercise of the powers conferred on the Financial Conduct Authority or the Prudential Regulation Authority under this Chapter.
(6BA) Paragraph 11 of Schedule 1 to the Bank of England Act 1998 (power to delegate) does not apply to the exercise of the powers conferred on the Bank of England under this Chapter.]²
(6C) An immunity notice may be given by the [Financial Conduct Authority, the Prudential Regulation Authority, the Bank of England]², the [Secretary of State for Business, Energy and Industrial Strategy]⁴ or a prosecutor designated by [any of them]² under subsection (4)(*e*), only with the consent of the Attorney General.]¹
(7) An immunity notice must not be given in relation to an offence under section 188 of the Enterprise Act 2002 (c 40) (cartel offences).

Amendments—¹ In sub-s (1) words substituted and words inserted, sub-ss (4)(*da*), (*db*), (6A)–(6C) inserted, in sub-s (4)(*e*) reference substituted by the Coroners and Justice Act 2009 s 113(1)–(4) with effect from 12 November 2009.
² Sub-s (4)(*da*)–(*dab*) substituted for former sub-s (4)(*da*), in sub-ss (6A), (6C), words substituted, and sub-ss (6B), (6BA) substituted for former sub-s (6B) by FSA 2012 s 114(1), Sch 18 para 106 with effect from 1 April 2013 by virtue of SI 2013/423 art 3, Schedule.
³ Sub-s (4)(*b*) repealed by the Public Bodies (Merger of the Director of Public Prosecutions and the Director of Revenue and Customs Prosecutions) Order, SI 2014/834 art 3(3) Sch 2 paras 40, 42 with effect from 27 March 2014.
⁴ In sub-ss (4)(*db*), (6A), (6C), words substituted by the Secretaries of State for Business, Energy and Industrial Strategy, for International Trade and for Exiting the European Union and the Transfer of Functions (Education and Skills) Order, SI 2016/992 art 10 with effect from 9 November 2016.
⁵ In sub-s (6B), words repealed and inserted by the Bank of England and Financial Services (Consequential Amendments) Regulations, SI 2017/80 reg 17 with effect from 1 March 2017.

CHAPTER 6

PROCEEDS OF CRIME

97 Confiscation orders by magistrates' courts

(1) The Secretary of State may by order make such provision as he considers appropriate for or in connection with enabling confiscation orders under—
  (*a*) Part 2 of the Proceeds of Crime Act 2002 (c 29) (confiscation: England and Wales), . . . ¹
  (*b*) . . . ¹
to be made by magistrates' courts in England and Wales . . . ¹.
[(1ZA) But an order under subsection (1) may not enable such a confiscation order to be made by any magistrates' court in respect of an amount exceeding £10,000.
(1ZB) The Secretary of State may by order amend subsection (1ZA) so as to substitute a different amount.]²
[(1A) The Department of Justice in Northern Ireland may by order make such provision as the Department considers appropriate for or in connection with enabling confiscation orders under Part 4 of the 2002 Act (confiscation: Northern Ireland) to be made by magistrates' courts in Northern Ireland.]¹

(2) But an order under subsection . . . [2] [. . . [2](1A)][1] may not enable such a confiscation order to be made by any magistrates' court in respect of an amount exceeding £10,000.

[(2A) The Department of Justice may by order amend subsection (2) so as to substitute a different amount.][2]

(3) An order under subsection (1) [or (1A)][1] may amend, repeal, revoke or otherwise modify any provision of Part 2 or 4 of the 2002 Act [as the case may be][1] or any other enactment relating to, or to things done under or for the purposes of, [that Part (or any provision of that Part)][1].

Amendments—[1]   In sub-s (1), para (*b*) and the preceding word, and words at the end repealed; sub-s (1A) inserted; words in sub-ss (2), (3) inserted; and words in sub-s (3) substituted by the Northern Ireland Act 1998 (Devolution of Policing and Justice Functions) Order, SI 2010/976 art 13, Sch 15 para 23 with effect from 12 April 2010 (the date on which the Northern Ireland Act 1998 (Amendment of Schedule 3) Order 2010, SI 2010/977 came into force: see SI 2010/976 art 1(2)).

[2]   Sub-ss (1ZA), (1ZB), (2A) inserted, and in sub-s (2), words repealed, by the Serious Crime Act 2015 s 40(1)–(4) with effect from 1 June 2015 (by virtue of SI 2015/820).

98 Civil recovery: freezing orders
(*inserts* PCA 2002 ss 245A–245D, 255A–255F and preceding crossheads)

99 Civil recovery: interim receivers' expenses etc
(1) The Proceeds of Crime Act 2002 (c 29) is amended as follows.

(2) (*inserts* PCA 2002 s 280(3), (4))

(3) (*inserts* PCA 2002 s 284(2), (3))

(4) (inserted PCA 2002 Sch 1 para 5(1A); *repealed by* the Serious Crime Act 2007 s 92, Sch 14).

100 Detention of seized cash: meaning of "48 hours"
(1) In the Proceeds of Crime Act 2002 (c 29), Chapter 3 of Part 5 (civil recovery of cash in summary proceedings) is amended as follows.

(2) (*inserts* PCA 2002 s 295(1A), (1B))

(3) (*amends* PCA 2002 ss 290(6), 296(1), 302(2))

101 Appeal in proceedings for forfeiture of cash
(1) (*substitutes* PCA 2002 s 299)

(2) This section does not apply to a decision of a court not to order the forfeiture of cash under section 298 of that Act taken before this section comes into force.

102 Money laundering: defence where overseas conduct is legal under local law
(1) In the Proceeds of Crime Act 2002 (c 29), Part 7 (money laundering) is amended as follows.

(2) (*inserts* PCA 2002 s 327(2A), (2B))

(3) (*inserts* PCA 2002 s 328(3), (4))

(4) (*inserts* PCA 2002 s 329(2A), (2B))

(5) (*inserts* PCA 2002 s 330(7A))

(6) (*inserts* PCA 2002 s 331(6A))

(7) (*inserts* PCA 2002 s 332(7))

103 Money laundering: threshold amounts
(1) The Proceeds of Crime Act 2002 (c 29) is amended as follows.

(2) (*inserts* PCA 2002 s 327(2C))

(3) (*inserts* PCA 2002 s 328(5))

(4) (*inserts* PCA 2002 s 329(2C))

(5) (*inserts* PCA 2002 s 339A)

(6) (*inserts* PCA 2002 s 340(14))

(7) (*amends* PCA 2002 s 459(4)(*a*), (6)(*a*))

104 Money laundering: disclosures to identify persons and property
(1) In the Proceeds of Crime Act 2002 (c 29), Part 7 (money laundering) is amended as follows.

(2) (*amends* PCA 2002 s 330(1))

(3) (*substitutes* PCA 2002 s 330(3A)–(6))

(4) (*substitutes* PCA 2002 s 331(3A)–(6))

(5) (*amends* PCA 2002 s 332(3))

(6) (*substitutes* PCA 2002 s 332(3A)–(6))

(7) (*inserts* PCA 2002 s 337(4A))

105 Money laundering: form and manner of disclosures
(1) In the Proceeds of Crime Act 2002 (c 29), Part 7 (money laundering) is amended as follows.

(2) (*amends* PCA 2002 ss 330(9)(*b*), 337(5)(*b*), 338(5)(*b*))

(3) (*inserts* PCA 2002 s 334(3))

(4) (*repeals* PCA 2002 s 338(1)(*b*))

(5) (*substitutes* PCA 2002 s 339(1A)–(3))

106 Money laundering: miscellaneous amendments
(1) In the Proceeds of Crime Act 2002, Part 7 (money laundering) is amended as follows.

(2) (*inserts* PCA 2002 s 330(9A))

(3) (*amends* PCA 2002 s 337(5)(*a*))

(4) (*amends* PCA 2002 s 338(1)(*c*))

(5) (*inserts* PCA 2002 s 338(2A))

(6) (*amends* PCA 2002 s 338(3))

107 Money laundering offences

(1) The Proceeds of Crime Act 2002 (c 29) is amended as follows.

(2) (*amends* PCA 2002 s 364(5))

(3) (*amends* PCA 2002 s 398(5))

(4) (*inserts* PCA 2002 s 415(1A))

108 International co-operation

(1) Part 11 of the Proceeds of Crime Act 2002 (c 29) (co-operation) is amended as follows.

(2) (*substitutes* PCA 2002 s 444(3)(*a*))

(3) (*inserts* PCA 2002 s 444(4))

(4) (*inserts* PCA 2002 s 447(3)(*aa*))

109 Minor and consequential amendments relating to Chapter 6

Schedule 6, which contains minor and consequential amendments relating to provisions of this Chapter, has effect.

PART 6

FINAL PROVISIONS

177 Interpretation

(1) . . . [1]

(2) In this Act "enactment" includes—

    (*a*) an enactment contained in or made under an Act of the Scottish Parliament or Northern Ireland legislation, and

    (*b*) an enactment comprised in subordinate legislation (within the meaning of the Interpretation Act 1978 (c 30)).

(3) In this Act references to enactments include enactments passed or made after the passing of this Act.

(4) Subsections (2) and (3) apply except where the context otherwise requires.

Amendment—[1]   Sub-s (1) repealed by the Crime and Courts Act 2013 s 15, Sch 8 paras 157, 164 with effect from 7 October 2013 by virtue of SI 2013/1682 art 3(*v*).

178 Commencement

(1) The following provisions come into force on the day on which this Act is passed—

    (*a*) sections 117(7) (and section 117(6) so far as relates to it), 158, 167, 172, 173, 176, 177, this section and section 179, and

    (*b*) Part 1 of Schedule 17 and (so far as it relates to that Part of that Schedule) section 174(2).

(2) Section 163(4) comes into force at the end of the period of three months beginning with the day on which this Act is passed.

(3) Sections 77 and 156 come into force on such day as the Scottish Ministers may by order appoint.

(4) So far as they extend to Scotland—

    (*a*) Chapter 1 of Part 2,

    (*b*) sections 79 to 81,

    (*c*) Chapter 4 of Part 2 (including Schedule 5),

    (*d*) sections 163 to 166, and

    (*e*) Schedule 14,

come into force on such day as the Scottish Ministers may by order appoint.

(5) So far as they relate—

    (*a*) to sections 113 and 115 of the Police Act 1997 (c 50) as those sections apply to Scotland;

    (*b*) to section 125 of that Act, to the Regulation of Care (Scotland) Act 2001 (asp 8), to the Protection of Children (Scotland) Act 2003 (asp 5) and to the Criminal Justice (Scotland) Act 2003 (asp 7),

section 174(2) and Schedule 17 come into force on such day as the Scottish Ministers may by order appoint.

(6) The following provisions come into force on such day as the Scottish Ministers may by order appoint after consulting the Secretary of State—

    (*a*) section 96 so far as it has effect for the purpose of conferring functions on the Scottish Ministers, and

    (*b*) section 171 and Schedule 15.

(7) The following provisions come into force on such day as the Secretary of State may by order appoint after consulting the Scottish Ministers—

    (*a*) sections 95, 98(2), 99(2) and (3), 100, 101 and 107, and

    (*b*) paragraphs 1 and 6 of Schedule 6, and section 109 so far as relating to those paragraphs.

[(7A) The following provisions, so far as they extend to Northern Ireland, come into force on such day as the Department of Justice in Northern Ireland may by order appoint—

(*a*) section 144 so far as it relates to Part 2 of Schedule 10,
(*b*) section 163(1),
(*c*) section 163(3) so far as it relates to paragraphs 4 and 10 of Schedule 14,
(*d*) Part 2 of Schedule 10, and
(*e*) paragraphs 4 and 10 of Schedule 14.][1]

(8) Otherwise, this Act comes into force on such day as the Secretary of State may by order appoint.

(9) Different days may be appointed for different purposes or different areas.

(10) The Secretary of State may by order make such provision as he considers appropriate for transitory, transitional or saving purposes in connection with the coming into force of any provision of this Act.

(11) The power conferred by subsection (10) is exercisable by the Scottish Ministers (rather than the Secretary of State) in connection with any provision of this Act which comes into force by order made by the Scottish Ministers.

[(12)][1]The power conferred by subsection (10) is exercisable by the Department of Justice in Northern Ireland (rather than the Secretary of State) in connection with any provision of this Act which comes into force by order made by the Department of Justice.

Amendments—[1]   Sub-ss (7A), (12) inserted by the Northern Ireland Act 1998 (Devolution of Policing and Justice Functions) Order, SI 2010/976 art 13, Sch 15 para 26 with effect from 12 April 2010 (the date on which the Northern Ireland Act 1998 (Amendment of Schedule 3) Order 2010, SI 2010/977 came into force: see SI 2010/976 art 1(2)).

179 Short title and extent

(1) This Act may be cited as the Serious Organised Crime and Police Act 2005.

(2) Subject to the following provisions, this Act extends to England and Wales only.

(3) The following extend also to Scotland—
(*a*) sections 1 to 54 [and 56 to][1] 58,
(*b*) sections 60 to 68, 70, [82][3] to 96, 98 to 106, 107(1) and (4) and 108,
(*c*) section 123,
(*d*) section 131,
(*e*) sections 150 to 153, 156(6), 158, 163(1) and (2), 164, 165(1) and (2), 166(2), 167 and 171(1),
(*f*) sections 172, 173, 176 to 178 and this section,
(*g*) Schedules 1, 3, 5 and 15.

(4) The following extend to Scotland only—
(*a*) section . . .[3] 107(3),
(*b*) sections 129 and 130(3),
(*c*) sections 156(1) to (5), 166(1) and 171(2).

(5) The following extend also to Northern Ireland—
(*a*) sections 1 to 54 [and 56 to][1] 58,
(*b*) sections 68, 71 to 75, [82][3] to 106, 107(1), (2) and (4) and 108,
(*c*) section 123(1),
(*d*) sections 128, 131 and 144,
(*e*) sections 150(1), 151, 163(1) and (2), 164, 165, 166(2) and 167,
(*f*) sections 172, 173, 176 to 178 and this section,
(*g*) Schedules 1, 3 and 5.

(6) The following extend to Northern Ireland only—
(*a*) section 55(2),
(*b*) . . .[2]
(*c*) section 130(2),
(*d*) Part 2 of Schedule 10.

(7) The following have the same extent as the enactments to which they relate—
(*a*) section 55(1) and Schedule 2,
(*b*) section 59 and Schedule 4,
(*c*) section 109 and Schedule 6,
(*d*) section 154,
(*e*) section 159 and Schedule 11,
(*f*) section 160 and Schedule 12,
(*g*) section 161(5) (so far as it has effect for the purposes of Part 2 of Schedule 13) and that Part of that Schedule,
(*h*) section 163(3) and Schedule 14,
(*i*) sections 169(5) and 170,
(j) (subject to subsection (8)) section 174(2) and Schedule 17.

(8) So far as Schedule 17 contains a repeal or revocation of an enactment which corresponds to the repeal or revocation of that enactment by another provision of this Act, that Schedule and section 174(2) have the same extent as that other provision.

(9) So far as they relate to any provision of this Act which extends to any place outside the United Kingdom, sections 172, 173, 177, 178 and this section also extend there.

(10) Subsection (2) does not apply to the following—

(*a*) section 168, or

(*b*) any provision of Schedule 7 which makes provision as to its extent.

Amendments—[1]   Words in sub-ss (3)(*a*), (5)(*a*) substituted by the Serious Organised Crime and Police Act 2005 (Amendment) Order, SI 2005/3496 arts 3, 4 with effect from 1 January 2006.

[2]   Sub-s (6)(*b*) repealed by the Serious Crime Act 2015 s 81(5), Sch 4 para 73(1), (5) with effect from 3 May 2015 (by virtue of SI 2015/820).

[3]   In sub-ss (3)(*b*), (5)(*b*), reference substituted, and in sub-s (4)(*a*), words repealed, by the Serious Crime Act 2015 s 81(5), Sch 4 para 73(1)–(3) with effect from 1 March 2016 (by virtue of SI 2016/148, reg 3(*f*), (*h*)).

FINANCE (NO 2) ACT 2005

(2005 Chapter 22)

ARRANGEMENT OF SECTIONS

Employee securities
12 Employee securities: anti-avoidance
Chapter 2 Scientific Research Organisations
14 Income tax deduction for payments to organisations
15 Corporation tax deduction for payments to organisations
Chapter 3 Authorised Investment Funds etc
17 Authorised unit trusts and open-ended investment companies
18 Section 17(3): specific powers
19 Section 17: commencement and procedure
20 Unauthorised unit trusts: chargeable gains
21 Unit trusts: treatment of accumulation units
22 Section 349B ICTA: exemption for distributions to PEP/ISA managers
Chapter 5 Chargeable Gains
Residence, location of assets etc
32 Temporary non-residents
33 Trustees both resident and non-resident in a year of assessment
34 Location of assets etc
Miscellaneous
35 Exercise of options etc
Chapter 6 Miscellaneous
Accounting practice and related matters
37 Accounting practice and related matters
Financial avoidance etc
38 Charges on income for the purposes of corporation tax
39 Avoidance involving financial arrangements
Financing of companies etc
40 Transfer pricing and loan relationships
44 Territories with a lower level of taxation: reduction of amount of local tax
Miscellaneous
45 Lloyd's underwriters: assessment and collection of tax
46 Energy Act 2004 and Health Protection Agency Act 2004
62 Groups
64 Held-over gains
65 Restrictions on set-off of pre-entry losses
Part 5: Miscellaneous Matters
67 Reorganisation of water and sewerage services in Northern Ireland
69 Abolition of statutory adjudicator for National Savings and Investments
Part 6: Supplementary Provisions
70 Repeals
71 Interpretation
72 Short title
Schedules:
Schedule 1 (see Tolley's Orange Tax Handbook)
Schedule 2 —Employee securities: anti-avoidance
Schedule 4 —Chargeable gains: location of assets etc
Schedule 5 —Chargeable gains: options
Schedule 6 —Accounting practice and related matters
Schedule 7 —Avoidance involving financial arrangements
Schedule 11 —Repeals

PART 2

INCOME TAX, CORPORATION TAX AND CAPITAL GAINS TAX

CHAPTER 1

PERSONAL TAXATION

Social security pension lump sums

7 Charge to income tax on lump sum

(1) A charge to income tax arises where a person becomes entitled to a social security pension lump sum.

(2) For the purposes of the Tax Acts (including subsection (5)) a social security pension lump sum—

(a) is to be treated as income, but

(b) is not to be taken into account in determining the total income of any person.

(*a*) section 55C of, and Schedule 5A to, SSCBA 1992, or

(*b*) section 55C of, and Schedule 5A to, SSCB(NI)A 1992;

"state pension lump sum" means a lump sum payable under—

[(*za*) section 8 of the Pensions Act 2014 or under any corresponding provision under the law of Northern Ireland,][1]

[(*zb*) regulations under section 10 of the Pensions Act 2014 which make provision corresponding or similar to section 8 of that Act or under any corresponding provision under the law of Northern Ireland,][2]

(*a*) section 55 of, and Schedule 5 to, SSCBA 1992, or

(*b*) section 55 of, and Schedule 5 to, SSCB(NI)A 1992.

(3) In section 8 and this section—

"NIA 1965" means the National Insurance Act 1965 (c 51);

"NIA(NI) 1966" means the National Insurance Act (Northern Ireland) 1966 (c 6 (NI));

"SSCBA 1992" means the Social Security Contributions and Benefits Act 1992 (c 4);

"SSCB(NI)A 1992" means the Social Security Contributions and Benefits (Northern Ireland) Act 1992 (c 7).

(4) Sections 7 and 8 and this section have effect in relation to the year 2006–07 and subsequent years of assessment.

Amendments—[1] In sub-s (2), in definition of "state pension lump sum" para (*za*) inserted by the Pensions Act 2014 s 23, Sch 12 paras 49, 51 with effect from 6 April 2016.

[2] In sub-s (2), in definition of "state pension lump sum" para (*zb*) inserted by the Pensions Act 2014 (Consequential and Supplementary Amendments) Order, SI 2016/224 art 6(1), (3) with effect from 6 April 2016.

10 Consequential amendments

(1) ITEPA 2003 is amended as follows.

(2) (*inserts* ITEPA 2003 s 577(1A)).

(3) (*amends* ITEPA 2003 s 683).

(4) (*inserts* ITEPA 2003 s 683(3A)).

(5) (*amends* ITEPA 2003 s 686(1)).

(6) (*inserts* ITEPA 2003 s 686(5)).

(7) (*amended* ITEPA 2003 Sch 1; *repealed* by FA 2009 s 126(6)(*b*)).

Employee securities

12 Employee securities: anti-avoidance

Schedule 2 contains amendments relating to employee securities.

CHAPTER 2

SCIENTIFIC RESEARCH ORGANISATIONS

14 Income tax deduction for payments to organisations

(1) Section 88 of ITTOIA 2005 (income tax deduction for payments to research associations etc) is amended as follows.

(2) (*amends* ITTOIA 2005 s 88(1)).

(3) (*repeals* ITTOIA 2005 s 88(4)(*a*)).

(4) (*amends* ITTOIA 2005 s 88(5)).

(5) This section has effect in relation to sums paid to an Association during any accounting period of the Association beginning on or after the day appointed under section 13(6).

15 Corporation tax deduction for payments to organisations

(1) Section 82B of ICTA (corporation tax deduction for payments to research associations etc) is amended as follows.

(2) (*amends* TA 1988 s 82B(1)).

(3) (*amends* TA 1988 s 82B(3)).

(4) This section has effect in relation to sums paid to an Association during any accounting period of the Association beginning on or after the day appointed under section 13(6).

CHAPTER 3

AUTHORISED INVESTMENT FUNDS ETC

17 Authorised unit trusts and open-ended investment companies

(1) The following provisions shall cease to have effect—

(*a*) sections 468H to 468Q of ICTA (authorised unit trusts),

(*b*) . . .[1]

(*c*) . . .[1]

(*d*) section 373(4) and (6) of ITTOIA 2005 (open-ended investment company: interest distributions), and

(*e*) section 376(4) and (6) of ITTOIA 2005 (authorised unit trust: interest distributions).

(2) In this Chapter "authorised investment funds" means—

FINANCE (NO 2) ACT 2005

(2005 Chapter 22)

ARRANGEMENT OF SECTIONS

Employee securities
12   Employee securities: anti-avoidance
Chapter 2 Scientific Research Organisations
14   Income tax deduction for payments to organisations
15   Corporation tax deduction for payments to organisations
Chapter 3 Authorised Investment Funds etc
17   Authorised unit trusts and open-ended investment companies
18   Section 17(3): specific powers
19   Section 17: commencement and procedure
20   Unauthorised unit trusts: chargeable gains
21   Unit trusts: treatment of accumulation units
22   Section 349B ICTA: exemption for distributions to PEP/ISA managers
Chapter 5 Chargeable Gains
Residence, location of assets etc
32   Temporary non-residents
33   Trustees both resident and non-resident in a year of assessment
34   Location of assets etc
Miscellaneous
35   Exercise of options etc
Chapter 6 Miscellaneous
Accounting practice and related matters
37   Accounting practice and related matters
Financial avoidance etc
38   Charges on income for the purposes of corporation tax
39   Avoidance involving financial arrangements
Financing of companies etc
40   Transfer pricing and loan relationships
44   Territories with a lower level of taxation: reduction of amount of local tax
Miscellaneous
45   Lloyd's underwriters: assessment and collection of tax
46   Energy Act 2004 and Health Protection Agency Act 2004
62   Groups
64   Held-over gains
65   Restrictions on set-off of pre-entry losses
Part 5: Miscellaneous Matters
67   Reorganisation of water and sewerage services in Northern Ireland
69   Abolition of statutory adjudicator for National Savings and Investments
Part 6: Supplementary Provisions
70   Repeals
71   Interpretation
72   Short title
Schedules:
Schedule 1 (see Tolley's Orange Tax Handbook)
Schedule 2 —Employee securities: anti-avoidance
Schedule 4 —Chargeable gains: location of assets etc
Schedule 5 —Chargeable gains: options
Schedule 6 —Accounting practice and related matters
Schedule 7 —Avoidance involving financial arrangements
Schedule 11 —Repeals

PART 2

INCOME TAX, CORPORATION TAX AND CAPITAL GAINS TAX

CHAPTER 1

PERSONAL TAXATION

Social security pension lump sums

7 Charge to income tax on lump sum

(1) A charge to income tax arises where a person becomes entitled to a social security pension lump sum.

(2) For the purposes of the Tax Acts (including subsection (5)) a social security pension lump sum—

  (*a*) is to be treated as income, but

  (*b*) is not to be taken into account in determining the total income of any person.

(3) The person liable to a charge under this section is the person ("P") entitled to the lump sum, whether or not P is resident . . . [4] or domiciled in the United Kingdom.

(4) The charge is imposed on P for the applicable year of assessment (see subsection (6)).

(5) A charge under this section [for a person who is [neither a Scottish taxpayer nor a Welsh taxpayer][7] in the applicable year of assessment][5] is a charge in respect of the amount of the lump sum at the following rate—

    (a) if P's [Step 3 income][1] for the applicable year of assessment is nil, 0%;

    (b) . . . [2]

    (c) if P's [Step 3 income][1] for that year of assessment [is greater than nil][2] but does not exceed the basic rate limit for that year, the basic rate . . . [5] for that year;

    (d) if P's [Step 3 income][1] for that year of assessment exceeds the basic rate limit for that year [but does not exceed the higher rate limit for that year][3], the higher rate . . . [5] for that year.

    [(e) if P's Step 3 income for that year of assessment exceeds the higher rate limit for that year, the additional rate . . . [5] for that year.][3]

[(5A) Where P is a Scottish taxpayer in the applicable year of assessment, a charge under this section is a charge in respect of the amount of the lump sum at the following rate—

    (a) if P's Step 3 income for the applicable year of assessment is nil, 0%;

    (b) *if P's Step 3 income for that year of assessment is greater than nil but does not exceed the Scottish basic rate limit for that year, the Scottish basic rate for that year;*[6]

    (c) if P's Step 3 income for that year of assessment [is greater than nil][6], the highest Scottish rate for that tax year that is [applicable to P's Step 3 income for that year][6].][5]

[(5B) Where P is a Welsh taxpayer in the applicable year of assessment, a charge under this section is a charge in respect of the amount of the lump sum at the following rate—

    (a) if P's step 3 income for the applicable year of assessment is nil, 0%;

    (b) *if P's step 3 income for that year of assessment is greater than nil but does not exceed the basic rate limit for that year, the Welsh basic rate for that year;*

    (c) if P's step 3 income for that year of assessment is greater than the basic rate limit but does not exceed the higher rate limit for that year, the Welsh higher rate for that year;

    (d) if P's step 3 income for that year of assessment is greater than the higher rate limit for that year, the Welsh additional rate for that year.][7]

(6) Section 8 makes provision as to the meaning of "the applicable year of assessment" for the purposes of this section.

(7) Section 9 contains further definitions and makes provision as to commencement.

(8) Section 10 contains consequential amendments.

[(9) For the purposes of this section P's "Step 3 income" means P's net income less allowances deducted at Step 3 of the calculation in section 23 of ITA 2007 (calculation of income tax liability).][1]

HMRC Manuals—Employment Income Manual EIM74651(social security pension lump sum: charge to income tax). EIM74652 (state pension lumpsum: rate of tax).

Amendments—[1]   Words in sub-s (5) inserted, and sub-s (9) inserted by ITA 2007 s 1027, Sch 1 paras 603, 604 with effect for income tax purposes from 6 April 2007, and corporation tax purposes for accounting periods ending after 5 April 2007.

[2]   In sub-s (5), para (*b*) repealed, and words in para (*c*) substituted, by FA 2008 s 5, Sch 1 para 64 with effect for the tax year 2008–09 and subsequent tax years.

[3]   In sub-s (5), in para (*d*), words inserted, and para (*e*) inserted, by FA 2009 s 6, Sch 2 paras 19, 23 with effect for the tax year 2010–11 and subsequent tax years. The powers conferred by the amendments made by FA 2009 Sch 2 may be exercised at any time on or after 21 July 2009 but not so as to make provision having effect before the tax year 2010–11 (FA 2009 Sch 2 para 25(1)).

[4]   Words in sub-s (3) repealed by FA 2013 s 219, Sch 46 paras 134, 135 with effect in relation to the tax year 2013–14 and any subsequent tax year.

[5]   In sub-s (5), words inserted, and in paras (*c*)–(*e*), words repealed, by the Scotland Act 2016 (Income Tax Consequential Amendments) Regulations, SI 2017/468 regs 2, 9 with effect in relation to 2017–18 (the tax year appointed under the Scotland Act 2016 section 13(15)(*b*)) and subsequent tax years.

[6]   In sub-s (5A), para (*b*) repealed, and in para (*c*), words substituted for words "exceeds the Scottish basic rate limit for that year" and "applicable to P", by the Scottish Rates of Income Tax (Consequential Amendments) Order, SI 2018/459 art 5 with effect for the tax year commencing on 6 April 2018 and subsequent tax years.

[7]   In sub-s (5) words substituted for words "not a Scottish tax payer", and sub-s (5B) inserted, by the Devolved Income Tax Rates (Consequential Amendments) Order, SI 2019/201 art 11 with effect in relation to the tax year commencing on 6 April 2019 and subsequent tax years.

8 Meaning of "applicable year of assessment" in section 7

(1) For the purposes of section 7 "the applicable year of assessment" has the meaning given by this section.

(2) Subject to subsections (5) to (7), the applicable year of assessment is—

    (a) the year of assessment in which the first benefit payment day falls, or

    (b) if P dies before the beginning of that year of assessment, the year of assessment in which P dies.

(3) For the purposes of subsection (2) "the first benefit payment day" is, subject to [subsections (4), (4A) and (4B)][2], the day as from which P's—

    (a) Category A or Category B retirement pension,

   (*b*) shared additional pension, or
   (*c*) graduated retirement benefit,

becomes payable following the period of deferment by virtue of which P's entitlement to the lump sum arises.

(4) But where—
   (*a*) the lump sum is a state pension lump sum to which P is entitled under paragraph 7A of Schedule 5 to SSCBA 1992 or paragraph 7A of Schedule 5 to SSCB(NI)A 1992 or a graduated retirement benefit lump sum to which P is entitled under a provision corresponding to either of those paragraphs, and
   (*b*) at the time of S's death, P was entitled to a Category A or Category B retirement pension or (as the case may be) graduated retirement benefit,

the first benefit payment day is the day on which S died; and for this purpose "S" is the person by virtue of whose period of deferment P's entitlement to the lump sum arises.

[(4A) In a case where the social security pension lump sum is a lump sum under section 8 of the Pensions Act 2014 or under any corresponding provision under the law of Northern Ireland, "the first benefit payment day" for the purposes of subsection (2) is the day as from which the lump sum becomes payable.]¹

[(4B) In a case where the social security pension lump sum is a lump sum under regulations under section 10 of the Pensions Act 2014 which make provision corresponding or similar to section 8 of that Act or under any corresponding provision under the law of Northern Ireland, "the first benefit payment day" for the purposes of subsection (2) is the day as from which the lump sum becomes payable.]²

(5) Subsections (6) and (7) apply where social security regulations make provision enabling the making of an election for a social security pension lump sum to be paid in the year of assessment ("the later year of assessment") next following that given by subsection (2).

(6) If such an election is made by P and is not revoked, the applicable year of assessment is—
   (*a*) the later year of assessment, or
   (*b*) if P dies before the beginning of that year of assessment, the year of assessment in which P dies.

(7) If—
   (*a*) P dies after the beginning of the later year of assessment,
   (*b*) by the time of P's death, P has not notified the Secretary of State as to whether or not P wishes to make such an election,
   (*c*) social security regulations make provision enabling the making of such an election in such a case by the personal representatives of P, and
   (*d*) P's personal representatives make such an election in accordance with the regulations,

the applicable year of assessment is the later year of assessment.

(8) For the purposes of determining the applicable year of assessment, it does not matter when the lump sum is actually paid.

(9) In this section—
    "Category A or Category B retirement pension" means Category A or Category B retirement pension under Part 2 of SSCBA 1992 or Part 2 of SSCB(NI)A 1992;
    "graduated retirement benefit" means graduated retirement benefit under section 36 or 37 of NIA 1965 or section 35 or 36 of NIA(NI) 1966;
    "shared additional pension" means shared additional pension under Part 2 of SSCBA 1992 or Part 2 of SSCB(NI)A 1992;
    "social security regulations" means any regulations under—
       (*a*) the Social Security Administration Act 1992 (c 5), or
       (*b*) the Social Security Administration (Northern Ireland) Act 1992 (c 8).

(10) This section is to be construed as one with section 7.

Amendments—¹ In sub-s (3), words substituted, and sub-s (4A) inserted, by the Pensions Act 2014 s 23, Sch 12 paras 49, 50 with effect from 6 April 2016.
² In sub-s (3), words substituted, and sub-s (4B) inserted, by the Pensions Act 2014 (Consequential and Supplementary Amendments) Order, SI 2016/224 art 6(1), (2) with effect from 6 April 2016.

9 Interpretation and commencement

(1) In sections 7 and 8 "social security pension lump sum" means—
   (*a*) a state pension lump sum,
   (*b*) a shared additional pension lump sum, or
   (*c*) a graduated retirement benefit lump sum.

(2) In section 8 and this section—
    "graduated retirement benefit lump sum" means a lump sum payable under—
       (*a*) section 36 or 37 of NIA 1965, or
       (*b*) section 35 or 36 of NIA(NI) 1966;
    "shared additional pension lump sum" means a lump sum payable under—

(*a*) section 55C of, and Schedule 5A to, SSCBA 1992, or

(*b*) section 55C of, and Schedule 5A to, SSCB(NI)A 1992;

"state pension lump sum" means a lump sum payable under—

[(*za*) section 8 of the Pensions Act 2014 or under any corresponding provision under the law of Northern Ireland,][1]

[(*zb*) regulations under section 10 of the Pensions Act 2014 which make provision corresponding or similar to section 8 of that Act or under any corresponding provision under the law of Northern Ireland,][2]

(*a*) section 55 of, and Schedule 5 to, SSCBA 1992, or

(*b*) section 55 of, and Schedule 5 to, SSCB(NI)A 1992.

(3) In section 8 and this section—

"NIA 1965" means the National Insurance Act 1965 (c 51);

"NIA(NI) 1966" means the National Insurance Act (Northern Ireland) 1966 (c 6 (NI));

"SSCBA 1992" means the Social Security Contributions and Benefits Act 1992 (c 4);

"SSCB(NI)A 1992" means the Social Security Contributions and Benefits (Northern Ireland) Act 1992 (c 7).

(4) Sections 7 and 8 and this section have effect in relation to the year 2006–07 and subsequent years of assessment.

Amendments—[1] In sub-s (2), in definition of "state pension lump sum" para (*za*) inserted by the Pensions Act 2014 s 23, Sch 12 paras 49, 51 with effect from 6 April 2016.

[2] In sub-s (2), in definition of "state pension lump sum" para (*zb*) inserted by the Pensions Act 2014 (Consequential and Supplementary Amendments) Order, SI 2016/224 art 6(1), (3) with effect from 6 April 2016.

10 Consequential amendments

(1) ITEPA 2003 is amended as follows.

(2) (*inserts* ITEPA 2003 s 577(1A)).

(3) (*amends* ITEPA 2003 s 683).

(4) (*inserts* ITEPA 2003 s 683(3A)).

(5) (*amends* ITEPA 2003 s 686(1)).

(6) (*inserts* ITEPA 2003 s 686(5)).

(7) (*amended* ITEPA 2003 Sch 1; *repealed* by FA 2009 s 126(6)(*b*)).

Employee securities

12 Employee securities: anti-avoidance

Schedule 2 contains amendments relating to employee securities.

CHAPTER 2
SCIENTIFIC RESEARCH ORGANISATIONS

14 Income tax deduction for payments to organisations

(1) Section 88 of ITTOIA 2005 (income tax deduction for payments to research associations etc) is amended as follows.

(2) (*amends* ITTOIA 2005 s 88(1)).

(3) (*repeals* ITTOIA 2005 s 88(4)(*a*)).

(4) (*amends* ITTOIA 2005 s 88(5)).

(5) This section has effect in relation to sums paid to an Association during any accounting period of the Association beginning on or after the day appointed under section 13(6).

15 Corporation tax deduction for payments to organisations

(1) Section 82B of ICTA (corporation tax deduction for payments to research associations etc) is amended as follows.

(2) (*amends* TA 1988 s 82B(1)).

(3) (*amends* TA 1988 s 82B(3)).

(4) This section has effect in relation to sums paid to an Association during any accounting period of the Association beginning on or after the day appointed under section 13(6).

CHAPTER 3
AUTHORISED INVESTMENT FUNDS ETC

17 Authorised unit trusts and open-ended investment companies

(1) The following provisions shall cease to have effect—

(*a*) sections 468H to 468Q of ICTA (authorised unit trusts),

(*b*) . . .[1]

(*c*) . . .[1]

(*d*) section 373(4) and (6) of ITTOIA 2005 (open-ended investment company: interest distributions), and

(*e*) section 376(4) and (6) of ITTOIA 2005 (authorised unit trust: interest distributions).

(2) In this Chapter "authorised investment funds" means—

(a) authorised unit trust schemes, and

(b) open-ended investment companies.

(3) The Treasury may, by regulations—

   (a) make provision about the treatment of authorised investment funds for the purposes of an enactment relating to taxation;

   (b) provide for the modification of an enactment relating to taxation in its application in relation to—

      (i) authorised investment funds,

      (ii) shareholders or unit holders in authorised investment funds, or

      (iii) transactions involving authorised investment funds;

   (c) impose requirements on persons responsible for the management of an authorised investment fund in relation to the provision of information, the form of accounts, the keeping of records or other administrative matters.

(4) For the purposes of this Chapter—

   (a) "unit trust scheme" has the meaning given by section 237 of the Financial Services and Markets Act 2000 (c 8),

   (b) a unit trust scheme is authorised in relation to an accounting period if an order under section 243 of the Financial Services and Markets Act 2000 is in force in relation to that scheme during the whole or part of that accounting period,

   (c) "unit holder" means a person entitled to a share of the investments subject to the trusts of a unit trust scheme,

   (d) a reference to a shareholder or unit holder includes a person beneficially entitled to shares or units (and a reference to owning units or shares shall be construed accordingly),

   (e) "open-ended investment company" means a company incorporated in the United Kingdom to which section 236 of the Financial Services and Markets Act 2000 applies,

   (f) "associate" has the meaning given by section 417 ICTA,

   (g) "net asset value" means the value of the assets of the authorised investment fund, after the deduction of specified liabilities,

   (h) a reference to a distribution includes investing an amount on behalf of a unit holder or shareholder in respect of his accumulation units or accumulation shares,

   (i) "distribution accounts" means accounts showing—

      (i) the total amount available for distribution to unit holders or shareholders, and

      (ii) how that amount is computed,

   (j) the "distribution date" for a distribution period in relation to an authorised investment fund means—

      (i) the date specified by or in accordance with the terms of the trust or the instrument of incorporation of the company for any distribution for that distribution period, or

      (ii) if no date is specified, the last day of that distribution period,

   (k) "distribution period" in relation to an authorised investment fund means a period by reference to which the total amount available for distribution to unit holders or shareholders is ascertained,

   (l) "umbrella company" has the meaning given by [section 615 of the Corporation Tax Act 2010][2],

   (m) "umbrella scheme" has the meaning given by [section 619 of the Corporation Tax Act 2010][2], and

   (n) [section 1122 of the Corporation Tax Act 2010][2] (connected persons) applies.

Regulations—Authorised Investment Funds (Tax) (Amendment) Regulations, SI 2012/519.
Authorised Investment Funds (Tax) (Amendment No 2) Regulations, SI 2012/1783.
Authorised Investment Funds (Tax) (Amendment No 3) Regulations, SI 2012/3043.
Authorised Investment Funds (Tax) (Amendment) Regulations, SI 2013/1772.
Authorised Investment Funds (Tax) (Amendment) (No 2) Regulations 2013/2994.
Real Estate Investment Trust (Amendments to the Corporation Tax Act 2010 and Consequential Amendments) Regulations, SI 2014/518.
Investment Transactions (Tax) Regulations, SI 2014/685.
Authorised Investment Funds (Tax) (Amendment) Regulations, SI 2015/485.
Corporate Interest Restriction (Consequential Amendments) Regulations, SI 2017/1227.
Amendments—[1]   Sub-s (1)(b), (c) repealed by CTA 2009 s 1325, Sch 3 Pt 1. CTA 2009 applies for accounting periods ending on or after 1 April 2009 (for corporation tax purposes) and for tax years 2009–10 onwards (for income and CGT purposes).
[2]   In paras (l), (m), (n), words substituted by CTA 2010 s 1177, Sch 1 para 479. CTA 2010 has effect for corporation tax purposes for accounting periods ending on or after 1 April 2010, and for income and capital gains tax purposes for the tax year 2010–11 and subsequent tax years.

18 Section 17(3): specific powers

(1) Regulations under section 17(3)(a) or (b) may make provision about distributions which may, in particular—

(a) require an authorised investment fund to comply with prescribed rules for determining (whether by reference to a formula or otherwise) what proportion of an amount shown in distribution accounts as available for distribution is to be distributed by way of dividends and what proportion is to be distributed by way of yearly interest;

(b) permit persons responsible for the management of an authorised investment fund to elect to distribute entirely by way of dividends;

(c) require distribution accounts to show the amount available for distribution—
   (i) by way of dividends;
   (ii) by way of yearly interest;

(d) allow a distribution of yearly interest for a distribution period to be deducted, in the prescribed manner, in computing the profits of the authorised investment fund for the accounting period in which the last day of that distribution period falls;

(e) make provision for determining the distribution date in relation to a distribution period of an authorised investment fund;

(f) permit distributions to be made, in prescribed circumstances, to or for the benefit of a person not . . . [5] resident in the United Kingdom without deducting tax;

(g) permit distributions to be made without deducting tax, in prescribed circumstances, to a person . . . [5] resident in the United Kingdom who is unlikely to be liable to pay an amount by way of income tax for the year of assessment in which the distribution is made;

(h) include provision, in respect of a unit holder or shareholder who is within the charge to corporation tax, about—
   (i) the liability to corporation tax resulting from receipt of a distribution, and
   (ii) the method of computing that liability.

(2) Regulations under section 17(3)(a) or (b) may, in particular—

(a) make special provision for loan relationships held by an authorised investment fund;

(b) make special provision for derivative contracts held by an authorised investment fund;

[(c) modify the meaning of "relevant holding" for the purposes of—
   (i) sections 490 and 492 of the Corporation Tax Act 2009 (loan relationships), and
   (ii) section 587 of that Act (derivative contracts).][2]

(d) make special provision in relation to the treatment of umbrella companies and umbrella schemes (or shareholders or unit holders in umbrella companies or umbrella schemes);

(e) prohibit action which favours a class of unit holders or shareholders.

(3) Regulations under section 17(3)(a) or (b) may[1], in particular—

(a) make special provision in relation to a person who, alone or together with associates or connected persons, owns (otherwise than as a nominee) units or shares, in a fund designated by the [Financial Conduct Authority][6] as a Qualified Investor Scheme, which represent 10% or more (or such other percentage as the regulations may specify) of the net asset value of the fund;

(b) include exceptions from provision made by virtue of paragraph (a) above including, in particular, an exception relating to units or shares held—
   (i) by a charity . . . [3]
   (ii) by a registered pension scheme (within the meaning of section 150 of FA 2004),
   [(iii) by an insurance company (within the meaning of section 65 of FA 2012) as assets for the purposes of its long-term business (within the meaning of section 63 of that Act),][4] or
   (iv) by such other persons, in such circumstances, as the regulations may specify.

(4) Regulations under section 17(3)(c) may, in particular, require persons responsible for the management of an authorised investment fund to supply information to, and make available books, documents and other records for inspection by, the Commissioners for Her Majesty's Revenue and Customs.

(5) Regulations under section 17(3) may in particular—

(a) amend a reference in an enactment to a provision repealed by section 17(1);

(b) make different provision for different circumstances;

(c) make incidental, consequential, supplemental or transitional provision.

Commentary—*Simon's Taxes* D7.551.

Regulations—Authorised Investment Funds (Tax) (Amendment) Regulations, SI 2012/519.

Authorised Investment Funds (Tax) (Amendment No 2) Regulations, SI 2012/1783.

Authorised Investment Funds (Tax) (Amendment No 3) Regulations, SI 2012/3043.

Authorised Investment Funds (Tax) (Amendment) Regulations, SI 2013/1772.

Authorised Investment Funds (Tax) (Amendment) (No 2) Regulations 2013/2994.

Real Estate Investment Trust (Amendments to the Corporation Tax Act 2010 and Consequential Amendments) Regulations, SI 2014/518.

Authorised Investment Funds (Tax) (Amendment) Regulations, SI 2015/485.

Corporate Interest Restriction (Consequential Amendments) Regulations, SI 2017/1227.

Amendments—[1] Words in sub-s (3) previously substituted by ITA 2007 s 1027, Sch 1 paras 603, 605 with effect for income tax purposes from 6 April 2007, and corporation tax purposes for accounting periods ending after 5 April 2007.

[2]   Sub-s (2)(*c*) substituted by CTA 2009 s 1322, Sch 1 para 688, 669. CTA 2009 applies for accounting periods ending on or after 1 April 2009 (for corporation tax purposes) and for tax years 2009–10 onwards (for income and CGT purposes).

[3]   In sub-s (3)(*b*)(i) words repealed by FA 2010 s 30, Sch 6 para 22 with effect from 1 April 2012 (SI 2012/736 art 16).

[4]   Sub-s (3)(*b*),(iii) substituted by FA 2012 s 146, Sch 16 paras 123, 124 with effect in relation to accounting periods of companies ending on or after 1 January 2013 (subject to transitional provisions in FA 2012 Sch 17). For accounting periods straddling 1 January 2013, see FA 2012 s 149.

[5]   Word in sub-s (1)(*f*), (*g*) repealed by FA 2013 s 219, Sch 46 paras 134, 136 with effect from 17 July 2013.

[6]   In sub-s (3)(*a*), words substituted by FSA 2012 s 114(1), Sch 18 para 108 with effect from 1 April 2013 by virtue of SI 2013/423 art 3, Schedule.

19 Section 17: commencement and procedure

(1) Section 17(1) shall come into force on such day as the Treasury may appoint by order.

(2) An order under subsection (1) may—

 (*a*) commence only a specified repeal;

 (*b*) commence different repeals at different times;

 (*c*) commence a repeal at different times for different purposes;

 (*d*) include savings.

(3) Regulations under section 17(3) shall be subject to annulment by a resolution of the House of Commons.

(4) But the first set of regulations under section 17(3) may not be made unless a draft has been laid before and approved by resolution of the House of Commons.

20 Unauthorised unit trusts: chargeable gains

(1) Section 100 of TCGA 1992 (exemption for authorised unit trusts, &c) shall be amended as follows.

(2) (*inserts* TCGA 1992 s 100(2A), (2B)).

(3) This section shall have effect for the year 2005–06 and subsequent years of assessment.

21 Unit trusts: treatment of accumulation units

(1) (*inserts* TCGA 1992 s 99B).

(2) This section shall have effect in relation to a disposal of units on or after 16th March 2005.

22 Section 349B ICTA: exemption for distributions to PEP/ISA managers

(1) Section 349B(4) of ICTA (requirement for individual to be entitled to income tax exemption) shall be amended as follows.

(2) (*amends* TA 1988 s 349B(4)(*a*)).

(3) (*repeals* TA 1988 s 349B(4)(*b*)).

(4) This section shall have effect in relation to payments made on or after 6 April 2005.

CHAPTER 5

CHARGEABLE GAINS

Residence, location of assets etc

32 Temporary non-residents

(1) Section 10A of TCGA 1992 is amended as follows.

(2) (*amends* TCGA 1992 s 10A(3)).

(3) (*amends* TCGA 1992 s 10A(8)).

(4) (*substitutes* TCGA 1992 s 10A(9)–(9B)).

(5) (*inserts* TCGA 1992 s 10A(9C)).

(6) (*repeals* TCGA 1992 s 10A(10)).

(7) The amendments in subsections (2)(*a*), (4), (5) and (6) have effect—

 (*a*) in any case in which the year of departure is, or (on the assumption that the amendment in subsection (4) had always had effect) would be, the year 2005–06 or a subsequent year of assessment; and

 (*b*) in any case in which—

 (i) the year of departure is, or (on that assumption) would be, the year 2004–05, and

 (ii) at a time in that year on or after 16th March 2005, the taxpayer was resident or ordinarily resident in the United Kingdom and was not Treaty non-resident (within the meaning given by section 10A(9A) of TCGA 1992, as inserted by subsection (4)).

(8) The amendment in subsection (2)(*b*) has effect in relation to relevant disposals made on or after 16th March 2005.

(9) The amendment in subsection (3) has effect for determining whether a disposal of an asset is a relevant disposal for the purposes of section 10A of TCGA 1992 in any case in which the person making the disposal acquired the asset on or after 16th March 2005.

33 Trustees both resident and non-resident in a year of assessment

(1) (*inserts* TCGA 1992 s 83A).

(2) The amendment made by this section has effect in relation to disposals made on or after 16th March 2005.

34 Location of assets etc

Schedule 4 (which makes provision in relation to the situation of assets for the purposes of TCGA 1992 and which makes minor amendments in that Act in relation to non-resident companies with United Kingdom permanent establishments) has effect.

Miscellaneous

35 Exercise of options etc

Schedule 5 (which makes provision, for the purposes of the taxation of chargeable gains, in relation to options) has effect.

CHAPTER 6

MISCELLANEOUS

Accounting practice and related matters

37 Accounting practice and related matters

Schedule 6 (accounting practice and related matters) has effect.

Financial avoidance etc

38 Charges on income for the purposes of corporation tax

(1) Section 338A of ICTA (meaning of "charges on income" for the purposes of corporation tax) is amended as follows.

(2) (*amends* TA 1988 s 338A).

(3) (*amended* TA 1988 s 125(1); *repealed by* ITA 2007 s 1031, Sch 3 Pt 1).

(4) (*amends* TA 1988 s 434A(2)(*a*)).

(5) (*amended* side-note to TA 1988 s 494); *repealed by* CTA 2010 s 1181, Sch 3 Pt 1).

(6) The amendment made by subsection (4) has effect for accounting periods beginning on or after 1st April 2004.

(7) The other amendments made by this section have effect in relation to payments made on or after the commencement date in respect of annuities or other annual payments.

(8) Where—

    (*a*) an accounting period of a company begins before, and ends on or after, the commencement date,

    (*b*) a payment in respect of an annuity or other annual payment is made by the company in that period but before the commencement date, and

    (*c*) the payment is deductible as a charge on income for the purposes of corporation tax,

subsection (9) applies.

(9) In any such case, so much of any amount as represents that payment—

    (*a*) is not deductible under section 75 of ICTA (expenses of management), and

    (*b*) is not to be brought into account under section 76 of that Act (expenses of insurance companies) as expenses payable,

for that or any subsequent accounting period.

(10) Subsection (12) applies in any case where—

    (*a*) a payment in respect of an annuity or other annual payment is made by a company on or after the commencement date, and

    (*b*) the condition in subsection (11) is satisfied.

(11) The condition is that the payment represents an amount which (apart from subsection (12))—

    (*a*) would not be deductible under section 75 of ICTA, or

    (*b*) would not fall to be brought into account under section 76 of that Act,

by reason only of section 337A(1)(b) of that Act (company's income from any source to be computed without any deduction in respect of charges on income) as it applies by virtue of section 338A(2)(a) of that Act.

(12) In any such case, the amount represented by the payment—

    (*a*) is deductible under section 75 of ICTA, or

    (*b*) falls to be brought into account under section 76 of that Act as expenses payable,

for the accounting period in which the payment is made.

(13) In this section "the commencement date" means 16th March 2005.

39 Avoidance involving financial arrangements

Schedule 7 (which makes provision in relation to tax avoidance involving financial arrangements) has effect.

Financing of companies etc

40 Transfer pricing and loan relationships

Schedule 8 (which amends Schedule 28AA to ICTA and Schedule 9 to FA 1996) has effect.

Insurance companies etc

42 Insurance companies etc

Schedule 9 (which makes provision about insurance companies etc) has effect.

44 Territories with a lower level of taxation: reduction of amount of local tax

(1) Section 750 of ICTA (controlled foreign companies: territories with a lower level of taxation) is amended as follows.

(2) (*amends* TA 1988 s 750(1)).

(3) (*inserts* TA 1988 s 750(1A), (1B)).

(4) The amendments made by this section have effect in relation to accounting periods of companies resident outside the United Kingdom beginning on or after 2nd December 2004.

(5) Where an accounting period of a company resident outside the United Kingdom—

    (*a*) would, without amendment, have ended on or after 2nd December 2004, but

    (*b*) is amended on or after that date so as to end before that date,

an accounting period of the company shall be deemed for the purposes of Chapter 4 of Part 17 of ICTA to have ended with 1st December 2004.

(6) In this section "accounting period" has the same meaning as in Chapter 4 of Part 17 of ICTA (see section 751).

Miscellaneous

45 Lloyd's underwriters: assessment and collection of tax

(1) (*repeals* FA 1993 s 173, Sch 19).

(2) (*amends* FA 1993 s 182(1)(*a*)).

(3) (*inserts* FA 1993 s 182(6)).

(4) (*repeals* FA 1994 s 221).

(5) (*amends* FA 1994 s 229).

(6) (*amends* FA 1994 s 229(1)(*a*)).

(7) (*inserts* FA 1994 s 229(2)).

(8) For the purpose of enabling the making of any regulations under—

    (*a*) section 182(1)(*a*) of FA 1993 (as amended by subsection (2)), or

    (*b*) section 229(1)(*a*) of FA 1994 (as amended by subsection (6)),

subsections (1) to (7) come into force on the day on which this Act is passed.

(9) Subject to that, those subsections come into force in accordance with provision made by the Treasury by order.

(10) Section 828(3) of ICTA shall not apply in relation to an order under subsection (9).

(11) The Commissioners for Her Majesty's Revenue and Customs may by regulations make such amendments, repeals or revocations in any enactment (including an enactment amended by this section) as appear to them to be appropriate in consequence of any one or more of the following—

    (*a*) any amendment made by this section;

    (*b*) the exercise by them of the power in section 182(1)(*a*) of FA 1993 (as amended by subsection (2));

    (*c*) the exercise by them of the power in section 229(1)(*a*) of FA 1994 (as amended by subsection (6)).

(12) Any power conferred by this section to make an order or regulations includes power to make—

    (*a*) different provision for different cases or different purposes, and

    (*b*) incidental, supplemental or transitional provision and savings.

(13) In this section—

    "enactment" includes an enactment comprised in subordinate legislation;

    "subordinate legislation" has the same meaning as in the Interpretation Act 1978 (c 30) (see section 21 of that Act).

46 Energy Act 2004 and Health Protection Agency Act 2004

(1) This section provides for certain enactments to cease to have effect which relate to—

    (*a*) the United Kingdom Atomic Energy Authority ("UKAEA"),

    (*b*) the National Radiological Protection Board ("NRPB"), or

    (*c*) pension schemes run by UKAEA.

(2) In ICTA the following provisions shall cease to have effect—

    (*a*) section 349B(3)(*g*) (no deduction of tax from certain payments to UKAEA);

    (*b*) section 349B(3)(*h*) (no deduction of tax from certain payments to NRPB);

    (*c*) section 512(1) and (3) (certain exemptions from income tax and corporation tax for UKAEA and NRPB);

    (*d*) section 512(2) (treatment of certain income of pension schemes run by UKAEA).

(3) In section 271(7) of TCGA 1992 (miscellaneous exemptions from tax in respect of chargeable gains)—

    (*a*) for "Memorial Fund, the" substitute "Memorial Fund and the";

(b) omit ", the United Kingdom Atomic Energy Authority";

(c) omit "and the National Radiological Protection Board";

(d) omit from "; and for the purposes" to the end of the subsection (treatment of gains accruing to pension schemes run by UKAEA).

(4) In subsection (2)—

(a) paragraph (a) has effect in relation to payments made on or after 1st April 2005;

(b) paragraph (b) has effect in relation to payments made after 1st April 2005;

(c) paragraph (c), so far as relating to UKAEA, has effect on and after 1st April 2005;

(d) paragraph (c), so far as relating to NRPB, has effect after 1st April 2005;

(e) paragraph (d) has effect in relation to income arising on or after 1st April 2005.

(5) In subsection (3)—

(a) paragraphs (a) and (c) have effect in relation to gains accruing after 1st April 2005;

(b) paragraphs (b) and (d) have effect in relation to gains accruing on or after 1st April 2005.

(6) The repeal of subsection (3)(g) of section 349B of ICTA does not affect the application of any other provision of that section in relation to UKAEA.

(7) Nothing in this section affects—

(a) any accounting period of UKAEA ending before 1st April 2005, or

(b) any accounting period of NRPB ending on or before 1st April 2005.

PART 4
EUROPEAN COMPANY STATUTE

51 Chargeable gains

(1) (*inserted* TCGA 1992 ss 140E–140G; *repealed by* CTA 2009 s 1325, Sch 3 Pt 1).

(2) Subsection (1) shall have effect in relation to the formation of an SE which occurs on or after 1st April 2005.

52 Intangible fixed assets

(1) (*inserts* FA 2002 Sch 29 para 85A).

(2) Subsection (1) shall have effect in relation to the formation of an SE which occurs on or after 1st April 2005.

53 Intangible fixed assets: permanent establishment in another member State

(1) (*inserts* FA 2002 Sch 29 para 87A).

(2) Subsection (1) shall have effect in relation to the formation of an SE which occurs on or after 1st April 2005.

56 Capital allowances

(1) (*inserts* CAA 2001 s 561A).

(2) Subsection (1) shall have effect in relation to a transfer made on or after 1st April 2005.

59 Consequential amendments

(1) (*amended* TA 1988 s 815A(1) *repealed by* TIOPA 2010 s 503, Sch 10 Pt 1).

(2) (*amended* TCGA 1992 s 35(3)(d)(i); *repealed by* FA 2008 s 8, Sch 2 para 70(h))

(3) (*amends* TCGA 1992 s 140A).

(4) (*amends* TCGA 1992 s 140C).

(5) (*amends* FA 2002 Sch 29 para 88(1), (5)).

(6) (*amends* FA 2002 Sch 29 para 127(1)(b)).

(7) Subsections (3) and (4) shall have effect in relation to an issue effected on or after 1st April 2005.

62 Groups

(1) (*inserts* TCGA 1992 s 170(10A)).

(2) Subsection (1) shall have effect in relation to the formation of an SE (including its formation by transformation) which occurs on or after 1st April 2005.

64 Held-over gains

(1) (*amends* TCGA 1992 s 116(11)).

(2) (*inserts* TCGA 1992 s 140(6B)).

(3) (*inserts* TCGA 1992 s 154(2A)).

(4) (*inserts* TCGA 1992 s 179(1B)).

(5) This section shall have effect in relation to the formation of an SE in accordance with Article 2 of Council Regulation (EC) 2157/2001 on the Statute for a European Company (Societas Europaea) which occurs on or after 1st April 2005.

65 Restrictions on set-off of pre-entry losses

(1) Schedule 7A to TCGA 1992 (restrictions on set-off of pre-entry losses) shall be amended as follows.

(2) (*amended* TCGA 1992 Sch 7A para 1(3A)(aa); *repealed by* FA 2011 s 46, Sch 11 para 10(d)).

(3) (*amended* TCGA 1992 Sch 7A para 1(3A); *repealed by* FA 2011 s 46, Sch 11 para 10(d)).

(4) (*amends* TCGA 1992 Sch 7A para 1(6)(a)).

(5) (*amended* TCGA 1992 Sch 7A para 9(6); *repealed* by FA 2011 s 46, Sch 11 para 10(*d*)).

(6) This section shall have effect in relation to the formation of an SE which occurs on or after 1st April 2005.

Commentary—*Simon's Taxes* **D7.505**.

PART 5
MISCELLANEOUS MATTERS

67 Reorganisation of water and sewerage services in Northern Ireland

(1) In this section "relevant transfer" means a transfer of property, rights or liabilities where—

    (*a*) the transfer is of property, rights or liabilities which—

        (i) are specified or described in or determined in accordance with a scheme, and

        (ii) consist of or include relevant property, rights or liabilities,

    (*b*) the transfer is from a Northern Ireland department or persons which include a Northern Ireland department to a company or companies specified in the scheme ("transferee company"), and

    (*c*) the transfer is effected by or under an enactment which—

        (i) is made after the coming into force of this section, and

        (ii) relates to the provision of water or sewerage services in Northern Ireland.

(2) In this section "relevant property, rights or liabilities" means property, rights or liabilities connected with the provision of any water or sewerage services.

(3) The Treasury may by regulations make provision for or in connection with varying the way in which a relevant tax or duty would, apart from the regulations, have effect in relation to, or in connection with, any of the following—

    (*a*) anything done for the purpose of, or under or in consequence of, a relevant transfer of relevant property, rights or liabilities from a Northern Ireland department to a transferee company;

    (*b*) any relevant property, rights or liabilities which are the subject of a relevant transfer from a Northern Ireland department to a transferee company;

    (*c*) any relevant property, rights or liabilities of a transferee company.

(4) The provision that may be made by the regulations includes provision for or in connection with any of the following—

    (*a*) a tax provision not to apply or to apply with modifications in prescribed cases or circumstances;

    (*b*) anything done to have or not to have a specified consequence for the purposes of a tax provision in prescribed cases or circumstances;

    (*c*) any relevant property, rights or liabilities which are the subject of a relevant transfer from a Northern Ireland department to a transferee company to be treated in a specified way for the purposes of a tax provision in prescribed cases or circumstances;

    (*d*) the withdrawal of relief (whether or not granted by virtue of the regulations), and the charging of tax, in prescribed cases or circumstances;

    (*e*) requiring or enabling the Secretary of State, with the consent of the Treasury, to determine or to specify the method to be used for determining anything (including amounts or values, or times or periods of time) which needs to be determined for the purposes of any tax provision (whether or not modified by the regulations) as it applies in relation to, or in connection with,—

        (i) anything done for the purpose of, or under or in consequence of, a relevant transfer of relevant property, rights or liabilities from a Northern Ireland department to a transferee company, or

        (ii) any relevant property, rights or liabilities which are the subject of a relevant transfer from a Northern Ireland department to a transferee company.

(5) A provision of regulations made by virtue only of subsection (3)(*c*) ("a subsection (3)(*c*) provision") (whether or not also by virtue of subsection (4)) shall not have effect for an accounting period of a transferee company unless the company is wholly owned by the Crown during the whole of that accounting period.

(6) Regulations under this section may provide that, for the purposes of a subsection (3)(*c*) provision, an accounting period of a transferee company shall be taken to have ended on the company ceasing to be wholly owned by the Crown.

(7) For the purposes of this section, a company shall be regarded as wholly owned by the Crown at any time when each of the issued shares in the company is held by, or by a nominee of,—

    (*a*) the Treasury,

    (*b*) the Secretary of State,

    (*c*) a Northern Ireland department, or

    (*d*) another company which is wholly owned by the Crown.

(8) In this section—

    "enactment" includes a provision comprised in—

(*a*) Northern Ireland legislation, or

(*b*) an instrument made under an enactment;

"prescribed" means prescribed by or determined in accordance with regulations under this section;

"relevant tax or duty" means income tax, corporation tax, capital gains tax, stamp duty or stamp duty reserve tax;

"tax provision" means a provision of an enactment about a relevant tax or duty.

(9) Any power to make regulations under this section is exercisable by statutory instrument.

(10) A statutory instrument containing regulations under this section shall be subject to annulment in pursuance of a resolution of the House of Commons.

(11) Any power to make regulations under this section includes power—

(*a*) to make different provision for different cases or circumstances;

(*b*) to make incidental, supplemental, consequential or transitional provision or savings.

Regulations—Transfer of the Northern Ireland Water Service (Tax) Regulations, SI 2007/766.

69 Abolition of statutory adjudicator for National Savings and Investments

(1) After the coming into force of this section, no further disputes shall be referred to a person appointed under section 84 of the Friendly Societies Act 1992 (c 40) (adjudicator for disputes under the National Savings Bank Act 1971 and the National Debt Act 1972).

(2) This section comes into force on 1st September 2005.

PART 6

SUPPLEMENTARY PROVISIONS

70 Repeals

(1) The enactments mentioned in Schedule 11 (which include provisions that are spent or of no practical utility) are repealed to the extent specified.

(2) The repeals specified in that Schedule have effect subject to the commencement provisions and savings contained or referred to in the notes set out in that Schedule.

71 Interpretation

In this Act—

"CAA 2001" means the Capital Allowances Act 2001 (c 2);

[CTA 2009" means the Corporation Tax Act 2009][2]

"FA", followed by a year, means the Finance Act of that year;

"ICTA" means the Income and Corporation Taxes Act 1988 (c 1);

["ITA 2007" means the Income Tax Act 2007;][1]

"ITEPA 2003" means the Income Tax (Earnings and Pensions) Act 2003 (c 1);

"ITTOIA 2005" means the Income Tax (Trading and Other Income) Act 2005 (c 5);

"TCGA 1992" means the Taxation of Chargeable Gains Act 1992 (c 12);

"VATA 1994" means the Value Added Tax Act 1994 (c 23);

"VERA 1994" means the Vehicle Excise and Registration Act 1994 (c 22).

Amendments—[1]   Entry inserted by ITA 2007 s 1027, Sch 1 paras 603, 606 with effect for income tax purposes from 6 April 2007, and corporation tax purposes for accounting periods ending after 5 April 2007.

[2]   Entry inserted by CTA 2009 s 1322, Sch 1 paras 668, 672. CTA 2009 applies for accounting periods ending on or after 1 April 2009 (for corporation tax purposes) and for tax years 2009–10 onwards (for income and capital gains tax purposes).

72 Short title

This Act may be cited as the Finance (No 2) Act 2005.

SCHEDULES

SCHEDULE 2

EMPLOYEE SECURITIES: ANTI-AVOIDANCE

Section 12

Introductory

1   ITEPA 2003 is amended as follows.

Rights under certain insurance contracts to be securities

2—(1) Section 420 (income and exemptions relating to securities: meaning of "securities" etc) is amended as follows.

(2) (*inserts* ITEPA 2003 s 240(1)(*aa*)).

(3) (*amends* ITEPA 2003 s 240(1)(*b*)).

(4) (*amends* ITEPA 2003 s 240(1)(*g*)).

(5) (*inserts* ITEPA 2003 s 240(1A), (1B)).

(6) (*amends* ITEPA 2003 s 240(5)).

(7) (*amends* ITEPA 2003 Sch 1 part 2).

(8) This paragraph has effect on and after 2nd December 2004 and applies in relation to rights under contracts of insurance acquired before that date, as well as those acquired on or after that date; and—

    (*a*) for the purposes of the application of Chapter 3B of Part 7 of ITEPA 2003 (securities with artificially enhanced market value) by reason of this paragraph in relation to rights under contracts of insurance acquired before that date, section 446O of that Act (meaning of "relevant period") has effect as if they were acquired on that date, and

    (*b*) for the purposes of section 420(1A)(*c*) of ITEPA 2003, section 50 of FA 2004 (meaning of "generally accepted accounting practice") has effect on and after that date, in spite of subsection (6) of that section.

Restricted securities

3   Chapter 2 of Part 7 (restricted securities) is amended as follows.

4—(1) (*amends* ITEPA 2003 s 424).

(2) (*amends* ITEPA 2003 s 424(1)).

(3) (*inserts* ITEPA 2003 s 424(2)).

(4) This paragraph has effect on and after 2nd December 2004 and applies in relation to employment-related securities acquired before that date, as well as those acquired on or after that date; and section 422 of ITEPA 2003 (application of Chapter 2 of Part 7) applies to employment-related securities in relation to which this paragraph has effect and which were acquired before that date with the omission of the words "at the time of the acquisition".

5—(1) (*inserts* ITEPA 2003 s 428(10)).

(2) This paragraph has effect where something such as is mentioned in section 428(10) of ITEPA 2003 has been done on or after 2nd December 2004.

6—(1) (*substitutes* ITEPA 2003 s 429(1A)).

(2) This paragraph has effect where something such as is mentioned in section 429(1A) of ITEPA 2003 has been done on or after 2nd December 2004.

7—(1) (*inserts* ITEPA 2003 s 431B).

(2) This paragraph has effect in relation to employment-related securities acquired on or after 2nd December 2004.

Convertible securities

8   Chapter 3 of Part 7 (convertible securities) is amended as follows.

9—(1) (*amends* ITEPA 2003 s 436(*a*)).

(2) (*amends* ITEPA 2003 s 437).

(3) (*inserts* ITEPA 2003 s 437(2)–(4)).

(4) This paragraph has effect in relation to acquisitions on or after 2nd December 2004.

10—(1) (*inserts* ITEPA 2003 s 440(3A)).

(2) This paragraph has effect on and after 2nd December 2004.

11—(1) (*substitutes* ITEPA 2003 s 443(1A)).

(2) This paragraph has effect where something such as is mentioned in section 443(1A) of ITEPA 2003 has been done on or after 2nd December 2004.

Securities acquired for less than market value

12   Chapter 3C of Part 7 (securities acquired for less than market value) is amended as follows.

13—(1) (*substitutes* ITEPA 2003 s 446R(1A)).

(2) This paragraph has effect where something such as is mentioned in section 446R(1A) of ITEPA 2003 has been done on or after 2nd December 2004.

14—(1) (*amends* ITEPA 2003 s 446U(1)).

(2) This paragraph has effect where something such as is mentioned in section 443U(1)(*c*) of ITEPA 2003 has been done on or after 2nd December 2004.

15—(1) (*inserts* ITEPA 2003 s 446UA).

(2) This paragraph has effect in relation to acquisitions on or after 2nd December 2004.

16—(1) Section 698 (PAYE: special charges on employment-related securities) is amended as follows.

(2) (*inserts* ITEPA 2003 s 698(1)(*ea*)).

(3) (*inserts* ITEPA 2003 s 698(6)(*da*)).

(4) This paragraph has effect on and after the day on which this Act is passed.

Post-acquisition benefits from securities

17 Chapter 4 of Part 7 (post-acquisition benefits from securities) is amended as follows.

18—(1) Section 447 (charge on other chargeable benefits from securities) is amended as follows.
(2) (*amends* ITEPA 2003 s 447(1)).
(3) (*substitutes* ITEPA 2003 s 447(4)).
(4) Sub-paragraph (2) has effect on and after 2nd December 2004 and sub-paragraph (3) has effect where something such as is mentioned in section 447(4) of ITEPA 2003 has been done on or after that date.

19—(1) (*substitutes* ITEPA 2003 s 449(1A)).
(2) This paragraph has effect where something such as is mentioned in section 449(1A) of ITEPA 2003 has been done on or after 2nd December 2004.

SCHEDULE 4
CHARGEABLE GAINS: LOCATION OF ASSETS ETC
Section 34

PART 1
LOCATION OF ASSETS

Designated international organisations

3—(1) Section 265 of TCGA 1992 is amended as follows.
(2) (*amends* TCGA 1992 s 265(3)).

Location of assets: general

4—(1) Section 275 of TCGA 1992 is amended as follows.
(2) (*amends* TCGA 1992 s 275).
(3) (*amends* TCGA 1992 s 275(1)(*d*)).
(4) (*inserts* TCGA 1992 s 275(1)(*da*)).
(5) (*amends* TCGA 1992 s 275(1)(*e*)).
(6) (*substitutes* TCGA 1992 s 275(1)(*h*)).
(7) (*substitutes* TCGA 1992 s 275(1)(*j*)).
(8) (*inserted* TCGA 1992 s 275(2)–(4); *repealed by* FA 2011 s 45, Sch 10 para 8(*c*)).

Location of certain intangible assets

5 (*inserts* TCGA 1992 ss 275A, 275B).

Location of assets: interests of co-owners

6 (*inserts* TCGA 1992 s 275C).

PART 2
MINOR AMENDMENTS: NON-RESIDENT COMPANY WITH UK
PERMANENT ESTABLISHMENT

Computation of losses

7—(1) Section 16 of TCGA 1992 is amended as follows.
(2) (*amends* TCGA 1992 s 16(3)).

Exemptions for disposals by companies with substantial shareholding

9—(1) Schedule 7AC to TCGA 1992 is amended as follows.
(2) (*amends* TCGA 1992 Sch 7AC para 3(2)(*c*)(ii)).

PART 3
COMMENCEMENT

Commencement

10—(1) The amendments made by Part 1 of this Schedule have effect for determining for the purposes of TCGA 1992—
(*a*) the situation of any asset, or
(*b*) whether the situation of any asset is in the United Kingdom,

at any time on or after 16th March 2005 (irrespective of when the asset was acquired by the person holding it).

(2) The amendment made by paragraph 7 has effect in relation to any loss accruing to a company in an accounting period ending on or after 16th March 2005.

(3) . . . [1]

(4) The amendment made by paragraph 9 has effect in relation to disposals on or after 16th March 2005.

Amendments—[1]   Sub-para (3) repealed by FA 2011 s 45, Sch 10 para 8(*c*) with effect in relation to any disposal of an asset by one company ("company B") to another company ("company A") made at a time when company B is a member of a group, if: (a) company A ceases to be a member of the group on or after 19 July 2011; or (b) where company A ceased to be such a member before 19 July 2011 in circumstances where TCGA 1992 s 179(6)–(8) applied, company A ceases to satisfy the conditions in TCGA 1992 s 179(7) on or after 19 July 2011.

Where an early commencement election is made in relation to a group, the effective date is 1 April 2011: see FA 2011 Sch 10 para 9(4)–(8).

SCHEDULE 5

CHARGEABLE GAINS: OPTIONS

Section 35

PART 1

APPLICATION OF MARKET VALUE RULE IN CASE OF EXERCISE OF OPTION

Application of market value rule in case of exercise of option

1—(1) Section 144ZA of TCGA 1992 is amended as follows.

(2) (*amends* TCGA 1992 s 144ZA(1)).

(3) (*amends* TCGA 1992 s 144ZA(4)).

(4) (*inserts* TCGA 1992 s 144ZA(4A)).

(5) (*substitutes* TCGA 1992 s 144ZA(5)).

Application of market value rule in case of exercise of option: exception

2   (*inserts* TCGA 1992 ss 144ZB–144ZD).

PART 2

MISCELLANEOUS AMENDMENTS RELATING TO SHARE OPTIONS ETC

Shares acquired on same day: election for alternative treatment

3—(1) Section 105A of TCGA 1992 is amended as follows.

(2) (*substitutes* TCGA 1992 s 105A(1)(*b*)(i), (ii)).

Employment-related securities options

4—(1) Section 149A of TCGA 1992 is amended as follows.

(2) (*substitutes* TCGA 1992 s 149A(1)(*b*)).

(3) (*amends* TCGA 1992 s 149A(1)(*c*)).

(4) The heading of the section accordingly becomes "Employment-related securities options".

Interpretation of TCGA 1992

5—(1) Section 288 of TCGA 1992 is amended as follows.

(2) (*amends* TCGA 1992 s 288(1A)).

PART 3

COMMENCEMENT

Commencement

6—(1) The amendments made by paragraphs 1 to 3 have effect in relation to cases where the option in question is exercised on or after 2nd December 2004 (whenever the option was acquired).

(2) The amendments made by paragraphs 4 and 5 have effect in relation to options granted on or after 2nd December 2004.

SCHEDULE 6

ACCOUNTING PRACTICE AND RELATED MATTERS

Section 37

Meaning of "statutory insolvency arrangement"

3—(1) (*substitutes* ITTOIA 2005 s 259).

(2) This amendment has effect for the tax year 2005–06 and subsequent tax years in relation to periods of account beginning on or after 1st January 2005.

Loan relationships with embedded derivatives

8—(1) (*amends* TCGA 1992 s 116(8A)).

(2) (*inserts* TCGA 1992 s 116(8B)).

(3) These amendments have effect in relation to transactions occurring after 26th May 2005.

SCHEDULE 7

AVOIDANCE INVOLVING FINANCIAL ARRANGEMENTS

Section 39

Consideration due after time of disposal: creditor relationships etc

7—(1) Section 48 of TCGA 1992 (consideration due after time of disposal) is amended as follows.

(2) (*amends* TCGA 1992 s 48).

(3) (*inserts* TCGA 1992 s 48(2)–(4)).

Corporate strips: manipulation of price: associated payment giving rise to loss

8   (*inserts* TCGA 1992 s 151D).

Money debts etc not arising from lending of money: discounts and profits from transactions

12—(1) Section 100 of FA 1996 (money debts etc not arising from the lending of money) is amended as follows.

(2) (*amends* FA 1996 s 100(1)(*c*)).

(3) (*inserts* FA 1996 s 100(1A)).

(4) (*amends* FA 1996 s 100(2)(*a*)).

(5) (*inserts* FA 1996 s 100(2ZA), (2ZB)).

(6) (*inserts* FA 1996 s 100(3A), (3B)).

(7) (*repeals* FA 1996 s 100(4)–(6), (8)).

(8) (*repeals* FA 1996 s 100(13)).

(9) In consequence of the amendments made by this paragraph, paragraph (*c*) of the Case III of Schedule D substituted for the purposes of corporation tax by section 18(3A) of ICTA (tax in respect of discount arising otherwise than in respect of a loan relationship) shall not have effect in relation to any discount arising in an accounting period beginning on or after the commencement date.

(10) Subject to sub-paragraph (9), the amendments made by this paragraph have effect in relation to any money debt to which a company is party as a creditor on or after the commencement date.

(11) Where, on or after the commencement date but in a period of account beginning before 1st January 2005, a company is party to a relationship to which section 100 of FA 1996 applies, then, in the application of that section for that period of account, subsection (2) of it shall have effect as follows—

    (*a*) paragraph (*a*) shall have effect in relation to—

        (i) any discount arising to the company from the money debt, and

        (ii) any profits, impairment of discount, or reversal of impairment of discount, arising to the company as mentioned in subsection (2ZA) of that section,

    as it has effect (or would have effect) in relation to interest payable to the company under the relationship,

    (*b*) paragraph (*b*) shall have effect as if the reference to interest included a reference to the matters mentioned in paragraph (*a*)(i) and (ii) above, and

    (*c*) the closing words shall have effect accordingly.

(12) None of the following shall be brought into account for the purposes of Chapter 2 of Part 4 of FA 1996 by virtue of this paragraph—

    (*a*) credits in respect of discount arising from a money debt, to the extent that the discount accrued before the commencement date;

    (*b*) credits in respect of profits arising as mentioned in section 100(2ZA)(*a*) or (*b*)(ii) of that Act where the related transaction took place before the commencement date;

  (*c*) debits in respect of any impairment arising in respect of discount arising from a money debt, to the extent that the discount accrued before the commencement date;

  (*d*) credits in respect of any reversal of any such impairment, to the extent that the discount accrued before the commencement date.

(13) In this paragraph "the commencement date" means 16th March 2005.

Capital redemption policies: removal of exclusion from loan relationships computations

14—(1) Schedule 9 to FA 1996 (loan relationships: special computational provisions) is amended as follows.

(2) (*repeals FA 1996 Sch 9 para 1A(1)(b)*).

(3) This paragraph has effect in relation to a capital redemption policy on and after 10th February 2005 (whenever the capital redemption policy was effected).

(4) Where a capital redemption policy—

  (*a*) is held by a company immediately before 10th February 2005, and

  (*b*) on or after that date, is, for the purposes of Chapter 2 of Part 4 of FA 1996 [or Part 5 of CTA 2009][1], a creditor relationship of the company,

sub-paragraphs (5) and (6) apply.

(5) In any such case, Chapter 2 of Part 13 of ICTA (life policies etc: chargeable events) shall have effect as if—

  (*a*) immediately before 10th February 2005, the company had assigned the whole of the rights conferred by the policy for money or money's worth, and

  (*b*) the value of the consideration for the assignment had been equal to what the carrying value of the creditor relationship would have been had an accounting period of the company ended on that date;

and Chapter 2 of Part 4 of FA 1996 [and Part 5 of CTA 2009][1] shall have effect as if, immediately after 9th February 2005, the company had acquired the creditor relationship at a cost equal to that carrying value.

(6) But if—

  (*a*) the accounting period in which the assignment is deemed to have happened ("the assignment period"), and

  (*b*) the accounting period in which the company ceases to be party to the creditor relationship ("the cessation period"),

are not the same accounting period, any gain which, by virtue of the deemed assignment, would have fallen to be brought into account in accordance with section 547(1)(b) of ICTA for the assignment period shall instead be brought into account for the cessation period.

(7) In this paragraph—

    "assignment", in relation to Scotland, means an assignation;

    "carrying value" has the same meaning as it has for the purposes of paragraph 19A of Schedule 9 to FA 1996, as it has effect for periods of account beginning on or after 1st January 2005.

Amendments—[1]   In sub-paras (4)(*b*), (5) words inserted by CTA 2009 ss 1322, Sch 1 paras 668, 674, Sch 3 Part 1. CTA 2009 applies for accounting periods ending on or after 1 April 2009 (for corporation tax purposes) and for tax years 2009–10 onwards (for income and capital gains tax purposes).

Relevant discounted securities: corporate strips

21—(1) Schedule 13 to FA 1996 (discounted securities: income tax) is amended as follows.

(2) (*amends FA 1996 Sch 13 para 3(1)*).

(3) (*amends FA 1996 Sch 13 para 4*).

(4) (*amends FA 1996 Sch 13 para 5*).

(5) (*inserts FA 1996 Sch 13 paras 13A–13D*).

(6) (*amends FA 1996 Sch 13 para 15*).

(7) (*amends FA 1996 Sch 13 para 15(1)*).

(8) The amendments made by this paragraph have effect in any case where a person acquires a corporate strip on or after 2nd December 2004 otherwise than in pursuance of an agreement entered into before that date.

Deeply discounted securities: corporate strips

25—(1) Chapter 8 of Part 4 of ITTOIA 2005 (profits from deeply discounted securities) is amended as follows.

(2) (*amends ITTOIA 2005 s 430(6)*).

(3) (*inserts ITTOIA 2005 s 437(5), (6)*).

(4) (*substitutes ITTOIA 2005 s 438(4)*).

(5) (*substitutes ITTOIA 2005 s 440(5)*).

(6) (*substitutes ITTOIA 2005 s 441(3)*).

(7) (*inserts* ITTOIA 2005 s 444(6)).

(8) (*inserts* ITTOIA 2005 ss 452A–452G).

(9) (*amends* abbreviations and defined expressions in ITTOIA 2005 Sch 4 Part 2).

(10) ITTOIA 2005 shall have effect as if it had been originally enacted with the amendments made by this paragraph.

SCHEDULE 9
INSURANCE COMPANIES ETC
Section 42

Transfers of business: modification of section 444AC of ICTA

7   (*amended* TA 1988 s 444AC; *repealed by* FA 2007 Sch 27 Pt 2(9) with effect in accordance with FA 2007 Sch 9).

Equalisation reserves for general business

9—(1) Section 444BA of ICTA is amended as follows.

(2) (*amends* TA 1988 s 444BA(11)).

(3) The amendment made by this paragraph has effect in relation to periods of account ending on or after 31st December 2004.

Relevant financial reinsurance contracts

11   (*amended* FA 1989 s 82C; *repealed by* FA 2007 Sch 27 Pt 2(9) with effect in accordance with FA 2007 Sch 9).

Transfers of business: references to accounting period ending with day of transfer

20—(1) Section 12 of ICTA (corporation tax: basis of, and periods for, assessment) is amended as follows.

(2) (*amended* TA 1988 s 12(7A); *repealed by* the Insurance Business Transfer Schemes (Amendment of the Corporation Tax Acts) Order, SI 2008/381 art 31, Sch Pt 1 with effect in relation to transfers of business taking place on or after 19 February 2008).

(3) (*inserted* TA 1988 s 12(7C); *repealed by* FA 2007 Sch 27 Pt 2(9) with effect in accordance with FA 2007 Sch 9) (Note, this para appears also to be *repealed* by the Insurance Business Transfer Schemes (Amendment of the Corporation Tax Acts) Order, SI 2008/381 art 31, Sch Pt 1 with effect in relation to transfers of business taking place on or after 19 February 2008).

(4) (*amended* TA 1988 s 444AB(3); *repealed by* FA 2007 Sch 27 Pt 2(9) with effect in accordance with FA 2007 Sch 9).

(5) (*amended* TA 1988 s 444ABA(3); *repealed by* FA 2007 Sch 27 Pt 2(9) with effect in accordance with FA 2007 Sch 9).

(6) (*inserts* TCGA 1992 s 213(10); *repealed* by the Insurance Business Transfer Schemes (Amendment of the Corporation Tax Acts) Order, SI 2008/381 art 31, Sch Pt 1 with effect in relation to transfers of business taking place on or after 19 February 2008).

(7) The amendments made by sub-paragraphs (2) to (5) have effect in relation to insurance business transfer schemes taking place on or after 16th March 2005.

(8) The amendment made by sub-paragraph (6) has effect where the accounting period for which the net amount represents an excess of losses over gains is an accounting period beginning on or after 1st January 2003.

FINANCE ACT 2006

(2006 Chapter 25)

ARRANGEMENT OF SECTIONS

Part 3: Income Tax, Corporation Tax and Capital Gains Tax
Chapter 1 Income Tax and Corporation Tax: Charge and Rate Bands
Income tax
23   Charge and rates for 2006–07
Corporation tax
24   Charge and main rate for financial year 2007
26   Abolition of corporation tax starting rate and non-corporate distribution rate
Chapter 2 Reliefs for Business
Group relief
27   Group relief where surrendering company not resident in UK
Research and development
Film tax relief
42   Film tax relief: further provisions
Films: withdrawal of existing reliefs
46   Films: withdrawal of existing reliefs (corporation tax)
47   Films: withdrawal of existing reliefs (income tax)
Supplementary provisions
53   Films and sound recordings: commencement and power to alter dates
Chapter 5 Personal Taxation
Mobile telephones and computers
60   Mobile telephones
61   Computer equipment
Eye care
62   Exemption for employees' eye tests and special glasses
Vouchers and tokens
63   Power to exempt use of vouchers or tokens to obtain exempt benefits
Holocaust victims
64   Payments to or in respect of victims of National-Socialist persecution
Chapter 6 The London Olympic Games and Paralympic Games
65   London Organising Committee
66   Section 65: supplementary
67   International Olympic Committee
68   Competitors and staff
Chapter 7 Chargeable Gains
Capital losses
70   Restrictions on companies buying losses or gains
71   Other avoidance involving losses accruing to companies
72   Repeal of s 106 of TCGA 1992
Insurance policies and annuities
73   Policies of insurance and non-deferred annuities
Capital gains tax
74   Exception to "bed and breakfasting" rules etc
Chapter 8 Avoidance: Miscellaneous
Financial instruments
76   Avoidance involving financial arrangements
83   Restrictions on use of losses etc: leasing partnerships
84   Disposal of plant or machinery subject to lease where income retained
85   Restrictions on effect of elections under section 266 of CAA 2001
Insurance companies and policyholders
87   Qualifying policies: altering method for calculating benefits
Settlements
88   Settlements, etc: chargeable gains
89   Settlements, etc: income
Investment reliefs
91   Venture capital schemes
Employment-related securities
92   Avoidance using options etc
PAYE
94   PAYE: retrospective notional payments
Nuclear decommissioning
99   Amendment of section 29 of the Energy Act 2004
100   Amendment of section 30 of the Energy Act 2004
Accounting practice
101   Securitisation companies

102 Accountancy change: spreading of adjustment

Part 4: Real Estate Investment Trusts

Groups

135 Transfer within group

Miscellaneous

137 Insurance companies

140 Penalties for failure to give notice, etc

143 Housing investment trusts: repeal

General

145 Commencement

Part 7: Pensions

158 Taxable property held by investment-regulated pension schemes

159 Recycling of lump sums

160 Inheritance tax

161 Miscellaneous

Part 9: Miscellaneous Provisions

International tax arrangements

173 International tax enforcement arrangements

175 Arrangements under section 173: recovery of debts

Part 10: Supplementary Provisions

178 Repeals

179 Interpretation

180 Short title

Schedules:

Schedule 1—Group relief where surrendering company not resident in UK

Schedule 3—Claims for relief for research and development

Schedule 5—Film tax relief: further provisions

Schedule 6—Avoidance involving financial arrangements

Schedule 7—Transfer of assets abroad

Schedule 8—Long funding leases of plant or machinery

Schedule 9—Leases of plant or machinery: miscellaneous amendments

Schedule 12—Settlements: amendment of TCGA 1992 etc

Schedule 13—Settlements: amendments to ICTA and ITTOIA 2005 etc

Schedule 14—Investment reliefs: venture capital schemes

Schedule 15—Accountancy change: spreading of adjustment

Schedule 21—Taxable property held by investment-regulated pension schemes

Schedule 22—Pension schemes: inheritance tax

Schedule 23—Pension schemes etc: miscellaneous

Schedule 26—Repeals

PART 3

INCOME TAX, CORPORATION TAX AND CAPITAL GAINS TAX

CHAPTER 1

INCOME TAX AND CORPORATION TAX: CHARGE AND RATE BANDS

Income tax

23 Charge and rates for 2006–07

Income tax shall be charged for the year 2006–07, and for that year—

(a) the starting rate shall be 10%;

(b) the basic rate shall be 22%;

(c) the higher rate shall be 40%.

Corporation tax

24 Charge and main rate for financial year 2007

Corporation tax shall be charged for the financial year 2007 at the rate of 30%.

26 Abolition of corporation tax starting rate and non-corporate distribution rate

(1), (2) (*repeal* TA 1988 ss 13AA, 13AB and Sch A2)

(3) (*amends* TA 1988 s 13A(1))

(4) (*amended* TA 1988 s 468(1A); *repealed by* CTA 2010 s 1181, Sch 3 Pt 1)

(5) (*amended* TA 1988 s 468A(1); *repealed by* CTA 2010 s 1181, Sch 3 Pt 1)

(6) (*amends* FA 1989 Sch 12 para 1(a))

(7) (*amends* FA 1998 Sch 8 para 8(1))

(8) The amendments made by this section have effect for the financial year 2006 and subsequent financial years (but see also subsections (9) to (11)).

(9) In the case of an accounting period (a "straddling period")—

(a) beginning before 1st April 2006, and

(*b*) ending on or after that date,

sections 13AA and 13AB of, and Schedule A2 to, ICTA ("the repealed provisions") apply as if the different parts of the straddling period falling in the different financial years were separate accounting periods.

(10) Where the rate of corporation tax charged on a company's basic profits for any such separate accounting period ending with 31st March 2006 is determined in accordance with any of the repealed provisions, section 13 of ICTA (small companies' relief) also so applies.

(11) For the purpose of treating different parts of the straddling period as separate accounting periods in accordance with subsections (9) and (10), the profits and basic profits of the straddling period are to be apportioned between those separate accounting periods.

CHAPTER 2

RELIEFS FOR BUSINESS

Group relief

27 Group relief where surrendering company not resident in UK

Schedule 1 (which makes provision in relation to group relief where the surrendering company is not resident in the United Kingdom) has effect.

29 Claims for relief for research and development

Schedule 3 (which amends Schedule 18 to FA 1998 in connection with claims for tax relief for expenditure on research and development) has effect.

42 Film tax relief: further provisions

(1) Schedule 5 to this Act contains further provisions about film tax relief.

(2) In that Schedule—

. . .¹

Part 2 provides for the certification of British films for the purposes of the relief;

Part 3 makes provision for claims for the relief;

. . .¹

Amendments—¹ In sub-s (2) words repealed by CTA 2009 ss 1322, 1326, Sch 1 paras 675, 677, Sch 3 Part 1. CTA 2009 applies for accounting periods ending on or after 1 April 2009 (for corporation tax purposes) and for tax years 2009–10 onwards (for income and capital gains tax purposes).

Films: withdrawal of existing reliefs

46 Films: withdrawal of existing reliefs (corporation tax)

(1) Sections 40A to 40D of F(No 2)A 1992 (treatment of expenditure on production or acquisition of film) do not apply—

(*a*) to production expenditure on a film that commences principal photography on or after [1st January 2007]¹;

(*b*) to acquisition expenditure—

(i) on a film that commences principal photography on or after [1st January 2007]¹, or

(ii) that is incurred on or after 1st October 2007 on a film (whenever made).

(2) Section 41 of that Act (preliminary expenditure) does not apply to expenditure incurred after the date on which this Act is passed.

(3) Section 42 of that Act and section 48 of F(No 2)A 1997 (special reliefs for British films) do not apply—

(*a*) to production expenditure on a film that commences principal photography on or after [1st January 2007]¹;

(*b*) to acquisition expenditure—

(i) on a film that commences principal photography on or after [1st January 2007]¹, or

(ii) that is incurred on or after 1st October 2007.

(4) References in this section to expenditure on the acquisition of a film, or to sums received from the disposal of a film, are to expenditure on the acquisition of, or sums received from the disposal of, the original master version of the film.

(5) For this purpose—

(*a*) "original master version" means the original negative, tape or disc;

(*b*) references to the original master version of a film include the original master version of the film soundtrack (if any);

(*c*) references to the original master version include any rights in the original master version that are held or acquired with it.

[(6) The provisions of sections 1181 to 1187 of CTA 2009 apply for the purposes of this section as if this section were contained in Part 15 of that Act.]²

Commentary—*Simon's Taxes* **D7.1202.**

Modification—Corporation Tax (Taxation of Films) (Transitional Provisions) Regulations, SI 2007/1050 (modification of this section in relation to films that commenced principal photography before 1 January 2007 but are not completed before that date).

Amendments—[1] Words in sub-ss (1), (3) substituted by the Finance Act 2006, Section 53(2) (Films and Sound Recordings: Power to alter Dates) Order, SI 2006/3265 art 2 with effect from 29 December 2006.
[2] Sub-s (6) inserted by CTA 2009 s 1322, Sch 1 paras 675, 679. CTA 2009 applies for accounting periods ending on or after 1 April 2009 (for corporation tax purposes) and for tax years 2009–10 onwards (for income and capital gains tax purposes).

47 Films: withdrawal of existing reliefs (income tax)

(1) Sections 134 and 135 of ITTOIA 2005 (treatment of expenditure on production or acquisition of film) do not apply—

- (a) to production expenditure on a film that commences principal photography on or after [1st January 2007][1];
- (b) to acquisition expenditure—
  - (i) on a film that commences principal photography on or after [1st January 2007][1], or
  - (ii) that is incurred on or after 1st October 2007 on a film (whenever made).

(2) Section 137 of that Act (preliminary expenditure) does not apply to expenditure incurred after the date on which this Act is passed.

(3) Sections 138 to 144 of that Act (special reliefs for British films) do not apply—

- (a) to production expenditure on a film that commences principal photography on or after [1st January 2007][1];
- (b) to acquisition expenditure—
  - (i) on a film that commences principal photography on or after [1st January 2007][1], or
  - (ii) that is incurred on or after 1st October 2007.

(4) References in this section to expenditure on the acquisition of a film, or to sums received from the disposal of a film, are to expenditure on the acquisition of, or sums received from the disposal of, the original master version of the film.

(5) For this purpose—

- (a) "original master version" means the original negative, tape or disc;
- (b) references to the original master version of a film include the original master version of the film soundtrack (if any);
- (c) references to the original master version include any rights in the original master version that are held or acquired with it.

[(6) The provisions of sections 1181 to 1187 of CTA 2009 apply for the purposes of this section as if this section were contained in Part 15 of that Act.][2]

Commentary—*Simon's Taxes* **D7.1202.**

Modification—Corporation Tax (Taxation of Films) (Transitional Provisions) Regulations, SI 2007/1050 (modification of this section in relation to films that commenced principal photography before 1 January 2007 but are not completed before that date).

Amendments—[1] Words in sub-ss (1), (3) substituted by the Finance Act 2006, Section 53(2) (Films and Sound Recordings: Power to alter Dates) Order, SI 2006/3265 art 2 with effect from 29 December 2006.
[2] Sub-s (6) inserted by CTA 2009 s 1322, Sch 1 paras 675, 679. CTA 2009 applies for accounting periods ending on or after 1 April 2009 (for corporation tax purposes) and for tax years 2009–10 onwards (for income and capital gains tax purposes).

Corporation tax treatment of sound recordings

Supplementary provisions

53 Films and sound recordings: commencement and power to alter dates

(1) The provisions of this Chapter come into force on such day as the Treasury may appoint by order.

(2) (spent)[1]

Regulations—Finance Act 2006, Section 53(1) (Films and Sound Recordings) (Appointed Day) Order, SI 2006/3399 (appointed day is 1 January 2007).

Amendments—[1] Sub-s (2) repealed by CTA 2009 ss 1322, 1326, Sch 1 paras 675, 682, Sch 3 Part 1. CTA 2009 applies for accounting periods ending on or after 1 April 2009 (for corporation tax purposes) and for tax years 2009–10 onwards (for income and capital gains tax purposes).

CHAPTER 5

PERSONAL TAXATION

Mobile telephones and computers

60 Mobile telephones

(1) (*inserts* ITEPA 2003 s 266(2)(*d*))

(2) (*inserts* ITEPA 2003 s 267(2)(*g*))

(3) (*substitutes* ITEPA 2003 s 319)

(4) This section has effect for the year 2006–07 and subsequent years of assessment.

(5) But the amendment made by subsection (3) does not cause any liability to income tax to arise in respect of the provision of a mobile telephone for an employee, or a member of an employee's family or household, if the mobile telephone was first provided to him before 6th April 2006.

61 Computer equipment

(1) (*repeals* ITEPA 2003 s 320)

(2) This section has effect for the year 2006–07 and subsequent years of assessment.

(3) But it does not cause any liability to income tax to arise in respect of the provision of computer equipment by making it available to an employee, or a member of an employee's family or household, if the computer equipment was first made available to him before 6th April 2006.

Eye care

62 Exemption for employees' eye tests and special glasses

(1) Part 4 of ITEPA 2003 (employment income: exemptions) is amended as follows.

(2) (*inserts* ITEPA 2003 s 320A)

(3) (*inserts* ITEPA 2003 s 266(3)(*f*))

(4) (*inserts* ITEPA 2003 s 267(2)(*h*))

(5) This section has effect for the year 2006–07 and subsequent years of assessment.

Vouchers and tokens

63 Power to exempt use of vouchers or tokens to obtain exempt benefits

(*inserts* ITEPA 2003 s 96A)

Holocaust victims

64 Payments to or in respect of victims of National-Socialist persecution

(1) (*amends* ITTOIA 2005 s 369(3)(*e*))

(2) (*inserts* ITTOIA 2005 s 756A)

(3) (*substitutes* ITTOIA 2005 s 783(2)–(2B) and *amends* ITTOIA 2005 s 783(3))

(4) (*inserts* ITTOIA 2005 s 268A)

(5) If at any time before claims could have been made under any qualifying compensation scheme—
    (*a*) a person beneficially entitled to a qualifying deposit has died, and
    (*b*) no information in respect of that deposit was contained in any account relating to that deceased person under any provision of IHTA 1984,
that deposit is to be ignored for all purposes of IHTA 1984.

(6) For this purpose "qualifying compensation scheme" and "qualifying deposit" have the same meaning as in section 756A of ITTOIA 2005.

(7) Subsection (2) has effect (and is deemed always to have had effect)—
    (*a*) for the year 1996-97, and
    (*b*) subsequent years of assessment.

(8) Subsection (4) has effect (and is deemed always to have had effect) in relation to disposals made on or after 6th April 1996; but no loss accruing on a disposal made before 6th April 2006 is, as a result of that subsection, to cease to be an allowable loss.

(9) In relation to any time before 6th April 2005 (the commencement of ITTOIA 2005)—
    (*a*) the section inserted by subsection (2) is to be treated as if it were inserted into ICTA (and as if, in subsection (5) of that section, "of ICTA" were omitted), and
    (*b*) any reference to that section in any enactment is to be read accordingly.

(10) In relation to the year 2005–06 or any earlier year of assessment, all such adjustments are to be made as are required to give effect to the exemptions conferred as a result of this section.

(11) But the adjustments are to be made only if the person entitled to the exemption makes a claim for the exemption on or before 31st January 2012.

(12) The adjustments may be made by discharge or repayment of tax, the making of an assessment or otherwise.

CHAPTER 6

THE LONDON OLYMPIC GAMES AND PARALYMPIC GAMES

65 London Organising Committee

(1) In this section "LOCOG" means the private company limited by guarantee incorporated on 22nd October 2004 with the Company Number 05267819 and with the name The London Organising Committee of the Olympic Games Limited.

(2) LOCOG shall be exempt from corporation tax.

(3) [The duties to deduct under Chapters 6, 7, 10 and 14 of Part 15 of ITA 2007 (deduction of income tax at source)][1] shall not apply to payments to LOCOG.

(4) A claim may be made for any repayment of income tax required as a result of an exemption conferred by this section.

(5) The Treasury may by regulations provide for subsections (2) to (4) to apply to a wholly-owned subsidiary of LOCOG (within the meaning of section 736 of the Companies Act 1985 (c 6)) as they apply to LOCOG.

(6) Subsection (7) applies if it appears to the Treasury—
    (*a*) that LOCOG has been or may have been, or is or may be, directly or indirectly connected with another person, or
    (*b*) has been or may have been, or is or may be, acting in association or co-operation with another person (whether by virtue of part-ownership, partnership, membership of a group or consortium or in any other way).

(7) The Treasury may make regulations—

    (*a*) restricting the application of a provision of this section to a specified extent;

    (*b*) removing or restricting an exemption or relief under an enactment relating to corporation tax, income tax or capital gains tax;

    (*c*) preventing a loss or expense of a specified kind from being used or treated in a specified way for purposes of corporation tax, income tax or capital gains tax;

    (*d*) wholly or to a specified extent preventing an allowance from being claimed for purposes of corporation tax, income tax or capital gains tax;

    (*e*) providing for a transfer of property to be disregarded, or treated in a specified way, for purposes of corporation tax, income tax or capital gains tax;

    (*f*) providing for specified action taken by LOCOG or the other person to have, or not to have, a specified effect for purposes of corporation tax, income tax or capital gains tax;

    (*g*) providing for an enactment relating to the treatment of groups of companies for purposes of corporation tax, income tax or capital gains tax to be wholly or partly disapplied or to be applied with modifications;

    (*h*) making any other provision which appears to the Treasury to be expedient for the purpose of preventing this section from being used or relied upon otherwise than in connection with the functions of LOCOG under the Host City Contract;

and provision made under any of paragraphs (b) to (h) may relate to LOCOG or to the other person mentioned in subsection (6).

(8) If it appears to the Treasury that LOCOG has undertaken, is undertaking or may undertake activities other than in pursuance of the Host City Contract, the Treasury may make regulations restricting the application of a provision of this section to a specified extent.

(9) Regulations under subsection (5) may include provision of a kind similar to that which may be made under subsection (7) or (8).

Amendments—[1] Words in sub-s (3) substituted by ITA 2007 s 1027, Sch 1 paras 610, 612 with effect for income tax purposes from 6 April 2007, and corporation tax purposes for accounting periods ending after 5 April 2007.

66 Section 65: supplementary

(1) Regulations under section 65(5) to (8)—

    (*a*) may make provision which applies generally or only in specified cases or circumstances,

    (*b*) may make different provision for different cases or circumstances,

    (*c*) may have retrospective effect, and

    (*d*) may include incidental, consequential or transitional provision.

(2) Regulations under section 65 shall be made by statutory instrument.

(3) Regulations under section 65(5)—

    (*a*) shall be subject to annulment in pursuance of a resolution of the House of Commons, or

    (*b*) if they include provision by virtue of section 65(9), may not be made unless a draft has been laid before and approved by resolution of the House of Commons.

(4) Regulations under section 65(7) or (8) may not be made unless a draft has been laid before and approved by resolution of the House of Commons.

(5) In section 65 "the Host City Contract" has the meaning given by section 1 of the London Olympic Games and Paralympic Games Act 2006.

(6) Section 65 shall be treated as having come into force on 22nd October 2004.

(7) The Treasury may by order made by statutory instrument repeal section 65 and this section.

67 International Olympic Committee

(1) The Treasury may make regulations—

    (*a*) providing for the International Olympic Committee to be treated for the purposes of corporation tax as not having a permanent establishment in the United Kingdom;

    (*b*) providing for the International Olympic Committee not to be chargeable to income tax or capital gains tax;

    (*c*) disapplying [the duties to deduct under Chapters 3, 6, 7, 10 and 14 of Part 15 of ITA 2007 (deduction of income tax at source)][1] to payments to the International Olympic Committee.

(2) The Treasury may make regulations—

    (*a*) providing for a specified person or class of person appearing to the Treasury to be owned or controlled by the International Olympic Committee to be treated for the purposes of corporation tax as not having a permanent establishment in the United Kingdom;

    (*b*) providing for a specified person or class of person appearing to the Treasury to be owned or controlled by the International Olympic Committee not to be chargeable to income tax or capital gains tax;

    (*c*) disapplying [the duties to deduct under Chapters 3, 6, 7, 10 and 14 of Part 15 of ITA 2007 (deduction of income tax at source][1] to payments to a specified person or class of person appearing to the Treasury to be owned or controlled by the International Olympic Committee.

(3) Regulations under this section—

    (*a*) may make provision which applies generally or only in specified cases or circumstances,

    (*b*) may make different provision for different cases or circumstances,

    (c) may have retrospective effect, and

    (d) may include incidental, consequential or transitional provision.

(4) Regulations under this section—

    (a) shall be made by statutory instrument, and

    (b) shall be subject to annulment in pursuance of a resolution of the House of Commons.

(5) A claim may be made for any repayment of income tax required as a result of an exemption conferred under this section.

Amendments—[1]   Words in sub-ss (1)(c), (2)(c) substituted by ITA 2007 s 1027, Sch 1 paras 610, 613 with effect for income tax purposes from 6 April 2007, and corporation tax purposes for accounting periods ending after 5 April 2007.

68 Competitors and staff

(1) The Treasury may make regulations—

    (a) exempting specified classes of person from income tax in respect of specified classes of income arising from participation in London Olympic events;

    (b) providing for specified classes of activity undertaken in connection with London Olympic events to be disregarded for purposes of corporation tax, income tax or capital gains tax;

    (c) providing for specified classes of activity in connection with London Olympic events to be disregarded in determining for fiscal purposes whether a person has a permanent establishment in the United Kingdom;

    (d) disapplying [the duties to deduct under Chapters 6, 7, 10 and 14 of Part 15 of ITA 2007 (deduction of income tax at source)][1] in consequence of provision made under paragraphs (a) to (c) above.

(2) The regulations may specify classes of person wholly or partly by reference to—

    (a) residence outside the United Kingdom, determined in such manner as the regulations may provide;

    (b) documents issued or authority given by such persons exercising functions in connection with the London Olympics as the regulations may provide.

(3) Regulations under this section—

    (a) may make provision which applies generally or only in specified cases or circumstances,

    (b) may make different provision for different cases or circumstances, and

    (c) may include incidental, consequential or transitional provision.

(4) Regulations under this section—

    (a) shall be made by statutory instrument, and

    (b) shall be subject to annulment in pursuance of a resolution of the House of Commons.

(5) In this section "London Olympic event" and "the London Olympics" have the meaning given by section 1 of the London Olympic Games and Paralympic Games Act 2006.

RegulationsLondon Olympic Games and Paralympic Games Tax Regulations, SI 2010/2913.

Amendments—[1]   Words in sub-s (1)(d) substituted by ITA 2007 s 1027, Sch 1 paras 610, 614 with effect for income tax purposes from 6 April 2007, and corporation tax purposes for accounting periods ending after 5 April 2007.

CHAPTER 7

CHARGEABLE GAINS

Capital losses

70 Restrictions on companies buying losses or gains

(1) TCGA 1992 is amended as follows.

(2) (*inserts* TCGA 1992 ss 184A–184F)

(3) (*amends* TCGA 1992 Sch 7A para 1(1))

(4) (*repeals* TCGA s 177B and Sch 7AA)

(5) (*amends* TCGA s 213(8H), (8I))

(6) The amendments made by this section, other than subsection (5), have effect for calculating the amount to be included in respect of chargeable gains in a company's total profits for any accounting period ending on or after 5th December 2005.

(7) But, in respect of any such accounting period, those amendments do not have effect in relation to the deduction of any loss from chargeable gains that accrue on any disposal made before 5th December 2005 unless that loss accrues on a disposal made on or after that date.

(8) For the purposes of those amendments, it does not matter whether a qualifying change of ownership in relation to a company occurs—

    (a) before 5th December 2005, or

    (b) on or after that date.

(9) [Subsections (10) to (12) apply][1] so long as each of the following conditions is met—

    (a) at any time ("the relevant time") before 5th December 2005 there is a qualifying change of ownership in relation to a company ("the relevant company") for the purposes of section 184A . . . of TCGA 1992,

    (b) the change of ownership occurs because the relevant company ceases to be a member of a group of companies at the relevant time (whether or not it also occurs for any other reason), (*c*) the principal company of that group has control of the relevant company at the relevant time and [immediately afterwards,][1]

[(*ca*) no qualifying change of ownership occurs at any time in relation to the principal company of that group for the purposes of section 184A of TCGA 1992 directly or indirectly in consequence of, or otherwise in connection with, any arrangements the main purpose, or one of the main purposes, of which is to secure a tax advantage falling within subsection (1)(*d*) of that section, and][1]

(*d*) . . . [1]

(*e*) a qualifying loss for the purposes of section 184A of TCGA 1992 . . . [1] accrues to the relevant company or any other company on a disposal made before 5th December 2005.

[(10) Subsection (2) of that section has effect in relation to that qualifying loss subject to the following modifications.

(11) That subsection has effect as if there were inserted at the end of it "unless the gains accrue to the company on a disposal of a pre-change asset".

(12) That subsection (modified as mentioned above) has effect as if the reference to a pre-change asset included an asset held before the relevant time by any company—

  (*a*) which, immediately before that time, was a member of the same group of companies as the relevant company, and

  (*b*) which, throughout the period beginning with that time and ending immediately after the making of the disposal referred to in that subsection, has remained under the control of the company which was the principal company of that group at the relevant time.

(13) Expressions which are used in subsections (9) to (12) have the same meaning as in sections 184A and 184C of TCGA 1992.][1]

Amendments—[1]   Words in sub-s (9) substituted, repealed and inserted, and sub-ss (10)–(13) substituted for sub-ss (10), (11) by FA 2007 ss 32(1), (4)–(6), (9), 114, Sch 27 Pt 2(4) with effect for disposals made on or after 21 March 2007; but the insertion of sub-s (9)(*ca*) has no effect in relation to disposals made before 9 May 2007.

71 Other avoidance involving losses accruing to companies

(1) (*inserts* TCGA 1992 ss 184G–184I)

(2), (3) (*amended* FA 1998 Sch 18 paras 25(1), 42(2A); *repealed by* TIOPA 2010 s 503, Sch 10 Pt 12)

(4) The amendments made by this section have effect in relation to chargeable gains accruing on any disposal that is made on or after 5th December 2005.

72 Repeal of s 106 of TCGA 1992

(1) (*repeals* TCGA 1992 s 106)

(2) (*amends* TCGA 1992 ss 104(2)(*b*), 105(2)(*b*), (*c*), 108(8), 110(1)(*b*), and FA 2000 Sch 15 para 93(6))

(3) The amendments made by this section have effect in relation to any disposal that is made on or after 5th December 2005.

Insurance policies and annuities

73 Policies of insurance and non-deferred annuities

(1) TCGA 1992 is amended as follows.

(2) (*substitutes* TCGA 1992 s 204)

(3) (*amends* TCGA 1992 s 237)

(4) The amendments made by this section have effect in relation to disposals made on or after 5th December 2005.

Capital gains tax

74 Exception to "bed and breakfasting" rules etc

(1) TCGA 1992 is amended as follows.

(2) (*inserts* TCGA 1992 s 106A(5A))

(3) (*inserts* TCGA 1992 s 288(7B))

(4) (*repeals* TCGA 1992 ss 10A(9A), 83A(5))

(5) The amendment made by subsection (2) has effect in relation to any acquisition made at any time on or after 22nd March 2006.

(6) The amendments made by subsections (3) and (4) have effect in relation to any time on or after 22nd March 2006.

CHAPTER 8
AVOIDANCE: MISCELLANEOUS
Film partnerships
Financial instruments

76 Avoidance involving financial arrangements

Schedule 6 (which makes provision in relation to tax avoidance involving financial arrangements) has effect.

International matters

78 Controlled foreign companies and treaty non-resident companies

(1) Section 90 of FA 2002 (controlled foreign companies and treaty non-resident companies) is amended as follows.

(2) (*substitutes* FA 2002 s 90(2)(*b*))

(3) (*inserts* FA 2002 s 90(3)–(8))

79 Transfer of assets abroad

Schedule 7 (which makes amendments of, or relating to, Chapter 3 of Part 17 of ICTA (transfer of assets abroad)) has effect.

Pre-owned assets

80 Restriction of exemption from charge to income tax

(1) Schedule 15 to FA 2004 (charge to income tax on benefits received by former owner of property) is amended as follows.

(2) (*amends* FA 2004 Sch 15 para 11(9) and *inserts* FA 2004 Sch 15 para 11(11)–(13))

(3) (*amends* FA 2004 Sch 15 para 21(2)(*b*) and *inserts* 21(3)(*a*)(iii))

(4) (*amends* FA 2004 Sch 15 para 22(2)(*b*))

(5) The amendments made by this section have effect—

    (*a*) for the part of the year 2005–06 beginning with 5th December 2005, and

    (*b*) for the year 2006–07 and subsequent years of assessment.

(6) If—

    (*a*) paragraph 11 of Schedule 15 to FA 2004 ceases, in consequence of the amendments made by this section, to apply to a person in relation to any property, and

    (*b*) that person dies before the day on which this Act is passed without making an election under paragraph 21 or 22 of that Schedule in relation to that property,

his personal representatives (within the meaning of IHTA 1984) may make any election under paragraph 21 or 22 of that Schedule that he might have made.

(7) If—

    (*a*) in consequence of the amendments made by this section a person makes an election under paragraph 21 or 22 of Schedule 15 to FA 2004,

    (*b*) that person dies before the day on which this Act is passed, and

    (*c*) an amount of inheritance tax would (but for this subsection) fall due before that day,

that amount is to be treated instead as falling due at the end of the period of 14 days beginning with that day.

(8) This section is deemed to have come into force on 5th December 2005.

CHAPTER 9
MISCELLANEOUS PROVISIONS
Leasing of plant or machinery

81 Leases of plant or machinery

(1) Schedule 8 (which makes provision in relation to leases of plant or machinery) has effect.

(2) Schedule 9 (which makes miscellaneous amendments relating to such leases) has effect.

Sale of lessors

83 Restrictions on use of losses etc: leasing partnerships

(*1*) (*amended* TA 1988 s 403(4); *repealed by* CTA 2010 ss 1177, 1181, Sch 1 paras 480, 482, Sch 3 Pt 1)

(*2*) (*inserted* TA 1988 ss 785ZA, 785ZB; *repealed by* CTA 2010 ss 1177, 1181, Sch 1 paras 480, 482, Sch 3 Pt 1)

(3) (*inserts* CAA 2001 s 261A)

(4) The amendments made by this section have effect in relation to any business carried on by a company in partnership in any accounting period of the partnership ending on or after 5th December 2005.

(5) But, in relation to any accounting period of the partnership beginning before 5th December 2005 and ending on or after that date, those amendments have effect only if—

    (*a*) the company starts to carry on the business in partnership on or after that date, or

    (*b*) a relevant change in the interest of the company in the business occurs on or after that date.

(6) A relevant change in the interest of the company in the business occurs at any time if—

    (*a*) immediately before that time its interest in the business during any accounting period of the partnership is determined on an allowable basis (within the meaning given by [section 887 of the Corporation Tax Act 2010][1]), and

    (*b*) immediately after that time its interest in the business during that period is not so determined.

Amendment—[1] In sub-s (6) (*a*) words substituted for words "section 785ZA of ICTA" by CTA 2010 ss 1177, 1181, Sch 1 paras 480, 482, Sch 3 Pt 1. CTA 2010 has effect for corporation tax purposes for accounting periods ending on or after 1 April 2010, and for income and capital gains tax purposes for the tax year 2010–11 and subsequent tax years.

84 Disposal of plant or machinery subject to lease where income retained

(1) CAA 2001 is amended as follows.

(2) (*amends* table in CAA 2001 s 66)

(3) (*inserts* CAA 2001 ss 228K–228M)

(4) (*amended* table in CAA 2001 Sch 1, Part 1; *repealed by* FA 2009 s 126(6)(*c*))

(5) The amendments made by this section have effect in relation to any disposal made on or after 5th December 2005.

(6) But any rentals that are receivable by the lessor before 22nd March 2006 are to be left out of account in calculating the income of the lessor's leasing business for corporation tax purposes.

85 Restrictions on effect of elections under section 266 of CAA 2001

(1) CAA 2001 is amended as follows.

(2) (*amends* CAA 2001 s 266)

(3) (*inserts* CAA 2001 s 267(6))

(4) (*inserts* CAA 2001 s 267A)

(5) The amendments made by this section have effect in relation to any succession occurring on or after 5th December 2005.

Insurance companies and policyholders

87 Qualifying policies: altering method for calculating benefits

(1) Schedule 15 to ICTA (provisions for determining whether an insurance policy is a "qualifying policy" for the purposes of the Tax Acts) is amended as follows.

(2) (*inserts* TA 1988 Sch 15 para 18(3)(*d*))

(3) (*inserts* TA 1988 Sch 15 para 22(3)(*c*))

(4) In the case of a variation effected as part of, or in connection with, an insurance business transfer scheme, the amendments made by this section are deemed always to have had effect.

(5) In any other case, the amendments made by this section have effect in relation to variations effected on or after 7th October 2005.

(6) In this section an "insurance business transfer scheme" means—

    (*a*) a scheme falling within section 105 of the Financial Services and Markets Act 2000 (c 8),

    (*b*) a scheme sanctioned by a court under Part 1 of Schedule 2C to the Insurance Companies Act 1982 (c 50), or

    (*c*) a scheme sanctioned by a court under section 49 of that Act or under any earlier enactment corresponding to that section,

and for the purposes of this subsection any reference to an enactment is a reference to the enactment as it had effect from time to time.

Settlements

88 Settlements, etc: chargeable gains

Schedule 12 (which amends TCGA 1992 in respect of settlors and trustees of settlements and makes other minor and consequential amendments) shall have effect.

89 Settlements, etc: income

Schedule 13 (which amends ICTA and ITTOIA 2005 in respect of settlors and trustees of settlements and makes other minor and consequential amendments) shall have effect.

Investment reliefs

91 Venture capital schemes

(1) Schedule 14 contains amendments of the provisions relating to—

    . . . .²,

    . . .¹

    the corporate venturing scheme.

(2) Those amendments have effect as mentioned in that Schedule.

Amendments—¹   Words in sub-s (1) repealed by ITA 2007 s 1031, Sch 3 Pt 1 with effect for income tax purposes from 6 April 2007, and corporation tax purposes for accounting periods ending after 5 April 2007.

²   Words in sub-s (1) repealed by ITA 2007 s 1031, Sch 3 Pt 2 with effect in relation to shares issued after 5 April 2007.

Employment-related securities

92 Avoidance using options etc

(1) Section 420 of ITEPA 2003 (meaning of securities etc) is amended as follows.

(2) (*amends* ITEPA 2003 s 420(1)(*f*))

(3) (*amends* ITEPA 2003 s 420(5)(*e*))

(4) (*amends* ITEPA 2003 s 420(8))

(5) This section has effect in relation to options acquired on or after 2nd December 2004; but subsection (4) also has effect in relation to an option acquired before that date where something is done on or after that date as part of the arrangements under which it was made available.

PAYE

94 PAYE: retrospective notional payments

(1) ITEPA 2003 is amended as follows.

(2) (*amends* ITEPA 2003 s 222(1)(*c*), (2), and *inserts* ITEPA 2003 s 222(4))

(3) (*amends* ITEPA 2003 s 684(2))

(4) (*amends* ITEPA 2003 s 710(7), and *inserts* ITEPA 2003 s 710(7A))

(5) The provisions of ITEPA 2003 amended by this section have effect in relation to notional payments treated by virtue of this Act as made before the date on which this Act is passed as if for the references to the date on which the Act is passed in—

    (*a*) section 222(4)(*a*),

    (*b*) paragraph (*a*) of the definition of "the relevant time" in section 684(2), and

    (*c*) section 710(7A)(*a*), (*b*) and (*c*),

there were substituted references to such date as the Commissioners for Her Majesty's Revenue and Customs may by order made by statutory instrument appoint.

Regulations—Finance Act 2006 (Section 94(5)) (PAYE—Retrospective Notional Payments—Appointment of Substituted Date) Order, SI 2007/1081 (for the purposes of sub-s (5) 6 April 2007 is appointed as the date substituted for the date on which FA 2006 was passed).

Nuclear decommissioning

99 Amendment of section 29 of the Energy Act 2004

(1) Section 29 of the Energy Act 2004 (c 20) (disregard for tax purposes of cancellation etc of decommissioning provisions) is amended as follows.

(2) (*amends* EA 2004 s 29(1))

(3) (*substitutes* EA 2004 s 29(3), (4))

(4) (*amends* EA 2004 s 29(5))

(5) (*inserts* EA 2004 s 29(5A))

(6) The amendments made by this section have effect in relation to accounting periods of a BNFL company ending on or after 22nd March 2006.

"BNFL company" has the same meaning as in section 29 of the Energy Act 2004 (c 20) as amended by this section.

Commentary—*Simon's Taxes* D1.369.

100 Amendment of section 30 of the Energy Act 2004

(1) Section 30 of the Energy Act 2004 (disregard for tax purposes of decommissioning provisions recognised by Nuclear Decommissioning Authority) is amended as follows.

(2) (*amends* EA 2004 s 30(1))

(3) (*substitutes* EA 2004 s 30(3))

(4) (*amends* EA 2004 s 30(4))

(5) (*amends* EA 2004 s 30(5))

(6) The amendments made by this section have effect in relation to accounting periods of the Nuclear Decommissioning Authority ending on or after 22nd March 2006.

Commentary—*Simon's Taxes* D1.369.

Accounting practice

101 Securitisation companies

(1) Section 83 of FA 2005 (application of accounting standards to securitisation companies) is amended as follows.

(2) (*amends* FA 2005 s 83(1)(*b*))

(3) (*inserts* FA 2005 s 83(3)(*e*))

(4) (*amends* FA 2005 s 83(5))

(5) (*amended* FA 2005 s 84); *repealed by* CTA 2010 s 1181 Sch 3 Pt 1.

(6) The amendments in this section shall be deemed always to have had effect, subject as follows.

(7) A company that would have been a securitisation company for the purposes of section 83 of FA 2005 if the amendments in this section had not been made, being either—

    (*a*) a note-issuing company that—

        (i) had become party as debtor to the capital market investment before 22nd March 2006, or

        (ii) had before that date entered into a binding arrangement to become a party as debtor to the capital market investment, or

    (*b*) another description of securitisation company by virtue of its connection with a company within paragraph (*a*),

may elect to be taxed as if the amendments in subsection (3) had not been made.

(8) Any such election must be made not later than 31st March 2007 and has effect for all relevant periods of account.

102 Accountancy change: spreading of adjustment

(1) Schedule 15 to this Act (accountancy change: spreading of adjustment) has effect.

(2) In that Schedule—

Part 1 makes provision for income tax purposes, and

Part 2 makes provision for corporation tax purposes.

(3) (*amends TA 1988 s 21B*)

PART 4
REAL ESTATE INVESTMENT TRUSTS

Regulations—Real Estate Investment Trusts (Breach of Conditions) Regulations, SI 2006/2864.
Real Estate Investment Trusts (Financial Statements of Group Real Estate Investment Trusts) Regulations, SI 2006/2865.
Real Estate Investment Trusts (Assessment and Recovery of Tax) Regulations, SI 2006/2867.

Introduction

135 Transfer within group
(*inserts TCGA 1992 s 171(2)(da)*)

Miscellaneous

137 Insurance companies
(*inserts TCGA 1992 s 212(1)(c)*)

140 Penalties for failure to give notice, etc
(*inserts words into second column of Table in* TMA 1970 s 98(5))

143 Housing investment trusts: repeal
(*repeals FA 1996 s 160 and Sch 30*)

General

145 Commencement
(1) . . . [1]

(2) Section 143 shall have effect in relation to accounting periods beginning on or after the day on which this Act is passed.

Amendment—[1] Sub-s (1) repealed by CTA 2010 ss 1177, 1181, Sch 1 paras 480, 483, Sch 3 Pt 1. CTA 2010 has effect for corporation tax purposes for accounting periods ending on or after 1 April 2010, and for income and capital gains tax purposes for the tax year 2010–11 and subsequent tax years.

PART 7
PENSIONS

158 Taxable property held by investment-regulated pension schemes
(1) Schedule 21 (taxable property held by investment-regulated pension schemes) has effect.

(2) This section and that Schedule are deemed to have come into force on 6th April 2006.

159 Recycling of lump sums
(1) (*inserts FA 2004 Sch 29 para 3A*)

(2) This section is deemed to have come into force on 6th April 2006.

160 Inheritance tax
(1) Schedule 22 (provisions about inheritance tax in relation to registered pension schemes) has effect.

(2) This section and that Schedule are deemed to have come into force on 6th April 2006.

161 Miscellaneous
(1) Schedule 23 (miscellaneous amendments relating to pension schemes etc) has effect.

(2) This section and that Schedule are deemed to have come into force on 6th April 2006.

PART 9
MISCELLANEOUS PROVISIONS

International tax arrangements

173 International tax enforcement arrangements
(1) If Her Majesty by Order in Council declares that—

(*a*) arrangements relating to international tax enforcement which are specified in the Order have been made in relation to any territory or territories outside the United Kingdom, and

(*b*) it is expedient that those arrangements have effect,

those arrangements have effect (and do so in spite of anything in any enactment or instrument).

(2) For the purposes of subsection (1) arrangements relate to international tax enforcement if they relate to any or all of the following—

(*a*) the exchange of information foreseeably relevant to the administration, enforcement or recovery of any UK tax or foreign tax;

(*b*) the recovery of debts relating to any UK tax or foreign tax;

(c) the service of documents relating to any UK tax or foreign tax.

(3) In this section—

"UK tax" means any tax or duty imposed under the domestic law of the United Kingdom, and "foreign tax" means any tax or duty imposed under the law of the territory, or any of the territories, in relation to which the arrangements have been made.

(4) Where any arrangements have effect by virtue of this section, no obligation of secrecy (whether imposed by statute or otherwise)—

(a) prevents any Minister of the Crown, or person with responsibilities in any government department, from disclosing to the Commissioners for Her Majesty's Revenue and Customs or any authorised Revenue and Customs official any information which is authorised to be disclosed in accordance with the arrangements to any authorised officer of the authorities of the territory, or any of the territories, in relation to which the arrangements have been made, or

(b) prevents the Commissioners for Her Majesty's Revenue and Customs or any authorised Revenue and Customs official from disclosing to any such authorised officer any information which is authorised to be so disclosed in accordance with the arrangements.

(5) But neither the Commissioners for Her Majesty's Revenue and Customs nor any authorised Revenue and Customs official may disclose any information in pursuance of any arrangements having effect by virtue of this section to any authorised officer of the authorities of the territory, or any of the territories, in relation to which the arrangements have been made unless satisfied that the authorities of the territory concerned are bound by, or have undertaken to observe, rules of confidentiality with respect to the information which are not less strict than those applying to it in the United Kingdom.

(6) An Order in Council made under this section revoking an earlier such Order may contain any transitional provisions that appear appropriate.

(7) An Order under this section is not to be submitted to Her Majesty in Council unless a draft of the Order has been laid before and approved by a resolution of the House of Commons.

(8) Any provisions which—

(a) are included in an Order in Council made under any of the provisions specified in subsection (10),

(b) are in force immediately before the passing of this Act, and

(c) could have been included in an Order in Council under this section had the Order in Council been made after that time,

have effect after that time as if included in an Order in Council under this section.

(9) If any such provisions relate to arrangements covering UK taxes or foreign taxes (or both) other than those in relation to which the Order in Council had effect, the provisions also have effect after the passing of this Act (by virtue of subsection (8)) in relation to those other UK taxes or foreign taxes (or both).

(10) The provisions referred to in subsection (8)(a) are—

(a) sections 788 and 815C of ICTA (international arrangements relating to income tax, corporation tax and capital gains tax and analogous foreign taxes), and

(b) sections 158 and 220A of IHTA 1984 (international arrangements relating to inheritance tax and analogous foreign taxes).

(11) In this section "Revenue and Customs official" has the same meaning as in section 18 of the Commissioners for Revenue and Customs Act 2005 (c 11) (confidentiality).

Regulations—International Mutual Administrative Assistance in Tax Matters Order 2007, SI 2007/2126.

Prospective amendments—Sub-ss (4)–(5) to be substituted for existing sub-ss (4), (5) by the Taxes (Amendments) (EU Exit) Regulations, SI 2019/689 reg 14(1), (2) with effect from Implementation Period completion day (see EU(WA)A 2020 Sch 5 para 1(1)). Sub-ss (4)–(5) to read as follows—

"(4) Where any arrangements have effect by virtue of this section, no obligation of secrecy (whether imposed by statute or otherwise) prevents a public authority or anyone acting on its behalf from making a disclosure to the Commissioners for Her Majesty's Revenue and Customs —

(a) for the purpose of giving effect, or enabling effect to be given, to the arrangements, or

(b) which is authorised in accordance with the arrangements.

(4A) Where any arrangements have effect by virtue of this section, no obligation of secrecy (whether imposed by statute or otherwise) prevents the Commissioners for Her Majesty's Revenue and Customs or any other authorised Revenue and Customs official from making a disclosure to a person outside the United Kingdom—

(a) for the purpose of giving effect, or enabling effect to be given, to the arrangements, or

(b) which is authorised in accordance with the arrangements.

(5) But information may not be disclosed by virtue of subsection (4A) unless the person making the disclosure is satisfied that the recipient of the information—

(a) will only use the information in a manner consistent with the purposes of the arrangements, and (*b*) is bound by, or has undertaken to observe, rules of confidentiality with respect to the information which are not less strict than those applying to it in the United Kingdom.".

175 Arrangements under section 173: recovery of debts

(1) The Treasury may by regulations make provision for the recovery in the United Kingdom of debts relating to any relevant foreign tax pursuant to arrangements having effect by virtue of section 173.

(2) "Relevant foreign tax" means any tax or duty—

(*a*) imposed under the law of a territory in relation to which such arrangements have been made, and

(*b*) covered by the arrangements.

(3) Regulations under this section may make provision for the taking of action to recover debts relating to any relevant foreign tax by way of legal proceedings, distress, diligence or otherwise.

(4) Such provision may in particular be made by applying, with any appropriate modifications, any enactment or rule of law that applies in relation to the recovery of any tax or duty imposed under the domestic law of the United Kingdom (including any enactment relating to penalties or interest on unpaid amounts).

(5) The power to make regulations under this section is exercisable by statutory instrument.

(6) A statutory instrument containing regulations under this section is subject to annulment in pursuance of a resolution of the House of Commons.

Regulations—Recovery of Foreign Taxes Regulations, SI 2007/3507.

Disclosure of information
177

(*see Orange Tax Handbook, VAT section*)

PART 10
SUPPLEMENTARY PROVISIONS

178 Repeals

(1) The enactments mentioned in Schedule 26 (which include provisions that are spent or of no practical utility) are repealed to the extent specified.

(2) The repeals specified in that Schedule have effect subject to the commencement provisions and savings contained or referred to in the notes set out in that Schedule.

179 Interpretation

In this Act—

"ALDA 1979" means the Alcoholic Liquor Duties Act 1979 (c 4);

"CAA 2001" means the Capital Allowances Act 2001 (c 2);

["CTA 2009" means the Corporation Tax Act 2009;][2]

"FA", followed by a year, means the Finance Act of that year;

"F(No 2)A", followed by a year, means the Finance (No 2) Act of that year;

"HODA 1979" means the Hydrocarbon Oil Duties Act 1979 (c 5);

"ICTA" means the Income and Corporation Taxes Act 1988 (c 1);

"IHTA 1984" means the Inheritance Tax Act 1984 (c 51);

["ITA 2007" means the Income Tax Act 2007;][1]

"ITEPA 2003" means the Income Tax (Earnings and Pensions) Act 2003 (c 1);

"ITTOIA 2005" means the Income Tax (Trading and Other Income) Act 2005 (c 5);

"OTA 1975" means the Oil Taxation Act 1975 (c 22);

"TCGA 1992" means the Taxation of Chargeable Gains Act 1992 (c 12);

"TMA 1970" means the Taxes Management Act 1970 (c 9);

"VATA 1994" means the Value Added Tax Act 1994 (c 23);

"VERA 1994" means the Vehicle Excise and Registration Act 1994 (c 22).

Amendments—[1] Entry inserted by ITA 2007 s 1027, Sch 1 paras 610, 622 with effect for income tax purposes from 6 April 2007, and corporation tax purposes for accounting periods ending after 5 April 2007.

[2] Entry inserted by CTA 2009 s 1322, Sch 1 paras 675, 692. CTA 2009 applies for accounting periods ending on or after 1 April 2009 (for corporation tax purposes) and for tax years 2009–10 onwards (for income and capital gains tax purposes).

180 Short title

This Act may be cited as the Finance Act 2006.

SCHEDULES

SCHEDULE 1

GROUP RELIEF WHERE SURRENDERING COMPANY NOT RESIDENT IN UK

Section 27

PART 2

AMENDMENTS OF OTHER ENACTMENTS

Claims for group relief

8   (*inserts* FA 1998 Sch 18 para 77)

PART 3

COMMENCEMENT

Commencement

9—(1) The amendments made by this Schedule, other than those made by paragraphs 4(2) and 5, have effect—

    (*a*) in relation to any accounting period of a claimant company beginning on or after 1st April 2006, and

    (*b*) in relation to any period ("the loss period") beginning on or after 1st April 2006 in which any loss or other amount arises to a non-resident company.

(2) If an accounting period (a "straddling period") of a claimant company begins before 1st April 2006 and ends on or after that date—

    (*a*) so much of the straddling period as falls before 1st April 2006, and

    (*b*) so much of the straddling period as falls on or after that date,

are to be treated as separate accounting periods for the purposes of the amendments made by this Schedule other than those made by paragraphs 4(2) and 5.

(3) The amount of the claimant company's profits for the straddling period is to be attributed, on an apportionment in accordance with this paragraph, to those separate accounting periods.

(4) If the loss period of the non-resident company begins before 1st April 2006 and ends on or after that date—

    (*a*) so much of the loss period as falls before 1st April 2006, and

    (*b*) so much of the loss period as falls on or after that date,

are to be treated as separate periods for the purposes of the amendments made by this Schedule other than those made by paragraphs 4(2) and 5.

(5) The amount of the loss or other amount of the non-resident company for the loss period is to be attributed, on an apportionment in accordance with this paragraph, to those separate periods.

(6) Any apportionment under this paragraph is to be made on a just and reasonable basis.

SCHEDULE 3

CLAIMS FOR RELIEF FOR RESEARCH AND DEVELOPMENT

Section 29

Introductory

1   Schedule 18 to FA 1998 (company tax returns, assessments and related matters) is amended as follows.

Claims to be included in return

2—(1) Paragraph 10 (other claims and elections to be included in return) is amended as follows.

(2) (*amends* FA 1998 Sch 18 para 10(2))

(3) (*inserted* FA 1998 Sch 18 para 10(2B); *repealed by* CTA 2009 s 1326, Sch 3 Pt 1)

(4) (*amended* FA 1998 Sch 18 para 10(3); *repealed by* CTA 2009 s 1326, Sch 3 Pt 1)

Claims for R&D tax relief

3   (*amends* FA 1998 Sch 18 para 83A)

4   (*amends* FA 1998 Sch 18 paras 83B–83E)

5   (*amends* FA 1998 Sch 18, Part 9A title)

Commencement and transitional provision

10   The amendments made by paragraphs 2 to 9 have effect in relation to accounting periods ending on or after 31st March 2006.

11—(1) This paragraph applies where a company is entitled to relief under Schedule 20 to FA 2000 or Schedule 12 or 13 to FA 2002 for any accounting period of the company falling within sub-paragraph (2).

(2) An accounting period of a company falls within this sub-paragraph if it ends on a day falling after 31st March 2002 but before 31st March 2006.

(3) Sub-paragraphs (4) and (5) apply to any claim by the company for such relief for an accounting period falling within sub-paragraph (2), other than a claim by the company for—

    (*a*)   an R&D tax credit under Schedule 20 to FA 2000, or

    (*b*)   a tax credit under Schedule 13 to FA 2002.

(4) A claim to which this sub-paragraph applies may be made, amended or withdrawn by the company at any time up to and including 31st March 2008.

(5) A claim to which this sub-paragraph applies may be made, amended or withdrawn by the company at a later date if an officer of Revenue and Customs allows it.

SCHEDULE 5
FILM TAX RELIEF: FURTHER PROVISIONS
Section 42

PART 2
CERTIFICATION OF BRITISH FILMS FOR PURPOSES OF FILM TAX RELIEF

15   (*substitutes* FiA 1985 s 6)

Modification—Corporation Tax (Taxation of Films) (Transitional Provisions) Regulations, SI 2007/1050 (new para 15A inserted in relation to films that commenced principal photography before 1 January 2007 but are not completed before that date).

16   (*amends* FiA 1985 Sch 1 heading)

17   (*substitutes* FiA 1985 Sch 1 para 1)

Modification—Corporation Tax (Taxation of Films) (Transitional Provisions) Regulations, SI 2007/1050 (this paragraph modified in relation to films that commenced principal photography before 1 January 2007 but are not completed before that date).

18   (*substitutes* FiA 1985 Sch 1 para 2)

19   (*substitutes* FiA 1985 Sch 1 para 3)

Modification—Corporation Tax (Taxation of Films) (Transitional Provisions) Regulations, SI 2007/1050 (this paragraph modified in relation to films that commenced principal photography before 1 January 2007 but are not completed before that date).

20   (*substitutes* FiA 1985 Sch 1 para 4(1) *for* sub-paras (1) to (3))

Modification—Corporation Tax (Taxation of Films) (Transitional Provisions) Regulations, SI 2007/1050 (new paragraphs 20A, 20B inserted in relation to films that commenced principal photography before 1 January 2007 but are not completed before that date).

21   (*substitutes* FiA 1985 Sch 1 para 5(1) and *inserts* FiA 1985 Sch 1 para 5(3))

22   (*amends* FiA 1985 Sch 1 para 9)

23   (*amends* FiA 1985 Sch 1 para 10)

PART 3
CONSEQUENTIAL AMENDMENTS
Interest

26—(1) Section 826 of ICTA (interest on tax overpaid etc) is amended as follows.

(2) (*inserts* TA 1988 s 826(1)(*f*))

(3) (*inserts* TA 1988 s 826(3C))

(4) (*amends* TA 1988 s 826(8A))

(5) (*amends* TA 1988 s 826(8BA))

Claim to be made in tax return

27   (*inserts* FA 1998 Sch 18 para 10(4))

Recovery of excessive film tax credit

28   (*amends* FA 1998 Sch 18 para 52(2), (5))

Claims for film tax credits

29 (*inserts* FA 1998 Sch 18 Part 9D)

SCHEDULE 6
AVOIDANCE INVOLVING FINANCIAL ARRANGEMENTS
Section 76

Repeal of rent factoring provisions

1—(1) (repeals TA 1988 ss 43A–43G)
(2) The amendment made by this paragraph has effect in relation to transactions entered into on or after 6th June 2006.

Dividend stripping: subsequent sales etc of rights to receive dividends etc

2—(1), (2) (*repeal* TA 1988 s 730(3))
(3) The amendment made by this paragraph has effect in relation to sales or other realisations on or after 20th January 2006.

Structured finance arrangements: chargeable gains treatment of acquisitions and disposals

9—(1) (*inserts* TCGA 1992 s 263D)
(2) The amendment made by this paragraph has effect in relation to disposals made on or after 6th June 2006.
(3) The amendment made by this paragraph also has effect in relation to any disposal made by a person before that date if the person makes a claim to that effect under this sub-paragraph.

Loan relationships: mandatory convertibles

10—*(1)–(3)* (*inserted* FA 1996 s 81(2)(c); *repealed by* CTA 2009 s 1326, Sch 3 Pt 1)
(4) The following provisions of this paragraph apply for the purposes of TCGA 1992 if—
  (*a*) a company is a party to a relationship on 22nd March 2006,
  (*b*) the relationship becomes a loan relationship on that date for the purposes of Chapter 2 of Part 4 of FA 1996 as a result of the amendments made by this paragraph,
  (*c*) the relationship is a creditor relationship of the company, and
  (*d*) immediately before that date the asset representing the relationship was a chargeable asset in relation to the company.
(5) The company is treated as if—
  (*a*) it had made a disposal of the asset representing the relationship immediately before 22nd March 2006, and
  (*b*) the disposal had been for a consideration equal to the fair value of the asset at that time (within the meaning given by section 103(1) of FA 1996).
(6) Any chargeable gain or loss accruing to the company on the disposal is treated as accruing to the company when it ceases to be a party to the relationship.
(7) For the purposes of this paragraph an asset is a chargeable asset in relation to the company at any time if any gain accruing to it on the disposal of the asset at that time would be a chargeable gain for the purposes of TCGA 1992.

SCHEDULE 7
TRANSFER OF ASSETS ABROAD
Section 79
INCOME AND CORPORATION TAXES ACT 1988
ITTOIA 2005

Gains from contracts for life insurance etc

7—(1)–(5) (*amend* ITTOIA 2005 s 468)
(5) The amendments made by this paragraph apply in relation to gains treated as arising on or after 5th December 2005.

SCHEDULE 8

LONG FUNDING LEASES OF PLANT OR MACHINERY

Section 81

PART 1

CAPITAL ALLOWANCES

Introductory

1   CAA 2001 is amended as follows.

Use for other qualifying activity of plant or machinery previously used for long funding leasing

2   (*inserts* CAA 2001 s 13A)

Expenditure on plant or machinery for long funding leasing not to be qualifying expenditure

3   (*inserts* CAA 2001 s 34A)

General exclusions applying to certain sections

4   (*amends* CAA 2001 s 46(2))

Commencement of leasing under long funding lease: disposal events and disposal values

5   (*amends* CAA 2001 s 61)

Lessee under long funding lease: capital allowances, disposal events and disposal values

6   (*inserts* CAA 2001 ss 70A–70E)

Interpretation of provisions relating to long funding leases

7   (*inserts* CAA 2001 Pt 2, Ch 6A, ss 70F–70YJ)

Cases in which short-life asset treatment is ruled out

8   (*amends* Table in CAA 2001 s 84)

Fixtures

9—(1) (*inserts* CAA 2001 s 172(2A))
(2) (*inserts* CAA 2001 s 172A)

PART 3

INCOME TAX

Introductory

12   ITTOIA 2005 is amended as follows.

Special rules for long funding leases

13   (*inserts* ITTOIA 2005 Pt 2 Ch 10A, ss 148A–148J)

Application of Chapter 10A for calculating the profits of a property business

14   (*amends* Table in ITTOIA 2005 s 272(2))

PART 4

COMMENCEMENT AND TRANSITIONAL PROVISIONS

Commencement

15—(1) The amendments made by this Schedule have effect in the case of a lease if—
    (*a*) Condition A is met, or
    (*b*) if Condition A is not met, Condition B is met,
unless the lease was finalised (see paragraph 23) before 21st July 2005 and on 17th May 2006 the lessor was within the charge to tax.

As respects any time before 18th May 2006, this sub-paragraph has effect with the omission of the words "and on 17th May 2006 the lessor was within the charge to tax".

This sub-paragraph is subject to sub-paragraphs (5) and (6).

(2) Condition A is that—

    (*a*) the lease is finalised on or after 1st April 2006, or

    (*b*) the commencement of the term of the lease is on or after that date,

and the lease is not an excepted lease (see paragraph 17).

(3) Condition B is that—

    (*a*) the commencement of the term of the lease was before 1st April 2006, but

    (*b*) the plant or machinery is on or after that date brought into use for the purposes of a qualifying activity carried on by the person concerned.

(4) The amendments made by this Schedule also have effect in relation to a lease, in the case of the lessor, if—

    (*a*) an election under paragraph 16 is in force in the case of the lease, and

    (*b*) the election has effect in the case of the lessor.

(5) Where the amendments made by this Schedule do not have effect in relation to a lease in the case of the lessor but—

    (*a*) there is a transfer of plant or machinery,

    (*b*) immediately before the transfer, the lessor is within the charge to tax, and

    (*c*) the transfer is in circumstances such that, if the amendments made by this Schedule did apply in relation to the lease, section 70W(4)(*b*) of CAA 2001 (transfers, assignments etc by lessor) would have effect in relation to the new lessor to treat the new lease as a lease which is not a long funding lease,

the amendments made by this Schedule do not have effect in relation to the new lease in the case of the new lessor.

In this sub-paragraph—

    "the new lease" means the lease that would be the new lease for the purposes of section 70W of CAA 2001, if that section applied;

    "the new lessor" means the person who would be the new lessor for the purposes of that section, if that section applied;

and section 70W(7) of CAA 2001 (construction of references to transfer of plant or machinery) also has effect for the purposes of this sub-paragraph.

(6) Where the amendments made by this Schedule do not have effect in relation to a lease in the case of the lessee but—

    (*a*) there is a transfer of plant or machinery,

    (*b*) immediately before the transfer, the lessee is within the charge to tax, and

    (*c*) the transfer is in circumstances such that, if the amendments made by this Schedule did apply in relation to the lease, section 70X(4)(*b*) of CAA 2001 (transfers, assignments etc by lessee) would have effect in relation to the new lessee to treat the new lease as a lease which is not a long funding lease,

the amendments made by this Schedule do not have effect in relation to the new lease in the case of the new lessee.

In this sub-paragraph—

    "the new lease" means the lease that would be the new lease for the purposes of section 70X of CAA 2001, if that section applied;

    "the new lessee" means the person who would be the new lessee for the purposes of that section, if that section applied;

and section 70X(7) of CAA 2001 (construction of references to transfer of plant or machinery) also has effect for the purposes of this sub-paragraph.

(7) In the application of section 70W(4)(*b*) or 70X(4)(*b*) of CAA 2001 for the purposes of sub-paragraph (5) or (6), the lease mentioned in the opening words of the sub-paragraph in question is to be regarded as a lease which is not a long funding lease.

HMRC Manuals—Business Leasing Manual, BLM23010 (defining long funding leases: basic rules for commencement and transition).

BLM23015 (transitional rules for commencement and transition).

BLM23020 (coming within the charge to tax on or after 1 April 2006).

Election for lease to be treated as long funding lease for tax purposes

16—(1) The Treasury may by regulations make provision enabling a person of a prescribed description who is, or is to be, the lessor under a plant or machinery lease of a prescribed description to make an election for the lease to be treated in his case as a long funding lease.

(2) The power to make regulations under this paragraph includes power to make provision for or in connection with any of the following—

    (*a*) any conditions that must be met if an election is, or is to be, made;

(b) whether an election is irrevocable;

(c) the date on and after which an election has effect;

(d) the manner in which an election is to be made.

(3) The power to make regulations under this paragraph includes—

(a) power to make provision having effect in relation to times before the making of the regulations (but not before 1st April 2006),

(b) power to make different provision for different cases,

(c) power to make incidental, consequential, supplemental, or transitional provision or savings.

(4) In this paragraph—

"election" means an election under this paragraph;

"long funding lease" means a lease which is a long funding lease for the purposes of Part 2 of CAA 2001;

"prescribed" means specified in, or determined in accordance with, regulations under this paragraph.

Regulations—Long Funding Leases (Elections) Regulations, SI 2007/304.

Excepted leases

17—(1) A lease is an excepted lease if the following conditions are met.

(2) Condition 1 is that before 21st July 2005 there was evidence in writing that there was agreement, or a common understanding, between the lessor's side and the lessee's side as to the principal terms of the lease (the "pre-existing heads of agreement").

The definitions of "the lessor's side", "the lessee's side" and "the principal terms" are in paragraph 27.

(3) Condition 2 is that the leased plant or machinery was under construction (see paragraph 24) before 1st April 2006.

(4) Condition 3 is that the lease has been finalised before 1st April 2007 (but see sub-paragraph (8)).

(5) Condition 4 is that the commencement of the term of the lease is before 1st April 2007 (but see sub-paragraph (8)).

(6) Condition 5 is that the lessee is the particular person or persons identified as such in the pre-existing heads of agreement.

(7) Condition 6 is that the principal terms of the lease are not (or, apart from section 70M of CAA 2001, would not be) materially different from those in the pre-existing heads of agreement.

(8) Sub-paragraphs (4) and (5) have effect with the substitution of "2009" for "2007" if the additional conditions in paragraph 18 are met.

HMRC Manuals—Business Leasing Manual, BLM23025 (defining long funding leases: excepted leases).

Extended time limit: the additional conditions

18—(1) The additional conditions mentioned in paragraph 17(8) are as follows.

(2) Condition A is that the commencement of the term of the lease is before 1st April 2009.

(3) Condition B is that, at the latest, the commencement of the term of the lease is as soon as is reasonably practicable after construction of the asset is substantially complete.

(4) Condition C is that construction of the asset proceeded continuously on and after 1st April 2006.

(5) Condition D is that construction of the asset proceeded at the normal pace for an asset of its type. For this purpose, "normal pace" is the pace required to construct the asset in a reasonable time without delays or interruptions and consistent with normal business practice.

(6) This paragraph is supplemented by paragraph 19.

HMRC Manuals—Business Leasing Manual, BLM23030 (defining long funding leases: extended time limits for excepted leases).

Events beyond the control of the parties etc

19—(1) Condition B, C or D in paragraph 18 is not failed by reason only of breaches due to events that meet the conditions in sub-paragraph (2).

(2) The conditions are that—

(a) the event is abnormal or unusual,

(b) the event is unforeseen, and could not reasonably have been foreseen, at the date when the main contract for the construction of the leased asset is entered into,

(c) the event is beyond the control of each of the principal parties,

(d) as respects the Condition in question, the consequences of the event could not have been avoided by the exercise of all due care, or the taking of all reasonable steps, by the principal parties or any of them.

(3) In this paragraph "the principal parties" are—

(a) the lessor's side,

(*b*) the lessee's side,

(*c*) the main constructor (see the definition in paragraph 27).

HMRC Manuals—Business Leasing Manual, BLM23035 (defining long funding leases: extended time limits for excepted leases: abnormal events).

Pre-existing heads of agreement relating to two or more assets

20—(1) This paragraph has effect for the purposes of this Part in any case where the pre-existing heads of agreement relates to two or more assets.

(2) The treatment of any of the assets varies according to whether the asset—

(*a*) is for use individually (see sub-paragraph (3)), or

(*b*) is a constituent asset of a combined asset (see sub-paragraph (4)).

(3) Where any of the assets is for use individually, this Part has effect in relation to that asset separately, as if it were the subject of—

(*a*) its own separate pre-existing heads of agreement, and

(*b*) if there is a finalised lease, its own separate finalised lease.

See sub-paragraph (5) for the method of determining the terms.

(4) Where any of the assets are constituent assets of a combined asset—

(*a*) the combined asset is to be regarded as a single asset, and

(*b*) the constituent assets are to be regarded as if they were instead component parts of that single asset,

and sub-paragraph (3) applies accordingly.

(5) For the purposes of sub-paragraph (3), the principles in sections 70L and 70M of CAA 2001 are to be applied, with any necessary modifications, for the purpose of determining the terms of—

(*a*) the deemed separate pre-existing heads of agreement, and

(*b*) the deemed separate finalised lease (if any).

Expenditure incurred before passing of this Act where lease is not an excepted lease

21—(1) This paragraph applies where the following conditions are met—

(*a*) a person incurs expenditure on the provision of plant or machinery for leasing under a long funding lease,

(*b*) some or all of that expenditure was incurred before the day on which this Act is passed,

(*c*) the long funding lease is not an excepted lease,

(*d*) before 21st July 2005 there was a pre-existing heads of agreement in the case of the long funding lease.

(2) In this paragraph—

(*a*) "the old expenditure" means so much of the expenditure as is expenditure incurred before the day on which this Act is passed, and

(*b*) "the new expenditure" means so much of the expenditure as is expenditure incurred on or after that day.

(3) Treat the old expenditure—

(*a*) as if it had been incurred on the provision of a separate asset for leasing under a separate long funding lease, and

(*b*) as if that separate long funding lease were an excepted lease.

(4) Treat the new expenditure as if it had been incurred on the provision of a separate asset for leasing under a separate long funding lease in relation to which the amendments made by this Schedule have effect.

That is without prejudice to the application of any provisions of this Part which treat that deemed separate long funding lease as if it were two or more leases.

(5) The rentals under the actual long funding lease are to be apportioned between the two deemed leases in such manner as is just and reasonable.

(6) This paragraph has effect for the purpose of determining liability to income tax or corporation tax in the case of any person who is or has been the lessor or the lessee under the actual long funding lease.

(7) Paragraph 22 has effect for determining when an amount of expenditure is to be treated for the purposes of this paragraph as incurred by the person mentioned in sub-paragraph (1).

HMRC Manuals—Business Leasing Manual, BLM23085 (expenditure incurred before 19 July 2006).

When expenditure is incurred for the purposes of paragraph 21

22—(1) This paragraph has effect for determining, for the purposes of paragraph 21, when an amount of expenditure is to be treated as incurred by the person mentioned in sub-paragraph (1) of that paragraph.

(2) The general rule is that an amount of expenditure is to be treated as incurred as soon as there is an unconditional obligation to pay it.

(3) The general rule applies even if the whole or a part of the expenditure is not required to be paid until a later date.

(4) There are the following exceptions to the general rule.

(5) If, under an agreement,—

    (*a*) an unconditional obligation to pay an amount of expenditure comes into being as a result of the giving of a certificate or any other event, and

    (*b*) the giving of the certificate, or other event, occurs before the day that falls one month after the passing of this Act,

the expenditure is to be treated as incurred on the day before the passing of this Act.

(6) If, under an agreement,—

    (*a*) there is an unconditional obligation to pay an amount of expenditure on a date earlier than accords with normal commercial usage, and

    (*b*) the sole or main benefit which might have been expected to be obtained thereby is that the amount would be treated, under the general rule, as incurred at an earlier time,

the amount is to be treated as incurred on the date on or before which it is required to be paid.

(7) If the terms of an agreement are varied on or after 22nd March 2006 with respect to the times for payment and—

    (*a*) apart from the variation, an unconditional obligation to pay an amount of expenditure would have come into being on or after the day on which this Act is passed, but

    (*b*) as a result of the variation, the unconditional obligation to pay the amount comes into being before that day,

the amount is to be treated as incurred on the date on which it would have been treated as incurred apart from the variation.

(8) Sub-paragraph (7) does not apply if the long funding lease mentioned in paragraph 21 was finalised before 22nd March 2006.

HMRC Manuals—Business Leasing Manual, BLM23085 (expenditure incurred before 19 July 2006).

When a lease is "finalised"

23—(1) For the purposes of this Part, a lease is "finalised" on the earliest day on which the following conditions are met.

(2) Condition 1 is that there is a contract in writing for the lease between the lessor and the lessee.

(3) Condition 2 is that either—

    (*a*) the contract is unconditional, or

    (*b*) if it is conditional, the conditions have been met.

(4) Condition 3 is that no terms remain to be agreed.

When an asset is "under construction"

24—(1) An asset is "under construction" at any time in the period which—

    (*a*) begins when construction of the asset begins, and

    (*b*) ends when construction of the asset is completed.

(2) An asset consisting of two or more component parts is to be taken to be under construction at any time after the start of construction of any of those component parts which meets the condition in subsection (3).

(3) The condition is that the component part has been identified as a component part of the particular asset before construction of the component part begins.

(4) Sub-paragraphs (1) and (2) are subject to sub-paragraph (5).

(5) The leased asset is not to be regarded as under construction at any time after the commencement of the term of the lease.

(6) This paragraph has effect for the purposes of this Part.

HMRC Manuals—Business Leasing Manual, BLM23070 (meaning of "construction").

Combined assets and constituent assets

25—(1) A "combined asset" is an asset which meets the conditions in sub-paragraph (2).

(2) The conditions are that—

    (*a*) the asset is for use individually,

    (*b*) it consists of two or more items of plant or machinery ("constituent assets"),

    (*c*) each of the constituent assets is constructed with a view to its use in conjunction with the others as a single asset (namely, the combined asset).

(3) Plant or machinery that can be used individually is not a constituent asset just because—

    (*a*) it is one of a number of assets of the same or a similar description,

    (*b*) each of those assets is intended for use individually, and

    (*c*) the use individually of those assets is to be co-ordinated to any extent.

(4) This paragraph has effect for the purposes of this Part.

HMRC Manuals—Business Leasing Manual, BLM23060–23065 (defining long funding leases: relating to two or more assets, with examples).

Mixed leases

26—(1) This paragraph applies in any case where there is a mixed lease (see section 70L of CAA 2001).

(2) In any such case, determine whether the mixed lease is an excepted lease.

(3) If the mixed lease is an excepted lease, section 70L of CAA 2001 and the amendments made by this Schedule accordingly do not have effect in relation to it.

(4) If the mixed lease is not an excepted lease, then apply sections 70L and 70M of CAA 2001 and determine separately in the case of each derived lease whether that derived lease is an excepted lease.

Interpretation of this Part

27—(1) In this Part—

"combined asset" is to be construed in accordance with paragraph 25;

"constituent asset" is to be construed in accordance with paragraph 25;

"finalise", in relation to a lease, is to be construed in accordance with paragraph 23;

"lease" includes—

    (a) a plant or machinery lease, and

    (b) a mixed lease,

and "lessor", "lessee" and other related expressions are to be construed accordingly;

"the lessee's side" means any of the following—

    (a) the lessee,

    (b) a person who controls (or is to control) the lessee,

    (c) any two or more persons who together control (or are to control) the lessee,

and for this purpose "control" has the meaning given by [section 574 of CAA 2001][1];

"the lessor's side" means any of the following—

    (a) the lessor,

    (b) a person who controls (or is to control) the lessor,

    (c) any two or more persons who together control (or are to control) the lessor,

and for this purpose "control" has the meaning given by [section 574 of CAA 2001][1];

"the main constructor" means the contractor under the main contract for the construction of the plant or machinery;

"pre-existing heads of agreement" is to be construed in accordance with paragraph 17(2);

"the principal terms", in relation to a lease, are the following—

    (a) the identity of the lessee;

    (b) the identity or description of the asset to be leased;

    (c) particulars, or a description, of the rentals payable under the lease;

    (d) particulars, or a description, of the term of the lease;

"qualifying activity" has the same meaning as in Part 2 of CAA 2001;

"under construction", in the case of an asset, is to be construed in accordance with paragraph 24.

(2) Chapter 6A of Part 2 of CAA 2001 (interpretation of that Part so far as relating to long funding leases) also applies for the purposes of this Part.

HMRC Manuals—Business Leasing Manual, BLM23050 (defining long funding leases: definition of "lessee's side", "lessor's side" and "lessee").

Amendments—[1] Words in sub-para (1) substituted by ITA 2007 s 1027, Sch 1 paras 610, 624 with effect for income tax purposes from 6 April 2007, and corporation tax purposes for accounting periods ending after 5 April 2007.

SCHEDULE 9

LEASES OF PLANT OR MACHINERY: MISCELLANEOUS AMENDMENTS

Section 81

TAXATION OF CHARGEABLE GAINS ACT 1992

Long funding leases: deemed disposals and re-acquisitions

4—(1) (*inserts* TCGA 1992 s 25A)

(2) The amendment made by this paragraph has effect where the commencement of the term of the lease is on or after 1st April 2006.

Restriction of losses: long funding leases of plant or machinery

5—(1) (*inserts* TCGA 1992 s 41A)

(2) The amendment made by this paragraph has effect in relation to disposals on or after 1st April 2006.

Definition of market value

6 (*amends* TCGA 1992 s 272(6))

FINANCE ACT 2000

Tonnage tax: introductory

8 Schedule 22 to FA 2000 (tonnage tax) is amended as follows.

Meaning of "finance costs"

9—(1) In Part 7 (the ring fence: general provisions) paragraph 63 (meaning of finance costs) is amended as follows.

(2) (*inserts* FA 2000 Sch 22 para 63(2)(*dd*))

(3) (*inserts* FA 2000 Sch 22 para 63(4))

(4) The amendments made by this paragraph have effect in relation to payments due on or after 1st April 2006.

Capital allowances: ship leasing

10—(1) Part 10 (the ring fence: capital allowances: ship leasing) is amended as follows.

(2) (*amends* FA 2000 Sch 22 para 89(1))

(3) (*inserts* FA 2000 Sch 22 paras 91A–91F)

(4) (*amends* FA 2000 Sch 22 para 93(1)(*b*))

(5) Paragraph 15 of Schedule 8 (commencement) also has effect in relation to the amendments made by this paragraph.

CAPITAL ALLOWANCES ACT 2001

Plant or machinery treated as owned by person entitled to benefit of contract etc

12—(1) Section 67 of CAA 2001 is amended as follows.

(2), (3) (*amend* CAA 2001 s 67)

(4) (*inserts* CAA 2001 s 67(2A)–(2C))

(5)–(7) (*Renumber* CAA 2001 s 67(5) as s 67(7) and *insert* s 67(6), (8)).

(8) The amendments made by this paragraph have effect in relation to contracts that are finalised (within the meaning of Part 4 of Schedule 8) on or after 1st April 2006.

Phasing out of overseas leasing rules

13 (*inserts* CAA 2001 s 105(2A))

Anti-avoidance: meaning of "finance lease"

14—(1) Section 219 of CAA 2001 (meaning of "finance lease" in Chapter 17 of Part 2) is amended as follows.

(2) (*amends* CAA 2001 s 219(1)(*b*)(ii))

(3) Paragraph 15 of Schedule 8 (commencement) also has effect in relation to the amendment made by this paragraph.

Capital allowances: allocation of expenditure to a chargeable period

15—(1) Section 220 of CAA 2001 is amended as follows.

(2) (*inserts* CAA 2001 s 220(A1))

(3) (*amends* CAA 2001 s 220(1))

(4) (*inserts* CAA 2001 s 220(3)–(11))

(5) In consequence of the amendments made by this paragraph, the italic cross-heading preceding section 219 becomes "Finance leases and certain operating leases".

(6) The amendments made by this paragraph have effect in relation to expenditure incurred on or after 1st April 2006.

SCHEDULE 12
SETTLEMENTS: AMENDMENT OF TCGA 1992 ETC
Section 88
PART 1
SETTLORS, TRUSTEES AND SETTLEMENTS
Basic trust concepts

1—(1) (*amends* TCGA 1992 s 68)

(2) (*inserts* TCGA 1992 ss 68A, 68B, 68C)

(3) The amendment of section 68 made by sub-paragraph (1) shall come into force on 6th April 2006 (in relation to settlements whenever created).

(4) Sections 68A and 68B (as inserted by sub-paragraph (2)) shall come into force on 6th April 2006 (in relation to settlements whenever created).

(5) Section 68C (as inserted by sub-paragraph (2)) shall have effect in respect of variations occurring on or after 6th April 2006 (irrespective of the date on which the deceased person died).

2—(1) (*substitutes* TCGA 1992 s 69(1)–(2E))

(2) This paragraph shall have effect—

    (*a*) for the purposes of determining the residence status of the trustees of a settlement (whenever created), from 6th April 2007, and

    (*b*) for any other purpose (in relation to settlements whenever created), from 6th April 2006.

Interests in settlements

4—(1) In section 169F of TCGA 1992 (meaning of "interest in a settlement" for purposes of sections 169B to 169D)—

    (*a*), (*b*)　(*amend* TCGA 1992 s 169F(1), (2)(*a*))

    (*c*), (*d*)　(*insert* TCGA 1992 s 169F(3A), (4A), (4B))

(2) Sub-paragraph (1) shall have effect for the purpose of determining whether for the purposes of sections 169B to 169D and 169F an individual is to be regarded as having an interest in a settlement (whenever created) on or after 6th April 2006.

(3) But sub-paragraph (1) shall not have effect in relation to section 169C if the relevant disposal (within the meaning of section 169C(1)) is made on or before 5th April 2006.

5—(1) (*inserts* TCGA 1992 Sch 4A para 7(5)(*c*))

(2) Sub-paragraph (1) shall have effect for the purpose of determining whether a settlor is regarded as having an interest in a settlement (whenever created) for the purposes of Schedule 4A to TCGA 1992 on or after 6th April 2006.

PART 2
SUB-FUND SETTLEMENTS

6—(1) (*inserts* TCGA 1992 s 69A)

(2) (*inserts* TCGA 1992 Sch 4ZA)

(3) This paragraph shall have effect in relation to years of assessment beginning on or after 6th April 2006 (but a sub-fund election may not be treated as having taken effect before 6th April 2006).

PART 3
CONSEQUENTIAL AND MINOR AMENDMENTS
Introduction

7　Paragraphs 8 to 45 amend TCGA 1992.

General

8—(1) (*amends* TCGA 1992 s 13(10))

(2) This paragraph shall have effect in relation to gains accruing on or after 6th April 2006.

9　(*substitutes* TCGA 1992 s 21(1)(*b*))

10—(1), (2) (*amend* TCGA 1992 s 60)

(3) This paragraph shall have effect from 6th April 2006.

11—(1) (*amends* TCGA 1992 s 63)

(2) (*inserts* TCGA 1992 s 63A)

(3) The provisions of this paragraph shall have effect in relation to a death occurring on or after 6th April 2006.

12—(1) (*amends* TCGA 1992 s 64(1))

(2) This paragraph shall have effect in relation to disposals made on or after 6th April 2006.

14—(1) (*amends* TCGA 1992 s 79B(1))

(2) This paragraph shall have effect in relation to gains accruing on or after 6th April 2006.

15—(1) (*amends* TCGA 1992 s 97(7))

(2) (*inserts* TCGA 1992 s 97(7A))

(3) This paragraph shall come into force on 6th April 2006 (in relation to settlements whenever created).

16—(1) (*amends* TCGA 1992 s 98(2))

(2) This paragraph shall come into force on 6th April 2006 (in relation to settlements whenever created).

17—(1) (*amends* TCGA 1992 s 104(1))

(2) This paragraph shall come into force on 6th April 2006.

18—(1) (*amends* TCGA 1992 s 109(2)(*a*))

(2) This paragraph shall come into force on 6th April 2006.

19—(1) (*amends* TCGA 1992 s 169D(5))

(2) This paragraph shall come into force on 6th April 2006.

20—(1) (*amends* TCGA 1992 s 217(3), (5))

(2) This paragraph shall have effect in relation to a transfer falling within section 216(1) which is effected on or after 6th April 2006.

21—(1) (*amends* TCGA 1992 s 227(2))

(2) This paragraph shall have effect in relation to disposals made on or after 6th April 2006.

22—(1) (*amends* TCGA 1992 s 228(5)(*b*))

(2) (*amends* TCGA 1992 s 228(7))

(3) Sub-paragraph (1) shall have effect in relation to arrangements which allow an acquisition to be made on or after 6th April 2006 (irrespective of when the arrangements were made).

(4) Sub-paragraph (2) shall have effect for the purposes of determining what constitutes a qualifying share ownership trust for the purpose of section 227 on or after 6th April 2006.

23—(1) (*amends* TCGA 1992 s 251(5))

(2) This paragraph shall have effect in relation to debts created on or after 6th April 2006.

24—(1) In section 283(4) (repayment supplements)—

    (*a*) (*substitutes* words in TCGA 1992 s 283(4))

    (*b*) (*repeals* words in TCGA 1992 s 283(4))

(2) Sub-paragraph (1)(*a*) shall have effect in relation to a repayment made on or after 6th April 2006.

(3) Sub-paragraph (1)(*b*) shall have effect in relation to a repayment made on or after 6th April 2006 (irrespective of the date on which the deceased person died).

25—(1) (*amends* TCGA 1992 s 286(3))

(2) (*inserts* TCGA 1992 s 286(3ZA))

(3) This paragraph shall come into force (in relation to settlements whenever created) on 6th April 2006.

26—(1) (*amends* Table of defined expressions in TCGA 1992 s 288(8))

(2) This paragraph shall come into force on 6th April 2006 (in relation to settlements whenever created).

28—(1) (*amends* TCGA 1992 Sch 1 para 1(6))

(2) (*amends* TCGA 1992 Sch 1 para 2(7))

(3) This paragraph shall have effect for the purposes of determining, for the purposes of Schedule 1, whether a person is a settlor in relation to a settlement (whenever created) on or after 6th April 2006.

Residence of trustees

30—(1) In each of the provisions set out in sub-paragraph (2) for "not resident or ordinarily resident in the United Kingdom" substitute "neither resident nor ordinarily resident in the United Kingdom".

(2) (*amends* TCGA 1992 ss 76(1B)(*a*), 86(2)(*a*), Sch 5A 2(1)(*c*), 3(1)(*a*) and 4(1)(*a*))

(3) (*amends* TCGA 1992 Sch 5A para (2)(1)(*d*))

(4) The amendments to sections 76(1B)(*a*) and 86(2)(*a*) shall come into force on 6th April 2007 (in relation to settlements whenever created).

(5) The amendments to paragraph 2(1)(*c*) and (*d*) of Schedule 5A shall have effect in relation to transfers of property made on or after 6th April 2007 (in relation to settlements whenever created).

(6) The amendments to paragraphs 3(1)(*a*) and 4(1)(*a*) of Schedule 5A shall have effect in relation to settlements created on or after 6th April 2007.

32   (*amends* TCGA 1992 s 83A(3))

33   Paragraphs 31 and 32 shall come into force on 6th April 2007 (in relation to settlements whenever created).

34—(1) In each of the provisions set out in sub-paragraph (2) for "resident or ordinarily resident in the United Kingdom" substitute " resident and ordinarily resident in the United Kingdom ".
(2) (*amended* TCGA 1992 ss 83A(4)(b), 85A(3), 87(2), Sch 4A para 5(2), Sch 4C paras 4(2) and 10(1) and (3), Sch 5A paras 3(1)(*b*) and 4(1)(*b*); *repealed in part by* FA 2008 s 25 Sch 7 para 114(*d*))
(3) The amendments to sections 83A(4)(*b*), 85A(3), 86(3) and 87(2), paragraph 5(2) of Schedule 4A and paragraphs 4(2) and 10(1) and (3) of Schedule 4C shall come into force on 6th April 2007 (in relation to settlements whenever created).
(4) The amendments to paragraphs 3(1)(*b*) and 4(1)(*b*) of Schedule 5A shall have effect in relation to settlements created on or after 6th April 2007.

35—(1) In each of the provisions set out in sub-paragraph (2)—
     (*a*)   for "resident in the United Kingdom during any part of the year or ordinarily resident in the United Kingdom during the year" substitute "resident and ordinarily resident in the United Kingdom during any part of the year", and
     (*b*)   for "such residence or ordinary residence" substitute "such residence and ordinary residence".
(2) Those provisions are—
     (*a*)–(*c*)   (*amend* TCGA 1992 ss 86(2)(*b*), 88(1), Sch 4C para 5(1))
(3) Sub-paragraph (2)(*c*) shall have effect in relation to a transfer of value made on or after 6th April 2007 (in relation to settlements whenever created).

36—(1) In each of the provisions set out in sub-paragraph (2) for "at no time resident or ordinarily resident in the United Kingdom" substitute "at no time resident and ordinarily resident in the United Kingdom".
(2) Those provisions are—
     (*a*)   (*amended* TCGA 1992 s 87(1); *repealed by* FA 2008 s 25 Sch 7 para 114(*d*))
     (*b*)   (*amends* TCGA 1992 Sch 4C para 4(1))
(3) Sub-paragraph (2)(*b*) shall have effect in relation to a transfer of value made on or after 6th April 2007 (in relation to settlements whenever created).

37—(1), (2) (*amend* TCGA 1992 s 169(3)(*a*), (*b*)(ii))
(3) This paragraph shall have effect in relation to relevant disposals (within the meaning given by section 169(2)) made on or after 6th April 2007 (in relation to settlements whenever created).

38   (*amends* TCGA 1992 Sch 1 para 2(7)(*a*))

39   (*amends* TCGA 1992 Sch 4A para 5(1))

40   (*amends* TCGA 1992 Sch 4C para 10(2))

41   Paragraphs 35 to 40 shall, unless otherwise expressly provided, come into force on 6th April 2007 (in relation to settlements whenever created).

Sub-fund settlements

42   (*inserts* TCGA 1992 s 73(1A))

43   (*inserts* TCGA 1992 s 286(3)(*d*), (*e*))

44—(1) (*inserts* TCGA 1992 Sch 1 para A1)
(2) (*inserts* TCGA 1992 Sch 1 para 3)

45   Paragraphs 42 to 44 shall have effect in relation to years of assessment beginning on or after 6th April 2006.

Amendments of other Acts

46—(1), (2) (*amend* TMA 1970 s 98 Table; *repealed in part by* Finance Act 2009 Schedule 47 (Consequential Amendments) Order, SI 2009/2035, Art 2 Schedule, para 60(*m*))
(3) This paragraph shall come into force on 6th April 2006.

48—(1) (*inserted* FA 2005 s 30(1A), (3A); *repealed by* FA 2008 s 8, Sch 2 para 21(*j*))
(2) (*substitutes* FA 2005 s 34(3)(*a*)–(*b*))
(3) (*substitutes* FA 2005 s 35(4)(*a*)–(*b*))
(4) (*inserts* FA 2005 s 37(7)–(9))

(5) This paragraph shall come into force on 6th April 2006 (in relation to vulnerable person elections whenever made).

SCHEDULE 13

SETTLEMENTS: AMENDMENTS TO ICTA AND ITTOIA 2005 ETC

Section 89

PART 1
PRINCIPAL AMENDMENTS

5—(1) (*substitutes* ITTOIA 2005 s 619(2))
(2) This paragraph shall have effect—
    (a) in relation to income which arises or is treated as arising on or after 6th April 2006, and
    (b) in relation to income which is paid to a minor child of the settlor, where the child is unmarried and is not in a civil partnership, on or after 6th April 2006 and in relation to which section 631 of ITTOIA 2005 applies (irrespective of when the income arose).

6—(1) (*inserts* ITTOIA 2005 s 685A)
(2) This paragraph shall have effect for payments in respect of income made on or after 6th April 2006.

PART 2
MINOR AND CONSEQUENTIAL AMENDMENTS

7 Paragraphs 8 to 26 amend ICTA.

8 (*repeals* TA 1988 s 220(2))

23 (*repeals* TA 1988 s 764)

27—(1) Paragraph 7 and paragraphs 9 to 26 shall come into force on 6th April 2006 (in relation to settlements whenever created).
(2) Paragraph 8 shall come into force on 6th April 2007 (in relation to settlements whenever created).

28—(1) FA 1989 shall be amended as follows.
(2) The following provisions shall cease to have effect—
    (a), (b) (*repeal* FA 1989 ss 68(2)(c), 71(4)(c)),
    (c) (*repeals* FA 1989 s 110)
(3) (*amends* FA 1989 s 68(2))
(4) (*amends* FA 1989 s 71(4))
(5) Sub-paragraph (2)(a) and (b) shall have effect in relation to payments made on or after 6th April 2006.
(6) Sub-paragraph (2)(c) shall have effect from 6th April 2007 (in relation to settlements whenever created).
(7) Sub-paragraphs (3) and (4) shall come into force on 6th April 2006.

30—(1) (*inserts* FA 1990 s 25(9)(b)(v); sub-para (b) *repealed by* ITA 2007 s 1031, Sch 3 Pt 1)
(2) This paragraph shall have effect for payments in respect of income made on or after 6th April 2006.

31—(1) (*amends* ITTOIA 2005 ss 417(2), 420, 420(1)(a) and (c))
(2) (*substitutes* ITTOIA 2005 s 623)
(3) This paragraph shall come into force on 6th April 2006 in respect of settlements whenever created, and in respect of loans or advances whenever made.

32—(1) (*repeals* ITTOIA 2005 ss 457(4), 568(5))
(2) (*amends* ITTOIA 2005 s 457(5))
(3) (*substitutes* ITTOIA 2005 s 467(7)(b))
(4) This paragraph shall have effect in relation to payments made on or after 6th April 2006 to the trustees of a settlement (whenever created).

33—(1)–(4) (*amend* ITTOIA 2005 ss 628, 630, 631)
(5) This paragraph shall come into force on 6th April 2006.

34—(1) (*inserts* ITTOIA s 629(8))
(2) This paragraph shall have effect in relation to payments made on or after 6th April 2004.

35—(1) FA 2005 shall be amended as follows.
(2) (*amends* FA 2005 ss 23(1)(a), (b), 24, 25(1)(a), 37(1))
(3) (*amends* FA 2005 s 25(3))
(4) (*amends* FA 2005 s 27(2)(b))

(5) (*repeals* FA 2005 s 42(5)(*b*))
(6) (*amends* FA 2005 s 43(4))
(7) This paragraph shall come into force on 6th April 2006.

36—(1) (*inserts* FA 2005 s 28A)
(2) This paragraph shall have effect in relation to payments made on or after 6th April 2004.

SCHEDULE 14
INVESTMENT RELIEFS: VENTURE CAPITAL SCHEMES

Section 91

PART 1
LIMITS ON GROSS ASSETS OF ISSUERS OF SHARES OR SECURITIES

Corporate venturing scheme

3—(1) (*amends* FA 2000 Sch 15 para 22(1) and (2))
(2) Sub-paragraph (1) has effect in relation to shares issued on or after 6th April 2006, subject to sub-paragraph (3).
(3) Sub-paragraph (1) does not have effect in relation to shares issued on or after 6th April 2006 to a person who subscribed for them before 22nd March 2006.

SCHEDULE 15
ACCOUNTANCY CHANGE: SPREADING OF ADJUSTMENT

Section 102

PART 1
INCOME TAX

Application of this Part of this Schedule

1—(1) This Part of this Schedule applies where—
  (*a*) there is a change of accounting approach from one period of account to the next in calculating the profits of a business for income tax purposes,
  (*b*) the later period of account ends on or after 22nd June 2005 and the basis on which the profits for that period are calculated is in accordance with UK GAAP (including SSAP 9 and Application Note G as interpreted by UITF 40), and
  (*c*) the earlier period of account ended before that date and the basis on which profits for that period were calculated was in accordance with UK GAAP (including SSAP 9 and Application Note G, but not as interpreted by UITF 40),
and has effect in relation to any adjustment income under Chapter 17 of Part 2 of ITTOIA 2005 attributable to the change of basis from that mentioned in paragraph (c) to that mentioned in paragraph (b).
(2) In relation to a period for which accounts are drawn up in accordance with international accounting standards, the references in sub-paragraph (1) to requirements of UK GAAP shall be read as references to the corresponding requirements of international accounting standards.
(3) In sub-paragraph (1)—
  "SSAP 9" means Statement of Standard Accounting Practice No 9 on Long-term contracts, issued by the Accounting Standards Board;
  "Application Note G" means Application Note G to Financial Reporting Standard 5 issued by the Accounting Standards Board in November 2003;
  "UITF 40" means Abstract No 40 on Revenue recognition and service contracts, issued by the Urgent Issues Task Force of the Accounting Standards Board on 10th March 2005.
(4) Any reference in this Part of this Schedule to the date on which the change of accounting approach was adopted is to the first day of the first period of account for which it was adopted.
(5) To determine the amount of adjustment income attributable to the change of basis mentioned in the closing words of sub-paragraph (1), assume that there was no other change of accounting approach.

Spreading of adjustment income

2—(1) The adjustment income shall be spread in accordance with the following rules.
(2) In each of the first three tax years beginning with that in which the whole amount of the adjustment income would otherwise be chargeable to tax, an amount equal to whichever is the less of—
  (*a*) one-third of the original amount of the adjustment income, and

(*b*) one-sixth of the profits of the business for that tax year,

is treated as arising and charged to tax.

(3) In the fourth and fifth tax years, if the whole of the adjustment income has not been charged to tax in previous tax years, an amount equal to whichever is the least of—

(*a*) the amount remaining untaxed,

(*b*) one-third of the original amount of the adjustment income, and

(*c*) one-sixth of the profits of the business for that tax year,

is treated as arising and charged to tax.

(4) In the sixth tax year so much (if any) of the adjustment income as has not previously been charged to tax is treated as arising and is charged to tax.

(5) For the purposes of this paragraph "the profits of the business" means the profits of the business as calculated for income tax purposes leaving out of account—

(*a*) any adjustment expenses under Chapter 17 of Part 2 of ITTOIA 2005, and

(*b*) any allowances or charges under CAA 2001.

(6) This paragraph has effect subject to—

(*a*) paragraph 3 (effect of cessation of business), and

(*b*) paragraph 4 (election to accelerate charge).

Effect of cessation of business

3   If before the whole of the adjustment income has been charged to tax the person permanently ceases to carry on the business in question, paragraph 2 continues to apply but with the omission of the alternative limit in sub-paragraph (2)(*b*) and (3)(*c*) referring to the profits of the business.

Election to accelerate charge

4—(1) A person who under paragraph 2 is liable to tax for a tax year [(Year 1)][1] on an amount of adjustment income may elect for an additional amount to be treated as arising in that tax year.

(2) The election must be made on or before the first anniversary of the [31st January of Year 2.][1]

(3) The election must specify the amount to be treated as income arising in the tax year (which may be any amount up to the whole of the adjustment income not previously charged to tax).

(4) If an election is made, paragraph 2 applies in relation to any subsequent tax year as if the original amount of adjustment income (as reduced by the previous application of this sub-paragraph) were reduced by the additional amount treated as arising in the tax year for which the election is made.

Amendments—[1]   Words in sub-para (1) inserted, and words in sub-para (2) substituted by FA 2007 ss 91(10), 92 with effect—

(a)   in relation to a return under TMA 1970 ss 8 or 8A, or a return under s 12AA for a partnership which includes one or more individuals, in respect of a return for a year of assessment beginning on or after 6 April 2007; and

(b)   in relation to a return under s 12AA for a partnership which includes one or more companies, in respect of a return for a relevant period beginning on or after 6 April 2007.

Liability of personal representatives

5—(1) This paragraph applies in the case of the death of a person who would otherwise have been liable to tax under this Part of this Schedule on adjustment income.

(2) The tax under this Part of this Schedule for which the person would otherwise have been liable—

(*a*) shall be assessed and charged on the personal representatives, and

(*b*) is a debt due from and payable out of the deceased's estate.

(3) The personal representatives may make any election under this Part of this Schedule that the deceased might have made.

Meaning of "business"

6   In this Part of this Schedule "business" means—

(*a*) a trade, profession or vocation, or

(*b*) a UK property business or overseas property business.

Application of provisions to partnerships

7—(1) This paragraph applies where the business is carried on by the person in partnership.

(2) The amounts chargeable to tax under this Part of this Schedule for any tax year are calculated as if the partnership were an individual resident in the United Kingdom.

(3) The person's share of the amount charged to tax is determined—

(*a*) for the first tax year, according to the profit-sharing arrangements for the twelve months ending immediately before the date on which the change of accounting practice was adopted;

(*b*) for any subsequent tax year, according to the profit-sharing arrangements for the twelve months immediately following the twelve months used to determine the person's share for the previous year.

An election under paragraph 4 (election to accelerate charge) in relation to a tax year must be made jointly by all the persons who have been members of the partnership in the relevant twelve month period and are chargeable to income tax.

(4) If paragraph 3 applies (effect of cessation of business), each partner's share of any amount charged to tax on or after the cessation is determined as follows—

- (a) if the cessation occurs on the date on which the change of accounting approach was adopted, according to the profit-sharing arrangements for the twelve months ending immediately before that date;
- (b) if the cessation occurs after that date, but on or before the first anniversary of that date, according to the profit-sharing arrangements for the period between that date and the date of cessation;
- (c) if the cessation occurs after the first anniversary of the date on which the change of accounting approach was adopted, according to the profit-sharing arrangements for the period between the immediately preceding anniversary of that date and the date of cessation.

An election under paragraph 4 after the cessation must be made by each former partner separately.

(5) For the purposes of this paragraph "profit-sharing arrangements" means the rights of the partners to share in the profits of the business for the period in question.

(6) In the case of a business carried on by a limited liability partnership the operation of this Part of this Schedule is not affected by the partnership's ceasing to be one carrying on a trade, profession or other business with a view to profit.

Cases where spreading already available

8   This Part of this Schedule does not apply to adjustment income to which section 238 of that Act applies (spreading on ending of special provision for barristers and advocates in early years of practice).

PART 2
CORPORATION TAX

Application of this Part of this Schedule

9—(1) This Part of this Schedule applies where—

- (a) there is a change of accounting approach from one period of account to the next in calculating the profits of a business for corporation tax purposes,
- (b) the later period of account ends on or after 22nd June 2005 and the basis on which the profits for that period are calculated is in accordance with UK GAAP (including SSAP 9 and Application Note G as interpreted by UITF 40), and
- (c) the earlier period of account ended before that date and the basis on which profits for that period were calculated was in accordance with UK GAAP (including SSAP 9 and Application Note G, but not as interpreted by UITF 40),

and has effect in relation to any positive adjustment under [Chapter 14 of Part 3 of or section 262 of CTA 2009][1] attributable to the change of basis from that mentioned in paragraph (c) to that mentioned in paragraph (b).

(2) In relation to a period for which accounts are drawn up in accordance with international accounting standards, the references in sub-paragraph (1) to requirements of UK GAAP shall be read as references to the corresponding requirements of international accounting standards.

(3) In this paragraph—

"SSAP 9" means Statement of Standard Accounting Practice No 9 on Long-term contracts, issued by the Accounting Standards Board;

"Application Note G" means Application Note G to Financial Reporting Standard 5 issued by the Accounting Standards Board in November 2003;

"UITF 40" means Abstract No 40 on Revenue recognition and service contracts, issued by the Urgent Issues Task Force of the Accounting Standards Board on 10th March 2005.

(4) Any reference in this Part of this Schedule to the date on which the change of accounting approach was adopted is to the first day of the first period of account for which it was adopted.

(5) To determine the amount of positive adjustment attributable to the change of basis mentioned in the closing words of sub-paragraph (1), assume that there was no other change of accounting approach.

Amendments—[1]   In sub-para (1) words substituted by CTA 2009 s 1322, Sch 1 paras 675, 696(1), (2). CTA 2009 applies for accounting periods ending on or after 1 April 2009 (for corporation tax purposes) and for tax years 2009–10 onwards (for income and capital gains tax purposes).

Spreading of adjustment

10—(1) The adjustment shall be spread in accordance with the following rules.

(2) In each of the first three accounting periods beginning with that in which the whole of the adjustment would otherwise be charged to tax, an amount equal to whichever is the less of—

    (*a*) one-third of the amount of the original adjustment, and

    (*b*) one-sixth of the profits of the business for that period,

is treated as arising and charged to tax.

(3) In the fourth and fifth accounting periods, if the whole of the adjustment has not been charged to tax in the previous periods, an amount equal to whichever is the least of—

    (*a*) the amount remaining untaxed,

    (*b*) one-third of the amount of the original adjustment, and

    (*c*) one-sixth of the profits of the business for that period,

is treated as arising and charged to tax.

(4) In the sixth accounting period so much (if any) of the adjustment as has not previously been charged to tax is treated as arising and is charged to tax.

(5) For the purposes of this paragraph "the profits of the business" means the profits of the business as calculated for corporation tax purposes leaving out of account—

    (*a*) any adjustment under [Chapter 14 of Part 3 of or section 262 of CTA 2009][1], and

    (*b*) any allowances or charges under CAA 2001.

(6) This paragraph has effect subject to—

    (*a*) paragraph 11 (accounting periods of less than twelve months),

    (*b*) paragraph 12 (effect of other events bringing accounting period to an end), and

    (*c*) paragraph 13 (election to accelerate charge).

Amendments—[1]   In sub-para (5)(*a*) words substituted by CTA 2009 s 1322, Sch 1 paras 675, 696(1), (3). CTA 2009 applies for accounting periods ending on or after 1 April 2009 (for corporation tax purposes) and for tax years 2009–10 onwards (for income and capital gains tax purposes).

Accounting periods of less than twelve months

11—(1) This paragraph applies where by reason of—

    (*a*) a change of accounting date,

    (*b*) the company entering administration (see [section 10 of CTA 2009][1]), or

    (*c*) an insurance business transfer scheme (see section 12(7A) and (7B) of that Act),

an accounting period to which paragraph 10 applies is a period of less than twelve months (a "short period").

(2) In relation to a short period the references in that paragraph to one-third of the amount of the original adjustment shall be read as references to the proportion of that amount that the period bears to twelve months.

(3) Where any of the accounting periods of the company falling within the period of six years following the change of accounting approach is a short period—

    (*a*) the rule in paragraph 10(3) applies in relation to every accounting period after the third and before that in which the sixth anniversary of the change of accounting approach falls, and

    (*b*) the rule in paragraph 10(4) applies in relation to the accounting period in which that anniversary falls.

Amendments—[1]   In sub-para (1)(*b*) words substituted by CTA 2009 s 1322, Sch 1 paras 675, 696(1), (4). CTA 2009 applies for accounting periods ending on or after 1 April 2009 (for corporation tax purposes) and for tax years 2009–10 onwards (for income and capital gains tax purposes).

Effect of other events bringing accounting period to an end

12—(1) If before the whole of the adjustment has been charged to tax an accounting period of the company ends by reason of—

    (*a*) the company ceasing to be within the charge to corporation tax,

    (*b*) the commencement of winding-up proceedings in respect of the company (see [section 12 of CTA 2009][1]),

the rule in paragraph 10(4) applies in relation to that accounting period.

(2) If the company permanently ceases to carry on the business in question (without there being any event within sub-paragraph (1) above), paragraph 10 continues to apply but with the omission of the alternative limit in sub-paragraph (2)(*b*) and (3)(*c*) referring to the profits of the business.

Amendments—[1]   In sub-para (1)(*b*) words substituted by CTA 2009 s 1322, Sch 1 paras 675, 696(1), (5). CTA 2009 applies for accounting periods ending on or after 1 April 2009 (for corporation tax purposes) and for tax years 2009–10 onwards (for income and capital gains tax purposes).

Election to accelerate charge

13—(1) A company that under paragraph 10 is liable to tax for an accounting period on any amount may elect for an additional amount to be treated as arising in that period.

(2) The election must be made on or before the first anniversary of the filing date for the company's company tax return for the accounting period for which the election is made.

(3) The election must specify the amount to be treated as arising in the accounting period (which may be any amount up to the whole of the adjustment not previously charged to tax).

(4) If an election is made, paragraph 10 applies in relation to any subsequent accounting period as if the amount of the original adjustment (as reduced by any previous application of this sub-paragraph) were reduced by the additional amount treated as arising in the accounting period for which the election is made.

Meaning of "business" etc

14—(1) In this Part of this Schedule "business" means—

    (*a*) a trade or vocation, or

    (*b*) a [UK property business][1] or overseas property business.

Amendments—[1] In sub-para (1)(*b*) words substituted by CTA 2009 s 1322, Sch 1 paras 675, 696(1), (6). CTA 2009 applies for accounting periods ending on or after 1 April 2009 (for corporation tax purposes) and for tax years 2009–10 onwards (for income and capital gains tax purposes).

Application of provisions to partnerships

15—(1) This paragraph applies where the business is carried on by the company in partnership.

(2) The amounts chargeable to tax under this Part of this Schedule are calculated as if the partnership were a company resident in the United Kingdom.

(3) The company's share of any such amount is determined by reference to the profit-sharing arrangements for the previous accounting period.

An election under paragraph 13 (election to accelerate charge) must be made jointly by all the persons who have been members of the partnership in the previous accounting period and are chargeable to corporation tax.

(4) If paragraph 12(2) applies (effect of cessation of business), each partner's share of any amount charged to tax on or after the cessation is determined as follows—

    (*a*) if the cessation occurs on the date on which the change of accounting approach was adopted, according to the profit-sharing arrangements for the twelve months ending immediately before that date;

    (*b*) if the cessation occurs after that date, but on or before the first anniversary of that date, according to the profit-sharing arrangements for the period between that date and the date of cessation;

    (*c*) if the cessation occurs after the first anniversary of the date on which the change of accounting approach was adopted, according to the profit-sharing arrangements for the period between the immediately preceding anniversary of that date and the date of cessation.

An election under paragraph 13 after the cessation must be made by each former partner separately.

(5) For the purposes of this paragraph "profit-sharing arrangements" means the rights of the partners to share in the profits of the business for the period in question.

(6) A change in the persons carrying on a business does not constitute the permanent cessation of the business for the purposes of this Part of this Schedule so long as a person carrying on the business immediately before the change continues to carry on the business immediately after the change.

(7) In the case of a business carried on by a limited liability partnership the operation of this Part of this Schedule is not affected by the partnership's ceasing to be one carrying on a trade, profession or other business with a view to profit.

(8) Nothing in this paragraph shall be read as affecting the operation of—

    (*a*) paragraph 19 of Schedule 9 to FA 1996 (loan relationships), or

    (*b*) paragraph 49 of Schedule 26 to FA 2002 (derivative contracts),

(under which certain debits and credits are not to be brought into account as if the partnership were a company).

SCHEDULE 18

OIL TAXATION: MARKET VALUE OF OIL

Section 146

PART 1

AMENDMENTS OF THE OIL TAXATION ACT 1975

(*see the PRT section in Part 3 of this publication*)

PART 2
AMENDMENTS OF OTHER ENACTMENTS
FINANCE (NO 2) ACT 1987

The designated fraction for the month

11—(1) Schedule 8 to F(No 2)A 1987 (amendments of Schedule 10 to FA 1987) is amended as follows.

(2) (*repeals* F(No 2)A 1987 Sch 8 para 5)

(3) The amendment made by this paragraph has effect for chargeable periods beginning on or after 1st July 2006.

INCOME AND CORPORATION TAXES ACT 1988

Valuation of oil disposed of or appropriated in certain circumstances.

12—(1) Section 493 of ICTA (valuation of oil disposed of or appropriated in certain circumstances) is amended as follows.

(2) (*inserted* TA 1988 s 493(A1)–(A3)); *repealed by* CTA 2010 s 1181, Sch 3 Pt 1.

(3)–(6) (*amended* TA 1988 s 493(1)–(4)); *repealed in part by* CTA 2010 s 1181, Sch 3 Pts1, 2.

(7) (*substituted* TA 1988 s 493(5)); *repealed by* CTA 2010 s 1181, Sch 3 Pt 2.

SCHEDULE 21
TAXABLE PROPERTY HELD BY INVESTMENT-REGULATED PENSION SCHEMES
Section 158

1   (*inserts* TCGA 1992 s 271(1B))

2   Part 4 of FA 2004 (pension schemes) is amended as follows.

3—(1) Section 160 (payments by registered pension schemes) is amended as follows.

(2) (*inserts* FA 2004 s 160(7A))

(3) (*amends* FA 2004 s 160(8))

4   (*inserts* FA 2004 s 173(7A))

5   (*inserts* FA 2004 s 174A)

6   (*inserts* FA 2004 ss 185A–185I)

7   (*inserts* FA 2004 s 186(2A))

8   (*inserts* FA 2004 s 239(6))

9   (*inserts* FA 2004 s 241(1)(*c*))

10   (*inserts* FA 2004 s 273ZA)

11   (*inserts* FA 2004 s 278(3A), (3B))

12   (*amends* table of defined expressions in FA 2004 s 280(2))

13   (*inserts* FA 2004 Sch 29A)

14—(1) Schedule 34 (non-UK schemes: application of certain charges) is amended as follows.

(2) (*amends* FA 2004 Sch 34 para 1(3)(*a*), (4))

(3) (*inserts* FA 2004 Sch 34 para 7A)

15   (*inserts* FA 2004 Sch 36 paras 37A–37I)

SCHEDULE 22
PENSION SCHEMES: INHERITANCE TAX
Section 160

Introductory

1   IHTA 1984 is amended as follows.

Dispositions

2   (*inserts* IHTA 1984 s 12(2A)–(2G) and amends s 12 heading)

Interpretation

10—(1) Section 272 (general interpretation) is amended as follows.

(2), (3) (*amended* IHTA 1984 s 272; *repealed* in part by FA 2011 s 65, Sch 16 para 84(*b*)(i))

SCHEDULE 23

PENSION SCHEMES ETC: MISCELLANEOUS

Section 161

Introduction

1   Part 4 of FA 2004 (pension schemes etc) is amended as follows.

Meaning of "pension credit member" etc: person dying before discharge of liability

2   (*amends* FA 2004 s 151(5))

Unauthorised payments: former members and sponsoring employers etc

3—(1) Section 160 (payments by registered pension schemes) is amended as follows.

(2) (*amends* FA 2004 s 160(1))

(3) In subsection (2)—

    (*a*)   (*amends* FA 2004 s 160(2)(*a*) and (*b*))

    (*b*)   (*amends* FA 2004 s 160(2)(*b*))

(4) (*amends* FA 2004 s 160(3) and (4))

4—(1) Section 161 (meaning of "payment" etc) is amended as follows.

(2) (*amends* FA 2004 s 161(5))

(3) (*amends* FA 2004 s 161(6) and (7))

5   (*amends* FA 2004 s 162(3) and (4))

6   (*amends* FA 2004 s 164)

7   (*amends* FA 2004 s 171(1) and (4))

8—(1) Section 173 (benefits) is amended as follows.

(2) (*amends* FA 2004 s 173(1))

(3) (*amends* FA 2004 s 173(3))

(4) (*amends* FA 2004 s 173(4))

(5) (*amends* FA 2004 s 173(7)(*b*))

(6) (*amends* FA 2004 s 173(9)(*a*))

9—(1) Section 174 (value shifting) is amended as follows.

(2) (*amends* FA 2004 s 174(1))

(3) (*amends* FA 2004 s 174(2))

10   (*amends* FA 2004 s 175)

11   (*amends* FA 2004 s 179(1), (5) and (6))

12   (*amends* FA 2004 s 180(1) and (4))

13   (*amends* FA 2004 s 181(1))

14   (*amends* FA 2004 s 208(2))

15   (*amends* FA 2004 s 209(3))

16—(1) Section 210 (surchargeable unauthorised member payments) is amended as follows.

(2) (*amends* FA 2004 s 210(1))

(3) (*amends* FA 2004 s 210(2), (4), (5) and (8))

(4) (*amends* FA 2004 s 210(9))

(5) (*amends* FA 2004 s 210(10))

17   (*amends* FA 2004 s 210211(1))

18   (*amends* FA 2004 s 212(3))

19—(1) Section 213 (surchargeable unauthorised employer payments) is amended as follows.

(2) (*amends* FA 2004 s 213(1))

(3) (*amends* FA 2004 s 213(2), (4), (5) and (8))

"Bridging" pensions

20—(1) Paragraph 2 of Schedule 28 (scheme pension) is amended as follows.
(2) *(substituted* FA 2004 Sch 28 para 2(4)(*c*); *repealed by* FA 2016 s 20(5)(*a*))
(3) *(substituted* FA 2004 Sch 28 para 2(5), (5A); *repealed by* FA 2016 s 20(5)(*a*))
(4) (*amends* FA 2004 Sch 28 para 2(8))

Pension commencement lump sum: scheme pensions under money purchase arrangements

22—(1) Paragraph 3 of Schedule 29 (pension commencement lump sum: applicable amount) is amended as follows.
(2) (*amends* FA 2004 Sch 29 para 3(6))
(3) (*inserts* FA 2004 Sch 29 para 3(7A)–(7C))
(4) (*amends* FA 2004 Sch 29 para 3(8))
(5) (*inserts* FA 2004 Sch 29 para 3(9)–(12))

23—(1) Paragraph 2 of that Schedule (the permitted maximum) is amended as follows.
(2) (*amends* FA 2004 Sch 29 para 2(6))
(3) (*inserts* FA 2004 Sch 29 para 2(6A), (6B))
(4) (*amends* FA 2004 Sch 29 para 2(7))

24—(1) Paragraph 29 of Schedule 36 (transitional provisions: applicable amount in cases of enhanced protection) is amended as follows.
(2) (*amends* FA 2004 Sch 36 para 29(3))
(3) (*amends* FA 2004 Sch 36 para 29(6))
(4) (*inserts* FA 2004 Sch 36 para 29(7A))

25—(1) Paragraph 34 of that Schedule (transitional provisions: entitlement to lump sums exceeding 25% of uncrystallised rights) is amended as follows.
(2) (*amends* FA 2004 Sch 36 para 34(2), inserted sub-para (7A))
(3) (*inserts* FA 2004 Sch 36 para 34(2), sub-para (7AA))
(4) (*amends* FA 2004 Sch 36 para 34(2), inserted sub-para (7B))
(5) (*amends* FA 2004 Sch 36 para 34(3))

26　(*amends* FA 2004 s 280(2))

Short service refund lump sum: protected rights etc

27　(*amends* FA 2004 Sch 29 para 5(1)(*d*)

Refund of excess contributions lump sum: excess relief at source

28—(1) Paragraph 6 of Schedule 29 (refund of excess contributions lump sum) is amended as follows.
(2) (*amends* FA 2004 Sch 29 para 6(4), (5))
(3) (*inserts* FA 2004 Sch 29 para 6(7))

Benefit crystallisation events: reaching 75 after designation for unsecured pension

30　(*amends* table in FA 2004 s 216(1))

Availability of individual's lifetime allowance: previous benefit crystallisation events

31—(1) Section 219 (availability of individual's lifetime allowance) is amended as follows.
(2) (*amends* FA 2004 s 219(4))
(3) (*inserts* FA 2004 s 219(4A))
(4) (*amends* FA 2004 s 219(5))

Overseas pension schemes: extension of migrant member relief

32—(1) Paragraph 4 of Schedule 33 (meaning of "relevant migrant member") is amended as follows.
(2) (*insert* FA 2004 Sch 33 para 4(2), (3))

Abatement

33　(*amends* FA 2004 s 279(1))

Amendments and transitionals

34—(1) Section 281 (minor and consequential amendments) is amended as follows.
(2) (*inserts* FA 2004 s 281(2A))

(3) (amends FA 2004 s 281(3))

(4) (inserted FA 2004 s 281(4)); repealed by FA 2009 s 75(3)(a).

35—(1) Section 283 (transitionals and savings) is amended as follows.

(2) (inserts FA 2004 s 283(3A)–(3C))

(3) (amends FA 2004 s 283(4) and (5))

Transitional provision: uncrystallised rights under paragraph 9 to include separate lump sums

36—(1) Paragraph 9 of Schedule 36 (uncrystallised rights under arrangement under pension scheme within paragraph 1(1)(a) to (d)) is amended as follows.

(2) (amends FA 2004 Sch 36 para 9(3))

(3) (inserts FA 2004 Sch 36 para 9(5A), (5B))

Transitional protection: taking account of death benefits

37 Schedule 36 (transitional provisions) is amended as follows.

38 *(inserts FA 2004 Sch 36 paras 11A–11D)*

39 *(inserts FA 2004 Sch 36 para 14(3)–(5))*

40 *(amends FA 2004 Sch 36 para 14(3)–(6))*

41 *(inserts FA 2004 Sch 36 para 15A)*

42 *(amends FA 2004 s 256(1))*

Transitional protection: right to take benefits before normal pension age

43—(1) Paragraph 22 of Schedule 36 (right to take benefits before normal minimum pension age: schemes within paragraph 1(1)(a) to (e) of Schedule 36) is amended as follows.

(2) (substitutes FA 2004 Sch 36 para 22(7)(b))

(3) (inserts FA 2004 Sch 36 para 22(7A)–(7J))

Transitional provisions: minor corrections

44 Schedule 36 (transitional provisions) is amended as follows.

45 *(amends FA 2004 Sch 36 paras 9(4)(a) and 26(3)(a))*

46 *(amends FA 2004 Sch 36 para 54(1)(b))*

GOVERNMENT OF WALES ACT 2006

2006 Chapter 32

ARRANGEMENT OF SECTIONS

Part 2: Functions
66   Provision of information to Treasury
66A   Provision of information to the Office for Budget Responsibility
Part 4: Acts of the Assembly
108A   Legislative competence
109A   Legislative competence: restriction relating to retained EU law
Part 4A: Taxation
Chapter 1 Introductory
116A   Overview of Part 4A
116B   Status of officials of body that collects and manages devolved taxes
116C   Power to add new devolved taxes
Chapter 2 Income tax
116D   Power to set Welsh rates for Welsh taxpayers]
116E   Welsh taxpayers
116F   Welsh taxpayers: Scottish parliamentarians
116G   Close connection with Wales or another part of the UK
116H   Days spent in Wales or another part of the UK]
116I   Supplemental powers to modify enactments]
116J   Reimbursement of expenses]
116K   Report by the Comptroller and Auditor General]
Chapter 3 Tax on Transactions Involving Interests in Land
116L, 116M   *(See Orange Tax Handbook Part 2)*
Chapter 4 Tax on Disposals to Landfill
116N   *(See Orange Tax Handbook Part 2)*
Part 6: Miscellaneous and Supplementary
Miscellaneous
156   English and Welsh texts of legislation
Supplementary
157   Orders and directions
157A   "Devolved Welsh authority"
157ZA   Explanatory statements in relation to certain regulations
158   Interpretation
161   Commencement
166   Short title
Schedules:
Schedule 7A—Reserved matters

An Act to make provision about the government of Wales.

PART 2
WELSH . . . GOVERNMENT

Amendments—In heading, word repealed by the Wales Act 2014 s 4(2)(*a*) with effect from 17 February 2015.

Functions

66 Provision of information to Treasury

Where it appears to the Treasury that any information in the possession, or under the control, of the Welsh Ministers is required for the exercise of any function by the Treasury, the Treasury may require the Welsh Ministers to provide the information to the Treasury in such form as the Treasury may reasonably specify.

[66A Provision of information to the Office for Budget Responsibility

(1) The Office for Budget Responsibility has a right of access at any reasonable time to all information held by—

(*a*) the Welsh Ministers, or

(*b*) any devolved Welsh authority within paragraph (*a*) or (*b*) of section 157A(1) that is specified in regulations made by the Secretary of State,

that it may reasonably require for the purpose of the performance of its duty under section 4 of the Budget Responsibility and National Audit Act 2011 (duty to examine and report on the sustainability of the public finances).

(2) The Office is entitled to require from any person holding or accountable for such information any assistance or explanation that the Office reasonably thinks necessary for that purpose.

(3) No regulations are to be made under subsection (1)(b) unless a draft of the statutory instrument containing them has been laid before, and approved by a resolution of, each House of Parliament.

(4) This section is subject to any enactment or rule of law that operates to prohibit or restrict the disclosure of information or the giving of any assistance or explanation.][1]

Amendments—[1]   Section 66A inserted by the Wales Act 2017 s 65 with effect from 1 April 2018 (by virtue of SI 2017/1179 reg 3(*m*)).

PART 4
ACTS OF THE ASSEMBLY

Power

[108A   Legislative competence

(1) An Act of the Assembly is not law so far as any provision of the Act is outside the Assembly's legislative competence.

(2) A provision is outside that competence so far as any of the following paragraphs apply—

> (*a*) it extends otherwise than only to England and Wales;
> (*b*) it applies otherwise than in relation to Wales or confers, imposes, modifies or removes (or gives power to confer, impose, modify or remove) functions exercisable otherwise than in relation to Wales;
> (*c*) it relates to reserved matters (see Schedule 7A);
> (*d*) it breaches any of the restrictions in Part 1 of Schedule 7B, having regard to any exception in Part 2 of that Schedule from those restrictions;
> (*e*) it is incompatible with the Convention rights or with EU law.

(3) But subsection (2)(*b*) does not apply to a provision that—

> (*a*) is ancillary to a provision of any Act of the Assembly or Assembly Measure or to a devolved provision of an Act of Parliament, and
> (*b*) has no greater effect otherwise than in relation to Wales, or in relation to functions exercisable otherwise than in relation to Wales, than is necessary to give effect to the purpose of that provision.

(4) For this purpose, a provision of an Act of Parliament is "devolved" if it would be within the Assembly's legislative competence if it were contained in an Act of the Assembly (ignoring any requirement for consent or consultation imposed under paragraph 8, 10 or 11 of Schedule 7B or otherwise).

(5) In determining what is necessary for the purposes of subsection (3), any power to make laws other than that of the Assembly is disregarded.

(6) The question whether a provision of an Act of the Assembly relates to a reserved matter is determined by reference to the purpose of the provision, having regard (among other things) to its effect in all the circumstances.

(7) For the purposes of this Act a provision is ancillary to another provision if it—

> (*a*) provides for the enforcement of the other provision or is otherwise appropriate for making that provision effective, or
> (*b*) is otherwise incidental to, or consequential on, that provision.][1]

Amendments—[1]   Section 108A substituted for s 108 by the Wales Act 2017 s 3(1) with effect from 1 April 2018 (by virtue of SI 2017/1179).

Prospective amendments—In sub-s (2)(*e*) words "in breach of the restriction in section 109A(1)" to be substituted for words "with EU law" by the European Union (Withdrawal) Act 2018 s 12(3) with effect from a date to be appointed.

[109A   Legislative competence: restriction relating to retained EU law

[(1) An Act of the Assembly cannot modify, or confer power by subordinate legislation to modify, retained EU law so far as the modification is of a description specified in regulations made by a Minister of the Crown.

(2) But subsection (1) does not apply to any modification so far as it would, immediately before [IP completion day][2], have been within the Assembly's legislative competence.

(3) No regulations are to be made under this section unless a draft of the statutory instrument containing them has been laid before, and approved by a resolution of, each House of Parliament.

(4) A Minister of the Crown must not lay a draft as mentioned in subsection (3) unless—

> (*a*) the Assembly has made a consent decision in relation to the laying of the draft, or
> (*b*) the 40 day period has ended without the Assembly having made such a decision.

(5) For the purposes of subsection (4) a consent decision is—

> (*a*) a decision to agree a motion consenting to the laying of the draft,
> (*b*) a decision not to agree a motion consenting to the laying of the draft, or
> (*c*) a decision to agree a motion refusing to consent to the laying of the draft;

and a consent decision is made when the Assembly first makes a decision falling within any of paragraphs (*a*) to (*c*) (whether or not it subsequently makes another such decision).

(6) A Minister of the Crown who is proposing to lay a draft as mentioned in subsection (3) must—

> (*a*) provide a copy of the draft to the Welsh Ministers, and
> (*b*) inform the Presiding Officer that a copy has been so provided.

(7) See also section 157ZA (duty to make explanatory statement about regulations under this section including a duty to explain any decision to lay a draft without the consent of the Assembly).

(8) No regulations may be made under this section after the end of the period of two years beginning with exit day.

(9) Subsection (8) does not affect the continuation in force of regulations made under this section at or before the end of the period mentioned in that subsection.

(10) Any regulations under this section which are in force at the end of the period of five years beginning with the time at which they came into force are revoked in their application to any Act of the Assembly which receives Royal Assent after the end of that period.

(11) Subsections (4) to (9) do not apply in relation to regulations which only relate to a revocation of a specification.

(12) In this section—

"the 40 day period" means the period of 40 days beginning with the day on which a copy of the draft instrument is provided to the Welsh Ministers,

and, in calculating that period, no account is to be taken of any time during which the Assembly is dissolved or during which it is in recess for more than four days.]¹

Amendments—¹   Section 109A inserted by the European Union (Withdrawal) Act 2018 s 12(4) with effect from 26 June 2018 for the purposes of making regulations under this section and with effect from a date to be appointed for remaining purposes.
²   In sub-s (2), words substituted for words "exit day" by the European Union (Withdrawal Agreement) Act 2020 s 46, Sch 5 paras 27, 29 with effect from exit day (31 January 2020 at 11pm) for the purposes of making regulations under this section (by virtue of SI 2020/75 reg 4(n)).

[PART 4A

TAXATION

CHAPTER 1

INTRODUCTORY

116A Overview of Part 4A

(1) In this Part[—

(a) Chapter 2 confers on the Assembly power to set rates of income tax to be paid by Welsh taxpayers, and

(b)] ² Chapters 3 and 4 specify particular taxes as devolved taxes about which the Assembly may make provision in the exercise of the power conferred by section 107(1).

(2) The power to make provision about a devolved tax is subject to the restrictions imposed by—

(a) subsection (3), and

(b) the other provisions of this Part.

(3) A devolved tax may not be imposed where to do so would be incompatible with any international obligations.

(4) In this Act "devolved tax" means a tax specified in this Part as a devolved tax.]¹

Amendments—¹   Sections 116A–116C inserted by the Wales Act 2014 s 6(1), (2) with effect from 17 February 2015.
²   In sub-s (1), words inserted by the Wales Act 2014 s 8(1), (2). Wales Act 2014 s 8 comes into force on 24 July 2018 and has effect in relation to the tax year 2019–20 (by virtue of SI 2018/892 arts 3, 5, 6). 2019–20 is appointed as the first tax year in relation to which a Welsh rate resolution may be made by the National Assembly for Wales under GOWA 2006 s 116D (SI 2018/892 art 6).

[116B Status of officials of body that collects and manages devolved taxes

(1) This section applies where an Act of the Assembly establishes a body that is to be responsible for the collection and management of devolved taxes (whether or not the body is also to be responsible for local government finance or any other matter).

(2) In this section "relevant official" means an officer or member of staff of the body mentioned in subsection (1) who has no functions other than functions relating to—

(a) the collection or management of devolved taxes, or

(b) local government finance.

(3) If an Act of the Assembly provides that service as a relevant official is service in the civil service of the State, that provision is [not to be regarded as falling outside the Assembly's legislative competence by virtue of section 108A(2)(b) or (c)²].

(4) In subsections (5) to (7), "relevant civil servant" means a relevant official whose service is service in the civil service of the State by virtue of provision of the kind mentioned in subsection (3).

(5) The Welsh Ministers must pay the salaries and expenses of relevant civil servants.

(6) The Welsh Ministers must make payments to the Minister for the Civil Service, at such times as the Minister for the Civil Service may determine, of such amounts as may be so determined in respect of—

(a) the provision of pensions, allowances or gratuities by virtue of section 1 of the Superannuation Act 1972 or section 1 of the Public Service Pensions Act 2013 to or in respect of persons who are or have been relevant civil servants, and

(b) the expenses incurred in administering those pensions, allowances and gratuities.

(7) The Welsh Ministers may make payments towards the provision of pensions, allowances or gratuities to or in respect of any person who is or has been a relevant civil servant.]¹

Amendments—[1]   Sections 116A–116C inserted by the Wales Act 2014 s 6(1), (2) with effect from 17 February 2015.
[2]   In sub-s (3), words substituted by the Wales Act 2017 s 69, Sch 6 paras 1, 6 with effect from 1 April 2018 (by virtue of SI 2017/1179 reg 3(n), (q)).

[116C Power to add new devolved taxes

(1) Her Majesty may by Order in Council amend this Part so as to—
    (a) specify, as an additional devolved tax, a tax of any description, or
    (b) make any other modifications of the provisions relating to devolved taxes which She considers appropriate.

(2) An Order in Council under this section may make such modifications of—
    (a) any enactment (including any enactment comprised in or made under this Act) or prerogative instrument, or
    (b) any other instrument or document,

as Her Majesty considers appropriate in connection with the provision made by the Order.

(3) No recommendation is to be made to Her Majesty in Council to make an Order in Council under this section unless a draft of the statutory instrument containing the Order has been laid before, and approved by a resolution of, each House of Parliament and the Assembly.

(4) The amendment of this Part by an Order in Council under this section does not affect—
    (a) the validity of an Act of the Assembly passed before the amendment comes into force, or
    (b) the previous or continuing operation of such an Act of the Assembly.][1]

Amendments—[1]   Sections 116A–116C inserted by the Wales Act 2014 s 6(1), (2) with effect from 17 February 2015.

[CHAPTER 2

INCOME TAX

116D Power to set Welsh rates for Welsh taxpayers

(1) The Assembly may by resolution (a "Welsh rate resolution") set one or more of the following—
    (a) a Welsh rate for the purpose of calculating the Welsh basic rate;
    (b) a Welsh rate for the purpose of calculating the Welsh higher rate;
    (c) a Welsh rate for the purpose of calculating the Welsh additional rate.

(2) See section 6B of the Income Tax Act 2007 for provision about the calculation of the Welsh basic, higher and additional rates and section 11B of that Act for provision about the income of Welsh taxpayers charged at those rates.

(3) A Welsh rate resolution applies—
    (a) for only one tax year, and
    (b) for the whole of that year.

(4) Any Welsh rate specified must be a whole number or half a whole number.

(5) A Welsh rate resolution—
    (a) must specify the tax year for which it applies,
    (b) must be made before the start of that tax year, and
    (c) must not be made more than 12 months before the start of that year.

(6) If a Welsh rate resolution is cancelled before the start of the tax year for which it is to apply—
    (a) the Income Tax Acts have effect for that year as if the resolution had never been made, and
    (b) the resolution may be replaced by another Welsh rate resolution.

(7) The standing orders must provide that only the First Minister or a Welsh Minister appointed under section 48 may move a motion for a Welsh rate resolution.][1]

Amendments—[1]   Chapter 2 (ss 116D–116K) inserted by the Wales Act 2014 s 8(1), (3). Wales Act 2014 s 8 comes into force on 24 July 2018 and has effect in relation to the tax year 2019–20 (by virtue of SI 2018/892 arts 3, 5, 6). 2019–20 is appointed as the first tax year in relation to which a Welsh rate resolution may be made by the National Assembly for Wales under GOWA 2006 s 116D (SI 2018/892 art 6).

[116E Welsh taxpayers

(1) For any tax year, a Welsh taxpayer is an individual (T)—
    (a) who is resident in the UK for income tax purposes for that year (see Schedule 45 to the Finance Act 2013), and
    (b) who, for that year, meets condition A, B or C.

(2) T meets condition A if T has a close connection with Wales (see section 116G).

(3) T meets condition B if—
    (a) T does not have a close connection with England, Scotland or Northern Ireland (see section 116G), and
    (b) T spends more days of that year in Wales than in any other part of the UK (see section 116H).

(4) T meets condition C if, for the whole or any part of the year, T is—
    (a) a member of Parliament for a constituency in Wales,
    (b) a member of the European Parliament for Wales, or
    (c) an Assembly member.

(5) Subsection (1) does not apply if T is a Scottish parliamentarian for the whole or any part of the year (see section 116F).

(6) For the purposes of subsection (5) and section 116F, T is a Scottish parliamentarian if T is a member as described in any of paragraphs (*a*) to (*c*) of section 80D(4) of the Scotland Act 1998 (definition of a Scottish taxpayer).

(7) In this Chapter "the UK" means the United Kingdom.]¹

Amendments—¹   Chapter 2 (ss 116D–116K) inserted by the Wales Act 2014 s 8(1), (3). Wales Act 2014 s 8 comes into force on 24 July 2018 and has effect in relation to the tax year 2019–20 (by virtue of SI 2018/892 arts 3, 5, 6). 2019–20 is appointed as the first tax year in relation to which a Welsh rate resolution may be made by the National Assembly for Wales under GOWA 2006 s 116D (SI 2018/892 art 6).

Prospective amendments—In sub-s (4), word "or" to be inserted at end of para (*a*), and para (*b*) and word "or" to be repealed, and in sub-s (6), words "paragraph (*a*) or (*c*)" to be substituted for words "any of paragraphs (*a*) to (*c*)", by the European Union (Withdrawal) Act 2018 s 12(12), Sch 3 paras 27, 41 with effect from a date to be appointed.

[116F Welsh taxpayers: Scottish parliamentarians

(1) An individual (T) who is a Scottish parliamentarian for the whole or any part of a tax year is a Welsh taxpayer for that tax year if—

    (*a*) T is resident in the UK for income tax purposes for that year (see Schedule 45 to the Finance Act 2013),

    (*b*) T meets condition C in section 116E for that year, and

    (*c*) T meets either of the following conditions for that year.

(2) T meets the first condition if—

    (*a*) the number of days in that year on which T is a member as described in any of paragraphs (*a*) to (*c*) of section 116E(4), exceeds

    (*b*) the number of days in that year on which T is a Scottish parliamentarian.

(3) T meets the second condition if—

    (*a*) the number of days in that year mentioned in paragraphs (*a*) and (*b*) of subsection (2) are the same, and

    (*b*) T meets condition A or B in section 116E for that year.]¹

Amendments—¹   Chapter 2 (ss 116D–116K) inserted by the Wales Act 2014 s 8(1), (3). Wales Act 2014 s 8 comes into force on 24 July 2018 and has effect in relation to the tax year 2019–20 (by virtue of SI 2018/892 arts 3, 5, 6). 2019–20 is appointed as the first tax year in relation to which a Welsh rate resolution may be made by the National Assembly for Wales under GOWA 2006 s 116D (SI 2018/892 art 6).

Prospective amendments—In sub-s (2)(*a*), words "paragraph (*a*) or (*c*)" to be substituted for words "any of paragraphs (*a*) to (*c*)" by the European Union (Withdrawal) Act 2018 s 12(12), Sch 3 paras 27, 42 with effect from a date to be appointed.

[116G Close connection with Wales or another part of the UK

(1) To find whether, for any year, T has a close connection with any part of the UK see—

    (*a*) subsection (2) (where T has only one place of residence in the UK), or

    (*b*) subsection (3) (where T has 2 or more places of residence in the UK).

(2) T has a close connection with a part of the UK if in that year—

    (*a*) T has only one place of residence in the UK,

    (*b*) that place of residence is in that part of the UK, and

    (*c*) for at least part of the year, T lives at that place.

(3) T has a close connection with a part of the UK if in that year—

    (*a*) T has 2 or more places of residence in the UK,

    (*b*) for at least part of the year, T's main place of residence in the UK is in that part of the UK,

    (*c*) the times in the year when T's main place of residence is in that part of the UK comprise (in aggregate) more of the year than the times when T's main place of residence is in each other part of the UK (considered separately), and

    (*d*) for at least part of the year, T lives at a place of residence in that part of the UK.

(4) In this section "place" includes a place on board a vessel or other means of transport.]¹

Amendments—¹   Chapter 2 (ss 116D–116K) inserted by the Wales Act 2014 s 8(1), (3). Wales Act 2014 s 8 comes into force on 24 July 2018 and has effect in relation to the tax year 2019–20 (by virtue of SI 2018/892 arts 3, 5, 6). 2019–20 is appointed as the first tax year in relation to which a Welsh rate resolution may be made by the National Assembly for Wales under GOWA 2006 s 116D (SI 2018/892 art 6).

[116H Days spent in Wales or another part of the UK

(1) T spends more days of a year in Wales than in any other part of the UK if (and only if) the number of days in the year on which T is in Wales at the end of the day exceeds each of the following—

    (*a*) the number of days in the year on which T is in England at the end of the day;

    (*b*) the number of days in the year on which T is in Scotland at the end of the day;

    (*c*) the number of days in the year on which T is in Northern Ireland at the end of the day.

(2) T is treated as not being in the UK at the end of a day if—

    (*a*) on that day T arrives in the UK as a passenger,

    (*b*) T departs from the UK on the next day, and

    (*c*) during the time between arrival and departure T does not engage in activities which are to a substantial extent unrelated to T's passage through the UK.]¹

Amendments—[1]   Chapter 2 (ss 116D–116K) inserted by the Wales Act 2014 s 8(1), (3). Wales Act 2014 s 8 comes into force
on 24 July 2018 and has effect in relation to the tax year 2019–20 (by virtue of SI 2018/892 arts 3, 5, 6). 2019–20 is appointed
as the first tax year in relation to which a Welsh rate resolution may be made by the National Assembly for Wales under
GOWA 2006 s 116D (SI 2018/892 art 6).

[116I Supplemental powers to modify enactments

(1) The Treasury may by order modify section 11B of the Income Tax Act 2007 (income charged at the Welsh basic, higher and additional rates) for the purpose of altering—

    (*a*) the definition of the income which is charged to income tax at the rates provided for under the section, or

    (*b*) the application of the section in relation to a particular class of income which is so charged.

(2) The Treasury may by order modify any enactment not contained in Chapter 2 of Part 2 of the Income Tax Act 2007 (rates at which income tax is charged) so that it makes provision, in relation to a Welsh taxpayer, by reference to the Welsh basic rate, the Welsh higher rate or the Welsh additional rate, instead of the basic rate, the higher rate or the additional rate.

(3) If the Treasury consider it necessary or expedient to do so, they may by order provide that—

    (*a*) a Welsh rate set by the Assembly for a tax year for the purpose of calculating the Welsh basic rate, Welsh higher rate or Welsh additional rate, or

    (*b*) the fact that a Welsh rate has not been set by the Assembly for a tax year for any one or more of those purposes,

does not require any change in the amounts repayable or deductible under PAYE regulations between the beginning of that year and such later date as may be specified in the order.

(4) The Treasury may by order make such modifications of any enactment as they consider necessary or expedient in consequence of or in connection with an order under subsection (1), (2) or (3).

(5) An order under this section may, to the extent that the Treasury consider it to be appropriate, take effect retrospectively from the beginning of the tax year in which the order is made.

(6) No order is to be made under subsection (1), (2) or (4) unless a draft of the statutory instrument containing it has been laid before, and approved by a resolution of, the House of Commons.

(7) A statutory instrument containing an order under subsection (3) is subject to annulment in pursuance of a resolution of the House of Commons.

(8) The power under subsection (1) does not include power to provide that any income which is—

    (*a*) savings income, or

    (*b*) dividend income which would otherwise be charged to income tax at a rate provided for under section 13 of the Income Tax Act 2007,

is income which is charged to income tax at a rate provided for under section 11B of that Act.][1]

Amendments—[1]   Chapter 2 (ss 116D–116K) inserted by the Wales Act 2014 s 8(1), (3). Wales Act 2014 s 8 comes into force
on 24 July 2018 and has effect in relation to the tax year 2019–20 (by virtue of SI 2018/892 arts 3, 5, 6). 2019–20 is appointed
as the first tax year in relation to which a Welsh rate resolution may be made by the National Assembly for Wales under
GOWA 2006 s 116D (SI 2018/892 art 6).

[116J Reimbursement of expenses

The Welsh Ministers may reimburse any Minister of the Crown or government department for administrative expenses incurred by virtue of this Chapter at any time after the passing of the Wales Act 2014 by the Minister or department.][1]

Amendments—[1]   Chapter 2 (ss 116D–116K) inserted by the Wales Act 2014 s 8(1), (3). Wales Act 2014 s 8 comes into force
on 24 July 2018 and has effect in relation to the tax year 2019–20 (by virtue of SI 2018/892 arts 3, 5, 6). 2019–20 is appointed
as the first tax year in relation to which a Welsh rate resolution may be made by the National Assembly for Wales under
GOWA 2006 s 116D (SI 2018/892 art 6).

[116K Report by the Comptroller and Auditor General

(1) The Comptroller and Auditor General must for each financial year prepare a report on the matters set out in subsection (2).

(2) Those matters are—

    (*a*) the adequacy of any of HMRC's rules and procedures put in place, in consequence of the Welsh rate provisions, for the purpose of ensuring the proper assessment and collection of income tax charged at rates determined under those provisions,

    (*b*) whether the rules and procedures described in paragraph (*a*) are being complied with,

    (*c*) the correctness of the sums brought to account by HMRC which relate to income tax which is attributable to a Welsh rate resolution, and

    (*d*) the accuracy and fairness of the amounts which are reimbursed to HMRC under section 116J (having been identified by it as administrative expenses incurred as a result of the charging of income tax as mentioned in paragraph (*a*)).

(3) "The Welsh rate provisions" are—

    (*a*) any provision made by or under this Chapter, and

    (*b*) any provision made by or under the Income Tax Acts relating to the Welsh basic rate, the Welsh higher rate or the Welsh additional rate.

(4) A report under this section may also include an assessment of the economy, efficiency and effectiveness with which HMRC has used its resources in carrying out relevant functions.

(5) "Relevant functions" are functions of HMRC in the performance of which HMRC incurs administrative expenses which are reimbursed to HMRC under section 116J (having been identified by it as administrative expenses incurred as a result of the charging of income tax as mentioned in subsection (2)(*a*)).

(6) HMRC must give the Comptroller and Auditor General such information as the Comptroller and Auditor General may reasonably require for the purposes of preparing a report under this section.

(7) A report prepared under this section must be laid before the Assembly not later than 31 January of the financial year following that to which the report relates.

(8) In this section "HMRC" means Her Majesty's Revenue and Customs.][1]

Amendments—[1]   Chapter 2 (ss 116D–116K) inserted by the Wales Act 2014 s 8(1), (3). Wales Act 2014 s 8 comes into force on 24 July 2018 and has effect in relation to the tax year 2019–20 (by virtue of SI 2018/892 arts 3, 5, 6). 2019–20 is appointed as the first tax year in relation to which a Welsh rate resolution may be made by the National Assembly for Wales under GOWA 2006 s 116D (SI 2018/892 art 6).

PART 6
MISCELLANEOUS AND SUPPLEMENTARY
Miscellaneous

156 English and Welsh texts of legislation

(1) The English and Welsh texts of—

    (*a*) any Assembly Measure or Act of the Assembly which is in both English and Welsh when it is enacted, or

    (*b*) any subordinate legislation which is in both English and Welsh when it is made,

are to be treated for all purposes as being of equal standing.

(2) The Welsh Ministers may by order provide in respect of any Welsh word or phrase that, when it appears in the Welsh text of any Assembly Measure or Act of the Assembly, or any subordinate legislation made under an Assembly Measure or Act of the Assembly or by the Welsh Ministers, it is to be taken as having the same meaning as the English word or phrase specified in relation to it in the order.

(3) No order is to be made under subsection (2) unless a draft of the statutory instrument containing it has been laid before, and approved by a resolution of, the Assembly.

(4) An Assembly Measure or Act of the Assembly, or any subordinate legislation made under an Assembly Measure or Act of the Assembly or by the Welsh Ministers, is to be construed in accordance with any order under subsection (2); but this is subject to anything to the contrary contained in the Assembly Measure, Act of the Assembly or subordinate legislation.

(5) This section applies in relation to subordinate legislation made by the First Minister or the Counsel General as in relation to subordinate legislation made by the Welsh Ministers.

Supplementary

157 Orders[, regulations] and directions

(1) Any power of a Minister of the Crown or the Welsh Ministers under this Act to make an order [or regulations][1] is exercisable by statutory instrument.

(2) Any such power and any power under this Act to make an Order in Council—

    (*a*) may be exercised so as to make different provision for different cases or classes of case or different purposes,

    (*b*) may be exercised so as to make provision which applies generally or subject to specified exemptions or exceptions or only in relation to specific cases or classes of case, and

    (*c*) includes power to make supplementary, incidental, consequential, transitory, transitional or saving provision.

(3) Any power conferred by this Act to give a direction includes power to vary or revoke the direction.

Orders—Welsh Ministers (Transfer of Functions) (Railways) Order, SI 2018/631.

Amendments—[1]   In heading and in sub-s (1), words inserted by the Wales Act 2017 s 69, Sch 6 paras 1, 8 with effect from 1 April 2018 (by virtue of SI 2017/1179 reg 3(*n*), (*q*)).

[157A "Devolved Welsh authority"

(1) In this Act "devolved Welsh authority" means—

    (*a*) a public authority that meets the conditions in subsection (2),

    (*b*) a public authority that is specified, or is of a description specified, in Schedule 9A (whether or not it meets those conditions), or

    (*c*) the governing body of an institution within the higher education sector (within the meaning of section 91(5) of the Further and Higher Education Act 1992) whose activities are carried on, or principally carried on, in Wales.

(2) A public authority meets the conditions in this section if its functions—

    (*a*) are exercisable only in relation to Wales, and

    (*b*) are wholly or mainly functions that do not relate to reserved matters.

(3) In determining for the purposes of this section whether functions of a public authority are exercisable only in relation to Wales, no account is taken of any function that—

    (*a*) is exercisable otherwise than in relation to Wales, and

    (*b*) could (apart from this paragraph) be conferred or imposed by provision falling within the Assembly's legislative competence (by virtue of section 108A(3)).

(4) Where the conditions in subsection (2) are relevant to determining whether a provision of an Act of the Assembly is within the Assembly's legislative competence, the time for assessing whether those conditions are met is the time when the Act is passed.

(5) Her Majesty may by Order in Council amend Schedule 9A—

    (*a*) so as to remove or revise an entry, or

    (*b*) so as to add or substitute a public authority whose functions—

        (i) are exercisable wholly or mainly in relation to Wales, and

        (ii) are wholly or mainly functions that do not relate to reserved matters.

(6) No recommendation is to be made to Her Majesty in Council to make an Order in Council under this section unless a draft of the statutory instrument containing the Order in Council has been laid before, and approved by a resolution of, each House of Parliament and the Assembly.

(7) Subsection (6) does not apply to a statutory instrument containing an Order in Council that only makes provision for—

    (*a*) the omission of an entry where the authority concerned has ceased to exist, or

    (*b*) the variation of an entry in consequence of a change of name or transfer of functions.

Such an Order in Council is subject to annulment in pursuance of a resolution of either House of Parliament.

(8) In this section "public authority" means a body, office or holder of an office that has functions of a public nature.][1]

Amendments—[1] Section 157A inserted by the Wales Act 2017 s 4(1) with effect from 1 April 2018 (by virtue of SI 2017/1179 reg 3(*a*)).

[157ZA Explanatory statements in relation to certain regulations

(1) This section applies where a draft of a statutory instrument containing regulations under section 80(8) or 109A is to be laid before each House of Parliament.

(2) Before the draft is laid, the Minister of the Crown who is to make the instrument—

    (*a*) must make a statement explaining the effect of the instrument, and

    (*b*) in any case where the Assembly has not made a decision to agree a motion consenting to the laying of the draft—

        (i) must make a statement explaining why the Minister has decided to lay the draft despite this, and

        (ii) must lay before each House of Parliament any statement provided for the purpose of this sub-paragraph to a Minister of the Crown by the Welsh Ministers giving the opinion of the Welsh Ministers as to why the Assembly has not made that decision.

(3) A statement of a Minister of the Crown under subsection (2) must be made in writing and be published in such manner as the Minister making it considers appropriate.

(4) For the purposes of this section, where a draft is laid before each House of Parliament on different days, the earlier day is to be taken as the day on which it is laid before both Houses.

(5) This section does not apply to a draft of an instrument which only contains regulations under section 80(8) or 109A which only relate to a revocation of a specification.][1]

Amendments—[1] Section 157ZA inserted by the European Union (Withdrawal) Act 2018 s 12(12), Sch 3 paras 27, 43 with effect from 26 June 2018 for the purposes of making regulations under ss 80(8) or 109A, and with effect from a date to be appointed for remaining purposes.

158 Interpretation

(1) In this Act (except where the context otherwise requires)—

    "[EU][2] law" means—

        (*a*) all the rights, powers, liabilities, obligations and restrictions from time to time created or arising by or under the [EU][2] Treaties, and

        (*b*) all the remedies and procedures from time to time provided for by or under the [EU][2] Treaties,

    "the Convention rights" has the same meaning as in the Human Rights Act 1998 (c 42),

    "cross-border body" means any body (including a government department) or undertaker exercising functions, or carrying on activities, in or with respect to Wales (or any part of Wales) and anywhere else,

    "enactment" includes an Assembly Measure, an Act of the Assembly and subordinate legislation (but see also subsection (2)),

    "English border area" means a part of England adjoining Wales (but not the whole of England),

    "financial year" means the twelve months ending with 31st March,

    "function" means power or duty,

    "government department" means any department of the Government of the United Kingdom,

    "international obligations" means any international obligations of the United Kingdom other than obligations to observe and implement [EU][2] law or the Convention rights,

"Minister of the Crown" includes the Treasury,

"modifications" includes amendments, repeals and revocations,

["property" includes rights and interests of any description,][4]

"subordinate legislation" has the same meaning as in the Interpretation Act 1978 (c 30) (including an instrument made under an Assembly Measure or Act of the Assembly),

"tribunal" means any tribunal in which legal proceedings may be brought, . . .[1]

"Wales" includes the sea adjacent to Wales out as far as the seaward boundary of the territorial sea[, and

"Welsh zone" means the sea adjacent to Wales which is—

    (*a*) within British fishery limits (that is, the limits set by or under section 1 of the Fishery Limits Act 1976), and

    (*b*) specified in an Order in Council under section 58 or an order under subsection (3)][1].

(2) In sections 95(3), 109(2)[, 116C(2)][, 150A(2)][3] and 151(2) "enactment" includes an Act of the Scottish Parliament and an instrument made under such an Act.

[(3) The Secretary of State may by order determine, or make provision for determining, for the purposes of the definitions of "Wales" and the "Welsh zone", any boundary between waters which are to be treated as parts of the sea adjacent to Wales, or sea within British fishery limits adjacent to Wales, and those which are not.][1]

(4) An Order in Council under section 58 may include any provision that may be included in an order under subsection (3).

(5) No order is to be made under subsection (3) unless a draft of the statutory instrument containing it has been laid before, and approved by a resolution of, each House of Parliament.

(6) Section 13 of the National Audit Act 1983 (c 44) (interpretation of references to the Committee of Public Accounts) applies for the purposes of this Act as for those of that Act.

Amendments—[1]   In sub-s (1), in definition of "tribunal", word repealed, definition "Welsh zone" and preceding word inserted, and sub-s (3) substituted, by the Marine and Coastal Access Act 2009 s 43(1), (2) with effect for certain purposes from 12 November 2009: (Marine and Coastal Access Act 2009, s 324(1)(*c*), (*d*), and for remaining purposes from 12 January 2010 (by virtue of SI 2009/3345, art 2, Schedule, para 7).

[2]   In sub-s (1), in definitions "EU law" and "international obligations", reference to "EU" substituted by Treaty of Lisbon (Changes in Terminology) Order, SI 2011/1043, art 6 with effect from 22 April 2011.

[3]   In sub-s (2), reference inserted by the Wales Act 2017 s 16(2) with effect from 31 March 2017.

[4]   In sub-s (1), definition of "property" inserted by the Wales Act 2017 s 69, Sch 6 paras 1, 9 with effect from 1 April 2018 (by virtue of SI 2017/1179 reg 3(*n*), (*q*)).

Prospective amendments—In sub-s (1), definition of "EU law" to be repealed, and in definition of "international obligations", words "EU law or" to be repealed, by the European Union (Withdrawal) Act 2018 s 12(12), Sch 3 paras 27, 44 with effect from a date to be appointed.

161 Commencement

(1) Subject as follows, this Act comes into force immediately after the ordinary election under section 3 of the Government of Wales Act 1998 (c 38) held in 2007 (referred to in this Act as "the 2007 election").

(2) The following provisions come into force on the day on which this Act is passed—

    paragraphs 5, 6 and 12 of Schedule 2,

    sections 95 and 96 and Schedule 5,

    section 109 and Schedule 7,

    section 119 and the repeal by Schedule 12 of section 81 of the Government of Wales Act 1998,

    section 120(3) and (7),

    section 125 and the repeal by Schedule 12 of section 86 of the Government of Wales Act 1998,

    sections 157 to 159,

    section 160(2) to (4),

    the amendment made by paragraph 61 of Schedule 10 in section 13 of the Political Parties, Elections and Referendums Act 2000 (c 41),

    this section,

    section 162 and Schedule 11,

    the repeal by Schedule 12 of section 12(1)(*d*) of the Government of Wales Act 1998, and

    sections 164 to 166.

(3) The following provisions come into force on 1st April 2007—

    sections 117 and 118 and the repeal by Schedule 12 of section 80 of the Government of Wales Act 1998,

    section 120(1) and (2), (4) to (6) and (8) and the repeal by Schedule 12 of section 84 of that Act,

    sections 121 and 122 and the repeal by Schedule 12 of section 82 of that Act,

    section 124 and the repeal by Schedule 12 of sections 85(1) and 89 of that Act,

    section 126,

    sections 128 and 129, and

    the amendments in the Local Government, Planning and Land Act 1980 (c 65), the Local Government Finance Act 1988 (c 41) and the Housing Act 1988 (c 50) made by Schedule 10.

(4) Subject to subsections (2), (3) and (6), the following provisions come into force immediately after the end of the initial period—

    (*a*) any provision of this Act so far as relating to functions of the Welsh Ministers, the First Minister, the Counsel General or the Assembly Commission,

    (*b*) any provision of this Act so far as relating to the Auditor General or the Comptroller and Auditor General,

    (*c*) any other provision consisting of an amendment made in the Government of Wales Act 1998 (c 38) by Schedule 10, and

    (*d*) the repeal by Schedule 12 of provisions falling to be repealed in consequence of any provision within paragraph (*a*), (*b*) or (*c*).

(5) In this Act "the initial period" means the period—

    (*a*) beginning with the day of the poll at the 2007 election, and

    (*b*) ending with the day on which the first appointment is made under section 46.

(6) The repeals by Schedule 12 of each of sections 83, 88, 93(8), 97 and 101A of the Government of Wales Act 1998 (and of the other provisions of that Act so far as relating to them) come into force when the section has been complied with for the financial year ending with 31st March 2007 (and earlier financial years); and sections 123, 131, 132 and 141 do not apply for that financial year.

(7) . . .¹

Amendments—¹   Sub-s (7) repealed by the Wales Act 2017 s 69, Sch 6 paras 1, 11 with effect from 1 April 2018 (by virtue of SI 2017/1179 reg 3(*n*), (*q*)).

166 Short title

This Act may be cited as the Government of Wales Act 2006.

[SCHEDULE 7A

RESERVED MATTERS

Section 108A

PART 1

GENERAL RESERVATIONS

The Constitution

1   The following aspects of the constitution are reserved matters—

    (a) the Crown, including succession to the Crown and a regency;

    (b) the union of the nations of Wales and England;

    (c) the Parliament of the United Kingdom.]¹

Amendments—¹   Schedule 7A substituted for previous Sch 7 by the Wales Act 2017 s 3(2) with effect from 1 April 2018 (by virtue of SI 2017/1179 reg 2).

[**2** (1) Paragraph 1 does not reserve—

    (a) Her Majesty's executive functions,

    (b) functions exercisable by any person acting on behalf of the Crown, or

    (c) the use of the Welsh Seal.

(2) Sub-paragraph (1) does not affect the reservation by paragraph 1 of the management (in accordance with any enactment regulating the use of land) of the Crown Estate.

(3) Sub-paragraph (1) does not affect the reservation by paragraph 1 of the functions of the Security Service, the Secret Intelligence Service and the Government Communications Headquarters.

(4) In this paragraph "executive function" does not include a function conferred or imposed by or by virtue of any legislation or the prerogative.]¹

Amendments—¹   Schedule 7A substituted for previous Sch 7 by the Wales Act 2017 s 3(2) with effect from 1 April 2018 (by virtue of SI 2017/1179 reg 2).

[**3** (1) Paragraph 1 does not reserve property belonging—

    (a) to Her Majesty in right of the Crown,

    (b) to Her Majesty in right of the Duchy of Lancaster, or

    (c) to the Duchy of Cornwall.

(2) Paragraph 1 does not reserve property belonging to any person acting on behalf of the Crown or held in trust for Her Majesty for the purposes of any person acting on behalf of the Crown.

(3) Sub-paragraphs (1) and (2) do not affect the reservation by paragraph 1 of—

    (a) the hereditary revenues of the Crown,

    (b) the royal arms and standard, or

    (c) the compulsory acquisition of property—

        (i) belonging to Her Majesty in right of the Crown;

        (ii) belonging to Her Majesty in right of the Duchy of Lancaster;

        (iii) belonging to the Duchy of Cornwall;

(iv) held or used by a Minister of the Crown or government department.][1]

Amendments—[1]   Schedule 7A substituted for previous Sch 7 by the Wales Act 2017 s 3(2) with effect from 1 April 2018 (by virtue of SI 2017/1179 reg 2).

[4 (1) Paragraph 1 does not reserve property held by Her Majesty in Her private capacity.

(2) Sub-paragraph (1) does not affect the reservation by paragraph 1 of the subject-matter of the Crown Private Estates Acts 1800 to 1873.][1]

Amendments—[1]   Schedule 7A substituted for previous Sch 7 by the Wales Act 2017 s 3(2) with effect from 1 April 2018 (by virtue of SI 2017/1179 reg 2).

[Single legal jurisdiction of England and Wales

8   (1) The following are reserved matters—

  (a) courts (including, in particular, their creation and jurisdiction);

  (b) judges (including, in particular, their appointment and remuneration);

  (c) civil or criminal proceedings (including, in particular, bail, costs, custody pending trial, disclosure, enforcement of orders of courts, evidence, sentencing, limitation of actions, procedure, prosecutors and remedies);

  (d) pardons for criminal offences;

  (e) private international law;

  (f) judicial review of administrative action.

(See also paragraphs 3 and 4 of Schedule 7B (restrictions on modifying private law and criminal law).)

(2) The reference to prosecutors in sub-paragraph (1)(c) does not prevent an Act of the Assembly from making provision about responsibility for the prosecution of devolved offences.

(3) Sub-paragraph (1) does not reserve—

  (a) welfare advice to courts in respect of family proceedings in which the welfare of children ordinarily resident in Wales is or may be in question;

  (b) representation in respect of such proceedings;

  (c) the provision of support (including information and advice), to children ordinarily resident in Wales and their families, in respect of such proceedings;

  (d) Welsh family proceedings officers.][1]

Amendments—[1]   Schedule 7A substituted for previous Sch 7 by the Wales Act 2017 s 3(2) with effect from 1 April 2018 (by virtue of SI 2017/1179 reg 2).

[Tribunals

9   (1) Tribunals, including—

  (a) their membership,

  (b) the appointment and remuneration of their members,

  (c) their functions and procedure, and

  (d) appeals against their decisions,

are a reserved matter.

(2) But this paragraph does not apply to a tribunal (a "devolved tribunal") all of whose functions are functions that—

  (a) are exercisable only in relation to Wales, and

  (b) do not relate to reserved matters.

(3) In the case of a tribunal which has functions that do not relate to reserved matters, sub-paragraph (1) does not reserve any function of deciding an appeal or application which—

  (a) relates to a matter that is not a reserved matter, and

  (b) is not an appeal against the decision of a tribunal (other than a devolved tribunal),

but it does reserve the tribunal's procedure in relation to that function.

(4) In determining for the purposes of this paragraph whether functions of a tribunal are exercisable only in relation to Wales, no account is taken of any function that—

  (a) is exercisable otherwise than in relation to Wales, and

  (b) could (apart from paragraph 8 of Schedule 7B) be conferred or imposed by provision falling within the Assembly's legislative competence (by virtue of section 108A(3)).

(5) Where the question whether this paragraph applies to a particular tribunal is relevant to determining whether a provision of an Act of the Assembly is within the Assembly's legislative competence, the time for deciding the question is the time when the Act is passed.][1]

Amendments—[1]   Schedule 7A substituted for previous Sch 7 by the Wales Act 2017 s 3(2) with effect from 1 April 2018 (by virtue of SI 2017/1179 reg 2).

[Foreign affairs etc

10   (1) International relations, regulation of international trade, and international development assistance and co-operation are reserved matters.

(2) In sub-paragraph (1) "international relations" includes—

(a) relations with territories outside the United Kingdom;

(b) relations with the EU and its institutions;

(c) relations with other international organisations.

(3) But sub-paragraph (1) does not reserve—

(a) observing and implementing international obligations, obligations under the Human Rights Convention and obligations under EU law, or

(b) assisting Ministers of the Crown in relation to any matter to which that sub-paragraph applies.

(4) In this paragraph "the Human Rights Convention" means—

(a) the Convention for the Protection of Human Rights and Fundamental Freedoms, agreed by the Council of Europe at Rome on 4th November 1950, and

(b) the Protocols to the Convention,

as they have effect for the time being in relation to the United Kingdom.]¹

Amendments—¹   Schedule 7A substituted for previous Sch 7 by the Wales Act 2017 s 3(2) with effect from 1 April 2018 (by virtue of SI 2017/1179 reg 2).

[PART 2
SPECIFIC RESERVATIONS

Preliminary

12   The matters to which any of the Sections in this Part apply are reserved matters.]¹

Amendments—¹   Schedule 7A substituted for previous Sch 7 by the Wales Act 2017 s 3(2) with effect from 1 April 2018 (by virtue of SI 2017/1179 reg 2).

[**13**   A Section applies to any matter described or referred to in it when read with any exceptions or interpretation provisions in that Section.]¹

Amendments—¹   Schedule 7A substituted for previous Sch 7 by the Wales Act 2017 s 3(2) with effect from 1 April 2018 (by virtue of SI 2017/1179 reg 2).

[**14**   Any exceptions or interpretation provisions in a Section relate only to that Section (so that an entry under the heading "Exceptions" does not affect any other Section).]¹

Amendments—¹   Schedule 7A substituted for previous Sch 7 by the Wales Act 2017 s 3(2) with effect from 1 April 2018 (by virtue of SI 2017/1179 reg 2).

[Reservations

Head A—Financial and Economic Matters
Section A1
A1 Fiscal, economic and monetary policy

15   Fiscal, economic and monetary policy, including the issue and circulation of money, taxes and excise duties, government borrowing and lending, control over United Kingdom public expenditure, the exchange rate and the Bank of England.

Exceptions

Devolved taxes, including their collection and management.

Local taxes to fund local authority expenditure (for example, council tax and non-domestic rates).

Section A3
A3 Financial services

17   Financial services, including investment business, banking and deposit-taking, collective investment schemes and insurance.

Section A4
A4 Financial markets

18   Financial markets, including listing and public offers of securities and investments, transfer of securities and insider dealing.

Section A5
A5 Dormant accounts

19   Distribution of money from dormant bank and building society accounts.

Section B22
B22 Charities and fund-raising

63   Charities.

64   Raising funds for charitable, benevolent or philanthropic purposes.
Interpretation
   "Funds" includes property other than money.
Head C—Trade and Industry
Section C1
C1 Business associations and business names

65   The creation, operation, regulation and dissolution of types of business association.

66   The regulation of the name under which an individual or business association carries on business.
Exception
   The creation, operation, regulation and dissolution of particular public bodies, or public bodies of a particular type, established by or under any enactment.
Interpretation
   "Business association" means any entity, whether or not a legal person, that is not an individual (including a body corporate, partnership or other unincorporated association) and is established for the purpose of carrying on any kind of business, whether or not for profit.
   "Business" includes the provision of benefits to the members of an association.
Section C2
C2 Insolvency and winding up

67   Insolvency.

68   Winding up solvent business associations.
Interpretation
   "Business association" has the same meaning as in Section C1.
Section F1
F1 Social security schemes

130   Social security schemes supported from public funds.

131   Requiring persons—
   (a) to establish and administer, or make payments to or in respect of, social security schemes, and
   (b) to keep records and supply information in connection with social security schemes.
Exceptions
   The provision by a local authority of financial assistance to or in respect of an individual in respect of costs of meeting his or her needs for care or support that the authority would otherwise meet in some other way (for example, by providing accommodation, facilities or services).
   The deferral of payment due to a local authority from an individual in respect of costs of, or financial assistance for, meeting that or another individual's needs for care or support.
Interpretation
   "Social security schemes" means schemes providing financial assistance for social security purposes to or in respect of individuals, including, in particular, providing such assistance to or in respect of individuals—
   (a) who qualify by reason of old age, survivorship, disability, sickness, incapacity, injury, unemployment, maternity or the care of children or others needing care,
   (b) who qualify by reason of low income, or
   (c) in relation to their housing costs.
   "Payments to or in respect of social security schemes" includes national insurance contributions.
Section F3
F3 Occupational and Personal Pensions

134   Occupational and personal pensions.
Exception
   Occupational and personal pension schemes for or in respect of—
   (a) Assembly members, the First Minister, Welsh Ministers appointed under section 48, the Counsel General and Deputy Welsh Ministers, and
   (b) members of local authorities,
   but pensions regulation in relation to such schemes is not excepted.

Interpretation

"Local authority" includes a fire and rescue authority, a National Park authority and a conservation board for an area of outstanding natural beauty.

"Occupational and personal pensions" includes pension protection.

"Pension" includes gratuities and allowances.

"Pensions regulation" means the regulation of occupational and personal pensions, including regulation in respect of members, employers, trustees or managers.

161 Government indemnities for objects on loan.

Section K4

K4 Property accepted in satisfaction of tax

162 Payments to Her Majesty's Revenue and Customs in respect of property accepted in satisfaction of tax and the disposal of such property.

Head L—Justice

Section L7

L7 Information rights

171 Public access to information held by a public authority.

Exception

Public access to information held by—

    (a) the Assembly,

    (b) the Assembly Commission,

    (c) the Welsh Government, or

    (d) any Welsh public authority,

        unless supplied by a Minister of the Crown or government department and held in confidence.

Interpretation

"Public authority" and "held by a public authority"—

    (a) in relation to environmental information, have the same meaning as in the Environmental Information Regulations 2004 (SI 2004/3391);

    (b) otherwise, have the meaning given by section 3 of the Freedom of Information Act 2000.

"Welsh public authority" has the meaning given by section 83 of that Act, but does not include a reserved authority within the meaning given by paragraph 8 of Schedule 7B to this Act.][1]

Amendments—[1]   Schedules 7A, 7B substituted for previous Sch 7 by the Wales Act 2017 s 3(2) with effect from 1 April 2018 (by virtue of SI 2017/1179 reg 2).

INCOME TAX ACT 2007

(2007 Chapter 3)

ARRANGEMENT OF SECTIONS

Part 1   Overview
1   Overview of Income Tax Acts
2   Overview of Act
Part 2   Basic Provisions
Chapter 1   Charges to Income Tax
3   Overview of charges to income tax
4   Income tax an annual tax
5   Income tax and companies
Chapter 2   Rates At Which Income Tax Is Charged
The rates
6   The basic rate, higher rate and additional rate
6A   The Scottish basic, higher and additional rates
6B   The Welsh basic, higher and additional rates
6C   The default basic, higher and additional rates
7   The starting rate for savings
7A   The savings basic, higher and additional rates
8   The dividend nil rate, dividend ordinary rate, dividend upper rate and dividend additional rate
9   The trust rate and dividend trust rate
Income charged at particular rates
9A   Overview of sections 10 to 15
10   Income charged at the basic, higher and additional rates: individuals
11   Income charged at the default basic rate: non-individuals
11A   Income charged at Scottish rates
11B   Income charged at the Welsh basic, higher and additional rates
11C   Income charged at the default basic, higher and additional rates: non-UK resident individuals
11D   Income charged at the savings basic, higher and additional rates
12   Income charged at the starting rate for savings
12A   Savings income charged at the savings nil rate
12B   Individual's entitlement to a savings allowance
13   Income charged at the dividend ordinary, dividend upper and dividend additional rates: individuals
13A   Income charged at the dividend nil rate
14   Income charged at the dividend ordinary rate: other persons
15   Income charged at the trust rate and the dividend trust rate
16   Savings and dividend income to be treated as highest part of total income
17   Repayment: tax paid at greater rate instead of starting rate for savings or savings nil rate
18   Meaning of "savings income"
19   Meaning of "dividend income"
Indexation of basic rate limit and starting rate limit for savings
21   Indexation of the basic rate limit and starting rate limit for savings
Chapter 3   Calculation of Income Tax Liability
22   Overview of Chapter
23   The calculation of income tax liability
24   Reliefs deductible at Step 2
24A   Limit on Step 2 deductions
25   Reliefs and allowances deductible at Steps 2 and 3: supplementary
26   Tax reductions
27   Order of deducting tax reductions: individuals
28   Order of deducting tax reductions: other persons
29   Tax reductions: supplementary
30   Additional tax
31   Total income: supplementary
32   Liability not dealt with in the calculation
Part 3   Personal Reliefs
Chapter 1   Introduction
33   Overview of Part
Chapter 2   Personal Allowance and Blind Person's Allowance
Introduction
34   Allowances under Chapter
Personal allowances
35   Personal allowance
Blind person's allowance

38   Blind person's allowance
39   Transfer of part of blind person's allowance to a spouse or civil partner
40   Election for transfer of allowance under section 39
Supplementary
41   Allowances in year of death
Chapter 3   Tax Reductions for Married Couples and Civil Partners: Persons Born Before
  6 April 1935
Introduction
42   Tax reductions under Chapter
43   Meaning of "the minimum amount"
44   Election for new rules to apply
Married couple's allowance
45   Marriages before 5 December 2005
46   Marriages and civil partnerships on or after 5 December 2005
Elections to transfer relief
47   Election by individual to transfer relief under section 45 or 46
48   Joint election to transfer relief under section 45 or 46
49   Election for partial transfer back of relief
50   Procedure for making and withdrawing elections under sections 47 to 49
Transfer of unused relief
51   Transfer of unused relief
52   Transfer back of unused relief
53   Transfer of unused relief: general
Supplementary
54   Tax reductions in the year of marriage or entry into civil partnership
55   Sections 45 to 53: supplementary
Chapter 3A   Transferable Tax Allowance for Married Couples and Civil Partners
Introduction
55A   Tax reduction under Chapter
Tax reduction
55B   Tax reduction: entitlement
Election to reduce personal allowance
55C   Election to reduce personal allowance
55D   Procedure for elections under section 55C
Supplementary
55E   Limitation on number of tax reductions and elections
Chapter 4   General
56   Residence etc of claimants
57   Indexation of allowances
58   Meaning of "adjusted net income"
Part 4   Loss Relief
Chapter 1   Introduction
59   Overview of Part
Chapter 2   Trade Losses
Introduction
60   Overview of Chapter
61   Non-partners: losses of a tax year
62   Partners: losses of a tax year etc
63   Prohibition against double counting
Trade loss relief against general income
64   Deduction of losses from general income
65   How relief works
Restriction on relief for uncommercial trades
66   Restriction on relief unless trade is commercial
Restriction on relief for "hobby" farming or market gardening
67   Restriction on relief in case of farming or market gardening
68   Reasonable expectation of profit
69   Whether trade is the same trade
70   Determining losses in previous tax years
Use of trading loss as CGT loss
71   Treating trade losses as CGT losses
Early trade losses relief
72   Relief for individuals for losses in first 4 years of trade
73   How relief works
74   Restrictions on relief unless trade is commercial etc
General restrictions on sideways relief and capital gains relief
74ZA   No relief for tax-generated losses
74A   Reliefs in any tax year not to exceed cap for tax year
74C   Meaning of "non-active capacity" for purposes of section 74A

74D   Meaning of "qualifying film expenditure" for purposes of sections 74ZA and 74A
Restriction on sideways relief and capital gains relief where cash basis applies
74E   No relief where cash basis used to calculate losses
Restrictions on sideways relief for certain capital allowances
75   Trade leasing allowances given to individuals
76   First-year allowances and annual investment allowances: introduction
77   First-year allowances: partnerships with companies
78   First-year allowances and annual investment allowances: arrangements to reduce tax
       liabilities
79   Capital allowances restrictions: supplementary
Restriction on sideways relief for specific trades
80   Ring fence income
82   Exploitation of films
Carry-forward trade loss relief
83   Carry forward against subsequent trade profits
84   How relief works
85   Use of trade-related interest and dividends if trade profits insufficient
86   Trade transferred to a company
87   Ring fence trades
88   Carry forward of certain interest as loss
Terminal trade loss relief
89   Carry back of losses on a permanent cessation of a trade
90   Losses that are "terminal losses"
91   How relief works
92   Use of trade-related interest and dividends if trade profits insufficient
93   Mineral extraction trade and carry back of balancing allowances
94   Carry back of certain interest as loss
Wholly foreign trades
95   Foreign trades etc: reliefs only against foreign income
Post-cessation trade relief
96   Post-cessation trade relief
97   Meaning of "qualifying payment"
98   Meaning of "qualifying event" etc
98A   Denial of relief for tax-generated payments or events
99   Reduction of relief for unpaid trade expenses
100   Prohibition against double counting
101   Treating excess post-cessation trade relief as CGT loss
Chapter 3   Restrictions On Trade Loss Relief for Certain Partners
Introduction
102   Overview of Chapter
103   Meaning of "sideways relief", "capital gains relief" and "firm"
103A   Meaning of "limited partner"
103B   Meaning of "non-active partner" etc
Limit on amount of sideways relief and capital gains relief
103C   Limit on reliefs in any tax year not to exceed cap for tax year
103D   Meaning of "qualifying film expenditure"
Limited partners
104   Restriction on reliefs for limited partners
105   Meaning of "contribution to the firm"
Members of LLPs
107   Restriction on reliefs for members of LLPs
108   Meaning of "contribution to the LLP"
109   Unrelieved losses brought forward
Non-active members of LLPs or other partnerships (apart from limited partnerships)
110   Restriction on reliefs for non-active partners in early tax years
111   Meaning of "contribution to the firm"
112   Meaning of "early tax year"
113   Unrelieved losses brought forward
Exclusion of amounts in calculating contribution to the firm or LLP
113A   Exclusion of amounts contributed to access relief
Power to exclude other amounts
114   Exclusion of amounts in calculating contribution to the firm or LLP
Restrictions for film trades carried on in partnership
115   Restrictions on reliefs for firms exploiting films
Partnerships with mixed membership etc
116A   Excess loss allocation to partners who are individuals
Chapter 4   Losses From Property Businesses
Introduction
117   Overview of Chapter

Carry-forward property loss relief
118   Carry forward against subsequent property business profits
119   How relief works
Property loss relief against general income
120   Deduction of property losses from general income
121   How relief works
122   Meaning of "the applicable amount of the loss"
123   Meaning of "the loss has a capital allowances connection" and "the business has a relevant agricultural connection"
124   Supplementary
Post-cessation property relief
125   Post-cessation property relief
126   Treating excess post-cessation property relief as CGT loss
Furnished holiday accommodation
127   UK furnished holiday lettings business treated as trade
127ZA   EEA furnished holiday lettings business treated as trade
Restrictions on relief
127A   No relief for tax-generated losses attributable to annual investment allowance
127B   No relief for tax-generated agricultural expenses
127BA   Restriction of relief: cash basis
127C   Excess loss allocation to partners who are individuals
Chapter 5   Losses in an Employment Or Office
128   Employment loss relief against general income
129   How relief works
130   Treating loss in employment or office as CGT loss
Chapter 6   Losses On Disposal of Shares
Share loss relief against general income
131   Share loss relief
132   Entitlement to claim
133   How relief works
Shares to which EIS relief is not attributable
134   Qualifying trading companies
135   Subscriptions for shares
136   Disposals of new shares
Qualifying trading companies: the requirements
137   The trading requirement
138   Ceasing to meet trading requirement because of administration or receivership
139   The control and independence requirement
140   The qualifying subsidiaries requirement
141   The property managing subsidiaries requirement
142   The gross assets requirement
143   The unquoted status requirement
144   Power to amend requirements by Treasury order
Qualifying trading companies: supplementary
145   Relief after an exchange of shares for shares in another company
146   Substitution of new shares for old shares
Limits on share loss relief and mixed holdings
147   Limits on share loss relief
148   Disposal of shares forming part of mixed holding
149   Section 148: supplementary
Miscellaneous and supplementary
150   Deemed time of issue for certain shares
151   Interpretation of Chapter
Chapter 7   Losses From Miscellaneous Transactions
Loss relief against miscellaneous income
152   Losses from miscellaneous transactions
153   How relief works
Deposit rights
154   Transactions in deposit rights
Supplementary
154A   Anti-avoidance
155   Time limit for claiming relief
Part 5   Enterprise Investment Scheme
Chapter 1   Chapter 1 Introduction
EIS relief
156   Meaning of "EIS relief" and commencement
157   Eligibility for EIS relief
157A   Risk-to-capital condition
158   Form and amount of EIS relief

Miscellaneous
159   Periods A, B and C
160   Overview of other Chapters of Part
161   Other tax reliefs relating to EIS
Chapter 2   The Investor
Introduction
162   Overview of Chapter
The requirements
163   The no connection with the issuing company requirement
164   The no linked loans requirement
164A   The existing shareholdings requirement
165   The no tax avoidance requirement
Meaning of connection with issuing company
166   Connection with issuing company
167   Employees, directors and partners
168   Directors excluded from connection
169   Directors qualifying for relief despite connection
170   Persons interested in capital etc of company
171   Persons subscribing for shares under certain arrangements
Chapter 3   General Requirements
Introduction
172   Overview of Chapter
The requirements
173   The shares requirement
173A   The maximum amount raised annually through risk finance investments requirement
173AA   Maximum risk finance investments at the issue date requirement
173AB   Maximum risk finance investments during period B requirement
174   The purpose of the issue requirement
175   The use of the money raised requirement
175A   The permitted maximum age requirement
176   The minimum period requirement
177   The no pre-arranged exits requirement
178   The no tax avoidance requirement
178A   The no disqualifying arrangements requirement
Meaning of "qualifying business activity"
179   Meaning of "qualifying business activity"
Chapter 4   The Issuing Company
Introduction
180   Overview of Chapter
The requirements
180A   The UK permanent establishment requirement
180B   The financial health requirement
181   The trading requirement
182   Ceasing to meet trading requirement because of administration or receivership
183   The issuing company to carry on the qualifying business activity requirement
184   The unquoted status requirement
185   The control and independence requirement
186   The gross assets requirement
186A   The number of employees requirement
187   The qualifying subsidiaries requirement
188   The property managing subsidiaries requirement
Definitions
189   Meaning of "qualifying trade"
190   Meaning of "qualifying 90% subsidiary"
191   Meaning of "qualifying subsidiary"
191A   Meaning of "permanent establishment"
Excluded activities
192   Meaning of "excluded activities"
193   Excluded activities: wholesale and retail distribution
194   Excluded activities: leasing of ships
195   Excluded activities: receipt of royalties and licence fees
196   Excluded activities: property development
196A   Excluded activities: shipbuilding
196B   Excluded activities: producing coal
196C   Excluded activities: producing steel
197   Excluded activities: hotels and comparable establishments
198   Excluded activities: nursing homes and residential care homes
198A   Excluded activities: export of electricity
199   Excluded activities: provision of services or facilities for another business

Chapter 5   Attribution of and Claims for EIS Relief
Attribution
201   Attribution of EIS relief to shares
Claims: general
202   Time for making claims for EIS relief
203   Entitlement to claim
Claims: supporting documents
204   Compliance certificates
205   Compliance statements
206   Appeal against refusal to authorise compliance certificate
207   Penalties for fraudulent certificate or statement etc
Chapter 6   Withdrawal Or Reduction of EIS Relief
Introduction
208   Overview of Chapter
Disposals
209   Disposal of shares
210   Cases where maximum EIS relief not obtained
211   Call options
212   Put options
Value received by investor
213   Value received by the investor
214   Value received: receipts of insignificant value
215   Meaning of "receipts of insignificant value"
216   When value is received
217   The amount of value received
218   Value received where there is more than one issue of shares
219   Value received where part of share issue treated as made in previous tax year
220   Cases where maximum EIS relief not obtained
221   Receipts of value by and from connected persons etc
222   Receipt of replacement value
223   Section 222: supplementary
Repayments etc of share capital to other persons
224   Repayments etc of share capital to other persons
225   Insignificant repayments ignored for purposes of section 224
226   Amount of repayments etc where there is more than one issue of shares
227   Single issue affecting more than one individual
228   Single issue treated as made partly in previous tax year
229   Maximum relief not obtained for share issue
230   Repayment of authorised minimum within 12 months
231   Restriction on withdrawal of relief under section 224
Miscellaneous
232   Acquisition of a trade or trading assets
233   Acquisition of share capital
234   Relief subsequently found not to have been due
Chapter 7   Withdrawal Or Reduction of EIS Relief: Procedure
Assessments and appeals
235   Assessments for the withdrawal or reduction of EIS relief
236   Appeals against section 234(3)(b) notices
237   Time limits for assessments
238   Cases where assessment not to be made
Interest
239   Date from which interest is chargeable
Information
240   Information to be provided by the investor
241   Information to be provided by the issuing company etc
242   Power to require information where section 240 or 241 applies or could have applied
243   Power to require information in other cases
244   Obligations of secrecy
Chapter 8   Supplementary and General
Disposals of shares
245   Transfers between spouses or civil partners
246   Identification of shares on a disposal
Acquisition of issuing company
247   Continuity of EIS relief where issuing company is acquired by new company
248   Carry over of obligations etc where EIS relief attributed to new shares
249   Substitution of new shares for old shares
Nominees etc
250   Nominees and bare trustees
251   Approved knowledge-intensive fund as nominee

Powers to amend
251A   Powers to amend Chapters 2 to 4 by Treasury regulations
Interpretation
252   Meaning of a company being "in administration" or "in receivership"
252A   Meaning of "knowledge-intensive company"
252B   Knowledge-intensive company reaching turnover of £200,000
253   Meaning of "associate"
254   Meaning of "disposal of shares"
255   Meaning of "issue of shares"
256   Meaning of "the termination date"
256A   Meaning of "the EIS original rate"
257   Minor definitions etc
Part 5A   Seed Enterprise Investment Scheme
Chapter 1   Introduction
SEIS relief
257A   Meaning of "SEIS relief" and commencement
257AA   Eligibility for SEIS relief
257AAA   Risk-to-capital condition
257AB   Form and amount of SEIS relief
Miscellaneous
257AC   Meaning of "period A" and "period B"
257AD   Overview of other Chapters of Part
257AE   CGT reliefs relating to SEIS
Chapter 2   The Investor
Introduction
257B   Overview of Chapter
The requirements
257BA   The no employee investors requirement
257BB   The no substantial interest in the issuing company requirement
257BC   The no related investment arrangements requirement
257BD   The no linked loan requirement
257BE   The no tax avoidance requirement
Meaning of substantial interest in a company
257BF   Persons with a substantial interest in a company
Chapter 3   General Requirements
Introduction
257C   Overview of Chapter
The requirements
257CA   The shares requirement
257CB   The purpose of the issue requirement
257CC   The spending of the money raised requirement
257CD   The no pre-arranged exits requirement
257CE   The no tax avoidance requirement
257CF   The no disqualifying arrangements requirement
Chapter 4   The Issuing Company
Introduction
257D   Overview of Chapter
The requirements
257DA   The trading requirement
257DB   Ceasing to meet trading requirement: administration etc
257DC   The issuing company to carry on the qualifying business activity
257DD   The UK permanent establishment requirement
257DE   The financial health requirement
257DF   The unquoted status requirement
257DG   The control and independence requirement
257DH   The no partnerships requirement
257DI   The gross assets requirement
257DJ   The number of employees requirement
257DK   No previous other risk capital scheme investments
257DL   The amount raised through the SEIS
257DM   The qualifying subsidiaries requirement
257DN   The property managing subsidiaries requirement
Chapter 5   Attribution and Claims for SEIS Relief
Attribution
257E   Attribution of SEIS relief to shares
Claims: general
257EA   Time for making claims for SEIS relief
257EB   Entitlement to claim
Claims: supporting documents

257EC   Compliance certificates

257ED   Compliance statements

257EE   Appeal against refusal to authorise compliance certificate

257EF   Penalties for fraudulent certificate or statement etc

257EG   Power to amend sections 257EC and 257ED

Chapter 6   Withdrawal or Reduction of SEIS Relief

Introduction

257F   Overview of Chapter

257FA   Disposal of shares

257FB   Cases where maximum SEIS relief not obtained

257FC   Call options

257FD   Put options

Value received by investor

257FE   Value received by the investor

257FF   Value received: receipts of insignificant value

257FG   Meaning of "a receipt of insignificant value"

257FH   When value is received

257FI   The amount of value received

257FJ   Value received where there is more than one issue

257FK   Value received where part of issue treated as made in previous tax year

257FL   Cases where maximum SEIS relief not obtained

257FM   Receipts of value by and from connected persons etc

257FN   Receipt of replacement value

257FO   Section 257FN: supplementary

Miscellaneous

257FP   Acquisition of trade or trading assets

257FQ   Acquisition of share capital

257FR   Relief subsequently found not to have been due

Chapter 7   Withdrawal or Reduction of SEIS Relief: Procedure

Assessments and appeals

257G   Assessments for the withdrawal or reduction of SEIS relief

257GA   Appeals against section 257FR(3)(b) notices

257GB   Time limits for assessments

257GC   Cases where assessments not to be made

Interest

257GD   Date from which interest is chargeable

Information

257GE   Information to be provided by the investor

257GF   Information to be provided by the issuing company etc

257GG   Power to require information where section 257GE or 257GF applies or could have applied

257GH   Power to require information in other cases

257GI   Obligations of secrecy

Chapter 8   Supplementary and General

Disposals of shares

257H   Transfers between spouses or civil partners

257HA   Identification of shares on a disposal

Acquisition of issuing company

257HB   Continuity of SEIS relief where issuing company is acquired by new company

257HC   Carry over of obligations etc where SEIS relief attributed to new shares

257HD   Substitution of new shares for old shares

Nominees etc

257HE   Nominees and bare trustees

Interpretation

257HF   Meaning of "new qualifying trade"

257HG   Meaning of "qualifying business activity"

257HH   Meaning of "disposal of shares"

257HI   Meaning of "issue of shares"

257HJ   Minor definitions

Part 5B   Tax Relief for Social Investments

Chapter 1   Introduction

257J   Meaning of "SI relief" and "social enterprise"

257JA   Form and amount of relief

257JB   Meaning of "community benefit society"

257JC   Charities that are trusts

257JD   Accreditation as a social impact contractor

257JE   Meaning of "social impact contract"

257JF   Accreditations: supplementary provisions

257JG   Period of accreditation as a social impact contractor

257JH   Functions of Ministers of the Crown under sections 257JD to 257JG
Chapter 2   Eligibility for Relief: Basic Rule and Key Definitions
Eligibility
257K   Eligibility for SI relief
Key definitions
257KA   Key to reading the rest of the Part
257KB   When investment is made, and "investment date"
257KC   "Shorter applicable period" and "longer applicable period"
Chapter 3   Eligibility: Conditions Relating to the Investor and the Investment
257L   Investment to be in new shares or new qualifying debt investments
257LA   Condition that the amount invested must have been paid over
257LB   The no pre-arranged exits requirements
257LC   The no risk avoidance requirement
257LD   The no linked loans requirement
257LDA   The existing investments requirement
257LE   The no tax avoidance requirement
257LEA   The no disqualifying arrangements requirement
257LF   Restrictions on being an employee, partner or paid director
257LG   The requirement not to be interested in capital etc of social enterprise
257LH   Requirement for no collusion with a non-qualifying investor
Chapter 4   Eligibility: Conditions Relating to the Social Enterprise
Conditions relating to the social enterprise: general
257M   The continuing to be a social enterprise requirement
257MC   The gross assets requirement
257MD   The unquoted status requirement
257ME   The control and independence requirements
257MF   The qualifying subsidiaries requirement
257MG   The property-managing subsidiaries requirement
257MH   The number of employees requirement
257MI   The no partnership requirement
257MIA   The financial health requirement
257MJ   The trading requirement
257MK   Ceasing to meet trading requirement: administration or receivership
257ML   The issue must be to raise money for chosen trade or preparing for it
257MM   Requirement to use money raised and to trade for minimum period
257MN   The social enterprise must carry on the chosen trade
Limits on amounts that may be invested
257MNA   Maximum amount where investment made in first 7 years
257MNB   Section 257MNA: supplementary
257MNC   Maximum amount for cases outside section 257MNA
257MND   Limit on investment in shorter applicable period
257MNE   Power to amend limits on amounts that may be invested
Interpretation of conditions relating to the social enterprise
257MP   Meaning of "qualifying trade"
257MQ   Meaning of "excluded activity"
257MQA   Excluded activities: nursing homes and residential care homes
257MR   Excluded activities: property development
257MT   Excluded activity: providing services or facilities for another business
257MU   Meaning of "qualifying subsidiary"
257MV   Meaning of "90% social subsidiary" of a social enterprise
257MW   Excluded activities: power to amend
Chapter 5   Attribution of Relief
257N   Attribution of SI relief to investments
Chapter 6   Claims for Relief
257P   Time for making claims for SI relief
257PA   Entitlement to claim
257PB   Compliance statements
257PC   Compliance certificates
257PD   Penalties for fraudulent certificate or statement etc
257PE   Power to amend Chapter
Chapter 7   Withdrawal or Reduction of SI Relief
Value received by the investor
257Q   Effect of the investor receiving value from the social enterprise
257QA   Value received: insignificant receipts
257QB   Value received where there is more than one issue of investments
257QC   Value received where part investment treated as made in previous tax year
257QD   Cases where maximum SI relief not obtained
257QE   When value is received
257QF   The amount of value received

257QG   Receipts of value by and from connected persons etc
257QH   Receipt of replacement value
257QI   Section 257QH: supplementary
Repayments etc of investments to other persons
257QJ   Repayments etc of share capital to other persons
257QK   Insignificant payments ignored for the purposes of section 257QJ
257QL   Amount of repayments etc if there is more than one issue of shares
257QM   Single issue affecting more than one individual
257QN   Single issue treated as made partly in previous tax year
257QO   Maximum relief not obtained for share issue
257QP   Repayment of authorised minimum within 12 months
Miscellaneous
257QQ   Acquisition of a trade or trading assets
257QR   Acquisition of share capital
257QS   Relief subsequently found not to have been due
Disposals
257R   Disposal of whole or part of the investment
257RA   Cases where maximum relief not obtained
257RB   Call options
257RC   Put options
Chapter 8   Withdrawal or Reduction of SI Relief: Procedure
Assessments and appeals
257S   Assessments for the withdrawal or reduction of SI relief
257SA   Appeals against section 257QS(3)(*b*) notices
257SB   Time limits for assessments
257SC   Cases where assessment not to be made
Interest
257SD   Date from which interest is chargeable
Information
257SE   Information to be provided by the investor
257SF   Information to be provided by the social enterprise etc
257SG   Power to require information in section 257SE or 257SF cases
257SH   Power to require information in other cases
257SI   Confidentiality
Chapter 9   Miscellaneous and Supplementary Provisions
257T   Transfers between spouses or civil partners
257TA   Identification of investments on a disposal
257TB   Meaning of a company being "in administration" or "in receivership"
257TC   Meaning of "associate"
257TD   Meaning of "control"
257TE   Minor definitions etc"
Part 6   Venture Capital Trusts
Chapter 1   Introduction
258   Overview of Part
259   Venture capital trusts and VCT approvals
260   Other tax reliefs relating to VCTs
Chapter 2   VCT Relief
Entitlement to relief
261   Eligibility for relief
262   Entitlement to claim relief
263   Form and amount of relief
264   No entitlement to relief if there is a linked loan
264A   Restricting relief where there is a linked sale
265   No entitlement to relief which would have been lost if it had already been obtained
Loss of relief
266   Loss of relief if shares disposed of within 5 years
267   Transfers of shares between spouses or civil partners
268   Loss of relief if VCT approval withdrawn
269   Loss of relief which is subsequently found not to have been due
270   Assessment on withdrawal or reduction of relief
Supplementary
271   Provision of information
272   Regulations as to procedure etc
273   Interpretation of Chapter
Chapter 3   VCT Approvals
Giving of approval
274   Requirements for the giving of approval
275   Alternative requirements for the giving of approval
276   Conditions relating to income

277 The 15% holding limit condition
278 Conditions relating to value of investments: general
279 Conditions relating to value of investments: qualifying holdings
280 Conditions relating to qualifying holdings and eligible shares
280A The 70% qualifying holdings condition: disposal of holding
280B The investment limits condition
280BA The minimum investment on further issue condition
280C The permitted maximum age condition
280D The no business acquisition condition
Withdrawal of approval
281 Withdrawal of VCT approval of a company
282 Withdrawal of VCT approval in cases for which provision made under section 280(3)
Supplementary
283 Time as from which VCT approval has effect
284 Power to make regulations as to procedure
285 Interpretation of Chapter
Chapter 4 Qualifying Holdings
Introduction
286 Qualifying holdings: introduction
The requirements
286ZA The risk-to-capital requirement
286A The UK permanent establishment requirement
286B The financial health requirement
287 The maximum qualifying investment requirement
288 The no guaranteed loan requirement
289 The proportion of eligible shares requirement
290 The trading requirement
291 The carrying on of a qualifying activity requirement
292 Ceasing to meet requirements because of administration or receivership
292A The maximum amount raised annually through risk finance investments requirement
292AA Maximum risk finance investments when relevant holding is issued requirement
292AB Maximum risk finance investments during the 5-year post-investment period requirement
293 The use of the money raised requirement
294 The relevant company to carry on the relevant qualifying activity requirement
294A The permitted company age requirement
295 The unquoted status requirement
296 The control and independence requirement
297 The gross assets requirement
297A The number of employees requirement
297B The proportion of skilled employees requirement
298 The qualifying subsidiaries requirement
299 The property managing subsidiaries requirement
299A The no disqualifying arrangements requirement
Definitions
300 Meaning of "qualifying trade"
301 Meaning of "qualifying 90% subsidiary"
302 Meaning of "qualifying subsidiary"
302A Meaning of "permanent establishment"
Excluded activities
303 Meaning of "excluded activities"
304 Excluded activities: wholesale and retail distribution
305 Excluded activities: leasing of ships
306 Excluded activities: receipt of royalties and licence fees
307 Excluded activities: property development
307A Excluded activities: shipbuilding
307B Excluded activities: producing coal
307C Excluded activities: producing steel
308 Excluded activities: hotels and comparable establishments
309 Excluded activities: nursing homes and residential care homes
309A Excluded activities: export of electricity
310 Excluded activities: provision of services or facilities for another business
Supplementary
312 Winding up of the relevant company
312A Power to require information relating to disqualifying arrangements
313 Interpretation of Chapter
Chapter 5 Powers: Winding Up and Mergers of VCTs
Winding up
314 Power to treat VCT-in-liquidation as VCT

315 Power to treat conditions for VCT approval as met with respect to VCT-in-liquidation
316 Power to make provision about distributions by VCT-in-liquidation
317 Power to facilitate disposal to VCT by VCT-in-liquidation
318 Power in respect of periods before and after winding up
319 Sections 314 to 318: supplementary
320 Meaning of "VCT-in-liquidation"
Mergers
321 Power to facilitate mergers of VCTs
322 Provision that may be made by regulations under section 321
323 Meaning of "merger" and "successor company"
Supplementary
324 Regulations under Chapter
325 Interpretation of Chapter
Chapter 6 Supplementary and General
Acquisitions for restructuring purposes
326 Restructuring to which sections 326A, 327 and 327A apply
326A Certain requirements of Chapter 3 to be treated as met
327 Certain requirements of Chapter 4 to be treated as met
327A Follow-on funding
328 Supplementary
Conversion of shares etc and company reorganisations
329 Conversion of convertible shares and securities
330 Power to facilitate company reorganisations etc involving exchange of shares
330A Nominees
Power to amend Part
330B Powers to amend Chapters 3 and 4 by Treasury regulations
Supplementary
331 Meaning of a company being "in administration" or "in receivership"
331A Meaning of "knowledge-intensive company"
331B Knowledge-intensive company reaching turnover of £200,000
332 Minor definitions etc
Part 7 Community Investment Tax Relief
Chapter 1 Introduction
CITR
333 Meaning of "CITR"
334 Eligibility for CITR
335 Form and amount of CITR
335A Carry forward of CITR
Miscellaneous
336 Meaning of "making an investment"
337 Determination of "the invested amount"
338 Meaning of "the 5 year period" and "the investment date"
339 Overview of other Chapters of Part
Chapter 2 Accredited Community Development Finance Institutions
340 Application and criteria for accreditation
341 Terms and conditions of accreditation
342 Period of accreditation
343 Delegation of Secretary of State's functions
Chapter 3 Qualifying Investments
344 Qualifying investments: introduction
345 Conditions to be met in relation to loans
346 Conditions to be met in relation to securities
347 Conditions to be met in relation to shares
348 Tax relief certificates
349 No pre-arranged protection against risks
Chapter 4 General Conditions
350 No control of CDFI by investor
351 Investor must have beneficial ownership
352 No acquisition of share in partnership
353 No tax avoidance purpose
Chapter 5 Claims for and Attribution of CITR
Claims
354 Loans: no claim after disposal or excessive repayments or receipts of value
355 Securities or shares: no claim after disposal or excessive receipts of value
356 No claim after loss of accreditation by the CDFI
Attribution
357 Attribution: general
358 Attribution: bonus shares
Chapter 6 Withdrawal or Reduction of CITR

Introduction
359   Overview of Chapter
Disposals
360   Disposal of loan during 5 year period
361   Disposal of securities or shares during 5 year period
Repayment of loans
362   Repayment of loan capital during 5 year period
Receipts of value
363   Value received by investor during 6 year period: loans
364   Value received by investor during 6 year period: securities or shares
365   Receipts of insignificant value to be added together
366   When value is received
367   The amount of value received
368   Value received if there is more than one investment
369   Effect of receipt of value on future claims for CITR
370   Receipts of value by or from connected persons
CITR not due
371   CITR subsequently found not to have been due
Manner of withdrawal or reduction
372   Manner of withdrawal or reduction of CITR
Chapter 7   Supplementary and General
Alternative finance arrangements
372A   Meaning of "loan" and "interest"
372B   Purchase and resale arrangements
372C   Deposit arrangements
372D   Profit share agency arrangements
Miscellaneous
373   Information to be provided by the investor
374   Disclosure
375   Nominees
376   Application for postponement of tax pending appeal
377   Identification of securities or shares on a disposal
Definitions
378   Meaning of "issue of securities or shares"
379   Meaning of "disposal"
380   Construction of references to being "held continuously"
381   Meaning of "associate"
382   Minor definitions etc
Part 8   Other Reliefs
Chapter 1   Interest Payments
The relief: introduction
383   Relief for interest payments
384   General restrictions on relief under Chapter
384A   Restriction on relief where arrangements minimise risk to borrower
384B   Restriction on relief where cash basis applies
385   General provisions about loans
386   Loans partly meeting requirements
387   Exclusion of double relief etc
Loans for plant or machinery
388   Loan to buy plant or machinery for partnership use
389   Eligibility requirements for interest on loans within section 388
390   Loan to buy plant or machinery for employment use
391   Eligibility requirements for interest on loans within section 390
Loans for interests in close companies
392   Loan to buy interest in close company
393   Eligibility requirements for interest on loans within section 392
393A   Close investment-holding companies
394   Meaning of "material interest" in section 393
395   Meaning of "associate" in section 394
Loans for interests in employee-controlled companies
396   Loan to buy interest in employee-controlled company
397   Eligibility requirements for interest on loans within section 396
Loans for investing in partnerships
398   Loan to invest in partnership
399   Eligibility requirements for interest on loans within section 398
399A   Property partnerships: restriction of relief for investment loan interest
399B   Property partnerships: tax reduction for non-deductible loan interest
400   Film partnerships
Loans for investing in co-operatives

401   Loan to invest in co-operative
402   Eligibility requirements for interest on loans within section 401
Loans for paying inheritance tax
403   Loan to pay inheritance tax
404   Eligibility requirements for interest on loans within section 403
405   Carry back and forward of relief for interest on loans within section 403
General and supplementary
406   Effect of recovery of capital in the case of some loans
407   Events counting as recovery of capital for section 406
408   Replacement loans
409   Business successions between partnerships
410   Other business successions and reorganisations
411   Ineligibility of interest where business is occupation of commercial woodlands
412   Information
Chapter 1A   Irrecoverable peer-to-peer loans
The relief
412A   Relief for irrecoverable peer-to-peer loans
412B   Claims for additional relief: sideways relief
412C   Claims for additional relief: carry-forward relief
412D   How carry-forward relief works
Supplementary provisions
412E   Subsequent recovery of peer-to-peer loans
412F   Assigned loans treated as made by the assignee etc
412G   Nominees etc
412H   Interaction with other reliefs
Interpretation
412I   Meaning of "loan", "peer-to-peer loan" and related terms
412J   Meaning of "operator" and related terms
Chapter 2   Gift Aid
The relief
413   Overview of Chapter
414   Relief for gifts to charity
414A   Tax reduction or charge if basic rate, and devolved basic rate, differ
415   Meaning of "grossed up amount"
416   Meaning of "qualifying donation"
417   Meaning of "benefits associated with a gift"
Restrictions on associated benefits
418   Restrictions on associated benefits
419   Gifts and benefits linked to periods of less than 12 months
Admission rights
420   Disregard of certain admission rights
421   Admission rights: supplementary
430   "Charity" to include exempt bodies
Chapter 3   Gifts of Shares, Securities and Real Property to Charities etc
Entitlement to relief
431   Relief for gifts of shares, securities and real property to charities etc
432   Meaning of "qualifying investment"
433   Meaning of "qualifying interest in land"
Amount of relief
434   The relievable amount
435   Incidental costs of making disposal
436   Consideration
Value of net benefit to charity
437   Value of net benefit to charity
438   Market value of qualifying investments
438A   Acquisition value of qualifying investments
439   Meaning of "disposal-related obligation"
440   Meaning and amount of "disposal-related liability"
Special provisions about qualifying interests in land
441   Certificate required from charity
442   Qualifying interests in land held jointly
443   Calculation of relievable amount where joint disposal of interest in land
444   Disqualifying events
Supplementary
445   Prohibition against double relief
446   "Charity" to include exempt bodies
Chapter 4   Annual Payments and Patent Royalties
447   Overview of Chapter
448   Relief for individuals

449 Relief for other persons
450 Other persons: payments ineligible for relief
452 The gross amount of a payment
Chapter 5 Qualifying Maintenance Payments
453 Tax reduction for qualifying maintenance payments
454 Meaning of "qualifying maintenance payment"
455 Child support maintenance payments
456 Payments under orders for recovery of benefit etc
Chapter 6 Miscellaneous Other Reliefs
Payments for life insurance etc
457 Payments to trade unions
458 Payments to police organisations
Chapter 10 Heritage Maintenance Settlements
Introduction
507 Overview of Chapter
Trustees' election in respect of income etc
508 Election by trustees
509 Change of circumstances during a tax year
Absence of election and income treated as income of settlor: special rules
510 Sums applied for property maintenance purposes
511 Prevention of double taxation: reimbursement of settlor
Application of property for non-heritage purposes: charge to tax
512 Charge to tax on some settlements
513 Income charged
514 Persons liable
515 Rate of tax
516 Transfer of property between settlements
517 Exemption for income treated as income of settlor
Part 9A Transactions in UK land
Introduction
517A Overview of Part
Amounts treated as profits of a trade
517B Disposals of land in the United Kingdom
517C Disposals of land: profits treated as trading profits
517D Disposals of property deriving its value from land in the United Kingdom
517E Disposals within section 517D: profits treated as trading profits
517F Profits and losses
Person to whom profits attributed
517G The chargeable person
Anti-fragmentation
517H Fragmented activities
Calculation of profit or gain on disposal
517I Calculation of surplus on a disposal of land
517J Apportionments
Arrangements for avoiding tax
517K Arrangements for avoiding tax
Exemptions
517L Gain attributable to period before intention to develop formed
517M Private residences
Other supplementary provisions
517N Tracing value
517O Relevance of transactions, arrangements, etc
Interpretation
517P "Another person"
517Q "Arrangement"
517R "Disposal"
517S "Land" and related expressions
517T References to realising a gain
517U Related parties
Part 10 Special Rules About Charitable Trusts etc
Introduction
518 Overview of Part
Gifts and other payments
520 Gifts entitling donor to gift aid relief: income tax treated as paid
521 Gifts entitling donor to gift aid relief: income tax liability and exemption
521A Gifts under payroll deduction schemes: income tax liability and exemption
522 Gifts of money from companies: income tax liability and exemption
523 Payments from other charities: income tax liability and exemption
Other exemptions

524   Exemption for profits etc of charitable trades
525   Meaning of "charitable trade"
526   Exemption for profits etc of small-scale trades
527   Exemption from charges under provisions to which section 1016 applies
528   Condition as to trading and miscellaneous incoming resources
529   Exemption for profits from fund-raising events
530   Exemption for profits from lotteries
531   Exemption for property income etc
532   Exemption for savings and investment income
533   Exemption for public revenue dividends
534   Exemption for transactions in deposits
535   Exemption for offshore income gains
536   Exemption for certain miscellaneous income
537   Exemption for income from estates in administration
Claims
538   Requirement to make claim
538A   Claims in relation to gift aid relief etc
Restrictions on exemptions
539   Restrictions on exemptions
540   The non-exempt amount
541   Attributing income to the non-exempt amount
542   How income is attributed to the non-exempt amount
Non-charitable expenditure
543   Meaning of "non-charitable expenditure"
544   Section 543: supplementary
545   Section 543(1)(*f*): meaning of expenditure
546   Section 543(1)(*f*): tax year in which certain expenditure treated as incurred
547   Section 543(1)(*f*): payment to body outside the UK
548   Section 543(1)(*i*) and (*j*): investments and loans
Approved charitable investments and loans
558   Approved charitable investments
559   Securities which are approved charitable investments
560   Conditions to be met for some securities
561   Approved charitable loans
Carry back of excess non-charitable expenditure
562   Excess expenditure treated as non-charitable expenditure of earlier years
563   Rules for attributing excess expenditure to earlier years
564   Adjustments in consequence of section 562
Part 10A   Alternative Finance Arrangements
Introduction
564A   Introduction
564B   Meaning of "financial institution"
Arrangements that are alternative finance arrangements
564C   Purchase and resale arrangements
564D   Diminishing shared ownership arrangements
564E   Deposit arrangements
564F   Profit share agency arrangements
564G   Investment bond arrangements
564H   Provision not at arm's length: exclusion of arrangements from sections 564C to 564G
Meaning of "alternative finance return"
564I   Purchase and resale arrangements
564J   Purchase and resale arrangements where return in foreign currency
564K   Diminishing shared ownership arrangements
564L   Other arrangements
Treatment of alternative finance return as interest etc
564M   Treatment of alternative finance return as interest for ITTOIA 2005
564N   Alternative finance return under arrangements for trade or property business purposes
564O   Relief for some alternative finance return under Chapter 1 of Part 8 etc
564P   Tax relief schemes and arrangements
564Q   Deduction of income tax at source under Part 15
Special rules for investment bond arrangements
564R   Treatment of discount
564S   Treatment of bond-holder and bond-issuer
564T   Treatment as securities
564U   Arrangements not unit trust scheme or offshore fund
Other rules
564V   Exclusion of alternative finance return from consideration for sale of assets
564W   Diminishing shared ownership arrangements not partnerships
564X   Treatment of principal under profit share agency arrangements

564Y   Provision not at arm's length: relevant return
Part 11ZA   Manufactured payments
614ZA   Overview of Part
614ZB   Key definitions
614ZC   Treatment of payer of manufactured payment
614ZD   Treatment of recipient of manufactured payment
Part 11A   Leasing Arrangements: Finance Leases and Loans
Chapter 1   Introduction
Introduction
614A   Overview of Part
Meaning of expressions about rent
614AA   Normal rent
614AB   Accountancy rental earnings
614AC   Rental earnings
Chapter 2   Finance Leases with Return in Capital Form
Introduction
614B   Arrangements to which this Chapter applies
614BA   Purposes of this Chapter
Leases to which this Chapter applies
614BB   Application of this Chapter
614BC   The conditions referred to in section 614BB(1)
614BD   Provisions supplementing section 614BC
614BE   The arrangements and circumstances referred to in section 614BC(8)
Current lessor taxed by reference to accountancy rental earnings
614BF   Current lessor taxed by reference to accountancy rental earnings
Reduction of taxable rent by cumulative rental excesses
614BG   Reduction of taxable rent by cumulative rental excesses: introduction
614BH   Meaning of "accountancy rental excess" and "cumulative accountancy rental excess"
614BI   Reduction of taxable rent by the cumulative accountancy rental excess
614BJ   Meaning of "normal rental excess" and "cumulative normal rental excess"
614BK   Reduction of taxable rent by the cumulative normal rental excess
Relief for bad debts by reduction of cumulative rental excesses
614BL   Relief for bad debts: reduction of cumulative accountancy rental excess
614BM   Recovery of bad debts following reduction under section 614BL
614BN   Relief for bad debts: reduction of cumulative normal rental excess
614BO   Recovery of bad debts following reduction under section 614BN
Effect of disposals
614BP   Effect of disposals of leases: general
614BQ   Assignments on which neither a gain nor a loss accrues
Capital allowances: claw-back of major lump sum
614BR   Effect of capital allowances: introduction
614BS   Cases where expenditure taken into account under Part 2, 5 or 8 of CAA 2001
614BT   Cases where expenditure taken into account under other provisions of CAA 2001
614BU   Capital allowances deductions: waste disposal and cemeteries
614BV   Capital allowances deductions: films and sound recordings
614BW   Contributors to capital expenditure
Schemes to which this Chapter does not at first apply
614BX   Pre-26 November 1996 schemes where this Chapter does not at first apply
614BY   Post-25 November 1996 schemes to which Chapter 3 applied first
Chapter 3   Other Finance Leases
Introduction
614C   Introduction to Chapter
614CA   Purpose of this Chapter
Leases to which this Chapter applies
614CB   Leases to which this Chapter applies
614CC   Current lessor taxed by reference to accountancy rental earnings
614CD   Application of provisions of Chapter 2 for purposes of this Chapter
Chapter 4   Supplementary provisions
614D   Pre-26 November 1996 schemes and post-25 November 1996 schemes
614DA   Time apportionment where periods of account do not coincide
614DB   Periods of account and related periods of account and tax years
614DC   Connected persons
614DD   Assets which represent the leased asset
614DE   Parent undertakings and consolidated group accounts
614DF   Assessments and adjustments
614DG   Interpretation
Part 12   Accrued Income Profits
Chapter 1   Introduction
615   Overview of Part

Chapter 2   Accrued Income Profits and Losses
Charge to tax
616   Charge to tax on accrued income profits
617   Income charged
618   Person liable
Securities to which Chapter applies
619   Meaning of "securities" and when securities are of the same kind
Transfers to which Chapter applies
620   Transactions which are transfers: general
621   Transferors and transferees
622   Application of Chapter to different kinds of transfer
623   Transfers with accrued interest
624   Transfers without accrued interest
625   Transfers with unrealised interest
626   Transfers of variable rate securities
627   Meaning of "variable rate securities"
Calculating accrued income profits and losses
628   Making accrued income profits and losses: general rule
629   Calculating accrued income profits and losses where section 628 applies
630   Making accrued income profits: settlement day outside interest period
631   Amount of accrued income profits where section 630 applies
The payments treated as made on transfers
632   Payment on transfer with accrued interest
633   Payment on transfer without accrued interest
634   Payment on transfer with unrealised interest
635   Payment on transfer of variable rate securities
Exception where there is a transfer to a legatee
636   Exception where there is a transfer to a legatee
Relief for losses
637   Accrued income losses treated as payments in next interest period
Excluded transferors and transferees
638   Excluded persons: disregard of certain payments and transfers
639   Small holdings: individuals
640   Small holdings: personal representatives
641   Small holdings: trustees of a disabled person's trusts
642   Traders
643   Non-residents
645   Charitable trusts etc
646   Pension scheme trustees
647   Makers of manufactured payments
Further transactions treated as transfers
648   Strips of gilt-edged securities
649   New securities issued with extra return
650   Trading stock appropriations etc
651   Owner becoming entitled to securities as trustee
652   Securities ceasing to be held on charitable trusts
Excluded transfers
653   Stock lending
654   Sale and repurchase arrangements
655   Transfers under sale and repurchase arrangements
656   Power to modify: non-standard sale and repurchase arrangements
657   Power to modify: redemption arrangements
658   Powers to modify: supplementary
Special rules about some calculations
659   Transfers with or without accrued interest: interest in default
660   Transfers with unrealised interest: interest in default
661   Successive transfers with unrealised interest in default
662   New securities issued with extra return: special rules about payments
663   Transfers without accrued interest to makers of manufactured payments
664   Foreign currency securities: sterling equivalent of payments on transfers
665   Foreign currency securities: unrealised interest payable in foreign currency
Nominees and trustees
666   Certain transfers by or to nominees or trustees treated as made by or to others
667   Trustees' accrued income profits treated as settlement income
Relief where transfer proceeds unremittable
668   Relief for unremittable transfer proceeds: general
669   Relief for unremittable transfer proceeds: section 630 profits
670   Withdrawal of relief
Individuals to whom remittance basis applies

ITA 2007

670A   Individuals to whom remittance basis applies

Interpretation

671   Meaning of "interest"
672   Meaning of "interest payment day"
673   Meaning of "interest period"
674   Meaning of "the settlement day"
675   The holding of securities
676   Nominal value of securities: general
677   Nominal value: foreign currency securities

Chapter 3   Exemptions Relating to Interest On Securities

678   Exemptions relating to interest on securities: preliminary
679   Interest on securities involving accrued income losses: general
680   Interest on securities involving accrued income losses: foreign trustees
681   Unrealised interest received by transferee after transfer

Part 12A   Sale and Lease-Back etc

Chapter 1   Payments Connected with Transferred Land

Overview

681A   Overview

Application of the Chapter

681AA   Transferor or associate becomes liable for payment of rent
681AB   Transferor or associate becomes liable for payment other than rent
681AC   Relevant income tax relief and relevant deduction from earnings

Relief: restriction and carrying forward

681AD   Relevant income tax relief: deduction not to exceed commercial rent
681AE   Deduction from earnings not to exceed commercial rent
681AF   Carrying forward parts of payments
681AG   Aggregation and apportionment of payments
681AH   Payments made for later periods

Interpretation etc

681AI   Exclusion of service charges etc
681AJ   Commercial rent: comparison with rent under a lease
681AK   Commercial rent: comparison with payments other than rent
681AL   Lease and rent
681AM   Associated persons
681AN   Land outside the UK

Chapter 2   New Lease of Land After Assignment or Surrender

Overview

681B   Overview

Application of the Chapter

681BA   New lease after assignment or surrender

Taxation of consideration

681BB   Taxation of consideration
681BC   Position where new lease does not include all original property

Relief for rent under new lease

681BD   Relief for rent under new lease

New lease treated as ending

681BE   New lease treated as ending
681BF   Position where rent reduces
681BG   Position where lease may be ended
681BH   Position where lease may be varied
681BI   Lease treated as ending: rentcharge

Lease varied to provide for increased rent

681BJ   Lease varied to provide for increased rent

Interpretation

681BK   Relevant income tax relief
681BL   Linked persons
681BM   Lease, lessee, lessor and rent

Chapter 3   Leased Trading Assets

Overview

681C   Overview

Application of the Chapter

681CA   Professions and vocations
681CB   Leased trading assets

Relief: restriction and carrying forward

681CC   Tax deduction not to exceed commercial rent
681CD   Long funding finance leases
681CE   Commercial rent

Interpretation

681CF   Lease

790 Overview of Chapter
Individuals in partnership: recovery of excess relief
791 Charge to tax on income treated as received under section 792
792 Partners claiming excess sideways or capital gains relief
793 Calculating the amount of income treated as received
794 Meaning of "the total amount of trade losses claimed" etc
795 Meaning of "post-1 December 2004 loss"
Individuals claiming relief for film-related trading losses
796 Charge to tax on income treated as received under section 797
797 Individuals claiming sideways or capital gains relief for film-related losses
798 Meaning of "non-taxable consideration" etc
799 Meaning of "disposal of a right of the individual to profits" etc
800 Meaning of "film-related losses" etc
801 Meaning of "capital contribution"
802 Exclusion of amounts in calculating capital contribution by a partner
803 Prohibition against double counting
Individuals in partnership claiming relief for licence-related trading losses
804 Charge to tax on income treated as received under section 805
805 Partners claiming relief for licence-related trading losses
806 Calculation of amount of income treated as received by the individual
807 Supplementary provision relating to calculation in section 806
808 Meaning of "disposal of the licence" etc
809 Other definitions
Chapter 5A Transfers of Income Streams
809AZA Application of Chapter
809AZB Value of transferred income stream treated as income
809AZC Exception: amount otherwise taxed
809AZD Exception: certain annuities
809AZE Exception: transfer by way of security
809AZF Partnership shares
809AZG Interpretation
Chapter 5AA Chapter 5AA Disposals of Income Streams through Partnerships
809AAZA Application of Chapter
809AAZB Relevant amount to be treated as income
Chapter 5B Chapter 5B Finance Arrangements
Type 1 arrangements
809BZA Type 1 finance arrangement defined
809BZB Certain tax consequences not to have effect
809BZC Payments treated as borrower's income
809BZD Deemed interest if borrower is not a partnership
809BZE Deemed interest if borrower is a partnership
Type 2 arrangements
809BZF Type 2 finance arrangement defined
809BZG Relevant change in relation to partnership
809BZH Certain tax consequences not to have effect
809BZI Deemed interest
Type 3 arrangements
809BZJ Type 3 finance arrangement defined
809BZK Certain tax consequences not to have effect
809BZL Deemed interest
Exceptions
809BZM Exceptions: preliminary
809BZN Exceptions
809BZO Exceptions: relevant person
809BZP Power to make further exceptions
Supplementary
809BZQ Accounts
809BZR Arrangements
809BZS Assets
Chapter 5C Loan or Credit Transactions
809CZA Loan or credit transaction defined
809CZB Certain payments treated as yearly interest
809CZC Tax charged on income transferred
Chapter 5D Disposals of Assets through Partnerships
809DZA Application of Chapter
809DZB Relevant amount to be treated as income
Chapter 5E Disguised investment management fees
809EZA Disguised investment management fees: charge to income tax
809EZB Meaning of "management fee" in section 809EZA

809EZC   Meaning of "carried interest" in section 809EZB

809EZD   Sums treated as "carried interest" for purposes of section 809EZB

809EZDA   Sums arising to connected persons other than companies

809EZDB   Sums arising to connected company or unconnected person

809EZE   Interpretation of Chapter

809EZF   Disguised investment management fees: anti-avoidance

809EZG   Disguised investment management fees: avoidance of double taxation

809EZH   Powers to amend Chapter

Chapter 5F   Income-Based Carried Interest

Income-based carried interest

809FZA   Overview

809FZB   Income based carried interest: general rule

Average holding period

809FZC   Average holding period

Average holding period: disposals

809FZD   Disposals

809FZE   Part disposals

809FZF   Unwanted short-term investments

Average holding period: derivatives and hedging

809FZG   Derivatives

809FZH   Hedging: exchange gains and losses

809FZI   Hedging: interest rates

Average holding period: aggregation of acquisitions and disposals

809FZJ   Significant interests

809FZK   Venture capital funds

809FZL   Significant equity stake funds

809FZM   Controlling equity stake funds

809FZN   Real estate funds

809FZO   Funds of funds

809FZP   Secondary funds

Direct lending funds

809FZQ   Direct lending funds

809FZR   Direct lending funds: exception

Conditionally exempt carried interest

809FZS   Conditionally exempt carried interest

809FZT   Carried interest which ceases to be conditionally exempt

Supplementary

809FZU   Employment-related securities

809FZV   "Loan to own" investments

809FZW   Anti-avoidance

809FZX   Treasury regulations

809FZY   "Reasonable to suppose"

Interpretation

809FZZ   Interpretation of Chapter 5F

Chapter 6   Avoidance Involving Leases of Plant and Machinery

809ZA   Plant and machinery leases: capital receipts to be treated as income

809Z2   Personal use rule

809Z3   Repair rule

809Z4   Temporary importation rule

809Z5   Notional remitted amount

809Z6   Exempt property: other interpretation

Interpretation of Chapter

809Z7   Meaning of "foreign income and gains" etc

809Z8   Meaning of "the disposal proceeds"

809Z9   Taking proceeds etc offshore or investing them

809Z10   General interpretation

Chapter 1   Limits On Liability to Income Tax of Non-UK Residents

Introduction

810   Overview of Chapter

Limit for non-UK resident individuals, trustees etc

811   Limit on liability to income tax of non-UK residents

812   Case where limit not to apply

812A   Temporary non-residents

813   Meaning of "disregarded income"

814   Meaning of "disregarded transaction income"

Limit for non-UK resident companies

815   Limit on liability to income tax of non-UK resident companies

816   Meaning of "disregarded company income"

The independent broker conditions

817   The independent broker conditions
The independent investment manager conditions
818   The independent investment manager conditions
819   Investment managers: the 20% rule
820   Meaning of "qualifying period"
821   Meaning of "relevant disregarded income"
822   Meaning of "beneficial entitlement"
823   Treatment of transactions where requirements of 20% rule not met
824   Application of 20% rule to collective investment schemes
Supplementary
825   Meaning of "disregarded savings and investment income"
826   Meaning of "disregarded annual payments"
827   Meaning of "investment manager" and "investment transaction"
828   Transactions through brokers and investment managers
Chapter 1A   Exemption for Persons not Domiciled in United Kingdom
828A   Introduction
828B   Conditions to be met
828C   The exemption
828D   Interpretation of Chapter
Chapter 2   Residence
833   Visiting forces etc
834   Residence of personal representatives
835   Residence rules for trustees
835A   Residence of companies
Chapter 2A   Domicile
835B   Domicile for income tax purposes of overseas electors
835BA   Deemed domicile
Chapter 2B   2B UK Representative of Non-UK Resident
Introduction
835C   Overview of Chapter
835D   Income tax chargeable on company's income: application
Branches and agencies
835E   Branch or agency treated as UK representative
835F   Trade or profession carried on in partnership
Persons who are not UK representatives
835G   Agents
835H   Brokers
835I   Investment managers
835J   Persons acting under alternative finance arrangements
835K   Lloyd's agents
The independent broker conditions
835L   The independent broker conditions
The independent investment manager conditions
835M   The independent investment manager conditions
835N   Investment managers: the 20% rule
835O   Meaning of "qualifying period", "relevant disregarded income" and "beneficial
        entitlement"
835P   Treatment of transactions where 20% rule not met
835Q   Application of 20% rule to collective investment schemes
Supplementary
835R   Supplementary provision
835S   Interpretation of Chapter
Chapter 2C   Income Tax Obligations and Liabilities Imposed on UK Representatives
835T   Introduction to Chapter
835U   Obligations and liabilities of UK representative
835V   Exceptions: notices and information
835W   Exceptions: criminal offences and penalties etc
835X   Indemnities
835Y   Meaning of "independent agent"
Chapter 3   Jointly Held Property
836   Jointly held property
837   Jointly held property: declarations of unequal beneficial interests
Chapter 4   Banks etc in Compulsory Liquidation
837A   Overview of Chapter
837B   Application of Chapter
837C   Charge to income tax on winding up receipts
837D   Transfer of rights to payment
837E   Allowable deductions
837F   Election to carry back

837G   Relationship of Chapter with other income tax provisions
837H   Interpretation of Chapter
Chapter 4   Other Miscellaneous Rules
838   Local authorities and local authority associations
838A   Asbestos compensation settlements
839   Issue departments of the Reserve Bank of India and the State Bank of Pakistan
840   Government securities held by non-UK resident central banks
841   Official agents of Commonwealth countries etc
842   European Economic Interest Groupings
843   Restriction of deductions for annual payments
844   Letters patent etc: exempting provisions
845   Extra return to be treated as interest etc
846   Interpretation of section 845
Part 15   Deduction of Income Tax At Source
Chapter 1   Introduction
847   Overview of Part
848   Income tax deducted at source treated as income tax paid by recipient
849   Interaction with other Income Tax Acts provisions
Chapter 2   Meaning of "relevant investment" for purposes of section 876
Introduction
850   Overview of Chapter
Deposit-takers and relevant investments
853   Meaning of "deposit-taker"
854   Power to prescribe persons as deposit-takers
855   Meaning of "investment" and "deposit"
856   Investments which are relevant investments
857   Investments to be treated as being or as not being relevant investments
Investments which are not relevant investments
863   General client account deposits
864   Qualifying uncertificated eligible debt security units
865   Qualifying certificates of deposit
866   Qualifying time deposits
867   Lloyd's premium trust funds
868   Investments held outside the United Kingdom
870   Other investments
Supplementary
872   Power to make orders amending Chapter
873   Discretionary or accumulation settlements
Chapter 3   Deduction From Certain Payments of Yearly Interest
Duty to deduct sums representing income tax
874   Duty to deduct from certain payments of yearly interest
Exceptions from duty to deduct
875   Interest paid by building societies
876   Interest paid by deposit-takers
877   UK public revenue dividends
878   Interest paid by banks
879   Interest paid on advances from banks
880   Interest paid on advances from building societies
881   National Savings Bank interest
882   Quoted Eurobond interest
883   Interest on loan to buy life annuity
884   Relevant foreign income
885   Authorised persons dealing in financial instruments
886   Interest paid by recognised clearing houses etc
887   Industrial and provident society payments
888   Statutory interest
888A   Qualifying private placements
888B   Designated dividends of investment trusts
888C   Interest distributions of certain open-ended investment companies
888D   Interest distribution of certain authorised unit trusts
888E   Interest on certain peer-to-peer lending
Chapter 4   Deduction From Payments in Respect of Building Society Securities
889   Payments in respect of building society securities
Chapter 5   Deduction From Payments of UK Public Revenue Dividends
Introduction
890   Overview of Chapter
891   Meaning of "UK public revenue dividend"
Duty to deduct sums representing income tax
892   Duty to deduct from certain UK public revenue dividends

Payments which are payable gross
893   Payments of UK public revenue dividends which are payable gross
894   Treasury directions
Deduction at source applications
895   Deduction at source application
896   Withdrawal of application
Regulations
897   Power to make regulations
Chapter 6   Deduction From Annual Payments and Patent Royalties
Introduction
898   Overview of Chapter
899   Meaning of "qualifying annual payment"
Duty to deduct from annual payments
900   Deduction from commercial payments made by individuals
901   Deduction from annual payments made by other persons
Duty to deduct from patent royalties
903   Deduction from patent royalties
Supplementary
904   Annual payments for dividends or non-taxable consideration
905   Interpretation of Chapter
Chapter 7   Deduction From Other Payments Connected with Intellectual Property
Certain royalties etc where usual place of abode of owner is abroad
906   Certain royalties etc where usual place of abode of owner is abroad
907   Meaning of "intellectual property"
908   Royalty payments etc made through UK resident agents
909   Royalty payments: further provision
Proceeds of a sale of patent rights
910   Proceeds of a sale of patent rights: payments to non-UK residents
Chapter 8   Chapters 6 and 7: Special Provision in Relation to Royalties
Deduction at special rates
911   Double taxation arrangements: deduction at treaty rate
912   Power to make directions disapplying section 911
913   Interpretation of sections 911 and 912
Discretion to make payments gross
914   EU companies: discretion to make payment gross
915   Power to make directions disapplying section 914
916   Duty of payee to notify if payment not exempt
917   Supplementary
Tax avoidance
917A   Tax avoidance arrangements
Chapter 9   Manufactured Payments
Manufactured dividends
918   Manufactured dividends on UK shares: Real Estate Investment Trusts
Manufactured interest
919   Manufactured interest on UK securities: payments by UK residents etc
Repos
925A   Creditor repos
925C   Actual payments ignored if section 925A or 925B applies
925D   Power to modify repo sections
925E   Cases where section 925D applies: non-standard repos
925F   Interpretation of the repo sections
Supplementary
926   Interpretation of Chapter
927   Regulation-making powers: general
Chapter 10   Deduction From Non-commercial Payments By Companies
928   Chargeable payments connected with exempt distributions
Chapter 11   Payments Between Companies Etc: Exception From Duties to Deduct
Introduction
929   Overview of Chapter
Exception from duties to deduct for excepted payments
930   Exception from duties to deduct sums representing income tax
931   Power to make directions disapplying section 930
932   Meaning of "qualifying partnership"
Excepted payments
933   UK resident companies
934   Non-UK resident companies
935   PEP and ISA managers
936   Recipients who are to be paid gross
937   Partnerships

Incorrect belief that payment is an excepted payment
938   Consequences of reasonable but incorrect belief
Chapter 12   Funding Bonds
939   Duty to retain bonds where issue treated as payment of interest
940   Exception from duty to retain bonds
Chapter 14   Tax Avoidance: Directions for Duty to Deduct to Apply
944   Directions for deduction from payments to non-UK residents
Chapter 15   Collection: Deposit-takers, Building Societies and Certain Companies
Introduction
945   Overview of Chapter
946   Payments within this section
947   Return periods
948   Meaning of "accounting period"
Returns of income tax
949   Payments in an accounting period
950   Payments otherwise than in an accounting period
Collection and payment of income tax
951   Collection and payment of income tax
Set-off
952   Conditions for a set-off claim
953   How a set-off claim works
954   Proceedings begun after a set-off claim is made
955   Proceedings begun before a set-off claim is made
Assessments and errors
956   Assessments where section 946 payment included in return
957   Assessments in other cases
958   Payer's duty to deliver amended return
959   Application of Income Tax Acts provisions about time limits for assessments
960   Further provisions about assessments
Supplementary
961   Relationship between Chapter and Income Tax Acts powers
962   Power to make regulations modifying Chapter
Chapter 16   Collection: Certain Payments By Other Persons
963   Collection of income tax on certain payments by other persons
963A   Power to make regulations modifying section 963
Chapter 17   Collection Through Self-assessment Return
964   Collection through self-assessment return
Chapter 18   Other Regimes Involving the Deduction of Income Tax At Source
Visiting performers
965   Overview of sections 966 to 970
966   Duty to deduct and account for sums representing income tax
967   Calculation of sums representing income tax
968   Treatment of sums representing income tax
969   Regulations
970   Supplementary
Non-resident landlords
971   Income tax due in respect of income of non-resident landlords
972   Regulations under section 971
Real Estate Investment Trusts
973   Income tax due in respect of distributions
974   Regulations under section 973
Chapter 19   General
Supplementary
975   Statements about deduction of income tax
975A   Statements about certain payments of interest
976   Arrangements for payments of interest less tax or at specified net rate
977   Payments to companies
978   Application to public departments
979   Designated international organisations: exceptions from duties to deduct
979A   FSCS payments representing interest
980   Derivative contracts: exception from duties to deduct
981   Foreign currency securities etc: exception from duties to deduct
982   Income tax is calculated by reference to gross amounts
Interpretation
983   Meaning of "deposit"
984   Meaning of "financial instrument"
985   Meaning of "qualifying certificate of deposit"
986   Meaning of "qualifying uncertificated eligible debt security unit"
987   Meaning of "quoted Eurobond"

Part 16   Income Tax Acts Definitions etc
Chapter 1   Definitions
988   Overview of Chapter
989   The definitions
990   Meaning of "Act"
991   Meaning of "bank"
992   Meaning of "company"
993   Meaning of "connected" persons
994   Meaning of "connected" persons: supplementary
995   Meaning of "control"
996   Meaning of "farming" and related expressions
997   Meaning of "generally accepted accounting practice" and related expressions
998   Meaning of "grossing up"
998A   Meaning of "hire-purchase agreement"
999   Meaning of "local authority"
1000   Meaning of "local authority association"
1001   Meaning of "offshore installation"
1002   Regulations about the meaning of "offshore installation"
1003   Meaning of "oil and gas exploration and appraisal"
1004   Meaning of "property investment LLP"
1005   Meaning of "recognised stock exchange" etc
1006   Meaning of "research and development"
1007   Meaning of "unit trust scheme"
1007A   Meaning of "permanent establishment"
Chapter 2   Other Income Tax Acts Provisions
1008   Scotland
1009   Sources of income within the charge to income tax or corporation tax
1011   References to married persons, or civil partners, living together
1012   Relationship between rules on highest part of total income
1013   Territorial sea of the United Kingdom
1014   Orders and regulations
1015   Territorial scope of charges under certain provisions to which section 1016 applies
1016   Table of provisions to which this section applies
Part 17   Definitions for Purposes of Act and Final Provisions
Definitions for the purposes of Act
1017   Abbreviated references to Acts
1018   "Act" to include Scottish and Northern Ireland legislation in some cases
1019   Meaning of "certificate of deposit"
1020   Claims and elections
1021   Application of definitions of "connected" persons and "control"
1022   Meaning of "debenture"
1023   Meaning of "double taxation arrangements"
1024   Meaning of "gilt-edged securities"
1025   Meaning of "modified net income"
1026   Meaning of "non-qualifying income" for the purposes of section 1025
Final provisions
1027   Minor and consequential amendments
1028   Power to make consequential provision
1029   Power to undo changes
1030   Transitional provisions and savings
1031   Repeals and revocations
1032   Index of defined expressions
1033   Extent
1034   Commencement
1035   Short title
SCHEDULES:
Schedule 1—Minor and consequential amendments
Schedule 2—Transitionals and savings
Schedule 3—Repeals and revocations
Schedule 4—Index of defined expressions

PART 1
OVERVIEW

1 Overview of Income Tax Acts

(1) The following Acts make provision about income tax—

    (*a*) ITEPA 2003 (which is about charges to tax on employment income, pension income and social security income [and makes provision for the high income child benefit charge][2]),

    (*b*) ITTOIA 2005 (which is about charges to tax on trading income, property income, savings and investment income and some other miscellaneous income), and

    (c) this Act (which contains the other main provisions about income tax).

(2) There are also provisions about income tax elsewhere: see in particular—

    (a) [Part 2 of TIOPA 2010][1] (double taxation relief),

    (b) CAA 2001 (allowances for capital expenditure), and

    (c) Part 4 of FA 2004 (pension schemes etc).

(3) Schedule 1 to the Interpretation Act 1978 (c 30) defines "the Income Tax Acts" (as all enactments relating to income tax).

Amendments—[1]   In sub-s (2)(a) words substituted by TIOPA 2010 s 501, Sch 8 paras 71, 72. TIOPA 2010 has effect for corporation tax purposes for accounting periods ending on or after 1 April 2010, for income and capital gains tax purposes for the tax year 2010–11 and subsequent tax years, and for petroleum revenue tax purposes for chargeable periods beginning on or after 1 July 2010.

[2]   Words in sub-s (1)(a) inserted by FA 2012 s 8, Sch 1 para 6(1), (2) with effect for the tax year 2012–13 and subsequent tax years.

2 Overview of Act

(1) This Act has 17 Parts.

(2) Part 2 contains basic provisions about income tax including—

    (a) provision about the annual nature of income tax (Chapter 1),

    (b) the rates at which income tax is charged (Chapter 2), and

    (c) the calculation of income tax liability (Chapter 3).

(3) Part 3 is about taxpayers' personal reliefs including—

    (a) personal allowances (Chapter 2),

    (b) blind persons' allowances (Chapter 2), and

    (c) tax reductions for married couples and civil partners (Chapter 3).

(4) Part 4 is about loss relief including relief for—

    (a) trade losses (Chapters 2 and 3),

    (b) losses from property businesses (Chapter 4),

    (c) losses in an employment or office (Chapter 5),

    (d) losses on disposal of shares (Chapter 6), and

    (e) losses from miscellaneous transactions (Chapter 7).

(5) Part 5 is about relief under the enterprise investment scheme.

[(5A) Part 5A is about relief under the seed enterprise investment scheme.][10]

[(5B) Part 5B is about relief for social investments.][14]

(6) Part 6 is about—

    (a) relief for investment in venture capital trusts, and

    (b) other matters relating to venture capital trusts.

(7) Part 7 is about community investment tax relief.

(8) Part 8 is about a variety of reliefs including relief for—

    (a) interest payments (Chapter 1),

    (b) gifts to charity including gift aid (Chapters 2 and 3),

    (c) annual payments . . . [11] (Chapter 4), and

    (d) maintenance payments (Chapter 5).

(9) Part 9 contains special rules about settlements and trustees including—

    (a) general provision about settlements and trustees (Chapter 2),

    (b) special income tax rates for trusts (Chapters 3, 4, 5 and 6),

    (c) rules about trustees' expenses (Chapters 4 and 8),

    (d) rules about trustees' discretionary payments (Chapter 7),

    (e) *rules about unauthorised unit trusts (Chapter 9), and*[13] and

    (f) rules about heritage maintenance settlements (Chapter 10).

[(9A) Part 9A is about the treatment of certain transactions in UK land.][18]

(10) Part 10 contains special rules about charitable trusts etc

[(10A) Part 10A is about alternative finance arrangements.][7]

(11) Part 11 is about manufactured payments and repos.[12]

[(11ZA) Part 11ZA is about manufactured payments.][12]

[(11A) Part 11A is about leasing arrangements involving finance leases or loans.][7]

(12) Part 12 is about accrued income profits.

[(12A) Part 12A is about sale and lease-back etc.][7]

(13) Part 13 is about tax avoidance in relation to—

    (a) transactions in securities (Chapter 1),

    (b) transfers of assets abroad (Chapter 2),

    (c) . . . [18]

    (d) sales of occupation income (Chapter 4), . . . [3]

    (e) trade losses (Chapter 5) [. . . [8]

    (f) transfers of income streams (Chapter 5A).][3]

    [(g) finance arrangements (Chapter 5B),

    (h) loan or credit transactions (Chapter 5C),][8]

    [(ha) disposals of assets through partnerships (Chapter 5D),][15] [(*hb*) disguised investment management fees (Chapter 5E),][16]

[(*hc*) income-based carried interest (Chapter 5F),][17]

[(*i*) leases of plant and machinery (Chapter 6), and

(*j*) tax relief for interest (Chapter 7).][4]

(14) Part 14 deals with some miscellaneous rules about income tax liability, including—

[(*za*) an alternative basis for charge (the remittance basis) for certain income and gains of certain individuals (Chapter A1),][1]

(*a*) limits on liability to income tax for non-UK residents (Chapter 1),

[(*aa*) exemption for persons not domiciled in United Kingdom (Chapter 1A),][2]

(*b*) special rules about residence [and domicile (Chapters 2 and 2A)][6], . . .[9]

[(*ba*) rules about UK representatives of non-UK residents (Chapters 2B and 2C),][9]

(*c*) rules about jointly held property (Chapter 3)[, and

(*d*) imposition of the charge to income tax on the receipts of certain types of company being wound up (Chapter 3A).][5]

(15) Part 15 is about the deduction of income tax at source.

(16) Part 16 contains definitions which apply for the purposes of the Income Tax Acts and other general provisions which apply for the purposes of those Acts.

(17) Part 17—

(*a*) contains provisions to be used in interpreting this Act,

(*b*) introduces Schedule 1 (minor and consequential amendments),

(*c*) introduces Schedule 2 (transitional provisions and savings),

(*d*) introduces Schedule 3 (repeals and revocations, including of spent enactments),

(*e*) introduces Schedule 4 (index of defined expressions that apply for the purposes of this Act),

(*f*) confers powers on the Treasury to make orders, and

(*g*) makes provision about the coming into force of this Act.

Amendments—[1]   Sub-s (14)(*za*) inserted by FA 2008 s 25, Sch 7 paras 74, 75 with effect for the tax year 2008–09 and subsequent tax years.

[2]   Sub-s (14)(*aa*) inserted by FA 2009 s 52(2) with effect for the tax year 2008–09 and subsequent tax years.

[3]   Sub-s (13)(*f*) inserted (and word "and" at the end of paragraph (*d*) repealed) by FA 2009 s 49, Sch 25, para 9(5) with effect in relation to transfers on or after 22 April 2009).

[4]   Sub-s (13)(*i*), (*j*) inserted by TIOPA 2010 s 371, Sch 7 paras 50, 51. TIOPA 2010 has effect for corporation tax purposes for accounting periods ending on or after 1 April 2010, for income and capital gains tax purposes for the tax year 2010–11 and subsequent tax years, and for petroleum revenue tax purposes for chargeable periods beginning on or after 1 July 2010.

[5]   Sub-s (14)(*d*) and preceding word "and" inserted by TIOPA 2010 s 371, Sch 7 paras 68, 69. TIOPA 2010 has effect for corporation tax purposes for accounting periods ending on or after 1 April 2010, for income and capital gains tax purposes for the tax year 2010–11 and subsequent tax years, and for petroleum revenue tax purposes for chargeable periods beginning on or after 1 July 2010.

[6]   In sub-s (14)(*b*) words substituted for words "(Chapter 2)" by TIOPA 2010 s 371, Sch 7 paras 75, 76. TIOPA 2010 has effect for corporation tax purposes for accounting periods ending on or after 1 April 2010, for income and capital gains tax purposes for the tax year 2010–11 and subsequent tax years, and for petroleum revenue tax purposes for chargeable periods beginning on or after 1 July 2010.

[7]   Sub-ss (10A), (11A), (12A) inserted by TIOPA 2010 s 501, Sch 8 paras 219, 220, 237, 238, 256, 257. TIOPA 2010 has effect for corporation tax purposes for accounting periods ending on or after 1 April 2010, for income and capital gains tax purposes for the tax year 2010–11 and subsequent tax years, and for petroleum revenue tax purposes for chargeable periods beginning on or after 1 July 2010.

[8]   In sub-s (13), in para (*e*) word "or" repealed, and paras (*g*), (*h*) inserted, by TIOPA 2010 ss 501, 503, Sch 8 paras 271, 272, Sch 10 Pt 10. TIOPA 2010 has effect for corporation tax purposes for accounting periods ending on or after 1 April 2010, for income and capital gains tax purposes for the tax year 2010–11 and subsequent tax years, and for petroleum revenue tax purposes for chargeable periods beginning on or after 1 July 2010.

[9]   In sub-s (14), in para (*b*) word "and" repealed, and para (*ba*) inserted, by TIOPA 2010 ss 501, 503, Sch 8 paras 280, 281, Sch 10 Pt 11. TIOPA 2010 has effect for corporation tax purposes for accounting periods ending on or after 1 April 2010, for income and capital gains tax purposes for the tax year 2010–11 and subsequent tax years, and for petroleum revenue tax purposes for chargeable periods beginning on or after 1 July 2010.

[10]   Sub-s (5A) inserted by FA 2012 s 38, Sch 6 paras 6, 7 with effect in relation to shares issued on or after 6 April 2012.

[11]   In sub-s (8)(*c*) words "and patent royalties" repealed by FA 2013 s 15(4) with effect in relation to payments made on or after 5 December 2012.

[12]   Sub-s (11) repealed, and sub-s (11ZA) inserted, by FA 2013 s 77, Sch 29 paras 16, 17 with effect from 1 January 2014.

[13]   Sub-s (9)(*e*) repealed by the Unauthorised Unit Trusts (Tax) Regulations, SI 2013/2819 reg 37(1), (2) with effect from 6 April 2014. Note that an unauthorised unit trust is not a non-exempt unauthorised unit trust, and these amendments do not apply in relation to the trust, if at all times in the period beginning with 24 May 2012 and ending with 5 April 2014 it had at least one unit holder which was, and at least one unit holder which was not, an eligible investor (ie a mixed unauthorised unit trust); this ceases to apply in relation to the trust if subsequently it no longer has any unit holders which are eligible investors (SI 2013/2819 reg 32).

[14]   Sub-s (5B) inserted by FA 2014 s 57, Sch 11 paras 3, 4 with effect from 17 July 2014.

[15]   Sub-s (13)(*ha*) inserted by FA 2015 s 21(2)(*a*) with effect from 26 March 2015.

[16]   Sub-s (13)(*hb*) inserted by FA 2015 s 21(2)(*b*) with effect in relation to sums arising on or after 6 April 2015 (whenever the arrangements under which the sums arise were made).

[17]   Sub-s (13)(*hc*) inserted by FA 2016 s 37(3) with effect in relation to sums of carried interest arising on or after 6 April 2016 (whenever the arrangements under which the sums arise were made).

[18]   Sub-s (9A) inserted by FA 2016 s 79(2), and sub-s (13)(c) repealed, with effect in relation to disposals on or after 5 July 2016 (FA 2016 s 82(1)), subject to transitional provisions for disposals to associated persons on or after 16 March 2016 and before 5 July 2016 (FA 2016 s 82(4)–(15)).

F(No 2)A 2017 s 39 provides that these amendments have effect (so far as they would not otherwise have effect) in relation to amounts that are recognised in GAAP accounts drawn up for any period of account beginning on or after 8 March 2017 or, in the case of a straddling period, amounts that would be recognised in GAAP accounts drawn up for a period of account beginning on 8 March 2017 and ending when the straddling period ends. "Straddling period" means a period of account beginning before 8 March 2017 and ending on or after that date.

PART 2
BASIC PROVISIONS

CHAPTER 1

CHARGES TO INCOME TAX

3 Overview of charges to income tax

(1) Income tax is charged under—

    (a) Part 2 of ITEPA 2003 (employment income),

    (b) Part 9 of ITEPA 2003 (pension income),

    (c) Part 10 of ITEPA 2003 (social security income),

    (d) Part 2 of ITTOIA 2005 (trading income),

    (e) Part 3 of ITTOIA 2005 (property income),

    (f) Part 4 of ITTOIA 2005 (savings and investment income), and

    (g) Part 5 of ITTOIA 2005 (miscellaneous income).

(2) Income tax is also charged under other provisions, including—

    (a) Chapter 5 of Part 4 of FA 2004 (registered pension schemes: tax charges),

    (b) section 7 of F(No 2)A 2005 (social security pension lump sums),

    (c) Part 10 of this Act (special rules about charitable trusts etc),

    (d) Chapter 2 of Part 12 of this Act (accrued income profits), *and*[1]

    (e) Part 13 of this Act (tax avoidance)[, and

    (f) Chapter 3A of Part 14 of this Act (banks etc in compulsory liquidation).][1]

Commentary—*Simon's Taxes* A1.131.

Derivation—TA 1988 s 1(1).

Amendments—[1]   Sub-s (2)(f) and preceding word "and" inserted, and word "and" immediately before sub-s (2)(e) repealed, by TIOPA 2010 ss 371, 503, Sch 7 paras 68, 70, Sch 10 Pt 12. TIOPA 2010 has effect for corporation tax purposes for accounting periods ending on or after 1 April 2010, for income and capital gains tax purposes for the tax year 2010–11 and subsequent tax years, and for petroleum revenue tax purposes for chargeable periods beginning on or after 1 July 2010.

4 Income tax an annual tax

(1) Income tax is charged for a year only if an Act so provides.

(2) A year for which income tax is charged is called a "tax year".

(3) A tax year begins on 6 April and ends on the following 5 April.

(4) "The tax year 2007–08" means the tax year beginning on 6 April 2007 (and any corresponding expression in which two years are similarly mentioned is to be read in the same way).

(5) Every assessment to income tax must be made for a tax year.

(6) Subsection (5) is subject to Chapter 15 of Part 15 (by virtue of which an assessment may relate to a return period).

Commentary—*Simon's Taxes* A1.125, A1.152.

[5 Income tax and companies

Section 3 of CTA 2009 disapplies the provisions of the Income Tax Acts relating to the charge to income tax in relation to income of a company (not accruing to it in a fiduciary or representative capacity) if—

    (a) the company is UK resident, or

    (b) the company is non-UK resident and [it is chargeable to corporation tax in respect of the income, or would be so chargeable but for an exemption.][2]][1]

Amendments—[1]   This section substituted by CTA 2009 s 1322, Sch 1 paras 699, 700. CTA 2009 applies for accounting periods ending on or after 1 April 2009 (for corporation tax purposes) and for tax years 2009–10 onwards (for income and capital gains tax purposes).

[2]   In para (b), words substituted for words "the income is within its chargeable profits as defined by section 19 of that Act (profits attributable to its permanent establishment in the United Kingdom)." by FA 2019 s 17, Sch 5 para 9 with effect from 6 April 2020, subject to transitional provisions in FA 2019 Sch 5 Pt 3 (paras 36–50).

CHAPTER 2

RATES AT WHICH INCOME TAX IS CHARGED

The rates

6 The . . . [1] basic rate[, higher rate and additional rate][2]

(1) The main rates at which income tax is charged are—

    (*a*) . . . [1]
    (*b*) the basic rate, . . . [3]
    (*c*) the higher rate[, and
    (*d*) the additional rate.][3]

(2) The . . . [1] basic rate[, higher rate and additional rate][2] for a tax year are the rates determined as such by Parliament for the tax year.

(3) For other rates at which income tax is charged see—

    (*za*) . . . [7]
    [(*zb*) section 6B *(Welsh basic, higher and additional rates),][9]*
    [(*zc*) section 6C *(default basic, higher and additional rates),][8]*
    [(*a*) section 7 (starting rate for savings [and savings nil rate][5]),][1]
    [(*aa*) section 7A *(savings basic, higher and additional rates),][8]*
    (*b*) section 8 ([dividend nil rate,][6] dividend ordinary rate[, dividend upper rate and dividend additional rate][3]), and
    (*c*) section 9 (trust rate and dividend trust rate).

[(4) See also section 80C of the Scotland Act 1998 which makes provision for the purposes of section 11A (income charged at Scottish rates).][7]

Commentary—*Simon's Taxes* **E1.101A**.
Amendments—[1]   Sub-s (1)(*a*), words in sub-s (2) and heading, repealed, and sub-s (3)(*a*) substituted, by FA 2008 s 5 with effect for the tax year 2008–09 and subsequent tax years.
[2]   In heading and in sub-s (2) words substituted for words "and higher rate" by FA 2009 s 6, Sch 2 paras 1, 2 with effect for the tax year 2010–11 and subsequent tax years.
[3]   In sub-s (1)(*b*), word "and" at end repealed, in sub-s (3)(*b*), words substituted for words "and dividend upper rate", sub-s (1)(*d*) and preceding word "and" inserted by FA 2009 s 6(1)–(3) with effect for the tax year 2010–11 and subsequent tax years.
[4]   Sub-s (3)(*za*) inserted by FA 2014 s 296, Sch 38 paras 1, 2(*b*) with effect in relation to the tax year 2016–17 (the tax year appointed by the Treasury under the Scotland Act 2012 s 25(5) by virtue of SI 2015/2000) and subsequent tax years.
[5]   Words in sub-s (3)(*a*) inserted by FA 2016 s 4(1), (2) with effect in relation to the tax year 2016–17 and subsequent tax years.
[6]   Words in sub-s (3)(*b*) inserted by FA 2016 s 5(1), (2) with effect in relation to the tax year 2016–17 and subsequent tax years.
[7]   Sub-s (3)(*za*) repealed, and sub-s (4) inserted, by the Scotland Act 2016 s 14(1)–(4) with effect in relation to the 2017–18 tax year (as appointed under the Scotland Act 2016 s 13(15)) and subsequent years by virtue of SI 2016/1161 reg 3.
[8]   Sub-s (3)(*zc*), (*aa*) inserted by FA 2016 s 6(1), (5) with effect in relation to the tax year 2017–18 (as appointed under the Scotland Act 2016 s 13(15)) and subsequent years by virtue of SI 2016/1161 reg 3, subject to transitional provisions (see FA 2016 s 6(24)–(30)).
[9]   Sub-s (3)(*zb*) inserted by the Wales Act 2014 s 9(1), (2). Wales Act 2014 s 9 comes into force on 24 July 2018 and has effect in relation to the tax year 2019–20 (by virtue of SI 2018/892 arts 3, 5, 6). 2019–20 is appointed as the first tax year in relation to which a Welsh rate resolution may be made by the National Assembly for Wales under GOWA 2006 s 116D (SI 2018/892 art 6).

[6B The Welsh basic, higher and additional rates

(1) The Welsh basic rate, the Welsh higher rate and the Welsh additional rate for a tax year are calculated as follows.

    Step 1

        Take the basic rate, higher rate or additional rate.

    Step 2

        Deduct 10 percentage points.

    Step 3

        Add the Welsh rate (if any) set by the National Assembly for Wales for that year for the purpose of calculating the Welsh basic rate, the Welsh higher rate or the Welsh additional rate (as the case may be).

(2) For provision about the setting of the Welsh rates, see Chapter 2 of Part 4A of the Government of Wales Act 2006.][1]

Commentary—*Simon's Taxes* **E1.101F, E7.222**.
Amendments—[1]   Section 6B inserted by the Wales Act 2014 s 9(1), (3). Wales Act 2014 s 9 comes into force on 24 July 2018 and has effect in relation to the tax year 2019–20 (by virtue of SI 2018/892 arts 3, 5, 6). 2019–20 is appointed as the first tax year in relation to which a Welsh rate resolution may be made by the National Assembly for Wales under GOWA 2006 s 116D (SI 2018/892 art 6).

[6C The default basic, higher and additional rates

The default basic rate, default higher rate and default additional rate for a tax year are the rates determined as such by Parliament for the tax year.][1]

Amendments—[1]   Section 6C inserted by FA 2016 s 6(1), (3) with effect in relation to the tax year 2017–18 (as appointed under the Scotland Act 2016 s 13(15)) and subsequent years by virtue of SI 2016/1161 reg 3, subject to transitional provisions (see FA 2016 s 6(24)–(30)).

[7 The starting rate for savings [and savings nil rate]

[(1)] The starting rate for savings is [0%][2].
[(2) The savings nil rate is 0%.][3]][1]

Commentary—*Simon's Taxes* **E1.1423A, T6.103**.

Derivation—TA 1988 s 1A(1B).

HMRC Manuals—Savings and Investment Manual SAIM1112 (tax on savings and investment income: changes to starting rate for savings).

Amendments—[1]   Section substituted by FA 2008 s 5, Sch 1 paras 1, 2 with effect for the tax year 2008–09 and subsequent tax years.

[2]   "0%" substituted for previous figure "10%" by FA 2014 s 3(1) with effect for the tax year 2015–16 and subsequent tax years.

[3]   Sub-s (1) numbered as such, and sub-s (2) and words in heading inserted, by FA 2016 s 4(1), (3) with effect in relation to the tax year 2016–17 and subsequent tax years.

[7A The savings basic, higher and additional rates

The savings basic rate, savings higher rate and savings additional rate for a tax year are the rates determined as such by Parliament for the tax year.][1]

Commentary—*Simon's Taxes* **T6.103**.

Amendments—[1]   Section 7A inserted by FA 2016 s 6(1), (4) with effect in relation to the tax year 2017–18 (as appointed under the Scotland Act 2016 s 13(15)) and subsequent years by virtue of SI 2016/1161 reg 3, subject to transitional provisions (see FA 2016 s 6(24)–(30)).

8 The [dividend nil rate,][2] dividend ordinary rate[, dividend upper rate and dividend additional rate][1]

[(A1) The dividend nil rate is 0%.][2]

(1) The dividend ordinary rate is [7.5%][2].

(2) The dividend upper rate is 32.5%.

[(3) The dividend additional rate is [38.1%][2].][1]

Commentary—*Simon's Taxes* **T6.104**.

Derivation—TA 1988 s 1B(2).

HMRC Manuals—Savings and Investment Manual SAIM1080 (the dividend 15/16 rates).

Amendments—[1]   In the heading, words substituted for words "and dividend upper rate", sub-s (3) inserted by FA 2009 s 6, Sch 2 paras 1, 3 with effect for the tax year 2010–11 and subsequent tax years.

[2]   Words in heading inserted, sub-s (A1) inserted, and figures in sub-ss (1), (3) substituted, by FA 2016 s 5(1), (3) with effect for the tax year 2016–17 and subsequent tax years.

9 The trust rate and dividend trust rate

(1) The trust rate is [45%][1].

(2) The dividend trust rate is [38.1%][2].

Commentary—*Simon's Taxes* **C4.210, T6.105**.

Derivation—TA 1988 s 686(1A).

HMRC Manuals—Savings and Investment Manual SAIM1080 (trusts and dividend trust 15/16 rates).

Amendments—[1]   In sub-s (1), "45%" substituted for "50%" by FA 2012 s 1(3)(*b*), (*c*) with effect for the tax year 2013–14 and subsequent tax years.

[2]   In sub-s (2), figure substituted by FA 2016 s 5(1), (4) with effect for the tax year 2016–17 and subsequent tax years.

Income charged at particular rates

[9A Overview of sections 10 to 15

The general effect of sections 10 to 15 is outlined in the following table—

Type of taxpayer	Rates payable on savings income	Rates payable on most dividend income	Rates payable on other income
UK resident individual who is neither a Scottish taxpayer nor a Welsh taxpayer	Savings rates	Dividend rates	Main rates
Scottish taxpayer	Savings rates	Dividend rates	Scottish rates
Welsh taxpayer	Savings rates	Dividend rates	Main rates while section 11B is not in force; Welsh rates if that section is in force
Non-UK resident individual	Savings rates	Dividend rates	Default rates
Non-individual, except that some trustees in some circumstances are subject instead to the trust rate or the dividend trust rate	Default basic rate	Dividend ordinary rate	Default basic rate

Note: the table does not address the effect of some exceptions referred to in sections 10 to 15.][1]

Commentary—*Simon's Taxes* **E1.101A**.

Amendments—[1]   Section 9A inserted by FA 2016 s 6(1), (2) with effect in relation to the tax year 2017–18 (as appointed under the Scotland Act 2016 s 13(15)) and subsequent years by virtue of SI 2016/1161 reg 3, subject to transitional provisions (see FA 2016 s 6(24)–(30)).

10 Income charged at the . . . .[2] basic[, higher and additional][3] rates: individuals

(1) . . .[2]

[(2) Income tax on an individual's income up to the basic rate limit is charged at the basic rate . . . [10] .][2]

(3) Income tax is charged at the higher rate on an individual's income above the basic rate limit [and up to the higher rate limit][3].

[(3A Income tax is charged at the additional rate on an individual's income above the higher rate limit.][3]

(4) This section is subject to—

    [section 11A (income charged at [Scottish][9] rates),][4]

    [section 11B (income charged at the Welsh basic, higher and additional rates),][11]

    [section 11C (income charged at the default basic, higher and additional rates: non-UK resident individuals),

    section 11D (savings income charged at the savings basic, higher and additional rates: individuals),

    section 12 (savings income charged at the starting rate for savings),][10]

    [section 12A (savings income charged at the savings nil rate),][7]

    section 13 (income charged at the dividend ordinary and dividend upper rates: individuals), and any other provisions of the Income Tax Acts which provide for income of an individual to be charged at different rates of income tax in some circumstances.

[(5) The basic rate limit is [£37,500][8] .][1]

[(5A) The higher rate limit is £150,000.][3]

[(6) The basic rate limit [and higher rate limit are][3] increased in some circumstances: see—

    (*a*) section 414(2) (gift aid relief), and

    (*b*) section 192(4) of FA 2004 (relief for pension contributions).

(7) See section 21 for indexation of the basic rate limit.][2]

Commentary—*Simon's Taxes* **E1.101A, T6.101**.

HMRC Manuals—Savings and Investment Manual SAIM2400 (taxation of interest).

Amendments—[1]   Sub-s (5) substituted by FA 2008 s 4 with effect for the tax year 2008–09 and subsequent tax years.

[2]   Sub-s (1), and words in sub-s (4), repealed, sub-s (2) substituted, and sub-ss (6), (7) inserted, by FA 2008 s 5, Sch 1 paras 1, 3 with effect for the tax year 2008–09 and subsequent tax years.

[3]   In sub-s (3), words at the end inserted, sub-ss (3A), (5A) inserted, in sub-s (6), words substituted for word "is", and in heading, words substituted for words "and higher" by FA 2009 s 6, Sch 2 paras 1, 4 with effect for the tax year 2010–11 and subsequent tax years.

[4]   In sub-s (4), words inserted FA 2014 s 296, Sch 38 paras 1, 4(*b*) with effect in relation to the tax year 2016–17 (the tax year appointed by the Treasury under the Scotland Act 2012 s 25(5) by virtue of SI 2015/2000) and subsequent tax years.

[7]   In sub-s (4), words inserted by FA 2016 s 4(1), (4) with effect in relation to the tax year 2016–17 and subsequent tax years.

[8]   In sub-s (5), figure substituted by FA 2019 s 5(1) with effect for the tax years 2019–20 and 2020–21. Figure was previously £34,500. ITA 2007 s 21 (indexation), so far as relating to the basic rate limit does not apply for 2019–20 and 2020–21 by virtue of FA 2019 s 5(5)(*a*).

[9]   In sub-s (4), word substituted by the Scotland Act 2016 s 14(1), (6) with effect in relation to the 2017–18 tax year (as appointed under the Scotland Act 2016 s 13(15)) and subsequent years by virtue of SI 2016/1161 reg 3.

[10]   In sub-s (2), words "(except to the extent that, in accordance with section 12, it is charged at the starting rate for savings)" repealed, and in sub-s (4), entries inserted, by FA 2016 s 6(1), (6), (7) with effect in relation to the tax year 2017–18 (as appointed under the Scotland Act 2016 s 13(15)) and subsequent tax years, subject to transitional provisions (see FA 2016 s 6(24)–(30)).

[11]   In sub-s (4), words inserted by the Wales Act 2014 s 9(1), (4). Wales Act 2014 s 9 comes into force on 24 July 2018 and has effect in relation to the tax year 2019–20 (by virtue of SI 2018/892 arts 3, 5, 6). 2019–20 is appointed as the first tax year in relation to which a Welsh rate resolution may be made by the National Assembly for Wales under GOWA 2006 s 116D (SI 2018/892 art 6).

11 Income charged at the [default basic rate: non-individuals][2]

(1) Income tax is charged at the [default][2] basic rate on the income of persons other than individuals.

(2) This section is subject to—

    . . .[1]

    section 14 (income charged at the dividend ordinary rate: other persons),

    Chapters 3 to 6 of Part 9 (which provide for some income of trustees to be charged at the dividend trust rate or at the trust rate), and

    any other provisions of the Income Tax Acts which provide for income of persons other than individuals to be charged at different rates of income tax in some circumstances.

Commentary—*Simon's Taxes* **C4.203**.

HMRC Manuals—Savings and Income Manual SAIM2400 (a person 'receiving' interest).

Amendments—[1]   Words in sub-s (2) repealed by FA 2008 s 5, Sch 1 paras 1, 4 with effect for the tax year 2008–09 and subsequent tax years.

[2]   In heading, words substituted for words "basic rate: other persons", and in sub-s (1), word inserted, by FA 2016 s 6(1), (8) with effect in relation to the tax year 2017–18 (as appointed under the Scotland Act 2016 s 13(15)) and subsequent years by virtue of SI 2016/1161 reg 3, subject to transitional provisions (see FA 2016 s 6(24)–(30)).

[11A Income charged at [Scottish][2] rates

[(1A) Income tax is charged at Scottish rates on the non-savings income of a Scottish taxpayer.][2]

(4) For the purposes of this section, "non-savings income" means income which is not savings income.

ITA 2007

(5) This section is subject to—

    section 13 (income charged at the dividend ordinary, upper and additional rates: individuals), and

    any provisions of the Income Tax Acts (apart from section 10) which provide for income of an individual to be charged at different rates of income tax in some circumstances.

(6) Section 16 has effect for determining [which part of a Scottish taxpayer's income consists of savings income]².]¹

Commentary—*Simon's Taxes* **E1.101C, E1.101A.**

Amendments—¹   This section inserted by FA 2014 s 296, Sch 38 paras 1, 5 with effect in relation to the tax year 2016–17 (the tax year appointed by the Treasury under the Scotland Act 2012 s 25(5) by virtue of SI 2015/2000) and subsequent tax years.
²   In section heading, word substituted, sub-s (1A) substituted for sub-ss (1)–(3), and in sub-s (6), words substituted, by the Scotland Act 2016 s 14(1), (7)–(10) with effect in relation to the tax year 2017–18 (as appointed under the Scotland Act 2016 s 13(15)) and subsequent years by virtue of SI 2016/1161 reg 3.

[11B Income charged at the Welsh basic, higher and additional rates

(1) Income tax is charged at the Welsh basic rate on the income of a Welsh taxpayer which—

    (a) is non-savings income, and

    (b) would otherwise be charged at the basic rate.

(2) Income tax is charged at the Welsh higher rate on the income of a Welsh taxpayer which—

    (a) is non-savings income, and

    (b) would otherwise be charged at the higher rate.

(3) Income tax is charged at the Welsh additional rate on the income of a Welsh taxpayer which—

    (a) is non-savings income, and

    (b) would otherwise be charged at the additional rate.

(4) For the purposes of this section, "non-savings income" means income which is not savings income.

(5) This section is subject to—

    section 13 (income charged at the dividend ordinary, upper and additional rates: individuals), and

    any provisions of the Income Tax Acts (apart from section 10) which provide for income of an individual to be charged at different rates of income tax in some circumstances.

(6) Section 16 has effect for determining the extent to which the non-savings income of a Welsh taxpayer would otherwise be charged at the basic, higher or additional rate.]¹

Commentary—*Simon's Taxes* **E1.101A.**

Amendments—¹   Section 11B inserted by the Wales Act 2014 s 9(1), (5). Wales Act 2014 s 9 comes into force on 24 July 2018 and has effect in relation to the tax year 2019–20 (by virtue of SI 2018/892 arts 3, 5, 6). 2019–20 is appointed as the first tax year in relation to which a Welsh rate resolution may be made by the National Assembly for Wales under GOWA 2006 s 116D (SI 2018/892 art 6).

[11C Income charged at the default basic, higher and additional rates: non- UK resident individuals

(1) Income tax on a non-UK resident individual's income up to the basic rate limit is charged at the default basic rate.

(2) Income tax is charged at the default higher rate on a non-UK resident individual's income above the basic rate limit and up to the higher rate limit.

(3) Income tax is charged at the default additional rate on a non-UK resident individual's income above the higher rate limit.

(4) Subsections (1) to (3) are subject to—

    section 11D (savings income charged at the savings basic, higher and additional rates),

    section 12 (savings income charged at the starting rate for savings),

    section 12A (savings income charged at the savings nil rate),

    section 13 (income charged at the dividend ordinary, upper and additional rates: individuals), and

    any other provisions of the Income Tax Acts (apart from section 10) which provide for income to be charged at different rates of income tax in some circumstances.]¹

Commentary—*Simon's Taxes* **E1.101A.**

Amendments—¹   Sections 11C, 11D inserted by FA 2016 s 6(1), (9) with effect in relation to the tax year 2017–18 (as appointed under the Scotland Act 2016 s 13(15)) and subsequent years by virtue of SI 2016/1161 reg 3, subject to transitional provisions (see FA 2016 s 6(24)–(30)).

[11D Income charged at the savings basic, higher and additional rates

(1) Income tax is charged at the savings basic rate on an individual's income which—

    (a) is saving income, and

    (b) would otherwise be charged at the basic rate or the default basic rate.

(2) Income tax is charged at the savings higher rate on an individual's income which—

    (a) is savings income, and

    (b) would otherwise be charged at the higher rate or the default higher rate.

(3) Income tax is charged at the savings additional rate on an individual's income which—

(a) is savings income, and

(b) would otherwise be charged at the additional rate or the default additional rate.

(4) Subsections (1) to (3)—

(a) have effect after sections 12 and 12A have been applied (so that any reference in subsections (1) to (3) to income which would otherwise be charged at a particular rate does not include income charged at the starting rate for savings or at the savings nil rate), and

(b) are subject to any other provisions of the Income Tax Acts (apart from sections 10 and 11C) which provide for income to be charged at different rates of income tax in some circumstances.

(5) Section 16 has effect for determining the extent to which an individual's savings income above the starting rate limit for savings would otherwise be charged at the basic, higher or additional rate or the default basic, default higher or default additional rate.

(6) In relation to an individual who is a Scottish taxpayer [or Welsh taxpayer]², references in this section to income which would otherwise be charged at a particular rate are to be read as references to income that would, if the individual were [neither a Scottish taxpayer nor a Welsh taxpayer]² (but were UK resident), be charged at that rate (and subsection (5) is to be read accordingly).]¹

Commentary—*Simon's Taxes* **E1.101C, E1.101A**.

Amendments—¹ Sections 11C, 11D inserted by FA 2016 s 6(1), (9) with effect in relation to the tax year 2017–18 (as appointed under the Scotland Act 2016 s 13(15)) and subsequent years by virtue of SI 2016/1161 reg 3, subject to transitional provisions (see FA 2016 s 6(24)–(30)).

² In sub-s (6), words inserted and words substituted for words "not a Scottish taxpayer", by the Devolved Income Tax Rates (Consequential Amendments) Order, SI 2019/201 arts 12(1), (2) with effect in relation to the tax year 2019–20 and subsequent tax years.

[12 Income charged at the starting rate for savings

(1) Income tax is charged at the starting rate for savings . . .² on so much of an individual's income up to the starting rate limit for savings [as—

(a) is savings income, and

(b) would otherwise be charged at the basic rate or the default basic rate]².

(2) This is subject to any provisions of the Income Tax Acts (apart from section 10) which provide for income of an individual to be charged at different rates of income tax in some circumstances.

(3) The starting rate limit for savings is [£5,000]³.

(4) See section 21 for indexation of the starting rate limit for savings.

(5) Section 16 has effect for determining the extent to which a person's income up to the starting rate limit for savings consists of savings income.]¹

Commentary—*Simon's Taxes* **E1.101A**.

Derivation—TA 1988 s 1A(1).

HMRC Manuals—Savings and Investment Manual SAIM1112 (changes to starting rate for savings - FY15/16).

Amendments—¹ Section 12 substituted by FA 2008 s 5, Sch 1 paras 1, 5 with effect for the tax year 2008–09 and subsequent tax years.

² In sub-s (1) words "(rather than the basic rate)" repealed, and words substituted for words "as is savings income", by FA 2016 s 6(10) with effect in relation to the tax year 2017–18 (as appointed under the Scotland Act 2016 s 13(15)) and subsequent years by virtue of SI 2016/1161 reg 3, subject to transitional provisions (see FA 2016 s 6(24)–(30)).

³ The amount specified in sub-s (3) for the tax year 2017–18 and subsequent tax years is £5,000 (FA 2017 s 4(1)). For tax years 2015–16 and 2016–17 the amount was £5,000 (FA 2014 s 3(2)). For 2014–15 the amount was £2,880. ITA 2007 s 21 (indexation), so far as relating to the starting rate limit for savings, does not apply for the tax years 2018–19 (FA 2018 s 5) 2017–18 (FA 2017 s 4(3)), or 2015–16 or 2016–17 (FA 2014 s 3(3)).

[12A Savings income charged at the savings nil rate

(1) This section applies in relation to an individual if—

(a) the amount of the individual's Step 3 income is greater than £L, where £L is the amount of the starting rate limit for savings, and

(b) when the individual's Step 3 income is split into two parts—

(i) one ("the individual's income up to the starting rate for savings") consisting of the lowest £L of the individual's Step 3 income, and

(ii) the other ("the individual's income above the starting rate limit for savings") consisting of the rest of the individual's Step 3 income,

some or all of the individual's income above the starting rate limit for savings consists of savings income (whether or not some or all of the individual's income up to the starting rate limit for savings consists of savings income).

(2) In this section—

£A is the amount of the individual's savings allowance (see section 12B),

"the excess" is so much of the individual's income above the starting rate limit for savings as consists of savings income, and

£X is the amount of the excess.

(3) If £X is less than or equal to £A, income tax is charged at the savings nil rate (rather than the basic, higher or additional rate) [or the default basic, default higher or default additional rate]² on the excess.

(4) If £X is more than £A, income tax is charged at the savings nil rate (rather than the basic, higher or additional rate) [or the default basic, default higher or default additional rate][2] on the lowest £A of the excess.

(5) Subsections (3) and (4) are subject to any provisions of the Income Tax Acts (apart from [sections 10 and 11C][2]) which provide for income to be charged at different rates of income tax in some circumstances.

(6) Section 16 has effect for determining the extent to which the individual's income above the starting rate limit for savings consists of savings income.

(7) For the purposes of this section, an individual's "Step 3 income" is the individual's net income less allowances deducted at Step 3 of the calculation in section 23.][1]

Commentary—*Simon's Taxes* **E1.101A**.
HMRC Manuals—Savings and Investment Manual SAIM1112 (changes to starting rate for savings - FY15/16).
Amendments—[1]   Section 12A inserted by FA 2016 s 4(1), (5) with effect in relation to the tax year 2016–17 and subsequent tax years.
[2]   In sub-ss (3), (4), words inserted, and in sub-s (5), words substituted for words "section 10", by FA 2016 s 6(1), (11) with effect in relation to the tax year 2017–18 (as appointed under the Scotland Act 2016 s 13(15)) and subsequent years by virtue of SI 2016/1161 reg 3, subject to transitional provisions (see FA 2016 s 6(24)–(30)).

[12B Individual's entitlement to a savings allowance

(1) Subsections (2) to (4) determine the amount of an individual's savings allowance for a tax year.

(2) If any of the individual's income for the year is additional-rate income, the individual's savings allowance for the year is nil.

(3) If—

    (*a*) any of the individual's income for the year is higher-rate income, and

    (*b*) none of the individual's income for the year is additional-rate income,

the individual's savings allowance for the year is £500.

(4) If none of the individual's income for the year is higher-rate income, the individual's savings allowance for the year is £1,000.

(5) The Treasury may by regulations substitute a different amount for the amount for the time being specified in subsection (2), (3) or (4); and regulations under this subsection that have effect for a tax year may be made at any time before the end of that tax year.

(6) If regulations under subsection (5) reduce any amount, the regulations may not be made unless a draft of the instrument containing them (whether alone or together with regulations under subsection (5) which increase any amount) has been laid before, and approved by a resolution of, the House of Commons.

(7) Section 1014(4) (negative procedure) does not apply to regulations under subsection (5) which increase any amount if—

    (*a*) the instrument containing them also contains regulations under subsection (5) which reduce any amount, and

    (*b*) a draft of the instrument has been laid before, and approved by a resolution of, the House of Commons.

(8) For the purposes of this section—

    (*a*) each of the following is "additional-rate income"—

        (i) income on which income tax is charged at the additional rate[, default additional rate][2] or dividend additional rate,

        (ii) income on which income tax would be charged at the additional rate[, or default additional rate,][2] but for section 12A (income charged at savings nil rate),

        (iii) income on which income tax would be charged at the dividend additional rate but for section 13A (income charged at dividend nil rate), and

        (iv) income of an individual who is a Scottish taxpayer or Welsh taxpayer which would, if the individual were not a Scottish taxpayer or Welsh taxpayer (as the case may be), be income on which income tax is charged at the additional rate [or default additional rate][2], and

    (*b*) each of the following is "higher-rate income"—

        (i) income on which income tax is charged at the higher rate[, default higher rate][2] or dividend upper rate,

        (ii) income on which income tax would be charged at the higher rate[, or default higher rate,][2] but for section 12A (income charged at savings nil rate),

        (iii) income on which income tax would be charged at the dividend upper rate but for section 13A (income charged at dividend nil rate), and

        (iv) income of an individual who is a Scottish taxpayer or Welsh taxpayer which would, if the individual were not a Scottish taxpayer or Welsh taxpayer (as the case may be), be income on which income tax is charged at the higher rate [or default higher rate][2].][1]

Commentary—*Simon's Taxes* **E1.101A**.
Amendments—[1]   Section 12B inserted by FA 2016 s 4(1), (5) with effect in relation to the tax year 2016–17 and subsequent tax years.

²   In sub-s (8)(*a*)(i), (ii), (iv), (*b*)(i), (ii), (iv), words inserted by FA 2016 s 6(1), (12) with effect in relation to the tax year 2017–18 (as appointed under the Scotland Act 2016 s 13(15)) and subsequent years by virtue of SI 2016/1161 reg 3, subject to transitional provisions (see FA 2016 s 6(24)–(30)).

13 Income charged at the dividend ordinary[, dividend upper and dividend additional] rates: individuals

(1) Income tax is charged at the dividend ordinary rate on an individual's income which—
- (*a*) is dividend income,
- (*b*) would otherwise be charged at the . . . ² basic rate [or the Welsh basic rate]⁶, . . . ⁵ and
- (*c*) is not relevant foreign income charged in accordance with section 832 of ITTOIA 2005 (relevant foreign income charged on the remittance basis).

(2) Income tax is charged at the dividend upper rate on an individual's income which—
- (*a*) is dividend income, . . . ¹
- (*b*) would otherwise be charged at the higher rate [or the Welsh higher rate,]⁶[, . . . ⁵ and
- (*c*) is not relevant foreign income charged in accordance with section 832 of ITTOIA 2005.]¹

[(2A) Income tax is charged at the dividend additional rate on an individual's income which—
- (*a*) is dividend income,
- (*b*) would otherwise be charged at the additional rate [or the Welsh additional rate,] . . . ⁶⁵ and
- (*c*) is not relevant foreign income charged in accordance with section 832 of ITTOIA 2005.]³

(3) Subsections (1) [to (2A)]³ are subject to any provisions of the Income Tax Acts (apart from section 10 [or 11A]⁴ [or 11B]⁶) which provide for income to be charged at different rates of income tax in some circumstances.

(4) Section 16 has effect for determining the extent to which an individual's dividend income would otherwise be charged at the . . . ² basic[, higher or additional]³ rate . . . ⁵ [or the Welsh basic, higher or additional rate]⁶.

[(5) In relation to an individual who is a Scottish taxpayer, references in this section to income that would otherwise be charged at a particular rate are to be read as references to income that would, if the individual were not a Scottish taxpayer, be charged at that rate (and subsection (4) is to be read accordingly).]⁵

Commentary—*Simon's Taxes* **E1.101A**.

HMRC Manuals—Savings and Investment Manual SAIM1080 (the dividend rates).

Amendments—¹   In sub-s (2), word "and" at the end of para (*a*) repealed, and para (*c*) and preceding word "and" inserted, by FA 2008 s 68 with effect for the tax year 2008–09 and subsequent tax years.
²   Words in sub-ss (1)(*b*), (4) repealed by FA 2008 s 5, Sch 1 paras 1, 6 with effect for the 2008–09 tax year and subsequent tax years.
³   Sub-s (2A) inserted; in sub-ss (3), (4), and section heading, words substituted by FA 2009 s 6, Sch 2 paras 1, 5 with effect for the tax year 2010–11 and subsequent tax years.
⁴   In sub-s (4) words inserted by FA 2014 s 296, Sch 38 paras 1, 6 with effect in relation to the tax year 2016–17 (the tax year appointed by the Treasury under the Scotland Act 2012 s 25(5) by virtue of SI 2015/2000) and subsequent tax years.
⁵   In sub-ss (1)(*b*), (2)(*b*), (2A)(*b*), (4), words repealed, and sub-s (5) inserted, by the Scotland Act 2016 s 14(1), (11) with effect in relation to the tax year 2017–18 (as appointed under the Scotland Act 2016 s 13(15)) and subsequent years by virtue of SI 2016/1161 reg 3.
⁶   In sub-ss (1)(*b*), (2)(*b*), (2A)(*b*), (3), (4), words inserted by the Wales Act 2014 s 9(1), (6). Wales Act 2014 s 9 comes into force on 24 July 2018 and has effect in relation to the tax year 2019–20 (by virtue of SI 2018/892 arts 3, 5, 6). 2019–20 is appointed as the first tax year in relation to which a Welsh rate resolution may be made by the National Assembly for Wales under GOWA 2006 s 116D (SI 2018/892 art 6).

[13A Income charged at the dividend nil rate

(1) Subsection (2) applies if, ignoring this section, at least some of an individual's income would be charged to income tax at the dividend ordinary rate, the dividend upper rate or the dividend additional rate.

(2) Income tax is charged at the dividend nil rate (rather than the dividend ordinary rate, dividend upper rate or dividend additional rate) on one or more amounts of the individual's income as follows—

Step 1

Identify the amount ("D") of the individual's income which would, ignoring this section, be charged at the dividend ordinary rate.

Rule 1A: If D is more than [£2,000]², the first [£2,000]² of D is charged at the dividend nil rate (rather than the dividend ordinary rate), and is the only amount charged at the dividend nil rate.

Rule 1B: If D is equal to [£2,000]², D is charged at the dividend nil rate (rather than the dividend ordinary rate), and is the only amount charged at the dividend nil rate.

Rule 1C: If D is less than [£2,000]² but more than nil, D is charged at the dividend nil rate (rather than the dividend ordinary rate).

Step 2

If D is less than [£2,000]², identify the amount ("U") of the individual's income which would, ignoring this section, be charged at the dividend upper rate.

Rule 2A: If the total of D and U is more than [£2,000]²—
- (*a*) the first £M of U is charged at the dividend nil rate (rather than the dividend upper rate), where £M is the difference between [£2,000]² and D, and

(*b*) the amounts charged under this Rule and Rule 1C are the only amounts charged at the dividend nil rate.

Rule 2B: If the total of D and U is equal to [£2,000][2], U is charged at the dividend nil rate (rather than the dividend upper rate), and the amounts charged under this Rule and Rule 1C are the only amounts charged at the dividend nil rate.

Rule 2C: If the total of D and U is less than [£2,000][2] but more than nil, U is charged at the dividend nil rate (rather than the dividend upper rate).

Step 3

If the total of D and U is less than [£2,000][2], identify the amount ("A") of the individual's income which would, ignoring this section, be charged at the dividend additional rate.

Rule 3A: If the total of D, U and A is more than [£2,000][2], the first £X of A is charged at the dividend nil rate (rather than the dividend additional rate), where £X is the difference between—

     [£2,000][2], and

     the total of D and U,

and the amounts charged under this Rule, and Rules 1C and 2C, are the amounts charged at the dividend nil rate.

Rule 3B: If the total of D, U and A is less than or equal to [£2,000][2], A is charged at the dividend nil rate (rather than the dividend additional rate), and the amounts charged under this Rule, and Rules 1C and 2C, are the amounts charged at the dividend nil rate.][1]

Commentary—*Simon's Taxes* **E1.101A**.

Amendments—[1]   Section 13A inserted by FA 2016 s 5(1), (5) with effect in relation to the tax year 2016–17 and subsequent tax years.

[2]   Figure substituted in each place by F(No 2)A 2017 s 8 with effect in relation to the tax year 2018–19 and subsequent tax years. Figure was previously £5,000.

14 Income charged at the dividend ordinary rate: other persons

(1) Income tax is charged at the dividend ordinary rate on the income of persons other than individuals which—

     (*a*) is dividend income,

     (*b*) would otherwise be charged at the basic rate, and

     (*c*) is not relevant foreign income charged in accordance with section 832 of ITTOIA 2005 (relevant foreign income charged on the remittance basis).

(2) This is subject to—

     Chapters 3 to 6 of Part 9 (which provide for some income of trustees to be charged at the dividend trust rate or at the trust rate),

     section 504(3) (treatment of income of unauthorised unit trust),[1] and

     any other provisions of the Income Tax Acts (apart from section 11) which provide for income of persons other than individuals to be charged at different rates of income tax in some circumstances.

Commentary—*Simon's Taxes* **C4.203**.

Amendments—[1]   In sub-s (2), entry relating to ITA 2007 s 504(3) repealed by the Unauthorised Unit Trusts (Tax) Regulations, SI 2013/2819 reg 37(1), (3) with effect from 6 April 2014. Note that an unauthorised unit trust is not a non-exempt unauthorised unit trust, and these amendments do not apply in relation to the trust, if at all times in the period beginning with 24 May 2012 and ending with 5 April 2014 it had at least one unit holder which was, and at least one unit holder which was not, an eligible investor (ie a mixed unauthorised unit trust); this ceases to apply in relation to the trust if subsequently it no longer has any unit holders which are eligible investors (SI 2013/2819 reg 32).

15 Income charged at the trust rate and the dividend trust rate

For the circumstances in which income tax is charged at the trust rate and the dividend trust rate, see Chapters 3 to 6 of Part 9.

16 Savings and dividend income to be treated as highest part of total income

(1) This section has effect for determining[—

     [(*za*) which part of a Scottish taxpayer's income consists of savings income,][4]

     [(*zb*) the rate at which income tax would be charged on the non-savings income of a Welsh taxpayer apart from section 11B,][6]

     (*a*) the extent to which a person's income up to the starting rate limit for savings consists of savings income,

     [(*aa*) the extent to which a person's income above the starting rate limit for savings consists of savings income,][3] and

     [(*ab*) the rate at which income tax would be charged on a person's savings income above the starting rate limit for savings apart from sections 11D and 12A,][5]

     (*b*) the rate at which income tax would be charged on a person's dividend income apart from section 13.][1]

(2) It also has effect for all other income tax purposes except for the purposes of—

     (*a*) section 491 (special rates not to apply to first slice of trustees' trust rate income), and

     (*b*) sections 535 to 537 of ITTOIA 2005 (gains from contracts for life insurance etc: top slicing relief).

(3) If a person has savings income but no dividend income, the savings income is treated as the highest part of the person's total income.

(4) If a person has dividend income but no savings income, the dividend income is treated as the highest part of the person's total income.

(5) If a person has both savings income and dividend income—

    (a) the savings income and dividend income are together treated as the highest part of the person's total income, and

    (b) the dividend income is treated as the higher part of that part of the person's total income.

(6) See section 1012 for the relationship between—

    (a) the rules in this section, and

    (b) other rules requiring particular income to be treated as the highest part of a person's total income.

(7) References in this section to dividend income do not include dividend income which is relevant foreign income charged in accordance with section 832 of ITTOIA 2005 (relevant foreign income charged on the remittance basis).

Commentary—*Simon's Taxes* **E1.101A, E1.101C, E1.101F, E7.222**.

HMRC Manuals—Savings and Investment Manual SAIM1090 (savings and dividend income).

Amendments—[1]   Words in sub-s (1) substituted by FA 2008 s 5, Sch 1 paras 1, 7 with effect for the 2008–09 tax year and subsequent tax years.

[2]   Sub-s (1)(*za*), which was to have been prospectively inserted by the Scotland Act 2012 s 26(1), (4) with effect in relation to the tax year 2016–17 (under Scotland Act 2012 s 25(5) by virtue of SI 2015/2000) and subsequent tax years (see Note above), substituted by FA 2014 s 296, Sch 38 paras 1, 7 with effect in relation to the tax year 2016–17 (the tax year appointed by the Treasury under the Scotland Act 2012 s 25(5) by virtue of SI 2015/2000) and subsequent tax years.

[3]   Sub-s (1)(*aa*) inserted by FA 2016 s 4(1), (6) with effect in relation to the tax year 2016–17 and subsequent tax years.

[4]   Sub-s (1)(*za*) substituted by the Scotland Act 2016 s 14(1), (12) with effect in relation to the tax year 2017–18 (as appointed under the Scotland Act 2016 s 13(15)) and subsequent years by virtue of SI 2016/1161 reg 3.

[5]   Sub-s (1)(*ab*) inserted by FA 2016 s 6(1), (13) with effect in relation to the tax year 2017–18 (as appointed under the Scotland Act 2016 s 13(15)) and subsequent years by virtue of SI 2016/1161 reg 3, subject to transitional provisions (see FA 2016 s 6(24)–(30)).

[6]   Sub-s (1)(*zb*) inserted by the Wales Act 2014 s 9(1), (7). Wales Act 2014 s 9 comes into force on 24 July 2018 and has effect in relation to the tax year 2019–20 (by virtue of SI 2018/892 arts 3, 5, 6). 2019–20 is appointed as the first tax year in relation to which a Welsh rate resolution may be made by the National Assembly for Wales under GOWA 2006 s 116D (SI 2018/892 art 6).

17 Repayment: tax paid at [greater] rate instead of [starting rate for savings] [or savings nil rate]

(1) This section applies if income tax [at a rate greater than the starting rate for savings][3] has been paid on income on which income tax is chargeable at the [starting rate for savings][1].

[(1A) This section also applies if income tax at a rate greater than the savings nil rate has been paid on income on which income tax is chargeable at the savings nil rate.][2]

(2) If a claim is made, any necessary repayment of tax must be made.

Commentary—*Simon's Taxes* **E1.101A**.

HMRC Manuals—Savings and Investment Manual SAIM1080 (savings income: basic rate tax is repayable).

Amendments—[1]   Words in sub-s (1) and heading substituted by FA 2008 s 5, Sch 1 paras 1, 8 with effect for the 2008–09 tax year and subsequent tax years.

[2]   Sub-s (1A) inserted, and words in heading substituted and inserted, by FA 2016 s 4(1), (7) with effect in relation to the tax year 2016–17 and subsequent tax years.

[3]   In sub-s (1), words substituted for words "at the basic rate" by FA 2016 s 6(1), (14) with effect in relation to the tax year 2017–18 (as appointed under the Scotland Act 2016 s 13(15)) and subsequent years by virtue of SI 2016/1161 reg 3, subject to transitional provisions (see FA 2016 s 6(24)–(30)).

18 Meaning of "savings income"

(1) This section applies for the purposes of the Income Tax Acts.

(2) "Savings income" is income—

    (a) which is within subsection (3) or (4), and

    (b) which is not relevant foreign income charged in accordance with section 832 of ITTOIA 2005 (relevant foreign income charged on the remittance basis).

(3) Income is within this subsection if it is—

    (a) income chargeable under Chapter 2 of Part 4 of ITTOIA 2005 (interest),

    (b) income chargeable under Chapter 7 of Part 4 of ITTOIA 2005 (purchased life annuity payments), other than income from annuities specified in section 718(2) of that Act (annuities purchased from certain life assurance premium payments or under wills etc),

    (c) income chargeable under Chapter 8 of Part 4 of ITTOIA 2005 (profits from deeply discounted securities), or

    (d) income chargeable under Chapter 2 of Part 12 of this Act (accrued income profits).

(4) Income is within this subsection if—

    (a) it is chargeable under Chapter 9 of Part 4 of ITTOIA 2005 (gains from contracts for life insurance etc), and (*b*) an individual is, or personal representatives are, liable for income tax on it (under section 465 or 466 of that Act).

Commentary—*Simon's Taxes* **E1.101A**.
HMRC Manuals—Savings and Investment Manual SAIM1080 (savings income meaning).

19 Meaning of "dividend income"
(1) This section applies for the purposes of the Income Tax Acts.
(2) "Dividend income" is income which is—
    (*a*) chargeable under Chapter 3 of Part 4 of ITTOIA 2005 (dividends etc from UK resident companies),
    (*b*) chargeable under Chapter 4 of that Part (dividends from non-UK resident companies),
    (*c*) chargeable under Chapter 5 of that Part (stock dividends from UK resident companies),
    (*d*) chargeable under Chapter 6 of that Part (release of loan to participator in close company), or
    (*e*) a relevant foreign distribution chargeable under Chapter 8 of Part 5 of ITTOIA 2005 (income not otherwise charged).
(3) In subsection (2) "relevant foreign distribution" means a distribution of a non-UK resident company which—
    (*a*) is not chargeable under Chapter 4 of Part 4 of ITTOIA 2005, but
    (*b*) would be chargeable under Chapter 3 of that Part if the company were UK resident.

Commentary—*Simon's Taxes* **C4.211**.
HMRC Manuals—Savings and Investment Manual SAIM5010 (dividends and other company distributions: dividend income).

[Indexation of basic rate limit and starting rate limit for savings][1]
Amendments—[1] Heading substituted by FA 2008 s 5, Sch 1 paras 1, 9 with effect for the 2008–09 tax year and subsequent tax years.

21 Indexation of the [basic rate limit and starting rate limit for savings][1]
(1) This section applies if the [consumer prices index][2] for the September before the start of a tax year is higher than it was for the previous September.
(2) . . .[1]
(3) The basic rate limit for the tax year is the amount found as follows.
    Step 1 Increase the basic rate limit for the previous tax year by the same percentage as the percentage increase in the [consumer prices index][2].
    Step 2 If the result of Step 1 is a multiple of £100, it is the basic rate limit for the tax year.
If the result of Step 1 is not a multiple of £100, round it up to the nearest amount which is a multiple of £100.
That amount is the basic rate limit for the tax year.
[(3A) The starting rate limit for savings for the tax year is the amount found as follows.
Step 1 Increase the starting rate limit for savings for the previous tax year by the same percentage as the percentage increase in the [consumer prices index][2].
Step 2 If the result of Step 1 is a multiple of £10, it is the starting rate limit for savings for the tax year.
If the result of Step 1 is not a multiple of £10, round it up to the nearest amount which is a multiple of £10.
That amount is the starting rate limit for savings for the tax year.][1]
(4) Subsections [(3) and (3A)][1] do not require a change to be made in the amounts deductible or repayable under PAYE regulations during the period beginning on 6 April and ending on 17 May in the tax year.
(5) Before the start of the tax year the Treasury must make an order replacing the amounts specified in [sections 10 and 12][1] with the amounts which, as a result of subsections [(3) and (3A)][1], are the [basic rate limit and starting rate limit for savings][1] for the tax year.
[(6) In this section "consumer prices index" means the all items consumer prices index published by the Statistics Board.][2]

Commentary—*Simon's Taxes* **E1.104**.
Amendments—[1] Sub-s (2) repealed, sub-s (3A) inserted, and words in sub-ss (4), (5) and heading substituted, by FA 2008 s 5, Sch 1 paras 1, 11 with effect from 21 July 2008.
[2] In sub-ss (1), (3), (3A), words substituted for words "retail prices index", and sub-s (6) inserted, by FA 2014 s 4(1), (2) with effect for the tax year 2015–16 and subsequent tax years.

CHAPTER 3
CALCULATION OF INCOME TAX LIABILITY

22 Overview of Chapter
(1) This Chapter deals with the calculation of a person's income tax liability for a tax year.
(2) But it does not deal with any income tax liability mentioned in section 32.
(3) This Chapter needs to be read with Chapter 1 of Part 14 (limits on liability to income tax of non-UK residents).

Commentary—*Simon's Taxes* E1.101, E1.113.
HMRC Manuals—Venture Capital Schemes Manual VCM31130 (SEIS income tax relief).

23 The calculation of income tax liability

To find the liability of a person ("the taxpayer") to income tax for a tax year, take the following steps.

Step 1 Identify the amounts of income on which the taxpayer is charged to income tax for the tax year.

The sum of those amounts is "total income".

Each of those amounts is a "component" of total income.

Step 2 Deduct from the components the amount of any relief under a provision listed in relation to the taxpayer in section 24 to which the taxpayer is entitled for the tax year.

See [sections 24A and 25][2] for further provision about the deduction of those reliefs.

The sum of the amounts of the components left after this step is "net income".

Step 3 Deduct from the amounts of the components left after Step 2 any allowances to which the taxpayer is entitled for the tax year under Chapter 2 of Part 3 of this Act . . . [1] (individuals: personal allowance and blind person's allowance).

See section 25 for further provision about the deduction of those allowances.

Step 4 Calculate tax at each applicable rate on the amounts of the components left after Step 3.

See Chapter 2 of this Part for the rates at which income tax is charged and the income charged at particular rates.

If the taxpayer is a trustee, see also Chapters 3 to 6 and 10 of Part 9 (special rules about settlements and trustees) for further provision about the income charged at particular rates.

[See also section 863I of ITTOIA 2005 which provides for certain partnership profits to be charged at the additional rate.][3]

Step 5 Add together the amounts of tax calculated at Step 4.

Step 6 Deduct from the amount of tax calculated at Step 5 any tax reductions to which the taxpayer is entitled for the tax year under a provision listed in relation to the taxpayer in section 26.

See sections 27 to 29 for further provision about the deduction of those tax reductions.

Step 7 Add to the amount of tax left after Step 6 any amounts of tax for which the taxpayer is liable for the tax year under any provision listed in relation to the taxpayer in section 30.

The result is the taxpayer's liability to income tax for the tax year.

Commentary—*Simon's Taxes* E1.902, E1.113.
Amendment—[1]   In Step 3 words "or section 257 or 265 of ICTA" repealed by FA 2009 s 5, Sch 1 para 6(*o*)(i) with effect for the tax year 2010–11 and subsequent tax years.
[2]   In Step 2 words substituted for words "section 25" by FA 2013 s 16, Sch 3 para 2(1), (2) with effect for the tax year 2013–14 and subsequent tax years, subject to transitional provisions in relation to loss relief claims for a tax year before 2013–14 in relation to losses made in 2013–14 or a later year (FA 2013 Sch 3 para 4).
[3]   Sentence at the end of Step 4 inserted by FA 2014 s 74, Sch 17 para 19 with effect for the tax year 2014–15 and subsequent tax years.

24 Reliefs deductible at Step 2

(1) If the taxpayer is an individual, the provisions referred to at Step 2 of the calculation in section 23 are—

(*a*) the following—

section 72 (early trade losses relief),

Chapter 6 of Part 4 (share loss relief),

Chapter 3 of Part 8 (gifts of shares, securities and real property to charities etc),

sections 457 and 458 of this Act or section 266(7) of ICTA (payments to trade unions or police organisations),

section 193(4) of FA 2004 (pension schemes: relief under net pay arrangement: excess relief), and

section 194(1) of FA 2004 (pension schemes: relief on making of claim), and

(*b*) the following—

section 64 (trade loss relief against general income),

section 83 (carry-forward trade loss relief),

section 89 (terminal trade loss relief),

section 96 (post-cessation trade relief),

section 118 (carry-forward property loss relief),

section 120 (property loss relief against general income),

section 125 (post-cessation property relief),

section 128 (employment loss relief against general income),

section 152 (loss relief against miscellaneous income),

Chapter 1 of Part 8 (interest payments),

> [Chapter 1A of Part 8 (irrecoverable peer-to-peer loans),][4]
>
> Chapter 4 of Part 8 (annual payments . . . [2]),
>
> section 574 (manufactured dividends on UK shares: payments by non-companies),
>
> section 579 (manufactured interest on UK securities: payments not otherwise deductible),
>
> Part 2 of CAA 2001 (plant and machinery allowances), in a case where the allowance is to be given effect under section 258 of that Act (special leasing of plant and machinery),
>
> . . . [1]
>
> Part 8 of CAA 2001 (patent allowances), in a case where the allowance is to be given effect under section 479 of that Act (persons having qualifying non-trade expenditure),
>
> section 555 of ITEPA 2003 (deduction for liabilities related to former employment),
>
> section 446 of ITTOIA 2005 (strips of government securities: relief for losses),
>
> section 454(4) of ITTOIA 2005 (listed securities held since 26 March 2003: relief for losses: persons other than trustees), and
>
> section 600 of ITTOIA 2005 (relief for patent expenses).

(2) In any other case, the provisions referred to at Step 2 of the calculation in section 23 are—

    (*a*) the provisions listed in subsection (1)(*b*), and

    (*b*) [regulation 18 of the Unauthorised Unit Trusts (Tax) Regulations 2013][3].

Commentary—*Simon's Taxes* **E1.113.**

Amendments—[1]   In sub-s (1)(*b*), entry repealed by FA 2008 s 84, Sch 27 para 27 with effect in relation to a transfer by the past owner (within the meaning of s 186) in a chargeable period beginning on or after—

    (a)   for corporation tax purposes, 1 April 2011, and

    (b)   for income tax purposes, 6 April 2011.

[2]   In sub-s (1)(*b*) words "and patent royalties" repealed by FA 2013 s 15(4)(*b*) with effect in relation to payments made on or after 5 December 2012.

[3]   In sub-s (2)(*b*), words substituted for words "section 505 (relief for trustees of unauthorised unit trust)" by the Unauthorised Unit Trusts (Tax) Regulations, SI 2013/2819 reg 37(1), (4) with effect from 6 April 2014. Note that an unauthorised unit trust is not a non-exempt unauthorised unit trust, and these amendments do not apply in relation to the trust, if at all times in the period beginning with 24 May 2012 and ending with 5 April 2014 it had at least one unit holder which was, and at least one unit holder which was not, an eligible investor (ie a mixed unauthorised unit trust); this ceases to apply in relation to the trust if subsequently it no longer has any unit holders which are eligible investors (SI 2013/2819 reg 32).

[4]   In sub-s (1)(*b*), entry inserted by FA 2016 s 32(3) with effect from 15 September 2016.

[24A Limit on Step 2 deductions

(1) If the taxpayer is an individual, there is a limit on certain deductions which may be made for the tax year at Step 2.

(2) The limit is determined as follows.

(3) Amount A must not exceed amount B.

(4) Amount A is—

    (*a*) the deductions for the tax year at Step 2 for the reliefs listed in subsection (6) taken together, less

    (*b*) so much of those deductions as fall within subsection (7).

(5) Amount B is—

    (*a*) £50,000, or

    (*b*) if more, 25% of the taxpayer's adjusted total income for the tax year (see subsection (8)).

(6) The reliefs are—

    (*a*) relief under section 64 (trade loss relief against general income);

    (*b*) relief under section 72 (early trade losses relief);

    (*c*) relief under section 96 (post-cessation trade relief);

    (*d*) relief under section 120 (property loss relief against general income);

    (*e*) relief under section 125 (post-cessation property relief);

    (*f*) relief under section 128 (employment loss relief against general income);

    (*g*) relief under Chapter 6 of Part 4 (share loss relief);

    (*h*) relief under Chapter 1 of Part 8 (interest payments);

    (*i*) relief under section 555 of ITEPA 2003 (deduction for liabilities relating to former employment);

    (*j*) relief under section 446 of ITTOIA 2005 (strips of government securities: relief for losses);

    (*k*) relief under section 454(4) of ITTOIA 2005 (listed securities held since 26 March 2003: relief for losses: persons other than trustees).

(7) The deductions falling within this subsection are—

    (*a*) deductions for amounts of relief so far as attributable to allowances under Part 3A of CAA 2001 (business premises renovation allowances);

    (*b*) deductions for amounts of relief under a provision mentioned in subsection (6)(*a*) to (*e*) so far as made from profits of the trade or business to which the relief in question relates;

(c) deductions for amounts of relief under the provision mentioned in subsection (6)(a) or (b) so far as attributable to a deduction allowed under section 205 or 220 of ITTOIA 2005 (deduction for overlap profit in final tax year or on change of accounting date);

(d) deductions for amounts of relief under the provision mentioned in subsection (6)(g)—

   (i) where the shares in question fall within section 131(2)(a) (qualifying shares to which EIS relief is attributable), or

   (ii) where SEIS relief is attributable to the shares in question as determined in accordance with Part 5A (seed enterprise investment scheme)[, or

   (iii) where SI relief is attributable to the shares in question as determined in accordance with Part 5B (income tax relief for social investments).][2]

(8) The taxpayer's "adjusted total income" for the tax year is calculated as follows.

Step 1

Take the amount of the taxpayer's total income for the tax year.

Step 2

Add back the amounts of any deductions allowed under Part 12 of ITEPA 2003 (payroll giving) in calculating the taxpayer's income which is charged to tax for the tax year.

Step 3

If the taxpayer is given relief in accordance with section 192 of FA 2004 (pension schemes: relief at source) in respect of any contribution paid in the tax year under a pension scheme, deduct the gross amount of the contribution.

The "gross" amount of a contribution is the amount of the contribution before deduction of tax under section 192(1) of FA 2004.

Step 4

If the taxpayer is entitled to a deduction for relief under section 193(4) or 194(1) of FA 2004 (pension schemes: excess relief under net payment arrangements or relief on making a claim) for the tax year, deduct the amount of the excess or contribution (as the case may be).

The result is the taxpayer's adjusted total income for the tax year.][1]

Commentary—_Simon's Taxes_ **E1.113**.
HMRC Manuals—Partnership Manual PM50200 (limited partnerships - restrictions on loss relief for limited partners).
Venture Capital Schemes Manual VCM74035 (limit on income tax reliefs).
Amendments—[1]   Section 24A inserted by FA 2013 s 16, Sch 3 para 1 with effect for the tax year 2013–14 and subsequent tax years, subject to transitional provisions in relation to loss relief claims for a tax year before 2013–14 in relation to losses made in 2013–14 or a later year. Note that in sub-s (6)(d) the reference to relief does not include relief in respect of a loss made in the tax year 2012–13 (FA 2013 Sch 3 paras 4, 5).
[2]   Sub-s (7)(d)(iii) and preceding word ", or" inserted by FA 2014 s 57, Sch 11 paras 3, 5 with effect from 17 July 2014.

25 Reliefs and allowances deductible at Steps 2 and 3: supplementary

(1) This section supplements the provisions about reliefs and allowances in Steps 2 and 3 of the calculation in section 23.

(2) At Steps 2 and 3, deduct the reliefs and allowances in the way which will result in the greatest reduction in the taxpayer's liability to income tax.

(3) Subsection (2) is subject to—

   section 65(2) to (4) (priority rule in relation to trade loss relief against general income),
   section 80(2) (ring fence income),
   section 83(3) and (4) (carry-forward trade loss relief against trade profits),
   section 89(3) (terminal trade loss relief against trade profits),
   section 93(2) (terminal trade loss relief and mineral extraction trade),
   section 95(2) (foreign trades etc reliefs only against qualifying foreign income),
   section 115(2) (restrictions on reliefs for firms exploiting films),
   section 118(3) and (4) (carry-forward property loss relief against property business profits),
   section 121(2) and (3) (priority rule in relation to property loss relief against general income),
   section 129(2) to (4) (priority rule in relation to employment loss relief against general income),
   section 133(4) (share loss relief against general income),
   section 152(4) and (7) (loss relief against miscellaneous income),
   [sections 412A(4), 412B(3) and 412C(3) (relief for irrecoverable peer-to-peer loans only against interest on certain loans),][2]
   sections 574(3) to (8) and 575 (manufactured dividends on UK shares: restrictions on deductions),
   section 579(2) to (5) and 580 (manufactured interest on UK securities: restrictions on deductions),
   section 258 of CAA 2001 (special leasing of plant or machinery),
   . . . [1]
   section 479 of that Act (persons having qualifying non-trade expenditure),
   section 601 of ITTOIA 2005 (how relief for patent expenses is given), and
   any other provision of the Income Tax Acts under which reliefs or allowances deductible at Step 2 or 3 are not permitted to be deducted from particular components of income or are required to be deducted from particular components of income or in a different order.

(4) A relief or allowance may be deducted at Step 2 or 3 only so far as there is sufficient income from which to deduct it.

(5) In deciding whether there is sufficient income from which to deduct a relief or allowance, reliefs and allowances already deducted at Step 2 or 3 must be taken into account.

(6) Nothing in Step 2 or 3 is to be read as permitting a relief or allowance to be deducted more than once.

Commentary—*Simon's Taxes* **E1.113**.

HMRC Manuals—Savings and Investment Manual SAIM1090 (reduction in the taxpayer's liability).

Amendments—[1]   In sub-s (3), entry repealed by FA 2008 s 84, Sch 27 para 27 with effect in relation to a transfer by the past owner (within the meaning of s 186) in a chargeable period beginning on or after—
    (a)   for corporation tax purposes, 1 April 2011, and
    (b)   for income tax purposes, 6 April 2011.
[2]   In sub-s (3), entry inserted by FA 2016 s 32(4) with effect from 15 September 2016.

26 Tax reductions

(1) If the taxpayer is an individual, the provisions referred to at Step 6 of the calculation in section 23 are—
    (a)   the following—

> Chapter 3 of Part 3 of this Act   . . . [1] (tax reductions for married couples and civil partners),
>
> [Chapter 3A of Part 3 of this Act (transferable tax allowance for married couples and civil partners),][6]
>
> Chapter 1 of Part 5 (EIS relief),
>
> [Chapter 1 of Part 5A (SEIS relief),][3]
>
> [Chapter 1 of Part 5B (relief for social investments),][5]
>
> Chapter 2 of Part 6 (VCT relief),
>
> Chapter 1 of Part 7 (community investment tax relief),
>
> [section 399B (relief for non-deductible interest on loan to invest in partnership with residential property business),][7]
>
> [section 414A(3) (gift aid where devolved basic rate is above basic rate),][10]
>
> section 453 (qualifying maintenance payments),
>
>   . . . [4]
>
> section 461 (spreading of patent royalty receipts),
>
> section 353(1A) of ICTA (relief for interest on loan to buy life annuity),
>
> [section 192A of FA 2004 (relief at source: additional relief),][8]
>
> [section 274A of ITTOIA 2005 (property business: relief for non-deductible costs of a dwelling-related loan),][7]
>
> section 535 of ITTOIA 2005 (top slicing relief), and
>
> section 539 of ITTOIA 2005 (relief for deficiencies), and

    (b)   the following—

>   . . . [2]
>   . . . [2]
>
> section 401 of ITTOIA 2005 (relief: [distribution repaying shares or security issued in earlier distribution][9]), . . . [2]
>
> sections 677 and 678 of ITTOIA 2005 (relief where foreign estates have borne UK income tax),
>
> [sections 2 and 6 of TIOPA 2010 (double taxation relief: relief by agreement), and section 18(1)(b) and (2) of TIOPA 2010 (relief for foreign tax where no double taxation arrangements).][2]

(2) In any other case, the provisions referred to at Step 6 of the calculation in section 23 are—
    (a)   the provisions listed in subsection (1)(b),
    [(aa)   section 274B of ITTOIA 2005 (trusts with accumulated or discretionary income derived from property business: relief for non-deductible costs of dwelling-related loans),][7] and
    (b)   section 26 of FA 2005 (trusts with vulnerable beneficiary: income tax relief).

Commentary—*Simon's Taxes* **E1.102**.

Amendments—[1]   In sub-s (1)(a) words "or section 257A, 257AB, 257BA or 257BB of ICTA" repealed by FA 2009 s 5, Sch 1 para 6(o)(ii) with effect for the tax year 2010–11 and subsequent tax years.
[2]   In sub-s (1)(b), entries for TA 1988 ss 788, 790, and word "and" preceding entry for ITTOIA 2005 ss 677, 678, repealed, and entries for TIOPA 2010 ss 2–6, 18(1)(b), (2) inserted, by TIOPA 2010 ss 501, 503, Sch 8 paras 71, 73, Sch 10 Pt 1. TIOPA 2010 has effect for corporation tax purposes for accounting periods ending on or after 1 April 2010, for income and capital gains tax purposes for the tax year 2010–11 and subsequent tax years, and for petroleum revenue tax purposes for chargeable periods beginning on or after 1 July 2010.
[3]   Entry in sub-s (1)(a) inserted by FA 2012 s 38, Sch 6 paras 6, 8 with effect in relation to shares issued on or after 6 April 2012.

4   In sub-s (1)(a), entry "section 459 of this Act or section 273 of ICTA (payments for benefit of family members)," repealed by FA 2012 s 227, Sch 39 para 32(2)(a) with effect for the tax year 2013–14 and subsequent tax years.

5   In sub-s (1)(a) entry inserted by FA 2014 s 57, Sch 11 paras 3, 6 with effect from 17 July 2014.

6   In sub-s (1)(a), entry inserted by FA 2014 s 11(3) with effect for the tax year 2015–16 and subsequent tax years.

7   Sub-s (2)(aa), and entries in sub-s (1)(a) inserted by F(No 2)A 2015 s 24(8), (9) with effect from 18 November 2015.

8   In sub-s (1)(a), words inserted by the Scottish Rate of Income Tax (Consequential Amendments) Order, SI 2015/1810 art 5(1), (2) with effect in relation to the tax year 2016–17 (the tax year appointed by the Treasury under the Scotland Act 2012 s 25(5) by virtue of SI 2015/2000) and subsequent tax years.

9   In sub-s (1)(b), words substituted by FA 2016 s 5, Sch 1 para 63(1), (2) with effect in relation to dividends paid or arising (or treated as paid), and other distributions made (or treated as made), in the tax year 2016-17 or at any later time.

10   In sub-s (1)(a) words inserted by the Devolved Income Tax Rates (Consequential Amendments) Order, SI 2019/201 arts 12(1), (3) with effect in relation to the tax year 2019–20 and subsequent tax years.

27 Order of deducting tax reductions: individuals

(1) This section makes provision about the order in which tax reductions are to be deducted at Step 6 of the calculation in section 23, if the taxpayer is an individual.

(2) Deduct the tax reductions in the order which will result in the greatest reduction in the taxpayer's liability to income tax for the tax year.

(3) Subsection (2) is subject to subsections (4) to (6).

(4) If the taxpayer is entitled to tax reductions for the tax year under more than one of the provisions listed in subsection (5), a tax reduction under a provision mentioned earlier in the list must be deducted before a tax reduction under a provision mentioned later in the list.

(5) The provisions are—

     Chapter 2 of Part 6 (VCT relief),

     Chapter 1 of Part 5 (EIS relief),

     [Chapter 1 of Part 5A (SEIS relief),][1]

     [Chapter 1 of Part 5B (relief for social investments),][4]

     Chapter 1 of Part 7 (community investment tax relief),

     section 353(1A) of ICTA (relief for interest on loan to buy life annuity),

     section 453 (qualifying maintenance payments),

     . . .[3]

     Chapter 3 of Part 3 of this Act . . .[1] (tax reductions for married couples and civil partners).

(6) If the taxpayer is entitled to a tax reduction under—

     (a) [sections 2 and 6 of TIOPA 2010][2] (double taxation arrangements: relief by agreement), or

     (b) [section 18(1)(b) and (2) of TIOPA 2010][2] (relief for foreign tax where no double taxation arrangements),

that tax reduction must be deducted after any other tax reduction to which the taxpayer is entitled for the tax year.

Commentary—*Simon's Taxes* **E1.102, E3.156, E3.211**.

HMRC Manuals—Venture Capital Schemes Manual VCM31130 (SEIS income tax relief).

VCM10530 (amount of EIS relief).

Amendments—[1] In sub-s (5) words repealed by FA 2009 s 5, Sch 1 para 6(o)(ii) with effect for the tax year 2010–11 and subsequent tax years.

2   In sub-s (6) words substituted by TIOPA 2010 s 501, Sch 8 paras 71, 74. TIOPA 2010 has effect for corporation tax purposes for accounting periods ending on or after 1 April 2010, for income and capital gains tax purposes for the tax year 2010–11 and subsequent tax years, and for petroleum revenue tax purposes for chargeable periods beginning on or after 1 July 2010.

3   In sub-s (5), entry repealed by FA 2012 s 227, Sch 39 para 32(2)(a) with effect for the tax year 2013–14 and subsequent tax years.

4   In sub-s (5), entry inserted by FA 2014 s 57, Sch 11 paras 3, 7 with effect from 17 July 2014.

28 Order of deducting tax reductions: other persons

(1) This section makes provision about the order in which tax reductions are to be deducted at Step 6 of the calculation in section 23, if the taxpayer is a person other than an individual.

(2) Deduct the tax reductions in the order which will result in the greatest reduction in the taxpayer's liability to income tax for the tax year.

(3) Subsection (2) is subject to subsections (4) and (5).

(4) If the taxpayer is entitled to a tax reduction under—

     (a) [sections 2 and 6 of TIOPA 2010][1] (double taxation arrangements: relief by agreement), or

     (b) [section 18(1)(b) and (2) of TIOPA 2010][1] (relief for foreign tax where no double taxation arrangements),

that tax reduction must be deducted after any other tax reduction to which the taxpayer is entitled for the tax year, subject to subsection (5).

(5) If the taxpayer is a trustee and is entitled to a tax reduction under section 26 of FA 2005 (trusts with vulnerable beneficiary: income tax relief) that tax reduction must be deducted after any other tax reduction to which the taxpayer is entitled for the tax year.

Commentary—*Simon's Taxes* **E1.102**.

Amendments—[1]   In sub-s (4), in para (*a*), (*b*), words substituted by TIOPA 2010 s 501, Sch 8 paras 71, 75. TIOPA 2010 has effect for corporation tax purposes for accounting periods ending on or after 1 April 2010, for income and capital gains tax purposes for the tax year 2010–11 and subsequent tax years, and for petroleum revenue tax purposes for chargeable periods beginning on or after 1 July 2010.

29 Tax reductions: supplementary

(1) This section supplements the provisions about tax reductions in Step 6 of the calculation in section 23.

(2) A tax reduction may be deducted at Step 6 only so far as there is sufficient tax calculated at Step 5 of the calculation from which to deduct it.

(3) In deciding whether there is sufficient tax calculated at Step 5 from which to deduct a tax reduction, tax reductions already deducted at Step 6 must be taken into account.

(4) Subsections (2) and (3) apply in addition to—

    (*a*) [sections 36(1) to (5) and (7) and 41 of TIOPA 2010][2] (limits on credit for foreign tax), and

    (*b*) any other provision of the Income Tax Acts that limits the amount of a tax reduction.

[(4A) If the taxpayer is an individual, the total of the tax reductions within subsection (4B) that are deducted at Step 6 must not be greater than—A − B

where—

    A is the amount of tax calculated at Step 5, and

    B is the total amount of the tax treated under section 414 (gift aid) as deducted from gifts made by the taxpayer in the tax year.

[(4B) A tax reduction is within this subsection if it is under—

    Chapter 1 of Part 5 (EIS relief),

    [Chapter 1 of Part 5A (SEIS relief),][3]

    [Chapter 1 of Part 5B (relief for social investments),][4]

    Chapter 2 of Part 6 (VCT relief), or

    Chapter 1 of Part 7 (community investment tax relief).

[(4C) Subsection (4A) applies in addition to subsections (2) and (3).][1]

(5) For the purposes of this Chapter, a person is treated as being entitled to a tax reduction under [sections 2 and 6 of TIOPA 2010][2] if the person is entitled to credit against income tax under double taxation arrangements.

Commentary—Simon's Taxes **E3.156, E1.102.**

Amendments—[1]   Sub-ss (4A)–(4C) inserted by the Income Tax Act 2007 (Amendment) (No 2) Order, SI 2009/2859 art 4(1), (2) with effect for income tax and capital gains tax purposes for the year 2007–08 and subsequent tax years, and for corporation tax purposes for accounting periods ending after 5 April 2007.

[2]   In sub-ss (4)(*a*), (5), words substituted by TIOPA 2010 s 501, Sch 8 paras 71, 76. TIOPA 2010 has effect for corporation tax purposes for accounting periods ending on or after 1 April 2010, for income and capital gains tax purposes for the tax year 2010–11 and subsequent tax years, and for petroleum revenue tax purposes for chargeable periods beginning on or after 1 July 2010.

[3]   In sub-s (4B), entry inserted by FA 2013 s 56(1), (2) with effect for the tax year 2013–14 and subsequent tax years.

[4]   In sub-s (4B), entry inserted by FA 2014 s 57, Sch 11 paras 3, 8 with effect from 17 July 2014.

30 Additional tax

(1) If the taxpayer is an individual, the provisions referred to at Step 7 of the calculation in section 23 are—

    [section 414A(4) read with section 414A(5) (gift aid where devolved basic rate is below basic rate),][5]

    section 424 (gift aid: charge to tax),

    [section 809ZN (tainted gift aid donations: charge to tax),

    section 809ZO (tainted charity donations by trustees: charge to tax),][1]

    section 205 of FA 2004 (pension schemes: the short service refund lump sum charge),

    section 206 of FA 2004 (pension schemes: the special lump sum death benefits charge),

    section 208(2)(*a*) of FA 2004 (pension schemes: the unauthorised payments charge),

    section 209(3)(*a*) of FA 2004 (pension schemes: the unauthorised payments surcharge),

    section 214 of FA 2004 (pension schemes: the lifetime allowance charge),

    section 227 of FA 2004 (pension schemes: the annual allowance charge), and

    section 7 of F(No 2)A 2005 (social security pension lump sum).

    [Chapter 8 of Part 10 of ITEPA 2003 (high income child benefit charge).][2]

    [section 192B of FA 2004 (relief at source: excessive relief given),][3]

[(2) If the taxpayer is a trustee, the provisions referred to at Step 7 of the calculation in section 23 are—

    section 496 (discretionary payments by trustees: tax pool adjustment),

    section 809ZN (tainted gift aid donations: charge to tax), and

    section 809ZO (tainted charity donations by trustees: charge to tax),][1]

Commentary—Simon's Taxes **E1.102A.**

Amendments—[1]   In sub-s (1), entries inserted and sub-s (2) substituted by FA 2011 s 27, Sch 3 paras 7, 8 with effect in relation to relievable charity donations made on or after 1 April 2011.

[2]   Words in sub-s (1) inserted by FA 2012 s 8, Sch 1 para 6(1), (3) with effect for the tax year 2012–13 and subsequent tax years.

[3]   In sub-s (1), words inserted by the Scottish Rate of Income Tax (Consequential Amendments) Order, SI 2015/1810 art 5(1), (3) with effect in relation to the tax year 2016–17 (the tax year appointed by the Treasury under the Scotland Act 2012 s 25(5) by virtue of SI 2015/2000) and subsequent tax years.

[4]   In sub-s (1), entry repealed by FA 2016 s 22, Sch 5 para 3(2) with effect in relation to lump sums paid after 15 September 2016.

[5]   In sub-s (1) words inserted by the Devolved Income Tax Rates (Consequential Amendments) Order, SI 2019/201 arts 12(1), (4) with effect in relation to the tax year 2019–20 and subsequent tax years.

31 Total income: supplementary

(1) This section applies for the purposes of calculating total income.

(2) Income from which a deduction in respect of income tax is to be made (or treated as made) at the basic [rate][2][, the Welsh basic rate][5] [or the Scottish basic rate][3] . . . [1] in force for a tax year is treated as income of that tax year.

(3) . . . [4]

(4) [Subsection (2) applies][4] even if all or part of the income, or the dividend or other distribution, accrued or will accrue in a different tax year.

(5) An assessment that has become final and conclusive for income tax purposes for a tax year is also final and conclusive for the purposes of calculating total income.

Commentary—*Simon's Taxes* **E1.112, A1.126.**

Amendments—[1]   Words in sub-s (2) repealed by FA 2008 s 5, Sch 1 paras 1, 12 with effect for the tax year 2008–09 and subsequent tax years

[2]   In sub-s (2) word inserted by FA 2014 s 11(4) with effect for the tax year 2015–16 and subsequent tax years.

[3]   In sub-s (2), words inserted by the Scottish Rate of Income Tax (Consequential Amendments) Order, SI 2015/1810 art 14(1), (2) with effect in relation to the tax year 2016–17 (the tax year appointed by the Treasury under the Scotland Act 2012 s 25(5) by virtue of SI 2015/2000) and subsequent tax years.

[4]   Sub-s (3) repealed, and words in sub-s (4) substituted, by FA 2016 s 5, Sch 1 para 63(1), (3) with effect in relation to dividends paid or arising (or treated as paid), and other distributions made (or treated as made), in the tax year 2016-17 or at any later time.

[5]   In sub-s (2) words inserted by the Devolved Income Tax Rates (Consequential Amendments) Order, SI 2019/201 arts 12(1), (5) with effect in relation to the tax year 2019–20 and subsequent tax years.

32 Liability not dealt with in the calculation

The liabilities referred to in section 22(2) are income tax liability—

     [under section 74C(5) (non-active traders: withdrawal of relief),][2]

     under section 79(1) (capital allowances restrictions: withdrawal of relief),

     under section 81(6) (dealings in commodity futures: withdrawal of relief),

     under [section 103B(5)][1] (non-active partners: withdrawal of relief),

     under section 235 (withdrawal or reduction of EIS relief),

     [under section 257G (withdrawal or reduction of SEIS relief),][4]

     [under section 257S (withdrawal or reduction of relief for social investments),][5]

     under sections 266 to 270 (withdrawal or reduction of VCT relief),

     under section 372 (withdrawal or reduction of CITR),

     under section 512 (heritage maintenance settlements: application of property for non-heritage purposes),

     under Chapter 1 of Part 13 (transactions in securities),

     under regulations made under section 918(4) (foreign payers of manufactured dividends: Real Estate Investment Trusts: the reverse charge),

     under section 920 or 923 (foreign payers of manufactured interest or manufactured overseas dividends: the reverse charge),

     under Chapter 15, 16 or 17 of Part 15 (deduction of tax at source: collection mechanisms),

     under section 804(5B)(a) of ICTA (recovery of excess credit for overseas tax),[3]

     under paragraph 11(3) of Schedule 20 to FA 1994 (recovery of excess credit for overseas tax: changes for facilitating self-assessment),

     of the person who is (or persons who are) the responsible person in relation to an employer-financed retirement benefits scheme under section 394(2) of ITEPA 2003,

     under Chapter 5 of Part 4 of FA 2004 (registered pension schemes: tax charges), except any liability under a provision mentioned in section 30(1), . . . [3]

     under section 682(4) of ITTOIA 2005 (assessments, adjustments and claims after the administration period), so far as the liability represents a tax reduction given effect at Step 6 of the calculation in section 23, [and

     under section 24(4) of TIOPA 2010 (recovery of excess credit for overseas tax).][3]

Amendments—[1]   Words substituted by FA 2007 s 26, Sch 4 para 5, 21 and deemed always to have had effect.

[2]   Words inserted by FA 2008 s 60, Sch 21 paras 1, 3 with effect in relation to any loss made by an individual in the tax year 2007–08 or any subsequent tax year (see FA 2008 Sch 21 para 6).

[3]   Entry for TA 1988 s 804(5B)(a), and word "and" preceding the entry for ITTOIA 2005 s 682(4), repealed, and entry for TIOPA 2010 s 24(4) and preceding word "and" inserted, by TIOPA 2010 ss 501, 503, Sch 8 paras 71, 77, Sch 10 Pt 1. TIOPA

2010 has effect for corporation tax purposes for accounting periods ending on or after 1 April 2010, for income and capital gains tax purposes for the tax year 2010–11 and subsequent tax years, and for petroleum revenue tax purposes for chargeable periods beginning on or after 1 July 2010.

4   Entry for s 257G inserted by FA 2013 s 56(1), (3) with effect for the tax year 2013–14 and subsequent tax years.
5   Entry for s 257S inserted by FA 2014 s 57, Sch 11 paras 3, 9 with effect from 17 July 2014.

PART 3
PERSONAL RELIEFS

CHAPTER 1
INTRODUCTION

33 Overview of Part

(1) This Part provides for personal reliefs.
(2) Chapter 2 provides for entitlement to a personal allowance and a blind person's allowance.
(3) Chapter 3 provides for tax reductions for married couples and civil partners [where a party to the marriage or civil partnership is born before 6 April 1935][1].
[(3A) Chapter 3A provides for a transferable tax allowance for married couples and civil partners.][1]
(4) Chapter 4 contains provision applicable for the purposes of Chapters 2[, 3 and 3A][1], in particular—
   (a) requirements about residence etc of claimants to allowances under Chapter 2 or tax reductions under Chapter 3 [or 3A][1], and
   (b) indexation of the amounts of [the allowances under Chapter 2 and tax reductions under Chapter 3][1].

Amendments—[1]   In sub-ss (3), (4)(a) words inserted, sub-s (3A) inserted, in sub-s (4), in the opening words, words substituted, and in sub-s (4)(b), words substituted, by FA 2014 s 11(5) with effect for the tax year 2015–16 and subsequent tax years.

CHAPTER 2

PERSONAL ALLOWANCE AND BLIND PERSON'S ALLOWANCE

Introduction

34 Allowances under Chapter

(1) In this Chapter—
   (a) [section 35 deals][2] with entitlement to a personal allowance,
   (b) section 38 deals with entitlement to a blind person's allowance, and
   (c) section 39 deals with the transfer of part of a blind person's allowance to a spouse or civil partner.

(2) An allowance under this Chapter is given effect at Step 3 of the calculation in section 23.
[(3) For the effect of section 809B (claim for remittance basis to apply) applying to an individual for a tax year, see section 809G (no entitlement to personal allowance or blind person's allowance).][1]

Amendments—[1]   Sub-s (3) inserted by FA 2008 s 25, Sch 7 paras 74, 76 with effect for the tax year 2008–09 and subsequent tax years.
2   In sub-s (1)(a), words substituted by FA 2015 s 5(3) with effect for the tax year 2016–17 and subsequent tax years.

Personal allowances

35 [Personal allowance]

[(1)] [1] An individual who makes a claim is entitled to a personal allowance of [£12,500][3] for a tax year if the individual [meets the requirements of section 56 (residence etc).][2]
[(2) For an individual whose adjusted net income exceeds £100,000, the allowance under subsection (1) is reduced by one-half of the excess.
(3) If the amount of any allowance that remains after the operation of subsection (2) would otherwise not be a multiple of £1, it is to be rounded up to the nearest amount which is a multiple of £1.
(4) For the meaning of "adjusted net income" see section 58.][1]

Commentary—*Simon's Taxes* **E1.910, E1.1416A, E1.1406.**
Amendments—[1]   Sub-s (1) numbered as such, and sub-ss (2)–(4) inserted, by FA 2009 s 4(1) with effect for the tax year 2010–11 and subsequent tax years.
2   Heading substituted, and words substituted for previous sub-s (1)(a), (b) by FA 2015 s 5(4) with effect for the tax year 2016–17 and subsequent tax years.
3   In sub-s (1), figure substituted by FA 2019 s 5(2) with effect for the tax years 2019–20 and 2020–21. For the tax year 2018–19, figure was £11,850. ITA 2007 s 57 (indexation), so far as relating to the personal allowance does not apply for 2019–20 and 2020–21 by virtue of FA 2019 s 5(5)(b).

Blind person's allowance

38 Blind person's allowance

(1) An individual who makes a claim is entitled to a blind person's allowance of [£2,500][1] for a tax year if the individual—
   (a) meets the first or second condition for the whole or part of the tax year, and
   (b) meets the requirements of section 56 (residence etc).

(2) The first condition is that the individual is[—

    (*a*) registered as a severely sight-impaired adult in a register kept under section 77(1) of the Care Act 2014 (registers kept by local authorities in England), or

    [(*b*) registered as a severely sight-impaired adult in a register kept under section 18(1) of the Social Services and Well-being (Wales) Act 2014 (registers kept by local authorities in Wales).][3]

(3) The second condition is that—

    (*a*) the individual is ordinarily resident in Scotland or Northern Ireland, and

    (*b*) because of the individual's blindness, the individual is unable to do any work for which eyesight is essential.

(4) If an individual who is entitled to a blind person's allowance for a particular tax year—

    (*a*) became registered . . . [3] [as a severely sight-impaired person in a register kept under section 77(1) of the Care Act 2014][2] [or section 18(1) of the Social Services and Well-being (Wales) Act 2014][3] in the tax year, but

    (*b*) obtained the evidence . . . [3] [of severe sight-impairment][2] on the basis of which the registration was made in the preceding tax year,

the individual is treated as having met the first condition for the whole of the preceding tax year.

Commentary—*Simon's Taxes* **E1.930, A86.**

Amendments—[1]   In sub-s (1), figure substituted by the Income Tax (Indexation) Order, SI 2020/343 art 2(*a*) with effect for the tax year 2020–21. Note that this fulfils the indexation requirement in s 57 that certain allowances and limits are increased by reference to the Consumer Prices Index. Figure was previously £2,450.

[2]   In sub-s (2), words inserted and repealed, and in sub-s (4)(*a*), (*b*), words inserted, by the Care Act 2014 and Children and Families Act 2014 (Consequential Amendments) Order, SI 2015/914 art 2, Schedule para 88 with effect from 1 April 2015 (see SI 2015/914 art 1(2): the Care Act 2015 s 1 came into force on 1 April 2015 by virtue of SI 2015/993).

[3]   Sub-s (2)(*b*) substituted, in sub-s (4)(*a*), words repealed and inserted, and in sub-s (4)(*b*), words repealed by the Social Services and Well-being (Wales) Act 2014 (Consequential Amendments) Regulations, SI 2016/413 reg 256 with effect from 6 April 2016.

39 Transfer of part of blind person's allowance to a spouse or civil partner

(1) This section applies to an individual who is entitled to a blind person's allowance under section 38 for a tax year if—

    (*a*) the individual is a person whose spouse or civil partner is living with the individual for the whole or any part of the tax year, and

    (*b*) the spouse or civil partner meets the requirements of section 56 (residence etc).

(2) If—

    (*a*) the allowance exceeds the individual's remaining relievable income,

    (*b*) the individual makes an election, and

    (*c*) the individual's spouse or civil partner makes a claim,

the individual's spouse or civil partner is entitled to an allowance for the tax year equal to the amount of the excess.

(3) The individual's remaining relievable income is the amount found by—

    (*a*) taking the amount of the individual's net income, and

    (*b*) subtracting any personal allowance to which the individual is entitled for the tax year.

Commentary—*Simon's Taxes* **E1.931, A4.327.**

40 Election for transfer of allowance under section 39

(1) An election under section 39—

    (*a*) must be made [not more than 4 years after the end of][1] the tax year to which it relates, and

    (*b*) cannot be withdrawn.

(2) If an individual makes an election for a tax year under section 39 the individual is treated as also giving notice under section 51(4) that section 51(1) (tax reductions for married couples and civil partners: transfer of unused relief) is to apply for the tax year.

Commentary—*Simon's Taxes* **E1.931.**

Amendments—[1]   In sub-s (1)(*a*), words substituted by FA 2008 s 118, Sch 39 paras 54, 55 with effect from 1 April 2010 (by virtue of SI 2009/403 art 2(2)), subject to transitional provisions in SI 2009/403 art 10(2) (where art 10 applies, the appointed day is 1 April 2012).

Supplementary

41 Allowances in year of death

(1) Any allowance to which an individual is entitled under this Chapter for any tax year, including the tax year in which the individual dies, is given in full.

(2) . . . [1]

(3) . . . [1]

Commentary—*Simon's Taxes* **E1.911.**

Amendments—[1]   Sub-ss (2), (3) repealed by FA 2012 s 4(1), (5) with effect for the tax year 2013–14 and subsequent tax years.

CHAPTER 3

TAX REDUCTIONS FOR MARRIED COUPLES AND CIVIL PARTNERS[: PERSONS BORN BEFORE 6 APRIL 1935]

Amendments—In heading to Chapter 3, words inserted by FA 2014 s 11(6) with effect for the tax year 2015–16 and subsequent tax years.

Introduction

42 Tax reductions under Chapter

(1) This Chapter contains provisions about entitlement to tax reductions in a case where a party to a marriage or civil partnership was born before 6 April 1935.

(2) Individuals are entitled to tax reductions under the following provisions of this Chapter—

    (*a*)   section 45 (marriages before 5 December 2005),

    (*b*)   section 46 (marriages and civil partnerships on or after 5 December 2005),

    (*c*)   section 47 (election by individual to transfer relief under section 45 or 46),

    (*d*)   section 48 (joint election to transfer relief under section 45 or 46),

    (*e*)   section 49 (election for partial transfer back of relief),

    (*f*)   section 51 (transfer of unused relief), and

    (*g*)   section 52 (transfer back of unused relief).

(3) The tax reductions under sections 45 to 49 are subject to section 54 (tax reductions in the year of marriage or entry into civil partnership).

(4) A tax reduction under this Chapter is given effect at Step 6 of the calculation in section 23.

[(5) For the effect of section 809B (claim for remittance basis to apply) applying to an individual for a tax year, see section 809G (no entitlement to tax reduction).][1]

Commentary—*Simon's Taxes* **E1.920**.

Amendments—[1]   Sub-s (5) inserted by FA 2008 s 25, Sch 7 paras 74, 77 with effect for the tax year 2008–09 and subsequent tax years.

43 Meaning of "the minimum amount"

In this Chapter "the minimum amount" means [£3,510][1].

Commentary—*Simon's Taxes* **T6.108**.

Amendments—[1]   Figure substituted by the Income Tax (Indexation) Order, SI 2020/343 art 2(*b*) with effect for the tax year 2020–21. Note that this fulfils the indexation requirement in s 57 that certain allowances and limits are increased by reference to the Consumer Prices Index. Figure was previously £3,450.

44 Election for new rules to apply

(1) In this Chapter "an election for the new rules to apply" means an election made by a husband and wife who got married before 5 December 2005 for the new rules to apply to them instead of the old rules.

(2) In subsection (1)—

    "the new rules" means the rules for relief under section 46 (marriages and civil partnerships on or after 5 December 2005), and

    "the old rules" means the rules for relief under section 45 (marriages before 5 December 2005).

(3) An election for the new rules to apply—

    (*a*)   must be made jointly by the parties to the marriage,

    (*b*)   must be made before the first tax year for which it is to be in force,

    (*c*)   continues in force in each subsequent tax year, and

    (*d*)   cannot be withdrawn.

Commentary—*Simon's Taxes* **E5.103**.

Married couple's allowance

45 Marriages before 5 December 2005

(1) If a man—

    (*a*)   makes a claim for a tax year, and

    (*b*)   meets the conditions set out in subsection (2),

he is entitled to a tax reduction for the tax year of 10% of the amount specified in subsection (3)(*a*) . . . [2].

(2) The conditions are that—

    (*a*)   for the whole or part of the tax year he is married and his wife is living with him,

    (*b*)   the marriage took place before 5 December 2005 and no election for the new rules to apply is in force for the tax year,

    (*c*)   he or his wife was born before 6 April 1935, and

    (*d*)   he meets the requirements of section 56 (residence etc).

(3) The amount is—

    (*a*)   [£9,075][1], if either the man or his wife is aged 75 or over at some time in the tax year, *and*

    (*b*)   . . . [2]

(4) For a man whose adjusted net income for the tax year exceeds [£30,200][1], the amounts specified in subsection (3) are reduced by [half the excess.][3]

(5) But subsection (4) does not reduce the amounts specified in subsection (3) below the minimum amount.

(6) For the meaning of "adjusted net income" see section 58.

Commentary—*Simon's Taxes* **E1.920, E1.910.**

Amendments—[1]   In sub-ss (3)(*a*), (4) figures substituted by the Income Tax (Indexation) Order, SI 2020/343 art 2(*c*), (*e*) with effect for the tax year 2020–21. Note that this fulfils the indexation requirement in s 57 that certain allowances and limits are increased by reference to the Consumer Prices Index. Figures were previously "£8,915" and "£29,600" respectively.

[2]   Words in sub-s (1) repealed by the Statute Law (Repeals) Act 2013 s 1, Sch 1 Pt 10 with effect from 31 January 2013. Note that sub-s (3)(*b*) and preceding word "and" also appears to have been repealed by the same Act with effect from the same date, although the wording in Sch 1 Pt 10 of that Act is not clear.

[3]   In sub-s (4), words substituted for previous paras (*a*), (*b*) by FA 2015 s 5(6) with effect for the tax year 2016–17 and subsequent tax years.

46 Marriages and civil partnerships on or after 5 December 2005

(1) If an individual—

    (*a*) makes a claim for a tax year, and

    (*b*) meets the conditions set out in subsection (2),

the individual is entitled to a tax reduction for the tax year of 10% of the amount specified in subsection (3)(a) . . . .[3]

(2) The conditions are that—

    (*a*) for the whole or part of the tax year the individual is married or in a civil partnership and is living with the spouse or civil partner,

    (*b*) the marriage took place, or the civil partnership was formed, on or after 5 December 2005 or, if the marriage took place before that date, an election for the new rules to apply is in force for the tax year,

    (*c*) the individual, or the spouse or civil partner, was born before 6 April 1935,

    (*d*) the individual meets the requirements of section 56 (residence etc), and

    (*e*) the individual's net income for the tax year exceeds that of the spouse or civil partner or, if they have the same amount of net income for the tax year, the individual is specified in an election as the person to be entitled to relief under this section for the year.

(3) The amount is—

    (*a*) [£9,075][1], if either the individual, or the spouse or civil partner, is aged 75 or over at some time in the tax year . . . .[3]

    (*b*) . . . .[3]

(4) For an individual whose adjusted net income for the tax year exceeds [£30,200][1], the amounts specified in subsection (3) are reduced by [half the excess.][4]

(5) But subsection (4) does not reduce the amounts specified in subsection (3) below the minimum amount.

(6) An election under subsection (2)(*e*)—

    (*a*) is to be made jointly by the parties to the marriage or civil partnership, and

    (*b*) is to be made [not more than 4 years after the end of][2] the tax year to which the election relates.

(7) For the meaning of "adjusted net income" see section 58.

Commentary—*Simon's Taxes* **E1.920, E5.103, E1.910.**

Amendments—[1]   In sub-ss (3)(*a*), (4), figures substituted by the Income Tax (Indexation) Order, SI 2020/343 art 2(*d*), (*e*) with effect for the tax year 2020–21. Note that this fulfils the indexation requirement in s 57 that certain allowances and limits are increased by reference to the Consumer Prices Index. Figures were previously "£8,915" and "£29,600" respectively.

[2]   In sub-s (6)(*b*), words substituted for words "on or before the fifth anniversary of the normal self-assessment filing date for", by FA 2008 s 118, Sch 39 paras 54, 56 with effect from 1 April 2010 (by virtue of SI 2009/403 art 2(2)), subject to transitional provisions in SI 2009/403 art 10(2) (where art 10 applies, the appointed day is 1 April 2012).

[3]   Words in sub-s (1), and sub-s (3)(*b*) and preceding word "and", repealed by the Statute Law (Repeals) Act 2013 s 1, Sch 1 Pt 10 with effect from 31 January 2013.

[4]   In sub-s (4), words substituted for previous paras (*a*), (*b*) by FA 2015 s 5(7) with effect for the tax year 2016–17 and subsequent tax years.

Elections to transfer relief

47 Election by individual to transfer relief under section 45 or 46

(1) If—

    (*a*) an individual's spouse or civil partner is entitled to a tax reduction under section 45 or 46 for a tax year, and

    (*b*) the individual meets the conditions set out in subsection (2),

the individual is entitled to a tax reduction for that tax year of 10% of half the minimum amount.

(2) The conditions are that the individual—

    (*a*) has made an election which is in force for the tax year,

    (*b*) makes a claim, and

    (*c*) meets the requirements of section 56 (residence etc).

(3) If an individual is entitled to a tax reduction under subsection (1), the tax reduction to which the individual's spouse or civil partner is entitled under section 45 or 46 is calculated for the tax year as if the appropriate amount were reduced by half the minimum amount.

(4) In subsection (3) "the appropriate amount" means—

    (a) if the individual's spouse is entitled to a tax reduction under section 45, the amount specified in section 45(3)(a) . . . [1], after any reductions under section 45(4) and 54(2), or

    (b) if the individual's spouse or civil partner is entitled to a tax reduction under section 46, the amount specified in section 46(3)(a) . . . [1], after any reductions under sections 46(4) and 54(2).

Commentary—*Simon's Taxes* **E1.924, E5.103**.

Modifications—ITA 2007 Sch 2 para 16 (modification of this section in relation to an individual if, immediately before 6 April 2007, the individual's spouse or civil partner is entitled to a tax reduction under TA 1988 s 257A or 257B).

Amendments—[1] Words in sub-s (4)(a), (b) repealed by the Statute Law (Repeals) Act 2013 s 1, Sch 1 Pt 10 with effect from 31 January 2013.

48 Joint election to transfer relief under section 45 or 46

(1) If—

    (a) an individual's spouse or civil partner is entitled to a tax reduction under section 45 or 46 for a tax year, and

    (b) the conditions set out in subsection (2) are met,

the individual is entitled to a tax reduction for that tax year of 10% of the minimum amount.

(2) The conditions are that—

    (a) the individual and the individual's spouse or civil partner have made a joint election which is in force for the tax year,

    (b) the individual makes a claim, and

    (c) the individual meets the requirements of section 56 (residence etc).

(3) If an individual is entitled to a tax reduction under subsection (1), the tax reduction to which the individual's spouse or civil partner is entitled under section 45 or 46 is calculated for the tax year as if the appropriate amount were reduced by the minimum amount.

(4) In subsection (3) "the appropriate amount" means—

    (a) if the individual's spouse is entitled to a tax reduction under section 45, the amount specified in section 45(3)(a) . . . [1], after any reductions under section 45(4) and 54(2), or

    (b) if the individual's spouse or civil partner is entitled to a tax reduction under section 46, the amount specified in section 46(3)(a) . . . [1], after any reductions under sections 46(4) and 54(2).

Commentary—*Simon's Taxes* **E1.924**.

Modification—ITA 2007 Sch 2 para 16 (modification of this section in relation to an individual if, immediately before 6 April 2007, the individual's spouse or civil partner is entitled to a tax reduction under TA 1988 ss 257A or 257B).

Amendments—[1] Words in sub-s (4)(a), (b) repealed by the Statute Law (Repeals) Act 2013 s 1, Sch 1 Pt 10 with effect from 31 January 2013.

49 Election for partial transfer back of relief

(1) If an individual whose spouse or civil partner is entitled under section 48(1) to a tax reduction for a tax year—

    (a) has made an election which is in force for the tax year, and

    (b) makes a claim,

the individual is entitled to a tax reduction for that tax year of 10% of half the minimum amount (in addition to any tax reduction to which the individual is entitled under section 45 or 46).

(2) The amount of the tax reduction to which the individual's spouse or civil partner is entitled under section 48(1) for that tax year is 10% of half the minimum amount (instead of 10% of the minimum amount).

Commentary—*Simon's Taxes* **E1.924**.

Modification—ITA 2007 Sch 2 para 17 (modification of this section in relation to an individual who, immediately before 6 April 2007, the individual's spouse or civil partner is entitled to a tax reduction under TA 1988 ss 257A or 257B).

50 Procedure for making and withdrawing elections under sections 47 to 49

(1) This section applies to elections under sections 47 to 49.

(2) An election—

    (a) must, except in the cases dealt with by subsection (3), be made before the first tax year in which it is to be in force, and

    (b) continues in force in each subsequent tax year until it is withdrawn.

(3) An election—

    (a) may be made in the first tax year in which it is to be in force if that is the tax year in which the marriage takes place or the civil partnership is formed, and

    (b) may be made in the first 30 days of the first tax year in which it is to be in force if appropriate notice is given before the tax year.

(4) In subsection (3), "appropriate notice" means notice given to an officer of Revenue and Customs by the individual or (in the case of a joint election) individuals concerned that it is intended to make the election.

(5) An election may be withdrawn only by—

    (*a*) a notice given by the individual or individuals by whom the election was made, or

    (*b*) a subsequent election under section 47, 48 or 49.

(6) If an election is withdrawn under subsection (5)(*a*), the withdrawal does not have effect until the tax year after the one in which the notice is given.

(7) A notice under subsection (5)(*a*)—

    (*a*) must be given to an officer of Revenue and Customs, and

    (*b*) must be in the form specified by the Commissioners for Her Majesty's Revenue and Customs.

Commentary—*Simon's Taxes* **E1.924**.

Transfer of unused relief

51 Transfer of unused relief

(1) If—

    (*a*) an individual's spouse or civil partner is entitled to a tax reduction under section 45 or 46 for a tax year,

    (*b*) the spouse or civil partner's MCA tax reductions are greater than the spouse or civil partner's comparable tax liability, and

    (*c*) the conditions set out in subsection (4) are met,

the individual is entitled to a tax reduction for that tax year equal to the unused part of the spouse or civil partner's MCA tax reductions.

(2) The spouse or civil partner's MCA tax reductions are the sum of—

    (*a*) the tax reduction to which the spouse or civil partner is entitled under section 45 or 46, and

    (*b*) any tax reduction under section 49 to which the spouse or civil partner is entitled for the tax year.

(3) The unused part of the spouse or civil partner's MCA tax reductions is equal to—

    (*a*) the spouse or civil partner's MCA tax reductions, less

    (*b*) the spouse or civil partner's comparable tax liability.

(4) The conditions are that—

    (*a*) the spouse or civil partner gives notice to an officer of Revenue and Customs that subsection (1) is to apply for the tax year,

    (*b*) the individual makes a claim, and

    (*c*) the individual meets the requirements of section 56 (residence etc).

(5) The tax reduction to which the individual is entitled under subsection (1) is in addition to any tax reduction to which the individual is entitled under section 47 or 48.

(6) The meaning of "comparable tax liability" is given in section 53.

Commentary—*Simon's Taxes* **E1.925**.

Modification—ITA 2007 Sch 2 para 16 (modification of this section in relation to an individual if, immediately before 6 April 2007, the individual's spouse or civil partner is entitled to a tax reduction under TA 1988 ss 257A or 257B).

52 Transfer back of unused relief

(1) If—

    (*a*) an individual's spouse or civil partner is entitled to a tax reduction under section 47 or 48 for a tax year,

    (*b*) the tax reduction is greater than the spouse or civil partner's comparable tax liability, and

    (*c*) the conditions set out in subsection (3) are met,

the individual is entitled to a tax reduction for that tax year equal to the unused part of the spouse or civil partner's tax reduction.

(2) The unused part of the spouse or civil partner's tax reduction is equal to—

    (*a*) the tax reduction to which the spouse or civil partner is entitled, less

    (*b*) the spouse or civil partner's comparable tax liability.

(3) The conditions are that—

    (*a*) the spouse or civil partner gives notice to an officer of Revenue and Customs that subsection (1) is to apply for the tax year, and

    (*b*) the individual makes a claim.

(4) The tax reduction to which the individual is entitled under subsection (1) is in addition to any tax reduction to which the individual is entitled under section 45, 46 or 49.

(5) The meaning of "comparable tax liability" is given in section 53.

Commentary—*Simon's Taxes* **E1.925**.

Modification—ITA 2007 Sch 2 para 17 (modification of this section in relation to an individual who, immediately before 6 April 2007, the individual's spouse or civil partner is entitled to a tax reduction under TA 1988 ss 257A or 257B).

53 Transfer of unused relief: general

(1) For the purposes of sections 51 and 52, the comparable tax liability of an individual is the amount of the individual's tax left after Step 6 of the calculation in section 23 for the tax year, making that calculation with the modifications set out in subsections (2) and (3).

(2) In making that calculation, do not deduct any tax reduction under—

   (a) [sections 2 and 6 of TIOPA 2010][2](double taxation arrangements: relief by agreement), or

   (b) [section 18(1)(b) and (2) of TIOPA 2010][2] (relief for foreign tax where there are no double taxation arrangements).

(3) If the individual's entitlement to a tax reduction under this Chapter is extinguished under section 423(4) (gift aid: restriction of reliefs) to any extent, deduct from the amount calculated in accordance with subsections (1) and (2) the amount by which the tax reduction is reduced.

(4) A notice under section 51 or 52—

   (a) must be given [not more than 4 years after the end of][1] the tax year to which it relates,

   (b) must be in the form specified by the Commissioners for Her Majesty's Revenue and Customs, and

   (c) cannot be withdrawn.

(5) For the purposes of this section a person is treated as being entitled to a tax reduction under [sections 2 and 6 of TIOPA 2010][2] if the person is entitled to credit against income tax under double taxation arrangements.

Commentary—*Simon's Taxes* **E1.925**.

Modification—ITA 2007 Sch 2 para 17 (modification of this section in relation to an individual who, immediately before 6 April 2007, the individual's spouse or civil partner is entitled to a tax reduction under TA 1988 ss 257A or 257B).

Amendments—[1]   In sub-s (4)(a), words substituted by FA 2008 s 118, Sch 39 paras 54, 57 with effect from 1 April 2010 (by virtue of SI 2009/403 art 2(2)), subject to transitional provisions in SI 2009/403 art 10(2) (where art 10 applies, the appointed day is 1 April 2012).

[2]   In sub-ss (2)(a), (b), (5), words substituted by TIOPA 2010 s 501, Sch 8 paras 71, 78. TIOPA 2010 has effect for corporation tax purposes for accounting periods ending on or after 1 April 2010, for income and capital gains tax purposes for the tax year 2010–11 and subsequent tax years, and for petroleum revenue tax purposes for chargeable periods beginning on or after 1 July 2010.

Supplementary

54 Tax reductions in the year of marriage or entry into civil partnership

(1) Subsection (2) applies if an individual—

   (a) gets married or enters into a civil partnership in a tax year, and

   (b) claims a tax reduction under section 45 or 46 for that tax year.

(2) In calculating the amount of the tax reduction (if any) to which the individual is entitled under that section, the amounts specified in section 45(3) or 46(3) (as applicable) are reduced by one twelfth for each month of the tax year which is a month ending before the date on which—

   (a) the marriage took place, or

   (b) the civil partnership was formed.

(3) The reference in subsection (2) to the amounts specified in section 45(3) or 46(3) is to those amounts after any reduction under section 45(4) or 46(4).

(4) But if—

   (a) the individual has previously been married or in a civil partnership in the same tax year, and

   (b) the conditions in section 45(2) or 46(2) are met in relation to the earlier marriage or civil partnership,

subsection (2) applies only if the claim is in respect of the later marriage or civil partnership.

(5) If a claim under section 47, 48 or 49 is for the tax year in which the marriage takes place, or the civil partnership is formed, the references in those sections to the minimum amount are to be read as references to the minimum amount reduced by one twelfth for each month of the tax year which is a month ending before the date on which—

   (a) the marriage took place, or

   (b) the civil partnership was formed.

(6) In this section, "month" means a period beginning with the sixth day of a calendar month and ending with the fifth day of the next calendar month.

Commentary—*Simon's Taxes* **E5.103, E1.920**.

55 Sections 45 to 53: supplementary

(1) An individual is not entitled to more than one tax reduction under sections 45 to 48 for a tax year (regardless of whether the individual is a party to more than one marriage or civil partnership in the tax year).

(2) For the purposes of sections 45 and 46 an individual is treated as having reached the age of 75 in a tax year if the individual was due to reach the age of 75 in the tax year, but dies in the tax year before reaching that age.

(3) Unless this Chapter provides otherwise, a tax reduction to which an individual is entitled under this Chapter for a tax year, including the tax year in which the individual dies, is given in full.

Commentary—*Simon's Taxes* **E1.920**.

[CHAPTER 3A

TRANSFERABLE TAX ALLOWANCE FOR MARRIED COUPLES AND CIVIL PARTNERS]

Amendments—Chapter 3A (ss 55A–55E) inserted by FA 2014 s 11(1), (2) with effect for the tax year 2015–16 and subsequent tax years.

[Introduction

55A Tax reduction under Chapter
(1) This Chapter contains provisions about the entitlement of a spouse or civil partner to a tax reduction in a case where the other party to the marriage or civil partnership has elected for a reduced personal allowance.
(2) A tax reduction under this Chapter is given effect at Step 6 of the calculation in section 23.
(3) For the effect of section 809B (claim for remittance basis to apply) applying to an individual for a tax year, see section 809G (no entitlement to tax reduction).][1]

Commentary—*Simon's Taxes* **E1.915**.
Amendments—[1]   Chapter 3A (ss 55A–55E) inserted by FA 2014 s 11(1), (2) with effect for the tax year 2015–16 and subsequent tax years.

[Tax reduction

55B Tax reduction: entitlement
(1) An individual is entitled to a tax reduction for a tax year of the appropriate percentage of the transferable amount if the conditions in subsection (2) are met.
(2) The conditions are that—
  [(a) the individual is the gaining party (see section 55C(1)(a)) in the case of an election under section 55C which is in force for the tax year,][8]
  (b) the individual is not, for the tax year, liable to tax at a rate other than the basic rate, [the default basic rate, the savings basic rate,][7] [the dividend nil rate,][6] [the Scottish basic rate,][4] [a Scottish rate below the Scottish basic rate, the Scottish intermediate rate,][9] [the Welsh basic rate,][10] the dividend ordinary rate[, the savings nil rate][5] or the starting rate for savings,
  [(ba) if for the tax year the individual is liable to tax at the dividend nil rate, the individual would for that year neither be liable to tax at the dividend upper rate, nor be liable to tax at the dividend additional rate, if section 13A (dividend nil rate) were omitted,][6]
  (c) the individual meets the requirements of section 56 (residence) for the tax year, and
  (d) neither the individual nor the [relinquishing][8] spouse or civil partner makes a claim for the tax year under section 45 (married couple's allowance: marriages before 5 December 2005) or section 46 (married couple's allowance: marriages and civil partnerships on or after 5 December 2005).
(3) "The appropriate percentage" is the basic rate [or default basic rate][7] [or, in the case of a Scottish taxpayer [or Welsh taxpayer][10], the Scottish basic rate][4] [or Welsh basic rate][10] at which the individual would be charged to income tax for the tax year to which the reduction relates.
(4) "The transferable amount"—
  (a) for the tax year 2015–16, is [£1,060][2], and
  (b) for the tax year 2016-17 and subsequent tax years, is 10% of the amount of personal allowance specified in section 35(1) for the tax year to which the reduction relates.
(5) If the transferable amount calculated in accordance with subsection (4)(b) would otherwise not be a multiple of £10, it is to be rounded up to the nearest amount which is a multiple of £10.
[(5A) In this section "the relinquishing spouse or civil partner", in relation to an election under section 55C, means the individual mentioned in section 55C(1)(a) by whom, or by whose personal representatives, the election is made.][8]
(6) If an individual is entitled to a tax reduction under subsection (1) [by reference to an election under section 55C][8], the personal allowance to which the [relinquishing][8] spouse or civil partner is entitled under section 35 . . . [3] is reduced for the tax year by the transferable amount.
(7) If an individual who is entitled to a tax reduction for a tax year under subsection (1) dies during that tax year, subsection (6) is to be ignored (but this does not affect the individual's entitlement to the tax reduction).][1]

Commentary—*Simon's Taxes* **E1.915**.
Amendments—[1]   Chapter 3A (ss 55A–55E) inserted by FA 2014 s 11(1), (2) with effect for the tax year 2015–16 and subsequent tax years.
[2]   In sub-s (4)(a), amount substituted by FA 2015 s 3(4) with effect for the tax year 2015–16 and subsequent tax years.
[3]   In sub-s (6), words repealed by FA 2015 s 5(8) with effect for the tax year 2016–17 and subsequent tax years.
[4]   In sub-s (2)(b), (3), words inserted by the Scottish Rate of Income Tax (Consequential Amendments) Order, SI 2015/1810 art 14(1), (3) with effect in relation to the tax year 2016–17 (the tax year appointed by the Treasury under the Scotland Act 2012 s 25(5) by virtue of SI 2015/2000) and subsequent tax years.
[5]   In sub-s (2)(b) words inserted by FA 2016 s 4(1), (8) with effect in relation to the tax year 2016–17 and subsequent tax years.
[6]   Words in sub-s (2)(b), and sub-s (2)(ba), inserted by FA 2016 s 5(1), (6) with effect in relation to the tax year 2016–17 and subsequent tax years.

ITA 2007

7   In sub-ss (2)(*b*), (3), words inserted by FA 2016 s 6(1), (15) with effect in relation to the tax year 2017–18 (as appointed under
     the Scotland Act 2016 s 13(15)) and subsequent years by virtue of SI 2016/1161 reg 3, subject to transitional provisions (see
     FA 2016 s 6(24)–(30)).
8   Sub-s (2)(*a*) substituted, words in sub-s (2)(*d*) substituted, sub-s (5A) inserted, and words in sub-s (6) inserted and substituted,
     by FA 2018 s 6(1)–(5). These amendments—
     –   are to be treated as having come into force on 29 November 2017;
     –   have effect in relation to elections made on or after that day; and
     –   so have effect even where a relevant death occurred on or before that day.
9   In sub-s (2)(*b*), words inserted by the Scottish Rates of Income Tax (Consequential Amendments) Order, SI 2018/459 art 6(1),
     (2) with effect for the tax year commencing on 6 April 2018 and subsequent tax years.
10   In sub-ss (2)(*b*), (3), words inserted by the Devolved Income Tax Rates (Consequential Amendments) Order, SI 2019/201
     arts 12(1), (6) with effect in relation to the tax year 2019–20 and subsequent tax years.

[Election to reduce personal allowance

55C Election to reduce personal allowance
(1) An individual may make an election for the purposes of section 55B if—
    (*a*) the individual is married to, or in a civil partnership with, the same person [("the gaining
           party")][8]—
           (i)   for the whole or part of the tax year concerned, and
           (ii) when the election is made [or, where the election is made after the death of one or each
                 of them, when they were last both living][8],
    (*b*) the individual is entitled to a personal allowance under section 35 . . . [2] for that tax year,
    (*c*) assuming the individual's personal allowance was reduced as set out in section 55B(6), the
           individual would not for that year be liable to tax at a rate other than the basic rate, [the
           default basic rate, the savings basic rate,][7] [the dividend nil rate,][5] [the Scottish basic rate,][3]
           [a Scottish rate below the Scottish basic rate, the Scottish intermediate rate,][9] [the Welsh
           basic rate,][10] the dividend ordinary rate[, the savings nil rate][4] or the starting rate for savings,
    [(*ca*) where on that assumption the individual would for the tax year be liable to tax at the
           dividend nil rate, the individual on that assumption would for that year neither be liable to tax
           at the dividend upper rate, nor be liable to tax at the dividend additional rate, if section 13A
           (dividend nil rate) were omitted,][5] and
    (*d*) where the individual meets the requirements of section 56 (residence) for the tax year by
           reason of meeting the condition in subsection (3) of that section, the individual meets the
           condition in subsection (2) of this section.
(2) The condition is that the individual's hypothetical net income for the tax year concerned is less
than the amount of the personal allowance to which the individual is entitled for that tax year under
section 35 . . . [2].
(3) For the purposes of subsection (2), an individual's "hypothetical net income" is the amount that
would be that individual's net income calculated at Step 2 of section 23 if that individual's income
tax liability were calculated on the basis that the individual—
    (*a*) was UK resident for the tax year concerned (and the year was not a split year),
    (*b*) was domiciled in the United Kingdom for that tax year,
    (*c*) in that tax year, did not fall to be regarded as resident in a country outside the United
           Kingdom for the purposes of double taxation arrangements having effect at the time, and
    (*d*) for that tax year, had made a claim for any available relief under section 6 of TIOPA 2010 (as
           required by subsection (6) of that section).
(4) An individual's hypothetical net income for a tax year is, to the extent that it is not sterling, to be
calculated by reference to the average exchange rate for the year ending on 31 March in the tax year
concerned.
[(5) The personal representatives of an individual may make any election for the purposes of
section 55B that the individual (if living) might make in relation to—
    (*a*) the tax year in which the individual dies, or
    (*b*) an earlier tax year.][8]][1]

Commentary—*Simon's Taxes* E1.915.
Amendments—[1]   Chapter 3A (ss 55A–55E) inserted by FA 2014 s 11(1), (2) with effect for the tax year 2015–16 and
    subsequent tax years.
2   In sub-ss (1)(*b*), (2), words repealed by FA 2015 s 5(9) with effect for the tax year 2016–17 and subsequent tax years.
3   In sub-s (1)(*c*), words inserted by the Scottish Rate of Income Tax (Consequential Amendments) Order, SI 2015/1810
    art 14(1), (4) with effect in relation to the tax year 2016–17 (the tax year appointed by the Treasury under the Scotland Act
    2012 s 25(5) by virtue of SI 2015/2000) and subsequent tax years.
4   In sub-s (1)(*c*) words inserted by FA 2016 s 4(1), (8) with effect in relation to the tax year 2016–17 and subsequent tax years.
5   Words in sub-s (1)(*c*), and sub-s (1)(*ca*), inserted by FA 2016 s 5(1), (7) with effect in relation to the tax year 2016–17 and
    subsequent tax years.
7   In sub-s (1)(*c*) words inserted by FA 2016 s 6(1), (16) with effect in relation to the tax year 2017–18 (as appointed under the
    Scotland Act 2016 s 13(15)) and subsequent years by virtue of SI 2016/1161 reg 3, subject to transitional provisions (see FA
    2016 s 6(24)–(30)).
8   Words in sub-s (1)(*a*) inserted, and sub-s (5) inserted, by FA 2018 s 6(1), (6)–(8). These amendments—
    –   are to be treated as having come into force on 29 November 2017;

      –   have effect in relation to elections made on or after that day; and

      –   so have effect even where a relevant death occurred on or before that day.

9   In sub-s (1)(*c*), words inserted by the Scottish Rates of Income Tax (Consequential Amendments) Order, SI 2018/459 art 6(1), (2) with effect for the tax year commencing on 6 April 2018 and subsequent tax years.

10   In sub-s (1)(*c*) words inserted by the Devolved Income Tax Rates (Consequential Amendments) Order, SI 2019/201 art 12(1), (7) with effect in relation to the tax year 2019–20 and subsequent tax years.

[55D Procedure for elections under section 55C

(1) An election under section 55C is to be made not more than 4 years after the end of the tax year to which it relates.

(2) If the conditions in paragraphs (*a*) to (*d*) of section 55C(1) continue to be met, an election continues in force in each subsequent tax year unless—

    (*a*) subsection (3) applies,

    (*b*) the election is withdrawn, or

    (*c*) it ceases to have effect under subsection (5).

(3) Where an election is made after the end of the tax year to which it relates [or is made after the death of either of the spouses or civil partners][2], the election has effect for the tax year to which it relates only (and accordingly does not continue in force for subsequent tax years under subsection (2)).

(4) An election may be withdrawn only by a notice given by the individual by whom the election was made[; an election made by an individual's personal representatives may not be withdrawn][2].

(5) If an individual's spouse or civil partner does not obtain a tax reduction under section 55B in respect of a tax year in which an election is in force the election ceases to have effect for subsequent tax years; but this does not prevent an individual making a further election for the purposes of section 55B(2)(*a*) (whether or not in relation to the same marriage or civil partnership).

(6) The withdrawal of an election under subsection (4) does not, except in the cases dealt with by subsection (7), have effect until the tax year after the one in which the notice is given.

(7) The withdrawal of an election under subsection (4) has effect for the tax year in which the notice is given if—

    (*a*) in a case where the individual concerned met the condition in section 55C(1)(*a*) by reason of being married, the marriage has come to an end in that tax year, or

    (*b*) in a case where the individual concerned met the condition in section 55C(1)(*a*) by reason of being in a civil partnership, the civil partnership has come to an end in that tax year.

(8) For the purposes of subsection (7)(*a*), a marriage comes to an end if any of the following is made in respect of it—

    (*a*) a decree absolute of divorce, a decree of nullity of marriage or a decree of judicial separation, or

    (*b*) in Scotland, a decree of divorce, a declarator of nullity or a decree of separation.

(9) For the purposes of subsection (7)(*b*), a civil partnership comes to an end if any of the following is made in respect of it—

    (*a*) a dissolution order or nullity order, which has been made final,

    (*b*) a separation order, or

    (*c*) in Scotland, a decree of dissolution, a declarator of nullity or a decree of separation.

(10) A notice under subsection (4) must—

    (*a*) be given to an officer of Revenue and Customs, and

    (*b*) must be in the form specified by the Commissioners for Her Majesty's Revenue and Customs.

(11) Paragraph 3(1)(*b*) of Schedule 1A to TMA 1970 (amendment of claims and elections) does not apply to an election under section 55C.][1]

Commentary—*Simon's Taxes* **E1.915**.

Amendments—[1] Chapter 3A (ss 55A–55E) inserted by FA 2014 s 11(1), (2) with effect for the tax year 2015–16 and subsequent tax years.

[2] Words in sub-ss (3), (4) inserted by FA 2018 s 6(1), (9)–(11). These amendments—

    –   are to be treated as having come into force on 29 November 2017;

    –   have effect in relation to elections made on or after that day; and

    –   so have effect even where a relevant death occurred on or before that day.

Prospective amendments—In sub-s (8), para (*a*) to be substituted, and para (*c*) and preceding word "or" to be inserted, and sub-s (12) to be inserted, by the Divorce, Dissolution and Separation Act 2020 s 6, Sch para 57 with effect from a date to be appointed. Sub-s (8)(*a*) to read as follows—

    "(*a*) in England and Wales, a divorce order which has been made final, a nullity of marriage order which has been made final, a judicial separation order or a corresponding decree,".

Sub-s (8)(*c*) to read as follows—

    "(*c*) in Northern Ireland, a decree absolute of divorce, a decree of nullity of marriage or a decree of judicial separation.".

Sub-s (12) to read as follows—

    "(12) In subsection (8) "corresponding decree" means any of the following—

    a decree absolute of divorce;

    a decree absolute of nullity of marriage;

a decree of judicial separation.".

[Supplementary

55E Limitation on number of tax reductions and elections

(1) An individual is not entitled to more than one tax reduction under section 55B for a tax year (regardless of whether the individual is a party to more than one marriage or civil partnership in the tax year).

(2) An individual is not entitled to have more than one election for the purposes of section 55B which operates for a tax year (regardless of whether the individual is a party to more than one marriage or civil partnership in the tax year).][1]

Commentary—*Simon's Taxes* **E1.915**.

Amendments—[1]   Chapter 3A (ss 55A–55E) inserted by FA 2014 s 11(1), (2) with effect for the tax year 2015–16 and subsequent tax years.

CHAPTER 4

GENERAL

56 Residence etc of claimants

(1) This section applies in relation to an individual who claims—

(*a*) an allowance under Chapter 2 (personal allowance and blind person's allowance) for a tax year, or

(*b*) a tax reduction under Chapter 3 [or 3A][2] (tax reductions for married couples and civil partners) for a tax year.

(2) The individual meets the requirements of this section if the individual—

(*a*) is UK resident for the tax year, or

(*b*) meets the condition in subsection (3).

(3) An individual meets the condition in this subsection if, at any time in the tax year, the individual—

[(*za*) is a national of an EEA state,][1]

(*a*) is resident in the Isle of Man or the Channel Islands,

(*b*) has previously resided in the United Kingdom and is resident abroad for the sake of the health of—

(i) the individual, or

(ii) a member of the individual's family who is resident with the individual,

(*c*) is a person who is or has been employed in the service of the Crown,

(*d*) is employed in the service of any territory under Her Majesty's protection,

(*e*) is employed in the service of a missionary society, or

(*f*) is a person whose late spouse or late civil partner was employed in the service of the Crown.

Commentary—*Simon's Taxes* **E1.910, E1.920, E6.125, E6.125, E6.125**.

Amendments—[1]   Sub-s (3)(*za*) inserted by FA 2008 s 70 with effect for the tax year 2008–09 and subsequent tax years.
[2]   In sub-s (1)(*b*), words inserted by FA 2014 s 11(7) with effect for the tax year 2015–16 and subsequent tax years.

Prospective amendments—In sub-s (3)(*za*), words "national of the United Kingdom or a" to be inserted after words "is a", by the Taxes (Amendments) (EU Exit) Regulations, SI 2020/332 reg 3 with effect from IP completion day.

57 Indexation of allowances

(1) This section provides for increases in the amounts specified in—

(*a*) section [35(1)][1] [(personal allowance)][6],

(*b*) section 36(1) (personal allowance for those aged 65 to 74),[2]

(*c*) section 37(1) (personal allowance for those aged 75 and over),[2]

(*d*) section 38(1) (blind person's allowance),

(*e*) section 43 (tax reductions for married couples and civil partners: the minimum amount),

(*f*) section 45(3)(*a*) . . .[3] (marriages before 5 December 2005),

(*g*) section 46(3)(*a*) . . .[3] (marriages and civil partnerships on or after 5 December 2005), and

(*h*) sections . . .[4] . . .[6] 45(4) and 46(4) (adjusted net income limit).

(2) It applies if the [consumer prices index][5] for the September before the start of a tax year is higher than it was for the previous September.

(3) For the tax year—

(*a*) the allowances specified in sections 35 [and][2] 38(1),

(*b*) the amounts specified in sections 45(3)(*a*) . . .[3] and 46(3)(*a*) . . .[3], and

(*c*) the minimum amount specified in section 43,

are found as follows.

Step 1 Multiply the allowance, amount or (as the case may be) the minimum amount for the previous tax year by the same percentage as the percentage increase in the [consumer prices index][5].

Step 2 If the result of Step 1 is a multiple of £10, it is the increase for the tax year.

If the result of Step 1 is not a multiple of £10, round it up to the nearest amount which is a multiple of £10.

That amount is the increase for the tax year.

>   *Step 3* Add the increase for the tax year to the allowance, amount or (as the case may be) the minimum amount for the previous tax year.

The result is the allowance, amount or (as the case may be) the minimum amount for the tax year.

(4) For the tax year, the adjusted net income limits specified in sections . . . [4] . . . [6] 45(4) and 46(4) are found as follows.

>   *Step 1* Increase the adjusted net income limit for the previous tax year by the same percentage as the percentage increase in the [consumer prices index][5].

>   *Step 2* If the result of Step 1 is a multiple of £100, it is the adjusted net income limit for the tax year.

If the result of Step 1 is not a multiple of £100, round it up to the nearest amount which is a multiple of £100.

That amount is the adjusted net income limit for the tax year.

(5) Subsections (1) to (4) do not require a change to be made in the amounts deductible or repayable under PAYE regulations during the period beginning on 6 April and ending on 17 May in the tax year.

(6) Before the start of the tax year the Treasury must make an order replacing the amounts specified in the provisions listed in subsection (1) with the amounts which, as a result of this section, are the allowances, amounts, the minimum amount and the adjusted net income limits for the tax year.

[(7) In this section "consumer prices index" means the all items consumer prices index published by the Statistics Board.][5]

(8) . . . [7]

Commentary—*Simon's Taxes* **E1.104, E1.902, E1.911**.
Orders—Income Tax (Indexation) Order, SI 2012/3047.
Income Tax (Indexation) Order, SI 2013/3088.
Income Tax (Indexation) Order, SI 2014/3273.
Income Tax (Indexation) Order, SI 2016/1175.
Income Tax (Indexation) Order, SI 2017/1184.
Income Tax (Indexation) Order, SI 2018/1150.
Income Tax (Indexation) Order, SI 2020/343.
Amendments—[1]   In sub-s (1)(*a*) figure substituted by FA 2009 s 4(3) with effect for the tax year 2011–12 and subsequent tax years.
[2]   In sub-s (1), in para (*a*), words substituted, and paras (*b*), (*c*) repealed; and in sub-s (3)(*a*), word substituted; by FA 2012 s 4(1), (6) with effect for the tax year 2013–14 and subsequent tax years.
[3]   Words in sub-ss (1)(*f*), (*g*), (3)(*b*) repealed by the Statute Law (Repeals) Act 2013 s 1, Sch 1 Pt 10 with effect from 31 January 2013.
[4]   In sub-s (1)(*a*), "1938" substituted for "1948", in sub-ss (1)(*h*), (4) "36(2)," repealed, by FA 2014 s 2(8) (as amended by FA 2015 s 3(3)) with effect for the tax year 2015–16 and subsequent tax years.
[5]   In sub-ss (2), (3), (4), words substituted, and sub-s (7) inserted, by FA 2014 s 4(1), (3) with effect for the tax year 2015–16 and subsequent tax years.
[6]   In sub-s (1)(*a*), words substituted, and in sub-ss (1)(*h*), (4), words repealed, by FA 2015 s 5(10) with effect for the tax year 2016–17 and subsequent tax years.
[7]   Sub-s (8) repealed by FA 2019 s 5(4)(*a*) with effect for the tax year 2019–20 and subsequent tax years.

58 Meaning of "adjusted net income"

(1) For the purposes of Chapters 2 and 3, an individual's adjusted net income for a tax year is calculated as follows.

>   *Step 1* Take the amount of the individual's net income for the tax year.

>   *Step 2* If in the tax year the individual makes, or is treated under section 426 as making, a gift that is a qualifying donation for the purposes of Chapter 2 of Part 8 (gift aid) deduct the grossed up amount of the gift.

>   *Step 3* If the individual is given relief in accordance with section 192 of FA 2004 (relief at source) in respect of any contribution paid in the tax year under a pension scheme, deduct the gross amount of the contribution.

>   *Step 4* Add back any relief under section 457 or 458 (payments to trade unions or police organisations) that was deducted in calculating the individual's net income for the tax year.

The result is the individual's adjusted net income for the tax year.

(2) The grossed up amount of a gift is the amount of the gift grossed up by reference to the basic rate for the tax year . . . [2].

(3) The gross amount of a contribution is the amount of the contribution before deduction of tax under section 192(1) of FA 2004.

[(4) Subsection (6) of section 809ZM (removal of income tax relief in respect of tainted donations etc) excludes certain donations from being deducted at step 2 in subsection (1).][1]

Commentary—*Simon's Taxes* **E1.920, E1.911**.
HMRC Manuals—PAYE Manual PAYE10010 (steps to calculate adjusted net income).

Amendments—[1]   Sub-s (4) inserted by FA 2011 s 27, Sch 3 paras 7, 9 with effect in relation to relievable charity donations made on or after 1 April 2011.

[2]   In sub-s (2) words "if for the tax year the individual is UK resident but not a Scottish taxpayer, by reference to the default basic rate for the tax year if for the tax year the individual is non-UK resident" repealed by the Scottish Rates of Income Tax (Consequential Amendments) Order, SI 2018/459 art 6(1), (3) with effect for the tax year commencing on 6 April 2018 and subsequent tax years.

PART 4

LOSS RELIEF

CHAPTER 1

INTRODUCTION

59 Overview of Part

(1) This Part provides for income tax relief for—

   (a) losses in a trade, profession or vocation (and certain post-cessation payments and events) (see Chapters 2 and 3),

   (b) losses in a UK property business or overseas property business (and, in the case of a UK property business, certain post-cessation payments and events) (see Chapter 4),

   (c) losses in an employment or office (see Chapter 5),

   (d) losses on a disposal of certain shares (see Chapter 6), and

   (e) losses in certain miscellaneous transactions (see Chapter 7).

(2) This Part needs to be read with Chapter 3 of Part 2 (calculation of income tax liability).

(3) For rules about the calculation of losses for the purposes of this Part, see—

   (a) section 26 of ITTOIA 2005 (losses of a trade, profession or vocation calculated on same basis as profits),

   (b) [sections 272 and 272ZA][1] of ITTOIA 2005 (which [apply][1] section 26 of that Act, so that losses of a UK property business or overseas property business are calculated on the same basis as profits),

   (c) section 11 of ITEPA 2003 (calculation of "net taxable earnings"), and

   (d) section 872 of ITTOIA 2005 (losses from miscellaneous transactions calculated on same basis as miscellaneous income).

Amendments—[1]   In sub-s (3)(b), words substituted for words "section 272" and word substituted for word "applies", by F(No 2)A 2017 s 16, Sch 2 paras 60, 61 with effect for the tax year 2017–18 and subsequent tax years, subject to transitional provisions in F(No 2)A 2017 Sch 2 para 64.

CHAPTER 2

TRADE LOSSES

Introduction

60 Overview of Chapter

(1) This Chapter—

   (a) provides for trade loss relief against general income (see sections 64 to 70),

   (b) provides for early trade losses relief (see sections 72 to 74),

   (c) contains provision restricting both those reliefs [and capital gains relief (see sections 74ZA][1] to 82),

   (d) provides for carry-forward trade loss relief (see sections 83 to 88),

   (e) provides for terminal trade loss relief (see sections 89 to 94),

   (f) contains restrictions on the above reliefs for trades, professions and vocations carried on wholly outside the United Kingdom (see section 95), and

   (g) provides for post-cessation trade relief (see sections 96 to 100).

(2) This Chapter is subject to paragraph 2 of Schedule 1B to TMA 1970 (claims for loss relief involving two or more years).

(3) For a rule treating an individual as starting or permanently ceasing to carry on a trade, profession or vocation for income tax purposes (including those of this Part), see—

   (a) section 17 of ITTOIA 2005 (effect of becoming or ceasing to be a UK resident), and

   (b) section 852(6) and (7) of ITTOIA 2005 (corresponding rule in the case of a trade or profession carried on by a firm).

(4) For the purposes of this Chapter sideways relief is—

   (a) trade loss relief against general income, or

   (b) early trade losses relief.

(5) References in this Chapter to a firm are to be read in the same way as references to a firm in Part 9 of ITTOIA 2005 (which contains special provision about partnerships).

Commentary—*Simon's Taxes* **E1.1001**.

HMRC Manuals—Business Income Manual BIM85010 (trade losses: types of relief - overview).

Amendments—[1]   In sub-s (1)(c) words substituted by FA 2010 s 24, Sch 3 paras 1, 2 with effect in relation to a loss if it arises directly or indirectly in consequence of, or otherwise in connection with—

(a)   arrangements which are entered into on or after 21 October 2009; or

(b)   any transaction forming part of arrangements which is entered into on or after that date,

This amendment does not have effect where arrangements were, or any such transaction was, entered into pursuant to an unconditional obligation in a contract made before 21 October 2009; see FA 2010 Sch 3 para 11(2), (3).

61 Non-partners: losses of a tax year

(1) This section applies if a trade, profession or vocation is carried on by a person otherwise than as a partner in a firm.

(2) For the purposes of this Chapter any reference to the person making a loss in the trade, profession or vocation in a tax year is to the person making a loss in the trade, profession or vocation in the basis period for the tax year.

(3) This section is subject to section 70 (restriction on trade loss relief against general income in case of farming or market gardening).

(4) For the rules about basis periods, see Chapter 15 of Part 2 of ITTOIA 2005.

(5) In particular, see the rule in section 206 of ITTOIA 2005 (restriction on bringing losses into account twice).

Commentary—*Simon's Taxes* **E1.1004**.

62 Partners: losses of a tax year etc

(1) This section applies if a trade or profession is carried on by a person as a partner in a firm.

(2) Any reference to a person making a loss in a trade or profession in a tax year is to the partner making a loss in the partner's notional trade in the basis period for the tax year (as to which, see sections 852 and 853 of ITTOIA 2005).

(3) Further—

(a)   any reference to a person making a claim for relief for a loss made in a trade or profession is to the partner making a claim for relief for a loss made in the partner's notional trade,

(b)   any reference to a basis period for a tax year is to the basis period for the partner's notional trade for the tax year,

(c)   any reference to the profits or losses of a partner's notional trade of a tax year is to the partner's share of the firm's profits or losses of the trade or profession treated for the purposes of Chapter 15 of Part 2 of ITTOIA 2005 as the profits or losses of the partner's notional trade in the basis period for the tax year,

(d)   any reference to a person starting to carry on a trade or profession is to the partner starting to carry on the notional trade in accordance with section 852(2) or (3) of ITTOIA 2005, and

(e)   any reference to a person permanently ceasing to carry on a trade or profession is to the partner permanently ceasing to carry on the notional trade in accordance with section 852(4) to (6) of ITTOIA 2005.

(4) In this section a partner's "notional trade" has the same meaning as in Part 9 of ITTOIA 2005.

(5) This section applies for the purposes of this Chapter and Chapter 3, except that it does not apply for the purposes of section 67(2) or sections 68 to 70 (restriction on trade loss relief against general income in case of farming or market gardening).

Commentary—*Simon's Taxes* **B7.504, B7.522, E1.1004**.
HMRC Manuals—Business Income Tax Manual BIM82255 (partner's notional trade).
Modifications—FA 2009 Sch 6 para 2(4) (for the purposes of the temporary carry-back of losses provisions in FA 2009 Sch 6, this section has effect as if FA 2009 Sch 6 para 1 were included in Part 4 Chapter 2 of ITA 2007).

63 Prohibition against double counting

If relief is given under any provision of this Chapter for a loss or part of a loss, relief is not to be given for—

(a)   the same loss, or

(b)   the same part of the loss,

under any other provision of this Chapter or of the Income Tax Acts.

Commentary—*Simon's Taxes* **B7.504, B7.522, E1.1002**.
Modifications—FA 2009 Sch 6 para 2(4) (for the purposes of the temporary carry-back of losses provisions in FA 2009 Sch 6, this section has effect as if FA 2009 Sch 6 para 1 were included in Part 4 Chapter 2 of ITA 2007).

Trade loss relief against general income

64 Deduction of losses from general income

(1) A person may make a claim for trade loss relief against general income if the person—

(a)   carries on a trade in a tax year, and

(b)   makes a loss in the trade in the tax year ("the loss-making year").

(2) The claim is for the loss to be deducted in calculating the person's net income—

(a)   for the loss-making year,

(b)   for the previous tax year, or

(c)   for both tax years.

(See Step 2 of the calculation in section 23.)

(3) If the claim is made in relation to both tax years, the claim must specify the tax year for which a deduction is to be made first.

(4) Otherwise the claim must specify either the loss-making year or the previous tax year.

(5) The claim must be made on or before the first anniversary of the normal self-assessment filing date for the loss-making year.

(6) Nothing in this section prevents a person who makes a claim specifying a particular tax year in respect of a loss from making a further claim specifying the other tax year in respect of the unused part of the loss.

(7) This section applies to professions and vocations as it applies to trades.

(8) This section needs to be read with—

> (*a*) section 65 (how relief works),
>
> (*b*) sections 66 to 70 (restrictions on the relief),
>
> [(*ba*) sections [74ZA]³ to 74D (general restrictions on relief),]¹
>
> [(*bb*) section 74E (restriction on the relief and early trade losses relief where cash basis applies),]⁴
>
> (*c*) sections 75 to 79 (restrictions on the relief and early trade losses relief in relation to capital allowances), [and]³
>
> (*d*) section 80 (restrictions on those reliefs in relation to ring fence income),
>
> (*e*) . . .³ and²
>
> (*f*) *section 734 of ICTA (restrictions on those reliefs in relation to bond-washing).²*

Commentary—*Simon's Taxes* **B5.417, B7.504, B7.522, E1.1002, E1.1004, E5.630, E5.622.**

HMRC Manuals—Company Taxation Manual CTM40200 (restriction of relief for farming companies). International Manual INTM165210 (losses - relief).

Business Income Manual BIM85015 (types of relief - relief against general income).

Amendments—¹   Sub-s (8)(*ba*) inserted by FA 2008 s 60, Sch 21 para 4 with effect in relation to any loss made by an individual in the tax year 2007–08 or any subsequent tax year (see FA 2008 Sch 21 para 6).

²   Sub-s (8)(*f*) and preceding word and repealed by FA 2008 s 66(4) with effect in accordance with FA 2008 s 66(8).

³   In sub-s (8)(*ba*) figure substituted, in sub-s (8)(*c*) word at the end inserted, and sub-s (8)(*e*) repealed, by FA 2010 s 24, Sch 3 paras 1, 3 with effect in relation to a loss if it arises directly or indirectly in consequence of, or otherwise in connection with—

> (a)   arrangements which are entered into on or after 21 October 2009; or
>
> (b)   any transaction forming part of arrangements which is entered into on or after that date,

This amendment does not have effect where arrangements were, or any such transaction was, entered into pursuant to an unconditional obligation in a contract made before 21 October 2009; see FA 2010 Sch 3 para 11(2), (3).

⁴   Sub-s (8)(*bb*) inserted by FA 2013 s 17, Sch 4 para 54(1), (2) with effect for the tax year 2013–14 and subsequent tax years, subject to the provisions of FA 2013 Sch 4 para 57 in relation to barristers and advocates.

65 How relief works

(1) This subsection explains how the deductions are to be made.

The amount of the loss to be deducted at any step is limited in accordance with [sections 24A and 25(4) and (5)]¹.

> *Step 1* Deduct the loss in calculating the person's net income for the specified tax year.
>
> *Step 2* This step applies only if the claim is made in relation to both tax years. Deduct the part of the loss not deducted at Step 1 in calculating the person's net income for the other tax year.

Other claims

If the loss has not been deducted in full at Steps 1 and 2, the person may use the part not so deducted in giving effect to any other relief under this Chapter (depending on the terms of the relief).

(2) There is a priority rule if a person—

> (*a*) makes a claim for trade loss relief against general income ("the first claim") in relation to the loss-making year, and
>
> (*b*) makes a separate claim in respect of a loss made in the following tax year in relation to the same tax year as the first claim.

(3) The rule is that priority is given to making deductions under the first claim.

(4) For this purpose a "separate claim" means—

> (*a*) a claim for trade loss relief against general income, or
>
> (*b*) a claim for employment loss relief against general income under section 128.

Commentary—*Simon's Taxes* **E1.1002, B5.175, E1.1006.**

Amendments—¹   In sub-s (1) words substituted for words "section 25(4) and (5)" by FA 2013 s 16, Sch 3 para 2(1), (3)(*a*) with effect for the tax year 2013–14 and subsequent tax years, subject to transitional provisions in relation to loss relief claims for a tax year before 2013–14 in relation to losses made in 2013–14 or a later year (FA 2013 Sch 3 para 4).

Restriction on relief for uncommercial trades

66 Restriction on relief unless trade is commercial

(1) Trade loss relief against general income for a loss made in a trade in a tax year is not available unless the trade is commercial.

(2) The trade is commercial if it is carried on throughout the basis period for the tax year—

> (*a*) on a commercial basis, and
>
> (*b*) with a view to the realisation of profits of the trade.

(3) If at any time a trade is carried on so as to afford a reasonable expectation of profit, it is treated as carried on at that time with a view to the realisation of profits.

(4) If the trade forms part of a larger undertaking, references to profits of the trade are to be read as references to profits of the undertaking as a whole.

(5) If there is a change in the basis period in the way in which the trade is carried on, the trade is treated as carried on throughout the basis period in the way in which it is carried on by the end of the basis period.

(6) The restriction imposed by this section does not apply to a loss made in the exercise of functions conferred by or under an Act.

(7) This section applies to professions and vocations as it applies to trades.

Commentary—*Simon's Taxes* **D1.1110, E1.1006, B5.175**.
HMRC Manuals—Business Income Manual BIM85701 (introduction).
BIM85705 (restriction of relief against general income - uncommercial trades - not on a commercial basis).
BIM85615 (test of commerciality).
BIM85710 (trade losses - uncommercial trades - not with a view to the realisation of profit).
BIM85715 (trade losses - change in conduct of trade).

Restriction on relief for "hobby" farming or market gardening

67 Restriction on relief in case of farming or market gardening

(1) This section applies if a loss is made in a trade of farming or market gardening in a tax year ("the current tax year").

(2) Trade loss relief against general income is not available for the loss if a loss, calculated without regard to capital allowances, was made in the trade in each of the previous 5 tax years (see section 70).

(3) This section does not prevent relief for the loss from being given if—
- (a) the carrying on of the trade forms part of, and is ancillary to, a larger trading undertaking,
- (b) the farming or market gardening activities meet the reasonable expectation of profit test (see section 68), or
- (c) the trade was started, or treated as started, at any time within the 5 tax years before the current tax year (see section 69 below, as well as section 17 of ITTOIA 2005).

Commentary—*Simon's Taxes* **B5.175, B5.175**.
HMRC Manuals—Business Income Manual BIM85645 (let-out where farming part of larger undertaking).
BIM85620 (restriction of relief after 5 years of losses).
BIM85650 (avoidance).

68 Reasonable expectation of profit

(1) This section explains how the farming or market gardening activities ("the activities") meet the reasonable expectation of profit test for the purposes of section 67.

(2) The test is decided by reference to the expectations of a competent farmer or market gardener (a "competent person") carrying on the activities.

(3) The test is met if—
- (a) a competent person carrying on the activities in the current tax year would reasonably expect future profits (see subsection (4)), but
- (b) a competent person carrying on the activities at the beginning of the prior period of loss (see subsection (5)) could not reasonably have expected the activities to become profitable until after the end of the current tax year.

(4) In determining whether a competent person carrying on the activities in the current tax year would reasonably expect future profits regard must be had to—
- (a) the nature of the whole of the activities, and
- (b) the way in which the whole of the activities were carried on in the current tax year.

(5) "The prior period of loss" means—
- (a) the 5 tax years before the current tax year, or
- (b) if losses in the trade, calculated without regard to capital allowances, were also made in successive tax years before those 5 tax years (see section 70), the period comprising both the successive tax years and the 5 tax years.

Commentary—*Simon's Taxes* **B5.175**.
HMRC Manuals—Business Income Manual BIM55725 (losses in stud farms).
BIM85640 (let-out for long term ventures).

69 Whether trade is the same trade

(1) This section applies for the purposes of sections 67 and 68.

(2) If there is a change in the persons carrying on a trade which involves all of the persons carrying it on before the change permanently ceasing to carry it on—
- (a) the trade is treated as permanently ceasing to be carried on, and
- (b) a new trade is treated as starting to be carried on,

at the date of the change (but see subsections (3) to (6)).

(3) A husband and wife are treated as the same person.

(4) Persons who are civil partners of each other are treated as the same person.

(5) A husband or wife is treated as the same person as—
- (a) a company of which either one of them has control, or

   (*b*) a company of which both have control.

(6) A person's civil partner is treated as the same person as—

   (*a*) a company of which either of the civil partners has control, or

   (*b*) a company of which both have control.

(7) "Control" [is to be read in accordance with sections 450 and 451 of CTA 2010][1].

Commentary—*Simon's Taxes* **B5.175**.

HMRC Manuals—Business Income Manual BIM85635 (notional cessations and re-commencements).
BIM85650 (avoidance).

Amendments—[1] In sub-s (7) words substituted by CTA 2010 s 1177, Sch 1 para 495. CTA 2010 has effect for corporation tax purposes for accounting periods ending on or after 1 April 2010, and for income and capital gains tax purposes for the tax year 2010–11 and subsequent tax years.

70 Determining losses in previous tax years

(1) This section applies for the purposes of sections 67(2) and 68(5) in determining whether a loss, calculated without regard to capital allowances, is made in the trade in any tax year before the current tax year.

(2) The loss made in a tax year before the current tax year is not taken to be the loss (if any) made in the basis period for the tax year, but is instead the loss made in the tax year itself.

(3) This loss is determined by reference to—

   (*a*) the profits or losses of periods of account of the trade (calculated for income tax purposes, but without regard to capital allowances), or

   (*b*) if (as a result of section 69) a person claiming the relief is treated as the same person as a company within the charge to corporation tax, the profits or losses of the company's accounting periods (calculated for corporation tax purposes, but without regard to capital allowances),

or by reference to both.

(4) If—

   (*a*) a period of account does not coincide with a tax year, or

   (*b*) an accounting period does not coincide with a tax year,

any of the steps in section 203(2) of ITTOIA 2005 may be taken to arrive at the profits or losses made in a tax year.

   For this purpose references in section 203(2) of that Act to basis periods are read as references to tax years and references to periods of account are read as including accounting periods.

(5) The steps must be taken in accordance with section 203(3) or (4) of ITTOIA 2005.

(6) A loss in a trade is calculated without regard to capital allowances by ignoring—

   (*a*) the allowances treated as expenses of the trade under CAA 2001, and

   (*b*) the charges treated as receipts of the trade under that Act.

Commentary—*Simon's Taxes* **B5.175**.

HMRC Manuals—Business Income Manual BIM85625 (operation of five year rule).
BIM85630 (loss considered is loss incurred in year to 5 April).

Use of trading loss as CGT loss

71 Treating trade losses as CGT losses

A person who cannot deduct all of a loss under a claim for trade loss relief against general income may be able to treat the unused part as an allowable loss for capital gains tax purposes: see sections 261B and 261C of TCGA 1992.

Commentary—*Simon's Taxes* **B7.504, B7.522, E1.1003, E5.622B**.

HMRC Manuals—Lloyds Manual LLM5380 (names: loss relief (except terminal losses).
Business Income Manual BIM85025 (trade losses: relief against chargeable gains).
BIM85030 (relief against chargeable gains: computation).
BIM85035 (gains subsequently relieved against capital gains).
Capital Gains Manual CG15801 (losses: deduction of trading losses).

Early trade losses relief

72 Relief for individuals for losses in first 4 years of trade

(1) An individual may make a claim for early trade losses relief if the individual makes a loss in a trade—

   (*a*) in the tax year in which the trade is first carried on by the individual, or

   (*b*) in any of the next 3 tax years.

(2) The claim is for the loss to be deducted in calculating the individual's net income for the 3 tax years before the one in which the loss is made (see Step 2 of the calculation in section 23).

(3) The claim must be made on or before the first anniversary of the normal self-assessment filing date for the tax year in which the loss is made.

(4) This section applies to professions and vocations as it applies to trades.

(5) This section needs to be read with—

   (*a*) section 73 (how relief works),

   (*b*) section 74 (restrictions on the relief [unless trade is commercial etc][1]),

[(*ba*) sections [74ZA][3] to 74D (general restrictions on relief),][1]
[(*bb*) section 74E (restriction on the relief and trade loss relief where cash basis applies),][4]
(*c*) sections 75 to 79 (restrictions on the relief and trade loss relief against general income in relation to capital allowances), [and][3]
(*d*) section 80 (restrictions on those reliefs in relation to ring fence income),
(*e*) . . . [3] and[2]
(*f*) section 734 of ICTA (restrictions on those reliefs in relation to bond-washing).[2]

Commentary—*Simon's Taxes* **E1.1021, E1.1429.**
HMRC Manuals—Business Income Manual BIM85045 (relief for losses in early years of trade).
Lloyds Manual LLM6150 (loss relief: partnership).
LLM5380 (loss relief: except terminal losses).
Amendments—[1]   Words in sub-s (5)(*b*), and sub-s (5)(*ba*) inserted, by FA 2008 s 60, Sch 21 para 5 with effect in relation to any loss made by an individual in the tax year 2007–08 or any subsequent tax year (see FA 2008 Sch 21 para 6).
[2]   Sub-s (5)(*f*) and preceding word "and" repealed by FA 2008 s 66(4) with effect in accordance with FA 2008 s 66(8).
[3]   In sub-s (5)(*ba*) figure substituted, in sub-s (5)(*c*) word at the end inserted, and sub-s (5)(*e*) repealed, by FA 2010 s 24, Sch 3 paras 1, 4 with effect in relation to a loss if it arises directly or indirectly in consequence of, or otherwise in connection with—
        (a)   arrangements which are entered into on or after 21 October 2009; or
        (b)   any transaction forming part of arrangements which is entered into on or after that date.
        This amendment does not have effect where arrangements were, or any such transaction was, entered into pursuant to an unconditional obligation in a contract made before 21 October 2009; see FA 2010 Sch 3 para 11(2), (3).
[4]   Sub-s (5)(*bb*) inserted by FA 2013 s 17, Sch 4 para 54(1), (3) with effect for the tax year 2013–14 and subsequent tax years, subject to the provisions of FA 2013 Sch 4 para 57 in relation to barristers and advocates.

73 How relief works

This section explains how the deductions are made for the 3 tax years mentioned in section 72(2). The amount of the loss to be deducted at any step is limited in accordance with [sections 24A and 25(4) and (5)][1].

> *Step 1* Deduct the loss in calculating the individual's net income for the earliest of the 3 tax years.
> *Step 2* Deduct any part of the loss not deducted at Step 1 in calculating the individual's net income for the next tax year.
> *Step 3* Deduct any part of the loss not deducted at Step 1 or 2 in calculating the individual's net income for the latest of the 3 tax years.

Other claims
If the loss has not been deducted in full at Steps 1 to 3, the individual may use the part not so deducted in giving effect to any other relief under this Chapter (depending on the terms of the relief).

Commentary—*Simon's Taxes* **E1.1021, B7.504, B7.522.**
Amendments—[1]   Words substituted for words "section 25(4) and (5)" by FA 2013 s 16, Sch 3 para 2(1), (3)(*b*) with effect for the tax year 2013–14 and subsequent tax years, subject to transitional provisions in relation to loss relief claims for a tax year before 2013–14 in relation to losses made in 2013–14 or a later year (FA 2013 Sch 3 para 4).

74 Restrictions on relief unless trade is commercial etc

(1) Early trade losses relief for a loss made by an individual in a trade in a tax year is not available unless the trade is commercial.
(2) The trade is commercial if it is carried on throughout the basis period for the tax year—
   (*a*) on a commercial basis, and
   (*b*) in such a way that profits of the trade could reasonably be expected to be made in the basis period or within a reasonable time afterwards.
(3) If the trade forms part of a larger undertaking, the reference to profits of the trade is to be read as a reference to profits of the undertaking as a whole.
(4) Early trade losses relief for a loss made by an individual is not available if—
   (*a*) the individual first carries on the trade at a time when the individual has a spouse or civil partner and is living with the spouse or civil partner,
   (*b*) the spouse or civil partner previously carried on the trade, and
   (*c*) the loss is made in a tax year falling after the relevant 4 year period.
(5) The relevant 4 year period comprises—
   (*a*) the tax year in which the spouse or civil partner first carried on the trade, and
   (*b*) the next 3 tax years.
(6) This section applies to professions and vocations as it applies to trades.

Commentary—*Simon's Taxes* **E1.1021, B7.504, B7.522.**
HMRC Manuals—Business Income Manual BIM85735 (uncommercial losses made in early years of trade).

[General restrictions on sideways relief and capital gains relief

[74ZA No relief for tax-generated losses

(1) This section applies if—
   (*a*) during a tax year a person carries on (alone or in partnership) a trade, profession or vocation ("the relevant activity"),
   (*b*) the person makes a loss in the relevant activity in that tax year, and

(*c*) the loss arises directly or indirectly in consequence of, or otherwise in connection with, relevant tax avoidance arrangements.

(2) No sideways relief or capital gains relief may be given to the person for the loss (but subject to subsection (5)).

(3) In subsection (1) "relevant tax avoidance arrangements" means arrangements—

    (*a*) to which the person is a party, and

    (*b*) the main purpose, or one of the main purposes, of which is the obtaining of a reduction in tax liability by means of sideways relief or capital gains relief.

(4) In subsection (3) "arrangements" includes any agreement, understanding, scheme, transaction or series of transactions (whether or not legally enforceable).

(5) This section has no effect in relation to any loss that derives wholly from qualifying film expenditure (see section 74D).

(6) For the purposes of this section—

    (*a*) capital gains relief is, in relation to a loss, the treatment of a loss as an allowable loss by virtue of section 261B of TCGA 1992 (use of trading loss as a CGT loss), and

    (*b*) capital gains relief is given for a loss when it is so treated.][1]

Commentary—*Simon's Taxes* **E1.1008, E1.1008, E1.1007**.

HMRC Manuals—Business Income Manual BIM85762 (tax-generated losses).

BIM85761 (no sideways relief for tax-generated losses).

Amendments—[1]　This section inserted by FA 2010 s 24, Sch 3 paras 1, 5 with effect in relation to a loss if it arises directly or indirectly in consequence of, or otherwise in connection with—

    (a)　arrangements which are entered into on or after 21 October 2009; or

    (b)　any transaction forming part of arrangements which is entered into on or after that date,

This amendment does not have effect where arrangements were, or any such transaction was, entered into pursuant to an unconditional obligation in a contract made before 21 October 2009; see FA 2010 Sch 3 para 11(2), (3).

74A Reliefs in any tax year not to exceed cap for tax year

(1) This section applies if—

    (*a*) during a tax year an individual carries on one or more trades, otherwise than as a partner in a firm, in a non-active capacity (see section 74C), and

    (*b*) the individual makes a loss in any of those trades (an "affected loss") in that tax year.

(2) There is a restriction on the amount of sideways relief and capital gains relief which (after applying the restrictions under the other provisions of this Chapter) may be given to the individual for any affected loss (but see subsections (7) and (8)).

(3) The restriction is that the total amount of the sideways relief and capital gains relief given to the individual for all the affected losses must not exceed the cap for that tax year.

(4) The cap for any tax year is £25,000.

(5) The Treasury may by order amend the sum for the time being specified in subsection (4).

(6) If—

    (*a*) in a tax year an individual makes a loss to which the restriction under section 103C (losses in trade carried on by non-active or limited partner) applies, and

    (*b*) sideways relief or capital gains relief is given to the individual for that loss,

the amount of the cap under this section for the tax year in the case of the individual is reduced by the amount of that loss.

(7) The restriction under this section does not apply to so much of any affected loss as derives from qualifying film expenditure (see section 74D).

(8) The restriction under this section does not affect the giving of sideways relief for a loss made in a trade against the profits of that trade.

(9) In this section "trade" does not include a trade which consists of the underwriting business of a member of Lloyd's (within the meaning of section 184 of FA 1993).

(10) For the purposes of this section—

    (*a*) capital gains relief is, in relation to a loss, the treatment of a loss as an allowable loss by virtue of section 261B of TCGA 1992 (use of trading loss as a CGT loss), and

    (*b*) capital gains relief is given for a loss when it is so treated.][1]

Commentary—*Simon's Taxes* **E1.1007**.

HMRC Manuals—Business Income Manual BIM85765 (non-active traders - overview).

BIM85766 (non-active traders – annual limit).

Amendments—[1]　Sections 74A–74D inserted by FA 2008 s 60, Sch 21 paras 1, 2 with effect in relation to any loss made by an individual in the tax year 2007–08 or any subsequent tax year. (For s 74B with effect in relation to any loss arising directly or indirectly in consequence of, or otherwise in connection with, relevant tax avoidance arrangements made on or after 12 March 2008). But this amendment does not have effect in relation to a loss made by an individual in a tax year the basis period for which ended before 12 March 2008: see FA 2008 Sch 21 para 6. (For s 74B this amendment does not have effect where arrangements were made pursuant to an unconditional obligation in a contract made before 12 March 2008; see FA 2008 Sch 21 para 7).

[74C Meaning of "non-active capacity" for purposes of [section 74A][2] etc

(1) For the purposes of [section 74A][2] an individual carries on a trade in a non-active capacity during a tax year if the individual—

   (*a*) carries on the trade at a time during the year, and

   (*b*) does not devote a significant amount of time to the trade in the relevant period for the tax year.

(2) For the purposes of this section an individual devotes a significant amount of time to a trade in the relevant period for a tax year if, in the relevant period, the individual spends an average of at least 10 hours a week personally engaged in activities of the trade and those activities are carried on—

   (*a*) on a commercial basis, and

   (*b*) with a view to the realisation of profits as a result of the activities.

(3) For this purpose "the relevant period" means the basis period for the tax year (unless the basis period is shorter than 6 months).

(4) If the basis period for the tax year is shorter than 6 months, "the relevant period" means—

   (*a*) the period of 6 months beginning with the date on which the individual first started to carry on the trade (if the basis period begins with that date), or

   (*b*) the period of 6 months ending with the date on which the individual permanently ceased to carry on the trade (if the basis period ends with that date).

(5) If—

   (*a*) any relief is given on the assumption that the individual devoted or will devote a significant amount of time to the trade in the relevant period for a tax year, but

   (*b*) the individual in fact failed or fails to do so,

the relief is withdrawn by the making of an assessment to income tax under this section.][1]

Commentary—*Simon's Taxes* **E1.1007**.

HMRC Manuals—Business Income Manual BIM85765 (meaning of 'non-active capacity')

Amendments—[1]   Sections 74A–74D inserted by FA 2008 s 60, Sch 21 paras 1, 2 with effect in relation to any loss made by an individual in the tax year 2007–08 or any subsequent tax year. (For s 74B with effect in relation to any loss arising directly or indirectly in consequence of, or otherwise in connection with, relevant tax avoidance arrangements made on or after 12 March 2008). But this amendment does not have effect in relation to a loss made by an individual in a tax year the basis period for which ended before 12 March 2008: see FA 2008 Sch 21 para 6. (For s 74B this amendment does not have effect where arrangements were made pursuant to an unconditional obligation in a contract made before 12 March 2008; see FA 2008 Sch 21 para 7).

[2]   In heading and sub-s (1) words substituted by FA 2010 s 24, Sch 3 paras 1, 7 with effect in relation to a loss if it arises directly or indirectly in consequence of, or otherwise in connection with—

   (a)   arrangements which are entered into on or after 21 October 2009; or

   (b)   any transaction forming part of arrangements which is entered into on or after that date.

This amendment does not have effect where arrangements were, or any such transaction was, entered into pursuant to an unconditional obligation in a contract made before 21 October 2009; see FA 2010 Sch 3 para 11(2), (3).

[74D Meaning of "qualifying film expenditure" for purposes of [sections 74ZA and 74A][2]

(1) For the purposes of [sections 74ZA and 74A][2] expenditure is qualifying film expenditure if—

   (*a*) it is deducted under a relevant film provision for the purposes of calculating the profits of a trade, or

   (*b*) it is incidental expenditure which (although not deducted under a relevant film provision) is incurred in connection with the production of a film, or the acquisition of the original master version of a film, in relation to which expenditure is so deducted.

(2) Expenditure is incidental if it is on management, administration or obtaining finance.

(3) The extent to which expenditure is within subsection (1)(*b*) is determined on a just and reasonable basis.

(4) For the purposes of [sections 74ZA and 74A][2] the amount of any loss that derives from qualifying film expenditure is determined on a just and reasonable basis.

(5) In this section—

   "the acquisition of the original master version of a film" has the same meaning as in Chapter 9 of Part 2 of ITTOIA 2005 (see sections 130 and 132 of that Act),

   "film" is to be read in accordance with paragraph 1 of Schedule 1 to the Films Act 1985, and

   "a relevant film provision" means any one of sections 137 to 140 of ITTOIA 2005 (relief for certified master versions of films).][1]

Commentary—*Simon's Taxes* **E1.1007, E1.1008**.

HMRC Manuals—Business Income Manual BIM56010 (old regime for films).

BIM85768 (trade losses - non-active traders - film-related expenditure).

Amendments—[1]   Sections 74A–74D inserted by FA 2008 s 60, Sch 21 paras 1, 2 with effect in relation to any loss made by an individual in the tax year 2007–08 or any subsequent tax year. (For s 74B with effect in relation to any loss arising directly or indirectly in consequence of, or otherwise in connection with, relevant tax avoidance arrangements made on or after 12 March 2008). But this amendment does not have effect in relation to a loss made by an individual in a tax year the basis period for which ended before 12 March 2008: see FA 2008 Sch 21 para 6. (For s 74B this amendment does not have effect where arrangements were made pursuant to an unconditional obligation in a contract made before 12 March 2008; see FA 2008 Sch 21 para 7).

[2]   In heading and sub-ss (1), (4) words substituted by FA 2010 s 24, Sch 3 paras 1, 8 with effect in relation to a loss if it arises directly or indirectly in consequence of, or otherwise in connection with—

   (a)   arrangements which are entered into on or after 21 October 2009; or

   (b)   any transaction forming part of arrangements which is entered into on or after that date.

This amendment does not have effect where arrangements were, or any such transaction was, entered into pursuant to an unconditional obligation in a contract made before 21 October 2009; see FA 2010 Sch 3 para 11(2), (3).

[Restriction on sideways relief and capital gains relief where cash basis applies

74E No relief where cash basis used to calculate losses

(1) This section applies if—

    (*a*) a person makes a loss in any trade in a tax year, and

    (*b*) an election under section 25A of ITTOIA 2005 (cash basis for small businesses) has effect in relation to the trade for that tax year.

(2) No sideways relief or capital gains relief may be given to the person for the loss.

(3) For the purposes of this section—

    (*a*) capital gains relief is, in relation to a loss, the treatment of a loss as an allowable loss by virtue of section 261B of TCGA 1992 (use of trading loss as a CGT loss), and

    (*b*) capital gains relief is given for a loss when it is so treated.][1]

Commentary—*Simon's Taxes* **E1.1003**.

HMRC Manuals—Business Income Manual BIM70005 (cash basis: overview).

Capital Gains Manual CG15470 (cash basis for small business: introduction).

CG15490 (cash basis: capital gains aspects: examples)

Amendments—[1] Section 74E inserted by FA 2013 s 17, Sch 4 para 54(1), (4) with effect for the tax year 2013–14 and subsequent tax years, subject to the provisions of FA 2013 Sch 4 para 57 in relation to barristers and advocates.

Restrictions on sideways relief for certain capital allowances

75 Trade leasing allowances given to individuals

(1) Sideways relief is not available to an individual for so much of a loss as derives from a trade leasing allowance unless the individual meets the time commitment test.

(2) A trade leasing allowance is an allowance made under Part 2 of CAA 2001 in respect of—

    (*a*) expenditure incurred on the provision of plant or machinery for leasing in the course of a trade, or

    (*b*) expenditure incurred on the provision for the purposes of a trade of an asset which is not to be leased but which is fee-producing.

(3) An asset is fee-producing if payments in the nature of—

    (*a*) royalties, or

    (*b*) licence fees,

are to arise from rights granted by the individual in connection with the asset.

(4) To meet the time commitment test conditions A and B must be met.

(5) Condition A is that the individual must carry on the trade for a continuous period of at least 6 months beginning or ending in the basis period for the tax year in which the loss was made ("the loss-making basis period").

(6) Condition B is that substantially the whole of the individual's time must be given to carrying on the trade—

    (*a*) for a continuous period of at least 6 months beginning or ending in the loss-making basis period (if the individual starts or permanently ceases to carry on the trade in the tax year (or does both)), or

    (*b*) throughout the loss-making basis period (in any other case).

Commentary—*Simon's Taxes* **B5.417**.

HMRC Manuals—Business Leasing Manual BLM01010 (anti-avoidance rules: sideways loss relief).

Business Income Manual BIM85730 (inclusion of capital allowances).

76 First-year allowances [and annual investment allowances][1]: introduction

Sideways relief is not available to an individual for so much of a loss as derives from [an annual investment allowance or][1] a first-year allowance under Part 2 of CAA 2001 if either section 77 or 78 applies.

Commentary—*Simon's Taxes* **B3.340C**.

HMRC Manuals—Business Income Manual BIM85750 (first year allowances and annual investment allowances).

Amendments—[1] Words inserted by FA 2008 s 74, Sch 24 paras 20, 21 with effect in relation to expenditure incurred on or after the relevant date: see FA 2008 Sch 24 para 23. The relevant date is—

    (a) for corporation tax purposes, 1 April 2008, and

    (b) for income tax purposes, 6 April 2008.

77 First-year allowances: partnerships with companies

(1) This section applies if—

    (*a*) the first-year allowance is in respect of expenditure incurred at any time on the provision of plant or machinery for leasing in the course of a qualifying activity, and

    (*b*) either the qualifying activity was at that time carried on by the individual in partnership with a company or arrangements have been made with a view to the activity being so carried on.

(2) It does not matter—

    (*a*) if the firm includes other partners, or

    (*b*) when the arrangements were made.

(3) For the purposes of this section—

(*a*) letting a ship on charter is treated as leasing the ship, and

(*b*) references to making arrangements include effecting schemes.

Commentary—*Simon's Taxes* **E1.1006, B5.417**.

HMRC Manuals—Business Income Manual BIM85750 (first year allowances and annual investment allowances).

78 First-year allowances [and annual investment allowances]¹: arrangements to reduce tax liabilities

(1) This section applies if—

(*a*) the [annual investment allowance or]¹ first-year allowance is made in connection with a relevant qualifying activity or a relevant asset (see subsections (2) and (3)), and

(*b*) arrangements within subsection (4) have been made.

(2) A qualifying activity is a relevant one if—

(*a*) at the time when the expenditure was incurred, the activity was carried on by the individual as a partner in a firm, or

(*b*) at a later time, it has been carried on by the individual as a partner in a firm or transferred to a person connected with the individual.

(3) An asset is a relevant one if, after the time when the expenditure was incurred, the asset was transferred by the individual—

(*a*) to a person connected with the individual, or

(*b*) to a person at a price lower than its market value.

(4) Arrangements are within this subsection if as a result of them—

(*a*) the sole benefit, or

(*b*) the main benefit,

that might be expected to arise to the individual from the transaction under which the expenditure was incurred is the obtaining of a reduction in tax liability by means of sideways relief.

(5) It does not matter when the arrangements were made.

(6) References to making arrangements include effecting schemes.

Commentary—*Simon's Taxes* **B3.340C, E1.1006, B5.417**.

HMRC Manuals—Business Income Manual BIM85750 (first year allowances and annual investment allowances).

Amendments—¹ Words in heading and in sub-s (1)(*a*) inserted by FA 2008 s 74, Sch 24 paras 20, 22 with effect in relation to expenditure incurred on or after the relevant date: see FA 2008 Sch 24 para 23. The relevant date is: (a) for corporation tax purposes, 1 April 2008, and (b) for income tax purposes, 6 April 2008.

79 Capital allowances restrictions: supplementary

(1) If relief is given in a case to which section 75 or 76 applies, the relief is withdrawn by the making of an assessment to income tax under this section.

(2) Expressions which are used—

(*a*) in any of sections 75 to 78, and

(*b*) in Part 2 of CAA 2001,

have the same meaning in those sections as in that Part.

Commentary—*Simon's Taxes* **B3.340C, E1.1006, B5.417**.

HMRC Manuals—Business Income Manual BIM85750 (first year allowances and annual investment allowances).

Restriction on sideways relief for specific trades

80 Ring fence income

(1) This section applies if—

(*a*) a person has income arising from oil extraction activities or oil rights ("ring fence income"), and

(*b*) the person makes a loss in any trade.

(2) Sideways relief for the loss is not to be given against the person's ring fence income except so far as the loss arises from oil extraction activities or oil rights.

(3) "Oil extraction activities" and "oil rights" have the [meaning given by sections 225A and 225B of ITTOIA 2005]¹.

Commentary—*Simon's Taxes* **E1.1006, D7.902**.

HMRC Manuals—Business Income Manual BIM85760 (income not eligible/losses not eligible).

Oil Taxation Manual OT21003 (definition of oil extraction activities).

OT21004 (definition of oil rights).

Amendments—¹ In sub-s (3), words substituted, by TIOPA 2010 s 501, Sch 8 paras 192, 193. TIOPA 2010 has effect for corporation tax purposes for accounting periods ending on or after 1 April 2010, for income and capital gains tax purposes for the tax year 2010–11 and subsequent tax years, and for petroleum revenue tax purposes for chargeable periods beginning on or after 1 July 2010.

82 Exploitation of films

In the case of a trade carried on by an individual which consists of or includes the exploitation of films—

(*a*) see [section 115]¹ for a restriction on sideways relief if the trade was carried on by the individual as a partner in a firm, and

(b) see section 796 for a charge to income tax if the individual made a loss in the trade (whether carried on alone or as a partner in a firm) for which sideways relief is claimed.

Commentary—*Simon's Taxes* **E1.1006**.
Amendments—[1] Words substituted by FA 2007 s 26, Sch 4 para 6, 21 and deemed always to have had effect.

Carry-forward trade loss relief

83 Carry forward against subsequent trade profits

(1) A person may make a claim for carry-forward trade loss relief if—
    (a) the person has made a loss in a trade in a tax year, and
    (b) relief for the loss has not been fully given under this Chapter or any other provision of the Income Tax Acts or under section 261B of TCGA 1992 (use of trading loss as a CGT loss).

(2) The claim is for the part of the loss for which relief has not been given under any such provision ("the unrelieved loss") to be deducted in calculating the person's net income for subsequent tax years (see Step 2 of the calculation in section 23).

(3) But a deduction for that purpose is to be made only from profits of the trade.

(4) In calculating a person's net income for a tax year, deductions under this section from the profits of a trade are to be made before deductions of any other reliefs from those profits.

(5) This section applies to professions and vocations as it applies to trades (and section 84 is to be read accordingly).

(6) This section needs to be read with—
    (a) section 84 (how relief works),
    (b) section 85 (use of trade-related interest and dividends if trade profits insufficient),
    (c) section 86 (trade transferred to a company),
    (d) section 87 (ring fence trades),
    (e) section 88 (carry forward of certain interest as loss), and
    (f) sections 17(3) and 852(7) of ITTOIA 2005 (effect of becoming or ceasing to be UK resident).

Commentary—*Simon's Taxes* **B7.522, E1.1014, E5.625**.
HMRC Manuals—Business Income Manual BIM85060 (types of relief - carry forward of losses).
International Manual INTM165220 (losses - relief under ITA2007/S83).

84 How relief works

This section explains how the deductions are to be made.
The amount of the unrelieved loss to be deducted at any step is limited in accordance with section 25(4) and (5).
    Step 1 Deduct the unrelieved loss from the profits of the trade of the next tax year.
    Step 2 Deduct from the profits of the trade of the following tax year the amount of the unrelieved loss not previously deducted.
    Step 3 Continue to apply Step 2 in relation to the profits of the trade of subsequent tax years until all the unrelieved loss is deducted.

Commentary—*Simon's Taxes* **E1.1015**.
Derivation—TA 1988 s 385(1).

85 Use of trade-related interest and dividends if trade profits insufficient

(1) This section applies if carry-forward trade loss relief cannot be fully given in relation to the profits of a trade of a tax year because (apart from this section) there are no profits, or insufficient profits, of the trade of the tax year.

(2) For the purposes of the relief any interest or dividends for the tax year that relate to the trade are treated as profits of the trade of the tax year.

(3) Interest or dividends for the tax year relate to the trade if they—
    (a) arise in the tax year, and
    (b) would be brought into account in calculating the profits of the trade but for the fact that they have been subjected to tax under other provisions of the Income Tax Acts.

Commentary—*Simon's Taxes* **B7.504, B7.522, E1.1010**.
Derivation—TA 1988 s 385(4).
HMRC Manuals—Business Income Manual BIM40810 (how chargeable).

86 Trade transferred to a company

(1) This section applies if—
    (a) a trade is carried on by an individual otherwise than as a partner in a firm or by individuals in partnership,
    (b) the trade is transferred to a company,
    (c) the consideration for the transfer is wholly or mainly the allotment of shares to the individual or individuals, and
    (d) in the case of any individual to whom, or to whose nominee or nominees, shares are so allotted, the individual's total income for a relevant tax year includes income derived by the individual from the company.

(2) For the purposes of carry-forward trade loss relief, the income so derived is treated as—

(*a*) profits of the trade of the relevant tax year carried on by the individual, or

(*b*) if the trade was carried on by the individual in partnership, profits of the individual's notional trade of the relevant tax year.

(3) The tax year in which the transfer is made is a relevant one if—

(*a*) the individual is the beneficial owner of the shares allotted as mentioned above, and

(*b*) the company carries on the trade,

throughout the period beginning with the date of the transfer and ending with the next 5 April.

(4) Otherwise a tax year is a relevant one if—

(*a*) the individual is the beneficial owner of the shares allotted as mentioned above, and

(*b*) the company carries on the trade,

throughout the tax year.

(5) The income derived from the company may be by way of dividends on the shares or otherwise.

(6) This section applies to businesses which are not trades as it applies to trades.

Commentary—*Simon's Taxes* B7.504, B7.522, E1.1012.

HMRC Manuals—Business Income Manual BIM85060 (types of relief - carry forward of losses)

87 Ring fence trades

(1) This section applies if—

(*a*) a person makes a loss in a tax year carrying on oil-related activities (within the meaning of section 16 of ITTOIA 2005),

(*b*) those activities are treated under that section as a separate trade for the tax year or a subsequent tax year,

(*c*) the person makes profits in a subsequent tax year from other activities, and

(*d*) the other activities and the oil-related activities would, but for that section, together form a single trade.

(2) For the purposes of carry-forward trade loss relief for the loss, the person may treat profits from the other activities in a subsequent tax year as if they were profits of the separate trade (despite section 16 of ITTOIA 2005).

Commentary—*Simon's Taxes* D7.902.

Derivation—TA 1988 s 492(4).

88 Carry forward of certain interest as loss

(1) This section applies if—

(*a*) an individual pays interest in a tax year which is eligible for relief under section 383 (as a result of section 388 or 398),

(*b*) the interest is an expense incurred wholly and exclusively for the purposes of a trade carried on wholly or partly in the United Kingdom, and

(*c*) relief under section 383 cannot be fully given in respect of the interest because there is no income or insufficient income in the tax year.

(2) For the purposes of carry-forward trade loss relief, the amount for which relief has not been given may be carried forward to subsequent tax years as if it were a loss made in the trade.

(3) This section applies to professions and vocations as it applies to trades.

Commentary—*Simon's Taxes* B2.446, B2.436, E1.1010.

Derivation—TA 1988 s 390.

Terminal trade loss relief

89 Carry back of losses on a permanent cessation of a trade

(1) A person may make a claim for terminal trade loss relief if the person—

(*a*) permanently ceases to carry on a trade in a tax year ("the final tax year"), and

(*b*) makes a terminal loss in the trade (see section 90).

(2) The claim is for the total amount of terminal losses made in the trade by the person ("the relievable loss") to be deducted in calculating the person's net income for the final tax year and the 3 previous tax years (see Step 2 of the calculation in section 23).

(3) But a deduction for that purpose is to be made only from profits of the trade.

(4) This section applies to professions and vocations as it applies to trades (and sections 90 and 91 are to be read accordingly).

(5) This section needs to be read with—

(*a*) section 91 (how relief works),

(*b*) section 92 (use of trade-related interest and dividends if trade profits insufficient),

(*c*) section 93 (mineral extraction trade and carry back of balancing allowances), and

(*d*) section 94 (carry back of certain interest as loss).

Commentary—*Simon's Taxes* E1.1022, E5.624.

HMRC Manuals—Business Income Manual BIM85055 (types of relief - terminal loss relief).

BIM85070 (claims involving more than one year).

90 Losses that are "terminal losses"

(1) Each of the following is a terminal loss made in the trade—

(a) the loss (if any) made in the trade in the period beginning with the start of the final tax year and ending with the cessation, and

(b) the loss (if any) made in the trade in the period consisting of so much of the previous tax year as falls in the 12 months prior to the cessation.

(2) The profit or loss of a period mentioned in subsection (1)(a) or (b) (a "terminal loss period") is determined by reference to the profits or losses of periods of account of the trade (calculated for income tax purposes).

(3) If no period of account coincides with a terminal loss period, any of the following steps may be taken if they are necessary in order to arrive at the profit or loss of the terminal loss period—

(a) apportioning the profit or loss of a period of account between the part of the period that falls in the terminal loss period and the part that does not, and

(b) adding the profit or loss of a period of account (or part of a period) to profits or losses of other periods of account (or parts).

(4) Section 203(3) and (4) of ITTOIA 2005 applies for the purposes of subsection (3) as it applies for the purposes of section 203(2) of that Act.

(5) If as a result of section 205 of ITTOIA 2005 a deduction is allowed for overlap profit in calculating the profits of the trade of the final tax year, that deduction is to be made in calculating the loss (if any) mentioned in subsection (1)(a) (and is therefore irrelevant for the purposes of subsection (1)(b)).

(6) In the case of a notional trade carried on by a partner in a firm—

(a) the periods of account of the notional trade are taken to be the periods of account of the actual trade, and

(b) the references in subsections (2) and (3) to the profits or losses of periods of account of the trade are to the partner's share of the profits or losses of the actual trade determined in accordance with sections 849 and 850 of ITTOIA 2005.

Commentary—*Simon's Taxes* **E1.1022**.
HMRC Manuals—Business Income Manual BIM85055 (types of relief - terminal loss relief).

91 How relief works

This section explains how the deductions are to be made.

The amount of the relievable loss to be deducted at any step is limited in accordance with section 25(4) and (5).

Step 1 Deduct the relievable loss from the profits of the trade of the final tax year.

Step 2 Deduct any part of the relievable loss not deducted at Step 1 from the profits of the trade of the previous tax year.

Step 3 Deduct any part of the relievable loss not deducted at Step 1 or 2 from the profits of the trade of the tax year before the previous one.

Step 4 Deduct any part of the relievable loss not deducted at Step 1, 2 or 3 from the profits of the trade of the tax year before that one.

Other claims

If the relievable loss has not been deducted in full at Steps 1 to 4, the person may use the part not so deducted in giving effect to any other relief under this Chapter (depending on the terms of the relief).

Commentary—*Simon's Taxes* **E1.1022**.
Derivation—TA 1988 s 388(3).

92 Use of trade-related interest and dividends if trade profits insufficient

(1) This section applies if terminal trade loss relief cannot be fully given in relation to the profits of a trade of a tax year because (apart from this section) there are no profits, or insufficient profits, of the trade of the tax year.

(2) For the purposes of the relief any interest or dividends for the tax year that relate to the trade are treated as profits of the trade of the tax year.

(3) Interest or dividends for the tax year relate to the trade if they—

(a) arise in the tax year, and

(b) would be brought into account in calculating the profits of the trade but for the fact that they have been subjected to tax under other provisions of the Income Tax Acts.

Commentary—*Simon's Taxes* **E1.1022**.
Derivation—TA 1988 s 388(4).
HMRC Manuals—Business Income Manual BIM40800 (interest and dividends: contents).

93 Mineral extraction trade and carry back of balancing allowances

(1) This section applies if—

(a) a person permanently ceases to carry on a mineral extraction trade, and

(b) the person makes a claim for terminal trade loss relief and a claim in respect of a balancing allowance under section 355 of CAA 2001.

(2) Terminal trade loss relief must be given before relief under section 355 of CAA 2001.

(3) In giving effect to the terminal trade loss relief, the balancing allowance is to be ignored.

(4) "Mineral extraction trade" has the same meaning as in Part 5 of CAA 2001 (see section 394 of that Act).

Commentary—*Simon's Taxes* **E1.1022**.
Derivation—TA 1988 s 389(2).
HMRC Manuals—Capital Allowances Manual CA50470 (MEA: balancing allowances: disposals and part disposals).

94 Carry back of certain interest as loss

(1) This section applies if—

    (a) an individual pays interest in a tax year which is eligible for relief under section 383 (as a result of section 388 or 398),

    (b) the interest is an expense incurred wholly and exclusively for the purposes of a trade carried on wholly or partly in the United Kingdom, and

    (c) relief under section 383 cannot be fully given in respect of the interest because there is no income or insufficient income in the tax year.

(2) For the purposes of terminal trade loss relief, the amount for which relief has not been given may be treated as a loss made in the trade at the date of payment.

(3) This section applies to professions and vocations as it applies to trades.

Commentary—*Simon's Taxes* **E1.1022**.
Derivation—TA 1988 s 390.

Wholly foreign trades

95 Foreign trades etc: reliefs only against foreign income

(1) This section applies if a person—

    (a) carries on a trade, profession or vocation wholly outside the United Kingdom, and

    (b) makes a loss in the trade, profession or vocation.

(2) In that case—

    (a) sideways relief for the loss is available only against the person's qualifying foreign income,

    (b) trade income relief for the loss is available only against the person's qualifying foreign trade income, and

    (c) section 261B of TCGA 1992 (use of trading loss as a CGT loss) does not apply in relation to the loss.

(3) "Trade income relief" means—

    (a) carry-forward trade loss relief, or

    (b) terminal trade loss relief.

(4) "Qualifying foreign income" means—

    (a) qualifying foreign trade income, or

    (b) income falling within section 23, 355, 575, 613, 615, 631 or 635 of ITEPA 2003 (foreign employment or pension income).

(5) "Qualifying foreign trade income" means the profits of any trade, profession or vocation carried on wholly outside the United Kingdom.

(6) But "qualifying foreign income" and "qualifying foreign trade income" do not include any income which is charged to income tax in accordance with section 832 of ITTOIA 2005 (relevant foreign income charged on the remittance basis).

Commentary—*Simon's Taxes* **E1.1025**.
HMRC Manuals—Business Income Manual BIM85760 (trade losses - income/losses not eligible).

Post-cessation trade relief

96 Post-cessation trade relief

(1) A person may make a claim for post-cessation trade relief if, after permanently ceasing to carry on a trade—

    (a) the person makes a qualifying payment, or

    (b) a qualifying event occurs in relation to a debt owed to the person,

and the payment is made, or the event occurs, within 7 years of that cessation.

(2) If the claim is made in respect of a payment, the claim is for the payment to be deducted in calculating the person's net income for the tax year in which the payment is made (see Step 2 of the calculation in section 23).

(3) If the claim is made in respect of an event, the claim is for the appropriate amount of the debt to be deducted in calculating the person's net income for the relevant tax year (see Step 2 of the calculation in section 23).

(4) The claim must be made on or before the first anniversary of the normal self-assessment filing date for the tax year for which the deduction is to be made.

(5) If—

    (a) the person is a company within the charge to income tax under Chapter 2 of Part 2 of ITTOIA 2005 in respect of a trade, and

    (b) the company ceases at any time to be within that tax charge in respect of the trade,

the company is treated for the purposes of this section as permanently ceasing to carry on the trade at that time.

(6) This section applies to professions and vocations as it applies to trades (and sections 97 and 98 are to be read accordingly).

(7) This section needs to be read with—
- (*a*) section 97 (meaning of "qualifying payment"),
- (*b*) section 98 (meaning of "qualifying event" etc),
- [(*ba*) section 98A (denial of relief for tax-generated payments or events),][1]
- (*c*) section 99 (reduction of relief for unpaid trade expenses), and
- (*d*) section 100 (prohibition against double counting).

Commentary—*Simon's Taxes* **B2.810, B2.805, B2.809.**
Derivation—TA 1988 s 109A(1) and s 110(1A) and (1B).
HMRC Manuals—Business Income Manual BIM90100 (post-cessation trade relief).
Amendments—[1]   Sub-s (7)(*ba*) inserted by FA 2012 s 9(1), (2) with effect in relation to payments made on or after 12 January 2012, except where they are made pursuant to an unconditional obligation in a contract made before that date, or events which occur on or after that date. "An unconditional obligation" means an obligation which may not be varied or extinguished by the exercise of a right (whether under the contract or otherwise): see FA 2012 s 9(7). ITA 2007 s 98 applies for determining when an event occurs: see FA 2012 s 9(8).

97 Meaning of "qualifying payment"

(1) For the purposes of section 96 a person makes a "qualifying payment" after permanently ceasing to carry on a trade if the person makes a payment wholly and exclusively for any of purposes A to D.

(2) A payment is made for purpose A if it is made—
- (*a*) in remedying defective work done, goods supplied or services provided in the course of the trade, or
- (*b*) by way of damages (whether awarded or agreed) in respect of defective work done, goods supplied or services provided in the course of the trade.

(3) A payment is made for purpose B if it is made in meeting the expenses of legal or other professional services in connection with a claim (a "claim about defects") that—
- (*a*) work done in the course of the trade was defective,
- (*b*) goods supplied in the course of the trade were defective, or
- (*c*) services provided in the course of the trade were defective.

(4) A payment is made for purpose C if it is made in insuring—
- (*a*) against liabilities arising out of any claim about defects, or
- (*b*) against the liability to meet the expenses of legal or other professional services in connection with any claim about defects.

(5) A payment is made for purpose D if it is made for the purpose of collecting a debt which was brought into account in calculating the profits of the trade.

Commentary—*Simon's Taxes* **B2.809, B2.805.**
Derivation—TA 1988 s 109A(2).
HMRC Manuals—Business Income Manual BIM90110 (post-cessation trade relief: meaning of qualifying payment).

98 Meaning of "qualifying event" etc

(1) This section explains for the purposes of section 96 what is meant by—
- (*a*) a "qualifying event" occurring in relation to a debt owed to a person who has permanently ceased to carry on a trade, and
- (*b*) "the appropriate amount of the debt" to be deducted in calculating a person's net income for "the relevant tax year".

(2) A qualifying event occurs in relation to a debt owed to the person if—
- (*a*) an unpaid debt was brought into account in calculating the profits of the trade,
- (*b*) the person is entitled to the benefit of the debt, and
- (*c*) the debt is released (in whole or in part) as part of a statutory insolvency arrangement (within the meaning of Part 2 of ITTOIA 2005).

The event occurs when the debt is released.

(3) The appropriate amount of the debt to be deducted is—
- (*a*) the amount released, or
- (*b*) if the person was entitled to only part of the benefit of the debt, the corresponding part of the amount released.

(4) The relevant tax year is the tax year in which the debt is released.

(5) A qualifying event also occurs in relation to a debt owed to the person if—
- (*a*) an unpaid debt was brought into account in calculating the profits of the trade,
- (*b*) the person is entitled to the benefit of the debt, and
- (*c*) the debt proves to be bad.

The event occurs when the debt proves to be bad.

(6) The appropriate amount of the debt to be deducted is—
- (*a*) the amount of the debt, or
- (*b*) if the person was entitled to only part of the benefit of the debt, the corresponding part of the amount of the debt.

(7) The relevant tax year is the tax year specified in the claim.

(8) The person making the claim may specify—
- (*a*) the tax year in which the debt proves to be bad, or

(*b*) a subsequent tax year throughout which the debt remains bad (so long as the tax year begins within 7 years of the cessation),

but, if the person has previously made a claim specifying a tax year in respect of the debt, the person may not specify another tax year in respect of it.

Commentary—*Simon's Taxes* B2.809.

HMRC Manuals—Business Income Manual BIM90115 (post-cessation trade relief: meaning of qualifying event).

[98A Denial of relief for tax-generated payments or events

(1) Post-cessation trade relief is not available to a person in respect of a payment or an event which is made or occurs directly or indirectly in consequence of, or otherwise in connection with, relevant tax avoidance arrangements (and, accordingly, no section 261D claim may be made in respect of the payment or event).

(2) For this purpose "relevant tax avoidance arrangements" means arrangements—

(*a*) to which the person is a party, and

(*b*) the main purpose, or one of the main purposes, of which is the obtaining of a reduction in tax liability as a result of the availability of post-cessation trade relief (whether by making a claim for that relief or a section 261D claim).

(3) In this section—

(*a*) "arrangements" includes any agreement, understanding, scheme, transaction or series of transactions (whether or not legally enforceable), and

(*b*) "section 261D claim" means a claim under section 261D of TCGA 1992.][1]

Commentary—*Simon's Taxes* B2.809, B2.810, B6.213.

HMRC Manuals—Business Income Manual BIM90120 (post-cessation trade relief: targeted anti-avoidance provision).

Amendments—[1]   This section inserted by FA 2012 s 9(1), (3) with effect in relation to payments made on or after 12 January 2012, except where they are made pursuant to an unconditional obligation in a contract made before that date, or events which occur on or after that date. "An unconditional obligation" means an obligation which may not be varied or extinguished by the exercise of a right (whether under the contract or otherwise): see FA 2012 s 9(7). ITA 2007 s 98 applies for determining when an event occurs: see FA 2012 s 9(8).

99 Reduction of relief for unpaid trade expenses

(1) This section applies for the purposes of post-cessation trade relief in respect of a person's trade if a deduction was made in calculating the profits of the trade for an expense not actually paid (an "unpaid expense").

(2) The amount of the person's relief for a tax year is reduced (but not below nil) by—

(*a*) the total amount of unpaid expenses at the end of the tax year, or

(*b*) if the person carried on the trade as a partner in a firm, the person's share of the total amount of unpaid expenses at the end of the tax year.

(3) But any unpaid expense which is taken into account in reducing the amount of the person's relief for a tax year is left out of account in making reductions for subsequent tax years.

(4) If the person actually pays an amount in respect of an unpaid expense taken into account in reducing the amount of the person's relief, the person is treated as making a qualifying payment for the purposes of section 96.

(5) The amount of the qualifying payment is—

(*a*) the amount actually paid, or

(*b*) if less, the amount of the reduction.

(6) This section applies to professions and vocations as it applies to trades.

Commentary—*Simon's Taxes* B2.809.

Derivation—TA 1988 s 109A(5).

HMRC Manuals—Business Income Manual BIM90100 (reduction for unpaid expenses).

100 Prohibition against double counting

(1) Post-cessation trade relief is not available for an amount for which relief is given, or is available, under any other provision of the Income Tax Acts.

(2) For this purpose—

(*a*) relief available under section 254 of ITTOIA 2005 (allowable deductions against post-cessation receipts) is treated as given for other amounts before any amount for which post-cessation trade relief is available, and

(*b*) relief under that section is treated as available if it would have been available but for the fact that the post-cessation receipts (against which the deductions would have been allowed) are exempt under section 524 of this Act.

Commentary—*Simon's Taxes* B2.810.

Derivation—TA 1988 s 109A(6).

HMRC Manuals—Business Income Manual BIM90090 (reliefs for post-cessation expenses -no double counting).

101 Treating excess post-cessation trade relief as CGT loss

A person who cannot deduct all of an amount under a claim for post-cessation trade relief may be able to treat the unused part as an allowable loss for capital gains tax purposes: see sections 261D and 261E of TCGA 1992.

Commentary—*Simon's Taxes* **B2.810, C1.502**.
HMRC Manuals—Business Income Manual BIM90090 (overview of reliefs for post-cessation expenses).

CHAPTER 3

RESTRICTIONS ON TRADE LOSS RELIEF FOR CERTAIN PARTNERS

Introduction

102 Overview of Chapter

(1) This Chapter restricts the amount of relief that may be given for any loss made by an individual in a trade carried on by the individual as—

    (*a*) a limited partner in any tax year (see sections [103A, 103C to 105, 113A and 114][1]),

    (*b*) a member of a limited liability partnership (an "LLP") in any tax year (see sections [103C, 103D, 107 to 109, 113A and 114)][1], or

    (*c*) a non-active partner [(see sections 103B to 103D and 110 to 114)][1].

(2) This Chapter also restricts the amount of relief that may be given for any loss made by an individual in a trade carried on by the individual as a partner in a firm if the trade consists of or includes the exploitation of films (see [section 115][1]).

[(2A) This Chapter also provides for no relief to be given for a loss made by an individual in a trade carried on by the individual as a partner in a firm in certain cases where some or all of the loss is allocated to the individual rather than a person who is not an individual (see section 116A).][2]

(3) This Chapter needs to be read with sections 791 to 795 (income tax charge recovering excess relief for losses made by individuals carrying on a trade in partnership).

(4) See also—

    (*a*) sections 796 to 803 (income tax charge in relation to individuals claiming relief for film-related trading losses), and

    (*b*) sections 804 to 809 (income tax charge in relation to individuals carrying on a trade in partnership claiming relief for licence-related trading losses).

Amendments—[1]   Words in sub-ss (1), (2) substituted by FA 2007 s 26, Sch 4 paras 7, 21 and deemed always to have had effect.
[2]   Sub-s (2A) inserted by FA 2014 s 74, Sch 17 para 8(1), (2) with effect in relation to losses made in the tax year 2014–15 and subsequent tax years, subject to transitional provisions in respect of accounting periods straddling 6 April 2014 (FA 2014 Sch 17 para 14).

103 Meaning of "sideways relief", "capital gains relief" and "firm"

(1) For the purposes of this Chapter sideways relief is—

    (*a*) trade loss relief against general income (see sections 64 to 70), or

    (*b*) early trade losses relief (see sections 72 to 74).

(2) For the purposes of this Chapter—

    (*a*) capital gains relief is, in relation to a loss, the treatment of the loss as an allowable loss by virtue of section 261B of TCGA 1992 (use of trading loss as a CGT loss), and

    (*b*) capital gains relief is given for a loss when it is so treated.

(3) References in this Chapter to a firm are to be read in the same way as references to a firm in Part 9 of ITTOIA 2005 (which contains special provision about partnerships).

HMRC Manuals—Business Income Manual BIM82601 (partnerships: introduction).

[103A Meaning of "limited partner"

(1) In this Chapter "limited partner" means an individual who carries on a trade—

    (*a*) as a limited partner in a limited partnership registered under the Limited Partnerships Act 1907,

    (*b*) as a partner in a firm who in substance acts as a limited partner in relation to the trade (see subsection (2)), or

    (*c*) while the condition mentioned in subsection (3) is met in relation to the individual.

(2) An individual in substance acts as a limited partner in relation to a trade if the individual—

    (*a*) is not entitled to take part in the management of the trade, and

    (*b*) is entitled to have any liabilities (or those beyond a certain limit) for debts or obligations incurred for the purposes of the trade met or reimbursed by some other person.

(3) The condition referred to in subsection (1)(*c*) is that—

    (*a*) the individual carries on the trade jointly with other persons,

    (*b*) under the law of a territory outside the United Kingdom, the individual is not entitled to take part in the management of the trade, and

    (*c*) under that law, the individual is not liable beyond a certain limit for debts or obligations incurred for the purposes of the trade.

(4) In the case of an individual who is a limited partner as a result of subsection (1)(*c*), references in this Chapter to the individual's firm are to be read as references to the relationship between the individual and the other persons mentioned in subsection (3)(*a*).][1]

Commentary—*Simon's Taxes* **B7.106**.
Derivation—TA 1988 s 109A(6).

HMRC Manuals—Partnership Manual PM10600 (overview of types of partnership).
Business Income Manual BIM82101 (partnership: overview).
BIM82615 (limited partners: meaning).
Amendments—[1]   This section inserted by FA 2007 s 26, Sch 4 paras 8, 21 and deemed always to have had effect.

[103B Meaning of "non-active partner" etc

(1) For the purposes of this Chapter an individual carries on a trade as a non-active partner during a tax year if the individual—

    (a) carries on the trade as a partner in a firm at a time during the year,

    (b) does not carry on the trade as a limited partner at any time during the year, and

    (c) does not devote a significant amount of time to the trade in the relevant period for the year.

(2) For the purposes of this Chapter an individual devotes a significant amount of time to a trade in the relevant period for a tax year if, in that period, the individual spends an average of at least 10 hours a week personally engaged in activities [of the trade and those activities are carried on—

    (a) on a commercial basis, and

    (b) with a view to the realisation of profits as a result of the activities.][2]

(3) For this purpose "the relevant period" means the basis period for the tax year (unless the basis period is shorter than 6 months).

(4) If the basis period for the tax year is shorter than 6 months, "the relevant period" means—

    (a) the period of 6 months beginning with the date on which the individual first started to carry on the trade (if the basis period begins with that date), or

    (b) the period of 6 months ending with the date on which the individual permanently ceased to carry on the trade (if the basis period ends with that date).

(5) If—

    (a) any relief is given on the assumption that the individual devoted or will devote a significant amount of time to the trade in the relevant period for a tax year, but

    (b) the individual in fact failed or fails to do so,

the relief is withdrawn by the making of an assessment to income tax under this section.][1]

Commentary—*Simon's Taxes* B7.522.
HMRC Manuals—Business Income Manual BIM82640 (non-active partners in early tax years).
BIM82645 (non-active partners in early tax years: example).
BIM56510 (non active partners ; meaning).
Amendments—[1]   This section inserted by FA 2007 s 26, Sch 4 paras 8, 21 and deemed always to have had effect.
[2]   Words in sub-s (2) substituted by FA 2008 s 61 with effect in relation to relevant periods ending on or after 12 March 2008.

[Limit on amount of sideways relief and capital gains relief

103C Limit on reliefs in any tax year not to exceed cap for tax year

(1) This section applies if an individual carries on one or more trades—

    (a) as a non-active partner in a firm during a tax year, or

    (b) as a limited partner in a firm at a time in that tax year,

and the individual makes a loss in any of those trades (an "affected loss") in that tax year.

(2) There is a restriction on the amount of sideways relief and capital gains relief which (after applying the restrictions under the other provisions of this Chapter) may be given to the individual for any affected loss (but see subsections (6) and (7)).

(3) The restriction is that the total amount of the sideways relief and capital gains relief given to the individual for all the affected losses must not exceed the cap for that tax year.

(4) The cap for any tax year is £25,000.

(5) The Treasury may by order amend the sum for the time being specified in subsection (4).

(6) The restriction under this section does not apply to so much of any affected loss as derives from qualifying film expenditure (see section 103D).

(7) The restriction under this section does not affect the giving of sideways relief for a loss made in a trade against the profits of that trade.

(8) In this section "trade" does not include a trade which consists of the underwriting business of a member of Lloyd's (within the meaning of section 184 of FA 1993).][1]

Commentary—*Simon's Taxes* B7.522, E1.1007, B7.522.
HMRC Manuals—Llyod Manual LLM6090 (conversion: Scottish limited partnerships: restriction of loss relief).
Business Income Manual BIM82611 (calculation of limit of relief: £25,000 annual limit).
BIM82105 (restriction of relief for limited partners).
Amendments—[1]   This section, and the heading preceding it, inserted by FA 2007 s 26, Sch 4 para 1 with effect for any loss made by an individual in a trade in 2007–08 or any subsequent tax year.

[103D Meaning of "qualifying film expenditure"

(1) For the purposes of this Chapter expenditure is qualifying film expenditure if—

    (a) it is deducted under a relevant film provision for the purposes of the calculation required by section 849 of ITTOIA 2005 (calculation of firm's profits or losses), or

    (b) it is incidental expenditure which (although not deducted under a relevant film provision) is incurred in connection with the production of a film, or the acquisition of the original master version of a film, in relation to which expenditure is so deducted.

(2) Expenditure is incidental if it is on management, administration or obtaining finance.

(3) The extent to which expenditure is within subsection (1)(*b*) is determined on a just and reasonable basis.

(4) For the purposes of this Chapter the amount of any loss that derives from qualifying film expenditure is determined on a just and reasonable basis.

(5) In this section—

"the acquisition of the original master version of a film" has the same meaning as in Chapter 9 of Part 2 of ITTOIA 2005 (see sections 130 and 132 of that Act),

"film" is to be read in accordance with paragraph 1 of Schedule 1 to the Films Act 1985, and

"a relevant film provision" means any one of sections 137 to 140 of ITTOIA 2005 (relief for certified master versions of films).][1]

Commentary—*Simon's Taxes* **B7.505.**
HMRC Manuals—Business Income Manual BIM82610 (qualifying film expenditure : meaning).
BIM56510 (qualifying film expenditure).
Amendments—[1]   This section inserted by FA 2007 s 26, Sch 4 paras 9, 21 and deemed always to have had effect.

Limited partners

104 Restriction on reliefs for limited partners

(1) This section applies if—

(*a*) at a time in a tax year ("the relevant tax year") an individual carries on a trade ("the relevant trade") as a limited partner in a firm, and

(*b*) the individual makes a loss in the relevant trade in the relevant tax year.

(2) There is a restriction on the amount of relief within subsection (3) which may be given to the individual for the loss.

(3) The relief within this subsection is—

(*a*) sideways relief against the individual's income apart from profits of the relevant trade, and

(*b*) capital gains relief.

(4) The restriction is that—

(*a*) the sum of the amount of the relief given and the total amount of all other relevant relief given, less

(*b*) the total amount of recovered relief,

must not exceed the individual's contribution to the firm as at the end of the basis period for the relevant tax year (see section 105).

(5) "Relevant relief" means sideways relief or capital gains relief given to the individual for—

(*a*) a loss made in the relevant trade in a tax year at a time during which the individual carries on that trade as a limited partner, or

(*b*) a loss made in the relevant trade in an early tax year during which the individual carries on that trade as a non-active partner . . . [1].

(6) "The total amount of recovered relief" means the total amount of income treated as received by the individual under section 792 (recovery of excess relief) as a result of the application of that section in relation to claims for relief for losses made by the individual in the relevant trade.

(7) If the firm is carrying on, or has carried on, other trades apart from the relevant trade, for the purpose of determining the total amount of all other relevant relief and the total amount of recovered relief—

(*a*) apply subsection (5) in relation to each other trade as well as the relevant trade and then add the results together, and

(*b*) apply subsection (6) as if the reference to the relevant trade were a reference to the relevant trade or any of the other trades.

Commentary—*Simon's Taxes* **B7.522.**
HMRC Manuals—Llyod Manual LLM6090 (conversion: Scottish limited partnerships: restriction of loss relief).
Business Income Manual BIM82105 (restriction of relief for limited partners).
BIM82610 (calculation of limit of relief: partners' capital contributions).
Amendments—[1]   Words in sub-s (5) repealed by FA 2007 s 26, Sch 4 paras 10, 21 and deemed always to have had effect.

105 Meaning of "contribution to the firm"

(1) For the purposes of section 104 the individual's contribution to the firm is the sum of amounts A and B.

(2) Amount A is the amount which the individual has contributed to the firm as capital less so much of that amount (if any) as is within subsection (4).

(3) In particular, the individual's share of any profits of the firm is to be included in the amount which the individual has contributed to the firm as capital so far as that share has been added to the firm's capital.

(4) An amount of capital is within this subsection if it is an amount which—

(*a*) the individual has previously drawn out or received back,

(*b*) the individual is or may be entitled to draw out or receive back at any time when the individual is carrying on a trade as a limited partner in the firm, or

(*c*) the individual is or may be entitled to require another person to reimburse to the individual.

(5) In subsection (4) any reference to drawing out or receiving back an amount is to doing so directly or indirectly but does not include drawing out or receiving back an amount which, because of its being drawn out or received back, is chargeable to income tax as profits of a trade.

(6) Amount B is the amount of the individual's total share of profits within subsection (7) except so far as—

    (*a*) that share has been added to the firm's capital, or

    (*b*) the individual has received that share in money or money's worth.

(7) Profits are within this subsection if they are from the relevant trade.

(8) In determining the amount of the individual's total share of profits within subsection (7) ignore the individual's share of any losses from the relevant trade which would (apart from this subsection) reduce that amount.

(9) In subsections (3), (7) and (8) any reference to profits or losses are to profits or losses calculated in accordance with generally accepted accounting practice (before any adjustment required or authorised by law in calculating profits or losses for income tax purposes).

(10) If the firm is carrying on, or has carried on, other trades apart from the relevant trade, subsections (7) and (8) have effect as if references to the relevant trade were references to the relevant trade or any of the other trades.

(11) This section needs to be read with [section 113A and any regulations made under section 114 (exclusion of amounts]¹ in calculating the individual's contribution to the firm for the purposes of section 104).

Commentary—*Simon's Taxes* **B7.522**.

HMRC Manuals—Business Income Manual BIM82105 (calculation of limit of relief: corporate partners).

Amendments—¹ Words in sub-s (11) substituted by FA 2007 s 26, Sch 4 paras 11, 21 and deemed always to have had effect.

Members of LLPs

107 Restriction on reliefs for members of LLPs

(1) This section applies if—

    (*a*) an individual carries on a trade ("the relevant trade") as a member of an LLP at a time in a tax year, and

    (*b*) the individual makes a loss in the relevant trade in the tax year ("the relevant tax year").

(2) But if the relevant tax year is an early tax year during which the individual carries on the relevant trade as a non-active partner¹ . . . —

    (*a*) this section does not apply, and

    (*b*) section 110 applies instead.

(3) There is a restriction on the amount of relief within subsection (4) which may be given to the individual for the loss.

(4) The relief within this subsection is—

    (*a*) sideways relief against the individual's income apart from profits of the relevant trade, and

    (*b*) capital gains relief.

(5) The restriction is that—

    (*a*) the sum of the amount of the relief given and the total amount of all other relevant relief given, less

    (*b*) the total amount of recovered relief,

must not exceed the individual's contribution to the LLP as at the end of the basis period for the relevant tax year (see section 108).

(6) "Relevant relief" means sideways relief or capital gains relief given to the individual for—

    (*a*) a loss made in the relevant trade in a tax year at a time during which the individual carries on that trade as a member of an LLP, or

    (*b*) a loss made in the relevant trade in an early tax year during which the individual carries on that trade as a non-active partner.

(7) "The total amount of recovered relief" means the total amount of income treated as received by the individual under section 792 (recovery of excess relief) as a result of the application of that section in relation to claims for relief for losses made by the individual in the relevant trade.

(8) If the LLP is carrying on, or has carried on, other trades apart from the relevant trade, for the purpose of determining the total amount of all other relevant relief and the total amount of recovered relief—

    (*a*) apply subsection (6) in relation to each other trade as well as the relevant trade and then add the results together, and

    (*b*) apply subsection (7) as if the reference to the relevant trade were a reference to the relevant trade or any of the other trades.

Commentary—*Simon's Taxes* **B7.522, E5.625A**.

HMRC Manuals—Business Income Manual BIM82135 (LLP: restriction of relief for LLP members).

BIM82625 (partnerships - LLP members restrictions).

Amendments—¹ Words in sub-s (2) repealed by FA 2007 s 26, Sch 4 paras 10, 21 and deemed always to have had effect.

108 Meaning of "contribution to the LLP"

(1) For the purposes of section 107 the individual's contribution to the LLP at any time ("the relevant time") is the sum of amounts A and B.

(2) Amount A is the amount which the individual has contributed to the LLP as capital less so much of that amount (if any) as is within subsection (5).

(3) In particular, the individual's share of any profits of the LLP is to be included in the amount which the individual has contributed to the LLP as capital so far as that share has been added to the LLP's capital.

(4) In subsection (3) the reference to profits is to profits calculated in accordance with generally accepted accounting practice (before any adjustment required or authorised by law in calculating profits for income tax purposes).

(5) An amount of capital is within this subsection if it is an amount which—

    (*a*) the individual has previously drawn out or received back,

    (*b*) the individual draws out or receives back during the period of 5 years beginning with the relevant time,

    (*c*) the individual is or may be entitled to draw out or receive back at any time when the individual is a member of the LLP, or

    (*d*) the individual is or may be entitled to require another person to reimburse to the individual.

(6) In subsection (5) any reference to drawing out or receiving back an amount is to doing so directly or indirectly but does not include drawing out or receiving back an amount which, because of its being drawn out or received back, is chargeable to income tax as profits of a trade.

(7) Amount B is the amount of the individual's liability on a winding up of the LLP so far as that amount is not included in amount A.

(8) For the purposes of subsection (7) the amount of the individual's liability on a winding up of the LLP is the amount which—

    (*a*) the individual is liable to contribute to the assets of the LLP in the event of its being wound up, and

    (*b*) the individual remains liable to contribute for the period of at least 5 years beginning with the relevant time (or until the LLP is wound up, if that happens before the end of that period).

(9) This section needs to be read with [section 113A and any regulations made under section 114 (exclusion of amounts)][1] in calculating the individual's contribution to the LLP for the purposes of section 107).

Commentary—*Simon's Taxes* **B7.522**.
HMRC Manuals—Business Income Manual BIM82625 (LLP member's capital contribution).
Amendments—[1]   Words in sub-s (9) substituted by FA 2007 s 26, Sch 4 paras 11, 21 and deemed always to have had effect.

109 Unrelieved losses brought forward

(1) This section applies for the purpose of determining an individual's entitlement to sideways relief and capital gains relief if—

    (*a*) the individual carries on a trade as a member of an LLP at a time during a tax year ("the current tax year"), and

    (*b*) as a result of section 107, sideways relief or capital gains relief has not been given to the individual for amounts of loss made in the trade in previous tax years as a member of the LLP.

(2) So far as they are not excluded by subsection (3), the amounts of loss mentioned in subsection (1)(*b*) are treated as having been made in the current tax year.

(3) An amount of loss is excluded so far as—

    (*a*) as a result of this section, sideways relief or capital gains relief has been given to the individual for the amount for years prior to the current tax year or would have been so given had a claim been made, or

    (*b*) other than as a result of this section, relief under the Income Tax Acts has been given to the individual for the amount for years prior to the current tax year or for the current tax year.

Commentary—*Simon's Taxes* **B7.522**.
HMRC Manuals—Business Income Manual BIM82625 (LLP members : losses).
BIM82635 (partnerships - LLP members: unrelieved amounts).

Non-active members of LLPs or other partnerships (apart from limited partnerships)

110 Restriction on reliefs for non-active partners in early tax years

(1) This section applies if—

    (*a*) an individual carries on a trade ("the relevant trade") as a non-active partner in a firm during an early tax year . . . [1], and

    (*b*) the individual makes a loss in the relevant trade in that tax year ("the relevant tax year").

(2) There is a restriction on the amount of relief within subsection (3) which may be given to the individual for the loss.

(3) The relief within this subsection is—

    (*a*) sideways relief against the individual's income apart from profits of the relevant trade, and

    (*b*) capital gains relief.

ITA 2007

(4) The restriction is that—

(a) the sum of the amount of the relief given and the total amount of all other relevant relief given, less

(b) the total amount of recovered relief,

must not exceed the individual's contribution to the firm as at the end of the basis period for the relevant tax year (see section 111).

(5) "Relevant relief" means sideways relief or capital gains relief given to the individual for—

(a) a loss made in the relevant trade in a tax year at a time during which the individual carries on that trade as a limited partner or as a member of an LLP, or

(b) a loss made in the relevant trade in an early tax year during which the individual carries on that trade as a non-active partner.

(6) "The total amount of recovered relief" means the total amount of income treated as received by the individual under section 792 (recovery of excess relief) as a result of the application of that section in relation to claims for relief for losses made by the individual in the relevant trade.

(7) If the firm is carrying on, or has carried on, other trades apart from the relevant trade, for the purpose of determining the total amount of all other relevant relief and the total amount of recovered relief—

(a) apply subsection (5) in relation to each other trade as well as the relevant trade and then add the results together, and

(b) apply subsection (6) as if the reference to the relevant trade were a reference to the relevant trade or any of the other trades.

(8) In this section "trade" does not include a trade which consists of the underwriting business of a member of Lloyd's (within the meaning of section 184 of FA 1993).

Commentary—*Simon's Taxes* **B7.522, B7.522, B7.522**.

HMRC Manuals—Business Income Manual BIM82640 (non-active partners in early tax years).

BIM82645 (non-active partners in early tax years: example).

Amendments—[1]   Words in sub-s (1)(a) repealed by FA 2007 s 26, Sch 4 paras 10, 21 and deemed always to have had effect.

111 Meaning of "contribution to the firm"

(1) For the purposes of section 110 the individual's contribution to the firm at any time ("the relevant time") is the sum of amount A and amount B and, if there is a winding up of the firm, amount C.

(2) Amount A is the amount which the individual has contributed to the firm as capital less so much of that amount (if any) as is within subsection (4).

(3) In particular, the individual's share of any profits of the firm is to be included in the amount which the individual has contributed to the firm as capital so far as that share has been added to the firm's capital.

(4) An amount of capital is within this subsection if it is an amount which—

(a) the individual has previously drawn out or received back,

(b) the individual draws out or receives back during the period of 5 years beginning with the relevant time,

(c) the individual is or may be entitled to draw out or receive back at any time when the individual is carrying on a trade as a partner in the firm, or

(d) the individual is or may be entitled to require another person to reimburse to the individual.

(5) In subsection (4) any reference to drawing out or receiving back an amount is to doing so directly or indirectly but does not include drawing out or receiving back an amount which, because of its being drawn out or received back, is chargeable to income tax as profits of a trade.

(6) Amount B is the amount of the individual's total share of profits within subsection (7) except so far as—

(a) that share has been added to the firm's capital, or

(b) the individual has received that share in money or money's worth.

(7) Profits are within this subsection if they are from the relevant trade.

(8) In determining the amount of the individual's total share of profits within subsection (7) ignore the individual's share of any losses from the relevant trade which would (apart from this subsection) reduce that amount.

(9) In subsections (3), (7) and (8) any reference to profits or losses are to profits or losses calculated in accordance with generally accepted accounting practice (before any adjustment required or authorised by law in calculating profits or losses for income tax purposes).

(10) If the firm is carrying on, or has carried on, other trades apart from the relevant trade, subsections (7) and (8) have effect as if references to the relevant trade were references to the relevant trade or any of the other trades.

Subsection (8) of section 110 applies for the purposes of this subsection as it applies for the purposes of that section.

(11) Amount C is the amount which the individual has contributed to the assets of the firm on its winding up so far as it is not included in amount A or B.

(12) This section needs to be read with [section 113A and any regulations made under section 114 (exclusion of amounts]¹ in calculating the individual's contribution to the firm for the purposes of section 110).

Commentary—*Simon's Taxes* **B7.522**.
HMRC Manuals—Business Income Manual BIM82135 (capital contribution: LLP).
Amendments—¹   Words in sub-s (12) substituted by FA 2007 s 26, Sch 4 paras 11, 21 and deemed always to have had effect.

112 [Meaning of "early tax year"]¹

(1)–(5) . . .   ¹

(6) In this Chapter "early tax year" means, in relation to an individual carrying on a trade—

    (*a*) the tax year in which the individual first started to carry on the trade, or

    (*b*) one of the next 3 tax years.

Commentary—*Simon's Taxes* **B7.522**.
HMRC Manuals—Business Income Manual BIM82640 (non-active partners in early tax years).
Amendments—¹   Sub-ss (1)–(5) repealed, and heading amended, by FA 2007 ss 26, 114, Sch 4 paras 13, 21 and Sch 27 Pt 2(1) and deemed always to have had effect.

113 Unrelieved losses brought forward

(1) This section applies for the purpose of determining an individual's entitlement to sideways relief and capital gains relief in relation to a trade if—

    (*a*) at a time during a tax year ("the current tax year") the individual carries on the trade as a partner in a firm or makes a contribution to the assets of a firm within subsection (2) on the firm's winding up, and

    (*b*) as a result of section 110, sideways relief or capital gains relief has not been given to the individual for amounts of loss made in the trade in previous tax years.

(2) A firm is within this subsection if the individual has carried on the trade as a partner in the firm.

(3) So far as they are not excluded by subsection (4), the amounts of loss mentioned in subsection (1)(*b*) are treated as having been made in the current tax year.

(4) An amount of loss is excluded so far as—

    (*a*) as a result of this section, sideways relief or capital gains relief has been given to the individual for the amount for years prior to the current tax year or would have been so given had a claim been made, or

    (*b*) other than as a result of this section, relief under the Income Tax Acts has been given to the individual for the amount for years prior to the current tax year or for the current tax year.

(5) For the purpose of applying sections 107 and 110 in relation to the amounts of loss treated by this section as having been made in the current tax year—

    (*a*) the individual is treated as having carried on the trade during the current tax year as a non-active partner in the firm, and

    (*b*) the current tax year is treated as if it were an early tax year in relation to the individual's carrying on of the trade.

(6) Subsection (7) applies if the individual—

    (*a*) made a contribution in the current tax year to the assets of the firm on its winding up, but

    (*b*) did not carry on the trade as a partner in the firm in the current tax year.

(7) If this subsection applies—

    (*a*) the restrictions under sections 66 and 74(1) do not apply in relation to the amounts of loss treated by this section as having been made in the current tax year, and

    (*b*) in the application of this Chapter in relation to those amounts of loss, section 110(4) has effect as if the words "the basis period for" were omitted.

(8) In subsection (1)(*b*) the reference to amounts of loss does not include amounts of loss which have been treated by section 109 as having been made in any previous tax year.

Commentary—*Simon's Taxes* **B7.522**.
HMRC Manuals—Business Income Manual BIM82650 (non-active partners in early tax years: unrelieved amounts).

[Exclusion of amounts in calculating contribution to the firm or LLP

113A Exclusion of amounts contributed to access relief

(1) An amount which an individual contributes to a firm as capital is to be excluded in calculating the individual's contribution to the firm for the purposes of section 104 or 110 if the contribution was made for a prohibited purpose (but see subsection (4)).

(2) If—

    (*a*) an individual carries on a trade as a member of an LLP at a time in a tax year,

    (*b*) the individual does not devote a significant amount of time to the trade in the relevant period for that year, and

    (*c*) the individual contributes an amount to the LLP as capital at any time in that year,

that amount is to be excluded in calculating the individual's contribution to the LLP for the purposes of section 107 if the contribution was made for a prohibited purpose (but see subsection (4)).

(3) For the purposes of this section a contribution is made for a prohibited purpose if the main purpose, or one of the main purposes, of making the contribution is the obtaining of a reduction in tax liability by means of sideways relief or capital gains relief.

(4) This section has no effect in relation to the application of any restriction under section 104, 107 or 110 to any loss that derives wholly from qualifying film expenditure.][1]

Commentary—*Simon's Taxes* **B7.522**.

HMRC Manuals—Business Income Manual BIM82615 (limited partners capital contributions).

Amendments—[1]   This section, and the heading preceding it, inserted by FA 2007 s 26, Sch 4 para 2 with effect for any amount contributed to a firm or LLP as capital on or after 2 March 2007. For this purpose—

(a)   an amount of money is not to be taken as contributed as capital to a firm or LLP until the money is paid to the firm or LLP, and

(b)   a right or other asset is not to be taken as contributed as capital to a firm or LLP until it is transferred to the firm or LLP.

However, these amendments have no effect in relation to any amount contributed by an individual on or after 2 March 2007 if—

(a)   the amount is contributed pursuant to an obligation in a contract made before that date, and

(b)   the obligation may not be varied or extinguished by the exercise of any right conferred on the individual (whether or not under the contract).

[Power to exclude other amounts][1]

Amendments—[1]   Heading substituted by FA 2007 s 26, Sch 4 paras 14, 21 and deemed always to have had effect.

114 Exclusion of amounts in calculating contribution to the firm or LLP

(1) The Commissioners for Her Majesty's Revenue and Customs may by regulations provide that any amount of a specified description is to be excluded in calculating—

(a) the individual's contribution to the firm for the purposes of section 104 or 110, or

(b) the individual's contribution to the LLP for the purposes of section 107.

(2) "Specified" means specified in the regulations.

(3) The regulations may—

(a) make provision having retrospective effect,

(b) contain incidental, supplemental, consequential and transitional provision and savings, and

(c) make different provision for different cases or purposes.

(4) The provision which may be made as a result of subsection (3)(b) includes provision amending or repealing any provision of an Act passed before FA 2005.

(5) No regulations may be made under this section unless a draft of them has been laid before and approved by a resolution of the House of Commons.

Commentary—*Simon's Taxes* **B7.522**.

HMRC Manuals—Business Income Manual BIM82615 (limited partners).

BIM82610 (partners' capital contributions).

Restrictions for film trades carried on in partnership

115 Restrictions on reliefs for firms exploiting films

(1) This section applies if—

(a) an individual carries on a trade as a partner in a firm at a time during a tax year,

(b) the trade consists of or includes the exploitation of films,

(c) the individual makes a loss in the trade in the tax year ("the affected tax year"),

(d) the individual does not devote a significant amount of time to the trade in the relevant period for the affected tax year . . .[1],

(e) the affected tax year is the one in which the individual first started to carry on the trade or is one of the next 3 tax years, and

(f) a relevant agreement existed at a time during the affected tax year which guaranteed the individual an amount of income (see subsections (5) to (9)).

(2) Sideways relief for the loss is not available to the individual, except against any of the individual's income which consists of profits of the trade.

(3) Capital gains relief for the loss is not available to the individual.

[(4) The restrictions under this section do not apply to so much of the loss (if any) as derives from qualifying film expenditure.][2]

(5) An agreement is relevant if—

(a) it is an agreement made with a view to the individual's carrying on the trade,

(b) it is an agreement made in the course of the individual's carrying it on, or

(c) it is related to an agreement falling within paragraph (a) or (b).

(6) An agreement is relevant whether or not the individual is or may be required under the agreement to contribute an amount to the trade.

(7) Agreements are related to one another if they are entered into under the same arrangement (regardless of when either agreement is entered into).

(8) A relevant agreement guarantees the individual an amount of income if it (or any part of it) is designed to secure the receipt by the individual of that amount (or at least that amount) of income.

(9) It does not matter when the amount of income is (or is to be) received.

(10) In this section "film" is to be read in accordance with paragraph 1 of Schedule 1 to the Films Act 1985 (c 21).

Commentary—*Simon's Taxes* **B7.505, B5.508, B5.505**.
HMRC Manuals—Business Income Manual BIM56510 (guaranteed income schemes).
Amendments—[1]   Words in sub-s (1)(*d*) repealed by FA 2007 s 26, Sch 4 paras 10, 21 and deemed always to have had effect.
[2]   Sub-s (4) substituted by FA 2007 s 26, Sch 4 paras 15, 21 and deemed always to have had effect.

[Partnerships with mixed membership etc

116A   Excess loss allocation to partners who are individuals
(1) Subsection (2) applies if—
    (*a*)   in a tax year, an individual ("A") makes a loss in a trade as a partner in a firm, and
    (*b*)   A's loss arises, wholly or partly—
        (i)   directly or indirectly in consequence of, or
        (ii)   otherwise in connection with,
    relevant tax avoidance arrangements.
(2) No relevant loss relief may be given to A for A's loss.
(3) In subsection (1)(*b*) "relevant tax avoidance arrangements" means arrangements—
    (*a*)   to which A is party, and
    (*b*)   the main purpose, or one of the main purposes, of which is to secure that losses of a trade are allocated, or otherwise arise, in whole or in part to A, rather than a person who is not an individual, with a view to A obtaining relevant loss relief.
(4) In subsection (3)(*b*) references to A include references to A and other individuals.
(5) For the purposes of subsection (3)(*b*) it does not matter if the person who is not an individual is not a partner in the firm or is unknown or does not exist.
(6) In this section—
    "arrangements" includes any agreement, understanding, scheme, transaction or series of transactions (whether or not legally enforceable), and
    "relevant loss relief" means—
        (*a*)   sideways relief,
        (*b*)   relief under section 83 (carry-forward trade loss relief),
        (*c*)   relief under section 89 (terminal trade loss relief), or
        (*d*)   capital gains relief.
(7) This section applies to professions as it applies to trades.][1]

HMRC Manuals—Business Income Manual BIM82950 (excess loss allocation).
BIM82955 (excess loss allocation: When do the restrictions apply?).
BIM82960 (excess loss allocation: the effect of the restrictions with example).
Amendments—[1]   Section 116A and preceding crosshead inserted by FA 2014 s 74, Sch 17 para 8(1), (3) with effect in relation to losses made in the tax year 2014–15 and subsequent tax years, subject to transitional provisions in respect of accounting periods straddling 6 April 2014 (FA 2014 Sch 17 para 14). This section does not apply in relation to the loss so far as it is apportioned to the part of the straddling period falling before 6 April 2014 (FA 2014 Sch 17 para 14(4)).

CHAPTER 4

LOSSES FROM PROPERTY BUSINESSES
Introduction

117   Overview of Chapter
(1) This Chapter—
    (*a*)   provides for losses made in a UK property business or overseas property business in a tax year to be carried forward for deduction from profits in subsequent tax years (see sections 118 and 119),
    (*b*)   provides in limited circumstances for relief against general income for losses made in a UK property business or overseas property business (see sections 120 to 124), and
    (*c*)   provides for relief for certain post-cessation payments and events in connection with a UK property business (see section 125).
(2) This Chapter also makes provision for a UK property business which consists of, or so far as it includes, the commercial letting of furnished holiday accommodation to be treated as a trade for the purposes of this Part (see section 127).
[(2A) This Chapter also makes provision for an overseas property business which consists of, or so far as it includes, the commercial letting of furnished holiday accommodation in one or more EEA states to be treated as a trade for the purposes of this Part (see section 127ZA).][2]
[(3) This Chapter also contains provision restricting relief under this Chapter (see [sections 127A [to 127C][4]][3]).][1]

Commentary—*Simon's Taxes* **B6.203**.
HMRC Manuals—Property Income Manual PIM4205 (losses: overview).
PIM4210(carry forward against the same rental business only).

Amendments—[1]   Sub-s (3) inserted by FA 2010 s 24(1), (2) with effect in relation to a loss if it arises directly or indirectly in consequence of, or otherwise in connection with—

    (a)   arrangements which are entered into on or after 24 March 2010; or

    (b)   any transaction forming part of arrangements which is entered into on or after that date.

This amendment does not have effect where the arrangements are, or any such transaction is, entered into pursuant to an unconditional obligation in a contract made before 24 March 2010; see FA 2010 s 25(6).

[2]   Sub-s (2A) inserted by FA 2011 s 52, Sch 14 para 3(1), (2) with effect in relation to the tax year 2011–12 and subsequent tax years.

[3]   In sub-s (3) words substituted by FA 2012 s 10(1), (2) with effect in relation to expenses arising directly or indirectly in consequence of, or otherwise in connection with—

    (a)   arrangements entered into on or after 13 March 2012; or

    (b)   any transaction forming part of arrangements entered into on or after that date.

This amendment does not have effect where the arrangements are, or any such transaction is, entered into pursuant to an unconditional obligation in a contract made before that date: see FA 2012 s 10(6). "An unconditional obligation" means an obligation which may not be varied or extinguished by the exercise of a right (whether under the contract or otherwise): see FA 2012 s 10(7).

[4]   In sub-s (3), words substituted for words "and 127B" by FA 2014 s 74, Sch 17 para 9(1), (2) with effect in relation to losses made in the tax year 2014–15 and subsequent tax years, subject to transitional provisions in respect of accounting periods straddling 6 April 2014 (FA 2014 Sch 17 para 14).

Carry-forward property loss relief

118 Carry forward against subsequent property business profits

(1) Relief is given to a person under this section if the person—

    (a) carries on a UK property business or overseas property business (alone or in partnership) in a tax year, and

    (b) makes a loss in the business in the tax year.

(2) The relief is given by deducting the loss in calculating the person's net income for subsequent tax years (see Step 2 of the calculation in section 23).

(3) But a deduction for that purpose is to be made only from profits of the business.

(4) In calculating a person's net income for a tax year, deductions under this section from the profits of a business are to be made before deductions of any other reliefs from those profits.

(5) No relief is to be given under this section so far as relief for the loss is given under section 120.

(6) This section needs to be read with section 119 (how relief works).

Commentary—*Simon's Taxes* **B6.203**.

HMRC Manuals—Property Income Manual PIM4210 (losses: set against future profits (IT)).

119 How relief works

This section explains how the deductions are to be made.

The amount of the loss to be deducted at any step is limited in accordance with section 25(4) and (5).

    Step 1 Deduct the loss from the profits of the business for the next tax year.

    Step 2 Deduct from the profits of the business for the following tax year the amount of the loss not previously deducted.

    Step 3 Continue to apply Step 2 in relation to the profits of the business for subsequent tax years until all the loss is deducted.

Commentary—*Simon's Taxes* **B6.203**.

HMRC Manuals—Property Income Manual PIM4210 (losses: set against future profits (IT)).

Property loss relief against general income

120 Deduction of property losses from general income

(1) A person may make a claim for property loss relief against general income if—

    (a) in a tax year ("the loss-making year") the person makes a loss in a UK property business or overseas property business (whether carried on alone or in partnership), and

    (b) the loss has a capital allowances connection or the business has a relevant agricultural connection.

(2) The claim is for the applicable amount of the loss to be deducted in calculating the person's net income—

    (a) for the loss-making year, or

    (b) for the next tax year.

  (See Step 2 of the calculation in section 23.)

(3) The claim must specify the tax year for which the deduction is to be made.

(4) But if the applicable amount of the loss is not deducted in full in giving effect to a claim for the specified tax year, the person may make a separate claim for property loss relief against general income for the other tax year.

(5) For this purpose "the other tax year" means the tax year which was not specified in the claim already made, but which could have been specified.

(6) This section needs to be read with—

    (a) section 121 (how relief works),

    (b) section 122 (meaning of "the applicable amount of the loss"), (*c*)   section 123 (meaning of "the loss has a capital allowances connection" and "the business has a relevant agricultural connection"), and

(*d*)   section 124 (supplementary).

[(7) See also section 127A (no relief for tax-generated losses attributable to annual investment allowance) [and section 127B (no relief for tax-generated agricultural expenses)][2] [and section 127BA (restriction of relief: cash basis)][3].][1]

Commentary—*Simon's Taxes* **B6.203**.
Derivation—TA 1988 ss 379A and 379B.
HMRC Manuals—Capital Allowances Manual CA11160 (sideways set-off of excess capital allowances - UK property business). Property Income Manual PIM4220 (losses: set against general income (IT)).
Amendments—[1]   Sub-s (7) inserted by FA 2010 s 24(1), (3) with effect in relation to a loss if it arises directly or indirectly in consequence of, or otherwise in connection with—
    (a)   arrangements which are entered into on or after 24 March 2010; or
    (b)   any transaction forming part of arrangements which is entered into on or after that date.
This amendment does not have effect where the arrangements are, or any such transaction is, entered into pursuant to an unconditional obligation in a contract made before 24 March 2010; see FA 2010 s 25(6).
[2]   Words inserted in sub-s (7) by FA 2012 s 10(1), (3) with effect in relation to expenses arising directly or indirectly in consequence of, or otherwise in connection with—
    (a)   arrangements entered into on or after 13 March 2012; or
    (b)   any transaction forming part of arrangements entered into on or after that date.
This amendment does not have effect where the arrangements are, or any such transaction is, entered into pursuant to an unconditional obligation in a contract made before that date: see FA 2012 s 10(6). "An unconditional obligation" means an obligation which may not be varied or extinguished by the exercise of a right (whether under the contract or otherwise): see FA 2012 s 10(7).
[3]   In sub-s (7), words inserted by F(No 2)A 2017 s 16, Sch 2 paras 60, 62(1), (2) with effect for the tax year 2017–18 and subsequent tax years, subject to transitional provisions in F(No 2)A 2017 Sch 2 para 64..

121   How relief works

(1) This subsection explains how the deductions are to be made.

The amount of the applicable amount of the loss to be deducted at any step is limited in accordance with [sections 24A and 25(4) and (5)][1].

> *Step 1* Deduct the applicable amount of the loss in calculating the person's net income for the specified tax year.
> *Step 2* This step applies if the applicable amount of the loss has not been deducted in full and the person makes a separate claim for the other tax year.

Deduct the part of the applicable amount of the loss not deducted at Step 1 in calculating the person's net income for the other tax year.

Other relief

If the applicable amount of the loss has not been deducted in full at Steps 1 and 2, relief is given under section 118 for the part not so deducted.

(2) There is a priority rule if—

(*a*)   a person makes a claim for property loss relief against general income ("the prior claim") in respect of a loss made in a tax year,

(*b*)   the prior claim specifies the next tax year as the one for which the deduction is to be made ("the relevant tax year"),

(*c*)   the person makes another claim for property loss relief against general income in respect of a loss made in the relevant tax year, and

(*d*)   that other claim also specifies the relevant tax year as the one for which the deduction is to be made.

(3) The rule is that priority is given to making deductions under the prior claim.

Commentary—*Simon's Taxes* **B6.203**.
Derivation—TA 1988 ss 379A and 379B.
HMRC Manuals—Property Income Manual PIM4220 (losses: relief).
Amendments—[1]   In sub-s (1) words substituted for words "section 25(4) and (5)" by FA 2013 s 16, Sch 3 para 2(1), (3)(*c*) with effect for the tax year 2013–14 and subsequent tax years, subject to transitional provisions in relation to loss relief claims for a tax year before 2013–14 in relation to losses made in 2013–14 or a later year (FA 2013 Sch 3 para 4).

122   Meaning of "the applicable amount of the loss"

(1) This section defines "the applicable amount of the loss" for the purposes of sections 120 and 121.

(2) "The applicable amount of the loss" is—

(*a*)   the amount of the loss, or

(*b*)   if less, the amount arising from the relevant connection (see subsections (3) to (5)).

(3) If—

(*a*)   the loss has a capital allowances connection, but

(*b*)   the business does not have a relevant agricultural connection,

the amount arising from the relevant connection is the amount ("the net capital allowances") by which the capital allowances exceed the charges under CAA 2001.

(4) If—

(*a*)   the business has a relevant agricultural connection, but

(b) the loss does not have a capital allowances connection,

the amount arising from the relevant connection is the amount of the allowable agricultural expenses.

(5) If—

    (a) the loss has a capital allowances connection, and

    (b) the business has a relevant agricultural connection,

the amount arising from the relevant connection is the sum of the net capital allowances and the amount of the allowable agricultural expenses.

Commentary—*Simon's Taxes* **B6.203**.
Derivation—TA 1988 ss 379A(4) and 379B.

123 Meaning of "the loss has a capital allowances connection" and "the business has a relevant agricultural connection"

(1) This section applies for the purposes of sections 120 and 122.

(2) The loss has a capital allowances connection if, in calculating the loss—

    (a) the amount of the capital allowances treated as expenses of the business, exceeds

    (b) the amount of any charges under CAA 2001 treated as receipts of the business.

[(2A) But any allowance under Part 2A of CAA 2001 (structures and buildings allowances) is to be ignored for the purposes of subsection (2).][1]

(3) The business has a relevant agricultural connection if—

    (a) the business is carried on in relation to land that consists of or includes an agricultural estate, and

    (b) allowable agricultural expenses deducted in calculating the loss are attributable to the estate.

(4) "Agricultural estate" means land—

    (a) which is managed as one estate, and

    (b) which consists of or includes land occupied wholly or mainly for purposes of husbandry.

(5) "Allowable agricultural expenses", in relation to an agricultural estate, means any expenses attributable to the estate which are deductible—

    (a) in respect of maintenance, repairs, insurance or management of the estate, and

    (b) otherwise than in respect of interest payable on a loan.

(6) But expenses attributable to the parts of the estate used wholly for purposes other than those of husbandry are to be ignored.

(7) And if parts of the estate are used both—

    (a) for purposes of husbandry, and

    (b) for other purposes,

the expenses in respect of those parts are to be reduced so far as those parts are used for the other purposes.

Commentary—*Simon's Taxes* **B6.203, B7.504, B7.522**.
Derivation—TA 1988 ss 379A and 379B.
HMRC Manuals—Property Income Manual PIM4220 (losses against other income: capital allowances and agricultural expenses).
Amendments—[1]   Sub-s (2A) inserted by the Capital Allowances (Structures and Buildings Allowances) Regulations, SI 2019/1087 reg 6 with effect from 5 July 2019. Note that the structures and buildings allowance in CAA 2001 Part 2A applies from 29 October 2018 (see CAA 2001 s 270AA).

124 Supplementary

(1) A claim for property loss relief against general income must be made on or before the first anniversary of the normal self-assessment filing date for the tax year specified in the claim.

(2) If a loss has previously been carried forward under section 118, the claim must be accompanied by the amendments of any return made under—

    (a) section 8 of TMA 1970, or

    (b) section 8A of TMA 1970,

that are necessary to give effect to section 118(5) (reducing the amount of the loss carried forward (if necessary, to nil)).

Commentary—*Simon's Taxes* **B6.203**.
Derivation—TA 1988 ss 379A(3) and 379B.

Post-cessation property relief

125 Post-cessation property relief

(1) A person may make a claim for post-cessation property relief if, after permanently ceasing to carry on a UK property business (whether carried on alone or in partnership)—

    (a) the person makes a qualifying payment, or

    (b) a qualifying event occurs in relation to a debt owed to the person, and the payment is made, or the event occurs, within 7 years of that cessation.

(2) If the claim is made in respect of a payment, the claim is for the payment to be deducted in calculating the person's net income for the tax year in which the payment is made (see Step 2 of the calculation in section 23).

(3) If the claim is made in respect of an event, the claim is for the appropriate amount of the debt to be deducted in calculating the person's net income for the relevant tax year (see Step 2 of the calculation in section 23).

(4) The claim must be made on or before the first anniversary of the normal self-assessment filing date for the tax year for which the deduction is to be made.

(5) If—

    (*a*) the person is a company within the charge to income tax under Chapter 3 of Part 3 of ITTOIA 2005 in respect of a UK property business, and

    (*b*) the company ceases at any time to be within that tax charge in respect of the business,

the company is treated for the purposes of this section as permanently ceasing to carry on the business at that time.

(6) The following provisions apply for the purposes of post-cessation property relief as they apply for the purposes of post-cessation trade relief (but as if any reference to a trade were to a UK property business)—

    (*a*) section 97 (meaning of "qualifying payment"),

    (*b*) section 98 (meaning of "qualifying event" etc),

    [(*ba*) section 98A (denial of relief for tax-generated payments or events),][1]

    (*c*) section 99 (reduction of relief for unpaid trade expenses), and

    (*d*) section 100 (prohibition against double counting).

Commentary—*Simon's Taxes* B6.213.
Derivation—TA 1988 ss 109A and 110.
HMRC Manuals—Property Income Manual PIM2510 (post-cessation receipts and expenditure).
Business Income Manual BIM90110 (post-cessation trade relief: meaning of qualifying payment).
BIM90115 (post-cessation trade relief: meaning of qualifying event).
Amendments—[1]   Sub-s (6)(*ba*) inserted by FA 2012 s 9(1), (4) with effect in relation to payments made on or after 13 March 2012, except where they are made pursuant to an unconditional obligation in a contract made before that date, or events which occur on or after that date. "An unconditional obligation" means an obligation which may not be varied or extinguished by the exercise of a right (whether under the contract or otherwise): see FA 2012 s 9(7). ITA 2007 s 98 applies for determining when an event occurs: see FA 2012 s 9(8).

126 Treating excess post-cessation property relief as CGT loss

A person who cannot deduct all of an amount under a claim for post-cessation property relief may be able to treat the unused part as an allowable loss for capital gains tax purposes: see sections 261D and 261E of TCGA 1992.

Commentary—*Simon's Taxes* B6.213.
HMRC Manuals—Business Income Manual BIM90130 (post-cessation receipts and expenses : set against chargeable gains).

Furnished holiday accommodation

127 UK furnished holiday lettings business treated as trade

(1) This section applies if, in a tax year, a person carries on a UK furnished holiday lettings business.

(2) "UK furnished holiday lettings business" means a UK property business which consists of, or so far as it includes, the commercial letting of furnished holiday accommodation (within the meaning of Chapter 6 of Part 3 of ITTOIA 2005).

(3) For the purposes of this Part (but as modified below) the person is treated instead as carrying on in the tax year a single trade—

    (*a*) which consists of every commercial letting of furnished holiday accommodation comprised in the person's UK furnished holiday lettings business, and

    (*b*) the profits of which are chargeable to income tax.

[(3A) Chapter 2 applies as if sections 64 to 82 and 89 to 95 were omitted.][1]

(7) If there is a letting of accommodation only part of which is furnished holiday accommodation, just and reasonable apportionments are to be made for the purpose of determining what is comprised in the trade treated as carried on.

Commentary—*Simon's Taxes* B6.401, E1.1434.
Derivation—TA 1988 s 504A.
HMRC Manuals—Property Income Manual PIM4105 (furnished holiday lettings :meaning and treatment).
Modifications—FA 2009 Sch 6 para 2(5) (for the purposes of the temporary carry-back of losses provisions in FA 2009 Sch 6, sub-ss (1)–(3) have effect as if FA 2009 Sch 6 para 1 were included in Part 4 of ITA 2007).
Amendments—[1]   Sub-s (3A) substituted for previous sub-ss (4)–(6) by FA 2011 s 52, Sch 14 para 3(1), (3) with effect in relation to the tax year 2011–12 and subsequent tax years.

[127ZA EEA furnished holiday lettings business treated as trade

(1) This section applies if, in a tax year, a person carries on an EEA furnished holiday lettings business.

(2) "EEA furnished holiday lettings business" means an overseas property business which consists of, or so far as it includes, the commercial letting of furnished holiday accommodation (within the meaning of Chapter 6 of Part 3 of ITTOIA 2005) in one or more EEA states.

(3) For the purposes of this Part (but as modified below) the person is treated instead as carrying on in the tax year a single trade—

    (*a*) which consists of every commercial letting of furnished holiday accommodation comprised in the person's EEA furnished holiday lettings business, and

    (*b*) the profits of which are chargeable to income tax.

(4) Chapter 2 applies as if sections 64 to 82 and 89 to 95 were omitted.

(5) If there is a letting of accommodation only part of which is furnished holiday accommodation, just and reasonable apportionments are to be made for the purpose of determining what is comprised in the trade treated as carried on.]¹

Commentary—*Simon's Taxes* **B6.401**.

Amendments—¹ This section inserted by FA 2011 s 52, Sch 14 para 3(1), (4) with effect in relation to the tax year 2011–12 and subsequent tax years.

[*Restrictions on relief*

127A No relief for tax-generated losses attributable to annual investment allowance

(1) This section applies if—

    (*a*) in a tax year a person makes a loss in a UK property business or overseas property business (whether carried on alone or in partnership),

    (*b*) the loss has a capital allowances connection (see section 123(2)), and

    (*c*) the loss arises directly or indirectly in consequence of, or otherwise in connection with, relevant tax avoidance arrangements.

(2) No property loss relief against general income may be given to the person for so much of the applicable amount of the loss as is attributable to an annual investment allowance.

(3) For the purposes of subsection (2), the applicable amount of the loss is to be treated as attributable to capital allowances before anything else and to an annual investment allowance before any other capital allowance.

(4) In subsection (1) "relevant tax avoidance arrangements" means arrangements—

    (*a*) to which the person is a party, and

    (*b*) the main purpose, or one of the main purposes, of which is being in a position to make use of an annual investment allowance in the obtaining of a reduction in tax liability by means of property loss relief against general income.

(5) In subsection (4) "arrangements" includes any agreement, understanding, scheme, transaction or series of transactions (whether or not legally enforceable).

(6) In this section "the applicable amount of the loss" has the meaning given by section 122.]¹

Commentary—*Simon's Taxes* **B6.203**.

Amendments—¹ This section and preceding cross-head inserted by FA 2010 s 25(1), (4) with effect in relation to a loss if it arises directly or indirectly in consequence of, or otherwise in connection with—

    (a)   arrangements which are entered into on or after 24 March 2010; or

    (b)   any transaction forming part of arrangements which is entered into on or after that date.

This amendment does not have effect where the arrangements are, or any such transaction is, entered into pursuant to an unconditional obligation in a contract made before 24 March 2010; see FA 2010 s 25(6).

[127B No relief for tax-generated agricultural expenses

(1) This section applies if—

    (*a*) in a tax year a person makes a loss in a UK property business or overseas property business (whether carried on alone or in partnership),

    (*b*) the business has a relevant agricultural connection for the purposes of section 120 (see section 123(3) to (7)), and

    (*c*) any allowable agricultural expenses deducted in calculating the loss arise directly or indirectly in consequence of, or otherwise in connection with, relevant tax avoidance arrangements.

(2) No property loss relief against general income may be given to the person for so much of the applicable amount of the loss as is attributable to expenses falling within subsection (1)(*c*).

(3) For the purposes of subsection (2), the applicable amount of the loss is to be treated as attributable to expenses falling within subsection (1)(*c*) before anything else.

(4) In subsection (1) "relevant tax avoidance arrangements" means arrangements—

    (*a*) to which the person is a party, and

    (*b*) the main purpose, or one of the main purposes, of which is the obtaining of a reduction in tax liability by means of property loss relief against general income.

(5) In subsection (4) "arrangements" includes any agreement, understanding, scheme, transaction or series of transactions (whether or not legally enforceable).

(6) In this section "the applicable amount of the loss" has the meaning given by section 122 and "allowable agricultural expenses" has the meaning given by section 123.]¹

Commentary—*Simon's Taxes* **B6.203**.

Amendments—¹ This section inserted by FA 2012 s 10(1), (4) with effect in relation to expenses arising directly or indirectly in consequence of, or otherwise in connection with—

    (a)   arrangements entered into on or after 13 March 2012; or

    (b)   any transaction forming part of arrangements entered into on or after that date.

This amendment does not have effect where the arrangements are, or any such transaction is, entered into pursuant to an unconditional obligation in a contract made before that date: see FA 2012 s 10(6). "An unconditional obligation" means an obligation which may not be varied or extinguished by the exercise of a right (whether under the contract or otherwise): see FA 2012 s 10(7).

[127BA Restriction of relief: cash basis

(1) This section applies if—

    (a) in a tax year a person makes a loss in a UK property business or overseas property business (whether carried on alone or in partnership), and

    (b) the profits of the business are calculated on the cash basis for the tax year (see section 271D of ITTOIA 2005).

(2) No property loss relief against general income may be given to the person for the loss.][1]

Commentary—*Simon's Taxes* **B6.203**.

Amendments—[1]   Section 127BA inserted by F(No 2)A 2017 s 16, Sch 2 para 60, 62(1), (3) with effect for the tax year 2017–18 and subsequent tax years, subject to transitional provisions in F(No 2)A 2017 Sch 2 para 64.

[127C Excess loss allocation to partners who are individuals

(1) Subsection (2) applies if—

    (a) in a tax year, an individual ("A") makes a loss in a UK property business or an overseas property business as a partner in a firm, and

    (b) A's loss arises, wholly or partly—

        (i) directly or indirectly in consequence of, or

        (ii) otherwise in connection with,

    relevant tax avoidance arrangements.

(2) No relevant loss relief may be given to A for A's loss.

(3) In subsection (1)(b) "relevant tax avoidance arrangements" means arrangements—

    (a) to which A is party, and

    (b) the main purpose, or one of the main purposes, of which is to secure that losses of a UK property business or an overseas property business are allocated, or otherwise arise, in whole or in part to A, rather than a person who is not an individual, with a view to A obtaining relevant loss relief.

(4) In subsection (3)(b) references to A include references to A and other individuals.

(5) For the purposes of subsection (3)(b) it does not matter if the person who is not an individual is not a partner in the firm or is unknown or does not exist.

(6) In this section—

    "arrangements" includes any agreement, understanding, scheme, transaction or series of transactions (whether or not legally enforceable), and

    "relevant loss relief" means relief under section 118 (carry-forward property loss relief) or section 120 (property loss relief against general income).][1]

HMRC Manuals—Business Income Manual BIM82955 (excess loss allocation: when do the restrictions apply?). BIM82960 (excess loss allocation: the effect of the restrictions?).

Amendments—[1]   Section 127C inserted by FA 2014 s 74, Sch 17 para 9(1), (3) with effect in relation to losses made in the tax year 2014–15 and subsequent tax years, subject to transitional provisions in respect of accounting periods straddling 6 April 2014 (FA 2014 Sch 17 para 14). This section does not apply in relation to the loss so far as it is apportioned to the part of the straddling period falling before 6 April 2014 (FA 2014 Sch 17 para 14(4)).

CHAPTER 5

LOSSES IN AN EMPLOYMENT OR OFFICE

128 Employment loss relief against general income

(1) A person may make a claim for employment loss relief against general income if the person—

    (a) is in employment or holds an office in a tax year, and

    (b) makes a loss in the employment or office in the tax year ("the loss-making year").

(2) The claim is for the loss to be deducted in calculating the person's net income—

    (a) for the loss-making year,

    (b) for the previous tax year, or

    (c) for both tax years.

    (See Step 2 of the calculation in section 23.)

(3) If the claim is made in relation to both tax years, the claim must specify the year for which a deduction is to be made first.

(4) Otherwise the claim must specify either the loss-making year or the previous tax year.

(5) The claim must be made on or before the first anniversary of the normal self-assessment filing date for the loss-making year.

[(5A) No claim may be made in respect of the loss if and to the extent that it is made as a result of anything done in pursuance of arrangements the main purpose, or one of the main purposes, of which is the avoidance of tax.][1]

(6) Nothing in this section prevents a person who makes a claim specifying a particular tax year in respect of a loss from making a further claim specifying the other tax year in respect of the unused part of the loss.

(7) This Chapter is subject to paragraph 2 of Schedule 1B to TMA 1970 (claims for loss relief involving two or more years).

(8) This section needs to be read with section 129 (how relief works).

Commentary—*Simon's Taxes* **E4.789A, E4.771.**
HMRC Manuals—Employment Income Manual, EIM36890 (set off of excess capital allowances against other income).
Business Income Manual BIM85090 (claims to relief - title to relief).
Amendments—[1]   Sub-s (5A) inserted by FA 2009 s 68(1) with effect—
    (a)   in relation to a loss made in the tax year 2009–10 or a subsequent tax year, and
    (b)   in relation to a loss made in the tax year 2008–09 if or to the extent that it is occasioned by an act or omission occurring on or after 12 January 2009. (FA 2009 s 68(2).)

129 How relief works

(1) This subsection explains how the deductions are to be made.

The amount of the loss to be deducted at any step is limited in accordance with [sections 24A and 25(4) and (5)][1].

    Step 1 Deduct the loss in calculating the person's net income for the specified tax year.

    Step 2 This step applies only if the claim is made in relation to both tax years. Deduct the part of the loss not deducted at Step 1 in calculating the person's net income for the other tax year.

(2) There is a priority rule if a person—
    (a) makes a claim for employment loss relief against general income ("the first claim") in relation to the loss-making year, and
    (b) makes a separate claim in respect of a loss made in the following tax year in relation to the same tax year as the first claim.

(3) The rule is that priority is given to making deductions under the first claim.

(4) For this purpose a "separate claim" means—
    (a) a claim for employment loss relief against general income, or
    (b) a claim for trade loss relief against general income (see sections 64 to 70).

Commentary—*Simon's Taxes* **E4.789A.**
Amendments—[1]   In sub-s (1) words substituted for words "section 25(4) and (5)" by FA 2013 s 16, Sch 3 para 2(1), (3)(d) with effect for the tax year 2013–14 and subsequent tax years, subject to transitional provisions in relation to loss relief claims for a tax year before 2013–14 in relation to losses made in 2013–14 or a later year (FA 2013 Sch 3 para 4).

130 Treating loss in employment or office as CGT loss

A person who cannot deduct all of a loss in an employment or office under a claim for employment loss relief against general income may be able to treat the unused part as an allowable loss for capital gains tax purposes: see sections 261B and 261C of TCGA 1992.

CHAPTER 6

LOSSES ON DISPOSAL OF SHARES

Share loss relief against general income

131 Share loss relief

(1) An individual is eligible for relief under this Chapter ("share loss relief") if—
    (a) the individual incurs an allowable loss for capital gains tax purposes on the disposal of any shares in any tax year ("the year of the loss"), and
    (b) the shares are qualifying shares.

This is subject to subsections (3) and (4) and section 136(2).

(2) Shares are qualifying shares for the purposes of this Chapter if—
    (a) EIS relief is attributable to them, or
    (b) if EIS relief is not attributable to them, they are shares in a qualifying trading company which have been subscribed for by the individual.

(3) Subsection (1) applies only if the disposal of the shares is—
    (a) by way of a bargain made at arm's length,
    (b) by way of a distribution in the course of dissolving or winding up the company,
    (c) a disposal within section 24(1) of TCGA 1992 (entire loss, destruction, dissipation or extinction of asset), or
    (d) a deemed disposal under section 24(2) of that Act (claim that value of the asset has become negligible).

(4) Subsection (1) does not apply to any allowable loss incurred on the disposal if—
    (a) the shares are the subject of an exchange or arrangement of the kind mentioned in section 135 or 136 of TCGA 1992 (company reconstructions etc), and
    (b) because of section 137 of that Act, the exchange or arrangement involves a disposal of the shares.

Commentary—*Simon's Taxes* **C1.501, E3.192, E1.1441, E3.701, E3.702, E3.707.**

HMRC Manuals—Venture Capital Schemes Manual VCM20130 (income tax relief for capital losses).
VCM74110 (deemed disposals where an asset is lost or destroyed).

132 Entitlement to claim

(1) An individual who is eligible for share loss relief may make a claim for the loss to be deducted in calculating the individual's net income—

    (*a*) for the year of the loss,

    (*b*) for the previous tax year, or

    (*c*) for both tax years.

    (See Step 2 of the calculation in section 23.)

(2) If the claim is made in relation to both tax years, the claim must specify the year for which a deduction is to be made first.

(3) Otherwise the claim must specify either the year of the loss or the previous tax year.

(4) The claim must be made on or before the first anniversary of the normal self-assessment filing date for the year of the loss.

Commentary—*Simon's Taxes* C1.501, E3.701.
HMRC Manuals—Venture Capital Schemes Manual VCM74020 (the claims procedure).

133 How relief works

(1) This subsection explains how the deductions are to be made.

    The amount of the loss to be deducted at any step is limited in accordance with [sections 24A and 25(4) and (5)][1].

    Step 1 Deduct the loss in calculating the individual's net income for the specified tax year.

    Step 2 This step applies only if the claim is made in relation to both tax years. Deduct the part of the loss not deducted at Step 1 in calculating the individual's net income for the other tax year.

(2) Subsection (1) is subject to sections 136(5) and 147 (which set limits on the amounts of share loss relief that may be obtained in particular cases).

(3) If an individual—

    (*a*) makes a claim for share loss relief against income ("the first claim") in relation to the year of the loss, and

    (*b*) makes a separate claim for share loss relief against income in respect of a loss made in the following tax year in relation to the same tax year as the first claim,

priority is to be given to making deductions under the first claim.

(4) Any share loss relief claimed in respect of any income has priority over any relief claimed in respect of that income under section 64 (deduction of losses from general income) or 72 (early trade losses relief).

(5) A claim for share loss relief does not affect any claim for a deduction under TCGA 1992 for so much of the allowable loss as is not deducted under subsection (1).

Commentary—*Simon's Taxes* E3.701.
Derivation—TA 1988 s 574(1) and (2).
HMRC Manuals—Venture Capital Schemes Manual VCM74030 (giving relief).
VCM74050 (interaction with CGT).
Amendments—[1]   In sub-s (1) words substituted for words "section 25(4) and (5)" by FA 2013 s 16, Sch 3 para 2(1), (3)(*e*) with effect for the tax year 2013–14 and subsequent tax years, subject to transitional provisions in relation to loss relief claims for a tax year before 2013–14 in relation to losses made in 2013–14 or a later year (FA 2013 Sch 3 para 4).

Shares to which EIS relief is not attributable

134 Qualifying trading companies

(1) In relation to shares to which EIS relief is not attributable (see section 131(2)(*b*)), a qualifying trading company is a company which meets each of conditions A to [C][2].

(2) Condition A is that the company either—

    (*a*) meets each of the following requirements on the date of the disposal—

        (i) the trading requirement (see section 137),

        (ii) the control and independence requirement (see section 139),

        (iii) the qualifying subsidiaries requirement (see section 140), and

        (iv) the property managing subsidiaries requirement (see section 141), or

    (*b*) has ceased to meet any of those requirements at a time which is not more than 3 years before that date and has not since that time been an excluded company, an investment company or a trading company.

(3) Condition B is that the company either—

    (*a*) has met each of the requirements mentioned in condition A for a continuous period of 6 years ending on that date or at that time, or

    (*b*) has met each of those requirements for a shorter continuous period ending on that date or at that time and has not before the beginning of that period been an excluded company, an investment company or a trading company.

(4) Condition C is that the company—

(a) met the gross assets requirement (see section 142) both immediately before and immediately after the issue of the shares in respect of which the share loss relief is claimed, and

(b) met the unquoted status requirement (see section 143) at the relevant time within the meaning of that section.

(5) . . .[1]

Commentary—*Simon's Taxes* **E3.704**.

Derivation—TA 1988 s 576(4).

HMRC Manuals—Venture Capital Schemes Manual VCM74320 (introduction).

VCM74990 (when requirements of condition a must be met).

VCM75000 (condition b).

VCM75100 (condition c: gross assets requirement).

VCM75110 (condition c: unquoted status requirement).

VCM75120 (condition d: relationship of issuing company to uk).

Modifications—ITA 2007 Sch 2 para 38(1) (modification of sub-s (2) above, in relation to shares issued before 17 March 2004), ITA 2007 Sch 2 para 38(2) (modification of this section in relation to shares issued before 6 April 1998).

ITA 2007 Sch 2 para 38(3),(4) (modification of sub-s (4) in relation to shares issued before 7 March 2001. For these purposes, shares issued on or after 5 April 1998, but before 7 March 2001, are treated as issued on or after 7 March 2001, in respect of any part of the relevant period which falls on or after that date).

Amendments—[1] Sub-s (5) repealed by FA 2020 s 38(1)(a) with effect in relation to disposals made on or after 24 January 2019.

[2] In sub-s (1) "C" substituted for "D" by FA 2020 s 38(2)(a)(i) with effect in relation to disposals made on or after 24 January 2019.

135 Subscriptions for shares

(1) This section has effect in relation to shares to which EIS relief is not attributable.

(2) An individual subscribes for shares in a company if they are issued to the individual by the company in consideration of money or money's worth.

(3) If—

(a) an individual ("A") subscribed for, or is treated under subsection (4) or this subsection as having subscribed for, any shares,

(b) A transferred the shares to another individual ("B") during their lives, and

(c) A was B's spouse or civil partner at the time of the transfer,

B is treated as having subscribed for the shares.

(4) If—

(a) an individual has subscribed for, or is treated under subsection (3) or this subsection as having subscribed for, any shares, and

(b) any corresponding bonus shares are subsequently issued to the individual,

the individual is treated as having subscribed for the bonus shares.

Commentary—*Simon's Taxes* **E3.707**.

HMRC Manuals—Venture Capital Schemes Manual VCM74060 (subscription for shares).

136 Disposals of new shares

(1) This section has effect in relation to shares to which EIS relief is not attributable.

(2) If—

(a) an individual disposes of shares ("the new shares"), and

(b) the new shares are, by virtue of section 127 of TCGA 1992 (reorganisation etc treated as not involving disposal), identified with other shares ("the old shares") previously held by the individual,

the individual is not eligible for share loss relief on the disposal of the new shares unless [condition A or B][1] is met.

This is subject to section 145(3).

(3) Condition A is that the individual would have been eligible for share loss relief on a disposal of the old shares—

(a) if the individual had incurred an allowable loss in disposing of them by way of a bargain made at arm's length on the occasion of the disposal that would have occurred but for section 127 of TCGA 1992, and

(b) where applicable, if this Chapter had then been in force.

(4) Condition B is that the individual gave for the new shares consideration in money or money's worth other than consideration of the kind mentioned in paragraph (a) or (b) of section 128(2) of TCGA 1992 ("new consideration").

(5) If the individual relies on condition B, the amount of share loss relief on the disposal of the new shares must not exceed the amount or value of the new consideration taken into account as a deduction in calculating the amount of the loss incurred on the disposal.

Commentary—*Simon's Taxes* **E3.709**.

HMRC Manuals—Venture Capital Schemes Manual VCM75390 (the effect on disposals of new shares).

Modifications—ITA 2007 Sch 2 para 39 (modification of this section in relation to new shares (see ITA 2007 s 145) issued before 6 April 2007).

Amendments—[1]   In sub-s (2) words substituted for words "one of conditions A and B" by CTA 2010 s 1177, Sch 1 para 496. CTA 2010 has effect for corporation tax purposes for accounting periods ending on or after 1 April 2010, and for income and capital gains tax purposes for the tax year 2010–11 and subsequent tax years.

Qualifying trading companies: the requirements

137 The trading requirement

(1) The trading requirement is that—

    (a) the company, ignoring any incidental purposes, exists wholly for the purpose of carrying on one or more qualifying trades, or

    (b) the company is a parent company and the business of the group does not consist wholly or as to a substantial part in the carrying on of non-qualifying activities.

(2) If the company intends that one or more other companies should become its qualifying subsidiaries with a view to their carrying on one or more qualifying trades—

    (a) the company is treated as a parent company for the purposes of subsection (1)(b), and

    (b) the reference in subsection (1)(b) to the group includes the company and any existing or future company that will be its qualifying subsidiary after the intention in question is carried into effect.

This subsection does not apply at any time after the abandonment of that intention.

(3) For the purpose of subsection (1)(b) the business of the group means what would be the business of the group if the activities of the group companies taken together were regarded as one business.

(4) For the purpose of determining the business of a group, activities are ignored so far as they are activities carried on by a mainly trading subsidiary otherwise than for its main purpose.

(5) For the purposes of determining the business of a group, activities of a group company are ignored so far as they consist in—

    (a) the holding of shares in or securities of a qualifying subsidiary of the parent company,

    (b) the making of loans to another group company,

    (c) the holding and managing of property used by a group company for the purpose of one or more qualifying trades carried on by a group company, or

    (d) the holding and managing of property used by a group company for the purpose of research and development from which it is intended—

        (i) that a qualifying trade to be carried on by a group company will be derived, or

        (ii) that a qualifying trade carried on or to be carried on by a group company will benefit.

(6) Any reference in subsection (5)(d)(i) or (ii) to a group company includes a reference to any existing or future company which will be a group company at any future time.

(7) In this section—

"excluded activities" has the meaning given by section 192 read with sections 193 to 199,

"group" means a parent company and its qualifying subsidiaries,

"group company", in relation to a group, means the parent company or any of its qualifying subsidiaries,

"incidental purposes" means purposes having no significant effect (other than in relation to incidental matters) on the extent of the activities of the company in question,

"mainly trading subsidiary" means a subsidiary which, apart from incidental purposes, exists wholly for the purpose of carrying on one or more qualifying trades, and any reference to the main purpose of such a subsidiary is to be read accordingly,

"non-qualifying activities" means—

    (a) excluded activities, and

    (b) activities (other than research and development) carried on otherwise than in the course of a trade,

"parent company" means a company that has one or more qualifying subsidiaries,

"qualifying subsidiary" is to be read in accordance with section 191,

"qualifying trade" has the meaning given by section 189, and

"research and development" has the meaning given by section 1006.

(8) In sections 189(1)(b) and 194(4)(c) (as applied by subsection (7) for the purposes of the definitions of "excluded activities" and "qualifying trade") "period B" means the continuous period that is relevant for the purposes of section 134(3).

[(9) In section 195 as applied by subsection (7) for the purposes mentioned in subsection (8), references to the issuing company are to be read as references to the company mentioned in subsection (1).][1]

Commentary—*Simon's Taxes* **E3.703, E3.129**.

HMRC Manuals—Venture Capital Schemes Manual VCM74610 (trading requirement :introduction).

VCM74620 (qualifying trades and excluded activities).

Modifications—ITA 2007 Sch 2 para 40(1) (modification of this section in relation to shares issued before 6 April 2007).

ITA 2007 Sch 2 para 40(2) (modification of this section in relation to shares issued before 6 April 2000).

ITA 2007 Sch 2 para 40(3) (this section does not apply in relation to shares issued before 6 April 1998).

Amendments—[1]   Sub-s (9) inserted by FA 2007 s 51, Sch 16 para 11(5). This amendment is deemed to have effect from 6 April 2007 by virtue of FA 2007 Sch 16 para 13, and is subject to transitional provisions in FA 2007 Sch 16 para 14.

138 Ceasing to meet trading requirement because of administration or receivership

(1) A company is not regarded as ceasing to meet the trading requirement merely because of anything done in consequence of the company or any of its subsidiaries being in administration or receivership.

This has effect subject to subsections (2) and (3).

(2) Subsection (1) applies only if—

(a) the entry into administration or receivership, and

(b) everything done as a result of the company concerned being in administration or receivership,

is for genuine commercial reasons, and is not part of a scheme or arrangement the main purpose or one of the main purposes of which is the avoidance of tax.

(3) A company ceases to meet the trading requirement if before the time that is relevant for the purposes of section 134(2)—

(a) a resolution is passed, or an order is made, for the winding up of the company or any of its subsidiaries (or, in the case of a winding up otherwise than under the Insolvency Act 1986 or the Insolvency (Northern Ireland) Order 1989, any other act is done for the like purpose), or

(b) the company or any of its subsidiaries is dissolved without winding up.

This is subject to subsection (4).

(4) Subsection (3) does not apply if—

(a) the winding up is for genuine commercial reasons, and is not part of a scheme or arrangement the main purpose or one of the main purposes of which is the avoidance of tax, and

(b) the company continues, during the winding up, to be a trading company.

(5) References in this section to a company being "in administration" or "in receivership" are to be read in accordance with section 252.

HMRC Manuals—Venture Capital Schemes Manual VCM74630 (effect of administration or receivership).

Modifications—ITA 2007 Sch 2 para 41(1) (modification of this section in relation to shares issued before 17 March 2004).

ITA 2007 Sch 2 para 41(2) (modification of sub-s (2) in relation to an administration order the petition for which was presented before 15 September 2003).

ITA 2007 Sch 2 para 41(3), (4) (modification of this section in relation to shares issued before 21 March 2000. In the application of ITA 2007 Sch 2 para 41(3) on or after 21 March 2000, shares issued on or after 6 April 1998, but before 21 March 2000, and to which EIS relief or relief under TCGA 1992 Sch 5B was attributable immediately before 21 March 2000, are treated as having been issued on or after 21 March 2000).

ITA 2007 Sch 2 para 41(5) (this section does not apply in relation to shares issued before 6 April 1998).

139 The control and independence requirement

(1) The control element of the requirement is that—

(a) the company must not control (whether on its own or together with any person connected with it) any company which is not a qualifying subsidiary of the company, and

(b) no arrangements must be in existence by virtue of which the company could fail to meet paragraph (a) (whether at a time during the continuous period that is relevant for the purposes of section 134(3) or otherwise).

(2) The independence element of the requirement is that—

(a) the company must not—

(i) be a 51% subsidiary of another company, or

(ii) be under the control of another company (or of another company and any other person connected with that other company), without being a 51% subsidiary of that other company, and

(b) no arrangements must be in existence by virtue of which the company could fail to meet paragraph (a) (whether at a time during the continuous period that is relevant for the purposes of section 134(3) or otherwise).

(3) This section is subject to section 145(3).

(4) In this section—

"arrangements" includes any scheme, agreement or understanding, whether or not legally enforceable,

"control", in subsection (1)(a), is to be read in accordance with [sections 450 and 451 of CTA 2010][1],

"qualifying subsidiary" is to be read in accordance with section 191.

Commentary—*Simon's Taxes* **E3.132**.

HMRC Manuals—Venture Capital Schemes Manual VCM74900 (control and independence requirement: introduction).

Modifications—ITA 2007 Sch 2 para 42(1) (modification of this section in relation to shares issued before 6 April 2007).

ITA 2007 Sch 2 para 42(2), (3) (modification of this section in relation to shares issued before 21 March 2000. In the application of ITA 2007 Sch 2 para 42(2) on or after 21 March 2000, shares issued on or after 6 April 1998, but before 21 March 2000, and to which EIS relief or relief under TCGA 1992 Sch 5B was attributable immediately before 21 March 2000, are treated as having been issued on or after 21 March 2000).

ITA 2007 Sch 2 para 42(4) (this section does not apply in relation to shares issued before 6 April 1998).

Amendments—[1]   In sub-s (4), in the definition of "control", words substituted by CTA 2010 s 1177, Sch 1 para 497. CTA 2010 has effect for corporation tax purposes for accounting periods ending on or after 1 April 2010, and for income and capital gains tax purposes for the tax year 2010–11 and subsequent tax years.

140 The qualifying subsidiaries requirement

(1) The qualifying subsidiaries requirement is that any subsidiary that the company has must be a qualifying subsidiary of the company.

(2) In this section "qualifying subsidiary" is to be read in accordance with section 191.

Commentary—*Simon's Taxes* E3.135.
Derivation—TA 1988 ss 293(3A), 308(1), 576(4A)(*d*).
HMRC Manuals—Venture Capital Schemes Manual VCM74920 (qualifying subsidiaries requirement: introduction).
VCM13130 (qualifying subsidiaries : meaning).
Modifications—ITA 2007 Sch 2 para 43 (this section does not apply in relation to shares issued before 6 April 1998).

141 The property managing subsidiaries requirement

(1) The property managing subsidiaries requirement is that any property managing subsidiary that the company has must be a qualifying 90% subsidiary of the company.

(2) In this section—

"property managing subsidiary" has the meaning given by section 188(2),

"qualifying 90% subsidiary" has the meaning given by section 190.

Commentary—*Simon's Taxes* E3.136.
Derivation—TA 1988 ss 293(6ZA), (6ZB), 576(4A).
HMRC Manuals—Venture Capital Schemes Manual VCM74950 (property managing subsidiaries requirement: introduction).
VCM13140 (property managing subsidiaries requirement).
VCM13080 (meaning of 'qualifying 90% subsidiary').
Modifications—ITA 2007 Sch 2 para 44 (this section does not apply in relation to shares issued before 17 March 2004).

142 The gross assets requirement

(1) The gross assets requirement in the case of a single company is that the value of the company's gross assets—

    (*a*) must not exceed £7 million immediately before the shares in respect of which the share loss relief is claimed are issued, and

    (*b*) must not exceed £8 million immediately afterwards.

(2) The gross assets requirement in the case of a parent company is that the value of the group assets—

    (*a*) must not exceed £7 million immediately before the shares in respect of which the share loss relief is claimed are issued, and

    (*b*) must not exceed £8 million immediately afterwards.

(3) The value of the group assets means the sum of the values of the gross assets of each of the members of the group, ignoring any that consist in rights against, or shares in or securities of, another member of the group.

(4) In this section—

"group" means a parent company and its qualifying subsidiaries,

"parent company" means a company that has one or more qualifying subsidiaries,

"qualifying subsidiary" is to be read in accordance with section 191, and

"single company" means a company that does not have one or more qualifying subsidiaries.

Commentary—*Simon's Taxes* E3.133.
Derivation—TA 1988 s 293(6A), (6B). (6C), 576(4A).
HMRC Manuals—Venture Capital Schemes Manual VCM75100 (gross assets requirement conditions).
Modifications—ITA 2007 Sch 2 para 45(1), (2) (modification of this section in relation to shares issued before 6 April 2006. For these purposes, shares issued on or after 6 April 2006 to a person who subscribed for them before 22 March 2006, are treated as having been issued before 6 April 2006).
ITA 2007 Sch 2 para 45(3) (this section does not apply in relation to shares issued before 6 April 1998).

143 The unquoted status requirement

(1) The unquoted status requirement is that, at the time ("the relevant time") at which the shares in respect of which the share loss relief is claimed are issued—

    (*a*) the company must be an unquoted company,

    (*b*) there must be no arrangements in existence for the company to cease to be an unquoted company, and

    (*c*) there must be no arrangements in existence for the company to become a subsidiary of another company ("the new company") by virtue of an exchange of shares, or shares and securities, if—

        (i) section 145 applies in relation to the exchange, and

        (ii) arrangements have been made with a view to the new company ceasing to be an unquoted company.

(2) The arrangements referred to in subsection (1)(*b*) and (*c*)(ii) do not include arrangements in consequence of which any shares, stocks, debentures or other securities of the company or the new company are at any subsequent time—

    (*a*) listed on a stock exchange that is a recognised stock exchange by virtue of an order made under section [1005(1)(*b*)][1], or

(b) listed on an exchange, or dealt in by any means, designated by an order made for the purposes of section 184(3)(b) or (c),

if the order was made after the relevant time.

(3) In this section—

"arrangements" includes any scheme, agreement or understanding, whether or not legally enforceable, and

"unquoted company" has the meaning given by section 184(2).

Commentary—*Simon's Taxes* **E3.131**.
Derivation—TA 1988 ss 293(1A), (1B), 312(1), (1E), 576(4A).
HMRC Manuals—Venture Capital Schemes Manual VCM75110 (condition c: unquoted status requirement).
Modifications—ITA 2007 Sch 2 para 46(1) (modification of this section in relation to shares issued before 7 March 2001. For circumstances in which shares which were issued before 7 March 2001 are to be treated as having been issued on or after that date, see ITA 2007 s 46(2), (3)).
ITA 2007 Sch 2 para 46(4) (this section does not apply in relation to shares issued before 6 April 1998).
Amendments—[1] Reference in sub-s (2)(a) substituted by FA 2007 s 109, Sch 26 para 12(1), (2) with effect from 19 July 2007.

144 Power to amend requirements by Treasury order

The Treasury may by order make such amendments of sections 137 to 143 as they consider appropriate.

HMRC Manuals—Venture Capital Schemes Manual VCM75130 (future changes to the conditions).
Modifications—ITA 2007 Sch 2 para 47 (this section does not apply in relation to shares issued before 6 April 1998).

Qualifying trading companies: supplementary

145 Relief after an exchange of shares for shares in another company

(1) This section and section 146 apply in relation to shares to which EIS relief is not attributable if—

(a) a company ("the new company") in which the only issued shares are subscriber shares acquires all the shares ("old shares") in another company ("the old company"),

(b) the consideration for the old shares consists wholly of the issue of shares ("new shares") in the new company,

(c) the consideration for the new shares of each description consists wholly of old shares of the corresponding description,

(d) new shares of each description are issued to the holders of old shares of the corresponding description in respect of and in proportion to their holdings, and

(e) by virtue of section 127 of TCGA 1992 as applied by section 135(3) of that Act (company reconstructions etc), the exchange of shares is not to be treated as involving a disposal of the old shares or an acquisition of the new shares.

In this subsection references to shares, except in the expressions "shares to which EIS relief is not attributable" and "subscriber shares", include securities.

(2) For the purposes of this Chapter the exchange of shares is not regarded as involving any disposal of the old shares or any acquisition of the new shares.

(3) Nothing in—

(a) section 136(2) (disposals of new shares), and

(b) section 139 (the control and independence requirement),

applies in relation to such an exchange of shares, or shares and securities, as is mentioned in subsection (1) or, in the case of section 139, arrangements with a view to such an exchange.

(4) For the purposes of this section old shares and new shares are of a corresponding description if, on the assumption that they were shares in the same company, they would be of the same class and carry the same rights.

(5) References in section 146 to "old shares", "new shares", "the old company" and "the new company" are to be read in accordance with this section.

Commentary—*Simon's Taxes* **E3.709**.
HMRC Manuals—Venture Capital Schemes Manual VCM75360 (more complex cases: shares received in exchange for other shares in a take-over: conditions for ITA07/S145 and S146 to apply).
VCM75370 (shares received in exchange for other shares in a take-over).
VCM23230 (EIS: deferral relief: share exchanges conditions).
VCM23250 (share exchange by company with subscriber shares only : example)
Modifications—ITA 2007 Sch 2 para 48(1) (modification of this section in relation to new shares issued before 6 April 2007).
ITA 2007 Sch 2 para 48(2) (this section does not apply in relation to shares issued before 6 April 1998).

146 Substitution of new shares for old shares

(1) Subsection (2) applies if, in the case of any new shares held by an individual or by a nominee for an individual, the old shares for which they were exchanged were shares—

(a) to which EIS relief was not attributable, and

(b) which had been subscribed for by the individual.

(2) This Chapter has effect in relation to any subsequent disposal or other event as if—

(a) the new shares had been subscribed for by the individual at the time when, and for the amount for which, the old shares were subscribed for by the individual,

(b) the new shares had been issued by the new company at the time when the old shares were issued to the individual by the old company, and

(c) any requirements of this Chapter which were met at any time before the exchange by the old company had been met at that time by the new company.

[(3) Nothing in subsection (2) applies in relation to section 195(7) as applied by section 137(7) for the purposes mentioned in section 137(8).][1]

Commentary—*Simon's Taxes* **E3.709**.

Derivation—TA 1988 s 304A(3) and (4).

HMRC Manuals—Venture Capital Schemes Manual VCM75360 (more complex cases: shares received in exchange for other shares in a take-over: conditions for ITA07/S145 and S146 to apply).

VCM75370 (shares received in exchange for other shares in a take-over).

Modifications—ITA 2007 Sch 2 para 49 (this section does not apply in relation to shares issued before 6 April 1998).

Amendments—[1] Sub-s (3) inserted by FA 2007 s 51, Sch 16 para 11(6). This amendment is deemed to have effect from 6 April 2007 by virtue of FA 2007 Sch 16 para 13, and is subject to transitional provisions in FA 2007 Sch 16 para 14.

Limits on share loss relief and mixed holdings

147 Limits on share loss relief

(1) Subsection (2) applies if—

(a) an individual disposes of any qualifying shares,

(b) those shares either—

  (i) form part of a section 104 holding . . . [1] at the time of the disposal, . . . [1]

  [(ii) at a time earlier than the time of the disposal but after 5 April 2008 formed part of a section 104 holding, or

  (iii) at a time earlier than that time and than 6 April 2008 formed part of an old section 104 holding or a 1982 holding, and][1]

(c) the individual makes a claim under section 132 in respect of a loss incurred on the disposal.

(2) The amount of share loss relief on the disposal is not to exceed the sums that would be allowed as deductions in calculating the amount of the loss if the qualifying shares had not formed part of the holding.

(3) Subsection (4) applies if—

(a) an individual disposes of any qualifying shares,

(b) the qualifying shares, and other shares that are not capable of being qualifying shares, are for the purposes of TCGA 1992 to be treated as acquired by a single transaction by virtue of section 105(1)(a) of that Act (disposal of shares acquired on same day etc), and

(c) the individual makes a claim under section 132 in respect of a loss incurred on the disposal.

(4) The amount of share loss relief on the disposal is not to exceed the sums that would be allowed as deductions in calculating the amount of the loss if—

(a) the qualifying shares were to be treated as acquired by a single transaction, and

(b) the other shares were not to be so treated.

(5) Subsection (6) applies if—

(a) an individual disposes of any qualifying shares,

(b) the qualifying shares (taken as a single asset), and other shares in the same company that are not capable of being qualifying shares (taken as a single asset), are for the purposes of TCGA 1992 to be treated as the same asset by virtue of section 127 of that Act (reorganisation etc treated as not involving disposal), and

(c) the individual makes a claim under section 132 in respect of a loss incurred on the disposal.

References in this subsection and subsection (6) to other shares in the same company include debentures of the same company.

(6) The amount of share loss relief on the disposal is not to exceed the sums that would be allowed as deductions in calculating the amount of the loss if the qualifying shares and the other shares in the same company were not to be treated as the same asset.

(7) In this section—

"section 104 holding" has the meaning given by section 104(3) of TCGA 1992 [and "old section 104 holding" is a holding that was a section 104 holding within the meaning of that provision as it applied in relation to disposals before 6 April 2008][1], and

"1982 holding" has the meaning given by section 109(1) of that Act [as it applied in relation to disposals before 6 April 2008][1].

(8) For the purposes of this section and section 148, shares to which EIS relief is not attributable are not capable of being qualifying shares at any time if—

(a) the individual acquired the shares otherwise than by subscription, [or][2]

(b) condition C in section 134(4) was not met in relation to the issue of the shares, . . . [2]

(c) . . . [2]

(9) For the purposes of subsection (5), shares to which EIS relief is not attributable are not capable of being qualifying shares at any time if they are shares of a different class from the shares mentioned in paragraph (a) of that subsection.

Commentary—*Simon's Taxes* **E3.708**.

HMRC Manuals—Venture Capital Schemes Manual VCM75200 (when relief is restricted: what to look out for).
VCM75410 (more complex cases: mixed holdings and part disposals: limiting share loss relief: first case).
VCM75420 (more complex cases: mixed holdings and part disposals: limiting share loss relief: second case).
VCM75430 (more complex cases: mixed holdings and part disposals: limiting share loss relief: third case).
VCM75400 (defined terms).
Amendments—[1]   In sub-s (1)(b), words in para (i) repealed, paras (ii), (iii) substituted for previous para (ii), and words in sub-s (7) inserted, by FA 2008 s 8, Sch 2 para 98 with effect in relation to disposals on or after 6 April 2008.
[2]   In sub-s (8), word "or" inserted in para (a), and para (c) and preceding word "or" repealed, by FA 2020 s 38(2)(a)(ii) with effect in relation to disposals made on or after 24 January 2019.

148 Disposal of shares forming part of mixed holding

(1) This section applies if an individual disposes of shares forming part of a mixed holding of shares, that is, a holding of shares in a company which includes—

    (a) shares that are not capable of being qualifying shares, and

    (b) other shares.

(2) Any question—

    (a) whether a disposal by the individual of shares forming part of the mixed holding is of qualifying shares, or

    (b) as to which of any qualifying shares acquired by the individual at different times such a disposal relates to,

is to be determined as provided by the following provisions of this section.

(3) Any such question as is mentioned in subsection (2) is to be determined—

    (a) except in a case falling within paragraph (b)—

        (i) in accordance with subsection (4), and

        (ii) in the case of shares which under that subsection are identified with the whole or any part of a section 104 holding . . . [1], in accordance with subsection (5),

    (b) in the case of a mixed holding which includes any of the following—

        [(ai) shares to which SEIS relief is attributable (as determined in accordance with Part 5A),][2]

        (i) shares issued before 1 January 1994 in respect of which relief has been given under Chapter 3 of Part 7 of ICTA (business expansion scheme) and has not been withdrawn,

        (ii) shares to which EIS relief is attributable, and

        (iii) shares to which deferral relief (within the meaning of Schedule 5B to TCGA 1992) is attributable,

        in accordance with subsection (6).

(4) For the purposes of subsection (3)(a)(i), the question is to be determined by identifying the shares disposed of in accordance with sections 105 to 105B and 106A of TCGA 1992.

(5) For the purposes of subsection (3)(a)(ii), the question is to be determined by treating the disposal and any previous disposal by the individual out of the section 104 . . . [1] holding as relating to shares acquired later rather than earlier.

(6) For the purposes of subsection (3)(b), the question is to be determined—

    (a) in relation to shares issued before 1 January 1994, as provided by subsections (3) to (4C) of section 299 of ICTA (as that section has effect in relation to shares so issued),

    (b) in relation to shares issued on or after that date and before 6 April 2007, as provided by subsections (6) to (6D) of that section (as that section has effect in relation to shares so issued), and

    (c) in relation to shares issued on or after 6 April 2007, as provided by section 246 of this Act.

(7) Any such question as is mentioned in subsection (2) which cannot be determined as provided by subsections (3) to (6) is to be determined on a just and reasonable basis.

(8) In this section "holding" means any number of shares of the same class held by one individual in the same capacity, growing or diminishing as shares of that class are acquired or disposed of.

    For this purpose—

    (a) shares are not to be treated as being of the same class unless they are so treated by the practice of a recognised stock exchange or would be so treated if dealt in on such an exchange, and

    (b) subsection (4) of section 104 of TCGA 1992 applies as it applies for the purposes of subsection (1) of that section.

(9) In this section "section 104 holding" [has][1] the same meaning as in section 147.

Commentary—*Simon's Taxes* **E3.708**.
HMRC Manuals—Venture Capital Schemes Manual VCM75440 (more complex cases: disposal of shares forming part of a mixed holding: introduction).
VCM75450 (more complex cases: disposal of shares forming part of a mixed holding: general case).
VCM75460 (more complex cases: disposal of shares forming part of a mixed holding: special case).
VCM75470 (more complex cases: disposal of shares forming part of a mixed holding: the 'just and reasonable' test).
VCM75490 (more complex cases: disposal of shares forming part of a mixed holding: other points).
Amendments—[1]   Words in sub-ss (3)(a)(ii), (5) repealed, and words in sub-s (9) substituted, by FA 2008 s 8, Sch 2 para 99 with effect in relation to disposals on or after 6 April 2008.

ITA 2007

²   In sub-s (3)(*b*), para (ai) inserted by FA 2013 s 16, Sch 3 para 2(1), (4) with effect for the tax year 2013–14 and subsequent tax years, subject to transitional provisions in relation to loss relief claims for a tax year before 2013–14 in relation to losses made in 2013–14 or a later year (FA 2013 Sch 3 para 4).

149 Section 148: supplementary

(1) In the case of a disposal of shares within section 148(3)(*b*)(ii) or (iii) to which section 105A of TCGA 1992 (election for alternative treatment: approved-scheme shares) applies—

 (*a*) section 299 of ICTA (identification of shares) has effect for the purposes of section 148(6)(*b*), and

 (*b*) section 246 of this Act has effect for the purposes of section 148(6)(*c*),

with the same modifications as those with which they have effect for the purposes of section 150A(4) of TCGA 1992 (enterprise investment schemes).

(2) In a case to which section 127 of TCGA 1992 (reorganisation etc treated as not involving disposal) applies (including a case where that section applies by virtue of an enactment relating to chargeable gains), shares included in the new holding are treated for the purposes of section 148 as acquired when the original shares were acquired.

(3) Any shares held or disposed of by a nominee or bare trustee for an individual are treated for the purposes of section 148 as held or disposed of by that individual.

(4) In this section "new holding" and "original shares" have the same meaning as in section 127 of TCGA 1992 (or, as the case may be, that section as applied by the enactment concerned).

Commentary—*Simon's Taxes* **E3.708**.

HMRC Manuals—Venture Capital Schemes Manual VCM75490 (more complex cases: disposal of shares forming part of a mixed holding: other points).

Miscellaneous and supplementary

150 Deemed time of issue for certain shares

(1) In this section "the relevant provisions" means—

 . . .¹

  section 142(1)(*a*) and (2)(*a*),
  section 143(1), and
  section 146(2)(*b*).

(2) If—

 (*a*) any shares were issued to an individual ("A") or are treated under subsection (3) or this subsection as having been issued to A at a particular time,

 (*b*) the shares are transferred by A to another individual ("B") during their lives, and

 (*c*) A was B's spouse or civil partner at the time of the transfer,

the shares are treated for the purposes of the relevant provisions as having been issued to B at the time they were issued to A or are treated as having been so issued.

(3) If—

 (*a*) any shares ("the original shares") have been issued to an individual, or are treated under subsection (2) or this subsection as having been issued to an individual at a particular time, and

 (*b*) any corresponding bonus shares are subsequently issued to the individual,

the bonus shares are treated for the purposes of the relevant provisions as having been issued at the time the original shares were issued to the individual or are treated as having been so issued.

Commentary—*Simon's Taxes* **E3.707**.

HMRC Manuals—Venture Capital Schemes Manual VCM75500 (deemed time of issue of shares transferred in certain circumstances and corresponding bonus shares).

Amendments—¹   In sub-s (1) entry relating to section 134(5)(*a*) repealed by FA 2020 s 38(2)(*a*)(iii) with effect in relation to disposals made on or after 24 January 2019.

151 Interpretation of Chapter

(1) In this Chapter (subject to subsections (2) to (8))—

  "bonus shares" means shares which are issued otherwise than for payment (whether in cash or otherwise),

  "civil partner" refers to one of two civil partners who are living together,

  "corresponding bonus shares", in relation to any shares, means bonus shares which—

 (*a*) are issued in respect of those shares, and

 (*b*) are in the same company, are of the same class, and carry the same rights, as those shares,

  "EIS relief" means—

 (*a*) EIS income tax relief under Part 5 of this Act, and

 (*b*) in relation to shares issued after 31 December 1993 and before 6 April 2007, relief under Chapter 3 of Part 7 of ICTA (enterprise investment scheme),

  "excluded company" means a company which—

 (*a*) has a trade which consists wholly or mainly of dealing in land, in commodities or futures or in shares, securities or other financial instruments, (*b*) has a trade which is not carried on on a commercial basis and in such a way that profits in the trade can reasonably be expected to be realised,

(*c*) is a holding company of a group other than a trading group, or

(*d*) is a building society or a [registered society][3],

"group" (except in sections 137 and 142) means a company which has one or more 51% subsidiaries together with that or those subsidiaries,

"holding company" means a company whose business consists wholly or mainly in the holding of shares or securities of companies which are its 51% subsidiaries,

["investment company" means a company—

(*a*) whose business consists wholly or mainly in the making of investments, and

(*b*) which derives the principal part of its income from the making of investments,][2]

"qualifying shares" has the meaning given by section 131(2),

["registered society" means—

(*a*) a registered society within the meaning of the Cooperative and Community Benefit Societies Act 2014,

(*b*) a society registered or treated as registered under the Industrial and Provident Societies Act (Northern Ireland) 1969, or

(*c*) an SCE formed in accordance with Council Regulation (EC) No 1435/2003 on the Statute for a European Cooperative Society,][3]

"shares"—

(*a*) includes stock, but

(*b*) does not include shares or stock not forming part of a company's ordinary share capital,

"share loss relief" has the meaning given by section 131(1),

"spouse" refers to one of two spouses who are living together,

"trading company" means a company other than an excluded company which is—

(*a*) a company whose business consists wholly or mainly of the carrying on of a trade or trades, or

(*b*) the holding company of a trading group,

"trading group" means a group the business of whose members, when taken together, consists wholly or mainly in the carrying on of a trade or trades, and

"the year of the loss" has the meaning given by section 131(1).

(2) For the purposes of the definition of "corresponding bonus shares" in subsection (1), shares are not treated as being of the same class unless they would be so treated if dealt in on [a recognised stock exchange][1].

(3) In section 148(3)(*b*) and (6) "shares" does not include stock.

(4) Except as provided by subsection (5), paragraph (*b*) of [the definition of shares in subsection (1)][2] does not apply in the definition of "excluded company" in subsection (1) or in sections 145(1) to (4) and 147(3) to (6), (8) and (9).

(5) Paragraph (*b*) of that definition applies in relation to the expression "shares to which EIS relief is not attributable" in section 145(1).

(6) The definition of "shares" in subsection (1) does not apply in sections 137(5)(*a*), 142(3) and 143(1)(*c*) and (2).

(7) For the purposes of the definition of "trading group" in subsection (1), any trade carried on by a subsidiary which is an excluded company is treated as not constituting a trade.

(8) For the purposes of this Chapter a disposal of shares which results in an allowable loss for capital gains tax purposes is treated as made at the time when the disposal is made or treated as made for the purposes of TCGA 1992.

Commentary—*Simon's Taxes* **D7.312**.

HMRC Manuals—Venture Capital Schemes Manual VCM71020 (share loss relief: definitions).

VCM71040 (spouse and trading company: definitions). .

Modifications—ITA 2007 Sch 2 para 50 (modification of this section in relation to shares issued before 6 April 1998).

Amendments—[1] Words in sub-s (2) substituted by FA 2007 s 109, Sch 26 para 12(1), (3) with effect from 19 July 2007.

[2] In sub-s (1) definition of "investment company" substituted, in sub-s (4) words substituted by CTA 2010 s 1177, Sch 1 para 498. CTA 2010 has effect for corporation tax purposes for accounting periods ending on or after 1 April 2010, and for income and capital gains tax purposes for the tax year 2010–11 and subsequent tax years.

[3] In sub-s (1), in definition of "excluded company" in para (*d*), words substituted for words "registered industrial and provident society", and definition substituted for definition of "registered industrial and provident society", by the Co-operative and Community Benefit Societies Act 2014 s 151, Sch 4 paras 104, 105 (as amended by FA 2014 Sch 39) with effect from 1 August 2014 and subject to transitional provisions and provisions preserving the continuity of the law in Sch 5 of that Act.

CHAPTER 7

LOSSES FROM MISCELLANEOUS TRANSACTIONS

Loss relief against miscellaneous income

152 Losses from miscellaneous transactions

[(1) If in a tax year ("the loss-making year") a person makes a loss in a relevant transaction, the person may make a claim for loss relief against relevant miscellaneous income.][1]

(2) A transaction is a relevant one if, assuming there were profits or other income arising from it—

    (*a*) those profits or that other income would be [income on which income tax is charged under, or by virtue of, a relevant section 1016 provision ("the relevant provision")][1], and

    (*b*) the person would be liable for income tax charged on those profits or that other income.

[(2A) A relevant section 1016 provision" means a provision to which section 1016 applies, other than—

    (*a*) regulation 17 of the Offshore Funds (Tax) Regulations 2009 (SI 2009/3001) (treatment of participants in non-reporting funds: charge to tax on disposal of asset), or

    (*b*) Chapter 9 of Part 4 of ITTOIA 2005 (gains from contracts for life insurance etc).][1]

(3) The claim is for the loss to be deducted in calculating the person's net income for the loss-making year and subsequent tax years (see Step 2 of the calculation in section 23).

(4) But a deduction for that purpose is to be made only from the person's [relevant][1] miscellaneous income.

(5) [The person's "relevant miscellaneous income", in relation to the loss,][1] is so much of the person's total income as is—

    (*a*) income or gains arising from transactions, and

    [(*b*) income on which income tax is charged under, or by virtue of, the relevant provision.][1]

This is subject to subsection (6).

(6) If the loss was made by the person as a partner in a partnership, the transactions covered by subsection (5)(*a*) are limited to transactions entered into by the partnership.

(7) In calculating a person's net income for a tax year, deductions under this section from the person's [relevant][1] miscellaneous income are to be made before deductions of any other reliefs from that [relevant][1] miscellaneous income.

(8) . . . [1]

(9) This section needs to be read with—

    (*a*) section 153 (how relief works),

    (*b*) section 154 (transactions in deposit rights), . . . [2]

    [(*ba*) section 154A (anti-avoidance), and][2]

    (*c*) section 155 (claims).

Commentary—*Simon's Taxes* **E1.588**.

Derivation—TA 1988 s 392.

HMRC Manuals—Savings And Investment Manual SAIM7120 (losses are relievable against profits from miscellaneous transactions).

Amendments—[1]   Sub-s (1) substituted; in sub-s(2)(*a*) words substituted; sub-s (2A) inserted; in sub-s (4) word inserted; in sub-s (5) words substituted and para (*b*) substituted; in sub-s (7) words inserted; and sub-s (8) repealed, by FA 2015 s 22(1), (2)(*a*)–(*h*) with effect for the tax year 2015–16 and subsequent tax years, and in relation to a loss whether it is made before, during or after that tax year.

[2]   In sub-s (9) word "and" at end of para (*b*) repealed and para (*ba*) inserted by FA 2015 s 22(1), (2)(*i*) with effect in relation to losses and income arising on or after 3 December 2014 directly or indirectly in consequence of, or otherwise in connection with, relevant tax avoidance arrangements (whenever the arrangements are made).

153 How relief works

This section explains how the deductions are to be made.

The amount of the loss to be deducted at any step is limited in accordance with section 25(4) and (5).

    Step 1 Deduct the loss from the [relevant][1] miscellaneous income for the loss-making year.

    Step 2 Deduct from the [relevant][1] miscellaneous income for the next tax year the amount of the loss not previously deducted.

    Step 3 Continue to apply Step 2 in relation to [relevant][1] miscellaneous income for subsequent tax years until all the loss is deducted.

Commentary—*Simon's Taxes* **E1.588**.

Amendments—[1]   Words inserted by FA 2015 s 22(1), (3) with effect for the tax year 2015–16 and subsequent tax years, and in relation to a loss whether it is made before, during or after that tax year.

Deposit rights

154 Transactions in deposit rights

(1) This section applies if—

    (*a*) a person makes a loss from the disposal or exercise of a right to receive an amount,

    (*b*) the disposal or exercise is a transaction in a deposit under Chapter 11 of Part 4 of ITTOIA 2005 (see subsection (2)), and

    (*c*) the person's total income for a tax year includes interest payable on the amount.

(2) The disposal or exercise is a transaction in a deposit under Chapter 11 of Part 4 of ITTOIA 2005 if, assuming there were a profit or gain from it, the profit or gain would be charged to tax under that Chapter.

(3) For the purposes of the giving of loss relief against [relevant][1] miscellaneous income for the loss mentioned in subsection (1)(*a*), the interest mentioned in subsection (1)(*c*) is treated as [relevant miscellaneous income, for the tax year, in relation to the loss.][1]

Commentary—*Simon's Taxes* **E1.588**.
Derivation—TA 1988 s 398.
HMRC Manuals—Savings And Investment Manual SAIM2520 (disposal of deposit rights: loss).
Amendments—[1] In sub-s (3) word inserted and words substituted by FA 2015 s 22(1), (4) with effect for the tax year 2015–16 and subsequent tax years, and in relation to a loss whether it is made before, during or after that tax year.

Supplementary

[154A Anti-avoidance
(1) Subsection (2) applies if—
  (*a*) a person makes a loss in a relevant transaction, and
  (*b*) that loss arises directly or indirectly in consequence of, or otherwise in connection with, relevant tax avoidance arrangements.
(2) The person is not to be given loss relief under section 152 for the loss.
(3) Subsection (4) applies if—
  (*a*) a person has income on which income tax is chargeable under, or by virtue of, a relevant section 1016 provision, and
  (*b*) that income arises directly or indirectly in consequence of, or otherwise in connection with, relevant tax avoidance arrangements.
(4) The person is not to be given loss relief against that income under section 152.
(5) In this section "relevant tax avoidance arrangements" means arrangements—
  (*a*) to which the person is party, and
  (*b*) the main purpose, or one of the main purposes, of which is to obtain a reduction in tax liability by means of loss relief under section 152.
(6) In subsection (5) "arrangements" includes any agreement, understanding, scheme, transaction or series of transactions (whether or not legally enforceable).][1]

Commentary—*Simon's Taxes* **E1.588**.
Modifications—By virtue of FA 2015 s 22(11), in relation to income arising on or after 3 December 2014 but before the beginning of the tax year 2015–16, s 154A has effect as if sub-s(3)(*a*) were to read as follows—

  "(*a*) a person has section 1016 income (within the meaning of section 152), and".

Amendments—[1] Section 154A inserted by FA 2015 s 22(1), (5) with effect in relation to losses and income arising on or after 3 December 2014 directly or indirectly in consequence of, or otherwise in connection with, relevant tax avoidance arrangements (whenever the arrangements are made), with sub-s (4) applying to loss relief under s 152 for losses whenever made.

155 Time limit for claiming relief
(1) So far as a claim for loss relief against [relevant][2] miscellaneous income concerns the amount of the loss for a tax year, it must be made [not more than 4 years after the end of][1] the tax year.
(2) But—
  (*a*) the question whether, and
  (*b*) if so, how much,
loss relief against [relevant][2] miscellaneous income should be given for a tax year may be the subject of a separate claim made [not more than 4 years after the end of][1] the tax year.

Commentary—*Simon's Taxes* **E1.588**.
Amendments—[1] In sub-ss (1), (2), words substituted for words "on or before the fifth anniversary of the normal self-assessment filing date for", by FA 2008 s 118, Sch 39 paras 54, 58 with effect from 1 April 2010 (by virtue of SI 2009/403 art 2(2)), subject to transitional provisions in SI 2009/403 art 10(2) (where art 10 applies, the appointed day is 1 April 2012).
[2] In each of sub-ss (1), (2), word inserted by FA 2015 s 22(1), (6), (8) with effect for the tax year 2015-16 and subsequent tax years, and in relation to a loss whether it is made before, during or after that tax year.

PART 5
ENTERPRISE INVESTMENT SCHEME

CHAPTER 1

INTRODUCTION
EIS relief

156 Meaning of "EIS relief" and commencement
(1) This Part provides for EIS income tax relief ("EIS relief"), that is, entitlement to tax reductions in respect of amounts subscribed by individuals for shares.
(2) In this Part "EIS" stands for the enterprise investment scheme.

ITA 2007

(3) In accordance with section 1034(3), this Part has effect only in relation to shares issued on or after 6 April 2007.

This is subject to Schedule 2 (transitional provisions and savings).

Commentary—*Simon's Taxes* **E3.101**.
HMRC Manuals—Venture Capital Schemes Manual VCM10510 (introduction to EIS income tax relief: overview).

157 Eligibility for EIS relief

(1) An individual ("the investor") is eligible for EIS relief in respect of an amount subscribed by the investor on the investor's own behalf for an issue of shares in a company ("the issuing company") if—

    [(*za*) the risk-to-capital condition is met (see section 157A),][3]

    (*a*) the shares ("the relevant shares") are issued to the investor,

    [(*aa*) the shares are issued before 6 April 2025,][2]

    (*b*) the investor is a qualifying investor in relation to the relevant shares (see Chapter 2),

    (*c*) the general requirements (including requirements as to the purpose of the issue of shares and the use of money raised) are met in respect of the relevant shares (see Chapter 3), and

    (*d*) the issuing company is a qualifying company in relation to the relevant shares (see Chapter 4).

[(1A) The Treasury may, by regulations, amend subsection (1)(*aa*) to substitute a different date for the date for the time being specified there.][2]

(2), (3) . . . [1]

Commentary—*Simon's Taxes* **E3.106, E3.116, E3.157, E3.182**.
HMRC Manuals—Venture Capital Schemes Manual VCM10520 (eligibility for EIS income tax relief).
Amendments—[1]   Sub-ss (2), (3) repealed by FA 2012 s 39, Sch 7 paras 1, 2 with effect in relation to shares issued on or after 6 April 2012.
[2] Sub-ss (1)(*aa*), (1A) inserted by F(No 2)A 2015 s 25, Sch 5 paras 1, 2 with effect from 18 November 2015.
[3] Sub-s (1)(*za*) inserted by FA 2018 s 14(1)(*a*) with effect for shares issued on or after 15 March 2018 (by virtue of SI 2018/931 reg 2(a)).

[157A Risk-to-capital condition

(1) The risk-to-capital condition is met if, having regard to all the circumstances existing at the time of the issue of the shares, it would be reasonable to conclude that—

    (*a*) the issuing company has objectives to grow and develop its trade in the long-term, and

    (*b*) there is a significant risk that there will be a loss of capital of an amount greater than the net investment return.

(2) For the purposes of subsection (1)(*b*)—

    (*a*) the risk is to be determined by reference to a loss of capital, and the net investment return, for the investors generally,

    (*b*) the reference to a loss of capital is to a loss of some or all of the amounts subscribed for the shares by the investors, and

    (*c*) the reference to the net investment return is to the net investment return to the investors (whether by way of income or capital growth) taking into account the value of EIS relief.

(3) For the purposes of subsection (1) the circumstances to which regard may be had include—

    (*a*) the extent to which the company's objectives include increasing the number of its employees or the turnover of its trade,

    (*b*) the nature of the company's sources of income, including the extent to which there is a significant risk of the company not receiving some or all of the income,

    (*c*) the extent to which the company has or is likely to have assets, or is or could become a party to arrangements for acquiring assets, that could be used to secure financing from any person,

    (*d*) the extent to which the activities of the company are sub-contracted to persons who are not connected with it,

    (*e*) the nature of the company's ownership structure or management structure, including the extent to which others participate in or devise the structure,

    (*f*) how any opportunity for investment in the company is marketed, and

    (*g*) the extent to which arrangements are in place under which opportunities for investments in the company are or may be marketed with, or otherwise associated with, opportunities for investments in other companies or entities.

(4) If the issuing company is a parent company—

    (*a*) any reference in this section to the company's trade is to what would be the trade of the group if the activities of the group companies taken together were regarded as one trade, and

    (*b*) any reference in subsection (3)(*a*) to (*e*) to the company is to any group company.][1]

Commentary—*Simon's Taxes* **E3.105**.
Amendments—[1]   Section 157A inserted by FA 2018 s 14(1)(*b*) with effect for shares issued on or after 15 March 2018 (by virtue of SI 2018/931 reg 2(a)).

158 Form and amount of EIS relief

(1) If an individual—

    (*a*) is eligible for EIS relief in respect of any amount subscribed for shares, and (*b*) makes a claim in respect of all or some of the shares included in the issue,

the individual is entitled to a tax reduction for the tax year in which the shares were issued ("the current year").

This is subject to the provisions of this Part.

(2) The amount of the tax reduction to which the individual is entitled is the amount equal to tax at the [EIS rate][1] for the current year on—

  (*a*) the amount or, as the case may be, the sum of the amounts subscribed for shares issued in that year in respect of which the individual is eligible for and claims EIS relief [(qualifying shares)][5], or

  (*b*) if less, [the allowable amount][5].

[(2ZA) The allowable amount is—

  (*a*) if the qualifying shares do not include any KIC shares: £1 million;

  (*b*) if the amount, or the sum of the amounts, subscribed for qualifying shares that are KIC shares is £1 million or more: £2 million;

  (*c*) if neither paragraph (*a*) nor paragraph (*b*) applies: £1 million plus the amount, or the sum of the amounts, subscribed for qualifying shares that are KIC shares.

(2ZB) In subsection (2ZA) "KIC shares" means shares in a company which, or in companies each of which, is a knowledge-intensive company at the time the shares are issued (see section 252A and subsection (6)).][5]

[(2A) In this Part "the EIS rate" means [30%][4].][1]

(3) The tax reduction is given effect at Step 6 of the calculation in section 23.

(4) . . . [2] if in the case of any issue of shares—

  (*a*) which are issued . . . [2] in the current year, and

  (*b*) in respect of the amount subscribed for which the individual is eligible for EIS relief,

the individual so claims, [subsections (1) to (2ZB)][5] apply as if, in respect of such part of that issue as may be specified in the claim, the shares had been issued in the preceding tax year; and the individual's liability to tax for both tax years is determined accordingly.

(5) . . . [3]

[(6) If the issuing company began to carry on a trade less than three years before the date the relevant shares are issued, section 252A as it applies for the purposes of this section has effect with the substitution of the following subsections for subsections (2) to (4A)—

  "(2) The first operating costs condition is that in at least one of the relevant three succeeding years at least 15% of the relevant operating costs constitute expenditure on research and development or innovation.

  (3) The second operating costs condition is that in each of the relevant three succeeding years at least 10% of the relevant operating costs constitute such expenditure.

  (4) In subsections (2) and (3)—

  "relevant operating costs" means—

         (*a*)   if the issuing company is a single company at the time the relevant shares are issued, the operating costs of that company, and

         (*b*)   if the issuing company is a parent company at the time the relevant shares are issued, the sum of—

      (i) the operating costs of the issuing company, and

      (ii) the operating costs of each company which is a qualifying subsidiary of the issuing company at that time, excluding a company's operating costs for any of the relevant three succeeding years during any part of which the company is not a qualifying subsidiary of the issuing company;

  "the relevant three succeeding years" means the three consecutive years the first of which begins with the date the relevant shares are issued."

(7) In subsection (6) "trade" includes—

  (*a*) any business or profession,

  (*b*) so far as not within paragraph (*a*), the carrying on of research and development activities from which it is intended a trade will be derived or will benefit,

  (*c*) preparing to carry on a trade.][5]

Commentary—*Simon's Taxes* **E3.102, E3.156**.
HMRC Manuals—Venture Capital Schemes Manual VCM10530 (form and amount of EIS income tax relief).
VCM20060 (EIS: investor's income tax liability).
Amendments—[1]   Words in sub-s (2) substituted and sub-s (2A) inserted, by FA 2008 s 5, Sch 1 paras 1, 13 with effect for the tax year 2008–09 and subsequent tax years.
[2]   In sub-s (4) words repealed by FA 2009 s 27, Sch 8 para 6(2) with effect in relation to shares issued in the tax year 2009–10 or a subsequent tax year.
[3]   Sub-s (5) repealed by FA 2009 s 27, Sch 8 para 6(3) with effect in relation to claims made under ITA 2007 s 158(4) in respect of shares issued in the tax year 2009–10 or a subsequent tax year.

ITA 2007

4   In sub-s (5), figure substituted by FA 2011 s 42(1), (2) with effect for the tax year 2011–12 and subsequent tax years. FA 2011 s 42 came into force on 13 October 2011 (SI 2011/2459 art 2).

5   In Sub-s (2)(*a*) words inserted, in sub-s (2)(*b*) words substituted for words "£1 million", in sub-s (4) words substituted for words "subsections (1) and (2)", and sub-ss (2ZA), (2ZB), (6), (7) inserted, by FA 2018 s 16, Sch 4 para 1 with effect for shares issued on or after 6 April 2018 (by virtue of SI 2018/931 reg 3(a)).

Miscellaneous

159 Periods A, B and C

(1) This section applies for the purposes of this Part in relation to any shares issued by a company.

(2) "Period A" means the period—

    (*a*) beginning—

        (i)   with the incorporation of the company, or

        (ii) if the company was incorporated more than two years before the date on which the shares were issued, two years before that date, and

    (*b*) ending immediately before the termination date relating to the shares (see section 256).

(3) "Period B" means the period—

    (*a*) beginning with the issue of the shares, and

    (*b*) ending immediately before the termination date relating to the shares.

(4) "Period C" means the period—

    (*a*) beginning 12 months before the issue of the shares, and

    (*b*) ending immediately before the termination date relating to the shares.

Commentary—*Simon's Taxes* **E3.104, E3.190, E3.1100.**

HMRC Manuals—Venture Capital Schemes Manual VCM10540 (periods A, B and C).

VCM23290 (EIS: deferral relief: meaning of relevant period).

VCM23310 (EIS: deferral relief: length of period).

160 Overview of other Chapters of Part

In this Part—

    (*a*) Chapter 5 provides for the attribution of EIS relief to shares and the making of claims for such relief,

    (*b*) Chapter 6 provides for EIS relief to be withdrawn or reduced in the circumstances mentioned in that Chapter,

    (*c*) Chapter 7 makes provision with respect to the procedure for the withdrawal or reduction of EIS relief, and

    (*d*) Chapter 8 contains supplementary and general provisions.

161 Other tax reliefs relating to EIS

(1) Chapter 6 of Part 4 (losses on disposal of shares) provides for relief against the income of an individual who incurs an allowable loss for capital gains tax purposes on a disposal of shares to which EIS relief is attributable.

(2) Subsection (3) of section 392 (loan to buy interest in close company) provides that subsection (2)(*a*) of that section does not apply if at any time—

    (*a*) the individual by whom the shares are acquired, or

    (*b*) that individual's spouse or civil partner,

makes a claim for EIS relief in respect of the shares.

(3) Section 150A of TCGA 1992 makes provision about gains or losses on the disposal of shares to which EIS relief is attributable.

(4) Schedule 5B to TCGA 1992 provides relief in respect of the re-investment under EIS of the proceeds of assets disposed of in circumstances where there would otherwise be a chargeable gain.

(5) . . . [1]

Amendments—[1]   Sub-s (5) repealed by FA 2008 s 8, Sch 2 para 54 with effect in relation to chargeable gains accruing or treated as accruing in the tax year 2008–09 or any subsequent tax year.

CHAPTER 2

THE INVESTOR

Introduction

162 Overview of Chapter

The investor is a qualifying investor in relation to the relevant shares if the requirements of this Chapter are met as to—

    (*a*) no connection with the issuing company (see section 163),

    (*b*) no linked loans (see section 164), . . . [1]

    [(*ba*) existing shareholdings (see section 164A), and][1]

    (*c*) no tax avoidance (see section 165).

Commentary—*Simon's Taxes* **E3.106.**

HMRC Manuals—Venture Capital Schemes Manual VCM11010 (the investor: overview).

Amendments—[1]   Word "and" at the end of para (*b*) repealed, and para (*ba*) inserted, by F(No 2)A 2015 s 25, Sch 5 paras 1, 3 with effect in relation to shares issued on or after 18 November 2015.

The requirements

163 The no connection with the issuing company requirement

(1) The investor must not be connected with the issuing company (whether before or after its incorporation) at any time during the period—

    (*a*) beginning two years before the issue of the shares, and

    (*b*) ending immediately before the termination date relating to the shares.

(2) This is subject to section 169(1).

Commentary—*Simon's Taxes* **E3.106**.

HMRC Manuals—Venture Capital Schemes Manual VCM11020 (no connection with the issuing company).

164 The no linked loans requirement

(1) No linked loan is to be made by any person, at any time in period A, to the investor or an associate of the investor.

(2) In this section "linked loan" means any loan which—

    (*a*) would not have been made, or

    (*b*) would not have been made on the same terms,

if the investor had not subscribed for the relevant shares, or had not been proposing to do so.

(3) References in this section to the making by any person of a loan to the investor or an associate of the investor include references—

    (*a*) to the giving by that person of any credit to the investor or any associate of the investor, and

    (*b*) to the assignment to that person of a debt due from the investor or any associate of the investor.

Commentary—*Simon's Taxes* **E3.113**.

HMRC Manuals—Venture Capital Schemes Manual VCM11030 (no linked loans).

VCM23470 (meaning of investment-linked loan).

[164A The existing shareholdings requirement

(1) If, at the time the relevant shares are issued, the investor holds any other shares in a company within subsection (2) ("C"), those other shares must be—

    (*a*) a risk finance investment, or

    (*b*) subscriber shares which—

        (i) were issued to, and have since they were issued been continuously held by, the investor, or

        (ii) were acquired by the investor at a time when C had not issued any shares other than subscriber shares and had not begun to carry on or make preparations for carrying on any trade or business.

(2) The companies referred to in subsection (1) are—

    (*a*) the issuing company, and

    (*b*) any company which is a qualifying subsidiary of the issuing company at the time the relevant shares are issued.

(3) Shares in a company are a "risk finance investment" if—

    (*a*) they are issued by the company to the investor, and

    (*b*) (at any time) the company provides a compliance statement under section 205, 257ED or 257PB in respect of the issue of shares which includes those shares.][1]

Commentary—*Simon's Taxes* **E3.115**.

HMRC Manuals—Venture Capital Schemes Manual 8110 (independent investor).

Amendments—[1]   This section inserted by F(No 2)A 2015 s 25, Sch 5 paras 1, 4 with effect in relation to shares issued on or after 18 November 2015.

165 The no tax avoidance requirement

The relevant shares must be subscribed for by the investor for genuine commercial reasons, and not as part of a scheme or arrangement the main purpose or one of the main purposes of which is the avoidance of tax.

Commentary—*Simon's Taxes* **E3.114**.

HMRC Manuals—Venture Capital Schemes Manual VCM11040 (no tax avoidance).

Meaning of connection with issuing company

166 Connection with issuing company

(1) For the purposes of this Chapter (except section 168(4)), an individual is connected with the issuing company if the individual or an associate of the individual is connected with that company under—

    (*a*) section 167 (employees, directors and partners),

    (*b*) section 170 (persons interested in capital etc of company), or

    (*c*) section 171 (persons subscribing for shares under certain arrangements).

[(1A) But see section 252A(12) for provision which disapplies section 168.][1]

(2) See too section 257(2).

Commentary—*Simon's Taxes* **E3.109, E3.111.**

Amendments—[1]   Sub-s (1A) inserted by F(No 2)A 2015 s 25, Sch 5 paras 1, 5 with effect in relation to shares issued on or after 18 November 2015.

167 Employees, directors and partners

(1) An individual is connected with the issuing company if the individual—

    (*a*) is an employee of—

        (i)   the issuing company,

        (ii)   any subsidiary of the issuing company, or

        (iii) a partner of the issuing company or any of its subsidiaries,

    (*b*) is a partner of—

        (i)   the issuing company, or

        (ii)   any subsidiary of the issuing company, or

    (*c*) subject to section 168, is a director of—

        (i)   the issuing company,

        (ii)   any subsidiary of the issuing company, or

        (iii) a company which is a partner of the issuing company or any of its subsidiaries.

(2) In subsection (1) "subsidiary", in relation to the issuing company, means a company which at any time in period A is a 51% subsidiary of the issuing company, whether or not it is such a subsidiary while the individual or associate concerned is such an employee, partner or director as is mentioned in that subsection.

(3) For the purposes of this section and sections 168 and 169, in the case of an individual ("A") who is both a director and an employee of a company—

    (*a*) references (however expressed) to A in A's capacity as a director of the company include A in A's capacity as an employee of the company, but

    (*b*) (apart from that) A is to be treated as a director, and not as an employee, of the company.

Commentary—*Simon's Taxes* **E3.109.**

HMRC Manuals—Venture Capital Schemes Manual VCM11050 (connection: employees, directors and partners).

168 Directors excluded from connection

(1) An individual is not connected with the issuing company under section 167 merely because the individual, or an associate of the individual, is a director of that or another company unless the individual or associate (or a partnership of which the individual or associate is a member)—

    (*a*) receives a payment from the issuing company or a related person during the period mentioned in section 163, or

    (*b*) is entitled to receive such a payment in respect of that period or any part of it.

(2) For the purposes of subsection (1) the following are ignored—

    (*a*) any payment or reimbursement of travelling or other expenses wholly, exclusively and necessarily incurred by the individual or an associate of the individual in the performance of the individual's or associate's duties as a director,

    (*b*) any interest which represents no more than a reasonable commercial return on money lent to the issuing company or a related person,

    (*c*) any dividend or other distribution which does not exceed a normal return on the investment,

    (*d*) any payment for the supply of goods which does not exceed their market value,

    (*e*) any payment of rent for any property occupied by the issuing company or a related person which does not exceed a reasonable and commercial rent for the property, and

    (*f*) any necessary and reasonable remuneration which meets the conditions in subsection (3).

(3) The conditions are that the remuneration—

    (*a*) is paid for services rendered to the issuing company or related person in the course of a trade or profession carried on wholly or partly in the United Kingdom (not being secretarial or managerial services or services of a kind provided by the person to whom they are rendered), and

    (*b*) is taken into account in calculating for tax purposes the profits of that trade or profession.

(4) In this section—

    (*a*) "related person", in relation to the issuing company, means—

        (i)   any company of which the individual or an associate of the individual is a director and which is a subsidiary or partner of the issuing company, or a partner of a subsidiary of the issuing company, and

        (ii)   any person connected with the issuing company or with a company falling within sub-paragraph (i), and

    (*b*) any reference to a payment to an individual includes a payment made to the individual indirectly or to the individual's order or for the individual's benefit.

(5) In this section and section 169 "subsidiary", in relation to the issuing company, means a company which at any time in period A is a 51% subsidiary of the issuing company.

Commentary—*Simon's Taxes* **E3.110.**

HMRC Manuals—Venture Capital Schemes Manual VCM11060 (connection: directors excluded).

169 Directors qualifying for relief despite connection

(1) Section 163(1) does not prevent the investor from being a qualifying investor despite the investor's connection with the issuing company at any time in period A relating to the relevant shares if—

    (a) the investor is connected with that company merely because of the investor, or the investor's associate—

        (i) being a director of, or of a company which is a partner of, the issuing company or a subsidiary of the issuing company, and

        (ii) being in receipt of, or entitled to receive, remuneration as such, and

    (b) conditions A and B and (where applicable) condition C are met.

(2) Condition A is that, in relation to the director ("D"), whether D is the investor or an associate of the investor—

    (a) D's remuneration, or

    (b) the remuneration to which D is entitled,

consists only of remuneration which is reasonable remuneration for services rendered to the company of which D is a director in D's capacity as such.

(3) Condition B is that the investor was issued with the relevant shares, or a previous issue of shares in the issuing company which meet the requirements of section 173(2), at a time when the investor had never been—

    (a) connected with the issuing company, or

    (b) involved in carrying on (whether on the investor's own account or as a partner, director or employee) the whole or any part of the trade, business or profession carried on by the issuing company or a subsidiary of that company.

(4) Condition C is that, if the issue of the relevant shares did not meet condition B, they were issued before[—

    (a) the termination date relating to the latest issue of shares which met that condition, or

    (b) if that issue is an issue in respect of which the investor is eligible for SEIS relief (within the meaning of Part 5A), before the date specified in section 257AC(4) in relation to the shares.][1]

(5) For the purposes of condition A any necessary and reasonable remuneration falling within section 168(2)(f) is to be left out of account.

(6) In this section "remuneration" includes any benefit or facility.

Commentary—*Simon's Taxes* E3.111.
HMRC Manuals—Venture Capital Schemes Manual VCM11070 (connection: directors qualifying for relief despite).
Amendments—[1]   Words in sub-s (4) substituted by FA 2012 s 38, Sch 6 paras 6, 10 with effect in relation to shares issued on or after 6 April 2012.

170 Persons interested in capital etc of company

(1) An individual is connected with the issuing company if the individual directly or indirectly possesses or is entitled to acquire more than 30% of—

    (a) the ordinary share capital of the company or any subsidiary of the company,

    (b) the . . . [2] issued share capital of the company or any such subsidiary, or

    (c) the voting power in the company or any such subsidiary.

(2) An individual is connected with the issuing company if the individual directly or indirectly possesses or is entitled to acquire such rights as would—

    (a) in the event of the winding up of the company or any subsidiary of the company, or

    (b) in any other circumstances,

entitle the individual to receive more than 30% of the assets of the company or subsidiary ("the company in question") which would then be available for distribution to equity holders of the company in question.

(3) For the purposes of subsection (2)—

    (a) the persons who are equity holders of the company in question, and

    (b) the percentage of the assets of the company in question to which the individual would be entitled,

are determined in accordance with [Chapter 6 of Part 5 of CTA 2010][1].

(4) In making that determination—

    (a) references in [section 166 of that Act to company A] are to be read as references to an equity holder, and

    (b) references in that [section] to a winding up are to be read as including references to any other circumstances in which assets of the company in question are available for distribution to its equity holders.

(5) An individual is not connected with a company merely because one or more shares in the company are held by the individual or by an associate of the individual, at a time when the company—

    (a) has not issued any shares other than subscriber shares, and (*b*) has not begun to carry on, or make preparations for carrying on, any trade or business.

(6) An individual is connected with the issuing company if the individual has control of the issuing company or of any subsidiary of that company.

(7) In this section "subsidiary", in relation to the issuing company, means a company which at any time in period A is a 51% subsidiary of the issuing company, whether or not it is such a subsidiary while the individual concerned has, or is entitled to acquire, such capital, voting power, rights or control as are mentioned in this section.

(8) . . . [2]

(9) For the purposes of this section—

    (*a*) an individual is treated as entitled to acquire anything which the individual is entitled to acquire at a future date or will at a future date be entitled to acquire, and

    (*b*) there is attributed to any individual any rights or powers of any other person who is an associate of the individual.

(10) . . . [2]

Commentary—*Simon's Taxes* **E3.107**.

HMRC Manuals—Venture Capital Schemes Manual VCM11080 (connection: persons interested in capital etc of company).

Amendments—[1]   In sub-s (3) words substituted for words "paragraphs 1 and 3 of Schedule 18 to ICTA", in sub-s (4)(a) words substituted for words "paragraph 3 of that Schedule to the first company" and in sub-s (4)(b) word substituted for word "paragraph" by CTA 2010 s 1177, Sch 1 para 499. CTA 2010 has effect for corporation tax purposes for accounting periods ending on or after 1 April 2010, and for income and capital gains tax purposes for the tax year 2010–11 and subsequent tax years.

[2]   Words in sub-s (1)(*b*) and the whole of sub-ss (8), (10) repealed, by FA 2012 s 39, Sch 7 paras 1, 4 with effect in relation to shares issued on or after 6 April 2012 (subject to transitional provisions in Sch 7 para 22(2)).

171 Persons subscribing for shares under certain arrangements

(1) This section applies if an individual ("A") subscribes for shares in a company ("the company") with which A is not connected under section 167 or 170.

(2) If—

    (*a*) A subscribes for the shares as part of an arrangement, and

    (*b*) the arrangement provides for another person to subscribe for shares in another company with which (assuming it to be the issuing company) A, or any other individual who is a party to the arrangement, is connected,

A is connected with the company under this section.

Commentary—*Simon's Taxes* **E3.106**.

HMRC Manuals—Venture Capital Schemes Manual VCM11090 (connection: persons subscribing for shares under certain arrangements).

CHAPTER 3

GENERAL REQUIREMENTS

Introduction

172 Overview of Chapter

The general requirements are met in respect of the relevant shares if the requirements of this Chapter are met as to—

    (*a*) the shares (see section 173),

    [(*aa*) the maximum amount raised annually through risk [finance investments][4] (see section 173A),][1]

    [(*aaa*) the maximum risk finance investments at the issue date (see section 173AA),

    (*aab*) the maximum risk finance investments at times during period B (see section 173AB),][4]

    [(*ab*) . . .][2]

    (*b*) the purpose of the issue (see section 174),

    (*c*) the use of the money raised (see section 175),

    [(*ca*) the permitted maximum age (see section 175A),][4]

    (*d*) the minimum period (see section 176),

    (*e*) no pre-arranged exits (see section 177), . . . [3]

    (*f*) no tax avoidance (see section 178)[, and

    (*g*) no disqualifying arrangements (see section 178A).][3]

Commentary—*Simon's Taxes* **E3.116**.

HMRC Manuals—Venture Capital Schemes Manual VCM12010 (general requirements: overview).

Amendments—[1]   Para (*aa*) inserted by FA 2007 s 51, Sch 16 para 5(1), (2) with effect from 19 July 2007. This amendment does not have effect in relation to shares issued to the managers of an approved fund which closed before that date: FA 2007 Sch 16 para 5(5), (6).

[2]   Para (*ab*) inserted by FA 2012 s 38, Sch 6 paras 6, 11 with effect in relation to shares issued on or after 6 April 2012 and repealed by F(No 2)A 2015, s 25, Sch 5 paras 1, 6(*c*) with effect in relation to shares issued on or after 6 April 2015.

[3]   Word "and" at the end of para (*e*) repealed and para (*g*) and preceding word "and" inserted, by FA 2012 s 39, Sch 7 paras 1, 5 with effect in relation to shares issued on or after 6 April 2012, subject to transitional provisions in FA 2012 Sch 7 para 22(2).

[4]   Words in para (*aa*) substituted for words "capital schemes", and paras (*aaa*), (*aab*), (*ca*) inserted, by F(No 2)A 2015, s 25, Sch 5 paras 1, 6(*a*), (*b*), (*d*) with effect in relation to shares issued on or after 18 November 2015.

The requirements

173 The shares requirement

(1) The relevant shares must meet—

   (a) the requirements of subsection (2), and

   (b) unless they are bonus shares, the requirements of subsection (3).

(2) Shares meet the requirements of this subsection if they are ordinary shares which do not, at any time during period B, carry—

   [(a) any present or future preferential right to dividends that is within subsection (2A),

   (aa) any present or future preferential right to a company's assets on its winding up,]¹ or

   (b) any present or future right to be redeemed.

[(2A) A preferential right to dividends carried by a share in a company is within this subsection if—

   (a) the amount of any dividends payable pursuant to the right, or the date or dates on which they are payable, depend to any extent on a decision of the company, the holder of the share or any other person, or

   (b) the amount of any dividends that become payable at any time pursuant to the right includes any amount that became payable at any earlier time pursuant to the right, but has not been paid.]¹

(3) Shares meet the requirements of this subsection if they—

   (a) are subscribed for wholly in cash, and

   (b) are fully paid up at the time they are issued.

(4) Shares are not fully paid up for the purposes of subsection (3)(b) if there is any undertaking to pay cash to any person at a future date in respect of the acquisition of the shares.

Commentary—*Simon's Taxes* **E3.117**.

HMRC Manuals—Venture Capital Schemes Manual VCM12020 (shares requirement).

Amendments—¹ Sub-s (2)(a), (aa) substituted for previous sub-s (2)(a), and sub-s (2A) inserted, by FA 2012 s 39, Sch 7 paras 1, 6 with effect in relation to shares issued on or after 6 April 2012 subject to transitional provisions in FA 2012 Sch 7 para 22(2).

[173A The maximum amount raised annually through risk [finance investments]⁵ requirement

(1) The total amount of relevant investments made in the issuing company in the year ending with the date the relevant shares are issued [must not exceed—.

   (a) if the company is a knowledge-intensive company at that date (see section 252A and subsection (5A)), £10 million, and

   (b) in any other case, £5 million.]⁶

[(2) In subsection (1), the reference to relevant investments made in the issuing company includes—

   (a) a relevant investment made in any company that has at any time in the year mentioned there been a 51% subsidiary of the issuing company (including investments made in such a company before it became such a subsidiary but, if it is not such a subsidiary at the end of that year, not those made after it last ceased to be such a subsidiary),

   (b) any other relevant investment made in a company to the extent that the money raised by the investment has been employed for the purposes of a trade carried on by another company that has at any time in that year been a 51% subsidiary of the issuing company (but, if it is not such a subsidiary at the end of that year, ignoring any money so employed after it last ceased to be such a subsidiary), and

   (c) any other relevant investment made in a company if—

     (i) the money raised by the investment has been employed for the purposes of a trade carried on by that company or another person, and

     (ii) in that year, after the investment was made, the trade (or a part of it) became a relevant transferred trade (see subsection (2B)).

(2A) If only a proportion of the money raised by a relevant investment is employed for the purposes of a trade which becomes a relevant transferred trade, the reference in subsection (2)(c) to the relevant investment is to be read as a reference to the corresponding proportion of that investment.

(2B) Where—

   (a) in the year mentioned in subsection (1) a trade is transferred—

     (i) to the issuing company,

     (ii) to a company that has at any time during that year been a 51% subsidiary of the issuing company, or

     (iii) to a partnership of which a company within subparagraph (i) or (ii) is a member,

   (including where it is transferred to a company within subparagraph (ii), or a partnership of which such a company is a member, in that year before the company became such a subsidiary but, if the company is not such a subsidiary at the end of that year, not where it is transferred to such a company or partnership after the company last ceased to be such a subsidiary), and

   (b) that trade or a part of it was previously (at any time) carried on by another person, the trade or part mentioned in paragraph (*b*) becomes a "relevant transferred trade" at the time it is transferred as mentioned in paragraph (*a*).][5]

(3) A "relevant investment" is made in a company if—

  (*a*) an investment (of any kind) in the company is made by a VCT, or

  (*b*) the company issues shares (money having been subscribed for them), and (at any time) the company provides—

     (i) a compliance statement under section 205, or

     [(ia) a compliance statement under section 257ED (seed enterprise investment scheme),][2]

     (ii) . . .[3]

in respect of the shares[, or

  [(*ba*) an investment is made in the company and (at any time) the company provides a compliance statement under section 257PB (tax relief for social investments) in respect of the investment, or][5]

  [(*c*) any other investment is made in the company which is aid received by it pursuant to a measure approved by the European Commission as compatible with Article 107 of the Treaty on the Functioning of the European Union in accordance with the principles laid down in the [European Commission's Guidelines on State aid to promote risk finance investment][5] (as those guidelines may be amended or replaced from time to time).][3]

(4) An investment within subsection (3)(*b*) is regarded as made when the shares are issued.][1]

[(5) Section 257KB applies in determining for those purposes when an investment within subsection (3)(*ba*) is made as it applies for the purposes of Part 5B (tax relief on social investments).

[(5A) If the issuing company began to carry on a trade less than three years before the date the relevant shares are issued, section 252A as it applies for the purposes of this section has effect with the substitution of the following subsections for subsections (2) to (4A)—

  "(2) The first operating costs condition is that in at least one of the relevant three succeeding years at least 15% of the relevant operating costs constitute expenditure on research and development or innovation.

  (3) The second operating costs condition is that in each of the relevant three succeeding years at least 10% of the relevant operating costs constitute such expenditure.

  (4) In subsections (2) and (3)—

    "relevant operating costs" means—

        (*a*) if the issuing company is a single company at the time the relevant shares are issued, the operating costs of that company, and

        (*b*) if the issuing company is a parent company at the time the relevant shares are issued, the sum of—

     (i) the operating costs of the issuing company, and

     (ii) the operating costs of each company which is a qualifying subsidiary of the issuing company at that time, excluding a company's operating costs for any of the relevant three succeeding years during any part of which the company is not a qualifying subsidiary of the issuing company;

  "the relevant three succeeding years" means the three consecutive years the first of which begins with the date the relevant shares are issued.][6]

(6) For the purposes of this section—

  (*a*) references to a trade include a part of a trade (and references to the carrying on of a trade are to be construed accordingly);

  (*b*) when determining the amount of money raised by a relevant investment which has been employed for the purposes of a trade such apportionments are to be made as are just and reasonable.

(7) In this section "trade" includes—

  (*a*) any business or profession,

  (*b*) so far as not within paragraph (*a*), the carrying on of research and development activities from which it is intended a trade will be derived or will benefit, and

  (*c*) preparing to carry on a trade.][5]

Commentary—*Simon's Taxes* **E3.118, E3.133.**

HMRC Manuals—Venture Capital Schemes Manual VCM12030 (maximum amount raised annually through risk capital schemes requirement).

8121 (a relevant investment: overview).

Amendments—[1] This section inserted by FA 2007 s 51, Sch 16 para 5(1), (3) with effect from 19 July 2007. This amendment does not have effect in relation to shares issued to the managers of an approved fund which closed before that date: FA 2007 Sch 16 para 5(5), (6).

[2] Sub-s (3)(*b*)(ia) inserted by FA 2012 s 38, Sch 6 paras 6, 12 with effect in relation to shares issued on or after 6 April 2012.

[3] Sub-s (3)(*b*)(ii) repealed and sub-s (3)(*c*) and preceding word "or" inserted, by FA 2012 s 39, Sch 7 paras 1, 7 (1), (3) with effect in relation to shares issued on or after 6 April 2012 subject to transitional provisions in FA 2012 Sch 7 para 22(2).

[5] Words in heading substituted for words "capital schemes", sub-ss (2)–(2B) substituted for previous sub-s (2), sub-ss (3)(*ba*), (5)–(7) inserted, and words in sub-s (3)(*c*) substituted for words "Community Guidelines on Risk Capital Investments in Small

ITA 2007

and Medium-sized Enterprises", by F(No 2)A 2015 s 25, Sch 5 paras 1, 7 with effect in relation to shares issued on or after 18 November 2015, but not so as to prevent shares issued before that day constituting "relevant investments" for the purposes of determining whether the requirements of this section are met in relation to shares issued on or after that day (F(No 2)A 2015 Sch 5 para 23(2)).

[6] In sub-s (1), words substituted for words "must not exceed £5 million", and sub-s (5A) inserted, by FA 2018 s 16, Sch 4 para 2 with effect for shares issued on or after 6 April 2018 (by virtue of SI 2018/931 reg 3(a).

[173AA Maximum risk finance investments at the issue date requirement

(1) The total amount of relevant investments made in the issuing company on or before the issue date must not exceed—

    (*a*) if the issuing company is a knowledge-intensive company at the issue date (see section 252A), £20 million, and

    (*b*) in any other case, £12 million.

(2) In subsection (1) the reference to relevant investments made in the issuing company includes—

    (*a*) any relevant investment made in any company that at the issue date is, or has at any time before that date been, a 51% subsidiary of the issuing company (including investments made in such a company before it became such a subsidiary but, if it is not such a subsidiary at the issue date, not investments made in it after it last ceased to be such a subsidiary),

    (*b*) any other relevant investment made in a company to the extent that the money raised by the investment has been employed for the purposes of a trade carried on by another company that has at any time before the issue date been a 51% subsidiary of the issuing company (but, if it is not such a subsidiary at that date, ignoring any money so employed after it last ceased to be such a subsidiary), and

    (*c*) any other relevant investment made in a company if—

        (i) the money raised by the investment has been employed for the purposes of a trade carried on by that company or another person, and

        (ii) after the investment was made, but on or before the issue date, that trade became a relevant transferred trade (see subsection (4)).

(3) If only a proportion of the money raised by a relevant investment is employed for the purposes of a trade which becomes a relevant transferred trade, the reference in subsection (2)(*c*) to the relevant investment is to be read as a reference to the corresponding proportion of that investment.

(4) Where—

    (*a*) at any time on or before the issue date, a trade is transferred—

        (i) to the issuing company,

        (ii) to a company that at the issue date is, or has at any time before that date been, a 51% subsidiary of the issuing company, or

        (iii) to a partnership of which a company within subparagraph (i) or (ii) is a member,

        (including where it is transferred to a company within subparagraph (ii), or a partnership of which such a company is a member, before the company became such a subsidiary but, if the company is not such a subsidiary at the issue date, not where it is transferred to such a company or partnership after the company last ceased to be such a subsidiary), and

    (*b*) the trade or a part of it was previously (at any time) carried on by another person,

the trade or part mentioned in paragraph (*b*) becomes a "relevant transferred trade" at the time it is transferred as mentioned in paragraph (*a*).

(5) In this section—

    "the issue date" means the date on which the relevant shares are issued;

    "relevant investment" has the meaning given by section 173A(3), and section 173A(4) and (5) (which determines when certain investments are made) applies for the purposes of this section;

and section 173A(6) and (7) (meaning of "trade" etc) applies for the purposes of this section as it applies for the purposes of section 173A.][1]

Commentary—*Simon's Taxes* **E3.118.**
HMRC Manuals—Venture Capital Schemes Manual 8121 (a relevant investment: overview).
8161 (knowledge-intensive company than other companies: conditions).
Amendments—[1]   Sections 173AA, 173AB inserted by F(No 2)A 2015 s 25, Sch 5 paras 1, 8 with effect in relation to shares issued on or after 18 November 2015, but not so as to prevent shares issued before that day constituting "relevant investments" for the purposes of determining whether the requirements of this section are met in relation to shares issued on or after that day (F(No 2)A 2015 Sch 5 para 23(2)).

[173AB Maximum risk finance investments during period B requirement

(1) The requirement of this section applies if condition A or B is met.

(2) Condition A is that—

    (*a*) a company becomes a 51% subsidiary of the issuing company at any time during period B,

    (*b*) all or part of the money raised by the issue of the relevant shares is employed for the purposes of a qualifying business activity which consists wholly or in part of a trade carried on by that company, and (*c*) that trade (or a part of it) was carried on by that company before it became a 51% subsidiary as mentioned in paragraph (*a*).

(3) Condition B is that all or part of the money raised by the issue of the relevant shares is employed for the purposes of a qualifying business activity which consists wholly or in part of a trade which, during period B, becomes a relevant transferred trade.

(4) The requirement of this section is that, at all times in period B, the total of the relevant investments made in the issuing company before the time in question ("the relevant time") must not exceed—

    (*a*) if the issuing company is a knowledge-intensive company at the issue date (see section 252A), £20 million, and

    (*b*) in any other case, £12 million.

(5) In subsection (4) the reference to relevant investments made in the issuing company includes—

    (*a*) any relevant investment made in any company that at any time before the relevant time has been a 51% subsidiary of the issuing company (including investments made in a company before it became such a subsidiary but, if it is not such a subsidiary at the relevant time, not investments made in it after it last ceased to be such a subsidiary),

    (*b*) any other relevant investment made in a company to the extent that the money raised by the investment has been employed for the purposes of a trade carried on by another company that has at any time before the relevant time been a 51% subsidiary of the issuing company (but, if it is not such a subsidiary at the relevant time, ignoring any money so employed after it last ceased to be such a subsidiary), and

    (*c*) any other relevant investments made in a company where—

        (i) the money raised by the investment has been employed for the purposes of a trade carried on by that company or another person, and

        (ii) after the investment was made, but before the relevant time, that trade (or a part of it) becomes a relevant transferred trade (see subsection (7)).

(6) If only a proportion of the money raised by a relevant investment is employed for the purposes of a trade which became a relevant transferred trade, the reference in subsection (5)(*c*) to the relevant investment is to be read as a reference to the corresponding proportion of that investment.

(7) Where—

    (*a*) before the relevant time, a trade is transferred—

        (i) to the issuing company,

        (ii) to a company that is at the relevant time, or has before that time been, a 51% subsidiary of the issuing company, or

        (iii) to a partnership of which a company within subparagraph (i) or (ii) is a member,

    (including where it is transferred to a company within subparagraph (ii), or a partnership of which such a company is a member, before the company became such a subsidiary but, if the company is not such a subsidiary at the relevant time, not where it is transferred to such a company or partnership after the company last ceased to be such a subsidiary), and

    (*b*) the trade or a part of it was previously (at any time) carried on by another person,

the trade or part mentioned in paragraph (*b*) becomes a "relevant transferred trade" at the time it is transferred as mentioned in paragraph (*a*).

(8) In this section—

    "the issue date" means the date on which the relevant shares are issued, and

    "relevant investment" has the meaning given by section 173A(3), and section 173A(4) and (5) (which determines when certain investments are made) applies for the purposes of this section;

and section 173A(6) and (7) (meaning of "trade" etc) applies for the purposes of this section as it applies for the purposes of section 173A.][1]

Commentary—*Simon's Taxes* **E3.118**.
HMRC Manuals—Venture Capital Schemes Manual 8121 (a relevant investment: overview).
8161 (knowledge-intensive company than other companies: conditions).
VCM12030 (EIS :relevant investments).
Amendments—[1]   Sections 173AA, 173AB inserted by F(No 2)A 2015 s 25, Sch 5 paras 1, 8 with effect in relation to shares issued on or after 18 November 2015, but not so as to prevent shares issued before that day constituting "relevant investments" for the purposes of determining whether the requirements of this section are met in relation to shares issued on or after that day (F(No 2)A 2015 Sch 5 para 23(2)).

174 The purpose of the issue requirement

[(1)] [1]The relevant shares (other than any of them which are bonus shares) must be issued in order to raise money for the purpose of a qualifying business activity [so as to promote business growth and development][1].

[(2) For this purpose "business growth and development" means the growth and development of—

    (*a*) if the issuing company is a single company, the business of that company, and

    (*b*) if the issuing company is a parent company, what would be the business of the group if the activities of the group companies taken together were regarded as one business.][1]

Commentary—*Simon's Taxes* E3.119, D6.813, E3.120, E3.130, E3.141.
HMRC Manuals—Venture Capital Schemes Manual VCM12050 (purpose of the issue requirement).
8130 (growth and development: meaning).
Amendments—[1]   Sub-s (1) numbered as such and words inserted, and sub-s (2) inserted, by F(No 2)A 2015 s 25, Sch 5 paras 1, 10 with effect in relation to shares issued on or after 18 November 2015.

175 The use of the money raised requirement

[(1) The requirement of this section is that all of the money raised by the issue of the relevant shares (other than any of them which are bonus shares) is, no later than the time mentioned in subsection (3), employed wholly for the purpose of the qualifying business activity for which it was raised.][1]

[(1ZA) Employing money raised by the issue of the relevant shares (whether on its own or together with other money) on the acquisition, directly or indirectly, of—

   (a) an interest in another company such that a company becomes a 51% subsidiary of the issuing company,
   (b) a further interest in a company which is a 51% subsidiary of the issuing company,
   (c) a trade,
   (d) intangible assets employed for the purposes of a trade, or
   (e) goodwill employed for the purposes of a trade,

does not amount to employing that money for the purposes of a qualifying business activity.

(1ZB) The Treasury may by regulations provide that subsection (1ZA) does not apply in relation to acquisitions of intangible assets which are of a description specified, or which occur in circumstances specified, in the regulations.

(1ZC) For the purposes of subsections (1ZA) and (1ZB)—

   "goodwill" has the same meaning as in Part 8 of CTA 2009 (see section 715(3));
   "intangible assets" means any asset which falls to be treated as an intangible asset in accordance with generally accepted accountancy practice;

and section 173A(6) and (7) (meaning of "trade" etc) applies as it applies for the purposes of section 173A.

(1A) Also, otherwise employing money on the acquisition of shares or stock in a company does not of itself amount to employing the money for the purposes of a qualifying business activity.][2]

(2) The [requirement in subsection (1) does][1] not fail to be met merely because an amount of money which is not significant is employed for another purpose.

(3) The time referred to in [subsection (1)][1] is—

   (a) the end of the period of [two years][1] beginning with the issue of the shares, or
   (b) in the case of money raised only for the purpose of an activity to which section 179(2) applies, the end of the period of [two years][1] beginning with—
       (i) the issue of the shares, or
       (ii) if later, the time when the company or a qualifying 90% subsidiary of the company begins to carry on the qualifying trade.

(4) In determining for the purposes of subsection (3)(b) when a qualifying trade is begun to be carried on by a qualifying 90% subsidiary of a company, any carrying on by it of the trade before it became such a subsidiary is ignored.

Commentary—*Simon's Taxes* E3.120, E3.141.
HMRC Manuals—Venture Capital Schemes Manual VCM12060 (use of the money raised requirement).
8140 (use of money: no business acquisitions).
Corporate Intangibles Research And Development Manual CIRD11070 (goodwill : definition).
CIRD11100 (intangible assets : definitions)
Amendments—[1]   Sub-s (1) substituted; in sub-ss (2), (3) words substituted by FA 2009 s 27, Sch 8 para 7 with effect in relation to shares issued on or after 22 April 2009.
[2]   Sub-ss (1ZA)–(1A) substituted for previous sub-s (1A) by F(No 2)A 2015 s 25, Sch 5 paras 1, 11 with effect in relation to shares issued on or after 18 November 2015. Sub-s (1A) was inserted by FA 2012 s 39, Sch 7 paras 1, 8, with effect in relation to shares issued on or after 6 April 2012 subject to transitional provisions in FA 2012 Sch 7 para 22(2).

[175A The permitted maximum age requirement

(1) The requirement of this section is that, if the relevant shares are issued after the initial investing period, condition A, B or C must be met.

(2) "The initial investing period" means—

   (a) where the issuing company is a knowledge-intensive company at the issue date, the period of 10 years [beginning with—
       (i) the relevant first commercial sale, or
       (ii) if the issuing company so elects, the date by reference to which that company is treated as reaching an annual turnover of £200,000 (see section 252B),][3] and
   (b) in any other case, the period of 7 years beginning with that sale.

(3) Condition A is that—

   (a) a relevant investment was made in the issuing company before the end of the initial investing period, and (*b*) some or all of the money raised by that investment was employed for the purposes of the relevant qualifying business activity (or a part of it).

(4) Condition B is that—

    (*a*) the total amount of relevant investments made in the issuing company in a period of 30 consecutive days which includes the issue date is at least 50% of the average turnover amount, and

    (*b*) the money raised by those investments is employed for the purpose of entering a new product or geographical market.

(5) Condition C is that—

    (*a*) condition B in subsection (4) or condition B in section 294A(4) (VCT: permitted company age requirement) was previously met in relation to one or more relevant investments made in the issuing company, and

    (*b*) some or all of the money raised by those investments was employed for the purposes of the relevant qualifying business activity.

(6) "The relevant first commercial sale" means the earliest of the following—

    (*a*) the first commercial sale made by the issuing company;

    (*b*) the first commercial sale made by a company that is at the issue date, or before that date has been, a 51% subsidiary of the issuing company (including a sale made by a company before it became such a subsidiary but, if it is not such a subsidiary at the issue date, not a sale made after it last ceased to be such a subsidiary);

    (*c*) the first commercial sale made by any person who previously (at any time) carried on a trade which was subsequently carried on, on or before the issue date, by—

        (i) the issuing company, or

        (ii) a company that is at the issue date, or before that date has been, a 51% subsidiary of the issuing company,

    (including a trade subsequently carried on by such a company before it became such a subsidiary but, if it is not such a subsidiary at the issue date, not a trade which it carried on only after it last ceased to be such a subsidiary);

    (*d*) the first commercial sale made by a company which becomes a 51% subsidiary of the issuing company after the issue date in circumstances where all or part of the money raised by the issue of the relevant shares is employed for the purposes of an activity carried on by that subsidiary (including a sale made by such a company before it became such a subsidiary);

    (*e*) the first commercial sale made by any person who previously (at any time) carried on a trade which was subsequently carried on by a company mentioned in paragraph (*d*) (including a trade carried on by such a company before it became such a subsidiary);

    (*f*) if the money raised by the issue of the relevant shares (or any part of it) is employed for the purposes of a trade which has been transferred, after the issue date, to the issuing company or a 51% subsidiary of that company (or a partnership of which the issuing company or such a subsidiary is a member), having previously (at any time) been carried on by another person, the first commercial sale made by that other person.

(7) "The average turnover amount" means one fifth of the total relevant turnover amount for the [relevant five year period.][2]

[(7A) Subject to subsection (7B), the relevant five year period is the five year period which ends immediately before the beginning of the last accounts filing period.

(7B) If the last accounts filing period ends more than 12 months before the issue date, the relevant five year period is the five year period which ends 12 months before the issue date.][2]

(8) In this section—

    "entering a new product or geographical market" has the same meaning as in Commission Regulation (EU) No 651/2014 (General block exemption Regulation);

    "first commercial sale" has the same meaning as in the European Commission's Guidelines on State aid to promote risk finance investments (as those guidelines may be amended or replaced from time to time);

    "the issue date" means the date on which the relevant shares are issued;

    "the last accounts filing period" means the last period for filing (within the meaning of section 442 of the Companies Act 2006) for the issuing company which ends before the date on which the relevant shares are issued;

    "relevant investment" has the meaning given by section 173A(3), and section 173A(4) and (5) (which determines when certain investments are made) applies for the purposes of this section;

    "relevant qualifying business activity" means the qualifying business activity for which the money raised by the issue of the relevant shares is employed;

    "the total relevant turnover amount" for a period is—

        (*a*) if the issuing company is a single company at the issue date, the sum of—

            (i) the issuing company's turnover for that period,

            (ii) if all or part of the money raised by the issue of the relevant shares is employed for the purposes of an activity carried on by a company which becomes a 51% subsidiary of the issuing company after the issue date, the turnover for that period of that subsidiary (or, if there is more than one, each of them), and

(iii) if all or part of the money raised by the issue of the relevant shares is employed for the purposes of a transferred trade, the turnover of that trade for so much of that period as falls before the trade became a transferred trade (except to the extent that it is already included in calculating the amounts within subparagraphs (i) and (ii));

(b) if the issuing company is a parent company at the issue date, the sum of—

(i) the issuing company's turnover for that period,

(ii) the turnover for that period of each company which at the issue date is a qualifying subsidiary of the issuing company,

(iii) if all or part of the money raised by the issue of the relevant shares is employed for the purposes of an activity carried on by a company which becomes a 51% subsidiary of the issuing company after the issue date, the turnover for that period of that subsidiary (or, if there is more than one, each of them), and

(iv) if all or part of the money raised by the issue of the relevant shares is employed for the purposes of a transferred trade, the turnover of that trade for so much of that period as falls before the trade became a transferred trade (except to the extent that it is already included in calculating the amounts within subparagraphs (i) to (iii));

"transferred trade" means a trade which has been transferred to the company which is carrying on the trade at the time the money raised by the issue of the relevant shares is employed or to a partnership of which that company is a member;

"turnover"—

(a) in relation to a company, has the meaning given by section 474(1) of the Companies Act 2006 and is to be determined by reference to the accounts of companies and amounts recognised for accounting purposes (and such apportionments of those amounts as are just and reasonable are to be made for the purpose of determining a company's turnover for a period);

(b) in relation to any other person carrying on a trade, also has the meaning given by section 474(1) of that Act (reading references in that provision to a company as references to the person) and is to be determined by reference to the accounts of the person and amounts recognised for accounting purposes (and such apportionments of those amounts as are just and reasonable are to be made for the purpose of determining a person's turnover for a period);

(c) in relation to a transferred trade carried on by a company or other person, means such proportion of the turnover of the company or other person as it is just and reasonable to attribute to the transferred trade;

and section 173A(6) and (7) (meaning of "trade" etc) applies for the purposes of this section as it applies for the purposes of section 173A.][1]

Commentary—*Simon's Taxes* **E3.120A**.
HMRC Manuals—Venture Capital Schemes Manual 8151 (the basic age condition: first commercial sale).
Amendments—[1]   This section inserted by F(No 2)A 2015 s 25, Sch 5 paras 1, 12 with effect in relation to shares issued on or after 18 November 2015, but not so as to prevent shares issued before that day constituting "relevant investments" for the purposes of determining whether the requirements of this section are met in relation to shares issued on or after that day (F(No 2)A 2015 Sch 5 para 23(2)).
[2]   Words in sub-s (7) substituted, and sub-ss (7A), (7B) inserted, by FA 2016 s 29(1). Subject to any election made under FA 2016 s 30 by the issuing company, these amendments are to be treated as always having had effect. If an election is made under s 30, the amendments made by s 29(1) do not apply in relation to shares issued by the relevant company in the period beginning with 18 November 2015 and ending with 5 April 2016. See FA 2016 s 30.
[3]   In sub-s (2)(a), words substituted for words "beginning with the relevant first commercial sale," by FA 2018 s 16, Sch 4 para 5 with effect for shares issued on or after 6 April 2018 (by virtue of SI 2018/931 reg 3(a)).

176 The minimum period requirement

(1) The issue of shares which includes the relevant shares must meet—

(a) the requirement of subsection (2) in a case where the money raised by an issue of shares is raised wholly for the purpose of a qualifying business activity falling within section 179(2),

(b) the requirement of subsection (3) in a case where the money raised by an issue of shares is raised wholly or partly for the purpose of a qualifying business activity falling within section 179(4).

(2) The requirement is that—

(a) the trade concerned must have been carried on for a period of at least 4 months ending at or after the time of the issue, and

(b) throughout that period—

(i) the trade must have been carried on by the issuing company or a qualifying 90% subsidiary of that company, and

(ii) the trade must not have been carried on by any other person.

(3) The requirement is that—

    (*a*) the research and development concerned must have been carried on for a period of at least 4 months ending at or after the time of the issue, and

    (*b*) throughout that period—

        (i) the research and development must have been carried on by the issuing company or a qualifying 90% subsidiary of that company, and

        (ii) the research and development must not have been carried on by any other person.

(4) If—

    (*a*) merely because of the issuing company or any other company being wound up, or dissolved without winding up—

        (i) the trade is carried on as mentioned in subsection (2), or

        (ii) the research and development is carried on as mentioned in subsection (3),

    for a period shorter than 4 months, and

    (*b*) the winding up or dissolution—

        (i) is for genuine commercial reasons, and

        (ii) is not part of a scheme or arrangement the main purpose or one of the main purposes of which is the avoidance of tax,

subsection (2) or, as the case may be, (3) has effect as if it referred to that shorter period.

(5) If—

    (*a*) merely because of anything done as a result of the issuing company or any other company being in administration or receivership—

        (i) the trade is carried on as mentioned in subsection (2), or

        (ii) the research and development is carried on as mentioned in subsection (3),

    for a period shorter than 4 months, and

    (*b*) the entry into administration or receivership, and everything done as a result of the company concerned being in administration or receivership—

        (i) is for genuine commercial reasons, and

        (ii) is not part of a scheme or arrangement the main purpose or one of the main purposes of which is the avoidance of tax,

subsection (2) or, as the case may be, (3) has effect as if it referred to that shorter period.

Commentary—*Simon's Taxes* **E3.121, E3.143, E3.159**.
HMRC Manuals—Venture Capital Schemes Manual VCM12070 (minimum period requirement).

177 The no pre-arranged exits requirement

(1) The issuing arrangements for the relevant shares must not include—

    (*a*) arrangements with a view to the subsequent repurchase, exchange or other disposal of those shares or of other shares in or securities of the issuing company,

    (*b*) arrangements for or with a view to the cessation of any trade which is being or is to be or may be carried on by the issuing company or a person connected with that company,

    (*c*) arrangements for the disposal of, or of a substantial amount (in terms of value) of, the assets of the issuing company or of a person connected with that company, or

    (*d*) arrangements the main purpose or one of the main purposes of which is (by means of any insurance, indemnity or guarantee or otherwise) to provide partial or complete protection for persons investing in shares in the issuing company against what would otherwise be the risks attached to making the investment.

[(2) The arrangements referred to in subsection (1)(*a*) do not include—

    (*a*) any arrangements with a view to such an exchange of shares, or shares and securities, as is mentioned in section 247(1), or

    (*b*) any arrangements with a view to any shares in the issuing company being exchanged for, or converted into, shares in that company of a different class.][1]

(3) The arrangements referred to in subsection (1)(*b*) and (*c*) do not include any arrangements applicable only on the winding up of a company except in a case where—

    (*a*) the issuing arrangements include arrangements for the company to be wound up, or

    (*b*) the arrangements are applicable on the winding up of the company otherwise than for genuine commercial reasons.

(4) The arrangements referred to in subsection (1)(*d*) do not include any arrangements which are confined to the provision—

    (*a*) for the issuing company itself, or

    (*b*) if the issuing company is a parent company that meets the trading requirement in section 181(2)(*b*), for the issuing company itself, for the issuing company itself and one or more of its subsidiaries or for one or more of its subsidiaries,

of any such protection against the risks arising in the course of carrying on its business as might reasonably be expected to be provided in normal commercial circumstances.

(5) In this section "the issuing arrangements" means—
- (*a*) the arrangements under which the shares are issued to the individual, and
- (*b*) any arrangements made before the issue of the shares to the individual in relation to or in connection with that issue.

Commentary—*Simon's Taxes* **E3.122**.

HMRC Manuals—Venture Capital Schemes Manual VCM12080 (no pre-arranged exists requirement).

Amendments—[1] Sub-s (2) substituted by F(No 2)A 2017 s 11(1), (2) with effect in relation to shares issued on or after 5 December 2016.

178 The no tax avoidance requirement

The relevant shares must be issued for genuine commercial reasons, and not as part of a scheme or arrangement the main purpose or one of the main purposes of which is the avoidance of tax.

Commentary—*Simon's Taxes* **E3.123**.

HMRC Manuals—Venture Capital Schemes Manual VCM12090 (no tax avoidance requirement).

[178A The no disqualifying arrangements requirement

(1) The relevant shares must not be issued, nor any money raised by the issue employed, in consequence or anticipation of, or otherwise in connection with, disqualifying arrangements.

(2) Arrangements are "disqualifying arrangements" if—
- (*a*) the main purpose, or one of the main purposes, of the arrangements to secure—
  - (i) that a qualifying business activity is or will be carried on by the issuing company or a qualifying 90% subsidiary of that company, and
  - (ii) that one or more persons (whether or not including any party to the arrangements) may obtain relevant tax relief in respect of shares issued by the issuing company which raise money for the purposes of that activity or that such shares may comprise part of the qualifying holdings of a VCT,
- (*b*) that activity is the relevant qualifying business activity, and
- (*c*) one or both of conditions A and B are met.

(3) Condition A is that, as a (direct or indirect) result of the money raised by the issue of the relevant shares being employed as required by section 175, an amount representing the whole or the majority of the amount raised is, in the course of the arrangements, paid to or for the benefit of a relevant person or relevant persons.

(4) Condition B is that, in the absence of the arrangements, it would have been reasonable to expect that the whole or greater part of the component activities of the relevant qualifying business activity would have been carried on as part of another business by a relevant person or relevant persons.

(5) For the purposes of this section it is immaterial whether the issuing company is a party to the arrangements.

(6) In this section—

"component activities" means—
- (*a*) if the relevant qualifying business activity is activity A (see section 179(2)), the carrying on of a qualifying trade or preparing to carry on such a trade, which constitutes that activity, and
- (*b*) if the relevant qualifying business activity is activity B (see section 179(4)), the carrying on of research and development which constitutes that activity;

[(*ba*) SI relief under Part 5B in respect of the shares;][2]

"qualifying holdings", in relation to the issuing company, is to be construed in accordance with section 286 (VCTs: qualifying holdings);

"relevant person" means a person who is a party to the arrangements or a person connected with such a party;

"relevant qualifying business activity" means the activity for the purposes of which the issue of the relevant shares raised money;

"relevant tax relief", in respect of shares, means one or more of the following—
- (*a*) EIS relief in respect of the shares;
- (*b*) SEIS relief under Part 5A in respect of the shares;
- (*c*) relief under Chapter 6 of Part 4 (losses on disposal of shares) in respect of the shares;
- (*d*) relief under section 150A or 150E of TCGA 1992 (enterprise investment scheme) in respect of the shares;
- (*e*) relief under Schedule 5B to that Act (enterprise investment scheme: reinvestment) in consequence of which deferral relief is attributable to the shares (see paragraph 19(2) of that Schedule);
- (*f*) relief under Schedule 5BB to that Act (seed enterprise investment scheme: re-investment) in consequence of which SEIS re-investment relief is attributable to the shares (see paragraph 4 of that Schedule).][1]

Commentary—*Simon's Taxes* **E3.124**.

HMRC Manuals—Venture Capital Schemes Manual VCM12100 (no disqualifying arrangements requirement).

Amendments—[1]   This section inserted by FA 2012 s 39, Sch 7 paras 1, 9, with effect in relation to shares issued on or after 6 April 2012, subject to transitional provisions in FA 2012 Sch 7 para 22(2).

[2]   Sub-s (6)(*ba*) inserted by F(No 2)A 2017 s 14, Sch 1 para 11(1), (2) with effect in relation to shares issued on or after 6 April 2017. This amendment does not have effect for the purposes of determining any question whether particular arrangements which include any transaction entered into before 6 April 2017 are "disqualifying arrangements" for the purposes of ss 178A, 257CF or 299A (F(No 2)A 2017 Sch 1 para 16(1), (3)).

Meaning of "qualifying business activity"

179 Meaning of "qualifying business activity"

(1) In this Part "qualifying business activity", in relation to the issuing company, means—

     (*a*)   activity A, or

     (*b*)   activity B,

if it is carried on by the company or a qualifying 90% subsidiary of the company.

. . . [2]

(2) Activity A is—

     (*a*)   the carrying on of a qualifying trade which, on the date the relevant shares are issued, the company or a qualifying 90% subsidiary of the company is carrying on, or

     (*b*)   the activity of preparing to carry on (or preparing to carry on and then carrying on) a qualifying trade—

         (i)   which, on that date, is intended to be carried on   . . . [1] by the company or such a subsidiary, and

         (ii)   which is begun to be carried on by the company or such a subsidiary within two years after that date.

(3) . . . [1]

(4) Activity B is the carrying on of research and development—

     (*a*)   which, on the date the relevant shares are issued, the company or a qualifying 90% subsidiary of the company is carrying on, or which the company or such a subsidiary begins to carry on immediately afterwards, and

     (*b*)   from which, on that date, it is intended—

         (i)   that a qualifying trade which the company or such a subsidiary will carry on   . . . [1] will be derived, or

         (ii)   that a qualifying trade which the company or such a subsidiary is carrying on, or will carry on,   . . . [1] will benefit.

(5) . . . [1]

(6) In determining—

     (*a*)   for the purposes of subsection (2)(*b*) when a qualifying trade is begun to be carried on by a qualifying 90% subsidiary of the company, or

     (*b*)   for the purposes of subsection (4)(*a*) when research and development is begun to be carried on by such a subsidiary,

any carrying on of the trade or, as the case may be, the research and development by it before it became such a subsidiary is ignored.

(7) References in subsection (2)(*b*)(i) or (4)(*b*) to a qualifying 90% subsidiary of the company include references to any existing or future company which will be such a subsidiary at any future time.

Commentary—*Simon's Taxes* **E3.141, E3.102, E3.142 , E3.150, E3.143**.

HMRC Manuals—Venture Capital Schemes Manual VCM12110 (meaning of 'qualifying business activity').

Amendments—[1]   In sub ss (2)(*b*)(i), (4)(*b*)(i), (ii) wordsrepealed, and sub-ss (3), (5) repealed, by F(No 3)A 2010 s 5, Sch 2 para 1(1), (2) with effect in relation to shares issued on or after 6 April 2011 (by virtue of SI 2011/662 art 2).

[2]   Words in sub-s (1) repealed by FA 2012 s 39, Sch 7 paras 1, 10, with effect in relation to shares issued on or after 6 April 2012 subject to transitional provisions in FA 2012 Sch 7 para 22(2).

CHAPTER 4

THE ISSUING COMPANY

Introduction

180 Overview of Chapter

The issuing company is a qualifying company in relation to the relevant shares if the requirements of this Chapter are met as to—

     [(*za*)   UK permanent establishment (see section 180A),

     (*zb*)   financial health (see section 180B),][2]

     (*a*)   trading (see section 181),

     (*b*)   the issuing company to carry on the qualifying business activity (see section 183),

     (*c*)   unquoted status (see section 184),

     (*d*)   control and independence (see section 185),

     (*e*)   gross assets (see section 186),

     [(*ea*)   number of employees (see section 186A),][1]

(*f*) qualifying subsidiaries (see section 187), and

(*g*) property managing subsidiaries (see section 188).

Commentary—*Simon's Taxes* **E3.126**.

HMRC Manuals—Venture Capital Schemes Manual VCM13010 (issuing company requirements: overview).

Amendments—[1]   Para (*ea*) inserted by FA 2007 s 51, Sch 16 para 2(1), (2). This amendment does not have effect for shares issued before 19 July 2007 or shares issued to the managers of an approved fund which closed before that day: FA 2007 Sch 16 para 2(4), (5).

[2]   Paras (*za*), (*zb*) inserted by F(No 3)A 2010 s 5, Sch 2 para 1(1), (3) with effect in relation to shares issued on or after 6 April 2011 (by virtue of SI 2011/662).

The requirements

[180A The UK permanent establishment requirement

(1) The issuing company must meet the UK permanent establishment requirement throughout period B.

(2) The UK permanent establishment requirement is that the issuing company has a permanent establishment in the United Kingdom.][1]

Commentary—*Simon's Taxes* **E3.127**.

HMRC Manuals—Venture Capital Schemes Manual VCM13020 (UK permanent establishment requirement).

Amendments—[1]   Sections 180A, 180B inserted by F(No 3)A 2010 s 5, Sch 2 para 1(1), (4) with effect in relation to shares issued on or after 6 April 2011 (by virtue of SI 2011/662).

[180B The financial health requirement

(1) The issuing company must meet the financial health requirement at the beginning of period B.

(2) The financial health requirement is that the issuing company is not in difficulty.

(3) The issuing company is "in difficulty" if it is reasonable to assume that it would be regarded as a firm in difficulty for the purposes of the Community Guidelines on State Aid for Rescuing and Restructuring Firms in Difficulty (2004/C 244/02).][1]

Commentary—*Simon's Taxes* **E3.128**.

HMRC Manuals—Venture Capital Schemes Manual VCM13040 (financial health requirement).

Amendments—[1]   Sections 180A, 180B inserted by F(No 3)A 2010 s 5, Sch 2 para 1(1), (4) with effect in relation to shares issued on or after 6 April 2011 (by virtue of SI 2011/662).

181 The trading requirement

(1) The issuing company must meet the trading requirement throughout period B.

(2) The trading requirement is that—

(*a*) the company, ignoring any incidental purposes, exists wholly for the purpose of carrying on one or more qualifying trades, or

(*b*) the company is a parent company and the business of the group does not consist wholly or as to a substantial part in the carrying on of non-qualifying activities.

(3) If the company intends that one or more other companies should become its qualifying subsidiaries with a view to their carrying on one or more qualifying trades—

(*a*) the company is treated as a parent company for the purposes of subsection (2)(*b*), and

(*b*) the reference in subsection (2)(*b*) to the group includes the company and any existing or future company that will be its qualifying subsidiary after the intention in question is carried into effect.

This subsection does not apply at any time after the abandonment of that intention.

(4) For the purpose of subsection (2)(*b*) the business of the group means what would be the business of the group if the activities of the group companies taken together were regarded as one business.

(5) For the purpose of determining the business of a group, activities are ignored so far as they are activities carried on by a mainly trading subsidiary otherwise than for its main purpose.

(6) For the purposes of determining the business of a group, activities of a group company are ignored so far as they consist in—

(*a*) the holding of shares in or securities of a qualifying subsidiary of the parent company,

(*b*) the making of loans to another group company,

(*c*) the holding and managing of property used by a group company for the purpose of one or more qualifying trades carried on by a group company, or

(*d*) the holding and managing of property used by a group company for the purpose of research and development from which it is intended—

(i) that a qualifying trade to be carried on by a group company will be derived, or

(ii) that a qualifying trade carried on or to be carried on by a group company will benefit.

(7) Any reference in subsection (6)(*d*)(i) or (ii) to a group company includes a reference to any existing or future company which will be a group company at any future time.

(8) In this section—

"incidental purposes" means purposes having no significant effect (other than in relation to incidental matters) on the extent of the activities of the company in question,

"mainly trading subsidiary" means a qualifying subsidiary which, apart from incidental purposes, exists wholly for the purpose of carrying on one or more qualifying trades, and any reference to the main purpose of such a subsidiary is to be read accordingly, and "non-qualifying activities" means—

    (*a*)   excluded activities, and

    (*b*)   activities (other than research and development) carried on otherwise than in the course of a trade.

(9) This section is supplemented by section 189 (meaning of "qualifying trade") and sections 192 to 199 (excluded activities).

Commentary—*Simon's Taxes* **E3.129**.

HMRC Manuals—Venture Capital Schemes Manual VCM13050 (the trading requirement).

182 Ceasing to meet trading requirement because of administration or receivership

(1) A company is not regarded as ceasing to meet the trading requirement merely because of anything done in consequence of the company or any of its subsidiaries being in administration or receivership.

    This has effect subject to subsections (2) and (3).

(2) Subsection (1) applies only if—

    (*a*)   the entry into administration or receivership, and

    (*b*)   everything done as a result of the company concerned being in administration or receivership,

is for genuine commercial reasons, and is not part of a scheme or arrangement the main purpose or one of the main purposes of which is the avoidance of tax.

(3) A company ceases to meet the trading requirement if before the end of period B—

    (*a*)   a resolution is passed, or an order is made, for the winding up of the company or any of its subsidiaries (or, in the case of a winding up otherwise than under the Insolvency Act 1986 (c 45) or the Insolvency (Northern Ireland) Order 1989 (SI 1989/2405 (NI 19)), any other act is done for the like purpose), or

    (*b*)   the company or any of its subsidiaries is dissolved without winding up.

    This is subject to subsection (4).

(4) Subsection (3) does not apply if the winding up or dissolution is for genuine commercial reasons, and is not part of a scheme or arrangement the main purpose or one of the main purposes of which is the avoidance of tax.

Commentary—*Simon's Taxes* **E3.129, E3.166**.

HMRC Manuals—Venture Capital Schemes Manual VCM13070 (ceasing to meet trading requirement because of administration or receivership).

183 The issuing company to carry on the qualifying business activity requirement

(1) The requirement of this section is met in relation to the issuing company if, at no time in period B, is any of the following—

    (*a*)   the relevant qualifying trade,

    (*b*)   relevant preparation work (if any), and

    (*c*)   relevant research and development (if any),

carried on by a person other than the issuing company or a qualifying 90% subsidiary of that company.

(2) Subsection (3) has effect for the purpose of determining whether the requirement of this section is met in relation to the issuing company in a case where relevant preparation work is carried out by that company or a qualifying 90% subsidiary of that company.

(3) The carrying on of the relevant qualifying trade by a company other than the issuing company or a subsidiary of that company is to be ignored if it takes place at any time in period B before the issuing company or any qualifying 90% subsidiary of that company begins to carry on that trade.

(4) The requirement of this section is not regarded as failing to be met in relation to the issuing company if, merely because of any act or event within subsection (5), the relevant qualifying trade—

    (*a*)   ceases to be carried on in period B by the issuing company or any qualifying 90% subsidiary of that company, and

    (*b*)   is subsequently carried on in that period by a person who is not at any time in period C connected with the issuing company.

(5) The following are acts and events within this subsection—

    (*a*)   anything done as a consequence of the issuing company or any other company being in administration or receivership, and

    (*b*)   the issuing company or any other company being wound up, or dissolved without being wound up.

(6) Subsection (4) applies only if—

    (*a*)   the entry into administration or receivership, and everything done as a consequence of the company concerned being in administration or receivership, or

    (*b*)   the winding up or dissolution,

is for genuine commercial reasons, and is not part of a scheme or arrangement the main purpose or one of the main purposes of which is the avoidance of tax.

(7) In this section—

"relevant preparation work" means preparations within section 179(2)(*b*) which are the subject of the qualifying business activity mentioned in section 174,

"the relevant qualifying trade" means the qualifying trade which is the subject of that qualifying business activity,

"relevant research and development" means—

(*a*) research and development within section 179(4) which is the subject of that qualifying business activity, and

(*b*) any other preparations for the carrying on of the qualifying trade which is the subject of that activity.

Commentary—*Simon's Taxes* **E3.130, E3.141, E3.1101**.

HMRC Manuals—Venture Capital Schemes Manual VCM13080 (issuing company to carry on the qualifying business activity requirement).

184 The unquoted status requirement

(1) At the beginning of period B—

(*a*) the issuing company must be an unquoted company,

(*b*) there must be no arrangements in existence for the issuing company to cease to be an unquoted company, and

(*c*) there must be no arrangements in existence for the issuing company to become a subsidiary of another company ("the new company") by virtue of an exchange of shares, or shares and securities, if—

(i) section 247 applies in relation to the exchange, and

(ii) arrangements have been made with a view to the new company ceasing to be an unquoted company.

(2) In this section "unquoted company" means a company none of whose shares, stocks, debentures or other securities are marketed to the general public.

(3) For the purposes of subsection (2), shares, stocks, debentures or other securities are marketed to the general public if they are—

(*a*) listed on [a recognised stock exchange,][1]

(*b*) listed on a designated exchange in a country outside the United Kingdom, or

(*c*) dealt in outside the United Kingdom by such means as may be designated.

(4) In subsection (3)(*b*) and (*c*) "designated" means designated by an order made by the Commissioners for Her Majesty's Revenue and Customs for the purposes of that provision.

(5) An order made for the purposes of subsection (3)(*b*) may designate an exchange by name, or by reference to any class or description of exchanges, including a class or description framed by reference to any authority or approval given in a country outside the United Kingdom.

(6) The arrangements referred to in subsection (1)(*b*) and (*c*)(ii) do not include arrangements in consequence of which any shares, stocks, debentures or other securities of the company are at any subsequent time—

(*a*) listed on a stock exchange that is a recognised stock exchange by virtue of an order made under section [1005(1)(*b*)][1], or

(*b*) listed on an exchange, or dealt in by any means, designated by an order made for the purposes of subsection (3)(*b*) or (*c*),

if the order was made after the beginning of period B.

Commentary—*Simon's Taxes* **E3.131, D8.316, E3.246**.

HMRC Manuals—Venture Capital Schemes Manual VCM13090 (unquoted status requirement). VCM75110 (unquoted company: meaning).

Amendments—[1] Words in sub-ss (3)(*a*), (6)(*a*) substituted by FA 2007 s 109, Sch 26 para 12(1), (4) with effect from 19 July 2007.

185 The control and independence requirement

(1) The control element of the requirement is that—

(*a*) the issuing company must not at any time in period B control (whether on its own or together with any person connected with it) any company which is not a qualifying subsidiary of the issuing company, and

(*b*) no arrangements must be in existence at any time in that period by virtue of which the issuing company could fail to meet paragraph (*a*) (whether during that period or otherwise).

(2) The independence element of the requirement is that—

(*a*) the issuing company must not at any time in period B—

(i) be a 51% subsidiary of another company, or

(ii) be under the control of another company (or of another company and any other person connected with that other company), without being a 51% subsidiary of that other company, and

(*b*) no arrangements must be in existence at any time in that period by virtue of which the issuing company could fail to meet paragraph (*a*) (whether during that period or otherwise).

(3) This section is subject to section 247(4) (exchange of shares).

Commentary—*Simon's Taxes* E3.132.
HMRC Manuals—Venture Capital Schemes Manual VCM13100 (control and independence requirement).

186 The gross assets requirement

(1) In the case of relevant shares issued by a single company, the value of the company's assets—

    (a) must not exceed [£15 million][1] immediately before the relevant share issue, and

    (b) must not exceed [£16 million][1] immediately afterwards.

(2) In the case of relevant shares issued by a parent company, the value of the group assets—

    (a) must not exceed [£15 million][1] immediately before the relevant share issue, and

    (b) must not exceed [£16 million][1] immediately afterwards.

(3) In this section—

    (a) the relevant share issue is the issue of shares in the company that includes the relevant shares, and

    (b) the value of the group assets is the sum of the values of the gross assets of each of the members of the group, ignoring any that consist in rights against, or shares in or securities of, another member of the group.

Commentary—*Simon's Taxes* E3.133.
HMRC Manuals—Venture Capital Schemes Manual VCM13110 (gross assets requirement).
Modifications—ITA 2007 Sch 2 para 58 (modification of this section in relation to shares issued to—
    (a)   a person who subscribed for them before 22 March 2006; or
    (b)   the managers of an investment fund approved for the purposes of ITA 2007 s 251 by the Commissioners for HMRC if—
        (i)   the fund was approved before 22 March 2006,
        (ii)   investments in the fund have been accepted before 6 April 2006, and
        (iii)   the shares are issued to the managers as nominee for an individual who has (whether or not before 6 April 2006) invested in the fund).
Amendments—[1]   In sub-ss (1)(a), (b), (2)(a),(b), figure substituted by FA 2012 s 39, Sch 7 paras 1, 11 with effect from 19 July 2012 (SI 2012/1896). This amendment has effect in relation to shares issued on or after 6 April 2012 (FA 2012 Sch 7 para 23(2)).

[186A The number of employees requirement

(1) If the issuing company is a single company, the full-time equivalent employee number for it must be less than [the permitted limit][2] when the relevant shares are issued.

(2) If the issuing company is a parent company, the sum of—

    (a) the full-time equivalent employee number for it, and

    (b) the full-time equivalent employee numbers for each of its qualifying subsidiaries,

must be less than [the permitted limit][2] when the relevant shares are issued.

(3) The full-time equivalent employee number for a company is calculated as follows—

Step 1 Find the number of full-time employees of the company.

Step 2 Add, for each employee of the company who is not a full-time employee, such fraction as is just and reasonable.

The result is the full-time equivalent employee number.

[(3A) "The permitted limit" means—

    (a) if the issuing company is a knowledge-intensive company (see section 252A) at the time the relevant shares are issued, 500, and

    (b) in any other case, 250.

(3B) The Treasury may by regulations amend subsection (3A)(a) or (b) by substituting a different number for the number for the time being specified there.][2]

(4) In this section references to an employee—

    (a) include a director, but

    (b) do not include—

        (i) an employee on maternity[, paternity[, shared parental or parental bereavement][3] leave, or

        (ii) a student on vocational training.][1]

Commentary—*Simon's Taxes* E3.134..
HMRC Manuals—Venture Capital Schemes Manual VCM13120 (number of employees requirement).
Amendments—[1]   This section inserted by FA 2007 s 51, Sch 16 para 2(1), (3) These amendments do not have effect for shares issued before 19 July 2007 or shares issued to the managers of an approved fund which closed before that day: FA 2007 Sch 16 para 2(4), (5).
[2]   In sub-ss (1), (2), words substituted for figure "250", and sub-ss (3A) and (3B) inserted, by F(No 2)A 2015 s 25, Sch 5 paras 1, 13 with effect in relation to shares issued on or after 18 November 2015. The figure of "250" was previously substituted by FA 2012 s 39, Sch 7 paras 1, 12 with effect from 19 July 2012 (SI 2012/1896); this amendment had effect in relation to shares issued on or after 6 April 2012 (FA 2012 Sch 7 para 23(2)).
[3]   In sub-s (4)(b)(i), words substituted for words "or shared parental" by the Parental Bereavement (Leave and Pay) Act 2018 s 1, Schedule paras 50, 51 with effect from 18 January 2020 (by virtue of SI 2020/45 reg 2).

187 The qualifying subsidiaries requirement

Any subsidiary that the issuing company has at any time in period B must be a qualifying subsidiary of the company.

Commentary—*Simon's Taxes* **E3.135**.
HMRC Manuals—Venture Capital Schemes Manual VCM13130 (qualifying subsidiaries requirement).

188 The property managing subsidiaries requirement

(1) Any property managing subsidiary that the issuing company has at any time in period B must be a qualifying 90% subsidiary of the company.

(2) "Property managing subsidiary" means a subsidiary of the company whose business consists wholly or mainly in the holding or managing of land or any property deriving its value from land.

(3) In subsection (2) references to property deriving its value from land include—

  (a) any shareholding in a company deriving its value directly or indirectly from land,
  (b) any partnership interest deriving its value directly or indirectly from land,
  (c) any interest in settled property deriving its value directly or indirectly from land, and
  (d) any option, consent or embargo affecting the disposition of land.

Commentary—*Simon's Taxes* **E3.136**.
HMRC Manuals—Venture Capital Schemes Manual VCM13140 (property managing subsidiaries requirement).
VCM13080 (meaning of qualifying 90% subsidiary).

Definitions

189 Meaning of "qualifying trade"

(1) For the purposes of this Part, a trade is a qualifying trade if—

  (a) it is conducted on a commercial basis and with a view to the realisation of profits, and
  (b) it does not at any time in period B consist wholly or as to a substantial part in the carrying on of excluded activities.

(2) References in this section and sections 192 to 198 to a trade are to be read without regard to the definition of "trade" in section 989.

Commentary—*Simon's Taxes* **E3.142**.
HMRC Manuals—Venture Capital Schemes Manual VCM13060 (meaning of 'qualifying trade').

190 Meaning of "qualifying 90% subsidiary"

(1) For the purposes of this Part, a company ("the subsidiary") is a qualifying 90% subsidiary of another company ("the relevant company") if the following conditions are met—

  (a) the relevant company possesses at least 90% of the issued share capital of, and at least 90% of the voting power in, the subsidiary,
  (b) the relevant company would—
    (i) in the event of a winding up of the subsidiary, or
    (ii) in any other circumstances,

    be beneficially entitled to receive at least 90% of the assets of the subsidiary which would then be available for distribution to equity holders of the subsidiary,
  (c) the relevant company is beneficially entitled to receive at least 90% of any profits of the subsidiary which are available for distribution to equity holders of the subsidiary,
  (d) no person other than the relevant company has control of the subsidiary, and
  (e) no arrangements are in existence by virtue of which any of the conditions in paragraphs (a) to (d) would cease to be met.

[(1A) For the purposes of this Part, a company ("company A") which is a subsidiary of another company ("company B") is a qualifying 90% subsidiary of a third company ("company C") if—

  (a) company A is a qualifying 90% subsidiary of company B, and company B is a qualifying 100% subsidiary of company C, or
  (b) company A is a qualifying 100% subsidiary of company B, and company B is a qualifying 90% subsidiary of company C.

(1B) For the purposes of subsection (1A), no account is to be taken of any control company C may have of company A.

(1C) For those purposes, a company ("company X") is a qualifying 100% subsidiary of another company ("company Y") at any time when the conditions in subsection (1)(a) to (e) would be met if—

  (a) company X were the subsidiary,
  (b) company Y were the relevant company, and
  (c) in subsection (1) for "at least 90%" in each place there were substituted "100%".][1]

(2) Subsections (3), (4) and (5) of section 191 (conditions not regarded as ceasing to be met because of winding up, dissolution, administration, receivership or arrangements for disposal not having tax avoidance as main purpose) apply in relation to the conditions in subsection (1)—

  (a) as they apply in relation to the conditions in subsection (2) of that section, but
  (b) with the omission from subsection (5) of "or (as the case may be) by another subsidiary".

(3) For the purposes of subsection (1)—

  (a) the persons who are equity holders of the subsidiary, and
  (b) the percentage of the assets of the subsidiary to which an equity holder would be entitled,

are to be determined in accordance with [Chapter 6 of Part 5 of CTA 2010][2].

(4) In making that determination—

    (*a*) references in [section 166 of that Act to company A][2] are to be read as references to an equity holder, and

    (*b*) references in that [section][2] to a winding up are to be read as including references to any other circumstances in which assets of the subsidiary are available for distribution to its equity holders.

Commentary—*Simon's Taxes* **E3.136**.

HMRC Manuals—Venture Capital Schemes Manual VCM13080 (meaning of 'qualifying 90% subsidiary').

VCM34040 (meaning : qualifying 90 percent subsidiary).

Amendments—[1]   Sub-ss (1A)–(1C) inserted by FA 2007 s 51, Sch 16 para 16(2). This amendment is deemed to have effect from 6 April 2007: FA 2007 Sch 16 para 18.

[2]   In sub-ss (3), (4)(*a*), (*b*) words substituted by CTA 2010 s 1177, Sch 1 para 500. CTA 2010 has effect for corporation tax purposes for accounting periods ending on or after 1 April 2010, and for income and capital gains tax purposes for the tax year 2010–11 and subsequent tax years.

191 Meaning of "qualifying subsidiary"

(1) For the purposes of this Part, a company ("the subsidiary") is a qualifying subsidiary of another company ("the relevant company") if the following conditions are met.

(2) The conditions are that—

    (*a*) the subsidiary is a 51% subsidiary of the relevant company,

    (*b*) no person other than the relevant company, or another of its subsidiaries, has control of the subsidiary, and

    (*c*) no arrangements are in existence by virtue of which either of the conditions in paragraphs (*a*) and (*b*) would cease to be met.

(3) The conditions do not cease to be met merely because the subsidiary or any other company is wound up, or dissolved without winding up, if the winding up or dissolution—

    (*a*) is for genuine commercial reasons, and

    (*b*) is not part of a scheme or arrangement the main purpose or one of the main purposes of which is the avoidance of tax.

(4) The conditions do not cease to be met merely because of anything done as a consequence of the subsidiary or any other company being in administration or receivership, if—

    (*a*) the entry into administration or receivership, and

    (*b*) everything done as a consequence of the company concerned being in administration or receivership,

is for genuine commercial reasons, and is not part of a scheme or arrangement the main purpose or one of the main purposes of which is the avoidance of tax.

(5) The conditions do not cease to be met merely because arrangements are in existence for the disposal by the relevant company or (as the case may be) by another subsidiary of all its interest in the subsidiary, if the disposal—

    (*a*) is to be for genuine commercial reasons, and

    (*b*) is not to be part of a scheme or arrangement the main purpose or one of the main purposes of which is the avoidance of tax.

Commentary—*Simon's Taxes* **E3.135, E3.136**.

HMRC Manuals—Venture Capital Schemes Manual VCM13130 (qualifying subsidiaries requirement).

VCM71020 (share loss relief: meaning of qualifying subsidiary).

VCM74940 (qualifying subsidiaries requirement : conditions).

VCM34140 (meaning of qualifying subsidiary).

Modifications—ITA 2007 Sch 2 para 51 (modification of this section in relation to shares issued before 17 March 2004).

CTA 2010 Sch 2 para 42 (modification of this section in relation to shares issued before 17 March 2004).

[191A Meaning of "permanent establishment"

(1) This section applies for the purposes of this Part.

(2) A company has a "permanent establishment" in the United Kingdom if (and only if)—

    (*a*) it has a fixed place of business there through which the business of the company is wholly or partly carried on, or

    (*b*) an agent acting on behalf of the company has and habitually exercises there authority to enter into contracts on behalf of the company.

(3) For the purposes of this section "fixed place of business" includes (without prejudice to the generality of that expression)—

    (*a*) a place of management,

    (*b*) a branch,

    (*c*) an office,

    (*d*) a factory,

    (*e*) a workshop,

    (*f*) a mine, an oil or gas well, a quarry or any other place of extraction of natural resources, and

    (*g*) a building site or construction or installation project.

(4) If the condition in subsection (5) is met, a company is not regarded as having a permanent establishment in the United Kingdom by reason of the fact that—

(a) a fixed place of business is maintained there for the purpose of carrying on activities for the company, or

(b) an agent carries on activities there for and on behalf of the company.

(5) The condition is that, in relation to the business of the company as a whole, the activities carried on are only of a preparatory or auxiliary character.

(6) For this purpose "activities of a preparatory or auxiliary character" include (without prejudice to the generality of that expression)—

(a) the use of facilities for the purpose of storage, display or delivery of goods or merchandise belonging to the company,

(b) the maintenance of a stock of goods or merchandise belonging to the company for the purpose of storage, display or delivery,

(c) the maintenance of a stock of goods or merchandise belonging to the company for the purpose of processing by another person, and

(d) purchasing goods or merchandise, or collecting information, for the company.

(7) A company is not regarded as having a permanent establishment in the United Kingdom by reason of the fact that it carries on business there through an agent of independent status (including a broker or a general commission agent) acting in the ordinary course of the agent's business.

(8) A company is not regarded as having a permanent establishment in the United Kingdom by reason of the fact that it controls a company that—

(a) is resident there, or

(b) carries on business there (whether through a permanent establishment or otherwise).

(9) The Treasury may by regulations amend this section.][1]

Commentary—*Simon's Taxes* **E3.127.**
HMRC Manuals—Venture Capital Schemes Manual VCM13030 (meaning of 'permanent establishment').
VCM34050 (UK permanent : meaning).
Amendments—[1]   Section 191A inserted by F(No 3)A 2010 s 5, Sch 2 para 1(1), (5) with effect in relation to shares issued on or after 6 April 2011 (by virtue of SI 2011/662 art 2).

Excluded activities

192 Meaning of "excluded activities"

(1) The following are excluded activities for the purposes of sections 181 and 189—

(a) dealing in land, in commodities or futures or in shares, securities or other financial instruments,

(b) dealing in goods otherwise than in the course of an ordinary trade of wholesale or retail distribution,

(c) banking, insurance, money-lending, debt-factoring, hire-purchase financing or other financial activities,

(d) leasing (including letting ships on charter or other assets on hire),

(e) receiving royalties or licence fees,

(f) providing legal or accountancy services,

(g) property development,

(h) farming or market gardening,

(i) holding, managing or occupying woodlands, any other forestry activities or timber production,

[(ia) shipbuilding,

(ib) producing coal,

(ic) producing steel,][1]

(j) operating or managing hotels or comparable establishments or managing property used as an hotel or comparable establishment,

(k) operating or managing nursing homes or residential care homes or managing property used as a nursing home or residential care home,   . . .[2]

[(ka) generating or exporting electricity or making electricity generating capacity available,

(kb) generating heat,

(kc) generating any form of energy not within paragraph (ka) or (kb),

(kd) producing gas or fuel, and][3]

(l) any activities which are excluded activities under section 199 (provision of services or facilities for another business).

(2) Subsection (1) is supplemented by the following provisions—

(a) section 193 (wholesale and retail distribution),

(b) section 194 (leasing of ships),

(c) section 195 (receipt of royalties and licence fees),

(d) section 196 (property development),

[(da) section 196A (shipbuilding),

(db) section 196B (producing coal),

(dc) section 196C (producing steel),][1]

(e) section 197 (hotels and comparable establishments),   . . .[2]

(*f*) section 198 (nursing homes and residential care homes), [and

(*g*) section 198A (export of electricity).][4]

(*h*)   . . . [4]

Commentary—*Simon's Taxes* **E3.142**.
HMRC Manuals—Venture Capital Schemes Manual VCM3000 (excluded activities: contents).
Modifications—ITA 2007 Sch 2 para 52 (modification of this section in relation to shares issued before 7 March 2001).
CTA 2010 Sch 2 para 43 (modification of this section in relation to shares issued before 6 April 2008, and shares issued before
  7 March 2001).
Amendments—[1]   Sub-ss (1)(*ia*)–(*ic*) and (2)(*da*)–(*dc*) inserted by FA 2008 s 32, Sch 11 paras 4, 5 with effect from 6 April 2008.
  This amendment does not have effect in relation to shares issued before that date (FA 2008 Sch 11 para 11).
[2]   Word "and" at the end of sub-ss (1)(*k*) and (2) (*e*) repealed, by FA 2012 s 39, Sch 7 paras 1, 13 with effect in relation to shares
  issued on or after 23 March 2011, subject to provisions relating to shares issued before 6 April 2012: see FA 2012 Sch 7
  para 24(2).
[3]   In sub-s (1), paras (*ka*)–(*kd*) substituted for previous paras (*ka*)–(*kc*) by FA 2016 s 28(1) with effect in relation to shares issued
  on or after 6 April 2016.
[4]   Sub-s (2)(*g*) and preceding word substituted, and sub-s (2)(*h*) repealed, by FA 2016 s 28(3)(*a*) with effect in relation to shares
  issued on or after 6 April 2016.

193 Excluded activities: wholesale and retail distribution

(1) This section supplements section 192(1)(*b*).

(2) In this section—

> (*a*) subsections (3) and (4) are for determining whether a trade is a trade of wholesale or retail
> distribution, and
>
> (*b*) subsections (5) and (6) are for determining whether a trade of wholesale or retail distribution
> is an ordinary trade of wholesale or retail distribution.

(3) A trade of wholesale distribution is one in which goods are offered for sale and sold to persons
for resale by them, or for processing and resale by them, to members of the general public for their
use or consumption.

(4) A trade of retail distribution is one in which goods are offered or exposed for sale and sold to
members of the general public for their use or consumption.

(5) A trade of wholesale or retail distribution is not an ordinary trade of wholesale or retail
distribution if—

> (*a*) it consists to a substantial extent—
>
> > (i)   in dealing in goods of a kind which are collected or held as an investment, or
> >
> > (ii) in that activity and any other excluded activity taken together, and
>
> (*b*) a substantial proportion of those goods are held for a period which is significantly longer than
> the period for which the trader would reasonably be expected to hold them while trying to
> dispose of them at their market value.

(6) In determining whether a trade of wholesale or retail distribution is an ordinary trade of
wholesale or retail distribution regard is to be had to the extent to which it has the following
features—

> (*a*) the goods are bought by the trader in quantities larger than those in which the trader sells
> them,
>
> (*b*) the goods are bought and sold by the trader in different markets,
>
> (*c*) the trader employs staff and incurs expenses in the trade in addition to the cost of the goods
> and, in the case of a trade carried on by a company, in addition to any remuneration paid to
> any person connected with it,
>
> (*d*) there are purchases from or sales to persons who are connected with the trader,
>
> (*e*) purchases are matched with forward sales or vice versa,
>
> (*f*) the goods are held by the trader for longer than is normal for goods of the kind in question,
>
> (*g*) the trade is carried on otherwise than at a place or places commonly used for wholesale or
> retail trade,
>
> (*h*) the trader does not take physical possession of the goods.

(7) In subsection (6)—

> (*a*) the features in paragraphs (*a*) to (*c*) are regarded as indications that the trade is an ordinary
> trade of wholesale or retail distribution, and
>
> (*b*) those in paragraphs (*d*) to (*h*) are regarded as indications to the contrary.

Commentary—*Simon's Taxes* **E3.145**.
HMRC Manuals—Venture Capital Schemes Manual VCM3030 ('ordinary' trade of wholesale or retail distribution).
Modifications—ITA 2007 Sch 2 para 53 (modification of this section in relation to shares issued before 6 April 2007).
CTA 2010 Sch 2 para 44 (modification of this section in relation to shares issued before 6 April 2008).

194 Excluded activities: leasing of ships

(1) This section supplements section 192(1)(*d*) so far as it relates to the leasing of ships other than
offshore installations or pleasure craft.

(2) In the following provisions "ship" accordingly means a ship other than an offshore installation or
a pleasure craft.

(3) If the requirements of subsection (4) are met, a trade is not to be regarded as consisting in the carrying on of excluded activities within section 192(1)(*d*) as a result only of its consisting in letting ships on charter.

(4) The requirements of this subsection are that—

   (*a*) every ship let on charter by the company carrying on the trade is beneficially owned by the company,

   (*b*) every ship beneficially owned by the company is registered in the United Kingdom,

   (*c*) throughout period B the company is solely responsible for arranging the marketing of the services of its ships, and

   (*d*) the conditions mentioned in subsection (5) are met in relation to every letting on charter by the company.

(5) The conditions referred to in subsection (4)(*d*) are—

   (*a*) the letting is for a period not exceeding 12 months and no provision is made at any time (whether in the charterparty or otherwise) for extending it beyond that period otherwise than at the option of the charterer,

   (*b*) no provision for the grant of a new letting to end more than 12 months after the provision is made (whether in the charterparty or otherwise) is in force during the period of the letting otherwise than at the option of the charterer,

   (*c*) the letting is by way of a bargain at arm's length between the company and a person who is not connected with it,

   (*d*) under the terms of the charter the company is responsible as principal—

      (i) for taking, throughout the period of the charter, management decisions in relation to the ship, other than those of a kind generally regarded by persons engaged in trade of the kind in question as matters of husbandry, and

      (ii) for defraying all expenses in connection with the ship throughout that period, or substantially all such expenses, other than those directly incidental to a particular voyage or to the employment of the ship during that period, and

   (*e*) no arrangements exist by virtue of which a person other than the company may be appointed to be responsible for the matters mentioned in paragraph (*d*) on behalf of the company.

(6) If in the case of the company carrying on the trade ("the letting company") the charterer is also a company and—

   (*a*) the charterer is a qualifying subsidiary of the letting company, or

   (*b*) the letting company is a qualifying subsidiary of the charterer, or

   (*c*) both companies are qualifying subsidiaries of a third company,

subsection (5) has effect with the omission of paragraph (c).

(7) If any of the requirements of subsection (4) is not met in relation to any lettings of ships, the trade is not, as a result, to be treated as consisting in the carrying on of excluded activities if—

   (*a*) those lettings, and

   (*b*) any other excluded activities

do not, taken together, amount to a substantial part of the trade.

(8) In this section "pleasure craft" means any ship of a kind primarily used for sport or recreation.

Commentary—*Simon's Taxes* E3.146.

HMRC Manuals—Venture Capital Schemes Manual VCM3050 (leasing including letting ships on charter or other assets on hire).

Modifications—ITA 2007 Sch 2 para 54 (modification of this section in relation to shares issued before 6 April 2007). CTA 2010 Sch 2 para 45 (modification of this section in relation to shares issued before 6 April 2008).

195 Excluded activities: receipt of royalties and licence fees

(1) This section supplements section 192(1)(*e*) (receipt of royalties and licence fees).

(2) If the requirement of subsection (3) is met, a trade is not to be regarded as consisting in the carrying on of excluded activities within section 192(1)(*e*) as a result only of its consisting to a substantial extent in the receiving of royalties or licence fees.

(3) The requirement of this subsection is that the royalties or licence fees (or all but for a part that is not a substantial part in terms of value) are attributable to the exploitation of relevant intangible assets.

(4) For this purpose an intangible asset is a "relevant intangible asset" if the whole or greater part (in terms of value) of it has been created—

   [(*a*) by the issuing company, or

   (*b*) by a company which was a qualifying subsidiary of the issuing company throughout a period during which it created the whole or greater part (in terms of value) of the intangible asset.][1]

(5) In the case of an intangible asset that is intellectual property, references to the creation of an asset by a company are to its creation in circumstances in which the right to exploit it vests in the company (whether alone or jointly with others).

(6) In this section—

   . . .[1]

"intangible asset" means any asset which falls to be treated as an intangible asset in accordance with generally accepted accountancy practice,

"intellectual property" means—

    (a) any patent, trade mark, registered design, copyright, design right, performer's right or plant breeder's right, or

    (b) any rights under the law of a country or territory outside the United Kingdom which correspond or are similar to those falling within paragraph (a).

[(7) If—

    (a) the issuing company acquired all the shares ("old shares") in another company ("the old company") at a time when the only shares issued in the issuing company were subscriber shares, and

    (b) the consideration for the old shares consisted wholly of the issue of shares in the issuing company,

references in subsection (4) to the issuing company include the old company.][1]

Commentary—*Simon's Taxes* **E3.148**.
HMRC Manuals—Venture Capital Schemes Manual VCM3060 (receiving royalties or licence fees).
Modifications—ITA 2007 Sch 2 para 55 (modification of this section in relation to shares issued before 6 April 2000).
CTA 2010 Sch 2 para 46–48 (modification of this section in relation to shares issued before 6 April 2007).
Amendments—[1]   Sub-s (4)(a), (b) substituted, in sub-s (6) the definition of "holding company" repealed, and sub-s (7) inserted, by FA 2007 ss 51, 114, Sch 16 para 11(7), Sch 27 Pt 2(16). These amendments are deemed to have effect from 6 April 2007 by virtue of FA 2007 Sch 16 para 13, and are subject to transitional provisions in FA 2007 Sch 16 para 14.

196 Excluded activities: property development

(1) This section supplements section 192(1)(g).

(2) "Property development" means the development of land—

    (a) by a company which has, or at any time has had, an interest in the land, and

    (b) with the sole or main object of realising a gain from the disposal of an interest in the land when it is developed.

(3) For this purpose "interest in land" means, subject to subsection (4)—

    (a) any estate, interest or right in or over land, including any right affecting the use or disposition of land, or

    (b) any right to obtain such an estate, interest or right from another which is conditional on the other's ability to grant it.

(4) References in this section to an interest in land do not include—

    (a) the interest of a creditor (other than a creditor in respect of a rentcharge) whose debt is secured by way of mortgage, an agreement for a mortgage or a charge of any kind over land, or

    (b) in the case of land in Scotland, the interest of a creditor in a charge or security of any kind over land.

Commentary—*Simon's Taxes* **E3.142**.
HMRC Manuals—Venture Capital Schemes Manual VCM3080 (property development).

[196A Excluded activities: shipbuilding

In section 192(1)(ia) "shipbuilding" has the same meaning as in the Framework on state aid to shipbuilding (2003/C 317/06), published in the Official Journal on 30 December 2003.][1]

Commentary—*Simon's Taxes* **E3.142**.
HMRC Manuals—Venture Capital Schemes Manual VCM3110 (shipbuilding).
Amendments—[1]   Sections 196A–196C inserted by FA 2008 s 32, Sch 11 paras 4, 6 with effect from 6 April 2008. This amendment does not have effect in relation to shares issued before that date (FA 2008 Sch 11 para 11).

[196B Excluded activities: producing coal

(1) This section supplements section 192(1)(ib).

(2) "Coal" has the meaning given by Article 2 of Council Regulation (EC) No. 1407/2002 (state aid to coal industry).

(3) The production of coal includes the extraction of it.][1]

Commentary—*Simon's Taxes* **E3.142**.
HMRC Manuals—Venture Capital Schemes Manual VCM3120 (producing coal).
Amendments—[1]   Sections 196A–196C inserted by FA 2008 s 32, Sch 11 paras 4, 6 with effect from 6 April 2008. This amendment does not have effect in relation to shares issued before that date (FA 2008 Sch 11 para 11).

[196C Excluded activities: producing steel

In section 192(1)(ic) "steel" means any of the steel products listed in Annex 1 to the Guidelines on national regional aid (2006/C 54/08), published in the Official Journal on 4 March 2006.][1]

Commentary—*Simon's Taxes* **E3.142**.
HMRC Manuals—Venture Capital Schemes Manual VCM3130 (producing steel).
Amendments—[1]   Sections 196A–196C inserted by FA 2008 s 32, Sch 11 paras 4, 6 with effect from 6 April 2008. This amendment does not have effect in relation to shares issued before that date (FA 2008 Sch 11 para 11).

197 Excluded activities: hotels and comparable establishments

(1) This section supplements section 192(1)(j).

(2) The reference to a comparable establishment is to a guest house, hostel or other establishment the main purpose of maintaining which is the provision of facilities for overnight accommodation (with or without catering services).

(3) The activities of a person are not to be taken to fall within section 192(1)(*j*) unless that person has an estate or interest in, or is in occupation of, the hotel or comparable establishment in question.

Commentary—*Simon's Taxes* **E3.142**.

HMRC Manuals—Venture Capital Schemes Manual VCM3140 (operating or managing hotels or comparable establishments).

198 Excluded activities: nursing homes and residential care homes

(1) This section supplements section 192(1)(*k*).

(2) "Nursing home" means any establishment which exists wholly or mainly for the provision of nursing care—

    (*a*) for persons suffering from sickness, injury or infirmity, or

    (*b*) for women who are pregnant or have given birth.

(3) "Residential care home" means any establishment which exists wholly or mainly for the provision of residential accommodation, together with board and personal care, for persons in need of personal care because of—

    (*a*) old age,

    (*b*) mental or physical disability,

    (*c*) past or present dependence on alcohol or drugs,

    (*d*) any past illnesses, or

    (*e*) past or present mental disorder.

(4) The activities of a person are not to be taken to fall within section 192(1)(*k*) unless that person has an estate or interest in, or is in occupation of, the nursing home or residential care home in question.

Commentary—*Simon's Taxes* **E3.142**.

HMRC Manuals—Venture Capital Schemes Manual VCM3150 (operating or managing nursing homes or residential care homes).

[198A Excluded activities: . . . export of electricity

(1) This section supplements section 192(1)(*ka*).

(2) Electricity is exported if it is exported onto a distribution system or transmission system (within the meaning of section 4 of the Electricity Act 1989).

(3)–(9) . . . ²]¹

Commentary—*Simon's Taxes* **E3.142, E3.149A**.

HMRC Manuals—Venture Capital Schemes Manual VCM3160 (subsidised generation or export of electricity).

Amendments—¹   This section inserted by FA 2012 s 39, Sch 7 paras 1, 14, with effect in relation to shares issued on or after 23 March 2011, subject to transitional arrangements for shares issued before 6 April 2012: see FA 2012 Sch 7 para 24(2).

²   Words in heading, and sub-ss (3)–(9), repealed, by FA 2016 s 28(3)(*b*) with effect in relation to shares issued on or after 6 April 2016.

199 Excluded activities: provision of services or facilities for another business

(1) Providing services or facilities for a business carried on by another person (other than a company of which the provider of the services or facilities is a qualifying subsidiary) is an excluded activity if—

    (*a*) the business consists wholly or as to a substantial part of activities falling within any of paragraphs (*a*) to [(*ka*)]² of section 192(1), and

    (*b*) a controlling interest in the business is held by a person who also has a controlling interest in the business carried on by the provider of the services or facilities.

(2) Subsections (3) to (5) explain what is meant by a controlling interest in a business for the purposes of subsection (1)(*b*).

(3) In the case of a business carried on by a company, a person ("A") has a controlling interest in the business if—

    (*a*) A controls the company,

    (*b*) the company is a close company and A or an associate of A is a director of the company and is either—

        (i) the beneficial owner of more than 30% of the ordinary share capital of the company, or

        (ii) able, directly or through the medium of other companies or by any other indirect means, to control more than 30% of that share capital, or

    (*c*) at least half the business could, in accordance with [section 942 of CTA 2010]¹, be regarded as belonging to A for the purposes of [section 941 of that Act]¹ of that Act (company reconstructions without a change of ownership).

(4) In any other case, a person has a controlling interest in a business if the person is entitled to at least half the assets used for, or of the income arising from, the business.

(5) For the purposes of this section—

    (*a*) any rights or powers of a person who is an associate of another are to be attributed to that other person, and

    (*b*) "business" includes any trade, profession or vocation.

Commentary—*Simon's Taxes* **E3.149**.
HMRC Manuals—Venture Capital Schemes Manual VCM3170 (provision of services or facilities for another business).
Modifications—ITA 2007 Sch 2 para 56 (modification of this section in relation to shares issued before 6 April 2007).
Amendments—[1]   In sub-s (3)(c) words substituted by CTA 2010 s 1177, Sch 1 para 501. CTA 2010 has effect for corporation tax purposes for accounting periods ending on or after 1 April 2010, and for income and capital gains tax purposes for the tax year 2010–11 and subsequent tax years.
[2]   Reference in sub-s (1)(a) substituted by FA 2012 s 39, Sch 7 paras 1, 15, with effect in relation to shares issued on or after 23 March 2011, subject to transitional arrangements for shares issued before 6 April 2012: see FA 2012 Sch 7 para 24(2).

CHAPTER 5

ATTRIBUTION OF AND CLAIMS FOR EIS RELIEF
Attribution

201 Attribution of EIS relief to shares

(1) References in this Part, in relation to any individual, to the EIS relief attributable to any shares or issue of shares are to be read as references to any reduction made in the individual's liability to income tax that is attributed to those shares or that issue in accordance with this section.

This is subject to the provisions of Chapters 6 and 7 providing for the withdrawal or reduction of EIS relief.

(2) If an individual's liability to income tax is reduced in any tax year, then—

    (a) if the reduction is obtained because of one issue of shares, the amount of the reduction is attributed to that issue, and

    (b) if the reduction is obtained because of two or more issues of shares, the amount of the reduction—

        (i) is apportioned between those issues in the same proportions as the amounts claimed by the individual in respect of each issue, and

        (ii) is attributed to those issues accordingly.

(3) If under this section an amount of any reduction of income tax is attributed to an issue of shares ("the original issue") to an individual, a proportionate part of that amount is attributed to each share in respect of which the claim was made.

(4) If corresponding bonus shares are issued to the individual in respect of any shares ("the original shares") to which EIS relief is attributed—

    (a) a proportionate part of the total amount attributed to the original shares immediately before the bonus shares are issued is attributed to each of the shares in the holding comprising the original shares and the bonus shares, and

    (b) after the issue of the bonus shares, this Part applies as if the original issue had included those shares.

(5) In subsection (4) "corresponding bonus shares" means bonus shares which are in the same company, of the same class, and carry the same rights as the original shares.

(6) If section 158(1) and (2) applies in the case of any issue of shares as if part of the issue had been issued in a previous tax year, this section has effect as if that part and the remainder were separate issues of shares (and that part had been issued on a day in the previous tax year).

(7) If, at a time when EIS relief is attributable to, or to any part of, any issue of shares, the relief falls to be withdrawn or reduced under Chapters 6 and 7—

    (a) if it falls to be withdrawn, the relief attributable to each of the shares in question is reduced to nil, and

    (b) if it falls to be reduced by any amount, the relief attributable to each of the shares in question is reduced by a proportionate part of that amount.

Commentary—*Simon's Taxes* **E3.160**.
HMRC Manuals—Venture Capital Schemes Manual VCM14020 (attribution of EIS relief to shares).

Claims: general

202 Time for making claims for EIS relief

(1) A claim for EIS relief in respect of shares issued by a company in any tax year may be made—

    (a) not earlier than the time the requirement in section 176(2) or (3) (trade etc must have been carried on for 4 months) is first met, and

    (b) not later than the fifth anniversary of the normal self-assessment filing date for the tax year.

(2) If section 158(1) and (2) applies in the case of any issue of shares as if part of the issue had been issued in a previous tax year, this section has effect as if that part and the remainder were separate issues of shares (and that part had been issued on a day in the previous tax year).

Commentary—*Simon's Taxes* **E3.121, E3.143, E3.159**.
HMRC Manuals—Venture Capital Schemes Manual VCM12070 (EIS: minimum period requirement under s.176).

203 Entitlement to claim

(1) The investor is entitled to make a claim for EIS relief in respect of the amount subscribed by the investor for the relevant shares if the investor has received from the issuing company a compliance certificate in respect of those shares.

(2) For the purposes of PAYE regulations no regard is to be had to EIS relief unless a claim for it has been duly made.

(3) No application may be made under section 55(3) or (4) of TMA 1970 (application for postponement of payment of tax pending appeal) on the ground that the investor is eligible for EIS relief unless a claim for the relief has been duly made by the investor.

Commentary—*Simon's Taxes* **E3.158, E3.159**.
HMRC Manuals—Venture Capital Schemes Manual VCM14150 (investor claims: conditions).
VCM23200 (EIS: deferral relief: claims procedure).

Claims: supporting documents

204 Compliance certificates

(1) A "compliance certificate" is a certificate which—
  (*a*) is issued by the issuing company in respect of the relevant shares,
  (*b*) states that, except so far as they fall to be met by or in relation to the investor, the requirements for EIS relief are for the time being met in relation to those shares, and
  (*c*) is in such form as the Commissioners for Her Majesty's Revenue and Customs may direct.

(2) Before issuing a compliance certificate in respect of the relevant shares, the issuing company must provide an officer of Revenue and Customs with a compliance statement in respect of the issue of shares which includes the relevant shares.

(3) The issuing company must not issue a compliance certificate without the authority of an officer of Revenue and Customs.

(4) If the issuing company, or a person connected with the issuing company, has given notice to an officer of Revenue and Customs under section 241 of this Act or paragraph 16(2) or (4) of Schedule 5B to TCGA 1992, a compliance certificate must not be issued unless the authority is given or renewed after the receipt of the notice.

(5) If an officer of Revenue and Customs—
  (*a*) has been requested to give or renew an authority to issue a compliance certificate, and
  (*b*) has decided whether or not to do so,
the officer must give notice of the officer's decision to the issuing company.

Commentary—*Simon's Taxes* **E3.158**.
HMRC Manuals—Venture Capital Schemes Manual VCM14090 (company procedures: company's statement on EIS1).

205 Compliance statements

(1) A "compliance statement" is a statement, in respect of an issue of shares, to the effect that, except so far as they fall to be met by or in relation to the individuals to whom shares included in that issue have been issued, the requirements for EIS relief (see section 157)—
  (*a*) are for the time being met in relation to the shares to which the statement relates, and
  (*b*) have been so met at all times since the shares were issued.

(2) In determining for the purposes of subsection (1) whether the requirements for EIS relief are met at any time in relation to the issue of shares, references in this Part to "the relevant shares" are read as references to the shares included in the issue.

(3) A compliance statement must be in such form as the Commissioners for Her Majesty's Revenue and Customs direct and must contain—
  (*a*) such additional information as the Commissioners reasonably require, including in particular information relating to the persons who have requested the issue of compliance certificates,
  (*b*) a declaration that the statement is correct to the best of the issuing company's knowledge and belief, and
  (*c*) such other declarations as the Commissioners may reasonably require.

(4) The issuing company may not provide an officer of Revenue and Customs with a compliance statement in respect of any shares issued by it in any tax year—
  (*a*) before the requirement in section 176(2) or (3) (trade etc must have been carried on for 4 months) is met, or
  (*b*) later than two years after the end of that tax year or, if that requirement is first met after the end of that tax year, later than two years after the requirement is first met.

Commentary—*Simon's Taxes* **E3.158**.
HMRC Manuals—Venture Capital Schemes Manual VCM14090 (company procedures: company's statement on EIS1).

206 Appeal against refusal to authorise compliance certificate

For the purpose of the provisions of TMA 1970 relating to appeals, the refusal of an officer of Revenue and Customs to authorise the issue of a compliance certificate is taken to be a decision disallowing a claim by the issuing company.

Commentary—*Simon's Taxes* **E3.158**.
HMRC Manuals—Venture Capital Schemes Manual VCM14130 (company procedures: refusal to authorise issue of EIS3).

207 Penalties for fraudulent certificate or statement etc

The issuing company is liable to a penalty not exceeding £3,000 if—
  (*a*) it issues a compliance certificate, or provides a compliance statement, which is made fraudulently or negligently, or

(*b*) it issues a compliance certificate in contravention of section 204(3) or (4).

Commentary—*Simon's Taxes* **E3.158**.
HMRC Manuals—Venture Capital Schemes Manual VCM14100 (the maximum penalty).

CHAPTER 6

WITHDRAWAL OR REDUCTION OF EIS RELIEF

Introduction

208 Overview of Chapter

This Chapter provides for EIS relief to be withdrawn or reduced under—
- (*a*) section 209 (disposal of shares),
- (*b*) section 211 (call options),
- (*c*) section 212 (put options),
- (*d*) section 213 (value received by the investor),
- (*e*) section 224 (repayments etc of share capital to other persons),
- (*f*) section 232 (acquisition of a trade or trading assets),
- (*g*) section 233 (acquisition of share capital), and
- (*h*) section 234 (relief subsequently found not to have been due).

Disposals

209 Disposal of shares

(1) This section applies if—
- (*a*) the investor disposes of any of the relevant shares,
- (*b*) the disposal takes place before period A ends, and
- (*c*) EIS relief is attributable to the shares.

(2) If the disposal is not made by way of a bargain made at arm's length, the EIS relief attributable to the shares must be withdrawn.

(3) If the disposal is made by way of a bargain made at arm's length, the EIS relief attributable to the shares must—
- (*a*) if it is greater than the amount given by the formula set out below, be reduced by that amount, and
- (*b*) in any other case, be withdrawn.

The formula is—

$$R \times EISR$$

where—

R is the amount or value of the consideration received by the investor for the shares, and
[EISR is the [EIS original rate]².][1]

(4) This section does not apply to a disposal of shares to which an amount of EIS relief is attributable if—
- (*a*) the disposal was made by an individual ("A") to another individual ("B"), and
- (*b*) A and B were married to, or were civil partners of, each other and living together at the time of the disposal.

(5) Section 246 contains rules for determining which shares of any class are treated as disposed of for the purposes of this section if the investor disposes of some but not all the shares of that class which are held by the investor.

[(6) Nothing in this section applies to a disposal of shares occurring as a result of the investor's death.][3]

Commentary—*Simon's Taxes* **E3.167, E3.190**.
HMRC Manuals—Venture Capital Schemes Manual VCM15015 (disposal of ESI shares).
Modifications—See FA 2011 s 42(8) (EIS relief attributable to shares obtained in 2007–08 or earlier, reference to "EIS original rate" in sub-s (3) to be read as a reference to "20%").
Amendments—[1]   In sub-s (3), in formula, "EISR" substituted for "S", and definition of EISR substituted for definition of "S" by FA 2008 s 5, Sch 1 paras 1, 14 with effect for the tax year 2008–09 and subsequent tax years.
[2]   In sub-s (3), words substituted for words "EIS rate" by FA 2011 s 42(3)(*a*) with effect for the tax year 2011–12 and subsequent tax years (subject to transitional provision in FA 2011 s 42(8)). FA 2011 s 42 came into force on 13 October 2011 (SI 2011/2459 art 2).
[3]   Sub-s (6) inserted by FA 2012 s 39, Sch 7 paras 1, 17 with effect from 17 July 2012.

210 Cases where maximum EIS relief not obtained

(1) If the investor's liability to income tax is reduced for any tax year in respect of any issue of shares and—
- (*a*) the amount of the reduction ("A"), is less than
- (*b*) the amount ("B") which is equal to tax at the [EIS original rate][1] on the amount on which the investor claims EIS relief in respect of the shares,

section 209(3) has effect in relation to a disposal of any of the shares as if the amount or value referred to as "R" were reduced by multiplying it by the fraction—

$$\frac{A}{B}$$

(2) If section 158(1) and (2) applies in the case of any issue of shares as if part of the issue had been issued in a previous tax year, subsection (1) has effect as if that part and the remainder were separate issues of shares (and that part had been issued on a day in the previous tax year).

(3) If the amount of EIS relief attributable to any of the relevant shares has been reduced before the EIS relief was obtained, the amount referred to in subsection (1) as A is to be treated for the purposes of that subsection as the amount that it would have been without that reduction.

(4) Subsection (3) does not apply to a reduction of EIS relief by virtue of section 201(4) (attribution of EIS relief if there is a corresponding issue of bonus shares).

Commentary—*Simon's Taxes* **E3.167**.

Modifications—See FA 2011 s 42(8) (EIS relief attributable to shares obtained in 2007–08 or earlier, reference to "EIS original rate" in sub-s (1)(*b*) to be read as a reference to "20%").

Amendments—[1] In sub-s (1)(*b*), words substituted for words "EIS rate" by FA 2011 s 42(3)(*b*) with effect for the tax year 2011–12 and subsequent tax years (subject to transitional provision in FA 2011 s 42(8)). FA 2011 s 42 came into force on 13 October 2011 (SI 2011/2459 art 2).

211 Call options

(1) This section applies if the investor grants an option which, if exercised, would bind the investor to sell any of the relevant shares.

(2) The grant of the option is treated for the purposes of section 209 as a disposal of the shares to which the option relates.

(3) Nothing in this section prejudices section 177 (no pre-arranged exits).

Commentary—*Simon's Taxes* **E3.167**.

HMRC Manuals—Venture Capital Schemes Manual VCM15020 (call and put options).

212 Put options

(1) This section applies if, at any time in period A, a person grants the investor an option which, if exercised, would bind the grantor to purchase any of the relevant shares.

(2) Any EIS relief attributable to the shares to which the option relates must be withdrawn.

(3) For the purposes of subsection (2) the shares to which an option relates are those which, if—

    (*a*) the option were exercised immediately after the grant, and

    (*b*) any shares in the issuing company acquired by the investor after the grant were disposed of immediately after being acquired,

would be treated for the purposes of section 209 as disposed of in pursuance of the option.

Commentary—*Simon's Taxes* **E3.167**.

HMRC Manuals—Venture Capital Schemes Manual VCM15020 (call and put options).

Value received by investor

213 Value received by the investor

(1) This section applies if the investor receives any value from the issuing company at any time in period C relating to the relevant shares.

(2) Any EIS relief attributable to the shares must—

    (*a*) if it is greater than the amount given by the formula set out below, be reduced by that amount, and

    (*b*) in any other case, be withdrawn.

The formula is—

$$R \times EISR$$

where—

    R is the amount of the value received by the investor, and

    [EISR is the [EIS original rate][2].][1]

(3) This section is subject to the following sections—

    (*a*) section 214 (value received: receipts of insignificant value),

    (*b*) section 218 (value received where there is more than one issue of shares),

    (*c*) section 219 (value received where part of share issue treated as made in previous tax year),

    (*d*) section 220 (cases where maximum EIS relief not obtained),

    (*e*) section 221 (receipts of value by and from connected persons etc), and

    (*f*) section 222 (receipt of replacement value).

Sections 218 to 220 are to be applied in the order in which they appear in this Part.

(4) Value received is to be ignored, for the purposes of this section, to the extent to which EIS relief attributable to the shares has already been withdrawn or reduced on its account.

(5) For the purposes of this section and sections 214 to 223, an individual who acquires any relevant shares on such a transfer as is mentioned in section 245 (spouses or civil partners) is treated as the investor.

Commentary—*Simon's Taxes* **E3.169**.

HMRC Manuals—Venture Capital Schemes Manual VCM15030 (value received by the investor: overview)

VCM15040 (value received by the investor: calculation of reduction of relief).

Modifications—See FA 2011 s 42(8) (EIS relief attributable to shares obtained in 2007–08 or earlier, reference to "EIS original rate" in sub-s (2) to be read as a reference to "20%").

Amendments—[1]   In sub-s (2), in formula, "EISR" substituted for "S", and definition of "EISR" substituted for definition of "S" by FA 2008 s 5, Sch 1 paras 1, 16 with effect for the tax year 2008–09 and subsequent tax years.

[2]   In sub-s (2), words substituted for words "EIS rate" by FA 2011 s 42(3)(*c*) with effect for the tax year 2011–12 and subsequent tax years (subject to transitional provision in FA 2011 s 42(8)). FA 2011 s 42 came into force on 13 October 2011 (SI 2011/2459 art 2).

214 Value received: receipts of insignificant value

(1) Section 213(2) does not apply if the receipt of value is a receipt of insignificant value.

This is subject to subsection (2).

(2) If—

    (*a*) value is received ("the relevant receipt") by the investor from the issuing company at any time in period C relating to the relevant shares,

    (*b*) the investor has received from the issuing company one or more receipts of insignificant value at a time or times—

        (i) during that period, but

        (ii) not later than the time of the relevant receipt, and

    (*c*) the total amount of the value of the receipts within paragraph (*a*) and (*b*) is not an amount of insignificant value,

the investor is treated for the purposes of this Chapter as if the relevant receipt had been a receipt of an amount of value equal to that total amount.

(3) A receipt does not fall within subsection (2)(*b*) if it has previously formed part of a total amount falling within subsection (2)(*c*).

Commentary—*Simon's Taxes* **E3.169**.

HMRC Manuals—Venture Capital Schemes Manual VCM15050 (value received by the investor: receipts of insignificant value).

215 Meaning of "receipts of insignificant value"

(1) This section applies for the purposes of section 214.

(2) "A receipt of insignificant value" means a receipt of an amount of insignificant value, that is, an amount of value which—

    (*a*) is not more than £1,000, or

    (*b*) if it is more than £1,000, is insignificant in relation to the amount subscribed by the investor for the relevant shares.

This is subject to subsection (3).

(3) If at any time in the period—

    (*a*) beginning 12 months before the issue of the relevant shares, and

    (*b*) ending at the end of the issue date,

repayment arrangements are in existence, no amount of value received by the investor is treated as a receipt of insignificant value.

(4) For this purpose "repayment arrangements" means arrangements which provide for the investor to receive, or to be entitled to receive, any value from the issuing company at any time in period C relating to the relevant shares.

(5) For the purposes of this section—

    (*a*) the references to the investor include references to any person who at any time in period C relating to the relevant shares is an associate of the investor (whether or not that person is such an associate at the material time), and

    (*b*) the reference in subsection (4) to the issuing company includes a reference to a person who at any time in period C relating to the relevant shares is connected with that company (whether or not that person is so connected at the material time).

Commentary—*Simon's Taxes* **E3.169**.

HMRC Manuals—Venture Capital Schemes Manual VCM15050 (value received by the investor: receipts of insignificant value).

216 When value is received

(1) This section applies for the purposes of sections 213 (value received by the investor) and 218 (value received where there is more than one issue of shares).

(2) The investor receives value from the issuing company at any time when the issuing company—

    (*a*) repays, redeems or repurchases any of its share capital or securities which belong to the investor or makes any payment to the investor for giving up the investor's right to any of the issuing company's share capital or any security on its cancellation or extinguishment, (*b*) repays, in pursuance of any arrangements for or in connection with the acquisition of the shares in respect of which EIS relief is claimed, any debt owed to the investor other than a debt which was incurred by the company—

    (i) on or after the date of issue of those shares, and

    (ii) otherwise than in consideration of the extinguishment of a debt incurred before that date,

(*c*) makes to the investor any payment for giving up on its extinguishment the investor's right to any debt, other than a debt in respect of a repayment of the kind mentioned in section 168(2)(*a*) or (*f*) (ignoring of certain expenses or remuneration) or an ordinary trade debt,

(*d*) releases or waives any liability of the investor to the issuing company or discharges or undertakes to discharge any liability of the investor to a third person,

(*e*) makes a loan or advance to the investor which has not been repaid in full before the issue of the shares in respect of which EIS relief is claimed,

(*f*) provides a benefit or facility for the investor,

(*g*) transfers an asset to the investor for no consideration or for consideration less than its market value or acquires an asset from the investor for consideration greater than its market value, or

(*h*) makes to the investor any other payment except—

    (i) a payment of a kind mentioned in any of the provisions of section 168(2) (ignoring of certain payments), or

    (ii) a payment in discharge of an ordinary trade debt.

(3) For the purposes of subsection (2)(*d*) the issuing company is to be treated as having released or waived a liability if the liability is not discharged within 12 months of the time when it ought to have been discharged.

(4) For the purposes of subsection (2)(*e*) the following is to be treated as if it were a loan made by the issuing company to the investor—

(*a*) the amount of any debt (other than an ordinary trade debt) incurred by the investor to the issuing company, and

(*b*) the amount of any debt due from the investor to a third party which has been assigned to the issuing company.

(5) The investor also receives value from the issuing company if—

(*a*) in respect of ordinary shares held by the investor any payment or asset is received in a winding up or in connection with a dissolution of the company, and

(*b*) the winding up or dissolution falls within section 182(4) (no tax avoidance).

(6) The investor also receives value from the issuing company if any person who would, for the purposes of section 163, be treated as connected with the company—

(*a*) purchases any of its share capital or securities which belong to the investor, or

(*b*) makes any payment to the investor for giving up any right in relation to any of the company's share capital or securities.

(7) If because of the investor's disposal of shares in a company any EIS relief attributable to those shares is withdrawn or reduced under section 209, the investor is not to be treated as receiving value from the company in respect of the disposal.

(8) The investor is not to be treated as receiving value from the issuing company merely because of the payment to the investor, or any associate of the investor, of any remuneration for services rendered to that company as a director if the remuneration is reasonable remuneration.

(9) Section 167(3) (director also an employee) applies for the purposes of subsection (8) as it applies for the purposes of section 167, and the reference in that subsection to the payment of remuneration includes the provision of any benefit or facility.

(10) In this section "ordinary trade debt" means any debt for goods or services supplied in the ordinary course of a trade or business if any credit given—

(*a*) is for not more than 6 months, and

(*b*) is not longer than that normally given to customers of the person carrying on the trade or business.

Commentary—*Simon's Taxes* **E3.169**.

HMRC Manuals—Venture Capital Schemes Manual VCM15060 (value received by the investor: when value is received). VCM15070 (value received by the investor: amount of value received).

217 The amount of value received

In a case falling within a provision listed in column 1 of the following table, the amount of value received for the purposes of sections 213 and 218 is given by the corresponding entry in column 2 of the table.

Provision	The amount of value received
Section 216(2)(*a*), (*b*) or (*c*)	The amount received by the investor or, if greater, the market value of the shares, securities or debt
Section 216(2)(*d*)	The amount of the liability

Provision	*The amount of value received*
Section 216(2)(*e*)	The amount of the loan or advance, less the amount of any repayment made before the issue of the relevant shares
Section 216(2)(*f*)	The cost to the issuing company of providing the benefit or facility, less any consideration given for it by the investor
Section 216(2)(*g*)	The difference between the market value of the asset and the consideration (if any) given for it
Section 216(2)(*h*)	The amount of the payment
Section 216(5)	The amount of the payment or the market value of the asset
Section 216(6)	The amount received by the investor or, if greater, the market value of the shares or securities

Commentary—*Simon's Taxes* **E3.169**.
HMRC Manuals—Venture Capital Schemes Manual VCM15060 (value received by the investor: when value is received). VCM15070 (value received by the investor: amount of value received).

218 Value received where there is more than one issue of shares

(1) This section applies if—
    (*a*) two or more issues of shares in the issuing company have been made to the investor which include shares in respect of which the investor obtains EIS relief, and
    (*b*) value is received by the investor at any time in the applicable periods for two or more of those issues.
(2) Section 213(2) has effect in relation to the shares included in each of the issues referred to in subsection (1)(*b*) as if the amount of value referred to as "R" were reduced by multiplying it by the fraction—

$$\frac{A}{B}$$

where—
    A is the amount on which the investor obtains EIS relief in respect of the shares included in the issue in question, and
    B is the sum of that amount and the corresponding amount or amounts in respect of the other issue or issues.
(3) For the purposes of subsection (1) "the applicable period" for an issue of shares is period C in relation to those shares.

Commentary—*Simon's Taxes* **E3.169**.
HMRC Manuals—Venture Capital Schemes Manual VCM15040 (value received by the investor: calculation of reduction of relief).

219 Value received where part of share issue treated as made in previous tax year

(1) This section applies if—
    (*a*) section 213(2) applies to an issue of shares, and
    (*b*) section 158(1) and (2) (form and amount of EIS relief) applies in the case of that issue as if part of the issue had been issued in a previous tax year.
(2) This subsection explains how the calculation under section 213(2) is to be made.
    Step 1 Apportion the amount referred to as "R" between the tax year in which the shares were issued and the previous tax year by multiplying that amount by the fraction—

$$\frac{A}{B}$$

where—
    A is the amount on which the investor obtains EIS relief in respect of the shares treated as issued in the tax year in question, and
    B is the sum of that amount and the corresponding amount in respect of the shares treated as issued in the other tax year.
    Step 2 In relation to each of the amounts ("R1" and "R2") so apportioned to the two tax years, calculate the amounts ("X1" and "X2") that would be given by the formula if there were separate issues of shares in those tax years.
    In calculating amounts X1 and X2, apply section 220 if appropriate but do not apply section 218.
    Step 3 Add amounts X1 and X2 together.
    The result is the required amount.

Commentary—*Simon's Taxes* **E3.169**.

220 Cases where maximum EIS relief not obtained

(1) If the investor's liability to income tax is reduced for any tax year in respect of any issue of shares and—

    (*a*) the amount of the reduction ("A"), is less than

    (*b*) the amount ("B") which is equal to income tax at the [EIS original rate][1] on the amount on which the investor claims EIS relief in respect of the shares,

section 213(2) has effect in relation to any value received as if the amount referred to as "R" were reduced by multiplying it by the fraction—

$$\frac{A}{B}$$

(2) If the amount of EIS relief attributable to any of the relevant shares has been reduced before the EIS relief was obtained, the amount referred to in subsection (1) as "A" is to be treated for the purposes of that subsection as the amount that it would have been without that reduction.

(3) Subsection (2) does not apply to a reduction of EIS relief by virtue of section 201(4) (attribution of EIS relief where there is a corresponding issue of bonus shares).

Commentary—*Simon's Taxes* **E3.169.**

HMRC Manuals—Venture Capital Schemes Manual VCM15040 (value received by the investor: calculation of reduction of relief).

Modifications—See FA 2011 s 42(8) (EIS relief attributable to shares obtained in 2007–08 or earlier, reference to "EIS original rate" in sub-s (2) to be read as a reference to "20%").

See FA 2011 s 42(8) (EIS relief attributable to shares obtained in 2007–08 or earlier, reference to "EIS original rate" in sub-s (1)(*b*) to be read as a reference to "20%").

Amendments—[1] In sub-s (1)(*b*), words substituted for words "EIS rate" by FA 2011 s 42(3)(*d*) with effect for the tax year 2011–12 and subsequent tax years (subject to transitional provision in FA 2011 s 42(8)). FA 2011 s 42 came into force on 13 October 2011 (SI 2011/2459 art 2).

221 Receipts of value by and from connected persons etc

In sections 213, 214 and 216 to 218—

    (*a*) any reference to a payment or transfer to the investor includes a reference to a payment or transfer made to the investor indirectly or to the investor's order or for the investor's benefit,

    (*b*) any reference to the investor includes a reference to an associate of the investor, and

    (*c*) any reference to the issuing company includes a reference to a person who at any time in period A relating to the relevant shares is connected with that company (whether or not that person is so connected at the material time).

Commentary—*Simon's Taxes* **E3.169.**

HMRC Manuals—Venture Capital Schemes Manual VCM15030 (value received by the investor: overview)

VCM15040 (example: receipt of value from connected persons).

VCM15050 (example: calculation of reduction of relief).

222 Receipt of replacement value

(1) If—

    (*a*) any EIS relief attributable to the relevant shares would, in the absence of this section, be reduced or withdrawn under section 213 because of a receipt of value within section 216(2) or (6) ("the original value"),

    (*b*) the original supplier receives value ("the replacement value") from the original recipient and the receipt is a qualifying receipt, and

    (*c*) the amount of the replacement value is at least the amount of the original value,

section 213 does not, because of the receipt of the original value, have effect to reduce or withdraw the EIS relief.

This is subject to section 223(1) and (2).

(2) For the purposes of this section—

    "the original recipient" means the person who receives the original value,

    "the original supplier" means the person from whom that value was received.

(3) If the amount of the original value is, by virtue of section 218, treated as reduced for the purposes of section 213(2) as it applies in relation to the relevant shares in question, the reference in subsection (1)(*c*) to the amount of the original value is to be read as a reference to the amount of that value ignoring the reduction.

(4) A receipt of the replacement value is a qualifying receipt for the purposes of subsection (1) if it arises—

    (*a*) because of the original recipient doing one or more of the following—

        (i) making a payment to the original supplier, other than a payment within paragraph (*c*) or a payment to which subsection (5) applies,

        (ii) acquiring any asset from the original supplier for a consideration the amount or value of which is more than the market value of the asset,

         (iii) disposing of any asset to the original supplier for no consideration or for a consideration the amount or value of which is less than the market value of the asset,

   (*b*)   if the receipt of the original value was within section 216(2)(*d*), because of an event the effect of which is to reverse the event which constituted the receipt of the original value, or

   (*c*)   if the receipt of the original value was within section 216(6), because of the original recipient repurchasing the share capital or securities in question, or (as the case may be) re-acquiring the right in question, for a consideration the amount or value of which is at least the amount of the original value.

(5) This subsection applies to—

   (*a*)   any payment for any goods, services or facilities, provided (whether in the course of trade or otherwise) by—

         (i)   the original supplier, or

         (ii)   any other person who, at any time in period C relating to the relevant shares, is an associate of, or is connected with, that supplier (whether or not the other person is such an associate, or is so connected, at the material time),

      which is reasonable in relation to the market value of those goods, services or facilities,

   (*b*)   any payment of any interest which represents no more than a reasonable commercial return on any money lent to—

         (i)   the original recipient, or

         (ii)   any person who, at any time in period C relating to the relevant shares, is an associate of that recipient (whether or not the person is such an associate at the material time),

   (*c*)   any payment for the acquisition of an asset which does not exceed its market value,

   (*d*)   any payment, as rent for any property occupied by—

         (i)   the original recipient, or

         (ii)   any person who, at any time in period C relating to the relevant shares, is an associate of that recipient (whether or not the person is such an associate at the material time),

      of an amount not exceeding a reasonable and commercial rent for the property,

   (*e*)   any payment in discharge of an ordinary trade debt, and

   (*f*)   any payment for shares in or securities of any company in circumstances that do not fall within subsection (4)(*a*)(ii).

(6) For the purposes of this section, the amount of the replacement value is—

   (*a*)   in a case within paragraph (*a*) of subsection (4), the sum of—

         (i)   the amount of any payment within sub-paragraph (i) of that paragraph, and

         (ii)   the difference between the market value of any asset to which sub-paragraph (ii) or (iii) of that paragraph applies and the amount or value of the consideration (if any) received for it,

   (*b*)   in a case within subsection (4)(*b*), the same as the amount of the original value, and

   (*c*)   in a case within subsection (4)(*c*), the amount or value of the consideration received by the original supplier.

      Section 217 applies for the purpose of determining the amount of the original value.

(7) In this section—

   (*a*)   any reference to a payment to a person (however expressed) includes a reference to a payment made to the person indirectly or to the person's order or for the person's benefit, and

   (*b*)   "ordinary trade debt" has the meaning given by section 216(10).

Commentary—*Simon's Taxes* **E3.170**.
HMRC Manuals—Venture Capital Schemes Manual VCM15080 (receipt of replacement value).

223 Section 222: supplementary

(1) The receipt of the replacement value by the original supplier is ignored for the purposes of section 222(1) to the extent to which it has previously been set (under that section) against a receipt of value to prevent any reduction or withdrawal of EIS relief under section 213.

(2) The receipt of the replacement value by the original supplier ("the event") is ignored for the purposes of section 222 if—

   (*a*)   the event occurs before period C relating to the relevant shares,

   (*b*)   if the event occurs after the time the original recipient receives the original value, it does not occur as soon after that time as is reasonably practicable in the circumstances, or

   (*c*)   if an appeal has been brought by the investor against an assessment to withdraw or reduce any EIS relief attributable to the relevant shares because of the receipt of the original value, the event occurs more than 60 days after the day on which the amount of relief which falls to be withdrawn has been finally determined.

      But nothing in section 222 or this section requires the replacement value to be received after the original value.

(3) This subsection applies if—

(a) the receipt of the replacement value by the original supplier is a qualifying receipt for the purposes of section 222(1), and

(b) in consequence of the receipt any receipts of value are ignored for the purposes of section 213 as that section applies in relation to the shares in question or any other shares subscribed for by the investor, and

(c) the event which gives rise to the receipt is (or includes) a subscription for shares by—

　　(i) the investor, or

　　(ii) any person who at any time in period C relating to the relevant shares is an associate of the investor (whether or not the person is such an associate at the material time).

(4) If either of the following applies—

(a) subsection (3), and

(b) paragraph 13C(3) of Schedule 5B to TCGA 1992 (which makes corresponding provision in relation to relief under that Schedule in respect of re-investment under EIS),

the person who subscribes for the shares is not to be eligible for any EIS relief in relation to those shares or any other shares in the same issue.

(5) In this section "the original recipient", "the original supplier" and "replacement value" have the same meaning as in section 222.

Commentary—*Simon's Taxes* E3.170.

Repayments etc of share capital to other persons

224 Repayments etc of share capital to other persons

(1) This section applies if any EIS relief is attributable to shares held by an individual and, at any time in period C, the issuing company or any subsidiary—

(a) repays, redeems or repurchases any of its share capital which belongs to any member other than—

　　(i) the individual, or

　　(ii) a person who falls within subsection (4), or

(b) makes any payment to any such member for giving up the member's right to any of the share capital of the company or subsidiary on its cancellation or extinguishment.

(2) The EIS relief must—

(a) if it is greater than the amount given by the formula set out below, be reduced by that amount, and

(b) in any other case, be withdrawn.

The formula is—

$$R \times EISR$$

where—

R is the amount received by the member, and

[EISR is the [EIS original rate]².]¹

(3) This section is subject to the following sections—

(a) section 225 (insignificant repayments ignored for the purposes of this section),

(b) section 226 (amount of repayments etc where there is more than one issue of shares),

(c) section 227 (single issue affecting more than one individual),

(d) section 228 (single issue treated as made partly in previous tax year),

(e) section 229 (maximum relief not obtained for share issue),

(f) section 230 (repayment of authorised minimum within 12 months), and

(g) section 231 (restriction on withdrawal of relief).

Sections 226 to 229 are to be applied in the order in which they appear in this Part.

(4) A person falls within this subsection if the repayment—

(a) causes any EIS relief attributable to that person's shares in the issuing company to be withdrawn or reduced by virtue of—

　　(i) section 209 (disposal of shares), or

　　(ii) section 216(2)(a) (receipt of value by virtue of repayment of share capital etc),

[(aa) causes any SEIS relief attributable to that person's shares in the issuing company to be withdrawn or reduced by virtue of—

　　(i) section 257FA (disposal of shares), or

　　(ii) section 257FH(2)(a) (receipt of value by virtue of repayment of share capital etc),]³

(b) causes any investment relief under Schedule 15 to FA 2000 (the corporate venturing scheme) attributable to that person's shares in the issuing company to be withdrawn or reduced by virtue of—

　　(i) paragraph 46 of that Schedule (disposal of shares), or

　　(ii) paragraph 49(1)(a) of that Schedule (receipt of value by virtue of repayment of share capital etc), or (*c*) gives rise to a qualifying chargeable event within the meaning of paragraph 14(4) of Schedule 5B to TCGA 1992 (EIS: deferral relief) in respect of that person's shares in the issuing company.

(5) A repayment is treated as having the effect mentioned in subsection (4)(*a*), [(*aa*),][3] (*b*) or (*c*) if it would have that effect were it not a receipt of insignificant value for the purposes of whichever of the following is applicable—

   (*a*) section 213,

   [(*aa*) section 257FE,][3]

   (*b*) paragraph 47 of Schedule 15 to FA 2000, and

   (*c*) paragraph 13 of Schedule 5B to TCGA 1992.

(6) A repayment is to be ignored, for the purposes of this section, to the extent to which EIS relief attributable to any shares has already been withdrawn or reduced on its account.

(7) In this section and sections 225 to 231—

   (*a*) "repayment" means a repayment, redemption, repurchase or payment mentioned in subsection (1)(*a*) or (*b*), and

   (*b*) references to a subsidiary of a company are references to a company which, at any time in period A relating to the shares in question, is a 51% subsidiary of the company, whether or not it is such a subsidiary at the time of the repayment.

Commentary—*Simon's Taxes* **E3.171**.

HMRC Manuals—Venture Capital Schemes Manual VCM15090 (repayments of share capital to other persons).

Modifications—See FA 2011 s 42(8) (EIS relief attributable to shares obtained in 2007–08 or earlier, reference to "EIS original rate" in sub-s (2) to be read as a reference to "20%").

Amendments—[1] In sub-s (2), in formula, "EISR" substituted for "S" and definition of "EISR" substituted for definition of "S", by FA 2008 s 5, Sch 1 paras 1, 18 with effect for the tax year 2008–09 and subsequent tax years.

[2] In sub-s (2), words substituted for words "EIS rate" by FA 2011 s 42(3)(*e*) with effect for the tax year 2011–12 and subsequent tax years (subject to transitional provision in FA 2011 s 42(8)). FA 2011 s 42 came into force on 13 October 2011 (SI 2011/2459 art 2).

[3] Sub-ss (4)(*aa*), (5)(*aa*) inserted, and word in sub-s (5), inserted by F(No 2)A 2015 s 25, Sch 5 paras 1, 15 with effect in relation to any repayment, redemption or repurchase of share capital, or payment to a member, on or after 6 April 2014.

225 Insignificant repayments ignored for purposes of section 224

(1) A repayment is ignored for the purposes of section 224 (repayments etc of share capital to other persons) if both—

   (*a*) the market value of the shares to which it relates ("the target shares") immediately before the event occurs, and

   (*b*) the amount received by the member in question,

are insignificant in relation to the market value of the remaining issued share capital of the issuing company (or, as the case may be, the subsidiary) immediately after the event occurs.

   This is subject to subsection (3).

(2) For the purposes of subsection (1) it is assumed that the target shares are cancelled at the time the repayment is made.

(3) Subsection (1) does not apply if repayment arrangements are in existence at any time in the period—

   (*a*) beginning 12 months before the issue of the relevant shares, and

   (*b*) ending at the end of the issue date.

(4) For this purpose "repayment arrangements" means arrangements which provide—

   (*a*) for a repayment by the issuing company or any subsidiary of that company (whether or not it is such a subsidiary at the time the arrangements are made), or

   (*b*) for anyone to be entitled to such a repayment,

at any time in period C relating to the relevant shares.

Commentary—*Simon's Taxes* **E3.171**.

HMRC Manuals—Venture Capital Schemes Manual VCM15100 (insignificant repayments ignored).

226 Amount of repayments etc where there is more than one issue of shares

(1) This section applies if, in relation to the same repayment, section 224(2) applies to EIS relief attributable to two or more issues of shares.

(2) Section 224(2) has effect in relation to the shares included in each of those issues as if the amount referred to as "R" were reduced by multiplying it by the fraction—

$$\frac{A}{B}$$

where—

   A is the amount on which EIS relief was obtained by the individuals in respect of shares which are included in the issue and to which EIS relief is or, but for section 224(2)(*b*), would be attributable, and

B is the sum of that amount and the corresponding amount or amounts in respect of the other issue or issues.

Commentary—*Simon's Taxes* E3.171.

227 Single issue affecting more than one individual

(1) This section applies if, in relation to the same repayment, section 224(2) applies to EIS relief attributable to shares held by two or more individuals.

(2) Section 224(2) has effect in relation to each individual as if the amount referred to as "R" were reduced by multiplying it by the fraction—

$$\frac{A}{B}$$

where—

A is the amount on which the individual obtains EIS relief in respect of the shares to which EIS relief is or, but for section 224(2)(b), would be attributable, and
B is the sum of that amount and the corresponding amount or amounts on which the other individual or individuals obtain EIS relief in respect of such shares.

Commentary—*Simon's Taxes* E3.171.

228 Single issue treated as made partly in previous tax year

(1) This section applies if—
   (a) section 224(2) applies to EIS relief attributable to shares held by an individual, and
   (b) part of the issue of shares has been treated as issued to the individual in a previous tax year for the purposes of section 158(1) and (2) (form and amount of EIS relief).

(2) This subsection explains how the calculation under section 224(2) is to be made.
   Step 1 Apportion the amount referred to as "R" between the tax year in which the shares were issued and the previous tax year by multiplying that amount by the fraction—

$$\frac{A}{B}$$

where—

   A is the amount on which the individual obtains EIS relief in respect of the shares treated as issued in the tax year in question, and
   B is the sum of that amount and the corresponding amount in respect of the shares treated as issued in the other tax year.

   Step 2 In relation to each of the amounts ("R1" and "R2") so apportioned to the two tax years, calculate the amounts ("X1" and "X2") that would be given by the formula if there were separate issues of shares in those tax years.
   In calculating amounts X1 and X2, apply section 229 if appropriate but do not apply section 226 or 227.
   Step 3 Add amounts X1 and X2 together.
   The result is the required amount.

Commentary—*Simon's Taxes* E3.171.

229 Maximum relief not obtained for share issue

(1) This section applies if section 224(2) applies to EIS relief attributable to shares held by an individual and—
   (a) the amount of the reduction ("A") in the individual's liability to income tax for any tax year in respect of the shares, is less than
   (b) the amount ("B") which is equal to income tax at the [EIS original rate][1] on the amount on which the individual claims EIS relief in respect of the shares.

(2) Section 224(2) has effect as if the amount referred to as "R" were reduced by multiplying it by the fraction—

$$\frac{A}{B}$$

(3) If the amount of EIS relief attributable to any of the relevant shares has been reduced before the EIS relief was obtained, the amount referred to in subsections (1) and (2) as "A" is to be treated for the purposes of those subsections as the amount that it would have been without that reduction.

(4) Subsection (3) does not apply to a reduction of EIS relief by virtue of section 201(4) (attribution of EIS relief where there is a corresponding issue of bonus shares).

Commentary—*Simon's Taxes* E3.171.

Modifications—See FA 2011 s 42(8) (EIS relief attributable to shares obtained in 2007–08 or earlier, reference to "EIS original rate" in sub-s (1)(*b*) to be read as a reference to "20%").

Amendments—[1]   In sub-s (1)(*b*), words substituted for words "EIS rate" by FA 2011 s 42(3)(*f*) with effect for the tax year 2011–12 and subsequent tax years (subject to transitional provision in FA 2011 s 42(8)). FA 2011 s 42 came into force on 13 October 2011 (SI 2011/2459 art 2).

230 Repayment of authorised minimum within 12 months

(1) This section applies if—

[(*a*) a company issues share capital ("the original shares") of nominal value equal to the authorised minimum (within the meaning of the Companies Act 2006) for the purposes of complying with section 761 of that Act (public company: requirement as to minimum share capital),][1]

(*b*) the registrar of companies issues the company with a certificate under that section.

(2) Section 224(2) does not apply in relation to any redemption of the original shares within 12 months of the date on which they were issued.

(3) . . . [1]

Commentary—*Simon's Taxes* **E3.171**.

Amendments—[1]   Sub-s (1)(*a*) substituted, and sub-s (3) repealed, by the Companies Act 2006 (Consequential Amendments) (Taxes and National Insurance) Order, SI 2008/954 arts 3, 38, 39, Schedule with effect from 6 April 2008.

231 Restriction on withdrawal of relief under section 224

(1) This section applies if, because of a repayment, any investment relief which is attributable under Schedule 15 to FA 2000 to any shares is withdrawn under paragraph 56(2) of that Schedule.

(2) For the purposes of this section "the relevant amount" is the amount determined by the formula—

$$A - 5B$$

where—

A is the amount of the repayment, and

B is the total amount of investment relief withdrawn because of the repayment.

(3) If the relevant amount does not exceed £1,000, the repayment is ignored for the purposes of section 224(1), unless repayment arrangements are in existence at any time in the period—

(*a*) beginning 12 months before the issue of the shares mentioned in subsection (1), and

(*b*) ending at the end of the issue date.

(4) For this purpose "repayment arrangements" means arrangements which provide—

(*a*) for a repayment by the issuing company or any subsidiary of that company, or

(*b*) for anyone to be entitled to such a repayment,

at any time.

(5) Subsection (4)(*a*) applies in relation to a subsidiary of the issuing company whether or not it is such a subsidiary when the arrangements were made.

(6) If the repayment is not ignored by virtue of subsection (3), the amount received because of the repayment is treated for the purposes of section 224(2) as an amount equal to the relevant amount.

(7) In this section—

(*a*) "investment relief" has the same meaning as in Schedule 15 to FA 2000 (corporate venturing scheme), and

(*b*) references to the withdrawal of investment relief include its reduction.

Commentary—*Simon's Taxes* **E3.171**.

Miscellaneous

232 Acquisition of a trade or trading assets

(1) Any EIS relief attributable to any shares in a company held by an individual is withdrawn if—

(*a*) at any time in period A, the company or any qualifying subsidiary—

    (i) begins to carry on as its trade, or as part of its trade, a trade which was previously carried on at any time in that period otherwise than by the company or any qualifying subsidiary, or

    (ii) acquires the whole, or the greater part, of the assets used for the purposes of a trade previously so carried on, and

(*b*) the individual is a person, or one of a group of persons, to whom subsection (2) or (3) applies.

(2) This subsection applies to any person or group of persons—

(*a*) to whom an interest amounting in total to more than a half share in the trade (as previously carried on) belonged at any time in period A, and

(*b*) who is or are a person or group of persons to whom such an interest in the trade carried on by the company belongs or has, at any such time, belonged.

(3) This subsection applies to any person or group of persons who—

(*a*) control or, at any time in period A, have controlled the company, and

    (b) is or are a person or group of persons who, at any such time, controlled another company which previously carried on the trade.

(4) For the purposes of subsection (2)—

    (a) [for the purpose of determining]¹ the person to whom a trade belongs and, if a trade belongs to two or more persons, their respective shares in [that trade—

        (i) apply section 941(6) of CTA 2010, and

        (ii) an interest in a trade belonging to a company may be treated in accordance with any of the options set out in section 942 of that Act, and"]¹

    (b) any interest, rights or powers of a person who is an associate of another person are treated as those of that other person.

(5) In determining whether any EIS relief attributable to any shares in the issuing company held by an individual who—

    (a) is a director of, or of a company which is a partner of, the issuing company or any qualifying subsidiary, and

    (b) is in receipt of, or entitled to receive, remuneration as such a director falling within section 169(2) (reasonable remuneration for services),

is to be withdrawn, the reference in subsection (3)(b), and (so far as relating to that provision) the reference in subsection (1)(a)(i), to any time in period A are to be read as references to any time before the end of period A.

(6) Section 167(3) (director also an employee) applies for the purposes of subsection (5) as it applies for the purposes of section 168, and in subsection (5) "remuneration" includes any benefit or facility.

(7) In this section "trade" includes any business or profession, and references to a trade previously carried on include references to part of such a trade.

Commentary—*Simon's Taxes* E3.172.

HMRC Manuals—Venture Capital Schemes Manual VCM15110 (acquisition of a trade or trading assets).

Amendments—¹ In sub-s (4)(a), words inserted and words substituted by CTA 2010 s 1177, Sch 1 para 502. CTA 2010 has effect for corporation tax purposes for accounting periods ending on or after 1 April 2010, and for income and capital gains tax purposes for the tax year 2010–11 and subsequent tax years.

233 Acquisition of share capital

(1) Any EIS relief attributable to any shares in a company held by an individual is withdrawn if—

    (a) the company comes to acquire all of the issued share capital of another company at any time in period A, and

    (b) the individual is a person, or one of a group of persons, to whom subsection (2) applies.

(2) This subsection applies to any person or group of persons who—

    (a) control or have, at any time in period A, controlled the company, and

    (b) is or are a person or group of persons who, at any such time, controlled the other company.

(3) In determining whether any EIS relief attributable to any shares in the issuing company held by an individual who—

    (a) is a director of, or of a company which is a partner of, the issuing company or any qualifying subsidiary, and

    (b) is in receipt of, or entitled to receive, remuneration as such a director falling within section 169(2),

is to be withdrawn, the reference in subsection (2)(b) to any time in period A is to be read as a reference to any time before the end of period A.

(4) Section 167(3) applies for the purposes of subsection (3) as it applies for the purposes of section 168, and in subsection (3) "remuneration" includes any benefit or facility.

Commentary—*Simon's Taxes* E3.172.

HMRC Manuals—Venture Capital Schemes Manual VCM15110 (acquisition of share capital from company owners).

234 Relief subsequently found not to have been due

(1) Any EIS relief obtained by the investor which is subsequently found not to have been due must be withdrawn.

(2) EIS relief obtained by the investor in respect of the relevant shares may not be withdrawn on the ground—

    (a) that the requirements of sections 174 and 175 (the purpose of the issue and use of money raised requirements) are not met in respect of the shares, or

    (b) that the issuing company is not a qualifying company in relation to the shares (see Chapter 4), unless the requirements of subsection (3) are met.

(3) The requirements of this subsection are met if either—

    (a) the issuing company has given notice under section 241, or paragraph 16(2) or (4) of Schedule 5B to TCGA 1992, (information to be provided by issuing company etc) in relation to the relevant issue of shares, or (*b*) an officer of Revenue and Customs has given notice to that company stating the officer's opinion that, because of the ground in question, the whole or any part of the EIS relief obtained by any individual in respect of shares included in the relevant issue of shares was not due.

(4) In this section "the relevant issue of shares" means the issue of shares in the issuing company which includes the relevant shares.

Commentary—*Simon's Taxes* **E3.173**.

HMRC Manuals—Venture Capital Schemes Manual VCM15120 (relief subsequently found not to have been due).

CHAPTER 7

WITHDRAWAL OR REDUCTION OF EIS RELIEF: PROCEDURE

Assessments and appeals

235 Assessments for the withdrawal or reduction of EIS relief

If any EIS relief which has been obtained falls to be withdrawn or reduced under Chapter 6, it must be withdrawn or reduced by the making of an assessment to income tax for the tax year for which the relief was obtained.

Commentary—*Simon's Taxes* **E3.174**.

HMRC Manuals—Venture Capital Schemes Manual VCM15140 (procedure: assessments).

236 Appeals against section 234(3)(b) notices

(1) For the purposes of the provisions of TMA 1970 relating to appeals, the giving of notice by an officer of Revenue and Customs under section 234(3)(*b*) is taken to be a decision disallowing a claim by the issuing company.

(2) If any issue has been determined on an appeal brought by virtue of paragraph 1A(6) of Schedule 5B to TCGA 1992 (appeal against notice that shares never have been, or have ceased to be, eligible shares), the determination is conclusive for the purposes of any appeal brought by virtue of subsection (1) on which that issue arises.

Commentary—*Simon's Taxes* **E3.173**.

237 Time limits for assessments

(1) An officer of Revenue and Customs may[1] . . . —

    (*a*) make an assessment for withdrawing or reducing the EIS relief attributable to any of the relevant shares, or

    (*b*) give a notice under section 234(3)(*b*),

[at any time not more than][1] 6 years after the end of the relevant tax year.

(2) In subsection (1) "the relevant tax year" means—

    (*a*) the tax year in which the time mentioned in section 175(3) (the use of money raised requirement) falls, or

    (*b*) the tax year in which the event which causes the EIS relief to be withdrawn or reduced occurs,

whichever is the later.

(3) Subsection (1) is without prejudice to section [36(1)(*a*)][1] of TMA 1970 [(loss of tax brought about deliberately etc)][1].

Commentary—*Simon's Taxes* **E3.174**.

HMRC Manuals—Venture Capital Schemes Manual VCM15150 (time limits for assessments).

Amendments—[1] In sub-s (1), word repealed and words substituted, in sub-s (3), figure substituted and words substituted by FA 2008 s 118, Sch 39 paras 54, 59 with effect from 1 April 2010 (by virtue of SI 2009/403 art 2(2)), subject to transitional provisions in SI 2009/403 art 10(2) (where art 10 applies, the appointed day is 1 April 2012).

238 Cases where assessment not to be made

(1) No assessment for withdrawing or reducing EIS relief in respect of shares issued to an individual may be made because of an event occurring after the individual's death.

(2) Subsection (3) applies if an individual has, by a disposal or disposals to which section 209(3) applies, disposed of all shares which—

    (*a*) have been issued to the individual by the issuing company, and

    (*b*) are shares—

        (i) to which EIS relief is attributable, or

        (ii) in relation to which period A has not come to an end.

(3) No assessment for withdrawing or reducing EIS relief in respect of those shares may be made because of any subsequent event unless the event occurs at a time when the individual is connected with the company within the meaning of section 166.

Commentary—*Simon's Taxes* **E3.174**.

Interest

239 Date from which interest is chargeable

(1) In its application to an assessment made by virtue of section 235 in the case of relief withdrawn or reduced by virtue of a provision listed [in subsection 2][1], section 86 of TMA 1970 (interest on overdue income tax) has effect as if the relevant date were [31 January next following the tax year for which the assessment is made][1].

[(2) The provisions are—

section 163,

section 164,

section 173A,

any of [sections 180A to 188][2],

section 209,

section 212(1),

section 213,

section 224,

section 232, and

section 233.][1]

Commentary—*Simon's Taxes* E3.175.

HMRC Manuals—Venture Capital Schemes Manual VCM15160 (ESI procedure to charge interest).

Amendments—[1]   In sub-s (1) words substituted and sub—s (1) substituted by FA 2009 s 105 with effect from 21 July 2009:
[2]   Words in sub-s (2) substituted by FA 2012 s 39, Sch 7 paras 1, 18. This amendment is treated as having come into effect on 6 April 2012: see FA 2012 Sch 7 para 25.

Information

240 Information to be provided by the investor

(1) This section applies if the investor has obtained EIS relief in respect of the relevant shares, and an event occurs as a result of which—

(*a*) the investor is not a qualifying investor in relation to the shares,

(*b*) the EIS relief falls to be withdrawn or reduced by virtue of section 164 (no linked loans requirement),

(*c*) the EIS relief falls to be withdrawn or reduced under—

(i)   section 209 (disposal of shares),

(ii)   section 211 (call options), or

(iii)   section 212 (put options), or

(*d*) the EIS relief falls to be withdrawn or reduced under section 213 (receipt of value by the investor), or would fall to be so withdrawn or reduced but for section 222 (receipt of replacement value).

(2) The investor must within 60 days of coming to know of the event give a notice to an officer of Revenue and Customs containing particulars of the event.

(3) If the investor—

(*a*) is required under this section to give notice of a receipt of value which is within section 213, or would be within that section but for section 222, and

(*b*) has knowledge of any replacement value received (or expected to be received) because of a qualifying receipt,

the notice must include particulars of that receipt of replacement value (or expected receipt).

(4) In subsection (3) "qualifying receipt" and "replacement value" are to be read in accordance with section 222.

Commentary—*Simon's Taxes* E3.181, A4.146.

HMRC Manuals—Venture Capital Schemes Manual VCM14210 (investor obligations to notify HMRC).

241 Information to be provided by the issuing company etc

(1) This section applies if the issuing company has provided an officer of Revenue and Customs with a compliance statement in respect of an issue of shares and an event occurs as a result of which—

[(*za*) a requirement of any of the following provisions is not met in respect of the shares included in the issue, or would not be met if EIS relief had been obtained in respect of those shares—

(i)   section 173A (the maximum amount raised annually through risk finance investments),

(ii)   section 173AA (the maximum amount raised through risk finance investments at the issue date),

(iii)   section 173AB (the maximum amount raised through finance investments during period B),

(iv)   section 175A (the permitted maximum age requirement),][1]

(*a*) the requirement of section 175 (the use of money raised) is not met in respect of any of the shares included in the issue, or would not be met if EIS relief had been obtained in respect of the shares in question,

(b) any provision of Chapter 4 has effect to prevent the issuing company being a qualifying company in relation to any of the shares included in the issue, or would have such an effect if EIS relief had been obtained in respect of the shares in question, or

(c) any provision of Chapter 6 which is listed in subsection (2) has effect to cause any EIS relief attributable to any of the shares included in the issue to be withdrawn or reduced, or—

    (i) would have such an effect if EIS relief had been obtained in respect of the shares in question, or

    (ii) in the case of section 213, would have such an effect but for section 222 (receipt of replacement value).

(2) The provisions are—

    (a) section 213 (value received by the investor),

    (b) section 224 (repayments etc of share capital to other persons),

    (c) section 232 (acquisition of a trade or trading assets), and

    (d) section 233 (acquisition of share capital).

(3) If this section applies—

    (a) the issuing company, and

    (b) any person connected with the issuing company who has knowledge of the matters mentioned in subsection (1),

must give a notice to an officer of Revenue and Customs containing particulars of the event.

(4) Any notice required to be given by the issuing company under subsection (3)(a) must be given—

    (a) within 60 days of the event, or

    (b) if the event is a receipt of value within section 216(2) from a person connected with the company (see section 221), within 60 days of the company coming to know of the event.

(5) Any notice required to be given by a person under subsection (3)(b) must be given within 60 days of the person coming to know of the event.

(6) If a person—

    (a) is required under this section to give notice of a receipt of value which is within section 213, or would be within that section but for section 222, and

    (b) has knowledge of any replacement value received (or expected to be received) because of a qualifying receipt,

the notice must include particulars of that receipt of replacement value (or expected receipt).

(7) In subsection (6) "qualifying receipt" and "replacement value" are to be read in accordance with section 222.

Commentary—*Simon's Taxes* **E3.181, A4.146** .

HMRC Manuals—Venture Capital Schemes Manual VCM14210 (company obligations to notify HMRC).

Amendments—[1]   Sub-s (1)(za) inserted by F(No 2)A 2015 s 25, Sch 5 paras 1, 16 with effect in relation to shares issued on or after 18 November 2015.

242 Power to require information where section 240 or 241 applies or could have applied

(1) This section applies if an officer of Revenue and Customs has reason to believe that a person—

    (a) has not given a notice which the person is required to give under section 240 or 241 in respect of any event,

    (b) has given or received value within the meaning of section 216(2) or (6) which, but for the fact that the amount given or received was an amount of insignificant value, would have triggered a requirement to give such a notice, or

    (c) has made or received any repayment within the meaning given by section 224(7) which, but for the fact that it falls to be ignored for the purposes of section 224 by virtue of section 225(1), would have triggered a requirement to give a notice under section 241.

(2) The officer may by notice require the person concerned to supply the officer, within such time as the officer may specify in the notice, with such information relating to the event as the officer may reasonably require for the purposes of this Part.

(3) The period specified in a notice under subsection (2) must be at least 60 days.

(4) In subsection (1)(b) the reference to an amount of insignificant value is construed in accordance with section 215(2).

Commentary—*Simon's Taxes* **E3.181, A4.146** .

HMRC Manuals—Venture Capital Schemes Manual VCM15170 (HMRC power to require information).

243 Power to require information in other cases

(1) Subsection (2) applies if EIS relief is claimed in respect of shares in a company, and an officer of Revenue and Customs has reason to believe that it may not be due because of any such arrangement or scheme as is mentioned in—

    (a) section 165 or 182(2) or (4) (no tax avoidance),

    (b) section 171 (persons subscribing for shares under certain arrangements),

    (c) section 176(4) or (5), 183(6) or 191(3), (4) or (5) (winding up, administration etc),

    (d) section 177(1) (no pre-arranged exits), . . . [1]

    [(da) section 178A (no disqualifying arrangements), or][1]

    (e) section 185(1) or (2), 190(1) or 191(2) (conditions ceasing to be met).

The reference in paragraph (*c*) to subsections (3), (4) and (5) of section 191 is to be read as including those subsections as applied by section 190(2).

(2) The officer may by notice require any person concerned to supply the officer within such time as may be specified in the notice with—

(*a*) a declaration in writing stating whether or not, according to the information which that person has or can reasonably obtain, any such arrangement or scheme exists or has existed, and

(*b*) such other information as the officer may reasonably require for the purposes of the provision in question and as that person has or can reasonably obtain.

(3) The period specified in a notice under subsection (2) must be at least 60 days.

(4) For the purposes of subsection (2), in a case falling within a provision listed in column 1 of the following table, the person concerned is given by the corresponding entry in column 2 of the table.

Provision	*The person concerned*
Subsection (1)(*a*)	The claimant, the company and any person controlling the company
Subsection (1)(*b*)	The claimant
Subsection (1)(*c*)	The claimant, the company, any other company in question and any person controlling the company or any other company in question
Subsection (1)(*d*)	The claimant, the company and any person connected with the company
[Subsection (1)(*da*)	The claimant, the company, any person controlling the company and any person whom an officer of Revenue and Customs has reason to believe may be a party to the arrangements in question][1]
Subsection (1)(*e*)	The company and any person controlling the company

References in this subsection to the claimant include references to any person to whom the claimant appears to have made such a transfer as is mentioned in section 245 (spouses or civil partners) of any of the shares in question.

(5) If EIS relief has been obtained in respect of shares in a company—

(*a*) any person who receives from the company any payment or asset which may constitute value received (by the person or another) for the purposes of section 213, and

(*b*) any person on whose behalf such a payment or asset is received,

must, if so required by an officer of Revenue and Customs, state whether the payment or asset so received is received on behalf of any other person and, if so, the name and address of that other person.

(6) If EIS relief has been claimed in respect of shares in a company—

(*a*) any person who holds or has held shares in the company, and

(*b*) any person on whose behalf any such shares are or were held,

must, if so required by an officer of Revenue and Customs, state whether the shares so held are or were held on behalf of any other person and, if so, the name and address of that other person.

Commentary—*Simon's Taxes* **E3.181, A4.146.**

HMRC Manuals—Venture Capital Schemes Manual VCM15170 (HMRC power to require information). VCM36170 (procedure: HMRC powers to obtain information).

Amendments—[1] Sub-s (1)(*da*) inserted and preceding word "or" repealed, and in sub-s (4) table entry inserted, by FA 2012 s 39, Sch 7 paras 1, 19, with effect in relation to shares issued on or after 6 April 2012, subject to transitional provisions in FA 2012 Sch 7 para 22(2).

244 Obligations of secrecy

No obligation of secrecy imposed by statute or otherwise prevents an officer of Revenue and Customs from disclosing to a company that EIS relief has been obtained or claimed in respect of a particular number or proportion of its shares.

Commentary—*Simon's Taxes* **E3.181.**

CHAPTER 8

SUPPLEMENTARY AND GENERAL

Disposals of shares

245 Transfers between spouses or civil partners

(1) This section applies if—

(*a*) shares to which an amount of EIS relief is attributable were issued to an individual ("A"),

(*b*) A transferred the shares to another individual ("B") during their lives,

(*c*) A was married to, or was the civil partner of, B at the time of the transfer, and

(*d*) section 209 (disposal of shares) does not apply to the transfer.

(2) This Part has effect, in relation to any subsequent disposal or other event, as if—

    (*a*) B were the individual who had subscribed for the shares,

    (*b*) the amount that B had subscribed for the shares were the amount that A had subscribed for them,

    (*c*) B's liability to income tax had been reduced in respect of the shares for the same tax year as that for which A's was so reduced,

    (*d*) the amount by which B's liability to income tax had been reduced in respect of the shares were the same as that by which A's liability to income tax had been so reduced, and

    (*e*) that amount of EIS relief had continued to be attributable to the shares despite the transfer.

(3) If the amount of EIS relief attributable to the shares had been reduced before the relief was obtained by A—

    (*a*) this Part has effect, in relation to any subsequent disposal or other event, as if the amount of EIS relief attributable to the shares transferred to B had been correspondingly reduced before the relief was obtained by B, and

    (*b*) sections 210(3), 220(2) and 229(3) apply in relation to B as they would have applied in relation to A.

(4) If, because of any such disposal or other event, an assessment for reducing or withdrawing EIS relief is to be made, the assessment is to be made on B.

Commentary—*Simon's Taxes* **E3.167**.

HMRC Manuals—Venture Capital Schemes Manual VCM16010 (transfers between spouses or civil partners).

246 Identification of shares on a disposal

(1) The rules in subsections (2) and (3) are for determining which shares of any class are treated as disposed of for the purposes of—

    (*a*) section 209 (disposal of shares), or

    (*b*) section 245 (spouses or civil partners),

if the investor disposes of some but not all of the shares of that class which the investor holds in a company.

(2) Shares acquired on an earlier day are treated as disposed of before shares acquired on a later day.

(3) Shares acquired on the same day are treated as disposed of in the following order—

    (*a*) first any to which [no EIS relief, deferral relief or SEIS relief][1] is attributable,

    [(*aa*) next any to which SEIS relief is attributable,][1]

    (*b*) next any to which deferral relief, but not EIS relief, is attributable,

    (*c*) next any to which EIS relief, but not deferral relief, is attributable, and

    (*d*) finally any to which both EIS relief and deferral relief are attributable.

(4) Any shares within paragraph (*c*) or (*d*) of subsection (3) which are treated by section 201(6) as issued on an earlier day are treated as disposed of before any other shares falling within that paragraph of subsection (3).

(5) The following—

    (*a*) any shares to which EIS relief is attributable and which were transferred to an individual as mentioned in section 245, and

    (*b*) any shares to which deferral relief, but not EIS relief, is attributable and which were acquired by an individual on a disposal to which section 58 of TCGA 1992 applies,

are treated for the purposes of subsections (2) and (3) as acquired by the individual on the day on which they were issued.

(6) In a case to which section 127 of TCGA 1992 applies (including the case where that section applies by virtue of an enactment relating to chargeable gains), shares included in the new holding are treated for the purposes of subsections (2) and (3) as acquired when the original shares were acquired.

(7) In this section—

    "deferral relief" has the same meaning as in Schedule 5B to TCGA 1992,

    "new holding" and "original shares" have the same meaning as in section 127 of TCGA 1992 (or, as the case may be, that section as applied by the enactment concerned).

    ["SEIS relief" means relief under Part 5A (seed enterprise investment scheme).][1]

Commentary—*Simon's Taxes* **E3.167, E3.191, E3.708**.

HMRC Manuals—Venture Capital Schemes Manual VCM16020 (identification of shares on a disposal).

VCM75460 (disposal of shares forming part of a mixed holding: special case).

Amendments—[1]   In sub-s (3)(*a*) words substituted, sub-s (3)(*aa*) inserted, and in sub-s (7) entry for "SEIS relief" inserted, by FA 2012 s 38, Sch 6 paras 6, 14 with effect in relation to shares issued on or after 6 April 2012.

Acquisition of issuing company

247 Continuity of EIS relief where issuing company is acquired by new company

(1) This section applies if—

    (*a*) a company ("the new company") in which the only issued shares are subscriber shares acquires all the shares ("old shares) in another company ("the old company"),

(b) the consideration for the old shares consists wholly of the issue of shares ("new shares") in the new company,

(c) the consideration for the new shares of each description consists wholly of old shares of the corresponding description,

(d) new shares of each description are issued to the holders of old shares of the corresponding description in respect of and in proportion to their holdings,

(e) at some time before the issue of the new shares—

    (i) the old company issued shares which meet the requirements of section 173(2), and

    (ii) a compliance certificate in respect of those shares was issued by that company for the purposes of subsection (1) of section 203 and in accordance with section 204, and

(f) before the issue of the new shares the Commissioners for Her Majesty's Revenue and Customs have, on the application of the new company or the old company, notified that company that they are satisfied that the exchange of shares—

    (i) will be effected for genuine commercial reasons, and

    (ii) will not form part of any such scheme or arrangements as are mentioned in section 137(1) of TCGA 1992 (schemes with avoidance purposes).

In this subsection references to shares, except in the expressions "subscriber shares" and "shares which meet the requirements of section 173(2)", include securities.

(2) Subsection (2) of section 138 of TCGA 1992 (procedure for advance clearance) applies for the purposes of subsection (1)(f) as it applies for the purposes of subsection (1) of that section.

(3) For the purposes of this Part—

(a) the exchange of shares is not regarded as involving any disposal of the old shares or any acquisition of the new shares, and

(b) any EIS relief which is attributable to any old shares is attributable instead to the new shares for which they are exchanged.

[(3A) In section 173AB(2)(a) and in the definition of "the total relevant turnover amount" in section 175A(7), references to a company becoming a 51% subsidiary of the issuing company after the issue date do not include a company becoming such a subsidiary as a result of an exchange of shares as mentioned in subsection (1).][1]

(4) Nothing in section 185 (the control and independence requirement) applies in relation to such an exchange of shares, or shares and securities, as is mentioned in subsection (1), or arrangements with a view to such an exchange.

(5) For the purposes of this section old shares and new shares are of a corresponding description if, on the assumption that they were shares in the same company, they would be of the same class and carry the same rights.

(6) References in sections 248 and 249 to "old shares", "new shares", "the old company" and "the new company" are to be read in accordance with this section.

Commentary—*Simon's Taxes* **E3.168, E3.193**.

HMRC Manuals—Venture Capital Schemes Manual 8170 (company re-organisations).

VCM16030 (acquisition of issuing company).

VCM20190 (EIS: share exchanges provisions for CGT purposes).

Amendments—[1] Sub-s (3A) inserted by F(No 2)A 2015 s 25, Sch 5 paras 1, 17 with effect in relation to shares issued on or after 18 November 2015.

248 Carry over of obligations etc where EIS relief attributed to new shares

(1) This section applies if, under section 247, any EIS relief which is attributable to any old shares becomes attributable instead to any new shares.

(2) This Part has effect as if anything which, under—

(a) section 203(1) (entitlement to claim),

(b) section 234(3) (relief subsequently found not to be due), or

(c) sections 241 to 244 (information to be provided),

has been done, or is required to be done, by or in relation to the old company had been done, or were required to be done, by or in relation to the new company.

(3) Any appeal brought by the old company against a notice under section 234(3)(b) may be prosecuted by the new company as if it had been brought by that company.

Commentary—*Simon's Taxes* **E3.168**.

HMRC Manuals—Venture Capital Schemes Manual VCM16030 (EIS: acquisition of issuing company or insertion of new holding company).

249 Substitution of new shares for old shares

(1) Subsection (2) applies if, in the case of any new shares held by an individual to which EIS relief becomes attributable under section 247, the old shares for which they were exchanged were subscribed for by and issued to the individual.

(2) This Part [(except section 195(7))][1] has effect as if—

(a) the new shares had been subscribed for by the individual at the time when, and for the amount for which, the old shares were subscribed for by the individual,

(b) the new shares had been issued to the individual by the new company at the time when the old shares were issued to the individual by the old company,

(c) the claim for EIS relief made in respect of the old shares had been made in respect of the new shares, and

(d) the individual's liability to income tax had been reduced in respect of the new shares for the same tax year as that for which the individual's liability was so reduced in respect of the old shares.

(3) Subsection (4) applies if, in the case of any new shares held by an individual to which EIS relief becomes so attributable under section 247, the old shares for which they were exchanged were transferred to the individual as mentioned in section 245.

(4) This Part [(except section 195(7))]^1 has effect in relation to any subsequent disposal or other event as if—

(a) the new shares had been subscribed for by the individual at the time when, and for the amount for which, the old shares were subscribed for,

(b) the new shares had been issued by the new company at the time when the old shares were issued by the old company,

(c) the claim for EIS relief made in respect of the old shares had been made in respect of the new shares, and

(d) the individual's liability to income tax had been reduced in respect of the new shares for the same tax year as that for which the liability of the individual who subscribed for the old shares was so reduced in respect of those shares.

Commentary—*Simon's Taxes* **E3.168**.

HMRC Manuals—Venture Capital Schemes Manual VCM16030 (EIS: acquisition of issuing company or insertion of new holding company).

Amendments—^{1} Words in sub-ss (2), (4) inserted, by FA 2007 ss 51, Sch 16 para 11(8). This amendment is deemed to have effect from 6 April 2007 by virtue of FA 2007 Sch 16 para 13, and is subject to transitional provisions in FA 2007 Sch 16 para 14.

Nominees etc

250 Nominees and bare trustees

(1) Shares subscribed for, issued to, held by or disposed of for an individual by a nominee are treated for the purposes of this Part as subscribed for, issued to, held by or disposed of by the individual.

(2) If shares have been issued to a bare trust for two or more beneficiaries, this Part has effect (with the necessary modifications) as if—

(a) each beneficiary had subscribed as an individual for all of those shares, and

(b) the amount subscribed by each beneficiary was equal to the total amount subscribed on the issue of those shares divided by the number of beneficiaries.

(3) In subsection (2) and section 251 "shares" means shares which meet the requirements of section 173(2).

Commentary—*Simon's Taxes* **E3.106, E3.182**.

HMRC Manuals—Venture Capital Scemes Manual VCM10520 (eligibility for EIS income tax relief). VCM16040 (nominees and bare trustees).

251 Approved [knowledge-intensive fund] as nominee

(1) [This section applies]^3 if an individual claims EIS relief in respect of shares in a company at a time when—

(a) the shares have been issued to the managers of [an approved knowledge-intensive fund]^3 as nominee for the individual,

(b) the fund has closed, that is to say, no further investments in the fund are to be accepted,
. . .^{3}

(c) the amounts which the managers have, as nominee for the individual, subscribed for shares issued within [12]^1 months after the closing of the fund represent at least [50%]^3 of the individual's investment in the fund.

[(d)   the amounts which the managers have, as nominee for the individual, subscribed for shares issued within 24 months after the closing of the fund represent at least 90% of the individual's investment in the fund,

(e) within that 24 month period at least 80% of the individual's investment in the fund is represented by shares in companies which are knowledge-intensive companies at the time the shares are issued, and

(f) the managers have met such conditions with respect to the provision of information to HMRC Commissioners as the Commissioners consider appropriate for the purposes of this section.]^3
. . .^{3}

[(1A) In this section "the managers of an approved knowledge-intensive fund" means the person or persons having the management of an investment fund—

(*a*) which is, in the opinion of HMRC Commissioners, a fund established for the purpose of investing wholly, or substantially wholly, in shares in companies which are knowledge-intensive companies at the time the shares are issued, and

(*b*) which is, having met such other conditions as HMRC Commissioners consider appropriate for the purposes of this section, approved by them for those purposes.][3]

(2) . . . [3] Section 158 (form and amount of EIS relief) and section 201 (attribution of EIS relief to shares) have effect as if—

(*a*) any reference to the tax year or other period in which the shares are issued were a reference to the tax year or other period in which the fund closes, and

(*b*) any reference to the time of the issue of the shares, or the time of the subscription for the shares, were a reference to the time of the closing of the fund.

[(2A) Accordingly, in a case where section 158 has effect with the modifications in subsection (2), the reference in section 158(4) to the issue of the shares in the preceding tax year is to the issue of the shares in the tax year preceding the tax year in which the fund closes (and references elsewhere in this Part to the issue of shares in a previous tax year are to be read accordingly).][3]

(3) . . . [2]

(4) If an individual claims EIS relief in respect of shares in a company which have been issued to the managers of [an approved knowledge-intensive fund][3] as nominee for the individual, section 203(1) (entitlement to claim) applies as if—

(*a*) it required the certificate referred to in that section to be issued by the company to the managers, and

(*b*) it provided that no claim for EIS relief may be made unless the person making the claim has received from the managers a certificate issued by the managers in accordance with subsection (5).

(5) A certificate is issued in accordance with this subsection if—

(*a*) it certifies that the managers hold compliance certificates issued to them by the companies concerned, for the purposes of section 203(1), in respect of the holding of shares shown on the managers' certificate, and

(*b*) it is in such form as [HMRC Commissioners][3] may authorise.

(6) The managers of [an approved knowledge-intensive fund][3] may be required by a notice given to them by an officer of Revenue and Customs to deliver to the officer, within the time limited by the notice, a return of the holdings of shares shown on certificates issued by them in accordance with subsection (5) in the tax year to which the return relates.

(7) Section 207 (penalties for fraudulent certificate or statement etc) does not apply in relation to any certificate issued by the managers of [an approved knowledge-intensive fund][3] for the purposes of subsection (4).

[(8) In this section "HMRC Commissioners" means the Commissioners for Her Majesty's Revenue and Customs.][3]

Commentary—*Simon's Taxes* **E3.182**.

HMRC Manuals—Venture Capital Schemes Manual VCM16050 (approved investment fund as nominee).

Amendments—[1]   Figure in sub-s (1)(*c*) substituted by FA 2007 s 51, Sch 16 para 19(1) with effect in relation to approved funds which closed or close on or after 7 October 2006.

[2]   Sub-s (3) repealed by FA 2012 s 39, Sch 7 paras 1, 20 with effect from 17 July 2012.

[3]   Amendments made by FA 2020 s 36 and treated as having come into force on 6 April 2020 in relation to funds that close on or after that date

[Powers to amend

251A Powers to amend Chapters 2 to 4 by Treasury regulations

(1) The Treasury may by regulations add to, repeal or otherwise amend any provision of—

(*a*) Chapter 2 (the requirements to be met in relation to the investor),

(*b*) Chapter 3 (the general requirements to be met in respect of the relevant shares), or

(*c*) Chapter 4 (the requirements to be met by the issuing company for it to be a qualifying company in relation to the relevant shares).

(2) Regulations under this section may—

(*a*) make different provision for different cases or purposes;

(*b*) contain incidental, supplemental, consequential and transitional provision and savings.

(3) The provision which may be made as a result of subsection (2)(*b*) includes provision amending any provision of this or any other Act (including an Act passed after this Act).

(4) Regulations under this section may, so long as they do not increase any person's liability to any tax, be made to have retrospective effect in relation to any time in the tax year in which they are made or the previous tax year.

(5) This section is without prejudice to any other power to amend any provision of this Part.

(6) A statutory instrument containing regulations under this section may not be made unless a draft of it has been laid before and approved by a resolution of the House of Commons.][1]

Commentary—*Simon's Taxes* **E3.101, E3.129, E3.131, E3.132, E3.145**.

Amendments—[1]   Section 251A and preceding cross-heading inserted by F(No 2)A 2015 s 25, Sch 5 paras 1, 18 with effect from 18 November 2015.

Interpretation

252 Meaning of a company being "in administration" or "in receivership"

(1) References in this Part to a company being "in administration" or "in receivership" are to be read as follows.

(2) A company is "in administration" if—

    (*a*) it is in administration within the meaning of Schedule B1 to the Insolvency Act 1986 (c 45) or Schedule B1 to the Insolvency (Northern Ireland) Order 1989 (SI 1989/2405 (NI 19)), or

    (*b*) there is in force in relation to it under the law of a country or territory outside the United Kingdom any appointment corresponding to an appointment of an administrator under either of those Schedules.

(3) A company is "in receivership" if there is in force in relation to it—

    (*a*) an order for the appointment of an administrative receiver, a receiver and manager or a receiver under Chapter 1 or 2 of Part 3 of the Insolvency Act 1986 or Part 4 of the Insolvency (Northern Ireland) Order 1989, or

    (*b*) any corresponding order under the law of a country or territory outside the United Kingdom.

Commentary—*Simon's Taxes* **E3.129.**

Modifications—ITA 2007 Sch 2 para 57(1)–(3) (modification of this section (as it applies for the purposes of ITA Pt 4 Chapter 6) in relation to an administration order under the Insolvency (Northern Ireland) Order 1989 Pt 3, the petition for which was presented before 6 April 2007; or any corresponding order under the law of a country or territory outside the United Kingdom the proceedings for which were instituted before that date).

ITA 2007 Sch 2 para 57(4) (modification of this section in relation to an administration order under the Insolvency Act 1986 Pt 2, the petition for which was presented before 15 September 2003).

ITA 2007 Sch 2 para 57(5), (6) (this section (as applied by ITA 2007 s 138(5)) does not apply in relation to shares issued before 21 March 2000. In the application of this provision on or after 21 March 2000, shares that were issued on or after 6 April 1998 but before 21 March 2000, and to which EIS relief or relief under TCGA 1992 Sch 5B was attributable immediately before 21 March 2000, are treated as having been issued on or after 21 March 2000).

CTA 2010 Sch 2 para 50(1)–(3) (modification of this section (as it applies for the purposes of CTA 2010 Pt 4 Chapter 5) in relation to an administration order under the Insolvency (Northern Ireland) Order, SI 1989/2405 Pt 3, the petition for which was presented before 6 April 2007; or any corresponding order under the law of a country or territory outside the United Kingdom the proceedings for which were instituted before that date).

CTA 2010 Sch 2 para 50(4) (modification of this section in relation to an administration order under the Insolvency Act 1986 Pt 2, the petition for which was presented before 15 September 2003)

CTA 2010 Sch 2 para 50(5) (this section (as applied by CTA 2010 s 80(5)) does not apply in relation to shares issued before 21 March 2000.

[252A Meaning of "knowledge-intensive company"

(1) For the purposes of this Part, the issuing company is a "knowledge-intensive company" at the time the relevant shares are issued if the company meets—

    (*a*) one or both of the operating costs conditions (see subsections (2) and (3)), and

    (*b*) one or both of—

        (i) the innovation condition (see subsection (5)), and

        (ii) the skilled employee condition (see subsection (8)).

(2) The first operating costs condition is that in at least one of the relevant three preceding years at least 15% of the relevant operating costs constituted expenditure on research and development or innovation.

(3) The second operating costs condition is that in each of the relevant three preceding years at least 10% of the relevant operating costs constituted such expenditure.

(4) In subsections (2) and (3)—

    "relevant operating costs" means—

    (*a*) if the issuing company is a single company at the time the relevant shares are issued, the operating costs of that company, and

    (*b*) if the issuing company is a parent company at the time the relevant shares are issued, the sum of—

        (i) the operating costs of the issuing company, and

        (ii) the operating costs of each company which is a qualifying subsidiary of the issuing company at that time;

    "the relevant three preceding years" [means, subject to subsection (4A), the three consecutive years the last of which ends immediately before the beginning of the last accounts filing period.][2]

[(4A) If the last accounts filing period ends more than 12 months before the date on which the relevant shares are issued, the relevant three preceding years are the three consecutive years the last of which ends 12 months before the date on which the relevant shares are issued.][2]

(5) "The innovation condition" is—

    (*a*) where the issuing company is a single company, that—

        (i) the issuing company is engaged in intellectual property creation at the time the relevant shares are issued, and

(ii) it is reasonable to assume that, within 10 years of the issue of the relevant shares, one or a combination of—

    (*a*) the exploitation of relevant intellectual property held by the company, and

    (*b*) business which results from new or improved products, processes or services utilising relevant intellectual property held by the company,

    will form the greater part of its business;

(*b*) where the issuing company is a parent company, that—

    (i) the parent company or one or more of its qualifying subsidiaries (or both that company and one or more of those subsidiaries) is or are engaged in intellectual property creation at the time the relevant shares are issued, and

    (ii) it is reasonable to assume that, within 10 years of the issue of the relevant shares, one or a combination of—

        (*a*) the exploitation of relevant intellectual property held by the parent company or any of its qualifying subsidiaries, and

        (*b*) business which results from new or improved products, processes or services utilising relevant intellectual property held by the parent company or any of its qualifying subsidiaries,

    will form the greater part of what would be the business of the group if the activities of the group companies taken together are regarded as one business.

(6) For the purposes of subsection (5), a company is engaged in intellectual property creation if—

    (*a*) relevant intellectual property is being created by the company, or has been created by it within the previous three years,

    (*b*) the company is taking, or preparing to take, steps in order that relevant intellectual property will be created by it, or

    (*c*) the company is carrying on activity which is the subject of a written evaluation which—

        (i) has been prepared by an independent expert, and

        (ii) includes a statement to the effect that, in the opinion of the expert, it is reasonable to assume that relevant intellectual property will, in the foreseeable future, be created by the company.

(7) For the purposes of this section—

    (*a*) intellectual property is "relevant" intellectual property, in relation to a company, if the whole or greater part (in terms of value) of it is created by the company, and

    (*b*) intellectual property is created by a company if it is created in circumstances in which the right to exploit it vests in the company (whether alone or jointly with others).

(8) "The skilled employee condition" is that throughout period B—

    (*a*) if the issuing company is a single company, the FTE skilled employee number is at least 20% of the FTE employee number, and

    (*b*) if the issuing company is a parent company, the FTE group skilled employee number is at least 20% of the FTE group employee number.

(9) But, in subsection (8), the reference to period B does not include any period during which the issuing company, by virtue of section 182 (companies in administration or receivership), is not regarded as having ceased to meet the trading requirement.

(10) In this section—

"FTE employee number" for a company is the full-time equivalent employee number determined in accordance with section 186A(3);

"FTE group employee number" means the sum of—

    (*a*) the FTE employee number for the issuing company, and

    (*b*) the FTE employee number for each of its qualifying subsidiaries;

"FTE group skilled employee number" means the sum of—

    (*a*) the FTE skilled employee number for the issuing company, and

    (*b*) the FTE skilled employee number for each of its qualifying subsidiaries;

"FTE skilled employee number" for a company is determined in accordance with section 186A(3) in the same way as the fulltime equivalent employee number except that only employees of the company who—

    (*a*) hold a relevant HE qualification, and

    (*b*) are engaged directly in research and development or innovation activities carried on—

        (i) if the issuing company is a single company, by that company, or

        (ii) if the issuing company is a parent company, by that company or any qualifying subsidiary of that company,

    are to be taken into account;

"independent expert", in relation to an evaluation of activity of a company, means an individual who—

    (*a*) is not connected with the issuing company,

    (*b*) holds a relevant HE qualification, and

    (*c*) is an expert in the area of research and development or innovation being or to be pursued by the company in question;

"intellectual property" has the meaning given by section 195(6);

"the last accounts filing period" means the last period for filing (within the meaning of section 442 of the Companies Act 2006) for the issuing company which ends before the date on which the relevant shares were issued;

        "operating costs", of a company for a period of account, means expenses of the company which are recognised as expenses in the company's profit and loss account or income statement for that period, other than expenses relating to transactions between that company and another company at a time when both companies are members of the same group (but see also subsection (11));

"relevant HE qualification" means—

    (*a*) a qualification which is at level 7, or a higher level, of the framework for higher education qualifications in England, Wales and Northern Ireland (as that framework may be amended or replaced from time to time),

    (*b*) a qualification which is at level 11, or a higher level, of the framework for qualifications of higher education institutions in Scotland (as that framework may be amended or replaced from time to time), or

    (*c*) a comparable qualification to one within paragraph (*a*) or (*b*).

(11) Such apportionments as are just and reasonable are to be made to amounts recognised in a company's profit and loss account or income statement for the purpose of determining the company's operating costs for a year.

(12) When determining whether an individual is connected with the issuing company for the purposes of this section, section 168 is to be ignored.

(13) The Treasury may by regulations amend this section for the purposes of adding, amending or removing a condition which must be met for a company to be a knowledge-intensive company.

(14) A statutory instrument containing regulations under subsection (13) may not be made unless a draft of it has been laid before and approved by a resolution of the House of Commons.][1]

Commentary—*Simon's Taxes* **E3.137.**

HMRC Manuals—Venture Capital Schemes Manual 8161 (knowledge intensive companies: overview).

Modifications—See ITA 2007 s 158(6), (7) (substitution of sub-ss (2)–(4A) as they apply for the purposes of s 158, where the issuing company began to carry on a trade less than three years before the date the relevant shares are issued).

See ITA 2007 s 173A(5A) (substitution of sub-ss (2)–(4A) as they apply for the purposes of s 173A, where the issuing company began to carry on a trade less than three years before the date the relevant shares are issued).

Amendments—[1] This section inserted by F(No 2)A 2015 s 25, Sch 5 paras 1, 19 with effect from 18 November 2015.

[2] In sub-s (4), in definition of "the relevant three preceding years", words substituted, and sub-s (4A) inserted, by FA 2016, s 29(2). Subject to any election made under FA 2016 s 30 by the issuing company, these amendments are to be treated as always having had effect. If an election is made under s 30, the amendments made by s 29(2) do not apply for the purposes of determining whether, at the date of issue of any shares issued by the company in the period beginning with 18 November 2015 and ending with 5 April 2016, the company is a knowledge-intensive company for the purposes of ITA 2007 Part 5. See FA 2016 s 30.

[252B Knowledge-intensive company reaching turnover of £200,000

(1) This section has effect for the purposes of section 175A(2)(*a*)(ii) (alternative initial investing period in case of knowledge-intensive company).

(2) Where—

    (*a*) the annual turnover of the issuing company in relation to an accounting period (see subsection (3)) is £200,000 or more, and

    (*b*) the annual turnover for the company in relation to each previous accounting period is less than £200,000,

the company is treated as reaching an annual turnover of £200,000 or more by reference to the specified date (see subsection (4)).

(3) The annual turnover in relation to an accounting period is—

    (*a*) the turnover for that accounting period (if the accounting period is for 12 months), or

    (*b*) the turnover for the period of 12 months ending when that accounting period ends (if not).

(4) The specified date is—

    (*a*) in the case of an accounting period of 12 months or less, the last day of that accounting period;

    (*b*) in the case of an accounting period of more than 12 months, the last day of the period of 12 months beginning when that accounting period begins.

(5) The turnover of the issuing company for a period ("the period") is treated for the purposes of this section as including the relevant turnover of any company that is a member of the same group as the issuing company during the whole or any part of the period (a "group company").

(6) The relevant turnover of a group company is—

ITA 2007

(*a*) its turnover for the period, if the group company is a member of the same group as the issuing company for the whole of the period;

(*b*) if the group company is a member of the same group as the issuing company for part of the period, its turnover for that part of the period.

(7) Any necessary apportionments of turnover are to be made, on a time basis according to the respective lengths of the periods in question, for the purposes of subsections (3)(*b*) and (6).

(8) In this section "turnover" has the meaning given by section 474(1) of the Companies Act 2006 and is to be determined by reference to—

(*a*) the accounts of the company, and

(*b*) amounts recognised for accounting purposes.]¹

Amendments—¹   Section 252B inserted by FA 2018 s 16, Sch 4 para 6 with effect for shares issued on or after 6 April 2018 (by virtue of SI 2018/931 reg 3(a)).

253 Meaning of "associate"

(1) In this Part "associate", in relation to a person, means—

(*a*) any relative or partner of that person,

(*b*) the trustee or trustees of any settlement in relation to which that person, or any relative of that person (living or dead), is or was a settlor, and

(*c*) if that person has an interest in any shares or obligations of a company which are subject to any trust or are part of the estate of a deceased person—

(i) the trustee or trustees of the settlement concerned or, as the case may be, the personal representatives of the deceased, and

(ii) if that person is a company, any other company which has an interest in those shares or obligations.

(2) In subsection (1)(*a*) and (*b*) "relative" means spouse or civil partner, ancestor or lineal descendant.

Commentary—*Simon's Taxes* **E3.108, D3.103**.

HMRC Manuals—Venture Capital Schemes Manual VCM11100 (meaning of 'associate').

254 Meaning of "disposal of shares"

(1) In this Part references to a disposal of shares include references to a disposal of an interest or right in or over shares.

(2) An individual is to be treated, for the purposes of this Part, as disposing of any shares which the individual is treated by virtue of section 136 of TCGA 1992 as exchanging for other shares.

Commentary—*Simon's Taxes* **E3.167, E3.193**.

HMRC Manuals—Venture Capital Schemes Manual VCM23250 (EIS: share exchanges: example).

255 Meaning of "issue of shares"

(1) In this Part—

(*a*) references (however expressed) to an issue of shares in any company are to such of the shares in the company as are of the same class and are issued on the same day, and

(*b*) references (however expressed) to an issue of shares in any company to an individual are to such of the shares in the company as are of the same class and are issued to the individual on the same day.

(2) Subsection (1)(*b*) has effect subject to sections 201(6), 202(2), 210(2), 219(1) and 228(1).

Commentary—*Simon's Taxes* **E3.802**.

256 Meaning of "the termination date"

(1) In this Part "the termination date", in relation to any shares issued by a company, means—

(*a*) the third anniversary of the issue date, or

(*b*) if—

(i) the money raised by the issue was raised wholly or mainly for the purpose of a qualifying business activity within section 179(2) (the issuing company or a qualifying 90% subsidiary of that company carrying on or preparing to carry on a qualifying trade), and

(ii) neither the issuing company nor any of its qualifying 90% subsidiaries had begun to carry on the trade in question on the issue date,

the third anniversary of the date on which the issuing company or any qualifying 90% subsidiary of that company begins to carry on that trade.

(2) In determining for the purposes of subsection (1) when a qualifying trade is begun to be carried on by a qualifying 90% subsidiary of a company, any carrying on of the trade by it before it became such a subsidiary is to be ignored.

Commentary—*Simon's Taxes* **E3.104, E3.1100, E3.190**.

HMRC Manuals—Venture Capital Schemes Manual VCM23070 (meaning of termination date).

[256A Meaning of "the EIS original rate"

In this Part "the EIS original rate", in relation to EIS relief, means the EIS rate for the tax year for which the EIS relief was obtained.]¹

Commentary—*Simon's Taxes* **E3.169, E3.171**.

Amendments[1]   Section 256A inserted by FA 2011 s 42(4) with effect for the tax year 2011–12 and subsequent tax years. FA 2011 s 42 came into force on 13 October 2011 (SI 2011/2459 art 2).

257 Minor definitions etc

(1) In this Part—

["arrangements" includes any scheme, agreement, understanding, transaction or series of transactions (whether or not legally enforceable);][3]

"bonus shares" means shares which are issued otherwise than for payment (whether in cash or otherwise),

"director" is read in accordance with [section 452 of CTA 2010][2],

"group" means a parent company and its qualifying subsidiaries,

"group company", in relation to a group, means the parent company or any of its qualifying subsidiaries,

"ordinary shares" means shares forming part of a company's ordinary share capital,

"parent company" means a company that has one or more qualifying subsidiaries and "single company" means a company that does not,

"period A", "period B" and "period C" have the meaning given by section 159, and

"research and development" has the meaning given by section 1006.

(2) Section 993 (connected persons) does not apply for the purposes of Chapter 2 (other than section 168(4)).

(3) Section 995 (control) does not apply for the purposes of the following provisions—

section 185(1)(*a*),

section 199(3)(*a*) and (*b*)(ii),

section 232(3),

section 233(2), and

section 243(4),

and in those provisions "control" is to be read in accordance with [sections 450 and 451 of CTA 2010][2].

(4) In this Part—

(*a*) references in any provision to the reduction of any EIS relief attributable to any shares include a reference—

  (i)   to the reduction of the relief to nil, and

  (ii)   if no relief has yet been obtained, to the reduction of the amount which apart from that provision would be the EIS relief, and

(*b*) references to the withdrawal of EIS relief in respect of any shares are—

  (i)   to the withdrawal of the EIS relief attributable to those shares, or

  (ii)   if no relief has yet been obtained, to ceasing to be eligible for EIS relief in respect of those shares.

(5) For the purposes of this Part shares in a company are not treated as being of the same class unless they would be so treated if dealt in on [a recognised stock exchange][1].

(6) For the purposes of this Part the market value at any time of any asset is the price which it might reasonably be expected to fetch on a sale at that time in the open market free from any interest or right which exists by way of security in or over it.

(7) In this Part—

(*a*) references to EIS relief obtained by an individual in respect of any shares include references to EIS relief obtained by the individual in respect of those shares at any time after the individual has disposed of them, and

(*b*) references to the withdrawal or reduction of EIS relief obtained by an individual in respect of any shares include references to the withdrawal or reduction of EIS relief obtained by the individual in respect of those shares at any such time.

(8) In the case of requirements that cannot be met until a future date, references in this Part to requirements being met for the time being are to nothing having occurred to prevent their being met.

Commentary—*Simon's Taxes* **D3.103, E3.143**.

HMRC Manuals—Venture Capital Schemes Manual VCM13100 (meaning of arrangements).

Capital Gains Manual CG50290 (definitions: bonus shares).

Company Taxation Manual CTM60180 (definition of a director).

Capital Allowance manual CA60200 (meaning of research and development).

Amendments—[1]   Words in sub-s (5) substituted by FA 2007 s 109, Sch 26 para 12(1), (5) with effect from 19 July 2007.

[2]   In sub-ss (1), (3), words substituted by CTA 2010 s 1177, Sch 1 para 503. CTA 2010 has effect for corporation tax purposes for accounting periods ending on or after 1 April 2010, and for income and capital gains tax purposes for the tax year 2010–11 and subsequent tax years.

[3]   In sub-s (1), definition of "arrangements" substituted by FA 2012 s 39, Sch 7 paras 1, 21. This amendment is treated as having come into force on 6 April 2012: see FA 2012 Sch 7 para 25.

[PART 5A

SEED ENTERPRISE INVESTMENT SCHEME]

Amendments—Part 5A (ss 257A–257HJ) inserted by FA 2012 s 38 Sch 6 para 1 with effect in relation to shares issued on or after 6 April 2012.

[CHAPTER 1

INTRODUCTION

SEIS relief

257A Meaning of "SEIS relief" and commencement

(1) This Part provides for SEIS income tax relief ("SEIS relief"), that is, entitlement to tax reductions in respect of amounts subscribed by individuals for shares in companies carrying on new businesses.

(2) In this Part "SEIS" stands for the seed enterprise investment scheme.

[(3) This Part has effect in relation to shares issued on or after 6 April 2012 only.][2]

(4) . . . [2][1]

Commentary—*Simon's Taxes* **E3.801**.

HMRC Manuals—Venture Capital Schemes Manual VCM31110 (SEIS: commencement).

Amendments—[1]   Part 5A (ss 257A–257HJ) inserted by FA 2012 s 38 Sch 6 para 1 with effect in relation to shares issued on or after 6 April 2012.

[2]   Sub-s (3) substituted and sub-s (4) repealed by FA 2014 s 54 with effect from 17 July 2014.

[257AA Eligibility for SEIS relief

An individual ("the investor") is eligible for SEIS relief in respect of an amount subscribed by the investor on the investor's own behalf for an issue of shares in a company ("the issuing company") if—

[(za) the risk-to-capital condition is met (see section 257AAA),][2]

(a) the shares ("the relevant shares") are issued to the investor,

(b) the investor is a qualifying investor in relation to the relevant shares (see Chapter 2),

(c) the general requirements (including requirements as to the purpose of the issue of shares and the use of money raised) are met in respect of the relevant shares (see Chapter 3), and

(d) the issuing company is a qualifying company in relation to the relevant shares (see Chapter 4).][1]

Commentary—*Simon's Taxes* **E3.802**.

HMRC Manuals—Venture Capital Schemes Manual VCM31120 (eligibility for SEIS income tax relief).

Amendments—[1]   Part 5A (ss 257A–257HJ) inserted by FA 2012 s 38 Sch 6 para 1 with effect in relation to shares issued on or after 6 April 2012.

[2]   Para (za) inserted by FA 2018 s 14(2)(a) with effect for shares issued on or after 15 March 2018 (by virtue of SI 2018/931 reg 2(a)).

[257AAA Risk-to-capital condition

(1) The risk-to-capital condition is met if, having regard to all the circumstances existing at the time of the issue of the shares, it would be reasonable to conclude that—

(a) the issuing company has objectives to grow and develop its trade in the long-term, and

(b) there is a significant risk that there will be a loss of capital of an amount greater than the net investment return.

(2) For the purposes of subsection (1)(b)—

(a) the risk is to be determined by reference to a loss of capital, and the net investment return, for the investors generally,

(b) the reference to a loss of capital is to a loss of some or all of the amounts subscribed for the shares by the investors, and

(c) the reference to the net investment return is to the net investment return to the investors (whether by way of income or capital growth) taking into account the value of SEIS relief.

(3) For the purposes of subsection (1) the circumstances to which regard may be had include—

(a) the extent to which the company's objectives include increasing the number of its employees or the turnover of its trade,

(b) the nature of the company's sources of income, including the extent to which there is a significant risk of the company not receiving some or all of the income,

(c) the extent to which the company has or is likely to have assets, or is or could become a party to arrangements for acquiring assets, that could be used to secure financing from any person,

(d) the extent to which the activities of the company are sub-contracted to persons who are not connected with it,

(e) the nature of the company's ownership structure or management structure, including the extent to which others participate in or devise the structure,

(f) how any opportunity for investment in the company is marketed, and

(g) the extent to which arrangements are in place under which opportunities for investments in the company are or may be marketed with, or otherwise associated with, opportunities for investments in other companies or entities.

(4) If the issuing company is a parent company—

    (*a*) any reference in this section to the company's trade is to what would be the trade of the group if the activities of the group companies taken together were regarded as one trade, and

    (*b*) any reference in subsection (3)(*a*) to (*e*) to the company is to any group company.][1]

Commentary—*Simon's Taxes* **E3.803**.

Amendments—[1] Section 257AAA inserted by FA 2018 s 14(2)(*b*) with effect for shares issued on or after 15 March 2018 (by virtue of SI 2018/931 reg 2(a)).

[257AB Form and amount of SEIS relief

(1) If an individual—

    (a) is eligible for SEIS relief in respect of any amount subscribed for shares, and

    (b) makes a claim in respect of all or some of the shares included in the issue,

the individual is entitled to a tax reduction for the tax year in which the shares were issued ("the current tax year").

   This is subject to the provisions of this Part.

(2) The amount of the tax reduction to which the individual is entitled is the amount equal to tax at the SEIS rate for the current tax year on—

    (a) the amount or, as the case may be, the sum of the amounts subscribed for shares issued in that year in respect of which the individual is eligible for and claims SEIS relief, or

    (b) if less, £100,000.

(3) In this Part "the SEIS rate" means 50%.

(4) The tax reduction is given effect at Step 6 of the calculation in section 23.

(5) If in the case of any issue of shares—

    (a) which are issued in the current tax year, and

    (b) in respect of the amount subscribed for which the individual is eligible for SEIS relief,

the individual so claims, subsections (1) and (2) apply as if, in respect of such part of that issue as may be specified in the claim, the shares had been issued in the preceding tax year, and the individual's liability to tax for both tax years is determined accordingly.][1]

Commentary—*Simon's Taxes* **E3.802**.

HMRC Manuals—Venture Capital Schemes Manual VCM31130 (limit of SEIS income tax relief).

Amendments—[1] Part 5A (ss 257A–257HJ) inserted by FA 2012 s 38 Sch 6 para 1 with effect in relation to shares issued on or after 6 April 2012.

[Miscellaneous

257AC Meaning of "period A" and "period B"

(1) This section applies for the purposes of this Part in relation to any shares issued by a company.

(2) "Period A" means the period—

    (a) beginning with the incorporation of the company, and

    (b) ending immediately before the termination date relating to the shares.

(3) "Period B" means the period—

    (a) beginning with the issue of the shares, and

    (b) ending immediately before the termination date relating to the shares.

(4) In this section "the termination date", in relation to the shares, means the third anniversary of the date on which the shares are issued.][1]

Commentary—*Simon's Taxes* **E3.802**.

HMRC Manuals—Venture Capital Schemes Manual VCM31140 (periods A and B: introduction).

Amendments—[1] Part 5A (ss 257A–257HJ) inserted by FA 2012 s 38 Sch 6 para 1 with effect in relation to shres issued on or after 6 April 2012.

[257AD Overview of other Chapters of Part

In this Part—

    (a) Chapter 5 provides for the attribution of SEIS relief to shares and the making of claims for such relief,

    (b) Chapter 6 provides for SEIS relief to be withdrawn or reduced in the circumstances mentioned in that Chapter,

    (c) Chapter 7 makes provision with respect to the procedure for the withdrawal or reduction of SEIS relief, and

    (d) Chapter 8 contains supplementary and general provisions.][1]

Commentary—*Simon's Taxes* **E3.802**.

Amendments—[1] Part 5A (ss 257A–257HJ) inserted by FA 2012 s 38 Sch 6 para 1 with effect in relation to shares issued on or after 6 April 2012.

[257AE CGT reliefs relating to SEIS

(1) Section 150E of TCGA 1992 makes provision about gains or losses on the disposal of shares to which SEIS relief is attributable.

(2) Schedule 5BB to that Act provides relief in respect of the reinvestment under SEIS of the proceeds of assets disposed of in circumstances where there would otherwise be a chargeable gain.][1]

Commentary—*Simon's Taxes* **E3.802**.

Amendments—[1]   Part 5A (ss 257A–257HJ) inserted by FA 2012 s 38 Sch 6 para 1 with effect in relation to shares issued on or after 6 April 2012.

[CHAPTER 2

THE INVESTOR]

Amendments—Part 5A (ss 257A–257HJ) inserted by FA 2012 s 38 Sch 6 para 1 with effect in relation to shares issued on or after 6 April 2012.

[Introduction

257B Overview of Chapter

The investor is a qualifying investor in relation to the relevant shares if the requirements of this Chapter are met as to—
  (a) no employee investors (see section 257BA),
  (b) no substantial interest in the issuing company (see section 257BB),
  (c) no related investment arrangements (see section 257BC),
  (d) no linked loans (see section 257BD), and
  (e) no tax avoidance (see section 257BE).][1]

Commentary—*Simon's Taxes* E3.805.
HMRC Manuals—Venture Capital Schemes Manual VCM32010 (qualifying investor: overview).
Amendments—[1]   Part 5A (ss 257A–257HJ) inserted by FA 2012 s 38 Sch 6 para 1 with effect in relation to shares issued on or after 6 April 2012.

[The requirements

257BA The no employee investors requirement

(1) Neither the investor nor an associate of the investor may, at any time during period B, be an employee of the issuing company or of any qualifying subsidiary of that company.
(2) For this purpose a person is not to be treated as an employee of the issuing company, or of any qualifying subsidiary of that company, at any time when the person is a director of that company.][1]

Commentary—*Simon's Taxes* E3.806.
HMRC Manuals—Venture Capital Schemes Manual VCM32020 (no employee investors).
Amendments—[1]   Part 5A (ss 257A–257HJ) inserted by FA 2012 s 38 Sch 6 para 1 with effect in relation to shares issued on or after 6 April 2012.

[257BB The no substantial interest in the issuing company requirement

The investor must not have a substantial interest in the issuing company at any time during period A.][1]

Commentary—*Simon's Taxes* E3.807.
HMRC Manuals—Venture Capital Schemes Manual VCM32030 (no substantial interest in the issuing company).
Amendments—[1]   Part 5A (ss 257A–257HJ) inserted by FA 2012 s 38 Sch 6 para 1 with effect in relation to shares issued on or after 6 April 2012.

[257BC The no related investment arrangements requirement

The investor ("P") must not subscribe for the relevant shares as part of an arrangement which provides for another person to subscribe for shares in another company in which P, or any other individual who is party to the arrangement, has a substantial interest.][1]

Commentary—*Simon's Taxes* E3.808.
HMRC Manuals—Venture Capital Schemes Manual VCM32040 (no related investment arrangements).
Amendments—[1]   Part 5A (ss 257A–257HJ) inserted by FA 2012 s 38 Sch 6 para 1 with effect in relation to shares issued on or after 6 April 2012.

[257BD The no linked loan requirement

(1) No linked loan is to be made by any person, at any time in period A, to the investor or an associate of the investor.
(2) In this section "linked loan" means any loan which—
  (a) would not have been made, or
  (b) would not have been made on the same terms,
if the investor had not subscribed for the relevant shares, or had not been proposing to do so.
(3) References in this section to the making by any person of a loan to the investor or an associate of the investor include a reference—
  (a) to the giving by that person of any credit to the investor or any associate of the investor, and
  (b) to the assignment to that person of a debt due from the investor or any associate of the investor.][1]

Commentary—*Simon's Taxes* E3.809.
HMRC Manuals—Venture Capital Schemes Manual VCM32050 (no linked loan).
Amendments—[1]   Part 5A (ss 257A–257HJ) inserted by FA 2012 s 38 Sch 6 para 1 with effect in relation to shares issued on or after 6 April 2012.

[257BE The no tax avoidance requirement
The relevant shares must be subscribed for by the investor for genuine commercial reasons, and not as part of a scheme or arrangement the main purpose or one of the main purposes of which is the avoidance of tax.][1]

Commentary—*Simon's Taxes* E3.810.
HMRC Manuals—Venture Capital Schemes Manual VCM32060 (no tax avoidance).
Amendments—[1]   Part 5A (ss 257A–257HJ) inserted by FA 2012 s 38 Sch 6 para 1 with effect in relation to shares issued on or after 6 April 2012.

[Meaning of substantial interest in a company

257BF Persons with a substantial interest in a company
(1) An individual has a substantial interest in a company if the individual directly or indirectly possesses or is entitled to acquire more than 30% of—
    (a) the ordinary share capital of the company or any subsidiary of the company,
    (b) the issued share capital of the company or any such subsidiary, or
    (c) the voting power in the company or any such subsidiary.
(2) An individual has a substantial interest in a company if the individual directly or indirectly possesses or is entitled to acquire such rights as would—
    (a) in the event of the winding up of the company or any subsidiary of the company, or
    (b) in any other circumstances,
entitle the individual to receive more than 30% of the assets of the company or subsidiary ("the company in question") which would then be available for distribution to equity holders of the company in question.
(3) For the purposes of subsection (2)—
    (a) the persons who are equity holders of the company in question, and
    (b) the percentage of the assets of the company in question to which the individual would be entitled,
are determined in accordance with Chapter 6 of Part 5 of CTA 2010.
(4) In making that determination—
    (a) references in section 166 of that Act to company A are to be read as references to an equity holder, and
    (b) references in that section to a winding up are to be read as including a reference to any other circumstances in which assets of the company in question are available for distribution to its equity holders.
(5) An individual does not have a substantial interest in a company merely because one or more shares in the company are held by the individual or by an associate of the individual, at a time when the company—
    (a) has not issued any shares other than subscriber shares, and
    (b) has not begun to carry on, or make preparations for carrying on, any trade or business.
(6) An individual has a substantial interest in a company if the individual has control of the company or any subsidiary of that company.
(7) For the purposes of this section—
    (a) an individual is treated as entitled to acquire anything which the individual is entitled to acquire at a future date or will at a future date be entitled to acquire, and
    (b) there is attributed to any individual any rights or powers of any other person who is an associate of the individual.
(8) In this section "subsidiary", in relation to a company, means a company which at any time in period A is a 51% subsidiary of the company, whether or not it is such a subsidiary while the individual concerned has, or is entitled to acquire, such capital, voting power, rights or control as are mentioned in this section.][1]

Commentary—*Simon's Taxes* E3.807.
HMRC Manuals—Venture Capital Schemes Manual VCM32030 (no substantial interest in the issuing company).
Amendments—[1]   Part 5A (ss 257A–257HJ) inserted by FA 2012 s 38 Sch 6 para 1 with effect in relation to shares issued on or after 6 April 2012.

[CHAPTER 3

GENERAL REQUIREMENTS]

Amendments—Part 5A (ss 257A–257HJ) inserted by FA 2012 s 38 Sch 6 para 1 with effect in relation to shares issued on or after 6 April 2012.

[Introduction

257C Overview of Chapter
The general requirements are met in respect of the relevant shares if the requirements of this Chapter are met as to—
    (a) the shares (see section 257CA),
    (b) the purpose of the issue (see section 257CB),

    (c) the spending of the money raised (see section 257CC),

    (d) no pre-arranged exits (see section 257CD),

    (e) no tax avoidance (see section 257CE), and

    (f) no disqualifying arrangements (see section 257CF).][1]

Commentary—*Simon's Taxes* **E3.815**.

HMRC Manuals—Venture Capital Schemes Manual VCM33010 (general requirements: overview).

Amendments—[1]   Part 5A (ss 257A–257HJ) inserted by FA 2012 s 38 Sch 6 para 1 with effect in relation to shares issued on or after 6 April 2012.

[The requirements

257CA The shares requirement

(1) The relevant shares must meet—

    (a) the requirements of subsection (2), and

    (b) unless they are bonus shares, the requirements of subsection (4).

(2) Shares meet the requirements of this subsection if they are ordinary shares which do not, at any time during period B, carry—

    (a) any present or future preferential right to dividends that is within subsection (3),

    (b) any present or future preferential right to a company's assets on its winding up, or

    (c) any present or future right to be redeemed.

(3) A preferential right to dividends carried by a share in a company is within this subsection if—

    (a) the amount of any dividends payable pursuant to the right, or the date or dates on which they are payable, depend to any extent on a decision of the company, the holder of the share or any other person, or

    (b) the amount of any dividends that become payable at any time pursuant to the right includes any amount that became payable at any earlier time pursuant to the right but has not been paid.

(4) Shares meet the requirements of this subsection if they—

    (a) are subscribed for wholly in cash, and

    (b) are fully paid up at the time they are issued.

(5) Shares are not fully paid up for the purposes of subsection (4)(b) if there is any undertaking to pay cash to any person at a future date in respect of the acquisition of the shares.][1]

Commentary—*Simon's Taxes* **E3.816**.

HMRC Manuals—Venture Capital Schemes Manual VCM33020 (shares requirement).

Amendments—[1]   Part 5A (ss 257A–257HJ) inserted by FA 2012 s 38 Sch 6 para 1 with effect in relation to shares issued on or after 6 April 2012.

[257CB The purpose of the issue requirement

(1) The relevant shares (other than any of them which are bonus shares) must be issued in order to raise money for the purposes of a qualifying business activity carried on, or to be carried on, by the issuing company or a qualifying 90% subsidiary of that company.

(2) For the meaning of "qualifying business activity" see section 257HG.][1]

Commentary—*Simon's Taxes* **E3.817**.

HMRC Manuals—Venture Capital Schemes Manual VCM33030 (purpose of the issue requirement).

Amendments—[1]   Part 5A (ss 257A–257HJ) inserted by FA 2012 s 38 Sch 6 para 1 with effect in relation to shares issued on or after 6 April 2012.

[257CC The spending of the money raised requirement

(1) The requirement of this section is that before the end of period B all of the money raised by the issue of the relevant shares (other than any of them which are bonus shares) is spent for the purposes of the qualifying business activity for which it was raised.

(2) Spending money on the acquisition of shares or stock in a company does not of itself amount to spending the money for the purposes of a qualifying business activity.

(3) This requirement does not fail to be met merely because an amount of money which is not significant is spent for another purpose or remains unspent at the end of period B.][1]

Commentary—*Simon's Taxes* **E3.818**.

HMRC Manuals—Venture Capital Schemes Manual VCM33040 (spending of the money raised requirement).

Amendments—[1]   Part 5A (ss 257A–257HJ) inserted by FA 2012 s 38 Sch 6 para 1 with effect in relation to shares issued on or after 6 April 2012.

[257CD The no pre-arranged exits requirement

(1) The issuing arrangements for the relevant shares must not include—

    (a) arrangements with a view to the subsequent repurchase, exchange or other disposal of those shares or of other shares in or securities of the issuing company,

    (b) arrangements for or with a view to the cessation of any trade which is being or is to be or may be carried on by the issuing company or a person connected with that company,

    (c) arrangements for the disposal of, or of a substantial amount (in terms of value) of, the assets of the issuing company or of a person connected with that company, or

(d)   arrangements the main purpose of which, or one of the main purposes of which, is (by means of any insurance, indemnity or guarantee or otherwise) to provide partial or complete protection for persons investing in shares in the issuing company against what would otherwise be the risks attached to making the investment.

[(2) The arrangements referred to in subsection (1)(*a*) do not include—

(*a*)   any arrangements with a view to such an exchange of shares, or shares and securities, as is mentioned in section 257HB(1), or

(*b*)   any arrangements with a view to any shares in the issuing company being exchanged for, or converted into, shares in that company of a different class.][2]

(3) The arrangements referred to in subsection (1)(b) and (c) do not include any arrangements applicable only on the winding up of a company except in a case where—

(a)   the issuing arrangements include arrangements for the company to be wound up, or

(b)   the arrangements are applicable to the winding up of the company otherwise than for genuine commercial reasons.

(4) The arrangements referred to in subsection (1)(d) do not include any arrangements which are confined to the provision—

(a)   for the issuing company itself, or

(b)   if the issuing company is a parent company that meets the trading requirement in section 257DA(2)(b), for the issuing company itself, for the issuing company itself and one or more of its subsidiaries or for one or more of its subsidiaries,

of any such protection against risks arising in the course of carrying on its business as might reasonably be expected to be provided in normal commercial circumstances.

(5) In this section "the issuing arrangements" means—

(a)   the arrangements under which the shares are issued to the individual,

(b)   any arrangements made, before the shares were issued, in relation to or in connection with the issue, and

(c)   if before the shares were issued information on pre-arranged exits was made available to any prospective subscribers for shares in the issuing company, any arrangements made during period B.

(6) For the purposes of subsection (5)(c) "information on pre-arranged exits" means any information indicating the possibility of making, during period B, arrangements of the kind described in paragraph (a), (b), (c) or (d) of subsection (1).][1]

Commentary—*Simon's Taxes* **E3.819**.

HMRC Manuals—Venture Capital Schemes Manual VCM33060 (no pre-arranged exits requirement).

Amendments—[1]   Part 5A (ss 257A–257HJ) inserted by FA 2012 s 38 Sch 6 para 1 with effect in relation to shares issued on or after 6 April 2012.

[2]   Sub-s (2) substituted by F(No 2)A 2017 s 11(1), (3) with effect in relation to shares issued on or after 5 December 2016.

[257CE The no tax avoidance requirement

The relevant shares must be issued for genuine commercial reasons, and not as part of a scheme or arrangement the main purpose or one of the main purposes of which is the avoidance of tax.][1]

Commentary—*Simon's Taxes* **E3.820**.

HMRC Manuals—Venture Capital Schemes Manual VCM33070 (no tax avoidance requirement).

Amendments—[1]   Part 5A (ss 257A–257HJ) inserted by FA 2012 s 38 Sch 6 para 1 with effect in relation to shares issued on or after 6 April 2012.

[257CF The no disqualifying arrangements requirement

(1) The relevant shares must not be issued, nor any money raised by the issue spent, in consequence or anticipation of, or otherwise in connection with, disqualifying arrangements.

(2) Arrangements are "disqualifying arrangements" if—

(*a*)   the main purpose, or one of the main purposes, of the arrangements is to secure—

(i)   that a qualifying business activity is or will be carried on by the issuing company or a qualifying 90% subsidiary of that company, and

(ii)   that one or more persons (whether or not including any party to the arrangements) may obtain relevant tax relief in respect of shares issued by the issuing company which raise money for the purposes of that activity or that such shares may comprise part of the qualifying holdings of a VCT,

(*b*)   that activity is the relevant qualifying business activity, and

(*c*)   one or both of conditions A and B are met.

(3) Condition A is that, as a (direct or indirect) result of the money raised by the issue of the relevant shares being spent as required by section 257CC, an amount representing the whole or the majority of the amount raised is, in the course of the arrangements, paid to or for the benefit of a relevant person or relevant persons.

(4) Condition B is that, in the absence of the arrangements, it would have been reasonable to expect that the whole or greater part of the component activities of the relevant qualifying business activity would have been carried on as part of another business by a relevant person or relevant persons.

(5) For the purposes of this section it is immaterial whether the issuing company is a party to the arrangements.

(6) In this section—

"component activities" means—

    (*a*) if the relevant qualifying business activity is activity A (see section 257HG(2)), the carrying on of a qualifying trade, or preparing to carry on such a trade, which constitutes that activity, and

    (*b*) if the relevant qualifying business activity is activity B (see section 257HG(4)), the carrying on of research and development which constitutes that activity;

    [(*ba*) if the relevant qualifying business activity is activity B (see section 257HG(4)), the carrying on of research and development which constitutes that activity;][2]

"qualifying holdings", in relation to the issuing company, is to be construed in accordance with section 286 (VCTs: qualifying holdings);

"relevant person" means a person who is a party to the arrangements or a person connected with such a party;

"relevant qualifying business activity" means the activity for the purposes of which the issue of the relevant shares raised money;

"relevant tax relief", in respect of shares, means one or more of the following—

    (*a*) SEIS relief in respect of the shares;

    (*b*) EIS relief in respect of the shares;

    (*c*) relief under Chapter 6 of Part 4 (losses on disposal of shares) in respect of the shares;

    (*d*) relief under section 150A or 150E of TCGA 1992 (enterprise investment scheme) in respect of the shares;

    (*e*) relief under Schedule 5B to that Act (enterprise investment scheme: re-investment) in consequence of which deferral relief is attributable to the shares (see paragraph 19(2) of that Schedule);

    (*f*) relief under Schedule 5BB to that Act (seed enterprise investment scheme: re-investment) in consequence of which SEIS re-investment relief is attributable to the shares (see paragraph 4 of that Schedule).][1]

Commentary—*Simon's Taxes* **E3.821**.

HMRC Manuals—Venture Capital Schemes Manual VCM33080 (no disqualifying arrangements).

Amendments—[1] Part 5A (ss 257A–257HJ) inserted by FA 2012 s 38 Sch 6 para 1 with effect in relation to shares issued on or after 6 April 2012.

[2] Sub-s (6)(*ba*) inserted by F(No 2)A 2017 s 14, Sch 1 para 11(1), (3) with effect in relation to shares issued on or after 6 April 2017. This amendment does not have effect for the purposes of determining any question whether particular arrangements which include any transaction entered into before 6 April 2017 are "disqualifying arrangements" for the purposes of ss 178A, 257CF or 299A (F(No 2)A 2017 Sch 1 para 16(1), (3)).

[CHAPTER 4

THE ISSUING COMPANY]

Amendments—Part 5A (ss 257A–257HJ) inserted by FA 2012 s 38 Sch 6 para 1 with effect in relation to shares issued on or after 6 April 2012.

[Introduction

257D Overview of Chapter

The issuing company is a qualifying company in relation to the relevant shares if the requirements of this Chapter are met as to—

    (a) trading (see section 257DA),

    (b) the issuing company's carrying on of the qualifying business activity (see section 257DC),

    (c) UK permanent establishment (see section 257DD),

    (d) financial health (see section 257DE),

    (e) unquoted status (see section 257DF),

    (f) control and independence (see 257DG),

    (g) no partnerships (see section 257DH),

    (h) gross assets (see section 257DI),

    (i) number of employees (see section 257DJ),

    (j) no previous other risk capital scheme investments (see section 257DK),

    (k) the amount raised through the SEIS (see section 257DL),

    (l) qualifying subsidiaries (see section 257DM), and

    (m) property managing subsidiaries (see section 257DN).][1]

Commentary—*Simon's Taxes* **E3.825**.

HMRC Manuals—Venture Capital Schemes Manual VCM34010 (issuing company requirements: overview).

Amendments—[1] Part 5A (ss 257A–257HJ) inserted by FA 2012 s 38 Sch 6 para 1 with effect in relation to shares issued on or after 6 April 2012.

[The requirements

257DA The trading requirement

(1) The issuing company must meet the trading requirement throughout period B.

(2) The trading requirement is that—

(a) the company, ignoring any incidental purposes, exists wholly for the purpose of carrying on one or more new qualifying trades (see section 257HF), or

(b) the company is a parent company and the business of the group does not consist wholly or as to a substantial part in the carrying on of non-qualifying activities.

(3) If the company intends that one or more other companies should become its qualifying subsidiaries with a view to their carrying on one or more new qualifying trades—

(a) the company is treated as a parent company for the purposes of subsection (2)(b), and

(b) the reference in subsection (2)(b) to the group includes the company and any existing or future company that will be its qualifying subsidiary after the intention in question is carried into effect.

This subsection does not apply at any time after the abandonment of that intention.

(4) For the purpose of subsection (2)(b) the business of the group means what would be the business of the group if the activities of the group companies taken together were regarded as one business.

(5) For the purpose of determining the business of a group, activities are ignored so far as they are activities carried on by a mainly trading subsidiary otherwise than for its main purpose.

(6) For the purposes of determining the business of a group, activities of a group company are ignored so far as they consist in—

(a) the holding of shares in or securities of a qualifying subsidiary of the parent company,

(b) the making of loans to another group company,

(c) the holding and managing of property used by a group company for the purpose of one or more qualifying trades carried on by a group company, or

(d) the holding and managing of property used by a group company for the purpose of research and development from which it is intended—

(i) that a qualifying trade to be carried on by a group company will be derived, or

(ii) that a qualifying trade carried on or to be carried on by a group company will benefit.

(7) Any reference in subsection (6)(d)(i) or (ii) to a group company includes a reference to any existing or future company which will be a group company at any future time.

(8) Where period B begins after the incorporation of the company, the requirement of subsection (2) must have been complied with since its incorporation; but for the purposes of that subsection any interval between the incorporation of the company and the time when it commenced business is to be ignored.

(9) In this section—

"incidental purposes" means purposes having no significant effect (other than in relation to incidental matters) on the extent of the activities of the company in question;

"mainly trading subsidiary" means a qualifying subsidiary which, apart from incidental purposes, exists wholly for the purpose of carrying on one or more qualifying trades, and any reference to the main purpose of such a subsidiary is to be read accordingly;

"non-qualifying activities" means—

(a) excluded activities (within the meaning of sections 192 to 199), and

(b) activities (other than research and development) carried on otherwise than in the course of a trade;

"qualifying trade" has the same meaning as in Part 5 (see sections 189 and 192 to 200).][1]

Commentary—*Simon's Taxes* **E3.826**.

HMRC Manuals—Venture Capital Schemes Manual VCM34020 (trading requirement).

Amendments—[1] Part 5A (ss 257A–257HJ) inserted by FA 2012 s 38 Sch 6 para 1 with effect in relation to shares issued on or after 6 April 2012.

[257DB Ceasing to meet trading requirement: administration etc

(1) A company is not regarded as ceasing to meet the trading requirement merely because of anything done in consequence of the company or any of its subsidiaries being in administration or receivership.

This is subject to subsections (2) and (3).

(2) Subsection (1) applies only if—

(a) the entry into administration or receivership, and

(b) everything done as a result of the company concerned being in administration or receivership,

is for genuine commercial reasons, and is not part of a scheme or arrangement the main purpose or one of the main purposes of which is the avoidance of tax.

(3) A company ceases to meet the trading requirement if before the end of period B—

(a) a resolution is passed, or an order is made, for the winding up of the company or any of its subsidiaries (or, in the case of a winding up otherwise than under the Insolvency Act 1986 or the Insolvency (Northern Ireland) Order 1989, any other act is done for the like purpose), or

(b) the company or any of its subsidiaries is dissolved without winding up.

This is subject to subsection (4).

(4) Subsection (3) does not apply if the winding up or dissolution is for genuine commercial reasons, and is not part of a scheme or arrangement the main purpose or one of the main purposes of which is the avoidance of tax.][1]

Commentary—*Simon's Taxes* **E3.827**.
HMRC Manuals—Venture Capital Schemes Manual VCM34030 (ceasing to meet trading requirement).
Amendments—[1]   Part 5A (ss 257A–257HJ) inserted by FA 2012 s 38 Sch 6 para 1 with effect in relation to shares issued on or after 6 April 2012.

[257DC The issuing company to carry on the qualifying business activity

(1) The requirement of this section is met in relation to the issuing company if, at no time in period B, is any of the following—

(a) the relevant new qualifying trade,

(b) relevant preparation work (if any), and

(c) relevant research and development (if any),

carried on by a person other than the issuing company or a qualifying 90% subsidiary of that company.

(2) Subsection (3) has effect for the purpose of determining whether the requirement of this section is met in relation to the issuing company in a case where relevant preparation work is carried out by that company or a qualifying 90% subsidiary of that company.

(3) The carrying on of the relevant new qualifying trade by a company other than the issuing company or a subsidiary of that company is to be ignored if it takes place at any time in period B before the issuing company or any qualifying 90% subsidiary of that company begins to carry on that trade.

(4) The requirement of this section is not regarded as failing to be met in relation to the issuing company if, merely because of any act or event within subsection (5), the relevant new qualifying trade—

(a) ceases to be carried on in period B by the issuing company or any qualifying 90% subsidiary of that company, and

(b) is subsequently carried on in that period by a person who is not at any time in period A connected with the issuing company.

(5) The following are acts and events within this subsection—

(a) anything done as a consequence of the issuing company or any other company being in administration or receivership, and

(b) the issuing company or any other company being wound up, or dissolved without being wound up.

(6) Subsection (4) applies only if—

(a) the entry into administration or receivership, and everything done as a consequence of the company concerned being in administration or receivership, or

(b) the winding up or dissolution,

is for genuine commercial reasons, and is not part of a scheme or arrangement the main purpose or one of the main purposes of which is the avoidance of tax.

(7) In this section—

"the relevant new qualifying trade" means the new qualifying trade which is the subject of that qualifying business activity;

"relevant preparation work" means preparations within section 257HG(2)(b) which are the subject of the qualifying business activity mentioned in section 257CB;

"relevant research and development" means—

(a) research and development within section 257HG(3) which is the subject of that qualifying business activity, and

(b) any other preparations for the carrying on of the new qualifying trade which is the subject of that activity.][1]

Commentary—*Simon's Taxes* **E3.828**.
HMRC Manuals—Venture Capital Schemes Manual VCM34040 (issuing company to carry on qualifying business activity).
Amendments—[1]   Part 5A (ss 257A–257HJ) inserted by FA 2012 s 38 Sch 6 para 1 with effect in relation to shares issued on or after 6 April 2012.

[257DD The UK permanent establishment requirement

(1) The issuing company must meet the UK permanent establishment requirement throughout period B.

(2) The UK permanent establishment requirement is that the issuing company has a permanent establishment in the United Kingdom.][1]

Commentary—*Simon's Taxes* **E3.829**.
HMRC Manuals—Venture Capital Schemes Manual VCM34050 (UK permanent establishment requirement).
Amendments—[1]   Part 5A (ss 257A–257HJ) inserted by FA 2012 s 38 Sch 6 para 1 with effect in relation to shares issued on or after 6 April 2012.

[257DE The financial health requirement
(1) The issuing company must meet the financial health requirement at the beginning of period B.
(2) The financial health requirement is that the issuing company is not in difficulty.
(3) The issuing company is "in difficulty" if it is reasonable to assume that it would be regarded as a firm in difficulty for the purposes of the Community Guidelines on State Aid for Rescuing and Restructuring Firms in Difficulty (2004/C 244/02).][1]

Commentary—*Simon's Taxes* E3.830.
HMRC Manuals—Venture Capital Schemes Manual VCM34060 (financial health requirement).
Amendments—[1]   Part 5A (ss 257A–257HJ) inserted by FA 2012 s 38 Sch 6 para 1 with effect in relation to shares issued on or after 6 April 2012.

[257DF The unquoted status requirement
(1) At the beginning of period B—
   (a) the issuing company must be an unquoted company,
   (b) there must be no arrangements in existence for the issuing company to cease to be an unquoted company, and
   (c) there must be no arrangements in existence for the issuing company to become a subsidiary of another company ("the new company") by virtue of an exchange of shares, or shares and securities, if—
      (i) section 257HB applies in relation to the exchange, and
      (ii) arrangements have been made with a view to the new company ceasing to be an unquoted company.
(2) In this section "unquoted company" means a company none of whose shares, stocks, debentures or other securities are marketed to the general public.
(3) For the purposes of subsection (2), shares, stock, debentures or other securities are marketed to the general public if they are—
   (a) listed on a recognised stock exchange,
   (b) listed on a designated exchange in a country outside the United Kingdom, or
   (c) dealt in outside the United Kingdom by such means as may be designated.
(4) In subsection (3)(b) and (c) "designated" means designated by an order made by the Commissioners for Her Majesty's Revenue and Customs for the purposes of that provision.
(5) An order made for the purposes of subsection (3)(b) may designate an exchange by name, or by reference to any class or description of exchanges, including a class or description framed by reference to any authority or approval given in a country outside the United Kingdom.
(6) The arrangements referred to in subsection (1)(b) and (c)(ii) do not include arrangements in consequence of which any shares, stocks, debentures or other securities of the company are at any subsequent time—
   (a) listed on a stock exchange that is a recognised stock exchange by virtue of an order made under section 1005(1)(b), or
   (b) listed on an exchange, or dealt in by any means, designated by an order made for the purposes of subsection (3)(b) or (c),
if the order was made after the beginning of period B.][1]

Commentary—*Simon's Taxes* E3.831.
HMRC Manuals—Venture Capital Schemes Manual VCM34070 (unquoted status requirement).
Amendments—[1]   Part 5A (ss 257A–257HJ) inserted by FA 2012 s 38 Sch 6 para 1 with effect in relation to shares issued on or after 6 April 2012.

[257DG The control and independence requirement
(1) The control element of the requirement is that—
   (a) the issuing company must not at any time in period A control (whether on its own or together with any person connected with it) any company which is not a qualifying subsidiary of the issuing company, and
   (b) no arrangements must be in existence at any time in that period by virtue of which the issuing company could fail to meet paragraph (a) (whether during that period or otherwise).
[(2) The independence element of the requirement is that—
   (a) the issuing company must not at any time in period A (ignoring any on-the-shelf period) be within subsection (2A), and
   (b) no arrangements must be in existence at any time in period A by virtue of which the issuing company could be within that subsection (whether during period A or otherwise).
(2A) The issuing company is within this subsection at any time if it is under the control of any other company (or of another company and any other person connected with that other company).
(2B) In subsection (2)(a) "on-the-shelf period" means a period during which the issuing company—
   (a) has not issued any shares other than subscriber shares, and
   (b) has not begun to carry on, or make preparations for carrying on, any trade or business.][2]
(3) This section is subject to section 257HB(4) (exchange of shares).][1]

Commentary—*Simon's Taxes* E3.832.
HMRC Manuals—Venture Capital Schemes Manual VCM34080 (control and independence requirement).

Amendments—[1]   Part 5A (ss 257A–257HJ) inserted by FA 2012 s 38 Sch 6 para 1 with effect in relation to shares issued on or after 6 April 2012.
[2]   Sub-ss (2)–(2B) substituted for previous sub-s (2) by FA 2013 s 56(1), (4) with effect in relation to shares issued on or after 6 April 2013.

[257DH The no partnerships requirement

(1) Neither the issuing company nor any qualifying 90% subsidiary of that company may, at any time during period A, be a member of a partnership.

(2) "Partnership" includes—

   (a) a limited liability partnership, and

   (b) an entity established under the law of a territory outside the United Kingdom of a similar character to a partnership,

and "member", in relation to a partnership, is to be read accordingly.][1]

Commentary—*Simon's Taxes* **E3.833**.
HMRC Manuals—Venture Capital Schemes Manual VCM34090 (no partnerships requirement).
Amendments—[1]   Part 5A (ss 257A–257HJ) inserted by FA 2012 s 38 Sch 6 para 1 with effect in relation to shares issued on or after 6 April 2012.

[257DI The gross assets requirement

(1) In the case of relevant shares issued by a single company, the value of the company's assets must not exceed £200,000 immediately before the relevant shares are issued.

(2) In the case of relevant shares issued by a parent company, the value of the group assets must not exceed £200,000 immediately before the relevant shares are issued.

(3) For the purposes of this section the value of the group assets is the sum of the values of the gross assets of each of the members of the group, ignoring any that consist in rights against, or shares in or securities of, another member of the group.][1]

Commentary—*Simon's Taxes* **E3.834**.
HMRC Manuals—Venture Capital Schemes Manual VCM34100 (gross assets requirement).
Amendments—[1]   Part 5A (ss 257A–257HJ) inserted by FA 2012 s 38 Sch 6 para 1 with effect in relation to shares issued on or after 6 April 2012.

[257DJ The number of employees requirement

(1) If the issuing company is a single company, the full-time equivalent employee number for it must be less than 25 when the relevant shares are issued.

(2) If the issuing company is a parent company, the sum of—

   (a) the full-time equivalent employee number for it, and

   (b) the full-time equivalent employee numbers for each of its qualifying subsidiaries,

must be less than 25 when the relevant shares are issued.

(3) The full-time equivalent employee number for a company is calculated as follows—

Step 1

Find the number of full-time employees of the company.

Step 2

Add, for each employee of the company who is not a full-time employee, such fraction as is just and reasonable.

The result is the full-time equivalent employee number.

(4) In this section references to an employee—

   (a) include a director, but

   (b) do not include—

      (i)   an employee on maternity[, paternity[, shared parental or parental bereavement][2] leave, or

      (ii) a student on vocational training.][1]

Commentary—*Simon's Taxes* **E3.835**.
HMRC Manuals—Venture Capital Schemes Manual VCM34110 (number of employees requirement).
Amendments—[1]   Part 5A (ss 257A–257HJ) inserted by FA 2012 s 38 Sch 6 para 1 with effect in relation to shares issued on or after 6 April 2012.
[2]   In sub-s (4)(b)(i), words substituted for words "or shared parental" by the Parental Bereavement (Leave and Pay) Act 2018 s 1, Schedule paras 50, 52 with effect from 18 January 2020 (by virtue of SI 2020/45 reg 2).

[257DK No previous other risk capital scheme investments

(1) The requirement of this section is that—

   (a) no EIS investment or VCT investment is or has been made in the issuing company on or before the day on which the relevant shares are issued, and

   (b) no EIS investment or VCT investment has been made on or before that day in a company which at the time the relevant shares are issued is a qualifying subsidiary of the issuing company.

(2) An "EIS investment" is made in the company if the company—

   (a) issues shares (money having been subscribed for them), and

   (b) (at any time) provides a compliance statement under section 205 in respect of the shares;

and the EIS investment is regarded as made when the shares are issued.

(3) A "VCT investment" is made in the company if an investment (of any kind) in the company is made by a VCT.][1]

Commentary—*Simon's Taxes* **E3.836**.

HMRC Manuals—Venture Capital Schemes Manual VCM34120 (no previous other risk capital scheme investments).

Amendments—[1]   Part 5A (ss 257A–257HJ) inserted by FA 2012 s 38 Sch 6 para 1 with effect in relation to shares issued on or after 6 April 2012.

[257DL The amount raised through the SEIS

(1) The sum of the following amounts must not exceed £150,000—
- (a) the amount of the SEIS investment made in the issuing company which includes the relevant shares ("the current investment"),
- (b) the amount of other SEIS investments made in the issuing company on the same day as the current investment,
- (c) the amount of any SEIS investments made in the issuing company during the period of 3 years ending immediately before that day, and
- (d) the total of any other aid which—
  - (i) is granted to the issuing company on the day the current investment is made or during that period, and
  - (ii) disregarding any SEIS investment within paragraph (a) or (b), would be de minimis aid.

(2) An "SEIS investment" is made in a company if—
- (a) the company issues shares (money having been subscribed for them), and
- (b) (at any time) the company provides a compliance statement under section 257ED in respect of the shares;

and an SEIS investment is made on the day when the shares are issued, and the amount of the investment is the amount subscribed for the shares.

(3) "De minimis aid" means de minimis aid within the meaning of Article 2 of Commission Regulation (EC) No 1998/2006 (de minimis aid).

The amount of the aid is the amount of the grant, or if the aid is not in the form of a grant, the gross grant equivalent amount (within the meaning of that Regulation).

(4) Subsection (5) applies where, in relation to the current investment—
- (a) the sum of the amounts mentioned in subsection (1) exceeds £150,000, but
- (b) the sum of the amounts in paragraphs (c) and (d) of that subsection does not exceed £150,000.

(5) In the case of the current investment and each other SEIS investment made in the issuing company on the same day (if any)—
- (a) the appropriate proportion of the shares in the issue constituting the investment and the remainder are to be treated as two separate issues for the purposes of this Part, and
- (b) the requirement in subsection (1) is to be treated as met in respect of the issue comprised of the appropriate proportion of the shares in the issue, but not in respect of the issue comprised of the remaining shares.

(6) "The appropriate proportion" of the shares is—

$$(A – B) / C$$

where—

    A is £150,000,

    B is the sum of the amounts in paragraphs (c) and (d) of subsection (1), and

    C is the sum of the amounts in paragraphs (a) and (b) of that subsection.][1]

Commentary—*Simon's Taxes* **E3.837**.

HMRC Manuals—Venture Capital Schemes Manual VCM34130 (amount raised through SEIS).

Amendments—[1]   Part 5A (ss 257A–257HJ) inserted by FA 2012 s 38 Sch 6 para 1 with effect in relation to shares issued on or after 6 April 2012.

[257DM The qualifying subsidiaries requirement

Any subsidiary that the issuing company has at any time in period B must be a qualifying subsidiary of the company.][1]

Commentary—*Simon's Taxes* **E3.838**.

HMRC Manuals—Venture Capital Schemes Manual VCM34140 (qualifying subsidiaries requirement).

Amendments—[1]   Part 5A (ss 257A–257HJ) inserted by FA 2012 s 38 Sch 6 para 1 with effect in relation to shares issued on or after 6 April 2012.

[257DN The property managing subsidiaries requirement

(1) Any property managing subsidiary that the issuing company has at any time in period B must be a qualifying 90% subsidiary of the company.

(2) "Property managing subsidiary" means a subsidiary of the company whose business consists wholly or mainly in the holding or managing of land or any property deriving its value from land.

(3) In subsection (2) references to property deriving its value from land include—
- (a) any shareholding in a company deriving its value directly or indirectly from land,
- (b) any interest in settled property deriving its value directly or indirectly from land, and

(c) any option, consent or embargo affecting the disposition of land.][1]

Commentary—*Simon's Taxes* **E3.839**.

HMRC Manuals—Venture Capital Schemes Manual VCM34150 (property managing subsidiaries requirement).

Amendments—[1] Part 5A (ss 257A–257HJ) inserted by FA 2012 s 38 Sch 6 para 1 with effect in relation to shares issued on or after 6 April 2012.

[CHAPTER 5

ATTRIBUTION AND CLAIMS FOR SEIS RELIEF]

Amendments—Part 5A (ss 257A–257HJ) inserted by FA 2012 s 38 Sch 6 para 1 with effect in relation to shares issued on or after 6 April 2012.

[Attribution

257E Attribution of SEIS relief to shares

(1) References in this Part, in relation to any individual, to the SEIS relief attributable to any shares or issue of shares are to be read as references to any reduction made in the individual's liability to income tax that is attributed to those shares or that issue in accordance with this section.

This is subject to the provisions of Chapters 6 and 7 providing for the withdrawal or reduction of SEIS relief.

(2) If an individual's liability to income tax is reduced in any tax year, then—

(a) if the reduction is obtained because of one issue of shares, the amount of the tax reduction is attributed to that issue, and

(b) if the reduction is obtained because of two or more issues of shares, the amount of the reduction—

(i) is apportioned between those issues in the same proportions as the amounts claimed by the individual in respect of each issue, and

(ii) is attributed to those issues accordingly.

(3) If under this section an amount of any reduction of income tax is attributed to an issue of shares ("the original issue"), a proportionate part of that amount is attributed to each share in respect of which the claim is made.

(4) If corresponding bonus shares are issued to the individual in respect of any shares ("the original shares") to which SEIS relief is attributed—

(a) a proportionate part of the total amount attributed to the original shares immediately before the bonus shares are issued is attributed to each of the shares in the holding comprising the original shares and the bonus shares, and

(b) after the issue of the bonus shares, this Part applies as if the original issue had included those shares.

(5) In subsection (4) "corresponding bonus shares" means bonus shares which are in the same company, of the same class, and carry the same rights as the original shares.

(6) If section 257AB(1) and (2) applies in the case of any issue of shares as if part of the issue had been issued in a previous tax year, this section has effect as if that part and the remainder were separate issues of shares (and that part had been issued on a day in the previous tax year).

(7) If, at a time when SEIS relief is attributable to, or to any part of, any issue of shares, the relief falls to be withdrawn or reduced under Chapters 6 and 7—

(a) if it falls to be withdrawn, the relief attributable to each of the shares in question is reduced to nil, and

(b) if it falls to be reduced by any amount, the relief attributable to each of the shares in question is reduced by a proportionate part of that amount.][1]

Commentary—*Simon's Taxes* **E3.845**.

HMRC Manuals—Venture Capital Schemes Manual VCM40150 (bonus issues).

VCM35020 (attribution of SEIS relief to shares).

Amendments—[1] Part 5A (ss 257A–257HJ) inserted by FA 2012 s 38 Sch 6 para 1 with effect in relation to shares issued on or after 6 April 2012.

[Claims: general

257EA Time for making claims for SEIS relief

(1) A claim for SEIS relief in respect of shares issued by a company in any tax year may not be made later than the fifth anniversary of the normal self-assessment filing date for the tax year.

(2) If section 257AB(1) and (2) applies in the case of any issue of shares as if part of the issue had been issued in a previous tax year, this section has effect as if that part and the remainder were separate issues of shares (and that part had been issued on a day in the previous tax year).][1]

Commentary—*Simon's Taxes* **E3.846**.

HMRC Manuals—Venture Capital Schemes Manual VCM35150 (investor claims: conditions).

Amendments—[1] Part 5A (ss 257A–257HJ) inserted by FA 2012 s 38 Sch 6 para 1 with effect in relation to shares issued on or after 6 April 2012.

[257EB Entitlement to claim

(1) The investor is entitled to make a claim for SEIS relief in respect of the amount subscribed by the investor for the relevant shares if the investor has received from the issuing company a compliance certificate in respect of those shares.

(2) For the purposes of PAYE regulations no regard is to be had to SEIS relief unless a claim for it has been duly made.

(3) No application may be made under section 55(3) or (4) of TMA 1970 (application for postponement of payment of tax pending appeal) on the ground that the investor is eligible for SEIS relief unless a claim for the relief has been duly made by the investor.][1]

Commentary—*Simon's Taxes* **E3.846**.

Amendments—[1]　Part 5A (ss 257A–257HJ) inserted by FA 2012 s 38 Sch 6 para 1 with effect in relation to shares issued on or after 6 April 2012.

[Claims: supporting documents

257EC Compliance certificates

(1) A "compliance certificate" is a certificate which—

    (a)　is issued by the issuing company in respect of the relevant shares,

    (b)　states that, except so far as they fall to be met by or in relation to the investor, the requirements for SEIS relief (see section 257AA) are for the time being met in relation to those shares, and

    (c)　is in such form as the Commissioners for Her Majesty's Revenue and Customs may direct.

(2) Before issuing a compliance certificate in respect of the relevant shares, the issuing company must provide an officer of Revenue and Customs with a compliance statement in respect of the issue of shares which includes the relevant shares.

(3) The issuing company must not issue a compliance certificate without the authority of an officer of Revenue and Customs.

(4) If the issuing company, or a person connected with the issuing company, has given notice to an officer of Revenue and Customs under section 257GF, a compliance certificate must not be issued unless the authority is given or renewed after the receipt of the notice.

(5) If an officer of Revenue and Customs—

    (a)　has been requested to give or renew an authority to issue a compliance certificate, and

    (b)　has decided whether or not to do so,

the officer must give notice of the officer's decision to the issuing company.][1]

Commentary—*Simon's Taxes* **E3.847**.

HMRC Manuals—Venture Capital Schemes Manual VCM35090 (company procedures: company's statement on SEIS1).

Amendments—[1]　Part 5A (ss 257A–257HJ) inserted by FA 2012 s 38 Sch 6 para 1 with effect in relation to shares issued on or after 6 April 2012.

[257ED Compliance statements

(1) A "compliance statement" is a statement, in respect of an issue of shares, to the effect that, except so far as they fall to be met by or in relation to the individuals to whom shares included in that issue have been issued, the requirements for SEIS relief (see section 257AA)—

    (a)　are for the time being met in relation to the shares to which the statement relates, and

    (b)　have been so met at all times since the shares were issued.

(2) In determining for the purposes of subsection (1) whether the requirements for SEIS relief are met at any time in relation to the issue of shares, references in this Part to the relevant shares are read as references to the shares included in the issue.

(3) A compliance statement must not be made in respect of an issue of shares before at least one of the following conditions is met—

    (a)　at least 70% of the money raised by the issue has been spent for the purposes of the qualifying business activity for which it was raised;

    (b)　the new qualifying trade which constitutes the qualifying business activity or to which that activity relates has been carried on by the issuing company or a qualifying 90% subsidiary of that company for at least 4 months.

(4) A compliance statement must be in such form as the Commissioners for Her Majesty's Revenue and Customs direct and must—

    (a)　state which of the conditions in subsection (3) is met at the time the statement is made,

    (b)　contain such additional information as the Commissioners reasonably require, including in particular information relating to the persons who have requested the issue of compliance certificates,

    (c)　contain a declaration that the statement is correct to the best of the issuing company's knowledge and belief, and

    (d)　contain such other declarations as the Commissioners may reasonably require.][1]

Commentary—*Simon's Taxes* **E3.847**.

HMRC Manuals—Venture Capital Schemes Manual VCM35080 (company procedures: overview).

Amendments—[1]　Part 5A (ss 257A–257HJ) inserted by FA 2012 s 38 Sch 6 para 1 with effect in relation to shares issued on or after 6 April 2012.

[257EE Appeal against refusal to authorise compliance certificate
For the purposes of the provisions of TMA 1970 relating to appeals, the refusal of an officer of Revenue and Customs to authorise the issue of a compliance certificate is taken to be a decision disallowing a claim by the issuing company.][1]
Commentary—*Simon's Taxes* E3.847.
HMRC Manuals—Venture Capital Schemes Manual VCM35130 (company procedures: refusal to authorise issue of SEIS3).
Amendments—[1]   Part 5A (ss 257A–257HJ) inserted by FA 2012 s 38 Sch 6 para 1 with effect in relation to shares issued on or after 6 April 2012.

[257EF Penalties for fraudulent certificate or statement etc
The issuing company is liable to a penalty not exceeding £3,000 if—
  (a) it issues a compliance certificate, or provides a compliance statement, which is made fraudulently or negligently, or
  (b) it issues a compliance certificate in contravention of section 257EC(3) or (4).][1]
Commentary—*Simon's Taxes* E3.847.
HMRC Manuals—Venture Capital Schemes Manual VCM35080 (penalties).
Amendments—[1]   Part 5A (ss 257A–257HJ) inserted by FA 2012 s 38 Sch 6 para 1 with effect in relation to shares issued on or after 6 April 2012.

[257EG Power to amend sections 257EC and 257ED
(1) The Treasury may by order make such amendments of sections 257EC and 257ED as they consider appropriate.
(2) An order under this section may include incidental, supplemental, consequential and transitional provision and savings.][1]
Commentary—*Simon's Taxes* E3.847.
Amendments—[1]   Part 5A (ss 257A–257HJ) inserted by FA 2012 s 38 Sch 6 para 1 with effect in relation to shares issued on or after 6 April 2012.

[CHAPTER 6

WITHDRAWAL OR REDUCTION OF SEIS RELIEF]
Amendments—Part 5A (ss 257A–257HJ) inserted by FA 2012 s 38 Sch 6 para 1 with effect in relation to shares issued on or after 6 April 2012.

[Introduction

257F Overview of Chapter
This Chapter provides for SEIS relief to be withdrawn or reduced under—
  (a) section 257FA (disposal of shares),
  (b) section 257FC (call options),
  (c) section 257FD (put options),
  (d) section 257FE (value received by the investor),
  (e) section 257FP (acquisition of a trade or trading asset),
  (f) section 257FQ (acquisition of share capital), and
  (g) section 257FR (relief subsequently found not to have been due).][1]
Commentary—*Simon's Taxes* E3.850.
Amendments—[1]   Part 5A (ss 257A–257HJ) inserted by FA 2012 s 38 Sch 6 para 1 with effect in relation to shares issued on or after 6 April 2012.

[257FA Disposal of shares
(1) This section applies if—
  (a) the investor disposes of any of the relevant shares,
  (b) the disposal takes place before period B ends, and
  (c) SEIS relief is attributable to the shares.
(2) If the disposal is not made by way of a bargain made at arm's length, the SEIS relief attributable to the shares must be withdrawn.
(3) If the disposal is made by way of a bargain made at arm's length, the SEIS relief attributable to the shares must—
  (a) if it is greater than the amount given by the formula set out below, be reduced by that amount, and
  (b) in any other case, be withdrawn.
The formula is—
R × SEISR
where—
    R is the amount or value of the consideration received by the investor for the shares, and
    SEISR is the SEIS rate.
(4) This section does not apply to a disposal of shares to which an amount of SEIS relief is attributable if—
  (a) the disposal was made by an individual ("A") to another individual ("B"), and

(b) A and B were married to, or were civil partners of, each other and living together at the time of the disposal.

(5) Section 257HA contains rules for determining which shares of any class are treated as disposed of for the purposes of this section if the investor disposes of some but not all of the shares of that class which are held by the investor.

(6) Nothing in this section applies to a disposal of shares occurring as a result of the investor's death.][1]

Commentary—*Simon's Taxes* **E3.850**.

HMRC Manuals—Venture Capital Schemes Manual VCM36020 (disposal of shares).

Amendments—[1] Part 5A (ss 257A–257HJ) inserted by FA 2012 s 38 Sch 6 para 1 with effect in relation to shares issued on or after 6 April 2012.

[257FB Cases where maximum SEIS relief not obtained

(1) If the investor's liability to income tax is reduced for any tax year in respect of any issue of shares and—

    (a) the amount of the reduction ("A"), is less than

    (b) the amount ("B") which is equal to tax at the SEIS rate on the amount on which the investor claims SEIS relief in respect of the shares,

section 257FA(3) has effect in relation to a disposal of any of the shares as if the amount or value referred to as "R" were reduced by multiplying it by the fraction—

A / B

(2) If section 257AB(1) and (2) applies in the case of any issue of shares as if part of the issue had been issued in a previous tax year, subsection (1) has effect as if that part and the remainder were separate issues of shares (and that part had been issued on a day in the previous tax year).

(3) If the amount of SEIS relief attributable to any of the relevant shares has been reduced before the SEIS relief was obtained, the amount referred to in subsection (1) as A is to be treated for the purposes of that subsection as the amount that it would have been without that reduction.

(4) Subsection (3) does not apply to a reduction of SEIS relief by virtue of section 257E(4) (attribution of SEIS relief if there is a corresponding issue of bonus shares).][1]

Commentary—*Simon's Taxes* **E3.850**.

HMRC Manuals—Venture Capital Schemes Manual VCM36020 (disposal of shares: maximum relief not obtained).

Amendments—[1] Part 5A (ss 257A–257HJ) inserted by FA 2012 s 38 Sch 6 para 1 with effect in relation to shares issued on or after 6 April 2012.

[257FC Call options

(1) This section applies if the investor grants an option which, if exercised, would bind the investor to sell any of the relevant shares.

(2) The grant of the option is treated for the purposes of section 257FA as a disposal of the shares to which the option relates.

(3) Nothing in this section prejudices section 257CD (no pre-arranged exits).][1]

Commentary—*Simon's Taxes* **E3.850**.

HMRC Manuals—Venture Capital Schemes Manual VCM36030 (call and put options).

Amendments—[1] Part 5A (ss 257A–257HJ) inserted by FA 2012 s 38 Sch 6 para 1 with effect in relation to shares issued on or after 6 April 2012.

[257FD Put options

(1) This section applies if, at any time in period A, a person grants the investor an option which, if exercised, would bind the grantor to purchase any of the relevant shares.

(2) Any SEIS relief attributable to the shares to which the option relates must be withdrawn.

(3) For the purposes of subsection (2) the shares to which an option relates are those which, if—

    (a) the option were exercised immediately after the grant, and

    (b) any shares in the issuing company acquired by the investor after the grant were disposed of immediately after being acquired,

would be treated for the purposes of section 257FA as disposed of in pursuance of the option.][1]

Commentary—*Simon's Taxes* **E3.850**.

HMRC Manuals—Venture Capital Schemes Manual VCM36030 (call and put options).

Amendments—[1] Part 5A (ss 257A–257HJ) inserted by FA 2012 s 38 Sch 6 para 1 with effect in relation to shares issued on or after 6 April 2012.

[Value received by investor

[257FE Value received by the investor

(1) This section applies if the investor receives any value from the issuing company at any time in period A relating to the relevant shares.

(2) Any SEIS relief attributable to the shares must—

    (a) if it is greater than the amount given by the formula set out below, be reduced by that amount, and

    (b) in any other case, be withdrawn.

The formula is—

R × SEISR

where—

> R is the amount of the value received by the investor, and
> SEISR is the SEIS rate.

(3) This section is subject to the following sections—

- (a) section 257FF (value received: receipts of insignificant value),
- (b) section 257FJ (value received where there is more than one issue of shares),
- (c) section 257FK (value received where part of share issue treated as made in previous tax year),
- (d) section 257FL (cases where maximum SEIS relief not obtained),
- (e) section 257FM (receipts of value by and from connected persons etc), and
- (f) section 257FN (receipt of replacement value).

Sections 257FJ to 257FL are to be applied in the order in which they appear in this Part.

(4) Value received is to be ignored, for the purposes of this section, to the extent to which SEIS relief attributable to the shares has already been withdrawn or reduced on its account.

(5) For the purposes of this section and sections 257FF to 257FO, an individual who acquires any relevant shares on such a transfer as is mentioned in section 257H (spouses or civil partners) is treated as the investor.][1]

Commentary—*Simon's Taxes* **E3.851**.

HMRC Manuals—Venture Capital Schemes Manual VCM36040 (value received by investor: overview).
VCM36050 (value received by investor: calculation of reduction of relief).

Amendments—[1]   Part 5A (ss 257A–257HJ) inserted by FA 2012 s 38 Sch 6 para 1 with effect in relation to shares issued on or after 6 April 2012.

[257FF Value received: receipts of insignificant value

(1) Section 257FE(2) does not apply if the receipt of value is a receipt of insignificant value.
This is subject to subsection (2).

(2) If—

- (a) value is received ("the relevant receipt") by the investor from the issuing company at any time in period A relating to the relevant shares,
- (b) the investor has received from the issuing company one or more receipts of insignificant value at a time or times—
    - (i)   during that period, but
    - (ii) not later than the time of the relevant receipt, and
- (c) the total value of the receipts within paragraphs (a) and (b) is not an amount of insignificant value,

the investor is treated for the purposes of this Chapter as if the relevant receipt had been a receipt of an amount of value equal to that total amount.

(3) A receipt does not fall within subsection (2)(b) if it has previously formed part of a total amount falling within subsection (2)(c).][1]

Commentary—*Simon's Taxes* **E3.851**.

HMRC Manuals—Venture Capital Schemes Manual VCM36060 (value received by investor: meaning of 'insignificant').

Amendments—[1]   Part 5A (ss 257A–257HJ) inserted by FA 2012 s 38 Sch 6 para 1 with effect in relation to shares issued on or after 6 April 2012.

[257FG Meaning of "a receipt of insignificant value"

(1) This section applies for the purposes of section 257FF.

(2) "A receipt of insignificant value" means a receipt of an amount of insignificant value, that is, an amount of value which—

- (a) is not more than £1,000, or
- (b) if it is more than £1,000, is insignificant in relation to the amount subscribed by the investor for the relevant shares.

This is subject to subsection (3).

(3) If at any time in the period—

- (a) beginning 12 months before the issue of the relevant shares, and
- (b) ending at the end of the issue date,

repayment arrangements are in existence, no amount of value received by the investor is treated as a receipt of insignificant value.

(4) For this purpose "repayment arrangements" means arrangements which provide for the investor to receive, or to be entitled to receive, any value from the issuing company at any time in period A relating to the relevant shares.

(5) For the purposes of this section—

- (a) the references in this section to the investor include a reference to any person who at any time in period A relating to the relevant shares is an associate of the investor (whether or not that person is such an associate at the material time), and

(b) the reference in subsection (4) to the issuing company includes a reference to a person who at any time in period A relating to the relevant shares is connected with that company (whether or not that person is so connected at the material time).][1]

Commentary—*Simon's Taxes* **E3.851**.

HMRC Manuals—Venture Capital Schemes Manual VCM36060 (value received by investor: meaning of 'insignificant').

Amendments—[1] Part 5A (ss 257A–257HJ) inserted by FA 2012 s 38 Sch 6 para 1 with effect in relation to shares issued on or after 6 April 2012.

[257FH When value is received

(1) This section applies for the purposes of sections 257FE (value received by the investor) and 257FJ (value received where there is more than one issue).

(2) The investor receives value from the issuing company at any time when the issuing company—

(a) repays, redeems or repurchases any of its share capital or securities which belong to the investor or makes any payment to the investor for giving up the investor's right to any of the issuing company's share capital or any security on its cancellation or extinguishment,

(b) repays, in pursuance of any arrangements for or in connection with the acquisition of the shares in respect of which SEIS relief is claimed, any debt owed to the investor other than a debt which was incurred by the company—

(i) on or after the date of issue of those shares, and

(ii) otherwise than in consideration of the extinguishment of a debt incurred before that date,

(c) makes to the investor any payment for giving up on its extinguishment the investor's right to any debt, other than a debt in respect of a payment of the kind mentioned in subsection (3)(a) or (f) or an ordinary trade debt,

(d) releases or waives any liability of the investor to the issuing company or discharges or undertakes to discharge any liability of the investor to a third person,

(e) makes a loan or advance to the investor which has not been repaid in full before the issue of the shares in respect of which SEIS relief is claimed,

(f) provides a benefit or facility for the investor,

(g) transfers an asset to the investor for no consideration or for consideration less than its market value or acquires an asset from the investor for consideration greater than its market value, or

(h) makes to the investor any other payment except—

(i) an excluded payment, or

(ii) a payment in discharge of an ordinary trade debt.

(3) "Excluded payment" means—

(a) any payment or reimbursement of travelling or other expenses, exclusively and necessarily incurred by the investor or an associate of the investor in the performance of the investor's or associate's duties as a director,

(b) any interest which represents no more than a reasonable commercial return on money lent to the issuing company or any person connected with that company,

(c) any dividend or other distribution which does not exceed a normal return on the investment,

(d) any payment for the supply of goods which does not exceed their market value,

(e) any payment of rent for any property occupied by the issuing company or a person connected with that company which does not exceed a reasonable and commercial rent for the property, and

(f) any necessary and reasonable remuneration which meets the conditions in subsection (4).

(4) The conditions are that the remuneration—

(a) is paid for services rendered to the issuing company or a person connected with that company in the course of a trade or profession (not being secretarial or managerial services or services of a kind provided by the person to whom they are rendered), and

(b) is taken into account in calculating for tax purposes the profits of that trade or profession.

(5) For the purposes of subsection (2)(d) the issuing company is to be treated as having released or waived a liability if the liability is not discharged within 12 months of the time when it ought to have been discharged.

(6) For the purposes of subsection (2)(e) the following is to be treated as if it were a loan made by the issuing company to the investor—

(a) the amount of any debt (other than an ordinary trade debt) incurred by the investor to the issuing company, and

(b) the amount of any debt due from the investor to a third party which has been assigned to the issuing company.

(7) The investor also receives value from the issuing company if—

(a) in respect of ordinary shares held by the investor any payment or asset is received in a winding up or in connection with a dissolution of the company, and

(b) the winding up or dissolution falls within section 257DB(4) (no tax avoidance).

(8) The investor also receives value from the issuing company if a person within subsection (9)—

(a) purchases any of its share capital or securities which belong to the investor, or

(b) makes any payment to the investor for giving up any right in relation to any of the company's share capital or securities.

(9) Those persons are—

(a) any person who has a substantial interest in the company within the meaning of section 257BB;

(b) any employee of the issuing company;

(c) any director of the issuing company.

(10) If because of the investor's disposal of shares in a company any SEIS relief attributable to those shares is withdrawn or reduced under section 257FA, the investor is not to be treated as receiving value from the company in respect of the disposal.

(11) The investor is not to be treated as receiving value from the issuing company merely because of the payment to the investor, or any associate of the investor, of any remuneration for services rendered to that company as a director if the remuneration is reasonable remuneration.

(12) For the purposes of subsection (11)—

(a) the reference in that subsection to the payment of remuneration includes a reference to the provision of any benefit or facility, and

(b) in the case of an individual who is both a director and an employee of a company, the reference in that subsection to services rendered to that company as a director includes a reference to services rendered to that company as an employee.

(13) In this section—

(a) "ordinary trade debt" means any debt for goods or services supplied in the ordinary course of a trade or business if any credit given—

(i) is for not more than 6 months, and

(ii) is not longer than that normally given to customers of the person carrying on the trade or business, and

(b) any reference to a payment to an individual includes a payment made to the individual indirectly or to the individual's order or for the individual's benefit.][1]

Commentary—*Simon's Taxes* **E3.851**.
HMRC Manuals—Venture Capital Schemes Manual VCM36070 (value received by investor: when value is received).
VCM36080 (payments not to be included).
Amendments—[1]   Part 5A (ss 257A–257HJ) inserted by FA 2012 s 38 Sch 6 para 1 with effect in relation to shares issued on or after 6 April 2012.

[257FI The amount of value received

In a case falling within a provision listed in column 1 of the following table, the amount of value received for the purposes of sections 257FE and 257FJ is given by the corresponding entry in column 2 of the table.

Provision	The amount of value received
Section 257FH(2)(a), (b) or (c)	The amount received by the investor or, if greater, the market value of the shares, securities or debt
Section 257FH(2)(d)	The amount of the liability
Section 257FH(2)(e)	The amount of the loan or advance, less the amount of any repayment made before the issue of the relevant shares
Section 257FH(2)(f)	The cost to the issuing company of providing the benefit or facility, less any consideration given for it by the investor
Section 257FH(2)(g)	The difference between the market value of the asset and the consideration (if any) given for it
Section 257FH(2)(h)	The amount of the payment
Section 257FH(7)	The amount of the payment or the market value of the asset
Section 257FH(8)	The amount received by the investor or, if greater, the market value of the shares or securities][1]

Commentary—*Simon's Taxes* **E3.851**.
HMRC Manuals—Venture Capital Scheme Manual VCM36070 (value received by investor: when value is received).
Amendments—[1]   Part 5A (ss 257A–257HJ) inserted by FA 2012 s 38 Sch 6 para 1 with effect in relation to shares issued on or after 6 April 2012.

[257FJ Value received where there is more than one issue

(1) This section applies if—

(a) two or more issues of shares in the issuing company have been made to the investor which include shares in respect of which the investor obtains SEIS relief, and

(b) value is received by the investor at any time in the applicable periods for two or more of those issues.

(2) Section 257FE(2) has effect in relation to the shares included in each of the issues referred to in subsection (1)(b) as if the amount of value referred to as "R" were reduced by multiplying it by the fraction—

A / B

where—

 A is the amount on which the investor obtains SEIS relief in respect of the shares included in the issue in question, and

 B is the sum of that amount and the corresponding amount or amounts in respect of the other issue or issues.

(3) For the purposes of subsection (1) "the applicable period" for an issue of shares is period A in relation to those shares.][1]

Commentary—*Simon's Taxes* **E3.851**.

HMRC Manuals—Venture Capital Schemes Manual VCM36050 (value received by investor: calculation of reduction of relief).

Amendments—[1]　Part 5A (ss 257A–257HJ) inserted by FA 2012 s 38 Sch 6 para 1 with effect in relation to shares issued on or after 6 April 2012.

[257FK　Value received where part of issue treated as made in previous tax year

(1) This section applies if—

 (a)　section 257FE(2) applies to an issue of shares, and

 (b)　section 257AB(1) and (2) (form and amount of SEIS relief) applies in the case of that issue as if part of the issue had been issued in a previous tax year.

(2) This subsection explains how the calculation under section 257FE(2) is to be made.

Step 1

Apportion the amount referred to as "R" between the tax year in which the shares were issued and the previous tax year by multiplying that amount by the fraction—

A / B

where—

 A is the amount on which the investor obtains SEIS relief in respect of the shares treated as issued in the tax year in question, and

 B is the sum of that amount and the corresponding amount in respect of the shares treated as issued in the other tax year.

Step 2

In relation to each of the amounts ("R1" and "R2") so apportioned to the two tax years, calculate the amounts ("X1" and "X2") that would be given by the formula if there were separate issues of shares in those tax years.

In calculating amounts X1 and X2, apply section 257FL if appropriate but do not apply section 257FJ.

Step 3

Add amounts X1 and X2 together.

The result is the required amount.][1]

Commentary—*Simon's Taxes* **E3.851**.

HMRC Manuals—Venture Capital Schemes Manual VCM36050 (value received by investor: calculation of reduction of relief).

Amendments—[1]　Part 5A (ss 257A–257HJ) inserted by FA 2012 s 38 Sch 6 para 1 with effect in relation to shares issued on or after 6 April 2012.

[257FL　Cases where maximum SEIS relief not obtained

(1) If the investor's liability to income tax is reduced for any tax year in respect of any issue of shares and—

 (a)　the amount of the reduction ("A"), is less than

 (b)　the amount ("B") which is equal to income tax at the SEIS rate on the amount on which the investor claims SEIS relief in respect of the shares,

section 257FE(2) has effect in relation to any value received as if the amount referred to as "R" were reduced by multiplying it by the fraction—

A / B

(2) If the amount of SEIS relief attributable to any of the relevant shares has been reduced before the SEIS relief was obtained, the amount referred to in subsection (1) as A is to be treated for the purposes of that subsection as the amount that it would have been without that reduction.

(3) Subsection (2) does not apply to a reduction of SEIS relief by virtue of section 257E(4) (attribution of SEIS relief where there is a corresponding issue of bonus shares).][1]

Commentary—*Simon's Taxes* **E3.851**.

HMRC Manuals—Venture Capital Schemes Manual VCM36050 (value received by investor: calculation of reduction of relief).

Amendments—[1]　Part 5A (ss 257A–257HJ) inserted by FA 2012 s 38 Sch 6 para 1 with effect in relation to shares issued on or after 6 April 2012.

[257FM　Receipts of value by and from connected persons etc

In sections 257FE, 257FF and 257FH to 257FJ—

 (a)　any reference to a payment or transfer to the investor includes a reference to a payment or transfer made to the investor indirectly or to the investor's order or for the investor's benefit,

(b) any reference to the investor includes a reference to an associate of the investor, and

(c) any reference to the issuing company includes a reference to a person who at any time in period A relating to the relevant shares is connected with that company (whether or not that person is so connected at the material time).][1]

Commentary—*Simon's Taxes* **E3.851**.
HMRC Manuals—Venture Capital Schemes Manual VCM36070 (value received by investor: when value is received).
Amendments—[1]   Part 5A (ss 257A–257HJ) inserted by FA 2012 s 38 Sch 6 para 1 with effect in relation to shares issued on or after 6 April 2012.

[257FN Receipt of replacement value

(1) If—

(a) any SEIS relief attributable to the relevant shares would, in the absence of this section, be reduced or withdrawn under section 257FE because of a receipt of value within section 257FH(2), (7) or (8) ("the original value"),

(b) the original supplier receives value ("replacement value") from the original recipient and the receipt is a qualifying receipt, and

(c) the amount of the replacement value is at least the amount of the original value,

section 257FE does not, because of the receipt of value, have effect to reduce or withdraw the SEIS relief.

This is subject to section 257FO(1) and (2).

(2) For the purposes of this section—

"the original recipient" means the person who receives the original value;

"the original supplier" means the person from whom that value was received.

(3) If the amount of the original value is, by virtue of section 257FJ, treated as reduced for the purposes of section 257FE(2) as it applies in relation to the relevant shares in question, the reference in subsection (1)(c) to the amount of the original value is to be read as a reference to the amount of that value ignoring the reduction.

(4) A receipt of the replacement value is a qualifying receipt for the purposes of subsection (1) if it arises—

(a) because of the original recipient doing one or more of the following—

(i)   making a payment to the original supplier, other than a payment within paragraph (c) or a payment to which subsection (5) applies,

(ii) acquiring any asset from the original supplier for a consideration the amount or value of which is more than the market value of the asset,

(iii) disposing of any asset to the original supplier for no consideration or for a consideration the amount or value of which is less than the market value of the asset,

(b) if the receipt of the original value was within section 257FH(2)(d), because of an event the effect of which is to reverse the event which constituted the receipt of the original value, or

(c) if the receipt of the original value was within section 257FH(8), because of the original recipient repurchasing the share capital or securities in question, or (as the case may be) re-acquiring the right in question, for a consideration the amount or value of which is at least the amount of the original value.

(5) This subsection applies to—

(a) any payment for any goods, services or facilities, provided (whether in the course of trade or otherwise) by—

(i)   the original supplier, or

(ii) any other person who, at any time in period A relating to the relevant shares, is an associate of, or is connected with, that supplier (whether or not the other person is such an associate, or is so connected, at the material time),

which is reasonable in relation to the market value of those goods, services or facilities,

(b) any payment of any interest which represents no more than a reasonable commercial return on any money lent to—

(i)   the original recipient, or

(ii) any person who, at any time in period A relating to the relevant shares, is an associate of that recipient (whether or not the person is such an associate at the material time),

(c) any payment for the acquisition of an asset which does not exceed its market value,

(d) any payment, as rent for any property occupied by—

(i)   the original recipient, or

(ii) any person who, at any time in period A relating to the relevant shares, is an associate of that recipient (whether or not the person is such an associate at the material time),

of an amount not exceeding a reasonable and commercial rent for the property,

(e) any payment in discharge of an ordinary trade debt, and

(f) any payment for shares in or securities of any company in circumstances that do not fall within subsection (4)(a)(ii).

(6) For the purposes of this section, the amount of the replacement value is—
   (a) in a case within paragraph (a) of subsection (4), the sum of—
      (i) the amount of any payment within sub-paragraph (i) of that paragraph, and
      (ii) the difference between the market value of any asset to which sub-paragraph (ii) or (iii) of that paragraph applies and the amount or value of the consideration (if any) received for it,
   (b) in a case within subsection (4)(b), the same as the amount of the original value, and
   (c) in a case within subsection (4)(c), the amount or value of the consideration received by the original supplier.
  Section 257FI applies for the purpose of determining the original value.
(7) In this section—
   (a) any reference to a payment to a person (however expressed) includes a reference to a payment made to the person indirectly or to the person's order or for the person's benefit, and
   (b) "ordinary trade debt" has the meaning given by section 257FH(13).][1]

Commentary—*Simon's Taxes* **E3.851**.
HMRC Manuals—Venture Capital Schemes Manual VCM36090 (receipt of replacement value).
Amendments—[1] Part 5A (ss 257A–257HJ) inserted by FA 2012 s 38 Sch 6 para 1 with effect in relation to shares issued on or after 6 April 2012.

[257FO Section 257FN: supplementary

(1) The receipt of the replacement value by the original supplier is ignored for the purposes of section 257FN(1) to the extent to which it has previously been set (under that section) against a receipt of value to prevent any reduction or withdrawal of SEIS relief under section 257FE.
(2) The receipt of the replacement value by the original supplier ("the event") is ignored for the purposes of section 257FN if—
   (a) the event occurs before period A relating to the relevant shares,
   (b) if the event occurs after the time the original recipient receives the original value, it does not occur as soon after that time as is reasonably practicable in the circumstances, or
   (c) if an appeal has been brought by the investor against an assessment to withdraw or reduce any SEIS relief attributable to the relevant shares because of the receipt of the original value, the event occurs more than 60 days after the day on which the amount of relief which falls to be withdrawn has been finally determined.
  But nothing in section 257FN or this section requires the replacement value to be received after the original value.
(3) This subsection applies if—
   (a) the receipt of the replacement value by the original supplier is a qualifying receipt for the purposes of section 257FN(1),
   (b) in consequence of the receipt, any receipts of value are ignored for the purposes of section 257FE as that section applies in relation to the shares in question or any other shares subscribed for by the investor, and
   (c) the event which gives rise to the receipt is (or includes) a subscription for shares by—
      (i) the investor, or
      (ii) any person who at any time in period A relating to the relevant shares is an associate of the investor (whether or not the person is such an associate at the material time).
(4) If subsection (3) applies, the person who subscribes for the shares is not to be eligible for any SEIS relief in relation to those shares or any other shares in the same issue.
(5) In this section "the original recipient", "the original supplier" and "replacement value" have the same meaning as in section 257FN.][1]

Commentary—*Simon's Taxes* **E3.851**.
HMRC Manuals—Venture Capital Schemes Manual VCM36090 (receipt of replacement value).
Amendments—[1] Part 5A (ss 257A–257HJ) inserted by FA 2012 s 38 Sch 6 para 1 with effect in relation to shares issued on or after 6 April 2012.

[Miscellaneous

257FP Acquisition of trade or trading assets

(1) Any SEIS relief attributable to any shares in a company held by an individual is withdrawn if—
   (a) at any time in period A, the company or any qualifying subsidiary—
      (i) begins to carry on as its trade, or as part of its trade, a trade which was previously carried on at any time in that period otherwise than by the company or any qualifying subsidiary, or
      (ii) acquires the whole, or the greater part, of the assets used for the purposes of a trade previously so carried on, and
   (b) the individual is a person, or one of a group of persons, to whom subsection (2) or (3) applies.
(2) This subsection applies to any person or group of persons—
   (a) to whom an interest amounting in total to more than a half share in the trade (as previously carried on) belonged at any time in period A, and

(b) who is a person or group of persons to whom such an interest in the trade carried on by the company belongs or has, at any such time, belonged.
(3) This subsection applies to any person or group of persons who—
   (a) controls or, at any time in period A, has controlled the company, and
   (b) at any such time, controlled another company which previously carried on the trade.
(4) For the purposes of subsection (2)—
   (a) for the purposes of determining the person to whom a trade belongs and, if a trade belongs to two or more persons, their respective shares in that trade—
      (i) apply section 941(6) of CTA 2010, and
      (ii) an interest in a trade belonging to a company may be treated in accordance with any of the options set out in section 942 of that Act, and
   (b) any interest, rights or powers of a person who is an associate of another person are treated as those of that other person.
(5) In this section "trade" includes any business or profession, and references to a trade previously carried on include references to part of such a trade.]¹

Commentary—*Simon's Taxes* E3.852.
HMRC Manuals—Venture Capital Schemes Manual VCM36100 (acquisition of trade).
Amendments—¹   Part 5A (ss 257A–257HJ) inserted by FA 2012 s 38 Sch 6 para 1 with effect in relation to shares issued on or after 6 April 2012.

[257FQ Acquisition of share capital
(1) Any SEIS relief attributable to any shares in a company held by an individual is withdrawn if—
   (a) the company comes to acquire all of the issued share capital of another company at any time in period A, and
   (b) the individual is a person, or one of a group of persons, to whom subsection (2) applies.
(2) This subsection applies to any person or group of persons who—
   (a) controls or, at any time in period A, has controlled the company, and
   (b) at any such time, controlled the other company.]¹

Commentary—*Simon's Taxes* E3.853.
HMRC Manuals—Venture Capital Schemes Manual VCM36110 (reduction of SEIS relief: acquisition of share capital).
Amendments—¹   Part 5A (ss 257A–257HJ) inserted by FA 2012 s 38 Sch 6 para 1 with effect in relation to shares issued on or after 6 April 2012.

[257FR Relief subsequently found not to have been due
(1) Any SEIS relief obtained by the investor which is subsequently found not to have been due must be withdrawn.
(2) SEIS relief obtained by the investor in respect of the relevant shares may not be withdrawn on the ground—
   (a) that the requirements of sections 257CB and 257CC (the purpose of the issue and use of money raised requirements) are not met in respect of the shares, or
   (b) that the issuing company is not a qualifying company in relation to the shares (see Chapter 4), unless the requirements of subsection (3) are met.
(3) The requirements of this subsection are met if either—
   (a) the issuing company has given notice under section 257GF (information to be provided by issuing company etc) in relation to the relevant issue of shares, or
   (b) an officer of Revenue and Customs has given notice to that company stating the officer's opinion that, because of the ground in question, the whole or any part of the SEIS relief obtained by any individual in respect of shares included in the relevant issue of shares was not due.
(4) In this section "the relevant issue of shares" means the issue of shares in the issuing company which includes the relevant shares.]¹

Commentary—*Simon's Taxes* E3.854.
HMRC Manuals—Venture Capital Schemes Manual VCM36120 (SEIS: relief subsequently found not to have been due).
Amendments—¹   Part 5A (ss 257A–257HJ) inserted by FA 2012 s 38 Sch 6 para 1 with effect in relation to shares issued on or after 6 April 2012.

[CHAPTER 7

WITHDRAWAL OR REDUCTION OF SEIS RELIEF: PROCEDURE]

Amendments—Part 5A (ss 257A–257HJ) inserted by FA 2012 s 38 Sch 6 para 1 with effect in relation to shares issued on or after 6 April 2012.

[Assessments and appeals

257G Assessments for the withdrawal or reduction of SEIS relief
If any SEIS relief which has been obtained falls to be withdrawn or reduced under Chapter 6, it must be withdrawn or reduced by the making of an assessment to income tax for the tax year for which the relief was obtained.]¹

Commentary—*Simon's Taxes* E3.860.

HMRC Manuals—Venture Capital Schemes Manual VCM36140 (withdrawal or reduction of relief: withdrawing relief).
Amendments—[1]   Part 5A (ss 257A–257HJ) inserted by FA 2012 s 38 Sch 6 para 1 with effect in relation to shares issued on or after 6 April 2012.

[257GA Appeals against section 257FR(3)(b) notices

For the purposes of the provisions of TMA 1970 relating to appeals, the giving of notice by an officer of Revenue and Customs under section 257FR(3)(b) is taken to be a decision disallowing a claim by the issuing company.][1]

Commentary—*Simon's Taxes* **E3.860**.
Amendments—[1]   Part 5A (ss 257A–257HJ) inserted by FA 2012 s 38 Sch 6 para 1 with effect in relation to shares issued on or after 6 April 2012.

[257GB Time limits for assessments

(1) An officer of Revenue and Customs may—
    (a) make an assessment for withdrawing or reducing the SEIS relief attributable to any of the relevant shares, or
    (b) give a notice under section 257FR(3),
at any time not more than 6 years after the end of the relevant tax year.
(2) In subsection (1) "the relevant tax year" means—
    (a) the tax year in which period B ends, or
    (b) the tax year in which the event which causes the SEIS relief to be withdrawn or reduced occurs,
whichever is the later.]
(3) Subsection (1) is without prejudice to section 36(1A) of TMA 1970 (loss of tax brought about deliberately etc).[1]

Commentary—*Simon's Taxes* **E3.860**.
HMRC Manuals—Venture Capital Schemes Manual VCM36150 (withdrawal or reduction of relief: procedure: time limits for assessments).
Amendments—[1]   Part 5A (ss 257A–257HJ) inserted by FA 2012 s 38 Sch 6 para 1 with effect in relation to shares issued on or after 6 April 2012.

[257GC Cases where assessments not to be made

(1) No assessment for withdrawing or reducing SEIS relief in respect of shares issued to an individual may be made because of an event occurring after the individual's death.
(2) Subsection (3) applies if an individual has, by a disposal or disposals to which section 257FA(3) applies, disposed of all shares which—
    (a) have been issued to the individual by the issuing company, and
    (b) are shares—
        (i) to which SEIS relief is attributable, or
        (ii) in relation to which period A has not come to an end.
(3) No assessment for withdrawing or reducing SEIS relief in respect of those shares may be made because of any subsequent event unless the event occurs at a time when the individual—
    (a) has a substantial interest in the company within the meaning of section 257BB,
    (b) is an employee of the issuing company, or
    (c) is a director of the issuing company.][1]

Commentary—*Simon's Taxes* **E3.860**.
Amendments—[1]   Part 5A (ss 257A–257HJ) inserted by FA 2012 s 38 Sch 6 para 1 with effect in relation to shares issued on or after 6 April 2012.

[Interest

257GD Date from which interest is chargeable

(1) In its application to an assessment made by virtue of section 257G in the case of relief withdrawn or reduced by virtue of a provision listed in subsection (2), section 86 of TMA 1970 (interest on overdue income tax) has effect as if the relevant date were 31 January next following the tax year in which the assessment is made.
(2) The provisions are—
    (a) section 257BB (no substantial interest in the issuing company),
    (b) section 257BD (no linked loan requirement),
    (c) sections 257DA to 257DN (Chapter 4 requirements),
    (d) section 257FA (disposal of shares),
    (e) section 257FD (put options),
    (f) section 257FE (receipt of value by the investor),
    (g) section 257FP (acquisition of a trade or trading asset),
    (h) section 257FQ (acquisition of share capital).][1]

Commentary—*Simon's Taxes* **E3.861**.
HMRC Manuals—Venture Capital Schemes Manual VCM36160 (SEIS procedure: date from which interest is chargeable).
Amendments—[1]   Part 5A (ss 257A–257HJ) inserted by FA 2012 s 38 Sch 6 para 1 with effect in relation to shares issued on or after 6 April 2012.

257GE Information to be provided by the investor

(1) This section applies if the investor has obtained SEIS relief in respect of the relevant shares, and an event occurs as a result of which—

    (a) the investor is not a qualifying investor in relation to the shares,

    (b) the SEIS relief falls to be withdrawn or reduced by virtue of section 257BD (no linked loans requirement),

    (c) the SEIS relief falls to be withdrawn or reduced under—

        (i)   section 257FA (disposal of shares),

        (ii) section 257FC (call options), or

        (iii) section 257FD (put options), or

    (d) the SEIS relief falls to be withdrawn or reduced under section 257FE (receipt of value by the investor), or would fall to be so withdrawn or reduced but for section 257FN (receipt of replacement value).

(2) The investor must within 60 days of coming to know of the event give a notice to an officer of Revenue and Customs containing particulars of the event.

(3) If the investor—

    (a) is required under this section to give notice of a receipt of value which is within section 257FE, or would be within that section but for section 257FN, and

    (b) has knowledge of any replacement value received (or expected to be received) because of a qualifying receipt,

the notice must include particulars of that receipt of replacement value (or expected receipt).

(4) In subsection (3) "qualifying receipt" and "replacement value" are to be read in accordance with section 257FN.]¹

Commentary—*Simon's Taxes* E3.862.

HMRC Manuals—Venture Capital Schemes Manual VCM35210 (obligation to notify HMRC of disqualifying events - investor obligations to notify HMRC).

Amendments—¹   Part 5A (ss 257A–257HJ) inserted by FA 2012 s 38 Sch 6 para 1 with effect in relation to shares issued on or after 6 April 2012.

[257GF Information to be provided by the issuing company etc

(1) This section applies if the issuing company has provided an officer of Revenue and Customs with a compliance statement in respect of an issue of shares and an event occurs as a result of which—

    (a) the requirement of section 257CC (spending of the money raised) is not met in respect of any of the shares included in the issue, or would not be met if SEIS relief had been obtained in respect of the shares in question,

    (b) any provision of Chapter 4 has effect to prevent the issuing company being a qualifying company in relation to any of the shares included in the issue, or would have such an effect if SEIS relief had been obtained in respect of the shares in question, or

    (c) any of the provisions of Chapter 6 mentioned in subsection (2) has effect to cause any SEIS relief attributable to any of the shares included in the issue to be withdrawn or reduced, or—

        (i)   would have such an effect if SEIS relief had been obtained in respect of the shares in question, or

        (ii) in the case of section 257FE, would have such an effect but for section 257FN (receipt of replacement value).

(2) The provision are—

    (a) section 257FE (value received by the investor),

    (b) section 257FP (acquisition of a trade or trading asset), and

    (c) section 257FQ (acquisition of share capital).

(3) If this section applies—

    (a) the issuing company, and

    (b) any person connected with the issuing company who has knowledge of the matters mentioned in subsection (1),

must give a notice to an officer of Revenue and Customs containing particulars of the event.

(4) Any notice required to be given by the issuing company under subsection (3)(a) must be given—

    (a) within 60 days of the event, or

    (b) if the event is a receipt of value within section 257FH(2) from a person connected with the company (see section 257FM), within 60 days of the company coming to know of the event.

(5) Any notice required to be given by a person under subsection (3)(b) must be given within 60 days of the person coming to know of the event.

(6) If a person—

    (a) is required under this section to give notice of a receipt of value which is within section 257FE, or would be within that section but for section 257FN, and

    (b) has knowledge of any replacement value received (or expected to be received) because of a qualifying receipt, the notice must include particulars of that receipt of replacement value (or expected receipt).

(7) In subsection (6) "qualifying receipt" and "replacement value" are to be read in accordance with section 257FN.][1]

Commentary—*Simon's Taxes* **E3.863**.

HMRC Manuals—Venture Capital Schemes Manual VCM35210 (obligation to notify HMRC of disqualifying events - company obligations to notify HMRC).

Amendments—[1]   Part 5A (ss 257A–257HJ) inserted by FA 2012 s 38 Sch 6 para 1 with effect in relation to shares issued on or after 6 April 2012.

[257GG Power to require information where section 257GE or 257GF applies or could have applied

(1) This section applies if an officer of Revenue and Customs has reason to believe that a person—

  (a) has not given a notice which the person is required to give under section 257GE or 257GF in respect of any event, or

  (b) has given or received value within the meaning of section 257FH(2) or (8) which, but for the fact that the amount given or received was an amount of insignificant value, would have triggered a requirement to give such a notice.

(2) The officer may by notice require the person concerned to supply the officer, within such time as the officer may specify in the notice, with such information relating to the event as the officer may reasonably require for the purposes of this Part.

(3) The period specified in a notice under subsection (2) must be at least 60 days.

(4) In subsection (1)(b), the reference to an amount of insignificant value is construed in accordance with section 257FG(2).][1]

Commentary—*Simon's Taxes* **E3.864**.

HMRC Manuals—Venture Capital Schemes Manual VCM36170 (HMRC powers to obtain information).

Amendments—[1]   Part 5A (ss 257A–257HJ) inserted by FA 2012 s 38 Sch 6 para 1 with effect in relation to shares issued on or after 6 April 2012.

[257GH Power to require information in other cases

(1) Subsection (2) applies if SEIS relief is claimed in respect of shares in a company, and an officer of Revenue and Customs has reason to believe that it may not be due because of any such arrangements or scheme as is mentioned in—

  (a) section 257BC (no related investment arrangements),

  (b) section 257BE or 257DB(2) or (4) (no tax avoidance),

  (c) section 257CD(1) (no pre-arranged exits),

  (d) section 257CF (no disqualifying arrangements),

  (e) section 257DB(4) (winding up, administration etc), or

  (f) section 257DG(1) or (2) (conditions ceasing to be met).

(2) The officer may by notice require any person concerned to supply the officer within such time as may be specified in the notice with—

  (a) a declaration in writing stating whether or not, according to the information which that person has or can reasonably obtain, any such arrangement or scheme exists or has existed, and

  (b) such other information as the officer may reasonably require for the purposes of the provision in question and as that person has or can reasonably obtain.

(3) The period specified in a notice under subsection (2) must be at least 60 days.

(4) For the purposes of subsection (2), in a case falling within a provision listed in column 1 of the following table, the person concerned is given by the corresponding entry in column 2 of the table.

Provision	The person concerned
Subsection (1)(a)	The claimant, the company and any person controlling the company
Subsection (1)(b)	The claimant
Subsection (1)(c)	The claimant, the company and any person connected with the company
Subsection (1)(d)	The claimant, the company, any person controlling the company and any person who an officer of Revenue and Customs has reason to believe may be a party to the arrangements in question
Subsection (1)(e)	The claimant, the company, any other company in question and any person controlling the company or any other company in question
Subsection (1)(f)	The company and any person controlling the company

References in this subsection to the claimant include references to any person to whom the claimant appears to have made such a transfer as is mentioned in section 257H (spouses or civil partners) of any of the shares in question.

(5) If SEIS relief has been obtained in respect of shares in a company—

(a) any person who receives from the company any payment or asset which may constitute value received (by the person or another) for the purposes of section 257FE, and

(b) any person on whose behalf such a payment or asset is received,

must, if so required by an officer of Revenue and Customs, state whether the payment or asset so received is received on behalf of any other person and, if so, the name and address of that other person.

(6) If SEIS relief has been claimed in respect of shares in a company—

(a) any person who holds or has held shares in the company, and

(b) any person on whose behalf any such shares are or were held,

must, if so required by an officer of Revenue and Customs, state whether the shares so held are or were held on behalf of any other person and, if so, the name and address of that other person.]¹

Commentary—*Simon's Taxes* **E3.864**.

HMRC Manuals—Venture Capital Schemes Manual VCM36170 (HMRC powers to obtain information).

Amendments—¹ Part 5A (ss 257A–257HJ) inserted by FA 2012 s 38 Sch 6 para 1 with effect in relation to shares issued on or after 6 April 2012.

[257GI Obligations of secrecy

No obligation of secrecy imposed by statute or otherwise prevents an officer of Revenue and Customs from disclosing to a company that SEIS relief has been obtained or claimed in respect of a particular number or proportion of its shares.]¹

Commentary—*Simon's Taxes* **E3.866**.

Amendments—¹ Part 5A (ss 257A–257HJ) inserted by FA 2012 s 38 Sch 6 para 1 with effect in relation to shares issued on or after 6 April 2012.

[CHAPTER 8

SUPPLEMENTARY AND GENERAL]

Amendments—Part 5A (ss 257A–257HJ) inserted by FA 2012 s 38 Sch 6 para 1 with effect in relation to shares issued on or after 6 April 2012.

[Disposals of shares

257H Transfers between spouses or civil partners

(1) This section applies if—

(a) shares to which an amount of SEIS relief is attributable were issued to an individual ("A"),

(b) A transferred the shares to another individual ("B") during their lives,

(c) A was married to, or was the civil partner of, B at the time of the transfer, and

(d) section 257FA (disposal of shares) does not apply to the transfer.

(2) This Part has effect, in relation to any subsequent disposal or other event, as if—

(a) B were the individual who had subscribed for the shares,

(b) the amount that B had subscribed for the shares were the amount that A had subscribed for them,

(c) B's liability to income tax had been reduced in respect of the shares for the same tax year as that for which A's was so reduced,

(d) the amount by which B's liability to income tax had been reduced in respect of the shares were the same as that by which A's liability to income tax had been so reduced, and

(e) that amount of SEIS relief had continued to be attributable to the shares despite the transfer.

(3) If the amount of SEIS relief attributable to the shares had been reduced before the relief was obtained by A—

(a) this Part has effect, in relation to any subsequent disposal or other event, as if the amount of SEIS relief attributable to the shares transferred to B had been correspondingly reduced before the relief was obtained by B, and

(b) sections 257FB(3) and 257FL(2) apply in relation to B as they would have applied in relation to A.

(4) If, because of any such disposal or other event, an assessment for reducing or withdrawing SEIS relief is to be made, the assessment is to be made on B.]¹

Commentary—*Simon's Taxes* **E3.870**.

HMRC Manuals—Venture Capital Schemes Manual VCM37010 (transfers between spouses or civil partners).

Amendments—¹ Part 5A (ss 257A–257HJ) inserted by FA 2012 s 38 Sch 6 para 1 with effect in relation to shares issued on or after 6 April 2012.

[257HA Identification of shares on a disposal

(1) The rules in subsections (2) and (3) are for determining which shares of any class are treated as disposed of for the purposes of—

(a) section 257FA (disposal of shares), or

(b) section 257H (spouses or civil partners),

if the investor disposes of some but not all of the shares of that class which the investor holds in a company.

(2) Shares acquired on an earlier day are treated as disposed of before shares acquired on a later day.

(3) Shares acquired on the same day are treated as disposed of in the following order—
- (a) first any to which no SEIS relief is attributable,
- (b) next any to which SEIS relief (but not SEIS re-investment relief) is attributable, and
- (c) next any to which SEIS relief and SEIS re-investment relief are attributable.

(4) Any shares to which SEIS relief is attributable and which were transferred to an individual as mentioned in section 257H are treated for the purposes of subsections (2) and (3) as acquired by the individual on the day on which they were issued.

(5) In a case to which section 127 of TCGA 1992 applies (including the case where that section applies by virtue of an enactment relating to chargeable gains), shares included in the new holding are treated for the purposes of subsections (2) and (3) as acquired when the original shares were acquired.

(6) In this section—
> "new holding" and "original shares" have the same meaning as in section 127 of TCGA 1992 (or, as the case may be, that section as applied by the enactment concerned);
> "SEIS re-investment relief" means relief under Schedule 5BB to TCGA 1992.]¹

Commentary—*Simon's Taxes* **E3.871**.
HMRC Manuals—Venture Capital Schemes Manual VCM37020 (identification of shares on a disposal)
Amendments—¹   Part 5A (ss 257A–257HJ) inserted by FA 2012 s 38 Sch 6 para 1 with effect in relation to shares issued on or after 6 April 2012.

[Acquisition of issuing company

257HB Continuity of SEIS relief where issuing company is acquired by new company

(1) This section applies if—
- (a) a company ("the new company") in which the only issued shares are subscriber shares acquires all the shares ("old shares") in another company ("the old company"),
- (b) the consideration for the old shares consists wholly of the issue of shares ("new shares") in the new company,
- (c) the consideration for the new shares of each description consists wholly of old shares of the corresponding description,
- (d) new shares of each description are issued to the holders of old shares of the corresponding description in respect of and in proportion to their holdings,
- (e) at some time before the issue of the new shares—
  - (i) the old company issued shares which meet the requirements of section 257CA(2), and
  - (ii) a compliance certificate in respect of those shares was issued by that company for the purposes of subsection (1) of section 257EB and in accordance with section 257EC, and
- (f) before the issue of the new shares the Commissioners for Her Majesty's Revenue and Customs have, on the application of the new company or the old company, notified that company that they are satisfied that the exchange of shares—
  - (i) will be effected for genuine commercial reasons, and
  - (ii) will not form part of any such scheme or arrangements as are mentioned in section 137(1) of TCGA 1992 (schemes with avoidance purposes).

In this subsection references to shares, except in the expressions "subscriber shares" and "shares which meet the requirements of section 257CA(2)", include securities.

(2) Subsection (2) of section 138 of TCGA 1992 (procedure for advance clearance) applies for the purposes of subsection (1)(f) as it applies for the purposes of subsection (1) of that section.

(3) For the purposes of this Part—
- (a) the exchange of shares is not regarded as involving any disposal of the old shares or any acquisition of the new shares, and
- (b) any SEIS relief which is attributable to any old shares is attributable instead to the new shares for which they are exchanged.

(4) Nothing in section 257DG (the control and independence requirement) applies in relation to such an exchange of shares, or shares and securities, as is mentioned in subsection (1), or arrangements with a view to such an exchange.

(5) For the purposes of this section old shares and new shares are of a corresponding description if, on the assumption that they were shares in the same company, they would be of the same class and carry the same rights.

(6) References in sections 257HC and 257HD to "old shares", "new shares", "the old company" and "the new company" are to be read in accordance with this section.]¹

Commentary—*Simon's Taxes* **E3.872**.
HMRC Manuals—Venture Capital Schemes Manual VCM37030 (supplementary and general: acquisition of issuing company).
Amendments—¹   Part 5A (ss 257A–257HJ) inserted by FA 2012 s 38 Sch 6 para 1 with effect in relation to shares issued on or after 6 April 2012.

[257HC Carry over of obligations etc where SEIS relief attributed to new shares

(1) This section applies if, under section 257HB, any SEIS relief which is attributable to any old shares becomes attributable instead to any new shares.

(2) This Part has effect as if anything which under—
  (a) section 257EB(1) (entitlement to claim),
  (b) section 257FR(3) (relief subsequently found not to be due), or
  (c) sections 257GF to 257GH (information to be provided),
has been done, or is required to be done, by or in relation to the old company had been done, or were required to be done, by or in relation to the new company.
(3) Any appeal brought by the old company against a notice under section 257FR(3)(b) may be prosecuted by the new company as if it had been brought by that company.][1]

Commentary—*Simon's Taxes* E3.872.
HMRC Manuals—Venture Capital Schemes Manual VCM37030 (supplementary and general: acquisition of issuing company).
Amendments—[1]   Part 5A (ss 257A–257HJ) inserted by FA 2012 s 38 Sch 6 para 1 with effect in relation to shares issued on or after 6 April 2012.

[257HD Substitution of new shares for old shares
(1) Subsection (2) applies if, in the case of any new shares held by an individual to which SEIS relief becomes attributable under section 257HB, the old shares for which they were exchanged were subscribed for by and issued to the individual.
(2) This Part has effect as if—
  (a) the new shares had been subscribed for by the individual at the time when, and for the amount for which, the old shares were subscribed for by the individual,
  (b) the new shares had been issued to the individual by the new company at the time when the old shares were issued to the individual by the old company,
  (c) the claim for SEIS relief made in respect of the old shares had been made in respect of the new shares, and
  (d) the individual's liability to income tax had been reduced in respect of the new shares for the same tax year as that for which the individual's liability was so reduced in respect of the old shares.
(3) Subsection (4) applies if, in the case of any new shares held by an individual to which SEIS relief becomes so attributable under section 257HB, the old shares for which they were exchanged were transferred to the individual as mentioned in section 257H.
(4) This Part has effect in relation to any subsequent disposal or other event as if—
  (a) the new shares had been subscribed for by the individual at the time when, and for the amount for which, the old shares were subscribed for,
  (b) the new shares had been issued by the new company at the time when the old shares were issued by the old company,
  (c) the claim for SEIS relief made in respect of the old shares had been made in respect of the new shares, and
  (d) the individual's liability to income tax had been reduced in respect of the new shares for the same tax year as that for which the liability of the individual who subscribed for the old shares was so reduced in respect of those shares.][1]

Commentary—*Simon's Taxes* E3.872.
HMRC Manuals—Venture Capital Schemes Manual VCM37030 (supplementary and general: acquisition of issuing company).
Amendments—[1]   Part 5A (ss 257A–257HJ) inserted by FA 2012 s 38 Sch 6 para 1 with effect in relation to shares issued on or after 6 April 2012.

[Nominees etc

257HE Nominees and bare trustees
(1) Shares subscribed for, issued to, held by or disposed of for an individual by a nominee are treated for the purposes of this Part as subscribed for, issued to, held by or disposed of by the individual.
(2) If shares have been issued to a bare trust for two or more beneficiaries, this Part has effect (with the necessary modifications) as if—
  (a) each beneficiary had subscribed as an individual for all of those shares, and
  (b) the amount subscribed by each beneficiary was equal to the total amount subscribed on the issue of those shares divided by the number of beneficiaries.
(3) In subsection (2) "shares" means shares which meet the requirements of section 257CA(2).][1]

Commentary—*Simon's Taxes* E3.873.
HMRC Manuals—Venture Capital Schemes Manual VCM37040 (nominees and bare trustees).
Amendments—[1]   Part 5A (ss 257A–257HJ) inserted by FA 2012 s 38 Sch 6 para 1 with effect in relation to shares issued on or after 6 April 2012.

[Interpretation

257HF Meaning of "new qualifying trade"
(1) For the purposes of this Part a qualifying trade carried on by the issuing company or a qualifying 90% subsidiary of that company ("the relevant company") is a "new qualifying trade" if (and only if)—
  (a) the trade does not begin to be carried on (whether by the relevant company or any other person) before the two year pre-investment period, and

(b) at no time before the relevant company begins to carry on the trade was any other trade being carried on by the issuing company or by any company that was a 51% subsidiary of the issuing company at the time in question.

(2) In this section—

"qualifying trade" has the same meaning as in Part 5 (see sections 189 and 192 to 200);

"two year pre-investment period" means the period of 2 years ending immediately before the day on which the relevant shares are issued.][1]

Commentary—*Simon's Taxes* **E3.826**.

HMRC Manuals—Venture Capital Schemes Manual VCM13060 (meaning of 'qualifying trade').

Amendments—[1]   Part 5A (ss 257A–257HJ) inserted by FA 2012 s 38 Sch 6 para 1 with effect in relation to shares issued on or after 6 April 2012.

[257HG Meaning of "qualifying business activity"

(1) In this Part "qualifying business activity", in relation to the issuing company, means—

  (a) activity A, or

  (b) activity B,

if it is carried on by the company or a qualifying 90% subsidiary of the company.

This is subject to subsection (3).

(2) Activity A is—

  (a) the carrying on of a new qualifying trade which, on the date the relevant shares are issued, the company or a qualifying 90% subsidiary of the company is carrying on, or

  (b) the activity of preparing to carry on (or preparing to carry on and then carrying on) a new qualifying trade—

    (i) which, on that date, is intended to be carried on by the company or such a subsidiary, and

    (ii) which is begun to be carried on by the company or such a subsidiary.

(3) Activity B is the carrying on of research and development—

  (a) which, on the date the relevant shares are issued, the company or a qualifying 90% subsidiary of the company is carrying on, or which the company or such a subsidiary begins to carry on immediately afterwards, and

  (b) from which, on that date, it is intended—

    (i) that a new qualifying trade which the company or such a subsidiary will carry on will be derived, or

    (ii) that a new qualifying trade which the company or such a subsidiary is carrying on, or will carry on, will benefit.

(4) For the purposes of subsection (3)(a), when research and development is begun to be carried on by a qualifying 90% subsidiary of the issuing company, any carrying on of the research and development by it before it became such a subsidiary is ignored.

(5) References in subsection (2)(b)(i) or (3)(b) to a qualifying 90% subsidiary of the issuing company include references to any existing or future company which will be such a subsidiary at any future time.][1]

Commentary—*Simon's Taxes* **E3.828, E3.817**.

HMRC Manuals—Venture Capital Schemes Manual VCM33050 (meaning of 'qualifying business activity').

Amendments—[1]   Part 5A (ss 257A–257HJ) inserted by FA 2012 s 38 Sch 6 para 1 with effect in relation to shares issued on or after 6 April 2012.

[257HH Meaning of "disposal of shares"

(1) In this Part references to a disposal of shares include a reference to a disposal of an interest or right in or over shares.

(2) An individual is to be treated, for the purposes of this Part, as disposing of any shares which the individual is treated by virtue of section 136 of TCGA 1992 as exchanging for other shares.][1]

Commentary—*Simon's Taxes* **E3.802**.

HMRC Manuals—Venture Capital Schemes Manual VCM36020 (SEIS: disposal of shares).

Amendments—[1]   Part 5A (ss 257A–257HJ) inserted by FA 2012 s 38 Sch 6 para 1 with effect in relation to shares issued on or after 6 April 2012.

[257HI Meaning of "issue of shares"

(1) In this Part—

  (a) references (however expressed) to an issue of shares in any company are to such of the shares in the company as are of the same class and issued on the same day, and

  (b) references (however expressed) to an issue of shares in any company to an individual are to such of the shares in the company as are of the same class and are issued to the individual in one capacity on the same day.

(2) Subsection (1)(b) has effect subject to sections 257E(6), 257EA(2), 257FB(2) and 257FK(1).][1]

Commentary—*Simon's Taxes* **E3.802**.

Amendments—[1]   Part 5A (ss 257A–257HJ) inserted by FA 2012 s 38 Sch 6 para 1 with effect in relation to shares issued on or after 6 April 2012.

[257HJ Minor definitions

(1) In this Part—

"arrangements" includes any scheme, agreement, understanding, transaction or series of transactions (whether or not legally enforceable);

"associate" has the same meaning as in Part 5 (see section 253);

"bonus shares" means shares which are issued otherwise than for payment (whether in cash or otherwise);

"director" is read in accordance with section 452 of CTA 2010;

"EIS relief" means relief under Part 5;

"group" means a parent company and its qualifying subsidiaries;

"group company", in relation to a group, means the parent company or any of its qualifying subsidiaries;

"ordinary shares" means shares forming part of a company's ordinary share capital;

"parent company" means a company that has one or more qualifying subsidiaries, and "single company" means a company that does not;

"permanent establishment" has the same meaning as in Part 5 (see section 191A);

"qualifying subsidiary" has the same meaning as in Part 5 (see section 191);

"qualifying 90% subsidiary" has the same meaning as in Part 5 (see section 190);

"research and development" has the meaning given by section 1006.

(2) Section 252 (meaning of a company being "in administration" or "in receivership") applies for the purposes of this Part.

(3) Section 995 (control) does not apply for the purposes of the following provisions—

(a) section 257DG(1)(a),

(b) section 257FP,

(c) section 257FQ,

(d) section 257GH(4);

and in those provisions "control" is to be read in accordance with sections 450 and 451 of CTA 2010.

(4) In this Part—

(a) references in any provision to the reduction of any SEIS relief attributable to any shares include a reference—

(i) to the reduction of the relief to nil, and

(ii) if no relief has yet been obtained, to the reduction of the amount which apart from that provision would be the SEIS relief, and

(b) references to the withdrawal of SEIS relief in respect of any shares are—

(i) to the withdrawal of the SEIS relief attributable to those shares, or

(ii) if no relief has yet been obtained, to ceasing to be eligible for SEIS relief in respect of those shares.

(5) For the purposes of this Part shares in a company are not treated as being of the same class unless they would be so treated if dealt in on a recognised stock exchange.

(6) For the purposes of this Part the market value at any time of any asset is the price which it might reasonably be expected to fetch on a sale at that time in the open market free from any interest or right which exists by way of security in or over it.

(7) In this Part—

(a) references to SEIS relief obtained by an individual in respect of any shares include a reference to SEIS relief obtained by the individual in respect of those shares at any time after the individual has disposed of them, and

(b) references to the withdrawal or reduction of SEIS relief obtained by an individual in respect of any shares include a reference to the withdrawal or reduction of SEIS relief obtained by the individual in respect of those shares at any time.

(8) In the case of requirements that cannot be met until a future date, references in this Part to requirements being met for the time being are to nothing having occurred to prevent their being met.][1]

Amendments—[1]   Part 5A (ss 257A–257HJ) inserted by FA 2012 s 38 Sch 6 para 1 with effect in relation to shares issued on or after 6 April 2012.

[PART 5B
TAX RELIEF FOR SOCIAL INVESTMENTS]

Commentary—*Simon's Taxes* **E3.901.**

Amendments—Part 5B (ss 257J–257TE) inserted by FA 2014 s 57 Sch 11 para 1 with effect from 17 July 2014.

[CHAPTER 1

INTRODUCTION

[257J Meaning of "SI relief" and "social enterprise"

(1) This Part provides for income tax relief for social investments ("SI relief"), that is, entitlement to tax reductions in respect of amounts invested in social enterprises by individuals.

(2) In this Part "social enterprise" means—

    (a) a community interest company,

    (b) a community benefit society (see section 257JB) that is not a charity,

    (c) a charity,

    (d) an accredited social impact contractor (see section 257JD), or

    (e) any other body prescribed, or of a description prescribed, by an order made by the Treasury.

(3) An order under subsection (2)(e) may make provision as to the bodies which are social enterprises for the purposes of this Part at times before the order comes into force or FA 2014 is passed but, where a body is a social enterprise for the purposes of this Part as a result of an order under subsection (2)(e) that has come into force, no subsequent order under subsection (2)(e) may undo that result in respect of times before the subsequent order comes into force.][1]

Amendments—[1]   Part 5B (ss 257J–257TE) inserted by FA 2014 s 57 Sch 11 para 1 with effect from 17 July 2014.

[257JA Form and amount of relief

(1) If an individual—

    (a) is eligible for SI relief in respect of any amount, and

    (b) makes a claim in respect of all or some of the amount,

the individual is entitled to a tax reduction for the tax year in which the amount was invested.

   This is subject to the provisions of this Part.

(2) The amount of the reduction to which an individual is entitled under this Part for any particular tax year is the amount equal to tax, at the SI rate for that year, on—

    (a) the amount or, as the case may be, the sum of the amounts invested in that year in respect of which the individual is eligible for and claims SI relief, or

    (b) if less, £1 million.

(3) The tax reduction is given effect at Step 6 in section 23.

(4) If an individual—

    (a) is eligible for and claims SI relief in respect of an amount, and

    (b) makes a claim for part of that amount to be treated for the purposes of subsections (1) and (2) as if it had been invested not in the tax year in which it was actually invested but in the preceding tax year,

those subsections apply, and the individual's liability to tax for both tax years is determined, in accordance with the claim.

(5) In this Part "the SI rate" means 30%.][1]

Commentary—*Simon's Taxes* **E3.901.**

Amendments—[1]   Part 5B (ss 257J–257TE) inserted by FA 2014 s 57 Sch 11 para 1 with effect from 17 July 2014.

[257JB Meaning of "community benefit society"

(1) In this Part "community benefit society" means a body that—

    (a) is registered as a community benefit society under the 2014 Act,

    (b) is a pre-commencement society (within the meaning of the 2014 Act) that meets the condition in section 2(2)(a)(ii) of the 2014 Act, or

    (c) is a society registered, or treated as registered, under section 1 of the Industrial and Provident Societies Act (Northern Ireland) 1969 in the case of which the condition in section 1(2)(b) of that Act is fulfilled,

and in respect of which the condition in subsection (2) is met.

(2) The condition is that—

    (a) the body is of a kind prescribed by regulation 5 of, and

    (b) the body's rules include a rule in the terms set out in Schedule 1 to,

the Community Benefit Societies (Restriction on Use of Assets) Regulations 2006 (SI 2006/264) or the Community Benefit Societies (Restriction on Use of Assets) Regulations (Northern Ireland) 2006 (S.R. 2006/258).

(3) The Treasury may by order amend this section for the purpose of—

    (a) replacing—

       (i) the condition in subsection (2), or

       (ii) the condition, or all or any of the conditions, for the time being replacing the condition in subsection (2),

    with one or more other conditions;

    (b) varying—

       (i) the condition in subsection (2), or

(ii) the condition, or any of the conditions, for the time being replacing the condition in subsection (2);

(c) dispensing with—

(i) the condition in subsection (2), or

(ii) the condition, or all or any of the conditions, for the time being replacing the condition in subsection (2).

(4) In this section—

"the 2014 Act" means the Co-operative and Community Benefit Societies Act 2014;

"the 2010 Act" means the Co-operative and Community Benefit Societies and Credit Unions Act 2010.

(5) While neither the 2014 Act, nor section 1 of the 2010 Act, is in force, subsection (1) of this section has effect as if for paragraphs (a) and (b) of that subsection there were substituted—

"(a)   is a society registered, or treated as registered, under section 1 of the Industrial and Provident Societies Act 1965 in the case of which the condition in section 1(2)(b) of that Act is fulfilled, or".

(6) If section 1 of the 2010 Act (registration of societies) comes into force before the 2014 Act comes into force then, with effect from the coming into force of that section and until the coming into force of the 2014 Act, subsection (1) of this section has effect as if for paragraphs (a) and (b) of that subsection there were substituted—

"(a)   is registered as a community benefit society under section 1 of the Industrial and Provident Societies Act 1965 ("the 1965 Act"),

(b)   is a pre-2010 Act society (as defined by section 4A(1) of the 1965 Act) that meets the condition in section 1(3) of the 1965 Act, or".

(7) In the event that section 2 of the 2010 Act (renaming of the 1965 Act) is brought into force before its repeal by the 2014 Act takes effect then, with effect from the coming into force of that section, subsections (5) and (6) of this section have effect as if, in the provisions which they substitute, the references to the Industrial and Provident Societies Act 1965 were references to the Co-operative and Community Benefit Societies and Credit Unions Act 1965.][1]

Amendments—[1]   Part 5B (ss 257J–257TE) inserted by FA 2014 s 57 Sch 11 para 1 with effect from 17 July 2014.

[257JC Charities that are trusts

In this Part (except section 257JD), a reference to a company includes a reference to a charity that is a trust.][1]

Commentary—*Simon's Taxes* **E3.902.**
Amendments—[1]   Part 5B (ss 257J–257TE) inserted by FA 2014 s 57 Sch 11 para 1 with effect from 17 July 2014.

[257JD Accreditation as a social impact contractor

(1) In this Part "accredited social impact contractor" means a company limited by shares that is accredited under this section as a social impact contractor.

(2) Applications for accreditation as a social impact contractor must be made to a Minister of the Crown in the form and manner specified by a Minister of the Crown.

(3) A Minister of the Crown is to accredit a company if, but only if, that Minister is satisfied that—

(a) the company has entered into a social impact contract (see section 257JE),

(b) the company is, and at all times since its incorporation has been, established—

(i) for the purpose of entering into and carrying out a social impact contract, or for that purpose and purposes incidental to it, but

(ii) for no other purpose, and

(c) the activities of the company in carrying out that contract will not consist wholly, or as to a substantial part, in excluded activities (see section 257MQ).

(4) If a Minister of the Crown is satisfied that the condition in subsection (3)(b) or (c) has ceased to be met in relation to a company that is an accredited social impact contractor, that Minister is to withdraw the company's accreditation with effect from the time the condition ceased to be met or a later time.][1]

Commentary—*Simon's Taxes* **E3.902.**
Amendments—[1]   Part 5B (ss 257J–257TE) inserted by FA 2014 s 57 Sch 11 para 1 with effect from 17 July 2014.

[257JE Meaning of "social impact contract"

(1) In this Part "social impact contract" means a contract that meets such criteria as may be specified in regulations made by the Treasury.

(2) The criteria which may be specified under subsection (1) include, in particular, criteria as to a party to the contract other than the company seeking accreditation.

(3) Criteria may be specified in regulations under subsection (1) by reference to material published by, or on behalf of, a Minister of the Crown after the making of the regulations (as well as by reference to material published before the making of the regulations).

(4) Regulations under subsection (1) may make different provision for different cases or circumstances or in relation to different areas.][1]

Commentary—*Simon's Taxes* **E3.902**.
Regulations—Tax Relief for Social Investments (Accreditation of Social Impact Contractor) Regulations, SI 2014/3066.
Tax Relief for Social Investments (Accreditation of Social Impact Contractor) (Amendment) Regulations, SI 2015/2051.
Amendments—[1]   Part 5B (ss 257J–257TE) inserted by FA 2014 s 57 Sch 11 para 1 with effect from 17 July 2014.

[257JF Accreditations: supplementary provisions

(1) An accreditation must be made so as to be conditional on compliance with—

    (*a*) any requirements imposed by or under regulations, and

    (*b*) any other requirements considered appropriate by the Minister of the Crown who is accrediting the company concerned.

(2) The requirements that may be imposed by virtue of subsection (1) include requirements relating to the provision of information.

(3) Regulations may—

    (*a*) make further provision about applications for accreditation,

    (*b*) make provision for the variation of an accreditation (including its provisions as to its duration),

    (*c*) make provision which, in a case where a company is or has been an accredited social impact contractor, imposes or authorises the imposition of requirements on the company, or on any other party to the social impact contract concerned, to provide information,

    (*d*) make provision about the consequences of a failure to comply with any requirement of an accreditation imposed by virtue of subsection (1) or with any requirement imposed by virtue of paragraph (*c*), including in particular—

        (i) provision for the withdrawal of the accreditation concerned with effect from the time of the failure or a later time, and

        (ii) provision for the imposition of penalties,

    (*e*) make provision for publication of information about an accreditation or accredited social impact contractor, and

    (*f*) make provision for reviews of, or for appeals to the tribunal against, any of the following—

        (i) a refusal to grant or vary an accreditation,

        (ii) the imposition of a requirement under subsection (1)(*b*),

        (iii) the withdrawal of an accreditation (whether under section 257JD(4) or by virtue of provision made under paragraph (*d*)(i)), and

        (iv) the imposition or amount of a penalty imposed by virtue of provision made under paragraph (*d*)(ii).

(4) Regulations under subsection (1) or (3) may—

    (*a*) make provision for the making of decisions by a Minister of the Crown as to any matter required to be decided for the purposes of the regulations,

    (*b*) be framed by reference to material published by, or on behalf of, a Minister of the Crown after the making of the regulations (as well as by reference to material published before the making of the regulations),

    (*c*) make different provision for different cases or circumstances or in relation to different areas, and

    (*d*) contain incidental, supplemental, consequential and transitional provision and savings.

(5) In this section—

    "accreditation" means accreditation under section 257JD, and

    "regulations" means regulations made by the Treasury.][1]

Commentary—*Simon's Taxes* **E3.902**.
Regulations—Tax Relief for Social Investments (Accreditation of Social Impact Contractor) Regulations, SI 2014/3066.
Tax Relief for Social Investments (Accreditation of Social Impact Contractor) (Amendment) Regulations, SI 2015/2051.
Amendments—[1]   Part 5B (ss 257J–257TE) inserted by FA 2014 s 57, Sch 11 para 1 with effect from 17 July 2014.

[257JG Period of accreditation as a social impact contractor

(1) An accreditation under section 257JD has effect for a period—

    (*a*) beginning with the day specified in the accreditation, and

    (*b*) of a length specified in, or determined in accordance with, the accreditation.

(2) The day specified under subsection (1)(*a*) in an accreditation may not be earlier than 6 April 2014 but subject to that—

    (*a*) may be, or be earlier than, the day it is decided to grant the accreditation (and in particular may be, or be earlier than, the day the application for the accreditation is made), and

    (*b*) may be earlier than the day section 257JD comes into force.

(3) This section has effect subject to sections 257JD(4) and 257JF(3)(*d*)(i) (withdrawal of accreditations).][1]

Commentary—*Simon's Taxes* **E3.902**.
Amendments—[1]   Part 5B (ss 257J–257TE) inserted by FA 2014 s 57, Sch 11 para 1 with effect from 17 July 2014.

[257JH Functions of Ministers of the Crown under sections 257JD to 257JG
(1) A Minister of the Crown may delegate any function given to a Minister of the Crown by or under sections 257JD to 257JG other than a power of the Treasury to make regulations.
(2) In those sections and this section "Minister of Crown" has the meaning given by section 8(1) of the Ministers of the Crown Act 1975.]¹

Commentary—*Simon's Taxes* E3.902.
Amendments—¹   Part 5B (ss 257J–257TE) inserted by FA 2014 s 57, Sch 11 para 1 with effect from 17 July 2014.

[CHAPTER 2

ELIGIBILITY FOR RELIEF: BASIC RULE AND KEY DEFINITIONS]

Commentary—*Simon's Taxes* E3.905.
Amendments—Part 5B (ss 257J–257TE) inserted by FA 2014 s 57 Sch 11 para 1 with effect from 17 July 2014.
[Eligibility

257K Eligibility for SI relief
(1) An individual ("the investor") who invests in a social enterprise is eligible for SI relief in respect of the amount invested if—
    (*a*) the investment is made—
        (i) by the investor on the investor's own behalf,
        (ii) on or after 6 April 2014, and
        (iii) before [6 April 2021]² (but see subsection (5)), and
    (*b*) the conditions set out in Chapters 3 and 4 are met.
(2) Subsection (1)(*b*) is subject to the provisions in sections 257LB and 257MJ to 257MN which provide for conditions set out in those sections not to apply where the social enterprise is an accredited social impact contractor.
(3) The investor is not eligible for SI relief in respect of the amount invested if—
    (*a*) the investor has obtained in respect of that amount, or any part of it, relief under—
        (i) Part 5 (enterprise investment scheme),
        (ii) Part 5A (seed enterprise investment scheme), or
        (iii) Part 7 (community investment tax relief), or
    (*b*) that amount, or any part of it, has under Schedule 5B to TCGA 1992 (enterprise investment scheme: re-investment) been set against a chargeable gain.
(4) Investments made by, subscribed for, issued to, held by or disposed of for an individual by a nominee are treated for the purposes of this Part as made by, subscribed for, issued to, held by or disposed of by the individual.
(5) The Treasury may by order substitute a later date for the date for time being specified in subsection (1)(*a*)(iii).]¹

Commentary—*Simon's Taxes* E3.901.
Amendments—¹   Part 5B (ss 257J–257TE) inserted by FA 2014 s 57, Sch 11 para 1 with effect from 17 July 2014.
²   In sub-s (1)(*a*)(iii), date substituted for date "6 April 2019" by F(No 2)A 2017 s 14, Sch 1 paras 1, 2 with effect from 16 November 2017.

[Key definitions

257KA Key to reading the rest of the Part
In the following provisions of this Part (except section 257N), a reference to—
    "the amount invested",
    "the investment",
    "the investor", or
    "the social enterprise",
is to be read in accordance with section 257K(1).]¹

Amendments—¹   Part 5B (ss 257J–257TE) inserted by FA 2014 s 57 Sch 11 para 1 with effect from 17 July 2014.

[257KB When investment is made, and "investment date"
(1) For the purposes of this Part "the investment date" means the date on which the investment is made.
(2) So far as the investment is in shares, for the purposes of this Part it is made when the shares are issued to the investor by the social enterprise.
(3) If the investment, so far as it is in qualifying debt investments (see section 257L), involves making the only advance covered by the debenture or debentures concerned, for the purposes of this Part it is made—
    (*a*) when the social enterprise issues the debenture or debentures to the investor, or
    (*b*) in a case where there is to be no such issuing, when the debenture or debentures, so far as relating to the advance, take effect between the social enterprise and the investor.
(4) If the investment, so far as it is in qualifying debt investments, involves making the first of multiple advances covered by the debenture or debentures concerned, for the purposes of this Part it is made—

(a) when the social enterprise issues the debenture or debentures to the investor, or

(b) in a case where there is to be no such issuing, when the debenture or debentures, so far as relating to all of those advances, take effect between the social enterprise and the investor.

(5) If the investment, so far as it is in qualifying debt investments, involves making the second of multiple advances covered by the debenture or debentures concerned, or a subsequent one of those advances, for the purposes of this Part it is made—

(a) when the amount of that advance is fully advanced in cash, or

(b) if later—

   (i) when the social enterprise issues the debenture or debentures to the investor, or

   (ii) in a case where there is to be no such issuing, when the debenture or debentures, so far as relating to all of those advances, takes effect between the social enterprise and the investor.

(6) For the purposes of subsections (3) to (5) "debenture" includes any instrument creating or acknowledging indebtedness.][1]

Commentary—*Simon's Taxes* E3.902.
Amendments—[1]   Part 5B (ss 257J–257TE) inserted by FA 2014 s 57 Sch 11 para 1 with effect from 17 July 2014.

[257KC "Shorter applicable period" and "longer applicable period"

(1) In this Part "the shorter applicable period" and "the longer applicable period" have the meaning given by this section.

(2) The shorter applicable period begins with the investment date.

(3) The longer applicable period begins with—

(a) the day on which the social enterprise is—

   (i) incorporated (if it is a body corporate), or

   (ii) established (in any other case), or

(b) if later, the day whose first anniversary is the investment date.

(4) Each of the periods ends with the third anniversary of the investment date.][1]

Commentary—*Simon's Taxes* E3.902.
Amendments—[1]   Part 5B (ss 257J–257TE) inserted by FA 2014 s 57 Sch 11 para 1 with effect from 17 July 2014.

[CHAPTER 3

ELIGIBILITY: CONDITIONS RELATING TO THE INVESTOR AND THE INVESTMENT]

Commentary—*Simon's Taxes* E3.905.
Amendments—Part 5B (ss 257J–257TE) inserted by FA 2014 s 57 Sch 11 para 1 with effect from 17 July 2014.

[257L Investment to be in new shares or new qualifying debt investments

(1) At all times during the shorter applicable period, the investment must be in—

(a) shares that meet conditions A and B and are issued to the investor by the social enterprise in return for the amount invested, or

(b) qualifying debt investments of which the investor is the holder in return for advancing the amount invested to the social enterprise.

(2) Condition A is that the shares must carry none of the following—

(a) a right to a return which, or any part of which, is a fixed amount;

(b) a right to a return which, or any part of which, is at a fixed rate;

(c) a right to a return which, or any part of which, is otherwise fixed by reference to the amount invested;

(d) a right to a return which, or any part of which, is fixed by reference to some other factor that is not contingent on successful financial performance by the social enterprise;

(e) a right to a return at a rate greater than a reasonable commercial rate.

(3) Condition B is that, for the purpose of determining the amounts due in respect of the shares to their holder in the event of the winding-up of the social enterprise—

(a) those amounts rank after all debts of the social enterprise except any due to holders of qualifying debt investments in the social enterprise in respect of their qualifying debt investments, and

(b) the shares do not rank above any other shares in the social enterprise.

(4) In this Part "qualifying debt investments", in relation to the social enterprise, means any debentures of the social enterprise in respect of which the following conditions are met—

(a) neither the principal of the debt concerned, nor any return on that, is charged on any assets,

(b) the rate of any such return is not greater than a reasonable commercial rate of return, and

(c) in the event of the winding-up of the social enterprise and so far as the law allows, any sums due in respect of the debt (whether principal or return)—

   (i) are subordinated to all other debts of the social enterprise except sums due in the case of other unsecured debentures of the social enterprise which rank equally,

   (ii) rank equally, if there are shares in the social enterprise and they all rank equally among themselves, with amounts due to share-holders in respect of their shares, and

(iii) rank equally, if there are shares in the social enterprise and they do not all rank equally, with amounts due in respect of their shares to the holders of shares that do not rank above any other shares.

(5) The condition in subsection (3)(*a*) or (4)(*c*)(i) is met even if the sums concerned do not rank after debts which are postponed—

(*a*) by rules under section 411 of the Insolvency Act 1986, or

(*b*) by or under any other enactment.

(6) For the purposes of subsection (4) "debenture" includes any instrument creating or acknowledging indebtedness.]¹

Commentary—*Simon's Taxes* E3.905.
Amendments—¹ Part 5B (ss 257J–257TE) inserted by FA 2014 s 57 Sch 11 para 1 with effect from 17 July 2014.

[257LA Condition that the amount invested must have been paid over

(1) So far as the investment is in shares—

(*a*) the shares must be subscribed for wholly in cash, and

(*b*) must be fully paid up at the time they are issued.

(2) If the investment, so far as it is in qualifying debt investments, involves making—

(*a*) the only advance covered by the debenture or debentures concerned, or

(*b*) one of multiple advances covered by the debenture or debentures concerned,

the full amount of that advance must have been advanced wholly in cash by the time the investment is made.

(3) For the purposes of this section—

(*a*) shares are not fully paid up, or

(*b*) the full nominal amount of qualifying debt investments has not been advanced,

if there is any undertaking to pay cash to any person at a future time in respect of the acquisition of the shares or investments.

(4) For the purposes of subsection (2) "debenture" includes any instrument creating or acknowledging indebtedness.]¹

Commentary—*Simon's Taxes* E3.905.
Amendments—¹ Part 5B (ss 257J–257TE) inserted by FA 2014 s 57 Sch 11 para 1 with effect from 17 July 2014.

[257LB The no pre-arranged exits requirements

(1) There must not at any time in the shorter applicable period be any arrangements in existence for the investment to be redeemed, repaid, repurchased, exchanged or otherwise disposed of in that period.

(2) The issuing arrangements for the investment must not include—

(*a*) arrangements for or with a view to the cessation of any trade which is being or is to be or may be carried on by the social enterprise or a person connected with the social enterprise, or

(*b*) arrangements for the disposal of, or of a substantial amount (in terms of value) of, the assets of the social enterprise or of a person connected with the social enterprise.

(3) The arrangements referred to in subsection (2)(*a*) and (*b*) do not include any arrangements applicable only on the winding-up of a company except in a case where—

(*a*) the issuing arrangements include arrangements for the company to be wound up, or

(*b*) the arrangements are applicable on the winding-up of the company otherwise than for genuine commercial reasons.

(4) In this section "the issuing arrangements" means—

(*a*) the arrangements under which the investor makes the investment, and

(*b*) any arrangements made before, and in relation to or in connection with, the making of the investment by the investor.]¹

(5) Subsections (2) to (4) do not apply if the social enterprise is an accredited social impact contractor.

Commentary—*Simon's Taxes* E3.905.
Amendments—¹ Part 5B (ss 257J–257TE) inserted by FA 2014 s 57, Sch 11 para 1 with effect from 17 July 2014.

[257LC The no risk avoidance requirement

(1) There must not at any time in the shorter applicable period be any arrangements in existence the main purpose or one of the main purposes of which is (by means of any insurance, indemnity, guarantee, hedging of risk or otherwise) to provide partial or complete protection for the investor against what would otherwise be the risks attached to making the investment.

(2) The arrangements referred to in subsection (1) do not include any arrangements which are confined to the provision—

(*a*) for the social enterprise itself, or

(*b*) if the social enterprise is a parent company that meets the trading requirement in section 257MJ(2)(*c*) or is a parent company that is an accredited social impact contractor—

(i) for the social enterprise itself,

(ii) for the social enterprise itself and one or more of its subsidiaries, or

(iii) for one or more of the subsidiaries of the social enterprise, of any such protection against the risks arising in the course of carrying on its business as might reasonably be expected to be provided in normal commercial circumstances.][1]

Commentary—*Simon's Taxes* E3.905.
Amendments—[1]   Part 5B (ss 257J–257TE) inserted by FA 2014 s 57, Sch 11 para 1 with effect from 17 July 2014.

[257LD The no linked loans requirement

(1) No linked loan is to be made by any person, at any time in the longer applicable period, to the investor or an associate of the investor.
(2) In this section "linked loan" means any loan which—
  (*a*) would not have been made, or
  (*b*) would not have been made on the same terms,
if the investor had not made the investment, or had not been proposing to do so.
(3) References in this section to the making by any person of a loan to the investor or an associate of the investor include—
  (*a*) references to the giving by that person of any credit to the investor or any associate of the investor, and
  (*b*) references to the assignment to that person of a debt due from the investor or any associate of the investor.][1]

Commentary—*Simon's Taxes* E3.905.
Amendments—[1]   Part 5B (ss 257J–257TE) inserted by FA 2014 s 57 Sch 11 para 1 with effect from 17 July 2014.

[257LDA The existing investments requirement

(1) If at the time immediately before the investment is made the investor holds any shares in or debentures of—
  (*a*) the social enterprise, or
  (*b*) a company which at that time is a qualifying subsidiary of the social enterprise,
those shares or debentures must be risk finance investments or (in the case of shares) permitted subscriber shares.
(2) A share or debenture is a "risk finance investment" for the purposes of this section if—
  (*a*) it is a share that was issued to the investor, or a debenture of which the investor is the holder in return for advancing an amount, and
  (*b*) at any time, a compliance statement under section 205, 257ED or 257PB is provided in respect of it or of shares or investments including it.
(3) Subscriber shares are "permitted subscriber shares" for the purposes of this section if—
  (*a*) they were issued to the investor and have been continuously held by the investor since they were issued, or
  (*b*) they were acquired by the investor at a time when the company which issued them—
    (i) had issued no shares other than subscriber shares, and
    (ii) had not begun to carry on or make preparations for carrying on any trade or business.
(4) In this section "debenture" is to be read in accordance with section 257L(6).][1]

Amendments—[1]   Section 257LDA inserted by F(No 2)A 2017 s 14, Sch 1 paras 1, 3 with effect in relation to investments made on or after 6 April 2017.

[257LE The no tax avoidance requirement

The investment must not be made as part of any arrangements the main purpose or one of the main purposes of which is the avoidance of tax.][1]

Commentary—*Simon's Taxes* E3.905, E3.931.
Amendments—[1]   Part 5B (ss 257J–257TE) inserted by FA 2014 s 57 Sch 11 para 1 with effect from 17 July 2014.

[257LEA The no disqualifying arrangements requirement

(1) The investment must not be made, and money raised by the social enterprise from the making of the investment must not be employed,—
  (*a*) in consequence or anticipation of disqualifying arrangements, or
  (*b*) otherwise in connection with disqualifying arrangements.
(2) Arrangements are "disqualifying arrangements" if—
  (*a*) the main purpose, or one of the main purposes, of the arrangements is to secure both that an activity is or will be carried on by the social enterprise or a 90% social subsidiary of the social enterprise and that—
    (i) one or more persons (whether or not including any party to the arrangements) may obtain relevant tax relief in respect of a qualifying investment which raises money for the purposes of that activity, or
    (ii) shares issued by the social enterprise which raise money for the purposes of that activity may comprise part of the qualifying holdings of a VCT,
  (*b*) that activity is the relevant qualifying activity, and
  (*c*) one or both of conditions A and B are met.

(3) Condition A is that, as a (direct or indirect) result of the money raised by the investment being employed as required by section 257MM, an amount representing the whole or the majority of the amount raised is, in the course of the arrangements, paid to or for the benefit of a relevant person or relevant persons.

(4) Condition B is that, in the absence of the arrangements, it would have been reasonable to expect that the whole or greater part of the component activities of the relevant qualifying activity would have been carried on as part of another business by a relevant person or relevant persons.

(5) For the purposes of this section it is immaterial whether the social enterprise is a party to the arrangements.

(6) In this section—

"90% social subsidiary" is to be read in accordance with section 257MV;

"component activities" means the carrying on of a qualifying trade or preparing to carry on such a trade, which constitutes the relevant qualifying activity;

a "qualifying investment" means—

(*a*) shares in the social enterprise, or

(*b*) a qualifying debt investment in the social enterprise (see section 257L);

"qualifying holdings", in relation to the social enterprise, is to be construed in accordance with section 286 (VCTs: qualifying holdings);

"relevant person" means a person who is a party to the arrangements or a person connected with such a party;

"relevant qualifying activity" means the qualifying trade or activity mentioned in section 257ML(1) for the purposes of which the investment raised money;

"relevant tax relief" has the meaning given by subsection (7).

(7) "Relevant tax relief"—

(*a*) in relation to a qualifying debt investment, means SI relief in respect of that investment;

(*b*) in relation to shares, means one or more of the following—

(i) SI relief in respect of the shares;

(ii) EIS relief (within the meaning of Part 5) in respect of the shares;

(iii) SEIS relief (within the meaning of Part 5A) in respect of the shares;

(iv) relief under Chapter 6 of Part 4 (losses on disposal of shares) in respect of the shares;

(v) relief under section 150A or 150E of TCGA 1992 (EIS and SEIS) in respect of the shares;

(vi) relief under Schedule 5B to that Act (EIS: reinvestment) in consequence of which deferral relief is attributable to the shares (see paragraph 19(2) of that Schedule);

(vii) relief under Schedule 5BB to that Act (SEIS: re-investment) in consequence of which SEIS re-investment relief is attributable to the shares (see paragraph 4 of that Schedule).][1]

Amendments—[1]   Section 257LEA inserted by F(No 2)A 2017 s 14, Sch 1 paras 1, 4 with effect in relation to investments made on or after 6 April 2017. Arrangements which include any transaction entered into before 6 April 2017 are not "disqualifying arrangements" for the purposes of this section (F(No 2)A 2017 para 14(4)).

[257LF Restrictions on being an employee, partner or paid director

(1) This section applies—

(*a*) to the investor, and

(*b*) to any individual who is an associate of the investor.

(2) An individual to whom this section applies must not at any time in the longer applicable period be—

(*a*) an employee of—

(i) the social enterprise,

(ii) any subsidiary of the social enterprise,

(iii) a partner of the social enterprise, or

(iv) a partner of any subsidiary of the social enterprise,

(*b*) a partner of—

(i) the social enterprise, or

(ii) any subsidiary of the social enterprise,

(*c*) a trustee of—

(i) the social enterprise, or

(ii) any subsidiary of the social enterprise, or

(*d*) a remunerated director of—

(i) the social enterprise, or

(ii) a linked company.

(3) In this section—

"linked company" means—

(*a*) a subsidiary of the social enterprise,

(*b*) a company which is a partner of the social enterprise, or

(*c*) a company which is a partner of a subsidiary of the social enterprise;

"related person" means—

(*a*) the social enterprise,

(*b*) a person connected with the social enterprise,

(*c*) a linked company of which the individual is a director, or

(*d*) a person connected with such a company;

"subsidiary", in relation to the social enterprise, means a company which at any time in the longer applicable period is a 51% subsidiary of the social enterprise (and such a company is therefore a subsidiary of the social enterprise for the purposes of this section even at times when it is not a 51% subsidiary of the social enterprise).

(4) For the purposes of subsection (2)(*d*), an individual who is a director of the social enterprise or a linked company is "remunerated" if the individual (or a partnership of which the individual is a member)—

(*a*) receives at any time in the longer applicable period a payment from a related person, or

(*b*) is entitled to receive a payment from a related person in respect of any time in the longer applicable period.

(5) For the purposes of subsection (4) the following are ignored—

(*a*) any payment or reimbursement of travelling or other expenses wholly, exclusively and necessarily incurred by the individual in the performance of the individual's duties as a director,

(*b*) any interest which represents no more than a reasonable commercial return on money lent to a related person,

(*c*) any dividend or other distribution which does not exceed a normal return on the investment,

(*d*) any payment for the supply of goods which does not exceed their market value,

(*e*) any payment of rent for any property occupied by a related person which does not exceed a reasonable and commercial rent for the property,

(*f*) any necessary and reasonable remuneration which—

    (i) is paid for services, rendered to a related person in the course of a trade or profession, that are not secretarial services and are not managerial services and are not services of a kind provided by the person to whom they are rendered, and

    (ii) is taken into account in calculating for tax purposes the profits of that trade or profession, and

(*g*) if condition A is met and (where applicable) condition B is also met, any other reasonable remuneration (including any benefit or facility) received by the individual, or to which the individual is entitled, for services rendered by the individual—

    (i) to the company (whether the social enterprise or a linked company) of which the individual is a director, and

    (ii) in the individual's capacity as a director of that company.

(6) Condition A is that the investor made the investment, or previously made another investment meeting the requirement in section 257L(1), at a time ("the qualifying time") when—

(*a*) the requirements of this section and sections 257LG and 257LH (even if the three sections were not then in force) would have been met even if each other reference in the three sections to any time in the longer applicable period were a reference to any time before the qualifying time, and

(*b*) the investor had never been involved in carrying on (whether on the investor's own account or as a partner, director or employee) the whole or any part of the trade, business or profession carried on by the social enterprise or a subsidiary of the social enterprise.

(7) Condition B is that—

(*a*) the investment did not meet condition A (but a previous investment did), and

(*b*) the investment was made before the third anniversary of the date when the investor last made an investment in the social enterprise which met condition A.

(8) References in this section to an individual in the individual's capacity as a director of a company include, if the individual is both a director and an employee of the company, references to the individual in the individual's capacity as an employee of the company but, apart from that, an individual who is both a director and an employee of a company is treated for the purposes of this section as a director, and not an employee, of the company.

(9) In subsections (2), (4) and (5) "director" does not include a trustee of a charity that is a trust.]¹

Commentary—*Simon's Taxes* **E3.906, E3.931.**
Amendments—¹ Part 5B (ss 257J–257TE) inserted by FA 2014 s 57 Sch 11 para 1 with effect from 17 July 2014.

[257LG The requirement not to be interested in capital etc of social enterprise

(1) This section applies—

(*a*) to the investor, and

(*b*) to any individual who is an associate of the investor.

(2) In this section "related company" means—

    (*a*) the social enterprise, or

    (*b*) a company which at any time in the longer applicable period is a 51% subsidiary of the social enterprise (and such a company is therefore a related company for the purposes of this section even at times when it is not a 51% subsidiary of the social enterprise).

(3) There must not be any time in the longer applicable period when an individual to whom this section applies has control of a related company.

(4) There must not be any time in the longer applicable period when an individual to whom this section applies directly or indirectly possesses or is entitled to acquire—

    (*a*) more than 30% of the ordinary share capital of a related company,

    (*b*) more than 30% of the loan capital of a related company, or

    (*c*) more than 30% of the voting power in a related company.

(5) For the purposes of subsections (3) and (4) ignore any shares in a related company held by the individual, or by an associate of the individual, at a time when that company—

    (*a*) has not issued any shares other than subscriber shares, and

    (*b*) has not begun to carry on, or make preparations for carrying on, any trade or business.

(6) For the purposes of this section, the loan capital of a company—

    (*a*) is treated as including any debt incurred by the company—

        (i) for any money borrowed or capital assets acquired by the company,

        (ii) for any right to receive income created in favour of the company, or

        (iii) for consideration the value of which to the company was (at the time when the debt was incurred) substantially less than the amount of the debt (including any premium on it), and

    (*b*) is treated as not including any debt incurred by the company by overdrawing an account with a person carrying on a business of banking if the debt arose in the ordinary course of that business.

(7) For the purposes of this section—

    (*a*) an individual is treated as entitled to acquire anything which the individual is entitled to acquire at a future date or will at a future date be entitled to acquire, and

    (*b*) there is attributed to any individual any rights or powers of any other person who is an associate of the individual.][1]

Commentary—*Simon's Taxes* **E3.906, E3.931**.
Amendments—[1]   Part 5B (ss 257J–257TE) inserted by FA 2014 s 57 Sch 11 para 1 with effect from 17 July 2014.

[257LH   Requirement for no collusion with a non-qualifying investor

There must not at any time in the longer applicable period be any arrangements—

    (*a*) as part of which—

        (i) the investor makes the investment, or

        (ii) the investor, or an individual who is an associate of the investor, makes any other investment in the social enterprise,

    (*b*) which provide for a person to make an investment in a company other than the social enterprise, where that person is not the individual ("A") who invests as mentioned in paragraph (*a*), and

    (*c*) to which there is a party (whether or not A) who is an individual in relation to whom not all of the requirements in sections 257LF and 257LG would be met if—

        (i) references in those sections to the investor were read as references to that individual, and

        (ii) references in those sections to the social enterprise were read as references to the company mentioned in paragraph (*b*).][1]

Commentary—*Simon's Taxes* **E3.906, E3.931**.
Amendments—[1]   Part 5B (ss 257J–257TE) inserted by FA 2014 s 57 Sch 11 para 1 with effect from 17 July 2014.

[CHAPTER 4

ELIGIBILITY: CONDITIONS RELATING TO THE SOCIAL ENTERPRISE]

Commentary—*Simon's Taxes* **E3.907**.
Amendments—Part 5B (ss 257J–257TE) inserted by FA 2014 s 57 Sch 11 para 1 with effect from 17 July 2014.

[Conditions relating to the social enterprise[: general]

257M   The continuing to be a social enterprise requirement

The social enterprise must be a social enterprise throughout the shorter applicable period.][1]

Commentary—*Simon's Taxes* **E3.909**.
Amendments—[1]   Part 5B (ss 257J–257TE) inserted by FA 2014 s 57, Sch 11 para 1 with effect from 17 July 2014.

[257MC   The gross assets requirement

(1) If the social enterprise is a single company, the value of its assets—

    (*a*) must not exceed £15 million immediately before the investment is made, and

    (*b*) must not exceed £16 million immediately after the investment is made.

(2) If the social enterprise is a parent company, the value of the group assets—

    (*a*) must not exceed £15 million immediately before the investment is made, and

    (*b*) must not exceed £16 million immediately after the investment is made.

(3) For the purposes of subsection (2), the value of the group assets is the sum of the values of the gross assets of each of the members of the group, ignoring any assets that consist in rights against, or shares in or securities of, another member of the group.]¹

Commentary—*Simon's Taxes* **E3.909**.
Amendments—¹   Part 5B (ss 257J–257TE) inserted by FA 2014 s 57 Sch 11 para 1 with effect from 17 July 2014.

[257MD The unquoted status requirement

(1) At the beginning of the shorter applicable period—

    (*a*) the social enterprise must not be a quoted company,

    (*b*) there must be no arrangements in existence for the social enterprise to become a quoted company, and

    (*c*) there must be no arrangements in existence for the social enterprise to become a subsidiary of a company ("the new company") by virtue of an exchange of shares, or shares and securities, if arrangements have been made with a view to the new company becoming a quoted company.

(2) For the purpose of this section, a company is a "quoted company" if any shares, stocks, debentures or other securities of the company are—

    (*a*) listed on a recognised stock exchange,

    (*b*) listed on a designated exchange in a country outside the United Kingdom, or

    (*c*) dealt in outside the United Kingdom by such means as may be designated.

(3) In subsection (2)(*b*) and (*c*) "designated" means designated by an order made by the Commissioners for Her Majesty's Revenue and Customs for the purposes of that provision.

(4) An order made for the purposes of subsection (2)(*b*) may designate an exchange by name, or by reference to any class or description of exchanges, including a class or description framed by reference to any authority or approval given in a country outside the United Kingdom.

(5) The arrangements referred to in subsection (1)(*b*), and the second arrangements referred to in subsection (1)(*c*), do not include arrangements in consequence of which any shares, stocks, debentures or other securities of the social enterprise or the new company (as the case may be) are at any subsequent time—

    (*a*) listed on a stock exchange that is a recognised stock exchange by virtue of an order under section 1005(1)(*b*), or

    (*b*) listed on an exchange, or dealt in by any means, designated by an order made for the purposes of subsection (2)(*b*) or (*c*),

if the order was made after the beginning of the shorter applicable period.]¹

Commentary—*Simon's Taxes* **E3.909**.
Amendments—¹   Part 5B (ss 257J–257TE) inserted by FA 2014 s 57 Sch 11 para 1 with effect from 17 July 2014.

[257ME The control and independence requirements

(1) The social enterprise must not at any time in the shorter applicable period control (whether on its own or together with any person connected with it) any company which is not a qualifying subsidiary of the social enterprise.

(2) The social enterprise must not at any time in the shorter applicable period—

    (*a*) be a 51% subsidiary of a company, or

    (*b*) be under the control of a company, or under the control of a company and a person connected with that company, without being a 51% subsidiary of the company.

(3) No arrangements must be in existence at any time in the shorter applicable period by virtue of which the social enterprise could fail to meet either or both of subsections (1) and (2) (whether during that period or otherwise).]¹

Commentary—*Simon's Taxes* **E3.909**.
Amendments—¹   Part 5B (ss 257J–257TE) inserted by FA 2014 s 57 Sch 11 para 1 with effect from 17 July 2014.

[257MF The qualifying subsidiaries requirement

Any subsidiary that the social enterprise has at any time in the shorter applicable period must be a qualifying subsidiary of the social enterprise.]¹

Commentary—*Simon's Taxes* **E3.909**.
Amendments—¹   Part 5B (ss 257J–257TE) inserted by FA 2014 s 57 Sch 11 para 1 with effect from 17 July 2014.

[257MG The property-managing subsidiaries requirement

(1) Any property-managing subsidiary that the social enterprise has at any time in the shorter applicable period must be a 90% social subsidiary of the social enterprise.

(2) In subsection (1) "property-managing subsidiary" means a subsidiary of the social enterprise whose business consists wholly or mainly in the holding or managing of land or any property deriving its value (directly or indirectly) from land.]¹

Commentary—*Simon's Taxes* **E3.909**.
Amendments—¹   Part 5B (ss 257J–257TE) inserted by FA 2014 s 57 Sch 11 para 1 with effect from 17 July 2014.

[257MH The number of employees requirement
(1) If the social enterprise is a single company, the full-time equivalent employee number for it must be less than [250]² when the investment is made.
(2) If the social enterprise is a parent company, the sum of—
  (*a*) the full-time equivalent employee number for it, and
  (*b*) the full-time equivalent employee number for each of its qualifying subsidiaries,
must be less than [250]² when the investment is made.
(3) The full-time equivalent employee number for a company is calculated by taking the number of full-time employees of the company and adding, for each employee of the company who is not a full-time employee, such fraction as is just and reasonable.
(4) In this section "employee"—
  (*a*) includes a director, but
  (*b*) does not include—
    (i)   an employee on maternity[, paternity or parental bereavement]³ leave, or
    (ii) a student on vocational training.]¹

Commentary—*Simon's Taxes* **E3.909.**
Amendments—¹   Part 5B (ss 257J–257TE) inserted by FA 2014 s 57 Sch 11 para 1 with effect from 17 July 2014.
²   In sub-ss (1), (2) number substituted for number "500", by F(No 2)A 2017 s 14, Sch 1 paras 1, 7 with effect in relation to investments made on or after 6 April 2017.
³   In sub-s (4)(*b*)(i), words substituted for words "or shared parental" by the Parental Bereavement (Leave and Pay) Act 2018 s 1, Schedule paras 50, 53 with effect from 18 January 2020 (by virtue of SI 2020/45 reg 2).

[257MI The no partnership requirement
(1) The requirements in this section apply during the shorter applicable period.
(2) The social enterprise must not be a member of any partnership.
(3) Each 90% social subsidiary of the social enterprise must not be a member of a partnership.]¹

Commentary—*Simon's Taxes* **E3.909.**
Amendments—¹   Part 5B (ss 257J–257TE) inserted by FA 2014 s 57 Sch 11 para 1 with effect from 17 July 2014.

[257MIA The financial health requirement
(1) The social enterprise must meet the financial health requirement at the beginning of the shorter applicable period.
(2) The financial health requirement is that the social enterprise is not in difficulty.
(3) The social enterprise is "in difficulty" if it is reasonable to assume that it would be regarded as a firm in difficulty for the purposes of the Community Guidelines on State Aid for Rescuing and Restructuring Firms in Difficulty (2004/C 244/02).]¹

Amendments—¹   Section 257MIA inserted by F(No 2)A 2017 s 14, Sch 1 paras 1, 8 with effect in relation to investments made on or after 6 April 2017.

[257MJ The trading requirement
(1) The social enterprise must meet the trading requirement throughout the shorter applicable period, but this does not apply if the social enterprise is an accredited social impact contractor.
(2) The trading requirement is that—
  (*a*) the social enterprise is a charity,
  (*b*) the social enterprise is a single company that is not a charity, and its business—
    (i)   does not, if things done for incidental purposes are ignored, consist to any extent in the carrying-on of non-trade activities, and
    (ii) does not consist wholly, or as to a substantial part, in the carrying-on of excluded activities, or
  (*c*) the social enterprise is a parent company that is not a charity, and the business of the group does not consist wholly, or as to a substantial part, in the carrying-on of non-qualifying activities.
(3) If the social enterprise intends that one or more companies should become its qualifying subsidiaries with a view to their carrying on one or more qualifying trades—
  (*a*) the social enterprise is treated as a parent company for the purposes of subsection (2)(*b*) and (*c*), and
  (*b*) the reference in subsection (2)(*c*) to the group includes the social enterprise and any existing or future company that will be its qualifying subsidiary after the intention in question is carried out,
but this subsection does not apply at any time after the abandonment of that intention.
(4) For the purposes of subsection (2)(*c*) "the business of the group" means what would be the business of the group if the activities of the group companies taken together were regarded as one business.
(5) For the purposes of determining the business of a group, activities of a group company are ignored so far as they are activities carried on by a mainly trading subsidiary otherwise than for its main purpose.

(6) For the purposes of determining the business of a group, activities of a group company are ignored so far as they consist in—
- (*a*) the holding of shares in or securities of a qualifying subsidiary of the parent company,
- (*b*) the making of loans to another group company, or
- (*c*) the holding and managing of property used by a group company for the purpose of one or more qualifying trades carried on by a group company.

(7) In this section—
"incidental purposes" means purposes having no significant effect (other than in relation to incidental matters) on the extent of the activities of the body in question;
"mainly trading subsidiary" means a qualifying subsidiary which, apart from incidental purposes, exists wholly for the purpose of carrying on one or more qualifying trades, and any reference to the main purpose of such a subsidiary is to be read accordingly, and
"non-qualifying activities" means—
- (*a*) excluded activities, and
- (*b*) activities, other than activities carried on by a charity, that are carried on otherwise than in the course of a trade, and

"non-trade activities" means activities which are neither of the following—
- (*a*) activities carried on in the course of a trade, and
- (*b*) activities carried on in the course of preparing to carry on a trade.]¹

Commentary—*Simon's Taxes* **E3.909**.
Amendments—¹ Part 5B (ss 257J–257TE) inserted by FA 2014 s 57, Sch 11 para 1 with effect from 17 July 2014.

[257MK Ceasing to meet trading requirement: administration or receivership
(1) The social enterprise is not regarded as ceasing to meet the trading requirement merely because of anything done in consequence of the social enterprise or any of its subsidiaries being in administration or receivership, but this is subject to subsections (2) and (3).
(2) Subsection (1) applies only if—
- (*a*) the entry into administration or receivership, and
- (*b*) everything done as a result of the company concerned being in administration or receivership,

is for genuine commercial reasons, and is not part of any arrangements the main purpose or one of the main purposes of which is the avoidance of tax.
(3) The social enterprise ceases to meet the trading requirement if before the end of the shorter applicable period—
- (*a*) a resolution is passed, or an order is made, for the winding-up of the social enterprise or any of its subsidiaries (or, in the case of a winding-up otherwise than under the Insolvency Act 1986 or the Insolvency (Northern Ireland) Order 1989 (SI 1989/2405 (NI 19)), any other act is done for the like purpose), or
- (*b*) the company or any of its subsidiaries is dissolved without winding-up,

but this is subject to subsection (4).
(4) Subsection (3) does not apply if the winding-up or dissolution is for genuine commercial reasons, and is not part of any arrangements the main purpose or one of the main purposes of which is the avoidance of tax.]¹

Commentary—*Simon's Taxes* **E3.909**.
Amendments—¹ Part 5B (ss 257J–257TE) inserted by FA 2014 s 57 Sch 11 para 1 with effect from 17 July 2014.

[257ML The issue must be to raise money for chosen trade or preparing for it
(1) The social enterprise must be a party to the making of the investment (so far as not in bonus shares) in order to raise money for the carrying-on, by the social enterprise or a 90% social subsidiary of the social enterprise, of—
- (*a*) a qualifying trade which on the investment date is carried on by the social enterprise or a 90% social subsidiary of the social enterprise, or
- (*b*) the activity of preparing to carry on (or preparing to carry on and then carrying on) a qualifying trade—
  - (i) which on the investment date is intended to be carried on by the social enterprise or a 90% social subsidiary of the social enterprise, and
  - (ii) which is begun to be carried by the social enterprise or such a subsidiary within 2 years after that date.

(2) In this Chapter—
- (*a*) the purpose within subsection (1) for which money is raised is referred to as "the funded purpose",
- (*b*) the qualifying trade mentioned in subsection (1)(*a*) or (*b*) is referred to as "the chosen trade", and
- (*c*) if the funded purpose is the carrying-on of the activity mentioned in subsection (1)(*b*), "relevant preparation work" means preparations that form the whole or part of the activity.

(3) In determining for the purposes of subsection (1)(*b*) when a qualifying trade is begun to be carried on by a 90% social subsidiary of the social enterprise, any carrying-on of the trade by it before it became such a subsidiary is ignored.

(4) The reference in subsection (1)(*b*)(i) to a 90% social subsidiary of the social enterprise includes a reference to any existing or future body which will be such a subsidiary at any future time.

(5) This section does not apply if the social enterprise is an accredited social impact contractor.]¹

Commentary—*Simon's Taxes* **E3.909**.
Amendments—¹   Part 5B (ss 257J–257TE) inserted by FA 2014 s 57, Sch 11 para 1 with effect from 17 July 2014.

[257MM Requirement to use money raised and to trade for minimum period

(1) All of the money raised by the social enterprise from the making of the investment must, no later than the end of 28 months beginning with the investment date, be employed wholly for the funded purpose.

(2) The chosen trade must have been carried on for a period of at least 4 months ending at or after the time the investment is made and, throughout that period, the trade—

    (*a*) must have been carried on by the social enterprise or a 90% social subsidiary of the social enterprise, and

    (*b*) must not have been carried on by any other person.

(3) Employing money on the acquisition of shares or stock in a body does not of itself amount to employing the money for the funded purpose.

[(3A) Employing money on the repayment of a loan does not amount to employing the money for the funded purpose.]²

(4) Subsection (1) does not fail to be met merely because an amount of money which is not significant is employed for other purposes.

(5) If—

    (*a*) merely because of the social enterprise or any other company being wound up, or dissolved without winding-up, the qualifying trade is carried on as mentioned in subsection (2) for a period shorter than 4 months, and

    (*b*) the winding-up or dissolution—

        (i) is for genuine commercial reasons, and

        (ii) is not part of any arrangements the main purpose or one of the main purposes of which is the avoidance of tax,

subsection (2) has effect as if it referred to that shorter period.

(6) If—

    (*a*) merely because of anything done as a result of the social enterprise or any other company being in administration or receivership, the chosen trade is carried on as mentioned in subsection (2) for a period shorter than 4 months, and

    (*b*) the entry into administration or receivership, and everything done as a result of the company concerned being in administration or receivership—

        (i) is for genuine commercial reasons, and

        (ii) is not part of any arrangements the main purpose or one of the main purposes of which is the avoidance of tax,

subsection (2) has effect as if it referred to that shorter period.

(7) If the social enterprise is an accredited social impact contractor, the preceding provisions of this section apply with the following modifications—

    (*a*) in subsection (1), for "28 months" substitute "24 months",

    (*b*) in that subsection, for "the funded purpose" substitute "the carrying out of the social impact contract concerned", and

    (*c*) omit subsections (2), (3), [(3A),]² (5) and (6).]¹

Commentary—*Simon's Taxes* **E3.909**.
Amendments—¹   Part 5B (ss 257J–257TE) inserted by FA 2014 s 57, Sch 11 para 1 with effect from 17 July 2014.
²   Sub-s (3A) inserted, in sub-s (7)(*c*), words inserted, by F(No 2)A 2017 s 14, Sch 1 paras 1, 9 with effect in relation to investments made on or after 6 April 2017.

[257MN The social enterprise must carry on the chosen trade

(1) There must not be a time in the shorter applicable period when—

    (*a*) the chosen trade, or

    (*b*) relevant preparation work,

is carried on by a person who is neither the social enterprise nor a 90% social subsidiary of the social enterprise.

(2) If relevant preparation work is carried out in the shorter applicable period by the social enterprise or a 90% social subsidiary of the social enterprise then, for the purposes of determining whether the requirement in subsection (1) is met, ignore any carrying-on of the chosen trade that takes place in that period before the trade begins to be carried on by a person who is the social enterprise or a 90% social subsidiary of the social enterprise.

(3) The requirement in subsection (1) is not regarded as failing to be met if, merely because of any act or event within subsection (4), the chosen trade—

    (*a*) ceases to be carried on in the shorter applicable period by the social enterprise or any 90% social subsidiary of the social enterprise, and

    (*b*) it is subsequently carried on in that period by a person who is not any time in the longer applicable period connected with the social enterprise.

(4) The acts and events within this subsection are—

    (*a*) anything done as a consequence of the social enterprise or any other company being in administration or receivership, and

    (*b*) the social enterprise or any other company being wound up, or dissolved without being wound up.

(5) Subsection (4) applies only if—

    (*a*) the entry into administration or receivership, and everything done as a consequence of the company concerned being in administration or receivership, or

    (*b*) the winding-up or dissolution,

is for genuine commercial reasons, and is not part of any arrangements the main purpose or one of the main purposes of which is the avoidance of tax.

(6) This section does not apply if the social enterprise is an accredited social impact contractor.][1]

Commentary—*Simon's Taxes* **E3.909.**

Amendments—[1]   Part 5B (ss 257J–257TE) inserted by FA 2014 s 57 Sch 11 para 1 with effect from 17 July 2014.

[Limits on amounts that may be invested

257MNA   Maximum amount where investment made in first 7 years

(1) This section applies where—

    (*a*) the investment is made before the end of the period of 7 years beginning with the relevant first commercial sale, or

    (*b*) the investment is made after that period but—

        (i)   a relevant investment was made in the social enterprise before the end of that period, and

        (ii) some or all of the money raised by that relevant investment was employed for the purposes of (or of part of) the qualifying activity for which the money raised by the investment is employed.

(2) Where this section applies, the total amount of relevant investments made in the social enterprise on or before the date when the investment is made must not exceed £1.5 million.

(3) The reference in subsection (2) to relevant investments "made in the social enterprise" is to be read with section 257MNB.

(4) In this section—

"qualifying activity" means—

    (*a*) a qualifying trade within paragraph (*a*) of section 257ML(1) carried on by the social enterprise or a 90% social subsidiary of the social enterprise, or

    (*b*) an activity within paragraph (*b*) of section 257ML(1) so carried on;

"the relevant first commercial sale" has the meaning given by section 175A(6), reading—

    (*a*) references to the issuing company as references to the social enterprise,

    (*b*) references to the issue date as references to the investment date, and

    (*c*) references to money raised by the issue of the relevant shares as references to money raised by the investment;

"relevant investment" has the meaning given by section 173A(3) (reading references in section 173A(3) to a company as including any social enterprise).

(5) Section 173A(4) and (5) apply to determine for the purposes of this section when a relevant investment is made.

(6) Where the social enterprise is an accredited social impact contractor—

    (*a*) the reference in subsection (1)(*a*) to the relevant first commercial sale is to be read as a reference to the date on which the social enterprise first entered into a social impact contract;

    (*b*) the reference in subsection (1)(*b*) to the qualifying activity mentioned there is to be read as a reference to the carrying out of the social impact contract for which the money raised by the investment is employed.

(7) For provision about maximum amounts where this section does not apply, see section 257MNC.][1]

Amendments—[1]   Sections 257MNA–257MNE and preceding cross-head inserted by F(No 2)A 2017 s 14, Sch 1 paras 1, 6(1), (3) with effect in relation to investments made on or after 6 April 2017. This amendment does not prevent investments made before 6 April 2017 from constituting "relevant investments" for any purpose of ss 257MNA–MND (F(No 2)A 2017 Sch 1 para 14(2)).

[257MNB   Section 257MNA: supplementary

(1) In section 257MNA(2) the reference to relevant investments "made in the social enterprise" includes—

(a) relevant investments made in a company which, at the material date, is or has been a 51% subsidiary of the social enterprise,

(b) any other relevant investment made in a company to the extent that the money raised by that relevant investment has been employed for the purposes of a trade carried on by another company ("company X") which, at the material date, is or has been a 51% subsidiary of the social enterprise, and

(c) any other relevant investment made in a company if—

(i) the money raised by that relevant investment has been employed for the purposes of a trade carried on by that company or another person, and

(ii) after that relevant investment was made, but on or before the material date, that trade became a transferred trade (see subsection (5)).

(2) The investments within paragraph (a) of subsection (1)—

(a) include investments made in a company mentioned in that paragraph before it became a 51% subsidiary of the social enterprise, but

(b) where a company mentioned in that paragraph is not a 51% subsidiary of the social enterprise at the material date, do not include any investments made in that company after it last ceased to be such a subsidiary.

(3) For the purposes of subsection (1)(b), where company X is not a 51% subsidiary of the social enterprise at the material date, any money employed after company X last ceased to be such a subsidiary is to be ignored.

(4) Where only a proportion of the money raised by a relevant investment is employed for the purposes of a trade which becomes a transferred trade, only the corresponding proportion of that relevant investment is to be treated as falling within subsection (1)(c).

(5) For the purposes of this section, if—

(a) on or before the material date a trade is transferred—

(i) to the social enterprise,

(ii) to a company which, at the material date, is or has been a 51% subsidiary of the social enterprise, or

(iii) to a partnership of which the social enterprise, or a company within sub-paragraph (ii), is a member, and

(b) the trade or part of it was at any time before the transfer carried on by another person,

the trade or part mentioned in paragraph (b) becomes a "transferred trade" when it is transferred as mentioned in paragraph (a).

(6) The cases within subsection (5)(a)—

(a) include the case where the trade is transferred to a company within subsection (5)(a)(ii), or a partnership of which such a company is a member, before the company became a 51% subsidiary of the social enterprise, but

(b) where a company within subsection (5)(a)(ii) is not a 51% subsidiary of the social enterprise at the material date, do not include the case where the trade is transferred to that company, or a partnership of which that company is a member, after that company last ceased to be such a subsidiary.

(7) In this section—

"the material date" means the date on which the investment is made;

"relevant investment" has the meaning given by section 173A(3) (reading references in section 173A(3) to a company as including any social enterprise).

(8) Section 173A(4) and (5) apply to determine for the purposes of this section when a relevant investment is made.

(9) Section 173A(6) and (7) (meaning of "trade" etc) apply also for the purposes of this section.]¹

Amendments—¹ Sections 257MNA–257MNE and preceding cross-head inserted by F(No 2)A 2017 s 14, Sch 1 paras 1, 6(1), (3) with effect in relation to investments made on or after 6 April 2017. This amendment does not prevent investments made before 6 April 2017 from constituting "relevant investments" for any purpose of ss 257MNA–MND (F(No 2)A 2017 Sch 1 para 14(2)).

[257MNC Maximum amount for cases outside section 257MNA

(1) This section applies where—

(a) the investment is made at any time after the period mentioned in section 257MNA(1)(a), and

(b) it is not the case that the conditions in section 257MNA(1)(b)(i) and (ii) are met.

(2) Where this section applies—

(a) the total amount of relevant investments made in the social enterprise on or before the date when the investment is made must not exceed £1.5 million, and

(b) the amount invested must not be more than the amount mentioned in subsection (3).

(3) That amount is the amount given by the formula—

$$((€200,000 - M) / (RCG + RSI)) - T$$

where—

T is the total of any relevant investments made in the social enterprise in the aid period,

M is the total of any de minimis aid, other than relevant investments, that is granted during the aid period—

    (*a*) to the social enterprise, or

    (*b*) to a qualifying subsidiary of the social enterprise at a time when it is such a subsidiary,

RCG is the highest rate at which capital gains tax is charged in the aid period, and

RSI is the highest SI rate in the aid period.

(4) In subsection (3) "the aid period" means the 3 years—

    (*a*) ending with the day on which the investment is made, but

    (*b*) in the case of that day, including only the part of the day before the investment is made.

(5) In this section "de minimis aid" means de minimis aid which fulfils the conditions laid down—

    (*a*) in Commission Regulation (EU) No. 1407/2013 (de minimis aid) as amended from time to time, or

    (*b*) in any EU instrument from time to time replacing the whole or any part of that Regulation.

(6) For the purposes of subsection (3), the amount of any de minimis aid is the amount of the grant or, if the aid is not in the form of a grant, the gross grant equivalent amount within the meaning of that Regulation as amended from time to time.

(7) For the purposes of subsection (3), if—

    (*a*) the investment or any relevant investment is made, or

    (*b*) any aid is granted,

in sterling or any other currency that is not the euro, its amount is to be converted into euros at an appropriate spot rate of exchange for the date on which the investment is made or the aid is paid.

(8) In this section "relevant investment" has the meaning given by section 173A(3) (reading references in section 173A(3) to a company as including any social enterprise).

(9) Section 173A(4) and (5) apply to determine for the purposes of this section when a relevant investment is made.

(10) Section 257MNB (which expands the meaning of "relevant investments made in the social enterprise") applies for the purposes of each of subsections (2) and (3) above as it applies for the purposes of section 257MNA(2).]¹

Amendments—¹   Sections 257MNA–257MNE and preceding cross-head inserted by F(No 2)A 2017 s 14, Sch 1 paras 1, 6(1), (3) with effect in relation to investments made on or after 6 April 2017. This amendment does not prevent investments made before 6 April 2017 from constituting "relevant investments" for any purpose of ss 257MNA–MND (F(No 2)A 2017 Sch 1 para 14(2)).

[257MND Limit on investment in shorter applicable period

(1) This section applies where condition A or condition B is met.

(2) Condition A is that—

    (*a*) a company becomes a 51% subsidiary of the social enterprise at any time during the shorter applicable period,

    (*b*) all or part of the money raised by the investment is employed for the purposes of a qualifying activity which consists wholly or partly of a trade carried on by that company, and

    (*c*) that trade (or part of it) was carried on by that company before it became a 51% subsidiary as mentioned in paragraph (*a*).

(3) Condition B is that all or part of the money raised by the investment is employed for the purposes of a qualifying activity which consists wholly or partly of a trade which, during the shorter applicable period, becomes a transferred trade (see subsection (9)).

(4) Where this section applies, at each time in the shorter applicable period ("the relevant time") the total of the relevant investments made in the social enterprise before that time must not exceed £1.5 million.

(5) In subsection (4) the reference to relevant investments "made in the social enterprise" includes—

    (*a*) relevant investments made in a company which at any time before the relevant time has been a 51% subsidiary of the social enterprise,

    (*b*) any other relevant investment made in a company to the extent that the money raised by that relevant investment has been employed for the purposes of a trade carried on by another company ("company X") which at any time before the relevant time has been a 51% subsidiary of the social enterprise, and

    (*c*) any other relevant investment made in a company if—

        (i) the money raised by that relevant investment has been employed for the purposes of a trade carried on by that company or another person, and

        (ii) after that relevant investment was made, but before the relevant time, that trade (or part of it) became a transferred trade.

(6) The investments within paragraph (*a*) of subsection (5)—

    (*a*) include investments made in a company mentioned in that paragraph before it became a 51% subsidiary of the social enterprise, but

(b) where a company mentioned in that paragraph is not a 51% subsidiary of the social enterprise at the relevant time, do not include any investments made in that company after it last ceased to be such a subsidiary.

(7) For the purposes of subsection (5)(b), where company X is not a 51% subsidiary of the social enterprise at the relevant time, any money employed after company X last ceased to be such a subsidiary is to be ignored.

(8) Where only a proportion of the money raised by a relevant investment is employed for the purposes of a trade which becomes a transferred trade, only the corresponding proportion of that relevant investment is to be treated as falling within subsection (5)(c).

(9) For the purposes of this section, if—
    (a) before the relevant time, a trade is transferred—
        (i) to the social enterprise,
        (ii) to a company which, at the relevant time, is or has been a 51% subsidiary of the social enterprise, or
        (iii) to a partnership of which the social enterprise, or a company within sub-paragraph (ii), is a member, and
    (b) the trade or part of it was at any time before the transfer carried on by another person,
the trade or part mentioned in paragraph (b) becomes a "transferred trade" when it is transferred as mentioned in paragraph (a).

(10) The cases within subsection (9)(a)—
    (a) include the case where the trade is transferred to a company within subsection (9)(a)(ii), or a partnership of which such a company is a member, before the company became a 51% subsidiary of the social enterprise, but
    (b) where a company within subsection (9)(a)(ii) is not a 51% subsidiary of the social enterprise at the relevant time, do not include the case where the trade is transferred to that company, or a partnership of which that company is a member, after that company last ceased to be such a subsidiary.

(11) In this section—
    "qualifying activity" has the same meaning as in section 257MNA (see subsection (4) of that section);
    "relevant investment" has the meaning given by section 173A(3) (reading references in section 173A(3) to a company as including any social enterprise).

(12) Section 173A(4) and (5) apply to determine for the purposes of this section when a relevant investment is made.

(13) Section 173A(6) and (7) (meaning of "trade" etc) apply also for the purposes of this section.]¹

Amendments—¹ Sections 257MNA–257MNE and preceding cross-head inserted by F(No 2)A 2017 s 14, Sch 1 paras 1, 6(1), (3) with effect in relation to investments made on or after 6 April 2017. This amendment does not prevent investments made before 6 April 2017 from constituting "relevant investments" for any purpose of ss 257MNA–MND (F(No 2)A 2017 Sch 1 para 14(2)).

[257MNE Power to amend limits on amounts that may be invested

(1) The Treasury may by regulations substitute a different figure for the figure for the time being specified in section 257MNA(2), 257MNC(2) or (3) or 257MND(4).

(2) Regulations under this section may make incidental, supplemental, consequential, transitional or saving provision.

(3) Regulations under this section may not be made unless a draft of the instrument containing them has been laid before, and approved by a resolution of, the House of Commons.]¹

Amendments—¹ Sections 257MNA–257MNE and preceding cross-head inserted by F(No 2)A 2017 s 14, Sch 1 paras 1, 6(1), (3) with effect in relation to investments made on or after 6 April 2017.

[Interpretation of conditions relating to the social enterprise

257MP Meaning of "qualifying trade"

(1) For the purposes of this Chapter, a trade is a qualifying trade if—
    (a) it is conducted on a commercial basis and with a view to the realisation of profits, and
    (b) it does not at any time in the shorter applicable period consist wholly or as to a substantial part in the carrying-on of excluded activities.

(2) References in this section and sections 257MQ to 257MT (excluded activities) to a trade are to be read without regard to the definition of "trade" in section 989.]¹

Commentary—*Simon's Taxes* **E3.908.**
Amendments—¹ Part 5B (ss 257J–257TE) inserted by FA 2014 s 57 Sch 11 para 1 with effect from 17 July 2014.

[257MQ Meaning of "excluded activity"

(1) The following are excluded activities for the purposes of sections 257JD, 257MJ and 257MP—
    (a) dealing in land, in commodities or futures or in shares, securities or other financial instruments,
    (b) banking, insurance, money-lending, debt-factoring, hire-purchase financing or other financial activities . . . ²,

[(*ba*) leasing (including letting ships on charter or other assets on hire),

(*bb*) receiving royalties or licence fees,

(*bc*) operating or managing nursing homes or residential care homes or managing property used as a nursing home or residential care home (see section 257MQA),

(*bd*) generating electricity, exporting electricity (see subsection (3)) or making electricity generating capacity available,

(*be*) generating heat,

(*bf*) generating any form of energy not within paragraph (*bd*) or (*be*),

(*bg*) producing gas or fuel,][2]

(*c*) property development (see section 257MR),

(*d*) activities in the fishery and aquaculture sector that is covered by Council Regulation (EC) No 104/2000 of 17 December 1999 on the common organisation of the markets in fishery and aquaculture products,

(*e*) the primary production of products listed in Annex I to the Treaty on the Functioning of the European Union (agricultural etc products), with the exception of products covered by Council Regulation (EC) No 104/2000 (fishery and aquaculture products),

(*f*) . . .[2]

(*g*) road freight transport for hire or reward, and

(*h*) providing services or facilities for a business carried on by another person (other than a company of which the provider of the services or facilities is a qualifying subsidiary) if—

   (i) the business consists wholly or as to a substantial part of activities falling within any of paragraphs (*a*) to (*g*), and

   (ii) a controlling interest (see section 257MT) in the business is held by a person who also has a controlling interest in the business carried on by the provider of the services or facilities.

(2) . . .[2]

[(3) For the purposes of subsection (1)(*bd*) electricity is exported if it is exported onto a distribution system or transmission system (within the meaning of section 4 of the Electricity Act 1989).][2]][1]

Commentary—*Simon's Taxes* **E3.908.**
Amendments—[1] Part 5B (ss 257J–257TE) inserted by FA 2014 s 57, Sch 11 para 1 with effect from 17 July 2014.
[2] In sub-s (1)(*b*), words repealed, sub-ss (1)(*ba*)–(*bg*), (3) inserted, and sub-ss (1)(*f*) (2) repealed, by F(No 2)A 2017 s 14, Sch 1 paras 1, 10(1)–(4). These amendments have effect—
  – so far as they apply for the purposes of s 257JD, from 6 April 2017; and
  – so far as they apply for the purposes of ss 257MJ, 257MP, in relation to investments made on or after 6 April 2017.

[257MQA Excluded activities: nursing homes and residential care homes

(1) This section supplements section 257MQ(1)(*bc*).

(2) "Nursing home" means any establishment which exists wholly or mainly for the provision of nursing care—

   (*a*) for persons suffering from sickness, injury or infirmity, or

   (*b*) for women who are pregnant or have given birth.

(3) "Residential care home" means any establishment which exists wholly or mainly for the provision of residential accommodation, together with board and personal care, for persons in need of personal care because of—

   (*a*) old age,

   (*b*) mental or physical disability,

   (*c*) past or present dependence on alcohol or drugs,

   (*d*) any past illnesses, or

   (*e*) past or present mental disorder.

(4) The activities of a person are not to be taken to fall within section 257MQ(1)(*bc*) unless that person has an estate or interest in, or is in occupation of, the nursing home or residential care home in question.][1]

Amendments—[1] Section 257MQA, inserted by F(No 2)A 2017 s 14, Sch 1 paras 1, 10(5). This amendment has effect—
  – so far as it applies for the purposes of s 257JD, from 6 April 2017; and
  – so far as it applies for the purposes of ss 257MJ, 257MP, in relation to investments made on or after 6 April 2017.

[257MR Excluded activities: property development

(1) For the purposes of section 257MQ(1)(c) "property development" means the development of land—

   (*a*) by a company which has, or at any time has had, an interest in the land, and

   (*b*) with the sole or main object of realising a gain from the disposal of an interest in the land when it is developed.

(2) For the purposes of subsection (1) "interest in land" means (subject to subsection (3))—

   (*a*) any estate, interest or right in or over land, including any right affecting the use or disposition of land, or

   (*b*) any right to obtain such an estate, interest or right from another which is conditional on the other's ability to grant it.

(3) References in this section to an interest in land do not include—

    (a) the interest of a creditor (other than a creditor in respect of a rentcharge) whose debt is secured by way of mortgage, an agreement for a mortgage or a charge of any kind over land, or

    (b) in the case of land in Scotland, the interest of a creditor in a charge or security of any kind over land.][1]

Commentary—*Simon's Taxes* **E3.908**.
Amendments—[1]   Part 5B (ss 257J–257TE) inserted by FA 2014 s 57 Sch 11 para 1 with effect from 17 July 2014.

[257MT Excluded activity: providing services or facilities for another business

(1) This section explains what is meant by a controlling interest in a business for the purposes of section 257MQ(1)(h).

(2) In the case of a business carried on by a company, a person ("A") has a controlling interest in the business if—

    (a) A controls the company,

    (b) the company is a close company and A, or an associate of A, is a director of the company and either—

        (i) is the beneficial owner of more than 30% of the ordinary share capital of the company, or

        (ii) is able, directly or through the medium of other companies or by any other indirect means, to control more than 30% of that share capital, or

    (c) at least half of the business could, in accordance with section 942 of CTA 2010, be regarded as belonging to A for the purposes of section 941 of CTA 2010 (company reconstructions without a change of ownership).

(3) In any other case, a person has a controlling interest in a business if the person is entitled to at least half of the assets used for, or of the income arising from, the business.

(4) For the purposes of this section—

    (a) any rights or powers of a person who is an associate of another are to be attributed to that other person, and

    (b) "business" includes any trade, profession or vocation.][1]

Commentary—*Simon's Taxes* **E3.908**.
Amendments—[1]   Part 5B (ss 257J–257TE) inserted by FA 2014 s 57 Sch 11 para 1 with effect from 17 July 2014.

[257MU Meaning of "qualifying subsidiary"

(1) For the purposes of this Part, a company ("the subsidiary") is a qualifying subsidiary of another company ("the parent") if—

    (a) the subsidiary is a 51% subsidiary of the parent,

    (b) no person other than the parent, or another of its subsidiaries, has control of the subsidiary, and

    (c) no arrangements are in existence as a result of which either of the conditions in paragraphs (a) and (b) would cease to be met.

(2) The conditions in subsection (1)(a) to (c) do not cease to be met merely because the subsidiary or any other company is wound up, or dissolved without winding up, if the winding-up or dissolution—

    (a) is for genuine commercial reasons, and

    (b) is not part of any arrangements the main purpose or one of the main purposes of which is the avoidance of tax.

(3) The conditions in subsection (1)(a) to (c) do not cease to be met merely because of anything done as a consequence of the subsidiary or another company being in administration, or receivership, if—

    (a) the entry into administration or receivership, and

    (b) everything done as a consequence of the company concerned being in administration or receivership,

is for genuine commercial reasons, and is not part of any arrangements the main purpose or one of the main purposes of which is the avoidance of tax.

(4) The conditions in subsection (1)(a) to (c) do not cease to be met merely because arrangements are in existence for the disposal by the parent or (as the case may be) by another subsidiary of all its interest in the subsidiary if the disposal—

    (a) is to be for genuine commercial reasons, and

    (b) is not to be part of any arrangements the main purpose or one of the main purposes of which is the avoidance of tax.][1]

Commentary—*Simon's Taxes* **E3.908**.
HMRC Manuals—Employee Tax Advantaged Share Scheme User Manual ETASSUM52040 (qualifying subsidiaries).
Amendments—[1]   Part 5B (ss 257J–257TE) inserted by FA 2014 s 57 Sch 11 para 1 with effect from 17 July 2014.

[257MV Meaning of "90% social subsidiary" of a social enterprise

(1) For the purposes of this Chapter, a company ("the subsidiary") is a 90% social subsidiary of another company ("the parent") if—

    (a) the subsidiary is a social enterprise,

(b) the parent possesses at least 90% of the issued share capital of, and at least 90% of the voting power in, the subsidiary,

(c) the parent would—

    (i) in the event of a winding-up of the subsidiary, or

    (ii) in any other circumstances,

be beneficially entitled to receive at least 90% of the assets of the subsidiary which would then be available for distribution to equity holders of the subsidiary,

(d) the parent is beneficially entitled to receive at least 90% of any profits of the subsidiary which are available for distribution to equity holders of the subsidiary,

(e) no person other than the parent has control of the subsidiary, and

(f) no arrangements are in existence as a result of which any of the conditions in paragraphs (a) to (e) would cease to be met.

(2) For the purposes of this Chapter, a company ("company A") which is a subsidiary of another company ("company B") is a 90% social subsidiary of a third company ("company C") if—

(a) company A is a 90% social subsidiary of company B, and company B is a 100% social subsidiary of company C, or

(b) company A is a 100% social subsidiary of company B, and company B is a 90% social subsidiary of company C.

(3) For the purposes of subsection (2) no account is to be taken of any control company C may have of company A.

(4) For the purposes of subsection (2), a company ("company X") is a 100% social subsidiary of another company ("company Y") at any time when the conditions in subsection (1)(a) to (f) would be met if—

(a) company X were the subsidiary,

(b) company Y were the parent, and

(c) in subsection (1) for "at least 90%" there were substituted "100%".

(5) The conditions in subsection (1)(a) to (f) do not cease to be met merely because of anything done as a consequence of the subsidiary or any other company being wound up, or dissolved without being wound up, if the winding-up or dissolution—

(a) is for genuine commercial reasons, and

(b) is not part of any arrangements the main purpose or one of the main purposes of which is the avoidance of tax.

(6) The conditions in subsection (1)(a) to (f) do not cease to be met merely because of anything done as a consequence of the subsidiary or any other company being in administration, or receivership, if—

(a) the entry into administration or receivership, and

(b) everything done as a consequence of the company concerned being in administration or receivership,

is for genuine commercial reasons, and is not part of any arrangements the main purpose or one of the main purposes of which is the avoidance of tax.

(7) The conditions in subsection (1)(a) to (f) do not cease to be met merely because any arrangements are in existence for the disposal by the parent of all its interest in the subsidiary if the disposal—

(a) is to be for genuine commercial reasons, and

(b) is not to be part of any arrangements the main purpose or one of the main purposes of which is the avoidance of tax.

(8) For the purposes of subsection (1)—

(a) the persons who are equity holders of the subsidiary, and

(b) the percentage of the assets of the subsidiary to which an equity holder would be entitled,

are to be determined in accordance with Chapter 6 of Part 5 of CTA 2010.

(9) In making that determination—

(a) references in section 166 of that Act to company A are to be read as references to an equity holder, and

(b) references in that section to winding up are to be read as including references to any other circumstances in which assets of the subsidiary are available for distribution to its equity holders.][1]

Commentary—*Simon's Taxes* **E3.908**.
Amendments—[1] Part 5B (ss 257J–257TE) inserted by FA 2014 s 57 Sch 11 para 1 with effect from 17 July 2014.

[257MW Excluded activities: power to amend

(1) The Treasury may by regulations add to, repeal or otherwise amend any provision of sections 257MQ to 257MT (excluded activities).

(2) Regulations under this section may—

(a) make different provision for different cases or purposes;

(b) contain incidental, supplemental, consequential and transitional provision and savings.

(3) So far as they cause an activity to cease to be an excluded activity, amendments made by regulations under this section may have effect in relation to times before they come into force, but not times before 6 April 2015.

(4) This section is without prejudice to any other power to amend any provision of this Part.]¹

Commentary—*Simon's Taxes* **E3.908**.

Amendments—¹   Section 257MW inserted by FA 2015 s 36, Sch 6 para 1 with effect from 26 March 2015.

[CHAPTER 5

ATTRIBUTION OF RELIEF]

Commentary—*Simon's Taxes* **E3.916**.

Amendments—Part 5B (ss 257J–257TE) inserted by FA 2014 s 57 Sch 11 para 1 with effect from 17 July 2014.

[257N Attribution of SI relief to investments

(1) References in this Part, in relation to any individual, to the SI relief attributable to any investment are to be read as references to any reduction made in the individual's liability to income tax that is attributed to that investment in accordance with this section.

This is subject to the provisions of this Part providing for the withdrawal or reduction of SI relief.

(2) If an individual's liability to income tax is reduced under this Part in any tax year, then—

  (*a*) if the reduction is obtained because of a single distinct investment, the amount of the reduction is attributed to that investment, and

  (*b*) if the reduction is obtained because of two or more distinct investments, the amount of the reduction—

    (i)   is apportioned between the distinct investments in the same proportions as the amounts claimed by the individual in respect of each of those investments, and

    (ii) is attributed to those investments accordingly.

(3) In this section "distinct investment" means an investment, made on a single day, in—

  (*a*) a single share or single qualifying debt investment, or

  (*b*) two or more shares, or two or more qualifying debt investments, where the shares or qualifying debt investments are in the same social enterprise and of the same class.

(4) If under this section an amount of any reduction in income tax is attributed to a distinct investment—

  (*a*) in the case of a distinct investment of the kind mentioned in subsection (3)(*a*), that amount is attributed to the share, or qualifying debt investment, concerned, and

  (*b*) in the case of a distinct investment of the kind mentioned in subsection (3)(*b*), a proportionate part of that amount is attributed to each of the shares, or qualifying debt investments, concerned.

(5) If corresponding bonus shares are issued to an individual in respect of any shares ("the original shares") to which SI relief is attributed—

  (*a*) a proportionate part of the total amount attributed to the original shares immediately before the bonus shares are issued is attributed to each of the shares in the holding comprising the original shares and the bonus shares, and

  (*b*) after the issue of the bonus shares, this Part applies as if those shares had been issued to the individual on the same day as the original shares.

(6) In subsection (5) "corresponding bonus shares" means bonus shares which are in the same company, of the same class, and carry the same rights, as the original shares.

(7) If section 257JA(1) and (2) apply in the case of any investment as if part of the amount invested had been invested in a previous tax year, this section has effect as if that part and the remainder had been invested by separate investments (and that part had been invested by an investment made on a day in the previous tax year).

(8) For the purposes of this section, shares or other investments in a company are not treated as being of the same class unless they would be so treated if dealt in on a recognised stock exchange.]¹

Commentary—*Simon's Taxes* **E3.911**.

Amendments—¹   Part 5B (ss 257J–257TE) inserted by FA 2014 s 57 Sch 11 para 1 with effect from 17 July 2014.

[CHAPTER 6

CLAIMS FOR RELIEF]

Commentary—*Simon's Taxes* **E3.911**.

Amendments—Part 5B (ss 257J–257TE) inserted by FA 2014 s 57 Sch 11 para 1 with effect from 17 July 2014.

[257P Time for making claims for SI relief

(1) A claim for SI relief in respect of the amount invested may be made—

  (*a*) not earlier than the time the requirement in section 257MM(2) (chosen trade must have been carried on for 4 months) is first met, and

  (*b*) not later than the fifth anniversary of the normal self-assessment filing date for the tax year in which the investment is made.

(2) If the social enterprise is an accredited social impact contractor, subsection (1) applies with the omission of its paragraph (*a*).

(3) If section 257JA(1) and (2) apply as if part of the amount invested had been invested in a previous tax year, subsection (1) has effect as if that part and the remainder had been invested by separate investments (and that part had been invested by an investment made on a day in the previous tax year).]¹

Commentary—*Simon's Taxes* **E3.911**.
Amendments—¹   Part 5B (ss 257J–257TE) inserted by FA 2014 s 57, Sch 11 para 1 with effect from 17 July 2014.

[257PA Entitlement to claim

(1) The investor is entitled to make a claim for SI relief in respect of the amount invested if the investor has received from the social enterprise a compliance certificate in respect of that amount.

(2) For the purposes of PAYE regulations, no regard is to be had to SI relief unless a claim for it has been duly made.

(3) No application may be under section 55(3) or (4) of TMA 1970 (application for postponement of payment of tax pending appeal) on the ground that the investor is entitled to SI relief unless a claim for the relief has been duly made by the investor.]¹

Commentary—*Simon's Taxes* **E3.911**.
Amendments—¹   Part 5B (ss 257J–257TE) inserted by FA 2014 s 57, Sch 11 para 1 with effect from 17 July 2014.

[257PB Compliance statements

(1) For the purposes of this Part, a "compliance statement" in respect of the investment is a statement by the social enterprise to the effect that, except so far as they fall to be met by or in relation to the individual, the requirements for SI relief—

    (*a*) are for the time being met in relation to the investment (or in relation to investments that include the investment), and

    (*b*) have been so met at all times since the investment was made.

(2) A compliance statement must be in such form as the Commissioners for Her Majesty's Revenue and Customs may direct and must contain—

    (*a*) such additional information as the Commissioners may reasonably require, including in particular information relating to the persons who have requested the issue of compliance certificates,

    (*b*) a declaration that the statement is correct to the best of the social enterprise's knowledge and belief, and

    (*c*) such other declarations as the Commissioners may reasonably require.

(3) The social enterprise may not provide an officer of Revenue and Customs with a compliance statement in respect of the investment—

    (*a*) before the requirement in section 257MM(2) (trade must have been carried for 4 months) is met, or

    (*b*) later than 2 years after the end of the tax year in which the investment is made or, if that requirement is first met after the end of that tax year, later than 2 years after the requirement is first met.

(4) If the social enterprise is an accredited social impact contractor, subsection (3) applies with the omission of its paragraph (*a*).]¹

Commentary—*Simon's Taxes* **E3.912**.
Amendments—¹   Part 5B (ss 257J–257TE) inserted by FA 2014 s 57, Sch 11 para 1 with effect from 17 July 2014.

[257PC Compliance certificates

(1) For the purposes of this Chapter, a "compliance certificate" is a certificate which—

    (*a*) is issued by the social enterprise in respect of the investment,

    (*b*) states that, except so far as they fall to be met by or in relation to the individual, the requirements for SI relief are for the time being met in relation to the investment, and

    (*c*) is in such form as the Commissioners for Her Majesty's Revenue and Customs may direct.

(2) Before issuing a compliance certificate, the social enterprise must provide an officer of Revenue and Customs with a compliance statement in respect of the investment.

(3) The social enterprise must not issue a compliance certificate without the authority of an officer of Revenue and Customs.

(4) If the social enterprise, or a person connected with the social enterprise, has under section 257SF given a notice to an officer of Revenue and Customs that relates (whether or not exclusively) to the investment, a compliance certificate must not be issued unless the authority mentioned in subsection (3) of this section is given or renewed after receipt of the notice.

(5) If—

    (*a*) an officer of Revenue and Customs has been requested to give or renew an authority to issue a compliance certificate, and

    (*b*) an officer of Revenue and Customs has decided whether or not to do so,

an officer of Revenue and Customs must give notice of the decision to the social enterprise.

(6) For the purposes of the provisions of TMA 1970 relating to appeals, the refusal of an officer of Revenue and Customs to authorise the issue of a compliance certificate is taken to be a decision disallowing a claim by the social enterprise.

(7) In the case of requirements that cannot be met until a future time, references in this section to requirements being met for the time being are to nothing having occurred to prevent their being met.][1]

Commentary—*Simon's Taxes* **E3.912**.
Amendments—[1]   Part 5B (ss 257J–257TE) inserted by FA 2014 s 57, Sch 11 para 1 with effect from 17 July 2014.

[257PD Penalties for fraudulent certificate or statement etc

The social enterprise is liable to a penalty not exceeding £3,000 if—

    (a) it issues a compliance certificate, or provides a compliance statement, which is made fraudulently or negligently, or

    (b) it issues a compliance certificate in contravention of section 257PC(3) or (4).][1]

Commentary—*Simon's Taxes* **E3.912**.
Amendments—[1]   Part 5B (ss 257J–257TE) inserted by FA 2014 s 57, Sch 11 para 1 with effect from 17 July 2014.

[257PE Power to amend Chapter

(1) The Treasury may by order amend this Chapter.

(2) An order under this section may include consequential, incidental or transitional provision or savings, including consequential amendments, repeals or revocations of provision made by or under an enactment (including this Act) whenever passed or made.

(3) An order under this section may make different provision for different cases or purposes.

(4) An order under this section may, in particular, make provision for persons to be liable to penalties whose amount, or maximum amount, does not exceed £3,000.][1]

Commentary—*Simon's Taxes* **E3.912**.
Amendments—[1]   Part 5B (ss 257J–257TE) inserted by FA 2014 s 57, Sch 11 para 1 with effect from 17 July 2014.

[CHAPTER 7

WITHDRAWAL OR REDUCTION OF SI RELIEF]

Commentary—*Simon's Taxes* **E3.915**.
Amendments—Part 5B (ss 257J–257TE) inserted by FA 2014 s 57, Sch 11 para 1 with effect from 17 July 2014.

[Value received by the investor

257Q Effect of the investor receiving value from the social enterprise

(1) If the investor receives any value from the social enterprise at any time in the longer applicable period, any SI relief given in respect of the investment must—

    (a) if it is greater than the amount given by the formula set out in subsection (2), be reduced by that amount, and

    (b) in any other case, be withdrawn.

(2) The formula is—

$$V \times R$$

where—

            V is the amount of the value received, and

            R is the SI rate for the tax year for which the SI relief was given.

(3) Subsections (1) and (2) are subject to—

    (a) section 257QA (value received: insignificant receipts),

    (b) section 257QB (value received where there is more than one issue of investments),

    (c) section 257QC (value received where part of investment treated as made in previous tax year),

    (d) section 257QD (cases where maximum SI relief not obtained),

    (e) section 257QG (receipts of value by and from connected persons etc), and

    (f) section 257QH (receipt of replacement value).

(4) Sections 257QB to 257QD are to be applied in the order in which they appear in this Part.

(5) Value received is to be ignored, for the purposes of this section, so far as SI relief attributable to the investment has already been withdrawn or reduced on its account.

(6) For the purposes of this section and sections 257QA to 257QI, an individual—

    (a) who acquires any part of the investment, and

    (b) who does so on such a transfer as is mentioned in section 257T (spouses or civil partners),

is treated as the investor.][1]

Commentary—*Simon's Taxes* **E3.917, E3.919**.
Amendments—[1]   Part 5B (ss 257J–257TE) inserted by FA 2014 s 57, Sch 11 para 1 with effect from 17 July 2014.

[257QA Value received: insignificant receipts

(1) In this section "insignificant receipt" means a receipt whose amount—

    (a) is not more than £1,000, or

    (b) is more than £1,000 but is insignificant in relation to the amount invested.

(2) Section 257Q(1) does not apply to an insignificant receipt, subject as follows.

(3) Section 257Q(1) applies to all receipts within the longer applicable period if, at any time on the investment date or in the preceding 12 months, arrangements are in existence providing for the investor to receive, or to be entitled to receive, value from the social enterprise at any time in the longer applicable period.

(4) Once section 257Q(1) has applied to a receipt, it applies also to all other receipts within the longer applicable period except any earlier insignificant receipts.

(5) The amount of the first receipt to which section 257Q(1) applies is treated as increased by the total amount of any earlier insignificant receipts.

(6) In subsection (3)—

    (a) the reference to the investor includes any person who at any time in the longer applicable period is an associate of the investor (whether or not an associate at the material time), and

    (b) the reference to the social enterprise includes any person who at any time in the longer applicable period is connected with the social enterprise (whether or not connected at the material time).][1]

Commentary—*Simon's Taxes* **E3.919**.
Amendments—[1]   Part 5B (ss 257J–257TE) inserted by FA 2014 s 57, Sch 11 para 1 with effect from 17 July 2014.

[257QB Value received where there is more than one issue of investments

(1) Subsection (3) applies if—

    (a) a time in the longer applicable period when the investor receives value from the social enterprise is within the period that for the purposes of this Part is the longer applicable period in relation to another investment in the social enterprise, and

    (b) that other investment is one for which the investor has SI relief.

(2) That other investment is an "overlapping investment" for the purposes of subsection (3).

(3) Section 257Q(2) has effect in relation to the investment as if the amount V were reduced by multiplying it by—

    I / T

    where—

         I is the amount on which the investor has SI relief in the case of the investment, and

         T is the total of that amount and the corresponding amount for each overlapping investment.][1]

Commentary—*Simon's Taxes* **E3.919**.
Amendments—[1]   Part 5B (ss 257J–257TE) inserted by FA 2014 s 57, Sch 11 para 1 with effect from 17 July 2014.

[257QC Value received where part of investment treated as made in previous tax year

(1) Subsection (2) applies if—

    (a) section 257Q(1) applies to a receipt, and

    (b) section 257JA(1) and (2) apply as if part of the amount invested had been invested in a previous tax year.

(2) The calculation under section 257Q(2) in relation to that receipt is to be made as follows—

Step 1

Apportion the amount referred to as "V" between the tax year in which the investment was made and the preceding tax year by multiplying that amount by—

    A / B

    where—

         A is the part of the amount invested on which the investor obtains SI relief for the tax year in question, and

         B is the sum of—

            (a) that part, and

            (b) the part of the amount invested on which the investor obtains SI relief for the other tax year.

Step 2

In relation to each of the amounts ("V1" and "V2") so apportioned to the two tax years, calculate the amounts ("X1" and "X2") that would be given by the formula if separate investments had been made in those tax years.

In calculating amounts X1 and X2, apply section 257QD if appropriate but do not apply section 257QB.

Step 3

Add amounts X1 and X2 together.

The result is the required amount.][1]

Commentary—*Simon's Taxes* **E3.919**.
Amendments—[1]   Part 5B (ss 257J–257TE) inserted by FA 2014 s 57, Sch 11 para 1 with effect from 17 July 2014.

[257QD Cases where maximum SI relief not obtained

(1) If the investor's liability to income tax is reduced for any tax year in respect of the investment and—

    (*a*) the amount of the reduction ("A"), is less than

    (*b*) the amount ("B") which is equal to income tax at the SI rate for that tax year on the amount on which the investor has SI relief in the case of the investment,

section 257Q(2) has effect in relation to any value received as if the amount referred to as "V" were reduced by multiplying it by—

    A / B

(2) If the amount of SI relief attributable to the investment has been reduced before the SI relief was obtained, the amount referred to in subsection (1) as "A" is to be treated for the purposes of that subsection as the amount that it would have been without that reduction.

(3) Subsection (2) does not apply to a reduction of SI relief as a result of section 257N(5) (attribution of SI relief where there is a corresponding issue of bonus shares).][1]

Commentary—*Simon's Taxes* E3.919.
Amendments—[1] Part 5B (ss 257J–257TE) inserted by FA 2014 s 57, Sch 11 para 1 with effect from 17 July 2014.

[257QE When value is received

(1) This section applies for the purposes of sections 257Q and 257QB.

(2) The investor receives value from the social enterprise at any time when the social enterprise—

    (*a*) repays, redeems or repurchases any investments in the social enterprise which belong to the investor, or makes any payment to the investor for giving up the investor's right to investments in the social enterprise on their cancellation or extinguishment,

    (*b*) repays, in pursuance of any arrangements for or in connection with the making of the investment, any debt owed to the investor other than a debt which was incurred by the social enterprise—

        (i) on or after the investment date, and

        (ii) otherwise than in consideration of the extinguishment of a debt incurred before that date,

    (*c*) makes to the investor any payment for giving up on its extinguishment the investor's right to any debt, other than—

        (i) a debt in respect of a repayment of the kind mentioned in section 257LF(5)(*a*) or (*f*), or

        (ii) an ordinary trade debt,

    (*d*) releases or waives any liability of the investor to the social enterprise or discharges or undertakes to discharge any liability of the investor to a third person,

    (*e*) makes a loan or advance to the investor which has not been repaid in full before the investment is made,

    (*f*) provides a benefit or facility for the investor by providing, at a price less than the arm's-length price or free of charge, goods or services for whose provision the social enterprise ordinarily makes a charge,

    (*g*) otherwise provides any benefit or facility for the investor,

    (*h*) transfers an asset to the investor for no consideration or for consideration less than its market value or acquires an asset from the investor for consideration greater than its market value, or

    (*i*) makes to the investor any other payment except—

        (i) a payment of a kind mentioned in section 257LF(5), or

        (ii) a payment in discharge of an ordinary trade debt.

(3) For the purposes of subsection (2)(*d*), the social enterprise is treated as having released or waived a liability if the liability is not discharged within 12 months of the time when it ought to have been discharged.

(4) For the purposes of subsection (2)(*e*), each of the following is treated as a loan made by the social enterprise to the investor—

    (*a*) the amount of any debt, other than an ordinary trade debt, incurred by the investor to the social enterprise, and

    (*b*) the amount of any debt due from the investor to a third party which has been assigned to the social enterprise.

(5) The investor also receives value from the social enterprise if—

    (*a*) in respect of ordinary shares, or qualifying debt investments, held by the investor any payment or asset is received in a winding-up or dissolution of the social enterprise, and

    (*b*) the winding-up or dissolution is for genuine commercial reasons, and is not part of any arrangements the main purpose or one of the main purposes of which is the avoidance of tax.

(6) The investor also receives value from the social enterprise if—

    (*a*) a person—

        (i) purchases any investments in the social enterprise which belong to the investor, or

        (ii) makes any payment to the investor for giving up any right in relation to any investments in the social enterprise, and (*b*) that person is an individual in relation to whom not all of the requirements in sections 257LF and 257LG would be met if references in those sections to the investor were read as references to that person.

(7) If, because of the investor's disposal of investments in the social enterprise, any SI relief attributable to those investments is withdrawn or reduced under section 257R, the investor is not to be treated as receiving value from the social enterprise in respect of the disposal.

(8) If the investor is a director of the social enterprise, the investor is not to be treated as receiving value from the social enterprise merely because of the payment to the investor of reasonable remuneration (including any benefit or facility) for any services rendered to the social enterprise as a director or employee.

(9) In this section "ordinary trade debt" means any debt for goods or services supplied in the ordinary course of a trade or business if any credit given—

(*a*) is for not more than 6 months, and

(*b*) is not for longer than that normally given to customers of the person carrying on the trade or business.][1]

Commentary—*Simon's Taxes* **E3.918**.
Amendments—[1]   Part 5B (ss 257J–257TE) inserted by FA 2014 s 57, Sch 11 para 1 with effect from 17 July 2014.

[257QF The amount of value received

In a case falling within a provision listed in column 1 of the following table, the amount of value received for the purposes of sections 257Q and 257QB is given by the corresponding entry in column 2 of the table.

Provision	The amount of value received
Section 257QE(2)(*a*), (*b*) or (*c*)	The amount received by the investor or, if greater, the market value of the investments or debt
Section 257QE(2)(*d*)	The amount of the liability
Section 257QE(2)(*e*)	The amount of the loan or advance, less the amount of any repayment made before the investment is made
Section 257QE(2)(*f*)	The arm's-length price for the goods or services, less any amount paid for them by the investor
Section 257QE(2)(*g*)	The cost to the social enterprise of providing the benefit or facility, less any consideration given for it by the investor
Section 257QE(2)(*h*)	The difference between the market value of the asset and the consideration (if any) given for it
Section 257QE(2)(*i*)	The amount of the payment
Section 257QE(5)	The amount of the payment or the market value of the asset
Section 257QE(6)	The amount received by the investor or, if greater, the market value of the investments][1]

Commentary—*Simon's Taxes* **E3.918**.
Amendments—[1]   Part 5B (ss 257J–257TE) inserted by FA 2014 s 57, Sch 11 para 1 with effect from 17 July 2014.

[257QG Receipts of value by and from connected persons etc

In sections 257Q, 257QA, 257QB, 257QE and 257QF—

(*a*) any reference to a payment or transfer to the investor includes a reference to a payment or transfer made to the investor indirectly or to the investor's order or for the investor's benefit,

(*b*) any reference to the investor includes a reference to an associate of the investor, and

(*c*) any reference to the social enterprise includes a reference to a person who at any time in the longer applicable period is connected with the social enterprise (whether or not that person is so connected at the material time).][1]

Commentary—*Simon's Taxes* **E3.918**.
Amendments—[1]   Part 5B (ss 257J–257TE) inserted by FA 2014 s 57, Sch 11 para 1 with effect from 17 July 2014.

[257QH Receipt of replacement value

(1) If—

(*a*) any SI relief attributable to the investment would, in the absence of this section, be reduced or withdrawn under section 257Q because of a receipt of value within section 257QE(2) or (6) ("the original value"),

(*b*) the original supplier receives value ("the replacement value") from the original recipient and the receipt is a qualifying receipt, and

(*c*) the amount of the replacement value is at least the amount of the original value,

section 257Q does not, because of the receipt of the original value, have effect to withdraw or reduce the SI relief.

This is subject to section 257QI(1) and (2).

(2) For the purposes of this section—

"the original recipient" means the person who receives the original value, and

"the original supplier" means the person from whom that value was received.

(3) If the amount of the original value is, by virtue of section 257QB, treated as reduced for the purposes of section 257Q(2) as it applies in relation to the investment, the reference in subsection (1)(*c*) to the amount of the original value is to be read as a reference to the amount of that value ignoring the reduction.

(4) A receipt of the replacement value is a qualifying receipt for the purposes of subsection (1) if it arises—

- (*a*) because of the original recipient doing one or more of the following—
  - (i)   making a payment to the original supplier, other than a payment within paragraph (*c*) or a payment to which subsection (5) applies,
  - (ii) acquiring any asset from the original supplier for a consideration the amount or value of which is more than the market value of the asset, and
  - (iii) disposing of any asset to the original supplier for no consideration or for a consideration the amount or value of which is less than the market value of the asset,
- (*b*) if the receipt of the original value was within section 257QE(2)(*d*), because of an event the effect of which is to reverse the event which constituted the receipt of the original value, or
- (*c*) if the receipt of the original value was within section 257QE(6), because of the original recipient repurchasing the investments in question, or (as the case may be) re-acquiring the right in question, for a consideration the amount or value of which is at least the amount of the original value.

(5) This subsection applies to—

- (*a*) any payment for any goods, services or facilities, provided (whether in the course of trade or otherwise) by—
  - (i)   the original supplier, or
  - (ii) any other person who at any time in the longer applicable period is an associate of, or is connected with, the original supplier (whether or not the person is such an associate, or is so connected, at the material time),

  which is reasonable in relation to the market value of those goods, services or facilities,
- (*b*) any payment of any interest which represents no more than a reasonable commercial return on any money lent to—
  - (i)   the original recipient, or
  - (ii) any other person who at any time in the longer applicable period is an associate of the original recipient (whether or not the person is such an associate at the material time),
- (*c*) any payment for the acquisition of an asset which does not exceed its market value,
- (*d*) any payment, as rent for any property occupied by—
  - (i)   the original recipient, or
  - (ii) any person who at any time in the longer applicable period is an associate of the original recipient (whether or not the person is such an associate at the material time),

  of an amount not exceeding a reasonable and commercial rent for the property,
- (*e*) any payment in discharge of an ordinary trade debt, and
- (*f*) any payment for shares in or securities of any company in circumstances that do not fall within subsection (4)(*a*)(ii).

(6) For the purposes of this section, the amount of the replacement value is—

- (*a*) in a case within paragraph (*a*) of subsection (4), the sum of—
  - (i)   the amount of any payment within sub-paragraph (i) of that paragraph, and
  - (ii) the difference between the market value of any asset to which sub-paragraph (ii) or (iii) of that paragraph applies and the amount or value of the consideration (if any) received for it,
- (*b*) in a case within subsection (4)(*b*), the same as the amount of the original value, and
- (*c*) in a case within subsection (4)(*c*), the amount or value of the consideration received by the original supplier.

Section 257QF applies for the purpose of determining the amount of the original value.

(7) In this section—

- (*a*) any reference to a payment to a person (however expressed) includes a reference to a payment made to the person indirectly or to the person's order or for the person's benefit, and
- (*b*) "ordinary trade debt" has the meaning given by section 257QE(9).]¹

Commentary—*Simon's Taxes* **E3.920**.

Amendments—¹ Part 5B (ss 257J–257TE) inserted by FA 2014 s 57, Sch 11 para 1 with effect from 17 July 2014.

[257QI Section 257QH: supplementary
(1) The receipt of the replacement value by the original supplier is ignored for the purposes of section 257QH(1) to the extent to which it has previously been set under section 257QH against a receipt of value to prevent any reduction or withdrawal of SI relief under section 257Q.
(2) The receipt of the replacement value by the original supplier ("the event") is ignored for the purposes of section 257QH if—
   (*a*) the event occurs before the longer applicable period,
   (*b*) where the event occurs after the time the original recipient receives the original value, it does not occur as soon after that time as is reasonably practicable in the circumstances, or
   (*c*) where an appeal has been brought by the investor against an assessment to withdraw or reduce any SI relief attributable to the investment because of the receipt of the original value, the event occurs more than 60 days after the day on which the amount of the relief which falls to be withdrawn has been finally determined.

But nothing in section 257QH or this section requires the replacement value to be received after the original value.
(3) This subsection applies if—
   (*a*) the receipt of the replacement value by the original supplier is a qualifying receipt for the purposes of section 257QH(1), and
   (*b*) in consequence of the receipt, any receipts of value are ignored for the purposes of section 257Q as that section applies in relation to the investment or any other investments made by the investor, and
   (*c*) the event which gives rise to the receipt is (or includes) the making of an investment by—
     (i) the investor, or
     (ii) any person who at any time in the longer applicable period is an associate of the investor (whether or not the person is such an associate at the material time).
(4) If subsection (3) applies, the person who makes the investment concerned is not to be eligible for SI relief in relation to the investment concerned or any other investments in the same issue.
(5) In this section "the original recipient", "the original supplier" and "replacement value" have the same meaning as in section 257QH.]¹
Commentary—*Simon's Taxes* E3.920.
Amendments—¹   Part 5B (ss 257J–257TE) inserted by FA 2014 s 57, Sch 11 para 1 with effect from 17 July 2014.

[Repayments etc of investments to other persons

257QJ Repayments etc of share capital to other persons
(1) This section applies if any SI relief is attributable to the whole or any part of the investment and, at any time in the longer applicable period, the social enterprise or any subsidiary—
   (*a*) repays, redeems or repurchases any of its share capital which belongs to any member other than—
     (i) the investor, or
     (ii) a person who falls within subsection (5), or
   (*b*) makes any payment to any such member for giving up the member's right to any of the share capital of the social enterprise or subsidiary on its cancellation or extinguishment.
(2) The SI relief must—
   (*a*) if it is greater than the amount given by the formula set out in subsection (3), be reduced by that amount, and
   (*b*) in any other case, be withdrawn.
(3) The formula is—

$$A \times R$$

  where—
      A is the amount received by the member, and
      R is the SI rate for the tax year for which the SI relief was given.
(4) This section is subject to sections 257QK to 257QP; and sections 257QL to 257QO are to be applied in the order in which they appear in this Part.
(5) A person falls within this subsection if the repayment causes any SI relief attributable to that person's shares in the social enterprise to be withdrawn or reduced by virtue of—
   (*a*) section 257QE(2)(*a*) (receipt of value by virtue of repayment of investments etc), or
   (*b*) section 257R (disposal of whole or part of the investment).
(6) A repayment is treated as having the effect mentioned in subsection (5)(*a*) if it would have that effect were it not an insignificant receipt; and here "insignificant receipt" is to be read in accordance with section 257QA(1).
(7) A repayment is to be ignored, for the purposes of this section, to the extent to which SI relief attributable to any shares has already been withdrawn or reduced on its account.
(8) In this section and sections 257QK to 257QP—
   (*a*) "repayment" means a repayment, redemption, repurchase or payment mentioned in subsection (1)(*a*) or (*b*), and

(*b*) references to a subsidiary of the social enterprise are references to a company which at any time in the longer applicable period is a 51% subsidiary of the social enterprise (whether or not it is such a subsidiary at the time of the repayment).][1]

Commentary—*Simon's Taxes* **E3.921**.
Amendments—[1]   Part 5B (ss 257J–257TE) inserted by FA 2014 s 57, Sch 11 para 1 with effect from 17 July 2014.

[257QK Insignificant payments ignored for the purposes of section 257QJ

(1) A repayment is ignored for the purposes of section 257QJ if both—
   (*a*) the market value of the shares to which it relates ("the target shares") immediately before the event occurs, and
   (*b*) the amount received by the member in question,
are insignificant in relation to the market value of the remaining issued share capital of the social enterprise, or (as the case may be) the subsidiary, immediately after the event occurs.
   This is subject to subsection (3).
(2) For the purposes of subsection (1) it is to be assumed that the target shares are cancelled at the time the repayment is made.
(3) Subsection (1) does not apply if repayment arrangements are in existence at any time in the period—
   (*a*) beginning 12 months before the investment date, and
   (*b*) ending at the end of the investment date.
(4) For this purpose "repayment arrangements" means arrangements which provide—
   (*a*) for a repayment by the social enterprise or any subsidiary of the social enterprise (whether or not it is such a subsidiary at the time the arrangements are made), or
   (*b*) for anyone to be entitled to such a repayment,
at any time in the longer applicable period.][1]

Commentary—*Simon's Taxes* **E3.921**.
Amendments—[1]   Part 5B (ss 257J–257TE) inserted by FA 2014 s 57, Sch 11 para 1 with effect from 17 July 2014.

[257QL Amount of repayments etc if there is more than one issue of shares

(1) This section applies if, in relation to the same repayment, section 257QJ(2) applies to SI relief attributable to two or more issues of shares.
(2) Section 257QJ(3) has effect in relation to the shares included in each of those issues as if the amount referred to as A were reduced by multiplying it by the fraction—

$$I / T$$

where—

   I is the amount on which SI relief was obtained by individuals in respect of shares which are included in the issue and to which SI relief is or, but for section 257QJ(2)(*b*), would be attributable, and

   T is the total of that amount and the corresponding amount or amounts in respect of the other issue or issues.][1]

Commentary—*Simon's Taxes* **E3.921**.
Amendments—[1]   Part 5B (ss 257J–257TE) inserted by FA 2014 s 57, Sch 11 para 1 with effect from 17 July 2014.

[257QM Single issue affecting more than one individual

(1) This section applies if, in relation to the same repayment, section 257QJ(2) applies to SI relief attributable to shares held by two or more individuals.
(2) Section 257QJ(3) has effect in relation to each individual as if the amount referred to as A were reduced by multiplying it by the fraction—

$$I / T$$

where—

   I is the amount on which the individual obtains SI relief in respect of the shares to which SI relief is or, but for section 257QJ(2)(*b*), would be attributable, and

   T is the total of that amount and the corresponding amount or amounts on which the other individual or individuals obtain SI relief in respect of such shares.][1]

Commentary—*Simon's Taxes* **E3.921**.
Amendments—[1]   Part 5B (ss 257J–257TE) inserted by FA 2014 s 57, Sch 11 para 1 with effect from 17 July 2014.

[257QN Single issue treated as made partly in previous tax year

(1) This section applies if—
   (*a*) section 257QJ(2) applies to SI relief attributable to shares held by an individual, and
   (*b*) part of the issue of shares has been treated as issued to the individual in a previous tax year for the purposes of section 257JA(1) and (2).
(2) This subsection explains how the calculation under section 257QJ(3) is to be made.
Step 1
Apportion the amount referred to as A between the tax year in which the shares were issued and the previous tax year by multiplying that amount by the fraction—

$$I / T$$

where—

      I is the amount on which the individual obtains SI relief in respect of the shares treated as issued in the tax year in question, and

      T is the total of that amount and the corresponding amount in respect of the shares treated as issued in the other tax year.

Step 2

In relation to each of the amounts ("A1" and "A2") so apportioned to the two tax years, calculate the amounts ("X1" and "X2") that would be given by the formula if there were separate issues of shares in those tax years.

In calculating amounts X1 and X2, apply section 257QO if appropriate but do not apply section 257QL or 257QM.

Step 3

Add amounts X1 and X2 together.

The result is the required amount.][1]

Commentary—*Simon's Taxes* **E3.921**.
Amendments—[1]   Part 5B (ss 257J–257TE) inserted by FA 2014 s 57, Sch 11 para 1 with effect from 17 July 2014.

[257QO Maximum relief not obtained for share issue

(1) This section applies if section 257QJ(2) applies to SI relief attributable to shares held by the investor and—

    (a) the amount of the reduction ("D") in the investor's liability to income tax for any tax year in respect of the shares, is less than

    (b) the amount given by—

          $I \times R$

          where—

I is the amount on which the investor claims SI relief in respect of the investment, and

R is the SI rate for the tax year for which the SI relief was given.

(2) Section 257QJ(3) has effect as if the amount referred to as A were reduced by multiplying it by the fraction—

      $D / (I \times R)$

(3) If the amount of SI relief attributable to any of the shares has been reduced before the SI relief was obtained, the amount referred to in subsections (1) and (2) as D is to be treated for the purposes of those subsections as the amount it would have been without that reduction.

(4) Subsection (3) does not apply to a reduction of SI relief by virtue of section 257N(5) (attribution of SI relief where there is a corresponding issue of bonus shares).][1]

Commentary—*Simon's Taxes* **E3.921**.
Amendments—[1]   Part 5B (ss 257J–257TE) inserted by FA 2014 s 57, Sch 11 para 1 with effect from 17 July 2014.

[257QP Repayment of authorised minimum within 12 months

(1) This section applies if—

    (a) a company issues share capital ("the original shares") of nominal value equal to the authorised minimum (within the meaning of the Companies Act 2006) for the purposes of complying with section 761 of that Act (public company: requirement as to minimum share capital), and

    (b) the registrar of companies issues the company with a certificate under that section.

(2) Section 257QJ(2) does not apply in relation to any redemption of the original shares within 12 months of the date on which they were issued.][1]

Commentary—*Simon's Taxes* **E3.921**.
Amendments—[1]   Part 5B (ss 257J–257TE) inserted by FA 2014 s 57, Sch 11 para 1 with effect from 17 July 2014.

[Miscellaneous

257QQ Acquisition of a trade or trading assets

(1) Any SI relief attributable to the investment is withdrawn if—

    (a) at any time in the longer applicable period, the social enterprise or any qualifying subsidiary—

       (i) begins to carry on as its trade, or as part of its trade, a trade which was previously carried on at any time in that period otherwise than by the social enterprise or any qualifying subsidiary, or

      (ii) acquires the whole, or the greater part, of the assets used for the purposes of a trade previously so carried on, and

    (b) the investor is a person, or one of a group of persons, to whom subsection (2) or (3) applies.

(2) This subsection applies to any person or group of persons—

    (a) to whom an interest amounting in total to more than a half share in the trade (as previously carried on) belonged at any time in the longer applicable period, and

    (b) who is or are a person or group of persons to whom such an interest in the trade carried on by the social enterprise belongs or has, at any such time, belonged.

(3) This subsection applies to any person or group of persons who—
- (a) control or, at any time in the longer applicable period, have controlled the social enterprise, and
- (b) is or are a person or group of persons who, at any such time, controlled another company which previously carried on the trade.

(4) For the purposes of subsection (2)—
- (a) for the purpose of determining the person to whom a trade belongs and, if a trade belongs to two or more persons, their respective shares in that trade—
  - (i) apply section 941(6) of CTA 2010, and
  - (ii) an interest in a trade belonging to a company may be treated in accordance with any of the options set out in section 942 of that Act, and
- (b) any interest, rights or powers of a person who is an associate of another person are treated as those of that other person.

(5) If the investor—
- (a) is a director of, or of a company which is a partner of, the social enterprise or any qualifying subsidiary, and
- (b) is in receipt of, or entitled to receive, remuneration as such a director falling within section 257LF(5)(g) (reasonable remuneration for services),

then, in determining whether any SI relief attributable to the investment is to be withdrawn, the reference in subsection (3)(b), and (so far as relating to that provision) the reference in subsection (1)(a)(i), to any time in the longer applicable period are to be read as references to any time before the end of the longer applicable period.

(6) Section 257LF(8) (director also an employee) applies for the purposes of subsection (5) as it applies for the purposes of section 257LF, and in subsection (5) "remuneration" includes any benefit or facility.

(7) In this section "trade" includes any business or profession, and references to a trade previously carried on include references to part of such a trade.]¹

Commentary—*Simon's Taxes* E3.922.
Amendments—¹ Part 5B (ss 257J–257TE) inserted by FA 2014 s 57, Sch 11 para 1 with effect from 17 July 2014.

[257QR Acquisition of share capital
(1) Any SI relief attributable to the investment is withdrawn if—
- (a) the social enterprise comes to acquire all of the issued share capital of another company at any time in the longer applicable period, and
- (b) the investor is a person, or one of a group of persons, to whom subsection (2) applies.

(2) This subsection applies to any person or group of persons who—
- (a) control or have, at any time in the longer applicable period, controlled the social enterprise, and
- (b) is or are a person or group of persons who, at any such time, controlled the other company.

(3) If the investor—
- (a) is a director of, or of a company which is a partner of, the social enterprise or any qualifying subsidiary, and
- (b) is in receipt of, or entitled to receive, remuneration as such a director falling within section 257LF(5)(g) (reasonable remuneration for services),

then, in determining whether any SI relief attributable to the investment is to be withdrawn, the reference in subsection (2)(b) to any time in the longer applicable period is to be read as a reference to any time before the end of the longer applicable period.

(4) Section 257LF(8) (director also an employee) applies for the purposes of subsection (3) as it applies for the purposes of section 257LF, and in subsection (3) "remuneration" includes any benefit or facility.]¹

Commentary—*Simon's Taxes* E3.923.
Amendments—¹ Part 5B (ss 257J–257TE) inserted by FA 2014 s 57, Sch 11 para 1 with effect from 17 July 2014.

[257QS Relief subsequently found not to have been due
(1) Any SI relief obtained by the investor which is subsequently found not to have been due must be withdrawn.

(2) SI relief obtained by the investor in respect of the investment may not be withdrawn on the ground that the requirements of Chapter 4 are not met unless the requirements of subsection (3) are met.

(3) The requirements of this subsection are met if either—
- (a) the social enterprise has given notice under section 257SF in relation to the investment (information to be provided by the social enterprise etc), or
- (b) an officer of Revenue and Customs has given notice to the social enterprise stating the officer's opinion that, because of the ground in question, the whole or any part of the SI relief attributable to the investment (whether alone or with other SI relief) was not due.]¹

Commentary—*Simon's Taxes* E3.924.

Amendments—[1]   Part 5B (ss 257J–257TE) inserted by FA 2014 s 57, Sch 11 para 1 with effect from 17 July 2014.

[Disposals

257R Disposal of whole or part of the investment

(1) This section applies if—

    (*a*) the investor disposes of the whole or part of the investment,

    (*b*) the disposal takes place before the shorter applicable period ends,

    (*c*) SI relief is attributable to the shares, or qualifying debt investments, disposed of,

    (*d*) the disposal is not to an individual who—

       (i)   is the spouse, or civil partner, of the investor, and

       (ii) is living together with the investor at the time of the disposal, and

    (*e*) the disposal does not occur as a result of the investor's death.

(2) If the disposal is not made by way of a bargain at arm's length, the SI relief attributable to those shares, or qualifying debt investments, must be withdrawn.

(3) If the disposal is made by way of a bargain at arm's length, the SI relief attributable to those shares or qualifying debt investments must—

    (*a*) if it is greater than the amount given by the formula set out in subsection (4), be reduced by that amount, and

    (*b*) in any other case, be withdrawn.

(4) The formula is—

$$C \times R$$

where—

         C is the amount or value of the consideration received by the investor for the shares or qualifying debt investments, and

         R is the SI rate for the tax year for which the SI relief was given.][1]

Commentary—*Simon's Taxes* **E3.925**.

Amendments—[1]   Part 5B (ss 257J–257TE) inserted by FA 2014 s 57, Sch 11 para 1 with effect from 17 July 2014.

[257RA Cases where maximum relief not obtained

(1) Subsection (2) applies if the investor's liability to income tax for any tax year is reduced under this Part in respect of the investment and—

    (*a*) the amount of the reduction ("D"), is less than

    (*b*) the amount given by—

$$A \times R$$

         where—

A is the amount on which the investor claims SI relief in respect of the investment, and

R is the SI rate for that tax year.

(2) Section 257R(3) and (4) have effect as if the amount or value referred to as C were reduced by multiplying it by the fraction—

$$D / (A \times R)$$

(3) If section 257JA(1) and (2) apply in the case of the investment as if part of it had been made in a previous tax year, subsections (1) and (2) of this section have effect as if that part and the remainder had been invested by separate investments (and that part had been invested by an investment made on a day in the previous tax year).

(4) If the amount of SI relief attributable to the investment or any part of it has been reduced before SI relief was obtained, the amount referred to in subsections (1) and (2) as D is to be treated for the purposes of those subsections as the amount that it would have been without that reduction.

(5) Subsection (4) does not apply to a reduction of SI relief by virtue of section 257N(5) (attribution of SI relief if there is a corresponding issue of bonus shares).][1]

Commentary—*Simon's Taxes* **E3.925**.

Amendments—[1]   Part 5B (ss 257J–257TE) inserted by FA 2014 s 57, Sch 11 para 1 with effect from 17 July 2014.

[257RB Call options

(1) This section applies if the investor grants an option which, if exercised, would bind the investor to sell the whole or part of investment.

(2) The grant of the option is treated for the purposes of section 257R as a disposal—

    (*a*) of the investment, or

    (*b*) (as the case may be) of the part of the investment to which the option relates.

(3) Nothing in this section prejudices section 257LB (no pre-arranged exits).][1]

Commentary—*Simon's Taxes* **E3.925**.

Amendments—[1]   Part 5B (ss 257J–257TE) inserted by FA 2014 s 57, Sch 11 para 1 with effect from 17 July 2014.

[257RC Put options

(1) This section applies if, at any time in the longer applicable period, a person grants the investor an option which, if exercised, would bind the grantor to purchase the whole or part of the investment.

(2) Any SI relief—

    (*a*) attributable to the investment, or

(*b*) (as the case may be) attributable to the part of the investment to which the option relates, must be withdrawn.

(3) For the purposes of subsection (2)(*b*), the part of the investment to which an option relates is the part which, if—

(*a*) the option were exercised immediately after the grant, and

(*b*) any investments made in the social enterprise by the investor after the grant were disposed of immediately after being made,

would be treated for the purposes of section 257R as disposed of in pursuance of the option.]¹

Commentary—*Simon's Taxes* **E3.925**.
Amendments—¹   Part 5B (ss 257J–257TE) inserted by FA 2014 s 57, Sch 11 para 1 with effect from 17 July 2014.

[CHAPTER 8

WITHDRAWAL OR REDUCTION OF SI RELIEF: PROCEDURE]

Commentary—*Simon's Taxes* **E3.930**.
Amendments—Part 5B (ss 257J–257TE) inserted by FA 2014 s 57, Sch 11 para 1 with effect from 17 July 2014.

[Assessments and appeals

257S Assessments for the withdrawal or reduction of SI relief

If any SI relief which has been obtained falls to be withdrawn or reduced under Chapter 7, it must be withdrawn or reduced by the making of an assessment to income tax for the tax year for which the relief was obtained.]¹

Commentary—*Simon's Taxes* **E3.930**.
Amendments—¹   Part 5B (ss 257J–257TE) inserted by FA 2014 s 57, Sch 11 para 1 with effect from 17 July 2014.

[257SA Appeals against section 257QS(3)(*b*) notices

For the purposes of the provisions of TMA 1970 relating to appeals, the giving of notice by an officer of Revenue and Customs under section 257QS(3)(*b*) is taken to be a decision disallowing a claim by the social enterprise.]¹

Commentary—*Simon's Taxes* **E3.924**.
Amendments—¹   Part 5B (ss 257J–257TE) inserted by FA 2014 s 57, Sch 11 para 1 with effect from 17 July 2014.

[257SB Time limits for assessments

(1) An officer of Revenue and Customs may—

(*a*) make an assessment for withdrawing or reducing the SI relief attributable to whole or any part of the investment, or

(*b*) give a notice under section 257QS(3)(*b*),

at any time not more than 6 years after the end of the relevant tax year.

(2) In subsection (1) "the relevant tax year" means—

(*a*) the tax year containing the end of the 28 months beginning with the investment date, or

(*b*) if later, the tax year in which occurs the event which causes the SI relief to be withdrawn or reduced.

(3) Subsection (1) is without prejudice to section 36(1A) of TMA 1970 (loss of tax brought about deliberately etc).]¹

Commentary—*Simon's Taxes* **E3.930**.
Amendments—¹   Part 5B (ss 257J–257TE) inserted by FA 2014 s 57, Sch 11 para 1 with effect from 17 July 2014.

[257SC Cases where assessment not to be made

(1) No assessment for withdrawing or reducing SI relief in respect of the investment may be made because of an event occurring after the investor's death.

(2) Subsection (3) applies if the investor has, by a disposal or disposals to which section 257R(3) applies, disposed of all investments which—

(*a*) have been made by the investor in the social enterprise, and

(*b*) are investments—

(i)   to which SI relief is attributable, or

(ii) have not been held by the investor until the end of the third anniversary of the date on which they were made.

(3) No assessment for withdrawing or reducing SI relief in respect of those investments may be made because of any subsequent event unless the event occurs at a time when the requirements of sections 257LF, 257LG and 257LH are not met in relation to the investor by reference to any of those investments.]¹

Commentary—*Simon's Taxes* **E3.930**.
Amendments—¹   Part 5B (ss 257J–257TE) inserted by FA 2014 s 57, Sch 11 para 1 with effect from 17 July 2014.

[Interest

257SD Date from which interest is chargeable

(1) In its application to an assessment made by virtue of section 257S in the case of relief withdrawn or reduced by virtue of a provision listed in subsection (2), section 86 of TMA 1970 (interest on overdue income tax) has effect as if the relevant date were 31 January next following the tax year for which the assessment is made.

(2) The provisions are—

section 257LD,
any of sections 257LF to 257LH,
any of sections 257M to 257MJ,
section 257MN,
section 257Q,
section 257QJ,
section 257QQ,
section 257QR,
section 257R, and
section 257RC.][1]

Commentary—*Simon's Taxes* **E3.930**.
Amendments—[1]   Part 5B (ss 257J–257TE) inserted by FA 2014 s 57, Sch 11 para 1 with effect from 17 July 2014.

[Information

257SE Information to be provided by the investor

(1) This section applies if the investor has obtained SI relief in respect of the investment, and an event occurs as a result of which—

(a) the SI relief falls to be withdrawn or reduced by virtue of any of sections 257LD, 257LF, 257LG and 257LH,

(b) the SI relief falls to be withdrawn or reduced under section 257Q (receipt of value), or would fall to be so withdrawn or reduced but for section 257QH (receipt of replacement value), or

(c) the SI relief falls to be withdrawn or reduced under any of sections 257R, 257RB and 257RC (disposals and options).

(2) The investor must within 60 days of coming to know of the event give a notice to an officer of Revenue and Customs containing particulars of the event.

(3) If the investor—

(a) is required under this section to give notice of a receipt of value which is within section 257Q, or would be within that section but for section 257QH, and

(b) has knowledge of any replacement value received (or expected to be received) because of a qualifying receipt,

the notice must include particulars of that receipt (or expected receipt).

(4) In subsection (3) "qualifying receipt" and "replacement value" are to be read in accordance with section 257QH.][1]

Commentary—*Simon's Taxes* **E3.931**.
Amendments—[1]   Part 5B (ss 257J–257TE) inserted by FA 2014 s 57, Sch 11 para 1 with effect from 17 July 2014.

[257SF Information to be provided by the social enterprise etc

(1) This section applies if the social enterprise has provided an officer of Revenue and Customs with a compliance statement in respect of the investment and an event occurs as a result of which—

(a) any of the requirements in sections 257M, 257MC to 257MK, 257MM(1) and 257MN is not met in respect of the investment, or

(b) any of sections 257Q, 257QJ, 257QQ and 257QR has effect to cause any SI relief attributable to the investment to be withdrawn or reduced, or—

(i)   would have such an effect if SI relief had been obtained in respect of the investment, or

(ii) in the case of section 257Q, would have such an effect but for section 257QH (receipt of replacement value).

(2) If this section applies—

(a) the social enterprise, and

(b) any person connected with the social enterprise who has knowledge of the matters mentioned in subsection (1),

must give a notice to an officer of Revenue and Customs containing particulars of the event.

(3) Any notice required to be given by the social enterprise under subsection (2)(a) must be given—

(a) within 60 days of the event, or

(b) if the event is a receipt of value within section 257QE(2) from a person connected with the social enterprise (see section 257QG), within 60 days of the social enterprise coming to know of the event.

(4) Any notice required to be given by a person under subsection (2)(b) must be given within 60 days of the person coming to know of the event.

(5) If a person—

(*a*) is required under this section to give notice of a receipt of value which is within section 257Q, or would be within that section but for section 257QH, and

(*b*) has knowledge of any replacement value received (or expected to be received) because of a qualifying receipt,

the notice must include particulars of that receipt of replacement value (or expected receipt).

(6) In subsection (5) "qualifying receipt" and "replacement value" are to be read in accordance with section 257QH.

(7) If the event mentioned in subsection (1) is one whose occurrence results in the requirement in section 257M not being met in respect of the investment, the references in subsections (2) and (3) to the social enterprise are to—

(*a*) the body concerned even though it has ceased to be a social enterprise, or

(*b*) the body into which the social enterprise has been converted.]¹

Commentary—*Simon's Taxes* **E3.931**.
Amendments—¹   Part 5B (ss 257J–257TE) inserted by FA 2014 s 57, Sch 11 para 1 with effect from 17 July 2014.

[257SG Power to require information in section 257SE or 257SF cases

(1) This section applies if an officer of Revenue and Customs has reason to believe that a person—

(*a*) has not given a notice which the person is required to give under section 257SE or 257SF in respect of any event,

(*b*) has given or received value within the meaning of section 257QE(2) or (6) which, but for the fact that the amount given or received was an insignificant receipt, would have triggered a requirement to give such a notice, or

(*c*) has made or received any repayment within the meaning given by section 257QJ(8) which, but for the fact that it falls to be ignored for the purposes of section 257QJ by virtue of section 257QK(1), would have triggered a requirement to give a notice under section 257SF.

(2) The officer may by notice require the person concerned to supply the officer, within such time as the officer may specify in the notice, with such information relating to the event as the officer may reasonably require for the purposes of this Part.

(3) The period specified in a notice under subsection (2) must be at least 60 days.

(4) In subsection (1)(*b*) the reference to an insignificant receipt is to be read in accordance with section 257QA(1).]¹

Commentary—*Simon's Taxes* **E3.931**.
Amendments—¹   Part 5B (ss 257J–257TE) inserted by FA 2014 s 57, Sch 11 para 1 with effect from 17 July 2014.

[257SH Power to require information in other cases

(1) Subsection (2) applies if SI relief is claimed in respect of the investment, and an officer of Revenue and Customs has reason to believe that it may not be due because of any such arrangements as are mentioned in section 257LB(1), 257LC, 257LE, [257LEA,]² 257LH, 257ME(3), 257MK(2) or (4), 257MM(5) or (6), 257MN(5), 257MU or 257MV(1), (5), (6) or (7).

(2) The officer may by notice require any person concerned to supply the officer within such time as may be specified in the notice with—

(*a*) a declaration in writing stating whether or not, according to the information which that person has or can reasonably obtain, any such arrangements exist or have existed, and

(*b*) such other information as the officer may reasonably require for the purposes of the provision in question and as that person has or can reasonably obtain.

(3) The period specified in a notice under subsection (2) must be at least 60 days.

(4) For the purposes of subsection (2), in the case of a provision listed in column 1 of the following table, the person concerned is given by the corresponding entry in column 2 of the table.

Provision	The person concerned
Section 257LB(1) or 257LC	The investor, the social enterprise and any person connected with the social enterprise
Section 257LE or 257MK(2) or (4)	The investor, the social enterprise and any person controlling the social enterprise
[Section 257LEA	The investor, the social enterprise, any person controlling the social enterprise and any person whom an officer of Revenue and Customs has reason to believe may be a party to the arrangements in question]²
Section 257LH	The investor
Section 257ME(3), 257MU(1) or 257MV(1)	The social enterprise and any person controlling the social enterprise
Section 257MM(5) or (6), 257MN(5), 257MU(2), (3) or (4) or 257MV(5), (6) or (7)	The investor, the social enterprise, any other company in question, and any person controlling the social enterprise or any other company in question

References in the table to the investor include references to any person to whom the investor appears to have made such a transfer as is mentioned in section 257T (spouses or civil partners) of the whole or part of the investment.

(5) If SI relief has been obtained in respect of the investment—

    (*a*) any person who receives from the social enterprise any payment or asset which may constitute value received (by the person or another) for the purposes of section 257Q, and

    (*b*) any person on whose behalf such a payment or asset is received,

must, if so required by an officer of Revenue and Customs, state whether the payment or asset so received is received on behalf of any other person and, if so, the name and address of that other person.

(6) If SI relief has been claimed in respect of the investment—

    (*a*) any person who holds or has held investments in the social enterprise, and

    (*b*) any person on whose behalf any such investments are or were held,

must, if so required by an officer of Revenue and Customs, state whether the investments so held are or were held on behalf of any other person and, if so, the name and address of that other person.]¹

Commentary—*Simon's Taxes* **E3.931**.

Amendments—¹   Part 5B (ss 257J–257TE) inserted by FA 2014 s 57, Sch 11 para 1 with effect from 17 July 2014.

²   In sub-s (1), words inserted, and in sub-s (4), table entry inserted, by F(No 2)A 2017 s 14, Sch 1 paras 1, 5 with effect in relation to investments made on or after 6 April 2017. Arrangements which include any transaction entered into before 6 April 2017 are not "disqualifying arrangements" for the purposes of ITA 2007 s 257LEA (F(No 2)A 2017 Sch 1 para 14(4)).

[257SI Confidentiality

(1) Section 18(1) of the Commissioners for Revenue and Customs Act 2005 does not prevent an officer of Revenue and Customs from disclosing to the social enterprise that SI relief has been obtained or claimed in respect of a particular number or proportion of any investments in it.

(2) Section 18(1) of the Commissioners for Revenue and Customs Act 2005 does not prevent—

    (*a*) disclosure to the Regulator of Community Interest Companies for the purposes of the Regulator's functions,

    (*b*) disclosure to a Minister of the Crown for the purposes of functions of a Minister of the Crown under sections 257JD to 257JG, or

    (*c*) disclosure to a person for the purposes of functions delegated to the person under section 257JH(1).

(3) Information disclosed in reliance on subsection (2) may not be further disclosed except—

    (*a*) with the consent of the Commissioners for Her Majesty's Revenue and Customs, or

    (*b*) if the disclosure is required by an enactment.

(4) Information originally disclosed in reliance on subsection (2)(*a*) may be disclosed in reliance on subsection (3)(*a*) only for the purposes of the Regulator's functions.

(5) Information originally disclosed in reliance on subsection (2)(*b*) or (*c*) may be disclosed in reliance on subsection (3)(*a*) only for the purposes of—

    (*a*) functions of a Minister of the Crown under sections 257JD to 257JG, or

    (*b*) functions delegated to a person under section 257JH(1).

(6) If, in contravention of subsections (3) to (5), any revenue and customs information relating to a person is disclosed and the identity of the person—

    (*a*) is specified in the disclosure, or

    (*b*) can be deduced from it,

section 19 of the Commissioners for Revenue and Customs Act 2005 (offence of wrongful disclosure) applies as it applies in relation to a disclosure of such information in contravention of section 20(9) of that Act.

(7) In subsection (6) "revenue and customs information relating to a person" has the meaning given by section 19(2) of that Act.

(8) Subject to subsections (3) and (5), no obligation as to confidentiality or other restriction on disclosure, whether imposed by an enactment or otherwise, prevents disclosure of relevant information—

    (*a*) to a Minister of the Crown for the purposes of functions of a Minister of the Crown under sections 257JD to 257JG,

    (*b*) to a person for the purposes of functions delegated to the person under section 257JH(1), or

    (*c*) to an officer of Revenue and Customs for the purpose of assisting Her Majesty's Revenue and Customs to discharge their functions under the Income Tax Acts so far as relating to matters arising under this Part.

(9) In subsection (8) "relevant information" means information obtained—

    (*a*) by a Minister of the Crown, or

    (*b*) by a person to whom functions have been delegated under section 257JH(1),

in the course of discharging functions under sections 257JD to 257JG.

(10) In this section "Minister of the Crown" has the meaning given by section 8(1) of the Ministers of the Crown Act 1975.]¹

Commentary—*Simon's Taxes* **E3.931**.
Amendments—[1]   Part 5B (ss 257J–257TE) inserted by FA 2014 s 57, Sch 11 para 1 with effect from 17 July 2014.

[CHAPTER 9

MISCELLANEOUS AND SUPPLEMENTARY PROVISIONS]

Amendments—Part 5B (ss 257J–257TE) inserted by FA 2014 s 57 Sch 11 para 1 with effect from 17 July 2014.

[257T Transfers between spouses or civil partners
(1) This section applies if—
   (a) the investor transfers the whole or part of the investment to another individual ("B") during their lives,
   (b) the investor was married to, or was the civil partner of, B at the time of the transfer, and
   (c) section 257R does not apply to the transfer.
(2) This Part (including subsection (1)) has effect, in relation to any subsequent disposal or other event, as if—
   (a) B were the investor as respects the transferred stake,
   (b) B's liability to income tax had been reduced in respect of the transferred stake for the same tax year as that for which the investor's was so reduced,
   (c) the amount by which B's liability to income tax had been reduced in respect of the transferred stake were the same as that by which the investor's liability had been so reduced, and
   (d) the same amount of SI relief had continued to be attributable to the transferred stake despite the transfer.
(3) If the amount of SI relief attributable to the transferred stake had been reduced before the relief was obtained by the investor—
   (a) this Part has effect, in relation to any subsequent disposal or other event, as if the amount of SI relief attributable to the transferred stake had been correspondingly reduced before the relief was obtained by B, and
   (b) section 257QD(2), 257QO(3) and 257RA(4) apply in relation to B as they would have applied in relation to the investor.
(4) If, because of any such disposal or other event, an assessment for reducing or withdrawing SI relief is to be made, the assessment is to be made on B.][1]

Commentary—*Simon's Taxes* **E3.925**.
Amendments—[1]   Part 5B (ss 257J–257TE) inserted by FA 2014 s 57, Sch 11 para 1 with effect from 17 July 2014.

[257TA Identification of investments on a disposal
(1) The rules in subsections (2) and (3) are for determining which investments of any class are treated as disposed of for the purposes of—
   (a) section 257R (disposal of the investment), or
   (b) section 257T (spouses or civil partners),
if the investor disposes of some but not all of the investments of that class which the investor holds in the social enterprise.
(2) Investments made on an earlier day are treated as disposed of before investments made on a later day.
(3) Investments made on the same day are treated as disposed of in the following order—
   (a) first, any to which neither SI relief nor hold-over relief is attributable,
   (b) next, any to which hold-over relief, but not SI relief, is attributable,
   (c) next, any to which SI relief, but not hold-over relief, is attributable, and
   (d) finally, any to which both SI relief and hold-over relief are attributable.
(4) Any investments within paragraph (c) or (d) of subsection (3) which are treated by section 257N(7) as issued on an earlier day are treated as disposed of before any other investments falling within that paragraph of subsection (3).
(5) The following—
   (a) any investments to which SI relief is attributable and which were transferred to an individual as mentioned in section 257T, and
   (b) any investments to which hold-over relief, but not SI relief, is attributable and which were acquired by an individual on a disposal to which section 58 of TCGA 1992 applies,
are treated for the purposes of subsections (2) and (3) as acquired by the individual on the day on which they were made.
(6) In a case to which section 127 of TCGA 1992 applies (including the case where that section applies by virtue of an enactment relating to chargeable gains), shares included in the new holding are treated for the purposes of subsections (2) and (3) as acquired when the original shares were acquired.
(7) In this section—
   "hold-over relief" means relief under Schedule 8B to TCGA 1992;
   "new holding" and "original shares" have the same meaning as in section 127 of TCGA 1992 (or, as the case may be, that section as applied by the enactment concerned).][1]

Commentary—*Simon's Taxes* **E3.925**.
Amendments—[1]   Part 5B (ss 257J–257TE) inserted by FA 2014 s 57, Sch 11 para 1 with effect from 17 July 2014.

[257TB Meaning of a company being "in administration" or "in receivership"

(1) References in this Part to a company being "in administration" or "in receivership" are to be read as follows.

(2) A company is "in administration" if—

    (*a*) it is in administration within the meaning of Schedule B1 to the Insolvency Act 1986 or Schedule B1 to the Insolvency (Northern Ireland) Order 1989 (SI 1989/2405 (N.I. 19)), or

    (*b*) there is in force in relation to it under the law of a country or territory outside the United Kingdom any appointment corresponding to an appointment of an administrator under either of those Schedules.

(3) A company is "in receivership" if there is in force in relation to it—

    (*a*) an order for the appointment of an administrative receiver, a receiver and manager or a receiver under Chapter 1 or 2 of Part 3 of the Insolvency Act 1986 or Part 4 of the Insolvency (Northern Ireland) Order 1989, or

    (*b*) any corresponding order under the law of a country or territory outside the United Kingdom.][1]

Commentary—*Simon's Taxes* **E3.902**.
Amendments—[1]   Part 5B (ss 257J–257TE) inserted by FA 2014 s 57, Sch 11 para 1 with effect from 17 July 2014.

[257TC Meaning of "associate"

(1) In this Part "associate", in relation to a person, means—

    (*a*) any relative or partner of the person,

    (*b*) the trustee or trustees of any settlement in relation to which the person, or any relative of the person (living or dead), is or was a settlor, and

    (*c*) if the person has an interest in any shares or obligations of a company which are subject to any trust or are part of the estate of a deceased person—

        (i) the trustee or trustees of the settlement concerned or, as the case may be, the personal representatives of the deceased, and

        (ii) if the person is a company, any other company which has an interest in those shares or obligations.

(2) In this section "relative" means spouse, civil partner, ancestor or lineal descendant.][1]

Commentary—*Simon's Taxes* **E3.902**.
Amendments—[1]   Part 5B (ss 257J–257TE) inserted by FA 2014 s 57, Sch 11 para 1 with effect from 17 July 2014.

[257TD Meaning of "control"

(1) In this Part "control" is to be read in accordance with sections 450 and 451 of CTA 2010 but as if "company" in those sections included a charity that is a trust.

(2) For the purposes of this Part, a charity that is a trust has "control" of another person if, as a result of the operation of subsection (1), the trustees (in their capacity as trustees of the trust) have, or any of them has, control of the person.

(3) A person has "control" of a charity that is a trust if—

    (*a*) the person is a trustee of the charity and some or all of the powers of the trustees of the charity could be exercised by—

        (i) the person acting alone, or

        (ii) by the person acting together with any other persons who are trustees of the charity and who are connected with the person,

    (*b*) the person, alone or together with other persons, has power to appoint or remove a trustee of the charity, or

    (*c*) the person, alone or together with other persons, has any power of approval or direction in relation to the carrying-out by the trustees of any of their functions.

(4) Subsection (3) is in addition to, and does not limit, subsection (1); and both of those subsections are subject to subsection (5).

(5) For the purposes of this Part, a regulator is to be treated as not having control of any company regulated by the regulator.

(6) Section 995 of this Act (control) does not apply for the purposes of this Part.][1]

Commentary—*Simon's Taxes* **E3.902**.
Amendments—[1]   Part 5B (ss 257J–257TE) inserted by FA 2014 s 57, Sch 11 para 1 with effect from 17 July 2014.

[257TE Minor definitions etc

(1) In this Part—

    "arrangements" (except as used, in sections 257LB and 257QK, in the expressions "issuing arrangements" and "repayment arrangements") includes any scheme, arrangement or understanding of any kind, whether or not legally enforceable, involving a single transaction or two or more transactions,

    "bonus shares" means shares which are issued otherwise than for payment (whether in cash or otherwise),

"compliance statement" has the meaning given by section 257PB,
"director"—

> (a) is read in accordance with section 452 of CTA 2010 but as if "company" in that
> section included a charity that is a trust, and

> (b) in relation to a charity that is a trust (but subject to section 257LF(9)), includes (in
> particular) each trustee of the trust,

"disposal", in relation to any shares or other investments, includes disposal of an interest or right
in or over them,
"group" means a parent company and its qualifying subsidiaries,
"group company", in relation to a group, means the parent company or any of its qualifying
subsidiaries,
"ordinary shares" means shares forming part of a company's ordinary share capital,
"parent company" means a company that has one or more qualifying subsidiaries,
"qualifying subsidiary" has the meaning given by section 257MU, and
"single company" means a company that does not have any qualifying subsidiaries.

(2) For the purposes of this Part, the market value at any time of any asset is the price which it might
reasonably be expected to fetch on a sale at that time in the open market free from any interest or
right which exists by way of security in or over it.]¹

Commentary—*Simon's Taxes* **E3.902, E3.908**.
Amendments—¹ Part 5B (ss 257J–257TE) inserted by FA 2014 s 57, Sch 11 para 1 with effect from 17 July 2014.

PART 6
VENTURE CAPITAL TRUSTS

Commentary—*Simon's Taxes* **E3.201, D8.201**.
Modification—ITA 2007 Sch 2 para 90 (transitional provisions and savings: modification of the provisions in this Part).

CHAPTER 1

INTRODUCTION

258 Overview of Part

In this Part—

> (a) Chapter 2 provides for VCT income tax relief ("VCT relief"), that is, entitlement to tax
> reductions in respect of amounts subscribed by individuals for shares issued to them by
> venture capital trusts,

> (b) Chapter 3 provides for VCT approvals,

> (c) Chapter 4 makes provision as to the meaning of "qualifying holding" for the purposes of
> Chapter 3,

> (d) Chapter 5 confers power for regulations to make provision in relation to the winding up and
> merger of venture capital trusts, and

> (e) Chapter 6 makes supplementary and general provision.

259 Venture capital trusts and VCT approvals

(1) In this Part "venture capital trust" means a company which—

> (a) is not a close company, and

> (b) is for the time being approved for the purposes of this Part by the Commissioners for Her
> Majesty's Revenue and Customs (see Chapter 3),

and "VCT" means a venture capital trust.

(2) In this Part "VCT approval" means an approval of a company for the purposes of this Part.

260 Other tax reliefs relating to VCTs

(1) Chapter 5 of Part 6 of ITTOIA 2005 (venture capital trust dividends) provides that, if conditions
are met, no liability to income tax arises in respect of dividends paid in respect of shares in a VCT.

(2) Section 100 of TCGA 1992 (exemption for venture capital trusts etc) provides that gains accruing
to a VCT are not to be chargeable gains.

(3) Section 151A of TCGA 1992 (venture capital trusts: reliefs) provides that a gain or loss accruing
to an individual on a qualifying disposal of any ordinary shares in a company which—

> (a) was a VCT at the time when the individual acquired the shares, and

> (b) is still a VCT at the time of the disposal,

is not to be a chargeable gain or, as the case may be, an allowable loss.

(4) Schedule 5C to TCGA 1992 (venture capital trusts: deferred charge on re-investment, but only in
relation to shares issued before 6 April 2004) provides that, if conditions are met, an
individual's unused qualifying expenditure on shares in a VCT may be set against what would
otherwise be chargeable gains.

CHAPTER 2
VCT RELIEF

Entitlement to relief

261 Eligibility for relief

(1) An individual ("A") is eligible for VCT relief for a tax year if—

    (*a*) a VCT issues eligible shares to A in that year,

    (*b*) the VCT issues the shares for raising money, and

    (*c*) A subscribes for the shares on A's own behalf.

(2) The amount in respect of which A is eligible for VCT relief for the tax year by reference to any shares is the amount subscribed by A for the shares.

(3) A is eligible for VCT relief by reference to any shares only if—

    [(*za*) the shares are issued before 6 April 2025,][1]

    (*a*) the shares are both subscribed for and issued—

        (i) for genuine commercial reasons, and

        (ii) not as part of a scheme or arrangement the main purpose or one of the main purposes of which is the avoidance of tax, and

    (*b*) A is at least 18 years old when the shares are issued.

(4) A is not eligible for VCT relief by reference to any shares if they are treated as issued to A by virtue of section 195(8) of FA 2003 (tax treatment of disposal by company of its own shares).

See section 271(4) for provision requiring the giving of notices about the effect of this subsection.

[(5) The Treasury may, by regulations, amend subsection (3)(*za*) to substitute a different date for the date for the time being specified there.][1]

Commentary—*Simon's Taxes* **E3.211**.

HMRC Manuals—Venture Capital Schemes Manual VCM51020 ('front-end' income tax relief: who can claim relief). VCM51040 ('front-end' income tax relief: when relief is not due).

Modifications—ITA 2007 Sch 2 para 59 (disapplication of sub-s (4) above in relation to shares acquired by a company before 1 December 2003).

Amendments—[1]   Sub-ss (3)(*za*), (5) inserted by F(No 2)A 2015 s 26, Sch 6 paras 1, 2 with effect from 18 November 2015.

262 Entitlement to claim relief

(1) An individual ("A") who is eligible for VCT relief by reference to shares issued in a tax year is entitled to claim VCT relief for that year.

(2) A is entitled to claim VCT relief in respect of the amount on which A is eligible for VCT relief by reference to all or some of the shares.

This is subject to subsection (3).

(3) A is not entitled to claim VCT relief for any tax year on an amount of more than £200,000.

Commentary—*Simon's Taxes* **E3.211**.

HMRC Manuals—Venture Capital Schemes Manual VCM51030 (how relief is claimed and calculated).

263 Form and amount of relief

(1) An individual who—

    (*a*) is entitled to claim VCT relief for a tax year, and

    (*b*) claims such relief for the year on any amount,

is entitled to a tax reduction for the year.

(2) The tax reduction is equal to 30% of the amount in respect of which the claim is made.

(3) The tax reduction is given effect at Step 6 of the calculation in section 23.

Commentary—*Simon's Taxes* **E3.211**.

HMRC Manuals—Venture Capital Schemes Manual VCM51030 (how relief is claimed and calculated).

Modifications—ITA 2007 Sch 2 para 60(1) (modification of sub-s (2) above in relation to shares issued before 6 April 2006). ITA 2007 Sch 2 para 60(2) (modification of sub-s (2) above in relation to shares issued before 6 April 2004).

264 No entitlement to relief if there is a linked loan

(1) An individual is not entitled to VCT relief by reference to any shares ("the relevant shares") if a linked loan is made by any person, at any time in the relevant period, to the individual or an associate of the individual.

(2) References in this section to the making by any person of a loan to an individual or any associate of the individual include references—

    (*a*) to the giving by that person of any credit to the individual or any associate of the individual, and

    (*b*) to the assignment to that person of any debt due from the individual or any associate of the individual.

(3) In this section—

    "linked loan" means a loan which—

        (*a*) would not have been made, or

        (*b*) would not have been made on the same terms,

    if the individual had not subscribed for the relevant shares or had not been proposing to do so, "the relevant period", in relation to VCT relief in respect of any shares in a company which is a VCT, means the period—

(*a*) beginning with—

(i) the incorporation of the company, or

(ii) if later, the date two years before the issue of the shares, and

(*b*) ending immediately before the fifth anniversary of that issue.

Commentary—*Simon's Taxes* **E3.211**.
HMRC Manuals—Venture Capital Schemes Manual VCM51040 ('front-end' income tax relief: when relief is not due).
Modifications—ITA 2007 Sch 2 para 61 (modification of sub-s (3) above in relation to shares issued before 6 April 2006).

[264A Restricting relief where there is a linked sale
(1) This section applies where—

(*a*) an individual subscribes for shares ("the relevant shares") in a VCT ("the VCT"), and

(*b*) there is at least one linked sale of other shares by the individual.

(2) For the purposes of this Part, the amount the individual subscribes for the shares is to be treated as reduced (but not below nil) by the total consideration given for the linked sales of other shares. This is subject to subsection (3).

(3) If a sale is linked in relation to more than one subscription for shares—

(*a*) the consideration for it is to be applied to reduce subscriptions under subsection (2) in the order in which the subscriptions are made, and

(*b*) accordingly, to the extent that any consideration has been used to reduce an earlier subscription, it is not available to reduce a later one.

(4) A sale of shares ("the sold shares") is "linked" if conditions A and B are met.

(5) Condition A is that the sold shares are in—

(*a*) the VCT, or

(*b*) [if subsection (7A) applies,]² a company which is (or later becomes) a successor or predecessor of the VCT.

(6) Condition B is that—

(*a*) the individual subscribes for the relevant shares in circumstances where—

(i) the purchase of the sold shares from the individual was conditional upon the individual subscribing for shares in the VCT, or

(ii) the individual's subscription for shares in the VCT was conditional upon that purchase, or

(*b*) the subscription for the relevant shares and the sale of the sold shares are within 6 months of each other (irrespective of which came first).

(7) A company ("company X") is a "successor or predecessor of the VCT" if—

(*a*) there is a merger of two or more companies for the purposes of Chapter 5 (see section 323) and—

(i) the VCT is one of the merged companies and company X is "the successor company" (as defined by that section), or

(ii) the VCT is "the successor company" and company X is one of the merged companies, or

(*b*) section 327 (effect of restructuring of VCT) applies and—

(i) the VCT is "the old company" and company X is "the new company" for the purposes of that section, or

(ii) company X is "the old company" and the VCT is "the new company" for those purposes.

[(7A) This subsection applies if—

(*a*) the date of the merger or restructuring referred to in subsection (7) ("D2") is before, or the same as, the date when the individual subscribes for the relevant shares ("D1"), or

(*b*) D2 is after D1 but no more than two years after, and either—

(i) the individual could reasonably be expected to know at the time of subscribing for the relevant shares that the merger or restructuring referred to in subsection (7) was likely to take place, or

(ii) the main purpose of the merger or restructuring, or one of its main purposes, is to enable individuals to obtain a tax advantage in connection with VCT relief.

(7B) For the purposes of subsection (7A)—

(*a*) the date of the merger or restructuring is the date of the issue of shares referred to in section 323(1)(*a*) or (2)(*a*) or section 326(2)(*a*) (or, if there is more than one such issue, the date of the first of them);

(*b*) a "tax advantage" includes—

(i) relief or increased relief from tax,

(ii) repayment or increased repayment of tax,

(iii) avoidance or reduction of a charge to tax or an assessment to tax, and

(iv) avoidance of a possible assessment to tax.]²

(8) This section does not apply if, or to the extent that, the subscription for the relevant shares is a result of the individual electing to reinvest dividends payable to the individual on shares in the VCT, in acquiring further shares in the VCT.][1]

Commentary—*Simon's Taxes* **E3.211**.
Amendments—[1]   Section 264A inserted by FA 2014 s 53, Sch 10 para 2 with effect in relation to claims for relief by reference to shares issued on or after 6 April 2014.
[2]   In sub-s (5)(*b*), words inserted, and sub-ss (7A), (7B) inserted, by FA 2018 s 17, Sch 5 para 1 with effect in relation to claims for relief by reference to shares issued on or after 6 April 2014.

265 No entitlement to relief which would have been lost if it had already been obtained

An individual is not entitled to VCT relief by reference to any shares if circumstances have arisen which would have resulted in the withdrawal or reduction of the relief, if that relief had already been obtained.

Commentary—*Simon's Taxes* **E3.212**.

Loss of relief

266 Loss of relief if shares disposed of within 5 years

(1) This section applies, subject to section 267 (spouses or civil partners), if an individual—
    (*a*) obtains VCT relief in respect of eligible shares in a VCT, and
    (*b*) makes a disposal of those shares within 5 years of their issue to the individual.
(2) In the case of a disposal that is made otherwise than by way of a bargain made at arm's length, any VCT relief obtained by reference to the shares which are disposed of is to be withdrawn.
(3) In the case of a disposal that is made by way of a bargain made at arm's length, any VCT relief obtained by reference to the shares disposed of must—
    (*a*) if it is greater than A, be reduced by A, and
    (*b*) in any other case, be withdrawn.
(4) A is 30% of the amount or value of the consideration which the individual receives for the shares.
(5) The rules in subsections (6) and (7) are for determining which eligible shares of any class are treated as disposed of for the purposes of—
    (*a*) this section, and
    (*b*) section 267,
if a person disposes of some but not all of the eligible shares of that class which the person holds in a company.
(6) Shares acquired on an earlier day are treated as disposed of before shares acquired on a later day.
(7) Shares acquired on the same day are treated as disposed of in the following order—
    (*a*) shares by reference to which VCT relief has not been obtained, and
    (*b*) shares by reference to which VCT relief has been obtained.

Commentary—*Simon's Taxes* **E3.221, E3.212**.
HMRC Manuals—Venture Capital Schemes Manual VCM51090 (withdrawing relief).
Modifications—ITA 2007 Sch 2 para 62(1) (modification of sub-ss (1), (4) above in relation to shares issued before 6 April 2006). ITA 2007 Sch 2 para 62(2) (modification of sub-s (4) above in relation to shares issued before 6 April 2004).

267 Transfers of shares between spouses or civil partners

(1) Section 266 does not apply in the case of any disposal of shares made by an individual to the individual's spouse or civil partner, if it is made at a time when they are living together.
(2) Subsection (3) applies if any eligible shares which—
    (*a*) have been issued to any individual ("the transferor"), and
    (*b*) are shares by reference to which any VCT relief has been obtained,
are transferred to the transferor's spouse or civil partner ("the transferee") by a disposal such as is mentioned in subsection (1).
(3) If this subsection applies, section 266 and subsection (2) have effect, in relation to any subsequent disposal or other event, as if—
    (*a*) the transferee were the person who had subscribed for the shares,
    (*b*) the shares had been issued to the transferee at the time when they were issued to the transferor,
    (*c*) there had been, in relation to the transferred shares, such a reduction by way of VCT relief in the transferee's liability to income tax as is equal to the actual reduction in respect of those shares of the transferor's liability, and
    (*d*) that deemed reduction were (despite the transfer) to be treated for the purposes of section 266 as an amount of VCT relief obtained by reference to the shares transferred.
(4) Any assessment for withdrawing or reducing VCT relief because of a disposal or other event falling within subsection (3) is to be made on the transferee.

Commentary—*Simon's Taxes* **E3.212**.

268 Loss of relief if VCT approval withdrawn

(1) This section applies if—
    (*a*) the approval of any company as a VCT is withdrawn, and

(b) the withdrawal of the approval is not one to which section 281(3) (VCT approval treated as never having been given) applies.

(2) Any person who, at the time when the withdrawal takes effect, is holding any shares issued by the company by reference to which VCT relief has been obtained is treated for the purposes of section 266 as having disposed of those shares—

(a) immediately before that time, and

(b) otherwise than by way of a bargain made at arm's length.

Commentary—Simon's Taxes **E3.212**.
HMRC Manuals—Venture Capital Schemes Manual VCM56030 (VCT winding-up: 'front-end' income tax relief).

269 Loss of relief which is subsequently found not to have been due

Any VCT relief obtained which is subsequently found not to have been due is to be withdrawn.

Commentary—Simon's Taxes **E3.212**.

270 Assessment on withdrawal or reduction of relief

(1) An assessment for withdrawing or reducing VCT relief under any of sections 266 to 269 must be made for the tax year for which the relief was obtained [, and may be made at any time not more than 6 years after the end of that tax year][1].

(2) No assessment for withdrawing or reducing VCT relief obtained by reference to shares issued to any individual may be made because of any event occurring after the individual's death.

Commentary—Simon's Taxes **E3.212**.
HMRC Manuals—Venture Capital Schemes Manual VCM56050 (VCT winding-up: deferral relief
Amendments—[1]   In sub-s (1) words inserted by FA 2014 s 53, Sch 10 para 1 with effect in relation to assessments made on or after 6 April 2014 (including those made for tax years ending before that date).

Supplementary

271 Provision of information

(1) If an event occurs that results in any VCT relief falling to be withdrawn or reduced, the individual by whom the relief was obtained must, within 60 days of coming to know of the event, give notice to an officer of Revenue and Customs containing particulars of the event.

(2), (3) . . . [1]

(4) If a company which is a VCT issues to any individual eligible shares to which section 261(4) applies, it must—

(a) at the time of the issue of those shares, give the individual a notice stating that the individual is not eligible for VCT relief by reference to those shares, and

(b) not later than 3 months after the issue of those shares, give a copy of that notice to an officer of Revenue and Customs.

(5) No obligation as to secrecy imposed by statute or otherwise prevents an officer of Revenue and Customs from disclosing to a VCT that VCT relief has been obtained by reference to a particular number or proportion of its shares.

Commentary—Simon's Taxes **E3.212**.
Amendments—[1]   Sub-ss (2), (3) repealed by the Finance Act 2009 Schedule 47 (Consequential Amendments) Order, SI 2009/2035, Art 2, Sch paras 46, 47 with effect from 13 August 2009.

272 Regulations as to procedure etc

(1) This section applies to VCT relief and relief for which the following provide—

(a) section 151A of TCGA 1992 (VCTs: reliefs),

(b) Schedule 5C to TCGA 1992 (VCTs: deferred charge on re-investment),

(c) Chapter 5 of Part 6 of ITTOIA 2005 (VCT dividends), and

(d) regulations under Chapter 5 of this Part.

(2) The Treasury may by regulations make such provision as they consider appropriate for—

(a) giving effect to relief to which this section applies, and

(b) preventing such relief from being given unless a claim is made in accordance with the regulations and such other requirements as may be imposed by the regulations have been met.

(3) Regulations under this section may make provision as to the manner in which, and the persons by whom, relief to which this section applies is to be claimed.

Commentary—Simon's Taxes **E3.234**.
Regulations—Venture Capital Trust (Amendment) Regulations, SI 2014/1929.
Venture Capital Trust (Amendment) Regulations, SI 2016/1192.

273 Interpretation of Chapter

(1) In this Chapter "eligible shares", in relation to a company which is a VCT, means ordinary shares in the VCT which, throughout the period of 5 years beginning on the date on which they are issued, carry—

(a) no present or future preferential right to dividends or to a company's assets on its winding up, and

(b) no present or future right to be redeemed.

(2) In this Chapter references to a disposal of shares include references to a disposal of an interest or right in or over shares.

Commentary—*Simon's Taxes* **E3.211**.
Modifications—ITA 2007 Sch 2 para 63(1) (modification of sub-s (1) above in relation to shares issued before 6 April 2007).
ITA 2007 Sch 2 para 63(2) (modification of sub-s (1) above in relation to shares issued before 6 April 2006).

CHAPTER 3

VCT APPROVALS

Giving of approval

274 Requirements for the giving of approval

(1) Subject to section 275, the Commissioners for Her Majesty's Revenue and Customs must not approve a company for the purposes of this Part unless it is shown to their satisfaction that the conditions mentioned in subsection (2)—

(*a*) are met in relation to the most recent complete accounting period of the company, and

(*b*) will be met in relation to the accounting period of the company which is current when the application for approval is made.

(2) The conditions applied by subsection (1) (which are also applied by section 275(1) and other provisions of this Chapter) are set out in column 2 of the following table together with, in column 1 of the table, the descriptions by which they are referred to.

In each of those conditions "the relevant period" means the accounting period that is relevant for the purposes of the particular provision by which the condition is applied.

Description	Condition
The listing condition	The shares making up the company's ordinary share capital (or, if there are such shares of more than one class, those of each class) have been or will be [[admitted to trading on a regulated market][3] throughout the relevant period][2]
The nature of income condition	The company's income in the relevant period has been or will be derived wholly or mainly from shares or securities
The income retention condition	The company has not retained or will not retain an amount which is greater than 15% of the income it derived or will derive in the relevant period from shares or securities
The 15% holding limit condition	No holding in any company, other than a VCT or a company that would qualify as a VCT but for the listing condition, has represented or will represent at any time during the relevant period more than 15% by value of the company's investments
The [80%][9] qualifying holdings condition	At least [80%][9] by value of the company's investments has been or will be represented throughout the relevant period by shares or securities included in qualifying holdings of the company
The [70%][4] eligible shares condition	At least [70%][4] by value of the company's qualifying holdings has been or will be represented throughout the relevant period by holdings of eligible shares
[The non-qualifying investments condition	The company has not made and will not make, in the relevant period, an investment which is neither of the following—
	(*a*) an investment that on the date it is made is included in the company's qualifying holdings;
	(*b*) an investment falling within subsection (3A).][7]
[The investment limits condition	The company has not made and will not make an investment, in the relevant period, in a company which breaches the permitted investment limits][5]
[The minimum investment on further issue condition	The company has not breached and will not breach, in the relevant period, the minimum investment on further issue condition][8]
[The permitted maximum age condition	The company has not made and will not make an investment, in the relevant period, in a company which breaches the permitted maximum age limit.
The no business acquisition condition	The company has not made and will not make an investment, in the relevant period, in a company which breaches the prohibition on business acquisitions.][6]

(3) The conditions mentioned in subsection (2) are supplemented as follows—

(*a*) the nature of income condition and the income retention condition by section 276,

(*b*) the 15% holding limit condition by section 277,

(*c*) the 15% holding limit condition, the [80%][9] qualifying holdings condition and the [70%][4] eligible shares condition by sections 278 and 279, . . . [1]

(*d*) the [80%][9] qualifying holdings condition and the [70%][4] eligible shares condition by section 280 [. . . [5]

(*e*) the [80%][9] qualifying holdings condition by section 280A][1][, . . . [6]

(*f*) the investment limits condition by [subsection [(3ZA)][7] and by][6] section 280B.][5]

[(*fa*) the minimum investment on further issue condition by section 280BA,][8]

[(*g*) the permitted maximum age condition by subsection [(3ZA)][7] and by section 280C, and

(*h*) the no business acquisition condition by subsection [(3ZA)][7] and by section 280D.][6]

(3ZA) In the second column of the table in subsection (2), in the entries for the investment limits condition, the permitted maximum age condition and the no business acquisition condition, any reference to an investment made by the company in a company does not include an investment falling within subsection (3A).][7]

[(3A) [An investment made by a company ("the investor") falls within this subsection if it is][7] any of the following investments—

(*a*) shares or units in an AIF (within the meaning given by regulation 3 of the Alternative Investment Fund Managers Regulations 2013) which may be repurchased or redeemed on 7 days' notice given by the investor;

(*b*) shares or units in a UCITS (within the meaning given by section 363A(4) of TIOPA 2010) which may be repurchased or redeemed on 7 days' notice given by the investor;

(*c*) ordinary shares or securities in a company which are acquired by [the investor][7] on a regulated market;

[(*d*) money in the investor's possession;

(*e*) a sum owed to the investor which—

(i) under section 285(4)(*b*) (read with section 285(5) and (6)) is to be regarded as an investment of the investor, and

(ii) is such that the investor's right mentioned in section 285(5)(*a*) may be exercised on 7 days' notice given by the investor.][7][6]

[(3B) In subsection (3A), any reference to a thing which may be done on 7 days' notice includes a case where that thing may be done—

(*a*) on less than 7 days' notice, or

(*b*) without notice.][7

[(4) In this section "regulated market" has the same meaning as in [Directive 2014/65/EU][10] of the European Parliament and of the Council on markets in financial instruments (see [Article 4.1.21][10]).

[(5) The Treasury may by regulations—

(*a*) amend the first entry in the table in subsection (2) (the listing condition),

(*b*) add, remove or amend an entry in the list of investments in subsection (3A),

(*ba*) amend or repeal subsection (3B) in consequence of any provision made under paragraph (*b*),][7

(*c*) amend this section so as to make provision to restrict the period for which an investment [falling within subsection (3A) may be held by the company][7, or

(*d*) amend subsection (4).][6][3

Commentary—*Simon's Taxes* **E3.230, E3.231, E3.232, E3.233, D8.205** .
HMRC Manuals—Venture Capital Schemes Manual VCM54020 (conditions for full approval).
Amendments—[1]   In sub-s (3)(*c*) word "and" repealed, and sub-s (3)(*e*) and preceding word "and" inserted by FA 2007 ss 51, 114, Sch 16 para 20(1), (2), (4), (5), Sch 27 Pt 2(16) with effect in relation to disposals made on or after 6 April 2007.
[2]   Words in sub-s (2) substituted by FA 2007 s 109, Sch 26 para 12(1), (6) with effect from 19 July 2007.
[3]   In sub-s (2), in column 2 of the first entry of the table, words substituted, and sub-ss (4), (5) inserted, by F(No 3)A 2010 s 5, Sch 2 para 2(1), (2)(*a*), (*d*) with effect in relation to accounting periods ending on or after 6 April 2011 (and in relation to shares issued at any time) (by virtue of SI 2011/662 art 2).
[4]   In sub-s (2), in columns 1 and 2 of the last entry of the table and in sub-s (3)(*c*), (*d*) figure substituted by F(No 3)A 2010 s 5, Sch 2 para 2(1), (2)(*b*), (*c*) with effect in relation to accounting periods ending on or after 6 April 2011 (by virtue of SI 2011/662). These amendments do not have effect in relation to shares or securities held by a company ("the investing company") if the shares or securities are issued before 6 April 2011 or are issued on or after that day and are acquired by the investing company by means of the investment of protected money (F(No 3)A 2010 Sch 2 para 6(2), (3)).
[5]   In sub-s (2), condition inserted, word "and" at the end of sub-s (3)(*d*) repealed, and sub-s (3)(*f*) and preceding word "and" inserted, by FA 2012 s 40, Sch 8 paras 1, 2 with effect in relation to investments made on or after 17 July 2012, subject to provisions relating to investments made before that date: see FA 2012 Sch 8 para 18(2).
[6]   In sub-s (2), conditions inserted; in sub-s (3)(*e*) word "and" repealed; in sub-s (3)(*f* words inserted; sub-ss (3)(*g*), (*h*), (3A) inserted; and sub-s (5) substituted; by F(No 2)A 2015 s 26, Sch 6 paras 1, 3 with effect in relation to investments made on or after 18 November 2015.
[7]   In sub-s (2), condition inserted; word in sub-s (3)(*f*), (*g*), (*h*) substituted; sub-ss (3ZA), (3B) inserted; words in sub-s (3A) substituted; sub-ss (3A)(*d*), (*e*), (5)(*ba*) inserted; and words in sub-s (5)(*c*) substituted; by FA 2016 s 31 with effect in relation to investments made on or after 6 April 2016.
[8]   In sub-s (2), condition inserted, and sub-s (3)(*fa*) inserted, by FA 2018 s 17, Sch 5 para 5 with effect in relation to money raised by a further issue that is made in an accounting period beginning on or after 6 April 2018 (by virtue of SI 2018/931 reg 4(*c*)).
[9]   In sub-s (2), in first and second columns of fifth entry (previously "the 70% qualifying holdings condition"), figure "80%" substituted for figure "70%", and in sub-s (3)(*c*)–(*e*), figure "80%" substituted for figure "70%", by FA 2018 s 17, Sch 5 paras 2, 3(*a*) with effect from 6 April 2019 (by virtue of SI 2018/931 reg 4(*a*)).
[10]   In sub-s (4) words substituted for words "Directive 2004/39/EC" and "Article 4.1(14)" by Financial Services and Markets Act 2000 (Markets in Financial Instruments) Regulations, SI 2017/701 reg 50(3), Sch 4 para 10 with effect from 3 January 2018 (see SI 2017/701 reg 1(6)). See also the commencement provisions for particular purposes in SI 2018/701 reg 1.

Prospective amendments—Sub-s (4) to be substituted by the Taxes (Amendments) (EU Exit) Regulations, SI 2019/689 reg 15(1), (2) with effect from Implementation Period completion day (see EU(WA)A 2020 Sch 5 para 1(1)). Sub-s (4) to read as follows—

"(4) In this section "regulated market" means—

(a) a UK regulated market within the meaning given by Article 2.1(13A) of Regulation (EU) No 600/2014 of the European Parliament and of the Council of 15 May 2014 on markets in financial instruments,

(b) an EU regulated market within the meaning given by Article 2.1(13B) of that Regulation, and

(c) a regulated market within the meaning given by Article 2.1(13) of that Regulation which is authorised and functions regularly and in accordance with Part 3 of the Financial Services (Markets in Financial Instruments) Act 2018 of Gibraltar."

Sub-s (4)(c), as inserted by SI 2019/689 above, to be substituted by the Taxes (Amendments) (EU Exit) (No 2) Regulations, SI 2019/818 reg 6(1), (2) with effect from Implementation Period completion day, immediately after the coming into force of SI 2019/689 (which also come into force on Implementation Period completion day (see EU(WA)A 2020 Sch 5 para 1(1)). Para (c) to read as follows—

" a (Gibraltar regulated market within the meaning given by Article 26(11)(b)(i) of that Regulation.".

275 Alternative requirements for the giving of approval

(1) This section applies if one or more of the conditions mentioned in section 274(2) are not met with respect to a company in relation to its most recent complete accounting period.

(2) The Commissioners for Her Majesty's Revenue and Customs may still approve the company for the purposes of this Part if they are satisfied that the condition or conditions in question—

(a) will be met in relation to the period mentioned in subsection (3), and

(b) will continue to be met in relation to accounting periods following that period.

(3) The period is—

(a) in relation to the listing condition, the nature of income condition, the income retention condition and the 15% holding limit condition, the accounting period of the company which is current when the application for approval is made, or its next accounting period,

(b) in relation to the [80%][2] qualifying holdings condition and the [70%][1] eligible shares condition, an accounting period of the company beginning no more than 3 years after the time when the approval is given or, if earlier, when the approval takes effect.

Commentary—*Simon's Taxes* **E3.230, D8.204**.
HMRC Manuals—Venture Capital Schemes Manual VCM54030 (conditions for provisional approval).
Amendments—[1] In sub-s (3)(b) figure substituted by F(No 3)A 2010 s 5, Sch 2 para 2(1), (3) with effect in relation to accounting periods ending on or after 6 April 2011 (by virtue of SI 2011/662). These amendments do not have effect in relation to shares or securities held by a company ("the investing company") if the shares or securities are issued before 6 April 2011 or are issued on or after that day and are acquired by the investing company by means of the investment of protected money (F(No 3)A 2010 Sch 2 para 6(2), (3)).
[2] In sub-s (3)(b), figure "80%" substituted for figure "70%" by FA 2018 s 17, Sch 5 para 3(b) with effect in relation to accounting periods beginning on or after 6 April 2019 (by virtue of SI 2018/931 reg 4(a)).

276 Conditions relating to income

(1) Subsections (2) and (3) apply in determining for the purposes of the nature of income condition and the income retention condition—

(a) the amount of a company's income, or

(b) the amount of income which a company derives from shares or securities.

(2) The amounts to be brought into account under [Part 5 of CTA 2009][2] in respect of the company's loan relationships are to be determined without reference to any debtor relationship of the company.

(3) The excess of any relevant credits over any relevant debits is to be treated as income which the company derives from shares or securities.

In this subsection "relevant credits" and "relevant debits" are credits and debits brought into account by virtue of [section 574 of CTA 2009 (non-trading credits and debits to be brought into account under Part 5 of that Act)][1].

(4) The income retention condition does not apply as regards an accounting period if the amount which the company would be required to distribute in order to meet that condition is less than—

(a) £10,000, or

(b) if the period is shorter than 12 months, a proportionately reduced amount.

(5) The income retention condition does not apply as regards an accounting period if—

(a) the company is required to retain income in respect of the period by virtue of a restriction imposed by law, and

(b) the amount of income which the company is so required to retain in respect of the period exceeds an amount equal to 15% of the income the company derives from shares or securities.

(6) Subsection (5) does not apply if—

(a) the amount of income the company retains in respect of the accounting period exceeds the amount of income it is required, by virtue of a restriction imposed by law, to retain in respect of the period, and

(b) the sum of the excess and any amount of income the company distributes in respect of the period is at least—

   (i) £10,000, or

   (ii) if the period is shorter than 12 months, a proportionately reduced amount.

Commentary—*Simon's Taxes* **E3.230, E3.231, E3.232**.

HMRC Manuals—Venture Capital Schemes Manual VCM54050 (nature of the income condition). VCM54060 (income retention condition).

Amendments—[1] In sub-s (3) words substituted by CTA 2009 s 1322, Sch 1 paras 699, 701. CTA 2009 applies for accounting periods ending on or after 1 April 2009 (for corporation tax purposes) and for tax years 2009–10 onwards (for income and capital gains tax purposes).

[2] In sub-s (2) words substituted by the Corporation Tax Act 2009 (Amendment) Order, SI 2009/2860 art 5 with effect for corporation tax purposes for accounting periods ending on or after 1 April 2009, and for income tax and capital gains tax purposes for the tax year 2009–10 and subsequent tax years.

277 The 15% holding limit condition

(1) If the 15% holding limit condition was met when a holding in a company was acquired or last added to, the condition is treated as continuing to be met until an addition is next made to it.

(2) "Holding in a company" means the shares or securities (whether of one class or more than one class) held in any one company.

(3) An addition is made to a holding in a company whenever the company whose holding it is—

   (a) acquires further shares or securities in the company, but

   (b) does not do so by being allotted shares or securities without becoming liable to give any consideration.

(4) For the purposes of this section—

   (a) holdings in companies which—

      (i) are members of a group, whether or not including the company whose holdings they are ("company A"), and

      (ii) are not excluded from the 15% holding limit condition,

   are to be treated as holdings in a single company, and

   (b) if company A is a member of a group, money owed to it by another member of the group is to be treated—

      (i) as a security of the latter held by company A, and

      (ii) accordingly as, or as part of, the holding of company A in the company owing the money.

For the purposes of this subsection "group" means a company and all companies which are its 51% subsidiaries.

(5) Subsection (6) applies if, in connection with a scheme of reconstruction—

   (a) a company issues shares or securities,

   (b) the shares or securities are issued to persons holding shares or securities in a second company in respect of and in proportion to (or as nearly as may be in proportion to) their holdings in the second company, and

   (c) those persons do not become liable to give any consideration for the shares or securities.

In this subsection "scheme of reconstruction" has the same meaning as in section 136 of TCGA 1992.

(6) For the purposes of this section—

   (a) a holding of the shares or securities in the second company, and

   (b) a corresponding holding of the shares or securities issued by the company,

are to be regarded as the same holding.

Commentary—*Simon's Taxes* **E3.233, E3.230**.

HMRC Manuals—Venture Capital Schemes Manual VCM54070 (15% holding limit condition).

Modifications—ITA 2007 Sch 2 para 64 (modification of this section in relation to shares or securities issued before 17 April 2002).

278 Conditions relating to value of investments: general

(1) This section and section 279 apply for the purposes of the 15% holding limit condition, the [80%][2] qualifying holdings condition and the [70%][1] eligible shares condition ("the relevant conditions").

(2) The value of a holding of investments of any description is to be taken, unless subsection (3) applies, to be its value when acquired.

(3) If, in the case of a holding of investments of any description—

   (a) the holding is added to by a further holding of investments of that description, or

   (b) any payment is made in discharge, in whole or in part, of any obligation attached to the holding that (by discharging the whole or any part of the obligation) increases the value of the holding, the value of the holding is to be taken to be its value immediately after the most recent addition or payment.

(4) For the purposes of this section an addition is made to a holding of investments of any description whenever the company whose holding it is—

    (*a*) acquires further investments of that description, but

    (*b*) does not do so by being allotted shares or securities in a company without becoming liable to give any consideration.

(5) Subsection (6) applies if, in connection with a scheme of reconstruction—

    (*a*) a company issues shares or securities,

    (*b*) the shares or securities are issued to persons holding shares or securities in a second company in respect of and in proportion to (or as nearly as may be in proportion to) their holdings in the second company, and

    (*c*) those persons do not become liable to give any consideration for the shares or securities.

In this subsection "scheme of reconstruction" has the same meaning as in section 136 of TCGA 1992.

(6) For the purposes of this section—

    (*a*) a holding of the shares or securities of any description in the second company, and

    (*b*) a corresponding holding of the shares or securities issued by the company,

are to be regarded as the same holding.

Commentary—*Simon's Taxes* **E3.240**.
HMRC Manuals—Venture Capital Schemes Manual VCM54160 (value of a holding).
VCM54190 (exchange of shares or securities in same company: valuation of new holding).
VCM54210 (exchange of shares or securities for those in another company: valuation of the new holding).
Modifications—ITA 2007 Sch 2 para 65(1), (2) (modification of this section if any question arises which would otherwise fall to be determined in accordance with this section, and is a question whether, in a case where a company ("company A") holds investments in a company ("company B") immediately before 6 April 2007, the 15% holding condition is met if there is an addition to the holding on or after that date).
ITA 2007 Sch 2 para 65(3) (modification of sub-s (5) above in relation to certain prescribed circumstances where investments were issued before 17 April 2002).
Amendments—[1] In sub-s (1) figure substituted by F(No 3)A 2010 s 5, Sch 2 para 2(1), (4) with effect in relation to accounting periods ending on or after 6 April 2011 (by virtue of SI 2011/662). These amendments do not have effect in relation to shares or securities held by a company ("the investing company") if the shares or securities are issued before 6 April 2011 or are issued on or after that day and are acquired by the investing company by means of the investment of protected money (F(No 3)A 2010 Sch 2 para 6(2), (3)).
[2] In sub-s (1), figure "80%" substituted for figure "70%" by FA 2018 s 17, Sch 5 para 3(*c*) with effect in relation to accounting periods beginning on or after 6 April 2019 (by virtue of SI 2018/931 reg 4(*a*)).

279 Conditions relating to value of investments: qualifying holdings

(1) If—

    (*a*) any shares ("new shares") are exchanged for other shares ("old shares") under arrangements in relation to which section 326 (restructuring arrangements) applies, and

    (*b*) those arrangements have not ceased by virtue of section 326(5) to be arrangements by reference to which requirements of Chapter 4 are treated as met,

the value of the new shares is taken to be the same as the value, when last valued in accordance with subsection (2) or (3) of section 278, of the old shares for which they are exchanged.

(2) In subsection (1)—

    (*a*) references to shares in a company include references to any securities of that company, and

    (*b*) the reference to the value of the new shares includes references to the value of those shares both—

        (i) at the time of their acquisition, and

        (ii) immediately after any subsequent addition to a holding of the new shares that is made under the arrangements.

(3) If—

    (*a*) shares ("new shares") are issued to a company as a result of the exercise by that company of any right of conversion attached to other shares, or securities, held by that company ("convertibles"), and

    (*b*) section 329 (conversion of convertible shares and securities) applies in relation to the issue of the new shares,

the value of the new shares at the time of their acquisition is taken to be the same as the value, when last valued in accordance with subsection (2) or (3) of section 278, of the convertibles for which they are exchanged.

(4) Regulations under section 330 may make provision for securing that if—

    (*a*) there is an exchange of shares to which regulations under section 330 apply, and

    (*b*) the new shares are treated by virtue of the regulations as meeting the requirements of Chapter 4, the value of the holding of the new shares, and of any original shares that are retained under the exchange, is taken to be an amount such that the requirements of the relevant conditions do not cease to be met because of the exchange.

(5) In subsection (4)—

    (a) "shares" includes securities, and

    (b) "exchange of shares", "new shares" and "original shares" have the same meaning as in section 330.

Commentary—*Simon's Taxes* E3.240.

280 Conditions relating to qualifying holdings and eligible shares

(1) Subsection (2) applies, subject to any regulations under subsection (3), if—

    (a) there has been an issue of ordinary share capital of a company ("the first issue"),

    (b) a VCT approval of that company has taken effect on or before the day of the making of the first issue, and

    (c) a further issue of ordinary share capital of that company has been made since the making of the first issue.

(2) If this subsection applies, the use to which the money raised by the further issue is put, and the use of any money deriving from that use, are ignored in determining whether either or both of the [80%][2] qualifying holdings condition and the [70%][1] eligible shares condition are, have been or will be met in relation to—

    (a) the accounting period in which the further issue is made, or

    (b) any later accounting period ending no more than 3 years after the making of the further issue.

(3) The Treasury may by regulations make provision for subsection (2)—

    (a) not to apply, or to be treated as not having applied, in specified cases, or

    (b) to apply, or to be treated as having applied, in specified cases—

        (i) only to a specified extent, or

        (ii) only if specified conditions (including conditions requiring approvals to be obtained) are met.

(4) Provision made by regulations under subsection (3) may (but need not) be made so that, in any particular case, subsection (2)—

    (a) does not apply, or is treated as not having applied, at prescribed times or with effect from a prescribed time, or

    (b) applies, or is treated as having applied, in accordance with provision made under subsection (3)(b) at prescribed times or with effect from a prescribed time.

(5) In subsection (3) "specified" means specified by regulations and in subsection (4) "prescribed" means specified by, or determined under, regulations.

(6) Section 324 applies in relation to—

    (a) regulations under subsection (3), and

    (b) any power conferred by that subsection,

as it applies in relation to regulations under Chapter 5 and a power conferred by any provision of that Chapter.

Commentary—*Simon's Taxes* E3.234.

HMRC Manuals—Venture Capital Schemes Manual VCM54170 (further share issues and 70% and 30% or 70% tests).

Modifications—ITA 2007 Sch 2 para 66 (disapplication of sub-s (3) above in relation to shares issued before 17 April 2002).

Amendments—[1]   In sub-s (2) figure substituted by F(No 3)A 2010 s 5, Sch 2 para 2(1), (5) with effect in relation to accounting periods ending on or after 6 April 2011 (by virtue of SI 2011/662). These amendments do not have effect in relation to shares or securities held by a company ("the investing company") if the shares or securities are issued before 6 April 2011 or are issued on or after that day and are acquired by the investing company by means of the investment of protected money (F(No 3)A 2010 Sch 2 para 6(2), (3)).

[2]   In sub-s (2), figure "80%" substituted for figure "70%" by FA 2018 s 17, Sch 5 para 3(d) with effect in relation to accounting periods beginning on or after 6 April 2019 (by virtue of SI 2018/931 reg 4(a)).

[280A The 70% qualifying holdings condition: disposal of holding

(1) This section applies if—

    (a) a company which is a VCT disposes of shares or securities ("the holding"),

    (b) the consideration for the disposal does not consist wholly of new qualifying holdings, and

    (c) the holding was comprised in the company's qualifying holdings throughout the 6 months ending immediately before the disposal.

(2) For the purpose of determining whether the [80%][2] qualifying holdings condition is, has been or will be met—

    (a) the company is to be treated as if it continued to hold the holding for the period of [12][3] months beginning with the disposal (but see subsection (4)), and

    (b) the value of the company's investments in that period is to be treated as reduced by the amount of any monetary consideration for the disposal.

(3) The value of the holding in the period mentioned in subsection (2)(a) is to be treated as equal to its value (determined in accordance with this Chapter) immediately before the disposal.

(4) If the consideration for the disposal includes new qualifying holdings, subsection (2)(*a*) has effect as if the reference to the holding were to the appropriate proportion of the holding (the value of which is that proportion of the value of the holding, determined in accordance with subsection (3)).
(5) The appropriate proportion is—

$$\frac{TC - NQH}{TC}$$

where—
>TC is the market value (at the time of the disposal) of the total consideration for the disposal, and
>NQH is the market value (at that time) of the new qualifying holdings.

(6) If at any time the value of the company's investments would by virtue of subsection (2)(*b*) be reduced to an amount less than the value of its qualifying holdings, the value of its investments at that time is to be treated as equal to the value of its qualifying holdings.
(7) "New qualifying holdings" means shares or securities which (on transfer to the company) are comprised in the company's qualifying holdings.
(8) If (and to the extent that) the holding was acquired with money the use of which is at any time ignored by virtue of section 280(2), subsections (2) to (6) do not apply in relation to that time.
(9) Nothing in this section applies in relation to disposals between companies that are merging (within the meaning of section 323).][1]

Commentary—*Simon's Taxes* **E3.234.**
HMRC Manuals—Venture Capital Schemes Manual VCM54100 (70% qualifying holdings condition: disregard of disposals). VCM54120 (70% qualifying holdings condition: disregard of disposals: qualifying holdings received).
Amendments—[1] This section inserted by FA 2007 s 51, Sch 16 para 20(1), (3)–(5) with effect in relation to disposals made on or after 6 April 2007.
[2] In sub-s (2), figure "80%" substituted for figure "70%" by FA 2018 s 17, Sch 5 para 3(*e*) with effect in relation to accounting periods beginning on or after 6 April 2019 (by virtue of SI 2018/931 reg 4(*a*)).
[3] In sub-s (2)(*a*), figure "12" substituted for figure "6" by FA 2018 s 17, Sch 5 para 4 with effect in relation to disposals made on or after 6 April 2019 (by virtue of SI 2018/931 reg 4(*b*)).

[280B The investment limits condition
(1) This section applies for the purposes of the investment limits condition.
(2) Where a company ("the investor") makes an investment ("the current investment") in another company ("the relevant company"), that investment breaches the permitted investment limits [if one or more of the following applies—
>(*a*) the total annual investment in the relevant company exceeds the amount for the time being specified in section 292A(1);
>(*b*) the total investment in the relevant company at the investment date exceeds the amount specified in—
>>(i) if the relevant company is a knowledge-intensive company (see section 331A) at the investment date, section 292AA(1)(*a*), and
>>(ii) in any other case, section 292AA(1)(*b*);
>(*c*) condition A or B is met and the total investment in the relevant company at any time during the 5-year post-investment period exceeds the amount specified in—
>>(i) if the relevant company is a knowledge-intensive company at the investment date, section 292AB(4)(*a*), and
>>(ii) in any other case, section 292AB(4)(*b*).][2]
[(2A) In this section—
>"the investment date" means the date the current investment is made;
>"the 5-year post-investment period" means the period of 5 years beginning with the day after the investment date.][2]
[(3) For the purposes of subsection (2)(*a*), the total annual investment in the relevant company is the sum of—
>(*a*) the amount of the current investment,
>(*b*) the total amount of other relevant investments made (whether or not by the investor), in the year ending with the day on which the current investment is made, in—
>>(i) the relevant company, or
>>(ii) a company that has at any time in that year been a 51% subsidiary of the relevant company,

>(including investments made in such a company before it became such a subsidiary but, if it is not such a subsidiary at the end of that year, not investments made in it after it last ceased to be such a subsidiary), and
>(*c*) the total amount of any other relevant investments (whether or not made by the investor) which are relevant imported investments.

(3A) For the purposes of subsection (2)(*b*), the total investment in the relevant company at the investment date is the sum of—

    (*a*) the amount of the current investment,

    (*b*) the total amount of other relevant investments made (whether or not by the investor), on or before the investment date, in—

        (i) the relevant company, or

        (ii) a company that is at the investment date, or has at any time before that date been, a 51% subsidiary of the relevant company,

    (including investments made in such a company before it became such a subsidiary but, if it is not such a subsidiary at the investment date, not investments made in it after it last ceased to be such a subsidiary), and

    (*c*) the total amount of any other relevant investments (whether or not made by the investor) which are relevant imported investments.

(3B) For the purposes of subsection (2)(*c*)—

    (*a*) condition A is that—

        (i) a company becomes a 51% subsidiary of the relevant company during the 5-year post-investment period,

        (ii) all or part of the money raised by the current investment is employed for the purposes of an activity which consists wholly or in part of a trade carried on by that company, and

        (iii) that trade (or a part of it) was carried on by that company before it became a 51% subsidiary as mentioned in sub-paragraph (i);

    (*b*) condition B is that all or part of the money raised by the current investment is employed for the purposes of an activity which consists wholly or in part of a trade which, during the 5-year post-investment period, becomes a relevant transferred trade (see subsection (3F)).

(3C) For the purposes of subsection (2)(*c*), the total investment in the relevant company at a time during the 5-year post-investment period ("the relevant time") is the sum of—

    (*a*) the amount of the current investment,

    (*b*) the total amount of other relevant investments made, before the relevant time (whether or not by the investor), in—

        (i) the relevant company, or

        (ii) a company that at the relevant time is, or before that time has been, a 51% subsidiary of the relevant company,

    (including investments made in such a company before it became such a subsidiary but, if it is not such a subsidiary at the relevant time, not investments made in it after it last ceased to be such a subsidiary), and

    (*c*) the total amount of any other relevant investments (whether or not made by the investor) which are relevant imported investments.

(3D) In this section "relevant imported investment" means—

    (*a*) a relevant investment

        (i) which is made in a company at a qualifying time, and

        (ii) the money raised by which is employed for the purposes of a trade carried on by another company that is, at a qualifying time, a 51% subsidiary of the relevant company (but, if at the latest possible qualifying time it has ceased to be such a subsidiary, ignoring any money so employed after it last ceased to be such a subsidiary), or

    (*b*) a relevant investment—

        (i) which is made in a company at a qualifying time, and

        (ii) the money raised by which is employed for the purposes of a trade carried on by that company or another person,

    where, at a qualifying time but after that investment was made, that trade (or a part of it) became a relevant transferred trade (see subsection (3F)).

(3E) In subsection (3D) "a qualifying time" means—

    (*a*) for the purposes of subsection (3), any time in the year mentioned in that subsection,

    (*b*) for the purposes of subsection (3A), any time on or before the investment date,

    (*c*) for the purposes of subsection (3C), any time before the relevant time.

(3F) For the purposes of this section if—

    (*a*) a trade is transferred—

        (i) to the relevant company,

        (ii) to a company that is a 51% subsidiary of the relevant company, or

        (iii) to a partnership of which a company within subparagraph (i) or (ii) is a member,

    (including where it is transferred to a company within subparagraph (ii), or a partnership of which such a company is a member, before the company became such a subsidiary), and

    (*b*) the trade, or a part of it, was previously (at any time) carried on by another person, the trade or part mentioned in paragraph (*b*) becomes a "relevant transferred trade" at the time it is transferred as mentioned in paragraph (*a*).][2]

(4) A "relevant investment" is made in a company if—

    (*a*) an investment (of any kind) in the company is made by a VCT,

    (*b*) the company issues shares (money having been subscribed for them), and (at any time) the company provides—

        (i) a compliance statement under section 205 (enterprise investment scheme), or

        (ii) a compliance statement under section 257ED (seed enterprise investment scheme), in respect of the shares, . . . [2]

    [(*ba*) an investment is made in the company and (at any time) the company provides a compliance statement under section 257PB (tax relief for social investments) in respect of the investment, or][2]

    (*c*) any other investment is made in the company which is aid received by it pursuant to a measure approved by the European Commission as compatible with Article 107 of the Treaty on the Functioning of the European Union in accordance with the principles laid down in the [European Commission's Guidelines on State aid to promote risk finance investment][2] (as those guidelines may be amended or replaced from time to time).

(5) For the purposes of subsections (2) [to (3E)][2], an investment within subsection (4)(*b*) is regarded as made when the shares are issued.

[(6) Section 257KB applies in determining for those purposes when an investment within subsection (4)(*ba*) is made as it applies for the purposes of Part 5B (tax relief on social investments).

(7) If only a proportion of the money raised by a relevant investment is employed for the purposes of a trade which became a relevant transferred trade as mentioned in subsection (3D), only the corresponding proportion of the relevant investment falls within that subsection.

(8) For the purposes of this section—

    (*a*) references to a trade include a part of a trade (and references to the carrying on of a trade are to be construed accordingly), and

    (*b*) when determining the amount of money raised by a relevant investment which has been employed for the purposes of a trade such apportionments are to be made as are just and reasonable.

(9) In this section "trade" includes—

    (*a*) any business or profession,

    (*b*) so far as not within paragraph (*a*), the carrying on of research and development activities from which it is intended a trade will be derived or will benefit, and

    (*c*) preparing to carry on a trade.][2]][1]

Commentary—*Simon's Taxes* **E3.235**

HMRC Manuals—Venture Capital Schemes Manual 8121 (funding limits for investee companies: overview). VCM54180 VCT: (investment limits condition).

Amendments—[1] This section inserted by FA 2012 s 40, Sch 8 paras 1, 3 with effect in relation to investments made on or after 17 July 2012, subject to provisions relating to investments made before that date: see FA 2012 Sch 8 para 18(2).

[2] Amendments made by F(No 2)A 2015 s 26, Sch 6 paras 1, 4 with effect in relation to investments made on or after 18 November 2015, but not so as to prevent investments made before that day constituting a "relevant investment" for the purposes of determining whether the investment limits condition in ITA 2007 s 274 is breached by an investment made on or after that day (F(No 2)A 2015 Sch 6 para 23(4))

[280BA The minimum investment on further issue condition

(1) A company breaches the minimum investment on further issue condition where—

    (*a*) there has been an issue of ordinary share capital of the company ("the first issue"),

    (*b*) a VCT approval of the company has taken effect on or before the day of the making of the first issue,

    (*c*) a further issue ("the further issue") of ordinary share capital of the company has been made since the making of the first issue, and

    (*d*) the company does not, on or before the relevant deadline, invest at least 30% of the money raised by the further issue in shares or securities which when held by the company are comprised in the company's qualifying holdings.

(2) The relevant deadline is the last day of the period of 12 months immediately following the end of the accounting period in which the further issue is made.][1]

Amendments—[1] Section 280BA inserted by FA 2018 s 17, Sch 5 para 6 with effect in relation to money raised by a further issue that is made in an accounting period beginning on or after 6 April 2018 (by virtue of SI 2018/931 reg 4(c)).

[280C The permitted maximum age condition

(1) This section applies for the purposes of the permitted maximum age condition.

(2) Where a company makes an investment in another company ("the relevant company"), that investment ("the current investment") breaches the permitted maximum age limits if—

    (*a*) the investment is made after the initial investing period, and

    (*b*) none of conditions A to C is met.

(3) "The initial investing period" means—

ITA 2007

(*a*) where the relevant company is a knowledge-intensive company on the investment date, the period of 10 years [beginning with—
  (i) the relevant first commercial sale, or
  (ii) if the relevant company so elects, the date by reference to which that company is treated as reaching an annual turnover of £200,000 (see section 331B),][3] and
(*b*) in any other case, the period of 7 years beginning with that sale.
(4) Condition A is that—
  (*a*) a relevant investment was made in the relevant company before the end of the initial investing period, and
  (*b*) some or all of the money raised by that investment was employed for the purposes of the same activities as the money raised by the current investment (or some of those activities).
(5) Condition B is that—
  (*a*) the sum of—
    (i) the amount of the current investment, and
    (ii) the total amount of any other relevant investments made in the relevant company in a period of 30 consecutive days which includes the investment date,
  is at least 50% of the average turnover amount, and
  (*b*) the money raised by the current investment and the investments mentioned in paragraph (*a*)(ii) is employed for the purpose of entering a new product or geographical market.
(6) Condition C is that—
  (*a*) condition B in subsection (5) or condition B in section 175A(4) (EIS: permitted company age requirement) was previously met in relation to one or more relevant investments made in the relevant company, and
  (*b*) some or all of the money raised by those investments was employed for the purposes of the same activities as the money raised by the current investment.
(7) "The relevant first commercial sale" means the earliest of the following—
  (*a*) the first commercial sale made by the relevant company,
  (*b*) the first commercial sale made by a company that is at the investment date, or before that date has been, a 51% subsidiary of the relevant company (including a sale made by a company before it became such a subsidiary but, if it is not such a subsidiary at the investment date, not a sale made after it last ceased to be such a subsidiary),
  (*c*) the first commercial sale made by any person who previously (at any time) carried on a trade which was subsequently carried on, on or before the investment date, by—
    (i) the relevant company, or
    (ii) a company that is at the investment date, or before that date has been, a 51% subsidiary of the relevant company,
  (including a trade subsequently carried on by such a company before it became such a subsidiary but, if it is not such a subsidiary at the investment date, not a trade which it carried on only after it last ceased to be such a subsidiary);
  (*d*) the first commercial sale made by a company which becomes a 51% subsidiary of the relevant company after the investment date in circumstances where all or part of the money raised by the current investment is employed for the purposes of an activity carried on by that subsidiary (including a sale made by such a company before it became such a subsidiary);
  (*e*) the first commercial sale made by any person who previously (at any time) carried on a trade which was subsequently carried on by a company mentioned in paragraph (*d*) (including a trade carried on by such a company before it became such a subsidiary);
  (*f*) if the money raised by the current investment or any part of it is employed for the purposes of a trade which has been transferred after the investment date to the relevant company or a 51% subsidiary of that company (or to a partnership of which the relevant company or such a subsidiary is a member), having previously been carried on (at any time) by another person, the first commercial sale made by that other person.
(8) "The average turnover amount" means one fifth of the total relevant turnover amount for the [relevant five year period.][2]
[(8A) Subject to subsection (8B), the relevant five year period is the five year period which ends immediately before the beginning of the last accounts filing period.
(8B) If the last accounts filing period ends more than 12 months before the investment date, the relevant five year period is the five year period which ends 12 months before the investment date.][2]
(9) In this section—
  "entering a new product or geographical market" has the same meaning as in Commission Regulation (EU) No 651/2014 (General block exemption Regulation);
  "first commercial sale" has the same meaning as in the European Commission's Guidelines on State aid to promote risk finance investments (as those guidelines may be amended or replaced from time to time);
  "the investment date" means the day on which the current investment is made;

"the last accounts filing period" means the last period for filing (within the meaning of section 442 of the Companies Act 2006) for the relevant company which ends before the date on which the current investment is made;

"relevant investment" has the meaning given by section 280B(4) (and section 280B(5) and (6) apply for the purposes of this section as they apply for section 280B(2) to (3E));

"the total relevant turnover amount" for a period is—

    (*a*) if the relevant company is a single company at the investment date, the sum of—

        (i) the relevant company's turnover for that period,

        (ii) if all or part of the money raised by the current investment is employed for the purposes of an activity carried on by a company which becomes a 51% subsidiary of the relevant company after the investment date, the turnover for that period of that subsidiary (or, if there is more than one, each of them), and

        (iii) if all or part of the money raised by the current investment is employed for the purposes of a transferred trade, the turnover of that trade for so much of that period as falls before the trade became a transferred trade (except to the extent that it is already included in calculating the amounts within sub-paragraphs (i) and (ii));

    (*b*) if the relevant company is a parent company at the investment date, the sum of—

        (i) the relevant company's turnover for that period,

        (ii) the turnover for that period of each company which at the investment date is a 51% subsidiary of the relevant company,

        (iii) if all or part of the money raised by the issue of the current investment is employed for the purposes of an activity carried on by a company which becomes a 51% subsidiary of the relevant company after the investment date, the turnover for that period of that subsidiary (or, if there is more than one, each of them), and

        (iv) if all or part of the money raised by the current investment is employed for the purposes of a transferred trade, the turnover of that trade for so much of that period as falls before the trade became a transferred trade (except to the extent that it is already included in calculating the amounts within sub-paragraphs (i) to (iii));

"transferred trade" means a trade which has been transferred to the company which is carrying on the trade at the time the money raised by the current investment is employed or to a partnership of which that company is a member;

"turnover"—

    (*a*) in relation to a company, has the meaning given by section 474(1) of the Companies Act 2006 and is to be determined by reference to the accounts of companies and amounts recognised for accounting purposes (and such apportionments of those amounts as are just and reasonable are to be made for the purpose of determining a company's turnover for a period);

    (*b*) in relation to any other person carrying on a trade, also has the meaning given by section 474(1) of that Act (reading references in that provision to a company as references to the person) and is to be determined by reference to the accounts of the person and amounts recognised for accounting purposes (and such apportionments of those amounts as are just and reasonable are to be made for the purpose of determining a person's turnover for a period);

    (*c*) in relation to a transferred trade carried on by a company or other person, means such proportion of the turnover of the company or other person as it is just and reasonable to attribute to the transferred trade;

and section 280B(8) and (9) (meaning of "trade" etc) applies for the purposes of this section as it applies for the purposes of section 280B.][1]

Commentary—*Simon's Taxes* **E3.237.**

HMRC Manuals—Venture Capital Schemes Manual 8151 (the basic age condition: first commercial sale).

Amendments—[1]   This section inserted by F(No 2)A 2015 s 26, Sch 6 paras 1, 5 with effect in relation to investments made on or after 18 November 2015, but not so as to prevent investments made before that day constituting a "relevant investment" for the purposes of determining whether the permitted maximum age condition in ITA 2007 s 274 is breached by an investment made on or after that day (F(No 2)A 2015 Sch 6 para 23(4)).

[2]   Words in sub-s (8) substituted, and sub-ss (8A), (8B) inserted, by FA 2016 s 29(3). Subject to any election made under FA 2016 s 30 by the issuing company, these amendments are to be treated as always having had effect. If an election is made under s 30, the amendments do not apply in relation to investments made in the relevant company in the period beginning with 18 November 2015 and ending with 5 April 2016: see FA 2016 s 30.

[3]   In sub-s (3)(*a*), words substituted for words "beginning with the relevant first commercial sale," by FA 2018 s 16, Sch 4 para 7 with effect for investments made on or after 6 April 2018 (by virtue of SI 2018/931 reg 3(a)).

[280D The no business acquisition condition

(1) This section applies for the purposes of the no business acquisition condition.

(2) Where a company makes an investment in another company ("the relevant company"), that investment breaches the prohibition on business acquisitions if any of the money raised by it is employed (whether on its own or together with other money) on the acquisition, directly or indirectly, of—

    (*a*) an interest in another company such that a company becomes a 51% subsidiary of the relevant company,

    (*b*) a further interest in a company which is a 51% subsidiary of the relevant company,

    (*c*) a trade,

    (*d*) intangible assets employed for the purposes of a trade, or

    (*e*) goodwill employed for the purposes of a trade.

(3) The Treasury may by regulations provide that subsection (2) does not apply in relation to acquisitions of intangible assets which are of a description specified, or which occur in circumstances specified, in the regulations.

(4) In this section—

    "goodwill" has the same meaning as in Part 8 of CTA 2009 (see section 715(3));

    "intangible assets" means any asset which falls to be treated as an intangible asset in accordance with generally accepted accountancy practice;

and section 280B(8) and (9) apply for the purposes of this section as they apply for the purposes of section 280B.][1]

Commentary—*Simon's Taxes* **E3.238.**
HMRC Manuals—Venture Capital Schemes Manual 8140 (use of money: no business acquisitions).
Amendments—[1]   This section inserted by F(No 2)A 2015 s 26, Sch 6 paras 1, 5 with effect in relation to investments made on or after 18 November 2015.

Withdrawal of approval

281 Withdrawal of VCT approval of a company

(1) The Commissioners for Her Majesty's Revenue and Customs ("the Commissioners") may withdraw the VCT approval of a company if at any time it appears to them that there are reasonable grounds for believing—

    (*a*) that the conditions for the approval of the company were not met at the time of the approval,

    (*b*) in a case where the Commissioners were satisfied for the purposes of section 274(1)(*b*) or 275(2) that any of the conditions mentioned in section 274(2) would be met in relation to any period, that the condition is one which will not be, or has not been, met in relation to that period,

    (*c*) in the case of a company approved under subsection (2) of section 275 (read with paragraph (*b*) of subsection (3) of that section), that the company has not met such other conditions as may be prescribed by regulations made by the Commissioners in relation to—

        (i) the period of 3 years mentioned in that paragraph, or

        (ii) any part of that period,

    (*d*) in a case where the use of any money falls to be ignored for any accounting period in accordance with section 280(2), that—

        (i) the first accounting period of the company for which the use of that money will not be ignored will be a period in relation to which any of the conditions mentioned in section 274(2) will fail to be met, or

        (ii) the company has not met such other conditions as may be prescribed by regulations made by the Commissioners in relation to, or to any part of, an accounting period for which the use of that money falls to be ignored, . . .[1]

    (*e*) that—

        (i) the company's most recent complete accounting period or its current one is a period in relation to which there has been or will be a failure of any of the conditions mentioned in section 274(2) to be met, and

        (ii) the failure was not or will not be one which, at the time of the approval, was allowed for in relation to that period by virtue of section 275(2).

    [(*f*) that, while it has been a VCT, the company has issued shares and, before the end of the restricted period, the company, other than for the purpose of redeeming or repurchasing any of those shares, has—

        (i) made a payment to all or any of its shareholders of an amount representing (directly or indirectly) a repayment of its share capital, whether that payment was made out of a reserve arising from a reduction of share capital or otherwise,

        (ii) where the shares were issued at a premium, made a payment to all or any of its shareholders of an amount representing (directly or indirectly) that premium or any part of it, whether that payment was made out of a share premium reserve or otherwise, or

(iii) used an amount which represents (directly or indirectly) the company's share capital or an amount by which that share capital has been diminished, or, where the shares were issued at a premium, that premium (or any part of it), to pay up new shares to be allotted to all or any of its shareholders.][1]

[(1A) In subsection (1)(*f*)—

    "payment"—

        (*a*) does not include any distribution of assets made in connection with the winding up of the company, but

        (*b*) does include every other description of distribution of the company's assets to its members,

    and for this purpose "distribution" includes (but is not limited to) a distribution within the meaning of section 989,

    "reduction of share capital" has the same meaning as in section 1027A(2) of CTA 2010, and

    "the restricted period" means the period of 3 years beginning at the end of the accounting period of the company in which the shares were issued.][1]

(2) Subject to subsections (3) and (4), the withdrawal of the approval of a company for the purposes of this Part has effect as from the time when notice of the withdrawal is given to the company.

(3) If, in the case of a company approved as a VCT in the exercise of the power conferred by section 275(2), the approval is withdrawn at a time before all of the conditions mentioned in section 274(2) have been met with respect to the company concerned—

    (*a*) in relation to a complete accounting period of 12 months, or

    (*b*) in relation to successive complete accounting periods constituting a continuous period of at least 12 months,

the withdrawal of the approval has the effect that the approval is for all purposes treated as never having been given.

(4) A notice withdrawing the approval of a company for the purposes of this Part may specify a time falling before the time mentioned in subsection (2) as the time from which the withdrawal is to be treated as having effect for the purposes of section 100 of TCGA 1992 (exemption for venture capital trusts etc).

But the time so specified must be no earlier than the beginning of the accounting period in relation to which it appears to the Commissioners that the condition by reference to which the approval is withdrawn has not been, or will not be, met.

(5) Despite any limitation on the time for making assessments, an assessment to any tax chargeable in consequence of the withdrawal of any VCT approval may be made at any time before the end of the period of 3 years beginning with the time when the notice of withdrawal is given.

Commentary—*Simon's Taxes* **E3.239, E3.241, E3.212**.

HMRC Manuals—Venture Capital Schemes Manual VCM54400 (withdrawal of approval: when approval may be withdrawn). VCM54420 (withdrawal of approval: effects of withdrawal of full approval).
VCM54440 (withdrawal of approval: withdrawal notices).

Amendments—[1] In sub-(1), word "or" at the end of para (*d*) repealed and para (*f*) inserted, sub-s (1A) inserted by FA 2014 s 53, Sch 10 para 3 with effect in relation to shares issued on or after 6 April 2014.

282 Withdrawal of VCT approval in cases for which provision made under section 280(3)

(1) The Treasury may by regulations make provision for withdrawal of VCT approval of a company to be treated—

    (*a*) in a case where the withdrawal is by reference to a condition for approval that would have been, or would be, met but for provision made under section 280(3), and

    (*b*) for the purposes of enactments specified by regulations,

as having taken effect as from a time specified in the notice of withdrawal that is earlier than the time when the notice is given to the company.

(2) Provision made under subsection (1) has effect subject to the provisions of section 281(4) (retrospective effect of notices of withdrawal of VCT approval) as to the earliest time that may be specified by such a notice.

(3) Section 324 applies in relation to—

    (*a*) regulations under subsection (1), and

    (*b*) any power conferred by that subsection,

as it applies in relation to regulations under Chapter 5 and a power conferred by any provision of that Chapter.

Commentary—*Simon's Taxes* **E3.237**.

Supplementary

283 Time as from which VCT approval has effect

(1) A VCT approval has effect as from the time specified in the approval.

(2) That time, if it falls before the time when the VCT approval is given, must be no earlier than the time when the application was made.

(3) If the Commissioners for Her Majesty's Revenue and Customs give a VCT approval, they may stipulate that the approval is to have effect as from the time when the application for the approval was made or any subsequent time.

Commentary—*Simon's Taxes* E3.230.

284 Power to make regulations as to procedure

[(1)] [1] Regulations under section 272 may make provision—

    (*a*) as to the making of applications for VCT approvals and otherwise as to the procedure to be followed in relation to any such applications and the giving of such approvals,

    [(*aa*) for and in connection with the making by a company of an application to the Commissioners for Her Majesty's Revenue and Customs ("the Commissioners") for relief in respect of a breach (including a future breach) of the conditions for its VCT approval to continue in force,][1]

    (*b*) as to the procedure to be followed in connection with the withdrawal of VCT approvals,

    (*c*) as to the obligations of a company which is a VCT if it should appear to the company—

        [(i) that the conditions for its VCT approval to continue in force are no longer met, or

        (ii) that it is likely that those conditions will cease to be met,][1]

    (*d*) as to the accounts, records, returns and other information to be kept, and provided or otherwise made available to the Commissioners . . . [1], by companies which are or have been VCTs and by persons [including nominees][2] who hold or have held shares in such companies, and

    (*e*) as to the persons liable to account for any tax becoming due where a VCT approval is withdrawn.

[(2) In subsection (1)(*aa*), the reference to relief in respect of a breach of the conditions mentioned there is to a determination by the Commissioners that they will not exercise their power to withdraw the company's VCT approval by reason of the breach for such period as they may determine (and subject to such conditions as they may determine).

(3) The provision that may be made by virtue of subsection (1)(*aa*) includes—

    (*a*) provision as to the procedure to be followed in relation to applications and determinations,

    (*b*) provision as to the grounds on which applications may be made or determined, and

    (*c*) provision conferring a discretion to be exercised by the Commissioners.][1]

Regulations—Venture Capital Trust (Amendment) Regulations, SI 2014/1929.
Venture Capital Trust (Amendment) Regulations, SI 2016/1192.
Amendments—[1] Sub-s (1) numbered as such, sub-ss (1)(*aa*), (2) inserted, words in sub-s (1)(*c*) substituted, and words in sub-s (1)(*d*) repealed, by FA 2007 ss 51, 114, Sch 16 para 21, Sch 27 Pt 2(16) with effect from 19 July 2007.
[2] In sub-s (1)(*d*) words inserted by FA 2014 s 53, Sch 10 para 5(2) with effect from 17 July 2014.

285 Interpretation of Chapter

(1) Chapter 4 has effect for interpreting references in this Chapter to a "qualifying holding".

(2) In this Chapter and the following Chapters of this Part "securities", in relation to a company, includes any liability of the company in respect of a loan . . . [2], except that it does not include—

    (*a*) any liability of the company in respect of a loan which has been made to the company on terms which allow any person to require—

        (i) the loan to be repaid, or

        (ii) any stock or security relating to the loan to be re-purchased or redeemed,

        within the period of 5 years from the making of the loan or, as the case may be, the issue of the stock or security, or

    (*b*) any stock or security relating to a loan which has been made to the company on terms which allow any person to require the loan to be repaid, or the stock or security to be re-purchased or redeemed, within that period[, or[2]

    (*c*) any liability of the company in respect of a loan to which subsection (2A) applies that has been made to the company.][2]

  But see sections 317(4) and 328(2).

[(2A) This subsection applies to a loan if—

    (*a*) the return on the loan represents more than a commercial rate of return, or

    (*b*) the loan is made on terms which grant to a person or allow a person to acquire—

        (i) any security or preferential rights in relation to assets of the company, or

        (ii) the ability to control the company.

In sub-paragraph (ii) "control" has the meaning given by sections 450 and 451 of CTA 2010.

(2B) The return on a loan is not to be treated as representing more than a commercial rate for the purposes of subsection (2A)(*a*) if—

    (*a*) the return on the loan during the period of 5 years from the making of the loan does not exceed 50% of the amount lent, and

    (*b*) the total return on the loan does not exceed—

        $N \times A \times 10\%$

        where—

N is the number of years (including any fraction) in the term of the loan;

A is the amount lent or, in a case where some of the loan is repaid during the term of the loan, the average amount outstanding during that term.

(2C) The Treasury may by regulations substitute a different figure for a figure that is at any time specified in subsection (2B)(*a*) or (*b*).

(2D) In subsections (2A)(*a*) and (2B) "return" means interest, fees, charges and other amounts payable in respect of the loan.

(2E) Where it is to any extent not known, before the end of the term of a loan, what amounts will be payable in respect of the loan—

    (*a*) subsections (2A)(*a*) and (2B) apply, until the relevant matters are ascertained, on the basis of what amounts can reasonably be expected to be payable;

    (*b*) when those matters are ascertained, any necessary adjustments must be made by making or amending assessments or by repayment or discharge of tax (regardless of any limitation on the time within which assessments or amendments may be made).][2]

[(3A) For the purposes of this Chapter, shares in a company are "eligible" unless they carry—

    (*a*) a present or future preferential right to dividends that is within subsection (3B),

    (*b*) a present or future preferential right to the company's assets on its winding up, or

    (*c*) a present or future right to be redeemed.

(3B) A preferential right to dividends carried by a share in a company is within this subsection if—

    (*a*) the amount of any dividends payable pursuant to the right, or the date or dates on which they are payable, depend to any extent on a decision of the company, the holder of the share or any other person, or

    (*b*) the amount of any dividends that become payable at any time pursuant to the right includes any amount that became payable at any earlier time pursuant to the right, but has not been paid.][1]

(4) Any reference in this Chapter to a company's investments is taken to include, so far as it would not otherwise do so—

    (*a*) money in the company's possession, and

    (*b*) any sum owed to the company by another person if the company has account-holder's rights over that sum.

(5) For the purposes of subsection (4)(*b*) a company has "account-holder's rights" over a sum owed to the company if—

    (*a*) the company has a right (whether or not the exercise of the right is subject to conditions) to require the other person to pay out the sum, or amounts out of the sum, to the company or at the company's direction, and

    (*b*) the sum is owed to the company—

        (i) as a result of amounts having been paid to the other person by or for the company, or

        (ii) as a result of the other person having identified a sum in respect of which the company may exercise such a right.

(6) Subsection (5) does not have effect to cause a company's investments to be taken to include anything to which the company is not beneficially entitled, but for this purpose a company is taken to be beneficially entitled to—

    (*a*) sums subscribed for shares issued by it, and

    (*b*) anything to which it is entitled that (directly or indirectly) represents such sums.

Commentary—*Simon's Taxes* **E3.245, E3.230, E3.231, E3.234, E3.259**.

HMRC Manuals—Venture Capital Schemes Manual VCM54090 (definition of 'securities', and references to a company's investments).

VCM54150 Definition of 'eligible shares' in a holding.

Modifications—ITA 2007 Sch 2 para 67 (modification of this section for the purposes of determining whether, at any time before 6 April 2007, the conditions mentioned in ITA 2007 s 274(2) are, will be or were met with respect to a company).

Amendments—[1]   Sub-ss (3A), (3B) substituted for sub-s (3) by F(No 3)A 2010 s 5, Sch 2 para 2(1), (6) with effect in relation to accounting periods ending on or after 6 April 2011 (by virtue of SI 2011/662). These amendments do not have effect in relation to shares or securities held by a company ("the investing company") if the shares or securities are issued before 6 April 2011 or are issued on or after that day and are acquired by the investing company by means of the investment of protected money (F(No 3)A 2010 Sch 2 para 6(2), (3)).

[2]   In sub-s (2), words "(whether secured or not)" repealed, sub-s (2)(*c*) and preceding word "or" inserted, and sub-ss (2A)–(2E) inserted, by FA 2018 s 17, Sch 5 para 7 with effect for loans made on or after 15 March 2018 (by virtue of SI 2018/931 reg 4(d)). For the purposes of these amendments, a loan is made on the day on which the amount lent, or (as the case may be) the first day on which any part of the amount lent, is paid or made available to the company (SI 2018/931 reg 5)).

CHAPTER 4

QUALIFYING HOLDINGS

Introduction

286 Qualifying holdings: introduction

(1) If any shares in or securities of any company ("the relevant company") are at any time held by another company ("the investing company"), this Chapter applies for determining whether and to what extent those shares or securities ("the relevant holding") are, for the purposes of Chapter 3, to be regarded as at that time comprised in the investing company's qualifying holdings.

(2) The relevant holding is to be regarded as comprised in the investing company's qualifying holding at any time if—

    (a) all the following requirements of this Chapter are met at that time in relation to the relevant company and the relevant holding, . . . [6]

    (b) the relevant holding consists of shares or securities which were first issued by the relevant company to the investing company and have been held by the investing company ever since[, and

    (c) those shares or securities were first issued by the relevant company in order to raise money for the purposes of promoting growth and development of—

        (i) if the relevant company is a single company, the business of that company, and

        (ii) if it is a parent company, what would be the business of the group if the activities of the group companies taken together were regarded as one business.][6]

(3) The requirements are those imposed as to—

    [(*1za*) risk to capital (see section 286ZA),][7]

    [(*za*) UK permanent establishment (see section 286A),

    (*zb*) financial health (see section 286B),][3]

    (*a*) maximum qualifying investment (see section 287),

    (*b*) no guaranteed loan (see section 288),

    (*c*) proportion of eligible shares (see section 289),

    (*d*) trading (see section 290),

    (*e*) the carrying on of a qualifying activity (see section 291),

    [(*ea*) the maximum amount raised annually through risk [finance investments][6] (see section 292A),][2]

    [(*eaa*) the maximum risk finance investments when the relevant holding is issued (see section 292AA),

    (*eab*) the maximum risk finance investments during the 5-year post-investment period (see section 292AB),][6]

    [(*eb*) . . .][4]

    (*f*) use of the money raised (see section 293),

    (*g*) the relevant company carrying on the relevant qualifying activity (see section 294),

    [(*ga*) the permitted company age requirement (see section 294A),][6]

    (*h*) unquoted status (see section 295),

    (*i*) control and independence (see section 296),

    (*j*) gross assets (see section 297),

    [(*ja*) number of employees (see section 297A),][1]

    [(*jb*) the proportion of skilled employees (see section 297B),][6]

    (*k*) qualifying subsidiaries (see section 298), . . . [5]

    (*l*) property managing subsidiaries (see section 299)[, and

    (*m*) no disqualifying arrangements (see section 299A).][5]

(4) Subject to section 293(7), subsection (5) applies if—

    (a) the requirements of section 287, 293 or 294 would be met as to only part of the money raised by the issue of the relevant holding, and

    (b) that holding is not otherwise capable of being treated as comprising separate holdings.

(5) If this subsection applies, this Chapter has effect in relation to the relevant holding as if it were two separate holdings consisting of—

    (a) a holding from which the part of the money mentioned in subsection (4)(a) was raised, and

    (b) a holding from which the remainder was raised.

Chapter 3 has effect as if the value of the relevant holding were to be apportioned between the two holdings treated as subsisting by this subsection.

Commentary—*Simon's Taxes* E3.245, E3.256.

HMRC Manuals—Venture Capital Schemes Manual VCM55010 (introduction).

Amendments—[1] Sub-s (3)(*ja*) inserted by FA 2007 s 51, Sch 16 para 3(1), (2) and deemed to have effect from 6 April 2007.

    By virtue of FA 2007 Sch 16 para 3(5)–(7), this amendment does not have effect in relation to—

    (a)   a relevant holding issued before that date; or

    (b)   a relevant holding acquired by a company ("the investing company") by means of the investment of protected money.

    The terms "relevant holding" and "protected money" are defined by FA 2007 Sch 16 para 3(6), (7).

2   Sub-s (3)(*ea*) inserted by FA 2007 s 51, Sch 16 para 6(1), (2), (4)–(6) and deemed to have effect from 6 April 2007. This amendment does not have effect in relation to an investment made by a VCT of protected money (defined by FA 2007 Sch 16 para 6(6)).

3   Sub-s (3)(*za*), (*zb*) inserted by F(No 3)A 2010 s 5, Sch 2 para 2(1), (7) with effect in relation to shares or securities issued on or after 6 April 2011 (by virtue of SI 2011/662 art 2).

4   Sub-s (3)(*eb*) inserted by FA 2012 s 38, Sch 6 paras 6, 15 with effect for the purpose of determining whether shares or securities issued on or after 6 April 2012 are to be regarded as comprised in a company's qualifying holdings, and repealed by F(No 2)A 2015 s 26, Sch 6 paras 1, 6(3)(*c*) with effect for the purposes of determining whether shares or securities issued on or after 6 April 2015 are to be so regarded.

5   Word "and" at the end of sub-s (3)(*k*) repealed and sub-s (3)(*m*) and preceding word "and" inserted, by FA 2012 s 40, Sch 8 paras 1, 4 with effect for the purpose of determining whether shares or securities issued on or after 6 April 2012 are to be regarded as comprised in a company's qualifying holdings, regardless of whether the disqualifying arrangements were entered into before or on or after 6 April 2012.

6   Word "and" at the end of sub-s (2)(*a*) repealed and sub-s (2)(*c*) and preceding word "and" inserted, in sub-s (3)(*ea*) substituted for words "capital schemes", and sub-s (3)(*eaa*), (*eab*), (*ga*), (*jb*) inserted, by F(No 2)A 2015 s 26, Sch 6 paras 1, 6 with effect for the purposes of determining whether shares or securities issued on or after 18 November 2015 are to be regarded as comprised in a company's qualifying holdings.

7   Sub-s (3)(*Iza*) inserted by FA 2018 s 14(3)(*a*) with effect for shares or securities issued on or after 15 March 2018 (by virtue of SI 2018/931 reg 2(b)).

[286ZA The risk-to-capital requirement

(1) The requirement of this section is that, having regard to all the circumstances existing at the time of the issue of the relevant holding, it would be reasonable to conclude that—

    (*a*) the relevant company has objectives to grow and develop its trade in the long-term, and

    (*b*) there is a significant risk that, for the investing company, there will be a loss of capital of an amount greater than its net investment return.

(2) For the purposes of subsection (1)(*b*)—

    (*a*) the reference to a loss of capital is to a loss of some or all of the amounts given in consideration for the relevant holding, and

    (*b*) the reference to the net investment return is to the net investment return to the investing company irrespective of whether the return takes the form of income, capital growth, fees or other payments or anything else.

(3) For the purposes of subsection (1) the circumstances to which regard may be had include—

    (*a*) the extent to which the company's objectives include increasing the number of its employees or the turnover of its trade,

    (*b*) the nature of the company's sources of income, including the extent to which there is a significant risk of the company not receiving some or all of the income,

    (*c*) the extent to which the company has or is likely to have assets, or is or could become a party to arrangements for acquiring assets, that could be used to secure financing from any person,

    (*d*) the extent to which the activities of the company are sub-contracted to persons who are not connected with it,

    (*e*) the nature of the company's ownership structure or management structure, including the extent to which others participate in or devise the structure,

    (*f*) how any opportunity for investment in the company is marketed, and

    (*g*) the extent to which arrangements are in place under which opportunities for investments in the company are or may be marketed with, or otherwise associated with, opportunities for investments in other companies or entities.

(4) If the relevant company is a parent company—

    (*a*) any reference in this section to the company's trade is to what would be the trade of the group if the activities of the group companies taken together were regarded as one trade, and

    (*b*) any reference in subsection (3)(*a*) to (*e*) to the company is to any group company.]

Amendments—[1]   Section 286ZA inserted by FA 2018 s 14(3)(*b*) with effect for shares or securities issued on or after 15 March 2018 (by virtue of SI 2018/931 art 2(b)).

The requirements

[286A The UK permanent establishment requirement

The requirement of this section, at any time on or after the issue of the relevant holding, is that the relevant company has a permanent establishment in the United Kingdom at all times from the issue of the holding to the time in question.][1]

Commentary—*Simon's Taxes* E3.247.

HMRC Manuals—Venture Capital Schemes Manual VCM55030 (UK permanent establishment requirement).

Amendments—[1]   Sections 286A, 286B inserted by F(No 3)A 2010 s 5, Sch 2 para 2(1), (8) with effect in relation to shares or securities issued on or after 6 April 2011 (by virtue of SI 2011/662 art 2).

[286B The financial health requirement

(1) The requirement of this section is that the relevant company is not, at the time of the issue of the relevant holding, in difficulty.

    (*b*)   the making of loans to another group company, or

    (*c*)   the holding and managing of property used by a group company for the purpose of one or more qualifying trades carried on by a group company, or

    (*d*)   the holding and managing of property used by a group company for the purpose of research and development from which it is intended—

       (i)   that a qualifying trade to be carried on by a group company will be derived, or

       (ii)   that a qualifying trade carried on or to be carried on by a group company will benefit.

(6) Any reference in sub-paragraph (i) or (ii) of subsection (5)(*d*) to a group company includes a reference to any existing or future company which will be a group company at any future time.

(7) In this section—

    "incidental purposes" means purposes having no significant effect (other than in relation to incidental matters) on the extent of the activities of the company in question,

    "mainly trading subsidiary" means a qualifying subsidiary which, apart from incidental purposes, exists wholly for the purpose of carrying on one or more qualifying trades, and any reference to the main purpose of such a subsidiary is to be read accordingly,

    "non-qualifying activities" means—

       (*a*)   excluded activities, and

       (*b*)   activities carried on otherwise than in the course of a trade.

(8) This section is supplemented by section 300 (meaning of "qualifying trade") and sections 303 to 310 (excluded activities).

Commentary—*Simon's Taxes* E3.247.

HMRC Manuals—Venture Capital Schemes Manual VCM55090 (trading requirement).

Modifications—ITA 2007 Sch 2 para 71 (for the purpose of determining whether shares or securities are to be regarded as comprised in a company's qualifying holdings, this section is modified in relation to shares or securities issued before 6 April 2007).

291 The carrying on of a qualifying activity requirement

(1) The requirement of this section, at any time on or after the issue of the relevant holding, is that a qualifying company (whether or not the same such company at every such time) must have been carrying on a qualifying activity at all times from the issue of the holding to the time in question.

(2) [Carrying on a qualifying trade][1] is a qualifying activity.

(3) Preparing to carry on a qualifying trade is a qualifying activity if, at the time when the relevant holding was issued, the trade was intended to be carried on . . . . [1] by a qualifying company.

    This is subject to subsections (4) and (5).

(4) The requirement of this section is not capable of being met by virtue of subsection (3) at any time after the end of the period of two years beginning with the issue of the relevant holding unless—

    (*a*)   the intended trade was begun to be carried on by a qualifying company before the end of that period, and

    (*b*)   at all times since the end of that period, a qualifying company (whether or not the same such company at every such time) has been carrying on a qualifying trade . . . . [1].

(5) The requirement of this section is also not capable of being met by virtue of subsection (3) at any time after the abandonment, within the period mentioned in subsection (4), of the intention in question.

(6) In determining for the purposes of subsection (4)(*a*) when the intended trade was begun to be carried on by a qualifying company which is a qualifying 90% subsidiary of the relevant company, any carrying on by it of the trade before it became such a subsidiary of the relevant company is ignored.

(7) In this section "qualifying company" means the relevant company or any qualifying 90% subsidiary of that company.

(8) The reference in subsection (7) to a qualifying company which is a qualifying 90% subsidiary of the relevant company includes, in its application to subsection (3), a reference to any existing or future qualifying company which will be a qualifying 90% subsidiary of the relevant company at any future time.

Commentary—*Simon's Taxes* E3.248.

HMRC Manuals—Venture Capital Schemes Manual VCM55110 (carrying on of a qualifying activity).

Modifications—ITA 2007 Sch 2 para 72(1) (for the purpose of determining whether shares or securities are to be regarded as comprised in a company's qualifying holdings, this section is modified in relation to shares or securities issued before 6 April 2007).

ITA 2007 Sch 2 para 72(2) (for the purpose of determining whether shares or securities are to be regarded as comprised in a company's qualifying holdings, this section is modified in relation to shares or securities issued before 17 March 2004).

Amendments—[1] In sub-s (2) words substituted, and in sub-ss (3), (4)(*b*) words repealed, by F(No 3)A 2010 s 5, Sch 2 para 2(1), (10) with effect in relation to shares or securities issued on or after 6 April 2011 (by virtue of SI 2011/662 art 2).

292 Ceasing to meet requirements because of administration or receivership

(1) A company is not regarded as ceasing to meet the requirement of section 290 or 291 merely because of anything done in consequence of its being in administration or receivership.

(2) Subsection (1) applies only if—

(*a*) the entry into administration or receivership, and

(*b*) everything done as a consequence of the company being in administration or receivership,

is for genuine commercial reasons, and is not part of a scheme or arrangement the main purpose or one of the main purposes of which is the avoidance of tax.

Commentary—*Simon's Taxes* **E3.265**.

HMRC Manuals—Venture Capital Schemes Manual VCM55120 (ceasing to meet requirements because of administration or receivership).

Modifications—ITA 2007 Sch 2 para 73 (for the purpose of determining whether shares or securities are to be regarded as comprised in a company's qualifying holdings, this section is modified in relation to shares or securities issued before 17 March 2004).

[292A The maximum amount raised annually through risk [finance investments][5] requirement

(1) The total amount of relevant investments made in the relevant company in the year ending with the date the relevant holding is issued [must not exceed—.

(*a*) if the company is a knowledge-intensive company at that date (see section 331A and subsection (6A)), £10 million, and

(*b*) in any other case, £5 million.][6]

[(2) In subsection (1), the reference to relevant investments made in the relevant company includes—

(*a*) relevant investments made in any company that has at any time in the year mentioned there been a 51% subsidiary of the relevant company (including investments made in such a company before it became such a subsidiary but, if it was not a subsidiary at the end of that year, not those made after it last ceased to be such a subsidiary),

(*b*) any other relevant investment made in a company to the extent that the money raised by the investment has been employed for the purposes of a trade carried on by another company that has at any time in that year been a 51% subsidiary of the relevant company (but, if it is not such a subsidiary at the end of that year, ignoring any money so employed after it last ceased to be such a subsidiary), and

(*c*) any other relevant investment made in a company if—

(i) the money raised by the investment has been employed for the purposes of a trade carried on by that company or another person, and

(ii) in that year, after that investment was made, the trade (or a part of it) became a relevant transferred trade (see subsection (2B)).

(2A) If only a proportion of the money raised by a relevant investment is employed for the purposes of a trade which becomes a relevant transferred trade, the reference in subsection (2)(*c*) to the relevant investment is to be read as a reference to the corresponding proportion of that investment.

(2B) Where—

(*a*) in the year mentioned in subsection (1) a trade is transferred—

(i) to the relevant company,

(ii) to a company that is, or has at any time during that year been, a 51% subsidiary of the relevant company, or

(iii) to a partnership of which a company within subparagraph (i) or (ii) is a member,

(including where it is transferred to a company within subparagraph (ii), or a partnership of which such a company is a member, at a time in the year before the company became such a subsidiary but not where it is transferred to such a company or partnership in that year after the company last ceased to be such a subsidiary), and

(*b*) that trade or a part of it was previously (at any time) carried on by another person,

the trade or part mentioned in paragraph (*b*) becomes a "relevant transferred trade" at the time it is transferred as mentioned in paragraph (*a*).][5]

(3) A "relevant investment" is made in a company if—

(*a*) an investment (of any kind) in the company is made by a VCT, or

(*b*) the company issues shares (money having been subscribed for them), and (at any time) the company provides—

(i) a compliance statement under section 205 (enterprise investment scheme), or

[(ia) a compliance statement under section 257ED (seed enterprise investment scheme),][2]

(ii) . . . [3]

in respect of the shares[, or

[(*ba*) an investment is made in the company and (at any time) the company provides a compliance statement under section 257PB (tax relief for social investments) in respect of the investment, or][5]

(*c*) any other investment is made in the company which is aid received by it pursuant to a measure approved by the European Commission as compatible with Article 107 of the Treaty on the Functioning of the European Union in accordance with the principles laid down in the [European Commission's Guidelines on State aid to promote risk finance investment][5] (as those guidelines may be amended or replaced from time to time).][3]

(4) For the purposes of subsections (1) [to (2B)]⁵, an investment within subsection (3)(*b*) is regarded as made when the shares are issued.

[(4A) Section 257KB applies in determining for those purposes when an investment within subsection (3)(*ba*) is made as it applies for the purposes of Part 5B (tax relief on social investments).]⁵

(5) Subsection (6) applies if, by virtue of the provision of a compliance statement under section 205[, 257ED or 257PB]⁵ above . . . ³, the requirement of this section is not met.

(6) The requirement is to be treated as having been met throughout the period—

    (*a*) beginning with the time the relevant holding was issued, and

    (*b*) ending with the time the compliance statement was provided.

[(6A) If the relevant company began to carry on a trade less than three years before the date the relevant holding is issued, section 331A as it applies for the purposes of this section has effect with the substitution of the following subsections for subsections (3) to (5A)—

    "(3) The first operating costs condition is that in at least one of the relevant three succeeding years at least 15% of the relevant operating costs constitute expenditure on research and development or innovation.

    (4) The second operating costs condition is that in each of the relevant three succeeding years at least 10% of the relevant operating costs constitute such expenditure.

    (5) In subsections (3) and (4)—

    "relevant operating costs" means—

            (*a*)   if the relevant company is a single company at the applicable time, the operating costs of that company, and

            (*b*)   if the relevant company is a parent company at the applicable time, the sum of—

        (i) the operating costs of the relevant company, and

        (ii) the operating costs of each company which is a qualifying subsidiary of the relevant company at that time, excluding a company's operating costs for any of the relevant three succeeding years during any part of which the company is not a qualifying subsidiary of the relevant company;

    "the relevant three succeeding years" means the three consecutive years the first of which begins with the date the relevant holding is issued.]⁶

[(7) Section 280B(8) and (9) (meaning of "trade" etc) applies for the purposes of this section as it applies for the purposes of section 280B.]⁵]¹

Commentary—*Simon's Taxes* **E3.235, E3.255**

HMRC Manuals—Venture Capital Schemes Manual VCM55130 (maximum amount to be raised annually through risk capital measures).

Amendments—¹   This section inserted by FA 2007 s 51, Sch 16 para 6(1), (3)–(6) and deemed to have effect from 6 April 2007. This amendment does not have effect in relation to an investment made by a VCT of protected money (defined by FA 2007 Sch 16 para 6(6)).

²   Sub-s (3)(*b*)(ia) inserted by FA 2012 s 38, Sch 6 paras 6, 16 with effect for the purpose of determining whether shares or securities issued on or after 6 April 2012 are to be regarded as comprised in a company's qualifying holdings.

³   Sub-s (3)(*b*)(ii) repealed, and sub-s (3)(*c*) and preceding word "or" inserted, by FA 2012 s 40, Sch 8 paras 1, 6(1), (3) with effect for the purpose of determining whether shares or securities issued on or after 6 April 2012 are to be regarded as comprised in a company's qualifying holdings.

⁵   Amendments made by F(No 2)A 2015 s 26, Sch 6 paras 1, 7 with effect for the purposes of determining whether shares or securities issued on or after 18 November 2015 are to be regarded as comprised in a company's qualifying holdings, but not so as to prevent investments made before that day constituting a "relevant investment" for the purposes of determining whether shares or securities issued on or after that day are to be so regarded (F(No 2)A 2015 Sch 6 para 23(4))

⁶   In sub-s (1), words substituted for words "must not exceed £5 million", and sub-s (6A) inserted, by FA 2018 s 16, Sch 4 para 3 with effect for investments made on or after 6 April 2018 (by virtue of SI 2018/931 reg 3(b).

[292AA Maximum risk finance investments when relevant holding is issued requirement

(1) The total amount of relevant investments made in the relevant company on or before the investment date must not exceed—

    (*a*) if the relevant company is a knowledge-intensive company at the investment date (see section 331A), £20 million, and

    (*b*) in any other case, £12 million.

(2) In subsection (1), the reference to relevant investments made in the relevant company includes—

    (*a*) relevant investments made in any company that is at the investment date, or has at any time before that date been, a 51% subsidiary of the relevant company (including investments made in such a company before it became such a subsidiary but, if it is not such a subsidiary at the investment date, not investments made in it after it last ceased to be such a subsidiary),

    (*b*) any other relevant investment made in a company to the extent that the money raised by the investment has been employed for the purposes of a trade carried on by another company that has at any time on or before the investment date been a 51% subsidiary of the relevant company (but, if it is not such a subsidiary at the investment date, ignoring any money so employed after it last ceased to be such a subsidiary), and

(c) any other relevant investment made in a company if—

    (i) the money raised by the investment has been employed for the purposes of a trade carried on by that company or another person, and

    (ii) after the investment was made, but on or before the investment date, that trade became a relevant transferred trade (see subsection (4)).

(3) If only a proportion of the money raised by a relevant investment is employed for the purposes of a trade which becomes a relevant transferred trade, the reference in subsection (2)(c) to the relevant investment is to be read as a reference to the corresponding proportion of that investment.

(4) Where—

    (a) at any time on or before the investment date, a trade is transferred—

        (i) to the relevant company,

        (ii) to a company that at the investment date is, or has at any time before that date been, a 51% subsidiary of the relevant company, or

        (iii) to a partnership of which a company within subparagraph (i) or (ii) is a member,

    (including where it is transferred to a company within subparagraph (ii), or a partnership of which such a company is a member, before the company became such a subsidiary but, if the company is not such a subsidiary at the investment date, not where it is transferred to such a company or partnership after the company last ceased to be such a subsidiary), and

    (b) the trade or a part of it was previously (at any time) carried on by another person,

the trade or part mentioned in paragraph (b) becomes a "relevant transferred trade" at the time it is transferred as mentioned in paragraph (a).

(5) In this section—

"the investment date" means the date the relevant holding is issued;

"relevant investment" has the meaning given by section 292A(3), and section 292A(4) and (4A) (which determine when certain investments are made) applies for the purposes of this section;

and section 280B(8) and (9) (meaning of "trade" etc) applies for the purposes of this section as it applies for the purposes of section 280B.

(6) Subsection (7) applies if, by virtue of the provision of a compliance statement under section 205, 257ED or 257PB, the requirement of this section is not met.

(7) The requirement is to be treated as having been met throughout the period—

    (a) beginning with the investment date, and

    (b) ending with the time the compliance statement was provided.][1]

Commentary—*Simon's Taxes* **E3.255**.

HMRC Manuals—Venture Capital Schemes Manual 8123 (lifetime limit on risk finance investments).

Amendments—[1]   Sections 292AA, 292AB inserted by F(No 2)A 2015 s 26, Sch 6 paras 1, 8 with effect for the purposes of determining whether shares or securities issued on or after 18 November 2015 are to be regarded as comprised in a company's qualifying holdings, but not so as to prevent investments made before that day constituting a "relevant investment" for the purposes of determining whether shares or securities issued on or after that day are to be so regarded (F(No 2)A 2015 Sch 6 para 23(4)).

[292AB Maximum risk finance investments during the 5-year post-investment period requirement

(1) The requirement of this section applies if condition A or B is met.

(2) Condition A is that—

    (a) a company becomes a 51% subsidiary of the relevant company at any time during the 5-year post-investment period,

    (b) all or part of the money raised by the issue of the relevant holding is employed for the purposes of a relevant qualifying activity which consists wholly or in part of a trade carried on by that company, and

    (c) that trade (or a part of it) was carried on by that company before it became a 51% subsidiary as mentioned in paragraph (a).

(3) Condition B is that all or part of the money raised by the issue of the relevant holding is employed for the purposes of a relevant qualifying activity which consists wholly or in part of a trade which, during the 5-year post-investment period, becomes a relevant transferred trade (see subsection (7)).

(4) The requirement of this section is that, at all times during the 5-year post-investment period, the total of the relevant investments made in the relevant company before the time in question ("the relevant time") must not exceed—

    (a) if the relevant company is a knowledge-intensive company at the investment date (see section 331A), £20 million, and

    (b) in any other case, £12 million.

(5) In subsection (4) the reference to relevant investments made in the relevant company includes—

(*a*) any relevant investment made in any company that has at any time before the relevant time been a 51% subsidiary of the relevant company (including investments made in that company before it became such a subsidiary but, if it is not such a subsidiary at the relevant time, not investments made in it after it last ceased to be such a subsidiary),

(*b*) any other relevant investment made in a company to the extent that the money raised by the investment has been employed for the purposes of a trade carried on by another company that has at any time before the relevant time been a 51% subsidiary of the relevant company (but, if it is not such a subsidiary at the relevant time, ignoring any money so employed after it last ceased to be such a subsidiary), and

(*c*) any other relevant investments made in a company where—

    (i) the money raised by the investment has been employed for the purposes of a trade carried on by that company or another person, and

    (ii) after that investment was made, but before the relevant time, that trade (or a part of it) became a relevant transferred trade (see subsection (7)).

(6) If only a proportion of the money raised by a relevant investment is employed for the purposes of a trade which became a relevant transferred trade, the reference in subsection (5)(*c*) to the relevant investment is to be read as a reference to the corresponding proportion of that investment.

(7) Where—

(*a*) a trade is transferred—

    (i) to the relevant company,

    (ii) to a company that at the relevant time is, or has before that time been, a 51% subsidiary of the relevant company, or

    (iii) to a partnership of which a company within subparagraph (i) or (ii) is a member,

(including where it is transferred to a company within subparagraph (ii), or a partnership of which such a company is a member, before the company became such a subsidiary but, if the company is not such a subsidiary at the relevant time, not where it is transferred to such a company or partnership after the company last ceased to be such a subsidiary), and

(*b*) the trade or a part of it was previously (at any time) carried on by another person,

the trade or part mentioned in paragraph (*b*) becomes a "relevant transferred trade" at the time it is transferred as mentioned in paragraph (*a*).

(8) In this section—

"5-year post-investment period" means the period of 5 years beginning with the day after the investment date;

"the investment date" means the date on which the relevant holding is issued;

"relevant investment" has the meaning given by section 292A(3), and section 292A(4) and (4A) (which determines when certain investments are made) applies for the purposes of this section;

and section 280B(8) and (9) (meaning of "trade" etc) applies for the purposes of this section as it applies for the purposes of section 280B.

(9) Subsection (10) applies if, by virtue of the provision of a compliance statement under section 205, 257ED or 257PB, the requirement of this section is not met.

(10) The requirement is to be treated as having been met throughout the period—

(*a*) beginning with the investment date, and

(*b*) ending with the time the compliance statement was provided.][1]

Commentary—*Simon's Taxes* **E3.255**.

HMRC Manuals—Venture Capital Schemes Manual 8123 (lifetime limit on risk finance investments).

Amendments—[1] Sections 292AA, 292AB inserted by F(No 2)A 2015 s 26, Sch 6 paras 1, 8 with effect for the purposes of determining whether shares or securities issued on or after 18 November 2015 are to be regarded as comprised in a company's qualifying holdings, but not so as to prevent investments made before that day constituting a "relevant investment" for the purposes of determining whether shares or securities issued on or after that day are to be so regarded (F(No 2)A 2015 Sch 6 para 23(4)).

293 The use of the money raised requirement

[(1) The requirement of this section is that—

(*a*) less than two years has passed since the trading time, or

(*b*) at least two years has passed since the trading time and all of the money raised by the issue of the relevant holding has been employed wholly for the purposes of a relevant qualifying activity.][1]

(2)–(4) . . .[1]

(5) In subsection (1) "the trading time" means whichever is applicable of the following—

(*a*) in a case where the requirement of section 291 was met in relation to the time when the relevant holding was issued and the relevant qualifying activity falls within subsection (2) of that section, the time when the relevant holding was issued, and

(b) in a case where that requirement was met in relation to that time and the relevant qualifying activity falls within subsection (3) of that section, the time when the condition in subsection (4)(a) of that section was met by a qualifying company beginning to carry on the intended trade.

[(5ZA) Employing money raised by the issue of the relevant holding (whether on its own or together with other money) on the acquisition, directly or indirectly, of—

(a) an interest in another company such that a company becomes a 51% subsidiary of the relevant company,

(b) a further interest in a company which is a 51% subsidiary of the relevant company,

(c) a trade,

(d) intangible assets employed for the purposes of a trade, or

(e) goodwill employed for the purposes of a trade,

does not amount to employing the money for the purposes of a relevant qualifying activity.

(5ZB) The Treasury may by regulations provide that subsection (5ZA) does not apply in relation to acquisitions of intangible assets which are of a description specified, or which occur in circumstances specified, in the regulations.

(5ZC) For the purposes of subsections (5ZA) and (5ZB)—

"goodwill" has the same meaning as in Part 8 of CTA 2009 (see section 715(3));

"intangible assets" means any asset which falls to be treated as an intangible asset in accordance with generally accepted accountancy practice;

and section 280B(8) and (9) (meaning of "trade" etc) applies for the purposes of this section as it applies for the purposes of section 280B.

(5A) Also, otherwise employing money on the acquisition of shares in a company does not of itself amount to employing the money for the purposes of a relevant qualifying activity.][2]

(6) For the purposes of this section money is not to be treated as employed otherwise than wholly for the purposes of a relevant qualifying activity if the only amount employed for other purposes is an amount which is not a significant amount.

(7) Nothing in section 286(5) requires any money whose use is ignored by virtue of subsection (6) to be treated as raised by a different holding.

(8) In this section—

"qualifying activity" and "qualifying company" have the same meaning as in section 291, and a qualifying activity is a "relevant qualifying activity" if—

(a) it was also a qualifying activity at the time when the relevant holding was issued, or

(b) it is a qualifying trade and preparing to carry it on was a qualifying activity at that time.

Commentary—*Simon's Taxes* E3.256.

HMRC Manuals—Venture Capital Schemes Manual 8140 (use of money: no business acquisitions). VCM55150 (employment of money raised).

Modifications—ITA 2007 Sch 2 para 74 (for the purpose of determining whether shares or securities are to be regarded as comprised in a company's qualifying holdings, this section is modified in relation to shares or securities issued before 17 March 2004).

Amendments—[1]   Sub-s (1) substituted, sub-ss (2)–(4) repealed by FA 2009 s 27, Sch 8 para 9 with effect in relation to shares or securities issued on or after 22 April 2009.

[2]   Sub-ss (5ZA)–(5A) substituted for previous sub-s (5A) by F(No 2)A 2015 s 26, Sch 6 paras 1, 10 with effect for the purposes of determining whether shares or securities issued on or after 18 November 2015 are to be regarded as comprised in a company's qualifying holdings. Sub-s (5A) was inserted by FA 2012 s 40, Sch 7 paras 1, 7. This amendment was treated as having come into force on 6 April 2012. It did not have effect in relation to an investment made by a VCT of protected money: see FA 2012 Sch 8 para 21(2), (3).

294 The relevant company to carry on the relevant qualifying activity requirement

(1) The requirement of this section is met if, at no time after the issue of the relevant holding, has the relevant qualifying activity in question been carried on by a person other than—

(a) the relevant company, or

(b) a qualifying 90% subsidiary of that company.

In this subsection "the relevant qualifying activity in question" means the relevant qualifying activity by reference to which the requirement of section 293 is met.

(2) The requirement of this section is not to be regarded as failing to be met merely because of the carrying on of the trade in question by a person other than the relevant company, or a qualifying subsidiary of that company, at any time—

(a) after the issue of the relevant holding, and

(b) before the relevant company, or any qualifying 90% subsidiary of that company, carries on that trade.

(3) The requirement of this section is not to be regarded as failing to be met merely because of the carrying on of the trade in question—

(a) by the partners in a partnership of which the relevant company, or a qualifying 90% subsidiary of that company, is a member, or

(b) by the parties to a joint venture to which the relevant company, or a qualifying 90% subsidiary of that company, is a party.

(4) The requirement of this section is not to be regarded as failing to be met if—
  (a) merely because of anything done as a consequence of the relevant company or any other company being in administration or receivership, or
  (b) merely because of the relevant company or any other company being wound up or dissolved without winding up,
the trade in question ceases to be carried on by the relevant company or a qualifying 90% subsidiary of that company and is subsequently carried on by a person who has not been connected, at any time after the date which is 12 months before the issue of the relevant holding, with the relevant company.
(5) Subsection (4) applies only if—
  (a) the entry into administration or receivership and everything done in consequence of the company concerned being in administration or receivership, or
  (b) the winding up or dissolution,
is for genuine commercial reasons and is not part of a scheme or arrangement the purpose or one of the main purposes of which is the avoidance of tax.
(6) In this section "the trade in question" means so much of the relevant qualifying activity mentioned in subsection (1) as consists of—
  (a) a trade which was being carried on at the time when the relevant holding was issued, or
  (b) a trade for the carrying on of which preparations were being made at that time.
(7) The definition of "relevant qualifying activity" in subsection (8) of section 293 applies for the purposes of this section as it applies for the purposes of that section.

Commentary—*Simon's Taxes* E3.256.
HMRC Manuals—Venture Capital Schemes Manual VCM55160 (company using the money).
Modifications—ITA 2007 Sch 2 para 75(1) (for the purpose of determining whether shares or securities are to be regarded as comprised in a company's qualifying holdings, this section is modified in relation to shares or securities issued before 6 April 2007).
ITA 2007 Sch 2 para 75(2) (for the purpose of determining whether shares or securities are to be regarded as comprised in a company's qualifying holdings, this section is modified in relation to shares or securities issued before 17 March 2004).

[294A The permitted company age requirement

(1) The requirement of this section is that, if the relevant holding is issued after the initial investing period, condition A, B or C must be met.
(2) "The initial investing period" means—
  (a) where the relevant company is a knowledge-intensive company at the investment date, the period of 10 years [beginning with—
    (i) the relevant first commercial sale, or
    (ii) if the relevant company so elects, the date by reference to which that company is treated as reaching an annual turnover of £200,000 (see section 331B),][3] and
  (b) in any other case, the period of 7 years beginning with that sale.
(3) Condition A is that—
  (a) a relevant investment was made in the relevant company before the end of the initial investing period, and
  (b) some or all of the money raised by that investment was employed for the purposes of the relevant qualifying activity (or a part of it).
(4) Condition B is that—
  (a) the total amount of relevant investments made in the relevant company in a period of 30 consecutive days which includes the investment date is at least 50% of the average turnover amount, and
    (b) the money raised by those investments is employed for the purpose of entering a new product or geographical market.
(5) Condition C is that—
  (a) condition B in subsection (4) or condition B in section 175A(4) (EIS: permitted company age requirement) was previously met in relation to one or more relevant investments made in the relevant company, and
  (b) some or all of the money raised by those investment was employed for the purposes of the relevant qualifying activity.
(6) "The relevant first commercial sale" means the earliest of the following—
  (a) the first commercial sale made by the relevant company,
  (b) the first commercial sale made by a company that is at the investment date, or before that date has been, a 51% subsidiary of the relevant company (including a sale made by a company before it became such a subsidiary but, if it is not such a subsidiary at the investment date, not a sale made after it last ceased to be such a subsidiary),
  (c) the first commercial sale made by any person who previously (at any time) carried on a trade which was subsequently carried on, on or before the investment date, by—
    (i) the relevant company, or
    (ii) a company that is at the investment date, or before that date has been, a 51% subsidiary of the relevant company,

(including a trade subsequently carried on by such a company before it became such a subsidiary but, if it not such a subsidiary at the investment date, not a trade which it carried on only after it last ceased to be such a subsidiary);

(*d*) the first commercial sale made by a company which becomes a 51% subsidiary of the relevant company after the investment date in circumstances where all or part of the money raised by the issue of the relevant holding is employed for the purposes of an activity carried on by that subsidiary (including a sale made by such a company before it became such a subsidiary);

    (*e*) the first commercial sale made by any person who previously (at any time) carried on a trade which was subsequently carried on by a company mentioned in paragraph (*d*) (including a trade carried on by such a company before it became such a subsidiary);

(*f*) if the money raised by the issue of the relevant holding (or any part of it) is employed for the purposes of a trade which has been transferred after the investment date to the relevant company or a 51% subsidiary of that company (or to a partnership of which the relevant company or such a subsidiary is a member), having previously (at any time) been carried on by another person, the first commercial sale made by that other person.

(7) "The average turnover amount" means one fifth of the total relevant turnover amount for the [relevant five year period.]²

[(7A) Subject to subsection (7B), the relevant five year period is the five year period which ends immediately before the beginning of the last accounts filing period.

(7B) If the last accounts filing period ends more than 12 months before the investment date, the relevant five year period is the five year period which ends 12 months before the investment date.]²

(8) In this section—

"entering a new product or geographical market" has the same meaning as in Commission Regulation (EU) No 651/2014 (General block exemption Regulation);

"first commercial sale" has the same meaning as in the European Commission's Guidelines on State aid to promote risk finance investments (as those guidelines may be amended or replaced from time to time);

"the investment date" means the date the relevant holding is issued;

"the last accounts filing period" means the last period for filing (within the meaning of section 442 of the Companies Act 2006) for the relevant company which ends before the date on which the relevant holding is issued;

"relevant investment" has the meaning given by section 292A(3), and section 292A(4) and (4A) (which determines when certain investments are made) applies for the purposes of this section;

"relevant qualifying activity" means the qualifying activity for which the money raised by the issue of the relevant holding is employed;

"the total relevant turnover amount" for a period is—

    (*a*) if the relevant company is a single company at the investment date, the sum of—

        (i) the relevant company's turnover for that period,

        (ii) if all or part of the money raised by the issue of the relevant shares is employed for the purposes of an activity carried on by a company which becomes a 51% subsidiary of the relevant company after the investment date, the turnover for that period of that subsidiary (or, if there is more than one, each of them), and

        (iii) if all or part of the money raised by the issue of the relevant shares is employed for the purposes of a transferred trade, the turnover of that trade for so much of that period as falls before the trade became a transferred trade (except to the extent that it is already included in calculating the amounts within subparagraphs (i) and (ii));

    (*b*) if the relevant company is a parent company at the investment date, the sum of—

        (i) the relevant company's turnover for that period,

        (ii) the turnover for that period of each company which at the investment date is a 51% subsidiary of the relevant company,

        (iii) if all or part of the money raised by the issue of the relevant holding is employed for the purposes of an activity carried on by a company which becomes a 51% subsidiary of the relevant company after the investment date, the turnover for that period of that subsidiary (or, if there is more than one, each of them), and

        (iv) if all or part of the money raised by the issue of the relevant shares is employed for the purposes of a transferred trade, the turnover of that trade for so much of that period as falls before the trade became a transferred trade (except to the extent that it is already included in calculating the amounts within subparagraphs (i) to (iii));

"transferred trade" means a trade which has been transferred to the company which is carrying on the trade at the time the money raised by the issue of the relevant holding is employed or to a partnership of which that company is a member;

"turnover"—

(a) in relation to a company, has the meaning given by section 474(1) of the Companies Act 2006 and is to be determined by reference to the accounts of companies and amounts recognised for accounting purposes (and such apportionments of those amounts as are just and reasonable are to be made for the purpose of determining a company's turnover for a period);

(b) in relation to any other person carrying on a trade, also has the meaning given by section 474(1) of that Act (reading references in that provision to a company as references to the person) and is to be determined by reference to the accounts of the person and amounts recognised for accounting purposes (and such apportionments of those amounts as are just and reasonable are to be made for the purpose of determining a person's turnover for a period);

(c) in relation to a transferred trade carried on by a company or other person, means such proportion of the turnover of the company or other person as it is just and reasonable to attribute to the transferred trade;

and section 280B(8) and (9) (meaning of "trade" etc) applies for the purposes of this section as it applies for the purposes of section 280B.][1]

Commentary—*Simon's Taxes* **E3.261**.

HMRC Manuals—Venture Capital Schemes Manual 8151 (the basic age condition: first commercial sale).

Amendments—[1]   This section inserted by F(No 2)A 2015 s 26, Sch 6 paras 1, 11 with effect for the purposes of determining whether shares or securities issued on or after 18 November 2015 are to be regarded as comprised in a company's qualifying holdings, but not so as to prevent investments made before that day constituting a "relevant investment" for the purposes of determining whether shares or securities issued on or after that day are to be so regarded (F(No 2)A 2015 Sch 6 para 23(4)).

[2]   Words in sub-s (7) substituted, and sub-ss (7A), (7B) inserted, by FA 2016 s 29(4). Subject to any election made under FA 2016 s 30 by the issuing company, these amendments are to be treated as always having had effect. If an election is made under s 30, the amendments do not apply for the purposes of determining whether the permitted company age requirement in this section is met in relation to any holding of shares or securities issued by the relevant company in the period beginning with 18 November 2015 and ending with 5 April 2016: see FA 2016 s 30.

[3]   In sub-s (2)(a), words substituted for words "beginning with the relevant first commercial sale," by FA 2018 s 16, Sch 4 para 8 with effect for investments made on or after 6 April 2018 (by virtue of SI 2018/931 reg 3(b)).

295 The unquoted status requirement

(1) The requirement of this section is that the relevant company must be an unquoted company.

(2) In this section "unquoted company" means a company none of whose shares, stocks, debentures or other securities are marketed to the general public.

(3) For the purposes of subsection (2), shares, stocks, debentures or other securities are marketed to the general public if they are—

(a) listed on [a recognised stock exchange,][1]

(b) listed on a designated exchange in a country outside the United Kingdom, or

(c) dealt in . . .[1] outside the United Kingdom by such means as may be designated.

(4) In subsection (3)(b) and (c) "designated" means designated by an order made by the Commissioners for Her Majesty's Revenue and Customs for the purposes of that provision.

(5) An order made for the purposes of subsection (3)(b) may designate an exchange by name, or by reference to any class or description of exchanges, including a class or description framed by reference to any authority or approval given in a country outside the United Kingdom.

(6) If—

(a) any shares in or securities of a company are included in the qualifying holdings of the investing company, and

(b) that company ceases to be an unquoted company at any time while the investing company is approved as a VCT,

the requirements of this section are to be treated, in relation to shares or securities acquired before that time, as continuing to be met for a period of 5 years after that time.

Commentary—*Simon's Taxes* **E3.246**.

Derivation—TA 1988 Sch 28B para 2.

HMRC Manuals—Venture Capital Schemes Manual VCM55180 (unquoted status requirement).

Amendments—[1]   Words in sub-s (3) substituted and repealed by FA 2007 ss 109, 114, Sch 26 para 12(1), (7), Sch 27 Pt 6(5) with effect from 19 July 2007.

296 The control and independence requirement

(1) The control element of the requirement is that—

(a) the relevant company must not control (whether on its own or together with any person connected with it) any company which is not a qualifying subsidiary of the relevant company, and

(b) no arrangements must be in existence by virtue of which the relevant company could fail to meet paragraph (a).

(2) The independence element of the requirement is that—

(a) the relevant company must not be under the control of another company (or of another company and any other person connected with that other company), and

(b) no arrangements must be in existence by virtue of which the relevant company could fail to meet paragraph (a).

(3) This section is subject to section 327(7) (exchange of shares).

Commentary—*Simon's Taxes* **E3.252**.
HMRC Manuals—Venture Capital Schemes Manual VCM55190 (control requirement).
VCM55200 (independence requirement).

297 The gross assets requirement

(1) The requirement of this section in the case of a relevant company that is a single company is that the value of the company's gross assets—

    (a) did not exceed [£15 million][1] immediately before the issue of the relevant holding, and

    (b) did not exceed [£16 million][1] immediately afterwards.

(2) The requirement of this section in the case of a relevant company that is a parent company is that the value of the group assets—

    (a) did not exceed [£15 million][1] immediately before the issue of the relevant holding, and

    (b) did not exceed [£16 million][1] immediately afterwards.

(3) The value of the group assets means the sum of the values of the gross assets of each of the members of the group, ignoring any that consist in rights against, or shares in or securities of, another member of the group.

Commentary—*Simon's Taxes* **E3.253**.
HMRC Manuals—Venture Capital Schemes Manual VCM55240 (gross assets test).
Amendments—[1]   In sub-ss (1)(a), (b), (2)(a),(b), figure substituted by FA 2012 s 40, Sch 8 paras 1, 8, with effect from 19 July 2012 (SI 2012/1901). These amendments have effect for the purpose of determining whether shares or securities issued on or after 6 April 2012 are to be regarded as comprised in a company's qualifying holdings.

[297A The number of employees requirement

(1) If the relevant company is a single company, the full-time equivalent employee number for it must be less than [the permitted limit][2] when the relevant holding is issued.

(2) If the relevant company is a parent company, the sum of—

    (a) the full-time equivalent employee number for it, and

    (b) the full-time equivalent employee numbers for each of its qualifying subsidiaries,

must be less than [the permitted limit][2] when the relevant holding is issued.

(3) The full-time equivalent employee number for a company is calculated as follows—

Step 1 Find the number of full-time employees of the company.

Step 2 Add, for each employee of the company who is not a full-time employee, such fraction as is just and reasonable.

    The result is the full-time equivalent employee number.

[[(3A) "The permitted limit" means—

    (a) if the relevant company is a knowledge-intensive company at the time the relevant holding is issued (see section 331A), 500, and

    (b) in any other case, 250.

(3B) The Treasury may by regulations amend subsection (3A)(a) or (b) by substituting a different number for the number for the time being specified there.][2]

(4) In this section references to an employee—

    (a) include a director, but

    (b) do not include—

        (i) an employee on maternity[, paternity[, shared parental or parental bereavement][3] leave, or

        (ii) a student on vocational training.][1]

Commentary—*Simon's Taxes* **E3.254**.
HMRC Manuals—Venture Capital Schemes Manual VCM55250 (employee numbers test).
Amendments—[1]   This section inserted by FA 2007 s 51, Sch 16 para 3(1), (3) and deemed to have effect from 6 April 2007 by virtue of FA 2007 Sch 16 para 3(5)–(7), this amendment does not have effect in relation to—

    (a)   a relevant holding issued before that date; or

    (b)   a relevant holding acquired by a company ("the investing company") by means of the investment of protected money.

    The terms "relevant holding" and "protected money" are defined by FA 2007 Sch 16 para 3(6), (7).

[2]   In sub-ss (1), (2), words substituted for figure "250", and sub-ss (3A) and (3B) inserted, by F(No 2)A 2015 s 26, Sch 6 paras 1, 12 with effect for the purposes of determining whether shares or securities issued on or after 18 November 2015 are to be regarded as comprised in a company's qualifying holdings. The figure of "250" was substituted by FA 2012 s 40, Sch 8 paras 1, 9 with effect from 19 July 2012 (by virtue of SI 2012/1901); this amendment had effect for the purpose of determining whether shares or securities issued on or after 6 April 2012 were to be so regarded.

[3]   In sub-s (4)(b)(i), words substituted for words "or shared parental" by the Parental Bereavement (Leave and Pay) Act 2018 s 1, Schedule paras 50, 54 with effect from 18 January 2020 (by virtue of SI 2020/45 reg 2).

[297B The proportion of skilled employees requirement

(1) The requirement of this section is that, where the conditions in subsection (2) are met, at all times in the period of 3 years beginning with the issue of the relevant holding—

(a) if the relevant company is a single company, the FTE skilled employee number must be at least 20% of the FTE employee number, and

(b) if the relevant company is a parent company, the FTE group skilled employee number must be at least 20% of the FTE group employee number.

(2) The conditions are that—

(a) the requirements one or more of sections [292A,][2] 292AA, 294A and 297A (the maximum risk finance investments when relevant holding is issued requirement and the number of employees requirement) is or are met only by reason of the relevant company being a knowledge-intensive company at the time the relevant holding was issued, and

(b) the innovation condition in section 331A(6) was not met by the relevant company at that time.

(3) The requirement of this section is not to be regarded as failing to be met at a time when the relevant company, by virtue of section 292 (companies in administration or receivership), is not regarded as having ceased to meet the trading requirement.

(4) In this section "FTE employee number", "FTE group employee number", "FTE skilled employee number" and "FTE group skilled employee number" have the meaning given by section 331A(10) (meaning of "knowledge-intensive company").][1]

Commentary—*Simon's Taxes* E3.254.

Amendments—[1]   This section inserted by F(No 2)A 2015 s 26, Sch 6 paras 1, 13 with effect for the purposes of determining whether shares or securities issued on or after 18 November 2015 are to be regarded as comprised in a company's qualifying holdings.

[2]   In sub-s (2)(a), reference "292A," inserted by FA 2018 s 16, Sch 4 para 4 with effect for investments made on or after 6 April 2018 (by virtue of SI 2018/931 reg 3(b).

298 The qualifying subsidiaries requirement

Any subsidiary that the relevant company has must be a qualifying subsidiary of the company.

Commentary—*Simon's Taxes* D8.320.

HMRC Manuals—Venture Capital Schemes Manual VCM55260 (qualifying subsidiaries requirement).

299 The property managing subsidiaries requirement

(1) Any property managing subsidiary that the relevant company has must be a qualifying 90% subsidiary of the company.

(2) "Property managing subsidiary" means a subsidiary of the relevant company whose business consists wholly or mainly in the holding or managing of land or any property deriving its value from land.

(3) In subsection (2) references to property deriving its value from land include—

(a) any shareholding in a company deriving its value directly or indirectly from land,

(b) any partnership interest deriving its value directly or indirectly from land,

(c) any interest in settled property deriving its value directly or indirectly from land, and

(d) any option, consent or embargo affecting the disposition of land.

Commentary—*Simon's Taxes* E3.252.

HMRC Manuals—Venture Capital Schemes Manual VCM55270 (property managing subsidiaries requirement).

[299A The no disqualifying arrangements requirement

(1) The relevant holding must not have been issued, nor any money raised by the issue employed, in consequence or anticipation of, or otherwise in connection with, disqualifying arrangements.

(2) Arrangements are "disqualifying arrangements" if—

(a) the main purpose, or one of the main purposes, of the arrangements is to secure—

(i) that a qualifying activity is or will be carried on by the relevant company, or a qualifying 90% subsidiary of that company, and

(ii) that shares or securities issued by the relevant company may be comprised in any company's qualifying holdings or that one or more persons may obtain relevant tax relief in respect of such shares which raise money for the purposes of that qualifying activity,

(b) that qualifying activity is the relevant qualifying activity by reference to which the requirement in section 293(1)(b) (money raised to be employed within two years for relevant qualifying activity) is met in relation to the relevant holding, and

(c) one or both of conditions A and B are met.

(3) Condition A is that, as a (direct or indirect) result of the money raised by the issue of the relevant holding being employed as required by section 293(1)(b), an amount representing the whole or the majority of the amount raised is, in the course of the arrangements, paid to or for the benefit of a relevant person or relevant persons.

(4) Condition B is that, in the absence of the arrangements, it would have been reasonable to expect that the whole or greater part of the component activities of the relevant qualifying activity would have been carried on as part of another business by a relevant person or relevant persons.

(5) For the purposes of this section it is immaterial whether the relevant company is a party to the arrangements.

(6) In this section—

"component activities" means—

(a) if the relevant qualifying activity is within section 291(2), the carrying on of a qualifying trade which constitutes that activity, and

(b) if the relevant qualifying activity is within section 291(3), the preparations to carry on a qualifying trade which constitute that activity;

"arrangements" includes any scheme, agreement, understanding, transaction or series of transactions (whether or not legally enforceable);

"relevant person" means a person who is a party to the arrangements or a person connected with such a party;

"qualifying activity" has the same meaning as in section 291;

"relevant tax relief", in respect of shares, means one or more of the following—

(a) relief under Chapter 6 of Part 4 (losses on disposal of shares) in respect of the shares;

(b) EIS relief (within the meaning of Part 5) in respect of the shares;

(c) SEIS relief (within the meaning of Part 5A) in respect of the shares;

[(ca) SI relief (within the meaning of Part 5B) in respect of the shares;][2]

(d) relief under section 150A or 150E of TCGA 1992 (enterprise investment scheme and seed enterprise investment scheme) in respect of the shares;

(e) relief under Schedule 5B to that Act in consequence of which deferral relief is attributable to the shares;

(f) relief under Schedule 5BB to that Act (seed enterprise investment scheme: re-investment) in consequence of which SEIS re-investment relief is attributable to the shares (see paragraph 4 of that Schedule).][1]

Commentary—*Simon's Taxes* **E3.260**.
HMRC Manuals—Venture Capital Schemes Manual VCM55280 (no disqualifying arrangements requirement).
Amendments—[1] This section inserted by FA 2012 s 40, Sch 8 paras 1, 10, with effect for the purpose of determining whether shares or securities issued on or after 6 April 2012 are to be regarded as comprised in a company's qualifying holdings. It does not matter whether the disqualifying arrangements were entered into before or on or after 6 April 2012: FA 2012 Sch 8 para 19(2).
[2] Sub-s (6)(ca) inserted by F(No 2)A 2017 s 14, Sch 1 para 11(1), (4) with effect for the purpose of determining whether shares or securities issued on or after 6 April 2017 are to be regarded as comprised in a company's qualifying holdings. This amendment does not have effect for the purposes of determining any question whether particular arrangements which include any transaction entered into before 6 April 2017 are "disqualifying arrangements" for the purposes of ss 178A, 257CF or 299A (F(No 2)A 2017 Sch 1 para 16(1), (3)).

Definitions

300 Meaning of "qualifying trade"

(1) For the purposes of this Chapter, a trade is a qualifying trade if—

(a) it is conducted on a commercial basis and with a view to the realisation of profits, and

(b) it does not consist wholly or as to a substantial part in the carrying on of excluded activities (see sections 303 to 310).

(2) The carrying on of any activities of research and development from which it is intended—

[(a) that a trade will be derived which will be a qualifying trade, or

(b) that a trade will benefit which is or will be a qualifying trade,][1]

is to be treated as the carrying on of a qualifying trade.

(3) But preparing to carry on such activities does not count as preparing to carry on a qualifying trade.

(4) References in this section to a trade are to be read without regard to the definition of "trade" in section 989.

Commentary—*Simon's Taxes* **E3.248**.
HMRC Manuals—Venture Capital Schemes Manual VCM55100 (meaning of 'qualifying trade').
Amendments—[1] Sub-s (2)(a), (b) substituted by F(No 3)A 2010 s 5, Sch 2 para 2(1), (11) with effect in relation to shares or securities issued on or after 6 April 2011 (by virtue of SI 2011/662 art 2).

301 Meaning of "qualifying 90% subsidiary"

(1) For the purposes of this Chapter, a company ("the subsidiary") is a qualifying 90% subsidiary of the relevant company at any time when the following conditions are met—

(a) the relevant company possesses at least 90% of the issued share capital of, and at least 90% of the voting power in, the subsidiary,

(b) the relevant company would—

(i) in the event of a winding up of the subsidiary, or

(ii) in any other circumstances,

be beneficially entitled to receive at least 90% of the assets of the subsidiary which would then be available for distribution to equity holders of the subsidiary,

(c) the relevant company is beneficially entitled to receive at least 90% of any profits of the subsidiary which are available for distribution to equity holders of the subsidiary,

(d) no person other than the relevant company has control of the subsidiary, and

ITA 2007

(*e*) no arrangements are in existence by virtue of which any of the conditions in paragraphs (*a*) to (*d*) would cease to be met.

[(1A) For the purposes of this Chapter, a company ("company A") which is a subsidiary of a company that is not the relevant company ("company B") is a qualifying 90% subsidiary of the relevant company if—

    (*a*) company A would be a qualifying 90% subsidiary of company B (if company B were the relevant company), and company B is a qualifying 100% subsidiary of the relevant company, or

    (*b*) company A is a qualifying 100% subsidiary of company B, and company B is a qualifying 90% subsidiary of the relevant company.

(1B) For the purposes of subsection (1A), no account is to be taken of any control the relevant company may have of company A.

(1C) For those purposes, a company ("company X") is a qualifying 100% subsidiary of another company ("company Y") at any time when the conditions in subsection (1)(*a*) to (*e*) would be met if—

    (*a*) company X were the subsidiary,

    (*b*) company Y were the relevant company, and

    (*c*) in subsection (1) for "at least 90%" in each place there were substituted "100%".][1]

(2) Subsections (3), (4) and (5) of section 302 apply in relation to the conditions in subsection (1)—

    (*a*) as they apply in relation to the conditions in subsection (2) of that section, but

    (*b*) with the omission from subsection (5) of "or (as the case may be) by another subsidiary of that company".

(3) For the purposes of subsection (1)—

    (*a*) the persons who are equity holders of the subsidiary, and

    (*b*) the percentage of the assets of the subsidiary to which an equity holder would be entitled,

are to be determined in accordance with [Chapter 6 of Part 5 of CTA 2010][2].

(4) In making that determination—

    (*a*) references in [section 166 of that Act to company A][2] are to be read as references to an equity holder, and

    (*b*) references in that [section][2] to a winding up are to be read as including references to any other circumstances in which assets of the subsidiary are available for distribution to its equity holders.

Commentary—*Simon's Taxes* **E3.252**.
HMRC Manuals—Venture Capital Schemes Manual VCM55170 (meaning of 'qualifying 90% subsidiary').
Amendments—[1] Sub-ss (1A)–(1C) inserted by FA 2007 s 51, Sch 16 para 17. This amendment is deemed to have effect from 6 April 2007: FA 2007 Sch 16 para 18.
[2] In sub-ss (3), (4)(*a*), (*b*), words substituted by CTA 2010 s 1177, Sch 1 para 504. CTA 2010 has effect for corporation tax purposes for accounting periods ending on or after 1 April 2010, and for income and capital gains tax purposes for the tax year 2010–11 and subsequent tax years.

302 Meaning of "qualifying subsidiary"

(1) For the purposes of this Chapter, a company ("the subsidiary") is a qualifying subsidiary of the relevant company if the following conditions are met.

(2) The conditions are that—

    (*a*) the subsidiary is a 51% subsidiary of the relevant company,

    (*b*) no person other than the relevant company, or another of its subsidiaries, has control of the subsidiary, and

    (*c*) no arrangements are in existence by virtue of which either of the conditions in paragraphs (*a*) and (*b*) would cease to be met.

(3) The conditions do not cease to be met merely because the subsidiary or any other company is wound up, if the winding up—

    (*a*) is for genuine commercial reasons, and

    (*b*) is not part of a scheme or arrangement the main purpose or one of the main purposes of which is the avoidance of tax.

(4) The conditions do not cease to be met merely because of anything done as a consequence of the subsidiary or any other company being in administration or receivership, if—

    (*a*) the entry into administration or receivership, and

    (*b*) everything done as a consequence of the company concerned being in administration or receivership,

is for genuine commercial reasons, and is not part of a scheme or arrangement the main purpose or one of the main purposes of which is the avoidance of tax.

(5) The conditions do not cease to be met merely because arrangements are in existence for the disposal by the relevant company or (as the case may be) by another subsidiary of that company of all its interest in the subsidiary, if the disposal—

    (*a*) is to be for genuine commercial reasons, and

(*b*) is not to be part of a scheme or arrangement the main purpose or one of the main purposes of which is the avoidance of tax.

Commentary—*Simon's Taxes* **E3.252**.
HMRC Manuals—Venture Capital Schemes Manual VCM55260 (qualifying subsidiaries requirement).

[302A Meaning of "permanent establishment"

(1) This section applies for the purposes of this Chapter.

(2) A company has a "permanent establishment" in the United Kingdom if (and only if)—

(*a*) it has a fixed place of business there through which the business of the company is wholly or partly carried on, or

(*b*) an agent acting on behalf of the company has and habitually exercises there authority to enter into contracts on behalf of the company.

(3) For the purposes of this section "fixed place of business" includes (without prejudice to the generality of that expression)—

(*a*) a place of management,

(*b*) a branch,

(*c*) an office,

(*d*) a factory,

(*e*) a workshop,

(*f*) a mine, an oil or gas well, a quarry or any other place of extraction of natural resources, and

(*g*) a building site or construction or installation project.

(4) If the condition in subsection (5) is met, a company is not regarded as having a permanent establishment in the United Kingdom by reason of the fact that—

(*a*) a fixed place of business is maintained there for the purpose of carrying on activities for the company, or

(*b*) an agent carries on activities there for and on behalf of the company.

(5) The condition is that, in relation to the business of the company as a whole, the activities carried on are only of a preparatory or auxiliary character.

(6) For this purpose "activities of a preparatory or auxiliary character" include (without prejudice to the generality of that expression)—

(*a*) the use of facilities for the purpose of storage, display or delivery of goods or merchandise belonging to the company,

(*b*) the maintenance of a stock of goods or merchandise belonging to the company for the purpose of storage, display or delivery,

(*c*) the maintenance of a stock of goods or merchandise belonging to the company for the purpose of processing by another person, and

(*d*) purchasing goods or merchandise, or collecting information, for the company.

(7) A company is not regarded as having a permanent establishment in the United Kingdom by reason of the fact that it carries on business there through an agent of independent status (including a broker or a general commission agent) acting in the ordinary course of the agent's business.

(8) A company is not regarded as having a permanent establishment in the United Kingdom by reason of the fact that it controls a company that—

(*a*) is resident there, or

(*b*) carries on business there (whether through a permanent establishment or otherwise).

(9) The Treasury may by regulations amend this section.][1]

Commentary—*Simon's Taxes* **E3.247**.
HMRC Manuals—Venture Capital Schemes Manual VCM55040 (meaning of 'permanent establishment').
Amendments—[1] Section 302A inserted by F(No 3)A 2010 s 5, Sch 2 para 2(1), (12) with effect in relation to shares or securities issued on or after 6 April 2011 (by virtue of SI 2011/662 art 2).

Excluded activities

303 Meaning of "excluded activities"

(1) The following are excluded activities for the purposes of sections 290 and 300—

(*a*) dealing in land, in commodities or futures or in shares, securities or other financial instruments,

(*b*) dealing in goods otherwise than in the course of an ordinary trade of wholesale or retail distribution,

(*c*) banking, insurance, money-lending, debt-factoring, hire-purchase financing or other financial activities,

(*d*) leasing (including letting ships on charter or other assets on hire),

(*e*) receiving royalties or licence fees,

(*f*) providing legal or accountancy services,

(*g*) property development,

(*h*) farming or market gardening,

(*i*) holding, managing or occupying woodlands, any other forestry activities or timber production,

[(*ia*) shipbuilding,

(*ib*) producing coal,

(*ic*) producing steel,]¹

(*j*)   operating or managing hotels or comparable establishments or managing property used as an hotel or comparable establishment,

(*k*)   operating or managing nursing homes or residential care homes or managing property used as a nursing home or residential care home, . . . ²

[(*ka*) generating or exporting electricity or making electricity generating capacity available,

(*kb*) generating heat,

(*kc*) generating any form of energy not within paragraph (*ka*) or (*kb*),

(*kd*) producing gas or fuel, and]³

(*l*)   any activities which are excluded activities under section 310 (provision of services or facilities for another business).

(2) Subsection (1) is supplemented by the following provisions—

(*a*) section 304 (wholesale and retail distribution),

(*b*) section 305 (leasing of ships),

(*c*) section 306 (receipt of royalties and licence fees),

(*d*) section 307 (property development),

[(*da*) section 307A (shipbuilding),

(*db*) section 307B (producing coal),

(*dc*) section 307C (producing steel),]¹

(*e*) section 308 (hotels and comparable establishments), . . . ²

(*f*) section 309 (nursing homes and residential care homes), [and

(*g*) section 309A (export of electricity).]⁴

(*h*) . . . ⁴

Commentary—*Simon's Taxes* **E3.248**.

HMRC Manuals—Venture Capital Schemes Manual VCM3010 (meaning of 'excluded activities'). VCM3000 (excluded activities: contents).

Amendments—¹   Sub-ss (1)(*ia*)–(*ic*) and (2)(*da*)–(*dc*) inserted by FA 2008 s 32, Sch 11 paras 7, 8 with effect from 6 April 2008. This amendment does not have effect in relation to:

    (a)   a relevant holding issued before that date, or

    (b)   a relevant holding acquired by a company ("the investing company") by means of the investment of protected money (FA 2008 Sch 11 para 12).

²   Word "and" at the end of sub-ss (1)(*k*) and (2)(*e*) repealed, and sub-s (2)(*g*) and preceding word "and" inserted, by FA 2012 s 40, Sch 8 paras 1, 11 with effect in relation to a relevant holding issued on or after 23 March 2011, subject to provisions relating to shares issued before 6 April 2012: see FA 2012 Sch 8 para 22(2).

³   In sub-s (1), paras (*ka*)–(*kd*) substituted for previous paras (*ka*)–(*kc*) by FA 2016 s 28(2) with effect in relation to relevant holdings issued on or after 6 April 2016.

⁴   Sub-s (2)(*g*) and preceding word substituted, and sub-s (2)(*h*) repealed, by FA 2016 s 28(4)(*a*) with effect in relation to relevant holdings issued on or after 6 April 2016.

304 Excluded activities: wholesale and retail distribution

(1) This section supplements section 303(1)(*b*).

(2) In this section—

(*a*) subsections (3) and (4) are for determining whether a trade is a trade of wholesale or retail distribution, and

(*b*) subsections (5) and (6) are for determining whether a trade of wholesale or retail distribution is an ordinary trade of wholesale or retail distribution.

(3) A trade of wholesale distribution is one in which goods are offered for sale and sold to persons for resale by them, or for processing and resale by them, to members of the general public for their use or consumption.

(4) A trade of retail distribution is one in which goods are offered or exposed for sale and sold to members of the general public for their use or consumption.

(5) A trade of wholesale or retail distribution is not an ordinary trade of wholesale or retail distribution if—

(*a*) it consists to a substantial extent—

(i)   in dealing in goods of a kind which are collected or held as an investment, or

(ii) in that activity and any other excluded activity taken together, and

(*b*) a substantial proportion of those goods are held for a period which is significantly longer than the period for which the trader would reasonably be expected to hold them while trying to dispose of them at their market value.

(6) In determining whether a trade of wholesale or retail distribution is an ordinary trade of wholesale or retail distribution regard is to be had to the extent to which it has the following features—

(*a*) the goods are bought by the trader in quantities larger than those in which the trader sells them,

(*b*) the goods are bought and sold by the trader in different markets,

(c) the trader employs staff and incurs expenses in the trade in addition to the cost of the goods and, in the case of a trade carried on by a company, in addition to any remuneration paid to any person connected with it,

(d) there are purchases or sales from or to persons who are connected with the trader,

(e) purchases are matched with forward sales or vice versa,

(f) the goods are held by the trader for longer than is normal for goods of the kind in question,

(g) the trade is carried on otherwise than at a place or places commonly used for wholesale or retail trade, and

(h) the trader does not take physical possession of the goods.

(7) In subsection (6)—

(a) the features in paragraphs (a) to (c) are regarded as indications that the trade is an ordinary trade of wholesale or retail distribution, and

(b) those in paragraphs (d) to (h) are regarded as indications to the contrary.

Commentary—*Simon's Taxes* **E3.249**.

HMRC Manuals—Venture Capital Schemes Manual VCM3030 (dealing in goods otherwise than in the course of an ordinary trade of wholesale or retail distribution).

305 Excluded activities: leasing of ships

(1) This section supplements section 303(1)(d) so far as it relates to the leasing of ships other than offshore installations or pleasure craft.

(2) In the following provisions "ship" accordingly means a ship other than an offshore installation or a pleasure craft.

(3) If the requirements of subsection (4) are met, a trade is not to be regarded as consisting in the carrying on of excluded activities within section 303(1)(d) as a result only of its consisting in letting ships on charter.

(4) The requirements of this subsection are that—

(a) every ship let on charter by the company carrying on the trade is beneficially owned by the company,

(b) every ship beneficially owned by the company is registered in the United Kingdom,

(c) the company is solely responsible for arranging the marketing of the services of its ships, and

(d) the conditions mentioned in subsection (5) are met in relation to every letting on charter by the company.

(5) The conditions referred to in subsection (4)(d) are—

(a) the letting is for a period not exceeding 12 months and no provision is made at any time (whether in the charterparty or otherwise) for extending it beyond that period otherwise than at the option of the charterer,

(b) no provision for the grant of a new letting to end more than 12 months after the provision is made (whether in the charterparty or otherwise) is in force during the period of the letting otherwise than at the option of the charterer,

(c) the letting is by way of a bargain at arm's length between the company and a person who is not connected with it,

(d) under the terms of the charter the company is responsible as principal—

(i) for taking, throughout the period of the charter, management decisions in relation to the ship, other than those of a kind generally regarded by persons engaged in trade of the kind in question as matters of husbandry, and

(ii) for defraying all expenses in connection with the ship throughout that period, or substantially all such expenses, other than those directly incidental to a particular voyage or to the employment of the ship during that period, and

(e) no arrangements exist by virtue of which a person other than the company may be appointed to be responsible for the matters mentioned in paragraph (d) on behalf of the company.

(6) If in the case of the company carrying on the trade ("the letting company") the charterer is also a company and—

(a) the charterer is a qualifying subsidiary of the letting company, or

(b) the letting company is a qualifying subsidiary of the charterer, or

(c) both companies are qualifying subsidiaries of a third company,

subsection (5) has effect with the omission of paragraph (c).

(7) If any of the requirements of subsection (4) is not met in relation to any lettings of ships, the trade is not, as a result, to be treated as consisting in the carrying on of excluded activities if—

(a) those lettings, and

(b) any other excluded activities

do not, taken together, amount to a substantial part of the trade.

(8) In this section "pleasure craft" means any ship of a kind primarily used for sport or recreation.

Commentary—*Simon's Taxes* **E3.250**.

HMRC Manuals—Venture Capital Schemes Manual VCM3050 (letting ships on charter or other assets on hire).

306 Excluded activities: receipt of royalties and licence fees
(1) This section supplements section 303(1)(*e*) (receipt of royalties and licence fees).
(2) If the requirement of subsection (3) is met, a trade is not to be regarded as consisting in the carrying on of excluded activities within section 303(1)(*e*) as a result only of its consisting to a substantial extent in the receiving of royalties or licence fees.
(3) The requirement of this subsection is that the royalties or licence fees (or all but for a part that is not a substantial part in terms of value) are attributable to the exploitation of relevant intangible assets.
(4) For this purpose an intangible asset is a "relevant intangible asset" if the whole or greater part (in terms of value) of it has been created—
  [(*a*) by the relevant company, or
  (*b*) by a company which was a qualifying subsidiary of the relevant company throughout a period during which it created the whole or greater part (in terms of value) of the intangible asset.][1]
(5) In the case of an intangible asset that is intellectual property, references to the creation of an asset by a company are to its creation in circumstances in which the right to exploit it vests in the company (whether alone or jointly with others).
(6) In this section—
  [1]

  "intangible asset" means any asset which falls to be treated as an intangible asset in accordance with generally accepted accountancy practice, and
  "intellectual property" means—
    (*a*) any patent, trade mark, registered design, copyright, design right, performer's right or plant breeder's right, or
    (*b*) any rights under the law of a country or territory outside the United Kingdom which correspond or are similar to those falling within paragraph (*a*).
[(7) If—
  (*a*) the relevant company acquired all the shares ("old shares") in another company ("the old company") at a time when the only shares issued in the relevant company were subscriber shares, and
  (*b*) the consideration for the old shares consisted wholly of the issue of shares in the relevant company,
references in subsection (4) to the relevant company include the old company.][1]
Commentary—*Simon's Taxes* **E3.251**.
HMRC Manuals—Venture Capital Schemes Manual VCM3060 (receiving royalties or licence fees).
Amendments—[1] Sub-s (4)(*a*), (*b*) substituted, in sub-s (6) the definition of "holding company" repealed, and sub-s (7) inserted, by FA 2007 ss 51, 114, Sch 16 para 12, Sch 27 Pt 2(16). This amendment is deemed to have effect from 6 April 2007 by virtue of FA 2007 Sch 16 para 13, and is subject to transitional provisions in FA 2007 Sch 16 para 14.

307 Excluded activities: property development
(1) This section supplements section 303(1)(*g*).
(2) "Property development" means the development of land—
  (*a*) by a company which has, or at any time has had, an interest in the land, and
  (*b*) with the sole or main object of realising a gain from the disposal of an interest in the land when it is developed.
(3) For this purpose "interest in land" means, subject to subsection (4)—
  (*a*) any estate, interest or right in or over land, including any right affecting the use or disposition of land, or
  (*b*) any right to obtain such an estate, interest or right from another which is conditional on the other's ability to grant it.
(4) References in this section to an interest in land do not include—
  (*a*) the interest of a creditor (other than a creditor in respect of a rentcharge) whose debt is secured by way of mortgage, an agreement for a mortgage or a charge of any kind over land, or
  (*b*) in the case of land in Scotland, the interest of a creditor in a charge or security of any kind over land.
Commentary—*Simon's Taxes* **E3.248**.
HMRC Manuals—Venture Capital Schemes Manual VCM3080 (property development).
Modification—ITA 2007 Sch 2 para 81 (for the purpose of determining whether shares or securities are to be regarded as comprised in a company's qualifying holdings, this section does not apply in relation to shares or securities acquired by the company by means of the investment of—
  (a)   money raised by the issue before 17 March 1998 of shares in or securities of the investing company, or
  (b)   money derived from the investment by that company of any such money).

[307A Excluded activities: shipbuilding
In section 303(1)(*ia*) "shipbuilding" has the same meaning as in the Framework on state aid to shipbuilding (2003/C 317/06), published in the Official Journal on 30 December 2003.][1]
Commentary—*Simon's Taxes* **E3.248**.

HMRC Manuals—Venture Capital Schemes Manual VCM3110 (shipbuilding).
Amendments—[1]   Sections 307A–307C inserted by FA 2008 s 32 Sch 11 paras 7, 9 with effect from 6 April 2008. This amendment does not have effect in relation to:

    (a)   a relevant holding issued before that date, or

    (b)   a relevant holding acquired by a company ("the investing company") by means of the investment of protected money (FA 2008 Sch 11 para 12).

[307B Excluded activities: producing coal

(1) This section supplements section 303(1)(*ib*).

(2) "Coal" has the meaning given by Article 2 of Council Regulation (EC) No 1407/2002 (state aid to coal industry).

(3) The production of coal includes the extraction of it.][1]

Commentary—*Simon's Taxes* **E3.248**.

HMRC Manuals—Venture Capital Schemes Manual VCM3120 (producing coal).

Amendments—[1]   Sections 307A–307C inserted by FA 2008 s 32 Sch 11 paras 7, 9 with effect from 6 April 2008. This amendment does not have effect in relation to:

    (a)   a relevant holding issued before that date, or

    (b)   a relevant holding acquired by a company ("the investing company") by means of the investment of protected money (FA 2008 Sch 11 para 12).

[307C Excluded activities: producing steel

In section 303(1)(*ic*) "steel" means any of the steel products listed in Annex 1 to the Guidelines on national regional aid (2006/C 54/08), published in the Official Journal on 4 March 2006.][1]

Commentary—*Simon's Taxes* **E3.248**.

HMRC Manuals—Venture Capital Schemes Manual VCM3130 (producing steel).

Amendments—[1]   Sections 307A–307C inserted by FA 2008 s 32 Sch 11 paras 7, 9 with effect from 6 April 2008. This amendment does not have effect in relation to:

    (a)   a relevant holding issued before that date, or

    (b)   a relevant holding acquired by a company ("the investing company") by means of the investment of protected money (FA 2008 Sch 11 para 12).

308 Excluded activities: hotels and comparable establishments

(1) This section supplements section 303(1)(*j*).

(2) The reference to a comparable establishment is to a guest house, hostel or other establishment the main purpose of maintaining which is the provision of facilities for overnight accommodation (with or without catering services).

(3) The activities of a person are not to be taken to fall within section 303(1)(*j*) unless that person has an estate or interest in, or is in occupation of, the hotel or comparable establishment in question.

Commentary—*Simon's Taxes* **E3.248**.

HMRC Manuals—Venture Capital Schemes Manual VCM3140 (operating or managing hotels or comparable establishments).

Modification—ITA 2007 Sch 2 para 81 (for the purpose of determining whether shares or securities are to be regarded as comprised in a company's qualifying holdings, this section does not apply in relation to shares or securities acquired by the company by means of the investment of—

    (a)   money raised by the issue before 17 March 1998 of shares in or securities of the investing company, or

    (b)   money derived from the investment by that company of any such money).

309 Excluded activities: nursing homes and residential care homes

(1) This section supplements section 303(1)(*k*).

(2) "Nursing home" means any establishment which exists wholly or mainly for the provision of nursing care—

    (*a*)   for persons suffering from sickness, injury or infirmity, or

    (*b*)   for women who are pregnant or have given birth.

(3) "Residential care home" means any establishment which exists wholly or mainly for the provision of residential accommodation, together with board and personal care, for persons in need of personal care because of—

    (*a*)   old age,

    (*b*)   mental or physical disability,

    (*c*)   past or present dependence on alcohol or drugs,

    (*d*)   any past illnesses, or

    (*e*)   past or present mental disorder.

(4) The activities of a person are not to be taken to fall within section 303(1)(*k*) unless that person has an estate or interest in, or is in occupation of, the nursing home or residential care home in question.

Commentary—*Simon's Taxes* **E3.248**.

HMRC Manuals—Venture Capital Schemes Manual VCM3150 (operating or managing nursing homes or residential care homes).

Modification—ITA 2007 Sch 2 para 81 (for the purpose of determining whether shares or securities are to be regarded as comprised in a company's qualifying holdings, this section does not apply in relation to shares or securities acquired by the company by means of the investment of—

    (a)   money raised by the issue before 17 March 1998 of shares in or securities of the investing company, or

    (b)   money derived from the investment by that company of any such money).

[309A Excluded activities: . . . export of electricity
(1) This section supplements section 303(1)(*ka*).
(2) Electricity is exported if it is exported onto a distribution system or transmission system (within the meaning of section 4 of the Electricity Act 1989).
(3)–(9) . . . ²]¹
Commentary—*Simon's Taxes* E3.248.
HMRC Manuals—Venture Capital Schemes Manual VCM3160 (subsidised generation or export of electricity).
Amendments—¹   This section inserted by FA 2012 s 40, Sch 8 paras 1, 12 with effect in relation to a relevant holding issued
   on or after 23 March 2011, subject to provisions relating to shares issued before 6 April 2012: see FA 2012 Sch 8 para 22(2).
²   Words in heading, and sub-ss (3)–(9), repealed, with effect in relation to relevant holdings issued on or after 6 April 2016.

310 Excluded activities: provision of services or facilities for another business
(1) Providing services or facilities for a business carried on by another person (other than a company of which the provider of the services or facilities is a qualifying subsidiary) is an excluded activity
if—
   (*a*) the business consists wholly or as to a substantial part of activities falling within any of
       paragraphs (*a*) to [(*ka*)]² of section 303(1), and
   (*b*) a controlling interest in the business is held by a person who also has a controlling interest in
       the business carried on by the provider of the services or facilities.
(2) Subsections (3) to (5) explain what is meant by a controlling interest in a business for the purposes of subsection (1)(*b*).
(3) In the case of a business carried on by a company, a person ("A") has a controlling interest in the business if—
   (*a*) A controls the company,
   (*b*) the company is a close company and A or an associate of A, being a director of the company,
       either—
       (i) is the beneficial owner of more than 30% of the ordinary share capital of the company, or
       (ii) is able, directly or through the medium of other companies or by any other indirect
           means, to control more than 30% of that share capital, or
   (*c*) at least half the business could, in accordance with section [section 942 of CTA 2010 (options
       for purposes of ownership condition)]¹, be regarded as belonging to A for the purposes of
       [section 941 of that Act (trade transfers without change of ownership: ownership condition)]¹.
(4) In any other case, a person has a controlling interest in a business if the person is entitled to at least half the assets used for, or of the income arising from, the business.
(5) For the purposes of this section—
   (*a*) any rights or powers of a person who is an associate of another are to be attributed to that
       other person, and
   (*b*) "business" includes any trade, profession or vocation.
Commentary—*Simon's Taxes* E3.248.
HMRC Manuals—Venture Capital Schemes Manual VCM3170 (provision of services or facilities for another business).
Modifications—ITA 2007 Sch 2 para 85(1) (for the purpose of determining whether shares or securities are to be regarded as
   comprised in a company's qualifying holdings, this section is modified in relation to shares or securities issued before 6 April
   2007).
ITA 2007 Sch 2 para 85(2) (for the purpose of determining whether shares or securities are to be regarded as comprised in a
   company's qualifying holdings, sub-s (1)(*a*) above is modified in relation to shares or securities acquired by the company by
   means of the investment of—
   (a)   money raised by the issue before 17 March 1998 of shares in or securities of the investing company, or
   (b)   money derived from the investment by that company of any such money).
Amendments—¹   In sub-s (3)(*c*), words substituted by CTA 2010 s 1177, Sch 1 para 505. CTA 2010 has effect for corporation
   tax purposes for accounting periods ending on or after 1 April 2010, and for income and capital gains tax purposes for the
   tax year 2010–11 and subsequent tax years.
²   In sub-s (1)(*a*) reference substituted by FA 2012 s 40, Sch 8 paras 1, 13 with effect in relation to a relevant holding issued
   on or after 23 March 2011, subject to provisions relating to shares issued before 6 April 2012: see FA 2012 Sch 8 para 22(2).

Supplementary

312 Winding up of the relevant company
None of the requirements of this Chapter is to be regarded, at a time when the relevant company is being wound up, as being, on that account, a requirement that is not met in relation to that company
if—
   (*a*) the requirements of this Chapter would be met in relation to that company apart from the
       winding up, and
   (*b*) the winding up is for genuine commercial reasons, and is not part of a scheme or arrangement
       the main purpose or one of the main purposes of which is the avoidance of tax.
Commentary—*Simon's Taxes* E3.265.
Modification—ITA 2007 Sch 2 para 86 (for the purpose of determining whether shares or securities are to be regarded as
   comprised in a company's qualifying holdings, this section is modified in relation to shares or securities issued before 17 March
   2004).

[312A Power to require information relating to disqualifying arrangements

(1) Subsection (2) applies if an officer of Revenue and Customs has reason to believe that the relevant company has issued the relevant holding to the investing company in consequence of, or otherwise in connection with, disqualifying arrangements (within the meaning of section 299A(2)).

(2) The officer may by notice require any person concerned to supply the officer within such time as may be specified in the notice with—

    (a) a declaration in writing stating whether or not, according to the information which that person has or can reasonably obtain, such arrangements exist or have existed, and

    (b) such other information as the officer may reasonably require for the purposes of section 299A and as that person has or can reasonably obtain.

(3) The period specified in a notice under subsection (2) must be at least 60 days.

(4) A "person concerned" means—

    (a) the relevant company,

    (b) the investing company,

    (c) any person connected with either of those companies, and

    (d) any person whom the officer has reason to believe is or was a party to the arrangements in question.][1]

Commentary—*Simon's Taxes* **E3.260**.
HMRC Manuals—Venture Capital Schemes Manual VCM55430 (information powers).
Amendments—[1]   This section inserted by FA 2012 s 40, Sch 8 paras 1, 15 with effect for the purpose of determining whether shares or securities issued on or after 6 April 2012 are to be regarded as comprised in a company's qualifying holdings, regardless of whether the disqualifying arrangements were entered into before or on or after 6 April 2012: see FA 2012 Sch 8 para 19(2).

313 Interpretation of Chapter

(1) In this Chapter—

    "the investing company" has the meaning given by section 286(1),

    "the relevant company" has the meaning given by section 286(1), and

    "the relevant holding" has the meaning given by section 286(1).

(2) References in this Chapter to the issue of any securities, in relation to any security consisting in a liability in respect of an unsecured loan, have effect as references to the making of the loan.

(3) References in sections 303 to 309 to a trade are to be read without regard to the definition of "trade" in section 989 (see also section 300(4)).

(4) For the purposes of sections 296 and 310(3) and (4), the question whether a person controls a company is to be determined in accordance with [sections 450 and 451 of CTA 2010][1] with the modification given by subsection (6).

(5) For the purposes of this Chapter [(other than section 312A)][3], section 993 (meaning of "connected persons") applies as if references to "control" in that section were to be read in accordance with [sections 450 and 451 of CTA 2010][1] with the modification given by subsection (6). [But section 993 does not apply for the purposes of the definition of "independent expert" in section 331A(10).][4]

(6) The modification is that, in determining whether a person controls a company, the following are to be ignored—

    (*a*) any person's possession of, or entitlement to acquire, fixed-rate preference shares in the company that do not carry voting rights, . . . [2]

    (*b*) any person's possession of, or entitlement to acquire, rights as a loan creditor of the company[, and

    (*c*) any right to dividends carried by shares in the company where the shares—

        (i) are eligible shares, and

        (ii) are held by the investing company.][2]

(7) In subsection (6) "fixed-rate preference shares" means shares which—

    (*a*) were issued wholly for new consideration,

    (*b*) do not carry any right either to conversion into shares or securities of any other description or to the acquisition of any additional shares or securities, and

    (*c*) do not carry any right to dividends other than dividends which—

        (i) are of a fixed amount or at a fixed rate per cent of the nominal value of the shares, and

        (ii) together with any sum paid on redemption, represent no more than a reasonable commercial return on the consideration for which the shares were issued,

and in paragraph (a) "new consideration" has the meaning given by [section 1115 of CTA 2010][1].

[(8) In subsection (6) "eligible shares" has the same meaning as in Chapter 3 (see section 285(3A) and (3B)).][2]

Commentary—*Simon's Taxes* **E3.248, E3.252, E3.249, E3.250**.
HMRC Manuals—Venture Capital Schemes Manual VCM55220 (meaning of 'relevant fixed rate preference shares'). VCM55210 (VCT: meaning of 'control').

Amendments—[1]   In sub-ss (4), (5), (7), words substituted by CTA 2010 s 1177, Sch 1 para 506. CTA 2010 has effect for corporation tax purposes for accounting periods ending on or after 1 April 2010, and for income and capital gains tax purposes for the tax year 2010–11 and subsequent tax years.

[2]   In sub-s (6)(*a*) word "and" repealed, sub-s (6)(*c*) and preceding word "and" inserted, and sub-s (8) inserted, by F(No 3)A 2010 s 5, Sch 2 para 2(1), (13) with effect in relation to shares issued at any time.

[3]   Words in sub-s (5) inserted by FA 2012 s 40, Sch 8 paras 1, 16 with effect for the purpose of determining whether shares or securities issued on or after 6 April 2012 are to be regarded as comprised in a company's qualifying holdings, regardless of whether the disqualifying arrangements were entered into before or on or after 6 April 2012: see FA 2012 Sch 8 para 19(2).

[4]   Words in sub-s (5) inserted by F(No 2)A 2015 s 26, Sch 6 paras 1, 15 with effect from 18 November 2015.

CHAPTER 5

POWERS: WINDING UP AND MERGERS OF VCTS

Winding up

314 Power to treat VCT-in-liquidation as VCT

(1) Regulations may make provision for tax enactments specified by the regulations to have effect as if—

  (*a*) a VCT-in-liquidation that is not a VCT were, or were during any prescribed period of its winding up, a VCT,

  (*b*) VCT approval withdrawn from a company—

    (i) at any time during the period when it is a VCT-in-liquidation, or

    (ii) at any time during a prescribed part of that period,

  were withdrawn at a prescribed time (and not at the time when it is actually withdrawn).

(2) In this section "prescribed" means specified by, or determined under, regulations.

Commentary—*Simon's Taxes* **E3.242**.

315 Power to treat conditions for VCT approval as met with respect to VCT-in-liquidation

(1) Regulations may make provision for conditions mentioned in section 274(2) (conditions for approval as a VCT) to be treated for the purposes of section 274(1) as met, or as conditions that will be met, with respect to a VCT-in-liquidation.

(2) Provision under subsection (1) may be made so as to apply in relation to a VCT-in-liquidation—

  (*a*) throughout its winding up, or

  (*b*) during prescribed periods of its winding up.

(3) Regulations may, for purposes of tax enactments specified by the regulations, make provision for VCT approval to be treated as having been withdrawn, with effect from a time specified by or determined under the regulations, from a VCT-in-liquidation from which the Commissioners for Her Majesty's Revenue and Customs would have power to withdraw such approval but for provision made under subsection (1).

316 Power to make provision about distributions by VCT-in-liquidation

(1) Regulations may make provision for tax enactments specified by the regulations—

  (*a*) to apply in relation to distributions from a VCT-in-liquidation (including, in particular, distributions in the course of dissolving it or winding it up),

  (*b*) not to apply in relation to such distributions,

  (*c*) to apply in relation to such distributions with modifications specified by the regulations.

(2) Provision under subsection (1) may be made so as to apply in relation to distributions from a VCT-in-liquidation made—

  (*a*) at any time during its winding up, or

  (*b*) during periods of its winding up specified by, or determined under, regulations.

317 Power to facilitate disposal to VCT by VCT-in-liquidation

(1) Regulations may make provision authorised by subsection (2) for cases where shares in or securities of a company are acquired by a VCT from a VCT-in-liquidation.

(2) The provision that may be made under subsection (1) for such a case is—

  (*a*) provision for conditions mentioned in section 274(2) (conditions for approval as a VCT) to be treated for the purposes of section 274(1) as met, or as conditions that will be met, with respect to the VCT in relation to periods ending after the acquisition,

  (*b*) provision for the shares or securities acquired to be treated, at times after the acquisition when they are held by the VCT, as meeting the requirements of Chapter 4 (provisions for determining whether shares or securities form part of qualifying holdings), and

  (*c*) provision for shares in the VCT issued in connection with the acquisition of the shares or securities from the VCT-in-liquidation and either—

    (i) issued to a person who is a member of the VCT-in-liquidation, or

    (ii) issued to the VCT-in-liquidation and distributed by it in the course of its winding up or dissolution to a person who is one of its members,

  to be treated, for the purposes of Schedule 5C to TCGA 1992 (VCTs: deferred charge on reinvestment), as representing shares in the VCT-in-liquidation held by that person.

(3) Provision under subsection (1) may be made so as to apply in relation to shares or securities acquired from a VCT-in-liquidation—

(*a*) at any time during its winding up, or

(*b*) during periods of its winding up specified by, or determined under, regulations.

(4) In this section "securities" means any securities and includes any liability that is a security in relation to a company because of section 285(2) (securities).

318 Power in respect of periods before and after winding up

(1) Any power under sections 314 to 317 to make provision in relation to a VCT-in-liquidation includes power to make corresponding or similar provision in relation to—

(*a*) a company for whose winding up an application has been made to a court and which is not a VCT-in-liquidation but would be if, at the time that the application was made, the court had ordered the company's winding up to commence at that time, or

(*b*) a company that has been a VCT-in-liquidation but no longer is a VCT-in-liquidation because it has been wound up.

(2) For the purposes of making provision in reliance on subsection (1), references in sections 314 to 317 (however expressed) to a VCT-in-liquidation's winding up, or the commencement or ending of its winding up, may be taken to be references to, or to the commencement or ending of, the extension period for a company to which subsection (1) applies.

(3) In this section—

"the extension period"—

(*a*) in relation to a company to which subsection (1)(*a*) applies, means the period beginning with the making of the application and ending with the earlier of its final determination and the company becoming a company that is being wound up, and

(*b*) in relation to a company to which subsection (1)(*b*) applies, means the period between the end of the company's winding up and the company's dissolution, and

"prescribed" means specified by, or determined under, regulations.

319 Sections 314 to 318: supplementary

(1) Provision made by regulations under sections 314 to 318 applies in cases, and subject to conditions, specified by regulations.

(2) Such provision may (but need not) be made so as to have effect in a particular case only for such period as may be specified by, or determined under, regulations.

(3) References in sections 314 to 318 to things done by a VCT-in-liquidation include things done by a liquidator of a VCT-in-liquidation.

Commentary—*Simon's Taxes* E3.242.

320 Meaning of "VCT-in-liquidation"

(1) In this Chapter "VCT-in-liquidation" means a company—

(*a*) that is being wound up (whether or not under the law of a part of the United Kingdom and whether under the law of one, or more than one, territory),

(*b*) that was a VCT immediately before the commencement of its winding up, and

(*c*) whose winding up is for genuine commercial reasons and is not part of a scheme or arrangement the main purpose or one of the main purposes of which is the avoidance of tax.

(2) Regulations may, for purposes of this Chapter, make provision as to when a company's winding up is to be treated as commencing or ending in a case where it is wound up otherwise than under the law of a part of the United Kingdom or otherwise than under the law of a single territory.

Commentary—*Simon's Taxes* E3.242.

HMRC Manuals—Venture Capital Schemes Manual VCM56010 (VCT winding-up: VCT-in-liquidation).

Mergers

321 Power to facilitate mergers of VCTs

(1) Regulations may make provision authorised by section 322 for cases where—

(*a*) there is a merger of two or more companies each of which is a VCT immediately before the merger begins to be effected, and

(*b*) the merger is for genuine commercial reasons and is not part of a scheme or arrangement the main purpose or one of the main purposes of which is the avoidance of tax.

(2) Provision made by regulations under subsection (1) applies—

(*a*) in cases, and

(*b*) subject to conditions (including conditions requiring approvals to be obtained),

specified by the regulations.

Regulations—Venture Capital Trust (Winding up and Mergers) (Tax) (Amendment) Regulations, SI 2015/361.

Commentary—*Simon's Taxes* E3.241.

322 Provision that may be made by regulations under section 321

(1) The provision that may be made under section 321(1) for a case where there is a merger of two or more companies ("the merging companies") is as follows.

(2) Provision for the successor company, or any of the merging companies, to be treated (whether at times before, during or after the merger) as a VCT for purposes of tax enactments specified by regulations.

(3) Provision for section 266 (loss of relief on disposal of VCT shares within 5 years of their issue) not to apply in the case of disposals of shares in a merging company made in the course of effecting the merger.

(4) Provision for such disposals not to be chargeable events for the purposes of Schedule 5C to TCGA 1992 (VCTs: deferred charge on re-investment).

(5) Provision for conditions mentioned in section 274(2) (conditions for approval as a VCT) to be treated (whether at times before, during or after the merger) for purposes of section 274(1) as met, or as conditions that will be met, with respect to the successor company or any of the merging companies.

[(5A) Provision for section 281(1)(*f*) (withdrawal of VCT approval where company has made a repayment of share capital etc) not to apply, or to apply subject to modifications, to the successor company or any of the merging companies, in relation to payments made, or amounts used to pay up new shares, in connection with or after the merger.][1]

(6) Provision for shares in or securities of a company that are acquired (whether at times before, during or after the merger) by the successor company from a merging company to be treated, at times after the acquisition when they are held by the successor company, as meeting requirements of Chapter 4 (provisions for determining whether shares or securities held by a VCT form part of its qualifying holdings).

(7) Provision for tax enactments specified by regulations to apply, with or without adaptations, in relation to the merger or transactions taking place (whether before, during or after the merger) in connection with the merger.

(8) Provision authorising disclosure for tax purposes connected with the merger—
- (*a*) by Her Majesty's Revenue and Customs,
- (*b*) to any of the merging companies or the successor company,
- (*c*) of any information provided to Her Majesty's Revenue and Customs by or on behalf of any of the merging companies or the successor company.

Regulations—Venture Capital Trust (Winding up and Mergers) (Tax) (Amendment) Regulations, SI 2015/361.
Derivation—FA 2002 Sch 33 para 9.
Cross-references—See FA 2016 s 180, Sch 24 Pt 2 (power to obtain information about tax advantages claimed under this Part which constitute the grant of State aid).
Amendments—[1] Sub-s (5A) inserted by FA 2014 s 53, Sch 10 para 4 with effect from 17 July 2014.

323 Meaning of "merger" and "successor company"

(1) For the purposes of this Chapter there is a merger of two or more companies ("the merging companies") if—
- (*a*) shares in one of the merging companies ("company A") are issued to members of the other merging company or companies, and
- (*b*) the shares issued to members of the other merging company or, in the case of each of the other merging companies, the shares issued to members of that other company, are issued—
  - (i) in exchange for their shares in that other company, or
  - (ii) by way of consideration for a transfer to company A of the whole or part of the business of that other company.

(2) For the purposes of this Chapter there is also a merger of two or more companies ("the merging companies") if—
- (*a*) shares in a company ("company B") that is not one of the merging companies are issued to members of the merging companies, and
- (*b*) in the case of each of the merging companies, the shares issued to members of that company are issued—
  - (i) in exchange for their shares in that company, or
  - (ii) by way of consideration for a transfer to company B of the whole or part of the business of that company.

(3) In this Chapter "the successor company"—
- (*a*) in relation to a merger such as is described in subsection (1), means the company that performs the role of company A, and
- (*b*) in relation to a merger such as is described in subsection (2), means the company that performs the role of company B.

Commentary—*Simon's Taxes* E3.241.
HMRC Manuals—Venture Capital Schemes Manual VCM57020 (VCT mergers: meaning of 'mergers' and 'successor company').

Supplementary

324 Regulations under Chapter

(1) Regulations under this Chapter may—

    (*a*) contain such administrative provisions (including provision for advance clearance and provision for the withdrawal of clearances) as appear to the Treasury to be necessary or appropriate,

    (*b*) authorise the Commissioners for Her Majesty's Revenue and Customs to give notice to any person requiring that person to provide such information, specified in the notice, as they may reasonably require in order to determine whether any conditions imposed by regulations under this Chapter are met,

    (*c*) make different provision for different cases,

    (*d*) contain incidental, supplemental, consequential and transitional provision and savings, and

    (*e*) include provision having retrospective effect.

(2) Without prejudice to any specific provision of this Chapter, a power conferred by any provision of this Chapter to make regulations includes power to provide for Her Majesty's Revenue and Customs to exercise a discretion in dealing with any matter.

Regulations—Venture Capital Trust (Winding up and Mergers) (Tax) (Amendment) Regulations, SI 2015/361.
Commentary—*Simon's Taxes* **E3.234**.

325 Interpretation of Chapter

In this Chapter—

    "regulations" means regulations made by the Treasury, and

    "tax enactments" means provisions of or made under—

        (*a*) the Tax Acts,

        (*b*) TCGA 1992 or any other enactment relating to capital gains tax, or

        (*c*) TMA 1970.

CHAPTER 6

SUPPLEMENTARY AND GENERAL

Acquisitions for restructuring purposes

326 Restructuring to which [sections 326A, 327 and 327A apply]

(1) [Sections 326A, 327 and 327A apply][2] if—

    (*a*) arrangements are made for a company ("the new company") to acquire all the shares ("old shares") in another company ("the old company"),

    (*b*) the acquisition provided for by the arrangements falls within subsection (2), and

    (*c*) the Commissioners for Her Majesty's Revenue and Customs have, before any exchange of shares takes place under the arrangements, given an approval notification.

(2) An acquisition of shares falls within this subsection if—

    (*a*) the consideration for the old shares consists wholly of the issue of shares ("new shares") in the new company,

    (*b*) new shares are issued in consideration of old shares only at times when there are no issued shares in the new company other than subscriber shares and new shares previously issued in consideration of old shares,

    (*c*) the consideration for new shares of each description consists wholly of old shares of the corresponding description, and

    (*d*) new shares of each description are issued to the holders of old shares of the corresponding description in respect of, and in proportion to, their holdings.

(3) For the purposes of subsection (1)(*c*) an approval notification is one which, on the application of either the old company or the new company, is given to the applicant company and states that the Commissioners for Her Majesty's Revenue and Customs are satisfied that the exchange of shares under the arrangements—

    (*a*) will be effected for genuine commercial reasons, and

    (*b*) will not form part of any such scheme or arrangements as are mentioned in section 137(1) of TCGA 1992 (schemes with avoidance purposes).

(4) [Nothing in section 326A treats any of the requirements of Chapter 3 as being met, and nothing in section 327 treats any of the requirement of Chapter 4 as being met][1] in relation to any new shares unless the matching old shares were first issued to the company holding them and have been held by that company from the time when they were issued until they are acquired by the new company.

(5) If, at any time after the arrangements first came into existence and before the new company acquired all the old shares, the arrangements—

    (*a*) cease to be arrangements for the acquisition of all the old shares by the new company, or

    (*b*) cease to be arrangements for an acquisition falling within subsection (2),

section [326A does not treat any requirement of Chapter 3 as being met and section][1] 327 does not treat any requirement of Chapter 4 as being met, and subsection (8) of that section does not apply, in the case of any new shares at any time after the arrangements have so ceased.

Commentary—*Simon's Taxes* **E3.263**.

HMRC Manuals—Venture Capital Schemes Manual VCM55290 (exchange for shares in new holding company). Venture Capital Schemes Manual 8170 (company reorganisations).

Modification—ITA 2007 Sch 2 para 87 (this section does not apply in relation to arrangements made, or rights of conversion exercised, before 16 June 1999).

Amendments—[1]   Words in sub-s (1) substituted for words "Section 327 applies", words in sub-s (4) substituted for words "Nothing in section 327 treats any of the requirements of Chapter 4 as being met", and words in sub-s (5) inserted, by F(No 2)A 2015 s 26, Sch 6 paras 1, 16 with effect from 18 November 2015.

[2]   In heading and sub-s (1), words substituted by F(No 2)A 2017 s 12(1), (2) with effect—
-     for the purposes of ITA 2007 s 280C, in relation to investments made on or after 6 April 2017; and
-     for the purposes of ITA 2007 s 294A, in relation to relevant holdings issued on or after 6 April 2017.

[326A Certain requirements of Chapter 3 to be treated as met

(1) If this section applies, subsections (2) to (6) have effect to determine the extent to which, and the time for which, the following conditions in Chapter 3 are met in relation to the old shares and the new shares—

> the investment limits condition (see section 280B);
> the permitted maximum age condition (see section 280C);
> the no business acquisition condition (see section 280D).

(2) If—

> (a) there is an exchange under the arrangements of any new shares for any old shares, and
> (b) those old shares are an investment in relation to which the investment limits condition, the permitted maximum age condition or the no business acquisition condition is (or is treated as being) met to any extent,

those conditions are to be treated as met to the same extent in relation to the matching new shares. See subsections (3) to (6) for further provision about when those conditions are treated as met in relation to the old shares.

(3) If—

> (a) the exchange occurs during the period of 5 years beginning with the day after the day on which the old shares were issued, and
> (b) those old shares are shares in relation to which section 280B(2)(c) applies,

section 280B(2)(c) is to be treated as applying in relation to the matching new shares.

(4) In determining whether section 280B(2)(c) applies in relation to the old shares—

> (a) condition A is treated as met if it would be met if the reference in section 280B(3B)(a)(i) to a company which becomes a 51% subsidiary of the relevant company during the 5-year post-investment period included a reference to a company which becomes a 51% subsidiary of the new company during that period otherwise than as a result of the exchange, and
> (b) in relation to investments made or trades transferred at or after the time of the exchange, references to the relevant company in section 280B(3C)(b) and (3F)(a) are to be read as references to the new company.

(5) The permitted maximum age condition is met in relation to the old shares if (and only if) it would be met if—

> (a) in section 280C(5)(a)(ii) and (6)(a) the references to relevant investments made in the relevant company included a reference to the relevant investments made in the new company,
> (b) in section 280C(7)(d) and (f) the references to the relevant company included a reference to the new company,
> (c) in paragraphs (a)(ii) and (b)(iii) of the definition of "the total relevant turnover amount" in section 280C(9) the reference to a company which becomes a 51% subsidiary of the relevant company after the investment date included a reference to a company which becomes a 51% subsidiary of the new company after that date otherwise than as a result of the exchange.

(6) The no business acquisition condition is met in relation to the old shares if (and only if) it would be met if, in section 280D(2), references to the relevant company were read as including a reference to the new company.][1]

HMRC Manuals—Venture Capital Schemes Manual 8170 (company reorganisations).

Amendments—[1]   This section inserted by F(No 2)A 2015 s 26, Sch 6 paras 1, 17 with effect from 18 November 2015.

327 Certain requirements of Chapter 4 to be treated as met

(1) If this section applies, subsections (2) to (8) have effect to determine the extent to which, and the times for which, the requirements of the following provisions of Chapter 4 are met in relation to the new shares—

> section 287 (the maximum qualifying investment requirement),
> section 289 (the proportion of eligible shares requirement),
> section 290 (the trading requirement),
> section 291 (the carrying on of a qualifying activity requirement),
> [section 292A (the maximum amount raised annually through risk finance investments requirement),

section 292AA (the maximum amount raised through risk finance investments when relevant holding is issued requirement),

section 292AB (the maximum risk finance investments during the 5-year post-investment period requirement),]²

section 293 (the use of the money raised requirement),

section 294 (the relevant company to carry on the relevant qualifying activity requirement),

[section 294A (the permitted company age requirement),]²

section 296 (the control and independence requirement), . . .¹

section 297 (the gross assets requirement) [. . .²

section 297A (the number of employees requirement)[,]¹ and

section 297B (the proportion of skilled employees requirement).]²

(2) If the requirements of sections 290 and 291 were met in relation to the old company and any old shares immediately before the beginning of the period for giving effect to the arrangements, then (so far as it would not otherwise be the case) those requirements are treated as being met in relation to the new company and the matching new shares at all times which—

    (*a*) fall in that period, and

    (*b*) do not fall after a time when (apart from the arrangements) those requirements would have ceased by virtue of—

        (i) section 291(4) or (5), or

        (ii) any cessation of a trade by any company,

to be met in relation to the old company and the matching old shares.

(3) For the purposes of section 291, the period of two years mentioned in subsection (4) of that section is treated, in the case of any new shares, as expiring at the same time as it would have expired (or by virtue of this subsection would have been treated as expiring) in the case of the matching old shares.

(4) Subject to subsection (5), if—

    (*a*) there is an exchange under the arrangements of any new shares for any old shares, and

    (*b*) those old shares are shares in relation to which the requirements of sections [292A, 292AA, 292AB,]² 293, 294[, 294A]² [, 297[, 297A and 297B]²]¹ were (or were treated as being) met to any extent immediately before the exchange,

those requirements are to be treated, at all times after that time, as met to the same extent in relation to the matching new shares.

[(4A) If—

    (*a*) there is an exchange under the arrangements of any new shares for any old shares,

    (*b*) that exchange occurs during the period of 5 years beginning with the day after the day on which the old shares were issued, and

    (*c*) those old shares are shares in relation to which the requirement of section 292AB (maximum risk finance investments during 5-year post-investment period) applies and is met,

that requirement is to be treated as applying and met in relation to the matching new shares.

(4B) But, where that requirement applies in relation to the old shares, it is met in relation to those shares if (and only if) it would be met were—

    (*a*) the first reference to the relevant company in section 292AB(4), and

    (*b*) the references to the relevant company in section 292AB(5) and (7)(*a*)(i),

read, in relation to times in that 5 year period which fall at or after the time of the exchange, as references to the new company.

(4C) For the purposes of subsections (4A) and (4B), the requirement in section 292AB is treated as applying in relation to the old shares if condition A or B in that section would be met if references in section 292AB(5) and (7)(*a*)(i) to the relevant company were read as references to the new company.

(4D) The requirement in section 293 (the use of money raised) is met in relation to the old shares if (and only if) it would be met if references to the relevant company in section 293(5ZA) were read as including a reference to the new company.

(4E) The requirement of section 294A (permitted company age) is met in relation to the old shares if (and only if) it would be met if—

    (*a*) in section 294A(4) the reference to relevant investments made in the relevant company included a reference to relevant investments made in the new company,

    (*b*) in section 294A(6)(*d*) and (*f*) the references to the relevant company included a reference to the new company,

    (*c*) in paragraphs (*a*)(ii) and (*b*)(iii) of the definition of "the total relevant turnover amount" in section 294A(8) the reference to a company which becomes a 51% subsidiary of the relevant company after the investment date included a reference to a company which becomes a 51% subsidiary of the new company after that date otherwise than as a result of the exchange.

(4F) If—

    (*a*) there is an exchange under the arrangements of any new shares for any old shares,

(b) that exchange occurs during the period of 3 years beginning with the issue of the old shares, and

(c) those old shares are shares in relation to which the requirement of section 297B (proportion of skilled employees requirement) is met,

that requirement is to be treated as met in relation to the matching new shares.

(4G) The requirement of section 297B is met in relation to the old shares if (and only if) it would be met in relation to those shares were references to the relevant company, in subsections (1) and (3) of that section (and, in the definitions of the terms mentioned in subsection (4) as they apply for the purposes of those subsections), read as references to the new company in relation to times in that 3 year period which fall at or after the exchange.]²

(5) If there is a time following any exchange under the arrangements of any new shares for any old shares when (apart from the arrangements) the requirement of section 293 would have ceased under—

(a) subsection (1) of that section, or

(b) this subsection,

to be met in relation to those old shares, that requirement ceases at that time to be met in relation to the matching new shares.

(6) For the purposes of section 287, any new shares acquired under the arrangements are to be treated as representing an investment which—

(a) raised the same amount of money as was raised (or, by virtue of this subsection, is treated as having been raised) by the issue of the matching old shares, and

(b) raised that amount by an issue of shares in the new company made at the time when the issue of the matching old shares took place (or, as the case may be, is treated as having taken place).

(7) In determining whether the requirements of section 296 are met in relation to the old company or the new company at a time in the period for giving effect to the arrangements, ignore both—

(a) the arrangements themselves, and

(b) any exchange of new shares for old shares that has already taken place under the arrangements.

(8) For the purposes of section 289, the value of the new shares, both—

(a) immediately after the time of their acquisition, and

(b) immediately after the time of any subsequent relevant event occurring by virtue of the arrangements,

is to be taken to be the same as the value, when last valued in accordance with that section, of the old shares for which they are exchanged.

Commentary—*Simon's Taxes* **E3.263**.

HMRC Manuals—Venture Capital Schemes Manual 8170 (company reorganisations).

Amendments—¹　Words in sub-s (1) inserted and repealed, and words in sub-s (4)(b) substituted, by FA 2007 ss 51, 114, Sch 16 para 3(1), (4), Sch 27 Pt 2(16) and deemed to have effect from 6 April 2007. By virtue of FA 2007 Sch 16 para 3(5)–(7), this amendment does not have effect in relation to—

　　(a)　a relevant holding issued before that date; or

　　(b)　a relevant holding acquired by a company ("the investing company") by means of the investment of protected money.

The terms "relevant holding" and "protected money" are defined by FA 2007 Sch 16 para 3(6), (7).

²　In sub-s (1), entries inserted and word "and" repealed, in sub-s (4), words inserted and words "and 297A" substituted for words ", 297A and 297B", and sub-ss (4A)–(4G) inserted, by F(No 2)A 2015 s 26, Sch 6 paras 1, 18 with effect from 18 November 2015.

[327A Follow-on funding

(1) Subsections (2) and (3) apply where—

(a) this section applies (see section 326(1)),

(b) the acquisition by the new company of all the old shares, which is provided for by the arrangements mentioned in section 326(1), takes place, and

(c) the acquisition falls within section 326(2).

(2) If, after the acquisition, another company makes an investment in the new company, section 280C (the permitted maximum age condition) has effect in relation to that investment as if—

(a) in subsection (4)(a) the reference to a relevant investment having been made in the relevant company before the end of the initial investing period included a reference to a relevant investment having been made in the old company before the acquisition and before the end of the initial investing period, and

(b) in subsection (6)(a) the reference to relevant investments made in the relevant company included a reference to relevant investments made in the old company before the acquisition.

(3) In relation to any relevant holding issued by the new company after the acquisition, section 294A (the permitted company age requirement) has effect as if—

(a) in subsection (3)(a) the reference to a relevant investment having been made in the relevant company before the end of the initial investing period included a reference to a relevant investment having been made in the old company before the acquisition and before the end of the initial investing period, and

(b) in subsection (5)(a) the reference to relevant investments made in the relevant company included a reference to relevant investments made in the old company before the acquisition.

(4) In subsection (3) "relevant holding" has the same meaning as in Chapter 4.][1]

Amendments—[1]   Section 327A inserted by F(No 2)A 2017 s 12(1), (3) with effect—
–   for the purposes of ITA 2007 s 280C, in relation to investments made on or after 6 April 2017; and
–   for the purposes of ITA 2007 s 294A, in relation to relevant holdings issued on or after 6 April 2017.

328 Supplementary

(1) Subject to subsection (2), references in sections 326 and 327 and this section, except in the expression "subscriber shares", to shares in a company include references to any securities of that company.

(2) For the purposes of subsection (1) a relevant security of the old company is not to be treated as a security of the old company if—

(a) the arrangements do not provide for the acquisition of the security by the new company, or

(b) such treatment prevents section 326(1)(b) from being met in connection with the arrangements.

(3) In subsection (2) "relevant security" means an instrument which is a security for the purposes of Chapter 4 merely because of section 285(2).

(4) References in section 327 to the period for giving effect to the arrangements are references to the period which—

(a) begins with the time when the arrangements first came into existence, and

(b) ends with the time when the new company completes its acquisition under the arrangements of all the old shares.

(5) For the purposes of sections 326 and 327 and this section—

(a) old shares and new shares are of a corresponding description if, were they shares in the same company, they would be of the same description, and

(b) old shares and new shares are matching shares in relation to each other if the old shares are the shares for which the new shares are exchanged under the arrangements.

Commentary—*Simon's Taxes* **E3.263**.
Modification—ITA 2007 Sch 2 para 87 (this section does not apply in relation to arrangements made, or rights of conversion exercised, before 16 June 1999).

Conversion of shares etc and company reorganisations

329 Conversion of convertible shares and securities

(1) This section applies if—

(a) shares have been issued to a company ("the investing company") by the exercise by it of any right of conversion attached to other shares or securities held by it ("the convertibles"),

(b) the shares so issued are in the same company as the convertibles to which the right was attached,

(c) the convertibles to which the right was attached were first issued to the investing company and were held by it from the time they were issued until converted, and

(d) the right was attached to the convertibles when they were first so issued and was not varied before it was exercised.

(2) If this section applies, subsections (3) and (4) have effect to determine the extent to which, and the times for which, the requirements of the following provisions of Chapter 4 are met in relation to the shares issued to the investing company by the exercise by it of the right of conversion—

section 287 (the maximum qualifying investment requirement),
section 289 (the proportion of eligible shares requirement),
section 291 (the carrying on of a qualifying activity requirement),
section 293 (the use of the money raised requirement),
section 294 (the relevant company to carry on the relevant qualifying activity requirement), and
section 297 (the gross assets requirement).

(3) Subsections (3) to (6) of section 327 apply in relation to the exchange of convertibles for shares by virtue of the exercise of the right of conversion as if—

(a) that exchange were an exchange, under any arrangements to which that section applies, of new shares for old shares, and

(b) the references in those subsections and section 328(5)(b) to the arrangements were references to the provision conferring the right of conversion.

(4) For the purposes of section 289 the value of the new shares immediately after the time of their acquisition by the investing company is to be taken as the same as the value, when last valued in accordance with that section, of the convertibles for which they are exchanged.

Commentary—*Simon's Taxes* **E3.264**.
HMRC Manuals—Venture Capital Schemes Manual VCM55300 (VCT: effect of conversion).

Modification—ITA 2007 Sch 2 para 87 (this section does not apply in relation to arrangements made, or rights of conversion exercised, before 16 June 1999).

330 Power to facilitate company reorganisations etc involving exchange of shares

(1) The Treasury may by regulations make provision for cases where—

    (a) a holding of shares or securities that meets the requirements of Chapter 4 is exchanged for other shares or securities,

    (b) the exchange is made for genuine commercial reasons and does not form part of a scheme or arrangement the main purpose or one of the main purposes of which is the avoidance of tax, and

    (c) the new shares or securities do not meet some or all of the requirements of Chapter 4,

providing that the new shares or securities are to be treated as meeting those requirements.

[(1A) The Treasury may by regulations make provision for the purposes of this Part for cases where—

    (a) a holding of shares or securities that does not meet the requirements of Chapter 4 is exchanged for other shares or securities not meeting those requirements, and

    (b) the exchange is made for genuine commercial reasons and does not form part of a scheme or arrangement the main purpose or one of the main purposes of which is the avoidance of tax.]^2

(2) The references in [subsections (1) and (1A)]^2 to an exchange of shares or securities include any form of company reorganisation or other arrangement which involves a holder of shares in or securities of a company receiving other shares or securities—

    (a) whether the original shares or securities are transferred, cancelled or retained, and

    (b) whether the new shares or securities are in or of the same or another company.

(3) [Regulations under subsection (1)]^2 must specify—

    (a) the cases in which, and conditions subject to which, they apply,

    (b) which requirements of Chapter 4 are to be treated as met, and

    (c) the period for which those requirements are to be treated as met.

[(3A) Regulations under subsection (1A) may, among other things, make provision—

    (a) for the new shares or securities to be treated in any respect in the same way as the original shares and securities for any period;

    (b) as to when the new shares or securities are to be regarded as having been acquired;

    (c) as to the valuation of the original or the new shares or securities.]^2

(4) [Regulations under this section]^2 may contain such administrative provisions (including provision for advance clearances) as appear to the Treasury to be necessary or appropriate.

(5) . . . ^{1}

(6) Regulations under this section—

    (a) may make different provision for different cases,

    (b) may contain incidental, supplemental, consequential and transitional provision and savings, and

    (c) [in the case of regulations under subsection (1)]^2 may include provision having retrospective effect.

HMRC Manuals—Venture Capital Schemes Manual VCM55310 (effect of reorganisation).

Regulations—Venture Capital Trust (Exchange of Shares and Securities) (Amendment) Regulations, SI 2018/109.

Modification—ITA 2007 Sch 2 para 88 (this section does not apply in relation to exchanges of shares or securities taking effect before 21 March 2000).

Amendments—^{1} Sub-s (5) repealed by Finance Act 2009 Schedule 47 (Consequential Amendments) Order, SI 2009/2035, Art 2, Schedule paras 46, 48 with effect from 13 August 2009.

^{2} Sub-ss (1A), (3A) inserted, in sub-s (2), words substituted for words "subsection (1)", in sub-ss (3), (4), words substituted for words "The regulations", and in sub-s (6)(c), words inserted, by F(No 2)A 2017 s 13, with effect from 16 November 2017.

[Nominees]

330A Nominees

Shares subscribed for, issued to, held by or disposed of for an individual by a nominee are treated for the purposes of this Part as subscribed for, issued to, held by or disposed of by the individual.]^1

Amendments—^{1} Section 330A and preceding cross-heading inserted by FA 2014 s 53, Sch 10 para 5(1) with effect from 17 July 2014.

[Power to amend Part]

330B Powers to amend Chapters 3 and 4 by Treasury regulations

(1) The Treasury may by regulations add to, repeal or otherwise amend any provision of Chapter 3 or 4.

(2) Regulations under this section may—

    (a) make different provision for different cases or purposes;

    (b) contain incidental, supplemental, consequential and transitional provision and savings.

(3) The provision which may be made as a result of subsection (2)(b) includes provision amending any provision of this or any other Act (including an Act passed after this Act).

(4) Regulations under this section may, so long as they do not increase any person's liability to any tax, be made to have retrospective effect in relation to any time in the tax year in which they are made or the previous tax year.

(5) This section is without prejudice to any other power to amend any provision of this Part.

(6) A statutory instrument containing regulations under this section may not be made unless a draft of it has been laid before and approved by a resolution of the House of Commons.][1]

Amendments—[1]   Section 330B and preceding cross-heading inserted by F(No 2)A 2015 s 26, Sch 6 paras 1, 19 with effect from 18 November 2015.

Supplementary

331 Meaning of a company being "in administration" or "in receivership"

(1) References in this Part to a company being "in administration" or "in receivership" are to be read as follows.

(2) A company is "in administration" if—

    (*a*) it is in administration within the meaning of Schedule B1 to the Insolvency Act 1986 (c 45) or Schedule B1 to the Insolvency (Northern Ireland) Order 1989 (SI 1989/2405 (NI 19)), or

    (*b*) there is in force in relation to it under the law of a country or territory outside the United Kingdom any appointment corresponding to an appointment of an administrator under either of those Schedules.

(3) A company is "in receivership" if there is in force in relation to it—

    (*a*) an order for the appointment of an administrative receiver, a receiver and manager or a receiver under Chapter 1 or 2 of Part 3 of the Insolvency Act 1986 or Part 4 of the Insolvency (Northern Ireland) Order 1989, or

    (*b*) any corresponding order under the law of a country or territory outside the United Kingdom.

Modifications—ITA 2007 Sch 2 para 89(1), (2) (modification of this section in relation to an administration order under the Insolvency (Northern Ireland) Order 1989 Pt 3, the petition for which was presented before 6 April 2007, or any corresponding order under the law of a country or territory outside the United Kingdom the proceedings for which were instituted before that date).

ITA 2007 Sch 2 para 89(3) (modification of this section in relation to an administration order under the Insolvency Act 1986 Pt 2 the petition for which was presented before 15 September 2003).

[331A Meaning of "knowledge-intensive company"

(1) For the purposes of this Part, the relevant company is a "knowledge-intensive company" at the applicable time if the company meets—

    (*a*) one or both of the operating costs conditions (see subsections (3) and (4)), and

    (*b*) one or both of—

        (i) the innovation condition (see subsection (6)), and

        (ii) the skilled employee condition (see subsection (9)).

(2) "The applicable time" means—

    (*a*) in relation to references to a knowledge-intensive company in section 280B or 280C, the date the current investment (within the meaning of the section in question) is made, and

    (*b*) in relation to any other reference to a knowledge-intensive company, the date the relevant holding is issued.

(3) The first operating costs condition is that in at least one of the relevant three preceding years at least 15% of the relevant operating costs constituted expenditure on research and development or innovation.

    (4) The second operating costs condition is that in each of the relevant three preceding years at least 10% of the relevant operating costs constituted such expenditure.

(5) In subsections (3) and (4)—

    "relevant operating costs" means—

        (*a*) if the relevant company is a single company at the applicable time, the operating costs of that company, and

        (*b*) if the relevant company is a parent company at the applicable time, the sum of—

            (i) the operating costs of the relevant company, and

            (ii) the operating costs of each company which is a qualifying subsidiary of the relevant company at that time;

    "the relevant three preceding years" [means, subject to subsection (5A), the three consecutive years the last of which ends immediately before the beginning of the last accounts filing period.][2]

[(5A) If the last accounts filing period ends more than 12 months before the applicable time, the relevant three preceding years are the three consecutive years the last of which ends 12 months before the applicable time.][2]

(6) "The innovation condition" is—

    (*a*) where the relevant company is a single company, that—

        (i) the relevant company is engaged in intellectual property creation at the applicable time, and

(ii) it is reasonable to assume that, within 10 years of the applicable time, one or a combination of—

    (a) the exploitation of relevant intellectual property held by the company, and

    (b) business which results from new or improved products, processes or services utilising relevant intellectual property held by the company,

will form the greater part of its business;

(b) where the relevant company is a parent company, that—

    (i) the parent company or one or more of its qualifying subsidiaries (or both that company and one or more of those subsidiaries) is or are engaged in intellectual property creation at the applicable time, and

    (ii) it is reasonable to assume that, within 10 years of the applicable time, one or a combination of—

        (a) the exploitation of relevant intellectual property held by the parent company or any of its qualifying subsidiaries, and

        (b) business which results from new or improved products, processes or services utilising relevant intellectual property held by the parent company or any of its qualifying subsidiaries,

will form the greater part of the business of the group, if the activities of the group companies taken together are regarded as one business.

(7) For the purposes of subsection (6), a company is engaged in intellectual property creation if—

    (a) relevant intellectual property is being created by the company, or has been created by it within the previous three years,

    (b) the company is taking, or preparing to take, steps in order that relevant intellectual property will be created by it, or

    (c) the company is carrying on activity which is the subject of a written evaluation which—

        (i) has been prepared by an independent expert, and

        (ii) includes a statement to the effect that, in the opinion of the expert, it is reasonable to assume that relevant intellectual property will, in the foreseeable future, be created by the company.

(8) For the purposes of this section—

    (a) intellectual property is "relevant" intellectual property, in relation to a company, if the whole or greater part (in terms of value) of it is created by the company, and

    (b) intellectual property is created by a company if it is created in circumstances in which the right to exploit it vests in the company (whether alone or jointly with others).

(9) "The skilled employee condition" is that at the applicable time—

    (a) if the relevant company is a single company, the FTE skilled employee number is at least 20% of the FTE employee number, and

    (b) if the relevant company is a parent company, the FTE group skilled employee number is at least 20% of the FTE group employee number.

(10) In this section—

"FTE employee number" for a company is the full-time equivalent employee number determined in accordance with section 297A(3);

"FTE group employee number" means the sum of—

    (a) the FTE employee number for the relevant company, and

    (b) the FTE employee number for each of its qualifying subsidiaries;

"FTE group skilled employee number" means the sum of—

    (a) the FTE skilled employee number for the relevant company, and

    (b) the FTE skilled employee number for each of its qualifying subsidiaries;

"FTE skilled employee number" for a company is determined in accordance with section 297A(3) in the same way as the fulltime equivalent employee number except that only employees of the company who—

    (a) hold a relevant HE qualification, and

    (b) are engaged directly in research and development or innovation activities carried on—

        (i) if the relevant company is a single company, by that company, or

        (ii) if the relevant company is a parent company, by that company or any qualifying subsidiary of that company,

are to be taken into account;

"independent expert", in relation to an evaluation of activity of a company, means an individual who—

    (a) is not connected with the relevant company,

    (b) holds a relevant HE qualification, and

    (c) is an expert in the area of research and development or innovation being or to be pursued by the company in question, and, for the purposes of paragraph (*a*), sections 167, 170 and 171 (but not section 168) apply to determine if an individual is connected with the relevant company (with references in those sections to the issuing company read as references to the relevant company);

"intellectual property" has the meaning given by section 306(6);

"the last accounts filing period" means the last period for filing (within the meaning of section 442 of the Companies Act 2006) for the relevant company which ends before the applicable time;

"operating costs", of a company for a period, means expenses of the company which are recognised as expenses in the company's profit and loss account or income statement for that period, other than expenses relating to transactions between that company and another company at a time when both companies are members of the same group (but see also subsection (11));

"relevant HE qualification" means—

    (*a*) a qualification which is at level 7, or a higher level, of the framework for higher education qualifications in England, Wales and Northern Ireland (as that framework may be amended or replaced from time to time),

    (*b*) a qualification which is at level 11, or a higher level, of the framework for qualifications of higher education institutions in Scotland (as that framework may be amended or replaced from time to time), or

    (*c*) a comparable qualification to one within paragraph (*a*) or (*b*).

(11) Such apportionments as are just and reasonable are to be made to amounts recognised in a company's profit and loss account or income statement for the purpose of determining the company's operating costs for a year.

(12) The Treasury may by regulations amend this section for the purposes of adding, amending or removing a condition which must be met for a company to be a knowledge-intensive company.

(13) A statutory instrument containing regulations under subsection (12) may not be made unless a draft of it has been laid before and approved by a resolution of the House of Commons.][1]

Commentary—*Simon's Taxes* **D8.243, E3.254**.

HMRC Manuals—Venture Capital Schemes Manual 8161 (knowledge intensive companies: overview).

Amendments—[1]   This section inserted by F(No 2)A 2015 s 26, Sch 6 paras 1, 20 with effect from 18 November 2015.

[2]   In sub-s (5), in definition of "the relevant three preceding years", words substituted, and sub-s (5A) inserted, by FA 2016, s 29(5). Subject to any election made under FA 2016 s 30 by the issuing company, these amendments are to be treated as always having had effect. If an election is made under s 30, the amendments do not apply for the purposes of determining whether at any time in the period beginning with 18 November 2015 and ending with 5 April 2016, which is the applicable time within the meaning given by this section, the relevant company is a knowledge-intensive company for the purposes of ITA 2007 Part 6: see FA 2016 s 30.

[331B Knowledge-intensive company reaching turnover of £200,000]

(1) This section has effect for the purposes of sections 280C(3)(*a*)(ii) and 294A(2)(*a*)(ii) (alternative initial investing period in case of knowledge-intensive company).

(2) Where—

    (*a*) the annual turnover of the relevant company in relation to an accounting period (see subsection (3)) is £200,000 or more, and

    (*b*) the annual turnover for the company in relation to each previous accounting period is less than £200,000,

the company is treated as reaching an annual turnover of £200,000 or more by reference to the specified date (see subsection (4)).

(3) The annual turnover in relation to an accounting period is—

    (*a*) the turnover for that accounting period (if the accounting period is for 12 months), or

    (*b*) the turnover for the period of 12 months ending when that accounting period ends (if not).

(4) The specified date is—

    (*a*) in the case of an accounting period of 12 months or less, the last day of that accounting period;

    (*b*) in the case of an accounting period of more than 12 months, the last day of the period of 12 months beginning when that accounting period begins.

(5) The turnover of the relevant company for a period ("the period") is treated for the purposes of this section as including the relevant turnover of any company that is a member of the same group as the relevant company during the whole or any part of the period (a "group company").

(6) The relevant turnover of a group company is—

    (*a*) its turnover for the period, if the group company is a member of the same group as the relevant company for the whole of the period;

    (*b*) if the group company is a member of the same group as the relevant company for part of the period, its turnover for that part of the period.

(7) Any necessary apportionments of turnover are to be made, on a time basis according to the respective lengths of the periods in question, for the purposes of subsections (3)(*b*) and (6).

(8) In this section "turnover" has the meaning given by section 474(1) of the Companies Act 2006 and is to be determined by reference to—

(*a*) the accounts of the company, and
(*b*) amounts recognised for accounting purposes.]¹

Amendments—¹   Section 331B inserted by FA 2018 s 16, Sch 4 para 9 with effect for investments made on or after 6 April 2018 (by virtue of SI 2018/931 reg 3(b).

332 Minor definitions etc

In this Part—

"associate" has the meaning given by section 253,

"company" includes any body corporate or unincorporated association but does not include a partnership, and is to be read in accordance with [section 99]³ of TCGA 1992 (unit trust schemes . . .³,¹),

"director" is read in accordance with [section 452 of CTA 2010]²,

"group" means a parent company and its qualifying subsidiaries,

"group company", in relation to a group, means the parent company or any of its qualifying subsidiaries,

"ordinary shares" means shares forming part of a company's ordinary share capital,

"parent company" means a company that has one or more qualifying subsidiaries and "single company" means a company that does not,

"research and development" has the meaning given by section 1006, and "shares" includes stock.

HMRC Manuals—Company Taxation Manual CTM60180 (definition of a director).
Capital Allowance Manual CA60200 (meaning of research and development).
Modification—ITA 2007 Sch 2 para 90 (transitional provisions and savings: modification of this provision).
Amendments—¹   In the definition of "company" words substituted and inserted by FA 2009 s 44, Sch 22 para 11(5) with effect in relation to the acquisition, holding and disposal of rights in a relevant offshore fund on or after the commencement day, subject to transitional provisions and modifications in FA 2009 paras 13–18. The commencement day" means—
    (a)   in relation to the acquisition, holding and disposal of rights by a person subject to the charge to capital gains tax, 1 December 2009, and
    (b)   in relation to the acquisition, holding and disposal of rights by a person subject to the charge to corporation tax, such day as the Treasury may by order appoint.
²   In definition of "director" words substituted by CTA 2010 s 1177, Sch 1 para 507. CTA 2010 has effect for corporation tax purposes for accounting periods ending on or after 1 April 2010, and for income and capital gains tax purposes for the tax year 2010–11 and subsequent tax years.
³   In definition of "company", words substituted for words "sections 99 and 103A" and words "and certain offshore funds" repealed, by the Collective Investment Schemes and Offshore Funds (Amendment of the Taxation of Chargeable Gains Act 1992) Regulations, SI 2017/1204 regs 2, 12 with effect in relation to disposals on or after 1 January 2018.

PART 7
COMMUNITY INVESTMENT TAX RELIEF
CHAPTER 1
INTRODUCTION
CITR

333 Meaning of "CITR"

This Part provides for community investment tax relief ("CITR"), that is, entitlement to tax reductions in respect of amounts invested by individuals in community development finance institutions.

Commentary—*Simon's Taxes* **E3.601**.
Derivation—FA 2002 Sch 16 para 51(1).
HMRC Manuals—Community Investment Tax Relief Manual CITM1010 (overview of the CITR scheme).

334 Eligibility for CITR

(1) An individual ("the investor") who makes an investment ("the investment") in a body is eligible for CITR in respect of the investment if—

    (*a*) that body is accredited as a community development finance institution under Chapter 2 at the time the investment is made,

    (*b*) the investment is a qualifying investment (see Chapter 3), and

    (*c*) the general conditions of Chapter 4 are met.

(2) In this Part references to "the CDFI" are to the body in which the investment is made.

Commentary—*Simon's Taxes* **E3.601**.
Derivation—FA 2002 Sch 16 para 1.
HMRC Manuals—Community Investment Tax Relief Manual CITM4005 (introduction).

335 Form and amount of CITR

(1) If the investor is eligible for CITR in respect of the investment, the investor may make a claim in respect of the investment for any one or more of the relevant tax years.

(2) If the investor makes a claim for a relevant tax year, the investor is entitled to a tax reduction for that year of 5% of the invested amount in respect of the investment for the year.

(3) For [the purposes of this section and section 335A][1] the "relevant" tax years are—

    (*a*) the tax year in which the investment date falls, and

    (*b*) each of the 4 subsequent tax years.

(4) The tax reduction is given effect at Step 6 of the calculation in section 23.

(5) The investor is entitled to make a claim for CITR for a relevant tax year if—

    (*a*) the investor considers that the conditions for the CITR are for the time being met, and

    (*b*) the investor has received a tax relief certificate (see section 348) relating to the investment from the CDFI,

but no claim may be made before the end of the tax year to which it relates.

(6) Subsection (5) is subject to the following provisions—

    (*a*) section 354 (loans: no claim after disposal or excessive repayments or receipts of value),

    (*b*) section 355 (securities or shares: no claim after disposal or excessive receipts of value), and

    (*c*) section 356 (no claim after loss of accreditation by CDFI).

Commentary—*Simon's Taxes* **E3.635, E3.630**.
Derivation—FA 2002 Sch 16 para 19.
HMRC Manuals—Community Investment Tax Relief Manual CITM6005 (individual investors - making a claim in respect of the investment).
CITM6010 (conditions for making a claim in respect of the investment).
CITM6030 (individual investors - effect of a claim).
Amendments-[1] In sub-s (3) words substituted by FA 2013 s 74, Sch 27 paras 1, 2 with effect in relation to investments made on or after 6 April 2013.

[335A Carry forward of CITR

(1) This section applies if—

    (*a*) the investor is entitled to a tax reduction for a relevant tax year under section 335 in respect of the investment, but

    (*b*) the amount of the tax reduction is not fully deducted at Step 6 for that relevant tax year.

(2) The amount ("the excess amount") not deducted is treated as follows.

(3) For each subsequent relevant tax year for which the investor—

    (*a*) is entitled to a tax reduction under section 335 in respect of the investment, and

    (*b*) makes a claim under this subsection,

the investor is also entitled to a tax reduction under this subsection which is given effect at Step 6.

(4) The amount of the tax reduction under subsection (3) for any relevant tax year is the excess amount so far as it has not been deducted at Step 6 for any earlier relevant tax year by virtue of that subsection.

(5) In this section "Step 6" means Step 6 of the calculation in section 23.][1]

Commentary—*Simon's Taxes* **E3.635**.

HMRC Manuals—Community Investment Tax Relief Manual CITM6031 (individual investors - effect of a claim - investments from 6 April 2013 - carry forward of unused relief).
Amendments—[1]   Section 335A inserted by FA 2013 s 74, Sch 27 paras 1, 3 with effect in relation to investments made on or after 6 April 2013.

Miscellaneous

336 Meaning of "making an investment"

(1) For the purposes of this Part, an individual makes an investment in a body at any time when—
   (a) the individual makes a loan (whether secured or unsecured) to the body, or
   (b) an issue of securities of or shares in the body, for which the individual has subscribed, is made to the individual.
(2) The following provisions of this section apply for the purposes of subsection (1)(a).
(3) An individual does not make a loan to a body if—
   (a) the body uses overdraft facilities provided by the individual, or
   (b) the individual subscribes for or otherwise acquires securities of the body.
(4) If the loan agreement authorises the body to draw down amounts of the loan over a period of time, the loan is treated as made at the time when the first amount is drawn down.

Commentary—*Simon's Taxes* **E3.610, E3.601**.
Derivation—FA 2002 Sch 16 para 2.

337 Determination of "the invested amount"

(1) This section applies for the purpose of determining "the invested amount" in respect of any loan, securities or shares included in the investment.
   This is subject to sections 363(2) and 369 (which adjust "the invested amount" in certain cases where value is received).
(2) In the case of a loan, the invested amount is—
   (a) for the tax year in which the investment date falls, the average capital balance for the first year of the 5 year period,
   (b) for the next tax year, the average capital balance for the second year of the 5 year period, and
   (c) for any subsequent tax year—
      (i) the average capital balance for the period of 12 months beginning with the anniversary of the investment date falling in the tax year concerned, or
      (ii) if less, the average capital balance for the period of 6 months beginning 18 months after the investment date.
(3) In the case of securities or shares, the invested amount for a tax year is the amount subscribed by the investor for the securities or shares.
(4) For the purposes of this section, the average capital balance of the loan for a period is the mean of the daily balances of capital outstanding during the period.

Commentary—*Simon's Taxes* **E3.637**.
Derivation—FA 2002 Sch 16 para 21.
HMRC Manuals—Community Investment Tax Relief Manual CITM6090 (determining the invested amount).

338 Meaning of "the 5 year period" and "the investment date"

In this Part—
   "the 5 year period" means the period of 5 years beginning with the investment date, and
   "the investment date" means the day the investment is made.

Commentary—*Simon's Taxes* **E3.655**.
Derivation—FA 2002 Sch 16 para 3.

339 Overview of other Chapters of Part

In this Part—
   (a) Chapter 5 provides for the making of claims for CITR and the attribution of CITR to investments,
   (b) Chapter 6 provides for CITR to be withdrawn or reduced in the circumstances mentioned in that Chapter, and
   (c) Chapter 7 contains supplementary and general provision.

CHAPTER 2

ACCREDITED COMMUNITY DEVELOPMENT FINANCE INSTITUTIONS

340 Application and criteria for accreditation

(1) Applications for accreditation as a community development finance institution must be made to the Secretary of State in the form and manner specified by the Secretary of State.
(2) The Secretary of State is to accredit a body if (and only if) the Secretary of State is satisfied—
   (a) that the body's principal objective is to provide (directly or indirectly)—
      (i) finance, or
      (ii) finance and access to business advice,

for enterprises for disadvantaged communities, and

(b) that the body meets any other criteria specified in regulations made by the Treasury.

(3) For the purposes of this section "enterprises for disadvantaged communities" include—

    (a) enterprises located in disadvantaged areas, and

    (b) enterprises owned or operated by, or designed to serve, members of disadvantaged groups.

(4) The criteria mentioned in paragraph (b) of subsection (2) may include criteria relating to the enterprises to which the body provides or proposes to provide finance or access to business advice.

(5) Regulations under that paragraph may make the provision authorised by that paragraph by reference to any material published by, or on behalf of, the Secretary of State (whether before or after the coming into force of this section).

[(5A) Regulations under that paragraph may include provision for the purposes of Part 7 of CTA 2010 in addition to provision made for the purposes of this Part.][1]

(6) Regulations under that paragraph—

    (a) may make different provision for different cases or circumstances or in relation to different areas, and

    (b) may, in particular, make different provision in the case of bodies whose principal objective in providing finance as mentioned in subsection (2)(a) is to invest directly in enterprises that meet the conditions of subsection (7).

(7) An enterprise meets the conditions of this subsection if it uses the money invested in it for the purposes of its business and either—

    (a) that business does not include the provision of finance for other enterprises, or

    (b) if it does, the nature and extent of such provision meets any conditions prescribed by regulations made by the Treasury.

(8) If the Secretary of State accredits a body of a kind mentioned in subsection (6)(b), the Secretary of State must specify in the accreditation that the body is accredited as a retail community development finance institution.

Commentary—*Simon's Taxes* **E3.605.**
Derivation—FA 2002 Sch 16 para 4.
HMRC Manuals—Community Investment Tax Relief Manual CITM2010 (accreditation: application for accreditation).
CITM2020 (accreditation: criteria for accreditation).
CITM2050 (accreditation: retail community development finance institutions).
Regulations—Community Investment Tax Relief (Accreditation of Community Development Finance Institutions) (Amendment) Regulations, SI 2013/417.
Amendments—[1]   Sub-s (5A) inserted by CTA 2010 s 1177, Sch 1 para 508. CTA 2010 has effect for corporation tax purposes for accounting periods ending on or after 1 April 2010, and for income and capital gains tax purposes for the tax year 2010–11 and subsequent tax years.

341 Terms and conditions of accreditation

(1) An accreditation under this Chapter must—

    (a) be made on—

        (i) any terms required by regulations, and

        (ii) any other terms the Secretary of State considers appropriate, and

    (b) be made conditional on compliance with—

        (i) any requirements imposed by regulations, and

        (ii) any other requirements the Secretary of State considers appropriate.

(2) The requirements that may be imposed by virtue of subsection (1)(b) include requirements relating to the provision of information.

(3) Regulations may—

    (a) make provision for appeals to the [tribunal][1] against refusals to grant accreditation under this Chapter,

    (b) make provision about the consequences of a failure to comply with any requirement of an accreditation, including—

        (i) provision for the withdrawal of the accreditation with effect from the time of the failure or a later time, and

        (ii) provision for the imposition of penalties,

    (c) make provision for the making of decisions by the Secretary of State as to any matter required to be decided for the purposes of the regulations,

    (d) make different provision for different cases or circumstances or in relation to different areas, and

    (e) contain incidental, supplemental, consequential and transitional provision and savings.

[(3A) Regulations under this section may include provision for the purposes of Part 7 of CTA 2010 in addition to provision made for the purposes of this Part.][2]

(4) In this section "regulations" means regulations made by the Treasury.

Commentary—*Simon's Taxes* **E3.605.**
Derivation—FA 2002 Sch 16 para 5.
HMRC Manuals—Community Investment Tax Relief Manual CITM2100 (accreditation: withdrawal of accreditation).

Regulations—Community Investment Tax Relief (Accreditation of Community Development Finance Institutions) (Amendment) Regulations, SI 2013/417.

Amendments—[1]   In sub-s (3)(*a*) word substituted by the Transfer of Tribunal Functions and Revenue and Customs Appeals Order, SI 2009/56 art 3, Sch 1 para 451 with effect from 1 April 2009.

[2]   Sub-s (3A) inserted by CTA 2010 s 1177, Sch 1 para 509. CTA 2010 has effect for corporation tax purposes for accounting periods ending on or after 1 April 2010, and for income and capital gains tax purposes for the tax year 2010–11 and subsequent tax years.

342 Period of accreditation

(1) An accreditation has effect for a period (an "accreditation period") of 3 years beginning on the day specified in the accreditation.

(2) Subject to subsection (4), the accreditation must not specify a day which is earlier than—

    (*a*) if the body is not accredited under this Chapter at the time the application is made, the day the accreditation is granted, and

    (*b*) if the body is so accredited, the time the body's current accreditation expires.

(3) Subsection (4) applies if—

    (*a*) the body is accredited at the time the application is made, and

    (*b*) it makes a request under this subsection.

(4) The new accreditation may specify that the existing accreditation is to be treated for the purposes of this Part (including subsection (2)(*b*)) as expiring immediately before the grant of the new accreditation (if it would otherwise expire at a later time).

(5) This section has effect subject to section 341(3)(*b*) (power to provide for the withdrawal of accreditation).

Commentary—*Simon's Taxes* E3.605.

Derivation—FA 2002 Sch 16 para 7.

HMRC Manuals—Community Investment Tax Relief Manual CITM2030 (accreditation: period of accreditation).

343 Delegation of Secretary of State's functions

The Secretary of State may delegate any functions conferred on the Secretary of State by or under this Chapter.

Commentary—*Simon's Taxes* E3.605.

Derivation—FA 2002 Sch 16 para 6.

CHAPTER 3

QUALIFYING INVESTMENTS

344 Qualifying investments: introduction

For the purposes of this Part the investment is a "qualifying investment" in the CDFI if—

    (*a*) the investment consists of—

        (i) a loan in relation to which the conditions of section 345 are met,

        (ii) securities in relation to which the conditions of section 346 are met, or

        (iii) shares in relation to which the conditions of section 347 are met,

    (*b*) the investor receives from the CDFI a valid tax relief certificate in relation to the investment (see section 348), and

    (*c*) the requirements of section 349 (no pre-arranged protection against risks) are met.

Commentary—*Simon's Taxes* E3.610.

Derivation—FA 2002 Sch 16 para 8.

HMRC Manuals—Community Investment Tax Relief Manual CITM4010 (meaning of qualifying investment).

345 Conditions to be met in relation to loans

(1) Condition A of this section is that either—

    (*a*) the CDFI receives from the investor, on the investment date, the full amount of the loan, or

    (*b*) if the loan agreement authorises the CDFI to draw down amounts of the loan over a period of time, the end of that period is not later than 18 months after the investment date.

(2) Condition B is that the loan must not carry any present or future right to be converted into or exchanged for a loan which is, or securities, shares or other rights which are, redeemable within the 5 year period.

(3) Condition C is that the loan must not have been made on terms that allow any person to require—

    (*a*) the repayment during the first two years of the 5 year period of any of the loan capital advanced in those two years,

    (*b*) the repayment during the third year of that period of more than 25% of the loan capital outstanding at the end of those two years,

    (*c*) the repayment before the end of the fourth year of that period of more than 50% of that loan capital, or

    (*d*) the repayment before the end of that period of more than 75% of that loan capital.

(4) Subsection (3) does not apply if the CDFI is required to make the repayment as a result of its failure to meet any obligation of the loan agreement which—

(*a*) is imposed merely because of the commercial risks to which the investor is exposed as lender under that agreement, and

(*b*) is no more likely to be breached than any obligation that might reasonably have been agreed in respect of the loan in the absence of this Part.

(5) The Treasury may by order substitute any other percentage for any percentage for the time being specified in subsection (3).

(6) Any such substitution is to have effect in relation to loans made by an individual on or after the date specified in the order.

Commentary—*Simon's Taxes* **E3.611**.
Derivation—FA 2002 Sch 16 para 9.
HMRC Manuals—Community Investment Tax Relief Manual CITM4020 (qualifying investments: loans).

346 Conditions to be met in relation to securities

(1) Condition A of this section is that the securities must be—

    (*a*) subscribed for wholly in cash, and

    (*b*) fully paid for on the investment date.

(2) Condition B is that the securities must not carry—

    (*a*) any present or future right to be redeemed within the 5 year period, or

    (*b*) any present or future right to be converted into or exchanged for a loan which is, or securities, shares or other rights which are, redeemable within that period.

(3) [For the purposes of subsection (1)(*b*), securities are not fully paid for][1] if there is any undertaking to pay cash to the CDFI at a future date in connection with the acquisition of the securities.

Commentary—*Simon's Taxes* **E3.612**.
Derivation—FA 2002 Sch 16 para 10.
HMRC Manuals—Community Investment Tax Relief Manual CITM4030 (conditions for securities to be treated as qualifying investment).
Amendments—[1]   In sub-s (3), words substituted by CTA 2010 s 1177, Sch 1 para 510. CTA 2010 has effect for corporation tax purposes for accounting periods ending on or after 1 April 2010, and for income and capital gains tax purposes for the tax year 2010–11 and subsequent tax years.

347 Conditions to be met in relation to shares

(1) Condition A of this section is that the shares must be—

    (*a*) subscribed for wholly in cash, and

    (*b*) fully paid up on the investment date.

(2) Condition B is that the shares must not carry—

    (*a*) any present or future right to be redeemed during the 5 year period, or

    (*b*) any present or future right to be converted into or exchanged for a loan which is, or securities, shares or other rights which are, redeemable within that period.

(3) Shares are not fully paid up for the purposes of subsection (1)(*b*) if there is any undertaking to pay cash to the CDFI at a future date in connection with the acquisition of the shares.

Commentary—*Simon's Taxes* **E3.613**.
Derivation—FA 2002 Sch 16 para 11.
HMRC Manuals—Community Investment Tax Relief Manual CITM4040 (conditions for shares to be treated as qualifying investment).

348 Tax relief certificates

(1) A "tax relief certificate" means a certificate issued by the CDFI in respect of the investment which is in the form specified by the Commissioners for Her Majesty's Revenue and Customs.

(2) The CDFI must not issue tax relief certificates under this section in respect of investments made in the CDFI in an accreditation period if the total value of—

    (*a*) those investments, and

    (*b*) any investments to which subsection (3) applies,

will exceed the limit for that period.

(3) This subsection applies to investments[1] *which*—

    (*a*) [which][1] have been made in the CDFI in the accreditation period, and

    (*b*) in respect of which the CDFI has issued tax relief certificates under [section 229 of CTA 2010][1] (which makes in relation to corporation tax provision corresponding to that made by this section).

(4) The limit for an accreditation period is—

    (*a*) £10 million if the CDFI is accredited for the period as a retail community development finance institution (see section 340(8)), and

    (*b*) £20 million in any other case.

(5) For the purposes of subsection (2) the value of an investment made in the CDFI is—

    (*a*) if the investment consists of a loan—

        (i) the amount of the loan, or

        (ii) if the loan agreement authorises the CDFI to draw down amounts of the loan over a period of time, the amount committed under the loan agreement, and

   (b) if the investment consists of securities or shares, the amount subscribed for them.

(6) The Treasury may by order substitute any other amount for any amount for the time being specified in subsection (4).

(7) Any such substitution is to have effect in relation to such accreditation periods as may be specified in the order; and those periods may, if the substitution increases [an amount][1] for the time being specified in subsection (4), include periods beginning before the order [comes into force][1].

(8) Any tax relief certificate issued in contravention of subsection (2) is invalid.

(9) A body is liable to a penalty of not more than £3,000 if it issues a tax relief certificate which is made fraudulently or negligently.

Commentary—*Simon's Taxes* **E3.614**.
Derivation—FA 2002 Sch 16 para 12.
HMRC Manuals—Community Investment Tax Relief Manual CITM4060 (issue of tax relief certificates).
CITM4070 (limit of issue of tax relief certificates).
Amendments—[1]   In sub-s (3) word repealed, in sub-s (3)(a) word inserted, and in sub-s (3)(b) words substituted, by CTA 2010
     ss 1177, 1181, Sch 1 para 511, Sch 3 Pt 2. CTA 2010 has effect for corporation tax purposes for accounting periods ending
     on or after 1 April 2010, and for income and capital gains tax purposes for the tax year 2010–11 and subsequent tax years.

349 No pre-arranged protection against risks

(1) Any arrangements—
   (a) under which the investment is made, or
   (b) made, before the investor makes the investment, in relation to or in connection with the making of the investment,
must not include excluded arrangements.

(2) For the purposes of subsection (1) "excluded arrangements"—
   (a) means arrangements the main purpose or one of the main purposes of which is (by means of any insurance, indemnity or guarantee or otherwise) to provide partial or complete protection for the investor against what would otherwise be the risks attached to making the investment, but
   (b) does not include any arrangements which are confined to the provision for the investor of any protection against those risks which might reasonably be expected to be provided for commercial reasons if the investment were made in the course of a business of banking.

(3) For the purposes of this section "arrangements" includes any scheme, agreement or understanding, whether or not legally enforceable.

Commentary—*Simon's Taxes* **E3.615**.
Derivation—FA 2002 Sch 16 para 13.
HMRC Manuals—Community Investment Tax Relief Manual CITM4050 (pre-arranged protection against risks).

CHAPTER 4

GENERAL CONDITIONS

350 No control of CDFI by investor

(1) The investor must not control the CDFI at any time during the 5 year period.

(2) In this section references to the investor include any person connected with the investor.

(3) If the CDFI is a body corporate, the question whether the investor controls the CDFI is, for the purposes of this section, determined in accordance with section 995.

   This is subject to subsection (6).

(4) In any other case the investor is treated, for those purposes, as having control of the CDFI if the investor has power to secure, as a result of—
   (a) the possession of voting power in the CDFI, or
   (b) any powers conferred by the constitution of, or any other document regulating, the CDFI,
that the affairs of the body are conducted in accordance with the investor's wishes.

   This is subject to subsections (5) and (6).

(5) If—
   (a) the CDFI is a partnership, and
   (b) the investor is a member of that partnership,
for the purposes of determining in accordance with this section whether the investor controls the CDFI, the other members of that partnership are not, as a result of their membership of the CDFI, treated as partners of the investor.

(6) In determining whether the investor controls the CDFI there are attributed to the investor (so far as it would not otherwise be the case)—
   (a) any rights or powers that the investor is entitled to acquire at a future date or will, at a future date, become entitled to acquire, and
   (b) any rights or powers which another person holds on behalf of the investor or may be required to exercise, by direction, on the investor's behalf.

Commentary—*Simon's Taxes* **E3.621**.
Derivation—FA 2002 Sch 16 para 14.

HMRC Manuals—Community Investment Tax Relief Manual CITM5010 (control of community development finance institution (CDFI) by the investor).

351 Investor must have beneficial ownership

(1) The investor must be the sole beneficial owner of the investment when it is made.

(2) If the investment consists of a loan, the person beneficially entitled to repayment of the loan is treated as the beneficial owner of the loan for the purposes of this Part.

Commentary—*Simon's Taxes* **E3.622**.
Derivation—FA 2002 Sch 16 para 15.
HMRC Manuals—Community Investment Tax Relief Manual CITM5020 (beneficial ownership).

352 No acquisition of share in partnership

(1) If the CDFI is a partnership, the investment must not consist of or include any amount of capital contributed by the investor on becoming a member of the partnership.

(2) For this purpose the amount of capital contributed by the investor on becoming a member of the partnership includes any amount which—

    (*a*) purports to be provided by the investor by way of loan capital, and

    (*b*) is accounted for as partners' capital in the accounts of the partnership.

Commentary—*Simon's Taxes* **E3.624**.
Derivation—FA 2002 Sch 16 para 17.
HMRC Manuals—Community Investment Tax Relief Manual CITM5040 (acquisition of partnership share).

353 No tax avoidance purpose

The investment must not be made as part of a scheme or arrangement the main purpose or one of the main purposes of which is the avoidance of tax.

Commentary—*Simon's Taxes* **E3.625**.
Derivation—FA 2002 Sch 16 para 18.
HMRC Manuals—Community Investment Tax Relief Manual CITM5050 (tax avoidance).

CHAPTER 5

CLAIMS FOR AND ATTRIBUTION OF CITR

Claims

354 Loans: no claim after disposal or excessive repayments or receipts of value

(1) If the investment consists of a loan, no claim may be made in respect of a tax year if—

    (*a*) the investor disposes of the whole or any part of the loan before the qualifying date relating to that year,

    (*b*) at any time after the investment is made but before that qualifying date, the amount of the capital outstanding on the loan is reduced to nil, or

    (*c*) before that qualifying date, paragraphs (*a*) and (*b*) of section 362(1) (repayments of loan in 5 year period exceeding permitted limits) apply in relation to the investment (whether by virtue of section 363 (receipts of value treated as repayments) or otherwise).

(2) For the purposes of subsection (1)(*a*) any repayment of the loan is to be ignored.

(3) For the purposes of this section the qualifying date relating to a tax year is the next anniversary of the investment date to occur after the end of that year.

Commentary—*Simon's Taxes* **E3.632**.
Derivation—FA 2002 Sch 16 para 22.
HMRC Manuals—Community Investment Tax Relief Manual CITM6100 (loans - disposal, excessive repayments, and receipt of value).

355 Securities or shares: no claim after disposal or excessive receipts of value

(1) If the investment consists of securities or shares, a claim made in respect of a tax year must relate only to those securities or shares held by the investor, as sole beneficial owner, continuously throughout the period—

    (*a*) beginning when the investment is made, and

    (*b*) ending immediately before the qualifying date relating to the tax year.

(2) No claim for CITR may be made in relation to a tax year if before the qualifying date relating to that year paragraphs (*a*) to (*d*) of section 364(1) (receipts of value in the [6][1] year period exceeding permitted limits) apply in relation to the investment or any part of it.

(3) For the purposes of this section the qualifying date relating to a tax year is the next anniversary of the investment date to occur after the end of that year.

Commentary—*Simon's Taxes* **E3.633**.
Derivation—FA 2002 Sch 16 para 23.
HMRC Manuals—Community Investment Tax Relief Manual CITM6110 (shares and securities - disposal and receipt of value).
Amendments—[1]   In sub-s (2), number substituted by CTA 2010 s 1177, Sch 1 para 512. CTA 2010 has effect for corporation tax purposes for accounting periods ending on or after 1 April 2010, and for income and capital gains tax purposes for the tax year 2010–11 and subsequent tax years.

356 No claim after loss of accreditation by the CDFI

(1) If the CDFI ceases to be accredited under Chapter 2 with effect from a time   . . . [1] within the 5 year period, no claim for CITR relating to the investment may be made by the investor—

    (a) for the relevant tax year, or

    (b) for any later tax year.

[(2) To find the relevant tax year proceed under the rest of this section, in which references to the time of accreditation ceasing are to the time with effect from which the CDFI ceases to be accredited.

(3) If the time of accreditation ceasing falls within the first year of the 5 year period, the relevant tax year is the year in which the investment date fell.

(4) In any other case the relevant tax year is—

    (a) the year in which fell the last anniversary of the investment date before the time of accreditation ceasing, or

    (b) if the time of accreditation ceasing itself falls on an anniversary of the investment date, the year in which that anniversary falls.][1]

Commentary—*Simon's Taxes* **E3.634**.

Derivation—FA 2002 Sch 16 para 24.

HMRC Manuals—Community Investment Tax Relief Manual CITM6120 (loss of accreditation by the CDFI).

Amendments—[1]   In sub-s (1) words repealed, sub-ss (2)–(4) substituted for former sub-s (2) by CTA 2010 ss 1177, 1181, Sch 1 para 513, Sch 3 Pt 1. CTA 2010 has effect for corporation tax purposes for accounting periods ending on or after 1 April 2010, and for income and capital gains tax purposes for the tax year 2010–11 and subsequent tax years.

Attribution

357 Attribution: general

(1) In this Part references to the CITR attributable to any loan, securities or shares in respect of a tax year are read as references to the reduction which—

    (a) is made in the investor's liability to income tax for that year, and

    (b) is attributed to that loan, or those securities or shares, in accordance with this section and section 358.

This is subject to the provisions of Chapter 6 for the withdrawal or reduction of CITR.

(2) Subsections (3) and (4) apply if the investor's liability to income tax is reduced for a tax year under this Part.

(3) If the reduction is obtained because of one loan, or securities or shares included in one issue, the amount of the tax reduction is attributed to that loan or those securities or shares.

(4) If the reduction is obtained because of a loan or loans, securities or shares included in two or more investments, the reduction—

    (a) is apportioned between the loan or loans, securities or shares in each of those investments in the same proportions as the invested amounts in respect of the loan or loans, securities or shares for the year, and

    (b) is attributed to that loan or those loans, securities or shares accordingly.

[(4A) In the case of CITR under section 335A, in subsection (4)(a) the reference to the year is to be read as a reference to the year mentioned in section 335A(1)(a).][1]

(5) If under this section an amount of any reduction of income tax is attributed to any securities in the same issue, a proportionate part of that amount is attributed to each security.

(6) If under this section an amount of any reduction of income tax is attributed to any shares in the same issue, a proportionate part of that amount is attributed to each of those shares.

(7) If CITR attributable to a loan or any securities or shares falls to be withdrawn under Chapter 6, the CITR attributable to that loan or each of those securities or shares is reduced to nil.

(8) If CITR attributable to any securities or shares falls to be reduced under that Chapter by any amount, the CITR attributable to each of those securities or shares is reduced by a proportionate part of that amount.

HMRC Manuals—Community Investment Tax Relief Manual CITM6140 (rules for attribution).

Amendments—[1]   Sub-s (4A) inserted by FA 2013 s 74, Sch 27 paras 1, 4 with effect in relation to investments made on or after 6 April 2013.

358 Attribution: bonus shares

(1) This section applies if—

    (a) corresponding bonus shares are issued to the investor in respect of any shares ("the original shares") included in the investment, and

    (b) the original shares have been continuously held by the investor, as sole beneficial owner, from the time they were issued until the issue of the bonus shares.

(2) A proportionate part of any amount attributed to the original shares, in respect of a tax year, immediately before the bonus shares are issued is attributed to each of the shares in the holding consisting of the original shares and the bonus shares, in respect of that year.

(3) After the issue of the bonus shares this Part applies as if—

    (a) the original issue had included the bonus shares, and

    (b) the bonus shares had been held by the investor, as sole beneficial owner, continuously from the time the original shares were issued until the bonus shares were issued.

(4) In this section—

"corresponding bonus shares" means bonus shares that are in the same company, are of the same class, and carry the same rights as the original shares,

"original issue" means the issue of shares forming the investment.

Derivation—FA 2002 Sch 16 para 26.
HMRC Manuals—Community Investment Tax Relief Manual CITM6140 (attribution).

CHAPTER 6

WITHDRAWAL OR REDUCTION OF CITR

Introduction

359 Overview of Chapter

(1) This Chapter provides for CITR to be withdrawn or reduced under—

    (*a*) section 360 (disposal of loan during 5 year period),

    (*b*) section 361 (disposal of securities or shares during 5 year period),

    (*c*) section 362 (repayment of loan capital during 5 year period),

    (*d*) section 363 (value received by investor during 6 year period: loans),

    (*e*) section 364 (value received by investor during 6 year period: securities or shares),

    (*f*) section 371 (CITR subsequently found not to have been due).

(2) This Chapter also provides for the manner in which CITR is to be withdrawn or reduced (see section 372).

(3) In this Chapter "the 6 year period" in relation to the investment is the period of 6 years beginning 12 months before the investment date.

HMRC Manuals—Community Investment Tax Relief Manual CITM7090 (value received - meaning of period of restriction).

Disposals

360 Disposal of loan during 5 year period

(1) If the investment consists of a loan and within the 5 year period—

    (*a*) the investor disposes of the whole of the investment, otherwise than by way of a permitted disposal, or

    (*b*) the investor disposes of a part of the investment,

any CITR attributable to the investment in respect of any tax year must be withdrawn.

(2) For the purposes of this section—

    (*a*) a disposal is "permitted" if—

        (i) it is by way of a distribution in the course of dissolving or winding up the CDFI,

        (ii) it is a disposal within section 24(1) of TCGA 1992 (entire loss, destruction, dissipation or extinction of asset),

        (iii) it is a deemed disposal under section 24(2) of that Act (claim that value of asset has become negligible), or

        (iv) it is made after the CDFI has ceased to be accredited under this Part, and

    (*b*) a full or partial repayment of the loan is not treated as giving rise to a disposal.

Commentary—*Simon's Taxes* E3.641.
Derivation—FA 2002 Sch 16 para 28.
HMRC Manuals—Community Investment Tax Relief Manual CITM7010 (disposal of loan).

361 Disposal of securities or shares during 5 year period

(1) This section applies if the investment consists of securities or shares and—

    (*a*) the investor disposes of the whole or any part of the investment ("the former investment") within the 5 year period,

    (*b*) the CDFI has not ceased to be accredited before the disposal, and

    (*c*) the disposal does not arise as a result of an event within section 366(1)(*a*) (repayment, redemption or repurchase of securities or shares included in the investment).

(2) If the disposal is not a qualifying disposal, any CITR attributable to the former investment in respect of any tax year must be withdrawn.

[(3) Subsections (3A) to (3H) apply if—

    (*a*) the disposal is a qualifying disposal, and

    (*b*) the investor has made a claim under section 335 in respect of the former investment for a tax year ("tax year X")[1].

(3A) Subsection (3B) applies if the total of the following CITR does not exceed A—

    (*a*) any CITR attributable to the former investment in respect of tax year X given under section 335, and

    (*b*) any CITR attributable to the former investment in respect of later tax years given under section 335A where tax year X is the tax year mentioned in section 335A(1)(*a*).

(3B) All CITR falling within subsection (3A)(*a*) or (*b*) must be withdrawn.

(3C) If the total of the CITR falling within subsection (3A)(*a*) or (*b*) exceeds A, that total must be reduced by A.

(3D) For the purposes of subsection (3C) CITR given in a later tax year must be reduced before CITR given in an earlier tax year.

(3E) For the purposes of subsections (3A) and (3C) "A" is an amount equal to 5% of the amount or value of the consideration (if any) which the investor receives for the former investment.

(3F) If—

    (a) the total of the CITR falling within subsection (3A)(a) or (b) ("B") is less than

    (b) the amount ("C") which is equal to 5% of the invested amount in respect of the former investment for tax year X,

"A" is to be reduced by multiplying it by the fraction—

B / C

(3G) If the amount of CITR attributable to the former investment in respect of a tax year has been reduced before the CITR is obtained, the amount referred to in subsection (3F) as B is to be treated for the purposes of that subsection as the amount it would have been without the reduction.

(3H) Subsection (3G) does not apply to a reduction by virtue of section 358 (attribution: bonus shares).]^2

(4) For the purposes of this section "qualifying disposal" means a disposal that is—

    (a) by way of a bargain made at arm's length, or

    (b) a permitted disposal (within the meaning of section 360).

(5)–(7) . . .^{2}

Commentary—*Simon's Taxes* **E3.642**.

HMRC Manuals—Community Investment Tax Relief Manual CITM7020 (disposal of shares or securities).

Amendments—^{1} In sub-s (3) words substituted for words "a tax year", and in sub-s (5) words substituted for words "any tax year" by CTA 2010 s 1177, Sch 1 para 514. CTA 2010 has effect for corporation tax purposes for accounting periods ending on or after 1 April 2010, and for income and capital gains tax purposes for the tax year 2010–11 and subsequent tax years. ^{2} Sub-ss (3)–(3H) substituted for previous sub-s (3) and sub-ss (5)–(7) repealed, by FA 2013 s 74, Sch 27 paras 1, 5 with effect in relation to investments made on or after 6 April 2013.

Repayment of loans

362 Repayment of loan capital during 5 year period

(1) If the investment consists of a loan and—

    (a) the average capital balance of the loan for the third, fourth or final year of the 5 year period is less than the permitted balance for the year in question, and

    (b) the difference between those balances is not an amount of insignificant value,

any CITR attributable to the investment in respect of any tax year must be withdrawn.

(2) For the purposes of this section—

    "the average capital balance" of the loan for a period is the mean of the daily balances of capital outstanding during that period, ignoring any non-standard repayments of the loan made in that period or at any earlier time, and

    "the permitted balance" of the loan is—

        (a) for the third year of the 5 year period, 75% of the average capital balance for the period of 6 months beginning 18 months after the investment date,

        (b) for the fourth year of that period, 50% of that balance, and

        (c) for the final year of that period, 25% of that balance.

(3) For the purposes of subsection (2) a repayment of the loan is a non-standard repayment if subsection (4) or (5) applies.

(4) This subsection applies if the repayment is made at the choice or discretion of the CDFI, and not as a direct or indirect consequence of any obligation provided for under the terms of the loan agreement.

(5) This subsection applies if the repayment is made as a result of the failure of the CDFI to meet any obligation of the loan agreement which—

    (a) is imposed merely because of the commercial risks to which the investor is exposed as lender under that agreement, and

    (b) is no more likely to be breached than any obligation that might reasonably have been agreed in respect of the loan in the absence of this Part.

(6) For the purposes of this section "an amount of insignificant value" means an amount which—

    (a) is not more than £1,000, or

    (b) if it is more than £1,000, is insignificant in relation to the average capital balance of the loan for the year of the 5 year period in question.

Commentary—*Simon's Taxes* **E3.643**.

Derivation—FA 2002 Sch 16 para 30.

HMRC Manuals—Community Investment Tax Relief Manual CITM7050 (repayments of loan capital).

Receipts of value

363 Value received by investor during 6 year period: loans

(1) This section applies if the investment consists of a loan and the investor receives any value (other than an amount of insignificant value) from the CDFI during the 6 year period.

(2) The investor is treated for the purposes of—

    (*a*) section 337 (determination of "invested amount"), and

    (*b*) section 362 (repayments of loan capital),

as having received a repayment of the loan of an amount equal to the amount of the value received.

(3) For those purposes the repayment is treated as made—

    (*a*) if the value is received in the first or second year of the 6 year period, at the beginning of that second year, and

    (*b*) if the value is received in a later year of that period, at the beginning of the year in question.

(4) For the purposes of section 362 the repayment is treated as a repayment other than a non-standard repayment (within the meaning of that section).

(5) For the purposes of this section "an amount of insignificant value" means an amount [of value][1] which—

    (*a*) is not more than £1,000, or

    (*b*) if it is more than £1,000, is insignificant in relation to the average capital balance of the loan for the year of the 6 year period in which the value is received.

(6) For the purposes of subsection (5)(*b*)—

    (*a*) "the average capital balance" of the loan for a year is the mean of the daily balances of capital outstanding during the year (ignoring the receipt of value in question), and

    (*b*) any value received in the first year of the 6 year period is treated as received at the beginning of the second year of that period.

(7) This section is subject to section 368 (value received if there is more than one investment).

(8) Value received is ignored, for the purposes of this section, so far as the CITR attributable to any loan, securities or shares in respect of any one or more tax years has already been reduced or withdrawn on its account.

Commentary—*Simon's Taxes* **E3.645**.

Derivation—FA 2002 Sch 16 para 31.

HMRC Manuals—Community Investment Tax Relief Manual CITM7070 (value received as repayment of loan).

Amendments—[1]   In sub-s (5) words inserted by CTA 2010 s 1177, Sch 1 para 515. CTA 2010 has effect for corporation tax purposes for accounting periods ending on or after 1 April 2010, and for income and capital gains tax purposes for the tax year 2010–11 and subsequent tax years.

364 Value received by investor during 6 year period: securities or shares

(1) This section applies if the investment consists of securities or shares and—

    (*a*) the investor receives any value (other than an amount of insignificant value) from the CDFI during the 6 year period,

    (*b*) the investment or a part of it is held by the investor at the time the value is received and has been held by the investor, as sole beneficial owner, continuously since the investment was made ("the continuing investment"),

    (*c*) the receipt is wholly or partly in excess of the permitted level of receipts in respect of the continuing investment, and

    (*d*) the amount of that excess ("the excess")[1] is not an amount of insignificant value.

(2) Any CITR attributable to the continuing investment in respect of any tax year must be withdrawn.

(3) For the purposes of subsection (1) the permitted level of receipts is exceeded if—

    (*a*) any amount of value is received by the investor (ignoring any amounts of insignificant value) in the first 3 years of the 6 year period, or

    (*b*) the total amount of value received by the investor (ignoring any amounts of insignificant value)—

        (i) before the beginning of the fifth year of that period, exceeds 25% of the invested capital,

        (ii) before the beginning of the final year of that period, exceeds 50% of the invested capital, or

        (iii) before the end of that period, exceeds 75% of the invested capital.

(4) In this section—

"the invested capital", in relation to the continuing investment, means the amount subscribed for the securities or shares concerned, and

"an amount of insignificant value" means an amount of value which—

    (*a*) is not more than £1,000, or

    (*b*) if it is more than £1,000, is insignificant in relation to the amount subscribed by the investor for the securities or shares included in the continuing investment.

(5) This section is subject to section 368 (value received if there is more than one investment).

(6) Value received is ignored, for the purposes of this section, so far as CITR attributable to any loan, securities or shares in respect of any one or more tax years has already been reduced or withdrawn on its account.

Commentary—*Simon's Taxes* **E3.646**.

Derivation—FA 2002 Sch 16 para 32.

HMRC Manuals—Community Investment Tax Relief Manual CITM7080 (value received – shares or securities).

Amendments—[1]   Words in sub-s (1)(*d*) repealed by CTA 2010 ss 1177, 1181, Sch 1 para 516, Sch 3 Pt 1. CTA 2010 has effect for corporation tax purposes for accounting periods ending on or after 1 April 2010, and for income and capital gains tax purposes for the tax year 2010–11 and subsequent tax years.

365 Receipts of insignificant value to be added together

(1) This section applies if—

    (*a*) value is received ("the relevant receipt") by the investor from the CDFI at any time during the 6 year period relating to the investment,

    (*b*) the investor has received from the CDFI one or more receipts of insignificant value at a time or times—

        (i) during that period, but

        (ii) not later than the time of the relevant receipt, and

    (*c*) the total amount of the value of the receipts within paragraph (*a*) and (*b*) is not an amount of insignificant value.

(2) The investor is treated for the purposes of this Part as if the relevant receipt had been a receipt of an amount of value equal to that total amount.

(3) A receipt does not fall within subsection (1)(*b*) if the whole or any part of it has previously formed part of a total amount falling within subsection (1)(*c*).

(4) For the purposes of this section "an amount of insignificant value" means an amount of value which—

    (*a*) is not more than £1,000, or

    (*b*) if it is more than £1,000, is insignificant in relation to the relevant amount.

(5) If the investment consists of a loan, the relevant amount for the purposes of subsection (4) is—

    (*a*) if the relevant receipt is received in the first or second year of the 6 year period, the average capital balance of the loan for the second year of that period, and

    (*b*) if the relevant receipt is received in a later year, the average capital balance of the loan for the year in question.

(6) For the purposes of subsection (5)—

    (*a*) the average capital balance of the loan for a year is the mean of the daily balances of capital outstanding during the year, and

    (*b*) the relevant receipt and any receipts within subsection (1)(*b*) are ignored when calculating the average capital balance for the year in question.

(7) If the investment consists of securities or shares, the relevant amount for the purposes of subsection (4) is—

    (*a*) if the relevant receipt is received in the first year of the 6 year period, the amount subscribed for the securities or shares, and

    (*b*) in any other case, the amount subscribed for such of the securities or shares as—

        (i) are held by the investor at the time the relevant receipt is received, and

        (ii) have been held by the investor, as sole beneficial owner, continuously since the investment was made.

[(8) This section is subject to section 368 (value received if there is more than one investment).][1]

Commentary—*Simon's Taxes* E3.644.

Derivation—FA 2002 Sch 16 para 34.

HMRC Manuals—Community Investment Tax Relief Manual CITM7100 (aggregation of receipts of insignificant value).

Amendments—[1]   Sub-s (8) inserted by CTA 2010 s 1177, Sch 1 para 517. CTA 2010 has effect for corporation tax purposes for accounting periods ending on or after 1 April 2010, and for income and capital gains tax purposes for the tax year 2010–11 and subsequent tax years.

366 When value is received

(1) For the purposes of this Chapter the investor receives value from the CDFI at any time when the CDFI—

    (*a*) repays, redeems or repurchases any securities or shares included in the investment,

    (*b*) releases or waives any liability of the investor to the CDFI or discharges, or undertakes to discharge, any liability of the investor to a third person,

    (*c*) makes a loan or advance to the investor which has not been repaid in full before the investment is made,

    (*d*) provides a benefit or facility for the investor or any associate of the investor,

    (*e*) disposes of an asset to the investor for no consideration or for a consideration of an amount or value which is less than the market value of the asset,

    (*f*) acquires an asset from the investor for a consideration of an amount or value which is more than the market value of the asset, or

    (*g*) makes a payment to the investor other than a qualifying payment.

(2) For the purposes of subsection (1)(*b*) the CDFI is treated as having released or waived a liability if the liability is not discharged within 12 months of the time when it ought to have been discharged.

(3) For the purposes of subsection (1)(*c*) the following are treated as loans made by the CDFI to the investor—

(*a*) the amount of any debt due from the investor to the CDFI (other than an ordinary trade debt), and

(*b*) the amount of any debt due from the investor to a third person which has been assigned to the CDFI.

(4) For the purposes of this section—

(*a*) references to a debt or liability do not, in relation to a person, include references to any debt or liability which would be discharged by the making by that person of a qualifying payment,

(*b*) references to a benefit or facility do not include references to any benefit or facility provided in circumstances such that, if a payment had been made of an amount equal to its value, that payment would have been a qualifying payment, and

(*c*) any reference to a payment or disposal to a person includes a reference to a payment or disposal made to that person indirectly or to that person's order or for that person's benefit.

(5) In subsection (4) references to "a person" include references to any other person who, at any time in the 6 year period, is connected with that person, whether or not the other person is so connected at the material time.

(6) In this section—

"qualifying payment" means—

(*a*) any payment by any person for any goods, services or facilities provided by the investor (in the course of the investor's trade or otherwise) which is reasonable in relation to the market value of those goods, services or facilities,

(*b*) the payment by any person of any interest which represents no more than a reasonable commercial return on money lent to that person,

(*c*) the payment by any company of any dividend or other distribution which does not exceed a normal return on any investment in shares in or securities of that company,

(*d*) any payment for the acquisition of an asset which does not exceed its market value,

(*e*) the payment by any person, as rent for any property occupied by the person, of an amount which is not more than a reasonable and commercial rent for the property, and

(*f*) a payment in discharge of an ordinary trade debt, and

"ordinary trade debt" means any debt for goods or services supplied in the ordinary course of a trade or business if any credit given—

(*a*) is for not more than 6 months, and

(*b*) is not longer than that normally given to customers of the person carrying on the trade or business.

Commentary—*Simon's Taxes* **E3.647.**
Derivation—FA 2002 Sch 16 para 35.
HMRC Manuals—Community Investment Tax Relief Manual CITM7110 (when value is received for the purposes of the CITR scheme how the amount of such value is established or calculated).
CITM7120 (when value is not received – meaning of qualifying payment).

367 The amount of value received

In a case falling within a provision listed in column 1 of the following table, the amount of value received for the purposes of this Chapter is given by the corresponding entry in column 2 of the table.

Provision	The amount of value received
Section 366(1)(*a*)	The amount received by the investor
Section 366(1)(*b*)	The amount of the liability
Section 366(1)(*c*)	The amount of the loan or advance, less the amount of any repayment made before the investment is made
Section 366(1)(*d*)	The cost to the CDFI of providing the benefit or facility, less any consideration given for it by the investor or any associate of the investor
Section 366(1)(*e*) or (*f*)	The difference between the market value of the asset and the consideration (if any) received for it
Section 366(1)(*g*)	The amount of the payment

Derivation—FA 2002 Sch 16 para 36.
HMRC Manuals—Community Investment Tax Relief Manual CITM7110 (when value is received).

368 Value received if there is more than one investment

(1) This section applies if—

(*a*) the investor makes two or more investments in the CDFI,

(*b*) the investor is eligible for and claims CITR in respect of those investments, and

(*c*) the investor receives value (other than value within section 366(1)(*a*)) which [is received]¹ within the 6 year periods relating to two or more of those investments.

(2) Sections 363, 364, 365 and 369 have effect in relation to each investment referred to in subsection (1)(*c*) as if the amount of the value received were reduced by multiplying it by the fraction—

$$\frac{A}{B}$$

where—
- (*a*) A is the appropriate amount in respect of the investment in question, and
- (*b*) B is the sum of that amount and the appropriate amount or amounts in respect of the other investment or investments.

(3) If the investment consists of a loan, the appropriate amount for the purposes of subsection (2) is—
- (*a*) if the value is received in the first or second year of the 6 year period, the average capital balance of the loan for the second year of that period, and
- (*b*) if the value is received in a later year, the average capital balance of the loan for the year in question.

(4) For the purposes of subsection (3)—
- (*a*) the average capital balance of the loan for a year is the mean of the daily balances of capital outstanding during the year, and
- (*b*) the receipt of value is ignored when calculating the average capital balance for the year in question.

(5) If the investment consists of securities or shares, the appropriate amount for the purposes of subsection (2) is—
- (*a*) if the value is received in the first year of the 6 year period, the amount subscribed for the securities or shares, and
- (*b*) in any other case, the amount subscribed for such of the securities or shares as—
  - (i) are held by the investor at the time the value is received, and
  - (ii) have been held by the investor, as sole beneficial owner, continuously since the investment was made.

Commentary—*Simon's Taxes* **E3.648**.
Derivation—FA 2002 Sch 16 para 37.
HMRC Manuals—Community Investment Tax Relief Manual CITM7130 (value received where there is more than one investment).
Amendments—[1] In sub-s (1)(*c*) words substituted by CTA 2010 s 1177, Sch 1 para 518. CTA 2010 has effect for corporation tax purposes for accounting periods ending on or after 1 April 2010, and for income and capital gains tax purposes for the tax year 2010–11 and subsequent tax years.

369 Effect of receipt of value on future claims for CITR

(1) This section applies if the investment consists of securities or shares and—
- (*a*) the investor receives any value (other than an amount of insignificant value) from the CDFI during the 6 year period, and
- (*b*) the investment or a part of it is held by the investor at the time the value is received and has been held by the investor, as sole beneficial owner, continuously since the investment was made ("the continuing investment"),

but no CITR attributable to the continuing investment is withdrawn under section 364 as a result of the receipt.

(2) For the purposes of calculating any CITR in respect of any securities or shares included in the continuing investment for any relevant tax year, the amount subscribed for the securities or shares included in the continuing investment is treated as reduced by the amount of the value received.

(3) For this purpose the "relevant" tax years are—
- (*a*) any tax year ending on or after the anniversary of the investment date immediately before the receipt of value, or
- (*b*) if the value was received on an anniversary of the investment date, any tax year ending on or after that anniversary.

(4) For the purposes of this section "an amount of insignificant value" means an amount of value which—
- (*a*) is not more than £1,000, or
- (*b*) if it is more than £1,000, is insignificant in relation to the amount subscribed by the investor for the securities or shares included in the continuing investment.

[(5) This section is subject to section 368 (value received if there is more than one investment).][1]
Commentary—*Simon's Taxes* **E3.646**.
Derivation—FA 2002 Sch 16 para 38.
HMRC Manuals—Community Investment Tax Relief Manual CITM7080 (value received – shares or securities).

Amendments—[1]   Sub-s (5) inserted by CTA 2010 s 1177, Sch 1 para 519. CTA 2010 has effect for corporation tax purposes for accounting periods ending on or after 1 April 2010, and for income and capital gains tax purposes for the tax year 2010–11 and subsequent tax years.

370 Receipts of value by or from connected persons

In sections 363 to 369, if the context permits, references to the investor or the CDFI include references to any person who at any time in the 6 year period relating to the investment is connected with the investor or, as the case may be, the CDFI, whether or not the person is connected at the material time.

Commentary—Simon's Taxes **E3.644**.
Derivation—FA 2002 Sch 16 para 39.
HMRC Manuals—Community Investment Tax Relief Manual CITM7140 (receipt of value by and from connected persons).

CITR not due

371 CITR subsequently found not to have been due

If any CITR has been obtained which is subsequently found not to have been due, the CITR must be withdrawn.

Manner of withdrawal or reduction

372 Manner of withdrawal or reduction of CITR

(1) This section applies if any CITR has been obtained which falls to be withdrawn or reduced under this Chapter.

(2) The CITR must be withdrawn or reduced by making an assessment to income tax for the tax year for which the CITR was obtained.

(3) No assessment may be made under subsection (2) because of any event occurring after the death of the investor.

[(4) An assessment under this paragraph may be made at any time not more than 6 years after the end of the tax year for which the relief was obtained.

(5) Subsection (4) is without prejudice to section 36(1A) of TMA 1970 (loss of tax brought about deliberately etc).][1]

Commentary—Simon's Taxes **E3.640**.
Derivation—FA 2002 Sch 16 para 27.
HMRC Manuals—Community Investment Tax Relief Manual CITM7005 (manner of withdrawal).
Amendments—[1]   Sub-ss (4), (5) inserted by FA 2008 s 118, Sch 39 paras 54, 60 with effect from 1 April 2010 (by virtue of SI 2009/403 art 2(2)), subject to transitional provisions in SI 2009/403 art 10(2) (where art 10 applies, the appointed day is 1 April 2012).

CHAPTER 7

SUPPLEMENTARY AND GENERAL

[Alternative finance arrangements

372A Meaning of "loan" and "interest"

(1) In this Part and regulations made under Chapter 2 of this Part—
    (a) references to a "loan" include references to alternative finance arrangements, and
    (b) references to "interest" include references to alternative finance return.

(2) In subsection (1)—
    "alternative finance arrangements" means arrangements to which any of the following applies—
        (a) section 564C (purchase and resale arrangements),
        (b) section 564E (deposit arrangements), and
        (c) section 564F (profit share agency arrangements), and
    "alternative finance return" has the meaning given by section 564I and 564L(1) and (2).

(3) Subsection (1) needs to be read with—
    (a) section 372B, in the case of arrangements to which section 564C applies,
    (b) section 372C, in the case of arrangements to which section 564E applies, and
    (c) section 372D, in the case of arrangements to which section 564F applies.][1]

Amendments—[1]   Section and preceding cross-head inserted by TIOPA 2010 s 365, Sch 2 paras 50, 51. TIOPA 2010 has effect for corporation tax purposes for accounting periods ending on or after 1 April 2010, for income and capital gains tax purposes for the tax year 2010–11 and subsequent tax years, and for petroleum revenue tax purposes for chargeable periods beginning on or after 1 July 2010.

[372B Purchase and resale arrangements

(1) This section applies if, under arrangements to which section 564C applies, a person ("the first purchaser") purchases an asset that is sold to another person ("the second purchaser").

(2) This Part and regulations made under Chapter 2 of this Part have effect in relation to the arrangements in accordance with subsections (3) to (9).

(3) The first purchaser is treated as making a loan to the second purchaser.

(4) The amount of the loan is treated as being equal to the first purchase price.

(5) If the arrangements provide that the first purchaser will transfer ownership of the asset to the second purchaser in instalments—

  (a) references to the loan being drawn down over a period of time include references to the asset being transferred to the second purchaser in instalments,

  (b) references to the date on which the first amount of the loan is drawn down include references to the date on which the first instalment is transferred to the second purchaser, and

  (c) references to the amount drawn down at a given date include references to the value of the instalments transferred at that date.

(6) In calculating the amount of capital outstanding on the loan, each payment of the second purchase price (or part of the second purchase price), as reduced by any amount of alternative finance return included within each payment, is treated as repayment of the loan capital.

(7) References to the beneficial owner of the loan include references to the person beneficially entitled to payment of the second purchase price.

(8) References to the disposal of the whole or any part of the loan include references to the disposal of the right to receive payment of the whole or any part of the outstanding second purchase price.

(9) If arrangements to which section 564C applies are, as a result of this section, qualifying investments under Chapter 3 of this Part, paragraph (f) of section 366(1) is to be ignored in relation to the arrangements concerned.

(10) In this section "the first purchase price" and "the second purchase price" have the same meaning as in section 564C.][1]

HMRC Manuals—CFM44060 (purchase and resale arrangements: tax treatment).

Amendments—[1]   Section inserted by TIOPA 2010 s 365, Sch 2 paras 50, 52. TIOPA 2010 has effect for corporation tax purposes for accounting periods ending on or after 1 April 2010, for income and capital gains tax purposes for the tax year 2010–11 and subsequent tax years, and for petroleum revenue tax purposes for chargeable periods beginning on or after 1 July 2010.

[372C Deposit arrangements

(1) This section applies if, under arrangements to which section 564E applies, a person ("the depositor") deposits money with a financial institution.

(2) This Part and regulations made under Chapter 2 of this Part have effect in relation to the arrangements in accordance with subsections (3) to (9).

(3) The depositor is treated as making a loan to the financial institution.

(4) The amount of the loan is treated as being equal to the money deposited under the arrangements.

(5) If the arrangements provide that the depositor will deposit a sum of money with the financial institution in instalments—

  (a) references to the loan being drawn down over a period of time include references to the depositor depositing a sum of money with the financial institution in instalments,

  (b) references to the date on which the first amount of the loan is drawn down include references to the date on which the first instalment is deposited with the financial institution, and

  (c) references to the amount drawn down at a given date include references to the value of the instalments deposited with the financial institution at that date.

(6) The capital outstanding on the loan is treated as being equal to the balance of the repayable deposit.

(7) References to any repayment of the loan include references to any repayment of the deposit.

(8) References to the beneficial owner of the loan include references to the person beneficially entitled to repayment of the deposit.

(9) References to the disposal of the whole or any part of the loan include references to the disposal of the right to receive repayment of the whole or any part of the deposit.

(10) In this section "financial institution" has the same meaning as in Part 10A (see section 564B).][1]

Amendments—[1]   Section inserted by TIOPA 2010 s 365, Sch 2 paras 50, 53. TIOPA 2010 has effect for corporation tax purposes for accounting periods ending on or after 1 April 2010, for income and capital gains tax purposes for the tax year 2010–11 and subsequent tax years, and for petroleum revenue tax purposes for chargeable periods beginning on or after 1 July 2010.

[372D Profit share agency arrangements

(1) This section applies if, under arrangements to which section 564F applies, a person ("the principal") appoints a financial institution as agent.

(2) This Part and regulations made under Chapter 2 of this Part have effect in relation to the arrangements in accordance with subsections (3) to (9).

(3) The principal is treated as making a loan to the agent.

(4) The amount of the loan is treated as being equal to the money provided by the principal to the agent under the arrangements.

(5) If the arrangements provide that the principal will provide a sum of money to the agent in instalments—

  (a) references to the loan being drawn down over a period of time include references to the principal providing a sum of money to the agent in instalments, (*b*) references to the date on which the first amount of the loan is drawn down include references to the date on which the first instalment is provided to the agent, and

   (*c*) references to the amount drawn down at a given date include references to the value of the instalments provided to the agent at that date.

(6) The capital outstanding on the loan is treated as being equal to the balance of the repayable money provided to the agent.

(7) References to any repayment of the loan include references to any repayment of the money provided to the agent.

(8) References to the beneficial owner of the loan include references to the person beneficially entitled to repayment of the money provided to the agent.

(9) References to the disposal of the whole or any part of the loan include references to the disposal of the right to receive repayment of the whole or any part of the money provided to the agent.

(10) In subsection (1) "financial institution" has the same meaning as in Part 10A (see section 564B).][1]

Commentary—*Simon's Taxes* **A1.303**.

Amendments—[1]   Section inserted by TIOPA 2010 s 365, Sch 2 paras 50, 54. TIOPA 2010 has effect for corporation tax purposes for accounting periods ending on or after 1 April 2010, for income and capital gains tax purposes for the tax year 2010–11 and subsequent tax years, and for petroleum revenue tax purposes for chargeable periods beginning on or after 1 July 2010.

Miscellaneous

373 Information to be provided by the investor

(1) If—

   (*a*) the investor has obtained CITR in respect of the investment, and

   (*b*) an event occurs because of which CITR attributable to the investment [in respect of][1] any tax year falls to be withdrawn or reduced by virtue of section 360, 361, 362 or 364,

the investor must give an officer of Revenue and Customs a notice containing particulars of the event.

(2) Subject to subsection (3), a notice under subsection (1) must be given not later than the normal self-assessment filing date for the tax year in which the event occurred.

(3) If—

   (*a*) the investor is required to give a notice as a result of the receipt of value by a person connected with the investor (see section 370), and

   (*b*) the end of the period of 60 days beginning when the investor comes to know of that event is later than the final notice date under subsection (2),

the notice must be given before the end of that 60 day period.

Commentary—*Simon's Taxes* **E3.649**.

Derivation—FA 2002 Sch 16 para 42.

HMRC Manuals—Community Investment Tax Relief Manual CITM6150 (information to be provided by the investor).

Amendments—[1]   In sub-s (1)(*b*) words substituted by CTA 2010 s 1177, Sch 1 para 520. CTA 2010 has effect for corporation tax purposes for accounting periods ending on or after 1 April 2010, and for income and capital gains tax purposes for the tax year 2010–11 and subsequent tax years.

374 Disclosure

(1) No obligation as to secrecy or other restriction on the disclosure of information imposed by statute or otherwise prevents the disclosure of information—

   (*a*) by the Secretary of State to an officer of Revenue and Customs for the purpose of assisting Her Majesty's Revenue and Customs to discharge their functions under the Income Tax Acts so far as relating to matters arising under this Part, or

   (*b*) by an officer of Revenue and Customs to the Secretary of State for the purpose of assisting the Secretary of State to discharge the Secretary of State's functions under this Part.

(2) Information obtained by such disclosure is not to be further disclosed except for the purposes of legal proceedings arising out of the functions referred to.

Commentary—*Simon's Taxes* **E3.651**.

Derivation—FA 2002 Sch 16 para 43.

HMRC Manuals—Community Investment Tax Relief Manual CITM6170 (disclosure of information).

375 Nominees

(1) For the purposes of this Part—

   (*a*) loans made by or to, or disposed of by, a nominee for a person are treated as made by or to, or disposed of by, that person, and

   (*b*) securities or shares subscribed for by, issued to, acquired or held by or disposed of by a nominee for a person are treated as subscribed for by, issued to, acquired or held by or disposed of by that person.

(2) For the purposes of subsection (1) references to things done by or to a nominee for a person include things done by or to a bare trustee for a person.

Commentary—*Simon's Taxes* **E3.652**.

Derivation—FA 2002 Sch 16 para 44.

HMRC Manuals—Community Investment Tax Relief Manual CITM6080 (nominees).

376 Application for postponement of tax pending appeal

No application may be made under section 55(3) or (4) of TMA 1970 (application for postponement of payment of tax pending appeal) on the ground that an individual is eligible for CITR unless a claim for the CITR has been duly made by the individual under this Part.

Commentary—*Simon's Taxes* E3.653.
Derivation—FA 2002 Sch 16 para 45.
HMRC Manuals—Community Investment Tax Relief Manual CITM6160 (postponement of tax pending appeal).

377 Identification of securities or shares on a disposal

(1) This section applies for the purpose of identifying the securities or shares disposed of in any case where—

    (*a*) the investor disposes of part of a holding of securities or shares ("the holding"), and

    (*b*) the holding includes securities or shares to which CITR is attributable in respect of one or more tax years that have been held continuously by the investor from the time they were issued until the disposal.

(2) Any disposal by the investor of securities or shares included in the holding which have been acquired by the investor on different days is treated as relating to those acquired on an earlier day rather than to those acquired on a later day.

(3) If there is a disposal by the investor of securities or shares included in the holding which have been acquired by the investor on the same day, any of those securities or shares—

    (*a*) to which CITR is attributable, and

    (*b*) which have been held by the investor continuously from the time they were issued until the time of disposal,

are treated as disposed of after any other securities or shares included in the holding which were acquired by the investor on that day.

(4) For the purposes of this section a holding of securities is any number of securities of a company which—

    (*a*) carry the same rights,

    (*b*) were issued under the same terms, and

    (*c*) are held by the investor in the same capacity.

It does not matter for this purpose that the number of the securities grows or diminishes as securities carrying those rights and issued under those terms are acquired or disposed of.

(5) For the purposes of this section a holding of shares is any number of shares in a company which—

    (*a*) are of the same class, and

    (*b*) are held by the investor in the same capacity.

It does not matter for this purpose that the number of the shares grows or diminishes as shares of that class are acquired or disposed of.

(6) In a case to which section 127 of TCGA 1992 (equation of original shares and new holding) applies, shares comprised in the new holding are to be treated for the purposes of subsections (2) and (3) as acquired when the original shares were acquired.

(7) In subsection (6)—

    (*a*) the reference to section 127 of TCGA 1992 includes a reference to that section as it is applied by virtue of any enactment relating to chargeable gains, and

    (*b*) "original shares" and "new holding" have the same meaning as in section 127 of TCGA 1992 or (as the case may be) that section as applied by virtue of the enactment in question.

Commentary—*Simon's Taxes* E3.654.
Derivation—FA 2002 Sch 16 para 47(1) to (4), (7) and (8).
HMRC Manuals—Community Investment Tax Relief Manual CITM7030 (identification of securities or shares on disposal).

Definitions

378 Meaning of "issue of securities or shares"

(1) In this Part—

    (*a*) references (however expressed) to an issue of securities of any body are to such securities of that body as carry the same rights and are issued under the same terms and on the same day, and

    (*b*) references (however expressed) to an issue of shares in any body are to such shares in that body as are of the same class and issued on the same day.

(2) In this Part references (however expressed) to an issue of securities of or shares in a body to an individual are to such of the securities or shares in an issue of securities of or shares in that body as are issued to that individual in one capacity.

Commentary—*Simon's Taxes* E3.655.
Derivation—FA 2002 Sch 16 para 46.
HMRC Manuals—Community Investment Tax Relief Manual CITM9020 (meaning of 'issue of securities or shares').

379 Meaning of "disposal"

(1) Subject to subsection (2), in this Part "disposal" is read in accordance with TCGA 1992, and related expressions are read accordingly.

(2) An investor is treated as disposing of any securities or shares which but for section 151BC(1) of TCGA 1992 the investor—

    (a) would be treated as exchanging for other securities or shares by virtue of section 136 of that Act, or

    (b) would be so treated but for section 137(1) of that Act (which restricts section 136 to genuine reconstructions).

Commentary—*Simon's Taxes* **E3.655**.
Derivation—FA 2002 Sch 16 para 48.
HMRC Manuals—Community Investment Tax Relief Manual CITM7040 (meaning of 'disposal').

380 Construction of references to being "held continuously"

(1) This section applies if for the purposes of this Part it becomes necessary to determine whether the investor has held the investment (or any part of it) continuously throughout any period.

(2) The investor is not treated as having held the investment (or any part of it) continuously throughout a period if the investor—

    (a) is treated, under any provision of TCGA 1992, as having disposed of and immediately re-acquired the investment (or part) at any time during the period, or

    (b) is treated as having disposed of the investment (or part) at any such time, by virtue of section 379(2).

Commentary—*Simon's Taxes* **E3.655**.
Derivation—FA 2002 Sch 16 para 49.
HMRC Manuals—Community Investment Tax Relief Manual CITM9030 (meaning of 'held continuously').

381 Meaning of "associate"

(1) In this Part "associate", in relation to a person, means—

    (a) any relative or partner of that person,

    (b) the trustee or trustees of any settlement in relation to which that person, or any relative of that person (living or dead), is or was a settlor, and

    (c) if that person has an interest in any shares or obligations of a company which are subject to any trust or are part of the estate of a deceased person—

        (i) the trustee or trustees of the settlement concerned or, as the case may be, the personal representatives of the deceased, and

        (ii) if that person is a company, any other company which has an interest in those shares or obligations.

(2) In subsection (1)(a) and (b) "relative" means spouse or civil partner, ancestor or lineal descendant.

(3) In subsection (1)(b) "settlor" and "settlement" have the same meaning as in Chapter 5 of Part 5 of ITTOIA 2005 (see section 620 of that Act).

Commentary—*Simon's Taxes* **E3.655**.
Derivation—FA 2002 Sch 16 para 50.
HMRC Manuals—Community Investment Tax Relief Manual CITM9010 (meaning of 'associate').

382 Minor definitions etc

(1) In this Part—

    "body" includes an unincorporated association, and

    "bonus shares" means shares which are issued otherwise than for payment (whether in cash or otherwise).

(2) For the purposes of this Part shares in a company are not treated as being of the same class unless they would be so treated if dealt in on [a recognised stock exchange][1].

(3) For the purposes of this Part the market value at any time of any asset is the price which it might reasonably be expected to fetch on a sale at that time in the open market free from any interest or right which exists by way of security in or over it.

(4) In this Part—

    (a) references to CITR obtained by the investor in respect of any investment (or part of an investment) include references to CITR obtained by the investor in respect of that investment (or part) at any time after the investor has disposed of it, and

    (b) references to the withdrawal or reduction of CITR obtained by the investor in respect of the investment (or any part of it) include references to the withdrawal or reduction of CITR obtained in respect of that investment (or part) at any such time.

(5) In the case of any condition that cannot be met until a future date—

    (a) references in this Part to a condition being met for the time being are to nothing having occurred to prevent its being met, and

    (b) references to its continuing to be met are to nothing occurring to prevent its being met.

Commentary—*Simon's Taxes* **E3.655**.

Amendments—[1]   Words in sub-s (2) substituted by FA 2007 s 109, Sch 26 para 12(1), (8) with effect from 19 July 2007.

PART 8
OTHER RELIEFS

CHAPTER 1

The relief: introduction

383 Relief for interest payments

(1) A person who pays interest in a tax year is entitled to relief for the tax year for the interest if—

    (*a*) the loan on which the interest is payable is a loan to which a provision specified in subsection (2) applies,

    (*b*) the interest is eligible for relief in accordance with this Chapter, and

    (*c*) the person makes a claim.

(2) The provisions are—

    (*a*) section 388 (loan to buy plant or machinery for partnership use),

    (*b*) section 390 (loan to buy plant or machinery for employment use),

    (*c*) section 392 (loan to buy interest in close company [etc][3]),

    (*d*) section 396 (loan to buy interest in employee-controlled company),

    (*e*) section 398 (loan to invest in partnership),

    (*f*) section 401 (loan to invest in co-operative), and

    (*g*) section 403 (loan to pay inheritance tax).

(3) The amount of the relief given under subsection (1) is equal to the amount of the interest eligible for relief.

(4) The relief is given by deducting that amount in calculating the person's net income for the tax year in which the interest is paid (see Step 2 of the calculation in section 23).

(5) This section is subject to—

    (*a*) section 384 (general restrictions on relief under this Chapter),

    [(*aa*) section 384B (restriction on relief where cash basis applies),][2]

    (*b*) section 385 (general provisions about loans),

    (*c*) section 386 (loans partly meeting requirements),

    (*d*) section 387 (exclusion of double relief etc), and

    (*e*) section 405 (carry back and forward of relief for interest on loans within section 403).

(6) See also [section 564O][1] (under which this Chapter applies as if arrangements [to which section 564C applies][1] were loans and alternative finance return were interest).

Commentary—*Simon's Taxes* **E1.820, B2.436.**

Derivation—TA 1988 ss 353, 359, 360, 361, 362 and 364.

HMRC Manuals—Savings and Investment Manual, SAIM10010 (relief for interest payments - introduction).

Amendments—[1]   In sub-s (6), words substituted by TIOPA 2010 s 501, Sch 8 paras 219, 222. TIOPA 2010 has effect for corporation tax purposes for accounting periods ending on or after 1 April 2010, for income and capital gains tax purposes for the tax year 2010–11 and subsequent tax years, and for petroleum revenue tax purposes for chargeable periods beginning on or after 1 July 2010.

[2]   Sub-s (5)(*aa*) inserted by FA 2013 s 17 Sch 4 para 55(1), (2) with effect for the tax year 2013–14 and subsequent tax years, subject to the provisions of FA 2013 Sch 4 para 57 in relation to barristers and advocates.

[3]   In sub-s (2)(*c*) word inserted by FA 2014 s 13(1), (4)(*a*) with effect in relation to interest paid in the tax year 2014–15 or in any subsequent tax year.

384 General restrictions on relief under Chapter

(1) Relief is not to be given under this Chapter for interest on a debt incurred—

    (*a*) by overdrawing an account, or

    (*b*) by debiting the account of any person as the holder of a credit card or under similar arrangements.

(2) If [the interest paid on a loan in a tax year exceeds a reasonable commercial amount of interest on the loan for the relevant period][1] relief is not to be given under this Chapter for so much of the interest as represents the excess.

[(3) The relevant period is the tax year or, if the loan exists for part only of the tax year, the part of the tax year for which the loan exists.

(4) A reasonable commercial amount of interest on the loan for the relevant period is an amount which, together with any interest paid before that period (other than unrelieved interest), represents a reasonable commercial rate of interest on the loan from the date it was made to the end of that period.

(5) "Unrelieved interest" means interest which because of subsection (2) is not eligible for relief under this Chapter.][1]

Commentary—*Simon's Taxes* **E1.820.**

Derivation—TA 1988 s 353(3).

HMRC Manuals—Savings and Investment Manual SAIM10020 (general conditions for relief for interest payments).

SAIM10060-10090 (interest paid in excess of a reasonable commercial rate, with examples).

ITA 2007

Amendments—[1]   In sub-s (2), words substituted, and sub-ss (3)–(5) inserted, by FA 2008 s 62, Sch 22 para 21 with effect in relation to interest paid on or after 9 October 2007; but in relation to interest paid in the period beginning with that date and ending with 5 April 2008, these amendments have effect as if the references in s 384(2) and (3) to a tax year were to that period.

[384A Restriction on relief where arrangements minimise risk to borrower

(1) Relief is not to be given under this Chapter for interest paid by a person on a loan if—

(a) the loan is made to the person ("the borrower") as part of arrangements which appear very likely to produce a post-tax advantage, and

(b) the arrangements seem to have been designed to reduce any income tax or capital gains tax to which the borrower (or any person whose circumstances are like those of the borrower) would be liable apart from the arrangements.

(2) Arrangements "appear very likely" to produce a post-tax advantage if (and only if) it would be reasonable to assume from either or both of—

(a) the likely effect of the arrangements, and

(b) the circumstances in which the arrangements, or any parts of the arrangements, are entered into or effected,

that there is no risk, or only an insignificant risk, that they will not produce a post-tax advantage.

(3) "Produce a post-tax advantage" means give rise to a sum or sums—

(a) payable to the borrower or a person connected with the borrower, or

(b) payable to any other person for the benefit of the borrower or a person connected with the borrower,

of an amount (or aggregate amount) which, after making the appropriate tax adjustments, is equal to or greater than the relevant amount.

(4) "The relevant amount" is the aggregate of—

(a) the amount required to meet the borrower's obligations in respect of the loan, and

(b) any amount which is used by the borrower in the same way as that which entitles the borrower to relief under this Chapter in respect of the loan and is not money lent to the borrower under any loan.

(5) If, with a view to securing that the condition in subsection (1)(a) is not met, the arrangements make provision for securing that, in all or any circumstances in which they do not produce a post-tax advantage, they will produce a broadly compensatory amount, the arrangements are to be regarded for the purposes of subsection (2) as making provision for securing the production of a post-tax advantage in those circumstances.

(6) "Produce a broadly compensatory amount" means give rise to a sum or sums payable as mentioned in subsection (3) of an amount (or aggregate amount) which, after making the appropriate tax adjustments, is not significantly less than the relevant amount.

(7) For the purposes of subsections (3) and (6) causing the value of an asset to be obtainable, directly or indirectly, by a person is to be treated as equivalent to giving rise to a sum payable to the person of an amount equal to that value.

(8) To make the appropriate tax adjustments for the purpose of subsection (3) or (6)—

(a) if A exceeds B, deduct the amount of the excess from the amount (or aggregate amount), and

(b) if B exceeds A, add the amount of the excess to the amount (or aggregate amount).

(9) For the purposes of subsection (8)—

A is the amount of any income tax, any capital gains tax and any tax under the law of a territory outside the United Kingdom to which the borrower is liable in consequence of the arrangements, and

B is the amount by which the borrower's liability to income tax and capital gains tax is (or apart from subsection (1) would be) reduced in consequence of the arrangements.

(10) Arrangements seem to have been designed to reduce any income tax or capital gains tax to which the borrower (or any person whose circumstances are like those of the borrower) would be liable apart from the arrangements if (and only if) it would be reasonable to assume from either or both of—

(a) the likely effect of the arrangements, and

(b) the circumstances in which the arrangements, or any parts of the arrangements, are entered into or effected,

that the arrangements, or any parts of the arrangements, are designed to do so.

(11) In this section "arrangements" means arrangements consisting of any number of agreements, understandings, schemes, transactions or other arrangements (whether or not legally enforceable); but in subsections (1)(a), (2), (5) and (9) the references to arrangements also include any related transactions.

(12) In subsection (11) "related transactions" means transactions in the case of which it is reasonable to assume from either or both of—

(a) the likely effect of the transactions, and

(b) the circumstances in which the transactions are entered into or effected,

that the transactions would not have been entered into or effected independently of the arrangements.

(13) Transactions are not prevented from being related transactions just because the transactions—

    (*a*) are not between the same parties, or

    (*b*) are not between parties to the arrangements.][1]

Commentary—*Simon's Taxes* **E1.820**.
HMRC Manuals—Savings and Investment Manual, SAIM10100 (arrangements minimising risk to borrower).
SAIM10110 (arrangements minimising risk to borrower: definitions).
SAIM10130 (arrangements minimising risk to borrower: examples).
Amendments—[1]   This section inserted by FA 2009 s 61, Sch 30 para 1 with effect in relation to interest paid on or after 19 March 2009.

[384B Restriction on relief where cash basis applies

(1) Relief is not to be given under this Chapter for a tax year for interest paid by a person on a relevant loan if the partnership to which the loan relates has made an election under section 25A of ITTOIA 2005 (cash basis for small businesses) for the tax year [or if the profits of a UK property business or overseas property business carried on by the partnership are calculated on the cash basis for the tax year (see section 271D of ITTOIA 2005)][2].

(2) A loan is a "relevant loan" if—

    (*a*) it is a loan to which section 388 applies (loan to buy plant or machinery for partnership use), or

    (*b*) it is a loan to which section 398 applies (loan to invest in partnership) and which is not used for purchasing a share in a partnership.][1]

Commentary—*Simon's Taxes* **E1.826, B2.436, E1.830**.
Amendments—[1]   Section 384B inserted by FA 2013 s 17, Sch 4 para 55(1), (3) with effect for the tax year 2013–14 and subsequent tax years, subject to the provisions of FA 2013 Sch 4 para 57 in relation to barristers and advocates.
[2]   In sub-s (1), words inserted by F(No 2)A 2017 s 16, Sch 2 para 60, 63 with effect for the tax year 2017–18 and subsequent tax years, subject to transitional provisions in F(No 2)A 2017 Sch 2 para 64.

385 General provisions about loans

(1) References in this Chapter to a loan being used or used in any way—

    (*a*) are references to the money lent being applied or, as the case may be, applied in that way, and

    (*b*) except in section 403 include references to a loan being used to meet expenditure already incurred or, as the case may be, already incurred on such a use.

(2) Sections 392, 396, 398, 401 and 403 apply to a loan only if it is made—

    (*a*) in connection with the use of money, and

    (*b*) on the occasion of its use or within what is in the circumstances a reasonable time from its use.

(3) Those sections apply to a loan only if the loan is used as mentioned in those sections without first having been used for another purpose.

(4) For the purposes of this Chapter the giving of credit for any money due from the purchaser under a sale is treated as the making of a loan used by the purchaser in making the purchase.

Commentary—*Simon's Taxes* **E1.820**.
Derivation—TA 1988 ss 359–362, 364 and 367.
HMRC Manuals—Savings and Investment Manual SAIM10020 (timing and use of the loan).

386 Loans partly meeting requirements

(1) If, at the time a loan ("the mixed loan") is used, only part of the mixed loan is a loan to which any of the provisions specified in section 383(2) apply, for the purposes of this Chapter that part ("the qualifying part") is treated as a loan to which the provision in question applies.

(2) Accordingly, the corresponding proportion of the interest on the mixed loan is eligible for relief.

(3) If a mixed loan is partly repaid, for the purposes of this Chapter the corresponding proportion of the repayment is treated as repaying the qualifying part (but see section 406(5)).

(4) In this section "the corresponding proportion" means the proportion that the qualifying part bears to the whole of the mixed loan at the time the mixed loan is used.

Commentary—*Simon's Taxes* **E1.820**.
HMRC Manuals—Savings and Investment Manual SAIM10020 (mixed loan).

387 Exclusion of double relief etc

(1) Interest for which relief is given under this Chapter is not allowable as a deduction for any other income tax purposes.

(2) No relief is given under this Chapter for any tax year for the payment of any interest taken into account in calculating the profits of—

    (*a*) any trade, profession or vocation,

    (*b*) any UK property business, or

    (*c*) any overseas property business.

(3) If interest is so taken into account, no relief is given under this Chapter for any relevant tax year for other interest on the same debt or liability.

(4) A tax year is a relevant one if the interest has been taken into account in calculating the profits of the trade, profession, vocation or business of the tax year.

(5) For the purposes of subsection (3) all interest which—

(*a*) is capable of being taken into account in calculating the profits of a trade, profession, vocation or business, and

(*b*) is payable by the same person on money advanced to the person on current account,

is treated as interest on the same debt.

(6) It does not matter whether the money is advanced—

(*a*) on one or more accounts, or

(*b*) by the same or separate banks or other persons.

(7) The reference in subsections (2) to (4) to interest taken into account is a reference to interest allowed as a deduction in an assessment which can no longer be varied (whether on appeal or otherwise).

Commentary—*Simon's Taxes* **E1.823, E1.821.**
HMRC Manuals—Savings and Investment Manual SAIM10020 (exclusion of double relief).

Loans for plant or machinery

388 Loan to buy plant or machinery for partnership use

(1) This section applies to a loan that is used for capital expenditure on the provision of plant or machinery to which subsection (2) applies.

(2) This subsection applies to plant or machinery if—

(*a*) it is in use for the purposes of a trade, profession or ordinary property business carried on by a partnership, and

(*b*) the partnership is entitled to a capital allowance or liable to a balancing charge in respect of it under section 264 of CAA 2001 (partnership using property of a partner) for the period of account in which the interest is paid.

(3) A partnership is treated as entitled to a capital allowance or liable to a balancing charge in respect of plant or machinery for a period of account ("the later period") for the purposes of subsection (2)(*b*) if—

(*a*) it has been so entitled or liable for a previous period of account, and

(*b*) no disposal value has been brought into account in respect of it in the later period or any earlier period of account.

(4) In this section and sections 389 and 390—

"capital expenditure" has the meaning given in section 4 of CAA 2001,

"period of account" has the same meaning as in that Act (see section 6(2) to (6) of that Act), and

"ordinary property business" has the same meaning as in Part 2 of that Act (see section 16 of that Act).

Commentary—*Simon's Taxes* **E1.826.**
HMRC Manuals—Savings and Investment Manual SAIM10200 (loans to buy plant or machinery).

389 Eligibility requirements for interest on loans within section 388

(1) Interest on a loan within section 388(1) is eligible for relief if conditions A and B are met.

(2) Condition A is that the interest is paid by an individual who is a member of the partnership referred to in section 388(2).

(3) Condition B is that the interest falls due and payable not later than 3 years after the end of the period of account in which the loan was made.

(4) If the machinery or plant is in use partly for the purposes of the trade, profession or ordinary property business carried on by the partnership referred to in section 388(2) ("trade purposes") and partly for other purposes, only part of the interest is eligible for relief.

(5) That part is such part as it is just and reasonable to attribute to trade purposes, having regard to all the relevant circumstances and, in particular, to the extent of the use for other purposes.

Commentary—*Simon's Taxes* **E1.826.**
HMRC Manuals—Savings and Investment Manual SAIM10200 (loans to buy plant or machinery).

390 Loan to buy plant or machinery for employment use

(1) This section applies to a loan that is used for capital expenditure on the provision of plant or machinery to which subsection (2) applies.

(2) This subsection applies to plant or machinery if—

(*a*) it is in use for the purposes of an office or employment held by an individual in the tax year,

(*b*) the plant or machinery belongs to the individual, and

(*c*) the individual is entitled to a capital allowance or liable to a balancing charge in respect of it under Part 2 of CAA 2001 for the tax year.

(3) An individual is treated as entitled to a capital allowance or liable to a balancing charge in respect of plant or machinery for a tax year ("the later year") for the purposes of subsection (2)(*c*) if—

(*a*) the individual has been so entitled or liable for a previous tax year, and

(*b*) no disposal value has been brought into account in respect of it in the later year or any earlier year.

(4) An individual is also treated as so entitled or liable for the purposes of this section if the individual would be so entitled or liable but for a contribution made by the individual's employer.

Commentary—*Simon's Taxes* **E1.826.**

HMRC Manuals—Savings and Investment Manual SAIM10200 (conditions for relief).

391 Eligibility requirements for interest on loans within section 390

(1) Interest on a loan within section 390(1) is eligible for relief if conditions A and B are met.

(2) Condition A is that the interest is paid by the individual referred to in section 390(2).

(3) Condition B is that the interest falls due and payable not later than 3 years after the end of the tax year in which the loan was made.

(4) If the machinery or plant is in use partly for the purposes of the office or employment referred to in section 390(2) ("employment purposes") and partly for other purposes, only part of the interest is eligible for relief.

(5) That part is such part as it is just and reasonable to attribute to employment purposes having regard to all the relevant circumstances and, in particular, to the extent of the use for other purposes.

Commentary—*Simon's Taxes* E1.826.
Derivation—TA 1988 s 359(3) and (4).
HMRC Manuals—Savings and Investment Manual SAIM10200 (timing of interest payment).

Loans for interests in close companies [etc]

392 Loan to buy interest in close company [etc][2]

(1) This section applies to a loan to an individual that is used in one or more of the ways specified in subsection (2).

(2) The ways are—

    (*a*) acquiring any part of the ordinary share capital of a close company that is not a close investment-holding company,

    (*b*) lending to such a company money which is used wholly and exclusively—

        (i) for the purposes of the business of the company, or

        (ii) for the purposes of the business of any associated company of the company which is also a close company that is not a close investment-holding company, or

    (*c*) repaying another loan to which this section applies.

(3) Subsection (2)(*a*) does not apply if at any time the individual by whom the shares are acquired or that individual's spouse or civil partner—

    (*a*) makes a claim for relief in respect of them under Part 5 of this Act or, in the case of shares issued before 6 April 2007, Chapter 3 of Part 7 of ICTA (enterprise investment scheme), or

    (*b*) makes a claim in respect of them under Schedule 5B to TCGA 1992 (enterprise investment scheme: reinvestment).

[(3A) Subsection (2) does not apply if at any time the individual by whom the shares are acquired or the money is lent, or that individual's spouse or civil partner, makes—

    (*a*) a claim under Part 5B of this Act for relief in respect of the amount invested in acquiring the shares or (as the case may be) in return for the debentures in respect of the money lent, or

    (*b*) a claim in respect of the amount under Schedule 8B to TCGA 1992 (hold-over relief for gains re-invested in social enterprises).

(3B) For the purposes of subsection (3A)(a) "debenture" includes any instrument creating or acknowledging indebtedness.][3]

(4) In this section and section 393—

    ["close company" includes a company which—

        (*a*) is resident in an EEA state other than the United Kingdom, and

        (*b*) if it were UK resident, would be a close company,][2]

    "close investment-holding company" [is to be read in accordance with [section 393A][2]][1], and "associated company" has the meaning given by [section 449 of CTA 2010][1].

(5) This section is subject to section 411 (ineligibility of interest where business is occupation of commercial woodlands).

Commentary—*Simon's Taxes* E1.827.
Derivation—TA 1988 s 360(1), (3A) and (4).
HMRC Manuals—Savings and Investment Manual SAIM10210 (interest in a close company).
Modifications—ITA 2007 Sch 2 para 91 (sub-s (3)(*a*) above does not apply if the shares were acquired before 14 March 1989).
ITA 2007 Sch 2 para 92 (sub-s (3)(*b*) above does not apply if the shares were acquired before 6 April 1989).
Amendments—[1] In sub-s (4), in definitions of "close investment-holding company", and "associated company", words substituted by CTA 2010 s 1177, Sch 1 para 521. CTA 2010 has effect for corporation tax purposes for accounting periods ending on or after 1 April 2010, and for income and capital gains tax purposes for the tax year 2010–11 and subsequent tax years.
[2] In preceding cross-heading, and in heading to s 392, word inserted, in sub-s (4), definition of "close company" inserted, and in definition of "close investment-holding company" words substituted, by FA 2014 s 13(1), (2), (4)(*b*), (*c*) with effect in relation to interest paid in the tax year 2014–15 or any subsequent tax year.
[3] Sub-ss (3A), (3B) inserted by FA 2014 s 57, Sch 11 paras 3, 10 with effect from 17 July 2014.
Prospective amendments—In sub-s (4), in para (*a*) of the definition of "close company", words "other than the United Kingdom" to be repealed by the Taxes (Amendments) (EU Exit) Regulations, SI 2019/689 reg 15(1), (3) with effect from Implementation Period completion day (see EU(WA)A 2020 Sch 5 para 1(1)).

393 Eligibility requirements for interest on loans within section 392

(1) Interest on a loan within section 392(1) to an individual is eligible for relief only if—

    (*a*) when the interest is paid the company is not a close investment-holding company, and

    (*b*) the capital recovery condition and either the full-time working conditions or the material interest conditions are met.

(2) The capital recovery condition is that in the period from the use of the loan to the payment of the interest the individual has not recovered any capital from the company, apart from any amount taken into account under section 406(2) (recovered capital that is treated as a repayment of the loan).

(3) The full-time working conditions are that—

    (*a*) when the interest is paid the individual holds part of the ordinary share capital of the company, and

    (*b*) in the period from the use of the loan to the payment of the interest the greater part of the individual's time has been spent in the actual management or conduct of the company or of an associated company of the company.

(4) The material interest conditions are that—

    (*a*) when the interest is paid the individual has a material interest in the company (see section 394), and

    (*b*) if the company exists wholly or mainly for the purpose of holding investments or other property, either—

       (i) the condition in subsection (3)(*b*) is met, or

       (ii) no property held by the company is used as a residence by the individual.

Commentary—*Simon's Taxes* **E1.827.**
Derivation—TA 1988 s 360(1), (2).
HMRC Manuals—Savings and Investment Manual SAIM10220 (interest in a close company: eligibility requirements).

[393A Close investment-holding companies

(1) For the purposes of sections 392 and 393, a close company ("the candidate company") is a close investment-holding company in an accounting period unless throughout the period it exists wholly or mainly for one or more of the permitted purposes set out in subsection (2).

    There is an exception to this rule in subsection (5).

(2) The candidate company exists for a permitted purpose so far as it exists—

    (*a*) for the purpose of carrying on a trade or trades on a commercial basis,

    (*b*) for the purpose of making investments in land, or estates or interests in land, in cases where the land is, or is intended to be, let commercially (see subsection (3)),

    (*c*) for the purpose of holding shares in and securities of, or making loans to, one or more companies each of which—

       (i) is a qualifying company, or

       (ii) falls within subsection (4),

    (*d*) for the purpose of co-ordinating the administration of two or more qualifying companies,

    (*e*) for the purpose of the making of investments as mentioned in paragraph (*b*)—

       (i) by one or more qualifying companies, or

       (ii) by a company which has control of the candidate company, or

    (*f*) for the purpose of a trade or trades carried on on a commercial basis—

       (i) by one or more qualifying companies, or

       (ii) by a company which has control of the candidate company.

(3) For the purposes of subsection (2)(*b*), any letting of land is taken to be commercial unless the land is let to—

    (*a*) a person connected with the candidate company ("a connected person"), or

    (*b*) a person who is—

       (i) the spouse or civil partner of a connected person,

       (ii) a relative of a connected person, or the spouse or civil partner of a relative of a connected person,

       (iii) the relative of the spouse or civil partner of a connected person, or

       (iv) the spouse or civil partner of a relative of a spouse or civil partner of the connected person.

(4) A company falls within this subsection (see subsection (2)(*c*)(ii)) if—

    (*a*) it is under the control of the candidate company or of a company which has control of the candidate company, and

    (*b*) it exists wholly or mainly for the purpose of holding shares in or securities of, or of making loans to, one or more qualifying companies.

(5) If a company is wound up and was not a close investment-holding company in the accounting period that ends (by virtue of section 12(2) of CTA 2009) immediately before the winding up starts, the company is not treated for the purposes of sections 392 and 393 as being a close investment-holding company in the subsequent accounting period.

(6) In this section "qualifying company" means a company which—

(*a*) is under the control of the candidate company or of a company which has control of the candidate company, and

(*b*) exists wholly or mainly for either or both of the purposes mentioned in subsection (2)(*a*) and (*b*).

(7) In this section—

"accounting period" has the meaning given by section 1119 of CTA 2010,

"close company" includes a company which—

(*a*) is resident in an EEA state other than the United Kingdom, and

(*b*) if it were UK resident, would be a close company,

"control" has the meaning given by section 450 of CTA 2010, and

"relative" means brother, sister, ancestor or lineal descendant.][1]

Commentary—*Simon's Taxes* **E1.827**.
Amendments—[1]   Section 393A inserted by FA 2014 s 13(1), (3) with effect in relation to interest paid in the tax year 2014–15 or any subsequent tax year.

Prospective amendments—In sub-s (7), in para (*a*) of the definition of "close company", words "other than the United Kingdom" to be repealed by the Taxes (Amendments) (EU Exit) Regulations, SI 2019/689 reg 15(1), (4) with effect from Implementation Period completion day (see EU(WA)A 2020 Sch 5 para 1(1)).

394 Meaning of "material interest" in section 393

(1) For the purposes of section 393(4)(*a*) an individual has a material interest in a company if a relevant person meets condition A or B.

(2) In this section "relevant person" means—

(*a*) the individual, either alone or with one or more associates (see section 395), or

(*b*) any associate of the individual with or without such other associates.

(3) Condition A is that the relevant person is the beneficial owner of, or able directly or indirectly to control, more than 5% of the ordinary share capital of the company.

(4) Condition B is that the relevant person possesses, or is entitled to acquire, such rights as would, in the event of the winding up of the company or in any other circumstances, give an entitlement to receive more than 5% of the assets which would then be available for distribution among the participators.

(5) In this section—

"control" [is to be read in accordance with sections 450 and 451 of CTA 2010][1], and

"participator" has the meaning given by [section 454 of CTA 2010][1].

Commentary—*Simon's Taxes* **E1.827**.
Derivation—TA 1988 s 360A(1).
HMRC Manuals—Savings and Investment Manual SAIM10240 (meaning of "material interest").
Amendments—[1]   In sub-s (5), in definitions of "control" and "participator", words substituted by CTA 2010 s 1177, Sch 1 para 522. CTA 2010 has effect for corporation tax purposes for accounting periods ending on or after 1 April 2010, and for income and capital gains tax purposes for the tax year 2010–11 and subsequent tax years.

395 Meaning of "associate" in section 394

(1) For the purposes of determining under section 394 whether an individual has a material interest in a company, in that section "associate", in relation to that individual and company, means—

(*a*) a relative or partner of the individual,

(*b*) the trustees of a settlement in relation to which—

(i) the individual is a settlor, or

(ii) a relative of the individual (living or dead) is or was a settlor,

(*c*) if the individual is interested in any shares or obligations of the company which are subject to a trust, the trustees of the settlement, and

(*d*) if the individual is interested in any shares or obligations of the company which are part of the estate of a deceased person, the personal representatives.

(2) But, despite subsection (1)(*c*), the trustees of an employee benefit trust are not regarded for the purposes of section 394 as the associates of an individual merely because the individual has an interest in shares or obligations of the company as a beneficiary of the trust, unless subsection (3) applies.

(3) This subsection applies if at any time after 26 July 1989 the individual, alone or with associates, or an associate of the individual, alone or with other such associates—

(*a*) has been the beneficial owner of more than 5% of the ordinary share capital of the company, or

(*b*) has been able directly or indirectly to control more than 5% of that share capital.

(4) In subsection (3) "associate" has the meaning given by section 549(4) of ITEPA 2003.

(5) Sections 552 to 554 of ITEPA 2003 (attribution of interests in company) apply for the purposes of subsection (3) in relation to the individual as they apply for the purposes of the provisions listed in section 549(2) of that Act in relation to an employee.

(6) In this section—

"control" [is to be read in accordance with sections 450 and 451 of CTA 2010][1], "employee benefit trust" has the meaning given by section 550 of ITEPA 2003 except that the reference in section 550(3) of that Act to 13 March 1989 is to be read as a reference to 26 July 1989, and

"relative" means spouse or civil partner, ancestor or lineal descendant or brother or sister.

Commentary—*Simon's Taxes* **E1.827.**
Derivation—TA 1988 s 360A(2), (4)–(7) and (10).
HMRC Manuals—Savings and Investment Manual SAIM10240 (meaning of "associate").
Modifications—ITA 2007 Sch 2 para 93 (modification of this section in relation to a loan made before 14 November 1986).
ITA 2007 Sch 2 para 94 (sub-s (2) above does not apply in relation to a loan made before 26 July 1989, and, for the purposes of this section, ITEPA 2003 s 550 (which defines "employee benefit trust" and is applied for the purposes of this section by sub-s (6) above) has effect as if ITEPA 2003 s 550 referred to that day instead of 13 March 1989).
Amendments—[1] In sub-s (6) words substituted by CTA 2010 s 1177, Sch 1 para 523. CTA 2010 has effect for corporation tax purposes for accounting periods ending on or after 1 April 2010, and for income and capital gains tax purposes for the tax year 2010–11 and subsequent tax years.

Loans for interests in employee-controlled companies

396 Loan to buy interest in employee-controlled company

(1) This section applies to a loan to an individual that is used in one or more of the ways specified in subsection (2).

(2) The ways are—
    [(a) acquiring part of the ordinary share capital of a company that first becomes an employee-controlled company—
        (i) after the date of acquisition, or
        (ii) not earlier than 12 months before that date, and][1]
    (b) repaying another loan to which this section applies.

(3) For the purposes of this section and section 397, a company is employee-controlled at any time when—
    (a) more than 50% of the issued ordinary share capital of the company is owned beneficially by persons who are full-time employees of the company, and
    (b) more than 50% of the voting power in the company is so owned.

(4) If an individual owns beneficially more than 10% of the issued ordinary share capital of, or voting power in, a company, for the purposes of subsection (3) the excess is treated as being owned by an individual who is not a full-time employee of the company.

(5) In this section and section 397 "full-time employee", in relation to a company, means an individual the greater part of whose time is spent working as an employee or director of the company or of a 51% subsidiary of the company.

(6) This section is subject to section 411 (ineligibility of interest where business is occupation of commercial woodlands).

Commentary—*Simon's Taxes* **E1.829.**
Derivation—TA 1988 s 361(3)–(8).
HMRC Manuals—Savings and Investment Manual SAIM10270 (interest in an employee controlled company).
Modifications—ITA 2007 Sch 2 para 95(1) (modification of this section in relation to a loan used before 6 April 1990 in one or more of the ways specified in sub-s (2) above).
ITA 2007 s 95(2) (if a loan within sub-s (2)(b) above was made on or after 6 April 1990, interest on the loan is eligible for relief under ITA 2007 s 383 only if interest on the original loan would have been allowable under TA 1988 s 353 after that date).
Amendments—[1] Sub-s (2)(a) substituted by the Income Tax Act 2007 (Amendment) (No 3) Order, SI 2007/3506 art 3(1), (2) with effect for income tax and capital gains tax purposes for the tax year 2007–08 and subsequent tax years, and for corporation tax purposes for accounting periods ending after 5 April 2007: SI 2007/3506 art 1(2).

397 Eligibility requirements for interest on loans within section 396

(1) Interest on a loan within section 396 to an individual is eligible for relief only if conditions A to D are met.

(2) Condition A is that the company is, throughout the period beginning with the date on which the shares are acquired and ending with the date on which the interest is paid ("the payment date")—
    [(a) an unquoted company that is resident in the United Kingdom or another EEA state and is not resident outside the European Economic Area, and][2]
    (b) a trading company or the holding company of a trading group.

(3) Condition B is that during the tax year in which the interest is paid the company either—
    (a) first becomes an employee-controlled company, or
    (b) is such a company throughout a period of at least 9 months.

(4) Condition C is that—
    (a) the individual is a full-time employee of the company throughout the period beginning with the date on which the loan is used ("the use date") and ending with the payment date, or
    (b) the individual ceased to be such an employee not more than 12 months before the payment date and was such an employee throughout the period beginning with the use date and ending with the date the individual ceased to be such an employee.

(5) Condition D is that in the period from the use of the loan to the payment of the interest the individual has not recovered any capital from the company, apart from any amount taken into account under section 406(2) (recovered capital that is treated as a repayment of the loan).

(6) In this section—

"holding company" means a company whose business (ignoring any trade carried on by it) consists wholly or mainly of the holding of shares or securities of one or more companies which are its 75% subsidiaries,

"trading company" means a company whose business consists wholly or mainly of the carrying on of a trade or trades,

"trading group" means a group the business of whose members taken together consists wholly or mainly of the carrying on of a trade or trades (taking a group to consist of a company with one or more 75% subsidiaries and those subsidiaries), and

"unquoted company" means a company none of whose shares is [included in the official UK list]².

Commentary—*Simon's Taxes* **E1.829**.

Derivation—TA 1988 s 361(3), (4) and (8).

HMRC Manuals—Savings and Investment Manual SAIM10270 (loan to buy interest in an employee controlled company: eligibility requirements).

Amendments—¹ Words in sub-s (6) substituted by FA 2007 s 109, Sch 26 para 12(1), (9) with effect from 19 July 2007.

² In sub-s (2), para (*a*) substituted by FA 2014 s 14(1) with effect in relation to interest paid in the tax year 2014–15 or any subsequent tax year.

Prospective amendments—In sub-s (2)(*a*) word "an" to be substituted for word "another" by the Taxes (Amendments) (EU Exit) Regulations, SI 2019/689 reg 15(1), (5) with effect from Implementation Period completion day (see EU(WA)A 2020 Sch 5 para 1(1)).

Loans for investing in partnerships

398 Loan to invest in partnership

(1) This section applies to a loan to an individual that is used in one or more of the ways specified in subsection (2).

(2) The ways are—

(*a*) purchasing a share in a partnership,

(*b*) contributing money to a partnership, by way of capital or premium, that is used wholly for the purposes of the trade or profession carried on by the partnership,

(*c*) advancing money to a partnership that is so used, and

(*d*) repaying another loan to which this section applies.

(3) This section is subject to section 411 (ineligibility of interest where business is occupation of commercial woodlands).

Commentary—*Simon's Taxes* **E1.830**.

Derivation—TA 1988 s 362(1).

HMRC Manuals—Savings and Investment Manual SAIM10280 (interest in a partnership: loan to invest in a partnership).

399 Eligibility requirements for interest on loans within section 398

(1) Interest on a loan within section 398 to an individual is eligible for relief only if conditions A and B are met.

(2) Condition A is that throughout the period from the use of the loan until the interest is paid the individual has been a member of the partnership otherwise than—

(*a*) as a limited partner in a limited partnership registered under the Limited Partnerships Act 1907 (c 24), or

(*b*) as a member of an investment LLP.

(3) Condition B is that in that period the individual has not recovered any capital from the partnership, apart from any amount taken into account under section 406(2) (recovered capital that is treated as a repayment of the loan).

(4) If section 400 (film partnerships) applies in a tax year, only 40% of the interest that would otherwise be eligible for relief for that year is eligible.

(5) For the purposes of subsection (2) an individual who is not a member of a partnership is treated as such a member if—

(*a*) the partnership carries on a profession,

(*b*) the individual is employed by the partnership in a senior capacity, and

(*c*) the individual is allowed—

    (i) to act independently in dealing with clients of the partnership, and

    (ii) to act generally in such a way as to be indistinguishable from the partners in relations with those clients.

(6) For the purposes of subsection (2) "investment LLP" means a limited liability partnership—

(*a*) whose business consists wholly or mainly of the making of investments, and

(*b*) the principal part of whose income is derived from investments,

and whether a limited liability partnership is an investment LLP is determined for each period of account of the partnership.

Commentary—*Simon's Taxes* **E1.830, E1.824, B7.401, E1.827B**.

HMRC Manuals—Savings and Investment Manual SAIM10290-10300 (eligiblility for interest on loans to invest in a partnership).

Modification—ITA 2007 Sch 2 para 96 (sub-s (4) above only applies if the interest accrued on or after 10 March 2006).

[399A Property partnerships: restriction of relief for investment loan interest

(1) This section applies to interest on a loan within section 398 if—

    (*a*) the partnership concerned carries on a property business, and

    (*b*) that property business or part of it is carried on for the purpose of generating income from—

        (i) land consisting of a dwelling-house or part of a dwelling-house, or

        (ii) an estate, interest or right in or over land within subparagraph (i).

(2) Subsections (3) to (6) have effect to restrict relief under section 383(1) for so much of the interest as is referable (on a just and reasonable apportionment) to the property business or (as the case may be) the part of it within subsection (1)(*b*).

(3) For the tax year 2017–18, the amount of that relief is 75% of what would be given apart from this section.

(4) For the tax year 2018–19, the amount of that relief is 50% of what would be given apart from this section.

(5) For the tax year 2019–20, the amount of that relief is 25% of what would be given apart from this section.

(6) For the tax year 2020–21 and subsequent tax years, that interest is not eligible for relief under this Chapter.

(7) Section 399(4) is to be applied in relation to the tax year to which subsection (3), (4) or (5) applies before that subsection is applied in relation to that tax year.

(8) Anything that in the course of a property business is done for creating (by construction or adaptation) a dwelling-house, or part of a dwelling-house, from which income is to be generated is, for the purposes of subsection (1)(*b*), to be treated as done for the purpose mentioned in subsection (1)(*b*).

(9) A property business, or part of a property business, that consists of the commercial letting of furnished holiday accommodation (as defined by Chapter 6 of Part 3 of ITTOIA 2005) is not within subsection (1)(*b*).

(10) A reference in this section to a "dwelling-house" includes any land occupied or enjoyed with it as its garden or grounds.

(11) In this section "property business" means a UK property business or an overseas property business.][1]

Commentary—*Simon's Taxes* **B6.202A**.

Amendments—[1]   Sections 399A, 399B inserted by F(No 2)A 2015 s 24(7) with effect from 18 November 2015.

[399B Property partnerships: tax reduction for non-deductible loan interest

(1) Subsections (2) and (3) apply if for a tax year an individual would be given relief for an amount ("the relievable amount") by section 383(1) but for section 399A.

(2) The individual is entitled to relief under this section for the tax year in respect of the relievable amount.

(3) The amount of the relief is given by—

    BR x the relievable amount

    where BR is the basic rate of income tax for the year.][1]

Commentary—*Simon's Taxes* **B6.202A**.

Amendments—[1]   Sections 399A, 399B inserted by F(No 2)A 2015 s 24(7) with effect from 18 November 2015.

400 Film partnerships

(1) This section applies in a tax year if—

    (*a*) the partnership ("the film partnership") carries on a trade,

    (*b*) the profits or losses of the trade are calculated in accordance with Chapter 9 of Part 2 of ITTOIA 2005 (films etc),

    (*c*) the loan is secured on an asset or activity of another partnership ("the investment partnership"),

    (*d*) the individual to whom the loan is made ("A") is or has been a member of the investment partnership, and

    (*e*) at any time in the year the proportion of the profits of the investment partnership to which A is entitled is less than the proportion of that partnership's capital contributed by A at that time.

(2) For the purposes of subsection (1)(*c*), a loan is secured on an asset or activity of a partnership if there is an arrangement—

    (*a*) under which such an asset may be used or relied upon wholly or partly to guarantee repayment of any part of the loan, or

    (*b*) because of which any part of the loan is expected to be repaid directly or indirectly out of assets held by or income accruing to the partnership.

(3) In subsection (1)(*e*)—

"profits" excludes any amount that would not be taken into account as, or for the purposes of calculating, income for income tax purposes, and

"partnership's capital" means—

    (a) anything that is, or in accordance with generally accepted accounting practice would be, accounted for as partners' capital or partners' equity, and

    (b) amounts lent to the partnership by partners or persons connected with partners.

(4) So far as the investment partnership's capital includes at any time any of the following amounts, they are treated as amounts contributed by A—

    (a) any amount A paid to acquire any interest in the partnership, so far as A retains the interest at that time,

    (b) any amount made available by A directly or indirectly to another person, so far as that person retains any interest in the partnership at that time,

    (c) any amount A lent to the partnership, so far as it has not been repaid at that time,

    (d) any amount A made available directly or indirectly to another person, so far as any amount that person lent to the partnership has not been repaid at that time, and

    (e) an amount made available in any other way prescribed by regulations made by the Commissioners for Her Majesty's Revenue and Customs.

(5) Regulations under subsection (4)(e)—

    (a) may make provision having retrospective effect,

    (b) may make provision generally or only in relation to specified cases or circumstances,

    (c) may make different provision for different cases or circumstances,

    (d) may make transitional, consequential or incidental provision, and

    (e) may be made only if a draft of them has been laid before and approved by a resolution of the House of Commons.

(6) In this section a reference to A includes a reference to a person connected with A.

(7) Section 993 (meaning of "connected" persons) applies for the purposes of this section with the omission of subsections (3) to (7).

Commentary—*Simon's Taxes* **B5.508, B5.505, E1.824**.

Derivation—FA 2006 s 75.

HMRC Manuals—Savings and Investment Manual SAIM10300 (restriction of relief).

Loans for investing in co-operatives

401 Loan to invest in co-operative

(1) This section applies to a loan to an individual that is used in one or more of the ways specified in subsection (2).

(2) The ways are—

    (a) acquiring shares in a body which is a co-operative,

    (b) lending money to any such body which is used wholly and exclusively for the purposes of the business of that body or of a subsidiary of that body, and

    (c) repaying another loan to which this section applies.

(3) In this Chapter—

    "co-operative" means a common ownership enterprise or a co-operative enterprise as defined in section 2 of the Industrial Common Ownership Act 1976 (c 78), and

    "subsidiary", in relation to a co-operative, has the same meaning as for the purposes of section 2 of that Act.

Commentary—*Simon's Taxes* **E1.828**.

HMRC Manuals—Savings and Investment Manual SAIM10330 (loan to invest in a co-operative).

Modifications—ITA 2007 Sch 2 para 97 (this section applies in relation to a loan used in one or more of the ways specified in sub-s (2)(a) or (b) above only if the loan was made after 10 March 1981, but sub-s (2)(c) above applies whenever the original loan was made).

402 Eligibility requirements for interest on loans within section 401

(1) Interest on a loan within section 401 to an individual is eligible for relief only if conditions A to C are met.

(2) Condition A is that when the interest is paid the body continues to be a co-operative.

(3) Condition B is that in the period from the use of the loan to the payment of the interest the greater part of the individual's time has been spent working as an employee of the body or of a subsidiary of the body.

(4) Condition C is that in that period the individual has not recovered any capital from the body, apart from any taken into account under section 406(2) (recovered capital that is treated as a repayment of the loan).

Commentary—*Simon's Taxes* **E1.828**.

Derivation—TA 1988 s 361(2).

HMRC Manuals—Savings and Investment Manual SAIM10330 (eligibility conditions).

Loans for paying inheritance tax

403 Loan to pay inheritance tax

(1) This section applies to a loan to the personal representatives of a deceased person if the loan is used—

    (*a*) in paying inheritance tax that meets the condition specified in subsection (2), or

    (*b*) in repaying another loan to which this section applies.

(2) The condition is that the personal representatives are obliged to pay the tax under section 226(2) of IHTA 1984 (obligation of personal representatives to pay tax on delivery of their account).

(3) A written statement appearing to be from an officer of Revenue and Customs is sufficient evidence—

    (*a*) of the amount of inheritance tax that meets the condition specified in subsection (2), and

    (*b*) of any statements relevant to its calculation.

(4) In this section references to inheritance tax include interest payable on that tax.

Commentary—*Simon's Taxes* **E1.832**.
HMRC Manuals—Savings and Investment Manual SAIM10350 (loans to pay inheritance tax).

404 Eligibility requirements for interest on loans within section 403

Interest on a loan within section 403(1) is eligible for relief only so far as it is paid in respect of a period ending within 12 months from the making of the loan used as mentioned in section 403(1)(*a*).

Commentary—*Simon's Taxes* **E1.832**.
HMRC Manuals—Savings and Investment Manual SAIM10350 (restriction on relief).

405 Carry back and forward of relief for interest on loans within section 403

(1) This section applies if relief for any interest on a loan within section 403(1) that is eligible for relief cannot be given for the tax year in which the interest is paid because there is not enough income in that year.

(2) The person paying the interest is entitled to relief for that interest—

    (*a*) for the preceding tax year, or

    (*b*) if there is not enough income in that year, for the tax year preceding it,

and so on.

(3) If relief cannot be given under subsection (2), it may instead be given—

    (*a*) for the tax year following that in which the interest is paid, or

    (*b*) if there is not enough income in that year, for the tax year following it,

and so on.

Commentary—*Simon's Taxes* **E1.832**.
Derivation—TA 1988 s 364(2).
HMRC Manuals—Savings and Investment Manual SAIM10350 (carry back and forward for interest).

General and supplementary

406 Effect of recovery of capital in the case of some loans

(1) This section applies if the individual to whom a loan is made to which section 392, 396, 398 or 401 applies recovers any amount of capital from the company, partnership or co-operative concerned at any time after the loan is used.

(2) The individual is treated for the purposes of this Chapter as having repaid that amount out of the loan at that time, whether or not such a repayment occurred.

(3) Accordingly, only part of the interest that, apart from any such repayment, would be payable on the loan for any period after that time and eligible for relief is so eligible.

(4) That part is so much of that interest as is attributable to the amount of the loan after the repayment.

(5) In the case of a loan to which section 386 applies (loans partly meeting requirements), subsection (3) applies instead of section 386(3) (under which repayments are apportioned between the qualifying and non-qualifying parts of such loans).

(6) The cases in which an individual is treated as having recovered an amount of capital for the purposes of this section are set out in section 407(1) to (3).

Commentary—*Simon's Taxes* **E1.831**.
HMRC Manuals—Savings and Investment Manual SAIM10250-10260 (the "capital recovery condition", with example). SAIM10310 (interest in a partnershp: recovery of capital).

407 Events counting as recovery of capital for section 406

(1) An individual is treated as having recovered an amount of capital from a company for the purposes of section 406 if—

    (*a*) the individual receives consideration of that amount or value—

        (i) for the sale, exchange or assignment of part of the ordinary share capital of the company,

        (ii) by way of repayment of part of that ordinary share capital, or

        (iii) for assigning a debt due to the individual from the company, or

    (*b*) the company repays that amount of a loan or advance from the individual.

(2) An individual is treated as having recovered an amount of capital from a partnership for those purposes if—

    (*a*) the individual receives consideration of that amount or value—

        (i) for the sale, exchange or assignment of part of the individual's interest in the partnership, or

        (ii) for assigning a debt due to the individual from the partnership, or

    (*b*) the partnership repays that amount of a loan or advance from the individual, or

    (*c*) the partnership returns that amount of capital to the individual.

(3) An individual is treated as having recovered an amount of capital from a co-operative for those purposes if—

    (*a*) the individual receives consideration of that amount or value—

        (i) for the sale, exchange or assignment of part of the individual's shares in the co-operative,

        (ii) by way of repayment of part of the individual's shares in the co-operative, or

        (iii) for assigning a debt due to the individual from the co-operative, or

    (*b*) the co-operative repays that amount of a loan or advance from the individual.

(4) A sale or assignment that is not a bargain made at arm's length is treated for the purposes of this section as being made for a consideration of an amount equal to the market value of what is disposed of.

Commentary—*Simon's Taxes* **E1.831**.
Derivation—TA 1988 s 363(2).
HMRC Manuals—Savings and Investment Manual SAIM10310-10320 (recovery of capital, with examples).
SAIM10330 (interest in a co-operative: recovery of capital).

408 Replacement loans

(1) This section applies to a replacement loan.

(2) In subsection (1) "replacement loan" means a loan to which section 392, 396, 398 or 401 applies because the loan is used in repaying another loan ("the replaced loan") to which that section applies.

(3) This Chapter, except for sections 385 and 386, applies to the replacement loan as if that loan and the replaced loan were a single loan (subject to subsection (5)).

(4) Accordingly, any restriction under section 406 (effect of recovery of capital in the case of some loans) which applies to the replaced loan applies to the replacement loan.

(5) But this Chapter, except for sections 385 and 386, applies as if references to the use of the loan were references to the use of the original loan.

Commentary—*Simon's Taxes* **E1.831**.
Derivation—TA 1988 s 363(4).
HMRC Manuals—Savings and Investment Manual SAIM10280 (interest in a partnerhsip: repaying another eligible loan).

409 Business successions between partnerships

(1) This section applies if—

    (*a*) a loan to which section 398 applies is made to an individual,

    (*b*) the partnership in question ("the old partnership") is dissolved,

    (*c*) on its dissolution another partnership of which the individual is a member ("the new partnership") is formed to carry on the whole or part of the undertaking carried on by the old partnership, and

    (*d*) interest payable on the loan for the period ending with the dissolution of the old partnership was eligible for relief (or would have been had any been payable).

(2) This Chapter applies as if the old partnership and the new partnership were the same partnership.

(3) Section 399(5) (salaried partners etc treated as partners) applies for the purposes of subsection (1)(*c*) as it applies for the purposes of section 399(2).

Commentary—*Simon's Taxes* **E1.831**.
HMRC Manuals—Savings and Investment Manual SAIM10340 (succession between partnerships).

410 Other business successions and reorganisations

(1) This subsection applies if—

    (*a*) a loan to which one of the business loan provisions or section 398 (loan to invest in partnership) applies is made to an individual ("the original loan"),

    (*b*) the company, partnership or co-operative in question is involved in a transaction as a result of which the individual acquires shares in or makes a loan to another company or a body that is a co-operative,

    (*c*) interest payable on the original loan for the period ending with the time of the transaction was eligible for relief (or would have been had any been payable), and

    (*d*) had the original loan been made at the time of the transaction and applied in acquiring the shares in or making the loan to the other company or the co-operative, the original loan would have fallen within one of the business loan provisions.

(2) If subsection (1) applies, from the time of the transaction referred to in subsection (1)(*b*) the original loan is treated as if it had been made and applied as mentioned in subsection (1)(*d*).

(3) In this section "the business loan provisions" means—

(a)   section 392 (loan to buy interest in close company),

(b)   section 396 (loan to buy interest in employee-controlled company), and

(c)   section 401 (loan to invest in co-operative).

Commentary—*Simon's Taxes* **B9.105**.

Changes in the law—See ITA 2007 EN Annex 1 Change 75. This change gives statutory effect to ESC A43 and extends it to cover partnership changes generally.

HMRC Manuals—Savings and Investment Manual SAIM10340 (other business successions and reorganisations).

411 Ineligibility of interest where business is occupation of commercial woodlands

(1) Interest that would be eligible for relief under this Chapter apart from this section is not eligible if—

(a)   the interest is on a loan to which section 392, 396 or 398 applies, and

(b)   the business carried on by the close company, employee-controlled company or partnership concerned consists of the occupation of commercial woodlands.

(2) If only part of the business consists in such occupation, only part of the interest is ineligible for the relief.

(3) That part is such part of the interest as it is just and reasonable to attribute to that part of the business having regard to all the relevant circumstances and, in particular, to the extent of the other part of the business.

(4) For the purposes of this section two or more businesses carried on by a company or partnership are to be regarded as a single business.

(5) In this section "commercial woodlands" means woodlands in the United Kingdom which are managed on a commercial basis and with a view to the realisation of profits.

Derivation—FA 1988 Sch 6 para 3.

HMRC Manuals—Savings and Investment Manual SAIM10020 (ineligibility of interest where business is occupation of commercial woodlands).

412 Information

(1) A person ("the payer") who claims relief under this Chapter for a payment of interest made in a tax year is entitled to request the person to whom the interest is paid to give the payer a statement in writing about that interest containing the information specified in subsection (3).

(2) That request must be in writing.

(3) The information is—

(a)   the date when the debt was incurred,

(b)   the amount of the debt when incurred,

(c)   the interest paid in the tax year, and

(d)   the name and address of the debtor.

(4) The person to whom the interest is paid has a duty to comply with a request under subsection (1) and that duty is enforceable by the payer.

(5) This section does not apply if the interest is paid to a building society or to a local authority.

Commentary—*Simon's Taxes* **E1.825**.

Derivation—TA 1988 s 366.

HMRC Manuals—Savings and Investment Manual SAIM10050 (information requirements).

[CHAPTER 1A

IRRECOVERABLE PEER-TO-PEER LOANS]

[The relief

412A Relief for irrecoverable peer-to-peer loans

(1) A person ("L") is entitled to relief under this section if—

(a)   L has made a peer-to-peer loan ("the relevant loan"),

(b)   the loan was made through an operator,

(c)   L has not assigned the right to recover the principal of the loan, and

(d)   any outstanding amount of the principal of the loan has, on or after 6 April 2015, become irrecoverable.

(2) But if the outstanding amount became irrecoverable before 6 April 2016 L is entitled to relief under this section only on the making of a claim.

(3) The relief is given by deducting the outstanding amount in calculating L's net income for the tax year in which the amount became irrecoverable (see Step 2 of the calculation in section 23).

(4) The deduction under this section is to be made only from income arising from the payment to L of interest on—

(a)   the relevant loan, and

(b)   any other loan within subsection (5) or (6).

(5) A loan is within this subsection if—

(a)   it is a peer-to-peer loan made by L, and

(b)   it was made through the operator through whom the relevant loan was made.

(6) A loan is within this subsection if—

(a) the loan was made by someone other than L,

(b) the right to receive interest on the loan has been assigned to L,

(c) the right was assigned through the operator through whom the relevant loan was made, and

(d) either—

    (i) L is a person within paragraph (a), (b) or (c) of section 412I(4), or

    (ii) the recipient of the loan is a person within one of those paragraphs and the loan is a personal or small loan.

(7) The amount deducted under this section is limited in accordance with section 25(4) and (5).

(8) In this section "irrecoverable" means irrecoverable other than by legal proceedings or by the exercise of any right granted by way of security for the loan.]¹

Commentary—*Simon's Taxes* **E1.407A**.

Amendments—¹   Chapter 1A (ss 412A–412J) inserted by FA 2016 s 32(1), (2) with effect from 15 September 2016.

[412B Claims for additional relief: sideways relief

(1) A person ("L") may make a claim for relief under this section if—

(a) L is entitled to relief under section 412A in respect of any outstanding amount of the principal of a loan ("the relevant loan"), but

(b) in the tax year in relation to which L is entitled to that relief ("the relevant year")—

    (i) L has no income of the kind mentioned in section 412A(4) from which to deduct the outstanding amount, or

    (ii) L has insufficient income of that kind to enable the outstanding amount to be deducted in full under that section.

(2) The claim is for the outstanding amount or (in a case within subsection (1)(b)(ii)) the part of the outstanding amount not capable of being deducted under section 412A to be deducted under this section in calculating L's net income for the relevant year.

(3) The deduction under this section is to be made only from income arising from the payment to L of interest on loans within subsection (4) or (5).

(4) A loan is within this subsection if—

(a) it is a peer-to-peer loan made by L, and

(b) it was made through an operator who is not the operator through whom the relevant loan was made.

(5) A loan is within this subsection if—

(a) the loan was made by someone other than L,

(b) the right to receive interest on the loan has been assigned to L,

(c) that right was assigned through an operator who is not the operator through whom the relevant loan was made, and

(d) either—

    (i) L is a person within paragraph (a), (b) or (c) of section 412I(4), or

    (ii) the recipient of the loan is a person within one of those paragraphs and the loan is a personal or small loan.

(6) The amount deducted under this section is limited in accordance with section 25(4) and (5).]¹

Commentary—*Simon's Taxes* **E1.407A**.

Amendments—¹   Chapter 1A (ss 412A–412J) inserted by FA 2016 s 32(1), (2) with effect from 15 September 2016.

[412C Claims for additional relief: carry-forward relief

(1) A person ("L") may make a claim for relief under this section if—

(a) L is entitled to relief under section 412A in respect of any outstanding amount of the principal of a loan ("the relevant loan"), but

(b) in the tax year in relation to which L is entitled to that relief ("the relevant year")—

    (i) L has no income of the kind mentioned in section 412A(4) or section 412B(3) from which to deduct the outstanding amount, or

    (ii) L has insufficient income of that kind to enable the outstanding amount to be deducted in full under those sections.

(2) The claim is for the outstanding amount or (in a case within subsection (1)(b)(ii)) the part of the outstanding amount not capable of being deducted under sections 412A and 412B to be deducted under this section in calculating L's net income for the four tax years following the relevant year.

(3) The deduction under this section is to be made only from income arising from the payment to L of interest on—

(a) the relevant loan, and

(b) any other loan within subsection (4) or (5).

(4) A loan is within this subsection if—

(a) it is a peer-to-peer loan made by L, and

(b) it was made through an operator (whether or not that operator is the operator through whom the relevant loan was made).

(5) A loan is within this subsection if—

(a) the loan was made by someone other than L,

   (*b*) the right to receive interest on the loan has been assigned to L,

   (*c*) that right was assigned through an operator (whether or not that operator is the operator through whom the relevant loan was made), and

   (*d*) either—

      (i) L is a person within paragraph (*a*), (*b*) or (*c*) of section 412I(4), or

      (ii) the recipient of the loan is a person within one of those paragraphs and the loan is a personal or small loan.

(6) This section needs to be read with section 412D (how relief works).][1]

Commentary—*Simon's Taxes* **E1.407A**.
Amendments—[1]   Chapter 1A (ss 412A–412J) inserted by FA 2016 s 32(1), (2) with effect from 15 September 2016.

[412D How carry-forward relief works

(1) This subsection explains how deductions are to be made under section 412C.
The amount to be deducted at any step is limited in accordance with section 25(4) and (5).
Step 1 Deduct the outstanding amount or (in a case within section 412C(1)(*b*)(ii)) the part of the outstanding amount not capable of being deducted under sections 412A and 412B from the lending income for the first tax year following the relevant year.
Step 2 Deduct from the lending income for the second tax year following the relevant year any part of the outstanding amount not previously deducted.
Step 3 Apply Step 2 in relation to the lending income for the third and fourth tax years following the relevant year, stopping if all of the outstanding amount is deducted.
(2) In this section—
    "lending income" means income of a kind mentioned in section 412C(3);
    "relevant year" has the meaning given by section 412C(1)(*b*).][1]

Commentary—*Simon's Taxes* **E1.407A**.
Amendments—[1]   Chapter 1A (ss 412A–412J) inserted by FA 2016 s 32(1), (2) with effect from 15 September 2016.

[Supplementary provisions

412E Subsequent recovery of peer-to-peer loans

(1) This section applies where—

   (*a*) any amount of the principal of a loan has been deducted under this Chapter in calculating a person's net income for a tax year, and

   (*b*) the person subsequently recovers that amount or any part of it.

(2) The amount recovered is to be treated for the purposes of this Act as if it were interest on the loan paid to the person at the time it was recovered.

(3) For the purposes of this section, a person is to be treated as recovering an amount if the person (or any other person at his or her direction) receives any money or money's worth—

   (*a*) in satisfaction of the person's right to recover that amount, or

   (*b*) in consideration of the person's assignment of the right to recover it;

and where a person assigns such a right otherwise than by way of a bargain made at arm's length the person shall be treated as receiving money or money's worth equal to the market value of the right at the time of the assignment.][1]

Commentary—*Simon's Taxes* **E1.407A**.
Amendments—[1]   Chapter 1A (ss 412A–412J) inserted by FA 2016 s 32(1), (2) with effect from 15 September 2016.

[412F Assigned loans treated as made by the assignee etc

(1) This section applies where—

   (*a*) a person ("A") is assigned the right to recover the principal of a loan,

   (*b*) the right is assigned through an operator ("O"),

   (*c*) A makes a payment in consideration of the assignment, and

   (*d*) A does not further assign the right.

(2) The loan is to be treated for the purposes of section 412A(1) as—

   (*a*) having been made by A, and

   (*b*) having been made through O.

(3) The amount (if any) of the principal of the loan which is treated as irrecoverable may not exceed the amount which is arrived at by—

   (*a*) taking the amount of the payment mentioned in subsection (1)(*c*), and

   (*b*) deducting any amount of the principal of the loan previously recovered by A.][1]

Commentary—*Simon's Taxes* **E1.407A**.
Amendments—[1]   Chapter 1A (ss 412A–412J) inserted by FA 2016 s 32(1), (2) with effect from 15 September 2016.

[412G Nominees etc

For the purposes of this Chapter—

   (*a*) a loan or a payment made by or to a nominee or bare trustee for a person is treated as made by or to that person, and

   (*b*) a right assigned by or to a nominee or bare trustee for a person is treated as assigned by or to that person.][1]

Amendments—[1]   Chapter 1A (ss 412A–412J) inserted by FA 2016 s 32(1), (2) with effect from 15 September 2016.

[412H Interaction with other reliefs

(1) Subsection (2) applies in relation to a loan if any person has obtained income tax relief (other than under this Chapter) which is properly attributable to the loan.

(2) The amount (if any) of the principal of the loan which is treated as irrecoverable may not exceed the amount which is arrived at by—

    (a) taking the amount of the principal of the loan, and

    (b) deducting the amount of the relief mentioned in subsection (1).][1]

Amendments—[1]   Chapter 1A (ss 412A–412J) inserted by FA 2016 s 32(1), (2) with effect from 15 September 2016.

[Interpretation

412I Meaning of "loan", "peer-to-peer loan" and related terms

(1) This section applies for the purposes of this Chapter.

(2) "Loan" means a loan of money which—

    (a) is made on genuine commercial terms, and

    (b) is not part of a scheme or arrangement the main purpose or one of the main purposes of which is to obtain a tax advantage (within the meaning given by section 208 of the FA 2013).

(3) A loan is a "peer-to-peer loan" only if it meets—

    (a) Condition A or B, and

    (b) Condition C.

(4) Condition A is that the person who made the loan is—

    (a) an individual,

    (b) a partnership which consists of—

        (i)   two or three persons, and

        (ii) at least one person who is not a body corporate, or

    (c) an unincorporated body of persons which—

        (i)   is not a partnership, and

        (ii) consists of at least one person who is not a body corporate.

(5) Condition B is that—

    (a) the recipient of the loan is a person within paragraph (a), (b) or (c) of subsection (4), and

    (b) the loan is a personal or small loan.

(6) Condition C is that, assuming interest were paid on the loan, the person who made the loan would (except for this Chapter) be liable for income tax charged on the interest.

(7) "Personal loan" means a loan which is not used wholly or predominantly for the purposes of a business carried on, or intended to be carried on, by the recipient of the loan.

(8) "Small loan" means a loan of £25,000 or less.[1]

Commentary—*Simon's Taxes* E1.407A.

Amendments—[1]   Chapter 1A (ss 412A–412J) inserted by FA 2016 s 32(1), (2) with effect from 15 September 2016.

412J Meaning of "operator" and related terms

(1) This section applies for the purposes of this Chapter.

(2) "Operator" means a person who—

    (a) has permission under Part 4A of FISMA 2000 to carry on a regulated activity specified in Article 36H of the Financial Services and Markets Act 2000 (Regulated Activities) Order 2001 (S.I. 2001/544) (operating an electronic system in relation to lending), or

    (b) has been granted equivalent permission under the law of a territory outside the United Kingdom that is within the European Economic Area.

(3) A loan is "made through" an operator if the person who makes the loan and the recipient of the loan enter the agreement under which the loan is made at the invitation of the operator.

(4) A right is "assigned through" an operator if the person who assigns the right and the person to whom the right is assigned enter the agreement under which the assignment takes effect at the invitation of the operator.

(5) A person is not to be treated as having entered an agreement at the invitation of an operator if the operator made the invitation otherwise than in the course of carrying on the activity to which the permission mentioned in subsection (2)(a) or (b) relates.][1]

Amendments—[1]   Chapter 1A (ss 412A–412J) inserted by FA 2016 s 32(1), (2) with effect from 15 September 2016.

CHAPTER 2

GIFT AID
The relief

413 Overview of Chapter

(1) This Chapter gives relief for some gifts of money to charities by individuals.

(2) The relief is set out in section 414.

(3) The Chapter contains provisions under which, in some circumstances—

    (a) the individual's entitlement to some other reliefs may be restricted (see section 423), and (*b*) the individual may be charged to income tax (see section 424).

(4) See section 430 for bodies that are treated as charities for the purposes of this Chapter.

[(4A) This Chapter is subject to section 809ZM (removal of income tax relief in respect of tainted charity donations etc).][2]

(5) For related reliefs for charities see Part 10 of [this Act and Part 11 of CTA 2010.][1]

[(6) For related reliefs for community amateur sports clubs see Chapter 9 of Part 13 of CTA 2010.][3]

Amendments—[1]   In sub-s (5) words substituted by CTA 2010 s 1177, Sch 1 para 524. CTA 2010 has effect for corporation tax purposes for accounting periods ending on or after 1 April 2010, and for income and capital gains tax purposes for the tax year 2010–11 and subsequent tax years.
[2]   Sub-s (4A) inserted by FA 2011 s 27, Sch 3 paras 7, 10 with effect in relation to relievable charity donations made on or after 1April 2011.
[3]   Sub-s (6) inserted by FA 2012 s 51, Sch 15 para 8.

414 Relief for gifts to charity

(1) An individual who makes a gift to a charity which is a qualifying donation is entitled to the relief set out in subsection (2).

(2) The Income Tax Acts have effect in their application to the individual for the tax year in which the gift is made as if—

(*a*) the gift had been made after deduction of [income tax at the basic rate, and][4]

(*b*) the basic rate limit [and the higher rate limit][2] (see [section 10][1]) [and additionally, in the case of a Scottish taxpayer, [the upper limit for the Scottish basic rate and the limits for any Scottish rates above the Scottish basic rate,][4]][3] were increased by an amount equal to the grossed up amount of the gift.

(3) See subsection (7) of section 535 of ITTOIA 2005 (gains from contracts for life insurance etc: top slicing relief) for provision about how relief under this Chapter is to be ignored for the purpose of calculating relief under that section.

Commentary—*Simon's Taxes* **E1.811**.
Derivation—FA 1990 s 25(6).
HMRC Manuals—Residence, Domicile And Remittance Basis Manual RDRM32450 (relief from tax for gifts of money to charities).
Capital Gains Manual CG21220 (extending the basic rate band).
Amendments—[1]   Words in sub-s (2) substituted by FA 2008 s 5, Sch 1 paras 1, 20 with effect for the tax year 2008–09 and subsequent tax years.
[2]   In sub-s (2)(*b*), words inserted by FA 2009 s 6, Sch 2 paras 1, 6 with effect for the tax year 2010–11 and subsequent tax years.
[3]   In sub-s (2)(*b*), words inserted by the Scotland Act 2016 (Income Tax Consequential Amendments) Regulations, SI 2017/468 regs 2, 10 with effect in relation to 2017–18 (the tax year appointed under the Scotland Act 2016 section 13(15)(*b*)) and subsequent tax years.
[4]   In sub-s (2)(*a*), (*b*), words substituted by the Scottish Rates of Income Tax (Consequential Amendments) Order, SI 2018/459 art 6(1), (4) with effect for the tax year commencing on 6 April 2018 and subsequent tax years.

[414A Tax reduction or charge if basic rate, and devolved basic rate, differ

(1) Subsections (3) and (4) apply if an individual makes a gift to a charity which is a qualifying donation, and for the tax year in which the gift is made—

(*a*) the individual is a Scottish taxpayer or a Welsh taxpayer,

(*b*) there is a difference between—

(i) the applicable devolved basic rate, and

(ii) the basic rate, and

(*c*) any of the individual's income is liable to the applicable devolved basic rate.

(2) In this section—

"the applicable devolved basic rate"—

(*a*) is the Scottish basic rate if the individual is a Scottish taxpayer, and

(*b*) is the Welsh basic rate if the individual is a Welsh taxpayer,

"the ADBR amount" is the amount of the individual's income liable to the applicable devolved basic rate, and

"the rate difference" means the difference between the basic rate and the applicable devolved basic rate.

(3) If, for the tax year in which the gift is made, the applicable devolved basic rate is above the basic rate—

(*a*) the individual is entitled to a tax reduction for that tax year,

(*b*) the tax reduction is given effect at Step 6 of the calculation in section 23,

(*c*) where the ADBR amount is more than or equal to the grossed up amount of the gift, the amount of the tax reduction is equal to the grossed up amount of the gift multiplied by the rate difference, and

(*d*) otherwise, the amount of the tax reduction is equal to the ADBR amount multiplied by the rate difference.

(4) If, for the tax year in which the gift is made, the applicable devolved basic rate is lower than the basic rate—

(*a*) income tax is charged under this subsection for that tax year,

(b) the individual is the person liable for the tax,

(c) where the ADBR amount is more than or equal to the grossed up amount of the gift, the amount of the tax is equal to the grossed up amount of the gift multiplied by the rate difference, and

(d) otherwise, the amount of the tax is the ADBR amount multiplied by the rate difference,

but see subsection (5).

(5) If, in the case of an individual (and ignoring this subsection), the total amount of tax charged under subsection (4) for a tax year is greater than the individual's section 414(2)(b) tax saving for that year, the total amount of that tax is limited so as to be equal to the individual's section 414(2)(b) tax saving for that year.

(6) For the purposes of subsection (5), the amount of an individual's "section 414(2)(b) tax saving" for a tax year is—

(a) if the amount calculated at Step 5 of the calculation in section 23 in the individual's case for that year is less than it would be were section 414(2)(b) not to have effect, equal to the difference, and

(b) otherwise is nil.][1]

Amendments—[1]   Section 414A inserted by the Devolved Income Tax Rates (Consequential Amendments) Order, SI 2019/201 arts 12(1), (8) with effect in relation to the tax year commencing on 6 April 2019 and subsequent tax years.

415 Meaning of "grossed up amount"
In this Chapter references to the grossed up amount of a gift are to the amount of the gift grossed up by reference to the basic rate for the tax year in which the gift is made . . . .[1].

Commentary—*Simon's Taxes* **E1.811**.
Derivation—FA 1990 s 25(12)(d).
Amendments—[1]   Words repealed by the Scottish Rates of Income Tax (Consequential Amendments) Order, SI 2018/459 art 6(1), (5) with effect for the tax year commencing on 6 April 2018 and subsequent tax years.

416 Meaning of "qualifying donation"
(1) A gift made to a charity by an individual is a qualifying donation for the purposes of this Chapter if—

(a) conditions A to [F][1] are met, and

(b) the individual[, or an intermediary representing the individual,][3] gives the charity [or an intermediary representing the charity,][3] a gift aid declaration relating to the gift (see section 428).

[(1A) For the purpose of subsection (1)(b) an intermediary is—

(a) a person authorised by the individual to give a gift aid declaration on behalf of that individual to the charity,

(b) a person authorised by a charity to receive a gift aid declaration on behalf of that charity, or

(c) a person authorised to perform both of the roles described in paragraphs (a) and (b).][3]

(2) Condition A is that the gift takes the form of a payment of a sum of money.

(3) Condition B is that the payment is not subject to any condition as to repayment.

(4) Condition C is that the payment is not a sum falling within section 713(3) of ITEPA 2003 (payroll deduction scheme).

(5) Condition D is that the payment is not deductible in calculating the individual's income from any source.

(6) Condition E is that the payment is not conditional on, associated with or part of an arrangement involving, the acquisition of property by the charity from the individual or a person connected with the individual.

An acquisition by way of gift is ignored for the purposes of this condition.

[(6A) Condition EA is that the payment is not by way of, and does not amount in substance to, waiver by the individual of entitlement to sums (whether of principal or return) due to the individual from the charity in respect of an amount—

(a) advanced to the charity, and

(b) in respect of which a person, whether or not the individual, has obtained relief under Part 5B (relief for social investments).][2]

(7) Condition F is that—

(a) there are no benefits associated with the gift, or

(b) there are benefits associated with the gift but the restrictions on those benefits are not breached.

See sections 417 to 421 for provision about benefits associated with gifts.

(8) . . . .[1]

Commentary—*Simon's Taxes* **E1.811, E1.811A**.
Amendments—[1]   In sub-s (1)(a) letter substituted, and sub-s (8) repealed, by FA 2010 s 32, Sch 8 para 3(1), (2) with effect in relation to gifts made on or after 6 April 2010.
[2]   Sub-s (6A) inserted by FA 2014 s 57, Sch 11 paras 3, 11 with effect from 17 July 2014.
[3]   In sub-s (1)(b) words inserted, and sub-s (1A) inserted, by FA 2015 s 20(1), (2) with effect in relation to gifts made on or after 6 April 2017 (by virtue of SI 2016/1010 reg 4.

417 Meaning of "benefits associated with a gift"

A benefit is associated with a gift for the purposes of this Chapter if it is received by the individual who makes the gift, or a person connected with the individual, in consequence of making the gift.

Commentary—*Simon's Taxes* **E1.811**.
Derivation—FA 1990 s 25(2), (4).

Restrictions on associated benefits

418 Restrictions on associated benefits

(1) For the purposes of section 416(7), the restrictions on benefits associated with a gift are breached if condition A or B is met.

(2) Condition A is that the total value of the benefits associated with the gift exceeds the variable limit, which is—

[(a) in a case where the amount of the gift is £100 or less, 25% of that amount, and
(b) in a case where the amount of the gift exceeds £100, the sum of £25 and 5% of the amount of the excess.]^2

(3) Condition B is that the sum of—

(a) the total value of the benefits associated with the gift, and
(b) the total value of the benefits (if any) associated with each relevant prior gift,

is more than [£2,500]^1.

(4) "Relevant prior gift" means a gift—

(a) which has already been made by the individual to the charity in the tax year, and
(b) which is a qualifying donation.

(5) This section needs to be read with sections 419 to 421.

Commentary—*Simon's Taxes* **E1.811**.
Amendments—^{1} Figure in sub-s (3) substituted by FA 2011 s 41(1) with effect in relation to gifts made on or after 6 April 2011.
^{2} In sub-s (2), paras (a), (b) substituted for previous paras (a)–(c) by FA 2019 s 40(1) with effect in relation to gifts made on or after 6 April 2019.

419 Gifts and benefits linked to periods of less than 12 months

(1) This section modifies the application of section 418(2) in relation to a gift if condition A, B, C or D is met.

(2) Condition A is that a benefit associated with the gift relates to a period of less than 12 months.

(3) Condition B is that a benefit associated with the gift consists of a right to receive benefits at intervals over a period of less than 12 months.

(4) Condition C is that a benefit associated with the gift is one of a series of benefits which are—

(a) received at intervals, and
(b) associated with a series of gifts made at intervals of less than 12 months.

(5) Condition D is that—

(a) a benefit associated with the gift is not one of a series of benefits received at intervals, and
(b) the gift is one of a series of gifts made at intervals of less than 12 months.

(6) If condition A, B or C is met, then for the purposes of section 418(2)—

(a) the value of the benefit is taken to be the annual equivalent of its actual value, and
(b) the amount of the gift is taken to be the annual equivalent of its actual amount.

(7) If condition D is met, the amount of the gift is taken for the purposes of section 418(2) to be the annual equivalent of its actual amount.

(8) The annual equivalent of the value of a benefit, or of the amount of a gift, is calculated as follows.

> *Step 1* Multiply the value or amount by 365.
> *Step 2* If condition A or B is met in relation to the benefit (and neither condition C nor condition D is met in relation to it), divide the result by the number of days in the period of less than 12 months referred to in subsection (2) or (as the case may be) subsection (3).

If condition C or D is met in relation to the benefit, divide the result by the average number of days in the intervals of less than 12 months referred to in subsection (4)(b) or (as the case may be) subsection (5)(b).

Commentary—*Simon's Taxes* **E1.811**.
Modification—ITA 2007 Sch 2 para 99 (modification of this section where a gift is made on or after 6 April 2007, and a benefit associated with the gift is received before that date or relates (wholly or partly) to a period falling before that date).

Admission rights

420 Disregard of certain admission rights

(1) A benefit associated with a gift is ignored for the purposes of this Chapter if the benefit consists of a relevant right of admission.

(2) "Right of admission" means a right which—

(a) benefits the individual who makes the gift or that individual and one or more members of that individual's family (whether or not the right must be exercised by all of them at the same time), (*b*) authorises admission to premises or property to which the public are admitted on payment of an admission fee, and

(*c*) authorises admission to those premises or that property without payment of the admission fee or on payment of a reduced fee.

(3) A right of admission is a relevant right of admission if—

(*a*) conditions A and B are met in relation to it, and

(*b*) either condition C or condition D is met in relation to it.

(4) Condition A is that the opportunity to make a gift and to receive the right of admission in consequence is available to the public.

(5) Condition B is that the right of admission is a right granted by the charity for the purpose of viewing property preserved, maintained, kept or created by a charity for its charitable purposes.

(6) The property mentioned in subsection (5) includes, in particular—

(*a*) buildings,

(*b*) grounds or other land,

(*c*) plants,

(*d*) animals,

(*e*) works of art (but not performances),

(*f*) artefacts, and

(*g*) property of a scientific nature.

(7) Condition C is that the right of admission applies, during a period of at least 12 months, at all times at which the public can obtain admission.

(8) Condition D is that—

(*a*) a member of the public could purchase the same right of admission, and

(*b*) the amount of the gift is greater by at least 10% than the amount the member of the public would have to pay.

(9) This section needs to be read with section 421.

Commentary—*Simon's Taxes* **E1.811**.
Derivation—FA 1990 s 25(5E) to (5I).

421 Admission rights: supplementary

(1) This section applies for the purposes of section 420.

(2) Condition C is to be treated as met even if the right does not apply on days which are specified by the charity as event days, provided no more than 5 days are so specified in relation to the applicable period.

(3) The applicable period is—

(*a*) the period during which the right applies, in the case of a right which applies for a period of 12 months, or

(*b*) each calendar year during all or part of which the right applies, in the case of a right which applies for a period of more than 12 months.

(4) An "event day" is a day on which an event is to take place on the premises to which the right relates.

(5) In condition D the "same right of admission" means a right relating to the same property, classes of persons and periods of time as the right received in consequence of the gift.

Commentary—*Simon's Taxes* **E1.811**.
Derivation—FA 1990 s 25(5I) and (5J).

Measures to ensure donor's liability not less than tax treated as deducted

423 Restriction of certain reliefs

(1) This section applies if—

(*a*) an individual makes one or more gifts to charities in a tax year which are qualifying donations, and

(*b*) amount A is greater than amount B.

(2) In this section—

"amount A" means the total amount of the tax treated as deducted from the gifts under section 414, and

"amount B" means the total amount of income tax and capital gains tax to which the individual is charged for the tax year (before applying this section).

(3) For the purposes of this section, the total amount of income tax to which the individual is charged for the tax year is the amount calculated in accordance with section 425.

(4) The individual's entitlement to the reliefs mentioned in subsection (5) is extinguished, so far as is necessary to ensure that the total amount of income tax and capital gains tax to which the individual is charged for the tax year (after applying this section)—

(*a*) is equal to amount A, or

(*b*) if that is not possible, falls short of amount A by as little as possible.

(5) The reliefs are—

(*a*) an allowance under Chapter 2 of Part 3 of this Act . . . . [1] (personal allowance and blind person's allowance),

(b) a tax reduction under Chapter 3 of Part 3 of this Act . . . [1] (tax reductions for married couples and civil partners), [and][2]

(c) relief under section 457 or 458 of this Act . . . [1] (payments to trade unions and police organisations), . . . [2]

(d) . . . [1] *(payments for benefit of family members).*[2]

Commentary—*Simon's Taxes* **E1.811.**

Amendments—[1] In sub-s (5) words repealed by FA 2009 s 5, Sch 1 para 6(*o*)(iii) with effect for the tax year 2010–11 and subsequent tax years.

[2] In sub-s (5)(*b*), word "and" inserted, and sub-s (5)(*d*) and preceding word "and" repealed, by FA 2012 s 227, Sch 39 para 32(2)(*b*) with effect for the tax year 2013–14 and subsequent tax years.

424 Charge to tax

(1) Income tax is charged under this section if—

    (a) an individual makes one or more gifts to charity in a tax year which are qualifying donations, and

    (b) amount A is greater than amount C.

(2) In this section—

"amount A" means the total amount of the tax treated as deducted from the gifts under section 414, and

"amount C" means the sum of—

    (a) the amount of income tax to which the individual is charged for the tax year, and

    [(b) the amount of capital gains tax to which the individual would be chargeable for the tax year if the following were ignored—

        (i) any relief under [sections 2 and 6 of TIOPA 2010][2] (double taxation arrangements: relief by agreement), and

        (ii) any relief under [section 18(1)(*b*) and (2) of TIOPA 2010][2] (relief for foreign tax where no double taxation arrangements).][1]

(3) For the purposes of this section, the total amount of income tax to which the individual is charged for the tax year is the amount calculated in accordance with section 425, after taking into account any restriction of relief under section 423.

(4) The amount of the tax charged under this section is equal to the difference between amount A and amount C.

(5) Tax charged under this section is charged for the tax year in which the gift or gifts are made.

(6) The person liable for any tax charged under this section is the individual.

Commentary—*Simon's Taxes* **E1.811.**

Derivation—FA 1990 s 25(8).

HMRC Manuals—Residence, Domicile and Remittance Basis Manual RDRM32450 (charitable donations and remittance basis charge).

Amendments—[1] In sub-s (2), in definition of "amount C", para (*b*) substituted by the Income Tax Act 2007 (Amendment) (No 2) Order, SI 2009/2859 art 4(1), (3) with effect for income tax and capital gains tax purposes for the year 2007–08 and subsequent tax years, and for corporation tax purposes for accounting periods ending after 5 April 2007.

[2] In sub-s (2), in definition of "amount C", in paras (*b*)(i), (*b*)(ii), words substituted by TIOPA 2010 s 501, Sch 8 paras 71, 79. TIOPA 2010 has effect for corporation tax purposes for accounting periods ending on or after 1 April 2010, for income and capital gains tax purposes for the tax year 2010–11 and subsequent tax years, and for petroleum revenue tax purposes for chargeable periods beginning on or after 1 July 2010.

425 Total amount of income tax to which individual charged for a tax year

(1) For the purposes of sections 423 and 424, the total amount of income tax to which an individual is charged for a tax year is the amount calculated as follows.

(2) Calculate the individual's liability to income tax for the tax year in accordance with section 23, as modified by subsection (3).

(3) In applying section 23—

    (a) at Step 6, ignore any tax reductions to which the individual is entitled for the tax year under a provision listed in subsection (4), and

    (b) ignore Step 7.

(4) The tax reductions to be ignored are tax reductions under—

    (a) section 453 (qualifying maintenance payments),

    (b) [sections 2 and 6 of TIOPA 2010][2] (double taxation arrangements: relief by agreement), or

    (c) [section 18(1)(*b*) and (2) of TIOPA 2010][2] (relief for foreign tax where no double taxation arrangements).

(5) From the amount calculated in accordance with subsections (2) to (4) deduct—

    (a) any tax treated as having been paid under—

        (i) section 399(2) . . . [3] of ITTOIA 2005 (distributions from UK resident companies etc on which there is no tax credit),

        (ii), (iii) . . . [3]

        (iv) section 530(1) of that Act (gains from contracts for life insurance), or

        (v) section 685A(3) of that Act (settlor-interested settlements), . . . [1] [and][3]

(b) any tax treated as deducted from estate income under section 656(3) or 657(4) of ITTOIA 2005, so far as that income is treated under section 679 of that Act as paid from sums within section [680(4)]⁴ of that Act, . . . ³

(c) . . . ³

(6) For the purposes of this section a person is treated as being entitled to a tax reduction under [sections 2 and 6 of TIOPA 2010]² if the person is entitled to credit against income tax under double taxation arrangements.

Commentary—*Simon's Taxes* **E1.811**.
Amendments—¹ Words "and" at end of sub-s (5)(a)(v) repealed, and sub-s (5)(c) inserted, by FA 2008 s 34, Sch 12 paras 23, 24 with effect for the tax year 2008–09 and subsequent tax years.
² In sub-ss (4)(b), (c), (6), words substituted by TIOPA 2010 s 501, Sch 8 paras 71, 80. TIOPA 2010 has effect for corporation tax purposes for accounting periods ending on or after 1 April 2010, for income and capital gains tax purposes for the tax year 2010–11 and subsequent tax years, and for petroleum revenue tax purposes for chargeable periods beginning on or after 1 July 2010.
³ In sub-s (5), words in para (a)(i), and whole of para (a)(ii), (iii), and para (c) and preceding word "and", repealed; and word "and" at end of para (a) inserted; by FA 2016 s 5, Sch 1 para 63(1), (4)(a), (b), (d) with effect for the tax year 2016-17 and subsequent tax years.
⁴ In sub-s (5)(b), words substituted by FA 2016 s 5, Sch 1 para 63(1), (4)(c) with effect: so far as relating to income within ITTOIA 2005 s 664(2)(c), in relation to stock dividend income treated as arising in the tax year 2016-17 or at any later time; and so far as relating to income within ITTOIA 2005 s 664(2)(d), in relation to amounts released or written off in the tax year 2016-17 or at any later time.

Election to carry back relief

426 Election by donor: gift treated as made in previous tax year

(1) If—
    (a) an individual makes a gift to a charity that is a qualifying donation, and
    (b) the condition in subsection (2) is met,
the individual may elect to be treated as if the gift had been made in the previous tax year ("year P").

(2) The condition is that the individual's charged amount for year P (see section 427) is at least equal to the increased total of gifts.

(3) If an election is made, sections 414 and 423 to 425 have effect in relation to the individual as if the gift were a qualifying donation made by the individual in year P.

(4) The increased total of gifts is the sum of—
    (a) the grossed up amount of the gift, and of any gifts that are the subject of the same election or an election made at the same time,
    (b) the sum of the grossed up amounts of any gifts to charities made by the individual in year P which—
        (i) are qualifying donations, and
        (ii) are not themselves treated as made in the tax year before year P because of an election under this section, and
    (c) the sum of the grossed up amounts of any gifts which, as a result of an earlier election under this section, are treated as made in year P.

(5) The grossed up amount of the gifts mentioned in paragraphs (a) and (c) of subsection (4) is to be determined as if the gifts were made in year P.

(6) An election must be made—
    (a) on or before the date on which the individual delivers a return for year P under section 8 of TMA 1970 (personal return), and
    (b) not later than the normal self-assessment filing date for year P.

(7) An election does not affect the position of the recipient of the gift (see section 520 (gifts to charitable trusts: income tax treated as paid) and [and sections 471 and 475 of CTA 2010 (charitable companies and eligible bodies: income tax treated as paid etc)).]¹

(8) . . . ²

Commentary—*Simon's Taxes* **E1.811**.
Modifications—ITA 2007 Sch 2 para 100 (modification of this section if in the tax year 2007–08 an individual makes a gift to a charity that is a qualifying donation for the purposes of ITA 2007 Pt 8 Chapter 2).
Amendments—¹ In sub-s (7) words substituted by CTA 2010 s 1177, Sch 1 para 525. CTA 2010 has effect for corporation tax purposes for accounting periods ending on or after 1 April 2010, and for income and capital gains tax purposes for the tax year 2010–11 and subsequent tax years.
² Sub-s (8) repealed by FA 2012 s 50(2)(a). This amendment is treated as having come into force on 6 April 2012.

Supplementary

427 Meaning of "charged amount"

(1) For the purposes of this Chapter, an individual's charged amount is the amount calculated as follows.

(2) Calculate the amount of the individual's modified net income for year X (see section 1025).

(3) Calculate the amount on which the individual is chargeable to capital gains tax for year X.

(4) Add together the amounts calculated under subsections (2) and (3). The result is the individual's charged amount for year X.

428 Meaning of "gift aid declaration"

(1) In this Chapter "gift aid declaration" means a declaration which—

    (*a*) is given in the manner specified by regulations made by the Commissioners for Her Majesty's Revenue and Customs, and

    (*b*) contains any information and any statements required by the regulations.

(2) The regulations may provide for declarations—

    (*a*) to have effect,

    (*b*) to cease to have effect, or

    (*c*) to be treated as never having had effect,

in any circumstances and for any purposes specified by the regulations.

[(3) The regulations may also require—

    (*a*) charities, or intermediaries within the meaning of section 416(1A), to keep records with respect to declarations received from individuals or from those intermediaries,

    (*b*) charities or intermediaries to produce, for inspection by an officer of Revenue and Customs, any records required to be kept by those charities or intermediaries by regulations made under paragraph (*a*), and

    (*c*) intermediaries to provide statements of account, and other specified information relating to declarations made, in such form and at such times as may be specified, to individuals who have authorised those intermediaries to give those declarations to charities on their behalf.

(4) The regulations may also make different provision for different cases or circumstances, including—

    (*a*) different provision for declarations made in a different manner or by different descriptions of persons, and

    (*b*) different provision depending on whether or not an intermediary, within the meaning of section 416(1A), is involved in the giving or receiving of the declaration.][1]

[(5) The regulations may also make provision—

    (*a*) for the imposition of a penalty of a specified amount (which must not exceed £3000) for a failure to comply with a specified requirement imposed by the regulations,

    (*b*) for the assessment and recovery of the penalty (which may include provision about the reduction of the penalty in specified circumstances), and

    (*c*) conferring a right of appeal against a decision that a penalty is payable.][2]

Commentary—*Simon's Taxes* **E1.811A**.
Regulations—Donations to Charity (Gift Aid Declarations) Regulations, SI 2016/1195.
Amendments—[1]　Sub-ss (3), (4) substituted for sub-s (3) by FA 2015 s 20(1), (3) with effect in relation to gifts made on or after 14 November 2016 (by virtue of SI 2016/1010 reg 2).
[2]　Sub-s (5) inserted by FA 2016 s 173 with effect from 14 November (by virtue of SI 2016/1010 reg 2).

430 "Charity" to include exempt bodies

(1) In this Chapter "charity" includes—

    (*a*) the Trustees of the National Heritage Memorial Fund, [and][2]

    (*b*) the Historic Buildings and Monuments Commission for England,

    (*c*) . . .[2]

    (*d*) a club that is registered as a community amateur sports club for the purposes of [Chapter 9 of Part 13 of CTA 2010][1].

(2) For the purposes of the application of section 414(1) in relation to clubs that are charities as a result of subsection (1)(*d*) of this section, membership fees are not gifts.

Commentary—*Simon's Taxes* **E1.810**.
Amendments—[1]　In sub-s (1)(*d*) words substituted by CTA 2010 s 1177, Sch 1 para 526. CTA 2010 has effect for corporation tax purposes for accounting periods ending on or after 1 April 2010, and for income and capital gains tax purposes for the tax year 2010–11 and subsequent tax years.
[2]　In sub-s (1)(*a*), word inserted, and sub-s (1)(*c*) repealed by the Public Bodies (Abolition of the National Endowment for Science, Technology and the Arts) Order, SI 2012/964 art 3(1), Schedule with effect from 1 April 2012.

CHAPTER 3

GIFTS OF SHARES, SECURITIES AND REAL PROPERTY TO CHARITIES ETC

Entitlement to relief

431 Relief for gifts of shares, securities and real property to charities etc

(1) An individual who disposes of the whole of the beneficial interest in a qualifying investment (see section 432) to a charity is entitled to relief if—

    (*a*) the disposal is otherwise than by way of a bargain made at arm's length, and

    (*b*) the individual makes a claim.

(2) The relief is given by deducting the relievable amount in calculating the individual's net income for the tax year in which the disposal is made (see Step 2 of the calculation in section 23).

(3) For the calculation of the relievable amount, see section 434.

(4) If the qualifying investment is a qualifying interest in land (see section 433), this section is subject to—
    section 441 (certificates),
    section 442 (qualifying interests in land held jointly),
    section 443 (calculation of relievable amount where joint disposal), and
    section 444 (disqualifying events).
(5) See section 446 for bodies that are treated as charities for the purposes of this Chapter.
(6) See subsection (7) of section 535 of ITTOIA 2005 (top slicing relief) for provision about how relief under this Chapter is to be ignored for the purpose of calculating relief under that section.
[(7) This Chapter is subject to section 809ZM (removal of income tax relief in respect of tainted charity donations etc).][1]

Commentary—*Simon's Taxes* E1.813.
Amendments—[1]   Sub-s (7) inserted by FA 2011 s 27, Sch 3 paras 7, 11 with effect in relation to relievable charity donations made on or after 1 April 2011.

432 Meaning of "qualifying investment"
(1) In this Chapter "qualifying investment" means—
    (a) shares or securities which are listed [on a recognised stock exchange or dealt in on any designated market in the United Kingdom][1],
    (b) units in an authorised unit trust,
    (c) shares in an open-ended investment company,
    (d) an interest in an offshore fund, and
    (e) a qualifying interest in land.
(2) In this section—
    ["designated" means designated by an order made by the Commissioners for Her Majesty's Revenue and Customs for the purposes of subsection (1)(a),][1]
    "offshore fund" has the same meaning as in Chapter 5 of Part 17 of ICTA (see sections 756A to 756C of that Act), and
    "open-ended investment company" is to be read in accordance with [sections 613 and 615 of CTA 2010][2].
[(3) An order under subsection (2) may—
    (a) designate a market by name or by reference to any class or description of market, and
    (b) vary or revoke a previous order under that subsection.][1]

Commentary—*Simon's Taxes* E1.813.
Amendments—[1]   Words in sub-s (1)(a) substituted; in sub-s (2), definition of "designated", and sub-s (3), inserted; by FA 2007 s 109, Sch 26 para 12(1), (10) with effect from 19 July 2007.
[2]   In sub-s (2) words substituted by CTA 2010 s 1177, Sch 1 para 527. CTA 2010 has effect for corporation tax purposes for accounting periods ending on or after 1 April 2010, and for income and capital gains tax purposes for the tax year 2010–11 and subsequent tax years.

433 Meaning of "qualifying interest in land"
(1) In this Chapter "qualifying interest in land" means—
    (a) a freehold interest in land in the United Kingdom, or
    (b) a leasehold interest in land in the United Kingdom which is a term of years absolute.
    This is subject to subsections (2) to (5).
(2) Subsection (3) applies if an individual with a beneficial interest in a freehold or leasehold interest mentioned in subsection (1)(a) or (b) makes a disposal to a charity of—
    (a) the whole of the beneficial interest, and
    (b) an easement, servitude, right or privilege so far as benefiting the land in question.
(3) The disposal mentioned in subsection (2)(b) is regarded for the purposes of this Chapter as a disposal by the individual of the whole of the individual's beneficial interest in a qualifying interest in land separate from the disposal mentioned in subsection (2)(a).
(4) If an individual who has a freehold or leasehold interest in land in the United Kingdom grants a lease for a term of years absolute to a charity of the whole or part of that land, the grant of the lease is regarded for the purposes of this Chapter as a disposal by the individual of the whole of the beneficial interest in the leasehold interest so granted.
(5) Neither an agreement to acquire a freehold interest nor an agreement for a lease is a qualifying interest in land.
(6) In the application of this section to Scotland—
    (a) references to a freehold interest in land are to the interest of the owner,
    (b) references to a leasehold interest in land which is a term of years absolute are to a tenant's right over or interest in a property subject to a lease,
    (c) references to an agreement for a lease do not include missives of let that constitute an actual lease, and
    (d) in subsection (4) the reference to granting a lease for a term of years absolute is to granting a lease.

Commentary—*Simon's Taxes* E1.813.

Derivation—TA 1988 s 587B(9A) to (9E).

Amount of relief

434 The relievable amount

(1) If the disposal is a gift, the relievable amount is given by the formula—

$$V + IC - B$$

where—

V is the value of the net benefit to the charity at, or immediately after, the time when the disposal is made, whichever is less,

IC is the amount of the incidental costs of making the disposal to the individual making it, and

B is the total value of any benefits received in consequence of making the disposal by the individual making the disposal or a person connected with the individual.

(2) If the disposal is at an undervalue, the relievable amount is given by the formula—

$$E + C - B$$

where—

E is the amount (if any) by which V (as defined in subsection (1)) exceeds the amount or value of the consideration for the disposal,

C is given by subsection (4), and

B is as defined in subsection (1).

(3) But if the amount given by the formula in subsection (1) or (2) is a negative amount, the relievable amount is nil.

(4) C is found by taking the following steps.

Step 1 Calculate the consideration for which the disposal is treated as made for the purposes of TCGA 1992 as a result of section 257(2)(*a*) of that Act (in case of disposal to charity etc, consideration to be such that no gain or loss accrues).

Step 2 Find the excess (if any) of the amount calculated at Step 1 over the amount or value of the consideration for the disposal.

If there is such an excess, C is the amount of that excess or, if less, the amount of the incidental costs of making the disposal to the individual making it.

If there is no such excess, C is nil.

(5) This section needs to be read with—

    (*a*) section 435 (incidental costs of making disposal),

    (*b*) section 436 (consideration), and

    (*c*) sections 437 to 440 (value of net benefit to charity).

Commentary—*Simon's Taxes* E1.813.
Derivation—TA 1988 s 587B(4) to (7).

435 Incidental costs of making disposal

References in section 434 to the incidental costs of making the disposal to the individual making it are to—

    (*a*) fees, commission or remuneration paid for the professional services of a surveyor, valuer, auctioneer, accountant, agent or legal adviser which are wholly and exclusively incurred by the individual for the purposes of the disposal,

    (*b*) costs of transfer or conveyance wholly and exclusively incurred by the individual for the purposes of the disposal,

    (*c*) costs of advertising to find a buyer, and

    (*d*) costs reasonably incurred in making any valuation or apportionment required for the purposes of this Chapter.

Commentary—*Simon's Taxes* E1.813.
Derivation—TA 1988 s 587B(9).

436 Consideration

(1) For the purposes of the formula in section 434(2) consideration for the disposal is brought into account—

    (*a*) without any discount for postponement of the right to receive any part of it,

    (*b*) in the first instance, without regard to a risk of any part of it being irrecoverable, and

    (*c*) in the first instance, without regard to the right to receive any part of it being contingent.

(2) If—

    (*a*) any part of the consideration so brought into account subsequently proves to be irrecoverable, and

    (*b*) a claim is made,

such adjustment as is required in consequence must be made.

(3) An adjustment under subsection (2) may be made by way of discharge or repayment of tax or otherwise.

Value of net benefit to charity

437 Value of net benefit to charity

(1) For the purposes of this Chapter the value of the net benefit to a charity is—

    (a) the [relevant][1] value of the qualifying investment, or

    (b) if the charity is, or becomes, subject to a disposal-related obligation, the [relevant][1] value of the qualifying investment reduced by the total amount of the disposal-related liabilities of the charity.

[(1A) In subsection (1) "relevant value" means—

    (a) where subsection (1B) applies, the lower of the market value and the acquisition value, and

    (b) otherwise, the market value.

(1B) This subsection applies where—

    (a) the qualifying investment, or anything from which it derives or which it represents (whether in whole or in part and whether directly or indirectly), was acquired by the individual making the disposal within the period of 4 years ending with the day on which the disposal is made,

    (b) the acquisition was made as part of a scheme, and

    (c) the main purpose, or one of the main purposes, of the individual in entering into the scheme was to obtain relief, or an increased amount of relief, under this Chapter.

(1C) In subsection (1B) "scheme" includes any scheme, arrangement or understanding of any kind, whether or not legally enforceable, involving a single transaction or two or more transactions.][1]

(2) This section is supplemented by—

    section 438 (market value of qualifying investments),

    [section 438A (acquisition value of qualifying investments),][1]

    section 439 (meaning of "disposal-related obligation"), and

    section 440 (meaning and amount of "disposal-related liability").

Commentary—*Simon's Taxes* E1.813.

Amendments—[1] In sub-ss (1)(a), (b) word substituted, sub-ss (1A)–(1C) inserted, and in sub-s (2) entry inserted, by FA 2010 s 31 Sch 7 paras 1, 2 with effect in relation to any disposal made to a charity on or after 15 December 2009.

438 Market value of qualifying investments

(1) The market value of a qualifying investment for the purposes of this Chapter is determined in accordance with sections 272 to 274 of TCGA 1992 (subject to Part 1 of Schedule 11 to that Act).

(2) But, in the case of an interest in an offshore fund for which separate buying and selling prices are published regularly by the managers of the fund, the market value for the purposes of this Chapter is equal to the buying price (that is the lower price) published on—

    (a) the day of the disposal, or

    (b) if none were published on that day, on the latest day on which the prices were published before that day.

[438A Acquisition value of qualifying investments

(1) For the purposes of this Chapter the acquisition value of a qualifying investment disposed of by an individual is—

    (a) where the qualifying investment was acquired by the individual within the period of 4 years ending with the day on which the disposal is made, the cost to the individual of acquiring it, or

    (b) where something from which the qualifying investment derives or which it represents was so acquired, such proportion of the cost to the individual of acquiring that thing as is just and reasonable to attribute to the qualifying investment.

(2) A reference in subsection (1) to the cost to the individual of an acquisition is to—

    (a) the consideration given by the individual for the acquisition, less

    (b) any amount that is received in connection with the acquisition, by the individual or a person connected with the individual, as part of the scheme in question.][1]

Commentary—*Simon's Taxes* E1.813.

Amendments—[1] This section inserted by FA 2010 s 31 Sch 7 paras 1, 3 with effect in relation to any disposal made to a charity on or after 15 December 2009.

439 Meaning of "disposal-related obligation"

(1) In this Chapter an obligation is a "disposal-related obligation", in relation to a qualifying investment, if condition A or condition B is met in relation to it.

(2) The obligation may be to any person (whether or not the individual making the disposal or a person connected with the individual).

(3) Condition A is that it is reasonable to suppose that the disposal of the qualifying investment to the charity would not have been made in the absence of the obligation.

(4) Condition B is that the obligation (whether in whole or in part) relates to, is framed by reference to, or is conditional on the charity receiving, the qualifying investment or a disposal-related investment.

(5) In applying condition A, all the circumstances must be taken into account (including, in particular, the difference in the value of the net benefit to the charity calculated under section 437(1)(*a*) and that value calculated under section 437(1)(*b*)).

(6) In subsection (4) "disposal-related investment" means any of the following—

    (*a*) an asset of the same class or description as the qualifying investment (irrespective of size, quantity or amount),

    (*b*) an asset derived from, or representing, the qualifying investment, whether in whole or in part and whether directly or indirectly, and

    (*c*) an asset from which the qualifying investment is derived, or which the qualifying investment represents, whether in whole or in part and whether directly or indirectly.

(7) In this Chapter "obligation" includes a reference to each of the following—

    (*a*) a scheme, arrangement or understanding of any kind, whether or not legally enforceable, and

    (*b*) a series of obligations (whether or not between the same parties).

Commentary—*Simon's Taxes* **E1.813**.
Derivation—TA 1988 s 587B(8B) to (8D) and (9).

440 Meaning and amount of "disposal-related liability"

(1) In this Chapter a liability is a "disposal-related liability" in the case of a qualifying investment if it is a liability of the charity under a disposal-related obligation in relation to the qualifying investment.

(2) If the disposal-related obligation is contingent, the amount to be brought into account for the purposes of section 437 at any time in respect of the disposal-related liability, so far as contingent, is—

    (*a*) if the contingency occurs, the amount or value of the liability actually incurred in consequence of the occurrence of the contingency, or

    (*b*) if the contingency does not occur, nil.

Commentary—*Simon's Taxes* **E1.813**.
Derivation—TA 1988 s 587B(8E) to (8G).

Special provisions about qualifying interests in land

441 Certificate required from charity

(1) This section applies if the qualifying investment is a qualifying interest in land.

(2) No individual may make a claim for relief under this Chapter unless the individual has received a certificate given by or on behalf of the charity.

(3) The certificate must—

    (*a*) describe the qualifying interest in land,

    (*b*) specify the date of the disposal, and

    (*c*) state that the charity has acquired the qualifying interest in land.

Commentary—*Simon's Taxes* **E1.813**.
Derivation—TA 1988 s 587C(1), (4) and (5).

442 Qualifying interests in land held jointly

(1) This section applies if the qualifying investment is a qualifying interest in land.

(2) It applies if two or more persons ("the owners")—

    (*a*) are jointly beneficially entitled to the qualifying interest in land, or

    (*b*) are, taken together, beneficially entitled in common to the qualifying interest in land.

(3) Relief under this Chapter is available if—

    (*a*) at least one of the owners is an individual, and

    (*b*) all the owners dispose of the whole of their beneficial interests in the qualifying interest in land to the charity.

(4) Relief under this Chapter is available to each of the owners who is an individual.

(5) The amount of relief under this Chapter to be given to an individual is such share of the relievable amount as is allocated to the individual by an agreement made between those owners who are—

    (*a*) individuals, or

    (*b*) qualifying companies.

(6) A company is a qualifying company if—

    (*a*) it is not itself a charity, *[and*

    (*b*) *it is not within section 587B(8)(a) of ICTA]*[1].

(7) If one or more of the owners is not an individual—

    (*a*) for the purpose of determining whether the owners' beneficial interests are disposed of as mentioned in subsection (3)(*b*) of this section, subsections (2) to (4) of section 433 apply as if references to an individual included a reference to a person who is not an individual, and

(b) the total amount of relief [given, because of the disposal of the qualifying interest in land, under this Chapter and as a result of Chapter 3 of Part 6 of CTA 2010][2] is not to exceed the relievable amount.

Commentary—*Simon's Taxes* **E1.813**.
Amendments—[1]   Sub-s (6)(b) and preceding word "and" repealed by FA 2007 s 114, Sch 27 Pt 2(10) with effect in accordance with FA 2007 Sch 10.
[2]   In sub-s (7)(b) words substituted by CTA 2010 s 1177, Sch 1 para 528. CTA 2010 has effect for corporation tax purposes for accounting periods ending on or after 1 April 2010, and for income and capital gains tax purposes for the tax year 2010–11 and subsequent tax years.

443 Calculation of relievable amount where joint disposal of interest in land

(1) This section applies for the purpose of calculating the relievable amount in a case where relief under this Chapter is available as a result of section 442(3).

(2) Calculate the relievable amount as if—
　(a) the owners were a single individual, and
　(b) the disposals of the owners' beneficial interests were a single disposal by that single individual of the whole of the beneficial interest in the qualifying interest in land.

(3) In particular, calculate the consideration mentioned at Step 1 in section 434(4) by—
　(a) calculating, for each owner, the consideration for which the disposal of the owner's beneficial interest is treated as made for the purposes of TCGA 1992 as a result of section 257(2)(a) of that Act, and
　(b) adding together all the consideration calculated under paragraph (a).

(4) Subsection (5) applies if one or more of the owners is neither—
　(a) an individual, nor
　(b) a qualifying company (see section 442(6)).

(5) In calculating the relievable amount make just and reasonable adjustments to reduce the relievable amount to reflect the fact that relief under this Chapter or [as a result of Chapter 3 of Part 6 of CTA 2010][2] is not available to that owner or to those owners.

[(6) If one or more of the owners is a company within paragraph (b) of section 587B(8) of ICTA, in calculating the relievable amount make just and reasonable adjustments to reduce the relievable amount to reflect the requirements of sub-paragraph (ii) of that paragraph.][1]

Commentary—*Simon's Taxes* **E1.813**.
Amendments—[1]   Sub-s (6) repealed by FA 2007 s 114, Sch 27 Pt 2(10) with effect in accordance with FA 2007 Sch 10.
[2]   In sub-s (5) words substituted for words "section 587B of ICTA" by CTA 2010 s 1177, Sch 1 para 529. CTA 2010 has effect for corporation tax purposes for accounting periods ending on or after 1 April 2010, and for income and capital gains tax purposes for the tax year 2010–11 and subsequent tax years.

444 Disqualifying events

(1) This section applies if the qualifying investment is a qualifying interest in land.

(2) If a disqualifying event occurs at any time in the provisional period, the following are treated as never having been entitled to relief under this Chapter in respect of the disposal of the qualifying interest in land—
　(a) in a case to which section 442 does not apply, the individual who made the disposal, or
　(b) in a case to which section 442 applies, each individual who is an owner.

(3) All such assessments and adjustments of assessments are to be made as are necessary to give effect to subsection (2).

(4) A disqualifying event occurs if a person mentioned in subsection (5) becomes, otherwise than for full consideration in money or money's worth—
　(a) entitled to an interest or right in relation to all or part of the land to which the disposal relates, or
　(b) party to an arrangement under which the person enjoys some right in relation to all or part of that land.

(5) The persons are—
　(a) in a case to which section 442 does not apply—
　　(i) the individual who made the disposal, or
　　(ii) a person connected with that individual, and
　(b) in a case to which section 442 applies—
　　(i) a person who is an owner, or
　　(ii) a person connected with such a person.

(6) A disqualifying event does not occur if a person becomes entitled to an interest or right as mentioned in subsection (4)(a) as a result of a disposition of property on death (whether the disposition is effected by will, under the law relating to intestacy or otherwise).

(7) "The provisional period" is the period beginning with the date of the disposal of the qualifying interest in land and ending with the fifth anniversary of the normal self-assessment filing date for the tax year in which the disposal was made.

Commentary—*Simon's Taxes* **E1.813**.
Derivation—TA 1988 s 587C(1) and (6) to (10).

Supplementary

445 Prohibition against double relief

(1) If a claim is made for relief under this Chapter in respect of a disposal—
  (*a*) section 108 of ITTOIA 2005 (gifts of trading stock to charities etc) does not apply in relation to the disposal, and
  (*b*) no relief in respect of the disposal is allowable under any other provision of the Income Tax Acts.

(2) For the effect on capital gains tax or corporation tax on chargeable gains where an individual is entitled to relief under this Chapter, see section 257(2A) to (2C) of TCGA 1992 (gifts to charities etc).

Commentary—*Simon's Taxes* **E1.813**.
Derivation—TA 1988 s 587B(2)(*b*).

446 "Charity" to include exempt bodies

In this Chapter "charity" includes—
  (*a*) the Trustees of the National Heritage Memorial Fund, [and][1]
  (*b*) the Historic Buildings and Monuments Commission for England, . . . [1]
  (*c*) . . . [1]

Amendments—[1]   Word in para (*a*) inserted, and para (*c*) and preceding word "and" repealed, by the Public Bodies (Abolition of the National Endowment for Science, Technology and the Arts) Order, SI 2012/964 art 3(1), Schedule, with effect from 1 April 2012.

CHAPTER 4

ANNUAL PAYMENTS . . .

Amendments—Words in heading repealed by FA 2013 s 15(4)(*c*) with effect in relation to payments made on or after 5 December 2012.

447 Overview of Chapter

(1) This Chapter gives relief for some of the payments from which sums representing income tax must be deducted under Chapter 6 of Part 15 (deduction from annual payments and patent royalties).

(2) For the payments which attract relief, see sections 448 and 449.

448 Relief for individuals

(1) This section applies to a payment made in a tax year if—
  (*a*) the person who makes it is an individual,
  (*b*) a sum representing income tax is required by section 900(2) . . . [2] (deduction from annual payments . . . [2]) to be deducted from it, and
  (*c*) the payment is not deductible in calculating the individual's income from any source.

(2) The individual is entitled to relief for the tax year equal to the gross amount of the payment.

(3) But this is subject to the restrictions in subsection (4) . . . [1].

(4) The total amount of relief given under this section to an individual for a tax year cannot be greater than the amount of the individual's modified net income for the tax year (see section 1025).

(5) The relief is given by deducting the amount of the relief in calculating the individual's net income for the tax year (see Step 2 of the calculation in section 23).

Commentary—*Simon's Taxes* **E1.802**.
HMRC Manuals—Savings and Investment Manual SAIM9060 (deduction of tax from annual payments).
Amendments—[1]   Words "and section 451" in sub-s (3) repealed by FA 2008 s 66(4) with effect in accordance with FA 2008 s 66(8).
[2]   In sub-s (1)(*b*), words repealed by FA 2013 s 15(1), (2) with effect in relation to payments made on or after 5 December 2012.

449 Relief for other persons

(1) This section applies to a payment made in a tax year if—
  (*a*) the person who makes it is not an individual,
  (*b*) a sum representing income tax is required by section 901(3) ...[2] (deduction from annual payments . . . [2]) to be deducted from it, and
  (*c*) the payment is not deductible in calculating the person's income from any source.

(2) The person who makes the payment is entitled to relief for the tax year equal to the gross amount of the payment.

(3) But this is subject to the restrictions in subsections (4) and (5) . . . [1].

(4) Relief is not given for the payment so far as it is ineligible for relief (see section 450).

(5) The total amount of relief given under this section to a person for a tax year cannot be greater than the amount of the person's modified net income for the tax year (see section 1025).

(6) The relief is given by deducting the amount of the relief in calculating the person's net income for the tax year (see Step 2 of the calculation in section 23).

Commentary—*Simon's Taxes* **C4.125**.
Amendments—[1]   Words "and section 451" in sub-s (3) repealed by FA 2008 s 66(4) with effect in accordance with FA 2008 s 66(8).
[2]   In sub-s (1)(*b*), words repealed by FA 2013 s 15(1), (3) with effect in relation to payments made on or after 5 December 2012.

450 Other persons: payments ineligible for relief

(1) This section sets out the circumstances in which a payment to which section 449 applies, or part of it, is ineligible for relief.

(2) The payment is ineligible for relief if, or so far as, it can lawfully be made only out of—

    (*a*) capital, or

    (*b*) income that is exempt from income tax.

(3) If the payment or any part of it is charged to capital, the payment or that part is ineligible for relief.

(4) If—

    (*a*) the person who makes the payment treats it or any part of it as made out of income that is exempt from income tax, and

    (*b*) the rights or obligations of any person are or may in the future be different from what they would have been if the payment or part had not been so treated,

the payment, or the part concerned, is ineligible for relief.

(5) If the payment or a part of it is not ultimately borne by the person who makes it, the payment or the part concerned is ineligible for relief.

(6) But subsection (5) does not apply to a payment or part of a payment if—

    (*a*) the person who makes the payment is liable to income tax on an amount, and

    (*b*) it is because the person receives that amount or benefits from it in some other way that the payment or the part concerned is not ultimately borne by that person.

Commentary—*Simon's Taxes* **E1.802**.

452 The gross amount of a payment

References in this Chapter to the gross amount of a payment are to the amount of the payment before deduction of the sum representing income tax deductible from it under Chapter 6 of Part 15 (deduction from annual payments and patent royalties).

HMRC Manuals—Savings and Investment Manual SAIM9060 (annual payments).

CHAPTER 5

QUALIFYING MAINTENANCE PAYMENTS

453 Tax reduction for qualifying maintenance payments

(1) An individual who makes a claim is entitled to a tax reduction for a tax year in which any qualifying maintenance payments made by the individual fall due.

(2) The amount of the tax reduction is 10% of—

    (*a*) the total amount of qualifying maintenance payments made by the individual which fall due in the tax year, or

    (*b*) if less, the amount specified in section 43 (tax reductions for married couples and civil partners: meaning of "the minimum amount").

(3) The tax reduction is given effect at Step 6 of the calculation in section 23.

Commentary—*Simon's Taxes* **E5.104, E1.806**.
Derivation—TA 1988 s 347B(2), (3) and (5A).

454 Meaning of "qualifying maintenance payment"

(1) For the purposes of section 453 a payment is a "qualifying maintenance payment" if conditions A to E are met.

(2) Condition A is that the payment is a periodical payment made by—

    (*a*) one of the parties to a marriage or civil partnership (including a marriage or civil partnership which has been dissolved or annulled) to or for the benefit of the other party and for the maintenance of the other party, or

    (*b*) one parent of a child to the child's other parent for the maintenance of the child by the other parent or by one person to another for the maintenance by the other of a relevant child of theirs.

(3) Condition B is that—

    (*a*) in a case falling within subsection (2)(*a*), either of the parties to the marriage or civil partnership was born before 6 April 1935, and

    (*b*) in a case falling within subsection (2)(*b*), either the person who made the payment, or the person to whom it is made, was born before that date.

(4) Condition C is that the payment is made—

    (*a*) under an order made by a court in a member State, or

    (*b*) under a written agreement the law applicable to which is the law of a member State or of a part of a member State.

(5) Condition D is that the payment is due at a time when—

    (*a*) in a case falling within subsection (2)(*a*)—

        (i) the two parties are not a married couple, or civil partners of each other, living together (see section 1011), and

    (ii) the party to whom or for whose benefit the payment is made has not entered into a new marriage or a new civil partnership, and

  (b) in a case falling within subsection (2)(b), the person making the payment and the person to whom the payment is made are not living together.

(6) Condition E is that relief from tax in respect of the payment is not available to the person making it under any provision of the Income Tax Acts other than section 453.

(7) In subsection (4) the reference to an order made by a court in a member State includes a reference to a maintenance calculation.

(8) "Maintenance calculation" means—

  (a) a maintenance calculation made under the Child Support Act 1991 (c 48), or

  (b) a maintenance assessment made under the Child Support (Northern Ireland) Order 1991 (SI 1991/2628 (NI 23)).

(9) In this section—

    "child" means a person under 21 years of age,

    "periodical payment" does not include an instalment of a lump sum, and

    "relevant child", in relation to any two persons, means a child who (not being a child who has been boarded out with them by a public authority or voluntary organisation) has been treated by both of them as a child of their family.

Commentary—*Simon's Taxes* **E5.105**.

Modification—ITA 2007 Sch 2 para 101 (transitional provisions and savings: modification of this section).

455 Child support maintenance payments

(1) Condition A in section 454(2) is treated as met in relation to a payment if—

  (a) it is a periodical payment made under a maintenance calculation by any person,

  (b) another person is, for the purposes of the Child Support Act 1991 or (as the case may be) the Child Support (Northern Ireland) Order 1991 (SI 1991/2628 (NI 23)), a parent of the child or children with respect to whom the calculation has effect,

  (c) the calculation was not made under section 7 of the Child Support Act 1991 (right of child in Scotland to apply for maintenance calculation), and

  (d) any of the conditions mentioned in subsection (2) is met.

(2) The conditions are that—

  (a) the payment is made to the Secretary of State in accordance with regulations made under section 29 of the Child Support Act 1991 by virtue of subsection (3)(a)(ii) of that section (collection of child support maintenance: payment to or through Secretary of State),

  (b) the payment is retained by the Secretary of State in accordance with regulations made under section 41 of that Act (arrears of child support maintenance),

  (c) the payment is made to the Department of Health, Social Services and Public Safety for Northern Ireland in accordance with regulations made under Article 29 of the Child Support (Northern Ireland) Order 1991 (SI 1991/2628 (NI 23)), by virtue of paragraph (3)(a)(ii) of that Article (collection of child support maintenance: payment to or through Department), or

  (d) the payment is retained by the Department of Health, Social Services and Public Safety for Northern Ireland in accordance with regulations made under Article 38 of that Order (arrears of child support maintenance).

(3) "Maintenance calculation" and "periodical payment" have the meanings given in section 454(8) and (9).

Commentary—*Simon's Taxes* **E5.106**.

Modification—ITA 2007 Sch 2 para 101 (transitional provisions and savings: modification of this section).

456 Payments under orders for recovery of benefit etc

(1) Condition A in section 454(2) is treated as met in relation to a payment made by any person if—

  (a) it is a periodical payment made to the Secretary of State or to the Department of Health, Social Services and Public Safety for Northern Ireland, and

  (b) it is made under a recovery of benefit order.

(2) A "recovery of benefit order" is—

  (a) one made under section 106 of the Social Security Administration Act 1992 (c 5) or section 101 of the Social Security Administration (Northern Ireland) Act 1992 (c 8) (recovery of expenditure on benefit from person liable for maintenance) in respect of income support claimed by any other person, or

  (b) one made by virtue of section 23 of the Jobseekers Act 1995 (c 18) or Article 25 of the Jobseekers (Northern Ireland) Order 1995 (SI 1995/ 2705 (NI 15)) (recovery of sums in respect of maintenance), in respect of an income-based jobseeker's allowance claimed by any other person.

(3) In subsection (2) "income-based jobseeker's allowance" has the same meaning as in—

  (a) the Jobseekers Act 1995, or

  (b) for Northern Ireland, the Jobseekers (Northern Ireland) Order 1995 (SI 1995/2705 (NI 15)).

(4) "Periodical payment" has the meaning given in section 454(9).

Commentary—*Simon's Taxes* **E5.107**.

Derivation—TA 1988 s 347B(12) and (13).

CHAPTER 6

MISCELLANEOUS OTHER RELIEFS

Payments for life insurance etc

457 Payments to trade unions

(1) An individual who makes a payment to a trade union in a tax year is entitled to relief for the tax year if—

    (*a*) part of the payment (the "qualifying amount") is attributable to the provision of superannuation, life insurance or funeral benefits,

    (*b*) the individual meets the requirements of section 460 (residence etc), and

    (*c*) the individual makes a claim.

(2) The amount of the relief is equal to half the qualifying amount.

(3) But the maximum amount of relief under this section to which an individual is entitled for a tax year is £100.

(4) The relief is given by deducting the amount of the relief in calculating the individual's net income for the tax year (see Step 2 of the calculation in section 23).

(5) "Trade union" has the meaning given by section 1 of the Trade Union and Labour Relations (Consolidation) Act 1992 (c 52).

Commentary—*Simon's Taxes* **D7.635**.

458 Payments to police organisations

(1) An individual who makes a payment to a police organisation in a tax year is entitled to relief for the tax year if—

    (*a*) part of the payment (the "qualifying amount") is attributable to the provision of superannuation, life insurance or funeral benefits,

    (*b*) the sum of the qualifying amounts for all the payments which the individual makes in the tax year is at least £20,

    (*c*) the individual meets the requirements of section 460 (residence etc), and

    (*d*) the individual makes a claim.

(2) The amount of the relief is equal to half the qualifying amount.

(3) But the maximum amount of relief under this section to which an individual is entitled for a tax year is £100.

(4) The relief is given by deducting the amount of the relief in calculating the individual's net income for the tax year (see Step 2 of the calculation in section 23).

(5) "Police organisation" means an organisation of persons in police service.

460 Residence etc of claimants

(1) This section applies in relation to an individual who claims—

    (*a*) relief under section 457 or 458 (payments to trade unions and police organisations) for a tax year, . . .[2]

    (*b*) . . .[2]

(2) The individual meets the requirements of this section if the individual—

    (*a*) is UK resident for the tax year, or

    (*b*) meets the condition in subsection (3).

(3) An individual meets the condition in this subsection if, at any time in the tax year, the individual—

    (*a*) is resident in the Isle of Man or the Channel Islands,

    (*b*) has previously resided in the United Kingdom and is resident abroad for the sake of the health of—

        (i) the individual, or

        (ii) a member of the individual's family who is resident with the individual,

    (*c*) is a person who is or has been employed in the service of the Crown,

    (*d*) is employed in the service of any territory under Her Majesty's protection,

    (*e*) is employed in the service of a missionary society, or

    (*f*) is a person whose late spouse or late civil partner was employed in the service of the Crown.

[(4) For the effect of section 809B (claim for remittance basis to apply) applying to an individual for a tax year, see section 809G (no entitlement under section 457 [or 458[2]).][1]

Amendments—[1] Sub-s (4) inserted by FA 2008 s 25, Sch 7 paras 74, 78 with effect for the tax year 2008–09 and subsequent tax years.

[2] Sub-s (1)(*b*) and preceding word "or" repealed, and in sub-s (4), words substituted, by FA 2012 s 227, Sch 39 para 32(2)(*c*) with effect for the tax year 2013–14 and subsequent tax years.

Patent royalty receipts

461 Spreading of patent royalty receipts

(1) A person who makes a claim is entitled to a tax reduction for a tax year in which the person receives a payment of a royalty or other sum if—

    (a) the payment is in respect of the use of a patent,

    (b) the use of the patent has extended over a period of two years or more, and

    (c) the payment is one from which a sum representing income tax is required to be deducted under section 903.

(2) The amount of the tax reduction is the difference between—

    (a) the amount of income tax payable by the person in respect of the payment, and

    (b) the total amount of income tax which would have been payable by the person in respect of the payment on the assumptions in subsection (3).

(3) Those assumptions are that—

    (a) the payment was made in a number of equal instalments at yearly intervals,

    (b) the last instalment was paid on the date on which the payment was in fact made, and

    (c) the number of instalments was the same as the number of complete years in the period over which the use of the patent extended, but subject to a maximum of 6.

(4) The tax reduction is given effect at Step 6 of the calculation in section 23.

Commentary—*Simon's Taxes* A4.437, B5.335.
Derivation—TA 1988 s 527.

PART 9

SPECIAL RULES ABOUT SETTLEMENTS AND TRUSTEES

CHAPTER 1
INTRODUCTION

462 Overview of Part

(1) This Part sets out special rules about settlements and trustees.

(2) Chapter 2 contains general provision about settlements and trustees, for example, definitions of expressions relating to settlements.

(3) Chapter 3 provides for income tax to be charged at the dividend trust rate or at the trust rate on certain amounts included in the net income of the trustees of a settlement.

(4) Chapter 4 provides—

    (a) for expenses of the trustees of a settlement to be set against the trustees' trust rate income (see section 463(2)), and

    (b) consequentially, for the amount of the trust rate income to be reduced.

(5) Chapter 5 qualifies section 479 (which is in Chapter 3) in the case of the trustees of [a Schedule 2][3] share incentive plan.

(6) Chapter 6 provides that the first slice of the trust rate income of the trustees of a settlement is not to be charged at the dividend trust rate or at the trust rate.

(7) Chapter 7 deals with the treatment of payments made by the trustees of a settlement in the exercise of a discretion.

This affects the way the trustees and the recipients of such payments are taxed.

(8) Chapter 8 deals with the treatment of expenses of the trustees of a settlement where income arising to the trustees is, before being distributed, the income of a person other than the trustees themselves.

This affects the way that other person is taxed on that income.

(9) Chapter 9 deals with unauthorised unit trusts. [2]

(10) Chapter 10 deals with heritage maintenance settlements.

(11) See also Part 10 for special rules about charitable trusts [and section 838A for special provision about asbestos compensation settlements][1].

(12) See also Chapter 4 of Part 2 of FA 2005 for provision about trusts with vulnerable beneficiaries.

Amendments—[1]   In sub-s (11) words inserted by F(No 3)A 2010 s 31, Sch 14 para 3(1), (2). This amendment is treated as having had effect for the tax year 2007–08 and subsequent tax years.

[2]   Sub-s (9) repealed by the Unauthorised Unit Trusts (Tax) Regulations, SI 2013/2819 reg 37(1), (5) with effect from 6 April 2014. Note that an unauthorised unit trust is not a non-exempt unauthorised unit trust, and these amendments do not apply in relation to the trust, if at all times in the period beginning with 24 May 2012 and ending with 5 April 2014 it had at least one unit holder which was, and at least one unit holder which was not, an eligible investor (ie a mixed unauthorised unit trust); this ceases to apply in relation to the trust if subsequently it no longer has any unit holders which are eligible investors (SI 2013/2819 reg 32).

[3]   In sub-s (5) words substituted by FA 2014 s 51, Sch 8 paras 68, 69 with effect from 6 April 2014. The effect of the FA 2014 changes on SIPs established before 6 April 2014 is set out in FA 2014 Sch 8 paras 91 to 96.

463 Interpretation of Part

(1) In this Part—

    "other income" means income which is neither dividend income nor savings income, and

    "the trustees of a settlement" does not include personal representatives.

(2) References in this Part to the trust rate income for a tax year of the trustees of a settlement are references to the trustees' net income for the tax year so far as it includes amounts on which income tax is charged at the dividend trust rate or at the trust rate (ignoring Chapters 4 and 6).

Commentary—*Simon's Taxes* C4.506.
Derivation—TA 1988 ss 686(6), 687(4).

464 Scottish trusts

(1) This section applies if—

    (a) income arises to trustees under a trust having effect under the law of Scotland,

    (b) the trustees are UK resident, and

    (c) a beneficiary under the trust ("B") would have an equitable right in possession to the income if the trust had effect under the law of England and Wales.

(2) B is treated for income tax purposes as having an equitable right in possession to the income (even though B has no such right under the law of Scotland).

Commentary—*Simon's Taxes* C4.207, C4.206, C4.501.
Derivation—FA 1993 s 118(1).

CHAPTER 2

GENERAL PROVISION ABOUT SETTLEMENTS AND TRUSTEES

Overview

465 Overview of Chapter and interpretation

(1) This Chapter contains general provision about settlements and trustees.

(2) Section 466 explains what is meant by references to settled property.

(3) Sections 467 to 473 explain what is meant by references to a settlor in relation to a settlement.

(4) Sections 474 to 476 treat the trustees of a settlement as a single and distinct person and set out rules in relation to the residence . . . [1] of that person.

(5) Section 477 relates to sub-fund elections under paragraph 1 of Schedule 4ZA to TCGA 1992.

(6) Section 478 is about references to settled property etc in regulations.

(7) For the purposes of this Chapter property is derived from other property if—

    (a) it derives (directly or indirectly and wholly or partly) from that other property or any part of that other property, and

    (b) in particular, if it derives (directly or indirectly and wholly or partly) from income from that other property or any part of that other property.

(8) In this Chapter "arrangements" includes any scheme, agreement or understanding, whether or not legally enforceable.

Commentary—*Simon's Taxes* C4.305.
Amendments—[1] In sub-s (4) words "and ordinary residence" repealed by FA 2013 s 219, Sch 46 paras 54, 55 with effect for the purposes of a person's tax liability to income tax for the tax year 2013–14 or any subsequent tax year, subject to savings in FA 2013 Sch 46 para 73.

Settled property

466 Meaning of "settled property" etc

(1) This section applies for the purposes of the Income Tax Acts, except so far as, in those Acts, the context otherwise requires.

(2) "Settled property" means any property held in trust other than property excluded by subsection (3).

(3) Property is excluded for the purposes of subsection (2) if—

    (a) it is held by a person as nominee for another person,

    (b) it is held by a person as trustee for another person who is absolutely entitled to the property as against the trustee, or

    (c) it is held by a person as trustee for another person who would be absolutely entitled to the property as against the trustee if that other person were not an infant or otherwise lacking legal capacity.

(4) References, however expressed, to property comprised in a settlement are references to settled property.

(5) A person is absolutely entitled to property as against a trustee if the person has the exclusive right to direct how the property is to be dealt with (subject to the trustees' right to use the property for the payment of duty, taxes, costs or other outgoings).

(6) References to a person who is or would be so entitled include references to two or more persons who are or would be jointly absolutely entitled as against the trustee.

Commentary—*Simon's Taxes* C4.305, C4.203.
Derivation—TA 1988 s 685A.
HMRC Manuals—Trusts, Settlements And Estates Manual TSEM1102 (meaning of settlement and related terms: 'settled property' for general income tax purposes).

Settlors

467 Meaning of "settlor" etc

(1) In the Income Tax Acts (except where the context otherwise requires) "settlor", in relation to a settlement, means the person, or any of the persons, who has made the settlement.

(2) In the Income Tax Acts (except where the context otherwise requires) a person is a settlor of property if—

    (*a*) the property is settled property because of—

        (i) the person's having made the settlement, or

        (ii) an event which leads to the person being treated by this Chapter as having made the settlement, or

    (*b*) the property derives from settled property within paragraph (*a*).

(3) A person ("S") is treated for the purposes of the Income Tax Acts as having made a settlement if—

    (*a*) S has made or entered into the settlement (directly or indirectly), or

    (*b*) the settled property, or property from which the settled property derives, is or includes property within subsection (4).

(4) Property is within this subsection if—

    (*a*) the settlement arose on S's death (whether by S's will, on S's intestacy or in any other way), and

    (*b*) immediately before S's death, the property was property of S—

        (i) which was disposable property (see section 468), or

        (ii) which represented S's severable share in any property to which S was beneficially entitled as joint tenant.

(5) In particular, S is treated for the purposes of the Income Tax Acts as having made a settlement if—

    (*a*) S has provided property for the purposes of the settlement (directly or indirectly), or

    (*b*) S has undertaken to do that.

(6) If a person ("A") makes or enters into a settlement in accordance with reciprocal arrangements with another person ("B")—

    (*a*) B is treated for the purposes of the Income Tax Acts as having made the settlement, and

    (*b*) A is not to be treated for the purposes of the Income Tax Acts as having made the settlement just because of the reciprocal arrangements.

(7) This section needs to be read with sections 469 to 473.

(8) This section and sections 469 to 473 do not apply for the purposes of Chapter 5 of Part 5 of ITTOIA 2005 (amounts treated as income of settlors).

Commentary—*Simon's Taxes* **C4.315.**

Derivation—TA 1988 s 685B.

HMRC Manuals—Stamp Taxes On Shares Manual STSM081050 (trusts and pension schemes: settlors).

Trusts, Settlements And Estates Manual TSEM1102 (meaning of settlement and related terms; 'settlor' for general income tax purposes).

468 Meaning of "disposable property"

(1) This section applies for the purposes of section 467(4)(*b*)(i).

(2) Property is disposable if S could have disposed of it by S's will.

(3) In working out whether any property could have been so disposed of—

    (*a*) make the assumptions mentioned in subsection (4), and

    (*b*) ignore the powers mentioned in subsection (5).

(4) Assume that—

    (*a*) S is of full age and capacity,

    (*b*) the property is situated in England and Wales, and

    (*c*) if S is not domiciled in the United Kingdom, S is domiciled in England and Wales.

(5) The powers to be ignored are—

    (*a*) any power of appointment giving S the right to dispose of the property, and

    (*b*) any testamentary power conferred by statute to dispose of entailed interests.

469 Person ceasing to be a settlor

(1) A person ("S") who is a settlor in relation to a settlement ceases to be so when the following condition is met.

(2) The condition is that—

    (*a*) no property of which S is the settlor is comprised in the settlement,

    (*b*) S has not undertaken to provide property (directly or indirectly) for the purposes of the settlement in the future, and

    (*c*) S has not made reciprocal arrangements with another person for that other person to enter into the settlement in the future.

Commentary—*Simon's Taxes* **C4.315.**

Derivation—TA 1988 s 685B(6).
HMRC Manuals—Stamp Taxes On Shares Manual STSM081050 (trusts and pension schemes: settlors).

470 Transfers between settlements

(1) Section 471 applies in relation to a transfer of property from the trustees of one settlement ("settlement 1") to the trustees of another settlement ("settlement 2") if the transfer—

    (*a*) is not for full consideration,

    (*b*) is not by way of a bargain made at arm's length, and

    (*c*) is not excluded by subsection (2).

(2) A transfer of property is excluded for the purposes of subsection (1) if—

    (*a*) it occurs only because of the assignment by a beneficiary under settlement 1 of an interest in that settlement to the trustees of settlement 2,

    (*b*) it occurs only because of the exercise of a general power of appointment, or

    (*c*) section 473(4) applies in relation to it.

(3) In this section "transfer of property" means—

    (*a*) a disposal of property by the trustees of settlement 1, and

    (*b*) the acquisition by the trustees of settlement 2 of—

        (i) property disposed of by the trustees of settlement 1, or

        (ii) property created by the disposal.

(4) For the purposes of subsection (3) there is an acquisition or disposal of property if there would be an acquisition or disposal of property for the purposes of TCGA 1992.

Commentary—*Simon's Taxes* **C4.316**.
Derivation—TCGA 1992 s 68B.

471 Identification of settlor following transfer covered by section 470

(1) If there is a transfer of property in relation to which this section applies, then the following subsections apply for the purposes of the Income Tax Acts, except so far as, in those Acts, the context otherwise requires.

(2) The settlor (or each settlor) of the property disposed of by the trustees of settlement 1 ("the disposed property") is treated from the time of the disposal as having made settlement 2.

(3) If there is more than one settlor of the disposed property, each of them is treated in relation to settlement 2 as the settlor of a proportionate part of the property acquired by the trustees of settlement 2 on the disposal.

(4) So far as the disposed property—

    (*a*) was provided for the purposes of settlement 1, or

    (*b*) was derived from property so provided,

the property acquired by the trustees of settlement 2 on the disposal is treated from the time of the disposal as having been provided for the purposes of settlement 2.

(5) If as a result of subsection (4), property ("the transferred property") is treated as having been provided for the purposes of settlement 2—

    (*a*) the person who provided the disposed property, or the property from which it was derived, for the purposes of settlement 1 is treated as having provided the transferred property for the purposes of settlement 2, and

    (*b*) if more than one person provided the disposed property, or the property from which it was derived, for the purposes of settlement 1, each of them is treated as having provided a proportionate part of the transferred property for the purposes of settlement 2.

Commentary—*Simon's Taxes* **C4.316**.
Derivation—TA 1988 s 685C.

472 Settlor where property becomes settled because of variation of will etc

(1) This section applies if—

    (*a*) a disposition of property following a person's death is varied, and

    (*b*) section 62(6) of TCGA 1992 applies in relation to the variation.

(2) If property becomes settled property because of the variation (and would not, but for the variation, have become settled property), a person within subsection (3) is treated for the purposes of the Income Tax Acts (except where the context otherwise requires)—

    (*a*) as having made the settlement, and

    (*b*) as having provided the property for the purposes of the settlement.

(3) The persons within this subsection are—

    (*a*) a person who immediately before the variation was entitled to the property, or to property from which it derived, absolutely as legatee,

    (*b*) a person who immediately before the variation would have been so entitled if that person had not been an infant or otherwise lacking legal capacity,

    (*c*) a person who, but for the variation, would have become so entitled, and

    (*d*) a person who, but for the variation, would have become so entitled if that person had not been an infant or otherwise lacking legal capacity.

(4) For the purposes of subsection (3)—

(*a*) "legatee" includes a person taking property—
    (i) under a testamentary disposition or on an intestacy or partial intestacy, whether beneficially or as trustee, or
    (ii) under a donatio mortis causa, and
(*b*) a person who is a legatee as a result of paragraph (*a*)(ii) is treated as acquiring the property when the donor dies.
(5) For the purposes of subsection (4)(*a*) property taken under a testamentary disposition or on an intestacy or partial intestacy includes any property appropriated by the personal representatives in or towards satisfaction of—
    (*a*) a pecuniary legacy, or
    (*b*) any other interest or share in the property devolving under the disposition or intestacy.
Commentary—*Simon's Taxes* **C4.317**.
Derivation—TA 1988 s 685D.

473 Deceased person as settlor where variation of will etc
(1) This section applies if—
    (*a*) a disposition of property following the death of a person ("D") is varied, and
    (*b*) section 62(6) of TCGA 1992 applies in relation to the variation.
(2) If—
    (*a*) property would have become comprised in a settlement within subsection (3), but
    (*b*) as a result of the variation, the property, or property derived from it, becomes comprised in another settlement,
D is treated for the purposes of the Income Tax Acts (except where the context otherwise requires) as having made the other settlement.
(3) A settlement is within this subsection if—
    (*a*) it arose on D's death (whether by D's will or on D's intestacy or in any other way), or
    (*b*) it was in existence immediately before D's death (whether or not D was a settlor in relation to it).
(4) If—
    (*a*) immediately before the variation property is comprised in a settlement and is property of which D is a settlor, and
    (*b*) immediately after the variation the property, or property derived from it, becomes comprised in another settlement,
D is treated for the purposes of the Income Tax Acts (except where the context otherwise requires) as having made the other settlement.
(5) A settlement treated as made by D as a result of this section is treated for the purposes of the Income Tax Acts as made by D immediately before D's death.
(6) But subsection (5) does not apply in relation to a settlement which arose on D's death.
Commentary—*Simon's Taxes* **C4.317**.
Derivation—TA 1988 s 685D.

Trustees

474 Trustees of settlement to be treated as a single and distinct person
(1) For the purposes of the Income Tax Acts (except where the context otherwise requires), the trustees of a settlement are together treated as if they were a single person (distinct from the persons who are the trustees of the settlement from time to time).
(2) If different parts of the settled property in relation to a settlement are vested in different bodies of trustees, subsection (1) and sections 475 and 476 apply in relation to the different bodies as if they were all one body.
(3) The cases covered by subsection (2) include cases where settled land (within the meaning of the Settled Land Act 1925 (c 18)) is vested in the tenant for life and investments representing capital money are vested in the trustees of the settlement.
Commentary—*Simon's Taxes* **C4.405, C4.203**.
Modification—ITA 2007 Sch 2 para 135(1), (2) (this section does not apply for the purposes of ITA 2007 ss 731–735 in relation to benefits received before 15 June 1989).

475 Residence of trustees
[(1) This section applies for income tax purposes and explains how to work out, in relation to the trustees of a settlement, whether or not the single person mentioned in section 474(1) is UK resident.][2]
(2) If at a time either condition A or condition B is met, then at that time the single person is [UK resident][2].
(3) If at a time neither condition A nor condition B is met, then at that time the single person is [non-UK resident][2].
(4) Condition A is met at a time if, at that time, all the persons who are trustees of the settlement are UK resident.
(5) Condition B is met at a time if at that time—

    (*a*) at least one person who is a trustee of the settlement is UK resident and at least one such person is non-UK resident, and

    (*b*) a settlor in relation to the settlement meets condition C (see section 476).

(6) If at a time a person ("T") who is a trustee of the settlement acts as trustee in the course of a business which T carries on in the United Kingdom through a branch, agency or permanent establishment there, then for the purposes of subsections (4) and (5) assume that T is UK resident at that time.

[(7) Subsection (8) applies if—

    (*a*) an individual becomes or ceases to be a trustee of the settlement during a tax year,

    (*b*) that year is a split year as respects the individual, and

    (*c*) the only period in that year when the individual is a trustee of the settlement falls wholly within the overseas part of the year.

(8) The individual is to be treated for the purposes of subsections (4) and (5) as if he or she had been non-UK resident for the year (and hence for the period in that year when he or she was a trustee of the settlement).

(9) But subsection (8) is subject to subsection (6) and, accordingly, an individual who is treated under subsection (8) as having been non-UK resident is, in spite of that, to be treated as UK resident whenever the individual acts as mentioned in subsection (6).][1]

Commentary—*Simon's Taxes* **C4.405**.

HMRC Manuals—Trusts, Settlements And Estates Manual TSEM10020 (trust residence for income tax and capital gains tax purposes – periods from 6 April 2007).

Modifications—ITA 2007 Sch 2 para 134(1), (2) (this section does not apply for the purposes of ITA 2007 ss 727–730 in relation to income payable before 15 June 1989).

ITA 2007 Sch 2 para 134(1), (3) (this section does not apply for the purposes of ITA 2007 ss 727–730 in relation to income payable on or after 15 June 1989 if—

    (a)   the individual received or became entitled to receive the capital sum mentioned in section 729(1) before that date, and

    (b)   the capital sum was wholly repaid or the right to it waived before 1 October 1989).

ITA 2007 Sch 2 para 135(1), (2) (this section does not apply for the purposes of ITA 2007 ss 731 to 735 in relation to benefits received before 15 June 1989).

Amendments—[1]   Sub-ss (7)–(9) inserted by FA 2013 s 218, Sch 45 para 103 with effect in calculating an individual's liability to income tax or capital gains tax for the tax year 2013–14 or any subsequent tax year, subject to transitional provisions and savings in FA 2013 Sch 45 paras 154–158.

[2]   Sub-s (1) substituted, words in sub-s (2) substituted for words "both UK resident and ordinarily UK resident" and words in sub-s (3) substituted for words "both non-UK resident and not ordinarily UK resident, " by FA 2013 s 219, Sch 46 paras 54, 56 with effect for the purposes of a person's tax liability to income tax for the tax year 2013–14 or any subsequent tax year, subject to savings in FA 2013 Sch 46 para 73.

476 How to work out whether settlor meets condition C

(1) This section applies for the purpose of working out whether a settlor ("S") in relation to a settlement meets condition C at a time.

(2) If—

    (*a*) the settlement arose on S's death (whether by S's will, on S's intestacy or in any other way), and

    (*b*) immediately before S's death, S was UK resident   . . . [1] or domiciled in the United Kingdom,

then S meets condition C from the time of S's death until S ceases to be a settlor in relation to the settlement.

(3) If—

    (*a*) the settlement is not within subsection (2)(*a*), and

    (*b*) at a time when S made the settlement (or is treated for the purposes of the Income Tax Acts as making the settlement), S was UK resident . . . [1] or domiciled in the United Kingdom,

then S meets condition C from that time until S ceases to be a settlor in relation to the settlement.

[(3A) Section 835BA (deemed domicile) applies for the purposes of subsections (2)(*b*) and (3)(*b*).][2]

(4) Further, if—

    (*a*) there is a transfer of property in relation to which section 471 applies,

    (*b*) S is a settlor in relation to settlement 2 as a result of that section, and

    (*c*) immediately before the disposal by the trustees of settlement 1, S meets condition C as a settlor in relation to settlement 1 as a result of subsection (2) or (3) or this subsection,

then S meets condition C as a settlor in relation to settlement 2 from the time S becomes such a settlor until S ceases to be such a settlor.

(5) "Settlement 1" and "settlement 2" are to be read in accordance with section 470(1).

Commentary—*Simon's Taxes* **C4.405**.

Amendments—[1]   In sub-ss (2)(*b*), (3)(*b*), words repealed by FA 2013 s 219, Sch 46 paras 54, 57 The amendment to sub-s (2)(*b*) applies where the person died on or after 6 April 2013 (FA 2013 Sch 46 para 57(4)). The amendment to sub-s (3)(*b*) applies where the settlement was made on or after 6 April 2013 (FA 2013 Sch 46 para 57(5)).

[2] Sub-s (3A) inserted by F(No 2)A 2017 s 29(2), Sch 8 paras 11, 12 with effect: (a) so far as relating to ITA 2007 s 476(2)(*b*), in relation to a settlor who dies on or after 6 April 2017; and (b) so far as relating to ITA 2007 s 476(3)(*b*), in relation to a settlement made on or after 6 April 2017.

Sub-funds

477 Sub-fund elections under Schedule 4ZA to TCGA 1992

(1) This section applies for the purposes of the Income Tax Acts (except so far as, in those Acts, the context otherwise requires) if the trustees of a settlement have made a sub-fund election under paragraph 1 of Schedule 4ZA to TCGA 1992.

(2) The sub-fund settlement is treated as a settlement that is created at the relevant time.

(3) Each trustee of the trusts on which property comprised in the sub-fund settlement is held is treated as a trustee of the sub-fund settlement.

(4) A person ("T") who is a trustee of the sub-fund settlement is treated, from the relevant time, as having ceased to be a trustee of the principal settlement unless T is also a trustee of trusts on which property comprised in the principal settlement is held.

(5) A person ("T") who is a trustee of the principal settlement is not to be treated as a trustee of the sub-fund settlement unless T is also a trustee of trusts on which property comprised in the sub-fund settlement is held.

(6) The trustees of the sub-fund settlement are treated as having become, at the relevant time, absolutely entitled to the property comprised in that settlement as against the trustees of the principal settlement.

(7) In this section—

"principal settlement" has the meaning given by paragraph 1 of Schedule 4ZA to TCGA 1992,
"the relevant time" means the time when the sub-fund election is treated as having taken effect under paragraph 2 of that Schedule,
"sub-fund election" has the meaning given by paragraph 2 of that Schedule, and
"sub-fund settlement" has the meaning given by paragraph 1 of that Schedule.

Commentary—*Simon's Taxes* **C4.601, C4.605**.
Derivation—TA 1988 s 685G.

Regulations

478 References to settled property etc in regulations

For the purposes of regulations (whenever made) made under a provision of the Income Tax Acts—

    (*a*) references to settled property, a settlor or trustees are to be read in accordance with this Chapter, and
    (*b*) references to the trustees of a trust are to be read as references to the trustees of a settlement.

CHAPTER 3
SPECIAL RATES FOR TRUSTEES' INCOME

479 Trustees' accumulated or discretionary income to be charged at special rates

(1) This section applies if—

    (*a*) accumulated or discretionary income arises to the trustees of a settlement, and
    (*b*) the income does not arise under a [charitable trust][1].

(2) Income tax is charged on the income at the rates referred to in this section instead of at the rates which would otherwise apply (for which see Chapter 2 of Part 2 (rates at which income tax is charged)).

(3) Income tax is charged on the income at the dividend trust rate so far as the income is dividend income.

(4) Otherwise, income tax is charged on the income at the trust rate.

(5) Section 488 disapplies this section in cases relating to [Schedule 2][2] share incentive plans.

Commentary—*Simon's Taxes* **C4.210**.
Amendments—[1] In sub-s (1)(*b*) words substituted by FA 2010 s 30, Sch 6 para 23(1), (2) with effect for the tax year 2012–13 and subsequent tax years (SI 2012/736 art 17).
[2] In sub-s (5) words substituted by FA 2014 s 51, Sch 8 paras 68, 70 with effect from 6 April 2014. The effect of the FA 2014 changes on SIPs established before 6 April 2014 is set out in FA 2014 Sch 8 paras 91 to 96.

480 Meaning of "accumulated or discretionary income"

(1) Income is accumulated or discretionary income so far as—

    (*a*) it must be accumulated, or
    (*b*) it is payable at the discretion of the trustees or any other person,

and it is not excluded by subsection (3).

(2) The cases covered by subsection (1)(*b*) include cases where the trustees have, or any other person has, any discretion over one or more of the following matters—

    (*a*) whether, or the extent to which, the income is to be accumulated,
    (*b*) the persons to whom the income is to be paid, and
    (*c*) how much of the income is to be paid to any person.

(3) Income is excluded for the purposes of subsection (1) so far as—

    (a) before being distributed, it is the income of any person other than the trustees,

    (b) it is income from property within subsection (4), or

    (c) it is income from service charges [which are paid in respect of dwellings in the United Kingdom and are held on trust.][1]

(4) Property is within this subsection if it—

    (a) is held for the purposes of a superannuation fund to which section 615(3) of ICTA (superannuation funds relating to undertakings outside the UK) applies, but

    (b) is not held as a member of a property investment LLP.

[(5) In subsection (3)(c) "service charges" has the meaning given by section 18 of the Landlord and Tenant Act 1985 (but as if that section also applied in relation to dwellings in Scotland and Northern Ireland).][1]

Commentary—*Simon's Taxes* **C4.210**.

Amendments—[1]   Words in sub-s (3)(c) substituted, and sub-s (5) substituted for original sub-ss (5), (6), by FA 2007 s 65 with effect from the tax year 2007–08.

481 Other amounts to be charged at special rates for trustees

(1) This section applies if—

    (a) the trustees of a settlement are liable for income tax on an amount of a type set out in section 482,

    (b) the trustees are not trustees of a unit trust scheme, and

    (c) the amount is not income arising under a [charitable trust][1].

(2) Income tax is charged on the amount at one of the rates referred to in this section instead of at the rate which would otherwise apply (for which see Chapter 2 of Part 2 (rates at which income tax is charged)).

This is subject to subsection (5).

(3) If the amount is within Type 1 [or Type12][2] as set out in section 482, income tax is charged on the amount at the dividend trust rate.

(4) Otherwise, income tax is charged on the amount at the trust rate.

(5) Income tax is not to be charged as mentioned in subsection (2) so far as the amount—

    (a) is accumulated or discretionary income,

    (b) would be accumulated or discretionary income apart from section 480(3)(a) or (c), or

    (c) is income from property within subsection (6).

(6) Property is within this subsection if it is held for the purposes of a superannuation fund to which section 615(3) of ICTA (superannuation funds relating to undertakings outside the UK) applies.

Commentary—*Simon's Taxes* **C4.208**.

Amendments—[1]   In sub-s (1)(c) words substituted by FA 2010 s 30, Sch 6 para 23(1), (3) with effect for the tax year 2012–13 and subsequent tax years (SI 2012/736 art 17).

[2]   In sub-s (3) words inserted by FA 2015 s 19(7) with effect in relation to things received on or after 6 April 2015 (even if the choice to receive them was made before that date).

482 Types of amount to be charged at special rates for trustees

The types of amount referred to in section 481 are as follows.

    Type 1 A payment—

        (a) which is made to the trustees or to which the trustees are entitled, and

        (b) which is made [by way of . . . [4] distribution][1] by a company on the redemption, repayment or purchase of shares in the company or on the purchase of rights to acquire such shares.

    Type 2 Accrued income profits treated as made by the trustees under section 628(5) or 630(2).

    Type 3 Income treated as arising to the trustees under [regulation 17 of the Offshore Funds (Tax) Regulations 2009 (SI 2009/3001)][2].

    Type 4 Income which the trustees are treated as receiving under section 68(2) or 71(4) of FA 1989 (which relate to employee share ownership trusts).

    Type 5 A sum to which Chapter 4 of Part 3 of ITTOIA 2005 (which provides for certain amounts to be treated as receipts of a property business) applies.

    Type 6 A profit in relation to which the trustees are liable for income tax under section 429 of ITTOIA 2005 (profits from deeply discounted securities).

    Type 7 A gain in relation to which the trustees are liable for income tax under section 467 of ITTOIA 2005 (gains from contracts for life insurance etc), other than a gain to which subsection (7) of that section applies.

    Type 8 A profit or gain in relation to which the trustees are liable for income tax under section 554 of ITTOIA 2005 (transactions in deposits).

    Type 9 A profit or gain—

        (a) in relation to which the trustees are liable for income tax under section 557 of ITTOIA 2005 (disposals of futures and options), and

        (b) which does not meet any of conditions A to C in section 568 of ITTOIA 2005.

Type 10 Proceeds in relation to which the trustees are liable for income tax under section 573 of ITTOIA 2005 (sales of foreign dividend coupons).

Type 11 Income treated as arising to the trustees under [Part 9A of this Act (transactions in land)][5].

[*Type 12* Income treated as arising to the trustees under section 396A of ITTOIA 2005 (arrangements offering a choice of income or capital return).][3]

Commentary—*Simon's Taxes* **C4.208**.

Amendments—[1]   Words in *Type 1(b)* inserted by FA 2007 s 55(2), (3) with effect in respect of payments made to the trustees of a settlement on or after 6 April 2006.

[2]   In the description of "Type 3", words substituted by the Offshore Funds (Tax) Regulations, SI 2009/3001 reg 129(1), (3) with effect for the purposes of income tax for the tax year 2009–10 and subsequent tax years and for distributions made on or after 1 December 2009; for the purposes of corporation tax, on income, for accounting periods ending on or after 1 December 2009 and for distributions made on or after that date and, on chargeable gains, in relation to disposals made on or after 1 December 2009; and for the purposes of capital gains tax, in relation to disposals made on or after 1 December 2009.

[3]   Entry relating to *Type 12* inserted by FA 2015 s 19(8) with effect in relation to things received on or after 6 April 2015 (even if the choice to receive them was made before that date).

[4]   In *Type 1(b)*, word repealed by FA 2016 s 5, Sch 1 para 63(1), (5) with effect in relation to dividends paid or arising (or treated as paid), and other distributions made (or treated as made), in the tax year 2016–17 or at any later time.

[5]   In *Type 11*, words substituted for words "Chapter 3 of Part 13 of this Act (tax avoidance: transactions in land)" by FA 2016 s 79(3) with effect in relation to disposals on or after 5 July 2016 (FA 2016 s 82(1)), subject to transitional provisions relating to disposals to associated persons on or after 16 March 2016 and before 5 July 2016 (FA 2016 s 82(4)–(15)).

F(No 2)A 2017 s 39 provides that this amendment has effect (so far as it would not otherwise have effect) in relation to amounts that are recognised in GAAP accounts drawn up for any period of account beginning on or after 8 March 2017 or, in the case of a straddling period, amounts that would be recognised in GAAP accounts drawn up for a period of account beginning on 8 March 2017 and ending when the straddling period ends. "Straddling period" means a period of account beginning before 8 March 2017 and ending on or after that date.

483 Sums paid by personal representatives to trustees

(1) This section applies if, during or at the end of the administration period for an estate—

    (a) the personal representatives pay the trustees of a settlement a sum representing income of the personal representatives, and

    (b) if this Chapter had applied to personal representatives, income tax would have been charged on that income at the dividend trust rate or at the trust rate.

(2) The sum is treated as—

    (a) being paid as income, and

    (b) having borne income tax at the applicable rate.

(3) In this section—

"administration period" has the meaning given by section 653 of ITTOIA 2005, and

"the applicable rate" means the rate referred to in section 663(1) of ITTOIA 2005 (the applicable rate for grossing up basic amounts of estate income).

Commentary—*Simon's Taxes* **C4.210**.

Derivation—TA 1988 s 686(6).

CHAPTER 4

TRUSTEES' EXPENSES AND SPECIAL RATES FOR TRUSTEES

484 Trustees' expenses to be set against trustees' trust rate income

(1) This section applies if the trustees of a settlement incur allowable expenses in a tax year ("the current tax year").

(2) The allowable expenses are to be set against the trustees' trust rate income for the current tax year in accordance with section 486.

(3) That is to be done before working out whether section 491 applies in relation to the trustees for the current tax year.

(4) So far as any of the trustees' trust rate income has an amount set against it in accordance with section 486, income tax is charged on it at the rate or rates which would apply apart from Chapter 3 (see Chapter 2 of Part 2).

(5) Expenses are allowable for the purposes of this Chapter only so far as—

    (a) they are expenses of the trustees, and

    (b) they are properly chargeable to income, ignoring the express terms of the settlement.

(6) Expenses are not allowable for the purposes of this Chapter if they are expenses which (apart from this section) have fallen, or may fall, to be taken into account for the purpose of calculating the trustees' liability to income tax for any tax year.

Commentary—*Simon's Taxes* **C4.205**.

HMRC Manuals—Trusts, Settlements And Estates Manual TSEM8220 (legislation - trustees' expenses to be set against trustees' trust rate income).

TSEM8225 (expenses of the trustees).

Modifications—ITA 2007 Sch 2 para 102 (modification of this section if the trustees of a settlement incur an allowable expense in a tax year prior to the tax year 2007–08).

485 Carry forward of unused expenses

(1) This section applies if (apart from this section) the trustees incur an allowable expense in a tax year prior to the current tax year ("the earlier tax year").

(2) For the purposes of this Chapter the trustees are treated as having incurred the allowable expense in the current tax year so far as conditions A and B are met in relation to the expense.

(3) Condition A is that the allowable expense could not be set against the trustees' trust rate income for the earlier tax year only because the trustees' trust rate income was insufficient or they had no trust rate income.

(4) Condition B is that the allowable expense has not been set against the trustees' trust rate income for a tax year prior to the current tax year as a result of this section.

HMRC Manuals—Trust Estates and Savings Manual TSEM8240 (how expenses are taken into account: basis of allowance).

486 How allowable expenses are to be set against trust rate income

(1) Take the following steps to determine how the allowable expenses are to be set against the trustees' trust rate income for the current tax year.

> *Step 1* Reduce the allowable expenses by the proportion of those expenses (if any) which is excluded in accordance with section 487.

References at Steps 3 to 6 below to the allowable expenses are references to the expenses as so reduced.

> *Step 2* Identify the type or types of income which make up the trust rate income. The possible types are dividend income, savings income and other income.

> *Step 3* If there is dividend income within subsection (2)—
>
> (a) gross up by reference to the dividend ordinary rate so much of the allowable expenses as is necessary to give a result equal to the amount of that income, or
>
> (b) if there are not enough allowable expenses to give that result, gross them all up by reference to that rate.

The grossed up amount is set against the dividend income within subsection (2).

> *Step 4* If there are remaining expenses and there is dividend income not within subsection (2)—
>
> (a) gross up by reference to the dividend ordinary rate so much of the remaining expenses as is necessary to give a result equal to the amount of that income, or
>
> (b) if there are not enough remaining expenses to give that result, gross them all up by reference to that rate.

The grossed up amount is set against the dividend income not within subsection (2).

For the purposes of this step "the remaining expenses" are the allowable expenses so far as they have not been grossed up at Step 3.

> *Step 5* If there are remaining expenses and there is savings income—
>
> (a) gross up by reference to the [basic rate][1] so much of the remaining expenses as is necessary to give a result equal to the amount of that income, or
>
> (b) if there are not enough remaining expenses to give that result, gross them all up by reference to that rate.

The grossed up amount is set against the savings income.

For the purposes of this step "the remaining expenses" are the allowable expenses so far as they have not been grossed up at Step 3 or 4.

> *Step 6* If there are remaining expenses and there is other income—
>
> (a) gross up by reference to the basic rate so much of the remaining expenses as is necessary to give a result equal to the amount of that income, or
>
> (b) if there are not enough remaining expenses to give that result, gross them all up by reference to that rate.

The grossed up amount is set against the other income.

For the purposes of this step "the remaining expenses" are the allowable expenses so far as they have not been grossed up at Step 3, 4 or 5.

(2) Income is within this subsection so far as it is—

(a) chargeable under Chapter 3 of Part 4 of ITTOIA 2005 (dividends etc from UK resident companies),

(b) chargeable under Chapter 5 of that Part (stock dividends from UK resident companies), or

(c) chargeable under Chapter 6 of that Part (release of loan to participator in close company).

(3) If income tax would, apart from Chapter 3, be charged on any income mentioned at Steps 3 to 6 at a rate different to the rate mentioned at the step in question, for the purpose of setting any expenses against that income, gross up the expenses by reference to the different rate instead of at the rate mentioned.

Commentary—*Simon's Taxes* **C4.210**.

HMRC Manuals—Trusts, Settlements And Estates Manual TSEM8250 (order of set-off).

Amendments—[1]   Words in sub-s (1), step 5, substituted by FA 2008 s 5, Sch 1 paras 1, 21 with effect for the tax year 2008–09 and subsequent tax years.

487 Non-UK resident trustees

(1) This section applies if a proportion of the income arising to the trustees in the current tax year is untaxed income.

(2) A proportion of the allowable expenses is excluded for the purposes of section 486.

(3) That proportion is the same as the proportion of the income arising to the trustees which is untaxed income.

(4) For the purposes of this section the income arising to the trustees is untaxed income so far as they are not liable to income tax on it wholly or partly because they—

   (a) have been non-UK resident, or

   (b) have been treated as resident in a territory outside the United Kingdom under double taxation arrangements.

(5) If the income tax charged on the income arising to the trustees is limited under Chapter 1 of Part 14 (limits on liability to income tax of non-UK residents), the untaxed income includes so much of the income so arising which is disregarded income (within the meaning of that Chapter) except so far as the disregarded income is within subsection (6).

(6) The disregarded income is within this subsection so far as—

   (a) sums representing income tax have been deducted from the income, [or][1]

   (b) sums representing income tax have been treated as deducted from or paid in respect of the income, . . . [1]

   (c) . . . [1]

Commentary—*Simon's Taxes* **C4.210**.

Amendments—[1]   In sub-s (6), para (c) and preceding word "or" repealed, and word "or" at end of para (a) inserted, by FA 2016 s 5, Sch 1 para 63(1), (6) with effect in relation to dividends paid or arising (or treated as paid), and other distributions made (or treated as made), in the tax year 2016-17 or at any later time.

CHAPTER 5

SHARE INCENTIVE PLANS

488 Application of section 479 to trustees of [Schedule 2] share incentive plans

(1) This section applies if—

   (a) income arises to the trustees of [a Schedule 2][1] share incentive plan, and

   (b) the income consists of dividends or other distributions in respect of shares held by the trustees in relation to which the requirements of Part 4 of Schedule 2 to ITEPA 2003 (. . . [1] share incentive plans: types of shares that may be awarded) are met.

(2) Section 479 applies in relation to the income only if and when condition A or condition B has been met.

(3) Condition A is that—

   (a) the applicable period in relation to the shares has ended, and

   (b) that period came to an end without the shares being awarded to a participant in accordance with the plan.

(4) Condition B is that the trustees disposed of the shares before the end of the applicable period in relation to the shares.

(5) For the purpose of determining whether shares are awarded to a participant within the applicable period in relation to them, shares acquired by the trustees at an earlier time are taken to be awarded to a participant before shares of the same class acquired by the trustees at a later time.

(6) References in this section to shares being awarded to a participant include references to the shares being acquired on behalf of the participant as dividend shares.

Commentary—*Simon's Taxes* **E4.538**.

Amendments—[1]   In heading, sub-s (1)(a) words substituted, and in sub-s (1)(b) word repealed, by FA 2014 s 51, Sch 8 paras 68, 71 with effect from 6 April 2014. The effect of the FA 2014 changes on SIPs established before 6 April 2014 is set out in FA 2014 Sch 8 paras 91 to 96.

489 "The applicable period" in relation to shares

(1) This section sets out how the applicable period in relation to any shares ("the relevant shares") is determined for the purposes of section 488.

(2) The length of the applicable period depends on whether any shares in the relevant company were readily convertible assets at the time the relevant shares were acquired by the trustees.

(3) If any were, the applicable period is the period of two years beginning with the acquisition date.

(4) If none were, the applicable period is—

   (a) the period of 5 years beginning with the acquisition date, or

   (b) if within that period any shares in the relevant company become readily convertible assets, the period of two years beginning with the date on which they did so,

whichever ends first.

(5) Subsections (2) to (4) are subject to subsection (6).

(6) If the relevant shares were acquired by the trustees by virtue of a payment in respect of which a deduction is allowed under [section 989 of CTA 2009][1] (deduction for contribution to plan trust), the applicable period is the period of 10 years beginning with the acquisition date.

(7) In this section—

"the acquisition date" means the date on which the trustees acquired the relevant shares,

"readily convertible assets" has, subject to subsection (8), the meaning given by sections 701 and 702 of ITEPA 2003, and

"the relevant company" means the company in which the relevant shares are shares.

(8) In determining for the purposes of this section whether shares are readily convertible assets, ignore any market for the shares that—

(*a*) is created by virtue of the trustees acquiring shares for the purposes of the [Schedule 2][2] share incentive plan, and

(*b*) exists solely for the purposes of that plan.

Commentary—*Simon's Taxes* **E4.538, C4.210**.

Modifications—ITA 2007 Sch 2 para 103 (modification of this section if the relevant shares were acquired by the trustees before 11 May 2001).

Amendments—[1]   In sub-s (6) words substituted by CTA 2009 s 1322, Sch 1 paras 699, 702. CTA 2009 applies for accounting periods ending on or after 1 April 2009 (for corporation tax purposes) and for tax years 2009–10 onwards (for income and capital gains tax purposes).

[2]   In sub-s (8)(*a*) words substituted by FA 2014 s 51, Sch 8 paras 68, 72 with effect from 6 April 2014. The effect of the FA 2014 changes on SIPs established before 6 April 2014 is set out in FA 2014 Sch 8 paras 91 to 96.

490 Interpretation of Chapter

(1) This Chapter forms part of the SIP code (see section 488 of ITEPA 2003 (. . . [1] share incentive plans)).

(2) Therefore expressions used in this Chapter and contained in the index at the end of Schedule 2 to ITEPA 2003 have the meaning indicated by that index.

(3) For the purposes of this Chapter shares which are subject to provision for forfeiture are treated as acquired by the trustees if and when the forfeiture occurs.

Amendment—[1]   In sub-s (1) word repealed by FA 2014 s 51, Sch 8 paras 68, 73 with effect from 6 April 2014. The effect of the FA 2014 changes on SIPs established before 6 April 2014 is set out in FA 2014 Sch 8 paras 91 to 96.

CHAPTER 6

TRUSTEES' FIRST SLICE OF TRUST RATE INCOME

491 Special rates not to apply to first slice of trustees' trust rate income

(1) If the trust rate income for a tax year of the trustees of a settlement is £1,000 or less, income tax is not charged on it at the dividend trust rate or at the trust rate.

(2) If the trustees' trust rate income is more than £1,000, income tax is not charged on the first £1,000 of it at the dividend trust rate or at the trust rate.

(3) Instead, income tax is charged on the trustees' trust rate income or the first £1,000 of it (as the case may be) at the rate or rates which would apply apart from Chapter 3 (see Chapter 2 of Part 2).

(4) For the purposes of subsection (2) apply the following rules in determining the type or types of income that make up the first £1,000 of the trustees' trust rate income.

Rule 1 If the trustees' trust rate income includes amounts on which income tax would be charged at the basic rate apart from Chapter 3, treat those amounts as the lowest part of the trust rate income.

Rule 2 If the trustees' trust rate income includes amounts on which income tax would be charged at the dividend ordinary rate apart from Chapter 3, treat those amounts as the highest part of the trust rate income.

(5) For the purposes of this section gains chargeable under Chapter 9 of Part 4 of ITTOIA 2005 (gains from contracts for life assurance etc) are treated as if they were savings income.

(6) Amounts on which income tax is not to be charged at the dividend trust rate or at the trust rate as a result of Chapter 4 are excluded from the trustees' trust rate income for the purposes of this section.

Commentary—*Simon's Taxes* **C4.210**.

Derivation—TA 1988 s 686D.

HMRC Manuals—Trusts, Settlements And Estates Manual TSEM3012 (standard rate band - income to which the band applies).

492 Cases where settlor has made more than one settlement

(1) The application of section 491 in relation to the trustees of a settlement ("the relevant settlement") for a tax year is modified in accordance with subsection (2) if the settlor in relation to the relevant settlement has made one or more other current settlements.

(2) References to £1,000 are to be read as references to—

(*a*) £200, or

(*b*) if greater, the settlor's threshold amount.

(3) The settlor's threshold amount is the amount calculated by dividing £1,000 by the number of current settlements (including the relevant settlement) made by the settlor.

(4) If there is more than one settlor in relation to the relevant settlement—

    (*a*) calculate the threshold amount of each of them, and

    (*b*) use the lowest of those threshold amounts for the purposes of subsection (2)(*b*).

(5) A settlement is current if it is in existence at a time during the tax year.

Commentary—*Simon's Taxes* **C4.210**.
Derivation—TA 1988 s 686E.
HMRC Manuals—Trust Estates and Savings Manual TSEM3012 (more than one settlement).

CHAPTER 7

DISCRETIONARY PAYMENTS

[Payments constituting income of beneficiary (other than employment income)][1]

Amendments—[1]   Crosshead inserted by the Enactment of Extra-Statutory Concessions Order 2010, SI 2010/157 art 3(1), (2) with effect for the tax year 2010–11 and subsequent tax years.

493 Discretionary payments by trustees

(1) Sections 494 and 495 apply for income tax purposes if—

    (*a*) in a tax year the trustees of a settlement make an annual payment to a person ("the beneficiary") in the exercise of a discretion (whether exercisable by the trustees or any other person),

    (*b*) the trustees are UK resident for the tax year, and

    (*c*) condition A or condition B is met.

(2) Condition A is that what is paid to the beneficiary is, only because of the payment, income of the beneficiary for income tax or corporation tax purposes. "Income" does not include employment income.

(3) Condition B is that the payment is treated for income tax purposes as the income of a settlor under section 629 of ITTOIA 2005 (income paid to relevant children of settlor).

"Settlor" is to be read in accordance with section 620 of ITTOIA 2005.

(4) The payment is referred to in sections 494 and 495 as "the discretionary payment".

(5) In this Chapter "payment" includes payment in money's worth.

Commentary—*Simon's Taxes* **C4.212, C4.506**.
HMRC Manuals—Trusts, Settlements And Estates Manual TSEM3490 (discretionary payments to a beneficiary).

494 Grossing up of discretionary payment and payment of income tax

(1) The discretionary payment is treated as if it were made after the deduction of a sum representing income tax at the trust rate on the grossed up amount of the discretionary payment.

(2) The grossed up amount of the discretionary payment is the actual amount of the discretionary payment grossed up by reference to the trust rate.

(3) The person mentioned in subsection (4) is treated as having paid income tax of an amount equal to the sum deducted as mentioned in subsection (1).

(4) That person is—

    (*a*) if condition A in section 493 is met, the beneficiary, and

    (*b*) if condition B in section 493 is met, the settlor.

Commentary—*Simon's Taxes* **C4.212, C4.507**.
Derivation—TA 1988 s 687(2).

495 Statement about deduction of income tax

(1) If the person who is treated as having paid income tax requests it in writing, the trustees must provide that person with a statement showing—

    (*a*) the grossed up amount of the discretionary payment,

    (*b*) the sum deducted as mentioned in section 494(1), and

    (*c*) the actual amount of the discretionary payment.

(2) A statement under this section must be in writing.

(3) The duty to comply with a request under this section is enforceable by the person who made it.

Commentary—*Simon's Taxes* **C4.212**.

496 Income tax charged on trustees

(1) Income tax is charged for a tax year if—

    (*a*) in the tax year the trustees of a settlement make payments as a result of which income tax is treated as having been paid under section 494, and

    (*b*) amount A is greater than amount B.

(2) Amount A is the total amount of the income tax treated under section 494 as having been paid.

(3) Amount B is the amount of the trustees' tax pool available for the tax year (see section 497).

(4) The amount of the tax charged under this section is equal to the difference between amounts A and B.

(5) The trustees are liable for the tax.

Commentary—*Simon's Taxes* **C4.212**.
HMRC Manuals—Trusts, Settlements And Estates Manual TSEM3023 (the tax pool - trustees pay excess tax).

[Payments constituting employment income of beneficiary

496A Discretionary payments by trustees: employment income

(1) Section 496B applies if—

  (*a*) in a tax year the trustees of a settlement make a discretionary employment income payment, and

  (*b*) the trustees are UK resident for the tax year.

(2) In this section and section 496B, "discretionary employment income payment" means a payment to a person ("the beneficiary") that—

  (*a*) is made in the exercise of a discretion (whether exercisable by the trustees or any other person),

  (*b*) is made out of income, and

  (*c*) meets conditions A and B.

(3) Condition A is that what is paid to the beneficiary—

  (*a*) is, only because of the payment, employment income of the beneficiary, but

  (*b*) is not exempt income (as defined in section 8 of ITEPA 2003).

(4) Condition B is that the payment is made at a time when the settlement is an employee benefit settlement.

(5) A settlement is an employee benefit settlement if the trusts on which the settled property is held do not permit the settled property to be applied otherwise than—

  (*a*) for the benefit of persons of one or more relevant classes, or

  (*b*) for the benefit of such persons and for charitable purposes.

(6) "Relevant class" means a class defined by reference to one or more of the following—

  (*a*) employment in a particular trade or profession,

  (*b*) employment by, or holding office with, a body carrying on a trade, profession or undertaking, or

  (*c*) marriage to or civil partnership with, or relationship to, or dependence on, persons of a class mentioned in paragraph (*a*) or (*b*).

(7) Where the trusts on which the settled property is held do not permit the settled property to be applied otherwise than as described in subsection (5) during a period (however defined), the settlement is an employee benefit settlement during (and only during) that period.][1]

Commentary—*Simon's Taxes* **C4.212**.

Amendments—[1]   Sections 496A, 496B and preceding cross-head inserted by the Enactment of Extra-Statutory Concessions Order 2010, SI 2010/157 art 3(1), (3) with effect in relation to payments made by trustees after 6 April 2010.

[496B   Relief for trustees

(1) The trustees of a settlement are entitled (on making a claim in respect of a tax year) to repayment of an amount of income tax equal to the lesser of amount A and amount B.

(2) Amount A is—

  $$TEI \times TR$$

where—

  TEI is the total of the amounts that are employment income of beneficiaries of the settlement because of discretionary employment income payments made in the tax year by the trustees, and TR is the trust rate in force for the tax year.

(3) Amount B is the amount of the trustees' tax pool available for the tax year (see section 497) reduced (but not so that is goes below nil) by the total amount of income tax (if any) treated under section 494 as having been paid as a result of payments made by the trustees in the tax year.

(4) A claim under this section may not be made before the end of the tax year to which it relates.][1]

Commentary—*Simon's Taxes* **C4.212**.

Amendments—[1]   Sections 496A, 496B and preceding cross-head inserted by the Enactment of Extra-Statutory Concessions Order 2010, SI 2010/157 art 3(1), (3) with effect in relation to payments made by trustees after 6 April 2010.

[Tax pool][1]

Amendments—[1]   Cross-head inserted by the Enactment of Extra-Statutory Concessions Order 2010, SI 2010/157 art 3(1), (4) with effect in relation to payments made by trustees after 6 April 2010.

497 Calculation of trustees' tax pool

(1) Take the following steps to calculate the amount of the trustees' tax pool available for a tax year ("the current tax year").

  This is subject to subsections (2) and (3).

  Step 1 Take the amount of the trustees' tax pool available for the previous tax year and deduct from that amount (but not so that it goes below nil)—

    [(*a*)][1] the total amount of income tax treated under section 494 as having been paid as a result of payments made by the trustees in the previous tax year[, and

    (*b*) the amount to which the trustees are entitled under section 496B in respect of the previous tax year.][1]

  Step 2 Add together all amounts of income tax for which the trustees are liable for the current tax year and which are of a type set out in section 498.

Step 3 Add the sum calculated at Step 2 to the amount resulting from Step 1.

(2) If the trustees were non-UK resident for the previous tax year, references in subsection (1) to the previous tax year are to be read as references to the last tax year prior to the current tax year for which the trustees were UK resident.

(3) If—

   (*a*)   the current tax year is the tax year during which the settlement is established, or

   (*b*)   the trustees have been UK resident for no tax year prior to the current tax year,

ignore Steps 1 and 3 and, accordingly, the trustees' tax pool available for the current tax year is the sum calculated at Step 2.

Commentary—*Simon's Taxes* **C4.212**.

Modifications—ITA 2007 Sch 2 para 104 (modification of this section in relation to the trustees of a settlement established prior to the tax year 2007–08 if the current tax year is 2007–08. The section is also modified if—

   (a)   the current tax year is a tax year subsequent to the tax year 2007–08, and

   (b)   the trustees have been UK resident for no tax year prior to the current tax year or the last tax year prior to the current tax year for which they were UK resident is a tax year prior to the tax year 2007–08).

Amendments—[1]   In sub-s (1), Step 1, word inserted after word "nil)" and words inserted at the end, by the Enactment of Extra-Statutory Concessions Order 2010, SI 2010/157 art 3(1), (5) with effect for the tax year 2011–12 and subsequent tax years.

498 Types of income tax for the purposes of section 497

(1) The types of amount referred to at Step 2 in section 497 are as follows.

   Type 1 The amount of any tax on income (other than income of a kind mentioned below in relation to Type [. . . [3] 3A][1]) charged at the dividend trust rate or at the trust rate.

   Type 2 . . . [3]

   Type 3 . . . [3]

   [*Type 3A* The amount of tax at the nominal rate on any amount in respect of which—

      (*a*)   the trustees are liable to income tax under section 467 of ITTOIA 2005 (gains from contracts for life insurance etc),

      (*b*)   the trustees are liable to income tax at the trust rate by virtue of section 482 above, and

      (*c*)   tax at the [basic rate][2] is treated as having been paid by virtue of section 530 of ITTOIA 2005 (life insurance).][1]

   Type 4 The amount of any tax on income on which tax is charged . . . [3] . . . [2] as a result of section 491.

   Type 5 The amount of tax on any income determined in accordance with section 26 of FA 2005 (special tax treatment for trusts for the benefit of vulnerable persons).

(2) . . . [3]

[(2A) In relation to Type 3A, the reference to the nominal rate is a reference to a rate equal to the difference between the trust rate and the [basic rate][2].][1]

(3) In relation to Types 1 to 4, references to income do not include income the tax on which is reduced in accordance with section 26 of FA 2005.

Commentary—*Simon's Taxes* **C4.212**.

Derivation—TA 1988 s 687(3), (3A).

HMRC Manuals—Trusts, Settlements And Estates Manual TSEM3021 (the tax pool - amounts entering).

Amendments—[1]   in sub-s (1) words in *Type 1* substituted, and *Type 3A* inserted; and sub-s (2A) inserted; by FA 2007 s 56 with effect in relation to gains arising to the trustees of a settlement on or after 6 April 2007.

[2]   In sub-s (1) words in *Type 3A* substituted, and words in *Type 4* repealed; and words in sub-s (2A) substituted; by FA 2008 s 5, Sch 1 paras 1, 22 with effect for the tax year 2008–09 and subsequent tax years.

[3]   In sub-s (1), words in *Types 1* and *4*, and whole of *Types 2* and *3*, repealed; and sub-s (2) repealed; by FA 2016 s 5, Sch 1 para 63(1), (7) with effect for the tax year 2016-17 and subsequent tax years.

CHAPTER 8

TRUSTEES' EXPENSES AND BENEFICIARY'S INCOME

499 Application of Chapter

(1) This Chapter applies if—

   (*a*)   in a tax year ("the current tax year") income arises to the trustees of a settlement, and

   (*b*)   before being distributed, some or all of that income is income of another person ("the beneficiary").

(2) It contains provision about how the beneficiary's income mentioned in subsection (1)(*b*) ("the beneficiary's income") can be reduced for income tax purposes by reference to expenses of the trustees.

500 Restrictions on use of trustees' expenses to reduce the beneficiary's income

(1) Expenses of the trustees can be used to reduce the beneficiary's income for income tax purposes only so far as—

   (*a*)   the expenses are incurred by the trustees in the current tax year or in an earlier tax year, and (*b*) as a result of the expenses being chargeable to income as mentioned in subsection (2) or (3), the beneficiary's entitlement to the beneficiary's income is reduced by reference to the expenses.

(2) Expenses are chargeable to income for the purposes of subsection (1)(*b*) if they are chargeable to income by the trustees under a term of the settlement (subject to any overriding law which prevents the expenses from being so chargeable).

(3) Expenses are also chargeable to income for the purposes of subsection (1)(*b*) if they—

(*a*) are not chargeable to income by the trustees under a term of the settlement, but

(*b*) are chargeable to income by the trustees in accordance with any law (subject to any overriding term of the settlement which prevents the expenses from being so chargeable).

(4) Expenses cannot be used to reduce the beneficiary's income for income tax purposes so far as they are expenses which have fallen, or may fall, to be taken into account for the purpose of calculating the trustees' liability to income tax for any tax year.

HMRC Manuals—Trusts, Settlements And Estates Manual TSEM8335 (IIP beneficiaries - tax law).

501 Non-UK resident beneficiaries

(1) This section applies if—

(*a*) expenses of the trustees are to be used to reduce the beneficiary's income for income tax purposes, and

(*b*) a proportion of the beneficiary's income is untaxed income (see section 502).

(2) A proportion of those expenses is not to be so used.

(3) That proportion is the same as the proportion of the beneficiary's income which is untaxed income.

(4) In subsection (3) the references to the beneficiary's income and untaxed income do not, in either case, include so much (if any) of that income as is equal to the amount of income tax, or of any foreign tax, for which the trustees are liable on that income.

(5) "Foreign tax" means any tax which—

(*a*) is of a similar character to income tax, and

(*b*) is imposed by the laws of a territory outside the United Kingdom.

502 Meaning of "untaxed income" in section 501

(1) For the purposes of section 501 the beneficiary's income is untaxed income so far as the beneficiary is not liable to income tax on it wholly or partly because the beneficiary—

(*a*) has been non-UK resident, or

(*b*) has been treated as resident in a territory outside the United Kingdom under double taxation arrangements.

(2) If the income tax charged on the beneficiary for the beneficiary's income is limited under Chapter 1 of Part 14 (limits on liability to income tax of non-UK residents), the untaxed income includes so much of the beneficiary's income which is disregarded income (within the meaning of that Chapter) except so far as the disregarded income is within subsection (3).

(3) The disregarded income is within this subsection so far as—

(*a*) sums representing income tax have been deducted from the income, [or][1]

(*b*) sums representing income tax have been treated as deducted from or paid in respect of the income, . . .[1]

(*c*) . . .[1]

Amendments—[1] In sub-s (3), para (*c*) and preceding word "or" repealed, and word "or" at end of para (*a*) inserted, by FA 2016 s 5, Sch 1 para 63(1), (8) with effect in relation to dividends paid or arising (or treated as paid), and other distributions made (or treated as made), in the tax year 2016-17 or at any later time.

503 How beneficiary's income is reduced

(1) This section applies if the beneficiary's income is to be reduced for income tax purposes by expenses of the trustees.

(2) The beneficiary's income is to be reduced in the following order—

first, reduce dividend income within subsection (3) (if any),

second, reduce dividend income not within that subsection (if any),

third, reduce savings income (if any), and

fourth, reduce other income (if any).

(3) Income is within this subsection so far as it is—

(*a*) chargeable under Chapter 3 of Part 4 of ITTOIA 2005 (dividends etc from UK resident companies),

(*b*) chargeable under Chapter 5 of that Part (stock dividends from UK resident companies), or

(*c*) chargeable under Chapter 6 of that Part (release of loan to participator in close company).

(4) If the trustees are liable for income tax charged on a component of the beneficiary's income at a particular rate, then any reduction of that component is to be made in accordance with the steps set out in subsection (5).

(5) Here are the steps.

Step 1 Deduct from the component the amount of income tax charged on it at the particular rate for which the trustees are liable.

Step 2 Take the result from Step 1 and reduce it (but not below nil) by the amount of the trustees' expenses so far as they have not already been used to reduce other components of the beneficiary's income.

Step 3 Take the result from Step 2 and gross it up by reference to the particular rate. The result is the reduced amount of the component of the beneficiary's income.

Commentary—*Simon's Taxes* **C4.508**.

CHAPTER 10

HERITAGE MAINTENANCE SETTLEMENTS

Introduction

507 Overview of Chapter

(1) This Chapter makes provision about income arising from heritage maintenance property comprised in a heritage maintenance settlement.

(2) In this Chapter—

"heritage body" means a body or charity of a kind mentioned in paragraph 3(1)(*a*)(ii) of Schedule 4 to IHTA 1984 (maintenance funds for historic buildings etc),

"heritage direction" means a direction under paragraph 1 of that Schedule,

"heritage maintenance property" means any property in respect of which a heritage direction has effect,

"heritage maintenance settlement" means a settlement which comprises heritage maintenance property, and

"property maintenance purpose" means any of the purposes mentioned in paragraph 3(1)(*a*)(i) of that Schedule.

(3) If a settlement comprises both heritage maintenance property and other property, the heritage maintenance property and the other property are treated as comprised in separate settlements for the purposes of Chapters 2 to 8 of this Part and the following provisions—

(*a*) sections 64 to 66 and sections 75 to 79 (trade loss relief against general income),

(*b*) sections 83 to 88 (carry-forward trade loss relief), and

(*c*) Chapter 5 of Part 5 of ITTOIA 2005.

Commentary—*Simon's Taxes* **C4.355**.
Derivation—TA 1988 ss 690, 691(1), 692(1), 693, 694(1).

Trustees' election in respect of income etc

508 Election by trustees

(1) The trustees of a heritage maintenance settlement may elect for this section to have effect for a tax year.

(2) If an election under subsection (1) has effect for a tax year, the rules in subsections (3) and (4) apply.

(3) Income arising in the year from the heritage maintenance property comprised in the settlement, which would otherwise be treated as income of the settlor under Chapter 5 of Part 5 of ITTOIA 2005, is not to be so treated.

(4) Any sum applied out of the heritage maintenance property in the year for a property maintenance purpose, which would otherwise be treated for income tax purposes as the income of a person—

(*a*) because of the person's interest in (or occupation of) the property in respect of which the sum is applied, or

(*b*) under section 633 of ITTOIA 2005 (capital sums paid to settlor by trustees of settlement), is not to be so treated.

(5) An election under subsection (1) must be made on or before the first anniversary of the normal self-assessment filing date for the tax year to which it relates.

Commentary—*Simon's Taxes* **C4.355**.
HMRC Manuals—Business Income Manual BIM58620 (historic houses: heritage maintenance settlements: reimbursement of settlor).
Capital Gains Manual CG35010 (settlor trusts: maintenance funds for historic buildings).

509 Change of circumstances during a tax year

(1) If a change of circumstances arises during a tax year—

(*a*) the part of the year before the change and the part of the year after the change are to be treated as separate tax years for the purposes of section 508, this section and section 510, and

(*b*) separate elections under section 508(1) may be made for each part.

(2) A change of circumstances arises if conditions A and B are met.

(3) Condition A is that for any part of the tax year—

(*a*) a heritage direction has effect, and

(*b*) income arising from the heritage maintenance property comprised in the settlement is treated as income of the settlor under Chapter 5 of Part 5 of ITTOIA 2005.

(4) Condition B is that for the remaining part of the year one or both of the following paragraphs applies—

    (*a*) no heritage direction has effect, and

    (*b*) no income arising from property comprised in the settlement is treated as income of the settlor under Chapter 5 of Part 5 of ITTOIA 2005.

Commentary—*Simon's Taxes* **C4.355**.
Derivation—TA 1988 s 691(5).

Absence of election and income treated as income of settlor: special rules

510 Sums applied for property maintenance purposes

(1) This section applies if—

    (*a*) income arises from the heritage maintenance property comprised in a heritage maintenance settlement in a tax year in respect of which no election is made under section 508,

    (*b*) the income is treated under Chapter 5 of Part 5 of ITTOIA 2005 as income of the settlor, and

    (*c*) a sum in excess of the income is applied for a property maintenance purpose in the year.

(2) Any such sum which is so applied in that year, which would otherwise be treated for income tax purposes as the income of a person—

    (*a*) because of the person's interest in (or occupation of) the property in respect of which the sum is applied, or

    (*b*) under section 633 of ITTOIA 2005 (capital sums paid to settlor by trustees of settlement), is not to be so treated.

Commentary—*Simon's Taxes* **C4.355**.
Derivation—TA 1988 s 691(3).

511 Prevention of double taxation: reimbursement of settlor

(1) This section applies to income arising from heritage maintenance property if—

    (*a*) the income is treated under Chapter 5 of Part 5 of ITTOIA 2005 as income of the settlor,

    (*b*) the income is applied in reimbursing the settlor for expenditure incurred by the settlor for a property maintenance purpose, and

    (*c*) the expenditure is deductible in calculating the profits of—

        (i) a trade, or

        (ii) a UK property business,

    carried on by the settlor.

(2) Any such income—

    (*a*) is not to be brought into account as a receipt in calculating the profits of that trade or business, and

    (*b*) is not to be treated as income of the settlor otherwise than under Chapter 5 of Part 5 of ITTOIA 2005.

Commentary—*Simon's Taxes* **C4.356**.
Derivation—TA 1988 s 692.
HMRC Manuals—Business Income Manual BIM58620 (historic houses: heritage maintenance settlements: reimbursement of settlor).

Application of property for non-heritage purposes: charge to tax

512 Charge to tax on some settlements

(1) Income tax is charged in respect of a heritage maintenance settlement on any of the occasions described in cases A to D, subject to sections 516 and 517.

(2) Case A is where any of the property comprised in the settlement (whether capital or income) is applied otherwise than—

    (*a*) for a property maintenance purpose, or

    (*b*) as respects income not so applied and not accumulated, for the benefit of a heritage body.

(3) Case B is where any of that property, on ceasing to be comprised in the settlement, devolves otherwise than on a heritage body.

(4) Case C is where the heritage direction ceases to have effect in respect of the settlement.

(5) Case D is where any of the property comprised in the settlement, on ceasing at any time to be comprised in the settlement—

    (*a*) devolves on a heritage body, and

    (*b*) at or before that time an interest under the settlement is or has been acquired for a consideration in money or money's worth by that or another such body.

(6) For the purposes of subsection (5)(*b*) any acquisition from another such body is to be ignored.

Commentary—*Simon's Taxes* **C4.357**.
Derivation—TA 1988 s 694(1), (5).

513 Income charged

(1) Tax is charged under section 512 on the whole of the income—

(a) which has arisen in the relevant period from the property comprised in the settlement, and

(b) which has not been applied (whether or not it has been first accumulated) for a property maintenance purpose or for the benefit of a heritage body.

(2) In this section "relevant period" means—

    (a) if tax has become chargeable under section 512 in respect of the settlement on a previous occasion, the period since the last occasion, and

    (b) in any other case, the period since the settlement took effect.

(3) Tax charged under section 512 is in addition to any tax otherwise chargeable.

(4) All the provisions of the Income Tax Acts relating to assessments and to the collection and recovery of income tax (so far as applicable) are to apply to that charge.

Commentary—*Simon's Taxes* **C4.357**.
Derivation—TA 1988 s 694(2), (4).

514 Persons liable

The persons liable for any tax charged under section 512 are the trustees of the settlement.

515 Rate of tax

Tax is charged under section 512 at the rate found by—

    (a) taking the [additional rate][1] for the tax year during which the charge arises, and

    (b) reducing it by the trust rate for that year.

Commentary—*Simon's Taxes* **C4.357**.
Amendments—[1]   In para (a), words substituted by FA 2009 s 6, Sch 2 paras 1, 7 with effect for the tax year 2010–11 and subsequent tax years.

516 Transfer of property between settlements

(1) This section applies if the whole of the property comprised in a settlement becomes comprised in another settlement because of a tax-free transfer.

(2) The occasion of charge under section 512, which would otherwise occur at the time of transfer, occurs when tax first becomes chargeable under that section in respect of any settlement comprising the transferred property ("the chargeable settlement").

(3) For the purposes of section 513(1) as it applies to the chargeable settlement, the relevant period is adjusted so that it begins—

    (a) on the occasion when tax last became chargeable under section 512 in respect of any previous settlement from which the property was transferred, or

    (b) if there has been no such occasion, when such previous settlement (or the first of them) took effect.

(4) In this section "tax-free transfer" means a transfer of property from one settlement into another in either of the following cases—

    (a) where paragraph 9(1) of Schedule 4 to IHTA 1984 provides (or, but for paragraph 9(4) of that Schedule, would provide) an exception from charge in respect of the property, or

    (b) where, both immediately before and immediately after the transfer, the property is heritage maintenance property.

Commentary—*Simon's Taxes* **C4.357**.
Derivation—TA 1988 s 694(6), (7).

517 Exemption for income treated as income of settlor

(1) Tax is not chargeable under section 512 in respect of income which is treated under section 624 or 629 of ITTOIA 2005 as income of the settlor.

(2) If such income arises in a tax year, any sums applied in the year—

    (a) for a property maintenance purpose, or

    (b) for the benefit of a heritage body,

are to be treated as paid first out of that income and, so far as there is any excess, out of income that does not fall within subsection (1).

Commentary—*Simon's Taxes* **C4.357**.
Derivation—TA 1988 s 694(3).

[PART 9A
TRANSACTIONS IN UK LAND]

[Introduction

517A Overview of Part

This Part contains provision about the income tax treatment of certain profits and gains realised from disposals concerned with land in the United Kingdom.][1]

Amendment—[1]   Part 9A (ss 517A–517U) inserted by FA 2016 s 79(1) with effect in relation to disposals on or after 5 July 2016 (FA 2016 s 82(1)), subject to transitional provisions relating to disposals to associated persons on or after 16 March 2016 and before 5 July 2016 (FA 2016 s 82(4)–(15)). F(No 2)A 2017 s 39 provides that this Part has effect (so far as it would not otherwise have effect) in relation to amounts that are recognised in GAAP accounts drawn up for any period of account beginning on or after 8 March 2017 or, in the case of a straddling period, amounts that would be recognised in GAAP accounts drawn up for a period of account beginning on 8 March 2017 and ending when the straddling period ends. "Straddling period" means a period of account beginning before 8 March 2017 and ending on or after that date.

[Amounts treated as profits of a trade

517B Disposals of land in the United Kingdom

(1) Section 517C(1) applies (subject to subsection (3) of that section) if—
> (a) a person within subsection (2)(a), (b) or (c) realises a profit or gain from a disposal of any land in the United Kingdom, and
> (b) any of conditions A to D is met in relation to the land.

(2) The persons referred to in subsection (1) are—
> (a) the person acquiring, holding or developing the land,
> (b) a person who is associated with the person in paragraph (a) at a relevant time, and
> (c) a person who is a party to, or concerned in, an arrangement within subsection (3).

(3) An arrangement is within this subsection if—
> (a) it is effected with respect to all or part of the land, and
> (b) it enables a profit or gain to be realised—
> > (i) by any indirect method, or
> > (ii) by any series of transactions.

(4) Condition A is that the main purpose, or one of the main purposes, of acquiring the land was to realise a profit or gain from disposing of the land.

(5) Condition B is that the main purpose, or one of the main purposes, of acquiring any property deriving its value from the land was to realise a profit or gain from disposing of the land.

(6) Condition C is that the land is held as trading stock.

(7) Condition D is that (in a case where the land has been developed) the main purpose, or one of the main purposes, of developing the land was to realise a profit or gain from disposing of the land when developed.

(8) In this section "relevant time" means any time in the period beginning when the activities of the project begin and ending 6 months after the disposal mentioned in subsection (1).

(9) In this section "the project" means all activities carried out for any of the following purposes—
> (a) the purposes of dealing in or developing the land, and
> (b) any other purposes mentioned in Conditions A to D.

(10) For the purposes of this section a person ("A") is associated with another person ("B") if—
> (a) A is connected with B by virtue of any of subsections (2) to (4) of section 993 (read in accordance with section 994), or
> (b) A is related to B (see section 517U).]¹

Amendment—¹ Part 9A (ss 517A–517U) inserted by FA 2016 s 79(1) with effect in relation to disposals on or after 5 July 2016 (FA 2016 s 82(1)), subject to transitional provisions relating to disposals to associated persons on or after 16 March 2016 and before 5 July 2016 (FA 2016 s 82(4)–(15)). F(No 2)A 2017 s 39 provides that this Part has effect (so far as it would not otherwise have effect) in relation to amounts that are recognised in GAAP accounts drawn up for any period of account beginning on or after 8 March 2017 or, in the case of a straddling period, amounts that would be recognised in GAAP accounts drawn up for a period of account beginning on 8 March 2017 and ending when the straddling period ends. "Straddling period" means a period of account beginning before 8 March 2017 and ending on or after that date.

[517C Disposals of land: profits treated as trading profits

(1) The profit or gain is to be treated for income tax purposes as profits of a trade carried on by the chargeable person.

(2) If the chargeable person is non-UK resident, that trade is the person's trade of dealing in or developing UK land (as defined in section 6B of ITTOIA 2005).

(3) But subsection (1) does not apply to a profit or gain so far as it would (apart from this section) be brought into account as income in calculating profits (of any person)—
> (a) for income tax purposes, or
> (b) for corporation tax purposes.

(4) The profits are treated as arising in the tax year in which the profit or gain is realised.

(5) This section applies in relation to gains which are capital in nature as it applies in relation to other gains.]¹

Amendment—¹ Part 9A (ss 517A–517U) inserted by FA 2016 s 79(1) with effect in relation to disposals on or after 5 July 2016 (FA 2016 s 82(1)), subject to transitional provisions relating to disposals to associated persons on or after 16 March 2016 and before 5 July 2016 (FA 2016 s 82(4)–(15)). F(No 2)A 2017 s 39 provides that this Part has effect (so far as it would not otherwise have effect) in relation to amounts that are recognised in GAAP accounts drawn up for any period of account beginning on or after 8 March 2017 or, in the case of a straddling period, amounts that would be recognised in GAAP accounts drawn up for a period of account beginning on 8 March 2017 and ending when the straddling period ends. "Straddling period" means a period of account beginning before 8 March 2017 and ending on or after that date.

[517D Disposals of property deriving its value from land in the United Kingdom

(1) Section 517E(1) applies (subject to subsection (3) of that section) if—
> (a) a person realises a profit or gain from a disposal of any property which (at the time of the disposal) derives at least 50% of its value from land in the United Kingdom,

(b) the person is a party to, or concerned in, an arrangement concerning some or all of the land mentioned in paragraph (a) ("the project land"), and

(c) the arrangement meets the condition in subsection (2).

(2) The condition is that the main purpose, or one of the main purposes, of the arrangement is to—

    (a) deal in or develop the project land, and

    (b) realise a profit or gain from a disposal of property deriving the whole or part of its value from that land.][1]

Amendment—[1]　Part 9A (ss 517A–517U) inserted by FA 2016 s 79(1) with effect in relation to disposals on or after 5 July 2016 (FA 2016 s 82(1)), subject to transitional provisions relating to disposals to associated persons on or after 16 March 2016 and before 5 July 2016 (FA 2016 s 82(4)–(15)). F(No 2)A 2017 s 39 provides that this Part has effect (so far as it would not otherwise have effect) in relation to amounts that are recognised in GAAP accounts drawn up for any period of account beginning on or after 8 March 2017 or, in the case of a straddling period, amounts that would be recognised in GAAP accounts drawn up for a period of account beginning on 8 March 2017 and ending when the straddling period ends. "Straddling period" means a period of account beginning before 8 March 2017 and ending on or after that date.

[517E Disposals within section 517D: profits treated as trading profits

(1) The relevant amount is to be treated for income tax purposes as profits of a trade carried on by the chargeable person.

(2) If the chargeable person is non-UK resident, that trade is the chargeable person's trade of dealing in or developing UK land.

(3) But subsection (1) does not apply to an amount so far as it would (apart from this section) be brought into account as income in calculating profits (of any person)—

    (a) for income tax purposes, or

    (b) for corporation tax purposes.

(4) The profits are treated as arising in the tax year in which the profit or gain is realised.

(5) In this section the "relevant amount" means so much (if any) of the profit or gain mentioned in section 517D(1) as is attributable, on a just and reasonable apportionment, to the relevant UK assets.

(6) In this section "the relevant UK assets" means any land in the United Kingdom from which the property mentioned in section 517D(1) derives any of its value (at the time of the disposal mentioned in that subsection).

(7) This section applies in relation to gains which are capital in nature as it applies in relation to other gains.][1]

Amendment—[1]　Part 9A (ss 517A–517U) inserted by FA 2016 s 79(1) with effect in relation to disposals on or after 5 July 2016 (FA 2016 s 82(1)), subject to transitional provisions relating to disposals to associated persons on or after 16 March 2016 and before 5 July 2016 (FA 2016 s 82(4)–(15)). F(No 2)A 2017 s 39 provides that this Part has effect (so far as it would not otherwise have effect) in relation to amounts that are recognised in GAAP accounts drawn up for any period of account beginning on or after 8 March 2017 or, in the case of a straddling period, amounts that would be recognised in GAAP accounts drawn up for a period of account beginning on 8 March 2017 and ending when the straddling period ends. "Straddling period" means a period of account beginning before 8 March 2017 and ending on or after that date.

[517F Profits and losses

(1) Sections 517B to 517E have effect as if they included provision about losses corresponding to the provision they make about profits and gains.

(2) Accordingly, in the following sections of this Part references to a "profit or gain" include a loss.][1]

Amendment—[1]　Part 9A (ss 517A–517U) inserted by FA 2016 s 79(1) with effect in relation to disposals on or after 5 July 2016 (FA 2016 s 82(1)), subject to transitional provisions relating to disposals to associated persons on or after 16 March 2016 and before 5 July 2016 (FA 2016 s 82(4)–(15)). F(No 2)A 2017 s 39 provides that this Part has effect (so far as it would not otherwise have effect) in relation to amounts that are recognised in GAAP accounts drawn up for any period of account beginning on or after 8 March 2017 or, in the case of a straddling period, amounts that would be recognised in GAAP accounts drawn up for a period of account beginning on 8 March 2017 and ending when the straddling period ends. "Straddling period" means a period of account beginning before 8 March 2017 and ending on or after that date.

[*Person to whom profits attributed*

517G The chargeable person

(1) For the purposes of sections 517C and 517E the general rule is that the "chargeable person" is the person ("P") that realises the profit or gain (as mentioned in section 517B(1) or 517D(1)).

(2) The general rule in subsection (1) is subject to the special rules in subsections (4) to (6).

(3) But those special rules do not apply in relation to a profit or gain to which section 517H(3) (fragmented activities) applies.

(4) If all or any part of the profit or gain accruing to P is derived from value provided directly or indirectly by another person ("B"), B is the "chargeable person".

(5) Subsection (4) applies whether or not the value is put at the disposal of P.

(6) If all or any part of the profit or gain accruing to P is derived from an opportunity of realising a profit or gain provided directly or indirectly by another person ("D"), D is "the chargeable person" (unless the case falls within subsection (4)).

(7) For the meaning of "another person" see section 517P.][1]

Amendment—[1]　Part 9A (ss 517A–517U) inserted by FA 2016 s 79(1) with effect in relation to disposals on or after 5 July 2016 (FA 2016 s 82(1)), subject to transitional provisions relating to disposals to associated persons on or after 16 March 2016 and before 5 July 2016 (FA 2016 s 82(4)–(15)). F(No 2)A 2017 s 39 provides that this Part has effect (so far as it would not otherwise have effect) in relation to amounts that are recognised in GAAP accounts drawn up for any period of account beginning on or after 8 March 2017 or, in the case of a straddling period, amounts that would be recognised in GAAP accounts drawn up for a period of account beginning on 8 March 2017 and ending when the straddling period ends. "Straddling period" means a period of account beginning before 8 March 2017 and ending on or after that date.

[Anti-fragmentation

517H Fragmented activities

(1) Subsection (3) applies if—

    (*a*) a person ("P") disposes of any land in the United Kingdom,

    (*b*) any of conditions A to D in section 517B is met in relation to the land, and

    (*c*) a person ("R") who is associated with P at a relevant time has made a relevant contribution to activities falling within subsection (2).

(2) The following activities fall within this subsection—

    (*a*) the development of the land,

    (*b*) any other activities directed towards realising a profit or gain from the disposal of the land.

(3) For the purposes of this Part, the profit or gain (if any) realised by P from the disposal is to be taken to be what that profit or gain would be if R were not a distinct person from P (and, accordingly, as if everything done by or in relation to R had been done by or in relation to P).

(4) Subsection (5) applies to any amount which is paid (directly or indirectly) by R to P for the purposes of meeting or reimbursing the cost of income tax which P is liable to pay as a result of the application of subsection (3) in relation to R and P.

(5) The amount—

    (*a*) is not to be taken into account in calculating profits or losses of either R or P for the purposes of income tax or corporation tax, and

    (*b*) is not for any purpose of the Corporation Tax Acts to be regarded as a distribution.

(6) In subsection (1) "relevant time" means any time in the period beginning when the activities of the project begin and ending 6 months after the disposal.

(7) For the purposes of this section any contribution made by P to activities falling within subsection (2) is a "relevant contribution" unless the profit made or to be made by P in respect of the contribution is insignificant having regard to the size of the project.

(8) In this section "contribution" means any kind of contribution, including, for example—

    (*a*) the provision of professional or other services, or

    (*b*) a financial contribution (including the assumption of a risk).

(9) For the purposes of this section R is "associated" with P if—

    (*a*) R is connected with P by virtue of any of subsections (2) to (4) of section 993 (read in accordance with section 994), or

    (*b*) R is related to P (see section 517U).

(10) In this section "the project" means all activities carried out for any of the following purposes—

    (*a*) the purposes of dealing in or developing the land, and

    (*b*) any other purposes mentioned in Conditions A to D in section 517B.][1]

Amendment—[1]   Part 9A (ss 517A–517U) inserted by FA 2016 s 79(1) with effect in relation to disposals on or after 5 July 2016 (FA 2016 s 82(1)), subject to transitional provisions relating to disposals to associated persons on or after 16 March 2016 and before 5 July 2016 (FA 2016 s 82(4)–(15)). F(No 2)A 2017 s 39 provides that this Part has effect (so far as it would not otherwise have effect) in relation to amounts that are recognised in GAAP accounts drawn up for any period of account beginning on or after 8 March 2017 or, in the case of a straddling period, amounts that would be recognised in GAAP accounts drawn up for a period of account beginning on 8 March 2017 and ending when the straddling period ends. "Straddling period" means a period of account beginning before 8 March 2017 and ending on or after that date.

[Calculation of profit or gain on disposal

517I Calculation of surplus on a disposal of land

For the purposes of this Part, the profit or gain (if any) from a disposal of any property is to be calculated according to the principles applicable for calculating the profits of a trade under Part 2 of ITTOIA 2005, subject to any modifications that may be appropriate (and for this purpose the same rules are to apply in calculating losses from a disposal as apply in calculating profits).][1]

Amendment—[1]   Part 9A (ss 517A–517U) inserted by FA 2016 s 79(1) with effect in relation to disposals on or after 5 July 2016 (FA 2016 s 82(1)), subject to transitional provisions relating to disposals to associated persons on or after 16 March 2016 and before 5 July 2016 (FA 2016 s 82(4)–(15)). F(No 2)A 2017 s 39 provides that this Part has effect (so far as it would not otherwise have effect) in relation to amounts that are recognised in GAAP accounts drawn up for any period of account beginning on or after 8 March 2017 or, in the case of a straddling period, amounts that would be recognised in GAAP accounts drawn up for a period of account beginning on 8 March 2017 and ending when the straddling period ends. "Straddling period" means a period of account beginning before 8 March 2017 and ending on or after that date.

[517J Apportionments

Any apportionment (whether of expenditure, consideration or any other amount) that is required to be made for the purposes of this Part is to be made on a just and reasonable basis.][1]

Amendment—[1]   Part 9A (ss 517A–517U) inserted by FA 2016 s 79(1) with effect in relation to disposals on or after 5 July 2016 (FA 2016 s 82(1)), subject to transitional provisions relating to disposals to associated persons on or after 16 March 2016 and before 5 July 2016 (FA 2016 s 82(4)–(15)). F(No 2)A 2017 s 39 provides that this Part has effect (so far as it would not otherwise have effect) in relation to amounts that are recognised in GAAP accounts drawn up for any period of account beginning on or after 8 March 2017 or, in the case of a straddling period, amounts that would be recognised in GAAP accounts drawn up for a period of account beginning on 8 March 2017 and ending when the straddling period ends. "Straddling period" means a period of account beginning before 8 March 2017 and ending on or after that date.

[Arrangements for avoiding tax

517K Arrangements for avoiding tax

(1) Subsection (3) applies if an arrangement has been entered into the main purpose or one of the main purposes of which is to enable a person to obtain a relevant tax advantage.

(2) In subsection (1) the reference to obtaining a relevant tax advantage includes obtaining a relevant tax advantage by virtue of any provisions of double taxation arrangements, but only in a case where the relevant tax advantage is contrary to the object and purpose of the provisions of the double taxation arrangements (and subsection (3) has effect accordingly, regardless of anything in section 6(1) of TIOPA 2010).

(3) The tax advantage is to be counteracted by means of adjustments.

(4) For this purpose adjustments may be made (whether by an officer of Revenue and Customs or by the person) by way of an assessment, the modification of an assessment, amendment or disallowance of a claim, or otherwise.

(5) In this section "relevant tax advantage" means an advantage in relation to income tax charged (or which would, if the tax advantage were not obtained, be charged) in respect of amounts treated as profits of a trade by virtue of this Part.

(6) In this section "advantage" includes—

   (*a*) a relief or increased relief from tax,

   (*b*) repayment or increased repayment of tax,

   (*c*) avoidance or reduction of a charge to tax or an assessment to tax,

   (*d*) avoidance of a possible assessment to tax,

   (*e*) deferral of a payment of tax or advancement of a repayment of tax, and

   (*f*) avoidance of an obligation to deduct or account for tax.][1]

Amendment—[1] Part 9A (ss 517A–517U) inserted by FA 2016 s 79(1) with effect in relation to disposals on or after 5 July 2016 (FA 2016 s 82(1)), subject to transitional provisions relating to disposals to associated persons on or after 16 March 2016 and before 5 July 2016 (FA 2016 s 82(4)–(15)). F(No 2)A 2017 s 39 provides that this Part has effect (so far as it would not otherwise have effect) in relation to amounts that are recognised in GAAP accounts drawn up for any period of account beginning on or after 8 March 2017 or, in the case of a straddling period, amounts that would be recognised in GAAP accounts drawn up for a period of account beginning on 8 March 2017 and ending when the straddling period ends. "Straddling period" means a period of account beginning before 8 March 2017 and ending on or after that date.

[Exemptions

517L Gain attributable to period before intention to develop formed

(1) Subsection (2) applies if—

   (*a*) subsection (1) of section 517C applies because Condition D in section 517B is met (land developed with purpose of realising a gain from its disposal when developed), and

   (*b*) part of the profit or gain mentioned in that subsection is fairly attributable to a period before the intention to develop was formed.

(2) Section 517C(1) has effect as if the person mentioned in section 517B(1) had not realised that part of the profit or gain.

(3) Subsection (4) applies if—

   (*a*) section 517E(1) applies, and

   (*b*) part of the profit or gain mentioned in section 517E(5) is fairly attributable to a period before the person mentioned in section 517D(1) was a party to, or concerned in, the arrangement in question.

(4) Section 517E has effect as if the person had not realised that part of the profit or gain.

(5) In applying this section account must be taken of the treatment under Part 2 of ITTOIA 2005 (trading income) of a person who appropriates land as trading stock.][1]

Amendment—[1] Part 9A (ss 517A–517U) inserted by FA 2016 s 79(1) with effect in relation to disposals on or after 5 July 2016 (FA 2016 s 82(1)), subject to transitional provisions relating to disposals to associated persons on or after 16 March 2016 and before 5 July 2016 (FA 2016 s 82(4)–(15)). F(No 2)A 2017 s 39 provides that this Part has effect (so far as it would not otherwise have effect) in relation to amounts that are recognised in GAAP accounts drawn up for any period of account beginning on or after 8 March 2017 or, in the case of a straddling period, amounts that would be recognised in GAAP accounts drawn up for a period of account beginning on 8 March 2017 and ending when the straddling period ends. "Straddling period" means a period of account beginning before 8 March 2017 and ending on or after that date.

[517M Private residences

No liability to income tax arises under this Part in respect of a gain accruing to an individual if—

   (*a*) the gain is exempt from capital gains tax as a result of sections 222 to 226 of TCGA 1992 (private residences), or

   (*b*) it would be so exempt but for section 224(3) of that Act (residences acquired partly with a view to making a gain).][1]

Amendment—[1] Part 9A (ss 517A–517U) inserted by FA 2016 s 79(1) with effect in relation to disposals on or after 5 July 2016 (FA 2016 s 82(1)), subject to transitional provisions relating to disposals to associated persons on or after 16 March 2016 and before 5 July 2016 (FA 2016 s 82(4)–(15)). F(No 2)A 2017 s 39 provides that this Part has effect (so far as it would not otherwise have effect) in relation to amounts that are recognised in GAAP accounts drawn up for any period of account beginning on or after 8 March 2017 or, in the case of a straddling period, amounts that would be recognised in GAAP accounts drawn up for a period of account beginning on 8 March 2017 and ending when the straddling period ends. "Straddling period" means a period of account beginning before 8 March 2017 and ending on or after that date.

[Other supplementary provisions

517N Tracing value

(1) This section applies if it is necessary to determine the extent to which the value of any property or right is derived from any other property or right for the purposes of this Part.

(2) Value may be traced through any number of companies, partnerships, trusts and other entities or arrangements.

(3) The property held by a company, partnership or trust must be attributed to the shareholders, partners, beneficiaries or other participants at each stage in whatever way is appropriate in the circumstances.

(4) In this section—

"partnership" includes an entity established under the law of a country or territory outside the United Kingdom of a similar nature to a partnership; and "partners", in relation to such arrangements, is to be construed accordingly;

"trust" includes arrangements—

(*a*) which have effect under the law of a country or territory outside the United Kingdom; and

(*b*) under which persons acting in a fiduciary capacity hold and administer property on behalf of other persons,

and "beneficiaries", in relation to such arrangements, is to be construed accordingly.]¹

Amendment—¹   Part 9A (ss 517A–517U) inserted by FA 2016 s 79(1) with effect in relation to disposals on or after 5 July 2016 (FA 2016 s 82(1)), subject to transitional provisions relating to disposals to associated persons on or after 16 March 2016 and before 5 July 2016 (FA 2016 s 82(4)–(15)). F(No 2)A 2017 s 39 provides that this Part has effect (so far as it would not otherwise have effect) in relation to amounts that are recognised in GAAP accounts drawn up for any period of account beginning on or after 8 March 2017 or, in the case of a straddling period, amounts that would be recognised in GAAP accounts drawn up for a period of account beginning on 8 March 2017 and ending when the straddling period ends. "Straddling period" means a period of account beginning before 8 March 2017 and ending on or after that date.

[517O Relevance of transactions, arrangements, etc

(1) In determining whether section 517C(1) or 517E(1) applies, account is to be taken of any method, however indirect, by which—

(*a*) any property or right is transferred or transmitted, or

(*b*) the value of any property or right is enhanced or diminished.

(2) Accordingly—

(*a*) the occasion of the transfer or transmission of any property or right, however indirect, and

(*b*) the occasion when the value of any property or right is enhanced,

may be an occasion on which section 517C(1) or 517E(1) applies.

(3) Subsections (1) and (2) apply in particular—

(*a*) to sales, contracts and other transactions made otherwise than for full consideration or for more than full consideration,

(*b*) to any method by which any property or right, or the control of any property or right, is transferred or transmitted by assigning—

(i) share capital or other rights in a company,

(ii) rights in a partnership, or

(iii) an interest in settled property,

(*c*) to the creation of an option affecting the disposition of any property or right and the giving of consideration for granting it,

(*d*) to the creation of a requirement for consent affecting such a disposition and the giving of consideration for granting it,

(*e*) to the creation of an embargo affecting such a disposition and the giving of consideration for releasing it, and

(*f*) to the disposal of any property or right on the winding up, dissolution or termination of a company, partnership or trust.]¹

Amendment—¹   Part 9A (ss 517A–517U) inserted by FA 2016 s 79(1) with effect in relation to disposals on or after 5 July 2016 (FA 2016 s 82(1)), subject to transitional provisions relating to disposals to associated persons on or after 16 March 2016 and before 5 July 2016 (FA 2016 s 82(4)–(15)). F(No 2)A 2017 s 39 provides that this Part has effect (so far as it would not otherwise have effect) in relation to amounts that are recognised in GAAP accounts drawn up for any period of account beginning on or after 8 March 2017 or, in the case of a straddling period, amounts that would be recognised in GAAP accounts drawn up for a period of account beginning on 8 March 2017 and ending when the straddling period ends. "Straddling period" means a period of account beginning before 8 March 2017 and ending on or after that date.

[Interpretation

517P "Another person"

(1) In this Part references to "other" persons are to be interpreted in accordance with subsections (2) to (4).

(2) A partnership or partners in a partnership may be regarded as a person or persons distinct from the individuals or other persons who are for the time being partners.

(3) The trustees of settled property may be regarded as persons distinct from the individuals or other persons who are for the time being the trustees.

(4) Personal representatives may be regarded as persons distinct from the individuals or other persons who are for the time being personal representatives.][1]

Amendment—[1]   Part 9A (ss 517A–517U) inserted by FA 2016 s 79(1) with effect in relation to disposals on or after 5 July 2016 (FA 2016 s 82(1)), subject to transitional provisions relating to disposals to associated persons on or after 16 March 2016 and before 5 July 2016 (FA 2016 s 82(4)–(15)). F(No 2)A 2017 s 39 provides that this Part has effect (so far as it would not otherwise have effect) in relation to amounts that are recognised in GAAP accounts drawn up for any period of account beginning on or after 8 March 2017 or, in the case of a straddling period, amounts that would be recognised in GAAP accounts drawn up for a period of account beginning on 8 March 2017 and ending when the straddling period ends. "Straddling period" means a period of account beginning before 8 March 2017 and ending on or after that date.

[517Q "Arrangement"

(1) In this Part "arrangement" (except in the phrase "double taxation arrangements") includes any agreement, understanding, scheme, transaction or series of transactions, whether or not legally enforceable.

(2) For the purposes of this Part any number of transactions may be regarded as constituting a single arrangement if—

    (*a*)   a common purpose can be discerned in them, or

    (*b*)   there is other sufficient evidence of a common purpose.][1]

Amendment—[1]   Part 9A (ss 517A–517U) inserted by FA 2016 s 79(1) with effect in relation to disposals on or after 5 July 2016 (FA 2016 s 82(1)), subject to transitional provisions relating to disposals to associated persons on or after 16 March 2016 and before 5 July 2016 (FA 2016 s 82(4)–(15)). F(No 2)A 2017 s 39 provides that this Part has effect (so far as it would not otherwise have effect) in relation to amounts that are recognised in GAAP accounts drawn up for any period of account beginning on or after 8 March 2017 or, in the case of a straddling period, amounts that would be recognised in GAAP accounts drawn up for a period of account beginning on 8 March 2017 and ending when the straddling period ends. "Straddling period" means a period of account beginning before 8 March 2017 and ending on or after that date.

[517R "Disposal"

(1) In this Part references to a "disposal" of any property include any case in which the property is effectively disposed of (whether wholly or in part, as mentioned in subsection (2))—

    (*a*)   by one or more transactions, or

    (*b*)   by any arrangement.

(2) For the purposes of this Part—

    (*a*)   references to a disposal of land or any other property include a part disposal of the property, and

    (*b*)   there is a part disposal of property ("the asset") where on a person making a disposal, any form of property derived from the asset remains undisposed of (including in cases where an interest or right in or over the asset is created by the disposal, as well as where it subsists before the disposal).][1]

Amendment—[1]   Part 9A (ss 517A–517U) inserted by FA 2016 s 79(1) with effect in relation to disposals on or after 5 July 2016 (FA 2016 s 82(1)), subject to transitional provisions relating to disposals to associated persons on or after 16 March 2016 and before 5 July 2016 (FA 2016 s 82(4)–(15)). F(No 2)A 2017 s 39 provides that this Part has effect (so far as it would not otherwise have effect) in relation to amounts that are recognised in GAAP accounts drawn up for any period of account beginning on or after 8 March 2017 or, in the case of a straddling period, amounts that would be recognised in GAAP accounts drawn up for a period of account beginning on 8 March 2017 and ending when the straddling period ends. "Straddling period" means a period of account beginning before 8 March 2017 and ending on or after that date.

[517S "Land" and related expressions

(1) In this Part "land" includes—

    (*a*)   buildings and structures,

    (*b*)   any estate, interest or right in or over land, and

    (*c*)   land under the sea or otherwise covered by water.

(2) In this Part references to property deriving its value from land include—

    (*a*)   any shareholding in a company deriving its value directly or indirectly from land,

    (*b*)   any partnership interest deriving its value directly or indirectly from land,

    (*c*)   any interest in settled property deriving its value directly or indirectly from land, and

    (*d*)   any option, consent or embargo affecting the disposition of land.][1]

Amendment—[1]   Part 9A (ss 517A–517U) inserted by FA 2016 s 79(1) with effect in relation to disposals on or after 5 July 2016 (FA 2016 s 82(1)), subject to transitional provisions relating to disposals to associated persons on or after 16 March 2016 and before 5 July 2016 (FA 2016 s 82(4)–(15)). F(No 2)A 2017 s 39 provides that this Part has effect (so far as it would not otherwise have effect) in relation to amounts that are recognised in GAAP accounts drawn up for any period of account beginning on or after 8 March 2017 or, in the case of a straddling period, amounts that would be recognised in GAAP accounts

ITA 2007

drawn up for a period of account beginning on 8 March 2017 and ending when the straddling period ends. "Straddling period" means a period of account beginning before 8 March 2017 and ending on or after that date.

[517T References to realising a gain

(1) For the purposes of sections 517B(1) and 517D(1) it does not matter whether the person ("P") realising the profit or gain in question realises it for P or another person.

(2) For the purposes of subsection (1), if, for example by a premature sale, a person ("A") directly or indirectly transmits the opportunity of realising a profit or gain to another person ("B"), A realises B's profit or gain for B.]¹

Amendment—¹   Part 9A (ss 517A–517U) inserted by FA 2016 s 79(1) with effect in relation to disposals on or after 5 July 2016 (FA 2016 s 82(1)), subject to transitional provisions relating to disposals to associated persons on or after 16 March 2016 and before 5 July 2016 (FA 2016 s 82(4)–(15)). F(No 2)A 2017 s 39 provides that this Part has effect (so far as it would not otherwise have effect) in relation to amounts that are recognised in GAAP accounts drawn up for any period of account beginning on or after 8 March 2017 or, in the case of a straddling period, amounts that would be recognised in GAAP accounts drawn up for a period of account beginning on 8 March 2017 and ending when the straddling period ends. "Straddling period" means a period of account beginning before 8 March 2017 and ending on or after that date.

[517U Related parties

(1) For the purposes of this Part a person ("A") is related to another person ("B")—

   (*a*) throughout any period for which A and B are consolidated for accounting purposes,

   (*b*) on any day on which the participation condition is met in relation to them, or

   (*c*) on any day on which the 25% investment condition is met in relation to them.

(2) A and B are consolidated for accounting purposes for a period if—

   (*a*) their financial results for a period are required to be comprised in group accounts,

   (*b*) their financial results for the period would be required to be comprised in group accounts but for the application of an exemption, or

   (*c*) their financial results for a period are in fact comprised in group accounts.

(3) In subsection (2) "group accounts" means accounts prepared under—

   (*a*) section 399 of the Companies Act 2006, or

   (*b*) any corresponding provision of the law of a territory outside the United Kingdom.

(4) The participation condition is met in relation to A and B ("the relevant parties") on a day if, within the period of 6 months beginning with that day—

   (*a*) one of the relevant parties directly or indirectly participates in the management, control or capital of the other, or

   (*b*) the same person or persons directly or indirectly participate in the management, control or capital of each of the relevant parties.

(5) The 25% investment condition is met in relation to A and B if—

   (*a*) one of them has a 25% investment in the other, or

   (*b*) a third person has a 25% investment in each of them.

(6) Section 259NC of TIOPA 2010 applies for the purposes of determining whether a person has a "25% investment" in another person for the purposes of this section as it applies for the purposes of section 259NB(2) of that Act.

(7) In Chapter 2 of Part 4 of TIOPA 2010, sections 157(2), 158(4), 159(2) and 160(2) (which are about the interpretation of references to direct and indirect participation) apply in relation to subsection (4) as they apply in relation to subsection (4) of section 259NA of that Act.]¹

Amendment—¹   Part 9A (ss 517A–517U) inserted by FA 2016 s 79(1) with effect in relation to disposals on or after 5 July 2016 (FA 2016 s 82(1)), subject to transitional provisions relating to disposals to associated persons on or after 16 March 2016 and before 5 July 2016 (FA 2016 s 82(4)–(15)). F(No 2)A 2017 s 39 provides that this Part has effect (so far as it would not otherwise have effect) in relation to amounts that are recognised in GAAP accounts drawn up for any period of account beginning on or after 8 March 2017 or, in the case of a straddling period, amounts that would be recognised in GAAP accounts drawn up for a period of account beginning on 8 March 2017 and ending when the straddling period ends. "Straddling period" means a period of account beginning before 8 March 2017 and ending on or after that date.

PART 10

SPECIAL RULES ABOUT CHARITABLE TRUSTS ETC

Introduction

518 Overview of Part

(1) This Part makes provision about some gifts and payments made to charitable trusts, including provision imposing charges to income tax and conferring exemptions from those charges (see sections 520 to 523).

(2) This Part also provides for some of the income of charitable trusts and others to be exempt from charges to income tax (see sections 524 to 537).

(3) In the provisions of this Part containing exemptions, references to total income of a charitable trust are to the total income of the trustees of the charitable trust concerned.

(4) See [sections 538 and 538A]¹ for provision about making claims for the exemptions under this Part.

(5) In the case of a charitable trust which has a non-exempt amount for a tax year (see section 540), the exemptions under this Part are subject to restrictions (see section 539).

(6) The non-exempt amount for a tax year depends on the charitable trust's attributable income and gains for the tax year and its non-charitable expenditure for the tax year (see sections 540 and 543 to 564).

Amendments—[1]   In sub-s (3) words substituted by FA 2010 s 32, Sch 8 para 5(1), (2) with effect from 8 April 2010.

Gifts and other payments

520 Gifts entitling donor to gift aid relief: income tax treated as paid

(1) This section applies if a gift is made to a charitable trust by an individual and the gift is a qualifying donation for the purposes of Chapter 2 of Part 8 (gift aid).

(2) The charitable trust is treated as receiving, under deduction of income tax at the basic rate for the tax year in which the gift is made, a gift of an amount equal to the grossed up amount of the gift.

(3) The grossed up amount of the gift is the amount of the gift grossed up by reference to the basic rate for the tax year in which the gift is made.

(4) The income tax treated as deducted is treated as income tax paid by the trustees of the charitable trust.

Commentary—*Simon's Taxes* **C5.117A**.
Derivation—FA 1990 s 25(10), (12).

521 Gifts entitling donor to gift aid relief: income tax liability and exemption

(1) This section applies if gifts are made to charitable trusts by individuals and the gifts are qualifying donations for the purposes of Chapter 2 of Part 8 (gift aid).

(2) Income tax is charged on the gifts under this section.

(3) It is charged on the grossed up amount of the gifts arising in the tax year.

(4) But a gift is not taken into account in calculating total income so far as it is applied to charitable purposes only.

(5) The grossed up amount of a gift is the amount of the gift grossed up by reference to the basic rate for the tax year in which the gift is made.

(6) The trustees of the charitable trust are liable for any tax charged under this section.

[(7) Schedule 19 to the Finance Act 2008 contains provision for transitional payments to charitable trusts in respect of gifts made in the tax years 2008–09 to 2010–11.][1]

Commentary—*Simon's Taxes* **C5.117A**.
Amendments—[1]   Sub-s (7) inserted by FA 2008 s 53, Sch 19 para 9 with effect from 21 July 2008.

[521A Gifts under payroll deduction schemes: income tax liability and exemption

(1) This section applies if gifts are made to charitable trusts by individuals and the gifts are donations for the purposes of Part 12 of ITEPA 2003 (payroll giving).

(2) Income tax is charged on the gifts under this section.

(3) It is charged on the full amount of the gifts arising in the tax year.

(4) But a gift is not taken into account in calculating total income so far as it is applied to charitable purposes only.

(5) The trustees of the charitable trust are liable for any tax charged under this section.][1]

Commentary—*Simon's Taxes* **C5.117A**.
Amendments—[1]   This section inserted by FA 2010 s 32, Sch 8 para 1(1) with effect in relation to gifts made on or after 24 March 2010.

522 Gifts of money from companies: income tax liability and exemption

(1) This section applies if gifts of sums of money are made to charitable trusts by companies.

(2) But this section does not apply to a gift of a sum of money made by a company that is itself a charity (see section 523).

(3) Income tax is charged on the gifts under this section.

(4) It is charged on the full amount of the gifts arising in the tax year.

(5) But a gift is not taken into account in calculating total income so far as it is applied to charitable purposes only.

(6) The trustees of the charitable trust are liable for any tax charged under this section.

Commentary—*Simon's Taxes* **C5.117A**.
Derivation—TA 1988 s 339(4).

523 Payments from other charities: income tax liability and exemption

(1) This section applies to payments which—
    (a) are received by charitable trusts from other charities,
    (b) are not made for full consideration in money or money's worth,
    (c) are not charged to income tax, apart from this section, and
    (d) are not of a description which (on a claim) would be exempt from income tax under any of the exemptions conferred by this Part.

(2) This section does not apply to a payment which arises from a source outside the United Kingdom.

(3) Income tax is charged under this section on the payments.

(4) It is charged on the full amount of the payments arising in the tax year.

(5) But a payment is not taken into account in calculating total income so far as it is applied to charitable purposes only.

(6) The amount charged under this section in the case of certain payments made by the trustees of a charitable trust in the exercise of a discretion is subject to section 494 (grossing up of discretionary payments from trusts).

(7) The trustees of the charitable trust are liable for any tax charged under this section.

Commentary—*Simon's Taxes* C5.117A.
Derivation—TA 1988 s 505(1)–(2).

Other exemptions

524 Exemption for profits etc of charitable trades

(1) The income mentioned in subsection (2) is not taken into account in calculating total income if conditions A and B are met.

(2) The income referred to in subsection (1) is—

    (a) the profits of a trade carried on by a charitable trust,

    (b) amounts treated as adjustment income of a charitable trust under section 228 of ITTOIA 2005 in respect of a trade carried on by the trust, and

    (c) post-cessation receipts arising from a trade carried on by a charitable trust which are received by the trustees of the trust or to which they are entitled.

(3) Condition A is—

    (a) in the case of the profits of a trade, that the profits are profits of a tax year in relation to which the trade is a charitable trade,

    (b) in the case of an amount treated as adjustment income, that the amount arises in a tax year in relation to which the trade is a charitable trade, and

    (c) in the case of a post-cessation receipt, that the trade was a charitable trade in relation to the tax year in which the cessation occurred.

See section 525 as to when a trade is a charitable trade in relation to a tax year.

(4) Condition B is that the profits are, or the amount or post-cessation receipt is, (as the case may be) applied to the purposes of the charitable trust only.

(5) Sections 232(1) and (2), 235 and 236 of ITTOIA 2005 (when adjustment income is treated as arising) apply for the purposes of subsection (3) as they apply for the purposes of Chapter 17 of Part 2 of that Act.

(6) In this section "post-cessation receipt" means an amount that is a post-cessation receipt for the purposes of Chapter 18 of Part 2 of ITTOIA 2005 (post-cessation receipts) (see sections 246 to 253 of that Act).

Commentary—*Simon's Taxes* C5.117D.

525 Meaning of "charitable trade"

(1) For the purposes of this Part a trade carried on by a charitable trust is a charitable trade in relation to a tax year if throughout the basis period for the tax year—

    (a) the trade is exercised in the course of carrying out a primary purpose of the charitable trust, or

    (b) the work in connection with the trade is mainly carried out by beneficiaries of the charitable trust.

(2) For the purposes of subsection (1)(a), if a trade is exercised partly in the course of carrying out a primary purpose of the charitable trust and partly otherwise, each part is to be treated as a separate trade.

(3) For the purposes of subsection (1)(b), if work in connection with a trade is carried out partly but not mainly by beneficiaries, the part in connection with which work is carried out by beneficiaries and the other part are to be treated as separate trades.

(4) If different parts of a trade are treated as separate trades under subsection (2) or (3), a just and reasonable apportionment is to be made for that purpose of—

    (a) expenses and receipts of the trade, and

    (b) any amounts which are treated as adjustment income under section 228 of ITTOIA 2005 in respect of the trade, or which are post-cessation receipts arising from the trade for the purposes of Chapter 18 of Part 2 of that Act.

(5) For the rules about basis periods, see Chapter 15 of Part 2 of ITTOIA 2005.

Commentary—*Simon's Taxes* C5.117D.

526 Exemption for profits etc of small-scale trades

(1) The income mentioned in subsection (2) is not taken into account in calculating total income if conditions A and B are met.

(2) The income referred to in subsection (1) is—

    (a) the profits of a trade carried on by a charitable trust,

    (b) amounts treated as adjustment income of a charitable trust under section 228 of ITTOIA 2005 in respect of a trade carried on by the trust, and

(c) post-cessation receipts arising from a trade carried on by a charitable trust which are received by the trustees of the trust or to which they are entitled.

(3) Subsection (1) does not apply in respect of—

    (a) profits of a trade that are, apart from this section, exempt from income tax chargeable under Part 2 of ITTOIA 2005,

    (b) amounts treated as adjustment income that are, apart from this section, exempt from income tax chargeable under Chapter 17 of Part 2 of that Act, or

    (c) post-cessation receipts that are, apart from this section, exempt from income tax chargeable under Chapter 18 of Part 2 of that Act.

(4) Condition A is—

    (a) in the case of the profits of a trade, that the profits are profits of a tax year in relation to which the condition specified in section 528 (condition as to trading and miscellaneous incoming resources) is met,

    (b) in the case of an amount treated as adjustment income, that the amount arises in such a tax year, and

    (c) in the case of a post-cessation receipt, that it is received in such a tax year.

(5) Condition B is that the profits are, or the amount or post-cessation receipt is, (as the case may be) applied to the purposes of the charitable trust only.

(6) Sections 232(1) and (2), 235 and 236 of ITTOIA 2005 (when adjustment income is treated as arising) apply for the purposes of subsection (4) as they apply for the purposes of Chapter 17 of Part 2 of that Act.

(7) In this section "post-cessation receipt" means an amount that is a post-cessation receipt for the purposes of Chapter 18 of Part 2 of that Act (post-cessation receipts) (see sections 246 to 253 of that Act).

Commentary—*Simon's Taxes* **C5.117E**.

527 Exemption from charges under provisions to which section 1016 applies

(1) Any income or gains of a charitable trust that is or are chargeable to income tax under or by virtue of any provision to which section 1016 applies is not or are not taken into account in calculating total income if conditions A and B are met.

(2) Subsection (1) does not apply in respect of any income or gains chargeable to income tax by virtue of any of—

    (a) [section 1086(2) of CTA 2010][1] (chargeable payments connected with exempt distributions),

    (b) *section 804 of that Act (double taxation relief),*[2]

    (c) Chapter 9 of Part 4 of ITTOIA 2005 (gains from contracts for life insurance etc),

    (d) Chapter 5 of Part 5 of that Act (settlements: amounts treated as income of settlor),[and][3]

    (e) . . .[3]

    (f) any other enactment specified in an order made by the Treasury.

(3) Subsection (1) does not apply in respect of any income that is, or gains that are, apart from this section, exempt from income tax chargeable under or by virtue of any provision to which section 1016 applies.

(4) Condition A is that the income is, or the gains are, for a tax year in relation to which the condition specified in section 528 is met.

(5) Condition B is that the income is, or the gains are, applied to the purposes of the charitable trust only.

Commentary—*Simon's Taxes* **C5.117F**.

Amendments—[1] In sub-s (2)(a) words substituted by CTA 2010 s 1177, Sch 1 para 530. CTA 2010 has effect for corporation tax purposes for accounting periods ending on or after 1 April 2010, and for income and capital gains tax purposes for the tax year 2010–11 and subsequent tax years.

[2] Sub-s (2)(b) repealed by TIOPA 2010 ss 501, 503, Sch 8 paras 71, 81, Sch 10 Pt 1. TIOPA 2010 has effect for corporation tax purposes for accounting periods ending on or after 1 April 2010, for income and capital gains tax purposes for the tax year 2010–11 and subsequent tax years, and for petroleum revenue tax purposes for chargeable periods beginning on or after 1 July 2010.

[3] In sub-s (2)(d), word inserted, and sub-s (2)(e) repealed, by FA 2016 s 79(4) with effect in relation to disposals on or after 5 July 2016 (FA 2016 s 82(1)), subject to transitional provisions relating to disposals to associated persons on or after 16 March 2016 and before 5 July 2016 (FA 2016 s 82(4)–(15)).

F(No 2)A 2017 s 39 provides that this amendment has effect (so far as it would not otherwise have effect) in relation to amounts that are recognised in GAAP accounts drawn up for any period of account beginning on or after 8 March 2017 or, in the case of a straddling period, amounts that would be recognised in GAAP accounts drawn up for a period of account beginning on 8 March 2017 and ending when the straddling period ends. "Straddling period" means a period of account beginning before 8 March 2017 and ending on or after that date.

528 Condition as to trading and miscellaneous incoming resources

(1) The condition in this section is met in relation to a tax year if—

    (a) the sum of the charitable trust's trading incoming resources and miscellaneous incoming resources for the tax year does not exceed the requisite limit for the tax year, or

    (b) the trustees of the charitable trust had, at the beginning of the tax year, a reasonable expectation that it would not do so.

(2) The charitable trust's "trading incoming resources" for the tax year are—

(a) the incoming resources which are required to be taken into account in calculating the profits of, or losses made in, the basis period for the tax year of any non-exempt trade carried on by the charitable trust, and

(b) the incoming resources which are treated as adjustment income under section 228 of ITTOIA 2005 in respect of such a trade, or which are post-cessation receipts arising from such a trade. "Post-cessation receipt" has the meaning given by section 526(7).

(3) For the purposes of subsection (2) a trade is a "non-exempt trade" if any profits of the trade would not, apart from section 526, be exempt from income tax chargeable under Part 2 of ITTOIA 2005.

(4) The charitable trust's "miscellaneous incoming resources" for the tax year are the incoming resources which are required to be taken into account in calculating non-exempt miscellaneous income or non-exempt miscellaneous losses for the tax year.

(5) In this section—

"non-exempt miscellaneous income" means income or gains chargeable to income tax under or by virtue of any provision to which section 1016 applies that is not, or are not, apart from section 526 or 527, exempt from income tax chargeable under or by virtue of that provision, and "non-exempt miscellaneous losses" means losses arising from a transaction which is of such a nature that if income or gains had arisen from it the income would have been non-exempt miscellaneous income.

(6) The requisite limit—

(a) is 25% of the charitable trust's total incoming resources for the tax year, but

(b) must not be less than [£8,000][1] or more than [£80,000][1].

Commentary—*Simon's Taxes* **C5.117E**.
Amendments—[1]   In sub-s (6)(b) figures substituted for "£5,000" and "£50,000" respectively, by FA 2019 s 41(1) with effect for the tax year 2019–20 and subsequent years.

529 Exemption for profits from fund-raising events

(1) The profits of a trade carried on by a charitable trust are not taken into account in calculating total income so far as they arise from a VAT-exempt event.

(2) Subsection (1) applies so far as the profits are [either applied for charitable purposes or transferred to another charity][1].

(3) An event is a VAT-exempt event if the supply of goods and services by the charitable trust in connection with the event would be exempt from value added tax under Group 12 of Schedule 9 to the Value Added Tax Act 1994 (c 23) (fund-raising events by charities and other qualifying bodies).

Commentary—*Simon's Taxes* **C5.117G**.
HMRC Manuals—Business Income Manual BIM24794 (voluntary organisations & charities: tax exemption). BIM24795 (conditions for exemption).
Amendments—[1]   In sub-s (2), words substituted by the Enactment of Extra-Statutory Concessions Order, SI 2011/1037 art 14 with effect in relation to profits applied or transferred on or after 6 April 2011 (SI 2011/1037 art 14(2)).

530 Exemption for profits from lotteries

(1) The profits accruing to a charitable trust from a lottery are not taken into account in calculating total income if conditions A and B are met.

(2) Condition A is that—

[(a)   the lottery is an exempt lottery within the meaning of the Gambling Act 2005 by virtue of Part 1 or 4 of Schedule 11 to that Act,

(ab)   the lottery is promoted in accordance with a lottery operating licence within the meaning of Part 5 of that Act, or][1]

(b)   the lottery is promoted and conducted in accordance with Article 133 or 135 of the Betting, Gaming, Lotteries and Amusements (Northern Ireland) Order 1985 (SI 1985/1204 (NI 11)).

(3) Condition B is that the profits are applied to the purposes of the charitable trust only.

Commentary—*Simon's Taxes* **C5.117H**.
Regulations—Finance Act 2007, Schedule 25 (Commencement and Transitional Provisions) Order, SI 2007/2532 art 3 (references to "lottery operating licence" include an operating licence which is treated as being held by a society by virtue of para 68 of the Gambling Act 2005 (Commencement No 6 and Transitional Provisions) Order 2006).
Amendments—[1]   Sub-s (2)(a), (ab) substituted for original sub-s (2)(a) by FA 2007 s 105, Sch 25 para 2 with effect from 1 September 2007: SI 2007/2532 art 2.

531 Exemption for property income etc

(1) Income which is chargeable to income tax under Part 2 of ITTOIA 2005 (trading income) as a result of section 261 of that Act is not taken into account in calculating total income so far as—

(a) it arises in respect of rents or other receipts from an estate, interest or right in or over land, and

(b) the estate, interest or right is vested in any person in trust for a charitable trust or for charitable purposes.

(2) Income which is chargeable to income tax under Part 3 of ITTOIA 2005 (property income) is not taken into account in calculating total income so far as—

(*a*)　it arises in respect of an estate, interest or right in or over land, and

(*b*)　the estate, interest or right is vested in any person in trust for a charitable trust or for charitable purposes.

[(2A) Distributions to which [section 548 of CTA 2010][2] (Real Estate Investment Trusts: distributions) applies and which are chargeable to income tax under Part 2 or Part 3 of ITTOIA 2005 are not taken into account in calculating total income so far as they arise in respect of shares vested in a person in trust for a charitable trust or for charitable purposes.][1]

(3)　Subsection (1) [to (2A)][1] apply so far as the income is applied to charitable purposes only.

Commentary—*Simon's Taxes* **C5.117I**.

Amendments—[1]　Sub-s (2A) inserted, and words in sub-s (3) substituted, by FA 2007 s 52, Sch 17 paras 1, 18 with effect in respect of—

　(a)　an accounting period, of a company to which Part 4 of FA 2006 (REITs) applies, which begins on or after 1 January 2007,

　(b)　an accounting period, of the principal company of a group to which that Part applies, which begins on or after 1 January 2007, and

　(c)　a distribution to which FA 2006 s 121 applies and which is received on or after 1 January 2007.

[2]　In sub-s (2A) words substituted by CTA 2010 s 1177, Sch 1 para 531. CTA 2010 has effect for corporation tax purposes for accounting periods ending on or after 1 April 2010, and for income and capital gains tax purposes for the tax year 2010–11 and subsequent tax years.

532 Exemption for savings and investment income

(1)　The income mentioned in subsection (2) is not taken into account in calculating total income if—

(*a*)　it is income of a charitable trust, or

(*b*)　it is required, under an Act, court judgment, charter, trust deed or will, to be applied to charitable purposes only.

(2)　The income referred to in subsection (1) is—

(*a*)　interest,

(*b*)　a dividend or other distribution of a UK resident company,

(*c*)　a dividend of a non-UK resident company,

(*d*)　an annuity payment under a purchased life annuity,

(*e*)　profits on the disposal of deeply discounted securities, or

(*f*)　income treated for the purposes of [regulation 15 of the Unauthorised Unit Trusts (Tax) Regulations 2013 as received by a unit holder from an exempt unauthorised unit trust.][1]

(3)　Subsection (1) applies only so far as the income falls within, and is dealt with under, Part 4 of ITTOIA 2005 (see section 366 of that Act as to provisions given priority over Part 4).

(4)　Subsection (1) applies so far as the income is applied to charitable purposes only.

(5)　In this section—

"deeply discounted security" has the same meaning as in Chapter 8 of Part 4 of ITTOIA 2005 (profits from deeply discounted securities) (see section 430 of that Act),

"disposal", in relation to a deeply discounted security, has the same meaning as in Chapter 8 of Part 4 of that Act (see section 437(1) of that Act),

"dividend", in relation to a UK resident company, has the same meaning as in Chapter 3 of Part 4 of that Act (dividends etc from UK resident companies etc) (see section 382(4) of that Act),

"interest" includes anything treated as interest for the purposes of Chapter 2 of Part 4 of that Act (interest), and

"purchased life annuity" has the same meaning as in Chapter 7 of Part 4 of that Act (purchased life annuity payments) (see section 423 of that Act).

Commentary—*Simon's Taxes* **C5.117J**.

Amendments—[1]　In sub-s (2)(*f*), words substituted by the Unauthorised Unit Trusts (Tax) Regulations, SI 2013/2819 reg 37(1), (7) with effect from 6 April 2014. Note that an unauthorised unit trust is not a non-exempt unauthorised unit trust, and this amendment does not apply in relation to the trust, if at all times in the period beginning with 24 May 2012 and ending with 5 April 2014 it had at least one unit holder which was, and at least one unit holder which was not, an eligible investor (ie a mixed unauthorised unit trust); this ceases to apply in relation to the trust if subsequently it no longer has any unit holders which are eligible investors (SI 2013/2819 reg 32).

533 Exemption for public revenue dividends

(1)　Public revenue dividends on securities which are in the name of trustees are not taken into account in calculating total income so far as the dividends are applicable and applied only for the repair of—

(*a*)　a cathedral, college, church or chapel, or

(*b*)　a building used only for the purposes of divine worship.

(2)　In this section "public revenue dividends" means—

(*a*)　income from securities which is payable out of the public revenue of the United Kingdom or Northern Ireland, or

(*b*)　income from securities issued by or on behalf of a government or a public or local authority in a country outside the United Kingdom.

Commentary—*Simon's Taxes* **C5.117K**.

Derivation—TA 1988 s 505(1), (1A).

534 Exemption for transactions in deposits

(1) Profits or gains arising to a charitable trust from the disposal of exempt deposit rights are not taken into account in calculating total income.

(2) Subsection (1) applies so far as the profits or gains are applied to charitable purposes only.

(3) For the purposes of this section, the exercise of an exempt deposit right is a disposal of it, except so far as the right is a right to receive interest.

(4) In this section "exempt deposit rights" means—

   (a) a right to receive, with or without interest, a principal amount stated in, or determined in accordance with, the current terms of issue of an eligible debt security, where in accordance with those terms the issue of uncertificated units of the eligible debt security corresponds to the issue of a certificate of deposit,

   (b) a right to receive the principal amount stated in a certificate of deposit, with or without interest, and

   (c) an uncertificated right to receive a principal amount, with or without interest, as a result of a deposit of money.

(5) In this section—

   "eligible debt security" has the meaning given in regulation 3(1) of the Uncertificated Securities Regulations 2001 (SI 2001/3755),

   "uncertificated", in relation to a unit, has the meaning given in regulation 3(1) of the Uncertificated Securities Regulations 2001,

   "uncertificated right" means a right in respect of which no certificate of deposit has been issued, although the person for the time being entitled to it is entitled to call for the issue of such a certificate, and

   "unit" has the meaning given in regulation 3(1) of the Uncertificated Securities Regulations 2001.

Commentary—*Simon's Taxes* **C5.117L**.
Derivation—TA 1988 ss 56, 56A.

535 Exemption for offshore income gains

(1) Offshore income gains accruing to a charitable trust are not taken into account in calculating total income.

(2) Subsection (1) applies if the gain is applicable and applied to charitable purposes only.

(3) In this section "offshore income gain" has the same meaning as in [Chapter 5 of Part 2 of the Offshore (Tax) Funds Regulations 2009 (SI 2009/3001)][1].

(4) See [regulation 31(3) to (5) of the Offshore Funds (Tax) Regulations 2009 (SI 2009/3001)][1], which—

   (a) applies where property held on charitable trusts ceases to be subject to charitable trusts, and

   (b) provides for any gain accruing under that subsection to be treated as an offshore income gain not accruing to a charity.

Commentary—*Simon's Taxes* **C5.117M**.
Amendments—[1]   In sub-ss (3), (4), words substituted for words by the Offshore Funds (Tax) Regulations, SI 2009/3001 reg 129(1), (4) with effect for the purposes of income tax for the tax year 2009–10 and subsequent tax years and for distributions made on or after 1 December 2009; for the purposes of corporation tax, on income, for accounting periods ending on or after 1 December 2009 and for distributions made on or after that date and, on chargeable gains, in relation to disposals made on or after 1 December 2009; and for the purposes of capital gains tax, in relation to disposals made on or after 1 December 2009.

536 Exemption for certain miscellaneous income

(1) The income mentioned in subsection (3) is not taken into account in calculating total income if—

   (a) it is income of a charitable trust, or

   (b) it is required, under an Act, court judgment, charter, trust deed or will, to be applied to charitable purposes only.

(2) Subsection (1) applies so far as the income is applied to charitable purposes only.

(3) The income referred to in subsection (1) is—

   (a) royalties and other income from intellectual property that do not fall within Chapter 2 of Part 2 of ITTOIA 2005 (receipts of a trade etc),

   (b) income derived from a relevant telecommunication right that is not income falling within Chapter 2 of Part 2 of ITTOIA 2005 (receipts of a trade etc),

   (c) annual payments charged to tax under Chapter 7 of Part 5 of ITTOIA 2005, and

   (d) relevant foreign distributions.

(4) In this section—

   "intellectual property" has the same meaning as in section 579 of ITTOIA 2005,

   "relevant foreign distribution" means a distribution of a non-UK resident company which—

      (a) is not chargeable to tax under Chapter 4 of Part 4 of ITTOIA 2005 (dividends from non-UK resident companies), but

(b) would be chargeable to tax under Chapter 3 of that Part of that Act (dividends etc from UK resident companies etc) if the company were a UK resident company, and

"relevant telecommunication right" has the same meaning as in Chapter 10 of Part 2 of that Act (trade profits: certain telecommunications rights) (see section 146 of that Act).

Commentary—*Simon's Taxes* **C5.117N**.

537 Exemption for income from estates in administration

(1) If the person liable under section 659 of ITTOIA 2005 for any income tax charged under section 649 of that Act (charge to tax on estate income) is the trustee of a charitable trust, the estate income is not taken into account in calculating total income.

(2) Subsection (1) applies so far as the estate income is applied to the purposes of the charitable trust only.

(3) In this section "estate income" has the same meaning as in Chapter 6 of Part 5 of ITTOIA 2005 (beneficiaries' income from estates in administration) (see section 649(2) of that Act).

Commentary—*Simon's Taxes* **C5.117O**.

Claims

538 Requirement to make claim

(1) The exemptions under this Part require a claim.

(2) Subsection (1) does not apply to an exemption under—
   (a) section 534 (exemption for transactions in deposits), or
   (b) section 535 (exemption for offshore income gains).

(3) . . .[2]

(4) . . .[1]

Commentary—*Simon's Taxes* **C5.141**.
Amendments—[1] Sub-s (4) repealed by the Transfer of Tribunal Functions and Revenue and Customs Appeals Order, SI 2009/56 art 3, Sch 1 para 452 with effect from 1 April 2009.
[2] Sub-s (3) repealed by FA 2012 s 50(2)(b). This amendment is treated as having come into force on 6 April 2012.

[538A Claims in relation to gift aid relief [etc]

[(A1) This section applies to claims for—
   (a) repayment of income tax treated as having been paid by virtue of section 520(4) (gift aid relief: income tax treated as paid by trustees of charitable trust), or
   (b) repayment of income tax deducted at source from income to which any of the following applies—
      (i) section 532 (exemption for savings and investment income),
      (ii) section 533 (exemption for public revenue dividends),
      (iii) section 536 (exemption for certain miscellaneous income), or
      (iv) section 537 (exemption for income from estates in administration).][2]

(1) This section [also][2] applies to claims for amounts to be exempt from tax [by virtue of—
   (a) section 521(4) (gifts entitling donor to gift aid relief: charitable trusts), or
   (b) any of the provisions mentioned in subsection (A1)(b).][2]

(2) A claim to which this section applies may be made—
   (a) to an officer of Revenue and Customs, or
   (b) by being included in a return under section 8A of TMA 1970 (trustee's self-assessment return).

(3) In this section—
   "free-standing claim" means a claim made as mentioned in subsection (2)(a), and
   "tax return claim" means a claim made as mentioned in subsection (2)(b).

(4) The Commissioners for Her Majesty's Revenue and Customs may by regulations make provision—
   (a) limiting the number of free-standing claims that may be made by a person in a tax year, or
   (b) requiring a claim for an amount below an amount specified in the regulations to be made as a tax return claim.

(5) The regulations may make different provision for different cases or purposes.][1]

Commentary—*Simon's Taxes* **C5.141**.
Amendments—[1] This section inserted by FA 2010 s 32, Sch 8 para 5(1), (3) with effect from 8 April 2010.
[2] Sub-s (A1), word in heading and words in sub-s (1) inserted, and sub-s (1)(a), (b) substituted for previous words, by FA 2012 s 51, Sch 15 para 1. These amendments are treated as having come into force on 8 April 2010.

Restrictions on exemptions

539 Restrictions on exemptions

(1) This section applies if a charitable trust has a non-exempt amount for a tax year (see section 540).

(2) The exemptions under this Part do not apply, and are treated as never having applied, to so much of any income of the charitable trust for the tax year as is attributed under section 541 to the non-exempt amount.

(3) Section 256(4) of TCGA 1992 contains corresponding restrictions which apply in relation to section 256(1) of that Act (gains accruing to charities not to be chargeable gains).

Commentary—*Simon's Taxes* C5.127, C5.124.

540 The non-exempt amount

(1) A charitable trust has a non-exempt amount for a tax year if it has—

    (*a*) non-charitable expenditure for the tax year (amount A), and

    (*b*) attributable income and gains for the tax year (amount B).

(2) The non-exempt amount for the tax year is—

    (*a*) amount A, or

    (*b*) if less, amount B.

(3) For the purposes of this Part—

    (*a*) a charitable trust's "attributable income" for a tax year is the charitable trust's income for the tax year that is exempt from income tax as a result of any of the exemptions under this Part,

    (*b*) a charitable trust's "attributable gains" for a tax year are any gains accruing to the charitable trust in the tax year that as a result of [section 256(1)][1] of TCGA 1992, are not chargeable gains, and

    (*c*) a charitable trust's "attributable income and gains" for a tax year is the sum of its attributable income for the tax year and its attributable gains for the tax year.

(4) In applying subsection (3)(*a*) ignore any restrictions on the exemptions under this Part which result from section 539(2).

(5) In applying subsection (3)(*b*) ignore any restriction on the exemption under section 256(1) of TCGA 1992 which results from section 256(4) of that Act.

Commentary—*Simon's Taxes* C5.127, C5.124.

Amendments—[1] Words in sub-s (3)(*b*) substituted by the Income Tax Act 2007 (Amendment) (No 3) Order, SI 2007/3506 art 3(1), (3) with effect for income tax and capital gains tax purposes for the tax year 2007–08 and subsequent tax years, and for corporation tax purposes for accounting periods ending after 5 April 2007: SI 2007/3506 art 1(2).

541 Attributing income to the non-exempt amount

(1) This section applies if a charitable trust has a non-exempt amount for a tax year.

(2) Attributable income of the charitable trust for the tax year may be attributed to the non-exempt amount but only so far as the non-exempt amount has not been used up.

(3) The non-exempt amount can be used up (in whole or in part) by—

    (*a*) attributable income being attributed to it under this section, or

    (*b*) attributable gains being attributed to it under section 256A of TCGA 1992.

(4) The whole of the non-exempt amount must be used up by—

    (*a*) attributable income being attributed to the whole of it under this section,

    (*b*) attributable gains being attributed to the whole of it under section 256A of TCGA 1992, or

    (*c*) a combination of attributable income being attributed to some of it under this section and attributable gains being attributed to the rest of it under section 256A of TCGA 1992.

(5) See section 542 for the way in which income is to be attributed to the non-exempt amount under this section.

Commentary—*Simon's Taxes* C5.127.

Derivation—TA 1988 s 505(4), (7).

542 How income is attributed to the non-exempt amount

(1) This section is about the ways in which attributable income can be attributed to a non-exempt amount under section 541.

(2) The trustees of the charitable trust may specify the attributable income that is to be attributed to the non-exempt amount.

(3) A specification under subsection (2) is made by notice to an officer of Revenue and Customs.

(4) Subsection (6) applies if—

    (*a*) an officer of Revenue and Customs requires the trustees of a charitable trust to make a specification under this section, and

    (*b*) the trustees have not given notice under subsection (3) of the specification before the end of the required period.

(5) The required period is 30 days beginning with the day on which the officer made the requirement.

(6) An officer of Revenue and Customs may determine the attributable income that is to be attributed to the non-exempt amount.

Commentary—*Simon's Taxes* C5.127.

Non-charitable expenditure

543 Meaning of "non-charitable expenditure"

(1) For the purposes of this Part a charitable trust's non-charitable expenditure for a tax year is—

    (*a*) any loss made in the tax year in a trade carried on by the charitable trust unless—

        (i) the trade is a charitable trade in relation to the tax year, or

    (ii) the trade is not a charitable trade in relation to the tax year but profits of the trade arising in the tax year would be exempt from income tax as a result of one of the exemptions in sections 526, 529 or 530,

  (b) any payment made in the tax year by the charitable trust in connection with a trade in circumstances where relief is available under section 96 (post-cessation trade relief) unless—

    (i) the trade was a charitable trade in relation to the tax year in which the cessation occurred, or

    (ii) the trade was not a charitable trade in relation to that tax year but profits of the trade arising immediately before the cessation would have been exempt from income tax as a result of one of the exemptions in sections 526, 529 or 530,

  (c) any loss made in the tax year in a trade, or in a UK property business or an overseas property business, carried on by the charitable trust, if—

    (i) the loss relates to land, and

    (ii) profits of the trade, or income of the business, generated from the land in the tax year would not be exempt from income tax as a result of the exemptions in section 531,

  (d) any payment made in the tax year by the charitable trust in connection with a trade or UK property business in circumstances where relief is available under section 96 or 125 (post-cessation trade or property relief), if—

    (i) the payment relates to land, and

    (ii) profits of the trade, or income of the business, generated from the land immediately before the cessation would not have been exempt from income tax as a result of the exemptions in section 531,

  (e) any loss made in the tax year in a miscellaneous transaction entered into by the charitable trust otherwise than in the course of carrying out a charitable purpose,

  (f) any expenditure incurred by the charitable trust in the tax year, not falling within paragraphs (b) or (d), which is not incurred for charitable purposes only and is not required to be taken into account in calculating—

    (i) the profits of, or losses made in, any trade, UK property business or overseas property business carried on by the charitable trust, or

    (ii) the profit or loss made in any miscellaneous transaction entered into by the charitable trust,

  (g) . . .¹

  (h) . . .¹

  (i) the amount of any of the charitable trust's funds that is invested in the tax year in an investment which is not an approved charitable investment (see section 558), and

  (j) any amount lent in the tax year by the charitable trust, if the loan is neither an investment nor an approved charitable loan (see section 561).

But anything which falls within more than one of the above paragraphs counts as non-charitable expenditure only once.

(2) An amount may also be non-charitable expenditure for a tax year as a result of section 562 (excess expenditure treated as non-charitable expenditure of earlier years).

(3) This section needs to be read with—

    section 525 (meaning of "charitable trade"),

    sections 544 to 548 (supplementary provision in relation to this section, in particular in relation to subsection (1)(f), (i) and (j)),

    sections 549 to 557 (transactions with substantial donors),

    section 558 (approved charitable investments), and

    section 561 (approved charitable loans).

Commentary—*Simon's Taxes* **C5.127**.

Modifications—ITA 2007 Sch 2 para 105 (sub-s (1)(g), (h) does not have effect in relation to—

  (a)   a transaction occurring before 22 March 2006, or

  (b)   a transaction entered into in pursuance of a contract made before 22 March 2006 (otherwise than in pursuance of a variation on or after that date).

Amendments—¹   Sub-s (1)(g), (h) repealed by FA 2011 s 27, Sch 3 paras 7, 12 with effect in relation to any transaction, other than an excluded transaction (as defined in FA 2011 Sch 3 para 27(3)) occurring on or after 1 April 2013.

544 Section 543: supplementary

(1) This section applies for the purposes of section 543.

(2) For rules about the calculation of losses, see—

  (a) section 26 of ITTOIA 2005 (losses of a trade calculated on same basis as profits),

  (b) section 272 of that Act (which applies section 26 of that Act, so that losses of a UK property business or overseas property business are calculated on the same basis as profits), and

  (c) section 872 of that Act (losses from miscellaneous transactions calculated on same basis as miscellaneous income).

(3) A transaction is a miscellaneous transaction if it is of such a nature that, if income or gains had arisen from it—

    (*a*) ignoring section 527 (exemption from charges under provisions to which section 1016 applies), it would have been charged to income tax under or by virtue of any provision to which section 1016 applies, and

    (*b*) the trustees of the charitable trust would have been liable for any tax so chargeable.

(4) References to a charitable trust making a loss in a trade in a tax year are to the charitable trust making a loss in the trade in the basis period for the tax year.

Commentary—*Simon's Taxes* **C5.127**.

Changes in the law—See ITA 2007 EN Annex 1 Change 98. This change clarifies the meaning of "non-charitable expenditure".

545 Section 543(1)(f): meaning of expenditure

(1) For the purposes of section 543(1)(*f*) "expenditure" includes expenditure of a capital nature.

(2) None of the following is "expenditure" for those purposes—

    (*a*) the investment of any of the charitable trust's funds,

    (*b*) the making of a loan by the charitable trust, or

    (*c*) the repayment by the charitable trust of the whole or a part of a loan made to it.

Commentary—*Simon's Taxes* **C5.127**.

Changes in the law—See ITA 2007 EN Annex 1 Change 98. This change clarifies the meaning of "non-charitable expenditure".

546 Section 543(1)(f): tax year in which certain expenditure treated as incurred

(1) This section applies for the purposes of section 543(1)(*f*).

(2) Subsection (3) applies to expenditure which is referable to commitments (whether or not of a contractual nature) that the charitable trust has entered into before or during a tax year.

(3) The expenditure is treated as incurred in the tax year if, had the charitable trust been required to draw up accounts that met the requirements mentioned in subsection (4), the expenditure would have been required to be taken into account in preparing those accounts.

(4) The requirements referred to in subsection (3) are—

    (*a*) that the accounts are drawn up for the tax year, and

    (*b*) that UK generally accepted accounting practice applies with respect to them.

Commentary—*Simon's Taxes* **C5.127**.

547 Section 543(1)(f): payment to body outside the UK

A payment made, or to be made, to a body situated outside the United Kingdom is non-charitable expenditure under section 543(1)(*f*) if—

    (*a*) it is incurred for charitable purposes only, but

    (*b*) the trustees of the charitable trust have not taken such steps as [the Commissioners for Her Majesty's Revenue and Customs consider][1] are reasonable in the circumstances to ensure that the payment will be applied for charitable purposes.

Commentary—*Simon's Taxes* **C5.127**.

Amendments—[1] In para (*b*) words inserted by FA 2010 s 32, Sch 8 para 2(1) with effect in relation to payments representing expenditure incurred on or after 24 March 2010.

548 Section 543(1)(i) and (j): investments and loans

(1) Subsection (2) applies if in a tax year a charitable trust—

    (*a*) realises the whole or part of an investment which was made in the tax year and is not an approved charitable investment (see section 558), or

    (*b*) is repaid the whole or part of a loan which was made in the tax year and is neither an investment nor an approved charitable loan (see section 561).

(2) Any further investment or lending in the tax year of the sum realised or repaid, so far as it does not exceed the sum originally invested or lent, is not non-charitable expenditure as a result of section 543(1)(i) or (j).

Commentary—*Simon's Taxes* **C5.127**.

Derivation—TA 1988 s 506(5).

Approved charitable investments and loans

558 Approved charitable investments

An investment is an approved charitable investment for the purposes of section 543 (meaning of "non-charitable expenditure") if it is an investment of any of the following types.

    Type 1 An investment to which section 559 applies.

    Type 2 An investment in a common investment fund established under—

        (*a*) section 22 of the Charities Act 1960 (c 58),

        (*b*) section 24 of the Charities Act 1993 (c 10),[

        (*bb*) section 96 of the Charities Act 2011, or][1]

        (*c*) section 25 of the Charities Act (Northern Ireland) 1964.

    Type 3 An investment in a common deposit fund established under—

        (*a*) section 22A of the Charities Act 1960, . . .[1]

        (*b*) section 25 of the Charities Act 1993[, or

   (*c*) section 100 of the Charities Act 2011.][1]

Type 4 An investment in a fund which—

   (*a*) is similar to a fund mentioned in relation to Type 2 or 3, and

   (*b*) is established for the exclusive benefit of charities by or under a provision relating to any particular charities or class of charities contained in an Act.

Type 5 An interest in land, other than an interest held as security for a debt.

Type 6 Any of the following issued by Her Majesty's Government in the United Kingdom—

   (*a*) bills,

   (*b*) Certificates of Tax Deposit,

   (*c*) Savings Certificates, and

   (*d*) Tax Reserve Certificates.

Type 7 Northern Ireland Treasury Bills.

Type 8 Units in a unit trust scheme (as defined in section 237(1) of FISMA 2000) or in a recognised scheme (as defined in section 237(3) of FISMA 2000).

    "Units" is defined in section 237(2) of FISMA 2000.

Type 9 A deposit with a bank (as defined in section 991)—

   (*a*) in respect of which interest is payable at a commercial rate, and

   (*b*) which is not made as part of an arrangement under which a loan is made by the bank to some other person.

Type 10 A deposit with—

   (*a*) the National Savings Bank,

   (*b*) a building society, or

   (*c*) a credit institution which operates on mutual principles and which is authorised by an appropriate governmental body in the territory in which the deposit is taken.

Type 11 Certificates of deposit (including uncertificated eligible debt security units as defined in section 986(3)).

Type 12 A loan or other investment as to which an officer of Revenue and Customs is satisfied, on a claim, that it is made for the benefit of the charitable trust and not for the avoidance of tax (whether by the trust or any other person).

Commentary—*Simon's Taxes* **C5.127**.

Amendments—[1]   Under heading "Type 2", para (*bb*) substituted for word at the end of para (*b*); and under heading "Type 3", word at the end of para (*a*) repealed and para (*c*) inserted by the Charities Act 2011 s 354, Sch 7 para 126 with effect from 14 March 2012.

559 Securities which are approved charitable investments

(1) The investments to which this section applies are investments in securities—

   (*a*) issued or guaranteed by the government of a member State of the European Union,

   (*b*) issued or guaranteed by the government or a governmental body of any territory or part of a territory,

   (*c*) issued by an international entity listed in the Annex to Council Directive 2003/48/EC (directive on taxation of interest payments),

   (*d*) issued by an entity meeting the four criteria set out at the end of that Annex,

   (*e*) issued by a building society,

   (*f*) issued by a credit institution which operates on mutual principles and which is authorised by an appropriate governmental body in the territory in which the securities are issued,

   (*g*) issued by an open-ended investment company,

   (*h*) issued by a company and listed on a recognised stock exchange, or

   (*i*) issued by a company but not listed on a recognised stock exchange.

(2) Subsection (1) is subject to section 560.

(3) In this section and in section 560—

    "debentures" includes—

      (*a*) debenture stock and bonds (whether constituting a charge on assets or not), and

      (*b*) loan stock or notes,

    "open-ended investment company" is to be read in accordance with [sections 613 and 615 of CTA 2010][1],

    "securities" includes shares and debentures, and

    "shares" includes stocks.

Commentary—*Simon's Taxes* **C5.127**.

Amendments—[1]   In sub-s (3), in definition of "open-ended investment company", words substituted by CTA 2010 s 1177, Sch 1 para 536. CTA 2010 has effect for corporation tax purposes for accounting periods ending on or after 1 April 2010, and for income and capital gains tax purposes for the tax year 2010–11 and subsequent tax years.

Prospective amendments—In sub-s (1)(*a*) after "by" words "Her Majesty's Government in the United Kingdom or by" to be inserted by the Taxes (Amendments) (EU Exit) Regulations, SI 2019/689 reg 15(1), (6) with effect from Implementation Period completion day (see EU(WA)A 2020 Sch 5 para 1(1)).

560 Conditions to be met for some securities

(1) Section 559 does not apply to an investment by virtue of subsection (1)(*b*), (*c*) or (*d*) of that section unless—

    (*a*) condition A is met in relation to the securities, and

    (*b*) if the securities are shares or debenture stock, condition B is met in relation to the securities.

    But see subsection (3) of this section.

(2) In the case of an investment in securities issued by a company which is incorporated, section 559 does not apply to the investment by virtue of subsection (1)(i) of that section unless—

    (*a*) condition A is met in relation to the securities,

    (*b*) if the securities are shares or debenture stock, condition B is met in relation to the securities, and

    (*c*) condition C is met in relation to the company.

    But see subsection (3) of this section.

(3) Conditions A and B need not be met if the securities are traded or quoted on a money market supervised by the government or a governmental body of any territory or part of a territory.

(4) Condition A is that the securities are traded or quoted on—

    (*a*) a recognised investment exchange (as defined in section 285(1) of FISMA 2000), or

    (*b*) an investment exchange which constitutes the principal or only market established in a territory on which securities admitted to official listing are dealt in or traded.

(5) Condition B is that—

    (*a*) the securities are fully paid up,

    (*b*) the terms of the issue of the securities require them to be fully paid up within the period of 9 months beginning with the day after the day on which they are issued, or

    (*c*) the securities are shares issued with no nominal value.

(6) Condition C is that—

    (*a*) throughout the last business day before the investment day, the company has total issued and paid up share capital of at least £1,000,000 (or the equivalent of £1,000,000 in some other currency), and

    (*b*) in each of the five years immediately before the calendar year in which the investment day falls, the company paid a dividend on all the shares issued by the company (excluding any shares issued after the dividend was declared and any shares which by their terms of issue did not rank for dividend for that year).

(7) For the purposes of the words in brackets in subsection (6)(*a*) use the exchange rate prevailing in the United Kingdom at the close of business on the last business day before the investment day.

(8) For the purposes of subsection (6)(*b*) a company formed—

    (*a*) to take over the business of another company or other companies, or

    (*b*) to acquire the securities of, or control of, another company or other companies,

is treated as having paid a dividend in any year in which a dividend has been paid by the other company or all of the other companies (as the case may be).

(9) It is irrelevant that the company is formed for other purposes in addition to those mentioned in paragraph (*a*) or (*b*) of subsection (8).

(10) In this section—

    "business day" means, in relation to an investment, a business day in the place where the investment is made, and

    "the investment day" means, in relation to an investment, the day on which the investment is made.

561 Approved charitable loans

(1) A loan is an approved charitable loan for the purposes of section 543 (meaning of "non-charitable expenditure") if it meets conditions A and B.

(2) Condition A is that the loan is not made by way of investment.

(3) Condition B is that either—

    (*a*) the loan is made to another charity for charitable purposes only,

    (*b*) it is made to a beneficiary of the charitable trust in the course of carrying out the purposes of the charitable trust,

    (*c*) it consists of money placed on current account with a bank otherwise than as part of an arrangement under which a loan is made by a bank to some other person, or

    (*d*) an officer of Revenue and Customs is satisfied, on a claim, that the loan is made for the benefit of the charitable trust and not for the avoidance of tax (whether by the charitable trust or by some other person).

(4) In this section "bank" has the meaning given by section 991.

Commentary—*Simon's Taxes* **C5.127**.
Derivation—TA 1988 Sch 20.

Carry back of excess non-charitable expenditure

562 Excess expenditure treated as non-charitable expenditure of earlier years

(1) This section applies if a charitable trust's non-charitable expenditure for a tax year exceeds its available income and gains for the tax year.

(2) The excess is the charitable trust's "excess expenditure" for the tax year.

(3) The charitable trust's excess expenditure for the tax year is treated for the purposes of this Part as non-charitable expenditure for earlier tax years so far as it can be attributed to earlier tax years under section 563.

(4) For the purposes of this Part a charitable trust's "available income and gains" for a tax year is the sum of—

    (*a*) the charitable trust's total income for the tax year (ignoring any restrictions on the exemptions under this Part which result from sections 539(2) and 541),

    (*b*) any chargeable gains accruing to the charitable trust in the tax year (ignoring any restriction on the exemption under section 256(1) of TCGA 1992 which results from section 256(4) of that Act),

    (*c*) the charitable trust's attributable income and gains for the tax year (see section 540), and

    (*d*) any non-taxable sums received by the charitable trust in the tax year.

(5) In subsection (4) "non-taxable sums" means donations, legacies and other sums of a similar nature which, ignoring exemptions from income tax under this Part and from capital gains tax under section 256 of TCGA 1992, are not liable to income tax or capital gains tax.

Commentary—*Simon's Taxes* **C5.127**.
Derivation—TA 1988 ss 505(3) and (5).

563 Rules for attributing excess expenditure to earlier years

(1) The rules in this section apply for attributing a charitable trust's excess expenditure for a tax year to earlier tax years under section 562.

(2) The excess expenditure for a tax year may be attributed to an earlier tax year if—

    (*a*) the earlier tax year ends not more than 6 years before the end of the tax year in question, and

    (*b*) the charitable trust's available income and gains for the earlier tax year exceed its non-charitable expenditure for the earlier tax year.

(3) If the conditions in subsection (2) are met in the case of more than one earlier tax year, the excess expenditure is to be attributed to a later tax year in priority to an earlier tax year.

(4) The amount of excess expenditure that is to be attributed to an earlier tax year must not be greater than the amount by which the charitable trust's available income and gains for the earlier tax year exceed its non-charitable expenditure for the earlier tax year.

(5) For the purposes of subsections (2)(*b*) and (4) the charitable trust's non-charitable expenditure for the earlier tax year includes any excess expenditure attributed to the earlier tax year as a result of a previous operation of this section, but ignores the attribution in question.

Commentary—*Simon's Taxes* **C5.127**.
Derivation—TA 1988 s 505(5) and (6).

564 Adjustments in consequence of section 562

Such adjustments must be made (whether by way of the making of assessments or otherwise) as may be required in consequence of section 562.

Commentary—*Simon's Taxes* **C5.127**.
Derivation—TA 1988 s 505(5).

[PART 10A
ALTERNATIVE FINANCE ARRANGEMENTS]

[*Introduction*

564A Introduction

(1) This Part—

    (*a*) contains provisions about the treatment as interest for certain income tax purposes of alternative finance return under alternative finance arrangements with financial institutions (see sections 564M to 564Q), and

    (*b*) contains some special provisions about the treatment of investment bond arrangements (see sections 564R to 564U) and some other rules about alternative finance arrangements (see sections 564V to 564Y).

(2) In this Part "alternative finance arrangements" means—

    (*a*) purchase and resale arrangements,

    (*b*) diminishing shared ownership arrangements,

    (*c*) deposit arrangements,

    (*d*) profit share agency arrangements, and

    (*e*) investment bond arrangements.

(3) In this Part—

    (*a*) "purchase and resale arrangements" means arrangements to which section 564C applies,

(b) "diminishing shared ownership arrangements" means arrangements to which section 564D applies,

(c) "deposit arrangements" means arrangements to which section 564E applies,

(d) "profit share agency arrangements" means arrangements to which section 564F applies, and

(e) "investment bond arrangements" means arrangements to which section 564G applies.

(4) For the meaning of "alternative finance return", see sections 564I to 564L.

(5) For the meaning of "financial institution", see section 564B.

(6) Also, see section 366 of TIOPA 2010 (power to extend this Part and other provisions to other arrangements by order).][1]

Commentary—*Simon's Taxes* A1.301.

HMRC Manuals—Business Income Manual BIM45780 (alternative finance arrangements - overview).

BIM45781 (alternative finance arrangements - tax treatment).

Corporate Finance Manual CFM44020 (the types of alternative finance arrangements).

Amendments—[1]   Section and preceding cross-head inserted by TIOPA 2010 s 365, Sch 2 paras 1, 2. TIOPA 2010 has effect for corporation tax purposes for accounting periods ending on or after 1 April 2010, for income and capital gains tax purposes for the tax year 2010–11 and subsequent tax years, and for petroleum revenue tax purposes for chargeable periods beginning on or after 1 July 2010.

[564B Meaning of "financial institution"

(1) In this Part "financial institution" means—

(a) a bank, as defined by section 991,

(b) a building society,

(c) a wholly-owned subsidiary—

(i) of a bank within paragraph (a), or

(ii) of a building society,

[(d) a person with permission under Part 4A of the Financial Services and Markets Act 2000 to enter into, or to exercise or have the right to exercise rights and duties under, a contract of the kind mentioned in paragraph 23 or paragraph 23B of Schedule 2 to that Act (credit agreements and contracts for hire of goods);][3]

(e) a bond-issuer, within the meaning of section 564G, but only in relation to any bond assets which are rights under purchase and resale arrangements, diminishing shared ownership arrangements or profit share agency arrangements,

(f) a person authorised in a jurisdiction outside the United Kingdom—

(i) to receive deposits or other repayable funds from the public, and

(ii) to grant credits for its own account,

(g) an insurance company as defined in [section 65 of FA 2012][2] or

(h) a person who is authorised in a jurisdiction outside the United Kingdom to carry on a business which consists of effecting or carrying out contracts of insurance or substantially similar business but not an insurance special purpose vehicle as defined in [section 139(1) of FA 2012][2].

[(1A) Subsection (1)(d) must be read with—

(a) section 22 of the Financial Services and Markets Act 2000,

(b) any relevant order under that section, and

(c) Schedule 2 to that Act.][3]

(2) For the purposes of subsection (1)(c) a company is a wholly-owned subsidiary of a bank or building society ("the parent") if it has no members except—

(a) the parent or persons acting on behalf of the parent, and

(b) the parent's wholly-owned subsidiaries or persons acting on behalf of the parent's wholly-owned subsidiaries.][1]

Commentary—*Simon's Taxes* A1.301.

HMRC Manuals—Corporate Finance Manual CFM44030 (definition of financial institution).

Modifications—See TIOPA 2010 Sch 9 para 39 (this section modified in relation to arrangements entered into before 15 October 2009).

FA 2013 s 143(3) (for the purposes of the annual tax on enveloped buildings, definition of "financial institution" in this section applies as if sub-s (1)(d) were repealed).

Amendments—[1]   Section inserted by TIOPA 2010 s 365, Sch 2 paras 1, 3. TIOPA 2010 has effect for corporation tax purposes for accounting periods ending on or after 1 April 2010, for income and capital gains tax purposes for the tax year 2010–11 and subsequent tax years, and for petroleum revenue tax purposes for chargeable periods beginning on or after 1 July 2010.

[2]   In sub-s (1), in paras (g), (h), words substituted for words "section 431(2) of ICTA" by FA 2012 s 146, Sch 16 paras 132, 133 with effect in relation to accounting periods of companies beginning on or after 1 January 2013 (subject to transitional provisions in FA 2012 Sch 17). For accounting periods straddling 1 January 2013, see FA 2012 s 149.

[3]   Sub-s (1)(d) substituted, and sub-s (1A) inserted by the Financial Services and Markets Act 2000 (Regulated Activities) (Amendment) (No 2) Order, SI 2013 1881 art 1(2), (6) with effect for certain purposes from 26 July 2013 and for remaining purposes, from 1 April 2014 (see SI 2013/1881 art 1).

[Arrangements that are alternative finance arrangements

564C Purchase and resale arrangements

(1) This section applies to arrangements if—

(a) they are entered into between two persons ("the first purchaser" and "the second purchaser"), one or both of whom are financial institutions, and

(b) under the arrangements—

(i) the first purchaser purchases an asset and sells it to the second purchaser,

(ii) the sale occurs immediately after the purchase or in the circumstances mentioned in subsection (2),

(iii) all or part of the second purchase price is not required to be paid until a date later than that of the sale,

(iv) the second purchase price exceeds the first purchase price, and

(v) the excess equates, in substance, to the return on an investment of money at interest.

(2) The circumstances are that—

(a) the first purchaser is a financial institution, and

(b) the asset referred to in subsection (1)(b)(i) was purchased by the first purchaser for the purpose of entering into arrangements within this section.

(3) In this section—

"the first purchase price" means the amount paid by the first purchaser in respect of the purchase, and

"the second purchase price" means the amount payable by the second purchaser in respect of the sale.

(4) This section is subject to section 564H (provision not at arm's length: exclusion of arrangements from this section and sections 564D to 564G).][1]

Commentary—*Simon's Taxes* **A1.302.**

HMRC Manuals—Corporate Finance Manual CFM4405 (purchase and resale agreement: conditions).

Amendments—[1] Section and preceding cross-head inserted by TIOPA 2010 s 365, Sch 2 paras 1, 4. TIOPA 2010 has effect for corporation tax purposes for accounting periods ending on or after 1 April 2010, for income and capital gains tax purposes for the tax year 2010–11 and subsequent tax years, and for petroleum revenue tax purposes for chargeable periods beginning on or after 1 July 2010.

[564D Diminishing shared ownership arrangements

(1) This section applies to arrangements if under them—

(a) a financial institution ("the first owner") acquires a beneficial interest in an asset,

(b) another person ("the eventual owner") also acquires a beneficial interest in it,

(c) the eventual owner is to make payments to the first owner amounting in aggregate to the consideration paid for the acquisition of the first owner's beneficial interest (but subject to any adjustment required for such a reduction as is mentioned in subsection (5)),

(d) the eventual owner is to acquire the first owner's beneficial interest (whether or not in stages) as a result of those payments,

(e) the eventual owner is to make other payments to the first owner (whether under a lease forming part of the arrangements or otherwise),

(f) the eventual owner has the exclusive right to occupy or otherwise to use the asset, and

(g) the eventual owner is exclusively entitled to any income, profit or gain arising from or attributable to the asset (including, in particular, an increase in its value).

(2) For the purposes of subsection (1)(a) it does not matter if—

(a) the first owner acquires its beneficial interest from the eventual owner,

(b) the eventual owner, or another person who is not the first owner, also has a beneficial interest in the asset, or

(c) the first owner also has a legal interest in it.

(3) Subsection (1)(f) does not prevent the eventual owner from granting an interest or right in relation to the asset if the conditions in subsection (4) are met.

(4) The conditions are that—

(a) the grant is not to—

(i) the first owner,

(ii) a person controlled by the first owner, or

(iii) a person controlled by a person who also controls the first owner, and

(b) the grant is not required by the first owner or arrangements to which the first owner is a party.

(5) Subsection (1)(g) does not prevent the first owner from—

(a) having responsibility for any reduction in the asset's value, or

(b) having a share in a loss arising out of any such reduction.

(6) This section is subject to section 564H (provision not at arm's length: exclusion of arrangements from section 564C, this section and sections 564E to 564G).][1]

Commentary—*Simon's Taxes* **A1.302.**

HMRC Manuals—Corporate Finance Manual CFM44070 (diminishing shared ownership arrangement: conditions).

Amendments—[1] Section inserted by TIOPA 2010 s 365, Sch 2 paras 1, 5. TIOPA 2010 has effect for corporation tax purposes for accounting periods ending on or after 1 April 2010, for income and capital gains tax purposes for the tax year 2010–11 and subsequent tax years, and for petroleum revenue tax purposes for chargeable periods beginning on or after 1 July 2010.

[564E Deposit arrangements

(1) This section applies to arrangements if under them—

    (*a*) a person ("the depositor") deposits money with a financial institution,

    (*b*) the money, together with money deposited with the institution by other persons, is used by it with a view to producing a profit,

    (*c*) from time to time the institution makes or credits a payment to the depositor out of profit resulting from the use of the money,

    (*d*) the payment is in proportion to the amount deposited by the depositor, and

    (*e*) the payments so made or credited by the institution equate, in substance, to the return on an investment of money at interest.

(2) This section is subject to section 564H (provision not at arm's length: exclusion of arrangements from sections 564C and 564D, this section and sections 564F and 564G).]¹

Commentary—*Simon's Taxes* **A1.303**.

HMRC Manuals—Savings and Investment Manual SAIM2250 (alternative finance return).

Corporate Finance Manual CFM44090 (deposit arrangements: conditions).

Amendments—¹   Section inserted by TIOPA 2010 s 365, Sch 2 paras 1, 6. TIOPA 2010 has effect for corporation tax purposes for accounting periods ending on or after 1 April 2010, for income and capital gains tax purposes for the tax year 2010–11 and subsequent tax years, and for petroleum revenue tax purposes for chargeable periods beginning on or after 1 July 2010.

[564F Profit share agency arrangements

(1) This section applies to arrangements if under them—

    (*a*) a person ("the principal") appoints an agent,

    (*b*) one or both of the principal and agent is a financial institution,

    (*c*) the agent uses money provided by the principal with a view to producing a profit,

    (*d*) the principal is entitled, to a specified extent, to profits resulting from the use of the money,

    (*e*) the agent is entitled to any additional profits resulting from its use (and may also be entitled to a fee paid by the principal), and

    (*f*) payments made because of the principal's entitlement to profits equate, in substance, to the return on an investment of money at interest.

(2) This section is subject to section 564H (provision not at arm's length: exclusion of arrangements from sections 564C to 564E, this section and section 564G).]¹

Commentary—*Simon's Taxes* **A1.303**.

HMRC Manuals—Savings and Investment Manual SAIM2250 (alternative finance return).

Corporate Finance Manual CFM44100 (profit share agency arrangements: conditions).

CFM44110 (example of profit share agency arrangements).

Modifications—See TIOPA 2010 Sch 9 para 39 (this section modified in relation to arrangements entered into before 15 October 2009).

Amendments—¹   Section inserted by TIOPA 2010 s 365, Sch 2 paras 1, 7. TIOPA 2010 has effect for corporation tax purposes for accounting periods ending on or after 1 April 2010, for income and capital gains tax purposes for the tax year 2010–11 and subsequent tax years, and for petroleum revenue tax purposes for chargeable periods beginning on or after 1 July 2010.

[564G Investment bond arrangements

(1) This section applies to arrangements if—

    (*a*) they provide for one person ("the bond-holder") to pay a sum of money ("the capital") to another ("the bond-issuer"),

    (*b*) they identify assets, or a class of assets, which the bond-issuer will acquire for the purpose of generating income or gains directly or indirectly ("the bond assets"),

    (*c*) they specify a period at the end of which they cease to have effect ("the bond term"),

    (*d*) the bond-issuer undertakes under the arrangements—

        (i) to dispose at the end of the bond term of any bond assets which are still in the bond-issuer's possession,

        (ii) to make a repayment of the capital ("the redemption payment") to the bond-holder during or at the end of the bond-term (whether or not in instalments), and

        (iii) to pay to the bond-holder other payments on one or more occasions during or at the end of the bond term ("additional payments"),

    (*e*) the amount of the additional payments does not exceed an amount which would be a reasonable commercial return on a loan of the capital,

    (*f*) under the arrangements the bond-issuer undertakes to arrange for the management of the bond assets with a view to generating income sufficient to pay the redemption payment and additional payments,

    (*g*) the bond-holder is able to transfer the rights under the arrangements to another person (who becomes the bondholder because of the transfer),

    (*h*) the arrangements are a listed security on a recognised stock exchange [or admitted to trading on a multilateral trading facility operated by an EEA-regulated recognised stock exchange]², and

    (*i*) the arrangements are wholly or partly treated in accordance with international accounting standards as a financial liability of the bond-issuer, or would be if the bond-issuer applied those standards.

(2) For the purposes of subsection (1)—

    (*a*) the bond-issuer may acquire bond assets before or after the arrangements take effect,

    (*b*) the bond assets may be property of any kind, including rights in relation to property owned by someone other than the bond-issuer,

    (*c*) the identification of the bond assets mentioned in subsection (1)(*b*) and the undertakings mentioned in subsection (1)(*d*) and (*f*) may (but need not) be described as, or accompanied by a document described as, a declaration of trust,

    (*d*) a reference to the management of assets includes a reference to disposal,

    (*e*) the bond-holder may (but need not) be entitled under the arrangements to terminate them, or participate in terminating them, before the end of the bond term,

    (*f*) the amount of the additional payments may be—

        (i) fixed at the beginning of the bond term,

        (ii) determined wholly or partly by reference to the value of or income generated by the bond assets, or

        (iii) determined in some other way,

    (*g*) if the amount of the additional payments is not fixed at the beginning of the bond term, the reference in subsection (1)(*e*) to the amount of the additional payments is a reference to the maximum amount of the additional payments,

    (*h*) the amount of the redemption payment may (but need not) be subject to reduction in the event of a fall in the value of the bond assets or in the rate of income generated by them, . . . [2]

    (*i*) entitlement to the redemption payment may (but need not) be capable of being satisfied (whether or not at the option of the bond-issuer or the bond-holder) by the issue or transfer of shares or other securities,

    [(*j*) a recognised stock exchange is an "EEA-regulated recognised stock exchange" if it is regulated in the European Economic Area, and

    (*k*) "multilateral trading facility" has the same meaning as in Article 4.1.22 of Directive 2014/65/EU of the European Parliament and of the Council of 15 May 2014 on markets in financial instruments.][2]

(3) This section is subject to section 564H (provision not at arm's length: exclusion of arrangements from sections 564C to 564F and this section).][1]

Commentary—*Simon's Taxes* **A1.302.**

HMRC Manuals—Savings and Investment Manual SAIM2250 (alternative finance return).

Corporate Finance Manual CFM44140 (investment bond arrangements: conditions).

CFM44130 (investment bond arrangements: example).

Amendments—[1]   Section inserted by TIOPA 2010 s 365, Sch 2 paras 1, 8. TIOPA 2010 has effect for corporation tax purposes for accounting periods ending on or after 1 April 2010, for income and capital gains tax purposes for the tax year 2010–11 and subsequent tax years, and for petroleum revenue tax purposes for chargeable periods beginning on or after 1 July 2010.

[2]   In sub-s (1)(*h*), words inserted, in sub-s (2)(*h*), word repealed, and sub-s (2)(*j*), (*k*) inserted, by FA 2018 s 34(2) with effect: (a) for corporation tax purposes, in relation to accounting periods beginning on or after 1 April 2018; and (b) for income tax and capital gains tax purposes, for the tax year 2018–19 and subsequent tax years.

Prospective amendments—In sub-s (1)(*h*) words "a regulated" to be substituted for words "an EEA-regulated", in sub-s (2)(*h*) word "and" to be inserted at the end, sub-s (2)(*j*) and (*k*) to be repealed, and sub-s (2A) to be inserted, by the Taxes (Amendments) (EU Exit) Regulations, SI 2019/689 reg 15(1), (7) with effect from Implementation Period completion day (see EU(WA)A 2020 Sch 5 para 1(1)). Sub-s (2A) to read as follows—

    "(2A) In subsection (1)—

    "regulated recognised stock exchange" means a recognised stock exchange that is regulated in the United Kingdom, the European Economic Area or Gibraltar;

    "multilateral trading facility" means—

        (*a*) a UK multilateral trading facility within the meaning given by Article 2.1(14A) of Regulation (EU) No 600/2014 of the European Parliament and of the Council of 15 May 2014 on markets in financial instruments,

        (*b*) an EU multilateral trading facility within the meaning given by Article 2.1(14B) of that Regulation, and

        (*c*) a multilateral system, operated by an investment firm or a market operator, which brings together multiple third-party buying and selling interests in financial instruments (in the system and in accordance with non-discretionary rules) in a way which results in a contract in accordance with Part 2 of the Financial Services (Markets in Financial Instruments) Act 2018 of Gibraltar,

    and in paragraph (*c*) "multilateral system", "investment firm", "market operator" and "financial instrument" have the same meanings as given by Articles 2.1(11), 2.1A, 2.1(10) and 2.1(9) respectively of that Regulation.".

In sub-s (2A), in definition of "multilateral trading facility", as inserted by SI 2019/689 above, para (*c*) to be substituted, and words from "and in paragraph (*c*)" to the end to be repealed, by the Taxes (Amendments) (EU Exit) (No 2) Regulations, SI 2019/818 reg 6(1), (3) with effect from Implementation Period completion day, immediately after the coming into force of SI 2019/689 (which also comes into force on Implementation Period completion day (see EU(WA)A 2020 Sch 5 para 1(1)). Para (*c*) to read as follows—

a Gibraltar multilateral trading facility within the meaning given by Article 26(11)(*b*)(ii) of that Regulation.".

[564H Provision not at arm's length: exclusion of arrangements from sections 564C to 564G
(1) Arrangements to which this section applies are not—
  (*a*) purchase and resale arrangements,
  (*b*) diminishing shared ownership arrangements,
  (*c*) deposit arrangements,
  (*d*) profit share agency arrangements, or
  (*e*) investment bond arrangements.
(2) This section applies to arrangements if—
  (*a*) apart from this section they would be alternative finance arrangements,
  (*b*) subsection (3) or (5) of section 147 of TIOPA 2010 (tax calculations to be based on arm's length, not actual, provision) requires the profits and losses of a person who is a party to the arrangements to be calculated for tax purposes as if the arm's length provision (within the meaning of that section) had been made or imposed rather than in accordance with the arrangements,
  (*c*) any person who is an affected person for the purposes of Part 4 of that Act ("the affected person") is entitled to—
    (i) relevant return in relation to the arrangements, or
    (ii) an amount representing relevant return in relation to them, and
  (*d*) the affected person is not subject—
    (i) to income tax or corporation tax, or
    (ii) to any corresponding tax under the law of a territory outside the United Kingdom,
  on the relevant return or the amount representing it.
(3) In this section "relevant return", in relation to arrangements, means any amount which would be alternative finance return if the arrangements were alternative finance arrangements.][1]
Commentary—*Simon's Taxes* A1.304.
HMRC Manuals—Corporate Finance Manual CFM44320 (alternative finance arrangements and transfer pricing).
Amendments—[1]   Section inserted by TIOPA 2010 s 365, Sch 2 paras 1, 9. TIOPA 2010 has effect for corporation tax purposes for accounting periods ending on or after 1 April 2010, for income and capital gains tax purposes for the tax year 2010–11 and subsequent tax years, and for petroleum revenue tax purposes for chargeable periods beginning on or after 1 July 2010.

[Meaning of "alternative finance return"

564I Purchase and resale arrangements
(1) In the case of purchase and resale arrangements, so much of the second purchase price as is specified under the following provisions of this section is alternative finance return for the purposes of this Part.
(2) If under the arrangements the whole of the second purchase price is paid on one day, the alternative finance return equals the amount by which the second purchase price exceeds the first purchase price.
(3) If under the arrangements the second purchase price is paid by instalments, the alternative finance return in each instalment equals the appropriate amount.
(4) The appropriate amount is an amount equal to the interest which would have been included in the instalment on the assumptions in subsection (5).
(5) The assumptions are that—
  (*a*) interest is payable on a loan by the first purchaser to the second purchaser of an amount equal to the first purchase price,
  (*b*) the total interest payable on the loan is equal to the amount by which the second purchase price exceeds the first purchase price,
  (*c*) the instalment is a part repayment of the principal of the loan with interest, and
  (*d*) the loan is made on arm's length terms and accounted for under generally accepted accounting practice.
(6) In this section expressions used in section 564C have the same meaning as in that section.][1]
Commentary—*Simon's Taxes* A1.302.
HMRC Manuals—Corporate Finance Manual CFM44060 (purchase and resale agreement: tax treatment).
Amendments—[1]   Section and preceding cross-head inserted by TIOPA 2010 s 365, Sch 2 paras 1, 10. TIOPA 2010 has effect for corporation tax purposes for accounting periods ending on or after 1 April 2010, for income and capital gains tax purposes for the tax year 2010–11 and subsequent tax years, and for petroleum revenue tax purposes for chargeable periods beginning on or after 1 July 2010.

[564J Purchase and resale arrangements where return in foreign currency
(1) If, in the case of purchase and resale arrangements, alternative finance return is paid in a currency other than sterling—
  (*a*) by or to a person other than a company, and
  (*b*) otherwise than for the purposes of a trade, profession or vocation or a property business, subsections (2) and (3) apply as respects that person.

(2) The amount of the excess referred to in section 564I(2) and (5)(*b*) and the appropriate amount for the purposes of section 564I(3) and (4) are to be calculated in that other currency.

(3) The amount of each payment of alternative finance return is to be translated into sterling at a spot rate of exchange for the day on which the payment is made.]¹

Commentary—*Simon's Taxes* A1.302.

Amendments—¹ Section inserted by TIOPA 2010 s 365, Sch 2 paras 1, 11. TIOPA 2010 has effect for corporation tax purposes for accounting periods ending on or after 1 April 2010, for income and capital gains tax purposes for the tax year 2010–11 and subsequent tax years, and for petroleum revenue tax purposes for chargeable periods beginning on or after 1 July 2010.

[564K Diminishing shared ownership arrangements

(1) In the case of diminishing shared ownership arrangements, payments by the eventual owner under the arrangements are alternative finance return for the purposes of this Part, except so far as subsection (2) or (3) applies to them.

(2) This subsection applies to the payments so far as they amount to payments of the kind described in section 564D(1)(*c*) (payments to be made by the eventual owner to the institution, amounting to the consideration paid for the acquisition of the institution's beneficial interest).

(3) This subsection applies to the payments so far as they amount to payments in respect of any arrangement fee or legal or other expenses which the eventual owner is required under the arrangements to pay.

(4) In this section "the eventual owner" has the same meaning as in section 564D.]¹

Commentary—*Simon's Taxes* A1.302.

HMRC Manuals—Corporate Finance Manual CFM44080 (diminishing shared ownership arrangements: tax treatment).

Amendments—¹ Section inserted by TIOPA 2010 s 365, Sch 2 paras 1, 12. TIOPA 2010 has effect for corporation tax purposes for accounting periods ending on or after 1 April 2010, for income and capital gains tax purposes for the tax year 2010–11 and subsequent tax years, and for petroleum revenue tax purposes for chargeable periods beginning on or after 1 July 2010.

[564L Other arrangements

(1) In the case of deposit arrangements, amounts paid or credited as mentioned in section 564E(1)(*c*) by a financial institution under the arrangements (payments to depositor out of profits resulting from use of money) are alternative finance return for the purposes of this Part.

(2) In the case of profit share agency arrangements, amounts paid or credited by a financial institution in accordance with such an entitlement as is mentioned in section 564F(1)(*d*) (principal's entitlement to profits under the arrangements) are alternative finance return for the purposes of this Part.

(3) In the case of investment bond arrangements, the additional payments under the arrangements are alternative finance return for the purposes of this Part, but subject to subsection (4).

(4) If any part of the additional payments in respect of investment bond arrangements equates in substance to discount, that part is not treated as alternative finance return for income tax purposes.

(5) In this section "additional payments" has the same meaning as in section 564G (see subsection (1)(*d*)(iii) of that section).

(6) For the treatment of the part of the additional payments to which subsection (4) applies, see section 564R (treatment of discount).]¹

Commentary—*Simon's Taxes* A1.303, A1.304.

HMRC Manuals—Corporate Finance Manual CFM44180 (investment bond arrangements: conditions: discounts).

Amendments—¹ Section inserted by TIOPA 2010 s 365, Sch 2 paras 1, 13. TIOPA 2010 has effect for corporation tax purposes for accounting periods ending on or after 1 April 2010, for income and capital gains tax purposes for the tax year 2010–11 and subsequent tax years, and for petroleum revenue tax purposes for chargeable periods beginning on or after 1 July 2010.

[Treatment of alternative finance return as interest etc

564M Treatment of alternative finance return as interest for ITTOIA 2005

(1) Alternative finance return is treated as interest for the purposes of ITTOIA 2005.

(2) References to interest in section 380 of that Act (funding bonds) include references to alternative finance return.]¹

Commentary—*Simon's Taxes* A1.304, A1.305.

HMRC Manuals—Corporate Finance Manual CFM44310 (other tax rules: deduction of tax).

Amendments—¹ Section and preceding cross-head inserted by TIOPA 2010 s 365, Sch 2 paras 1, 14. TIOPA 2010 has effect for corporation tax purposes for accounting periods ending on or after 1 April 2010, for income and capital gains tax purposes for the tax year 2010–11 and subsequent tax years, and for petroleum revenue tax purposes for chargeable periods beginning on or after 1 July 2010.

[564N Alternative finance return under arrangements for trade or property business purposes

(1) This section applies so far as a person is a party to alternative finance arrangements for the purposes of—

 (*a*) a trade, profession or vocation carried on by that person, or

 (*b*) a property business of that person.

(2) Alternative finance return paid by that person is treated as an expense of the trade, profession, vocation or business.

(3) In section 58 of ITTOIA 2005—

 (*a*) references to a loan include references to alternative finance arrangements, and (*b*) references to interest include references to alternative finance return.][1]

Commentary—*Simon's Taxes* A1.304.

Amendments—[1]   Section inserted by TIOPA 2010 s 365, Sch 2 paras 1, 15. TIOPA 2010 has effect for corporation tax purposes for accounting periods ending on or after 1 April 2010, for income and capital gains tax purposes for the tax year 2010–11 and subsequent tax years, and for petroleum revenue tax purposes for chargeable periods beginning on or after 1 July 2010.

[564O Relief for some alternative finance return under Chapter 1 of Part 8 etc

(1) Chapter 1 of Part 8 of this Act (interest payments) has effect as if—

(*a*) purchase and resale arrangements involved the making of a loan, and

(*b*) alternative finance return were interest.

(2) Section 412 (information) has effect accordingly.][1]

Commentary—*Simon's Taxes* A1.304.

HMRC Manuals—Corporate Finance Manual CFM44310 (other tax rules: deduction of tax).

Amendments—[1]   Section inserted by TIOPA 2010 s 365, Sch 2 paras 1, 16. TIOPA 2010 has effect for corporation tax purposes for accounting periods ending on or after 1 April 2010, for income and capital gains tax purposes for the tax year 2010–11 and subsequent tax years, and for petroleum revenue tax purposes for chargeable periods beginning on or after 1 July 2010.

[564P Tax relief schemes and arrangements

Section 809ZG (tax relief schemes and arrangements) applies to alternative finance return as it applies to interest.][1]

Commentary—*Simon's Taxes* A1.305.

Amendments—[1]   Section inserted by TIOPA 2010 s 365, Sch 2 paras 1, 17. TIOPA 2010 has effect for corporation tax purposes for accounting periods ending on or after 1 April 2010, for income and capital gains tax purposes for the tax year 2010–11 and subsequent tax years, and for petroleum revenue tax purposes for chargeable periods beginning on or after 1 July 2010.

[564Q Deduction of income tax at source under Part 15

(1) Chapter 2 of Part 15 [and section 876][2] (deduction of income tax at source: [exception for deposit-takers][2]), and Chapter 19 of that Part so far as it has effect for the purposes of Chapter 2 of that Part [and section 876][2], have effect as if—

(*a*) relevant alternative finance arrangements were a deposit,

(*b*) for the purposes of section 866(2)(*a*) such arrangements were a deposit consisting of a loan, and

(*c*) alternative finance return payable under such arrangements were interest.

(2) For the purposes of subsection (1) alternative finance arrangements are relevant unless they are purchase and resale arrangements where the second purchaser is not a financial institution.

(3) In subsection (2) "the second purchaser" has the same meaning as in section 564C.

(4) In Chapter 12 of Part 15 (funding bonds) references to interest include references to alternative finance return.

(5) Chapters 3 to 5 of Part 15 [except section 876][2], and Chapter 19 of that Part so far as it has effect for the purposes of [those provisions][2], apply to alternative finance return as they apply to interest.][1]

Commentary—*Simon's Taxes* A1.305.

HMRC Manuals—Corporate Finance Manual CFM44310 (other tax rules: deduction of tax).

Amendments—[1]   Section inserted by TIOPA 2010 s 365, Sch 2 paras 1, 18. TIOPA 2010 has effect for corporation tax purposes for accounting periods ending on or after 1 April 2010, for income and capital gains tax purposes for the tax year 2010–11 and subsequent tax years, and for petroleum revenue tax purposes for chargeable periods beginning on or after 1 July 2010.

[2]   Words in sub-ss (1), (5) inserted and substituted by FA 2016 s 39, Sch 6 paras 3, 20 with effect in relation to alternative finance return paid on or after 6 April 2016.

[Special rules for investment bond arrangements

564R Treatment of discount

(1) This section applies if any part of the additional payments in respect of investment bond arrangements is excluded from being alternative finance return by section 564L(4) because it equates in substance to discount.

(2) That part is treated in accordance with section 381 of ITTOIA 2005 (discounts) unless subsection (3) applies.

(3) If the arrangements are deeply discounted securities for the purposes of Chapter 8 of Part 4 of that Act (profits from deeply discounted securities), that part is treated in accordance with that Chapter.

(4) In this section "additional payments" has the same meaning as in section 564G of this Act (see subsection (1)(*d*)(iii) of that section).][1]

HMRC Manuals—Corporate Finance Manual CFM44180 (investment bond arrangements: conditions: discounts).

Amendments—[1]   Section and preceding cross-head inserted by TIOPA 2010 s 365, Sch 2 paras 1, 19. TIOPA 2010 has effect for corporation tax purposes for accounting periods ending on or after 1 April 2010, for income and capital gains tax purposes for the tax year 2010–11 and subsequent tax years, and for petroleum revenue tax purposes for chargeable periods beginning on or after 1 July 2010.

[564S Treatment of bond-holder and bond-issuer

(1) This section applies for the purposes of the Income Tax Acts and irrespective of the position for other purposes.

(2) The bond-holder under investment bond arrangements is not treated as having a legal or beneficial interest in the bond assets.

(3) The bond-issuer under such arrangements is not treated as a trustee of the bond assets.

(4) Profits accruing to the bond-issuer in connection with the bond assets are profits of the bond-issuer and not of the bond-holder (and do not arise to the bond-issuer in a fiduciary or representative capacity).

(5) Payments made by the bond-issuer by way of redemption payment or additional payment are not made in a fiduciary or representative capacity.

(6) The bond-holder is not entitled to relief for capital expenditure in connection with the bond assets.

(7) Expressions used in this section have the same meaning as in section 564G.][1]

Commentary—*Simon's Taxes* **A1.304**.

HMRC Manuals—Corporate Finance Manual CFM44240 (investment bond arrangements: tax treatment of bond assets).

Amendments—[1] Section inserted by TIOPA 2010 s 365, Sch 2 paras 1, 20. TIOPA 2010 has effect for corporation tax purposes for accounting periods ending on or after 1 April 2010, for income and capital gains tax purposes for the tax year 2010–11 and subsequent tax years, and for petroleum revenue tax purposes for chargeable periods beginning on or after 1 July 2010.

[564T Treatment as securities

(1) Investment bond arrangements are securities for the purposes of the Income Tax Acts (including Chapters 1 to 5 of Part 7 of ITEPA 2003).

(2) For those purposes—

    (*a*) a reference in an enactment to redemption is to be taken as a reference to making the redemption payment, and

    (*b*) a reference in an enactment to interest is to be taken as a reference to alternative finance return.

(3) In subsection (2) "the redemption payment" has the same meaning as in section 564G (see subsection (1)(d)(ii) of that section).][1]

HMRC Manuals—Corporate Finance Manual CFM44250 (investment bond arrangements: tax treatment of bond assets as securities).

Amendments—[1] Section inserted by TIOPA 2010 s 365, Sch 2 paras 1, 21. TIOPA 2010 has effect for corporation tax purposes for accounting periods ending on or after 1 April 2010, for income and capital gains tax purposes for the tax year 2010–11 and subsequent tax years, and for petroleum revenue tax purposes for chargeable periods beginning on or after 1 July 2010.

[564U Arrangements not unit trust scheme or offshore fund

Investment bond arrangements are not—

    (*a*) a unit trust scheme for the purposes of section 1007 of this Act, or

    (*b*) an offshore fund for the purposes of section 354 of TIOPA 2010 so far as relating to income tax.][1]

HMRC Manuals—Corporate Finance Manual CFM44250 (investment bond arrangements: tax treatment of bond assets as securities).

Amendments—[1] Section inserted by TIOPA 2010 s 365, Sch 2 paras 1, 22. TIOPA 2010 has effect for corporation tax purposes for accounting periods ending on or after 1 April 2010, for income and capital gains tax purposes for the tax year 2010–11 and subsequent tax years, and for petroleum revenue tax purposes for chargeable periods beginning on or after 1 July 2010.

[Other rules

564V Exclusion of alternative finance return from consideration for sale of assets

(1) If under purchase and resale arrangements an asset is sold by one party to the arrangements to the other party, the alternative finance return is excluded in determining the consideration for the sale and purchase of the asset for the purposes of the Income Tax Acts (apart from section 564C).

(2) If under diminishing shared ownership arrangements an asset is sold by one party to the arrangements to the other party, the alternative finance return is excluded in determining the consideration for the sale and purchase of the asset for the purposes of the Income Tax Acts (apart from section 564D).

(3) If under investment bond arrangements an asset is sold by one party to the arrangements to the other party, the alternative finance return is excluded in determining the consideration for the sale and purchase of the asset for the purposes of the Income Tax Acts (apart from section 564G).

(4) Subsections (1) to (3) do not affect the operation of any provision of the Tax Acts or TCGA 1992 that provides that the consideration for a sale or purchase is taken for any purpose to be an amount other than the actual consideration.][1]

Commentary—*Simon's Taxes* **A1.304**.

HMRC Manuals—Corporate Finance Manual CFM44290 (other tax rules: capital allowances and capital gains).

Amendments—[1] Section and preceding cross-head inserted by TIOPA 2010 s 365, Sch 2 paras 1, 23. TIOPA 2010 has effect for corporation tax purposes for accounting periods ending on or after 1 April 2010, for income and capital gains tax purposes for the tax year 2010–11 and subsequent tax years, and for petroleum revenue tax purposes for chargeable periods beginning on or after 1 July 2010.

[564W Diminishing shared ownership arrangements not partnerships

Diminishing shared ownership arrangements are not treated as a partnership for the purposes of the Income Tax Acts.][1]

Commentary—*Simon's Taxes* **A1.302**.
Amendments—[1]   Section inserted by TIOPA 2010 s 365, Sch 2 paras 1, 24. TIOPA 2010 has effect for corporation tax purposes for accounting periods ending on or after 1 April 2010, for income and capital gains tax purposes for the tax year 2010–11 and subsequent tax years, and for petroleum revenue tax purposes for chargeable periods beginning on or after 1 July 2010.

[564X Treatment of principal under profit share agency arrangements

(1) The principal under profit share agency arrangements is not treated for the purposes of the Income Tax Acts as entitled to profits to which the agent is entitled in accordance with section 564F(1)(*e*).

(2) And the agent under such arrangements is treated for those purposes as entitled to those profits and the profits specified in section 564F(1)(*d*).

(3) In this section "the principal" and "the agent" are to be read in accordance with section 564F.][1]

Commentary—*Simon's Taxes* **A1.303**.
HMRC Manuals—Corporate Finance Manual CFM44110 (example of profit share agency arrangements).
Amendments—[1]   Section inserted by TIOPA 2010 s 365, Sch 2 paras 1, 25. TIOPA 2010 has effect for corporation tax purposes for accounting periods ending on or after 1 April 2010, for income and capital gains tax purposes for the tax year 2010–11 and subsequent tax years, and for petroleum revenue tax purposes for chargeable periods beginning on or after 1 July 2010.

[564Y Provision not at arm's length: relevant return

(1) This section applies if arrangements to which section 564H (provision not at arm's length: exclusion of arrangements from sections 564C to 564G) applies would, but for that section, be alternative finance arrangements.

(2) A person paying relevant return under the arrangements is not entitled to—
(*a*) any deduction in respect of the relevant return in calculating profits or other income for income tax purposes, or
(*b*) any deduction in respect of the relevant return in calculating net income.

(3) In this section "relevant return" has the same meaning as in section 564H (see subsection (3) of that section).][1]

Commentary—*Simon's Taxes* **A1.304**.
HMRC Manuals—Corporate Finance Manual CFM44320 (alternative finance arrangements and transfer pricing).
Amendments—[1]   Section inserted by TIOPA 2010 s 365, Sch 2 paras 1, 26. TIOPA 2010 has effect for corporation tax purposes for accounting periods ending on or after 1 April 2010, for income and capital gains tax purposes for the tax year 2010–11 and subsequent tax years, and for petroleum revenue tax purposes for chargeable periods beginning on or after 1 July 2010.

[PART 11ZA
MANUFACTURED PAYMENTS]

[614ZA Overview of Part

This Part deals with the application of the Income Tax Acts to manufactured payment relationships and payments representative of dividends or interest.]

Amendments—Part 11ZA (ss 614ZA–614ZD) inserted by FA 2013 s 77, Sch 29 para 1 with effect in relation to any payment representative of a dividend or interest which is made on or after 1 January 2014.

[614ZB Key definitions

(1) For the purposes of the Income Tax Acts a person has a manufactured payment relationship if conditions A to C are met.

(2) Condition A is that under any arrangements—
(*a*) an amount is payable by or to the person, or
(*b*) any other benefit is given by or to the person (including the release of the whole or part of any liability to pay an amount).

(3) Condition B is that the arrangements relate to the transfer of securities.

(4) Condition C is that the amount or value of the other benefit—
(*a*) is representative of a dividend or interest on the securities, or
(*b*) will fall to be treated as representative of such a dividend or interest when it is paid or given.

(5) In subsection (2) the reference to an amount being payable, or other benefit being given, by the person includes a reference to an amount being payable, or other benefit being given, by another person on behalf of the person in question.

(6) In this Part—
    "manufactured payment", in relation to a manufactured payment relationship, means an amount, or the value of a benefit, within subsection (2), and
    "securities" means—
    (*a*) shares in a company, and
    (*b*) loan stock or any similar security (whether the security is of the government of the United Kingdom, any other government, any public or local authority in the United Kingdom or elsewhere, or any other company or body).]

Commentary—*Simon's Taxes* **D9.702**.
HMRC Manuals—Corporate Finance Manual CFM74430 (overview of manufactured payments).
Amendments—Part 11ZA (ss 614ZA–614ZD) inserted by FA 2013 s 77, Sch 29 para 1 with effect in relation to any payment representative of a dividend or interest which is made on or after 1 January 2014.

[614ZC Treatment of payer of manufactured payment

(1) This section applies where a person has a manufactured payment relationship under which a manufactured payment is paid by or on behalf of the person.

(2) No deduction is allowed in respect of the manufactured payment in calculating any profits or other income of the person for income tax purposes (subject to subsection (3)).

(3) Subsection (2) does not apply in relation to the person so far as the manufactured payment is brought into account under Part 2 of ITTOIA 2005 in calculating the profits of a trade carried on by the person.

(4) But nothing in subsection (3) affects the question whether (apart from that provision) a deduction in calculating the profits of a trade carried on by the person is allowed.]

Commentary—*Simon's Taxes* **D9.703**.

HMRC Manuals—Corporate Finance Manual CFM74440 (payments made).

Amendments—Part 11ZA (ss 614ZA–614ZD) inserted by FA 2013 s 77, Sch 29 para 1 with effect in relation to any payment representative of a dividend or interest which is made on or after 1 January 2014.

[614ZD Treatment of recipient of manufactured payment

(1) Subsection (2) applies if a person has a manufactured payment relationship under which a manufactured payment is payable to the person.

(2) For the purposes of the charge to income tax on the person's income, the Income Tax Acts apply to the person as if the manufactured payment were a dividend or interest on the securities (as the case may require).

(3) Subsection (2) is subject to subsections (4) [and (5)][2].

(4) Subsection (2) does not apply in relation to the person so far as the manufactured payment is brought into account under Part 2 of ITTOIA 2005 in calculating the profits of a trade carried on by the person.

(5) Subsection (2) does not apply in relation to the person for the purposes of determining entitlement to double taxation relief in respect of any dividend or interest.

(6) . . . [2]

(7) For the purposes of this section "double taxation relief" means any relief given under or as a result of Part 2 of TIOPA 2010.][1]

Commentary—*Simon's Taxes* **D9.703A**.

HMRC Manuals—Corporate Finance Manual CFM4440 (tax treatment of manufactured payments).

Amendments—[1]　Part 11ZA (ss 614ZA–614ZD) inserted by FA 2013 s 77, Sch 29 para 1 with effect in relation to any payment representative of a dividend or interest which is made on or after 1 January 2014.

[2]　Words in sub-s (3) substituted, and sub-s (6) repealed, by FA 2016 s 5, Sch 1 para 63(1), (9) with effect in relation to manufactured payments made on or after 6 April 2016.

[PART 11A

LEASING ARRANGEMENTS: FINANCE LEASES AND LOANS]

[CHAPTER 1

INTRODUCTION][1]

Amendments—[1]　Chapter 1 (ss 614A–614AC) inserted by TIOPA 2010 s 367, Sch 3 paras 1, 2. TIOPA 2010 has effect for corporation tax purposes for accounting periods ending on or after 1 April 2010, for income and capital gains tax purposes for the tax year 2010–11 and subsequent tax years, and for petroleum revenue tax purposes for chargeable periods beginning on or after 1 July 2010.

[Introduction

614A Overview of Part

(1) This Part makes provision for the purposes of income tax about the taxation of leasing arrangements.

(2) Chapter 2 makes provision in relation to certain arrangements involving the lease of assets where the conditions in section 614BC are or have been met, so far as the lease is not regarded as a long-funding lease for the purposes of Part 2 of CAA 2001 in accordance with Chapter 6A of that Part (see sections 614BB to 614BE).

(3) Chapter 3 makes provision in relation to arrangements involving the lease of assets that are not within Chapter 2, so far as the lease is not so regarded (see sections 614C and 614CB).

(4) The remaining provisions of this Chapter explain some expressions about rent for the purposes of this Part.

(5) Chapter 4 contains further provisions supplementing this Part, including more about its interpretation.][1]

Amendments—[1]　Sections 614A–614AC inserted by TIOPA 2010 s 367, Sch 3 paras 1, 2. TIOPA 2010 has effect for corporation tax purposes for accounting periods ending on or after 1 April 2010, for income and capital gains tax purposes for the tax year 2010–11 and subsequent tax years, and for petroleum revenue tax purposes for chargeable periods beginning on or after 1 July 2010.

ITA 2007

[Meaning of expressions about rent

614AA Normal rent

(1) For the purposes of this Part, the "normal rent" in respect of a lease for a period of account of the lessor ("L") is the amount specified in subsection (2).

(2) That amount is the amount that L would, apart from this Part, bring into account as rent from the lease that arises to L in that period of account for the purpose of determining L's liability to income tax for the related tax year or years.]

(3) For the meaning of "related tax year", see section 614DB(4).[1]

Amendments—[1] Sections 614A–614AC inserted by TIOPA 2010 s 367, Sch 3 paras 1, 2. TIOPA 2010 has effect for corporation tax purposes for accounting periods ending on or after 1 April 2010, for income and capital gains tax purposes for the tax year 2010–11 and subsequent tax years, and for petroleum revenue tax purposes for chargeable periods beginning on or after 1 July 2010.

[614AB Accountancy rental earnings

(1) For the purposes of this Part, the "accountancy rental earnings" in respect of a lease for a period of account of the lessor ("L") is the greatest of the amounts specified in subsection (2).

(2) Those amounts are—

   (a) the rental earnings for that period in respect of the lease in L's case,

   (b) the rental earnings for that period in respect of the lease in the case of a person connected with L, and

   (c) the rental earnings for that period in respect of the lease for the purposes of consolidated group accounts of a group of companies of which L is a member.

(3) For the meaning of "the rental earnings", see section 614AC.][1]

Commentary—*Simon's Taxes* **B5.416.**
Amendments—[1] Sections 614A–614AC inserted by TIOPA 2010 s 367, Sch 3 paras 1, 2. TIOPA 2010 has effect for corporation tax purposes for accounting periods ending on or after 1 April 2010, for income and capital gains tax purposes for the tax year 2010–11 and subsequent tax years, and for petroleum revenue tax purposes for chargeable periods beginning on or after 1 July 2010.

[614AC Rental earnings

(1) In this Part "the rental earnings" for any period in respect of a lease of an asset in the case of any person or any consolidated group accounts is the amount specified in subsection (2).

(2) That amount is the amount that falls for accounting purposes to be treated, in accordance with generally accepted accounting practice, as the gross return for that period on investment in respect of a finance lease or loan in respect of the leasing arrangements.

(3) For the meaning of "for accounting purposes", see section 614DG.][1]

Commentary—*Simon's Taxes* **B5.416.**
Amendments—[1] Sections 614A–614AC inserted by TIOPA 2010 s 367, Sch 3 paras 1, 2. TIOPA 2010 has effect for corporation tax purposes for accounting periods ending on or after 1 April 2010, for income and capital gains tax purposes for the tax year 2010–11 and subsequent tax years, and for petroleum revenue tax purposes for chargeable periods beginning on or after 1 July 2010.

[CHAPTER 2

FINANCE LEASES WITH RETURN IN CAPITAL FORM]

[Introduction

614B Arrangements to which this Chapter applies

(1) This Chapter applies to arrangements involving the lease of an asset that meet conditions A and B.

(2) Condition A is that in accordance with generally accepted accounting practice the arrangements fall to be treated as a finance lease or loan.

(3) Condition B is that the effect of the arrangements is that some or all of the return on investment in respect of the finance lease or loan—

   (a) is or may be in the form of a sum that is not rent, and

   (b) would not, apart from this Part and Part 21 of CTA 2010, be wholly brought into account for tax purposes as rent from the lease of the asset.

(4) It does not matter—

   (a) when the arrangements are or have been entered into, or

   (b) whether they are or have been entered into by companies or other persons.][1]

Amendments—[1] Sections 614B–614BY inserted by TIOPA 2010 s 367, Sch 3 paras 1, 3. TIOPA 2010 has effect for corporation tax purposes for accounting periods ending on or after 1 April 2010, for income and capital gains tax purposes for the tax year 2010–11 and subsequent tax years, and for petroleum revenue tax purposes for chargeable periods beginning on or after 1 July 2010.

[614BA Purposes of this Chapter

(1) This section sets out the main purposes of this Chapter where there are any arrangements to which this Chapter applies.

(2) The first main purpose is to charge any person entitled to the lessor's interest under the lease of the asset to income tax on amounts of income determined as mentioned in subsections (3) and (4).

(3) The amounts referred to in subsection (2) are determined by reference to the amounts that fall for accounting purposes to be treated, in accordance with generally accepted accounting practice, as the income return on and after 26 November 1996 on investment in respect of the finance lease or loan.

(4) The amounts referred to in subsection (2) are also determined taking into account the substance of the matter as a whole, including, in particular, the state of affairs—

(a) as between connected persons, or

(b) within a group of companies,

as reflected or falling to be reflected in accounts of any of those persons or in consolidated group accounts.

(5) The second main purpose of this Chapter is, if the sum mentioned in section 614B(3)(a) that is not rent falls due, to recover by reference to that sum the whole or any part of the capital expenditure reliefs.

(6) In subsection (5) "the capital expenditure reliefs" means any reliefs, allowances or deductions that are or have been allowed or made in respect of capital expenditure incurred in respect of the leased asset.][1]

Amendments—[1]   Sections 614B–614BY inserted by TIOPA 2010 s 367, Sch 3 paras 1, 3. TIOPA 2010 has effect for corporation tax purposes for accounting periods ending on or after 1 April 2010, for income and capital gains tax purposes for the tax year 2010–11 and subsequent tax years, and for petroleum revenue tax purposes for chargeable periods beginning on or after 1 July 2010.

[Leases to which this Chapter applies

614BB Application of this Chapter

(1) This Chapter applies if—

(a) a lease of an asset is or has been granted, and

(b) the conditions in section 614BC are or have been met in relation to the lease at some time in a period of account of the current lessor.

(2) But this Chapter does not apply so far as, in relation to the current lessor, the lease falls to be regarded as a long funding lease for the purposes of Part 2 of CAA 2001 (plant and machinery allowances) in accordance with Chapter 6A of that Part (interpretation of provisions about long funding leases) (see section 70G of that Act).

(3) If the conditions in section 614BC have been met at some time in a period of account of the person who was at that time the lessor, they are taken to continue to be met for the purposes of this Chapter unless and until one of the conditions in subsection (4) is met.

(4) The conditions are that—

(a) the asset ceases to be leased under the lease, or

(b) the lessor's interest under the lease is assigned to a person who is not connected with any of the persons specified in subsection (5).

(5) Those persons are—

(a) the assignor,

(b) any person who was the lessor at some time before the assignment, and

(c) any person who at some time after the assignment becomes the lessor pursuant to arrangements made by a person who was the lessor, or was connected with the lessor, at some time before the assignment.

(6) If at any time the person who was the lessor at that time was a person within the charge to corporation tax on income, the reference in subsection (3) to the conditions in section 614BC having been met at that time includes a reference to the conditions in section 902 of CTA 2010 having been so met.

(7) Nothing in subsection (3) prevents this Chapter from applying again in relation to the lease where the lessor's interest is assigned if the conditions for its application are met after the assignment.][1]

Commentary—*Simon's Taxes* B5.416.

Amendments—[1]   Sections 614B–614BY inserted by TIOPA 2010 s 367, Sch 3 paras 1, 3. TIOPA 2010 has effect for corporation tax purposes for accounting periods ending on or after 1 April 2010, for income and capital gains tax purposes for the tax year 2010–11 and subsequent tax years, and for petroleum revenue tax purposes for chargeable periods beginning on or after 1 July 2010.

[614BC The conditions referred to in section 614BB(1)

(1) This section sets out the conditions required by section 614BB(1) to be met for this Chapter to apply (conditions A to E).

(2) Condition A is that at the relevant time—

(a) the leasing arrangements fall for accounting purposes to be treated, in accordance with generally accepted accounting practice, as a finance lease or a loan, and

(b) subsection (3) or (4) applies.

(3) This subsection applies if the lessor ("L"), or a person connected with L, falls for accounting purposes to be treated, in accordance with generally accepted accounting practice, as the finance lessor in relation to the finance lease or loan.

(4) This subsection applies if the finance lease or loan falls for accounting purposes to be treated, in accordance with generally accepted accounting practice, as subsisting for the purposes of consolidated group accounts of a group of companies of which L is a member.

(5) Condition B is that, under the leasing arrangements, there is or may be payable to L, or to a person connected with L, a sum (a "major lump sum") that is not rent but falls for accounting purposes to be treated, in accordance with generally accepted accounting practice—

    (*a*) as to part, as repayment of some or all of the investment in respect of a finance lease or loan, and

    (*b*) as to part, as a return on investment in respect of a finance lease or loan.

(6) Condition C is that not all of that part of the sum that falls within subsection (5)(*b*) would, apart from this Chapter, fall to be brought into account for income tax purposes in tax years ending with the relevant tax year as the normal rent from the lease for periods of account of L.

(7) Condition D is that, in relation to L at the relevant time—

    (*a*) the period of account of L in which the relevant time falls, or

    (*b*) an earlier period of account of L during which L was the lessor,

is a period of account for which the accountancy rental earnings in respect of the lease exceed the normal rent for the period.

(8) Condition E is that at the relevant time—

    (*a*) arrangements within section 614BE(1) exist, or

    (*b*) paragraph (*a*) does not apply and circumstances within section 614BE(3) exist.

(9) Section 614BD supplements this section.][1]

Commentary—*Simon's Taxes* **B3.340E, B5.416.**

Amendments—[1] Sections 614B–614BY inserted by TIOPA 2010 s 367, Sch 3 paras 1, 3. TIOPA 2010 has effect for corporation tax purposes for accounting periods ending on or after 1 April 2010, for income and capital gains tax purposes for the tax year 2010–11 and subsequent tax years, and for petroleum revenue tax purposes for chargeable periods beginning on or after 1 July 2010.

[614BD Provisions supplementing section 614BC

(1) In section 614BC—

    "the relevant tax year", in relation to a major lump sum, means—

        (*a*) the tax year which is related to the period of account of the lessor ("L") in which the major lump sum is or may be payable in accordance with the leasing arrangements, or

        (*b*) if there are two or more such tax years, the latest of them, and

    "the relevant time" means the time as at which it must be determined for the purposes of section 614BB(1) or (3) whether the conditions in section 614BC are or, as the case may be, were met.

(2) For the meaning of a tax year being related to a period of account, see section 614DB(4).

(3) Subsection (4) applies for determining the normal rent for a period of account for the purpose of determining whether condition D in section 614BC is met as respects L unless subsection (5) applies.

(4) Rent that falls to be brought into account for income tax purposes as it falls due is treated—

    (*a*) as accruing evenly throughout the period to which, in accordance with the terms of the lease, each payment falling due relates, and

    (*b*) as falling due as it so accrues.

(5) This subsection applies if any such payment as is mentioned in subsection (4)(*a*) falls due more than 12 months after the time at which any of the rent to which that payment relates is treated as accruing under subsection (4)(*a*).][1]

Amendments—[1] Sections 614B–614BY inserted by TIOPA 2010 s 367, Sch 3 paras 1, 3. TIOPA 2010 has effect for corporation tax purposes for accounting periods ending on or after 1 April 2010, for income and capital gains tax purposes for the tax year 2010–11 and subsequent tax years, and for petroleum revenue tax purposes for chargeable periods beginning on or after 1 July 2010.

[614BE The arrangements and circumstances referred to in section 614BC(8)

(1) The arrangements referred to in section 614BC(8)(*a*) are arrangements under which—

    (*a*) the lessee or a person connected with the lessee may acquire, whether directly or indirectly, the leased asset or an asset representing the leased asset from the lessor or a person connected with the lessor, and

    (*b*) in connection with that acquisition, the lessor or a person connected with the lessor may receive, whether directly or indirectly, a qualifying lump sum from the lessee or a person connected with the lessee.

(2) In this section "qualifying lump sum" means any sum that is not rent but at least part of which would fall for accounting purposes to be treated, in accordance with generally accepted accounting practice, as a return on investment in respect of a finance lease or loan.

(3) The circumstances referred to in section 614BC(8)(*b*) are circumstances which make it more likely—

    (*a*) that the events described in subsection (4) will occur, than

    (*b*) that the event described in subsection (5) will occur.

(4) The events mentioned in subsection (3)(*a*) are—

(a) that the lessee or a person connected with the lessee will acquire, whether directly or indirectly, the leased asset or an asset representing the leased asset from the lessor or a person connected with the lessor, and

(b) that, in connection with that acquisition, the lessor or a person connected with the lessor will receive, whether directly or indirectly, a qualifying lump sum from the lessee or a person connected with the lessee.

(5) The event mentioned in subsection (3)(b) is that, before any such acquisition as is mentioned in subsection (4) takes place, the leased asset or, as the case may be, the asset representing the leased asset, will have been acquired, in a sale on the open market, by an independent third party.

(6) In subsection (5) "independent third party" means a person who—

(a) is not the lessor or the lessee, and

(b) is not connected with either of them.

(7) For the meaning of an asset representing the leased asset, see section 614DD.][1]

Amendments—[1] Sections 614B–614BY inserted by TIOPA 2010 s 367, Sch 3 paras 1, 3. TIOPA 2010 has effect for corporation tax purposes for accounting periods ending on or after 1 April 2010, for income and capital gains tax purposes for the tax year 2010–11 and subsequent tax years, and for petroleum revenue tax purposes for chargeable periods beginning on or after 1 July 2010.

[Current lessor taxed by reference to accountancy rental earnings

614BF Current lessor taxed by reference to accountancy rental earnings

(1) This section applies if, in the case of any period of account of the current lessor ("L")—

(a) this Chapter applies in relation to the lease, and

(b) the accountancy rental earnings in respect of the lease for that period of account exceed the normal rent for that period.

(2) For income tax purposes, L is treated as if in that period of account L had been entitled to, and there had arisen to L, rent from the lease of an amount equal to those accountancy rental earnings (instead of the normal rent referred to in subsection (1)(b)).

(3) Such rent from the lease of an asset is treated for income tax purposes—

(a) as if it had accrued at an even rate throughout so much of the period of account as falls within the period for which the asset is leased, and

(b) as if L had become entitled to it as it accrued.][1]

Commentary—_Simon's Taxes_ **B5.416**.

Amendments—[1] Sections 614B–614BY inserted by TIOPA 2010 s 367, Sch 3 paras 1, 3. TIOPA 2010 has effect for corporation tax purposes for accounting periods ending on or after 1 April 2010, for income and capital gains tax purposes for the tax year 2010–11 and subsequent tax years, and for petroleum revenue tax purposes for chargeable periods beginning on or after 1 July 2010.

Reduction of taxable rent by cumulative rental excesses

[614BG Reduction of taxable rent by cumulative rental excesses: introduction

(1) This section and sections 614BH to 614BK provide for reductions of the taxable rent of a current lessor ("L") under a lease to which this Chapter applies.

(2) In this section and sections 614BH to 614BK "taxable rent", in relation to a period of account of L, means the amount that would, apart from those sections, be treated for income tax purposes as rent from the lease that arises to L in that period of account for the purpose of determining L's liability to tax for the related tax year or years.

(3) The reductions of taxable rent under sections 614BH to 614BK depend on there being—

(a) a cumulative accountancy rental excess for the period of account of L in question, or

(b) a cumulative normal rental excess for the period of account of L in question.

(4) For the meaning of "cumulative accountancy rental excess" and "cumulative normal rental excess", see sections 614BH and 614BJ respectively.][1]

Amendments—[1] Sections 614B–614BY inserted by TIOPA 2010 s 367, Sch 3 paras 1, 3. TIOPA 2010 has effect for corporation tax purposes for accounting periods ending on or after 1 April 2010, for income and capital gains tax purposes for the tax year 2010–11 and subsequent tax years, and for petroleum revenue tax purposes for chargeable periods beginning on or after 1 July 2010.

[614BH Meaning of "accountancy rental excess" and "cumulative accountancy rental excess"

(1) For the purposes of this Chapter, there is an "accountancy rental excess" in relation to the lease for a period of account of the current lessor ("L") if the taxable rent in relation to the lease for the period is as a result of section 614BF (current lessor taxed by reference to accountancy rental earnings) an amount equal to the accountancy rental earnings.

(2) The amount of the accountancy rental excess for the period is equal to the difference between the accountancy rental earnings for the period and the normal rent for the period.

(3) But if the taxable rent for the period is reduced under section 614BK (reduction of taxable rent by the cumulative normal rental excess), there is only an accountancy rental excess for the period if—

(a) the accountancy rental earnings, reduced by an amount equal to the reduction under that section, exceed

(b) the normal rent.

(4) And in that case the amount of the accountancy rental excess for the period is equal to that excess.

(5) In this Chapter the "cumulative accountancy rental excess", in relation to the lease and a period of account of L, means so much of the total of the accountancy rental excesses for previous periods of account of L (as increased under section 614BM: recovery of bad debts following reduction under section 614BL) as has not been—

    (*a*) set off under section 614BI (reduction of taxable rent by the cumulative accountancy rental excess) against the taxable rent for any such previous period,

    (*b*) reduced under section 614BL (relief for bad debts: reduction of cumulative accountancy rental excess), or

    (*c*) set off under section 37A of TCGA 1992 (consideration on disposal of certain leases) against the consideration for a disposal.][1]

Amendments—[1] Sections 614B–614BY inserted by TIOPA 2010 s 367, Sch 3 paras 1, 3. TIOPA 2010 has effect for corporation tax purposes for accounting periods ending on or after 1 April 2010, for income and capital gains tax purposes for the tax year 2010–11 and subsequent tax years, and for petroleum revenue tax purposes for chargeable periods beginning on or after 1 July 2010.

[614BI Reduction of taxable rent by the cumulative accountancy rental excess

(1) This section applies if a period of account of the current lessor ("L") is one for which—

    (*a*) the normal rent in relation to the lease exceeds the accountancy rental earnings, and

    (*b*) there is a cumulative accountancy rental excess.

(2) The taxable rent for the period of account is reduced by setting against it the cumulative accountancy rental excess (but not so as to reduce that rent below the amount of the accountancy rental earnings).

(3) But see section 614BL(3) and (4) (under which the amount of the cumulative accountancy rental excess which may be set against the taxable rent is limited in some circumstances).[1]

Amendments—[1] Sections 614B–614BY inserted by TIOPA 2010 s 367, Sch 3 paras 1, 3. TIOPA 2010 has effect for corporation tax purposes for accounting periods ending on or after 1 April 2010, for income and capital gains tax purposes for the tax year 2010–11 and subsequent tax years, and for petroleum revenue tax purposes for chargeable periods beginning on or after 1 July 2010.

[614BJ Meaning of "normal rental excess" and "cumulative normal rental excess"

(1) For the purposes of this Chapter, there is a "normal rental excess" in relation to a lease for any period of account of the current lessor ("L") throughout which the leasing arrangements fall for accounting purposes to be treated, in accordance with generally accepted accounting practice, as a finance lease or loan if—

    (*a*) the normal rent for the period, exceeds

    (*b*) the accountancy rental earnings for the period.

(2) The amount of the normal rental excess for that period is equal to that excess.

(3) But if the taxable rent for the period is reduced under section 614BI (reduction of taxable rent by the cumulative accountancy rental excess), there is only a normal rental excess for the period if—

    (*a*) the normal rent, reduced by an amount equal to the reduction under that section, exceeds

    (*b*) the accountancy rental earnings.

(4) And in that case the amount of the normal rental excess for the period is equal to that excess.

(5) In this Chapter "cumulative normal rental excess", in relation to the lease and a period of account of L, means so much of the total of the normal rental excesses for previous periods of account of L (as increased under section 614BO: recovery of bad debts following reduction under section 614BN) as has not been—

    (*a*) set off under section 614BK (reduction of taxable rent by the cumulative normal rental excess) against the taxable rent for any such previous period, or

    (*b*) reduced under section 614BN (relief for bad debts: reduction of cumulative normal rental excess).][1]

Amendments—[1] Sections 614B–614BY inserted by TIOPA 2010 s 367, Sch 3 paras 1, 3. TIOPA 2010 has effect for corporation tax purposes for accounting periods ending on or after 1 April 2010, for income and capital gains tax purposes for the tax year 2010–11 and subsequent tax years, and for petroleum revenue tax purposes for chargeable periods beginning on or after 1 July 2010.

[614BK Reduction of taxable rent by the cumulative normal rental excess

(1) This section applies if a period of account of the current lessor ("L") is one for which—

    (*a*) the taxable rent in relation to the lease is as a result of section 614BF (current lessor taxed by reference to accountancy rental earnings) an amount equal to the accountancy rental earnings, and

    (*b*) there is a cumulative normal rental excess.

(2) The taxable rent for the period of account is reduced by setting against it the cumulative normal rental excess (but not so as to reduce that rent below the amount of the normal rent).

(3) But see section 614BN(3) and (4) (under which the amount of the cumulative normal rental excess which may be set against the taxable rent is limited in some circumstances).][1]

Commentary—*Simon's Taxes* **B5.416**.

Amendments—[1] Sections 614B–614BY inserted by TIOPA 2010 s 367, Sch 3 paras 1, 3. TIOPA 2010 has effect for corporation tax purposes for accounting periods ending on or after 1 April 2010, for income and capital gains tax purposes for the tax year 2010–11 and subsequent tax years, and for petroleum revenue tax purposes for chargeable periods beginning on or after 1 July 2010.

[Relief for bad debts by reduction of cumulative rental excesses

614BL Relief for bad debts: reduction of cumulative accountancy rental excess

(1) This section applies if in relation to the lease for any period of account of the current lessor—

    (a) there is a cumulative accountancy rental excess, and

    (b) a bad debt deduction falls to be made in respect of rent from the lease.

(2) If for that period—

    (a) the accountancy rental earnings in relation to the lease exceed the normal rent, and

    (b) the amount of the bad debt deduction exceeds the amount of the accountancy rental earnings,

the cumulative accountancy rental excess for that period is reduced by the amount of the excess of that deduction over those earnings (but not so as to reduce the amount of that rental excess below nil).

(3) Subsections (4) and (5) apply if for that period the accountancy rental earnings in relation to the lease do not exceed the normal rent.

(4) The amount of the cumulative accountancy rental excess that may be set against the taxable rent for that period under section 614BI(2) (reduction of taxable rent by the cumulative accountancy rental excess) is limited to the amount (if any) by which the normal rent exceeds the bad debt deduction.

(5) If for that period the bad debt deduction exceeds the normal rent, the cumulative accountancy rental excess for that period is reduced by the amount of that excess (but not so as to reduce the amount of that rental excess below nil).

(6) In this section—

    "bad debt deduction", in relation to a period of account of the lessor, means the total of any sums falling within section 35(1)(a), (b) or (c) of ITTOIA 2005 in respect of amounts in respect of rents from the lease of the asset which are deductible as expenses for that period, and

    "taxable rent" has the meaning given in section 614BG(2).][1]

Commentary—*Simon's Taxes* B5.416.

Amendments—[1] Sections 614B–614BY inserted by TIOPA 2010 s 367, Sch 3 paras 1, 3. TIOPA 2010 has effect for corporation tax purposes for accounting periods ending on or after 1 April 2010, for income and capital gains tax purposes for the tax year 2010–11 and subsequent tax years, and for petroleum revenue tax purposes for chargeable periods beginning on or after 1 July 2010.

[614BM Recovery of bad debts following reduction under section 614BL

(1) This section applies if in relation to the lease—

    (a) the cumulative accountancy rental excess for any period of account of the current lessor ("L") has been reduced under section 614BL(2) or (5) because of a bad debt deduction,

    (b) in a subsequent period of account of L, an amount ("the relevant credit") is recovered or credited in respect of the amount which constituted the bad debt deduction, and

    (c) there is a cumulative accountancy rental excess for that subsequent period.

(2) The cumulative accountancy rental excess for the subsequent period is increased.

(3) If the relevant credit does not exceed the total of the reductions under section 614BL(2) or (5), the increase is by the relevant credit.

(4) Otherwise, the increase is limited to that total.

(5) In this section "bad debt deduction" has the meaning given in section 614BL(6).][1]

Amendments—[1] Sections 614B–614BY inserted by TIOPA 2010 s 367, Sch 3 paras 1, 3. TIOPA 2010 has effect for corporation tax purposes for accounting periods ending on or after 1 April 2010, for income and capital gains tax purposes for the tax year 2010–11 and subsequent tax years, and for petroleum revenue tax purposes for chargeable periods beginning on or after 1 July 2010.

[614BN Relief for bad debts: reduction of cumulative normal rental excess

(1) This section applies if in relation to the lease for any period of account of the current lessor—

    (a) there is a cumulative normal rental excess, and

    (b) a bad debt deduction falls to be made in respect of rent from the lease.

(2) If for that period—

    (a) the accountancy rental earnings in the case of the lease do not exceed the normal rent, and

    (b) the amount of the bad debt deduction exceeds the amount of that rent,

the cumulative normal rental excess for that period is reduced by the amount of the excess of that deduction over that rent (but not so as to reduce the amount of that rental excess below nil).

(3) Subsections (4) and (5) apply if for that period the accountancy rental earnings in relation to the lease exceed the normal rent.

(4) The amount of the cumulative normal rental excess that may be set against the taxable rent for that period under section 614BK (reduction of taxable rent by the cumulative normal rental excess) is limited to the amount (if any) by which the accountancy rental earnings exceed the bad debt deduction.

(b) within a group of companies,

as reflected or falling to be reflected in accounts of any of those persons or in consolidated group accounts.]¹

Amendments—¹   Sections 614C–614CD inserted by TIOPA 2010 s 367, Sch 3 paras 1, 4. TIOPA 2010 has effect for corporation tax purposes for accounting periods ending on or after 1 April 2010, for income and capital gains tax purposes for the tax year 2010–11 and subsequent tax years, and for petroleum revenue tax purposes for chargeable periods beginning on or after 1 July 2010.

[Leases to which this Chapter applies

614CB Leases to which this Chapter applies

(1) This Chapter applies if—

    (a) a lease of an asset is or has been granted on or after 26 November 1996,

    (b) the lease forms part of a post-25 November 1996 scheme,

    (c) condition A in section 614BC is or has been met at some time on or after 26 November 1996 in relation to the lease in a period of account of the current lessor ("L"), and

    (d) Chapter 2 does not apply in relation to the lease because of the other conditions in that section not all being, or having been, met as mentioned in section 614BB.

(2) For the meaning of "forming part of a post-25 November 1996 scheme", see section 614D.

(3) This Chapter does not apply so far as, in relation to L, the lease falls to be regarded as a long funding lease for the purposes of Part 2 of CAA 2001 (plant and machinery allowances) in accordance with Chapter 6A of that Part (interpretation of provisions about long funding leases) (see section 70G of that Act).

(4) If condition A in section 614BC has been met at any time on or after 26 November 1996 in a period of account of the person who was at that time the lessor, it is taken to continue to be met unless and until one of the conditions in subsection (5) is met.

(5) The conditions are that—

    (a) the asset ceases to be leased under the lease, or

    (b) the lessor's interest under the lease is assigned to a person who is not connected with any of the persons specified in subsection (6).

(6) Those persons are—

    (a) the assignor,

    (b) any person who was the lessor at some time before the assignment, and

    (c) any person who at some time after the assignment becomes the lessor pursuant to arrangements made by a person who was the lessor, or was connected with the lessor, at some time before the assignment.

(7) If at any time the person who was the lessor at that time was a person within the charge to corporation tax on income—

    (a) the reference in subsection (4) to condition A in section 614BC having been met at that time includes a reference to condition A in section 902 of CTA 2010 having been so met, and

    (b) the reference in subsection (1)(d) to the other conditions in section 614BC not having been met as mentioned in section 614BB includes a reference to the other conditions in section 902 of that Act not having been met as mentioned in section 901 of that Act.

(8) Nothing in subsection (4) prevents this Chapter from applying again in relation to the lease where the lessor's interest is assigned if the conditions for its application are met after the assignment.]¹

Commentary—*Simon's Taxes* **B5.416.**

Amendments—¹   Sections 614C–614CD inserted by TIOPA 2010 s 367, Sch 3 paras 1, 4. TIOPA 2010 has effect for corporation tax purposes for accounting periods ending on or after 1 April 2010, for income and capital gains tax purposes for the tax year 2010–11 and subsequent tax years, and for petroleum revenue tax purposes for chargeable periods beginning on or after 1 July 2010.

[Current lessor taxed by reference to accountancy rental earnings

614CC Current lessor taxed by reference to accountancy rental earnings

(1) This section applies if, in the case of any period of account of the current lessor ("L")—

    (a) this Chapter applies in relation to the lease, and

    (b) the accountancy rental earnings in respect of the lease for that period of account exceed the normal rent for that period.

(2) For income tax purposes, L is treated as if in that period of account L had been entitled to, and there had arisen to L, rent from the lease of an amount equal to those accountancy rental earnings (instead of the normal rent referred to in subsection (1)(b)).

(3) Such rent from the lease of an asset is treated for income tax purposes—

    (a) as if it had accrued at an even rate throughout so much of the period of account as falls within the period for which the asset is leased, and

    (b) as if L had become entitled to it as it accrued.]¹

Amendments—¹   Sections 614C–614CD inserted by TIOPA 2010 s 367, Sch 3 paras 1, 4. TIOPA 2010 has effect for corporation tax purposes for accounting periods ending on or after 1 April 2010, for income and capital gains tax purposes for the tax year 2010–11 and subsequent tax years, and for petroleum revenue tax purposes for chargeable periods beginning on or after 1 July 2010.

Amendments—[1]   Sections 614B–614BY inserted by TIOPA 2010 s 367, Sch 3 paras 1, 3. TIOPA 2010 has effect for corporation tax purposes for accounting periods ending on or after 1 April 2010, for income and capital gains tax purposes for the tax year 2010–11 and subsequent tax years, and for petroleum revenue tax purposes for chargeable periods beginning on or after 1 July 2010.

[Relief for bad debts by reduction of cumulative rental excesses

614BL Relief for bad debts: reduction of cumulative accountancy rental excess

(1) This section applies if in relation to the lease for any period of account of the current lessor—

(*a*) there is a cumulative accountancy rental excess, and

(*b*) a bad debt deduction falls to be made in respect of rent from the lease.

(2) If for that period—

(*a*) the accountancy rental earnings in relation to the lease exceed the normal rent, and

(*b*) the amount of the bad debt deduction exceeds the amount of the accountancy rental earnings,

the cumulative accountancy rental excess for that period is reduced by the amount of the excess of that deduction over those earnings (but not so as to reduce the amount of that rental excess below nil).

(3) Subsections (4) and (5) apply if for that period the accountancy rental earnings in relation to the lease do not exceed the normal rent.

(4) The amount of the cumulative accountancy rental excess that may be set against the taxable rent for that period under section 614BI(2) (reduction of taxable rent by the cumulative accountancy rental excess) is limited to the amount (if any) by which the normal rent exceeds the bad debt deduction.

(5) If for that period the bad debt deduction exceeds the normal rent, the cumulative accountancy rental excess for that period is reduced by the amount of that excess (but not so as to reduce the amount of that rental excess below nil).

(6) In this section—

"bad debt deduction", in relation to a period of account of the lessor, means the total of any sums falling within section 35(1)(*a*), (*b*) or (*c*) of ITTOIA 2005 in respect of amounts in respect of rents from the lease of the asset which are deductible as expenses for that period, and

"taxable rent" has the meaning given in section 614BG(2).][1]

Commentary—*Simon's Taxes* **B5.416**.

Amendments—[1]   Sections 614B–614BY inserted by TIOPA 2010 s 367, Sch 3 paras 1, 3. TIOPA 2010 has effect for corporation tax purposes for accounting periods ending on or after 1 April 2010, for income and capital gains tax purposes for the tax year 2010–11 and subsequent tax years, and for petroleum revenue tax purposes for chargeable periods beginning on or after 1 July 2010.

[614BM Recovery of bad debts following reduction under section 614BL

(1) This section applies if in relation to the lease—

(*a*) the cumulative accountancy rental excess for any period of account of the current lessor ("L") has been reduced under section 614BL(2) or (5) because of a bad debt deduction,

(*b*) in a subsequent period of account of L, an amount ("the relevant credit") is recovered or credited in respect of the amount which constituted the bad debt deduction, and

(*c*) there is a cumulative accountancy rental excess for that subsequent period.

(2) The cumulative accountancy rental excess for the subsequent period is increased.

(3) If the relevant credit does not exceed the total of the reductions under section 614BL(2) or (5), the increase is by the relevant credit.

(4) Otherwise, the increase is limited to that total.

(5) In this section "bad debt deduction" has the meaning given in section 614BL(6).][1]

Amendments—[1]   Sections 614B–614BY inserted by TIOPA 2010 s 367, Sch 3 paras 1, 3. TIOPA 2010 has effect for corporation tax purposes for accounting periods ending on or after 1 April 2010, for income and capital gains tax purposes for the tax year 2010–11 and subsequent tax years, and for petroleum revenue tax purposes for chargeable periods beginning on or after 1 July 2010.

[614BN Relief for bad debts: reduction of cumulative normal rental excess

(1) This section applies if in relation to the lease for any period of account of the current lessor—

(*a*) there is a cumulative normal rental excess, and

(*b*) a bad debt deduction falls to be made in respect of rent from the lease.

(2) If for that period—

(*a*) the accountancy rental earnings in the case of the lease do not exceed the normal rent, and

(*b*) the amount of the bad debt deduction exceeds the amount of that rent,

the cumulative normal rental excess for that period is reduced by the amount of the excess of that deduction over that rent (but not so as to reduce the amount of that rental excess below nil).

(3) Subsections (4) and (5) apply if for that period the accountancy rental earnings in relation to the lease exceed the normal rent.

(4) The amount of the cumulative normal rental excess that may be set against the taxable rent for that period under section 614BK (reduction of taxable rent by the cumulative normal rental excess) is limited to the amount (if any) by which the accountancy rental earnings exceed the bad debt deduction.

(5) If for that period the bad debt deduction exceeds the accountancy rental earnings, the cumulative normal rental excess for that period is reduced by the amount of the excess (but not so as to reduce the amount of that rental excess below nil).

(6) In this section, in relation to a period of account of the lessor—

"bad debt deduction" has the meaning given in section 614BL(6), and

"taxable rent" has the meaning given in section 614BG(2).][1]

Amendments—[1]   Sections 614B–614BY inserted by TIOPA 2010 s 367, Sch 3 paras 1, 3. TIOPA 2010 has effect for corporation tax purposes for accounting periods ending on or after 1 April 2010, for income and capital gains tax purposes for the tax year 2010–11 and subsequent tax years, and for petroleum revenue tax purposes for chargeable periods beginning on or after 1 July 2010.

[614BO Recovery of bad debts following reduction under section 614BN

(1) This section applies if in relation to the lease—

   (a) the cumulative normal rental excess for any period of account of the current lessor ("L") has been reduced under section 614BN(2) or (5) as a result of a bad debt deduction,

   (b) in a subsequent period of account of L, an amount ("the relevant credit") is recovered or credited in respect of the amount which constituted the bad debt deduction, and

   (c) there is a cumulative normal rental excess for that subsequent period.

(2) The cumulative normal rental excess for the subsequent period is increased.

(3) If the relevant credit does not exceed the total of the reductions under section 614BN(2) or (5), the increase is by the relevant credit.

(4) Otherwise, the increase is limited to that total.

(5) In this section "bad debt deduction" has the meaning given in section 614BL(6).][1]

Amendments—[1]   Sections 614B–614BY inserted by TIOPA 2010 s 367, Sch 3 paras 1, 3. TIOPA 2010 has effect for corporation tax purposes for accounting periods ending on or after 1 April 2010, for income and capital gains tax purposes for the tax year 2010–11 and subsequent tax years, and for petroleum revenue tax purposes for chargeable periods beginning on or after 1 July 2010.

[Effect of disposals

614BP Effect of disposals of leases: general

(1) This section applies if the current lessor ("L") or a person connected with L disposes of—

   (a) the lessor's interest under the lease,

   (b) the leased asset, or

   (c) an asset representing the leased asset (see section 614DD).

(2) This Part has effect as if immediately before the disposal a period of account of L ended and another began.

(3) If—

   (a) two or more disposals within subsection (1) are made at the same time, and

   (b) there is any cumulative accountancy rental excess for any period of account of L in which the disposal occurs,

subsection (2) has effect in relation to those disposals as if they together constituted a single disposal.

(4) In this section "dispose" and "disposal" are to be read in accordance with TCGA 1992.

(5) In cases where there is any cumulative accountancy rental excess for L's period of account in which the disposal occurs, section 37A of that Act (consideration on disposal of certain leases) makes provision for the purposes of that Act about the reduction of the consideration for the disposal by that excess in determining if a gain has accrued.][1]

Amendments—[1]   Sections 614B–614BY inserted by TIOPA 2010 s 367, Sch 3 paras 1, 3. TIOPA 2010 has effect for corporation tax purposes for accounting periods ending on or after 1 April 2010, for income and capital gains tax purposes for the tax year 2010–11 and subsequent tax years, and for petroleum revenue tax purposes for chargeable periods beginning on or after 1 July 2010.

[614BQ Assignments on which neither a gain nor a loss accrues

(1) This section applies if—

   (a) the current lessor ("L") assigns the lessor's interest under the lease, and

   (b) the assignment is a disposal on which, as a result of any of the no gain/no loss provisions, neither a gain nor a loss accrues.

(2) This Part has effect as if—

   (a) a period of account of L ("L's period") ended with the assignment, and

   (b) a period of account of the assignee ("A's period") began with the assignment.

(3) Any cumulative accountancy rental excess for L's period becomes the cumulative accountancy rental excess for A's period.

(4) Any cumulative normal rental excess for L's period becomes the cumulative normal rental excess for A's period.

(5) If the assignee is a company subject to the charge to corporation tax on income, so far as this section relates to the assignee, it applies for the purposes of Part 21 of CTA 2010 as it would otherwise apply for the purposes of this Part.

(6) In this section "the no gain/no loss provisions" has the same meaning as in TCGA 1992 (see section 288(3A) of that Act).][1]

Amendments—[1]   Sections 614B–614BY inserted by TIOPA 2010 s 367, Sch 3 paras 1, 3. TIOPA 2010 has effect for corporation tax purposes for accounting periods ending on or after 1 April 2010, for income and capital gains tax purposes for the tax year 2010–11 and subsequent tax years, and for petroleum revenue tax purposes for chargeable periods beginning on or after 1 July 2010.

[Capital allowances: claw-back of major lump sum

614BR Effect of capital allowances: introduction

(1) This section and sections 614BS to 614BW apply if an occasion occurs on which a major lump sum falls to be paid in relation to the lease of the asset.

(2) In those sections the occasion is called "the relevant occasion".][1]

Amendments—[1]   Sections 614B–614BY inserted by TIOPA 2010 s 367, Sch 3 paras 1, 3. TIOPA 2010 has effect for corporation tax purposes for accounting periods ending on or after 1 April 2010, for income and capital gains tax purposes for the tax year 2010–11 and subsequent tax years, and for petroleum revenue tax purposes for chargeable periods beginning on or after 1 July 2010.

[614BS Cases where expenditure taken into account under Part 2, 5 or 8 of CAA 2001

(1) This section applies if capital expenditure incurred by the current lessor ("L") in respect of the leased asset is or has been taken into account for the purposes of any allowance or charge under—

(a) Part 2 of CAA 2001 (plant and machinery allowances),

(b) Part 5 of that Act (mineral extraction allowances), or

(c) Part 8 of that Act (patent allowances).

(2) The Part of that Act in question ("the relevant Part") has effect as if the relevant occasion were an event ("the relevant event") as a result of which a disposal value is to be brought into account of an amount equal to the amount or value of the major lump sum (but subject to any applicable limiting provision).

(3) In this section "limiting provision" means a provision to the effect that the disposal value of the asset in question is not to exceed an amount ("the limit") described by reference to capital expenditure incurred in respect of the asset.

(4) Subsection (5) applies if—

(a) as a result of subsection (2), a disposal value ("the relevant disposal value") falls or has fallen to be brought into account by a person in respect of the leased asset for the purposes of the relevant Part, and

(b) a limiting provision has effect in the case of that Part.

(5) The limiting provision has effect (so far as it would not otherwise do so), in relation to the relevant disposal value and any simultaneous or later disposal value, as if—

(a) it did not limit any particular disposal value, but

(b) it limited the total amount of all the disposal values brought into account for the purposes of the relevant Part by L in respect of the leased asset.

(6) In subsection (5) "simultaneous or later disposal value" means any disposal value which falls to be brought into account by L in respect of the leased asset as a result of any event occurring at the same time as, or later than, the relevant event.][1]

Commentary—*Simon's Taxes* **B3.340E**.

Amendments—[1]   Sections 614B–614BY inserted by TIOPA 2010 s 367, Sch 3 paras 1, 3. TIOPA 2010 has effect for corporation tax purposes for accounting periods ending on or after 1 April 2010, for income and capital gains tax purposes for the tax year 2010–11 and subsequent tax years, and for petroleum revenue tax purposes for chargeable periods beginning on or after 1 July 2010.

[614BT Cases where expenditure taken into account under other provisions of CAA 2001

(1) This section applies if any allowance is or has been given in respect of capital expenditure incurred by the current lessor ("L") in respect of the leased asset under any provision of CAA 2001 other than—

(a) Part 2 of CAA 2001 (plant and machinery allowances),

(b) Part 5 of that Act (mineral extraction allowances), or

(c) Part 8 of that Act (patent allowances).

(2) The amount specified in subsection (3) is treated, in relation to L, as if it were a balancing charge to be made on L for the chargeable period in which the relevant occasion falls.

(3) That amount is an amount equal to—

(a) the total of the allowances given as mentioned in subsection (1) (so far as not previously recovered or withdrawn), or

(b) if it is less, the amount or value of the major lump sum.

(4) In this section "chargeable period" has the meaning given by section 6 of CAA 2001.][1]

Amendments—[1]   Sections 614B–614BY inserted by TIOPA 2010 s 367, Sch 3 paras 1, 3. TIOPA 2010 has effect for corporation tax purposes for accounting periods ending on or after 1 April 2010, for income and capital gains tax purposes for the tax year 2010–11 and subsequent tax years, and for petroleum revenue tax purposes for chargeable periods beginning on or after 1 July 2010.

[614BU Capital allowances deductions: waste disposal and cemeteries

(1) This section applies if any deduction is or has been allowed to the current lessor ("L") in respect of capital expenditure incurred in connection with the leased asset as a result of—

(a) section 165 or 168 of ITTOIA 2005 (preparation and restoration expenditure in relation to waste disposal site), or

(b) section 170 of that Act (cemeteries and crematoria: deduction for capital expenditure).

(2) L is treated as if trading receipts arose to L from the trade in question on the relevant occasion.

(3) The amount of those receipts is equal to the lesser of—

(a) the amount or value of the major lump sum, and

(b) the deductions previously allowed.][1]

Amendments—[1] Sections 614B–614BY inserted by TIOPA 2010 s 367, Sch 3 paras 1, 3. TIOPA 2010 has effect for corporation tax purposes for accounting periods ending on or after 1 April 2010, for income and capital gains tax purposes for the tax year 2010–11 and subsequent tax years, and for petroleum revenue tax purposes for chargeable periods beginning on or after 1 July 2010.

[614BV Capital allowances deductions: films and sound recordings

(1) This section applies if—

(a) any relevant deduction has been allowed to the current lessor ("L") in respect of expenditure incurred in connection with the leased asset, and

(b) the amount or value of the major lump sum exceeds so much of that sum as was treated as receipts of a revenue nature under section 134(2) of ITTOIA 2005 (disposal proceeds of original master version of film or sound recording treated as receipt of a revenue nature).

(2) In subsection (1) "relevant deduction" means any deduction as a result of—

(a) section 135 of ITTOIA 2005 (allocation of expenditure on master versions of films or sound recordings to periods), or

(b) section 138, 138A, 139 or 140 of that Act (relief for production or acquisition expenditure in respect of films).

(3) L is treated as if receipts of a revenue nature arose to L from the trade or business in question on the relevant occasion.

(4) The amount of those receipts is equal to the excess mentioned in subsection (1)(b).][1]

Amendments—[1] Sections 614B–614BY inserted by TIOPA 2010 s 367, Sch 3 paras 1, 3. TIOPA 2010 has effect for corporation tax purposes for accounting periods ending on or after 1 April 2010, for income and capital gains tax purposes for the tax year 2010–11 and subsequent tax years, and for petroleum revenue tax purposes for chargeable periods beginning on or after 1 July 2010.

[614BW Contributors to capital expenditure

(1) This section applies if—

(a) section 614BS or 614BT applies in relation to a leased asset,

(b) allowances are or have been made to a person ("the contributor") as a result of sections 537 to 542 of CAA 2001 (allowances in respect of contributions to capital expenditure), and

(c) those allowances are or were in respect of the contributor's contribution of a capital sum to expenditure on the provision of the leased asset.

(2) Section 614BS or, as the case may be, section 614BT has effect in relation to the contributor and those allowances as it has effect in relation to the current lessor and allowances in respect of capital expenditure incurred by the current lessor in respect of the leased asset.][1]

Commentary—*Simon's Taxes* **B3.340E**.

Amendments—[1] Sections 614B–614BY inserted by TIOPA 2010 s 367, Sch 3 paras 1, 3. TIOPA 2010 has effect for corporation tax purposes for accounting periods ending on or after 1 April 2010, for income and capital gains tax purposes for the tax year 2010–11 and subsequent tax years, and for petroleum revenue tax purposes for chargeable periods beginning on or after 1 July 2010.

[Schemes to which this Chapter does not at first apply

614BX Pre-26 November 1996 schemes where this Chapter does not at first apply

(1) This section applies if—

(a) the lease of an asset forms part of a pre-26 November 1996 scheme, but

(b) the conditions in section 614BC become met after 26 November 1996.

(2) For the meaning of "forming part of a pre-26 November 1996 scheme", see section 614D.

(3) This Part has effect as if—

(a) a period of account ("period 1") of the current lessor ("L") ended immediately before the time at which those conditions become met,

(b) another period of account of L ("period 2") began immediately before that time and ended immediately after that time, and

(c) another period of account of L began immediately after that time.

(4) If, on the continuous application assumption (see subsection (9)), there would be an amount of cumulative accountancy rental excess for period 2, that amount is the cumulative accountancy rental excess for period 2.

(5) If subsection (4) applies, L is treated for income tax purposes as if in period 1 L had been entitled to, and there had arisen to L, rent from the lease of an amount equal to that cumulative accountancy rental excess.

(6) The amount of rent mentioned in subsection (5)—

(a) is in addition to any other rent from the lease for period 1, and (*b*) is left out of account for the purposes of section 614BF (current lessor taxed by reference to accountancy rental earnings).

(7) Rent within subsection (5) is treated for income tax purposes as if it had accrued and L had become entitled to it immediately before the end of period 1.

(8) If, on the continuous application assumption, there would be an amount of cumulative normal rental excess for period 2, that amount is the cumulative normal rental excess for period 2.

(9) In this section "the continuous application assumption" means the assumption that this Chapter (other than this section) had applied in the case of the lease at all times on or after 26 November 1996.

(10) If at any time the person who was the lessor at that time was a person within the charge to corporation tax on income, the reference in subsection (9) to this Chapter (other than this section) includes a reference to Chapter 2 of Part 21 of CTA 2010 (other than section 923 of that Act).][1]

Commentary—*Simon's Taxes* **B5.416**.

Amendments—[1] Sections 614B–614BY inserted by TIOPA 2010 s 367, Sch 3 paras 1, 3. TIOPA 2010 has effect for corporation tax purposes for accounting periods ending on or after 1 April 2010, for income and capital gains tax purposes for the tax year 2010–11 and subsequent tax years, and for petroleum revenue tax purposes for chargeable periods beginning on or after 1 July 2010.

[614BY Post-25 November 1996 schemes to which Chapter 3 applied first

(1) This section applies if—
  (*a*) the conditions in section 614BC become met in the case of the lease of the asset, and
  (*b*) immediately before those conditions become met, Chapter 3 applied.

(2) Subsection (3) applies for the purpose of determining—
  (*a*) the cumulative accountancy rental excess for any period of account ending after those conditions become met, or
  (*b*) the cumulative normal rental excess for any such period.

(3) This Part has effect as if this Chapter had applied in relation to the lease at any time when Chapter 3 applied in relation to it.

(4) If at any time the person who was the lessor at that time was a person within the charge to corporation tax on income—
  (*a*) the reference in subsection (1)(*a*) to the conditions in section 614BC becoming met at that time includes a reference to the conditions in section 902 of CTA 2010 becoming so met,
  (*b*) the reference in subsection (1)(*b*) to Chapter 3 applying immediately before that time includes a reference to Chapter 3 of Part 21 of that Act so applying, and
  (*c*) the reference in subsection (3) to Chapter 3 applying at that time includes a reference to Chapter 3 of that Part so applying.][1]

Amendments—[1] Sections 614B–614BY inserted by TIOPA 2010 s 367, Sch 3 paras 1, 3. TIOPA 2010 has effect for corporation tax purposes for accounting periods ending on or after 1 April 2010, for income and capital gains tax purposes for the tax year 2010–11 and subsequent tax years, and for petroleum revenue tax purposes for chargeable periods beginning on or after 1 July 2010.

[CHAPTER 3

OTHER FINANCE LEASES]

[Introduction]

614C Introduction to Chapter

(1) This Chapter applies to arrangements involving the lease of an asset that—
  (*a*) fall to be treated, in accordance with generally accepted accounting practice, as a finance lease or loan, but
  (*b*) are not arrangements to which Chapter 2 applies.

(2) It does not matter whether the arrangements are or have been entered into by companies or other persons.][1]

Amendments—[1] Sections 614C–614CD inserted by TIOPA 2010 s 367, Sch 3 paras 1, 4. TIOPA 2010 has effect for corporation tax purposes for accounting periods ending on or after 1 April 2010, for income and capital gains tax purposes for the tax year 2010–11 and subsequent tax years, and for petroleum revenue tax purposes for chargeable periods beginning on or after 1 July 2010.

[614CA Purpose of this Chapter

(1) The main purpose of this Chapter where there are arrangements to which this Chapter applies is to charge a person entitled to the lessor's interest under the lease of the asset to income tax on amounts of income determined as mentioned in subsection (2).

(2) The amounts referred to in subsection (1) are determined by reference to the amounts that fall for accounting purposes to be treated, in accordance with generally accepted accounting practice, as the income return on and after 26 November 1996 on investment in respect of the finance lease or loan.

(3) The amounts referred to in subsection (1) are also determined taking into account the substance of the matter as a whole, including, in particular, the state of affairs—
  (*a*) as between connected persons, or

(*b*) within a group of companies,

as reflected or falling to be reflected in accounts of any of those persons or in consolidated group accounts.][1]

Amendments—[1]   Sections 614C–614CD inserted by TIOPA 2010 s 367, Sch 3 paras 1, 4. TIOPA 2010 has effect for corporation tax purposes for accounting periods ending on or after 1 April 2010, for income and capital gains tax purposes for the tax year 2010–11 and subsequent tax years, and for petroleum revenue tax purposes for chargeable periods beginning on or after 1 July 2010.

[Leases to which this Chapter applies

614CB Leases to which this Chapter applies

(1) This Chapter applies if—

    (*a*) a lease of an asset is or has been granted on or after 26 November 1996,

    (*b*) the lease forms part of a post-25 November 1996 scheme,

    (*c*) condition A in section 614BC is or has been met at some time on or after 26 November 1996 in relation to the lease in a period of account of the current lessor ("L"), and

    (*d*) Chapter 2 does not apply in relation to the lease because of the other conditions in that section not all being, or having been, met as mentioned in section 614BB.

(2) For the meaning of "forming part of a post-25 November 1996 scheme", see section 614D.

(3) This Chapter does not apply so far as, in relation to L, the lease falls to be regarded as a long funding lease for the purposes of Part 2 of CAA 2001 (plant and machinery allowances) in accordance with Chapter 6A of that Part (interpretation of provisions about long funding leases) (see section 70G of that Act).

(4) If condition A in section 614BC has been met at any time on or after 26 November 1996 in a period of account of the person who was at that time the lessor, it is taken to continue to be met unless and until one of the conditions in subsection (5) is met.

(5) The conditions are that—

    (*a*) the asset ceases to be leased under the lease, or

    (*b*) the lessor's interest under the lease is assigned to a person who is not connected with any of the persons specified in subsection (6).

(6) Those persons are—

    (*a*) the assignor,

    (*b*) any person who was the lessor at some time before the assignment, and

    (*c*) any person who at some time after the assignment becomes the lessor pursuant to arrangements made by a person who was the lessor, or was connected with the lessor, at some time before the assignment.

(7) If at any time the person who was the lessor at that time was a person within the charge to corporation tax on income—

    (*a*) the reference in subsection (4) to condition A in section 614BC having been met at that time includes a reference to condition A in section 902 of CTA 2010 having been so met, and

    (*b*) the reference in subsection (1)(*d*) to the other conditions in section 614BC not having been met as mentioned in section 614BB includes a reference to the other conditions in section 902 of that Act not having been met as mentioned in section 901 of that Act.

(8) Nothing in subsection (4) prevents this Chapter from applying again in relation to the lease where the lessor's interest is assigned if the conditions for its application are met after the assignment.][1]

Commentary—*Simon's Taxes* **B5.416.**

Amendments—[1]   Sections 614C–614CD inserted by TIOPA 2010 s 367, Sch 3 paras 1, 4. TIOPA 2010 has effect for corporation tax purposes for accounting periods ending on or after 1 April 2010, for income and capital gains tax purposes for the tax year 2010–11 and subsequent tax years, and for petroleum revenue tax purposes for chargeable periods beginning on or after 1 July 2010.

[Current lessor taxed by reference to accountancy rental earnings

614CC Current lessor taxed by reference to accountancy rental earnings

(1) This section applies if, in the case of any period of account of the current lessor ("L")—

    (*a*) this Chapter applies in relation to the lease, and

    (*b*) the accountancy rental earnings in respect of the lease for that period of account exceed the normal rent for that period.

(2) For income tax purposes, L is treated as if in that period of account L had been entitled to, and there had arisen to L, rent from the lease of an amount equal to those accountancy rental earnings (instead of the normal rent referred to in subsection (1)(*b*)).

(3) Such rent from the lease of an asset is treated for income tax purposes—

    (*a*) as if it had accrued at an even rate throughout so much of the period of account as falls within the period for which the asset is leased, and

    (*b*) as if L had become entitled to it as it accrued.][1]

Amendments—[1]   Sections 614C–614CD inserted by TIOPA 2010 s 367, Sch 3 paras 1, 4. TIOPA 2010 has effect for corporation tax purposes for accounting periods ending on or after 1 April 2010, for income and capital gains tax purposes for the tax year 2010–11 and subsequent tax years, and for petroleum revenue tax purposes for chargeable periods beginning on or after 1 July 2010.

[Application of provisions of Chapter 2 for purposes of this Chapter

614CD Application of provisions of Chapter 2 for purposes of this Chapter

Sections 614BG to 614BQ apply for the purposes of this Chapter as they apply for the purposes of Chapter 2, but taking the references in sections 614BH(1) and 614BK(1)(*a*) to section 614BF as references to section 614CC.][1]

Amendments—[1]   Sections 614C–614CD inserted by TIOPA 2010 s 367, Sch 3 paras 1, 4. TIOPA 2010 has effect for corporation tax purposes for accounting periods ending on or after 1 April 2010, for income and capital gains tax purposes for the tax year 2010–11 and subsequent tax years, and for petroleum revenue tax purposes for chargeable periods beginning on or after 1 July 2010.

[CHAPTER 4

SUPPLEMENTARY PROVISIONS]

[614D Pre-26 November 1996 schemes and post-25 November 1996 schemes

(1) For the purposes of this Part, a lease of an asset—

   (*a*) forms part of a pre-26 November 1996 scheme if (and only if) the conditions in subsection (2) or (3) are met, and

   (*b*) in any other case, forms part of a post-25 November 1996 scheme.

(2) The conditions in this subsection are that—

   (*a*) a contract in writing for the lease of the asset was made before 26 November 1996,

   (*b*) either—

     (i) the contract was unconditional, or

     (ii) if the contract was conditional, the conditions were met before that date, and

   (*c*) no terms remain to be agreed on or after that date.

(3) The conditions in this subsection are that—

   (*a*) a contract in writing for the lease of the asset was made before 26 November 1996,

   (*b*) the condition in subsection (2)(*b*) or (*c*) was not met in the case of the contract,

   (*c*) either—

     (i) the contract was unconditional, or

     (ii) if the contract was conditional, the conditions were met before the end of the finalisation period or within such further period as the Commissioners for Her Majesty's Revenue and Customs may allow in the particular case,

   (*d*) no terms remain to be agreed after the end of the finalisation period or such further period as those Commissioners may so allow, and

   (*e*) the contract in its final form was not materially different from the contract as it stood when it was made before 26 November 1996.

(4) In subsection (3) "the finalisation period" means the period which ended with the later of—

   (*a*) 31 January 1997, and

   (*b*) the end of the period of six months beginning with the day after that on which the contract was made as mentioned in subsection (3)(*a*).][1]

Amendments—[1]   Sections 614D–614DG inserted by TIOPA 2010 s 367, Sch 3 paras 1, 5. TIOPA 2010 has effect for corporation tax purposes for accounting periods ending on or after 1 April 2010, for income and capital gains tax purposes for the tax year 2010–11 and subsequent tax years, and for petroleum revenue tax purposes for chargeable periods beginning on or after 1 July 2010.

[614DA Time apportionment where periods of account do not coincide

(1) Subsection (2) applies if a period of account of the lessor ("L") does not coincide with a period of account of a person connected with L.

(2) Any amount which falls for the purposes of this Part to be found for L's period of account but by reference to the connected person is found by making such apportionments as may be necessary between two or more periods of account of the connected person.

(3) Subsection (4) applies if a period of account of L does not coincide with a period for which consolidated group accounts of a group of companies of which L is a member fall to be prepared.

(4) Any amount which falls for the purposes of this Part to be found for L's period of account but by reference to the consolidated group accounts is found by making such apportionments as may be necessary between two or more periods for which consolidated group accounts of the group fall to be prepared.

(5) Any apportionment under subsection (2) or (4) must be made in proportion to the number of days in the respective periods that fall within L's period of account.][1]

Amendments—[1]   Sections 614D–614DG inserted by TIOPA 2010 s 367, Sch 3 paras 1, 5. TIOPA 2010 has effect for corporation tax purposes for accounting periods ending on or after 1 April 2010, for income and capital gains tax purposes for the tax year 2010–11 and subsequent tax years, and for petroleum revenue tax purposes for chargeable periods beginning on or after 1 July 2010.

[614DB Periods of account and related periods of account and tax years

(1) In this Part "period of account" means a period for which accounts are made up.

(2) Except for the purposes of sections 614BB to 614BE and subsection (3), in this Part "period of account" does not include a period that begins before 26 November 1996.

(3) But this Part applies in relation to a period of account that begins before 26 November 1996 and ends on or after that date as if—

(a) so much of the period as falls before that date, and

(b) so much of the period as falls on or after that date,

were separate periods of account.

(4) For the purposes of this Part, a tax year is related to a period of account if the tax year consists of or includes the whole or any part of the period of account.

(5) For the purposes of this Part a period of account is related to a tax year if the tax year is related to the period of account.]¹

Amendments—¹ Sections 614D–614DG inserted by TIOPA 2010 s 367, Sch 3 paras 1, 5. TIOPA 2010 has effect for corporation tax purposes for accounting periods ending on or after 1 April 2010, for income and capital gains tax purposes for the tax year 2010–11 and subsequent tax years, and for petroleum revenue tax purposes for chargeable periods beginning on or after 1 July 2010.

[614DC Connected persons

(1) For the purposes of this Part in its application as a result of any leasing arrangements, if a person ("A") is connected with another ("B") at some time during the relevant period A is treated as being connected with B throughout that period.

(2) The relevant period is the period that—

(a) begins at the earliest time at which any of the arrangements were made, and

(b) ends when the current lessor finally ceases to have an interest in the asset or any arrangements relating to it.]¹

Amendments—¹ Sections 614D–614DG inserted by TIOPA 2010 s 367, Sch 3 paras 1, 5. TIOPA 2010 has effect for corporation tax purposes for accounting periods ending on or after 1 April 2010, for income and capital gains tax purposes for the tax year 2010–11 and subsequent tax years, and for petroleum revenue tax purposes for chargeable periods beginning on or after 1 July 2010.

[614DD Assets which represent the leased asset

(1) For the purposes of this Part, the assets described in subsection (2) are treated as representing the leased asset.

(2) Those assets are—

(a) any asset derived from the leased asset or created out of it,

(b) any asset from which the leased asset was derived or out of which the leased asset was created,

(c) any asset derived from or created out of an asset within paragraph (b), and

(d) any asset that derives the whole or a substantial part of its value from the leased asset or an asset that itself represents the leased asset.]¹

Amendments—¹ Sections 614D–614DG inserted by TIOPA 2010 s 367, Sch 3 paras 1, 5. TIOPA 2010 has effect for corporation tax purposes for accounting periods ending on or after 1 April 2010, for income and capital gains tax purposes for the tax year 2010–11 and subsequent tax years, and for petroleum revenue tax purposes for chargeable periods beginning on or after 1 July 2010.

[614DE Parent undertakings and consolidated group accounts

(1) This Part has effect in relation to a body corporate that—

(a) is a parent undertaking, but

(b) for accounting purposes is not required to prepare consolidated group accounts in accordance with generally accepted accounting practice,

as if it were so required.

(2) For the purposes of subsection (1) it does not matter where the body corporate is incorporated.

(3) In subsection (1) "parent undertaking" is to be read in accordance with section 1162 of the Companies Act 2006.]¹

Amendments—¹ Sections 614D–614DG inserted by TIOPA 2010 s 367, Sch 3 paras 1, 5. TIOPA 2010 has effect for corporation tax purposes for accounting periods ending on or after 1 April 2010, for income and capital gains tax purposes for the tax year 2010–11 and subsequent tax years, and for petroleum revenue tax purposes for chargeable periods beginning on or after 1 July 2010.

[614DF Assessments and adjustments

All such assessments and adjustments must be made as are necessary to give effect to this Part.]¹

Amendments—¹ Sections 614D–614DG inserted by TIOPA 2010 s 367, Sch 3 paras 1, 5. TIOPA 2010 has effect for corporation tax purposes for accounting periods ending on or after 1 April 2010, for income and capital gains tax purposes for the tax year 2010–11 and subsequent tax years, and for petroleum revenue tax purposes for chargeable periods beginning on or after 1 July 2010.

[614DG Interpretation

In this Part, unless the context otherwise requires—

"accountancy rental earnings" has the meaning given by section 614AB(1),

"accountancy rental excess" is to be read—

(*a*) for the purposes of Chapter 2, in accordance with section 614BH(1) to (4), and

(*b*) for the purposes of Chapter 3, in accordance with section 614BH(1) to (4) as it has effect as a result of section 614CD,

"asset" means any form of property or rights,

"asset representing the leased asset" is to be read in accordance with section 614DD,

"cumulative accountancy rental excess" is to be read—

(*a*) for the purposes of Chapter 2, in accordance with section 614BH(5), and

(*b*) for the purposes of Chapter 3, in accordance with section 614BH(5) as it has effect as a result of section 614CD,

"cumulative normal rental excess" is to be read—

(*a*) for the purposes of Chapter 2, in accordance with section 614BJ(5), and

(*b*) for the purposes of Chapter 3, in accordance with section 614BJ(5) as it has effect as a result of section 614CD,

"the current lessor", in relation to a lease of an asset, means the person who is for the time being entitled to the lessor's interest under the lease,

"finance lessor" means a person who for accounting purposes is treated, in accordance with generally accepted accounting practice, as the person with—

(*a*) the grantor's interest in relation to a finance lease, or

(*b*) the lender's interest in relation to a loan,

"for accounting purposes" means for the purposes of—

(*a*) accounts of companies incorporated in any part of the United Kingdom, or

(*b*) consolidated group accounts for groups all the members of which are companies so incorporated,

"lease"—

(*a*) in relation to land, includes an underlease, sublease, tenancy or licence, and any agreement for a lease, underlease, sublease, tenancy or licence and, in the case of land outside the United Kingdom, any interest corresponding to a lease as so defined, and

(*b*) in relation to any form of property or right other than land, means any kind of agreement or arrangement under which payments are made for the use of, or otherwise in respect of, an asset,

and "rent" is to be read accordingly,

"the leasing arrangements", in relation to a lease of an asset, means—

(*a*) the lease,

(*b*) any arrangements relating to or connected with the lease, and

(*c*) any other arrangements of which the lease forms part,

and includes a reference to any of the leasing arrangements,

"the lessee", in relation to a lease of an asset, means (except in the expression "the lessee's interest under the lease") the person entitled to the lessee's interest under the lease,

"the lessor", in relation to a lease of an asset, means (except in the expression "the lessor's interest under the lease") the person entitled to the lessor's interest under the lease,

"major lump sum" is to be read in accordance with section 614BC(5),

"normal rent" is to be read in accordance with section 614AA,

"normal rental excess" is to be read—

(*a*) for the purposes of Chapter 2, in accordance with section 614BJ(1) to (4), and

(*b*) for the purposes of Chapter 3, in accordance with section 614BJ(1) to (4) as it has effect as a result of section 614CD,

"period of account" is to be read in accordance with section 614DB(1) to (3),

"post-25 November 1996 scheme" is to be read in accordance with section 614D(1)(*b*),

"pre-26 November 1996 scheme" is to be read in accordance with section 614D(1)(*a*),

"related period of account" is to be read in accordance with section 614DB(5),

"related tax year" is to be read in accordance with section 614DB(4),

"the rental earnings", in relation to a lease of an asset and any period, has the meaning given by section 614AC, and

"sum" includes any money or money's worth (and "pay" and related expressions are to be read accordingly).][1]

Amendments—[1]   Sections 614D–614DG inserted by TIOPA 2010 s 367, Sch 3 paras 1, 5. TIOPA 2010 has effect for corporation tax purposes for accounting periods ending on or after 1 April 2010, for income and capital gains tax purposes for the tax year 2010–11 and subsequent tax years, and for petroleum revenue tax purposes for chargeable periods beginning on or after 1 July 2010.

PART 12
ACCRUED INCOME PROFITS

CHAPTER 1
INTRODUCTION

615 Overview of Part

(1) This Part makes provision about—

    (*a*) accrued income profits and losses, and

    (*b*) exemptions which apply where there is interest on securities.

(2) In this Part "accrued income profits" means profits which under Chapter 2 are treated as made where securities which carry or have carried interest are transferred.

(3) See sections 628, 630 and 670(2) and (3) for when such profits are treated as made.

(4) In this Part "accrued income losses" means losses which under Chapter 2 are treated as made where securities which carry or have carried interest are transferred.

(5) See section 628 for when such losses are treated as made.

(6) For the meaning of "securities", "transfer" and "interest", see sections 619, 620 and 671 respectively.

Derivation—TA 1988 ss 714, 716, 723.

HMRC Manuals—Savings and Investment Manual SAIM4030 (outline of the legislation).

CHAPTER 2

ACCRUED INCOME PROFITS AND LOSSES

Charge to tax

616 Charge to tax on accrued income profits

Income tax is charged on accrued income profits.

Derivation—TA 1988 ss 714(2), 716(2), (3), 723(4).

HMRC Manuals—Savings and Investment Manual SAIM4010 (the charge to tax under the accrued income scheme). SAIM4030 (outline of the legislation - the basic rules).

617 Income charged

(1) Tax is charged under this Chapter on the full amount of the accrued income profits treated as made in the tax year.

(2) Accrued income profits within section 628(5) (profits treated as made where the settlement day falls within an interest period) are treated as made in the tax year in which the last day of the interest period in which the profits are treated as made falls.

(3) Accrued income profits within section 630(2) (profits treated as made where the settlement day falls after the end of the securities' last interest period) are treated as made in the tax year in which the settlement day for the transfer falls.

(4) Accrued income profits within section 670(2) or (3) (withdrawal of relief for unremittable transfer proceeds) are treated as made in the tax year in which the proceeds cease to be unremittable.

(5) Section 668(5) (when proceeds are unremittable) applies for the purposes of subsection (4) as it applies for the purposes mentioned in section 668(5).

(6) For the meaning of "interest period" and "the settlement day", see sections 673 and 674 respectively.

[(7) Subsection (1) is subject to section 832 of ITTOIA 2005 (relevant foreign income charged on remittance basis).][1]

Commentary—*Simon's Taxes* **D9.420**.

HMRC Manuals—Savings and Investment Manual SAIM4030 (outline of the legislation - the basic rules).

Amendments—[1]   Sub-s (7) inserted by FA 2008 s 25, Sch 7 para 157 with effect in relation to transfers of securities where the settlement day is on or after 6 April 2008.

618 Person liable

(1) The person liable for any tax charged under this Chapter is the person treated as making the accrued income profits.

(2) But see section 666 (under which nominees and trustees may be disregarded).

Derivation—TA 1988 ss 714(2), (2B), 716(3), (3B), 723(4).

HMRC Manuals—Savings and Investment Manual SAIM4030 (outline of the legislation - the basic rules).

Securities to which Chapter applies

619 Meaning of "securities" and when securities are of the same kind

(1) In this Chapter "securities" includes—

    (*a*) any loan stock or similar security other than an excluded security, and

    (*b*) shares in a building society which are qualifying shares for the purposes of section 117(4) of TCGA 1992 (qualifying corporate bonds),

but (subject to paragraph (b)) it does not include any shares in a company.

(2) For the purposes of subsection (1)(*a*), it does not matter—

   (*a*) whether the security is of the government of the United Kingdom, any other government, any public or local authority in the United Kingdom or elsewhere, or any company or other body,

   (*b*) whether or not the security is secured,

   (*c*) whether or not the security carries a right to interest of a fixed amount or at a fixed rate percentage of the nominal value of the security, or

   (*d*) whether or not the security is in bearer form.

(3) In this section "excluded securities" means—

   (*a*) national savings certificates (including Ulster Savings Certificates as defined in section 693(7) of ITTOIA 2005),

   (*b*) war savings certificates,

   (*c*) uncertificated eligible debt security units as defined in section 986,

   (*d*) certificates of deposit (see section 1019),

   (*e*) a security which is a right falling within section 552(1)(*c*) of ITTOIA 2005 at the time of the transfer in question,

   (*f*) a security that meets the redemption conditions (see subsection (5)), and

   (*g*) a security that is a deeply discounted security within the meaning of Chapter 8 of Part 4 of ITTOIA 2005.

(4) But subsection (3)(*g*) does not include a security if, on its transfer, Chapter 8 of Part 4 of ITTOIA 2005 would apply subject to the rules in sections 454 to 456 of that Act (listed securities held since 26 March 2003).

(5) The redemption conditions are that—

   (*a*) the security is redeemable,

   (*b*) the amount payable on its redemption exceeds its issue price, and

   (*c*) no return other than the amount of that excess is payable on it.

(6) Securities are treated as being of the same kind for the purposes of this Chapter if they—

   (*a*) are treated as being of the same kind by the practice of a recognised stock exchange, or

   (*b*) would be so treated if dealt in on such an exchange.

Commentary—*Simon's Taxes* D9.402.

Derivation—TA 1988 s 710.

HMRC Manuals—Savings and Investment Manual SAIM4040 (definition of "securities").

Transfers to which Chapter applies

620 Transactions which are transfers: general

(1) References in this Chapter to the transfer of securities are—

   (*a*) to the transfer of securities by way of sale, exchange, gift or otherwise,

   (*b*) to the conversion of securities in any case where there is no transfer of the securities within paragraph (*a*),

   [(*c*) to the redemption of variable rate securities in any case where there has been a transfer of the securities at any time before redemption, or][1]

   (*d*) to a transaction or event treated as a transfer under—

      (i) section 648(1) or (3) (strips of gilt-edged securities),

      (ii) section 649(4) (new securities issued with extra return),

      (iii) section 650(2), (4) or (6) (trading stock appropriations etc),

      (iv) section 651(2) (owner becoming entitled to securities as trustee), or

      (v) section 652(2) (securities ceasing to be held on charitable trusts).

(2) But subsection (1)(*a*) does not include—

   (*a*) the vesting of securities in personal representatives on death, or

   (*b*) the transfer of a security to which Chapter 8 of Part 4 of ITTOIA 2005 applies subject to the rules in sections 454 to 456 of that Act.

(3) For the purposes of this Chapter—

   (*a*) a transfer of securities under an agreement takes place when the agreement is made, and

   (*b*) the person to whom they are to be transferred under the agreement becomes entitled to them at that time.

(4) But in the case of a conversion of securities within subsection (1)(*b*), the transfer takes place on the day of the conversion.

(5) And in the case of a redemption of securities within subsection (1)(*c*), the transfer takes place on the day of the redemption.

(6) Subsection (1) is subject to—

   section 648(7) (transactions forming part of exchanges concerning strips of gilt-edged securities),

   section 653 (stock lending), and

   section 655 (transfers under sale and repurchase arrangements).

(7) In this Chapter "conversion", in relation to securities, has the meaning given by section 132 of TCGA 1992.

(a) the total amount ("A") of the payments treated under this Chapter as made to the person in the interest period in question in respect of transfers of securities of the particular kind, and

(b) the total amount ("B") of the payments treated under this Chapter as made by the person in that period in respect of such transfers.

(5) A person is treated as making accrued income profits in an interest period as a result of transfers of securities of a particular kind if A exceeds B.

(6) A person is treated as making accrued income losses in an interest period as a result of transfers of securities of a particular kind if B exceeds A.

(7) For the payments that are treated as made on transfers of different kinds, see—

section 632 (payment on transfer with accrued interest),

section 633 (payment on transfer without accrued interest),

section 634 (payment on transfer with unrealised interest),

section 635 (payment on transfer of variable rate securities), and

section 637(2) (accrued income losses treated as payment on transfer in next interest period).

(8) See also—

section 638(2) (no account to be taken of any payment treated as made by or to excluded transferor or transferee), and

Chapter 3 (exemptions relating to interest on securities).

Commentary—*Simon's Taxes* **D9.420**.
Derivation—TA 1988 s 714.
HMRC Manuals—Savings and Investment Manual SAIM4110 (accrued income profits: general rule).
SAIM4120 (accrued income profits and losses: reliefs for losses).
SAIM4130 (accrued income profits and losses: examples).
SAIM4260 (special calculation for payments).

629 Calculating accrued income profits and losses where section 628 applies

(1) If section 628(5) applies, the amount of the accrued income profits treated as made is equal to the excess mentioned in section 628(5).

(2) If section 628(6) applies, the amount of the accrued income losses treated as made is equal to the excess mentioned in section 628(6).

Commentary—*Simon's Taxes* **D9.420**.
Derivation—TA 1988 ss 714 and 716.

630 Making accrued income profits: settlement day outside interest period

(1) This section applies if—

(a) there is a transfer of securities with unrealised interest or a transfer of variable rate securities, and

(b) the settlement day for the transfer falls after the end of the only or last interest period of the securities.

(2) The transferor is treated as making accrued income profits.

(3) See also—

section 638(3) (no account to be taken of transfer if transferor is excluded transferor), and

section 681 (exemption for unrealised interest received by transferee after transfer).

Commentary—*Simon's Taxes* **D9.426**.
HMRC Manuals—Savings and Investment Manual SAIM4110 (accrued income profits: settlement day outside the interest period).

631 Amount of accrued income profits where section 630 applies

(1) In the case of a transfer of securities with unrealised interest to which section 630 applies, the amount of the accrued income profits treated as made is equal to the unrealised interest.

(2) Subsection (1) is subject to section 660 (transfers with unrealised interest: interest in default).

(3) In the case of a transfer of variable rate securities to which section 630 applies, the amount of the accrued income profits treated as made is such amount as is just and reasonable.

Commentary—*Simon's Taxes* **D9.414, D9.426**.
Derivation—TA 1988 ss 716(3) and 717(9).
HMRC Manuals—Savings and Investment Manual SAIM4110 (accrued income profits: settlement day outside the interest period).

The payments treated as made on transfers

632 Payment on transfer with accrued interest

(1) In the case of a transfer of securities with accrued interest, for the purposes of this Chapter a payment is treated as made by the transferee to the transferor in the interest period in which the settlement day falls.

(2) The amount of that payment depends on whether the transfer is under an arrangement by which the transferee accounts to the transferor separately—

(a) for the consideration for the securities, and

(b) for gross interest accruing to the settlement day.

(3) If the transfer is under such an arrangement, the amount of the payment is the amount of gross interest which the transferee accounts for.

(2) For the purposes of subsection (1)(*a*), it does not matter—

    (*a*) whether the security is of the government of the United Kingdom, any other government, any public or local authority in the United Kingdom or elsewhere, or any company or other body,

    (*b*) whether or not the security is secured,

    (*c*) whether or not the security carries a right to interest of a fixed amount or at a fixed rate percentage of the nominal value of the security, or

    (*d*) whether or not the security is in bearer form.

(3) In this section "excluded securities" means—

    (*a*) national savings certificates (including Ulster Savings Certificates as defined in section 693(7) of ITTOIA 2005),

    (*b*) war savings certificates,

    (*c*) uncertificated eligible debt security units as defined in section 986,

    (*d*) certificates of deposit (see section 1019),

    (*e*) a security which is a right falling within section 552(1)(*c*) of ITTOIA 2005 at the time of the transfer in question,

    (*f*) a security that meets the redemption conditions (see subsection (5)), and

    (*g*) a security that is a deeply discounted security within the meaning of Chapter 8 of Part 4 of ITTOIA 2005.

(4) But subsection (3)(*g*) does not include a security if, on its transfer, Chapter 8 of Part 4 of ITTOIA 2005 would apply subject to the rules in sections 454 to 456 of that Act (listed securities held since 26 March 2003).

(5) The redemption conditions are that—

    (*a*) the security is redeemable,

    (*b*) the amount payable on its redemption exceeds its issue price, and

    (*c*) no return other than the amount of that excess is payable on it.

(6) Securities are treated as being of the same kind for the purposes of this Chapter if they—

    (*a*) are treated as being of the same kind by the practice of a recognised stock exchange, or

    (*b*) would be so treated if dealt in on such an exchange.

Commentary—*Simon's Taxes* **D9.402**.
Derivation—TA 1988 s 710.
HMRC Manuals—Savings and Investment Manual SAIM4040 (definition of "securities").

Transfers to which Chapter applies

620 Transactions which are transfers: general

(1) References in this Chapter to the transfer of securities are—

    (*a*) to the transfer of securities by way of sale, exchange, gift or otherwise,

    (*b*) to the conversion of securities in any case where there is no transfer of the securities within paragraph (*a*),

    [(*c*) to the redemption of variable rate securities in any case where there has been a transfer of the securities at any time before redemption, or][1]

    (*d*) to a transaction or event treated as a transfer under—

        (i) section 648(1) or (3) (strips of gilt-edged securities),

        (ii) section 649(4) (new securities issued with extra return),

        (iii) section 650(2), (4) or (6) (trading stock appropriations etc),

        (iv) section 651(2) (owner becoming entitled to securities as trustee), or

        (v) section 652(2) (securities ceasing to be held on charitable trusts).

(2) But subsection (1)(*a*) does not include—

    (*a*) the vesting of securities in personal representatives on death, or

    (*b*) the transfer of a security to which Chapter 8 of Part 4 of ITTOIA 2005 applies subject to the rules in sections 454 to 456 of that Act.

(3) For the purposes of this Chapter—

    (*a*) a transfer of securities under an agreement takes place when the agreement is made, and

    (*b*) the person to whom they are to be transferred under the agreement becomes entitled to them at that time.

(4) But in the case of a conversion of securities within subsection (1)(*b*), the transfer takes place on the day of the conversion.

(5) And in the case of a redemption of securities within subsection (1)(*c*), the transfer takes place on the day of the redemption.

(6) Subsection (1) is subject to—

    section 648(7) (transactions forming part of exchanges concerning strips of gilt-edged securities),

    section 653 (stock lending), and

    section 655 (transfers under sale and repurchase arrangements).

(7) In this Chapter "conversion", in relation to securities, has the meaning given by section 132 of TCGA 1992.

Commentary—*Simon's Taxes* **D9.403**.
HMRC Manuals—Savings and Investment Manual SAIM4050 (meaning of "transfer").
SAIM4160 (examples of transfers with and without accrued interest).
Amendments—[1]   Sub-s (1)(c) substituted by the Income Tax Act 2007 (Amendment) (No 2) Order, SI 2007/1820 art 4(1), (2) with effect from 17 July 2007.

621 Transferors and transferees

(1) In this Chapter "transferor" and "transferee" are to be read in accordance with section 620 (but this is subject to subsections (2) to (4)).

(2) In the case of a conversion of securities within section 620(1)(b)—

    (a) the person who was entitled to the securities immediately before the conversion is treated as the transferor, but

    (b) no one is treated as the transferee.

(3) In the case of a redemption of securities within section 620(1)(c)—

    (a) the person who was entitled to the securities immediately before the redemption is treated as the transferor, but

    (b) no one is treated as the transferee.

(4) The following provisions also contain rules about who is the transferor or the transferee for certain transfers—

    section 648(1) to (4) (strips of gilt-edged securities),

    section 649(4) and (5) (new securities issued with extra return),

    section 650 (trading stock appropriations etc),

    section 651(2) and (3) (owner becoming entitled to securities as trustee),

    section 652(2) and (3) (securities ceasing to be held on charitable trusts), and

    section 666 (certain transfers by or to nominees or trustees treated as made by or to others).

(5) See also sections 638 to 647 (excluded transferors and transferees).

Commentary—*Simon's Taxes* **D9.403**.
Derivation—TA 1988 ss 710(13), 717(8).
HMRC Manuals—Savings and Investment Manual SAIM4050 (conversion).

622 Application of Chapter to different kinds of transfer

(1) Different rules apply under this Chapter for the different kinds of transfer specified in subsection (2).

(2) The transfers are—

    (a) transfers with accrued interest (see section 623),

    (b) transfers without accrued interest (see section 624),

    (c) transfers with unrealised interest (see section 625), and

    (d) transfers of variable rate securities (see section 626).

(3) If a transfer is both a transfer with unrealised interest and a transfer of a kind specified in subsection (2)(a), (b) or (d), both the provisions of this Chapter applicable to transfers with unrealised interest and the provisions applicable to the other kind of transfer apply to the transfer.

623 Transfers with accrued interest

(1) The general rule is that securities are transferred with accrued interest for the purposes of this Chapter if they are transferred with the right to receive interest payable—

    (a) in a case where the settlement day is an interest payment day, on the settlement day, and

    (b) in any other case, on the first interest payment day after the settlement day.

(2) But, in the case of the transfers specified in subsection (3), subsection (4) applies instead of subsection (1).

(3) The transfers are those treated as made under—

    (a) section 620(1)(b) (conversion),

    (b) section 650 (trading stock appropriations etc),

    (c) section 651 (owner becoming entitled to securities as trustee), and

    (d) section 652 (securities ceasing to be held on charitable trusts).

(4) If the person treated as the transferor had the right to receive interest payable as mentioned in subsection (1)(a) or (b), the securities are treated as transferred with accrued interest.

(5) This section is subject to section 626 (transfers of variable rate securities).

(6) See also—

    section 648(6) (certain exchanges of strips treated as transfers with accrued interest), and

    section 649(4) (issue of new securities with extra return treated as transfer with accrued interest).

Commentary—*Simon's Taxes* **D9.427, D9.410**.
Derivation—TA 1988 s 711.
HMRC Manuals—Savings and Investment Manual SAIM4060 (transfers with accrued interest)..
SAIM4160 (examples of transfers with and without accrued interest).

624 Transfers without accrued interest

(1) The general rule is that securities are transferred without accrued interest for the purposes of this Chapter if they are transferred without the right to receive interest payable as mentioned in section 623(1)(*a*) or (*b*).

(2) But, in the case of the transfers specified in subsection (3), subsection (4) applies instead of subsection (1).

(3) The transfers are those treated as made under—

    (*a*) section 620(1)(*b*) (conversion),

    (*b*) section 650 (trading stock appropriations etc),

    (*c*) section 651 (owner becoming entitled to securities as trustee), and

    (*d*) section 652 (securities ceasing to be held on charitable trusts).

(4) If the person treated as the transferor did not have the right to receive interest payable as mentioned in section 623(1)(*a*) or (*b*), the securities are treated as transferred without accrued interest.

(5) This section is subject to section 626 (transfers of variable rate securities).

(6) See also section 648(5) (certain exchanges of strips treated as transfers without accrued interest).

Commentary—*Simon's Taxes* **D9.427, D9.410**.
HMRC Manuals—Savings and Investment Manual SAIM4060 (transfers without accrued interest).

625 Transfers with unrealised interest

(1) For the purposes of this Chapter securities are transferred with unrealised interest if they are transferred with the right to receive interest payable on an interest payment day falling before the settlement day.

(2) Such interest is referred to in this Chapter as "unrealised interest".

Commentary—*Simon's Taxes* **D9.414, D9.410**.
Derivation—TA 1988 s 716(1).
HMRC Manuals—Savings and Investment Manual SAIM4060 (transfers with unrealised interest).

626 Transfers of variable rate securities

(1) Sections 623 and 624 do not apply to transfers of variable rate securities.

(2) Such transfers are not treated as transfers with accrued interest or transfers without accrued interest.

Commentary—*Simon's Taxes* **D9.426**.
HMRC Manuals—Savings and Investment Manual SAIM4060 (transfers of variable rate securities).
SAIM4180 (variable rate securities).

627 Meaning of "variable rate securities"

(1) For the purposes of this Chapter securities are "variable rate securities" unless their terms of issue provide that throughout the period from issue to redemption (whenever redemption might occur) they are to carry interest at a rate which falls into one, and one only, of the categories specified in subsection (2).

(2) The categories are—

    (*a*) a fixed rate which is the same throughout the period,

    (*b*) a rate which bears the same fixed relationship to a standard published base rate throughout the period, and

    (*c*) a rate which bears the same fixed relationship to a published index of prices throughout the period.

(3) In subsection (2) "published index of prices" means the retail prices index or any similar general index of prices which is published by the government of any territory outside the United Kingdom or by an agent of such a government.

(4) In determining whether new securities (within the meaning of section 649 (new securities issued with extra return)) are variable rate securities, the interest payable on them on the first interest payment day after their issue is treated as payable in respect of the period beginning with the relevant period and ending with that day.

(5) In subsection (4) "the relevant period" has the meaning given by section 649(8).

Commentary—*Simon's Taxes* **D9.426, D9.425**.
Derivation—TA 1988 ss 717(1)–(3), 726A(2), (7), (8).
HMRC Manuals—Savings and Investment Manual SAIM4180 (variable rate securities).

Calculating accrued income profits and losses

628 Making accrued income profits and losses: general rule

(1) This section sets out the general rule for determining whether a person is treated as making accrued income profits or accrued income losses where securities are transferred by or to the person.

(2) This section does not apply in a case where section 630 applies.

(3) A separate calculation is to be made for each kind of security that is transferred by or to the person and for each interest period of each such kind of security.

(4) Each such calculation is to find—

(*a*) the total amount ("A") of the payments treated under this Chapter as made to the person in the interest period in question in respect of transfers of securities of the particular kind, and

(*b*) the total amount ("B") of the payments treated under this Chapter as made by the person in that period in respect of such transfers.

(5) A person is treated as making accrued income profits in an interest period as a result of transfers of securities of a particular kind if A exceeds B.

(6) A person is treated as making accrued income losses in an interest period as a result of transfers of securities of a particular kind if B exceeds A.

(7) For the payments that are treated as made on transfers of different kinds, see—

section 632 (payment on transfer with accrued interest),

section 633 (payment on transfer without accrued interest),

section 634 (payment on transfer with unrealised interest),

section 635 (payment on transfer of variable rate securities), and

section 637(2) (accrued income losses treated as payment on transfer in next interest period).

(8) See also—

section 638(2) (no account to be taken of any payment treated as made by or to excluded transferor or transferee), and

Chapter 3 (exemptions relating to interest on securities).

Commentary—*Simon's Taxes* **D9.420**.
Derivation—TA 1988 s 714.
HMRC Manuals—Savings and Investment Manual SAIM4110 (accrued income profits: general rule).
SAIM4120 (accrued income profits and losses: reliefs for losses).
SAIM4130 (accrued income profits and losses: examples).
SAIM4260 (special calculation for payments).

629 Calculating accrued income profits and losses where section 628 applies

(1) If section 628(5) applies, the amount of the accrued income profits treated as made is equal to the excess mentioned in section 628(5).

(2) If section 628(6) applies, the amount of the accrued income losses treated as made is equal to the excess mentioned in section 628(6).

Commentary—*Simon's Taxes* **D9.420**.
Derivation—TA 1988 ss 714 and 716.

630 Making accrued income profits: settlement day outside interest period

(1) This section applies if—

(*a*) there is a transfer of securities with unrealised interest or a transfer of variable rate securities, and

(*b*) the settlement day for the transfer falls after the end of the only or last interest period of the securities.

(2) The transferor is treated as making accrued income profits.

(3) See also—

section 638(3) (no account to be taken of transfer if transferor is excluded transferor), and

section 681 (exemption for unrealised interest received by transferee after transfer).

Commentary—*Simon's Taxes* **D9.426**.
HMRC Manuals—Savings and Investment Manual SAIM4110 (accrued income profits: settlement day outside the interest period).

631 Amount of accrued income profits where section 630 applies

(1) In the case of a transfer of securities with unrealised interest to which section 630 applies, the amount of the accrued income profits treated as made is equal to the unrealised interest.

(2) Subsection (1) is subject to section 660 (transfers with unrealised interest: interest in default).

(3) In the case of a transfer of variable rate securities to which section 630 applies, the amount of the accrued income profits treated as made is such amount as is just and reasonable.

Commentary—*Simon's Taxes* **D9.414, D9.426**.
Derivation—TA 1988 ss 716(3) and 717(9).
HMRC Manuals—Savings and Investment Manual SAIM4110 (accrued income profits: settlement day outside the interest period).

The payments treated as made on transfers

632 Payment on transfer with accrued interest

(1) In the case of a transfer of securities with accrued interest, for the purposes of this Chapter a payment is treated as made by the transferee to the transferor in the interest period in which the settlement day falls.

(2) The amount of that payment depends on whether the transfer is under an arrangement by which the transferee accounts to the transferor separately—

(*a*) for the consideration for the securities, and

(*b*) for gross interest accruing to the settlement day.

(3) If the transfer is under such an arrangement, the amount of the payment is the amount of gross interest which the transferee accounts for.

(4) If—

  (*a*) the transfer is not under such an arrangement, and

  (*b*) the settlement day is itself an interest payment day for the securities,

the amount of the payment is the amount of interest payable on the securities on that day.

(5) If—

  (*a*) the transfer is not under such an arrangement, and

  (*b*) the settlement day is not an interest payment day for the securities, the amount of the payment is an amount equal to—

$$I \times \frac{A}{B}$$

where—

I is the interest payable on the securities on the first interest payment day after the settlement day ("the payment day"),

A is the number of days in the period beginning with the first day on which that interest accrues and ending with the settlement day, and

B is the number of days in the period beginning with the first day on which that interest accrues and ending with the payment day.

(6) For the purposes of subsection (5), the first day on which that interest accrues is taken to be—

  (*a*) the day after the last interest payment day before the settlement day, or

  (*b*) if there was no interest payment day before the settlement day, the first day of the first interest period of the securities.

(7) In a case where no one is treated as the transferor (see sections 648(4) and 649(5)), this section has effect as if—

  (*a*) in subsection (1) the words "to the transferor" were omitted, and

  (*b*) subsections (2), (3), (4)(*a*) and (5)(*a*) were omitted.

(8) In a case where no one is treated as the transferee (see sections 621(2) and (3) and 648(2)), this section has effect as if—

  (*a*) in subsection (1) the words "by the transferee" were omitted, and

  (*b*) subsections (2), (3), (4)(*a*) and (5)(*a*) were omitted.

(9) Subsections (2) to (5) are subject to section 662 (new securities issued with extra return: special rules about payments).

(10) Subsections (4) and (5) are subject to section 659 (transfers with or without accrued interest: interest in default).

Commentary—*Simon's Taxes* **D9.411**.

Derivation—TA 1988 s 713.

HMRC Manuals—Savings and Investment Manual SAIM4140 (payments on transfer with accrued interest).

SAIM4160 (examples of transfers with and without accrued interest).

SAIM4400 (payment into separate accounts of capital and accrued income elements).

SAIM4290 (special calculations: interest in default).

633 Payment on transfer without accrued interest

(1) In the case of a transfer of securities without accrued interest, for the purposes of this Chapter a payment is treated as made by the transferor to the transferee in the interest period in which the settlement day falls.

(2) The amount of that payment depends on whether the transfer is under an arrangement by which the transferor accounts to the transferee for gross interest accruing from the settlement day to the next interest payment day.

(3) If the transfer is under such an arrangement, the amount of the payment is the amount of gross interest which the transferor accounts for.

(4) If—

  (*a*) the transfer is not under such an arrangement, and

  (*b*) the settlement day is itself an interest payment day for the securities,

the amount of the payment is nil.

(5) If—

  (*a*) the transfer is not under such an arrangement, and

  (*b*) the settlement day is not an interest payment day for the securities,

the amount of the payment is an amount equal to—

$$I \times \frac{A}{B}$$

where—

I is the interest payable on the securities on the first interest payment day after the settlement day ("the payment day"),

A is the number of days in the period beginning with the day after the settlement day and ending with the payment day, and

B is the number of days in the period beginning with the first day on which that interest accrues and ending with the payment day.

(6) For the purposes of subsection (5), the first day on which that interest accrues is taken to be—

    (*a*) the day after the last interest payment day before the settlement day, or

    (*b*) if there is no interest payment day before the settlement day, the first day of the first interest period of the securities.

(7) In a case where no one is treated as the transferor (see section 648(4)), this section has effect as if—

    (*a*) in subsection (1) the words "by the transferor" were omitted, and

    (*b*) subsections (2), (3), (4)(*a*) and (5)(*a*) were omitted.

(8) In a case where no one is treated as the transferee (see sections 621(2) and (3) and 648(2)), this section has effect as if—

    (*a*) in subsection (1) the words "to the transferee" were omitted, and

    (*b*) subsections (2), (3), (4)(*a*) and (5)(*a*) were omitted.

(9) Subsection (5) is subject to section 659 (transfers with or without accrued interest: interest in default).

(10) See also section 663(2) (reduction of amount of payment under this section where transfer to maker of manufactured payments).

Commentary—*Simon's Taxes* **D9.412**.
Derivation—TA 1988 s 713.
HMRC Manuals—Savings and Investment Manual SAIM4150 (payments on transfer without accrued interest).
SAIM4160 (examples of transfers with and without accrued interest).

634 Payment on transfer with unrealised interest

(1) In the case of a transfer of securities with unrealised interest where the settlement day falls within an interest period, for the purposes of this Chapter a payment is treated as made to the transferor in that period.

(2) The amount of the payment is equal to the unrealised interest.

(3) Subsection (2) is subject to section 660 (transfers with unrealised interest: interest in default).

(4) No one is treated as making the payment.

(5) Accordingly, the payment is not brought into account in determining whether the transferee is treated as making accrued income profits or losses under section 628.

(6) But see section 681 (exemption for unrealised interest received by transferee after transfer).

(7) See section 630 for the rules that apply to transfers of securities with unrealised interest where the settlement day falls outside an interest period.

Commentary—*Simon's Taxes* **D9.414**.
Derivation—TA 1988 s 716.
HMRC Manuals—Savings and Investment Manual SAIM4170 (payment on transfer with "unrealised interest").
SAIM4350 (unrealised interest received after transfer).

635 Payment on transfer of variable rate securities

(1) In the case of a transfer of variable rate securities where the settlement day falls within an interest period, for the purposes of this Chapter a payment is treated as made to the transferor in that period.

(2) The amount of the payment is such amount as is just and reasonable.

(3) No one is treated as making the payment.

(4) Accordingly, the payment is not brought into account in determining whether the transferee is treated as making accrued income profits or losses under section 628.

(5) See section 630 for the rules that apply to transfers of variable rate securities where the settlement day falls outside an interest period.

Commentary—*Simon's Taxes* **D9.426**.
Derivation—TA 1988 s 717.
HMRC Manuals—Savings and Investment Manual SAIM4180 (the transferor is taxable on transfers of variable rate securities, and euroconversion).

Exception where there is a transfer to a legatee

636 Exception where there is a transfer to a legatee

(1) This section applies if—

    (*a*) an individual who is entitled to securities dies, and

    (*b*) the securities are transferred by the personal representatives to a legatee.

(2) If the securities are transferred in the interest period in which the death occurs, no payment is treated as made under this Chapter as a result of the transfer.

(3) If the securities are variable rate securities and the deceased dies after the end of the only or last interest period of the securities, no accrued income profits are treated as made under section 630(2).

(4) In this section "legatee" includes any person taking (whether beneficially or as trustee)—

(*a*) under a testamentary disposition, or

(*b*) on an intestacy or partial intestacy.

(5) Such a person includes a person taking as a result of an appropriation by personal representatives in or towards the satisfaction of a legacy or other interest or share in the deceased's property.

Commentary—*Simon's Taxes* **D9.430**.

HMRC Manuals—Savings and Investment Manual SAIM4190 (no accrued income scheme charge on death).

Relief for losses

637 Accrued income losses treated as payments in next interest period

(1) This section applies if—

(*a*) a person is treated as making accrued income losses in an interest period as a result of transfers of securities, and

(*b*) the period does not end with an interest payment day.

(2) For the purposes of this Chapter the person is treated as making a payment on a transfer of the securities in the next interest period equal to the amount of the losses.

(3) For cases where the period does end with an interest payment day, see sections 678 to 680 (exemptions for interest on securities involving accrued income losses).

Commentary—*Simon's Taxes* **D9.421**.

Derivation—TA 1988 s 714.

HMRC Manuals—Savings and Investment Manual SAIM4130 (accrued income profits and losses, with examples).
SAIM4120 (losses treated as payments in the next interest period).

Excluded transferors and transferees

638 Excluded persons: disregard of certain payments and transfers

(1) This section applies if there is a transfer of securities in relation to which a person ("P") is an excluded transferor or excluded transferee.

(2) In determining whether P has made accrued income profits or accrued income losses under section 628 (making accrued income profits and losses: general rule) and the amount of any such profits or losses, no account is to be taken of any payment treated as made by or to P on the transfer.

(3) In determining whether P has made accrued income profits under section 630 (making accrued income profits: settlement day outside interest period) and the amount of any such profits, no account is to be taken of the transfer if P is an excluded transferor in relation to it.

(4) For the cases where a person is an excluded transferor or excluded transferee in relation to a transfer, see—

     section 639 (small holdings: individuals),

     section 640 (small holdings: personal representatives),

     section 641 (small holdings: trustees of a disabled person's trusts),

     section 642 (traders),

     section 643 (non-residents),

     section 644 (individuals to whom the remittance basis applies),

     section 645 (charitable trusts etc),

     section 646 (pension scheme trustees), and

     section 647 (makers of manufactured payments).

(5) Whether a person is an excluded transferee is also relevant to the application of section 681 (exemption for unrealised interest received by transferee after transfer).

Derivation—TA 1988 s 715.

HMRC Manuals—Savings and Investment Manual SAIM4200 (excluded persons).

639 Small holdings: individuals

(1) In relation to a transfer with accrued interest or transfer without accrued interest, an individual is an excluded transferor or excluded transferee unless the nominal value of securities held by the individual exceeds £5,000 on any day—

(*a*) in the tax year in which the interest period ends, or

(*b*) in the previous tax year.

(2) In relation to a transfer with unrealised interest, an individual is an excluded transferor or excluded transferee unless the nominal value of securities held by the individual exceeds £5,000 on any day—

(*a*) in the tax year in which the settlement day falls, or

(*b*) in the previous tax year.

(3) In relation to a transfer of variable rate securities, an individual is an excluded transferor unless the nominal value of securities held by the individual exceeds £5,000 on any day in the relevant tax year or the previous tax year.

(4) In subsection (3) "the relevant tax year" means—

(*a*) if the settlement day falls in an interest period, the tax year in which the interest period ends, or

(*b*) otherwise, the tax year in which the settlement day falls.

(5) For the purposes of this section, if—

(*a*) an individual holds securities at a particular time, and

(*b*) any interest on them which became payable at that time would be treated for income tax purposes as part of another individual's income,

each of those individuals is treated as holding at that time the securities which the other holds, as well as those which that individual actually holds.

Commentary—*Simon's Taxes* **D9.435**.

HMRC Manuals—Savings and Investment Manual SAIM4210 (small holdings exclusion with examples).

640 Small holdings: personal representatives

(1) In relation to a transfer with accrued interest or transfer without accrued interest of securities that form part of a deceased person's estate, the deceased's personal representatives are an excluded transferor or excluded transferee unless the nominal value of securities held by the deceased's personal representatives as such exceeds £5,000 on any day—

(*a*) in the tax year in which the interest period ends, or

(*b*) in the previous tax year.

(2) In relation to a transfer with unrealised interest of securities that form part of a deceased person's estate, the deceased's personal representatives are an excluded transferor or excluded transferee unless the nominal value of securities held by the deceased's personal representatives as such exceeds £5,000 on any day—

(*a*) in the tax year in which the settlement day falls, or

(*b*) in the previous tax year.

(3) In relation to a transfer of variable rate securities that form part of a deceased person's estate, the deceased's personal representatives are an excluded transferor unless the nominal value of securities held by the deceased's personal representatives as such exceeds £5,000 on any day in the relevant tax year or the previous tax year.

(4) In subsection (3) "the relevant tax year" has the meaning given by section 639(4).

Commentary—*Simon's Taxes* **D9.435**.

HMRC Manuals—Savings and Investment Manual SAIM4210 (small holdings exclusion - personal representatives).

641 Small holdings: trustees of a disabled person's trusts

(1) In relation to a transfer with accrued interest or transfer without accrued interest of securities held on a disabled person's trusts, the trustees of the settlement are an excluded transferor or excluded transferee unless the nominal value of securities held by the trustees of the settlement as such exceeds £5,000 on any day—

(*a*) in the tax year in which the interest period ends, or

(*b*) in the previous tax year.

(2) In relation to a transfer with unrealised interest of securities held on a disabled person's trusts, the trustees of the settlement are an excluded transferor or excluded transferee unless the nominal value of securities held by the trustees of the settlement as such exceeds £5,000 on any day—

(*a*) in the tax year in which the settlement day falls, or

(*b*) in the previous tax year.

(3) In relation to a transfer of variable rate securities held on a disabled person's trusts, the trustees of the settlement are an excluded transferor unless the nominal value of securities held by the trustees of the settlement as such exceeds £5,000 on any day in the relevant tax year or the previous tax year.

(4) In this section—

"disabled person's trusts" means trusts falling within [paragraph 3 of Schedule 1C][1] to TCGA 1992 (application of annual exempt amount), and

"the relevant tax year" has the meaning given by section 639(4).

Commentary—*Simon's Taxes* **D9.435**.

HMRC Manuals—Savings and Investment Manual SAIM4210 (small holdings and disabled trusts).

Amendments—[1] In sub-s (4) words substituted for words "paragraph 1(1) of Schedule 1" by FA 2019 s 13, Sch 1 paras 99, 100 with effect for capital gains tax purposes for the tax year 2019–20 and subsequent tax years, and for corporation tax purposes for accounting periods beginning on or after 6 April 2019. These amendments also have effect for corporation tax purposes in relation to disposals made on or after 6 April 2019 (whether in their application to accounting periods beginning on, and ending on or after, that date or to later accounting periods). See also transitional provisions in FA 2019 Sch 1 paras 121–126.

642 Traders

(1) In relation to a transfer of securities by a person carrying on a trade, the person is an excluded transferor if the transfer is taken into account for income tax purposes in calculating the profits or losses of the trade.

(2) In relation to a transfer of securities at any time to a person carrying on a trade, the person is an excluded transferee if, had the transfer been made by the person at that time, it would have been taken into account for income tax purposes in calculating the profits or losses of the trade.

Commentary—*Simon's Taxes* **D9.428, D9.437**.

Derivation—TA 1988 ss 715(1)(*a*) and 715(2)(*a*).

HMRC Manuals—Savings and Investment Manual SAIM4220 (other excluded persons - financial traders).

643 Non-residents

(1) A person is—

    (*a*) an excluded transferor in relation to a transfer by the person, and

    (*b*) an excluded transferee in relation to a transfer to the person,

if the person is non-UK resident throughout the tax year in which the transfer occurs . . . [1].

(2) In the case of a person who is carrying on a trade in the United Kingdom through a branch or agency during any part of that year ("a UK branch trader"), subsection (1) is subject to subsections (3) and (4).

(3) A UK branch trader is not an excluded transferor under subsection (1) if the securities transferred were situated in the United Kingdom and used or held for the purposes of the branch or agency at or before the time of the transfer.

(4) A UK branch trader is not an excluded transferee under subsection (1) if the securities transferred were situated in the United Kingdom at the time of the transfer and were acquired for use by or for the purposes of the branch or agency.

(5) In this section "branch or agency" has the meaning given by [section 1B(5)][2] of TCGA 1992.

(6) The place where securities are situated is determined for the purposes of this section in accordance with sections 275(1) and (2)(*b*) and 275C of TCGA 1992.

(7) Further provision about trustees who are non-UK resident is made in section 667 (trustees' accrued income profits treated as settlement income).

Commentary—*Simon's Taxes* **D9.436**.
Derivation—TA 1988 s 715(1)(*f*) and (2)(*b*).
HMRC Manuals—Savings and Investment Manual SAIM4230 (other excluded persons - non-residents).
Amendments—[1]   In sub-s (1) words "and is not ordinarily UK resident during that year" repealed by FA 2013 s 219, Sch 46 paras 54, 58 with effect for the purposes of a person's tax liability to income tax for the tax year 2013–14 or any subsequent tax year, subject to savings in FA 2013 Sch 46 para 73.
[2]   In sub-s (5) words substituted for words "section 10(6)" by FA 2019 s 13, Sch 1 paras 99, 101 with effect for capital gains tax purposes for the tax year 2019–20 and subsequent tax years, and for corporation tax purposes for accounting periods beginning on or after 6 April 2019. These amendments also have effect for corporation tax purposes in relation to disposals made on or after 6 April 2019 (whether in their application to accounting periods beginning on, and ending on or after, that date or to later accounting periods). See also transitional provisions in FA 2019 Sch 1 paras 121–126.

645 Charitable trusts etc

(1) A person is—

    (*a*) an excluded transferor in relation to a transfer of securities by the person, and

    (*b*) an excluded transferee in relation to a transfer of securities to the person,

if condition A or B is met.

(2) Condition A is that if the person—

    (*a*) became entitled to any interest on the securities, and

    (*b*) applied it for charitable purposes only,

exemption could be granted in respect of the interest under section 532 (exemption for certain savings and investment income that belongs to a charitable trust and is applicable and applied to charitable purposes only).

(3) Condition B is that if the person—

    (*a*) became entitled to any interest on the securities, and

    (*b*) applied it for the purposes mentioned in section 533 (exemption for public revenue dividends that are applied only for the repair of college or church buildings etc),

exemption could be granted in respect of the interest under that section.

(4) For the transfer treated as occurring where charitable trusts over securities cease, see section 652 (securities ceasing to be held on charitable trusts).

Commentary—*Simon's Taxes* **D9.438**.
Derivation—TA 1988 s 715(1)(*d*) and (2)(*b*).
HMRC Manuals—Savings and Investment Manual SAIM4220 (other excluded persons - charities).

646 Pension scheme trustees

A person is—

    (*a*) an excluded transferor in relation to a transfer of securities by the person, and

    (*b*) an excluded transferee in relation to a transfer of securities to the person,

if, were the person to become entitled to interest on the securities, exemption in respect of it would be allowable under section 186 of FA 2004 (exemption for income from investments held for the purposes of a registered pension scheme).

Commentary—*Simon's Taxes* **D9.439**.
Derivation—TA 1988 s 715(1)(k) and (2)(*b*).
HMRC Manuals—Savings and Investment Manual SAIM4220 (registered pension schemes).

647 Makers of manufactured payments

(1) This section applies if the manufactured payments conditions are met.

(2) The manufactured payments conditions are that—

    (*a*) securities are transferred without accrued interest to a person ("the seller"),

(b) the seller makes a contract for the sale of securities of that kind ("the seller's contract"), and

(c) any contract under which the securities are transferred to the seller, or the seller's contract itself, is a manufactured payments contract.

(3) The seller is an excluded transferee in relation to the transfer to the seller if the nominal value of the securities subject to the seller's contract equals or exceeds that of the securities transferred to the seller.

(4) The seller is an excluded transferor in relation to the transfer of securities under the seller's contract.

(5) See section 663 (transfers without accrued interest to makers of manufactured payments) for cases where that nominal value is less than that of the securities transferred to the seller.

[(6) In this section "manufactured payments contract" means a contract under which—

(a) the seller is required to pay another person an amount which is representative of a periodical payment of interest on UK securities under an arrangement between them for the transfer of the securities, or

(b) the seller is required to pay another person an amount which is representative of an overseas dividend on overseas securities under an arrangement between them for the transfer of the securities.

(7) In this section—

(a) "overseas securities" means shares, stock or other securities issued by—

(i) a government, local authority or other public authority of a territory outside the United Kingdom, or

(ii) another non-UK resident body of persons, and includes shares in a non-UK resident company,

(b) "overseas dividend" means any interest, dividend or other annual payment payable in respect of overseas securities, and

(c) "UK securities" means securities of—

(i) the government of the United Kingdom,

(ii) a local authority in the United Kingdom,

(iii) another public authority in the United Kingdom, or

(iv) a UK resident company or other UK resident body,

but does not include shares in a UK resident company.][1]

Commentary—*Simon's Taxes* **D9.431**.
Derivation—TA 1988 s 715(6).
HMRC Manuals—Savings and Investment Manual SAIM4220 (makers of manufactured payments).
Amendments—[1] Sub-ss (6), (7) substituted for previous sub-s (6) by FA 2013 s 77, Sch 29 paras 16, 19 with effect from 1 January 2014.

Further transactions treated as transfers

648 Strips of gilt-edged securities

(1) The exchange of a gilt-edged security for strips of that security is treated for the purposes of this Chapter as a transfer of the security by the person who exchanges the security.

(2) But no one is treated as the transferee.

(3) The exchange of strips of a gilt-edged security for a single gilt-edged security consolidating those strips is treated for the purposes of this Chapter as a transfer of the single security to the person who exchanges those strips.

(4) But no one is treated as the transferor.

(5) An exchange within subsection (1) or (3) is treated as a transfer without accrued interest if it is made at any time after the balance has been struck for a dividend on the security but before the day on which that dividend is payable.

(6) In any other case, such an exchange is treated as a transfer with accrued interest.

(7) If an exchange is treated as a transfer under subsection (1) or (3), any transaction forming part of the exchange is not itself a transfer for the purposes of this Chapter.

(8) In this section "strip" has the meaning given by section 444 of ITTOIA 2005.

(9) For the meaning of "gilt-edged security", see section 1024.

Commentary—*Simon's Taxes* **D9.429**.
Derivation—TA 1988 s 722A.
HMRC Manuals—Savings and Investment Manual SAIM4250 (special types of transfer: gilt strips).

649 New securities issued with extra return

(1) This section applies if—

(a) securities ("old securities") of a particular kind are issued by way of an original issue of securities of that kind,

(b) on a later occasion securities ("new securities") of the same kind are issued,

(c) a sum ("the extra return") is payable in respect of the new securities by the issuer of them to reflect the fact that interest is accruing on the old securities, (*d*) the issue price of the new securities includes an element (whether or not separately identified) representing payment for the extra return, and

(*e*) the extra return is equal to the amount of interest mentioned in subsection (2).

(2) The amount of interest referred to in subsection (1)(*e*) is—

(*a*) the amount of interest payable for the relevant period on so many old securities as there are new, or

(*b*) if there are more new securities than old, the amount of interest which would be so payable if there were as many old securities as new.

(3) This section does not apply if the new securities are variable rate securities.

(4) The new securities are treated as transferred with accrued interest to the person to whom they are issued on the new issue day.

(5) But no one is treated as the transferor.

(6) For the purposes of this Chapter, the settlement day for the transfer is taken to be the new issue day.

(7) See section 662 for the amount of the payment treated as made in the case of the transfer.

(8) In this section—

"the relevant period" is the period beginning with the day after—

(*a*) the only or last interest payment day before the new issue day, or

(*b*) if there is no interest payment day before the new issue day, the day on which the old securities are issued,

and ending with the new issue day, and

"the new issue day" is the day on which the new securities are issued.

Commentary—*Simon's Taxes* **D9.425**.
Derivation—TA 1988 s 726A.
HMRC Manuals—Savings and Investment Manual SAIM4260 (special types of transfer: new issues of securities).

650 Trading stock appropriations etc

(1) Subsection (2) applies if a person—

(*a*) acquires securities otherwise than as trading stock of a trade the person carries on, and

(*b*) appropriates the securities as trading stock for the purposes of such a trade (whether on the start of the trade or otherwise).

(2) The person is treated for the purposes of this Chapter as transferring the securities otherwise than in the course of the trade, and re-acquiring them in the course of the trade, on the day of appropriation.

(3) Subsection (4) applies if securities—

(*a*) form part of the trading stock of a person's trade, and

(*b*) are appropriated by the person for any other purpose.

(4) The person is treated for the purposes of this Chapter as transferring the securities in the course of the trade, and re-acquiring them otherwise than in the course of the trade, on the day of appropriation.

(5) Subsection (6) applies if securities—

(*a*) form part of the trading stock of a person's trade, and

(*b*) are retained by the person on ceasing to carry on the trade.

(6) The person is treated for the purposes of this Chapter as transferring the securities in the course of the trade, and re-acquiring them otherwise than in the course of the trade, on the day of cessation.

(7) See sections 623(2) to (4) and 624(2) to (4) for cases where securities are treated as transferred with or without accrued interest where this section applies.

Commentary—*Simon's Taxes* **D9.428** .
Derivation—TA 1988 s 722.
HMRC Manuals—Savings and Investment Manual SAIM4270 (appropriations to and from trading stock).

651 Owner becoming entitled to securities as trustee

(1) This section applies if a person entitled to securities otherwise than as trustee becomes trustee of them.

(2) The person is treated for the purposes of this Chapter as transferring the securities at the time the person becomes trustee of them.

(3) The transfer is treated as being made—

(*a*) by the person in a capacity other than trustee, and

(*b*) to the person and, if there are any other trustees, to the others in the capacity of trustees.

(4) See sections 623(2) to (4) and 624(2) to (4) for cases where securities are treated as transferred with or without accrued interest where this section applies.

Commentary—*Simon's Taxes* **D9.432**.
Derivation—TA 1988 s 720.
HMRC Manuals—Savings and Investment Manual SAIM4270 (owner becoming entitled to securities as trustee).

652 Securities ceasing to be held on charitable trusts

(1) This section applies if securities held on charitable trusts cease to be subject to those trusts.

(2) The trustees are treated for the purposes of this Chapter as transferring the securities at the time when the securities cease to be so subject.

(3) The transfer is treated as being made by the trustees in their capacity as charitable trustees to themselves in another capacity.

(4) See sections 623(2) to (4) and 624(2) to (4) for cases where securities are treated as transferred with or without accrued interest where this section applies.

Commentary—*Simon's Taxes* **D9.438**.
Derivation—TA 1988 s 715(3).
HMRC Manuals—Savings and Investment Manual SAIM4270 (securities ceasing to be held on charitable trusts).

Excluded transfers

653 Stock lending

This Chapter does not apply to transfers of securities in circumstances such that any disposal and acquisition are disregarded for the purposes of capital gains tax as a result of section 263B(2) of TCGA 1992 (capital gains tax exemption for disposals in pursuance of stock lending arrangements).

Commentary—*Simon's Taxes* **D9.431**.
Derivation—TA 1988 s 727.
HMRC Manuals—Savings and Investment Manual SAIM4280 (excluded transfers - stock lending).
Corporate Finance Manual CFM74140 (capital gains : transfers of securities under stock loans - accrued income scheme).

654 Sale and repurchase arrangements

(1) This section applies for the purposes of sections 655 to 658.

(2) There is a sale and repurchase arrangement in respect of securities if the securities are transferred under an agreement to sell them and—

 (*a*) the transferor ("T") or a person connected with T is required to buy back the securities by the agreement or a related agreement,

 (*b*) T or a person connected with T is required to buy back the securities as a result of the exercise of an option acquired under the agreement or a related agreement, or

 (*c*) T or a person connected with T exercises an option to buy back the securities which was acquired under the agreement or a related agreement.

(3) Agreements are related for the purposes of this section if they are entered into in pursuance of the same arrangement (regardless of the date on which either agreement is entered into).

(4) References in this section to buying back securities include—

 (*a*) buying similar securities, and

 (*b*) in the case of a person connected with T, buying the securities sold by T or similar securities.

(5) Subsection (4) applies even if the person buying the securities has not held them before.

(6) References in sections 656 and 657 to repurchase are to be read accordingly.

(7) Securities are similar for the purposes of subsection (4) if they give their holders—

 (*a*) the same rights against the same persons as to capital and interest, and

 (*b*) the same remedies to enforce those rights.

(8) Subsection (7) applies even if there is a difference in—

 (*a*) the total nominal amounts of the securities,

 (*b*) the form in which they are held, or

 (*c*) the manner in which they can be transferred.

Commentary—*Simon's Taxes* **D9.431**.
Modifications—ITA 2007 Sch 2 para 126(3) (modification of this section for the purpose of determining whether (for the purposes of ITA 2007 s 655) there is a sale and repurchase arrangement in respect of the securities).
ITA 2007 Sch 2 para 126(4), (5) (modification of this section for the purpose of determining whether (for the purposes of section 656) there is a sale and repurchase arrangement in respect of the securities, and for the purpose of determining whether (for the purposes of ITA 2007 s 657) the case involves redemption arrangements).

655 Transfers under sale and repurchase arrangements

(1) If there is a sale and repurchase arrangement in respect of securities, this Chapter does not apply to the transfer by T or the transfer back under the arrangement.

(2) But subsection (1) does not apply if section 608 prevents section 607 (treatment of price differences under repos) from applying in relation to the arrangement.

Commentary—*Simon's Taxes* **D9.431**.
Derivation—TA 1988 s 727A.
HMRC Manuals—Savings and Investment Manual SAIM4280 (transfers under sale and repurchase agreements : "repos").
Modifications—ITA 2007 Sch 2 para 125 (this section applies only if—

 (a) in the case of overseas securities (within the meaning given in ITA 2007 Pt 11), the agreement to sell the securities mentioned in ITA 2007 s 654(2) is entered into after 5 November 1996, and

 (b) in any other case, the agreement to sell the securities so mentioned is entered into after 30 April 1995).

ITA 2007 Sch 2 para 126(1), (2) (modification of this section if the agreement to sell the securities mentioned in ITA 2007 s 654(2) was made before 9 April 2003).

656 Power to modify: non-standard sale and repurchase arrangements

(1) The Treasury may by regulations provide for section 655 to apply with modifications in relation to cases involving non-standard sale and repurchase arrangements.

(2) A case involves a non-standard sale and repurchase arrangement if—
    (*a*) there is a sale and repurchase arrangement in respect of securities,
    (*b*) T makes a sale of the securities under the agreement to sell them ("the original sale"),
    (*c*) the securities are UK shares, UK securities or overseas securities, and
    (*d*) any of conditions A to E is met in relation to the sale and repurchase arrangement.
(3) Condition A is that—
    (*a*) the obligation to buy back the securities is not performed, or
    (*b*) the option to buy them back is not exercised.
(4) Condition B is that provision is made by or under an agreement for different or additional UK shares, UK securities or overseas securities to be treated as (or as included with) representative securities.
(5) Condition C is that provision is made by or under an agreement for any UK shares, UK securities or overseas securities to be treated as not included with representative securities.
(6) Condition D is that provision is made by or under an agreement for the sale price or repurchase price to be decided or varied wholly or partly by reference to post-agreement fluctuations.
(7) Condition E is that provision is made by or under an agreement for a person to be required, in a case where there are post-agreement fluctuations, to make a payment in the period—
    (*a*) beginning immediately after the making of the agreement for the original sale, and
    (*b*) ending when the repurchase price becomes due.
(8) "Post-agreement fluctuations" are fluctuations in the value of—
    (*a*) securities transferred in pursuance of the original sale, or
    (*b*) representative securities,
which occur in the period after the making of the agreement for the original sale.
(9) "Representative securities" are UK shares, UK securities or overseas securities which, for the purposes of the repurchase, are to represent securities transferred in pursuance of the original sale.

Commentary—*Simon's Taxes* **D9.431**.
Derivation—TA 1988 s 737E.

657 Power to modify: redemption arrangements

(1) The Treasury may by regulations provide for section 655 to apply with modifications in relation to cases involving redemption arrangements.
(2) A case involves redemption arrangements if—
    (*a*) arrangements, corresponding to those made in cases where there is a sale and repurchase arrangement in respect of securities, are made by an agreement, or one or more related agreements, in relation to securities that are to be redeemed in the period after their sale,
    (*b*) the securities are UK shares, UK securities or overseas securities, and
    (*c*) the arrangements are such that the seller or a person connected with the seller (instead of being required to repurchase the securities or acquiring an option to do so) is granted rights in respect of the benefits that will result from the redemption.

Commentary—*Simon's Taxes* **D9.431**.
Derivation—TA 1988 s 737E.

658 Powers to modify: supplementary

(1) Regulations under section 656 or 657 may make different provision for different cases.
(2) Regulations under either section may contain incidental, supplemental, consequential and transitional provision and savings.
(3) In this section and sections 656 and 657 "modifications" includes exceptions and omissions.
(4) Accordingly, a power in sections 656 and 657 to provide for a provision to apply with modifications in relation to a particular case includes power to provide for the provision not to apply in relation to that case.
[(5) Subsections (6) to (10) apply for the purposes of sections 656 and 657 and this section.
(6) "UK shares" means shares in a UK resident company.
(7) "UK securities" means securities of—
    (*a*) the government of the United Kingdom,
    (*b*) a local authority in the United Kingdom,
    (*c*) another public authority in the United Kingdom, or
    (*d*) a UK resident company or other UK resident body.
(8) But "UK securities" does not include UK shares.
(9) "Overseas securities" means shares, stock or other securities issued by—
    (*a*) a government, local authority or other public authority of a territory outside the United Kingdom, or
    (*b*) another non-UK resident body of persons.
(10) "Overseas securities" includes shares in a non-UK resident company.][1]

Commentary—*Simon's Taxes* **D9.431**.
Amendments—[1] Sub-ss (5)–(10) substituted for previous sub-s (5) by FA 2013 s 77, Sch 29 paras 16, 20 with effect from 1 January 2014.

Special rules about some calculations

659 Transfers with or without accrued interest: interest in default

(1) This section applies if—

    (a) the amount of the payments treated as made on a transfer of securities is to be determined under section 632(4) or (5), 633(5) or 662(4) (cases where interest is not accounted for separately),

    (b) there has been a failure to pay interest due on the securities, and

    (c) as a result of the failure, on the interest payment day which is or follows the settlement day the value of the right to receive the interest payable on the securities is less than the interest payable.

(2) The calculation under section 632(4) or (5), 633(5) or 662(4) is to be made by reference to that value instead of the interest.

Commentary—*Simon's Taxes* **D9.446**.
Derivation—TA 1988 s 718.
HMRC Manuals—Savings and Investment Manual SAIM4290 (cases where the issuer has defaulted on interest).

660 Transfers with unrealised interest: interest in default

(1) This section applies if—

    (a) securities are transferred with unrealised interest,

    (b) there has been a failure to pay interest due on the securities transferred, and

    (c) as a result of the failure, on the day of the transfer the value of the right to receive the unrealised interest ("the unrealised interest value") is less than the unrealised interest.

(2) The amount of the payment treated as made to the transferor under section 634(2) is taken to be the unrealised interest value instead of the amount of the unrealised interest.

(3) The amount of accrued income profits under section 631(1) is taken to be the unrealised interest value instead of the amount of the unrealised interest.

(4) Subsections (2) and (3) are subject to section 661 (successive transfers with unrealised interest in default).

(5) For the purposes of this section and section 661, a person is treated as transferring securities of a particular kind which the person acquired later before securities of that kind acquired earlier.

(6) See also section 681 (exemption for unrealised interest received by transferee after transfer).

Commentary—*Simon's Taxes* **D9.447**.
Derivation—TA 1988 s 719.
HMRC Manuals—Savings and Investment Manual SAIM4290 (transfers with unrealised interest).

661 Successive transfers with unrealised interest in default

(1) The amount taken as the unrealised interest value for the purposes of section 660(2) or (3) is reduced if the person ("T") who makes the transfer referred to in section 660(1) also acquired the securities with the right to receive unrealised interest.

(2) The amount of the reduction depends on whether subsection (3) applies.

(3) This subsection applies if—

    (a) T has received, as transferee, some or all of that unrealised interest, and

    (b) T is liable for income tax on it for the tax year in which it was received.

(4) If subsection (3) applies, the reduction is equal to the value on the day of the transfer to T of the right to receive the unrealised interest ("the earlier value") less the total so received.

(5) If subsection (3) does not apply, the reduction is equal to the earlier value.

(6) But if the reduction under subsection (4) or (5) exceeds the amount mentioned in subsection (1), that amount is treated as reduced to nil.

Commentary—*Simon's Taxes* **D9.447**.
Derivation—TA 1988 s 719(4).
HMRC Manuals—Savings and Investment Manual SAIM4290 (successive transfers with unrealised interest in default).
Modification—ITA 2007 Sch 2 para 127 (this section does not apply if the transferor's acquisition was before 28 February 1986).

662 New securities issued with extra return: special rules about payments

(1) In the case of a transfer treated as made under section 649 (new securities issued with extra return), the amount of the payment treated as made under section 632(1) (payment on transfer with accrued interest) is not determined under section 632(2) to (5).

(2) Instead, that amount depends on whether under the issue arrangements the person to whom the new securities are issued accounts to the issuer separately—

    (a) for the extra return, and

    (b) for the rest of the issue price.

(3) If the person does account for them separately, the amount of the payment is the amount of the extra return separately accounted for.

(4) If the person does not account for them separately, the amount of the payment is an amount equal to—

$$I \times \frac{A}{B}$$

where—

    I is the interest payable on the new securities on the first interest payment day after the new issue day ("the payment day"),

    A is the number of days in the relevant period, and

    B is the number of days in the period beginning with the first day of the relevant period and ending with the payment day.

(5) Subsection (4) is subject to section 659 (transfers with or without accrued interest: interest in default).

(6) In this section "the extra return", "the new issue day", "new securities" and "the relevant period" have the same meaning as in section 649.

Commentary—*Simon's Taxes* **D9.425**.

Derivation—TA 1988 s 726A.

HMRC Manuals—Savings and Investment Manual SAIM4260 (special calculation for payments).

663 Transfers without accrued interest to makers of manufactured payments

(1) This section applies if—

    (a) the manufactured payments conditions are met (see section 647(2)), and

    (b) the nominal value of the securities subject to the seller's contract is less than that of the securities transferred to the seller.

(2) The amount of the payment treated as made to the seller under section 633 on the transfer of the securities to the seller is reduced.

(3) The reduction is by so much of that amount as is attributable to securities ("the matched securities") of a nominal value equal to that of the securities subject to the seller's contract.

(4) If there is more than one transfer of securities to the seller, those transferred to the seller earlier are treated as the matched securities before those transferred later.

(5) In this section "the seller" and "the seller's contract" have the same meaning as in section 647.

(6) For cases where subsection (1)(b) does not apply, see section 647(3) (under which the seller is treated as an excluded transferee).

Commentary—*Simon's Taxes* **D9.431**.

Derivation—TA 1988 s 715(6) and (7).

HMRC Manuals—Savings and Investment Manual SAIM4220 (other excluded persons: makers of manufactured payments).

664 Foreign currency securities: sterling equivalent of payments on transfers

(1) The sterling equivalent of the amount of the payment treated as made on a transfer of securities is determined in accordance with this section if interest on the securities is payable in a currency other than sterling ("a foreign currency").

(2) If the payment is determined under section 632(3), 633(3) or 662(3) (transfers under an arrangement by which interest is accounted for separately), the amount of the payment depends on whether the sterling equivalent of the interest separately accounted for is shown in an agreement for transfer.

(3) If the sterling equivalent is so shown, the amount of the payment is taken to be that sterling equivalent.

(4) If the sterling equivalent is not so shown, the amount is taken to be the sterling equivalent on the settlement day of the interest separately accounted for.

(5) If the amount of the payment treated as made is determined under any other provision (except section 660 (transfers with unrealised interest: interest in default)), the amount is taken to be its sterling equivalent on the settlement day.

(6) For the purposes of this section, the sterling equivalent of an amount or value in a foreign currency is to be calculated by reference to the London closing rate of exchange for the day concerned.

Commentary—*Simon's Taxes* **D9.413**.

Derivation—TA 1988 ss 713(7), (8), 716(6) and 726A(5).

HMRC Manuals—Savings and Investment Manual SAIM4310 (foreign securities: translation into sterling).

665 Foreign currency securities: unrealised interest payable in foreign currency

(1) This section applies if unrealised interest is payable in a currency other than sterling ("a foreign currency").

(2) For the purposes of section 631(1) (amount of accrued income profits where settlement day outside interest period) the amount of the unrealised interest is taken to be its sterling equivalent on the settlement day.

(3) For the purposes of sections 660 (transfers with unrealised interest: interest in default) and 661 (successive transfers with unrealised interest in default), the value on any day of the right to receive unrealised interest is the sterling equivalent on that day of that value in the foreign currency.

(4) For the purposes of those sections unrealised interest received in a foreign currency is taken to be the sterling equivalent on the day of receipt of the amount received.

(5) For the purposes of this section, the sterling equivalent of an amount or value in a foreign currency is to be calculated by reference to the London closing rate of exchange for the day concerned.

Derivation—TA 1988 ss 713(7), (8), 716(6) and 726A(5).
HMRC Manuals—Savings and Investment Manual SAIM4310 (foreign securities: translation into sterling).
SAIM4350 (unrealised interest payable in a foreign currency).

Nominees and trustees

666 Certain transfers by or to nominees or trustees treated as made by or to others

(1) Transfers of securities by or to a person as nominee for another person ("A") are treated for the purposes of this Chapter as transfers by or to A.

(2) Transfers of securities by or to a person ("T") as trustee for another person ("B") are treated for the purposes of this Chapter as transfers by or to B if B is absolutely entitled as against T.

(3) For the purposes of subsection (2) where T is the transferor, B is absolutely entitled as against T if immediately before the transfer B has the exclusive right to direct how the securities are to be dealt with.

(4) For the purposes of subsection (2) where T is the transferee, B is absolutely entitled as against T if immediately after the transfer B has that exclusive right.

(5) For the purposes of subsections (3) and (4), a right to direct how securities are to be dealt with is treated as an exclusive right despite being subject to satisfying any outstanding charge, lien or other right of the trustee to resort to the securities for payment of duty, taxes, costs or other outgoings.

(6) Subsection (1) applies to a transfer of securities by or to a person as nominee for two or more persons as it applies to a transfer of securities by or to a person as nominee for one person, taking the references to A as references to the two or more persons.

(7) This section applies to a transfer of securities by or to a person as trustee for two or more persons as it applies to a transfer of securities as trustee for one person, taking—

    (a) the references to B as references to the two or more persons, and

    (b) the references to B being absolutely entitled as references to the two or more persons being jointly absolutely entitled.

(8) The fact that a person is an infant or otherwise lacks legal capacity is to be disregarded in determining for the purposes of this section whether the person is absolutely entitled as against T.

Commentary—*Simon's Taxes* D9.403, D9.432.
Derivation—TA 1988 s 720.
HMRC Manuals—Savings and Investment Manual SAIM4320 (nominees and bare trusts).

667 Trustees' accrued income profits treated as settlement income

(1) If the trustees of a settlement are treated as making qualifying accrued income profits, those profits are to be taken to be income arising under the settlement for the purposes of Chapter 5 of Part 5 of ITTOIA 2005 (settlements: amounts treated as income of settlor).

(2) Subsection (3) applies if the trustees of a settlement—

    (a) are non-UK resident or domiciled outside the United Kingdom throughout a tax year in which an interest period or part of an interest period falls, and

    (b) would have been treated as making an amount or an additional amount of qualifying accrued income profits in the interest period if the trustees had been UK resident or domiciled in the United Kingdom during a part of each such tax year.

(3) The amount or additional amount of qualifying accrued income profits that the trustees would have been treated as making is to be taken to be income arising under the settlement for the purposes of Chapter 5 of Part 5 of ITTOIA 2005.

(4) In this section—

    (a) "qualifying accrued income profits" means accrued income profits which are treated as made—

        (i) under section 628(5), or

        (ii) under section 630(2) in respect of a transfer of variable rate securities, and

    (b) in any case where there are no trustees of a settlement, references to such trustees are to any persons entitled to securities comprised in the settlement.

(5) In the case of qualifying accrued income profits within subsection (4)(a)(ii)—

    (a) the reference in subsection (2)(a) to an interest period is to the period—

        (i) beginning with the day after the last day of the only or last interest period of the securities, and

        (ii) ending with the settlement day, and

    (b) the reference in subsection (2)(b) to making qualifying accrued income profits in the interest period is to be read as making them in the tax year in which settlement day falls.

Commentary—*Simon's Taxes* D9.432.

HMRC Manuals—Savings and Investment Manual SAIM4320 (trusts where the settler may benefit).

Relief where transfer proceeds unremittable

668 Relief for unremittable transfer proceeds: general

(1) This section applies if—

    (*a*)   a person is liable for income tax on accrued income profits,

    (*b*)   the profits are calculated by reference to payments treated as made to the person in an interest period,

    (*c*)   the payments are so treated as a result of the person making transfers of foreign securities of a particular kind, and

    (*d*)   the proceeds of the transfers are unremittable in the tax year.

(2) If the person makes a claim for relief under this section—

    (*a*)   the profits are reduced by the amount of the payments treated as made to the person, or

    (*b*)   if that amount exceeds the profits, the profits are reduced to nil.

(3) But see section 670 (withdrawal of relief).

(4) In this section and section 669 "foreign securities" means securities which are situated outside the United Kingdom.

(5) For the purposes of this section and sections 669 and 670, proceeds of transfers of foreign securities are unremittable in relation to a person if the person is prevented from transferring them to the United Kingdom because of—

    (*a*)   the laws of the territory where the securities are situated,

    (*b*)   executive action of its government, or

    (*c*)   the impossibility of obtaining there currency that could be transferred to the United Kingdom.

(6) For the purposes of this section the place where securities are situated is to be determined in accordance with sections 275(1) and (2)(*b*) and 275C of TCGA 1992.

(7) Any claim under this section must be made [not more than 4 years after the end of][1] the tax year for which the profits would be chargeable to tax if no claim were made.

(8) A person's personal representatives may make any claim under this section which the person might have made.

Commentary—*Simon's Taxes* **D9.445**.

HMRC Manuals—Savings and Investment Manual SAIM4340 (relief for unremittable transfers).

Amendments—[1]   In sub-s (7), words substituted by FA 2008 s 118, Sch 39 paras 54, 61 with effect from 1 April 2010 (by virtue of SI 2009/403 art 2(2)), subject to transitional provisions in SI 2009/403 art 10(2) (where art 10 applies, the appointed day is 1 April 2012).

669 Relief for unremittable transfer proceeds: section 630 profits

(1) This section applies if—

    (*a*)   a person is liable for income tax on accrued income profits within section 630(2) (making accrued income profits: settlement day outside interest period),

    (*b*)   the person is so liable as a result of making transfers of foreign securities of a particular kind, and

    (*c*)   the proceeds of the transfers are unremittable in the tax year.

(2) If the person makes a claim for relief under this section the profits are reduced to nil.

(3) But see section 670 (withdrawal of relief).

(4) Any claim under this section must be made [not more than 4 years after the end of][1] the tax year for which the profits would be chargeable to tax if no claim were made.

(5) A person's personal representatives may make any claim under this section which the person might have made.

Commentary—*Simon's Taxes* **D9.445**.

HMRC Manuals—Savings and Investment Manual SAIM4340 (relief for unremittable transfers).

Amendments—[1]   In sub-s (4), words substituted by FA 2008 s 118, Sch 39 paras 54, 62 with effect from 1 April 2010 (by virtue of SI 2009/403 art 2(2)), subject to transitional provisions in SI 2009/403 art 10(2) (where art 10 applies, the appointed day is 1 April 2012).

670 Withdrawal of relief

(1) This section applies if—

    (*a*)   a claim under section 668(2) or 669(2) has been made in relation to profits, and

    (*b*)   the proceeds of the transfers cease to be unremittable.

(2) The claimant is treated as making accrued income profits of an amount equal to the reduction under that section.

(3) If the claimant has died, the claimant's personal representatives are so treated.

[Individuals to whom remittance basis applies

670A Individuals to whom remittance basis applies

(1) This section applies if—

    (*a*)   accrued income profits are made by an individual as a result of a transfer of foreign securities, and

(b) section 809B, 809D or 809E (remittance basis) applies to the individual for the tax year in which the profits are made.

(2) Treat the accrued income profits as relevant foreign income of the individual.

(3) For the purposes of Chapter A1 of Part 14 (remittance basis)—

    (a) if the individual is the transferor—

        (i) treat any consideration for the transfer as deriving from the accrued income profits, and

        (ii) if on the transfer the individual does not receive consideration of an amount equal to (or exceeding) the market value of the securities, treat the securities as deriving from the accrued income profits, and

    (b) if the individual is the transferee, treat the securities as deriving from the accrued income profits.

(4) For the purposes of this section securities are "foreign" if income from them would be relevant foreign income.]¹

Commentary—*Simon's Taxes* **D9.439**.

HMRC Manuals—Savings and Investment Manual SAIM4380 (remittance basis).

Amendments—¹   Section 670A inserted by FA 2008 s 25, Sch 7 para 159 with effect in relation to transfers of securities where the settlement day is on or after 6 April 2008.

Interpretation

671 Meaning of "interest"

(1) In this Chapter "interest" includes dividends and any other return (however described).

(2) But it does not include a return consisting of the difference between the amount payable on a security's redemption and its issue price.

Commentary—*Simon's Taxes* **D9.404**.

Derivation—TA 1988 s 711(9).

HMRC Manuals—Savings and Investment Manual SAIM4070 ('interest' excludes premiums and discounts).

672 Meaning of "interest payment day"

(1) In this Chapter "interest payment day", in relation to securities of any kind, means a day on which interest on those securities is payable.

(2) If a particular payment of interest may be made on one of a number of days, the first of them is the interest payment day.

Commentary—*Simon's Taxes* **D9.404**.

Derivation—TA 1988 s 711(2).

HMRC Manuals—Savings and Investment Manual SAIM4070 (interest payment day).

673 Meaning of "interest period"

(1) The general rule is that for the purposes of this Chapter—

    (a) the first interest period of securities of any kind begins with the day after that on which those securities are first issued and ends with the first interest payment day or, if it is earlier, the expiry of 12 months, and

    (b) any other interest period of those securities begins with the day after the last day of their previous interest period and ends with the next interest payment day or, if it is earlier, the expiry of 12 months.

(2) Subsection (1) is subject to subsections (3) and (4).

(3) The last interest period of securities of any kind ends with the last interest payment day for those securities, unless subsection (4) applies.

(4) An interest period of securities of any kind in which either of the events specified in subsection (5) occurs is treated as ending on the day on which it would have ended apart from that event.

(5) The events are—

    (a) a conversion of those securities, and

    (b) if those securities are gilt-edged securities, the exchange of those securities for strips of those securities.

(6) In this section "strip" has the meaning given by section 444 of ITTOIA 2005.

(7) See also section 667(5) (construction of reference to "interest period" in section 667(2)).

Commentary—*Simon's Taxes* **D9.404**.

HMRC Manuals—Savings and Investment Manual SAIM4070 (meaning of "interest period", with example).

SAIM4160 (examples of transfers with and without accrued interest).

674 Meaning of "the settlement day"

(1) For the purposes of this Chapter the settlement day for a transfer of securities in accordance with the rules of a recognised market is—

    (a) the day on which the transferee agrees to settle, or

    (b) if the transferee may settle on one of a number of days, the day on which settlement actually occurs.

(2) The settlement day for a transfer of securities which is not in accordance with such rules is determined in accordance with subsection (3), (4) or (6) (and see also section 649(6): settlement day where new securities issued with extra return).

(3) If—

    (*a*) the consideration for the transfer is money alone, and

    (*b*) the transferee agrees to pay the whole of it on or before the first interest payment day after an agreement for the transfer is made,

the settlement day is the day on which the transferee agrees to make the payment or, if payment may be made on one of a number of days, or on a number of different days, the latest of them.

(4) If—

    (*a*) there is no consideration for the transfer, or

    (*b*) the transfer is a transfer because of a provision specified in subsection (5),

the settlement day is the day on which the securities are transferred.

(5) The provisions are—

    section 620(1)(*b*) or (*c*) (conversion, or redemption of variable rate securities),

    section 648(1) or (3) (exchanges relating to strips of gilt-edged securities),

    section 650 (trading stock appropriations etc),

    section 651 (owner becoming entitled to securities as trustee), and

    section 652 (securities ceasing to be held on charitable trusts).

(6) If neither subsection (3) nor (4) applies, the settlement day is such day as an officer of Revenue and Customs decides.

[(7) On any appeal that is notified to the tribunal, the jurisdiction of the tribunal includes jurisdiction to affirm or replace such a decision.]¹

Commentary—*Simon's Taxes* **D9.404**.

Derivation—TA 1988 s 712.

HMRC Manuals—Savings and Investment Manual SAIM4160 (examples of transfers with and without accrued interest).

Amendments—¹ Sub-s (7) substituted by the Transfer of Tribunal Functions and Revenue and Customs Appeals Order, SI 2009/56 art 3, Sch 1 para 454 with effect from 1 April 2009.

675 The holding of securities

(1) For the purposes of this Chapter, a person holds securities—

    (*a*) at a particular time if the person is entitled to them at that time, and

    (*b*) on a particular day if the person is entitled to them throughout that day or becomes and does not cease to be entitled to them on that day.

(2) A person acquires securities when the person becomes entitled to them.

(3) If a Scottish partnership carries on a trade or business—

    (*a*) any partnership dealings are treated as dealings by the partners and not by the partnership as such, and

    (*b*) the partners are treated as being entitled to securities held by the partnership.

Commentary—*Simon's Taxes* **D9.404**.

Derivation—TA 1988 s 710(7), (8) and (10).

HMRC Manuals—Savings and Investment Manual SAIM4090 (meaning of "holdings").

676 Nominal value of securities: general

(1) If the interest on securities is expressed to be payable by reference to a given value, for the purposes of this Chapter their nominal value is that value.

(2) In any other case, the nominal value of securities for those purposes is their price when they were issued.

(3) See section 677 if the nominal value of the securities is expressed in a currency other than sterling.

Commentary—*Simon's Taxes* **D9.404**.

Derivation—TA 1988 s 710(11).

HMRC Manuals—Savings and Investment Manual SAIM4100 (definitions: nominal value).

677 Nominal value: foreign currency securities

(1) If the nominal value of securities is expressed in a currency other than sterling ("a foreign currency"), for the purposes of this Chapter their nominal value on any day is taken to be the sterling equivalent on that day of that value.

(2) For the purposes of this section, the sterling equivalent of a value in a foreign currency is to be calculated by reference to the London closing rate of exchange for the day concerned.

Commentary—*Simon's Taxes* **D9.404**.

Derivation—TA 1988 s 710(12).

HMRC Manuals—Savings and Investment Manual SAIM4310 (foreign securities: translation into sterling).

CHAPTER 3

EXEMPTIONS RELATING TO INTEREST ON SECURITIES

678 Exemptions relating to interest on securities: preliminary

(1) This Chapter confers exemptions relating to interest on securities.

(2) Expressions used in this Chapter and in Chapter 2 have the same meaning as in that Chapter.

(3) Accordingly, for the meanings of the following expressions see the sections indicated—

"interest" see section 671,
"interest payment day" see section 672,
"interest period" see section 673,
"makes accrued income losses" see section 628(6),
"securities" see section 619,
"transfer with unrealised interest" see section 625(1),
"transferee" see section 621,
"transfer" see section 620, and
"unrealised interest" see section 625(2).

(4) Section 666 (certain transfers by or to nominees or trustees treated as made by or to others) applies for the purposes of this Chapter as it applies for the purposes of Chapter 2.

HMRC Manuals—Savings and Investment Manual SAIM4350 (exemptions from income tax on interest on AIS securities).

679 Interest on securities involving accrued income losses: general

(1) This section applies if—
  (a) a person is liable for income tax on interest on securities of any kind which is due at the end of an interest period of the securities,
  (b) in that period accrued income losses are made as a result of transfers of those securities, and
  (c) the period ends with an interest payment day.
(2) No liability to income tax arises in respect of the interest to the extent that it does not exceed the losses.
(3) If, apart from this subsection, a person would be entitled to the exemption under this section in more than one tax year, the person is so entitled only in the tax year in which the interest period ends.
(4) For cases where the interest period does not end with an interest payment day, see section 637 (accrued income losses treated as payments in next interest period).

Commentary—*Simon's Taxes* D9.421.
HMRC Manuals—Savings and Investment Manual SAIM4120 (relief for accrued income losses).
SAIM4350 (accrued income losses).

680 Interest on securities involving accrued income losses: foreign trustees

(1) This section applies if—
  (a) the trustees of a settlement are non-UK resident or domiciled outside the United Kingdom throughout a tax year in which an interest period or part of an interest period of securities falls,
  (b) the trustees' income is or includes interest from those securities,
  (c) the interest falls due at the end of that interest period, and
  (d) had the trustees been UK resident, or domiciled in the United Kingdom, during a part of each such tax year the interest would have been wholly or partly exempt from income tax under section 679.
(2) No liability to income tax arises as a result of Chapter 5 of Part 5 of ITTOIA 2005 (settlements: amounts treated as income of settlor) in respect of so much of the interest as would have been exempt from income tax under section 679.
(3) For cases where the interest period does not end with an interest payment day, see section 637 (accrued income losses treated as payments in next interest period).

Commentary—*Simon's Taxes* D9.432.
HMRC Manuals—Savings and Investment Manual SAIM4350 (accrued income losses of foreign trustees),

681 Unrealised interest received by transferee after transfer

(1) This section applies if—
  (a) securities are transferred with unrealised interest,
  (b) the transferee is not an excluded transferee in relation to the transfer for the purposes of Chapter 2 (see sections 638 to 647),
  (c) the transferee receives some or all of the unrealised interest, and
  (d) apart from this section, the transferee would be liable to income tax on the unrealised interest.
(2) No liability to income tax arises in respect of the unrealised interest received by the transferee, unless conditions A and B are met.
(3) Condition A is that section 660 (transfers with unrealised interest: interest in default) applies on the transfer.
(4) Condition B is that the unrealised interest received by the transferee exceeds the residual value of the interest.
(5) In this section "the residual value of the interest" means—
  (a) the value on the day of the transfer of the right to receive the unrealised interest, less
  (b) the total amount of any of that unrealised interest received previously by the transferee.
(6) If conditions A and B are met, no liability to income tax arises in respect of the unrealised interest to the extent that it does not exceed the residual value of the interest.
(7) Section 665 (foreign currency securities: unrealised interest payable in foreign currency) applies for the purposes of this section as it applies for the purposes of sections 660 and 661.

Commentary—*Simon's Taxes* **D9.448**.
HMRC Manuals—Savings and Investment Manual SAIM4290 (transfers with unrealised interest).
SAIM4350 (Unrealised interest received after transfer).
SAIM4170 (payments on transfers with unrealised interest).
Modification—ITA 2007 Sch 2 para 128 (modification of this section if the transfer of securities within sub-s (1)(*a*) above occurred before 19 March 1986).

[PART 12A
SALE AND LEASE-BACK ETC]

[CHAPTER 1

PAYMENTS CONNECTED WITH TRANSFERRED LAND][1]

Amendments—[1]   Chapter 1 (ss 681A–681AN) inserted by TIOPA 2010 s 368, Sch 4 paras 1, 2. TIOPA 2010 has effect for corporation tax purposes for accounting periods ending on or after 1 April 2010, for income and capital gains tax purposes for the tax year 2010–11 and subsequent tax years, and for petroleum revenue tax purposes for chargeable periods beginning on or after 1 July 2010.

[Overview

681A Overview

This Chapter provides that in certain circumstances where a transfer is made regarding land, and the transferor or an associate becomes liable to make a payment connected with the land, income tax relief for the payment is restricted.][1]

Amendments—[1]   Sections 681A–681AN inserted by TIOPA 2010 s 368, Sch 4 paras 1, 2. TIOPA 2010 has effect for corporation tax purposes for accounting periods ending on or after 1 April 2010, for income and capital gains tax purposes for the tax year 2010–11 and subsequent tax years, and for petroleum revenue tax purposes for chargeable periods beginning on or after 1 July 2010.

[Application of the Chapter

681AA Transferor or associate becomes liable for payment of rent

(1) Section 681AD has effect if—
  (*a*) land, or an estate or interest in land, is transferred,
  (*b*) the transferor, or a person associated with the transferor, becomes liable to make a payment of rent under a lease of the land or part of it, and
  (*c*) a deduction by way of relevant income tax relief (see section 681AC) is allowed for the payment.
(2) Section 681AE has effect if—
  (*a*) land, or an estate or interest in land, is transferred,
  (*b*) the transferor, or a person associated with the transferor, becomes liable to make a payment of rent under a lease of the land or part of it, and
  (*c*) a relevant deduction from earnings (see section 681AC) is allowed for the payment.
(3) The reference in subsection (1)(*a*) or (2)(*a*) to a transfer of an estate or interest in land includes a reference to any of the following—
  (*a*) the granting of a lease or another transaction involving the creation of a new estate or interest in the land,
  (*b*) the transfer of the lessee's interest under a lease by surrender or forfeiture of the lease, and
  (*c*) a transaction or series of transactions affecting land or an estate or interest in land, such that some person is the owner or one of the owners before and after the transaction or transactions but another person becomes or ceases to be one of the owners.
(4) In relation to a transaction or series of transactions mentioned in subsection (3)(*c*), a person is to be regarded as a transferor for the purposes of this Chapter if the person—
  (*a*) is an owner before the transaction or transactions, and
  (*b*) is not the sole owner afterwards.
(5) The liability mentioned in subsection (1)(*b*) or (2)(*b*) is one resulting from—
  (*a*) a lease of the land or part of it granted (at the time of the transfer or later) by the transferee to the transferor, or
  (*b*) another transaction or series of transactions affecting the land or an estate or interest in it.
(6) The liability mentioned in subsection (1)(*b*) or (2)(*b*) is one arising at the time of the transfer or later.
(7) The reference in subsection (1)(*a*) or (2)(*a*) to a transfer does not include a transfer on or before 14 April 1964.][1]

Commentary—*Simon's Taxes* **B5.247**.
HMRC Manuals—Business Income Manual BIM61310 (meaning of transfer).
Amendments—[1]   Sections 681A–681AN inserted by TIOPA 2010 s 368, Sch 4 paras 1, 2. TIOPA 2010 has effect for corporation tax purposes for accounting periods ending on or after 1 April 2010, for income and capital gains tax purposes for the tax year 2010–11 and subsequent tax years, and for petroleum revenue tax purposes for chargeable periods beginning on or after 1 July 2010.

[681AB Transferor or associate becomes liable for payment other than rent

(1) Section 681AD has effect if—

(*a*) land, or an estate or interest in land, is transferred,

(*b*) the transferor, or a person associated with the transferor, becomes liable to make a payment which is not rent under a lease but is otherwise connected with the land or part of it (whether it is a payment under a rentcharge or under some other transaction), and

(*c*) a deduction by way of relevant income tax relief (see section 681AC) is allowed for the payment.

(2) Section 681AE has effect if—

(*a*) land, or an estate or interest in land, is transferred,

(*b*) the transferor, or a person associated with the transferor, becomes liable to make a payment which is not rent under a lease but is otherwise connected with the land or part of it (whether it is a payment under a rentcharge or under some other transaction), and

(*c*) a relevant deduction from earnings (see section 681AC) is allowed for the payment.

(3) The reference in subsection (1)(*a*) or (2)(*a*) to a transfer of an estate or interest in land includes a reference to any of the following—

(*a*) the granting of a lease or another transaction involving the creation of a new estate or interest in the land,

(*b*) the transfer of the lessee's interest under a lease by surrender or forfeiture of the lease, and

(*c*) a transaction or series of transactions affecting land or an estate or interest in land, such that some person is the owner or one of the owners before and after the transaction or transactions but another person becomes or ceases to be one of the owners.

(4) In relation to a transaction or series of transactions mentioned in subsection (3)(*c*), a person is to be regarded as a transferor for the purposes of this Chapter if the person—

(*a*) is an owner before the transaction or transactions, and

(*b*) is not the sole owner afterwards.

(5) The liability mentioned in subsection (1)(*b*) or (2)(*b*) is one resulting from a transaction or series of transactions affecting the land or an estate or interest in it.

(6) The liability mentioned in subsection (1)(*b*) or (2)(*b*) is one arising at the time of the transfer or later.

(7) The reference in subsection (1)(*a*) or (2)(*a*) to a transfer does not include a transfer on or before 14 April 1964.][1]

Commentary—*Simon's Taxes* **B5.247**.

HMRC Manuals—Business Income Manual BIM61310 (extended meaning of transfer).

Amendments—[1]   Sections 681A–681AN inserted by TIOPA 2010 s 368, Sch 4 paras 1, 2. TIOPA 2010 has effect for corporation tax purposes for accounting periods ending on or after 1 April 2010, for income and capital gains tax purposes for the tax year 2010–11 and subsequent tax years, and for petroleum revenue tax purposes for chargeable periods beginning on or after 1 July 2010.

[681AC Relevant income tax relief and relevant deduction from earnings

(1) For the purposes of this Chapter each of the following is a deduction by way of relevant income tax relief—

(*a*) a deduction in calculating profits or losses of a trade, profession or vocation for income tax purposes,

(*b*) a deduction in calculating the profits of a UK property business for income tax purposes, and

(*c*) a deduction in calculating any loss for which relief is given under section 152 (losses from miscellaneous transactions), or in calculating profits or other income or gains chargeable to income tax under or by virtue of any provision to which section 1016 applies.

(2) For the purposes of this Chapter each of the following is a relevant deduction from earnings—

(*a*) a deduction under section 336 of ITEPA 2003 (expenses), and

(*b*) a deduction from earnings in calculating losses in an employment for income tax purposes.][1]

Commentary—*Simon's Taxes* **B5.247**.

Amendments—[1]   Sections 681A–681AN inserted by TIOPA 2010 s 368, Sch 4 paras 1, 2. TIOPA 2010 has effect for corporation tax purposes for accounting periods ending on or after 1 April 2010, for income and capital gains tax purposes for the tax year 2010–11 and subsequent tax years, and for petroleum revenue tax purposes for chargeable periods beginning on or after 1 July 2010.

[Relief: restriction and carrying forward]

681AD Relevant income tax relief: deduction not to exceed commercial rent

(1) The rules in subsection (3) apply to the calculation of the deduction by way of relevant income tax relief allowed in a relevant period—

(*a*) for the non-excluded element of the payment within section 681AA(1) or 681AB(1), or

(*b*) if there are two or more such payments, for the non-excluded elements of those payments.

(2) For the purposes of this section—

(*a*) in relation to a deduction within section 681AC(1)(*a*) "relevant period" means—

(i) a period of account of the trade, profession or vocation concerned, or

   (ii) if no accounts of the trade, profession or vocation are drawn up for a period, the basis period of a tax year,

   (*b*) in relation to a deduction within section 681AC(1)(*b*) or (*c*) "relevant period" means—

      (i) a period of account of the business or person concerned, or

      (ii) if no accounts of the business are drawn up for a period or the person does not draw up accounts for a period, a tax year, and

   (*c*) the non-excluded element of a payment is the element of the payment not excluded under section 681AI (service charges etc).

(3) The rules are—

Rule 1—meaning of amount E

For any relevant period, amount E (which may be nil) is the expense or total expenses to be brought, in accordance with generally accepted accounting practice, into account in the period in respect of—

   (*a*) the non-excluded element of the payment, or

   (*b*) the non-excluded elements of the payments.

Rule 2—calculations

For every relevant period—

   (*a*) calculate the total of amount E for the period and amount E for every previous relevant period ending on or after the date of the transfer mentioned in section 681AA(1)(*a*) or 681AB(1)(*a*),

   (*b*) calculate the total of the deductions by way of relevant income tax relief for every previous relevant period ending on or after the date of that transfer, and

   (*c*) subtract the total at (*b*) from the total at (*a*) to give the cumulative unrelieved expenses for the period.

Rule 3—meaning of post-spread period

A relevant period is a post-spread period if for that relevant period, and every later relevant period, there are no payments within section 681AA(1) or 681AB(1).

Rule 4—the deduction allowed in a relevant period

If a relevant period is not a post-spread period, the deduction allowed for the period is equal to the cumulative unrelieved expenses for the period, but is the commercial rent for the period if that is less (see section 681AJ or 681AK).

Rule 5—relevant periods in which no deduction allowed

If a relevant period is a post-spread period, no deduction is allowed for the period.]¹

Commentary—*Simon's Taxes* **B5.247**.

HMRC Manuals—Business Income Manual BIM61315 (restriction to the allowable deduction and the carry forward of disallowed amounts).

Amendments—¹   Sections 681A–681AN inserted by TIOPA 2010 s 368, Sch 4 paras 1, 2. TIOPA 2010 has effect for corporation tax purposes for accounting periods ending on or after 1 April 2010, for income and capital gains tax purposes for the tax year 2010–11 and subsequent tax years, and for petroleum revenue tax purposes for chargeable periods beginning on or after 1 July 2010.

[Certain deductions from earnings: restriction and carrying forward of relief

681AE Deduction from earnings not to exceed commercial rent

(1) Subsection (3) applies to the calculation of the relevant deduction from earnings allowed for the non-excluded element of the payment within section 681AA(2) or 681AB(2).

(2) For the purposes of this section the non-excluded element of a payment is the element of the payment not excluded under section 681AI (service charges etc).

(3) The deduction must not exceed the commercial rent for the period for which the payment is made (see section 681AJ or 681AK).]¹

Commentary—*Simon's Taxes* **B5.247**.

Amendments—¹   Sections 681A–681AN inserted by TIOPA 2010 s 368, Sch 4 paras 1, 2. TIOPA 2010 has effect for corporation tax purposes for accounting periods ending on or after 1 April 2010, for income and capital gains tax purposes for the tax year 2010–11 and subsequent tax years, and for petroleum revenue tax purposes for chargeable periods beginning on or after 1 July 2010.

[681AF Carrying forward parts of payments

(1) This section applies if—

   (*a*) section 681AE has effect, and

   (*b*) conditions A and B are met.

(2) Condition A is that under section 681AE part of a payment which would otherwise be allowed as a relevant deduction from earnings is not allowed.

(3) Condition B is that one or more later payments are made, by the transferor or a person associated with the transferor, under—

   (*a*) the lease (if section 681AE has effect because of section 681AA(2)), or

   (*b*) the rentcharge or other transaction mentioned in section 681AB(2)(*b*) (if section 681AE has effect because of section 681AB(2)).

(4) The part of the payment mentioned in subsection (2) may be carried forward and treated for the purposes of a relevant deduction from earnings as if it were made—

   (*a*) when the next of the later payments is made, and

(*b*) for the period for which that later payment is made.

(5) So far as a part of a payment carried forward under this section is not allowed as a relevant deduction from earnings, it may be carried forward again under this section.]¹

Commentary—*Simon's Taxes* **B5.247**.

Amendments—¹   Sections 681A–681AN inserted by TIOPA 2010 s 368, Sch 4 paras 1, 2. TIOPA 2010 has effect for corporation tax purposes for accounting periods ending on or after 1 April 2010, for income and capital gains tax purposes for the tax year 2010–11 and subsequent tax years, and for petroleum revenue tax purposes for chargeable periods beginning on or after 1 July 2010.

[681AG Aggregation and apportionment of payments

(1) This section applies for the purposes of section 681AE.

(2) If more than one payment is made for the same period, the payments must be taken together.

(3) If payments are made for periods which overlap—
   (*a*) the payments must be apportioned, and
   (*b*) the apportioned payments which belong to the common part of the overlapping periods must be taken together.

(4) References in subsections (2) and (3) to payments include references to parts of payments which under section 681AF are treated as if made later than they were made.]¹

Commentary—*Simon's Taxes* **B5.247**.

Amendments—¹   Sections 681A–681AN inserted by TIOPA 2010 s 368, Sch 4 paras 1, 2. TIOPA 2010 has effect for corporation tax purposes for accounting periods ending on or after 1 April 2010, for income and capital gains tax purposes for the tax year 2010–11 and subsequent tax years, and for petroleum revenue tax purposes for chargeable periods beginning on or after 1 July 2010.

[681AH Payments made for later periods

(1) This section applies for the purposes of sections 681AE to 681AG.

(2) For the purposes of this section the relevant year (in relation to a payment) is the year which begins with the date it is made.

(3) If a payment is made for a period all of which is after the relevant year, it must be treated as made for the relevant year.

(4) If a payment is made for a period part of which is after the relevant year, it must be treated as if a corresponding part of it was made for the relevant year (and no part for a later period).]¹

Commentary—*Simon's Taxes* **B5.247**.

Amendments—¹   Sections 681A–681AN inserted by TIOPA 2010 s 368, Sch 4 paras 1, 2. TIOPA 2010 has effect for corporation tax purposes for accounting periods ending on or after 1 April 2010, for income and capital gains tax purposes for the tax year 2010–11 and subsequent tax years, and for petroleum revenue tax purposes for chargeable periods beginning on or after 1 July 2010.

[Interpretation etc

681AI Exclusion of service charges etc

(1) This section applies for the purposes of sections 681AD and 681AE.

(2) A payment must be excluded so far as it is in respect of any of the following—
   (*a*) services,
   (*b*) the use of relevant assets, and
   (*c*) rates usually borne by the tenant.

(3) The amount excluded must be just and reasonable.

(4) If a lease or agreement contains provisions fixing the payments or parts of payments which are in respect of services or the use of assets, those provisions are not conclusive.

(5) A relevant asset is any description of property or rights other than land or an interest in land.]¹

Commentary—*Simon's Taxes* **B5.247**.

HMRC Manuals—Business Income Manual BIM61315 (restriction to the allowable deduction and the carry forward of disallowed amounts).

Amendments—¹   Sections 681A–681AN inserted by TIOPA 2010 s 368, Sch 4 paras 1, 2. TIOPA 2010 has effect for corporation tax purposes for accounting periods ending on or after 1 April 2010, for income and capital gains tax purposes for the tax year 2010–11 and subsequent tax years, and for petroleum revenue tax purposes for chargeable periods beginning on or after 1 July 2010.

[681AJ Commercial rent: comparison with rent under a lease

(1) Subsection (3) applies—
   (*a*) for the purpose of making a comparison under rule 4 of section 681AD(3) if section 681AD has effect because of section 681AA(1), and
   (*b*) for the purpose of making a comparison under section 681AE(3) if section 681AE has effect because of section 681AA(2).

(2) In this section "the actual lease" means the lease mentioned in section 681AA(1)(*b*) or (2)(*b*).

(3) The commercial rent is the rent which might be expected to be paid under a lease, of the land in respect of which the payment mentioned in section 681AA(1)(*b*) or (2)(*b*) is made, which—
   (*a*) was negotiated in the open market when the actual lease was created,
   (*b*) is of the same duration as the actual lease,

(c) is subject to the terms and conditions of the actual lease as respects liability for maintenance and repairs, and

(d) provides for rent payable at uniform intervals and at an appropriate rate.

(4) Rent is payable at an appropriate rate if—

     (a) it is payable at a uniform rate, or

     (b) in a case where the rent payable under the actual lease is rent at a progressive rate (and such that the amount of rent payable for a year is never less than the amount payable for a previous year), it progresses by gradations proportionate to those provided by the actual lease.][1]

Commentary—*Simon's Taxes* **B5.247**.

HMRC Manuals—Business Income Manual BIM61305 (definition of 'commercial rent').

Amendments—[1] Sections 681A–681AN inserted by TIOPA 2010 s 368, Sch 4 paras 1, 2. TIOPA 2010 has effect for corporation tax purposes for accounting periods ending on or after 1 April 2010, for income and capital gains tax purposes for the tax year 2010–11 and subsequent tax years, and for petroleum revenue tax purposes for chargeable periods beginning on or after 1 July 2010.

[681AK Commercial rent: comparison with payments other than rent

(1) Subsection (2) applies—

     (a) for the purpose of making a comparison under rule 4 of section 681AD(3) if section 681AD has effect because of section 681AB(1), and

     (b) for the purpose of making a comparison under section 681AE(3) if section 681AE has effect because of section 681AB(2).

(2) The commercial rent is the rent which might be expected to be paid under a lease, of the land in respect of which the payment mentioned in section 681AB(1)(b) or (2)(b) is made, which—

     (a) was negotiated in the open market when the rentcharge or other transaction mentioned in section 681AB(1)(b) or (2)(b) was effected,

     (b) is a tenant's repairing lease, and

     (c) is of an appropriate duration.

(3) A tenant's repairing lease is a lease where the lessee is under an obligation to maintain and repair the whole (or substantially the whole) of the premises comprised in the lease.

(4) To see whether a lease is of an appropriate duration, take the period over which payments are to be made under the rentcharge or other transaction, and—

     (a) if that period is 200 years or more (or the obligation to make the payments is perpetual) an appropriate duration is 200 years, or

     (b) if that period is less than 200 years, an appropriate duration is the same duration as that period.][1]

Commentary—*Simon's Taxes* **B5.247**.

HMRC Manuals—Business Income Manual BIM61305 (definition of 'commercial rent').

Amendments—[1] Sections 681A–681AN inserted by TIOPA 2010 s 368, Sch 4 paras 1, 2. TIOPA 2010 has effect for corporation tax purposes for accounting periods ending on or after 1 April 2010, for income and capital gains tax purposes for the tax year 2010–11 and subsequent tax years, and for petroleum revenue tax purposes for chargeable periods beginning on or after 1 July 2010.

[681AL Lease and rent

(1) This section applies for the purposes of this Chapter.

(2) A reference to a lease includes a reference to any of the following—

     (a) an underlease, sublease, tenancy or licence, and

     (b) an agreement for a lease, underlease, sublease, tenancy or licence, and

     (c) in the case of land outside the United Kingdom, an interest corresponding to a lease (as defined here).

(3) A reference to rent includes a reference to any payment under a lease.

(4) A reference to rent under a lease includes a reference to expenses which the tenant under the lease is treated as incurring in respect of the land subject to the lease under any of—

     (a) sections 61 to 67 of ITTOIA 2005 (land occupied for trade purposes), and

     (b) sections 292 to 297 of that Act (taxed leases).

(5) Expenses within subsection (4) must be treated as having been paid as soon as they were incurred.][1]

Commentary—*Simon's Taxes* **B5.247**.

Amendments—[1] Sections 681A–681AN inserted by TIOPA 2010 s 368, Sch 4 paras 1, 2. TIOPA 2010 has effect for corporation tax purposes for accounting periods ending on or after 1 April 2010, for income and capital gains tax purposes for the tax year 2010–11 and subsequent tax years, and for petroleum revenue tax purposes for chargeable periods beginning on or after 1 July 2010.

[681AM Associated persons

(1) This section applies for the purposes of this Chapter.

(2) The following persons are associated with one another—

     (a) the transferor in an affected transaction and the transferor in another affected transaction, if the two persons are acting in concert or if the two transactions are in any way reciprocal, and

     (b) any person who is an associate of either of those associated transferors.

(3) Two or more bodies corporate are associated with one another if they participate in, or are incorporated for the purposes of, a scheme—

(a) for the reconstruction of any body or bodies corporate, or

(b) for the amalgamation of any two or more bodies corporate.

(4) Persons are associated with one another if they are associates as defined in section 681DL (relatives, settlements, persons controlling bodies, joint owners etc).

(5) In subsection (2) "affected transaction" means a transaction within—

(a) section 681AA(1) or (2) or 681AB(1) or (2), or

(b) section 835(1) or (2) or 836(1) or (2) of CTA 2010.]¹

Amendments—¹   Sections 681A–681AN inserted by TIOPA 2010 s 368, Sch 4 paras 1, 2. TIOPA 2010 has effect for corporation tax purposes for accounting periods ending on or after 1 April 2010, for income and capital gains tax purposes for the tax year 2010–11 and subsequent tax years, and for petroleum revenue tax purposes for chargeable periods beginning on or after 1 July 2010.

[681AN Land outside the UK

In the case of land outside the United Kingdom, expressions in this Chapter relating to interests in land and their disposition must be taken to relate to corresponding interests and dispositions.]¹

Amendments—¹   Sections 681A–681AN inserted by TIOPA 2010 s 368, Sch 4 paras 1, 2. TIOPA 2010 has effect for corporation tax purposes for accounting periods ending on or after 1 April 2010, for income and capital gains tax purposes for the tax year 2010–11 and subsequent tax years, and for petroleum revenue tax purposes for chargeable periods beginning on or after 1 July 2010.

[CHAPTER 2

NEW LEASE OF LAND AFTER ASSIGNMENT OR SURRENDER]¹

[Overview

681B Overview

(1) This Chapter provides that in certain circumstances where a lease of land is assigned or surrendered and another lease is granted or assigned—

(a) consideration received for the assignment or surrender of the first lease is taxed as a receipt of a trade, profession or vocation or charged to income tax, and

(b) tax relief is allowed for rent under the other lease.

(2) The Chapter provides that in certain circumstances where a lease is varied it is treated as surrendered and another lease is treated as granted.]¹

HMRC Manuals—Business Income Manual BIM61340 (special arrangements).

Amendments—¹   Sections 681B–681BM inserted by TIOPA 2010 s 368, Sch 4 paras 1, 3. TIOPA 2010 has effect for corporation tax purposes for accounting periods ending on or after 1 April 2010, for income and capital gains tax purposes for the tax year 2010–11 and subsequent tax years, and for petroleum revenue tax purposes for chargeable periods beginning on or after 1 July 2010.

[Application of the Chapter

681BA New lease after assignment or surrender

(1) This Chapter has effect if each of conditions A to E is met.

(2) Condition A is that—

(a) a person ("L") is a lessee of land under a lease which has 50 years or less to run ("the original lease"), and

(b) L is entitled in respect of the rent under the original lease to a deduction by way of relevant income tax relief.

(3) Condition B is that—

(a) L assigns the original lease to another person or surrenders it to L's landlord, and

(b) the consideration for the assignment or surrender would not (apart from this Chapter) be taxable except as capital in L's hands.

(4) Condition C is that—

(a) another lease ("the new lease") is granted, or assigned, to L or a person linked to L, and

(b) the new lease is for a term of 15 years or less.

(5) Condition D is that the new lease—

(a) is of all or part of the land which was the subject of the original lease, or

(b) includes all or part of the land which was the subject of the original lease.

(6) Condition E is that neither L nor a person linked to L had, before 22 June 1971, a right enforceable at law or in equity to the grant of the new lease.

(7) If each of conditions A to D is met but condition E is not met, see the relevant provisions in Schedule 2 to CTA 2010 and Schedule 9 to TIOPA 2010.]¹

Commentary—Simon's Taxes B5.248.

HMRC Manuals—Business Income Manual BIM61335 (new lease after assignment or surrender).

Amendments—[1]   Sections 681B–681BM inserted by TIOPA 2010 s 368, Sch 4 paras 1, 3. TIOPA 2010 has effect for corporation tax purposes for accounting periods ending on or after 1 April 2010, for income and capital gains tax purposes for the tax year 2010–11 and subsequent tax years, and for petroleum revenue tax purposes for chargeable periods beginning on or after 1 July 2010.

[Taxation of consideration

681BB Taxation of consideration

(1) An appropriate amount must be found under subsection (3) or (4) of—
    (*a*) the consideration received by L for the assignment or surrender, or
    (*b*) each instalment of the consideration (if it is paid in instalments).

(2) For the purposes of the Income Tax Acts the appropriate amount must be treated in accordance with subsections (6) to (8) and not as a capital receipt.

(3) If the term of the new lease is one year or less, the appropriate amount of the consideration or instalment is the whole of it.

(4) If the term of the new lease is more than one year, the appropriate amount of the consideration or instalment is the proportion of it found by the formula—

$$(16 - N)/15$$

(5) In subsection (4) N is the term of the new lease expressed in years (taking part of a year as an appropriate proportion of a year).

(6) The way the appropriate amount must be treated depends on whether the following conditions are met—
    (*a*) the consideration is received by L in the course of a trade, profession or vocation, and
    (*b*) the rent payable by L, or a person linked to L, under the new lease is allowable as a deduction in calculating profits or losses of a trade, profession or vocation for tax purposes.

(7) If the conditions are met the appropriate amount must be treated as a receipt of the trade, profession or vocation mentioned in subsection (6)(*a*).

(8) If the conditions are not met the appropriate amount must be treated as an amount chargeable to income tax.

(9) If income tax is charged under subsection (8)—
    (*a*) it must be charged on the proportion of the appropriate amount arising in the tax year,
    (*b*) the person liable for the tax is L, and
    (*c*) the amount charged must be treated for income tax purposes as an amount of income.][1]

Commentary—*Simon's Taxes* **B5.248.**
Amendments—[1]   Sections 681B–681BM inserted by TIOPA 2010 s 368, Sch 4 paras 1, 3. TIOPA 2010 has effect for corporation tax purposes for accounting periods ending on or after 1 April 2010, for income and capital gains tax purposes for the tax year 2010–11 and subsequent tax years, and for petroleum revenue tax purposes for chargeable periods beginning on or after 1 July 2010.

[681BC Position where new lease does not include all original property

(1) This section applies for the purposes of section 681BB if the property which is the subject of the new lease does not include all the property which was the subject of the original lease.

(2) The consideration received by L must be treated as reduced to the portion of it found under subsection (3).

(3) The portion is that which is reasonably attributable to such part of the original property as—
    (*a*) consists of the property which is the subject of the new lease, or
    (*b*) is included in the property which is the subject of the new lease.

(4) The original property is the property which was the subject of the original lease.][1]

Commentary—*Simon's Taxes* **B5.248.**
Amendments—[1]   Sections 681B–681BM inserted by TIOPA 2010 s 368, Sch 4 paras 1, 3. TIOPA 2010 has effect for corporation tax purposes for accounting periods ending on or after 1 April 2010, for income and capital gains tax purposes for the tax year 2010–11 and subsequent tax years, and for petroleum revenue tax purposes for chargeable periods beginning on or after 1 July 2010.

[Relief for rent under new lease

681BD Relief for rent under new lease

(1) This section applies if the rent under the new lease is payable by a person within the charge to income tax.

(2) This section also applies if—
    (*a*) Chapter 2 of Part 19 of CTA 2010 (provision for corporation tax corresponding to this Chapter) has effect, and
    (*b*) the rent under the new lease is payable by a person within the charge to income tax.

(3) The provisions of ITTOIA 2005 providing for deductions or allowances by way of income tax relief in respect of payments of rent apply in relation to the rent under the new lease.

(4) In subsection (2), and in subsection (3) as applied by subsection (2), references to the new lease and rent are to be read as in Chapter 2 of Part 19 of CTA 2010.][1]

Commentary—*Simon's Taxes* **B5.248.**

Amendments—[1]   Sections 681B–681BM inserted by TIOPA 2010 s 368, Sch 4 paras 1, 3. TIOPA 2010 has effect for corporation tax purposes for accounting periods ending on or after 1 April 2010, for income and capital gains tax purposes for the tax year 2010–11 and subsequent tax years, and for petroleum revenue tax purposes for chargeable periods beginning on or after 1 July 2010.

[New lease treated as ending

681BE New lease treated as ending

(1) Sections 681BF to 681BH treat the new lease as ending in certain circumstances for the purposes of this Chapter.

(2) If any of those provisions apply in a given case, and the new lease is treated as ending on different dates, it must be treated as ending on the earlier or earliest of them.][1]

Commentary—*Simon's Taxes* **B5.248.**

Amendments—[1]   Sections 681B–681BM inserted by TIOPA 2010 s 368, Sch 4 paras 1, 3. TIOPA 2010 has effect for corporation tax purposes for accounting periods ending on or after 1 April 2010, for income and capital gains tax purposes for the tax year 2010–11 and subsequent tax years, and for petroleum revenue tax purposes for chargeable periods beginning on or after 1 July 2010.

[681BF Position where rent reduces

(1) If the rent for a relevant period exceeds the rent for the following comparable period, the term of the new lease must be treated as ending on the date when the relevant period ends.

(2) For the purposes of this section—

   (*a*) a relevant period is a rental period of the new lease ending before its fifteenth anniversary,

   (*b*) the following comparable period (in relation to a relevant period) is the rental period which is of the same duration as the relevant period and which begins on the day following the end of the relevant period,

   (*c*) the rent for a period is the total rent payable under the new lease in respect of the period,

   (*d*) a rental period is a period in respect of which a payment of rent is to be made, and

   (*e*) the fifteenth anniversary of the new lease is the fifteenth anniversary of the date on which its term begins.

(3) For the purposes of this section—

   (*a*) all rental periods of a quarter must be treated as being of the same duration, and

   (*b*) all rental periods of a month must be treated as being of the same duration.][1]

Commentary—*Simon's Taxes* **B5.248** .

Amendments—[1]   Sections 681B–681BM inserted by TIOPA 2010 s 368, Sch 4 paras 1, 3. TIOPA 2010 has effect for corporation tax purposes for accounting periods ending on or after 1 April 2010, for income and capital gains tax purposes for the tax year 2010–11 and subsequent tax years, and for petroleum revenue tax purposes for chargeable periods beginning on or after 1 July 2010.

[681BG Position where lease may be ended

(1) This section applies if under the new lease the lessor, or L or a person linked to L, has power to end the lease before the end of the term for which it was granted.

(2) The term of the lease must be treated as ending on the earliest date with effect from which the lessor, or L or a person linked to L, could end the lease by exercising the power.][1]

Commentary—*Simon's Taxes* **B5.248.**

Amendments—[1]   Sections 681B–681BM inserted by TIOPA 2010 s 368, Sch 4 paras 1, 3. TIOPA 2010 has effect for corporation tax purposes for accounting periods ending on or after 1 April 2010, for income and capital gains tax purposes for the tax year 2010–11 and subsequent tax years, and for petroleum revenue tax purposes for chargeable periods beginning on or after 1 July 2010.

[681BH Position where lease may be varied

(1) This section applies if under the new lease L, or a person linked to L, has power to vary, in a manner beneficial to L or a person linked to L, obligations under the lease that are obligations of L or a person linked to L.

(2) The term of the lease must be treated as ending on the earliest date with effect from which L, or a person linked to L, could vary the obligations by exercising the power.][1]

Commentary—*Simon's Taxes* **B5.248.**

Amendments—[1]   Sections 681B–681BM inserted by TIOPA 2010 s 368, Sch 4 paras 1, 3. TIOPA 2010 has effect for corporation tax purposes for accounting periods ending on or after 1 April 2010, for income and capital gains tax purposes for the tax year 2010–11 and subsequent tax years, and for petroleum revenue tax purposes for chargeable periods beginning on or after 1 July 2010.

[681BI Lease treated as ending: rentcharge

(1) Subsection (2) applies if a rentcharge payable by L, or a person linked to L, is secured on all or part of the property subject to the new lease.

(2) For the purposes of sections 681BF to 681BH the rent payable under the new lease must be treated as equal to the sum of the rentcharge and the rent payable under the lease.][1]

Commentary—*Simon's Taxes* **B5.248.**

ITA 2007

Amendments—[1]   Sections 681B–681BM inserted by TIOPA 2010 s 368, Sch 4 paras 1, 3. TIOPA 2010 has effect for corporation tax purposes for accounting periods ending on or after 1 April 2010, for income and capital gains tax purposes for the tax year 2010–11 and subsequent tax years, and for petroleum revenue tax purposes for chargeable periods beginning on or after 1 July 2010.

[Lease varied to provide for increased rent

681BJ   Lease varied to provide for increased rent

(1) This section applies if each of conditions A to D is met.

(2) Condition A is that—

    (*a*)   a person ("the lessee") is a lessee of land under a lease which has 50 years or less to run ("the original lease"), and

    (*b*)   the lessee is entitled in respect of the rent under the original lease to a deduction by way of relevant income tax relief.

(3) Condition B is that (by agreement with the landlord) the lessee varies the original lease.

(4) Condition C is that under the variation—

    (*a*)   the lessee agrees to pay a rent greater than that payable under the original lease, and

    (*b*)   the lessee agrees to pay the greater rent in return for a consideration which would not (apart from this Chapter) be taxable except as capital in the lessee's hands.

(5) Condition D is that under the variation the period during which the greater rent is to be paid ends 15 years or less after the date on which—

    (*a*)   the consideration is paid to the lessee, or

    (*b*)   the last instalment of the consideration is paid to the lessee (if it is paid in instalments).

(6) If this section applies the lessee must be treated for the purposes of this Chapter—

    (*a*)   as having surrendered the original lease for the consideration mentioned in subsection (4)(*b*), and

    (*b*)   as having been granted a new lease for a term of 15 years or less but otherwise on the terms of the original lease varied as mentioned in subsection (3).][1]

Commentary—*Simon's Taxes* **B5.248**.

Amendments—[1]   Sections 681B–681BM inserted by TIOPA 2010 s 368, Sch 4 paras 1, 3. TIOPA 2010 has effect for corporation tax purposes for accounting periods ending on or after 1 April 2010, for income and capital gains tax purposes for the tax year 2010–11 and subsequent tax years, and for petroleum revenue tax purposes for chargeable periods beginning on or after 1 July 2010.

[Interpretation

681BK   Relevant income tax relief

For the purposes of this Chapter each of the following is a deduction by way of relevant income tax relief—

    (*a*)   a deduction in calculating profits or losses of a trade, profession or vocation for income tax purposes,

    (*b*)   a deduction in calculating the profits of a UK property business for income tax purposes,

    (*c*)   a deduction in calculating any loss for which relief is given under section 152 (losses from miscellaneous transactions), or in calculating profits or other income or gains chargeable to income tax under or by virtue of any provision to which section 1016 applies, and

    (*d*)   a deduction from earnings allowed under section 336 of ITEPA 2003 (expenses) or allowed in calculating losses in an employment for income tax purposes.][1]

Amendments—[1]   Sections 681B–681BM inserted by TIOPA 2010 s 368, Sch 4 paras 1, 3. TIOPA 2010 has effect for corporation tax purposes for accounting periods ending on or after 1 April 2010, for income and capital gains tax purposes for the tax year 2010–11 and subsequent tax years, and for petroleum revenue tax purposes for chargeable periods beginning on or after 1 July 2010.

[681BL   Linked persons

(1) In this Chapter references to a person linked to L are to a person who is—

    (*a*)   a partner of L,

    (*b*)   an associate of L, or

    (*c*)   an associate of a partner of L.

(2) "Associate" must be read in accordance with section 681DL (relatives, settlements, persons controlling bodies, joint owners etc).][1]

Amendments—[1]   Sections 681B–681BM inserted by TIOPA 2010 s 368, Sch 4 paras 1, 3. TIOPA 2010 has effect for corporation tax purposes for accounting periods ending on or after 1 April 2010, for income and capital gains tax purposes for the tax year 2010–11 and subsequent tax years, and for petroleum revenue tax purposes for chargeable periods beginning on or after 1 July 2010.

[681BM   Lease, lessee, lessor and rent

(1) This section applies for the purposes of this Chapter.

(2) "Lease" includes—

    (*a*)   an agreement for a lease, and

    (*b*)   any tenancy.

(3) "Lease" does not include a mortgage.

(4) A reference to a lessee or lessor—

(*a*) is to be read in accordance with subsections (2) and (3), and

(*b*) includes a reference to the successors in title of a lessee or lessor.

(5) "Rent" includes a payment by a tenant for work to maintain or repair leased premises which the lease does not require the tenant to carry out; and "premises" here includes land.

(6) In the application of this section to Scotland "mortgage" means—

(*a*) a standard security, or

(*b*) a heritable security, as defined in the Conveyancing (Scotland) Act 1924 but including a security constituted by ex facie absolute disposition or assignation.]¹

Commentary—*Simon's Taxes* **B5.248**.

Amendments—¹   Sections 681B–681BM inserted by TIOPA 2010 s 368, Sch 4 paras 1, 3. TIOPA 2010 has effect for corporation tax purposes for accounting periods ending on or after 1 April 2010, for income and capital gains tax purposes for the tax year 2010–11 and subsequent tax years, and for petroleum revenue tax purposes for chargeable periods beginning on or after 1 July 2010.

[CHAPTER 3

LEASED TRADING ASSETS]¹

Amendments—¹   Chapter 3 (ss 681C–681CG) inserted by TIOPA 2010 s 368, Sch 4 paras 1, 4. TIOPA 2010 has effect for corporation tax purposes for accounting periods ending on or after 1 April 2010, for income and capital gains tax purposes for the tax year 2010–11 and subsequent tax years, and for petroleum revenue tax purposes for chargeable periods beginning on or after 1 July 2010.

[Overview

681C Overview

This Chapter provides that, in certain circumstances where a payment is made under a lease of a trading asset, income tax relief for the payment is restricted.]¹

HMRC Manuals—Business Income Manual BIM61201 (leased trading assets - overview).

Amendments—¹   Sections 681C–681CG inserted by TIOPA 2010 s 368, Sch 4 paras 1, 4. TIOPA 2010 has effect for corporation tax purposes for accounting periods ending on or after 1 April 2010, for income and capital gains tax purposes for the tax year 2010–11 and subsequent tax years, and for petroleum revenue tax purposes for chargeable periods beginning on or after 1 July 2010.

[Application of the Chapter

681CA Professions and vocations

In this Chapter a reference to a trade includes a reference to a profession or vocation.]¹

Commentary—*Simon's Taxes* **B5.413**.

Amendments—¹   Sections 681C–681CG inserted by TIOPA 2010 s 368, Sch 4 paras 1, 4. TIOPA 2010 has effect for corporation tax purposes for accounting periods ending on or after 1 April 2010, for income and capital gains tax purposes for the tax year 2010–11 and subsequent tax years, and for petroleum revenue tax purposes for chargeable periods beginning on or after 1 July 2010.

[681CB Leased trading assets

(1) Section 681CC has effect if—

(*a*) condition A is met, and

(*b*) condition B or C is met.

(2) Condition A is that—

(*a*) a payment is made by a person under a lease of a relevant asset, and

(*b*) a deduction is allowed for the payment in calculating the profits of a trade for income tax purposes.

(3) Condition B is that—

(*a*) at a time before the lease's creation the asset was used for the purposes of the trade, and

(*b*) when it was so used it was owned by the person then carrying on the trade.

(4) Condition C is that—

(*a*) at a time before the lease's creation the asset was used for the purposes of another trade,

(*b*) when it was so used it was owned by the person then carrying on the other trade, and

(*c*) when it was so used, or later, that person was carrying on the trade mentioned in subsection (2).

(5) The reference in subsection (2)(*a*) to a lease does not include a lease created on or before 14 April 1964.

(6) In this section references to a person carrying on a trade are to the person carrying on the trade for the time being.]¹

Commentary—*Simon's Taxes* **B5.413**.

HMRC Manuals—Business Income Manual BIM61240 (leased trading assets).

Amendments—¹   Sections 681C–681CG inserted by TIOPA 2010 s 368, Sch 4 paras 1, 4. TIOPA 2010 has effect for corporation tax purposes for accounting periods ending on or after 1 April 2010, for income and capital gains tax purposes for the tax year 2010–11 and subsequent tax years, and for petroleum revenue tax purposes for chargeable periods beginning on or after 1 July 2010.

[Relief: restriction and carrying forward

681CC Tax deduction not to exceed commercial rent

(1) The rules in subsection (3) apply to the calculation of the deduction by way of relevant income tax relief allowed in a relevant period—

    (*a*) for the non-excluded element of the payment within section 681CB(2), or

    (*b*) if there are two or more such payments, for the non-excluded elements of those payments.

(2) For the purposes of this section—

    (*a*) "relevant period" means—

        (i) a period of account of the trade, or

        (ii) if no accounts of the trade are drawn up for a period, the basis period of a tax year, and

    (*b*) the non-excluded element of a payment is the element of the payment not excluded under section 681CD (long funding finance leases).

(3) The rules are—

Rule 1—meaning of amount E

For any relevant period, amount E (which may be nil) is the expense or total expenses to be brought, in accordance with generally accepted accounting practice, into account in the period in respect of—

    (*a*) the non-excluded element of the payment, or

    (*b*) the non-excluded elements of the payments.

Rule 2—calculations

For every relevant period—

    (*a*) calculate the total of amount E for the period and amount E for every previous relevant period ending on or after the date of the creation of the lease mentioned in section 681CB(2)(*a*),

    (*b*) calculate the total of the deductions by way of relevant income tax relief for every previous relevant period ending on or after that date, and

    (*c*) subtract the total at (*b*) from the total at (*a*) to give the cumulative unrelieved expenses for the period.

Rule 3—meaning of post-spread period

A relevant period is a post-spread period if for that relevant period, and every later relevant period, there are no payments within section 681CB(2).

Rule 4—the deduction allowed in a relevant period

If a relevant period is not a post-spread period, the deduction allowed for the period is equal to the cumulative unrelieved expenses for the period, but is the commercial rent for the period if that is less (see section 681CE).

Rule 5—relevant periods in which no deduction allowed

If a relevant period is a post-spread period, no deduction is allowed for the period.][1]

Commentary—*Simon's Taxes* **B5.413**.

HMRC Manuals—Business Income Manual BIM61250 (calculation of tax deduction).

Amendments—[1] Sections 681C–681CG inserted by TIOPA 2010 s 368, Sch 4 paras 1, 4. TIOPA 2010 has effect for corporation tax purposes for accounting periods ending on or after 1 April 2010, for income and capital gains tax purposes for the tax year 2010–11 and subsequent tax years, and for petroleum revenue tax purposes for chargeable periods beginning on or after 1 July 2010.

[681CD Long funding finance leases

(1) This section applies for the purposes of section 681CC.

(2) A payment must be excluded so far as, in the case of the lessee, it is to be regarded in accordance with Chapter 6A of Part 2 of CAA 2001 as a payment under a lease which is a long funding finance lease for the purposes of that Part.][1]

Commentary—*Simon's Taxes* **B5.413**.

Amendments—[1] Sections 681C–681CG inserted by TIOPA 2010 s 368, Sch 4 paras 1, 4. TIOPA 2010 has effect for corporation tax purposes for accounting periods ending on or after 1 April 2010, for income and capital gains tax purposes for the tax year 2010–11 and subsequent tax years, and for petroleum revenue tax purposes for chargeable periods beginning on or after 1 July 2010.

[681CE Commercial rent

(1) Subsection (3) applies for the purpose of making a comparison under rule 4 of section 681CC(3).

(2) In this section "the actual lease" means the lease mentioned in section 681CB(2)(*a*).

(3) The commercial rent is the rent which might at the relevant time be expected to be paid under a lease of the asset if—

    (*a*) the lease were for the rest of the asset's expected normal working life,

    (*b*) the rent were payable at uniform intervals and at a uniform rate, and

    (*c*) the rent gave a reasonable return for the asset's market value at the relevant time, taking account of the actual lease's terms and conditions.

(4) The relevant time is the time when the actual lease was created.

(5) An asset's expected normal working life is the period which might be expected, when it is first put into use, to pass before it is finally put out of use as being unfit for further use.

(6) In applying subsection (5) it must be assumed that the asset will be used in the normal way, and to the normal extent, throughout the period.

(7) If the asset is used at the same time partly for the purposes of the trade mentioned in section 681CB(2)(*b*) and partly for other purposes, the commercial rent as defined in subsection (3) is to be determined by reference to what would be paid for such partial use.][1]

Commentary—*Simon's Taxes* **B5.413**.

HMRC Manuals—Business Income Manual BIM61245 (meaning of 'commercial rent').

Amendments—[1]   Sections 681C–681CG inserted by TIOPA 2010 s 368, Sch 4 paras 1, 4. TIOPA 2010 has effect for corporation tax purposes for accounting periods ending on or after 1 April 2010, for income and capital gains tax purposes for the tax year 2010–11 and subsequent tax years, and for petroleum revenue tax purposes for chargeable periods beginning on or after 1 July 2010.

[Interpretation

681CF Lease

(1) This section applies for the purposes of this Chapter.

(2) A lease is (in relation to an asset) an agreement or arrangement under which payments are made for the use of or otherwise in respect of the asset.

(3) In particular it includes an agreement or arrangement under which the payments (or any of them) represent instalments of a purchase price or payments towards it.][1]

Commentary—*Simon's Taxes* **B5.410**.

Amendments—[1]   Sections 681C–681CG inserted by TIOPA 2010 s 368, Sch 4 paras 1, 4. TIOPA 2010 has effect for corporation tax purposes for accounting periods ending on or after 1 April 2010, for income and capital gains tax purposes for the tax year 2010–11 and subsequent tax years, and for petroleum revenue tax purposes for chargeable periods beginning on or after 1 July 2010.

[681CG Relevant asset

For the purposes of this Chapter a relevant asset is any description of property or rights other than land or an interest in land.][1]

Commentary—*Simon's Taxes* **B5.410**.

Amendments—[1]   Sections 681C–681CG inserted by TIOPA 2010 s 368, Sch 4 paras 1, 4. TIOPA 2010 has effect for corporation tax purposes for accounting periods ending on or after 1 April 2010, for income and capital gains tax purposes for the tax year 2010–11 and subsequent tax years, and for petroleum revenue tax purposes for chargeable periods beginning on or after 1 July 2010.

[CHAPTER 4

LEASED ASSETS: CAPITAL SUMS][1]

Amendments—[1]   Chapter 4 (ss 681D–681DP) inserted by TIOPA 2010 s 368, Sch 4 paras 1, 5. TIOPA 2010 has effect for corporation tax purposes for accounting periods ending on or after 1 April 2010, for income and capital gains tax purposes for the tax year 2010–11 and subsequent tax years, and for petroleum revenue tax purposes for chargeable periods beginning on or after 1 July 2010.

[Overview

681D Overview

This Chapter provides that in certain circumstances where a payment is made under a lease of an asset, and a capital sum is obtained in respect of an interest in the asset, income tax is charged on an amount not greater than the capital sum.][1]

HMRC Manuals—Business Income Manual BIM61205 (capital sums: overview).

Amendments—[1]   Sections 681D–681DP inserted by TIOPA 2010 s 368, Sch 4 paras 1, 5. TIOPA 2010 has effect for corporation tax purposes for accounting periods ending on or after 1 April 2010, for income and capital gains tax purposes for the tax year 2010–11 and subsequent tax years, and for petroleum revenue tax purposes for chargeable periods beginning on or after 1 July 2010.

[Application of the Chapter

681DA Application of the Chapter

This Chapter applies if—

    (*a*) condition A is met (see section 681DB), and

    (*b*) condition B, C, D or E is met (see section 681DC).][1]

Amendments—[1]   Sections 681D–681DP inserted by TIOPA 2010 s 368, Sch 4 paras 1, 5. TIOPA 2010 has effect for corporation tax purposes for accounting periods ending on or after 1 April 2010, for income and capital gains tax purposes for the tax year 2010–11 and subsequent tax years, and for petroleum revenue tax purposes for chargeable periods beginning on or after 1 July 2010.

[681DB Payment under lease

(1) Condition A is that—

    (*a*) a payment is made under a lease of a relevant asset, and

    (*b*) the payment is one for which a deduction by way of relevant tax relief is allowed.

(2) Condition A is not met if section 681CC (leased trading assets: tax deductions)—

    (*a*) applies to the payment, or

    (*b*) would apply to it but for its being excluded under section 681CD (long funding finance leases).

(3) Condition A is not met if section 865 of CTA 2010 (provision for corporation tax corresponding to section 681CC)—

    (*a*) applies to the payment, or

    (*b*) would apply to it but for its being excluded under section 866 of that Act (long funding finance leases).

(4) The reference in subsection (1)(*a*) to a lease does not include a lease created on or before 14 April 1964.]¹

Amendments—¹   Sections 681D–681DP inserted by TIOPA 2010 s 368, Sch 4 paras 1, 5. TIOPA 2010 has effect for corporation tax purposes for accounting periods ending on or after 1 April 2010, for income and capital gains tax purposes for the tax year 2010–11 and subsequent tax years, and for petroleum revenue tax purposes for chargeable periods beginning on or after 1 July 2010.

[681DC   Sum obtained

(1) Condition B is that the person making the payment—

    (*a*) obtains a capital sum in respect of the lessee's interest in the lease, and

    (*b*) is within the charge to income tax.

(2) Condition C is that an associate of the person making the payment—

    (*a*) obtains a capital sum by way of consideration in respect of the lessee's interest in the lease, and

    (*b*) is within the charge to income tax.

(3) Condition D is that—

    (*a*) the lessor's interest in the lease, or any other interest in the asset, belongs to an associate of the person making the payment,

    (*b*) the associate obtains a capital sum in respect of the interest, and

    (*c*) the associate is within the charge to income tax.

(4) Condition E is that—

    (*a*) the lessor's interest in the lease, or any other interest in the asset, belongs to an associate of the person making the payment,

    (*b*) an associate of that associate obtains a capital sum by way of consideration in respect of the interest, and

    (*c*) the associate obtaining the sum is within the charge to income tax.

(5) Condition B, C, D or E may be met before, at or after the time when the payment is made.

(6) Condition B or C is not met if—

    (*a*) the lease is a hire-purchase agreement for plant or machinery, and

    (*b*) the capital sum is required to be brought into account as the whole or part of the disposal value of the plant or machinery under section 68 of CAA 2001.

(7) Condition D or E is not met if—

    (*a*) the capital sum is obtained in respect of the lessee's interest in the lease,

    (*b*) the lease is a hire-purchase agreement for plant or machinery, and

    (*c*) the capital sum is required to be brought into account as the whole or part of the disposal value of the plant or machinery under section 68 of CAA 2001.]¹

Commentary—*Simon's Taxes* **B5.411, B5.414.**

HMRC Manuals—Business Income Manual BIM61215 (meaning of 'capital sum').

BIM61220 (associated persons).

Amendments—¹   Sections 681D–681DP inserted by TIOPA 2010 s 368, Sch 4 paras 1, 5. TIOPA 2010 has effect for corporation tax purposes for accounting periods ending on or after 1 April 2010, for income and capital gains tax purposes for the tax year 2010–11 and subsequent tax years, and for petroleum revenue tax purposes for chargeable periods beginning on or after 1 July 2010.

[Charge to income tax]

681DD   Charge to income tax

(1) The person obtaining the capital sum is charged to income tax, for the tax year in which the sum is obtained, on the amount given by subsection (2).

(2) That amount is—

    (*a*) the amount of the payment for which a deduction by way of relevant tax relief is allowed, or

    (*b*) the total amount of such payments (if more than one).

(3) But subsections (1) and (2) have effect subject to—

    (*a*) subsections (4) to (7), and

    (*b*) section 681DE(3) (hire-purchase agreements).

(4) The amount on which tax is charged under this section is not to exceed the capital sum obtained (but see section 681DE(4)).

(5) Subsection (6) applies if—

    (*a*) income tax is charged under this section in respect of a capital sum, and

    (*b*) a payment or part of a payment is taken into account in deciding the amount on which the tax is charged.

(6) The payment or part must be left out of account in deciding—

    (*a*) whether income tax is to be charged under this section in respect of another capital sum, and (*b*) the amount on which the tax is to be charged (if any is to be charged).

(7) The order in which subsections (5) and (6) are applied is the order in which capital sums are obtained.

(8) An amount on which income tax is charged under this section is treated for income tax purposes as an amount of income.]¹

Commentary—*Simon's Taxes* **B5.410, B5.411** .

Amendments—¹   Sections 681D–681DP inserted by TIOPA 2010 s 368, Sch 4 paras 1, 5. TIOPA 2010 has effect for corporation tax purposes for accounting periods ending on or after 1 April 2010, for income and capital gains tax purposes for the tax year 2010–11 and subsequent tax years, and for petroleum revenue tax purposes for chargeable periods beginning on or after 1 July 2010.

[681DE Hire-purchase agreements

(1) This section applies if—

   (*a*) the lease is a hire-purchase agreement (as defined in section 998A), and

   (*b*) the capital sum is obtained in respect of the lessee's interest in the lease (whether it is obtained by the person making the payment or by an associate).

(2) Find the total of the following amounts—

   (*a*) so much of any payment made under the lease by the person obtaining the capital sum as is not a payment for which a deduction by way of relevant tax relief is allowed, and

   (*b*) if the lessee's interest was assigned to the person obtaining the capital sum, any capital payment made by that person as consideration for the assignment.

(3) If the total of the amounts found under subsection (2) is equal to or greater than the capital sum, income tax is not charged under section 681DD in respect of the capital sum.

(4) If the total of those amounts is less than the capital sum, in applying section 681DD(4) that total must be deducted from the capital sum.

(5) If the capital sum is the consideration for part only of the lessee's interest in the lease—

   (*a*) any amount found under subsection (2) (and still unallowed) must be reduced to a just and reasonable proportion of it, and

   (*b*) in calculating that proportion account must be taken of the degree to which the payments mentioned in subsection (2) have contributed to the value of what is disposed of in return for the capital sum.

(6) Subsection (7) applies if—

   (*a*) more than one capital sum is (or is treated as) obtained by the same person in respect of the lessee's interest in the lease, and

   (*b*) in arriving at a total under subsection (2) a payment is taken into account in respect of one of the capital sums.

(7) So far as the payment is so taken into account it must not be taken into account in applying subsection (2) to another of the capital sums.

(8) The order in which subsections (6) and (7) are applied is the order in which capital sums are obtained.

(9) If the capital sum is obtained by the personal representatives of a deceased person, the reference in subsection (2)(*a*) to any payment made under the lease by the person obtaining the capital sum includes any payment made under the lease by the deceased.]¹

Commentary—*Simon's Taxes* **B5.414** .

Amendments—¹   Sections 681D–681DP inserted by TIOPA 2010 s 368, Sch 4 paras 1, 5. TIOPA 2010 has effect for corporation tax purposes for accounting periods ending on or after 1 April 2010, for income and capital gains tax purposes for the tax year 2010–11 and subsequent tax years, and for petroleum revenue tax purposes for chargeable periods beginning on or after 1 July 2010.

[681DF Adjustments where sum obtained before payment made

(1) This section applies if a capital sum is obtained as mentioned in section 681DC and later a payment is made as mentioned in section 681DB.

(2) Adjustments must be made if they are needed to give effect to a charge to income tax under section 681DD in respect of the capital sum.

(3) An adjustment may be made within the period ending with the fifth anniversary of the 31 January following the tax year in which the payment is made.

(4) Subsection (3) applies despite any time limit specified in the Income Tax Acts.]¹

Commentary—*Simon's Taxes* **B5.411**.

Amendments—¹   Sections 681D–681DP inserted by TIOPA 2010 s 368, Sch 4 paras 1, 5. TIOPA 2010 has effect for corporation tax purposes for accounting periods ending on or after 1 April 2010, for income and capital gains tax purposes for the tax year 2010–11 and subsequent tax years, and for petroleum revenue tax purposes for chargeable periods beginning on or after 1 July 2010.

[Obtaining of sum

681DG Sum obtained in respect of interest

A reference in this Chapter to a sum obtained in respect of an interest in an asset (whether the lessee's interest in a lease of the asset or the lessor's interest or any other interest) includes a reference to—

(*a*) insurance money obtained in respect of the interest, and

(*b*) sums representing money or money's worth obtained in respect of the interest by a transaction or series of transactions disposing of it.][1]

Commentary—*Simon's Taxes* **B5.412** .

Amendments—[1]   Sections 681D–681DP inserted by TIOPA 2010 s 368, Sch 4 paras 1, 5. TIOPA 2010 has effect for corporation tax purposes for accounting periods ending on or after 1 April 2010, for income and capital gains tax purposes for the tax year 2010–11 and subsequent tax years, and for petroleum revenue tax purposes for chargeable periods beginning on or after 1 July 2010.

[681DH Sum obtained in respect of lessee's interest

(1) This section applies to a reference in this Chapter to a sum obtained in respect of the lessee's interest in a lease of an asset.

(2) The reference includes a reference to sums representing the consideration in money or money's worth obtained on any of the following occasions—

(*a*) a surrender of the interest to the lessor,

(*b*) an assignment of the lease, and

(*c*) the creation of a sublease or another interest out of the lease.

(3) The reference also includes a reference to sums representing money or money's worth obtained in respect of the interest by a transaction or series of transactions under which the lessee's rights are merged in any way with the lessor's rights or with any other rights as respects the asset.

(4) Subsection (3) applies so far as the money or money's worth is attributable to the lessee's rights under the lease.][1]

Commentary—*Simon's Taxes* **B5.412** .

Amendments—[1]   Sections 681D–681DP inserted by TIOPA 2010 s 368, Sch 4 paras 1, 5. TIOPA 2010 has effect for corporation tax purposes for accounting periods ending on or after 1 April 2010, for income and capital gains tax purposes for the tax year 2010–11 and subsequent tax years, and for petroleum revenue tax purposes for chargeable periods beginning on or after 1 July 2010.

[681DI Disposal of interest to associate

(1) This section applies for the purposes of this Chapter if a person disposes of an interest in an asset to a person who is the first person's associate (and the interest may be the lessee's interest in a lease of the asset or the lessor's interest or any other interest).

(2) The person disposing of the interest must be treated as obtaining in respect of it the greatest of—

(*a*) the sum in fact obtained by the person,

(*b*) the value of the interest in the open market, and

(*c*) the value of the interest to the person to whom it is in effect transferred.

(3) The disposal—

(*a*) may be direct or indirect, and

(*b*) may be effected by a transaction or series of transactions described in section 681DG(*b*) or 681DH(3).][1]

Commentary—*Simon's Taxes* **B5.412** .

HMRC Manuals—Business Income Manual BIM61220 (associated persons).

Amendments—[1]   Sections 681D–681DP inserted by TIOPA 2010 s 368, Sch 4 paras 1, 5. TIOPA 2010 has effect for corporation tax purposes for accounting periods ending on or after 1 April 2010, for income and capital gains tax purposes for the tax year 2010–11 and subsequent tax years, and for petroleum revenue tax purposes for chargeable periods beginning on or after 1 July 2010.

[Apportionment

681DJ Apportionment of payments made and of sums obtained

(1) This section applies for the purposes of this Chapter.

(2) Subsection (3) applies if—

(*a*) a payment is made,

(*b*) it is one for which a deduction by way of relevant tax relief is allowed, and

(*c*) it is made by persons carrying on a trade or profession in partnership.

(3) The payment must be apportioned in a manner which is just and reasonable.

(4) Subsection (5) applies if—

(*a*) a sum is obtained in respect of an interest in an asset,

(*b*) the sum is obtained by persons carrying on a trade or profession in partnership, and

(*c*) the asset is and continues to be used for the purposes of the trade or profession.

(5) The sum must be apportioned between the partners in the shares in which they are entitled to the profits of the trade or profession at the time the sum is obtained.

(6) Subsection (7) applies if—

(*a*) a sum is obtained in respect of an interest in an asset, and

(*b*) the sum is obtained by persons jointly entitled to the interest.

(7) The sum must be apportioned according to their respective rights in the interest.

(8) Subsections (6) and (7) are subject to subsections (4) and (5).][1]

Commentary—*Simon's Taxes* **B5.412** .

HMRC Manuals—Business Income Manual BIM61225 (joint interests).

Amendments—[1]   Sections 681D–681DP inserted by TIOPA 2010 s 368, Sch 4 paras 1, 5. TIOPA 2010 has effect for corporation tax purposes for accounting periods ending on or after 1 April 2010, for income and capital gains tax purposes for the tax year 2010–11 and subsequent tax years, and for petroleum revenue tax purposes for chargeable periods beginning on or after 1 July 2010.

[681DK Manner of apportionment

(1) Subsections (2) and (3) apply if—

    (a) a payment or sum is to be apportioned under section 681DJ or under section 880 of CTA 2010,

    (b) at the time of the apportionment it appears that it is material to the liability to tax (whether income tax or corporation tax, and for whatever period) of two or more persons (in this section referred to collectively as "the set"),

    (c) a question arises as to the manner in which the payment or sum is to be apportioned, and

    (d) at the time of the apportionment, it appears that the apportionment is material to the income tax liability (for whatever period) of—

        (i) a person, or some two or more persons, in the set, or

        (ii) all the persons in the set.

(2) For the purposes of income tax of the person or persons mentioned in subsection (1)(d), the question is to be determined in the same way as an appeal.

(3) All the persons in the set are entitled to be a party to the proceedings.][1]

Commentary—*Simon's Taxes* **B5.412** .

Amendments—[1]   Sections 681D–681DP inserted by TIOPA 2010 s 368, Sch 4 paras 1, 5. TIOPA 2010 has effect for corporation tax purposes for accounting periods ending on or after 1 April 2010, for income and capital gains tax purposes for the tax year 2010–11 and subsequent tax years, and for petroleum revenue tax purposes for chargeable periods beginning on or after 1 July 2010.

[Interpretation

681DL Associates

(1) This section applies for the purposes of this Chapter.

(2) Persons are associates if they are associated with each other.

(3) The following are associated with each other—

    (a) an individual and the individual's spouse or civil partner or relative,

    (b) an individual and a spouse or civil partner of a relative of the individual,

    (c) an individual and a relative of the individual's spouse or civil partner,

    (d) an individual and a spouse or civil partner of a relative of the individual's spouse or civil partner.

(4) The following are associated with each other—

    (a) a person as trustee of a settlement and an individual who (in relation to the settlement) is a settlor, and

    (b) a person as trustee of a settlement and a person associated with an individual who (in relation to the settlement) is a settlor.

(5) The following are associated with each other—

    (a) a person and a body of persons of which the person has control,

    (b) a person and a body of persons of which persons associated with the person have control,

    (c) a person and a body of persons of which the person and persons associated with the person have control,

    (d) two or more bodies of persons associated with the same person under paragraphs (a) to (c).

(6) In relation to a disposal by joint owners, the joint owners and any person associated with any of them are associated with each other.

(7) For the purposes of this section—

    (a) a relative is a brother, sister, ancestor or lineal descendant,

    (b) a body of persons includes a partnership, and

    (c) "settlement" and "settlor" have the meanings given by section 620 of ITTOIA 2005.][1]

Commentary—*Simon's Taxes* **B5.411** .

HMRC Manuals—Business Income Manual BIM61220 (meaning of associated persons).

Amendments—[1]   Sections 681D–681DP inserted by TIOPA 2010 s 368, Sch 4 paras 1, 5. TIOPA 2010 has effect for corporation tax purposes for accounting periods ending on or after 1 April 2010, for income and capital gains tax purposes for the tax year 2010–11 and subsequent tax years, and for petroleum revenue tax purposes for chargeable periods beginning on or after 1 July 2010.

[681DM Capital sum

For the purposes of this Chapter a capital sum is any sum of money, or any money's worth, except so far as it or any part of it—

    (a) is to be treated for income tax purposes as a receipt to be taken into account in calculating the profits or losses of a trade, profession or vocation, or

    (b) is (apart from this Chapter) chargeable to income tax under or by virtue of any provision to which section 1016 applies.][1]

Commentary—*Simon's Taxes* **B5.410**.

HMRC Manuals—Business Income Manual BIM61205 (definition of capital sum).
Amendments—[1]   Sections 681D–681DP inserted by TIOPA 2010 s 368, Sch 4 paras 1, 5. TIOPA 2010 has effect for corporation tax purposes for accounting periods ending on or after 1 April 2010, for income and capital gains tax purposes for the tax year 2010–11 and subsequent tax years, and for petroleum revenue tax purposes for chargeable periods beginning on or after 1 July 2010.

[681DN Lease

(1) This section applies for the purposes of this Chapter.

(2) A lease is (in relation to an asset) an agreement or arrangement under which payments are made for the use of or otherwise in respect of the asset.

(3) In particular it includes an agreement or arrangement under which the payments (or any of them) represent instalments of a purchase price or payments towards it.][1]

Commentary—*Simon's Taxes* **B5.410**.
Amendments—[1]   Sections 681D–681DP inserted by TIOPA 2010 s 368, Sch 4 paras 1, 5. TIOPA 2010 has effect for corporation tax purposes for accounting periods ending on or after 1 April 2010, for income and capital gains tax purposes for the tax year 2010–11 and subsequent tax years, and for petroleum revenue tax purposes for chargeable periods beginning on or after 1 July 2010.

[681DO Relevant asset

For the purposes of this Chapter a relevant asset is any description of property or rights other than land or an interest in land.][1]

Commentary—*Simon's Taxes* **B5.410**.
Amendments—[1]   Sections 681D–681DP inserted by TIOPA 2010 s 368, Sch 4 paras 1, 5. TIOPA 2010 has effect for corporation tax purposes for accounting periods ending on or after 1 April 2010, for income and capital gains tax purposes for the tax year 2010–11 and subsequent tax years, and for petroleum revenue tax purposes for chargeable periods beginning on or after 1 July 2010.

[681DP Relevant tax relief

For the purposes of this Chapter each of the following is a deduction by way of relevant tax relief—

    (*a*) a deduction in calculating profits or losses of a trade for corporation tax purposes,

    (*b*) a deduction in calculating any loss for which relief is given under section 91 of CTA 2010 (losses from miscellaneous transactions), or in calculating profits or gains chargeable to corporation tax under or by virtue of any provision to which section 1173 of CTA 2010 applies (miscellaneous charges),

[(*c*) a deduction of an amount which for the purposes of section 73 of FA 2012 is adjusted BLAGAB management expenses of an insurance company for an accounting period,][2]

    (*d*) a deduction under section 1219 of CTA 2009 (expenses of management of a company's investment business),

    (*e*) a deduction in calculating profits or losses of a trade, profession or vocation for income tax purposes,

    (*f*) a deduction in calculating any loss for which relief is allowed under section 152 (losses from miscellaneous transactions), or in calculating profits or other income or gains chargeable to income tax under or by virtue of any provision to which section 1016 applies, and

    (*g*) a deduction from earnings allowed under section 336 of ITEPA 2003 (expenses) or allowed in calculating losses in an employment for income tax purposes.][1]

Commentary—*Simon's Taxes* **B5.410, B5.414**.
HMRC Manuals—Business Income Manual BIM61210 (tax-relieved payments).
Amendments—[1]   Sections 681D–681DP inserted by TIOPA 2010 s 368, Sch 4 paras 1, 5. TIOPA 2010 has effect for corporation tax purposes for accounting periods ending on or after 1 April 2010, for income and capital gains tax purposes for the tax year 2010–11 and subsequent tax years, and for petroleum revenue tax purposes for chargeable periods beginning on or after 1 July 2010.
[2]   Para (*c*) substituted by FA 2012 s 146, Sch 16 paras 132, 134 with effect in relation to accounting periods of companies beginning on or after 1 January 2013 (subject to transitional provisions in FA 2012 Sch 17). For accounting periods straddling 1 January 2013 see FA 2012 s 149.

PART 13

TAX AVOIDANCE

CHAPTER 1

TRANSACTIONS IN SECURITIES

[Introduction

682 Overview of Chapter

This Chapter makes provision for counteracting income tax advantages from transactions in securities.][1]

HMRC Manuals—Company Taxation Manual CTM36805 (counteracting tax advantage from transactions in securities).
Amendments—[1]   Sections 682–687 substituted for former ss 682–694 by FA 2010 s 38, Sch 12 paras 1, 2 with effect in relation to income tax advantages obtained on or after 24 March 2010.

[683 Provisions of Chapter

(1) Sections 684 to 687 specify when a person is liable to counteraction of income tax advantages from transactions in securities.

(2) Sections 695 to 700 make provision about the procedure for counteraction of such income tax advantages.

(3) Sections 701 and 702 make provision for a clearance procedure.

(4) Section 705 makes provision for appeals against counteraction notices.

(5) Sections 712 deals with cases in which a person liable to counteraction dies.

(6) Section 713 contains interpretative provisions.]¹

Amendments—¹   Sections 682–687 substituted for former ss 682–694 by FA 2010 s 38, Sch 12 paras 1, 2 with effect in relation to income tax advantages obtained on or after 24 March 2010.

[Person liable to counteraction of income tax advantages

684 Person liable to counteraction of income tax advantage

(1) This section applies to a person [("the party")]² where—

    (*a*) the person is a party to a transaction in securities or two or more transactions in securities (see subsection (2)),

    (*b*) the circumstances are covered by section 685 and not excluded by section 686,

    (*c*) the main purpose, or one of the main purposes, of . . . ² the transaction in securities, or any of the transactions in securities, is to obtain an income tax advantage, and

    (*d*) [the party or any other person]² obtains an income tax advantage in consequence of the transaction or the combined effect of the transactions.

(2) In this Chapter "transaction in securities" means a transaction, of whatever description, relating to securities, and includes in particular—

    (*a*) the purchase, sale or exchange of securities,

    (*b*) issuing or securing the issue of new securities,

    (*c*) applying or subscribing for new securities, . . . ²

    (*d*) altering or securing the alteration of the rights attached to securities,

    [(*e*) a repayment of share capital or share premium, and

    (*f*) a distribution in respect of securities in a winding up.]²

(3) Section 687 defines "income tax advantage".

[(4) This section is subject to no-counteraction notices issued under section 698A.]³]¹

Commentary—Simon's Taxes **D9.117, D9.101.**

HMRC Manuals—Company Taxation Manual CTM36810 (transaction in securities).

Amendments—¹   Sections 682–687 substituted for former ss 682–694 by FA 2010 s 38, Sch 12 paras 1, 2 with effect in relation to income tax advantages obtained on or after 24 March 2010.

²   In the opening words of sub-s (1), words inserted; in sub-s (1)(*c*) words "the person in being a party to" repealed; in sub-s (1)(*d*), words substituted for words "the person"; at the end of sub-s (2)(*c*), word "and" repealed; and sub-s (2)(*e*), (*f*) inserted; by FA 2016 s 33(1)–(3) with effect in relation to a transaction occurring on or after 6 April 2016 or a series of transactions any one or more of which occurs on or after that date. Accordingly, ITA 2007 Part 13 Chapter 1 has effect without these amendments in relation to a tax advantage obtained on or after 6 April 2016 in consequence of a transaction occurring before that date or a series of transactions all of which occur before that date (FA 2016 s 33(9)).

    Where before 6 April 2016 a person provided particulars to the Commissioners for HMRC under ITA 2007 s 701 in respect of a transaction or transactions, any one or more of which occurs on or after 6 April 2016, is notified under that section that no counteraction notice ought to be served, and the effect of the amendments made by FA 2016 s 33 is that such notification should not have been given, the notification is void and ITA 2007 s 702(2) does not apply in relation to the transaction or transactions (FA 2016 s 33(10)).

³   Sub-s (4) substituted by FA 2016 s 34(1), (7) with effect in relation to a transaction occurring on or after 6 April 2016 or a series of transactions any one or more of which occurs on or after that date. Accordingly, ITA 2007 Part 13 Chapter 1 has effect without this amendment in relation to a tax advantage obtained on or after 6 April 2016 in consequence of a transaction occurring before that date or a series of transactions all of which occur before that date (FA 2016 s 34(9)).

[685 Receipt of consideration in connection with distribution by or assets of close company

(1) The circumstances covered by this section are circumstances where condition A or condition B is met.

(2) Condition A is that, as a result of the transaction in securities or any one or more of the transactions in securities, [a relevant person]² receives relevant consideration in connection with—

    (*a*) the distribution, transfer or realisation of assets of a close company,

    (*b*) the application of assets of a close company in discharge of liabilities, or

    (*c*) the direct or indirect transfer of assets of one close company to another close company,

and [the relevant person]² does not pay or bear income tax on the consideration (apart from this Chapter).

(3) Condition B is that—

    (*a*) [a relevant person]² receives relevant consideration in connection with the transaction in securities or any one or more of the transactions in securities,

    (*b*) two or more close companies are concerned in the transaction or transactions in securities concerned, and (*c*) [the relevant person][2] does not pay or bear income tax on the consideration (apart from this Chapter).

[(3A) In subsections (2) and (3) "relevant person" means—

    (*a*) the party, or

    (*b*) any person other than the party in relation to whom the condition in section 684(1)(*d*) is met.][2]

(4) In a case within subsection (2)(*a*) or (*b*) "relevant consideration" means consideration which—

    (*a*) is or represents the value of—

        (i)   assets which are available for distribution by way of dividend by the company, or

        (ii) assets which would have been so available apart from anything done by the company,

    (*b*) is received in respect of future receipts of the company, or

    (*c*) is or represents the value of trading stock of the company.

(5) In a case within subsection (2)(*c*) or (3) "relevant consideration" means consideration which consists of any share capital or any security issued by a close company and which is or represents the value of assets which—

    (*a*) are available for distribution by way of dividend by the company,

    (*b*) would have been so available apart from anything done by the company, or

    (*c*) are trading stock of the company.

(6) . . . [2]

(7) So far as subsection (2)(*c*) or (3) relates to share capital other than redeemable share capital, it applies only so far as the share capital is repaid (on a winding up or otherwise); and for this purpose any distribution made in respect of any shares on a winding up or dissolution of the company is to be treated as a repayment of share capital.

[(7A) The references in subsection (4)(*a*)(i) and (ii) to assets do not include assets shown to represent return of sums paid by subscribers on the issue of securities merely because the law of the country in which the company is incorporated allows assets of that description to be available for distribution by way of dividend.

(7B) The references in subsections (4)(*a*)(i) and (5)(*a*) to assets which are available for distribution by way of dividend by the company include assets which are available for distribution to the company by way of dividend by any other company it controls.][2]

(8) References in this section to the receipt of consideration include references to the receipt of any money or money's worth.

(9) In this section—

    "security" includes securities not creating or evidencing a charge on assets;

    "share" includes stock and any other interest of a member in a company.][1]

Commentary—*Simon's Taxes* **D9.118** .

HMRC Manuals—Company Taxation Manual CTM36820 (circumstances where condition A or condition B are met). CTM36822 (condition A). CTM36823 (condition B).

Amendments—[1]   Sections 682–687 substituted for former ss 682–694 by FA 2010 s 38, Sch 12 paras 1, 2 with effect in relation to income tax advantages obtained on or after 24 March 2010.

[2]   In the opening words of sub-s (2), words substituted for words "the person"; in the closing words of sub-s (2), words inserted; in sub-s (3)(*a*), (*c*) words substituted for words "the person"; sub-s (3A) inserted; sub-s (6) repealed; and sub-ss (7A), (7B) inserted; by FA 2016 s 33(1), (4) with effect in relation to a transaction occurring on or after 6 April 2016 or a series of transactions any one or more of which occurs on or after that date. Accordingly, ITA 2007 Part 13 Chapter 1 has effect without these amendments in relation to a tax advantage obtained on or after 6 April 2016 in consequence of a transaction occurring before that date or a series of transactions all of which occur before that date (FA 2016 s 33(9)).

Where before 6 April 2016 a person provided particulars to the Commissioners for HMRC under ITA 2007 s 701 in respect of a transaction or transactions, any one or more of which occurs on or after 6 April 2016, is notified under that section that no counteraction notice ought to be served, and the effect of the amendments made by FA 2016 s 33 is that such notification should not have been given, the notification is void and ITA 2007 s 702(2) does not apply in relation to the transaction or transactions (FA 2016 s 33(10)).

[686 Excluded circumstances: fundamental change of ownership]

(1) Circumstances are excluded by this section if—

    (*a*) immediately before the transaction in securities (or the first of the transactions in securities) [the party][2] holds shares or an interest in shares in the close company, and

    (*b*) there is a fundamental change of ownership of the close company.

[(2) There is a fundamental change of ownership of the close company if, as a result of the transaction or transactions in securities, the condition in subsection (3) is met.

(3) The condition in this subsection is that the original shareholder or original shareholders taken together with any associate or associates—

    (*a*) do not directly or indirectly hold more than 25% of the ordinary share capital of the close company,

    (*b*) do not directly or indirectly hold shares in the close company carrying an entitlement to more than 25% of the distributions which may be made by the close company, and

    (*c*) do not directly or indirectly hold shares in the close company carrying more than 25% of the total voting rights in the close company.

(4) In this section "original shareholder" means a person who, immediately before the transaction in securities (or the first of the transactions in securities), held any ordinary share capital of the close company.

(5) For the purposes of this section, shares of or share capital in the close company which are held by a person controlled by an original shareholder, or by two or more original shareholders taken together, count as shares or share capital held by that original shareholder or those original shareholders.][2]][1]

Commentary—*Simon's Taxes* **D9.119** .

HMRC Manuals—Company Taxation Manual CTM36830 (excluded circumstances).

Amendments—[1]   Sections 682–687 substituted for former ss 682–694 by FA 2010 s 38, Sch 12 paras 1, 2 with effect in relation to income tax advantages obtained on or after 24 March 2010.

[2]   Words in sub-s (1)(a), and sub-ss (2)–(5), substituted, by FA 2016 s 33(1), (5) with effect in relation to a transaction occurring on or after 6 April 2016 or a series of transactions any one or more of which occurs on or after that date. Accordingly, ITA 2007 Part 13 Chapter 1 has effect without these amendments in relation to a tax advantage obtained on or after 6 April 2016 in consequence of a transaction occurring before that date or a series of transactions all of which occur before that date (FA 2016 s 33(9)).

Where before 6 April 2016 a person provided particulars to the Commissioners for HMRC under ITA 2007 s 701 in respect of a transaction or transactions, any one or more of which occurs on or after 6 April 2016, is notified under that section that no counteraction notice ought to be served, and the effect of the amendments made by FA 2016 s 33 is that such notification should not have been given, the notification is void and ITA 2007 s 702(2) does not apply in relation to the transaction or transactions (FA 2016 s 33(10)).

[687 Income tax advantage

(1) For the purposes of this Chapter [a person][3] obtains an income tax advantage if—

     (a) the amount of any income tax which would be payable by the person in respect of the relevant consideration if it constituted a . . . [2] distribution exceeds the amount of any capital gains tax payable in respect of it, or

     (b) income tax would be payable by the person in respect of the relevant consideration if it constituted a . . . [2] distribution and no capital gains tax is payable in respect of it.

(2) So much of the relevant consideration as exceeds the maximum amount that could in any circumstances have been paid to the person [or an associate of the person][3] by way of a . . . [2] distribution at the time when [Condition A or B in section 685 is met][3] is to be left out of account for the purposes of subsection (1).

(3) The amount of the income tax advantage is the amount of the excess or (if no capital gains tax is payable) the amount of the income tax which would be payable.

(4) In this section[—

     (a) "distribution" does not include a distribution which is a distribution for the purposes of the Corporation Tax Acts only because it falls within paragraph C or D in section 1000(1) of CTA 2010 (redeemable share capital or security issued as bonus in respect of shares in, or securities of, the company), and

     (b)][2] "relevant consideration" has the same meaning as in section 685.][1]

Commentary—*Simon's Taxes* **D9.117**.

HMRC Manuals—Company Taxation Manual CTM36815 (definition: income tax advantage).

Amendments—[1]   Sections 682–687 substituted for former ss 682–694 by FA 2010 s 38, Sch 12 paras 1, 2 with effect in relation to income tax advantages obtained on or after 24 March 2010.

[2]   Word in sub-ss (1)(a), (b), (2) repealed, and words in sub-s (4) inserted, by FA 2016 s 5, Sch 1 para 63(1), (10) with effect where the relevant consideration is received in the tax year 2016-17 or at any later time.

[3]   In sub-s (1), words substituted for words "the person"; in sub-s (2), words inserted and words substituted for words "the relevant consideration is received", by FA 2016 s 33(1), (6) with effect in relation to a transaction occurring on or after 6 April 2016 or a series of transactions any one or more of which occurs on or after that date. Accordingly, ITA 2007 Part 13 Chapter 1 has effect without these amendments in relation to a tax advantage obtained on or after 6 April 2016 in consequence of a transaction occurring before that date or a series of transactions all of which occur before that date (FA 2016 s 33(9)).

Where before 6 April 2016 a person provided particulars to the Commissioners for HMRC under ITA 2007 s 701 in respect of a transaction or transactions, any one or more of which occurs on or after 6 April 2016, is notified under that section that no counteraction notice ought to be served, and the effect of the amendments made by FA 2016 s 33 is that such notification should not have been given, the notification is void and ITA 2007 s 702(2) does not apply in relation to the transaction or transactions (FA 2016 s 33(10)).

Procedure for counteraction of income tax advantages

[695 Notice of enquiry

(1) An officer of Revenue and Customs may enquire into a transaction or transactions if—

     (a) the officer has reason to believe that section 684 (person liable to counteraction of income tax advantage) may apply to a person ("the taxpayer") in respect of the transaction or transactions, and

     (b) the officer notifies the taxpayer of his intention to do so.

(2) The notification may be given at any time not more than 6 years after the end of the tax year to which the income tax advantage in question relates.][1]

Commentary—*Simon's Taxes* **D9.132, D9.134**.

Amendments—[1]   This section substituted by FA 2016 s 34(1), (2) with effect in relation to a transaction occurring on or after 6 April 2016 or a series of transactions any one or more of which occurs on or after that date. Accordingly, ITA 2007 Part 13 Chapter 1 has effect without this amendment in relation to a tax advantage obtained on or after 6 April 2016 in consequence of a transaction occurring before that date or a series of transactions all of which occur before that date (FA 2016 s 34(9)).

698 Counteraction notices

[(1) If on an enquiry under section 695 an officer of Revenue and Customs determines that section 684 applies to the taxpayer, the income tax advantage in question is to be counteracted by adjustments, unless the officer is of the opinion that no counteraction is required.][2]

(2) The adjustments required to be made to counteract the income tax advantage and the basis on which they are to be made are to be specified in a notice served on the person by an officer of Revenue and Customs.

(3) In this Chapter such a notice is referred to as a "counteraction notice".

(4) Any of the following adjustments may be specified—

    (*a*)   an assessment,

    (*b*)   the nullifying of a right to repayment,

    (*c*)   the requiring of the return of a repayment already made, or

    (*d*)   the calculation or recalculation of profits or gains or liability to income tax.

[(5) An assessment may be made in accordance with a counteraction notice at any time (without regard to any time limit on making the assessment that would otherwise apply).][2]

(6) This section is subject to—

    . . .[1]

    section 700 (timing of assessments . . .[1]), and

    section 702(2) (effect of clearance notification under section 701).

(7) But no other provision in the Income Tax Acts is to be read as limiting the powers conferred by this section.

Commentary—*Simon's Taxes* **D9.101, D9.134.**

Amendments—[1]   In sub-s (6) entry repealed and words in entry relating to s 700 repealed by FA 2010 s 38, Sch 12 paras 1, 3 with effect in relation to income tax advantages obtained on or after 24 March 2010.

[2]   Sub-ss (1), (5) substituted by FA 2016 s 34(1), (4), (5) with effect in relation to a transaction occurring on or after 6 April 2016 or a series of transactions any one or more of which occurs on or after that date. Accordingly, ITA 2007 Part 13 Chapter 1 has effect without these amendments in relation to a tax advantage obtained on or after 6 April 2016 in consequence of a transaction occurring before that date or a series of transactions all of which occur before that date (FA 2016 s 34(9)).

[698A No-counteraction notices

(1) If on an enquiry under section 695 an officer of Revenue and Customs is of the opinion that no counteraction is required, the officer must serve notice on the person (a "no-counteraction notice") stating that no counteraction is required and why.

(2) The taxpayer may apply to the tribunal for a direction requiring an officer of Revenue and Customs to issue one of the following within a specified period—

    (*a*)   a counteraction notice;

    (*b*)   a no-counteraction notice.

(3) Any such application is to be subject to the relevant provisions of Part 5 of TMA 1970 (see, in particular, section 48(2)(*b*) of that Act).

(4) The tribunal must give the direction applied for unless satisfied that there are reasonable grounds for not serving either a counteraction notice or a no-counteraction notice within a specified period.][1]

Commentary—*Simon's Taxes* **D9.134.**

Amendments—[1]   Section 698A inserted by FA 2016 s 34(1), (6) with effect in relation to a transaction occurring on or after 6 April 2016 or a series of transactions any one or more of which occurs on or after that date. Accordingly, Chapter 1 of Part 13 of ITA 2007 has effect without this amendment in relation to a tax advantage obtained on or after 6 April 2016 in consequence of a transaction occurring before that date or a series of transactions all of which occur before that date (FA 2016 s 34(9)).

700 Timing of assessments . . .[1]

(1) This section applies if section 684 (person liable to counteraction of income tax advantage) applies to a person because the person is in a position to obtain or has obtained an income tax advantage by falling within the circumstances mentioned in [685(2)(*c*) or (3)][1] when share capital is repaid.

(2) An assessment to income tax made in accordance with a counteraction notice must be an assessment for the tax year in which the repayment occurs.

(3) The references in this section to the repayment of share capital include references to any distribution made in respect of any shares in a winding up or dissolution of the company.

(4) In subsection (3) "shares" includes stock and any other interest of a member in a company.

Commentary—*Simon's Taxes* **D9.118.**

Amendments—[1]   In sub-s (1) words substituted and in heading, words repealed, by FA 2010 s 38, Sch 12 paras 1, 5 with effect in relation to income tax advantages obtained on or after 24 March 2010.

Clearance procedure . . .[1]

Amendments—[1]   Words repealed by FA 2010 s 38, Sch 12 paras 1, 6. This amendment is treated as having come into force on 1 April 2009.

701 Application for clearance of transactions

(1) A person may provide the Commissioners for Her Majesty's Revenue and Customs with particulars of a transaction or transactions effected or to be effected by the person in order to obtain a notification about them under this section.

(2) If the Commissioners consider that the particulars, or any further information provided under this subsection, are insufficient for the purposes of this section, they must notify the person what further information they require for those purposes within 30 days of receiving the particulars or further information.

(3) If any such further information is not provided within 30 days from the notification, or such further time as the Commissioners allow, they need not proceed further under this section.

(4) The Commissioners must notify the person whether they are satisfied that the transaction or transactions, as described in the particulars, were or will be such that no counteraction notice ought to be served about the transaction or transactions.

(5) The notification must be given within 30 days of receipt of the particulars, or, if subsection (2) applies, of all further information required.

Commentary—*Simon's Taxes* **B9.116, D9.120**.
Derivation—TA 1988 s 707(1).
HMRC Manuals—Company Taxation Manual CTM36845 (response to a clearance application).

702 Effect of clearance notification under section 701

(1) This section applies if the Commissioners for Her Majesty's Revenue and Customs notify a person under section 701 that they are satisfied that a transaction or transactions, as described in the particulars provided under that section, were or will be such that no counteraction notice ought to be served about the transaction or transactions.

(2) No such notice may be served on the person in respect of the transaction or transactions.

(3) But the notification does not prevent such a notice being served on the person in respect of transactions including not only the ones to which the notification relates but also others.

(4) The notification is void if the particulars and any further information given under section 701 about the transaction or transactions do not fully and accurately disclose all facts and considerations which are material for the purposes of that section.

Commentary—*Simon's Taxes* **D9.121**.
Derivation—TA 1988 s 707.

Appeals

705 Appeals against counteraction notices

(1) A person on whom a counteraction notice has been served may appeal . . . [1] on the grounds that—

    (*a*) section 684 (person liable to counteraction of income tax advantage) does not apply to the person in respect of the transaction or transactions in question, or

    (*b*) the adjustments directed to be made are inappropriate.

(2) Such an appeal may be made only by giving notice to the Commissioners for Her Majesty's Revenue and Customs within 30 days of the service of the counteraction notice.

(3) On an appeal under this section [that is notified to the tribunal, the tribunal][1] may—

    (*a*) affirm, vary or cancel the counteraction notice, or

    (*b*) affirm, vary or quash an assessment made in accordance with the notice.

(4) But the bringing of an appeal under this section . . . [1] does not affect—

    (*a*) the validity of the counteraction notice, or

    (*b*) the validity of any other thing done under or in accordance with section 698 (counteraction notices),

pending the determination of the proceedings.

Commentary—*Simon's Taxes* **D9.135**.
Amendments—[1]   In sub-s (1), (4), words repealed, and in sub-s (3), words substituted by the Transfer of Tribunal Functions and Revenue and Customs Appeals Order, SI 2009/56 art 3, Sch 1 para 459 with effect from 1 April 2009.

Supplementary

712 Application of Chapter where individual within section 684 dies

(1) This section applies if an individual to whom section 684 (person liable to counteraction of income tax advantage) applies (or may apply) has died.

(2) Any notice or notification to the individual under this Chapter may be given to the individual's personal representatives.

(3) The provisions of this Chapter relating to any such notice or notification, to the making of a statutory declaration, to rights of appeal and to the giving of information must be read accordingly.

Commentary—*Simon's Taxes* **D9.130**.
Derivation—TA 1988 s 703(11).
HMRC Manuals—Company Taxation Manual CTM36825 (personal representatives).

713 Interpretation of Chapter

[(1)] In this Chapter—

["associate" is to be construed in accordance with section 681DL, but as if subsection (4) of that section also included, as persons associated with each other, a person as trustee of a settlement and an individual, where one or more beneficiaries of the settlement are connected or associated with the individual,][3]

["close company" includes a company that would be a close company if it were resident in the United Kingdom,][1]

"company" includes any body corporate,

"dividends" includes references to other . . . [2] distributions and to interest,

"securities"—

    (*a*) includes shares and stock, and

    (*b*) in relation to a company not limited by shares (whether or not it has a share capital) also includes a reference to the interest of a member of the company as such, whatever the form of that interest,

"trading stock" has the meaning given by section 174 of ITTOIA 2005, and
. . .

[(2) In the definition of "dividends" given by subsection (1), "other distributions" does not include a distribution which is a distribution for the purposes of the Corporation Tax Acts only because it falls within paragraph C or D in section 1000(1) (redeemable share capital or security issued as bonus in respect of shares in, or securities of, the company).][2]

Commentary—*Simon's Taxes* **D9.117**
Derivation—TA 1988 s 709(2).
HMRC Manuals—Company Taxation Manual CTM36810 (definition: securities).
Amendments—[1]   Definition inserted and definition repealed by FA 2010 s 38, Sch 12 paras 1, 7 with effect in relation to income tax advantages obtained on or after 24 March 2010.
[2]   Sub-s (1) numbered as such, word in definition of "dividends" repealed, and sub-s (2) inserted, by FA 2016 s 5, Sch 1 para 63(1), (11) with effect in relation to dividends paid or arising (or treated as paid), and other distributions made (or treated as made), in the tax year 2016-17 or at any later time.
[3]   Definition inserted by FA 2016 s 33(1), (7) with effect in relation to a transaction occurring on or after 6 April 2016 or a series of transactions any one or more of which occurs on or after that date. See FA 2016 s 33(9) in relation to a tax advantage obtained on or after 6 April in consequence of a transaction or series of transactions occurring before that date.

CHAPTER 2

TRANSFER OF ASSETS ABROAD

Commentary—*Simon's Taxes* **C4.438**.
Modification—ITA 2007 Sch 2 para 138 (in relation to transfers and associated operations on or after 20 March 1990 and before 30 November 1993, a body corporate regarded as resident in a territory outside the United Kingdom for the purposes of any double taxation arrangements is treated as if it were resident outside the United Kingdom for the purposes of this Chapter).

Introduction

714 Overview of Chapter

(1) This Chapter imposes a charge to income tax on—

    (*a*) individuals to whom income is treated as arising under section 721 (individuals with power to enjoy income as a result of relevant transactions),

    (*b*) individuals to whom income is treated as arising under section 728 (individuals receiving capital sums as a result of relevant transactions), and

    (*c*) individuals to whom income is treated as arising under section 732 (non-transferors receiving a benefit as a result of relevant transactions).

(2) The charges apply only if a relevant transfer occurs, and they operate by reference to income of a person abroad that is connected with the transfer or another relevant transaction.

(3) For the meaning of "relevant transaction", "relevant transfer" and "person abroad", see sections 715, 716 and 718 respectively.

(4) In this Chapter references to individuals include their spouses or civil partners.

Commentary—*Simon's Taxes* **E1.1110**.

715 Meaning of "relevant transaction"

(1) A transaction is a relevant transaction for the purposes of this Chapter if it is—

    (*a*) a relevant transfer, or

    (*b*) an associated operation.

(2) For the meaning of "relevant transfer" and "associated operation", see sections 716 and 719 respectively.

Commentary—*Simon's Taxes* **E1.1111**.
Derivation—TA 1988 s 741B(2).

716 Meaning of "relevant transfer" and "transfer"

(1) A transfer is a relevant transfer for the purposes of this Chapter if—

    (*a*) it is a transfer of assets, and

    (*b*) as a result of—

     (i) the transfer,

     (ii) one or more associated operations, or

     (iii) the transfer and one or more associated operations, income becomes payable to a person abroad.

(2) In this Chapter "transfer", in relation to rights, includes the creation of the rights.

(3) For the meaning of "assets", see section 717.

Commentary—*Simon's Taxes* E1.1110, 1113.

Modification—ITA 2007 Sch 2 para 141(1) (in relation to any time before 5 December 2005, the reference in sub-s (1)(*b*) above to income which becomes payable to a person abroad does not include income that becomes so payable just as a result of one or more associated operations).

717 Meaning of "assets" etc

In this Chapter—

     (*a*) "assets" includes property or rights of any kind, and

     (*b*) references to assets representing any assets, income or accumulations of income include references to—

         (i) shares in or obligations of any company to which the assets, income or accumulations are or have been transferred, or

         (ii) obligations of any other person to whom the assets, income or accumulations are or have been transferred.

Commentary—*Simon's Taxes* E1.1110.

Derivation—TA 1988 s 742(9).

718 Meaning of "person abroad" etc

(1) [In this Chapter "person abroad" means—

     (*a*) a person who is resident outside the United Kingdom, or

     (*b*) an individual who is domiciled outside the United Kingdom.][2]

(2) For the purposes of this Chapter, the following persons are treated as resident outside the United Kingdom—

     (*a*) . . .[2]

     (*b*) the person treated as [non-UK resident][1] under section 475(3) (trustees of settlements), and

     (*c*) persons treated as non-UK resident under section 834(4) (personal representatives).

[(3) Section 835BA (deemed domicile) applies for the purposes of subsection (1)(*b*).][3]

Commentary—*Simon's Taxes* E1.1112.

Amendments—[1]   Words in sub-s (2)(*b*) substituted for words "neither UK resident nor ordinarily UK resident" by FA 2013 s 219, Sch 46 paras 54, 59 with effect for the purposes of a person's tax liability to income tax for the tax year 2013–14 or any subsequent tax year, subject to savings in FA 2013 Sch 46 para 73. This section has effect, in relation to an individual who was resident in the UK for the tax year 2012–13 but was not ordinarily resident there at the end of that tax year, for a qualifying tax year, as if these amendments had not been made. This saving applies only if service in the employment in question began before the start of the tax year 2013–14. See FA 2013 Sch 46 para 73.

[2]   Sub-s (1) substituted and sub-s (2)(*a*) repealed by FA 2013 s 26, Sch 10 paras 1, 2 with effect in relation to times on or after 6 April 2012.

[3]   Sub-s (3) inserted by F(No 2)A 2017 s 29(2), Sch 8 paras 11, 13 with effect in relation to the tax year 2017–18 and subsequent tax years.

719 Meaning of "associated operation"

(1) In this Chapter "associated operation", in relation to a transfer of assets, means an operation of any kind effected by any person in relation to—

     (*a*) any of the assets transferred,

     (*b*) any assets directly or indirectly representing any of the assets transferred,

     (*c*) the income arising from any assets within paragraph (*a*) or (*b*), or

     (*d*) any assets directly or indirectly representing the accumulations of income arising from any assets within paragraph (*a*) or (*b*).

(2) It does not matter whether the operation is effected before, after or at the same time as the transfer.

Commentary—*Simon's Taxes* E1.1111.

Modification—ITA 2007 Sch 2 para 141(2) (modification of this section in relation to any time before 5 December 2005).

Charge where power to enjoy income

720 Charge to tax on income treated as arising under section 721

(1) The charge under this section applies for the purpose of preventing the avoiding of liability to income tax by individuals who are . . .[2] UK resident by means of relevant transfers.

(2) Income tax is charged on income treated as arising to such an individual under section 721 (individuals with power to enjoy income as a result of relevant transactions).

(3) Tax is charged under this section on the amount of income treated as arising in the tax year.

(4) But see section 724 (special rules where benefit provided out of income of person abroad) [and section 726 (non-UK domiciled individuals to whom remittance basis applies)][1].

(5) The person liable for any tax charged under this section is the individual to whom the income is treated as arising.

(6) For rules about the reduction in the amount charged in some circumstances and the availability of deductions and reliefs, see—

      section 725 (reduction in amount charged where controlled foreign company involved), and

      section 746 (deductions and reliefs where individual charged under this section or section 727).

(7) For exemptions from the charge under this section, see sections 736 to [742A][3] (exemptions where no tax avoidance purpose or genuine commercial transaction[, etc][3]).

Commentary—*Simon's Taxes* **E1.1120**.
Amendments—[1]   Words in sub-s (4) inserted by FA 2008 s 25, Sch 7 paras 163, 164 with effect for the tax year 2008–09 and subsequent tax years.
[2]   In sub-s (1), word "ordinarily" repealed by FA 2013 s 219, Sch 46 paras 54, 60 with effect for the purposes of a person's tax liability to income tax for the tax year 2013–14 or any subsequent tax year, subject to savings in FA 2013 Sch 46 para 73. This section has effect, in relation to an individual who was resident in the UK for the tax year 2012–13 but was not ordinarily resident there at the end of that tax year, for a qualifying tax year, as if these amendments had not been made. This saving applies only if service in the employment in question began before the start of the tax year 2013–14. See FA 2013 Sch 46 para 73.
[3]   In sub-s (7), reference substituted and word inserted by FA 2013 s 26, Sch 10 paras 1, 3 with effect for the tax year 2012–13 and subsequent tax years.

721 Individuals with power to enjoy income as a result of relevant transactions

(1) Income is treated as arising to such an individual as is mentioned in section 720(1) in a tax year for income tax purposes if [conditions A to C][1] are met.

(2) Condition A is that the individual has power in the tax year to enjoy income of a person abroad as a result of—

    (*a*)   a relevant transfer,

    (*b*)   one or more associated operations, or

    (*c*)   a relevant transfer and one or more associated operations.

(3) Condition B is that the income [of the person abroad][2] would be chargeable to income tax if it were the individual's and received by the individual in the United Kingdom.

[(3A) Condition C is that the individual is UK resident for the tax year.][1]

[[(3B) The amount of the income treated as arising under subsection (1) is (subject to sections 724 and 725) given by the following rules—

    Rule 1

    The amount is equal to the amount of the income of the person abroad if the individual—

       (*a*)   is domiciled in the United Kingdom at any time in the tax year, or

       (*b*)   is at any time in the tax year regarded for the purposes of section 718(1)(*b*) as domiciled in the United Kingdom as a result of section 835BA having effect because of Condition A in that section being met.

    Rule 2

    In any other case, the amount is equal to so much of the income of the person abroad as is not protected foreign-source income (see section 721A).

(3BA) In a case in which rule 2 of subsection (3B) applies, so much of the income of the person abroad as is protected foreign-source income for the purposes of that rule counts as "protected income" for the purposes of section 733A(1)(*b*)(i).][3]

(3C) Subsection (1) does not apply if—

    (*a*)   the individual is liable for income tax charged on the income of the person abroad by virtue of a charge not contained in this Chapter, and

    (*b*)   all that income tax has been paid.][2]

(4) For the purposes of subsection (2), it does not matter whether the income [of the person abroad][2] may be enjoyed immediately or only later.

(5) It does not matter for the purposes of this section—

    (*a*)   . . . [2]

    [(*b*)   whether the individual is UK resident for the tax year in which the relevant transfer is made (if different from the tax year mentioned in subsection (1)), or][1]

    (*c*)   whether the avoiding of liability to income tax is a purpose for which the transfer is effected.

(6) For the circumstances in which an individual is treated as having the power to enjoy income for the purposes of this section, see section 722.

Commentary—*Simon's Taxes* **E1.1120, 1128**.
Derivation—TA 1988 ss 739(1) to (2) and 742(1B).
HMRC Manuals—International Manual INTM600020 ("income charge").
Modifications—ITA 2007 Sch 2 para 140 (sub-s (5)(*b*), (*c*) above does not apply if the income arose before 26 November 1996).
ITA 2007 Sch 2 para 141(3) (in relation to any time before 5 December 2005, the reference in sub-s (2) above to income which an individual has power to enjoy does not include income which the individual has power to enjoy just as a result of one or more associated operations).
Amendments—[1]   In sub-s (1), words substituted for words "conditions A and B", sub-s (3A) inserted, and sub-s (5)(*b*) substituted, by FA 2013 s 219, Sch 46 paras 54, 61 with effect for the purposes of a person's tax liability to income tax for the tax year 2013–14 or any subsequent tax year, subject to savings in FA 2013 Sch 46 para 73.

This section has effect, in relation to an individual who was resident in the UK for the tax year 2012–13 but was not ordinarily resident there at the end of that tax year, for a qualifying tax year, as if these amendments had not been made. This saving applies only if service in the employment in question began before the start of the tax year 2013–14. See FA 2013 Sch 46 para 73.

2   In sub-ss (3), (4), words inserted, sub-ss (3B), (3C) inserted, and sub-s (5)(*a*) repealed, by FA 2013 s 26, Sch 10 para 10 with effect for the tax year 2013–14 and subsequent tax years. The insertion of sub-s (3C) has effect only if the income of the person abroad arises to that person on or after 6 April 2013. The repeal of sub-s (5)(*a*) has no effect in relation to income arising to a person abroad before 6 April 2013 (FA 2013 Sch 10 para 21). The other amendments apply in relation to relevant transfers occurring before 6 April 2013 as well as to relevant transfers occurring on or after that date (FA 2013 Sch 10 para 20(2)).

3   Sub-ss (3B), (3BA) substituted for sub-s (3B) by F(No 2)A 2017 s 29(2), Sch 8 paras 27, 28 with effect for the tax year 2017–18 and subsequent tax years.

[721A Meaning of "protected foreign-source income" in section 721

(1) This section has effect for the purposes of rule 2 of section 721(3B) (cases where the individual is not UK domiciled and is not deemed domiciled by virtue of Condition A in section 835BA).

(2) The income of the person abroad is "protected foreign-source income" so far as it is within subsection (3) or (4).

(3) Income is within this subsection if—

    (*a*) it would be relevant foreign income if it were the individual's,

    (*b*) the person abroad is the trustees of a settlement,

    (*c*) the trustees are non-UK resident for the tax year,

    (*d*) when the settlement is created, the individual is—

        (i) not domiciled in the United Kingdom, and

        (ii) if the settlement is created on or after 6 April 2017, not deemed domiciled in the United Kingdom, and

    (*e*) no property or income is provided directly or indirectly for the purposes of the settlement by the individual, or by the trustees of any other settlement of which the individual is a beneficiary or settlor, at a time in the period—

        (i) beginning with the start of 6 April 2017 or, if later, the creation of the settlement, and

        (ii) ending with the end of the tax year,

    when the individual is domiciled or deemed domiciled in the United Kingdom.

(4) Income is within this subsection if—

    (*a*) it would be relevant foreign income if it were the individual's,

    (*b*) the person abroad is a company,

    (*c*) the trustees of a settlement—

        (i) are participators in the person abroad, or

        (ii) are participators in the first in a chain of two or more companies where the last company in the chain is the person abroad and where each company in the chain (except the last) is a participator in the next company in the chain,

    (*d*) the individual's power to enjoy the income results from the trustees being participators as mentioned in paragraph (*c*)(i) or (ii),

    (*e*) the trustees are not UK resident for the tax year,

    (*f*) when the settlement is created, the individual is—

        (i) not domiciled in the United Kingdom, and

        (ii) if the settlement is created on or after 6 April 2017, not deemed domiciled in the United Kingdom, and

    (*g*) no property or income is provided directly or indirectly for the purposes of the settlement by the individual, or by the trustees of any other settlement of which the individual is a beneficiary or settlor, at a time in the period—

        (i) beginning with the start of 6 April 2017 or, if later, the creation of the settlement, and

        (ii) ending with the end of the tax year,

    when the individual is domiciled or deemed domiciled in the United Kingdom.

(5) For the purposes of subsections (3)(*e*) and (4)(*g*), the addition of value to property comprised in the settlement is to be treated as the direct provision of property for the purposes of the settlement.

(6) Section 721B (tainting) contains further provision for the purposes of subsections (3)(*e*) and (4)(*g*).

(7) In this section—

    "participator", in relation to a company, has the meaning given by section 454 of CTA 2010;

    "deemed domiciled" means regarded for the purposes of section 718(1)(*b*) as domiciled in the United Kingdom as a result of section 835BA of ITA 2007 having effect.][1]

Amendments—[1] Sections 721A, 721B inserted by F(No 2)A 2017 s 29(2), Sch 8 paras 27, 29 with effect for the tax year 2017–18 and subsequent tax years.

[721B Section 721A: tainting

(1) This section applies for the purposes of subsections (3)(*e*) and (4)(*g*) of section 721A.

(2) Ignore—

(a) property or income provided under a transaction, other than a loan, where the transaction is entered into on arm's length terms,

(b) property or income provided, otherwise than under a loan, without any intention by the person providing it to confer a gratuitous benefit on any person,

(c) the principal of a loan which is made to the trustees of the settlement on arm's length terms,

(d) the payment of interest to the trustees of the settlement under a loan made by them on arm's length terms,

(e) repayment to the trustees of the settlement of the principal of a loan made by them,

(f) property or income provided in pursuance of a liability incurred by any person before 6 April 2017, and

(g) where the settlement's expenses relating to taxation and administration for a tax year exceed its income for that year, property or income provided towards meeting that excess if the value of any such property and income is not greater than the amount of—

    (i) the excess, or

    (ii) if greater, the amount by which such expenses exceed the amount of such expenses which may be paid out of the settlement's income.

(3) Where—

(a) a loan is made to the trustees of the settlement by the settlor or the trustees of a settlement connected with the settlor, and

(b) the loan is on arm's length terms, but

(c) a relevant event occurs,

the principal of the loan is to be regarded as having been provided to the trustees at the time of that event (despite subsection (2)).

(4) In subsection (3) "relevant event" means—

(a) capitalisation of interest payable under the loan,

(b) any other failure to pay interest in accordance with the terms of the loan, or

(c) variation of the terms of the loan such that they cease to be arm's length terms.

(5) Subsection (6) applies (subject to subsection (7)) where—

(a) the settlor becomes deemed domiciled in the United Kingdom on or after 6 April 2017,

(b) before the date on which the settlor becomes deemed domiciled in the United Kingdom ("the deemed domicile date"), a loan has been made to the trustees of the settlement by—

    (i) the settlor, or

    (ii) the trustees of a settlement connected with the settlor,

(c) the loan is not entered into on arm's length terms, and

(d) any amount that is outstanding under the loan on the deemed domicile date ("the outstanding amount") is payable or repayable on demand on or after that date.

(6) Where this subsection applies, the outstanding amount is to be regarded as property directly provided on the deemed domicile date by the lender for the purposes of the settlement (despite subsection (2)).

(7) But if the deemed domicile date is 6 April 2017, subsection (6) does not apply if—

(a) the principal of the loan is repaid, and all interest payable under the loan is paid, before 6 April 2018, or

(b) the loan becomes a loan on arm's length terms before 6 April 2018 and—

    (i) before that date interest is paid to the lender in respect of the period beginning with 6 April 2017 and ending with 5 April 2018 as if those arm's length terms had been terms of the loan in relation to that period, and

    (ii) interest continues to be payable from 6 April 2018 in accordance with those terms.

(8) For the purposes of this section, a loan is on "arm's length terms"—

(a) in the case of a loan made to the trustees of a settlement, only if interest at the official rate or more is payable at least annually under the loan;

(b) in the case of a loan made by the trustees of a settlement, only if any interest payable under the loan is payable at no more than the official rate.

(9) For the purposes of this section—

a settlement is "connected" with a person if the person is the settlor or a beneficiary of it;

"deemed domiciled" has the same meaning as in section 721A;

"official rate", in relation to interest, means the rate of interest applicable from time to time under section 178 of FA 1989 for the purposes of Chapter 7 of Part 3 of ITEPA 2003.][1]

Amendments—[1]   Sections 721A, 721B inserted by F(No 2)A 2017 s 29(2), Sch 8 paras 27, 29 with effect for the tax year 2017–18 and subsequent tax years.

722 When an individual has power to enjoy income of person abroad

(1) For the purposes of section 721, an individual is treated as having power to enjoy income of a person abroad if any of the enjoyment conditions are met.

(2) In subsection (1) "the enjoyment conditions" means conditions A to E as specified in section 723.

(3) In determining whether an individual has power to enjoy income for the purposes of section 721, regard must be had to the substantial result and effect of all the relevant transactions.

(4) In making that determination all benefits which may at any time accrue to the individual as a result of the transfer and any associated operations must be taken into account, irrespective of—

    (a) the nature or form of the benefits, or

    (b) whether the individual has legal or equitable rights in respect of the benefits.

Commentary—*Simon's Taxes* **E1.1121**.
Derivation—TA 1988 s 742(2) and (3).

723 The enjoyment conditions

(1) Condition A is that the income is in fact so dealt with by any person as to be calculated at some time to enure for the benefit of the individual, whether in the form of income or not.

(2) Condition B is that the receipt or accrual of the income operates to increase the value to the individual—

    (a) of any assets the individual holds, or

    (b) of any assets held for the individual's benefit.

(3) Condition C is that the individual receives or is entitled to receive at any time any benefit provided or to be provided out of the income or related money.

(4) In subsection (3) "related money" means money which is or will be available for the purpose of providing the benefit as a result of the effect or successive effects—

    (a) on the income, and

    (b) on any assets which directly or indirectly represent the income,

of the associated operations referred to in section 721(2).

(5) Condition D is that the individual may become entitled to the beneficial enjoyment of the income if one or more powers are exercised or successively exercised.

(6) For the purposes of subsection (5) it does not matter—

    (a) who may exercise the powers, or

    (b) whether they are exercisable with or without the consent of another person.

(7) Condition E is that the individual is able in any manner to control directly or indirectly the application of the income.

Commentary—*Simon's Taxes* **E1.1122–1126**.
Derivation—TA 1988 s 742(2).

724 Special rules where benefit provided out of income of person abroad

(1) This section applies if an individual has power to enjoy income of a person abroad for the purposes of section 721 because of receiving any such benefit as is referred to in section 723(3) (benefit provided out of income of person abroad).

(2) Despite anything in section 720, the individual is liable to income tax under that section for the tax year in which the benefit is received on [an amount equal to][1] the whole of the amount or value of that benefit.

(3) But subsection (2) does not apply so far as it is shown that the benefit derives directly or indirectly from income [by reference to][1] which the individual has already been charged to income tax for that tax year or a previous tax year [under this Chapter][1].

Commentary—*Simon's Taxes* **E1.1124**.
Amendments—[1] In sub-ss (2), (3) words substituted and in sub-s (3) words inserted by FA 2013 s 26, Sch 10 para 11 with effect for the tax year 2013–14 and subsequent tax years. The amendments have effect in relation to relevant transfers occurring before 6 April 2013 as well as relevant transfers occurring on or after that date (FA 2013 s 26, Sch 10 para 20(2)).

725 Reduction in amount charged where controlled foreign company involved

[(1) This section applies if—

    (a) under Part 9A of TIOPA 2010 (controlled foreign companies), the CFC charge is charged in relation to a CFC's accounting period, . . . [2]

    (b) an amount of income is treated as arising to an individual under section 721 for a tax year, and

    (c) the income mentioned in section 721(2) is or includes a sum forming part of the CFC's chargeable profits for that accounting period.][2]

(2) The amount of income so treated is reduced by—

$$S \times \frac{CA}{CP}$$

where—

    S is the sum forming part of the [CFC's][1] chargeable profits for that accounting period,

    CA is the [CFC's chargeable profits for that accounting period so far as apportioned to chargeable companies at step 3 in section 371BC(1) of TIOPA 2010], and

    CP is the [CFC's][1] chargeable profits for that accounting period.

[(2A) In a case in which section 724 applies, the reference to S in the formula in subsection (2) is to be read as a reference to X% of S.

(2B) "X%" is determined as follows—

100% x (A / I)

where—

     A is the amount on which the individual is liable as determined under section 724(2), and

     I is the amount of the income mentioned in section 721(2).][2]

[(3) Terms used in this section which are defined in Part 9A of TIOPA 2010 have the same meaning as in that Part.][1]

Commentary—*Simon's Taxes* E1.1128.

Modification—FA 2013 Sch 10 para 12(4), (5) (modification of amendment to sub-s (1) made by FA 2013 Sch 10 para 12(2) in cases where the amendments made by FA 2012 Sch 20 para 22 are ignored in accordance with para 50(9) of that Schedule).

Amendments—[1]   Sub-ss (1), (3) substituted, in sub-s (2), in definitions of "S" and "CP", words substituted for words "controlled foreign company's", and in definition of "CA" words substituted for words "chargeable amount", by FA 2012 s 180, Sch 20 para 22 with effect in relation to accounting periods of CFCs beginning on or after 1 January 2013. This is subject to savings in FA 2012 Sch 20 para 50(9) which provides, broadly, that the amendments in question will not take effect until an accounting period under the new CFC rules in TIOPA 2010 Part 9A begins.

[2]   in sub-s (1), paras (*b*), (*c*) substituted for previous word "and", and preceding word "and", and sub-ss (2A), (2B) inserted, by FA 2013 s 26, Sch 10 para 12(1)–(3) with effect for the tax year 2013–14 and subsequent tax years (subject to the modification of the amendments to sub-s (1) in accordance with FA 2013 Sch 10 para 12(4), (5) in relation to cases where the changes made by FA 2012 Sch 20 para 22 are ignored). The amendments have effect in relation to relevant transfers occurring before 6 April 2013 as well as relevant transfers occurring on or after that date (FA 2013 s 26, Sch 10 para 20(2)).

[726 Non-UK domiciled individuals to whom remittance basis applies

[(1) This section applies in relation to income treated under section 721 as arising to an individual in a tax year ("the deemed income") if section 809B, 809D or 809E (remittance basis) applies to the individual for that year.][3]

(2) For the purposes of this section the deemed income is "foreign" if (and to [the corresponding extent][4] that) the income mentioned in section 721(2) would be relevant foreign income if it were the individual's.

(3) Treat the foreign deemed income as relevant foreign income of the individual.

(4) For the purposes of Chapter A1 of Part 14 (remittance basis) treat so much of the income within section 721(2) as would be relevant foreign income if it were the individual's as deriving from the foreign deemed income.

[(5) In the application of section 832 of ITTOIA 2005 to the foreign deemed income, subsection (2) of that section has effect with the omission of paragraph (*b*).][2]][1]

[(6) In addition, where the tax year in which any foreign deemed income arises is earlier than the tax year 2017-18, section 832 of ITTOIA 2005 does not apply to the foreign deemed income so far as it—

     (*a*)   is remitted to the United Kingdom in the tax year 2017-18 or a later tax year, and

     (*b*)   is transitionally protected income.

(7) In subsection (6)—

     "remitted to the United Kingdom" is to be read in accordance with Chapter A1 of Part 14, and "transitionally protected income" means any foreign deemed income where the income mentioned in section 721(2)—

         (*a*)   arises in a tax year earlier than the tax year 2017-18,

         (*b*)   would be protected foreign-source income as defined by section 721A if section 721A—

             (i)   had effect for tax years earlier than the tax year 2017-18, and

             (ii)   so had effect with the omission of its subsections (3)(*e*), (4)(*g*), (5) and (6), and

         (*c*)   has not prior to 6 April 2017 been distributed by the trustees of the settlement concerned.][5]

Commentary—*Simon's Taxes* E1.1127.

Amendments—[1]   Section 726 substituted by FA 2008 s 25, Sch 7 paras 163, 165 with effect for the tax year 2008–09 and subsequent tax years.

[2]   Sub-s (5) inserted by FA 2013 s 218, Sch 45 para 91(1), (2) with effect in calculating an individual's liability to income tax or capital gains tax for the tax year 2013–14 or any subsequent tax year, subject to transitional provisions and savings in FA 2013 Sch 45 paras 154–158.

[3]   Sub-s (1) substituted by FA 2013 s 219, Sch 46 para 19 with effect in relation to an individual's foreign income and gains for the tax year 2013–14 or any subsequent tax year, subject to transitional provisions in FA 2013 Sch 46 para 26.

[4]   In sub-s (2), words substituted by FA 2013 s 26, Sch 10 para 13 with effect for the tax year 2013–14 and subsequent tax years. The substitution has effect in relation to relevant transfers occurring before 6 April 2013 as well as in relation to relevant transfers occurring on or after that date (FA 2013 Sch 10 para 20(2)).

[5]   Sub-ss (6), (7) inserted by F(No 2)A 2017 s 29(2), Sch 8 paras 27, 30 with effect for the tax year 2017–18 and subsequent tax years.

Charge where capital sums received

727 Charge to tax on income treated as arising under section 728

(1) The charge under this section applies for the purpose of preventing the avoiding of liability to income tax by individuals who are . . . [2] UK resident by means of relevant transfers.

(2) Income tax is charged on income treated as arising to such an individual under section 728 (individuals receiving capital sums as a result of relevant transactions).

(3) Tax is charged under this section on the amount of income treated as arising in the tax year.

[(3A) But see section 730 (non-UK domiciled individuals to whom remittance basis applies).][1]

(4) The person liable for any tax charged under this section is the individual to whom the income is treated as arising.

(5) For exemptions from the charge under this section, see sections 736 to [742A][3] (exemptions where no tax avoidance purpose or genuine commercial transaction[, etc][3]).

(6) For rules about the availability of deductions and reliefs where income is charged under this section, see section 746 (deductions and reliefs where individual charged under section 720 or this section).

HMRC Manuals—International Manual INTM600020 ("income charge").

Amendments—[1]   Sub-s (3A) inserted by FA 2008 s 25, Sch 7 paras 163, 166 with effect for the tax year 2008–09 and subsequent tax years.

[2]   In sub-s (1), word "ordinarily" repealed by FA 2013 s 219, Sch 46 paras 54, 62 with effect for the purposes of a person's tax liability to income tax for the tax year 2013–14 or any subsequent tax year, subject to savings in FA 2013 Sch 46 para 73. This section has effect, in relation to an individual who was resident in the UK for the tax year 2012–13 but was not ordinarily resident there at the end of that tax year, for a qualifying tax year, as if these amendments had not been made. This saving applies only if service in the employment in question began before the start of the tax year 2013–14. See FA 2013 Sch 46 para 73.

[3]   In sub-s (5), reference substituted and word inserted by FA 2013 s 26, Sch 10 paras 1, 4 with effect for the tax year 2012–13 and subsequent tax years.

728 Individuals receiving capital sums as a result of relevant transactions

(1) Income is treated as arising to such an individual as is referred to in section 727(1) in a tax year for income tax purposes if—

   (*a*) income has become the income of a person abroad as a result of—

      (i) a relevant transfer,

      (ii) one or more associated operations, or

      (iii) a relevant transfer and one or more associated operations, . . . [1]

   (*b*) the capital receipt conditions are met in respect of the individual in the tax year (see section 729)[, and

   (*c*) the individual is UK resident for the tax year.][1]

[(1A) The amount of the income treated as arising under subsection (1) is (subject to subsection (2)) given by the following rules—

Rule 1

The amount is equal to the amount of the income of the person abroad if the individual—

(*a*) is domiciled in the United Kingdom at any time in the tax year, or

(*b*) is at any time in the tax year regarded for the purposes of section 718(1)(*b*) as domiciled in the United Kingdom as a result of section 835BA having effect because of Condition A in that section being met.

Rule 2

In any other case, the amount is equal to so much of the income of the person abroad as is not protected foreign-source income (see section 729A).

(1B) In a case in which rule 2 of subsection (1A) applies, so much of the income of the person abroad as is protected foreign-source income for the purposes of that rule counts as "protected income" for the purposes of section 733A(1)(*b*)(i).][3]

(2) Section 725 (reduction in amount charged where controlled foreign company involved) applies for determining the amount of income treated as arising under subsection (1) as [if—

   (*a*) in subsection (1) of that section—

      (i) the reference to section 721 were a reference to this section, and

      (ii) the reference to section 721(2) were a reference to subsection (1)(*a*) of this section, and

   (*b*) subsections (2A) and (2B) of that section were omitted.][2]

[(2A) Subsection (1) does not apply if—

   (*a*) the individual is liable for income tax charged on the income of the person abroad by virtue of a charge not contained in this Chapter, and

   (*b*) all that income tax has been paid.][2]

(3) It does not matter for the purposes of this section—

   (*a*) . . . [2]

   [(*b*) whether the individual is UK resident for the tax year in which the relevant transfer abroad is made (if different from the tax year mentioned in subsection (1)), or][1]

   (*c*) whether the avoiding of liability to income tax is a purpose for which that transfer is effected.

Commentary—*Simon's Taxes* **E1.1130**.

Modifications—ITA 2007 Sch 2 para 140 (sub-s (3)(*b*), (*c*) above does not apply if the income arose before 26 November 1996). ITA 2007 Sch 2 para 141(4), (5) (In relation to any time before 5 December 2005, the reference in sub-s (1)(*a*) to income which has become the income of a person abroad does not include income that has become such income just as a result of one or more associated operations).

Amendments—[1]   In sub-s (1)(*a*)(iii), word "and" repealed, sub-s (1)(*c*) and preceding word "and" inserted, and sub-s (3)(*b*) substituted, by FA 2013 s 219, Sch 46 paras 54, 63 with effect for the purposes of a person's tax liability to income tax for the tax year 2013–14 or any subsequent tax year, subject to savings in FA 2013 Sch 46 para 73. This section has effect, in relation to an individual who was resident in the UK for the tax year 2012–13 but was not ordinarily resident there at the end of that tax year, for a qualifying tax year, as if these amendments had not been made. This saving applies only if service in the employment in question began before the start of the tax year 2013–14. See FA 2013 Sch 46 para 73).

[2]   Sub-ss (1A), (2A) inserted, in sub-s (2), paras (*a*), (*b*) substituted for words "it applies for determining the amount so treated under section 721(1)", and in sub-s (3), para (*a*) repealed by FA 2013 s 26, Sch 10 para 14 with effect in relation to the tax year 2013–14 and subsequent tax years. The insertion of sub-s (2A) has effect only if the income of the person abroad arises to that person on or after 6 April 2013 and the repeal of sub-s (3)(*a*) has no effect in relation to income arising to a person abroad before 6 April 2013. The other amendments have effect in relation to relevant transfers occurring before 6 April 2013 as well as relevant transfers occurring on or after that date (FA 2013 Sch 10 para 20(2), 21).

[3]   Sub-ss (1A), (1B) substituted for sub-s (1A) by F(No 2)A 2017 s 29(2), Sch 8 paras 27, 31 with effect for the tax year 2017–18 and subsequent tax years.

729 The capital receipt conditions

(1) For the purposes of section 728(1), the capital receipt conditions are met in respect of the individual in a tax year ("the relevant year") if—

    (*a*) either—

        (i) in the relevant year the individual receives or is entitled to receive any capital sum, whether before or after the relevant transfer, or

        (ii) in any earlier tax year the individual has received any capital sum, whether before or after the relevant transfer, and

    (*b*) the payment of that sum is (or, in the case of an entitlement, would be) in any way connected with any relevant transaction.

(2) But subsection (1)(*a*)(ii) does not apply merely because of the receipt of a sum by way of loan if the loan is wholly repaid before the relevant year begins.

(3) In subsection (1) "capital sum" means—

    (*a*) any sum paid or payable by way of loan or repayment of a loan, and

    (*b*) any other sum paid or payable—

        (i) otherwise than as income, and

        (ii) not for full consideration in money or money's worth.

(4) For the purposes of subsection (1), a sum is treated as a capital sum which the individual ("A") receives or is entitled to receive if another person receives or is entitled to receive it—

    (*a*) at A's direction, or

    (*b*) as a result of the assignment by A of A's right to receive it.

Commentary—*Simon's Taxes* **E1.1131**.

[729A Meaning of "protected foreign-source income" in section 728

(1) This section has effect for the purposes of rule 2 of section 728(1A) (cases where the individual is not UK domiciled and is not deemed domiciled by virtue of Condition A in section 835BA).

(2) The income of the person abroad is "protected foreign-source income" so far as it is within subsection (3) or (4).

(3) Income is within this subsection if—

    (*a*) it would be relevant foreign income if it were the individual's,

    (*b*) the person abroad is the trustees of a settlement,

    (*c*) the trustees are non-UK resident for the tax year,

    (*d*) when the settlement is created, the individual is—

        (i) not domiciled in the United Kingdom, and

        (ii) if the settlement is created on or after 6 April 2017, not deemed domiciled in the United Kingdom, and

    (*e*) no property or income is provided directly or indirectly for the purposes of the settlement by the individual, or by the trustees of any other settlement of which the individual is a beneficiary or settlor, at a time in the period—

        (i) beginning with the start of 6 April 2017 or, if later, the creation of the settlement, and

        (ii) ending with the end of the tax year,

    when the individual is domiciled or deemed domiciled in the United Kingdom.

(4) Income is within this subsection if—

    (*a*) it would be relevant foreign income if it were the individual's,

    (*b*) the person abroad is a company,

    (*c*) the trustees of a settlement—

        (i) are participators in the person abroad, or

(ii) are participators in the first in a chain of two or more companies where the last company in the chain is the person abroad and where each company in the chain (except the last) is a participator in the next company in the chain,

(*d*) the condition in paragraph (*c*) is met as a result of a relevant transaction (whether or not it is also met otherwise than as a result of a relevant transaction),

(*e*) the income has become the income of the person abroad as a result of that relevant transaction,

(*f*) the trustees are not UK resident for the tax year,

(*g*) when the settlement is created, the individual is—

(i) not domiciled in the United Kingdom, and

(ii) if the settlement is created on or after 6 April 2017, not deemed domiciled in the United Kingdom, and

(*h*) no property or income is provided directly or indirectly for the purposes of the settlement by the individual, or by the trustees of any other settlement of which the individual is a beneficiary or settlor, at a time in the period—

(i) beginning with start of 6 April 2017 or, if later, the creation of the settlement, and

(ii) ending with the end of the tax year,

when the individual is domiciled or deemed domiciled in the United Kingdom.

(5) For the purposes of subsections (3)(*e*) and (4)(*h*), the addition of value to property comprised in the settlement is to be treated as the direct provision of property for the purposes of the settlement.

(6) Section 721B (tainting) applies for the purposes of subsections (3)(*e*) and (4)(*h*) as it applies for the purposes of section 721A(3)(*e*) and (4)(*g*).

(7) In this section—

"participator", in relation to a company, has the meaning given by section 454 of CTA 2010, and "deemed domiciled" means regarded for the purposes of section 718(1)(*b*) as domiciled in the United Kingdom as a result of section 835BA of ITA 2007 having effect.]¹

Amendments—[1]   Section 729A inserted by F(No 2)A 2017 s 29(2), Sch 8 paras 27, 32 with effect for the tax year 2017–18 and subsequent tax years.

[730 Non-UK domiciled individuals to whom remittance basis applies

[(1) This section applies in relation to income treated under section 728 as arising to an individual in a tax year ("the deemed income") if section 809B, 809D or 809E (remittance basis) applies to the individual for that year.]³

(2) For the purposes of this section the deemed income is "foreign" if (and to [the corresponding extent]⁴ that) the income mentioned in section 728(1)(*a*) would be relevant foreign income if it were the individual's.

(3) Treat the foreign deemed income as relevant foreign income of the individual.

(4) For the purposes of Chapter A1 of Part 14 (remittance basis) treat so much of the income within section 728(1)(*a*) as would be relevant foreign income if it were the individual's as deriving from the foreign deemed income.]¹

[(5) In the application of section 832 of ITTOIA 2005 to the foreign deemed income, subsection (2) of that section has effect with the omission of paragraph (*b*).]²

[(6) In addition, where the tax year in which any foreign deemed income arises is earlier than the tax year 2017-18, section 832 of ITTOIA 2005 does not apply to the foreign deemed income so far as it—

(*a*) is remitted to the United Kingdom in the tax year 2017-18 or a later tax year, and

(*b*) is transitionally protected income.

(7) In subsection (6)—

"remitted to the United Kingdom" is to be read in accordance with Chapter A1 of Part 14, and "transitionally protected income" means any foreign deemed income where the income mentioned in section 728(1)(*a*)—

(*a*) arises in a tax year earlier than the tax year 2017-18,

(*b*) would be protected foreign-source income as defined by section 729A if section 729A—

(i) had effect for tax years earlier than the tax year 2017-18, and

(ii) so had effect with the omission of its subsections (3)(*e*), (4)(*h*), (5) and (6), and

(*c*) has not prior to 6 April 2017 been distributed by the trustees of the settlement concerned.]⁵

Commentary—*Simon's Taxes* E1.1132.

Amendments—[1]   Section 730 substituted by FA 2008 s 25, Sch 7 paras 163, 167 with effect for the tax year 2008–09 and subsequent tax years.

²   Sub-s (5) inserted by FA 2013 s 218 Sch 45 para 91(1), (3) with effect in calculating an individual's liability to income tax or capital gains tax for the tax year 2013–14 or any subsequent tax year, subject to transitional provisions and savings in FA 2013 Sch 45 paras 154–158.

³   Sub-s (1) substituted by FA 2013 s 219, Sch 46 para 20 with effect in relation to an individual's foreign income and gains for the tax year 2013–14 or any subsequent tax year, subject to transitional provisions in FA 2013 Sch 46 para 26.

[4]   In sub-s (2) words substituted by FA 2013 s 26, Sch 10 para 15 with effect for the tax year 2013–14 and subsequent tax years. This amendment has effect in relation to relevant transfers occurring before 6 April 2013 as well as relevant transfers occurring on or after that date (FA 2013 Sch 10 para 20(2)).

[5]   Sub-ss (6), (7) inserted by F(No 2)A 2017 s 29(2), Sch 8 paras 27, 33 with effect for the tax year 2017–18 and subsequent tax years.

Charge where benefit received

731 Charge to tax on income treated as arising under section 732

(1) Income tax is charged on income treated as arising to an individual under section 732 ([individuals][3] receiving a benefit as a result of relevant transactions).

[(1A) But where the individual is non-UK resident for the tax year in which a benefit is received, there is a charge to tax under this section on any matched deemed income—

    (*a*) only so far as that matched deemed income would under section 735A (if it applied also for this purpose) be matched with an amount of relevant income that is protected income for the purposes of section 733A(1)(*b*)(i) (see sections 721(3BA) and 728(1B)), and

    (*b*) only if—

        (i) the individual is the settlor of the settlement concerned, or

        (ii) the benefit is received by the individual at a time when the individual is a close member of the family of the settlor of that settlement.

(1B) For the purposes of subsection (1A)—

    (*a*) "matched deemed income" means income which—

        (i) is treated by section 732 as arising to the individual, and

        (ii) would, if section 735A applied also for this purpose, be matched under that section with the benefit, and

    (*b*) a person is a close member of the family of the settlor of a settlement if the person is—

        (i) the settlor's spouse or civil partner, or

        (ii) a child of the settlor, or of a person within sub-paragraph (i), if the child has not reached the age of 18;

and section 733A(7) (persons living together) applies also for the purposes of paragraph (*b*).][3]

[(1C) Subsection (1A) does not restrict the charge to tax under this section on income treated as arising to the individual by section 733C or 733E (onward gifts: recipient or settlor treated as individual to whom income is treated as arising).][4]

(2) Tax is charged under this section on the amount of income treated as arising for the tax year.

[(2A) But see [sections 735, 735B and 735C][4] (non-UK domiciled individuals to whom remittance basis applies).][1]

(3) The person liable for any tax charged under this section is the individual to whom the income is treated as arising[, but this is subject to section 733A][3].

(4) For exemptions from the charge under this section, see sections 736 to [742A][2] (exemptions where no tax avoidance purpose or genuine commercial transaction[, etc][2]).

HMRC Manuals—International Manual INTM600030 ("benefits charge").

Amendments—[1]   Sub-s (2A) inserted by FA 2008 s 25, Sch 7 paras 163, 168 with effect for the tax year 2008–09 and subsequent tax years.

[2]   In sub-s (4), reference substituted and word inserted by FA 2013 s 26, Sch 10 paras 1, 5 with effect for the tax year 2012–13 and subsequent tax years.

[3]   In sub-s (1), word substituted for word "non-transferors", sub-ss (1A), (1B) inserted, and in sub-s (3), words inserted, by F(No 2)A 2017 s 29(2), Sch 8 paras 27, 34 with effect for the tax year 2017–18 and subsequent tax years.

[4]   Sub-s (1C) inserted, and in sub-s (2A), words substituted, by FA 2018 s 35, Sch 10 paras 12, 13 with effect for the tax year 2018–19 and subsequent tax years.

732 [Individuals] receiving a benefit as a result of relevant transactions

(1) This section applies if—

    (*a*) a relevant transfer occurs,

    (*b*) an individual [receives a benefit in a tax year][2],

    (*c*) the benefit is provided out of assets which are available for the purpose as a result of—

        (i) the transfer, or

        (ii) one or more associated operations,

    [(*d*) where there is a time in the year when the individual is relevantly domiciled, the individual is not liable to income tax under section 720 or 727 by reference to the transfer, and][2]

    (*e*) the individual is not liable to income tax[, under any provision that is none of section 731 of this Act and sections 643A, 643J and 643L of ITTOIA 2005,][3] on the amount or value of the benefit . . .[3].

(2) Income is treated as arising to the individual for income tax purposes for any tax year for which section 733 provides that income arises.

(3) Also see that section for the amount of income treated as arising for any such tax year.

[(4) For the purposes of subsection (1)(*d*), the individual is "relevantly domiciled" at any time if at that time—

    (*a*) the individual is domiciled in the United Kingdom, or

(b) the individual is regarded for the purposes of section 718(1)(b) as domiciled in the United Kingdom as a result of section 835BA having effect because of Condition A in that section being met.][2]

Commentary—*Simon's Taxes* E1.1141, C4.438.

Modification—ITA 2007 Sch 2 para 133 (transitional provisions and savings).

Amendments—[1]   In sub-s (1)(b) words substituted for words "ordinarily UK resident receives a benefit" by FA 2013 s 219, Sch 46 paras 54, 64 with effect for the purposes of a person's tax liability to income tax for the tax year 2013–14 or any subsequent tax year, subject to savings in FA 2013 Sch 46 para 73. This section has effect, in relation to an individual who was resident in the UK for the tax year 2012–13 but was not ordinarily resident there at the end of that tax year, for a qualifying tax year, as if these amendments had not been made. This saving applies only if service in the employment in question began before the start of the tax year 2013–14. See FA 2013 Sch 46 para 73.

[2]   In heading, word substituted for word "non-transferors", in sub-s (1)(b) words substituted for words "who is UK resident for a tax year receives a benefit in that tax year", sub-s (1)(d) substituted, and sub-s (4) inserted, by F(No 2)A 2017 s 29(2), Sch 8 paras 27, 35(1)–(4) with effect for the tax year 2017–18 and subsequent tax years.

[3]   In sub-s (1)(e), words inserted and repealed by FA 2018 s 35, Sch 10 paras 12, 14 with effect for the tax year 2018–19 and subsequent tax years.

733 Income charged under section 731

(1) To find the amount (if any) of the income treated as arising under section 732(2) for any tax year in respect of benefits provided as mentioned in section 732(1)(c) take the following steps.

> *Step 1* Identify the amount or value of such benefits received by the individual in the tax year and in any earlier tax years in which section 732 has applied.
>
> The sum of those amounts and values is "the total benefits".
>
> *Step 2* Deduct from the total benefits the total amount of income treated as arising to the individual under section 732(2) for earlier tax years as a result of the relevant transfer or associated operations [except that, where any of that income is matched deemed income for the purposes of section 731(1A), that matched deemed income is to be deducted only so far as it is matched deemed income on which tax has been charged under section 731 for an earlier tax year][1].
>
> The result is "the total untaxed benefits".
>
> *Step 3* Identify the amount of any income which—
>
> > (a) arises in the tax year to a person abroad, and
> >
> > (b) as a result of the relevant transfer or associated operations can be used directly or indirectly for providing a benefit for the individual.
>
> That amount is "the relevant income of the tax year" in relation to the individual and the tax year.
>
> *Step 4* Add together the relevant income of the tax year and the relevant income of earlier tax years in relation to the individual (identified as mentioned in Step 3). The sum of those amounts is "total relevant income".
>
> *Step 5* Deduct from total relevant income—
>
> > (a) the amount deducted at Step 2, and
> >
> > (b) any other amount which may not be taken into account because of section 743(1) and (2) (no duplication of charges).
>
> The result is "the available relevant income".
>
> *Step 6* Compare the total untaxed benefits and the available relevant income.
>
> The amount of the income treated as arising under section 732(2) for any tax year is the total untaxed benefits unless the available relevant income is lower. If the available relevant income is lower, it is the amount of income treated as so arising.

(2) Subsection (1) is subject to section 734 (reduction in amount charged: previous capital gains tax charge).

(3) See also section 740(5) to (7) (which makes provision about relevant income and benefits where relevant transactions include both transactions before 5 December 2005 and transactions after 4 December 2005 and exemptions under this Chapter cease to apply).

Commentary—*Simon's Taxes* E1.1141.

Modifications—ITA 2007 Sch 2 para 133 (transitional provisions and savings).

ITA 2007 Sch 2 para 135(3)–(5) (transitional provisions and savings).

ITA 2007 Sch 2 para 137(3)–(5) (transitional provisions and savings).

Amendments—[1]   In sub-s (1), Step 2, words inserted by F(No 2)A 2017 s 29(2), Sch 8 paras 27, 35(5) with effect for the tax year 2017–18 and subsequent tax years.

[733A Settlor liable for section 731 charge on closely-related beneficiary

(1) Subsections (2) and (3) apply if—

(a) an amount of income is treated as arising to an individual under section 732 for a tax year,

(b) under section 735A (if it applied also for this purpose) that amount would be matched—

> (i) with an amount of relevant income that is protected income for the purposes of this sub-paragraph (see sections 721(3BA) and 728(1B)), and

    (ii) with a benefit received by the individual at a time when the individual was a close member (see subsection (7)) of the family of the settlor of the settlement concerned,

  (c) there is no time in the year when the trustees of the settlement are resident in the United Kingdom,

  (d) there is a time in the year when the settlor is resident in the United Kingdom,

  (e) there is no time in the year when the settlor is domiciled in the United Kingdom, and

  (f) there is no time in the year when the settlor is regarded for the purposes of section 718(1)(b) as domiciled in the United Kingdom as a result of section 835BA having effect because of Condition A in that section being met.

(2) If—

  (a) the individual is not resident in the United Kingdom at any time in the year, or

  (b) section 809B, 809D or 809E (remittance basis) applies to the individual for the year and none of the amount mentioned in subsection (1)(a) of this section is remitted to the United Kingdom in the year,

the settlor is liable for the tax charged under section 731 on that amount as if that amount were income arising to the settlor in the year (and the individual is not liable in any later year for income tax on that amount).

(3) If—

  (a) section 809B, 809D or 809E (remittance basis) applies to the individual for the year, and

  (b) part only of the amount mentioned in subsection (1)(a) of this section is remitted to the United Kingdom in the year,

the settlor is liable for the tax charged under section 731 on the remainder of that amount as if that remainder were income arising to the settlor in the year (and the individual is not liable in any later year for income tax on that remainder).

(4) The amount mentioned in subsection (1)(a) may be the whole, or part only, of the amount treated as arising to the individual under section 732 for the year in the case of the relevant transfer and its associated operations.

(5) Where any tax for which the settlor is liable as a result of subsection (2) or (3) is paid, the settlor is entitled to recover the amount of the tax from the individual.

(6) For the purpose of recovering that amount, the settlor is entitled to require an officer of Revenue and Customs to give the settlor a certificate specifying—

  (a) the amount of the income concerned, and

  (b) the amount of tax paid,

and any such certificate is conclusive evidence of the facts stated in it.

(7) For the purposes of subsection (1)(b)(ii), a person is a close member of the family of the settlor [at any time if the settlor is living at that time and—

  (a) the person is the settlor's spouse or civil partner at that time, or

  (b) the person—

    (i) is a child of the settlor, or of a person who at that time is the settlor's spouse or civil partner, and

    (ii) at that time has not reached the age of 18.][2]

[(8) For the purposes of subsection (7), two people living together as if they were a married couple or civil partners are treated as if they were spouses or civil partners of each other.][3]

(9) Sections 809L to 809Z6 (remittance basis: rules about when income is remitted, including rule treating pre-arising remittances of deemed income as made when the income arises) apply for the purposes of this section.][1]

Amendments—[1]   Section 733A inserted by F(No 2)A 2017 s 29(2), Sch 8 paras 27, 36 with effect for the tax year 2017–18 and subsequent tax years.

[2]   Words in sub-s (7) substituted by FA 2018 s 35, Sch 10 paras 12, 15 with effect for the tax year 2017–18 and subsequent tax years (FA 2018 Sch 10 para 21(5)).

[3]   Sub-s (8) substituted by the Civil Partnership (Opposite-sex Couples) Regulations, SI 2019/1458 reg 29(1), (2) with effect from 2 December 2019.

[733B Recipients of onward gifts

(1) Sections 733C to 733E apply if—

  (a) an amount of income is treated as arising under section 732 to an individual ("the original beneficiary") in a tax year ("the arising year") but neither by section 733C nor by section 733E,

  (b) under section 735A (if it applied also for this purpose) that amount would be matched—

    (i) with an amount of relevant income that is protected income for the purposes of section 733A(1)(b)(i) (see sections 721(3BA) and 728(1B)), and

    (ii) with the whole or part of a benefit received by the original beneficiary,

  (c) at the time that benefit is received by the original beneficiary ("the distribution time")—

    (i) there are arrangements, or there is an intention, as regards the (direct or indirect) passing-on of the whole or part of that benefit to another person, and

(ii) it is reasonable to expect that, in the event of the whole or part of that benefit being passed on to another person as envisaged by the arrangements or intention, that other person will be UK resident when they receive at least part of what is passed on to them,

(*d*) the original beneficiary makes, directly or indirectly, a gift ("the onward payment") to a person ("the subsequent recipient")—

(i) at the distribution time, or at any later time in the 3 years beginning with the start time, or

(ii) at any time before the distribution time and, it is reasonable to assume, in anticipation of receipt of the benefit mentioned in paragraph (*b*)(ii),

(*e*) the gift is of or includes—

(i) the whole or part of the benefit mentioned in paragraph (*b*)(ii),

(ii) anything that (wholly or in part, and directly or indirectly) derives from, or represents, the whole or part of that benefit, or

(iii) any other property, but only if the benefit mentioned in paragraph (*b*)(ii) is provided with a view to enabling or facilitating, or otherwise in connection with, the making of the gift of the property to the subsequent recipient,

(*f*) except where an individual is liable as a result of section 733A(2) or (3) for the tax charged under section 731 on the amount mentioned in paragraph (*a*), either—

(i) the original beneficiary is non-UK resident for the arising year, or

(ii) section 809B or 809D or 809E (remittance basis) applies to the original beneficiary for the arising year and none of the amount mentioned in paragraph (*a*) is relevantly remitted before the end of the charging year, and

(*g*) where an individual is liable as a result of section 733A(2) or (3) for the tax charged under section 731 on the amount mentioned in paragraph (*a*), section 809B or 809D or 809E applies to that individual for the arising year and none of the amount mentioned in paragraph (*a*) is relevantly remitted before the end of the charging year.

(2) If—

(*a*) the amount mentioned in subsection (1)(*a*) is not treated as arising by section 733D (and neither by section 733C nor by section 733E),

(*b*) except where an individual is liable as a result of section 733A(2) or (3) for the tax charged under section 731 on that amount, section 809B or 809D or 809E applies to the original beneficiary for the arising year,

(*c*) where an individual is liable as a result of section 733A(2) or (3) for the tax charged under section 731 on that amount, section 809B or 809D or 809E applies to that individual for the arising year, and

(*d*) part only of that amount is relevantly remitted before the end of the charging year,

subsection (1)(*a*) is to be treated as referring instead only to the remainder of that amount.

(3) The original beneficiary is not liable to tax for any year after the charging year on so much of the amount mentioned in subsection (1)(*a*) as is—

(*a*) treated as arising to the subsequent recipient by section 733C, or

(*b*) treated as arising to the settlor by section 733E;

and the settlor is not is liable under section 733A(2) or (3) to tax for any year after the charging year on so much of the amount mentioned in subsection (1)(*a*) as is treated as arising to the subsequent recipient by section 733C.

(4) For the purposes of subsection (1)(*d*)(i)—

(*a*) if the amount mentioned in subsection (1)(*a*) is not one that is treated as arising by section 733D, "the start time" is the time the benefit mentioned in subsection (1)(*b*) is provided to the original beneficiary, and

(*b*) if the amount mentioned in subsection (1)(*a*) is one that is treated as arising by section 733D in connection with the operation of this section on a previous occasion, "the start time" is the time given by this subsection as the start time on that occasion.

(5) Where the onward payment is made as mentioned in subsection (1)(*d*)(ii), the onward payment is to be treated—

(*a*) for the purposes of the provisions of this section following subsection (1)(*d*), and

(*b*) for the purposes of sections 733C to 733E,

as made immediately after, and in the tax year containing, the distribution time.

(6) Where subsection (1)(*d*) and (*e*) are met in any case, it is to be presumed (unless the contrary is shown) that subsection (1)(*c*) is also met in that case.

(7) In this section—

"arrangements" includes any agreement, understanding, scheme, transaction or series of transactions (whether or not legally enforceable),

"the charging year" means the gift year or, if later, the matching year,

"gift" includes any benefit,

"the gift year" means the tax year in which the onward payment is made, but see subsection (5), "make", in relation to a gift that is a benefit, means provide,

"the matching year" means the first tax year in which the matching mentioned in subsection (1)(*b*) would occur,

"relevantly remitted" means remitted to the United Kingdom in a tax year for which the original beneficiary is UK resident but, where an individual is liable as a result of section 733A(2) or (3) for the tax charged under section 731 on the amount mentioned in subsection (1)(*a*), means remitted to the United Kingdom in a tax year for which that individual is UK resident, and

"the settlor" means the settlor of the settlement, mentioned in section 721A(3) or (4) or 729A(3) or (4), which because of subsection (1)(*b*)(i) is the settlement concerned.

(8) Sections 742C to 742E (value of benefit provided to a person) apply in relation to the onward payment as if references in those sections to a benefit provided were references to a gift made.

(9) Sections 809L to 809Z6 (remittance basis: rules about when income is remitted, including rule treating pre-arising remittances of deemed income as made when the income arises)—

(*a*) apply for the purposes of this section and sections 733C to 733E, and

(*b*) apply for those purposes in relation to references to remittance of the onward payment as if the onward payment were relevant foreign income of the subsequent recipient.]¹

Commentary—*Simon's Taxes* **E1.1144.**

Amendments—¹   Sections 733B–733E inserted by FA 2018 s 35, Sch 10 paras 12, 16 with effect only in relation to onward payments made on or after 6 April 2018. These sections have effect in relation to an onward payment made on or after that date even where the onward payment is referable to a benefit received before that date (FA 2018 Sch 10 para 21(4)).

[733C Cases where income treated as arising to recipient of onward gift

(1) Subsection (3) applies if—

(*a*) this section applies (see section 733B(1)), and

(*b*) the subsequent recipient is UK resident for the gift year, and

(*c*) the subsequent recipient is UK resident for the matching year if that is later than the gift year, and

(*d*) none of sections 809B, 809D and 809E applies to the subsequent recipient for the charging year.

(2) Subsection (3) also applies if—

(*a*) this section applies (see section 733B(1)), and

(*b*) the subsequent recipient is UK resident for the gift year, and

(*c*) the subsequent recipient is UK resident for the matching year if that is later than the gift year, and

(*d*) section 809B, 809D or 809E applies to the subsequent recipient for the charging year, and

(*e*) the whole, or part only, of the onward payment is remitted to the United Kingdom in the charging year.

(3) Section 731 has effect—

(*a*) as if the subsequent recipient were an individual to whom income is treated as arising under section 732 for the charging year, and

(*b*) as if, subject to subsection (4), the amount of that income—

(i) were equal to the amount or value of so much of the onward payment as is within any of sub-paragraphs (i) to (iii) of section 733B(1)(*e*), or

(ii) were, where this subsection applies because of subsection (2) and part only of that much of the onward payment is remitted to the United Kingdom in the charging year, equal to the amount or value of that part.

(4) The amount given by subsection (3) (before adjustment under this subsection) is to be adjusted as follows—

(*a*) deduct any part of the amount on which the subsequent recipient is liable to income tax otherwise than under this section, and

(*b*) if following any adjustment under paragraph (*a*) the amount exceeds the amount mentioned in section 733B(1)(*a*), deduct the excess.]¹

Commentary—*Simon's Taxes* **E1.1144.**

Amendments—¹   Sections 733B–733E inserted by FA 2018 s 35, Sch 10 paras 12, 16 with effect only in relation to onward payments made on or after 6 April 2018. These sections have effect in relation to an onward payment made on or after that date even where the onward payment is referable to a benefit received before that date (FA 2018 Sch 10 para 21(4)).

[733D Cases where deemed income attributed to recipient of onward gift

(1) Subsection (3) applies if this section applies (see section 733B(1)) and—

(*a*) the subsequent recipient is non-UK resident for the gift year, or

(*b*) the matching year is later than the gift year and the subsequent recipient is UK resident for the gift year but non-UK resident for the matching year.

(2) Subsection (3) also applies if—

(*a*) this section applies (see section 733B(1)), and

(*b*) the subsequent recipient is UK resident for the gift year, and

(*c*) the subsequent recipient is UK resident for the matching year if that is later than the gift year, and (*d*) section 809B, 809D or 809E applies to the subsequent recipient for the charging year, and

(*e*) none, or part only, of the onward payment is remitted to the United Kingdom in the charging year.

(3) Section 733B(1)(*a*) has effect—

    (*a*) as if the subsequent recipient were an individual to whom income is treated as arising under section 732 for the charging year, and

    (*b*) as if, subject to subsection (4), the amount of that income—

        (i) were equal to the amount or value of so much of the onward payment as is within any of sub-paragraphs (i) to (iii) of section 733B(1)(*e*) and is not treated as arising to someone other than the subsequent recipient as a result of the operation of section 733E, or

        (ii) were, where this subsection applies because of subsection (2) and part only of that much of the onward payment is remitted to the United Kingdom in the charging year, equal to the amount or value of the remainder of that much of the onward payment.

(4) The amount given by subsection (3) (before adjustment under this subsection) is to be adjusted as follows: if that amount exceeds the amount mentioned in section 733B(1)(*a*) in the case of the original beneficiary, deduct the excess.

(5) Where the amount mentioned in section 733B(1)(*a*) is one treated as arising by this section in connection with the operation of section 733B and this section on a previous occasion, section 733B(1) has effect—

    (*a*) with the omission of its paragraphs (*b*) and (*c*),

    (*b*) as if the reference in its paragraph (*d*) to the benefit mentioned in its paragraph (*b*)(ii) were, instead, to what was the onward payment on that previous occasion,

    (*c*) as if the references in its paragraph (*d*) to the distribution time were, instead, to the time when that onward payment was made, and

    (*d*) as if the references in its paragraph (*e*) to the benefit mentioned in its paragraph (*b*)(ii) were, instead, to so much of that onward payment as was on that previous occasion within any of sub-paragraphs (i) to (iii) of its paragraph (*e*).][1]

Commentary—*Simon's Taxes* E1.1144.

Amendments—[1]   Sections 733B–733E inserted by FA 2018 s 35, Sch 10 paras 12, 16 with effect only in relation to onward payments made on or after 6 April 2018. These sections have effect in relation to an onward payment made on or after that date even where the onward payment is referable to a benefit received before that date (FA 2018 Sch 10 para 21(4)).

[733E Cases where settlor liable following onward gift

(1) Subsection (3) applies if—

    (*a*) this section applies (see section 733B(1)),

    (*b*) the subsequent recipient is a close member of the settlor's family when the onward payment is made,

    (*c*) the subsequent recipient is UK resident for the charging year,

    (*d*) section 809B, 809D or 809E applies to the subsequent recipient for the charging year,

    (*e*) none, or part only, of the onward payment is remitted to the United Kingdom in the charging year,

    (*f*) there is a time in the charging year when the settlor is UK resident,

    (*g*) there is no time in the charging year when the settlor is domiciled in the United Kingdom, and

    (*h*) there is no time in the charging year when the settlor is regarded for the purposes of section 718(1)(*b*) as domiciled in the United Kingdom as a result of section 835BA having effect because of Condition A in that section being met.

(2) Subsection (3) also applies if—

    (*a*) this section applies (see section 733B(1)),

    (*b*) the subsequent recipient is a close member of the settlor's family when the onward payment is made,

    (*c*) the subsequent recipient is non-UK resident for the charging year,

    (*d*) there is a time in the charging year when the settlor is UK resident,

    (*e*) there is no time in the charging year when the settlor is domiciled in the United Kingdom, and

    (*f*) there is no time in the charging year when the settlor is regarded for the purposes of section 718(1)(*b*) as domiciled in the United Kingdom as a result of section 835BA having effect because of Condition A in that section being met.

(3) Section 731 applies—

    (*a*) as if the settlor were an individual to whom income is treated as arising under section 732 for the charging year, and

    (*b*) as if, subject to subsection (4), the amount of that income—

        (i) were equal to the amount or value of so much of the onward payment as is within any of sub-paragraphs (i) to (iii) of section 733B(1)(*e*), or

ITA 2007

    (ii) were, where this subsection applies because of subsection (1) in a case where part only of that much of the onward payment is remitted to the United Kingdom in the charging year, equal to the amount or value of the remainder of that much of the onward payment.

(4) The amount given by subsection (3)(*b*) (before adjustment under this subsection) is to be adjusted as follows—

    (*a*) deduct any part of the amount on which the settlor is liable to income tax otherwise than under this section, and

    (*b*) if following any adjustment under paragraph (*a*) the amount exceeds the amount mentioned in section 733B(1)(*a*), deduct the excess.

(5) Where any tax for which the settlor is liable as a result of subsections (3) and (4) is paid, the settlor is entitled to recover the amount of the tax from the subsequent recipient.

(6) For the purpose of recovering that amount, the settlor is entitled to require an officer of Revenue and Customs to give the settlor a certificate specifying—

    (*a*) the amount of the income concerned, and

    (*b*) the amount of tax paid,

and any such certificate is conclusive evidence of the facts stated in it.

(7) In this section—

    (*a*) "the settlor" means the settlor of the settlement, mentioned in section 721A(3) or (4) or 729A(3) or (4), which because of section 733B(1)(*b*)(i) is the settlement concerned, and

    (*b*) "close member", in relation to the family of the settlor, is to be read in accordance with section 733A(7) and (8).][1]

Commentary—*Simon's Taxes* E1.1144.
Amendments—[1]   Sections 733B–733E inserted by FA 2018 s 35, Sch 10 paras 12, 16 with effect only in relation to onward payments made on or after 6 April 2018. These sections have effect in relation to an onward payment made on or after that date even where the onward payment is referable to a benefit received before that date (FA 2018 Sch 10 para 21(4)).

734 Reduction in amount charged: previous capital gains tax charge

(1) This section applies if—

    (*a*) benefits provided as mentioned in section 732(1)(*c*) are received in a tax year,

    (*b*)   . . .[3]

    (*c*)   . . .[3] and

    [(*d*) chargeable gains are treated by section 87, 87K, 87L or 89(2) of, or paragraph 8 of Schedule 4C to, TCGA 1992 as accruing to a person in that or a subsequent tax year by reference (direct or indirect) to the whole or part of any benefits so provided.][3]

(2) For any tax year after one in which such chargeable gains are so treated, the amount of income treated as arising to the individual under section 732(2) in respect of benefits provided as mentioned in section 732(1)(*c*) as a result of the transfer or operations in question is calculated as follows.

(3) The amount is calculated under section 733(1) as if the total untaxed benefits were reduced by the amount of those gains.

(4) In this section "the total untaxed benefits" [has][3] the same meaning as in section 733(1) (see [Step 2][3]).

[(5) References in this section to chargeable gains treated as accruing to an individual include offshore income gains treated as arising to the individual (see [regulations 20 and 22 to 24 of the Offshore Funds (Tax) Regulations 2009 (SI 2009/3001)][2]).][1]

Commentary—*Simon's Taxes* E1.1142.
Amendments—[1]   Sub-s (5) inserted by FA 2008 s 25, Sch 7 para 97 with effect for the tax year 2008–09 and subsequent tax years.
[2]   In sub-s (5), words substituted by the Offshore Funds (Tax) Regulations, SI 2009/3001 reg 129(1), (5) with effect for the purposes of income tax for the tax year 2009–10 and subsequent tax years and for distributions made on or after 1 December 2009; for the purposes of corporation tax, on income, for accounting periods ending on or after 1 December 2009 and for distributions made on or after that date and, on income, in relation to disposals made on or after 1 December 2009; and for the purposes of capital gains tax, in relation to disposals made on or after 1 December 2009.
[3]   Sub-s (1)(*b*), (*c*) repealed, sub-s (1)(*d*) substituted, and words in sub-s (4) substituted, by FA 2018 s 35, Sch 10 paras 12, 17 with effect for the tax year 2018–19 and subsequent tax years.

[734A Reduction in amount charged: previous settlements charge

(1) This section applies if—

    (*a*) benefits provided as mentioned in section 732(1)(*c*) are received in a tax year, and

    (*b*) income is treated by section 643A, 643J or 643L of ITTOIA 2005 as arising to a person in that or a subsequent tax year by reference (direct or indirect) to the whole or part of any benefits so provided.

(2) For any tax year after one in which such income is so treated, the amount of income treated as arising to the individual under section 732(2) in respect of benefits provided as mentioned in section 732(1)(*c*) as a result of the transfer or operations in question is calculated as follows.

(3) The amount is calculated under section 733(1) as if the total untaxed benefits were reduced by the amount of that income.

(4) In this section "the total untaxed benefits" has the same meaning as in section 733(1) (see Step 2).][1]

Amendments—[1] Section 734A inserted by FA 2018 s 35, Sch 10 paras 12, 18 with effect for the tax year 2018–19 and subsequent tax years.

[735 Non-UK domiciled individuals to whom remittance basis applies

[(1) This section applies in relation to income treated under section 732 as arising to an individual in a tax year ("the deemed income") if section 809B, 809D or 809E (remittance basis) applies to the individual for that year.][3]

(2) For the purposes of this section the deemed income is "foreign" if (and to the extent that) the relevant income to which it relates would be relevant foreign income if it were the individual's.

(3) Treat the foreign deemed income as relevant foreign income of the individual.

(4) For the purposes of Chapter A1 of Part 14 (remittance basis) treat relevant income, or a benefit, that relates to any part of the foreign deemed income as deriving from that part of the foreign deemed income.][1]

[(5) In the application of section 832 of ITTOIA 2005 to the foreign deemed income, subsection (2) of that section has effect with the omission of paragraph (b).][2]

Commentary—*Simon's Taxes* **E1.1141, 1143.**

Amendments—[1] Sections 735, 735A substituted for previous s 735 by FA 2008 s 25, Sch 7 paras 163, 169 with effect for the tax year 2008–09 and subsequent tax years.

[2] Sub-s (5) inserted by FA 2013 s 218, Sch 45 para 91(1), (4) with effect in calculating an individual's liability to income tax or capital gains tax for the tax year 2013–14 or any subsequent tax year, subject to transitional provisions and savings in FA 2013 Sch 45 paras 154–158.

[3] Sub-s (1) substituted by FA 2013 s 219, Sch 46 para 21 with effect in relation to an individual's foreign income and gains for the tax year 2013–14 or any subsequent tax year, subject to transitional provisions in FA 2013 Sch 46 para 26.

[735A Section 735: relevant income and benefits relating to foreign deemed income

(1) For the purposes of section 735—

   (a) place the benefits mentioned in Step 1 in the order in which they were received by the individual (starting with the earliest benefit received),

   (b) deduct from those benefits so much of any benefit within section 734(1)(b) as gives rise as mentioned in section 734(1)(d) to chargeable gains or offshore income gains,

   (c) place the income mentioned in Step 3 for the tax years mentioned in Step 4 ("the relevant income") in the order determined under subsection (3),

   (d) deduct from that income any income that may not be taken into account because of section 743(1) or (2) (no duplication of charges),

   (e) place the income treated under section 732(2) as arising to the individual in respect of the benefits in the order in which it is treated as arising (starting with the earliest income treated as having arisen), and

   (f) treat the income mentioned in paragraph (e) as related to—

      (i) the benefits, and

      (ii) the relevant income,

by matching that income with the benefits and the relevant income (in the orders mentioned in paragraphs (a), (c) and (e)).

(2) In subsection (1) references to a step are to a step in section 733(1).

(3) The order referred to in subsection (1)(c) is arrived at by taking the following steps.

Step 1 Find the relevant income for the earliest tax year (of the tax years referred to in subsection (1)(c)).

Step 2 Place so much of that income as is not foreign in the order in which it arose (starting with the earliest income to arise).

Step 3 After that, place so much of that income as is foreign in the order in which it arose (starting with the earliest income to arise).

Step 4 Repeat Steps 1 to 3.

   For this purpose, read references to the relevant income for the earliest tax year as references to the relevant income for the first tax year after the last tax year in relation to which those Steps have been undertaken.

(4) For the purposes of subsection (3) relevant income is "foreign" where it would be relevant foreign income if it were the individual's.

(5) For those purposes treat income for a period as arising immediately before the end of the period.

(6) Subsection (1)(d) does not apply if the income may not be taken into account because the individual[, or as a result of section 733A another person,][2] has been charged to income tax under section 731 by reason of the income.][1]

Commentary—*Simon's Taxes* **E1.1141.**

Amendments—[1] Sections 735, 735A substituted for previous s 735 by FA 2008 s 25, Sch 7 paras 163, 169 with effect for the tax year 2008–09 and subsequent tax years.

[2] In sub-s (6), words inserted by F(No 2)A 2017 s 29(2), Sch 8 paras 27, 37 with effect for the tax year 2017–18 and subsequent tax years.

[735B Settlor liable under section 733A and remittance basis applies

(1) This section applies in relation to income if—

   (*a*) the income is treated by section 732 as arising to an individual ("the beneficiary") for a tax year,

   (*b*) another individual ("the settlor") is under section 733A(2) or (3) liable for tax on the income, and

   (*c*) section 809B, 809D or 809E (remittance basis) applies to the settlor for that year.

(2) The income ("the transferred-liability deemed income") is treated as relevant foreign income of the settlor.

(3) If, for the purposes of section 735 as it applies in relation to the beneficiary, any benefit or relevant income relates to any part of the transferred-liability deemed income then, for the purposes of Chapter A1 of Part 14 as it applies in relation to the settlor, that benefit or relevant income is to be treated as deriving from that part of the transferred-liability deemed income.

(4) In the application of section 832 of ITTOIA 2005 in relation to the income, subsection (2) of that section has effect with the omission of its paragraph (*b*).][1]

Amendments—[1]   Section 735B inserted by F(No 2)A 2017 s 29(2), Sch 8 paras 27, 38 with effect for the tax year 2017–18 and subsequent tax years.

[735C Person liable under section 733C or 733E and remittance basis applies

(1) This section applies in relation to income if—

   (*a*) the income is treated as arising to an individual for a tax year—

      (i) as a result of the operation of section 733C(3) and (4) where section 733C(3) applies because of section 733C(2), or

      (ii) as a result of the operation of section 733E, and

   (*b*) section 809B, 809D or 809E (remittance basis) applies to the individual for that year.

(2) The income is treated as relevant foreign income of the individual.

(3) For the purposes of Chapter A1 of Part 14 (remittance basis) treat the onward payment, or (as the case may be) the part of it whose amount or value is equal to the amount of the income, as deriving from the income.

(4) In the application of section 832 of ITTOIA 2005 in relation to the income, subsection (2) of that section has effect with the omission of its paragraph (*b*).][1]

Amendments—[1]   Section 735C inserted by FA 2018 s 35, Sch 10 paras 12, 19 with effect only in relation to onward payments made on or after 6 April 2018. This section has effect in relation to an onward payment made on or after that date even where the onward payment is referable to a benefit received before that date.

Exemptions: no tax avoidance purpose or genuine commercial transaction

736 Exemptions: introduction

(1) Sections 737 to [742A][1] deal with exemptions from liability under this Chapter.

(2) Some exemptions apply according to whether the relevant transactions are all pre-5 December 2005 transactions or all post-4 December 2005 transactions or include both (see sections 737, 739 and 740).

[(2A) The exemption given by section 742A applies only in the case of a relevant transaction effected on or after 6 April 2012.][1]

(3) In this section and sections 737 to 742—

   "post-4 December 2005 transaction" means a relevant transaction effected on or after 5 December 2005, and

   "pre-5 December 2005 transaction" means a relevant transaction effected before 5 December 2005.

HMRC Manuals—International Manual INTM600040 (exemption from liability).

Amendments—[1]   In sub-s (1), reference substituted and sub-s (2A) inserted by FA 2013 s 26, Sch 10 paras 1, 6 with effect for the tax year 2012–13 and subsequent tax years.

737 Exemption: all relevant transactions post-4 December 2005 transactions

(1) This section applies if all the relevant transactions are post-4 December 2005 transactions.

(2) An individual is not liable to income tax under this Chapter for the tax year by reference to the relevant transactions if the individual satisfies an officer of Revenue and Customs—

   (*a*) that Condition A is met, or

   (*b*) in a case where Condition A is not met, that Condition B is met.

(3) Condition A is that it would not be reasonable to draw the conclusion, from all the circumstances of the case, that the purpose of avoiding liability to taxation was the purpose, or one of the purposes, for which the relevant transactions or any of them were effected.

(4) Condition B is that—

   (*a*) all the relevant transactions were genuine commercial transactions (see section 738), and

   (*b*) it would not be reasonable to draw the conclusion, from all the circumstances of the case, that any one or more of those transactions was more than incidentally designed for the purpose of avoiding liability to taxation.

(5) In determining the purposes for which the relevant transactions or any of them were effected, the intentions and purposes of any person within subsection (6) are to be taken into account.

(6) A person is within this subsection if, whether or not for consideration, the person—

(*a*) designs or effects, or

(*b*) provides advice in relation to,

the relevant transactions or any of them.

(7) In this section—

"revenue" includes taxes, duties and national insurance contributions,

"taxation" includes any revenue for whose collection and management the Commissioners for Her Majesty's Revenue and Customs are responsible.

(8) If—

(*a*) apart from this subsection, an associated operation would not be taken into account for the purposes of this section, and

(*b*) the conditions in subsections (2) to (4) are not met if it is taken into account, because of—

(i) the associated operation, or

(ii) the associated operation taken together with any other relevant transactions,

it must be taken into account for those purposes.

Commentary—*Simon's Taxes* E1.1151.
Derivation—TA 1988 ss 741A(1)–(4), (7), (8) and s 741B(4).

738 Meaning of "commercial transaction"

(1) For the purposes of section 737, a relevant transaction is a commercial transaction only if it meets the conditions in subsections (2) and (3).

(2) It must be effected—

(*a*) in the course of a trade or business and for its purposes, or

(*b*) with a view to setting up and commencing a trade or business and for its purposes.

(3) It must not—

(*a*) be on terms other than those that would have been made between persons not connected with each other dealing at arm's length, or

(*b*) be a transaction that would not have been entered into between such persons so dealing.

(4) For the purposes of subsection (2), making investments, managing them or making and managing them is a trade or business only so far as—

(*a*) the person by whom it is done, and

(*b*) the person for whom it is done,

are persons not connected with each other and are dealing at arm's length.

Commentary—*Simon's Taxes* E1.1151.
Derivation—TA 1988 s 741A(5) to (7).

739 Exemption: all relevant transactions pre-5 December 2005 transactions

(1) This section applies if all the relevant transactions are pre-5 December 2005 transactions.

(2) An individual is not liable for income tax under this Chapter for the tax year by reference to the relevant transactions if the individual satisfies an officer of Revenue and Customs that condition A or B is met.

(3) Condition A is that the purpose of avoiding liability to taxation was not the purpose, or one of the purposes, for which the relevant transactions or any of them were effected.

(4) Condition B is that the transfer and any associated operations—

(*a*) were genuine commercial transactions, and

(*b*) were not designed for the purpose of avoiding liability to taxation.

Commentary—*Simon's Taxes* E1.1152.

740 Exemption: relevant transactions include both pre-5 December 2005 and post-4 December 2005 transactions

(1) This section applies if the relevant transactions include both pre-5 December transactions and post-4 December transactions.

(2) An individual is not liable to tax under this Chapter for the tax year by reference to the relevant transactions if—

(*a*) the condition in section 737(2) (exemption where all relevant transactions are post-4 December 2005 transactions) is met by reference to the post-4 December 2005 transactions, and

(*b*) the condition in section 739(2) (exemption where all relevant transactions are pre-5 December 2005 transactions) is met by reference to the pre-5 December transactions.

(3) If subsection (2)(*b*) applies but subsection (2)(*a*) does not, this Chapter applies with the modifications in subsections (4) to (6).

(4) For the purposes of sections 720 to 730, any income arising before 5 December 2005 must not be brought into account as income of the person abroad.

(5) In determining the relevant income of an earlier tax year for the purposes of section 733(1) (see Step 4), it does not matter whether that year was a year for which the individual was not liable under section 731 because of section 739 or this section.

(6) For the purposes of Step 1 in section 733(1), a benefit received by the individual in or before the tax year 2005–06 is to be left out of account.

(7) But, in the case of a benefit received in the tax year 2005–06, subsection (6) applies only so far as, on a time apportionment basis, the benefit fell to be enjoyed in any part of the year that fell before 5 December 2005.

Commentary—*Simon's Taxes* **E1.1153**.
Derivation—TA 1988 ss 741B(5) and 741C(1) to (6) and (8).

741 Application of section 742 (partial exemption)

(1) Section 742 (partial exemption where later associated operations fail conditions) applies if—
  (a) an individual is liable to tax because of section 720 or 727 for a tax year (the "taxable year") because condition B in section 737(4) (genuine commercial transaction: post-4 December 2005 transactions) is not met, and
  (b) subsections (2) and (3) apply.
(2) This subsection applies if—
  (a) since the relevant transfer there has been at least one tax year for which the individual was not so liable by reference to the relevant transactions effected before the end of the year, and
  (b) the individual was not so liable for that year because—
    (i) condition B in section 737(4) was met, or
    (ii) condition B in section 739(4) (genuine commercial transaction: pre-5 December 2005 transactions) was met.
(3) This subsection applies if the income by reference to which the individual is liable to tax for the taxable year is attributable—
  (a) partly to relevant transactions by reference to which one of those conditions was met for the last exempt tax year, and
  (b) partly to associated operations not falling within paragraph (a).
(4) For the purposes of this section a tax year is exempt if—
  (a) it is one of the tax years mentioned in subsection (2), and
  (b) there is no earlier tax year for which the individual was liable to tax because of section 720 or 727 by reference to the relevant transactions or any of them.
(5) References in this section to a person being liable to tax for a tax year because of section 720 or 727 include references to the individual being so liable had any income been treated as arising to the individual for that year under section 721 or 728.

Commentary—*Simon's Taxes* **E1.1154**.
Derivation—TA 1988 s 741D(1)–(5) and (9).

742 Partial exemption where later associated operations fail conditions

(1) If this section applies, the individual is liable to tax under this Chapter only in respect of part of the income for which the individual would otherwise be liable.
(2) That part is so much of the income as appears to an officer of Revenue and Customs to be justly and reasonably attributable to the operations mentioned in section 741(3)(b) in all the circumstances of the case.
(3) Those circumstances include how far those operations or any of them directly or indirectly affect—
  (a) the nature or amount of any person's income, or
  (b) any person's power to enjoy any income.

Commentary—*Simon's Taxes* **E1.1154**.
Derivation—TA 1988 s 741D(6) and (7).

[742A Post-5 April 2012 transactions: exemption for genuine transactions

(1) Subsection (2) applies for the purpose of determining the liability of an individual to tax under this Chapter by reference to a relevant transaction if—
  (a) the transaction is effected on or after 6 April 2012, and
  (b) conditions A and B are met.
(2) Income is to be left out of account so far as the individual satisfies an officer of Revenue and Customs that it is attributable to the transaction.
(3) Condition A is that—
  (a) were, viewed objectively, the transaction to be considered to be a genuine transaction having regard to any arrangements under which it is effected and any other relevant circumstances, and
  (b) were the individual to be liable to tax under this Chapter by reference to the transaction,
the individual's liability to tax would, in contravention of a relevant treaty provision, constitute an unjustified and disproportionate restriction on a freedom protected under that relevant treaty provision.
(4) In subsection (3) "relevant treaty provision" means—
  (a) Title II or IV of Part Three of the Treaty on the Functioning of the European Union,
  (b) Part II or III of the EEA agreement, or
  (c) the provision of any subsequent treaty replacing a provision mentioned in paragraph (a) or (b).

(5) Condition B is that the individual satisfies an officer of Revenue and Customs that, viewed objectively, the transaction must be considered to be a genuine transaction having regard to any arrangements under which it is effected and any other relevant circumstances.

(6) Without prejudice to the generality of subsection (3)(a) or (5), in order for the transaction to be considered to be a genuine transaction the transaction must not—

  (a) be on terms other than those that would have been made between persons not connected with each other dealing at arm's length, or

  (b) be a transaction that would not have been entered into between such persons so dealing,

having regard to any arrangements under which the transaction is effected and any other relevant circumstances.

(7) Subsection (8) applies if any asset or income falling within subsection (12) is used for the purposes of, or is received in the course of, activities carried on in a territory outside the United Kingdom by a person ("the relevant person") through a business establishment which the relevant person has in that territory.

(8) Without prejudice to the generality of subsection (3)(a) or (5), in order for the transaction to be considered to be a genuine transaction the activities mentioned in subsection (7) must consist of the provision by the relevant person of goods or services to others on a commercial basis and involve—

  (a) the use of staff in numbers, and with competence and authority,

  (b) the use of premises and equipment, and

  (c) the addition of economic value, by the relevant person, to those to whom the goods or services are provided,

commensurate with the size and nature of those activities.

(9) In subsection (8)(a) "staff" means employees, agents or contractors of the relevant person.

(10) To determine if a person has a "business establishment" in a territory outside the United Kingdom, apply sections 1141, 1142(1) and 1143 of CTA 2010 as if in those provisions—

  (a) references to a company were to a person, and

  (b) references to a permanent establishment were to a business establishment.

(11) Subsection (6) does not apply if—

  (a) the relevant transfer is made by an individual who makes it wholly—

   (i) for personal reasons (and not commercial reasons), and

   (ii) for the personal benefit (and not the commercial benefit) of other individuals, and

  (b) no consideration is given (directly or indirectly) for the relevant transfer or otherwise for any benefit received by any individual mentioned in paragraph (a)(ii),

and all assets and income falling within subsection (12) are dealt with accordingly.

(12) The assets and income falling within this subsection are—

  (a) any of the assets transferred by the relevant transfer;

  (b) any assets directly or indirectly representing any of the assets transferred;

  (c) any income arising from any assets within paragraph (a) or (b);

  (d) any assets directly or indirectly representing the accumulations of income arising from any assets within paragraph (a) or (b).

(13) In subsections (11) and (12) references to the relevant transfer are to—

  (a) if the transaction mentioned in subsection (1) is a relevant transfer, the transfer, or

  (b) if the transaction so mentioned is an associated operation, the relevant transfer to which it relates.

(14) Subsection (15) applies if—

  (a) subsection (2) would apply in relation to a transaction but for the individual being unable to satisfy an officer of Revenue and Customs for the purposes of condition B that the transaction meets the requirements set out in subsection (6), but

  (b) the individual does satisfy an officer of Revenue and Customs that those requirements are met in relation to a part of the transaction.

(15) Subsection (2) applies as if the reference to the transaction were to that part of the transaction.][1]

Commentary—*Simon's Taxes* **E1.1155.**

Amendments—[1]   This section inserted by FA 2013 s 26, Sch 10 paras 1, 7 with effect for the tax year 2012–13 and subsequent tax years.

[Value of certain benefits

742B Value of certain benefits

Sections 742C to 742E apply where it is necessary, for the purpose of calculating a charge to income tax under the preceding provisions of this Chapter, to determine the value of a benefit provided to a person by way of—

  (a) a payment by way of loan (see section 742C),

  (b) making available movable property without any transfer of the property in it (see section 742D), or

  (c) making available land for use without transferring the whole interest in it (see section 742E).][1]

Amendments—[1]   Sections 742B–742E and preceding cross-head inserted by F(No 2)A 2017 s 31, Sch 9 para 2 with effect in relation to capital payments or benefits received in the tax year 2017–18 and subsequent tax years.

[742C Value of benefit provided by a payment by way of loan

(1) The value of the benefit provided to a person (P) by a payment by way of loan to P is, for each tax year in which the loan is outstanding, the amount (if any) by which—

    (*a*) the amount of interest that would have been payable in that year on the loan if interest had been payable on the loan at the official rate, exceeds

    (*b*) the amount of interest (if any) actually paid by P in that year on the loan.

(2) In this section and section 742D the "official rate", in relation to interest, means the rate applicable from time to time under section 178 of the Finance Act 1989 for the purposes of Chapter 7 of Part 3 of ITEPA 2003.][1]

Amendments—[1]   Sections 742B–742E and preceding cross-head inserted by F(No 2)A 2017 s 31, Sch 9 para 2 with effect in relation to capital payments or benefits received in the tax year 2017–18 and subsequent tax years.

[742D Value of benefit provided by making movable property available

(1) The value of the benefit provided by making movable property available, without any transfer of the property in it, to a person (P) is, for each tax year in which the benefit is provided to P—

$$((CC \times R \times D) / Y) - T$$

    where—

        CC is the capital cost of the movable property on the date when the property is first made available to P in the tax year,

        D is the number of days in the tax year on which the property is made available to P (the relevant period),

        R is the official rate of interest for the relevant period (but see subsection (3)),

        T is the total of the amounts (if any) paid in the tax year by P—

    (*a*) to the person providing the benefit, in respect of the availability of the movable property, or

    (*b*) so far as not within paragraph (*a*), in respect of the repair, insurance, maintenance or storage of the movable property, and

        Y is the number of days in the tax year.

(2) In subsection (1), in the meaning of CC, the "capital cost" of the movable property means an amount equal to the total of—

    (*a*) the amount which is the greater of—

        (i) the amount or value of the consideration given for the acquisition of the movable property by, or on behalf of, the person (*a*) providing the benefit, and

        (ii) its market value at the time of that acquisition, and

    (*b*) the amount of any expenditure wholly and exclusively incurred by, or on behalf of, A for the purpose of enhancing the value of the movable property.

(3) If the official rate of interest changes during the relevant period, then in subsection (1) R is the average official rate of interest for the period calculated as follows.

    Step 1

    Multiply each official rate of interest in force during the relevant period by the number of days when it is in force.

    Step 2

    Add together the products found in Step 1.

    Step 3

    Divide the total found in Step 2 by the number of days in the relevant period.

(4) In subsections (1) and (2), "movable property" means any tangible movable property other than money.][1]

Amendments—[1]   Sections 742B–742E and preceding cross-head inserted by F(No 2)A 2017 s 31, Sch 9 para 2 with effect in relation to capital payments or benefits received in the tax year 2017–18 and subsequent tax years.

[742E Value of benefit provided by making land available

(1) The value of the benefit provided by making land available for the use of a person (P) is, for each tax year in which the benefit is provided to P, the amount by which—

    (*a*) the rental value of the land for the period of the tax year during which the land is made available to P, exceeds

    (*b*) the total of the amounts (if any) paid in the tax year by P—

        (i) to the person providing the benefit, in respect of the availability of the land, or

        (ii) so far as not within sub-paragraph (i), in respect of costs of repair, insurance or maintenance relating to the land.

(2) Subsection (1) does not apply in the case where the person providing the benefit transfers the whole of the person's interest in the land to P.

(3) In subsection (1) "the rental value" of the land for a period means the rent which would have been payable for the period if the land had been let to P at an annual rent equal to the annual value.

(4) For the purposes of subsection (3) "the annual value" of land is the rent that might reasonably be expected to be obtained on a letting from year to year if—

    (*a*) the tenant undertook to pay all taxes, rates and charges usually paid by a tenant, and

    (*b*) the landlord undertook to bear the costs of the repairs and insurance and the other expenses (if any) necessary for maintaining the property in a state to command that rent.

(5) For the purposes of subsection (4) that rent—

    (*a*) is to be taken to be the amount that might reasonably be expected to be so obtained in respect of a letting of the land, and

    (*b*) is to be calculated on the basis that the only amounts that may be deducted in respect of services provided by the landlord are amounts in respect of the costs to the landlord of providing any relevant services.

(6) In subsection (5) "relevant service" means a service other than the repair, insurance or maintenance of the property.][1]

Amendments—[1]   Sections 742B–742E and preceding cross-head inserted by F(No 2)A 2017 s 31, Sch 9 para 2 with effect in relation to capital payments or benefits received in the tax year 2017–18 and subsequent tax years.

General

743 No duplication of charges

(1) No amount of income may be taken into account more than once in charging income tax under this Chapter.

(2) If there is a choice about the persons in relation to whom any amount of income may be taken into account in charging income tax under this Chapter, it is to be taken into account—

    (*a*) in relation to such one or more of them as appears to an officer of Revenue and Customs to be just and reasonable, and

    (*b*) if more than one, in such respective proportions as appears to the officer to be just and reasonable.

[(2A) Subsection (2B) applies if—

    (*a*) in the case of an individual, an amount of income is taken into account in charging income tax under section 720 or 727, and

    (*b*) the individual subsequently receives that income.

(2B) The income received is treated as not being the individual's income for income tax purposes.][1]

(3) For the meaning of references in [this section][1] to an amount of income taken into account in charging tax, see section 744.

(4) . . .[1]

Commentary—*Simon's Taxes* E1.1150.

Amendments—[1]   Sub-ss (2A), (2B) inserted, in sub-s (3), words substituted, and sub-s (4) repealed, by FA 2013 s 26, Sch 10 para 16 with effect for the tax year 2013–14 and subsequent tax years. These amendments have effect in relation to relevant transfers occurring before 6 April 2013 as well as relevant transfers occurring on or after that date (FA 2013 Sch 10 para 20(2)).

744 Meaning of taking income into account in charging income tax for section 743

(1) References in section [743][1] (no duplication of charges) to an amount of income taken into account in charging income tax are to be read as follows.

(2) In the case of tax charged on income under section 720 (charge where income enjoyed as a result of relevant transactions)—

    (*a*) if section 724(1) (benefit provided out of income of person abroad) applies, they are references to an amount of the income out of which the benefit is provided equal to the amount . . .[1] charged, and

    (*b*) otherwise they are references to the amount of [the income mentioned in section 721(2)][1].

(3) In the case of tax charged on income under section 727 (charge where capital sums received as a result of relevant transactions), they are references to the amount of [the income mentioned in section 728(1)(*a*)][1].

(4) In the case of tax charged under section 731 (charge to tax on income treated as arising to non-transferors where benefit received as a result of relevant transfers), they are references to the amount of relevant income taken into account under section 733 (income charged under section 731) in calculating the amount to be charged in respect of the benefit for the tax year in question.

Amendments—[1]   In sub-s (1), reference substituted, in sub-s (2)(*a*), words repealed, and in sub-ss (2)(*b*), (3), words substituted, by FA 2013 s 26, Sch 10 para 17 with effect for the tax year 2013–14 and subsequent tax years. These amendments have effect in relation to relevant transfers occurring before 6 April 2013 as well as relevant transfers occurring on or after that date (FA 2013 Sch 10 para 20(2)).

745 Rates of tax applicable to income charged under sections 720 and 727 etc

(1) Income tax at the basic rate, [or][4] the [starting rate for savings][1] [when that rate is more than 0%,][3] . . .[4] is not charged under section 720 or 727 in respect of any income [if (and to the corresponding extent that) the income mentioned in section 721(2) or 728(1)(*a*)][2] has borne tax at that rate by deduction or otherwise.

[(1A) Income tax at a Scottish rate above 0% and below, or equal to, the basic rate is not charged under section 720 or 727 in respect of any income if (and to the corresponding extent that) the income mentioned in section 721(2) or 728(1)(a) has borne tax at the basic rate.][5]

[(1B) Income tax at the Welsh basic rate when that rate is above 0% and below, or equal to, the basic rate is not charged under section 720 or 727 in respect of any income if (and to the corresponding extent that) the income mentioned in section 721(2) or 728(1)(*a*) has borne tax at the basic rate.][6]

(2) [Subsections (1)[, (1A) and (1B)][6] do][5] not affect the tax charged if section 724(2) applies (benefit provided out of income of person abroad charged in year of receipt).

[(3) Subsection (4) applies to income treated as arising to an individual under section 721 or 728 so far as [[none of subsections (1), (1A) and (1B)][6] applies][5] to it.

(4) The charge to income tax under section 720 or 727 operates by treating the income as if it were income within section 19(2) (meaning of "dividend income") if the income mentioned in section 721(2) or 728(1)(*a*) would be dividend income were it the income of the individual.][2]

Commentary—*Simon's Taxes* **E1.1124, E1.1160.**

Amendments—[1]   Words in sub-s (1) substituted by FA 2008 s 5, Sch 1 paras 1, 24 with effect for the tax year 2008–09 and subsequent tax years.

[2]   In sub-s (1) words substituted, and sub-ss (3), (4) substituted by FA 2013 s 26, Sch 10 para 18 with effect for the tax year 2013–14 and subsequent tax years. These amendments have effect in relation to relevant transfers occurring before 6 April 2013 as well as relevant transfers occurring on or after that date (FA 2013 Sch 10 para 20(2)).

[3]   Words in sub-s (1) inserted by FA 2016 s 4(1), (9) with effect for the tax year 2016–17 and subsequent tax years.

[4]   In sub-s (1), word inserted and words repealed by FA 2016 s 5, Sch 1 para 63(1), (12) with effect for the tax year 2016-17 and subsequent tax years.

[5]   Sub-s (1A) inserted, in sub-s (2), words substituted for words "Subsection (1) does", and in sub-s (3), words substituted for words "subsection (1) does not apply", by the Scottish Rates of Income Tax (Consequential Amendments) Order, SI 2018/459 art 6(1), (6) with effect for the tax year commencing on 6 April 2018 and subsequent tax years.

[6]   Sub-s (1B) inserted, in sub-s (2) words substituted for words "and (1A) ", and in sub-s (3) words substituted for words "neither of subsections (1) and (1A)", by the Devolved Income Tax Rates (Consequential Amendments) Order, SI 2019/201 arts 12(1), (9) with effect in relation to the tax year commencing on 6 April 2019 and subsequent tax years.

746 Deductions and reliefs where individual charged under section 720 or 727

(1) This section applies for the purpose of calculating the liability to income tax of an individual charged under section 720 or 727.

[(2) For the purpose of determining the deductions and reliefs allowed to the individual, the individual is to be treated as if the individual had actually received the amount by reference to which the income treated as arising to the individual under section 721 or 728 is determined.][1]

Commentary—*Simon's Taxes* **E1.1120.**

Amendments—[1]   Sub-s (2) substituted by FA 2013 s 26, Sch 10 para 19 with effect for the tax year 2013–14 and subsequent tax years. These amendments have effect in relation to relevant transfers occurring before 6 April 2013 as well as relevant transfers occurring on or after that date (FA 2013 Sch 10 para 20(2)).

747 Amounts corresponding to accrued income profits and related interest

(1) This subsection applies if a person—

    (*a*) would have been treated as—

        (i) making qualifying accrued income profits, or

        (ii) making qualifying accrued income profits of a greater amount,

        in an interest period, but

    (*b*) is not so treated because of being resident or domiciled outside the United Kingdom throughout any tax year in which the interest period (or part of it) falls.

(2) If subsection (1) applies, this Chapter applies as if the amount which the person would be treated as making or, as the case may be, the additional amount were income becoming payable to the person.

(3) Accordingly, any reference in this Chapter to income of (or payable or arising to) a person abroad must be read as including a reference to such an amount.

(4) This subsection applies if income consisting of interest which falls due at the end of an interest period—

    (*a*) would have been income as respects which a person is entitled to an exemption, or an exemption of a greater amount, from liability to income tax under section 679 (interest on securities involving accrued income losses: general), but

    (*b*) is not such income because it is income of a person who is resident or domiciled outside the United Kingdom throughout any tax year in which the interest period (or part of it) falls.

(5) If subsection (4) applies, for the purposes of this Chapter the interest is treated as reduced by the amount of the exemption or, as the case may be, the additional exemption.

(6) In this section—

    (*a*) expressions which are also used in Chapter 2 of Part 12 (accrued income profits) have the same meaning as in that Chapter (but see subsection (7)), and

    (*b*) "qualifying accrued income profits" means accrued income profits which are treated as made—

        (i) under section 628(5), or

(ii) under section 630(2) in respect of a transfer of variable rate securities.

(7) In the case of qualifying accrued income profits within sub-paragraph (ii) of the definition of that expression in subsection (6)(*b*)—

    (*a*) references in subsection (1)(*a*) to making qualifying accrued income profits in an interest period are to be read as making them in the tax year in which the settlement day falls, and

    (*b*) the reference in subsection (1)(*b*) to the interest period is to the period—

        (i) beginning with the day after the last day of the only or last interest period of the securities, and

        (ii) ending with the settlement day.

Commentary—*Simon's Taxes* **E1.1113, D9.451**.

Supplementary

748 Power to obtain information

(1) An officer of Revenue and Customs may by notice require any person to provide the officer with such particulars as the officer may reasonably require for the purposes of this Chapter.

(2) The officer may direct the time within which the particulars must be provided and that time must be at least 30 days.

(3) The particulars which a person must provide under this section, if required to do so by a notice under subsection (1), include particulars about—

    (*a*) transactions with respect to which the person is or was acting on behalf of others,

    (*b*) transactions which in the opinion of the officer should properly be investigated for the purposes of this Chapter even though in the person's opinion no liability to income tax arises under this Chapter, and

    (*c*) whether the person has taken or is taking any part and, if so, what part in transactions of a description specified in the notice.

(4) A [relevant lawyer][1] is not treated as having taken part in a transaction for the purposes of subsection (3)(*c*) merely because of giving professional advice to a client about it.

[(4A In this section "relevant lawyer" means a barrister, advocate, solicitor or other legal representative communications with whom may be the subject of a claim to professional privilege or, in Scotland, protected from disclosure in legal proceedings on grounds of confidentiality of communication.][1]

(5) This section is subject to—

    section 749 (restrictions on particulars to be provided by [relevant lawyers][1]), and

    section 750 (restrictions on particulars to be provided by banks).

Commentary—*Simon's Taxes* **E1.1161**.

Amendments—[1]   In sub-ss (4), (5), words substituted, and sub-s (4A) inserted, by the Legal Services Act 2007 s 208, Sch 21 paras 157, 158 with effect from 1 January 2010 (by virtue of SI 2010/3250, art 2(*h*)).

749 Restrictions on particulars to be provided by [relevant lawyers][1]

(1) In relation to anything done by a [relevant lawyer][1] on behalf of a client who does not consent to the information otherwise required from the [relevant lawyer][1] under section 748 being provided, the [relevant lawyer][1] may not be compelled under that section to do more than—

    (*a*) state that the [relevant lawyer][1] is or was acting on behalf of a client, and

    (*b*) give the name and address of the client and any relevant person.

(2) In the case of anything done by the [relevant lawyer][1] in connection with the transfer of any asset by or to an individual who is . . . [2] UK resident to or by a body corporate to which subsection (6) applies, the transferor and the transferee are relevant persons.

(3) In the case of anything done by the [relevant lawyer][1] in connection with any associated operation in relation to any such transfer, the persons concerned in the associated operations are relevant persons.

(4) In the case of anything done by the [relevant lawyer][1] in connection with the formation or management of a body corporate to which subsection (6) applies, the body corporate is a relevant person.

(5) In the case of anything done by the [relevant lawyer][1] in connection with—

    (*a*) the creation of any settlement as a result of which income becomes payable to a person abroad, or

    (*b*) the execution of the trusts of any such settlement,

the settlor and that person are relevant persons.

(6) This subsection applies to bodies corporate resident or incorporated outside the United Kingdom which—

    (*a*) are, or if UK resident would be, close companies, and

    (*b*) are not companies whose business consists wholly or mainly of the carrying on of a trade or trades.

[(7) In this section—]

"relevant lawyer" means a barrister, advocate, solicitor or other legal representative communications with whom may be the subject of a claim to professional privilege or, in Scotland, protected from disclosure in legal proceedings on grounds of confidentiality of communication;

"settlement" and "settlor" have the meanings given by section 620 of ITTOIA 2005.][1]

(8) In the application of this section to Scotland, any reference to the trusts of a settlement is a reference to the purposes of the settlement.

Commentary—*Simon's Taxes* **E1.1161**.

Modifications—ITA 2007 Sch 2 para 139 (so far as sub-s (6) above applies for the purposes of sub-s (2) or (3), it applies in relation to transfers and associated operations on or after 20 March 1990 and before 30 November 1993, with the modifications set out in ITA 2007 Sch 2 para 139(2)).

Amendments—[1]   In heading and asection text, words substituted, and sub-s (7) substituted by the Legal Services Act 2007 s 208, Sch 21 paras 157, 159 with effect from from 1 January 2010 (by virtue of SI 2010/3250, art 2(h)).

[2]   In sub-s (2), word "ordinarily" repealed by FA 2013 s 219, Sch 46 paras 54, 65(1) with effect only where the transfer is made or, in the case of an associated operation, the transfer is made and the associated operation is effected on or after 6 April 2013. This section has effect, in relation to an individual who was resident in the UK for the tax year 2012–13 but was not ordinarily resident there at the end of that tax year, for a qualifying tax year, as if these amendments had not been made. This saving applies only if service in the employment in question began before the start of the tax year 2013–14. See FA 2013 Sch 46 para 73.

750 Restrictions on particulars to be provided by banks

(1) Section 748 does not oblige a bank to provide any particulars of any ordinary banking transactions between the bank and a customer carried out in the ordinary course of banking business, unless subsection (2) or (3) applies.

(2) This subsection applies if the bank has acted or is acting on behalf of the customer in connection with—

    (*a*) the creation of any settlement as a result of which income becomes payable to a person abroad, or

    (*b*) the execution of the trusts of any such settlement.

(3) This subsection applies if the bank has acted or is acting on behalf of the customer in connection with the formation or management of a body corporate to which section 749(6) applies.

(4) In this section—

    "bank" has the meaning given by section 991, and

    "settlement" has the meaning given by section 620 of ITTOIA 2005.

(5) In the application of this section to Scotland, any reference to the trusts of a settlement is a reference to the purposes of the settlement.

Commentary—*Simon's Taxes* **E1.1161**.
Derivation—TA 1988 s 745(5) to (6).

751 [The Tribunal's][1] jurisdiction on appeals

[On any appeal that is notified to the tribunal, the jurisdiction of the tribunal][1] includes jurisdiction to affirm or replace any decision taken by an officer of Revenue and Customs in exercise of the officer's functions under—

    (*a*) section 737 (exemption: all relevant transactions post-4 December 2005 transactions),

    (*b*) section 738 (meaning of "commercial transaction"),

    (*c*) section 739 (exemption: all relevant transactions pre-5 December 2005 transactions),

    (*d*) section 742 (partial exemption where later associated operations fail conditions),

    [(*da*) section 742A (post-5 April 2012 transactions: exemption for genuine transactions),][2]

    (*e*) section 743(2) (no duplication of charges: choice of persons in relation to whom income is taken into account).

Commentary—*Simon's Taxes* **E1.1161**.

Amendments—[1]   Words in the heading and words at the beginning substituted by the Transfer of Tribunal Functions and Revenue and Customs Appeals Order, SI 2009/56 art 3, Sch 1 para 461 with effect from 1 April 2009.

[2]   Para (*da*) inserted by FA 2013 s 26, Sch 10 paras 1, 8 with effect for the tax year 2012–13 and subsequent tax years.

CHAPTER 4

SALES OF OCCUPATION INCOME

Introduction

773 Overview of Chapter

(1) This Chapter imposes a charge to income tax—

    (*a*) on individuals to whom income is treated as arising under section 778 (income arising where capital amount other than derivative property or right obtained), and

    (*b*) on individuals to whom income is treated as arising under section 779 (income arising where derivative property or right obtained).

(2) Income is treated as arising under those sections only if—

    (*a*) transactions are effected or arrangements made to exploit the earning capacity of an individual in an occupation, and (*b*) the main object or one of the main objects of the transactions or arrangements is the avoidance or reduction of liability to income tax.

Commentary—*Simon's Taxes* **E1.1201**.
Derivation—TA 1988 s 775(1).
HMRC Manuals—Business Income Manual BIM100351 (introduction to sale of income in exchange for 'capital amount').

774 Meaning of "occupation"

In this Chapter references to an occupation, in relation to an individual, are references to any activities of a kind undertaken in a profession or vocation, regardless of whether the individual—
(*a*) is carrying on a profession or vocation on the individual's own account, or
(*b*) is an employee or office-holder.

Commentary—*Simon's Taxes* **E1.1201**.
Derivation—TA 1988 s 775(3).
HMRC Manuals—Business Income Manual BIM100360 (occupation).

775 Priority of other tax provisions

This Chapter has effect subject to—
(*a*) Chapter 5 of Part 5 of ITTOIA 2005 (settlements: amounts treated as income of settlor), and
(*b*) any other provision of the Tax Acts treating income as belonging to a particular person.

Commentary—*Simon's Taxes* **E1.1207**.
Derivation—TA 1988 s 777(10).
HMRC Manuals—Business Income Manual BIM60305 (priority of other tax provisions).

Charge on sale of occupation income

776 Charge to tax on sale of occupation income

(1) Income tax is charged on income treated as arising under—
(*a*) section 778 (income arising where capital amount other than derivative property or right obtained), or
(*b*) section 779 (income arising where derivative property or right obtained).
(2) Tax is charged under this section on the full amount of income treated as arising in the tax year.
(3) The person liable for any tax charged under this section is the individual to whom the income is treated as arising.
(4) This section is subject to section 784 (exemption for sales of going concerns).

Commentary—*Simon's Taxes* **E1.1201**.
Derivation—TA 1988 s 775(2A).

777 Conditions for sections 778 and 779 to apply

(1) Sections 778 and 779 apply only if conditions A to C are met in respect of an individual.
(2) Condition A is that the individual carries on an occupation wholly or partly in the United Kingdom.
(3) Condition B is that transactions are effected or arrangements made to exploit the individual's earning capacity in the occupation by putting another person (see section 782) in a position to enjoy—
(*a*) all or part of the income or receipts derived from the individual's activities in the occupation, or
(*b*) anything derived directly or indirectly from such income or receipts.
(4) The reference in subsection (3) to income or receipts derived from the individual's activities includes a reference to payments for any description of copyright or licence or franchise or other right deriving its value from the individual's activities (including past activities).
(5) Condition C is that as part of, or in connection with, or in consequence of, the transactions or arrangements a capital amount is obtained by the individual for the individual or another person.
(6) For the purposes of subsection (5), the cases where an individual ("A") obtains a capital amount for another person ("B") include cases where A has put B in a position to receive the capital amount by providing B with something of value derived, directly or indirectly, from A's activities in the occupation.
(7) In this Chapter "capital amount" means an amount in money or money's worth which does not fall to be included in a calculation of income for [purposes of the Tax Acts otherwise than as a result of][1] this Chapter.

Commentary—*Simon's Taxes* **E1.1201A, E1.1201**.
Derivation—TA 1988 ss 775(1), (3), and (7)–(9) and 777(13).
HMRC Manuals—Business Income Manual BIM100370 (tax year).
BIM100365 (capital amount).
Amendments—[1]   In sub-s (7) words substituted by the Income Tax Act 2007 (Amendment) (No 2) Order, SI 2009/2859 art 4(1), (5) with effect for income tax and capital gains tax purposes for the year 2007–08 and subsequent tax years, and for corporation tax purposes for accounting periods ending after 5 April 2007.

778 Income arising where capital amount other than derivative property or right obtained

(1) This section applies if the capital amount obtained as mentioned in section 777(5) does not consist of—

(*a*) property which derives substantially the whole of its value from the individual's activities, or

(*b*) a right which does so.

(2) The capital amount is treated for income tax purposes as income arising to the individual.

(3) The income is treated as arising in the tax year in which the capital amount is receivable.

(4) A capital amount is not regarded as having become receivable by a person for the purposes of this section until the person can effectively enjoy or dispose of it.

Commentary—*Simon's Taxes* E1.1202.

HMRC Manuals—Business Income Manual BIM100370 (tax year).

779 Income arising where derivative property or right obtained

(1) This section applies if—

(*a*) the capital amount obtained as mentioned in section 777(5) consists of—

    (i) property which derives substantially the whole of its value from the activities of an individual, or

    (ii) a right which does so, and

(*b*) the property or right is sold or otherwise realised.

(2) For the purposes of subsection (1), it does not matter whether the capital amount is obtained on one occasion or on two or more occasions (for example, because the individual acquires a stock option and subsequently exercises it).

(3) Income of an amount equal to the proceeds of sale or the realised value is treated for income tax purposes as income arising to the individual.

(4) The income is treated as arising in the tax year in which the property or right is sold or otherwise realised.

Commentary—*Simon's Taxes* E1.1202.

Derivation—TA 1988 s 775(2) and (7).

HMRC Manuals—Business Income Manual BIM100355 (conditions needed before the sale of income legislation can operate).

Further provisions relevant to the charge

780 Transactions, arrangements, sales and realisations relevant for Chapter

(1) For the purposes of this Chapter, account is to be taken of any method, however indirect, by which—

(*a*) any property or right is transferred or transmitted, or

(*b*) the value of any property or right is enhanced or diminished.

(2) Accordingly—

(*a*) the occasion of the transfer or transmission of any property or right however indirect, and

(*b*) the occasion when the value of any property or right is enhanced,

may be an occasion when tax is charged under this Chapter.

(3) Subsections (1) and (2) apply in particular—

(*a*) to sales, contracts and other transactions made otherwise than for full consideration or for more than full consideration,

(*b*) to any method by which any property or right, or the control of any property or right, is transferred or transmitted by assigning—

    (i) share capital or other rights in a company,

    (ii) rights in a partnership, or

    (iii) an interest in settled property,

(*c*) to the creation of an option and the giving of consideration for granting it,

(*d*) to the creation of a requirement for consent and the giving of consideration for granting it,

(*e*) to the creation of an embargo affecting the disposition of any property or right and the giving of consideration for releasing it, and

(*f*) to the disposal of any property or right on the winding up, dissolution or termination of a company, partnership or trust.

Commentary—*Simon's Taxes* E1.1203.

Derivation—TA 1988 s 777(2) and (3).

781 Tracing value

(1) This section applies if it is necessary to determine the extent to which the value of any property or right is derived from any other property or right for the purposes of this Chapter.

(2) Value may be traced through any number of companies, partnerships and trusts.

(3) The property held by a company, partnership or trust must be attributed to the shareholders, partners or beneficiaries at each stage in such manner as is appropriate in the circumstances.

Commentary—*Simon's Taxes* E1.1201A.

Derivation—TA 1988 s 777(5).

782 Meaning of "other person"

(1) For the purposes of this Chapter references to other persons are to be read in accordance with subsections (2) to (4).

(2) A partnership or partners in a partnership may be regarded as a person or persons distinct from the individuals or other persons who are for the time being partners.

(3) The trustees of settled property may be regarded as persons distinct from the individuals or other persons who are for the time being trustees.

(4) Personal representatives may be regarded as persons distinct from the individuals or other persons who are for the time being personal representatives.

Commentary—*Simon's Taxes* **E1.1201A**.
Derivation—TA 1988 s 777(7).

783 Valuations and apportionments

(1) All such valuations are to be made as are appropriate to give effect to this Chapter.

(2) For the purposes of this Chapter, any expenditure, receipt, consideration or other amount may be apportioned by such method as is just and reasonable in the circumstances.

Commentary—*Simon's Taxes* **E1.1201**.
Derivation—TA 1988 s 777(6).

Exemption for sales of going concerns

784 Exemption for sales of going concerns

(1) This section applies if a capital amount is obtained from the disposal—
  (a) of assets (including any goodwill) of a profession or vocation,
  (b) of a share in a partnership which is carrying on a profession or vocation, or
  (c) of shares in a company.

(2) An individual is not liable to income tax under this Chapter in respect of the capital amount so far as the going concern condition is met (see subsections (4) and (5)).

(3) Subsection (2) is subject to section 785 (restriction on exemption: sales of future earnings).

(4) In the case of a disposal within subsection (1)(a) or (b), the going concern condition is that the value of what is disposed of at the time of disposal is attributable to the value of the profession or vocation as a going concern.

(5) In the case of a disposal within subsection (1)(c), the going concern condition is that the value of what is disposed of at the time of disposal is attributable to the value of the company's business as a going concern.

(6) In subsection (5) the reference to the company's business includes a reference to the business of any other company in which it holds shares directly or indirectly.

Commentary—*Simon's Taxes* **E1.1204**.
Derivation—TA 1988 s 775(4) and (6).
HMRC Manuals—Business Income Manual BIM100365 (capital amount).

785 Restriction on exemption: sales of future earnings

(1) This section applies if the value as a going concern mentioned in section 784(4) or (5) is derived to a material extent from prospective income or receipts derived directly or indirectly from the individual's activities in the occupation.

(2) The exemption under section 784 applies to the value so derived only if the future earnings condition is met.

(3) The future earnings condition is met if, ignoring all capital amounts, the individual will receive full consideration for the prospective income or receipts, whether as a partner in a partnership or as an employee or otherwise.

(4) The references in subsections (1) and (3) to income or receipts include references to payments for any description of copyright, licence, franchise or other right deriving its value from the individual's activities (including past activities).

Commentary—*Simon's Taxes* **E1.1204**.

Recovery of tax

786 Recovery of tax where consideration receivable by person not assessed

(1) This section applies if a person ("A") is assessed to tax under this Chapter in respect of consideration receivable by another person ("B").

(2) Consideration is not regarded as having become receivable by B for this purpose until B can effectively enjoy or dispose of it.

(3) A is entitled to recover from B any part of the tax which A has paid.

(4) If any part of the tax remains unpaid at the end of the period of 6 months beginning with the date when it became due and payable, it is recoverable from B as if B were the person assessed.

(5) Subsection (4) does not affect the right to recover the tax from A.

(6) For the purposes of this section, any income which an individual is treated as having as a result of this Chapter (the "occupation income") is treated as the highest part of the individual's total income.

(7) But if in the tax year—
  (a) more than one capital amount is treated as the individual's occupation income, or
  (b) the individual is also treated as having income as a result of Chapter 3 (transactions in land),

only a just and reasonable proportion of each capital amount treated as occupation income is to be treated as the highest part of the individual's total income.

(8) See section 1012 for the relationship between—

    (*a*) the rules in subsections (6) and (7), and

    (*b*) other rules requiring particular income to be treated as the highest part of a person's total income.

Commentary—*Simon's Taxes* E1.1205.

HMRC Manuals—Business Income Manual BIM100370 (recovery of tax).

787 Recovery of tax: certificates of tax paid etc

(1) For the purposes of section 786(3), an officer of Revenue and Customs must, if requested to do so, produce a certificate specifying—

    (*a*) the amount of income in respect of which tax has been paid, and

    (*b*) the amount of tax paid.

(2) The certificate is conclusive evidence of any facts stated in it.

(3) See also section 944 (under which directions may be given for payments within this Chapter to non-UK residents to be subject to a duty to deduct income tax).

Commentary—*Simon's Taxes* E1.1205.

Derivation—TA 1988 s 777(8).

Interpretation

789 Minor definitions

In this Chapter—

    "company" includes any body corporate, and

    "share" includes stock.

Commentary—*Simon's Taxes* E1.1208.

Derivation—TA 1988 s 777(13).

CHAPTER 5

AVOIDANCE INVOLVING TRADING LOSSES

Introduction

790 Overview of Chapter

(1) This Chapter imposes charges to income tax on—

    (*a*) individuals who are treated as receiving income under section 792 (individuals in partnership claiming excess relief),

    (*b*) individuals who are treated as receiving income under section 797 (individuals claiming relief for film-related trading losses), and

    (*c*) individuals who are treated as receiving income under section 805 (individuals in partnership claiming relief for licence-related trading losses).

(2) The charges apply if (among other things) the individual makes a loss in a trade for which the individual claims sideways relief or capital gains relief.

(3) For the purposes of this Chapter sideways relief is—

    (*a*) trade loss relief against general income (see sections 64 to 70), or

    (*b*) early trade losses relief (see sections 72 to 74).

(4) For the purposes of this Chapter—

    (*a*) capital gains relief is, in relation to a loss, the treatment of the loss as an allowable loss by virtue of section 261B of TCGA 1992 (use of trading loss as a CGT loss), and

    (*b*) capital gains relief is claimed for a loss when a claim under that section is made in relation to the loss.

(5) References in this Chapter to a firm are to be read in the same way as references to a firm in Part 9 of ITTOIA 2005 (which contains special provision about partnerships).

Individuals in partnership: recovery of excess relief

791 Charge to tax on income treated as received under section 792

(1) Income tax is charged on income treated as received by an individual under section 792.

(2) Tax is charged under this section on the amount of the income treated as received in the tax year.

(3) The person liable for any tax charged under this section is the individual treated as receiving the income.

Derivation—FA 2005 s 74(4).

HMRC Manuals—Business Income Manual BIM82675 (partnerships: recovery of excess relief).

792 Partners claiming excess sideways or capital gains relief

(1) This section applies if—

    (*a*) an individual carrying on a trade ("the relevant trade") as a partner in a firm makes post-1 December 2004 losses in the relevant trade for which the individual claims relief within subsection (2),

(b) any of sections 104, 107 and 110 applies in relation to the relief (whether or not any of those sections restricts the amount of the relief), and

(c) after the individual makes the claim or claims, a chargeable event occurs.

(2) The relief within this subsection is—

(a) sideways relief but only if the whole or part of the relief is claimed against income of the individual apart from profits of the relevant trade, and

(b) capital gains relief.

(3) A chargeable event occurs whenever—

(a) the amount of the individual's contribution to the firm is reduced as a result of the application of regulations made under section 114, and

(b) that reduction in the individual's contribution to the firm immediately results in—

(i) the total amount of trade losses claimed (less any reclaimed relief) becoming greater than the contribution, or

(ii) an increase in the amount by which the total amount of trade losses claimed (less any reclaimed relief) exceeds the contribution.

(4) The individual is treated as receiving an amount of income every time a chargeable event occurs. The income is treated as arising otherwise than as profits of a trade.

(5) The amount of the income is calculated in accordance with section 793.

(6) If—

(a) the firm is carrying on, or has carried on, more than one trade, and

(b) subsection (1)(a) and (b) applies in relation to losses made by the individual in one or more of those trades as a partner in the firm,

the firm's trades are taken together for the purpose of determining whether a chargeable event occurs at any time after a claim in relation to any of those losses has been made and, if one does occur, the amount of income treated as received by the individual at that time.

See section 794(6) for modifications giving effect to this.

(7) References in this section to an individual being a partner in a firm include a reference to an individual being a limited partner within the meaning of section [103A][1] as a result of subsection (1)(c) of that section.

(8) And, accordingly, in the case of an individual who is such a limited partner, in this section and in sections 793 to 795 references to the individual's firm are references to the relationship between the individual and the other persons mentioned in section [103A(3)(a)][1].

Commentary—*Simon's Taxes* B7.522.
HMRC Manuals—Business Income Manual BIM82675 (partnerships - recovery of excess relief).
Amendments—[1]   Section numbers in sub-ss (7), (8) substituted by FA 2007 s 26, Sch 4 paras 17, 21 and deemed always to have had effect.

793 Calculating the amount of income treated as received

(1) The amount of income treated as received by the individual under section 792 when the chargeable event occurs is the lowest of amounts A to C.

(2) Amount A is the amount by which the individual's contribution to the firm is reduced as a result of the application of regulations made under section 114.

(3) Amount B is the amount given by—

(a) taking, at the time immediately after the chargeable event occurs, the total amount of trade losses claimed that are post-1 December 2004 losses, and

(b) reducing that amount (but not below nil) by any reclaimed relief.

(4) Amount C is the amount given by—

(a) taking the amount by which, at the time immediately after the chargeable event occurs, the total amount of trade losses claimed exceeds the individual's contribution to the firm, and

(b) reducing that amount (but not below nil) by any reclaimed relief.

Commentary—*Simon's Taxes* B7.522.
HMRC Manuals—Business Income Manual BIM82675 (partnerships: amount chargeable).

794 Meaning of "the total amount of trade losses claimed" etc

(1) In sections 792 and 793 "the total amount of trade losses claimed" means the total amount of losses within subsection (2) for which the individual has claimed sideways relief or capital gains relief.

(2) The losses within this subsection are losses made by the individual in the relevant trade—

(a) in a tax year at a time during which the individual carries on the relevant trade as a limited partner or as a member of an LLP, or

(b) in an early tax year during which the individual carries on the relevant trade as a non-active partner.

Expressions used in this subsection are to be read as if contained in Chapter 3 of Part 4.

(3) In sections 792 and 793 "reclaimed relief" means the total amount of income treated as received by the individual under section 792 as a result of that section being previously applied in relation to claims for relief for losses made by the individual in the relevant trade.

(4) In sections 792 and 793 "the individual's contribution to the firm" at any time means the individual's contribution to the firm or the LLP (as the case may be) at that time as calculated for the purposes of the relevant restriction provision.

(5) The "relevant restriction provision" means—

    (a) whichever of sections 104, 107 and 110 applied as mentioned in section 792(1)(b), or

    (b) if more than one of those sections applied as mentioned in section 792(1)(b), the section which so applied to the amount of relief which could be given for the loss most recently made by the individual in the relevant trade.

(6) In a case to which section 792(6) applies, for the purpose of determining the total amount of trade losses claimed, the amount of the reclaimed relief and the relevant restriction provision—

    (a) apply subsections (1) and (2) in relation to each of the trades that the firm is carrying on, or has carried on, and then add the results together, and

    (b) apply subsections (3) and (5)(b) as if references to the relevant trade were references to any of the trades that the firm is carrying on, or has carried on.

But if a trade is of the kind mentioned in section 110(8), do not apply subsection (2)(b) in relation to it.

795 Meaning of "post-1 December 2004 loss"

(1) For the purposes of sections 792 and 793 a "post-1 December 2004 loss" means—

    (a) any loss made by an individual in a trade in a tax year the basis period for which begins on or after 2 December 2004, or

    (b) the post-1 December 2004 part of any loss made by an individual in a trade in a tax year the basis period for which includes 2 December 2004 (but begins before that date).

(2) The "post-1 December 2004 part" of any loss made by an individual in a trade means the individual's share of any losses made by the relevant firm in the trade in the period—

    (a) beginning with 2 December 2004, and

    (b) ending with the end of the basis period for the tax year concerned.

(3) For this purpose "the relevant firm" means the firm in which the individual carried on the trade, and—

    (a) the losses of that firm are calculated as if that period were one for which profits and losses had to be calculated for the purposes of section 849 of ITTOIA 2005 (calculation of firm's profits or losses), and

    (b) the individual's share of the losses is determined in accordance with the individual's interest in the firm during that period.

(4) In this section "basis period", in relation to an individual with a notional trade, means the basis period for the notional trade (within the meaning of Part 9 of ITTOIA 2005).

Derivation—FA 2005 s 76.

HMRC Manuals—Business Income Manual BIM82675 (losses sustained after 1 december 2004).

Individuals claiming relief for film-related trading losses

796 Charge to tax on income treated as received under section 797

(1) Income tax is charged on income treated as received by an individual under section 797.

(2) Tax is charged under this section on the amount of the income treated as received in the tax year.

(3) The person liable for any tax charged under this section is the individual treated as receiving the income.

Commentary—*Simon's Taxes* B7.522.

Derivation—FA 2004 s 119(4).

HMRC Manuals—Business Income Manual BIM56515 (individual exit schemes : overview).

797 Individuals claiming sideways or capital gains relief for film-related losses

(1) This section applies if—

    (a) an individual makes a film-related loss (see section 800) in a trade for which the individual claims sideways relief or capital gains relief (a "relevant claim"),

    (b) there is a disposal of a right of the individual to profits arising from the trade (a "relevant disposal") (see section 799), and

    (c) an exit event occurs.

(2) An exit event occurs whenever—

    (a) the individual receives any non-taxable consideration (see section 798) for a relevant disposal, or

    (b) an increase in the individual's claimed film-related losses (see section 800) or a decrease in the individual's capital contribution (see section 801) results in—

        (i) those losses becoming greater than that contribution, or

        (ii) an increase in the amount by which those losses exceed that contribution.

(3) The individual is treated as receiving an amount of income every time a chargeable event occurs.

The income is treated as arising otherwise than as profits of the trade.

(4) A chargeable event occurs whenever—

(a) the individual makes a relevant claim (if by that time a relevant disposal and an exit event have occurred),

(b) a relevant disposal occurs (if by that time an exit event has occurred and the individual has made a relevant claim), or

(c) an exit event occurs (if by that time a relevant disposal has occurred and the individual has made a relevant claim).

(5) The amount of income treated as received when a chargeable event occurs is equal to the sum of—

(a) the total amount or value of all non-taxable consideration received by the individual for relevant disposals, and

(b) the amount (if any) by which the individual's claimed film-related losses exceed the individual's capital contribution.

The calculation in this subsection is made immediately after the chargeable event occurs and is subject to section 803.

(6) For the purposes of this section it does not matter—

(a) if the individual (or anyone else) is still carrying on the trade when a chargeable event occurs, or

(b) if the individual receives both non-taxable and taxable consideration for a relevant disposal.

Commentary—*Simon's Taxes* **B5.508**.
HMRC Manuals—Business Income Manual BIM56520 (individual exit schemes: who is affected by the legislation?).
BIM56525 (individual exit schemes: exit events).
BIM56535 (individual exit schemes: the exit charge - the 'chargeable event').

798 Meaning of "non-taxable consideration" etc

(1) This section applies for the purposes of section 797.

(2) Consideration is non-taxable if (apart from section 796) it is not chargeable to income tax.

(3) Non-taxable consideration from which a deduction within subsection (4) is made is treated as received free of the deduction.

(4) A deduction is within this subsection if it is in consideration of any person's agreeing to, or facilitating, any relevant disposal or exit event.

Commentary—*Simon's Taxes* **B5.508**.
Derivation—FA 2004 ss 122(3) and 123(2).
HMRC Manuals—Business Income Manual BIM56525 (non-taxable consideration).

799 Meaning of "disposal of a right of the individual to profits" etc

(1) For the purposes of section 797 any reference to a disposal of a right of an individual to profits arising from a trade includes, in particular, any of events A to D.

(2) Event A is the disposal, giving up or loss by—

(a) the individual, or

(b) a firm in which the individual is a partner,

of a right arising from the trade to income (or any part of any income).

It does not matter if the right is disposed of, given up or lost as part of a larger disposal, giving up or loss.

(3) Event B is the disposal, giving up or loss of the individual's interest in a firm that carries on the trade (including the dissolution of the firm).

(4) Event C is a default in the payment of income to which—

(a) the individual, or

(b) a firm in which the individual is a partner,

has a right arising from the trade.

(5) Event D is a change in the individual's entitlement to any profits or losses arising from the trade the effect of which is that—

(a) the individual's share of any profits is reduced (including to nil), or

(b) the individual becomes entitled to a share, or a greater share, of any losses without becoming entitled to a corresponding share of profits.

(6) The changes covered by event D include cases where there is an agreement under which the individual is entitled—

(a) to a particular share of any profits or losses arising from the trade in a period (including a nil share), and

(b) to a different share of any such profits or losses in a succeeding period (including a nil share).

(7) In such cases the change in the individual's entitlement is treated for the purposes of section 797 as occurring at the beginning of the succeeding period.

Commentary—*Simon's Taxes* **B5.508**.
Derivation—FA 2004 s 120.
HMRC Manuals—Business Income Manual BIM56530 (individual exit schemes: disposals).

800 Meaning of "film-related losses" etc

(1) This section applies for the purposes of sections 797, 801 and 802.

(2) A loss is a "film-related loss" if the calculation of profits or losses that it results from is made in accordance with any provision of Chapter 9 of Part 2 of ITTOIA 2005.

(3) "The individual's claimed film-related losses" means—

   (a) the total amount of film-related losses made by the individual in the trade so far as they are losses for which the individual has made a relevant claim, less

   (b) the amount of any relevant recovered relief.

(4) "The amount of any relevant recovered relief" means—

   (a) amount A, or

   (b) if less, amount B.

(5) Amount A is the total amount of income treated as received by the individual under section 792 (recovery of excess relief) as a result of the application of that section in relation to claims for relief for losses made by the individual in the trade.

(6) Amount B is the total amount of film-related losses within subsection (7) for which the individual has made a relevant claim.

(7) A loss is within this subsection if it is made by the individual in the trade—

   (a) in a tax year at a time during which the individual carries on the trade as a member of an LLP or as a limited partner, or

   (b) in an early tax year during which the individual carries on the trade as a non-active partner.

(8) Expressions used in subsection (7) are to be read as if contained in Chapter 3 of Part 4.

(9) Subsection (10) applies if—

   (a) the individual has made a relevant claim for a film-related loss made in the trade as a partner in a firm, and

   (b) the firm is carrying on, or has carried on, more than one trade.

(10) For the purpose of determining the individual's claimed film-related losses—

   (a) apply subsection (3)(a) in relation to each of the trades and then add the results together,

   (b) apply subsection (5) as if the reference to the trade were a reference to any of the trades, and

   (c) apply subsections (6) and (7) in relation to each of the trades and then add the results together.

Commentary—*Simon's Taxes* **B5.508**.

HMRC Manuals—Business Income Manual BIM56520 (film related losses).

801 Meaning of "capital contribution"

(1) This section applies for the purposes of section 797.

(2) The individual's capital contribution is the amount which the individual has contributed to the trade as capital less so much of that amount (if any) as is within subsection (6).

   This is subject to subsection (3).

(3) If the individual has made a relevant claim for a film-related loss made in the trade as a partner in a firm, the individual's capital contribution is the amount which the individual has contributed to the firm as capital less so much of that amount (if any) as is within subsection (6).

(4) In particular, the individual's share of any profits of the firm is to be included for the purposes of subsection (3) in the amount which the individual has contributed to the firm as capital so far as that share has been added to the firm's capital.

(5) In subsection (4) the reference to profits are to profits calculated in accordance with generally accepted accounting practice (before any adjustment required or authorised by law in calculating profits for income tax purposes).

(6) An amount of capital is within this subsection if it is an amount which—

   (a) the individual has previously drawn out or received back,

   (b) the individual is entitled to draw out or receive back,

   (c) another person has reimbursed to the individual, or

   (d) the individual is entitled to require another person to reimburse to the individual.

(7) But if a chargeable event occurs, anything treated for the purposes of section 797(5)(a) as consideration received by the individual for a relevant disposal is not to be treated as capital within subsection (6) in calculating the individual's capital contribution for the purposes of section 797(5)(b).

(8) In this section—

   (a) any reference to drawing out, receiving back or reimbursing an amount is to doing so directly or indirectly,

   (b) any reference to drawing out or receiving back an amount does not include drawing out or receiving back an amount which, because of its being drawn out or received back, is chargeable to income tax as profits of a trade, and

   (c) any reference to reimbursing an amount includes discharging or assuming all or part of a liability of the individual,

but the express provision made by paragraph (c) does not affect what counts as the receipt back or reimbursement of an amount.

(9) This section needs to be read with any regulations made under section 802 (specified amounts to be excluded in calculating a partner's capital contribution for the purposes of section 797).

Commentary—*Simon's Taxes* **B5.508**.
HMRC Manuals—Business Income Manual BIM56540 (capital contribution to the trade).

802 Exclusion of amounts in calculating capital contribution by a partner

(1) This section applies if an individual makes a relevant claim for a film-related loss made by the individual in a trade as a partner in a firm.

(2) The Commissioners for Her Majesty's Revenue and Customs may by regulations provide that any amount of a specified description is to be excluded in calculating the individual's capital contribution for the purposes of section 797.

(3) "Specified" means specified in the regulations.

(4) The regulations may—

    (a) make provision having retrospective effect,

    (b) contain incidental, supplemental, consequential and transitional provision and savings, and

    (c) make different provision for different cases or purposes.

(5) The provision which may be made as a result of subsection (4)(b) includes provision amending or repealing any provision of an Act passed before FA 2005.

(6) No regulations may be made under this section unless a draft of them has been laid before and approved by a resolution of the House of Commons.

Commentary—*Simon's Taxes* **B5.508**.
HMRC Manuals—Business Income Manual BIM56545 (capital contributions not at risk).

803 Prohibition against double counting

(1) Subsections (2) and (3) apply for the purpose of calculating the amount of income received under section 797 on a chargeable event in respect of the individual and the trade.

(2) If chargeable events have previously occurred in respect of the individual and the trade, any consideration taken into account in calculating the amount of income received on an earlier chargeable event is left out of account.

(3) If chargeable events have previously occurred in respect of the individual and the trade, the amount of income received as a result of section 797(5)(b) is reduced (but not below nil) by the total amount of income received on earlier chargeable events as a result of that provision.

(4) In a case to which section 800(10) (cases in which firm is carrying on, or has carried on, more than one trade) applies—

    (a) subsections (2) and (3) of this section have effect as if references to the trade were references to any of the firm's trades, and

    (b) if chargeable events in respect of the individual and any of the firm's trades occur at the same time, to find the total amount of income received under section 797 at that time on those chargeable events—

        (i) calculate separately the income received on each chargeable event ignoring the other chargeable events,

        (ii) add the results from sub-paragraph (i) together, and

        (iii) reduce the total amount of income resulting from sub-paragraph (ii) so far as necessary to ensure that no amount is included more than once in that total.

Commentary—*Simon's Taxes* **B5.508**.
HMRC Manuals—Business Income Manual BIM56535 (the exit charge).

Individuals in partnership claiming relief for licence-related trading losses

804 Charge to tax on income treated as received under section 805

(1) Income tax is charged on income treated as received by an individual under section 805.

(2) Tax is charged under this section on the amount of the income treated as received in the tax year.

(3) The person liable for any tax charged under this section is the individual treated as receiving the income.

Commentary—*Simon's Taxes* **B5.646B**.
Derivation—FA 2004 s 127(2).
HMRC Manuals—Business Income Manual BIM82685 (partnerships: license-related losses: exit charge - chargeable amount).

805 Partners claiming relief for licence-related trading losses

(1) This section applies if—

    (a) an individual carries on a trade as a non-active partner during an early tax year,

    (b) the individual makes a loss in the trade in that tax year for which the individual claims sideways relief or capital gains relief (a "relevant claim"),

    (c) the loss derives to any extent from expenditure incurred in the trade in exploiting a licence acquired in carrying on the trade, and

    (d) there is a relevant disposal of the licence.

(2) For the purposes of this section and section 806 there is a relevant disposal of the licence whenever the individual receives non-taxable consideration for—

    (a) a disposal of the licence, or

    (b) a disposal of a right to income under an agreement related to or containing the licence.

(3) If one or more chargeable events occur in any tax year, the individual is treated as receiving an amount of income in the tax year.

The income is treated as arising otherwise than as profits of the trade.

(4) For the purposes of this section and section 806 a chargeable event occurs whenever—

    (a) there is a relevant disposal of the licence (if by that time the individual has made a relevant claim), or

    (b) the individual makes a relevant claim (if by that time there has been a relevant disposal of the licence).

(5) For the purposes of this section and section 806 consideration is non-taxable if—

    (a) (apart from section 804) it is not chargeable to income tax, and

    (b) its receipt is not an exit event for the purposes of section 797.

(6) For the purposes of this section and section 806 it does not matter—

    (a) if the individual (or anyone else) is still carrying on the trade when a chargeable event occurs,

    (b) if the individual receives both non-taxable and taxable consideration for a relevant disposal of the licence, or

    (c) if a relevant disposal of the licence is part of a larger disposal.

Commentary—*Simon's Taxes* **B5.646B**.

HMRC Manuals—Business Income Manual BIM82685 (partnerships: licence-related losses).

806 Calculation of amount of income treated as received by the individual

The amount of income treated under section 805 as received by the individual in the tax year is calculated by taking the following steps.

    Step 1 Calculate, at the end of the tax year, the total amount of the claimed losses (so far as relating to the licence) made by the individual in the trade in any early tax year during which the individual carried on the trade as a non-active partner.

    Step 2 Calculate, at the end of the tax year, the total amount of the profits (so far as relating to the licence) made by the individual in the trade in any tax year.

    Step 3 Deduct the total calculated at Step 2 from the total calculated at Step 1.

    The result is "the net licence-related loss".

    If the net licence-related loss is nil or a negative figure—

    (a) the income treated as received in the tax year is nil, and

    (b) ignore Steps 4 and 5.

    Step 4 Calculate, at the end of the tax year, the total amount or value of all non-taxable consideration received by the individual for relevant disposals (including consideration received in previous tax years).

    Step 5 Deduct from—

    (a) the net licence-related loss, or

    (b) if less, the total calculated at Step 4,

    the total amount of all income treated under section 805 as received by the individual in previous tax years as a result of chargeable events.

    The result is the amount of the income treated as received in the tax year. (If the result is a negative figure, the income is nil.)

Commentary—*Simon's Taxes* **B5.646B**.

807 Supplementary provision relating to calculation in section 806

(1) This section applies for the purposes of section 806.

(2) For the purposes of Step 1, the amount of a loss made in a tax year that relates to the licence is so much of the loss in the tax year as derives from expenditure incurred in the trade in exploiting the licence.

(3) The amount of the loss that derives from such expenditure is determined on a just and reasonable basis.

(4) For the purposes of Step 1, a loss is a claimed loss if the individual has claimed sideways relief or capital gains relief for the loss.

(5) For the purposes of Step 2, the amount of profits made in a tax year that relates to the licence is so much of the individual's profits from the trade in the tax year as derives from income arising from an agreement related to or containing the licence.

(6) The amount of the profits that derives from such income is determined on a just and reasonable basis.

Commentary—*Simon's Taxes* **B5.646B**.

808 Meaning of "disposal of the licence" etc

(1) For the purposes of section 805 any reference to—

    (a) a disposal of a licence acquired in carrying on a trade, or

    (b) a disposal of a right to income under an agreement related to or containing a licence acquired in carrying on a trade ("a licence-related agreement"),

includes, in particular, any of events A to E.

(2) Event A is the revocation of the licence.

(3) Event B is the disposal, giving up or loss of—

    (a) a right under the licence, or

    (b) a right to income (or any part of any income) under a licence-related agreement,

by the individual or by a firm in which the individual is a partner.

It does not matter if the right is disposed of, given up or lost as part of a larger disposal, giving up or loss.

(4) Event C is the disposal, giving up or loss of the individual's interest in a firm that has the licence or a right to income under a licence-related agreement (including the dissolution of the firm).

(5) Event D is a default in the payment of income to which—

    (a) the individual, or

    (b) a firm in which the individual is a partner,

has a right under a licence-related agreement.

(6) Event E is a change in the individual's entitlement to any profits or losses relating to the licence the effect of which is that—

    (a) the individual's share of any profits is reduced (including to nil), or

    (b) the individual becomes entitled to a share, or a greater share, of any losses without becoming entitled to a corresponding share of profits.

(7) The changes covered by event E include cases where there is an agreement under which the individual is entitled—

    (a) to a particular share of any profits or losses relating to the licence in a period (including a nil share), and

    (b) to a different share of any such profits or losses in a succeeding period (including a nil share).

(8) In such cases the change in the individual's entitlement is treated for the purposes of section 805 as occurring at the beginning of the succeeding period.

(9) For the purposes of this section—

    (a) references to any profits relating to the licence are to any profits deriving to any extent from income to which the individual has a right under a licence-related agreement, and

    (b) references to any losses relating to the licence are to losses deriving to any extent from expenditure incurred in exploiting the licence.

Commentary—*Simon's Taxes* **B5.646B**.
Derivation—FA 2004 s 129.
HMRC Manuals—Business Income Manual BIM82685 (partnerships: license-related losses: disposal of licence).

809 Other definitions

(1) References in sections 805 and 806 to an individual carrying on a trade as a non-active partner in an early tax year are to be read as if those sections were contained in Chapter 3 of Part 4 (see, in particular, section [103B][1]).

(2) But for that purpose, section [103B(1)(b)][1] (which contains a requirement that the individual does not carry on the trade as a limited partner at any time during the tax year) is treated as if it were omitted.

(3) For the purposes of sections 805 to 808 an agreement is related to a licence if the agreement and licence are entered into under the same arrangement (regardless of when the agreement or licence is entered into).

(4) For the purposes of sections 805 to 808 an agreement, or part of an agreement, is not prevented from being a licence merely because it imposes an obligation to do a thing (rather than merely gives authority to do it).

References to exploiting a licence are to be read in that light.

Commentary—*Simon's Taxes* **B5.646B**.
Derivation—FA 2004 ss 126, 127(7) and 130.
HMRC Manuals—Business Income Manual BIM82685 (partnerships: license-related losses).
Amendments—[1]   Section numbers in sub-ss (1), (2) substituted by FA 2007 s 26, Sch 4 paras 18, 21 and deemed always to have had effect.

[CHAPTER 5A

TRANSFERS OF INCOME STREAMS

809AZA Application of Chapter

(1) This Chapter applies where—

    (a) a person within the charge to income tax ("the transferor") makes a transfer to another person ("the transferee") of a right to relevant receipts (see subsection (2)), and

    (b) (subject to subsection (3)) the transfer of the right is not a consequence of the transfer to the transferee of an asset from which the right to relevant receipts arises.

(2) "Relevant receipts" means any income—

    (a) which (but for the transfer) would be charged to income tax as income of the transferor, or (*b*) which (but for the transfer) would be brought into account in calculating profits of the transferor for the purposes of income tax.

(3) Despite paragraph (*b*) of subsection (1), this Chapter applies if the transfer of the right is a consequence of the transfer to the transferee of all rights under an agreement for annual payments; and for the purposes of that paragraph the transfer of an asset under a sale and repurchase agreement is not to be regarded as a transfer of the asset.

(4) Section 809AZB makes provision as to the consequences of this Chapter applying.

(5) For exclusions from this Chapter, see—

    (*a*) section 809AZC (amount otherwise taxed),

    (*b*) section 809AZD (certain annuities), and

    (*c*) section 809AZE (transfer by way of security).

(6) Section 809AZF makes special provision about transfers of partnership shares.

(7) Section 809AZG contains supplementary provisions.][1]

Commentary—*Simon's Taxes* **E1.468**.

Amendments—[1]   Sections 809AZA–809AZG inserted by FA 2009 s 49, Sch 25 para 7 with effect in relation to transfers on or after 22 April 2009.

[809AZB Value of transferred income stream treated as income

(1) The relevant amount (see subsection (2)) is to be treated as income of the transferor chargeable to income tax in the same way and to the same extent as that in which the relevant receipts—

    (*a*) would have been chargeable to income tax, or

    (*b*) would have been brought into account in calculating any profits for the purposes of income tax,

but for the transfer of the right to relevant receipts.

(2) The relevant amount is—

    (*a*) (except where paragraph (*b*) applies) the amount of the consideration for the transfer of the right, or

    (*b*) where the amount of any such consideration is substantially less than the market value of the right at the time when the transfer takes place (or where there is no consideration for the transfer of the right), the market value of the right at that time.

(3) The income under subsection (1) is to be treated as arising in the chargeable period of the transferor in which the transfer takes place.

(4) But subsection (5) applies if (apart from the transfer) any of the relevant receipts—

    (*a*) would have been brought into account in accordance with Part 2 or 3 of ITTOIA 2005 (trading income and property income) in calculating any profits for the purposes of income tax, and

    (*b*) in accordance with generally accepted accounting practice, would have been recognised otherwise than wholly in the chargeable period in which the transfer takes place.

(5) If this subsection applies, the income under subsection (1) is to be treated as arising—

    (*a*) to the extent that it does not exceed the amount of the consideration for the transfer of the right, in the chargeable period or periods for which, in accordance with generally accepted accounting practice, the consideration for the transfer is recognised for accounting purposes in a profit and loss account or income statement of the transferor, and

    (*b*) otherwise, in the chargeable period or periods for which, in accordance with generally accepted accounting practice, the consideration for the transfer would be so recognised if it were of an amount equal to the market value of the right at the time when the transfer takes place.

(6) But if in a case where the transferor is a company it at any time becomes reasonable to assume that the income (to any extent) is not, or would not be, treated by subsection (5) as arising in an accounting period of the transferor, the income is to that extent to be treated as arising immediately before that time.][1]

Commentary—*Simon's Taxes* **B7.401**.

HMRC Manuals—Savings and Investment Manual SAIM11030 (transfers of income streams: non-corporate transferors).

Amendments—[1]   Sections 809AZA–809AZG inserted by FA 2009 s 49, Sch 25 para 7 with effect in relation to transfers on or after 22 April 2009.

[809AZC Exception: amount otherwise taxed

This Chapter does not apply if and to the extent that the income under section 809AZB(1) is (apart from this Chapter)—

    (*a*) charged to tax as income of the transferor,

    (*b*) brought into account in calculating the profits of the transferor, or

    (*c*) brought into account under CAA 2001.][1]

Amendments—[1]   Sections 809AZA–809AZG inserted by FA 2009 s 49, Sch 25 para 7 with effect in relation to transfers on or after 22 April 2009.

[809AZD Exception: certain annuities

This Chapter does not apply to a transfer of a right to—

    (*a*) annual payments under a life annuity as defined in section 473(2) of ITTOIA 2005, or

(b) annual payments under an annuity which is pension income within the meaning of Part 9 of ITEPA 2003 (see section 566(2) of that Act).][1]

Amendments—[1]   Sections 809AZA–809AZG inserted by FA 2009 s 49, Sch 25 para 7 with effect in relation to transfers on or after 22 April 2009.

[809AZE Exception: transfer by way of security

(1) This Chapter does not apply if—
   (a) the consideration for the transfer is the advance under a type 1 finance arrangement, and
   (b) the transferor is, or is a member of a partnership which is, the borrower in relation to the arrangement.
(2) This Chapter does not apply if—
   (a) the consideration for the transfer is the advance under a type 2 finance arrangement or a type 3 finance arrangement, and
   (b) the transferor is a member of the partnership which receives that advance under the arrangement.
(3) In this section—
   "type 1 finance arrangement" has the meaning given for the purposes of Chapter 5B by section 809BZA,
   "type 2 finance arrangement" has the meaning given for the purposes of Chapter 5B by section 809BZF, and
   "type 3 finance arrangement" has the meaning given for the purposes of Chapter 5B by section 809BZJ.][1]

Commentary—*Simon's Taxes* **D9.301A**.
Amendments—[1]   This section substituted by TIOPA 2010 s 501, Sch 8 paras 271, 273. TIOPA 2010 has effect for corporation tax purposes for accounting periods ending on or after 1 April 2010, for income and capital gains tax purposes for the tax year 2010–11 and subsequent tax years, and for petroleum revenue tax purposes for chargeable periods beginning on or after 1 July 2010.

[809AZF Partnership shares

(1) For the purposes of this Chapter a transfer of a right to relevant receipts consisting of the reduction in a transferor's share in the profits or losses of a partnership is to be regarded as a consequence of a transfer of an asset from which the right arose (that is, the partnership property) . . . .[2]
(2), (3) . . .[2]][1]

Amendments—[1]   Sections 809AZA–809AZG inserted by FA 2009 s 49, Sch 25 para 7 with effect in relation to transfers on or after 22 April 2009.
[2]   In sub-s (1), words repealed, and sub-ss (2), (3) repealed, by FA 2014 s 74, Sch 17 paras 22, 23 with effect for cases where the transfer of a right to relevant receipts occurs on or after 6 April 2014.

[809AZG Interpretation

(1) For the purposes of this Chapter—
   (a) the grant or surrender of a lease of land is to be regarded as a transfer of the land, and
   (b) the disposal of an interest in an oil licence (within the meaning of section 809 of CTA 2009) is to be regarded as a transfer of the oil licence.
(2) The Treasury may by order make other provision for securing that other transactions are to be regarded as transfers of assets for those purposes.
(3) In this Chapter—
   (a) references to a transfer include sale, exchange, gift and assignment (or assignation) and any other arrangement which equates in substance to a transfer, and
   (b) references to a transfer taking place are, in the case of an arrangement other than a sale, exchange, gift or assignment (or assignation), to the making of the arrangement.
(4) A transfer to or by any partnership of which the transferor or transferee is a member, and a transfer to the trustees of any trust of which the transferor is a beneficiary, counts as a transfer in relation to which this Chapter applies.][1]

Amendments—[1]   Sections 809AZA–809AZG inserted by FA 2009 s 49, Sch 25 para 7 with effect in relation to transfers on or after 22 April 2009.

[CHAPTER 5AA

DISPOSALS OF INCOME STREAMS THROUGH PARTNERSHIPS]

[809AAZA Application of Chapter

(1) This Chapter applies (subject to subsection (2)) if directly or indirectly in consequence of, or otherwise in connection with, arrangements involving a person within the charge to income tax ("the transferor") and another person ("the transferee")—
   (a) there is, or is in substance, a disposal of a right to relevant receipts by the transferor to the transferee,
   (b) the disposal is effected (wholly or partly) by or through a partnership ("the relevant partnership"),

(c) at any time—
- (i) the transferor is a member of the relevant partnership or of a partnership associated with the relevant partnership, and
- (ii) the transferee is a member of the relevant partnership or of a partnership associated with the relevant partnership, and
- (d) the main purpose, or one of the main purposes, of one or more steps taken in effecting the disposal is the obtaining of a tax advantage for any person.

(2) This Chapter does not apply if—
- (a) the transferor is the spouse or civil partner of the transferee and they are living together, or
- (b) the transferor is a brother, sister, ancestor or lineal descendant of the transferee.

(3) In subsection (1)(a) the reference to a disposal of a right to relevant receipts includes anything constituting a disposal of such a right for the purposes of TCGA 1992.

(4) For the purposes of subsection (1)(b) the disposal might, in particular, be effected by an acquisition or disposal of, or an increase or decrease in, an interest in the relevant partnership (including a share of the profits or assets of the relevant partnership or an interest in such a share).

(5) For the purposes of subsection (1)(c) it does not matter if the transferor and the transferee are not members of a partnership as mentioned at the same time.

(6) For the purposes of subsection (1)(c) a partnership is "associated" with the relevant partnership if—
- (a) it is a member of the relevant partnership, or
- (b) it is a member of a partnership which is associated with the relevant partnership (whether by virtue of paragraph (a) or this paragraph).

(7) In subsections (1)(c) and (5) references to the transferor include a person connected with the transferor and references to the transferee include a person connected with the transferee.

(8) In this Chapter—
"arrangements" includes any agreement, understanding, scheme, transaction or series of transactions (whether or not legally enforceable),
"partnership" includes a limited liability partnership whether or not section 863(1) of ITTOIA 2005 applies in relation to it,
"relevant receipts" means any income—
- (a) which (but for the disposal) would be charged to income tax as income of the transferor (whether directly or as a member of a partnership), or
- (b) which (but for the disposal) would be brought into account as income in calculating profits of the transferor (whether directly or as a member of a partnership) for income tax purposes, and
"tax advantage" means a tax advantage, as defined in section 1139 of CTA 2010, in relation to income tax or the charge to corporation tax on income.][1]

Commentary—*Simon's Taxes* **B7.401**.
Amendments—[1]   Chapter 5AA (ss 809AAZA, 809AAZB) inserted by FA 2014 s 74, Sch 17 paras 22, 24 with effect for cases where the arrangements mentioned in ITA 2007 s 809AAZA(1) are made on or after 6 April 2014.

[809AAZB Relevant amount to be treated as income

(1) The relevant amount is to be treated as income of the transferor chargeable to income tax in the same way and to the same extent as that in which the relevant receipts—
- (a) would have been chargeable to income tax as income of the transferor, or
- (b) would have been brought into account as income in calculating profits of the transferor for income tax purposes,

but for the disposal.

(2) In subsection (1) "the relevant amount" is to be read in accordance with section 809AZB(2) and section 809AZB(3) to (6) applies for the purpose of determining when income under subsection (1) is treated as arising.

(3) For this purpose, in section 809AZB(2) to (6) references to the transfer of the right are to be read as references to the disposal of the right.

(4) If, apart from this subsection and section 809DZB(3)—
- (a) both this Chapter and Chapter 5D would apply in relation to the disposal, and
- (b) Chapter 5D would give a greater amount of income of the transferor chargeable to income tax,

this Chapter is not to apply in relation to the disposal.][1]

Commentary—*Simon's Taxes* **B7.401**.
Amendments—[1]   Chapter 5AA (ss 809AAZA, 809AAZB) inserted by FA 2014 s 74, Sch 17 paras 22, 24 with effect for cases where the arrangements mentioned in ITA 2007 s 809AAZA(1) are made on or after 6 April 2014.

[CHAPTER 5B
FINANCE ARRANGEMENTS][1]

Amendments—

1   Chapter 5B (ss 809BZA–809BZS) inserted by TIOPA 2010 s 369, Sch 5 paras 1–6. TIOPA 2010 has effect for corporation
    tax purposes for accounting periods ending on or after 1 April 2010, for income and capital gains tax purposes for the tax year
    2010–11 and subsequent tax years, and for petroleum revenue tax purposes for chargeable periods beginning on or after 1 July
    2010.

[Type 1 arrangements

809BZA Type 1 finance arrangement defined

(1) For the purposes of this Chapter an arrangement is a type 1 finance arrangement if conditions A
and B are met.

(2) Condition A is that under the arrangement—

    (*a*) a person ("the borrower") receives money or another asset ("the advance") from another
person ("the lender"),

    (*b*) the borrower or a person connected with the borrower makes a disposal of an asset ("the
security") to or for the benefit of the lender or a person connected with the lender, and

    (*c*) the lender or a person connected with the lender is entitled to payments in respect of the
security.

[(2A) For the purposes of subsection (2)(*c*) it does not matter if an entitlement of the lender or a
person connected with the lender is subject to any condition.][2]

(3) Condition B is that in accordance with generally accepted accounting practice—

    (*a*) the borrower's accounts for the period in which the advance is received record a financial
liability in respect of it, and

    (*b*) the payments reduce the amount of the financial liability.

(4) If the borrower is a partnership the reference to the borrower's accounts includes a reference to
the accounts of any member of the partnership.

(5) For the purposes of this section the borrower and the lender are not connected with one another.][1]

Commentary—*Simon's Taxes* **D1.793**.

Amendments—[1]   Sections 809BZA–809BZE inserted by TIOPA 2010 s 369, Sch 5 paras 1, 2. TIOPA 2010 has effect for
    corporation tax purposes for accounting periods ending on or after 1 April 2010, for income and capital gains tax purposes
    for the tax year 2010–11 and subsequent tax years, and for petroleum revenue tax purposes for chargeable periods beginning
    on or after 1 July 2010.
[2]   Sub-s (2A) inserted by FA 2012 s 48, Sch 13 paras 32, 33 with effect in relation to arrangements whenever made, subject to
    transitional provisions in FA 2012 Sch 13 para 42(2)–(4).

[809BZB Certain tax consequences not to have effect

(1) This section applies if a type 1 finance arrangement would have the relevant effect (ignoring this
section).

(2) The arrangement is not to have that effect.

(3) The relevant effect is that—

    (*a*) an amount of income on which the borrower or a person connected with the borrower would
otherwise have been charged to income tax is not so charged,

    (*b*) an amount which would otherwise have been brought into account in calculating for income
tax purposes any income of the borrower or of a person connected with the borrower is not
so brought into account, or

    (*c*) the borrower or a person connected with the borrower becomes entitled to an income
deduction.

(4) But if the borrower is a partnership the relevant effect is that—

    (*a*) an amount of income on which a member of the partnership would otherwise have been
charged to income tax is not so charged,

    (*b*) an amount which would otherwise have been brought into account in calculating for income
tax purposes any income of a member of the partnership is not so brought into account, or

    (*c*) a member of the partnership becomes entitled to an income deduction.

(5) For the purposes of this section the borrower and the lender are not connected with one another.

(6) An income deduction is—

    (*a*) a deduction in calculating income for income tax purposes, or

    (*b*) a deduction from total income.][1]

Commentary—*Simon's Taxes* **D1.793**.

Amendments—[1]   Sections 809BZA–809BZE inserted by TIOPA 2010 s 369, Sch 5 paras 1, 2. TIOPA 2010 has effect for
    corporation tax purposes for accounting periods ending on or after 1 April 2010, for income and capital gains tax purposes
    for the tax year 2010–11 and subsequent tax years, and for petroleum revenue tax purposes for chargeable periods beginning
    on or after 1 July 2010.

[809BZC Payments treated as borrower's income

(1) This section applies if—

(a) a type 1 finance arrangement would not have the relevant effect (ignoring section 809BZB(2)),

(b) that arrangement would not have the corresponding corporation-tax effect (ignoring section 759(2) of CTA 2010), and

(c) the borrower is—

   (i) within the charge to income tax, or

   (ii) a partnership at least one member of which is within the charge to income tax.

(2) The payments mentioned in section 809BZA(2)(c) must be treated for income tax purposes as income of the borrower payable in respect of the security.

(3) Subsection (2) applies whether or not the payments are also the income of another person for tax purposes.

(4) Subsections (3) to (6) of section 809BZB (meaning of relevant effect) apply for the purposes of this section as for those of that.

(5) In subsection (1)(b) "the corresponding corporation-tax effect" means the relevant effect as defined by section 759(3) to (6) of CTA 2010 (provision for corporation tax corresponding to section 809BZB(3) to (6)).][1]

Commentary—*Simon's Taxes* **D1.793**.

Amendments—[1]   Sections 809BZA–809BZE inserted by TIOPA 2010 s 369, Sch 5 paras 1, 2. TIOPA 2010 has effect for corporation tax purposes for accounting periods ending on or after 1 April 2010, for income and capital gains tax purposes for the tax year 2010–11 and subsequent tax years, and for petroleum revenue tax purposes for chargeable periods beginning on or after 1 July 2010.

[809BZD Deemed interest if borrower is not a partnership

(1) This section applies if—

(a) there is a type 1 finance arrangement,

(b) the borrower is not a partnership,

(c) the arrangement is prevented by section 809BZB from having the relevant effect in relation to the borrower, or section 809BZC applies to the borrower, and

(d) in accordance with generally accepted accounting practice the borrower's accounts record an amount as a finance charge in respect of the advance.

(2) For income tax purposes the borrower may treat the amount as interest payable on a loan.

(3) If an amount is treated as interest ("deemed interest") under subsection (2), to find out when it is paid—

(a) treat the payments mentioned in section 809BZA(2)(c) as consisting of amounts for repaying the advance and amounts ("the interest elements") in respect of interest on the advance,

(b) treat the interest elements of the payments as paid when the payments are paid, and

(c) treat the deemed interest as paid at the times when the interest elements are treated as paid.][1]

Commentary—*Simon's Taxes* **D1.793**.

Amendments—[1]   Sections 809BZA–809BZE inserted by TIOPA 2010 s 369, Sch 5 paras 1, 2. TIOPA 2010 has effect for corporation tax purposes for accounting periods ending on or after 1 April 2010, for income and capital gains tax purposes for the tax year 2010–11 and subsequent tax years, and for petroleum revenue tax purposes for chargeable periods beginning on or after 1 July 2010.

[809BZE Deemed interest if borrower is a partnership

(1) This section applies if each of conditions A to C is met.

(2) Condition A is that—

(a) there is a type 1 finance arrangement, and

(b) the borrower is a partnership.

(3) Condition B is that—

(a) the arrangement is prevented by section 809BZB from having the relevant effect in relation to a person who is a member of the partnership, or

(b) section 809BZC applies to the partnership (in which event "the person" in subsections (4) and (5) means the person within the charge to income tax who is a member of the partnership).

(4) Condition C is that in accordance with generally accepted accounting practice the person's accounts, or the partnership's accounts, record an amount as a finance charge in respect of the advance.

(5) For income tax purposes the person may treat the amount as interest payable by the partnership on a loan.

(6) If an amount is treated as interest ("deemed interest") under subsection (5), to find out when it is paid—

(a) treat the payments mentioned in section 809BZA(2)(c) as consisting of amounts for repaying the advance and amounts ("the interest elements") in respect of interest on the advance,

(b) treat the interest elements of the payments as paid when the payments are paid, and

(c) treat the deemed interest as paid at the times when the interest elements are treated as paid.][1]

Commentary—*Simon's Taxes* **D1.793**.

Amendments—[1]   Sections 809BZA–809BZE inserted by TIOPA 2010 s 369, Sch 5 paras 1, 2. TIOPA 2010 has effect for corporation tax purposes for accounting periods ending on or after 1 April 2010, for income and capital gains tax purposes for the tax year 2010–11 and subsequent tax years, and for petroleum revenue tax purposes for chargeable periods beginning on or after 1 July 2010.

[Type 2 arrangements

809BZF Type 2 finance arrangement defined

(1) For the purposes of this Chapter an arrangement is a type 2 finance arrangement if conditions A and B are met.

(2) Condition A is that—

  (a) under the arrangement a person ("the transferor") makes a disposal of an asset ("the security") to a partnership,

  (b) the transferor [or a person connected with the transferor][2] is a member of the partnership immediately after the disposal (whether or not a member immediately before it),

  (c) under the arrangement the partnership receives money or another asset ("the advance") from another person ("the lender"),

  (d) there is a relevant change in relation to the partnership (see section 809BZG), and

  (e) under the arrangement the share in the partnership's profits of the person involved in the change is determined by reference (wholly or partly) to payments in respect of the security.

[(2A) For the purposes of subsection (2)(e) it does not matter if any determination of the share in the partnership's profits of the person involved in the relevant change as mentioned is subject to any condition.][2]

(3) Condition B is that in accordance with generally accepted accounting practice—

  (a) the partnership's accounts for the period in which the advance is received record a financial liability in respect of it, and

  (b) the payments reduce the amount of the financial liability.

(4) The reference to the partnership's accounts includes a reference to the transferor's accounts.][1]

Commentary—*Simon's Taxes* **D1.794**.
Amendments—[1]   Sections 809BZF–809BZI inserted by TIOPA 2010 s 369, Sch 5 paras 1, 3. TIOPA 2010 has effect for corporation tax purposes for accounting periods ending on or after 1 April 2010, for income and capital gains tax purposes for the tax year 2010–11 and subsequent tax years, and for petroleum revenue tax purposes for chargeable periods beginning on or after 1 July 2010.
[2]   Words in sub-s (2)(b) and the whole of sub-s (2A) inserted by FA 2012 s 48, Sch 13 paras 32, 34 with effect in relation to arrangements whenever made, subject to transitional provisions in FA 2012 Sch 13 para 42(2)–(4).

[809BZG Relevant change in relation to partnership

(1) For the purposes of this Chapter there is a relevant change in relation to a partnership if condition A or condition B is met.

(2) Condition A is that in connection with the arrangement the lender or a person connected with the lender becomes a member of the partnership at any time.

(3) Condition B is that—

  (a) in connection with the arrangement there is at any time a change in a member's share in the partnership's profits, and

  (b) the member is the lender or a person connected with the lender or a person who in connection with the arrangement becomes at any time connected with the lender.

(4) An event occurs in connection with the arrangement if it occurs directly or indirectly in consequence of it or otherwise in connection with it.

(5) If there is a relevant change in relation to a partnership, a reference in this Chapter to the person involved in the change is—

  (a) if it is condition A that is met, to the person who becomes a member of the partnership, and

  (b) if it is condition B that is met, to the member of the partnership in whose share in the partnership's profits there is a change.][1]

Commentary—*Simon's Taxes* **D1.794**.
Amendments—[1]   Sections 809BZF–809BZI inserted by TIOPA 2010 s 369, Sch 5 paras 1, 3. TIOPA 2010 has effect for corporation tax purposes for accounting periods ending on or after 1 April 2010, for income and capital gains tax purposes for the tax year 2010–11 and subsequent tax years, and for petroleum revenue tax purposes for chargeable periods beginning on or after 1 July 2010.

[809BZH Certain tax consequences not to have effect

(1) This section applies if—

  (a) there is a type 2 finance arrangement, and

  (b) any relevant change in relation to the partnership would have the relevant effect (ignoring this section).

(2) In such a case—

  (a) Part 9 of ITTOIA 2005 (partnerships) is to have effect in relation to the transferor [or the person connected with the transferor][2] as if the relevant change in relation to the partnership had not occurred, and

  (b) accordingly the finance arrangement is not to have the relevant effect.

(3) The relevant effect is that—

   (*a*) an amount of income on which the transferor [or the person connected with the transferor][2] would otherwise have been charged to income tax is not so charged,

   (*b*) an amount which would otherwise have been brought into account in calculating for income tax purposes any income of the transferor [or the person connected with the transferor][2] is not so brought into account, or

   (*c*) the transferor [or the person connected with the transferor][2] becomes entitled to an income deduction.

(4) In deciding whether subsection (1)(*b*) is met assume that amounts of income equal to the payments mentioned in section 809BZF(2)(*e*) were payable to the partnership before the relevant change in relation to it occurred.

(5) An income deduction is—

   (*a*) a deduction in calculating income for income tax purposes, or

   (*b*) a deduction from total income.]¹

Commentary—*Simon's Taxes* **D1.794**.

Amendments—¹ Sections 809BZF–809BZI inserted by TIOPA 2010 s 369, Sch 5 paras 1, 3. TIOPA 2010 has effect for corporation tax purposes for accounting periods ending on or after 1 April 2010, for income and capital gains tax purposes for the tax year 2010–11 and subsequent tax years, and for petroleum revenue tax purposes for chargeable periods beginning on or after 1 July 2010.

² Words inserted by FA 2012 s 48, Sch 13 paras 32, 35 with effect in relation to arrangements whenever made, subject to transitional provisions in FA 2012 Sch 13 para 42(2)–(4).

[809BZI Deemed interest

(1) This section applies if—

   (*a*) there is a type 2 finance arrangement,

   (*b*) the transferor is a person within the charge to income tax, and

   (*c*) in accordance with generally accepted accounting practice the partnership's accounts record an amount as a finance charge in respect of the advance.

(2) For income tax purposes the transferor may treat the amount as interest payable by the transferor on a loan.

(3) The reference in subsection (1) to the partnership's accounts includes a reference to the transferor's accounts.

(4) If an amount is treated as interest ("deemed interest") under subsection (2), to find out when it is paid—

   (*a*) treat the payments mentioned in section 809BZF(2)(*e*) as consisting of amounts for repaying the advance and amounts ("the interest elements") in respect of interest on the advance,

   (*b*) treat the interest elements of the payments as paid when the payments are paid, and

   (*c*) treat the deemed interest as paid at the times when the interest elements are treated as paid.]¹

Commentary—*Simon's Taxes* **D1.794**.

Amendments—¹ Sections 809BZF–809BZI inserted by TIOPA 2010 s 369, Sch 5 paras 1, 3. TIOPA 2010 has effect for corporation tax purposes for accounting periods ending on or after 1 April 2010, for income and capital gains tax purposes for the tax year 2010–11 and subsequent tax years, and for petroleum revenue tax purposes for chargeable periods beginning on or after 1 July 2010.

[Type 3 arrangements

809BZJ Type 3 finance arrangement defined

(1) For the purposes of this Chapter an arrangement is a type 3 finance arrangement if conditions A and B are met.

(2) Condition A is that—

   (*a*) a partnership holds an asset ("the security") as a partnership asset at any time before the arrangement is made,

   (*b*) under the arrangement the partnership receives money or another asset ("the advance") from another person ("the lender"),

   (*c*) there is a relevant change in relation to the partnership (see section 809BZG), and

   (*d*) under the arrangement the share in the partnership's profits of the person involved in the change is determined by reference (wholly or partly) to payments in respect of the security.

[(2A) For the purposes of subsection (2)(*d*) it does not matter if any determination of the share in the partnership's profits of the person involved in the relevant change as mentioned is subject to any condition.]²

(3) Condition B is that in accordance with generally accepted accounting practice—

   (*a*) the partnership's accounts for the period in which the advance is received record a financial liability in respect of it, and

   (*b*) the payments reduce the amount of the financial liability.

(4) The reference to the partnership's accounts includes a reference to the accounts of any person who is a member of the partnership immediately before the arrangement is made.]¹

Commentary—*Simon's Taxes* **D1.794**.

Amendments—[1]   Sections 809BZJ–809BZL inserted by TIOPA 2010 s 369, Sch 5 paras 1, 4. TIOPA 2010 has effect for corporation tax purposes for accounting periods ending on or after 1 April 2010, for income and capital gains tax purposes for the tax year 2010–11 and subsequent tax years, and for petroleum revenue tax purposes for chargeable periods beginning on or after 1 July 2010.

[2]   Sub-s (2A) inserted by FA 2012 s 48, Sch 13 paras 32, 36 with effect in relation to arrangements whenever made, subject to transitional provisions in FA 2012 Sch 13 para 42(2)–(4).

[809BZK Certain tax consequences not to have effect

(1) This section applies if—

    (*a*) there is a type 3 finance arrangement, and

    (*b*) any relevant change in relation to the partnership would have the relevant effect (ignoring this section).

(2) The relevant effect is that—

    (*a*) an amount of income on which a relevant member would otherwise have been charged to income tax is not so charged,

    (*b*) an amount which would otherwise have been brought into account in calculating for income tax purposes any income of a relevant member is not so brought into account, or

    (*c*) a relevant member becomes entitled to an income deduction.

(3) A relevant member is a person who—

    (*a*) was a member of the partnership immediately before the relevant change in relation to it occurred, and

    (*b*) is not the lender.

(4) If this section applies—

    (*a*) Part 9 of ITTOIA 2005 (partnerships) is to have effect in relation to any relevant member as if the relevant change in relation to the partnership had not occurred, and

    (*b*) accordingly the finance arrangement is not to have the relevant effect.

(5) In deciding whether subsection (1)(*b*) is met assume that amounts of income equal to the payments mentioned in section 809BZJ(2)(*d*) were payable to the partnership before the relevant change in relation to it occurred.

(6) An income deduction is—

    (*a*) a deduction in calculating income for income tax purposes, or

    (*b*) a deduction from total income.][1]

Commentary—*Simon's Taxes* **D1.794**.

Amendments—[1]   Sections 809BZJ–809BZL inserted by TIOPA 2010 s 369, Sch 5 paras 1, 4. TIOPA 2010 has effect for corporation tax purposes for accounting periods ending on or after 1 April 2010, for income and capital gains tax purposes for the tax year 2010–11 and subsequent tax years, and for petroleum revenue tax purposes for chargeable periods beginning on or after 1 July 2010.

[809BZL Deemed interest

(1) This section applies if—

    (*a*) there is a type 3 finance arrangement,

    (*b*) a relevant member is a person within the charge to income tax, and

    (*c*) in accordance with generally accepted accounting practice the partnership's accounts record an amount as a finance charge in respect of the advance.

(2) For income tax purposes the relevant member may treat the amount as interest payable by the partnership on a loan.

(3) The reference in subsection (1) to the partnership's accounts includes a reference to the accounts of any relevant member.

(4) If an amount is treated as interest ("deemed interest") under subsection (2), to find out when it is paid—

    (*a*) treat the payments mentioned in section 809BZJ(2)(*d*) as consisting of amounts for repaying the advance and amounts ("the interest elements") in respect of interest on the advance,

    (*b*) treat the interest elements of the payments as paid when the payments are paid, and

    (*c*) treat the deemed interest as paid at the times when the interest elements are treated as paid.

(5) A relevant member is a person who—

    (*a*) was a member of the partnership immediately before the relevant change in relation to it occurred, and

    (*b*) is not the lender.][1]

Commentary—*Simon's Taxes* **D1.794**.

Amendments—[1]   Sections 809BZJ–809BZL inserted by TIOPA 2010 s 369, Sch 5 paras 1, 4. TIOPA 2010 has effect for corporation tax purposes for accounting periods ending on or after 1 April 2010, for income and capital gains tax purposes for the tax year 2010–11 and subsequent tax years, and for petroleum revenue tax purposes for chargeable periods beginning on or after 1 July 2010.

[Exceptions

809BZM Exceptions: preliminary

(1) Sections 809BZN to 809BZP make provision for finance arrangement codes not to apply in certain circumstances.

(2) For the purposes of those sections each of the following groups of provisions is a finance arrangement code—

    (*a*) sections 809BZA to 809BZE (type 1 arrangements),

    (*b*) sections 809BZF to 809BZI (type 2 arrangements), and

    (*c*) sections 809BZJ to 809BZL (type 3 arrangements).][1]

Commentary—*Simon's Taxes* **D7.1102**.

Amendments—[1] Sections 809BZM–809BZP inserted by TIOPA 2010 s 369, Sch 5 paras 1, 5. TIOPA 2010 has effect for corporation tax purposes for accounting periods ending on or after 1 April 2010, for income and capital gains tax purposes for the tax year 2010–11 and subsequent tax years, and for petroleum revenue tax purposes for chargeable periods beginning on or after 1 July 2010.

[809BZN Exceptions

(1) A finance arrangement code does not apply if the whole of the advance under the arrangement—

    (*a*) is charged to tax on a relevant person as an amount of income,

    (*b*) is brought into account in calculating for tax purposes any income of a relevant person, or

    (*c*) is brought into account for the purposes of any provision of CAA 2001 as a disposal receipt, or proceeds from a balancing event or disposal event, of a relevant person.

(2) Treat subsection (1)(*c*) as not met if—

    (*a*) the receipt gives rise, or proceeds give rise, to a balancing charge, and

    (*b*) the amount of the balancing charge is limited by any provision of CAA 2001.

(3) A finance arrangement code does not apply if at all times the whole of the advance under the arrangement—

    (*a*) is a debtor relationship of a relevant person for the purposes of Part 5 of CTA 2009 (loan relationships), or

    (*b*) would be a debtor relationship of a relevant person for those purposes if that person were a company within the charge to corporation tax.

(4) In subsection (3) references to a debtor relationship do not include references to a relationship to which Chapter 2 of Part 6 of CTA 2009 applies (relevant non-lending relationships).

(5) A finance arrangement code does not apply so far as—

    (*a*) section 263A of TCGA 1992 applies in relation to the arrangement (agreements for sale and repurchase of securities), or

    (*b*) Schedule 13 to FA 2007 or Chapter 10 of Part 6 of CTA 2009 applies in relation to the arrangement (sale and repurchase of securities, and repos).

(6) A finance arrangement code does not apply so far as Part 10A of this Act, Chapter 4 of Part 4 of TCGA 1992 or Chapter 6 of Part 6 of CTA 2009 has effect in relation to the arrangement (alternative finance arrangements).

(7) A finance arrangement code does not apply so far as the security is plant or machinery which is the subject of a sale and finance leaseback.

(8) For the purposes of subsection (7) apply section 221 of CAA 2001 to determine whether plant or machinery is the subject of a sale and finance leaseback.

(9) A finance arrangement code does not apply so far as sections 228B and 228C of CAA 2001 (finance leaseback) apply in relation to the arrangement.

[(9A) A finance arrangement code does not apply if the arrangement is a right-of-use lease—

    (*a*) under which the relevant person is a lessee, and

    (*b*) which, were that person required under generally accepted accounting practice to determine whether the lease falls to be treated in the accounts of that person as a finance lease or loan, would not fall to be so treated.

(9B) In subsection (9A) "right-of-use lease" has the same meaning as in Part 2 of CAA 2001 (see section 70YI(1) of that Act).][2]

(10) Section 809BZO defines a relevant person for the purposes of this section.][1]

Commentary—*Simon's Taxes* **D1.793, D1.794**.

Amendments—[1] Sections 809BZM–809BZP inserted by TIOPA 2010 s 369, Sch 5 paras 1, 5. TIOPA 2010 has effect for corporation tax purposes for accounting periods ending on or after 1 April 2010, for income and capital gains tax purposes for the tax year 2010–11 and subsequent tax years, and for petroleum revenue tax purposes for chargeable periods beginning on or after 1 July 2010.

[2] Sub-ss (9A), (9B) inserted by FA 2019 s 36, Sch 14 para 3 with effect in relation to periods of account beginning on or after 1 January 2019.

[809BZO Exceptions: relevant person

(1) This section defines a relevant person for the purposes of section 809BZN.

(2) If (apart from sections 809BZN and 809BZP) sections 809BZA to 809BZE would apply, each of the following is a relevant person—

    (*a*) the borrower, and

    (*b*) a person connected with the borrower or (if the borrower is a partnership) a member of the partnership.

(3) If (apart from sections 809BZN and 809BZP) sections 809BZF to 809BZI would apply, the transferor is a relevant person.

(4) If (apart from sections 809BZN and 809BZP) sections 809BZJ to 809BZL would apply, a relevant member as there defined is a relevant person.

(5) For the purposes of subsection (2)(*b*) the persons connected with the borrower include any persons who under section 993 (meaning of "connected") are connected with the borrower.]¹

Commentary—*Simon's Taxes* **D1.793**.
Amendments—¹   Sections 809BZM–809BZP inserted by TIOPA 2010 s 369, Sch 5 paras 1, 5. TIOPA 2010 has effect for corporation tax purposes for accounting periods ending on or after 1 April 2010, for income and capital gains tax purposes for the tax year 2010–11 and subsequent tax years, and for petroleum revenue tax purposes for chargeable periods beginning on or after 1 July 2010.

[809BZP Power to make further exceptions

(1) The Treasury may make regulations prescribing other circumstances in which a finance arrangement code is not to apply.
(2) The regulations may amend sections 809BZN and 809BZO.
(3) The power to make regulations includes—
  (*a*) power to make provision that has effect in relation to times before the making of the regulations (but not times before 6 June 2006),
  (*b*) power to make different provision for different cases or different purposes, and
  (*c*) power to make incidental, supplemental, consequential and transitional provision and savings.]¹

Commentary—*Simon's Taxes* **D1.793**, **D1.794**.
Amendments—¹   Sections 809BZM–809BZP inserted by TIOPA 2010 s 369, Sch 5 paras 1, 5. TIOPA 2010 has effect for corporation tax purposes for accounting periods ending on or after 1 April 2010, for income and capital gains tax purposes for the tax year 2010–11 and subsequent tax years, and for petroleum revenue tax purposes for chargeable periods beginning on or after 1 July 2010.

[Supplementary

809BZQ Accounts

(1) This section applies for the purposes of this Chapter.
(2) A reference to the accounts of a person includes (if the person is a company) a reference to the consolidated group accounts of a group of companies of which it is a member.
(3) In determining whether accounts record an amount as a financial liability in respect of an advance, assume that the period in which the advance is received ended immediately after the receipt of the advance.
(4) If a person does not draw up accounts in accordance with generally accepted accounting practice, assume that the person drew up the accounts in accordance with that practice.]¹

Commentary—*Simon's Taxes* **D1.793**.
Amendments—¹   Sections 809BZQ–809BZS inserted by TIOPA 2010 s 369, Sch 5 paras 1, 6. TIOPA 2010 has effect for corporation tax purposes for accounting periods ending on or after 1 April 2010, for income and capital gains tax purposes for the tax year 2010–11 and subsequent tax years, and for petroleum revenue tax purposes for chargeable periods beginning on or after 1 July 2010.

[809BZR Arrangements

A reference in this Chapter to an arrangement includes a reference to an agreement or understanding (whether or not legally enforceable).]¹

Commentary—*Simon's Taxes* **D1.793**, **D1.794**.
Amendments—¹   Sections 809BZQ–809BZS inserted by TIOPA 2010 s 369, Sch 5 paras 1, 6. TIOPA 2010 has effect for corporation tax purposes for accounting periods ending on or after 1 April 2010, for income and capital gains tax purposes for the tax year 2010–11 and subsequent tax years, and for petroleum revenue tax purposes for chargeable periods beginning on or after 1 July 2010.

[809BZS Assets

(1) This section applies for the purposes of this Chapter.
(2) A reference to a person receiving an asset includes—
  (*a*) a reference to the person obtaining (directly or indirectly) the value of an asset or otherwise deriving (directly or indirectly) a benefit from it, and
  (*b*) a reference to the discharge (in whole or part) of a liability of the person.
(3) A reference to a disposal of an asset includes a reference to anything constituting a disposal of it for the purposes of TCGA 1992.
(4) A reference to payments in respect of an asset includes—
  (*a*) a reference to payments in respect of another asset substituted for it under the arrangement, and
  (*b*) a reference to obtaining (directly or indirectly) the value of an asset or otherwise deriving (directly or indirectly) a benefit from it.]¹

Commentary—*Simon's Taxes* **D1.793**, **D1.794** .
Amendments—¹   Sections 809BZQ–809BZS inserted by TIOPA 2010 s 369, Sch 5 paras 1, 6. TIOPA 2010 has effect for corporation tax purposes for accounting periods ending on or after 1 April 2010, for income and capital gains tax purposes for the tax year 2010–11 and subsequent tax years, and for petroleum revenue tax purposes for chargeable periods beginning on or after 1 July 2010.

[CHAPTER 5C

LOAN OR CREDIT TRANSACTIONS][1]

Amendments—[1]   Chapter 5C (ss 809CZA–809CZC) inserted by TIOPA 2010 s 369, Sch 5 paras 1, 7. TIOPA 2010 has effect for corporation tax purposes for accounting periods ending on or after 1 April 2010, for income and capital gains tax purposes for the tax year 2010–11 and subsequent tax years, and for petroleum revenue tax purposes for chargeable periods beginning on or after 1 July 2010.

[809CZA Loan or credit transaction defined

(1) This section defines a loan or credit transaction for the purposes of sections 809CZB and 809CZC.

(2) A transaction is a loan or credit transaction if it is—

   (*a*) effected with reference to the lending of money or the varying of the terms on which money is lent, or

   (*b*) effected with a view to enabling or facilitating an arrangement concerning the lending of money or the varying of the terms on which money is lent.

(3) A transaction is a loan or credit transaction if it is—

   (*a*) effected with reference to the giving of credit or the varying of the terms on which credit is given, or

   (*b*) effected with a view to enabling or facilitating an arrangement concerning the giving of credit or the varying of the terms on which credit is given.

(4) Subsection (2) has effect whether the transaction is effected—

   (*a*) between the lender and borrower,

   (*b*) between either of them and a person connected with the other, or

   (*c*) between a person connected with one and a person connected with the other.

(5) Subsection (3) has effect whether the transaction is effected—

   (*a*) between the creditor and debtor,

   (*b*) between either of them and a person connected with the other, or

   (*c*) between a person connected with one and a person connected with the other.][1]

Commentary—*Simon's Taxes* **E1.824.**
Amendments—[1]   Sections 809CZA–809CZC inserted by TIOPA 2010 s 369, Sch 5 paras 1, 7. TIOPA 2010 has effect for corporation tax purposes for accounting periods ending on or after 1 April 2010, for income and capital gains tax purposes for the tax year 2010–11 and subsequent tax years, and for petroleum revenue tax purposes for chargeable periods beginning on or after 1 July 2010.

[809CZB Certain payments treated as yearly interest

(1) This section applies if a loan or credit transaction provides for a payment which is not interest but is—

   (*a*) an annuity or other annual payment falling within Part 5 of ITTOIA 2005 and chargeable to income tax otherwise than as relevant foreign income, or

   (*b*) an annuity or other annual payment which is from a source in the United Kingdom and chargeable to corporation tax under [Chapter 7 of Part 10 of CTA 2009 (annual payments not otherwise charged) or regulation 15 of the Unauthorised Unit Trusts (Tax) Regulations 2013.][2]

(2) The payment must be treated for the purposes of the Income Tax Acts as if it were a payment of yearly interest (see, in particular, section 874).][1]

Commentary—*Simon's Taxes* **E1.824.**
Amendments—[1]   Sections 809CZA–809CZC inserted by TIOPA 2010 s 369, Sch 5 paras 1, 7. TIOPA 2010 has effect for corporation tax purposes for accounting periods ending on or after 1 April 2010, for income and capital gains tax purposes for the tax year 2010–11 and subsequent tax years, and for petroleum revenue tax purposes for chargeable periods beginning on or after 1 July 2010.
[2]   In sub-s (1)(*b*), words substituted by the Unauthorised Unit Trusts (Tax) Regulations, SI 2013/2819 reg 37(1), (8) with effect from 6 April 2014. Note that an unauthorised unit trust is not a non-exempt unauthorised unit trust, and these amendments do not apply in relation to the trust, if at all times in the period beginning with 24 May 2012 and ending with 5 April 2014 it had at least one unit holder which was, and at least one unit holder which was not, an eligible investor (ie a mixed unauthorised unit trust); this ceases to apply in relation to the trust if subsequently it no longer has any unit holders which are eligible investors (SI 2013/2819 reg 32).

[809CZC Tax charged on income transferred

(1) This section applies if—

   (*a*) under a loan or credit transaction a person transfers income arising from property,

   (*b*) the person is not, as a result of Chapter 5B (finance arrangements), chargeable to income tax on the income transferred, and

   (*c*) the person is within the charge to income tax.

(2) In such a case—

   (*a*) income tax is charged under this section,

   (*b*) the tax is charged on an amount equal to the full amount of the income transferred,

   (*c*) the tax is charged for the tax year in which the transfer takes place, and

   (*d*) the person who transfers the income is liable for the tax.

(3) This section does not prejudice the liability of any other person to tax.

(4) For the purposes of this section a person transfers income if the person surrenders, waives or forgoes it.

(5) Subsection (6) applies for the purposes of this section if—

    (*a*) credit is given for the purchase price of property, and

    (*b*) the rights attaching to the property are such that the buyer's rights to income from the property are suspended or restricted during the life of the debt.

(6) The buyer must be treated as surrendering income of an amount equal to the income the buyer in effect forgoes by obtaining the credit.

(7) For the purposes of this section an amount of income payable subject to deduction of income tax must be taken as the amount before deduction of tax.]¹

Commentary—*Simon's Taxes* **E1.824**.

Modification—TIOPA 2010 Sch 9 para 44 (modification of this section in relation to a transfer before 22 April 2009).

Amendments—¹ Sections 809CZA–809CZC inserted by TIOPA 2010 s 369, Sch 5 paras 1, 7. TIOPA 2010 has effect for corporation tax purposes for accounting periods ending on or after 1 April 2010, for income and capital gains tax purposes for the tax year 2010–11 and subsequent tax years, and for petroleum revenue tax purposes for chargeable periods beginning on or after 1 July 2010.

[CHAPTER 5D

DISPOSALS OF ASSETS THROUGH PARTNERSHIPS]

[809DZA Application of Chapter

(1) This Chapter applies if conditions A and B are met.

(2) Condition A is (subject to subsection (3)) that directly or indirectly in consequence of, or otherwise in connection with, arrangements involving a person within the charge to income tax ("the transferor") and another person ("the transferee")—

    (*a*) there is, or is in substance, a disposal of an asset ("the transferred asset") by the transferor to the transferee,

    (*b*) the disposal is effected (wholly or partly) by or through a partnership ("the relevant partnership"),

    (*c*) at any time—

        (i) the transferor is a member of the relevant partnership or of a partnership associated with the relevant partnership, and

        (ii) the transferee is a member of the relevant partnership or of a partnership associated with the relevant partnership, and

    (*d*) the main purpose, or one of the main purposes, of one or more steps taken in effecting the disposal is the obtaining of a tax advantage for any person.

(3) Condition A is not met if—

    (*a*) the transferor is the spouse or civil partner of the transferee and they are living together, or

    (*b*) the transferor is a brother, sister, ancestor or lineal descendant of the transferee.

(4) In subsection (2)(*a*) the reference to a disposal of an asset includes anything constituting a disposal of an asset for the purposes of TCGA 1992.

(5) For the purposes of subsection (2)(*b*) the disposal might, in particular, be effected by an acquisition or disposal of, or an increase or decrease in, an interest in the relevant partnership (including a share of the profits or assets of the relevant partnership or an interest in such a share).

(6) For the purposes of subsection (2)(*c*) it does not matter if the transferor and the transferee are not members of a partnership as mentioned at the same time.

(7) For the purposes of subsection (2)(*c*) a partnership is "associated" with the relevant partnership if—

    (*a*) it is a member of the relevant partnership, or

    (*b*) it is a member of a partnership which is associated with the relevant partnership (whether by virtue of paragraph (*a*) or this paragraph).

(8) In subsections (2)(*c*) and (6) references to the transferor include a person connected with the transferor and references to the transferee include a person connected with the transferee.

(9) Condition B is that it is reasonable to assume that, had the transferred asset instead been disposed of directly by the transferor to the transferee, the relevant amount (or any part of it)—

    (*a*) would have been chargeable to income tax as income of the transferor, or

    (*b*) would have been brought into account as income in calculating profits of the transferor for income tax purposes.

(10) In this Chapter "the relevant amount" means the amount of the consideration received by the transferor for the disposal.

(11) If the transferor receives—

    (*a*) no consideration for the disposal, or

    (*b*) consideration which is substantially less than the market value of the transferred asset, assume for the purposes of subsection (10) that the transferor receives consideration of an amount equal to the market value of the transferred asset.

(12) In subsection (11) references to the market value of the transferred asset are to that value at the time of the disposal.

(13) In this Chapter—

"arrangements" includes any agreement, understanding, scheme, transaction or series of transactions (whether or not legally enforceable),

"partnership" includes a limited liability partnership whether or not section 863(1) of ITTOIA 2005 applies in relation to it, and

"tax advantage" means a tax advantage, as defined in section 1139 of CTA 2010, in relation to income tax or the charge to corporation tax on income.][1]

Commentary—*Simon's Taxes* **B7.142** .

Amendments—[1]   Chapter 5D (ss 809DZA, 809DZB) inserted by FA 2014 s 74, Sch 17 paras 22, 25 with effect for cases where the arrangements mentioned in ITA 2007 s 809DZA(2) are made on or after 6 April 2014.

[809DZB Relevant amount to be treated as income

(1) The relevant amount is to be treated as income of the transferor chargeable to income tax in the same way and to the same extent as that in which it—

(*a*) would have been chargeable to income tax as income of the transferor, or

(*b*) would have been brought into account as income in calculating profits of the transferor for income tax purposes,

as mentioned in section 809DZA(9).

(2) Section 809AZB(3) to (6) applies for the purpose of determining when income under subsection (1) is treated as arising (reading references to the transfer of the right as references to the disposal of the transferred asset).

(3) If, apart from this subsection and section 809AAZB(4)—

(*a*) both this Chapter and Chapter 5AA would apply in relation to the disposal, and

(*b*) Chapter 5AA would give the same amount, or a greater amount, of income of the transferor chargeable to income tax,

this Chapter is not to apply in relation to the disposal.][1]

Commentary—*Simon's Taxes* **B7.142** .

Amendments—[1]   Chapter 5D (ss 809DZA, 809DZB) inserted by FA 2014 s 74, Sch 17 paras 22, 25 with effect for cases where the arrangements mentioned in ITA 2007 s 809DZA(2) are made on or after 6 April 2014.

[CHAPTER 5E

DISGUISED INVESTMENT MANAGEMENT FEES]

[809EZA Disguised investment management fees: charge to income tax

(1) Where one or more disguised fees arise to an individual in a tax year from one or more investment schemes (whether or not by virtue of the same arrangements), the individual is liable for income tax for the tax year in respect of the disguised fee or fees as if—

(*a*) the individual were carrying on a trade for the tax year,

(*b*) the disguised fee or fees were the profits of the trade of the tax year, and

(*c*) the individual were the person receiving or entitled to those profits.

(2) For the purposes of subsection (1) the trade is treated as carried on—

(*a*) in the United Kingdom, to the extent that the individual performs the relevant services in the United Kingdom;

(*b*) outside the United Kingdom, to the extent that the individual performs the relevant services outside the United Kingdom;

and for this purpose "the relevant services" means the investment management services by virtue of which the disguised fee or fees arise to the individual in the tax year.

[(2A) Subsection (2B) applies instead of subsections (1) and (2) where—

(*a*) one or more disguised fees arise to an individual in a tax year ("the relevant tax year") from one or more investment schemes (whether or not by virtue of the same arrangements),

(*b*) the disguised fees consist of carried interest which is income-based carried interest,

(*c*) the individual is UK resident in the relevant tax year,

(*d*) before the relevant tax year, the individual was not UK resident for a period of at least five consecutive tax years ("the period of non-residence"), and

(*e*) either—

(i) the relevant tax year is the first tax year immediately after the end of the period of non-residence, or

(ii) the relevant tax year is the second, third, or fourth tax year after the end of that period and the individual has been UK resident in all the intervening tax years.

(2B) To the extent that the income-based carried interest arises by virtue of pre-arrival services, the individual is liable for income tax for the relevant tax year in respect of it as if—

(*a*) in relation to pre-arrival services performed in the United Kingdom—

  (i) the individual were carrying on a trade for the relevant year consisting of the performance of those services,

  (ii) the income-based carried interest, so far as arising by virtue of those services, were profits of that trade, and

  (iii) the individual were the person receiving or entitled to those profits, and

(*b*) in relation to pre-arrival services performed outside the United Kingdom—

  (i) the individual were carrying on a trade for the relevant tax year consisting of the performance of those services,

  (ii) the income-based carried interest, so far as arising by virtue of those services, were profits of that trade, and

  (iii) the individual were the person receiving or entitled to those profits.]

(2C) In subsection (2B) "pre-arrival services" means investment management services performed before the end of the period of non-residence.][4]

(3) For the purposes of this Chapter a "disguised fee" arises to an individual in a tax year from an investment scheme if—

(*a*) the individual [at any time performs or is to perform][3] investment management services directly or indirectly in respect of the scheme under any arrangements,

(*b*) ...[3]

(*c*) under the arrangements, a management fee arises to the individual . . .[2] from [an investment scheme][3] in the tax year (see section 809EZB), and

(*d*) some or all of the management fee is untaxed;

and the amount of the disguised fee is so much of the management fee as is untaxed.

(4) For the purposes of subsection (3) the management fee is "untaxed" if and to the extent that the fee would not (apart from this section)—

(*a*) be charged to tax under ITEPA 2003 as employment income of the individual for any tax year, or

(*b*) be brought into account in calculating the profits of a trade of the individual for the purposes of income tax for any tax year.

(5) In subsection (4) "trade" includes profession or vocation.

(6) In this Chapter "investment scheme" means—

(*a*) a collective investment scheme, or

(*b*) an investment trust.][1]

[(7) The reference in subsection (6)(*a*) to a collective investment scheme includes—

(*a*) arrangements which permit an external investor to participate in investments acquired by the collective investment scheme without participating in the scheme itself, and

(*b*) arrangements under which sums arise to an individual performing investment management services in respect of the collective investment scheme without those sums arising from the scheme itself.][3]

Commentary—*Simon's Taxes* **B5.646**.

Amendments—[1]   Chapter 5E (ss 809EZA–809EZH) inserted by FA 2015 s 21(1) with effect in relation to sums arising on or after 6 April 2015 (whenever the arrangements under which the sums arise were made).

[2]   In sub-s (3)(*c*) words "directly or indirectly" repealed by F(No 2)A 2015 s 45(2) with effect in relation to sums other than carried interest arising on or after 22 October 2015, (whenever the arrangements under which the sums arise were made), and carried interest arising on or after 22 October 2015 under any arrangements, unless the carried interest arises in connection with the disposal of an asset or assets of a partnership or partnerships before that date.

[3]   In sub-s (3)(*a*), (*c*) words substituted, sub-s (3)(*b*) repealed, and sub-s (7) inserted, by FA 2016 s 36(1)–(3) with effect in relation to sums arising on or after 6 April 2016 (whenever the arrangements under which the sums arise were made).

[4]   Sub-ss (2A)–(2C) inserted by FA 2016 s 38 with effect in relation to sums of carried interest arising on or after 6 April 2016 (whenever the arrangements under which the sums arise were made).

[809EZB Meaning of "management fee" in section 809EZA

(1) Subject as follows, for the purposes of section 809EZA "management fee" means any sum (including a sum in the form of a loan or advance or an allocation of profits) except so far as the sum constitutes—

(*a*) a repayment (in whole or part) of an investment made directly or indirectly by the individual in the scheme,

(*b*) an arm's length return on an investment made directly or indirectly by the individual in the scheme, or

[*c*] carried interest which is not income-based carried interest (see sections 809EZC and 809EZD for carried interest, and Chapter 5F for income-based carried interest).][3]

(2) For the purposes of subsection (1)(*b*) a return on an investment is "an arm's length return" if—

(*a*) the return is on an investment which is of the same kind as investments in the scheme made by external investors,

(*b*) the return on the investment is reasonably comparable to the return to external investors on those investments, and

(c) the terms governing the return on the investment are reasonably comparable to the terms governing the return to external investors on those investments.

[(2A) For the purposes of subsection (2)(b), the return on the investment is reasonably comparable to the return to external investors on the investments referred to in subsection (2)(a) if (and only if)—

    (a) the rate of return on the investment is reasonably comparable to the rate of return to external investors on those investments, and

    (b) any other factors relevant to determining the size of the return on the investment are reasonably comparable to the factors determining the size of the return to external investors on those investments.][2]

(3) In this Chapter "sum" includes any money or money's worth (and other expressions are to be construed accordingly).

(4) Where—

    (a) a sum in the form of money's worth arises to the individual from the scheme in the ordinary course of the scheme's business, and

    (b) the individual gives the scheme money in exchange for the sum,

the sum constitutes a "management fee" only to the extent that its market value at the time it arises exceeds the amount of the money given by the individual.][1]

Commentary—*Simon's Taxes* **B5.646**.

Amendments—[1]   Chapter 5E (ss 809EZA–809EZH) inserted by FA 2015 s 21(1) with effect in relation to sums arising on or after 6 April 2015 (whenever the arrangements under which the sums arise were made).

[2]   Sub-s (2A) inserted by F(No 2)A 2015 s 44(1) with effect in relation to sums arising on or after 8 July 2015 (whenever the arrangements under which the sums arise were made).

[3]   Sub-s (1)(c) substituted by FA 2016 s 37(1) with effect in relation to sums of carried interest arising on or after 6 April 2016 (whenever the arrangements under which the sums arise were made).

[809EZC Meaning of "carried interest" in section 809EZB

(1) For the purposes of section 809EZB "carried interest" means a sum which arises to the individual under the arrangements by way of profit-related return.

This is subject to subsections (3) to (8) (sums where no significant risk of not arising); and see also section 809EZD (sums treated as carried interest).

(2) A sum which arises to the individual under the arrangements does so by way of "profit-related return" if under the arrangements—

    (a) the sum is to, or may, arise only if—

        (i) there are profits for a period on the investments, or on particular investments, made for the purposes of the scheme, or

        (ii) there are profits arising from a disposal of the investments, or of particular investments, made for those purposes,

    (b) the amount of the sum which is to, or may, arise is variable, to a substantial extent, by reference to those profits, and

    (c) returns to external investors are also determined by reference to those profits;

but where any part of the sum does not meet these conditions, that part is not to be regarded as arising by way of "profit-related return".

(3) Where—

    (a) one or more sums ("actual sums") arise to the individual under the arrangements by way of profit-related return in a tax year, and

    (b) there was no significant risk that a sum of at least a certain amount ("the minimum amount") would not arise to the individual,

so much of the actual sum, or of the aggregate of the actual sums, as is equal to the minimum amount is not "carried interest".

(See subsections (7) and (8) as to how the minimum amount is to be apportioned between the actual sums where more than one actual sum arises in the tax year.)

(4) For the purposes of subsection (3)(b) assess the risk both—

    (a) in relation to each actual sum (and the investments to which it relates) individually, taking into account also any other sums that might have arisen to the individual under the arrangements instead of that sum, and

    (b) in relation to the actual sum or sums and any other sums that might have arisen to the individual under the arrangements by way of profit-related return in the tax year (and the investments to which all those sums relate) taken as a whole;

(so that, in a particular case, some of the minimum amount may arise by assessing the risk in accordance with paragraph (a) and some by assessing it in accordance with paragraph (b)).

(5) For the purposes of subsection (3)(b) assess the risk as at the latest of—

    (a) the time when the individual becomes party to the arrangements,

    (b) the time when the individual begins to perform investment management services directly or indirectly in respect of the scheme under the arrangements, and

(c) the time when a material change is made to the arrangements so far as relating to the sums which are to, or may, arise to the individual.

(6) For the purposes of subsection (3)(*b*) ignore any risk that a sum is prevented from arising to the individual (by reason of insolvency or otherwise).

(7) Where more than one actual sum arises in the tax year, the minimum amount is to be apportioned between the actual sums as follows for the purposes of subsection (3)—

(a) so much of the minimum amount as is attributable to a particular actual sum is to be apportioned to that actual sum, and

(b) so much of the minimum amount as is not attributable to any particular actual sum is to be apportioned between the actual sums on a just and reasonable basis.

(8) For the purpose of subsection (7) any part of the minimum amount is attributable to a particular actual sum to the extent that there was no significant risk that that part would not arise to the individual in relation to that actual sum, assessing the risk in accordance with subsection (4)(*a*).][1]

Commentary—*Simon's Taxes* **B5.646.**

Amendments—[1]   Chapter 5E (ss 809EZA–809EZH) inserted by FA 2015 s 21(1) with effect in relation to sums arising on or after 6 April 2015 (whenever the arrangements under which the sums arise were made).

[809EZD Sums treated as "carried interest" for purposes of section 809EZB

(1) A sum falling within subsection (2) or (3)—

(a) is to be assumed to meet the requirements of section 809EZC, and

(b) accordingly, is to be treated as constituting "carried interest" for the purposes of section 809EZB.

(2) A sum falls within this subsection if, under the arrangements, it is to, or may, arise to the individual out of profits on the investments made for the purposes of the scheme, but only after—

(a) all, or substantially all, of the investments in the scheme made by the participants have been repaid to the participants, and

(b) each external investor has received a preferred return on all, or substantially all, of the investor's investments in the scheme.

(3) A sum falls within this subsection if, under the arrangements, it is to, or may, arise to the individual out of profits on a particular investment made for the purposes of the scheme, but only after—

(a) all, or substantially all, of the relevant investments made by participants have been repaid to those participants, and

(b) each of those participants who is an external investor has received a preferred return on all, or substantially all, of the investor's relevant investments;

and for this purpose "relevant investments" means those investments in the scheme to which the particular investment made for the purposes of the scheme is attributable.

(4) In this section "preferred return" means a return of not less than the amount that would be payable on the investment by way of interest if—

(a) compound interest were payable on the investment for the whole of the period during which it was invested in the scheme, and

(b) the interest were calculated at a rate of 6% per annum, with annual rests.][1]

Commentary—*Simon's Taxes* **B5.646.**

Amendments—[1]   Chapter 5E (ss 809EZA–809EZH) inserted by FA 2015 s 21(1) with effect in relation to sums arising on or after 6 April 2015 (whenever the arrangements under which the sums arise were made).

[809EZDA Sums arising to connected persons other than companies

(1) This section applies in relation to an individual ("A") if—

(a) a sum arises to a person ("B") who is connected with A,

(b) B is not a company,

(c) income tax is not charged on B in respect of the sum by virtue of this Chapter,

(d) capital gains tax is not charged on B in respect of the sum by virtue of Chapter 5 of Part 3 of TCGA 1992, and

(e) the sum does not arise to A apart from this section.

(2) The sum referred to in subsection (1)(*a*) arises to A for the purposes of this Chapter.

(3) Where a sum arises to A by virtue of this section, it arises to A at the time the sum referred to in subsection (1)(*a*) arises to B.

(4) Section 993 (meaning of "connected") applies for the purposes of this section, but as if—

(a) subsection (4) of that section were omitted, and

(b) partners in a partnership in which A is also a partner were not "associates" of A for the purposes of sections 450 and 451 of CTA 2010 ("control").][1]

Commentary—*Simon's Taxes* **B5.646.**

Amendments—[1]   Sections 809EZDA, 809EZDB inserted by F(No 2)A 2015 s 45(1) with effect in relation to sums other than carried interest arising on or after 22 October 2015, (whenever the arrangements under which the sums arise were made), and carried interest arising on or after 22 October 2015 under any arrangements, unless the carried interest arises in connection with the disposal of an asset or assets of a partnership or partnerships before that date.

[809EZDB Sums arising to connected company or unconnected person

(1) This section applies in relation to an individual ("A") if—

   (*a*) a sum arises to—

      (i) a company connected with A, or

      (ii) a person not connected with A,

   (*b*) any of the enjoyment conditions is met, and

   (*c*) the sum does not arise to A apart from this section.

(2) The enjoyment conditions are—

   (*a*) the sum, or part of the sum, is in fact so dealt with by any person as to be calculated at some time to enure for the benefit of A or a person connected with A;

   (*b*) the arising of the sum operates to increase the value to A or a person connected with A of any assets which—

      (i) A or the connected person holds, or

      (ii) are held for the benefit of A or the connected person;

   (*c*) A or a person connected with A receives or is entitled to receive at any time any benefit provided or to be provided out of the sum or part of the sum;

   (*d*) A or a person connected with A may become entitled to the beneficial enjoyment of the sum or part of the sum if one or more powers are exercised or successively exercised (and for these purposes it does not matter who may exercise the powers or whether they are exercisable with or without the consent of another person);

   (*e*) A or a person connected with A is able in any manner to control directly or indirectly the application of the sum or part of the sum.

In this subsection, in a case where the sum referred to in subsection (1)(*a*) arises to a company connected with A, references to a person connected with A do not include that company.

(3) There arises to A for the purposes of this Chapter—

   (*a*) the sum referred to in subsection (1)(*a*), or

   (*b*) if the enjoyment condition in subsection (2)(*a*), (*c*), (*d*) or (*e*) is met in relation to part of the sum, that part of that sum, or

   (*c*) if the enjoyment condition in subsection (2)(*b*) is met, such part of that sum as is equal to the amount by which the value of the assets referred to in that condition is increased.

(4) Where a sum (or part of a sum) arises to A by virtue of this section, it arises to A at the time it arises to the person referred to in subsection (1)(*a*)(i) or (ii) (whether the enjoyment condition was met at that time or at a later date).

(5) In determining whether any of the enjoyment conditions is met in relation to a sum or part of a sum—

   (*a*) regard must be had to the substantial result and effect of all the relevant circumstances, and

   (*b*) all benefits which may at any time accrue to a person as a result of the sum arising as specified in subsection (1)(*a*) must be taken into account, irrespective of—

      (i) the nature or form of the benefits, or

      (ii) whether the person has legal or equitable rights in respect of the benefits.

(6) The enjoyment condition in subsection (2)(*b*), (*c*) or (*d*) is to be treated as not met if it would be met only by reason of A holding shares or an interest in shares in a company.

(7) The enjoyment condition in subsection (2)(*a*) or (*e*) is to be treated as not met if the sum referred to in subsection (1)(*a*) arises to a company connected with A and—

   (*a*) the company is liable to pay corporation tax in respect of its profits and the sum is included in the computation of those profits, or

   (*b*) paragraph (*a*) does not apply but—

      (i) the company is a CFC and the exemption in Chapter 14 of Part 9A of TIOPA 2010 applies for the accounting period in which the sum arises, or

      (ii) the company is not a CFC but, if it were, that exemption would apply for that period.

In this subsection "CFC" has the same meaning as in Part 9A of TIOPA 2010.

(8) But subsections (6) and (7) do not apply if the sum referred to in subsection (1)(*a*) arises to the company referred to in subsection (1)(*a*)(i) or the person referred to in subsection (1)(*a*)(ii) as part of arrangements where—

   (*a*) it is reasonable to assume that in the absence of the arrangements the sum or part of the sum would have arisen to A or an individual connected with A, and

   (*b*) it is reasonable to assume that the arrangements have as their main purpose, or one of their main purposes, the avoidance of a liability to pay income tax, capital gains tax, inheritance tax or corporation tax.

(9) The condition in subsection (8)(*b*) is to be regarded as met in a case where the sum is applied directly or indirectly as an investment in a collective investment scheme.

(10) Section 993 (meaning of "connected") applies for the purposes of this section, but as if—

   (*a*) subsection (4) of that section were omitted, and

   (*b*) partners in a partnership in which A is also a partner were not "associates" of A for the purposes of sections 450 and 451 of CTA 2010 ("control").][1]

Commentary—*Simon's Taxes* **B5.646.**
Amendments—[1]   Sections 809EZDA, 809EZDB inserted by F(No 2)A 2015 s 45(1) with effect in relation to sums other than carried interest arising on or after 22 October 2015, (whenever the arrangements under which the sums arise were made), and carried interest arising on or after 22 October 2015 under any arrangements, unless the carried interest arises in connection with the disposal of an asset or assets of a partnership or partnerships before that date.

[809EZE Interpretation of Chapter

(1) In this Chapter—
"arrangements" includes any agreement, understanding, scheme, transaction or series of transactions (whether or not legally enforceable);
"collective investment scheme" has the meaning given by section 235 of FISMA 2000;
"external investor", in relation to an investment scheme and any arrangements, means a participant in the scheme other than—
  (*a*) an individual who [at any time performs or is to perform][2] investment management services directly or indirectly in respect of the scheme, or
  (*b*) a person through whom sums are to, or may, arise directly or indirectly to such an individual from the scheme under the arrangements;
"investment management services", in relation to an investment scheme, includes—
  (*a*) seeking funds for the purposes of the scheme from participants or potential participants,
  (*b*) researching potential investments to be made for the purposes of the scheme,
  (*c*) acquiring, managing or disposing of property for the purposes of the scheme, and
  (*d*) acting for the purposes of the scheme with a view to assisting a body in which the scheme has made an investment to raise funds;
"investment trust" means a company in relation to which conditions A to C in section 1158 of CTA 2010 are met (or treated as met); and for this purpose "company" has the meaning given by section 1121 of CTA 2010;
"market value" has the same meaning as in TCGA 1992 (see sections 272 and 273 of that Act);
"participant"—
  (*a*) in relation to a collective investment scheme, is construed in accordance with section 235 of FISMA 2000;
  (*b*) in relation to an investment trust, means a member of the investment trust;
"profits", in relation to an investment made for the purposes of an investment scheme, means profits (including unrealised profits) arising from the acquisition, holding, management or disposal of the investment (taking into account items of a revenue nature and items of a capital nature).
(2) In this Chapter a reference to an investment made by a person in an investment scheme is a reference to a contribution by the person (whether by way of capital, loan or otherwise) towards the property subject to the scheme (but does not include a sum committed but not yet invested).
(3) For the purposes of subsection (2) a person who holds a share in an investment scheme which is a company limited by shares and who acquired the share from a person other than the scheme is to be taken to have made a contribution towards the property subject to the scheme equal to—
  (*a*) the consideration given by the person for the acquisition of the share, or
  (*b*) if less, the market value of the share at the time of the acquisition.
(4) In this Chapter, in relation to an investment scheme which is a company limited by shares—
  (*a*) references to a repayment of, or a return on, an investment in the scheme include a repayment of, or a return on, an investment represented by a share in the scheme resulting from—
    (i) the purchase of the share by the scheme,
    (ii) the redemption of the share by the scheme,
    (iii) the distribution of assets in respect of the share on the winding up of the scheme, or
    (iv) any similar process;
  (*b*) references to a return on an investment in the scheme include a dividend or similar distribution in respect of a share in the scheme representing the investment.][1]

Amendments—[1]   Chapter 5E (ss 809EZA–809EZH) inserted by FA 2015 s 21(1) with effect in relation to sums arising on or after 6 April 2015 (whenever the arrangements under which the sums arise were made).
[2]   In sub-s (1) in the definition of "external investor" words substituted by FA 2016 s 36(4) with effect in relation to sums arising on or after 6 April 2016 (whenever the arrangements under which the sums arise were made).

[809EZF Disguised investment management fees: anti-avoidance

In determining whether section 809EZA applies in relation to an individual, no regard is to be had to any arrangements the main purpose, or one of the main purposes, of which is to secure that that section does not apply in relation to—
  (*a*) the individual, or
  (*b*) the individual and one or more other individuals.][1]

Commentary—*Simon's Taxes* **B5.646.**
Amendments—[1]   Chapter 5E (ss 809EZA–809EZH) inserted by FA 2015 s 21(1) with effect in relation to sums arising on or after 6 April 2015 (whenever the arrangements under which the sums arise were made).

[809EZG Disguised investment management fees: avoidance of double taxation
(1) This section applies where—
  (a) income tax is charged on an individual by virtue of section 809EZA in respect of a disguised fee, and
  (b) at any time, a tax (whether income tax or another tax) is charged on the individual [or another person][2] otherwise than by virtue of section 809EZA in relation to the disguised fee.
(2) This section also applies where—
  (a) income tax is charged on an individual by virtue of section 809EZA in respect of a disguised fee which arises to the individual under the arrangements by way of a loan or advance,
  (b) at any time, a tax (whether income tax or another tax) is charged on the individual in relation to another sum which arises to the individual under the arrangements, and
  (c) some or all of the loan or advance has to be repaid as a result of the other sum having arisen to the individual.
(3) In order to avoid a double charge to tax, the individual may make a claim for one or more consequential adjustments to be made in respect of the tax charged as mentioned in subsection (1)(b) or (2)(b).
(4) On a claim under this section an officer of Revenue and Customs must make such of the consequential adjustments claimed (if any) as are just and reasonable.
(5) The value of any consequential adjustments must not exceed the lesser of the income tax charged on the individual as mentioned in subsection (1)(a) or (2)(a) and—
  (a) where subsection (1) applies, the tax charged as mentioned in subsection (1)(b);
  (b) where subsection (2) applies, the tax charged as mentioned in subsection (2)(b) in relation to so much of the other sum as does not exceed the amount of the loan or advance that has to be repaid as mentioned in subsection (2)(c).
(6) Consequential adjustments may be made—
  (a) in respect of any period,
  (b) by way of an assessment, the modification of an assessment, the amendment of a claim, or otherwise, and
  (c) despite any time limit imposed by or under any enactment.][1]

Commentary—*Simon's Taxes* **B5.646**.
Amendments—[1]   Chapter 5E (ss 809EZA–809EZH) inserted by FA 2015 s 21(1) with effect in relation to sums arising on or after 6 April 2015 (whenever the arrangements under which the sums arise were made).
[2]   In sub-s (1)(b) words inserted by F(No 2)A 2015 s 44(2) with effect in relation to sums arising on or after 8 July 2015 (whenever the arrangements under which the sums arise were made).

[809EZH Powers to amend Chapter
(1) The Treasury may by regulations amend this Chapter—
  (a) so as to change the definition of "investment scheme" for the purposes of this Chapter;
  (b) so as to change the definition of "participant" for those purposes;
  (c) so as to change what is "carried interest" for the purposes of section 809EZB.
(2) Regulations under this section may—
  (a) make different provision for different purposes, and
  (b) contain incidental, supplemental, consequential and transitional provision and savings.
(3) A statutory instrument containing regulations under this section to which subsection (4) applies may not be made unless a draft of the instrument has been laid before and approved by a resolution of the House of Commons.
(4) This subsection applies if the regulations contain any provision which has or may have the effect of increasing any person's liability to tax.
(5) Any other statutory instrument containing regulations under this section is subject to annulment in pursuance of a resolution of the House of Commons.][1]

Commentary—*Simon's Taxes* **B5.646**.
Amendments—[1]   Chapter 5E (ss 809EZA–809EZH) inserted by FA 2015 s 21(1) with effect in relation to sums arising on or after 6 April 2015 (whenever the arrangements under which the sums arise were made).

[CHAPTER 5F

INCOME-BASED CARRIED INTEREST
Income-based carried interest

809FZA Overview
(1) This Chapter determines when carried interest arising to an individual from an investment scheme is "income-based carried interest" for the purposes of Chapter 5E (and, in particular, section 809EZB(1)(c)).
(2) Section 809FZB contains the general rule, under which the extent to which carried interest is income-based carried interest depends on the average holding period of the investment scheme.
(3) Sections 809FZC to 809FZP contain further provision relating to average holding periods.
(4) Sections 809FZQ and 809FZR contain a particular rule for direct lending funds.

(5) Sections 809FZS and 809FZT contain an exception to the general rule for carried interest which is conditionally exempt from income tax.

(6) Sections 809FZU to 809FZZ contain supplementary and interpretative provision.

(7) Nothing in this Chapter affects the liability to any tax of—

   (*a*) the investment scheme, or

   (*b*) external investors in the investment scheme.][1]

Amendments—[1]   Chapter 5F (ss 809FZA–809FZZ) inserted by FA 2016 s 37(2) with effect in relation to sums of carried interest arising on or after 6 April 2016 (whenever the arrangements under which the sums arise were made).

[809FZB Income based carried interest: general rule

(1) "Income-based carried interest" is the relevant proportion of a sum of carried interest arising to an individual from an investment scheme.

(2) The relevant proportion is determined by reference to the investment scheme's average holding period as follows.

Average holding period	Relevant proportion
Less than 36 months	100%
At least 36 months but less than 37 months	80%
At least 37 months but less than 38 months	60%
At least 38 months but less than 39 months	40%
At least 39 months but less than 40 months	20%
40 months or more	0%

(3) This section is subject to the following provisions of this Chapter.][1]

Commentary—*Simon's Taxes* **B5.646**.

Amendments—[1]   Chapter 5F (ss 809FZA–809FZZ) inserted by FA 2016 s 37(2) with effect in relation to sums of carried interest arising on or after 6 April 2016 (whenever the arrangements under which the sums arise were made).

Average holding period

[809FZC Average holding period

(1) The average holding period of an investment scheme, in relation to a sum of carried interest, is the average length of time for which relevant investments have been held for the purposes of the scheme.

(2) In this section, "relevant investments" means investments—

   (*a*) which are made for the purposes of the scheme, and

   (*b*) by reference to which the carried interest is calculated.

(3) The average holding period is calculated by reference to the time the carried interest arises.

(4) It is calculated as follows.

Step 1

For each relevant investment, multiply the value invested at the time the investment was made by the length of time for which the investment has been held.

Step 2

Add together the amounts produced under *step 1* in respect of all relevant investments.

Step 3

Divide the amount produced under *step 2* by the total value invested in all relevant investments.

(5) Disregard intermediate holdings or intermediate holding structures (including intermediate investment schemes) by or through which investments are made or held—

   (*a*) when identifying, for the purpose of determining the average holding period of an investment scheme, what relevant investments are held for the purposes of an investment scheme, and

   (*b*) for any other purpose relating to the determination of the average holding period.

This is subject to the following provisions of this Chapter.

(6) In this section, references to the length of time for which a relevant investment has been held are—

   (*a*) in the case of an investment which has been disposed of before the carried interest arises, references to the time for which it was held before being disposed of, and

   (*b*) in any other case, references to the time for which it has been held up to the time the carried interest arises.

(7) For the purposes of this Chapter, carried interest which is deferred carried interest in relation to a person within the meaning of section 103KG of TCGA 1992 is to be treated as arising to that person at the time it would have arisen had it not been deferred as specified in section 103KG(3)(*a*) or (*b*) of that Act.

(8) Sections 809FZD to 809FZP apply for the purposes of determining the average holding period of an investment scheme.][1]

Commentary—*Simon's Taxes* **B5.646**.

Amendments—[1]   Chapter 5F (ss 809FZA–809FZZ) inserted by FA 2016 s 37(2) with effect in relation to sums of carried interest arising on or after 6 April 2016 (whenever the arrangements under which the sums arise were made).

Average holding period: disposals

[809FZD Disposals

(1) An investment or part of an investment is disposed of where—

(a) there is a disposal of the investment or the part of the investment for the purposes of the investment scheme,

(b) there is a disposal for the purposes of the investment scheme of an intermediate holding or intermediate holding structure (including an intermediate investment scheme) by or through which the investment is held, or

(c) in any other case, there is a deemed disposal under subsection (2).

(2) There is a deemed disposal of an investment or part of an investment under this subsection where—

(a) under any arrangements—

(i) the scheme in substance closes its position on the investment or the part of the investment, or

(ii) the scheme ceases to be exposed to risks and rewards in the respect of the investment or the part of the investment, and

(b) it is reasonable to suppose that the arrangements were designed to secure that result.

(3) In the case of a disposal of part of a holding of securities in a company which are of the same class, suppose for the purposes of determining which investments have been disposed of that the disposal affects the securities in the order in which they were acquired (that is, on a first in first out basis).

(4) The references in subsection (1)(a) and (b) to a disposal are to something which is a disposal for the purposes of TCGA 1992; but for the purposes of subsection (1)(a) disregard section 116 of TCGA 1992 (which disapplies sections 127 to 130 of that Act in relation to qualifying corporate bonds).][1]

Amendments—[1]   Chapter 5F (ss 809FZA–809FZZ) inserted by FA 2016 s 37(2) with effect in relation to sums of carried interest arising on or after 6 April 2016 (whenever the arrangements under which the sums arise were made).

[809FZE Part disposals

(1) Where there is a disposal of part of an investment, the part disposed of and the part not disposed of are to be treated as two separate investments which were made at the same time.

(2) The value of each of those two separate investments is the appropriate proportion of the value first invested in the whole investment.

(3) The appropriate proportion is the proportion of the value of the part in question to the value of the whole investment at the time of the disposal.

(4) The disposal of part of an asset includes the disposal of an interest in or right over the asset (and "part disposed of" is to be construed accordingly).][1]

Amendments—[1]   Chapter 5F (ss 809FZA–809FZZ) inserted by FA 2016 s 37(2) with effect in relation to sums of carried interest arising on or after 6 April 2016 (whenever the arrangements under which the sums arise were made).

[809FZF Unwanted short-term investments

(1) The making and disposal of an investment for the purposes of an investment scheme are to be disregarded if—

(a) the investment is an unwanted short-term investment, and

(b) the unwanted short-term investment is excludable.

(2) An investment is an unwanted short-term investment where—

(a) the investment is made as part of a transaction under which one or more other investments are made for the purposes of the scheme,

(b) the value of the investment does not exceed that of the other investments taken together,

(c) it is reasonable to suppose that the investment had to be made in order for the other investments to be made,

(d) at the time the investment is made, managers of the scheme have a firm, settled and evidenced intention to dispose of the investment for the purposes of the scheme within the relevant period,

(e) the investment is disposed of for the purposes of the scheme within the relevant period, and

(f) any profit resulting from the disposal has no bearing on whether a sum of carried interest arises or on the amount of any sum of carried interest which does arise.

(3) An unwanted short-term investment is excludable if it constitutes—

(a) an investment in land,

(b) an investment in securities in an unlisted company,

(c) the making of a direct loan where the other investments specified in subsection (2)(b) are shares or other securities in an unlisted company, or

(d) the making of a direct loan which is a qualifying loan within the meaning given by section 809FZR(2).

(4) In subsection (2)(e) "relevant period" means—

(a) for an investment within subsection (3)(a), 12 months;

(b) for an investment within subsection (3)(b) or (c), 6 months;

(c) for an investment within subsection (3)(d), 120 days.

(5) But if at any time it becomes reasonable to suppose that, when the scheme ceases to invest, 25% or more of the capital of the investment scheme will have been invested in unwanted short-term investments which are excludable, subsection (1) does not apply to any investment made subsequently for the purposes of the scheme.]¹

Amendments—¹ Chapter 5F (ss 809FZA–809FZZ) inserted by FA 2016 s 37(2) with effect in relation to sums of carried interest arising on or after 6 April 2016 (whenever the arrangements under which the sums arise were made).

Average holding period: derivatives and hedging

[809FZG Derivatives

(1) A derivative contract entered into for the purposes of an investment scheme is an investment, subject to the following provisions of this section.

(2) The value invested in the derivative contract is—

(a) where the contract is an option, the cost of acquiring the option (whether from the grantor or another person),

(b) where the contract is a future, the price specified in the contract for the underlying subject matter, or

(c) where the contract is a contract for differences, the notional principal of the contract.

(3) But where entering into a derivative contract constitutes a deemed disposal of an investment or part of an investment by virtue of section 809FZD(2)(a)(ii)—

(a) the derivative contract is not an investment, and

(b) the subsequent disposal of the derivative contract without a corresponding disposal of the investment or part investment is to be regarded as the making of a new investment to the extent that the scheme becomes materially exposed to risks and rewards in respect of the investment or part investment.

(4) For the purposes of this Chapter, references to disposal, in the case of a derivative contract, include any of the following events (to the extent that the event is not otherwise a disposal under section 809FZD(1) or (2))—

(a) the expiry of the contract,

(b) the termination of the contract (whether or not in accordance with its terms),

(c) the disposal, substantial variation, loss or cancellation of the investment scheme's rights under the contract, and

(d) in the case of a derivative contract which is an option, the exercise of the option,

but do not include the renewal of the contract with the same counterparty on substantially the same terms.

(5) The substantial variation of an investment scheme's rights under a derivative contract constitutes (in addition to the disposal of the contract as originally entered into (see subsection (4)(c)) a new investment consisting of the contract as varied.]¹

Amendments—¹ Chapter 5F (ss 809FZA–809FZZ) inserted by FA 2016 s 37(2) with effect in relation to sums of carried interest arising on or after 6 April 2016 (whenever the arrangements under which the sums arise were made).

[809FZH Hedging: exchange gains and losses

(1) This section applies where—

(a) an investment scheme has a hedging relationship between a relevant instrument and a relevant investment, and

(b) the hedging relationship relates to exchange gains or losses.

(2) In this section—

"relevant instrument" means a derivative contract or a liability representing a loan relationship, and

"relevant investment" means—

(a) where the relevant instrument is a derivative contract, an investment made for the purposes of the scheme or a liability representing a loan relationship;

(b) where the relevant instrument is a liability representing a loan relationship, an investment made for the purposes of the scheme.

(3) An investment scheme has a hedging relationship between a relevant instrument and a relevant investment if or to the extent that—

(a) the instrument and the investment are designated by the scheme as a hedge, or

(b) in any other case, the instrument is intended to act as a hedge of exposure to—

(i) changes in fair value of the investment or an identified portion of the investment, or

(ii) variability in cash flows,

where the exposure is attributable to exchange gains or losses and could affect profit or loss of the investment scheme.

(4) Entering into the hedging relationship is not a deemed disposal of the relevant investment under section 809FZD(2).

(5) The relevant instrument is not an investment for the purposes of the investment scheme to the extent that the conditions in subsection (3)(*a*) and (*b*) are met.

(6) But the termination of the hedging relationship is the making of an investment constituting the relevant instrument if or to the extent that that instrument continues to subsist.][1]

Amendments—[1]　　Chapter 5F (ss 809FZA–809FZZ) inserted by FA 2016 s 37(2) with effect in relation to sums of carried interest arising on or after 6 April 2016 (whenever the arrangements under which the sums arise were made).

[809FZI Hedging: interest rates

(1) This section applies where an investment scheme has a hedging relationship between—
  (*a*) an interest rate contract, and
  (*b*) a qualifying investment held for the purposes of the fund.

(2) An investment scheme has a hedging relationship between an interest rate contract and a qualifying investment if or to the extent that—
  (*a*) the interest rate contract and the investment are designated by the scheme as a hedge, or
  (*b*) in any other case, the interest rate contract is intended to act as a hedge of exposure to—
    (i) changes in fair value of the investment or an identified portion of the investment, or
    (ii) variability in cash flows,

  where the exposure is attributable to interest rates and could affect profit or loss of the investment scheme.

(3) Entering into the hedging relationship is not a deemed disposal of the relevant investment under section 809FZD(2).

(4) The interest rate contract is not an investment for the purposes of the investment scheme to the extent that the conditions in subsection (2)(*a*) and (*b*) are met.

(5) But the termination of the hedging relationship is the making of an investment constituting the interest rate contract if or to the extent that the interest rate contract continues to subsist.

(6) In this section "qualifying investment" means—
  (*a*) money placed at interest,
  (*b*) securities (excluding shares issued by companies),
  (*c*) alternative finance arrangements, and
  (*d*) a liability representing a loan relationship.][1]

Amendments—[1]　　Chapter 5F (ss 809FZA–809FZZ) inserted by FA 2016 s 37(2) with effect in relation to sums of carried interest arising on or after 6 April 2016 (whenever the arrangements under which the sums arise were made).

Average holding period: aggregation of acquisitions and disposals

[809FZJ Significant interests

(1) Where an investment scheme has a controlling interest in a trading company or the holding company of a trading group—
  (*a*) any investment made for the purposes of the scheme in that company after the time when the controlling interest was acquired is to be regarded as having been made at that time, and
  (*b*) any disposal for the purposes of the scheme of an investment in the company after the time the controlling interest was acquired is to be regarded as not being made until a relevant disposal is made.

(2) In subsection (1)(*b*) "relevant disposal", in relation to a company, means a disposal which (apart from subsection (1)) has the effect that the investment scheme ceases to have a 40% interest in the company.

(3) For the purposes of this section, in determining whether an investment scheme has a controlling interest or a 40% interest in a company, any share capital of the company which is held for the purposes of an associated investment scheme is to be regarded as held for the purposes of the investment scheme.][1]

Amendments—[1]　　Chapter 5F (ss 809FZA–809FZZ) inserted by FA 2016 s 37(2) with effect in relation to sums of carried interest arising on or after 6 April 2016 (whenever the arrangements under which the sums arise were made).

[809FZK Venture capital funds

(1) Where a venture capital fund has a relevant interest in a trading company or the holding company of a trading group—
  (*a*) any venture capital investment made for the purposes of the scheme in the company after the time the relevant interest was acquired (and before a relevant disposal) is to be regarded as having been made at the time the relevant interest was acquired, and
  (*b*) any disposal for the purposes of the scheme of a venture capital investment in the company after that time is to be regarded as not being made until—
    (i) a relevant disposal is made, or
    (ii) the scheme director condition ceases to be met.

(2) For the purposes of subsection (1) a venture capital fund has a relevant interest in a company if

(a) by virtue of its venture capital investments the fund has at least a 5% interest in the company, or

(b) venture capital investments held for the purposes of the scheme in the company have a value of more than £1 million.

(3) For the purposes of subsection (1) "relevant disposal" means a disposal which (apart from subsection (1)) has the effect that the venture capital fund has disposed of more than 80% of the greatest amount invested at any one time in the company for the purposes of the fund.

(4) In this Chapter, "venture capital fund" means an investment scheme in relation to which the condition in subsection (5) is met.

(5) The condition is that when the scheme starts to invest it is reasonable to suppose that over the investing life of the scheme—

(a) at least two-thirds of the total value invested for the purposes of the scheme will be invested in venture capital investments, and

(b) at least two-thirds of the total value invested for the purposes of the scheme will be invested in investments which are held for 40 months or more.

(6) In determining whether subsection (5)(b) is met in relation to an investment scheme, apply the rule in subsection (1) to the scheme.

(7) In this section, "venture capital investment", in relation to an investment scheme, means an investment in a trading company or the holding company of a trading group where—

(a) at the time the investment is made the company is unlisted and is likely to remain so,

(b) at least 75%of the total value of the investment is invested in—

(i) newly issued shares or

(ii) newly issued securities convertible into shares,

(c) the investment is used in a trade carried on by the trading company or the trading group—

(i) to support its growth, or

(ii) for the development of new products or services,

and is not used directly or indirectly to acquire shares in the company which are not newly issued,

(d) if the investment is the first investment made in the company for the purposes of the scheme, the trading company or group has not carried on that trade for more than 7 years, and

(e) the scheme director condition is met.

(8) In this Chapter, the scheme director condition, in relation to an investment scheme and a company, is that—

(a) the scheme (or the scheme and one or more investment schemes acting together) are entitled to appoint a director ("the scheme director") of—

(i) the company, or

(ii) a company which controls the company, and

(b) the scheme director is entitled to exercise rights within subsection (9).

(9) Those rights are rights which—

(a) are rights conferred under contractual arrangements—

(i) to which some or all of the investors in the company are parties, and

(ii) which it would be reasonable to suppose would not otherwise be capable of being exercised by the scheme director,

(b) relate to the conduct of the business and affairs of the company, and

(c) are at least equivalent to the rights which it is reasonable to suppose a prudent investor would have obtained on making an investment in the company at arm's length of the same size and nature as that held in the company for the purposes of the investment scheme.

(10) In determining whether the condition in subsection (2)(a) or (b) is met in relation to a venture capital fund, any share capital of a company which is held for the purposes of an associated investment scheme is to be regarded as held for the purposes of the venture capital fund.][1]

Amendments—[1]   Chapter 5F (ss 809FZA–809FZZ) inserted by FA 2016 s 37(2) with effect in relation to sums of carried interest arising on or after 6 April 2016 (whenever the arrangements under which the sums arise were made).

[809FZL Significant equity stake funds

(1) Where a significant equity stake fund has a significant equity stake investment in a trading company or the holding company of a trading group—

(a) any investment made for the purposes of the fund in that company made after the time the significant equity stake investment was acquired is to be regarded as having been made at that time, and

(b) any disposal for the purposes of the fund of an investment in the company after that time is to be regarded as not being made until—

(i) a relevant disposal is made, or

(ii) the scheme director condition ceases to be met.

(2) In subsection (1)(b) "relevant disposal" means a disposal which (apart from subsection (1)) has the effect that the significant equity stake fund ceases to have a 15% interest in the company.

(3) In this Chapter, "significant equity stake fund" means an investment scheme—
  (*a*) which is not a venture capital fund, and
  (*b*) in relation to which the condition in subsection (4) is met.
(4) The condition is that when the scheme starts to invest it is reasonable to suppose that over the investing life of the scheme—
  (*a*) more than 50% of the total value invested for the purposes of the scheme will be invested in investments which are significant equity stake investments, and
  (*b*) more than 50% of that value will be invested in investments which are held for 40 months or more.
(5) In determining whether subsection (4)(*b*) is met in relation to an investment scheme, apply the rule in subsection (1) to the scheme.
(6) In this section, "significant equity stake investment", in relation to an investment scheme, means an investment in a trading company or the holding company of a trading group where—
  (*a*) at the time the investment is made, the company is unlisted and likely to remain so,
  (*b*) by virtue of the investment (on its own or with other investments) the scheme has a 20% interest in the company, and
  (*c*) the scheme director condition is met.
(7) For the purposes of this section, in determining whether a significant equity stake fund has an interest of a particular percentage in a company, any share capital of the company which is held for the purposes of an associated investment scheme is to be regarded as held for the purposes of the significant equity stake fund.][1]

Amendments—[1]   Chapter 5F (ss 809FZA–809FZZ) inserted by FA 2016 s 37(2) with effect in relation to sums of carried interest arising on or after 6 April 2016 (whenever the arrangements under which the sums arise were made).

[809FZM Controlling equity stake funds

(1) Where a controlling equity stake fund has a 25% interest in a trading company or the holding company of a trading group—
  (*a*) any investment made for the purposes of the controlling equity stake fund in the company after the time the 25% interest was acquired is to be regarded as having been made at that time, and
  (*b*) any disposal for the purposes of the controlling equity stake fund of an investment in the company after that time is to be regarded as not being made until a relevant disposal is made.
(2) In subsection (1)(*b*), "relevant disposal", in relation to a company, means a disposal which (apart from subsection (1)) has the effect that the controlling equity stake fund ceases to have a 25% interest in the company.
(3) In this Chapter, "controlling equity stake fund" means an investment scheme—
  (*a*) which is not a venture capital fund or significant equity stake fund, and
  (*b*) in relation to which the condition in subsection (4) is met.
(4) The condition is that when the scheme starts to invest it is reasonable to suppose that, over the investing life of the scheme—
  (*a*) more than 50% of the total value invested for the purposes of the scheme will be invested in investments which are controlling interests in trading companies or holding companies of trading groups, and
  (*b*) more than 50% of the total value invested for the purposes of the scheme will be invested in investments which are held for 40 months or more.
(5) In determining whether subsection (4)(*b*) is met in relation to an investment scheme, apply the rule in subsection (1) to the scheme.
(6) For the purposes of this section, in determining whether a controlling equity stake fund has a controlling interest or an interest of a particular percentage in a company, any share capital of the company which is held for the purposes of an associated investment scheme is to be regarded as held for the purposes of the controlling equity stake fund.][1]

Amendments—[1]   Chapter 5F (ss 809FZA–809FZZ) inserted by FA 2016 s 37(2) with effect in relation to sums of carried interest arising on or after 6 April 2016 (whenever the arrangements under which the sums arise were made).

[809FZN Real estate funds

(1) Where a real estate fund has a major interest in any land—
  (*a*) any investment made for the purposes of the fund in that land after the time the major interest was acquired is to be regarded as having been made at that time, and
  (*b*) any disposal for the purposes of the fund of an investment in the land after that time is to be regarded as not being made until a relevant disposal is made.
(2) In subsection (1)(*b*) "relevant disposal" means a disposal which (apart from subsection (1)) has the effect that the real estate fund has disposed of more than 50% of the greatest amount invested at any one time in the land for the purposes of the real estate fund.
(3) Where a real estate fund has a major interest in any land ("the original land") and subsequently acquires a major interest in any adjacent land—
  (*a*) the acquisition is an investment in the original land for the purposes of subsection (1)(*a*), and

(b) after the acquisition, the adjacent land is to be regarded as part of the original land for the purposes of subsections (1) and (2).

(4) In this Chapter, "real estate fund" means an investment scheme—

    (a) which is not a venture capital fund, significant equity stake fund or controlling equity stake fund, and

    (b) in relation to which the condition in subsection (5) is met.

(5) The condition is that when the scheme starts to invest it is reasonable to suppose that over the investing life of the scheme—

    (a) more than 50% of the total value invested for the purposes of the scheme will be invested in land, and

    (b) more than 50% of the total value invested for the purposes of the scheme will be invested in investments which are held for 40 months or more.

(6) In determining whether subsection (5)(b) is met in relation to an investment scheme, apply the rule in subsection (1) to the scheme.][1]

Amendments—[1]   Chapter 5F (ss 809FZA–809FZZ) inserted by FA 2016 s 37(2) with effect in relation to sums of carried interest arising on or after 6 April 2016 (whenever the arrangements under which the sums arise were made).

[809FZO Funds of funds

(1) Section 809FZC(5) (disregard of intermediate holdings and holding structures) does not apply to an investment made for the purposes of a fund of funds in a collective investment scheme (and, accordingly, such an investment is regarded as an investment in the collective investment scheme itself).

(2) Subsection (1) does not apply in relation to a fund of funds in relation to a collective investment scheme if it is reasonable to suppose that the main purpose or one of the main purposes of the making of any investment in any collective investment scheme for the purposes of the fund of funds is to reduce the proportion of carried interest arising to any person which is income-based carried interest.

(3) Where by virtue of subsection (1) a fund of funds has a significant investment in a collective investment scheme ("the underlying scheme")—

    (a) any qualifying investment made for the purposes of the fund in the underlying scheme after the time the significant investment was acquired is to be regarded as having been made at that time, and

    (b) any disposal for the purposes of the fund of a qualifying investment in the underlying scheme after that time is to be regarded as not being made until a relevant disposal is made.

(4) In subsection (3)(b) "relevant disposal", in relation to an underlying scheme, means a disposal which (apart from subsection (3)) has the effect that—

    (a) the fund of funds has (by virtue of disposals of its interest in the underlying scheme) disposed of at least 50% of the greatest amount invested for its purposes at any one time in the underlying scheme, or

    (b) the fund of fund's investment in the underlying scheme is worth less than whichever is the greater of—

        (i) £1 million, or

        (ii) 5% of the total value of the investments made before the disposal for the purposes of the fund of funds in the underlying scheme.

(5) In this Chapter, "fund of funds" means an investment scheme in relation to which the condition in subsection (6) is met.

(6) The condition is that when the scheme starts to invest it is reasonable to suppose that over the investing life of the scheme—

    (a) substantially all of the total value invested for the purposes of the scheme will be invested in collective investment schemes of which the scheme holds less than 50% by value,

    (b) more than 50% of the total value invested for the purposes of the scheme will be invested in investments which are held for 40 months or more, and

    (c) more than 75% of the total value invested in the scheme will be invested by external investors.

(7) In determining whether subsection (6)(b) is met in relation to an investment scheme, apply the rule in subsection (3) to the scheme.

(8) In this section, "significant investment", in relation to a collective investment scheme, means—

    (a) an investment of a least £1 million in the scheme, or

    (b) an investment of at least 5% of the total amounts raised or to be raised from external investors in the scheme.

(9) In this section, "qualifying investment" means an investment made for the purposes of an investment scheme in a collective investment scheme ("the underlying scheme") where—

    (a) the investment is held on the same terms as other investments made by external investors in the underlying scheme,

    (b) the fund of funds, together with any connected funds, does not hold more than 30% by value of the underlying scheme,

    (c) the underlying scheme has not made an investment in the fund of funds, (*d*) no person providing investment management services to the underlying scheme provides investment management services to the fund of funds, and

   (*e*) it is reasonable to suppose that the investment in the underlying scheme is not part of arrangements the main purpose or one of the main purposes of which is to reward any person involved in providing investment management services to the underlying scheme or a scheme connected with that underlying scheme.]¹

Amendments—¹   Chapter 5F (ss 809FZA–809FZZ) inserted by FA 2016 s 37(2) with effect in relation to sums of carried interest arising on or after 6 April 2016 (whenever the arrangements under which the sums arise were made).

[809FZP Secondary funds

(1) Section 809FZC(5) (disregard of intermediate holdings and holding structures) does not apply to investments acquired for the purposes of a secondary fund in a collective investment scheme (and, accordingly, such an investment is regarded as an investment in the collective investment scheme itself).

(2) Subsection (1) does not apply in relation to a secondary fund in relation to a collective investment scheme if it is reasonable to suppose that the main purpose or one of the main purposes of the making of any investment in any collective investment scheme for the purposes of the secondary fund is to reduce the proportion of carried interest arising to any person which is income-based carried interest.

(3) Where by virtue of subsection (1) a secondary fund has a significant investment in a collective investment scheme ("the underlying scheme")—

   (*a*) any qualifying investment acquired for the purposes of the fund in the underlying scheme after the time when the significant investment is acquired is to be regarded as having been made at that time, and

   (*b*) any disposal for the purposes of the fund of a qualifying investment in the underlying scheme after that time is to be regarded as not being made until a relevant disposal is made.

(4) In subsection (3)(*b*) "relevant disposal" means a disposal which (apart from subsection (3)) has the effect that—

   (*a*) the secondary fund has (by virtue of disposals of its interest in the underlying scheme) disposed of at least 50% of the greatest amount invested for its purposes at any one time in the underlying scheme, or

   (*b*) the secondary fund's investment in the underlying scheme is worth less than whichever is the greater of—

      (i) £1 million, or

      (ii) 5% of the total value of the investments held immediately before the disposal for the purposes of the secondary fund in the underlying scheme.

(5) In this Chapter, "secondary fund" means an investment scheme in relation to which the condition in subsection (6) is met.

(6) The condition is that when the scheme starts to invest it is reasonable to suppose that over the investing life of the scheme—

   (*a*) substantially all of the total value invested for the purposes of the scheme will be in the acquisition of investments in, or the acquisition of portfolios of investments from, unconnected collective investment schemes,

   (*b*) more than 50% of the total value invested for the purposes of the scheme will be invested in investments which are held for 40 months or more, and

   (*c*) more than 75% of the total amount invested in the scheme will be invested by external investors.

(7) In determining whether subsection (6)(*b*) is met in relation to an investment scheme, apply the rule in subsection (3) to the scheme.

(8) In this section, "significant interest", in relation to a collective investment scheme, means—

   (*a*) an investment of at least £1 million in the scheme, or

   (*b*) an investment of at least 5% of the total amounts raised or to be raised from external investors in the scheme.

(9) In this section, "qualifying investment" means an investment in a collective investment scheme ("the underlying scheme") acquired for the purposes of a secondary fund where—

   (*a*) the investment acquired was originally made on the same terms as investments in the underlying scheme made by external investors,

   (*b*) the terms on which the investment was acquired or investments made in the underlying scheme were made by external investors have not significantly changed since the investment was acquired,

   (*c*) the secondary fund, together with any connected funds, does not hold more than 30% by value of the underlying scheme,

   (*d*) no person providing investment management services to the underlying scheme provides investment management services to the secondary fund, and

(e) it is reasonable to suppose that the investment in the underlying scheme is not part of arrangements the main purpose or one of the main purposes of which is to reward any person involved in providing investment management services to the underlying scheme or a scheme connected with that underlying scheme.][1]

Amendments—[1]   Chapter 5F (ss 809FZA–809FZZ) inserted by FA 2016 s 37(2) with effect in relation to sums of carried interest arising on or after 6 April 2016 (whenever the arrangements under which the sums arise were made).

Direct lending funds

[809FZQ Direct lending funds

(1) Carried interest arising from an investment scheme which is a direct lending fund is income-based carried interest in its entirety. Subsections (2) to (4) apply for the purposes of this Chapter.

(2) A direct lending fund is an investment scheme—

    (a) which is not a venture capital fund, significant equity stake fund, controlling equity stake fund or real estate fund, and

    (b) in relation to which it is reasonable to suppose that, when the scheme ceases to invest, a majority of the investments made for the purposes of the scheme (calculated by reference to value invested) will have been direct loans made by the scheme.

(3) An investment scheme makes a direct loan if for the purposes of the scheme money is advanced at interest or for any other return determined by reference to the time value of money.

(4) The acquisition of a direct loan is to be regarded as the making of a direct loan if the loan is acquired within the period of 120 days beginning with the day on which the money is first advanced.][1]

Commentary—*Simon's Taxes* **B5.646.**

Amendments—[1]   Chapter 5F (ss 809FZA–809FZZ) inserted by FA 2016 s 37(2) with effect in relation to sums of carried interest arising on or after 6 April 2016 (whenever the arrangements under which the sums arise were made).

[809FZR Direct lending funds: exception

(1) Section 809FZQ does not apply to carried interest arising from a direct lending fund if—

    (a) the fund is a limited partnership,

    (b) the carried interest is a sum falling within section 809EZD(2) or (3), and

    (c) it is reasonable to suppose that, when investments cease to be made for the purposes of the fund, at least 75% of the direct loans made by the fund (calculated by reference to value advanced) will have been qualifying loans.

(2) In this section "qualifying loan" means a direct loan made by an investment scheme where—

    (a) the borrower is not connected with the investment scheme,

    (b) the money is advanced under a genuine commercial loan agreement negotiated at arm's length,

    (c) repayments are fixed and determinable,

    (d) maturity is fixed,

    (e) the scheme has the positive intention and ability to hold the loan to maturity, and

    (f) the relevant term of the loan is at least four years.

(3) In this section "relevant term", in relation to a loan, means the period which—

    (a) begins with the time when the money is advanced, and

    (b) ends with the time by which, under the terms of the loan, at least 75% of the principal due under the loan must be repaid.

(4) For the purposes of determining the average holding period of a scheme, where—

    (a) a qualifying loan made by an investment scheme is repaid by the borrower to any extent before the end of 40 months from the time the loan is made, and

    (b) it is reasonable to suppose that the borrower's decision to repay was not affected by considerations relating to the application of this Chapter,

the loan is, to the extent it is repaid by the borrower before the end of 40 months from the time it is made, to be treated as held for 40 months.

(5) In determining for the purposes of subsection (1)(b) whether a sum falls within section 809EZD(2) or (3), read section 809EZD(4)(b) as if the reference to 6% were to 4%.

(6) Section 809FZB applies to carried interest to which, by virtue of subsection (1), section 809FZQ does not apply.][1]

Amendments—[1]   Chapter 5F (ss 809FZA–809FZZ) inserted by FA 2016 s 37(2) with effect in relation to sums of carried interest arising on or after 6 April 2016 (whenever the arrangements under which the sums arise were made).

Conditionally exempt carried interest

[809FZS Conditionally exempt carried interest

(1) Carried interest which—

    (a) arises to an individual from an investment scheme, and

    (b) is conditionally exempt from income tax,

is to be treated as if it were not income-based carried interest to any extent.

(2) Carried interest is conditionally exempt from income tax if Conditions A to D are met.

(3) Condition A is that the carried interest arises to the individual in the period of—

    (*a*) four years beginning with the day on which the scheme starts to invest, or

    (*b*) ten years beginning with that day if the carried interest is calculated on the realisation model.

(4) Condition B is that the carried interest would, apart from this section, be income-based carried interest to any extent.

(5) Condition C is that it is reasonable to suppose that, were the carried interest to arise to the individual at the relevant time (but by reference to the same relevant investments), it would not be income-based carried interest to any extent.

(6) The "relevant time" is whichever is the earliest of—

    (*a*) the time when it is reasonable to suppose that the investment scheme will be wound up;

    (*b*) the end of the period of four years beginning with the time when it is reasonable to suppose that the scheme will cease to invest;

    (*c*) the end of the period of—

        (i) four years beginning with the day on which the sum of carried interest arises to the individual, or

        (ii) ten years beginning with that day if the carried interest was calculated on the realisation model;

    (*d*) the end of the period of four years beginning with the end of the period by reference to which the amount of the carried interest was determined.

(7) Subsection (5) does not affect what would otherwise be the time at which an investment is disposed of for the purposes of this Chapter.

(8) Condition D is that the individual makes a claim under this section for the carried interest to be conditionally exempt from income tax.][1]

Commentary—*Simon's Taxes* **B5.646**.
Amendments—[1]   Chapter 5F (ss 809FZA–809FZZ) inserted by FA 2016 s 37(2) with effect in relation to sums of carried interest arising on or after 6 April 2016 (whenever the arrangements under which the sums arise were made).

[809FZT Carried interest which ceases to be conditionally exempt

(1) Carried interest which is conditionally exempt from income tax ceases to be conditionally exempt from income tax at whichever is the earliest of—

    (*a*) the time when the investment scheme is wound up;

    (*b*) the end of the period of four years beginning with the time the scheme ceases to invest;

    (*c*) the end of the period of—

        (i) four years beginning with the day on which the sum of carried interest arises to the individual, or

        (ii) ten years beginning with that day if the carried interest was calculated on the realisation model;

    (*d*) the end of the period of four years beginning with the end of the period by reference to which the amount of the carried interest is determined;

    (*e*) the time at which Condition C in section 809FZS(5) ceases to be met.

(2) Carried interest which ceases to be conditionally exempt from income tax is to be treated as having been income-based carried interest at the time it arose to the individual if or to the extent that, had it arisen to the individual at the time it ceased to be conditionally exempt (but in relation to the same relevant investments) it would have been income-based carried interest.

(3) All such assessments and adjustments of assessments are to be made as are necessary to give effect to subsection (2).

(4) Any amount paid by way of capital gains tax in respect of carried interest which is conditionally exempt from income tax is to be treated as if it had been paid in respect of any income tax liability arising under subsection (2).][1]

Commentary—*Simon's Taxes* **B5.646**.
Amendments—[1]   Chapter 5F (ss 809FZA–809FZZ) inserted by FA 2016 s 37(2) with effect in relation to sums of carried interest arising on or after 6 April 2016 (whenever the arrangements under which the sums arise were made).

Supplementary

[809FZU Employment-related securities

This Chapter does not apply in relation to carried interest arising to an individual in respect of employment-related securities as defined by section 421B(8) of ITEPA 2003.][1]

Commentary—*Simon's Taxes* **B5.646**.
Amendments—[1]   Chapter 5F (ss 809FZA–809FZZ) inserted by FA 2016 s 37(2) with effect in relation to sums of carried interest arising on or after 6 April 2016 (whenever the arrangements under which the sums arise were made).

[809FZV "Loan to own" investments

(1) This section applies where—

    (*a*) an investment scheme acquires a debt,

    (*b*) the debt is to any extent uncollectable or otherwise impaired,

    (*c*) the debt is acquired at a discount with a view to securing direct or indirect ownership of any assets which are—

        (i) owned by a company which is the debtor in respect of the debt, or

(ii) subject to a security interest in respect of the debt, and

(*d*) the fund acquires ownership of the assets within three months of the acquisition of the debt.

(2) For the purposes of this Chapter—

(*a*) the debt and the assets are to be treated as a single investment, and

(*b*) the value invested in that single investment is the amount paid for the debt.

(3) In this section "security interest" means an interest or right (other than a rentcharge) held for the purpose of securing the payment of money or the performance of any obligation.]¹

Amendments—¹   Chapter 5F (ss 809FZA–809FZZ) inserted by FA 2016 s 37(2) with effect in relation to sums of carried interest arising on or after 6 April 2016 (whenever the arrangements under which the sums arise were made).

[809FZW Anti-avoidance

(1) For the purposes mentioned in subsection (2), no regard is to be had to any arrangements the main purpose of which, or one of the main purposes of which, is to reduce the proportion of carried interest which is income-based carried interest.

(2) The purposes referred to in subsection (1) are—

(*a*) determining the average holding period, or

(*b*) determining whether an investment scheme is a venture capital fund, significant equity stake fund, controlling equity stake fund, real estate fund, fund of funds or secondary fund.

(3) In determining to what extent carried interest is income-based carried interest, no regard is to be had to any arrangements the main purpose, or one of the main purposes, of which is to secure that section 809EZA(1) (charge to income tax) does not apply in relation to some or all of the carried interest.]¹

Amendments—¹   Chapter 5F (ss 809FZA–809FZZ) inserted by FA 2016 s 37(2) with effect in relation to sums of carried interest arising on or after 6 April 2016 (whenever the arrangements under which the sums arise were made).

[809FZX Treasury regulations

(1) The Treasury may by regulations make—

(*a*) provision relating to the calculation of the average holding period in some or all cases;

(*b*) provision repealing, or restricting the application of, section 809FZU (employment-related securities).

(2) The provision referred to in subsection (1)(*a*) includes in particular—

(*a*) provision for a method of calculating that period which is different from that in section 809FZC;

(*b*) provision as to what is and is not to be regarded as an investment;

(*c*) provision as to when an investment is to be regarded as made or disposed of;

(*d*) anti-avoidance provision.

(3) Regulations under this section may—

(*a*) amend this Chapter;

(*b*) make different provision for different purposes;

(*c*) contain incidental, supplemental, consequential and transitional provision and savings.]¹

Amendments—¹   Chapter 5F (ss 809FZA–809FZZ) inserted by FA 2016 s 37(2) with effect in relation to sums of carried interest arising on or after 6 April 2016 (whenever the arrangements under which the sums arise were made).

[809FZY "Reasonable to suppose"

(1) For the purposes of this Chapter, in determining what it is reasonable to suppose in relation to an investment scheme, regard is to be had to all the circumstances.

(2) Those circumstances include in particular any prospectus or other document which—

(*a*) is made available to external investors in the investment scheme, and

(*b*) on which external investors may reasonably be supposed to have relied or been able to rely.]¹

Amendments—¹   Chapter 5F (ss 809FZA–809FZZ) inserted by FA 2016 s 37(2) with effect in relation to sums of carried interest arising on or after 6 April 2016 (whenever the arrangements under which the sums arise were made).

Interpretation

[809FZZ Interpretation of Chapter 5F

(1) In this Chapter—

"5% interest", "15% interest", "20% interest", "25% interest" and "40% interest" are to be construed in accordance with subsection (4);

"act together": two or more investment schemes act together in relation to a company if—

(*a*) they enter into contractual arrangements (with or without other persons) in relation to the conduct of the company's affairs,

(*b*) the arrangements are negotiated on arm's length terms, and

(*c*) the investment schemes act together to secure greater control or influence over the company's affairs than they would be able to secure individually;

"alternative finance arrangements" has the same meaning as in Part 6 of CTA 2009 (see section 501(2) of that Act);

"arrangements" has the same meaning as in Chapter 5E (see section 809EZE);

"associated": two (or more) investment schemes are "associated if—

(a) the same or substantially the same individuals provide investment management services to both schemes;

(b) the investment schemes have the same or substantially the same investments, and

(c) the schemes act together in relation to all or substantially all of the investments they acquire;

"carried interest" has the same meaning as in section 809EZB (see sections 809EZC and 809EZD);

"collective investment scheme" has the same meaning as in Chapter 5E (see section 809EZE);

"connected" and "unconnected" are to be construed in accordance with subsections (6) and (7);

"contract for differences" has the same meaning as in Part 7 of CTA 2009 (see section 582 of that Act);

"controlling equity stake fund" has the meaning given in section 809FZM;

"controlling interest" has the meaning given in subsection (3);

"derivative contract" has the same meaning as in Part 7 of CTA 2009 (but see below);

"designated" has the same meaning as for accounting purposes;

"direct lending fund" and "direct loan" have the meanings given in section 809FZQ;

"exchange gain or loss" is to be construed in accordance with section 475 of CTA 2009;

"external investor" has the same meaning as in Chapter 5E (see section 809EZE);

"fund of funds" has the meaning given in section 809FZO;

"future" has the same meaning as in Part 7 of CTA 2009 (see section 581 of that Act);

"interest rate contract" means—

(a) a derivative contract whose underlying subject-matter is, or includes, interest rates, or

(b) a swap contract in which payments fall to be made by reference to a rate of interest;

"investing life" is to be construed in accordance with subsection (2);

"investment" does not include—

(a) cash awaiting investment, or

(b) cash representing the proceeds of the disposal of an investment, where the cash is to be distributed as soon as reasonably practicable to investors in the scheme;

"investment scheme" has the same meaning as in Chapter 5E (see section 809EZA(6));

"limited partnership" means—

(a) a limited partnership registered under the Limited Partnerships Act 1907,

(b) a limited liability partnership formed under the Limited Liability Partnerships Act 2000 or the Limited Liability Partnerships Act (Northern Ireland) 2002 (c.12 (N.I.)), or

(c) a firm or entity of a similar character to any of those mentioned in paragraph (a) or (b) formed under the law of a country or territory outside the United Kingdom;

"loan relationship" has the meaning given by section 302 of CTA 2009 (but see below);

"major interest", in relation to land, has the meaning given by section 96 of the Value Added Tax Act 1994;

"option" has the same meaning as in Part 7 of CTA 2009, disregarding section 580(2) of that Act;

"real estate fund" has the meaning given by section 809FZN;

"realisation model": a sum of carried interest is calculated on the "realisation model" if it falls within section 809EZD(2) or (3) (disregarding section 809EZD(2)(b) and (3)(b));

"scheme director condition" has the meaning given by section 809FZK(8) and (9);

"secondary fund" has the meaning given by section 809FZP;

"significant equity stake fund" has the meaning given by section 809FZL;

"sum" has the same meaning as in Chapter 5E (see section 809EZB(3));

"trading company" and "trading group" have the meanings given by paragraphs 20 and 21 of Schedule 7AC to TCGA 1992;

"underlying subject matter" has the same meaning as in Part 7 of CTA 2009;

"unlisted": a company is unlisted if—

(a) no shares of any class issued by the company are listed on any stock exchange, and

(b) there are no other trading arrangements in place in respect of shares of any class issued by the company;

"venture capital fund" has the meaning given by section 809FZK.

(2) In this Chapter—

(a) references to when a scheme starts or ceases to invest are to the time when investments start or cease to be made for the purposes of the scheme, and

(b) references to the investing life of the scheme are to the time between when a scheme starts and ceases to invest.

(3) For the purposes of this Chapter, an investment scheme has a controlling interest in a company if share capital of the company is held for the purposes of the scheme which—

(a) amounts to more than 50% of the ordinary share capital of the company, and

(b) carries an entitlement to more than 50% of—
    (i) voting rights in the company,
    (ii) profits available for distribution to shareholders, and
    (iii) assets of the company available for distribution to shareholders in a winding-up.
(4) For the purposes of this Chapter, an investment scheme has an interest of a particular percentage in a company (for example, a 40% interest) if share capital of the company is held for the purposes of the scheme which—
    (a) amounts to at least that percentage of the ordinary share capital of the company, and
    (b) carries an entitlement to at least that percentage of—
        (i) voting rights in the company,
        (ii) profits available for distribution to shareholders, and
        (iii) assets of the company available for distribution to shareholders in a winding-up.
(5) For the purposes of subsections (3) and (4) any share capital held by a company controlled by an investment scheme is to be regarded as held for the purposes of the investment scheme.
(6) For the purposes of this Chapter, an investment scheme (a) is connected with another investment scheme or person (b) if—
    (a) A directly or indirectly has control of B, or
    (b) the same person, directly or indirectly, has control of A and B.
(7) For the purposes of subsection (6) "control"—
    (a) in the case of control of a company, is to be read in accordance with sections 450 and 451 of CTA 2010;
    (b) in the case of control of a partnership, has the meaning given in section 995(3);
    (c) in the case of control of an investment scheme which is not a company or partnership, or of any other person which is not a company or partnership, means the ability to secure that the affairs of that scheme or other person are conducted in accordance with one's wishes.
(8) For the purposes of the definition of "derivative contract", read Part 7 of CTA 2009 as if—
    (a) references to a company were references to an investment scheme, and
    (b) references to a contract of a company were references to a contract for the purposes of an investment scheme.
(9) For the purposes of the definition of "loan relationship", read Part 5 of CTA 2009 as if—
    (a) references to a company were references to an investment scheme, and
    (b) references to a loan relationship of a company were references to a loan relationship for the purposes of an investment scheme.][1]

Amendments—[1]   Chapter 5F (ss 809FZA–809FZZ) inserted by FA 2016 s 37(2) with effect in relation to sums of carried interest arising on or after 6 April 2016 (whenever the arrangements under which the sums arise were made).

[CHAPTER 6

AVOIDANCE INVOLVING LEASES OF PLANT AND MACHINERY

809ZA Plant and machinery leases: capital receipts to be treated as income
(1) This section applies if—
    (a) there is an unconditional obligation, under a lease of plant or machinery or a relevant arrangement, to make a relevant capital payment (at any time), or
    (b) a relevant capital payment is made under such a lease or arrangement otherwise than in pursuance of such an obligation.
(2) The lessor is treated for income tax purposes as receiving income attributable to the lease of an amount equal to the amount of the capital payment.
[(3) If subsection (1)(a) applies, the income is treated as income for the period of account in which there is first an obligation of the kind mentioned there.
(4) If subsection (1)(b) applies, the income is treated as income for the period of account in which the capital payment is made.
(5) For the meaning of "capital payment" and "relevant capital payment", see section 809ZE.
(6) For the meaning of other expressions used in this section or section 809ZC, 809ZD or 809ZE, see section 809ZF.][2]][1]

Commentary—*Simon's Taxes* **B5.415A**.
Amendments—[1]   Sections 809ZA–809ZD inserted by FA 2008 s 55, Sch 20 para 2(1) with effect in relation to:
    (a)   cases where there is first an obligation of the kind mentioned in ITA 2007 s 809ZA(1)(a) on or after 13 December 2007, and
    (b)   capital payments within subsection (1)(b) of that section made on or after that date.
    Where conditions in para (a) or (b) of s 809ZA(1) were met before 12 March 2008 see FA 2008 Sch 20 para 2(3).
[2]   Sub-s (3)–(6) substituted for former sub-s (3) by CTA 2010 s 1177, Sch 1 para 548. CTA 2010 has effect for corporation tax purposes for accounting periods ending on or after 1 April 2010, and for income and capital gains tax purposes for the tax year 2010–11 and subsequent tax years.

[809ZC Section 809ZA: lease of plant and machinery and other property
(1) This section applies if section 809ZA applies in relation to a lease of plant or machinery and other property (see [section 809ZF(3)][2]).
(2) The relevant capital payment is to be apportioned, on a just and reasonable basis, between—
   (a) the plant and machinery, and
   (b) the other property.
(3) If the income (if any) received by the lessor that is attributable to any of the plant or machinery is chargeable to tax under Part 3 of ITTOIA 2005 (property income), treat that plant or machinery as falling within subsection (2)(b) (and not subsection (2)(a)).
(4) Section 809ZA(2) has effect as if the reference to the amount of the capital payment were to such amount as is apportioned under subsection (2) in respect of the plant or machinery within subsection (2)(a).][1]

Commentary—*Simon's Taxes* **B5.415A**.
Amendments—[1]   Sections 809ZA–809ZD inserted by FA 2008 s 55, Sch 20 para 2(1) with effect in relation to:
   (a)   cases where there is first an obligation of the kind mentioned in ITA 2007 s 809ZA(1)(a) on or after 13 December 2007, and
   (b)   capital payments within subsection (1)(b) of that section made on or after that date.
Where conditions in para (a) or (b) of s 809ZA(1) were met before 12 March 2008 see FA 2008 Sch 20 para 2(3).
[2]   In sub-s (1) words substituted by CTA 2010 s 1177, Sch 1 para 550. CTA 2010 has effect for corporation tax purposes for accounting periods ending on or after 1 April 2010, and for income and capital gains tax purposes for the tax year 2010–11 and subsequent tax years.

[809ZD Section 809ZA: expectation that relevant capital payment will not be paid
(1) This section applies for income tax purposes if—
   (a) section 809ZA applies by virtue of subsection (1)(a) of that section, and
   (b) at any time, the lessor reasonably expects that the relevant capital payment will not be paid (or will not be paid in full).
(2) For the purposes of calculating the profits of the lessor, a deduction is allowed for the period of account which includes that time.
(3) The amount of the deduction is equal to the amount reasonably expected not to be paid.
(4) No other deduction is allowed in respect of the matters mentioned in subsection (1).][1]

Commentary—*Simon's Taxes* **B5.415A**.
Amendments—[1]   Sections 809ZA–809ZD inserted by FA 2008 s 55, Sch 20 para 2(1) with effect in relation to:
   (a)   cases where there is first an obligation of the kind mentioned in ITA 2007 s 809ZA(1)(a) on or after 13 December 2007, and
   (b)   capital payments within subsection (1)(b) of that section made on or after that date.
Where conditions in para (a) or (b) of s 809ZA(1) were met before 12 March 2008 see FA 2008 Sch 20 para 2(3).

[809ZE "Capital payment", "relevant capital payment" etc
(1) This section gives the meaning of "capital payment", "relevant capital payment" and references to payment for the purposes of sections 809ZA to 809ZD and this section.
(2) "Capital payment" means any payment except one which, if made to the lessor—
   (a) would fall to be included in a calculation of the lessor's income for income tax purposes, or
   (b) would so fall but for section 148A of ITTOIA 2005 (rental earnings under long funding finance lease).
(3) A capital payment, in relation to a lease or relevant arrangement, is "relevant" if condition A or B is met (but this is subject to subsections (6) and (7)).
(4) Condition A is that the capital payment is payable (or paid), directly or indirectly, by or on behalf of the lessee to the lessor or another person on the lessor's behalf in connection with—
   (a) the grant, assignment, novation or termination of the lease, or
   (b) any provision of the lease or relevant arrangement (including the variation or waiver of any such provision).
(5) Condition B is that rentals payable under the lease are less than, or payable later than, they might reasonably be expected to be if there were no obligation to make the capital payment and it were not made.
(6) A capital payment is not "relevant" so far as it—
   (a) reduces the amount of expenditure incurred by the lessor for the purposes of CAA 2001 in respect of the plant or machinery in question or would reduce it but for section 536 of that Act (contributions not made by public bodies and not eligible for tax relief), or
   (b) is compensation for loss resulting from damage to, or damage caused by, the plant or machinery in question.
(7) If—
   (a) a capital payment is an initial payment under a long funding lease for the purposes of Part 2 of CAA 2001 (see section 70YI of that Act), and
   (b) under section 61 of that Act (disposal events and disposal values) the commencement of the term of the lease (as defined in section 70YI of that Act) is an event that requires the lessor to bring a disposal value into account,

the capital payment is only "relevant" so far as it exceeds the amount that is the disposal value for the purposes of Part 2 of that Act.

(8) References to payment include the provision of value by any means other than the making of a payment.

(9) Accordingly—

(a) references to the making of a payment include the passing of value by any other means, and

(b) references to the amount of the payment include the value passed.]¹

Commentary—*Simon's Taxes* **B5.415A**.
Amendments—¹   Sections 809ZE, 809ZF inserted by CTA 2010 s 1177, Sch 1 para 551. CTA 2010 has effect for corporation tax purposes for accounting periods ending on or after 1 April 2010, and for income and capital gains tax purposes for the tax year 2010–11 and subsequent tax years.

[809ZF Further interpretation of section 809ZA etc

(1) This section applies for the purposes of sections 809ZA to 809ZE and this section.

(2) "Lease" includes—

(a) a licence, and

(b) the letting of a ship or aircraft on charter or the letting of any other asset on hire,

and "lessor" and "lessee" must be read accordingly.

(3) "Lease of plant or machinery" includes a lease of plant or machinery and other property, but does not include a lease to which subsection (4) or (5) applies.

(4) This subsection applies to a lease if any income attributable to it and received by the lessor would be chargeable to tax under Part 3 of ITTOIA 2005 (property income).

(5) This subsection applies to a lease of plant or machinery if the lessor has incurred on the plant or machinery what would be qualifying expenditure within the meaning of Part 2 of CAA 2001 but for section 34A of that Act (expenditure on plant or machinery for long funding leasing not qualifying expenditure).

(6) "Relevant arrangement" means any agreement or arrangement relating to a lease of plant or machinery, including one made before the lease is entered into or after it has ended.

(7) Accordingly, "lessor" and "lessee" include prospective and former lessors and lessees.]¹

Commentary—*Simon's Taxes* **B5.415A**.
Amendments—¹   Sections 809ZE, 809ZF inserted by CTA 2010 s 1177, Sch 1 para 551. CTA 2010 has effect for corporation tax purposes for accounting periods ending on or after 1 April 2010, and for income and capital gains tax purposes for the tax year 2010–11 and subsequent tax years.

[809ZFA Consideration for taking over payment obligations as lessee treated as income

(1) This section applies where under any arrangements—

(a) a person within the charge to income tax (P) agrees to take over obligations of another person (Q) as lessee under a lease of plant or machinery,

(b) as a result of that agreement P, or a person connected with P, becomes entitled to income deductions (whether deductions in calculating income or from total profits), and

(c) a payment is payable to P, or a person connected with P, by way of consideration for that agreement.

(2) The payment is treated for the purposes of income tax as income received by P in the tax year in which P takes over the obligations mentioned in subsection (1)(a).

(3) Subsection (2) does not apply if and to the extent that the consideration is (apart from this section)—

(a) charged to tax on P, or a person connected with P, as an amount of income,

(b) brought into account in calculating for tax purposes any income of P or a person connected with P, or

(c) brought into account for the purposes of any provision of CAA 2001 as a disposal receipt, or proceeds from a balancing event or disposal event, of P or a person connected with P.

(4) It does not matter how P takes over the obligations of Q (whether by assignment, novation, variation or replacement of the contract, by operation of law or otherwise).

(5) In this section—

"arrangements" include any scheme, arrangement, understanding, transaction or series of transactions (whether or not legally enforceable);

"lease of plant or machinery" means any kind of agreement or arrangement under which sums are paid for the use of, or otherwise in respect of, plant or machinery;

"payment" includes the provision of any benefit, the assumption of any liability or the transfer of money or money's worth (and "payable" is to be construed accordingly),;

"payment by way of consideration" includes a payment made, directly or indirectly, in consequence of or otherwise in connection with, the agreement mentioned in subsection (1)(a), where it is reasonable to assume the agreement would not have been made unless the arrangements included provision for the payment.

(6) Any priority rule (other than section 212(1) of FA 2013 (general anti-abuse rule to have priority over other rules)) has effect subject to this section, despite the terms of the priority rule.

(7) For that purpose "priority rule" is a rule (however expressed) to the effect that particular provisions have effect to the exclusion of, or otherwise in priority to, anything else.

(8) An example of a priority rule is section 6(1) of TIOPA 2010 (effect to be given to double taxation arrangements despite anything in any enactment).][1]

Amendments—[1]   Section 809ZFA inserted by FA 2016 s 68(2) with effect in relation to agreements of the kind mentioned in CTA 2010 s 894A(1)(a) or ITA 2007 s 809ZFA made on or after 25 November 2015.

[CHAPTER 7

AVOIDANCE INVOLVING OBTAINING TAX RELIEF FOR INTEREST][1]

Amendments—[1]   Chapter 7 (s 809ZG) inserted by TIOPA 2010 s 371, Sch 7 paras 50, 52. TIOPA 2010 has effect for corporation tax purposes for accounting periods ending on or after 1 April 2010, for income and capital gains tax purposes for the tax year 2010–11 and subsequent tax years, and for petroleum revenue tax purposes for chargeable periods beginning on or after 1 July 2010.

[809ZG Tax relief schemes and arrangements

(1) Relief is not to be given under any provision of the Income Tax Acts to a person in respect of a payment of interest if a tax relief scheme has been effected, or tax relief arrangements have been made, in relation to the transaction under which the interest is paid.

(2) Subsection (1) applies whether the tax relief scheme is effected, or the tax relief arrangements are made, before or after the transaction.

(3) A scheme is a tax relief scheme in relation to a transaction for the purposes of subsection (1) if it is such that the sole or main benefit that might be expected to accrue to the person from the transaction is the obtaining of a reduction in tax liability by means of relief under the Income Tax Acts.

(4) Arrangements are tax relief arrangements in relation to a transaction for the purposes of subsection (1) if they are such that the sole or main benefit that might be expected to accrue to the person from the transaction is the obtaining of a reduction in tax liability by means of relief under the Income Tax Acts.

(5) In this section "relief" means relief by way of—
   (a) deduction in calculating profits or gains, or
   (b) deduction or set off against income.][1]

Commentary—*Simon's Taxes* **E1.824, B5.415B.**
Amendments—[1]   Section inserted by TIOPA 2010 s 371, Sch 7 paras 50, 52. TIOPA 2010 has effect for corporation tax purposes for accounting periods ending on or after 1 April 2010, for income and capital gains tax purposes for the tax year 2010–11 and subsequent tax years, and for petroleum revenue tax purposes for chargeable periods beginning on or after 1 July 2010.

[CHAPTER 8

TAINTED CHARITY DONATIONS]

Commentary—*Simon's Taxes* **C5.127AA.**
Amendments—This Chapter inserted by FA 2011 s 27, Sch 3 para 1 with effect in relation to relievable charity donations made on or after 1 April 2011.

[Introduction

809ZH Overview of Chapter

(1) This Chapter makes provision for removing entitlement to income tax reliefs, and counteracting income tax advantages, where a person makes a relievable charity donation which is a tainted donation.

(2) See section 257A of TCGA 1992 and Part 21C of CTA 2010 for the removal of entitlement to other reliefs where a person makes a relievable charity donation which is a tainted donation.][1]

Commentary—*Simon's Taxes* **C5.127AA.**
HMRC Manuals—Business Income Manual BIM45160 (relief for gifts of trading stock to charities and other bodies: tainted charity donations).
Amendments—[1]   This Chapter inserted by FA 2011 s 27, Sch 3 para 1 with effect in relation to relievable charity donations made on or after 1 April 2011.

[809ZI Relievable charity donations

(1) In this Chapter "relievable charity donation" means a gift or other disposal which—
   (a) is made by a person to a charity, and
   (b) is eligible for tax relief.

(2) A gift or other disposal is eligible for tax relief if one or both of the following apply—
   (a) (ignoring the tainted donation provisions) tax relief would be available in respect of it under a relevant relieving provision;
   (b) the charity is entitled to claim a repayment of tax in respect of it.

(3) "The tainted donation provisions" are—
   (a) this Chapter,
   (b) section 257A of TCGA 1992 (tainted charity donations: disapplication of section 257), and

(c) Part 21C of CTA 2010 (tainted charity donations: removal of corporation tax reliefs).

(4) The following are "relevant relieving provisions"—

(a) section 257 of TCGA 1992 (gifts of chargeable assets),

(b) section 63(2)(a), (aa) and (ab) of CAA 2001 (gifts of plant and machinery),

(c) Part 12 of ITEPA 2003 (payroll giving),

(d) section 108 of ITTOIA 2005 (gifts of trading stock),

(e) Chapters 2 and 3 of Part 8 of this Act (gift aid and gifts of shares),

(f) section 105 of CTA 2009 (gifts of trading stock), and

(g) Part 6 of CTA 2010 (charitable donations relief).

(5) For the purposes of this Chapter, an amount of income which arises under a UK settlement and to which a charity is entitled under the terms of the settlement is to be regarded as an amount gifted to the charity by the trustees of the settlement.

"UK settlement" has the same meaning as in section 628 of ITTOIA 2005.][1]

Commentary—*Simon's Taxes* **C5.127AA, E1.810**.

Amendments—[1]   This Chapter inserted by FA 2011 s 27, Sch 3 para 1 with effect in relation to relievable charity donations made on or after 1 April 2011.

[Tainted donations

809ZJ Tainted donations

(1) For the purposes of this Chapter, a relievable charity donation is a tainted donation if (and only if) Conditions A, B and C are met.

(2) Condition A is that—

(a) a linked person enters into arrangements (whether before or after the donation is made), and

(b) it is reasonable to assume from either or both of—

(i) the likely effects of the donation and the arrangements, and

(ii) the circumstances in which the donation is made and the circumstances in which the arrangements are entered into,

that the donation would not have been made and the arrangements would not have been entered into independently of one another.

(3) "Linked person" means—

(a) the person who made the donation ("the donor"), or

(b) a person connected with the donor at a relevant time.

(4) In subsection (3) "relevant time" means a time during the period which begins with the earliest, and ends with the latest, of the following times—

(a) the time when the arrangements are entered into as mentioned in subsection (2);

(b) the time when the relievable charity donation is made;

(c) the time when the arrangements are first materially implemented.

(5) Condition B is that the main purpose, or one of the main purposes, of the linked person in entering into the arrangements is to obtain a financial advantage—

(a) directly or indirectly from the charity to which the donation is made or a connected charity,

(b) for one or more linked persons who are not charities (each of whom is referred to in this Chapter as "a potentially advantaged person").

(6) Condition C is that the donor is not—

(a) a qualifying charity-owned company, or

(b) a relevant housing provider linked with the charity to which the donation is made.

(7) For the purposes of subsection (6)(b) a relevant housing provider is linked with the charity if (and only if)—

(a) one is wholly owned, or subject to control, by the other, or

(b) both are wholly owned, or subject to control, by the same person.

(8) In this section—

"qualifying charity-owned company", in relation to a relievable charity donation, means a company which—

(a) is wholly owned by one or more charities, at least one of which is the charity to which the donation is made or a connected charity, and

(b) has not previously been under the control of, and does not carry on a trade or business previously carried on by, one or more of the following—

(i) a potentially advantaged person;

(ii) a person (other than a charity) who, at any time within the period of 4 years ending with the day on which paragraph (a) was first satisfied, was connected with a person who is a potentially advantaged person;

"relevant housing provider" means a body which is—

(a) a non-profit registered provider of social housing, or

(b) entered on a register maintained under section 1 of the Housing Act 1996, section 20 of the Housing (Scotland) Act 2010 (asp 17) or Article 14 of the Housing (Northern Ireland) Order 1992 (S.I. 1992/ 1725 (N.I. 15)).

(9) Section 200 of CTA 2010 (company wholly owned by a charity) applies for the purposes of subsection (8), and for those purposes references in that section to "charity" include a registered club within the meaning of section 658(6) of that Act.

(10) This section is subject to section 809ZL (certain financial advantages to be ignored).][1]

Commentary—*Simon's Taxes* **C5.127AA**.
Modification —See FA 2011 Sch 3 para 31 (modification of definition of "relevant housing provider" in sub-s (8) prior to coming into force of s 20 of the Housing (Scotland) Act 2010).
Amendments—[1]   This Chapter inserted by FA 2011 s 27, Sch 3 para 1 with effect in relation to relievable charity donations made on or after 1 April 2011.

[809ZK Circumstances in which financial advantage deemed to be obtained

(1) This section applies for the purposes of Condition B.

(2) Subsection (3) applies where the arrangements entered into by the linked person (as mentioned in Condition A) involve a transaction to which—

    (*a*) that or any other linked person ("X"), and

    (*b*) another person ("Y"),

are parties.

(3) X obtains a financial advantage from the charity to which the donation is made or a connected charity if—

    (*a*) the terms of the transaction are less beneficial to Y or more beneficial to X (or both) than those which might reasonably be expected in a transaction concluded between parties dealing at arm's length, or

    (*b*) the transaction is not of a kind which a person dealing at arm's length and in place of Y might reasonably be expected to make.

(4) Nothing in this section is intended to limit the circumstances in which a linked person may be regarded as obtaining a financial advantage for the purposes of section 809ZJ.

(5) In this section—

    "Condition A" and "Condition B" have the same meaning as in section 809ZJ;

    "linked person" has the meaning given by section 809ZJ(3);

    "transaction" includes (for example)—

        (*a*) the sale or letting of property,

        (*b*) the provision of services,

        (*c*) the exchange of property,

        (*d*) the provision of a loan or any other form of financial assistance, and

        (*e*) investment in a business.][1]

Commentary—*Simon's Taxes* **C5.127AA**.
Amendments—[1]   This Chapter inserted by FA 2011 s 27, Sch 3 para 1 with effect in relation to relievable charity donations made on or after 1 April 2011.

[809ZL Certain financial advantages to be ignored

(1) When determining whether a relievable charity donation is a tainted donation, a financial advantage within subsection (2), (3), (4) or (5) is to be ignored.

(2) A financial advantage is within this subsection if the person for whom it is obtained applies the advantage for charitable purposes only.

(3) A financial advantage is within this subsection if (ignoring the tainted donation provisions) it is—

    (*a*) a benefit associated with a gift which is a qualifying donation for the purposes of Chapter 2 of Part 8 (gift aid), or

    (*b*) a benefit associated with a payment which is a qualifying payment for the purposes of Chapter 2 of Part 6 of CTA 2010 (charitable donations relief: payments to charity).

(4) A financial advantage is within this subsection if (ignoring the tainted donation provisions)—

    (*a*) the relievable charity donation is a disposal in respect of which tax relief would be available under Chapter 3 of Part 8 of this Act (gifts of shares, securities and real property to charities etc) or Chapter 3 of Part 6 of CTA 2010 (charitable donations: certain disposals to charity), and

    (*b*) the advantage is a benefit the value of which would be taken into account in determining the relievable amount in respect of the disposal for the purposes of the Chapter in question.

(5) A financial advantage is within this subsection if (ignoring the tainted donation provisions)—

    (*a*) the relievable charity donation is a gift in respect of which tax relief would be available under section 108 of ITTOIA 2005 or section 105 of CTA 2009 (gifts of trading stock to charities etc), and

    (*b*) the advantage is a benefit attributable to the making of the gift in respect of which an amount would be brought into account under section 109 of ITTOIA 2005 or section 108 of CTA 2009 (receipt of benefits by donor or connected person).

(6) In this section—

    "benefit associated with a gift" has the meaning given by section 417;

    "benefit associated with a payment" has the meaning given by section 196 of CTA 2010;

    "the tainted donation provisions" has the meaning given by section 809ZI(3).][1]

Commentary—*Simon's Taxes* **C5.127AA**.
Amendments—[1]   This Chapter inserted by FA 2011 s 27, Sch 3 para 1 with effect in relation to relievable charity donations made on or after 1 April 2011.

[Removal of reliefs and imposition of charge to tax

809ZM Removal of income tax relief in respect of tainted donations etc

(1) This section applies where a tainted donation is made by a person.

(2) Where (ignoring this Chapter) income tax relief would be available in respect of the tainted donation, that relief is not available.

(3) Where—

(a) (ignoring this Chapter) income tax relief would be available in respect of an associated donation, and

(b) entitlement to that relief is not withdrawn by subsection (2),

that relief is not available.

(4) In this section—

"associated donation", in relation to a tainted donation, means a relievable charity donation made—

(a) in accordance with the relevant arrangements, and

(b) by a person, other than—

(i) a qualifying charity-owned company in relation to that relievable charity donation, or

(ii) a relevant housing provider linked (within the meaning of section 809ZJ(7)) with the charity to which that donation is made;

"income tax relief" means relief under—

(a) section 63(2)(a), (aa) or (ab) of CAA 2001 (gifts of plant and machinery), so far as it applies in relation to income tax,

(b) Part 12 of ITEPA 2003 (payroll giving),

(c) section 108 of ITTOIA 2005 (gifts of trading stock),

(d) Chapter 2 of Part 8 of this Act (gift aid), or

(e) Chapter 3 of that Part (gifts of shares etc);

"qualifying charity-owned company" has the meaning given by section 809ZJ(8) (except that paragraph (b) of that definition does not apply);

"relevant housing provider" has the meaning given by section 809ZJ(8);

"the relevant arrangements", in relation to a tainted donation, means the arrangements by reference to which Conditions A and B in section 809ZJ are met.

(5) Where entitlement to relief is withdrawn under this section in respect of a donation—

(a) subsections (6) and (7) apply if the relief is under Chapter 2 of Part 8 (gift aid), and

(b) subsection (8) applies if the relief is under Part 12 of ITEPA 2003 (payroll giving).

(6) For the purposes of Step 2 in section 58(1), the donation is not a qualifying donation for the purposes of Chapter 2 of Part 8.

(7) But—

(a) the donation remains a qualifying donation for the purposes of—

(i) Part 10 (special rules about charitable trusts etc),

(ii) section 899(5) (meaning of "qualifying annual payment"),

(iii) Chapter 2 of Part 11 of CTA 2010 (charitable companies: gifts and other payments),

(iv) section 664 of that Act (community amateur sports clubs: exemption for interest and gift aid income), and

(b) accordingly, section 414(2)(a) (donation treated as made after deduction of basic rate income tax) applies for the purposes of section 520(4) (income tax treated as deducted to be treated as income tax paid by charitable trust).

(8) The donation remains a donation for the purposes of Part 12 of ITEPA 2003 for the purposes of—

(a) section 521A (gifts under payroll deduction scheme: income tax liability and exemption), and

(b) section 472A of CTA 2010 (gifts under payroll reduction scheme: corporation tax liability and exemption).][1]

Commentary—*Simon's Taxes* **C5.127AA**.
Amendments—[1]   This Chapter inserted by FA 2011 s 27, Sch 3 para 1 with effect in relation to relievable charity donations made on or after 1 April 2011.

[809ZN Income tax charge where gift aid is withdrawn

(1) Income tax is charged under this section if—

(a) a person makes a tainted donation in a tax year,

(b) (ignoring this Chapter) relief would have been available under Chapter 2 of Part 8 in respect of the tainted donation or an associated donation ("the gift aid donation"), and

(c) the charity to which the gift aid donation is made is entitled to claim a repayment of tax in respect of that donation.

(2) The amount of the tax charged under this section is equal to the amount of the repayment of tax which the charity is entitled to claim in respect of the gift aid donation (whether or not such a claim is made).

(3) Each of the persons mentioned in subsection (4) is liable for any tax charged under this section, and the liability of those persons is joint and several.

(4) The persons are—

(*a*) the donor in respect of the gift aid donation,

(*b*) if different, the donor in respect of the tainted donation,

(*c*) each potentially advantaged person under the relevant arrangements relating to the tainted donation, and

(*d*) any charity to which the gift aid donation or (if different) the tainted donation is made, or any connected charity, which falls within subsection (5).

(5) A charity falls within this subsection if the charity—

(*a*) is or was party to the relevant arrangements relating to the tainted donation, and

(*b*) was aware, at the time it entered into those arrangements, that a linked person was entering (or had entered or was likely to enter) into the arrangements in circumstances falling within Condition B in section 809ZJ.

(6) No liability to income tax arises under this section in respect of a repayment of tax, if (and to the extent that) the repayment is itself repaid to the Commissioners for Her Majesty's Revenue and Customs under any other provision of the Tax Acts.

(7) In this section—

"associated donation" has the same meaning as in section 809ZM;

"linked person" has the same meaning as in section 809ZJ;

"the relevant arrangements" has the same meaning as in section 809ZM.][1]

Commentary—*Simon's Taxes* **C5.127AA**.
Amendments—[1]   This Chapter inserted by FA 2011 s 27, Sch 3 para 1 with effect in relation to relievable charity donations made on or after 1 April 2011.

[809ZO Income tax charge where payment of trust income to charity

(1) Income tax is charged under this section if—

(*a*) a person makes a tainted donation in a tax year,

(*b*) the tainted donation or an associated donation is a payment by the trustees of a settlement of income arising under the settlement ("the trust donation"), and

(*c*) the charity to which the trust donation is made is entitled to claim a repayment of tax in respect of that donation.

(2) The amount of the tax charged under this section is equal to the amount of the repayment of tax which the charity is entitled to claim in respect of the trust donation (whether or not such a claim is made).

(3) Each of the persons mentioned in subsection (4) is liable for any tax charged under this section, and the liability of those persons is joint and several.

(4) The persons are—

(*a*) the trustees of the settlement who made the trust donation,

(*b*) if different, the donor in respect of the tainted donation,

(*c*) if section 628 or 630 of ITTOIA 2005 (gifts from settlor-interested trusts etc) applies in relation to the income out of which the trust donation is made, the settlor in relation to the settlement,

(*d*) each potentially advantaged person under the relevant arrangements relating to the tainted donation,

(*e*) any beneficiary of the settlement who is party to those arrangements, and

(*f*) any charity to which the trust donation or (if different) the tainted donation is made, or any connected charity, which falls within subsection (5).

(5) A charity falls within this subsection if—

(*a*) the charity is or was party to the relevant arrangements relating to the tainted donation, and

(*b*) the charity was aware, at the time it entered into those arrangements, that a linked person was entering (or had entered or was likely to enter) into the arrangements in circumstances falling within Condition B in section 809ZJ.

(6) No liability to income tax arises under this section in respect of a repayment of tax if that repayment is itself repaid to the Commissioners for Her Majesty's Revenue and Customs under any other provision of the Tax Acts.

(7) In this section—

"associated donation" has the same meaning as in section 809ZM;

"linked person" has the same meaning as in section 809ZJ;

"the relevant arrangements" has the same meaning as in section 809ZM;

"settlement" and "settlor" have the same meaning as in Chapter 5 of Part 5 of ITTOIA 2005 (see section 620 of that Act).][1]

Commentary—*Simon's Taxes* **C5.127AA**.

Amendments—[1]   This Chapter inserted by FA 2011 s 27, Sch 3 para 1 with effect in relation to relievable charity donations made on or after 1 April 2011.

[Supplementary

809ZP Connected charities

For the purposes of this Chapter, a "connected charity" in relation to another charity means a charity which is connected with that other charity in a matter relating to the structure, administration or control of either charity.][1]

Commentary—*Simon's Taxes* **C5.127AA**.
Amendments—[1]   This Chapter inserted by FA 2011 s 27, Sch 3 para 1 with effect in relation to relievable charity donations made on or after 1 April 2011.

[809ZQ Connected persons

(1) Section 993 (meaning of "connected" persons) applies for the purposes of this Chapter—
    (a) subject to section 809ZP, and
    (b) as if, after subsection (7) there were inserted the provision in subsection (2).
(2) That provision is—
"(8) A person who is a beneficiary of a settlement is connected with—
    (a) a person in the capacity as trustee of the settlement, and
    (b) the settlor in relation to the settlement.
(9) For the purposes of this section—
    [(a) two people living together as if they were a married couple or civil partners are treated as if they were spouses or civil partners of each other, and][2]
    (c) "close company" includes a company that would be a close company if it were resident in the United Kingdom."][1]

Commentary—*Simon's Taxes* **C5.127AA**.
Amendments—[1]   This Chapter inserted by FA 2011 s 27, Sch 3 para 1 with effect in relation to relievable charity donations made on or after 1 April 2011.
[2]   In sub-s (2), in the inserted sub-s (9), paras (a) and (b) substituted by the Civil Partnership (Opposite-sex Couples) Regulations, SI 2019/1458 reg 29(1), (3) with effect from 2 December 2019.

[809ZR Minor definitions

(1) In this Chapter—
    "arrangements" includes any scheme, arrangement or understanding of any kind, whether or not legally enforceable, involving a single transaction or two or more transactions;
    "charity" includes a registered club within the meaning of section 658(6) of CTA 2010 (meaning of "community amateur sports club" and "registered club").
(2) In this Chapter, in the case of a charitable trust, references to a charity being entitled to a repayment of, or liable to pay, tax are to be read as references to the trustees of the trust being so entitled or liable.][1]

Commentary—*Simon's Taxes* **C5.127AA**.
Amendments—[1]   This Chapter inserted by FA 2011 s 27, Sch 3 para 1 with effect in relation to relievable charity donations made on or after 1 April 2011.

PART 14

INCOME TAX LIABILITY: MISCELLANEOUS RULES

[CHAPTER A1

REMITTANCE BASIS

Introduction

809A Overview of Chapter

This Chapter provides for an alternative basis of charge in the case of individuals who are not domiciled in the United Kingdom . . . ².]¹

Commentary—*Simon's Taxes* **E4.1319, E4.15, E1.1436A.**
Amendments—¹   Chapter 1A, ss 809A–809Z7 inserted by FA 2008 s 25, Sch 7 para 1 with effect for the tax year 2008–09 and subsequent tax years.
²   Words "or are not ordinarily UK resident" repealed by FA 2013 s 219, Sch 46 paras 1, 2 with effect in relation to an individual's foreign income and gains for the tax year 2013–14 or any subsequent tax year, subject to savings in FA 2013 Sch 46 para 26.

[Application of remittance basis

809B Claim for remittance basis to apply

(1) This section applies to an individual for a tax year if the individual—

(*a*) is UK resident [for that year]²,
(*b*) is not domiciled in the United Kingdom in that year   . . . ³, and
(*c*) makes a claim under this section for that year.

[(1A) Section 835BA (deemed domicile) applies for the purposes of subsection (1)(*b*).]⁴

(2) . . . ³

(3) Sections 42 and 43 of TMA 1970 (procedure and time limit for making claims), except section 42(1A) of that Act, apply in relation to a claim under this section as they apply in relation to a claim for relief.]¹

Commentary—*Simon's Taxes* **C1.603, E6.324–E6.332, E5.308** .
HMRC Manuals—Employment-Related Securities Manual ERSM160500 (new rules for general earnings).
ERSM160825 (conditions for non-domiciled employees).
ERSM160845 (conditions for not- ordinarily resident employees).
ERSM160860 (non-resident year).
ERSM160910 (just and reasonable override).
Residence, Domicile and Remittance Basis Manual RDRM31220 (using the remittance basis – automatic versus claim).
RDRM32010 (remittance basis: who can claim - status conditions).
Amendments—¹   Chapter A1, ss 809A–809Z7 inserted by FA 2008 s 25, Sch 7 para 1 with effect for the tax year 2008–09 and subsequent tax years.
²   Words in sub-s (1)(*a*) substitutedby FA 2013 s 218, Sch 45 para 152(1), (2) with effect from 17 July 2013
³   In sub-s (1)(*b*), words "or is not ordinarily UK resident in that year" repealed and sub-s (2) repealed by FA 2013 s 219, Sch 46 paras 1, 3 with effect in relation to an individual's foreign income and gains for the tax year 2013–14 or any subsequent tax year, subject to savings in FA 2013 Sch 46 para 26.
⁴   Sub-s (1A) inserted by F(No 2)A 2017 s 29(2), Sch 8 paras 11, 14(1), (2) with effect in relation to the tax year 2017–18 and subsequent tax years, subject to F(No 2)A 2017 Sch 8 paras 15, 16.

[809C Claim for remittance basis by long-term UK resident: nomination of foreign income and gains to which section 809H(2) is to apply

(1) This section applies to an individual for a tax year if the individual—

(*a*) is aged 18 or over in that year, and
[(*b*) meets . . . ⁵ the 12-year residence test or the 7-year residence test for that year.]³

(*1ZA*) *An individual meets the 17-year residence test for a tax year if the individual has been UK resident in at least 17 of the 20 tax years immediately preceding that year.*⁵

[(1A) An individual meets the 12-year residence test for a tax year if the individual—

[(*a*) *does not meet the 17-year residence test for that year, but*⁵
(*b*) has been UK resident in at least 12 of the 14 tax years immediately preceding that year.]⁴

(1B) An individual meets the 7-year residence test for a tax year if the individual—

(*a*) does not meet . . . ⁵ the 12-year residence test for that year, but
(*b*) has been UK resident in at least 7 of the 9 tax years immediately preceding that year.]³

(2) A claim under section 809B by the individual for that year must contain a nomination of the income or chargeable gains of the individual for that year to which section 809H(2) is to apply.

(3) The income or chargeable gains nominated must be part (or all) of the individual's foreign income and gains for that year.

(4) The income and chargeable gains nominated must be such that the relevant tax increase does not exceed[—

(*za*) *for an individual who meets the 17-year residence test for that year, £90,000;*⁵
(*a*) for an individual who meets the 12-year residence test for that year, [£60,000]⁴;
(*b*) for an individual who meets the 7-year residence test for that year, £30,000.]³

(5) "The relevant tax increase" is—

(a) the total amount of income tax and capital gains tax payable by the individual for that year, minus

(b) the total amount of income tax and capital gains tax that would be payable by the individual for that year apart from section 809H(2).

[(5A) The references to income tax in subsection (5) do not include income tax under section 424 (gift aid).][2]

(6) See section 809Z7 for the meaning of an individual's foreign income and gains for a tax year.][1]

Commentary—*Simon's Taxes* **E6.324**.

HMRC Manuals—Residence, Domicile and Remittance Basis Manual RDRM32210 (long-term residents and the remittance basis charge - overview).

RDRM32220 (counting years of UK residence (seven out of nine)).

RDRM32310 (nomination of foreign income and gains).

Amendments—[1]　Chapter A1, ss 809A–809Z7 inserted by FA 2008 s 25, Sch 7 para 1 with effect for the tax year 2008–09 and subsequent tax years.

[2]　Sub-s (5A) inserted by FA 2009 s 51, Sch 27 para 2 with effect for the tax year 2008–09 and subsequent tax years.

[3]　Sub-s (1)(b) substituted; sub-s (4)(a), (b) substituted; and sub-ss (1A), (1B) inserted; by FA 2012 s 47, Sch 12 paras 1, 2 with effect for the tax year 2012–13 and subsequent tax years.

[4]　In sub-s (1B)(a), words inserted, and in sub-s (4)(a), figure substituted by FA 2015 s 24(1), (2) with effect for the tax year 2015–16 and subsequent tax years.

[5]　In sub-s (1)(b), words "the 17-year residence test," repealed, in sub-s (1B)(a), words "the 17-year residence test or" repealed, and sub-ss (1ZA), (1A)(a), (4)(za) repealed, by F(No 2)A 2017 s 29(2), Sch 8 paras 11, 14(1), (3) with effect in relation to the tax year 2017–18 and subsequent tax years, subject to F(No 2)A 2017 Sch 8 paras 15, 16.

[809D Application of remittance basis without claim where unremitted foreign income and gains under £2,000

(1) This section applies to an individual for a tax year if—

(a) the individual is UK resident [for that year][3],

(b) the individual is not domiciled in the United Kingdom in that year . . . , and[4]

(c) the amount of the individual's unremitted foreign income and gains for that year is less than £2,000

[unless condition A or condition B is met][2].

[(1A) Condition A is that . . . [4] conditions A to F in section 828B are met.

(1B) Condition B is that the individual gives notice in a return under section 8 of TMA 1970 that this section is not to apply in relation to the individual for that year.][2]

(2) The amount of an individual's "unremitted" foreign income and gains for a tax year is—

(a) the total amount of what would (if this section applied) be the individual's foreign income and gains for that year, minus

(b) the total amount of those income and gains that are remitted to the United Kingdom in that year.][1]

Commentary—*Simon's Taxes* **E6.324–E6.332**.

HMRC Manuals—Residence, Domicile and Remittance Basis Manual RDRM31190 (remittance basis users below the £2,000 threshold, with examples).

RDRM32105 (exceptions to the claim requirements - overview).

RDRM32135 (exception to rule, with example).

RDRM32260 (long-term UK residents, with example).

RDRM32110 (un-remitted foreign income and gains below £2,000 threshold).

Amendments—[1]　Chapter A1, ss 809A–809Z7 inserted by FA 2008 s 25, Sch 7 para 1 with effect for the tax year 2008–09 and subsequent tax years.

[2]　In sub-s (1) words at the end inserted, and sub-ss (1A), (1B) inserted, by FA 2009 s 51, Sch 27 para 3 with effect for the tax year 2008–09 and subsequent tax years.

[3]　Words in sub-s (1)(a) substituted by FA 2013 s 218, Sch 45 para 152(1), (3) with effect from 17 July 2013.

[4]　In sub-s (1)(b) words "or is not ordinarily UK resident in that year" repealed, and in sub-s (1A) words "the individual is not domiciled in the United Kingdom in that year and" repealed, by FA 2013 s 219, Sch 46 paras 1, 4 with effect in relation to an individual's foreign income and gains for the tax year 2013–14 or any subsequent tax year, subject to savings in FA 2013 Sch 46 para 26.

[809E Application of remittance basis without claim: other cases

(1) This section applies to an individual for a tax year if—

(a) the individual is UK resident [for that year][3],

(b) the individual is not domiciled in the United Kingdom in that year . . . ,[4]

[(c) for that year the individual either has no UK income or gains or has no UK income and gains other than taxed investment income not exceeding £100,][2]

(d) no relevant income or gains are remitted to the United Kingdom in that year, and

(e) either—

(i) the individual has been UK resident in not more than 6 of the 9 tax years immediately preceding that year, or

(ii) the individual is under 18 throughout that year

[unless the individual gives notice in a return under section 8 of TMA 1970 that this section is not to apply in relation to the individual for that year][2].

ITA 2007

[(1A) Section 835BA (deemed domicile) applies for the purposes of subsection (1)(*b*).][5]

(2) For the purposes of subsection (1)(*c*) the individual's "UK income and gains" for the tax year are the individual's income and chargeable gains for that year other than what would (if this section applied) be the individual's foreign income and gains for that year.

[(2A) For the purposes of subsection (1)(*c*) "taxed investment income" means UK income or gains consisting of payments within section 946 from which a sum representing income tax has been deducted.][2]

(3) For the purposes of subsection (1)(*d*) "relevant" income and gains are—

    (*a*) what would (if this section applied) be the individual's foreign income and gains for the tax year mentioned in subsection (1), and

    (*b*) the individual's foreign income and gains for every other tax year for which section 809B or 809D or this section applies to the individual.][1]

Commentary—*Simon's Taxes* E6.324–E6.332, E5.308 .
HMRC Manuals—Residence, Domicile and Remittance Basis Manual RDRM31410–31420 (transitional provisions).
RDRM31450 (relevant foreign income).
RDRM32140 (accessing the remittance basis: exceptions to the claim requirements: application of remittance basis without claim - other cases).
RDRM32105 (exceptions to the claim requirements).
RDRM32520 (temporary non residents: qualifying conditions).
RDRM32510 (temporary non residents: relevant foreign income).
Amendments—[1]   Chapter A1, ss 809A–809Z7 inserted by FA 2008 s 25, Sch 7 para 1 with effect for the tax year 2008–09 and
    subsequent tax years.
    In subs (3)(*b*), the reference to a tax year for which s 809B, 809D or 809E applies to an individual includes a tax year (not
    later than 2007–08) in which the individual was UK resident but was not domiciled or ordinarily resident in the UK. In relation
    to such a tax year, the reference to the individual's foreign income and gains only includes the individual's relevant foreign
    income if the individual made a claim under ITTOIA 2005 s 831 for the year, or TA 1988 s 65(5) applied in relation to the
    individual for the year (FA 2008 Sch 7 para 85).
[2]   Sub-s (1)(*c*) substituted, words at the end of sub-s (1) inserted, and sub-s (2A) inserted, by FA 2009 s 51, Sch 27 para 4 with
    effect for the tax year 2008–09 and subsequent tax years.
[3]   Words in sub-s (1)(*a*) substituted by FA 2013 s 218, Sch 45 para 152(1), (4) with effect from 17 July 2013.
[4]   In sub-s (1)(*b*) words "or is not ordinarily UK resident in that year" repealed by FA 2013 s 219, Sch 46 paras 1, 5 with effect
    in relation to an individual's foreign income and gains for the tax year 2013–14 or any subsequent tax year, subject to savings
    in FA 2013 Sch 46 para 26.
[5]   Sub-s (1A) inserted by F(No 2)A 2017 s 29(2), Sch 8 paras 11, 14(1), (4) with effect in relation to the tax year 2017–18 and
    subsequent tax years, subject to F(No 2)A 2017 Sch 8 paras 15, 16.

[Effect of section 809B, 809D or 809E applying

809F Effect on what is chargeable

(1) This section applies if section 809B, 809D or 809E applies to an individual for a tax year.

(2) The individual's relevant foreign earnings for that year are charged in accordance with section 22 or 26 of ITEPA 2003.

(3) The individual's relevant foreign income for that year is charged in accordance with section 832 of ITTOIA 2005.

(4) [The][3] individual's foreign chargeable gains for that year are charged in accordance with [paragraph 1 of Schedule 1 to TCGA 1992][4].

(5) For the effect on amounts which count as employment income of the individual under certain provisions of Part 7 of ITEPA 2003 (employment-related securities), see Chapter 5A of Part 2 of that Act.

[(5A) For the effect on amounts which count as employment income under Chapter 2 of Part 7A of ITEPA 2003, see sections 554Z9 to 554Z11 of that Act.][2]

(6) Nothing in this section applies in relation to nominated income or chargeable gains (see section 809H).][1]

Commentary—*Simon's Taxes* E6.324.
HMRC Manuals—Residence, Domicile and Remittance Basis Manual RDRM31110 (nominated income or gains).
Amendments—[1]   Chapter A1, ss 809A–809Z7 inserted by FA 2008 s 25, Sch 7 para 1 with effect for the tax year 2008–09 and
    subsequent tax years.
[2]   Sub-s (5A) inserted by FA 2011 s 26, Sch 2 paras 40, 41 with effect in relation to relevant steps taken on or after 6 April 2011,
    subject to transitional provisions in FA 2011 Sch 2 paras 53–59.
[3]   In sub-s (4) word substituted for words "If the individual is not domiciled in the United Kingdom in that year, the" by FA
    2013 s 219, Sch 46 para 22 with effect in relation to an individual's foreign income and gains for the tax year 2013–14 or any
    subsequent tax year, subject to transitional provisions in FA 2013 Sch 46 para 26.
[4]   In sub-s (4) words substituted for words "section 12 of TCGA 1992" by FA 2019 s 13, Sch 1 paras 99, 102 with effect for
    capital gains tax purposes for the tax year 2019–20 and subsequent tax years, and for corporation tax purposes for accounting
    periods beginning on or after 6 April 2019. These amendments also have effect for corporation tax purposes in relation to
    disposals made on or after 6 April 2019 (whether in their application to accounting periods beginning on, and ending on or
    after, that date or to later accounting periods). See also transitional provisions in FA 2019 Sch 1 paras 121–126.

809G Claim for remittance basis: effect on allowances etc

(1) This section applies if section 809B (claim for remittance basis to apply) applies to an individual for a tax year.

(2) For that year, the individual is not entitled to—

    (*a*) any allowance under Chapter 2 of Part 3 (personal allowance and blind person's allowance),

    (*b*) any tax reduction under Chapter 3 of that Part (tax reductions for married couples and civil partners), . . . [3]

    [(*ba*) any tax reduction under Chapter 3A of that Part (transferable tax allowance for married couples and civil partners), or][3]

    (*c*) any relief under section 457 [or 458][2] (payments for life insurance etc).

(3) See also [section 1K(6)][4] of TCGA 1992 (no annual exempt amount for chargeable gains).][1]

Commentary—*Simon's Taxes* **E6.324, E6.125**.

HMRC Manuals—Residence, Domicile and Remittance Basis Manual RDRM32040 (loss of personal allowances and annual exempt amount with examples).

RDRM32050 (loss of personal allowances - exceptions for dual residents).

Amendments—[1]   Chapter A1, ss 809A–809Z7 inserted by FA 2008 s 25, Sch 7 para 1 with effect for the tax year 2008–09 and subsequent tax years.

[2]   In sub-s (2)(*c*) words substituted for words ", 458 or 459" by FA 2012 s 227, Sch 39 para 32(2)(*d*) with effect for the tax year 2013–14 and subsequent tax years.

[3]   In sub-s (2), word "or" following para (*b*) repealed and para (*ba*) inserted, by FA 2014 s 11(8) with effect for the tax year 2015–16 and subsequent tax years.

[4]   In sub-s (3) words substituted for words "section 3(1A)" by FA 2019 s 13, Sch 1 paras 99, 103 with effect for capital gains tax purposes for the tax year 2019–20 and subsequent tax years, and for corporation tax purposes for accounting periods beginning on or after 6 April 2019. These amendments also have effect for corporation tax purposes in relation to disposals made on or after 6 April 2019 (whether in their application to accounting periods beginning on, and ending on or after, that date or to later accounting periods). See also transitional provisions in FA 2019 Sch 1 paras 121–126.

809H Claim for remittance basis by long-term UK resident: charge

(1) This section applies if—

    (*a*) section 809B (claim for remittance basis to apply) applies to an individual for a tax year ("the relevant tax year"),

    (*b*) the individual is aged 18 or over in the relevant tax year, and

    [(*c*) the individual meets . . . [6] the 12-year residence test or the 7-year residence test for the relevant tax year.][3]

[(1A) See section [809C . . . [6], (1A)][4] and (1B) for when an individual meets . . . [6] the 12-year residence test or the 7-year residence test for a tax year.][3]

(2) Income tax is charged on nominated income, and capital gains tax is charged on nominated chargeable gains, as if section 809B did not apply to the individual for the relevant tax year (and neither did section 809D).

(3) "Nominated" income or chargeable gains means income or chargeable gains nominated under section 809C in the individual's claim under section 809B for the relevant tax year.

[(3A) If the individual is a Scottish taxpayer for the relevant tax year, the individual is to be treated for the purpose of calculating income tax charged by virtue of subsection (2) as if the individual were not a Scottish taxpayer for that year.][5]

[(3B) If the individual is a Welsh taxpayer for the relevant tax year, the individual is to be treated for the purpose of calculating income tax charged by virtue of subsection (2) as if the individual were not a Welsh taxpayer for that year.][7]

(4) If the relevant tax increase would otherwise be less than [the applicable amount][3], subsection (2) has effect as if—

    (*a*) in addition to the income and gains actually nominated under section 809C in the individual's claim under section 809B for the relevant tax year, an amount of income had been nominated so as to make the relevant tax increase equal to [the applicable amount][3], and

    (*b*) the individual's income for that year were such that such a nomination could have been made (if that is not the case).

(5) "The relevant tax increase" is—

    (*a*) the total amount of income tax and capital gains tax payable by the individual for the relevant tax year, minus

    (*b*) the total amount of income tax and capital gains tax that would be payable by the individual for the relevant tax year apart from subsection (2).

[(5A) The references to income tax in subsection (5) do not include income tax under section 424 (gift aid).][2]

[(5B) "The applicable amount" is—

    [(*za*) if the individual meets the 17-year residence test for the relevant tax year, £90,000;][6]

    (*a*) if the individual meets the 12-year residence test for the relevant tax year, [£60,000][4];

    (*b*) if the individual meets the 7-year residence test for the relevant tax year, £30,000.][3]

(6) Nothing in subsection (4) affects what is regarded, for the purposes of section 809I or 809J, as nominated under section 809C.][1]

Commentary—*Simon's Taxes* **E6.324H, E6.324** .

HMRC Manuals—Residence, Domicile and Remittance Basis Manual RDRM32310 (nomination of foreign income and gains - overview).

RDRM32360 (insufficient nomination - automatic additional nomination of income under ITA07 s809H(4)).

RDRM32370 (example - insufficient nomination).

Amendments—[1]   Chapter A1, ss 809A–809Z7 inserted by FA 2008 s 25, Sch 7 para 1 with effect for the tax year 2008–09 and subsequent tax years.

[2]   Sub-s (5A) inserted by FA 2009 s 51, Sch 27 para 5 with effect for the tax year 2008–09 and subsequent tax years.

[3]   Sub-s (1)(c) substituted; words in sub-s (4) substituted; and sub-s (1A), (5B) inserted; by FA 2012 s 47, Sch 12 paras 1, 3 with effect for the tax year 2012–13 and subsequent tax years.

[4]   In sub-ss (1)(c), (1A) words inserted, and in sub-s (5B) para (za) inserted and in para (a) figure substituted for "£50,000", by FA 2015 s 24(1), (3) with effect for the tax year 2015–16 and subsequent tax years.

[5]   Sub-s (3A), which was to have been as prospectively inserted by the Scotland Act 2012 s 26(1), (4) with effect from a date to be appointed (see note above), substituted by FA 2014 s 296, Sch 38 paras 1, 8 with effect in relation to the tax year 2016–17 (the tax year appointed by the Treasury under the Scotland Act 2012 s 25(5) by virtue of SI 2015/2000) and subsequent tax years.

[6]   In sub-s (1)(c), words "the 17-year residence test," repealed, in sub-s (1A)(a), reference "(1ZA)" repealed and words "the 17-year residence test" repealed, and sub-s (5B)(za) repealed, by F(No 2)A 2017 s 29(2), Sch 8 paras 11, 14(1), (5) with effect in relation to the tax year 2017–18 and subsequent tax years, subject to F(No 2)A 2017 Sch 8 paras 15, 16.

[7]   Sub-s (3B) inserted by the Wales Act 2014 s 9(1), (8). Wales Act 2014 s 9 comes into force on 24 July 2018 and has effect in relation to the tax year 2019–20 (by virtue of SI 2018/892 arts 3, 5, 6). 2019–20 is appointed as the first tax year in relation to which a Welsh rate resolution may be made by the National Assembly for Wales under GOWA 2006 s 116D (SI 2018/892 art 6).

[809I Remittance basis charge: income and gains treated as remitted

(1) This section applies if—

    (a) any of an individual's nominated income and gains is remitted to the United Kingdom in a tax year, . . . [2]

    (b) any of the individual's remittance basis income and gains has not been remitted to the United Kingdom in or before that year[, and

    [the (c) £10 test is met for that year.][2]

(2) Income tax and capital gains tax are charged, for that year and subsequent tax years, as if the income and chargeable gains treated under section 809J as remitted to the United Kingdom by the individual in that tax year had been so remitted (and income and chargeable gains of the individual that were actually remitted in that year had not been).

(3) An individual's "nominated income and gains" are the total income and chargeable gains nominated by the individual under section 809C for the tax year mentioned in subsection (1)(a) or any earlier tax year [(each such year for which the individual has made a nomination under that section being referred to as a "nomination year")][2].

(4) An individual's "remittance basis income and gains" are the foreign income and gains of the individual for all the tax years (up to and including the tax year mentioned in subsection (1)(a)) for which section 809B, 809D or 809E applies to the individual, apart from the individual's nominated income and gains.][1]

[(5) The £10 test is met for the tax year mentioned in subsection (1)(a) ("year X") if, taking each nomination year separately, the cumulative total as respects at least one nomination year exceeds £10.

(6) In relation to a nomination year—

    (a) "the cumulative total" means the sum, for all the tax years in aggregate up to and including year X, of the amounts of relevant income and gains remitted to the United Kingdom in those tax years from that nomination year, and

    (b) "relevant income and gains" means the income and chargeable gains nominated by the individual under section 809C for that nomination year.][2]

Commentary—*Simon's Taxes* **E6.324H**.

HMRC Manuals—Residence, Domicile and Remittance Basis Manual RDRM35120 (application of ordering rules to remittances of nominated income or gains).

RDRM35140 (remittances of nominated income or gains - miscellaneous).

RDRM35115 (simplification of the treatment of nominated income - ITA07/S809i).

Amendments—[1]   Chapter A1, ss 809A–809Z7 inserted by FA 2008 s 25, Sch 7 para 1 with effect for the tax year 2008–09 and subsequent tax years.

[2]   Sub-ss (1)(c) and preceding word "and", (5), (6), and words in sub-s (3), inserted, and word "and" at the end of sub-s (1)(a) repealed, by FA 2012 s 47, Sch 12 paras 1, 20 with effect for determining whether this section applies for the tax year 2012–13 or any subsequent tax year.

[809J Section 809I: order of remittances

(1) If section 809I applies, the following steps are to be taken for the purpose of determining the income or gains treated in a tax year ("the relevant tax year") as remitted to the United Kingdom by the individual.

Step 1 Find the total amount of—

    (a) the individual's nominated income and gains, and

    (b) the individual's remittance basis income and gains,

that have been remitted to the United Kingdom in the relevant tax year.

   This amount is "the relevant amount".

Step 2 Find the amount of foreign income and gains of the individual for the relevant tax year (other than income or chargeable gains nominated under section 809C) that is within each of the categories of income and gains in paragraphs (*a*) to (*h*) of subsection (2).

If none of sections 809B, 809D and 809E apply to the individual for that year, treat those amounts as nil (and accordingly go to step 6).

Step 3 Find the earliest paragraph for which the amount determined under step 2 is not nil.

If that amount does not exceed the relevant amount, treat the individual as having remitted the income or gains within that paragraph (and for that tax year).

Otherwise, treat the individual as having remitted the relevant proportion of each kind of income or gains within that paragraph (and for that tax year).

"The relevant proportion" is the relevant amount divided by the amount determined under step 2 for that paragraph.

Step 4 Reduce the relevant amount by the amount taken into account under step 3.

Step 5 If the relevant amount (as reduced under step 4) is not nil, start again at step 3.

In step 3, read the reference to the earliest paragraph of the kind mentioned there as a reference to the earliest such paragraph which has not previously been taken into account under that step.

Step 6 If the relevant amount (as reduced) is not nil once steps 3 to 5 have been undertaken in relation to all paragraphs of subsection (2) for which the amount determined under step 2 is not nil, start again at step 2.

In step 2, read the reference to the foreign income and gains of the individual for the relevant tax year as a reference to such of the foreign income and gains of the individual for the appropriate tax year as had not been remitted by the beginning of the relevant tax year.

"The appropriate tax year" is the latest tax year which is—
  (*a*) before the last tax year for which step 2 has been undertaken, and
  (*b*) a tax year for which section 809B, 809D or 809E applies to the individual.
(2) The kinds of income and gains are—
  (*a*) relevant foreign earnings (other than those subject to a foreign tax),
  (*b*) foreign specific employment income (other than income subject to a foreign tax),
  (*c*) relevant foreign income (other than income subject to a foreign tax),
  (*d*) foreign chargeable gains (other than gains subject to a foreign tax),
  (*e*) relevant foreign earnings subject to a foreign tax,
  (*f*) foreign specific employment income subject to a foreign tax,
  (*g*) relevant foreign income subject to a foreign tax, and
  (*h*) foreign chargeable gains subject to a foreign tax.
(3) In this section the individual's "nominated income and gains" are the total income and chargeable gains nominated by the individual under section 809C for the relevant tax year or any earlier tax year.
(4) In step 1 of subsection (1) the individual's "remittance basis income and gains" are the foreign income and gains of the individual for all the tax years (up to and including the relevant tax year) for which section 809B, 809D or 809E applies to the individual, apart from the individual's nominated income and gains.
(5) In step 6 of subsection (1) the reference to income or gains being remitted is—
  (*a*) as respects any tax year before section 809I applies, to income or gains being remitted to the
          United Kingdom, and
  (*b*) as respects any tax year in relation to which that section applies, to income or gains treated
          under this section as so remitted.
(6) In subsection (2) "foreign tax" means any tax chargeable under the law of a territory outside the United Kingdom.]¹

Commentary—*Simon's Taxes* **E6.324H.**
HMRC Manuals—Residence, Domicile and Remittance Basis Manual RDRM35130 (order of remittances). RDRM35160 (ordering rules - example).
Amendments—¹   Chapter 1A, ss 809A–809Z7 inserted by FA 2008 s 25, Sch 7 para 1 with effect for the tax year 2008–09 and subsequent tax years.

[Remittance of income and gains: introduction

809K Sections 809L to 809Z6: introduction

(1) Sections 809L to 809Z6 apply for the purposes of—
  (*a*) this Chapter,
  (*b*) sections 22 and 26 of ITEPA 2003 (relevant foreign earnings charged on remittance basis),
  [(*c*) Chapter 5B of Part 2 of that Act (taxable specific income from employment-related securities
          etc: internationally mobile employees),]⁴
  [(*ca*) sections 554Z9 to 554Z11 of that Act (employment income provided through third parties
          charged on remittance basis),]².
  (*d*) section 832 of ITTOIA 2005 (relevant foreign income charged on remittance basis), and
  [(*e*) Schedule 1 to TCGA 1992 (UK resident individuals not domiciled in UK).]⁵
(2) Those sections—

(a) explain what is meant by income or chargeable gains being "remitted to the United Kingdom" (sections 809L to 809O),

(b) provide for the calculation of the amount remitted (section 809P),

(c) contain rules for attributing transfers from mixed funds to particular kinds of income and capital (sections 809Q to 809S),

(d) contain supplementary provision for certain cases (sections 809T and 809U), and

(e) treat income or chargeable gains as not remitted to the United Kingdom in certain cases (sections [809UA]³ to 809Z6).]¹

Amendments—¹   Chapter A1, ss 809A–809Z7 inserted by FA 2008 s 25, Sch 7 para 1 with effect for the tax year 2008–09 and subsequent tax years.

²   Sub-s (1)(*ca*) inserted by FA 2011 s 26, Sch 2 paras 40, 42 with effect in relation to relevant steps taken on or after 6 April 2011, subject to transitional provisions in FA 2011 Sch 2 paras 53–59.

³   In sub-s (2)(*e*), reference substituted by FA 2013 s 21(1), (2) with effect in relation to payments on account made in respect of the tax year 2012–13 and subsequent tax years.

⁴   Sub-s (1)(*c*) substituted by FA 2014 s 52, Sch 9 para 29 with effect from 6 April 2015 in relation to employment-related securities and employment-related securities options irrespective of the date of acquisition, subject to any transitional provision or savings that the Treasury may make by regulations under FA 2014 Sch 9 para 49.

⁵   Sub-s (1)(*e*) substituted by FA 2019 s 13, Sch 1 paras 99, 104 with effect for capital gains tax purposes for the tax year 2019–20 and subsequent tax years, and for corporation tax purposes for accounting periods beginning on or after 6 April 2019. These amendments also have effect for corporation tax purposes in relation to disposals made on or after 6 April 2019 (whether in their application to accounting periods beginning on, and ending on or after, that date or to later accounting periods). See also transitional provisions in FA 2019 Sch 1 paras 121–126.

[Remittance of income and gains: meaning of "remitted to the United Kingdom"

809L Meaning of "remitted to the United Kingdom"

(1) An individual's income is, or chargeable gains are, "remitted to the United Kingdom" if—

(a) conditions A and B are met,

(b) condition C is met, or

(c) condition D is met.

(2) Condition A is that—

(a) money or other property is brought to, or received or used in, the United Kingdom by or for the benefit of a relevant person, or

(b) a service is provided in the United Kingdom to or for the benefit of a relevant person.

(3) Condition B is that—

(a) the property, service or consideration for the service is (wholly or in part) the income or chargeable gains,

(b) the property, service or consideration—

(i) derives (wholly or in part, and directly or indirectly) from the income or chargeable gains, and

(ii) in the case of property or consideration, is property of or consideration given by a relevant person,

(c) the income or chargeable gains are used outside the United Kingdom (directly or indirectly) in respect of a relevant debt, or

(d) anything deriving (wholly or in part, and directly or indirectly) from the income or chargeable gains is used as mentioned in paragraph (c).

(4) Condition C is that qualifying property of a gift recipient—

(a) is brought to, or received or used in, the United Kingdom, and is enjoyed by a relevant person,

(b) is consideration for a service that is enjoyed in the United Kingdom by a relevant person, or

(c) is used outside the United Kingdom (directly or indirectly) in respect of a relevant debt.

(5) Condition D is that property of a person other than a relevant person (apart from qualifying property of a gift recipient)—

(a) is brought to, or received or used in, the United Kingdom, and is enjoyed by a relevant person,

(b) is consideration for a service that is enjoyed in the United Kingdom by a relevant person, or

(c) is used outside the United Kingdom (directly or indirectly) in respect of a relevant debt,

in circumstances where there is a connected operation.

(6) In a case where subsection (4)(a) or (b) or (5)(a) or (b) applies to the importation or use of property, the income or chargeable gains are taken to be remitted at the time the property or service is first enjoyed by a relevant person by virtue of that importation or use.

(7) In this section "relevant debt" means a debt that relates (wholly or in part, and directly or indirectly) to—

(a) property falling within subsection (2)(a),

(b) a service falling within subsection (2)(b),

(c) qualifying property dealt with as mentioned in subsection (4)(a),

(d) a service falling within subsection (4)(b),

(e) qualifying property dealt with as mentioned in subsection (5)(a), or (*f*) a service falling within subsection (5)(*b*).

(8) . . . [2]

(9) The cases in which [property (including income or chargeable gains) is used in respect of a debt include cases where the property is][2] used to pay interest on the debt.

(10) This section is subject to sections 809V to 809Z6 (property treated as not remitted to the United Kingdom).][1]

Commentary—*Simon's Taxes* **E6.324C.**
HMRC Manuals—Employment Income Manual EIM40302 (meaning of "remitted to the United Kingdom").
Capital Gains Manual CG25341(remittance basis: meaning of remitted to the united kingdom: basic meaning).
CG25342 (remittance basis: meaning of remitted to the united kingdom: gifts of money and assets).
CG25343(remittance basis: meaning of remitted to the united kingdom: other reciprocal arrangements).
Employment Related Securities Manual ERSM161110 (ERSM161110 2015: what Is remittance).
ERSM162920 (what is remittance).
Residence, Domicile and Remittance Basis Manual RDRM31480–31500 (relevant persons and foreign income and gains and offshore loans: transitional provisions, with example).
RDRM33020–33040 (meaning of "remittance" and "relevant debt").
RDRM33100–33170 (details regarding Conditions A and B, with examples).
RDRM33210–33295 (detail regarding Condition C – gift recipients).
RDRM33410–33490 (Condition D details, with examples).
RDRM35010 (amounts remitted).
RDRM35020-35030 (remittances of foreign income or chargeable gains, with examples).
RDRM35040-35050 (remittances in respect of relevant debt).
RDRM35060-35070 (Condition C – examples of remittances).
RDRM35080 (example of Condition D remittance).
RDRM35210 (Conditions C and D and mixed funds).
Amendments—[1]   Chapter A1, ss 809A–809Z7 inserted by FA 2008 s 25, Sch 7 para 1 with effect for the tax year 2008–09 and subsequent tax years. [2] sub-s (8) repealed, and in sub-s (9) words substituted by FA 2009 s 51, Sch 27 para 6 with effect from 22 April 2009.

[809M Meaning of "relevant person"

(1) This section applies for the purposes of [this Chapter][5].
(2) A "relevant person" is—
   (*a*) the individual,
   (*b*) the individual's husband or wife,
   (*c*) the individual's civil partner,
   (*d*) a child or grandchild of a person falling within any of paragraphs (*a*) to (*c*), if the child or grandchild has not reached the age of 18,
   (*e*) a close company in which a person falling within any other paragraph of this subsection is a participator [or a company which is a 51% subsidiary of such a close company][2],
   (*f*) a company in which a person falling within any other paragraph of this subsection is a participator, and which would be a close company if it were resident in the United Kingdom, [or a company which is a 51% subsidiary of such a company,][4]
   (*g*) the trustees of a settlement of which a person falling within any other paragraph of this subsection is a beneficiary, or
   (*h*) a body connected with such a settlement.
(3) For that purpose—
   [(*a*) two people living together as if they were a married couple or civil partners are treated as if they were spouses or civil partners of each other,][6]
   (*c*) "close company" [is to be read in accordance with Chapter 2 of Part 10 of CTA 2010 (see in particular section 439 of that Act)][3],
   [(*ca*) "participator", in relation to a close company, means a person who is a participator in relation to the company for the purposes of [section 455 of CTA 2010 (see sections 454 and 455(5) of][3] that [Act) and, in relation to a company that would be a close company if it were resident in the United Kingdom, means a person who would be such a participator if it were a close company,][4],
   (*cb*) "51% subsidiary" has the same meaning as in the Corporation Tax Acts (see [Chapter 3 of Part 24 of CTA 2010][3]),][2]
   (*d*) "settlement" and "settlor" have the same meaning as in Chapter 2 of Part 9,
   (*e*) "beneficiary", in relation to a settlement, means any person who receives, or may receive, any benefit under or by virtue of the settlement,
   (*f*) "trustee" has the same meaning as in section 993 (see, in particular, section 994(3)), and
   (*g*) a body is "connected with" a settlement if the body falls within section 993(3)(*c*), (*d*), (*e*) or (*f*) as regards the settlement.][1]

Commentary—*Simon's Taxes* **E6.324C.**
HMRC Manuals—Residence, Domicile and Remittance Basis Manual RDRM33030 (further meaning of "relevant person").
Amendments—[1]   Chapter A1, ss 809A–809Z7 inserted by FA 2008 s 25, Sch 7 para 1 with effect for the tax year 2008–09 and subsequent tax years.
[2]   In sub-s (2)(*e*) words at the end inserted, and sub-s (3)(*ca*), (*cb*) inserted, by FA 2009 s 51, Sch 27 para 7 with effect from 22 April 2009.

[3]   In sub-s (3)(*c*), (*ca*), (*cb*) words substituted by CTA 2010 s 1177, Sch 1 para 552. CTA 2010 has effect for corporation tax purposes for accounting periods ending on or after 1 April 2010, and for income and capital gains tax purposes for the tax year 2010–11 and subsequent tax years.

[4]   In sub-s (2)(*f*) words inserted, and in sub-s (3)(*ca*) words substituted, by FA 2010 s 33. These amendments are treated as having come into force on 6 April 2010.

[5]   Words in sub-s (1) substituted by FA 2012 s 47, Sch 12 paras 1, 13 with effect where the relevant event (as defined in ITA 2007 s 809VA) or the ceasing to be exempt property (as defined in ITA 2007 s 809Y) occurs on or after 6 April 2012.

[6]   Sub-s (3)(a) and (b) substituted by the Civil Partnership (Opposite-sex Couples) Regulations, SI 2019/1458 reg 29(1), (4) with effect from 2 December 2019.

[809N Section 809L: gift recipients, qualifying property and enjoyment

(1) This section applies for the purposes of determining whether or not income or chargeable gains of an individual are remitted to the United Kingdom by virtue of condition C in section 809L.

(2) A "gift recipient" means a person, other than a relevant person, to whom the individual makes a gift of money or other property that—

    (*a*)   is income or chargeable gains of the individual, or

    (*b*)   derives (wholly or in part, and directly or indirectly) from income or chargeable gains of the individual.

(3) The question of whether or not a person is a relevant person is to be determined by reference to the time when a gift is made.

(4) But, if a person to whom a gift is made subsequently becomes a relevant person, the person ceases to be a gift recipient.

(5) The individual "makes a gift of" property if the individual disposes of the property—

    (*a*)   for no consideration, or

    (*b*)   for consideration less than the full consideration in money or money's worth that would be given if the disposal were by way of a bargain made at arm's length;

but, in a case falling in paragraph (b), the individual is to be taken to make a gift of only so much of the property as exceeds the consideration actually given.

(6) A reference to the individual making a gift of property includes a case where—

    (*a*)   the individual retains an interest in the property, or

    (*b*)   an interest, right or arrangement enables or entitles the individual to benefit from the property.

(7) "Qualifying property", in relation to a gift recipient, is—

    (*a*)   the property that the individual gave to the gift recipient,

    (*b*)   anything that derives (wholly or in part, and directly or indirectly) from that property, or

    (*c*)   any other property, but only if it is dealt with as mentioned in section 809L(4)(*a*), (*b*) or (*c*) by virtue of an operation which is effected—

       (i)   with reference to the gift of the property to the gift recipient, or

       (ii)   with a view to enabling or facilitating the gift of the property to the gift recipient to be made.

(8) In subsection (7)—

    (*a*)   the reference in paragraph (*b*) to anything deriving from property, and

    (*b*)   the reference in paragraph (*c*) to other property,

includes a thing, or property, that does not belong to the individual but which the individual is enabled or entitled to benefit from by virtue of any interest, right or arrangement.

(9) Enjoyment by a relevant person of property or a service is to be disregarded in any of these cases—

    (*a*)   if the property or service is enjoyed virtually to the entire exclusion of all relevant persons,

    (*b*)   if full consideration in money or money's worth is given by a relevant person for the enjoyment, or

    (*c*)   the property or service is enjoyed by relevant persons in the same way, and on the same terms, as it may be enjoyed by the general public or by a section of the general public.][1]

Commentary—*Simon's Taxes* **E6.324C**.

HMRC Manuals—Residence, Domicile and Remittance Basis Manual RDRM33230–33280 (detail regarding gift recipients, with examples).

Amendments—[1]   Chapter A1, ss 809A–809Z7 inserted by FA 2008 s 25, Sch 7 para 1 with effect for the tax year 2008–09 and subsequent tax years.

    This section has effect in relation to an individual's income and chargeable gains for the tax year 2007–08 or any earlier tax year as if—

    (a)   the reference in sub-s (2) to a relevant person were to the individual;

    (b)   sub-ss (3), (4) were omitted; and

    (c)   the references in sub-s (9) to a relevant person, all relevant persons, or relevant persons were to the individual (FA 2008 Sch 7 para 87).

[809O Section 809L: dealings where there is a connected operation

(1) This section applies for the purposes of determining whether or not income or chargeable gains of an individual are remitted to the United Kingdom by virtue of condition D in section 809L.

(2) For the purposes of section 809L(5), the question of whether or not the person whose property is dealt with as mentioned in paragraph (*a*), (*b*) or (*c*) of section 809L(5) is a relevant person is to be determined by reference to the time when the property is so dealt with.

(3) A "connected operation", in relation to property dealt with as mentioned in section 809L(5)(*a*), (*b*) or (*c*), means an operation which is effected—

    (*a*) with reference to a qualifying disposition, or

    (*b*) with a view to enabling or facilitating a qualifying disposition.

(4) A "qualifying disposition" is a disposition that—

    (*a*) is made by a relevant person,

    (*b*) is made to, or for the benefit of, the person whose property is dealt with as mentioned in section 809L(5)(*a*), (*b*) or (*c*), and

    (*c*) is a disposition of money or other property that is, or derives (wholly or in part, and directly or indirectly) from, income or chargeable gains of the individual.

(5) But a disposition of property is not a qualifying disposition if the disposition is, or is part of, the giving of full consideration in money or money's worth for the dealing that falls within section 809L(5)(*a*), (*b*) or (*c*).

(6) Enjoyment by a relevant person of property or a service is to be disregarded in any of these cases—

    (*a*) if the property or service is enjoyed virtually to the entire exclusion of all relevant persons,

    (*b*) if full consideration in money or money's worth is given by a relevant person for the enjoyment, or

    (*c*) the property or service is enjoyed by relevant persons in the same way, and on the same terms, as it may be enjoyed by the general public or by a section of the general public.][1]

Commentary—*Simon's Taxes* **E6.324C**.

HMRC Manuals—Residence, Domicile and Remittance Basis Manual RDRM33420–33490 (qualifying disposal and connected operation, with examples).

RDRM35080 (example of Condition D remittance).

Amendments—[1]   Chapter A1, ss 809A–809Z7 inserted by FA 2008 s 25, Sch 7 para 1 with effect for the tax year 2008–09 and subsequent tax years.

This section has effect in relation to an individual's income and chargeable gains for the tax year 2007–08 or any earlier tax year as if—

    (a)   sub-s (2) were omitted; and

    (b)   the references in sub-ss (4), (6) to a relevant person, all relevant persons, or relevant persons were to the individual (FA 2008 Sch 7 para 88).

[Remittance of income and gains: amount remitted

809P Section 809L: amount remitted

(1) The amount of income or chargeable gains remitted to the United Kingdom is to be determined as follows.

(2) If the property, service or consideration is the income or chargeable gains, the amount remitted is equal to the amount of the income or chargeable gains.

(3) If the property, service or consideration derives from the income or chargeable gains, the amount remitted is equal to the amount of income or chargeable gains from which the property, service or consideration derives.

(4) If the income or chargeable gains are used as mentioned in section 809L(3)(*c*), the amount remitted is equal to the amount of income or chargeable gains used; but this is subject to subsection (10).

(5) If anything deriving from the income or chargeable gains is used as mentioned in section 809L(3)(*c*), the amount remitted is equal to the amount of income or chargeable gains from which what is used derives; but this is subject to subsection (10).

(6) In a case falling within section 809L(4)(*a*) or (*b*), the amount remitted is equal to the amount of the relevant income or chargeable gains.

(7) In a case falling within section 809L(4)(*c*), the amount remitted is equal to the amount of the relevant income or chargeable gains; but this is subject to subsection (10).

(8) In a case falling within section 809L(5)(*a*) or (*b*), the amount remitted is equal to the amount of the income or chargeable gains referred to in section 809O(4)(*c*).

(9) In a case falling within section 809L(5)(*c*), the amount remitted is equal to the amount of the income or chargeable gains referred to in section 809O(4)(*c*); but this is subject to subsection (10).

(10) If the debt is only partly in respect of the property or service, the amount remitted is (if it would otherwise be greater) limited to the amount the debt would be if it were wholly in respect of the property or service.

(11) In subsections (6) and (7) "relevant income or chargeable gains" means—

    (*a*) if the qualifying property falls within section 809N(7)(*a*), the income or gains—

        (i) of which the qualifying property consists, or

        (ii) from which the qualifying property derives;

    (*b*) if the qualifying property falls within section 809N(7)(*b*), the income or gains—

        (i) of which the property given to the gift recipient consisted, or

    (ii) from which that property derived;

  (c) if the qualifying property falls within section 809N(7)(c), the income or gains—

    (i) of which the property given to the gift recipient consists, or

    (ii) from which that property derives.

(12) If the amount remitted (taken together with any amount previously remitted) would otherwise exceed the amount of the income or chargeable gains, the amount remitted is limited to the amount which (when taken together with any amount previously remitted) is equal to the amount of the income or chargeable gains.][1]

[(13) If the property forms part of a set only part of which is in the United Kingdom, the amount remitted is such portion of what it would have been had the complete set been brought to, or received or used in, the United Kingdom when the part was as is just and reasonable (having regard to the part of the set which is there).][2]

Commentary—Simon's Taxes **E6.327, C1.603**.

HMRC Manuals—Residence, Domicile and Remittance Basis Manual RDRM35040 and 35070 (remittances in respect of relevant debt, with examples).

RDRM35010 (quantification: remittances of cash or property).

Amendments—[1]   Chapter A1, ss 809A–809Z7 inserted by FA 2008 s 25, Sch 7 para 1 with effect for the tax year 2008–09 and subsequent tax years.

[2]   Sub-s (13) inserted by FA 2009 s 51, Sch 27 para 8 with effect from 22 April 2009.

[Remittance of income and gains: transfers from mixed funds

809Q Sections 809L and 809P: transfers from mixed funds

(1) This section applies for the purposes mentioned in subsection (2) where condition A in section 809L is met and—

  (a) the property or consideration for the service is (wholly or in part), or derives (wholly or in part, and directly or indirectly) from, a transfer from a mixed fund, or

  (b) a transfer from a mixed fund, or anything deriving (wholly or in part, and directly or indirectly) from such a transfer, is used as mentioned in section 809L(3)(c).

[(1A) But this section must be read subject to section 809RA.][2]

(2) The purposes referred to in subsection (1) are—

  (a) determining whether condition B in section 809L is met, and

  (b) if it is met, determining (under section 809P) the amount of income or chargeable gains remitted.

(3) The extent to which the transfer is of the individual's income or chargeable gains is to be determined as follows.

Step 1 For each of the categories of income and capital in paragraphs (a) to (i) of subsection (4), find (applying section 809R) the amount of income or capital of the individual for the relevant tax year in the mixed fund immediately before the transfer.

"The relevant tax year" is the tax year in which the transfer occurs.

Step 2 Find the earliest paragraph for which the amount determined under step 1 is not nil.

If that amount does not exceed the amount of the transfer, treat the transfer as containing the income or capital within that paragraph (and for that tax year).

Otherwise, treat the transfer as containing the relevant proportion of each kind of income or capital within that paragraph (and for that tax year).

"The relevant proportion" is the amount of the transfer divided by the amount determined under step 1 for that paragraph.

Step 3 Treat the amount of the transfer as reduced by the amount taken into account under step 2.

Step 4 If the amount of the transfer (as reduced under step 3) is not nil, start again at step 2.

In step 2, read the reference to the earliest paragraph of the kind mentioned there as a reference to the earliest such paragraph which has not previously been taken into account under that step in relation to the transfer.

Step 5 If the amount of the transfer (as reduced under step 3) is not nil once steps 2 and 3 have been undertaken in relation to all paragraphs of subsection (4) for which the amount determined under step 1 is not nil, start again at step 1.

In step 1, read the reference to the relevant tax year as a reference to the tax year immediately before the last tax year for which step 1 has been undertaken in relation to the transfer.

(4) The kinds of income and capital are—

  (a) employment income (other than income within paragraph (b), (c) or (f)),

  (b) relevant foreign earnings (other than income within paragraph (f)),

  (c) foreign specific employment income (other than income within paragraph (f)),

  (d) relevant foreign income (other than income within paragraph (g)),

  (e) foreign chargeable gains (other than chargeable gains within paragraph (h)),

  (f) employment income subject to a foreign tax,

  (g) relevant foreign income subject to a foreign tax,

  (h) foreign chargeable gains subject to a foreign tax, and

(*i*)   income or capital not within another paragraph of this subsection.

(5) In subsection (4) "foreign tax" means any tax chargeable under the law of a territory outside the United Kingdom.

(6) In this section "mixed fund" means money or other property which, immediately before the transfer, contains or derives from—

(*a*)   more than one of the kinds of income and capital mentioned in subsection (4), or

(*b*)   income or capital for more than one tax year.

(7) References in this section to the amount of the transfer include the market value of it.

(8) References in this section and section 809R to anything deriving from income or capital within paragraph (*i*) of subsection (4) do not include—

(*a*)   income or gains within any of paragraphs (*a*) to (*h*) of that subsection, or

(*b*)   anything deriving from such income or gains.]¹

Commentary—*Simon's Taxes* **E6.328, E5.308** .

HMRC Manuals—Employment Income Manual EIM40305 (transfers from an offshore 'mixed fund' account under SP1/09). Residence, Domicile and Remittance Basis Manual RDRM33510 (analysing the account).

RDRM33515 (detailed example involving joint accounts).

RDRM33580 (mixed fund remittances and interaction with capital gains rules, with example).

RDRM35220-35290 (remittances from mixed funds).

RDRM35410-35470 (compostition of mixed funds: offshore transfers and debt, with examples).

Capital Gains Manual CG25386 (remittance basis: mixed funds: ordering rules: details).

CG25387 (remittance basis: mixed funds: ordering rules: example).

Amendments—¹   Chapter A1, ss 809A–809Z7 inserted by FA 2008 s 25, Sch 7 para 1 with effect for the tax year 2008–09 and subsequent tax years.

Sections 809Q–809S do not apply for the purposes of determining whether income or chargeable gains for the tax year 2007–08 or any earlier tax year are remitted to the UK (or the amount of any such income or chargeable gains so remitted) (FA 2008 Sch 7 para 89).

²   Sub-s (1A) inserted by FA 2013 s 19, Sch 6 paras 4, 5 with effect in relation to transfers from a mixed fund that are made in the tax year 2013–14 or any subsequent tax year.

[809R Section 809Q: composition of mixed fund

(1) This section applies for the purposes of step 1 of section 809Q(3) (composition of mixed fund).

(2) Treat property which derives wholly or in part (and directly or indirectly) from an individual's income or capital for a tax year as consisting of or containing that income or capital.

(3) If a debt relating (wholly or in part, and directly or indirectly) to property is at any time satisfied (wholly or in part) by—

(*a*)   an individual's income or capital for a tax year, or

(*b*)   anything deriving (directly or indirectly) from such income or capital,

from that time treat the property as consisting of or containing the income or capital if and to the extent that it is just and reasonable to do so.

(4) Treat an offshore transfer from a mixed fund as containing the appropriate proportion of each kind of income or capital in the fund immediately before the transfer.

"The appropriate proportion" means the amount (or market value) of the transfer divided by the market value of the mixed fund immediately before the transfer.

(5) A transfer from a mixed fund is an "offshore transfer" for the purposes of subsection (4) if and to the extent that section 809Q does not apply in relation to it.

(6) Treat a transfer from a mixed fund as an "offshore transfer" (and section 809Q as not applying in relation to it, if it otherwise would do) if and to the extent that, at the end of a tax year in which it is made—

(*a*)   section 809Q does not apply in relation to it, and

(*b*)   on the basis of the best estimate that can reasonably be made at that time, section 809Q will not apply in relation to it.

(7) In this section 'mixed fund' means money or other property containing or deriving from—

(*a*)   more than one of the kinds of income and capital mentioned in section 809Q(4), or

(*b*)   income or capital for more than one tax year.

(8) If section 809Q applies in relation to part of a transfer, apply that section in relation to that part before applying subsection (4) in relation to the rest of the transfer.

(9) If section 809Q applies in relation to more than one transfer from a mixed fund, when undertaking step 1 in relation to the second or any subsequent transfer take into account the effect of step 2 of section 809Q(3) (composition of transfer) as it applied in relation to each earlier transfer.]¹

Commentary—*Simon's Taxes* **E6.328**.

HMRC Manuals—Residence, Domicile and Remittance Basis Manual RDRM33580 (example of an offshore transfer).

RDRM35230-35250 (remittances from mixed funds).

RDRM35410-35470 (composition of mixed funds: offshore transfers and debt, with examples).

Amendments—¹   Chapter A1, ss 809A–809Z7 inserted by FA 2008 s 25, Sch 7 para 1 with effect for the tax year 2008–09 and subsequent tax years.

Sections 809Q–809S do not apply for the purposes of determining whether income or chargeable gains for the tax year 2007–08 or any earlier tax year are remitted to the UK (or the amount of any such income or chargeable gains so remitted) (FA 2008 Sch 7 para 89).

[809RA Special mixed fund rules for certain employment cases

(1) This section applies if—

    (*a*) an individual has general earnings from an employment for a tax year,

    (*b*) those earnings include both general earnings within section 15(1) of ITEPA 2003 ("section 15(1) earnings") and general earnings within section 26(1) of that Act ("section 26(1) earnings"),

    (*c*) at least some of the section 15(1) earnings, or sums deriving (wholly or in part, and directly or indirectly) from at least some of the section 15(1) earnings, are paid into an account in that tax year at a time (a "relevant time") when the account is a qualifying account of the individual, and

    (*d*) at least some of the section 26(1) earnings, or sums deriving (wholly or in part, and directly or indirectly) from at least some of the section 26(1) earnings, are also paid into the account in that tax year at a relevant time.

(2) If this section applies, the composition of each transfer made from the account in that tax year at a relevant time is to be determined as follows—

Step 1 Suppose that all the condition A transfers made from the account in the tax year at a relevant time had been a single transfer made from the account at the end of the tax year.

Step 2 Suppose that all the other transfers made from the account in the tax year at a relevant time had been a single offshore transfer made at the end of the tax year immediately after the single transfer mentioned in step 1.

Step 3 Applying those suppositions—

    (*a*) find under section 809Q(3) the extent to which the single transfer mentioned in step 1 is of the individual's income or chargeable gains, and

    (*b*) find under section 809R(4) the content of the single offshore transfer mentioned in step 2.

Step 4 Each transfer made from the account in the tax year at a relevant time is to be treated as containing the specified proportion of each kind of income or capital contained in the relevant deemed transfer.

"The specified proportion" is the amount of the transfer divided by the amount of the relevant deemed transfer.

"The relevant deemed transfer" is—

    (*a*) if the transfer is a condition A transfer, the single transfer mentioned in step 1, and

    (*b*) otherwise, the single offshore transfer mentioned in step 2.

(3) Subsection (2) applies in determining the composition of a transfer for the purposes of sections 809Q and 809R but it does not otherwise affect the date on which a transfer is considered to occur for the purposes of this Chapter.

(4) If the tax year is the tax year in which the account becomes a qualifying account, for the purpose of applying section 809Q(3) in relation to the single transfer mentioned in step 1 of subsection (2), treat the part of the tax year falling before the qualifying date for the account as a separate tax year.

(5) If the account ceases to be a qualifying account of the individual during the tax year other than as a result of a breach of the deposit rule—

    (*a*) subsection (2) has effect as if references to the end of the tax year were to the end of the day on which the account ceases to be a qualifying account, and

    (*b*) for the purpose of applying section 809Q(3) in relation to the single transfer mentioned in step 1 of subsection (2), treat the part of the tax year falling after the day mentioned in paragraph (*a*) as a separate tax year.

(6) A transfer from the account is a "condition A transfer" if and to the extent that—

    (*a*) condition A in section 809L is met, and

    (*b*) either—

        (i) the property or consideration for the service is (wholly or in part), or derives (wholly or in part, and directly or indirectly) from, the transfer, or

        (ii) the transfer, or anything deriving (wholly or in part, and directly or indirectly) from the transfer, is used as mentioned in section 809L(3)(*c*).

(7) A transfer from the account is an "other transfer" if and to the extent that it is not a condition A transfer.

(8) Treat a transfer as an "other transfer" if and to the extent that, at the end of the tax year—

    (*a*) it is not a condition A transfer, and

    (*b*) on the basis of the best estimate that can reasonably be made at that time, it will not become a condition A transfer.

(9) If the account ceases to be a qualifying account of the individual during the tax year other than as a result of a breach of the deposit rule, subsection (8) has effect as if the reference to the end of the tax year were to the end of the day on which the account ceases to be a qualifying account.

(10) "Qualifying account" and "the qualifying date" for an account are defined in section 809RB.

(11) For the purposes of this section and sections 809RB to 809RD—

    (*a*) "employment" is to be read in accordance with section 4(1) of ITEPA 2003, and includes an office (as read in accordance with section 5(3) of that Act), (*b*) whether general earnings are "for" a tax year is to be determined as for the purposes of the employment income Parts of ITEPA 2003 (see section 3(2) of that Act),

(*c*) a reference to anything "paid into" an account includes anything credited to the account by whatever means, and

(*d*) references to a breach of the deposit rule are to be read in accordance with section 809RC.][1]

Commentary—*Simon's Taxes* **E4.1318**.

HMRC Manuals—Employment Related Securities Manual ERSM162910 (special mixed fund rules for certain employment cases).

ERSM161105 (2015: special mixed fund rules for certain employment cases).

Amendments—[1]   Sections 809RA–809RD inserted by FA 2013 s 19, Sch 6 paras 4, 6 with effect in relation to transfers from a mixed fund that are made in the tax year 2013–14 or any subsequent tax year.

[809RB Qualifying accounts

(1) An individual may by notice to the Commissioners nominate an account to be a qualifying account of the individual for the purposes of section 809RA.

(2) The notice must specify the qualifying date for the account.

(3) "The qualifying date" for the account is the first date on which there is paid into the account sums falling within subsection (4) which (in total) are more than £10.

(4) A sum falls within this subsection if it is, or derives wholly (whether directly or indirectly) from, general earnings of the individual from an employment for a tax year which is a relevant tax year in relation to the employment.

(5) A tax year is a "relevant" tax year in relation to an employment if the general earnings which the individual has for the tax year from the employment include both general earnings within section 15(1) of ITEPA 2003 and general earnings within section 26(1) of that Act.

(6) The individual may withdraw the nomination by giving a further notice to the Commissioners, specifying the date with effect from which the nomination is withdrawn.

(7) A notice under subsection (1) or (6) must be in writing and include such information as the Commissioners may reasonably require.

(8) A notice under subsection (1) or (6) must be given no later than—

(*a*) 31 January in the tax year following the tax year in which falls, as the case may be—

    (i) the qualifying date for the account, or

    (ii) the date with effect from which the nomination is withdrawn, or

(*b*) such later date as the Commissioners may allow.

(9) If an individual nominates an account under this section, the account is a "qualifying account" of the individual throughout the period—

(*a*) beginning with the qualifying date, and

(*b*) ending with the date before the earliest of the following dates—

    (i) the date on which the account is closed or ceases to be an ordinary bank account held by and for the benefit of the individual (alone or jointly with others);

    (ii) the date with effect from which the nomination is withdrawn under this section;

    (iii) the qualifying date for another qualifying account of the individual;

    (iv) 6 April in a tax year in which there is a breach of the deposit rule which is not remedied or cannot be remedied;

    (v) 6 April in a tax year for which the individual has no general earnings within section 26(1) of ITEPA 2003.

(10) The account is not to be a qualifying account at all if—

(*a*) at any time on the qualifying date, the account is not an ordinary bank account held by and for the benefit of the individual (alone or jointly with others), or

(*b*) immediately before the qualifying date, the account has a credit balance of more than £10.

(11) The account is not to be a qualifying account at all if the qualifying date falls in a tax year—

(*a*) for which the individual has no general earnings within section 26(1) of ITEPA 2003, or

(*b*) in which there is a breach of the deposit rule which is not remedied or cannot be remedied.

(12) Subsection (9)(*b*)(iv) or (11)(*b*) (as relevant) is to be ignored if the breach occurs on or after a date falling within subsection (9)(*b*)(i) to (iii).

(13) If, apart from this subsection, an individual might have nominated two or more accounts for which the qualifying date would be the same, the individual may nominate only one of those accounts.

(14) If, apart from this subsection, an account would be a qualifying account of two or more individuals at any time, it is not to be a qualifying account of either or any of them at that time or any other time.

(15) For the purposes of this section an account is an "ordinary bank account" if it is a cash account in a bank (whether a current or savings account) where sums standing to the credit of the account from time to time represent a debt owed by the bank to the account-holder.][1]

Commentary—*Simon's Taxes* **E4.1318**.

Amendments—[1]   Sections 809RA–809RD inserted by FA 2013 s 19, Sch 6 paras 4, 6 with effect in relation to transfers from a mixed fund that are made in the tax year 2013–14 or any subsequent tax year.

[809RC Breaches of the deposit rule

(1) There is a breach of the deposit rule if a prohibited sum is paid into the account on or after the qualifying date.

(2) A breach of the deposit rule is remedied if, within 30 days beginning with the day on which the individual became or ought reasonably to have become aware of the payment of the prohibited sum, the required amount is transferred out of the account by way of a single one-off transfer.

(3) "The required amount" is an amount equal to—

    (*a*) the prohibited sum, plus

    (*b*) all the other prohibited sums (if any) that have been paid into the account since that sum was paid in.

(4) If there are 3 breaches of the deposit rule in any 12 month period, subsection (2) does not apply to the third breach and, accordingly, the third breach cannot be remedied.

(5) The payment of a prohibited sum ("the later prohibited sum") into the account does not result in a breach of the deposit rule if—

    (*a*) a breach resulting from an earlier payment of a prohibited sum into the account is remedied, and

    (*b*) the later prohibited sum is represented by the required amount in relation to that breach.

(6) A "prohibited sum" is anything other than a sum that is, or derives wholly (whether directly or indirectly) from, any of the following kinds of income or capital—

    (*a*) general earnings of the individual from an employment for a tax year which is a relevant tax year in relation to the employment,

    (*b*) general earnings of the individual from an employment which consist of money and are paid in a tax year which is a relevant tax year in relation to the employment,

    (*c*) an amount of specific employment income which, by virtue of Part 6, 7 or 7A of ITEPA 2003 or any other enactment, counts as employment income of the individual in respect of an employment for a tax year which is a relevant tax year in relation to the employment,

    (*d*) interest on the account, or

    (*e*) consideration for the disposal of employment-related securities or employment-related securities options in the circumstances described in subsection (7).

(7) The circumstances are—

    (*a*) the securities or options were acquired pursuant to a right or opportunity available by reason of an employment of the individual,

    (*b*) the disposal is or occurs in conjunction with, or as soon as reasonably practicable after, a relevant event involving those securities or options, and

    (*c*) the tax year in which the relevant event occurs is a relevant tax year in relation to the employment.

(8) For the purposes of subsection (7) each of the following is a "relevant event"—

    (*a*) the acquisition mentioned in subsection (7)(*a*), and

    (*b*) any event on the occurrence of which an amount (if positive) counts as employment income by virtue of Part 7 of ITEPA 2003 or would do so but for—

        (i) section 421E or 474 of that Act (exclusions: residence etc), or

        (ii) an election under section 430 or 431 of that Act.

(9) For the purposes of this section a tax year is a "relevant" tax year in relation to an employment if—

    (*a*) the individual has general earnings from the employment for the tax year,

    (*b*) those earnings include both general earnings within section 15(1) of ITEPA 2003 ("section 15(1) earnings") and general earnings within section 26(1) of that Act ("section 26(1) earnings"),

    (*c*) at least some of the section 15(1) earnings, or sums deriving (wholly or in part, and directly or indirectly) from at least some of the section 15(1) earnings, are paid into the account in the tax year, and

    (*d*) at least some of the section 26(1) earnings, or sums deriving (wholly or in part, and directly or indirectly) from at least some of the section 26(1) earnings, are also paid into the account in the tax year.

(10) For the purposes of this section—

    (*a*) "employment-related securities" has the meaning given in section 421B(8) of ITEPA 2003, and

    (*b*) "employment-related securities options" has the meaning given in section 471(5) of that Act.][1]

Commentary—*Simon's Taxes* E4.1318.

Amendments—[1] Sections 809RA–809RD inserted by FA 2013 s 19, Sch 6 paras 4, 6 with effect in relation to transfers from a mixed fund that are made in the tax year 2013–14 or any subsequent tax year.

[809RD Effect where 30-day deadline is met

(1) This section applies if the required amount in relation to a breach of the deposit rule was transferred out of the account in accordance with section 809RC(2).

(2) Sections 809Q and 809R have effect as if—

    (a) the intervening transactions had never taken place, and

    (b) each prohibited sum represented by the required amount had instead been transferred directly (at the time that sum was paid into the qualifying account) into the account or other property into which the required amount was transferred by virtue of the single one-off transfer.

(3) Each of the following is an "intervening transaction"—

    (a) each payment into the qualifying account of a prohibited sum represented by the required amount, and

    (b) the single one-off transfer out of the qualifying account.

(4) If it is supposed under step 1 or 2 of section 809RA(2) that a single transfer had been made in the intervening period, re-apply section 809Q or 809R in relation to that transfer taking account of subsection (2).

(5) "The intervening period" is the period—

    (a) beginning with the day on which the breach occurred, and

    (b) ending with the day on which the single one-off transfer was made in accordance with section 809RC(2).

(6) If more than one transfer of a sum equal to the required amount was transferred out of the qualifying account within the 30-day grace period, the first of those transfers is assumed to be the single one-off transfer.

(7) "The 30-day grace period" is the period of 30 days mentioned in section 809RC(2).][1]

Commentary—*Simon's Taxes* E4.1318.

Amendments—[1] Sections 809RA–809RD inserted by FA 2013 s 19, Sch 6 paras 4, 6 with effect in relation to transfers from a mixed fund that are made in the tax year 2013–14 or any subsequent tax year.

[809S Section 809Q: anti-avoidance

(1) This section applies if, by reason of an arrangement the main purpose (or one of the main purposes) of which is to secure an income tax advantage or capital gains tax advantage, a mixed fund would otherwise be regarded as containing income or capital within any of paragraphs (f) to (i) of section 809Q(4).

(2) Treat the mixed fund as containing so much (if any) of the income or capital as is just and reasonable.

(3) "Arrangement" includes any scheme, understanding, transaction or series or transactions (whether or not enforceable).

[(4) Income tax advantage" means—

    (a) a relief from income tax or increased relief from income tax,

    (b) a repayment of income tax or increased repayment of income tax,

    (c) the avoidance or reduction of a charge to income tax or an assessment to income tax, or

    (d) the avoidance of a possible assessment to income tax.

. . . [3]

(4A) For the purposes of subsection (4)(c) and (d) it does not matter whether the avoidance or reduction is effected—

    (a) by receipts accruing in such a way that the recipient does not pay or bear income tax on them, or

    (b) by a deduction in calculating profits or gains.][2]

(5) "Capital gains tax advantage" means—

    (a) a relief from capital gains tax or increased relief from capital gains tax,

    (b) a repayment of capital gains tax or increased repayment of capital gains tax,

    (c) the avoidance or reduction of a charge to capital gains tax or an assessment to capital gains tax, or

    (d) the avoidance of a possible assessment to capital gains tax.][1]

Commentary—*Simon's Taxes* E6.328.

HMRC Manuals—Residence, Domicile and Remittance Basis Manual RDRM35480 (anti-avoidance provisions).

Amendments—[1]   Chapter A1, ss 809A–809Z7 inserted by FA 2008 s 25, Sch 7 para 1 with effect for the tax year 2008–09 and subsequent tax years.

Sections 809Q–809S do not apply for the purposes of determining whether income or chargeable gains for the tax year 2007–08 or any earlier tax year are remitted to the UK (or the amount of any such income or chargeable gains so remitted) (FA 2008 Sch 7 para 89).

[2]   Sub-ss (4), (4A) substituted for former sub-s (4) by FA 2010 s 38, Sch 12 para 11 with effect in relation to income tax advantages obtained on or after 24 March 2010.

[3]   In sub-s (4), words repealed by FA 2016 s 5, Sch 1 para 63(1), (13) with effect in relation to dividends paid or arising (or treated as paid), and other distributions made (or treated as made), in the tax year 2016-17 or at any later time.

[Remittance of income and gains: supplementary

809T Foreign chargeable gains accruing on disposal made [otherwise][2] than for full consideration

(1) This section applies if—

    (a) foreign chargeable gains accrue to an individual on the disposal of an asset, and (*b*) the individual does not receive consideration for the disposal of an amount [at least]² equal to the market value of the asset.

(2) For the purposes of this Chapter treat the asset as deriving from the chargeable gains.]¹

Commentary—*Simon's Taxes* **E6.329**.
HMRC Manuals—Residence, Domicile and Remittance Basis Manual RDRM31180 (elaboration on this section, with examples).
Capital Gains Manual CG25344 (remittance basis: disposals other than for full consideration).
Amendments—¹   Chapter A1, ss 809A–809Z7 inserted by FA 2008 s 25, Sch 7 para 1 with effect for the tax year 2008–09 and subsequent tax years.
²   In heading word substituted, and in sub-s (1)(*b*) words inserted, by FA 2009 s 51, Sch 27 para 9 with effect from 22 April 2009.

[809U Deemed income or gains not to be regarded as remitted before time when they are treated as arising or accruing

Where—

   (*a*) income or foreign chargeable gains are treated as arising or accruing, and

   (*b*) by virtue of anything done in relation to anything regarded as deriving from the income or chargeable gains, the income or chargeable gains would otherwise be regarded as remitted to the United Kingdom before the time when they are treated as arising or accruing, treat the income or chargeable gains as remitted to the United Kingdom at that time.]¹

Commentary—*Simon's Taxes* **E6.329**.
HMRC Manuals—Residence, Domicile and Remittance Basis Manual RDRM35510 (timing of remittance: deemed income and gains).
Amendments—¹   Chapter A1, ss 809A–809Z7 inserted by FA 2008 s 25, Sch 7 para 1 with effect for the tax year 2008–09 and subsequent tax years.

[Relief for money used to pay tax etc]

[809UA Money used for payments on account

(1) Subsection (2) applies to income or chargeable gains of an individual if—

   (*a*) the income or gains would (but for subsection (2)) be regarded as remitted to the United Kingdom by virtue of the bringing of money to the United Kingdom,

   (*b*) the money is brought to the United Kingdom by way of direct payments to the Commissioners on account of income tax,

   (*c*) the tax year ("tax year 2") in respect of which the payments on account are made is a tax year for which section 809H (remittance basis charge for long-term UK resident) does not apply as respects the individual, and

   (*d*) that section applied as respects the individual for the previous tax year ("tax year 1").

(2) The relevant amount of income or chargeable gains is to be treated as not remitted to the United Kingdom if money equal to the relevant amount is taken offshore by—

   (*a*) the 15 March following the end of tax year 2, or

   (*b*) such later date as the Commissioners may allow on a claim made by the individual.

(3) A claim under subsection (2)(*b*)—

   (*a*) may be made only if the individual has made and delivered a return under section 8 of TMA 1970 for tax year 2 and reasonably expects to receive from the Commissioners a repayment of tax paid in respect of that tax year, and

   (*b*) may be made no later than the 5 April following the end of tax year 2.

(4) Money that is taken offshore in accordance with subsection (2) is to be treated as having the same composition of kinds of income and capital as the money used to make the payments on account.

(5) In this section "the relevant amount" means the lower of the following—

   (*a*) the amount brought to the United Kingdom as mentioned in subsection (1)(*b*), and

   (*b*) the applicable amount (as defined in section 809H) for tax year 1.]¹

Commentary—*Simon's Taxes* **E4.1319, E4.15, E6.329**.
Amendments—¹   This section inserted by FA 2013 s 21(1), (3) with effect in relation to payments on account made in respect of the tax year 2012–13 and subsequent tax years.

[809V Money paid to the Commissioners

(1) Subsection (2) applies to income or chargeable gains of an individual if—

   (*a*) the income or gains would (but for subsection (2)) be regarded as remitted to the United Kingdom by virtue of the bringing of money to the United Kingdom,

   (*b*) the money is brought to the United Kingdom by way of one or more direct payments to the Commissioners, and

   (*c*) the payments are made in relation to a tax year to which section 809H applies as regards the individual.

(2) The income or chargeable gains are to be treated as not remitted to the United Kingdom to the extent that the payments do not exceed the applicable amount (as defined in section 809H).

(3) Subsection (2) does not apply to payments if or to the extent that they are repaid by the Commissioners.]¹

Commentary—*Simon's Taxes* **E6.329**.

HMRC Manuals—Residence, Domicile and Remittance Basis Manual RDRM34020-34030 (money paid directly to HMRC and repayment by HMRC, with examples).
RDRM35140 (remittance basis charge and section ITA07/s809V).
Amendments—Cross-head substituted by FA 2012 s 47, Sch 12 paras 1, 6 with effect where the relevant event (as defined in ITA 2007 s 809VA) or the ceasing to be exempt property (as defined in ITA 2007 s 809Y) occurs on or after 6 April 2012.
[1]   This section substituted by FA 2012 s 47, Sch 12 paras 1, 4 with effect for the tax year 2012–13 and subsequent tax years.

[Business investment relief

809VA Money or other property used to make investments
(1) Subsection (2) applies if—
    (*a*) a relevant event occurs,
    (*b*) but for subsection (2), income or chargeable gains of an individual would be regarded as remitted to the United Kingdom by virtue of that event, and
    (*c*) the individual makes a claim for relief under this section.
(2) The income or gains are to be treated as not remitted to the United Kingdom.
(3) A "relevant event" occurs if money or other property—
    (*a*) is used by a relevant person to make a qualifying investment, or
    (*b*) is brought to or received in the United Kingdom in order to be used by a relevant person to make a qualifying investment.
(4) Subsection (1)(*b*) includes a case where income or gains would be treated under section 809Y as remitted to the United Kingdom by virtue of the relevant event.
(5) Subsection (2) applies by virtue of subsection (3)(*b*) to the extent only that the investment is made within the period of 45 days beginning with the day on which the money or other property is brought to or received in the United Kingdom.
(6) Where some but not all of the money or other property is used to make the investment within that 45-day period, the part of the income or gains to which subsection (2) applies is to be determined on a just and reasonable basis.
(7) Subsection (2) does not apply if the relevant event occurs, or the investment is made, as part of or as a result of a scheme or arrangement the main purpose or one of the main purposes of which is the avoidance of tax.
(8) A claim for relief under this section must be made on or before the first anniversary of the 31 January following the tax year in which the income or gains would, but for subsection (2), be regarded as remitted to the United Kingdom by virtue of the relevant event.][1]
Commentary—*Simon's Taxes* **E6.333A, E6.333B**.
HMRC Manuals—Residence, Domicile and Remittance Basis Manual RDRM34320 (relevant events).
RDRM34310 (an introduction).
Amendments—[1]   Sections 809VA–809VO inserted by FA 2012 s 47, Sch 12 paras 1, 7 with effect where the relevant event (as defined in ITA 2007 s 809VA) or the ceasing to be exempt property (as defined in ITA 2007 s 809Y) occurs on or after 6 April 2012.

[809VB Failure to invest within 45 days
(1) This section applies to any portion of the income or gains to which section 809VA(2) does not apply because the investment was not made within the period mentioned in section 809VA(5) ("the 45-day period").
(2) That portion is to be treated as not remitted to the United Kingdom to the extent that the remaining money or other property is taken offshore within the 45-day period.
(3) Where some but not all of the remaining money or other property is taken offshore within the 45-day period, the part of the income or gains to which subsection (2) applies is to be determined on a just and reasonable basis.
(4) If any remaining money or other property is taken offshore within the 45-day period, nothing in subsection (2) prevents anything subsequently done in relation to it (or anything deriving from it) from counting as a remittance of the underlying income or gains to the United Kingdom at the time when the thing is subsequently done.
(5) A reference to the "remaining" money or other property is to so much of the money or other property brought to or received in the United Kingdom as is not used within the 45-day period to make the investment (which may in some cases be all of it).][1]
Commentary—*Simon's Taxes* **E6.333A, E6.333B**.
HMRC Manuals—Residence, Domicile and Remittance Basis Manual RDRM34370 (failure to invest within 45 days).
Amendments—[1]   Sections 809VA–809VO inserted by FA 2012 s 47, Sch 12 paras 1, 7 with effect where the relevant event (as defined in ITA 2007 s 809VA) or the ceasing to be exempt property (as defined in ITA 2007 s 809Y) occurs on or after 6 April 2012.

[809VC Qualifying investments
(1) For the purposes of section 809VA, a person makes an investment if—
    (*a*) shares in a company are issued to [or acquired by][2] the person, or
    (*b*) the person makes a loan (secured or unsecured) to a company.
(2) The company is referred to as "the target company".

(3) The shares or the person's rights under the loan (or both) forming the subject of the investment are referred to as "the holding".

(4) The investment counts as a "qualifying investment" if conditions A and B are met when the investment is made.

(5) Conditions A and B are defined in sections 809VD and 809VF.

(6) A reference in this section to "shares" includes any securities.

(7) If a loan agreement authorises a company to draw down amounts of a loan over a period of time—

    (*a*) entry into the agreement does not count for the purposes of this section as the making of a loan, but

    (*b*) a separate loan is to be treated as made each time an amount is drawn down under the agreement.

(8) Accordingly—

    (*a*) a separate investment is treated as made each time an amount is drawn down under the agreement, and

    (*b*) the reference in subsection (3) to the person's rights under the loan applies only to so much of the person's rights as relate to the drawdown of that particular amount.][1]

Commentary—*Simon's Taxes* **E6.333A, E6.333B**.

HMRC Manuals—Residence, Domicile and Remittance Basis Manual RDRM34330 (qualifying investments - overview).

Amendments—[1] Sections 809VA–809VO inserted by FA 2012 s 47, Sch 12 paras 1, 7 with effect where the relevant event (as defined in ITA 2007 s 809VA) or the ceasing to be exempt property (as defined in ITA 2007 s 809Y) occurs on or after 6 April 2012.

[2] In sub-s (1)(*a*), words inserted by F(No 2)A 2017 s 15(1), (2) with effect where the relevant event, as defined in ITA 2007 s 809VA, occurs on or after 6 April 2017.

[809VD Condition A

(1) Condition A is that the target company is—

    (a) an eligible trading company,

    (b) an eligible stakeholder company, . . . [2]

    [(ba) an eligible hybrid company, or][2]

    (c) an eligible holding company.

(2) A company is an "eligible trading company" if—

    (a) it is a private limited company,

    (b) it carries on one or more commercial trades or is preparing to do so within the next [5][2] years, and

    (c) carrying on commercial trades is all or substantially all of what it does (or of what it is reasonably expected to do once it begins trading).

(3) A company is an "eligible stakeholder company" if—

    (a) it is a private limited company,

    (b) it exists wholly for the purpose of making investments in eligible trading companies (ignoring any minor or incidental purposes), and

    (c) it holds one or more such investments or is preparing to do so within the next [5][2] years.

[(3A) A company is an "eligible hybrid company" if—

    (a) it is a private limited company,

    (b) it is not an eligible trading company or an eligible stakeholder company,

    (c) it carries on one or more commercial trades or is preparing to do so within the next 5 years,

    (d) it holds one or more investments in eligible trading companies or is preparing to do so within the next 5 years, and

    (e) carrying on commercial trades and making investments in eligible trading companies are all or substantially all of what it does (or of what it is reasonably expected to do once it begins operating).][2]

(4) The [references in subsections (3) and (3A)][2] to making investments is to be read in accordance with section 809VC.

(5) A company is an "eligible holding company" if—

    (a) it is a member of an eligible trading group or of an eligible group that is reasonably expected to become an eligible trading group within the next [5][2] years,

    (b) an eligible trading company in the group is a 51% subsidiary of it, and

    (c) if the ordinary share capital that it owns in the eligible trading company is owned indirectly, each intermediary in the series is also a member of the group.

(6) "Group" means a parent company and its 51% subsidiaries.

(7) "Parent company" means a company that—

    (a) has one or more 51% subsidiaries, but

    (b) is not itself a 51% subsidiary of any company.

(8) A group is an "eligible group" if the parent company and each of its 51% subsidiaries are private limited companies.

(9) A group is an "eligible trading group" if—

    (a) it is an eligible group, and

(b) carrying on commercial trades is all or substantially all of what the group does (taking the activities of its members as a whole).

(10) The reference in subsection (5) to owning ordinary share capital indirectly is to be read in accordance with section 1155 of CTA 2010.

(11) A company is a "private limited company" if—

(a) it is a body corporate whose liability is limited,

(b) it is not a limited liability partnership, and

(c) none of its shares are listed on a recognised stock exchange.]¹

Commentary—*Simon's Taxes* **E6.330F** .

HMRC Manuals—Residence, Domicile and Remittance Basis Manual RDRM34340 (qualifying investments - condition A overview).

RDRM34345 (condition A: eligible trading company).

RDRM34350 (condition A: eligible stakeholder company).

RDRM34355 (condition A: eligible holding company).

Amendments—¹ Sections 809VA–809VO inserted by FA 2012 s 47, Sch 12 paras 1, 7 with effect where the relevant event (as defined in ITA 2007 s 809VA) or the ceasing to be exempt property (as defined in ITA 2007 s 809Y) occurs on or after 6 April 2012.

² In sub-s (1)(*b*), word repealed; sub-ss (1)(*ba*) (3A) inserted; in sub-ss (2)(*b*), (3)(*c*), (5)(*a*), figure substituted for figure "2"; and in sub-s (4), words substituted for words "reference in subsection (3)", by F(No 2)A 2017 s 15(1), (3) with effect where the relevant event, as defined in ITA 2007 s 809VA, occurs on or after 6 April 2017.

[809VE Commercial trades

(1) Section 809VD is to be read in accordance with this section.

(2) A reference to a "trade" also includes—

(a) anything that is treated for corporation tax purposes as if it were a trade, and

(b) a business carried on for generating income from land (as defined in section 207 of CTA 2009).

(3) A trade is a "commercial trade" if it is conducted on a commercial basis and with a view to the realisation of profits.

(4) The carrying on of activities of research and development from which it is intended that a commercial trade will be derived, or will benefit, is to be treated as the carrying on of a commercial trade.

(5) But preparing to carry on activities within subsection (4) is not to be treated as the carrying on of a commercial trade.

[(6) A company which is a partner in a partnership is not to be regarded as carrying on a trade carried on by the partnership.]²]¹

Commentary—*Simon's Taxes* **E6.330F** .

HMRC Manuals—Residence, Domicile and Remittance Basis Manual RDRM34345 (condition A - eligible trading company). RDRM34430 (potentially chargeable events - 2-year start-up rule).

Amendments—¹ Sections 809VA–809VO inserted by FA 2012 s 47, Sch 12 paras 1, 7 with effect where the relevant event (as defined in ITA 2007 s 809VA) or the ceasing to be exempt property (as defined in ITA 2007 s 809Y) occurs on or after 6 April 2012.

² Sub-s (6) inserted by F(No 2)A 2017 s 15(1), (4) with effect where the relevant event, as defined in ITA 2007 s 809VA, occurs on or after 6 April 2017.

[809VF Condition B

(1) Condition B is that no relevant person has (directly or indirectly) obtained or become entitled to obtain any related benefit, and no relevant person expects to obtain any such benefit.

(2) A "benefit"—

(a) includes the provision of anything that would not be provided to the relevant person in the ordinary course of business, or would be provided but on less favourable terms, but

(b) does not include the provision of anything provided to the relevant person in the ordinary course of business and on arm's length terms.

(3) A benefit is "related" if—

(a) it is directly or indirectly attributable to the making of the investment (whether it is obtained before or after the investment is made), or

(b) it is reasonable to assume that the benefit would not be available in the absence of the investment.

(4) For the purposes of subsection (2)—

(a) a reference to the provision of anything is to the provision of anything in money or money's worth, including property, capital, goods or services of any kind, and

(b) "provision" includes any arrangement that allows a person to enjoy or benefit from the thing in question (whether temporarily or permanently).]¹

Commentary—*Simon's Taxes* **E6.333A, E6.333B**.

HMRC Manuals—Residence, Domicile and Remittance Basis Manual RDRM34360 (qualifying investment - condition B).

Amendments—¹ Sections 809VA–809VO inserted by FA 2012 s 47, Sch 12 paras 1, 7 with effect where the relevant event (as defined in ITA 2007 s 809VA) or the ceasing to be exempt property (as defined in ITA 2007 s 809Y) occurs on or after 6 April 2012.

[809VG Income or gains treated as remitted following certain events

(1) Subsection (2) applies if—

    (a) income or chargeable gains are treated under section 809VA(2) as not remitted to the United Kingdom as a result of a qualifying investment,

    (b) a potentially chargeable event occurs after the investment is made, and

    (c) the appropriate mitigation steps are not taken within the grace period allowed for each step.

(2) The affected income or gains are to be treated as having been remitted to the United Kingdom immediately after the end of the relevant grace period.

(3) Where the step required by section 809VI(2)(a) is not taken within the grace period allowed for that step, "the relevant grace period" is the grace period allowed for that step.

(4) Otherwise, "the relevant grace period" is the grace period allowed for the step required by section 809VI(1) or (2)(b).

(5) "The affected income or gains" means such portion of the income or gains mentioned in subsection (1)(a) as reflects the portion of the investment affected by the potentially chargeable event.

(6) The portion of the investment affected is—

    (a) if the potentially chargeable event is a disposal of a part of the holding (or a part of the remaining holding), a portion equal to the portion of the holding (or remaining holding) being disposed of, and

    (b) otherwise, the whole of the investment.

(7) Sections 809VN (order of disposals etc) and 809VO (investments made from mixed funds) make further provision for the purposes of this section.

(8) If a qualifying investment is made using the money or other property mentioned in section 809VA(3) together with other funds—

    (a) that investment is to be treated as two separate investments, one made using the money or other property mentioned in section 809VA(3) and one made using the other funds, and

    (b) references in the business investment provisions to "the investment" and "the holding" relate only to the investment made using the money or other property mentioned in section 809VA(3).

(9) If the potentially chargeable event mentioned in subsection (1)(b) is not the first such event to affect the investment, the income or gains mentioned in subsection (1)(a) do not include, as respects that investment—

    (a) any part already treated under subsection (2) as remitted to the United Kingdom as a result of an earlier event,

    (b) any part contained in amounts already taken offshore or reinvested by way of appropriate mitigation steps following an earlier event, or

    (c) any part contained in amounts already used to make a tax deposit without which an amount mentioned in paragraph (b) would not have been enough to satisfy section 809VI(1) or (2)(b) (see section 809VK).][1]

Commentary—*Simon's Taxes* **E6.333A, E6.333B**.

HMRC Manuals—Residence, Domicile and Remittance Basis Manual RDRM34470 (amount of foreign income or gains remitted).

RDRM34535 (order of disposals: qualifying and non qualifying investments).

Amendments—[1] Sections 809VA–809VO inserted by FA 2012 s 47, Sch 12 paras 1, 7 with effect where the relevant event (as defined in ITA 2007 s 809VA) or the ceasing to be exempt property (as defined in ITA 2007 s 809Y) occurs on or after 6 April 2012.

[809VH Meaning of "potentially chargeable event"

(1) For the purposes of section 809VG, a "potentially chargeable event" occurs if—

    (a) the target company is for the first time neither an eligible trading company nor an eligible stakeholder [nor an eligible hybrid company][2] company nor an eligible holding company,

    (b) the relevant person who made the investment ("P") disposes of all or part of the holding,

    (c) the extraction of value rule is breached, or

    (d) the [5-year][2] start-up rule is breached.

(2) The extraction of value rule is breached if—

    (a) value (in money or money's worth) is received by or for the benefit of P or another relevant person,

    [(b) the value is received from any person in circumstances that are directly or indirectly attributable to the investment, and][2]

    (c) the value is received other than by virtue of a disposal that is itself a potentially chargeable event.

(3) But the extraction of value rule is not breached merely because a relevant person receives value that—

    (a) is treated for income tax or corporation tax purposes as the receipt of income or would be so treated if that person were liable to such tax, and

    (b) is paid or provided to the person in the ordinary course of business and on arm's length terms.

(4) Each of the following is an "involved company"—

    (a) the target company,

(b) if the target company is an eligible stakeholder company, any eligible trading company in which it has made or intends to make an investment,

(c) if the target company is an eligible holding company, any eligible trading company that is a 51% subsidiary of it, and

(d) any company that is connected with a company within paragraph (a), (b) or (c).[2]

(5) The [5-year][2] start-up rule is breached if—

(a) immediately after the end of the period of [5][2] years beginning with the day on which the investment was made, the target company is non-operational, or

(b) at any time after the end of that period, the target company becomes non-operational.

(6) The target company is "non-operational" at any time when—

(a) it is an eligible trading company but is not trading,

(b) it is an eligible stakeholder company but—

(i) it holds no investments in eligible trading companies, or

(ii) none of the eligible trading companies in which it holds investments is trading, ...[2]

[(ba) it is an eligible hybrid company but is not trading and—

(i) it holds no investments in eligible trading companies, or

(ii) none of the eligible trading companies in which it holds investments is trading, or][2]

(c) it is an eligible holding company but—

(i) the group of which it is a member is not an eligible trading group, or

(ii) none of its 51% subsidiaries in the eligible trading group of which it is a member is an eligible trading company that is trading.

(7) In subsection (6), "trading" means carrying on one or more commercial trades (including the carrying on of any activities treated under section 809VE(4) as the carrying on of a commercial trade).

(8) If consideration for a disposal of all or part of the holding is or is to be paid in instalments, the disposal is to be treated for the purposes of this section as if it were separate disposals, one for each instalment (and each giving rise to a separate potentially chargeable event).

(9) An event listed in subsection (1) does not count as a potentially chargeable event if it is due to an insolvency step taken for genuine commercial reasons (but this does not prevent the extraction of any value in connection with the insolvency step from counting as a potentially chargeable event).

(10) For the purposes of subsection (9), an insolvency step is taken if—

(a) the target company enters into administration or receivership or is wound up or dissolved,

(b) the target company is an eligible stakeholder [or an eligible hybrid company][2] company and any eligible trading company in which it holds an investment enters into administration or receivership or is wound up or dissolved,

(c) the target company is an eligible holding company and any eligible trading company in the group that is a 51% subsidiary of it enters into administration or receivership or is wound up or dissolved, or

(d) a similar step is taken in relation to a company mentioned in paragraph (a), (b) or (c) under the law of a country or territory outside the United Kingdom.][1]

Commentary—*Simon's Taxes* E6.330F .

HMRC Manuals—Residence, Domicile and Remittance Basis Manual RDRM34390 (potentially chargeable events - overview).
RDRM34410 (potentially chargeable events - ceasing to be an eligible company).
RDRM34420 (potentially chargeable events - the extraction of value rule).
RDRM34400 (potentially chargeable events - disposal of all or part of a holding).
RDRM34430 (potentially chargeable events - 2- year start-up rule).

Amendments—[1]   Sections 809VA–809VO inserted by FA 2012 s 47, Sch 12 paras 1, 7 with effect where the relevant event (as defined in ITA 2007 s 809VA) or the ceasing to be exempt property (as defined in ITA 2007 s 809Y) occurs on or after 6 April 2012.

[2]   Amendments made by F(No 2)A 2017 s 15(1), (5) with effect where the relevant event, as defined in ITA 2007 s 809VA, occurs on or after 6 April 2017

[809VI The appropriate mitigation steps

(1) If the potentially chargeable event is a disposal of all or part of the holding, the appropriate mitigation steps are regarded as taken if the whole of the disposal proceeds have been taken offshore or reinvested.

(2) For any other case, the appropriate mitigation steps are regarded as taken if—

(a) P has disposed of the entire holding (or so much of it as P retains when the potentially chargeable event occurs), and

(b) the whole of the disposal proceeds have been taken offshore or re-invested.

(3) But if the disposal proceeds exceed X, subsections (1) and (2)(b) apply only to so much of the proceeds as is equal to X.

(4) "X" is—

(a) the sum originally invested, less

(b) so much of that sum as has, on previous occasions involving the same investment—

    (i) been taken into account in determining the affected income or gains under section 809VG(2),

    (ii) been taken offshore or re-invested in order to avoid the application of that section, or

    (iii) been used to make a tax deposit without which the amount actually taken offshore or re-invested would not have been enough to satisfy subsection (1) or (2)(b) (see section 809VK).

(5) "The sum originally invested" means the amount of the money, or the market value of the other property, used to make the investment.

(6) Market value is to be assessed for these purposes as at the date of the relevant event (see section 809VA).

(7) Proceeds are "re-invested" if a relevant person uses them to make another qualifying investment (or the proceeds are themselves a qualifying investment) whether in the same or a different company.

(8) In cases where a breach of the extraction of value rule occurs in connection with the winding-up or dissolution of the target company—

    (a) subsection (2)(a) does not apply,

    (b) the reference in subsection (2)(b) to the disposal proceeds is to the value received, and

    (c) references in this section and in succeeding provisions of the business investment provisions to the disposal proceeds are to be read as references to the value received.][1]

Commentary—*Simon's Taxes* **E6.333A, E6.333B**.

HMRC Manuals—Residence, Domicile and Remittance Basis Manual RDRM34440 (appropriate mitigation steps).

Amendments—[1] Sections 809VA–809VO inserted by FA 2012 s 47, Sch 12 paras 1, 7 with effect where the relevant event (as defined in ITA 2007 s 809VA) or the ceasing to be exempt property (as defined in ITA 2007 s 809Y) occurs on or after 6 April 2012.

[809VJ The grace period allowed for the appropriate mitigation steps

(1) The grace period allowed for the step mentioned in section 809VI(2)(a) is the period of 90 days beginning—

    (a) if the potentially chargeable event is a breach of the extraction of value rule, with the day on which the value is received, and

    (b) otherwise, with the day on which a relevant person first became aware or ought reasonably to have become aware of the potentially chargeable event.

(2) The grace period allowed for the step mentioned in section 809VI(1) and (2)(b) is the period of 45 days beginning with the day on which the disposal proceeds first became available for use by or for the benefit of P or any other relevant person.

[(2A) But subsection (2B) applies instead of subsections (1) and (2) where the potentially chargeable event is a breach of the 5-year start-up rule by virtue of section 809VH(5)(*b*).

(2B) The grace period allowed for the steps mentioned in section 809VI(2)(*a*) and (2)(*b*) is the period of 2 years beginning with the day on which a relevant person first became aware or ought reasonably to have become aware of the potentially chargeable event referred to in subsection (2A).][2]

(3) An officer of Revenue and Customs may agree in a particular case to extend the grace period allowed for an appropriate mitigation step in exceptional circumstances.

(4) An officer of Revenue and Customs may agree in a particular case to extend the grace period allowed for an appropriate mitigation step in circumstances specified in regulations made by the Commissioners.

(5) Regulations under subsection (4) may have effect in relation to investments made before the day on which the regulations are made.

(6) Nothing in subsection (4) or in regulations made under it limits the power conferred by subsection (3).

(7) The powers conferred on officers of Revenue and Customs by subsections (3) and (4) include power to agree to extend a grace period for a length of time that is indefinite but is capable of becoming definite by means identified in the agreement (such as the satisfaction of conditions).][1]

Commentary—*Simon's Taxes* **E6.333A, E6.333B**.

HMRC Manuals—Residence, Domicile and Remittance Basis Manual RDRM34480 (grace periods).

Regulations—Business Investment Relief Regulations, SI 2012/1898.

Amendments—[1] Sections 809VA–809VO inserted by FA 2012 s 47, Sch 12 paras 1, 7 with effect where the relevant event (as defined in ITA 2007 s 809VA) or the ceasing to be exempt property (as defined in ITA 2007 s 809Y) occurs on or after 6 April 2012.

[2] Sub-ss (2A), (2B) inserted, by F(No 2)A 2017 s 15(1), (6) with effect where the relevant event, as defined in ITA 2007 s 809VA, occurs on or after 6 April 2017.

[809VK Retention of funds to meet CGT liabilities

(1) This section applies if—

    (a) there is a disposal of all or part of the holding,

    (b) the disposal counts as a potentially chargeable event or is part of the appropriate mitigation steps taken in consequence of a potentially chargeable event,

    (c) a chargeable gain (but not a loss) accrues to P on the disposal,

    (d) P is chargeable to capital gains tax (but not corporation tax) in respect of that gain, and

    (e) the actual disposal proceeds are less than Y.

(2) The difference between the actual disposal proceeds and Y is referred to in this section as "the shortfall".

(3) "The actual disposal proceeds" means the disposal proceeds but disregarding section 809Z8(4).

(4) "Y" is the sum of—

(a) the amount (if any) that would, but for this section, be required to be taken offshore or re-invested in order to satisfy section 809VI(1) or (2)(b), and

(b) the amount found by applying the highest potential CGT rate to the amount (computed in accordance with TCGA 1992) of the chargeable gain accruing to P on the disposal.

[(5) The highest potential CGT rate is the highest rate specified in section 1H of TCGA 1992 (regardless of the type of the chargeable gain or, if P is an individual, the rate of income tax at which P's income is chargeable).]²

(6) If this section applies, the amount that is required to be taken offshore or re-invested in order to satisfy section 809VI(1) or (2)(b) is reduced by the permitted amount.

(7) "The permitted amount" is so much of the shortfall as is used, within the grace period allowed for taking the disposal proceeds offshore or re-investing them, to make a deposit in respect of which a certificate of tax deposit is issued to P under section 12 of the National Loans Act 1968.

(8) A reduction may not be made under subsection (6) unless—

(a) when details of the deposit are confirmed to Her Majesty's Revenue and Customs, the confirmation letter states that this section is intended to apply to the deposit, and

(b) the amount of the deposit is no greater than the shortfall.]¹

Commentary—*Simon's Taxes* **E6.333A, E6.333B.**

HMRC Manuals—Residence, Domicile and Remittance Basis Manual RDRM34510 (CTD - amount that can be deposited).

Amendments—¹　　Sections 809VA–809VO inserted by FA 2012 s 47, Sch 12 paras 1, 7 with effect where the relevant event (as defined in ITA 2007 s 809VA) or the ceasing to be exempt property (as defined in ITA 2007 s 809Y) occurs on or after 6 April 2012.

² 　Sub-s (5) substituted by FA 2019 s 13, Sch 1 paras 99, 105 with effect for capital gains tax purposes for the tax year 2019–20 and subsequent tax years, and for corporation tax purposes for accounting periods beginning on or after 6 April 2019. These amendments also have effect for corporation tax purposes in relation to disposals made on or after 6 April 2019 (whether in their application to accounting periods beginning on, and ending on or after, that date or to later accounting periods). See also transitional provisions in FA 2019 Sch 1 paras 121–126.

[809VL　Effect of taking appropriate mitigation steps within grace period

(1) This section explains the effect for the purposes of this Chapter in cases where section 809VG(2) does not apply because the appropriate mitigation steps were taken within the grace period allowed for each step.

(2) If disposal proceeds were taken offshore as part of those steps, nothing in section 809VA(2) prevents anything subsequently done in relation to those proceeds (or anything deriving from them) from counting as a remittance of the underlying income or gains to the United Kingdom at the time when the thing is subsequently done.

(3) If disposal proceeds were re-invested as part of those steps—

(a) the underlying income or gains continue to be treated under section 809VA(2) as not remitted to the United Kingdom, and

(b) the business investment provisions apply to the reinvestment as they apply to the original investment.

(4) In the application of the business investment provisions to the reinvestment—

(a) treat the potentially chargeable event mentioned in section 809VG(1)(b) as the relevant event,

(b) treat the underlying income or gains as the income or gains treated under section 809VA(2) as not remitted to the United Kingdom as a result of the re-investment, and

(c) treat the amount used to make the re-investment as the sum originally invested.

(5) If the re-investment is made using more than the minimum amount of disposal proceeds required to satisfy section 809VI(1) or (2)(b)—

(a) that investment is to be treated as two separate investments, one made using the minimum amount of disposal proceeds and one made using the excess, and

(b) references in the business investment provisions to "the investment" and "the holding" relate only to the investment made using the minimum amount of disposal proceeds.

(6) "The underlying income or gains" means the affected income or gains (within the meaning of section 809VG) or, if one part of the disposal proceeds is taken offshore and the other part re-invested, a corresponding proportion of the affected income or gains.

(7) A further claim must be made in accordance with section 809VA in respect of the re-investment and, if no such claim is made on or before the first anniversary of the 31 January following the tax year in which the re-investment was made, section 809VG(2) applies, as respects the original investment, as if the appropriate mitigation steps had not been taken within the grace period allowed for each step.

(8) Section 809VM makes further provision in cases involving a tax deposit.]¹

Commentary—*Simon's Taxes* **E6.333A, E6.333B.**

ITA 2007

Amendments—[1] Sections 809VA–809VO inserted by FA 2012 s 47, Sch 12 paras 1, 7 with effect where the relevant event (as defined in ITA 2007 s 809VA) or the ceasing to be exempt property (as defined in ITA 2007 s 809Y) occurs on or after 6 April 2012.

[809VM Cases involving tax deposits

(1) This section applies in cases where—

    (a) section 809VG(2) did not apply because the appropriate mitigation steps were taken within the grace period allowed for each step,

    (b) the amount required to be taken offshore or re-invested in order to satisfy section 809VI(1) or (2)(b) had been reduced under section 809VK, and

    (c) but for that reduction, the amount that was actually taken offshore or re-invested would not have been enough to satisfy section 809VI(1) or (2)(b).

(2) The tax deposit that gave rise to the reduction is referred to in this section as "the tax deposit".

(3) Use of the tax deposit to pay the relevant tax liability does not count as remitting the underlying income or gains to the United Kingdom (and, accordingly, section 809VA(2) continues to apply to the income or gains).

(4) If any of the CTD conditions is breached, the underlying income or gains are to be treated as having been remitted to the United Kingdom immediately after the day on which the breach occurs.

(5) "The underlying income or gains" means such portion of the affected income or gains (within the meaning of section 809VG) as is—

    (a) represented by the payment, in the case of subsection (3), or

    (b) affected by the breach, in the case of subsection (4).

(6) The CTD conditions are as follows—

    (a) the tax deposit must not be used to pay a tax liability other than the relevant tax liability,

    (b) if any of the tax deposit is withdrawn by the depositor, the amount withdrawn must be taken offshore or re-invested within the period of 45 days beginning with the day on which the withdrawal was made, and

    (c) any part of the tax deposit that has been neither used to pay a tax liability nor withdrawn by the due date must be withdrawn by the depositor and taken offshore or reinvested within the period of 45 days beginning with that date.

(7) Where the CTD conditions were not breached because the requisite amount was taken offshore or re-invested within the 45-day period mentioned in subsection (6)(b) or (c)—

    (a) section 809VL applies to the amount taken offshore or reinvested as it applies to disposal proceeds, but

    (b) read the reference in section 809VL(4)(a) to the potentially chargeable event as a reference to—

        (i) the withdrawal, in a case within subsection (6)(b), and

        (ii) the due date, in a case within subsection (6)(c).

(8) For the purposes of this section—

    (a) "the relevant tax liability" means P's liability to capital gains tax for the tax year in which the disposal took place,

    (b) "the due date" means the date by which the relevant tax liability is required to be paid,

    (c) "re-invested" has the meaning given in section 809VI(7), and

    (*d*) references to withdrawal include repayment for whatever reason.][1]

Amendments—[1] Sections 809VA–809VO inserted by FA 2012 s 47, Sch 12 paras 1, 7 with effect where the relevant event (as defined in ITA 2007 s 809VA) or the ceasing to be exempt property (as defined in ITA 2007 s 809Y) occurs on or after 6 April 2012.

[809VN Order of disposals etc

(1) Subsection (2) applies if at any time income or chargeable gains of an individual are treated under section 809VA as not remitted to the United Kingdom as a result of—

    (a) more than one qualifying investment made in the same target company,

    (b) more than one qualifying investment made in companies in the same eligible trading group, or

    (c) qualifying investments made in an eligible trading company and in an eligible stakeholder company [or eligible hybrid company][2] that holds investments in that trading company.

(2) In the application of section 809VG at that time—

    (a) treat the investments and holdings as if they were a single qualifying investment and a single holding, and

    (b) assume that a disposal of all or part of that deemed single holding affects the deemed single investment in the order in which the qualifying investments were made (that is to say, on a first in, first out basis).

(3) Subsection (4) applies if at any time—

    (a) income or chargeable gains of an individual are treated under section 809VA as not remitted to the United Kingdom as a result of one or more qualifying investments,

    (b) in addition to that investment or those investments, a relevant person holds at least one other investment in the same target company, the same eligible trading group or a related eligible company, and

    (c) that other investment is not a qualifying investment.

(4) In the application of section 809VG at that time—

    (a) treat the investments and holdings as if they were a single investment and a single holding, and

    (b) assume that a disposal of all or part of that deemed single holding is a disposal of a holding from a qualifying investment until the holdings from all the qualifying investments have been disposed of.

(5) The reference to a "related eligible company"—

    (a) in relation to an eligible trading company, is to an eligible stakeholder company [or eligible hybrid company]² that holds investments in that company, and

    (b) in relation to an eligible stakeholder company [or eligible hybrid company]², is to an eligible trading company in which that company holds investments.

(6) Subsections (2) and (4) apply whether the investments in question are held by the same relevant person or different ones.]¹

HMRC Manuals—Residence, Domicile and Remittance Basis Manual RDRM34530 (order of disposals: multiple qualifying investments).

Amendments—¹ Sections 809VA–809VO inserted by FA 2012 s 47, Sch 12 paras 1, 7 with effect where the relevant event (as defined in ITA 2007 s 809VA) or the ceasing to be exempt property (as defined in ITA 2007 s 809Y) occurs on or after 6 April 2012.

² In sub-ss (1)(c), (5)(a), (b), words inserted by F(No 2)A 2017 s 15(1), (7) with effect where the relevant event, as defined in ITA 2007 s 809VA, occurs on or after 6 April 2017.

[809VO Investments made from mixed funds

(1) This section applies if—

    (a) but for section 809VA(2), income or gains would have been remitted to the United Kingdom by virtue of a relevant event, and

    (b) section 809Q (transfers from mixed funds) would have applied in determining the amount that would have been so remitted.

(2) The relevant event counts as an offshore transfer for the purposes of section 809R(4).

(3) The holding is to be treated as containing a proportion of each kind of income and capital contained in the invested property equal to the fixed proportion.

(4) "The fixed proportion" is the proportion of that kind of income or capital contained in the invested property by virtue of subsection (2).

(5) "The invested property" means the money or other property used to make the investment.

(6) Subsection (7) applies in cases where—

    (a) section 809VG(2) does not apply because an amount is taken offshore, re-invested or used to make a tax deposit, or

    (b) section 809VM(4) does not apply because an amount is taken offshore or re-invested.

(7) The amount taken offshore, re-invested or used to make a tax deposit is treated, immediately after that step, as containing the fixed proportion of each kind of income and capital contained in the holding.

(8) In cases where section 809VG(2) applies—

    (a) the affected income or gains are so much of the fixed amount of each kind of income or gain mentioned in subsection (1)(a) as reflects the portion of the investment affected by the potentially chargeable event (see section 809VG(6)),

    (b) "the fixed amount" is the amount of that kind of income or gain that the holding is treated as containing by virtue of subsection (3), and

    (c) section 809Q does not apply in determining the affected income or gains.

(9) Section 809R(2) and (3) and section 809S apply for the purposes of this section.]¹

Commentary—*Simon's Taxes* **E6.333A, E6.333B.**

HMRC Manuals—Residence, Domicile and Remittance Basis Manual RDRM34540 (mixed funds).

Amendments—¹ Sections 809VA–809VO inserted by FA 2012 s 47, Sch 12 paras 1, 7 with effect where the relevant event (as defined in ITA 2007 s 809VA) or the ceasing to be exempt property (as defined in ITA 2007 s 809Y) occurs on or after 6 April 2012.

[Relief for certain UK services]

Amendments—Cross-head inserted by FA 2012 s 47, Sch 12 paras 1, 8 with effect where the relevant event (as defined in ITA 2007 s 809VA) or the ceasing to be exempt property (as defined in ITA 2007 s 809Y) occurs on or after 6 April 2012.

[809W Consideration for certain services

(1) This section applies to income or chargeable gains if—

    (*a*) the income or gains would (but for subsection (2)) be regarded as remitted to the United Kingdom because conditions A and B in section 809L are met,

    (*b*) condition A in section 809L is met because a service is provided in the United Kingdom ("the relevant UK service"), and

(c) condition B in section 809L is met because section 809L(3)(a) or (b) applies to the consideration for the relevant UK service ("the relevant consideration").

(2) The income or chargeable gains are to be treated as not remitted to the United Kingdom if the following conditions are met; but this is subject to subsection (5).

(3) Condition A is that the relevant UK service relates wholly or mainly to property situated outside the United Kingdom.

(4) Condition B is that the whole of the relevant consideration is given by way of one or more payments to one or more bank accounts held outside the United Kingdom by or on behalf of the person who provides the relevant UK service.

(5) Subsection (2) does not apply if the relevant UK service relates (to any extent) to the provision in the United Kingdom of—

(a) a benefit that is treated as deriving from the income by virtue of section 735, or

(b) a relevant benefit within the meaning of section 87B of TCGA 1992 that is treated as deriving from the chargeable gains by virtue of that section.

(6) Sections 275 to 275C of TCGA 1992 (location of assets) apply for the purposes of subsection (3) as they apply for the purposes of TCGA 1992.][1]

Commentary—*Simon's Taxes* **E6.329**.

HMRC Manuals—Residence, Domicile and Remittance Basis Manual RDRM34040-34060 (relevant services provided in the UK, with many examples).

Amendments—[1] Chapter A1, ss 809A–809Z7 inserted by FA 2008 s 25, Sch 7 para 1 with effect for the tax year 2008–09 and subsequent tax years.

[Exempt property relief]

Amendments—Cross-head inserted by FA 2012 s 47, Sch 12 paras 1, 9 with effect where the relevant event (as defined in ITA 2007 s 809VA) or the ceasing to be exempt property (as defined in ITA 2007 s 809Y) occurs on or after 6 April 2012.

[809X Exempt property

(1) Exempt property which is brought to, or received or used in, the United Kingdom in circumstances in which section 809L(2)(a) applies is to be treated as not remitted to the United Kingdom.

(2) Subsections (3) to (5) set out the cases in which property is exempt property.

(3) Property is exempt property if it meets the public access rule (see [section 809Z)][3].

(4) Clothing, footwear, jewellery and watches . . . [2] are exempt property if they meet the personal use rule (see section 809Z2).

(5) Property . . . [2] is exempt property if—

(a) the property meets the repair rule (see section 809Z3),

(b) the property meets the temporary importation rule (see section 809Z4), or

(c) the notional remitted amount (see section 809Z5) is less than £1,000.][1]

Commentary—*Simon's Taxes* **E6.330**.

HMRC Manuals—Residence, Domicile and Remittance Basis Manual RDRM34070 (exempt property)

Amendments—[1] Chapter A1, ss 809A–809Z7 inserted by FA 2008 s 25, Sch 7 para 1 with effect for the tax year 2008–09 and subsequent tax years.

[2] In sub-ss (4), (5), words repealed by FA 2009 s 51, Sch 27 para 10 with effect for the tax year 2008–09 and subsequent tax years.

[3] In sub-s (3) words substituted by FA 2013 s 20, Sch 7 paras 1, 2 with effect in relation to property that is not in the UK on 6 April 2013, as from that date, and in relation to property that is in the UK on that date, as from the time when it ceases to be in the UK or is lost or stolen. Note that, in the case of property that is in the UK on 6 April 2013 but ceases to be in the UK by virtue of being lost or stolen, any period that is a period of importation in relation to the property for the purposes of s 809Z4 of this Act ends with the time at which it is lost or stolen.

[809Y Property that ceases to be exempt property treated as remitted

(1) Property that ceases to be exempt property is to be treated as having been remitted to the United Kingdom at the time it ceases to be exempt property.

(2) Property ceases to be exempt property in [any][3] of the following cases.

(3) The first case is where the whole or part of the exempt property is sold, or otherwise converted into money, whilst it is in the United Kingdom.

(4) The second case is where the property—

(a) is exempt property only because it meets one or more of the relevant rules,

(b) ceases to meet that rule, or all of those rules, whilst it is in the United Kingdom, and

(c) does not meet any other relevant rule.

[(4A) Where exempt property has been lost, stolen or destroyed, the first and second cases do not apply in relation to the property during any period—

(a) beginning with the time at which it was lost, stolen or destroyed, and

(b) (if lost or stolen) ending with the time at which it is recovered.

(4B) The third case is where a compensation payment is released in respect of exempt property that has been lost, stolen or destroyed.][3]

(5) In this section—

"money" includes—

(a) a traveller's cheque,

   (*b*) a promissory note,
   (*c*) a bill of exchange, and
   (*d*) any other—
       (i) instrument that is evidence of a debt, or
       (ii) voucher, stamp or similar token or document which is capable of being exchanged
            for money, goods or services, and
   "relevant rule" means—
       (*a*) the public access rule,
       (*b*) the personal use rule,
       (*c*) the repair rule, and
       (*d*) the temporary importation rule.]¹

[(6) Subsection (1) does not apply to property that ceases to be exempt property [by virtue of the first
or second case]³ if—
   (*a*) the property, or anything into which it is converted, is used by a relevant person to make a
          qualifying investment within the period of 45 days beginning with the day on which it ceased
          to be exempt property, and
   (*b*) the remittance basis user makes a claim for relief under this subsection on or before the first
          anniversary of the 31 January following the tax year in which the property ceases to be
          exempt property.
(7) The reference in subsection (6)(*a*) to anything into which property is converted is—
   (*a*) if the property is disposed of, the disposal proceeds, and
   (*b*) if the property is converted into money in some other way, the money into which it is
          converted, (including where the disposal or conversion occurs after the property ceases to be
          exempt property).
(8) If subsection (1) does not apply by virtue of subsection (6)—
   (*a*) the property (or thing into which it was converted) used to make the investment is to be
          treated as containing or deriving from an amount of each kind of income and gain mentioned
          in section 809Q(4)(*a*) to (*h*) equal to the fixed amount,
   (*b*) the income or gains treated under section 809X as not remitted to the United Kingdom
          continue to be treated as not remitted to the United Kingdom even though the property has
          ceased to be exempt property, and
   (*c*) the business investment provisions apply to the income and gains as they apply to income or
          gains treated under section 809VA(2) as not remitted to the United Kingdom.
(9) "The fixed amount" is the amount of that kind of income or gain contained in the property when
it was brought to, or received or used in, the United Kingdom (as mentioned in section 809X).
(10) If the investment is made using more than just the property (or thing into which it was
converted), treat only the part made using the property (or thing into which it was converted) as "the
investment" for the purposes of the business investment provisions.]²

Commentary—*Simon's Taxes* **E6.330, E4.1319, E4.15, E6.330A.**
HMRC Manuals—Residence, Domicile and Remittance Basis Manual RDRM34080 (exemptions: property ceasing to be exempt
   property).
Amendments—¹   Chapter A1, ss 809A–809Z7 inserted by FA 2008 s 25, Sch 7 para 1 with effect for the tax year 2008–09 and
   subsequent tax years.
²   Sub-ss (6)–(10) inserted by FA 2012 s 47, Sch 12 paras 1, 10 with effect where the relevant event (as defined in ITA 2007
   s 809VA) or the ceasing to be exempt property (as defined in ITA 2007 s 809Y) occurs on or after 6 April 2012.
³   In sub-s (2), word substituted, sub-ss (4A), (4B) inserted, and in sub-s (6) words inserted, by FA 2013 s 20, Sch 7 paras 1,
   3 with effect in relation to property that is lost, stolen or destroyed on or after 6 April 2013.

[809YA Exception to section 809Y: proceeds taken offshore or invested
(1) Section 809Y(1) does not apply to property if—
   (a) it ceases to be exempt property because the whole of it is sold whilst it is in the United
        Kingdom, and
   (b) conditions A to F are met.
(2) Condition A is that the sale is to a person other than a relevant person.
(3) Condition B is that the sale is by way of a bargain made at arm's length.
(4) Condition C is that, once the sale is completed, no relevant person—
   (a) has any interest in the property,
   (b) is able or entitled to benefit from the property by virtue of any interest, right or arrangement,
        or
   (c) has any right (whether conditional or unconditional) to acquire any interest mentioned in
        paragraph (a) or ability or entitlement mentioned in paragraph (b).
(5) Condition D is that the whole of the disposal proceeds are released (whether in one go or in
instalments) on or before the final deadline.
(6) "The final deadline" is the first anniversary of the 5 January following the tax year in which the
property ceases to be exempt property (within the meaning of section 809Y).
(7) Condition E is that—

(a) the whole of the disposal proceeds are taken offshore or used by a relevant person to make a qualifying investment within the period of 45 days beginning with the day on which the proceeds are released, or

(b) if the disposal proceeds are paid in instalments, each instalment is taken offshore or used by a relevant person to make a qualifying investment within the period of 45 days beginning with the day on which the instalment is released.

(8) But if any of the disposal proceeds are released in the period of 45 days ending with the final deadline, Condition E is satisfied, as respects those proceeds, only if they are taken offshore or used by a relevant person to make a qualifying investment on or before the final deadline.

(9) Condition F is that, if Condition E is satisfied wholly or in part by using disposal proceeds to make a qualifying investment, the remittance basis user makes a claim for relief under section 809YC(2) on or before the first anniversary of the 31 January following the tax year in which the property is sold.

(10) For the purposes of this section, proceeds or instalments are "released" on the day on which they first become available for use by or for the benefit of any relevant person.

(11) This section does not apply if the sale is made as part of or as a result of a scheme or arrangement the main purpose or one of the main purposes of which is the avoidance of tax.]¹

Commentary—*Simon's Taxes* E6.330, E6.333A, E6.333B.
HMRC Manuals—Residence, Domicile and Remittance Basis Manual RDRM34240 (sales of exempt property).
Amendments—¹ Sections 809YA–809YD inserted by FA 2012 s 47, Sch 12 paras 1, 18 with effect in relation to exempt property that is sold on or after 6 April 2012 (including property sold pursuant to a contract entered into before that date so long as the contract only becomes unconditional on or after that date).

[809YB Condition E: supplementary

(1) An officer of Revenue and Customs may agree in a particular case to extend any period within which disposal proceeds (or instalments) must be taken offshore or used by a relevant person to make a qualifying investment in order to satisfy Condition E.

(2) The power to agree to an extension is exercisable only in exceptional circumstances and only if the remittance basis user requests such an extension.]¹

Commentary—*Simon's Taxes* E6.333A, E6.333B.
Amendments—¹ Sections 809YA–809YD inserted by FA 2012 s 47, Sch 12 paras 1, 18 with effect in relation to exempt property that is sold on or after 6 April 2012 (including property sold pursuant to a contract entered into before that date so long as the contract only becomes unconditional on or after that date).

[809YC Effect of disapplying section 809Y

(1) This section has effect if section 809Y(1) does not apply to property by virtue of section 809YA.

(2) The income and gains treated under section 809X as not remitted to the United Kingdom continue to be treated after the sale as not remitted to the United Kingdom even though the property has ceased to be exempt property.

(3) But nothing in subsection (2) prevents anything done in relation to any part of the disposal proceeds after that part is taken offshore (or used to make a qualifying investment) from counting as a remittance of the underlying income or gains to the United Kingdom at the time when the thing is done.

(4) Treat the disposal proceeds as containing or deriving from an amount of each kind of income and gain mentioned in section 809Q(4)(a) to (h) equal to the amount of that kind of income or gain contained in the exempt property when it was brought to, or received or used in, the United Kingdom (as mentioned in section 809X).

(5) Where Condition E was met by using the disposal proceeds to make a qualifying investment—

(a) the business investment provisions apply to the income and gains that continue, by virtue of subsection (2), to be treated as not remitted as they apply to income or gains that are treated under section 809VA(2) as not remitted, and

(b) if the investment was made using more than just the disposal proceeds, treat only the part of the investment made using the disposal proceeds as "the investment" for the purposes of those provisions.]¹

HMRC Manuals—Residence, Domicile and Remittance Basis Manual RDRM34240 (sales of exempt property).
RDRM34270 (exempt property: taking proceeds offshore or investing them).
RDRM34320 (relevant events).
Amendments—¹ Sections 809YA–809YD inserted by FA 2012 s 47, Sch 12 paras 1, 18 with effect in relation to exempt property that is sold on or after 6 April 2012 (including property sold pursuant to a contract entered into before that date so long as the contract only becomes unconditional on or after that date).

[809YD Chargeable gains accruing on sales of exempt property

(1) This section applies to an individual ("P") if—

(a) a chargeable gain (but not a loss) accrues to a person on a sale of exempt property,

(b) but for section 809YA, section 809Y(1) would have applied to the property by virtue of the sale, and

(c) P is either—

(i) the person to whom the gain accrues, or

      (ii) a person to whom a part of the gain is treated as accruing under [section 3][3] of TCGA 1992 (members of non-resident companies).

(2) The relevant UK gain is to be treated for the purposes of this Chapter as if—
    (a) it were a foreign chargeable gain of P, and
    (b) in the case of section 809E, it were not part of P's UK income and gains.

(3) Accordingly, if section 809F applies to P for the applicable tax year . . . .[2], the relevant UK gain is charged in accordance with [paragraph 1 of Schedule 1 to TCGA 1992][3] as if it were a foreign chargeable gain.

(4) The relevant UK gain is—
    (a) in a case falling within subsection (1)(c)(i), the gain accruing to P,
    (b) in a case falling within subsection (1)(c)(ii), the part of the gain treated as accruing to P.

(5) The applicable tax year is—
    (a) if [section 1M][3] of TCGA 1992 (temporary non-residents) applies in P's case and the relevant UK gain is within subsection (2) of that section, [the tax year that consists of or includes the period of return][3] as defined in that section,
    (b) otherwise, the tax year in which the relevant UK gain accrues.

(6) In applying this Chapter to the relevant UK gain—
    (a) treat the amount of any gains mentioned in section 809Q(4)(e) contained in the disposal proceeds by virtue of section 809YC(4) as increased by the amount of the relevant UK gain,
    (b) disregard section 809U, and
    (c) anything done in relation to any part of the disposal proceeds before the part is taken offshore or used to make a qualifying investment (or both) does not count as a remittance to the United Kingdom of any of the relevant UK gain.

(7) The relevant UK gain is to be treated for the purposes of the following provisions of TCGA 1992 as if it [accrued on the disposal of a foreign asset (within the meaning of Schedule 1 to TCGA 1992)][3]—
    [(a) section 1M,
    (b) section 3D, and
    (c) Schedule 1.][3]

(8) This section has effect despite [section 3D(2)][3] of TCGA 1992.

(9) This section does not apply with respect to a chargeable gain if P gives notice to Her Majesty's Revenue and Customs under this subsection.

(10) A notice under subsection (9)—
    (a) must be in writing and must identify the gain in question,
    (b) must be given on or before the first anniversary of the 31 January following the applicable tax year, and
    (c) may not be revoked after that first anniversary.][1]

HMRC Manuals—Residence, Domicile and Remittance Basis Manual RDRM34280 (chargeable gains on sales of exempt property).

Amendments—[1] Sections 809YA–809YD inserted by FA 2012 s 47, Sch 12 paras 1, 18 with effect in relation to exempt property that is sold on or after 6 April 2012 (including property sold pursuant to a contract entered into before that date so long as the contract only becomes unconditional on or after that date).

[2] In sub-s (3) words "and P is not domiciled in the United Kingdom in that year" repealed by FA 2013 s 219, Sch 46 para 23 with effect in relation to an individual's foreign income and gains for the tax year 2013–14 or any subsequent tax year, subject to transitional provisions in FA 2013 Sch 46 para 26.

[3] In sub-s (1)(c)(ii), words substituted for words "section 13"; in sub-s (3), words substituted for words "section 12 of TCGA 1992"; in sub-s (5)(a), words substituted for words "section 10A" and "the year of return"; in sub-s (7), words substituted for words "fell within the definition of foreign chargeable gains in section 12(4) of that Act", and paras (a)–(c) substituted for previous paras (a)–(d); and in sub-s (8), words substituted for words "section 14A(2)"; by FA 2019 s 13, Sch 1 paras 99, 106 with effect for capital gains tax purposes for the tax year 2019–20 and subsequent tax years, and for corporation tax purposes for accounting periods beginning on or after 6 April 2019. These amendments also have effect for corporation tax purposes in relation to disposals made on or after 6 April 2019 (whether in their application to accounting periods beginning on and, ending on or after, that date or to later accounting periods). See also transitional provisions in FA 2019 Sch 1 paras 121–126.

[809YE Exception to section 809Y: gifts to the nation]
(1) Section 809Y(1) does not apply to property if—
    (a) it ceases to be exempt property in the second case mentioned in that section, and
    (b) by no later than the time when it ceases to be exempt property, it has been donated in the circumstances described in paragraph 1 of Schedule 14 to FA 2012 (gifts to the nation).

(2) Where section 809Y(1) does not apply to property by virtue of this section, the property is to continue to be treated as not remitted to the United Kingdom even though it no longer meets any of the relevant rules.][1]

Commentary—*Simon's Taxes* **E6.330A**.
Amendments—[1] This section inserted by FA 2012 s 49, Sch 14 para 35 with effect from 17 July 2012.

[809YF Exception to section 809Y: compensation taken offshore or invested]
(1) Section 809Y(1) does not apply to property if—

(*a*) it ceases to be exempt property because a compensation payment in respect of it is released, and

(*b*) conditions A and B are met.

(2) Condition A is that the whole of the compensation payment is taken offshore or used by a relevant person to make a qualifying investment within the period of 45 days beginning with the day on which the payment is released.

(3) Condition B is that, if Condition A is satisfied wholly or in part by using the compensation payment to make a qualifying investment, the remittance basis user makes a claim for relief under subsection (4) on or before the first anniversary of the 31 January following the tax year in which the payment is released.

(4) If section 809Y(1) does not apply to property by virtue of subsection (1), the income and gains treated under section 809X as not remitted to the United Kingdom continue to be treated after the compensation payment is released as not remitted to the United Kingdom even though the property has ceased to be exempt property.

(5) But nothing in subsection (4) prevents anything done in relation to any part of the compensation payment after that payment is taken offshore (or used to make a qualifying investment) from counting as a remittance of the underlying income or gains to the United Kingdom at the time when the thing is done.

(6) Treat the compensation payment as containing or deriving from an amount of each kind of income and gain mentioned in section 809Q(4)(*a*) to (*h*) equal to the amount of that kind of income or gain contained in the exempt property when it was brought to, or received or used in, the United Kingdom (as mentioned in section 809X).

(7) Where Condition A was met by using the compensation payment to make a qualifying investment—

(*a*) the business investment provisions apply to the income and gains that continue, by virtue of subsection (4), to be treated as not remitted as they apply to income or gains that are treated under section 809VA(2) as not remitted, and

(*b*) if the investment was made using more than just the compensation payment, treat only the part of the investment made using the payment as "the investment" for the purposes of those provisions.][1]

Commentary—*Simon's Taxes* **E6.330**.
Amendments—[1]   Section 809YF inserted by FA 2013 s 20, Sch 7 paras 1, 4 with effect in relation to property that is lost, stolen or destroyed on or after 6 April 2013.

[809Z Public access rule: general

(1) Property meets the public access rule if conditions [B and C][2] are met.

(2) . . .[2]

(3) Condition B is that—

(*a*) the property is available for public access at an approved establishment,

(*b*) the property is to be available for public access at an approved establishment and, in connection with its being so available, is in transit to, or in storage at, public access rule premises, or

(*c*) the property has been available for public access at an approved establishment and, in connection with its having been so available, is in transit from, or in storage at, public access rule premises.

(4) Property is "available for public access" at an approved establishment if the property is—

(*a*) on public display at the establishment,

(*b*) held by the establishment and made available to the public on request for viewing or for educational use, or

(*c*) held by the establishment for public exhibition in connection with the sale of the property.

(5) An "approved establishment" is—

(*a*) an approved museum, gallery or other institution within the meaning of Group 9 of Schedule 2 to the Value Added Tax (Imported Goods) Relief Order 1984, or

(*b*) any other person, premises or institution designated (or of a description designated) by the Commissioners.

(6) "Public access rule premises" are—

(*a*) premises in the United Kingdom at which the property is to be, or has been, available for public access, or

(*b*) other commercial premises in the United Kingdom used by the approved establishment for the storage of property in advance of its being, or after its having been, available for public access at the approved establishment.

(7) Condition C is that, during the relevant period, the property meets condition B for no more than—

(*a*) two years, or

(*b*) such longer period as the Commissioners may specify.

(8) "The relevant period" means the period—

   (*a*) beginning with the importation of the property, and

   (*b*) ending when it ceases to be in the United Kingdom after that importation.

[(8A) But if the property is lost or stolen—

   (*a*) the relevant period ends with the time at which it is lost or stolen, and

   (*b*) a new relevant period begins with its importation or the time at which it is recovered.][3]

(9) "Importation" means the property being brought to, or received or used in, the United Kingdom in circumstances in which section 809L(2)(*a*) applies.

(10) . . . [2]][1]

Commentary—*Simon's Taxes* **E6.330**.

HMRC Manuals—Residence, Domicile and Remittance Basis Manual RDRM34100-34160 (explanation of Conditions A-D, with examples).

Amendments—[1]   Chapter A1, ss 809A–809Z7 inserted by FA 2008 s 25, Sch 7 para 1 with effect for the tax year 2008–09 and subsequent tax years.

[2]   In sub-s (1), references substituted, and sub-ss (2), (10) repealed, by FA 2013 s 20, Sch 7 paras 1, 5(1)–(3), (5) with effect in relation to property that is not in the UK on 6 April 2013, as from that date, and in relation to property that is in the UK on that date, as from the time when it ceases to be in the UK or is lost or stolen. Note that, in the case of property that is in the UK on 6 April 2013 but ceases to be in the UK by virtue of being lost or stolen, any period that is a period of importation in relation to the property for the purposes of s 809Z4 of this Act ends with the time at which it is lost or stolen.

[3]   Sub-s (8A) inserted by FA 2013 s 20, Sch 7 paras 1, 5(1), (4) with effect in relation to property that is lost, stolen or destroyed on or after 6 April 2013.

[809Z2 Personal use rule

(1) Clothing, footwear, jewellery or watches meet the personal use rule if they—

   (*a*) are property of a relevant person, and

   (*b*) are for the personal use of a relevant individual.

(2) In this section—

   (*a*) . . . [2]

   (*b*) "relevant individual" means an individual who is a relevant person by virtue of section 809M(2)(*a*), (*b*), (*c*) or (*d*) (the individual with income or gains, or a husband, wife, civil partner, child or grandchild).][1]

Commentary—*Simon's Taxes* **E6.330, E6.330B**.

HMRC Manuals—Residence, Domicile and Remittance Basis Manual RDRM34170 (example of personal use rule).

Amendments—[1]   Chapter A1, ss 809A–809Z7 inserted by FA 2008 s 25, Sch 7 para 1 with effect for the tax year 2008–09 and subsequent tax years.

[2]   Sub-s (2)(*a*) repealed by FA 2012 s 47, Sch 12 paras 1, 11 with effect where the relevant event (as defined in ITA 2007 s 809VA) or the ceasing to be exempt property (as defined in ITA 2007 s 809Y) occurs on or after 6 April 2012.

[809Z3 Repair rule

(1) Property meets the repair rule for the whole of the relevant period if, during the whole of that period, the property meets the repair conditions.

(2) Property meets the repair rule for a part of the relevant period if—

   (*a*) during the whole of that part of that period, the property meets the repair conditions, and

   (*b*) during the whole of the other part of that period, or the whole of each other part of that period, the property meets the repair conditions or the public access rule.

(3) Property meets the repair conditions if the property—

   (*a*) is under repair or restoration,

   (*b*) is in transit from a place outside the United Kingdom to repair rule premises, in transit between such premises, or in storage at such premises, in advance of repair or restoration, or

   (*c*) is in storage at such premises, in transit between such premises, or in transit from such premises to a place outside the United Kingdom, following repair or restoration.

(4) "Repair rule premises" means—

   (*a*) premises in the United Kingdom that are to be used, or have been used, for the repair or restoration referred to in subsection (3)(*b*) or (*c*), or

   (*b*) other commercial premises in the United Kingdom used by the restorer for the storage of property in advance of, or following, repair or restoration of property by the restorer.

(5) "Restorer" means the person who is to carry out, or has carried out, the repair or restoration referred to in subsection (3)(*b*) or (*c*).

(6) Property meets the repair conditions, or the public access rule, during the whole of a period, or the whole of part of a period, if the property meets those conditions or that rule—

   (*a*) on the whole of, or on part of, the first day of that period or part period,

   (*b*) on the whole of, or on part of, the last day of that period or part period, and

   (*c*) on the whole of each other day of that period or part period.

(7) "The relevant period" has the same meaning as in section 809Z.][1]

Commentary—*Simon's Taxes* **E6.330, E6.330C**.

HMRC Manuals—Residence, Domicile and Remittance Basis Manual RDRM34190 (examples involving the repair rule). RDRM34200 (allowable repair premises).

Amendments—[1]   Chapter A1, ss 809A–809Z7 inserted by FA 2008 s 25, Sch 7 para 1 with effect for the tax year 2008–09 and subsequent tax years.

ITA 2007

[809Z4 Temporary importation rule

(1) Property meets the temporary importation rule if the total number of countable days [(subject to any increase under subsection (3B))][3] is 275 or fewer.

(2) A "countable day" is a day on which, or on part of which, the property is in the United Kingdom by virtue of being brought to, or received or used in, the United Kingdom in circumstances in which section 809L(2)(a) applies (whether the current case, or a past case, when the property was so brought, received or used).

(3) A day is not a countable day if, on that day or any part of that day—
  [(za) the property meets the public access rule,][4]
  (a) the property meets the personal use rule,
  (b) the property meets the repair rule, . . . [2]
  [(ba) subsection (3A) applies to the property,][3]
  (c) the notional remitted amount in relation to the property is less than £1,000 [or
  (d) all or any part of the income or chargeable gains contained in the property (or from which the property derives) is treated, or continues to be treated, under section 809VA(2), 809Y(8)(b)[, 809YC(2) or 809YF(4)][3] as not remitted to the United Kingdom.][2]

[(3A) This subsection applies to the property if—
  (a) it is not available to be used or enjoyed in the United Kingdom by or for the benefit of a relevant person because it has been lost, stolen or destroyed,
  (b) (if lost or stolen) it has not been recovered, and
  (c) no compensation payment has been released in respect of it.

(3B) If—
  (a) property that has been lost or stolen is recovered,
  (b) the first day after the day on which it is recovered is a countable day, and
  (c) excluding that countable day there have already been 231 or more countable days in relation to the property,
the number of countable days specified in subsection (1) is read as being increased by the number necessary for there to be 45 countable days beginning with the countable day mentioned in paragraph (b).][3]

(4)–(10) . . . [4]][1]

Commentary—*Simon's Taxes* E6.330, E6.330D.
HMRC Manuals—Residence, Domicile and Remittance Basis Manual RDRM34210 (exempt property - temporary importation rule).
RDRM34220 (temporary importation rule - countable days).
RDRM34230 (temporary importation rule - period of importation).
Amendments—[1] Chapter A1, ss 809A–809Z7 inserted by FA 2008 s 25, Sch 7 para 1 with effect for the tax year 2008–09 and subsequent tax years.
[2] Sub-s (3)(d) and preceding word "or" inserted, and word "or" at the end of sub-s (3)(b) repealed, by FA 2012 s 47, Sch 12 paras 1, 12 with effect where the relevant event (as defined in ITA 2007 s 809VA) or the ceasing to be exempt property (as defined in ITA 2007 s 809Y) occurs on or after 6 April 2012.
[3] In sub-s (1), words inserted, in sub-s (3), para (ba) inserted and in para (d) references substituted for reference "or 809YC(2)", and sub-ss (3A), (3B) inserted, by FA 2013 s 20, Sch 7 paras 1, 7(1), (2), (3)(b), (c), (4) with effect in relation to property that is lost, stolen or destroyed on or after 6 April 2013.
[4] Sub-s (3)(za) inserted and sub-ss (4)–(10) repealed, by FA 2013 s 20, Sch 7 paras 1, 7(1), (3)(a), (5) with effect in relation to property that is not in the UK on 6 April 2013, as from that date, and in relation to property that is in the UK on that date, as from the time when it ceases to be in the UK or is lost or stolen. Note that, in the case of property that is in the UK on 6 April 2013 but ceases to be in the UK by virtue of being lost or stolen, any period that is a period of importation in relation to the property for the purposes of s 809Z4 of this Act ends with the time at which it is lost or stolen.

[809Z5 Notional remitted amount

(1) The "notional remitted amount", in relation to property, is the amount . . . [2] that would be taken to be remitted to the United Kingdom in relation to the property (if section 809X did not apply in relation to the property).

(2), (3) . . . [2]][1]

Commentary—*Simon's Taxes* E6.330, E6.330E.
HMRC Manuals—Residence, Domicile and Remittance Basis Manual RDRM34180 (notional remitted amount less than £1,000).
Amendments—[1] Chapter A1, ss 809A–809Z7 inserted by FA 2008 s 25, Sch 7 para 1 with effect for the tax year 2008–09 and subsequent tax years.
[2] In sub-s (1) words repealed by FA 2009 s 51, Sch 27 para 11(1), (2) with effect for the tax year 2008–09 and subsequent tax years; sub-ss (2), (3) repealed by FA 2009 s 51, Sch 27 para 11(1), (3) with effect from 22 April 2009.

[809Z6 Exempt property: other interpretation

(1) This section applies for the purposes of sections 809X to 809Z5.
(2) "Property" does not include money.
(3) In subsection (2) "money" includes—
  (a) a traveller's cheque,
  (b) a promissory note,
  (c) a bill of exchange, and

(*d*) any other—

    (i) instrument that is evidence of a debt, or

    (ii) voucher, stamp or similar token or document which is capable of being exchanged for money, goods or services.

(4) References to property being in the United Kingdom are references to the property—

    (*a*) being in the United Kingdom after being brought to, or received in, the United Kingdom in circumstances in which section 809L(2)(*a*) applies, or

    (*b*) being used in the United Kingdom in circumstances in which section 809L(2)(*a*) applies.]¹

[(5) References to property being lost, stolen or destroyed are to the property being lost, stolen or destroyed whilst in the United Kingdom.

(6) "Compensation payment", in relation to property that has been lost, stolen or destroyed, means any payment of compensation (whether under an insurance policy or otherwise) in respect of the property.

(7) A compensation payment is "released" on the day on which it first becomes available for use in the United Kingdom by or for the benefit of any relevant person.

(8) Property that has been lost or stolen is "recovered" on the day on which it becomes available to be used or enjoyed in the United Kingdom by or for the benefit of a relevant person.]²

Commentary—*Simon's Taxes* **E6.330, E6.330E**.
Amendments—¹   Chapter A1, ss 809A–809Z7 inserted by FA 2008 s 25, Sch 7 para 1 with effect for the tax year 2008–09 and subsequent tax years.
²   Sub-ss (5)–(8) inserted by FA 2013 s 20, Sch 7 para 8 with effect in relation to property that is lost, stolen or destroyed on or after 6 April 2013.

[Interpretation of Chapter

809Z7 [Meaning of "foreign income and gains" etc]

(1) This section applies for the purposes of this Chapter.

(2) An individual's "foreign income and gains" for a tax year are—

    (*a*) the individual's relevant foreign earnings for that year,

    (*b*) the individual's foreign specific employment income for that year,

    (*c*) the individual's relevant foreign income for that year, and

    (*d*) ⁴ the individual's foreign chargeable gains for that year.

(3) An individual's "relevant foreign earnings" for a tax year are—

    (*a*) if the individual [does not meet the requirement of section 26A of ITEPA 2003 for]⁴ that year, the individual's chargeable overseas earnings for that year, and

    (*b*) otherwise, the individual's general earnings within section 26(1) of ITEPA 2003 for that year (non-UK earnings).

[(4) An individual's "foreign specific employment income" for a tax year ("the relevant tax year") consists of the income (if any) within subsections (4A) and (4B).

(4A) The income within this subsection is the individual's specific employment income for the relevant tax year so far as it consists of [securities income that is "foreign" for the purposes of section 41F]⁵ of ITEPA 2003.

(4B) The income within this subsection is any income, or any part of any income, of the individual—

    (*a*) to which section 554Z9(2) or 554Z10(2) of ITEPA 2003 applies, and

    (*b*) which consists of the value of a relevant step, or a part of the value of a relevant step, which is "for" the relevant tax year as determined under section 554Z4 of ITEPA 2003.]²

(5) An individual's "foreign chargeable gains" for a tax year [are the chargeable gains accruing to the individual in that year on the disposal of foreign assets (within the meaning of Schedule 1 to TCGA 1992)]⁶.

(6) In subsection (3)(*a*) "chargeable overseas earnings" has the same meaning as in section 22 of ITEPA 2003 (see section 23 of that Act).

(7) . . . ³.]¹

Commentary—*Simon's Taxes* **E6.330, E6.324**.
HMRC Manuals—Residence, Domicile and Remittance Basis Manual RDRM31120–31130 (relevant foreign earnings and foreign specific employment income).
Amendments—¹   Chapter A1, ss 809A–809Z7 inserted by FA 2008 s 25, Sch 7 para 1 with effect for the tax year 2008–09 and subsequent tax years.
²   Sub-ss (4A), (4B) and (4C) substituted for previous sub-s (4) by FA 2011 s 26, Sch 2 paras 40, 43 with effect in relation to relevant steps taken on or after 6 April 2011, subject to transitional provisions in FA 2011 Sch 2 paras 53–59.
³   Heading substituted and sub-s (7) repealed by FA 2012 s 47, Sch 12 paras 1, 14, 15 with effect where the relevant event (as defined in ITA 2007 s 809VA) or the ceasing to be exempt property (as defined in ITA 2007 s 809Y) occurs on or after 6 April 2012.
⁴   In sub-s (2)(*d*) words "if the individual is not domiciled in the United Kingdom in that year," repealed and in sub-s (3)(*a*) words substituted for words "is ordinarily UK resident in" by FA 2013 s 219, Sch 46 para 24 with effect in relation to an individual's foreign income and gains for the tax year 2013–14 or any subsequent tax year, subject to transitional provisions in FA 2013 Sch 46 para 26.
⁵   In sub-s (4A), words substituted for words "foreign securities income for the purposes of section 41A" by the Finance Act 2014, Schedule 9 (Consequential Amendment) Regulations, SI 2016/74 reg 2 with effect from 17 February 2016.

ITA 2007

[6]   In sub-s (5) words substituted for words "are the foreign chargeable gains (within the meaning of section 12(4) of TCGA 1992) accruing to the individual in that year." by FA 2019 s 13, Sch 1 paras 99, 107 with effect for capital gains tax purposes for the tax year 2019–20 and subsequent tax years, and for corporation tax purposes for accounting periods beginning on or after 6 April 2019. These amendments also have effect for corporation tax purposes in relation to disposals made on or after 6 April 2019 (whether in their application to accounting periods beginning on, and ending on or after, that date or to later accounting periods). See also transitional provisions in FA 2019 Sch 1 paras 121–126.

[809Z8 Meaning of "the disposal proceeds"

(1) In this Chapter, in relation to a sale or other disposal, "the disposal proceeds" means—
   (a) the consideration for the disposal, less
   (b) any agency fees that are deducted before the consideration is paid or otherwise made available to or for the benefit of the person making the disposal ("the transferor") or any other relevant person.

(2) The following rules apply in determining the consideration for the disposal.

(3) If the consideration is provided in the form of anything other than money, the amount of the consideration is the market value of the thing at the time of the disposal.

(4) If the disposal is made other than by way of a bargain made at arm's length, the disposal is deemed to be made for a consideration equal to the market value, immediately before the disposal, of the thing being disposed of.

(5) Without limiting the generality of subsection (4), a disposal made to another relevant person or to a person connected with a relevant person is treated in all cases as made other than by way of a bargain at arm's length.

(6) In subsection (1), "agency fees" means fees and other incidental costs of the disposal that are charged to the transferor by any person by or through whom the disposal is effected, but excluding any such fees or costs that—
   (a) are charged to the transferor by another relevant person, or
   (b) are to be passed on to or otherwise applied for the benefit of a relevant person.

(7) The exclusion mentioned in subsection (6) does not apply to the extent that the fees or costs—
   (a) relate to a service actually provided by the relevant person to the transferor in connection with effecting the disposal, and
   (b) do not exceed the amount that would be charged for that service if it were provided in the ordinary course of business and on arm's length terms.][1]

Commentary—*Simon's Taxes* **E6.330**.

HMRC Manuals—Residence, Domicile and Remittance Basis Manual RDRM34260 (exempt property: disposal proceeds; agency fees).

RDRM34450 (disposal proceeds).

Amendments—[1]   Sections 809Z8–809Z10 inserted by FA 2012 s 47, Sch 12 paras 1, 16 with effect where the relevant event (as defined in ITA 2007 s 809VA) or the ceasing to be exempt property (as defined in ITA 2007 s 809Y) occurs on or after 6 April 2012.

[809Z9 Taking proceeds etc offshore or investing them

(1) This section applies to a provision of this Chapter that is satisfied if something (for example, disposal proceeds) is taken offshore or used by a relevant person to make a qualifying investment.

(2) Things are to be regarded as "taken offshore" if (and only if) they are taken outside the United Kingdom such that, on leaving the United Kingdom, they cease to be available—
   (a) to be used or enjoyed in the United Kingdom by or for the benefit of a relevant person, or
   (b) to be used or enjoyed in any other way that would count as remitting income or gains to the United Kingdom.

(3) If—
   (a) the thing required to be taken offshore or invested is money, and
   (b) it is paid temporarily into an account pending satisfaction of the provision,
the provision is satisfied only if the money actually taken offshore or invested is taken from the same account.

(4) If the thing required to be taken offshore or invested is something in money's worth, the provision may be satisfied—
   (a) by taking the thing offshore or investing it, or
   (b) by taking offshore or investing money or other property of the equivalent value.

(5) "The equivalent value" is the market value of the thing in money's worth, assessed as at the date of the sale or other disposal in relation to which the provision is triggered.

(6) If the consideration for a disposal is deemed under section 809Z8(4), the provision may be satisfied by taking offshore or investing money or other property of a value equal to—
   (a) the amount of the deemed consideration, less
   (b) any agency fees (within the meaning of section 809Z8) that are deducted before the actual consideration is paid or otherwise made available to or for the benefit of a relevant person.

(7) Subsections (4)(b) and (6) do not apply in the case of other property of the equivalent value if the other property is—
   (a) exempt property under section 809X,
   (b) consideration for the disposal of any such exempt property, or

    (c)   consideration for the disposal of all or part of the holding (see section 809VC) relating to a qualifying investment.

(8) Money or other property taken offshore or invested in accordance with subsection (4)(b) or (6) is to be treated for the purposes of this Chapter—

    (a)   as deriving from the thing required to be taken offshore or invested, and

    (b)   as having the same composition of kinds of income and capital as that thing.

(9) A provision to which this section applies may be satisfied—

    (a)   by taking the whole thing offshore or investing the whole thing, or

    (b)   by taking one part offshore and investing the other part.

(10) References in this section to something being "invested" are to something being used by a relevant person to make a qualifying investment.

(11) The provisions to which this section applies include [sections 809UA(2) and 809VB(2), but in those cases[2]]—

    (a)   disregard references in this section to investment, and

    (b)   [in the case of section 809VB(2),][2] the assessment date for the purposes of subsection (5) is the date of the relevant event (see section 809VA(3)(b)).][1]

Commentary—*Simon's Taxes* E6.330.

HMRC Manuals—Residence, Domicile and Remittance Basis Manual RDRM34270 (exempt property: taking proceeds offshore or investing them).

RDRM34460 (taking proceeds offshore or investing them).

Amendments—[1]   Sections 809Z8–809Z10 inserted by FA 2012 s 47, Sch 12 paras 1, 16 with effect where the relevant event (as defined in ITA 2007 s 809VA) or the ceasing to be exempt property (as defined in ITA 2007 s 809Y) occurs on or after 6 April 2012.

[2]   In sub-s (11), words substituted and words inserted, by FA 2013 s 21(1), (4) with effect in relation to payments on account made in respect of the tax year 2012–13 and subsequent tax years.

[809Z10 General interpretation

In this Chapter—

    "the business investment provisions" means sections 809VA to 809VO;

    "the Commissioners" means the Commissioners for Her Majesty's Revenue and Customs;

    "market value" has the same meaning as in TCGA 1992 (see in particular sections 272 and 273 of that Act);

    "qualifying investment" has the meaning given by section 809VC (and references to making a qualifying investment are to be read in accordance with that section);

    "relevant person" has the meaning given by section 809M;

    "the remittance basis user", in relation to income or chargeable gains of an individual, means that individual.][1]

Amendments—[1]   Sections 809Z8–809Z10 inserted by FA 2012 s 47, Sch 12 paras 1, 16 with effect where the relevant event (as defined in ITA 2007 s 809VA) or the ceasing to be exempt property (as defined in ITA 2007 s 809Y) occurs on or after 6 April 2012.

CHAPTER 1

LIMITS ON LIABILITY TO INCOME TAX OF NON-UK RESIDENTS

Introduction

810 Overview of Chapter

(1) This Chapter provides for limits on the liability to income tax of non-UK residents.

(2) See sections 811 to 814 in the cases of—

    (a)   a non-UK resident, other than a company, and

    (b)   a non-UK resident company liable as a trustee.

(3) See sections 815 and 816 in the case of a non-UK resident company which is liable otherwise than as a trustee.

[(4) In relation to an individual—

    (a)   a reference in this Chapter to a non-UK resident's liability to income tax is a reference to the liability of someone who is non-UK resident for the tax year for which the liability arises, and

    (b)   accordingly, enactments under which income arising to a UK resident in the overseas part of a split year is treated as arising to a non-UK resident are of no relevance to this Chapter.][1]

Commentary—*Simon's Taxes* E6.126.

Amendments—[1]   Sub-s (4) inserted by FA 2013 s 218, Sch 45 para 150(1), (5) with effect from 17 July 2013.

Limit for non-UK resident individuals, trustees etc

811 Limit on liability to income tax of non-UK residents

(1) This section applies to income tax to which—

    (a)   a non-UK resident, other than a company, is liable, or

    (b)   a non-UK resident company is liable as a trustee.

(2) Subsection (1) is subject to section 812 (case where limit not to apply).

(3) The non-UK resident's liability to income tax for a tax year is limited to the sum of amounts A and B.

(4) Amount A is the sum of—

   (*a*) any sums representing income tax deducted from the non-UK resident's disregarded income for the tax year (see section 813), [and][3]

   (*b*) any sums representing income tax that are treated as deducted from or paid in respect of that income, . . .[3]

   (*c*) . . .[3]

(5) Amount B is the amount that, apart from this section, would be the non-UK resident's liability to income tax for the tax year, if the following were left out of account—

   (*a*) the non-UK resident's disregarded income for the tax year, and

   (*b*) any relief mentioned in subsection (6) to which the non-UK resident is entitled for the tax year as a result of—

      (i) section 56(3) or 460(3) of this Act . . .[1] (residence etc of claimants), or

      (ii) double taxation arrangements.

(6) The reliefs referred to in subsection (5) are—

   (*a*) an allowance under Chapter 2 of Part 3 of this Act . . .[1] (personal allowance and blind person's allowance),

   (*b*) a tax reduction under Chapter 3 of Part 3 of this Act . . .[1] (tax reductions for married couples and civil partners),

   (*c*) relief under section 457 or 458 of this Act (payments to trade unions and police organisations),

   (*d*) . . . and[2]

   (*e*) relief under section 266 of ICTA (life assurance premiums).

Commentary—*Simon's Taxes* **E6.125, E6.126.**

Derivation—FA 1995 s 128(1), (2), (4), (12).

HMRC Manuals—International Manual INTM269180 (limit to income tax charge on non-residents).

Savings and Investment Manual SAIM1170 (limit on tax liability of non-resident's savings and investment income, with example).

Amendments—[1]   In sub-s (5)(*b*)(i), words repealed by FA 2009 s 5, Sch 1 paras 1, 6(*o*)(iv) with effect for the tax year 2010–11 and subsequent tax years.

[2]   Sub-s (6)(*d*) (but not the word "and" at the end) repealed by FA 2012 s 227, Sch 39 para 32(2)(*e*) with effect for the tax year 2013–14 and subsequent tax years.

[3]   Sub-s (4)(*c*) and preceding word "and" repealed, and word "and" at end of sub-s (4)(*a*) inserted, by FA 2016 s 5, Sch 1 para 63(1), (14) with effect in relation to dividends paid or arising (or treated as paid), and other distributions made (or treated as made), in the tax year 2016-17 or at any later time.

Prospective amendments—Sub-s (6)(*e*) and the preceding word "and" to be repealed by FA 2012 s 227, Sch 39 para 28(1) with effect from a date to be appointed.

812 Case where limit not to apply

(1) Section 811 does not apply to income tax to which non-UK resident trustees are liable for a tax year, if there is a beneficiary of the trust who is—

   (*a*) an individual who is . . .[1] UK resident, or

   (*b*) a UK resident company.

(2) For the purposes of subsection (1) a person is a beneficiary of the trust if—

   (*a*) the person is an actual or potential beneficiary of the trust, and

   (*b*) condition A or B is met in relation to the person.

(3) Condition A is that the person is, or will or may become, entitled under the trust to receive some or all of any income under the trust.

(4) Condition B is that some or all of any income under the trust may be paid to or used for the benefit of the person in the exercise of a discretion conferred by the trust.

(5) The references in subsections (3) and (4) to any income under the trust include a reference to any capital under the trust so far as it represents amounts originally received by the trustees as income.

Commentary—*Simon's Taxes* **E6.125, E6.126.**

Amendments—[1]   In sub-s (1)(*a*), word "ordinarily" repealed by FA 2013 s 219, Sch 46 paras 54, 66 with effect for the purposes of a person's tax liability to income tax for the tax year 2013–14 or any subsequent tax year, subject to savings in FA 2013 Sch 46 para 73.

[812A Temporary non-residents

(1) This section applies if—

   (*a*) an individual is temporarily non-resident,

   (*b*) the individual's liability to income tax for a tax year is limited under section 811,

   (*c*) that tax year ("the non-resident year") falls within the temporary period of non-residence, and

   (*d*) the individual's income for that tax year includes relevant investment income.

(2) The total income (see Step 1 of the calculation in section 23) on which the individual is charged to income tax for the year of return is to be increased by an amount equal to the amount of that relevant investment income.

(3) But the notional UK tax on that relevant investment income is to be allowed as a credit against the individual's liability to income tax for the year of return under Step 6 of the calculation in section 23.

(4) Income is "relevant investment income" if—

    (a) it is chargeable under Chapter 3 or 5 of Part 4 of ITTOIA 2005 (dividends etc from UK resident companies and stock dividends from UK resident companies),

    (b) the distributing company is a close company, and

    (c) the income arises or is treated as arising to the individual because the individual was at a relevant time—

        (i) a material participator in that company, or

        (ii) an associate of a material participator in the company.

(5) But income within subsection (4) in the form of a cash or stock dividend is not "relevant investment income" to the extent that the dividend is paid, or the share capital is issued, in respect of post-departure trade profits.

(6) "Post-departure trade profits" are—

    (a) trade profits of the distributing company arising in an accounting period that begins after the start of the temporary period of non-residence, and

    (b) so much of any trade profits of the distributing company arising in an accounting period that straddles the start of that temporary period as is attributable (on a just and reasonable basis) to a time after the start of that temporary period.

(7) The "notional UK tax" on relevant investment income is—

    (a) the total of any sums in respect of that income that were included within amount A in determining the limit under section 811, less

    (b) any credit for foreign tax paid in respect of that income that was allowed under Chapter 2 of Part 2 of TIOPA 2010 against the individual's liability to income tax for the non-resident year.

(8) The following matters are to be determined on a just and reasonable basis—

    (a) the extent to which a dividend is paid, or share capital is issued, in respect of post-departure trade profits, and

    (b) the extent to which a sum included within amount A is a sum in respect of relevant investment income.

(9) Nothing in any double taxation arrangements is to be read as preventing the individual from being chargeable to income tax by virtue of this section (or as preventing a charge to that tax from arising as a result).

(10) Part 4 of Schedule 45 to FA 2013 (statutory residence test: anti-avoidance) explains—

    (a) when an individual is to be regarded as "temporarily non-resident", and

    (b) what "the temporary period of non-residence", "the year of departure" and "the period of return" mean.

(11) In this section—

    "associate" and "participator" have the same meanings as in Part 10 of CTA 2010 (see sections 448 and 454);

    "the distributing company" means the UK resident company mentioned in section 383(1) or, as the case may be, 410(1) of ITTOIA 2005;

    "material participator" means a participator who has a material interest in the company, as defined in section 457 of CTA 2010;

    "relevant time" means—

        (a) any time in the year of departure or, if the year of departure is a split year as respects the individual, the UK part of that year, or

        (b) any time in one or more of the 3 tax years preceding that year;

    "trade profits of the distributing company" means the profits of any trade carried on by the distributing company, as calculated in accordance with Part 3 of CTA 2009 (trading income);

    "year of return" means the tax year consisting of or including the period of return.][1]

Commentary—*Simon's Taxes* E6.126.

Amendments—[1]　Section 812A inserted by FA 2013 s 218, Sch 45 para 138 with effect if the year of departure (as defined in FA 2013 Sch 45 Pt 4) is the tax year 2013–14 or any subsequent tax year, subject to transitional provisions and savings in FA 2013 Sch 45 paras 154–158.

813 Meaning of "disregarded income"

(1) For the purposes of this Chapter income arising to a non-UK resident is "disregarded income" if it is—

    (a) disregarded savings and investment income (see section 825),

    (b) disregarded annual payments (see section 826),

    (c) disregarded pension income,

    (d) disregarded social security income,

    (e) disregarded transaction income (see section 814), or

(*f*) income of such other description as the Treasury may by regulations designate for the purposes of this section.

(2) But income in relation to which the non-UK resident has a UK representative for the purposes of [Chapter 2B][1] is not disregarded income.

(3) Income is "disregarded pension income" if it is chargeable under Part 9 of ITEPA 2003 (pension income) because any of the following provisions of that Act applies to it—

     section 577 (UK social security pensions),

     section 579A (pensions under registered pension schemes) (but see subsection (4) below),

     section 609 (annuities for the benefit of dependants),

     section 610 (annuities under non-registered occupational pension schemes), or

     section 611 (annuities in recognition of another's services).

(4) Income chargeable under Part 9 of ITEPA 2003 because section 579A of that Act applies to it is disregarded pension income only if the registered pension scheme in question—

     (*a*) falls within paragraph 1(1)(*f*) of Schedule 36 to FA 2004, and

     (*b*) was, immediately before 6 April 2006, a retirement annuity contract to which section 605 of ITEPA 2003 applied.

(5) Income is "disregarded social security income" if—

     (*a*) it is a taxable benefit listed in Table A in section 660 of ITEPA 2003, other than income support or jobseeker's allowance, and

     (*b*) it is chargeable under Part 10 of that Act (social security income).

Commentary—*Simon's Taxes* **E6.127**.

Amendments—[1] In sub-s (2), words substituted for words "section 126 of, and Schedule 23 to, FA 1995 (UK representatives of non-UK residents)", by TIOPA 2010 s 501, Sch 8 paras 280, 282. TIOPA 2010 has effect for corporation tax purposes for accounting periods ending on or after 1 April 2010, for income and capital gains tax purposes for the tax year 2010–11 and subsequent tax years, and for petroleum revenue tax purposes for chargeable periods beginning on or after 1 July 2010.

814 Meaning of "disregarded transaction income"

(1) Subsection (2) applies if a non-UK resident carries on (alone or in partnership) a business through a broker in the United Kingdom.

(2) Income is "disregarded transaction income", subject to subsection (6), if—

     (*a*) it is transaction income, and

     (*b*) the independent broker conditions are met in relation to the transaction in question.

(3) Subsection (4) applies if a non-UK resident carries on (alone or in partnership) a business through an investment manager in the United Kingdom.

(4) Income is "disregarded transaction income", subject to subsection (6), if—

     (*a*) it is transaction income, and

     (*b*) the independent investment manager conditions are met in relation to the transaction in question.

(5) In this Chapter "transaction income", in relation to a transaction carried out through a broker or investment manager in the United Kingdom on behalf of a non-UK resident, means income which arises to the non-UK resident from—

     (*a*) so much of the non-UK resident's business carried on (alone or in partnership) through the broker or investment manager as relates to the transaction, or

     (*b*) property or rights which, as a result of the transaction, are used by, or held by or for, the broker or investment manager on behalf of the non-UK resident.

(6) Income is not disregarded transaction income if it is chargeable to income tax in accordance with section 171(2) of FA 1993 (profits of the underwriting business of a member of Lloyd's).

(7) This section needs to be read with—

     section 817 (the independent broker conditions),

     sections 818 to 824 (the independent investment manager conditions),

     section 827 (meaning of "investment manager" and "investment transaction"), and

     section 828 (transactions through brokers and investment managers).

Commentary—*Simon's Taxes* **E6.127**.

Derivation—FA 1995 ss 127(1), (15), 128(3)(*d*).

Limit for non-UK resident companies

815 Limit on liability to income tax of non-UK resident companies

(1) This section applies to income tax to which a non-UK resident company is liable, otherwise than as a trustee.

(2) The non-UK resident company's liability to income tax for a tax year is limited to the sum of amounts A and B.

(3) Amount A is the sum of—

     (*a*) any amounts representing income tax deducted from the non-UK resident company's disregarded company income for the tax year, [and][1]

     (*b*) any amounts representing income tax that are treated as deducted from or paid in respect of that income, . . . [1]

     (*c*) . . . [1]

(4) Amount B is the amount that, apart from this section, would be the non-UK resident company's liability to income tax for the tax year if the non-UK resident company's disregarded company income for the tax year were left out of account.

Commentary—*Simon's Taxes* **D4.122**.

HMRC Manuals—International Manual INTM269180 (limit to income tax charge on non-residents).

Amendments—[1]   Sub-s (3)(c) and preceding word "and" repealed, and word "and" at end of sub-s (3)(a) inserted, by FA 2016 s 5, Sch 1 para 63(1), (15) with effect in relation to dividends paid or arising (or treated as paid), and other distributions made (or treated as made), in the tax year 2016-17 or at any later time.

816 Meaning of "disregarded company income"

(1) For the purposes of this Chapter income arising to a non-UK resident company is "disregarded company income" if it is—

    (a) disregarded savings and investment income (see section 825),

    (b) disregarded annual payments (see section 826),

    [(c) income arising from a transaction carried out through a broker in the United Kingdom acting as an agent of independent status in the ordinary course of the broker's business,

    (d) income arising from a transaction carried out through an investment manager in the United Kingdom acting as an agent of independent status in the ordinary course of the investment manager's business, or][1]

    (e) income of such other description as the Treasury may by regulations designate for the purposes of this section.

[(2) A broker is regarded for the purposes of subsection (1)(c) as an agent of independent status acting in the ordinary course of the broker's business in relation to a transaction carried out on behalf of a non-UK resident company in the course of that company's trade if, and only if, the independent broker conditions are met in relation to the transaction (see section 817).

(3) An investment manager is regarded for the purposes of subsection (1)(d) as an agent of independent status acting in the ordinary course of the investment manager's business in relation to an investment transaction carried out on behalf of a non-UK resident company in the course of that company's trade if, and only if, the independent investment manager conditions are met in relation to the investment transaction (see sections 818 to 824).

(4) This section needs to be read with—

    section 827 (meaning of "investment manager" and "investment transaction"), and

    section 828 (transactions through brokers and investment managers).][1]

Commentary—*Simon's Taxes* **D4.122**.

Amendments—[1]   Sub-s (1)(c), (d) substituted, and sub-ss (2)–(4) substituted for previous sub-s (2), by the Income Tax Act 2007 (Amendment) (No 3) Order, SI 2007/3506 art 3(1), (4) with effect for income tax and capital gains tax purposes for the tax year 2007–08 and subsequent tax years, and for corporation tax purposes for accounting periods ending after 5 April 2007: SI 2007/3506 art 1(2).

The independent broker conditions

817 The independent broker conditions

(1) The independent broker conditions are met in relation to a transaction carried out on behalf of a non-UK resident by a broker in the United Kingdom if—

    (a) conditions A to D are met, if this section applies for the purposes of section 813, or

    (b) conditions A to C and E are met, if this section applies for the purposes of section 816.

(2) Condition A is that at the time of the transaction the broker is carrying on the business of a broker.

(3) Condition B is that the transaction is carried out . . . [1] in the ordinary course of that business.

(4) Condition C is that the remuneration which the broker receives in respect of the transaction for the provision of the services of a broker to the non-UK resident is not less than is customary for that class of business.

(5) Condition D is that the broker does not fall for the purposes of [Chapter 2B of this Part, or of Chapter 1 of Part 7A of TCGA 1992,][1] to be treated as a UK representative of the non-UK resident in relation to any other income which is chargeable to income tax, or amounts which are chargeable to capital gains tax, for the same tax year as the transaction income.

(6) Condition E is that the broker does not fall to be treated as a permanent establishment of the non-UK resident company in relation to any other transaction of any kind carried out in the same accounting period of the non-UK resident company as the transaction in question.

Commentary—*Simon's Taxes* **E6.125**, **E6.128**.

Amendments—[1]   In sub-s (3), words repealed, and in sub-s (5), words substituted for words , by TIOPA 2010 ss 501, 503, Sch 8 paras 280, 283, Sch 10 Pt 11. TIOPA 2010 has effect for corporation tax purposes for accounting periods ending on or after 1 April 2010, for income and capital gains tax purposes for the tax year 2010–11 and subsequent tax years, and for petroleum revenue tax purposes for chargeable periods beginning on or after 1 July 2010.

The independent investment manager conditions

818 The independent investment manager conditions

(1) The independent investment manager conditions are met in relation to an investment transaction carried out on behalf of a non-UK resident by an investment manager in the United Kingdom [if conditions A to E are met.][1]

(2) Condition A is that at the time of the transaction the investment manager is carrying on a business of providing investment management services.

(3) Condition B is that the transaction is carried out in the ordinary course of that business.

(4) Condition C is that, when the investment manager acts on behalf of the non-UK resident in relation to the transaction, the relationship between them, having regard to its legal, financial and commercial characteristics, is a relationship between persons carrying on independent businesses dealing with each other at arm's length.

(5) Condition D is that the requirements of the 20% rule are met (see section 819).

(6) Condition E is that the remuneration which the investment manager receives in respect of the transaction for the provision of investment management services to the non-UK resident is not less than is customary for that class of business.

(7), (8) . . . [1]

Commentary—*Simon's Taxes* **E6.125, E6.129**.
Derivation—FA 1995 ss 127(1), (3), 128(3) and FA 2003 s 151(2), Sch 26 paras 3(1), (2), 7(2).
HMRC Manuals—International Manual INTM269060 (investment manager exemption: conditions).
Amendments—[1]   Words in sub-s (1) substituted, and sub-ss (7), (8) repealed, by FA 2008 s 38, Sch 16 para 10 with effect for the tax year 2008–09 and subsequent tax years.

819 Investment managers: the 20% rule

(1) The requirements of the 20% rule are met if conditions A and B are met.

(2) Condition A is that in relation to a qualifying period it has been or is the intention of the investment manager and the persons connected with the investment manager that at least 80% of the non-UK resident's relevant disregarded income should consist of amounts to which none of them has a beneficial entitlement.

(3) Condition B is that, so far as there is a failure to fulfil that intention, that failure—

    (*a*) is attributable (directly or indirectly) to matters outside the control of the investment manager and persons connected with the investment manager, and

    (*b*) does not result from a failure by any of them to take such steps as may be reasonable for mitigating the effect of those matters in relation to the fulfilment of that intention.

(4) This section needs to be read with—

    section 820 (meaning of "qualifying period"),

    section 821 (meaning of "relevant disregarded income"), and

    section 822 (meaning of "beneficial entitlement").

Commentary—*Simon's Taxes* **E6.129**.
Derivation—FA 1995 s 127(4) and FA 2003 Sch 26 para 4(1).
HMRC Manuals—"International Manual INTM269110 (investment managers: the 20% rule). "

820 Meaning of "qualifying period"

(1) This section applies for the purposes of this Chapter.

(2) If section 819 applies for the purposes of section 813, a "qualifying period" means—

    (*a*) the tax year in which the transaction income is chargeable to income tax, or

    (*b*) a period of not more than 5 years comprising two or more tax years including that one.

(3) If section 819 applies for the purposes of section 816, a "qualifying period" means—

    (*a*) the accounting period of the non-UK resident company in which the transaction in question is carried out, or

    (*b*) a period of not more than 5 years comprising two or more complete accounting periods including that one.

Commentary—*Simon's Taxes* **E6.125, E6.129**.
Derivation—FA 1995 s 127(7) and FA 2003 Sch 26 para 4(2).
HMRC Manuals—"International Manual INTM269110 (investment managers: the 20% rule). "

821 Meaning of "relevant disregarded income"

(1) This section applies for the purposes of this Chapter.

(2) If section 819 applies for the purposes of section 813, the "relevant disregarded income" of the non-UK resident for the qualifying period is the total of the non-UK resident's income for the tax years comprised in the qualifying period which derives from the transactions mentioned in subsection (4).

(3) If section 819 applies for the purposes of section 816, the "relevant disregarded income" of the non-UK resident company for the qualifying period is the total of the non-UK resident company's income for the accounting periods comprised in the qualifying period which derives from the transactions mentioned in [subsection (5)][1].

(4) The transactions referred to in [subsection (2)][1] are investment transactions—

    (*a*) carried out by the investment manager on the non-UK resident's behalf, and (*b*) in relation to which the independent investment manager conditions are met, ignoring the requirements of the 20% rule.

[(5) The transactions referred to in subsection (3) are transactions—

    (*a*) carried out by the investment manager on the non-UK resident company's behalf, and

    (*b*) in relation to which the investment manager does not fall to be treated as a permanent establishment of the non-UK resident company, ignoring the requirements of the 20% rule.][1]

Commentary—*Simon's Taxes* **E6.129**.

Amendments—[1]   In sub-ss (3), (4) references substituted, and sub-s (5) inserted, by the Income Tax Act 2007 (Amendment) Order, SI 2009/23 art 5(1), (3) with effect for income tax and capital gains tax purposes for the tax year 2007–08 and subsequent tax years, and for corporation tax purposes for accounting periods ending after 5 April 2007.

822 Meaning of "beneficial entitlement"

(1) This section applies for the purposes of this Chapter.

(2) A person has a "beneficial entitlement" to relevant disregarded income if the person has or may acquire a beneficial entitlement that is, or would be, attributable to the relevant disregarded income as a result of having an interest or other rights mentioned in subsection (3).

(3) The interests and rights referred to in subsection (2) are—

    (*a*) an interest (whether or not an interest giving a right to an immediate payment of a share in the profits or gains) in property in which the whole or any part of the relevant disregarded income is represented, or

    (*b*) an interest in, or other rights in relation to, the non-UK resident.

Commentary—*Simon's Taxes* **E6.129**.

Derivation—FA 1995 s 127(6) and FA 2003 Sch 26 para 4(4).

823 Treatment of transactions where requirements of 20% rule not met

(1) This section applies in the case of an investment transaction in relation to which the independent investment manager conditions are met, except for the requirements of the 20% rule.

(2) This Chapter has effect as if the requirements of that rule were met in relation to the transaction but only in relation to—

    (*a*) so much of the transaction income of the non-UK resident as falls within subsection (3), if this section applies for the purposes of section 813, or

    (*b*) so much of the income of the non-UK resident company deriving from the transaction as falls within subsection (3), if this section applies for the purposes of section 816.

(3) Income falls within this subsection if it does not represent income—

    (*a*) which is relevant disregarded income of the non-UK resident, and

    (*b*) to which the investment manager or a person connected with the investment manager has or has had any beneficial entitlement.

Commentary—*Simon's Taxes* **E6.129**.

HMRC Manuals—International Manual INTM269155 (the 20% rule: consequences of not meeting the rule).

824 Application of 20% rule to collective investment schemes

(1) This section applies if amounts arise or accrue to the non-UK resident as a participant in a collective investment scheme.

(2) It applies for the purposes of determining whether the requirements of the 20% rule are met in relation to a transaction carried out for the purposes of the scheme [(so far as the transaction is one in respect of which such amounts so arise or accrue)][1].

(3) In applying this section make the following assumptions—

    (*a*) that all the transactions carried out for the purposes of the scheme are carried out on behalf of a company ("the assumed company") which is—

        (i) constituted for the purposes of the scheme, and

        (ii) non-UK resident, and

    (*b*) that the participants do not have any rights in respect of the amounts arising or accruing in respect of those transactions, other than the rights which, if they held shares in the assumed company, would be their rights as shareholders.

(4) If the scheme is such that the assumed company would not be regarded for tax purposes as carrying on a trade in the United Kingdom in relation to the appropriate relevant period, the requirements of the 20% rule are treated as met in relation to a transaction carried out for the purposes of the scheme.

(5) If the scheme is such that the assumed company would be so regarded for tax purposes, sections 819 to 823 have effect in relation to a transaction carried out for the purposes of the scheme with the modifications in subsection (6).

(6) The modifications are—

    (*a*) for references to the non-UK resident substitute references to the assumed company, and '

    (*b*) for references to the non-UK resident's relevant disregarded income for a qualifying period substitute references to the sum of the amounts that would, for relevant periods comprised in the qualifying period, be chargeable to tax on the assumed company as profits deriving from the transactions—

     (i)   carried out by the investment manager, and

     (ii)   assumed to be carried out on behalf of the company.

(7) In this section—

    "the appropriate relevant period" is—

     (*a*)   the tax year in which the transaction income is chargeable to income tax, if this section applies for the purposes of section 813, or

     (*b*)   the accounting period in which the transaction is carried out, if this section applies for the purposes of section 816,

    "collective investment scheme" has the meaning given by section 235 of FISMA 2000,

    "participant", in relation to a collective investment scheme, is construed in accordance with that section, and

    "relevant period" means—

     (*a*)   a tax year, if this section applies for the purposes of section 813, or

     (*b*)   an accounting period, if this section applies for the purposes of section 816.

Commentary—*Simon's Taxes* **E6.129**.

Amendments—[1]   In sub-s (2), words inserted by TIOPA 2010 s 501, Sch 8 paras 280, 284. TIOPA 2010 has effect for corporation tax purposes for accounting periods ending on or after 1 April 2010, for income and capital gains tax purposes for the tax year 2010–11 and subsequent tax years, and for petroleum revenue tax purposes for chargeable periods beginning on or after 1 July 2010.

Supplementary

825 Meaning of "disregarded savings and investment income"

(1) For the purposes of this Chapter income is "disregarded savings and investment income" if—

     (*a*)   it is chargeable under Chapter 3 or 5 of Part 4 of ITTOIA 2005 (dividends etc from UK resident companies and stock dividends from UK resident companies), or

     (*b*)   it is within subsection (2) and is not relevant foreign income.

(2) Income is within this subsection if it is chargeable under—

     (*a*)   Chapter 2 of Part 4 of ITTOIA 2005 (interest),

     (*b*)   Chapter 7 of that Part (purchased life annuity payments),

     (*c*)   Chapter 8 of that Part (profits from deeply discounted securities),

     (*d*)   *Chapter 10 of that Part (distributions from unauthorised unit trusts), or*[1]

     (*e*)   Chapter 11 of that Part (transactions in deposits)[, or

     (*f*)   regulation 15 of the Unauthorised Unit Trusts (Tax) Regulations 2013.][1]

Commentary—*Simon's Taxes* **E6.127**.

HMRC Manuals—International Manual INTM269180 (limit to income tax charge on non-residents).

Amendments—[1]   In sub-s (2), para (*d*) repealed, and para (*f*) and preceding word inserted, by the Unauthorised Unit Trusts (Tax) Regulations, SI 2013/2819 reg 37(1), (9) with effect from 6 April 2014. Note that an unauthorised unit trust is not a non-exempt unauthorised unit trust, and these amendments do not apply in relation to the trust, if at all times in the period beginning with 24 May 2012 and ending with 5 April 2014 it had at least one unit holder which was, and at least one unit holder which was not, an eligible investor (ie a mixed unauthorised unit trust); this ceases to apply in relation to the trust if subsequently it no longer has any unit holders which are eligible investors (SI 2013/2819 reg 32).

826 Meaning of "disregarded annual payments"

For the purposes of this Chapter income is "disregarded annual payments" if it is not relevant foreign income and is chargeable under—

     (*a*)   section 579 of ITTOIA 2005, so far as it relates to annual payments (royalties etc from intellectual property),

     (*b*)   Chapter 4 of Part 5 of that Act, so far as it relates to annual payments (certain telecommunication rights: non-trading income), or

     (*c*)   Chapter 7 of Part 5 of that Act (annual payments not otherwise charged).

Commentary—*Simon's Taxes* **E6.127**.

Derivation—FA 1995 s 128(3)(*a*) and FA 2003 s 151(2)(*a*).

827 Meaning of "investment manager" and "investment transaction"

(1) In this Chapter "investment manager" means a person who provides investment management services.

[(2) In this section "investment transaction" means any transaction of a description specified for the purposes of this section in regulations made by the Commissioners for Her Majesty's Revenue and Customs.

(3) Provision made in regulations under subsection (2) may, in particular, have effect in relation to the tax year current on the day on which the regulations are made.][1]

(2) In this Chapter "investment transaction" means—

     (*a*)   transactions in shares, stock, futures contracts, options contracts or securities of any description not mentioned in this paragraph, but excluding futures contracts or options contracts relating to land,

     (*b*)   transactions consisting in the buying or selling of any foreign currency or in the placing of money at interest, and

(c) such other transactions as the Treasury may by regulations designate for the purposes of this section.

(3) For the purposes of subsection (2) a contract is not prevented from being a futures contract or an options contract by the fact that a party is or may be entitled to receive or liable to make, or entitled to receive and liable to make, only a payment of a sum (as opposed to a transfer of assets other than money) in full settlement of all obligations.

Commentary—*Simon's Taxes* **E6.129**.
Derivation—FA 1995 s 127(12), (13) and FA 2003 Sch 26 paras 3(1), (3), (4).
HMRC Manuals—International Manual INTM269070 (definition of "investment transaction").
Regulations—Investment Manager (Specified Transactions) Regulations 2009 (issued May 2009).
Investment Manager (Specified Transactions) Regulations 2014 (issued April 2014).
Amendments—[1]   Sub-ss (2), (3) substituted by FA 2008 s 38, Sch 16 paras 4, 5 with effect from 21 July 2008. However, the original sub-ss (2), (3), and any regulations made under them, continue to have effect until such time as the first regulations under the new regulation-making power come into force: FA 2008 Sch 16 para 11(5).

828 Transactions through brokers and investment managers

(1) For the purposes of this Chapter a person is regarded as carrying out a transaction on behalf of another if the person—
    (a) undertakes the transaction, whether on behalf of or to the account of the other, or
    (b) gives instructions for it to be so carried out by another.

(2) In the case of a person who acts as a broker or investment manager as part only of a business, this Chapter has effect as if that part were a separate business.

Commentary—*Simon's Taxes* **E6.128, E6.127, E6.129**.
Derivation—FA 1995 s 127(14), (15) and FA 2003 Sch 26 para 7(1), (4).

[CHAPTER 1A

EXEMPTION FOR PERSONS NOT DOMICILED IN UNITED KINGDOM

828A Introduction

This Chapter provides for an exemption from liability to income tax for an individual for a tax year if—
    (a) the individual is UK resident in the tax year but not domiciled in the United Kingdom in the tax year,
    (b) section 809B does not apply to the individual for the tax year, and
    (c) conditions A to F in section 828B are met.][1]

Commentary—*Simon's Taxes* **E6.340, E4.1319, E4.15**.
HMRC Manuals—Residence, Domicile and Remittance Basis Manual RDRM32070 (small amounts of foreign employment income).
RDRM32110 (unremitted foreign income and gains below £2,000 threshold).
Amendments—[1]   Chapter 1A, ss 828A–828D inserted by FA 2009 s 52(1) with effect for the tax year 2008–09 and subsequent tax years.

[828B Conditions to be met

(1) Condition A is that in the tax year the individual has income from an employment the duties of which are performed wholly or partly in the United Kingdom.
(2) Condition B is that, if the individual's income for the tax year consists of or includes relevant foreign earnings—
    (a) the amount of the relevant foreign earnings does not exceed £10,000, and
    (b) all of that amount is subject to a foreign tax.
(3) Condition C is that, if the individual's income for the tax year consists of or includes income that is relevant foreign income by virtue of section 830(2)(e) of ITTOIA 2005—
    (a) the amount of that income does not exceed £100, and
    (b) all of that amount is subject to a foreign tax.
(4) Condition D is that the individual has no other foreign income and gains for the tax year.
(5) Condition E is that the individual would not for the tax year be liable to income tax at a rate other than the basic rate[, the savings basic rate][4][, the savings nil rate][3] [, [a Scottish rate below the Scottish basic rate,][5] the Scottish basic rate][2][, the Scottish intermediate rate][5][, the Welsh basic rate][6] or the starting rate for savings if this Chapter did not apply to the individual for the tax year.
(6) Condition F is that the individual does not make a return under section 8 of TMA 1970 for the tax year.][1]

Commentary—*Simon's Taxes* **E6.341, E1.101E, E1.101F, E7.222, E6.340**.
HMRC Manuals—Residence, Domicile and Remittance Basis Manual RDRM32070 (small amounts of foreign employment income).
Amendments—[1]   Chapter 1A, ss 828A–828D inserted by FA 2009 s 52(1) with effect for the tax year 2008–09 and subsequent tax years.
[2]   In sub-s (5), words inserted by FA 2014 s 296, Sch 38 para 9 with effect in relation to the tax year 2016–17 (the tax year appointed by the Treasury under the Scotland Act 2012 s 25(5) by virtue of SI 2015/2000) and subsequent tax years.
[3]   In sub-s (5), words inserted by FA 2016 s 4(1), (10) with effect in relation to the tax year 2016–17 and subsequent tax years.

[4]   In sub-s (5), words inserted by FA 2016 s 6(1), (20) with effect in relation to the tax year 2017–18 (as appointed under the Scotland Act 2016 s 13(15)) and subsequent years by virtue of SI 2016/1161 reg 3, subject to transitional provisions (see FA 2016 s 6(24)–(30)). The Agreement between the Scottish Government and the UK Government on the Scottish Government's fiscal framework confirms that full devolution of income tax rates and thresholds for non-savings and non-dividend income will commence in April 2017.

[5]   In sub-s (5), words inserted by the Scottish Rates of Income Tax (Consequential Amendments) Order, SI 2018/459 art 6(1), (7) with effect for the tax year commencing on 6 April 2018 and subsequent tax years.

[6]   In sub-s (5), words inserted by the Wales Act 2014 s 9(1), (9). Wales Act 2014 s 9 comes into force on 24 July 2018 and has effect in relation to the tax year 2019–20 (by virtue of SI 2018/892 arts 3, 5, 6). 2019–20 is appointed as the first tax year in relation to which a Welsh rate resolution may be made by the National Assembly for Wales under GOWA 2006 s 116D (SI 2018/892 art 6).

[828C The exemption

(1) The exemption is given by deducting the relevant amount from what would otherwise be the amount of the individual's liability to income tax for the tax year under section 23.

(2) "The relevant amount" is so much of the amount of the individual's liability to income tax as is attributable to the individual's foreign income or gains for the tax year.

(3) But if for the tax year the individual's total income is reduced by any deductions which fall to be made at Step 3 of the calculation in section 23 from the individual's foreign income or gains for the tax year, subsection (2) has effect as if the individual's foreign income or gains for the tax year were reduced by the amount of the deductions.

(4) And if the individual is entitled under—

    (*a*)   [sections 2 and 6 of TIOPA 2010][2] (double taxation arrangements: relief by agreement), or

    (*b*)   [section 18(1)(*b*) and (2)][2] of that Act (relief for foreign tax where no double taxation arrangements),

to a tax reduction in respect of the individual's foreign income or gains for the tax year, what would otherwise be the relevant amount is reduced by the amount of that reduction.][1]

Commentary—*Simon's Taxes* **E6.340**.

Amendments—[1]   Chapter 1A, ss 828A–828D inserted by FA 2009 s 52(1) with effect for the tax year 2008–09 and subsequent tax years.

[2]   In sub-s (4), (*a*), (*b*), words substituted by TIOPA 2010 s 501, Sch 8 paras 71, 83. TIOPA 2010 has effect for corporation tax purposes for accounting periods ending on or after 1 April 2010, for income and capital gains tax purposes for the tax year 2010–11 and subsequent tax years, and for petroleum revenue tax purposes for chargeable periods beginning on or after 1 July 2010.

[828D Interpretation of Chapter

(1) This section applies for the purposes of this Chapter.

(2) "Employed" and "employment" have the same meaning as in the employment income Parts of ITEPA 2003: see Chapter 1 of Part 2 of that Act.

(3) "Foreign income and gains", in relation to an individual, means what would be the individual's foreign income and gains for the purposes of Chapter A1 of this Part if section 809B applied to the individual (see section 809Z7(2)).

(4) "Foreign tax" means any tax chargeable under the law of a territory outside the United Kingdom.

(5) "Relevant foreign earnings", in relation to an individual, means what would be the individual's relevant foreign earnings for the purposes of Chapter A1 of this Part if section 809B applied to the individual (see section 809Z7(3)).][1]

Commentary—*Simon's Taxes* **E6.341**.

Amendments—[1]   Chapter 1A, ss 828A–828D inserted by FA 2009 s 52(1) with effect for the tax year 2008–09 and subsequent tax years.

CHAPTER 2

RESIDENCE

833 Visiting forces [etc]

(1) This section applies to an individual who—

    (*a*)   is a member of a visiting force of a designated country or of a civilian component of such a force,

    (*b*)   is in the United Kingdom, but only because of being a member of the force or the civilian component, and

    (*c*)   is not a British citizen, a British overseas territories citizen, a British National (Overseas) or a British Overseas citizen.

(2) For the purposes of subsection (1)—

    (*a*)   members of the armed forces of a designated country who are attached to a designated [international military][2] headquarters are treated as a visiting force of that country, and

    (*b*)   whether an individual is a member of a civilian component of such a force is to be determined accordingly.

[(2A) This section also applies to an individual within subsection (3) or (3A).][2]

(3) [An individual is within this subsection if the individual—][2]

(*a*) is of a category for the time being agreed between Her Majesty's Government in the United Kingdom and the other members of the North Atlantic Council,

(*b*) is employed by a designated allied headquarters,

(*c*) is in the United Kingdom, but only because of being employed by the designated allied headquarters, and

(*d*) is not a British citizen, a British overseas territories citizen, a British National (Overseas) or a British Overseas citizen.

[(3A) An individual is within this subsection if the individual—

(*a*) belongs to the EU civilian staff,

(*b*) is in the United Kingdom, but only because of serving as part of that staff, and

(*c*) is not a British citizen, a British overseas territories citizen, a British National (Overseas) or a British Overseas citizen.][2]

(4) If this section applies to an individual throughout a period, the period is not treated for income tax purposes as—

(*a*) a period of residence in the United Kingdom, or

(*b*) creating a change of the individual's residence or domicile.

(5) Subsection (4) does not affect the operation of section 56 or 460 of this Act . . . [1] (residence etc of claimants) in relation to an individual for any tax year.

(6) Subsections (1) to (3) are to be interpreted as if—

(*a*) they were in Part 1 of the Visiting Forces Act 1952 (c 67), and

(*b*) references in that Act to a country to which a provision of that Act applies were references to a designated country.

(7) In this section—

"allied headquarters" means an international military headquarters established under the North Atlantic Treaty, . . . [2]

"designated" means designated for the purpose in question by or under an Order in Council made for giving effect to an international agreement[, and

"the EU civilian staff" means—

(*a*) civilian personnel seconded by a member State to an EU institution for the purposes of activities (including exercises) relating to the preparation for, and execution of, tasks mentioned in Article 43(1) of the Treaty on European Union (tasks relating to a common security and defence policy), as amended from time to time, and

(*b*) civilian personnel (other than locally hired personnel)—

(i) made available to the EU by a member State to work with designated international military headquarters or a force of a designated country, or

(ii) otherwise made available to the EU by a member State for the purposes of activities of the kind referred to in paragraph (*a*).][2]

Commentary—*Simon's Taxes* E5.403, A1.109, E4.1313, E4.1314, I9.328.

Orders—Visiting Forces and International Military Headquarters (NATO and PfP) (Tax Designation) Order, SI 2012/3071.

Amendments—[1] In sub-s (5), words repealed by FA 2009 s 5, Sch 1 paras 1, 6(*o*)(v) with effect for the tax year 2010–11 and subsequent tax years.

[2] In heading, sub-ss (2)(*a*), (3), words substituted; sub-ss (2A), (3A) inserted; in sub-s (7) definition of "the EU civilian staff" and preceding word inserted, and word repealed, by FA 2012 s 220, Sch 37 para 5 with effect from 17 July 2012.

834 Residence of personal representatives

(1) This section applies for income tax purposes if the personal representatives of a deceased person ("D") include one or more persons who are UK resident and one or more persons who are non-UK resident.

(2) If the following condition is met, the person or persons who are non-UK resident are treated, in their capacity as personal representatives, as UK resident.

(3) The condition is that when D died D was UK resident . . . [1] or domiciled in the United Kingdom.

(4) If that condition is not met, the person or persons who are UK resident are treated, in their capacity as personal representatives, as non-UK resident.

[(5) Section 835BA (deemed domicile) applies for the purposes of subsection (3).][2]

Commentary—*Simon's Taxes* C4.104.

HMRC Manuals—International Manual INTM340080 (residence of personal representatives).

Trusts, Settlements and Estates Manual TSEM7358 (mixed residence personal representatives).

Modifications—ITA 2007 Sch 2 para 136(1), (2) (this section does not apply for the purposes of ITA 2007 ss 727 to 730 in relation to income payable before 15 June 1989).

ITA 2007 Sch 2 para 136(1), (3) (this section does not apply for the purposes of sections 727 to 730 in relation to income payable on or after 15 June 1989 if

(a) the individual received or became entitled to receive the capital sum mentioned in section 729(1) before that date, and

(b) the capital sum was wholly repaid or the right to it waived before 1 October 1989).

ITA 2007 Sch 2 para 137(1), (2) (this section does not apply for the purposes of ITA 2007 ss 731 to 735 in relation to benefits received before 15 June 1989).

ITA 2007

Amendments—[1]   In sub-s (3) words repealed by FA 2013 s 219, Sch 46 paras 54, 67(1) with effect where D died on or after 6 April 2013.

[2]   Sub-s (5) inserted by F(No 2)A 2017 s 29(2), Sch 8 paras 11, 17 with effect in relation to the tax year 2017–18 and subsequent tax years.

835 Residence rules for trustees . . .[1]

(1) See sections 475 and 476 for rules about the residence of the trustees of a settlement.

(2) . . .[1]

Amendments—[1]   Words in heading repealed, and sub-s (2) repealed, by CTA 2009 ss 1322, 1326, Sch 1 paras 699, 705, Sch 3 Part 1. CTA 2009 applies for accounting periods ending on or after 1 April 2009 (for corporation tax purposes) and for tax years 2009–10 onwards (for income and capital gains tax purposes).

[835A Residence of companies

Chapter 3 of Part 2 of CTA 2009 (rules for determining residence of companies) applies for the purposes of the Income Tax Acts as it applies for the purposes of the Corporation Tax Acts.][1]

Commentary—*Simon's Taxes* **D4.101, D4.102.**

Amendments—[1]   This section inserted by CTA 2009 s 1322, Sch 1 paras 699, 706. CTA 2009 applies for accounting periods ending on or after 1 April 2009 (for corporation tax purposes) and for tax years 2009–10 onwards (for income and capital gains tax purposes).

[CHAPTER 2A

DOMICILE][1]

Amendments—[1]   Chapter 2A (s 835B) inserted by TIOPA 2010 s 371, Sch 7 para 77. TIOPA 2010 has effect for corporation tax purposes for accounting periods ending on or after 1 April 2010, for income and capital gains tax purposes for the tax year 2010–11 and subsequent tax years, and for petroleum revenue tax purposes for chargeable periods beginning on or after 1 July 2010.

[835B Domicile for income tax purposes of overseas electors

(1) In determining for income tax purposes where a person is domiciled, disregard any relevant electoral action taken by the person (whether taken before, on or after the day on which TIOPA 2010 is passed).

(2) For the purposes of this section, relevant electoral action is taken by a person if—

(*a*) the person does anything with a view to, or in connection with, being registered as an overseas elector, or

(*b*) the person, when registered as an overseas elector, votes in any election at which the person is entitled to vote as a result of being registered as an overseas elector.

(3) For the purposes of this section, a person is registered as an overseas elector if the person is—

(*a*) registered in any register of parliamentary electors in pursuance of such a declaration as is mentioned in section 1(1)(*a*) of the Representation of the People Act 1985 (extension of parliamentary franchise to certain non-resident British citizens), or

(*b*) registered under section 3 of that Act (certain non-resident peers entitled to vote at European Parliamentary elections).

(4) Subsection (1) does not prevent regard being had, in determining a person's domicile at any time, to any relevant electoral action taken by the person if—

(*a*) the person's domicile at that time is being determined for the purpose of ascertaining that or any other person's liability to income tax, and

(*b*) the person whose liability is being ascertained wishes regard to be had to that action.

(5) If a person's domicile is determined in accordance with any such wishes, that domicile is to be regarded as having been determined for the purpose only of ascertaining the liability concerned.][1]

Commentary—*Simon's Taxes* **I9.206.**

Amendments—[1]   Section inserted by TIOPA 2010 s 371, Sch 7 para 77. TIOPA 2010 has effect for corporation tax purposes for accounting periods ending on or after 1 April 2010, for income and capital gains tax purposes for the tax year 2010–11 and subsequent tax years, and for petroleum revenue tax purposes for chargeable periods beginning on or after 1 July 2010.

Prospective amendments—Sub-s (3)(*b*) and the preceding "or" to be repealed by the European Parliamentary Elections Etc (Repeal, Revocation, Amendment and Saving Provisions) (United Kingdom and Gibraltar) (EU Exit) Regulations, SI 2018/1310 reg 4, Sch 1, Pt 1 with effect from Implementation Period completion day (see EU(WA)A 2020 Sch 5 para 1(1)).

[835BA Deemed domicile

(1) This section has effect for the purposes of the provisions of the Income Tax Acts or TCGA 1992 which apply this section.

(2) An individual not domiciled in the United Kingdom at a time in a tax year ("the relevant tax year") is to be regarded as domiciled in the United Kingdom at that time if—

(*a*) condition A is met, or

(*b*) condition B is met.

(3) Condition A is that—

(*a*) the individual was born in the United Kingdom,

(*b*) the individual's domicile of origin was in the United Kingdom, and

(*c*) the individual is UK resident for the relevant tax year.

(4) Condition B is that the individual has been UK resident for at least 15 of the 20 tax years immediately preceding the relevant tax year.

(5) But Condition B is not met if—

    (a) the individual is not UK resident for the relevant tax year, and

    (b) there is no tax year beginning after 5 April 2017 and preceding the relevant tax year in which the individual was UK resident.][1]

Commentary—*Simon's Taxes* **E6.308**.
Amendments—[1]   Section 835BA inserted by F(No 2)A 2017 s 29(1) with effect from 16 November 2017.

[CHAPTER 2B

UK REPRESENTATIVE OF NON-UK RESIDENT]

[Introduction

835C Overview of Chapter

(1) This Chapter provides for a branch or agency to be treated as the UK representative of a non-UK resident in respect of certain amounts chargeable to income tax.

(2) For obligations and liabilities in relation to income tax imposed on a branch or agency which under this Chapter is treated as the UK representative of a non-UK resident, see Chapter 2C.][1]

Commentary—*Simon's Taxes* **A1.302**.
HMRC Manuals—International Manual INTM269010 (non-residents trading in the UK: through UK investment managers, brokers or lloyd's agents: introduction).
Amendments—[1]   Section and preceding cross-head inserted by TIOPA 2010 s 370, Sch 6 para 1. TIOPA 2010 has effect for corporation tax purposes for accounting periods ending on or after 1 April 2010, for income and capital gains tax purposes for the tax year 2010–11 and subsequent tax years, and for petroleum revenue tax purposes for chargeable periods beginning on or after 1 July 2010.

[835D Income tax chargeable on company's income: application

This Chapter does not apply in relation to income tax chargeable on income of a company otherwise than as a trustee.][1]

Commentary—*Simon's Taxes* **B2.125**.
Amendments—[1]   Section inserted by TIOPA 2010 s 370, Sch 6 para 2. TIOPA 2010 has effect for corporation tax purposes for accounting periods ending on or after 1 April 2010, for income and capital gains tax purposes for the tax year 2010–11 and subsequent tax years, and for petroleum revenue tax purposes for chargeable periods beginning on or after 1 July 2010.

[Branches and agencies

835E Branch or agency treated as UK representative

(1) This section applies if a non-UK resident carries on (alone or in partnership) any trade, profession or vocation through a branch or agency in the United Kingdom.

(2) The branch or agency is the UK representative of the non-UK resident in relation to—

    (a) the amount of any income from the trade, profession or vocation that arises (directly or indirectly) through or from the branch or agency, and

    (b) the amount of any income from property or rights which are used by, or held by or for, the branch or agency.

(3) The following rules are to be applied for the purposes of subsection (2) and Chapter 2C in relation to an amount within that subsection.

Rule 1

The UK representative continues to be the UK representative of the non-UK resident in relation to the amount even after ceasing to be a branch or agency through which the non-UK resident carries on the trade, profession or vocation concerned.

Rule 2

The UK representative is treated in relation to the amount as a distinct and separate person from the non-UK resident (if the representative would not otherwise be so treated).

Rule 3

If the branch or agency is carried on by persons in partnership, the partnership, as such, is treated in relation to the amount as the UK representative of the non-UK resident.

(4) For further rules that apply where a trade or profession carried on by a non-UK resident in the United Kingdom is carried on in partnership, see section 835F.

(5) This section needs to be read with sections 835G to 835K (which provide for descriptions of persons who are not to be regarded as the UK representative of a non-UK resident if certain conditions are met).][1]

Commentary—*Simon's Taxes* **B2.125**.
HMRC Manuals—International Manual INTM268020 (non-residents trading in the UK: who can be the non-resident's UK representative?).
Amendments—[1]   Section and preceding cross-head inserted by TIOPA 2010 s 370, Sch 6 para 3. TIOPA 2010 has effect for corporation tax purposes for accounting periods ending on or after 1 April 2010, for income and capital gains tax purposes for the tax year 2010–11 and subsequent tax years, and for petroleum revenue tax purposes for chargeable periods beginning on or after 1 July 2010.

[835F Trade or profession carried on in partnership

(1) Subsection (2) applies if a trade or profession carried on by a non-UK resident through a branch or agency in the United Kingdom is carried on by the non-UK resident in partnership.

(2) The trade or profession carried on through the branch or agency is, for the purposes of section 835E and Chapter 2C, to be treated as including the notional trade or profession.

(3) Subsection (4) applies (in addition to subsection (2) if that subsection also applies) if—

    (*a*) a trade or profession carried on by a non-UK resident in the United Kingdom is carried on by the non-UK resident in partnership, and

    (*b*) any member of the partnership is resident in the United Kingdom.

(4) The notional trade or profession is, for the purposes of section 835E and Chapter 2C, to be treated as being a trade carried on in the United Kingdom through the partnership as such.

(5) In this section "the notional trade or profession" means the notional trade from which the non-UK resident's share in the partnership's profits or losses is treated for the purposes of section 852 of ITTOIA 2005 as deriving.][1]

Commentary—*Simon's Taxes* **B2.125**.

HMRC Manuals—International Manual INTM268020 (non-residents trading in the UK: partnerships can be the UK representative of a non-resident).

Amendments—[1]   Section inserted by TIOPA 2010 s 370, Sch 6 para 4. TIOPA 2010 has effect for corporation tax purposes for accounting periods ending on or after 1 April 2010, for income and capital gains tax purposes for the tax year 2010–11 and subsequent tax years, and for petroleum revenue tax purposes for chargeable periods beginning on or after 1 July 2010.

[Persons who are not UK representatives

835G Agents

(1) This section applies if a non-UK resident carries on (alone or in partnership) a business through an agent in the United Kingdom.

(2) The agent is not the UK representative of the non-UK resident in relation to an amount within section 835E(2) arising to the non-UK resident from—

    (*a*) so much of the non-UK resident's business as relates to disregarded transactions, or

    (*b*) property or rights which, as a result of disregarded transactions, are used by, or held by or for, the agent on behalf of the non-UK resident.

(3) "Disregarded transactions" are transactions—

    (*a*) carried out through the agent in the United Kingdom, and

    (*b*) in respect of which the agent does not act in the course of carrying on a regular agency for the non-UK resident.][1]

Commentary—*Simon's Taxes* **B2.125**.

Amendments—[1]   Section and preceding cross-head inserted by TIOPA 2010 s 370, Sch 6 para 5. TIOPA 2010 has effect for corporation tax purposes for accounting periods ending on or after 1 April 2010, for income and capital gains tax purposes for the tax year 2010–11 and subsequent tax years, and for petroleum revenue tax purposes for chargeable periods beginning on or after 1 July 2010.

[835H Brokers

(1) This section applies if a non-UK resident carries on (alone or in partnership) a business through a broker in the United Kingdom.

(2) The broker is not the UK representative of the non-UK resident in relation to an amount within section 835E(2) if—

    (*a*) the amount is transaction income in relation to a transaction carried out through the broker in the United Kingdom on behalf of the non-UK resident, and

    (*b*) the independent broker conditions are met in relation to the transaction (see section 835L).

(3) In subsection (2) "transaction income", in relation to a transaction carried out through a broker in the United Kingdom on behalf of a non-UK resident, has the same meaning as in Chapter 1 (see section 814(5)).][1]

Commentary—*Simon's Taxes* **B2.125**.

Amendments—[1]   Section inserted by TIOPA 2010 s 370, Sch 6 para 6. TIOPA 2010 has effect for corporation tax purposes for accounting periods ending on or after 1 April 2010, for income and capital gains tax purposes for the tax year 2010–11 and subsequent tax years, and for petroleum revenue tax purposes for chargeable periods beginning on or after 1 July 2010.

[835I Investment managers

(1) This section applies if a non-UK resident carries on (alone or in partnership) a business through an investment manager in the United Kingdom.

(2) The investment manager is not the UK representative of the non-UK resident in relation to an amount within section 835E(2) if—

    (*a*) the amount is transaction income in relation to an investment transaction carried out through the investment manager in the United Kingdom on behalf of the non-UK resident, and

    (*b*) the independent investment manager conditions are met in relation to the investment transaction (see section 835M).

(3) In subsection (2) "transaction income", in relation to a transaction carried out through an investment manager in the United Kingdom on behalf of a non-UK resident, has the same meaning as in Chapter 1 (see section 814(5)).][1]

Commentary—*Simon's Taxes* **B2.125**.
Amendments—[1]   Section inserted by TIOPA 2010 s 370, Sch 6 para 7. TIOPA 2010 has effect for corporation tax purposes
for accounting periods ending on or after 1 April 2010, for income and capital gains tax purposes for the tax year 2010–11
and subsequent tax years, and for petroleum revenue tax purposes for chargeable periods beginning on or after 1 July 2010.

[835J Persons acting under alternative finance arrangements

(1) Subsection (2) applies if an amount within section 835E(2) arising to a non-UK resident consists
of alternative finance return.

(2) Neither of the following is the UK representative of the non-UK resident in relation to the
amount—

  (a) the other party to the alternative finance arrangements,

  (b) any other person acting for the non-UK resident in relation to the alternative finance
       arrangements.

(3) In subsection (1) "alternative finance return" means alternative finance return within the
application of section 564I, 564K or 564L(2) or (3).

(4) In subsection (2) the reference to "the alternative finance arrangements" is a reference to the
alternative finance arrangements under which the alternative finance return mentioned in subsection
(1) arises.][1]

Commentary—*Simon's Taxes* **B2.125, A1.302**.
HMRC Manuals—Corporate Finance Manual CFM44280 (alternative finance arrangements and non-residents).
Amendments—[1]   Section inserted by TIOPA 2010 s 370, Sch 6 para 8. TIOPA 2010 has effect for corporation tax purposes
for accounting periods ending on or after 1 April 2010, for income and capital gains tax purposes for the tax year 2010–11
and subsequent tax years, and for petroleum revenue tax purposes for chargeable periods beginning on or after 1 July 2010.

[835K Lloyd's agents

(1) This section applies if—

  (a) a non-UK resident ("X") is a member of Lloyd's, and

  (b) an amount within section 835E(2) arises to X from X's underwriting business.

(2) A person who has been X's members' agent or the managing agent of the syndicate in question
is not the UK representative of X in relation to the amount or to matters connected with the amount.

(3) For the purposes of this section—

  (a) X is a member of Lloyd's if X is a member within the meaning of Chapter 3 of Part 2 of FA
       1993, and

  (b) "members' agent" and "managing agent" are to be construed in accordance with section 184
       of that Act.][1]

Commentary—*Simon's Taxes* **B2.125**.
HMRC Manuals—International Manual INTM269040 (non-residents trading in the UK: through UK investment managers,
brokers or lloyd's agents: lloyd's members' agents).
Amendments—[1]   Section inserted by TIOPA 2010 s 370, Sch 6 para 9. TIOPA 2010 has effect for corporation tax purposes
for accounting periods ending on or after 1 April 2010, for income and capital gains tax purposes for the tax year 2010–11
and subsequent tax years, and for petroleum revenue tax purposes for chargeable periods beginning on or after 1 July 2010.

[The independent broker conditions

835L The independent broker conditions

(1) The independent broker conditions are met in relation to a transaction carried out on behalf of a
non-UK resident by a broker in the United Kingdom if conditions A to D are met.

(2) Condition A is that at the time of the transaction the broker is carrying on the business of a
broker.

(3) Condition B is that the transaction is carried out in the ordinary course of that business.

(4) Condition C is that the remuneration which the broker receives in respect of the transaction for
the provision of the services of a broker to the non-UK resident is not less than is customary for that
class of business.

(5) Condition D is that the broker does not fall (apart from this subsection) to be treated under this
Chapter, or under Chapter 1 of Part 7A of TCGA 1992, as a UK representative of the non-UK
resident in relation to any amounts that—

  (a) are not included in transaction income in relation to the transaction (see section 835H(2) and
       (3)), and

  (b) are chargeable to tax for the same tax year as that transaction income.][1]

Commentary—*Simon's Taxes* **B2.125**.
HMRC Manuals—International Manual INTM269050 (non-residents trading in the UK: through UK investment managers,
brokers or lloyd's agents: brokers - conditions to be met).
Amendments—[1]   Section and preceding cross-head inserted by TIOPA 2010 s 370, Sch 6 para 10. TIOPA 2010 has effect for
corporation tax purposes for accounting periods ending on or after 1 April 2010, for income and capital gains tax purposes
for the tax year 2010–11 and subsequent tax years, and for petroleum revenue tax purposes for chargeable periods beginning
on or after 1 July 2010.

[The independent investment manager conditions

835M The independent investment manager conditions

(1) The independent investment manager conditions are met in relation to an investment transaction carried out on behalf of a non-UK resident by an investment manager in the United Kingdom if conditions A to E are met.

(2) Condition A is that at the time of the transaction the investment manager is carrying on a business of providing investment management services.

(3) Condition B is that the transaction is carried out in the ordinary course of that business.

(4) Condition C is that, when the investment manager acts on behalf of the non-UK resident in relation to the transaction, the relationship between them, having regard to its legal, financial and commercial characteristics, is a relationship between persons carrying on independent businesses dealing with each other at arm's length.

(5) Condition D is that the requirements of the 20% rule are met (see section 835N).

(6) Condition E is that the remuneration which the investment manager receives in respect of the transaction for the provision of investment management services to the non-UK resident is not less than is customary for that class of business.]¹

Commentary—*Simon's Taxes* **B2.125**.

HMRC Manuals—International Manual INTM269060 (investment manager exemption: conditions to be met).

Amendments—¹   Section and preceding cross-head inserted by TIOPA 2010 s 370, Sch 6 para 11. TIOPA 2010 has effect for corporation tax purposes for accounting periods ending on or after 1 April 2010, for income and capital gains tax purposes for the tax year 2010–11 and subsequent tax years, and for petroleum revenue tax purposes for chargeable periods beginning on or after 1 July 2010.

[835N Investment managers: the 20% rule

(1) The requirements of the 20% rule are met if conditions A and B are met.

(2) Condition A is that, in relation to a qualifying period, it has been or is the intention of the investment manager and the persons connected with the investment manager that at least 80% of the non-UK resident's relevant disregarded income should consist of amounts to which none of them has a beneficial entitlement.

(3) Condition B is that, so far as there is a failure to fulfil that intention, that failure—

(a) is attributable (directly or indirectly) to matters outside the control of the investment manager and persons connected with the investment manager, and

(b) does not result from a failure by any of them to take such steps as may be reasonable for mitigating the effect of those matters in relation to the fulfilment of that intention.]¹

Commentary—*Simon's Taxes* **B2.125**.

HMRC Manuals—International Manual INTM269110 (investment managers: the 20% rule).

Amendments—¹   Section inserted by TIOPA 2010 s 370, Sch 6 para 12. TIOPA 2010 has effect for corporation tax purposes for accounting periods ending on or after 1 April 2010, for income and capital gains tax purposes for the tax year 2010–11 and subsequent tax years, and for petroleum revenue tax purposes for chargeable periods beginning on or after 1 July 2010.

[835O Meaning of "qualifying period", "relevant disregarded income" and "beneficial entitlement"

(1) This section applies for the purposes of this Chapter.

(2) A "qualifying period" means—

(a) the tax year in which the transaction income mentioned in section 835I(2) is chargeable to tax, or

(b) a period of not more than 5 years comprising two or more tax years including that one.

(3) The "relevant disregarded income" of the non-UK resident for a qualifying period is the total of the non-UK resident's income for the tax years comprised in the qualifying period which derives from investment transactions—

(a) carried out by the investment manager on the non-UK resident's behalf, and

(b) in relation to which the independent investment manager conditions are met, ignoring the requirements of the 20% rule.

(4) A person has a "beneficial entitlement" to relevant disregarded income if the person has or may acquire a beneficial entitlement that is, or would be, attributable to the relevant disregarded income as a result of having an interest or other rights mentioned in subsection (5).

(5) The interests and rights referred to in subsection (4) are—

(a) an interest (whether or not an interest giving a right to an immediate payment of a share in the profits or gains) in property in which the whole or any part of the relevant disregarded income is represented, or

(b) an interest in, or other rights in relation to, the non-UK resident.]¹

Commentary—*Simon's Taxes* **B2.125**.

Amendments—¹   Section inserted by TIOPA 2010 s 370, Sch 6 para 13. TIOPA 2010 has effect for corporation tax purposes for accounting periods ending on or after 1 April 2010, for income and capital gains tax purposes for the tax year 2010–11 and subsequent tax years, and for petroleum revenue tax purposes for chargeable periods beginning on or after 1 July 2010.

[835P Treatment of transactions where 20% rule not met

(1) This section applies in the case of an investment transaction in relation to which the independent investment manager conditions are met, except for the requirements of the 20% rule.

(2) This Chapter has effect as if the requirements of that rule were met in relation to the transaction, but only in relation to so much of the transaction income in relation to the transaction (see section 835I(2) and (3)) as does not represent an amount—

    (*a*) which is relevant disregarded income of the non-UK resident, and

    (*b*) to which the investment manager or a person connected with the investment manager has or has had any beneficial entitlement.][1]

Commentary—*Simon's Taxes* **B2.125**.

Amendments—[1] Section inserted by TIOPA 2010 s 370, Sch 6 para 14. TIOPA 2010 has effect for corporation tax purposes for accounting periods ending on or after 1 April 2010, for income and capital gains tax purposes for the tax year 2010–11 and subsequent tax years, and for petroleum revenue tax purposes for chargeable periods beginning on or after 1 July 2010.

[835Q Application of 20% rule to collective investment schemes

(1) This section applies if amounts arise or accrue to the non-UK resident as a participant in a collective investment scheme.

(2) It applies for the purposes of determining whether the requirements of the 20% rule are met in relation to a transaction carried out for the purposes of the scheme (so far as the transaction is one in respect of which amounts so arise or accrue).

(3) In applying this section make the following assumptions—

    (*a*) that all the transactions carried out for the purposes of the scheme are carried out on behalf of a company ("the assumed company") which is—

        (i) constituted for the purposes of the scheme, and

        (ii) non-UK resident, and

    (*b*) that the participants do not have any rights in respect of the amounts arising or accruing in respect of those transactions, other than the rights which, if they held shares in the assumed company, would be their rights as shareholders.

(4) If the scheme is such that the assumed company would not be regarded for tax purposes as carrying on a trade in the United Kingdom in relation to the tax year in which the transaction income mentioned in section 835I(2) is chargeable to tax, the requirements of the 20% rule are treated as met in relation to a transaction carried out for the purposes of the scheme.

(5) If the scheme is such that the assumed company would be so regarded for tax purposes, sections 835N to 835P have effect in relation to a transaction carried out for the purposes of the scheme with the modifications in subsection (6).

(6) The modifications are—

    (*a*) for references to the non-UK resident substitute references to the assumed company, and

    (*b*) for references to the non-UK resident's relevant disregarded income for a qualifying period substitute references to the sum of the amounts that would, for tax years comprised in the qualifying period, be chargeable to tax on the assumed company as profits deriving from the transactions—

        (i) carried out by the investment manager, and

        (ii) assumed to be carried out on behalf of the company.

(7) In this section—

"collective investment scheme" has the meaning given by section 235 of FISMA 2000, and

"participant", in relation to a collective investment scheme, is construed in accordance with that section.][1]

Commentary—*Simon's Taxes* **B2.125**.

HMRC Manuals—International Manual INTM269155 (the 20% rule: consequences of not meeting the rule).

Amendments—[1] Section inserted by TIOPA 2010 s 370, Sch 6 para 15. TIOPA 2010 has effect for corporation tax purposes for accounting periods ending on or after 1 April 2010, for income and capital gains tax purposes for the tax year 2010–11 and subsequent tax years, and for petroleum revenue tax purposes for chargeable periods beginning on or after 1 July 2010.

[Supplementary

835R Supplementary provision

(1) For the purposes of this Chapter a person is to be regarded as carrying out a transaction on behalf of another if the person—

    (*a*) undertakes the transaction, whether on behalf of or to the account of the other, or

    (*b*) gives instructions for it to be so carried out by another.

(2) In the case of a person who acts as a broker or investment manager as part only of a business, this Chapter has effect as if that part were a separate business.][1]

Commentary—*Simon's Taxes* **B2.125**.

Amendments—[1] Section and preceding cross-head inserted by TIOPA 2010 s 370, Sch 6 para 16. TIOPA 2010 has effect for corporation tax purposes for accounting periods ending on or after 1 April 2010, for income and capital gains tax purposes for the tax year 2010–11 and subsequent tax years, and for petroleum revenue tax purposes for chargeable periods beginning on or after 1 July 2010.

[835S Interpretation of Chapter

(1) This section applies for the purposes of this Chapter.

(2) "Branch or agency" means any factorship, agency, receivership, branch or management.

(3) "Investment manager" has the same meaning as in Chapter 1 (see section 827).

(4) "Investment transaction" means any transaction of a description specified for the purposes of this section in regulations made by the Commissioners for Her Majesty's Revenue and Customs.

(5) Provision made in regulations under subsection (4) may, in particular, have effect in relation to the tax year current on the day on which the regulations are made.][1]

Commentary—*Simon's Taxes* **B2.125, B2.125**.

Regulations—Investment Manager (Specified Transactions) Regulations 2014 (issued April 2014).

Amendments—[1]   Section inserted by TIOPA 2010 s 370, Sch 6 para 17. TIOPA 2010 has effect for corporation tax purposes for accounting periods ending on or after 1 April 2010, for income and capital gains tax purposes for the tax year 2010–11 and subsequent tax years, and for petroleum revenue tax purposes for chargeable periods beginning on or after 1 July 2010.

[CHAPTER 2C

INCOME TAX OBLIGATIONS AND LIABILITIES IMPOSED ON UK REPRESENTATIVES]

[835T Introduction to Chapter

(1) This Chapter applies to the enactments relating to income tax so far as they make provision for or in connection with the assessment, collection and recovery of tax, or of interest on tax.

(2) Those enactments have effect in accordance with section 835U in relation to amounts in respect of which a branch or agency is to be treated as the UK representative of a non-UK resident under Chapter 2B.

(3) In this section "enactment" includes an enactment contained in subordinate legislation within the meaning of the Interpretation Act 1978.][1]

Amendments—[1]   Section inserted by TIOPA 2010 s 370, Sch 6 para 18. TIOPA 2010 has effect for corporation tax purposes for accounting periods ending on or after 1 April 2010, for income and capital gains tax purposes for the tax year 2010–11 and subsequent tax years, and for petroleum revenue tax purposes for chargeable periods beginning on or after 1 July 2010.

[835U Obligations and liabilities of UK representative

(1) The obligations and liabilities of a non-UK resident are to be treated, for the purposes of the enactments to which this Chapter applies, as if they were also the obligations and liabilities of the UK representative of the non-UK resident.

(2) Subsection (3) applies if—

(a) the UK representative of a non-UK resident discharges an obligation or liability imposed by this section that corresponds to one to which the non-UK resident is subject, or

(b) a non-UK resident discharges an obligation or liability that corresponds to one to which the non-UK resident's UK representative is subject by virtue of this section.

(3) The corresponding obligation or liability—

(a) of the non-UK resident (in a case within subsection (2)(a)), or

(b) of the UK representative (in a case within subsection (2)(b)),

is discharged.

(4) A non-UK resident is bound, as if they were the non-UK resident's own, by acts or omissions of the non-UK resident's UK representative in the discharge of the obligations and liabilities imposed on the representative by this section.

(5) This section is subject to sections 835V and 835W.][1]

Commentary—*Simon's Taxes* **B2.125**.

Amendments—[1]   Section inserted by TIOPA 2010 s 370, Sch 6 para 19. TIOPA 2010 has effect for corporation tax purposes for accounting periods ending on or after 1 April 2010, for income and capital gains tax purposes for the tax year 2010–11 and subsequent tax years, and for petroleum revenue tax purposes for chargeable periods beginning on or after 1 July 2010.

[835V Exceptions: notices and information

(1) An obligation or liability attaching to a non-UK resident ("X") by reason of a notice or other document having been given or served on X does not also attach to the UK representative of X by virtue of section 835U unless the notice or other document (or a copy of it) has been given to or served on the representative.

(2) An obligation or liability attaching to X by reason of a request or demand having been received by X does not also attach to the UK representative of X by virtue of section 835U unless the representative has been notified of the request or demand.

(3) Subsection (4) applies to obligations relating to the provision of information that are imposed on the UK representative of X by section 835U in a case where the representative is X's independent agent.

(4) The obligations do not require the UK representative to do anything except so far as it is practicable for the representative to do so.

(5) For this purpose, the representative must act to the best of the representative's knowledge and belief after taking all reasonable steps to obtain the necessary information.

(6) An obligation of X to provide information is not discharged by virtue of section 835U in a case where the UK representative of X has discharged the obligation only so far as required by subsection (4) of this section.

(7) X is not bound by virtue of section 835U by mistakes in information provided by the UK representative of X in discharging, so far as required under subsection (4) of this section, an obligation imposed on the representative by section 835U unless—

    (*a*) the mistake is the result of an act or omission of X, or

    (*b*) the mistake is one to which X consented or in which X connived.

(8) In this section "information" includes anything contained in a return, self-assessment, account, statement or report required to be provided to the Commissioners for Her Majesty's Revenue and Customs or to any officer of Revenue and Customs.][1]

Commentary—*Simon's Taxes* **B2.125**.

Amendments—[1]   Section inserted by TIOPA 2010 s 370, Sch 6 para 20. TIOPA 2010 has effect for corporation tax purposes for accounting periods ending on or after 1 April 2010, for income and capital gains tax purposes for the tax year 2010–11 and subsequent tax years, and for petroleum revenue tax purposes for chargeable periods beginning on or after 1 July 2010.

[835W Exceptions: criminal offences and penalties etc

(1) A person is not by virtue of section 835U liable to be proceeded against for a criminal offence unless the person—

    (*a*) committed the offence, or

    (*b*) consented to or connived in its commission.

(2) An independent agent of a non-UK resident is not by virtue of section 835U liable to any civil penalty or surcharge in respect of an act or omission if conditions A and B are met.

(3) Condition A is that the act or omission is not—

    (*a*) an act or omission of the independent agent, or

    (*b*) an act or omission to which the agent consented or in which the agent connived.

(4) Condition B is that the independent agent is able to show that the amount of the penalty or surcharge will not be recoverable out of the sums mentioned in section 835X(3) (after being indemnified for any other liabilities under section 835X).][1]

Commentary—*Simon's Taxes* **B2.125**.

Amendments—[1]   Section inserted by TIOPA 2010 s 370, Sch 6 para 21. TIOPA 2010 has effect for corporation tax purposes for accounting periods ending on or after 1 April 2010, for income and capital gains tax purposes for the tax year 2010–11 and subsequent tax years, and for petroleum revenue tax purposes for chargeable periods beginning on or after 1 July 2010.

[835X Indemnities

(1) An independent agent of a non-UK resident is entitled to be indemnified for the amount of any liability of the non-UK resident which the agent has discharged by virtue of section 835U.

(2) An independent agent of a non-UK resident is entitled to retain, from the sums mentioned in subsection (3), amounts sufficient to meet any liabilities which by virtue of section 835U the agent has discharged or to which the agent is subject.

(3) The sums are those which—

    (*a*) (ignoring subsection (2)) are due from the independent agent to the non-UK resident, or

    (*b*) are received by the independent agent on behalf of the non-UK resident.][1]

Commentary—*Simon's Taxes* **B2.125**.

Amendments—[1]   Section inserted by TIOPA 2010 s 370, Sch 6 para 22. TIOPA 2010 has effect for corporation tax purposes for accounting periods ending on or after 1 April 2010, for income and capital gains tax purposes for the tax year 2010–11 and subsequent tax years, and for petroleum revenue tax purposes for chargeable periods beginning on or after 1 July 2010.

[835Y Meaning of "independent agent"

(1) In this Chapter "independent agent", in relation to a non-UK resident ("X"), means a person who is the UK representative of X in respect of any agency in which the person is acting on behalf of X in an independent capacity.

(2) For this purpose a person does not act in an independent capacity on behalf of X unless the relationship between them, having regard to its legal, financial and commercial characteristics, is a relationship between persons carrying on independent businesses dealing with each other at arm's length.][1]

Commentary—*Simon's Taxes* **B2.125**.

Amendments—[1]   Section inserted by TIOPA 2010 s 370, Sch 6 para 23. TIOPA 2010 has effect for corporation tax purposes for accounting periods ending on or after 1 April 2010, for income and capital gains tax purposes for the tax year 2010–11 and subsequent tax years, and for petroleum revenue tax purposes for chargeable periods beginning on or after 1 July 2010.

CHAPTER 3

JOINTLY HELD PROPERTY

836 Jointly held property

(1) This section applies if income arises from property held in the names of individuals—

    (*a*) who are married to, or are civil partners of, each other, and

    (*b*) who live together.

(2) The individuals are treated for income tax purposes as beneficially entitled to the income in equal shares.

(3) But this treatment does not apply in relation to any income within any of the following exceptions.

Exception A Income to which neither of the individuals is beneficially entitled.

Exception B Income in relation to which a declaration by the individuals under section 837 has effect (unequal beneficial interests).

Exception C Income to which Part 9 of ITTOIA 2005 applies (partnerships).

Exception D Income arising from a UK property business which consists of, or so far as it includes, the commercial letting of furnished holiday accommodation (within the meaning of Chapter 6 of Part 3 of ITTOIA 2005).

[*Exception DA* Income arising from an overseas property business which consists of, or so far as it includes, the commercial letting of furnished holiday accommodation (within the meaning of Chapter 6 of Part 3 of ITTOIA 2005) in one or more EEA states.][2]

Exception E Income consisting of a distribution arising from property consisting of—

    (*a*)   shares in or securities of a close company to which one of the individuals is beneficially entitled to the exclusion of the other, or

    (*b*)   such shares or securities to which the individuals are beneficially entitled in equal or unequal shares.

"Shares" and "securities" have the same meaning as in [section 1117 of CTA 2010][1].

Exception F Income to which one of the individuals is beneficially entitled so far as it is treated as a result of any other provision of the Income Tax Acts as—

    (*a*)   the income of the other individual, or

    (*b*)   the income of a third party.

Commentary—*Simon's Taxes* **E5.103A, E5.115, B6.401, D6.651**.
HMRC Manuals—Residence, Domicile and Remittance Basis Manual RDRM33510 (joint income and remittance basis).
Savings and Investment Manual SAIM2420 (taxation of joint accounts and election for actual entitlement taxation).
Amendments—[1]   In sub-s (3) words substituted by CTA 2010 s 1177, Sch 1 para 553. CTA 2010 has effect for corporation tax purposes for accounting periods ending on or after 1 April 2010, and for income and capital gains tax purposes for the tax year 2010–11 and subsequent tax years.
[2]   In sub-s (3), Exception DA inserted by FA 2011 s 52, Sch 14 para 3(1), (5) with effect in relation to the tax year 2011–12 and subsequent tax years.

837 Jointly held property: declarations of unequal beneficial interests

(1) The individuals may make a joint declaration under this section if—

    (*a*)   one of them is beneficially entitled to the income to the exclusion of the other, or

    (*b*)   they are beneficially entitled to the income in unequal shares,

and their beneficial interests in the income correspond to their beneficial interests in the property from which it arises.

(2) The declaration must state the beneficial interests of the individuals in—

    (*a*)   the income to which the declaration relates, and

    (*b*)   the property from which that income arises.

(3) The declaration has effect only if notice of it is given to an officer of Revenue and Customs—

    (*a*)   in such form and manner as the Commissioners for Her Majesty's Revenue and Customs may prescribe, and

    (*b*)   within the period of 60 days beginning with the date of the declaration.

(4) The declaration has effect in relation to income arising on or after the date of the declaration.

(5) The declaration continues to have effect until such time (if any) as there is a change in the beneficial interests of the individuals in either—

    (*a*)   the income to which the declaration relates, or

    (*b*)   the property from which that income arises.

Commentary—*Simon's Taxes* **E5.103A**.
Derivation—TA 1988 ss 282A, 282B.
HMRC Manuals—Residence, Domicile and Remittance Basis Manual RDRM33510 (joint income and remittance basis).

[CHAPTER 3A]

BANKS ETC IN COMPULSORY LIQUIDATION[1]

Amendments—[1]   Chapter 3A (ss 837A–837H) inserted by TIOPA 2010 s 371, Sch 7 paras 68, 71. TIOPA 2010 has effect for corporation tax purposes for accounting periods ending on or after 1 April 2010, for income and capital gains tax purposes for the tax year 2010–11 and subsequent tax years, and for petroleum revenue tax purposes for chargeable periods beginning on or after 1 July 2010.

[837A Overview of Chapter

(1) This Chapter provides for the receipts of certain types of company being wound up to be charged to income tax.

(2) For provision charging the receipts of such companies to corporation tax, see Chapter 6 of Part 13 of CTA 2010.][1]

Amendments—[1] Sections 837A–837H inserted by TIOPA 2010 s 371, Sch 7 paras 68, 71. TIOPA 2010 has effect for corporation tax purposes for accounting periods ending on or after 1 April 2010, for income and capital gains tax purposes for the tax year 2010–11 and subsequent tax years, and for petroleum revenue tax purposes for chargeable periods beginning on or after 1 July 2010.

[837B Application of Chapter
(1) This Chapter applies if—
    (a) a company is being or has been wound up by the court in the United Kingdom, and
    (b) conditions A, B and C are met.
(2) Condition A is that the company was, at any time within the period mentioned in subsection (5), lawfully carrying on a business of accepting deposits as—
    (a) a person of the kind mentioned in paragraph (b) of the definition of "bank" in section 991(2) (persons with permission under Part 4 of FISMA 2000 to accept deposits), or
    (b) a permitted EEA credit institution.
(3) Condition B is that the company has permanently ceased to carry on the trade that included the business of accepting deposits (the "deposit-taking trade").
(4) Condition C is that the company is insolvent and—
    (a) was so when the winding up proceedings started, or
    (b) became so at any time in the period of 12 months following the day on which those proceedings started.
(5) The period referred to in subsection (2) is the period of 12 months ending with the earlier of—
    (a) the day on which the winding up proceedings started, and
    (b) the day on which the company permanently ceased to carry on the deposit-taking trade.
(6) In subsection (2)(b) a "permitted EEA credit institution" means an EEA firm of the kind mentioned in paragraph 5(b) of Schedule 3 to FISMA 2000 (credit institutions authorised by home state regulator) which has permission to accept deposits under paragraph 15 of that Schedule.][1]

Amendments—[1] Sections 837A–837H inserted by TIOPA 2010 s 371, Sch 7 paras 68, 71. TIOPA 2010 has effect for corporation tax purposes for accounting periods ending on or after 1 April 2010, for income and capital gains tax purposes for the tax year 2010–11 and subsequent tax years, and for petroleum revenue tax purposes for chargeable periods beginning on or after 1 July 2010.

Prospective amendments—In sub-s (2)(a) word ", or" at the end to be repealed, and sub-ss (2)(b) and (6) to be repealed, by the Taxes (Amendments) (EU Exit) Regulations, SI 2019/689 reg 15(1), (8) with effect from Implementation Period completion day (see EU(WA)A 2020 Sch 5 para 1(1)). These amendments do not apply where a person qualifies for authorisation under FSMA 2000 Sch 3 by virtue of SI 2001/3084 (see SI 2019/689 reg 41(f)). These amendments do not apply in determining whether condition A in sub-s (2) is met by reference to a time before the amendments come into force (see SI 2019/689 reg 44).

[837C Charge to income tax on winding up receipts
(1) Winding up receipts arising from the deposit-taking trade are chargeable to income tax.
(2) Subsection (1) applies in relation to a winding up receipt only so far as its value was not brought into account in calculating the profits of the trade of any period before the permanent cessation of the trade.
(3) A "winding up receipt" means (subject to subsection (4)) a sum received by the company or its liquidator after—
    (a) the start of the winding up proceedings, or
    (b) if later, the permanent cessation of the deposit-taking trade.
(4) The following are not winding up receipts—
    (a) a sum received on behalf of a person entitled to the sum to the exclusion of the company and its liquidator, and
    (b) a sum realised by the transfer of an asset required to be valued under section 173 of ITTOIA 2005 (valuation of trading stock on cessation).][1]

Amendments—[1] Sections 837A–837H inserted by TIOPA 2010 s 371, Sch 7 paras 68, 71. TIOPA 2010 has effect for corporation tax purposes for accounting periods ending on or after 1 April 2010, for income and capital gains tax purposes for the tax year 2010–11 and subsequent tax years, and for petroleum revenue tax purposes for chargeable periods beginning on or after 1 July 2010.

[837D Transfer of rights to payment
(1) This section applies if—
    (a) the company or its liquidator transfers for value to another person the right to receive a sum arising from the deposit-taking trade, and
    (b) the sum is one which, if received by the company or its liquidator, would be a winding up receipt.
(2) If the transfer is at arm's length, this Chapter has effect as if the amount or value of the consideration for the transfer were a winding up receipt arising from the deposit-taking trade.
(3) If the transfer is not at arm's length, this Chapter has effect as if the value of the right transferred as between parties at arm's length were a winding up receipt arising from the deposit-taking trade.][1]

Commentary—*Simon's Taxes* **D7.725.**

Amendments—[1]   Sections 837A–837H inserted by TIOPA 2010 s 371, Sch 7 paras 68, 71. TIOPA 2010 has effect for corporation tax purposes for accounting periods ending on or after 1 April 2010, for income and capital gains tax purposes for the tax year 2010–11 and subsequent tax years, and for petroleum revenue tax purposes for chargeable periods beginning on or after 1 July 2010.

[837E Allowable deductions

(1) In calculating the amount on which income tax is charged under this Chapter for a tax year, deductions are allowed in accordance with this section from the amount which would otherwise be chargeable to income tax under this Chapter.

(2) A deduction is allowed for the total sum of all losses, expenses and debits within subsection (3) that are incurred during or before the tax year (but subject to subsections (4) and (5)).

(3) The losses, expenses and debits within this subsection are those which, if the company carrying on the deposit-taking trade had not permanently ceased to do so—

    (*a*) would have been deducted in calculating the profits of the trade for income or corporation tax purposes, or

    (*b*) would have been deducted from or set off against the profits of the trade for income or corporation tax purposes.

(4) No deduction is allowed if the loss, expense or debit arises directly or indirectly from the cessation itself.

(5) A loss, expense or debit is only within subsection (3) if incurred—

    (*a*) after the start of the winding up proceedings or, if later, the permanent cessation of the deposit-taking trade, or

    (*b*) in the case of a loss, at or before the permanent cessation of the deposit-taking trade.

(6) No deduction for an amount is allowed under this section if the amount has already been allowed (whether under this section or under any other provision of the Tax Acts).][1]

Amendments—[1]   Sections 837A–837H inserted by TIOPA 2010 s 371, Sch 7 paras 68, 71. TIOPA 2010 has effect for corporation tax purposes for accounting periods ending on or after 1 April 2010, for income and capital gains tax purposes for the tax year 2010–11 and subsequent tax years, and for petroleum revenue tax purposes for chargeable periods beginning on or after 1 July 2010.

[837F Election to carry back

(1) This section applies if a winding up receipt arising from the deposit-taking trade is received in a tax year beginning no later than 6 years after the company permanently ceased to carry on the trade.

(2) The company or its liquidator may elect that the income tax chargeable under this Chapter in respect of the receipt is to be charged as if the receipt has been received on the date of the cessation.

(3) The election must be made before the end of the period of two years beginning immediately after the end of the tax year in which the receipt is received.

(4) If an election is made under this section an assessment to income tax must be made accordingly (regardless of anything in the Income Tax Acts).][1]

Amendments—[1]   Sections 837A–837H inserted by TIOPA 2010 s 371, Sch 7 paras 68, 71. TIOPA 2010 has effect for corporation tax purposes for accounting periods ending on or after 1 April 2010, for income and capital gains tax purposes for the tax year 2010–11 and subsequent tax years, and for petroleum revenue tax purposes for chargeable periods beginning on or after 1 July 2010.

[837G Relationship of Chapter with other income tax provisions

If a winding up receipt arising from the deposit-taking trade is chargeable to income tax under this Chapter it is not chargeable to income tax under any other provision.][1]

Amendments—[1]   Sections 837A–837H inserted by TIOPA 2010 s 371, Sch 7 paras 68, 71. TIOPA 2010 has effect for corporation tax purposes for accounting periods ending on or after 1 April 2010, for income and capital gains tax purposes for the tax year 2010–11 and subsequent tax years, and for petroleum revenue tax purposes for chargeable periods beginning on or after 1 July 2010.

[837H Interpretation of Chapter

(1) This section applies for the purposes of this Chapter.

(2) There is the permanent cessation of a company's trade if—

    (*a*) the company ceases to carry on the trade, or

    (*b*) the company ceases to be within the charge to corporation tax in respect of the trade,

whether or not the trade is in fact ceased.

(3) A company is insolvent at any time if at that time—

    (*a*) it is unable to pay its debts as they fall due, or

    (*b*) the value of its assets is less than the amount of its liabilities (including its contingent and prospective liabilities).

(4) "Company" means—

    (*a*) a company as defined in section 1(1) of the Companies Act 2006, or

    (*b*) an unregistered company as defined in section 220 of the Insolvency Act 1986 or Article 184 of the Insolvency (Northern Ireland) Order 1989 (SI 1989/2405 (NI 19)).

(5) For the meaning of "deposit-taking trade" and "winding up receipt", see sections 837B(3) and 837C(3) respectively.][1]

Amendments—[1] Sections 837A–837H inserted by TIOPA 2010 s 371, Sch 7 paras 68, 71. TIOPA 2010 has effect for corporation tax purposes for accounting periods ending on or after 1 April 2010, for income and capital gains tax purposes for the tax year 2010–11 and subsequent tax years, and for petroleum revenue tax purposes for chargeable periods beginning on or after 1 July 2010.

CHAPTER 4

OTHER MISCELLANEOUS RULES

838 Local authorities and local authority associations

(1) A local authority in the United Kingdom is not liable to income tax in respect of its income.

(2) A local authority association in the United Kingdom is not liable to income tax in respect of its income.

(3) Tax is repayable as a result of subsection (1) or (2) only if a claim for repayment is made.

Commentary—Simon's Taxes **B1.445, D1.201A, B5.659, B5.651**.
Derivation—TA 1988 s 519.
HMRC Manuals—Company Taxation Manual CTM40855 (local authorities: introduction).

[838A Asbestos compensation settlements

(1) The trustees of an asbestos compensation settlement are not liable to income tax in respect of the income of the trustees.

(2) In this section "asbestos compensation settlement" means a settlement—

    (a) the sole or main purpose of which is making compensation payments to or in respect of individuals who have, or had before their death, an asbestos-related condition, and

    (b) which is made before 24 March 2010 in pursuance of an arrangement within subsection (3).

(3) An arrangement is within this subsection if it is—

    (a) a voluntary arrangement that has taken effect under Part 1 of the Insolvency Act 1986 or Part 2 of the Insolvency (Northern Ireland) Order 1989,

    (b) a compromise or arrangement that has taken effect under section 425 of the Companies Act 1985, Article 418 of the Companies (Northern Ireland) Order 1986 or Part 26 of the Companies Act 2006, or

    (c) an arrangement or compromise of a kind corresponding to any of those mentioned in paragraph (a) or (b) that has taken effect under, or as a result of, the law of a country or territory outside the United Kingdom.][1]

Commentary—Simon's Taxes **C4.203**.
Amendments—[1] This section inserted by F(No 3)A 2010 s 31, Sch 14 para 3(1), (3). This amendment is treated as having had effect for the tax year 2007–08 and subsequent tax years.

839 Issue departments of the Reserve Bank of India and the State Bank of Pakistan

No liability to income tax arises in respect of the income of the issue department of—

    (a) the Reserve Bank of India constituted under an Act of the Indian legislature called the Reserve Bank of India Act 1934, or

    (b) the State Bank of Pakistan constituted under orders made under section 9 of the Indian Independence Act 1947 (c 30).

Commentary—Simon's Taxes **C1.222, D1.231**.
Derivation—TA 1988 s 517.

840 Government securities held by non-UK resident central banks

(1) No liability to income tax arises in respect of income from securities which is—

    (a) income payable out of the public revenue of the United Kingdom, and

    (b) income of a bank, or the issue department of a bank, to which this section applies for the time being.

(2) But subsection (1) does not prevent the income from being taken into account in calculating profits, gains or losses of a business carried on in the United Kingdom.

(3) Her Majesty may by Order in Council direct that this section applies to a bank or its issue department if it appears to Her Majesty that the bank—

    (a) is non-UK resident, and

    (b) is entrusted by the government of a territory outside the United Kingdom with the custody of the territory's principal foreign exchange reserves.

(4) No recommendation may be made to Her Majesty in Council to make an order under this section unless a draft of the order has been laid before and approved by a resolution of the House of Commons.

Commentary—Simon's Taxes **A1.106, D1.232**.
Derivation—TA 1988 s 516.

841 Official agents of Commonwealth countries etc

(1) This section applies if an individual is employed in the United Kingdom as an official agent for—

    (a) a country mentioned in Schedule 3 to the British Nationality Act 1981 (c 61) (which contains a list of Commonwealth countries) or the Republic of Ireland, or

    (b) a state or province of a country within paragraph (a).

(2) If conditions A and B are met, the individual is entitled to the same immunity from income tax as that to which a member of the staff of a mission is entitled under the Diplomatic Privileges Act 1964 (c 81).

(3) Condition A is that the individual has been certified—
    (*a*) to be ordinarily resident outside the United Kingdom, and
    (*b*) to be UK resident solely for the purposes of the individual's functions as an official agent.

(4) The certification must have been done by (as the case may be)—
    (*a*) the High Commissioner of the country for which the individual is an official agent, or
    (*b*) the Agent-General of the state or province for which the individual is an official agent.

(5) In subsection (4)(*a*) "High Commissioner" includes the head of the mission of the country in question by whatever name called.

(6) Condition B is that the individual's functions as an official agent are not performed in connection with a trade, business or other undertaking carried on for the purposes of profit.

(7) In this section "head of the mission" and "a member of the staff of a mission" are to be read in accordance with the Diplomatic Privileges Act 1964.

Commentary—*Simon's Taxes* **E5.401B**.
Derivation—TA 1988 s 320(2)–(4).

842 European Economic Interest Groupings

(1) The following rules about European Economic Interest Groupings apply for the purposes of charging income tax—
    Rule 1 A grouping is treated as acting as the agent of its members.
    Rule 2 The activities of a grouping are treated as those of its members acting jointly.
    Rule 3 Each member of a grouping is treated as having a share of the grouping's property, rights and liabilities.
    Rule 4 Any trade or profession carried on by the grouping is treated as carried on in partnership by the members of the grouping.

(2) For the purposes of Rule 3, a member's share of any property, rights or liabilities of a grouping is determined according to the contract under which the grouping is established.

(3) If the contract does not provide for this, the member's share is determined by reference to the share of the profits of the grouping to which the member is entitled under the contract.

(4) If the contract does not provide for this either, the members are treated as having equal shares of the property, rights and liabilities of the grouping.

(5) "European Economic Interest Grouping" means a European Economic Interest Grouping formed under Council Regulation (EEC) No 2137/85 of 25 July 1985, whether registered in Great Britain, Northern Ireland or elsewhere.

Commentary—*Simon's Taxes* **D4.501, C1.609, D4.502**.
HMRC Manuals—Business Income Manual BIM82160 (partnerships: EEIGS - background).
Prospective amendments—In the heading, at the beginning, words "UK Economic Interest Groupings and" to be inserted, in sub-s (1) after "rules about" words "UK Economic Interest Groupings and" to be inserted, and sub-s (5) to be substituted, by the Taxes (Amendments) (EU Exit) Regulations, SI 2019/689 reg 15(1), (9) with effect from Implementation Period completion day (see EU(WA)A 2020 Sch 5 para 1(1)). Sub-s (5) to read as follows—
    "(5) "European Economic Interest Grouping" means a grouping registered in a member State and formed in pursuance of Council Regulation (EEC) No. 2137/85 of 25 July 1985 on the European Economic Interest Grouping as it has effect in EU law.".

843 Restriction of deductions for annual payments

In calculating a person's income from any source, no deduction is allowed for an annual payment to which section 904 applies (annual payments for dividends or non-taxable consideration).

Commentary—*Simon's Taxes* **E1.802**.
Derivation—TA 1988 s 125(1).
HMRC Manuals—Savings and Investment Manual SAIM8080 (annual payments made for dividends or non-taxable consideration).

844 Letters patent etc: exempting provisions

(1) No provision in letters patent granted by the Crown is to be construed as conferring exemption from income tax.

(2) Subsection (1) applies whether the letters patent are granted before or after the date on which this Act is passed.

(3) Any provision of the letters patent purporting to override the effect of subsection (1) is void.

Commentary—*Simon's Taxes* **E1.520**.
Derivation—TA 1988 s 829(4).

845 Extra return to be treated as interest etc

(1) This section applies if—
    (*a*) securities ("old securities") of a particular kind are issued by way of an original issue of securities of that kind,
    (*b*) on a later occasion securities ("new securities") of the same kind are issued,

(c) a sum ("the extra return") is payable in respect of the new securities by the issuer of them to reflect the fact that interest is accruing on the old securities,

(d) the issue price of the new securities includes an element (whether or not separately identified) representing payment for the extra return, and

(e) the extra return is equal to the amount of interest mentioned in subsection (2).

(2) The amount of interest referred to in subsection (1)(e) is—

(a) the amount of interest payable for the relevant period on so many old securities as there are new, or

(b) if there are more new securities than old, the amount of interest which would be so payable if there were as many old securities as new.

(3) A sum paid or payable by way of the extra return is treated for income tax purposes as if it were paid or payable as interest (so far as it would not be treated in that way apart from this subsection).

(4) No relief for the extra return is to be given to the issuer of the new securities.

Commentary—*Simon's Taxes* **D9.1105**.
Derivation—TA 1988 s 587A(1)–(3).

846 Interpretation of section 845

(1) This section applies for the purposes of section 845.

(2) Securities are of the same kind if they—

(a) are treated as being of the same kind by the practice of a recognised stock exchange, or

(b) would be so treated if dealt in on a recognised stock exchange.

(3) "The relevant period" is the period—

(a) beginning with the day mentioned in subsection (4), and

(b) ending with the day ("the new issue day") on which the new securities are issued.

(4) The day referred to in subsection (3)(a) is the day after—

(a) the last (or only) interest payment day before the new issue day, or

(b) if there is no interest payment day before the new issue day, the day on which the old securities are issued.

(5) In subsection (4) "interest payment day" means a day on which interest is payable under the old securities.

(6) "Relief" means relief by way of deduction in calculating amounts of income charged to income tax or in calculating net income.

Commentary—*Simon's Taxes* **D9.1105**.
Derivation—TA 1988 s 587A(3)–(6).

PART 15

DEDUCTION OF INCOME TAX AT SOURCE

Commentary—*Simon's Taxes* **A4.401–A4.475**.

CHAPTER 1

INTRODUCTION

847 Overview of Part

(1) This Part deals with deduction of income tax at source.

(2) The following Chapters contain duties to deduct sums representing income tax from certain payments—

(a) . . . [2]

(b) Chapter 3 (certain payments of yearly interest),

(c) Chapter 4 (payments in respect of building society securities),

(d) Chapter 5 (payments of UK public revenue dividends),

(e) Chapter 6 (annual payments and patent royalties),

(f) Chapter 7 (other payments connected with intellectual property),

(g) Chapter 9 (manufactured payments), and

(h) Chapter 10 (non-commercial payments by companies).

(3) Chapters 6 and 7 are subject to Chapter 8 which makes special provision in relation to the deduction of sums representing income tax from royalty payments.

(4) Chapter 11 contains provision disapplying some of the duties to deduct where payments are made between companies etc

(5) The following Chapters contain further provision in connection with the deduction (or deemed deduction) of sums representing income tax from certain payments (or deemed payments)—

[(za) Chapter 2 (interpretation of section 876 in Chapter 3: exception for deposit-takers),][2]

(a) Chapter 12 (funding bonds),

(b) Chapter 13 (unauthorised unit trusts),[1] and

(c) Chapter 14 (tax avoidance: directions for deductions from payments to non-UK residents).

(6) Chapters 15 to 17 contain provision about the collection of income tax in respect of payments from which sums are required to be deducted (or from which sums are treated as deducted) under the preceding Chapters.

(7) Chapter 18 deals with regimes involving the deduction of income tax at source which apply in the case of—

   (a) visiting performers,

   (b) non-resident landlords, and

   (c) Real Estate Investment Trusts.

(8) Chapter 19 makes general provision for this Part including—

   (a) provision about the giving of statements about deduction of income tax,

   (b) provision about payments where the recipient is a company or where the payer is a public department, and

   (c) exceptions from duties to deduct for payments made by designated international organisations, some payments under derivative contracts and for some payments of interest on foreign currency securities.

(9) The following provisions also deal with deduction of income tax at source—

   (a) Part 11 of ITEPA 2003 (Pay As You Earn), and

   (b) Chapter 3 of Part 3 of FA 2004 (construction industry scheme).

Amendments—[1]   Sub-s (5)(b) repealed by the Unauthorised Unit Trusts (Tax) Regulations, SI 2013/2819 reg 37(1), (10) with effect from 6 April 2014. Note that an unauthorised unit trust is not a non-exempt unauthorised unit trust, and these amendments do not apply in relation to the trust, if at all times in the period beginning with 24 May 2012 and ending with 5 April 2014 it had at least one unit holder which was, and at least one unit holder which was not, an eligible investor (ie a mixed unauthorised unit trust); this ceases to apply in relation to the trust if subsequently it no longer has any unit holders which are eligible investors (SI 2013/2819 reg 32).

[2]   Sub-s (2)(a) repealed, and sub-s (5)(za) inserted, by FA 2016 s 39, Sch 6 para 21 with effect in relation to interest paid or credited on or after 6 April 2016, and dividends or other distributions paid by a building society on or after that date.

848 Income tax deducted at source treated as income tax paid by recipient

(1) A sum representing income tax which is deducted (or treated as deducted) under this Part from a payment is treated as income tax paid by the recipient.

(2) The sum is accordingly taken into account under sections 59B and 59D of TMA 1970 (see also paragraph 8 of Schedule 18 to FA 1998) in determining the income tax or corporation tax payable by, or repayable to, the recipient.

(3) But this section does not apply to income tax deducted at source under section 966 (visiting performers) or 971 (non-resident landlords).

(4) In relation to income tax deducted at source under section 941 (unauthorised unit trusts), this section is subject to section 943A (treatment of cases involving double tax relief).[1]

Commentary—*Simon's Taxes* **E1.513**.

Derivation—TA 1988 ss 348(1), 349(1) and ITTOIA 2005 ss 426, 550, 602, 618, 686(1).

HMRC Manuals—Savings and Investment Manual SAIM9010 (deduction of tax: introduction).

Amendments—[1]   Sub-s (4) inserted by FA 2010 s 40, Sch 13 para 2 with effect in relation to payments treated under ITA 2007 s 941(2) as made on or after 21 October 2009 and repealed by the Unauthorised Unit Trusts (Tax) Regulations, SI 2013/2819 reg 37(1), (11) with effect from 6 April 2014. Note that an unauthorised unit trust is not a non-exempt unauthorised unit trust, and this repeal does not apply in relation to the trust, if at all times in the period beginning with 24 May 2012 and ending with 5 April 2014 it had at least one unit holder which was, and at least one unit holder which was not, an eligible investor (ie a mixed unauthorised unit trust); this ceases to apply in relation to the trust if subsequently it no longer has any unit holders which are eligible investors (SI 2013/2819 reg 32).

849 Interaction with other Income Tax Acts provisions

(1) Regulations made under [section 7 of TIOPA 2010 (double taxation arrangements: general regulations)][1] make provision disapplying or otherwise affecting duties to deduct under this Part in circumstances where relief is available under double taxation arrangements.

(2) Sections 821 and 822 of ICTA make provision in relation to under-deductions and over-deductions from some payments which are made before the passing of the relevant annual Act imposing income tax and corporation tax.

(3) In accordance with section 783 of ITTOIA 2005 (general disregard of exempt income for income tax purposes), any payment (or part of a payment) which is exempt from income tax as a result of Part 6 of ITTOIA 2005 is ignored for the purposes of the duties under this Part.

   This is subject to any express or implied provision to the contrary.

(4) [Section 564Q (deduction of income tax at source under this Part) makes][1] provision for Chapters 2 to 5, 12 and 19 to have effect in relation to alternative finance arrangements.

(5) For exceptions from the duties to deduct under Chapters 3, 6, 7, 10 and 14 in connection with the London Olympic Games and Paralympic Games see—

   (a) Chapter 6 of Part 3 of FA 2006, and

   (b) regulations made under that Chapter.

Amendments—[1]   In sub-ss (1), (4), words substituted by TIOPA 2010 s 501, Sch 8 paras 71, 84, 219, 222. TIOPA 2010 has effect for corporation tax purposes for accounting periods ending on or after 1 April 2010, for income and capital gains tax purposes for the tax year 2010–11 and subsequent tax years, and for petroleum revenue tax purposes for chargeable periods beginning on or after 1 July 2010.

CHAPTER 2
[MEANING OF "RELEVANT INVESTMENT" FOR PURPOSES OF SECTION 876]

Introduction

850 Overview of Chapter

[(1) This Chapter has effect for the purposes of section 876 (duty under section 874 to deduct tax from payments of yearly interest: exception for deposit-takers).][1]

(2) . . . [1]

(3) Sections 853 to 856 set out some basic concepts, so that—

    (*a*) section 853 defines "deposit-taker" (and section 854 allows the Treasury by order to prescribe persons as deposit-takers),

    (*b*) section 855 defines "investment" and "deposit", and

    (*c*) section 856 explains which investments are relevant investments.

(4) Section 856 is subject to—

    (*a*) section 857 (which sets out when investments must be treated as relevant and when they may be treated as not relevant), and

    (*b*) sections [863][1] to 870 (which describe various kinds of investment which are not relevant investments).

(5) Sections [872 and][1] 873 contain supplementary provisions.

(6) For the purposes of this [Chapter, crediting][1] interest counts as paying it.

Commentary—*Simon's Taxes* **A4.402, A4.405.**

HMRC Manuals—Savings and Investment Manual SAIM9020 (interest etc. paid by 'deposit takers').

Amendments—[1] Sub-s (1) substituted, sub-s (2) repealed, and words in sub-ss (4)(*b*), (5), (6) substituted, by FA 2016 s 39, Sch 6 paras 3, 5 with effect in relation to interest paid or credited on or after 6 April 2016, and dividends or other distributions paid by a building society on or after that date.

Deposit-takers and relevant investments

853 Meaning of "deposit-taker"

(1) In this Chapter [and section 876][3] "deposit-taker" means—

    (*a*) the Bank of England, or

    (*b*) a person to whom one of the following subsections or section 854 applies.

(2) This subsection applies to a person—

    (*a*) who has permission under Part 4 of FISMA 2000 to accept deposits which are relevant investments, and

    (*b*) who is not—

        (i) a building society,

        (ii) a society registered within the meaning of the Friendly Societies Act 1974 (c 46) or incorporated under the Friendly Societies Act 1992 (c 40),

        (iii) a society registered as a credit union under [the Co-operative and Community Benefit Societies Act 2014][2] or the Credit Unions (Northern Ireland) Order 1985 (SI 1985/1205 (NI 12)), or

        (iv) an insurance company within the meaning of section 275 of FA 2004.

(3) This subsection applies to a company [as defined in section 1(1) of the Companies Act 2006 (c 46)[1]]—

    (*a*) in respect of which a resolution has been passed by a local authority under—

        (i)   section 48(3) of the Banking Act 1979 (c 37), or

        (ii) section 103(3) of the Banking Act 1987 (c 22), and

    (*b*) which is exempt from the prohibition in section 19 of FISMA 2000 on accepting deposits which are relevant investments.

(4) This subsection applies to a local authority.

(5) This subsection applies to an EEA firm which—

    (*a*) is of the kind mentioned in paragraph 5(*b*) of Schedule 3 to FISMA 2000 (EEA passport rights), and

    (*b*) has permission under paragraph 15 of that Schedule to accept deposits (as a result of qualifying for authorisation under paragraph 12(1) of that Schedule).

(6) This subsection applies to a person—

    (*a*) who is authorised for the purposes of FISMA 2000, and

    (*b*) whose business consists wholly or mainly of dealing in financial instruments as principal.

    For the meaning of "financial instrument", see section 984.

Commentary—*Simon's Taxes* **A4.402, D7.701.**

HMRC Manuals—Corporate Finance Manual CFM75040 (deposit-taker).

Amendments—[1] In para (3) words substituted by the Companies Act 2006 (Consequential Amendments) (Taxes and National Insurance) Order, SI 2009/1890 art 3(2)(*b*) with effect from 1 October 2009.

[2] In sub-s (2)(*b*)(iii) words substituted for words "the Industrial and Provident Societies Act 1965" by the Co-operative and Community Benefit Societies Act 2014 s 151, Sch 4 paras 104, 108 with effect from 1 August 2014 and subject to transitional provisions and provisions preserving the continuity of the law in Sch 5 of that Act.

[3] Words in sub-s (1) inserted by FA 2016 s 39, Sch 6 paras 3, 7 with effect in relation to interest paid or credited on or after 6 April 2016, and dividends or other distributions paid by a building society on or after that date.

Prospective amendments—Sub-s (5) to be repealed by the Taxes (Amendments) (EU Exit) Regulations, SI 2019/689 reg 15(1), (10) with effect from Implementation Period completion day (see EU(WA)A 2020 Sch 5 para 1(1)). This amendment does not apply where a person qualifies for authorisation under FSMA 2000 Sch 3 by virtue of SI 2001/3084 (see SI 2019/689 reg 41(*f*)).

854 Power to prescribe persons as deposit-takers

(1) This section applies to a person who receives deposits in the course of carrying on business or activities and—

    (*a*) is for the time being prescribed by order by the Treasury for the purposes of this section, or

    (*b*) is a member of a class of persons which is for the time being so prescribed.

(2) An order under this section may prescribe a person or class of person—

    (*a*) in relation to all deposits which are relevant investments, or

    (*b*) in relation to deposits which are relevant investments of a kind specified in the order.

(3) If a person is prescribed only in relation to deposits which are relevant investments of a kind specified in the order, the reference in section [876(1)(*b*)][1] to "relevant investment" is to be read as a reference only to relevant investments of the kind so specified.

Commentary—*Simon's Taxes* **A1.106, A4.402, D7.701**.
Derivation—TA 1988 ss 481(2)(*f*), 482(10).
HMRC Manuals—Savings and Investment Manual SAIM9020 (interest etc. paid by 'deposit takers').
Amendments—[1] Words in sub-s (3) substituted by FA 2016 s 39, Sch 6 paras 3, 9 with effect in relation to interest paid or credited on or after 6 April 2016, and dividends or other distributions paid by a building society on or after that date.

855 Meaning of "investment" and "deposit"

[(1) In this Chapter, and section 876, "investment" means a deposit with a deposit-taker.][1]

(2) In this Chapter "deposit" means a sum of money paid on terms which mean that it will be repaid (with or without interest)—

    (*a*) on demand, or

    (*b*) at a time or in circumstances agreed by or on behalf of the person who pays it and the person who receives it.

Commentary—*Simon's Taxes* **A4.406**.
Derivation—TA 1988 s 480A(1), 481(3) and SI 1990/2231 regs 2, 3.
HMRC Manuals—Savings and Investment Manual SAIM9020 (interest etc. paid by 'deposit takers').
Amendments—[1] Sub-s (1) substituted by FA 2016 s 39, Sch 6 paras 3, 9 with effect in relation to interest paid or credited on or after 6 April 2016, and dividends or other distributions paid by a building society on or after that date.

856 Investments which are relevant investments

(1) An investment is a relevant investment for the purposes of [section 876][1] if it meets—

    (*a*) the individual interest condition (see subsection (3)),

    (*b*) the Scottish partnership condition (see subsection (4)),

    (*c*) the personal representative condition (see subsection (5)), or

    (*d*) the settlement condition (see subsection (6)).

(2) But an investment is not a relevant investment if any of sections [863][1] to 870 prevent it from being a relevant investment.

(3) An investment meets the individual interest condition if the only persons beneficially entitled to interest on the investment are individuals.

(4) An investment meets the Scottish partnership condition if—

    (*a*) a Scottish partnership is beneficially entitled to all interest on the investment, and

    (*b*) that partnership consists only of individuals.

(5) An investment meets the personal representative condition if personal representatives are entitled to any interest on the investment and they receive it in that capacity.

(6) An investment meets the settlement condition if all interest on the investment is income arising to the trustees of a discretionary or accumulation settlement and they receive it in that capacity.

For the meaning of "discretionary or accumulation settlement", see section 873(1).

Commentary—*Simon's Taxes* **A4.406, A4.407, A4.408, A4.409, A4.410**.
Amendments—[1] Words in sub-ss (1), (2) substituted by FA 2016 s 39, Sch 6 paras 3, 10 with effect in relation to interest paid or credited on or after 6 April 2016, and dividends or other distributions paid by a building society on or after that date.

857 Investments to be treated as being or as not being relevant investments

(1) A deposit-taker . . . [1] must treat every investment with it as a relevant investment unless satisfied that the investment is not a relevant investment.

(2) If a deposit-taker . . . [1] is satisfied that an investment is not a relevant investment, it may continue to treat the investment as not being a relevant investment until subsection (3) applies.

(3) This subsection applies when the deposit-taker . . . [1] has information which can reasonably be taken to indicate that the investment is or may be a relevant investment.

Commentary—*Simon's Taxes* **A4.406**.
Amendments—[1] Words "or building society" in each place repealed by FA 2016 s 39, Sch 6 paras 3, 11 with effect in relation to interest paid or credited on or after 6 April 2016, and dividends or other distributions paid by a building society on or after that date.

[Investments] which are not relevant investments

863 General client account deposits

(1) An investment is not a relevant investment if it is a general client account deposit.

(2) An investment is a general client account deposit for the purposes of this section if—

    (*a*) it is a deposit held by a deposit-taker . . . [1] in a client account, and

    (*b*) provision made under any enactment requires the person whose account it is to make payments representing interest to some or all of the clients for whom, or on whose account, that person received the sums deposited in the account.

(3) But an investment is not a general client account deposit if the account in which it is held is identified by the deposit-taker . . . [1] as one in which sums are held only for one or more particular clients of the person whose account it is.

Commentary—*Simon's Taxes* **A4.406, B5.670**.

Derivation—TA 1988 s 481(5), 482(6) and SI 1990/2231 regs 2(1) and 4(1).

HMRC Manuals—Savings and Investment Manual SAIM9020 (not all investments are 'relevant investments').

Amendments—[1]　In heading before s 863, word substituted, and in sub-ss (2), (3), words "or building society" repealed, by FA 2016 s 39, Sch 6 paras 3, 14 with effect in relation to interest paid or credited on or after 6 April 2016, and dividends or other distributions paid by a building society on or after that date.

864 Qualifying uncertificated eligible debt security units

An investment is not a relevant investment if it is a deposit in respect of which a deposit-taker . . . [1] has issued a qualifying uncertificated eligible debt security unit (see section 986).

Commentary—*Simon's Taxes* **A4.406**.

Amendments—[1]　Words "or building society" repealed by FA 2016 s 39, Sch 6 paras 3, 14 with effect in relation to interest paid or credited on or after 6 April 2016, and dividends or other distributions paid by a building society on or after that date.

865 Qualifying certificates of deposit

An investment is not a relevant investment if it is a deposit in respect of which a deposit-taker . . . [1] has issued a qualifying certificate of deposit (see section 985).

Commentary—*Simon's Taxes* **A4.406**.

HMRC Manuals—Corporate Finance Manual CFM75060 (qualifying certificates of deposit and qualifying time deposits).

Amendments—[1]　Words "or building society" repealed by FA 2016 s 39, Sch 6 paras 3, 14 with effect in relation to interest paid or credited on or after 6 April 2016, and dividends or other distributions paid by a building society on or after that date.

866 Qualifying time deposits

(1) An investment is not a relevant investment if it is a qualifying time deposit [made before 6 April 2012][1].

(2) An investment is a qualifying time deposit for the purposes of this section if—

    (*a*) it is a deposit consisting of a loan of at least £50,000,

    (*b*) the terms of the deposit require its repayment at a specified time within 5 years beginning with the date on which it is made,

    (*c*) those terms do not make provision for the transfer of the right to repayment, and

    (*d*) those terms prevent partial withdrawals of, or additions to, the deposit.

(3) If a deposit is denominated in a foreign currency, subsection (2)(*a*) has effect as if it referred to an amount which is at least the equivalent in that currency of £50,000 at the time the deposit is made.

Commentary—*Simon's Taxes* **A4.406**.

HMRC Manuals—Corporate Finance Manual CFM75060 (qualifying certificates of deposit and qualifying time deposits).

Amendments—[1]　Words inserted in sub-s (1) by FA 2012 s 18. This amendment is treated as having come into force on 6 April 2012.

867 Lloyd's premium trust funds

(1) An investment is not a relevant investment if it forms part of a premium trust fund of an underwriting or former underwriting member of Lloyd's.

(2) In this section "premium trust fund" has the meaning given in section 184 of FA 1993.

Commentary—*Simon's Taxes* **A4.406**.

Derivation—TA 1988 s 481(5) and FA 1993 ss 183(2), 184(1) and SI 1990/2231 regs 2(1) and 4(1).

868 Investments held outside the United Kingdom

(1) An investment with a deposit-taker is not a relevant investment if—

    (*a*) the deposit-taker is UK resident for income tax purposes or corporation tax purposes, and

    (*b*) the investment is held at a branch of the deposit-taker situated outside the United Kingdom.

(2) An investment with a deposit-taker is not a relevant investment if—

    (*a*) the deposit-taker is non-UK resident for income tax purposes or corporation tax purposes, and

    (*b*) the investment is not held at a branch of the deposit-taker situated in the United Kingdom.

(3) . . . [2]

(4) For the purposes of this section an investment is held at a branch of a deposit-taker . . . [1] if the investment is recorded in its books as a liability of that branch.

Commentary—*Simon's Taxes* **A4.406**.

Amendments—[1]   Words "or building society" in sub-s (4) repealed by FA 2016 s 39, Sch 6 paras 3, 14 with effect in relation to interest paid or credited on or after 6 April 2016, and dividends or other distributions paid by a building society on or after that date.

[2]   Sub-s (3) repealed by FA 2016 s 39, Sch 6 paras 3, 15 with effect in relation to interest paid or credited on or after 6 April 2016, and dividends or other distributions paid by a building society on or after that date.

870 Other investments

(1) An investment with a deposit-taker is not a relevant investment if—

(a) it is a loan made by a deposit-taker in the ordinary course of its business or activities,

(b) it is a debt on a security which is listed on a recognised stock exchange, or

(c) it is a debt on a debenture issued by the deposit-taker (see section 1022).

(2) . . .[1]

Commentary—*Simon's Taxes* **A4.406**.

Amendments—[1]   Sub-s (2) repealed by FA 2016 s 39, Sch 6 paras 3, 15 with effect in relation to interest paid or credited on or after 6 April 2016, and dividends or other distributions paid by a building society on or after that date.

872 Power to make orders amending Chapter

(1) The Treasury may by order amend this Chapter for the purposes of providing that investments of a kind specified in the order are, or are not, relevant investments.

(2) An order under this section [may amend this Chapter[1]]—

(a) in [its application][1] to all deposit-takers, or

(b) in [its application][1] to such deposit-takers or classes of deposit-taker as the order may specify.

(3) An order under this section may contain incidental, supplemental, consequential and transitional provision and savings.

(4) . . .[1]

(5) . . .[1]

Amendments—[1]   Words in sub-s (2) substituted, and sub-ss (4), (5) repealed, by FA 2016 s 39, Sch 6 paras 3, 17 with effect in relation to interest paid or credited on or after 6 April 2016, and dividends or other distributions paid by a building society on or after that date.

873 Discretionary or accumulation settlements

(1) A settlement is a discretionary or accumulation settlement for the purposes of this Chapter if any income arising to the trustees would (unless treated as income of the settlor) be to any extent income within subsection (2) for the tax year in which it arises.

(2) Income is within this subsection so far as it is—

(a) accumulated or discretionary income as defined in section 480 (other than income arising under a [charitable trust][1] or an unauthorised unit trust in relation to which [regulation 12 of the Unauthorised Unit Trusts (Tax) Regulations 2013][2] applies), or

(b) an amount of a type set out in section 482 (unless the trust is a unit trust scheme or the amount is income arising under a [charitable trust][1] only or is excluded by section 481(5)).

(3)–(6) . . .[3]

Amendments—[1]   In sub-s (2)(a), (b) words substituted by FA 2010 s 30, Sch 6 para 23(1), (5) with effect for the tax year 2012–13 and subsequent tax years (SI 2012/736 art 17).

[2]   In sub-s (2)(a), words substituted for words "section 504" by the Unauthorised Unit Trusts (Tax) Regulations, SI 2013/2819 reg 37(1), (12) with effect from 6 April 2014. Note that an unauthorised unit trust is not a non-exempt unauthorised unit trust, and these amendments do not apply in relation to the trust, if at all times in the period beginning with 24 May 2012 and ending with 5 April 2014 it had at least one unit holder which was, and at least one unit holder which was not, an eligible investor (ie a mixed unauthorised unit trust); this ceases to apply in relation to the trust if subsequently it no longer has any unit holders which are eligible investors (SI 2013/2819 reg 32).

[3]   Sub-ss (3)–(6) repealed by FA 2016 s 39, Sch 6 paras 3, 18 with effect in relation to interest paid or credited on or after 6 April 2016, and dividends or other distributions paid by a building society on or after that date.

CHAPTER 3

DEDUCTION FROM CERTAIN PAYMENTS OF YEARLY INTEREST

Duty to deduct sums representing income tax

874 Duty to deduct from certain payments of yearly interest

(1) This section applies if a payment of yearly interest arising in the United Kingdom is made—

(a) by a company,

(b) by a local authority,

(c) by or on behalf of a partnership of which a company is a member, or

(d) by any person to another person whose usual place of abode is outside the United Kingdom.

(2) The person by or through whom the payment is made must, on making the payment, deduct from it a sum representing income tax on it at the [basic rate][1] in force for the tax year in which it is made.

(3) But see—

(a) sections 875 to [888E][5] as to circumstances in which the duty to deduct a sum under this section is disapplied, and

(b) Chapter 11 (payments between companies etc) for a further exception from the duty to deduct under this section.

(4) See also regulations made under section 17(3) of F(No 2)A 2005 (authorised investment funds)—

(a) for provision treating certain amounts shown in the distribution accounts of authorised investment funds as payments of yearly interest, and

(b) for exceptions from the duty to deduct under this section which would otherwise apply to such payments.

(5) For the purposes of subsection (1) the following are to be treated as payments of yearly interest—

(a) a payment of interest made by a [registered society][4] in respect of any mortgage, loan, loan stock or deposit, and

(b) any interest, dividend, bonus or other sum payable to a shareholder of such a society by reference to the amount of the shareholder's holding in the share capital of the society.

[(5A) For the purposes of subsection (1) a payment of interest which is payable to an individual in respect of compensation is to be treated as a payment of yearly interest (irrespective of the period in respect of which the interest is paid).

(5B) But the Commissioners for Her Majesty's Revenue and Customs may make regulations which provide that subsection (5A) does not apply in the circumstances prescribed in the regulations.][2]

(6) For the purposes of subsection (1)—

(a) a payment made by a company in a fiduciary or representative capacity is not to be treated as a payment made by the company, and

(b) a payment made by a local authority in a fiduciary or representative capacity is not to be treated as a payment made by the local authority.

[(6A) In determining for the purposes of subsection (1) whether a payment of interest arises in the United Kingdom no account is to be taken of the location of any deed which records the obligation to pay the interest.][3]

(7) For provision about the collection of income tax in respect of a payment from which a sum must be deducted under this section—

(a) see Chapter 15 if the person making the payment is a UK resident company, and

(b) otherwise see Chapter 16.

Commentary—*Simon's Taxes* A4.421–A4.425, A1.109, A1.114, A4.141, B5.670, B7.401, E1.827B, D5.102, D7.626, D8.177, I9.243 .

HMRC Manuals—Savings and Investment Manual SAIM9070 (what is yearly interest?).
SAIM9080 (meaning of "place of abode").
Company Taxation Manual CTM35210 (payments made before 1 April 2001).
CTM35215 (payments made on or after 1 April 2001).
CTM48862 (deduction of tax from property authorised investment fund distributions).
Business Income Manual BIM65805 (solicitors' rules regarding interest on client account money).
International Manual INTM152060 (double taxation agreements and domestic law).
SAIM9080 (meaning of "place of abode").

Amendments—[1] Words in sub-s (2) substituted by FA 2008 s 5, Sch 1 paras 1, 26 with effect for the tax year 2008–09 and subsequent tax years.

[2] Sub-ss (5A), (5B) inserted by FA 2013 s 27, Sch 11 paras 1, 2 with effect in relation to any payment of interest by a building society which is made on or after 1 September 2013 and in relation to any other payment of interest which is made on or after 1 October 2013.

[3] Sub-s (6A) inserted by FA 2013 s 27, Sch 11 para 5 with effect in relation to any payment of interest which is made on or after 17 July 2013.

[4] In sub-s (5)(a) words substituted for words "registered industrial and provident society" by the Co-operative and Community Benefit Societies Act 2014 s 151, Sch 4 paras 104, 109 with effect from 1 August 2014 and subject to transitional provisions and provisions preserving the continuity of the law in Sch 5 of that Act.

[5] In sub-s (3)(a) reference substituted for reference "888" by FA 2017 s 11, Sch 5 para 4 with effect from 27 April 2017.

Exceptions from duty to deduct

875 Interest paid by building societies

The duty to deduct a sum representing income tax under section 874 does not apply to a payment of interest made by a building society [unless it is treated as a payment of yearly interest by virtue of section 874(5A)][1].

Commentary—*Simon's Taxes* A4.425, A4.141.
TA 1988 s 349(2).
HMRC Manuals—Savings and Investment Manual SAIM9116 (banks and building societies).
Company Taxation Manual CTM35210 (exemptions from deducting tax on certain payments).
Amendments—[1] Words inserted by FA 2013 s 27, Sch 11 paras 1, 3 with effect in relation to any payment of interest by a building society which is made on or after 1 September 2013 and in relation to any other payment of interest which is made on or after 1 October 2013.

876 Interest paid by deposit-takers

[(1) The duty to deduct a sum representing income tax under section 874 does not apply to a payment of interest on an investment if—

(a) the payment is made by a deposit-taker, and

(b) when the payment is made, the investment is a relevant investment.

(1A) In this section "deposit-taker", "investment" and "relevant investment" have the meaning given by Chapter 2.][1]

Commentary—*Simon's Taxes* **A4.425, A4.406**.
Amendments—[1]   Sub-ss (1), (1A) substituted by FA 2016 s 39, Sch 6 para 2 with effect in relation to interest paid on or after 6 April 2016.

877 UK public revenue dividends

The duty to deduct a sum representing income tax under section 874 does not apply to a payment of interest [that is][1] a UK public revenue dividend [(as defined by section 891)][1].

Commentary—*Simon's Taxes* **A4.425**.
HMRC Manuals—Savings and Investment Manual SAIM9140 (UK public revenue dividends).
Amendments—[1]   Words substituted for words "in respect of", and words inserted, by FA 2016 s 39, Sch 6 para 26 with effect from 15 September 2016.

878 Interest paid by banks

(1) The duty to deduct a sum representing income tax under section 874 does not apply to a payment of interest made by a bank if that payment is made in the ordinary course of its business.
[(1A) But that duty does apply to such a payment if it is treated as a payment of yearly interest by virtue of section 874(5A).][1]
(2) Section 991 (meaning of "bank") applies for the purposes of this section.

Commentary—*Simon's Taxes* **A4.425, A4.426, D7.701**.
HMRC Manuals—Corporate Finance Manual CFM75100 (interest paid in the ordinary course of banking business).
Modifications—ITA 2007 Sch 2 para 163 (modification of this section in relation to interest payable on an advance made before 29 April 1996).
Amendments—[1]   Sub-s (1A) inserted by FA 2013 s 27, Sch 11 paras 1, 4 with effect in relation to any payment of interest by a building society which is made on or after 1 September 2013 and in relation to any other payment of interest which is made on or after 1 October 2013.

879 Interest paid on advances from banks

(1) The duty to deduct a sum representing income tax under section 874 does not apply to a payment of interest on an advance from a bank if, at the time when the payment is made, the person beneficially entitled to the interest is within the charge to corporation tax as respects the interest [or is a bank that would be within the charge to corporation tax as respects the interest apart from section 18A of CTA 2009][1].
(2) Section 991 (meaning of "bank") applies for the purposes of this section.
(3) Subsection (1) applies to the European Investment Bank as if the words from "if" to the end were omitted.
(4) An order under subsection (2)(*e*) of section 991 designating an international organisation as a bank may provide that subsection (1) applies to the organisation with the modification mentioned in subsection (3).

Commentary—*Simon's Taxes* **A4.425, A4.426**.
HMRC Manuals—International Manual INTM287050 (interest paid on advances from banks).
Corporate Finance Manual CFM75110 (advances by a bank).
Modifications—ITA 2007 Sch 2 para 164(1)–(3) (modification of this section in relation to interest payable before 29 April 1996).
ITA 2007 Sch 2 para 164(4)–(6) (transitional provisions and savings).
Amendments—[1]   In sub-s (1) words inserted by FA 2011 s 48, Sch 13 paras 18, 19 with effect from 19 July 2011, subject to transitional provisions in FA 2011 Sch 13 paras 32–37.

880 Interest paid on advances from building societies

The duty to deduct a sum representing income tax under section 874 does not apply to a payment of interest on an advance from a building society.

Commentary—*Simon's Taxes* **A4.421, A4.425**.
Derivation—TA 1988 s 477A(7).

881 National Savings Bank interest

The duty to deduct a sum representing income tax under section 874 does not apply to a payment of interest on deposits with the National Savings Bank.

Commentary—*Simon's Taxes* **A4.425**.
Derivation—TA 1998 s 349(3).

882 Quoted Eurobond interest

The duty to deduct a sum representing income tax under section 874 does not apply to a payment of interest on a quoted Eurobond (see section 987).

Commentary—*Simon's Taxes* **A4.425, D9.801**.
Derivation—TA 1988 s 349(3).
HMRC Manuals—Company Taxation Manual CTM35218 (application of the eurobond exemption).

883 Interest on loan to buy life annuity

The duty to deduct a sum representing income tax under section 874 does not apply to a payment of interest to which section 369 of ICTA applies (interest on loan to buy life annuity payable under deduction of tax).

Commentary—*Simon's Taxes* **A4.425, A1.304**.
Derivation—TA 1988 s 349(3).

884 Relevant foreign income

(1) The duty to deduct a sum representing income tax under section 874 does not apply to a payment of interest which is chargeable to income tax as relevant foreign income.

(2) For the meaning of "relevant foreign income", see section 989.

Commentary—*Simon's Taxes* **A4.425**.
Derivation—TA 1988 s 349(3).
HMRC Manuals—Savings and Investment Manual SAIM9090 (duty to deduct tax from interest with a UK source).

885 Authorised persons dealing in financial instruments

(1) The duty to deduct a sum representing income tax under section 874 does not apply to a payment of interest made by a person authorised for the purposes of FISMA 2000 if—

    (a) the person's business consists wholly or mainly of dealing in financial instruments as principal, and

    (b) the payment is made by that person in the ordinary course of that business.

(2) For the meaning of "financial instrument", see section 984.

Commentary—*Simon's Taxes* **A4.425**.
HMRC Manuals—Company Taxation Manual CTM35215 (categories of recipient).

886 Interest paid by recognised clearing houses etc

(1) The duty to deduct a sum representing income tax under section 874 does not apply to a payment of interest made by a [relevant entity][2] if—

    (a) the [relevant entity][2] is carrying on business as the provider of a central counterparty clearing service [or as a central securities depository][3], and

    (b) the interest is paid in the ordinary course of that business, on margin or other collateral deposited with it by users of the service [or central securities depository][3].

(2) The duty to deduct a sum representing income tax under section 874 does not apply to interest treated by virtue of section 607 (treatment of price differences under repos)[, or paragraph 5 of Schedule 13 to FA 2007 (relief for borrower for finance charges in case of debtor repos and debtor quasi-repos),][1] as paid by an [relevant entity][2] in respect of contracts made by it as the provider of a central counterparty clearing service [or as a central securities depository][3].

(3) In this section—

    "central counterparty clearing service" means the service provided by [a relevant entity][2] to the parties to a transaction where there are contracts between each of the parties and the RCH or RIE (in place of, or as an alternative to, a contract directly between the parties), and

    [""relevant entity", means any of the following (as defined for the purposes of FISMA 2000 by section 285 of that Act)—

        (a) a recognised clearing house;

        (b) a recognised investment exchange;

        (c) an EEA central counterparty;

        (d) a third country central counterparty;][2]

        [(e) a recognised CSD;

        (f) an EEA CSD;

        (g) a third country CSD.][3]

Commentary—*Simon's Taxes* **A4.425**.
Amendments—[1]   In sub-s (2), words inserted by FA 2007 s 47, Sch 14 paras 21, 24 with effect in relation to an arrangement that comes into force on or after 1 October 2007: SI 2007/2483 art 3.
[2]   In sub-ss (1), (2), words substituted, in sub-s (3), words in definition of "central counterparty clearing service" substituted, definition of "recognised clearing house" and "recognised investment exchange" repealed and definition inserted by the Financial Services and Markets Act 2000 (Over the Counter Derivatives, Central Counterparties and Trade Repositories) Regulations, SI 2013/504 reg 24 with effect from 1 April 2013.
[3]   In sub-ss (1)(a), (b), (2) words inserted, and sub-s (3)(e)–(g) inserted, by the Central Securities Depositories Regulations 2017/1064 reg 10, Schedule para 12 with effect from 28 November 2017.
Prospective amendments—In sub-s (3), in the definition of "relevant entity", paragraphs (c) and (f) to be repealed, by the Financial Services (Miscellaneous) (Amendment) (EU Exit) Regulations, SI 2019/710 reg 4 with effect from Implementation Period completion day (see EU(WA)A 2020 Sch 5 para 1(1)).

887 [Payments made by registered societies]

(1) The duty to deduct a sum representing income tax under section 874 does not apply to either of the following payments if they are payable to a person whose usual place of abode is in the United Kingdom—

    (a) a payment of interest made by a [registered society][2] in respect of any mortgage, loan, loan stock or deposit, or

    (b) any interest, dividend, bonus or other sum payable to a shareholder of such a society by reference to the amount of the shareholder's holding in the share capital of the society.

(2) A [registered society][2] must, within 3 months after the end of each of its accounting periods, deliver to an officer of Revenue and Customs a return containing the information mentioned in subsection (3).

(3) That information is—

   (*a*) the name and place of residence of every person to whom the society has, as a result of this section, made one or more payments in the period amounting in total to at least £15 without deducting a sum (or sums) representing income tax, and

   (*b*) the amount so paid in the period to each of those persons.

(4) See [section 500(2) of CTA 2009][1] as to the consequences of not making a return as required by subsection (2).

[(5) In this Chapter "registered society" means—

   (*a*) a registered society within the meaning of the Co-operative and Community Benefit Societies Act 2014,

   (*b*) a society registered or treated as registered under the Industrial and Provident Societies Act (Northern Ireland) 1969,

   (*c*) a society registered as a credit union under the Credit Unions (Northern Ireland) Order 1985 (S.I. 1985/1205 (N.I. 12)), or

   (*d*) an SCE formed in accordance with Council Regulation (EC) No 1435/2003 on the Statute for a European Cooperative Society.][2]

(6) For the purposes of this section crediting interest (or amounts treated as interest) counts as paying it.

Commentary—*Simon's Taxes* **A4.425, A4.427, A1.109, A4.143, A6.709, B1.438, D7.626**.

Derivation—TA 1988 s 486(2), (3), (6), (12).

HMRC Manuals—Company Taxation Manual CTM40162 (returns required to be made by credit unions).
CTM40430 (interest paid by registered society).
CTM40525 (returns of gross payments).

Amendments—[1]   In sub-s (4), words substituted by TIOPA 2010 s 501, Sch 8 paras 306, 307. TIOPA 2010 has effect for corporation tax purposes for accounting periods ending on or after 1 April 2010, for income and capital gains tax purposes for the tax year 2010–11 and subsequent tax years, and for petroleum revenue tax purposes for chargeable periods beginning on or after 1 July 2010.

[2]   Heading substituted for previous heading "Industrial and provident society payments", in sub-ss (1)(*a*), (2) words substituted for words "registered industrial and provident society", and sub-s (5) substituted, by the Co-operative and Community Benefit Societies Act 2014 s 151, Sch 4 paras 104, 110 (as amended by FA 2014 Sch 39) with effect from 1 August 2014 and subject to transitional provisions and provisions preserving the continuity of the law in Sch 5 of that Act.

888 Statutory interest

The duty to deduct a sum representing income tax under section 874 does not apply to a payment of interest made by virtue of the contractual term implied by section 1(1) of the Late Payment of Commercial Debts (Interest) Act 1998 (c 20) (statutory interest).

Commentary—*Simon's Taxes* **A4.421, A4.425**.

Changes in the law—See ITA 2007 EN Annex 1 Change 136. This change makes specific provision that payments of "statutory interest" are not subject to deduction of tax under s 874.

HMRC Manuals—Savings and Investment Manual SAIM9070 (statutory interest).

[888A Qualifying private placements

(1) The duty to deduct a sum representing income tax under section 874 does not apply to a payment of interest on a qualifying private placement.

(2) "Qualifying private placement" means a security—

   (*a*) which represents a loan relationship to which a company is a party as debtor,

   (*b*) which is not listed on a recognised stock exchange, and

   (*c*) in relation to which such other conditions as the Treasury may specify by regulations are met.

(3) The conditions which may be specified under subsection (2)(*c*) include conditions relating to—

   (*a*) the security itself,

   (*b*) the loan relationship represented by the security,

   (*c*) the terms on which, or circumstances under which, the security or loan relationship is entered into,

   (*d*) the company which is party to the loan relationship as debtor,

   (*e*) any person by or through whom a payment of interest on the security is made, or

   (*f*) the holder of the security.

(4) Regulations under this section may make provision about the consequences of failing to make a deduction under section 874, in respect of a payment of interest on a security, in cases where the person required to make the deduction had a reasonable, but mistaken, belief that the security was a qualifying private placement.

(5) Regulations under this section may—

   (*a*) make different provision for different cases;

   (*b*) contain incidental, supplemental, consequential and transitional provision and savings.

(6) In this section "loan relationship" has the same meaning as in Part 5 of CTA 2009.][1]

Commentary—*Simon's Taxes* **A4.425**.

Regulations—Qualifying Private Placement Regulations, SI 2015/2002.

Amendments—[1]   Section 888A inserted by FA 2015 s 23 with effect from 1 January 2016 (by virtue of SI 2015/2035). Note that any power conferred on the Treasury under this section to make regulations came into force on 26 March 2015.

[888B Designated dividends of investment trusts

The duty to deduct a sum representing income tax under section 874 does not apply to a dividend so far as it is treated as a payment of yearly interest by regulations under section 45 of FA 2009 (dividends designated by investment trust or prospective investment trust).][1]

Commentary—*Simon's Taxes* **A4.425, D7.339**.

Amendments—[1]   Sections 888B–888D inserted by FA 2017 s 11, Sch 5 para 1 with effect in relation to amounts treated as payments of yearly interest made on or after 6 April 2017.

[888C Interest distributions of certain open-ended investment companies

The duty to deduct a sum representing income tax under section 874 does not apply to a payment of yearly interest under section 373 of ITTOIA 2005 (in the case of certain open-ended investment companies, payments of yearly interest treated as made where distributable amount shown in accounts as yearly interest).][1]

Commentary—*Simon's Taxes* **A4.425, D7.339, D8.131, D8.141**.

Amendments—[1]   Sections 888B–888D inserted by FA 2017 s 11, Sch 5 para 1 with effect in relation to amounts treated as payments of yearly interest made on or after 6 April 2017.

[888D Interest distribution of certain authorised unit trusts

The duty to deduct a sum representing income tax under section 874 does not apply to a payment of yearly interest under section 376 of ITTOIA 2005 (in the case of certain authorised unit trusts, payments of yearly interest treated as made where distributable amount shown in accounts as yearly interest).][1]

Commentary—*Simon's Taxes* **A4.425, D7.339, D8.131, D8.141**.

Amendments—[1]   Sections 888B–888D inserted by FA 2017 s 11, Sch 5 para 1 with effect in relation to amounts treated as payments of yearly interest made on or after 6 April 2017.

[888E Interest on certain peer-to-peer lending

(1) The duty to deduct a sum representing income tax under section 874 does not apply to a payment of interest on an amount of peer-to-peer lending.

(2) In subsection (1) "peer-to-peer lending" means credit in relation to which the condition in subsection (4) is met.

(3) In this section—

"original borrower", in relation to any credit, means the person to whom the credit is originally provided,

"credit" includes a cash loan and any other form of financial accommodation, and

"original lender", in relation to any credit, means the person who originally provides the credit.

(4) The condition is that—

(a) the original borrower and the original lender enter the agreement under which the credit is provided at the invitation of a person ("the operator"),

(b) the operator makes the invitation in the course of, or in connection with, operating an electronic system,

(c) the operator's operation of the electronic system is an activity specified in article 36H(1) or (2D) of the Order (operating an electronic system in relation to lending), and

(d) the operator has permission under Part 4A of FISMA 2000 to carry on that activity.

(5) For the purposes of subsection (4), it does not matter if the agreement mentioned in subsection (4)(a) is not an article 36H agreement (as defined in article 36H of the Order).

(6) The Commissioners for Her Majesty's Revenue and Customs may by regulations make such amendments of the preceding provisions of this section as they consider appropriate in consequence of—

(a) the Order, or any part of it, being replaced (or further replaced) by provision in another instrument, or

(b) any amendment of the Order or any such other instrument.

(7) In this section "the Order" means the Financial Services and Markets Act 2000 (Regulated Activities) Order 2001 (S.I. 2001/544).][1]

Commentary—*Simon's Taxes* **A4.425, E1.407A**.

Amendments—[1]   Section 888E inserted by FA 2017 s 11, Sch 5 para 3 with effect in relation to payments of interest made on or after 6 April 2017..

CHAPTER 4

DEDUCTION FROM PAYMENTS IN RESPECT OF BUILDING SOCIETY SECURITIES

889 Payments in respect of building society securities

(1) This section applies to any payment made in a tax year if—

(a) it is a payment of a dividend or interest in respect of a security issued by a building society, and

(b) conditions A and B are met in relation to the security.

(2) Condition A is that the security was listed or capable of being listed on a recognised stock exchange at the time the dividend or interest became payable.

(3) Condition B is that the security is not—
- (a) a qualifying certificate of deposit (see section 985),
- (b) a qualifying uncertificated eligible debt security unit (see section 986), or
- (c) a quoted Eurobond (see section 987).

(4) The person by or through whom the payment is made must, on making it, deduct from it a sum representing income tax on it at the [basic rate][1] in force for the tax year.

(5) For provision about the collection of income tax in respect of a payment from which a sum must be deducted under this section—
- (a) see Chapter 15 if the person making the payment is a UK resident company, and
- (b) otherwise see Chapter 16.

(6) See also Chapter 11 (payments between companies) for an exception from the duty to deduct sums representing income tax under this section.

(7) In this section—
> "dividend" includes any distribution (whether or not described as a dividend), and
> "security" includes a share (and, in particular, a permanent interest bearing share as defined in section 117 of TCGA 1992).

Commentary—*Simon's Taxes* **A4.429, A4.141, D7.803**.
HMRC Manuals—Company Taxation Manual CTM49370 (deduction of income tax from interest on marketable securities). Savings and Investment Manual SAIM9140 (building societies securities).
International Manual INTM342140 (permanent interest bearing shares).
Amendments—[1]   Words in sub-s (4) substituted by FA 2008 s 5, Sch 1 paras 1, 27 with effect for the tax year 2008–09 and subsequent tax years.

CHAPTER 5

DEDUCTION FROM PAYMENTS OF UK PUBLIC REVENUE DIVIDENDS

Introduction

890 Overview of Chapter

(1) This Chapter contains provision about the deduction of sums representing income tax from payments of UK public revenue dividends.

(2) Section 891 defines "UK public revenue dividend".

(3) Section 892 contains a duty to deduct sums representing income tax from payments of UK public revenue dividends unless they are payable gross.

(4) Sections 893 and 894 explain when such payments are payable gross.

(5) Sections 895 and 896 make provision for the making, and withdrawal, of applications for payments to be subject to the duty to deduct under this Chapter.

(6) Section 897 contains a regulation-making power in connection with payments from which sums must be deducted under this Chapter.

891 Meaning of "UK public revenue dividend"

In this Chapter "UK public revenue dividend" means any income from securities which—
- (a) is paid out of the public revenue of the United Kingdom or Northern Ireland, but
- (b) is not interest on local authority stock.

Commentary—*Simon's Taxes* **A4.425**.
Derivation—TA 1988 s 349(4).
HMRC Manuals—Savings and Investment Manual SAIM9140 (UK public revenue dividends).

Duty to deduct sums representing income tax

892 Duty to deduct from certain UK public revenue dividends

(1) This section has effect if—
- (a) a payment of a UK public revenue dividend is made, and
- (b) it is not payable gross under section 893.

(2) The person by or through whom the payment is made must, on making the payment, deduct from it a sum representing income tax on it at the [basic rate][1] in force for the tax year in which it is made.

(3) For provision about the collection of income tax in respect of a payment from which a sum must be deducted under this section—
- (a) see Chapter 15 if the person making the payment is a UK resident company, and
- (b) otherwise see Chapter 16.

Commentary—*Simon's Taxes* **A4.141**.
Amendments—[1]   Words in sub-s (2) substituted by FA 2008 s 5, Sch 1 paras 1, 28 with effect for the tax year 2008–09 and subsequent tax years.

Payments which are payable gross

893 Payments of UK public revenue dividends which are payable gross

(1) A payment of a UK public revenue dividend is payable gross if—
- (a) it is a payment of interest on gross-paying government securities, and

(b) no deduction at source application has effect in respect of the securities at the time the payment is made (see section 895).

(2) In this Chapter "gross-paying government securities" means—

(a) gilt-edged securities (see section 1024),

[(aa) securities, so far as they are not gilt-edged securities, issued or treated as issued under—

    (i) the National Loans Act 1939, or

    (ii) the National Loans Act 1968,][1] or

(b) securities which are the subject of a Treasury direction under section [894(3)][1].

Commentary—*Simon's Taxes* **A4.425, A4.425**.

HMRC Manuals—Savings and Investment Manual SAIM9140 (UK public revenue dividends).

Amendments—[1]   In sub-s (2), para (aa) inserted, and words in para (b) substituted, by FA 2016 s 39, Sch 6 para 27(1), (2) with effect in relation to interest paid on or after 6 April 2016.

894 Treasury directions

(1), (2)   . . . [1]

(3) The Treasury may, at the request of the Department of Finance and Personnel for Northern Ireland, direct that any securities issued under section 11(1)(c) of the Exchequer and Financial Provisions Act (Northern Ireland) 1950 (c 3 (NI)) are gross-paying government securities.

(4) In relation to any securities which are gross-paying government securities by virtue of a direction under subsection (3)—

(a) references in sections 895 and 896 to "the Registrar" are to be read as references to the bank in the books of which the securities are registered or inscribed, and

(b) references in those sections to the Treasury are to be read as references to the Department of Finance and Personnel for Northern Ireland.

(5) A direction under subsection . . . [1] (3) in respect of any securities may provide that the direction is to have effect in relation only to payments of interest on the securities made on or after a date specified in the direction.

Commentary—*Simon's Taxes* **A4.425**.

Amendments—[1]   Sub-ss (1), (2) repealed, and in sub-s (5) words repealed, by FA 2016 s 39, Sch 6 para 27(1), (3) with effect in relation to interest paid on or after 6 April 2016.

Deduction at source applications

895 Deduction at source application

(1) The holder of registered gross-paying government securities may make a deduction at source application in respect of the securities.

(2) A deduction at source application in respect of any securities is an application—

(a) for payments of interest on those securities to be subject to the duty to deduct sums representing income tax under section 892,

(b) made to the Registrar, and

(c) made in such form as the Registrar may, with the approval of the Treasury, prescribe.

(3) A deduction at source application in respect of any securities has effect from the date which is one month after the date on which it is made until—

(a) the securities cease to be registered in the name of the person who made the application, or

(b) the application ceases to have effect under section 896 following its withdrawal in accordance with that section.

(4) If any registered gross-paying government securities are held on trust, the holders of the securities may make a deduction at source application in respect of them without the consent of any other person.

(5) Subsection (4) applies despite anything in the instrument creating the trust.

(6) In this Chapter—

"registered" means—

(a) entered in the register of the Registrar, or

(b) entered in a register maintained in accordance with regulations under [section 785 of the Companies Act 2006 (provision enabling procedures for evidencing and transferring title),][1] and

"the Registrar" means the person or persons appointed in accordance with regulations under section 47(1)(b) of FA 1942 (see regulation 3 of the Government Stock Regulations 2004 (SI 2004/1611)).

Commentary—*Simon's Taxes* **A4.425, A4.425**.

Modifications—ITA 2007 Sch 2 para 165 (if any person holds any gilt-edged securities in relation to which a direction was given under TA 1988 s 50(1) at any time before 6 April 1998, and that person at any time before that date made an application under TA 1988 s 50(2) with respect to those securities, the person is treated as having made a deduction at source application under this section in respect of the securities which (unless withdrawn) is treated as having effect from that date).

Amendments—[1]   In sub-s (6), in definition of "registered", para (b), words substituted by the Companies Act 2006 (Consequential Amendments) (Taxes and National Insurance) Order, SI 2008/954 arts 38, 40 with effect from 6 April 2008.

896 Withdrawal of application

(1) A deduction at source application may be withdrawn by notice given to the Registrar by the holder of the securities.

(2) The notice must be given in such form as the Registrar may, with the approval of the Treasury, prescribe.

(3) If withdrawn, a deduction at source application ceases to have effect on the date which is one month after the date on which the notice of withdrawal is received by the Registrar.

Commentary—*Simon's Taxes* A4.425.
Derivation—TA 1988 s 50(5).

Regulations

897 Power to make regulations

(1) The Commissioners for Her Majesty's Revenue and Customs may by regulations—

    (*a*) make provision as to the time and manner in which persons are to account for and pay income tax in respect of payments from which they are required to deduct sums representing income tax under section 892, and

    (*b*) otherwise modify the provisions of section 892 and Chapters 15 and 16 in their application to such payments.

(2) Regulations under this section may—

    (*a*) make different provision for different descriptions of UK public revenue dividend and for different circumstances, and

    (*b*) contain incidental, supplemental, consequential and transitional provision and savings.

(3) The Commissioners for Her Majesty's Revenue and Customs must not make any regulations under this section unless a draft of them has been laid before and approved by a resolution of the House of Commons.

Commentary—*Simon's Taxes* A4.425.
Derivation—TA 1988 s 350A.

CHAPTER 6

DEDUCTION FROM ANNUAL PAYMENTS AND PATENT ROYALTIES

Introduction

898 Overview of Chapter

(1) This Chapter deals with the deduction of sums representing income tax from—

    (*a*) qualifying annual payments, and

    (*b*) royalties or other sums paid in respect of the use of patents.

(2) See also—

    (*a*) Chapter 11 (payments between companies etc) for an exception from the duties to deduct sums representing income tax under this Chapter,

    (*b*) Chapter 4 of Part 8, which gives relief for certain payments from which sums representing income tax must be deducted under this Chapter, and

    (*c*) section 615(3) of ICTA (exemption from tax in respect of certain pensions) which contains a further exception from the duties to deduct sums representing income tax under this Chapter.

(3) If a payment to which a provision of this Chapter applies is also one to which section 906 applies, it is treated as not being a payment to which a provision of this Chapter applies.

Commentary—*Simon's Taxes* A4.432, E1.801.

899 Meaning of "qualifying annual payment"

(1) In this Chapter "qualifying annual payment" means an annual payment that meets the conditions in subsections (2) to (5).

(2) The payment must arise in the United Kingdom.

(3) If the recipient is a person other than a company, the payment must be—

    (*a*) a payment charged to income tax under—

      (i) Chapter 7 of Part 4 of ITTOIA 2005 (purchased life annuity payments),

      (ii) section 579 of that Act (royalties etc from intellectual property),

      (iii) Chapter 4 of Part 5 of that Act (certain telecommunication rights: non-trading income), or

      (iv) Chapter 7 of Part 5 of that Act (annual payments not otherwise charged), or

    (*b*) a payment charged to income tax under Part 9 of ITEPA 2003 because section 609 or 611 of that Act applies to it (certain employment-related annuities).

(4) If the recipient is a company, the payment must be—

    (*a*) a payment charged to income tax as mentioned in subsection (3)(*a*), or

    (*b*) a payment [which is—

      (i) required to be brought into account under Part 5 of CTA 2009 (loan relationships) as a non-trading credit, or

(ii) from a source in the United Kingdom and chargeable to corporation tax under [Chapter 7 of Part 10 of that Act (annual payments not otherwise charged) or regulation 15 of the Unauthorised Unit Trusts (Tax) Regulations 2013]³.]¹

(5) The payment must not be—

(a) interest,

[(b) a payment which is a qualifying payment for the purposes of Chapter 2 of Part 6 of CTA 2010 (certain payments to charity),]²

(c) a payment which is a qualifying donation for the purposes of Chapter 2 of Part 8 (gift aid),

(d) a payment in relation to which income tax is treated as having been paid under section 494(3) (income tax treated as paid by beneficiary or settlor in relation to discretionary trust),

(e) a payment which would fall within paragraph (d) but for the fact that the trustees making the payment are non-UK resident, or

(f) an annual payment to which section 904 applies (annual payments for dividends or non-taxable consideration).

Commentary—*Simon's Taxes* A4.432, A4.608, B5.332, C5.1277AA, E1.801, E1.802.
HMRC Manuals—Savings and Investment Manual SAIM9120 (meaning of annual payment).
Amendments—¹ In sub-s (4)(b) words substituted by CTA 2009 s 1322, Sch 1 paras 699, 707. CTA 2009 applies for accounting periods ending on or after 1 April 2009 (for corporation tax purposes) and for tax years 2009–10 onwards (for income and capital gains tax purposes).
² Sub-s (5)(b) substituted by CTA 2010 s 1177, Sch 1 para 554. CTA 2010 has effect for corporation tax purposes for accounting periods ending on or after 1 April 2010, and for income and capital gains tax purposes for the tax year 2010–11 and subsequent tax years.
³ In sub-s (4)(b)(ii), words substituted by the Unauthorised Unit Trusts (Tax) Regulations, SI 2013/2819 reg 37(1), (13) with effect from 6 April 2014. Note that an unauthorised unit trust is not a non-exempt unauthorised unit trust, and this amendment does not apply in relation to the trust, if at all times in the period beginning with 24 May 2012 and ending with 5 April 2014 it had at least one unit holder which was, and at least one unit holder which was not, an eligible investor (ie a mixed unauthorised unit trust); this ceases to apply in relation to the trust if subsequently it no longer has any unit holders which are eligible investors (SI 2013/2819 reg 32).

Duty to deduct from annual payments

900 Deduction from commercial payments made by individuals

(1) This section applies to any payment made in a tax year if—

(a) it is a qualifying annual payment,

(b) the person who makes it is an individual, and

(c) it is made for genuine commercial reasons in connection with the individual's trade, profession or vocation.

(2) The individual must, on making the payment, deduct from it a sum representing income tax on it at the basic rate in force for the tax year.

(3) Income tax equal to the sum required to be deducted is to be collected through the individual's self-assessment return (see Chapter 17).

Commentary—*Simon's Taxes* A4.433, E1.103, B5.332, E1.805, E1.802, E1.801.
HMRC Manuals—Savings and Investment Manual SAIM9120 (deduction of tax).
SAIM9060 (annual payments).

901 Deduction from annual payments made by other persons

(1) This section applies to any payment made in a tax year if—

(a) it is a qualifying annual payment, and

(b) the person who makes it is not an individual.

(2) But this section does not apply if—

(a) an individual's personal representatives make the payment,

(b) the individual would have been liable to make it if the individual had not died, and

(c) the payment would not have been made for genuine commercial reasons in connection with the individual's trade, profession or vocation, had it been made by the individual.

(3) If the person who makes the payment has some modified net income for the tax year (see section 1025)—

(a) the person must, on making it, deduct from it a sum representing income tax on it at the basic rate in force for the tax year, and

(b) income tax equal to the sum required to be deducted is to be collected through the person's self-assessment return (see Chapter 17).

(4) If the person who makes the payment has no modified net income for the tax year the person by or through whom the payment is made must, on making it, deduct from it a sum representing income tax on it at [the basic rate in force for the tax year in which the payment is made]¹.

(5) For provision about the collection of income tax in respect of a payment from which a sum must be deducted under subsection (4)—

(a) see Chapter 15 if the person making the payment is a UK resident company, and

(b) otherwise see Chapter 16.

Commentary—*Simon's Taxes* A4.434, A4.141, C4.125, B5.332, C4.207, E1.801, E1.429.
HMRC Manuals—Savings and Investment Manual SAIM9120 (deduction of tax).

Company Taxation Manual CTM49390 (return periods for building societies where the interest is on annuities or other annual payments).

Amendments—[1]   Words in sub-s (4) substituted by FA 2008 s 5, Sch 1 paras 1, 29 with effect for the tax year 2008–09 and subsequent tax years.

Duty to deduct from patent royalties

903 Deduction from patent royalties

(1) This section applies to any payment made in a tax year if—

    (*a*) it is a payment of a royalty or other sum in respect of the use of a patent, and

    (*b*) it meets the conditions in subsections (2) to (4).

(2) The payment must not be—

    (*a*) a qualifying annual payment, or

    (*b*) an annual payment to which section 904 applies (annual payments for dividends or non-taxable consideration).

(3) The payment must arise in the United Kingdom.

(4) The payment must be one that is charged to income tax or corporation tax.

(5) If the person who makes the payment is an individual—

    (*a*) the person must, on making the payment, deduct from it a sum representing income tax on it at the basic rate in force for the tax year, and

    (*b*) income tax equal to the sum required to be deducted is to be collected through the person's self-assessment return (see Chapter 17).

(6) If the person who makes the payment is not an individual, and has some modified net income for the tax year (see section 1025)—

    (*a*) the person must, on making the payment, deduct from it a sum representing income tax on it at the basic rate in force for the tax year, and

    (*b*) income tax equal to the sum required to be deducted is to be collected through the person's self-assessment return (see Chapter 17).

(7) If the person who makes the payment—

    (*a*) is not an individual, and

    (*b*) has no modified net income for the tax year,

the person by or through whom the payment is made must, on making it, deduct from it a sum representing income tax on it at the basic rate in force for the tax year.

(8) See Chapter 8 which makes special provision in relation to royalties (double taxation arrangements: deduction at treaty rate and EU companies: discretion to pay gross).

(9) For provision about the collection of income tax in respect of a payment from which a sum must be deducted under subsection (7)—

    (*a*) see Chapter 15 if the person making the payment is a UK resident company, and

    (*b*) otherwise see Chapter 16.

Commentary—Simon's Taxes **A4.436, B5.316, B5.332, A4.141, B5.341, A4.435.**

HMRC Manuals—Savings and Investment Manual SAIM9130 (deduction of tax from patent royalties).

International Manual INTM441140 (taxation at source for payment of royalties by UK company).

Supplementary

904 Annual payments for dividends or non-taxable consideration

(1) For the purposes of section 899(5)(*f*) and 903(2)(*b*) this section applies to an annual payment which meets the conditions in subsections (2) to (7).

[(2) The payment must be—

    (*a*) a payment charged to income tax under Part 5 of ITTOIA 2005 (miscellaneous income), or

    (*b*) a payment which is—

        (i) required to be brought into account under Part 5 of CTA 2009 (loan relationships) as a non-trading credit, or

        (ii) from a source in the United Kingdom and chargeable to corporation tax under [Chapter 7 of Part 10 of that Act (annual payments not otherwise charged) or regulation 15 of the Unauthorised Unit Trusts (Tax) Regulations 2013][2].][1]

(3) The payment must be made under a liability incurred for consideration in money or money's worth all or any of which—

    (*a*) consists of a dividend or the right to receive a dividend, or

    (*b*) is not required to be brought into account in calculating for the purposes of income tax or corporation tax the income of the person making the payment.

(4) The payment must not be a payment of income—

    (*a*) which arises under a settlement made by one party to a marriage or civil partnership by way of provision for the other—

        (i) after the dissolution or annulment of the marriage or civil partnership, or

        (ii) while they are separated under an order of a court, or under a separation agreement, or if the separation is likely to be permanent, and

    (*b*) which is payable to, or applicable for the benefit of, the other party.

(5) The payment must not be made by an individual for genuine commercial reasons in connection with the individual's trade, profession or vocation.

(6) The payment must not be made to an individual under a liability incurred at any time in consideration of the individual surrendering, assigning or releasing an interest in settled property to or in favour of a person with a subsequent interest.

(7) The payment must not be a payment of an annuity granted in the ordinary course of a business of granting annuities.

(8) In the application of this section to Scotland the reference in subsection (6) to settled property is to be read as a reference to property held in trust.

Commentary—*Simon's Taxes* A4.439, E1.801, E1.802.
Derivation—TA 1988 s 125.
HMRC Manuals—Savings and Investment Manual SAIM8080 (annual payments made for dividends on non-taxable consideration).
Amendments—[1] Sub-s (2) substituted by CTA 2009 s 1322, Sch 1 paras 699, 708. CTA 2009 applies for accounting periods ending on or after 1 April 2009 (for corporation tax purposes) and for tax years 2009–10 onwards (for income and capital gains tax purposes).
[2] In sub-s (2)(b)(ii), words substituted by the Unauthorised Unit Trusts (Tax) Regulations, SI 2013/2819 reg 37(1), (14) with effect from 6 April 2014. Note that an unauthorised unit trust is not a non-exempt unauthorised unit trust, and these amendments do not apply in relation to the trust, if at all times in the period beginning with 24 May 2012 and ending with 5 April 2014 it had at least one unit holder which was, and at least one unit holder which was not, an eligible investor (ie a mixed unauthorised unit trust); this ceases to apply in relation to the trust if subsequently it no longer has any unit holders which are eligible investors (SI 2013/2819 reg 32).

905 Interpretation of Chapter

In this Chapter "individual" includes a Scottish partnership if at least one partner is an individual.

Commentary—*Simon's Taxes* A4.434, 435, A4.433, A4.439.
Derivation—TA 1988 s 347A(6).

CHAPTER 7

DEDUCTION FROM OTHER PAYMENTS CONNECTED WITH INTELLECTUAL PROPERTY

Certain royalties etc where usual place of abode of owner is abroad

906 Certain royalties etc where usual place of abode of owner is abroad

[(1) This section applies to any payment made in a tax year where condition A or condition B is met.
(2) Condition A is that—
  (a) the payment is a royalty, or a payment of any other kind, for the use of, or the right to use, intellectual property (see section 907),
  (b) the usual place of abode of the owner of the intellectual property is outside the United Kingdom, and
  (c) the payment is charged to income tax or corporation tax.
(3) Condition B is that—
  (a) the payment is a payment of sums payable periodically in respect of intellectual property,
  (b) the person entitled to those sums ("the assignor") assigned the intellectual property to another person,
  (c) the usual place of abode of the assignor is outside the United Kingdom, and
  (d) the payment is charged to income tax or corporation tax.][1]
(4) But this section does not apply if the payment is made in respect of copies of works, or articles, which have been exported from the United Kingdom for distribution outside the United Kingdom.
(5) The person by or through whom the payment is made must, on making it, deduct from it a sum representing income tax on it at the basic rate in force for the tax year.
(6) See—
  (a) Chapter 8 which makes special provision in relation to royalties (double taxation arrangements: deduction at treaty rate and EU companies: discretion to pay gross), and
  (b) Chapter 11 (payments between companies etc) for an exception from the duty to deduct sums representing income tax under this section.
(7) For provision about the collection of income tax in respect of a payment from which a sum must be deducted under this section—
  (a) see Chapter 15 if the person making the payment is a UK resident company, and
  (b) otherwise see Chapter 16.
(8) If a payment to which this section applies is also one to which a provision of Chapter 6 applies, it is treated as not being a payment to which a provision of Chapter 6 applies.

Commentary—*Simon's Taxes* A4.441, B5.317–B5.325, A1.109, A4.141, B3.103.
Amendments—[1] Sub-ss (1)–(3) substituted by FA 2016 s 40(1), (2) with effect for payments made on or after 28 June 2016. In determining whether s 906 applies to a payment, no regard is to be had to any arrangements the main purpose of which, or one of the main purposes of which, is to avoid the effect of these amendments (FA 2016 s 40(5)). Transitional provisions also apply in relation to arrangements which are so disregarded (FA 2016 s 40(6)–(8)).

[907 Meaning of "intellectual property"

(1) In section 906 "intellectual property" means—

   (a) copyright of literary, artistic or scientific work,

   (b) any patent, trade mark, design, model, plan, or secret formula or process,

   (c) any information concerning industrial, commercial or scientific experience, or

   (d) public lending right in respect of a book.

(2) In this section "copyright of literary, artistic or scientific work" does not include copyright in—

   (a) a cinematographic film or video recording, or

   (b) the sound-track of a cinematographic film or video recording, except so far as it is separately exploited.][1]

Amendments—[1]   Section 907 substituted by FA 2016 s 40(1), (3) with effect for payments made on or after 28 June 2016.
Commentary—*Simon's Taxes* **B5.317, A4.441.**

908 Royalty payments etc made through UK resident agents

(1) If—

   (a) a payment to which section 906 applies is made through an agent who is UK resident, and

   (b) the agent is entitled as against the owner of the right to deduct a sum as commission for services provided,

section 906(5) and Chapters 8 (deduction at special rates), 15 and 16 (collection) apply as if the amount of the payment were the amount net of the sum deductible as commission.

(2) But if the person by or through whom the payment is made does not know the commission is payable, or does not know its amount—

   (a) the sum representing income tax required to be deducted under section 906 must be calculated in the first instance on the total amount of the payment, and

   (b) the return to be made under Chapter 15 or the account of the payment under Chapter 16, must be based on that total amount.

Commentary—*Simon's Taxes* **A4.441, B5.317.**
Derivation—TA 1988 ss 536(3), (4), 537B(3), (4).

909 Royalty payments: further provision

(1) A payment to which section 906 applies is treated for all income and corporation tax purposes as made when it is made by the first person who makes it, not when it is made by or through any other person.

(2) If, under section 906, a sum representing income tax must be deducted from a payment, any agreement to make the payment without deduction of that sum is void.

(3) Section 906—

   (a) applies to payments on account of royalties as it applies to payments of royalties, and

   (b) applies to payments on account of sums payable periodically as it applies to payments of sums payable periodically.

Commentary—*Simon's Taxes* **A4.441, B5.317.**
Derivation—TA 1988 ss 536(1), (5), (6), 537B(1), (5), (6).

Proceeds of a sale of patent rights

910 Proceeds of a sale of patent rights: payments to non-UK residents

(1) This section applies if a non-UK resident sells the whole or part of any patent rights and is chargeable in respect of the sale—

   (a) to income tax under section 587 of ITTOIA 2005, or

   (b) to corporation tax under [section 912 of CTA 2009][1].

(2) The person by or through whom the proceeds of the sale are paid must, on making any payment of—

   (a) the proceeds, or

   (b) an instalment of the proceeds,

deduct from it a sum representing income tax on the chargeable amount at the basic rate in force for the tax year in which the payment is made.

(3) In subsection (2) "the chargeable amount" means—

   (a) so much of the proceeds or instalment as consists of a capital sum, less

   (b) any incidental expenses of the sale which are deducted before payment.

(4) Sections 597 to 599 of ITTOIA 2005 (licences connected with patents etc) apply for the purposes of this section as they apply for the purposes of sections 587 to 596 of that Act.

(5) Section 4 of CAA 2001 (meaning of "capital sums" etc) applies in relation to this section as it applies in relation to that Act.

(6) For further provision about the sum required to be deducted, see—

   (a) section 595 of ITTOIA 2005 (certain rules affecting the seller's income tax position do not affect the amount to be deducted), and

   (b) [section 919 of CTA 2009][1] (certain rules affecting the seller's corporation tax position do not affect the amount to be deducted).

(7) See Chapter 11 (payments between companies etc) for an exception from the duty to deduct sums representing income tax under this section.

(8) For provision about the collection of income tax in respect of a payment from which a sum must be deducted under this section—

> (*a*) see Chapter 15 if the person making the payment is a UK resident company, and
>
> (*b*) otherwise see Chapter 16.

Commentary—*Simon's Taxes* **A4.141, A4.437, A4.442, B3.602, B5.334–B5.336.**
Amendments—[1]   In sub-ss (1)(*b*), (6)(*b*), words substituted by CTA 2009 s 1322, Sch 1 paras 699, 709. CTA 2009 applies for accounting periods ending on or after 1 April 2009 (for corporation tax purposes) and for tax years 2009–10 onwards (for income and capital gains tax purposes).

CHAPTER 8

CHAPTERS 6 AND 7: SPECIAL PROVISION IN RELATION TO ROYALTIES
Deduction at special rates

911 Double taxation arrangements: deduction at treaty rate

(1) This section applies if—

> (*a*) a company pays a royalty from which it is required to deduct a sum representing income tax under Chapter 6 or 7,
>
> (*b*) the income tax in respect of the payment is collectible under Chapter 15 or 16, and
>
> (*c*) the company reasonably believes that, at the time the payment is made, the payee is entitled to relief in respect of the payment under double taxation arrangements.

(2) The company may calculate the sum to be deducted from the payment under Chapter 6 or 7 by reference to the treaty rate.

(3) But, if the payee is not at the time entitled to such relief, this Part has effect as if subsection (2) had never applied in relation to the payment.

(4) In this section "the treaty rate" means the rate of income tax appropriate to the payee under the arrangements.

Commentary—*Simon's Taxes* **A4.445, B5.318, D4.804A.**
Derivation—TA 1988 s 349E(1), (2), (5).
HMRC Manuals—Company Taxation Manual CTM35270 (royalties paid by companies under double taxation agreements). International Manual INTM400010 (details regarding the EU interest and royalties directive).

912 Power to make directions disapplying section 911

(1) This section applies if an officer of Revenue and Customs is not satisfied that the payee will be entitled to relief under double taxation arrangements in respect of one or more payments of royalties that a company is to make.

(2) The officer may direct the company that section 911 is not to apply to the payment or payments.

(3) A direction under subsection (2) may be varied or revoked by a later direction.

Commentary—*Simon's Taxes* **A4.445, B5.318.**

913 Interpretation of sections 911 and 912

(1) In sections 911 and 912 "royalty" includes—

> (*a*) a payment received as consideration for the use of, or the right to use, a copyright, patent, trade mark, design, process or information, and
>
> (*b*) the proceeds of the sale of the whole or part of any patent rights.

(2) In sections 911 and 912 "payee" means the person beneficially entitled to the income in respect of which the payment is made.

Commentary—*Simon's Taxes* **A4.445, B5.318.**
Derivation—TA 1988 349E(1), (5).
HMRC Manuals—Company Taxation Manual CTM35270 (definition of royalty payment).

Discretion to make payments gross

914 EU companies: discretion to make payment gross

(1) This section applies if—

> (*a*) a company makes a royalty payment and, at the time the payment is made, the company reasonably believes that the payment is exempt from income tax as a result of section 758 of ITTOIA 2005 (exemption for certain interest and royalty payments), but
>
> (*b*) there is a duty to deduct a sum representing income tax from the payment under section 903(7) or 906 if the payment is not in fact exempt.

(2) The company may make the payment without deducting a sum representing income tax under section 903(7) or 906 (as the case may be).

(3) But if the payment is not in fact exempt from income tax as a result of section 758 of ITTOIA 2005, this Part has effect as if subsection (2) had never applied in relation to the payment.

Commentary—*Simon's Taxes* **A4.454, B5.319.**
Derivation—FA 2004 s 101(1), (2).
HMRC Manuals—International Manual INTM400010 (details regarding the EU interest and royalties directive). INTM400090 (treatment of royalties under the directive).

915 Power to make directions disapplying section 914

(1) This section applies if an officer of Revenue and Customs is not satisfied that one or more payments to be made by a company will be exempt from income tax as a result of section 758 of ITTOIA 2005 (exemption for certain interest and royalty payments).

(2) The officer may direct the company that section 914 is not to apply to the payment or payments.

(3) A direction under subsection (2) may be varied or revoked by a later direction.

Commentary—*Simon's Taxes* **A4.454, B5.319**.

916 Duty of payee to notify if payment not exempt

(1) This section applies if before a payment of a royalty is made, the company beneficially entitled to the income in respect of which the payment is to be made—

(a) believed that the payment was exempt from income tax as a result of section 758 of ITTOIA 2005 (exemption for certain interest and royalty payments), but

(b) has subsequently become aware that any of conditions A to C in that section have ceased to be met.

(2) The company must without delay notify—

(a) an officer of Revenue and Customs, and

(b) the company which is to make the payment.

Commentary—*Simon's Taxes* **A4.454, B5.319**.

917 Supplementary

(1) If section 763 of ITTOIA 2005 (special relationships) applies, sections 914 to 916 have effect in relation to only so much of the payment as does not exceed the arm's length amount (within the meaning of that section).

(2) Expressions used in sections 914 to 916 and in sections 757 to 767 of ITTOIA 2005 have the same meaning in sections 914 to 916 as in those sections.

Commentary—*Simon's Taxes* **A4.454, B5.319**.

Derivation—FA 2004 s 101(8), (9).

[Tax avoidance

917A Tax avoidance arrangements

(1) This section applies if and to the extent that—

(a) a person ("the payer") makes an intellectual property royalty payment,

(b) the payment is received by a person ("the payee") who is connected with the payer, and

(c) the payment is made under DTA tax avoidance arrangements.

(2) Any duty under Chapter 6 or 7 to deduct a sum representing income tax at any rate applies without regard to any double taxation arrangements.

(3) Any income tax deducted by virtue of subsection (2) may not be set off under section 967 or 968 of CTA 2010.

(4) In this section—

"arrangements" (except in the phrase "double taxation arrangements") includes any agreement, understanding, scheme, transaction or series of transactions, whether or not legally enforceable; "DTA tax avoidance arrangements" means arrangements where, having regard to all the circumstances, it is reasonable to conclude that—

(a) the main purpose, or one of the main purposes, of the arrangements was to obtain a tax advantage by virtue of any provisions of a double taxation arrangement, and

(b) obtaining that tax advantage is contrary to the object and purpose of those provisions;

"intellectual property royalty payment" means a payment referred to in section 906(2)(a) or (3)(a);

"receive" means receive—

(a) directly or indirectly;

(b) by one payment or by a series of payments;

"tax advantage" is to be construed in accordance with section 208 of FA 2013.

(5) For the purposes of this section the payer is connected with the payee if the participation condition is met as between them.

(6) Section 148 of TIOPA 2010 (when the participation condition is met) applies for the purposes of subsection (5) as for the purposes of section 147(1)(b) of that Act, but as if references to the actual provision were to the provision made or imposed between the payer and the payee in respect of the arrangements under which the payment is made.][1]

Commentary—*Simon's Taxes* **A4.445, E1.503, D1.1429**.

Amendments—[1]   Section 917A inserted by FA 2016 s 41 with effect in respect of a payment made on or after 17 March 2016 under arrangements entered into at any time (including arrangements entered into before that date).

CHAPTER 9
MANUFACTURED PAYMENTS
Manufactured dividends

918 Manufactured dividends on UK shares: Real Estate Investment Trusts

(1) This section applies if—

[(a) a person pays a manufactured payment as mentioned in section 614ZC(1) and the amount payable is representative of a dividend (a "manufactured dividend"), and][3]

(b) the manufactured dividend is representative of a dividend which is—

[(i) paid by a company UK REIT in respect of profits or gains (or both) of the company's property rental business, or

(ii) paid by the principal company of a group UK REIT in respect of profits or gains (or both) of property rental business of members of the group.][1]

(2) This section applies only so far as the manufactured dividend is representative of such a dividend.

(3) If the payer—

(a) is UK resident, or

(b) pays the manufactured dividend in the course of a trade carried on through a branch or agency in the United Kingdom,

regulations under section 973 apply to the payer as they apply to a [company UK REIT][1], with any necessary modifications.

[(3A) But subsection (3) does not apply if—

(a) the manufactured dividend is paid by a UK resident company in the course of a trade carried on through a permanent establishment in a territory outside the United Kingdom, and

(b) section 18A of CTA 2009 has effect in relation to the company for the accounting period in which it is paid.][2]

(4) The Treasury may by regulations provide, in a case where the payer—

[(a) is non-UK resident and pays the manufactured dividend otherwise than in the course of a trade carried on through a branch or agency in the United Kingdom, or

(b) is a UK resident company and pays the manufactured dividend in the course of a trade carried on through a permanent establishment in a territory outside the United Kingdom and section 18A of CTA 2009 has effect in relation to the company for the accounting period in which it is paid,][2]

for a United Kingdom recipient of the manufactured dividend to be liable to account for and pay income tax in respect of it.

(5) A United Kingdom recipient is a recipient who—

(a) is UK resident, or

(b) is non-UK resident but receives the manufactured dividend for the purposes of a trade carried on by the recipient through a branch or agency in the United Kingdom.

[(5A) But a UK resident is not a United Kingdom recipient if—

(a) it is a UK resident company which receives the manufactured dividend for the purposes of a trade carried on by the recipient through a permanent establishment in a territory outside the United Kingdom, and

(b) section 18A of CTA 2009 has effect in relation to the company for the accounting period in which it is received.][2]

(6) The amount of income tax which the recipient may be liable to account for and pay under regulations under subsection (4) is equal to the amount of the sum representing income tax which the payer would have been required to deduct in accordance with regulations under section 973.

(7) For the purposes of—

(a) regulations under section 973 as applied by subsection (3), and

(b) regulations under subsection (4),

the "gross amount" of a manufactured dividend to which this section applies is equal to the gross amount of the dividend of which it is representative.

[(8) In subsection (1) "gains" includes chargeable gains.][1]

Commentary—*Simon's Taxes* **D9.703A, D9.705.**

Amendments—[1] Sub-s (1)(b)(i), (ii) substituted, in sub-s (3) words substituted, and sub-s (8) inserted by CTA 2010 s 1177, Sch 1 para 555. CTA 2010 has effect for corporation tax purposes for accounting periods ending on or after 1 April 2010, and for income and capital gains tax purposes for the tax year 2010–11 and subsequent tax years.

[2] Sub-ss (3A), (5A) inserted, and sub-s (4)(a), (b) substituted, by FA 2011 s 48, Sch 13 paras 18, 20 with effect from 19 July 2011, subject to transitional provisions in FA 2011 Sch 13 paras 32–37.

[3] Sub-s (1)(a) substituted by FA 2013 s 77, Sch 29 paras 16, 21 with effect from 1 January 2014.

Manufactured interest

919 Manufactured interest on UK securities: payments by UK residents etc

[(1) This section applies if—

(a) a person pays a manufactured payment as mentioned in section 614ZC(1),

(b) the amount payable is representative of interest on UK securities ("manufactured interest"), and
(c) the person—
    (i) is UK resident, or
    (ii) pays the manufactured interest in the course of a trade carried on in the United Kingdom through a branch or agency.][3]

[(1A) But this section does not apply if—
(a) the manufactured interest is paid by a UK resident company in the course of a trade carried on through a permanent establishment in a territory outside the United Kingdom, and
(b) section 18A of CTA 2009 has effect in relation to the company for the accounting period in which it is paid.][2]

(2) The payer of the manufactured interest must, on making the payment, deduct from the gross amount of the manufactured interest a sum representing income tax on it at the [basic rate][1] in force for the tax year in which the payment is made.

(3) The "gross amount" of manufactured interest is equal to the gross amount of the interest of which it is representative.

(4) This section is subject (in particular) to—
  . . .[3]

    section 921 (cases where interest on underlying securities paid gross), and
    Chapter 11 (payments between companies etc: exception from duties to deduct).

(5) For provision about the collection of income tax in respect of a payment from which a sum must be deducted under this section—
(a) see Chapter 15 if the payer of the manufactured interest is a company, and
(b) otherwise see Chapter 16.

[(6) In subsection (1) "UK securities" means securities of—
(a) the government of the United Kingdom,
(b) a local authority in the United Kingdom,
(c) another public authority in the United Kingdom, or
(d) a UK resident company or other UK resident body.

(7) But "UK securities" does not include shares in a UK resident company.

(8) In this section "securities" includes loan stock or any similar security.][3]

Commentary—*Simon's Taxes* **D9.711, 712, A4.144, A4.465, D9.703.**
Derivation—TA 1988 s 4(1A) and Sch 23A para 3.
HMRC Manuals—Corporate Finance Manual CFM74340 (manufactured payments made before 1 January 2014).
CFM74430 (manufactured payments made on or after 1 January 2014).
Amendments—[1]   Words in sub-s (2) substituted by FA 2008 s 5, Sch 1 paras 1, 31 with effect for the tax year 2008–09 and subsequent tax years.
[2]   Sub-s (1A) inserted by FA 2011 s 48, Sch 13 paras 18, 21 with effect from 19 July 2011, subject to transitional provisions in FA 2011 Sch 13 paras 32–37.
[3]   Sub-s (1) substituted, in sub-s (4) words repealed, and sub-ss (6)–(8) inserted, by FA 2013 s 77, Sch 29 paras 16, 22 with effect from 1 January 2014.

921 Cases where interest on underlying securities paid gross

(1) This section applies to manufactured interest which is representative of interest on—
(a) gilt-edged securities, or
(b) securities which are not gilt-edged securities but on which the interest is payable without deduction of income tax.

(2) Section 919(2) does not require any deduction of a sum representing income tax to be made on the payment of the manufactured interest.

(3) In this section ["manufactured interest" has the same meaning as in section 919.][1]

Commentary—*Simon's Taxes* **D9.711, 712, A4.425, D9.703.**
Amendments—[1]   In sub-s (3), words substituted by FA 2013 s 77, Sch 29 paras 16, 24 with effect from 1 January 2014.

Manufactured overseas dividends

[Repos

925A Creditor repos

(1) Subsection (2) applies if a company ("the lender") has a creditor repo for the purposes of Chapter 10 of Part 6 of CTA 2009 (see section 543 of that Act).

(2) Sections 918[, 919 and 921][2] have effect in relation to the lender while the arrangement is in force as if—
(a) the lender paid the borrower amounts which are representative of the income payable on the securities that are initially sold,
(b) the payments were made under requirements of the arrangement, and
(c) the payments were made on the dates on which the income is payable.

(3) For the purposes of subsection (2), an arrangement is in force from the time when the securities are initially sold until the earlier of—
(a) the time when the subsequent sale of the securities, or similar securities, takes place, and

(b) the time when it becomes apparent that that sale will not take place.][1]

Commentary—*Simon's Taxes* **D9.1001**.

Derivation—FA 2007 Sch 13 para 13.

HMRC Manuals—Corporate Finance Manual CFM46530 (repos: manufactured payments: requirement to deduct tax).

Modification—TIOPA 2010 Sch 9 para 45 (modification of this section in relation to an arrangement that comes into force before 1 October 2007).

Amendments—[1]   Sections 925A–925F and preceding cross-head inserted by TIOPA 2010 s 371, Sch 7 paras 111, 112. TIOPA 2010 has effect for corporation tax purposes for accounting periods ending on or after 1 April 2010, for income and capital gains tax purposes for the tax year 2010–11 and subsequent tax years, and for petroleum revenue tax purposes for chargeable periods beginning on or after 1 July 2010.

[2]   In sub-s (2) words substituted by FA 2013 s 77, Sch 29 paras 16, 26 with effect from 1 January 2014.

[925C Actual payments ignored if section 925A . . . applies

If section 925A(2) . . .[2] applies, any payment actually made under an arrangement which is representative of any income payable on any securities is to be treated for the purposes of sections 918[, 919 and 921][2] as if it had not been made.][1]

Commentary—*Simon's Taxes* **D9.1001**.

Modification—TIOPA 2010 Sch 9 para 45 (modification of this section in relation to an arrangement that comes into force before 1 October 2007).

Amendments—[1]   Sections 925A–925F and preceding cross-head inserted by TIOPA 2010 s 371, Sch 7 paras 111, 112. TIOPA 2010 has effect for corporation tax purposes for accounting periods ending on or after 1 April 2010, for income and capital gains tax purposes for the tax year 2010–11 and subsequent tax years, and for petroleum revenue tax purposes for chargeable periods beginning on or after 1 July 2010.

[2]   In heading, words repealed, and in section text, words repealed and substituted, by FA 2013 s 77, Sch 29 paras 16, 28 with effect from 1 January 2014.

[925D Power to modify repo sections

(1) The Treasury may by regulations provide for all or any of the provisions of sections 925A to 925F to apply with modifications in relation to—

    (a) cases to which section 925E (non-standard repo cases) applies, or

    (b) cases involving redemption arrangements, or

    (c) both of those cases.

(2) A case involves redemption arrangements if—

    (a) arrangements, corresponding to those made in cases where a company has a repo, are made in relation to securities that are to be redeemed in the period after their sale, and

    (b) the arrangements are such that a person (instead of having the right or obligation to buy those securities, or similar or other securities, at any subsequent time) has a right or obligation in respect of the benefits which will result from the redemption.

(3) The regulations may make incidental, supplemental, consequential and transitional provision and savings.

(4) In this section "modifications" includes exceptions and omissions.

(5) For the purposes of subsection (2)(a) and section 925E(1), a company has a repo if—

    (a) for the purposes of Chapter 10 of Part 6 of CTA 2009—

        (i)   it has a creditor repo (see section 543 of that Act),

        (ii) it has a creditor quasi-repo (see section 544 of that Act),

        (iii) it has a debtor repo (see section 548 of that Act), or

        (iv) it has a debtor quasi-repo (see section 549 of that Act), or

    (b) as a result of section 547 of that Act, the company has a creditor repo for the purposes of section 546 of that Act.][1]

Commentary—*Simon's Taxes* **A3.204**.

Modification—TIOPA 2010 Sch 9 para 45 (modification of this section in relation to an arrangement that comes into force before 1 October 2007).

Amendments—[1]   Sections 925A–925F and preceding cross-head inserted by TIOPA 2010 s 371, Sch 7 paras 111, 112. TIOPA 2010 has effect for corporation tax purposes for accounting periods ending on or after 1 April 2010, for income and capital gains tax purposes for the tax year 2010–11 and subsequent tax years, and for petroleum revenue tax purposes for chargeable periods beginning on or after 1 July 2010.

[925E Cases where section 925D applies: non-standard repos

(1) This section applies to a case if—

    (a) a company has a repo,

    (b) there has been a sale of the securities under the arrangement or arrangements by reference to which the company has the repo, and

    (c) any of conditions A to C is met.

(2) Condition A is that those securities, or similar or other securities, are not subsequently bought under the arrangement or arrangements.

(3) Condition B is that provision is made by or under an arrangement for different or additional securities to be treated as, or as included with, securities which, for the purposes of the subsequent purchase, are to represent those initially sold.

(4) Condition C is that provision is made by or under an arrangement for securities to be treated as not so included.

(5) Section 925D(5) interprets references in subsection (1) to a company having a repo.][1]

Commentary—*Simon's Taxes* **D9.1001**.

Modification—TIOPA 2010 Sch 9 para 45 (modification of this section in relation to an arrangement that comes into force before 1 October 2007).

Amendments—[1]   Sections 925A–925F and preceding cross-head inserted by TIOPA 2010 s 371, Sch 7 paras 111, 112. TIOPA 2010 has effect for corporation tax purposes for accounting periods ending on or after 1 April 2010, for income and capital gains tax purposes for the tax year 2010–11 and subsequent tax years, and for petroleum revenue tax purposes for chargeable periods beginning on or after 1 July 2010.

[925F Interpretation of the repo sections

(1) This section applies for the purposes of sections 925A to 925E and this section.

(2) "Arrangement" includes any agreement or understanding (whether or not legally enforceable).

(3) It does not matter whether or not provision of any arrangement conferring a right or imposing an obligation on any person to buy any securities is subject to any conditions.

(4) "Securities" means shares, stock or other securities issued by—

    (a) the government of the United Kingdom,

    (b) any public or local authority in the United Kingdom,

    (c) any UK resident company or other UK resident body,

    (d) a government or public or local authority of a territory outside the United Kingdom, or

    (e) any other body of persons not resident in the United Kingdom.

(5) Securities are similar if they give their holders—

    (a) the same rights against the same persons as to capital, interest and dividends, and

    (b) the same remedies to enforce those rights.

(6) Subsection (5) applies even if there is a difference in—

    (a) the total nominal amounts of the securities,

    (b) the form in which they are held, or

    (c) the manner in which they can be transferred.

(7) If—

    (a) a person ("A") buys securities (or has a right or obligation to buy securities), but

    (b) the securities are (or are to be) held for the benefit of another person ("B"),

B (not A) is treated as buying (or having the right or obligation to buy) the securities.

(8) If—

    (a) a person ("C") sells securities, but

    (b) the proceeds of the sale are held for the benefit of another person ("D"),

D (not C) is treated as selling the securities.][1]

Modification—TIOPA 2010 Sch 9 para 45 (modification of this section in relation to an arrangement that comes into force before 1 October 2007).

Amendments—[1]   Sections 925A–925F and preceding cross-head inserted by TIOPA 2010 s 371, Sch 7 paras 111, 112. TIOPA 2010 has effect for corporation tax purposes for accounting periods ending on or after 1 April 2010, for income and capital gains tax purposes for the tax year 2010–11 and subsequent tax years, and for petroleum revenue tax purposes for chargeable periods beginning on or after 1 July 2010.

Supplementary

926 Interpretation of Chapter

(1), (1A) . . . [1]

(2) References in this Chapter to a trade carried on through a branch or agency are to be read, in relation to a company, as references to a trade carried on through a permanent establishment.

Modification—TIOPA 2010 Sch 9 para 45 (modification of sub-s (1A) in relation to an arrangement that comes into force before 1 October 2007).

Amendments—[2]   Sub-ss (1), (1A) repealed by FA 2013 s 77, Sch 29 paras 16, 29 with effect from 1 January 2014.

927 Regulation-making powers: general

Regulations under this Chapter may make different provision for different cases.

CHAPTER 10

DEDUCTION FROM NON-COMMERCIAL PAYMENTS BY COMPANIES

928 Chargeable payments connected with exempt distributions

(1) This section applies to any payment chargeable to tax under [section 1086 of CTA 2010][1] (chargeable payments made within 5 years of an exempt distribution).

(2) The person by or through whom the payment is made must, on making the payment, deduct from it a sum representing income tax on it at the basic rate in force for the tax year in which it is made.

(3) See Chapter 11 (payments between companies etc) for an exception from the duty to deduct sums representing income tax under this section.

(4) For provision about the collection of income tax in respect of a payment from which a sum must be deducted under this section—

(a) see Chapter 15 if the person making the payment is a UK resident company, and

(b) otherwise see Chapter 16.

(5) In this section "payment" does not include a transfer of money's worth that is treated as a payment for the purposes of [sections 1086 to 1090 of CTA 2010 (see section 1086(6) of that Act)][1].

Commentary—*Simon's Taxes* **A4.141, A4.459**.

Derivation—TA 1988 ss 4, 214(1), 349(1).

HMRC Manuals—Company Taxation Manual CTM17290 (treatment of chargeable payment).

Amendments—[1] In sub-ss (1), (5) words substituted by CTA 2010 s 1177, Sch 1 para 556. CTA 2010 has effect for corporation tax purposes for accounting periods ending on or after 1 April 2010, and for income and capital gains tax purposes for the tax year 2010–11 and subsequent tax years.

CHAPTER 11

PAYMENTS BETWEEN COMPANIES ETC: EXCEPTION FROM DUTIES TO DEDUCT

Introduction

929 Overview of Chapter

(1) This Chapter makes provision allowing some payments made by companies, local authorities and qualifying partnerships to be paid gross where they would otherwise be subject to specified duties to deduct sums representing income tax under this Part.

(2) Section 930 disapplies specified duties to deduct where a payment is made by a company, local authority or qualifying partnership which reasonably believes that the payment is an excepted payment.

(3) Section 931 confers power on an officer of Revenue and Customs to disapply section 930 by direction.

(4) Section 932 defines "qualifying partnership".

(5) Sections 933 to 937 make provision as to when a payment is an excepted payment.

(6) Section 938 deals with what happens when a company, local authority or qualifying partnership makes a payment without deducting a sum representing income tax under a reasonable but incorrect belief that the payment is an excepted payment.

Commentary—*Simon's Taxes* **A4.425**.

Derivation—TA 1988 ss 349A–349D.

Exception from duties to deduct for excepted payments

930 Exception from duties to deduct sums representing income tax

(1) The duties to deduct sums representing income tax mentioned in subsection (2) do not apply to a payment if—

(a) it is made by a company, local authority or qualifying partnership, and

(b) at the time the payment is made, the company, authority or partnership reasonably believes that it is an excepted payment.

(2) The duties to deduct are those under—

(a) section 874(2) (certain payments of yearly interest),

(b) section 889(4) (payments in respect of building society securities),

(c) section 901(4) (annual payments made by persons other than individuals),

(d) section 903(7) (patent royalties),

(e) section 906(5) (certain royalty payments etc where the owner lives abroad),

(f) section 910(2) (proceeds of a sale of patent rights paid to non-UK residents),

(g) section 919(2) (manufactured interest on UK securities: payments by UK residents etc), and

(h) section 928(2) (chargeable payments connected with exempt distributions).

(3) Subsection (1) has effect subject to any directions under section 931.

(4) Subsection (1) does not apply to a payment made by a company, or qualifying partnership, acting as trustee or agent for another person.

Commentary—*Simon's Taxes* **A4.460, A4.571, D5.102, D5.127**.

Derivation—TA 1988 s 349A.

HMRC Manuals—Company Taxation Manual CTM35215 (types of payment).

Partnership Manual PM60700 (deduction of income tax at source for qualifying partnerships).

931 Power to make directions disapplying section 930

(1) An officer of Revenue and Customs may give a direction to a company, local authority or qualifying partnership directing that section 930 is not to apply in relation to any payment that—

(a) is made by the company, authority or partnership after the giving of the direction, and

(b) is specified in the direction or is of a description so specified.

(2) A direction under this section may be given only if the officer has reasonable grounds for believing, as respects each payment to which the direction relates, that the payment will not be an excepted payment at the time it is made.

(3) A direction under this section may be varied or revoked by a later direction.

(4) A variation or revocation of a direction under this section has effect only in relation to payments made after the date of the variation or revocation.

Commentary—*Simon's Taxes* **A4.460**.

932 Meaning of "qualifying partnership"

For the purposes of this Chapter a partnership is a "qualifying partnership" if any partner in the partnership is a company or a local authority.

Excepted payments

933 UK resident companies

A payment is an excepted payment if the person beneficially entitled to the income in respect of which the payment is made is a UK resident company.

Commentary—*Simon's Taxes* **A2.204, A4.460**.
Derivation—TA 1988 s 349B(1).
HMRC Manuals—International Manual INTM287020 (foreign permanent establishments of UK companies: payments subject to deduction of tax)
Company Taxation Manual CTM47540 (exception to this rule).

934 Non-UK resident companies

(1) A payment is an excepted payment if each of the following conditions is met in relation to the payment.

(2) The person beneficially entitled to the income in respect of which the payment is made must be a non-UK resident company.

(3) The non-UK resident company must carry on a trade in the United Kingdom through a permanent establishment.

(4) The payment must be one that is required to be brought into account in calculating the chargeable profits (within the meaning given by [section 19 of CTA 2009][1]) of the non-UK resident company.

Commentary—*Simon's Taxes* **A4.460**.
Amendments—[1]   In sub-s (4) words substituted by CTA 2009 s 1322, Sch 1 paras 699, 710. CTA 2009 applies for accounting periods ending on or after 1 April 2009 (for corporation tax purposes) and for tax years 2009–10 onwards (for income and capital gains tax purposes).

935 PEP and ISA managers

(1) A payment is an excepted payment if each of the following conditions is met in relation to the payment.

(2) The person to whom the payment is made must be, or must be the nominee of, the plan manager of a plan of a kind to which regulations under Chapter 3 of Part 6 of ITTOIA 2005 (income from individual investment plans) apply.

(3) The plan manager must receive the payment in respect of investments under the plan.

Commentary—*Simon's Taxes* **A4.460**.
Derivation—TA 1988 s 349B(4).

936 Recipients who are to be paid gross

(1) A payment is an excepted payment if it is made to, or to the nominee of, a recipient who is specified in subsection (2) as a recipient who is to be paid gross.

(2) The following recipients are to be paid gross—

    (*a*) a local authority,

    (*b*) a health service body within the meaning of [section 986 of CTA 2010][1],

    (*c*) a public office or department of the Crown other than one mentioned in section 978(2),

    (*d*) a charity,

    (*e*) a body for the time being mentioned in [section 468 of CTA 2010][1] (bodies that are allowed the same exemption from tax as charitable companies the whole income of which is applied to charitable purposes),

    [(*f*)   a body which is an association for the purposes of section 469(1)(*a*) of CTA 2010 (scientific research associations) and complies with the conditions in subsections (2) and (3) of that section,][1]

    (*g*) the scheme administrator of a registered pension scheme,

    (*h*) the sub-scheme administrator of a sub-scheme which forms part of a split scheme pursuant to the Registered Pensions (Splitting of Schemes) Regulations 2006 (SI 2006/569),

    (*i*)   the trustees of a scheme entitled to exemption under section 613(4) of ICTA (Parliamentary pension funds), and

    (*j*)   the persons entitled to receive the income of a fund entitled to exemption under section 614(3) of ICTA (certain colonial, etc pension funds).

(3) The Treasury may by order amend this section so as to add to, restrict or otherwise alter the persons or bodies who are to be paid gross.

Commentary—*Simon's Taxes* **A4.460**.
Derivation—TA 1988 s 349B(3), (8).
HMRC Manuals—Company Taxation Manual CTM47550 (exceptions to obligation to deduct tax).
Amendments—[1]   In sub-s (2)(*b*), (*e*) words substituted, and sub-s (2)(*f*) substituted by CTA 2010 s 1177, Sch 1 para 557. CTA 2010 has effect for corporation tax purposes for accounting periods ending on or after 1 April 2010, and for income and capital gains tax purposes for the tax year 2010–11 and subsequent tax years.

937 Partnerships

(1) A payment is an excepted payment if each of the following conditions are met.

(2) A partnership must be beneficially entitled to the income in respect of which the payment is made.

(3) Each partner in the partnership must be—

   (*a*) a person or body mentioned in section 936, or

   (*b*) a person or body to whom one of subsections (4) to (6) applies.

(4) This subsection applies to a UK resident company.

(5) This subsection applies to a company that—

   (*a*) is non-UK resident,

   (*b*) carries on a trade in the United Kingdom through a permanent establishment, and

   (*c*) is required to bring into account, in calculating its chargeable profits (within the meaning of [section 19 of CTA 2009][1]), the whole of any share of the payment that is attributable to it because of [Part 17 of that Act][1].

(6) This subsection applies to the European Investment Fund.

(7) The Treasury may by order amend this section to add to, restrict or otherwise alter the persons or bodies falling within subsection (3)(*b*).

Commentary—*Simon's Taxes* **A4.460**.
Derivation—TA 1988 s 349B(6), (7), (8).
HMRC Manuals—Savings and Investment Manual SAIM9070 (yearly interest paid to partnerships).
Company Taxation Manual CTM35215 (payments made on or after 1 April 2001).
Amendments—[1] In sub-s (5)(*c*) words substituted by CTA 2009 s 1322, Sch 1 paras 699, 711. CTA 2009 applies for accounting periods ending on or after 1 April 2009 (for corporation tax purposes) and for tax years 2009–10 onwards (for income and capital gains tax purposes).

Incorrect belief that payment is an excepted payment

938 Consequences of reasonable but incorrect belief

(1) This section applies if—

   (*a*) a payment is made by a company, local authority or qualifying partnership without a sum representing income tax on the payment being deducted from it,

   (*b*) at the time the payment is made, the company, authority or partnership reasonably believes that it is an excepted payment,

   (*c*) one of the duties to deduct sums representing income tax mentioned in section 930(2) would apply to the payment if the company did not so believe, and

   (*d*) the payment is not an excepted payment at the time it is made.

(2) This Part has effect in relation to the payment as if section 930(1) had never disapplied the duties to deduct mentioned in section 930(2).

Commentary—*Simon's Taxes* **A4.460**.
Derivation—TA 1988 s 349D.

CHAPTER 12

FUNDING BONDS

939 Duty to retain bonds where issue treated as payment of interest

(1) This section applies if—

   (*a*) there is an issue of funding bonds to a creditor in respect of a liability to pay interest on a debt incurred by a government, public institution, other public authority or body corporate,

   (*b*) by virtue of [section 413 of CTA 2009][3] or section 380 of ITTOIA 2005, the issue is treated as if it were a payment of an amount of interest ("the deemed interest"), and

   (*c*) the person by or through whom the bonds are issued is required, under this Part, to deduct a sum representing income tax from the deemed interest.

(2) The person by or through whom the bonds are issued must retain bonds the value of which is, at the time of their issue, equal to income tax on the deemed interest at the [basic rate][1] in force for the tax year in which the bonds are issued.

(3) A person who retains bonds in accordance with subsection (2) is treated as complying with the duty to deduct a sum representing income tax from the deemed interest.

(4) The person may tender the bonds retained in satisfaction of any income tax to be collected from the person in respect of the deemed interest under Chapter 15 or 16.

[(4A) If bonds are tendered in accordance with subsection (4), the Commissioners for Her Majesty's Revenue and Customs may tender the bonds in satisfaction of any amount that is payable by the Commissioners to the relevant creditor in connection with the relevant debt.

(4B) For the purposes of subsection (4A)—

   (*a*) "relevant creditor" and "relevant debt" mean the creditor and the debt mentioned in subsection (1)(*a*), and

   (*b*) a bond is to be taken to have the same value that it had at the time of its issue.

(4C) If bonds that are to be tendered in accordance with subsection (4) or (4A) are subject to restrictions on their tender or transfer, the restrictions do not prevent the bonds from being—

(*a*) tendered in accordance with that subsection, or

(*b*) transferred from the person tendering them to the person to whom they are tendered.][2]

(5) . . .[2]

(6) In this Chapter "funding bonds" includes any bonds, stocks, shares, securities or certificates of indebtedness [(but does not include any instrument providing for payment in the form of goods or services or a voucher)][4].

Commentary—*Simon's Taxes* A4.423, A4.472.

HMRC Manuals—Savings and Investment Manual SAIM2210 (funding bonds, with example).

Corporate Finance Manual CFM37420 (steps to account for deduction of tax at source by issuer).

Amendments—[1] Words in sub-s (2) substituted by FA 2008 s 5, Sch 1 paras 1, 31 with effect for the tax year 2008–09 and subsequent tax years.

[2] Sub-ss (4A)–(4C) inserted, and sub-s (5) repealed, by FA 2008 s 134(1)–(3) with effect in relation to funding bonds issued on or after 12 March 2008.

[3] In sub-s (1)(*b*) words substituted by CTA 2009 s 1322, Sch 1 paras 699, 712. CTA 2009 applies for accounting periods ending on or after 1 April 2009 (for corporation tax purposes) and for tax years 2009–10 onwards (for income and capital gains tax purposes).

[4] In sub-s (6) words inserted by FA 2013 s 27, Sch 11 para 8 with effect in relation to any payment of interest made on or after 17 July 2013.

940 Exception from duty to retain bonds

(1) This section applies if an issue of funding bonds is treated as a payment of interest ("the deemed interest") as mentioned in section 939(1) and—

(*a*) the person by or through whom the bonds are issued is required to retain bonds under section 939(2), but

(*b*) it is impracticable for the person to do so.

(2) The duty to deduct a sum representing income tax from the deemed interest under this Part does not apply if the person tells the Commissioners for Her Majesty's Revenue and Customs—

(*a*) the names and addresses of the persons to whom the bonds have been issued, and

(*b*) the amount of the bonds issued to each person.

(3) Accordingly—

(*a*) the duty to retain bonds under section 939(2) does not apply, and

(*b*) the provisions in Chapters 15 and 16 about the collection of income tax in respect of the deemed interest do not apply.

[940A No appropriate bond or combination of bonds

(1) This section applies if—

(*a*) the Commissioners for Her Majesty's Revenue and Customs hold one or more bonds tendered in accordance with section 939(4),

(*b*) the Commissioners wish to tender bonds in accordance with section 939(4A) in satisfaction of an amount payable to the relevant creditor, and

(*c*) the Commissioners consider that they do not hold a bond, or combination of bonds, that is appropriate for satisfying the amount payable.

(2) If requested to do so by the Commissioners, the bond issuer must secure that the Commissioners hold a bond, or combination of bonds, that the Commissioners consider to be appropriate for satisfying the amount payable.

(3) If requested to do so by the bond issuer, a person must assist the bond issuer to comply with subsection (2).

(4) The duty under subsection (2), or under subsection (3), does not apply if it would be impracticable for the bond issuer, or the other person, to comply with the duty.

(5) The matters which the Commissioners may take into account when considering whether or not a bond or combination of bonds is appropriate for satisfying the amount payable include—

(*a*) the value of a bond at the time of its issue,

(*b*) the interest which the relevant creditor, or any other person, has in a bond (including the nature or size of the interest), and

(*c*) the terms on which a bond is issued.

(6) For the purposes of this section—

(*a*) "bond issuer" means the person by or through whom bonds were issued, and

(*b*) "relevant creditor" and "relevant debt" have the same meanings as in section 939(4A).][1]

Amendments—[1] Section 940A inserted by FA 2008 s 134(4) with effect in relation to funding bonds issued on or after 12 March 2008.

CHAPTER 14

TAX AVOIDANCE: DIRECTIONS FOR DUTY TO DEDUCT TO APPLY

944 Directions for deduction from payments to non-UK residents

(1) This section applies if it appears to an officer of Revenue and Customs that any person entitled to an amount taxable under—

(a) . . . [1]

(b) Chapter 4 of [Part 13][1] (tax avoidance: sales of occupation income),

is non-UK resident.

(2) The officer may, in relation to any payment forming the whole or part of that amount, direct that the person by or through whom the payment is made must, on making it, deduct from it a sum representing income tax on it at the basic rate in force for the tax year in which the payment is made.

(3) Subsection (2) does not affect the final liability of the person entitled to the amount mentioned in subsection (1) including any liability under section 768(4) or 786(4) (recovery of tax where consideration receivable by person not assessed).

(4) For provision about the collection of income tax in respect of a payment from which a sum must be deducted under subsection (2)—

(a) see Chapter 15 if the person making the payment is a UK resident company, and

(b) otherwise see Chapter 16.

Commentary—*Simon's Taxes* **A4.141, E1.1206.**

HMRC Manuals—Business Income Manual BIM100375 (deduction of tax from payments).

Amendments—[1] Sub-s (1)(a) repealed, and in sub-s (1)(b), words substituted for words "that Part", by FA 2016 s 79(6) with effect in relation to disposals on or after 5 July 2016 (FA 2016 s 82(1)), subject to transitional provisions for disposals to associated persons on or after 16 March 2016 and before 5 July 2016 (FA 2016 s 82(4)–(15)).

F(No 2)A 2017 s 39 provides that these amendments have effect (so far as they would not otherwise have effect) in relation to amounts that are recognised in GAAP accounts drawn up for any period of account beginning on or after 8 March 2017 or, in the case of a straddling period, amounts that would be recognised in GAAP accounts drawn up for a period of account beginning on 8 March 2017 and ending when the straddling period ends. "Straddling period" means a period of account beginning before 8 March 2017 and ending on or after that date.

CHAPTER 15

COLLECTION: DEPOSIT-TAKERS, BUILDING SOCIETIES AND CERTAIN COMPANIES

Introduction

945 Overview of Chapter

(1) This Chapter provides—

(a) for persons who have made payments within section 946 ("section 946 payments") to make returns of the payments, and

(b) for the collection of income tax in respect of those payments.

(2) Sections 947 and 948 contain definitions and other provisions in relation to the following basic concepts used in the Chapter: "return period" and "accounting period".

(3) Section 949 requires persons who have made section 946 payments to deliver returns of those payments made in return periods falling within accounting periods, and section 950 requires such persons to deliver returns of those payments made otherwise than in accounting periods.

(4) Section 951 explains—

(a) how much income tax is due from persons in respect of section 946 payments made by them, and

(b) when that income tax must be paid.

(5) Sections 952 to 955 allow persons who have made section 946 payments to make claims for income tax they have suffered to be set off against income tax payable by them in respect of the payments.

(6) Sections 956 to 960 explain what happens in cases where income tax payable in respect of section 946 payments is not paid when it is due, or where returns are incomplete or incorrect.

(7) Sections 961 and 962 contain supplementary provisions.

(8) For further provisions applying to returns and set-off claims under this Chapter, see TMA 1970 (in particular section 113(1) (returns) and section 42 and Schedule 1A (claims)).

946 Payments within this section

The payments within this section are—

(a) . . . [1]

(b) a payment from which a UK resident company is required to deduct a sum representing income tax under—

(i) section 874(2) (payments of yearly interest),

(ii) section 889(4) (payments in respect of building society securities),

(iii) section 892(2) (certain payments of UK public revenue dividends),

(iv) section 901(4) (annual payments made by persons other than individuals),

    (v) section 903(7) (patent royalties),

    (vi) section 906(5) (royalty payments etc where the owner lives abroad),

    (vii) section 910(2) (proceeds of a sale of patent rights paid to non-UK residents),

    (viii) section 928(2) (chargeable payments connected with exempt distributions), or

    (ix) section 944(2) (directions for deduction from payments to non-UK residents), and

  (*c*) a payment from which a company is required to deduct a sum representing income tax under section 919(2) (manufactured interest on UK securities: payments by UK residents etc).

Commentary—*Simon's Taxes* **D5.510, A4.144, A4.466**.

HMRC Manuals—Company Tax Manual CTM35050 (accounting for tax deducted from interest etc).

Amendments—[1] Para (*a*) repealed by FA 2016 s 39, Sch 6 para 22 with effect in relation to interest paid or credited on or after 6 April 2016, and dividends or other distributions paid by a building society on or after that date.

947 Return periods

(1) For the purposes of this Chapter, the return periods which fall within a person's accounting period are determined as follows.

(2) If at least one quarter date falls within the accounting period, each of the following is a return period which falls within the accounting period—

  (*a*) any complete quarter which falls within the accounting period, and

  (*b*) any part of the accounting period which is not a complete quarter and which—

    (i) ends with the first (or only) quarter date in that period, or

    (ii) begins immediately after the last (or only) quarter date in that period.

(3) If no quarter date falls within the accounting period, the accounting period itself is to be treated as a return period which falls within the accounting period.

(4) In this section—

    "quarter" means a period of three months ending—

      (*a*) unless paragraph (*b*) applies, with the last day of March, June, September or December, or

      (*b*) if the person mentioned in subsection (1) is a building society, with the last day of February, May, August or November, and

    "quarter date" means—

      (*a*) unless paragraph (*b*) applies, the last day of March, June, September or December, or

      (*b*) if the person mentioned in subsection (1) is a building society, the last day of February, May, August or November.

Commentary—*Simon's Taxes* **A4.144, A4.466**.

HMRC Manuals—Company Taxation Manual CTM49380 (return periods for building societies where interest if from marketable securities). CTM35110 (return period).

948 Meaning of "accounting period"

(1) In this Chapter "accounting period", in relation to a deposit-taker who is not a company, means a period for which the deposit-taker's accounts are drawn up. "Deposit-taker" has the same meaning as in Chapter 2 (see section 853).

(2) See [Chapter 2 of Part 2 of CTA 2009 (accounting periods)][1] for provision about accounting periods of companies.

Amendments—[1] In sub-s (2) words substituted by CTA 2009 s 1322, Sch 1 paras 699, 714. CTA 2009 applies for accounting periods ending on or after 1 April 2009 (for corporation tax purposes) and for tax years 2009–10 onwards (for income and capital gains tax purposes).

Returns of income tax

949 Payments in an accounting period

(1) This section applies if a person makes a section 946 payment on a date which falls within an accounting period of the person.

(2) The person must deliver a return to an officer of Revenue and Customs for each return period—

  (*a*) which falls within the accounting period, and

  (*b*) in which the person makes a section 946 payment.

(3) The person must deliver the return within 14 days after the end of the return period to which it relates.

(4) The return must show the amount of—

  (*a*) any section 946 payments made by the person in the return period, and

  (*b*) the income tax payable by the person in respect of those payments (see section 951).

Commentary—*Simon's Taxes* **A4.144, A4.465, A4.466, A4.466**.

HMRC Manuals—Company Taxation Manual CTM35115 (collection of tax on annual payments of returns). CTM35120 (date tax payable).

950 Payments otherwise than in an accounting period

(1) This section applies if a person makes a section 946 payment on a date which does not fall within an accounting period of the person.

(2) The person must deliver a return to an officer of Revenue and Customs within 14 days after the date on which the payment is made.
(3) The return must show the amount of—
  (a) the payment, and
  (b) the income tax payable by the person in respect of that payment (see section 951).

Commentary—*Simon's Taxes* **A4.144, A4.466, D5.510**.
HMRC Manuals—Company Taxation Manual CTM35140 (payment made otherwise than in an accounting period).

Collection and payment of income tax

951 Collection and payment of income tax
(1) Income tax in respect of a section 946 payment is due, from the person who makes the payment, on the date by which the return on which the payment must be included is required to be delivered.
(2) The income tax due is equal to the sum which the person is required to deduct from the payment under the applicable provision mentioned in section 946.
(3) The income tax is payable by the person without an officer of Revenue and Customs making any assessment.

Commentary—*Simon's Taxes* **A4.144, A4.466**.
HMRC Manuals—International Manual INTM413220 (assessing the unpaid income tax).

Set-off

952 Conditions for a set-off claim
(1) A person who makes a section 946 payment may make a set-off claim if conditions A and B are met at the end of a return period which falls within an accounting period of the person.
(2) Condition A is that in the return period the person has—
  (a) made a section 946 payment, or
  (b) received a payment on which the person has suffered income tax by deduction.
(3) Condition B is that at the end of the return period there is—
  (a) a net amount of income tax suffered (see subsection (4)), and
  (b) a net amount of income tax payable (see subsection (5)).
(4) There is a net amount of income tax suffered at the end of a return period if—
  (a) the person has received any payments on which income tax has been suffered by deduction in the return period or in any previous return period which falls within the accounting period, and
  (b) the amount of income tax so suffered by the person on those payments exceeds the amount of such income tax treated as repaid for the accounting period to date as a result of any previous set-off claim.
(5) There is a net amount of income tax payable at the end of a return period if—
  (a) the person has made any section 946 payments in the return period or in any previous return period which falls within the accounting period, and
  (b) the amount of income tax payable by the person in respect of those payments exceeds the amount of such income tax treated as paid for the accounting period to date as a result of any previous set-off claim.

Commentary—*Simon's Taxes* **A4.466**.
HMRC Manuals—Company Taxation Manual CTM49365 (set off by a company).
CTM49428 (taxed interest received by building societies).
CTM35125 (set off of tax suffered by deduction).

953 How a set-off claim works
(1) A set-off claim is a claim for the net amount of income tax suffered at the end of the return period to be set off against the net amount of income tax payable at the end of the return period.
(2) The effect of a claim is that, to the extent of the set-off—
  (a) the income tax comprised in the net amount of income tax suffered is treated as repaid, and
  (b) the income tax comprised in the net amount of income tax payable is treated as paid.
(3) Accordingly—
  (a) any liability of the person making the set-off claim to pay any of the income tax treated as paid under subsection (2)(b) is discharged, and
  (b) any of that income tax which has been paid is to be repaid to the person.
(4) A set-off claim must be made in a return under section 949 for the return period.
(5) A return may be made under that section for the purposes of making a set-off claim despite the fact that the person making the claim may not have made any section 946 payments in the return period.
(6) Income tax suffered which is taken into account in a set-off claim may not also be taken into account for the purposes of—
  (a) [section 967 of CTA 2010][1] (income tax deducted from payments to UK resident company to be set off against corporation tax), or
  (b) [section 968][1] of that Act (income tax deducted from payments to non-UK resident company to be set off against corporation tax).

(7) Income tax suffered by a deposit-taker is to be taken into account in a set-off claim only if the payment on which the income tax is suffered is to be taken into account in calculating the deposit-taker's liability to corporation tax. "Deposit-taker" has the same meaning as in Chapter 2 (see section 853).

Commentary—*Simon's Taxes* **A4.466**.
HMRC Manuals—Company Taxation Manual CTM35250 (set off claim for a company).
Amendments—[1]   In sub-s (6)(*a*), (*b*) words substituted by CTA 2010 s 1177, Sch 1 para 558. CTA 2010 has effect for corporation tax purposes for accounting periods ending on or after 1 April 2010, and for income and capital gains tax purposes for the tax year 2010–11 and subsequent tax years.

954 Proceedings begun after a set-off claim is made
(1) If a set-off claim has been made no proceedings for collecting income tax which would have to be discharged if the claim were allowed may be brought until the claim is finally determined.
(2) Subsection (1) does not affect the date when the income tax is due.
(3) Any income tax underpaid as a result of this section must be paid when the claim is finally determined.
(4) In this section "proceedings" includes proceedings by way of distraint or attachment.

Commentary—*Simon's Taxes* **A4.466**.
Derivation—TA 1988 Sch 16 para 6.

955 Proceedings begun before a set-off claim is made
(1) This section applies if—
    (*a*) a person has made a set-off claim, and
    (*b*) before the claim was made, proceedings were brought for collecting income tax assessed, or interest on income tax assessed, under section 956 or 957.
(2) No effect is to be given to the set-off claim so as to affect or delay the collection or recovery of the income tax, or of interest on that income tax, until the claim is finally determined.
(3) Any income tax overpaid as a result of this section must be repaid when the claim is finally determined.
(4) In this section "proceedings" includes proceedings by way of distraint or attachment [or under Schedule 12 to the Tribunals, Courts and Enforcement Act 2007 (taking control of goods)][1].

Commentary—*Simon's Taxes* **A4.466**.
Derivation—TA 1988 Sch 16 para 6.

AMENDMENTS—
[1]   In sub-s (4), words inserted by the Tribunals, Courts and Enforcement Act 2007 s 62(3), Sch 13 para 157 with effect from 6 April 2014 (by virtue of SI 2014/768 art 2(1)(*b*)).

Assessments and errors

956 Assessments where section 946 payment included in return
(1) This section applies if any income tax in respect of a section 946 payment which is included in a return under this Chapter has not been paid at or before the date mentioned in section 951.
(2) An officer of Revenue and Customs may make an assessment on the person who made the payment.
(3) Income tax may be assessed under this section whether or not it has been paid when the assessment is made.

Commentary—*Simon's Taxes* **A4.466, A4.466**.
Derivation—TA 1988 Sch 16 para 4(1).
HMRC Manuals—Company Taxation Manual CTM35150 (unpaid tax).

957 Assessments in other cases
(1) This section applies if an officer of Revenue and Customs thinks—
    (*a*) that there is a section 946 payment which should have been included in a return under this Chapter and which has not been so included, or
    (*b*) that a return under this Chapter is otherwise incorrect.
(2) An officer of Revenue and Customs may make an assessment, to the best of the officer's judgement, on the person who made the return, or who should have made one.

Commentary—*Simon's Taxes* **A4.466**.
HMRC Manuals—Company Taxation Manual CTM35135 (items included in error).
CTM35145 (relevant payments not returned).

958 Payer's duty to deliver amended return
(1) This section applies if a person who has made a section 946 payment becomes aware that—
    (*a*) anything which should have been included in a return delivered by the person under this Chapter has not been so included,
    (*b*) anything which should not have been included in a return delivered by the person under this Chapter has been so included, or
    (*c*) any other error has occurred in a return delivered by the person under this Chapter.

(2) The person must deliver an amended return correcting the error to an officer of Revenue and Customs without delay.

(3) If the person delivers an amended return such assessments, adjustments, set-offs or payments or repayments of income tax as are necessary for achieving the objective mentioned in subsection (4) must be made.

(4) The objective is that the resulting liabilities to income tax (including interest on unpaid or overpaid income tax) of the person or any other person are the same as they would have been if a correct return had been delivered.

Commentary—*Simon's Taxes* **A4.465, D5.510.**

HMRC Manuals—Company Taxation Manual CTM35130 (amended return where company becomes aware of an error).

959 Application of Income Tax Acts provisions about time limits for assessments

(1) This section deals with the application of the provisions of the Income Tax Acts about time limits for making assessments.

(2) So far as the provisions refer or relate to—

(a) the tax year for which an assessment is made, or

(b) the year to which an assessment relates,

they apply to assessments under this Chapter despite the fact that an assessment under this Chapter may relate to a return period which is not a tax year.

(3) Subsection (4) applies if an assessment under this Chapter relates to income tax due in respect of a payment required to be included in a return for a return period under section 949 (payments in an accounting period).

(4) In that case, for the purposes of the provisions mentioned in subsection (1), the assessment is treated as made for the tax year in which the return period ends.

(5) Subsection (6) applies if an assessment under this Chapter relates to income tax due in respect of a payment required to be included in a return under section 950 (payments otherwise than in an accounting period).

(6) In that case, for the purposes of the provisions mentioned in subsection (1), the assessment is treated as made for the tax year in which payment is made.

Commentary—*Simon's Taxes* **A4.466.**

Derivation—TA 1988 Sch 16 paras 10(1) and 11.

HMRC Manuals—Company Taxation Manual CTM35160 (time limits provisions).

960 Further provisions about assessments

(1) Income tax assessed on a person under this Chapter is due on the date mentioned in section 951 and an appeal against the assessment does not affect the date when the income tax is due under that section.

(2) On the determination of an appeal against an assessment under this Chapter any income tax overpaid must be repaid.

(3) Any income tax assessable under any one or more of the provisions of this Chapter may be included in a single assessment if all the income tax is due on the same date.

Commentary—*Simon's Taxes* **A4.466.**

Derivation—TA 1988 Sch 16 para 10.

HMRC Manuals—Company Taxation Manual CTM35160 (time limits provisions).

CTM35155 (composite assessments).

Supplementary

961 Relationship between Chapter and Income Tax Acts powers

Nothing in this Chapter affects any powers conferred by the Income Tax Acts for the recovery of income tax by means of an assessment or otherwise.

Commentary—*Simon's Taxes* **A4.466.**

Derivation—TA 1988 Sch 16 para 11.

HMRC Manuals—Company Taxation Manual CTM35170 (due and payable date on assessments).

962 Power to make regulations modifying Chapter

(1) The Commissioners for Her Majesty's Revenue and Customs may by regulations modify, replace or supplement any of the provisions of this Chapter for the purpose of regulating the time and manner in which persons making section 946 payments—

(a) are to account for and pay income tax which is to be collected from them in respect of those payments, and

(b) are to be repaid income tax in respect of payments received by them.

(2) In particular, regulations under this section may, in relation to income tax for which a person is liable to account,—

(a) modify any provision of Parts 2 to 6 of TMA 1970, or

(b) apply any such provision with or without modifications.

(3) Regulations under this section may—

(a) make different provision for different kinds of payer,

(b) make different provision for different circumstances, and

(c) authorise the Commissioners for Her Majesty's Revenue and Customs, if they think there are special circumstances justifying it, to make special arrangements in relation to—

   (i) income tax for which a person is liable to account, or

   (ii) the repayment of income tax suffered by a person.

(4) Regulations under this section may contain incidental, supplemental, consequential and transitional provision and savings.

(5) The Commissioners for Her Majesty's Revenue and Customs must not make any regulations under this section unless a draft of them has been laid before and approved by a resolution of the House of Commons.

(6) References in this Act and in any other enactment to any of the provisions of this Chapter are to be read as references to those provisions as modified, replaced or supplemented by provision made by regulations under this section.

CHAPTER 16
COLLECTION: CERTAIN PAYMENTS BY OTHER PERSONS

963 Collection of income tax on certain payments by other persons

(1) This section makes provision for the collection of income tax in respect of—

  (a) a payment from which a person other than a UK resident company is required to deduct a sum representing income tax under—

    (i) section 874(2) (certain payments of yearly interest),

    (ii) section 889(4) (payments in respect of building society securities),

    (iii) section 892(2) (certain payments of UK public revenue dividends),

    (iv) section 901(4) (annual payments made by persons other than individuals),

    (v) section 903(7) (patent royalties),

    (vi) section 906(5) (royalty payments etc where the owner lives abroad),

    (vii) section 910(2) (proceeds of a sale of patent rights paid to non-UK residents),

    (viii) section 928(2) (chargeable payments connected with exempt distributions), or

    (ix) section 944(2) (directions for deduction from payments to non-UK residents), and

  (b) a payment from which a person other than a company is required to deduct a sum representing income tax under section 919(2) (manufactured interest for UK securities: payments by UK residents etc).

(2) The person required to deduct the sum must deliver to an officer of Revenue and Customs an account of the payment without delay.

(3) An officer of Revenue and Customs may make an assessment on that person for income tax equal to the sum required to be deducted.

(4) The provisions of the Income Tax Acts relating to—

  (a) persons chargeable to income tax,

  (b) income tax assessments, and

  (c) the collection and recovery of income tax,

apply (unless excluded expressly or by implication) to the assessment, collection and recovery of income tax which is assessable on persons under this section.

Commentary—*Simon's Taxes* A4.465, A4.141, A4.330, A4.441, A4.442, B5.334, B5.317.

HMRC Manuals—Savings and Investment Manual SAIM9170 (collection other than through self assessment).

[963A Power to make regulations modifying section 963

(1) The Commissioners for Her Majesty's Revenue and Customs may by regulations modify, replace or supplement any provision of section 963(2) to (4).

(2) Regulations under this section may only be made for the purpose of regulating the time at and manner in which persons making payments within section 963(1)(a) or (b) are to account for and pay income tax which is to be collected from them in respect of those payments.

(3) In particular, regulations under this section may, in relation to income tax for which a person is liable to account—

  (a) modify any provision of Parts 2 to 6 of TMA 1970, or

  (b) apply any such provision with or without modifications.

(4) Regulations under this section may—

  (a) make different provision for different kinds of payer,

  (b) make different provision for different circumstances, and

  (c) authorise the Commissioners for Her Majesty's Revenue and Customs, if they think there are special circumstances justifying it, to make special arrangements in relation to income tax for which a person is liable to account.

(5) Regulations under this section may contain incidental, supplemental, consequential and transitional provision and savings.

(6) The Commissioners for Her Majesty's Revenue and Customs must not make any regulations under this section unless a draft of them has been laid before and approved by a resolution of the House of Commons.

(7) References in this Act and in any other enactment to any of the provisions of section 963(2) to (4) are to be read as references to those provisions as modified, replaced or supplemented by provision made by regulations under this section.]¹

Amendments—¹   This section inserted by F(No 3)A 2010 s 8 with effect from 16 December 2010.

CHAPTER 17

COLLECTION THROUGH SELF-ASSESSMENT RETURN

964 Collection through self-assessment return

(1) This section applies if—

    (a) a person makes a payment from which the person is required to deduct a sum representing income tax, and

    (b) income tax equal to the sum required to be deducted is, under section 900(3), 901(3) or 903(5) or (6), to be collected through the person's self-assessment return.

(2) . . .²

(3) The income tax is to be treated for the purposes of TMA 1970 as if it were income tax charged on the person or trustee.

(4) Accordingly, the income tax must be taken into account for the purposes of—

    (a) the person's or trustee's return under section 8 or 8A of TMA 1970, and

    (b) the person's or trustee's assessment to income tax under section 9 of that Act,

(in addition to the person or trustee's income tax liability calculated in accordance with Chapter 3 of Part 2 (calculation of income tax liability)).

(5) . . .¹

Commentary—*Simon's Taxes* **A4.465, A4.330, E1.804**.

HMRC Manuals—Savings and Investment Manual SAIM9160 (collection through self assessment).

Amendments—¹   Sub-s (5) repealed by FA 2008 s 69 with effect for the purpose of calculating the amount of any payments to be made under TMA 1970 s 59A on account of liability to income tax for the tax year 2008–09 and subsequent tax years.
²   Sub-s (2) repealed by the Unauthorised Unit Trusts (Tax) Regulations, SI 2013/2819 reg 37(1), (16) with effect from 6 April 2014.

Prospective amendments—In sub-s (4)(b), words "that section" to be substituted for words "section 9 of that Act" by F(No 2)A 2017 s 61(1), Sch 14 para 36 with effect from a day to be appointed.

CHAPTER 18

OTHER REGIMES INVOLVING THE DEDUCTION OF INCOME TAX AT SOURCE

Visiting performers

965 Overview of sections 966 to 970

(1) Sections 966 to 970 make provision for the payment of sums representing income tax to the Commissioners for Her Majesty's Revenue and Customs where certain payments or transfers are made in connection with activities performed in the United Kingdom by non-UK resident entertainers, sportsmen and sportswomen.

(2) See also—

    [section 1309 of CTA 2009]¹ (entertainers and sportsmen) which makes provision in relation to such payments or transfers for the purposes of corporation tax,

    Chapter 8 of Part 2 of ITEPA 2003 (application of provisions to workers under arrangements made by intermediaries), in particular section 48(2) (exclusions from the scope of the Chapter), and

    sections 13 and 14 of ITTOIA 2005 (trades and trade profits: visiting performers).

Amendments—¹   In sub-s (2) words substituted by CTA 2009 s 1322, Sch 1 paras 699, 715. CTA 2009 applies for accounting periods ending on or after 1 April 2009 (for corporation tax purposes) and for tax years 2009–10 onwards (for income and capital gains tax purposes).

966 Duty to deduct and account for sums representing income tax

(1) This section applies if—

    (a) an entertainer, sportsman or sportswoman of a prescribed description ("a performer") who is non-UK resident for a tax year performs a relevant activity in the United Kingdom in the tax year, and

    (b) a payment or transfer connected with the relevant activity is made.

(2) It does not matter—

    (a) whether the payment or transfer is made to the performer or anyone else, or

    (b) when the payment or transfer is made.

(3) If a payment within subsection (1)(*b*) is made the person who makes the payment must, on making it, deduct from it a sum representing income tax and account to the Commissioners for Her Majesty's Revenue and Customs for the sum.

(4) If a transfer within subsection (1)(*b*) is made the person who makes the transfer must account to the Commissioners for Her Majesty's Revenue and Customs for a sum representing income tax.

(5) See section 967 as to the calculation of the sums representing income tax mentioned in subsections (3) and (4).

(6) This section does not apply to payments or transfers of such a kind as may be prescribed.

(7) In this section—

    (*a*) "relevant activity" means an activity of a prescribed description, and

    (*b*) a payment or transfer is connected with a relevant activity if it has a connection of a prescribed kind with that activity.

Commentary—*Simon's Taxes* **D4.132, E4.1001A, E5.802**.

Regulations—London Olympic Games and Paralympic Games Tax Regulations, SI 2010/2913.

Income Tax (Removal of Ordinary Residence) Regulations, SI 2013/605.

Modifications—FA 2013 s 8(4) (this section does not apply to any payment or transfer which gives rise to income benefiting from the exemption under FA 2013 s 8(1) (persons exempt from income tax in respect of certain income arising in connection with the London Anniversary Games)).

FA 2013 s 9(4) (this section does not apply to any payment or transfer which gives rise to income benefiting from the exemption under FA 2013 s 9(1) (persons exempt from income tax in respect of certain income arising in connection with the Glasgow Commonwealth Games)).

Major Sporting Events (Income Tax Exemption) Regulations, SI 2016/771 regs 6, 10 (this section does not apply to any payment or transfer which gives rise to income benefiting from the exemption under SI 2016/771 regs 3, 7 (persons exempt from income tax in respect of income arising in connection with the London Anniversary Games and the World Athletics Championships)).

967 Calculation of sums representing income tax

(1) The sums representing income tax mentioned in section 966(3) and (4) are to be calculated in accordance with prescribed rules.

(2) But the sums must not exceed the relevant proportion of the payment concerned or of the value of what is transferred.

"Relevant proportion" means a proportion equal to the basic rate of income tax for the tax year in which the payment or transfer is made.

(3) Regulations made by the Treasury may provide, in relation to a transfer to which section 966 applies, that for the purposes of the Tax Acts the value of what is transferred is to be calculated in accordance with prescribed rules.

(4) In particular, rules may include provision—

    (*a*) for the calculation of an amount representing the actual value of what is transferred,

    (*b*) for that amount to be treated as a net amount corresponding to a gross amount from which income tax at the basic rate has been deducted, and

    (*c*) for the gross amount to be taken to be the value of what is transferred.

Commentary—*Simon's Taxes* **A3.204, E5.802, E5.803, E5.804**.

Regulations—Income Tax (Entertainers and Sportsmen) (Amendment) Regulations, SI 2012/1359.

968 Treatment of sums representing income tax

(1) This section applies if, in accordance with section 966(3) or (4), a person pays a sum to the Commissioners for Her Majesty's Revenue and Customs.

(2) The sum is treated as paid on account of a liability of another person to income tax or corporation tax.

(3) The liability and the other person are to be found in accordance with prescribed rules.

(4) If the sum exceeds the liability concerned, the Commissioners must pay so much of the sum as is appropriate to the other person.

(5) If no liability is found, the Commissioners must pay the sum to the recipient of the relevant payment or transfer.

(6) The relevant payment or transfer is the payment or transfer—

    (*a*) to which section 966 applies, and

    (*b*) which gave rise to the payment of the sum.

(7) A reference to a sum in this section does not include anything representing interest.

Commentary—*Simon's Taxes* **E5.808**.

Derivation—TA 1988 ss 555(8)–(11).

969 Regulations

(1) The Treasury may by regulations—

    (*a*) make provision enabling the Commissioners for Her Majesty's Revenue and Customs to serve notices requiring persons who make payments or transfers to which section 966 applies to give them prescribed information in respect of such payments or transfers,

(b) make provision requiring persons who make payments or transfers to which section 966 applies to make, at prescribed times and for prescribed periods, returns to the Commissioners containing prescribed information about payments or transfers and the income tax for which those persons are accountable in respect of them,

(c) make provision for the collection and recovery of such income tax, for assessments and claims to be made in respect of it, and for the payment of interest on it, and

(d) adapt, or modify the effect of, any enactment relating to income tax for the purpose of making any provision mentioned in paragraphs (a) to (c).

(2) The Treasury may also by regulations make provision generally for giving effect to this section and sections 966 to 968 (including different provision for different cases or descriptions of case).

Commentary—*Simon's Taxes* **E5.801**.

Derivation—TA 1988 ss 555(7), 558(5).

Regulations—Income Tax (Entertainers and Sportsmen) (Amendment) Regulations, SI 2012/1359.

970 Supplementary

(1) For the purposes of the Tax Acts a payment to which section 966 applies is treated as if it were not reduced by the deduction of a sum representing income tax under that section.

(2) An officer of Revenue and Customs may disclose, to any person who appears to the officer to have an interest in the matter, information relevant to determining whether section 966 applies to a payment or transfer.

(3) An officer is not precluded from doing so by any obligation as to secrecy imposed by statute or otherwise.

(4) In this section and sections 966 to 969—

(a) references to a payment include references to a payment by way of loan of money, and

(b) references to a transfer do not include references to a transfer of money but, subject to that, include references to—

(i) a temporary transfer (as by way of loan), and

(ii) a transfer of a right (whether or not a right to receive money).

(5) In sections 966 to 969 "prescribed" means prescribed by regulations made by the Treasury.

Commentary—*Simon's Taxes* **E5.802, E5.803, E5.809**.

Regulations—London Olympic Games and Paralympic Games Tax Regulations, SI 2010/2913.

Income Tax (Entertainers and Sportsmen) (Amendment) Regulations, SI 2012/1359.

Income Tax (Removal of Ordinary Residence) Regulations, SI 2013/605.

Non-resident landlords

971 Income tax due in respect of income of non-resident landlords

(1) The Commissioners for Her Majesty's Revenue and Customs may by regulations make provision for—

(a) the collection, from non-resident landlord representatives of a prescribed description, of prescribed amounts of income tax in respect of non-resident landlord income, and

(b) the assessment and recovery of the income tax on or from such persons.

(2) "Non-resident landlord income" means income of a person whose usual place of abode is outside the United Kingdom ("the non-resident") and which is or may become [chargeable as the profits of a UK property business under Chapter 3 of Part 3 of ITTOIA 2005 or Chapter 3 of Part 4 of CTA 2009.][1]

(3) "Non-resident landlord representative" means—

(a) a person by whom any sums are payable to the non-resident which are to be treated as receipts of a [UK property business (within the meaning of Chapter 2 of Part 3 of ITTOIA 2005 or Chapter 2 of Part 4 of CTA 2009)][1] carried on by the non-resident, or

(b) a person who acts on behalf of the non-resident in connection with the management or administration of any such business.

(4) A non-resident landlord representative who must pay prescribed amounts of income tax to the Commissioners for Her Majesty's Revenue and Customs under regulations under this section is entitled—

(a) to be indemnified by the non-resident for all such payments, and

(b) to retain out of any sums otherwise due from the representative to the non-resident, or received by the representative on behalf of the non-resident, sums representing income tax sufficient for meeting any liabilities under the regulations to make such payments.

(5) Subsection (4)(b) applies whether the liability is one which the representative has discharged or to which the representative is subject.

Commentary—*Simon's Taxes* **A4.135, B6.217**.

Regulations—Taxation of Income from Land (Non-residents) (Amendment) Regulations, SI 2020/151.

Amendments—[1] In sub-ss (2), (3) words substituted by CTA 2009 s 1322, Sch 1 paras 699, 716. CTA 2009 applies for accounting periods ending on or after 1 April 2009 (for corporation tax purposes) and for tax years 2009–10 onwards (for income and capital gains tax purposes).

972 Regulations under section 971

(1) Regulations under section 971 may, in particular, include all or any of the following provisions—

- (a) provision for the amount of any income tax in respect of non-resident landlord income, which is to be paid to the Commissioners for Her Majesty's Revenue and Customs, to be calculated by reference to prescribed factors,
- (b) provision for the determination in accordance with the regulations of the period for which, the circumstances in which and the times at which any payments are to be made to the Commissioners,
- (c) provision for requiring the payment of interest on amounts which are not paid to the Commissioners at the times required under the regulations,
- (d) provision as to the certificates to be given in prescribed circumstances to the non-resident by a non-resident landlord representative, and as to the particulars to be included in any such certificate,
- (e) provision for the making of repayments of income tax to the non-resident and for such repayments to be made in prescribed cases to non-resident landlord representatives,
- (f) provision for the payment of interest by the Commissioners on sums repaid under the regulations,
- (g) provision for the rights and obligations arising under the regulations to depend on the giving of such notices and the making of such claims and determinations as may be prescribed,
- (h) provision for the making and determination of applications for requirements of the regulations not to apply in certain cases, and for the variation or revocation, in prescribed cases, of the determinations made on such applications,
- (i) provision for appeals with respect to questions arising under the regulations,
- (j) provision requiring non-resident landlord representatives within section 971(3)(b) who are of a prescribed description to register with the Commissioners,
- (k) provision requiring persons registered with the Commissioners and other non-resident landlord representatives of a prescribed description to make returns and supply prescribed information to the Commissioners and to make available prescribed books, documents and other records for inspection on behalf of the Commissioners,
- (l) provision for the partnership, as such, to be treated as the non-resident landlord representative if a liability to make a payment under the regulations arises from amounts payable or things done in the course of a business carried on by persons in partnership, and
- (m) provision which, in relation to payments of income tax to be made by virtue of section 971 or to sums retained in respect of such payments, applies (with or without modifications) any enactment or subordinate legislation having effect apart from section 971 with respect to cases in which tax is or is treated as deducted from any income.

(2) Interest required to be paid by regulations under section 971 is to be paid without deduction of a sum representing income tax and is not to be taken into account in calculating any income, profits or losses for any tax purposes.

(3) Regulations under section 971 may—

- (a) make different provision for different cases, and
- (b) contain incidental, supplemental, consequential and transitional provision and savings.

(4) Provision made by virtue of subsection (3)(b) may, in particular, in connection with any other provision made by regulations under section 971, modify the operation in any case of section 59A of TMA 1970 (payments on account of income tax).

(5) In this section and section 971 "prescribed" means prescribed by, or determined by an officer of Revenue and Customs in accordance with, regulations made by the Commissioners for Her Majesty's Revenue and Customs under section 971.

(6) See [section 548(7) of CTA 2010,][1] which prevents certain distributions of Real Estate Investment Trusts being non-resident landlord income for the purposes of regulations under section 971.

Commentary—*Simon's Taxes* **B6.217**.

Amendments—[1] In sub-s (6) words substituted by CTA 2010 s 1177, Sch 1 para 559. CTA 2010 has effect for corporation tax purposes for accounting periods ending on or after 1 April 2010, and for income and capital gains tax purposes for the tax year 2010–11 and subsequent tax years.

Real Estate Investment Trusts

973 Income tax due in respect of distributions

(1) The Treasury may make regulations providing for the assessment, collection and recovery of income tax where—

- (a) a distribution to which subsection (2) or (3) applies is made, and
- (b) tax is or may become chargeable in respect of the distribution (whether by virtue of [section 548(5) or (6) of CTA 2010][1] (distributions: liability to tax) or otherwise).

(2) This subsection applies to a distribution if—

- (a) it is made by a [company UK REIT][1], and
- (b) it is a distribution of profits or gains (or of both) of [the company's property rental business][1].

(3) This subsection applies to a distribution if—

    (a) it is made by the principal company of a [group UK REIT][1], and

    [(b) it is a distribution of amounts shown in the financial statement under section 532(2)(a) of CTA 2010 (statement of group's property rental business) as—

        (i) profits or gains (or both) of UK members of the group, or

        (ii) profits or gains (or both) of UK property rental business of non-UK members of the group.][1]

[(3A) In this section, section 974 and any regulations under this section, "distribution" is to be read in accordance with section 554A of CTA 2010 (meaning of "distribution").

(3B) Section 599A of CTA 2010 (amount of distribution consisting of share capital issued in lieu of cash dividend) applies for the purposes of this section, section 974 and any regulations under this section as it applies for the purposes of Part 12 of that Act (Real Estate Investment Trusts).][2]

[(4) In this section—

    "company UK REIT" and "group UK REIT" have the same meaning as in Part 12 of CTA 2010 (see sections 523(5) and 524(5) of that Act),

    "group" and "principal company" have the same meaning as in Part 12 of CTA 2010 (see section 606 of that Act), and

    "property rental business" and "UK property rental business" have the same meaning as in Part 12 of CTA 2010 (see sections 519 and 520 of that Act).][1]

(5) References in this section to a [UK or non-UK company are to be read in accordance with Part 12 of CTA 2010 (see section 521 of that Act).][1].

(6) In this section "gains" includes chargeable gains.

[(7) In relation to references to profits of property rental business, see section 549A of CTA 2010.][3]

Commentary—*Simon's Taxes* A3.204, D7.1128.

HMRC Manuals—Guidance on Real Estate Investment Trusts Manual GREIT09160 (manufactured payments: deduction of tax).

Regulations—Authorised Investment Funds (Tax) (Amendment) Regulations, SI 2009/2036.

Amendments—[1] In sub-ss (1)(b), (2), (3)(a), (5), words substituted, and sub-ss (3)(b), (4) substituted by CTA 2010 s 1177, Sch 1 para 560. CTA 2010 has effect for corporation tax purposes for accounting periods ending on or after 1 April 2010, and for income and capital gains tax purposes for the tax year 2010–11 and subsequent tax years.

[2] Sub-ss (3A), (3B) inserted by F(No 3)A 2010 s 10, Sch 4 para 2 with effect in relation to distributions made on or after 16 December 2010.

[3] Sub-s (7) inserted by FA 2013 s 39, Sch 19 para 12 with effect from 17 July 2013.

974 Regulations under section 973

(1) Regulations under section 973 may, in particular—

    (a) require a company to deduct sums representing income tax at the basic rate before payment of distributions,

    (b) specify classes of shareholder to whom distributions may be made without deduction of such sums,

    (c) make provision about the calculation of the sums to be deducted by a company,

    (d) require a company to account for income tax equal to the sums deducted,

    (e) apply an enactment (with or without modification) in respect of cases where a sum representing income tax is deducted or treated as deducted from income,

    (f) specify the time at which a distribution is to be treated as made by a company,

    (g) specify periods in respect of which payments of income tax are to be made,

    (h) specify times at which payments of income tax are to be made,

    (i) make provision about the making of claims and determinations in respect of over-payment or under-payment (which may include provision for appeals),

    (j) include provision requiring the payment of interest in respect of late payments of income tax (which may—

        (i) provide for payment without deduction of sums representing income tax,

        (ii) allow interest paid as a deduction from profits of the company's [property rental business][1]),

    (k) require a company to provide a shareholder with a statement in writing containing specified information,

    (l) make provision about the repayment to a shareholder of sums deducted and paid to the Commissioners for Her Majesty's Revenue and Customs in respect of income tax,

    (m) make provision for the payment of interest in respect of repayments under paragraph (l),

    (n) require notices to be given by or to a company,

    (o) require a company to make returns, and

    (p) require a company to make records available to the Commissioners for Her Majesty's Revenue and Customs for inspection.

(2) A reference in subsection (1) to a distribution in respect of profits of [property rental business][1] includes a distribution made after [the company or group (as the case may be) has ceased to be a UK REIT][1].

(3) A distribution which is treated as having been made by virtue of [section 530(6) of CTA 2010][1] is also to be treated as having been made for the purposes of regulations under section 973.

(4) Regulations under section 973—
  (*a*) may make provision which applies generally or only in specified cases or circumstances,
  (*b*) may make different provision for different cases or circumstances, and
  (*c*) may contain incidental, supplemental, consequential and transitional provision and savings.

(5) In subsections (1) and (2), so far as they apply to cases within section 973(1)(*a*), "profits" includes gains (including chargeable gains).

[(6) In this section—
  "property rental business" has the same meaning as in Part 12 of CTA 2010 (see section 519 of that Act), and
  "UK REIT" has the same meaning as in Part 12 of CTA 2010 (see section 518(4) of that Act).][1]

[(7) In relation to references to profits of property rental business, see section 549A of CTA 2010.][2]

Commentary—*Simon's Taxes* **D7.1128**.
HMRC Manuals—Guidance on Real Estate Investment Trusts Manual GREIT09160 (manufactured payments: deduction of tax).
Regulations—Authorised Investment Funds (Tax) (Amendment) Regulations, SI 2009/2036.
Amendments—[1] In sub-ss (1)(*j*)(ii), (2), (3) words substituted, and sub-s (6) substituted by CTA 2010 s 1177, Sch 1 para 561. CTA 2010 has effect for corporation tax purposes for accounting periods ending on or after 1 April 2010, and for income and capital gains tax purposes for the tax year 2010–11 and subsequent tax years.
[2] Sub-s (7) inserted by FA 2013 s 39, Sch 19 para 12 with effect from 17 July 2013.

CHAPTER 19

GENERAL

Supplementary

975 Statements about deduction of income tax
(1) Subsection (2) applies if[—
  (*a*)] a person makes a payment from which a sum representing income tax must be deducted under any provision of Chapters 2 to 7 or under section 919 or 928[, and
  (*b*) the person is not under a duty to provide a statement under section 975A][1].

(2) If the recipient requests it in writing, the person must provide the recipient with a statement showing—
  (*a*) the gross amount of the payment,
  (*b*) the amount of the sum deducted, and
  (*c*) the actual amount paid.

(3) Subsection (4) applies if the trustees of an unauthorised unit trust are treated as making a deemed payment to a unit holder ("U").[2]

(4) If U requests it in writing, the trustees must provide U with a statement showing—
  (*a*) the gross amount of the payment,
  (*b*) the amount of the deemed deduction from the payment, and
  (*c*) the amount of the payment after the deemed deduction.[2]

(5) A statement under this section must be in writing.

(6) The duty to comply with a request under subsection (2) . . . [2] is enforceable by the recipient . . . [2].

(7) In this section "deemed deduction", "deemed payment" and "the gross amount" have the same meanings as in Chapter 13 (see section 941(6)).[2]

Commentary—*Simon's Taxes* **A4.472**.
HMRC Manuals—Company Taxation Manual CTM47540 (taxation of investors within the charge to income tax). CTM75090 (certificates).
Savings and Investment Manual, SAIM6120 (collective investment schemes: tax statements).
SAIM9117 (certificate of tax deducted).
Amendments—[1] In sub-s (1), para (*a*) designated as such, and para (*b*) and preceding word inserted, by FA 2013 s 27, Sch 11 para 9 with effect in relation to any payment of interest made on or after 17 July 2013.
[2] Sub-ss (3), (4), (7) repealed, and in sub-s (6) words "or (4)" and "or U (as the case may be)" repealed, by the Unauthorised Unit Trusts (Tax) Regulations, SI 2013/2819 reg 37(1), (17) with effect from 6 April 2014. Note that an unauthorised unit trust is not a non-exempt unauthorised unit trust, and these amendments do not apply in relation to the trust, if at all times in the period beginning with 24 May 2012 and ending with 5 April 2014 it had at least one unit holder which was, and at least one unit holder which was not, an eligible investor (ie a mixed unauthorised unit trust); this ceases to apply in relation to the trust if subsequently it no longer has any unit holders which are eligible investors (SI 2013/2819 reg 32).

[975A Statements about certain payments of interest
(1) Subsection (2) applies if a person makes a payment of interest of which the whole or part is in the form of goods or services or a voucher.

(2) The person must provide the recipient of the payment with a statement showing—
  (*a*) the gross amount of the payment,
  (*b*) the amount of the sum deducted under any provision of Chapters 2 to 7 or under section 919 or 928 (if any),
  (*c*) the actual amount paid, and
  (*d*) the date on which the payment was made.

(3) The amounts mentioned in paragraphs (*a*) to (*c*) of subsection (2) are to be calculated in accordance with section 370A of ITTOIA 2005.

(4) Subsection (5) applies where a person—

    (*a*) is treated as making a payment of an amount of interest ("the deemed interest") by virtue of section 413 of CTA 2009 or section 380 of ITTOIA 2005 (funding bonds), and

    (*b*) is under a duty under section 939(2) to retain funding bonds equal in value to income tax on the deemed interest at the basic rate.

(5) The person must provide the recipient of the funding bonds with a statement showing—

    (*a*) the gross amount of the deemed interest,

    (*b*) the sum representing income tax which the person is treated under section 939(3) as having deducted by retaining funding bonds,

    (*c*) the amount of the deemed interest after the deduction of that sum, and

    (*d*) the date on which the deemed interest is treated as being paid.

(6) The amount of the deemed interest is to be calculated in accordance with section 413 of CTA 2009 or section 380 of ITTOIA 2005, as the case may require.

(7) A statement under this section must be provided in writing to the recipient on the date that the payment is made or (as the case may be) the date that the deemed interest is treated as being paid.

(8) The duty to comply with this section is enforceable by the recipient.

(9) In this section—

    (*a*) references to a voucher are to a voucher, stamp or similar document or token which is capable of being exchanged for money, goods or services, and

    (*b*) "funding bonds" has the same meaning as in Chapter 12 (see section 939(6)).][1]

Commentary—*Simon's Taxes* **A4.472**.

HMRC Manuals—Savings and Investment Manual SAIM9117 (certificate of tax deducted).

Amendments—[1] This section inserted by FA 2013 s 27, Sch 11 para 10 with effect in relation to any payment of interest made on or after 17 July 2013.

976 Arrangements for payments of interest less tax or at specified net rate

(1) This section applies if—

    (*a*) provision is made for the payment of interest, and

    (*b*) the interest is payable without deduction of a sum representing income tax.

(2) It applies—

    (*a*) whenever the provision was made, and

    (*b*) whether it was made orally or in writing.

(3) If the provision is for the payment of interest "less tax" (or uses words to similar effect) it is to be read as if the words "less tax" (or the equivalent words) were not included.

(4) Subsection (5) applies if the provision is (however worded)—

    (*a*) for the payment of interest to which subsection (6) applies, and

    (*b*) for that interest to be paid at such a rate ("the gross rate") that the amount of interest payable at that rate is, after deduction of a sum representing income tax, equal to the amount of interest payable at a specified rate ("the net rate").

(5) In that case the provision is to be read as if it were for the payment of interest at the gross rate.

(6) This subsection applies to—

    (*a*) interest on which the recipient is chargeable to income tax, which falls within Chapter 2 of Part 4 of ITTOIA 2005 but which is not relevant foreign income, or

    [(*b*) interest which is required to be brought into account under Part 5 of CTA 2009 (loan relationships) as a non-trading credit of the recipient.][1]

Commentary—*Simon's Taxes* **A4.421, A4.471**.

Amendments—[1] Sub-s (6)(*b*) substituted by CTA 2009 s 1322, Sch 1 paras 699, 717. CTA 2009 applies for accounting periods ending on or after 1 April 2009 (for corporation tax purposes) and for tax years 2009–10 onwards (for income and capital gains tax purposes).

977 Payments to companies

(1) The provisions of this Part relating to the deduction from payments of sums representing income tax are not affected by the fact that the recipient is a company not chargeable to income tax on the payment.

(2) References in subsection (1) to payments received by a company—

    (*a*) include payments received by another person on behalf of or in trust for the company, but

    (*b*) do not include payments received by the company on behalf of or in trust for another person.

(3) For further provision about payments received by companies, see—

    (*a*) sections 7(2) and 11(3) of ICTA (set-off of income tax deducted at source against liability to corporation tax), and

    (*b*) section 952 (set-off of income tax suffered against income tax payable under Chapter 15).

978 Application to public departments

(1) This Part applies in relation to payments made by public offices and departments of the Crown except as mentioned in subsection (2).

(2) This Part does not apply to payments made by public offices and departments of—

    (a) any country mentioned in Schedule 3 to the British Nationality Act 1981 (c 61) (which contains a list of Commonwealth countries) or the Republic of Ireland, or

    (b) any state or province of a country within paragraph (a).

Commentary—*Simon's Taxes* **A1.601, A4.460, E4.1134**.

Derivation—TA 1988 s 829(1), (3).

979 Designated international organisations: exceptions from duties to deduct

(1) The Treasury may by order designate for the purposes of this section any international organisation of which the United Kingdom is a member.

(2) The duty to deduct under section 874 (duty to deduct from certain payments of yearly interest) does not apply to a payment of interest made by—

    (a) an organisation designated under subsection (1), or

    (b) a partnership of which an organisation so designated is a member.

(3) None of the duties to deduct under Chapters 6, 7 (deduction from annual payments, patent royalties and other payments connected with intellectual property) and 14 (directions for duty to deduct to apply in tax avoidance cases) apply to a payment made by an organisation designated under subsection (1).

(4) The duties to deduct under sections 919(2) and 922(2) do not apply in a case where the payer of the manufactured interest or (as the case may be) the manufactured overseas dividend is an organisation designated under subsection (1).

Commentary—*Simon's Taxes* **A4.425, D1.240**.

[979A FSCS payments representing interest

(1) This section applies where a payment is made under the FSCS representing interest net of an amount equal to a sum representing income tax that would have been deducted on the payment of interest but for the circumstances giving rise to the making of payments under the FSCS.

(2) A payment of the relevant gross amount is treated as having been made under the FSCS after there has been deducted from it a sum representing income tax of that amount.

(3) That sum is accordingly taken into account under section 59B of TMA 1970 in determining the income tax payable by, or repayable to, the recipient.

(4) "The relevant gross amount" means the aggregate of the amount of the payment representing interest which is made and that sum.

(5) If the recipient requests it in writing, the scheme manager of the FSCS must provide the recipient with a statement showing—

    (a) the relevant gross amount,

    (b) the amount of the sum treated as deducted, and

    (c) the amount of the payment representing interest.

(6) The duty to comply with a request under subsection (5) is enforceable by the recipient.

(7) In this section—

    "the FSCS" means the Financial Services Compensation Scheme (established under Part 15 of the Financial Services and Markets Act 2000);

    "payment representing interest" has the same meaning as in section 380A of ITTOIA 2005.][1]

Commentary—*Simon's Taxes* **E1.410A**.

HMRC Manuals—Savings and Investment Manual SAIM2100-2110 (interest payable from the Financial Services Compensation Scheme, with examples).

Amendments—[1] This section inserted by FA 2009 s 33 with effect in relation to payments made on or after 6 October 2008.

980 Derivative contracts: exception from duties to deduct

(1) Despite the provisions of this Part, a company is not required to deduct a sum representing income tax from a payment made under a derivative contract to which this section applies.

(2) This section applies to a derivative contract if profits and losses arising from it are calculated in accordance with [Part 7 of CTA 2009][1].

Commentary—*Simon's Taxes* **D1.875, D1.892**.

Derivation—FA 2002 Sch 26 para 51.

HMRC Manuals—Corporate Finance Manual CFM72680 (deduction of tax).

Amendments—[1] In sub-s (2) words substituted by CTA 2009 s 1322, Sch 1 paras 699, 718. CTA 2009 applies for accounting periods ending on or after 1 April 2009 (for corporation tax purposes) and for tax years 2009–10 onwards (for income and capital gains tax purposes).

981 Foreign currency securities etc: exception from duties to deduct

Despite the provisions of this Part there is no duty to deduct a sum representing income tax from a payment of interest within section 755(1) of ITTOIA 2005 (interest on foreign currency securities etc owned by non-UK residents).

[981A Offshore receipts in respect of intangible property: exception from duties to deduct

Despite the provisions of this Part there is no duty to deduct a sum representing income tax from a payment charged to income tax under Chapter 2A of Part 5 of ITTOIA 2005 (offshore receipts in respect of intangible property).][1]

Amendments—[1]   This section inserted by Income Tax (Trading and Other Income) Act 2005 (Amendments to Chapter 2A of Part 5) Regulations, SI 2019/1452 reg 15 with effect for the tax year 2019–20 and subsequent tax years.

982 Income tax is calculated by reference to gross amounts

If any provision of this Part requires the deduction from a payment of a sum representing income tax at a specified rate, the rate is to be applied to the gross payment, that is to the payment before deduction of a sum representing income tax under this Part.

Interpretation

983 Meaning of "deposit"

In this Chapter "deposit" means a sum of money paid on terms which mean that it will be repaid (with or without interest)—

  (a) on demand, or

  (b) at a time or in circumstances agreed by or on behalf of the person who pays it and the person who receives it.

984 Meaning of "financial instrument"

(1) In this Part "financial instrument" includes—

  (a) any money,

  (b) any shares or securities,

  (c) an option, future or contract for differences if its underlying subject-matter is (or is primarily) one or more financial instruments, and

  (d) an instrument the underlying subject-matter of which is (or is primarily) creditworthiness.

(2) For the purposes of subsection (1) if the effect of an instrument depends on an index or factor, the "underlying" subject-matter of the instrument is the matter by reference to which the index or factor is determined.

Commentary—*Simon's Taxes* **D1.893**.
Derivation—TA 1988 s 349(5), (6).

985 Meaning of "qualifying certificate of deposit"

(1) In this Part "qualifying certificate of deposit" means a certificate of deposit under which—

  (a) the amount payable is at least £50,000, exclusive of interest, and

  (b) that amount is payable at a specified time within 5 years beginning with the date on which the deposit is made.

(2) If an amount is denominated in a foreign currency, subsection (1)(a) has effect as if it referred to an amount which is at least the equivalent in that currency of £50,000 at the time the deposit is made.

(3) For the meaning of "certificate of deposit", see section 1019.

986 Meaning of "qualifying uncertificated eligible debt security unit"

(1) In this Part "qualifying uncertificated eligible debt security unit" means an uncertificated eligible debt security unit under which—

  (a) the amount payable is at least £50,000, exclusive of interest, and

  (b) that amount is payable at a specified time within 5 years beginning with the date on which the deposit is made.

(2) If an amount is denominated in a foreign currency, subsection (1)(a) has effect as if it referred to an amount which is at least the equivalent in that currency of £50,000 at the time the deposit is made.

(3) In this section "uncertificated eligible debt security unit" means an uncertificated unit of an eligible debt security where the issue of the unit corresponds, in accordance with the current terms of issue of the eligible debt security, to the issue of a certificate of deposit.

(4) In subsection (3)—

  (a) "eligible debt security",

  (b) "uncertificated" (in relation to a unit), and

  (c) "unit",

have the meanings given by regulation 3(1) of the Uncertificated Securities Regulations 2001 (SI 2001/3755).

(5) For the meaning of "certificate of deposit", see section 1019.

Commentary—*Simon's Taxes* **A4.406**.

987 Meaning of "quoted Eurobond"

[(1)] [1] In this Part "quoted Eurobond" means a security, including a share (in particular any permanent interest bearing share as defined in section 117 of TCGA 1992), that—

  (a) is issued by a company,

  (b) is listed on a recognised stock exchange [or admitted to trading on a multilateral trading facility operated by an EEA-regulated recognised stock exchange][1], and

  (c) carries a right to interest.

[(2) For the purposes of this section—

  (a) a recognised stock exchange is an "EEA-regulated recognised stock exchange" if it is regulated in the European Economic Area, and (*b*) "multilateral trading facility" has the same meaning as in Article 4.1.22 of Directive 2014/65/EU of the European Parliament and of the Council of 15 May 2014 on markets in financial instruments.][1]

Commentary—*Simon's Taxes* **A1.304, D9.801.**
HMRC Manuals—International Manual INTM342160 (eurobonds).
Company Taxation Manual CTM35218 (application of the eurobond exemption).
Amendments—[1] Sub-s (1) numbered as such, in sub-s (1)(*b*), words inserted, and sub-s (2) inserted, by FA 2018 s 34(1) with effect in relation to payments made on or after 1 April 2018.
Prospective amendments—In sub-s (1)(*b*) words "a regulated" to be substituted for words "an EEA-regulated", and sub-s (2) to be substituted, by the Taxes (Amendments) (EU Exit) Regulations, SI 2019/689 reg 15(1), (11) with effect from Implementation Period completion day (see EU(WA)A 2020 Sch 5 para 1(1)). Sub-s (2) to read as follows—

"(2) For the purposes of this section—

(*a*) "regulated recognised stock exchange" means a recognised stock exchange that is regulated in the United Kingdom, the European Economic Area or Gibraltar, and

(*b*) "multilateral trading facility" means—

(i) a UK multilateral trading facility within the meaning given by Article 2.1(14A) of Regulation (EU) No 600/2014 of the European Parliament and of the Council of 15 May 2014 on markets in financial instruments,

(ii) an EU multilateral trading facility within the meaning given by Article 2.1(14B) of that Regulation, and

(iii) a multilateral system, operated by an investment firm or a market operator, which brings together multiple third-party buying and selling interests in financial instruments (in the system and in accordance with non-discretionary rules) in a way which results in a contract in accordance with Part 2 of the Financial Services (Markets in Financial Instruments) Act 2018 of Gibraltar,

and in sub-paragraph (iii) "multilateral system", "investment firm", "market operator" and "financial instrument" have the same meanings as given by Articles 2.1(11), 2.1A, 2.1(10) and 2.1(9) respectively of that Regulation."

In sub-s (2)(*b*), as inserted by SI 2019/689 above, para (iii) to be substituted, and words from "and in sub-paragraph (iii)" to the end to be repealed, by the Taxes (Amendments) (EU Exit) (No 2) Regulations, SI 2019/818 reg 6(1), (4) with effect from Implementation Period completion day, immediately after the coming into force of SI 2019/689 (which also comes into force on Implementation Period completion day (see EU(WA)A 2020 Sch 5 para 1(1)). Para (iii) to read as follows—

a Gibraltar multilateral trading facility within the meaning given by Article 26(11)(*b*)(ii) of that Regulation.".

PART 16
INCOME TAX ACTS DEFINITIONS ETC

CHAPTER 1

DEFINITIONS

988 Overview of Chapter
(1) This Chapter contains definitions which apply for the purposes of the Income Tax Acts, except where, in those Acts, the context otherwise requires.
(2) To find a definition go first to section 989, which sets out some of the definitions in full.
(3) If a definition is not set out in full in section 989, the section indicates where it is set out in full.
(4) In some cases it is stated that a definition does not apply for the purposes of specified provisions of the Income Tax Acts (see, for example, sections 990(2), 992(3) and 1007(4)).
(5) And in some cases it is stated that a definition has effect only for the purposes of specific provisions of the Income Tax Acts (see, for example, sections 991, 993, 995 and 1006).

989 The definitions
The following definitions apply for the purposes of the Income Tax Acts—
"Act" has the meaning given by section 990,
["additional rate" means the rate of income tax determined in pursuance of section 6(2),][8]
"authorised unit trust" is to be read in accordance with [sections 616 and 619 of CTA 2010][9],
"bank" is to be read in accordance with section 991,
"basic rate" means the rate of income tax determined in pursuance of section 6(2),
"basic rate limit" has the meaning given by section [10][5],
"body of persons" means any body politic, corporate or collegiate and any company, fraternity, fellowship [and][9] society of persons whether corporate or not corporate,
"building society" means a building society within the meaning of the Building Societies Act 1986 (c 53),
"capital allowance" means any allowance under CAA 2001,
"the Capital Allowances Act" means CAA 2001,
"chargeable gain" has the same meaning as in TCGA 1992,
"chargeable period" means an accounting period of a company or a tax year,

. . . [11],

"close company" [is to be read in accordance with Chapter 2 of Part 10 of CTA 2010 (see in particular section 439 of that Act)][9],

"company" has the meaning given by section 992,

"connected", in relation to two persons being connected with one another, is to be read in accordance with sections 993 and 994,

"control", in relation to the control of a body corporate or a partnership, is to be read in accordance with section 995,

["default additional rate" means the rate of income tax of that name determined pursuant to section 6C,

"default basic rate" means the rate of income tax of that name determined pursuant to section 6C,

"default higher rate" means the rate of income tax of that name determined pursuant to section 6C,][21]

"distribution" has the [meaning given by Chapters 2 to 5 of Part 23 of CTA 2010[, disregarding section 1027A of that Act][13]][9],

["dividend additional rate" means the rate of income tax specified in section 8(3),][8]

"dividend income" has the meaning given by section 19,

["dividend nil rate" means the rate of income tax specified in section 8(A1),][19]

"dividend ordinary rate" means the rate of income tax specified in section 8(1),

"dividend trust rate" means the rate of income tax specified in section 9(2),

"dividend upper rate" means the rate of income tax specified in section 8(2),

"farming" has the meaning given by section 996,

"for accounting purposes" has the meaning given by section 997(4),

"forestry" is to be read in accordance with section 996,

"generally accepted accounting practice" has the meaning given by section 997(1) and (3),

"grossing up" is to be read in accordance with section 998,

"higher rate" means the rate of income tax determined in pursuance of section 6(2),

["higher rate limit" has the meaning given by section 10,][8]

["hire-purchase agreement" is to be read in accordance with section 998A,][12]

"international accounting standards" has the meaning given by section 997(5),

"local authority" has the meaning given by section 999,

"local authority association" has the meaning given by section 1000,

"market gardening" has the meaning given by section 996,

"net income" has the meaning given by section 23 (see Step 2 in that section),

"non-UK resident" means not resident in the United Kingdom (and references to a non-UK resident or a non-UK resident person are to a person who is not resident there),

"normal self-assessment filing date", in relation to a tax year, means the 31 January following the tax year,

"notice" means notice in writing or in a form authorised (in relation to the case in question) by directions under [section 43E(1) of TMA 1970][10],

"offshore installation" has the meaning given by sections 1001 and 1002,

"oil and gas exploration and appraisal" has the meaning given by section 1003,

"ordinary share capital", in relation to a company, means all the company's issued share capital (however described), other than capital the holders of which have a right to a dividend at a fixed rate but have no other right to share in the company's profits,

["the overseas part", in relation to a split year, has the meaning given in Part 3 of Schedule 45 to FA 2013 (statutory residence test: split year treatment);][16]

"overseas property business" has the meaning given by Chapter 2 of Part 3 of ITTOIA 2005,

"period of account"—

  (a) in relation to a person, means any period for which the person draws up accounts, and

  (b) in relation to a trade, profession, vocation or other business, means any period for which the accounts of the business are drawn up,

. . . [14],

"personal representatives" in relation to a person who has died, means—

  (a) in the United Kingdom, persons responsible for administering the estate of the deceased, and

  (b) in a territory outside the United Kingdom, those persons having functions under its law equivalent to those of administering the estate of the deceased,

"profits or gains" does not include chargeable gains,

"property investment LLP" has the meaning given by section 1004,

. . . [7]

"qualifying policy" means a policy of insurance which is a qualifying policy for the purposes of Chapter 1 of Part 7 of ICTA,

"recognised stock exchange" has the meaning given by section 1005, "registered pension scheme" has the meaning given by section 150(2) of FA 2004,

"relevant foreign income" has the meaning given by section 830(1) to (3) of ITTOIA 2005 but also includes, for any purpose mentioned in any provision listed in section 830(4) of that Act, income treated as relevant foreign income for that purpose by that provision,

"research and development" is to be read in accordance with section 1006,

"retail prices index" means—

    (*a*) the general index of retail prices (for all items) published by the [Statistics Board][2], or

    (*b*) if that index is not published for a relevant month, any substituted index or index figures published by [the Board][2],

["savings additional rate" means the rate of income tax of that name determined pursuant to section 7A,][21]

["savings allowance" has the meaning given by section 12B,][18]

["savings basic rate" means the rate of income tax of that name determined pursuant to section 7A,

"savings higher rate" means the rate of income tax of that name determined pursuant to section 7A,][21]

"savings income" has the meaning given by section 18,

. . .[3]

. . .[6]

["savings nil rate" means the rate of income tax specified in section 7(2),][18]

"scheme administrator", in relation to a pension scheme, has the meaning given by section 270 of FA 2004 (but see also sections 271 to 274 of that Act),

[. . .[20]

"Scottish basic rate" [in relation to a tax year, means the Scottish basic rate set by a Scottish rate resolution for that year][20],

. . .[20]

["Scottish intermediate rate", in relation to a tax year, means any Scottish rate for that year which is named "intermediate" by the Scottish rate resolution setting it,][22]

["Scottish rate" in relation to a tax year, means a rate set by a Scottish rate resolution for that year,

""Scottish rate resolution" means a resolution of the Scottish Parliament under section 80C of the Scotland Act 1998,][20]

"Scottish taxpayer" has the same meaning as in Chapter 2 of Part 4A of the Scotland Act 1998,][17]

"settled property" (together with references to property comprised in a settlement) is to be read in accordance with section 466,

"settlor" is to be read in accordance with sections 467 to 473,

["shares, stock or other securities included in the official UK list" is to be read in accordance with section 1005,

"shares, stock or other securities listed on a recognised stock exchange" is to be read in accordance with section 1005,][1]

["split year", in relation to an individual, means a tax year that, as respects that individual, is a split year within the meaning of Part 3 of Schedule 45 to FA 2013 (statutory residence test: split year treatment);][16]

["starting rate for savings" [means the rate of income tax specified in section 7(1)][18],

"starting rate limit for savings" has the meaning given by section 12,][3]

"stepchild", in relation to a civil partner, is to be read in accordance with section 246 of the Civil Partnership Act 2004 (c 33),

"51% subsidiary", in relation to bodies corporate, has the same meaning as in the Corporation Tax Acts (see [Chapter 3 of Part 24 of CTA 2010][9]),

"75% subsidiary", in relation to bodies corporate, has the same meaning as in the Corporation Tax Acts (see [Chapter 3 of Part 24 of CTA 2010][9]),

["tax", if neither income tax nor corporation tax is specified, means either of those taxes,][9]

. . .[7]

"tax year" has the meaning given by section 4(2),

"the tax year 2007-08" (and any corresponding expression in which two years are similarly mentioned) has the meaning given by section 4(4),

"total income" has the meaning given by section 23 (see Step 1 in that section and also section 31),

["trade of dealing in or developing UK land", in relation to a non-UK resident person, has the meaning given by section 6B of ITTOIA 2005,][11]

"trade" includes any venture in the nature of trade,

["tribunal" means the First-tier Tribunal or, where determined by or under Tribunal Procedure Rules, the Upper Tribunal,][5]

"trust rate" means the rate of income tax specified in section 9(1),

"UK generally accepted accounting practice" has the meaning given by section 997(2),

["the UK part", in relation to a split year, has the meaning given in Part 3 of Schedule 45 to FA 2013 (statutory residence test: split year treatment);][16]

"UK property business" has the meaning given by Chapter 2 of Part 3 of ITTOIA 2005,

"UK resident" means resident in the United Kingdom (and references to a UK resident or a UK resident person are to a person who is resident there),

"umbrella scheme" is to be read in accordance with [section 619 of CTA 2010][9],

"unauthorised unit trust" means a unit trust scheme which is neither an authorised unit trust nor an umbrella scheme,

"unit holder" is to be read in accordance with [sections 616 and 619 of CTA 2010][9],

"unit trust scheme" has the meaning given by section 1007,

"venture capital trust" and "VCT" have the same meaning as in Part 6 (see section 259(1)),

["Welsh additional rate" means the rate of income tax of that name calculated in accordance with section 6B,

["Welsh basic rate" means the rate of income tax of that name calculated in accordance with section 6B,]

["Welsh higher rate" means the rate of income tax of that name calculated in accordance with section 6B,]

["Welsh taxpayer" has the same meaning as in Chapter 2 of Part 4A of the Government of Wales Act 2006][25]

"woodlands" has the meaning given by section 996,

"year of assessment" means a tax year, and

"the year 1988-1989" means the tax year 1988-1989 (and any corresponding expression in which two years are similarly mentioned is to be read in the same way).

Commentary—*Simon's Taxes* **A1.152, A1.153, A1.154, A1.155, B1.401.**

HMRC Manuals—Business Income Manual BIM20060 (definition of trade).

Amendments—[1]   Definitions of "shares, stock or other securities included in the official UK list" and "shares, stock or other securities listed on a recognised stock exchange" inserted by FA 2007 s 109, Sch 26 para 12(1), (12) with effect from 19 July 2007.

[2]   Words in definition of "retail prices index" substituted by the Statistics and Registration Service Act 2007 s 60(1), Sch 3 para 16 with effect from 1 April 2008: SI 2008/839, art 2.

[3]   Words in definition of "basic rate limit" substituted, definition of "savings rate" repealed, and definitions of "starting rate" and "starting rate limit" substituted, by FA 2008 s 5, Sch 1 paras 1, 33 with effect for the tax year 2008–09 and subsequent tax years.

[5]   Definition of "tribunal" inserted by the Transfer of Tribunal Functions and Revenue and Customs Appeals Order, SI 2009/56 art 3, Sch 1 para 462 with effect from 1 April 2009.

[6]   Definition of "Schedule A business" repealed by CTA 2009 ss 1322, 1326, Sch 1 paras 699, 719, Sch 3 Part 1. CTA 2009 applies for accounting periods ending on or after 1 April 2009 (for corporation tax purposes) and for tax years 2009–10 onwards (for income and capital gains tax purposes).

[7]   Definitions of "qualifying distribution" and "tax credit" repealed by FA 2016 s 5, Sch 1 para 63(1), (16) with effect in relation to dividends paid or arising (or treated as paid), and other distributions made (or treated as made), in the tax year 2016–17 or at any later time.

[8]   Definitions of "additional rate", "dividend additional rate" and "higher rate limit" inserted by FA 2009 s 6, Sch 2 paras 1, 8 with effect for the tax year 2010–11 and subsequent tax years.

[9]   Definitions amended, definition of "tax" substituted by CTA 2010 s 1177, Sch 1 para 562. CTA 2010 has effect for corporation tax purposes for accounting periods ending on or after 1 April 2010, and for income and capital gains tax purposes for the tax year 2010–11 and subsequent tax years.

[10]   In the definition of "notice" words substituted for words "section 118 of FA 1998" by TIOPA 2010 s 371, Sch 7 paras 91, 92. TIOPA 2010 has effect for corporation tax purposes for accounting periods ending on or after 1 April 2010, for income and capital gains tax purposes for the tax year 2010–11 and subsequent tax years, and for petroleum revenue tax purposes for chargeable periods beginning on or after 1 July 2010.

[11]   Definition of "trade of dealing in or developing UK land" inserted by FA 2016 s 78(5) with effect in relation to disposals on or after 5 July 2016 (FA 2016 s 82(1)), subject to transitional provisions relating to disposals to associated persons on or after 16 March 2016 and before 5 Jluy 2016 (FA 2016 s 82(4)–(15)).

F(No 2)A 2017 s 39 provides that this amendment has effect (so far as it would not otherwise have effect) in relation to amounts that are recognised in GAAP accounts drawn up for any period of account beginning on or after 8 March 2017 or, in the case of a straddling period, amounts that would be recognised in GAAP accounts drawn up for a period of account beginning on 8 March 2017 and ending when the straddling period ends. "Straddling period" means a period of account beginning before 8 March 2017 and ending on or after that date.

[12]   Definition of "hire-purchase agreement" inserted by TIOPA 2010 s 501, Sch 8 paras 256, 258. TIOPA 2010 has effect for corporation tax purposes for accounting periods ending on or after 1 April 2010, for income and capital gains tax purposes for the tax year 2010–11 and subsequent tax years, and for petroleum revenue tax purposes for chargeable periods beginning on or after 1 July 2010.

[13]   In definition of "distribution" words inserted by F(No 3)A 2010 s 9, Sch 3 para 2 with effect in relation to distributions made on or after 1 July 2009. Note that if a company so elects, F(No 3)A 2010 Sch 3 has effect in relation to a relevant distribution (a distribution made before 22 June 2010) received by the company as if the amendments made by paras 1–4 were of no effect, and paras 5(2) and 6 were of no effect. Such an election has effect only in relation to such distributions as are specified in the election (F(No 3)A 2010 Sch 3 para 7).

[14]   Definition of "permanent establishment" repealed by F(No 3)A 2010 s 5, Sch 2 para 3(1), (2) with effect in relation to shares or securities issued on or after 6 April 2011 (by virtue of SI 2011/662 art 2).

[15]   Definition of "charity" repealed by FA 2010 s 30, Sch 6 para 23(1), (6). This repeal, so far as it applies for purposes other than those of ITA 2007 Part 8 Chapter 2, comes into force for the tax year 2012–13 and subsequent tax years (SI 2012/736 art 18).

[16]   Definitions of "the overseas part", "split year" and "the UK part" inserted by FA 2013 s 218, Sch 45 para 107 with effect in calculating an individual's tax liability to income tax or capital gains tax for the tax year 2013–14 or any subsequent tax year, subject to transitional provisions and savings in FA 2013 Sch 45 paras 154–158.

[17]   Definitions of "Scottish additional rate", "Scottish basic rate" "Scottish higher rate" and "Scottish taxpayer" inserted by FA 2014 s 296, Sch 38 paras 1, 10(*b*) with effect in relation to the tax year 2016–17 (the tax year appointed by the Treasury under the Scotland Act 2012 s 25(5) by virtue of SI 2015/2000) and subsequent tax years.

[18]   Definitions of "savings allowance" and "savings nil rate" inserted, and in definition of "starting rate of savings" words substituted, by FA 2016 s 4(1), (11) with effect in relation to the tax year 2016–17 and subsequent tax years.

[19]   Definition of "dividend nil rate" inserted by FA 2016 s 5(1), (8) with effect in relation to the tax year 2016–17 and subsequent tax years.

[20]   Definitions of "Scottish additional rate" and "Scottish higher rate" repealed, in definition of "Scottish basic rate", words substituted, and definitions of "Scottish rate", "Scottish rate resolution" inserted, by the Scotland Act 2016 s 14(1), (13) with effect in relation to the tax year 2017–18 (as appointed under the Scotland Act 2016 s 13(15)) and subsequent years by virtue of SI 2016/1161 reg 3.

[21]   Definitions of "default additional rate", "default basic rate", "default higher rate", "savings additional rate", "savings basic rate" and "savings higher rate" inserted by FA 2016 s 6(1), (21) with effect in relation to the tax year 2017–18 (as appointed under the Scotland Act 2016 s 13(15)) and subsequent years by virtue of SI 2016/1161 reg 3, subject to transitional provisions (see FA 2016 s 6(24)–(30)). The Agreement between the Scottish Government and the UK Government on the Scottish Government's fiscal framework confirms that full devolution of income tax rates and thresholds for non-savings and non-dividend income will commence in April 2017.

[22]   Definition of "Scottish intermediate rate" inserted by the Scottish Rates of Income Tax (Consequential Amendments) Order, SI 2018/459 art 6(1), (8) with effect for the tax year commencing on 6 April 2018 and subsequent tax years.

[23]   Definitions of "Welsh additional rate", "Welsh basic rate", "Welsh higher rate", and "Welsh taxpayer" inserted by the Wales Act 2014 s 9(1), (10). Wales Act 2014 s 9 comes into force on 24 July 2018 and has effect in relation to the tax year 2019–20 (by virtue of SI 2018/892 arts 3, 5, 6). 2019–20 is appointed as the first tax year in relation to which a Welsh rate resolution may be made by the National Assembly for Wales under GOWA 2006 s 116D (SI 2018/892 art 6).

Prospective amendments—Definition of "qualifying policy" to be substituted by FA 2012 s 227, Sch 39 para 28(2) with effect from a date to be appointed. Definition as substituted to read—

> "'qualifying policy' is to be read in accordance with Schedule 15 to ICTA,".

990 Meaning of "Act"

(1) In the Income Tax Acts "Act" includes Northern Ireland legislation.

(2) This section does not apply for the purposes of—

    (*a*) this Act (see instead section 1018), or

    (*b*) ITTOIA 2005 (see instead sections 879 and 880 of that Act).

991 Meaning of "bank"

(1) This section has effect for the purposes of the provisions of the Income Tax Acts which apply this section.

(2) "Bank" means—

    (*a*) the Bank of England,

    (*b*) a person who has permission under [Part 4A][2] of FISMA 2000 to accept deposits (but see subsection (3) for exclusions),

    (*c*) an EEA firm of the kind mentioned in paragraph 5(*b*) of Schedule 3 to FISMA 2000 which has permission under paragraph 15 of that Schedule to accept deposits (as a result of qualifying for authorisation under paragraph 12(1) of that Schedule),

    (*d*) the European Investment Bank, and

    (*e*) an international organisation designated as a bank for the purposes of this section by an order made by the Treasury.

(3) The reference to a person who has permission under [Part 4A][2] of FISMA 2000 to accept deposits does not include—

    (*a*) a building society,

    (*b*) a society registered within the meaning of the Friendly Societies Act 1974 (c 46) or incorporated under the Friendly Societies Act 1992 (c 40),

    (*c*) a society registered as a credit union under [the Co-operative and Community Benefit Societies Act 2014][3] or the Credit Unions (Northern Ireland) Order 1985 (SI 1985/1205 (NI 12)), or

    (*d*) an insurance company within the meaning of section 275 of FA 2004.

(4) The Treasury may designate an international organisation for the purposes of this section only if the United Kingdom is a member of the organisation.

[(5) An order under subsection (2)(*e*) may include provision for a designation to have effect only in relation to the application of this section by a provision specified in the order.][1]

Commentary—*Simon's Taxes* **D7.701, A4.426.**

HMRC Manuals—Corporate Finance Manual CFM14060 (regulated entities: definition of a 'bank').

Amendments—[1] Sub-s (5) inserted by CTA 2010 s 1177, Sch 1 para 563. CTA 2010 has effect for corporation tax purposes for accounting periods ending on or after 1 April 2010, and for income and capital gains tax purposes for the tax year 2010–11 and subsequent tax years.

[2] In sub-ss (2)(b), (c) words substituted by the Financial Services (Banking Reform) Act 2013 s 141, Sch 10 para 6 with effect from 1 March 2014 (by virtue of SI 2014/377).

[3] In sub-s (3)(c), words substituted for words "the Industrial and Provident Societies Act 1965" by the Co-operative and Community Benefit Societies Act 2014 s 151, Sch 4 paras 104, 111 with effect from 1 August 2014 and subject to transitional provisions and provisions preserving the continuity of the law in Sch 5 of that Act.

Prospective amendments—Sub-s (2)(c) to be repealed by the Taxes (Amendments) (EU Exit) Regulations, SI 2019/689 reg 15(1), (12) with effect from Implementation Period completion day (see EU(WA)A 2020 Sch 5 para 1(1)). This amendment does not apply where a person qualifies for authorisation under FSMA 2000 Sch 3 by virtue of SI 2001/3084 (see SI 2019/689 reg 41(f)).

992 Meaning of "company"

(1) In the Income Tax Acts "company" means any body corporate or unincorporated association, but does not include a partnership, a local authority or a local authority association.

(2) Subsection (1) needs to be with read with [section 617 of CTA 2010 (authorised unit trust treated as UK resident company)][1].

(3) This section does not apply for the purposes of—

    (a) Part 6 (venture capital trusts),

    (b) Chapters 1, 3 and 4 of Part 13 (transactions in securities and land and sales of income from occupation), and

    (c) sections 993 and 994 (meaning of "connected" persons).

Commentary—*Simon's Taxes* **A1.155, D1.201.**

HMRC Manuals—Employment Income Manual EIM11371 (meaning of company where it owns homes outside the UK).

Amendments—[1] In sub-s (2) words substituted by CTA 2010 s 1177, Sch 1 para 564. CTA 2010 has effect for corporation tax purposes for accounting periods ending on or after 1 April 2010, and for income and capital gains tax purposes for the tax year 2010–11 and subsequent tax years.

993 Meaning of "connected" persons

(1) This section has effect for the purposes of the provisions of the Income Tax Acts which apply this section.

(2) An individual ("A") is connected with another individual ("B") if—

    (a) A is B's spouse or civil partner,

    (b) A is a relative of B,

    (c) A is the spouse or civil partner of a relative of B,

    (d) A is a relative of B's spouse or civil partner, or

    (e) A is the spouse or civil partner of a relative of B's spouse or civil partner.

(3) A person, in the capacity as trustee of a settlement, is connected with—

    (a) any individual who is a settlor in relation to the settlement,

    (b) any person connected with such an individual,

    (c) any close company whose participators include the trustees of the settlement,

    (d) any non-UK resident company which, if it were UK resident, would be a close company whose participators include the trustees of the settlement,

    (e) any body corporate controlled (within the meaning of section 995) by a company within paragraph (c) or (d),

    (f) if the settlement is the principal settlement in relation to one or more sub-fund settlements, a person in the capacity as trustee of such a sub-fund settlement, and

    (g) if the settlement is a sub-fund settlement in relation to a principal settlement, a person in the capacity as trustee of any other sub-fund settlements in relation to the principal settlement.

(4) A person who is a partner in a partnership is connected with—

    (a) any partner in the partnership,

    (b) the spouse or civil partner of any individual who is a partner in the partnership, and

    (c) a relative of any individual who is a partner in the partnership.

But this subsection does not apply in relation to acquisitions or disposals of assets of the partnership pursuant to genuine commercial arrangements.

(5) A company is connected with another company if—

    (a) the same person has control of both companies,

    (b) a person ("A") has control of one company and persons connected with A have control of the other company,

    (c) A has control of one company and A together with persons connected with A have control of the other company, or

    (d) a group of two or more persons has control of both companies and the groups either consist of the same persons or could be so regarded if (in one or more cases) a member of either group were replaced by a person with whom the member is connected.

(6) A company is connected with another person ("A") if—

    (a) A has control of the company, or

    (b) A together with persons connected with A have control of the company.

(7) In relation to a company, any two or more persons acting together to secure or exercise control of the company are connected with—

   (a) one another, and

   (b) any person acting on the directions of any of them to secure or exercise control of the company.

Commentary—*Simon's Taxes* **A1.156, B5.404.**

HMRC Manuals—Pensions Tax Manual PTM027000 (meaning of connected with).

994 Meaning of "connected" persons: supplementary

(1) In section 993 and this section—

   "company" includes any body corporate or unincorporated association, but does not include a partnership (and see also subsection (2)),

   "control" is to be read in accordance with [sections 450 and 451 of CTA 2010][1] (except where otherwise indicated),

   "principal settlement" has the meaning given by paragraph 1 of Schedule 4ZA to TCGA 1992,

   "relative" means brother, sister, ancestor or lineal descendant,

   "settlement" has the same meaning as in Chapter 5 of Part 5 of ITTOIA 2005 (see section 620 of that Act), and

   "sub-fund settlement" has the meaning given by paragraph 1 of Schedule 4ZA to TCGA 1992.

(2) For the purposes of section 993—

   (a) a unit trust scheme is treated as if it were a company, and

   (b) the rights of the unit holders are treated as if they were shares in the company.

(3) For the purposes of section 993 "trustee", in the case of a settlement in relation to which there would be no trustees apart from this subsection, means any person—

   (a) in whom the property comprised in the settlement is for the time being vested, or

   (b) in whom the management of that property is for the time being vested.

   Section 466(4) does not apply for the purposes of this subsection.

(4) If any provision of section 993 provides that a person ("A") is connected with another person ("B"), it also follows that B is connected with A.

Commentary—*Simon's Taxes* **A1.156, B5.404.**

Amendments—[1]   In sub-s (1) in defintion of "control", words substituted by CTA 2010 s 1177, Sch 1 para 565. CTA 2010 has effect for corporation tax purposes for accounting periods ending on or after 1 April 2010, and for income and capital gains tax purposes for the tax year 2010–11 and subsequent tax years.

995 Meaning of "control"

(1) This section has effect for the purposes of the provisions of the Income Tax Acts which apply this section.

(2) In relation to a body corporate ("company A"), "control" means the power of a person ("P") to secure—

   (a) by means of the holding of shares or the possession of voting power in relation to that or any other body corporate, or

   (b) as a result of any powers conferred by the articles of association or other document regulating that or any other body corporate,

that the affairs of company A are conducted in accordance with P's wishes.

(3) In relation to a partnership, "control" means the right to a share of more than half the assets, or of more than half the income, of the partnership.

Commentary—*Simon's Taxes* **A1.156.**

HMRC Manuals—Community Investment Tax Relief Manual CITM5010 (meaning of control).

996 Meaning of "farming" and related expressions

(1) In the Income Tax Acts "farming" means the occupation of land wholly or mainly for the purposes of husbandry, but does not include market gardening (see subsection (5)).

(2) In subsection (1) "husbandry" includes—

   (a) hop growing, and

   (b) the breeding and rearing of horses and the grazing of horses in connection with those activities.

(3) For the purposes of the Income Tax Acts the cultivation of short rotation coppice is regarded as husbandry and not as forestry.

(4) In the Income Tax Acts "woodlands" does not include land on which short rotation coppice is cultivated.

(5) In the Income Tax Acts "market gardening" means the occupation of land as a garden or nursery for the purpose of growing produce for sale.

(6) For the purposes of this section "short rotation coppice" means a perennial crop of tree species planted at high density, the stems of which are harvested above ground level at intervals of less than 10 years.

(7) In the application of this section for the purposes of section 192(1) or 303(1) of this Act or paragraph 16 of Schedule 5 to ITEPA 2003—

(*a*) both references to the occupation of land, and the reference to land on which short rotation coppice is cultivated, refer to land in the United Kingdom, and

(*b*) the reference to the cultivation of such coppice refers to its cultivation in the United Kingdom.[1]

Commentary—*Simon's Taxes* **A1.158, B5.101** .

HMRC Manuals—Business Income Manual BIM55051 (definition of 'farming').

BIM55120 (short rotation coppice treated as farming).

Amendments—[1]   Sub-s (7) repealed by F(No 2)A 2015 s 28(1) with effect as regards its application: (a) for the purposes of ITA 2007 s 192(1), in relation to shares issued on or after 18 November 2015; (b) for the purposes of ITA 2007 s 303(1), for the purposes of determining whether shares or securities issued on or after 18 November 2015 are to be regarded as comprised in a company's qualifying holdings; and (c) for the purposes of ITEPA 2003 Sch 5 para 16, in relation to options granted on or after 18 November 2015.

997 Meaning of "generally accepted accounting practice" and related expressions

(1) In the Income Tax Acts "generally accepted accounting practice" means UK generally accepted accounting practice.

This is subject to subsection (3).

(2) In the Income Tax Acts "UK generally accepted accounting practice"—

(*a*) means generally accepted accounting practice in relation to accounts of UK companies (other than IAS accounts) that are intended to give a true and fair view, and

(*b*) has the same meaning in relation to—

(i) individuals,

(ii) entities other than companies, and

(iii) companies that are not UK companies,

as it has in relation to UK companies.

(3) In relation to the affairs of a company or other entity that prepares IAS accounts, in the Income Tax Acts "generally accepted accounting practice" means generally accepted accounting practice in relation to IAS accounts.

(4) In the Income Tax Acts "for accounting purposes" means for the purposes of accounts drawn up in accordance with generally accepted accounting practice.

(5) In the Income Tax Acts "international accounting standards" has the same meaning as in the Corporation Tax Acts (see [section 1127 of CTA 2010][1]).

(6) In this section—

"IAS accounts" means accounts prepared in accordance with international accounting standards, and

"UK companies" means companies incorporated or formed under the law of a part of the United Kingdom.

Commentary—*Simon's Taxes* **B2.102, B3.702**.

HMRC Manuals—Business Income Manual BIM31015 (tax meaning of 'generally accepted accountancy practice').

Amendments—[1]   In sub-s (5) words substituted by CTA 2010 s 1177, Sch 1 para 566. CTA 2010 has effect for corporation tax purposes for accounting periods ending on or after 1 April 2010, and for income and capital gains tax purposes for the tax year 2010–11 and subsequent tax years.

998 Meaning of "grossing up"

(1) In the Income Tax Acts references to grossing up by reference to a rate of tax are to calculating the amount ("the grossed up amount") which after deduction of income tax at that rate would equal the amount to be grossed up ("the net amount").

(2) The grossed up amount is the sum of the net amount and the tax deducted.

(3) The grossed up amount may also be expressed as—

$$GA = NA + \left(NA \times \frac{R}{100 - R} \right)$$

where—

GA is the grossed up amount,

NA is the net amount, and

R is the percentage rate of tax by reference to which the net amount is to be grossed up.

[998A Meaning of "hire-purchase agreement"

(1) This section applies for the purposes of the provisions of the Income Tax Acts which apply this section.

(2) A hire-purchase agreement is an agreement in whose case each of conditions A to C is met.

(3) Condition A is that under the agreement goods are bailed (or in Scotland hired) in return for periodical payments by the person to whom they are bailed (or hired).

ITA 2007

(4) Condition B is that under the agreement the property in the goods will pass to the person to whom they are bailed (or hired) if the terms of the agreement are complied with and one or more of the following events occurs—

(*a*) the exercise of an option to purchase by that person,

(*b*) the doing of another specified act by any party to the agreement,

(*c*) the happening of another specified event.

(5) Condition C is that the agreement is not a conditional sale agreement.

(6) In subsection (5) "conditional sale agreement" means an agreement for the sale of goods under which—

(*a*) the purchase price or part of it is payable by instalments, and

(*b*) the property in the goods is to remain in the seller (even though they are to be in the possession of the buyer) until conditions specified in the agreement are met (whether as to the payment of instalments or otherwise).][1]

Commentary—*Simon's Taxes* **B5.414**.

Amendments—[1] This section inserted by TIOPA 2010 s 501, Sch 8 paras 256, 259. TIOPA 2010 has effect for corporation tax purposes for accounting periods ending on or after 1 April 2010, for income and capital gains tax purposes for the tax year 2010–11 and subsequent tax years, and for petroleum revenue tax purposes for chargeable periods beginning on or after 1 July 2010.

999 Meaning of "local authority"

(1) In the Income Tax Acts "local authority", in relation to England and Wales, means—

(*a*) a billing authority as defined in [section 1(2)][1] of the Local Government Finance Act 1992 (c 14),

(*b*) a precepting authority as defined in [section 69(1) of that Act][1],

(*c*) a body with power to issue a levy (by virtue of regulations under section 74 of the Local Government Finance Act 1988 (c 41)),

(*d*) a body with power to issue a special levy (by virtue of regulations under section 75 of that Act),

(*e*) a fire and rescue authority in Wales constituted by a scheme under section 2 of the Fire and Rescue Services Act 2004 (c 21) or a scheme to which section 4 of that Act applies,

(*f*) an authority with power to make or determine a rate, or

(*g*) a residuary body established by order under section 22(1) of the Local Government Act 1992 (c 19).

(2) In the Income Tax Acts "local authority", in relation to Scotland, means—

(*a*) a council constituted under section 2 of the Local Government etc (Scotland) Act 1994 (c 39),

(*b*) a joint board or committee within the meaning of the Local Government (Scotland) Act 1973 (c 65), or

(*c*) an authority with power to requisition any sum from a council such as is mentioned in paragraph (*a*).

[(3) In the Income Tax Acts "local authority", in relation to Northern Ireland, means a district council constituted under section 1 of the Local Government Act (Northern Ireland) 1972 (c 9 (NI)).][1]

(4) In this section "rate" means a rate—

(*a*) whose proceeds are applicable for public local purposes, and

(*b*) which is leviable by reference to the value of land or property.

Commentary—*Simon's Taxes* **D1.201A**.

Amendments—[1] In sub-s (1)(*a*), (*b*) words substituted, and sub-s (3) substituted by CTA 2010 s 1177, Sch 1 para 567. CTA 2010 has effect for corporation tax purposes for accounting periods ending on or after 1 April 2010, and for income and capital gains tax purposes for the tax year 2010–11 and subsequent tax years.

1000 Meaning of "local authority association"

(1) In the Income Tax Acts "local authority association" means any incorporated or unincorporated association which meets conditions A and B.

(2) Condition A is that all of its members are local authorities, groups of local authorities or local authority associations.

(3) Condition B is that its purpose, or primary purpose, is to protect and further the general interests of local authorities or any description of local authorities.

[(4) For the purposes of condition A, if a member ("M") of a local authority association is a representative of, or is appointed by, a local authority, group of local authorities or a local authority association, the authority, group or association concerned (rather than M) is to be treated as a constituent member of the local authority association.][1]

Commentary—*Simon's Taxes* **D1.201A**.

Amendments—[1] Sub-s (4) substituted for former sub-ss (4), (5) by CTA 2010 s 1177, Sch 1 para 568. CTA 2010 has effect for corporation tax purposes for accounting periods ending on or after 1 April 2010, and for income and capital gains tax purposes for the tax year 2010–11 and subsequent tax years.

1001 Meaning of "offshore installation"

(1) In the Income Tax Acts "offshore installation" means a structure which is, is to be, or has been, put to a relevant use while in water (see subsections (3) and (4)).

(2) But a structure is not an offshore installation if—
- (a) it has permanently ceased to be put to a relevant use,
- (b) it is not, and is not to be, put to any other relevant use, and
- (c) since permanently ceasing to be put to a relevant use, it has been put to a use which is not relevant.

(3) A use is a relevant use if it is—
- (a) for the purposes of exploiting mineral resources by means of a well,
- (b) for the purposes of exploration with a view to exploiting mineral resources by means of a well,
- (c) for the storage of gas in or under the shore or the bed of any waters,
- (d) for the recovery of gas so stored,
- (e) for the conveyance of things by means of a pipe, or
- (f) mainly for the provision of accommodation for individuals who work on or from a structure which is, is to be, or has been, put to any of the above uses while in water.

(4) For the purposes of this section references to a structure being put to a use while in water are to the structure being put to a use while—
- (a) standing in any waters,
- (b) stationed (by whatever means) in any waters, or
- (c) standing on the foreshore or other land intermittently covered with water.

(5) In this section "structure" includes a ship or other vessel.

Commentary—*Simon's Taxes* **E3.146**.
Derivation—TA 1988 s 837C.
HMRC Manuals—Employment Income Manual EIM33103 (definition and detail of offshore installations).
EIM33110 (discussion of relevant cases).

1002 Regulations about the meaning of "offshore installation"

(1) The Treasury may by regulations make provision as to the meaning of "offshore installation" in the Income Tax Acts.

(2) The regulations may—
- (a) add to, amend or repeal any provision of section 1001,
- (b) make different provision for different purposes, and
- (c) contain incidental, supplemental, consequential and transitional provision and savings.

1003 Meaning of "oil and gas exploration and appraisal"

(1) In the Income Tax Acts "oil and gas exploration and appraisal" means activities carried out for the purpose of—
- (a) searching for petroleum anywhere in an area,
- (b) ascertaining a petroleum-bearing area's extent or characteristics, or
- (c) ascertaining its reserves of petroleum,

so that it may be determined whether the petroleum is suitable for commercial exploitation.

(2) In this section "petroleum" has the meaning given by section 1 of the Petroleum Act 1998 (c 17).

Commentary—*Simon's Taxes* **B3.711**.
Derivation—TA 1988 s 837B.

1004 Meaning of "property investment LLP"

(1) In the Income Tax Acts "property investment LLP" means a limited liability partnership—
- (a) whose business consists wholly or mainly in the making of investments in land, and
- (b) the principal part of whose income is derived from investments in land.

(2) Whether a limited liability partnership is a property investment LLP is determined for each period of account of the partnership.

Commentary—*Simon's Taxes* **B7.107, B7.107**.
Derivation—TA 1988 s 832(1), 842B.
HMRC Manuals—Business Income Manual BIM82155 (liability partnership (LLP): property investment LLP).

[1005 Meaning of "recognised stock exchange" etc

(1) In the Income Tax Acts "recognised stock exchange" means—
- (a) any market of a recognised investment exchange which is for the time being designated as a recognised stock exchange for the purposes of this section by an order made by the Commissioners for Her Majesty's Revenue and Customs, and
- (b) any market outside the United Kingdom which is for the time being so designated.

(2) An order under subsection (1) may—
- (a) designate a market by name or by reference to any class or description of market (including, in the case of a market outside the United Kingdom, one framed by reference to any authority or approval given in a country outside the United Kingdom),
- (b) contain incidental, supplemental, consequential and transitional provision and savings, and
- (c) vary or revoke a previous order under that subsection.

[(2A) An order under subsection (1) may designate a stock exchange for the purposes of this section in its application to section 564G of this Act, section 151N of TCGA 1992 and section 507 of CTA 2009 only.]²

(3) References in the Income Tax Acts to securities which are listed on a recognised stock exchange are to securities—

(a) which are admitted to trading on that exchange, and

(b) which are included in the official UK list or are officially listed in a qualifying country outside the United Kingdom in accordance with provisions corresponding to those generally applicable in EEA states.

(4) For this purpose "qualifying country outside the United Kingdom" means any country outside the United Kingdom in which there is a recognised stock exchange.

(5) References in the Income Tax Acts to securities which are included in the official UK list are to securities which are included in the official list (within the meaning of Part 6 of FISMA 2000) in accordance with the provisions of that Part.

(6) In this section—

"recognised investment exchange" has the same meaning as in FISMA 2000 (see section 285), and

"securities" includes shares and stock.]¹

Commentary—*Simon's Taxes* **A1.159, C2.1010.**
Amendments—¹   This section substituted by FA 2007 s 109, Sch 26 para 1 with effect from 19 July 2007.
²   Sub-s (2A) inserted by TIOPA 2010 s 365, Sch 2 paras 50, 55. TIOPA 2010 has effect for corporation tax purposes for accounting periods ending on or after 1 April 2010, for income and capital gains tax purposes for the tax year 2010–11 and subsequent tax years, and for petroleum revenue tax purposes for chargeable periods beginning on or after 1 July 2010.

1006 Meaning of "research and development"

(1) This section has effect for the purposes of the provisions of the Income Tax Acts which apply this section.

(2) "Research and development" means activities that fall to be treated as research and development in accordance with generally accepted accounting practice. This is subject to subsection (3).

(3) The Treasury may by regulations specify activities which—

(a) are to be treated as being "research and development" for the purposes of this section, or

(b) are to be treated as not being "research and development" for the purposes of this section.

(4) The regulations may—

(a) make provision by reference to guidelines issued by the Secretary of State, and

(b) contain incidental, supplemental, consequential and transitional provision and savings.

(5) Unless otherwise expressly provided, "research and development" does not include oil and gas exploration and appraisal.

Commentary—*Simon's Taxes* **B2.467, B3.708, E3.143.**
Derivation—TA 1988 s 837A.
HMRC Manuals—Venture Capital Manual VCM71020 (research and development).

1007 Meaning of "unit trust scheme"

(1) In the Income Tax Acts "unit trust scheme" has the meaning given by section 237 of FISMA 2000.

This is subject to subsection (2).

[(2) The Treasury may, in relation to a unit trust scheme within the meaning given by section 237 of FISMA 2000 whose trustees are UK resident, by regulations provide that the scheme is not to be a unit trust scheme for the purposes of the definition in section 989 of "unauthorised unit trust" if it is within a specified description.]¹

(3) The regulations may contain incidental, supplemental, consequential and transitional provision and savings.

(4) This section does not apply for the purposes of section 558 (approved charitable investments).

Commentary—*Simon's Taxes* **D8.175, D8.178.**
Derivation—TA 1988 ss 469(7), (8), 832(1).
HMRC Manuals—Savings and Income Manual SAIM6050 (unauthorised unit trusts: definition of 'unit trust scheme').
Amendments—¹   Sub-s (2) substituted by the Income Tax Act 2007 (Amendment) Order, SI 2009/23 art 5(1), (5) with effect for income tax and capital gains tax purposes for the tax year 2007–08 and subsequent tax years, and for corporation tax purposes for accounting periods ending after 5 April 2007.

[1007A Meaning of "permanent establishment"

(1) In the Income Tax Acts "permanent establishment", in relation to a company, is to be read in accordance with Chapter 2 of Part 24 of CTA 2010.

(2) This section does not apply for the purposes of—

(a) Part 5 of this Act (see instead section 191A), or

(b) Chapter 4 of Part 6 of this Act (see instead section 302A).]¹

Commentary—*Simon's Taxes* **A1.153.**
Amendments—¹   Section 1007A inserted by F(No 3)A 2010 s 5, Sch 2 para 3(1), (3) with effect in relation to shares or securities issued on or after 6 April 2011 (by virtue of SI 2011/662 art 2).

CHAPTER 2

OTHER INCOME TAX ACTS PROVISIONS

1008 Scotland

(1) In the application of the Income Tax Acts to Scotland—

"assignment" means an assignation,

"estate in land" includes the land, and

"surrender" includes renunciation.

(2) In the application of the Income Tax Acts to Scotland, any reference to property or rights being held on trust or on trusts is a reference to the property or rights being held in trust.

Commentary—*Simon's Taxes* **E1.831**.

Derivation—TA 1988 ss 363(3), 832(1) and ITTOIA 2005 s 879.

1009 Sources of income within the charge to income tax or corporation tax

In the Income Tax Acts a source of income is within the charge to income tax or corporation tax if that tax—

(a) is chargeable on the income arising from it, or

(b) would be so chargeable if there were any income arising from it,

and references to a person, or income, being within the charge to income tax or corporation tax are to be read in the same way.

1011 References to married persons, or civil partners, living together

Individuals who are married to, or are civil partners of, each other are treated for the purposes of the Income Tax Acts as living together unless—

(a) they are separated under an order of a court of competent jurisdiction,

(b) they are separated by deed of separation, or

(c) they are in fact separated in circumstances in which the separation is likely to be permanent.

Commentary—*Simon's Taxes* **E5.102, E1.920, E5.105, E5.115**.

HMRC Manuals—Capital Gains Manual CG22070 (transfer of assets between husband and wife: living together).

1012 Relationship between rules on highest part of total income

(1) This section makes provision about the relationship between rules requiring particular income to be treated as the highest part of a person's total income.

(2) It has effect for the purposes of the Income Tax Acts except sections 535 to 537 of ITTOIA 2005 (gains from contracts for life insurance etc: top slicing relief).

(3) If more than one of the provisions listed in subsection (4) applies in relation to a person, a provision mentioned earlier in the list has priority over a provision mentioned later in the list.

(4) The provisions are—

section 465A of ITTOIA 2005 (gains from contracts for life insurance etc to be treated as highest part of total income),

[section 685A(5A) of ITTOIA 2005 (payments from trustees of settlor-interested settlements to be treated as highest part of total income),][1]

section 404A of ITEPA 2003 (payments and other benefits on termination of employment to be treated as highest part of total income), and

section 16 (savings and dividend income to be treated as highest part of total income).

(5) The provisions listed in subsection (4) have priority over—

section 619A(2) of ITTOIA 2005 (income treated as highest part of settlor's total income),

section 768(6) and (7) (income treated as arising under Chapter 3 of Part 13 to be treated as highest part of total income),

section 786(6) and (7) (income treated as arising under Chapter 4 of Part 13 to be treated as highest part of total income), and

any other provisions of the Income Tax Acts requiring income of any description to be treated as the highest part of a person's total income.

(6) The effect of one provision having priority over another is that the second provision has effect subject to the first.

Commentary—*Simon's Taxes* **C4.350**.

HMRC Manuals—Savings and Income Manual SAIM1090 (savings and dividend income).

Amendments—[1]   Entry in sub-s (4) inserted by FA 2008 s 67(2) with effect for the tax year 2006–07 and subsequent tax years.

1013 Territorial sea of the United Kingdom

The territorial sea of the United Kingdom is treated for the purposes of the Income Tax Acts as part of the United Kingdom.

Commentary—*Simon's Taxes* **A1.109, E6.101**.

HMRC Manuals—Employment Income Manual EIM40032 (extension of meaning of the United Kingdom).

EIM67105 (territorial extension of the charge to tax on employment income).

1014 Orders and regulations

(1) This section applies to all powers under the Income Tax Acts of the Treasury or the Commissioners for Her Majesty's Revenue and Customs to make orders or regulations, other than excluded powers.

(2) All powers under the following are excluded—

    (*a*) ICTA (see instead section 828 of that Act),

    (*b*) section 178(5) of FA 1989 (setting of rates of interest),

    [(*ba*) section 127(12) of FA 1995,]$^{2,\,4}$

    (*c*) CAA 2001 (see instead section 570B of that Act),

    (*d*) ITEPA 2003 (see instead section 717 of that Act),

    (*e*) Part 4 of FA 2004 (see instead section 282 of that Act),

    (*f*) ITTOIA 2005 (see instead section 873 of that Act),

    [(*fa*) TIOPA 2010 (see instead section [499]^9 of that Act), and]^5

    (*g*) the following provisions of this Act—

        (i) section 184(3)(*b*) and (*c*) (EIS: the unquoted status requirement (designated exchanges etc)),

        (ii) section 295(3)(*b*) and (*c*) (venture capital trusts: the unquoted status requirement (designated exchanges etc)),

        [(iia) section 432(2) (gifts of shares, securities and real property to charities etc: meaning of "qualifying investment"),]^1 . . . ^{2}

        [(iib) section 827(2) (meaning of "investment transaction"), . . . ^{4}]^2

        [(iic) section 835S(4) (meaning of "investment transaction"), and]^4

        (iii) section [1005(1)]^1 (meaning of "recognised stock exchange").

(3) Any orders or regulations made under a power to which this section applies must be made by statutory instrument.

(4) Any orders or regulations made under a power to which this section applies are subject to annulment in pursuance of a resolution of the House of Commons.

(5) Subsection (4) does not apply if the order or regulations are made under—

    (*a*) section 73A of FA 2004 (exemption for designated international organisations), or

    (*b*) any of the following provisions of this Act—

        (i) section 21(5) (indexation of [basic rate limit and starting rate limit for saving]^3),

        (ii) section 57 (indexation of allowances),

        (iia) . . . ^{8}

        (iii) section 114 or 802 (exclusion of amounts in calculating individual's contribution to the firm),

        [(iiia) section 257MNE (social investment relief: amendment of limits on investments),]^{10}

        (iv) section 400(4)(*e*) (amounts treated as contributed by an individual to investment partnership capital),

        (v) section 897 (UK public revenue dividends: regulations about collection of income tax),

        (vi) section 962 (regulations modifying Chapter 15 of Part 15),

        (vii) section 979 (designated international organisations: exceptions from duties to deduct),

        (viii) section 991(2)(*e*) (meaning of "bank"), or

        (ix) section 1030(2) (power to make transitional or saving provision in connection with coming into force of this Act).

(6) Further, subsection (4) does not apply—

    (*a*) if any other Parliamentary procedure is expressly provided to apply in relation to the order or regulations, or

    [(*b*) if the order or regulations provide for any provision of the Income Tax Acts to come into force or have effect in accordance with the order or regulations,]^7

and is also subject to any other provision to the contrary.

Commentary—*Simon's Taxes* **A1.106, D7.701**.

Amendments—^{1} Sub-s (2)(*g*)(iia) inserted, and reference in sub-s (2)(*g*)(iii) substituted, by FA 2007 s 109, Sch 26 para 12(1), (14) with effect from 19 July 2007.

^{2} Sub-s (2)(*ba*), (*g*)(iib) inserted, and word in Sub-s (2)(*g*)(iia) repealed, by FA 2008 s 38 Sch 16 paras 2(2), 6(2), (3) with effect from 21 July 2008.

^{3} Words in sub-s (5)(*b*)(i) substituted by FA 2008 s 5, Sch 1 paras 1, 34 with effect for the tax year 2008–09 and subsequent tax years.

^{4} In sub-s (2), para (*ba*) repealed, in para (*g*)(iib) word "and" repealed, and para (*g*)(iic) inserted, by TIOPA 2010 ss 501, 503, Sch 8 paras 280, 285, Sch 10 Pt 11. TIOPA 2010 has effect for corporation tax purposes for accounting periods ending on or after 1 April 2010, for income and capital gains tax purposes for the tax year 2010–11 and subsequent tax years, and for petroleum revenue tax purposes for chargeable periods beginning on or after 1 July 2010.

^{5} Sub-s (2)(*fa*) inserted by TIOPA 2010 s 501, Sch 8 paras 326, 327. TIOPA 2010 has effect for corporation tax purposes for accounting periods ending on or after 1 April 2010, for income and capital gains tax purposes for the tax year 2010–11 and subsequent tax years, and for petroleum revenue tax purposes for chargeable periods beginning on or after 1 July 2010.

^{6} Sub-s (5)(*b*)(iiia) inserted by FA 2014 s 57, Sch 11 paras 3, 12 with effect from 17 July 2014.

[7] Sub-s (6)(*b*) substituted by FA 2015 s 125(2) with effect only in relation to powers conferred on and after 26 March 2015.

[8] Sub-s (5)(*b*)(iia) repealed by FA 2019 s 5(4)(*a*) with effect for the tax year 2019–20 and subsequent tax years.

[9] In sub-s (2)(*fa*), reference substituted for reference "372" by F(No 2)A 2017 s 20, Sch 5 para 10(4)(*b*) with effect in relation to periods of account of worldwide groups that begin on or after 1 April 2017, subject to commencement and transitional provisions in Sch 5 paras 27–35. In relation to periods of account that straddle 1 April 2017, see Sch 5 para 25(4)–(11).

[10] Sub-s (5)(*a*)(iiia), substituted by F(No 2)A 2017 s 14, Sch 1 paras 1, 6(4) with effect in relation to investments made on or after 6 April 2017.

1015 Territorial scope of charges under certain provisions to which section 1016 applies

(1) This section applies in relation to any amount chargeable to income tax under or by virtue of any provision—

 (*a*) to which section 1016 applies, and

 (*b*) which is listed in Part 2 or 3 of the table in that section (provisions not in ITTOIA 2005).

(2) An amount arising to a UK resident is chargeable to tax whether or not it is from a source in the United Kingdom.

(3) An amount arising to a non-UK resident is chargeable to tax only if it is from a source in the United Kingdom.

(4) References in this section to amounts which are from a source in the United Kingdom include, in the case of any amount which does not have a source, references to amounts which have a comparable connection to the United Kingdom.

(5) This section is subject to any express or implied provision to the contrary in any provision of the Income Tax Acts.

1016 Table of provisions to which this section applies

(1) In the Income Tax Acts references to any provision to which this section applies are references to any provision listed in the following table so far as it relates to income tax (but subject to any applicable limitation in subsections (3) and (4)).

(2) This is the table—

Part 1

Provisions of ITTOIA 2005	Description
Chapter 18 of Part 2	Post-cessation receipts: trades, professions and vocations
Chapter 8 of Part 3	Rent receivable in connection with a UK section 12(4) concern
Chapter 9 of Part 3	Rent receivable for UK electric-line wayleaves
Chapter 10 of Part 3	Post-cessation receipts: UK property businesses
Chapter 2 of Part 4	Interest
Chapter 9 of Part 4	Gains from contracts for life insurance etc
Chapter 11 of Part 4	Transactions in deposits
Chapter 12 of Part 4	Disposals of futures and options involving guaranteed returns
Section 579	Royalties and other income from intellectual property
Section 583	Income from disposals of know-how
Section 587	Income from sales of patent rights
Chapter 3 of Part 5	Films and sound recordings: non-trade businesses
Chapter 4 of Part 5	Certain telecommunication rights: non-trading income
Chapter 5 of Part 5	Settlements: amounts treated as income of settlor
Section 682(4)	Adjustments after the administration period
Chapter 8 of Part 5	Income not otherwise charged
Section 844(4)	Withdrawal of relief for unremittable foreign income after source ceases

Part 2

Provisions of this Act	Description
Chapter 2 of Part 12	Accrued income profits
[Section 681BB(8) and (9)	New lease after assignment or surrender][4]
[Section 681DD	Leased assets: capital sums][4]
Section 720, 727 or 731	Transfer of assets abroad
. . .[5]	. . .[5]
Section 776	Sales of occupation income
Section 796	Individuals benefited by film relief

Provisions of this Act	Description
Section 804	Losses derived from exploiting licence: individuals in partnership
[Section 809CZC(2)	Income transferred under a loan or credit transaction][4]

Part 3

Other provisions	Description
Section 214(1)(ab) of ICTA[3]	Chargeable payments connected with exempt distributions[3]
Section 571(1) of ICTA	Cancellation of certificates: schemes for rationalising industry
Section 730(4) of ICTA[1]	Transfers of income arising from securities[1]
Section 761(1)(b)(i) of ICTA	Offshore income gains[2]
Section 774(1) of ICTA	Transactions between dealing company and associated company
Section 780(3A)(a) of ICTA	Sale and lease-back (taxation of consideration received)[4]
Section 781(1) of ICTA	Assets leased to traders and others[4]
Section 786(5)(a) of ICTA	Transactions associated with loans or credit[4]
Section 68(2) of FA 1989	Employee share ownership trust (chargeable event)
Section 71(4) of FA 1989	Employee share ownership trust (borrowing)
Section 258(4) of CAA 2001	Special leasing
Section 479(4) of CAA 2001	Persons having qualifying non-trade expenditure
Section 394(2) of ITEPA 2003	Charge on administrator of non-approved pension scheme
Section 476(5) of ITEPA 2003	Charge on occurrence of chargeable event
[Regulation 17 of the Offshore Funds (Tax) Regulations 2009 (SI 2009/3001)	Offshore income gains][2]
[Section 1086(2) of CTA 2010][3]	Chargeable payments connected with exempt distributions

(3) For the purposes of this section—

    (*a*) any reference to any provision of ITTOIA 2005 does not include that provision so far as relating to relevant foreign income,

    (*b*) the reference to Chapter 2 of Part 4 of ITTOIA 2005 is a reference to that Chapter only so far as relating to an issue of funding bonds where—

        (i) the issue is treated under section 380 of that Act as a payment of interest, and

        (ii) the person by or through whom they are issued is required to retain bonds under section 939(2) of this Act but it is impracticable for the person to do so,

    (*c*) the reference to Chapter 9 of Part 4 of ITTOIA 2005 is a reference to that Chapter only so far as relating to gains—

        (i) which are from a policy or contract specified in section 531(3) of that Act, and

        (ii) which do not fall within section 532 or 534 of that Act,

    (*d*) the reference to section 579 of ITTOIA 2005 does not include that section so far as relating to any annual payment,

    (*e*) the reference to Chapter 4 of Part 5 of ITTOIA 2005 does not include that Chapter so far as relating to any annual payment, and

    (*f*) the reference to Chapter 5 of Part 5 of ITTOIA 2005 does not include that Chapter so far as relating to income which falls within section 619(3) of that Act.

(4) For the purposes of this section the reference to section 720 or 727 of this Act does not include those sections so far as relating to income falling within subsection (3) of section 745.

Amendments—[1]   Words repealed by FA 2009 s 49, Sch 25, para 9(3)(*h*) with effect in relation to transfers on or after 22 April 2009.

[2]   In sub-s (2), in Part 3 of the Table, entry relating to TA 1988 s 761(1)(*b*)(i) repealed, and entry inserted, by the Offshore Funds (Tax) Regulations, SI 2009/3001 regs 13(2), 129(1), (6), Sch 2 with effect for the purposes of income tax for the tax year 2009–10 and subsequent tax years and for distributions made on or after 1 December 2009; for the purposes of corporation tax, on income, for accounting periods ending on or after 1 December 2009 and for distributions made on or after that date and, on chargeable gains, in relation to disposals made on or after 1 December 2009; and for the purposes of capital gains tax, in relation to disposals made on or after 1 December 2009.

[3]   In sub-s (2), in Part 3 of the Table, entry repealed and entry inserted by CTA 2010 ss 1177, 1181, Sch 1 para 569, Sch 3 Pt 1. CTA 2010 has effect for corporation tax purposes for accounting periods ending on or after 1 April 2010, and for income and capital gains tax purposes for the tax year 2010–11 and subsequent tax years.

4   In sub-s (2), in Part 2 of the Table, entries inserted, and in Part 3 of the Table entries for TA 1988 s 780(3A)(a) and TA 1988 s 781(1) repealed, by TIOPA 2010 ss 501, 503, 271, 274, Sch 8 paras 256, 260, Sch 10 Pts 9, 10. TIOPA 2010 has effect for corporation tax purposes for accounting periods ending on or after 1 April 2010, for income and capital gains tax purposes for the tax year 2010–11 and subsequent tax years, and for petroleum revenue tax purposes for chargeable periods beginning on or after 1 July 2010.

5   In sub-s (2), in Part 2 of the Table, entry relating to Chapter 3 of Part 13 repealed by FA 2016 s 79(7) with effect in relation to disposals on or after 5 July 2016 (FA 2016 s 82(1)), subject to transitional provisions for disposals to associated persons on or after 16 March 2016 and before 5 July 2016 (FA 2016 s 82(4)–(15)). F(No 2)A 2017 s 39 provides that this amendment has effect (so far as it would not otherwise have effect) in relation to amounts that are recognised in GAAP accounts drawn up for any period of account beginning on or after 8 March 2017 or, in the case of a straddling period, amounts that would be recognised in GAAP accounts drawn up for a period of account beginning on 8 March 2017 and ending when the straddling period ends. "Straddling period" means a period of account beginning before 8 March 2017 and ending on or after that date.

PART 17

DEFINITIONS FOR PURPOSES OF ACT AND FINAL PROVISIONS

Definitions for the purposes of Act

1017 Abbreviated references to Acts

In this Act—

    "CAA 2001" means the Capital Allowances Act 2001 (c 2),

    ["CTA 2009" means the Corporation Tax Act 2009][1]

    ["CTA 2010" means the Corporation Tax Act 2010][2]

    "FA", followed by a year, means the Finance Act of that year,

    "F(No 2)A", followed by a year, means the Finance (No 2) Act of that year,

    "FISMA 2000" means the Financial Services and Markets Act 2000 (c 8),

    "ICTA" means the Income and Corporation Taxes Act 1988 (c 1),

    "IHTA 1984" means the Inheritance Tax Act 1984 (c 51),

    "ITEPA 2003" means the Income Tax (Earnings and Pensions) Act 2003 (c 1),

    "ITTOIA 2005" means the Income Tax (Trading and Other Income) Act 2005 (c 5),

    "TCGA 1992" means the Taxation of Chargeable Gains Act 1992 (c 12),

    ["TIOPA 2010" means the Taxation (International and Other Provisions) Act 2010, and][3]

    "TMA 1970" means the Taxes Management Act 1970 (c 9).

Amendments—[1]   Definition of "CTA 2009" inserted by CTA 2009 s 1322, Sch 1 paras 699, 720. CTA 2009 applies for accounting periods ending on or after 1 April 2009 (for corporation tax purposes) and for tax years 2009–10 onwards (for income and capital gains tax purposes).

[2]   Definition of "CTA 2010" inserted by CTA 2010 s 1177, Sch 1 para 570. CTA 2010 has effect for corporation tax purposes for accounting periods ending on or after 1 April 2010, and for income and capital gains tax purposes for the tax year 2010–11 and subsequent tax years.

[3]   Definition of "TIOPA 2010" inserted by TIOPA 2010 s 501, Sch 8 paras 326, 328. TIOPA 2010 has effect for corporation tax purposes for accounting periods ending on or after 1 April 2010, for income and capital gains tax purposes for the tax year 2010–11 and subsequent tax years, and for petroleum revenue tax purposes for chargeable periods beginning on or after 1 July 2010.

1018 "Act" to include Scottish and Northern Ireland legislation in some cases

(1) In the following provisions of this Act, "Act" includes an Act of the Scottish Parliament—

    section 66 (restriction on relief unless trade is commercial),

    section 532 (exemption for savings and investment income),

    section 536 (exemption for miscellaneous income),

    section 558 (approved charitable investments),

    section 1028 (power to make consequential provision), and

    section 1029 (power to undo changes).

(2) In the following provisions of this Act, "Act" includes Northern Ireland legislation—

    section 66 (restriction on relief unless trade is commercial),

    section 114 (exclusion of amounts in calculating contribution to the firm),

    section 532 (exemption for savings and investment income),

    section 536 (exemption for miscellaneous income),

    section 558 (approved charitable investments),

    section 802 (exclusion of amounts in calculating partner's capital contribution),

    section 1028 (power to make consequential provision), and

    section 1029 (power to undo changes).

1019 Meaning of "certificate of deposit"

In this Act "certificate of deposit" means a document—

    (*a*) relating to the deposit of money in any currency,

    (*b*) recognising an obligation to pay a stated principal amount to bearer or to order, with or without interest, and

    (*c*) by the delivery of which, with or without endorsement, the right to receive that stated amount, with or without interest, is transferable.

1020 Claims and elections

(1) In this Act any reference to a claim or election is to a claim or election in writing or in any form authorised (in relation to the case in question) by directions under [section 43E(1) of TMA 1970][1].

(2) For further information about claims and elections, see TMA 1970 [more generally (but in)][1] particular, section 42(2), (10) and (11) and Schedule 1A).

Amendments—[1]   In sub-ss (1), (2) words substituted by TIOPA 2010 s 371, Sch 7 paras 91, 93. TIOPA 2010 has effect for corporation tax purposes for accounting periods ending on or after 1 April 2010, for income and capital gains tax purposes for the tax year 2010–11 and subsequent tax years, and for petroleum revenue tax purposes for chargeable periods beginning on or after 1 July 2010.

1021 Application of definitions of "connected" persons and "control"

(1) Section 993 (meaning of "connected" persons) applies for the purposes of this Act unless otherwise indicated.

(2) Section 995 (meaning of "control") applies for the purposes of this Act unless otherwise indicated.

1022 Meaning of "debenture"

(1) In this Act "debenture" has the meaning given by [section 738 of the Companies Act 2006][1].

[(1A) For the meaning of "debenture" in sections 257KB(3) to (5), 257L(4), 257LA(2) and 392(3A)(a), see also sections 257KB(6), 257L(6), 257LA(4) and 392(3B).][2]

(2) This section does not apply for the purposes of sections 559, 560 and 691.

Amendments—[1]   Words in sub-s (1) substituted by the Companies Act 2006 (Consequential Amendments) (Taxes and National Insurance) Order, SI 2008/954 arts 38, 41 with effect from 6 April 2008.
[2]   Sub-s (1A) inserted by FA 2014 s 57, Sch 11 paras 3, 13 with effect from 17 July 2014.

1023 Meaning of "double taxation arrangements"

In this Act "double taxation arrangements" means arrangements which have effect under [section 2(1) of TIOPA 2010][1].

Amendments—[1]   Words substituted by TIOPA 2010 s 501, Sch 8 paras 71, 85. TIOPA 2010 has effect for corporation tax purposes for accounting periods ending on or after 1 April 2010, for income and capital gains tax purposes for the tax year 2010–11 and subsequent tax years, and for petroleum revenue tax purposes for chargeable periods beginning on or after 1 July 2010.

1024 Meaning of "gilt-edged securities"

In this Act "gilt-edged securities" means any securities which—

    (*a*)   are gilt-edged securities for the purposes of TCGA 1992 (see Schedule 9 to that Act), or

    (*b*)   will be such securities on the making of an order under paragraph 1 of that Schedule, if the making of the order is anticipated in the prospectus under which the securities were issued.

Commentary—*Simon's Taxes* **A4.425**.
Derivation—TA 1988 ss 50(7), 722A(5) and Sch 23A para 3A(2).
HMRC Manuals—Capital Gains Manual CG54900 (gilt-edged securities).

1025 Meaning of "modified net income"

(1) For the purposes of this Act a person's modified net income for a tax year ("year X") is the person's net income for year X calculated in accordance with Steps 1 and 2 of section 23 (calculation of income tax liability) as modified by subsection (2).

(2) In applying Steps 1 and 2 of section 23, ignore—

    (*a*)   any non-qualifying income included in the person's total income (see section 1026),

    (*b*)   any relief under Chapter 2 of Part 4 for a loss incurred or treated as incurred, or a payment made, in a tax year later than year X,

    (*c*)   any reliefs to which the person may be entitled under Chapter 4 of Part 8,

    (*d*)   any adjustment of profits resulting from a claim under Chapter 16 of Part 2 of ITTOIA 2005 (averaging profits of farmers and creative artists), if year X is [any earlier tax year][2] in relation to which the claim is made,

    (*e*)   any adjustment resulting from an election under section 257 of ITTOIA 2005 (election to carry back post-cessation receipts), and

    (*f*)   any relief or adjustment resulting from the making, amendment or revocation of a claim for relief, if the claim, amendment or revocation would have been out of time but for section 224(4) of ITTOIA 2005 (averaging profits of farmers and creative artists: extension of deadline for claiming other reliefs).

(3) This section applies for the purposes of section 427 as if subsection (2)(*c*) were omitted.

(4) This section applies for the purposes of Chapter 9 of Part 9 and Chapter 13 of Part 15 as if for subsection (2)(c) there were substituted—

        "(c)   any reliefs to which the person may be entitled under section 505,".[1]

(5) In this section "claim" includes an election or notice.

Commentary—*Simon's Taxes* **A4.434**.

Amendments—[1]   Sub-s (4) repealed by the Unauthorised Unit Trusts (Tax) Regulations, SI 2013/2819 reg 37(1), (18) with effect from 6 April 2014. Note that an unauthorised unit trust is not a non-exempt unauthorised unit trust, and this amendment does not apply in relation to the trust, if at all times in the period beginning with 24 May 2012 and ending with 5 April 2014 it had at least one unit holder which was, and at least one unit holder which was not, an eligible investor (ie a mixed unauthorised unit trust); this ceases to apply in relation to the trust if subsequently it no longer has any unit holders which are eligible investors (SI 2013/2819 reg 32).

[2] Words in sub-s (2)(*d*) substituted by FA 2016 s 25(9) with effect for the tax year 2016-17 and subsequent tax years.

1026 Meaning of "non-qualifying income" for the purposes of section 1025

For the purposes of section 1025 an amount included in a person's total income is non-qualifying income if it is—

(*a*) income on which income tax is treated as paid under section 399(2) . . . [2] of ITTOIA 2005 (distributions [to non-UK resident persons][2]),

(*b*), (*c*) . . . [2]

(*d*) income on which an individual is liable to income tax as a result of section 465 of ITTOIA 2005 or trustees are so liable as a result of section 467 of that Act (gains from contracts for life insurance etc), being income to which section 530 of that Act applies (income tax treated as paid etc),

(*e*) income which is included in the aggregate income of an estate as a result of section 664(2)(*c*), (*d*) or (*e*) of ITTOIA 2005 (income arising to personal representatives and corresponding to income within paragraph (*b*), (*c*) or (*d*)), [or][1]

(*f*) income on which income tax is treated as paid under section 685A(3) of ITTOIA 2005 (settlor-interested settlements), . . . [1]

(*g*) *an amount that a person is treated as having received under section 804(5B) of ICTA (double taxation relief: special rules about overlap profit).*[1]

Commentary—*Simon's Taxes* **A4.434**.
Amendments—[1] Word "or" inserted after para (*e*), and para (*g*) and preceding word "or" repealed, by TIOPA 2010 ss 501, 503, Sch 8 paras 71, 86, Sch 10 Pt 1. TIOPA 2010 has effect for corporation tax purposes for accounting periods ending on or after 1 April 2010, for income and capital gains tax purposes for the tax year 2010–11 and subsequent tax years, and for petroleum revenue tax purposes for chargeable periods beginning on or after 1 July 2010.
[2] Words in para (*a*) repealed and substituted, and paras (*b*), (*c*) repealed, by FA 2016 s 5, Sch 1 para 63(1), (17) with effect for the tax year 2016-17 and subsequent tax years.

Final provisions

1027 Minor and consequential amendments

Schedule 1 (minor and consequential amendments) has effect.

1028 Power to make consequential provision

(1) The Treasury may by order make such provision as the Treasury consider appropriate in consequence of this Act.

(2) The power conferred by subsection (1) may not be exercised after 5 April 2010.

(3) An order under this section may amend, repeal or revoke any provision made by or under an Act.

(4) An order under this section may contain provision having retrospective effect.

(5) An order under this section may contain incidental, supplemental, consequential and transitional provision and savings.

Orders—Income Tax Act 2007 (Amendment) Order 2010, SI 2010/558.

1029 Power to undo changes

(1) The Treasury may by order make such provision as the Treasury consider appropriate, in relation to a case in which the Treasury consider that a provision of this Act changes the effect of the law, for the purpose of returning the effect of the law to what it was immediately before 6 April 2007.

(2) The power conferred by subsection (1) may not be exercised after 5 April 2010.

(3) An order under this section may amend, repeal or revoke any provision made by or under this Act or by or under any other Act.

(4) An order under this section may contain provision having retrospective effect.

(5) An order under this section may contain incidental, supplemental, consequential and transitional provision and savings.

Orders—Income Tax Act 2007 (Amendment) (No 2) Order, SI 2009/2859.
Income Tax Act 2007 (Amendment) Order 2010, SI 2010/558.

1030 Transitional provisions and savings

(1) Schedule 2 (transitional provisions and savings) has effect.

(2) The Treasury may by order make such transitional or saving provision as the Treasury consider appropriate in connection with the coming into force of this Act.

(3) An order under subsection (2) may contain provision having retrospective effect.

(4) At any time before section 1014 of this Act (orders and regulations) comes into force, section 828(4) of ICTA (order-making powers excluded from negative resolution procedure) has effect as if it included a reference to an order made under subsection (2) of this section.

1031 Repeals and revocations

Schedule 3 (repeals and revocations, including of spent enactments) has effect.

1032 Index of defined expressions

(1) Schedule 4 (index of defined expressions that apply for the purposes of this Act) has effect.

(2) That Schedule lists the places where some of the expressions used in this Act are defined or otherwise explained.

1033 Extent

(1) This Act extends to England and Wales, Scotland and Northern Ireland (but see subsection (2)).

(2) An amendment, repeal or revocation contained in Schedule 1 or 3 has the same extent as the provision amended, repealed or revoked.

1034 Commencement

(1) This Act comes into force on 6 April 2007 and has effect—

    (a) for income tax purposes, for the tax year 2007–08 and subsequent tax years, and

    (b) for corporation tax purposes, for accounting periods ending after 5 April 2007.

(2) Subsection (1) is subject to subsections (3) and (4).

(3) The following—

    (a) Part 5 (enterprise investment scheme),

    (b) Part 3 of Schedule 1 (consequential amendment associated with Part 5), and

    (c) Part 2 of Schedule 3 (repeals so associated),

do not have effect in relation to shares issued before 6 April 2007.

This is subject to Schedule 2 (transitional provisions and savings).

(4) Subsection (1) does not apply to the following provisions of this Act (which therefore come into force on the day on which this Act is passed)—

    (a) in Part 15, section 852, and

    (b) in this Part, sections 1017, 1018, 1028, 1029, 1030(2) to (4) and 1033, this section and section 1035.

1035 Short title

This Act may be cited as the Income Tax Act 2007.

SCHEDULES

SCHEDULE 1

MINOR AND CONSEQUENTIAL AMENDMENTS

Section 1027

SCHEDULE 2

TRANSITIONALS AND SAVINGS

Section 1034

PART 1

GENERAL PROVISIONS

Continuity of the law: general

1   The repeal of provisions and their enactment in a rewritten form by this Act does not affect the continuity of the law.

2   Paragraph 1 does not apply to any change made by this Act in the effect of the law.

3   Any subordinate legislation or other thing which—

    (a) has been made or done, or has effect as if made or done, under or for the purposes of a superseded enactment so far as it applied for relevant tax purposes, and

    (b) is in force or effective immediately before the commencement of the corresponding rewritten provision,

has effect after that commencement as if made or done under or for the purposes of the rewritten provision.

4—(1) Any reference (express or implied) in this Act, another enactment or an instrument or document to a rewritten provision is to be read as including, in relation to times, circumstances or purposes in relation to which any corresponding superseded enactment had effect for relevant tax purposes, a reference to the superseded enactment so far as applying for those relevant tax purposes.

(2) Any reference (express or implied) in this Act, another enactment or an instrument or document to—

    (a) things done under or for the purposes of a rewritten provision, or

    (b) things falling to be done under or for the purposes of a rewritten provision,

is to be read as including, in relation to times, circumstances or purposes in relation to which any corresponding superseded enactment had effect for relevant tax purposes, a reference to things done or falling to be done under or for the purposes of the superseded enactment so far as applying for those relevant tax purposes.

5—(1) Any reference (express or implied) in any enactment, instrument or document to a superseded enactment in its application for relevant tax purposes is to be read, so far as is required for those relevant tax purposes, as including, in relation to times, circumstances or purposes in relation to which any corresponding rewritten provision has effect, a reference to the rewritten provision.

(2) Any reference (express or implied) in any enactment, instrument or document to—

    (a) things done under or for the purposes of a superseded enactment in its application for relevant tax purposes, or

    (b) things falling to be done under or for the purposes of a superseded enactment in its application for relevant tax purposes,

is to be read, so far as is required for those relevant tax purposes, as including, in relation to times, circumstances or purposes in relation to which any corresponding rewritten provision has effect, a reference to things done or falling to be done under or for the purposes of the rewritten provision.

6—(1) Paragraphs 1 to 5 have effect instead of section 17(2) of the Interpretation Act 1978 (c 30) (but are without prejudice to any other provision of that Act).

(2) Paragraphs 4 and 5 apply only so far as the context permits.

General saving for old transitional provisions and savings

7—(1) The repeal by this Act of a transitional or saving provision relating to the coming into force of a provision rewritten in this Act does not affect the operation of the transitional or saving provision, so far as it is not specifically rewritten in this Act but remains capable of having effect in relation to the corresponding provision of this Act.

(2) The repeal by this Act of an enactment previously repealed subject to savings does not affect the continued operation of those savings.

(3) The repeal by this Act of a saving on the previous repeal of an enactment does not affect the operation of the saving so far as it is not specifically rewritten in this Act but remains capable of having effect.

Partnerships involving companies

8—(1) References in this Act to any person are to be read, in the case of a person acting in partnership with other persons of whom at least one is a company chargeable to corporation tax, as references to all the partners so far as is required for the purposes of preserving the continuity of the law.

(2) References to a company or other person in any provision amended in its application for corporation tax purposes by this Act are to be read, in the case of a company acting in partnership with other persons of whom at least one is not a company, as references to all the partners so far as is required for the purposes of preserving the continuity of the law.

Interpretation

9—(1) In this Part—

    "enactment" includes subordinate legislation (within the meaning of the Interpretation Act 1978 (c 30)),

    "relevant tax purposes" means, in relation to a superseded enactment, tax purposes for which the enactment has been rewritten by this Act, and

    "superseded enactment" means an earlier enactment which has been rewritten by this Act for certain tax purposes (whether it applied only for those purposes or for those and other tax purposes).

(2) References in this Part to the repeal of a provision include references to its revocation and to its express or implied disapplication for income tax purposes of this Act.

(3) References in this Part to tax purposes are not limited to income tax purposes.

PART 2
CHANGES IN THE LAW

10—(1) This paragraph applies if, in the case of any person—

    (a) a thing is done or an event occurs before 6 April 2007, and

    (b) because of a change in the law made by this Act, the tax consequences of that thing or event for the relevant period are different from what they would otherwise have been.

(2) If that person so elects, this Act applies with such modifications as may be necessary to secure that the tax consequences for the relevant period are the same as they would have been if the change in the law had not been made.

(3) In sub-paragraphs (1) and (2) "the relevant period" means—

    (*a*) for income tax purposes, any period of account beginning before and ending on or after 6 April 2007, and

    (*b*) for corporation tax purposes, any accounting period beginning before and ending on or after 6 April 2007.

(4) If this paragraph applies in the case of two or more persons in relation to the same thing or event, an election made under this paragraph by any one of those persons is of no effect unless a corresponding election is made by the other or each of the others.

(5) An election under this paragraph must be made—

    (*a*) for income tax purposes, on or before the first anniversary of the normal self-assessment filing date for the tax year in which the period of account ends, and

    (*b*) for corporation tax purposes, not later than two years after the end of the accounting period.

PART 3
RATES AT WHICH INCOME TAX IS CHARGED

11   In relation to a tax year before 2007–08—

    (*a*) references in this Act, another enactment or an instrument or document to the savings rate are to be read as references to the lower rate, and

    (*b*) references in this Act, another enactment or an instrument or document to the trust rate are to be read as references to the rate applicable to trusts.

12   In relation to the tax year 2007–08 or any subsequent tax year—

    (*a*) references in an enactment, instrument or document to the lower rate are to be read as references to the savings rate, and

    (*b*) references in an enactment, instrument or document to the rate applicable to trusts are to be read as references to the trust rate.

13   In this Part "enactment" includes subordinate legislation (within the meaning of the Interpretation Act 1978 (c 30)).

PART 5
LOSSES (EXCEPT LOSSES ON DISPOSAL OF SHARES)

General: carry forward loss reliefs

18—(1) The repeal by this Act of the superseded carry forward provisions does not alter the effect of those provisions so far as they determine—

    (*a*) whether, and

    (*b*) to what extent,

relief for any loss made (or treated as made) in a tax year before the tax year 2007–08 is to be given for the tax year 2007–08 or any subsequent tax year.

(2) But any relief for the loss (or any part of the loss) which is given for the tax year 2007–08 or any subsequent tax year is to be given in accordance with the relevant provisions of Part 4 of this Act.

(3) In this paragraph "the superseded carry forward provisions" means—

    (*a*) sections 379A and 379B of ICTA (carry forward of loss in Schedule A business or overseas property business),

    (*b*) sections 385, 387, 390 and 391 (so far as applying to section 385) of ICTA (carry forward of loss in trade, profession or vocation),

    (*c*) section 392(2)(*b*) and (5) of ICTA (carry forward of miscellaneous loss), and

    (*d*) any provision inserting or amending, or affecting the application of, any of the above provisions.

Trade loss relief against general income

19—(1) This paragraph applies for the purposes of section 64 if the loss is made in the tax year 2007–08.

(2) Relief for the loss can be given for the tax year 2006–07.

(3) Sub-paragraphs (4) and (5) apply if relief for the loss is claimed for the tax year 2006–07.

(4) If relief is to be given, the relief is given in the way it would have been given had it been given under section 380(1)(*b*) of ICTA ignoring this Act (and section 65 of this Act is to be read accordingly).

(5) Section 72 of FA 1991 applies as if the relief had been claimed under section 380(1)(*b*) of ICTA.

20—(1) This paragraph applies if—

    (*a*) a person makes a loss ("the 2006–07 loss") in a trade in the tax year 2006–07,

(b) relief under section 380 of ICTA is not available for the 2006–07 loss because of section 384(1) of that Act,

(c) the person makes a loss ("the 2007–08 loss") in the trade in the tax year 2007–08,

(d) (apart from this paragraph) relief under section 64 of this Act is not available for the 2007–08 loss because of section 66 of this Act,

(e) the basis period for the tax year 2007–08 overlaps with the tax year 2006–07, and

(f) ignoring this Act, section 384(1) of ICTA would not have prevented relief under section 380 of that Act being available for the 2007–08 loss.

(2) Section 66 of this Act is not to apply in relation to the 2007–08 loss.

(3) This paragraph applies to professions and vocations as it applies to trades.

Early trade losses relief

21—(1) This paragraph applies for the purposes of section 72 if the loss is made in the tax year 2007–08, 2008–09 or 2009-10.

(2) Relief for the loss can be given for one or more of the tax years 2004–05, 2005–06 and 2006–07 (depending on the tax year in which the loss is made).

(3) If relief for the loss is to be given for one or more of those tax years, the relief is given in the way in which it would have been given had it been given under section 381 of ICTA ignoring this Act (and section 73 of this Act is to be read accordingly).

22—(1) This paragraph applies if—

(a) a person makes a loss ("the 2006–07 loss") in a trade in the tax year 2006–07,

(b) relief under section 381 of ICTA is not available for the 2006–07 loss because of subsection (4) of that section,

(c) the person makes a loss ("the 2007–08 loss") in the trade in the tax year 2007–08,

(d) (apart from this paragraph) relief under section 72 of this Act is not available for the 2007–08 loss because of section 74(1) of this Act,

(e) the basis period for the tax year 2007–08 overlaps with the tax year 2006–07, and

(f) ignoring this Act, subsection (4) of section 381 of ICTA would not have prevented relief under that section being available for the 2007–08 loss.

(2) Section 74(1) of this Act is not to apply in relation to the 2007–08 loss.

(3) This paragraph applies to professions and vocations as it applies to trades.

Sideways relief: trade leasing allowances given to individuals

23—(1) This paragraph applies if—

(a) a person makes a loss ("the 2006–07 loss") in a trade in the tax year 2006–07,

(b) relief under section 380 or 381 of ICTA is not available for the 2006–07 loss (or for part of it) because of section 384(6) of that Act,

(c) the person makes a loss ("the 2007–08 loss") in the trade in the tax year 2007–08,

(d) (apart from this paragraph) relief under section 64 or 72 of this Act is not available for the 2007–08 loss (or for part of it) because of section 75 of this Act,

(e) the basis period for the tax year 2007–08 overlaps with the tax year 2006–07, and

(f) ignoring this Act, section 384(6) of ICTA would not have prevented relief under section 380 or 381 of that Act being available for the 2007–08 loss (or for the part).

(2) Section 75 of this Act is not to apply in relation to the 2007–08 loss (or to the part).

Sideways relief: dealings in commodity futures

24   Section 81 does not apply if the arrangements mentioned in that section were made wholly before 6 April 1976.

Terminal trade loss relief

25—(1) This paragraph applies for the purposes of section 89 if the final tax year is the tax year 2007–08, 2008–09 or 2009–10.

(2) Relief for the terminal losses in question can be given for one or more of the tax years 2004–05, 2005–06 and 2006–07 (depending on which tax year is the final tax year).

(3) If relief for the terminal losses is to be given for one or more of those tax years, the relief is given in the way in which it would have been given had it been given under section 388 of ICTA ignoring this Act (and section 91 of this Act is to be read accordingly).

Post-cessation trade loss relief and post-cessation property relief

26   The events covered by section 98(5) (including as applied by section 125(6)(b)) include events—

(a) which occur before the tax year 2007–08, and

(b) in relation to which no claim is made under section 109A of ICTA.

Reliefs for limited partners not to exceed contribution to the firm

27—(1) The relief covered by section 104(5) includes—

(a) relief given for a loss as a result of section 380 or 381 of ICTA,

(b) any amount that, ignoring this Act, would have been included in the individual's aggregate amount in relation to the trade for the purposes of section 117 of ICTA as a result of paragraph 22(3) of Schedule 2 to CAA 2001, and

(c) the treatment of a loss as an allowable loss by virtue of section 72 of FA 1991.

(2) The income covered by section 104(6) includes amounts treated as received as a result of the application of section 74 of FA 2005.

Reliefs for members of LLPs not to exceed contribution to the LLP

28—(1) The relief covered by section 107(6) includes—

(a) relief given for a loss as a result of section 380 or 381 of ICTA, and

(b) the treatment of a loss as an allowable loss by virtue of section 72 of FA 1991.

(2) The income covered by section 107(7) includes amounts treated as received as a result of the application of section 74 of FA 2005.

Members of LLPs: carry-forward of losses

29—(1) The amounts of loss covered by section 109(1)(b) include amounts of loss which, as a result of section 117 of ICTA (as applied by section 118ZB of that Act), are not—

(a) relieved under section 380 or 381 of ICTA, or

(b) treated as an allowable loss by virtue of section 72 of FA 1991.

(2) In section 109(3)—

(a) references to section 109 include references to section 118ZD of ICTA,

(b) references to sideways relief include references to relief under section 380 or 381 of ICTA, and

(c) references to capital gains relief include references to the treatment of a loss as an allowable loss by virtue of section 72 of FA 1991.

Reliefs for non-active partners not to exceed contribution to the firm

30—(1) The relief covered by section 110(5) includes—

(a) relief given for a loss as a result of section 380 or 381 of ICTA, and

(b) the treatment of a loss as an allowable loss by virtue of section 72 of FA 1991.

(2) Sub-paragraph (1) is subject to paragraph 33.

(3) The income covered by section 110(6) includes amounts treated as received as a result of the application of section 74 of FA 2005.

Non-active partners: carry-forward of losses

31—(1) The amounts of loss covered by section 113(1)(b) include amounts of loss which, as a result of section 118ZE of ICTA, are not—

(a) relieved under section 380 or 381 of ICTA, or

(b) treated as an allowable loss by virtue of section 72 of FA 1991.

(2) In section 113(4)—

(a) references to section 113 include references to section 118ZI of ICTA,

(b) references to sideways relief include references to relief under section 380 or 381 of ICTA, and

(c) references to capital gains relief include references to the treatment of a loss as an allowable loss by virtue of section 72 of FA 1991.

(3) In section 113(8) the reference to section 109 includes a reference to section 118ZD of ICTA.

Restriction on reliefs for non-active partners: pre-10 February 2004 events

32 In Chapter 3 of Part 4 any reference to an early tax year in relation to an individual carrying on a trade does not include a tax year the basis period for which ends before 10 February 2004.

33—(1) Sub-paragraphs (2) to (9) set out relief which is not covered by section 110(5) (relevant relief).

(2) Relief is not covered if it is given for a loss made in a trade in a tax year the basis period for which ends before 10 February 2004.

(3) Sub-paragraphs (4) to (9) apply if the individual carried on a trade in a tax year the basis period for which includes 10 February 2004.

(4) Relief given for a loss made in the trade is not covered so far as the loss derives from an allowance or deduction within sub-paragraph (5).

(5) An allowance or deduction is within this sub-paragraph if it is—

    (*a*) a capital allowance in respect of expenditure incurred before 10 February 2004 which is treated as an expense of the trade, or

    (*b*) a deduction in respect of expenditure incurred before 10 February 2004 under section 42(1) of F(No 2)A 1992 or any of sections 138 to 140 of ITTOIA 2005.

(6) For the purposes of sub-paragraph (4) the amount of a loss that derives from an allowance or deduction within sub-paragraph (5) is determined on a just and reasonable basis.

(7) Relief given for a loss made in the trade is not covered so far as it is given for the pre-announcement allowance in relation to the trade.

(8) "Pre-announcement allowance" is to be read in accordance with section 118ZJ(4) and (6) to (8) of ICTA.

(9) For that purpose, references to the first restricted year are to be read as references to the tax year mentioned in sub-paragraph (3).

If sub-paragraph (3) covers more than one tax year, the first restricted year is the first of the tax years covered.

(10) Sub-paragraph (11) applies for the purpose of applying the restriction in section 110(4) (relevant relief not to exceed contribution to the firm) in relation to an individual if before 10 February 2004 the individual contributed an amount of capital to the firm.

(11) That amount of capital is reduced (but not below nil)—

    (*a*) by the amount of relief (if any) to be left out of account for the purposes of section 110(5) as a result of paragraph 32 or this paragraph (ignoring sub-paragraph (4)), and

    (*b*) by any pre-announcement allowance so far as—

        (i) relief has not been given for the allowance, and

        (ii) had relief been given for the allowance, the relief would have to be left out of account for the purposes of section 110(5)(*b*) as mentioned in paragraph (*a*).

Regulations under section 114

34—(1) The provision which may be made in regulations under section 114 does not include provision affecting the amount of relief that may be given for a loss made in a trade that is not a post-1 December 2004 loss (as determined in accordance with section 795).

(2) The repeal by this Act of sections 118ZN and 118ZO of ICTA (or any provision inserting or amending, or affecting the application of, those sections) does not affect the power of the Commissioners for Her Majesty's Revenue and Customs to make regulations under section 118ZN having effect before the tax year 2007–08.

Application of existing regulations under sections 114 and 802

35—(1) After the commencement of sections 114 and 802, the Partnerships (Restrictions on Contributions to a Trade) Regulations 2005 (SI 2005/2017) have effect as if made under those sections.

(2) The Regulations so have effect subject to the following modifications.

(3) They have effect as if in regulation 2—

    (*a*) in the definition of "bank" for "section 840A of ICTA" there were substituted "section 991 of ITA 2007",

    (*b*) for the definition of "contribution to the relevant trade" there were substituted—

""capital contribution"—

        (*a*)   for the purposes of section 114 of ITA 2007, means the contribution to the firm for the purposes of section 104 or 110 of that Act or the contribution to the LLP for the purposes of section 107 of that Act, and

        (*b*)   for the purposes of section 802 of ITA 2007, has the meaning given by section 801(3) of that Act;", and

    (*c*) for the definition of "ICTA" there were substituted—

""ITA 2007" means the Income Tax Act 2007;".

(4) They have effect as if in regulations 3 to 6 for "contribution to the relevant trade", wherever occurring, there were substituted "capital contribution".

(5) They have effect as if—

    (*a*) in regulation 3(*a*) for "section 118ZN of ICTA" there were substituted "section 114(1)(*a*) and (*b*) of ITA 2007", and

    (*b*) in regulation 3(*b*) for the words from "section 119" to the end there were substituted "section 797 of ITA 2007 as mentioned in section 802(2) of that Act".

(6) They have effect as if in regulation 6(*c*) for "the trade" there were substituted "a trade".

Losses in an employment or office

36—(1) This paragraph applies for the purposes of section 128 if the loss is made in the tax year 2007–08.

(2) Relief for the loss can be given for the tax year 2006–07.

(3) Sub-paragraphs (4) and (5) apply if relief for the loss is claimed for the tax year 2006–07.

(4) If relief is to be given, the relief is given in the way it would have been given had it been given under section 380(1)(*b*) of ICTA ignoring this Act (and section 129 of this Act is to be read accordingly).

(5) Section 72 of FA 1991 applies as if the relief had been claimed under section 380(1)(*b*) of ICTA.

Loss relief against miscellaneous income: Case VI losses

37—(1) This paragraph applies if a person makes a loss in any transaction—

    (*a*) which was of such a nature that, if any profits had arisen from it, the person would have been liable to income tax under Case VI of Schedule D for any tax year before the tax year 2005–06, and

    (*b*) which did not fall within section 34, 35 or 36 of ICTA.

(2) So far as relief for the loss has not previously been given, the loss (or the unused part of it) is to be treated as a loss available for deduction in accordance with section 153.

PART 6
LOSSES ON DISPOSAL OF SHARES

Qualifying trading companies

38—(1) In relation to shares issued before 17 March 2004, section 134(2)(*a*) applies with the omission of sub-paragraph (iv) and the "and" immediately before it.

(2) In relation to shares issued before 6 April 1998, section 134 applies with the substitution for subsections [(2) to (4)]³ of—

  "(2)   Condition A is that the company either—

    (*a*)   is a trading company on the date of the disposal, or

    (*b*)   has ceased to be a trading company at a time which is not more than 3 years before that date and has not since that time been an excluded company or an investment company.

  (3)   Condition B is that the company either—

    (*a*)   has been a trading company for a continuous period of 6 years ending on that date or at that time, or

    (*b*)   has been a trading company for a shorter continuous period ending on that date or [at that time and has not before]¹ the beginning of that period been an excluded company or an investment company.

  (4)   Condition C is that none of the shares in the company has been listed on a recognised stock exchange at any time in the period—

    (*a*)   beginning with the incorporation of the company or, if later, 12 months before the date on which the shares in question were subscribed for, and

    (*b*)   ending with the date on which the shares are disposed of.

  (5)   . . .³

(3) In relation to shares issued before 7 March 2001, section 134(4)(*b*) applies with the substitution for "at the relevant time" of "throughout the relevant period".

(4) For the purposes of sub-paragraph (3), shares that were issued—

    (*a*)   . . .¹ after 5 April 1998, but

    (*b*)   before 7 March 2001,

are treated as having been issued on or after 7 March 2001 in respect of any part of the relevant period which falls on or after that date.

(5)   . . .²

Amendments—¹   Words in sub-para (2), in substituted sub-s (3)(*b*), substituted, and words in sub-para (4)(*a*) revoked, by the Income Tax Act 2007 (Amendment) Order, SI 2007/940 art 2(1), (2) with effect for income tax purposes from 2007–08, and for corporation tax purposes for accounting periods ending after 5 April 2007: SI 2007/940 art 1(2).

²   Sub-para (5) repealed by CTA 2010 s 1181, Sch 3 Pt 1. CTA 2010 has effect for corporation tax purposes for accounting periods ending on or after 1 April 2010, and for income and capital gains tax purposes for the tax year 2010–11 and subsequent tax years.

³   In sub-para (2), words substituted for words "(2) to (5)", and the substituted ITA 2007 s 134(5) repealed, by FA 2020 s 38(2)(*a*)(iv) with effect in relation to disposals made on or after 24 January 2019.

Disposals of new shares

39—(1) In relation to new shares issued before 6 April 2007, section 136(2) applies with the omission of "This is subject to section 145(3)."

(2) In this paragraph "new shares" is to be read in accordance with section 145.

The trading requirement

40—(1) In relation to shares issued before 6 April 2007, section 137 applies with the following modifications—

(*a*) the omission of subsection (2),

(*b*) in subsection (5), the omission of paragraph (*d*)(ii) and the "or" immediately before it, and

(*c*) the omission of subsection (6).

(2) In relation to shares issued before 6 April 2000, section 137 applies with the substitution for the definition of "research and development" in subsection

(7) of—

""research and development" means any activity which is intended to result in a patentable invention (within the meaning of the Patents Act 1977) or in a computer program."

(3) Section 137 does not apply in relation to shares issued before 6 April 1998.

(4) . . . [1]

Amendments—[1]   Sub-para (4) repealed by CTA 2010 s 1181, Sch 3 Pt 1. CTA 2010 has effect for corporation tax purposes for accounting periods ending on or after 1 April 2010, and for income and capital gains tax purposes for the tax year 2010–11 and subsequent tax years.

Ceasing to meet trading requirement because of administration or receivership

41—(1) In relation to shares issued before 17 March 2004, section 138 applies with the following modifications—

(*a*) in subsection (1), the omission of "merely" and the substitution for "the company or any of its subsidiaries" of "its",

(*b*) in subsection (2)(*b*), the omission of "concerned",

(*c*) in subsection (3)(*a*), the omission of "or any of its subsidiaries",

(*d*) in subsection (3)(*b*), the omission of "or any of its subsidiaries", and

(*e*) in subsection (4), the omission of "is", in the second place where it occurs.

(2) In relation to an administration order the petition for which was presented before 15 September 2003, section 138(2) applies with the substitution for paragraph (*a*) of—

"(*a*)   the making of the order in question, and".

(3) In relation to shares issued before 21 March 2000, section 138 applies with the omission of subsections (1) and (2).

(4) In the application of sub-paragraph (3) on or after 21 March 2000, shares—

(*a*) that were issued on or after 6 April 1998 but before 21 March 2000, and

(*b*) to which EIS relief or relief under Schedule 5B to TCGA 1992 was attributable immediately before 21 March 2000,

are treated as having been issued on or after 21 March 2000.

(5) Section 138 does not apply in relation to shares issued before 6 April 1998.

(6) . . . [1]

Amendments—[1]   Sub-para (6) repealed by CTA 2010 s 1181, Sch 3 Pt 1. CTA 2010 has effect for corporation tax purposes for accounting periods ending on or after 1 April 2010, and for income and capital gains tax purposes for the tax year 2010–11 and subsequent tax years.

The control and independence requirement

42—(1) In relation to shares issued before 6 April 2007, section 139(1)(*a*) applies with the omission of "of the company".

(2) In relation to shares issued before 21 March 2000, section 139 applies with the following modifications—

(*a*) the substitution for subsections (1) to (3) of—

"(1)   The control element of the requirement is that—

(*a*)   the company must not control (or together with any person connected with it control) another company or have a 51% subsidiary, and

(*b*)   no arrangements must be in existence by virtue of which the company could fail to meet paragraph (*a*).

(2)   The independence element of the requirement is that—

      (*a*)   the company must not be under the control of another company (or another company and any other person connected with that company) or be a 51% subsidiary of another company, and

      (*b*)   no arrangements must be in existence by virtue of which the company could fail to meet paragraph (*a*).

(3) This section is subject to section 145(3); and nothing in subsection (1) prevents the company having one or more qualifying subsidiaries.", and

  (*b*) in subsection (4) the omission of the definition of "arrangements" and, in the definition of "control", the omission of "in subsection (1)(*a*)".

(3) In the application of sub-paragraph (2) on or after 21 March 2000, shares—

  (*a*) that were issued on or after 6 April 1998 but before 21 March 2000, and

  (*b*) to which EIS relief or relief under Schedule 5B to TCGA 1992 was attributable immediately before 21 March 2000,

are treated as having been issued on or after 21 March 2000.

(4) Section 139 does not apply in relation to shares issued before 6 April 1998.

(5), (6) . . . [1]

Amendments—[1]   Sub-paras (5), (6) repealed by CTA 2010 s 1181 Sch 3 Pt 1. CTA 2010 has effect for corporation tax purposes for accounting periods ending on or after 1 April 2010, and for income and capital gains tax purposes for the tax year 2010–11 and subsequent tax years.

The qualifying subsidiaries requirement

43—(1) Section 140 does not apply in relation to shares issued before 6 April 1998.

(2) . . . [1]

Amendments—[1]   Sub-para (2) repealed by CTA 2010 s 1181, Sch 3 Pt 1. CTA 2010 has effect for corporation tax purposes for accounting periods ending on or after 1 April 2010, and for income and capital gains tax purposes for the tax year 2010–11 and subsequent tax years.

The property managing subsidiaries requirement

44—(1) Section 141 does not apply in relation to shares issued before 17 March 2004.

(2) . . . [1]

Amendments—[1]   Sub-para (2) repealed by CTA 2010 s 1181, Sch 3 Pt 1. CTA 2010 has effect for corporation tax purposes for accounting periods ending on or after 1 April 2010, and for income and capital gains tax purposes for the tax year 2010–11 and subsequent tax years.

The gross assets requirement

45—(1) In relation to shares issued before 6 April 2006, section 142 applies with the substitution in subsections (1) and (2)—

  (*a*) of "£15 million" for "£7 million", and

  (*b*) of "£16 million" for "£8 million".

(2) For the purposes of sub-paragraph (1) shares issued on or after 6 April 2006 to a person who subscribed for them before 22 March 2006 are treated as having been issued before 6 April 2006.

(3) Section 142 does not apply in relation to shares issued before 6 April 1998.

(4) . . . [1]

Amendments—[1]   Sub-para (4) repealed by CTA 2010 s 1181 Sch 3 Pt 1. CTA 2010 has effect for corporation tax purposes for accounting periods ending on or after 1 April 2010, and for income and capital gains tax purposes for the tax year 2010–11 and subsequent tax years.

The unquoted status requirement

46—(1) In relation to shares issued before 7 March 2001, section 143 applies with the following modifications—

  (*a*) the substitution for subsection (1) of—

"(1) The unquoted status requirement is that the company must be an unquoted company throughout the relevant period.",

  (*b*) the substitution for subsection (2) of—

"(2) If the company is an unquoted company at the time when any shares are issued, it is not treated for the purposes of this section as ceasing to be an unquoted company in relation to those shares at any subsequent time merely because any shares, stocks, debentures or other securities of the company are at that time—

      (*a*)   listed on an exchange designated by an order made for the purposes of section 184(3)(*b*), or

      (*b*)   dealt in by any means designated by an order made for the purposes of section 184(3)(*c*), if the order was made after the shares were issued.", and

(*c*) in subsection (3) the substitution for the definition of "arrangements" of—

""the relevant period" means the period—

    (*a*)   beginning with the incorporation of the company or, if later, the date one year before the issue of the shares in question, and

    (*b*)   ending with the date of the disposal."

(2) For the purposes of sub-paragraph (1)(*a*) and (*c*), shares that were issued—

(*a*) . . . [1] after 5 April 1998, but

(*b*) before 7 March 2001,

are treated as having been issued on or after 7 March 2001 in respect of any part of the relevant period which falls on or after that date.

(3) In the application of sub-paragraph (1)(*b*) on or after 7 March 2001, shares—

(*a*) that were issued . . . [1] after 5 April 1998 but before 7 March 2001, and

(*b*) to which EIS relief or relief under Schedule 5B to TCGA 1992 was attributable immediately before 7 March 2001,

are treated as having been issued on or after 7 March 2001.

(4) Section 143 does not apply in relation to shares issued before 6 April 1998.

(5), (6) . . . [2]

Amendments—[1]   Words in sub-paras (2)(*a*), (3)(*a*) revoked by the Income Tax Act 2007 (Amendment) Order, SI 2007/940 art 2(1), (3) with effect for income tax purposes from 2007–08, and for corporation tax purposes for accounting periods ending after 5 April 2007: SI 2007/940 art 1(2).

[2]   Sub-paras (5), (6) repealed by CTA 2010 s 1181, Sch 3 Pt 1. CTA 2010 has effect for corporation tax purposes for accounting periods ending on or after 1 April 2010, and for income and capital gains tax purposes for the tax year 2010–11 and subsequent tax years.

Power to amend requirements by Treasury order

47—(1) Section 144 does not apply in relation to shares issued before 6 April 1998.

(2) . . . [1]

Amendments—[1]   Sub-para (2) repealed by CTA 2010 s 1181, Sch 3 Pt 1. CTA 2010 has effect for corporation tax purposes for accounting periods ending on or after 1 April 2010, and for income and capital gains tax purposes for the tax year 2010–11 and subsequent tax years.

Relief after an exchange of shares for shares in another company

48—(1) In relation to new shares issued before 6 April 2007, section 145 applies with—

(*a*) the substitution for subsection (1)(*e*) of—

    "(*e*)   before the issue of the new shares, the Commissioners for Her Majesty's Revenue and Customs have, on the application of the new company or the old company, notified that company that the exchange of shares—

        (i)   will be effected for genuine commercial reasons, and

        (ii)   will not form part of any such scheme or arrangement as is mentioned in section 137(1) of TCGA 1992.", and

(*b*) the omission of subsection (3)(*a*).

(2) Section 145 does not apply in relation to shares issued before 6 April 1998.

(3), (4) . . . [1]

Amendments—[1]   Sub-paras (3), (4) repealed by CTA 2010 s 1181 Sch 3 Pt 1. CTA 2010 has effect for corporation tax purposes for accounting periods ending on or after 1 April 2010, and for income and capital gains tax purposes for the tax year 2010–11 and subsequent tax years.

Substitution of new shares for old shares

49—(1) Section 146 does not apply in relation to shares issued before 6 April 1998.

(2) . . . [1]

Amendments—[1]   Sub-para (2) repealed by CTA 2010 s 1181, Sch 3 Pt 1. CTA 2010 has effect for corporation tax purposes for accounting periods ending on or after 1 April 2010, and for income and capital gains tax purposes for the tax year 2010–11 and subsequent tax years.

Interpretation of Chapter

50—(1) In relation to shares issued before 6 April 1998, section 151 applies with the following modifications—

(*a*) in the definition of "excluded company" in subsection (1), the substitution for "in land, in commodities or futures or in shares, securities or other financial instruments" of "in shares, securities, land, trades or commodity futures",

(*b*) in subsection (7), the insertion after "excluded company" of "or is a non-UK resident".

(2), (3) . . . [1]

Amendments—[1]   Sub-paras (2), (3) repealed by CTA 2010 s 1181 Sch 3 Pt 1. CTA 2010 has effect for corporation tax purposes for accounting periods ending on or after 1 April 2010, and for income and capital gains tax purposes for the tax year 2010–11 and subsequent tax years.

Meaning of "qualifying subsidiary"

51—(1) In relation to shares issued before 17 March 2004, section 191 (as applied by sections 137(7), 139(4), 140(2) and 142(4)) applies with the following modifications—

   (a) in subsection (1), the insertion at the end of "and, except as provided by subsection (3), continue to be met until the time that is relevant for the purposes of section 134(2)",

   (b) in subsection (2), the substitution for paragraph (a) of—

      "(a)   the relevant company, or another of its subsidiaries, possesses at least 75% of the issued share capital of, and at least 75% of the voting power in, the subsidiary,

      (aa)   the relevant company, or another of its subsidiaries, would in the event of a winding up of the subsidiary, or in any other circumstances, be beneficially entitled to receive at least 75% of the assets of the subsidiary which would then be available for distribution to the equity holders of the subsidiary,

      (ab)   the relevant company, or another of its subsidiaries, is beneficially entitled to at least 75% of any profits of the subsidiary which are available for distribution to the equity holders of the subsidiary,",

   (c) in paragraph (c) of subsection (2), the substitution for "either of the conditions in paragraphs (a) and (b)" of "any of the conditions in paragraphs (a), (aa), (ab) and (b)",

   (d) in subsection (3), the substitution for "any other company" of "the relevant company" and the substitution for the words from "the winding up or dissolution" to the end of that subsection of—

      "(a)   the winding up or dissolution is for genuine commercial reasons, and not part of a scheme or arrangement the main purpose or one of the main purposes of which is the avoidance of tax,

      (b)   the net assets, if any, of the subsidiary or, as the case may be, the relevant company are distributed to its members, or dealt with as bona vacantia, before the time that is relevant for the purposes of section 134(2) or, in the case of a winding up, the end (if later) of 3 years from the commencement of the winding up.",

   (e) the omission of subsection (4),

   (f) in subsection (5), the substitution for "arrangements are in existence for" of "of" and the insertion after "another subsidiary" of "within the continuous period that is relevant for the purposes of section 134(3)",

   (g) in subsection (5)(a), the omission of "to be",

   (h) in subsection (5)(b), the substitution for "is not to be" of "not", and

   (i) after subsection (5), the insertion of—

"(6)   The persons who are equity holders of a subsidiary, and the percentage of the assets of a subsidiary to which an equity holder would be entitled, is to be determined in accordance with [Chapter 6 of Part 5 of CTA 2010][1], taking—

      (a)   references in [section 166 of that Act to company A][1] as references to an equity holder, and

      (b)   references to a winding up as including references to any other circumstances in which assets of the subsidiary are available for distribution to its equity holders."

(2), (3) . . . [1]

Amendments—[1]   In sub-para (1)(i), in the inserted sub-s (6) words substituted, in the inserted sub-s (6)(a) words substituted, and sub-paras (2), (3) repealed by CTA 2010 ss 1177, 1181, Sch 1 para 571, Sch 3 Pt 1. CTA 2010 has effect for corporation tax purposes for accounting periods ending on or after 1 April 2010, and for income and capital gains tax purposes for the tax year 2010–11 and subsequent tax years.

Meaning of "excluded activities"

52—(1) In relation to shares issued before 7 March 2001, section 192(1) (as applied by section 137(7)) applies with the insertion after paragraph (c) of—

      "(ca)   oil extraction activities (within the meaning of Chapter 5 of Part 12 of ICTA),".

(2) In the application of sub-paragraph (1) on or after 7 March 2001, shares—

   (a) that were issued on or after 6 April 1998 but before 7 March 2001, and

   (b) to which EIS relief or relief under Schedule 5B to TCGA 1992 was attributable immediately before 7 March 2001,

are treated as having been issued on or after 7 March 2001.

(3) . . . [1]

Amendments—[1]   Sub-para (3) repealed by CTA 2010 s 1181, Sch 3 Pt 1. CTA 2010 has effect for corporation tax purposes for accounting periods ending on or after 1 April 2010, and for income and capital gains tax purposes for the tax year 2010–11 and subsequent tax years.

Excluded activities: wholesale and retail distribution

53—(1) In relation to shares issued before 6 April 2007, section 193(5)(*b*) (as applied by section 137(7)) applies with the following modifications—

    (*a*) the insertion after "held" of "by the company", and

    (*b*) the substitution for "the trader" of "a vendor".

(2) . . . [1]

Amendments—[1]   Sub-para (2) repealed by CTA 2010 s 1181 Sch 3 Pt 1. CTA 2010 has effect for corporation tax purposes for accounting periods ending on or after 1 April 2010, and for income and capital gains tax purposes for the tax year 2010–11 and subsequent tax years.

Excluded activities: leasing of ships

54—(1) In relation to shares issued before 6 April 2007, section 194 (as applied by the definition of "non-qualifying activities" in section 137(7)) applies with the omission of subsection (7).

(2) In relation to shares issued before 6 April 2004, section 194 (as applied by section 137(7)) applies with the following modifications—

    (*a*) in subsection (1), the substitution for "offshore installations" of "oil rigs",

    (*b*) in subsection (2), the substitution for "offshore installation" of "oil rig", and

    (*c*) in subsection (8), the insertion after "this section" of—

      ""oil rig" means any ship which is an offshore installation for the purposes of the Mineral Workings (Offshore Installations) Act 1971,".

(3) . . . [1]

Amendments—[1]   Sub-para (3) repealed by CTA 2010 s 1181, Sch 3 Pt 1. CTA 2010 has effect for corporation tax purposes for accounting periods ending on or after 1 April 2010, and for income and capital gains tax purposes for the tax year 2010–11 and subsequent tax years.

Excluded activities: receipt of royalties and licence fees

55—(1) In relation to shares issued before 6 April 2000, Chapter 6 of Part 4 applies with the substitution for section 195 (as applied by section 137(7)) of—

"195 Excluded activities: receipt of royalties and licence fees

(1) This section supplements section 192(1)(*e*) (receipt of royalties and licence fees).

(2) A trade is not to be regarded as consisting in the carrying on of excluded activities within section 192(1)(*e*) as a result only of it consisting to a substantial extent in the receiving of royalties or licence fees if—

    (*a*)   the company carrying on the trade is engaged throughout the relevant period in—

        (i)   the production of films, or

        (ii)   the production of films and the distribution of films produced by it in the relevant period, and

    (*b*)   all royalties and licence fees received by it in the relevant period are in respect of films produced by it in that period or sound recordings in relation to such films or other products arising from such films.

(3) A trade is not to be regarded as consisting in the carrying on of excluded activities within section 192(1)(*e*) as a result only of it consisting to a substantial extent in the receiving of royalties or licence fees if—

    (*a*)   the company carrying on the trade is engaged in research and development throughout the relevant period, and

    (*b*)   all royalties and licence fees received by it in the relevant period are attributable to research and development which it has carried out.

(4) In this section "the relevant period" means the continuous period that is relevant for the purposes of section 134(3)."

(2), (3) . . . [1]

Amendments—[1]   Sub-paras (2), (3) repealed by CTA 2010 s 1181 Sch 3 Pt 1. CTA 2010 has effect for corporation tax purposes for accounting periods ending on or after 1 April 2010, and for income and capital gains tax purposes for the tax year 2010–11 and subsequent tax years.

Excluded activities: provision of services or facilities for another business

56—(1) In relation to shares issued before 6 April 2007, section 199 (as applied by section 137(7)) applies with the following modifications—

(*a*) in subsections (1) to (4), the substitution of "trade" for "business", wherever it occurs, and

(*b*) in subsection (5) the substitution for paragraph (*b*) of—

"(*b*)   references to a trade, in relation to the provider of the services or facilities, are to be read without regard to the definition of "trade" in section 989, and

(*c*)   "trade", in relation to the other person, includes any business, profession or vocation".

(2) . . . [1]

Amendments—[1]   Sub-para (2) repealed by CTA 2010 s 1181, Sch 3 Pt 1. CTA 2010 has effect for corporation tax purposes for accounting periods ending on or after 1 April 2010, and for income and capital gains tax purposes for the tax year 2010–11 and subsequent tax years.

Meaning of a company being "in administration"

57—(1) Sub-paragraph (2) applies in relation to—

(*a*) an administration order under Part 3 of the Insolvency (Northern Ireland) Order 1989 the petition for which was presented before 6 April 2007, or

(*b*) any corresponding order under the law of a country or territory outside the United Kingdom the proceedings for which were instituted before that date.

(2) Section 252 (as it applies for the purposes of Chapter 6 of Part 4) applies with the substitution for subsection (2) of—

"(2)   A company is "in administration" if—

(*a*)   it is in administration within the meaning of Schedule B1 to the Insolvency Act 1986, or

(*b*)   there is in force in relation to it—

(i)   an administration order under Part 3 of the Insolvency (Northern Ireland) Order 1989, or

(ii)   any corresponding order under the law of a country or territory outside the United Kingdom."

(3) For the purposes of sub-paragraph (2), section 252 applies for the purposes of Chapter 6 of Part 4 in any case where—

(*a*) it is applied by section 138(5),

(*b*) it applies for the purposes of section 190 as applied by section 141(2), or

(*c*) it applies for the purposes of section 191 as applied by section 137(7), 139(4), 140(2) or 142(4).

(4) In relation to an administration order under Part 2 of the Insolvency Act 1986 the petition for which was presented before 15 September 2003, section 252 (as applied by section 138(5)) applies with the substitution for subsection (2) of—

"(2)   A company is "in administration" if there is in force in relation to it—

(*a*)   an administration order under Part 2 of the Insolvency Act 1986 or Part 3 of the Insolvency (Northern Ireland) Order 1989, or

(*b*)   any corresponding order under the law of a country or territory outside the United Kingdom."

(5) Section 252 (as applied by section 138(5)) does not apply in relation to shares issued before 21 March 2000.

(6) In the application of sub-paragraph (5) on or after 21 March 2000, shares—

(*a*) that were issued on or after 6 April 1998 but before 21 March 2000, and

(*b*) to which EIS relief or relief under Schedule 5B to TCGA 1992 was attributable immediately before 21 March 2000,

are treated as having been issued on or after 21 March 2000.

(7), (8) . . . [1]

Amendments—[1]   Sub-paras (7), (8) repealed by CTA 2010s 1181, Sch 3 Pt 1. CTA 2010 has effect for corporation tax purposes for accounting periods ending on or after 1 April 2010, and for income and capital gains tax purposes for the tax year 2010–11 and subsequent tax years.

[Application in relation to corresponding bonus shares

57A   (1) For the purposes of this Part of this Schedule, if—

(*a*) any shares ("the original shares") have been issued to an individual before a particular date, or are treated under this paragraph as having been issued to the individual before a particular date, and

(*b*) any corresponding bonus shares are issued to the individual on or after that date,

the bonus shares are treated as having been issued at the time the original shares were issued to the individual or are treated as having been so issued.

(2) In this paragraph "bonus shares" and "corresponding bonus shares" have the same meaning as in Chapter 6 of Part 4.][1]

Amendments—[1]   Paragraph 57A and preceding cross-head inserted by CTA 2010 s 1177, Sch 1 para 571. CTA 2010 has effect for corporation tax purposes for accounting periods ending on or after 1 April 2010, and for income and capital gains tax purposes for the tax year 2010–11 and subsequent tax years.

PART 7
ENTERPRISE INVESTMENT SCHEME

The gross assets requirement

58—(1) In relation to shares to which sub-paragraph (2) or (3) applies, section 186 applies with the substitution in subsections (1) and (2)—

(a) of "£15 million" for "£7 million", and

(b) of "£16 million" for "£8 million".

(2) This sub-paragraph applies to shares issued to a person who subscribed for them before 22 March 2006.

(3) This sub-paragraph applies to shares issued to the managers of an investment fund approved for the purposes of section 251 by the Commissioners for Her Majesty's Revenue and Customs if—

(a) the fund was approved before 22 March 2006,

(b) investments in the fund have been accepted before 6 April 2006, and

(c) the shares are issued to the managers as nominee for an individual who has (whether or not before 6 April 2006) invested in the fund.

PART 8
VENTURE CAPITAL TRUSTS

Eligibility for relief

59   Section 261(4) does not apply in relation to shares acquired by a company before 1 December 2003.

Form and amount of relief

60—(1) In relation to shares issued before 6 April 2006, section 263(2) applies with the substitution of "tax at the higher rate for the tax year on" for "30% of".

(2) In relation to shares issued before 6 April 2004, section 263(2) applies with the substitution of "the savings rate" for "the higher rate".

No entitlement to relief if there is a linked loan

61   In relation to shares issued before 6 April 2006, section 264(3) applies with the substitution, in paragraph (b) of the definition of "the relevant period", of "the third anniversary" for "the fifth anniversary".

Loss of relief if shares disposed of within 5 years

62—(1) In relation to shares issued before 6 April 2006—

(a) subsection (1) of section 266 applies with the substitution of "3 years" for "5 years", and

(b) subsection (4) of that section applies with the omission of "30% of" and the insertion at the end of "multiplied by the higher rate for the tax year in which the shares were issued".

(2) In relation to shares issued before 6 April 2004, section 266(4) applies with the substitution of "the savings rate" for "the higher rate".

Interpretation of Chapter 2

63—(1) In relation to shares issued before 6 April 2007, section 273(1) applies as if it gave "eligible shares" the same meaning as that given by paragraph 6(1) of Schedule 15B to ICTA at the time of the issue of the shares.

(2) In relation to shares issued before 6 April 2006, section 273(1) applies with the substitution of "3 years" for "5 years".

The 15% holding limit condition

64   In relation to shares or securities issued before 17 April 2002, section 277(5) applies with the following modifications—

(a) the insertion after "reconstruction", in the first place where it occurs, of "or amalgamation", and

(b) the omission of the words from "In this subsection" to the end.

Conditions relating to value of investments

65—(1) Sub-paragraph (2) applies if any question arises which—

(a) would otherwise fall to be determined in accordance with section 278, and

(b) is a question whether, in a case where a company ("company A") holds investments in a company ("company B") immediately before 6 April 2007, the 15% holding condition is met if there is an addition to the holding on or after that date.

(2) Any such question is to be determined in accordance with—

(a) section 842AA(11)(c) of ICTA, and

(b) section 842(3) and (4) of that Act as applied by that provision,

until such time as company A ceases to hold investments in company B.

(3) Except in a case to which sub-paragraph (2) applies, section 278(5) applies in relation to investments issued before 17 April 2002 with the following modifications—

(a) the insertion after "reconstruction", in the first place where it occurs, of "or amalgamation", and

(b) the omission of the words from "In this subsection" to the end.

Conditions relating to qualifying holdings and eligible shares: supplementary

66 Section 280(3) does not apply in relation to shares issued before 17 April 2002.

Interpretation of Chapter 3

67 Section 285 applies with the omission of subsections (4) to (6) for the purposes of determining whether, at any time before 6 April 2007, the conditions mentioned in section 274(2) are, will be or were met with respect to a company.

The maximum qualifying investment requirement

68 For the purpose of determining whether shares or securities are to be regarded as comprised in a company's qualifying holdings, section 287(3)(b) does not apply in relation to shares or securities issued before 6 April 2007.

The no guaranteed loan requirement

69 For the purpose of determining whether shares or securities are to be regarded as comprised in a company's qualifying holdings, section 288 does not apply in relation to shares or securities acquired [before 6 April 2018][1] by a company by means of the investment of—

(a) money raised by the issue before 2 July 1997 of shares in or securities of the investing company, or

(b) money derived from the investment by that company of any such money.

Amendments—[1] Words inserted by FA 2018 s 17, Sch 5 para 8(1), (2) with effect from 6 April 2018 (by virtue of SI 2018/931 reg 4(e)).

The proportion of eligible shares requirement

70—(1) If at any time the requirement of section 289—

(a) would be met in relation to a relevant holding and a company if none of the old investments were held by the investing company at that time, but

(b) would not otherwise be met,

that section applies in relation to that holding as if the old investments were not held by the investing company at that time.

(2) In sub-paragraph (1) "old investments" means shares in or securities of the relevant company acquired [before 6 April 2018][1] by means of the investment of—

(a) money raised by the issue before 2 July 1997 of shares in or securities of the investing company, or

(b) money derived from the investment by that company of any such money.

Amendments—[1] In sub-para (2), words inserted by FA 2018 s 17, Sch 5 para 8(1), (3) with effect from 6 April 2018 (by virtue of SI 2018/931 reg 4(e)).

The trading requirement

71 For the purpose of determining whether shares or securities are to be regarded as comprised in a company's qualifying holdings, section 290 applies in relation to shares or securities issued before 6 April 2007 with the following modifications—

(*a*) the omission of subsections (2) and (6), and

(*b*) in subsection (5)(*d*), the omission of sub-paragraph (ii) and the "or" immediately before it.

The carrying on of a qualifying activity requirement

72—(1) For the purpose of determining whether shares or securities are to be regarded as comprised in a company's qualifying holdings, section 291 applies in relation to shares or securities issued before 6 April 2007 with the omission of subsection (8).

(2) For the purpose of determining whether shares or securities are to be regarded as comprised in a company's qualifying holdings, section 291 applies in relation to shares or securities issued before 17 March 2004 with the following modifications—

(*a*) in subsection (1), the substitution for "a qualifying company (whether or not the same such company at every such time)" of "the qualifying company",

(*b*) in subsection (3), the substitution for "was intended to be carried on" of "it intended to carry on" and the omission of "by a qualifying company",

(*c*) in subsection (4)(*a*), the substitution for "a qualifying company" of "the qualifying company",

(*d*) in subsection (4)(*b*), the substitution for "at all times since the end of that period, a qualifying company (whether or not the same such company at every such time) has" of "the qualifying company has at all times since the end of that period", and

(*e*) the omission of subsection (6).

Ceasing to meet the requirement because of administration or receivership

73 For the purpose of determining whether shares or securities are to be regarded as comprised in a company's qualifying holdings, section 292(1) applies in relation to shares or securities issued before 17 March 2004 with the omission of "merely".

The use of the money raised requirement

74 For the purpose of determining whether shares or securities are to be regarded as comprised in a company's qualifying holdings, section 293 applies in relation to shares or securities issued before 17 March 2004 with the following modifications—

(*a*) in subsection (2), the substitution for "has been or is intended to be employed" of "is money which the qualifying company has employed or intends to employ", and

(*b*) in subsection (5)(*b*), the substitution for "a qualifying company" of "the qualifying company".

The relevant company to carry on the relevant qualifying activity requirement

75—(1) For the purpose of determining whether shares or securities are to be regarded as comprised in a company's qualifying holdings, section 294 applies in relation to shares or securities issued before 6 April 2007 with the following modifications—

(*a*) in subsections (1) and (6) the substitution for "relevant qualifying activity" of "qualifying activity",

(*b*) in subsection (1) the substitution for "section 293" of "section 291", and

(*c*) the omission of subsection (7).

(2) For the purpose of determining whether shares or securities are to be regarded as comprised in a company's qualifying holdings, Chapter 4 of Part 6 of this Act applies in relation to shares or securities issued before 17 March 2004 with the substitution for section 294 of—

"294 Further requirements as to the money raised by the investment in question

(1) If—

    (*a*)   the relevant company is a parent company, and

    (*b*)   the business of the group does not consist wholly or as to a substantial part in the carrying on of non-qualifying activities,

the requirements of this section are not met unless one or more of the following conditions is met.

(2) Condition A is that the trader company meets the requirement of section 290(1)(*a*).

(3) Condition B is that the trader company would meet that requirement if its purposes were ignored so far as they consist in the carrying on of activities in section 290(5).

(4) Condition C is that the trader company is a [qualifying 90% subsidiary of the relevant company][1] and—

    (*a*)   apart from incidental purposes, it exists wholly for the purposes of carrying on activities such as those in section 290(5)(*c*) and (*d*), or

    (*b*)   it has no profits for the purposes of corporation tax and no part of its business consists in the making of investments.

(5) In this section—

"the business of the group" has the same meaning as it has for the purposes of subsection (1)(*b*) of section 290,

"incidental purposes" and "non-qualifying activities" have the same meaning as in that section,

"the trader company" means the company (whether the relevant company or a qualifying subsidiary of the relevant company) carrying on the qualifying activity which meets the requirement of section 291."

Amendments—[1]   In sub-s (2), in inserted s 294(4), words substituted by the Income Tax Act 2007 (Amendment) (No 2) Order, SI 2007/1820 art 4(1), (3) with effect from 17 July 2007.

The gross assets requirement

76—(1) For the purpose of determining whether shares or securities are to be regarded as comprised in a company's qualifying holdings, section 297 applies in relation to shares or securities issued on or after 6 April 1998 and before 6 April 2006 with the substitution in subsections (1) and (2)—

    (*a*) of "£15 million" for "£7 million", and

    (*b*) of "£16 million" for "£8 million".

(2) For the purposes of sub-paragraph (1) any shares or securities acquired by a company at any time by means of the investment of—

    (*a*) money raised by the issue before 6 April 2006 of shares in or securities of the investing company, or

    (*b*) money derived from the investment by that company of any such money,

are treated as having been issued before 6 April 2006.

(3) For the purpose of determining whether shares or securities are to be regarded as comprised in a company's qualifying holdings, section 297 applies in relation to shares or securities issued before 6 April 1998 with the substitution in subsections (1) and (2)—

    (*a*) of "£10 million" for "£7 million", and

    (*b*) of "£11 million" for "£8 million".

The property managing subsidiaries requirement

77   For the purpose of determining whether shares or securities are to be regarded as comprised in a company's qualifying holdings, section 299 does not apply in relation to shares or securities issued before 17 March 2004.

Meaning of "qualifying trade"

78   For the purpose of determining whether shares or securities are to be regarded as comprised in a company's qualifying holdings, section 300 applies in relation to shares or securities issued before 6 April 2007 with the following modifications—

    (*a*) in subsection (2), the omission of paragraph (*b*) and the "or" immediately before it, and

    (*b*) the omission of subsection (3).

Meaning of "qualifying 90% subsidiary"

79   For the purpose of determining whether shares or securities are to be regarded as comprised in a company's qualifying holdings, section 301 does not apply in relation to shares or securities issued before 17 March 2004.

Meaning of "qualifying subsidiary"

80   For the purpose of determining whether shares or securities are to be regarded as comprised in a company's qualifying holdings, section 302 applies in relation to shares or securities issued before 17 March 2004 with the following modifications—

    (*a*) the substitution for subsection (2)(*a*) of—

        "(*a*)   the relevant company, or another of its subsidiaries, possesses at least 75% of the issued share capital of, and at least 75% of the voting power in, the subsidiary,

        (*aa*)   the relevant company, or another of its subsidiaries, would in the event of a winding up of the subsidiary, or in any other circumstances, be beneficially entitled to receive at least 75% of the assets of the subsidiary which would then be available for distribution to the equity holders of the subsidiary,

        (*ab*)   the relevant company, or another of its subsidiaries, is beneficially entitled to at least 75% of any profits of the subsidiary which are available for distribution to the equity holders of the subsidiary,",

    (*b*) in subsection (2)(*c*), the substitution for "either of the conditions in paragraphs (*a*) and (*b*)" of "any of the conditions in paragraphs (*a*), (*aa*), (*ab*) and (*b*)",

(c) in subsection (3), the omission of "or any other company" and the substitution for paragraphs (*a*) and (*b*) of "is for genuine commercial reasons, and not part of a scheme or arrangement the main purpose or one of the main purposes of which is the avoidance of tax",

(d) the omission of subsection (4),

(e) in subsection (5), the substitution for paragraphs (*a*) and (*b*) of "is to be for genuine commercial reasons, and not part of a scheme or arrangement the main purpose or one of the main purposes of which is the avoidance of tax",

(f) after subsection (5) the insertion of—

"(6) For the purposes of this section the persons who are equity holders of a subsidiary, and the percentage of the assets of the subsidiary to which an equity holder would be entitled, is to be determined in accordance with [Chapter 6 of Part 5 of CTA 2010][1], taking—

> (*a*)   references in [section 166 of that Act to company A][1] as references to the equity holder, and
>
> (*b*)   references to a winding up as including references to any other circumstances in which assets of the subsidiary are available for distribution to its equity holders."

Amendments—[1]   In para (f), in the inserted sub-s (6), words substituted for words by CTA 2010 s 1177, Sch 1 para 571. CTA 2010 has effect for corporation tax purposes for accounting periods ending on or after 1 April 2010, and for income and capital gains tax purposes for the tax year 2010–11 and subsequent tax years.

Meaning of "excluded activities"

81 For the purpose of determining whether shares or securities are to be regarded as comprised in a company's qualifying holdings at any time, section 303(1)(*g*) to (k) (and accordingly sections 307 to 309) do not apply in relation to shares or securities acquired [before 6 April 2018][1] by the company by means of the investment of—

(a) money raised by the issue before 17 March 1998 of shares in or securities of the investing company, or

(b) money derived from the investment by that company of any such money.

Amendments—[1]   Words inserted by FA 2018 s 17, Sch 5 para 8(1), (4) with effect from 6 April 2018 (by virtue of SI 2018/931 reg 4(e)).

Excluded activities: wholesale and retail distribution

82 For the purpose of determining whether shares or securities are to be regarded as comprised in a company's qualifying holdings, section 304 applies in relation to shares or securities issued before 6 April 2007 with the following modifications—

(a) in subsection (5)(*b*), the insertion after "held" of "by the company" and the substitution for "the trader" of "a vendor", and

(b) in subsection (6), the substitution for "of wholesale or retail distribution", in the first place where it occurs, of "carried on by any person" and the substitution for "the trader", in each place where it occurs, of "that person".

Excluded activities: leasing of ships

83—(1) For the purpose of determining whether shares or securities are to be regarded as comprised in a company's qualifying holdings, section 305 as applied by the definition of "non-qualifying activities" in section 290(8) applies in relation to shares or securities issued before 6 April 2007 with the omission of subsection (7).

(2) For the purpose of determining whether shares or securities are to be regarded as comprised in a company's qualifying holdings, section 305 applies in relation to shares or securities issued before 6 April 2004 with the following modifications—

(a) in subsection (1), the substitution for "offshore installations" of "oil rigs",

(b) in subsection (2), the substitution for "offshore installation" of "oil rig",

(c) in subsection (8), the insertion after "this section" of—

""oil rig" means any ship which is an offshore installation for the purposes of the Mineral Workings (Offshore Installations) Act 1971,".

Excluded activities: receipt of royalties and licence fees

84 For the purpose of determining whether shares or securities are to be regarded as comprised in a company's qualifying holdings, section 306 applies in relation to shares or securities issued before 6 April 2000 with the substitution for subsections (2) to (6) of—

"(2) If the requirement of subsection (3) or (4) is met, a trade is not to be regarded as consisting in the carrying on of excluded activities within section 303(1)(*e*) as a result only of its consisting to a substantial extent in the receiving of royalties of licence fees.

ITA 2007

(3) The requirement of this subsection is that—
    (*a*)   the company carrying on the trade is engaged in—
        (i)   the production of films, or
        (ii)   the production of films and the distribution of films produced by it since the issue of the relevant holding, and
    (*b*)   all royalties and licence fees received by it are in respect of—
        (i)   films produced by it since the issue of the relevant holding,
        (ii)   sound recordings in relation to such films, or
        (iii)   other products arising from such films.
(4) The requirement of this subsection is that—
    (*a*)   the company carrying on the trade is engaged in research and development, and
    (*b*)   all royalties and licence fees received by it are attributable to research and development which it has carried out."

Excluded activities: provision of services or facilities for another business

85—(1) For the purpose of determining whether shares or securities are to be regarded as comprised in a company's qualifying holdings, section 310 applies in relation to shares or securities issued before 6 April 2007 with the following modifications—
    (*a*)   in subsections (1) to (4), the substitution of "trade" for "business", wherever it occurs, and
    (*b*)   in subsection (5) the substitution for paragraph (*b*) of—
        "(*b*)   "trade" includes business, profession or vocation where what is carried on is carried on by a person other than a company."
(2) For the purpose of determining whether shares or securities are to be regarded as comprised in a company's qualifying holdings at any time, section 310(1)(*a*) applies in relation to shares or securities acquired by the company by means of the investment of—
    (*a*)   money raised by the issue before 17 March 1998 of shares in or securities of the investing company, or
    (*b*)   money derived from the investment by that company of any such money,
with the substitution for "paragraphs (a) to (k)" of "paragraphs (a) to (f)".

Winding up of the relevant company

86 For the purpose of determining whether shares or securities are to be regarded as comprised in a company's qualifying holdings, section 312(*b*) applies in relation to shares or securities issued before 17 March 2004 with the substitution for "is not" of "not".

Acquisitions for restructuring purposes etc

87 Sections 326 to 329 do not apply in relation to arrangements made, or rights of conversion exercised, before 16 June 1999.

Power to facilitate company reorganisations

88 Section 330 does not apply in relation to exchanges of shares or securities taking effect before 21 March 2000.

Meaning of a company being "in administration"

89—(1) Sub-paragraph (2) applies in relation to—
    (*a*)   an administration order under Part 3 of the Insolvency (Northern Ireland) Order 1989 the petition for which was presented before 6 April 2007, or
    (*b*)   any corresponding order under the law of a country or territory outside the United Kingdom the proceedings for which were instituted before that date.
(2) Section 331 applies with the substitution for subsection (2) of—
    "(2)   A company is "in administration" if—
    (*a*)   it is in administration within the meaning of Schedule B1 to the Insolvency Act 1986, or
    (*b*)   there is in force in relation to it—
        (i)   an administration order under Part 3 of the Insolvency (Northern Ireland) Order 1989, or
        (ii)   any corresponding order under the law of a country or territory outside the United Kingdom."

(3) In relation to an administration order under Part 2 of the Insolvency Act 1986 the petition for which was presented before 15 September 2003, section 331 applies with the substitution for subsection (2) of—

"(2)   A company is "in administration" if there is in force in relation to it—

(*a*)   an administration order under Part 2 of the Insolvency Act 1986 or Part 3 of the Insolvency (Northern Ireland) Order 1989, or

(*b*)   any corresponding order under the law of a country or territory outside the United Kingdom."

Meaning of "company", "shares" and "research and development" in Part 6

90—(1) This paragraph applies in relation to the meaning of "company", "shares" and "research and development" in Part 6 (see section 332).

(2) If—

(*a*)   a company holds investments of any description in an entity immediately before 6 April 2007, and

(*b*)   the entity is a company for any purposes of the Part 6 provisions but not for the corresponding purposes of the ICTA provisions,

any question whether the entity is a company for those purposes of the Part 6 provisions is to be determined in accordance with the ICTA provisions until such time as the company ceases to hold investments of that description.

(3) If—

(*a*)   a company holds investments of any description in an entity immediately before 6 April 2007, and

(*b*)   the investments are shares for any purposes of either of the following—

(i)   the Part 6 provisions, and

(ii)   the ICTA provisions,

but not for the corresponding purposes of the other set of provisions,

any question whether the investments are shares for those purposes of the Part 6 provisions is to be determined in accordance with the ICTA provisions until such time as the company ceases to hold investments of that description.

(4) In sub-paragraphs (2) and (3)—

"the ICTA provisions" means section 842AA of ICTA (VCT approvals) and Schedule 28B to that Act (qualifying holdings),

"the Part 6 provisions" means Chapter 3 of Part 6 (VCT approvals) and Chapter 4 of that Part (qualifying holdings).

(5) For the purpose of determining whether any shares or securities are to be regarded as comprised in a company's qualifying holdings, section 332 applies in relation to shares issued before 6 April 2000 with the substitution for the definition of "research and development" of—

""research and development" means any activity which is intended to result in a patentable invention (within the meaning of the Patents Act 1977) or in a computer program."

PART 9

OTHER RELIEFS

Interest: loans for interests in close companies

91   Section 392(3)(*a*) does not apply if the shares were acquired before 14 March 1989.

92   Section 392(3)(*b*) does not apply if the shares were acquired before 6 April 1989.

93—(1) In relation to a loan made before 14 November 1986—

(*a*)   section 395(1)(*c*) applies with the substitution for "the trustees of" of "any person (other than the individual) interested in", and

(*b*)   section 395(1)(*d*) applies with the substitution for "the personal representatives" of "any person (other than the individual) interested in the estate".

(2) No individual is an associate because of sub-paragraph (1)(*a*) if the trust relates exclusively to a registered pension scheme.

(3) No individual is an associate because of sub-paragraph (1)(*a*) if—

(*a*)   the trust—

(i)   is exclusively for the benefit of the employees, or the employees and directors, of the company or their dependants, and

(ii)   is not wholly or mainly for the benefit of the directors or their relatives, and

(*b*)   the individual—

    (i)   is not (either alone or with relatives) the beneficial owner of more than 5% of the company's ordinary share capital, and

    (ii)   could not become so as a result of the operation of the trust.

(4) For the purposes of sub-paragraph (3)(*b*), charitable trusts that may arise on the failure or determination of other trusts are ignored.

(5) In relation to any time before 6 April 2006, sub-paragraph (2) applies as if the reference to a registered pension scheme were a reference to an exempt approved scheme, as defined in section 592 of ICTA.

94   Section 395(2) does not apply in relation to a loan made before 26 July 1989, and, for the purposes of that section, section 550 of ITEPA 2003 (which defines "employee benefit trust" and is applied for the purposes of section 395 by section 395(6)) has effect as if section 550 of ITEPA 2003 referred to that day instead of 13 March 1989.

Interest: loans for interests in employee-controlled companies

95—(1) In relation to a loan used before 6 April 1990 in one or more of the ways specified in section 396(2)—

    (*a*)   section 396 applies as if—

        (i)   the reference in subsection (3) to full-time employees included a reference to full-time employees' spouses,

        (ii)   the references in subsection (4) to an individual included a reference to an individual's spouse, unless the individual and the individual's spouse are both full-time employees of the company within the meaning of section 396(5), and

    (*b*)   section 397(4) applies as if references to the individual included references to the individual's spouse.

(2) If a loan within section 396(2)(*b*) was made on or after that date, interest on the loan is eligible for relief under section 383 only if interest on the original loan would have been allowable under section 353 of ICTA after that date.

Interest relief: film partnerships

96   Section 399(4) (restriction on relief for interest on loans for purchasing interest in some film partnerships) only applies if the interest accrued on or after 10 March 2006.

Interest: loans for investing in co-operatives

97   Section 401 applies in relation to a loan used in one or more of the ways specified in subsection (2)(*a*) or (*b*) of that section only if the loan was made after 10 March 1981, but subsection (2)(*c*) of that section applies whenever the original loan was made.

Gift aid: restrictions on associated benefits

99—(1) This paragraph applies if—

    (*a*)   a gift is made on or after 6 April 2007, and

    (*b*)   a benefit associated with the gift is received before that date or relates (wholly or partly) to a period falling before that date.

(2) Step 2 of the calculation in section 419(8) is to be read as if the words "(and neither condition C nor condition D is met in relation to it)" were omitted.

Gift aid: election to carry back relief

100—(1) This paragraph applies if in the tax year 2007–08 an individual makes a gift to a charity that is a qualifying donation for the purposes of Chapter 2 of Part 8.

(2) Section 426 has effect with the substitution for subsections (2) and (3) of—

    "(2)   The condition is that in year P the grossed up amount of the gift would, if made in year P, be payable out of profits or gains brought into charge to income tax or capital gains tax.

    (3)   If an election is made, section 25(6) to (9A) of FA 1990 have effect in relation to the individual as if the gift were a qualifying donation (within the meaning of section 25 of FA 1990) made in year P."

(3) Section 426 has effect with the omission of subsections (4) and (5).

Qualifying maintenance payments: maintenance assessments

101—(1) This paragraph applies for the purposes for which, on the day on which this Act comes into force, the amendments to section 347B of ICTA made by paragraph 8(1) and (2) of Schedule 3 to the Child Support, Pensions and Social Security Act 2000 (c 19) (maintenance assessments superseded by maintenance calculations) do not have effect.

(2) Until a day is appointed for any of those purposes under this paragraph, section 454 and 455 have effect for that purpose as if—

    (a) in section 454(7) and section 455(1)(a), (b), (c) and (3) for "calculation" there were substituted "assessment", and

    (b) for section 454(8) there were substituted—

"(8) In this section "maintenance assessment" means a maintenance assessment made under the Child Support Act 1991 or the Child Support (Northern Ireland) Order 1991."

(3) The power to appoint a day under this paragraph is exercisable by the Secretary of State by order made by statutory instrument and different days may be appointed for different purposes (including different days for different areas).

PART 10
SPECIAL RULES ABOUT SETTLEMENTS AND TRUSTEES

Trustees' expenses to be set against trustees' trust rate income

102—(1) This paragraph applies if the trustees of a settlement incur an allowable expense (see section 484) in a tax year prior to the tax year 2007–08.

(2) So far as the trustees have not paid the expense, the expense cannot, under Chapter 4 of Part 9, be set against the trustees' trust rate income for any tax year.

(3) So far as the expense is paid by the trustees in a tax year ("the relevant tax year") after the tax year 2006–07, the expense is treated for the purposes of sections 484(1) and 485(1) as if it were incurred in the relevant tax year.

(4) So far as the expense is paid by the trustees in a tax year prior to the tax year 2007–08, section 485 applies in relation to the expense with the following modifications.

(5) It applies as if for subsection (3) there were substituted—

"(3)   Condition A is—

    (a)   that section 686(2AA) of ICTA could not be applied in relation to the allowable expense so as to reduce the trustees' liability to tax for the tax year in which the trustees paid the expense, and

    (b)   that was the case only because the trustees' section 686 income for that year was insufficient or they had no section 686 income for that year.

"Section 686 income" means income to which section 686 of ICTA applies."

(6) It applies as if for subsection (4) there were substituted—

"(4)   Condition B is that—

    (a)   for no tax year prior to the tax year 2007–08 has the allowable expense been used to reduce the trustees' liability to tax, and

    (b)   the allowable expense has not been set against the trustees' trust rate income for a tax year prior to the current tax year as a result of this section."

Share incentive plans: definition of "applicable period"

103—(1) This paragraph applies for the purposes of section 489 if the relevant shares (see subsection (1) of that section) were acquired by the trustees before 11 May 2001.

(2) That section applies in relation to those shares with the following modifications.

(3) It applies as if subsection (2) were omitted.

(4) It applies as if in subsection (3) the words "If any were" were omitted.

(5) It applies as if in subsection (4)—

    (a) for "If none were" there were substituted "But if when the trustees acquired the relevant shares none of the shares in the relevant company were readily convertible assets", and

    (b) in paragraph (b) for "any shares in the relevant company" there were substituted "the relevant shares".

(6) It applies as if in subsection (5) for "(2) to" there were substituted "(3) and".

Discretionary payments: trustees' tax pool

104—(1) Section 497 applies with the following modifications in relation to the trustees of a settlement established prior to the tax year 2007–08 if the current tax year is the tax year 2007–08.

(2) It also so applies if—

    (a) the current tax year is a tax year subsequent to the tax year 2007–08, and

    (b) the trustees have been UK resident for no tax year prior to the current tax year or the last tax year prior to the current tax year for which they were UK resident is a tax year prior to the tax year 2007–08.

(3) It applies as if in subsection (1) for Step 1 there were substituted—

"*Step 1*

Take the amount of the trustees' final section 687(3) tax pool and deduct from that amount (but not so that it goes below nil) the total of all tax (if any) treated under section 687(2)(*a*) of ICTA as being paid as a result of payments made by the trustees in the tax year 2006–07.

"The amount of the trustees' final section 687(3) tax pool" is the total amount—

(*a*) available to the trustees under section 687(3) of ICTA for setting against tax assessable on them under section 687(2)(*b*) of that Act for the tax year 2006–07, or

(*b*) which would have been so available had tax been so assessable."

(4) It applies as if subsections (2) and (3) were omitted.

PART 11
SPECIAL RULES ABOUT CHARITABLE TRUSTS ETC
Non-charitable expenditure

107—(1) This paragraph applies if, as a result of sections 562 to 564, an amount of expenditure for the tax year 2007–2008 or any subsequent tax year ("the carry back tax year") is treated as non-charitable expenditure for the tax year 2005–2006 or any earlier tax year.

(2) The amount of relief or exemption to be disallowed in respect of the tax year 2005–2006 or any earlier tax year is not to exceed the amount which would have been disallowed in respect of that tax year if—

(*a*) sections 562 to 564 had not applied in relation to the carry back tax year, and

(*b*) the amount of expenditure for the carry back tax year to be treated as non-charitable expenditure for an earlier tax year had instead been calculated in accordance with the provisions mentioned in sub-paragraph (3).

(3) Those provisions are—

(*a*) sections 505 and 506 of ICTA, and

(*b*) Part 3 of Schedule 20 to that Act,

as those provisions would have had effect in relation to the carry back tax year if the amendments made to them by section 55 of FA 2006 had not been made and the amendments made to them by this Act had not been made.

PART 13
ACCRUED INCOME PROFITS
Sale and repurchase arrangements

125—(1) Section 655 applies only if—

(*a*) in the case of overseas securities, the agreement to sell the securities mentioned in section 654(2) is entered into after 5 November 1996, and

(*b*) in any other case, the agreement to sell the securities so mentioned is entered into after 30 April 1995.

(2) In sub-paragraph (1) "overseas securities" has the same meaning as in Part 11 (see section 567).

126—(1) This paragraph applies if the agreement to sell the securities mentioned in section 654(2) was made before 9 April 2003.

(2) Section 655 has effect with the omission of subsection (2).

(3) For the purpose of determining whether (for the purposes of section 655) there is a sale and repurchase arrangement in respect of the securities, section 654(2) has effect with the omission of paragraph (*b*).

(4) Sub-paragraph (5) applies—

(*a*) for the purpose of determining whether (for the purposes of section 656) there is a sale and repurchase arrangement in respect of the securities, and

(*b*) for the purpose of determining whether (for the purposes of section 657) the case involves redemption arrangements.

(5) Section 654(2) has effect with the substitution for paragraphs (*b*) and (*c*) of

"or

(*b*) T or a person connected with T acquires, under the agreement or a related agreement, an option to buy back the securities."

Successive transfers with unrealised interest in default

127 Section 661 does not apply if the transferor's acquisition was before 28 February 1986.

Unrealised interest received by transferee after transfer within Chapter 2 of Part 12

128 If the transfer of securities within section 681(1)(*a*) occurred before 19 March 1986, section 681(1) has effect with the omission of paragraph (*b*).

PART 14

TAX AVOIDANCE

Transactions in securities: general

129—(1) Despite anything in this Act, Chapter 1 of Part 17 of ICTA (cancellation of tax advantages from certain transactions in securities) continues to apply so far as required for the purposes of notices under section 703(3) of that Act requiring adjustments to be made affecting tax years before the tax year 2007–08; and a counteraction notice under Chapter 1 of Part 13 (transactions in securities) may not require such an adjustment to be made.

(2) Subject to that, Chapter 1 of Part 13 applies—

    (*a*) whether or not the transaction or transactions, in consequence of which, or of the combined effect of which, the tax advantage has been or will be obtained, occur on or after 6 April 2007, and

    (*b*) whether or not the tax year to which that advantage relates ("the tax advantage year") is a year before the tax year 2007–08,

but see section 698(5) (under which no assessments may be made as a result of a counteraction notice later than 6 years after the tax advantage year).

(3) This paragraph is to be interpreted as if it were part of Chapter 1 of Part 13.

Transactions in securities: meaning of relevant companies for the purposes of sections 689 and 690

130—(1) In its application to a transaction in securities that took place before 29 April 1996 or two or more transactions in securities the first of which took place before that date, section 691(1)(*b*)(i) (meaning of "relevant company") applies with the substitution for the words "listed in the Official List of" of the words "authorised to be dealt in on".

(2) In its application to a transaction in securities that took place before 1 January 1997 or two or more transactions in securities the first of which took place before that date, section 691(1) applies as if the companies referred to in paragraph (*b*) included companies none of whose shares or stocks are dealt in on the Unlisted Securities Market regularly or from time to time.

(3) In this paragraph "companies" and "transaction in securities" have the same meaning as in Chapter 1 of Part 13 (see section 713).

Transactions in securities: statement of case by tribunal for opinion of High Court or Court of Session

131 If a tribunal has made a determination under section 705(3) of ICTA (determination on rehearing of appeal against notice under section 703 of ICTA) within 30 days before 6 April 2007, the appellant or an officer of Revenue and Customs may require the tribunal to state and sign a case under section 707(2) of this Act, despite not having declared dissatisfaction with the determination.

Transactions in securities: appeals to House of Lords

132—(1) This paragraph applies until paragraph 47 of Schedule 9 to the Constitutional Reform Act 2005 (c 4) comes into force.

(2) Section 710 has effect until that time as if—

    (*a*) references in subsections (1), (2) and (4) to the Supreme Court were references to the House of Lords, and

    (*b*) in subsection (3) the words "unless leave has been given under and in accordance with section 1 of the Administration of Justice (Appeals) Act 1934" were substituted for the words "except with the leave of the Court of Appeal or the Supreme Court".

(3) Section 711(4) has effect until that time as if the reference to the Supreme Court were a reference to the House of Lords.

Transfers of assets abroad: non-transferors receiving benefit-exclusion of income arising before 10 March 1981

133—(1) Section 732 (non-transferors receiving a benefit as a result of relevant transactions) applies whenever the relevant transfer referred to in that section took place.

(2) But the relevant income referred to in section 733(1) (by reference to which the amount of income treated as arising under section 732 is determined) does not include income that arose before 10 March 1981.

Transfers of assets abroad: whether trustees are "persons abroad"

134—(1) This paragraph deals with whether section 475 (residence of trustees) applies in determining if the single person mentioned in section 474 is a person abroad (as defined in section 718) for the purposes of sections 727 to 730 (charge where individuals receive capital sums as a result of transfers of assets abroad etc) (and accordingly whether section 718(2)(*b*) applies for those purposes).

(2) Section 475 does not apply for the purposes of sections 727 to 730 in relation to income payable before 15 June 1989.

(3) Section 475 does not apply for the purposes of sections 727 to 730 in relation to income payable on or after 15 June 1989 if—

    (*a*) the individual received or became entitled to receive the capital sum mentioned in section 729(1) before that date, and

    (*b*) the capital sum was wholly repaid or the right to it waived before 1 October 1989.

(4) In sub-paragraph (3) "capital sum" has the meaning given in section 729, and subsection (4) of that section applies for the purposes of that sub-paragraph as it applies for the purposes of section 729(1).

135—(1) Sub-paragraph (2) deals with whether section 474 (trustees of settlement to be treated as a single and distinct person) and section 475 (residence of trustees) apply for the purposes of sections 731 to 735 (charge where benefit received) (and accordingly whether section 718(2)(*b*) applies for those purposes).

(2) Sections 474 and 475 do not apply for the purposes of sections 731 to 735 in relation to benefits received before 15 June 1989.

(3) Sub-paragraphs (4) and (5) apply for the purposes of section 733 (income charged under section 731) in finding the amount of income treated as arising under section 732(2) in respect of benefits received on or after 15 June 1989.

(4) In determining the relevant income of an earlier tax year for the purposes of section 733(1) (see Step 4), income that arose to the trustees of a settlement before 6 April 1989 is treated as arising to persons abroad if one or more of the trustees were resident outside the United Kingdom, even though one or more were not so resident.

(5) But sub-paragraph (4) does not apply if the trustees have been charged to tax on that income.

Transfers of assets abroad: whether personal representatives are "persons abroad"

136—(1) This paragraph deals with whether section 834 (residence of personal representatives) applies in determining if personal representatives are persons abroad (as defined in section 718) for the purposes of sections 727 to 730 (charge where individuals receive capital sums as a result of transfers of assets abroad etc) (and accordingly whether section 718(2)(*c*) applies for those purposes).

(2) Section 834 does not apply for the purposes of sections 727 to 730 in relation to income payable before 15 June 1989.

(3) Section 834 does not apply for the purposes of sections 727 to 730 in relation to income payable on or after 15 June 1989 if—

    (*a*) the individual received or became entitled to receive the capital sum mentioned in section 729(1) before that date, and

    (*b*) the capital sum was wholly repaid or the right to it waived before 1 October 1989.

(4) In sub-paragraph (3) "capital sum" has the meaning given in section 729, and subsection (4) of that section applies for the purposes of that sub-paragraph as it applies for the purposes of section 729(1).

137—(1) Sub-paragraph (2) deals with whether section 834 (residence of personal representatives) applies for the purposes of sections 731 to 735 (charge where individuals receive a benefit as a result of transfers of assets abroad etc) (and accordingly whether section 718(2)(*c*) applies for those purposes).

(2) Section 834 does not apply for the purposes of sections 731 to 735 in relation to benefits received before 15 June 1989.

(3) Sub-paragraphs (4) and (5) apply for the purposes of section 733 (income charged under section 731) in finding the amount of income treated as arising under section 732(2) in respect of benefits received on or after 15 June 1989.

(4) In determining the relevant income of an earlier tax year for the purposes of section 733(1) (see Step 4), income that arose to personal representatives before 6 April 1989 is treated as arising to persons abroad if one or more of them were resident outside the United Kingdom, even though one or more were not so resident.

(5) But sub-paragraph (4) does not apply if the personal representatives have been charged to tax on that income.

Transfers of assets abroad: company residence for transfers between 20 March 1990 and 29 November 1993

138—(1) In relation to transfers and associated operations on or after 20 March 1990 and before 30 November 1993, a body corporate regarded as resident in a territory outside the United Kingdom for the purposes of any double taxation arrangements is treated as if it were resident outside the United Kingdom for the purposes of Chapter 2 of Part 13 (transfer of assets abroad).

(2) In this paragraph "transfers" and "associated operations" have the same meaning as in Chapter 2 of Part 13 (see sections 716 and 719 respectively).

Transfers of assets abroad: information powers concerning transfers between 20 March 1990 and 29 November 1993 involving companies

139—(1) So far as section 749(6) (restrictions on information to be provided under section 748) applies for the purposes of section 749(2) or (3), it applies in relation to transfers and associated operations on or after 20 March 1990 and before 30 November 1993 with the modification specified in sub-paragraph (2).

(2) The modification is that the reference to bodies corporate resident outside the United Kingdom includes a reference to bodies corporate regarded as resident in a territory outside the United Kingdom for the purposes of any double taxation arrangements.

Transfers of assets abroad: income arising before 26 November 1996

140   Sections 721(5)(b) and (c) and 728(3)(b) and (c) do not apply if the income arose before 26 November 1996.

Transfers of assets abroad: meaning of "associated operation" and consideration of associated operations alone

141—(1) In relation to any time before 5 December 2005, the reference in section 716(1)(b) (meaning of "relevant transfer") to income which becomes payable to a person abroad does not include income that becomes so payable just as a result of one or more associated operations.

(2) In relation to any time before 5 December 2005, section 719 (meaning of "associated operation") applies as if subsection (2) were omitted.

(3) In relation to any time before 5 December 2005, the reference in section 721(2) (individuals with power to enjoy income as a result of relevant transactions) to income which an individual has power to enjoy does not include income which the individual has power to enjoy just as a result of one or more associated operations.

(4) In relation to any time before 5 December 2005, the reference in section 728(1)(a) (individuals receiving capital sums as a result of relevant transactions) to income which has become the income of a person abroad does not include income that has become such income just as a result of one or more associated operations.

(5) In this paragraph—

   (a) "associated operation" has the meaning given in section 719, and

   (b) references to power to enjoy income are to be read in accordance with section 722 (when an individual has power to enjoy income of a person abroad).

Individuals in partnership: recovery of excess relief

142   In section 792(1)—

   (a) the reference to the claiming of relief includes a reference to the claiming of relief as mentioned in section 74(1)(a) and (b) of FA 2005, and

   (b) the reference to sections 104, 107 and 110 includes a reference to section 117 of ICTA (including as applied by section 118ZB of that Act) and section 118ZE of that Act.

143—(1) The losses covered by section 794(1) and (2) in relation to a trade include losses within section 74(5) of FA 2005 made in the trade.

(2) The income covered by section 794(3) includes amounts treated as received as a result of the application of section 74 of FA 2005.

(3) Sub-paragraph (4) applies for the purposes of section 794(5) if, as a result of paragraph 142(b), the relevant restriction provision would be section 117 of ICTA (including as applied by section 118ZB of that Act) or section 118ZE of that Act.

(4) The relevant restriction provision is instead taken to be—

   (a) in the case of section 117 of ICTA (other than as applied by section 118ZB of that Act), section 104,

   (b) in the case of section 117 of ICTA (as applied by section 118ZB of that Act), section 107, and

   (c) in the case of section 118ZE of ICTA, section 110.

(5) In section 794(6) the reference to subsection (2)(*b*) includes a reference to section 74(11)(*b*) of FA 2005.

Individuals claiming relief for film-related trading losses

144—(1) The claims covered by section 797(1)(*a*) include claims within section 119(1)(*a*) of FA 2004.
(2) For the purposes of section 797—
   (*a*) a "relevant disposal" does not include a disposal which was made before 10 December 2003, and
   (*b*) an event occurring before the tax year 2007–08 is an "exit event" if (and only if) it is an "exit event" for the purposes of section 119 of FA 2004.

145—(1) The losses covered by section 800(3)(*a*) include losses in relation to which a claim is made as mentioned in section 121(1)(*a*) or (*b*) of FA 2004.
(2) The income covered by section 800(5) includes amounts treated as received as a result of the application of section 74 of FA 2005.
(3) The losses covered by section 800(6) in relation to a trade include losses within section 121(1A)(*b*) of FA 2004 made in the trade.
(4) In section 800(9) the reference to the making of a claim includes a reference to the making of a claim as mentioned in section 122A(1) of FA 2004.

146 In section 801(3) the reference to the making of a claim includes a reference to the making of a claim as mentioned in section 122A(1) of FA 2004.

147—(1) In section 802(1) the reference to the making of a claim includes a reference to the making of a claim as mentioned in section 122A(1) of FA 2004.
(2) The repeal by this Act of section 122A of FA 2004 (or any provision inserting or amending, or affecting the application of, that section) does not affect the power of the Commissioners for Her Majesty's Revenue and Customs to make regulations under that section having effect before the tax year 2007–08.

148—(1) After the commencement of section 802, the Partnerships (Restrictions on Contributions to a Trade) Regulations 2006 (SI 2006/1639) have effect as if made under that section.
(2) The Regulations so have effect subject to the following modifications.
(3) They have effect as if in regulation 2—
   (*a*) for the definition of "ICTA" there were substituted— " "ITA 2007" means the Income Tax Act 2007;", and
   (*b*) for the definition of "relevant individual" there were substituted—
   " "relevant individual" means—
      (*a*) a limited partner (within the meaning given by section [103A][1] of ITA 2007),
      (*b*) a member of a limited liability partnership, or
      (*c*) a non-active partner (within the meaning given by section [103B][1] of ITA 2007),

   where the partnership carries on a trade in which the individual makes a film-related loss (as defined in section 800(2) of ITA 2007) for which the individual makes a claim as mentioned in section 802(1) of that Act;".
(4) They have effect as if in regulation 3(*a*) for "section 120 of the Finance Act 2004" there were substituted "section 799 of ITA 2007".
(5) They have effect as if in regulation 4—
   (*a*) for "contribution to the trade", wherever occurring, there were substituted "capital contribution",
   (*b*) for "section 119(2)(*b*) or (*c*) of the Finance Act 2004", wherever occurring, there were substituted "section 797(2)(*b*) of ITA 2007", and
   (*c*) for paragraph (*c*)(ii) there were substituted—
      "(ii) the amount of income treated as received in accordance with section 797(5) of that Act."
(6) See paragraph 35 of this Schedule for provision about the effect of the Partnerships (Restrictions on Contributions to a Trade) Regulations 2005 (SI 2005/2017) after the commencement of section 802.

Amendments—[1] Section numbers in sub-para (3)(*b*) substituted by FA 2007 s 26, Sch 4 paras 19, 21 and deemed always to have had effect.

149—(1) In section 803 references to chargeable events include events that are chargeable events for the purposes of section 119 of FA 2004.

(2) Accordingly, the total amount of income mentioned in section 803(3) is to include any income treated as received as a result of section 119(5)(*b*) of FA 2004.

Individuals in partnership: exit charge

150—(1) The losses covered by section 805(1)(*b*) include losses in relation to which a claim is made as mentioned in section 126(1)(*c*) of FA 2004.

(2) The disposals covered by section 805(2)(*a*) and (*b*) do not include disposals made before 10 February 2004.

151—(1) In section 806 at Step 4 non-taxable consideration received before 10 February 2004 is excluded.

(2) In section 806 at Step 5—

    (*a*) the reference to section 805 includes a reference to section 127 of FA 2004, and

    (*b*) the reference to chargeable events includes a reference to chargeable events for the purposes of section 127 of FA 2004.

152—(1) This paragraph applies for the purposes of sections 805 to 807 if the individual carried on the trade at any time before 26 March 2004.

(2) Any reference to expenditure incurred in the trade in exploiting the licence does not include expenditure incurred before 10 February 2004.

153 The losses covered by section 807(4) include losses in relation to which a claim has been made as mentioned in section 128(2)(*a*) or (*b*) of FA 2004.

HMRC Manuals—Part 14, Chapter 1A: Residence, Domicile and Remittance Basis Manual, RDRM30005 (the remittance basis).

PART 15

DEDUCTION OF INCOME TAX AT SOURCE

Deduction by deposit-takers: qualifying certificates of deposit

157—(1) This paragraph applies to a certificate of deposit which was issued by a deposit-taker before 13 March 1984 on terms which provide for interest to be payable on the deposit at any time after 5 April 1985 (whether or not interest is payable on it before that date).

(2) The certificate of deposit is to be treated as a qualifying certificate of deposit for the purposes of section 865.

Deduction by deposit-takers: qualifying time deposits

158—(1) This paragraph applies to a deposit with a deposit-taker which—

    (*a*) was made before 6 July 1984, and

    (*b*) meets the condition in sub-paragraph (2).

(2) The condition is that the deposit is made on terms which—

    (*a*) do not make provision for the transfer of the right to repayment,

    (*b*) prevent partial withdrawals of, or additions to, the deposit, and

    (*c*) require the deposit-taker—

        (i) to repay the sum at the end of a specified period ending after 5 April 1985, or

        (ii) if interest is payable only when the deposit is repaid, to repay the sum on demand or on notice.

(3) The deposit is to be treated as a qualifying time deposit for the purposes of section 866.

Deduction by deposit-takers and building societies: saving for regulations

159—(1) This paragraph applies to regulations which—

    (*a*) were made under section 477A(1) to (2A) of ICTA (building societies: regulations for deduction of tax),

    (*b*) were in force immediately before the commencement of the repeal of those provisions by this Act, and

    (*c*) could have been made under section 17 of TMA 1970 as amended by this Act, if those amendments had been in force at the time the regulations were made.

(2) The regulations have effect after the commencement of the repeal of section 477A(1) to (2A) of ICTA as if made under section 17 of TMA 1970 as amended by this Act.

160—(1) This paragraph applies to regulations about the making of declarations to building societies which—

    (*a*) were made under section 477A(1) to (2A) of ICTA,

    (*b*) were in force immediately before the commencement of the repeal of those provisions by this Act, and

(c) could have been made under section 132 or 133 of FA 1999 (electronic communications), if provision about the making of declarations to building societies had precluded to any extent the use of electronic communications for that purpose at the time that the regulations were made.

(2) The regulations have effect after the commencement of the repeal of section 477A(1) to (2A) of ICTA as if made under section 132 and 133 of FA 1999.

(3) Regulations under sections 132 and 133 of FA 1999 may make any provision in relation to Chapter 2 of Part 15 of this Act which they could have made if that Chapter had come into force before those sections.

Deduction by deposit-takers, building societies etc: collection of tax

161 Chapter 15 of Part 15 has effect for return periods which—

    (a) fall within accounting periods ending on or after 6 April 2007, and

    (b) end on or after that date.

162—(1) This paragraph applies to a payment—

    (a) which is made in an accounting period beginning before 6 April 2007 and ending on or after that date, and

    (b) which was made before 6 April 2007, but which would have been a payment within section 946 if it had been made on or after that date.

(2) A payment to which this paragraph applies is to be treated as a payment within section 946 if it is made in a return period which—

    (a) falls within the accounting period,

    (b) begins before 6 April 2007, and

    (c) ends on or after that date.

(3) In addition, a payment to which this paragraph applies which was made in an earlier return period which falls within the accounting period is to be treated as a payment within section 946.

Deduction from certain payments of yearly interest: interest paid by banks

163—(1) In the case of payments of interest to which this paragraph applies, section 878 (exceptions from duty to deduct: interest paid by banks) has effect with the modification in sub-paragraph (2).

(2) The modification is the substitution for subsections (1) and (2) of that section of "The duty to deduct a sum representing income tax under section 874 does not apply to a payment of interest by a bank carrying on a genuine banking business in the United Kingdom."

(3) This paragraph applies to interest payable on an advance made before 29 April 1996.

Deduction from certain payments of yearly interest: interest paid on advances from banks

164—(1) In the case of payments of interest to which this paragraph applies, section 879 (exceptions from duty to deduct: interest paid on advances from banks) has effect with the modification in sub-paragraph (2).

(2) The modification is the substitution for subsections (1) to (4) of that section of "The duty to deduct a sum representing income tax under section 874 does not apply to a payment of interest in the United Kingdom on an advance from a bank carrying on a genuine banking business in the United Kingdom."

(3) This paragraph applies to interest payable before 29 April 1996.

(4) In the case of an institution which—

    (a) immediately before 29 April 1996 was not treated for the purposes of section 349(3)(a) of ICTA as a bank carrying on a genuine banking business in the United Kingdom, and

    (b) on that day fell within the definition of "bank" given by section 840A of ICTA,

this paragraph applies to interest payable on an advance made before that day.

(5) In the case of an institution which—

    (a) immediately before 29 April 1996 was treated for the purposes of section 349(3)(a) of ICTA as a bank carrying on a genuine banking business in the United Kingdom, and

    (b) on that day did not fall within the definition of "bank" given by section 840A(1) of ICTA,

this paragraph applies to the interest mentioned in sub-paragraph (6).

(6) That interest is any interest payable on an advance made before 29 April 1996, if at the time when the interest is paid the person beneficially entitled to the interest is within the charge to corporation tax as respects the interest.

Deduction from certain UK public revenue dividends

165—(1) This paragraph applies if—

    (a) any person holds any gilt-edged securities in relation to which a direction was given under section 50(1) of ICTA at any time before 6 April 1998, and

(b) that person at any time before that date made an application under section 50(2) of that Act with respect to those securities.

(2) The person is treated as having made a deduction at source application under section 895 in respect of the securities which (unless withdrawn) is treated as having effect from that date.

166—(1) This paragraph applies in relation to any gilt-edged securities issued before 6 April 1998 which—

(a) are securities the interest on which, if paid immediately before that date, would have fallen to be paid after deduction of income tax, and

(b) are registered within the meaning of section 895 but are not securities in relation to which any direction under section 50 of ICTA was given before that date.

(2) Chapter 5 of Part 15 has effect as if the appropriate person had made a deduction at source application under section 895 in respect of the securities so as to enable that application to have effect from (and including) that date.

(3) In sub-paragraph (2) "the appropriate person" means—

(a) in the case of securities transferred before 6 April 1998 but after the time when the balance was struck for a dividend on them falling due on or after that date, the person who held the securities at the time when the balance was struck,

(b) in any other case, the person holding the securities in question immediately before 6 April 1998.

Non-resident landlords

169—(1) Sub-paragraph (2) applies to any references in the Taxation of Income from Land (Non-residents) Regulations 1995 (SI 1995/2902) to payments to be made to the Board in respect of tax that is or may become chargeable as the income from a business of a non-resident (as defined in those regulations).

(2) On and after 6 April 2007 those references are to be read as references to income tax to be paid to the Commissioners for Her Majesty's Revenue and Customs in respect of non-resident landlord income (as defined in section 971(2)).

Interpretation

170 Expressions used in this Part of this Schedule and in Part 15 have the same meaning as they have in Part 15.

PART 16
OTHER PROVISIONS

Old references to surtax and standard rate tax

171 The repeal by this Act of section 819 of ICTA has no effect in relation to any instrument (of whatever nature), will or codicil made before the date on which this Act comes into force.

Section 820 of ICTA

172 Section 820 of ICTA (application of Income Tax Acts from year to year) applies to this Act as if this Act were in force on the day before 6 April 2007.

SCHEDULE 3
REPEALS AND REVOCATIONS

Section 1031

SCHEDULE 4
INDEX OF DEFINED EXPRESSIONS

Section 1032

[accountancy rental earnings (in Part 11A)	section 614AB(1)][12]
[accountancy rental excess (in Chapter 2 of Part 11A)	section 614BH(1) to (4)][12]
[accountancy rental excess (in Chapter 3 of Part 11A)	section 614BH(1) to (4), as it has effect as a result of section 614CD][12]
accounting period (in relation to a deposit-taker who is not a company) (in Chapter 15 of Part 15)	section 948(1)
[accounts (in Chapter 5B of Part 13)	section 809BZQ][12]

accreditation period (in Part 7)   section 342(1)

accrued income losses (in Part 12)   section 615(4)

accrued income profits (in Part 12)   section 615(2)

accumulated or discretionary income (in Chapter 3 of Part 9)   section 480

[acquisition value of a qualifying investment (in Chapter 3 of Part 8)   section 438A][8]

Act   section 1018

[additional rate   section 6(2) (as applied by section 989)][11]

adjusted net income (in Chapters 2 and 3 of Part 3)   section 58

[alternative finance arrangements (in Part 10A)   section 564A(2)][12]

[alternative finance return (in Part 10A)   sections 564I to 564L][12]

arrangements (in Part 5)   section 257(1)

[arrangements (in Part 5A)   section 257HJ(1)][18]

arrangements (in Chapter 2 of Part 9)   section 465(8)

[arrangements (in Chapter 5B of Part 13)   section 809BZR][12]

[arrangements (in Chapter 5E of Part 13)   section 809EZE(1)][24]

[arrangements (in Chapter 8 of Part 13)   section 809ZR][15]

[asset (in Part 11A)   section 614DG][12]

[asset representing the leased asset (in Part 11A)   section 614DD][12]

assets (in Chapter 2 of Part 13)   section 717

assignment (in the application of this Act to Scotland)   section 1008(1)

associate (in Part 5)   section 253

[associate (in Part 5A)   section 257HJ(1)][18]

associate (in Part 6)   section 253 (as applied by section 332)

associate (in Part 7)   section 381

[associated (in Chapter 1 of Part 12A)   section 681AM][12]

associated operation (in Chapter 2 of Part 13)   section 719

[associates (in Chapter 4 of Part 12A)   section 681DL][12]

attributable income (in Part 10)   section 540(3)

attributable gains (in Part 10)   section 540(3)

attributable income and gains (in Part 10)   section 540(3)

authorised unit trust   section 989

available income and gains (in Part 10)   section 562(4)

basic rate   section 6(2) (as applied by section 989)

basic rate limit   section [10][11] (as applied by section 989)

beneficial entitlement (in Chapter 1 of Part 14)   section 822

[beneficial entitlement (in Chapter 2B of Part 14)   section 835O(4)][12]

the beneficiary (in Chapter 8 of Part 9)   section 499(1)(*b*)

the beneficiary's income (in Chapter 8 of Part 9)   section 499(2)

. . .[28]   . . .[28]

benefits associated with a gift (in Chapter 2 of Part 8)   section 417

body (in Part 7)   section 382(1)

body of persons   section 989

bonus shares (in Chapter 6 of Part 4)   section 151(1)

bonus shares (in Part 5)   section 257(1)

[bonus shares (in Part 5A)   section 257HJ(1)][18]

bonus shares (in Part 7)   section 382(1)

[branch or agency (in Chapter 2B of Part 14)   section 835S(2)][12]

building society   section 989

. . .[21]   . . .[21]

. . .[6]   . . .[6]

. . .[6]   . . .[6]

. . .[6]   . . .[6]

capital (in Chapter 3 of Part 13)	section 772(1)
capital allowance	section 989
capital amount (in Chapter 4 of Part 13)	section 777(7)
capital gains relief (in Chapter 3 of Part 4)	section 103(2)
capital gains relief (in Chapter 5 of Part 13)	section 790(4)
[capital sum (in Chapter 4 of Part 12A)	section 681DM][12]
the CDFI (in Part 7)	sections 334(2) and 370
certificate of deposit	section 1019
chargeable gain	section 989
chargeable period	section 989
charged amount (in Chapter 2 of Part 8)	section 427
charitable trade ...[17]	section 525
charitable trust (in Part 10)	[paragraph 1 of Schedule 6 to FA 2010][17]
charity	[paragraph 1 of Schedule 6 to FA 2010][17]
charity (in Chapter 2 of Part 8)	[paragraph 1 of Schedule 6 to FA 2010][17](and see also section 430)
charity (in Chapter 3 of Part 8)	[paragraph 1 of Schedule 6 to FA 2010][17](and see also section 446)
[charity (in Chapter 8 of Part 13)	paragraph 1 of Schedule 6 to FA 2010 (and see also section 809ZR)][15]
CITR (in Part 7)	section 333
civil partner (in Chapter 6 of Part 4)	section 151(1)
claim	section 1020
close company	section 989
[close company (in Chapter 1 of Part 13)	section 713][9]
[collective investment scheme (in Chapter 5E of Part 13)	section 809EZE(1)][24]
company (except in Part 6, Chapters 1, 3 and 4 of Part 13 and sections 993 and 994)	section 992
company (in Part 6)	section 332
company (in Chapter 1 of Part 13)	section 713
company (in Chapter 3 of Part 13)	section 772(3)
[company (in Chapter 3A of Part 14)	section 837H(4)][7]
company (in Chapter 4 of Part 13)	section 789
company in administration (in Part 5)	section 252(2)
company in administration (in Part 6)	section 331(2)
company in receivership (in Part 5)	section 252(3)
company in receivership (in Part 6)	section 331(3)
. . . [21]	[section 591(1)][6]
[. . . [20]][6]	. . . [20]
[company UK REIT (in Chapter 9 of Part 15)][6]	[section 591(1) (as applied by section 926(1))][6]
compliance certificate (in Part 5)	section 204(1)
[compliance certificate (in Part 5A)	section 257EC(1)][18]
compliance statement (in Part 5)	section 205(1)
[compliance statement (in Part 5A)	section 257ED(1)][18]
connected (in relation to two persons being connected with one another)	section 993 as applied by section 1021(1) (but see exceptions and alternative provision in sections 166 to 171, 257(2) and 313(5) and (6))

control	section 995 as applied by section 1021(2) (but see exceptions and alternative provision in sections 69(7), 139(2), 257(3),[257HJ(3),][18] 313(4) and (6), 394(5), 395(6), 691(4) and 994(1))
conversion (in Part 12)	section 620(7)
co-operative (in Chapter 1 of Part 8)	section 401(3)
corresponding bonus shares (in Chapter 6 of Part 4)	section 151(1)
counteraction notice (in Chapter 1 of Part 13)	section 698(3)
[cumulative accountancy rental excess (in Chapter 2 of Part 11A)	section 614BH(5)][12]
[cumulative accountancy rental excess (in Chapter 3 of Part 11A)	section 614BH(5), as it has effect as a result of section 614CD][12]
[cumulative normal rental excess (in Chapter 2 of Part 11A)	section 614BJ(5)][12]
[cumulative normal rental excess (in Chapter 3 of Part 11A)	section 614BJ(5), as it has effect as a result of section 614CD][12]
[the current lessor (in Part 11A)	section 614DG][12]
the current tax year (in Chapter 8 of Part 9)	section 499
debenture (except in sections 559, 560 and 691)	section 1022
[deduction by way of relevant income tax relief (in Chapter 1 of Part 12A)	section 681AC(1)][12]
[deduction by way of relevant income tax relief (in Chapter 2 of Part 12A)	section 681BK][12]
[deduction by way of relevant tax relief (in Chapter 4 of Part 12A)	section 681DP][12]
deemed deduction (in Chapter 13 of Part 15)[22]	*section 941(6)*[22]
deemed income (in Chapter 13 of Part 15) [22]	*section 941(6)*[22]
deemed payment (in Chapter 13 of Part 15) [22]	*section 941(6)* [22]
[default additional rate	section 6C (as applied by section 989)
default basic rate	section 6C (as applied by section 989)
default higher rate	section 6C (as applied by section 989)][30]
deposit (in Chapter 2 of Part 15)	section 855(2)
deposit (in Chapter 19 of Part 15)	section 983
deposit-taker (in Chapter 2 of Part 15 [and section 876][28])	section 853
[deposit-taking trade (in Chapter 3A of Part 14)	section 837B(3)][7]
director (in Part 5)	section 257(1)
[director (in Part 5A)	section 257HJ(1)][18]
director (in Part 6)	section 332
discretionary or accumulation settlement (in Chapter 2 of Part 15)	section 873(1)
[disguised fee (in Chapter 5E of Part 13)	section 809EZA(3)][24]
disposal (in Part 7)	section 379
[disposal of an asset (in Chapter 5B of Part 13)	section 809BZS(3)][12]
disposal of shares (in Part 5)	section 254
[disposal of shares (in Part 5A)	section 257HH)][18]
disposal-related liability (in Chapter 3 of Part 8)	section 440
disposal-related obligation (in Chapter 3 of Part 8)	section 439
disposing of land (in Chapter 3 of Part 13)	section 753
[dispositions of interests in land outside the United Kingdom (in Chapter 1 of Part 12A)	section 681AN][12]
disregarded annual payments (in Chapter 1 of Part 14)	section 826
disregarded company income (in Chapter 1 of Part 14)	section 816
disregarded income (in Chapter 1 of Part 14)	section 813(1)
disregarded pension income (in Chapter 1 of Part 14)	section 813(3)
disregarded savings and investment income (in Chapter 1 of Part 14)	section 825
disregarded social security income (in Chapter 1 of Part 14)	section 813(5)
disregarded transaction income (in Chapter 1 of Part 14)	section 814

distribution . . . [20]

. . . [20]

. . . [28]

dividends (in Chapter 1 of Part 13)

[dividend additional rate

dividend income

dividend ordinary rate

dividend trust rate

dividend upper rate

[the donor (in Chapter 8 of Part 13)

double taxation arrangements

early tax year (in Chapter 3 of Part 4)

EIS (in Part 5)

[EIS (in Part 5A)

[EIS original rate (in Part 5)

[EIS rate (in Part 5)

EIS relief (in Chapter 6 of Part 4)

EIS relief (in Part 5)

election

eligible for EIS relief (in Part 5)

eligible shares (in Chapter 2 of Part 6)

eligible shares (in Chapter 3 of Part 6)

the [70%][13] eligible shares condition (in Chapter 3 of Part 6)

employment income

excluded company (in Chapter 6 of Part 4)

[external investor (in Chapter 5E of Part 13)

farming

[finance lessor (in Part 11A)

financial instrument (in Part 15)

firm (in Chapter 2 of Part 4)

firm (in Chapter 3 of Part 4)

firm (in Chapter 5 of Part 13)

the 5 year period (in Part 7)

[for accounting purposes (in Part 11A)

foreign element (in Chapter 13 of Part 15)[22]

. . . [6]

. . . [6]

. . . [6]

generally accepted accounting practice

gift aid declaration (in Chapter 2 of Part 8)

gilt-edged securities

gross amount of a payment (in Chapter 4 of Part 8)

. . . [21]

. . . [20]

gross amount (in Chapter 9 of Part 15)

the gross amount (in Chapter 13 of Part 15)[22]

grossing up

grossed up amount (in Chapter 2 of Part 8)

gross-paying government securities (in Chapter 5 of Part 15)

group (in Chapter 6 of Part 4 (except in sections 137 and 142))

group (in Part 5)

section 989

. . . [20]

. . . [28]

section 713

section 8(3) (as applied by section 989)][11]

section 19

section 8(1) (as applied by section 989)

section 9(2) (as applied by section 989)

section 8(2) (as applied by section 989)

section 809ZJ(3)][15]

section 1023

section 112(6)

section 156(2)

section 257HJ(1)][18]

section 256A][16]

section 158(2A)][3]

section 151(1)

section 156(1)

section 1020

section 157(1)

section 273(1)

section [285(3A) and (3B)][13]

section 274(2)

section 7 of ITEPA 2003

section 151(1)

section 809EZE(1)][24]

section 996

section 614DG][12]

section 984

section 60(5)

section 103(3)

section 790(5)

section 338

section 614DG][12]

section 943B[22]

. . . [6]

. . . [6]

. . . [6]

section 997(1) and (3)

section 428

section 1024

section 452

. . . [21]

. . . [20]

section 589 (as applied by section 926(1))

section 941(6)[22]

section 998

section 415

section 893(2)

section 151(1)

section 257(1)

[group (in Part 5A)	section 257HJ(1)][18]
group (in Part 6)	section 332
. . . [21]	. . . [21]
. . . [20]	. . . [20]
group (in Chapter 9 of Part 15)	section 591(1) (as applied by section 926(1))
group company (in Part 5)	section 257(1)
[group company (in Part 5A)	section 257HJ(1)][18]
group company (in Part 6)	section 332
. . . [21]	. . . [21]
. . . [20]	. . . [20]
[group UK REIT (in Chapter 9 of Part 15)][6]	[section 591(1) (as applied by section 926(1))][6]
heritage body (in Chapter 10 of Part 9)	section 507(2)
heritage direction (in Chapter 10 of Part 9)	section 507(2)
heritage maintenance property (in Chapter 10 of Part 9)	section 507(2)
heritage maintenance settlement (in Chapter 10 of Part 9)	section 507(2)
higher rate	section 6(2) (as applied by section 989)
[higher rate limit	section 10 (as applied by section 989)][11]
holding company (in Chapter 6 of Part 4)	section 151(1)
the 15% holding limit condition (in Chapter 3 of Part 6)	section 274(2)
the income retention condition (in Chapter 3 of Part 6)	section 274(2)
income tax advantage (in Chapter 1 of Part 13)	section [687][9]
[independent agent (in Chapter 2C of Part 14)	section 835Y][12]
the independent broker conditions (in Chapter 1 of Part 14)	section 817
[the independent broker conditions (in Chapter 2B of Part 14)	section 835L][12]
the independent investment manager conditions (in Chapter 1 of Part 14)	section 818
[the independent investment manager conditions (in Chapter 2B of Part 14)	section 835M][12]
individual (in Chapter 2 of Part 13)	section 714(4)
individual (in Chapter 6 of Part 15)	section 905
interest (in Part 12)	section 671
interest payment day (in Part 12)	section 672
interest period (in Part 12)	section 673
[interests in land outside the United Kingdom (in Chapter 1 of Part 12A)	section 681AN][12]
the invested amount (in Part 7)	section 337
the investing company (in Chapter 4 of Part 6)	section 286(1)
investment (in Chapter 2 of Part 15 [and section 876][28])	section 855(1)
the investment (in Part 7)	section 334(1)
investment company (in Chapter 6 of Part 4)	section 151(1)
the investment date (in Part 7)	section 338
[investment (in investment scheme) (in Chapter 5E of Part 13)	section 809EZE(2)][24]
[investment management services (in Chapter 5E of Part 13)	section 809EZE(1)][24]
investment manager (in Chapter 1 of Part 14)	section 827(1)
[investment manager (in Chapter 2B of Part 14)	section 835S(3)][12]
[investment scheme (in Chapter 5E of Part 13)	section 809EZA(6)][24]
investments (in relation to a company) (in Chapter 3 of Part 6)	section 285(4)
investment transaction (in Chapter 1 of Part 14)	section 827(2)
[investment transaction (in Chapter 2B of Part 14)	section 835S(4)][12]
[investment trust (in Chapter 5E of Part 13)	section 809EZE(1)][24]
the investor (in Part 5)	section 157(1)
the investor (in Part 7)	sections 334(1) and 370
[issue of shares (in Part 5A)	section 257HI][18]
the issuing company (in Part 5)	section 157(1)
[lease (in Chapter 1 of Part 12A)	section 681AL(2)][12]

[lease (in Chapter 2 of Part 12A)	section 681BM(2), (3)][12]
[lease (in Chapter 3 of Part 12A)	section 681CF][12]
[lease (in Chapter 4 of Part 12A)	section 681DN][12]
[lease (in Part 11A)	section 614DG][12]
[lessee (in Chapter 2 of Part 12A)	section 681BM(4)][12]
[the leasing arrangements (in Part 11A)	section 614DG][12]
[the lessee (in Part 11A)	section 614DG][12]
[lessor (in Chapter 2 of Part 12A)	section 681BM(4)]][12]
[the lessor (in Part 11A)	section 614DG][12]
limited partner (in Chapter 3 of Part 4)	section [103A][1]
[linked (in relation to a person) (in Chapter 2 of Part 12A)	section 681BL][12]
the listing condition (in Chapter 3 of Part 6)	section 274(2)
living together (in relation to married couples and civil partners)	section 1011
local authority	section 999
local authority association	section 1000
[major lump sum (in Part 11A)	section 614BC(5)][12]
. . .[21]	. . .[21]
. . .[21]	. . .[21]
. . .[20]	. . .[20]
manufactured dividend (in Chapter 9 of Part 15)	section 573(1)(*a*) (as applied by section 926(1))
. . .[21]	. . .[21]
manufactured interest (in Chapter 9 of Part 15)	section 578(1)(*a*) (as applied by section 926(1))
. . .[21]	. . .[21]
manufactured overseas dividend (in Chapter 9 of Part 15)	section 581(1)(*a*) (as applied by section 926(1))
market gardening	section 996
market value (of an asset) (in Part 5)	section 257(6)
[market value (in Part 5A)	section 257HJ(6)][18]
[market value (in Chapter 5E of Part 13)	section 809EZE(1)][24]
market value (of an asset) (in Part 7)	section 382(3)
market value of a qualifying investment (in Chapter 3 of Part 8)	section 438
modified net income	section 1025
the nature of income condition (in Chapter 3 of Part 6)	section 274(2)
net income	section 23 (see Step 2) (as applied by section 989)
[new qualifying trade (in Part 5A)	section 257HF][18]
nominal value of securities (in Part 12)	sections 676 and 677
non-active partner (in Chapter 3 of Part 4)	section [103B][1]
non-charitable expenditure (in Part 10)	section 543
non-UK resident (and references to a non-UK resident or a non-UK resident person)	section 989
[normal rent (in Part 11A)	section 614AA][12]
[normal rental excess (in Chapter 2 of Part 11A)	section 614BJ(1) to (4)][12]
[normal rental excess (in Chapter 3 of Part 11A)	section 614BJ(1) to (4), as it has effect as a result of section 614CD][12]
normal self-assessment filing date	section 989
notice	section 989
obligation (in Chapter 3 of Part 8)	section 439(7)
occupation (in Chapter 4 of Part 13)	section 774
offshore installation	sections 1001 and 1002
oil and gas exploration and appraisal	section 1003
ordinary share capital	section 989
ordinary shares (in Part 5)	section 257(1)
[ordinary shares (in Part 5A)	section 257HJ(1)][18]

ITA 2007

ordinary shares (in Part 6)	section 332
other income (in Part 9)	section 463
other person (in Chapter 3 of Part 13)	section 763
other person (in Chapter 4 of Part 13)	section 782
. . . [21]	. . . [21]
. . . [21]	. . . [21]
[the overseas part	section 989][19]
overseas property business	Chapter 2 of Part 3 of IT-TOIA 2005 (as applied by section 989)
. . . [21]	. . . [21]
. . . [21]	. . . [21]
. . . [21]	. . . [21]
. . . [21]	. . . [21]
parent company (in Part 5)	section 257(1)
[parent company (in Part 5A)	section 257HJ(1)][18]
parent company (in Part 6)	section 332
[participant (in Chapter 5E of Part 13)	section 809EZE(1)][24]
[pay (in Part 11A)	section 614DG][12]
payment (in Chapter 7 of Part 9)	section 493(5)
[payments in respect of an asset (in Chapter 5B of Part 13)	section 809BZS(4)][12]
[period A, period B (in Part 5A)	section 257AC][18]
period A, period B, period C (in Part 5)	section 159(2), (3), (4)
period of account	section 989
[period of account (in Part 11A)	section 614DB(1) to (3)][12]
[permanent establishment (except in Part 5 and Chapter 4 of Part 6)	section 1007A
permanent establishment (in Part 5)	section 191A
[permanent establishment (in Part 5A)	section 257HJ(1)][18]
permanent establishment (in Chapter 4 of Part 6)	section 302A][14]
person abroad (in Chapter 2 of Part 13)	section 718
personal representatives	section 989
[person involved in a relevant change (in Chapter 5B of Part 13)	section 809BZG(5)][12]
[person receiving an asset (in Chapter 5B of Part 13)	section 809BZS(2)][12]
[post-25 November 1996 scheme (in Part 11A)	section 614D(1)(b)][12]
[potentially advantaged person (in Chapter 8 of Part 13)	section 809ZJ(5)][15]
[prescribed (in Chapter 2 of Part 11)	section 591(1)
[pre-26 November 1996 scheme (in Part 11A)	section 614D(1)(a)][12]
. . . [21]	. . . [21]
. . . [20]	. . . [20]
. . . [21]	. . . [21]
[profits (on investment made for purposes of investment scheme) (in Chapter 5E of Part 13)	section 809EZE(1)][24]
profits or gains	section 989
property deriving its value from land (in Chapter 3 of Part 13)	section 772(2)
property investment LLP	section 1004
property maintenance purpose (in Chapter 10 of Part 9)	section 507(2)
. . . [21]	. . . [21]
. . . [20]	. . . [20]
. . . [21]	. . . [21]
qualifying annual payment (in Chapter 6 of Part 15)	section 899
qualifying business activity (in Part 5)	section 179
[qualifying business activity (in Part 5A)	section 257HG][18]
qualifying certificate of deposit (in Part 15)	section 985
qualifying company (in Part 5)	section 180
. . . [27]	. . . [27]
qualifying donation (in Chapter 2 of Part 8)	section 416

[qualifying film expenditure (in Chapter 3 of Part 4)	section 103D][1]
qualifying holding (in Chapter 3 of Part 6)	Chapter 4 of Part 6
the [80%][33] qualifying holdings condition (in Chapter 3 of Part 6)	section 274(2)
qualifying interest in land (in Chapter 3 of Part 8)	section 433
qualifying investor (in Part 5)	section 162
qualifying investment (in Part 7)	section 344
qualifying investment (in Chapter 3 of Part 8)	section 432
qualifying partnership (in Chapter 11 of Part 15)	section 932
qualifying period (in Chapter 1 of Part 14)	section 820
[qualifying period (in Chapter 2B of Part 14)	section 835O(2)][12]
qualifying shares (in Chapter 6 of Part 4)	section 131(2)
qualifying subsidiary (in Part 5)	section 191
[qualifying subsidiary (in Part 5A)	section 257HJ(1)][18]
qualifying subsidiary (in Chapter 4 of Part 6)	section 302
qualifying 90% subsidiary (in Part 5)	section 190
[qualifying 90% subsidiary (in Part 5A)	section 257HJ(1)][18]
qualifying 90% subsidiary (in Chapter 4 of Part 6)	section 301
qualifying trade (in Part 5)	section 189(1)
qualifying trade (in Chapter 4 of Part 6)	section 300
qualifying uncertificated eligible debt security unit (in Part 15)	section 986
quoted Eurobond (in Part 15)	section 987
recognised stock exchange	section 1005
registered (in Chapter 5 of Part 15)	section 895(6)
. . .	. . . [23]
registered pension scheme	section 150(2) of FA 2004 (as applied by section 989)
[registered society (in Chapter 6 of Part 4)	section 151(1)][23]
[registered society (in Chapter 3 of Part 15)	section 887(5)][23]
the Registrar (in Chapter 5 of Part 15)	section 895(6)
regulations (in Chapter 5 of Part 6)	section 325
. . . [21]	section 571
[related period of account (in Part 11A)	section 614DB(5)][12]
[related tax year (in Part 11A)	section 614DB(4)][12]
[relevant asset (in Chapter 3 of Part 12A)	section 681CG][12]
[relevant asset (in Chapter 4 of Part 12A)	section 681DO][12]
[relevant change in relation to a partnership (in Chapter 5B of Part 13)	section 809BZG][12]
the relevant company (in Chapter 4 of Part 6)	section 286(1)
[relevant deduction from earnings (in Chapter 1 of Part 12A)	section 681AC(2)][12]
relevant disregarded income (in Chapter 1 of Part 14)	section 821
[relevant disregarded income (in Chapter 2B of Part 14)	section 835O(3)][12]
relevant foreign income	section 989
the relevant holding (in Chapter 4 of Part 6)	section 286(1)
. . . [28]	. . . [28]
the relevant shares (in Part 5)	section 157(1)
relevant transaction (in Chapter 2 of Part 13)	section 715
relevant transfer (in Chapter 2 of Part 13)	section 716(1)
. . . [21]	. . . [21]
[relievable charity donation (in Chapter 8 of Part 13)	section 809ZI(1)][15]
[rent (in Chapter 1 of Part 12A)	section 681AL(3), (4)][12]
[rent (in Chapter 2 of Part 12A)	section 681BM(5)][12]
[rent (in Part 11A)	section 614DG][12]
[the rental earnings (in Part 11A)	section 614AC][12]
. . . [21]	. . . [21]
. . . [20]	. . . [20]
[repayment of, and return on, investment in certain investment schemes (in Chapter 5E of Part 13)	section 809EZE(4)][24]

retail prices index	section 989
[research and development (in Part 5A)	section 257HJ(1)][18]
. . .[21]	. . .[21]
[savings additional rate	section 7A (as applied by section 989)][30]
[savings allowance	section 12B][26]
[savings basic rate	section 7A (as applied by section 989)
savings higher rate	section 7A (as applied by section 989)][30]
savings income	section 18
[savings nil rate	section 7][26]
. . .[3]	. . .[3]
. . .[4]	. . .[4]
scheme administrator	section 989
. . .[29]	. . .[29]
[Scottish basic rate	section [989)][2925]
. . .[29]	. . .[29]
[Scottish intermediate rate	section 989][31]
[Scottish rate	section 989
Scottish rate resolution	section 989][29]
[Scottish taxpayer	section 989][25]
section 946 payment (in Chapter 15 of Part 15)	section 945(1)
securities (in relation to a company) (in Chapters 3 to 6 of Part 6, but see sections 317(4) and 328(2))	section 285(2)
securities (in Part 12)	section 619
securities (in Chapter 1 of Part 13)	section 713
securities of the same kind (in Part 12)	section 619(6)
[SEIS (in Part 5A)	section 257A(2)][18]
settled property	section 466 (as applied by section 989)
settlor	sections 467 to 473 (as applied by section 989)
share (in Chapter 3 of Part 13)	section 772(3)
share (in Chapter 4 of Part 13)	section 789
shares (in Chapter 6 of Part 4)	section 151(1)
shares (in Part 6)	section 332
share loss relief (in Chapter 6 of Part 4)	section 131(1)
[shares, stock or other securities included in the official UK list	section 1005
shares, stock or other securities listed on a recognised stock exchange	section 1005][2]
sideways relief (in Chapter 2 of Part 4)	section 60(4)
sideways relief (in Chapter 3 of Part 4)	section 103(1)
sideways relief (in Chapter 5 of Part 13)	section 790(3)
single company (in Part 5)	section 257(1)
[single company (in Part 5A)	section 257HJ(1)][18]
single company (in Part 6)	section 332
the 6 year period (in Chapter 6 of Part 7)	section 359(3)
[split year	section 989][19]
spouse (in Chapter 6 of Part 4)	section 151(1)
[starting rate for savings	section 7][3]
[starting rate limit for savings	section 12][3]
. . .[21]	. . .[21]
subsidiary (in Chapter 1 of Part 8)	section 401(3)
51% subsidiary	section 989
75% subsidiary	section 989
the successor company (in Chapter 5 of Part 6)	section 323(3)
[sum (in Part 11A)	section 614DG][12]

[sum (in Chapter 5E of Part 13)	section 809EZB(3)][24]
[sum obtained in respect of an interest in an asset (in Chapter 4 of Part 12A)	section 681DG][12]
[sum obtained in respect of the lessee's interest in a lease of an asset (in Chapter 4 of Part 12A)	section 681DH][12]
surrender (in the application of this Act to Scotland)	section 1008
[tainted donation (in Chapter 8 of Part 13)	section 809ZJ][15]
. . .[27]	. . .[27]
tax enactments (in Chapter 5 of Part 6)	section 325
tax relief certificate (in Part 7)	section 348(1)
tax year	section 4(2) (as applied by section 989)
the tax year 2007–08 etc	section 4(4) (as applied by section 989
the termination date (in relation to shares) (in Part 5)	section 256
total income	sections 23 (see Step 1) and 31 (as applied by section 989)
trade (except in Parts 5 and 6)	section 989
trade (in Part 5)	section 989 (but see sections 189(2) and 232(7))
trade (in Part 6)	section 989 (but see sections 300(4) and 313(3))
. . .[21]	. . .[21]
trade carried on through a branch or agency (in Chapter 9 of Part 15)	section 926(2)
trading company (in Chapter 6 of Part 4)	section 151(1)
trading group (in Chapter 6 of Part 4)	section 151(1)
trading stock (in Chapter 1 of Part 13)	section [684(2)][9]
transaction income (in Chapter 1 of Part 14)	section 814(5)
transaction in securities (in Chapter 1 of Part 13)	section [684(2)][9]
. . .[21]	. . .[21]
transfer (of securities) (in Part 12)	section 620
transfer (in Chapter 2 of Part 13)	section 716(2)
[transfer (in Chapter 5A of Part13)	section 809AZF(3)][5]
transfer with accrued interest (in Part 12)	section 623
transfer with unrealised interest (in Part 12)	section 625
transfer without accrued interest (in Part 12)	section 624
transferee (in Part 12)	section 621
transferor (in Part 12)	section 621
[transfer taking place (in Chapter 5A of Part 13)	section 809AZF(3)][5]
trust rate	section 9(1) (as applied by section 989)
the trustees of a settlement (in Part 9)	section 463
[type 1 finance arrangement (in Chapter 5B of Part 13)	section 809BZA][12]
[type 2 finance arrangement (in Chapter 5B of Part 13)	section 809BZF][12]
[type 3 finance arrangement (in Chapter 5B of Part 13)	section 809BZJ][12]
UK generally accepted accounting practice	section 997(2)
[the UK part	section 989][19]
UK property business	Chapter 2 of Part 3 of ITTOIA 2005 (as applied by section 989)
UK public revenue dividend (in Chapter 5 of Part 15)	section 891
UK resident (and references to a UK resident or a UK resident person)	section 989
. . .[21]	. . .[21]
. . .[21]	. . .[21]
umbrella scheme	section 989
unauthorised unit trust	section 989
unit holder	section 989
unit trust scheme	section 1007

United Kingdom	section 1013
unrealised interest (in Part 12)	section 625
the value of the net benefit to a charity (in Chapter 3 of Part 8)	section 437
variable rate securities (in Part 12)	section 627
VCT	section 259(1) (as applied by section 989)
VCT approval (in Part 6)	section 259(2)
VCT-in-liquidation (in Chapter 5 of Part 6)	section 320
VCT relief (in Part 6)	section 258
venture capital trust	section 259(1) (as applied by section 989)
[Welsh additional rate	section 6B (as applied by section 989)
Welsh basic rate	section 6B (as applied by section 989)
Welsh higher rate	section 6B (as applied by section 989)
Welsh taxpayer	section 989][32]
[winding up receipt (in Chapter 3A of Part 14)	section 837C(3)][7]
woodlands	section 996
the year of the loss (in Chapter 6 of Part 4)	section 131(1)[10]

Amendments—[1]   Section numbers substituted and definition inserted by FA 2007 s 26, Sch 4 paras 20, 21 and deemed always to have had effect.

[2]   Entries inserted by FA 2007 s 109, Sch 26 para 12(15) with effect from 19 July 2007.

[3]   Entry "EIS rate (in Part 5)" inserted, entries "starting rate for savings" and "starting rate limit for savings" substituted, and entry "savings rate" repealed, by FA 2008 s 5, Sch 1 paras 1, 36 with effect for the tax year 2008–09 and subsequent tax years.

[4]   Entry "Schedule A business" repealed by CTA 2009 ss 1322, 1326, Sch 1 paras 699, 721, Sch 3 Part 1. CTA 2009 applies for accounting periods ending on or after 1 April 2009 (for corporation tax purposes) and for tax years 2009–10 onwards (for income and capital gains tax purposes).

[5]   Entries inserted by FA 2009 s 49, Sch 25, para 9(7),(8) with effect in relation to transfers on or after 22 April 2009.

[6]   Entries inserted and repealed by CTA 2010 ss 1177, 1181, Sch 1 para 572, Sch 3 Pt 1. CTA 2010 has effect for corporation tax purposes for accounting periods ending on or after 1 April 2010, and for income and capital gains tax purposes for the tax year 2010–11 and subsequent tax years.

[7]   Entries inserted by TIOPA 2010 s 371, Sch 7 paras 68, 72. TIOPA 2010 has effect for corporation tax purposes for accounting periods ending on or after 1 April 2010, for income and capital gains tax purposes for the tax year 2010–11 and subsequent tax years, and for petroleum revenue tax purposes for chargeable periods beginning on or after 1 July 2010.

[8]   Entry inserted by FA 2010 s 31 Sch 7 paras 1, 4 with effect in relation to any disposal made to a charity on or after 15 December 2009.

[9]   Entry inserted and in entries relating to "income tax advantage (in Chapter 1 of Part 13)" and "transaction in securities (in Chapter 1 of Part 13)" figure substituted by FA 2010 s 38, Sch 12 para 12 with effect in relation to income tax advantages obtained on or after 24 March 2010.

[10]   Entries inserted by FA 2010 s 40, Sch 13 para 3 with effect in relation to payments treated under ITA 2007 s 941(2) as made on or after 21 October 2009.

[11]   Entries inserted and in entry for "basic rate limit" figure substituted for figure "20(2)", by FA 2009 s 6, Sch 2 paras 1, 9 with effect for the tax year 2010–11 and subsequent tax years. The powers conferred by the amendments made by FA 2009 Sch 2 may be exercised at any time on or after 21 July 2009 but not so as to make provision having effect before the tax year 2010–11 (FA 2009 Sch 2 para 25(1)).

[12]   Entries inserted by TIOPA 2010 s 501, Sch 8 paras 219, 223, 237, 239. TIOPA 2010 has effect for corporation tax purposes for accounting periods ending on or after 1 April 2010, for income and capital gains tax purposes for the tax year 2010–11 and subsequent tax years, and for petroleum revenue tax purposes for chargeable periods beginning on or after 1 July 2010.

[13]   In column 2 of entry for "eligible shares (in Chapter 3 of Part 6)" words substituted for words "285(3)", and in column 1 of entry for "the 30% eligible shares condition (in Chapter 3 of Part 6)" figure substituted for figure "30%", by F(No 3)A 2010 s 5, Sch 2 para 4(1)–(3) with effect in relation to accounting periods ending on or after 6 April 2011 (by virtue of SI 2011/662 art 2). These amendments do not have effect in relation to shares or securities held by a company ("the investing company") if the shares or securities are issued before 6 April 2011 or are issued on or after that day and are acquired by the investing company by means of the investment of protected money (F(No 3)A 2010 Sch 2 para 6(2), (3)).

[14]   Entries for "permanent establishment" substituted by F(No 3)A 2010 s 5, Sch 2 para 4(1), (4) with effect in relation to shares or securities issued on or after 6 April 2011 (by virtue of SI 2011/662 art 2).

[15]   Entries inserted by FA 2011 s 27, Sch 3 paras 7, 15 with effect in relation to relievable charity donations made on or after 1 April 2011.

[16]   Entry inserted by FA 2011 s 42(5) with effect for the tax year 2011–12 and subsequent tax years. FA 2011 s 42 came into force on 13 October 2011 (SI 2011/2459 art 2).

[17]   In entry for "charitable trust" words repealed and words substituted, in entries for "charity", "charity (in Chapter 2 of Part 8)" and "charity (in Chapter 3 of Part 8)", words substituted, by FA 2010 s 30, Sch 6 para 23(1), (7) with effect for the tax year 2012–13 and subsequent tax years (SI 2012/736 art 17).

[18]   Entries inserted, and in the entry for "control", reference inserted in the second column by FA 2012 s 38, Sch 6 paras 6, 18 with effect in relation to shares issued on or after 6 April 2012.

19   Entries inserted by FA 2013 s 218, Sch 45 para 108 with effect in calculating an individual's tax liability to income tax or capital gains tax for the tax year 2013–14 or any subsequent tax year, subject to transitional provisions and savings in FA 2013 Sch 45 paras 154–158.

20   Entries repealed in entry for "distribution", words repealed, by FA 2013 s 28, Sch 12 para 15(1), (5) with effect for the tax year 2013–14 and subsequent tax years.

21   Entries repealed by FA 2013 s 77, Sch 29 paras 16, 32 with effect from 1 January 2014.

22   Entries repealed by the Unauthorised Unit Trusts (Tax) Regulations, SI 2013/2819 reg 37(1), (19) with effect from 6 April 2014. Note that an unauthorised unit trust is not a non-exempt unauthorised unit trust, and these amendments do not apply in relation to the trust, if at all times in the period beginning with 24 May 2012 and ending with 5 April 2014 it had at least one unit holder which was, and at least one unit holder which was not, an eligible investor (ie a mixed unauthorised unit trust); this ceases to apply in relation to the trust if subsequently it no longer has any unit holders which are eligible investors (SI 2013/2819 reg 32).

23   Entries for "registered industrial and provident society" repealed, and entries inserted, by the Co-operative and Community Benefit Societies Act 2014 s 151, Sch 4 paras 104, 112 with effect from 1 August 2014 and subject to transitional provisions and provisions preserving the continuity of the law in Sch 5 of that Act.

24   Entries inserted by FA 2015 s 21(3) with effect in relation to sums arising on or after 6 April 2015 (whenever the arrangements under which the sums arise were made).

25   Entries inserted by FA 2014 s 296, Sch 38 paras 1, 11 with effect in relation to the tax year 2016–17 (the tax year appointed by the Treasury under the Scotland Act 2012 s 25(5) by virtue of SI 2015/2000) and subsequent tax years.

26   Entries inserted by FA 2016 s 4(1), (12) with effect in relation to the tax year 2016–17 and subsequent tax years.

27   Entries repealed by FA 2016 s 5, Sch 1 para 63(1), (19) with effect in relation to dividends paid or arising (or treated as paid), and other distributions made (or treated as made), in the tax year 2016-17 or at any later time.

28   Words inserted, and entries repealed, by FA 2016 s 39, Sch 6 para 24 with effect in relation to interest paid or credited on or after 6 April 2016, and dividends or other distributions paid by a building society on or after that date.

29   Entries for "Scottish additional rate" and "Scottish higher rate" repealed, in entry relating to the Scottish basic rate, words substituted, and entries inserted, by the Scotland Act 2016 s 14(1), (14) with effect in relation to the tax year 2017–18 (as appointed under the Scotland Act 2016 s 13(15)) and subsequent years by virtue of SI 2016/1161 reg 3.

30   Entries inserted by FA 2016 s 6(1), (22) with effect in relation to the tax year 2017–18 (as appointed under the Scotland Act 2016 s 13(15)) and subsequent years by virtue of SI 2016/1161 reg 3, subject to transitional provisions (see FA 2016 s 6(24)–(30)). The Agreement between the Scottish Government and the UK Government on the Scottish Government's fiscal framework confirms that full devolution of income tax rates and thresholds for non-savings and non-dividend income will commence in April 2017.

31   Entry for "Scottish intermediate rate" inserted by the Scottish Rates of Income Tax (Consequential Amendments) Order, SI 2018/459 art 6(1), (9) with effect for the tax year commencing on 6 April 2018 and subsequent tax years.

32   Entries for "Welsh additional rate", "Welsh basic rate", "Welsh higher rate", and "Welsh taxpayer" inserted by the Wales Act 2014 s 9(1), (11). Wales Act 2014 s 9 comes into force on 24 July 2018 and has effect in relation to the tax year 2019–20 (by virtue of SI 2018/892 arts 3, 5, 6). 2019–20 is appointed as the first tax year in relation to which a Welsh rate resolution may be made by the National Assembly for Wales under GOWA 2006 s 116D (SI 2018/892 art 6).

33   In entry for "the 80% qualifying holdings condition", figure "80%" substituted for previous figure "70%" by FA 2018 s 17, Sch 5 para 3(*f*) with effect in relation to accounting periods beginning on or after 6 April 2019 (by virtue of SI 2018/931 reg 4(*a*)).

FINANCE ACT 2007

(2007 Chapter 11)

CONTENTS

Part 1: Charges, Rates, Thresholds etc
Income tax
1   Charge and rates for 2007–08
Corporation tax
2   Charge and main rates for financial year 2008
Part 2: Environment
Energy-saving: houses
18   Extension of income tax deduction for expenditure on energy-saving items
Domestic microgeneration
20   Income tax exemption for domestic microgeneration
21   Renewables obligation certificates for domestic microgeneration
Part 3: Income Tax, Corporation Tax and Capital Gains Tax
Anti-avoidance
25   Managed service companies
26   Restrictions on trade loss relief for partners
27   Extension of restrictions on allowable capital losses
29   Life policies etc: effect of rebated or reinvested commission
30   Avoidance involving financial arrangements
31   Companies carrying on business of leasing plant or machinery
32   Restrictions on companies buying losses or gains: tax avoidance schemes
33   Lloyd's corporate members: restriction of group relief
34   Employee benefit contributions
Insurance and friendly societies
38   Insurance companies: gross roll-up business etc
39   Insurance companies: basis of taxation etc
40   Insurance companies: transfers etc
41   Insurance companies: miscellaneous
42   Technical provisions made by general insurers
43   Lloyd's: cessation of business by corporate members
45   Tax exempt business of friendly societies
46   Purchased life annuities: self-assessment
Repos
47   Sale and repurchase of securities
CFCs
48   Controlled foreign companies
Venture capital schemes etc
51   Venture capital schemes etc
REITs
52   Real Estate Investment Trusts
Trusts
55   Trust income
56   Trust gains on contracts for life insurance
Other corporation tax measures
57   Offshore funds
58   Election out of special film rules for film production companies
59   Securitisation companies
Other income tax measures
60   Gift aid: limits
61   Enterprise management incentives: excluded activities
62   Benefits code: whether employment is "lower-paid employment"
63   Armed forces redundancy schemes
64   Armed forces: the Operational Allowance
65   Service charge income
66   Charge on benefits received by former owner of property: late elections
67   Unpaid remuneration and employee benefit contributions
Part 4: Pensions
68   Abolition of contributions relief for life assurance premium contributions
69   Alternatively secured pensions etc
70   Miscellaneous
Part 6: Investigation, Administration etc
Investigation etc
82   Criminal investigations: powers of Revenue and Customs
83   Northern Ireland criminal investigations

84   Sections 82 and 83: supplementary
85   Criminal investigations: Scotland
86   Search warrants
87   Cross-border exercise of powers
Filing dates
88   Personal tax returns
89   Trustee's tax return
90   Partnership tax returns
91   Consequential amendments
92   Commencement
Other administration
93   Mandatory electronic filing of returns
94   Mandatory electronic payment
95   Payment by cheque
96   Enquiry into returns
97   Penalties for errors
Part 7: Miscellaneous
Other miscellaneous measures
105   Amendments connected with Gambling Act 2005
106   (not reproduced)
107   Limitation period in old actions for mistake of law relating to direct tax
108   Disclosure of tax avoidance schemes
109   Meaning of "recognised stock exchange" etc
110   Mergers Directive: regulations
111   (not reproduced)
112   Updating references to Standing Committees
Part 8: Final Provisions
113   Interpretation
114   Repeals
115   Short title
Schedules
Schedule 3—Managed service companies
Schedule 4—Restrictions on trade loss relief for partners
Schedule 5—Avoidance involving financial arrangements
Schedule 6—Companies carrying on business of leasing plant or machinery
Schedule 7—Insurance business: gross roll-up business etc
Schedule 8—Insurance companies: basis of taxation etc
Schedule 9—Insurance companies: transfers etc
Schedule 10—Insurance companies: miscellaneous
Schedule 11—Technical provisions made by general insurers
Schedule 13—Sale and repurchase of securities
Schedule 14—Sale and repurchase of securities: minor and consequential amendments
Schedule 15—Controlled foreign companies
Schedule 16—Venture capital schemes etc
Schedule 17—Real Estate Investment Trusts
Schedule 18—Pensions schemes: abolition of relief for life assurance premium contributions etc
Schedule 19—Alternatively secured pensions and transfer lump sum death benefit etc
Schedule 20—Pension schemes etc: miscellaneous
Schedule 22—Amendments and repeals consequential on extension of HMRC powers
Schedule 23—Extension of HMRC powers: Scotland
Schedule 24—Penalties for errors
Schedule 25—Amendments connected with Gambling Act 2005
Schedule 26—Meaning of "recognised stock exchange" etc
Schedule 27—Repeals

PART 1
CHARGES, RATES, THRESHOLDS ETC
Income tax

1 Charge and rates for 2007–08

Income tax is charged for the tax year 2007–08; and for that tax year—

    (a) the starting rate is 10%,

    (b) the basic rate is 22%, and

    (c) the higher rate is 40%.

Corporation tax

2 Charge and main rates for financial year 2008

(1) Corporation tax is charged for the financial year 2008; and for that year the rate of corporation tax is—

(a) 28% on profits of companies other than ring fence profits, and

(b) 30% on ring fence profits of companies.

(2) In this section "ring fence profits" has the same meaning as in Chapter 5 of Part 12 of ICTA (see section 502(1) and (1A)).

PART 2
ENVIRONMENT

Energy-saving: houses

18 Extension of income tax deduction for expenditure on energy-saving items

(1) Section 312 of ITTOIA 2005 (deduction for expenditure on energy-saving items) is amended as follows.

(2) (*amends* ITTOIA 2005 s 312(1)(*b*))

(3) (*amends* ITTOIA 2005 s 312(1)(*c*))

(4) (*inserts* ITTOIA 2005 s 313(6))

(5) (*inserts* ITTOIA 2005 s 314(3))

(6) The amendments made by subsections (2) and (4) have effect in relation to expenditure incurred on or after 6th April 2007.

(7) The amendment made by subsection (5) is deemed always to have had effect.

(8) Regulations under section 314 of ITTOIA 2005 made on or after the day on which this Act is passed but before 31st December 2007 may include provision having effect in relation to expenditure incurred on or after 6th April 2007.

Commentary—*Simon's Taxes* **B6.207**.

HMRC Manuals—Property Income Manual PIM2072 (main types of expenses: landlord's energy savings allowances).

Domestic microgeneration

20 Income tax exemption for domestic microgeneration

(1) (*inserts* ITTOIA 2005 s 782A)

(2) The amendment made by subsection (1) has effect for the tax year 2007–08 and subsequent tax years.

Commentary—*Simon's Taxes* **E1.586**.

HMRC Manuals—Business Income Manual BIM40520 (income tax exemption for domestic microgeneration).

21 Renewables obligation certificates for domestic microgeneration

(1) (*inserts* ITTOIA 2005 s 782B)

(2) (*inserts* TCGA 1992 s 263AZA)

(3) The amendment made by subsection (1) has effect for the tax year 2007–08 and subsequent tax years.

(4) The amendment made by subsection (2) has effect in relation to disposals on or after 6th April 2007.

Commentary—*Simon's Taxes* **C3.1808, E1.586**.

HMRC Manuals—Business Income Manual BIM40530 (renewable obligation certificates for domestic microgeneration).

PART 3
INCOME TAX, CORPORATION TAX AND CAPITAL GAINS TAX

Anti-avoidance

25 Managed service companies

(1) Schedule 3 contains provision about managed service companies.

(2) That Schedule is deemed to have come into force on 6th April 2007.

Commentary—*Simon's Taxes* **E4.901, E4.910**.

HMRC Manuals—Employment Status Manual ESM3505 (managed service companies: introduction and background). ESM3510 (meaning of managed service companies).

26 Restrictions on trade loss relief for partners

Schedule 4 contains provision restricting reliefs for losses made by individuals carrying on trades in partnership.

Commentary—*Simon's Taxes* **B7.522, B7.522**.

HMRC Manuals—Partnership Manual PM50200 (restriction on loss relief for limited partners). Business Income Manual BIM82600 (partnership loss relief restrictions: contents).

27 Extension of restrictions on allowable capital losses

(1) TCGA 1992 is amended as follows.

(2) (*amends* TCGA 1992 s 8(2) and *repeals* TCGA 1992 s 8(2A)–(2C))

(3) (*inserts* TCGA 1992 s 16A)

(4) In section 288(1) (interpretation), in the definition of "allowable loss", after "16" insert ", 16A".

(5) (*amended* ICTA 1988 s 834(1); (*repealed by* CTA 2010 s 1181, Sch 3 Pt 1)

(6) The amendments made by this section have effect in relation to losses accruing on disposals made on or after 6th December 2006.

Commentary—*Simon's Taxes* **C1.501, C4.227**.
HMRC Manuals—Capital Gains Manual CG48205 (restrictions on capital losses: qualifying losses).
CG15835 (losses: targeted anti-avoidance rule from 6 December 2006).

29 Life policies etc: effect of rebated or reinvested commission

(1) (inserted TA 1988 ss 548A, 548B; *repealed by* FA 2008 s 36, Sch 14 para 17)
(2) (inserts TA 1988 s 552(13))
(3) (inserts ITTOIA 2005 ss 541A, 541B)
(4) The amendments made by this section have effect in relation to a policy or contract if—
    (a) it is made on or after 21st March 2007, or
    (b) on or after that date, any of its terms are varied, or a right under it is exercised, so as to increase the benefits under it.

Commentary—*Simon's Taxes* **E1.542B**.

30 Avoidance involving financial arrangements

Schedule 5 contains provision in relation to tax avoidance involving financial arrangements.

Commentary—*Simon's Taxes* **C4.325, C4.330, D9.737, D1.793, D1.794**.

31 Companies carrying on business of leasing plant or machinery

Schedule 6 contains provision in relation to companies carrying on a business of leasing plant or machinery.

Commentary—*Simon's Taxes* **B3.340CA, D6.330**.

32 Restrictions on companies buying losses or gains: tax avoidance schemes

(1) TCGA 1992 is amended as follows.
(2) (amends TCGA 1992 s 184A(2))
(3) (amends TCGA 1992 s 184B(2))
(4) Section 70 of FA 2006 (which inserted sections 184A to 184F of TCGA 1992) is amended as follows.
(5) (amends FA 2006 s 70(9))
(6) (substitutes FA 2006 s 70(10)–(13))
(7) The amendment made by subsection (2) has effect in relation to gains accruing on disposals made on or after 21st March 2007.
(8) The amendment made by subsection (3) has effect in relation to losses accruing on disposals made on or after that date.
(9) The amendments made by subsections (5) and (6) have effect in relation to disposals made on or after that date; but the amendment made by subsection (5)(*d*) has no effect in relation to disposals made before 9th May 2007.

Commentary—*Simon's Taxes* **C1.502, D2.403**.
HMRC Manuals—Capital Gains Manual CG47020 (anti-loss buying rules in finance act 2006: contents).
CG47320 (anti-gain buying rules in finance act 2006: contents).

33 Lloyd's corporate members: restriction of group relief

(1) (inserts FA 1994 s 227A)
(2) The amendment made by subsection (1) has effect in relation to any case where the corporate member (as the surrendering company) and the other company (as the claimant company) first meet the conditions in section 402(2) or (3) of ICTA on or after 21st March 2007.

HMRC Manuals—Lloyd's Manual LLM4250 (restriction of group relief).

34 Employee benefit contributions

(1)–(6) (amended FA 2003 Sch 24 paras 1(1), 2–5, 9(1); *repealed by* CTA 2009 s 1326, Sch 3 Pt 1)
(7) Part 2 of ITTOIA 2005 (trading income) is amended as follows.
(8) (substitutes ITTOIA 2005 s 38(1))
(9) (substitutes ITTOIA 2005 s 39(1))
(10) (amends ITTOIA 2005 s 41)
(11) (amends ITTOIA 2005 s 42(1), (3), (5))
(12) (amends ITTOIA 2005 s 44(1))
(13) The amendments made by this section have effect in relation to employee benefit contributions made on or after 21st March 2007.

Commentary—*Simon's Taxes* **B2.422**.
HMRC Manuals—Business Income Manual BIM44525 (specific deductions: used with accident benefit schemes).
BIM44585 (timing of deductions for contributions: what it applies to).
BIM44590 (timing of deductions for contributions: structure of the legislation).
BIM44615 (timing of deductions for contributions: payments 'out of' contributions).

Insurance and friendly societies

38 Insurance companies: gross roll-up business etc

(1) Part 1 of Schedule 7 contains provisions relating to gross roll-up business, capital redemption business and miscellaneous minor matters relating to insurance companies.
(2) The amendments made by that Part of that Schedule have effect—

(8) The amendment made by subsection (4) has effect in relation to account periods (within the meaning of Chapter 5 of Part 17 of ICTA) beginning on or after 1st January 2007.

(9) The amendment made by subsection (5) has effect in relation to transactions on or after 6th April 2007.

Commentary—*Simon's Taxes* C1.620.

HMRC Manuals—Company Taxation Manual CTM48135 (offshore funds).

Amendments—[1]   Sub-ss (6), (7) repealed by CTA 2010 s 1181, Sch 3 Pt 1. CTA 2010 has effect for corporation tax purposes for accounting periods ending on or after 1 April 2010, and for income and capital gains tax purposes for the tax year 2010–11 and subsequent tax years.

58 Election out of special film rules for film production companies

(1) (inserted FA 2006 s 32(7)–(10); *repealed by* CTA 2009 s 1326, Sch 3 Pt 1)

(2) (*inserts* FA 1998 Sch 18 para 10(5))

HMRC Manuals—Film Production Company Manual FPC10500 (legislation). FPC10110 (election not to be regarded as FPC).

59 Securitisation companies

(1) Section 83 of FA 2005 (continued application of old UK GAAP to securitisation companies during transitional period) is amended as follows.

(2) (*amends* FA 2005 s 83(1)(*b*) and *inserts* FA 2005 s 83(7A), (7B))

(4) . . . [1]

(5) (*amended* FA 2005 s 84(3)(*d*)); *repealed by* CTA 2010 s 1181, Sch 3 Pt 1.

(6) (*substituted* FA 2005 s 84(5)); *repealed by* CTA 2010 s 1181, Sch 3 Pt 1.[1]

Commentary—*Simon's Taxes* D7.1301, D7.1302.

HMRC Manuals—Corporate Finance Manual CFM72370 (periods beginning on or after 1 January 2007: the regulations; meaning of a 'securitisation company').

CFM72210 (securitisation: periods beginning on or after 1 January 2005: overview of the interim regime).

CFM72260 (securitisation: periods beginning on or after 1 January 2005: the interim regime: continuation after 2008).

Amendments—[1]   Sub-s (4) repealed by CTA 2010 s 1181, Sch 3 Pt 1. CTA 2010 has effect for corporation tax purposes for accounting periods ending on or after 1 April 2010, and for income and capital gains tax purposes for the tax year 2010–11 and subsequent tax years.

Other income tax measures

60 Gift aid: limits

(1) (*amends* ITA 2007 s 418(2)(*c*), (3))[1]

(2) (*amended* TA 1988 s 339(3B)(*b*), (3DA)(*c*)); *repealed by* CTA 2010 s 1181, Sch 3 Pt 1.

(3) The amendment made by subsection (1) has effect in relation to gifts made on or after 6th April 2007.

(4) The amendment made by subsection (2) has effect in relation to gifts made in an accounting period ending on or after 6th April 2007.

Commentary—*Simon's Taxes* E1.811.

Amendments[1]   Sub-s (1)(*b*) repealed by FA 2011 s 41(3) with effect in relation to gifts made on or after 6 April 2011.

61 Enterprise management incentives: excluded activities

(1) In Part 3 of Schedule 5 to ITEPA 2003 (enterprise management incentives: qualifying companies), in paragraph 19 (excluded activities: receipt of royalties or licence fees)—

   (*a*)   (*substitutes* ITEPA 2003 Sch 5 para 19(4)(*a*), (*b*))

   (*b*)   (*inserts* ITEPA 2003 Sch 5 para 19(8))

(2) The amendments made by subsection (1) have effect in relation to options granted on or after 6th April 2007.

(3) They also have effect in relation to a qualifying option within subsection (4), for the purpose of determining at any time on or after that date whether an activity is an excluded activity.

(4) An option is within this subsection if it was granted before 6th April 2007 and, immediately before that date—

   (*a*)   it had not been exercised, and

   (*b*)   no disqualifying event had occurred in relation to it.

(5) Subsection (6) applies in respect of an option within subsection (4) if—

   (*a*)   immediately before 6th April 2007—

      (i)   the right to exploit an intangible asset ("the asset") was vested in the relevant company or a subsidiary of it (in either case, alone or jointly with others), and

      (ii)   the asset was a relevant intangible asset,

   (*b*)   at any time on or after that date, an activity carried on by the relevant company or a subsidiary of it would be an excluded activity by reason only of the receipt of royalties or licence fees attributable to the exploitation of the asset, and

   (*c*)   the activity would not be an excluded activity if the amendments made by subsection (1) had not been made.

(6) The activity is to be treated, in relation to the option, as not being an excluded activity at that time.

Commentary—Simon's Taxes **E4.545**.

HMRC Manuals—Employee Tax Advantaged Share Scheme Manual ETASSUM52100 - 52180 (enterprise management incentives: excluded activities).

62 Benefits code: whether employment is "lower-paid employment"

(1) (*repeals* ITEPA 2003 s 219(5), (6))

(2) The repeal made by subsection (1) has effect for the tax year 2007–08 and subsequent tax years.

Commentary—Simon's Taxes **E4.602A**.

HMRC Manuals—Employment Income Manual EIM20105 (extra statutory concession A104 superseded by section 62 FA2007).

63 Armed forces redundancy schemes

(1) (*inserts* ITEPA 2003 s 411(2))

(2) The amendments made by subsection (1) have effect for the tax year 2006–07 and subsequent tax years.

HMRC Manuals—Employment Income Manual EIM13720 (exceptions: terminal grants, payments and benefits to members of HM forces).

64 Armed forces: the Operational Allowance

(1) (*inserts* ITEPA 2003 s 297A)

(2) The amendment made by subsection (1) has effect in relation to payments whenever made.

Commentary—Simon's Taxes **E4.1181**.

HMRC Manuals—Tax Credit Technical Manual TCTM04203 (income: armed forces travel and operational allowances).

65 Service charge income

(1) Section 480 of ITA 2007 (meaning of "accumulated or discretionary income") is amended as follows.

(2) (*amends* ITA 2007 s 480(3)(*c*))

(3) (*substitutes* ITA 2007 s 480(5))

(4) The amendments made by this section have effect for the tax year 2007–08 and subsequent tax years.

Commentary—Simon's Taxes **C4.210**.

66 Charge on benefits received by former owner of property: late elections

(1) (*substitutes* FA 2004 Sch 15 para 23(3))

(2) The amendment made by subsection (1) is deemed to have come into force on 21st March 2007.

Commentary—Simon's Taxes **I3.746**.

67 Unpaid remuneration and employee benefit contributions

(1) Section 31 of ITTOIA 2005 (relationship between rules prohibiting and allowing deductions: trading income) is amended as follows.

(2) (*amends* ITTOIA 2005 s 31(1)(*b*))

(3) (*amends* ITTOIA 2005 s 31(3))

(4) Section 274 of ITTOIA 2005 (provision corresponding to section 31 of that Act in case of property income) is amended as follows.

(5) (*amends* ITTOIA 2005 s 274(1)(*b*))

(6) (*amends* ITTOIA 2005 s 274(3))

(7) The amendments made by this section have effect for the tax year 2007–08 and subsequent tax years.

Commentary—Simon's Taxes **B2.302, B2.303, B2.401**.

HMRC Manuals—Business Income Manual BIM42080 (deductions: general: interaction between prohibitive and permissive rules).

PART 4
PENSIONS

68 Abolition of contributions relief for life assurance premium contributions

Schedule 18 contains provisions denying relief for contributions made by or on behalf of members in respect of life assurance premiums.

Commentary—Simon's Taxes **E7.222**.

69 Alternatively secured pensions etc

Schedule 19 contains provisions about alternatively secured pensions and transfer lump sum death benefit etc

HMRC Manuals—Inheritance Tax Manual IHTM17350 - 17451 (alternatively secured pensions).

70 Miscellaneous

Schedule 20 contains miscellaneous provisions about registered pension schemes and employer-financed retirement benefits schemes.

Commentary—Simon's Taxes **E7.202, E7.204, E7.208, E7.245, E7.252**.

PART 6
INVESTIGATION, ADMINISTRATION ETC

Investigation etc

82 Criminal investigations: powers of Revenue and Customs

(1) Section 114 of the Police and Criminal Evidence Act 1984 (c 60) (application of Act to customs and excise) is amended as follows.

(2) (*amends* PACE 1984 s 114(2)(*a*))

(3), (4) (*amend* PACE 1984 s 114(2)(*b*))

(5) (*amends* PACE 1984 s 114(2)(*b*)(i) inserted section 14A))

(6) (*inserts* PACE 1984 s 114(2)(*b*)(i) inserted section 14B)

(7) (*amends* PACE 1984 s 114(2)(*c*))

(8) (*inserts* PACE 1984 s 114(2)(*d*), (*e*))

(9) (*inserts* PACE 1984 s 114(2A))

(10) (*substitutes* PACE 1984 s 114(3))

(11) The heading of section 114 accordingly becomes "**Application of Act to Revenue and Customs**".

Commentary—*Simon's Taxes* **A6.306, A6.315, A6.1102**.

Orders—Finance Act 2007 (Sections 82 to 84 and Schedule 23) (Commencement) Order 2007, SI 2007/3166 (this section comes into force on 8 November 2007).

83 Northern Ireland criminal investigations

(*amends* and *modifies* the Police and Criminal Evidence (Northern Ireland) Order, SI 1989/1341 (NI 12) art 85)

Commentary—*Simon's Taxes* **A6.1102**.

HMRC Manuals—Hydrocarbon Oils Strategy Manual HCOS4275 (contact with offenders).

Orders—Finance Act 2007 (Sections 82 to 84 and Schedule 23) (Commencement) Order 2007, SI 2007/3166 (this section comes into force on 8 November 2007).

84 Sections 82 and 83: supplementary

(1) (*repeals* CRCA 2005 Sch 2 paras 7, 9)

(2) Nothing in section 6 or 7 of CRCA 2005 (initial functions) restricts the functions in connection with which officers of Revenue and Customs may exercise a power under—

    (*a*) the Police and Criminal Evidence Act 1984 by virtue of section 114 of that Act (as amended by section 82 above), or

    (*b*) the Police and Criminal Evidence (Northern Ireland) Order 1989 by virtue of Article 85 of that Order (as amended by section 83 above).

(3) But neither an order under section 114 of the Police and Criminal Evidence Act 1984 nor an order under Article 85 of the Police and Criminal Evidence (Northern Ireland) Order 1989 has effect in relation to a matter specified in section 54(4)(b) or (f) of, or in paragraphs 3, 7, 10, [14][1] to 15, 19 or 24 to 29 of Schedule 1 to, CRCA 2005 (former Inland Revenue matters).[2]

(4) Schedule 22 contains amendments and repeals consequential on extension of police powers to Revenue and Customs.

(5) Sections 82 and 83 and this section come into force in accordance with provision made by the Treasury by order.

(6) The power to make an order under subsection (5) is exercisable by statutory instrument.

Commentary—*Simon's Taxes* **A6.1102**.

Orders—Finance Act 2007 (Sections 82 to 84 and Schedule 23) (Commencement) Order 2007, SI 2007/3166 (this section comes into force on 8 November 2007, except for sub-s (4), which comes into force on 1 December 2007).

Amendments—[1] In sub-s (3), reference substituted by the Employment Act 2008 s 12(1) with effect from 6 April 2009 (by virtue of SI 2009/603 arts 2, 3).

[2] Sub-s (3) repealed by the Criminal Finances Act 2017 s 18(5) with effect from 27 June 2017.

85 Criminal investigations: Scotland

Schedule 23 contains provision for Scotland about the investigation of offences by Her Majesty's Revenue and Customs.

Commentary—*Simon's Taxes* **A6.1102, A6.1103**.

HMRC Manuals—Hydrocarbon Oils Strategy Manual HCOS4275 (contact with offenders).

Orders—Finance Act 2007 (Sections 82 to 84 and Schedule 23) (Commencement) Order 2007, SI 2007/3166 (Schedule 23 comes into force on 1 December 2007).

86 Search warrants

(*inserts* PACE 1984 s 8(7))

87 Cross-border exercise of powers

(1) This section relates to the Criminal Justice and Public Order Act 1994 (c 33).

(2) Sections 136 to 139 (execution of warrants and powers of arrest and search) shall apply to an officer of Revenue and Customs as they apply to a constable; and for that purpose—

   (*a*) a reference to a constable (including a reference to a constable of a police force in England and Wales, a constable of a police force in Scotland or a constable of a police force in Northern Ireland) shall be treated as a reference to an officer of Revenue and Customs, and

   (*b*) a reference to a police station, or a designated police station, includes a reference to an office of Revenue and Customs or (in England and Wales and Northern Ireland) a designated office of Revenue and Customs.

[(2A) In the application of section 137C where a person is arrested under section 137A by an officer of Revenue and Customs in respect of a specified offence that is being investigated by an officer of Revenue and Customs—

   (*a*) subsection (2)(*b*) is to be read as if (instead of requiring the detention to be authorised by both an officer of at least the rank of inspector in the arresting force and an officer of at least the rank of inspector in the investigating force) it required the detention to be authorised by an officer of Revenue and Customs of at least the grade equivalent to the rank of inspector;

   (*b*) subsection (2)(*c*) is to be read as if (instead of requiring the detention to be authorised by both an officer of a rank above that of inspector in the arresting force and an officer of a rank above that of inspector in the investigating force) it required the detention to be authorised by an officer of Revenue and Customs of a grade above that equivalent to the rank of inspector;

   (*c*) subsection (3) is omitted;

   (*d*) in subsections (4) and (5), the reference to an officer of the investigating force is to be read as a reference to an officer of Revenue and Customs;

   (*e*) in subsection (6), the reference to an appropriate officer in the investigating force is to be read as a reference to an appropriate officer of Revenue and Customs (as defined by subsection (7));

   (*f*) subsection (6)(*a*) is omitted;

   (*g*) in subsection (7)(*b*), the reference to an officer of at least the rank of inspector is to be read as a reference to an officer of Revenue and Customs of at least the equivalent grade;

   (*h*) in subsection (7)(*c*), the reference to an officer of a rank above that of inspector is to be read as a reference to an officer of Revenue and Customs of above the equivalent grade;

   (*i*) subsections (8) to (10) are omitted.

(2B) Where section 137C applies in accordance with subsection (2A), Schedule 7B applies with the following modifications—

   (*a*) any reference to a constable in the arresting force is to be read as a reference to an officer of Revenue and Customs;

   (*b*) any reference to an officer of at least, or above, a particular rank in the investigating force is to be read as a reference to an officer of Revenue and Customs of at least, or above, the equivalent grade;

   (*c*) any reference to the arresting force or to the investigating force (otherwise than in relation to a description of officer in the force) is to be read as a reference to officers of Revenue and Customs;

   (*d*) instead of the modification made by paragraph 9, section 42 of the Criminal Justice (Scotland) Act 2016 is to be read as if the references in subsections (1)(c)(ii) and (3)(b) to the police were references to officers of Revenue and Customs;

   (*e*) the Schedule is to be read as if it also provided for references in the provisions applied by section 137D(2)(*d*), (3)(*d*) and (4)(*d*) to a police station to include references to an office of Revenue and Customs.

(2C) In the application of section 137C where a person is arrested under section 137A by an officer of Revenue and Customs in respect of a specified offence other than one that is being investigated by an officer of Revenue and Customs—

   (*a*) any reference to an officer of at least, or above, the rank of inspector in the arresting force is to be read as a reference to an officer of Revenue and Customs of at least, or above, the equivalent grade;

   (*b*) the reference in subsection (6)(*a*) to the arresting force is to be read as a reference to any officer of Revenue and Customs.

(2D) Where section 137C applies in accordance with subsection (2C), Schedule 7B applies with the following modifications—

   (*a*) any reference to a constable in the arresting force is to be read as a reference to an officer of Revenue and Customs;

   (*b*) any reference to the arresting force (otherwise than in relation to a description of officer in the force) is to be read as a reference to officers of Revenue and Customs;

   (*c*) instead of the modification made by paragraph 9, section 42 of the Criminal Justice (Scotland) Act 2016 is to be read as if the references in subsections (1)(*c*)(ii) and (3)(*b*) to the police were references to officers of Revenue and Customs;

   (*d*) the Schedule is to be read as if it also provided for references in the provisions applied by section 137D(2)(*d*), (3)(*d*) and (4)(*d*) to a police station to include references to an office of Revenue and Customs.]³

[(2E) In the application of those sections to an officer of Revenue and Customs—

(*a*) sections 136(4B) and 137(7B) apply with the omission of the words from "and, if the constable" to the end;

(*b*) section 137ZA applies with the omission of subsection (6).][4]

[(3) In the application of section 138 to an officer of Revenue and Customs—

(*a*) subsection (1B) shall be treated as if it provided as follows—

"(1B) Where a person is arrested under subsection (2) of the principal section but not charged in connection with an offence, subsections (2) to (9) of section 25A of the Criminal Law (Consolidation) (Scotland) Act 1995 (right of suspects to have access to a solicitor) apply with the following modifications—

    (*a*)   omit the references to "other premises or place" in subsections (2) and (6);

    (*b*)   the right under subsection (2) arises when the person is arrested;

    (*c*)   the reference in subsection (2)(*b*) to the office of Revenue and Customs where the person is being detained is to be read as a reference to the police station to which the person is to be taken; and

    (*d*)   subsection (6) is to be read as requiring that the person be informed of the rights under section 25A(2) and (3) on being arrested."

(*b*) in subsection (2), the references to the 1995 Act and to section 14(1) of that Act are to be treated as references to the Criminal Law (Consolidation) (Scotland) Act 1995 ("the Consolidation Act") and to section 24(1) of that Act;

(*c*) subsection (2A) is to be treated as if it provided as follows—

"(2A) Those provisions are—

    (*a*)   section 24(2) to (8A) (detention and questioning at office of Revenue and Customs);

    (*b*)   sections 24A and 24B (extension of period of detention under section 24);

    (*c*)   section 25 (right to have someone informed when detained);

    (*d*)   section 25A(2) to (9) (right of access to solicitor)"

(*d*) in subsection (6) the reference to the 1995 Act is to be treated as a reference to the Consolidation Act;

(*e*) in subsection 7—

    (i) the reference to section 14 is to be treated as a reference to section 24 of the Consolidation Act; and

    (ii) the reference to subsections (6) and (9) of section 14 is to be treated as a reference to subsections (5) and (8) of section 24;

(*f*) in subsection 8—

    (i) the reference to section 15 is to be treated as a reference to section 25 of the Consolidation Act;

    (ii) paragraph (*a*) is to be treated as if it provided as follows—

    (*a*)   "in subsection (1)—

        (i)   the words "other premises or place" (in both places) are to be treated as if they referred to a police station;

        (ii)   the reference in paragraph (*a*) to other premises is to be treated as a reference to a police station:"

    (iii) paragraph (*b*) does not apply;

    (iv) the references in paragraph (*c*)(i) and (iii) to the right under subsection (1)(*b*) are to be treated as references to the right under section 25(1) to have someone informed when detained;

    (v) the reference in paragraph (*c*)(ii) to subsection (1)(*b*) is to be treated as a reference to section 25(1);

    (vi) the reference in paragraph (*c*)(iii) to subsection (2) is to be treated as a reference to the words in section 25(1) beginning "and the person shall be informed";

    (vii) the reference to subsection (4) is to be treated as a reference to section 25(2); and

(*g*) in subsection 9—

    (i) the reference to section 15A is to be treated as a reference to section 25A;

    (ii) paragraph (*a*) is to be treated as if it provided as follows—

    (*a*)   "the words "other premises or place" in subsections (2) and (6) are to be treated as referring to a police station;"

    ; and

    (iii) in paragraph (*b*)(iii) the reference to section 15A(2) and (3) is to be treated as a reference to section 25A(2) and (3).][1]

(4) An officer of Revenue and Customs may exercise a power under sections 136 to 139 [in the exercise of any function of the Commissioners for Her Majesty's Revenue and Customs or of officers of Revenue and Customs, within the meaning of the Commissioners for Revenue and Customs Act 2005 (see section 51(2) to (2B) of that Act)][2].

(5) In subsection (2)—

"office of Revenue and Customs" means premises wholly or partly occupied by Her Majesty's Revenue and Customs, and

"designated office of Revenue and Customs" has the meaning given by an order under section 114 of the Police and Criminal Evidence Act 1984 (c 60) (power to extend provisions to HMRC) or, in Northern Ireland, by an order under Article 85 of the Police and Criminal Evidence (Northern Ireland) Order 1989 (SI 1989/1341 (NI 12)) (power to extend Order to HMRC).

(6) (*inserts* Criminal Justice and Public Order Act 1994 s 136(9))

Commentary—*Simon's Taxes* A6.1102.

Amendments—[1] Sub-s (3) substituted by the Criminal Procedure (Legal Assistance, Detention and Appeals) (Scotland) Act 2010 (Consequential Provisions) Order, SI 2011/1739 art 7 with effect from 15 July 2011. Note that this amendment does not affect the operation of CJPO 1994 ss 136–139 (as they apply to HMRC officers by virtue of FA 1987 s 87 as it has effect immediately before 15 July 2011) in relation to a person arrested or detained under s 137(2) of that Act (as it applies to such officers,) where the arrest occurred or the period of detention began before that time.

[2] In sub-s (4), words substituted by the Policing and Crime Act 2017 s 118 with effect from 1 March 2018 (by virtue of SI 2018/227 reg 2(*f*)).

[3] Sub-ss (2A)–(2D) inserted by the Policing and Crime Act 2017 s 119, Sch 17 para 9 with effect from 1 March 2018 (by virtue of SI 2018/227 reg 2(*g*)).

[4] Sub-s (2E) inserted, and sub-s (3) repealed, by the Criminal Justice (Scotland) Act 2016 (Consequential Provisions) Order, SI 2018/46 art 19 with effect from 25 January 2018 (being the later of (a) the day after the day on which SI 2018/46 was made (ie 17 January 2018), and (b) the date of repeal of the Criminal Procedure (Scotland) Act 1995 s 14 (25 January 2018)).

Filing dates

88 Personal tax returns

(1) Section 8 of TMA 1970 (personal tax return) is amended as follows.

(2) (*amends* TMA 1970 s 8(1)(*a*))

(3) (*repeals* TMA 1970 s 8(1A))

(4) (*inserts* TMA 1970 s 8(1D)–(1H))

Commentary—*Simon's Taxes* E1.202A.

HMRC Manuals—Self Assessment Legal Framework Manual SALF203 (personal tax returns).

Compliance Operational Guidance Manual COG931720 (primary and secondary legislation for SA).

89 Trustee's tax return

(1) Section 8A of TMA 1970 (trustee's tax return) is amended as follows.

(2) (*amends* TMA 1970 s 8A(1)(*a*))

(3) (*repeals* TMA 1970 s 8A(1A))

(4) (*inserts* TMA 1970 s 8A(1B)–(1F))

Commentary—*Simon's Taxes* C4.245, E1.210, E1.212.

HMRC Manuals—Self Assessment Legal Framework Manual SALF805 (self assessment for trustees).

90 Partnership tax returns

(1) (*substitutes* TMA 1970 s 12AA(4)–(4E))

(2) (*substitutes* TMA 1970 s 12AA(5)–(5E))

HMRC Manuals—Self Assessment Legal Framework Manual SALF503 (partnership tax returns).

91 Consequential amendments

(1) (*amends* TMA 1970 s 9(2)(*a*), (*b*))

(2) (*substitutes* TMA 1970 s 9ZA(3))

(3) (*amends* TMA 1970 s 9(6))

(4) (*substitutes* TMA 1970 s 12ABA(4))

(5) (*substitutes* TMA 1970 s 28C(6))

(6) (*amended* TMA 1970 s 33A(1), (2), (9)); *repealed by* FA 2008 s 118, Sch 39 para 65(*e*))

(7) (*amends* TMA 1970 s 93(10))

(8) (*inserts* TMA 1970 s 93A(7A), (7B))

(9) (*amends* TMA 1970 s 93A(8))

(10) (*amends* FA 2006 Sch 15 para 4(1), (2))

Commentary—*Simon's Taxes* E1.202A, E1.222, E1.264.

92 Commencement

(1) Sections 88 to 91 have effect—

(*a*) in relation to a return under section 8 or 8A of TMA 1970, or a return under section 12AA of that Act for a partnership which includes one or more individuals, in respect of a return for a year of assessment beginning on or after 6th April 2007, and

(*b*) in relation to a return under section 12AA of that Act for a partnership which includes one or more companies, in respect of a return for a relevant period beginning on or after 6th April 2007.

(2) In subsection (1)(*b*) "relevant period" means a period in respect of which a return is required.

Commentary—*Simon's Taxes* C4.245, E1.202A.

Other administration

93 Mandatory electronic filing of returns

(1) Section 135 of FA 2002 (mandatory electronic filing) is amended as follows.

(2) (*inserts* FA 2002 s 135(7)(*ba*))

(3) (*amends* FA 2002 s 135(10))

(4) Section 76 of VATA 1994 (assessment) is amended as follows.

(5)–(9) (see *Orange Tax Handbook*)

Commentary—*Simon's Taxes* **A4.171, E4.11152**.

94 Mandatory electronic payment

(1) Section 204 of FA 2003 (mandatory electronic payment by large employers) is amended as follows.

(2) (*substitutes* FA 2003 s 204(1), (2))

(3) (*amends* FA 2003 s 204(5)(*b*))

(4) (*amends* FA 2003 s 204(6)(*a*))

(5) (*amends* FA 2003 s 204(8))

(6) (*amends* FA 2003 s 204(12))

(7) (*amends* heading to FA 2003 s 204)

(8) (*amends* FA 2003 s 205(1))

Commentary—*Simon's Taxes* **A4.613, E4.11152**.
HMRC Manuals—Debt Management and Banking Manual DMBM523570 (mandatory electronic payments).

95 Payment by cheque

(1) The Commissioners may make regulations providing for a payment to HMRC made by cheque to be treated as made when the cheque clears, as defined in the regulations.

(2) Section 70A of TMA 1970 (payment by cheque treated as made on receipt by HMRC) is subject to regulations under subsection (1).

(3) Regulations under subsection (1)—

    (*a*) may make provision generally or only for specified purposes,

    (*b*) may make different provision for different purposes, and

    (*c*) may include incidental, consequential or transitional provision.

(4) Regulations under subsection (1)—

    (*a*) shall be made by statutory instrument, and

    (*b*) shall be subject to annulment in pursuance of a resolution of the House of Commons.

(5) In this section—

    (*a*) "the Commissioners" means the Commissioners for Her Majesty's Revenue and Customs, and

    (*b*) "HMRC" means Her Majesty's Revenue and Customs.

(6) (*inserts* FA 2003 s 204(13))

(7) (*inserts* TMA 1970 s 70A(3))

(8) (see *Orange Tax Handbook*)

Commentary—*Simon's Taxes* **A4.613, E4.11132**.
HMRC Manuals—Self Assessment Legal Framework Manual SALF309 (payments by cheque treated as made in receipt by HMRC).

96 Enquiry into returns

(1) (*amends* TMA 1970 s 9A(2)(*a*))

(2) (*amends* TMA 1970 s 12AC(2)(*a*))

(3) (*amends* FA 1998 Sch 18 para 24(2))

(4) (*inserts* FA 1998 Sch 18 para 24(6), (7))

(5) The amendments made by subsections (1) and (2) apply to returns which relate to the tax year 2007–08 or a later tax year.

(6) The amendments made by subsections (3) and (4) apply to returns which relate to accounting periods ending after 31st March 2008.

Commentary—*Simon's Taxes* **A6.401, A6.401**.
HMRC Manuals—Self Assessment Manual SAM31001 (compliance: enquiry work: introduction).

97 Penalties for errors

(1) Schedule 24 contains provisions imposing penalties on taxpayers who—

    (*a*) make errors in certain documents sent to HMRC, or

    (*b*) unreasonably fail to report errors in assessments by HMRC.

(2) That Schedule comes into force in accordance with provision made by the Treasury by order.

(3) An order—

    (*a*) may commence a provision generally or only for specified purposes,

    (*b*) may make different provision for different purposes, and

    (*c*) may include incidental, consequential or transitional provision.

(4) The power to make an order is exercisable by statutory instrument.

Commentary—*Simon's Taxes* **E1.1328, E4.816D**.

HMRC Manuals—Compliance Handbook Manual CH81011 (commencement date for FA 2007 penalties).
CH81070 (conditions for penalty for inaccuracy).
Orders—Finance Act 2007, Schedule 24 (Commencement and Transitional Provisions) Order 2008, SI 2008/568.

PART 7
MISCELLANEOUS

Other miscellaneous measures

105 Amendments connected with Gambling Act 2005

Schedule 25 contains amendments that are consequential on, or otherwise connected with, the Gambling Act 2005 (c 19).

107 Limitation period in old actions for mistake of law relating to direct tax

(1) Section 32(1)(c) of the Limitation Act 1980 (c 58) (extended period for bringing action in case of mistake) does not apply in relation to any action brought before 8th September 2003 for relief from the consequences of a mistake of law relating to a taxation matter under the care and management of the Commissioners of Inland Revenue.

(2) Subsection (1) has effect regardless of how the grounds on which the action was brought were expressed and of whether it was also brought otherwise than for such relief.

(3) But subsection (1) does not have effect in relation to an action, or so much of an action as relates to a cause of action, if—

    (a) the action, or cause of action, has been the subject of a judgment of the House of Lords given before 6th December 2006 as to the application of section 32(1)(c) in relation to such relief, or

    (b) the parties to the action are, in accordance with a group litigation order, bound in relation to the action, or cause of action, by a judgment of the House of Lords in another action given before that date as to the application of section 32(1)(c) in relation to such relief.

(4) If the judgment of any court was given on or after 6th December 2006 but before the day on which this Act is passed, the judgment is to be taken to have been what it would have been had subsections (1) to (3) been in force at all times since the action was brought (and any defence of limitation which would have been available had been raised).

(5) And any payment made to satisfy a liability under the judgment which (in consequence of subsection (4)) is to be taken not to have been imposed is repayable (with interest from the date of the payment).

[(5A) Subsection (1) also does not have effect in relation to an action, or so much of an action as relates to a cause of action, if the consequences of a mistake of law to which the action, or cause of action, relates is the charging of tax contrary to EU law.][1]

(6) In this section—

    "group litigation order" means an order of a court providing for the case management of actions which give rise to common or related issues of fact or law, and

    "judgment" includes order (and "given" includes made).

Commentary—*Simon's Taxes* A1.706, A2.206.
Amendments—[1] Sub-s (5A) inserted by FA 2014 s 299 with effect in relation to actions brought, and causes of action arising, before, on or after 17 July 2014.

108 Disclosure of tax avoidance schemes

(1) Part 7 of FA 2004 (disclosure of tax avoidance schemes) is amended as follows.

(2) (*inserts* FA 2004 s 306A)

(3) (*inserts* FA 2004 s 307(6))

(4) (*inserts* FA 2004 s 308A)

(5) (*inserts* FA 2004 s 313A, 313B)

(6) (*inserts* FA 2004 s 314A)

(7) (*inserts* FA 2004 s 317A)

(8) (*amends* FA 2004 s 318(1))

(9) (*inserts* TMA 1970 s 98C(2)(e), (2A)–(2F))

(10) The amendments made by this section come into force on the passing of this Act; and—

    (a) . . .[1]

    (b) a power under Part 7 of FA 2004 as amended by this section may be exercised in relation to, or by virtue of, matters arising wholly or partly before the passing of this Act.

Commentary—*Simon's Taxes* A7.241, A7.244, A7.261.
Amendments—[1] Sub-s (10)(a) repealed by the Transfer of Tribunal Functions and Revenue and Customs Appeals Order, SI 2009/56 art 3, Sch 1 para 465 with effect from 1 April 2009.

109 Meaning of "recognised stock exchange" etc

Schedule 26 contains—

    (a) new definitions of "recognised stock exchange" for the purposes of the Tax Acts and TCGA 1992,

    (b) provision for the valuation for the purposes of TCGA 1992 of certain shares or securities listed on recognised stock exchanges,

(c) provision for the valuation for the purposes of Chapter 8 of Part 4 of ITTOIA 2005 of strips and securities exchanged for strips, and

(d) minor and consequential amendments in relation to stock exchanges.

110 Mergers Directive: regulations

(1) The Treasury may by regulations make provision about—

    (a) the tax consequences of a merger to form an SE or SCE,

    (b) the tax consequences of a merger where—

      (i) each party to the merger is resident in a member State, and

      (ii) the parties are not all resident in the same member State,

    (c) the tax consequences of a transfer between companies of a business or part of a business, where—

      (i) each party to the transfer is resident in a member State, and

      (ii) the parties are not all resident in the same member State,

    (d) the tax consequences of a share exchange to which section 135 of TCGA 1992 (exchange of securities) applies where companies A and B are resident in different member States,

    (e) the residence of an SE or SCE.

(2) Regulations may, in particular, make provision—

    (a) about the taxation of chargeable gains (including conferring relief from taxation in relation to transfers or mergers which satisfy specified conditions),

    (b) conferring relief from taxation on a distribution of a company which satisfies specified conditions,

    (c) about the treatment of securities issued on a transfer or merger,

    (d) about the treatment of loan relationships,

    (e) about the treatment of derivative contracts,

    (f) about the treatment of intangible fixed assets, and

    (g) about capital allowances.

(3) Regulations may make provision only if the Treasury think it necessary or expedient for the purposes of complying with the United Kingdom's obligations under the Mergers Directive.

(4) In this section—

    "the Mergers Directive" means Council Directive [2009/133/EC][1].

    "SCE" means an SCE formed in accordance with Council Regulation (EC) 1435/2003 on the Statute for a European Cooperative Society, and

    "SE" means an SE formed in accordance with Council Regulation (EC) 2157/2001 on the Statute for a European Company.

(5) Regulations under this section may—

    (a) amend the Taxes Acts,

    (b) make incidental or consequential amendments of enactments other than the Taxes Acts,

    (c) make provision having retrospective effect,

    (d) make provision generally or only for specified cases or circumstances,

    (e) make different provision for different cases or circumstances,

    (f) make incidental, consequential or transitional provision.

(6) In this section "the Taxes Acts" has the meaning given by section 118(1) of TMA 1970.

Regulations—Corporation Tax (Implementation of the Mergers Directive) Regulations, SI 2007/3186.
Corporation Tax (Implementation of the Mergers Directive) Regulations, SI 2008/1579.
Amendments—[1]   In sub-s (4), in the definition of "the Mergers Directive" words substituted for "90/43/EEC" by the Corporation Tax (Implementation of the Mergers Directive) Regulations SI 2011/1431 reg 3 with effect from 1 July 2011.

112 Updating references to Standing Committees

(1) (*amends* PCTA 1968 s 1(4)(*b*))

(2) (see *Orange Tax Handbook*)

PART 8
FINAL PROVISIONS

113 Interpretation

(1) In this Act—

    "BGDA 1981" means the Betting and Gaming Duties Act 1981 (c 63),

    "CAA 2001" means the Capital Allowances Act 2001 (c 2),

    "CEMA 1979" means the Customs and Excise Management Act 1979 (c 2),

    "CRCA 2005" means the Commissioners for Revenue and Customs Act 2005 (c 11),

    ["CTA 2009" means the Corporation Tax Act 2009;][1]

    "ICTA" means the Income and Corporation Taxes Act 1988 (c 1),

    "IHTA 1984" means the Inheritance Tax Act 1984 (c 51),

    "ITA 2007" means the Income Tax Act 2007 (c 3),

    "ITEPA 2003" means the Income Tax (Earnings and Pensions) Act 2003 (c 1),

    "ITTOIA 2005" means the Income Tax (Trading and Other Income) Act 2005 (c 5),

"TCGA 1992" means the Taxation of Chargeable Gains Act 1992 (c 12),

"TMA 1970" means the Taxes Management Act 1970 (c 9),

"VATA 1994" means the Value Added Tax Act 1994 (c 23), and

"VERA 1994" means the Vehicle Excise and Registration Act 1994 (c 22).

(2) In this Act—

"FA", followed by a year, means the Finance Act of that year, and

"F(No 2)A", followed by a year, means the Finance (No 2) Act of that year.

Amendments—[1]   Definition of "CTA 2009" inserted by CTA 2009 s 1322, Sch 1 paras 722, 723. CTA 2009 applies for accounting periods ending on or after 1 April 2009 (for corporation tax purposes) and for tax years 2009–10 onwards (for income and capital gains tax purposes).

114 Repeals

Schedule 27 contains repeals.

115 Short title

This Act may be cited as the Finance Act 2007.

SCHEDULES

SCHEDULE 3

MANAGED SERVICE COMPANIES

Section 25

PART 1

AMENDMENTS OF ITEPA 2003

1   ITEPA 2003 is amended as follows.

2   (*substitutes* ITEPA 2003 s (5)(*a*))

3   (*inserts* ITEPA 2003 s 48(2)(*aa*))

4   (*inserts* ITEPA 2003 ss 61A–61J)

5   (*inserts* ITEPA 2003 s 218(1)(*e*))

6   (*inserts* ITEPA 2003 s 688A)

7   (*amends* ITEPA 2003 s 717(4))

8   (*inserts* definitions into ITEPA 2003 Sch 1 Pt 2)

PART 2

CALCULATION OF PROFITS OF MSCS: DEDUCTION FOR DEEMED EMPLOYMENT PAYMENTS

Deduction for deemed employment payments for income tax purposes

9   (*inserts* ITTOIA 2005 s 164A)

SCHEDULE 4

RESTRICTIONS ON TRADE LOSS RELIEF FOR PARTNERS

Section 26

Limit on amount of sideways relief and capital gains relief available in any tax year

1—(1) (*inserts* ITA 2007 s 103C)

(2) The amendment made by sub-paragraph (1) has effect in relation to any loss made by an individual in a trade in the tax year 2007–08 or any subsequent tax year.

(3) But, in the case of a loss made by an individual in a trade in a tax year the basis period for which begins before 2nd March 2007 (a "straddling basis period"), the amount of that loss for the purposes of section 103C of ITA 2007 is—

(*a*) the amount of sideways relief and capital gains relief which (after applying the restrictions under the other provisions of Chapter 3 of Part 4 of that Act) may be given to the individual for that loss, less

(*b*) the amount (if any) of the pre-announcement loss.

(4) "The pre-announcement loss" is determined as follows.

(5) Calculate the profits or losses of the straddling basis period, but without regard to capital allowances and qualifying film expenditure (within the meaning of section 103D of ITA 2007).

(6) If that calculation produces a loss and the individual has made a contribution of an amount as capital to the firm or LLP in question—

    (a) on or before the start of the straddling basis period, or

    (b) after the start of that period but before 2nd March 2007,

apportion the loss produced by that calculation to the part of the straddling basis period which begins with the relevant date and falls before 2nd March 2007 in proportion to the number of days in that part.

(7) Calculate so much of the loss of the straddling basis period as derives from relevant pre-announcement capital expenditure.

(8) The pre-announcement loss is the sum of—

    (a) the amount of the loss apportioned under sub-paragraph (6) (if any), and

    (b) so much of the loss of the straddling basis period (if any) as derives from relevant pre-announcement capital expenditure.

(9) In sub-paragraph (6) "the relevant date" means—

    (a) in any case where a contribution was made on or before the start of the straddling basis period, the start of that period, and

    (b) in any other case, the date on which the contribution was made or, if more than one contribution was made, the date on which the first contribution was made.

(10) For the purposes of this paragraph the amount of the loss of the straddling basis period that derives from relevant pre-announcement capital expenditure is determined on a just and reasonable basis.

(11) In this paragraph "relevant pre-announcement capital expenditure" means—

    (a) any capital allowance in respect of expenditure paid before 2nd March 2007, and

    (b) any capital allowance in respect of expenditure paid on or after that date pursuant to an unconditional obligation in a contract made before that date,

and for this purpose "an unconditional obligation" means an obligation which may not be varied or extinguished by the exercise of any right conferred on the firm or LLP in question (whether or not under the contract).

(12) For the purposes of this paragraph—

    (a) an amount of money is not to be taken as contributed as capital to a firm or LLP until the money is paid to the firm or LLP, and

    (b) a right or other asset is not to be taken as contributed as capital to a firm or LLP until it is transferred to the firm or LLP.

(13) Section 62 of ITA 2007 (partners: losses of a tax year etc) applies for the purposes of this paragraph as it applies for the purposes of Chapter 3 of Part 4 of that Act.

Disregard of contributions made for purpose of accessing sideways relief and capital gains relief

2—(1) (*inserts* ITA 2007 s 113A)

(2) The amendment made by sub-paragraph (1) has effect in relation to any amount contributed to a firm or LLP as capital on or after 2nd March 2007 (but see sub-paragraph (4)).

(3) For this purpose—

    (a) an amount of money is not to be taken as contributed as capital to a firm or LLP until the money is paid to the firm or LLP, and

    (b) a right or other asset is not to be taken as contributed as capital to a firm or LLP until it is transferred to the firm or LLP.

(4) The amendment made by sub-paragraph (1) has no effect in relation to any amount contributed by an individual on or after 2nd March 2007 if—

    (a) the amount is contributed pursuant to an obligation in a contract made before that date, and

    (b) the obligation may not be varied or extinguished by the exercise of any right conferred on the individual (whether or not under the contract).

Provision corresponding to paragraphs 1 and 2 for tax year 2006–07

3—(1) ICTA has effect, in relation to any loss made by an individual in a trade in the tax year 2006–07 the basis period for which ends on or after 2nd March 2007, as if provision corresponding to section 103C of ITA 2007 were included in Chapter 7 of Part 4 of ICTA.

(2) Sub-paragraphs (3) to (13) of paragraph 1 apply for the purposes of sub-paragraph (1) above.

(3) ICTA has effect for the tax year 2006–07 as if provision corresponding to section 113A of ITA 2007 were included in that Chapter.

(4) Sub-paragraphs (2) to (4) of paragraph 2 apply for the purposes of sub-paragraph (3) above.

(5) The provisions which are treated by this paragraph as included in Chapter 7 of Part 4 of ICTA have effect as if—

    (a) any reference in section 103C of ITA 2007 to sideways relief were to relief under section 380 or 381 of ICTA, (*b*) any reference in section 103C of ITA 2007 to capital gains relief in relation to a loss were to the treatment of the loss as an allowable loss by virtue of section 72 of FA 1991,

(*c*) any reference in section 103C or 113A of ITA 2007 to any provision of Chapter 3 of Part 4 of ITA 2007 were to the corresponding provision of Chapter 7 of Part 4 of ICTA, and

(*d*) any reference in section 113A of ITA 2007 to a contribution to a firm or an LLP were to a contribution to a trade carried on by the firm or LLP,

and references in paragraphs 1(3) to (13) and 2(2) to (4) to any of those expressions are to be read accordingly.

Consequential amendments

4 ITA 2007 is amended as follows.

5 (*amends* ITA 2007 s 32)

6 (*amends* ITA 2007 s 82(*a*))

7—(1) Section 102 (overview of Chapter 3 of Part 4) is amended as follows.
(2) (*amends* ITA 2007 s 102(1))
(3) (*amends* ITA 2007 s 102(2)).

8 (*inserts* ITA 2007 ss 103A, 103B)

9 (*inserts* ITA 2007 s 103D)

10 (*amends* ITA 2007 ss 104(5), 107(2), 110(1)(*a*), (115(1)(*d*))

11 (*amends* ITA 2007 s 105(11), 108(9), 111(12))

12 (*repeals* ITA 2007 s 106)

13 (*amends* heading to ITA 2007 s 112 and *repeals* ITA 2007 s 112(1)–(5))

14 (*substitutes* cross heading before ITA 2007 s 114)

15 (*substitutes* ITA 2007 s 115(4))

16 (*repeals* ITA 2007 s 116)

17 (*amends* ITA 2007 s 792(7), (8))

18 (*amends* ITA 2007 s 809(1), (2))

19 (*amends* ITA 2007 Sch 2 para 148(3)(*b*))

20 (*amends* ITA 2007 Sch 4 index of defined expressions)

21 The amendments made by paragraphs 5 to 20 are deemed always to have had effect.

SCHEDULE 5

AVOIDANCE INVOLVING FINANCIAL ARRANGEMENTS

Section 30

Amounts not forming part of a company's income

1—(1) ICTA is amended as follows.
(2) (*repeals* TA 1988 s 347A(1)(b) , as it had effect before ITA 2007)
(3) The amendment made by sub-paragraph (2) has effect in relation to payments made on or after 6th December 2006 but before 6th April 2007.
(4) (*repeals* TA 1988 s 347A (as amended by ITA 2007))
(5) The amendment made by sub-paragraph (4) has effect in relation to payments made on or after 6th April 2007.

2—(1) (*repeals* TA 1988 s 660C(4))
(2) The amendment made by sub-paragraph (1) has effect in relation to accounting periods ending on or after 6th March 2007.
(3) But income which arises in an accounting period beginning before that date is to be chargeable to corporation tax as a result of that amendment only if it arises on or after that date.

8—(1) Section 263E of TCGA 1992 (structured finance arrangements) is amended as follows.
(2) (*amends* TCGA 1992 s 263E(2))
(3) (*amends* TCGA 1992 s 263E(3))
(4) (*inserts* TCGA 1992 s 263E(4A))
(5) (*amends* TCGA 1992 s 263E(5))

(6) The amendments made by this paragraph have effect in relation to disposals made on or after 6th March 2007.

(7) The amendments made by this paragraph also have effect in relation to any disposal made by a person before that date if the person makes a claim to that effect under this sub-paragraph.

Options and groups of companies

10—(1) (*inserts* TCGA 1992 s 171(2)(*db*))

(2) The amendment made by sub-paragraph (1) has effect in relation to cases where the option is exercised on or after 6th March 2007 (whenever the option was granted).

Plant or machinery subject to a lease and finance leaseback

17—(1) Chapter 17 of Part 2 of CAA 2001 (plant and machinery allowances: anti-avoidance) is amended as follows.

(2) (*amends* CAA 2001 s 228A(2))

(3) (*amends* CAA 2001 s 228F(1), (8), and *repeals* CAA 2001 s 228F(4))

(4) (*amended* TA 1988 s 774E(5)(*b*)); *repealed by* CTA 2010 s 1181, Sch 3 Pt 2, TIOPA 2010 s 503, Sch 10 Pt 10.

(5) The amendments made by this paragraph have effect in relation to post-commencement rentals that fall to be taken into account in calculating for tax purposes the income or profits for any post-commencement period of account.

(6) In this paragraph—

"post-commencement period of account" means any period of account ending on or after 6th December 2006, and

"post-commencement rental" means—

(*a*) any amount receivable on or after 6th December 2006 in respect of any period beginning on or after that date, or

(*b*) the appropriate fraction of any amount receivable on or after that date in respect of any period beginning before, and ending on or after, that date,

but does not include any amount received before that date.

(7) For this purpose the "appropriate fraction", in relation to any amount received in respect of any period, means the fraction—

$$\frac{\text{PCP}}{\text{WP}}$$

where—

"PCP" means the number of days in the part of the period falling on or after 6th December 2006, and

"WP" means the number of days in the whole of the period.

(8) Sub-paragraph (9) applies if the amounts that, in accordance with section 228D of CAA 2001 as applied by section 228F of that Act, fall to be taken into account in calculating for tax purposes the income or profits for any post-commencement period of account comprise both post-commencement rentals and other amounts.

(9) For the purposes of section 228D of CAA 2001 as applied by section 228F of that Act, the amount of the gross earnings is taken to be so much of the gross earnings as, on a just and reasonable basis, relates to those other amounts. "Gross earnings" has the meaning given by section 228D(5) of CAA 2001.

SCHEDULE 7

INSURANCE BUSINESS: GROSS ROLL-UP BUSINESS ETC

Section 38

PART 1

AMENDMENTS

Taxes Management Act 1970 (c 9)

1   (*amends* TMA 1970 s 98)

Income and Corporation Taxes Act 1988 (c 1)

2   ICTA is amended as follows.

4   (*repeals* TA 1988 s 333B)

5   (*repeals* TA 1988 s 403E(3))

7   (*amends* TA 1988 s 431A(3)(*a*))

15   (*repeals* TA 1988 s 432AB(6))

18   (*repeals* TA 1988 s 432D)

20   (*amends* TA 1988 s 432F(2);)

24   (*repeals* TA 1988 s 436)

27   (*repeals* TA 1988 s 438B)

28   (*repeals* TA 1988 s 438C)

29   (*repeals* TA 1988 s 439)

30   (*repeals* TA 1988 s 439B)

34   (*repeals* TA 1988 s 441)

39   (*repeals* TA 1988 ss 458 and 458A)

41   (*repeals* TA 1988 s 461(3A))

42   (*repeals* TA 1988 s 461B(2A))

47—(1) Section 755A (treatment of chargeable profits and creditable tax apportioned to company carrying on life assurance business) is amended as follows.
(2) (*amends* TA 1988 s 755A(4))
(3) (*amends* TA 1988 s 755A(6)(*c*))
(4) (*substitutes* TA 1988 s 755A(13)(*a*), (*ba*))

55   (*repeals* TA 1988 Sch 19AA)

Taxation of Chargeable Gains Act 1992 (c 12)

60   TCGA 1992 is amended as follows.

61   (*amends* TCGA 1992 s 204(10))

62   (*repeals* TCGA 1992 s 210B(6)(*b*) and *amends* TCGA 1992 s 210B(8))

63   (*amends* TCGA 1992 s 212(2))

64   (*amends* TCGA 1992 s 213(1A))

Capital Allowances Act 2001 (c 2)

68   CAA 2001 is amended as follows.

69—(1) Section 255 (apportionment of allowances and charges) is amended as follows.
(2) (*substitutes* CAA 2001 s 255(1)–(1B))
(3) (*repeals* CAA 2001 s 255(2))
(4) (*amends* CAA 2001 s 255(3))

70—(1) Section 256 (different giving effect rules for different categories of business) is amended as follows.
(2) (*amends* CAA 2001 s 256(3))
(3) (*amends* CAA 2001 s 256(4))

71—(1) Section 545 (investment assets) is amended as follows.
(2) (*amends* CAA 2001 s 545(3))
(3) (*amends* CAA 2001 s 545(5))

Finance Act 2002 (c 23)

73   FA 2002 is amended as follows.

Income Tax (Trading and Other Income) Act 2005 (c 5)

76   ITTOIA 2005 is amended as follows.

77   (*amends* ITTOIA 2005 s 473(2))

79   (*amends* ITTOIA 2005 Sch 2 para 118(2))

PART 2
TRANSITIONAL PROVISIONS

Amendments—

This para repealed by FA 2012 s 146, Sch 16 para 247(*p*)(i) with effect in relation to accounting periods of companies beginning on or after 1 January 2013 (subject to transitional provisions in FA 2012 Sch 17). For accounting periods straddling 1 January 2013, see FA 2012 s 149.

"Section 432F(2) excesses"

84   *Where there is a subsection (2) excess (within the meaning of section 432F of ICTA) for any category of business of an insurance company in the period of account immediately preceding the commencement period it shall be taken to be, or form part of, the subsection (2) excess falling to be carried forward under subsection (3) of that section (as amended by this Schedule) and used in a post-commencement period.*

Commentary—*Simon's Taxes* **D7.5122**.

This para repealed by FA 2012 s 146, Sch 16 para 247(*p*)(i) with effect in relation to accounting periods of companies beginning on or after 1 January 2013 (subject to transitional provisions in FA 2012 Sch 17). For accounting periods straddling 1 January 2013, see FA 2012 s 149.

[[Losses transferred under section 444AZA]

85—(1) This paragraph applies where a loss   . . . [2] is treated by virtue of section 444AZA of ICTA as a loss of the transferee   . . . [2].

(2) Where any [losses so treated][2] would (assuming the transferor had continued to carry on the business transferred after the transfer) have been losses to which paragraph 81(1) would have applied, the amount of such losses to be treated as [losses of the transferee][2] in any period of account must not exceed—

$$\text{GRBP} \times \frac{\text{PBTL}}{\text{GRBTL}}$$

where—

    "GRBP" has the same meaning as in section 444AZA(2) of ICTA,

    "PBTL" is the mean of the opening and closing liabilities of the transferred pension business for the period of account, and

    "GRBTL" is the mean of the opening and closing liabilities of the transferred gross roll-up business for the period of account.][1]

Amendments—[1]   Paras 85, 86 inserted by the Insurance Business Transfer Schemes (Amendment of the Corporation Tax Acts) Order, SI 2008/381 art 30 with effect in relation to transfers of business taking place on or after 1 January 2007. This amendment does not have any effect in relation to periods of account earlier than those which are current on 19 February 2008: SI 2008/381 art 1(5).

[2]   In cross-head and sub-para (2), words substituted, and in sub-para (1) words repealed, by CTA 2009 s 1322, Sch 1 paras 699, 725(1)–(3). CTA 2009 applies for accounting periods ending on or after 1 April 2009 (for corporation tax purposes) and for tax years 2009–10 onwards (for income and capital gains tax purposes).

[[Losses transferred under section 444AZB]

86—(1) This paragraph applies where section 444AZB of ICTA has effect in relation to a transferee and the circumstances specified in sub-paragraph (2) or (3) below apply.

(2) The circumstances are that—

    (*a*) the profits of the life assurance business of the transferee for the period of account immediately preceding the first period of account beginning on or after 1st January 2007 were chargeable to tax in accordance with Case I of Schedule D by virtue of section 439A of ICTA, and

    (*b*) in that period, the transferee carried on pension business.

(3) The circumstances are that—

    (*a*) paragraph 29 of Schedule 8 applies in relation to the transferee, and

    (*b*) the transferee has an unused pension business loss within the meaning given by paragraph 81(4).

(4) The appropriate fraction of any amount treated by virtue of section 444AZB(2) of ICTA as a loss of the transferee (a "[gross roll-up business][2] loss") available to be set off against profits chargeable under section 436A of ICTA is to be treated for the purposes of paragraph 81 as an unused pension business loss.

(5) The relevant fraction of any [gross roll-up business]² loss is to be treated for the purposes of paragraph 82 as an unused non-pension business loss.

(6) In this paragraph "the appropriate fraction", in relation to a period of account, is—

$$\frac{PBTL}{TL}$$

where—

"PBTL" is the mean of the opening and closing liabilities of the transferred pension business for the period of account, and

"TL" is the mean of the opening and closing liabilities of the transferred life assurance business for the period of account.

(7) In this paragraph the "the relevant fraction", in relation to a period of account, is—

$$\frac{NPBTL}{TL}$$

where—

"NPBTL" is the mean of the opening and closing liabilities of the transferred gross roll- up business which is not pension business for the period of account, and

"TL" is the mean of the opening and closing liabilities of the transferred life assurance business for the period of account.]¹

Amendments—¹   Paras 85, 86 inserted by the Insurance Business Transfer Schemes (Amendment of the Corporation Tax Acts) Order, SI 2008/381 art 30 with effect in relation to transfers of business taking place on or after 1 January 2007. This amendment does not have any effect in relation to periods of account earlier than those which are current on 19 February 2008: SI 2008/381 art 1(5).

²   In cross-head and in sub-paras (4), (5,) words substituted by CTA 2009 s 1322, Sch 1 paras 722, 725(1), (4), (5). CTA 2009 applies for accounting periods ending on or after 1 April 2009 (for corporation tax purposes) and for tax years 2009–10 onwards (for income and capital gains tax purposes).

SCHEDULE 8
INSURANCE COMPANIES: BASIS OF TAXATION ETC

Section 39

PART 1
AMENDMENTS

Income and Corporation Taxes Act 1988 (c 1)

1   ICTA is amended as follows.

7   (*repeals* TA 1988 s 439A)

10   (*amends* TA 1988 s 755A(2), (6)(*a*))

Finance Act 1991 (c 31)

17   (*amends* FA 1991 Sch 7 para 16(1))

Taxation of Chargeable Gains Act 1992 (c 12)

18   (*repeals* TCGA 1992 s 212(7A))

Finance (No 2) Act 1992 (c 48)

19   (*repeals* F(No 2)A 1992 s 65)

Finance Act 1998 (c 36)

21   (*substitutes* FA 1998 Sch 18 para 84(1) and *amends* preceding cross-heading)

Capital Allowances Act 2001 (c 2)

22   CAA 2001 is amended as follows.

23   (*substitutes* CAA 2001 s 256(1)(*b*))

24   (*substitutes* CAA 2001 s 257(2)(*a*), (*b*))

SCHEDULE 9

INSURANCE COMPANIES: TRANSFERS ETC

Section 40

Definition of "insurance business transfer scheme"

1—*(1)* (*substituted* definition "insurance business transfer scheme" in TA 1988 s 431(2); *repealed by* FA 2012 s 146, Sch 16 para 247(*p*)(iii))
(2) In consequence of sub-paragraph (1), omit—
    (*a*) (*amends* TA 1988 s 12(7B))
    (*b*) (*repeals* TA 1988 s 444AB(11))
    (*c*) (*amends* TA 1988 s 444AC(11))
    (*d*) (*repeals* TA 1988 s 460(10B))
    (*e*) (*amends* TA 1988 Sch 9 para 12(9))
    (*f*) (*repeals* CAA 2001 s 560(5)(*b*))
    ((*g*) (*repealed* FA 2002 Sch 26 para 28(5); *repealed by* FA 2012 s 146, Sch 16 para 247(*p*)(iii))
    ((*h*) (*amended* FA 2002 Sch 29 para 89(3); *repealed by* FA 2012 s 146, Sch 16 para 247(*p*)(iii)))
(3) (inserted TA 1988 s 431(2ZG), (2ZH)); *repealed* by FA 2012 s 146, Sch 16 para 247(*p*)(iii))
(4) (amends FA 2002 s 66(4)(*a*), (5), and *repeals* FA 2002 s 66(6), (7))
(5) (amends FA 2002 Sch 22 para 10(1)(a), (4), and *repeals* FA 2002 Sch 22 para 10(5), (6))

Transfer schemes: expenses, losses etc

2—(1) Section 444A of ICTA (transfers of business: expenses, losses and section 432F(2) excesses) is amended as follows.
(2) (*amends* TA 1988 s 444A(1))
(3) (*repeals* TA 1988 s 444A(7), (8))

Repeal of FA s 82C

9   (*repeals* FA 1989 s 82C)

Transfers and demutualisations: losses where assets added to long-term insurance fund

11—(1) FA 1989 is amended as follows.
(2) Omit—
    (*a*) (*repeals* FA 1989 s 83(3)–(7) and *amends* FA 1989 s 83(8))
    (*b*) (*repeals* FA 1989 s 83AA)
    (*c*) (*repeals* FA 1989 s 83AB)
(3) (*amended* FA 1989 s 83B(3); *repealed by* FA 2012 s 146, Sch 16 para 247(*p*)(iii) with effect in accordance with FA 2012 ss 148, 149.)

Transfer schemes: old annuity contracts

13—(1) Paragraph 16 of Schedule 7 to FA 1991 (transitional relief for old general annuity contracts) is amended as follows.
(2) (*amends* FA 1991 Sch 7 para 16(7))
(3) (*inserts* FA 1991 Sch 7 para 16(8))

Transfer schemes: no gain/no loss

14—(1) TCGA 1992 is amended as follows.
(2) (*substitutes* TCGA 1992 s 211(2), (3))
(3) . . .
Amendments—Sub-para (3) repealed by FA 2008 s 8, Sch 2 para 70(*i*) with effect in relation to disposals made on or after 6 April 2008.

Commencement

17—(1) The amendments made by paragraphs 1 to 3 and 13 to 15 have effect in relation to periods of account beginning on or after 1st January 2007.
(2) The amendments made by paragraphs 4, 6 to [10(5),]¹ 11 and 12 have effect in accordance with provision made by an order made by the Treasury.
(3) But the amendments made by paragraphs 11 and 12 also have effect—
    [(*a*)]   ¹ in relation to periods of account beginning on or after 1st January 2007 where the transfer of business or demutualisation concerned took place before 21st March 2007 [and

(*b*) in relation to periods of account ending after 30 June 2008 where the transfer of business or demutualisation concerned took place on or after 21 March 2007 and before 1 July 2008.]¹

(4) The amendment made by paragraph 5 has effect in relation to transfers of business with a transfer date after 21st March 2007.

[(4A) The amendment made by paragraph 9 has effect in relation to contracts entered into in a period of account beginning on or after 1 January 2008.]¹

(5) The amendment made by paragraph 10(2) has effect in relation to transfers taking place on or after 6th December 2006.

[(6) The amendments made by paragraph 10(3) and (4) have effect in relation to assets transferred on or after 1 January 2008.]¹

Commentary—*Simon's Taxes* **D7.5221**.
Amendments—¹ In sub-para (2), words substituted , in sub-s (3) para (*a*) numbered as such and para (*b*) inserted, and sub-ss (4A), (6) inserted by FA 2008 s 43, Sch 17 para 38 with effect from 21 July 2008.

SCHEDULE 10
INSURANCE COMPANIES: MISCELLANEOUS
Section 41
"Structural" assets

2—(1) (*inserted* FA 1989 s 83XA; *repealed* by FA 2012 s 146, Sch 16 para 247(*p*)(iv) with effect in accordance with FA 2012 ss 148, 149)
(2) (*repeals* TA 1988 s 444ACA)
(3) (*amends* TA 1988 s 432E(2A) and *repeals* TA 1988 s 432E(2A)(*b*))
(4) (*inserts* TCGA 1992 s 211(2A))
(5) (*inserts* TCGA 1992 Sch 7AC para 17(4A))

Losses on disposal of authorised investment fund assets to connected manager

3 (*inserts* TCGA 1992 s 210C)

Tidying up of TCGA 1992

5—(1) TCGA 1992 is amended as follows.
(2) (*amends* TCGA 1992 s 210B(6)(*a*))
(3) (*repeals* TCGA 1992 ss 212(2A), 214, 214A)

Correction of erroneous repeal

7 The repeals made by Schedule 3 to ITA 2007 in paragraph 11 of Schedule 6 to FA 1990 are deemed never to have had effect; but Schedule 3 to ITA 2007 is deemed to have included the repeal of the words before the paragraphs in sub-paragraph (1) of that paragraph.

Non-profit companies, non-profit funds and with-profits funds

8—(1) (*inserts* definitions of "non-profit company", "non-profit fund" and "with-profits fund" in TA 1988 s 431(2))
(2) (*repeals* definitions of "non-profit company" and "non-profit fund" in TA 1988 s 432YA(5), FA 1989 ss 82D(5), 83YA(8), (11) (definition of "with-profits fund"), 83A(6), and words in s 83A(2)(*b*), (3D)(*b*))

Internal linked funds and net value

9—(1) (*inserts* definitions of "internal linked fund" and "net value" in TA 1988 s 431(2))
(2) (*repeals* definition of "internal linked fund" in TA 1988 s 432ZA(6), TA 1988 s 432A(9A), definition of "internal linked fund" in TCGA 1992 s 210B(8), and FA 1996 Sch 11 para 3A(6))

Fair value

10—(1) (*inserts* definition of "fair value" in TA 1988 s 431(2))
(2) In section 440 of ICTA (transfer of assets etc)—
    (*a*) (*amends* TA 1988 s 440(1), (2))
    (*b*) (*repeals* TA 1988 s 440(5))
(3) (*repeals* TA 1988 s 444AB(6), words in TA 1988 s 444AC(11), s 444AD(5), FA 1989 s 83(8)(*a*) (in "fair value"), and s 83YB(5))

Generalisation of definitions

14—(1) Omit the following provisions.
(2) In ICTA—

  (*a*) (words in TA 1988 s 12(7B) *repealed*)

  (*b*) (words in TA 1988 s 76(15) *repealed*)

  (*c*) (definition of "life assurance business" in TA 1988 s 587B(9) *repealed*)

  (*d*) (definition of "long-term insurance fund" in TA 1988 755A(12) *repealed*)

  (*e*) (TA 1988 s 804F *repealed*)

  (*f*) (definition of "insurance company" in TA 1988 Sch 28AA para 14(1) *repealed*)

(3) (*repeals* FA 1989 s 90A and words in FA 1989 s 85(2A) and s 89(6))

(4) (*amends* FA 1991 Sch 7 para 16(7))

(5) (*repeals* TCGA 1992 s 214BA, and Sch 7AC para 17(5))

(6) (*repeals* FA 1996 s 88(7), words in s 87A(2), Sch 9 para 20(3)(*b*), definitions in Sch 9 para 12(9), Sch 11 para 6)

(7) (*repeals* words in FA 1998 Sch 18 para 13(3))

(8) (*repeals* CAA 2001 ss 257(3), 544(5) and 560(5)(*a*), (*c*))

(9) (*repeals definitions in FA 2001 Sch 22 para 31(1)*)

(10) In FA 2002—

  (*a*) (*repeals* words in FA 2002 s 66(5))

  (*b*) (*repeals* definition in FA 2002 Sch 12 para 19(1))

  (*c*) (*repeals words in FA 2002 Sch 22 para 10(4)*)

  (*d*) (*repeals FA 2002 Sch 26 para 12(15), (16), words in para 12(1), and definitions in para 54(1)*)

  (*e*) (*repeals* FA 2002 Sch 29 para 89(3) (definition of "contracts of long-term insurance"), and para 138(1))

(11) (*repeals* definitions in FA 2003 Sch 23 para 30 and entries in FA 2003 Sch 23 para 31)

(12) (*repeals* FA 2006 s 134(4)(*c*))

Amendments—Sub-paras (9), (10), (*c*), (*d*) repealed by CTA 2009 s 1326, Sch 3 Pt 1. CTA 2009 applies for accounting periods ending on or after 1 April 2009 (for corporation tax purposes) and for tax years 2009–10 onwards (for income and capital gains tax purposes).

Minor changes

15—(1) (*amended* TA 1988 s 432ZA(5); *repealed* by FA 2012 s 146, Sch 16 para 247(*p*)(iv) with effect in accordance with FA 2012 ss 148, 149)

(2) (*amended* TA 1988 s 434A(2A); *repealed* by FA 2012 s 146, Sch 16 para 247(*p*)(iv) with effect in accordance with FA 2012 ss 148, 149)

(3) (*amended* heading to FA 1989 s 88; *repealed* by FA 2012 s 146, Sch 16 para 247(*p*)(iv) with effect in accordance with FA 2012 ss 148, 149)

(4) (*amends* FA 1991 Sch 7 para 17(4) and *repeals* sub-paras (4A), (5))

Obsolete etc provisions

16—(1) Omit the following provisions (which are obsolete or of limited value).

(2) (*amends* TMA 1970 s 98)

(3) In ICTA—

  (*a*) (*amends* TA 1988 s 76(7) Step 3)

  (*b*) (*repeals* TA 1988 s 440(2A) and (2B))

  (*c*) (*repeals* TA 1988 s 442(4))

  (*d*) (*repeals* TA 1988 s 443)

  (*e*) (*repeals* TA 1988 s 444)

  (*f*) (*repeals* TA 1988 s 587B(8))

  (*g*) (*repeals* TA 1988 s 807A(4), (5)(*b*) and words in (6)(*a*))

(4) In FA 1989—

  (*a*) (*repeals* FA 1989 s 84(2), (3), (5), (6))

  (*b*) (*repeals* words in FA 1989 s 85(3))

  (*c*) (*repeals* FA 1989 s 86(3), (3A) and words in (10))

  (*d*) (*repeals* FA 1989 s 87)

(5) In FA 1996—

  (*a*) (*repeals* FA 1996 Sch 11 para 1(1), (2))

  (*b*) (*repeals* FA 1996 Sch 11 para 4(6))

  (*c*) (*repeals* FA 1996 Sch 11 para 5)

  (*d*) (*repeals* FA 1996 Sch 15 para 1(3))

(6) (*repeals* FA 1997 Sch 12 para 18)

(7) (*repeals* FA 1998 Sch 18 para 86)

(8) (*repeals FA 1999 Sch 6 para 4*)

(9) (*repeals* FA 2001 s 87(3), (4))

(10) (repeals FA 2002 Sch 13 paras 22, 23, 25(3), and, para 27 definition of "life assurance business")

Amendments—Sub-paras (8), (10) repealed by CTA 2009 s 1326, Sch 3 Pt 1. CTA 2009 applies for accounting periods ending on or after 1 April 2009 (for corporation tax purposes) and for tax years 2009–10 onwards (for income and capital gains tax purposes).

Commencement

17—(1) The amendment made by paragraph 1 has effect on and after 10th May 2007.
(2) The amendments made by paragraphs 2, 4(2) and (4), 5, 6 and 8 to 15 have effect in relation to periods of account beginning on or after 1st January 2007.
(3) But the amendment made by paragraph 2(4) does not apply where the transfer of business concerned took place before 10th May 2007.
(4) The amendment made by paragraph 3 has effect in relation to losses accruing in a period of account beginning on or after 1st January 2007.
(5) The amendment made by paragraph 4(3) has effect in relation to periods of account beginning on or after 1st January 2005.

SCHEDULE 11
TECHNICAL PROVISIONS MADE BY GENERAL INSURERS
Section 42

Restriction on amount of technical provisions made by general insurers

1—(1) This paragraph applies if a general insurer makes any technical provisions for a period of account.
(2) The amount of the technical provisions stated in the accounts for that period is to be taken into account in the calculation for tax purposes of the profits of the general insurer's trade for that period unless an officer of Revenue and Customs considers that that amount exceeds the appropriate amount.
(3) In that case—
    (*a*) the excess is not to be taken into account in that calculation, and
    (*b*) the profits of the general insurer's trade for the next period of account are to be adjusted accordingly for tax purposes.
(4) "The appropriate amount" means such amount as is determined in accordance with regulations made by the Commissioners for Her Majesty's Revenue and Customs to be the appropriate amount to be taken into account in that calculation.
(5) Any such determination must be made by reference to the time at which the technical provisions are made.

Regulations—The General Insurers' Technical Provisions (Appropriate Amount) (Tax) Regulations, SI 2009/1926).

Enforcement

2—(1) This paragraph applies if an officer of Revenue and Customs gives a notice of enquiry under paragraph 24(1) of Schedule 18 to FA 1998 to a general insurer.
(2) The officer may by notice require the general insurer (at the general insurer's own expense) to provide the officer with a report as to whether (and, if so, the extent to which) the amount of any technical provisions stated in the accounts for any period covered by the company tax return into which the enquiry is made exceeds the appropriate amount.
(3) The report must cover such matters, and be in such form, as the officer may reasonably require for the purposes of the enquiry.
(4) The report must be made by a person who is appointed by the general insurer unless the officer requires the report to be made instead by another person.
(5) As soon as the general insurer appoints a person to make the report, the general insurer must give a notice to the officer specifying that person.
(6) A notice under sub-paragraph (2) must specify the time (which must not be less than 30 days) within which the general insurer is to comply with it.
[(7) The following provisions of Schedule 36 to FA 2008 (information and inspection powers) apply in relation to a notice under sub-paragraph (2) as they apply in relation to a taxpayer notice under that Schedule—
    (a) paragraphs 29 and 32 (right to appeal), and
    (b) Part 7 (penalties).][1]

Amendments—[1] Sub-para (7) substituted for previous sub-paras (7), (8) by Finance Act 2009 Schedule 47 (Consequential Amendments) Order, SI 2009/2035, Art 2, Schedule para 53 with effect from 13 August 2009.

Supplementary

3—(1) In paragraph 1 "general insurer" means—

    (*a*) a company within the charge to corporation tax which carries on general business,

    [(*b*) a CFC (within the meaning of Part 9A of the Taxation (International and Other Provisions) Act 2010) which carries on general business, or][2]

    (*c*) members of a Lloyd's syndicate who carry on general business.

(2) In paragraph 2 "general insurer" means—

    (*a*) a company within the charge to corporation tax which carries on general business, or

    [(*b*) a company which for the purposes of Part 9A of the Taxation (International and Other Provisions) Act 2010 has an interest in a CFC (within the meaning of that Part) which carries on general business.][2]

(3) For the purposes of sub-paragraphs (1) and (2) "general business" means business which consists of the effecting or carrying out of contracts that fall within Part 1 of Schedule 1 to the Financial Services and Markets Act 2000 (Regulated Activities) Order 2001 (SI 2001/544).

(4) In the case of members of a Lloyd's syndicate, references in paragraph 1 to any accounts for a period are to the return of the syndicate's profits or loss for that period under regulation 4 of the Lloyd's Underwriters (Tax) Regulations 2005 (SI 2005/3338).

(5) In paragraph 1 "period of account"—

    (*a*) except in the case of members of a Lloyd's syndicate, means a period of account for which an account is made up, and

    (*b*) in the case of members of a Lloyd's syndicate, means an underwriting year in which profits or losses are declared for an earlier underwriting year.

(6) In paragraphs 1 and 2 "technical provisions", except in the case of members of a Lloyd's syndicate, means any of the following—

    (*a*) provisions for claims outstanding,

    (*b*) provisions for unearned premiums, and

    (*c*) provisions for unexpired risks.

(7) In paragraphs 1 and 2 "technical provisions", in the case of members of a Lloyd's syndicate ("the syndicate"), means—

    (*a*) so much of the reinsurance to close amounts of the members, and

    (*b*) so much of the provisions made by an open Lloyd's syndicate of which any member of the syndicate is a member for claims outstanding, unearned premiums and unexpired risks,

as may be determined by or under regulations made by the Commissioners for Her Majesty's Revenue and Customs.

(8) For this purpose—

    (*a*) the reference to reinsurance to close amounts of any member of a Lloyd's syndicate is to any consideration which, in accordance with the rules or practice of Lloyd's, is given (or any amount which, in accordance with those rules or practice, is treated as consideration given) by the member in respect of the liabilities arising from the member's underwriting business in an underwriting year for the purpose of closing the accounts of the business for that year, and

    (*b*) a Lloyd's syndicate is an "open" Lloyd's syndicate at any time after the end of its closing year if, at that time, the accounts of its business for the underwriting year for which it was formed have not been closed,

and in paragraph (b) "closing year" has the same meaning as in Chapter 3 of Part 2 of FA 1993 or Chapter 5 of Part 4 of FA 1994.

(9) In this paragraph—

    "Lloyd's syndicate" means a syndicate of underwriting members of Lloyd's formed for an underwriting year, and

    "underwriting year" means the calendar year.

(10) In this paragraph references to provisions for claims outstanding, unearned premiums and unexpired risks have the same meaning as in [Schedule 3 to the Large and Medium-sized Companies and Groups (Accounts and Reports) Regulations 2008][1].

(11) The Commissioners for Her Majesty's Revenue and Customs may by regulations—

    (*a*) provide in prescribed circumstances for paragraph 1 not to apply in relation to any member of a Lloyd's syndicate, or

    (*b*) provide in prescribed circumstances for a reduction in relation to any member of a Lloyd's syndicate of the amount which (as a result of that paragraph) is not to be taken into account in the calculation mentioned in sub-paragraph (2) of that paragraph.

(12) The Treasury may by regulations amend sub-paragraphs (1) to (3) (definition of "general insurer").

(13) In the event of any changes in the rules or practice of Lloyd's, the Commissioners for Her Majesty's Revenue and Customs may by regulations make such amendments of paragraph 1 and this paragraph as appear to the Commissioners to be expedient having regard to those changes.

(14) Regulations under section 182(1)(*a*) of FA 1993 or section 229(1)(*a*) of FA 1994 (assessment and collection of tax charged in case of Lloyd's underwriters) may, in particular, include provision applying paragraph 2 with modifications in the case of members of a Lloyd's syndicate.

(15) Regulations under paragraph 1 or this paragraph may—

    (*a*) make different provision for different purposes, and

    (*b*) make supplementary, incidental, consequential and transitional provision.

Regulations—The General Insurers' Technical Provisions (Appropriate Amount) (Tax) Regulations, SI 2009/1926.

Amendments—[1]   Words in sub-para (10) substituted by the Companies Act 2006 (Consequential Amendments) (Taxes and National Insurance) Order, SI 2008/954 arts 42 with effect for periods of account beginning on or after 6 April 2008.

[2]   Sub-paras (1)(*b*), (2)(*b*) substituted, by FA 2012 s 180, Sch 20 para 23 with effect in relation to accounting periods of CFCs beginning on or after 1 January 2013. This is subject to savings in FA 2012 Sch 20 para 50(9) which provides, broadly, that the amendments in question will not take effect until an accounting period under the new CFC rules in TIOPA 2010 Part 9A begins.

Repeal of section 107 of FA 2000

4   (*repeals* FA 2000 s 107)

Commencement

5—(1) Paragraphs 1 to 3 have effect in relation to periods of account ending on or after the day on which this Act is passed.

(2) The repeal of section 107 of FA 2000 made by paragraph 4 has effect as follows.

(3) The repeal of—

    (*a*) subsections (1) to (3) of that section (technical provisions made by a general insurer proving to be excessive or insufficient),

    (*b*) subsections (5) to (8) and (10) of that section so far as relating to those subsections, and

    (*c*) subsections (9) and (12)(*a*) of that section (which relate to those subsections),

has effect in relation to any amount that would otherwise have been treated as a receipt or an expense of a trade in computing for tax purposes the profits of the trade for any period of account ending on or after the day on which this Act is passed.

(4) The repeal of—

    (*a*) subsection (4) of that section (election for any part of technical provisions not to be taken into account in a period of account),

    (*b*) subsections (5) to (8) and (10) of that section so far as relating to that subsection, and

    (*c*) subsection (12)(*b*) of that section (which relates to that subsection),

has effect so that no election may be made under that subsection in respect of technical provisions made by a general insurer for any period of account which begins on or after that day.

(5) There is a restriction in relation to any election made by a general insurer under that subsection in respect of technical provisions made by the general insurer for the final election period.

(6) The restriction is that the amount of the part of those provisions which the general insurer elects not to be taken into account in computing for tax purposes the profits of the general insurer's trade for that period must not exceed 10% of the total amount of those provisions.

(7) In sub-paragraph (5) "the final election period", in relation to any general insurer, means the general insurer's first period of account ending on or after the day on which this Act is passed.

SCHEDULE 13

SALE AND REPURCHASE OF SECURITIES

Section 47

Commentary—*Simon's Taxes* **D9.1001** .

Order—Finance Act 2007 (Schedules 13 and 14) Order 2007, SI 2007/2483 (Sch 13 has effect in relation to an arrangement that comes into force on or after 1 October 2007).

Purpose of Schedule

1—(1) The purpose of this Schedule is to secure that in the case of an arrangement—

    (*a*) which involves the sale of securities and the subsequent purchase of securities, and

    (*b*) which equates, in substance, to a transaction for the lending of money at interest from or to a company (with the securities which were sold as collateral for the loan),

the charge to corporation tax in that case [in respect of chargeable gains][1] reflects the fact that the arrangement equates, in substance, to such a transaction.

(2) But this is not to be read as preventing the rules in this Schedule about corporation tax in respect of chargeable gains from having no effect in relation to debtor quasi-repos and creditor quasi-repos.

Commentary—*Simon's Taxes* **D9.1001** .

Amendments—[1]   In sub-s (1), words inserted by CTA 2009 s 1322, Sch 1 paras 722, 726(1), (2). CTA 2009 applies for accounting periods ending on or after 1 April 2009 (for corporation tax purposes) and for tax years 2009–10 onwards (for income and capital gains tax purposes).

Ignoring sale and subsequent purchase for purposes of chargeable gains: debtor repos

6—(1) This paragraph applies if—

    (*a*) a company ("the borrower") has a debtor repo, and

    (*b*) the borrower (having sold the securities under the arrangement to the lender) is the only person with the right or obligation under the arrangement to buy those or similar securities at any subsequent time.

(2) The sale of the securities, and the subsequent purchase of those or similar securities, by the borrower under the arrangement are to be ignored for the purposes of corporation tax in respect of chargeable gains (but see sub-paragraph (5)).

(3) If at any time after the initial sale of the securities—

    (*a*) it becomes apparent that the borrower will not subsequently buy those or similar securities under the arrangement, or

    (*b*) the accounting condition ceases to be met,

the borrower is to be treated for the purposes of corporation tax in respect of chargeable gains as disposing of the securities at that time for a consideration equal to their market value at that time.

(4) The accounting condition ceases to be met if, in accordance with generally accepted accounting practice, the accounts of the borrower for any period after the one in which the advance is received do not record a financial liability in respect of the advance (except as a result of the subsequent purchase of the securities or similar securities).

(5) If sub-paragraph (3) applies because the accounting condition ceases to be met, any subsequent purchase of those or similar securities by the borrower under the arrangement is not to be ignored for the purposes of corporation tax in respect of chargeable gains as a result of this paragraph.

(6) For the purposes of this paragraph references to the borrower include a partnership of which the borrower is a member.

Commentary—*Simon's Taxes* **D9.1006, D9.1030**.

Modification—Sale and Repurchase of Securities (Modification of Schedule 13 to the Finance Act 2007) Regulations, SI 2007/2485 reg 2 (in certain non-standard repo cases, where securities are substituted for other securities, references in this para to "securities or similar securities" to include a reference to the substituted securities).

Sale and Repurchase of Securities (Modification of Schedule 13 to the Finance Act 2007) Regulations, SI 2007/2485 reg 4(1) (modification of sub-paras (3)–(5) where Sch 13 para 2, as modified by SI 2007/2485 reg 3, applies).

Ignoring purchase and subsequent sale for purposes of chargeable gains: creditor repos

11—(1) This paragraph applies if—

    (*a*) a company ("the lender") has a creditor repo, and

    (*b*) the lender (having bought the securities under the arrangement from the borrower) is the only person with the right or obligation under the arrangement to sell those or similar securities at any subsequent time.

(2) The purchase of the securities, and the subsequent sale of those or similar securities, by the lender under the arrangement are to be ignored for the purposes of corporation tax in respect of chargeable gains (but see sub-paragraph (5)).

(3) If at any time after the initial purchase of the securities—

    (*a*) it becomes apparent that the lender will not subsequently sell those or similar securities under the arrangement, or

    (*b*) the accounting condition ceases to be met,

the lender is to be treated for the purposes of corporation tax in respect of chargeable gains as acquiring the securities at that time for a consideration equal to their market value at that time.

(4) The accounting condition ceases to be met if, in accordance with generally accepted accounting practice, the accounts of the lender for any period after the one in which the advance is made do not record a financial asset in respect of the advance (except as a result of the subsequent sale of the securities or similar securities).

(5) If sub-paragraph (3) applies because the accounting condition ceases to be met, any subsequent sale of those or similar securities by the lender under the arrangement is not to be ignored for the purposes of corporation tax in respect of chargeable gains as a result of this paragraph.

(6) For the purposes of this paragraph references to the lender include a partnership of which the lender is a member.

Commentary—*Simon's Taxes* **D9.1008**.

Modification—Sale and Repurchase of Securities (Modification of Schedule 13 to the Finance Act 2007) Regulations, SI 2007/2485 reg 2 (in certain non-standard repo cases, where securities are substituted for other securities, references in this para to "securities or similar securities" to include a reference to the substituted securities).

Sale and Repurchase of Securities (Modification of Schedule 13 to the Finance Act 2007) Regulations, SI 2007/2485 reg 4(1) (modification of sub-paras (3)–(5) where Sch 13 para 7, as modified by SI 2007/2485 reg 3, applies).

Interpretation etc

14—(1) In this Schedule—

"arrangement" includes any agreement or understanding (whether or not legally enforceable),

"creditor quasi-repo" has the meaning given by [section 544 of CTA 2009][1],

"creditor repo" has the meaning given by [section 543 of CTA 2009][1],

"debtor quasi-repo" has the meaning given by [section 549 of CTA 2009][1],

"debtor repo" has the meaning given by [section 548 of CTA 2009][1],

"discharge", in relation to a liability, means the discharge of the liability in whole or in part (and "discharged" is to be read accordingly),

"the loan relationship rules" means the provisions of [Part 5 of CTA 2009][1],

"market value" has the same meaning as in TCGA 1992,

"overseas dividend", in relation to overseas securities, means any interest, dividend or other annual payment payable in respect of the securities,

"overseas securities" means shares, stock or other securities issued by—

    (*a*) a government or public or local authority of a territory outside the United Kingdom, or

    (*b*) any other body of persons not resident in the United Kingdom,

"securities" (except in the definition of "overseas securities") means shares, stock or other securities issued by—

    (*a*) the government of the United Kingdom,

    (*b*) any public or local authority in the United Kingdom, or

    (*c*) any company or other body resident in the United Kingdom,

  or overseas securities, and

"tax advantage" has the meaning given by section 840ZA of ICTA.

(2) For the purposes of this Schedule references to a person's receiving any asset include the person's obtaining directly or indirectly the value of any asset or otherwise deriving directly or indirectly any benefit from it.

(3) For the purposes of this Schedule—

    (*a*) in any case where a person buys securities (or has a right or obligation to buy securities) but the securities are (or are to be) held for another person's benefit, that other person is treated as buying (or having the right or obligation to buy) the securities, and

    (*b*) in any case where a person sells securities but the proceeds of the sale are held for another person's benefit, that other person is treated as selling the securities.

(4) For the purposes of this Schedule securities are similar if they entitle their holders to—

    (*a*) the same rights against the same persons as to capital, interest and dividends, and

    (*b*) the same remedies for the enforcement of those rights,

in spite of any difference in the total nominal amounts of the respective securities or in the form in which they are held or the manner in which they can be transferred.

(5) For the purposes of this Schedule it does not matter whether or not provision of any arrangement conferring a right or imposing an obligation on any person to buy any securities is subject to any conditions.

(6) For the purposes of this Schedule an arrangement is in force from the time when the securities are initially sold until the earlier of—

    (*a*) the time when the relevant repurchase takes place, and

    (*b*) the time when it becomes apparent that that repurchase will not take place.

(7) For this purpose "the relevant repurchase" means—

    (*a*) in the case of a debtor repo, the subsequent buying of the securities or similar securities,

    (*b*) in the case of a debtor quasi-repo, the subsequent buying of the securities or other securities by the borrower, the receipt of the asset from the borrower or (as the case may be) the discharge of the liability to the borrower,

    (*c*) in the case of a creditor repo, the subsequent sale of the securities or similar securities, and

    (*d*) in the case of a creditor quasi-repo, the subsequent sale of the securities or other securities by the lender, the receipt of the asset from the lender or (as the case may be) the discharge of the liability to the lender.

(8) Any reference in this Schedule to an amount being recognised in determining a company's profit or loss for a period is to an amount being recognised for accounting purposes—

    (*a*) in the company's profit and loss account or income statement,

    (*b*) in the company's statement of recognised gains and losses or statement of changes in equity, or

    (*c*) in any other statement of items brought into account in calculating the company's profits and losses for that period.

(9) In determining for the purposes of this Schedule whether an amount is recorded as a financial asset or liability in respect of the advance it is to be assumed that the period of account in which the advance is received or made ended immediately after the receipt or making of the advance.

(10) For the purposes of paragraphs 6(4) and 11(4)—

    (*a*) any period of account in which the advance is received or made is treated as if it ended immediately after the receipt or making of the advance, and

    (*b*) a new period of account is treated as beginning immediately after the end of that period.

(11) If any person does not draw up accounts in accordance with generally accepted accounting practice, this Schedule applies as if the accounts had been drawn up by the person in accordance with that practice.

Commentary—*Simon's Taxes* **D9.1001** , **D9.1006**.

Amendments—[1]　　The following amendments made in sub-para (1) by CTA 2009 s 1322, Sch 1 paras 722, 726(1), (4)—

    –　　in definition of "creditor quasi-repo" words substituted for words "paragraph 8";

    –　　in definition of "creditor repo" words substituted for words "paragraph 7";

    –　　in definition of "debtor quasi-repo" words substituted for words "paragraph 3";

    –　　in definition of "debtor repo" words substituted for words "paragraph 2";

    –　　in definition of "loan relationship rules" words substituted for words "Chapter 2 of Part 4 of FA 1996".

CTA 2009 applies for accounting periods ending on or after 1 April 2009 (for corporation tax purposes) and for tax years 2009–10 onwards (for income and capital gains tax purposes).

Power to modify Schedule

15—(1) The Treasury may by regulations provide for all or any of the provisions of this Schedule to apply with modifications in relation to either or both of the following cases—

    (*a*) non-standard repo cases (see sub-paragraphs (2) to (5)), and

    (*b*) cases involving redemption arrangements (see sub-paragraph (6)).

(2) A case is a non-standard repo case if—

    (*a*) a company has a repo,

    (*b*) there has been a sale of the securities under the arrangement or arrangements by reference to which the company has the repo, and

    (*c*) any of conditions A to C are met in relation to the repo.

(3) Condition A is that those securities, or similar or other securities, are not subsequently bought under the arrangement or arrangements.

(4) Condition B is that provision is made by or under an arrangement for different or additional securities to be treated as, or as included with, securities which, for the purposes of the subsequent purchase, are to represent those initially sold.

(5) Condition C is that provision is made by or under an arrangement for securities to be treated as not so included.

(6) A case involves redemption arrangements if—

    (*a*) arrangements, corresponding to those made in cases where a company has a repo, are made in relation to securities that are to be redeemed in the period after their sale, and

    (*b*) the arrangements are such that a person (instead of having the right or obligation to buy those securities, or similar or other securities, at any subsequent time) has a right or obligation in respect of the benefits that will result from the redemption.

(7) The regulations may—

    (*a*) make different provision for different cases, and

    (*b*) contain incidental, supplemental, consequential and transitional provision and savings.

(8) Regulations about paragraph 6 or 11 may, in particular, include modifications of TCGA 1992 in relation to cases where, as a result of the regulations, any acquisition or disposal is excluded from those which are to be ignored for the purposes of corporation tax in respect of chargeable gains.

(9) In this paragraph—

    "modifications" include exceptions and omissions, and

    "repo" means—

        (*a*) a debtor repo or debtor quasi-repo, or

        (*b*) a creditor repo or creditor quasi-repo (including anything treated, as a result of [section 547 of CTA 2009][1], as a creditor repo for the purposes of [section 546 of that Act][1]).

Regulations—Sale and Repurchase of Securities (Modification of Schedule 13 to the Finance Act 2007) Regulations 2007, SI 2007/2485.

Amendments—[1]　　In sub-para (9)(*b*), words substituted by CTA 2009 s 1322, Sch 1 paras 722, 726(1), (5). CTA 2009 applies for accounting periods ending on or after 1 April 2009 (for corporation tax purposes) and for tax years 2009–10 onwards (for income and capital gains tax purposes).

SCHEDULE 14

SALE AND REPURCHASE OF SECURITIES: MINOR
AND CONSEQUENTIAL AMENDMENTS

Section 47

Order—Finance Act 2007 (Schedules 13 and 14) Order 2007, SI 2007/2483 (the amendments made by Sch 14, except those made by paras 10 and 18, have effect in relation to an arrangement that comes into force on or after 1 October 2007).

Income and Corporation Taxes Act 1988 (c 1)

1   ICTA is amended as follows.

4   (*repeals* TA 1988 ss 730A, 730B)

5   (*repeals* TA 1988 s 730BB)

7   (*repeals* TA 1988 ss 737A–737C)

8   (*repeals* TA 1988 s 737E)

Taxation of Chargeable Gains Act 1992 (c 12)

11   TCGA 1992 is amended as follows.

12—(1) Section 263A (agreements for sale and repurchase of securities) is amended as follows.
(2) (*amends* TCGA 1992 s 263A(1))
(3) (*inserts* TCGA 1992 s 263A(1A), (1B))
(4) (*repeals* TCGA 1992 s 263A(2))
(5) (*substitutes* TCGA 1992 s 263A(5), (6))
(6) (*amends* heading to TCGA 1992 s 263A)

13—(1) (*substitutes* TCGA 1992 Sch 7AC para 12)

Finance Act 1994 (c 9)

19   (*substitutes* FA 1994 s 229(1)(*ca*)(ii))

Finance Act 2006 (c 25)

20   (*repeals* FA 2006 s 139(5))

Income Tax Act 2007 (c 3)

21   ITA 2007 is amended as follows.

24   (*amends* ITA 2007 s 886(2))

SCHEDULE 15

CONTROLLED FOREIGN COMPANIES

Section 48

Imputation of chargeable profits and creditable tax of controlled foreign companies

1—(1) Section 747 of ICTA (imputation of chargeable profits and creditable tax of controlled foreign companies) is amended as follows.
(2) (*inserts* TA 1988 s 747(3A))
(3) (*inserts* TA 1988 s 747(5A))

Residence

2   (*inserts* TA 1988 s 749(10))

Elections and designations under section 749: supplementary provisions

3   (*inserts* TA 1988 s 749A(9))

Territories with a lower level of taxation

4   (*inserts* TA 1988 s 750(3)(*ab*))

Reduction in chargeable profits for certain activities of EEA business establishments

5   (*inserts* TA 1988 ss 751A, 751B)

Interpretation

6 (*inserts* TA 1988 s 756(1A), (1B))

Exempt activities test

7—(1) Part 2 of Schedule 25 to ICTA (supplementary provision in relation to cases where apportionment under section 747(3) does not apply: exempt activities) is amended as follows.
(2) (*inserts* TA 1988 Sch 25 para 5(1A))
(3) (*amends* TA 1988 Sch 25 para 8(1))
(4) (*inserts* TA 1988 Sch 25 para 8(5), (6))

Abolition of public quotation exemption

8—(1) (*repeals* TA 1988 s (1)(c))
(2) (*repeals* TA 1988 Sch 25 Part 3)

Discovery assessments

9 (*amends* FA 1998 Sch 18 44(3))

Commencement

10—(1) The amendments made by this Schedule have effect in relation to accounting periods of controlled foreign companies beginning on or after 6th December 2006.
(2) In the case of an accounting period (a "straddling period") of a controlled foreign company—
(*a*) beginning before 6th December 2006, and
(*b*) ending on or after that date,
the amendments made by this Schedule have effect as if, for the purposes of Chapter 4 of Part 17 of ICTA, so much of the straddling period as falls before that date, and so much of the straddling period as falls on or after that date, were separate accounting periods.
(3) The company's chargeable profits for the straddling period, and its creditable tax (if any) for that period, are to be apportioned to the two separate accounting periods on a just and reasonable basis.
(4) Each of the following expressions—
"accounting period",
"chargeable profits",
"controlled foreign company", and
"creditable tax",
has the same meaning in this paragraph as in Chapter 4 of Part 17 of ICTA.

SCHEDULE 16
VENTURE CAPITAL SCHEMES ETC

Section 51

PART 1
LIMIT ON NUMBER OF EMPLOYEES OF COMPANY IN WHICH INVESTMENT IS MADE

Corporate venturing scheme

1—(1) Part 3 of Schedule 15 to FA 2000 (requirements as to issuing company) is amended as follows.
(2) (*inserts* FA 2000 Sch 15 para 15(*fa*))
(3) (*inserts* FA 2000 Sch 15 para 22A)
(4) The amendments made by this paragraph do not have effect in relation to shares issued before the day on which this Act is passed.

Enterprise investment scheme

2—(1) Chapter 4 of Part 5 of ITA 2007 (the issuing company) is amended as follows.
(2) (*inserts* ITA 2007 s 180(*ea*))
(3) (*inserts* ITA 2007 s 186A)
(4) The amendments made by this paragraph do not have effect in relation to—
(*a*) shares issued before the day on which this Act is passed, or
(*b*) shares issued to the managers of an approved fund which closed before that day.
(5) For the purposes of sub-paragraph (4)(*b*)—
(*a*) "the managers of an approved fund" has the same meaning as in section 251 of ITA 2007, and

(*b*) the reference to shares issued to the managers of an approved fund is to shares issued to those managers as nominee for an individual who has invested in the fund.

Venture capital trusts

3—(1) Part 6 of ITA 2007 is amended as follows.

(2) (*inserts* ITA 2007 s 286(3)(*ja*))

(3) (*inserts* ITA 2007 s 297A)

(4) (*amends* ITA 2007 s 327(1), (4)(*b*))

(5) This paragraph is deemed to have come into force on 6th April 2007.

(6) The amendments made by this paragraph do not have effect in relation to—

(*a*) a relevant holding issued before that date, or

(*b*) a relevant holding acquired by a company ("the investing company") [before 6 April 2018][1] by means of the investment of protected money.

(7) For the purposes of sub-paragraph (6)(*b*), "protected money" is—

(*a*) money raised by the issue before 6th April 2007 of shares in or securities of the investing company, or

(*b*) money derived from the investment of such money.

Amendments—[1] In sub-para (6)(*b*), words inserted by FA 2018 s 17, Sch 5 para 9 with effect from 6 April 2018 (by virtue of SI 2018/931 reg 4(e)).

PART 2

LIMIT ON AMOUNT RAISED ANNUALLY BY COMPANY THROUGH RISK CAPITAL SCHEMES

Corporate venturing scheme

4—(1) Schedule 15 to FA 2000 is amended as follows.

(2) (*inserts* FA 2000 Sch 15 para 34(*aa*))

(3) (*inserts* FA 2000 Sch 15 para 35A)

(4) (*inserts* FA 2000 Sch 15 para (1)(*a*)(ia))

Enterprise investment scheme

5—(1) Part 5 of ITA 2007 is amended as follows.

(2) (*inserts* ITA 2007 s 172(*aa*))

(3) (*inserts* ITA 2007 s 173A)

(4) (*amends* ITA 2007 s 239(1))

(5) The amendments made by this paragraph do not have effect in relation to shares issued to the managers of an approved fund which closed before the day on which this Act is passed.

(6) Paragraph 2(5) (meaning of "the managers of an approved fund" etc) applies for the purposes of sub-paragraph (5).

Venture capital trusts

6—(1) Chapter 4 of Part 6 of ITA 2007 (qualifying holdings) is amended as follows.

(2) (*inserts* ITA 2007 s 286(3)(*ea*))

(3) (*inserts* ITA 2007 s 292A)

(4) This paragraph is deemed to have come into force on 6th April 2007.

(5) The amendments made by this paragraph do not have effect in relation to an investment made by a VCT of protected money.

(6) "Protected money" means—

(*a*) money raised by the issue on or before 5th April 2007 of shares in or securities of the VCT, and

(*b*) money derived from the investment of such money.

Enterprise investment scheme: reinvestment

7—(1) Schedule 5B to TCGA 1992 is amended as follows.

(2) (*inserts* TCGA 1992 Sch 5B para 1(2)(*da*), (6), (7))

(3) (*amends* TCGA 1992 Sch 5B para 1A(1))

Transitional provision

8—(1) This paragraph applies for the purposes of—

(*a*) paragraph 35A of Schedule 15 to FA 2000,

(*b*) section 173A of ITA 2007 (including that section as applied by paragraph 1(6) of Schedule 5B to TCGA 1992), and

    (c) section 292A of ITA 2007.

(2) References to investments made by a VCT do not include—

    (a) investments made on or before 5th April 2007,

    (b) investments of protected money (as defined by paragraph 6(6)).

(3) References to shares in respect of which compliance statements are provided do not include—

    (a) shares issued before the day on which this Act is passed, or

    (b) shares issued to the managers of an approved fund which closed before that day.

(4) Paragraph 2(5) (meaning of "the managers of an approved fund" etc) applies for the purposes of sub-paragraph (3)(b) above.

PART 3

EXCLUDED ACTIVITIES: RECEIPT OF ROYALTIES AND LICENCE FEES

Corporate venturing scheme

9—(1) Paragraph 29 of Schedule 15 to FA 2000 is amended as follows.

(2) (*substitutes* FA 2000 Sch 15 para 29(3)(a), (b))

(3) (*inserts* FA 2000 Sch 15 para 29(7))

10   (*amends* FA 2000 Sch 15 para 86(2))

Enterprise investment scheme

11—(1) In section 297 of ICTA (qualifying trades)—

    (a) (*substitutes* TA 1988 s 297(5)(a), (b))

    (b) (*repeals* TA 1988 s 297(5A)(b), (c))

    (c) (*inserts* TA 1988 s 297(5D))

(2) (*amends* TA 1988 s 304A(3), (4))

(3) (*inserted* TA 1988 s 576B(9)); *repealed by* CTA 2010 s 1181, Sch 3 Pt 1.

(4) (*inserted* TA 1988 s 576K(4)); *repealed by* CTA 2010 s 1181, Sch 3 Pt 1.

(5) (*inserts* ITA 2007 s 137(9))

(6) (*inserts* ITA 2007 s 146(3))

(7) (*substitutes* ITA 2007 s 195(4)(a), (b), *repeals* definition in ITA 2007 s 195(6), *inserts* ITA 2007 s 195(7))

(8) (*amends* ITA 2007 s 249(2), (4))

Venture capital trusts

12—(1) Section 306 of ITA 2007 (qualifying holdings) is amended as follows.

(2) (*substitutes* ITA 2007 s 306(4)(a), (b))

(3) (*repeals* definition in ITA 2007 s 306(6))

(4) (*inserts* ITA 2007 s 306(7))

Commencement

13   This Part of this Schedule is deemed to have come into force on 6th April 2007.

Transitional provision

14—(1) This paragraph applies if—

    (a) shares in or securities of a company ("the company") were issued before 6th April 2007,

    (b) immediately before that date—

        (i) the right to exploit an intangible asset ("the asset") was vested in the company or a subsidiary of it (in either case, whether alone or jointly with others), and

        (ii) the asset was a relevant intangible asset,

    (c) at any time on or after that date, an activity carried on by the company or a subsidiary of it would be an excluded activity by reason only of the receipt of royalties or licence fees attributable to the exploitation of the asset, and

    (d) the activity would not be an excluded activity if the amendments made by this Part of this Schedule had not been made.

(2) The activity is to be treated, in relation to those shares or securities, as not being an excluded activity at that time.

(3) In sub-paragraphs (1) and (2), references to an excluded activity are to be read—

    (a) for the purposes of Chapter 3 of Part 7 of ICTA (including any provision of that Chapter as applied by any other provision), as references to—

        (i) an activity within section 293(3B)(a) of ICTA, or

        (ii) an activity within subsection (2) of section 297 of ICTA which causes a trade to fail to comply with that section,

(b) for the purposes of Schedule 15 to FA 2000, as references to an excluded activity other than the receiving of royalties or licence fees within paragraph 29 of that Schedule in circumstances where the requirements of sub-paragraph (2) of that paragraph are met.

PART 4
MEANING OF "QUALIFYING 90% SUBSIDIARY"

Corporate venturing scheme

15—(1) Schedule 15 to FA 2000 is amended as follows.

(2) In paragraph 23 (trading activities requirement), omit sub-paragraphs (10) and (11).

(3) (*inserts FA 2000 Sch 15 para 23A*)

(4) (*amends FA 2000 Sch 15 para 103*)

Enterprise investment scheme etc

16—(1) In Chapter 3 of Part 7 of ICTA—

    (a) (*substitutes TA 1988 s 289(9)*)

    (b) (*amends TA 1988 s 312(1)*)

(2) (*inserts ITA 2007 s 190(1A)–(1C)*)

Venture capital trusts

17   (*inserts ITA 2007 s 301(1A)–(1C)*)

Commencement

18   This Part of this Schedule is deemed to have come into force on 6th April 2007.

PART 5
OTHER AMENDMENTS

EIS: approved investment funds

19—(1) (*amends ITA 2007 s 251(1)(c)*)

(2) The amendment made by this paragraph has effect in relation to approved funds which closed or close on or after 7 October 2006.

VCTs: disposal of holding

20—(1) Chapter 3 of Part 6 of ITA 2007 (VCT approvals) is amended as follows.

(2) (*inserts ITA 2007 s 274(3)(e)*)

(3) (*inserts ITA 2007 s 280A*)

(4) This paragraph is deemed to have come into force on 6th April 2007.

(5) The amendments made by this paragraph have effect in relation to disposals made on or after that date.

VCTs: power to make regulations as to breaches of conditions

21—(1) In section 284 of ITA 2007 (power to make regulations as to procedure), in the existing provision (which becomes subsection (1))—

    (a) (*inserts ITA 2007 s 284(1)(aa)*)

    (b) (*substitutes ITA 2007 s 284(1)(c)(i), (ii)*)

    (c) (*amends ITA 2007 s 284(1)(d)*)

(2) (*inserts ITA 2007 s 284(2), (3)*)

SCHEDULE 17
REAL ESTATE INVESTMENT TRUSTS

Section 52

18   (*inserts ITA 2007 s 531(2A), and amends ITA 2007 s 531(3)*)

SCHEDULE 18
PENSIONS SCHEMES: ABOLITION OF RELIEF FOR LIFE ASSURANCE
PREMIUM CONTRIBUTIONS ETC

Section 68

Introduction

1   Part 4 of FA 2004 (pension schemes etc) is amended as follows.

Life assurance premium contributions not to be relievable pension contributions

2   (*inserts* FA 2004 s 188(3)(*aa*))

Life assurance premium contributions

3   (*inserts* FA 2004 s 195A)

Commencement: schemes other than occupational pension schemes

4—(1) In relation to contributions under any pension scheme that is not an occupational pension scheme, the amendments made by this Schedule have effect in relation to contributions paid on or after 6th April 2007.

(2) But they do not have effect in relation to such contributions paid at any time if the contributions are treated as paid in respect of premiums under a policy of insurance which at that time is a protected policy (see paragraph 5).

5—(1) This paragraph specifies when a policy of insurance is a protected policy in a case where the rights under it are held for the purposes of a pension scheme that is not an occupational pension scheme.

(2) A policy of insurance within sub-paragraph (3) or (4) is a protected policy but only until a relevant event occurs (see sub-paragraphs (5) and (6)).

(3) A policy of insurance is within this sub-paragraph if—

    (*a*) it is issued in respect of insurances made before 6th December 2006,

    (*b*) the pension scheme became a registered pension scheme before that date, and

    (*c*) rights under the policy became held for the purposes of the pension scheme before that date.

(4) A policy of insurance is within this sub-paragraph if—

    (*a*) it is issued in respect of insurances made before 1st August 2007,

    (*b*) the pension scheme became a registered pension scheme before that date,

    (*c*) rights under the policy became held for the purposes of the pension scheme before that date,

    (*d*) the policy was issued in pursuance of a proposal made in writing (by whatever means) and received by or on behalf of the insurer before the appropriate date,

    (*e*) the amount of the benefits payable under the policy (at the latest of the time when the insurances were made, the pension scheme was registered or rights under the policy became held for the purposes of the pension scheme) is no more than the amount applied for in the proposal,

    (*f*) the period for which benefits are so payable (at the latest of those times) is no longer than the period specified in the proposal, and

    (*g*) the policy is not a protected policy by virtue of sub-paragraph (3).

(5) In sub-paragraph (4)(*d*) "the appropriate date" means—

    (*a*) 13th April 2007, in any case where, on the day of the making of the insurances in respect of which the policy of insurance was issued, the rights of the individual under the pension scheme included an actual or prospective entitlement to a pension, and

    (*b*) 14th December 2006, in any other case.

(6) For the purposes of sub-paragraph (2) a "relevant event" occurs if, after the relevant time, the terms of the policy are varied so as to—

    (*a*) increase the benefits payable under the policy, or

    (*b*) extend the period during which benefits are so payable.

(7) But where, on the day of the variation, the rights of the individual under the pension scheme included an actual or prospective entitlement to a pension, a relevant event does not occur by virtue of the variation if it was made in pursuance of a proposal made in writing (by whatever means) and received by or on behalf of the insurer before 13th April 2007.

(8) "The relevant time"—

    (*a*) in the case of a policy of insurance within sub-paragraph (3) which is issued in respect of insurances made before 6th April 2006, is 20th March 2007,

    (*b*) in the case of any other policy of insurance within sub-paragraph (3), is 5th December 2006, and

    (*c*) in the case of a policy of insurance within sub-paragraph (4), is the time when it became a protected policy.

Commencement: occupational pension schemes

6—(1) In relation to contributions under any occupational pension scheme, the amendments made by this Schedule have effect in relation to contributions paid on or after 1st August 2007.

(2) But they do not have effect in relation to such contributions paid at any time if the contributions are treated as paid in respect of premiums under a policy of insurance which at that time is a protected policy (see paragraph 7).

7—(1) This paragraph specifies when a policy of insurance is a protected policy in a case where the rights under it are held for the purposes of an occupational pension scheme.

(2) A policy of insurance within sub-paragraph (3) or (4) is a protected policy but only until a relevant event occurs (see sub-paragraphs (5) to (7)).

(3) A policy of insurance is within this sub-paragraph if—

    (*a*) it is issued in respect of insurances made before 21st March 2007,

    (*b*) the pension scheme became a registered pension scheme before that date, and

    (*c*) rights under the policy became held for the purposes of the pension scheme before that date.

(4) A policy of insurance is within this sub-paragraph if—

    (*a*) it is issued in respect of insurances made before 1st August 2007,

    (*b*) the pension scheme became a registered pension scheme before that date,

    (*c*) rights under the policy became held for the purposes of the pension scheme before that date,

    (*d*) the policy was issued in pursuance of a proposal made in writing (by whatever means) and received by or on behalf of the insurer before 29th March 2007,

    (*e*) the amount of the benefits payable under the policy (at the latest of the time when the insurances were made, the pension scheme was registered or rights under the policy became held for the purposes of the pension scheme) is no more than the amount applied for in the proposal,

    (*f*) the period for which benefits are so payable (at the latest of those times) is no longer than the period specified in the proposal, and

    (*g*) the policy is not a protected policy by virtue of sub-paragraph (3).

(5) For the purposes of sub-paragraph (2) a "relevant event" occurs if, after the relevant time, the terms of the policy are varied so as to—

    (*a*) increase the benefits payable under the policy, or

    (*b*) extend the period during which benefits are so payable.

(6) "The relevant time"—

    (*a*) in the case of a policy of insurance within sub-paragraph (3), is 20th March 2007, and

    (*b*) in the case of a policy of insurance within sub-paragraph (4), is the time when it became a protected policy.

(7) A variation of the terms of a policy made in order to comply with the [Equality Act 2010, so far as relating to age,][1] Employment Equality (Age) Regulations 2006 (SI 2006/1031) or Employment Equality (Age) Regulations (Northern Ireland) 2006 (S.R. 2006/261) (or any regulations amending or replacing [those Regulations][1]) is to be ignored for the purposes of sub-paragraph (5).

Amendments—[1]   In sub-para (7) words substituted in both places by the Equality Act 2010, s 211(1), Sch 26 para 95(a) with effect from 1 October 2010 by virtue of SI 2010/2317, art 2(1), (15)(b), (e)(xi), subject to savings: see SI 2010/2279 art 15.

Power to amend commencement provisions

8—(1) The Commissioners for Her Majesty's Revenue and Customs may by regulations amend paragraphs 4 to 7.

(2) Regulations under sub-paragraph (1) having the effect of limiting the contributions which are life assurance premium contributions may be made so as to have effect in relation to times before they are made.

SCHEDULE 19

ALTERNATIVELY SECURED PENSIONS AND TRANSFER LUMP SUM DEATH BENEFIT ETC

Section 69

Introduction

1   Part 4 of FA 2004 (pension schemes etc) is amended as follows.

Alternatively secured pension: guaranteed pension and maximum

2—(1) In section 165(1) (pension rules) is amended as follows.

(2) (*amends* FA 2004 s 165(1) pension rule 2)

(3) (*amended* FA 2004 s 165(1) pension rule 7; *repealed* by FA 2011 s 65, Sch 16 para 84(*c*)(i))

3   (*repeals* FA 2004 Sch 28 para 12(3), (4))

Abolition of transfer lump sum death benefit

5　(*repeals* FA 2004 s 168(1)(*g*))

6　(*repeals* FA 2004 s 172B(5)(*a*))

7　(*repeals* FA 2004 s 188(5)(*b*))

8　(*amends* FA 2004 s 280(2))

9　(*repeals* FA 2004 Sch 29 para 19) benefit).

10　(*repeals* FA 2004 Sch 36 para 17A(1)(*c*), and amends para 17A(2))

Increase in rights on death

12—(1) Section 172B (increase in rights of connected person on death) is amended as follows.
(2) (*amended* FA 2004 s 172B(2)(*b*); *repealed by* FA 2011 s 65, Sch 16 para 84(*c*)(i))
(3) (*amends* FA 2004 s 172B(4))
(4) (*amends* FA 2004 s 172B(7)(*a*))
(5) (*inserted* FA 2004 s 172B(8A); *repealed by* FA 2011 s 65, Sch 16 para 84(*c*)(i))

Charity lump sum death benefit

16—(1) Paragraph 18 of Schedule 29 (charity lump sum death benefit) is amended as follows.
(2) (*amended* FA 2004 Sch 29 para 18(1)(*c*); *repealed by* FA 2011 s 65, Sch 16 para 84(*c*)(i))
(3) (*amended* FA 2004 Sch 29 para 18(1)(*d*); *repealed by* FA 2011 s 65, Sch 16 para 84(*c*)(i))
(4) (*amended* FA 2004 Sch 29 para 18(2)(*d*); *repealed by* FA 2011 s 65, Sch 16 para 84(*c*)(i))
(5) (*amends* FA 2004 Sch 29 para 18(2)(*e*))
(6) (*amended* FA 2004 Sch 29 para 18(4); *repealed by* FA 2011 s 65, Sch 16 para 84(*c*)(i))

Discharge of liability to scheme chargeable payment

17　(*amends* FA 2004 s 268(6))

Non-UK schemes

18—(1) Schedule 34 (non-UK schemes application of certain charges) is amended as follows.
(2) (*amends* FA 2004 Sch 34 para 1(6))
(3) (*amends* FA 2004 Sch 34 para 4(3))
(4) (*inserted* FA 2004 Sch 34 para 7ZA; *repealed by* FA 2011 s 65, Sch 16 para 84(*c*)(i))

Inheritance tax

19　IHTA 1984 is amended as follows.

27　In Schedule 2 (provisions applying on reduction of tax), omit paragraph 6A.

Consequential amendment

28—(1) Section 636A of ITEPA 2003 (exemption for certain lump sums under registered pension schemes) is amended as follows.
(2) (*repeals* ITEPA 2003 s 636A(1)(*f*))
(3) (*amends* ITEPA 2003 s 636A(7))

Commencement

29—(1) The amendments made by paragraphs 2(2) and 3 have effect in relation to deaths of members of registered pension schemes occurring on or after 6th April 2007.
(2) . . . [1]
(3) The amendments made by paragraphs 5 to 10, 18(2) and (3) and 28 have effect in relation to lump sum death benefits paid in respect of members of schemes whose deaths occur on or after 6th April 2007.
(4), (5) . . . [1]
(6) The amendments made by paragraph 16(3) and (5) have effect in relation to charity lump sum death benefits paid on or after 6th April 2007.
(7) The amendment made by paragraph 17 is deemed to have come into force on 6th April 2007.
(8) The amendments made by paragraphs 19 to 27 have effect in relation to deaths, cases where scheme administrators become aware of deaths and cessations of dependency occurring on or after 6th April 2007.

Amendments—[1]　Sub-paras (2), (4), (5) repealed by FA 2011 s 65, Sch 16 para 84(*c*)(i) with effect for the tax year 2011–12 and subsequent tax years, subject to transitional provisions in FA 2011 Sch 16 Pt 3.

SCHEDULE 20
PENSION SCHEMES ETC: MISCELLANEOUS
Section 70
Introduction

1   Part 4 of FA 2004 (pension schemes etc) is amended as follows.

Persons by whom registered pension schemes may be established

2—(1) Section 154 (persons by whom registered pension scheme may be established) is amended as follows.
(2) (*substitutes* FA 2004 s 154(1))
(3) (*inserts* FA 2004 s 154(2A))
(4) (*repeals* FA 2004 s 154(3))
(5) (*amends* FA 2004 s 154(4))

3   (*repeals* FA 2004 s 155)

4   (*amends* FA 2004 s 273(5)(*a*), (7))

Unauthorised payments reduced by amount of scheme sanction charge

5   (*inserts* FA 2004 s 160(4A), (4B))

Surrenders

6—(1) Section 172A (surrender) is amended as follows.
(2) (*inserts* FA 2004 s 172A(5)(*da*), (*db*))
(3) (*amends* FA 2004 s 172A(10))
(4) (*inserts* FA 2004 s 172A(10A))

Scheme pensions where ill-health condition met

7—(1) Schedule 28 (pension rules) is amended as follows.
(2) (*substitutes* FA 2004 Sch 28 para 2(4))
(3) (*amends* FA 2004 Sch 28 para 2A(2))

Unsecured and dependants' unsecured pensions: reference periods

8—(1) Schedule 28 (pension rules) is amended as follows.
(2) (*substitutes* FA 2004 Sch 28 para 10(1)–(1C))
(3) (*substitutes* FA 2004 Sch 28 para 24(1)–(1C))

Pension commencement lump sums

9   (*amends* FA 2004 s 166(2)(*a*))

10   (*amends* FA 2004 s 219(7))

11—(1) Schedule 29 (authorised lump sums) is amended as follows.
(2) In paragraph 1(1) (conditions to be met if lump sum is to be pension commencement lump sum)—
    (*a*) (*substitutes* FA 2004 Sch 29 para 1(1)(*a*)(*aa*))
    (*b*) (*amends* FA 2004 Sch 29 para 1(1)(*c*))
    (*c*) (*repeals* FA 2004 Sch 29 para 1(1)(*e*))
(3) (*amended* FA 2004 Sch 29 para 1(6); *repealed by* FA 2011 s 65, Sch 16 para 84(*c*)(ii))
(4) (*inserts* FA 2004 Sch 29 para 2(5A))

Winding-up lump sums

12—(1) Paragraph 10 of Schedule 29 (winding-up lump sums) is amended as follows.
(2) (*amends* FA 2004 Sch 29 para 10(1)(*c*))
(3) In sub-paragraph (3)—
    (*a*) (*amends* FA 2004 Sch 29 para 10(3))
    (*b*) (*repeals* FA 2004 Sch 29 para 10(3)(*a*))

Taxable property held by investment-regulated pension schemes: indirect holdings in REITs

14—(1) Schedule 29A (taxable property held by investment-regulated pension schemes) is amended as follows.

(2) (*amends* FA 2004 Sch 29A para 20(1)(*b*))
(3) In paragraph 22 (REITs)—
    (*a*) (*amends* FA 2004 Sch 29A para 22(1))
    (*b*) (*repeals* FA 2004 Sch 29A para 22(2))
(4) (*amends* FA 2004 Sch 29A para 24(1))
(5) (*amends* FA 2004 Sch 29A para 25(2))

Transitional provision: primary protection

15   (*inserts* FA 2004 Sch 36 para 11D(2A)–(2C))

Transitional provision: enhanced protection

16   Schedule 36 (transitional provision) is amended as follows.

17—(1) Paragraph 12 (when enhanced protection ceases) is amended as follows.
(2) (*amends* FA 2004 Sch 36 para 12(2)(*c*))
(3) (*inserts* FA 2004 Sch 36 para 12(2A)–(2C))
(4) (*amends* FA 2004 Sch 36 para 12(7))
(5) (*amends* FA 2004 Sch 36 para 12(8)(*a*))
(6) (*inserts* FA 2004 Sch 36 para 12(8)(*c*), (*d*))
(7) (*inserts* FA 2004 Sch 36 para 12(8A), (8B))
(8) In sub-paragraph (9)—
    (*a*) (*amends* FA 2004 Sch 36 para 12(9)(*a*))
    (*b*) (*amends* FA 2004 Sch 36 para 12(9)(*b*))
    (*c*) (*inserts* FA 2004 Sch 36 para 12(9)(*c*))
(9) (*inserts* FA 2004 Sch 36 para 12(10))

18   (*inserts* FA 2004 Sch 36 para 14(3A)–(3D))

19—(1) Paragraph 15 (relevant benefit accrual) is amended as follows.
(2) (*amends* FA 2004 Sch 36 para 15(2))
(3) (*amends* FA 2004 Sch 36 para 15(7))

Inheritance tax: lump sum death benefits

20   (*inserts* IHTA 1984 s 58(2A))

Benefits under employer-financed retirement benefits schemes

21   (*inserts* ITEPA 2003 s 393B(4A))

Consequential amendments

22—(1) (*amends* FA 2004 s 167(2))
(2) (*amends* FA 2004 s 280(2))

23—(1) (*amends* PSA 1993 s 1(1)(*b*))
(2) In section 1(1) of the Pension Schemes (Northern Ireland) Act 1993 (c 49) (categories of pension schemes), in paragraph (*b*) of the definition of "personal pension scheme", omit "any of the paragraphs of".

Commencement

24—(1) The amendments made by paragraphs 2 to 4 and 23 are deemed to have come into force on 6th April 2007.
(2) The amendment made by paragraph 5 has effect in relation to payments made on or after 6th April 2007.
(3) The amendments made by paragraphs 6, 7(2), 9 to 11, 15 to 19 and 22 are deemed always to have had effect.
(4) The amendment made by paragraph 7(3) has effect in relation to reductions occurring on or after 6th April 2007.
(5) The amendments made by paragraph 8 have effect in relation to notifications given on or after 6th December 2006.
(6) The amendments made by paragraph 12 have effect in relation to lump sums paid on or after 6th April 2006.
(7) The amendments made by paragraph 13 have effect in relation to deaths occurring on or after 6th April 2006.
(8) The amendments made by paragraph 14 are deemed to have come into force on 1st January 2007.

(9) The amendment made by paragraph 20 has effect in relation to lump sum death benefits paid on or after 6th April 2006.

SCHEDULE 22

AMENDMENTS AND REPEALS CONSEQUENTIAL ON EXTENSION OF HMRC POWERS

Section 84

Order—Finance Act 2007 (Sections 82 to 84 and Schedule 23) (Commencement) Order, SI 2007/3166 art 3(*a*) (FA 2007 s 84(4) comes into force on 1 December 2007).

PART 1
AMENDMENTS

1   (*amends* TMA 1970 s 20D(1))

2   (*amends* CJPA 2001 s 67)

PART 2
REPEALS

3   The provisions listed below are omitted.

4   (*repeals* TMA 1970 ss 20C, 20CC, and *amends* TMA 1970 s 118)

5   (*repeals* CEMA 1979 s 118C(3)(*c*) (gaming duty) and *amends* CEMA 1979 s 118C(4)(*b*) and (5))

6   (*repeals* BGDA 1981 Sch 1 para 16, Sch 3 para 17, Sch 4 para 17)

7   (*repeals* FA 1989 s 148(4))

8   (*repeals* VATA 1994 s 72(9), Sch 11 para 10(3)–(6))

9   (*repeals* FA 1994 Sch 7 para 4(2)–(7))

10   (*repeals* FA 1996 Sch 5 paras 5, 6)

11   (*repeals* FA 2000 Sch 6 paras 97, 130)

12   (*repeals* FA 2001 Sch 6 para 6, Sch 7 para 7)

13—(1) (*repeals* CJPA 2001 ss 57(1)(*c*), 63(2)(*e*), 65(3))
(2) (*repeals* CJPA 2001 Sch 1 paras 13, 28, 29, 57, 58, 61, 72)

14   (*repeals* TCA 2002 s 36(2) and (3))

15   (*repeals* PCA 2002 s 323(3)(*e*), (*f*))

16   (*repeals* FA 2003 Sch 13 Pt 7)

17   (*repeals* CRCA 2005 ss 13(3)(*b*), (*c*), 14(2)(*b*) and (*c*))

SCHEDULE 23

EXTENSION OF HMRC POWERS: SCOTLAND

Section 85

Orders—Finance Act 2007 (Sections 82 to 84 and Schedule 23) (Commencement) Order 2007, SI 2007/3166 (this Schedule comes into force on 1 December 2007).

Criminal Justice and Police Act 2001 (c 16)

11   The Criminal Justice and Police Act 2001 is amended as follows.

12   (*inserts* CJPA 2001 s 63(2)(*ga*))

13   (*amends provisions outside the scope of this publication*)

14—(1) The amendments made by this Schedule come into force in accordance with provision made by the Treasury by order.
(2) The power to make an order under this paragraph is exercisable by statutory instrument.

SCHEDULE 24

PENALTIES FOR ERRORS

Section 97

HMRC Manuals—Compliance Handbook Manual, CH81000–84974 (HMRC Compliance Handbook Manual chapter on penalties for inaccuracies).

PART 1

LIABILITY FOR PENALTY

Error in taxpayer's document

1—(1) A penalty is payable by a person (P) where—

(*a*) P gives HMRC a document of a kind listed in the Table below, and

(*b*) Conditions 1 and 2 are satisfied.

(2) Condition 1 is that the document contains an inaccuracy which amounts to, or leads to—

(*a*) an understatement of [a][1] liability to tax,

(*b*) a false or inflated statement of a loss . . . .[1], or

(*c*) a false or inflated claim to repayment of tax.

(3) Condition 2 is that the inaccuracy was [careless (within the meaning of paragraph 3) or deliberate on P's part][1].

(4) Where a document contains more than one inaccuracy, a penalty is payable for each inaccuracy.

Tax	Document
Income tax or capital gains tax	Return under section 8 of TMA 1970 (personal return).
Income tax or capital gains tax	Return under section 8A of TMA 1970 (trustee's return).
Income tax or capital gains tax	Return, statement or declaration in connection with a claim for an allowance, deduction or relief.
Income tax or capital gains tax	Accounts in connection with ascertaining liability to tax.
Income tax or capital gains tax	Partnership return.
Income tax or capital gains tax	Statement or declaration in connection with a partnership return.
Income tax or capital gains tax	Accounts in connection with a partnership return.
[Apprenticeship levy	Return under regulations under section 105 of FA 2016.][7]
[Capital gains tax	Return under [Schedule 2 to FA 2019][9].][6]
[Income tax	Return under section 254 of FA 2004.][1]
Income tax	Return for the purposes of PAYE regulations.
Construction industry deductions	Return for the purposes of regulations under section 70(1)(a) of FA 2004 in connection with deductions on account of tax under the Construction Industry Scheme.
Corporation tax	Company tax return under paragraph 3 of Schedule 18 to FA 1998.
Corporation tax	Return, statement or declaration in connection with a claim for an allowance, deduction or relief.
Corporation tax	Accounts in connection with ascertaining liability to tax.
[Digital services tax	DST return under paragraph 2 of Schedule 8 to FA 2020.][10]
VAT	VAT return under regulations made under paragraph 2 of Schedule 11 to VATA 1994.
VAT	Return, statement or declaration in connection with a claim.
[VAT	Return under a special scheme.][5]
[Insurance premium tax	Return under regulations under section 54 of FA 1994.
Insurance premium tax	Return, statement or declaration in connection with a claim.
Inheritance tax	Account under section 216 or 217 of IHTA 1984.
Inheritance tax	Information or document under regulations under section 256 of IHTA 1984.
Inheritance tax	Statement or declaration in connection with a deduction, exemption or relief.
Stamp duty land tax	Return under section 76 of FA 2003.
Stamp duty reserve tax	Return under regulations under section 98 of FA 1986.
[Annual tax on enveloped dwellings	Annual tax on enveloped dwellings return.
Annual tax on enveloped dwellings	Return of adjusted chargeable amount.][4]

Tax	Document
Petroleum revenue tax	Return under paragraph 2 of Schedule 2 to the Oil Taxation Act 1975.
[Petroleum revenue tax	Statement or declaration in connection with a claim under paragraph 13A of Schedule 2 to the Oil Taxation Act 1975.][2]
Petroleum revenue tax	Statement or declaration in connection with a claim under Schedule 5, 6, 7 or 8 to the Oil Taxation Act 1975.
Petroleum revenue tax	Statement under section 1(1)(a) of the Petroleum Revenue Tax Act 1980.
[Soft drinks industry levy	Return under regulations under section 52 of FA 2017][8]
Aggregates levy	Return under regulations under section 25 of FA 2001.
Climate change levy	Return under regulations under paragraph 41 of Schedule 6 to FA 2000.
Landfill tax	Return under regulations under section 49 of FA 1996.
Air passenger duty	Return under section 38 of FA 1994.
Alcoholic liquor duties	Return under regulations under section 13, 49, 56 or 62 of the Alcoholic Liquor Duties Act 1979.
Alcoholic liquor duties	Statement or declaration in connection with a claim for repayment of duty under section 4(4) of FA 1995.
Tobacco products duty	Return under regulations under section 7 of the Tobacco Products Duties Act 1979.
Hydrocarbon oil duties	Return under regulations under section 21 of the Hydrocarbon Oil Duties Act 1979.
Excise duties	Return under regulations under section 93 of CEMA 1979.
Excise duties	Return under regulations under section 100G or 100H of CEMA 1979.
Excise duties	Statement or declaration in connection with a claim.
General betting duty	Return under regulations under paragraph 2 of Schedule 1 to BGDA 1981.
Pool betting duty	Return under regulations under paragraph 2A of Schedule 1 to BGDA 1981.
Bingo duty	Return under regulations under paragraph 9 of Schedule 3 to BGDA 1981.
Lottery duty	Return under regulations under section 28(2) of FA 1993.
Gaming duty	Return under directions under paragraph 10 of Schedule 1 to FA 1997.
Remote gaming duty	Return under regulations under section 26K of BGDA 1981.][1]
[Machine games duty	Return under regulations under paragraph 18 of Schedule 24 to FA 2012.][3]
[Any of the taxes mentioned above][1]	Any document which is likely to be relied upon by HMRC to determine, without further inquiry, a question about—
	(a) P's liability to tax,
	(b) payments by P by way of or in connection with tax,
	(c) any other payment by P (including penalties), or
	(d) repayments, or any other kind of payment or credit, to P.

[(4A) In this paragraph "return under a special scheme" means any of the following, so far as relating to supplies of services treated as made in the United Kingdom—

    (a) a special accounting return under paragraph 11 of Schedule 3B;

    (b) a value added tax return submitted under any provision of the law of a member State other than the United Kingdom which implements Article 364 of the VAT Directive (as substituted by Article 5(11) of the Amending Directive);

    (c) a value added tax return submitted under any provision of the law of a member State other than the United Kingdom which implements Article 369f of the VAT Directive (as inserted by Article 5(15) of the Amending Directive).

(4B) A value added tax return mentioned in paragraph (*b*) or (*c*) of subparagraph (4A) is regarded for the purposes of sub-paragraph (1) as given to HMRC when it is submitted to the authority to whom it is required to be submitted.

(4C) In sub-paragraph (4A)—

"the VAT Directive" means Directive 2006/112/EC;

"the Amending Directive" means Council Directive 2008/8/EC.][5]

(5) In relation to a return under paragraph 2 of Schedule 2 to the Oil Taxation Act 1975 [or a statement or declaration under paragraph 13A of that Schedule][2], references in this Schedule to P include any person who, after the giving of the return for a taxable field (within the meaning of that Act), becomes the responsible person for the field (within the meaning of that Act).][1]

HMRC Manuals—Compliance Handbook Manual, CH81011–81013 (penalties for inaccuracies: commencement date for penalties).

CH81060 (penalties for inaccuracies: which documents do penalties for inaccuracies apply to).

CH81070 (conditions for penalty for inaccuracy).

Modifications—FA 2007 Sch 24 has effect as if, in the Table in this para, the list of taxes included bank payroll tax and the list of documents included a bank payroll tax return (FA 2010 s 22, Sch 1 para 37(1)).

Amendments—[1]   In sub-para (2), word substituted and words repealed, in sub-para (3), words substituted, in the table, entries inserted, in the last entry in column 1 words substituted, and sub-para (5) inserted, by FA 2008 s 122, Sch 40 paras 1, 2 with effect from 1 April 2009 (by virtue of SI 2009/571 art 2). In their application in relation to penalties payable under paras 1, 1A of this Schedule, the entries inserted in the table (by FA 2008 Sch 40 para 2(4), (5)) shall have effect in relation to—

    (a)   relevant documents—

           (i)   which relate to tax periods commencing on or after 1 April 2009, and

           (ii)   for which the filing date is on or after 1 April 2010;

    (b)   relevant documents relating to all claims for repayments of relevant tax made on or after 1 April 2010 which are not related to a tax period;

    (c)   relevant documents produced under regulations under IHTA 1984 s 256 where the date of death is on or after 1 April 2009; and

    (d)   in any other case, relevant documents given where a person's liability to pay relevant tax arises on or after 1 April 2010 (SI 2009/571 arts 3, 4).

In their application in relation to assessments falling within para 2 of this Schedule, the entries inserted in the table (by FA 2008 Sch 40 para 2(4), (5)) shall have effect in relation to tax periods commencing on or after 1 April 2009, where the filing date for the relevant document is on or after 1 April 2010 (SI 2009/571 art 5).

[2]   In table, entry inserted, and in sub-para (5) words inserted, by F(No 3)A 2010 s 28, Sch 12 Pt 2 para 12 with effect in relation to claims made on or after 1 April 2011.

[3]   In table, entry inserted by FA 2012 s 191, Sch 24 para 29 with effect in relation to the playing of machine games on or after 1 February 2013

[4]   In table, entries inserted by FA 2013 s 164, Sch 34 para 6 with effect from 17 July 2013.

[5]   In para 1, third entry for VAT inserted, and sub-paras (4A)–(4C) inserted, by FA 2014 s 103, Sch 22 para 19 with effect in relation to supplies made on or after 1 January 2015.

[6]   In table, entry inserted by FA 2015 s 37, Sch 7 para 56(1), (2) with effect in relation to disposals made on or after 6 April 2015.

[7]   In table, entry inserted by FA 2016 s 113(1), (2) with effect from 6 April 2017 (by virtue of SI 2017/355).

[8]   In table, entry relating to soft drinks industry inserted by FA 2017 s 56, Sch 11 para 3 with effect from 6 April 2018 (by virtue of SI 2018/467).

[9]   In table, in entry relating to capital gains tax, words substituted for words "section 12ZB of TMA 1970 (NRCGT return)" by FA 2019 s 14, Sch 2 para 27(1), (2) with effect in relation to disposals made on or after 6 April 2019.

[10]   In table, entry relating to digital services tax inserted by FA 2020 s 70, Sch 10 para 3 with effect from 22 July 2020.

Prospective amendments—In the table, the third entry relating to VAT to be repealed, and sub-paras (4A)–(4C) to be repealed, by the Taxation (Cross-border Trade) Act 2018 s 43, Sch 8 para 111 with effect from a date to be appointed.

[Error in taxpayer's document attributable to another person

1A—(1) A penalty is payable by a person (T) where—

    (*a*)   another person (P) gives HMRC a document of a kind listed in the Table in paragraph 1,

    (*b*)   the document contains a relevant inaccuracy, and

    (*c*)   the inaccuracy was attributable to T deliberately supplying false information to P (whether directly or indirectly), or to T deliberately withholding information from P, with the intention of the document containing the inaccuracy.

(2) A "relevant inaccuracy" is an inaccuracy which amounts to, or leads to—

    (*a*)   an understatement of a liability to tax,

    (*b*)   a false or inflated statement of a loss, or

    (*c*)   a false or inflated claim to repayment of tax.

(3) A penalty is payable under this paragraph in respect of an inaccuracy whether or not P is liable to a penalty under paragraph 1 in respect of the same inaccuracy.][1]

HMRC Manuals—Compliance Handbook Manual, CH81011–81013 (penalties for inaccuracies: commencement date for penalties).

CH84545 (other penalty issues: agent acting – inaccuracy attributable to another person).

CH81075 (penalties for inaccuracies: inaccuracy due to another person).

CH81165–81166 (inaccuracy attributable to another person).

CH81167–81168 (intentions of another person, with examples).

CH81110 (penalties for inaccuracies: the four types of inaccuracy).
Amendment—[1]   Paragraph 1A inserted by FA 2008 s 122, Sch 40 paras 1, 3 with effect from 1 April 2009 (by virtue of SI 2009/571 art 2).

Under-assessment by HMRC

2—(1) A penalty is payable by a person (P) where—
    (a) an assessment issued to P by HMRC understates P's liability to [a relevant tax][1], and
    (b) P has failed to take reasonable steps to notify HMRC, within the period of 30 days beginning with the date of the assessment, that it is an under-assessment.
(2) In deciding what steps (if any) were reasonable HMRC must consider—
    (a) whether P knew, or should have known, about the under-assessment, and
    (b) what steps would have been reasonable to take to notify HMRC.
[(3) In sub-paragraph (1) "relevant tax" means any tax mentioned in the Table in paragraph 1.][1]
[(4) In this paragraph (and in Part 2 of this Schedule so far as relating to this paragraph)—
    (a) "assessment" includes determination, and
    (b) accordingly, references to an under-assessment include an under-determination.][2]

HMRC Manuals—Compliance Handbook Manual, CH81011–81013 (penalties for inaccuracies: commencement date for penalties).
CH81090 (penalties for inaccuracies: under assessment by HMRC).
CH81170 (under assessment by HMRC).
Amendments—[1]   In sub-para (1), words substituted, and sub-para (3) substituted, by FA 2008 s 122, Sch 40 paras 1, 4 with effect from 1 April 2009 (by virtue of SI 2009/571 art 2).
[2]   Sub-para (4) inserted by FA 2009 s 109, Sch 57 para 2 with effect from 21 July 2009.

Degrees of culpability

3—(1) [For the purposes of a penalty under paragraph 1, inaccuracy in][1] a document given by P to HMRC is—
    (a) "careless" if the inaccuracy is due to failure by P to take reasonable care,
    (b) "deliberate but not concealed" if the inaccuracy is deliberate [on P's part][1] but P does not make arrangements to conceal it, and
    (c) "deliberate and concealed" if the inaccuracy is deliberate [on P's part][1] and P makes arrangements to conceal it (for example, by submitting false evidence in support of an inaccurate figure).
(2) An inaccuracy in a document given by P to HMRC, which was neither careless nor deliberate [on P's part][1] when the document was given, is to be treated as careless if P—
    (a) discovered the inaccuracy at some later time, and
    (b) did not take reasonable steps to inform HMRC.
[(3) Paragraph 47 of Schedule 19 to FA 2016 (special measures for persistently unco-operative large businesses) provides for certain inaccuracies to be treated, for the purposes of this Schedule, as being due to a failure by P to take reasonable care.][2]

HMRC Manuals—Compliance Handbook Manual, CH81080 (penalties for inaccuracies: inaccuracy discovered after document sent to HMRC).
CH81120–81140 (what is reasonable care, with examples at CH81131).
CH81141–81142 (correction of errors for indirect taxes).
CH81145 (examples of careless inaccuracy).
CH81150–81151 (deliberate but not concealed inaccuracy, with examples).
CH81160–81161 (deliberate and concealed inaccuracy, with examples).
CH81110 (penalties for inaccuracies: the four types of inaccuracy).
Amendments—[1]   In sub-para (1), words substituted, and in sub-paras (1), (2), words inserted, by FA 2008 s 122, Sch 40 paras 1, 5 with effect from 1 April 2009 (by virtue of SI 2009/571 art 2).
[2]   Sub-para (3) inserted by FA 2016 s 161, Sch 19 para 48 with effect in relation to financial years beginning on or after 15 September 2016.

[*Errors related to avoidance arrangements*

3A   (1) This paragraph applies where a document of a kind listed in the Table in paragraph 1 is given to HMRC by a person ("P") and the document contains an inaccuracy which—
    (a) falls within paragraph 1(2), and
    (b) arises because the document is submitted on the basis that particular avoidance arrangements (within the meaning of paragraph 3B) had an effect which in fact they did not have.
(2) It is to be presumed that the inaccuracy was careless, within the meaning of paragraph 3, unless—
    (a) the inaccuracy was deliberate on P's part, or
    (b) P satisfies HMRC or (on an appeal notified to the tribunal) the tribunal that P took reasonable care to avoid inaccuracy.

(3) In considering whether P took reasonable care to avoid inaccuracy, HMRC and (on an appeal notified to the tribunal) the tribunal must take no account of any evidence of any reliance by P on advice where the advice is disqualified.

(4) Advice is "disqualified" if any of the following applies—

    (*a*) the advice was given to P by an interested person;

    (*b*) the advice was given to P as a result of arrangements made between an interested person and the person who gave the advice;

    (*c*) the person who gave the advice did not have appropriate expertise for giving the advice;

    (*d*) the advice took no account of P's individual circumstances;

    (*e*) the advice was addressed to, or given to, a person other than P;

but this is subject to sub-paragraphs (5) and (7).

(5) Where (but for this sub-paragraph) advice would be disqualified under any of paragraphs (*a*) to (*c*) of sub-paragraph (4), the advice is not disqualified under that paragraph if at the relevant time P—

    (*a*) has taken reasonable steps to find out whether the advice falls within that paragraph, and

    (*b*) reasonably believes that it does not.

(6) In sub-paragraph (4) "an interested person" means—

    (*a*) a person, other than P, who participated in the avoidance arrangements or any transaction forming part of them, or

    (*b*) a person who for any consideration (whether or not in money) facilitated P's entering into the avoidance arrangements.

(7) Where (but for this sub-paragraph) advice would be disqualified under paragraph (*a*) of sub-paragraph (4) because it was given by a person within sub-paragraph (6)(*b*), the advice is not disqualified under that paragraph if—

    (*a*) the person giving the advice had appropriate expertise for giving it,

    (*b*) the advice took account of P's individual circumstances, and

    (*c*) at the time when the question whether the advice is disqualified arises—

        (i) Condition E in paragraph 3B(5) is met in relation to the avoidance arrangements, but

        (ii) none of Conditions A to D in paragraph 3B(5) is or has at any time been met in relation to them.

(8) If the document mentioned in sub-paragraph (1) is given to HMRC by P as a personal representative of a deceased person ("D")—

    (*a*) sub-paragraph (4) is to be read as if—

        (i) the references in paragraphs (*a*) and (*b*) to P were to P or D;

        (ii) the reference in paragraph (*d*) to P were to D, and

        (iii) the reference in paragraph (*e*) to a person other than P were to a person who is neither P nor D,

    (*b*) sub-paragraph (6) is to be read as if—

        (i) the reference in paragraph (*a*) to P were a reference to the person to whom the advice was given, and

        (ii) the reference in paragraph (*b*) to P were to D (or, where P also participated in the avoidance arrangements, P or D), and

    (*c*) sub-paragraph (7) is to be read as if the reference in paragraph (*b*) to P were to D.

(9) In this paragraph—

    "arrangements" includes any agreement, understanding, scheme, transaction or series of transactions (whether or not legally enforceable);

    "the relevant time" means the time when the document mentioned in sub-paragraph (1) is given to HMRC;

    "the tribunal" has the same meaning as in paragraph 17 (see paragraph 17(5A)).][1]

Commentary—*Simon's Taxes* A4.512.
Amendments—[1]   Paragraphs 3A, 3B inserted by F(No 2)A 2017 s 64(1), (2) with effect in relation to any document of a kind listed in the Table in FA 2007 Sch 24 para 1 which is given to HMRC on or after 16 November 2017 and which relates to a tax period beginning on or after 6 April 2017 and ending on or after 16 November 2017. "Tax period", and the reference to giving a document to HMRC have the same meaning as in FA 2007 Sch 24 para 28 (F(No 2)A 2017 s 64(6)).

[**3B** (1) In paragraph 3A "avoidance arrangements" means, subject to sub-paragraph (3), arrangements which fall within sub-paragraph (2).

(2) Arrangements fall within this sub-paragraph if, having regard to all the circumstances, it would be reasonable to conclude that the obtaining of a tax advantage was the main purpose, or one of the main purposes, of the arrangements.

(3) Arrangements are not avoidance arrangements for the purposes of paragraph 3A if (although they fall within sub-paragraph (2))—

    (*a*) they are arrangements which accord with established practice, and (*b*) HMRC had, at the time the arrangements were entered into, indicated its acceptance of that practice.

(4) If, at any time, any of Conditions A to E is met in relation to particular arrangements—

    (*a*) for the purposes of this Schedule the arrangements are to be taken to fall within (and always to have fallen within) sub-paragraph (2), and

    (*b*) in relation to the arrangements, sub-paragraph (3) (and the reference to it in sub-paragraph (1)) are to be treated as omitted.

This does not prevent arrangements from falling within sub-paragraph (2) other than by reason of one or more of Conditions A to E being met.

(5) Conditions A to E are as follows—

    (*a*) Condition A is that the arrangements are DOTAS arrangements within the meaning given by section 219(5) and (6) of FA 2014;

    (*b*) Condition B is that the arrangements are disclosable VAT arrangements or disclosable indirect tax arrangements for the purposes of Schedule 18 to FA 2016 (see paragraphs 8A to 9A of that Schedule);

    (*c*) Condition C is that both of the following apply—

        (i) P has been given a notice under a provision mentioned in sub-paragraph (6) stating that a tax advantage arising from the arrangements is to be counteracted, and

        (ii) that tax advantage has been counteracted under section 209 of FA 2013;

    (*d*) Condition D is that a follower notice under section 204 of FA 2014 has been given to P by reference to the arrangements (and not withdrawn) and—

        (i) the necessary corrective action for the purposes of section 208 of FA 2014 has been taken in respect of the denied advantage, or

        (ii) the denied advantage has been counteracted otherwise than as mentioned in sub-paragraph (i);

    (*e*) Condition E is that a tax advantage asserted by reference to the arrangements has been counteracted (by an assessment, an amendment of a return or claim, or otherwise) on the basis that an avoidance-related rule applies in relation to P's affairs.

(6) The provisions referred to in sub-paragraph (5)(*c*)(i) are—

    (*a*) paragraph 12 of Schedule 43 to FA 2013 (general anti-abuse rule: notice of final decision);

    (*b*) paragraph 8 or 9 of Schedule 43A to that Act (pooled or bound arrangements: notice of final decision);

    (*c*) paragraph 8 of Schedule 43B to that Act (generic referrals: notice of final decision).

(7) In sub-paragraph (5)(*d*) the reference to giving a follower notice to P includes giving a partnership follower notice in respect of a partnership return in relation to which P is a relevant partner; and for the purposes of this sub-paragraph—

    (*a*) "relevant partner" has the meaning given by paragraph 2(5) of Schedule 31 to FA 2014;

    (*b*) a partnership follower notice is given "in respect of" the partnership return mentioned in paragraph 2(2)(*a*) or (*b*) of that Schedule.

(8) For the purposes of sub-paragraph (5)(*d*) it does not matter whether the denied advantage has been dealt with—

    (*a*) wholly as mentioned in one or other of sub-paragraphs (i) and (ii) of sub-paragraph (5)(*d*), or

    (*b*) partly as mentioned in one of those sub-paragraphs and partly as mentioned in the other;

and "the denied advantage" has the same meaning as in Chapter 2 of Part 4 of FA 2014 (see section 208(3) of and paragraph 4(3) of Schedule 31 to that Act).

(9) For the purposes of sub-paragraph (5)(*e*) a tax advantage has been "asserted by reference to" the arrangements if a return, claim or appeal has been made by P on the basis that the tax advantage results from the arrangements.

(10) In this paragraph—

    "arrangements" has the same meaning as in paragraph 3A;

    "avoidance-related rule" has the same meaning as in Part 4 of Schedule 18 to FA 2016 (see paragraph 25 of that Schedule);

    a "tax advantage" includes—

        (*a*) relief or increased relief from tax,

        (*b*) repayment or increased repayment of tax,

        (*c*) avoidance or reduction of a charge to tax or an assessment to tax,

        (*d*) avoidance of a possible assessment to tax,

        (*e*) deferral of a payment of tax or advancement of a repayment of tax,

        (*f*) avoidance of an obligation to deduct or account for tax, and

        (*g*) in relation to VAT, anything which is a tax advantage for the purposes of Schedule 18 to FA 2016 under paragraph 5 of that Schedule.][1]

Commentary—*Simon's Taxes* **A4.512.**

Amendments—[1]   Paragraphs 3A, 3B inserted by F(No 2)A 2017 s 64(1), (2) with effect in relation to any document of a kind listed in the Table in FA 2007 Sch 24 para 1 which is given to HMRC on or after 16 November 2017 and which relates to a tax period beginning on or after 6 April 2017 and ending on or after 16 November 2017. "Tax period", and the reference to giving a document to HMRC have the same meaning as in FA 2007 Sch 24 para 28 (F(No 2)A 2017 s 64(6)).

PART 2
AMOUNT OF PENALTY

Standard amount

[4   (1) This paragraph sets out the penalty payable under paragraph 1.

(2) If the inaccuracy is in category 1, the penalty is—

    (a) for careless action, 30% of the potential lost revenue,

    (b) for deliberate but not concealed action, 70% of the potential lost revenue, and

    (c) for deliberate and concealed action, 100% of the potential lost revenue.

(3) If the inaccuracy is in category 2, the penalty is—

    (a) for careless action, 45% of the potential lost revenue,

    (b) for deliberate but not concealed action, 105% of the potential lost revenue, and

    (c) for deliberate and concealed action, 150% of the potential lost revenue.

(4) If the inaccuracy is in category 3, the penalty is—

    (a) for careless action, 60% of the potential lost revenue,

    (b) for deliberate but not concealed action, 140% of the potential lost revenue, and

    (c) for deliberate and concealed action, 200% of the potential lost revenue.

(5) Paragraph 4A explains the 3 categories of inaccuracy.]¹

HMRC Manuals—Compliance Handbook Manual, CH82120 (penalties for inaccuracies: introduction to amount of penalty).

Amendments—[1]   Paras 4–4D substituted for previous para 4 by FA 2010 s 35 Sch 10 paras 1, 2 with effect from 6 April 2011 (by virtue of SI 2011/975 art 2(1)). Note that these changes do not have effect in relation to documents given to HMRC, and assessments issued by HMRC, in relation to a tax period commencing on or before 5 April 2011 (SI 2011/975 art 3).

Prospective amendments—Sub-para (1A) to be inserted, in sub-para (2), figures "37.5%" to be substituted for "30%", "87.5%" to be substituted for "70%" and "125%" to be substituted for "100%", and in sub-para (5), figure "4" to be substituted for figure "3", by FA 2015 s 120, Sch 20 paras 1, 2 with effect from a day to be appointed. Sub-para (1A) as inserted to read as follows—

    "(1A) If the inaccuracy is in category 0, the penalty is—

    (a)   for careless action, 30% of the potential lost revenue,

    (b)   for deliberate but not concealed action, 70% of the potential lost revenue, and

    (c)   for deliberate and concealed action, 100% of the potential lost revenue.".

[4A   (1) An inaccuracy is in category 1 if—

    (a) it involves a domestic matter, or

    (b) it involves an offshore matter and—

        (i) the territory in question is a category 1 territory, or

        (ii) the tax at stake is a tax other than income tax or capital gains tax.

(2) An inaccuracy is in category 2 if—

    (a) it involves an offshore matter [or an offshore transfer]²,

    (b) the territory in question is a category 2 territory, and

    (c) the tax at stake is income tax[, capital gains tax or inheritance tax]².

(3) An inaccuracy is in category 3 if—

    (a) it involves an offshore matter [or an offshore transfer]²,

    (b) the territory in question is a category 3 territory, and

    (c) the tax at stake is income tax[, capital gains tax or inheritance tax]².

(4) An inaccuracy "involves an offshore matter" if it results in a potential loss of revenue that is charged on or by reference to—

    (a) income arising from a source in a territory outside the UK,

    (b) assets situated or held in a territory outside the UK,

    (c) activities carried on wholly or mainly in a territory outside the UK, or

    (d) anything having effect as if it were income, assets or activities of a kind described above.

[(4A) Where the tax at stake is inheritance tax, assets are treated for the purposes of sub-paragraph (4) as situated or held in a territory outside the UK if they are so situated or held immediately after the transfer of value by reason of which inheritance tax becomes chargeable.

(4B) An inaccuracy "involves an offshore transfer" if—

    (a) it does not involve an offshore matter,

    (b) it is deliberate (whether or not concealed) and results in a potential loss of revenue,

    (c) the tax at stake is income tax, capital gains tax or inheritance tax, and

    (d) the applicable condition in paragraph 4AA is satisfied.]²

(5) An inaccuracy "involves a domestic matter" if it results in a potential loss of revenue [and does not involve either an offshore matter or an offshore transfer][2].

(6) If a single inaccuracy is in more than one category (each referred to as a "relevant category")—

    (*a*) it is to be treated for the purposes of this Schedule as if it were separate inaccuracies, one in each relevant category according to the matters [or transfers][2] that it involves, and

    (*b*) the potential lost revenue is to be calculated separately in respect of each separate inaccuracy.

(7) "Category 1 territory", "category 2 territory" and "category 3 territory" are defined in paragraph 21A.

(8) "Assets" has the meaning given in section 21(1) of TCGA 1992, but also includes sterling.][1]

Amendments—[1]   Paras 4–4D substituted for previous para 4 by FA 2010 s 35 Sch 10 paras 1, 2 with effect from 6 April 2011 (by virtue of SI 2011/975 art 2(1)). Note that these changes do not have effect in relation to documents given to HMRC, and assessments issued by HMRC, in relation to a tax period commencing on or before 5 April 2011 (SI 2011/975 art 3).

[2]   In sub-paras (2)(*a*), (3)(*a*), (6)(*a*), words inserted, in sub-paras (2)(*c*). (3)(*c*), (5), words substituted, and sub-paras (4A), (4B) inserted by FA 2015 s 120, Sch 20 paras 1, 3(3)–(7) with effect from 1 April 2016 (by virtue of SI 2016/456 art 3) in relation to documents given to HMRC relating to—
-    for the purposes of inheritance tax, a transfer of value made on or after that date; and
-    for the purposes of income tax and capital gains tax, a tax year commencing on or after 6 April 2016).

Prospective amendments—The following amendments to be made by FA 2015 s 120, Sch 20 paras 1, 3(1), (2), (8) with effect from a day to be appointed—
-    sub-paras (A1), (1) to be substituted for sub-para (1);
-    in sub-para (7), words ""Category 0 territory", "category 1" to be substituted for words ""Category 1".

Sub-paragraphs (A1), (1) as substituted to read as follows—

    "(A1) An inaccuracy is in category 0 if—

    (a)   it involves a domestic matter,

    (b)   it involves an offshore matter or an offshore transfer, the territory in question is a category 0 territory and the tax at stake is income tax, capital gains tax or inheritance tax, or

    (c)   it involves an offshore matter and the tax at stake is a tax other than income tax, capital gains tax or inheritance tax.

    (1) An inaccuracy is in category 1 if—

    (a)   it involves an offshore matter or an offshore transfer,

    (b)   the territory in question is a category 1 territory, and

    (c)   the tax at stake is income tax, capital gains tax or inheritance tax.".

[4AA (1) This paragraph makes provision in relation to offshore transfers.

(2) Where the tax at stake is income tax, the applicable condition is satisfied if the income on or by reference to which the tax is charged, or any part of the income—

    (*a*) is received in a territory outside the UK, or

    (*b*) is transferred before the filing date to a territory outside the UK.

(3) Where the tax at stake is capital gains tax, the applicable condition is satisfied if the proceeds of the disposal on or by reference to which the tax is charged, or any part of the proceeds—

    (*a*) are received in a territory outside the UK, or

    (*b*) are transferred before the filing date to a territory outside the UK.

(4) Where the tax at stake is inheritance tax, the applicable condition is satisfied if—

    (*a*) the disposition that gives rise to the transfer of value by reason of which the tax becomes chargeable involves a transfer of assets, and

    (*b*) after that disposition but before the filing date the assets, or any part of the assets, are transferred to a territory outside the UK.

(5) In the case of a transfer falling within sub-paragraph (2)(*b*), (3)(*b*) or (4)(*b*), references to the income, proceeds or assets transferred are to be read as including references to any assets derived from or representing the income, proceeds or assets.

(6) In relation to an offshore transfer, the territory in question for the purposes of paragraph 4A is the highest category of territory by virtue of which the inaccuracy involves an offshore transfer.

(7) "Filing date" means the date when the document containing the inaccuracy is given to HMRC.

(8) "Assets" has the same meaning as in paragraph 4A.][1]

Amendments—[1]   Paragraph 4AA inserted by FA 2015 s 120, Sch 20 paras 1, 4 with effect from 1 April 2016 (by virtue of SI 2016/456 art 3) in relation to documents given to HMRC relating to—
-    for the purposes of inheritance tax, a transfer of value made on or after that date; and
-    for the purposes of income tax and capital gains tax, a tax year commencing on or after 6 April 2016).

[4B The penalty payable under paragraph 1A is 100% of the potential lost revenue.][1]

Amendments—[1]   Paras 4–4D substituted for previous para 4 by FA 2010 s 35 Sch 10 paras 1, 2 with effect from 6 April 2011 (by virtue of SI 2011/975 art 2(1)). Note that these changes do not have effect in relation to documents given to HMRC, and assessments issued by HMRC, in relation to a tax period commencing on or before 5 April 2011 (SI 2011/975 art 3).

[4C The penalty payable under paragraph 2 is 30% of the potential lost revenue.][1]

Amendments—[1]   Paras 4–4D substituted for previous para 4 by FA 2010 s 35 Sch 10 paras 1, 2 with effect from 6 April 2011 (by virtue of SI 2011/975 art 2(1)). Note that these changes do not have effect in relation to documents given to HMRC, and assessments issued by HMRC, in relation to a tax period commencing on or before 5 April 2011 (SI 2011/975 art 3).

[4D   Paragraphs 5 to 8 define "potential lost revenue".]**[1]**

Amendments—[1]   Paras 4–4D substituted for previous para 4 by FA 2010 s 35 Sch 10 paras 1, 2 with effect from 6 April 2011 (by virtue of SI 2011/975 art 2(1)). Note that these changes do not have effect in relation to documents given to HMRC, and assessments issued by HMRC, in relation to a tax period commencing on or before 5 April 2011 (SI 2011/975 art 3).

Potential lost revenue: normal rule

5—(1) "The potential lost revenue" in respect of an inaccuracy in a document [(including an inaccuracy attributable to a supply of false information or withholding of information)]**[1]** or a failure to notify an under-assessment is the additional amount due or payable in respect of tax as a result of correcting the inaccuracy or assessment.

(2) The reference in sub-paragraph (1) to the additional amount due or payable includes a reference to—

    (*a*)   an amount payable to HMRC having been erroneously paid by way of repayment of tax, and

    (*b*)   an amount which would have been repayable by HMRC had the inaccuracy or assessment not been corrected.

(3) In sub-paragraph (1) "tax" includes national insurance contributions.

(4) The following shall be ignored in calculating potential lost revenue under this paragraph—

    (*a*)   group relief, and

    [(*b*)   any relief under [section 458 of CTA 2010]**[3]** (relief in respect of repayment etc of loan) which is deferred under [subsection (5)]**[3]** of that section;]**[2]**

(but this sub-paragraph does not prevent a penalty being charged in respect of an inaccurate claim for relief).

HMRC Manuals—Compliance Handbook Manual, CH82160–82161 (penalties for inaccuracies: single inaccuracy with examples of potential lost revenue).
CH82162 (examples of potential lost revenue for an under assessment).
Amendments—[1]   In sub-para (1), words inserted by FA 2008 s 122, Sch 40 paras 1, 7 with effect from 1 April 2009 (by virtue of SI 2009/571 art 2).
[2]   Sub-para (4)(*b*) substituted by FA 2009 s 109, Sch 57 para 3 with effect from 21 July 2009.
[3]   In sub-para (4)(*b*) words substituted by CTA 2010 s 1177, Sch 1 paras 573, 575. CTA 2010 has effect for corporation tax purposes for accounting periods ending on or after 1 April 2010, and for income and capital gains tax purposes for the tax year 2010–11 and subsequent tax years.

Potential lost revenue: multiple errors

6—(1) Where P is liable to a penalty [under paragraph 1]**[1]** in respect of more than one inaccuracy, and the calculation of potential lost revenue under paragraph 5 in respect of each inaccuracy depends on the order in which they are corrected—

    (*a*)   careless inaccuracies shall be taken to be corrected before deliberate inaccuracies, and

    (*b*)   deliberate but not concealed inaccuracies shall be taken to be corrected before deliberate and concealed inaccuracies.

(2) In calculating potential lost revenue where P is liable to a penalty [under paragraph 1]**[1]** in respect of one or more understatements in one or more documents relating to a tax period, account shall be taken of any overstatement in any document given by P which relates to the same tax period.

(3) In sub-paragraph (2)—

    (*a*)   "understatement" means an inaccuracy that satisfies Condition 1 of paragraph 1, and

    (*b*)   "overstatement" means an inaccuracy that does not satisfy that condition.

(4) For the purposes of sub-paragraph (2) overstatements shall be set against understatements in the following order—

    (*a*)   understatements in respect of which P is not liable to a penalty,

    (*b*)   careless understatements,

    (*c*)   deliberate but not concealed understatements, and

    (*d*)   deliberate and concealed understatements.

(5) In calculating [for the purposes of a penalty under paragraph 1]**[1]** potential lost revenue in respect of a document given by or on behalf of P no account shall be taken of the fact that a potential loss of revenue from P is or may be balanced by a potential over-payment by another person (except to the extent that an enactment requires or permits a person's tax liability to be adjusted by reference to P's).

HMRC Manuals—Compliance Handbook Manual, CH82180–82250 (penalties for inaccuracies: more than one inaccuracy and when inaccuracies should or should not be grouped).
CH82260 (overstatements, with a worked example).
CH82270 (calculating potential lost revenue for multiple inaccuracies).
CH82271 (calculating potential lost revenue for multiple inaccuracies – employer and contractor issues).

CH82272 (example of allocating overstatements to potential lost revenue).
Amendments—[1]   In sub-paras (1), (2), (5) words inserted, by FA 2008 s 122, Sch 40 paras 1, 8 with effect from 1 April 2009 (by virtue of SI 2009/571 art 2).

Potential lost revenue: losses

7—(1) Where an inaccuracy has the result that a loss is wrongly recorded for purposes of direct tax and the loss has been wholly used to reduce the amount due or payable in respect of tax, the potential lost revenue is calculated in accordance with paragraph 5.

(2) Where an inaccuracy has the result that a loss is wrongly recorded for purposes of direct tax and the loss has not been wholly used to reduce the amount due or payable in respect of tax, the potential lost revenue is—

    (a) the potential lost revenue calculated in accordance with paragraph 5 in respect of any part of the loss that has been used to reduce the amount due or payable in respect of tax, plus

    (b) 10% of any part that has not.

(3) Sub-paragraphs (1) and (2) apply both—

    (a) to a case where no loss would have been recorded but for the inaccuracy, and

    (b) to a case where a loss of a different amount would have been recorded (but in that case sub-paragraphs (1) and (2) apply only to the difference between the amount recorded and the true amount).

(4) Where an inaccuracy has the effect of creating or increasing an aggregate loss recorded for a group of companies—

    (a) the potential lost revenue shall be calculated in accordance with this paragraph, and

    (b) in applying paragraph 5 in accordance with sub-paragraphs (1) and (2) above, group relief may be taken into account (despite paragraph 5(4)(a)).

(5) The potential lost revenue in respect of a loss is nil where, because of the nature of the loss or P's circumstances, there is no reasonable prospect of the loss being used to support a claim to reduce a tax liability (of any person).

HMRC Manuals—Compliance Handbook Manual, CH82310–82320 (calculating the penalty: losses used and not used).
CH82330 (losses available for potential lost revenue calculation).
CH82331 (losses available – income tax example).
CH82332 (losses available – capital gains tax example).
CH82333 (losses available – corporation tax example).
CH82340–82341 (aggregate group profits).
CH82342–82345 (worked examples of understatements and overstatements of profits creating or increasing and aggregate loss).
CH82350 (losses and when to assess a penalty).
CH82370–82371 (losses where there is no reasonable prospect of use, with example).

Potential lost revenue: delayed tax

8—(1) Where an inaccuracy resulted in an amount of tax being declared later than it should have been ("the delayed tax"), the potential lost revenue is—

    (a) 5% of the delayed tax for each year of the delay, or

    (b) a percentage of the delayed tax, for each separate period of delay of less than a year, equating to 5% per year.

(2) This paragraph does not apply to a case to which paragraph 7 applies.

HMRC Manuals—Compliance Handbook Manual, CH82390 (calculating the penalty: delayed tax and potential lost revenue).
CH82395 and 82396 (examples of tax declared late).
CH82397 (capital allowances example of delayed tax).

Reductions for disclosure

9—[(A1) Paragraph 10 provides for reductions in penalties—

    (a) under paragraph 1 where a person discloses an inaccuracy that involves a domestic matter,

    (b) under paragraph 1A where a person discloses a supply of false information or withholding of information, and

    (c) under paragraph 2 where a person discloses a failure to disclose an under-assessment.

(A2) Paragraph 10A provides for reductions in penalties under paragraph 1 where a person discloses an inaccuracy that involves an offshore matter or an offshore transfer.

(A3) Sub-paragraph (1) applies where a person discloses—

    (a) an inaccuracy that involves a domestic matter,

    (b) a careless inaccuracy that involves an offshore matter,

    (c) a supply of false information or withholding of information, or

    (d) a failure to disclose an under-assessment.][3]

(1) A person discloses an inaccuracy[, a supply of false information or withholding of information,][1] or a failure to disclose an under-assessment by—

    (a) telling HMRC about it,

(b) giving HMRC reasonable help in quantifying the inaccuracy[, the inaccuracy attributable to the [supply of false information][2] or withholding of information, or the][1] under-assessment, and

(c) allowing HMRC access to records for the purpose of ensuring that the inaccuracy[, the inaccuracy attributable to the [supply of false information][2] or withholding of information, or the][1] under-assessment is fully corrected.

[(1A) Sub-paragraph (1B) applies where a person discloses—

(a) a deliberate inaccuracy (whether concealed or not) that involves an offshore matter, or

(b) an inaccuracy that involves an offshore transfer.

(1B) A person discloses the inaccuracy by—

(a) telling HMRC about it,

(b) giving HMRC reasonable help in quantifying the inaccuracy,

(c) allowing HMRC access to records for the purpose of ensuring that the inaccuracy is fully corrected, and

(d) providing HMRC with additional information.

(1C) The Treasury must make regulations setting out what is meant by "additional information" for the purposes of sub-paragraph (1B)(d).

(1D) Regulations under sub-paragraph (1C) are to be made by statutory instrument.

(1E) An instrument containing regulations under sub-paragraph (1C) is subject to annulment in pursuance of a resolution of the House of Commons.][3]

(2) Disclosure—

(a) is "unprompted" if made at a time when the person making it has no reason to believe that HMRC have discovered or are about to discover the inaccuracy[, the supply of false information or withholding of information, or the under-assessment][1], and

(b) otherwise, is "prompted".

(3) In relation to disclosure "quality" includes timing, nature and extent.

[(4) Paragraph 4A(4) to (5) applies to determine whether an inaccuracy involves an offshore matter, an offshore transfer or a domestic matter for the purposes of this paragraph.][3]

HMRC Manuals—Compliance Handbook Manual, CH82410 (calculating the penalty: penalty reductions for disclosure).
CH82420–82422 (unprompted and prompted disclosure, with examples).
CH82430–82431 (quality of disclosure).
CH82432 (calculating the reduction for disclosure example).
CH82440–82460 (quality of disclosure: telling, helping and giving access),
CH82470 (maximum and minimum penalties for each type of behaviour).
Regulations—Penalties Relating to Offshore Matters and Offshore Transfers (Additional Information) Regulations, SI 2017/345.
Amendments—[1]   In sub-para (1), words inserted, in paras (b), (c), words substituted, and in sub-para (2)(a), words substituted, by FA 2008 s 122, Sch 40 paras 1, 9 with effect from 1 April 2009 (by virtue of SI 2009/571 art 2).
[2]   In sub-para (1)(b), (c), words substituted by FA 2009 s 109, Sch 57 para 4 with effect from 21 July 2009.
[3]   Sub-paras (A1)–(A3) substituted for sub-para (A1); in sub-para (1), words substituted; and sub-paras (1A)–(1E), (4) inserted, by FA 2016 s 163, Sch 21 paras 1, 2 with effect, by virtue of SI 2017/259 regs 2, 3: (a) for inheritance tax purposes, in relation to transfers of value made on or after 1 April 2017; (b) for income tax and capital gains tax purposes, in relation to any tax year commencing on or after 6 April 2016; and (c) for the purpose of making regulations, from 8 March 2017.

[**10**—(1) If a person who would otherwise be liable to a penalty of a percentage shown in column 1 of the Table (a "standard percentage") has made a disclosure, HMRC must reduce the standard percentage to one that reflects the quality of the disclosure.

(2) But the standard percentage may not be reduced to a percentage that is below the minimum shown for it—

(a) in the case of a prompted disclosure, in column 2 of the Table, and

(b) in the case of an unprompted disclosure, in column 3 of the Table.

[Standard %	Minimum % for prompted disclosure	Minimum % for unprompted disclosure
30%	15%	0%
70%	35%	20%
100%	50%	30%][2]

HMRC Manuals—Compliance Handbook Manual, CH82500–82512 (calculating the penalty: how to calculate the penalty with examples).
Amendments—[1]   This para substituted by FA 2010 s 35 Sch 10 paras 1, 3 with effect from 6 April 2011 (by virtue of SI 2011/975 art 2(1)). Note that these changes do not have effect in relation to documents given to HMRC, and assessments issued by HMRC, in relation to a tax period commencing on or before 5 April 2011 (SI 2011/975 art 3).
[2]   In sub-para (2), Table substituted by FA 2016 s 163, Sch 21 paras 1, 3 with effect, by virtue of SI 2017/259 regs 2, 3: (a) for inheritance tax purposes, in relation to transfers of value made on or after 1 April 2017; and (b) for income tax and capital gains tax purposes, in relation to any tax year commencing on or after 6 April 2016.

[10A—(1) If a person who would otherwise be liable to a penalty of a percentage shown in column 1 of the Table (a "standard percentage") has made a disclosure, HMRC must reduce the standard percentage to one that reflects the quality of the disclosure.

(2) But the standard percentage may not be reduced to a percentage that is below the minimum shown for it—

(*a*) in the case of a prompted disclosure, in column 2 of the Table, and

(*b*) in the case of an unprompted disclosure, in column 3 of the Table.

Standard %	Minimum % for prompted disclosure	Minimum % for unprompted disclosure
30%	15%	0%
37.5%	18.75%	0%
45%	22.5%	0%
60%	30%	0%
70%	45%	30%
87.5%	53.75%	35%
100%	60%	40%
105%	62.5%	40%
125%	72.5%	50%
140%	80%	50%
150%	85%	55%
200%	110%	70%][1]

Amendments—[1] Paragraph 10A inserted by FA 2016 s 163, Sch 21 paras 1, 4 with effect, by virtue of SI 2017/259 regs 2, 3—
– for inheritance tax purposes, in relation to transfers of value made on or after 1 April 2017; and
– for income tax and capital gains tax purposes, in relation to any tax year commencing on or after 6 April 2016.

Special reduction

11—(1) If they think it right because of special circumstances, HMRC may reduce a penalty under paragraph 1[, 1A][1] or 2.

(2) In sub-paragraph (1) "special circumstances" does not include—

(*a*) ability to pay, or

(*b*) the fact that a potential loss of revenue from one taxpayer is balanced by a potential over-payment by another.

(3) In sub-paragraph (1) the reference to reducing a penalty includes a reference to—

(*a*) staying a penalty, and

(*b*) agreeing a compromise in relation to proceedings for a penalty.

HMRC Manuals—Compliance Handbook Manual, CH82490 (calculating the penalty: guidance regarding special reduction).
Amendments—[1] In sub-para (1) reference inserted, by FA 2008 s 122, Sch 40 paras 1, 10 with effect from 1 April 2009 (by virtue of SI 2009/571 art 2).

Interaction with other penalties [and late payment surcharges]

12—(1) The final entry in the Table in paragraph 1 excludes a document in respect of which a penalty is payable under section 98 of TMA 1970 (special returns).

(2) The amount of a penalty for which P is liable under paragraph 1 or 2 in respect of a document relating to a tax period shall be reduced by the amount of any other penalty [incurred by P, or any surcharge for late payment of tax imposed on P, if the amount of the penalty or surcharge is determined by reference to the same tax liability.][1]

[(2A) In sub-paragraph (2) "any other penalty" does not include a penalty under Part 4 of FA 2014 (penalty where corrective action not taken after follower notice etc).][3] [or Schedule 22 to FA 2016 (asset-based penalty)][4]

(3) In the application of section 97A of TMA 1970 (multiple penalties) no account shall be taken of a penalty under paragraph 1 or 2.

[(4) Where penalties are imposed under paragraphs 1 and 1A in respect of the same inaccuracy, the aggregate of the amounts of the penalties must not exceed the relevant percentage of the potential lost revenue.

(5) The relevant percentage is—

[(*za*) if the penalty imposed under paragraph 1 is for an inaccuracy in category 0, 100%,][5]

(*a*) if the penalty imposed under paragraph 1 is for an inaccuracy in category 1, [125%][5],

(*b*) if the penalty imposed under paragraph 1 is for an inaccuracy in category 2, 150%, and

(*c*) if the penalty imposed under paragraph 1 is for an inaccuracy in category 3, 200%.][2]

HMRC Manuals—Compliance Handbook Manual, CH84960 (interaction with other penalties: penalties for inaccurate documents other than returns).
CH84970–84972 (more than one penalty/surcharge on the same tax with examples).
Regulations—Penalties Relating to Offshore Matters and Offshore Transfers (Additional Information) Regulations, SI 2017/345.
Amendments—[1]   In sub-para (2), words substituted, and words inserted at end of heading, by FA 2008 s 122, Sch 40 paras 1, 11 with effect from 1 April 2009 (by virtue of SI 2009/571 art 2).
[2]   Sub-paras (4), (5) substituted for previous sub-para (4) by FA 2010 s 35 Sch 10 paras 1, 4 with effect from 6 April 2011 (by virtue of SI 2011/975 art 2(1)). Note that these changes do not have effect in relation to documents given to HMRC, and assessments issued by HMRC, in relation to a tax period commencing on or before 5 April 2011 (SI 2011/975 art 3).
[3]   Sub-para (2A) inserted by FA 2014 s 233, Sch 33 para 3 with effect from 17 July 2014.
[4]   Words in sub-para (2A) inserted by FA 2016 Sch 22 para 20 with effect: (a) for income tax and CGT purposes, in relation to tax years commencing on or after 6 April 2016; and (b) for IHT purposes, in relation to transfers of value made on or after 1 April 2017,
(by virtue of SI 2017/277 reg 2).
[5]   Sub-para (5)(za) inserted, and in sub-para (5)(a), figure "125%" substituted for "100%", by FA 2015 s 120, Sch 20 paras 1, 6 with effect: (a) for inheritance tax purposes, in relation to transfers of value (within the meaning of IHTA 1984 s 3) made on or after that day; and (b) for income tax and capital gains tax purposes, in relation to any tax year commencing on or after 6 April 2016.

PART 3
PROCEDURE

Assessment

13—(1) [Where a person][1] becomes liable for a penalty under paragraph 1[, 1A][1] or 2 HMRC shall—

   (a)   assess the penalty,

   (b)   [notify the person][1], and

   (c)   state in the notice a tax period in respect of which the penalty is assessed [(subject to sub-paragraph (1ZB))][3].

[(1ZA)   Sub-paragraph (1ZB) applies where—

   (a)   a person is at any time liable for two or more penalties relating to PAYE returns, or for two or more penalties relating to CIS returns, [or for two or more penalties relating to apprenticeship levy returns,][4] and

   (b)   the penalties ("the relevant penalties") are assessed in respect of more than one tax period ("the relevant tax periods").

(1ZB)   A notice under sub-paragraph (1) in respect of any of the relevant penalties may, instead of stating the tax period in respect of which the penalty is assessed, state the tax year or the part of a tax year to which the penalty relates.

(1ZC)   For that purpose, a relevant penalty relates to the tax year or the part of a tax year in which the relevant tax periods fall.

(1ZD)   For the purposes of sub-paragraph (1ZA)—

    "a PAYE return" means a return for the purposes of PAYE regulations;

    "a CIS return" means a return for the purposes of regulations under section 70(1)(a) of FA 2004 in connection with deductions on account of tax under the Construction Industry Scheme.][3]

        ["an apprenticeship levy return" means a return under regulations under section 105 of FA 2016;][4]

[(1A)   A penalty under paragraph 1, 1A or 2 must be paid before the end of the period of 30 days beginning with the day on which notification of the penalty is issued.][1]

(2)   An assessment—

   (a)   shall be treated for procedural purposes in the same way as an assessment to tax (except in respect of a matter expressly provided for by this Act),

   (b)   may be enforced as if it were an assessment to tax, and

   (c)   may be combined with an assessment to tax.

(3)   An assessment of a penalty under paragraph 1[or 1A][1] must be made [before the end of the][1] period of 12 months beginning with—

   (a)   the end of the appeal period for the decision correcting the inaccuracy, or

   (b)   if there is no assessment [to the tax concerned][1] within paragraph (a), the date on which the inaccuracy is corrected.

(4)   An assessment of a penalty under paragraph 2 must be made [before the end of the period of 12 months beginning with—

   (a)   the end of the appeal period for the assessment of tax which corrected the understatement, or

   (b)   if there is no assessment within paragraph (a), the date on which the understatement is corrected.][1]

(5)   For the purpose of sub-paragraphs (3) and (4) a reference to an appeal period is a reference to the period during which—

(*a*) an appeal could be brought, or

(*b*) an appeal that has been brought has not been determined or withdrawn.

(6) Subject to sub-paragraphs (3) and (4), a supplementary assessment may be made in respect of a penalty if an earlier assessment operated by reference to an underestimate of potential lost revenue.

[(7) In this Part of this Schedule references to an assessment to tax, in relation to inheritance tax and stamp duty reserve tax, are to a determination.][2]

HMRC Manuals—Compliance Handbook Manual, CH83020–83030 (processing the penalty: penalty assessments and what they must include).

CH83040 (when you should assess a penalty).

CH83050 (supplementary penalties).

CH83060 (enforcement of penalties).

Amendments—[1]   In sub-para (1), words substituted and words inserted, sub-para (1A) inserted, in sub-para (3), words inserted and words substituted , and in sub-para (4), words substituted, by FA 2008 s 122, Sch 40 paras 1, 12 with effect from 1 April 2009 (by virtue of SI 2009/571 art 2).

[2]   Sub-s (7) inserted by FA 2009 s 109, Sch 57 para 5 with effect from 21 July 2009.

[3]   Words in sub-para (1)(*c*) inserted, and sub-paras (1ZA)–(1ZD) inserted, by FA 2013 s 230, Sch 50 para 1 with effect in relation to any assessment of a penalty under this Schedule made on or after 17 July 2013.

[4]   In sub-para (1ZA), words inserted, and in sub-para (1ZD), entry inserted by FA 2016 s 113(1), (3) with effect from 6 April 2017 (by virtue of SI 2017/355).

Suspension

14—(1) HMRC may suspend all or part of a penalty for a careless inaccuracy under paragraph 1 by notice in writing to P.

(2) A notice must specify—

(*a*) what part of the penalty is to be suspended,

(*b*) a period of suspension not exceeding two years, and

(*c*) conditions of suspension to be complied with by P.

(3) HMRC may suspend all or part of a penalty only if compliance with a condition of suspension would help P to avoid becoming liable to further penalties under paragraph 1 for careless inaccuracy.

(4) A condition of suspension may specify—

(*a*) action to be taken, and

(*b*) a period within which it must be taken.

(5) On the expiry of the period of suspension—

(*a*) if P satisfies HMRC that the conditions of suspension have been complied with, the suspended penalty or part is cancelled, and

(*b*) otherwise, the suspended penalty or part becomes payable.

(6) If, during the period of suspension of all or part of a penalty under paragraph 1, P becomes liable for another penalty under that paragraph, the suspended penalty or part becomes payable.

HMRC Manuals—Compliance Handbook Manual, CH83110–83120 (suspension of a penalty).

Appeal

15—(1) [A person may][1] appeal against a decision of HMRC that a penalty is payable [by the person][1].

(2) [A person may][1] appeal against a decision of HMRC as to the amount of a penalty payable [by the person][1].

(3) [A person may][1] appeal against a decision of HMRC not to suspend a penalty payable [by the person][1].

(4) [A person may][1] appeal against a decision of HMRC setting conditions of suspension of a penalty payable [by the person][1].

HMRC Manuals—Compliance Handbook Manual, CH84010–84020 (appeals against a penalty: types of appeal and entitlement to appeal).

Amendments—[1]   Words substituted by FA 2008 s 122, Sch 40 paras 1, 13 with effect from 1 April 2009 (by virtue of SI 2009/571 art 2).

[**16**—(1) An appeal under this Part of this Schedule shall be treated in the same way as an appeal against an assessment to the tax concerned (including by the application of any provision about bringing the appeal by notice to HMRC, about HMRC review of the decision or about determination of the appeal by the First-tier Tribunal or Upper Tribunal).

[(2) Sub-paragraph (1) does not apply—

(*a*) so as to require P to pay a penalty before an appeal against the assessment of the penalty is determined, or

(*b*) in respect of any other matter expressly provided for by this Act.][2]][1]

HMRC Manuals—Compliance Handbook Manual, CH84070 (appeals against a penalty: which Tribunal will hear the appeal and procedures).

Amendments—[1]   Paragraph 16 substituted by the Transfer of Tribunal Functions and Revenue and Customs Appeals Order, SI 2009/56 art 3, Sch 1 para 466 with effect from 1 April 2009. The previous substitution made by FA 2008 therefore effectively never took place.
[2]   Sub-para (2) substituted by FA 2009 s 109, Sch 57 para 6 with effect from 21 July 2009.

17—(1) On an appeal under paragraph 15(1) the . . . [1] tribunal may affirm or cancel HMRC's decision.

(2) On an appeal under paragraph 15(2) the . . . [1] tribunal may—

    (a) affirm HMRC's decision, or

    (b) substitute for HMRC's decision another decision that HMRC had power to make.

(3) If the . . . [1] tribunal substitutes its decision for HMRC's, the . . . [1] tribunal may rely on paragraph 11—

    (a) to the same extent as HMRC (which may mean applying the same percentage reduction as HMRC to a different starting point), or

    (b) to a different extent, but only if the . . . [1] tribunal thinks that HMRC's decision in respect of the application of paragraph 11 was flawed.

(4) On an appeal under paragraph 15(3)—

    (a) the . . . [1] tribunal may order HMRC to suspend the penalty only if it thinks that HMRC's decision not to suspend was flawed, and

    (b) if the . . . [1] tribunal orders HMRC to suspend the penalty—

        (i) P may appeal [1] against a provision of the notice of suspension, and

        (ii) the . . . [1] tribunal may order HMRC to amend the notice.

(5) On an appeal under paragraph 15(4) the . . . [1] tribunal—

    (a) may affirm the conditions of suspension, or

    (b) may vary the conditions of suspension, but only if the . . . [1] tribunal thinks that HMRC's decision in respect of the conditions was flawed.

[(5A) In this paragraph "tribunal" means the First-tier Tribunal or Upper Tribunal (as appropriate by virtue of paragraph 16(1)).][1]

(6) In sub-paragraphs (3)(b), (4)(a) and (5)(b) "flawed" means flawed when considered in the light of the principles applicable in proceedings for judicial review.

(7) Paragraph 14 (see in particular paragraph 14(3)) is subject to the possibility of an order under this paragraph.

HMRC Manuals—Compliance Handbook Manual, CH84030–84040 (appeals against a penalty: appeals against the imposition or amount of a penalty).
CH84050 (appeals against the decision not to suspend a penalty).
CH84060 (appeals against the conditions set for penalty suspension).
CH84080 (flawed decision).
Amendment—[1]   In sub-paras (1), (2), (3), (4)(a), (4)(b) in the first place, (4)(b)(ii), (5) in each place, word "appellate" repealed, in para (4)(b) (i) words "to the appellate tribunal" repealed; sub-para (5A) inserted by the Transfer of Tribunal Functions and Revenue and Customs Appeals Order, SI 2009/56 art 3, Sch 1 para 467 with effect from 1 April 2009.

PART 4

MISCELLANEOUS

Agency

18—(1) P is liable under paragraph 1(1)(a) where a document which contains a careless inaccuracy (within the meaning of paragraph 3) is given to HMRC on P's behalf.

(2) In paragraph 2(1)(b) and (2)(a) a reference to P includes a reference to a person who acts on P's behalf in relation to tax.

(3) Despite sub-paragraphs (1) and (2), P is not liable to a penalty [under paragraph 1 or 2][1] in respect of anything done or omitted by P's agent where P satisfies HMRC that P took reasonable care to avoid inaccuracy (in relation to paragraph 1) or unreasonable failure (in relation to paragraph 2).

(4) In paragraph 3(1)(a) (whether in its application to a document given by P or, by virtue of sub-paragraph (1) above, in its application to a document given on P's behalf) a reference to P includes a reference to a person who acts on P's behalf in relation to tax.

(5) In paragraph 3(2) a reference to P includes a reference to a person who acts on P's behalf in relation to tax.

[(6) Paragraph 3A applies where a document is given to HMRC on behalf of P as it applies where a document is given to HMRC by P (and in paragraph 3B(9) the reference to P includes a person acting on behalf of P).][2]

HMRC Manuals—Compliance Handbook Manual, CH84520–84530 (other penalty issues: agent acting).
CH84540 (reliance on use of an agent to avoid an inaccuracy).
CH84545 (agent acting – inaccuracy attributable to another person).
Amendments—[1]   In sub-para (3), words inserted by FA 2008 s 122, Sch 40 paras 1, 15 with effect from 1 April 2009 (by virtue of SI 2009/571 art 2).

²   Sub-para (6) inserted by F(No 2)A 2017 s 64(1), (3) with effect in relation to any document of a kind listed in the Table in FA 2007 Sch 24 para 1 which is given to HMRC on or after 16 November 2017 and which relates to a tax period beginning on or after 6 April 2017 and ending on or after 16 November 2017. "Tax period", and the reference to giving a document to HMRC have the same meaning as in FA 2007 Sch 24 para 28 (F(No 2)A 2017 s 64(6)).

Companies: officers' liability

19—(1) Where a penalty under paragraph 1 is payable by a company for a deliberate inaccuracy which was attributable to an officer [of the company, the officer is liable to pay such portion of the penalty (which may be 100%) as HMRC]¹ may specify by written notice to the officer.
(2) Sub-paragraph (1) does not allow HMRC to recover more than 100% of a penalty.
(3) In the application of sub-paragraph (1) to a body corporate [other than a limited liability partnership]² "officer" means—
- (*a*) a director (including a shadow director within the meaning of section 251 of the Companies Act 2006 (c 46)), . . . ²
- [(*aa*) a manager, and]²
- (*b*) a secretary.

[(3A) In the application of sub-paragraph (1) to a limited liability partnership, "officer" means a member.]²
(4) In the application of sub-paragraph (1) in any other case "officer" means—
- (*a*) a director,
- (*b*) a manager,
- (*c*) a secretary, and
- (*d*) any other person managing or purporting to manage any of the company's affairs.

[(5) Where HMRC have specified a portion of a penalty in a notice given to an officer under sub-paragraph (1)—
- (*a*) paragraph 11 applies to the specified portion as to a penalty,
- (*b*) the officer must pay the specified portion before the end of the period of 30 days beginning with the day on which the notice is given,
- (*c*) paragraph 13(2), (3) and (5) apply as if the notice were an assessment of a penalty,
- (*d*) a further notice may be given in respect of a portion of any additional amount assessed in a supplementary assessment in respect of the penalty under paragraph 13(6),
- (*e*) paragraphs 15(1) and (2), 16 and 17(1) to (3) and (6) apply as if HMRC had decided that a penalty of the amount of the specified portion is payable by the officer, and
- (*f*) paragraph 21 applies as if the officer were liable to a penalty.]¹

[(6) In this paragraph "company" means any body corporate or unincorporated association, but does not include a partnership, a local authority or a local authority association.]²

HMRC Manuals—Compliance Handbook Manual, CH84610 (company penalties: officer of a company liable to a penalty).
CH84611 (deliberate action by officer of the company).
CH84620 (what is a company).
CH84625 (who is an officer of the company).
CH84630 (notice of liability).
CH84640 (amount of officer's liability).
CH84650 (personal gain).
CH84660 (insolvency or imminent insolvency).

Amendments—¹   In sub-para (1), words substituted, and sub-para (5) substituted, by FA 2008 s 122, Sch 40 paras 1, 16 with effect from 1 April 2009 (by virtue of SI 2009/571 art 2).
²   In sub-para (3) words inserted; word "or" repealed and para (*aa*) inserted; sub-paras (3A), (6) inserted, by FA 2009 s 109, Sch 57 para 7 with effect from 21 July 2009.

Partnerships

20—(1) This paragraph applies where P is liable to a penalty under paragraph 1 for an inaccuracy in or in connection with a partnership return.
(2) Where the inaccuracy affects the amount of tax due or payable by a partner of P, the partner is also liable to a penalty ("a partner's penalty").
(3) Paragraphs 4 to 13 and 19 shall apply in relation to a partner's penalty (for which purpose a reference to P shall be taken as a reference to the partner).
(4) Potential lost revenue shall be calculated separately for the purpose of P's penalty and any partner's penalty, by reference to the proportions of any tax liability that would be borne by each partner.
(5) Paragraph 14 shall apply jointly to P's penalty and any partner's penalties.
(6) P may bring an appeal under paragraph 15 in respect of a partner's penalty (in addition to any appeal that P may bring in connection with the penalty for which P is liable).

HMRC Manuals—Compliance Handbook Manual, CH84720 (partnership penalties: partnerships and self assessment).
CH84730 (liable partners).
CH84740–84741 (calculating potential lost revenue, with example for partnerships).

CH84750–84760 (suspended penalties and appeals against penalties).

Double jeopardy

21 [A person is][1] not liable to a penalty under paragraph 1[, 1A][1] or 2 in respect of an inaccuracy or failure in respect of which [the person has][1] been convicted of an offence.

HMRC Manuals—Compliance Handbook Manual, CH84900 (partnership penalties: double jeopardy).
Amendments—[1] Words substituted and reference inserted, by FA 2008 s 122, Sch 40 paras 1, 17 with effect from 1 April 2009 (by virtue of SI 2009/571 art 2).

[21ZA (1) A person is not liable to a penalty under paragraph 1 in respect of an inaccuracy if—

(a) the inaccuracy involves a claim by the person to exercise or rely on a VAT right (in relation to a supply) that has been denied or refused by HMRC as mentioned in subsection (4) of section 69C of VATA 1994, and

(b) the person has been assessed to a penalty under that section (and the assessment has not been successfully appealed against or withdrawn).

(2) In sub-paragraph (1)(a) "VAT right" has the same meaning as in section 69C of VATA 1994.][1]

Amendments—[1] Paragraph 21ZA inserted by F(No 2)A 2017 s 68(1), (6) with effect from 16 November 2017.

PART 5
GENERAL

[*Classification of territories*

21A—(1) A category 1 territory is a territory designated as a category 1 territory by order made by the Treasury.

(2) A category 2 territory is a territory that is neither—

(a) a category 1 territory, nor

(b) a category 3 territory.

(3) A category 3 territory is a territory designated as a category 3 territory by order made by the Treasury.

(4) In considering how to classify a territory for the purposes of this paragraph, the Treasury must have regard to—

(a) the existence of any arrangements between the UK and that territory for the exchange of information for tax enforcement purposes,

(b) the quality of any such arrangements (in particular, whether they provide for information to be exchanged automatically or on request), . . . [2]

(c) the benefit that the UK would be likely to obtain from receiving information from that territory, were such arrangements to exist with it,

(d) the existence of any other arrangements between the UK and that territory for co-operation in the area of taxation, and

(e) the quality of any such other arrangements (in particular, the extent to which the co-operation provided for in them assists or is likely to assist in the protection of revenue raised from taxation in the UK).][2]

(5) An order under this paragraph is to be made by statutory instrument.

(6) Subject to sub-paragraph (7), an instrument containing an order under this paragraph is subject to annulment in pursuance of a resolution of the House of Commons.

(7) If the order is—

(a) the first order to be made under sub-paragraph (1), or

(b) the first order to be made under sub-paragraph (3),

it may not be made unless a draft of the instrument containing it has been laid before, and approved by a resolution of, the House of Commons.

(8) An order under this paragraph does not apply to inaccuracies in a document given to HMRC (or, in a case within paragraph 3(2), inaccuracies discovered by P) before the date on which the order comes into force.][1]

Orders—Penalties, Offshore Income etc. (Designation of Territories) Order, SI 2011/976.
Penalties, Offshore Income etc. (Designation of Territories) (Amendment) Order, SI 2013/1618.
Amendments—[1] Paras 21A, 21B inserted by FA 2010 s 35 Sch 10 paras 1, 5 with effect from 6 April 2011 (by virtue of SI 2011/975 art 2(1)). Note that these changes do not have effect in relation to documents given to HMRC, and assessments issued by HMRC, in relation to a tax period commencing on or before 5 April 2011 (SI 2011/975 art 3).
[2] Word "and" at the end of sub-para (4)(b) repealed, and sub-para (4)(d), (e) inserted, by FA 2012 s 219 with effect from 17 July 2012.
Prospective amendments—Sub-para (A1) to be inserted before sub-para (1), and sub-paras (2), (7) to be substituted, by FA 2015 s 120, Sch 20 paras 1, 7 with effect from a day to be appointed. Sub-para (A1) as inserted to read as follows—

"(A1) A category 0 territory is a territory designated as a category 0 territory by order made by the Treasury.".

Sub-para (2) as substituted to read as follows—

"(2) A category 2 territory is a territory that is not any of the following—

(a)   a category 0 territory;

(b)   a category 1 territory;

(c)   a category 3 territory.".

Sub-para (7) as substituted to read as follows—

"(7) An instrument containing (whether alone or with other provisions) the first order to be made under sub-paragraph (A1) may not be made unless a draft of the instrument has been laid before, and approved by a resolution of, the House of Commons.".

[Location of assets etc

21B—(1) The Treasury may by regulations make provision for determining for the purposes of paragraph 4A where—

(*a*)   a source of income is located,

(*b*)   an asset is situated or held, or

(*c*)   activities are wholly or mainly carried on.

[(1A) The Treasury may by regulations make provision for determining for the purposes of paragraph 4AA where—

(*a*)   income is received or transferred,

(*b*)   the proceeds of a disposal are received or transferred, or

(*c*)   assets are transferred.][2]

(2) Different provision may be made for different cases and for income tax[, capital gains tax and inheritance tax][2].

(3) Regulations under this paragraph are to be made by statutory instrument.

(4) An instrument containing regulations under this paragraph is subject to annulment in pursuance of a resolution of the House of Commons.][1]

Amendments—[1]   Paras 21A, 21B inserted by FA 2010 s 35 Sch 10 paras 1, 5 with effect from 6 April 2011 (by virtue of SI 2011/975 art 2(1)). Note that these changes do not have effect in relation to documents given to HMRC, and assessments issued by HMRC, in relation to a tax period commencing on or before 5 April 2011 (SI 2011/975 art 3).

[2]   Sub-para (1A) inserted, and in sub-para (2), words substituted by FA 2015 s 120, Sch 20 paras 1, 8 with effect from 1 April 2016 (by virtue of SI 2016/456 art 3) in relation to documents given to HMRC relating to: (a) for the purposes of inheritance tax, a transfer of value made on or after that date; and (b) for the purposes of income tax and capital gains tax, a tax year commencing on or after 6 April 2016.

[Treatment of certain payments on account of tax

21C   In paragraphs 1(2) and 5 references to "tax" are to be interpreted as if amounts payable under [Schedule 2 to FA 2019][3] [and amounts payable on account of apprenticeship levy][2] were tax.][1]

Amendments—[1]   Paragraph 21C inserted by FA 2015 s 37, Sch 7 para 56(1), (3) with effect in relation to disposals made on or after 6 April 2015.

[2]   Words inserted by FA 2016 s 113(1), (4) with effect from 6 April 2017 (by virtue of SI 2017/355).

[3]   Words substituted for words "section 59AA(2) of TMA 1970 (non-resident CGT disposals: payments on account of capital gains tax)" by FA 2019 s 14, Sch 2 para 27(1), (3) with effect in relation to disposals made on or after 6 April 2019.

Interpretation

22   Paragraphs 23 to [27][1] apply for the construction of this Schedule.

Amendments—[1]   Reference substituted by FA 2008 s 122, Sch 40 paras 1, 18 with effect from 1 April 2009 (by virtue of SI 2009/571 art 2).

23   HMRC means Her Majesty's Revenue and Customs.

[**23A**   "Tax", without more, includes duty.][1]

Amendments—[1]   Paragraph 23A inserted by FA 2008 s 122, Sch 40 paras 1, 19 with effect from 1 April 2009 (by virtue of SI 2009/571 art 2).

[**23B**   "UK" means the United Kingdom, including the territorial sea of the United Kingdom.][1]

Amendments—[1]   This para inserted by FA 2010 s 35 Sch 10 paras 1, 6 with effect from 6 April 2011 (by virtue of SI 2011/975 art 2(1)). Note that these changes do not have effect in relation to documents given to HMRC, and assessments issued by HMRC, in relation to a tax period commencing on or before 5 April 2011 (SI 2011/975 art 3).

24   An expression used in relation to income tax has the same meaning as in the Income Tax Acts.

25   An expression used in relation to corporation tax has the same meaning as in the Corporation Tax Acts.

26   An expression used in relation to capital gains tax has the same meaning as in the enactments relating to that tax.

27   An expression used in relation to VAT has the same meaning as in VATA 1994.

28   In this Schedule—

(*a*)   a reference to corporation tax includes a reference to tax or duty which by virtue of an enactment is assessable or chargeable as if it were corporation tax,

(*b*)   a reference to tax includes reference to construction industry deductions under Chapter 3 of Part 3 of FA 2004,

(*c*)   "direct tax" means—

     (i)   income tax,

     (ii)   capital gains tax, . . . [1]

     (iii)   corporation tax, [and

     (iv)   petroleum revenue tax,][1]

(*d*)   a reference to understating liability to VAT includes a reference to overstating entitlement to a VAT credit,

[(*da*)   references to an assessment to tax, in relation to inheritance tax, means a determination,][1,3]

(*e*)   a reference to a loss includes a reference to a charge, expense, deficit and any other amount which may be available for, or relied on to claim, a deduction or relief,

(*f*)   a reference to repayment of tax includes a reference to allowing a credit [against tax or to a payment of a corporation tax credit][1],

[(*fa*)   "corporation tax credit" means—

     (i)   an R&D tax credit under [Chapter 2 or 7 of Part 13 of CTA 2009][2],

     [(ia)   an R&D expenditure credit under Chapter 6A of Part 3 of CTA 2009,][4]

     (ii)   a land remediation tax credit or life assurance company tax credit under [Chapter 3 or 4 respectively of Part 14 of CTA 2009][2],

     (iii)   *a tax credit under Schedule 13 to FA 2002 (vaccine research etc),*[2]

     (iv)   a film tax credit under [Chapter 3 of Part 15 of CTA 2009][2], . . . [5]

     [(iva)   a television tax credit under Chapter 3 of Part 15A of that Act,

     (ivb)   a video game tax credit under Chapter 3 of Part 15B of that Act, . . . [6]][5]

     [(ivc)   a theatre tax credit under section 1217K of that Act, . . . [7]][6]

     [(ivd)   an orchestra tax credit under Chapter 3 of Part 15D of that Act, . . . [8]][7]

     [(ive)   a museums and galleries exhibition tax credit under Chapter 3 of Part 15E of that Act, or][8]

     (v)   a first-year tax credit under Schedule A1 to CAA 2001,][1]

(*g*)   "tax period" means a tax year, accounting period or other period in respect of which tax is charged,

(*h*)   a reference to giving a document to HMRC includes a reference to communicating information to HMRC in any form and by any method (whether by post, fax, email, telephone or otherwise),

(*i*)   a reference to giving a document to HMRC includes a reference to making a statement or declaration in a document,

(*j*)   a reference to making a return or doing anything in relation to a return includes a reference to amending a return or doing anything in relation to an amended return, and

(*k*)   a reference to action includes a reference to omission.

HMRC Manuals—Compliance Handbook Manual, CH81050 (penalties for inaccuracies: what is meant by "giving a document").

CH81071 (what is a "repayment of tax").

Amendments—[1]   In sub-para (*c*), word "and" after para (ii) repealed, after para (iii) word "and" inserted, and para (iv) inserted, sub-paras (*da*), (*fa*) inserted, and in sub-para (*f*), words inserted, by FA 2008 s 122, Sch 40 para 20 with effect from 1 April 2009 (by virtue of SI 2009/571 art 2).

[2]   In sub-para (*fa*)(i), (ii), (iv), words substituted and sub-para (*fa*)(iii) repealed by CTA 2009 ss 1322, 1326, Sch 1 paras 722, 727, Sch 3 Part 1. CTA 2009 applies for accounting periods ending on or after 1 April 2009 (for corporation tax purposes) and for tax years 2009–10 onwards (for income and capital gains tax purposes).

[3]   Sub-para (*da*) repealed by FA 2009 s 109, Sch 57 para 8 with effect from 21 July 2009.

[4]   Sub-para (*fa*)(ia) inserted by FA 2013 s 35, Sch 15 para 8 with effect in relation to expenditure incurred on or after 1 April 2013.

[5]   In sub-para (*fa*), word "or" at end of para (iv) repealed and paras (iva), (ivb) inserted, by FA 2013 s 36, Sch 18 para 7. The amendments made by Sch 18 come into force as follows—

     –   so far as relating to television tax relief on 19 July 2013 (by virtue of SI 2013/1817 art 2(2)); and

     –   so far as relating to video game development, with effect from 1 April 2014 (by virtue of SI 2014/1962 art 2(3)).

Those amendments have effect in relation to accounting periods beginning on or after the "relevant day", subject to transitional provisions. The "Relevant day" is defined as follows—.

     –   in the case of amendments relating to CTA 2009 Part 15A (as inserted by FA 2013 Sch 16), 1 April 2013, and

     –   in the case of amendments relating to CTA 2009 Part 15B (as inserted by FA 2013 Sch 17), 1 April 2014 (by virtue of SI 2014/1962 art 2(3)).).

See FA 2013 Sch 18 paras 22, 23 for commencement provisions.

[6]   In sub-para (*fa*), word "or" at the end of para (ivb) repealed, and para (ivc) inserted, by FA 2014 s 36, Sch 4 para 8 with effect in relation to accounting periods beginning on or after 1 September 2014, subject to transitional provisions for accounting periods straddling that date (FA 2014 Sch 4 para 17). SI 2014/2228 reg 2 provides that the amendments made by FA 2014 Sch 4 come into force on 22 August 2014 (other than the power to make regulations under Sch 4 para 16(1) which came into force on 17 July 2014).

[7]   In sub-para (*fa*), word "or" at the end of para (ivc) repealed, and para (ivd) inserted, by FA 2016 s 54, Sch 8 para 8 with effect in relation to accounting periods beginning on or after 1 April 2016, subject to transitional provisions for accounting periods straddling that date (FA 2016 Sch 8 para 17). Note that any power conferred on the Treasury by FA 2016 Sch 8 to make regulations came into force on 15 September 2016 (FA 2016 Sch 8 para 16).

[8]   In sub-para (*fa*), word "or" at end of para (ivd) repealed, and para (ive) inserted, by F(No 2)A 2017 s 21, Sch 6 para 8 with effect in relation to accounting periods beginning on or after 1 April 2017.

Consequential amendments

29   The following provisions are omitted—

(*a*)   (*repeals* TMA 1970 ss 95, 95A, 97, 98A(4))

(*b*)   (*repeals* TMA 1970 ss 100A(1), 103(2))

(*c*)   (*repeals*FA 1998 Sch 18 paras 20, 89)

(*d*)   (*repeals* VATA 1994 ss 60, 61, 63, 64)

30   In [paragraphs 7 and 7B][1] of Schedule 1 to the Social Security Contributions and Benefits Act 1992 (c 4) (penalties) a reference to a provision of TMA 1970 shall be construed as a reference to this Schedule so far as is necessary to preserve its effect.

Amendments—[1]   Words substituted by FA 2009 s 109, Sch 57 para 9 with effect from 21 July 2009.

31   In [paragraphs 7 and 7B][1] of Schedule 1 to the Social Security Contributions and Benefits (Northern Ireland) Act 1992 (c 7) (penalties) a reference to a provision of TMA 1970 shall be construed as a reference to this Schedule so far as is necessary to preserve its effect.

Amendments—[1]   Words substituted by FA 2009 s 109, Sch 57 para 9 with effect from 21 July 2009.

SCHEDULE 25

AMENDMENTS CONNECTED WITH GAMBLING ACT 2005

Section 105

PART 1

AMENDMENTS OF THE TAX ACTS

Exemption from income tax for profits of charitable trusts from certain lotteries

2   (*substitutes* ITA 2007 s 530(2)(*a*), (*ab*))

PART 6

COMMENCEMENT

23—(1) Paragraphs 3, 4, 6, 7(1) and (5), 11(1) and (2), 13, 15, 16 and 20(1) and (6) and this paragraph come into force on the day on which this Act is passed.

(2) The other provisions of this Schedule come into force in accordance with provision made by the Treasury by order.

(3) The power to make an order under this paragraph is exercisable by statutory instrument.

(4) An order under this paragraph—

(*a*)   may make different provision for different purposes, and

(*b*)   may contain transitional provision and savings.

Regulations—Finance Act 2007, Schedule 25 (Commencement and Transitional Provisions) Order 2007 (gives a commencement date of 1 September 2007 for the provisions of this Schedule).

SCHEDULE 26

MEANING OF "RECOGNISED STOCK EXCHANGE" ETC

Section 109

Meaning of "recognised stock exchange" etc in Tax Acts and TCGA 1992

1   (*substitutes* ITA 2007 s 1005)

TRIBUNALS, COURTS AND ENFORCEMENT ACT 2007

(2007 Chapter 15)

ARRANGEMENT OF SECTIONS

Part 1: Tribunals and Inquiries
Chapter 1 Tribunal Judiciary: Independence and Senior President
1   Independence of tribunal judiciary
2   Senior President of Tribunals
Chapter 2 First-tier Tribunal and Upper Tribunal
Establishment
3   The First-tier Tribunal and the Upper Tribunal
Members and composition of tribunals
4   Judges and other members of the First-tier Tribunal
5   Judges and other members of the Upper Tribunal
6   Certain judges who are also judges of First-tier Tribunal and Upper Tribunal
6A   Certain judges who are also judges of the First-tier Tribunal
7   Chambers: jurisdiction and Presidents
8   Senior President of Tribunals: power to delegate
Review of decisions and appeals
9   Review of decision of First-tier Tribunal
10   Review of decision of Upper Tribunal
11   Right to appeal to Upper Tribunal
12   Proceedings on appeal to Upper Tribunal
13   Right to appeal to Court of Appeal etc
14   Proceedings on appeal to Court of Appeal etc
14A   Appeal to Supreme Court: grant of certificate by Upper Tribunal
14B   Appeal to Supreme Court: permission to appeal
14C   Appeal to Supreme Court: exclusions
"Judicial review"
15   Upper Tribunal's "judicial review" jurisdiction
16   Application for relief under section 15(1)
17   Quashing orders under section 15(1): supplementary provision
18   Limits of jurisdiction under section 15(1)
19   Transfer of judicial review applications from High Court
20   Transfer of judicial review applications from the Court of Session
20A   Procedural steps where application transferred
21   Upper Tribunal's "judicial review" jurisdiction: Scotland
Miscellaneous
22   Tribunal Procedure Rules
23   Practice directions
24   Mediation
25   Supplementary powers of Upper Tribunal
26   First-tier Tribunal and Upper Tribunal: sitting places
27   Enforcement
28   Assessors
29   Costs or expenses
Use of live video or audio links: public participation & offences of recording etc
29ZA   Enabling the public to see and hear proceedings
29ZB   Offences of recording or transmission in relation to broadcasting
29ZC   Offences of recording or transmitting participation through live link
29ZD   Interpretation
Chapter 2A Exercise of Tribunal Functions by Authorised Persons
29A   Meaning of "authorised person" and "judicial office holder"
29B   Directions and independence: authorised persons
29C   Protection of authorised persons
29D   Costs or expenses in legal proceedings: authorised persons
29E   Indemnification of authorised persons
Chapter 3 Transfer of Tribunal Functions
30   Transfer of functions of certain tribunals
31   Transfers under section 30: supplementary powers
32   Power to provide for appeal to Upper Tribunal from tribunals in Wales
33   Power to provide for appeal to Upper Tribunal from tribunals in Scotland
34   Power to provide for appeal to Upper Tribunal from tribunals in Northern Ireland
35   Transfer of Ministerial responsibilities for certain tribunals
36   Transfer of powers to make procedural rules for certain tribunals
37   Power to amend lists of tribunals in Schedule 6
38   Orders under sections 30 to 36: supplementary
Chapter 4 Administrative Matters in respect of Certain Tribunals

39   The general duty
40   Tribunal staff and services
41   Provision of accommodation
42   Fees
43   Report by Senior President of Tribunals
Chapter 6 Supplementary
46   Delegation of functions by Lord Chief Justice etc
47   Co-operation in relation to judicial training, guidance and welfare
48   Consequential and other amendments, and transitional provisions
49   Orders and regulations under Part 1: supplemental and procedural provisions
Part 3: Enforcement by Taking Control of Goods
Chapter 1 Procedure
62   Enforcement by taking control of goods
63   Enforcement agents
64   Certificates to act as an enforcement agent
65   Common law rules replaced
66   Pre-commencement enforcement not affected
67   Transfer of county court enforcement
68   Magistrates' courts warrants of control
69   County court warrants of control etc
70   Power of High Court to stay execution
Chapter 3 General
88   Abolition of Crown preference
89   Application to the Crown
90   Regulations
Part 4: Enforcement of Judgments and Orders
Attachment of earnings orders
91   Attachment of earnings orders: deductions at fixed rates
92   Attachment of earnings orders: finding the debtor's current employer
Charging orders
93   Payment by instalments: making and enforcing charging orders
94   Charging orders: power to set financial thresholds
Information requests and orders
95   Application for information about action to recover judgment debt
96   Action by the court
97   Departmental information requests
98   Information orders
99   Responding to a departmental information request
100   Information order: required information not held etc
101   Using the information about the debtor
102   Offence of unauthorised use or disclosure
103   Regulations
104   Interpretation
105   Application and transitional provision
Part 8: General
146   Repeals
147   Extent
148   Commencement
149   Short title
Schedules
Schedule 1—Senior President of Tribunals
Schedule 2—Judges and Other Members of the First-tier Tribunal
Schedule 3—Judges and Other Members of the Upper Tribunal
Schedule 4—Chambers and Chamber Presidents: Further Provision
Schedule 5—Procedure in First-tier Tribunal and Upper Tribunal
Schedule 6—Tribunals for the Purposes of Sections 30 to 36
Schedule 10—Amendments relating to Judicial Appointments
Schedule 12—Taking Control of Goods
Schedule 13—Taking Control of Goods: Amendments
Schedule 23—Repeals

PART 1

TRIBUNALS AND INQUIRIES

CHAPTER 1

TRIBUNAL JUDICIARY: INDEPENDENCE AND SENIOR PRESIDENT

1 Independence of tribunal judiciary

(*Inserts* Constitutional Reform Act 2005 s 3(7A), (7B) with effect from 19 September 2007: SI 2007/2709 art 2)

2 Senior President of Tribunals

(1) Her Majesty may, on the recommendation of the Lord Chancellor, appoint a person to the office of Senior President of Tribunals.

(2) Schedule 1 makes further provision about the Senior President of Tribunals and about recommendations for appointment under subsection (1).

(3) A holder of the office of Senior President of Tribunals must, in carrying out the functions of that office, have regard to—

    (*a*) the need for tribunals to be accessible,

    (*b*) the need for proceedings before tribunals—

        (i) to be fair, and

        (ii) to be handled quickly and efficiently,

    (*c*) the need for members of tribunals to be experts in the subject-matter of, or the law to be applied in, cases in which they decide matters, and

    (*d*) the need to develop innovative methods of resolving disputes that are of a type that may be brought before tribunals.

(4) In subsection (3) "tribunals" means—

    (*a*) the First-tier Tribunal,

    (*b*) the Upper Tribunal,

    (*c*) employment tribunals,

    (*d*) the Employment Appeal Tribunal, and

    (*e*) the Asylum and Immigration Tribunal.

Commentary—*Simon's Taxes* **A3.704**.

CHAPTER 2

FIRST-TIER TRIBUNAL AND UPPER TRIBUNAL

Establishment

3 The First-tier Tribunal and the Upper Tribunal

(1) There is to be a tribunal, known as the First-tier Tribunal, for the purpose of exercising the functions conferred on it under or by virtue of this Act or any other Act.

(2) There is to be a tribunal, known as the Upper Tribunal, for the purpose of exercising the functions conferred on it under or by virtue of this Act or any other Act.

(3) Each of the First-tier Tribunal, and the Upper Tribunal, is to consist of its judges and other members.

(4) The Senior President of Tribunals is to preside over both of the First-tier Tribunal and the Upper Tribunal.

(5) The Upper Tribunal is to be a superior court of record.

Commentary—*Simon's Taxes* **A5.611, A5.616**.

HMRC Manuals—Appeals, Reviews and Tribunals Manual ARTG8020 (composition of tribunals).

Members and composition of tribunals

4 Judges and other members of the First-tier Tribunal

(1) A person is a judge of the First-tier Tribunal if the person—

    (*a*) is a judge of the First-tier Tribunal by virtue of appointment under paragraph 1(1) of Schedule 2,

    (*b*) is a transferred-in judge of the First-tier Tribunal (see section 31(2)),

    (*c*) is a judge of the Upper Tribunal,

    [(*ca*) is within section 6A,][1]

    (*d*) is a member of the Asylum and Immigration Tribunal appointed under paragraph 2(1)(*a*) to (*d*) of Schedule 4 to the Nationality, Immigration and Asylum Act 2002 (c 41) (legally qualified members) and is not a judge of the Upper Tribunal, or

    (*e*) is a member of a panel of [Employment Judges][1] of employment tribunals.

(2) A person is also a judge of the First-tier Tribunal, but only as regards functions of the tribunal in relation to appeals such as are mentioned in subsection (1) of section 5 of the Criminal Injuries Compensation Act 1995 (c 53), if the person is an adjudicator appointed under that section by the Scottish Ministers.

(3) A person is one of the other members of the First-tier Tribunal if the person—

    (*a*) is a member of the First-tier Tribunal by virtue of appointment under paragraph 2(1) of Schedule 2,

    (*b*) is a transferred-in other member of the First-tier Tribunal (see section 31(2)),

    (*c*) is one of the other members of the Upper Tribunal, or

    (*d*) is a member of a panel of members of employment tribunals that is not a panel of [Employment Judges][1] of employment tribunals.

(4) Schedule 2—

contains provision for the appointment of persons to be judges or other members of the First-tier Tribunal, and

makes further provision in connection with judges and other members of the First-tier Tribunal.

Commentary—*Simon's Taxes* **A3.709**.

Amendments—[1]   Sub-s (1)(*ca*) inserted, and in sub-ss (1)(*e*), (3)(*d*), words substituted for word "chairmen" by the Crime and Courts Act 2013 s 21, Sch 14 paras 6, 7 with effect from 1 October 2013 (by virtue of SI 2013/2200).

5 Judges and other members of the Upper Tribunal

(1) A person is a judge of the Upper Tribunal if the person—

(*a*)   is the Senior President of Tribunals,

(*b*)   is a judge of the Upper Tribunal by virtue of appointment under paragraph 1(1) of Schedule 3,

(*c*)   is a transferred-in judge of the Upper Tribunal (see section 31(2)),

(*d*)   is a member of the Asylum and Immigration Tribunal appointed under paragraph 2(1)(*a*) to (*d*) of Schedule 4 to the Nationality, Immigration and Asylum Act 2002 (c 41) (legally qualified members) who—

(i)   is the President or a Deputy President of that tribunal, or

(ii)   has the title Senior Immigration Judge but is neither the President nor a Deputy President of that tribunal,

(*e*)   is the Chief Social Security Commissioner, or any other Social Security Commissioner, appointed under section 50(1) of the Social Security Administration (Northern Ireland) Act 1992 (c 8),

(*f*)   is a Social Security Commissioner appointed under section 50(2) of that Act (deputy Commissioners),

(*g*)   is within section 6(1),

(*h*)   is a deputy judge of the Upper Tribunal (whether under paragraph 7 of Schedule 3 or under section 31(2)), or

(*i*)   is a Chamber President or a Deputy Chamber President, whether of a chamber of the Upper Tribunal or of a chamber of the First-tier Tribunal, and does not fall within any of paragraphs (*a*) to (*h*).

(2) A person is one of the other members of the Upper Tribunal if the person—

(*a*)   is a member of the Upper Tribunal by virtue of appointment under paragraph 2(1) of Schedule 3,

(*b*)   is a transferred-in other member of the Upper Tribunal (see section 31(2)),

(*c*)   is a member of the Employment Appeal Tribunal appointed under section 22(1)(*c*) of the Employment Tribunals Act 1996 (c 17), or

(*d*)   is a member of the Asylum and Immigration Tribunal appointed under paragraph 2(1)(*e*) of Schedule 4 to the Nationality, Immigration and Asylum Act 2002 (members other than "legally qualified members").

(3) Schedule 3—

contains provision for the appointment of persons to be judges (including deputy judges), or other members, of the Upper Tribunal, and

makes further provision in connection with judges and other members of the Upper Tribunal.

6 Certain judges who are also judges of First-tier Tribunal and Upper Tribunal

(1) A person is within this subsection (and so, by virtue of sections 4(1)(*c*) and 5(1)(*g*), is a judge of the First-tier Tribunal and of the Upper Tribunal) if the person—

[(*za*)   is the Lord Chief Justice of England and Wales,

(*zb*)   is the Master of the Rolls,

(*zc*)   is the President of the Queen's Bench Division of the High Court in England and Wales,

(*zd*)   is the President of the Family Division of the High Court in England and Wales,

(*ze*)   is the Chancellor of the High Court in England and Wales,][1]

(*a*)   is an ordinary judge of the Court of Appeal in England and Wales (including the vice-president, if any, of either division of that Court),

(*b*)   is a Lord Justice of Appeal in Northern Ireland,

(*c*)   is a judge of the Court of Session,

[(*da*)   is a deputy judge of the High Court in England and Wales,

(*db*)   is the Judge Advocate General,][1]

(*d*)   is a puisne judge of the High Court in England and Wales or Northern Ireland,

(*e*)   is a circuit judge,

[(*ea*)   is a Recorder,][2]

(*f*)   is a sheriff in Scotland,

(*g*)   is a county court judge in Northern Ireland,

(*h*)   is a district judge in England and Wales or Northern Ireland, . . .[2]

(*i*)   is a District Judge (Magistrates' Courts).

[(*j*)   is the President of Employment Tribunals (England and Wales), (*k*)   is the President of Employment Tribunals (Scotland),

(*l*)   is the Vice President of Employment Tribunals (Scotland), or

(*m*) is a Regional Employment Judge.][2]

(2) References in subsection (1)(*c*) to (*i*) to office-holders do not include deputies or temporary office-holders.

Amendments—[1]   Sub-s (1)(*za*)–(*ze*), (*da*), (*db*) inserted by the Crime and Courts Act 2013 s 21, Sch 14 paras 6, 8 with effect from 1 October 2013 (by virtue of SI 2013/2200).

[2]   Sub-s (1)(*ea*), (*j*)–(*m*) inserted, and word "or" at end of sub-s (1)(*h*) repealed, by the Courts and Tribunals (Judiciary and Functions of Staff) Act 2018 s 1(2) with effect from 20 February 2019.

[6A   Certain judges who are also judges of the First-tier Tribunal

A person is within this section (and so, by virtue of section 4(1)(ca), is a judge of the First-tier Tribunal) if the person—

(*a*)   is a deputy Circuit judge,

(*b*)   . . . [2]

(*c*)   is a person who holds an office listed—

     (i)   in the first column of the table in section 89(3C) of the Senior Courts Act 1981 (senior High Court Masters etc), or

     (ii) in column 1 of Part 2 of Schedule 2 to that Act (High Court Masters etc),

(*d*)   is a deputy district judge appointed under section 102 of that Act or section 8 of the County Courts Act 1984,

(*e*)   is a Deputy District Judge (Magistrates' Courts), or

(*f*)   is a person appointed under section 30(1)(*a*) or (*b*) of the Courts-Martial (Appeals) Act 1951 (assistants to the Judge Advocate General).][1]

Amendments—[1]   Section 6A inserted by the Crime and Courts Act 2013 s 21, Sch 14 paras 6, 9 with effect from 1 October 2013 (by virtue of SI 2013/2200).

[2]   Sub-s (1)(*b*) repealed by the Courts and Tribunals (Judiciary and Functions of Staff) Act 2018 s 1(3) with effect from 20 February 2019.

7   Chambers: jurisdiction and Presidents

(1) The Lord Chancellor may, with the concurrence of the Senior President of Tribunals, by order make provision for the organisation of each of the First-tier Tribunal and the Upper Tribunal into a number of chambers.

(2) There is—

(*a*)   for each chamber of the First-tier Tribunal, and

(*b*)   for each chamber of the Upper Tribunal,

to be a person, or two persons, to preside over that chamber.

[(3) A person may at a particular time—

(*a*)   preside over more than one chamber of the First-tier Tribunal;

(*b*)   preside over more than one chamber of the Upper Tribunal;

(*c*)   preside over—

     (i)   one or more chambers of the First-tier Tribunal, and

     (ii) one or more chambers of the Upper Tribunal.][2]

(4) A person appointed under this section to preside over a chamber is to be known as a Chamber President.

(5) Where two persons are appointed under this section to preside over the same chamber, any reference in an enactment to the Chamber President of the chamber is a reference to a person appointed under this section to preside over the chamber.

(6) The Senior President of Tribunals may (consistently with [subsection (2)][2]) appoint a person who is the Chamber President of a chamber to preside instead, or to preside also, over another chamber.

(7) The [Senior President of Tribunals][1] may (consistently with [subsection (2)][2]) appoint a person who is not a Chamber President to preside over a chamber.

(8) Schedule 4 (eligibility for appointment under subsection (7), appointment of Deputy Chamber Presidents and Acting Chamber Presidents, assignment of judges and other members of the First-tier Tribunal and Upper Tribunal, and further provision about Chamber Presidents and chambers) has effect.

(9) Each of the Lord Chancellor and the Senior President of Tribunals may, with the concurrence of the other, by order—

(*a*)   make provision for the allocation of the First-tier Tribunal's functions between its chambers;

(*b*)   make provision for the allocation of the Upper Tribunal's functions between its chambers;

(*c*)   amend or revoke any order made under this subsection.

Commentary—*Simon's Taxes* **A3.704**.

Orders—First-tier Tribunal and Upper Tribunal (Chambers) (Amendment) Order, SI 2009/196 (*note: revoked except for art 9 transitional provisions*).

First-tier Tribunal and Upper Tribunal (Chambers) Order, SI 2010/2655.

First-tier Tribunal and Upper Tribunal (Chambers) (Amendment) Order 2011, SI 2011/2342.

First-tier Tribunal and Upper Tribunal (Chambers) (Amendment) Order, SI 2012/1673,

First-tier Tribunal and Upper Tribunal (Chambers) (Amendment) Order, SI 2013/1187.
First-tier Tribunal and Upper Tribunal (Chambers) (Amendment No 2) Order, SI 2013/2068.
First-tier Tribunal and Upper Tribunal (Chambers) (Amendment) Order, SI 2014/1901.
First-tier Tribunal and Upper Tribunal (Chambers) (Amendment) Order, SI 2015/1563.
First-tier Tribunal and Upper Tribunal (Chambers) (Amendment) Order, SI 2017/722.
First-tier Tribunal and Upper Tribunal (Chambers) (Amendment No 2) Order, SI 2017/1169.
First-tier Tribunal and Upper Tribunal (Chambers) (Amendment) Order, SI 2018/509.
First-tier Tribunal and Upper Tribunal (Chambers) (Amendment) Order, SI 2020/137.

Amendments—[1]   In sub-s (7), words substituted for words "Lord Chancellor" by the Crime and Courts Act 2013 s 20, Sch 13 paras 42, 43 with effect from 1 October 2013 (by virtue of SI 2013/2200).

[2]   Sub-s (3) substituted, and in sub-ss (6) and (7) words substituted for words "subsections (2) and (3)", by the Courts and Tribunals (Judiciary and Functions of Staff) Act 2018 s 1(4) with effect from 20 February 2019.

8 Senior President of Tribunals: power to delegate

(1) The Senior President of Tribunals may delegate any function he has in his capacity as Senior President of Tribunals—

    (*a*) to any judge, or other member, of the Upper Tribunal or First-tier Tribunal;

    (*b*) to staff appointed under section 40(1).

[(1A) A function under paragraph 1(1) or 2(1) of Schedule 2 may be delegated under subsection (1) only to a Chamber President of a chamber of the Upper Tribunal.][1]

(2) Subsection (1) does not apply to functions of the Senior President of Tribunals [under any of the following—

    section 7(7);

    section 7(9);

    [section 29B;][2]

    [section 29D;;][2]

    paragraph 2(1) of Schedule 3;

    paragraph 7(1) of Schedule 3;

    paragraph 2 of Schedule 4;

    paragraph 5(1) and (3) of Schedule 4;

    paragraph 5(5) to (8) of Schedule 4;

    paragraph 5A(2)(a) of Schedule 4;

    paragraph 5A(3)(a) of Schedule 4;

    [paragraph 3 of Schedule 5.][2]][1]

(3) A delegation under subsection (1) is not revoked by the delegator's becoming incapacitated.

(4) Any delegation under subsection (1) that is in force immediately before a person ceases to be Senior President of Tribunals continues in force until varied or revoked by a subsequent holder of the office of Senior President of Tribunals.

(5) The delegation under this section of a function shall not prevent the exercise of the function by the Senior President of Tribunals.

Amendments—[1]   Sub-s (1A) inserted, and in sub-s (2), words substituted for words "under section 7(9)" by the Crime and Courts Act 2013 s 20, Sch 13 paras 42, 44(1), (2) with effect from 1 October 2013 (by virtue of SI 2013/2200).

[2]   In sub-s (2), entries inserted by the Courts and Tribunals (Judiciary and Functions of Staff) Act 2018 s 3, Schedule paras 39, 40 with effect from 6 April 2020 (by virtue of SI 2020/24 reg 3(*b*)).

Review of decisions and appeals

9 Review of decision of First-tier Tribunal

(1) The First-tier Tribunal may review a decision made by it on a matter in a case, other than a decision that is an excluded decision for the purposes of section 11(1) (but see subsection (9)).

(2) The First-tier Tribunal's power under subsection (1) in relation to a decision is exercisable—

    (*a*) of its own initiative, or

    (*b*) on application by a person who for the purposes of section 11(2) has a right of appeal in respect of the decision.

(3) Tribunal Procedure Rules may—

    (*a*) provide that the First-tier Tribunal may not under subsection (1) review (whether of its own initiative or on application under subsection (2)(*b*)) a decision of a description specified for the purposes of this paragraph in Tribunal Procedure Rules;

    (*b*) provide that the First-tier Tribunal's power under subsection (1) to review a decision of a description specified for the purposes of this paragraph in Tribunal Procedure Rules is exercisable only of the tribunal's own initiative;

    (*c*) provide that an application under subsection (2)(*b*) that is of a description specified for the purposes of this paragraph in Tribunal Procedure Rules may be made only on grounds specified for the purposes of this paragraph in Tribunal Procedure Rules;

    (*d*) provide, in relation to a decision of a description specified for the purposes of this paragraph in Tribunal Procedure Rules, that the First-tier Tribunal's power under subsection (1) to review the decision of its own initiative is exercisable only on grounds specified for the purposes of this paragraph in Tribunal Procedure Rules.

(4) Where the First-tier Tribunal has under subsection (1) reviewed a decision, the First-tier Tribunal may in the light of the review do any of the following—

    (*a*) correct accidental errors in the decision or in a record of the decision;

    (*b*) amend reasons given for the decision;

    (*c*) set the decision aside.

(5) Where under subsection (4)(*c*) the First-tier Tribunal sets a decision aside, the First-tier Tribunal must either—

    (*a*) re-decide the matter concerned, or

    (*b*) refer that matter to the Upper Tribunal.

(6) Where a matter is referred to the Upper Tribunal under subsection (5)(*b*), the Upper Tribunal must re-decide the matter.

(7) Where the Upper Tribunal is under subsection (6) re-deciding a matter, it may make any decision which the First-tier Tribunal could make if the First-tier Tribunal were re-deciding the matter.

(8) Where a tribunal is acting under subsection (5)(*a*) or (6), it may make such findings of fact as it considers appropriate.

(9) This section has effect as if a decision under subsection (4)(*c*) to set aside an earlier decision were not an excluded decision for the purposes of section 11(1), but the First-tier Tribunal's only power in the light of a review under subsection (1) of a decision under subsection (4)(*c*) is the power under subsection (4)(*a*).

(10) A decision of the First-tier Tribunal may not be reviewed under subsection (1) more than once, and once the First-tier Tribunal has decided that an earlier decision should not be reviewed under subsection (1) it may not then decide to review that earlier decision under that subsection.

(11) Where under this section a decision is set aside and the matter concerned is then re-decided, the decision set aside and the decision made in re-deciding the matter are for the purposes of subsection (10) to be taken to be different decisions.

Commentary—*Simon's Taxes* **A3.713, A5.610, A5.613, I11.343A.**

Rules—Tribunal Procedure (First-tier Tribunal) (Social Entitlement Chamber) Rules, SI 2008/2685.
Tribunal Procedure (First-tier Tribunal) (War Pensions and Armed Forces Compensation Chamber) Rules, SI 2008/2686.
Tribunal Procedure (First-tier Tribunal) (Health, Education and Social Care Chamber) Rules, SI 2008/2699.
Tribunal Procedure (First-tier Tribunal) (Tax Chamber) Rules, SI 2009/273.
Tribunal Procedure (First-tier Tribunal) (General Regulatory Chamber) Rules, SI 2009/1976.
Tribunal Procedure (Amendment) Rules, SI 2010/43.
Tribunal Procedure (Upper Tribunal) (Amendment) Rules, SI 2010/747.
Tribunal Procedure (First-tier Tribunal) (Property Chamber) Rules, SI 2013/1169.
Tribunal Procedure (First-tier Tribunal) (Immigration and Asylum Chamber) Rules, SI 2014/2604.

10 Review of decision of Upper Tribunal

(1) The Upper Tribunal may review a decision made by it on a matter in a case, other than a decision that is an excluded decision for the purposes of section 13(1) (but see subsection (7)).

(2) The Upper Tribunal's power under subsection (1) in relation to a decision is exercisable—

    (*a*) of its own initiative, or

    (*b*) on application by a person who for the purposes of section 13(2) has a right of appeal in respect of the decision.

(3) Tribunal Procedure Rules may—

    (*a*) provide that the Upper Tribunal may not under subsection (1) review (whether of its own initiative or on application under subsection (2)(*b*)) a decision of a description specified for the purposes of this paragraph in Tribunal Procedure Rules;

    (*b*) provide that the Upper Tribunal's power under subsection (1) to review a decision of a description specified for the purposes of this paragraph in Tribunal Procedure Rules is exercisable only of the tribunal's own initiative;

    (*c*) provide that an application under subsection (2)(*b*) that is of a description specified for the purposes of this paragraph in Tribunal Procedure Rules may be made only on grounds specified for the purposes of this paragraph in Tribunal Procedure Rules;

    (*d*) provide, in relation to a decision of a description specified for the purposes of this paragraph in Tribunal Procedure Rules, that the Upper Tribunal's power under subsection (1) to review the decision of its own initiative is exercisable only on grounds specified for the purposes of this paragraph in Tribunal Procedure Rules.

(4) Where the Upper Tribunal has under subsection (1) reviewed a decision, the Upper Tribunal may in the light of the review do any of the following—

    (*a*) correct accidental errors in the decision or in a record of the decision;

    (*b*) amend reasons given for the decision;

    (*c*) set the decision aside.

(5) Where under subsection (4)(*c*) the Upper Tribunal sets a decision aside, the Upper Tribunal must re-decide the matter concerned.

(6) Where the Upper Tribunal is acting under subsection (5), it may make such findings of fact as it considers appropriate.

(7) This section has effect as if a decision under subsection (4)(*c*) to set aside an earlier decision were not an excluded decision for the purposes of section 13(1), but the Upper Tribunal's only power in the light of a review under subsection (1) of a decision under subsection (4)(*c*) is the power under subsection (4)(*a*).

(8) A decision of the Upper Tribunal may not be reviewed under subsection (1) more than once, and once the Upper Tribunal has decided that an earlier decision should not be reviewed under subsection (1) it may not then decide to review that earlier decision under that subsection.

(9) Where under this section a decision is set aside and the matter concerned is then re-decided, the decision set aside and the decision made in re-deciding the matter are for the purposes of subsection (8) to be taken to be different decisions.

Commentary—*Simon's Taxes* A5.617, I11.352A.

Rules—Tribunal Procedure (Upper Tribunal) (Lands Chamber) Rules, SI 2010/2600.

11 Right to appeal to Upper Tribunal

(1) For the purposes of subsection (2), the reference to a right of appeal is to a right to appeal to the Upper Tribunal on any point of law arising from a decision made by the First-tier Tribunal other than an excluded decision.

(2) Any party to a case has a right of appeal, subject to subsection (8).

(3) That right may be exercised only with permission (or, in Northern Ireland, leave).

(4) Permission (or leave) may be given by—

    (*a*) the First-tier Tribunal, or

    (*b*) the Upper Tribunal,

on an application by the party.

(5) For the purposes of subsection (1), an "excluded decision" is—

    (*a*) any decision of the First-tier Tribunal on an appeal made in exercise of a right conferred by the Criminal Injuries Compensation Scheme in compliance with section 5(1)(*a*) of the Criminal Injuries Compensation Act 1995 (c 53) (appeals against decisions on reviews),

    [(*aa*) any decision of the First-tier Tribunal on an appeal made in exercise of a right conferred by the Victims of Overseas Terrorism Compensation Scheme in compliance with section 52(3) of the Crime and Security Act 2010,][1]

    (*b*) any decision of the First-tier Tribunal on an appeal under [section 27(3) or (5), 79(5) or (7) or 111(3) or (5) of the Data Protection Act 2018][4] (appeals against national security certificate),

    (*c*) any decision of the First-tier Tribunal on an appeal under section 60(1) or (4) of the Freedom of Information Act 2000 (c 36) (appeals against national security certificate),

    [(*ca*) any decision of the First-tier Tribunal under section 88, 89(3) or 92(3) of the Tax Collection and Management (Wales) Act 2016 (anaw 6) (approval for Welsh Revenue Authority to issue certain information notices),

    (*cb*) any decision of the First-tier Tribunal under section 108 of that Act (approval for Welsh Revenue Authority to inspect premises),][2]

    [(*cc*) any decision of the First-tier Tribunal under section 181E or 181F of that Act (appeals relating to postponement requests),][3]

    (*d*) a decision of the First-tier Tribunal under section 9—

        (i) to review, or not to review, an earlier decision of the tribunal,

        (ii) to take no action, or not to take any particular action, in the light of a review of an earlier decision of the tribunal,

        (iii) to set aside an earlier decision of the tribunal, or

        (iv) to refer, or not to refer, a matter to the Upper Tribunal,

    (*e*) a decision of the First-tier Tribunal that is set aside under section 9 (including a decision set aside after proceedings on an appeal under this section have been begun), or

    (*f*) any decision of the First-tier Tribunal that is of a description specified in an order made by the Lord Chancellor.

(6) A description may be specified under subsection (5)(*f*) only if—

    (*a*) in the case of a decision of that description, there is a right to appeal to a court, the Upper Tribunal or any other tribunal from the decision and that right is, or includes, something other than a right (however expressed) to appeal on any point of law arising from the decision, or

    (*b*) decisions of that description are made in carrying out a function transferred under section 30 and prior to the transfer of the function under section 30(1) there was no right to appeal from decisions of that description.

(7) Where—

    (*a*) an order under subsection (5)(*f*) specifies a description of decisions, and

    (*b*) decisions of that description are made in carrying out a function transferred under section 30,

the order must be framed so as to come into force no later than the time when the transfer under section 30 of the function takes effect (but power to revoke the order continues to be exercisable after that time, and power to amend the order continues to be exercisable after that time for the purpose of narrowing the description for the time being specified).

(8) The Lord Chancellor may by order make provision for a person to be treated as being, or to be treated as not being, a party to a case for the purposes of subsection (2).

Commentary—*Simon's Taxes* **A1.106, A5.601, A5.605, A5.611, A5.631, E8.1005, I11.351, I11.351A**.

HMRC Manuals—Business Income Manual BIM37045 (appeal to be a point of law).

Appeals, Reviews and Tribunals Manual ARTG8990 (HMRC does not accept the decision of the tribunal).

Orders—Appeals (Excluded Decisions) Order, SI 2009/275.

Tribunals, Courts and Enforcement Act 2007 (Miscellaneous Provisions) Order, SI 2010/41.

Amendments—[1]   Sub-s (5)(*aa*) inserted by the Crime and Security Act 2010 s 48(4), Sch 2 para 5 with effect from 8 April 2010 (Crime and Security Act 2010 s 59(2)(*b*)).

[2]   Sub-s (5)(*ca*), (*cb*) inserted by the Tax Collection and Management (Wales) Act 2016 s 116(1) with effect from 25 January 2018 (by virtue of SI 2018/33).

[3]   Sub-s (5)(*cc*) inserted by the Tax Collection and Management (Wales) Act 2016 s 181I(1) with effect from 1 April 2018 (by virtue of SI 2018/34).

[4]   In sub-s (5)(*b*), words substituted for words "section 28(4) or (6) of the Data Protection Act 1998 (c 29)" by the Data Protection Act 2018 s 211(1)(*a*), Sch 19 paras 130, 131 with effect from 25 May 2018 (by virtue of SI 2018/625 reg 2(1)(*g*)).

12 Proceedings on appeal to Upper Tribunal

(1) Subsection (2) applies if the Upper Tribunal, in deciding an appeal under section 11, finds that the making of the decision concerned involved the making of an error on a point of law.

(2) The Upper Tribunal—

    (*a*) may (but need not) set aside the decision of the First-tier Tribunal, and

    (*b*) if it does, must either—

        (i) remit the case to the First-tier Tribunal with directions for its reconsideration, or

        (ii) re-make the decision.

(3) In acting under subsection (2)(*b*)(i), the Upper Tribunal may also—

    (*a*) direct that the members of the First-tier Tribunal who are chosen to reconsider the case are not to be the same as those who made the decision that has been set aside;

    (*b*) give procedural directions in connection with the reconsideration of the case by the First-tier Tribunal.

(4) In acting under subsection (2)(*b*)(ii), the Upper Tribunal—

    (*a*) may make any decision which the First-tier Tribunal could make if the First-tier Tribunal were re-making the decision, and

    (*b*) may make such findings of fact as it considers appropriate.

Commentary—*Simon's Taxes* **A5.613, I11.351B**.

Commencement—Tribunals, Courts and Enforcement Act 2007 (Commencement No 6 and Transitional Provisions) Order, SI 2008/2696 art 5(*a*) (this section comes into force on 3 November 2008).

Modification—See the Mental Health Act 1983, s 78A (as inserted by SI 2008/2833, art 9(1), Sch 3, paras 39, 60) (in relation to the application with modifications of this section to appeals from the Mental Health Review Tribunal for Wales).

13 Right to appeal to Court of Appeal etc

(1) For the purposes of subsection (2), the reference to a right of appeal is to a right to appeal to the relevant appellate court on any point of law arising from a decision made by the Upper Tribunal other than an excluded decision.

(2) Any party to a case has a right of appeal, subject to subsection (14).

(3) That right may be exercised only with permission (or, in Northern Ireland, leave).

(4) Permission (or leave) may be given by—

    (*a*) the Upper Tribunal, or

    (*b*) the relevant appellate court,

on an application by the party.

(5) An application may be made under subsection (4) to the relevant appellate court only if permission (or leave) has been refused by the Upper Tribunal.

(6) The Lord Chancellor may, as respects an application under subsection (4) that falls within subsection (7) and for which the relevant appellate court is the Court of Appeal in England and Wales or the Court of Appeal in Northern Ireland, by order make provision for permission (or leave) not to be granted on the application unless the Upper Tribunal or (as the case may be) the relevant appellate court considers—

    (*a*) that the proposed appeal would raise some important point of principle or practice, or

    (*b*) that there is some other compelling reason for the relevant appellate court to hear the appeal.

[(6A) Rules of court may make provision for permission not to be granted on an application under subsection (4) to the Court of Session that falls within subsection (7) unless the court considers—

    (*a*) that the proposed appeal would raise some important point of principle [or practice][2], or

    (*b*) that there is some other compelling reason for the court to hear the appeal.][1]

(7) An application falls within this subsection if the application is for permission (or leave) to appeal from any decision of the Upper Tribunal on an appeal under section 11.

(8) For the purposes of subsection (1), an "excluded decision" is—

    (*a*) any decision of the Upper Tribunal on an appeal under [section 27(3) or (5), 79(5) or (7) or 111(3) or (5) of the Data Protection Act 2018][5] (appeals against national security certificate),

(b) any decision of the Upper Tribunal on an appeal under section 60(1) or (4) of the Freedom of Information Act 2000 (c 36) (appeals against national security certificate),

[(*ba*) any decision of the Upper Tribunal under section 88, 89(3) or 92(3) of the Tax Collection and Management (Wales) Act 2016 (anaw 6) (approval for Welsh Revenue Authority to issue certain information notices),

(*bb*) any decision of the Upper Tribunal under section 108 of that Act (approval for Welsh Revenue Authority to inspect premises),][3]

[(*bc*) any decision of the First-tier Tribunal under section 181E or 181F of that Act (appeals relating to postponement requests),][4]

(c) any decision of the Upper Tribunal on an application under section 11(4)(*b*) (application for permission or leave to appeal),

(d) a decision of the Upper Tribunal under section 10—

(i) to review, or not to review, an earlier decision of the tribunal,

(ii) to take no action, or not to take any particular action, in the light of a review of an earlier decision of the tribunal, or

(iii) to set aside an earlier decision of the tribunal,

(e) a decision of the Upper Tribunal that is set aside under section 10 (including a decision set aside after proceedings on an appeal under this section have been begun), or

(f) any decision of the Upper Tribunal that is of a description specified in an order made by the Lord Chancellor.

(9) A description may be specified under subsection (8)(*f*) only if—

(a) in the case of a decision of that description, there is a right to appeal to a court from the decision and that right is, or includes, something other than a right (however expressed) to appeal on any point of law arising from the decision, or

(b) decisions of that description are made in carrying out a function transferred under section 30 and prior to the transfer of the function under section 30(1) there was no right to appeal from decisions of that description.

(10) Where—

(a) an order under subsection (8)(*f*) specifies a description of decisions, and

(b) decisions of that description are made in carrying out a function transferred under section 30,

the order must be framed so as to come into force no later than the time when the transfer under section 30 of the function takes effect (but power to revoke the order continues to be exercisable after that time, and power to amend the order continues to be exercisable after that time for the purpose of narrowing the description for the time being specified).

(11) Before the Upper Tribunal decides an application made to it under subsection (4), the Upper Tribunal must specify the court that is to be the relevant appellate court as respects the proposed appeal.

(12) The court to be specified under subsection (11) in relation to a proposed appeal is whichever of the following courts appears to the Upper Tribunal to be the most appropriate—

(a) the Court of Appeal in England and Wales;

(b) the Court of Session;

(c) the Court of Appeal in Northern Ireland.

(13) In this section except subsection (11), "the relevant appellate court", as respects an appeal, means the court specified as respects that appeal by the Upper Tribunal under subsection (11).

(14) The Lord Chancellor may by order make provision for a person to be treated as being, or to be treated as not being, a party to a case for the purposes of subsection (2).

(15) Rules of court may make provision as to the time within which an application under subsection (4) to the relevant appellate court must be made.

Commentary—*Simon's Taxes* A5.617, I11.109, I11.315, I11.352B, I11.352C, I11.352D, I11.354, I11.355.

HMRC Manuals—Business Income Manual BIM37045 (appeal to be a point of law).

Compliance Handbook Manual CH182680 (approval by tribunal).

Orders—Appeals from the Upper Tribunal to the Court of Appeal Order, SI 2008/2834 (made under sub-s (6)).

Appeals (Excluded Decisions) Order, SI 2009/275 (made under sub-s (8)(*f*)).

Tribunals, Courts and Enforcement Act 2007 (Miscellaneous Provisions) Order, SI 2010/41 (made under sub-s (8)(f)).

Act of Sederunt (Rules of the Court of Session Amendment No 5) (Miscellaneous), SSI 2013/238 (made under sub-s (6A)).

Amendments—[1]   Sub-s (6A) inserted by the Crime and Courts Act 2013 s 23 with effect from 7 October 2013 (by virtue of SI 2013/1725, art 3(*b*)).

[2]   In sub-s (6A)(*a*), words inserted by the Criminal Justice and Courts Act 2015 s 83(2)with effect from 13 April 2015 (by virtue of SI 2015/778).

[3]   Sub-s (8)(*ba*), (*bb*) inserted by the Tax Collection and Management (Wales) Act 2016 s 116(2) with effect from 25 January 2018 (by virtue of SI 2018/33).

[4]   Sub-s (8)(*bc*) inserted by the Tax Collection and Management (Wales) Act 2016 s 181I(2) with effect from 1 April 2018 (by virtue of SI 2018/34).

[5]   In sub-s (8)(*a*), words substituted for words "section 28(4) or (6) of the Data Protection Act 1998 (c 29)" by the Data Protection Act 2018 s 211(1)(*a*), Sch 19 paras 130, 132 with effect from 25 May 2018 (by virtue of SI 2018/625 reg 2(1)(*g*)).

14 Proceedings on appeal to Court of Appeal etc

(1) Subsection (2) applies if the relevant appellate court, in deciding an appeal under section 13, finds that the making of the decision concerned involved the making of an error on a point of law.

(2) The relevant appellate court—

    (a) may (but need not) set aside the decision of the Upper Tribunal, and

    (b) if it does, must either—

        (i) remit the case to the Upper Tribunal or, where the decision of the Upper Tribunal was on an appeal or reference from another tribunal or some other person, to the Upper Tribunal or that other tribunal or person, with directions for its reconsideration, or

        (ii) re-make the decision.

(3) In acting under subsection (2)(b)(i), the relevant appellate court may also—

    (a) direct that the persons who are chosen to reconsider the case are not to be the same as those who—

        (i) where the case is remitted to the Upper Tribunal, made the decision of the Upper Tribunal that has been set aside, or

        (ii) where the case is remitted to another tribunal or person, made the decision in respect of which the appeal or reference to the Upper Tribunal was made;

    (b) give procedural directions in connection with the reconsideration of the case by the Upper Tribunal or other tribunal or person.

(4) In acting under subsection (2)(b)(ii), the relevant appellate court—

    (a) may make any decision which the Upper Tribunal could make if the Upper Tribunal were re-making the decision or (as the case may be) which the other tribunal or person could make if that other tribunal or person were re-making the decision, and

    (b) may make such findings of fact as it considers appropriate.

(5) Where—

    (a) under subsection (2)(b)(i) the relevant appellate court remits a case to the Upper Tribunal, and

    (b) the decision set aside under subsection (2)(a) was made by the Upper Tribunal on an appeal or reference from another tribunal or some other person,

the Upper Tribunal may (instead of reconsidering the case itself) remit the case to that other tribunal or person, with the directions given by the relevant appellate court for its reconsideration.

(6) In acting under subsection (5), the Upper Tribunal may also—

    (a) direct that the persons who are chosen to reconsider the case are not to be the same as those who made the decision in respect of which the appeal or reference to the Upper Tribunal was made;

    (b) give procedural directions in connection with the reconsideration of the case by the other tribunal or person.

(7) In this section "the relevant appellate court", as respects an appeal under section 13, means the court specified as respects that appeal by the Upper Tribunal under section 13(11).

Commentary—*Simon's Taxes* I11.352D.

[14A Appeal to Supreme Court: grant of certificate by Upper Tribunal

(1) If the Upper Tribunal is satisfied that—

    (a) the conditions in subsection (4) or (5) are fulfilled in relation to the Upper Tribunal's decision in any proceedings, and

    (b) as regards that decision, a sufficient case for an appeal to the Supreme Court has been made out to justify an application under section 14B,

the Upper Tribunal may grant a certificate to that effect.

(2) The Upper Tribunal may grant a certificate under this section only on an application made by a party to the proceedings.

(3) The Upper Tribunal may grant a certificate under this section only if the relevant appellate court as regards the proceedings is—

    (a) the Court of Appeal in England and Wales, or

    (b) Court of Appeal in Northern Ireland.

(4) The conditions in this subsection are that a point of law of general public importance is involved in the decision of the Upper Tribunal and that point of law is—

    (a) a point of law that—

        (i) relates wholly or mainly to the construction of an enactment or statutory instrument, and

        (ii) has been fully argued in the proceedings and fully considered in the judgment of the Upper Tribunal in the proceedings, or

    (b) a point of law—

        (i) in respect of which the Upper Tribunal is bound by a decision of the relevant appellate court or the Supreme Court in previous proceedings, and

        (ii) that was fully considered in the judgments given by the relevant appellate court or, as the case may be, the Supreme Court in those previous proceedings.

(5) The conditions in this subsection are that a point of law of general public importance is involved in the decision of the Upper Tribunal and that—

   (*a*) the proceedings entail a decision relating to a matter of national importance or consideration of such a matter,

   (*b*) the result of the proceedings is so significant (whether considered on its own or together with other proceedings or likely proceedings) that, in the opinion of the Upper Tribunal, a hearing by the Supreme Court is justified, or

   (*c*) the Upper Tribunal is satisfied that the benefits of earlier consideration by the Supreme Court outweigh the benefits of consideration by the Court of Appeal.

(6) Before the Upper Tribunal decides an application made to it under this section, the Upper Tribunal must specify the court that would be the relevant appellate court if the application were an application for permission (or leave) under section 13.

(7) In this section except subsection (6) and in sections 14B and 14C, "the relevant appellate court", as respects an application, means the court specified as respects that application by the Upper Tribunal under subsection (6).

(8) No appeal lies against the grant or refusal of a certificate under subsection (1).][1]

Amendments—[1] Sections 14A–14C inserted by the Criminal Justice and Courts Act 2015 s 64 with effect from 8 August 2016 (see SI 2016/717 art 3(a)).

[14B Appeal to Supreme Court: permission to appeal

(1) If the Upper Tribunal grants a certificate under section 14A in relation to any proceedings, a party to those proceedings may apply to the Supreme Court for permission to appeal directly to the Supreme Court.

(2) An application under subsection (1) must be made—

   (*a*) within one month from the date on which that certificate is granted, or

   (*b*) within such time as the Supreme Court may allow in a particular case.

(3) If on such an application it appears to the Supreme Court to be expedient to do so, the Supreme Court may grant permission for such an appeal.

(4) If permission is granted under this section—

   (*a*) no appeal from the decision to which the certificate relates lies to the relevant appellate court, but

   (*b*) an appeal lies from that decision to the Supreme Court.

(5) An application under subsection (1) is to be determined without a hearing.

(6) Subject to subsection (4), no appeal lies to the relevant appellate court from a decision of the Upper Tribunal in respect of which a certificate is granted under section 14A until—

   (*a*) the time within which an application can be made under subsection (1) has expired, and

   (*b*) where such an application is made, that application has been determined in accordance with this section.][1]

Amendments—[1] Sections 14A–14C inserted by the Criminal Justice and Courts Act 2015 s 64 with effect from 8 August 2016 (see SI 2016/717 art 3(a)).

[14C Appeal to Supreme Court: exclusions

(1) No certificate may be granted under section 14A in respect of a decision of the Upper Tribunal in any proceedings where, by virtue of any enactment (other than sections 14A and 14B), no appeal would lie from that decision of the Upper Tribunal to the relevant appellate court, with or without the permission (or leave) of the Upper Tribunal or the relevant appellate court.

(2) No certificate may be granted under section 14A in respect of a decision of the Upper Tribunal in any proceedings where, by virtue of any enactment, no appeal would lie from a decision of the relevant appellate court on that decision of the Upper Tribunal to the Supreme Court, with or without the permission (or leave) of the relevant appellate court or the Supreme Court.

(3) Where no appeal would lie to the relevant appellate court from the decision of the Upper Tribunal except with the permission (or leave) of the Upper Tribunal or the relevant appellate court, no certificate may be granted under section 14A in respect of a decision of the Upper Tribunal unless it appears to the Upper Tribunal that it would be a proper case for giving permission (or leave) to appeal to the relevant appellate court.

(4) No certificate may be granted under section 14A in respect of a decision or order of the Upper Tribunal made by it in the exercise of its jurisdiction to punish for contempt.][1]

Amendments—[1] Sections 14A–14C inserted by the Criminal Justice and Courts Act 2015 s 64 with effect from 8 August 2016 (see SI 2016/717 art 3(a)).

"Judicial review"

15 Upper Tribunal's "judicial review" jurisdiction

(1) The Upper Tribunal has power, in cases arising under the law of England and Wales or under the law of Northern Ireland, to grant the following kinds of relief—

   (*a*) a mandatory order;

   (*b*) a prohibiting order;

   (*c*) a quashing order;

    (*d*) a declaration;

    (*e*) an injunction.

(2) The power under subsection (1) may be exercised by the Upper Tribunal if—

    (*a*) certain conditions are met (see section 18), or

    (*b*) the tribunal is authorised to proceed even though not all of those conditions are met (see section 19(3) and (4)).

(3) Relief under subsection (1) granted by the Upper Tribunal—

    (*a*) has the same effect as the corresponding relief granted by the High Court on an application for judicial review, and

    (*b*) is enforceable as if it were relief granted by the High Court on an application for judicial review.

(4) In deciding whether to grant relief under subsection (1)(*a*), (*b*) or (*c*), the Upper Tribunal must apply the principles that the High Court would apply in deciding whether to grant that relief on an application for judicial review.

(5) In deciding whether to grant relief under subsection (1)(*d*) or (*e*), the Upper Tribunal must—

    (*a*) in cases arising under the law of England and Wales apply the principles that the High Court would apply in deciding whether to grant that relief under section 31(2) of the Supreme Court Act 1981 (c 54) on an application for judicial review, and

    (*b*) in cases arising under the law of Northern Ireland apply the principles that the High Court would apply in deciding whether to grant that relief on an application for judicial review.

[(5A) In cases arising under the law of England and Wales, subsections (2A) and (2B) of section 31 of the Senior Courts Act 1981 apply to the Upper Tribunal when deciding whether to grant relief under subsection (1) as they apply to the High Court when deciding whether to grant relief on an application for judicial review.

(5B) If the tribunal grants relief in reliance on section 31(2B) of the Senior Courts Act 1981 as applied by subsection (5A), the tribunal must certify that the condition in section 31(2B) as so applied is satisfied.][1]

(6) For the purposes of the application of subsection (3)(*a*) in relation to cases arising under the law of Northern Ireland—

    (*a*) a mandatory order under subsection (1)(*a*) shall be taken to correspond to an order of mandamus,

    (*b*) a prohibiting order under subsection (1)(*b*) shall be taken to correspond to an order of prohibition, and

    (*c*) a quashing order under subsection (1)(*c*) shall be taken to correspond to an order of certiorari.

Commentary—*Simon's Taxes* A3.706, A5.611.

Amendments—[1] Sub-ss (5A), (5B) inserted by the Criminal Justice and Courts Act 2015 s 84(4) with effect from 8 August 2016 (SI 2016/717 art 3(c)).

16 Application for relief under section 15(1)

(1) This section applies in relation to an application to the Upper Tribunal for relief under section 15(1).

(2) The application may be made only if permission (or, in a case arising under the law of Northern Ireland, leave) to make it has been obtained from the tribunal.

(3) The tribunal may not grant permission (or leave) to make the application unless it considers that the applicant has a sufficient interest in the matter to which the application relates.

[(3C) In cases arising under the law of England and Wales, when considering whether to grant permission to make the application, the tribunal—

    (a) may of its own initiative consider whether the outcome for the applicant would have been substantially different if the conduct complained of had not occurred, and

    (b) must consider that question if the respondent asks it to do so.

(3D) In subsection (3C) "the conduct complained of" means the conduct (or alleged conduct) of the respondent that the applicant claims justifies the tribunal in granting relief.

(3E) If, on considering the question mentioned in subsection (3C)(a) and (b), it appears to the tribunal to be highly likely that the outcome for the applicant would not have been substantially different, the tribunal must refuse to grant permission.

(3F) The tribunal may disregard the requirement in subsection (3E) if it considers that it is appropriate to do so for reasons of exceptional public interest.

(3G) If the tribunal grants permission in reliance on subsection (3F), the tribunal must certify that the condition in subsection (3F) is satisfied.][1]

(4) Subsection (5) applies where the tribunal considers—

    (a) that there has been undue delay in making the application, and

    (b) that granting the relief sought on the application would be likely to cause substantial hardship to, or substantially prejudice the rights of, any person or would be detrimental to good administration.

(5) The tribunal may—

    (a) refuse to grant permission (or leave) for the making of the application;

(*b*) refuse to grant any relief sought on the application.

(6) The tribunal may award to the applicant damages, restitution or the recovery of a sum due if—

(*a*) the application includes a claim for such an award arising from any matter to which the application relates, and

(*b*) the tribunal is satisfied that such an award would have been made by the High Court if the claim had been made in an action begun in the High Court by the applicant at the time of making the application.

[(6A) In cases arising under the law of England and Wales, subsections (2A) and (2B) of section 31 of the Senior Courts Act 1981 apply to the Upper Tribunal as regards the making of an award under subsection (6) as they apply to the High Court as regards the making of an award under section 31(4) of the Senior Courts Act 1981.

(6B)If the tribunal makes an award in reliance on section 31(2B) of the Senior Courts Act 1981 as applied by subsection (6A), the tribunal must certify that the condition in section 31(2B) as so applied is satisfied.]¹

(7) An award under subsection (6) may be enforced as if it were an award of the High Court.

(8) Where—

(*a*) the tribunal refuses to grant permission (or leave) to apply for relief under section 15(1),

(*b*) the applicant appeals against that refusal, and

(*c*) the Court of Appeal grants the permission (or leave),

the Court of Appeal may go on to decide the application for relief under section 15(1).

(9) Subsections (4) and (5) do not prevent Tribunal Procedure Rules from limiting the time within which applications may be made.

Commentary—*Simon's Taxes* **A5.301A**.

Rules—Tribunal Procedure (Upper Tribunal) Rules, SI 2008/2698 (made under sub-s (9)).

Tribunal Procedure (Amendment) Rules, SI 2009/274 (made under sub-s (9)).

Tribunal Procedure (Upper Tribunal) (Lands Chamber) Rules, SI 2010/2600 (made under sub-s (9)).

Amendments—¹ Sub-ss (3C)–(3G), (6A), (6B) inserted by the Criminal Justice and Courts Act 2015 s 84(5), (6) with effect from 8 August 2016 (SI 2016/717 art 3(3)).

Prospective amendments—In sub-s (3), text following the word "unless" to be designated para (*a*), para (*b*) and preceding word ", and" to be inserted, and sub-ss (3A), (3B) to be inserted, by the Criminal Justice and Courts Act 2015 s 85(3), (4) with effect from a date to be appointed. Para (*b*) as inserted to read as follows—

"(*b*) in cases arising under the law of England and Wales, the applicant has provided the tribunal with any information about the financing of the application that is specified in Tribunal Procedure Rules for the purposes of this paragraph.".

Sub-ss (3A), (3B) as inserted to read as follows—

"(3A) The information that may be specified for the purposes of subsection (3)(b) includes—

(a) information about the source, nature and extent of financial resources available, or likely to be available, to the applicant to meet liabilities arising in connection with the application, and

(b) if the applicant is a body corporate that is unable to demonstrate that it is likely to have financial resources available to meet such liabilities, information about its members and about their ability to provide financial support for the purposes of the application.

(3B) Tribunal Procedure Rules under subsection (3)(b) that specify information identifying those who are, or are likely to be, sources of financial support must provide that only a person whose financial support (whether direct or indirect) exceeds, or is likely to exceed, a level set out in the rules has to be identified.

This subsection does not apply to rules that specify information described in subsection (3A)(b).".

17 Quashing orders under section 15(1): supplementary provision

(1) If the Upper Tribunal makes a quashing order under section 15(1)(*c*) in respect of a decision, it may in addition—

(*a*) remit the matter concerned to the court, tribunal or authority that made the decision, with a direction to reconsider the matter and reach a decision in accordance with the findings of the Upper Tribunal, or

(*b*) substitute its own decision for the decision in question.

(2) The power conferred by subsection (1)(*b*) is exercisable only if—

(*a*) the decision in question was made by a court or tribunal,

(*b*) the decision is quashed on the ground that there has been an error of law, and

(*c*) without the error, there would have been only one decision that the court or tribunal could have reached.

(3) Unless the Upper Tribunal otherwise directs, a decision substituted by it under subsection (1)(*b*) has effect as if it were a decision of the relevant court or tribunal.

18 Limits of jurisdiction under section 15(1)

(1) This section applies where an application made to the Upper Tribunal seeks (whether or not alone)—

(*a*) relief under section 15(1), or

(*b*) permission (or, in a case arising under the law of Northern Ireland, leave) to apply for relief under section 15(1).

(2) If Conditions 1 to 4 are met, the tribunal has the function of deciding the application.

(3) If the tribunal does not have the function of deciding the application, it must by order transfer the application to the High Court.

(4) Condition 1 is that the application does not seek anything other than—

    (a) relief under section 15(1);

    (b) permission (or, in a case arising under the law of Northern Ireland, leave) to apply for relief under section 15(1);

    (c) an award under section 16(6);

    (d) interest;

    (e) costs.

(5) Condition 2 is that the application does not call into question anything done by the Crown Court.

(6) Condition 3 is that the application falls within a class specified for the purposes of this subsection in a direction given in accordance with Part 1 of Schedule 2 to the Constitutional Reform Act 2005 (c 4).

(7) The power to give directions under subsection (6) includes—

    (a) power to vary or revoke directions made in exercise of the power, and

    (b) power to make different provision for different purposes.

(8) Condition 4 is that the judge presiding at the hearing of the application is either—

    (a) a judge of the High Court or the Court of Appeal in England and Wales or Northern Ireland, or a judge of the Court of Session, or

    (b) such other persons as may be agreed from time to time between the Lord Chief Justice, the Lord President, or the Lord Chief Justice of Northern Ireland, as the case may be, and the Senior President of Tribunals.

(9) Where the application is transferred to the High Court under subsection (3)—

    (a) the application is to be treated for all purposes as if it—

        (i) had been made to the High Court, and

        (ii) sought things corresponding to those sought from the tribunal, and

    (b) any steps taken, permission (or leave) given or orders made by the tribunal in relation to the application are to be treated as taken, given or made by the High Court.

(10) Rules of court may make provision for the purpose of supplementing subsection (9).

(11) The provision that may be made by Tribunal Procedure Rules about amendment of an application for relief under section 15(1) includes, in particular, provision about amendments that would cause the application to become transferable under subsection (3).

(12) For the purposes of subsection (9)(a)(ii), in relation to an application transferred to the High Court in Northern Ireland—

    (a) an order of mandamus shall be taken to correspond to a mandatory order under section 15(1)(a),

    (b) an order of prohibition shall be taken to correspond to a prohibiting order under section 15(1)(b), and

    (c) an order of certiorari shall be taken to correspond to a quashing order under section 15(1)(c).

Commentary—*Simon's Taxes* A5.301A, A5.614, I11.373.

Rules—Tribunal Procedure (Upper Tribunal) (Amendment) Rules, SI 2011/2343 (made under sub-s (11)).

19 Transfer of judicial review applications from High Court

(1) Section 31A inserted into the Supreme Court Act 1981 (c 54)

(2) Section 25A inserted into the Judicature (Northern Ireland) Act 1978 (c 23)

(3) Where an application is transferred to the Upper Tribunal under 31A of the Supreme Court Act 1981 (c 54) or section 25A of the Judicature (Northern Ireland) Act 1978 (transfer from the High Court of judicial review applications)—

    (a) the application is to be treated for all purposes as if it—

        (i) had been made to the tribunal, and

        (ii) sought things corresponding to those sought from the High Court,

    (b) the tribunal has the function of deciding the application, even if it does not fall within a class specified under section 18(6), and

    (c) any steps taken, permission given, leave given or orders made by the High Court in relation to the application are to be treated as taken, given or made by the tribunal.

(4) Where—

    (a) an application for permission is transferred to the Upper Tribunal under section 31A of the Supreme Court Act 1981 (c 54) and the tribunal grants permission, or

    (b) an application for leave is transferred to the Upper Tribunal under section 25A of the Judicature (Northern Ireland) Act 1978 (c 23) and the tribunal grants leave,

the tribunal has the function of deciding any subsequent application brought under the permission or leave, even if the subsequent application does not fall within a class specified under section 18(6).

(5) Tribunal Procedure Rules may make further provision for the purposes of supplementing subsections (3) and (4).

(6) For the purposes of subsection (3)(*a*)(ii), in relation to an application transferred to the Upper Tribunal under section 25A of the Judicature (Northern Ireland) Act 1978—

    (*a*) a mandatory order under section 15(1)(*a*) shall be taken to correspond to an order of mandamus,

    (*b*) a prohibiting order under section 15(1)(*b*) shall be taken to correspond to an order of prohibition, and

    (*c*) a quashing order under section 15(1)(*c*) shall be taken to correspond to an order of certiorari.

Commentary—*Simon's Taxes* A5.301A.

Rules—Tribunal Procedure (Upper Tribunal) (Amendment) Rules, SI 2011/2343 (made under sub-s (5)).

20 Transfer of judicial review applications from the Court of Session

(1) Where an application is made to the supervisory jurisdiction of the Court of Session, the Court—

    (*a*) must, if Conditions 1 [and 2 are met, and]²[. . .

    (*aa*) ¹ . . . ²

    (*b*) may, if Conditions 1 [and 3] are met, but Condition 2 is not,

by order transfer the application to the Upper Tribunal.

(2) Condition 1 is that the application does not seek anything other than an exercise of the supervisory jurisdiction of the Court of Session.

(3) Condition 2 is that the application falls within a class specified for the purposes of this subsection by act of sederunt made with the consent of the Lord Chancellor.

(4) Condition 3 is that the subject matter of the application is not a devolved Scottish matter.

(5) . . . ²

(5A) . . . ²

(6) There may not be specified under subsection (3) any class of application which includes an application the subject matter of which is a devolved Scottish matter.

(7) For the purposes of this section, the subject matter of an application is a devolved Scottish matter if it—

    (*a*) concerns the exercise of functions in or as regards Scotland, and

    (*b*) does not relate to a reserved matter within the meaning of the Scotland Act 1998 (c 46).

(8) In subsection (2), the reference to the exercise of the supervisory jurisdiction of the Court of Session includes a reference to the making of any order in connection with or in consequence of the exercise of that jurisdiction.

Orders—Act of Sederunt (Transfer of Judicial Review Applications from the Court of Session), SSI 2008/357 (made under sub-s (3)).

Amendments—¹ Sub-s (1)(*aa*) substituted for word "and" at the end of sub-s (1)(*a*), sub-s 5A inserted by the Borders, Citizenship and Immigration Act 2007 s 53(3) with effect from 8 August 2011 (by virtue of SI 2011/1741

² In sub-s (1)(*a*), words substituted for words ", 2 and 4 are met", sub-ss (1)(*aa*), (5), (5A) repealed, and in sub-s (1)(*b*), words substituted for words ", 3 and 4" by the Crime and Courts Act 2013 s 22(2) with effect from 7 October 2013 (by virtue of SI 2013/1725, art 3(*b*)).

[20A Procedural steps where application transferred

(1) This section applies where the Court of Session transfers an application under section 20(1).

(2) It is for the Upper Tribunal to determine—

    (*a*) whether the application has been made timeously, and

    (*b*) whether to grant permission for the application to proceed under section 27B of the Court of Session Act 1988 ("the 1988 Act") (requirement for permission).

(3) Accordingly—

    (*a*) the Upper Tribunal has the same powers in relation to the application as the Court of Session would have had in relation to it under sections 27A to 27C of the 1988 Act,

    (*b*) sections 27C and 27D of that Act apply in relation to a decision of the Upper Tribunal under section 27B(1) of that Act as they apply in relation to such a decision of the Court of Session.

(4) The references in section 27C(3) and (4) of the 1988 Act (oral hearings where permission refused) to a different Lord Ordinary from the one who granted or refused permission are to be read as references to different members of the Tribunal from those of whom it was composed when it refused or granted permission.]¹

Amendments—¹ Section 20A inserted by the Courts Reform (Scotland) Act 2014 (Consequential Provisions and Modifications) Order, SI 2015/700 art 7 with effect from 22 September 2015 (being the same day as the Courts Reform (Scotland) Act 2014 s 89 came into force (by virtue of SSI 2015/247 art 2, Schedule): see SI 2015/700 arts 1, 8.

21 Upper Tribunal's "judicial review" jurisdiction: Scotland

(1) The Upper Tribunal has the function of deciding applications transferred to it from the Court of Session under section 20(1).

(2) The powers of review of the Upper Tribunal in relation to such applications are the same as the powers of review of the Court of Session in an application to the supervisory jurisdiction of that Court.

(3) In deciding an application by virtue of subsection (1), the Upper Tribunal must apply principles that the Court of Session would apply in deciding an application to the supervisory jurisdiction of that Court.

(4) An order of the Upper Tribunal by virtue of subsection (1)—

    (*a*) has the same effect as the corresponding order granted by the Court of Session on an application to the supervisory jurisdiction of that Court, and

    (*b*) is enforceable as if it were an order so granted by that Court.

(5) Where an application is transferred to the Upper Tribunal by virtue of section 20(1), any steps taken or orders made by the Court of Session in relation to the application (other than the order to transfer the application under section 20(1)) are to be treated as taken or made by the tribunal.

(6) Tribunal Procedure Rules may make further provision for the purposes of supplementing subsection (5).

Miscellaneous

22 Tribunal Procedure Rules

(1) There are to be rules, to be called "Tribunal Procedure Rules", governing—

    (*a*) the practice and procedure to be followed in the First-tier Tribunal, and

    (*b*) the practice and procedure to be followed in the Upper Tribunal.

(2) Tribunal Procedure Rules are to be made by the Tribunal Procedure Committee.

(3) In Schedule 5—

    Part 1 makes further provision about the content of Tribunal Procedure Rules,

    Part 2 makes provision about the membership of the Tribunal Procedure Committee,

    Part 3 makes provision about the making of Tribunal Procedure Rules by the Committee, and

    Part 4 confers power to amend legislation in connection with Tribunal Procedure Rules.

(4) Power to make Tribunal Procedure Rules is to be exercised with a view to securing—

    (*a*) that, in proceedings before the First-tier Tribunal and Upper Tribunal, justice is done,

    (*b*) that the tribunal system is accessible and fair,

    (*c*) that proceedings before the First-tier Tribunal or Upper Tribunal are handled quickly and efficiently,

    (*d*) that the rules are both simple and simply expressed, and

    (*e*) that the rules where appropriate confer on members of the First-tier Tribunal, or Upper Tribunal, responsibility for ensuring that proceedings before the tribunal are handled quickly and efficiently.

(5) In subsection (4)(*b*) "the tribunal system" means the system for deciding matters within the jurisdiction of the First-tier Tribunal or the Upper Tribunal.

Commentary—*Simon's Taxes* A3.711.

Rules—Tribunal Procedure (First-tier Tribunal) (Social Entitlement Chamber) Rules, SI 2008/2685.
Tribunal Procedure (First-tier Tribunal) (War Pensions and Armed Forces Compensation Chamber) Rules, SI 2008/2686.
Tribunal Procedure (First-tier Tribunal) (Social Entitlement Chamber) Rules, SI 2008/2685.
Tribunal Procedure (First-tier Tribunal) (War Pensions and Armed Forces Compensation Chamber) Rules, SI 2008/2686.
Tribunal Procedure (Upper Tribunal) Rules, SI 2008/2698.
Tribunal Procedure (First-tier Tribunal) (Tax Chamber) Rules, SI 2009/273.
Tribunal Procedure (Amendment) Rules, SI 2009/274.
Tribunal Procedure (Amendment No 2) Rules, SI 2009/1975.
Tribunal Procedure (First-tier Tribunal) (General Regulatory Chamber) Rules, SI 2009/1976.
Tribunal Procedure (Amendment) Rules, SI 2010/43.
Tribunal Procedure (Amendment No 2) Rules, SI 2010/44.
Tribunal Procedure (Upper Tribunal) (Amendment) Rules, SI 2010/747.
Tribunal Procedure (Upper Tribunal) (Lands Chamber) Rules, SI 2010/2600.
Tribunal Procedure (Amendment No 3) Rules, SI 2010/2653.
Tribunal Procedure (Amendment) Rules 2011, SI 2011/651.
Tribunal Procedure (Amendment) Rules, SI 2012/500.
Tribunal Procedure (Amendment No 2) Rules, SI 2012/1363.
Tribunal Procedure (Upper Tribunal) (Amendment) Rules, SI 2012/2890.
Tribunal Procedure (Amendment) Rules, SI 2013/477.
Tribunal Procedure (Amendment No 2) Rules 2013/606.
Tribunal Procedure (Amendment No 3) Rules, SI 2013/1188 (amendments to the Tribunal Procedure (Upper Tribunal) (Lands Chamber) Rules, SI 2010/2600 only).
Tribunal Procedure (First-tier Tribunal) (Property Chamber) Rules, SI 2013/1169.
Tribunal Procedure (Amendment No 3) Rules, SI 2013/1188.
Tribunal Procedure (Amendment No 4) Rules, SI 2013/2067.
Tribunal Procedure (Amendment) Rules, SI 2014/514.
Tribunal Procedure (Amendment No 2) Rules, SI 2014/1505.
Tribunal Procedure (Amendment No 3) Rules, SI 2014/2128.
Tribunal Procedure (First-tier Tribunal) (Immigration and Asylum Chamber) Rules, SI 2014/2604.
Tribunal Procedure (Amendment) Rules, SI 2015/1510.
Tribunal Procedure (Amendment) Rules, SI 2017/723.
Tribunal Procedure (Amendment No 2) Rules, SI 2017/1168.
Tribunal Procedure (Amendment) Rules, SI 2018/511.
Tribunal Procedure (Amendment No 2) Rules, SI 2018/1053.
Tribunal Procedure (Amendment) Rules, SI 2019/925.
Tribunal Procedure (Coronavirus) (Amendment) Rules, SI 2020/416.

23 Practice directions

(1) The Senior President of Tribunals may give directions—

    (*a*) as to the practice and procedure of the First-tier Tribunal;

    (*b*) as to the practice and procedure of the Upper Tribunal.

(2) A Chamber President may give directions as to the practice and procedure of the chamber over which he presides.

(3) A power under this section to give directions includes—

    (*a*) power to vary or revoke directions made in exercise of the power, and

    (*b*) power to make different provision for different purposes (including different provision for different areas).

(4) Directions under subsection (1) may not be given without the approval of the Lord Chancellor.

(5) Directions under subsection (2) may not be given without the approval of—

    (*a*) the Senior President of Tribunals, and

    (*b*) the Lord Chancellor.

(6) Subsections (4) and (5)(*b*) do not apply to directions to the extent that they consist of guidance about any of the following—

    (*a*) the application or interpretation of the law;

    (*b*) the making of decisions by members of the First-tier Tribunal or Upper Tribunal.

(7) Subsections (4) and (5)(*b*) do not apply to directions to the extent that they consist of criteria for determining which members of the First-tier Tribunal or Upper Tribunal may be chosen to decide particular categories of matter; but the directions may, to that extent, be given only after consulting the Lord Chancellor.

Commentary—*Simon's Taxes* I11.331D.

24 Mediation

(1) A person exercising power to make Tribunal Procedure Rules or give practice directions must, when making provision in relation to mediation, have regard to the following principles—

    (*a*) mediation of matters in dispute between parties to proceedings is to take place only by agreement between those parties;

    (*b*) where parties to proceedings fail to mediate, or where mediation between parties to proceedings fails to resolve disputed matters, the failure is not to affect the outcome of the proceedings.

(2) Practice directions may provide for members to act as mediators in relation to disputed matters in a case that is the subject of proceedings.

(3) The provision that may be made by virtue of subsection (2) includes provision for a member to act as a mediator in relation to disputed matters in a case even though the member has been chosen to decide matters in the case.

(4) Once a member has begun to act as a mediator in relation to a disputed matter in a case that is the subject of proceedings, the member may decide matters in the case only with the consent of the parties.

(5) Staff appointed under section 40(1) may, subject to their terms of appointment, act as mediators in relation to disputed matters in a case that is the subject of proceedings.

(6) In this section—

    "member" means a judge or other member of the First-tier Tribunal or a judge or other member of the Upper Tribunal;

    "practice direction" means a direction under section 23(1) or (2);

    "proceedings" means proceedings before the First-tier Tribunal or proceedings before the Upper Tribunal.

25 Supplementary powers of Upper Tribunal

(1) In relation to the matters mentioned in subsection (2), the Upper Tribunal—

    (*a*) has, in England and Wales or in Northern Ireland, the same powers, rights, privileges and authority as the High Court, and

    (*b*) has, in Scotland, the same powers, rights, privileges and authority as the Court of Session.

(2) The matters are—

    (*a*) the attendance and examination of witnesses,

    (*b*) the production and inspection of documents, and

    (*c*) all other matters incidental to the Upper Tribunal's functions.

(3) Subsection (1) shall not be taken—

    (*a*) to limit any power to make Tribunal Procedure Rules;

    (*b*) to be limited by anything in Tribunal Procedure Rules other than an express limitation.

(4) A power, right, privilege or authority conferred in a territory by subsection (1) is available for purposes of proceedings in the Upper Tribunal that take place outside that territory (as well as for purposes of proceedings in the tribunal that take place within that territory).

Commentary—*Simon's Taxes* A5.612, I11.351B.

26 First-tier Tribunal and Upper Tribunal: sitting places
Each of the First-tier Tribunal and the Upper Tribunal may decide a case—
- (*a*) in England and Wales,
- (*b*) in Scotland, or
- (*c*) in Northern Ireland,

even though the case arises under the law of a territory other than the one in which the case is decided.

27 Enforcement
(1) A sum payable in pursuance of a decision of the First-tier Tribunal or Upper Tribunal made in England and Wales—
- (*a*) shall be recoverable as if it were payable under an order of [the county court][1] in England and Wales;
- (*b*) shall be recoverable as if it were payable under an order of the High Court in England and Wales.

(2) An order for the payment of a sum payable in pursuance of a decision of the First-tier Tribunal or Upper Tribunal made in Scotland (or a copy of such an order certified in accordance with Tribunal Procedure Rules) may be enforced as if it were an extract registered decree arbitral bearing a warrant for execution issued by the sheriff court of any sheriffdom in Scotland.

(3) A sum payable in pursuance of a decision of the First-tier Tribunal or Upper Tribunal made in Northern Ireland—
- (*a*) shall be recoverable as if it were payable under an order of [the county court][1] in Northern Ireland;
- (*b*) shall be recoverable as if it were payable under an order of the High Court in Northern Ireland.

(4) This section does not apply to a sum payable in pursuance of—
- (*a*) an award under section 16(6), or
- (*b*) an order by virtue of section 21(1).

(5) The Lord Chancellor may by order make provision for subsection (1) or (3) to apply in relation to a sum of a description specified in the order with the omission of one (but not both) of paragraphs (*a*) and (*b*).

(6) Tribunal Procedure Rules—
- (*a*) may make provision as to where, for purposes of this section, a decision is to be taken to be made;
- (*b*) may provide for all or any of subsections (1) to (3) to apply only, or not to apply except, in relation to sums of a description specified in Tribunal Procedure Rules.

Amendments—[1] In sub-s (1)(*a*), words substituted for words "a county court" by the Crime and Courts Act 2013 s 17, Sch 9 para 52 with effect from 22 April 2014 (by virtue of SI 2014/954 art 2(*c*)).

28 Assessors
(1) If it appears to the First-tier Tribunal or the Upper Tribunal that a matter before it requires special expertise not otherwise available to it, it may direct that in dealing with that matter it shall have the assistance of a person or persons appearing to it to have relevant knowledge or experience.

(2) The remuneration of a person who gives assistance to either tribunal as mentioned in subsection (1) shall be determined and paid by the Lord Chancellor.

(3) The Lord Chancellor may—
- (*a*) establish panels of persons from which either tribunal may (but need not) select persons to give it assistance as mentioned in subsection (1);
- (*b*) under paragraph (*a*) establish different panels for different purposes;
- (*c*) after carrying out such consultation as he considers appropriate, appoint persons to a panel established under paragraph (*a*);
- (*d*) remove a person from such a panel.

29 Costs or expenses
(1) The costs of and incidental to—
- (*a*) all proceedings in the First-tier Tribunal, and
- (*b*) all proceedings in the Upper Tribunal,

shall be in the discretion of the Tribunal in which the proceedings take place.

(2) The relevant Tribunal shall have full power to determine by whom and to what extent the costs are to be paid.

(3) Subsections (1) and (2) have effect subject to Tribunal Procedure Rules.

(4) In any proceedings mentioned in subsection (1), the relevant Tribunal may—
- (*a*) disallow, or
- (*b*) (as the case may be) order the legal or other representative concerned to meet,

the whole of any wasted costs or such part of them as may be determined in accordance with Tribunal Procedure Rules.

(5) In subsection (4) "wasted costs" means any costs incurred by a party—

    (*a*) as a result of any improper, unreasonable or negligent act or omission on the part of any legal or other representative or any employee of such a representative, or

    (*b*) which, in the light of any such act or omission occurring after they were incurred, the relevant Tribunal considers it is unreasonable to expect that party to pay.

(6) In this section "legal or other representative", in relation to a party to proceedings, means any person exercising a right of audience or right to conduct the proceedings on his behalf.

(7) In the application of this section in relation to Scotland, any reference in this section to costs is to be read as a reference to expenses.

Commentary—*Simon's Taxes* **A5.501, A5.618, I11.361A, I11.361B, A5.619**.

HMRC Manuals—Appeals, Reviews and Tribunals Manual ARTG8660 (tribunals rights to award costs - first tier tribunal). ARTG8665 (tribunals right to award costs - upper tribunal).

Rules—Tribunal Procedure (First-tier Tribunal) (Social Entitlement Chamber) Rules, SI 2008/2685 (made under sub-s (3)).

Tribunal Procedure (First-tier Tribunal) (War Pensions and Armed Forces Compensation Chamber) Rules, SI 2008/2686 (made under sub-para (3)).

Tribunal Procedure (Upper Tribunal) Rules, SI 2008/2698 (made under sub-ss (3), (4)).

Tribunal Procedure (First-tier Tribunal) (Health, Education and Social Care Chamber) Rules, SI 2008/2699 (made under sub-ss (2), (3)).

Tribunal Procedure (First-tier Tribunal) (Tax Chamber) Rules, SI 2009/273 (made under sub-s (3)).

Tribunal Procedure (Amendment) Rules, SI 2009/274 (made under sub-ss (3), (4)).

Tribunal Procedure (Amendment No 2) Rules, SI 2009/1975 (made under sub-s (3)).

Tribunal Procedure (First-tier Tribunal) (General Regulatory Chamber) Rules, SI 2009/1976 (made under sub-ss (3), (4)).

Tribunal Procedure (Amendment) Rules, SI 2010/43 (made under sub-ss (3), (4)).

Tribunal Procedure (Upper Tribunal) (Amendment) Rules, SI 2010/747 (made under sub-ss (3), (4)).

Tribunal Procedure (Upper Tribunal) (Lands Chamber) Rules, SI 2010/2600 (made under sub-ss (3), (4)).

Tribunal Procedure (Amendment) Rules, SI 2013/477.

Tribunal Procedure (First-tier Tribunal) (Property Chamber) Rules, SI 2013/1169 (made under sub-ss (3), (4)).

Tribunal Procedure (Amendment No 3) Rules, SI 2013/1188 (amendments to the Tribunal Procedure (Upper Tribunal) (Lands Chamber) Rules, SI 2010/2600 only).

Tribunal Procedure (Amendment) Rules, SI 2014/514.

Tribunal Procedure (First-tier Tribunal) (Immigration and Asylum Chamber) Rules, SI 2014/2604 (made under sub-ss (3), (4)).

[Use of live video or audio links: public participation & offences of recording etc]

29ZA Enabling the public to see and hear proceedings

(1) If the First-tier Tribunal or Upper Tribunal directs that tribunal proceedings are to be conducted wholly as video proceedings, that Tribunal—

    (*a*) may direct that the proceedings are to be broadcast (in the manner specified in the direction) for the purpose of enabling members of the public to see and hear the proceedings;

    (*b*) may direct that a recording of the proceedings is to be made (in the manner specified in the direction) for the purpose of enabling that Tribunal to keep an audio-visual record of the proceedings.

(2) If the First-tier Tribunal or Upper Tribunal directs that tribunal proceedings are to be conducted wholly as audio proceedings, that Tribunal—

    (*a*) may direct that the proceedings are to be broadcast (in the manner specified in the direction) for the purpose of enabling members of the public to hear the proceedings;

    (*b*) may direct that a recording of the proceedings is to be made (in the manner specified in the direction) for the purpose of enabling that Tribunal to keep an audio record of the proceedings.

(3) A direction under this section may relate to the whole, or to part, of the proceedings concerned.]

Modifications—Sections 29ZA–29ZD treated as inserted by the Coronavirus Act 2020 s 55, Sch 25 para 2 with effect for a period of two years beginning with 25 March 2020, subject to the powers in ss 88–92 and 98.

[29ZB Offences of recording or transmission in relation to broadcasting

(1) It is an offence for a person to make, or attempt to make—

    (*a*) an unauthorised recording, or

    (*b*) an unauthorised transmission,

of an image or sound which is being broadcast in accordance with a direction under section 29ZA.

(2) It is an offence for a person to make, or attempt to make—

    (*a*) an unauthorised recording, or

    (*b*) an unauthorised transmission,

of an image of, or sound made by, another person while the other person is viewing or listening to a broadcast made in accordance with a direction under section 29ZA.

(3) It is a defence for a person charged with an offence under subsection (1) or (2) to prove that, at the time of the actual or attempted recording or transmission of the image or sound concerned—

    (*a*) he or she was not in designated live-streaming premises, and

    (*b*) he or she did not know, and could not reasonably have known, that the image or sound was—

        (i) being broadcast in accordance with a direction under section 29ZA (in the case of an offence under subsection (1)), or

      (ii) an image of, or sound made by, another person while the other person was viewing or listening to a broadcast made in accordance with a direction under section 29ZA (in the case of an offence under subsection (2)).

(4) A person guilty of an offence under this section is liable on summary conviction to a fine not exceeding level 3 on the standard scale.

(5) For the purposes of this section it does not matter whether a person making, or attempting to make, a recording or transmission intends the recording or transmission, or anything comprised in it, to be seen or heard by any other person.

(6) For the purposes of this section a recording or transmission is "unauthorised" unless it is—

    (*a*) authorised by a direction under section 29ZA,

    (*b*) otherwise authorised (generally or specifically) by the Tribunal in which the proceedings concerned are being conducted, or

    (*c*) authorised (generally or specifically) by the Lord Chancellor.]

Modifications—Sections 29ZA–29ZD treated as inserted by the Coronavirus Act 2020 s 55, Sch 25 para 2 with effect for a period of two years beginning with 25 March 2020, subject to the powers in ss 88–92 and 98.

[29ZC Offences of recording or transmitting participation through live link

(1) It is an offence for a person to make, or attempt to make—

    (*a*) an unauthorised recording, or

    (*b*) an unauthorised transmission,

of an image or sound which is being transmitted through a live video link or transmitted through a live audio link.

(2) It is an offence for a person (P) to make, or attempt to make—

    (*a*) an unauthorised recording, or

    (*b*) an unauthorised transmission,

of an image of, or sound made by, any person (whether P or another person) while that person is participating in tribunal proceedings through a live video link or a live audio link.

(3) It is a defence for a person charged with an offence under subsection (1) or (2) to prove that, at the time of the actual or attempted recording or transmission, he or she did not know, and could not reasonably have known, that the image or sound concerned—

    (*a*) was being transmitted through a live video link or through a live audio link (in the case of an offence under subsection (1)), or

    (*b*) was an image of, or sound made by, a person while that person was participating in tribunal proceedings through a live video link or a live audio link (in the case of an offence under subsection (2)).

(4) A person guilty of an offence under this section is liable on summary conviction to a fine not exceeding level 3 on the standard scale.

(5) For the purposes of this section it does not matter whether a person making, or attempting to make, a recording or transmission intends the recording or transmission, or anything comprised in it, to be seen or heard by any other person.

(6) For the purposes of this section a recording or transmission is "unauthorised" unless it is—

    (*a*) authorised (generally or specifically) by the Tribunal in which the proceedings concerned are being conducted, or

    (*b*) authorised (generally or specifically) by the Lord Chancellor.]

Modifications—Sections 29ZA–29ZD treated as inserted by the Coronavirus Act 2020 s 55, Sch 25 para 2 with effect for a period of two years beginning with 25 March 2020, subject to the powers in ss 88–92 and 98.

[29ZD Interpretation

(1) This section applies for the purposes of sections 29ZA to 29ZC (and this section).

(2) The following expressions have the meanings given—

    "tribunal proceedings" means any proceedings in the First-tier Tribunal or Upper Tribunal;

    "designated live-streaming premises" means premises that are designated by the Lord Chancellor for the purposes of this section as premises provided by the Lord Chancellor for the purpose of enabling members of the public to see and hear, or hear, proceedings that are broadcast in accordance with directions under section 29ZA;

    "recording" means a recording on any medium—

        (*a*) of a single image, a moving image or any sound, or

        (*b*) from which a single image, a moving image or any sound may be produced or reproduced;

    "transmission" means any transmission by electronic means of a single image, a moving image or any sound (and "transmitted" is to be construed accordingly).

(3) A "live video link", in relation to a person (P) taking part in proceedings, is a live television link or other arrangement which—

    (*a*) enables P to see and hear all other persons taking part in the proceedings who are not in the same location as P, and

(b) enables all other persons taking part in the proceedings who are not in the same location as P to see and hear P.

(4) Proceedings are conducted wholly as video proceedings if—

    (a) directions have been given for all of the persons taking part in the proceedings to do so through a live video link, and

    (b) all of those persons take part in the proceedings in accordance with those directions.

(5) A "live audio link", in relation to a person (P) taking part in proceedings, is a live telephone link or other arrangement which—

    (a) enables P to hear all other persons taking part in the proceedings who are not in the same location as P, and

    (b) enables all other persons taking part in the proceedings who are not in the same location as P to hear P.

(6) Proceedings are conducted wholly as audio proceedings if—

    (a) directions have been given for all of the persons taking part in the proceedings to do so through a live audio link, and

    (b) all of those persons take part in the proceedings in accordance with those directions.

(7) An image or sound is transmitted—

    (a) through a live video link if it is transmitted as part of a person's participation in tribunal proceedings through a live video link;

    (b) through a live audio link if it is transmitted as part of a person's participation in tribunal proceedings through a live audio link.]

Modifications—Sections 29ZA–29ZD treated as inserted by the Coronavirus Act 2020 s 55, Sch 25 para 2 with effect for a period of two years beginning with 25 March 2020, subject to the powers in ss 88–92 and 98.

[CHAPTER 2A

EXERCISE OF TRIBUNAL FUNCTIONS BY AUTHORISED PERSONS

[29A Meaning of "authorised person" and "judicial office holder"

In this Chapter—

    "authorised person" means a person authorised under paragraph 3 of Schedule 5 to exercise functions of the First-tier Tribunal or Upper Tribunal;

    "judicial office holder" has the meaning given by section 109(4) of the Constitutional Reform Act 2005.][1]

Amendments—[1] Chapter 2A (ss 29A–29E) inserted by the Courts and Tribunals (Judiciary and Functions of Staff) Act 2018 s 3, Schedule paras 39, 41 with effect from 10 January 2020 for the purpose of making regulations, and from 6 April 2020 for all remaining purposes (by virtue of SI 2020/24 regs 2, 3).

[29B Directions and independence: authorised persons

(1) The Senior President of Tribunals may give directions to an authorised person.

(2) Apart from such directions, an authorised person exercising a function by virtue of paragraph 3 of Schedule 5 is not subject to the direction of the Lord Chancellor or any other person when exercising the function.

(3) The Senior President of Tribunals may delegate to one or more of the following the Senior President of Tribunals' functions under subsection (1)—

    (a) a judicial office holder;

    (b) a person appointed under section 2(1) of the Courts Act 2003 or section 40(1) of this Act.

(4) A person to whom functions of the Senior President of Tribunals are delegated under subsection (3)(b) is not subject to the direction of any person other than—

    (a) the Senior President of Tribunals, or

    (b) a judicial office holder nominated by the Senior President of Tribunals,

when exercising the functions.

(5) Subsections (3) to (5) of section 8 apply to—

    (a) a delegation under subsection (3) of this section, and

    (b) a nomination under subsection (4) of this section,

as they apply to a delegation under subsection (1) of that section.][1]

Amendments—[1] Chapter 2A (ss 29A–29E) inserted by the Courts and Tribunals (Judiciary and Functions of Staff) Act 2018 s 3, Schedule paras 39, 41 with effect from 10 January 2020 for the purpose of making regulations, and from 6 April 2020 for all remaining purposes (by virtue of SI 2020/24 regs 2, 3).

[29C Protection of authorised persons

(1) No action lies against an authorised person in respect of what the person does or omits to do—

    (a) in the execution of the person's duty as an authorised person exercising, by virtue of paragraph 3 of Schedule 5, functions of a tribunal, and

    (b) in relation to a matter within the person's jurisdiction.

(2) An action lies against an authorised person in respect of what the person does or omits to do—

    (a) in the purported execution of the person's duty as an authorised person exercising, by virtue of paragraph 3 of Schedule 5, functions of a tribunal, but

(b) in relation to a matter not within the person's jurisdiction,

if, but only if, it is proved that the person acted in bad faith.

(3) If an action is brought in a court in Scotland in circumstances in which subsection (1) or (2) provides that no action lies, the court in which the action is brought—

(a) may, on the application of the defender, dismiss the action, and

(b) if it does so, may find the person bringing the action liable in expenses.

(4) If an action is brought in any other court in circumstances in which subsection (1) or (2) provides that no action lies, the court in which the action is brought—

(a) may, on the application of the defendant, strike out the proceedings in the action, and

(b) if it does so, may if it thinks fit order the person bringing the action to pay costs.][1]

Amendments—[1]   Chapter 2A (ss 29A–29E) inserted by the Courts and Tribunals (Judiciary and Functions of Staff) Act 2018 s 3, Schedule paras 39, 41 with effect from 10 January 2020 for the purpose of making regulations, and from 6 April 2020 for all remaining purposes (by virtue of SI 2020/24 regs 2, 3).

[29D Costs or expenses in legal proceedings: authorised persons

(1) A court may not order an authorised person to pay costs in any proceedings in respect of what the person does or omits to do in the execution (or purported execution) of the person's duty as an authorised person exercising, by virtue of paragraph 3 of Schedule 5, a function of a tribunal.

(2) But subsection (1) does not apply in relation to any proceedings in which an authorised person—

(a) is being tried for an offence or is appealing against a conviction, or

(b) is proved to have acted in bad faith in respect of the matters giving rise to the proceedings.

(3) A court which is prevented by subsection (1) from ordering an authorised person to pay costs in any proceedings may instead order the Lord Chancellor to make a payment in respect of the costs of a person in the proceedings.

(4) The Lord Chancellor may, after consulting the Senior President of Tribunals, make regulations specifying—

(a) circumstances in which a court must or must not exercise the power conferred on it by subsection (3), and

(b) how the amount of any payment ordered under subsection (3) is to be determined.

(5) The power to make regulations under subsection (4) includes power to make—

(a) any supplementary, incidental or consequential provision, and

(b) any transitory, transitional or saving provision,

which the Lord Chancellor considers necessary or expedient.

(6) The Senior President of Tribunals may delegate the Senior President of Tribunals' functions under subsection (4) to a person who is a judicial office holder.

(7) Subsections (3) to (5) of section 8 apply to a delegation under subsection (6) of this section as they apply to a delegation under subsection (1) of that section.

(8) In the application of this section to Scotland—

(a) references to a court ordering an authorised person to pay costs are to be read as references to a court finding an authorised person liable in expenses, and

(b) the second reference to costs in subsection (3) is to be read as a reference to expenses.][1]

Amendments—[1]   Chapter 2A (ss 29A–29E) inserted by the Courts and Tribunals (Judiciary and Functions of Staff) Act 2018 s 3, Schedule paras 39, 41 with effect from 10 January 2020 for the purpose of making regulations, and from 6 April 2020 for all remaining purposes (by virtue of SI 2020/24 regs 2, 3).

[29E Indemnification of authorised persons

(1) "Indemnifiable amounts", in relation to an authorised person, means—

(a) costs which the person reasonably incurs in or in connection with proceedings in respect of anything done or omitted to be done in the exercise (or purported exercise) of the person's duty as an authorised person,

(b) costs which the person reasonably incurs in taking steps to dispute a claim which might be made in such proceedings,

(c) damages awarded against the person or costs ordered to be paid by the person in such proceedings, or

(d) sums payable by the person in connection with a reasonable settlement of such proceedings or such a claim.

(2) The Lord Chancellor must indemnify an authorised person in respect of indemnifiable amounts if, in respect of the matters giving rise to the proceedings or claim, the person acted reasonably and in good faith.

(3) The Lord Chancellor may indemnify an authorised person in respect of other indemnifiable amounts unless it is proved, in respect of the matters giving rise to the proceedings or claim, that the person acted in bad faith.

(4) Any question whether, or to what extent, an authorised person is to be indemnified under this section is to be determined by the Lord Chancellor.

(5) The Lord Chancellor may, if an authorised person claiming to be indemnified so requests, make a determination for the purposes of this section with respect to—

(a) costs such as are mentioned in subsection (1)(a) or (b), or

    (b) sums such as are mentioned in subsection (1)(d),

before the costs are incurred or the settlement in connection with which the sums are payable is made.

(6) But a determination under subsection (5) before costs are incurred—

    (a) is subject to such limitations (if any) as the Lord Chancellor thinks proper and to the subsequent determination of the costs reasonably incurred, and

    (b) does not affect any other determination which may fall to be made in connection with the proceedings or claim in question.

(7) In the application of this section to Scotland, references to costs are to be read as references to expenses.]¹

Amendments—¹   Chapter 2A (ss 29A–29E) inserted by the Courts and Tribunals (Judiciary and Functions of Staff) Act 2018 s 3, Schedule paras 39, 41 with effect from 10 January 2020 for the purpose of making regulations, and from 6 April 2020 for all remaining purposes (by virtue of SI 2020/24 regs 2, 3).

CHAPTER 3

TRANSFER OF TRIBUNAL FUNCTIONS

30 Transfer of functions of certain tribunals

(1) The Lord Chancellor may by order provide for a function of a scheduled tribunal to be transferred—

    (*a*) to the First-tier Tribunal,

    (*b*) to the Upper Tribunal,

    (*c*) to the First-tier Tribunal and the Upper Tribunal with the question as to which of them is to exercise the function in a particular case being determined by a person under provisions of the order,

    (*d*) to the First-tier Tribunal to the extent specified in the order and to the Upper Tribunal to the extent so specified,

    (*e*) to the First-tier Tribunal and the Upper Tribunal with the question as to which of them is to exercise the function in a particular case being determined by, or under, Tribunal Procedure Rules,

    (*f*) to an employment tribunal,

    (*g*) to the Employment Appeal Tribunal,

    (*h*) to an employment tribunal and the Employment Appeal Tribunal with the question as to which of them is to exercise the function in a particular case being determined by a person under provisions of the order, or

    (*i*) to an employment tribunal to the extent specified in the order and to the Employment Appeal Tribunal to the extent so specified.

(2) In subsection (1) "scheduled tribunal" means a tribunal in a list in Schedule 6 that has effect for the purposes of this section.

(3) The Lord Chancellor may, as respects a function transferred under subsection (1) or this subsection, by order provide for the function to be further transferred as mentioned in any of paragraphs (*a*) to (*i*) of subsection (1).

(4) An order under subsection (1) or (3) may include provision for the purposes of or in consequence of, or for giving full effect to, a transfer under that subsection.

(5) A function of a tribunal may not be transferred under subsection (1) or (3) if, or to the extent that, the provision conferring the function—

    (*a*) would be within the legislative competence of the Scottish Parliament if it were included in an Act of that Parliament, or

    (*b*) would be within the legislative competence of the Northern Ireland Assembly if it were included in an Act of that Assembly.

(6) Subsection (5) does not apply to—

    (*a*) the Secretary of State's function of deciding appeals under section 41 of the Consumer Credit Act 1974 (c 39),

    (*b*) functions of the Consumer Credit Appeals Tribunal,

    (*c*) the Secretary of State's function of deciding appeals under section 7(1) of the Estate Agents Act 1979 (c 38), or

    (*d*) functions of an adjudicator under section 5 of the Criminal Injuries Compensation Act 1995 (c 53) (but see subsection (7)).

(7) Functions of an adjudicator under section 5 of the Criminal Injuries Compensation Act 1995 (c 53), so far as they relate to Scotland, may be transferred under subsection (1) or (3) only with the consent of the Scottish Ministers.

(8) A function of a tribunal may be transferred under subsection (1) or (3) only with the consent of the Welsh Ministers if any relevant function is exercisable in relation to the tribunal by the Welsh Ministers (whether by the Welsh Ministers alone, or by the Welsh Ministers jointly or concurrently with any other person).

(9) In subsection (8) "relevant function", in relation to a tribunal, means a function which relates—
  (a) to the operation of the tribunal (including, in particular, its membership, administration, staff, accommodation and funding, and payments to its members or staff), or
  (b) to the provision of expenses and allowances to persons attending the tribunal or attending elsewhere in connection with proceedings before the tribunal.

Commentary—*Simon's Taxes* **A5.601**.
Orders—Transfer of Tribunal Functions Order, SI 2008/2833 (made under sub-ss (1), (4)).
Transfer of Tribunal Functions and Revenue and Customs Appeals Order, SI 2009/56 (made under sub-ss (1), (4)).
Transfer of Tribunal Functions (Lands Tribunal and Miscellaneous Amendments) Order, SI 2009/1307 (made under sub-ss (1), (4)).
Transfer of Functions of the Charity Tribunal Order, SI 2009/1834 (made under sub-ss (1), (4)).
Transfer of Functions of the Consumer Credit Appeals Tribunal Order, SI 2009/1835 (made under sub-ss (1), (4)).
Transfer of Functions (Estate Agents Appeals and Additional Scheduled Tribunal) Order, SI 2009/1836 (made under sub-ss (1), (4)).
Transfer of Functions (Transport Tribunal and Appeal Panel) Order, SI 2009/1885 (made under sub-ss (1), (4)).
Transfer of Functions of the Asylum and Immigration Tribunal Order, SI 2010/21 (made under sub-ss (1), (4)).
Transfer of Tribunal Functions Order, SI 2010/22 (made under sub-ss (1), (4)).
Transfer of Tribunal Functions Order, SI 2013/1036 (made under sub-s (1)).
Transfer of Tribunal Functions (Mobile Homes Act 2013 and Miscellaneous Amendments) Order, SI 2014/1900 (made under sub-ss (1)(e), (4)).
Transfer of Tribunal Functions (Transport Tribunal) Order, SI 2015/65 (made under sub-ss (1)(b), (4)).

31 Transfers under section 30: supplementary powers

(1) The Lord Chancellor may by order make provision for abolishing the tribunal by whom a function transferred under section 30(1) is exercisable immediately before its transfer.
(2) The Lord Chancellor may by order make provision, where functions of a tribunal are transferred under section 30(1), for a person—
  (a) who is the tribunal (but is not the Secretary of State), or
  (b) who is a member of the tribunal, or
  (c) who is an authorised decision-maker for the tribunal,
to (instead or in addition) be the holder of an office specified in subsection (3).
(3) Those offices are—
  (a) transferred-in judge of the First-tier Tribunal,
  (b) transferred-in other member of the First-tier Tribunal,
  (c) transferred-in judge of the Upper Tribunal,
  (d) transferred-in other member of the Upper Tribunal, and
  (e) deputy judge of the Upper Tribunal.
(4) Where functions of a tribunal are transferred under section 30(1), the Lord Chancellor must exercise the power under subsection (2) so as to secure that each person who immediately before the end of the tribunal's life—
  (a) is the tribunal,
  (b) is a member of the tribunal, or
  (c) is an authorised decision-maker for the tribunal,
becomes the holder of an office specified in subsection (3) with effect from the end of the tribunal's life (if the person is not then already the holder of such an office).
(5) Subsection (4) does not apply in relation to a person—
  (a) by virtue of the person's being the Secretary of State, or
  (b) by virtue of the person's being a Commissioner for the general purposes of the income tax;
and a reference in subsection (4) to the end of a tribunal's life is to when the tribunal is abolished or (without being abolished) comes to have no functions.
(6) For the purposes of this section, a person is an "authorised decision-maker" for a tribunal if—
  (a) the tribunal is listed in column 1 of an entry in the following Table, and
  (b) the person is of the description specified in column 2 of that entry.

(1) Tribunal	(2) Authorised decision-maker
Adjudicator to Her Majesty's Land Registry	Member of the Adjudicator's staff who is authorised by the Adjudicator to carry out functions of the Adjudicator which are not of an administrative character
The Secretary of State as respects his function of deciding appeals under section 41 of the Consumer Credit Act 1974 (c 39)	Person who is a member of a panel under regulation 24 of the Consumer Credit Licensing (Appeals) Regulations 1998 (SI 1998/1203)
The Secretary of State as respects his function of deciding appeals under section 7(1) of the Estate Agents Act 1979 (c 38)	Person appointed, at any time after 2005, under regulation 19(1) of the Estate Agents (Appeals) Regulations 1981 (SI 1981/1518) to hear an appeal on behalf of the Secretary of State

(7) Where a function of a tribunal is transferred under section 30(1), the Lord Chancellor may by order provide for procedural rules in force immediately before the transfer to have effect, or to have effect with appropriate modifications, after the transfer (and, accordingly, to be capable of being varied or revoked) as if they were—

(a) Tribunal Procedure Rules, or

(b) employment tribunal procedure regulations, or Appeal Tribunal procedure rules, within the meaning given by section 42(1) of the Employment Tribunals Act 1996 (c 17).

(8) In subsection (7)—

"procedural rules" means provision (whether called rules or not)—

(a) regulating practice or procedure before the tribunal, and

(b) applying for purposes connected with the exercise of the function;

"appropriate modifications" means modifications (including additions and omissions) that appear to the Lord Chancellor to be necessary to secure, or expedient in connection with securing, that the procedural rules apply in relation to the exercise of the function after the transfer.

(9) The Lord Chancellor may, in connection with provision made by order under section 30 or the preceding provisions of this section, make by order such incidental, supplemental, transitional or consequential provision, or provision for savings, as the Lord Chancellor thinks fit, including provision applying only in relation to cases selected by a member—

(a) of the First-tier Tribunal,

(b) of the Upper Tribunal,

(c) of the Employment Appeal Tribunal, or

(d) of a panel of members of employment tribunals.

(10) Subsections (1), (2) and (7) are not to be taken as prejudicing the generality of subsection (9).

Commentary—*Simon's Taxes* **A5.601**.

Orders—Tribunals, Courts and Enforcement Act 2007 (Transitional and Consequential Provisions) Order, SI 2008/2683 (made under sub-s (9)).

Tribunals, Courts and Enforcement Act 2007 (Commencement No 6 and Transitional Provisions) Order, SI 2008/2696 (made under sub-s (9)).

Transfer of Tribunal Functions Order, SI 2008/2833 (made under sub-ss (1), (2), (9)).

Transfer of Tribunal Functions and Revenue and Customs Appeals Order, SI 2009/56 (made under sub-ss (1), (2), (9)).

Transfer of Tribunal Functions (Lands Tribunal and Miscellaneous Amendments) Order, SI 2009/1307 (made under sub-ss (1), (2), (7), (9)).

Transfer of Functions of the Charity Tribunal Order, SI 2009/1834 (made under sub-ss (1), (2), (9)).

Transfer of Functions of the Consumer Credit Appeals Tribunal Order, SI 2009/1835 (made under sub-ss (1), (2), (9)).

Transfer of Functions (Estate Agents Appeals and Additional Scheduled Tribunal) Order, SI 2009/1836 (made under sub-ss (2), (9)).

Transfer of Functions (Transport Tribunal and Appeal Panel) Order, SI 2009/1885 (made under sub-ss (2), (9)).

Transfer of Functions of the Asylum and Immigration Tribunal Order, SI 2010/21 (made under sub-ss (1), (2), (7), (9)).

Transfer of Tribunal Functions Order, SI 2010/22 (made under sub-ss (1), (2), (9)).

Tribunals, Courts and Enforcement Act 2007 (Miscellaneous Provisions) Order, SI 2010/41 (made under sub-s (9)).

Transfer of Tribunal Functions Order, SI 2013/1036.

Transfer of Tribunal Functions (Mobile Homes Act 2013 and Miscellaneous Amendments) Order 2014, SI 2014/1900 (made under sub-s (9)).

32 Power to provide for appeal to Upper Tribunal from tribunals in Wales

(1) Subsection (2) applies if—

(a) a function is transferred under section 30(1)(a), (c), (d) or (e) in relation to England but is not transferred under section 30(1) in relation to Wales, or

(b) a function that is not exercisable in relation to Wales is transferred under section 30(1)(a), (c), (d) or (e) in relation to England and, although there is a corresponding function that is exercisable in relation to Wales, that corresponding function is not transferred under section 30(1) in relation to Wales.

(2) The Lord Chancellor may by order—

(a) provide for an appeal against a decision to be made to the Upper Tribunal instead of to the court to which an appeal would otherwise fall to be made where the decision is made in exercising, in relation to Wales, the function mentioned in subsection (1)(a) or (as the case may be) the corresponding function mentioned in subsection (1)(b);

(b) provide for a reference of any matter to be made to the Upper Tribunal instead of to the court to which a reference would otherwise fall to be made where the matter arises in exercising, in relation to Wales, the function mentioned in subsection (1)(a) or (as the case may be) the corresponding function mentioned in subsection (1)(b).

(3) The Lord Chancellor may by order provide for an appeal against a decision of a scheduled tribunal to be made to the Upper Tribunal, instead of to the court to which an appeal would otherwise fall to be made, where the decision is made by the tribunal in exercising a function in relation to Wales.

(4) In subsection (3) "scheduled tribunal" means a tribunal in a list in Schedule 6 that has effect for the purposes of that subsection.

(5) An order under subsection (2) or (3)—

  (*a*) may include provision for the purposes of or in consequence of, or for giving full effect to, provision made by the order;

  (*b*) may include such incidental, supplemental, transitional or consequential provision or savings as the Lord Chancellor thinks fit.

Orders—Transfer of Tribunal Functions Order, SI 2008/2833 (made under sub-ss (3), (5)).
Transfer of Tribunal Functions Order, SI 2013/1036.

33 Power to provide for appeal to Upper Tribunal from tribunals in Scotland

(1) Subsection (2) applies if—

  (*a*) a function is transferred under section 30(1)(*a*), (*c*), (*d*) or (*e*) in relation to England (whether or not also in relation to Wales) but is not transferred under section 30(1) in relation to Scotland,

  (*b*) an appeal may be made to the Upper Tribunal against any decision, or any decision of a particular description, made in exercising the transferred function in relation to England, and

  (*c*) no appeal may be made against a corresponding decision made in exercising the function in relation to Scotland.

(2) The Lord Chancellor may by order provide for an appeal against any such corresponding decision to be made to the Upper Tribunal.

(3) An order under subsection (2)—

  (*a*) may include provision for the purposes of or in consequence of, or for giving full effect to, provision made by the order;

  (*b*) may include such incidental, supplemental, transitional or consequential provision or savings as the Lord Chancellor thinks fit.

(4) An order under subsection (2) does not cease to have effect, and power to vary or revoke the order does not cease to be exercisable, just because either or each of the conditions in subsection (1)(*b*) and (*c*) ceases to be satisfied in relation to the function and decisions concerned.

Orders—Transfer of Tribunal Functions Order, SI 2008/2833 (made under sub-ss (2), (3)).

34 Power to provide for appeal to Upper Tribunal from tribunals in Northern Ireland

(1) Subsection (2) applies if—

  (*a*) a function is transferred under section 30(1)(*a*), (*c*), (*d*) or (*e*) in relation to England (whether or not also in relation to Wales) but is not transferred under section 30(1) in relation to Northern Ireland,

  (*b*) an appeal may be made to the Upper Tribunal against any decision, or any decision of a particular description, made in exercising the transferred function in relation to England, and

  (*c*) no appeal may be made against a corresponding decision made in exercising the function in relation to Northern Ireland.

(2) The Lord Chancellor may by order provide for an appeal against any such corresponding decision to be made to the Upper Tribunal.

(3) An order under subsection (2)—

  (*a*) may include provision for the purposes of or in consequence of, or for giving full effect to, provision made by the order;

  (*b*) may include such incidental, supplemental, transitional or consequential provision or savings as the Lord Chancellor thinks fit.

(4) An order under subsection (2) does not cease to have effect, and power to vary or revoke the order does not cease to be exercisable, just because either or each of the conditions in subsection (1)(*b*) and (*c*) ceases to be satisfied in relation to the function and decisions concerned.

Orders—Transfer of Tribunal Functions Order, SI 2008/2833 (made under sub-ss (2), (3)).

35 Transfer of Ministerial responsibilities for certain tribunals

(1) The Lord Chancellor may by order—

  (*a*) transfer any relevant function, so far as that function is exercisable by a Minister of the Crown—

    (i) to the Lord Chancellor, or

    (ii) to two (or more) Ministers of the Crown of whom one is the Lord Chancellor;

  (*b*) provide for any relevant function that is exercisable by a Minister of the Crown other than the Lord Chancellor to be exercisable by the other Minister of the Crown concurrently with the Lord Chancellor;

  (*c*) provide for any relevant function that is exercisable by the Lord Chancellor concurrently with another Minister of the Crown to cease to be exercisable by the other Minister of the Crown.

(2) In this section "relevant function" means a function, in relation to a scheduled tribunal, which relates—

  (*a*) to the operation of the tribunal (including, in particular, its membership, administration, staff, accommodation and funding, and payments to its members or staff), or

  (*b*) to the provision of expenses and allowances to persons attending the tribunal or attending elsewhere in connection with proceedings before the tribunal.

(3) In subsection (2) "scheduled tribunal" means a tribunal in a list in Schedule 6 that has effect for the purposes of this section.

(4) A relevant function may not be transferred under subsection (1) if, or to the extent that, the provision conferring the function—

(a) would be within the legislative competence of the Scottish Parliament if it were included in an Act of that Parliament, or

(b) would be within the legislative competence of the Northern Ireland Assembly if it were included in an Act of that Assembly.

(5) Subsection (4) does not apply to any relevant function of the Secretary of State—

(a) under section 41 of the Consumer Credit Act 1974 (c 39) (appeals), or

(b) under section 7 of the Estate Agents Act 1979 (c 38) (appeals).

(6) Any reference in subsection (1) to a Minister of the Crown includes a reference to a Minister of the Crown acting jointly.

(7) An order under subsection (1)—

(a) may relate to a function either wholly or in cases (including cases framed by reference to areas) specified in the order;

(b) may include provision for the purposes of, or in consequence of, or for giving full effect to, the transfer or (as the case may be) other change as regards exercise;

(c) may include such incidental, supplementary, transitional or consequential provision or savings as the Lord Chancellor thinks fit;

(d) may include provision for the transfer of any property, rights or liabilities of the person who loses functions or whose functions become shared with the Lord Chancellor.

(8) An order under subsection (1), so far as it—

(a) provides under paragraph (a) for the transfer of a function, or

(b) provides under paragraph (b) for a function to become exercisable by the Lord Chancellor, or

(c) provides under paragraph (c) for a function to cease to be exercisable by a Minister of the Crown other than the Lord Chancellor,

may not, after that transfer or other change has taken place, be revoked by another order under that subsection.

(9) Section 1 of the 1975 Act (power to transfer Ministerial functions) does not apply to a function of the Lord Chancellor—

(a) so far as it is a function transferred to the Lord Chancellor under subsection (1)(a),

(b) so far as it is a function exercisable by the Lord Chancellor as a result of provision under subsection (1)(b), or

(c) so far as it is a function that has become exercisable by the Lord Chancellor alone as a result of provision under subsection (1)(c).

(10) In this section—

"Minister of the Crown" has the meaning given by section 8(1) of the 1975 Act but includes the Commissioners for Her Majesty's Revenue and Customs;

"the 1975 Act" means the Ministers of the Crown Act 1975 (c 26).

Orders—Transfer of Tribunal Functions Order, SI 2013/1036.

36 Transfer of powers to make procedural rules for certain tribunals

(1) The Lord Chancellor may by order transfer any power to make procedural rules for a scheduled tribunal to—

(a) himself, or

(b) the Tribunal Procedure Committee.

(2) A power may not be transferred under subsection (1) if, or to the extent that, the provision conferring the power—

(a) would be within the legislative competence of the Scottish Parliament if it were included in an Act of that Parliament, or

(b) would be within the legislative competence of the Northern Ireland Assembly if it were included in an Act of that Assembly.

(3) Subsection (2) does not apply to—

(a) power conferred by section 40A(3) . . . [1] of the Consumer Credit Act 1974 (c 39) (power to make provision with respect to appeals), or

(b) power conferred by section 7(3) of the Estate Agents Act 1979 (c 38) (duty of Secretary of State to make regulations with respect to appeals under section 7(1) of that Act).

(4) An order under subsection (1)(b)—

(a) may not alter any parliamentary procedure relating to the making of the procedural rules concerned, but

(b) may otherwise include provision for the purpose of assimilating the procedure for making them to the procedure for making Tribunal Procedure Rules.

(5) An order under subsection (1)(b) may include provision requiring the Tribunal Procedure Committee to make procedural rules for purposes notified to it by the Lord Chancellor.

(6) An order under this section—

(*a*) may relate to a power either wholly or in cases (including cases framed by reference to areas) specified in the order;

(*b*) may include provision for the purposes of or in consequence of, or for giving full effect to, the transfer;

(*c*) may include such incidental, supplementary, transitional or consequential provision or savings as the Lord Chancellor thinks fit.

(7) A power to make procedural rules for a tribunal that is exercisable by the Tribunal Procedure Committee by virtue of an order under this section must be exercised by the committee with a view to securing—

(*a*) that the system for deciding matters within the jurisdiction of that tribunal is accessible and fair,

(*b*) that proceedings before that tribunal are handled quickly and efficiently,

(*c*) that the rules are both simple and simply expressed, and

(*d*) that the rules where appropriate confer on persons who are, or who are members of, that tribunal responsibility for ensuring that proceedings before that tribunal are handled quickly and efficiently.

(8) In this section—

"procedural rules", in relation to a tribunal, means provision (whether called rules or not) regulating practice or procedure before the tribunal;

"scheduled tribunal" means a tribunal in a list in Schedule 6 that has effect for the purposes of this section.

Orders—Transfer of Tribunal Functions Order, SI 2013/1036.
Amendments—[1]   Words "or 41(2)" repealed by TCEA 2007 s 146, Sch 23 Pt 1 with effect from 3 November 2008 (by virtue of SI 2008/2696 art 5(i), (vii)).

37 Power to amend lists of tribunals in Schedule 6

(1) The Lord Chancellor may by order amend Schedule 6—

(*a*) for the purpose of adding a tribunal to a list in the Schedule;

(*b*) for the purpose of removing a tribunal from a list in the Schedule;

(*c*) for the purpose of removing a list from the Schedule;

(*d*) for the purpose of adding to the Schedule a list of tribunals that has effect for the purposes of any one or more of sections 30, 32(3), 35 and 36.

(2) The following rules apply to the exercise of power under subsection (1)—

(*a*) a tribunal may not be added to a list, or be in an added list, if the tribunal is established otherwise than by or under an enactment;

(*b*) a tribunal established by an enactment passed or made after the last day of the Session in which this Act is passed must not be added to a list, or be in an added list, that has effect for the purposes of section 30;

(*c*) if any relevant function is exercisable in relation to a tribunal by the Welsh Ministers (whether by the Welsh Ministers alone, or by the Welsh Ministers jointly or concurrently with any other person), the tribunal may be added to a list, or be in an added list, only with the consent of the Welsh Ministers;

(*d*) a tribunal may be in more than one list.

(3) In subsection (2)(*c*) "relevant function", in relation to a tribunal, means a function which relates—

(*a*) to the operation of the tribunal (including, in particular, its membership, administration, staff, accommodation and funding, and payments to its members or staff), or

(*b*) to the provision of expenses and allowances to persons attending the tribunal or attending elsewhere in connection with proceedings before the tribunal.

(4) In subsection (1) "tribunal" does not include an ordinary court of law.

(5) In this section "enactment" means any enactment whenever passed or made, including an enactment comprised in subordinate legislation (within the meaning of the Interpretation Act 1978 (c 30)).

Orders—Transfer of Tribunal Functions Order, SI 2008/2833 (made under sub-s (1)).
Transfer of Functions (Estate Agents Appeals and Additional Scheduled Tribunal) Order, SI 2009/1836 (made under sub-s (1)(a)).

Amendment to Schedule 6 to the Tribunals, Courts and Enforcement Act 2007 Order, SI 2010/20 (made under sub-s (1)(a)).
Amendments to Schedule 6 to the Tribunals, Courts and Enforcement Act 2007 Order, SI 2013/1034.

38 Orders under sections 30 to 36: supplementary

(1) Provision in an order under any of sections 30 to 36 may take the form of amendments, repeals or revocations of enactments.

(2) In this section "enactment" means any enactment whenever passed or made, including an enactment comprised in subordinate legislation (within the meaning of the Interpretation Act 1978).

(3) Any power to extend enactments to a territory outside the United Kingdom shall have effect as if it included—

(*a*) power to extend those enactments as they have effect with any amendments and repeals made in them by orders under any of sections 30 to 36, and

(*b*) power to extend those enactments as if any amendments and repeals made in them under those sections had not been made.

Orders—Transfer of Functions of the Asylum and Immigration Tribunal Order, SI 2010/21.

Transfer of Tribunal Functions (Lands Tribunal and Miscellaneous Amendments) Order, SI 2009/1307).

Transfer of Tribunal Functions Order, SI 2013/1036.

Transfer of Tribunal Functions (Transport Tribunal) Order, SI 2015/65.

CHAPTER 4

ADMINISTRATIVE MATTERS IN RESPECT OF CERTAIN TRIBUNALS

39 The general duty

(1) The Lord Chancellor is under a duty to ensure that there is an efficient and effective system to support the carrying on of the business of—

(*a*) the First-tier Tribunal,

(*b*) the Upper Tribunal,

(*c*) employment tribunals,

(*d*) the Employment Appeal Tribunal, and

(*e*) the Asylum and Immigration Tribunal,

and that appropriate services are provided for those tribunals (referred to in this section and in sections 40 and 41 as "the tribunals").

(2) Any reference in this section, or in section 40 or 41, to the Lord Chancellor's general duty in relation to the tribunals is to his duty under subsection (1).

(3) The Lord Chancellor must annually prepare and lay before each House of Parliament a report as to the way in which he has discharged his general duty in relation to the tribunals.

40 Tribunal staff and services

(1) The Lord Chancellor may appoint such staff as appear to him appropriate for the purpose of discharging his general duty in relation to the tribunals.

(2) Subject to subsections (3) and (4), the Lord Chancellor may enter into such contracts with other persons for the provision, by them or their sub-contractors, of staff or services as appear to him appropriate for the purpose of discharging his general duty in relation to the tribunals.

(3) The Lord Chancellor may not enter into contracts for the provision of staff to discharge functions which involve making judicial decisions or exercising any judicial discretion.

(4) The Lord Chancellor may not enter into contracts for the provision of staff to carry out the administrative work of the tribunals unless an order made by the Lord Chancellor authorises him to do so.

(5) Before making an order under subsection (4) the Lord Chancellor must consult the Senior President of Tribunals as to what effect (if any) the order might have on the proper and efficient administration of justice.

(6) An order under subsection (4) may authorise the Lord Chancellor to enter into contracts for the provision of staff to discharge functions—

(*a*) wholly or to the extent specified in the order,

(*b*) generally or in cases or areas specified in the order, and

(*c*) unconditionally or subject to the fulfilment of conditions specified in the order.

Orders—Contracting Out (Administrative Work of Tribunals) Order, SI 2009/121 (made under sub-s (4)).

41 Provision of accommodation

(1) The Lord Chancellor may provide, equip, maintain and manage such tribunal buildings, offices and other accommodation as appear to him appropriate for the purpose of discharging his general duty in relation to the tribunals.

(2) The Lord Chancellor may enter into such arrangements for the provision, equipment, maintenance or management of tribunal buildings, offices or other accommodation as appear to him appropriate for the purpose of discharging his general duty in relation to the tribunals.

(3) The powers under—

(*a*) section 2 of the Commissioners of Works Act 1852 (c 28) (acquisition by agreement), and

(*b*) section 228(1) of the Town and Country Planning Act 1990 (c 8) (compulsory acquisition),

to acquire land necessary for the public service are to be treated as including power to acquire land for the purpose of its provision under arrangements entered into under subsection (2).

(4) In this section "tribunal building" means any place where any of the tribunals sits, including the precincts of any building in which it sits.

42 Fees

(1) The Lord Chancellor may by order prescribe fees payable in respect of—

(*a*) anything dealt with by the First-tier Tribunal,

(*b*) anything dealt with by the Upper Tribunal,

    (*c*) anything dealt with by the Asylum and Immigration Tribunal,

    (*d*) anything dealt with by an added tribunal, and

    (*e*) mediation conducted by staff appointed under section 40(1).

(2) An order under subsection (1) may, in particular, contain provision as to—

    (*a*) scales or rates of fees;

    (*b*) exemptions from or reductions in fees;

    (*c*) remission of fees in whole or in part.

(3) In subsection (1)(*d*) "added tribunal" means a tribunal specified in an order made by the Lord Chancellor.

(4) A tribunal may be specified in an order under subsection (3) only if—

    (*a*) it is established by or under an enactment, whenever passed or made, and

    (*b*) is not an ordinary court of law.

(5) Before making an order under this section, the Lord Chancellor must consult—

    (*a*) the Senior President of Tribunals, ...[1]

    (*b*) . . .[1]

(6) The making of an order under subsection (1) requires the consent of the Treasury except where the order contains provision only for the purpose of altering amounts payable by way of fees already prescribed under that subsection.

(7) The Lord Chancellor must take such steps as are reasonably practicable to bring information about fees under subsection (1) to the attention of persons likely to have to pay them.

(8) Fees payable under subsection (1) are recoverable summarily as a civil debt.

(9) Subsection (8) does not apply to the recovery in Scotland of fees payable under this section.

(10) . . .[1]

Orders—Upper Tribunal (Lands Chamber) Fees Order, SI 2009/1114 (made under sub-s (1)(b)).
First-tier Tribunal (Gambling) Fees Order, SI 2010/42.
First-tier Tribunal (Gambling) Fees (Amendment) Order, SI 2010/633.
Upper Tribunal (Lands Chamber) Fees (Amendment) Order, SI 2010/2601 (made under sub-s (1)(b)).
Upper Tribunal (Immigration and Asylum Chamber) (Judicial Review) (England and Wales) Fees Order, SI 2011/2344.
First-tier Tribunal (Immigration and Asylum Chamber) Fees Order, SI 2011/2841.
First-tier Tribunal (Property Chamber) Fees Order, SI 2013/1179 (made under sub-ss (1)(a), (2)).
Upper Tribunal (Lands Chamber) Fees (Amendment) Order, SI 2013/1199 (made under sub-ss (1)(b), (2)).
Added Tribunals (Employment Tribunals and Employment Appeal Tribunal) Order, SI 2013/1892 (made under sub-s (3)).
Employment Tribunals and the Employment Appeal Tribunal Fees Order, SI 2013/1893 (made under sub-ss (1)(d), (2)).
Upper Tribunal (Immigration and Asylum Chamber) (Judicial Review) (England and Wales) Fees (Amendment) Order, SI 2013/2069.
Courts and Tribunals Fee Remissions Order, SI 2013/2302.
First-tier Tribunal (Property Chamber) Fees (Amendment) Order, SI 2014/182.
Courts and Tribunals Fees (Miscellaneous Amendments) Order, SI 2014/590.
Upper Tribunal (Immigration and Asylum Chamber) (Judicial Review) (England and Wales) Fees (Amendment) Order, SI 2014/878.
Transfer of Tribunal Functions (Mobile Homes Act 2013 and Miscellaneous Amendments) Order, SI 2014/1900 (made under sub-s (1)).
Employment Tribunals and the Employment Appeal Tribunal Fees (Amendment) Order, SI 2015/414 (made under sub-ss (1)(d), (2)).
Civil Proceedings, Family Proceedings and Upper Tribunal Fees (Amendment) Order, SI 2016/402 (made under sub-ss (1)(b), (2)).
Court of Appeal and Upper Tribunal (Lands Chamber) Fees (Amendment) Order, SI 2016/434 (made under sub-ss (1)(b), (2)).
Civil Proceedings, First-tier Tribunal, Upper Tribunal and Employment Tribunals Fees (Amendment) Order, SI 2016/807 (made under sub-ss (1)(a), (b), (d), (2)).
Amendments—[1]   Sub-ss (5)(*b*) and word preceding it, (10) repealed by Public Bodies (Abolition of Administrative Justice and Tribunals Council) Order, Si 2013/2042 art 2(2), Schedule para 32 with effect from 19 August 2013.

43 Report by Senior President of Tribunals

(1) Each year the Senior President of Tribunals must give the Lord Chancellor a report covering, in relation to relevant tribunal cases—

    (*a*) matters that the Senior President of Tribunals wishes to bring to the attention of the Lord Chancellor, and

    (*b*) matters that the Lord Chancellor has asked the Senior President of Tribunals to cover in the report.

(2) The Lord Chancellor must publish each report given to him under subsection (1).

(3) In this section "relevant tribunal cases" means—

    (*a*) cases coming before the First-tier Tribunal,

    (*b*) cases coming before the Upper Tribunal,

    (*c*) cases coming before the Employment Appeal Tribunal, . . .[1]

    (*d*) cases coming before employment tribunals[, and

    (*e*) cases coming before the Asylum and Immigration Tribunal.][1]

Amendments—[1]   Word "and" in sub-s (3)(*c*) repealed, and sub-s (3)(*e*) and preceding word "and" inserted, by the UK Borders Act 2007 ss 56, 58, Schedule, with effect from 1 April 2008: SI 2008/309, art 4(*g*).

CHAPTER 6
SUPPLEMENTARY

46 Delegation of functions by Lord Chief Justice etc

(1) The Lord Chief Justice of England and Wales may nominate a judicial office holder (as defined in section 109(4) of the Constitutional Reform Act 2005) to exercise any of his functions under the provisions listed in subsection (2).

(2) The provisions are—

paragraphs 3(4) and 6(3)(*a*) of Schedule 2;
paragraphs 3(4) and 6(3)(*a*) of Schedule 3;
paragraphs 2(2) and 5(5) of Schedule 4;
paragraphs 21(2), 22, 24 and 25(2)(*a*) of Schedule 5.

(3) The Lord President of the Court of Session may nominate any of the following to exercise any of his functions under the provisions listed in subsection (4)—

(*a*) a judge who is a member of the First or Second Division of the Inner House of the Court of Session;
(*b*) the Senior President of Tribunals.

(4) The provisions are—

paragraphs 3(2) and 6(3)(*b*) of Schedule 2;
paragraphs 3(2) and 6(3)(*b*) of Schedule 3;
paragraphs 2(3) and 5(6) of Schedule 4;
paragraphs 23, 24, 25(2)(*b*) and (*c*) and 28(1)(*b*) of Schedule 5.

(5) The Lord Chief Justice of Northern Ireland may nominate any of the following to exercise any of his functions under the provisions listed in subsection (6)—

(*a*) the holder of one of the offices listed in Schedule 1 to the Justice (Northern Ireland) Act 2002 (c 26);
(*b*) a Lord Justice of Appeal (as defined in section 88 of that Act);
(*c*) the Senior President of Tribunals.

(6) The provisions are—

paragraphs 3(3) and 6(3)(*c*) of Schedule 2;
paragraphs 3(3) and 6(3)(*c*) of Schedule 3;
paragraphs 2(4) and 5(7) of Schedule 4;
paragraphs 24 and 25(2)(*c*) of Schedule 5.

[(7) In Schedules 2 to 4 "senior judge" means—

(*a*) the Lord Chief Justice of England and Wales,
(*b*) the Lord President of the Court of Session,
(*c*) the Lord Chief Justice of Northern Ireland, or
(*d*) the Senior President of Tribunals.][1]

Amendments—[1]   Sub-s (7) inserted by the Crime and Courts Act 2013 s 20, Sch 13 paras 42, 44(3) with effect from 1 October 2013 (by virtue of SI 2013/2200).

47 Co-operation in relation to judicial training, guidance and welfare

(1) Persons with responsibilities in connection with a courts-related activity, and persons with responsibilities in connection with the corresponding tribunals activity, must co-operate with each other in relation to the carrying-on of those activities.

(2) In this section "courts-related activity" and "corresponding tribunals activity" are to be read as follows—

(*a*) making arrangements for training of judiciary of a territory is a courts-related activity, and the corresponding tribunals activity is making arrangements for training of tribunal members;
(*b*) making arrangements for guidance of judiciary of a territory is a courts-related activity, and the corresponding tribunals activity is making arrangements for guidance of tribunal members;
(*c*) making arrangements for the welfare of judiciary of a territory is a courts-related activity, and the corresponding tribunals activity is making arrangements for the welfare of tribunal members.

(3) Subsection (1) applies to a person who has responsibilities in connection with a courts-related activity only if—

(*a*) the person is the chief justice of the territory concerned, or
(*b*) what the person does in discharging those responsibilities is done (directly or indirectly) on behalf of the chief justice of that territory.

(4) Subsection (1) applies to a person who has responsibilities in connection with a corresponding tribunals activity only if—

(*a*) the person is the Senior President of Tribunals [or the President of Welsh Tribunals][2], or
(*b*) what the person does in discharging those responsibilities is done (directly or indirectly) on behalf of the Senior President of Tribunals [or the President of Welsh Tribunals][2].

(5) For the purposes of this section—

(*a*) "territory" means—

(i) England and Wales,
(ii) Scotland, or
(iii) Northern Ireland;
(b) the "chief justice"—
    (i) of England and Wales is the Lord Chief Justice of England and Wales,
    (ii) of Scotland is the Lord President of the Court of Session, and
    (iii) of Northern Ireland is the Lord Chief Justice of Northern Ireland;
(c) a person is a "tribunal member" if the person is—
    (i) a judge, or other member, of the First-tier Tribunal or Upper Tribunal,
    (ii) a judge, or other member, of the Employment Appeal Tribunal,
    (iii) a member of a panel of members of employment tribunals (whether or not a panel of [Employment Judges][1]), . . . [2]
    (iv) any member of the Asylum and Immigration Tribunal[, or
    (v) a judge, or other member, of a tribunal listed in section 59 of the Wales Act 2017 (the Welsh tribunals).][2]

Amendments—[1] In sub-s (5)(c)(iii), words substituted by the Crime and Courts Act 2013 s 21, Sch 14 para 13(1) with effect from 1 October 2013 (by virtue of SI 2013/2200).
[2] In sub-s (4)(a), (b), words inserted, and in sub-s (5)(c), word at the end of sub-para (iii) repealed, and sub-para (v) and preceding word inserted, by the Wales Act 2017 s 69, Sch 6 para 68 with effect from 1 April 2018 (by virtue of SI 2017/1179 reg 3(n), (r)), being the later of 10 July 2017 and the commencement date of regulations made under the Wales Act 2017 Sch 5 para 7(1).

48 Consequential and other amendments, and transitional provisions
(1) Schedule 8, which makes—
    amendments consequential on provisions of this Part, and
    other amendments in connection with tribunals and inquiries,
has effect.
(2) Schedule 9, which contains transitional provisions, has effect.

49 Orders and regulations under Part 1: supplemental and procedural provisions
(1) Power—
(a) of the Lord Chancellor to make an order, or regulations, under this Part,
(b) of the Senior President of Tribunals to make an order under section 7(9), or
(c) of the Scottish Ministers, or the Welsh Ministers, to make an order under paragraph 25(2) of Schedule 7,
is exercisable by statutory instrument.
(2) The Statutory Instruments Act 1946 (c 36) shall apply in relation to the power to make orders conferred on the Senior President of Tribunals by section 7(9) as if the Senior President of Tribunals were a Minister of the Crown.
(3) Any power mentioned in subsection (1) includes power to make different provision for different purposes.
(4) Without prejudice to the generality of subsection (3), power to make an order under section 30 or 31 includes power to make different provision in relation to England, Scotland, Wales and Northern Ireland respectively.
(5) [None of the orders or regulations mentioned in subsection (6) may be made unless a draft of the statutory instrument containing the order or regulations][1] (whether alone or with other provision) has been laid before, and approved by a resolution of, each House of Parliament.
(6) [The orders and regulations][1] are—
(a) an order under section 11(8), 13(6) or (14), 30, 31(1), 32, 33, 34, 35, 36, 37 or 42(3);
[(aa) regulations under section 29D(4);][1]
(b) an order under paragraph 15 of Schedule 4;
(c) an order under section 42(1)(a) to (d) that provides for fees to be payable in respect of things for which fees have never been payable;
(d) an order under section 31(2), (7) or (9), or paragraph 30(1) of Schedule 5, that contains provision taking the form of an amendment or repeal of an enactment comprised in an Act.
(7) A statutory instrument that—
(a) contains—
    (i) an order mentioned in subsection (8), or
    (ii) regulations under Part 3 of Schedule 9, and
(b) is not subject to any requirement that a draft of the instrument be laid before, and approved by a resolution of, each House of Parliament,
is subject to annulment in pursuance of a resolution of either House of Parliament.
(8) Those orders are—
(a) an order made by the Lord Chancellor under this Part;
(b) an order made by the Senior President of Tribunals under section 7(9).

(9) A statutory instrument that contains an order made by the Scottish Ministers under paragraph 25(2) of Schedule 7 is subject to annulment in pursuance of a resolution of the Scottish Parliament.

(10) A statutory instrument that contains an order made by the Welsh Ministers under paragraph 25(2) of Schedule 7 is subject to annulment in pursuance of a resolution of the National Assembly for Wales.

Orders—First-tier Tribunal (Property Chamber) Fees Order, SI 2013/1179 (made under sub-s (3)).
Upper Tribunal (Lands Chamber) Fees (Amendment) Order, SI 2013/1199 (made under sub-s (3)).
Employment Tribunals and the Employment Appeal Tribunal Fees Order, SI 2013/1893 (made under sub-s (3)).
Courts and Tribunals Fees (Miscellaneous Amendments) Order, SI 2014/590 (made under sub-s (3)).
Civil Proceedings, Family Proceedings and Upper Tribunal Fees (Amendment) Order, SI 2016/402 (made under sub-s (3)).
Court of Appeal and Upper Tribunal (Lands Chamber) Fees (Amendment) Order, SI 2016/434 (made under sub-s (3)).
Amendments—[1]   In sub-s (5) words substituted for words "No order mentioned in subsection (6) is to be made unless a draft
of the statutory instrument containing it", in sub-s (6) words substituted for words "Those orders", and sub-para (6)(*aa*)
inserted, by the Courts and Tribunals (Judiciary and Functions of Staff) Act 2018 s 3, Schedule paras 39, 42 with effect from
10 January 2020 for the purpose of making regulations, and from 6 April 2020 for all remaining purposes (by virtue of SI
2020/24 regs 2, 3).

PART 3
ENFORCEMENT BY TAKING CONTROL OF GOODS

CHAPTER 1

PROCEDURE

62 Enforcement by taking control of goods

(1) Schedule 12 applies where an enactment, writ or warrant confers power to use the procedure in that Schedule (taking control of goods and selling them to recover a sum of money).

(2) The power conferred by a writ or warrant of control to recover a sum of money, and any power conferred by a writ or warrant of possession or delivery to take control of goods and sell them to recover a sum of money, is exercisable only by using that procedure.

(3) Schedule 13—

    (*a*) amends some powers previously called powers to distrain, so that they become powers to use that procedure;

    (*b*) makes other amendments relating to Schedule 12 and to distress or execution.

(4) The following are renamed—

    (*a*) writs of fieri facias, except writs of fieri facias de bonis ecclesiasticis, are renamed writs of control;

    (*b*) warrants of execution are renamed warrants of control;

    (*c*) warrants of distress, unless the power they confer is exercisable only against specific goods, are renamed warrants of control.

Note—This section does not extend to Scotland (s 147(2)).

63 Enforcement agents

(1) This section and section 64 apply for the purposes of Schedule 12.

(2) An individual may act as an enforcement agent only if one of these applies—

    (*a*) he acts under a certificate under section 64;

    (*b*) he is exempt;

    (*c*) he acts in the presence and under the direction of a person to whom paragraph (*a*) or (*b*) applies.

(3) An individual is exempt if he acts in the course of his duty as one of these—

    (*a*) a constable;

    (*b*) an officer of Revenue and Customs;

    [(*ba*) a person authorised to use the procedure in Schedule 12 by the Welsh Revenue Authority (or by a person to whom the Welsh Revenue Authority has delegated the function of authorising the use of the procedure);][1]

    (*c*) a person appointed under section 2(1) of the Courts Act 2003 (c 39) (court officers and staff).

(4) An individual is exempt if he acts in the course of his duty as an officer of a government department.

(5) For the purposes of an enforcement power conferred by a warrant, an individual is exempt if in relation to the warrant he is a civilian enforcement officer, as defined in section 125A of the Magistrates' Courts Act 1980 (c 43).

(6) A person is guilty of an offence if, knowingly or recklessly, he purports to act as an enforcement agent without being authorised to do so by subsection (2).

(7) A person guilty of an offence under this section is liable on summary conviction to a fine not exceeding level 5 on the standard scale.

Note—This section does not extend to Scotland (s 147(2)).

Amendments—[1]   Sub-s (3)(*ba*) inserted by the Tax Collection and Management (Wales) Act 2016 s 170(2) with effect from 25 January 2018 (by virtue of SI 2018/33 art 2(*h*)).

64 Certificates to act as an enforcement agent
(1) A certificate may be issued under this [section by a judge of the county court][1]
(2) The Lord Chancellor must make regulations about certificates under this section.
(3) The regulations may in particular include provision—
- (*a*) for fees to be charged for applications;
- (*b*) for certificates to be issued subject to conditions, including the giving of security;
- (*c*) for certificates to be limited to purposes specified by or under the regulations;
- (*d*) about complaints against holders of certificates;
- (*e*) about suspension and cancellation of certificates;
- (*f*) to modify or supplement Schedule 12 for cases where a certificate is suspended or cancelled or expires;
- (*g*) requiring courts to make information available relating to certificates.

(4) A certificate under section 7 of the Law of Distress Amendment Act 1888 (c 21) which is in force on the coming into force of this section has effect as a certificate under this section, subject to any provision made by regulations.

Regulations—Certification of Enforcement Agents Regulations, SI 2014/421.
Taking Control of Goods and Certification of Enforcement Agents (Amendment) (No. 2) (Coronavirus) Regulations, SI 2020/614.
Note—This section does not extend to Scotland (s 147(2)).
Amendments—[1]   In sub-s (1), words substituted by the Crime and Courts Act 2013 s 17, Sch 9 paras 45, 46 with effect from 22 April 2014 (by virtue of SI 2014/954 art 2(*c*)).

65 Common law rules replaced
(1) This Chapter replaces the common law rules about the exercise of the powers which under it become powers to use the procedure in Schedule 12.
(2) The rules replaced include—
- (*a*) rules distinguishing between an illegal, an irregular and an excessive exercise of a power;
- (*b*) rules that would entitle a person to bring proceedings of a kind for which paragraph 66 of Schedule 12 provides (remedies available to the debtor);
- (*c*) rules of replevin;
- (*d*) rules about rescuing goods.

Note—This section does not extend to Scotland (s 147(2)).

66 Pre-commencement enforcement not affected
Where—
- (*a*) by any provision of this Part a power becomes a power to use the procedure in Schedule 12, and
- (*b*) before the commencement of that provision, goods have been distrained or executed against, or made subject to a walking possession agreement, under the power,

this Part does not affect the continuing exercise of the power in relation to those goods.

Note—This section does not extend to Scotland (s 147(2)).

67 Transfer of county court enforcement
In section 85(2) of the County Courts Act 1984 (c 28) (under which writs of control give the district judge, formerly called the registrar, power to execute judgments or orders for payment of money) for "the registrar shall be" substitute "any person authorised by or on behalf of the Lord Chancellor is".

Note—This section does not extend to Scotland (s 147(2)).

68 Magistrates' courts warrants of control
Section 125ZA inserted into the Magistrates' Courts Act 1980 (c 43).

Note—This section does not extend to Scotland (s 147(2)).

69 County court warrants of control etc
Section 99 of the County Courts Act 1984 substituted.

Note—This section does not extend to Scotland (s 147(2)).

70 Power of High Court to stay execution
(1) If, at any time, the High Court is satisfied that a party to proceedings is unable to pay—
- (*a*) a sum recovered against him (by way of satisfaction of the claim or counterclaim in the proceedings or by way of costs or otherwise), or
- (*b*) any instalment of such a sum,

the court may stay the execution of any writ of control issued in the proceedings, for whatever period and on whatever terms it thinks fit.

(2) The court may act under subsection (1) from time to time until it appears that the cause of the inability to pay has ceased.

(3) In this section a party to proceedings includes every person, whether or not named as a party, who is served with notice of the proceedings or attends them.

Note—This section does not extend to Scotland (s 147(2)).

CHAPTER 2

RENT ARREARS RECOVERY

(not reproduced)

CHAPTER 3
GENERAL

88 Abolition of Crown preference

Crown preference for the purposes of execution against goods is abolished.

Note—This section does not extend to Scotland (s 147(2)).

89 Application to the Crown

(1) This Part binds the Crown.

(2) But the procedure in Schedule 12 may not be used—

   (*a*) to recover debts due from the Crown,

   (*b*) to take control of or sell goods of the Crown (including goods owned by the Crown jointly or in common with another person), or

   (*c*) to enter premises occupied by the Crown.

Note—This section does not extend to Scotland (s 147(2)).

90 Regulations

(1) In this Part—

   "prescribed" means prescribed by regulations;

   "regulations" means regulations made by the Lord Chancellor.

(2) The following apply to regulations under this Part.

(3) Any power to make regulations is exercisable by statutory instrument.

(4) . . .[1]

(5) . . .[1] a statutory instrument containing regulations is subject to annulment in pursuance of a resolution of either House of Parliament.

(6) Regulations may include any of these that the Lord Chancellor considers necessary or expedient—

   (*a*) supplementary, incidental or consequential provision;

   (*b*) transitory, transitional or saving provision.

(7) Regulations may make different provision for different cases.

Regulations—Taking Control of Goods and Certification of Enforcement Agents (Amendment) (No. 2) (Coronavirus) Regulations, SI 2020/614.

Note—This section does not extend to Scotland (s 147(2)).

Amendments—[1] Sub-s (4) repealed, and in sub-s (5), words "In any other case" repealed by the Crime and Courts Act 2013 s 25(1), (8) with effect from 15 July 2013 (by virtue of SI 2013/1725 art 2(*d*)).

PART 4

ENFORCEMENT OF JUDGMENTS AND ORDERS

Attachment of earnings orders

91 Attachment of earnings orders: deductions at fixed rates

(1) Schedule 15 makes amendments to the Attachment of Earnings Act 1971 (c 32).

(2) Those amendments are about the basis on which periodical deductions are to be made under an attachment of earnings order.

(3) In particular, they provide that deductions under certain orders are to be made in accordance with a fixed deductions scheme made by the Lord Chancellor (rather than in accordance with Part I of Schedule 3 to the 1971 Act).

92 Attachment of earnings orders: finding the debtor's current employer

(1) Sections 15A–15D inserted into the Attachment of Earnings Act 1971.

(2) This section applies in relation to any attachment of earnings order, whether made before or after the commencement of this section.

(3) In relation to an offence committed before the commencement of section 154(1) of the Criminal Justice Act 2003 (c 44), the reference in section 15B(10)(*b*) of the Attachment of Earnings Act 1971 (c 32) to 12 months is to be read as a reference to 6 months.

Note—This section does not extend to Scotland (s 147(2)).

Charging orders

93 Payment by instalments: making and enforcing charging orders

(1) Subsections (2), (3) and (4) make amendments to the Charging Orders Act 1979 (c 53).

(2) In section 1 (charging orders), after subsection (5) insert—

"(6)   Subsections (7) and (8) apply where, under a judgment or order of the High Court or a county court, a debtor is required to pay a sum of money by instalments.

(7)   The fact that there has been no default in payment of the instalments does not prevent a charging order from being made in respect of that sum.

(8)   But if there has been no default, the court must take that into account when considering the circumstances of the case under subsection (5)."

(3) In section 3 (provisions supplementing sections 1 and 2), after subsection (4) insert—

"(4A)   Subsections (4C) to (4E) apply where—

  (*a*)   a debtor is required to pay a sum of money in instalments under a judgment or order of the High Court or a county court (an "instalments order"), and

  (*b*)   a charge has been imposed by a charging order in respect of that sum.

(4B)   In subsections (4C) to (4E) references to the enforcement of a charge are to the making of an order for the enforcement of the charge.

(4C)   The charge may not be enforced unless there has been default in payment of an instalment under the instalments order.

(4D)   Rules of court may—

  (*a*)   provide that, if there has been default in payment of an instalment, the charge may be enforced only in prescribed cases, and

  (*b*)   limit the amounts for which, and the times at which, the charge may be enforced.

(4E)   Except so far as otherwise provided by rules of court under subsection (4D)—

  (*a*)   the charge may be enforced, if there has been default in payment of an instalment, for the whole of the sum of money secured by the charge and the costs then remaining unpaid, or for such part as the court may order, but

  (*b*)   the charge may not be enforced unless, at the time of enforcement, the whole or part of an instalment which has become due under the instalments order remains unpaid."

(4) In section 6(2) (meaning of references to judgment or order of High Court or county court), for "section 1" substitute "sections 1 and 3".

(5) In section 313(4) of the Insolvency Act 1986 (c 45) (charge on bankrupt's home: certain provisions of section 3 of Charging Orders Act 1979 to apply), for the words before "section 3" substitute "Subsection (1), (2), (4), (5) and (6) of".

(6) This section does not apply in a case where a judgment or order of the High Court or a county court under which a debtor is required to pay a sum of money by instalments was made, or applied for, before the coming into force of this section.

Note—This section does not extend to Scotland (s 147(2)).

94 Charging orders: power to set financial thresholds

Section 3A of the Charging Orders Act 1979 (c 53) inserted.

Note—This section does not extend to Scotland (s 147(2)).

Information requests and orders

95 Application for information about action to recover judgment debt

(1) A person who is the creditor in relation to a judgment debt may apply to the High Court[, the family court][1] or a county court for information about what kind of action it would be appropriate to take in court to recover that particular debt.

(2) An application under subsection (1) must comply with any provision made in regulations about the making of such applications.

Note—This section does not extend to Scotland (s 147(2)).

Amendments—[1]   In sub-s (1), words inserted by the Crime and Courts Act 2013 (Family Court: Consequential Provision) Order, SI 2014/605 arts 22, 23 with effect from 22 April 2014 (being the date on which the Crime and Courts Act 2013, s 17(3) is brought fully into force by virtue of SI 2014/954, art 2(*a*), see SI 2014/605, art 1).

96 Action by the court

(1) This section applies if the creditor in relation to a judgment debt makes an application for information under section 95.

(2) The relevant court may make one or more of the following in relation to the debtor—

  (*a*)   a departmental information request;

  (*b*)   an information order.

(3) The relevant court may exercise its powers under subsection (2) only if it is satisfied that to do so will help it to deal with the creditor's application.

(4) Before exercising its powers under subsection (2), the relevant court must give notice to the debtor that the court intends to make a request or order.

(5) The relevant court may not make a departmental information request to the Commissioners unless regulations are in force that have been made under section 102(4) and (7) and relate to the use or disclosure of debtor information disclosed by the Commissioners.

(6) The relevant court may disclose such information (including information identifying the debtor) as it considers necessary to assist the recipient of a request or order to comply with the request or order.

(7) A disclosure under subsection (6) is not to be taken to breach any restriction on the disclosure of information (however imposed).

(8) Nothing in this section is to be taken to prejudice any power that exists apart from this section to request or order the disclosure of information.

Note—This section does not extend to Scotland (s 147(2)).

97 Departmental information requests

(1) A departmental information request is a request for the disclosure of information held by, or on behalf of, a government department.

(2) The request is to be made to the Minister of the Crown, or other person, who is in charge of the department.

(3) In the case of a request made to the designated Secretary of State, the disclosure of some or all of the following information may be requested—

    (a) the full name of the debtor;

    (b) the address of the debtor;

    (c) the date of birth of the debtor;

    (d) the national insurance number of the debtor;

    (e) prescribed information.

(4) In the case of a request made to the Commissioners, the disclosure of some or all of the following information may be requested—

    (a) whether or not the debtor is employed;

    (b) the name and address of the employer (if the debtor is employed);

    (c) the national insurance number of the debtor;

    (d) prescribed information.

(5) In the case of any other request, the disclosure of prescribed information may be requested.

(6) In this section—

    "designated Secretary of State" means the Secretary of State designated for the purpose of this section by regulations;

    "government department" does not include the following—

        (a) any part of the Scottish Administration;

        (b) a Northern Ireland department;

        (c) the Welsh Assembly Government or any member of staff appointed under section 52 of the Government of Wales Act 2006 (c 32);

    "prescribed information", in relation to a departmental information request, means information that falls within the category or categories of information (if any) prescribed by regulations in relation to the department to which the request relates.

Note—This section does not extend to Scotland (s 147(2)).

Reference to the Welsh Assembly Government is to be read as, or as including, a reference to the Welsh Government, unless the context requires otherwise (Wales Act 2014 s 4(4)(a)).

98 Information orders

(1) An information order is an order of the relevant court which—

    (a) specifies a prescribed person ("the information discloser"),

    (b) specifies prescribed information relating to the debtor ("the required information"), and

    (c) orders the information discloser to disclose the required information to the relevant court.

(2) In subsection (1) "prescribed" means prescribed in regulations.

(3) Regulations under this section may be made by reference to—

    (a) particular persons or particular descriptions of person (or both);

    (b) particular information or particular descriptions of information (or both).

(4) Regulations may, in particular, be made under this section so as to ensure that—

    (a) an information order made against a particular person, or a person of a particular description, may order that person to disclose only particular information, or information of a particular description;

    (b) an information order that orders the disclosure of particular information, or information of a particular description, may only be made against a particular person, or a person of a particular description.

(5) Regulations under this section must not make provision that would allow the relevant court to order—

    (a) the disclosure of information by the debtor, or

    (b) the disclosure of information held by, or on behalf of, a government department.

Note—This section does not extend to Scotland (s 147(2)).

99 Responding to a departmental information request

(1) This section applies if the relevant court makes a departmental information request.

(2) The recipient of the request may disclose to the relevant court any information (whether held by the department or on its behalf) that the recipient considers is necessary to comply with the request.

(3) A disclosure under subsection (2) is not to be taken to breach any restriction on the disclosure of information (however imposed).

(4) Nothing in this section is to be taken to prejudice any power that exists apart from this section to disclose information.

Note—This section does not extend to Scotland (s 147(2)).

100 Information order: required information not held etc

(1) An information discloser is not to be regarded as having breached an information order because of a failure to disclose some or all of the required information, if that failure is for one of the permitted reasons.

(2) These are the permitted reasons—
     (a) the information provider does not hold the information;
     (b) the information provider is unable to ascertain whether the information is held, because of the way in which the information order identifies the debtor;
     (c) the disclosure of the information would involve the information discloser in unreasonable effort or expense.

(3) It is to be presumed that a failure to disclose required information is for a permitted reason if—
     (a) the information discloser gives the relevant court a certificate that complies with subsection (4), and
     (b) there is no evidence that the failure is not for a permitted reason.

(4) The certificate must state—
     (a) which of the required information is not being disclosed;
     (b) what the permitted reason is, or permitted reasons are, for the failure to disclose that information.

(5) Any reference in this section to the information discloser holding, or not holding, information includes a reference to the information being held, or not being held, on the information discloser's behalf.

Note—This section does not extend to Scotland (s 147(2)).

101 Using the information about the debtor

(1) This section applies if—
     (a) the creditor in relation to a judgment debt makes an application for information under section 95, and
     (b) information ("debtor information") is disclosed to the relevant court in compliance with a request or order made under section 96.

(2) The relevant court may use the debtor information for the purpose of making another request or order under section 96 in relation to the debtor.

(3) The relevant court may use the debtor information for the purpose of providing the creditor with information about what kind of action (if any) it would be appropriate to take in court (whether the relevant court or another court) to recover the judgment debt.

(4) If the creditor takes any action in the relevant court to recover the judgment debt, the relevant court may use the debtor information in carrying out functions in relation to that action.

(5) If the creditor takes any action in another court to recover the judgment debt—
     (a) the relevant court may disclose the debtor information to the other court, and
     (b) the other court may use that information in carrying out functions in relation to that action.

(6) Debtor information may be used or disclosed under any of subsections (3) to (5) only if—
     (a) regulations about such use or disclosure of information are in force, and
     (b) the use or disclosure complies with those regulations.

(7) In addition, if the debtor information was disclosed by the Commissioners, the information may be used or disclosed under any of subsections (3) to (5) only with the consent of the Commissioners.

(8) Consent for the purposes of subsection (7) may be given—
     (a) in relation to particular use or a particular disclosure, or
     (b) in relation to use, or a disclosure made, in such circumstances as may be specified or described in the consent.

(9) The use or disclosure of information in accordance with this section is not to be taken to breach any restriction on the use or disclosure of information (however imposed).

(10) Nothing in this section is to be taken to prejudice any power that exists apart from this section to use or disclose information.

Note—This section does not extend to Scotland (s 147(2)).

102 Offence of unauthorised use or disclosure

(1) This section applies if—
     (a) an application is made under section 95 in relation to recovery of a judgment debt ("the relevant judgment debt"),

(*b*) a departmental information request or an information order is made in consequence of that application, and

(*c*) information ("debtor information") is disclosed in accordance with the request or order.

(2) A person to whom the debtor information is disclosed commits an offence if he—

(*a*) uses or discloses the debtor information, and

(*b*) the use or disclosure is not authorised by any of subsections (3) to (6).

(3) The use or disclosure of the debtor information is authorised if it is in accordance with section 101.

(4) The use or disclosure of the debtor information is authorised if it is—

(*a*) in accordance with an enactment or order of court, or

(*b*) for the purposes of any proceedings before a court,

and it is in accordance with regulations.

(5) The use or disclosure of the debtor information is authorised if the information has previously been lawfully disclosed to the public.

(6) The use or disclosure of the debtor information is authorised if it is in accordance with rules of court that comply with regulations under subsection (7).

(7) Regulations may make provision about the circumstances, if any, in which rules of court may allow access to, or the supply of, information disclosed in accordance with a department information request or an information order.

(8) It is a defence for a person charged with an offence under subsection (2) to prove that he reasonably believed that the use or disclosure was lawful.

(9) A person guilty of an offence under subsection (2) is liable—

(*a*) on conviction on indictment, to imprisonment for a term not exceeding two years, to a fine or to both;

(*b*) on summary conviction, to imprisonment for a term not exceeding twelve months, to a fine not exceeding the statutory maximum, or to both.

Note—This section does not extend to Scotland (s 147(2)).

103 Regulations

(1) It is for the Lord Chancellor to make information regulations.

(2) But the Lord Chancellor may make the following regulations only with the agreement of the Commissioners—

(*a*) regulations under section 97(4)(*d*);

(*b*) regulations under section 102(4) or (7) so far as the regulations relate to the use or disclosure of debtor information disclosed by the Commissioners.

(3) Information regulations are to be made by statutory instrument.

(4) A statutory instrument containing information regulations may not be made unless a draft of the instrument has been laid before and approved by a resolution of each House of Parliament.

(5) But subsection (4) does not apply in the case of a statutory instrument that contains only—

(*a*) regulations under section 95, or

(*b*) regulations under section 97 which designate a Secretary of State for the purpose of that section.

(6) In such a case, the statutory instrument is subject to annulment in pursuance of a resolution of either House of Parliament.

(7) In this section "information regulations" means regulations under any of sections 95 to 102.

Note—This section does not extend to Scotland (s 147(2)).

104 Interpretation

(1) This section applies for the purposes of sections 95 to 103.

(2) In those provisions—

"Commissioners" means the Commissioners for Her Majesty's Revenue and Customs;

"creditor", in relation to a judgment debt, means—

(*a*) the person to whom the debt is payable (whether directly or through [any court,]¹ an officer of any court or another person);

(*b*) where the debt is payable under an administration order (within the meaning of Part 6 of the County Courts Act 1984 (c 28)), any one of the creditors scheduled to the order;

"debtor", in relation to a judgment debt, means the person by whom the debt is payable;

"departmental information request" has the meaning given by section 97;

"information" means information held in any form;

"information discloser", in relation to an information order, has the meaning given by section 98(1)(*a*);

"information order" has the meaning given by section 98;

"judgment debt" means either of the following—

(*a*) a sum which is payable under a judgment or order enforceable by the High Court[, the family court]¹ or a county court;

(*b*) a sum which, by virtue of an enactment, is recoverable as if it were payable under a judgment or order of the High Court[, the family court][1] or of a county court (including a sum which is so recoverable because a court so orders);

"required information", in relation to an information order, has the meaning given by section 98(1)(*b*);

"relevant court", in relation to an application under section 95, means the court to which the application is made

(3) Any reference to information held on behalf of a government department, or on behalf of an information discloser, includes a reference to any information which—

(*a*) is held by a person who provides services to the department or to the information discloser, and

(*b*) is held by that person in connection with the provision of those services.

Note—This section does not extend to Scotland (s 147(2)).

Amendments—[1]   In sub-s (2), words in definitions of "creditor" and "judgment debt", inserted by the Crime and Courts Act 2013 (Family Court: Consequential Provision) Order, SI 2014/605 arts 22, 24 with effect from 22 April 2014 (being the date on which the Crime and Courts Act 2013, s 17(3) is brought fully into force by virtue of SI 2014/954, art 2(*a*), see SI 2014/605, art 1).

105 Application and transitional provision

(1) Sections 95 to 104 apply in relation to any judgment debt, whether it became payable, or recoverable, before or after the commencement of those sections.

(2) In relation to an offence committed before the commencement of section 154(1) of the Criminal Justice Act 2003 (c 44), the reference in section 102(9)(*b*) to 12 months is to be read as a reference to 6 months.

Note—This section does not extend to Scotland (s 147(2)).

PART 8
GENERAL

146 Repeals

Schedule 23 contains repeals.

147 Extent

(1) Parts 1, 2 and 6 and this Part extend to England and Wales, Scotland and Northern Ireland.

(2) The other provisions of this Act extend only to England and Wales.

(3) Subsections (1) and (2) are subject to subsections (4) and (5).

(4) Unless provided otherwise, amendments, repeals and revocations in this Act extend to any part of the United Kingdom to which the provisions amended, repealed or revoked extend.

(5) The following extend also to the Isle of Man—

(*a*) section 143(1) and (2),

(*b*) the repeal by this Act of any provision specified in Part 6 of Schedule 23 that extends to the Isle of Man,

(*c*) sections 145 and 148(5) to (7) so far as relating to—

(i) section 143(1) and (2), and

(ii) the provisions of this Act by which the repeals mentioned in paragraph (*b*) are effected, and

(*d*) this section and section 149.

148 Commencement

(1) Section 60 comes into force at the end of the period of two months beginning with the day on which this Act is passed.

(2) The provisions of Chapter 3 of Part 5 come into force in accordance with provision made by the Lord Chancellor or the Secretary of State by order.

(3) The provisions of Part 6 come into force, except as provided by subsection (4), in accordance with provision made by the Secretary of State by order.

(4) The provisions of Part 6 come into force, in so far as they extend to Scotland, in accordance with provision made by the Scottish Ministers by order.

(5) The remaining provisions of this Act, except sections 53, 55, 56, 57, 145, 147, 149, this section and Schedule 11, come into force in accordance with provision made by the Lord Chancellor by order.

(6) An order under this section may make different provision for different purposes.

(7) The power to make an order under this section is exercisable by statutory instrument.

Orders—Tribunals, Courts and Enforcement Act 2007 (Commencement No 1) Order, SI 2007/2709.

Tribunals, Courts and Enforcement Act 2007 (Commencement No 2) Order, SI 2007/3613.

Tribunals, Courts and Enforcement Act 2007 (Commencement) (Scotland) Order, SSI 2008/150 (in relation to Scotland only).

Tribunals, Courts and Enforcement Act 2007 (Commencement No 3) Order, SI 2008/749.

Tribunals, Courts and Enforcement Act 2007 (Commencement No 4) Order, SI 2008/1158.

Tribunals, Courts and Enforcement Act 2007 (Commencement No 5 and Transitional Provisions) Order, SI 2008/1653.
Tribunals, Courts and Enforcement Act 2007 (Commencement No 6 and Transitional Provisions) Order, SI 2008/2696.
Tribunals, Courts and Enforcement Act 2007 (Commencement No 7) Order, SI 2009/382.
Tribunals, Courts and Enforcement Act 2007 (Commencement No 8) Order, SI 2012/1312.
Tribunals, Courts and Enforcement Act 2007 (Commencement No 9) Order, SI 2013/1739.
Tribunals, Courts and Enforcement Act 2007 (Commencement No 10) Order, SI 2013/2043.
Tribunals, Courts and Enforcement Act 2007 (Commencement No 11) Order, SI 2014/768.

149 Short title

This Act may be cited as the Tribunals, Courts and Enforcement Act 2007.

SCHEDULES

SCHEDULE 1

SENIOR PRESIDENT OF TRIBUNALS

Section 2

PART 1

RECOMMENDATIONS FOR APPOINTMENT

Duty to fill vacancies

1—(1) If there is a vacancy in the office of Senior President of Tribunals, the Lord Chancellor must recommend a person for appointment to that office.
(2) Sub-paragraph (1) does not apply to a vacancy while the Lord Chief Justice of England and Wales agrees that it may remain unfilled.

The two routes to a recommendation: agreement under this paragraph or selection under Part 2

2—(1) Before the Lord Chancellor may recommend a person for appointment to the office of Senior President of Tribunals, the Lord Chancellor must consult—
    (*a*) the Lord Chief Justice of England and Wales,
    (*b*) the Lord President of the Court of Session, and
    (*c*) the Lord Chief Justice of Northern Ireland.
(2) Sub-paragraphs (3) and (4) apply if—
    (*a*) the outcome of consultation under sub-paragraph (1) is agreement between—
        (i) the Lord Chancellor,
        (ii) the Lord Chief Justice of England and Wales,
        (iii) the Lord President of the Court of Session, and
        (iv) the Lord Chief Justice of Northern Ireland,
        as to the person to be recommended, and
    (*b*) the person is—
        (i) an ordinary judge of the Court of Appeal in England and Wales,
        (ii) a judge of the Court of Session who is a member of the First or Second Division of the Inner House of that Court, or
        (iii) a Lord Justice of Appeal in Northern Ireland.
(3) The Lord Chancellor must recommend the person for appointment to the office of Senior President of Tribunals, subject to sub-paragraph (4).
(4) Where the person—
    (*a*) declines to be recommended, or does not agree within a time specified to him for that purpose, or
    (*b*) is otherwise not available within a reasonable time to be recommended,
the Lord Chancellor must, instead of recommending the person for appointment, consult afresh under sub-paragraph (1).
(5) If the Lord Chancellor has consulted under sub-paragraph (1) but sub-paragraphs (3) and (4) do not apply following that consultation, the Lord Chancellor must make a request to the Judicial Appointments Commission for a person to be selected for recommendation for appointment to the office of Senior President of Tribunals.

PART 2

SELECTION BY THE JUDICIAL APPOINTMENTS COMMISSION

Eligibility for selection

3   A person is eligible for selection in pursuance of a request under paragraph 2(5) only if—
    (*a*) he satisfies the judicial-appointment eligibility condition on a 7-year basis,

(*b*) he is an advocate or solicitor in Scotland of at least seven years' standing, or

(*c*) he is a barrister or solicitor in Northern Ireland of at least seven years' standing.

The selection process

4 Section 75A–75G inserted into Constitutional Reform Act 2005.

Commencement—Tribunals, Courts and Enforcement Act 2007 (Commencement No 1) Order, SI 2007/2709 art 2(*g*) (paras 1–11 come into force on 19 September 2007).

Withdrawal and modification of requests under paragraph 2(5)

5—(1) Section 95 of the Constitutional Reform Act 2005 (c 4) (withdrawal and modification of requests) is amended as follows.

(2) In subsection (1) (application of section), after "87" insert "or paragraph 2(5) of Schedule 1 to the Tribunals, Courts and Enforcement Act 2007".

(3) In subsection (4) (limitation on withdrawal of request under subsection (2)(*c*)), after "73(2)," insert "75E(2),".

PART 3
TERMS OF OFFICE

Tenure, removal, resignation etc

6—(1) If—

(*a*) a person appointed to the office of Senior President of Tribunals is appointed on terms that provide for him to retire from the office at a particular time specified in those terms ("the end of the fixed-term"), and

(*b*) the end of the fixed-term is earlier than the time at which the person is required by the 1993 Act to retire from the office,

the person shall, if still holding the office at the end of the fixed-term, vacate the office at the end of the fixed-term.

(2) Subject to sub-paragraph (1) (and to the 1993 Act), a person appointed to the office of Senior President of Tribunals shall hold that office during good behaviour, subject to a power of removal by Her Majesty on an address presented to Her by both Houses of Parliament.

(3) It is for the Lord Chancellor to recommend to Her Majesty the exercise of the power of removal under sub-paragraph (2).

(4) In this paragraph "the 1993 Act" means the Judicial Pensions and Retirement Act 1993 (c 8).

7—(1) Sub-paragraph (2) applies to a person appointed to the office of Senior President of Tribunals on a recommendation made under paragraph 2(3).

(2) The person ceases to be Senior President of Tribunals if he ceases to fall within paragraph 2(2)(*b*).

8 A person who holds the office of Senior President of Tribunals may at any time resign that office by giving the Lord Chancellor notice in writing to that effect.

9—(1) The Lord Chancellor, if satisfied by means of a medical certificate that a person holding the office of Senior President of Tribunals—

(*a*) is disabled by permanent infirmity from the performance of the duties of the office, and

(*b*) is for the time being incapacitated from resigning the office,

may, subject to sub-paragraph (2), by instrument under his hand declare the person to have vacated the office; and the instrument shall have the like effect for all purposes as if the person had on the date of the instrument resigned the office.

(2) A declaration under sub-paragraph (1) with respect to a person shall be of no effect unless it is made with the concurrence of—

(*a*) the Lord Chief Justice of England and Wales,

(*b*) the Lord President of the Court of Session, and

(*c*) the Lord Chief Justice of Northern Ireland.

Remuneration, allowances and expenses

10 The Lord Chancellor may pay to the Senior President of Tribunals such amounts (if any) as the Lord Chancellor may determine by way of—

(*a*) remuneration;

(*b*) allowances;

(*c*) expenses.

Oaths

11—(1) A person appointed to the office of Senior President of Tribunals must take the required oaths in the presence of—

(a) the Lord Chief Justice of England and Wales, or

(b) another holder of high judicial office (as defined in section 60(2) of the Constitutional Reform Act 2005 (c 4)) who is nominated by the Lord Chief Justice of England and Wales for the purpose of taking the oaths from the person.

(2) Sub-paragraph (1) applies whether or not the person has previously taken the required oaths after accepting another office.

(3) In this paragraph "the required oaths" means—

(a) the oath of allegiance, and

(b) the judicial oath,

as set out in the Promissory Oaths Act 1868 (c 72).

PART 4

CERTAIN FUNCTIONS OF THE SENIOR PRESIDENT

Meaning of "tribunal member"

12—(1) For the purposes of this Part of this Schedule, each of the following is a "tribunal member"—

(a) a judge, or other member, of the First-tier Tribunal or Upper Tribunal,

(b) any member of the Asylum and Immigration Tribunal,

(c) a member of a panel of members of employment tribunals (whether or not a panel of [Employment Judges][1]),

(d) a judge, or other member, of the Employment Appeal Tribunal, and

(e) a person who is, or is a member of, a tribunal in a list in Schedule 6 that has effect for the purposes of section 30.

(2) In this Part of this Schedule "tribunals" means—

(a) the First-tier Tribunal,

(b) the Upper Tribunal,

(c) the Asylum and Immigration Tribunal,

(d) employment tribunals,

(e) the Employment Appeal Tribunal, and

(f) any tribunal in a list in Schedule 6 that has effect for the purposes of section 30.

Amendments—[1]   In sub-para (1)(c), words substituted for word "chairmen" by the Crime and Courts Act 2013 s 21, Sch 14 para 13(1) with effect from 1 October 2013 (by virtue of SI 2013/2200).

Representations to Parliament

13   The Senior President of Tribunals may lay before Parliament written representations on matters that appear to him to be matters of importance relating—

(a) to tribunal members, or

(b) otherwise to the administration of justice by tribunals.

Representation of views of tribunal members

14   The Senior President of Tribunals is responsible for representing the views of tribunal members to Parliament, to the Lord Chancellor and to Ministers of the Crown generally.

SCHEDULE 2

JUDGES AND OTHER MEMBERS OF THE FIRST-TIER TRIBUNAL

Section 4

Power to appoint judges of First-tier Tribunal

1—(1) The [Senior President of Tribunals][1] may appoint a person to be one of the judges of the First-tier Tribunal.

(2) A person is eligible for appointment under sub-paragraph (1) only if the person—

(a) satisfies the judicial-appointment eligibility condition on a 5-year basis,

(b) is an advocate or solicitor in Scotland of at least five years' standing,

(c) is a barrister or solicitor in Northern Ireland of at least five years' standing, or

(d) in the [opinion of the Senior President of Tribunals][1], has gained experience in law which makes the person as suitable for appointment as if the person satisfied any of paragraphs (a) to (c).

(3) Section 52(2) to (5) (meaning of "gain experience in law") apply for the purposes of sub-paragraph (2)(*d*), but as if section 52(4)(*i*) referred to the [Senior President of Tribunals][1] instead of to the relevant decision-maker.

Amendments—[1]   In sub-paras (1), (3), words substituted for words "Lord Chancellor", and in sub-para (2)(*d*), words substituted for words "Lord Chancellor's opinion" by the Crime and Courts Act 2013 s 20, Sch 13 paras 42, 45(1)–(4) with effect from 1 October 2013 (by virtue of SI 2013/2200).

Power to appoint other members of First-tier Tribunal

2—(1) The [Senior President of Tribunals][1] may appoint a person to be one of the members of the First-tier Tribunal who are not judges of the tribunal.

(2) A person is eligible for appointment under sub-paragraph (1) only if the person has qualifications prescribed in an order made by the Lord Chancellor with the concurrence of the Senior President of Tribunals.

Orders—Qualifications for Appointment of Members to the First-tier Tribunal and Upper Tribunal Order, SI 2008/2692.
Qualifications for Appointment of Members to the First-tier Tribunal and Upper Tribunal (Amendment) Order, SI 2009/1592.
Qualifications for Appointment of Members to the First-tier Tribunal and Upper Tribunal (Amendment) Order, SI 2012/897.
Qualifications for Appointment of Members to the First-tier Tribunal and Upper Tribunal (Amendment) Order, SI 2013/1185.
Amendments—[1]   In sub-para (1), words substituted for words "Lord Chancellor" by the Crime and Courts Act 2013 s 20, Sch 13 paras 42, 45(1), (2) with effect from 1 October 2013 (by virtue of SI 2013/2200).

Appointed and transferred-in judges and other members: removal from office

3—(1) This paragraph applies to any power by which—

   (*a*) a person appointed under paragraph 1(1) or 2(1),

   (*b*) a transferred-in judge of the First-tier Tribunal, or

   (*c*) a transferred-in other member of the First-tier Tribunal,

may be removed from office.

(2) If the person exercises functions wholly or mainly in Scotland, the power may be exercised only with the concurrence of the Lord President of the Court of Session.

(3) If the person exercises functions wholly or mainly in Northern Ireland, the power may be exercised only with the concurrence of the Lord Chief Justice of Northern Ireland.

(4) If neither of sub-paragraphs (2) and (3) applies, the power may be exercised only with the concurrence of the Lord Chief Justice of England and Wales.

Terms of appointment

4—(1) This paragraph applies—

   (*a*) to a person appointed under paragraph 1(1) or 2(1),

   (*b*) to a transferred-in judge of the First-tier Tribunal, and

   (*c*) to a transferred-in other member of the First-tier Tribunal.

(2) If the terms of the person's appointment provide that he is appointed on a salaried (as opposed to fee-paid) basis, the person may be removed from office—

   (*a*) only by the Lord Chancellor (and in accordance with paragraph 3), and

   (*b*) only on the ground of inability or misbehaviour.

[(2A) If the terms of the person's appointment provide that the person is appointed on a fee-paid basis, the person may be removed from office—

   (*a*) only by the Lord Chancellor (and in accordance with paragraph 3), and

   (*b*) only on—

      (i) the ground of inability or misbehaviour, or

      (ii) a ground specified in the person's terms of appointment.

(2B) If the period (or extended period) for which the person is appointed ends before—

   (*a*) the day on which the person attains the age of 70, or

   (*b*) if different, the day that for the purposes of section 26 of the Judicial Pensions and Retirement Act 1993 is the compulsory retirement date for the office concerned in the person's case,

then, subject to sub-paragraph (2C), the Lord Chancellor must extend the period of the person's appointment (including a period already extended under this sub-paragraph) before it ends.

(2C) Extension under sub-paragraph (2B)—

   (*a*) requires the person's agreement,

   (*b*) is to be for such period as the Lord Chancellor considers appropriate, and

   (*c*) may be refused on—

      (i) the ground of inability or misbehaviour, or

      (ii) a ground specified in the person's terms of appointment,

     but only with any agreement of a senior judge (see section 46(7)), or a nominee of a senior judge, that may be required by those terms.][1]

(3) Subject to [the preceding provisions of this paragraph (but subject in the first place][1] to the Judicial Pensions and Retirement Act 1993 (c 8)), the person is to hold and vacate office in accordance with the terms of his appointment[, which are to be such as the Lord Chancellor may determine][1].

Amendments—[1]   Sub-paras (2A)–(2C) inserted, and in sub-para (3), words substituted for words "sub-paragraph (2) (and" and words inserted by the Crime and Courts Act 2013 s 20, Sch 13 paras 42, 45(1), (5), (6) with effect from 1 October 2013 (by virtue of SI 2013/2200).

Remuneration, allowances and expenses

5—(1) Sub-paragraph (2) applies—

    (*a*) to a person appointed under paragraph 1(1) or 2(1),

    (*b*) to a transferred-in judge of the First-tier Tribunal, and

    (*c*) to a transferred-in other member of the First-tier Tribunal.

(2) The Lord Chancellor may pay to a person to whom this sub-paragraph applies such amounts (if any) as the Lord Chancellor may determine by way of—

    (*a*) remuneration;

    (*b*) allowances;

    (*c*) expenses.

Certain judges neither appointed under paragraph 1(1) nor transferred in

6—(1) In this paragraph "judge by request of the First-tier Tribunal" means a person who is a judge of the First-tier Tribunal but who—

    (*a*) is not the Senior President of Tribunals,

    (*b*) is not a judge of the First-tier Tribunal appointed under paragraph 1(1),

    (*c*) is not a transferred-in judge of the First-tier Tribunal,

    (*d*) is not a Chamber President, or Acting Chamber President or Deputy Chamber President, of a chamber of the First-tier Tribunal,

    (*e*) is not a judge of the First-tier Tribunal by virtue of section 4(1)(*e*) (chairman of employment tribunal),

    (*f*) is not a judge of the First-tier Tribunal by virtue of section 4(1)(*d*) or by virtue of the combination of sections 4(1)(*c*) and 5(1)(*d*) (legally qualified member of Asylum and Immigration Tribunal), and

    (*g*) is not a judge of the First-tier tribunal by virtue of section 4(2) (criminal injuries compensation adjudicator appointed by the Scottish Ministers).

(2) A judge by request of the First-tier Tribunal may act as a judge of the First-tier Tribunal only if requested to do so by the Senior President of Tribunals.

(3) Such a request made to a person who is a judge of the First-tier Tribunal by virtue of the combination of sections 4(1)(*c*) and 5(1)(*g*) may be made only with—

    (*a*) the concurrence of the Lord Chief Justice of England and Wales where the person is—

        (i) an ordinary judge of the Court of Appeal in England and Wales,

        (ii) a puisne judge of the High Court in England and Wales,

        (iii) a circuit judge,

        (iv) a district judge in England and Wales, . . .[1]

        (v) a District Judge (Magistrates' Courts);

        [(vi) the Master of the Rolls,

        (vii) the President of the Queen's Bench Division of the High Court of England and Wales,

        (viii) the President of the Family Division of that court,

        (ix) the Chancellor of that court,

        (x) a deputy judge of that court, or

        (xi) the Judge Advocate General;][1]

    (*b*) the concurrence of the Lord President of the Court of Session where the person is—

        (i) a judge of the Court of Session, or

        (ii) a sheriff;

    (*c*) the concurrence of the Lord Chief Justice of Northern Ireland where the person is—

        (i) a Lord Justice of Appeal in Northern Ireland,

        (ii) a puisne judge of the High Court in Northern Ireland,

        (iii) a county court judge in Northern Ireland, or

        (iv) a district judge in Northern Ireland.

[(3A) A request made under sub-paragraph (2) to a person who is a judge of the First-tier Tribunal by virtue of section 4(1)(ca) may be made only with the concurrence of the Lord Chief Justice of England and Wales.][1]

(4) Sub-paragraph (5) applies—

(*a*) to a judge by request of the First-tier Tribunal,

(*b*) to a person who is a judge of the First-tier Tribunal by virtue of section 4(1)(*e*) (chairman of employment tribunal), and

(*c*) to a person who is a judge of the First-tier Tribunal by virtue of section 4(1)(*d*) or by virtue of the combination of sections 4(1)(*c*) and 5(1)(*d*) (legally qualified member of Asylum and Immigration Tribunal).

(5) The Lord Chancellor may pay to a person to whom this sub-paragraph applies such amounts (if any) as the Lord Chancellor may determine by way of—

(*a*) remuneration;

(*b*) allowances;

(*c*) expenses.

Amendments—[1]   In sub-para (3)(*a*)(iv), word "or" at the end repealed, and sub-paras (3)(*a*)(vi)–(xi), (3A) inserted by the Crime and Courts Act 2013 s 21, Sch 14 paras 6, 10 with effect from 1 October 2013 (by virtue of SI 2013/2200).

Other members neither appointed under paragraph 2(1) nor transferred in

7—(1) In this paragraph "ex officio member of the First-tier Tribunal" means a person who is a member of the First-tier Tribunal by virtue of—

(*a*) section 4(3)(*d*) (members of employment tribunals who are not [Employment Judges][1]),

(*b*) the combination of sections 4(3)(*c*) and 5(2)(*c*) (members of Employment Appeal Tribunal appointed under section 22(1)(*c*) of the Employment Tribunals Act 1996), or

(*c*) the combination of sections 4(3)(*c*) and 5(2)(*d*) (members of Asylum and Immigration Tribunal who are not legally qualified members).

(2) The Lord Chancellor may pay to an ex officio member of the First-tier Tribunal such amounts (if any) as the Lord Chancellor may determine by way of—

(*a*) remuneration;

(*b*) allowances;

(*c*) expenses.

Amendments—[1]   In sub-para (1)(*a*), words substituted for word "chairmen" by the Crime and Courts Act 2013 s 21, Sch 14 para 13(1) with effect from 1 October 2013 (by virtue of SI 2013/2200).

Training etc

8   The Senior President of Tribunals is responsible, within the resources made available by the Lord Chancellor, for the maintenance of appropriate arrangements for the training, guidance and welfare of judges and other members of the First-tier Tribunal (in their capacities as such judges and other members).

Oaths

9—(1) Sub-paragraph (2) applies to a person ("J")—

(*a*) who is appointed under paragraph 1(1) or 2(1), or

(*b*) who becomes a transferred-in judge, or a transferred-in other member, of the First-tier Tribunal and has not previously taken the required oaths after accepting another office.

(2) J must take the required oaths before—

(*a*) the Senior President of Tribunals, or

(*b*) an eligible person who is nominated by the Senior President of Tribunals for the purpose of taking the oaths from J.

(3) A person is eligible for the purposes of sub-paragraph (2)(*b*) if any one or more of the following paragraphs applies to him—

(*a*) he holds high judicial office (as defined in section 60(2) of the Constitutional Reform Act 2005 (c 4));

(*b*) he holds judicial office (as defined in section 109(4) of that Act);

(*c*) he holds (in Scotland) the office of sheriff.

(4) In this paragraph "the required oaths" means (subject to sub-paragraph (5))—

(*a*) the oath of allegiance, and

(*b*) the judicial oath,

as set out in the Promissory Oaths Act 1868 (c 72).

(5) Where it appears to the Lord Chancellor that J will carry out functions as a judge or other member of the First-tier Tribunal wholly or mainly in Northern Ireland, the Lord Chancellor may direct that in relation to J "the required oaths" means—

(*a*) the oath as set out in section 19(2) of the Justice (Northern Ireland) Act 2002 (c 26), or

(*b*) the affirmation and declaration as set out in section 19(3) of that Act.

SCHEDULE 3

JUDGES AND OTHER MEMBERS OF THE UPPER TRIBUNAL

Section 5

Power to appoint judges of Upper Tribunal

1—(1) Her Majesty, on the recommendation of the Lord Chancellor, may appoint a person to be one of the judges of the Upper Tribunal.

(2) A person is eligible for appointment under sub-paragraph (1) only if the person—

    (*a*) satisfies the judicial-appointment eligibility condition on a 7-year basis,

    (*b*) is an advocate or solicitor in Scotland of at least seven years' standing,

    (*c*) is a barrister or solicitor in Northern Ireland of at least seven years' standing, or

    (*d*) in the [opinion of the Senior President of Tribunals][1], has gained experience in law which makes the person as suitable for appointment as if the person satisfied any of paragraphs (*a*) to (*c*).

(3) Section 52(2) to (5) (meaning of "gain experience in law") apply for the purposes of sub-paragraph (2)(*d*), but as if section 52(4)(*i*) referred to the [Senior President of Tribunals][1] instead of to the relevant decision-maker.

Amendments—[1] In sub-para (2)(*d*), words substituted for words "Lord Chancellor's opinion", and in sub-para (3), words substituted for words "Lord Chancellor" by the Crime and Courts Act 2013 s 20, Sch 13 para 30 with effect from 1 October 2013 (by virtue of SI 2013/2200).

Power to appoint other members of Upper Tribunal

2—(1) The [Senior President of Tribunals][1] may appoint a person to be one of the members of the Upper Tribunal who are not judges of the tribunal.

(2) A person is eligible for appointment under sub-paragraph (1) only if the person has qualifications prescribed in an order made by the Lord Chancellor with the concurrence of the Senior President of Tribunals.

Orders—Qualifications for Appointment of Members to the First-tier Tribunal and Upper Tribunal Order, SI 2008/2692.

Qualifications for Appointment of Members to the First-tier Tribunal and Upper Tribunal (Amendment) Order, SI 2009/1592 (made under para 2(2)).

Qualifications for Appointment of Members to the First-tier Tribunal and Upper Tribunal (Amendment) Order, SI 2012/897.

Qualifications for Appointment of Members to the First-tier Tribunal and Upper Tribunal (Amendment) Order, SI 2013/1185.

Amendments—[1] In sub-para (1), words substituted for words "Lord Chancellor" by the Crime and Courts Act 2013 s 20, Sch 13 paras 42, 46(1), (2) with effect from 1 October 2013 (by virtue of SI 2013/2200).

Appointed and transferred-in judges and other members: removal from office

3—(1) This paragraph applies to any power by which—

    (*a*) a person appointed under paragraph 1(1) or 2(1),

    (*b*) a transferred-in judge of the Upper Tribunal,

    [(*ba*) a person who is a deputy judge of the Upper Tribunal (whether by appointment under paragraph 7(1) or as a result of provision under section 31(2)), or][1]

    (*c*) a transferred-in other member of the Upper Tribunal,

may be removed from office.

(2) If the person exercises functions wholly or mainly in Scotland, the power may be exercised only with the concurrence of the Lord President of the Court of Session.

(3) If the person exercises functions wholly or mainly in Northern Ireland, the power may be exercised only with the concurrence of the Lord Chief Justice of Northern Ireland.

(4) If neither of sub-paragraphs (2) and (3) applies, the power may be exercised only with the concurrence of the Lord Chief Justice of England and Wales.

Amendments—[1] Sub-para (1)(*ba*) inserted by the Crime and Courts Act 2013 s 20, Sch 13 paras 42, 46(1), (3) with effect from 1 October 2013 (by virtue of SI 2013/2200).

Terms of appointment

4—(1) This paragraph applies—

    (*a*) to a person appointed under paragraph 1(1) or 2(1),

    (*b*) to a transferred-in judge of the Upper Tribunal, and

    (*c*) to a transferred-in other member of the Upper Tribunal.

(2) If the terms of the person's appointment provide that he is appointed on a salaried (as opposed to fee-paid) basis, the person may be removed from office—

    (*a*) only by the Lord Chancellor (and in accordance with paragraph 3), and

    (*b*) only on the ground of inability or misbehaviour.

[(2A) If the terms of the person's appointment provide that the person is appointed on a fee-paid basis, the person may be removed from office—

(a) only by the Lord Chancellor (and in accordance with paragraph 3), and
(b) only on—
  (i) the ground of inability or misbehaviour, or
  (ii) a ground specified in the person's terms of appointment.
(2B) If the period (or extended period) for which the person is appointed ends before—
  (a) the day on which the person attains the age of 70, or
  (b) if different, the day that for the purposes of section 26 of the Judicial Pensions and Retirement Act 1993 is the compulsory retirement date for the office concerned in the person's case,
then, subject to sub-paragraph (2C), the Lord Chancellor must extend the period of the person's appointment (including a period already extended under this sub-paragraph) before it ends.
(2C) Extension under sub-paragraph (2B)—
  (a) requires the person's agreement,
  (b) is to be for such period as the Lord Chancellor considers appropriate, and
  (c) may be refused on—
    (i) the ground of inability or misbehaviour, or
    (ii) a ground specified in the person's terms of appointment,

  but only with any agreement of a senior judge (see section 46(7)), or a nominee of a senior judge, that may be required by those terms.][1]
(3) Subject to [the preceding provisions of this paragraph (but subject in the first place][1] to the Judicial Pensions and Retirement Act 1993 (c 8)), the person is to hold and vacate office as a judge, or other member, of the Upper Tribunal in accordance with the terms of his appointment[, which are to be such as the Lord Chancellor may determine][1].

Amendments—[1] Sub-paras (2A)–(2C) inserted, and in sub-para (3), words substituted for words "sub-paragraph (2) (and" and words inserted by the Crime and Courts Act 2013 s 20, Sch 13 paras 42, 46(1), (4), (5) with effect from 1 October 2013 (by virtue of SI 2013/2200).

Remuneration, allowances and expenses

5—(1) Sub-paragraph (2) applies—
  (a) to a person appointed under paragraph 1(1) or 2(1),
  (b) to a transferred-in judge of the Upper Tribunal, and
  (c) to a transferred-in other member of the Upper Tribunal.
(2) The Lord Chancellor may pay to a person to whom this sub-paragraph applies such amounts (if any) as the Lord Chancellor may determine by way of—
  (a) remuneration;
  (b) allowances;
  (c) expenses.

Certain judges neither appointed under paragraph 1(1) nor transferred in

6—(1) In this paragraph "judge by request of the Upper Tribunal" means a person who is a judge of the Upper Tribunal but—
  (a) is not the Senior President of Tribunals,
  (b) is not a judge of the Upper Tribunal appointed under paragraph 1(1),
  (c) is not a transferred-in judge of the Upper Tribunal,
  (d) is not a judge of the Upper Tribunal by virtue of section 5(1)(d) (legally qualified member of Asylum and Immigration Tribunal),
  (e) is not a deputy judge of the Upper Tribunal, and
  (f) is not a Chamber President, or Acting Chamber President or Deputy Chamber President, of a chamber of the Upper Tribunal.
(2) A judge by request of the Upper Tribunal may act as a judge of the Upper Tribunal only if requested to do so by the Senior President of Tribunals.
(3) Such a request made to a person who is a judge of the Upper Tribunal by virtue of section 5(1)(g) may be made only with—
  (a) the concurrence of the Lord Chief Justice of England and Wales where the person is—
    (i) an ordinary judge of the Court of Appeal in England and Wales,
    (ii) a puisne judge of the High Court in England and Wales,
    (iii) a circuit judge,
    (iv) a district judge in England and Wales, . . . [1]
    [(vi) the Master of the Rolls,
    (vii) the President of the Queen's Bench Division of the High Court of England and Wales,
    (viii) the President of the Family Division of that court,

(ix) the Chancellor of that court,

(x) a deputy judge of that court, or

(xi) the Judge Advocate General;][1]

(v) a District Judge (Magistrates' Courts);

(b) the concurrence of the Lord President of the Court of Session where the person is—

(i) a judge of the Court of Session, or

(ii) a sheriff;

(c) the concurrence of the Lord Chief Justice of Northern Ireland where the person is—

(i) a Lord Justice of Appeal in Northern Ireland,

(ii) a puisne judge of the High Court in Northern Ireland,

(iii) a county court judge in Northern Ireland, or

(iv) a district judge in Northern Ireland.

(4) The Lord Chancellor may pay to a judge by request of the Upper Tribunal, or a person who is a judge of the Upper Tribunal by virtue of section 5(1)(d), such amounts (if any) as the Lord Chancellor may determine by way of—

(a) remuneration;

(b) allowances;

(c) expenses.

Amendments—[1]   In sub-para (3)(a)(iv), word "or" at the end repealed, and sub-para (3)(a)(vi)–(xi) inserted by the Crime and Courts Act 2013 s 21, Sch 14 paras 6, 10(1) with effect from 1 October 2013 (by virtue of SI 2013/2200).

Deputy judges of the Upper Tribunal

7—(1) The [Senior President of Tribunals][1] may appoint a person to be a deputy judge of the Upper Tribunal for such period as the Lord Chancellor considers appropriate.

(2) A person is eligible for appointment under sub-paragraph (1) only if he is eligible to be appointed under paragraph 1(1) (see paragraph 1(2)).

(3) [The following provisions of this paragraph][1] apply—

(a) to a person appointed under sub-paragraph (1), and

(b) to a person who becomes a deputy judge of the Upper Tribunal as a result of provision under section 31(2).

[(3A) The person may be removed from office—

(a) only by the Lord Chancellor (and in accordance with paragraph 3), and

(b) only on—

(i) the ground of inability or misbehaviour, or

(ii) a ground specified in the person's terms of appointment.

(3B) If the period (or extended period) for which the person is appointed ends before—

(a) the day on which the person attains the age of 70, or

(b) if different, the day that for the purposes of section 26 of the Judicial Pensions and Retirement Act 1993 is the compulsory retirement date for the office concerned in the person's case,

then, subject to sub-paragraph (3C), the Lord Chancellor must extend the period of the person's appointment (including a period already extended under this sub-paragraph) before it ends.

(3C) Extension under sub-paragraph (3B)—

(a) requires the person's agreement,

(b) is to be for such period as the Lord Chancellor considers appropriate, and

(c) may be refused on—

(i) the ground of inability or misbehaviour, or

(ii) a ground specified in the person's terms of appointment,

but only with any agreement of a senior judge (see section 46(7)), or a nominee of a senior judge, that may be required by those terms.

(4) Subject to the previous provisions of this paragraph (but subject in the first place to the Judicial Pensions and Retirement Act 1993), a person is to hold and vacate office as a deputy judge of the Upper Tribunal in accordance with the person's terms of appointment, which are to be such as the Lord Chancellor may determine.][1]

(5) The Lord Chancellor may pay to a person to whom this sub-paragraph applies such amounts (if any) as the Lord Chancellor may determine by way of—

(a) remuneration;

(b) allowances;

(c) expenses.

Amendments—[1]   In sub-para (1), words substituted for words "Lord Chancellor" in the first place; in sub-para (3), words substituted for words "Subparagraphs (4) and (5)"; and sub-paras (3A)–(4) substituted for former sub-para (4) by the Crime and Courts Act 2013 s 20, Sch 13 paras 42, 46(1), (6)–(8) with effect from 1 October 2013 (by virtue of SI 2013/2200).

Other members neither appointed under paragraph 2(1) nor transferred in

8—(1) In this paragraph "ex officio member of the Upper Tribunal" means—

    (*a*) a person who is a member of the Upper Tribunal by virtue of section 5(2)(*c*) (member of Employment Appeal Tribunal appointed under section 22(1)(*c*) of the Employment Tribunals Act 1996 (c 17)), or

    (*b*) a person who is a member of the Upper Tribunal by virtue of section 5(2)(*d*) (member of the Asylum and Immigration Tribunal who is not a legally qualified member).

(2) The Lord Chancellor may pay to an ex officio member of the Upper Tribunal such amounts (if any) as the Lord Chancellor may determine by way of—

    (*a*) remuneration;

    (*b*) allowances;

    (*c*) expenses.

Training etc

9   The Senior President of Tribunals is responsible, within the resources made available by the Lord Chancellor, for the maintenance of appropriate arrangements for the training, guidance and welfare of judges and other members of the Upper Tribunal (in their capacities as such judges and other members).

Oaths

10—(1) Sub-paragraph (2) applies to a person ("J")—

    (*a*) who is appointed under paragraph 1(1), 2(1) or 7(1), or

    (*b*) who—

        (i) becomes a transferred-in judge, or a transferred-in other member, of the Upper Tribunal, or

        (ii) becomes a deputy judge of the Upper Tribunal as a result of provision under section 31(2),

        and has not previously taken the required oaths after accepting another office.

(2) J must take the required oaths before—

    (*a*) the Senior President of Tribunals, or

    (*b*) an eligible person who is nominated by the Senior President of Tribunals for the purpose of taking the oaths from J.

(3) A person is eligible for the purposes of sub-paragraph (2)(*b*) if any one or more of the following paragraphs applies to him—

    (*a*) he holds high judicial office (as defined in section 60(2) of the Constitutional Reform Act 2005 (c 4));

    (*b*) he holds judicial office (as defined in section 109(4) of that Act);

    (*c*) he holds (in Scotland) the office of sheriff.

(4) In this paragraph "the required oaths" means (subject to sub-paragraph (5))—

    (*a*) the oath of allegiance, and

    (*b*) the judicial oath,

as set out in the Promissory Oaths Act 1868 (c 72).

(5) Where it appears to the Lord Chancellor that J will carry out functions as a judge or other member of the Upper Tribunal wholly or mainly in Northern Ireland, the Lord Chancellor may direct that in relation to J "the required oaths" means—

    (*a*) the oath as set out in section 19(2) of the Justice (Northern Ireland) Act 2002 (c 26), or

    (*b*) the affirmation and declaration as set out in section 19(3) of that Act.

SCHEDULE 4

CHAMBERS AND CHAMBER PRESIDENTS: FURTHER PROVISION

Section 7

PART 1

CHAMBER PRESIDENTS: APPOINTMENT, DELEGATION, DEPUTIES AND FURTHER PROVISION

Eligibility for appointment as Chamber President [under section 7(7)][1]

1   A person is eligible for appointment under section 7(7) only if—

    (*a*) he is a judge of the Upper Tribunal, or

(*b*) he does not fall within paragraph (*a*) but is eligible to be appointed under paragraph 1(1) of Schedule 3 as a judge of the Upper Tribunal (see paragraph 1(2) of that Schedule).

Amendments—[1]   In cross-head preceding this para, words substituted for words " by Lord Chancellor" by the Crime and Courts Act 2013 s 20, Sch 13 paras 42, 47(1), (2) with effect from 1 October 2013 (by virtue of SI 2013/2200).

Appointment as Chamber President [under section 7(7)][1]*: consultation and nomination*

2—(1) The [Senior President of Tribunals must consult the Lord Chancellor before the Senior President of Tribunals][1] appoints under section 7(7) a person within—

section 6(1)(*a*) (ordinary judge of Court of Appeal in England and Wales),

section 6(1)(*b*) (Lord Justice of Appeal in Northern Ireland),

section 6(1)(*c*) (judge of the Court of Session), or

section 6(1)(*d*) (puisne judge of the High Court in England and Wales or Northern Ireland).

(2) If the [Senior President of Tribunals][1], in exercise of his power under section 7(7) in a particular case, wishes that the person appointed should be drawn from among the ordinary judges of the Court of Appeal in England and Wales or the puisne judges of the High Court in England and Wales, the [Senior President of Tribunals][1] must first ask the Lord Chief Justice of England and Wales to nominate one of those judges for the purpose.

(3) If the [Senior President of Tribunals][1], in exercise of his power under section 7(7) in a particular case, wishes that the person appointed should be drawn from among the judges of the Court of Session, the [Senior President of Tribunals][1] must first ask the Lord President of the Court of Session to nominate one of those judges for the purpose.

(4) If the [Senior President of Tribunals][1], in exercise of his power under section 7(7) in a particular case, wishes that the person appointed should be drawn from among the Lords Justices of Appeal in Northern Ireland or the puisne judges of the High Court in Northern Ireland, the [Senior President of Tribunals][1] must first ask the Lord Chief Justice of Northern Ireland to nominate one of those judges for the purpose.

[(4A) The Senior President of Tribunals may make a request under subparagraph (2), (3) or (4) only with the Lord Chancellor's concurrence.][1]

(5) If a judge is nominated under sub-paragraph (2), (3) or (4) in response to a request under that sub-paragraph, the [Senior President of Tribunals][1] must appoint the nominated judge as Chamber President of the chamber concerned.

Amendments—[1]   In cross-head preceding this para, words substituted for words "by Lord Chancellor", in sub-para (1), words substituted for words "Lord Chancellor must consult the Senior President of Tribunals before the Lord Chancellor", in sub-paras (2)–(5) in each place, words substituted for words "Lord Chancellor", and sub-para (4A) inserted by the Crime and Courts Act 2013 s 20, Sch 13 paras 42, 47(1)–(6) with effect from 1 October 2013 (by virtue of SI 2013/2200).

Chamber Presidents: duration of appointment, remuneration etc

3—(1) A Chamber President is to hold and vacate office as a Chamber President in accordance with the terms of his appointment as a Chamber President [but subject to paragraph 5A (and subject in the first place][1] to the Judicial Pensions and Retirement Act 1993 (c 8))[, and those terms are to be such as the Lord Chancellor may determine][1].

(2) The Lord Chancellor may pay to a Chamber President such amounts (if any) as the Lord Chancellor may determine by way of—

(*a*) remuneration;

(*b*) allowances;

(*c*) expenses.

Amendments—[1]   In sub-para (1), words substituted for words "(subject", and words inserted by the Crime and Courts Act 2013 s 20, Sch 13 paras 42, 47(1), (7) with effect from 1 October 2013 (by virtue of SI 2013/2200).

Delegation of functions by Chamber Presidents

4—(1) The Chamber President of a chamber of the First-tier Tribunal or Upper Tribunal may delegate any function he has in his capacity as the Chamber President of the chamber—

(*a*) to any judge, or other member, of either of those tribunals;

(*b*) to staff appointed under section 40(1).

(2) A delegation under sub-paragraph (1) is not revoked by the delegator's becoming incapacitated.

(3) Any delegation made by a person under sub-paragraph (1) that is in force immediately before the person ceases to be the Chamber President of a chamber continues in force until subsequently varied or revoked by another holder of the office of Chamber President of that chamber.

(4) The delegation under sub-paragraph (1) of a function shall not prevent the exercise of the function by the Chamber President of the chamber concerned.

(5) In this paragraph "delegate" includes further delegate.

Deputy Chamber Presidents

5—(1) The [Senior President of Tribunals][1] may appoint a person who is not a Deputy Chamber President of a chamber to be a Deputy Chamber President of a chamber.

(2) The Senior President of Tribunals may appoint a person who is a Deputy Chamber President of a chamber to be instead, or to be also, a Deputy Chamber President of another chamber.

(3) The power under sub-paragraph (1) is exercisable in any particular case only if the [Senior President of Tribunals][1]

    (*a*) has consulted the [Lord Chancellor][1] about whether a Deputy Chamber President should be appointed for the chamber concerned, and

    (*b*) considers, in the light of the consultation, that a Deputy Chamber President of the chamber should be appointed.

(4) A person is eligible for appointment under sub-paragraph (1) only if—

    (*a*) he is a judge of the Upper Tribunal by virtue of appointment under paragraph 1(1) of Schedule 3,

    (*b*) he is a transferred-in judge of the Upper Tribunal (see section 31(2)),

    (*c*) he is a judge of the Upper Tribunal by virtue of—

             section 5(1)(*d*) (legally qualified member of Asylum and Immigration Tribunal),

             section 5(1)(*e*) (Social Security Commissioner for Northern Ireland),

             section 5(1)(*g*) (certain judges of courts in the United Kingdom), or

             section 5(1)(*h*) (deputy judge of the Upper Tribunal), or

    (*d*) he falls within none of paragraphs (*a*) to (*c*) but is eligible to be appointed under paragraph 1(1) of Schedule 3 as a judge of the Upper Tribunal (see paragraph 1(2) of that Schedule).

(5) If the [Senior President of Tribunals][1], in exercise of his power under sub-paragraph (1) in a particular case, wishes that the person appointed should be drawn from among the ordinary judges of the Court of Appeal in England and Wales or the puisne judges of the High Court in England and Wales, the [Senior President of Tribunals][1] must first ask the Lord Chief Justice of England and Wales to nominate one of those judges for the purpose.

(6) If the [Senior President of Tribunals][1], in exercise of his power under sub-paragraph (1) in a particular case, wishes that the person appointed should be drawn from among the judges of the Court of Session, the Lord Chancellor must first ask the Lord President of the Court of Session to nominate one of those judges for the purpose.

(7) If the [Senior President of Tribunals][1], in exercise of his power under sub-paragraph (1) in a particular case, wishes that the person appointed should be drawn from among the Lords Justices of Appeal in Northern Ireland or the puisne judges of the High Court in Northern Ireland, the [Senior President of Tribunals][1] must first ask the Lord Chief Justice of Northern Ireland to nominate one of those judges for the purpose.

[(7A) The Senior President of Tribunals may make a request under sub-paragraph (5), (6) or (7) only with the Lord Chancellor's concurrence.][1]

(8) If a judge is nominated under sub-paragraph (5), (6) or (7) in response to a request under that sub-paragraph, the [Senior President of Tribunals][1] must appoint the nominated judge as a Deputy Chamber President of the chamber concerned.

(9) A Deputy Chamber President is to hold and vacate office as a Deputy Chamber President in accordance with the terms of his appointment [but subject to paragraph 5A (and subject in the first place][1] to the Judicial Pensions and Retirement Act 1993 (c 8))[, and those terms are to be such as the Lord Chancellor may determine][1].

(10) The Lord Chancellor may pay to a Deputy Chamber President such amounts (if any) as the Lord Chancellor may determine by way of—

    (*a*) remuneration;

    (*b*) allowances;

    (*c*) expenses.

(11) In sub-paragraphs (1) and (2) "chamber" means chamber of the First-tier Tribunal or chamber of the Upper Tribunal.

Amendments—[1]   In sub-paras (1), (3), (5)–(8), words substituted in each place for words "Lord Chancellor"; in sub-para (3)(*a*), words substituted for words "Senior President of Tribunals"; sub-para (7A) inserted; and in sub-para (9), words substituted for word "(subject" and words inserted by the Crime and Courts Act 2013 s 20, Sch 13 paras 42, 47(1), (8)–(13) with effect from 1 October 2013 (by virtue of SI 2013/2200).

[Chamber Presidents and Deputies: removal from office and extension of appointment

5A—(1) This paragraph applies to a person—

    (*a*) appointed under section 7(6) or (7) as a Chamber President, or

    (*b*) appointed under paragraph 5(1) or (2) as a Deputy Chamber President of a chamber.

(2) If the terms of the person's appointment provide that the person is appointed otherwise than on a fee-paid basis, the person may be removed from office—

    (*a*) only by the Lord Chancellor with the concurrence of the Senior President of Tribunals, and

    (*b*) only on the ground of inability or misbehaviour.

(3) If the terms of the person's appointment provide that the person is appointed on a fee-paid basis, the person may be removed from office—

    (*a*) only by the Lord Chancellor with the concurrence of the Senior President of Tribunals, and

    (*b*) only on—

        (i) the ground of inability or misbehaviour, or

        (ii) a ground specified in the person's terms of appointment.

(4) If the period (or extended period) for which the person is appointed ends before—

    (*a*) the day on which the person attains the age of 70, or

    (*b*) if different, the day that for the purposes of section 26 of the Judicial Pensions and Retirement Act 1993 is the compulsory retirement date for the office concerned in the person's case,

then, subject to sub-paragraph (5), the Lord Chancellor must extend the period of the person's appointment (including a period already extended under this sub-paragraph) before it ends.

(5) Extension under sub-paragraph (4)—

    (*a*) requires the person's agreement,

    (*b*) is to be for such period as the Lord Chancellor considers appropriate, and

    (*c*) may be refused on—

        (i) the ground of inability or misbehaviour, or

        (ii) a ground specified in the person's terms of appointment,

        but only with any agreement of a senior judge (see section 46(7)), or a nominee of a senior judge, that may be required by those terms.][1]

Amendments—[1] Para 5A inserted by the Crime and Courts Act 2013 s 20, Sch 13 paras 42, 47(1), (14) with effect from 1 October 2013 (by virtue of SI 2013/2200).

Acting Chamber Presidents

6—(1) If in the case of a particular chamber of the First-tier Tribunal or Upper Tribunal there is no-one appointed under section 7 to preside over the chamber, the Senior President of Tribunals may appoint a person to preside over the chamber during the vacancy.

(2) A person appointed under sub-paragraph (1) is to be known as an Acting Chamber President.

(3) A person who is the Acting Chamber President of a chamber is to be treated as the Chamber President of the chamber for all purposes other than—

    (*a*) the purposes of this paragraph of this Schedule, and

    (*b*) the purposes of the Judicial Pensions and Retirement Act 1993 (c 8).

(4) A person is eligible for appointment under sub-paragraph (1) only if he is eligible for appointment as a Chamber President.

(5) An Acting Chamber President is to hold and vacate office as an Acting Chamber President in accordance with the terms of his appointment.

(6) The Lord Chancellor may pay to an Acting Chamber President such amounts (if any) as the Lord Chancellor may determine by way of—

    (*a*) remuneration;

    (*b*) allowances;

    (*c*) expenses.

Guidance

7   The Chamber President of a chamber of the First-tier Tribunal or the Upper Tribunal is to make arrangements for the issuing of guidance on changes in the law and practice as they relate to the functions allocated to the chamber.

Oaths

8—(1) Sub-paragraph (2) applies to a person ("the appointee")—

    (*a*) appointed under section 7(7) as a Chamber President,

    (*b*) appointed under paragraph 5(1) as a Deputy Chamber President of a chamber, or

    (*c*) appointed as an Acting Chamber President.

(2) The appointee must take the required oaths before—

    (*a*) the Senior President of Tribunals, or

    (*b*) an eligible person who is nominated by the Senior President of Tribunals for the purpose of taking the oaths from the appointee.

(3) A person is eligible for the purposes of sub-paragraph (2)(*b*) if any one or more of the following paragraphs applies to him—

    (*a*) he holds high judicial office (as defined in section 60(2) of the Constitutional Reform Act 2005 (c 4));

    (*b*) he holds judicial office (as defined in section 109(4) of that Act);

    (*c*) he holds (in Scotland) the office of sheriff.

(4) Sub-paragraph (2) does not apply to the appointee if he has previously taken the required oaths in compliance with a requirement imposed on him under paragraph 9 of Schedule 2 or paragraph 10 of Schedule 3.

(5) In this paragraph "the required oaths" means (subject to sub-paragraph (6))—

    (*a*) the oath of allegiance, and

    (*b*) the judicial oath,

as set out in the Promissory Oaths Act 1868 (c 72).

(6) Where it appears to the Lord Chancellor that the appointee will carry out functions under his appointment wholly or mainly in Northern Ireland, the Lord Chancellor may direct that in relation to the appointee "the required oaths" means—

    (*a*) the oath as set out in section 19(2) of the Justice (Northern Ireland) Act 2002 (c 26), or

    (*b*) the affirmation and declaration as set out in section 19(3) of that Act.

PART 2

JUDGES AND OTHER MEMBERS OF CHAMBERS: ASSIGNMENT AND JURISDICTION

Assignment is function of Senior President of Tribunals

9—(1) The Senior President of Tribunals has—

    (*a*) the function of assigning judges and other members of the First-tier Tribunal (including himself) to chambers of the First-tier Tribunal, and

    (*b*) the function of assigning judges and other members of the Upper Tribunal (including himself) to chambers of the Upper Tribunal.

(2) The functions under sub-paragraph (1) are to be exercised in accordance with the following provisions of this Part of this Schedule.

Deemed assignment of Chamber Presidents and Deputy Chamber Presidents

10—(1) The Chamber President, or a Deputy Chamber President, of a chamber—

    (*a*) is to be taken to be assigned to that chamber;

    (*b*) may be assigned additionally to one or more of the other chambers;

    (*c*) may be assigned under paragraph (*b*) to different chambers at different times.

(2) Paragraphs 11(1) and (2) and 12(2) and (3) do not apply to assignment of a person who is a Chamber President or a Deputy Chamber President.

(3) In sub-paragraph (1) "chamber" means chamber of the First-tier Tribunal or the Upper Tribunal.

Assigning members of First-tier Tribunal to its chambers

11—(1) Each person who is a judge or other member of the First-tier Tribunal by virtue of appointment under paragraph 1(1) or 2(1) of Schedule 2 or who is a transferred-in judge, or transferred-in other member, of the First-tier Tribunal—

    (*a*) is to be assigned to at least one of the chambers of the First-tier Tribunal, and

    (*b*) may be assigned to different chambers of the First-tier Tribunal at different times.

(2) A judge or other member of the First-tier Tribunal to whom sub-paragraph (1) does not apply—

    (*a*) may be assigned to one or more of the chambers of the First-tier Tribunal, and

    (*b*) may be assigned to different chambers of the First-tier Tribunal at different times.

(3) The Senior President of Tribunals may assign a judge or other member of the First-tier Tribunal to a particular chamber of the First-tier Tribunal only with the concurrence—

    (*a*) of the Chamber President of the chamber, and

    (*b*) of the judge or other member.

(4) The Senior President of Tribunals may end the assignment of a judge or other member of the First-tier Tribunal to a particular chamber of the First-tier Tribunal only with the concurrence of the Chamber President of the chamber.

(5) Sub-paragraph (3)(*a*) does not apply where the judge, or other member, concerned is not assigned to any of the chambers of the First-tier Tribunal.

(6) Sub-paragraphs (3)(*a*) and (4) do not apply where the judge concerned is within section 6(1)(*a*) to (*d*) (judges of Courts of Appeal, Court of Session and High Courts).

(7) Sub-paragraphs (3) and (4) do not apply where the judge concerned is the Senior President of Tribunals himself.

Assigning members of Upper Tribunal to its chambers

12—(1) Sub-paragraph (2) applies to a person if—

   (a) he is a judge of the Upper Tribunal by virtue of appointment under paragraph 1(1) of Schedule 3, or

   (b) he is a transferred-in judge of the Upper Tribunal, or

   (c) he is a deputy judge of the Upper Tribunal, or

   (d) he is a member of the Upper Tribunal by virtue of appointment under paragraph 2(1) of Schedule 3, or

   (e) he is a transferred-in other member of the Upper Tribunal.

(2) Each person to whom this sub-paragraph applies—

   (a) is to be assigned to at least one of the chambers of the Upper Tribunal, and

   (b) may be assigned to different chambers of the Upper Tribunal at different times.

(3) A judge or other member of the Upper Tribunal to whom sub-paragraph (2) does not apply—

   (a) may be assigned to one or more of the chambers of the Upper Tribunal, and

   (b) may be assigned to different chambers of the Upper Tribunal at different times.

(4) The Senior President of Tribunals may assign a judge or other member of the Upper Tribunal to a particular chamber of the Upper Tribunal only with the concurrence—

   (a) of the Chamber President of the chamber, and

   (b) of the judge or other member.

(5) The Senior President of Tribunals may end the assignment of a judge or other member of the Upper Tribunal to a particular chamber of the Upper Tribunal only with the concurrence of the Chamber President of the chamber.

(6) Sub-paragraph (4)(a) does not apply where the judge, or other member, concerned is not assigned to any of the chambers of the Upper Tribunal.

(7) Sub-paragraphs (4)(a) and (5) do not apply where the judge concerned is within section 6(1)(a) to (d) (judges of Courts of Appeal, Court of Session and High Courts).

(8) Sub-paragraphs (4) and (5) do not apply where the judge concerned is the Senior President of Tribunals himself.

Policy of Senior President of Tribunals as respects assigning members to chambers etc

13—(1) The Senior President of Tribunals must publish a document recording the policy adopted by him in relation to—

   (a) the assigning of persons to chambers in exercise of his functions under paragraph 9,

   (b) the assigning of persons to act as members of the Asylum and Immigration Tribunal in exercise of his functions under paragraphs 5A and 5B of Schedule 4 to the Nationality, Immigration and Asylum Act 2002 (c 41), and

   (c) the nominating of persons to act as members of panels of members of employment tribunals in exercise of his functions under any such provision as is mentioned in section 5D(1) of the Employment Tribunals Act 1996 (c 17).

(2) That policy must be such as to secure—

   (a) that appropriate use is made of the knowledge and experience of the judges and other members of the First-tier Tribunal and Upper Tribunal, and

   (b) that, in the case of a chamber (of the First-tier Tribunal or Upper Tribunal) whose business consists of, or includes, cases likely to involve the application of the law of Scotland or Northern Ireland, sufficient knowledge and experience of that law is to be found among persons assigned to the chamber.

(3) No policy may be adopted by the Senior President of Tribunals for the purposes of sub-paragraph (1) unless the Lord Chancellor concurs in the policy.

(4) The Senior President of Tribunals must keep any policy adopted for the purposes of sub-paragraph (1) under review.

Choosing members to decide cases

14—(1) The First-tier Tribunal's function, or the Upper Tribunal's function, of deciding any matter in a case before the tribunal is to be exercised by a member or members of the chamber of the tribunal to which the case is allocated.

(2) The member or members must be chosen by the Senior President of Tribunals.

(3) A person choosing under sub-paragraph (2)—

   (a) must act in accordance with any provision under paragraph 15;

   (b) may choose himself.

(4) In this paragraph "member", in relation to a chamber of a tribunal, means a judge or other member of the tribunal who is assigned to the chamber.

Composition of tribunals

15—(1) The Lord Chancellor must by order make provision, in relation to every matter that may fall to be decided by the First-tier Tribunal or the Upper Tribunal, for determining the number of members of the tribunal who are to decide the matter.

(2) Where an order under sub-paragraph (1) provides for a matter to be decided by a single member of a tribunal, the order—

(a) must make provision for determining whether the matter is to be decided by one of the judges, or by one of the other members, of the tribunal, and

(b) may make provision for determining, if the matter is to be decided by one of the other members of the tribunal, what qualifications (if any) that other member must have.

(3) Where an order under sub-paragraph (1) provides for a matter to be decided by two or more members of a tribunal, the order—

(a) must make provision for determining how many (if any) of those members are to be judges of the tribunal and how many (if any) are to be other members of the tribunal, and

(b) may make provision for determining—

(i) if the matter is to be decided by persons who include one or more of the other members of the tribunal, or

(ii) if the matter is to be decided by two or more of the other members of the tribunal,

what qualifications (if any) that other member or any of those other members must have.

(4) A duty under sub-paragraph (1), (2) or (3) to provide for the determination of anything may be discharged by providing for the thing to be determined by the Senior President of Tribunals, or a Chamber President, in accordance with any provision made under that sub-paragraph.

(5) Power under paragraph (b) of sub-paragraph (2) or (3) to provide for the determination of anything may be exercised by giving, to the Senior President of Tribunals or a Chamber President, power to determine that thing in accordance with any provision made under that paragraph.

(6) Where under sub-paragraphs (1) to (4) a matter is to be decided by two or more members of a tribunal, the matter may, if the parties to the case agree, be decided in the absence of one or more (but not all) of the members chosen to decide the matter.

(7) Where the member, or any of the members, of a tribunal chosen to decide a matter does not have any qualification that he is required to have under sub-paragraphs (2)(b), or (3)(b), and (5), the matter may despite that, if the parties to the case agree, be decided by the chosen member or members.

(8) Before making an order under this paragraph, the Lord Chancellor must consult the Senior President of Tribunals.

(9) In this paragraph "qualification" includes experience.

Orders—First-tier Tribunal and Upper Tribunal (Composition of Tribunal) Order, SI 2008/2835.

First-tier Tribunal and Upper Tribunal (Composition of Tribunal) (Amendment) Order, SI 2018/606.

SCHEDULE 5

PROCEDURE IN FIRST-TIER TRIBUNAL AND UPPER TRIBUNAL

Section 22

Rules—Tribunal Procedure (Amendment) Rules, SI 2015/1510.

Tribunal Procedure (Amendment) Rules, SI 2017/723.

Tribunal Procedure (Amendment No 2) Rules, SI 2017/1168.

Tribunal Procedure (Amendment) Rules, SI 2018/511.

Tribunal Procedure (Amendment) Rules, SI 2019/925.

Tribunal Procedure (Coronavirus) (Amendment) Rules, SI 2020/416.

PART 1

TRIBUNAL PROCEDURE RULES

Introductory

1—(1) This Part of this Schedule makes further provision about the content of Tribunal Procedure Rules.

(2) The generality of section 22(1) is not to be taken to be prejudiced by—

(a) the following paragraphs of this Part of this Schedule, or

(b) any other provision (including future provision) authorising or requiring the making of provision by Tribunal Procedure Rules.

(3) In the following paragraphs of this Part of this Schedule "Rules" means Tribunal Procedure Rules.

Concurrent functions

2   Rules may make provision as to who is to decide, or as to how to decide, which of the First-tier Tribunal and Upper Tribunal is to exercise, in relation to any particular matter, a function that is exercisable by the two tribunals on the basis that the question as to which of them is to exercise the function is to be determined by, or under, Rules.

Delegation of functions to staff

3—(1) Rules may provide for functions—

  (*a*) of the First-tier Tribunal, or

  (*b*) of the Upper Tribunal,

to be exercised by staff appointed under section [2(1) of the Courts Act 2003 or section 40(1) of this Act][1].

(2) In making provision of the kind mentioned in sub-paragraph (1) in relation to a function, Rules may (in particular)—

  (*a*) provide for the function to be exercisable by a member of staff only if the member of staff is, or is of a description, specified in exercise of a discretion conferred by Rules;

  (*b*) provide for the function to be exercisable by a member of staff only if the member of staff is approved, or is of a description approved, for the purpose by a person specified in Rules.

[(3) A person may exercise functions by virtue of this paragraph only if authorised to do so by the Senior President of Tribunals.

(4) An authorisation under this paragraph—

  (a) may be subject to conditions, and

  (b) may be varied or revoked by the Senior President of Tribunals at any time.

(5) The Senior President of Tribunals may delegate to one or more of the following the Senior President of Tribunals' functions under the preceding provisions of this paragraph—

  (a) a judicial office holder;

  (b) a person appointed under section 2(1) of the Courts Act 2003 or section 40(1) of this Act.

(6) A person to whom functions of the Senior President of Tribunals are delegated under sub-paragraph (5)(b) is not subject to the direction of any person other than—

  (a) the Senior President of Tribunals, or

  (b) a judicial office holder nominated by the Senior President of Tribunals,

when exercising the functions.

(7) Subsections (3) to (5) of section 8 apply to—

  (a) a delegation under sub-paragraph (5), and

  (b) a nomination under sub-paragraph (6),

as they apply to a delegation under subsection (1) of that section.

(8) In this paragraph—

    "function" does not include—

      (a) any function so far as its exercise involves authorising a person's committal to prison or arrest;

      (b) any function of granting an injunction;

    "judicial office holder" has the meaning given by section 109(4) of the Constitutional Reform Act 2005.][1]

Amendments—[1]   In sub-para (1) words substituted for words "40(1)", and sub-paras (3)–(8) inserted, by the Courts and Tribunals (Judiciary and Functions of Staff) Act 2018 s 3, Schedule paras 39, 43, 44 with effect from 10 January 2020 for the purpose of making regulations, and from 6 April 2020 for all remaining purposes (by virtue of SI 2020/24 regs 2, 3).

Time limits

4   Rules may make provision for time limits as respects initiating, or taking any step in, proceedings before the First-tier Tribunal or the Upper Tribunal.

Repeat applications

5   Rules may make provision restricting the making of fresh applications where a previous application in relation to the same matter has been made.

Tribunal acting of its own initiative

6   Rules may make provision about the circumstances in which the First-tier Tribunal, or the Upper Tribunal, may exercise its powers of its own initiative.

Hearings

7 Rules may—

　(a) make provision for dealing with matters without a hearing;

　(b) make provision as respects allowing or requiring a hearing to be in private or as respects allowing or requiring a hearing to be in public.

Proceedings without notice

8 Rules may make provision for proceedings to take place, in circumstances described in Rules, at the request of one party even though the other, or another, party has had no notice.

Representation

9 Rules may make provision conferring additional rights of audience before the First-tier Tribunal or the Upper Tribunal.

Evidence, witnesses and attendance

10—(1) Rules may make provision about evidence (including evidence on oath and administration of oaths).

(2) Rules may modify any rules of evidence provided for elsewhere, so far as they would apply to proceedings before the First-tier Tribunal or Upper Tribunal.

(3) Rules may make provision, where the First-tier Tribunal has required a person—

　(a) to attend at any place for the purpose of giving evidence,

　(b) otherwise to make himself available to give evidence,

　(c) to swear an oath in connection with the giving of evidence,

　(d) to give evidence as a witness,

　(e) to produce a document, or

　(f) to facilitate the inspection of a document or any other thing (including any premises),

for the Upper Tribunal to deal with non-compliance with the requirement as though the requirement had been imposed by the Upper Tribunal.

(4) Rules may make provision for the payment of expenses and allowances to persons giving evidence, producing documents, attending proceedings or required to attend proceedings.

Use of information

11—(1) Rules may make provision for the disclosure or non-disclosure of information received during the course of proceedings before the First-tier Tribunal or Upper Tribunal.

(2) Rules may make provision for imposing reporting restrictions in circumstances described in Rules.

Costs and expenses

12—(1) Rules may make provision for regulating matters relating to costs, or (in Scotland) expenses, of proceedings before the First-tier Tribunal or Upper Tribunal.

(2) The provision mentioned in sub-paragraph (1) includes (in particular)—

　(a) provision prescribing scales of costs or expenses;

　(b) provision for enabling costs to undergo detailed assessment in England and Wales by a county court or the High Court;

　(c) provision for taxation in Scotland of accounts of expenses by an Auditor of Court;

　(d) provision for enabling costs to be taxed in Northern Ireland in a county court or the High Court;

　(e) provision for costs or expenses—

　　(i) not to be allowed in respect of items of a description specified in Rules;

　　(ii) not to be allowed in proceedings of a description so specified;

　(f) provision for other exceptions to either or both of subsections (1) and (2) of section 29.

Set-off and interest

13—(1) Rules may make provision for a party to proceedings to deduct, from amounts payable by him, amounts payable to him.

(2) Rules may make provision for interest on sums awarded (including provision conferring a discretion or provision in accordance with which interest is to be calculated).

Tribunal	Enactment
[Tribunal	Section 704 of the Income Tax Act 2007 (c 3)][1]
Umpire or deputy umpire	Paragraph 5 of Schedule 2 to the Reserve Forces (Safeguard of Employment) Act 1985
VAT and duties tribunal	Schedule 12 to the Value Added Tax Act 1994 (c 23)

Amendments—[1]   Entries inserted by the Transfer of Tribunal Functions Order, SI 2008/2833 art 2 with effect from 3 November 2008.

[2]   Entries inserted by the Amendments to Schedule 6 to the Tribunals, Courts and Enforcement Act 2007 Order, SI 2013/1034 art 2.

[3]   Entry relating to the "Claims Management Services Tribunal" repealed by the Financial Services and Markets Act 2000 (Claims Management Activity) Order, SI 2018/1253 art 94 with effect from 1 April 2019. This amendment extends to England, Wales and Scotland.

PART 2
TRIBUNALS FOR THE PURPOSES OF SECTIONS 30 AND 35

Tribunal	Enactment
Adjudicator	Section 5 of the Criminal Injuries Compensation Act 1995 (c 53)

PART 3
TRIBUNALS FOR THE PURPOSES OF SECTIONS 30 AND 36

Tribunal	Enactment
Adjudicator to Her Majesty's Land Registry	Section 107 of the Land Registration Act 2002 (c 9)
Charity Tribunal	Section 2A of the Charities Act 1993 (c 10)
Consumer Credit Appeals Tribunal	Section 40A of the Consumer Credit Act 1974 (c 39)
Financial Services and Markets Tribunal	Section 132 of the Financial Services and Markets Act 2000 (c 8)
Gambling Appeals Tribunal	Section 140 of the Gambling Act 2005 (c 19)
Immigration Services Tribunal	Section 87 of the Immigration and Asylum Act 1999 (c 33)
Lands Tribunal	Section 1(1)(b) of the Lands Tribunal Act 1949 (c 42)
Pensions Appeal Tribunal in England and Wales	Paragraph 1(1) of the Schedule to the Pensions Appeal Tribunals Act 1943 (c 39)
Pensions Regulator Tribunal	Section 102 of the Pensions Act 2004 (c 35)
Commissioner for the special purposes of the Income Tax Acts	Section 4 of the Taxes Management Act 1970 (c 9)

PART 4
TRIBUNALS FOR THE PURPOSES OF SECTION 30

Tribunal	Enactment
[3]	[3]
[4]	[4]
Antarctic Act Tribunal	Regulation 11 of the Antarctic Regulations 1995 (SI 1995/490)
Appeal tribunal	Part 2 of Schedule 9 to the Scheme set out in Schedule 2 to the Firefighters' Pension Scheme Order 1992 (SI 1992/129)
[Asylum and Immigration Tribunal	Section 81 of the Nationality, Immigration and Asylum Act 2002(b)][2]
Asylum Support Adjudicator	Section 102 of the Immigration and Asylum Act 1999
Case tribunal, or interim case tribunal, drawn from the Adjudication Panel for England	Section 76 of the Local Government Act 2000 (c 22)
Family Health Services Appeal Authority	Section 49S of the National Health Service Act 1977 (c 49)
Insolvency Practitioners Tribunal[6]	*Section 396(1) of the Insolvency Act 1986 (c 45)*[6]

Tribunal	Enactment
Appeals Tribunal	Part 3 of the Local Authorities (Code of Conduct) (Local Determination) Regulations 2003 (SI 2003/1483)
[Panel	Section 189(6) of the Greater London Authority Act 1999][1]
Plant Varieties and Seeds Tribunal	Section 42 of the Plant Varieties Act 1997 (c 66)
Tribunal	Rule 6 of the model provisions with respect to appeals as applied with modifications by the Chemical Weapons (Licence Appeal Provisions) Order 1996 (SI 1996/3030)
Tribunal	Health Service Medicines (Price Control Appeals) Regulations 2000 (SI 2000/124)
Tribunal	Section 706 of the Income and Corporation Taxes Act 1988 (c 1)
. . .[5]	. . .[5]
Tribunal	Part 1 of Schedule 3 to the Misuse of Drugs Act 1971 (c 38)
Tribunal	Regulation H6(3) of the Police Pensions Regulations 1987 (SI 1987/257)
Tribunal	Section 9 of the Protection of Children Act 1999 (c 14)

Amendments—[1]   Entry for "panel" inserted by the Transfer of Functions (Estate Agents Appeals and Additional Scheduled Tribunal) Order, SI 2009/1836 art 4 with effect from 8 July 2009.

[2]   Entry inserted by the Amendment to Schedule 6 to the Tribunals, Courts and Enforcement Act 2007 Order 2010, SI 2010/21 art 2 with effect from 14 February 2010.

[3]   Entry relating to "Agricultural Land Tribunal" repealed by the Amendments to Schedule 6 to the Tribunals, Courts and Enforcement Act 2007 Order, SI 2013/1034 art 3.

[4]   Entry relating to "Aircraft and Shipbuilding Industries Arbitration Tribunal" repealed by the Public Bodies (Abolition of the Aircraft and Shipbuilding Industries Arbitration Tribunal) Order, SI 2013/686 art 3, Sch 1, para 9 with effect from 22 March 2013.

[5]   Entry relating to "Section 150 of the Mines and Quarries Act 1954" repealed by the Mines Regulations, SI 2014/3248 reg 74(1), Sch 3 Pt 2 with effect from 6 April 2015.

[6]   Entry relating to "Insolvency Practitioners Tribunal" repealed by the Deregulation Act 2015 s 19, Sch 6 para 22(1), (16)(a) with effect from 1 October 2015 (by virtue of SI 2015/1732 art 2(e)(vi)). Where immediately before 1 October 2015, an individual has applied for authorisation under the Insolvency Act 1986 s 392 or holds an authorisation granted under the Insolvency Act 1986 s 393, this amendment has no effect for the transitional period (SI 2015/1732 art 7), as defined by the Deregulation Act 2015 Sch 6 para 23. The transitional period is the period of one year beginning on 1 October 2015.

PART 5

TRIBUNALS FOR THE PURPOSES OF SECTIONS 35 AND 36

Tribunal	Enactment
Employment Appeal Tribunal	Section 20 of the Employment Tribunals Act 1996 (c 17)

PART 6

TRIBUNALS FOR THE PURPOSES OF SECTION 35

Tribunal	Enactment
Employment tribunal	Section 1 of the Employment Tribunals Act 1996

PART 7

TRIBUNALS FOR THE PURPOSES OF SECTION 32(3)

Tribunal	Enactment
Case tribunal, or interim case tribunal, drawn from the Adjudication Panel for Wales	Section 76 of the Local Government Act 2000 (c 22)
[Agricultural Land Tribunal for Wales	Section 73 of the Agriculture Act 1947 (c. 48)][1]

Tribunal	Enactment
Appeals Tribunal	Local Government Investigations (Functions of Monitoring Officers and Standards Committees) (Wales) Regulations 2001 (SI 2001/2281)
Mental Health Review Tribunal for Wales	Section 65(1) and (1A)(b) of the Mental Health Act 1983 (c 20)
[Rent assessment committees for areas in Wales	Section 65 of, and Schedule 10 to, the Rent Act 1977 (c. 42)][1]
Special Educational Needs Tribunal for Wales	Section 336ZA of the Education Act 1996 (c 56)
Tribunal	Section 27 of, and Schedule 3 to, the Education Act 2005 (c 18)

Amendments—[1]   Entries inserted by the Amendments to Schedule 6 to the Tribunals, Courts and Enforcement Act 2007 Order, SI 2013/1034 art 4.

Prospective amendments—Entry relating to "Special Educational Needs Tribunal for Wales" to be repealed by the Additional Learning Needs and Education Tribunal (Wales) Act 2018 s 96, Sch 1 para 13 with effect from a date to be appointed.

SCHEDULE 10

AMENDMENTS RELATING TO JUDICIAL APPOINTMENTS

Section 50

PART 1

AMENDMENTS

. . .

8—(1) Section 4(2) of the Taxes Management Act 1970 (c 9) (Special Commissioners) is amended as follows.

(2) For paragraph (*a*) substitute—

"(*a*)   he satisfies the judicial-appointment eligibility condition on a 7-year basis;".

(3) In paragraphs (*b*) and (*c*), for "10" substitute "7".

. . .

19—(1) Paragraph 1(1)(*a*) of Schedule 7 to the Insolvency Act 1986 (c 45) (members of Insolvency Practitioners Tribunal) is amended as follows.

(2) For sub-paragraph (i) substitute—

"(i)   satisfy the judicial-appointment eligibility condition on a 5-year basis;".

(3) In sub-paragraph (ii), for "7" substitute "5".

Amendments—Para 19 repealed by the Deregulation Act 2015 s 19, Sch 6, para 22(1), (16)(*b*) with effect from 1 October 2015 (SI 2015/1732 art 2(e)(vi)). Transitional provisions apply until 30 September 2016 (see SI 2015/1732 art 7).

24—(1) Schedule 12 to the Value Added Tax Act 1994 (c 23) is amended as follows.

(2) In paragraph 2(2) (President of VAT and duties tribunals)—

(*a*) for paragraph (*a*) substitute—

"(*a*)   a person who satisfies the judicial-appointment eligibility condition on a 7-year basis;", and

(*b*) in paragraphs (*b*) and (*c*), for "10" substitute "7".

(3) In paragraph 7(4) (panel of chairmen)—

(*a*) for paragraph (*a*) substitute—

"(*a*)   a person who satisfies the judicial-appointment eligibility condition on a 5-year basis; or", and

(*b*) in paragraph (*b*) and in the words after that paragraph, for "7" substitute "5".

. . .

35—(1) The Land Registration Act 2002 (c 9) is amended as follows.

(2) In section 107(2) (Adjudicator to Her Majesty's Land Registry), for the words from "have" to the end substitute "satisfy the judicial-appointment eligibility condition on a 7-year basis."

(3) In paragraph 4(2) of Schedule 9 (delegation by adjudicator of non-administrative functions to staff), for the words from "has" to the end substitute "satisfies the judicial-appointment eligibility condition on a 7-year basis."

36—(1) Paragraph 1 of Schedule 2 to the Enterprise Act 2002 (c 40) is amended as follows.

(2) In sub-paragraph (1) (President of Competition Appeal Tribunal)—

(*a*) for paragraph (*a*) substitute—

"(*a*)   he satisfies the judicial-appointment eligibility condition on a 7-year basis;", and

(*b*) in paragraphs (*b*) and (*c*), for "10" substitute "7".

(3) In sub-paragraph (2) (chairmen)—
> (*a*) for paragraph (*a*) substitute—
>> "(*a*)   he satisfies the judicial-appointment eligibility condition on a 5-year basis;", and
> (*b*) in paragraphs (*b*) and (*c*), for "7" substitute "5".

. . .

41—(1) Section 25 of the Constitutional Reform Act 2005 (c 4) (judges of the Supreme Court) is amended as follows.
(2) In subsection (1), for paragraph (*b*) and the word "or" immediately preceding it substitute—
>> "(*b*)   satisfied the judicial-appointment eligibility condition on a 15-year basis, or
>> (*c*)   been a qualifying practitioner for a period of at least 15 years."
(3) In subsection (2), omit paragraph (*a*).

42   In paragraph 1(2) of Schedule 3 to the Education Act 2005 (c 18) (Chairman of tribunal hearing appeals under section 27 of that Act), for the words from "have a" to the end substitute "satisfy the judicial-appointment eligibility condition on a 5-year basis."

SCHEDULE 12

TAKING CONTROL OF GOODS

Section 62(1)

Note—This Schedule does not extend to Scotland (s 147(2)).

PART 1
INTRODUCTORY

The procedure

1—(1) Using the procedure in this Schedule to recover a sum means taking control of goods and selling them to recover that sum in accordance with this Schedule and regulations under it.
(2) In this Schedule a power to use the procedure to recover a particular sum is called an "enforcement power".
(3) The following apply in relation to an enforcement power.
(4) "Debt" means the sum recoverable.
(5) "Debtor" means the person liable to pay the debt or, if two or more persons are jointly or jointly and severally liable, any one or more of them.
(6) "Creditor" means the person for whom the debt is recoverable.

Enforcement agents

2—(1) In this Schedule "enforcement agent" means an individual authorised by section 63(2) to act as an enforcement agent.
(2) Only an enforcement agent may take control of goods and sell them under an enforcement power.
(3) An enforcement agent, if he is not the person on whom an enforcement power is conferred, may act under the power only if authorised by that person.
(4) In relation to goods taken control of by an enforcement agent under an enforcement power, references to the enforcement agent are references to any person for the time being acting as an enforcement agent under the power.

General interpretation

3—(1) In this Schedule—
> "amount outstanding" is defined in paragraph 50(3);
> "control" (except in paragraph 5(4)(*a*)) means control under an enforcement power;
> "controlled goods" means goods taken control of that—
>> (*a*) have not been sold or abandoned,
>> (*b*) if they have been removed, have not been returned to the debtor (unless subject to a controlled goods agreement), and
>> (*c*) if they are goods of another person, have not been returned to that person;
> "controlled goods agreement" has the meaning given by paragraph 13(4);
> "co-owner" in relation to goods of the debtor means a person other than the debtor who has an interest in the goods, but only if the enforcement agent—
>> (*a*) knows that the person has an interest in the particular goods, or
>> (*b*) would know, if he made reasonable enquiries;
> "the court", unless otherwise stated, and subject to rules of court, means—
>> (*a*) the High Court, in relation to an enforcement power under a writ of the High Court;

    (*b*) a county court, in relation to an enforcement power under a warrant issued by a county court;

    (*c*) in any other case, a magistrates' court;

"disposal" and related expressions, in relation to securities, are to be read in accordance with paragraph 48(2);

"exempt goods" means goods that regulations exempt by description or circumstances or both;

"goods" means property of any description, other than land;

"interest" means a beneficial interest;

"money" means money in sterling or another currency;

"premises" means any place, and in particular includes—

    (*a*) a vehicle, vessel, aircraft or hovercraft;

    (*b*) a tent or movable structure;

"securities" includes bills of exchange, promissory notes, bonds, specialties and securities for money.

(2) In this Schedule—

    (*a*) references to goods of the debtor or another person are references to goods in which the debtor or that person has an interest, but

    (*b*) references to goods of the debtor do not include references to trust property in which either the debtor or a co-owner has an interest not vested in possession.

Regulations—Taking Control of Goods Regulations, SI 2013/1894.

PART 2
THE PROCEDURE

Binding property in the debtor's goods

4—(1) For the purposes of any enforcement power, the property in all goods of the debtor, except goods that are exempt goods for the purposes of this Schedule or are protected under any other enactment, becomes bound in accordance with this paragraph.

(2) Where the power is conferred by a writ issued from the High Court the writ binds the property in the goods from the time when it is received by the person who is under a duty to endorse it.

(3) Where the power is conferred by a warrant to which section 99 of the County Courts Act 1984 (c 28) or section 125ZA of the Magistrates' Courts Act 1980 (c 43) applies, the warrant binds the property in the goods from the time when it is received by the person who is under a duty to endorse it under that section.

(4) Where sub-paragraphs (2) and (3) do not apply but notice is given to the debtor under paragraph 7(1), the notice binds the property in the goods from the time when the notice is given.

Effect of property in goods being bound

5—(1) An assignment or transfer of any interest of the debtor's in goods while the property in them is bound for the purposes of an enforcement power—

    (*a*) is subject to that power, and

    (*b*) does not affect the operation of this Schedule in relation to the goods, except as provided by paragraph 61 (application to assignee or transferee).

(2) Sub-paragraph (1) does not prejudice the title to any of the debtor's goods that a person acquires—

    (*a*) in good faith,

    (*b*) for valuable consideration, and

    (*c*) without notice.

(3) For the purposes of sub-paragraph (2)(*a*), a thing is to be treated as done in good faith if it is in fact done honestly (whether it is done negligently or not).

(4) In sub-paragraph (2)(*c*) "notice" means—

    (*a*) where the property in the goods is bound by a writ or warrant, notice that the writ or warrant, or any other writ or warrant by virtue of which the goods of the debtor might be seized or otherwise taken control of, had been received by the person who was under a duty to endorse it and that goods remained bound under it;

    (*b*) where the property in the goods is bound by notice under paragraph 7(1), notice that that notice had been given and that goods remained bound under it.

(5) In sub-paragraph (4)(*a*) "endorse" in relation to a warrant to which section 99 of the County Courts Act 1984 (c 28) or section 125ZA of the Magistrates' Courts Act 1980 (c 43) applies, means endorse under that section.

Time when property ceases to be bound

6—(1) For the purposes of any enforcement power the property in goods of the debtor ceases to be bound in accordance with this paragraph.
(2) The property in any goods ceases to be bound—
    (*a*) when the goods are sold;
    (*b*) in the case of money used to pay any of the amount outstanding, when it is used.
(3) The property in all goods ceases to be bound when any of these happens—
    (*a*) the amount outstanding is paid, out of the proceeds of sale or otherwise;
    (*b*) the instrument under which the power is exercisable ceases to have effect;
    (*c*) the power ceases to be exercisable for any other reason.

Notice of enforcement

7—(1) An enforcement agent may not take control of goods unless the debtor has been given notice.
(2) Regulations must state—
    (*a*) the minimum period of notice;
    (*b*) the form of the notice;
    (*c*) what it must contain;
    (*d*) how it must be given;
    (*e*) who must give it.
(3) The enforcement agent must keep a record of the time when the notice is given.
(4) If regulations authorise it, the court may order in prescribed circumstances that the notice given may be less than the minimum period.
(5) The order may be subject to conditions.
Regulations—Taking Control of Goods Regulations, SI 2013/1894.

Time limit for taking control

8—(1) An enforcement agent may not take control of goods after the prescribed period.
(2) The period may be prescribed by reference to the date of notice of enforcement or of any writ or warrant conferring the enforcement power or any other date.
(3) Regulations may provide for the period to be extended or further extended by the court in accordance with the regulations.
Regulations—Taking Control of Goods Regulations, SI 2013/1894.
Taking Control of Goods and Certification of Enforcement Agents (Amendment) (No. 2) (Coronavirus) Regulations, SI 2020/614.

Goods which may be taken

9   An enforcement agent may take control of goods only if they are—
    (*a*) on premises that he has power to enter under this Schedule, or
    (*b*) on a highway.

10   An enforcement agent may take control of goods only if they are goods of the debtor.

11—(1) Subject to paragraphs 9 and 10 and to any other enactment under which goods are protected, an enforcement agent—
    (*a*) may take control of goods anywhere in England and Wales;
    (*b*) may take control of any goods that are not exempt.
(2) Regulations may authorise him to take control of exempt goods in prescribed circumstances, if he provides the debtor with replacements in accordance with the regulations.

Value of goods taken

12—(1) Unless sub-paragraph (2) applies, an enforcement agent may not take control of goods whose aggregate value is more than—
    (*a*) the amount outstanding, and
    (*b*) an amount in respect of future costs, calculated in accordance with regulations.
(2) An enforcement agent may take control of goods of higher value on premises or on a highway, only to the extent necessary, if there are not enough goods of a lower value within a reasonable distance—
    (*a*) on a highway, or
    (*b*) on premises that he has power to enter under this Schedule, either under paragraph 14 or under an existing warrant.
(3) For the purposes of this paragraph goods are above a given value only if it is or ought to be clear to the enforcement agent that they are.

(4) Sub-paragraph (1) does not affect the power to keep control of goods if they rise in value once they have been taken.

Ways of taking control

13—(1) To take control of goods an enforcement agent must do one of the following—

(a) secure the goods on the premises on which he finds them;

(b) if he finds them on a highway, secure them on a highway, where he finds them or within a reasonable distance;

(c) remove them and secure them elsewhere;

(d) enter into a controlled goods agreement with the debtor.

(2) Any liability of an enforcement agent (including criminal liability) arising out of his securing goods on a highway under this paragraph is excluded to the extent that he acted with reasonable care.

(3) Regulations may make further provision about taking control in any of the ways listed in sub-paragraph (1), including provision—

(a) determining the time when control is taken;

(b) prohibiting use of any of those ways for goods by description or circumstances or both.

(4) A controlled goods agreement is an agreement under which the debtor—

(a) is permitted to retain custody of the goods,

(b) acknowledges that the enforcement agent is taking control of them, and

(c) agrees not to remove or dispose of them, nor to permit anyone else to, before the debt is paid.

Regulations—Taking Control of Goods Regulations, SI 2013/1894.
Taking Control of Goods (Fees) Regulations, SI 2014/1.
Taking Control of Goods and Certification of Enforcement Agents (Amendment) (No. 2) (Coronavirus) Regulations, SI 2020/614.

Entry without warrant

14—(1) An enforcement agent may enter relevant premises to search for and take control of goods.

(2) Where there are different relevant premises this paragraph authorises entry to each of them.

(3) This paragraph authorises repeated entry to the same premises, subject to any restriction in regulations.

(4) If the enforcement agent is acting under section 72(1) (CRAR), the only relevant premises are the demised premises.

(5) . . .[1]

(6) Otherwise premises are relevant if the enforcement agent reasonably believes that they are the place, or one of the places, where the debtor—

(a) usually lives, or

(b) carries on a trade or business.

Regulations—Taking Control of Goods Regulations, SI 2013/1894.
Taking Control of Goods and Certification of Enforcement Agents (Amendment) (No. 2) (Coronavirus) Regulations, SI 2020/614.
Amendments—[1]   Sub-s (5) repealed by FA 2008 s 129, Sch 43 para 10(2) with effect from 6 April 2014 (by virtue of SI 2014/906 art 2).

Entry under warrant

15—(1) If an enforcement agent applies to the court it may issue a warrant authorising him to enter specified premises to search for and take control of goods.

(2) Before issuing the warrant the court must be satisfied that all these conditions are met—

(a) an enforcement power has become exercisable;

(b) there is reason to believe that there are goods on the premises that the enforcement power will be exercisable to take control of if the warrant is issued;

(c) it is reasonable in all the circumstances to issue the warrant.

(3) The warrant authorises repeated entry to the same premises, subject to any restriction in regulations.

Regulations—Taking Control of Goods Regulations, SI 2013/1894.
Taking Control of Goods and Certification of Enforcement Agents (Amendment) (No. 2) (Coronavirus) Regulations, SI 2020/614.

Re-entry

16—(1) This paragraph applies where goods on any premises have been taken control of and have not been removed by the enforcement agent.

(2) The enforcement agent may enter the premises to inspect the goods or to remove them for storage or sale.

(3) This paragraph authorises repeated entry to the same premises.

(3) No further step may be taken under the enforcement power concerned.

(4) For the purposes of this paragraph the amount outstanding is reduced by the value of any controlled goods consisting of money required to be used to pay that amount, and sub-paragraph (2) does not apply to that money.

59—(1) This paragraph applies if a further step is taken despite paragraph 58(3).

(2) The enforcement agent is not liable unless he had notice, when the step was taken, that the amount outstanding had been paid in full.

(3) Sub-paragraph (2) applies to a related party as to the enforcement agent.

(4) If the step taken is sale of any of the goods the purchaser acquires good title unless, at the time of sale, he or the enforcement agent had notice that the amount outstanding had been paid in full.

(5) A person has notice that the amount outstanding has been paid in full if he would have found it out if he had made reasonable enquiries.

(6) Sub-paragraphs (2) to (4) do not affect any right of the debtor or a co-owner to a remedy against any person other than the enforcement agent or a related party.

(7) In this paragraph, "related party" has the meaning given by paragraph 65(4).

Third party claiming goods

60—(1) This paragraph applies where a person makes an application to the court claiming that goods taken control of are his and not the debtor's.

(2) After receiving notice of the application the enforcement agent must not sell the goods, or dispose of them (in the case of securities), unless directed by the court under this paragraph.

(3) The court may direct the enforcement agent to sell or dispose of the goods if the applicant fails to make, or to continue to make, the required payments into court.

(4) The required payments are—

- (*a*) payment on making the application (subject to sub-paragraph (5)) of an amount equal to the value of the goods, or to a proportion of it directed by the court;
- (*b*) payment, at prescribed times (on making the application or later), of any amounts prescribed in respect of the enforcement agent's costs of retaining the goods.

(5) If the applicant makes a payment under sub-paragraph (4)(*a*) but the enforcement agent disputes the value of the goods, any underpayment is to be—

- (*a*) determined by reference to an independent valuation carried out in accordance with regulations, and
- (*b*) paid at the prescribed time.

(6) If sub-paragraph (3) does not apply the court may still direct the enforcement agent to sell or dispose of the goods before the court determines the applicant's claim, if it considers it appropriate.

(7) If the court makes a direction under sub-paragraph (3) or (6)—

- (*a*) paragraphs 38 to 49, and regulations under them, apply subject to any modification directed by the court;
- (*b*) the enforcement agent must pay the proceeds of sale or disposal into court.

(8) In this paragraph "the court", subject to rules of court, means—

- (*a*) the High Court, in relation to an enforcement power under a writ of the High Court;
- (*b*) a county court, in relation to an enforcement power under a warrant issued by a county court;
- (*c*) in any other case, the High Court or a county court.

Regulations—Taking Control of Goods Regulations, SI 2013/1894.

Application to assignee or transferee

61—(1) This Schedule applies as follows where an interest of the debtor's in goods is assigned or transferred while the property in the goods is bound for the purposes of an enforcement power, and the enforcement agent—

- (*a*) knows that the assignee or transferee has an interest in the particular goods, or
- (*b*) would know, if he made reasonable enquiries.

(2) These apply as if the assignee or transferee were a co-owner of the goods with the debtor—

- (*a*) paragraph 34 (inventory);
- (*b*) paragraph 36 (valuation);
- (*c*) paragraphs 39 to 41 (sale);
- (*d*) paragraph 59(6) (remedies after payment of amount outstanding).

(3) If the interest of the assignee or transferee was acquired in good faith, for valuable consideration and without notice, paragraph 50(6) applies as if "co-owner" included the assignee or transferee.

(4) If the interest of the assignee or transferee was not acquired in good faith, for valuable consideration and without notice, the enforcement agent must pay any surplus under paragraph 50(5) to the assignee or transferee and to the debtor (if he retains an interest).

(5) If the surplus is payable to two or more persons it must be paid in shares proportionate to their interests.

(6) Paragraph 5(3) and (4) ("good faith" and "notice") apply for the purposes of this paragraph.

Costs

62—(1) Regulations may make provision for the recovery by any person from the debtor of amounts in respect of costs of enforcement-related services.

(2) The regulations may provide for recovery to be out of proceeds or otherwise.

(3) The amount recoverable under the regulations in any case is to be determined by or under the regulations.

(4) The regulations may in particular provide for the amount, if disputed, to be assessed in accordance with rules of court.

(5) "Enforcement-related services" means anything done under or in connection with an enforcement power, or in connection with obtaining an enforcement power, or any services used for the purposes of a provision of this Schedule or regulations under it.

Regulations—Taking Control of Goods (Fees) Regulations, SI 2014/1.

Limitation of liability for sale or payment of proceeds

63—(1) Any liability of an enforcement agent or related party to a lawful claimant for the sale of controlled goods is excluded except in two cases.

(2) The first exception is where at the time of the sale the enforcement agent had notice that the goods were not the debtor's, or not his alone.

(3) The second exception is where before sale the lawful claimant had made an application to the court claiming an interest in the goods.

(4) A lawful claimant in relation to goods is a person who has an interest in them at the time of sale, other than an interest that was assigned or transferred to him while the property in the goods was bound for the purposes of the enforcement power.

64—(1) Any liability of an enforcement agent or related party to a lawful claimant for paying over proceeds is excluded except in two cases.

(2) The first exception is where at the time of the payment he had notice that the goods were not the debtor's, or not his alone.

(3) The second exception is where before that time the lawful claimant had made an application to the court claiming an interest in the goods.

(4) A lawful claimant in relation to goods is a person who has an interest in them at the time of sale.

65—(1) Paragraphs 63 and 64—

    (*a*) do not affect the liability of a person other than the enforcement agent or a related party;

    (*b*) do not apply to the creditor if he is the enforcement agent.

(2) The following apply for the purposes of those paragraphs.

(3) The enforcement agent or a related party has notice of something if he would have found it out if he had made reasonable enquiries.

(4) A related party is any person who acts in exercise of an enforcement power, other than the creditor or enforcement agent.

(5) "The court" has the same meaning as in paragraph 60.

Remedies available to the debtor

66—(1) This paragraph applies where an enforcement agent—

    (*a*) breaches a provision of this Schedule, or

    (*b*) acts under an enforcement power under a writ, warrant, liability order or other instrument that is defective.

(2) The breach or defect does not make the enforcement agent, or a person he is acting for, a trespasser.

(3) But the debtor may bring proceedings under this paragraph.

(4) Subject to rules of court, the proceedings may be brought—

    (*a*) in the High Court, in relation to an enforcement power under a writ of the High Court;

    (*b*) in a county court, in relation to an enforcement power under a warrant issued by a county court;

    (*c*) in any other case, in the High Court or a county court.

(5) In the proceedings the court may—

    (*a*) order goods to be returned to the debtor;

    (*b*) order the enforcement agent or a related party to pay damages in respect of loss suffered by the debtor as a result of the breach or of anything done under the defective instrument.

(6) A related party is either of the following (if different from the enforcement agent)—

    (*a*) the person on whom the enforcement power is conferred,

    (*b*) the creditor.

(7) Sub-paragraph (5) is without prejudice to any other powers of the court.

(8) Sub-paragraph (5)(*b*) does not apply where the enforcement agent acted in the reasonable belief—

    (*a*) that he was not breaching a provision of this Schedule, or

    (*b*) (as the case may be) that the instrument was not defective.

(9) This paragraph is subject to paragraph 59 in the case of a breach of paragraph 58(3).

Remedies available to the creditor

67   If a debtor wrongfully interferes with controlled goods and the creditor suffers loss as a result, the creditor may bring a claim against the debtor in respect of the loss.

Offences

68—(1) A person is guilty of an offence if he intentionally obstructs a person lawfully acting as an enforcement agent.

(2) A person is guilty of an offence if he intentionally interferes with controlled goods without lawful excuse.

(3) A person guilty of an offence under this paragraph is liable on summary conviction to—

    (*a*) imprisonment for a term not exceeding 51 weeks, or

    (*b*) a fine not exceeding level 4 on the standard scale, or

    (*c*) both.

(4) In relation to an offence committed before the commencement of section 281(5) of the Criminal Justice Act 2003 (c 44), the reference in sub-paragraph (3)(*a*) to 51 weeks is to be read as a reference to 6 months.

Relation to insolvency provisions

69   This Schedule is subject to sections 183, 184 and 346 of the Insolvency Act 1986 (c 45).

SCHEDULE 13
TAKING CONTROL OF GOODS: AMENDMENTS
Section 62(3)

. . .

Taxes Management Act 1970 (c 9)

32   The Taxes Management Act 1970 is amended as follows.

34   (*inserts* TMA 1970 s 62(4))

. . .

Commencement—Tribunals, Courts and Enforcement Act 2007 (Commencement No 11) Order, SI 2014/768 art 2(1)(*b*) (Sch 13 comes into force on 6 April 2014).

Social Security Administration Act 1992 (c 5)

101   The Social Security Administration Act 1992 is amended as follows.

Value Added Tax Act 1994 (c 23)

117   The Value Added Tax Act 1994 is amended as follows.

118   (*amends*VATA 1994 s 48(7A))Ireland,".

120   (*substitutes* VATA 1994 s 68(5))

Finance Act 1996 (c 8)

122   Schedule 5 to the Finance Act 1996 (landfill tax) is amended as follows.

124   (*substitutes* FA 1996 Sch 5 para 24(4))

Finance Act 1997 (c 16)

126—(1) Section 51 of the Finance Act 1997 (enforcement by distress) is amended as follows.

(2) (*inserted* FA 1997 s 51(A1); *repealed by* FA 2008 s 129, Sch 43 para 11(*d*))

(3) (*amends* FA 1997 s 51(1)).

(4) (*repeals* FA 1997 s 51(7))

Finance Act 2000 (c 17)

135   Schedule 6 to the Finance Act 2000 (climate change levy) is amended as follows.

137 (*substitutes* FA 2000 Sch 6 para 90(5))

Finance Act 2001 (c 9)

139 Schedule 5 to the Finance Act 2001 (aggregates levy: recovery and interest) is amended as follows.

141 (*substitutes* FA 2000 Sch 5 para 15(5))

Income Tax Act 2007 (c 3)

157 (*amends* ITA 2007 s 955(4)).

SCHEDULE 23

REPEALS

Section 146

PART 1

TRIBUNALS AND INQUIRIES

Reference	Extent of repeal or revocation
Taxes Management Act 1970 (c 9)	Sections 2 to 3A.
	In section 5(1), the words "General Commissioner or".
	In section 6—
	(a) in subsection (1), the words "a General Commissioner or" and the words ", or before a General Commissioner"; and
	(b) subsection (2).
	In section 56(3), the words "the clerk to".
	Section 115(4).
Superannuation Act 1972 (c 11)	In Schedule 6, paragraph 77.
Finance Act 1972 (c 41)	Section 130.
Consumer Credit Act 1974 (c 39)	In Schedule A1, paragraph 11.
House of Commons Disqualification Act 1975 (c 24)	In Schedule 1, in Part 2—
	(a) the entry relating to the Council on Tribunals, and
	(b) the entry relating to the Scottish Committee of the Council on Tribunals.
Northern Ireland Assembly Disqualification Act 1975 (c 25)	In Schedule 1, in Part 2—
	(a) the entry relating to the Council on Tribunals, and
	(b) the entry relating to the Scottish Committee of the Council on Tribunals.
Race Relations Act 1976 (c 74)	In Schedule 1A, in Part 2, the entry relating to the Council on Tribunals.
Estate Agents Act 1979 (c 38)	Section 24(2).
Finance Act 1988 (c 39)	Section 134(1).
Food Safety Act 1990 (c 16)	In section 26(2)—
	(a) in paragraph (e), the words "or to a tribunal constituted in accordance with the regulations," and
	(b) paragraph (f).
	Section 37(2)(a).
	Section 47.
Finance (No 2) Act 1992 (c 48)	In section 75(1), paragraph (a).
	In Schedule 16, paragraph 2.
Tribunals and Inquiries Act 1992 (c 53)	Sections 1 to 5, 6(1) to (3), (6) and (7) and 8.
	In section 13—
	(a) subsection (2), and
	(b) in subsection (5)(c), the words "the reference in section 8(1) to the Foreign Compensation Commission and".
	Section 14(1A).

Reference	Extent of repeal or revocation
	In section 16(1), in the definition of "decision", "procedural rules" and "working", the words ", "procedural rules" and "working"".
	In Schedule 1, paragraph 19.
Judicial Pensions and Retirement Act 1993 (c 8)	In section 1(1), the word "and" at the end of paragraph (c).
	Section 12(1)(b).
Employment Tribunals Act 1996 (c 17)	Section 26.
	In section 27(1)—
	(a) in paragraph (b), the word "and" at the end,
	(b) paragraph (c), and
	(c) the words after "persons within paragraph (a) or (b)".
Social Security Act 1998 (c 14)	In Schedule 7, in paragraph 118(1), "subsection (3) of" and the words after "1992".
Social Security Contributions (Transfer of Functions, Etc.) Act 1999 (c 2)	In Schedule 7, paragraph 1.
Access to Justice Act 1999 (c 22)	Sections 101 to 103.
Social Security Contributions (Transfer of Functions, etc) (Northern Ireland) Order 1999 (SI 1999/671)	In Schedule 6, in paragraph 1, the words "section 2(1) (appointment of General Commissioners),".
Scotland Act 1998 (Cross-Border Public Authorities) (Adaptation of Functions etc) Order 1999 (SI 1999/1747)	Schedule 9.
Scotland Act 1998 (Transfer of Functions to the Scottish Ministers etc) Order 1999 (SI 1999/1750)	In Schedule 1, the entry in respect of sections 2(3), 2(6) and 3(4) of the Taxes Management Act 1970.
Freedom of Information Act 2000 (c 36)	In Schedule 1, in Part 6, the entry relating to the Council on Tribunals and the entry relating to the Scottish Committee of the Council on Tribunals.
Financial Services and Markets Act 2000 (Consequential Amendments and Repeals) Order 2001 (SI 2001/3649)	Article 335(3).
Justice (Northern Ireland) Act 2002 (c 26)	In each of Schedules 1 and 6, the entry relating to the panel of persons appointed under section 6(1) of the Tribunals and Inquiries Act 1992 to act as chairmen of tribunals that sit in Northern Ireland.
Nationality, Immigration and Asylum Act 2002 (c 41)	In Schedule 4, paragraphs 9 and 10(b) and (c).
Scottish Public Services Ombudsman Act 2002 (Consequential Provisions and Modifications) Order 2004 (SI 2004/1823)	Article 14.
Constitutional Reform Act 2005 (c 4)	In Schedule 4, paragraph 64.
	In Schedule 5, in the amendment made by paragraph 122(5), and in the amendment made by paragraph 126(5), the entry relating to the panel of persons appointed under section 6(1) of the Tribunals and Inquiries Act 1992 to act as chairmen of tribunals that sit in Northern Ireland.
	In Schedule 7, in Part A of the list in paragraph 4—
	(a) the entry for section 6(2), (8) and (9) of the Tribunals and Inquiries Act 1992, and
	(b) the entry for paragraph 7(4) of Schedule 5 to that Act.
	In Schedule 12, in paragraph 4(4)(a), the words "or no other except that of General Commissioner,".
	In Schedule 14, in Part 2, the entry relating to General Commissioner for a division in England and Wales.
	In Schedule 14, in Part 3, the entry relating to members of panels appointed under section 6(1) of the Tribunals and Inquiries Act 1992.
Tribunals, Courts and Enforcement Act 2007 (c 15)	In section 36(3)(a), the words "or 41(2)".
	In Schedule 8, paragraph 26.

PART 2
JUDICIAL APPOINTMENTS

Reference	Extent of repeal
Courts and Legal Services Act 1990 (c 41)	In Schedule 10—
	(a) paragraph 4,
	(b) in paragraph 6(1), the words "paragraph 13(1) of" and the words after "1947", and
	(c) paragraphs 24, 26, 32, 49, 50(2)(b) and 57.
Judicial Pensions and Retirement Act 1993 (c 8)	In Schedule 5—
	(a) in the entry for a deputy district judge appointed under section 102 of the Supreme Court Act 1981, the words "for a district registry", and
	(b) in the entry for a deputy district judge appointed under section 8 of the County Courts Act 1984, the words "for a county court district".
Child Support Act 1991 (c 48)	In section 54, the definition of "general qualification".
Social Security Act 1998 (c 14)	In Schedule 4, paragraph 1(3).
Enterprise Act 2002 (c 40)	In Schedule 2, paragraph 1(4).
Constitutional Reform Act 2005 (c 4)	Section 25(2)(a).
	In Schedule 3, paragraph 2(3).
	In Schedule 14, in Part 2—
	(a) in the entry relating to a deputy district judge in a district registry of the High Court, the words "in a district registry of the High Court", and
	(b) in the entry relating to a deputy district judge for a county court district, the words "for a county court district".
	In Schedule 14, in Part 3, the entries relating to—
	(a) Member of the Special Immigration Appeals Commission;
	(b) Chairman of the Special Immigration Appeals Commission;
	(c) Member of the Proscribed Organisations Appeal Commission;
	(d) Chairman of the Proscribed Organisations Appeal Commission;
	(e) Member of the Pathogens Access Appeal Commission; and
	(f) Chairman of the Pathogens Access Appeal Commission.

PART 3
ENFORCEMENT BY TAKING CONTROL OF GOODS

Reference	Extent of repeal
Inclosure Act 1773 (c 81)	In section 4, the words from "rendering" to the end.
	In section 16, the words from "rendering" to the end.
Sale of Farming Stock Act 1816 (c 50)	The whole Act.
Judgments Act 1838 (c 110)	Section 12.
Compulsory Purchase Act 1965 (c 56)	Section 13(5).
	Section 29.
Sea Fisheries Act 1968 (c 77)	In section 12(3), the words from "as they apply" to the end.
Criminal Justice Act 1972 (c 71)	In section 66(2), the words from ""sentence of imprisonment"" to the end.
Magistrates' Courts Act 1980 (c 43)	In section 125(2), the words from "This subsection" to the end.
	Section 125D(3)(c).
	Section 151.

Reference	Extent of repeal
	In Schedule 4A, paragraph 3.
British Fishing Boats Act 1983 (c 8)	In section 5(3), the words from "as they apply" to the end.
County Courts Act 1984 (c 28)	Section 85(3).
	Section 87(2).
	Sections 89 to 91.
	Sections 93 to 100.
	Sections 102 and 103.
	Section 123.
	In section 126—
	(a) in subsection (3) the words from "but" to the end;
	(b) in subsection (4) ""bailiff"".
	In section 147(1) the definition of "bailiff".
Finance Act 1984 (c 43)	Section 16.
Local Government Finance Act 1988 (c 41)	In Schedule 9, paragraph 3(2)(b).
Child Support Act 1991 (c 48)	Section 35(2) to (8).
Social Security Administration Act 1992 (c 5)	Section 121A(2) to (8) and (10).
Local Government Finance Act 1992 (c 14)	In Schedule 4—
	(a) paragraph 7;
	(b) in paragraph 8(1)(a) the words from "an authority" to "paragraph 7 above";
	(c) paragraph 12(1)(c);
	(d) paragraph 19(3).
Finance Act 1997 (c 16)	Section 51(7).
Courts Act 2003 (c 39)	In Schedule 7, paragraph 8(5).
Traffic Management Act 2004 (c 18)	Section 82(3)(a).
	Section 83.

(2007 Chapter 27)

[30 October 2007]

PART 3

OTHER MEASURES TO PREVENT OR DISRUPT SERIOUS AND OTHER CRIME

CHAPTER 2

PROCEEDS OF CRIME

Assets Recovery Agency

74 Abolition of Assets Recovery Agency and redistribution of functions etc

(1) The Assets Recovery Agency and the corporation sole that is its Director shall cease to exist on such day as the Secretary of State may by order appoint.

(2) The following Parts of Schedule 8 (abolition of Assets Recovery Agency and its Director) have effect—

 (*a*) Part 1 (abolition of confiscation functions);

 (*b*) Part 2 (transfer to SOCA and prosecution authorities of civil recovery functions);

 (*c*) Part 3 (transfer to SOCA of Revenue functions and power to abolish those functions);

 (*d*) Part 4 (transfer of investigation functions);

 (*e*) Part 5 (transfer of accreditation and training functions to National Policing Improvement Agency);

 (*f*) Part 6 (other amendments to the Proceeds of Crime Act 2002 (c 29)); and

 (*g*) Part 7 (amendments to other enactments).

(3) Schedule 9 (which makes provision about the transfer of the Director and staff of the Agency, and property, rights and liabilities of the Director and the Agency, to SOCA and the National Policing Improvement Agency) has effect.

(4) In this section and Schedules 8 and 9 "SOCA" means the Serious Organised Crime Agency.

Orders—Serious Crime Act 2007 (Commencement No 1) Order, SI 2008/219 art 3 (sub-ss (1), (3) came into force on 1 March 2008; sub-s (2)(*d*), (*g*) came into force on 1 March 2008 in so far as they relate to Sch 8 paras 115, 169 of this Act).
Serious Crime Act 2007 (Commencement No 2 and Transitional and Transitory Provisions and Savings) Order, SI 2008/755 (sub-ss (2), (4) came into force, to the extent not already in force, on 1 April 2008, subject to transitional provisions and savings in SI 2008/755 arts 3–14).

85 Disclosure of information by Revenue and Customs

(1) This section applies to information held as mentioned in section 18(1) of the Commissioners for Revenue and Customs Act 2005 (c 11) (confidentiality).

(2) Information to which this section applies may be disclosed by or with the authority of the Commissioners of Revenue and Customs—

 (*a*) to the Criminal Assets Bureau in Ireland ("the CAB") for the purpose of enabling or assisting the CAB to exercise any of its functions in connection with any matter within subsection (3); or

 (*b*) to any specified public authority (in the United Kingdom or elsewhere)—

   (i) for the purpose of enabling or assisting the public authority to exercise any of its functions in connection with any matter within subsection (3); or

   (ii) (if the specifying order so provides) for the purpose of enabling or assisting the public authority to exercise any of its functions in connection with any matter within that subsection that is specified, or of a description specified, in the order.

(3) The matters within this subsection are—

 (*a*) the identification of proceeds of crime;

 (*b*) the bringing of civil proceedings for enforcement purposes in relation to proceeds of crime; and

 (*c*) the taking of other action in relation to proceeds of crime.

(4) Information disclosed in accordance with subsection (2) must not be further disclosed except—

 (*a*) in connection with the exercise of any of the functions of the CAB or a specified public authority in connection with any matter within subsection (3) (or, in a subsection (2)(*b*)(ii) case, any such matter as is mentioned there); and

 (*b*) with the consent of the Commissioners of Revenue and Customs or an authorised officer of the Commissioners of Revenue and Customs.

(5) For the purposes of this section any consent or authorisation may be general or specific.

(6) If a person in the United Kingdom discloses, in contravention of subsection (4), any revenue and customs information relating to a person whose identity—

 (*a*) is specified in the disclosure; or

 (*b*) can be deduced from it;

section 19 of the 2005 Act (wrongful disclosure) applies in relation to that disclosure as it applies in relation to a disclosure of such information in contravention of section 20(9) of that Act.

(7) Any reference in this section to a disclosure to the CAB or a specified public authority is a reference to a disclosure to such person, or to persons of such description, as may be specified in relation to the CAB or the public authority (as the case may be).

(8) Nothing in this section authorises any disclosure of information which—

   (a) contravenes [the data protection legislation][1]; or

   (b) is prohibited by [any of Parts 1 to 7 or Chapter 1 of Part 9 of the Investigatory Powers Act 2016][2].

(9) In this section—

"the 2005 Act" means the Commissioners for Revenue and Customs Act 2005 (c 11);

"assets" means property of any description, wherever situated;

"civil proceedings" means civil proceedings of whatever nature and whether brought in the United Kingdom or elsewhere;

"Commissioners of Revenue and Customs" means the Commissioners for Her Majesty's Revenue and Customs;

["the data protection legislation" has the same meaning as in the Data Protection Act 2018 (see section 3 of that Act);][1]

"enforcement purposes", in relation to the proceeds of crime, means with a view to—

   (a) recovering, forfeiting or freezing assets constituting proceeds of crime; or

   (b) otherwise depriving persons (to any extent) of, or of access to, such assets or the benefit of such assets;

"functions" includes powers, duties and objectives, and references to the exercise of functions include the pursuit of objectives;

"proceeds of crime" means assets derived, or suspected to be derived, directly or indirectly from criminal conduct (wherever occurring);

"public authority" means any body or person discharging functions of a public nature;

"revenue and customs information relating to a person" has the meaning given by section 19(2) of the 2005 Act;

"specified" means specified in an order made by the Treasury; and

"the specifying order", in relation to a specified public authority, means the order specifying the authority for the purposes of this section.

Orders—Serious Crime Act 2007 (Commencement No 1) Order, SI 2008/219 art 2 (this section came into force on 15 February 2008).

Serious Crime Act 2007 (Disclosure of Information by Revenue and Customs) Order 2008, SI 2008/403 (made under sub-s (7)).

Amendments—[1]   In sub-s (8)(a) words substituted for words "the Data Protection Act 1998 (c. 29)", and in sub-s (9) definition of "the data protection legislation" inserted, by the Data Protection Act 2018 s 211, Sch 19 para 143, 146 with effect from 25 May 2018 (by virtue of SI 2018/625 reg 2(1)(g)).

[2]   In sub-s (8)(b), words substituted for words "Part 1 of the Regulation of Investigatory Powers Act 2000 (c. 23)" by the Investigatory Powers Act 2016 s 271(1), Sch 10 para 19(1), (3) with effect from 27 June 2018 (by virtue of SI 2018/652 reg 12(g)(iii)).

88 Extension of investigatory powers of Revenue and Customs

Schedule 12 (which makes provision about the regulation of investigatory powers of Her Majesty's Revenue and Customs) has effect.

Orders—Serious Crime Act 2007 (Commencement No 1) Order, SI 2008/219 art 2 (this section came into force on 15 February 2008).

92 Repeals and revocations

Schedule 14 (which contains repeals and revocations) has effect.

Orders—Serious Crime Act 2007 (Commencement No 1) Order, SI 2008/219 art 2(c). This section came into force on 15 February 2008 in so far as it relates to the entry in Schedule 14 relating to the Commissioners for Revenue and Customs Act 2005 Sch 2 paras 1, 11.

94 Commencement

(1) The preceding provisions of this Act (other than sections 89, 90, 91(2) and (3) and 93 and the provisions specified in subsection (4) but, subject to this, including the Schedules) come into force on such day as the Secretary of State may by order appoint; and different days may be appointed for different purposes.

(2) The Secretary of State must consult the Scottish Ministers before making an order under subsection (1) in relation to—

   (a) section 75(1);

   (b) paragraph 2 of Schedule 10; or

   (c) paragraph 24 of that Schedule.

(3) The provisions of this Act specified in subsection (4) come into force on such day as the Scottish Ministers may by order appoint; and different days may be appointed for different purposes.

(4) Those provisions are—

   (a) section 75(4) and (5);

   (b) section 76(4) to (6);

   (c) section 86;

(d) paragraphs 14 to 23 and, so far as extending to Scotland, paragraph 25 of Schedule 10; and

(e) so far as relating to the provisions falling within paragraph (d) above, paragraph 1 of that Schedule and section 77.

95 Short title

This Act may be cited as the Serious Crime Act 2007.

SCHEDULE 1
SERIOUS OFFENCES

Sections 2 and 3

PART 1
SERIOUS OFFENCES IN ENGLAND AND WALES

Offences in relation to public revenue [etc]

8—(1) An offence under section 170 of the Customs and Excise Management Act 1979 (c 2) (fraudulent evasion of duty etc) so far as not falling within paragraph 1(2)(c) or 3(1)(b) above.

(2) An offence under section 72 of the Value Added Tax Act 1994 (c 23) (fraudulent evasion of VAT etc).

(3) An offence under [section 106A of the Taxes Management Act 1970][1] (fraudulent evasion of income tax).

(4) An offence under section 35 of the Tax Credits Act 2002 (c 21) (tax credit fraud).

(5) An offence at common law of cheating in relation to the public revenue.

[(6) An offence under section 45 or 46 of the Criminal Finances Act 2017 (failure to prevent the facilitation of UK tax evasion offences or foreign tax evasion offences).][2]

Amendments—[1]   In sub-para 3 words substituted for words "section 144 of the Finance Act 2000 (c 17)" by TIOPA 2010 s 371, Sch 7 paras 100, 101(1), (2). TIOPA 2010 has effect for corporation tax purposes for accounting periods ending on or after 1 April 2010, for income and capital gains tax purposes for the tax year 2010–11 and subsequent tax years, and for petroleum revenue tax purposes for chargeable periods beginning on or after 1 July 2010.

[2]   In heading, word inserted, and sub-para (6) inserted, by the Criminal Finances Act 2017 s 51(2)(a) with effect from 30 September 2017 (by virtue of SI 2017/739).

[PART 1A
SERIOUS OFFENCES IN SCOTLAND

[Money laundering

16F—(1) An offence under any of the following provisions of the Proceeds of Crime Act 2002—

(a) section 327 (concealing etc criminal property);

(b) section 328 (facilitating the acquisition etc of criminal property by or on behalf of another);

(c) section 329 (acquisition, use and possession of criminal property).][1]

Amendments—[1]   This para inserted by the Serious Crime Act 2015 s 46, Sch 1 paras 1, 31 with effect from March 2016 (by virtue of SI 2016/148 reg 3(d), (g)).

[Offences in relation to public revenue [etc]

16G—(1) An offence under section 170 of the Customs and Excise Management Act 1979 (fraudulent evasion of duty etc) so far as not falling within paragraph 16A(2)(c) or 16C(2)(b) above.

(2) An offence under section 72 of the Value Added Tax Act 1994 (fraudulent evasion of VAT etc).

(3) An offence under section 106A of the Taxes Management Act 1970 (fraudulent evasion of income tax).

(4) An offence under section 35 of the Tax Credits Act 2002 (tax credit fraud).][1]

[(5) An offence under section 45 or 46 of the Criminal Finances Act 2017 (failure to prevent the facilitation of UK tax evasion offences or foreign tax evasion offences).][2]][1]

Amendments—[1]   This para inserted by the Serious Crime Act 2015 s 46, Sch 1 paras 1, 31 with effect from March 2016 (by virtue of SI 2016/148 reg 3(d), (g)).

[2]   In heading, word inserted, and sub-para (5) inserted, by the Criminal Finances Act 2017 s 51(2)(b) with effect from 30 September 2017 (by virtue of SI 2017/739).

SCHEDULE 8
ABOLITION OF ASSETS RECOVERY AGENCY AND ITS DIRECTOR
Section 74(2)

PART 1
ABOLITION OF CONFISCATION FUNCTIONS

Orders—Serious Crime Act 2007 (Commencement No 2 and Transitional and Transitory Provisions and Savings) Order, SI 2008/755 (Sch 8 came into force, to the extent not already in force, on 1 April 2008 subject to transitional provisions and savings in SI 2008/755 arts 3–14).

1   The Proceeds of Crime Act 2002 (c 29) is amended as follows.

. . .

84   In Schedule 10 (tax), in paragraph 1—
    (*a*) in paragraph (*a*) for ", 50 or 52" substitute "or 50"; and
    (*b*) in paragraph (*c*) for ", 198 or 200" substitute "or 198".

PART 3
TRANSFER OR ABOLITION OF REVENUE FUNCTIONS

92   The Proceeds of Crime Act 2002 (c 29) is amended in accordance with paragraphs 93 to 101.

93—(1) Section 317 (Director's general Revenue functions) is amended as follows.
(2)-(9) Word "Director's" substituted for word "SOCA's" and words "the Director" substituted for word "SOCA".

94—(1) Section 318 (Revenue functions regarding employment) is amended as follows.
(2)-(5) Words "the Director" substituted for word "SOCA".

95—(1) Section 319 (source of income) is amended as follows.
(2) In subsection (1)—
    (*a*) for "the Director" substitute "SOCA";
    (*b*) for "him" substitute "it"; and
    (*c*) for "he" substitute "SOCA".
(3) In subsection (2) for "the Director" substitute "SOCA".
(4) In subsection (3)—
    (*a*) for "the Director" substitute "SOCA"; and
    (*b*) for "him" substitute "SOCA".

96—(1) Section 320 (appeals) is amended as follows.
(2) In subsection (1) for "the Director" substitute "SOCA".
(3) In subsection (2)—
    (*a*) for "the Director" substitute "SOCA"; and
    (*b*) for "his" substitute "its".

97—(1) Section 321 (Director's functions: transfers of value) is amended as follows.
(2) In the heading for "Director's" substitute "SOCA's".
(3) In subsection (1)—
    (*a*) for "the Director" substitute "SOCA"; and
    (*b*) in paragraph (*b*) for "it" substitute "the transfer of value".
(4)-(8) Words "the Director" substituted for word "SOCA".

98—(1) Section 322 (Director's functions: certain settlements) is amended as follows.
(2) In the heading for "Director's" substitute "SOCA's".
(3) In subsection (1) for "the Director" substitute "SOCA".
(4) In subsection (2)—
    (*a*) for "the Director", in both places where it appears, substitute "SOCA"; and
    (*b*) in paragraph (*c*) for "he" substitute "SOCA".
(5)-(8) Words "the Director" substituted for word "SOCA".

99—(1) Section 324 (exercise of Revenue functions) is amended as follows.
(2) In subsection (1) for "the Director" substitute "SOCA".
(3) In subsection (2) for "Paragraph (*b*) of section 1(6)" substitute "Section 2B(2)".
(4) In subsection (3) for "The Director" substitute "SOCA".
(5) In subsection (4) for "The Director" substitute "SOCA".
(6) In subsection (5)—
    (*a*) for "The Director" substitute "SOCA"; and
    (*b*) for "they" substitute "the Board".

100—(1) Section 325 (declarations) is amended as follows.

(2) Omit subsection (1).

(3) For subsection (2) substitute—

"(2) Every member of SOCA's staff who is assigned to carry out any of SOCA's functions under this Part must, as soon as practicable after being so assigned, make a declaration in the form set out in Schedule 8 before a person nominated by the Director General of SOCA for the purpose."

102 The Secretary of State may by order—

(a) repeal Part 6 of the Proceeds of Crime Act 2002 (c 29); and

(b) make such amendment, repeal or revocation of any provision made by or under any enactment (including this Schedule to this Act) as appears to the Secretary of State to be appropriate in consequence of the repeal of Part 6 of the Act of 2002.

PART 5
TRANSFER OF ACCREDITATION AND TRAINING FUNCTIONS

120—(1) Section 3 of the Proceeds of Crime Act 2002 (c 29) (accreditation and training) is amended as follows.

(2) In subsection (1)—

(a) for "Director" substitute "National Policing Improvement Agency"; and

(b) for "establish" substitute "provide".

(3) Omit subsection (6).

(4) In subsection (7) for "Director" substitute "National Policing Improvement Agency".

(5) Omit subsection (8).

PART 6
OTHER AMENDMENTS TO 2002 ACT

121 The Proceeds of Crime Act 2002 is amended as follows.

122 In the heading for Part 1 for "Assets Recovery Agency" substitute "Introductory".

123 Omit sections 1 and 2 (the Assets Recovery Agency, its Director and the Director's general functions).

124 (*inserts* PCA 2002 ss 2A–2C)

125 Omit sections 4 and 5 (co-operation and advice and assistance for Secretary of State).

126 In section 330(4)(b) (failure to disclose: regulated sector) for "the Serious Organised Crime Agency" substitute "SOCA".

127 In section 331(4) (failure to disclose: nominated officers in the regulated sector) for "the Serious Organised Crime Agency" substitute "SOCA".

128 In section 332(4) (failure to disclose: other nominated officers) for "the Serious Organised Crime Agency" substitute "SOCA".

129 In section 336(2)(a), (3)(a) and (4)(a) (nominated officer: consent) for "the Serious Organised Crime Agency" substitute "SOCA".

130 In section 340(13) (interpretation: Part 7) for "the Serious Organised Crime Agency" substitute "SOCA".

Police Reform Act 2002 (c 30)

160 Section 10(9) inserted to the Police Reform Act 2002.

161 Section 26A(4A) of that Act (SOCA) inserted.

Commissioners for Revenue and Customs Act 2005 (c 11)

164 In section 21(1)(b) of the Commissioners for Revenue and Customs Act 2005 (disclosure to prosecuting authority)—

(a) omit "or" at the end of sub-paragraph (i); and

(b) after sub-paragraph (ii) insert", or

"(iii) in the case of the Director of Revenue and Customs Prosecutions, to exercise his functions under, or in relation to, Part 5 or 8 of the Proceeds of Crime Act 2002 (c 29)."

166 In section 37(1) of that Act (prosecutors) after "section 35" insert " (excluding any function mentioned in subsection (4A) of that section)".

167—(1) Section 40 of that Act (confidentiality) is amended as follows.
(2) Subsection (2)(*ca*) and (*cb*), inserted.
(3) Subsection (10A) inserted.

Serious Organised Crime and Police Act 2005 (c 15)

169 (*inserts* SOCPA 2005 s 2A)

Orders—Serious Crime Act 2007 (Commencement No 1) Order, SI 2008/219 art 3 (this section came into force on 1 March 2008).

172—(1) Section 33 (disclosure of information by SOCA) of that Act is amended as follows.
(2) Subsection (2)(ca)–(ce) inserted.
(3) Sub-ss (2A)-(2D) inserted.

173 Section 35(1A) inserted.

SCHEDULE 12

REVENUE AND CUSTOMS: REGULATION OF INVESTIGATORY POWERS

Section 88

Orders—Serious Crime Act 2007 (Commencement No 1) Order, SI 2008/219 art 2 (Sch 12 came into force on 15 February 2008).

Commissioners for Revenue and Customs Act 2005 (c 11)

30 The following paragraphs of Schedule 2 to the Commissioners for Revenue and Customs Act 2005 (which restrict the class of functions in connection with which certain powers may be used) shall cease to have effect—
   (*a*) paragraph 1 (Wireless Telegraphy Act 2006 (c 36), s. 48); and
   (*b*) paragraph 11 (Regulation of Investigatory Powers Act 2000 (c 23), ss. 6(2)(*h*), 32(6)(m), 49(1)(*e*) and 54 and Sched. 2, paras. 2(3) and 4(2)).

31 Nothing in section 6 or 7 of the Commissioners for Revenue and Customs Act 2005 (initial functions) restricts the functions in connection with which Her Majesty's Revenue and Customs may exercise a power under an enactment amended by this Schedule.

SCHEDULE 14

REPEALS AND REVOCATIONS

Section 92

Title	Extent of repeal or revocation
Proceeds of Crime Act 2002 (c 29)	Sections 1 and 2.
	Section 3(6) and (8).
	Sections 4 and 5.
	Section 325(1).
Commissioners for Revenue and Customs Act 2005 (c 11)	In section 21(1)(*b*), the word "or" at the end of sub-paragraph (i).
	Paragraphs 1 and 11 of Schedule 2.
	Paragraph 98 of Schedule 4.
Tribunals, Courts and Enforcement Act 2007 (c 15)	In Schedule 13, paragraph 145.

Orders—Serious Crime Act 2007 (Commencement No 1) Order, SI 2008/219 art 2 (repeals relating to CRCA 2005 Sch 2 paras 1, 11 came into force on 15 February 2008).

FINANCE ACT 2008

(2008 Chapter 9)

CONTENTS

Part 1: Charges, Rates, Allowances, Reliefs etc
Income tax
1   Charge and main rates for 2008–09
2   Personal allowance for those aged under 65
3   Personal allowances for those aged 65 and over
4   Basic rate limit
5   Abolition of starting and savings rates and creation of starting rate for savings
Corporation tax
6   Charge and main rates for financial year 2009
Capital gains tax
8   Rate etc
9   Entrepreneurs' relief
Inheritance tax
10   (see Part 3 of this work)
Part 2: Income Tax, Corporation Tax and Capital Gains Tax – General
Residence and domicile
24   Periods of residence
25   Remittance basis
Venture capital schemes etc
32   Venture capital schemes
33   Enterprise management incentives: qualifying companies
Other business and investment measures
34   Tax credits for certain foreign distributions
36   Company gains from investment life insurance contracts etc
37   Trade profits: changes in trading stock
38   Non-residents: investment managers
39   Dormant bank and building society accounts
40   Individual investment plan regulations
Insurance companies and friendly societies
43   Insurance companies etc
Employment matters
45   Homes outside UK owned through company etc
46   In-work and return to work credits and payments
47   Company cars: lower threshold for CO2 emissions figure
48   Van fuel benefit
49   Employment-related securities etc: deductible amounts etc
50   Employment-related securities: repeal of obsolete provisions
51   Armed forces: the Council Tax Relief
52   Greater London Authority: severance payments
Charities etc
53   Gift aid: payments to charities
Leasing
55   Leases of plant or machinery
Double taxation arrangements
58   UK residents and foreign partnerships
Other anti-avoidance provisions
60   Restrictions on trade loss relief for individuals
61   Non-active partners
62   Financial arrangements avoidance
63   Manufactured payments
64   Controlled foreign companies
66   Repeal of obsolete anti-avoidance provisions
Miscellaneous
67   Income of beneficiaries under settlor-interested settlements
68   Income charged at dividend upper rate
69   Payments on account of income tax
70   Allowances etc for non-resident nationals of an EEA state
Part 3: Capital Allowances
Plant and machinery: qualifying expenditure
71   Thermal insulation of buildings
72   Expenditure on required fire precautions
73   Integral features
Plant and machinery: annual investment allowance
74   Annual investment allowance

Plant and machinery: first-year allowances
75   First-year allowance for small and medium-sized enterprises discontinued
76   Repeal of spent first-year allowances
77   Cars with low carbon dioxide emissions
78   Gas refuelling stations
Plant and machinery: writing-down allowances and pools
80   Main rate of writing down allowance
81   Small pools
82   Special rate expenditure and the special rate pool
83   Existing long-life asset expenditure treated as special rate expenditure
Industrial and agricultural buildings allowances
84   Abolition of allowances from 2011
Supplementary provision
88   Power to make consequential and transitional provision
Part 4: Pensions
90   Spreading of relief on indirect contributions
91   Inheritance etc of tax-relieved pension savings
92   Pension schemes: further provision
Part 6: Oil
Petroleum revenue tax
102   Meaning of "participator"
103   Abandonment expenditure: default by participator met by former participator
106   Returns of relevant sales of oil
107   Elections for oil fields to become non-taxable
Corporation tax
108   Capital allowances: plant and machinery for use in ring fence trade
109   Capital allowances: decommissioning expenditure
110   Capital allowances: abandonment expenditure after ceasing ring fence trade
111   Losses: set off against profits of earlier accounting periods
Part 7: Administration
Chapter 1 Information etc
New information etc powers
113   Information and inspection powers
114   Computer records etc
Other measures
115   Record-keeping
116   Disclosure of tax avoidance schemes
Chapter 2 Time Limits for Claims and Assessments etc
General
118   Time limits for assessments, claims etc
Income tax and corporation tax
119   Correction and amendment of tax returns
Chapter 3 Penalties
122   Penalties for errors
123   Penalties for failure to notify etc
Chapter 4 Appeals etc
Reviews and appeals etc: general
124   HMRC decisions etc: reviews and appeals
Chapter 5 Payment and Enforcement
Taking control of goods etc
127   Enforcement by taking control of goods: England and Wales
128   Summary warrant: Scotland
129   Consequential provision and commencement
Set off
131   No set-off where insolvency procedure has been applied
132   VAT: requirement to set-off
133   Set-off etc where right to be paid a sum has been transferred
134   Retained funding bonds: tender by Commissioners
Other measures
135   Interest on unpaid tax in case of disaster etc of national significance
136   Fee for payment
137   County court proceedings
138   Certificates of debt
Supplementary
139   Interpretation of Chapter
Part 8 Miscellaneous
Alternative finance arrangements
154   Stamp duty and stamp duty reserve tax: alternative finance investment bonds
155   Alternative property finance: anti-avoidance

157   Government borrowing: alternative finance arrangements
Payments from Exchequer accounts
158   Power of Treasury to make payments
159   Payments from certain Exchequer accounts: mechanism
Other matters
160   Power to give statutory effect to concessions
163   National savings
Part 9 Final Provisions
165   Interpretation
166   Short title
Schedules:
Schedule 1—Abolition of starting and savings rates and creation of starting rate for savings
Schedule 2—Capital gains tax reform
Schedule 3—Entrepreneurs' relief
Schedule 7—Remittance basis
Schedule 11—Venture capital schemes
Schedule 12—Tax credit for certain foreign distributions
Schedule 14—Company gains from investment life insurance contracts: consequential amend-
       ments etc
Schedule 15—Changes in trading stock
Schedule 16—Non-residents: investment managers
Schedule 17—Insurance companies etc
Schedule 19—Reduction of basic rate of income tax: transitional relief for gift aid charities
Schedule 20—Leases of plant or machinery
Schedule 21—Restriction on loss relief for non-active traders
Schedule 22—Avoidance involving financial arrangements
Schedule 23—Manufactured payments: anti-avoidance
Schedule 24—Annual investment allowance
Schedule 26—Special rate expenditure and the special rate pool
Schedule 27—Abolition of allowances: consequential amendments and savings
Schedule 28—Inheritance of tax-relieved pension savings
Schedule 29—Further provision about pension schemes
Schedule 33—PRT: elections for oil fields to become non-taxable
Schedule 34—Oil decommissioning expenditure: consequential amendments
Schedule 35—Set off against oil profits: minor and consequential amendments
Schedule 36—Information and inspection powers
Schedule 37—Record-keeping
Schedule 38—Disclosure of tax avoidance schemes
Schedule 39—Time limits for assessments, claims etc
Schedule 40—Penalties: amendments of Schedule 24 to FA 2007
Schedule 41—Penalties: failure to notify and certain VAT and excise wrongdoing
Schedule 43—Taking control of goods etc: consequential provision
Schedule 44—Certificates of debt: consequential provision
Schedule 46—Government borrowing: alternative finance arrangements

PART 1
CHARGES, RATES, ALLOWANCES, RELIEFS ETC
Income tax

1 Charge and main rates for 2008–09

(1) Income tax is charged for the tax year 2008–09.

(2) For that tax year—

    (*a*) the basic rate is 20%, and

    (*b*) the higher rate is 40%.

2 Personal allowance for those aged under 65

(1) For the tax year 2008–09 the amount specified in—

    (*a*) section 35 of ITA 2007, . . .

    (*b*) *section 257(1) of ICTA,*[1]

(personal allowance for those aged under 65) is replaced with "£6,035".

(2) Accordingly—

    (*a*) section 57 of ITA 2007, so far as relating to the amount specified in section 35 of that Act,

      . . .

    (*b*) *section 257C of ICTA, so far as relating to the amount specified in section 257(1) of that Act,*[1]

(indexation) do not apply for the tax year 2008–09.

(3) This section does not require a change to be made in the amounts deductible or repayable under PAYE regulations before 7 September 2008.

Commentary—*Simon's Taxes* **E1.910, E1.104, E1.911.**

Amendments—[1]   In sub-ss (1), (2), para (*b*) and preceding word "and" repealed by FA 2009 s 5, Sch 1 paras 1, 6(*p*)(i) with effect for the tax year 2010–11 and subsequent tax years.

3 Personal allowances for those aged 65 and over

(1) For the tax year 2008–09—

    (*a*) the amount specified in section 36(1) of ITA 2007 . . . [1] (personal allowance for those aged 65 to 74) is replaced with "£9,030", and

    (*b*) the amount specified in section 37(1) of ITA 2007 . . . [1] (personal allowance for those aged 75 and over) is replaced with "£9,180".

(2) Accordingly—

    (*a*) section 57 of ITA 2007, so far as relating to the amounts specified in sections 36(1) and 37(1) of that Act, . . .

    (*b*) *section 257C of ICTA, so far as relating to the amounts specified in section 257(2) and (3) of that Act,*[1]

(indexation) do not apply for the tax year 2008–09.

Commentary—*Simon's Taxes* **E1.911**.

Amendments—[1]   In sub-s (1), words "and section 257(2) of ICTA" and "and section 257(3) of ICTA" and, in sub-s (2), para (*b*) and preceding word "and", repealed, by FA 2009 s 5, Sch 1 paras 1, 6(*p*)(ii) with effect for the tax year 2010–11 and subsequent tax years.

4 Basic rate limit

(1) (*substitutes* ITA 2007 s 10(5))

(2) The amendment made by subsection (1) has effect for the tax year 2008–09 and subsequent tax years.

(3) But until 7 September 2008 for the purpose of ascertaining the amounts deductible or repayable under PAYE regulations it may be assumed that the figure specified in section 10(5) of ITA 2007 for the tax year 2008–09 is £36,000.

Commentary—*Simon's Taxes* **E1.101A**.

5 Abolition of starting and savings rates and creation of starting rate for savings

(1)–(5) (*amend* ITA 2007 s 6 heading and sub-s (2); *repeal* ITA 2007 s 6(1)(*a*); *substitute* ITA 2007 s (3)(*a*))

(5) Accordingly, in the heading omit "**starting rate,**".

(6) The amendments made by this section have effect for the tax year 2008–09 and subsequent tax years.

(7) Schedule 1 contains provision in connection with—

    (*a*) the abolition of the starting rate and the savings rate, and

    (*b*) the creation of the starting rate for savings.

Commentary—*Simon's Taxes* **E1.101A**.

Corporation tax

6 Charge and main rates for financial year 2009

(1) Corporation tax is charged for the financial year 2009.

(2) For that year the rate of corporation tax is—

    (*a*) 28% on profits of companies other than ring fence profits, and

    (*b*) 30% on ring fence profits of companies.

(3) In subsection (2) "ring fence profits" has the ["meaning given by section 276 of CTA 2010]".[1]

Commentary—*Simon's Taxes* **T4.101, D1.1204**.

HMRC Manuals—Oil Taxation Manual OT21001(introduction to the ring fence).

Amendments—[1]   In sub-s (3) words substituted for words "same meaning as in Chapter 5 of Part 12 of ICTA (see section 502(1) and (1A))" by CTA 2010 s 1177, Sch 1 paras 576, 577. CTA 2010 has effect for corporation tax purposes for accounting periods ending on or after 1 April 2010, and for income and capital gains tax purposes for the tax year 2010–11 and subsequent tax years.

Capital gains tax

8 Rate etc

(1) (*substitutes* TCGA 1992 s 4)

(2) Schedule 2 contains further provision for and in connection with the reform of capital gains tax.

(3) The amendment made by subsection (1) has effect for the tax year 2008–09 and subsequent tax years.

Commentary—*Simon's Taxes* **T3.104**.

HMRC Manuals—Capital Gains Manual CG10246 (rates of tax).

9 Entrepreneurs' relief

Schedule 3 contains provision for and in connection with entrepreneurs' relief.

Commentary—*Simon's Taxes* **T3.107**.

HMRC Manuals—Capital Gains Manual CG63950 (entrepreneurs' relief: contents).

PART 2
INCOME TAX, CORPORATION TAX AND CAPITAL GAINS TAX—GENERAL

Residence and domicile

24 Periods of residence
(1) Section 831 of ITA 2007 (foreign income of individuals in United Kingdom for temporary purpose) is amended as follows.
(2) (*substitutes* ITA 2007 s 831(1)((*b*))
(3) (*inserts* ITA 2007 s 831(1A), (1B))
(4) (*inserts* ITA 2007 s 832(1A), (1B))
(5) Section 9 of TCGA 1992 (residence, including temporary residence) is amended as follows.
(6) (*amends* TCGA 1992 s 9(3))
(7) (*inserts* TCGA 1992 s 9(5), (6))
(8) The amendments made by this section have effect for the tax year 2008–09 and subsequent tax years.

Commentary—*Simon's Taxes* **E6.124F, E4.1335, C1.201**.
HMRC Manuals—Capital Gains Manual CG26155 (arrival in and departure from UK: temporary non-residence: meaning of terms – year of departure 2012-13 or earlier).

25 Remittance basis
Schedule 7 contains provision for and in connection with the revision of the remittance basis.
Commentary—*Simon's Taxes* **E4.1319, E4.15**.
HMRC Manuals—Capital Gains Manual CG25340 (remittance basis).

32 Venture capital schemes
Schedule 11 contains provision about venture capital schemes.
Commentary—*Simon's Taxes* **E3.248**.
HMRC Manuals—Venture Capital Schemes Manual VCM50000 (venture capital trust (VCT) scheme).

33 Enterprise management incentives: qualifying companies
(1) Part 3 of Schedule 5 to ITEPA 2003 (enterprise management incentives: qualifying companies) is amended as follows.
(2) (*amends* ITEPA 2003 Sch 5 para 8)
(3) (*inserts* ITEPA 2003 Sch 5 para 12A)
(4) (*inserts* ITEPA 2003 Sch 5 para 16(*ia*)–(*ic*))
(5) (*inserts* ITEPA 2003 Sch 5 paras 20A–20C)
(6) The amendments made by this section have effect in relation to options granted on or after the day on which this Act is passed.

Commentary—*Simon's Taxes* **E4.545**.
HMRC Manuals—Employee Tax Advantaged Share Scheme User Manual ETASSUM52010 (introduction).

Other business and investment measures

34 Tax credits for certain foreign distributions
(1) Schedule 12 contains provision about tax credits for certain foreign distributions.
(2) The amendments made by that Schedule have effect for the tax year 2008–09 and subsequent tax years.

Commentary—*Simon's Taxes* **D9.726, D5.202**.
HMRC Manuals—Savings And Investment Manual SAIM5104 (tax credits on foreign distributions).

36 Company gains from investment life insurance contracts etc
(1) Schedule 13 contains provisions about company gains from investment life insurance contracts.[1]
(2) Schedule 14 contains amendments and repeals consequential on that Schedule etc

Amendments—[1]   Sub-s (1) repealed by CTA 2009 ss 1322, 1326, Sch 1 paras 728, 730, Sch 3 Part 1. CTA 2009 applies for accounting periods ending on or after 1 April 2009 (for corporation tax purposes) and for tax years 2009–10 onwards (for income and capital gains tax purposes).

37 Trade profits: changes in trading stock
(1) Schedule 15 contains provision about the effect of certain changes in trading stock on the calculation of profits of trades for the purposes of income tax or corporation tax.
(2) The amendments made by that Schedule have effect in relation to changes in trading stock occurring on or after 12 March 2008.
(3) In subsection (2) "change in trading stock" means—
    (*a*) in relation to new section 172B of ITTOIA 2005, or paragraph 6 of Schedule 15, an appropriation of trading stock,
    (*b*) in relation to new section 172C of ITTOIA 2005, or paragraph 7 of Schedule 15, a thing becoming trading stock,
    (*c*) in relation to new section 172D of ITTOIA 2005, or paragraph 8 of Schedule 15, a disposal of trading stock, and

(*d*) in relation to new section 172E of ITTOIA 2005, or paragraph 9 of Schedule 15, an acquisition of trading stock.

Commentary—*Simon's Taxes* **B2.205**.
HMRC Manuals—Business Income Manual BIM33630 (stock).

38 Non-residents: investment managers

Schedule 16 contains provision about—

(*a*) the eligibility of an investment manager to be the UK representative of a non-resident, or an agent of independent status in relation to a non-resident, and

(*b*) profits or income of non-residents that are to be disregarded if derived from certain investment transactions carried out by investment managers.

Commentary—*Simon's Taxes* **D4.123, B2.125**.
HMRC Manuals—International Manual INTM269060 (non-residents trading in the UK: investment manager exemption: conditions).

39 Dormant bank and building society accounts

(1) The Commissioners for Her Majesty's Revenue and Customs may by regulations—

(*a*) . . . [1]

(*b*) modify Chapters 2 and 3 of Part 15 of ITA 2007 (deduction of income tax on interest payments at source) in relation to such interest, and

(*c*) provide that, for the purposes of Chapter 2 of Part 4 of ITTOIA 2005 (charge to income tax on interest), such interest is to be treated as not being paid until the time (if any) at which the balance of the dormant account is paid out following a claim made by virtue of section 1(2)(*b*) or 2(2)(*b*) of the 2008 Act.

(2) A relevant dormant account is a dormant account the balance of which is to be, or has been, transferred—

(*a*) to an authorised reclaim fund, with the result that section 1 of the 2008 Act will apply, or applies, in relation to the account, or

(*b*) to an authorised reclaim fund and one or more charities, with the result that section 2 of the 2008 Act will apply, or applies, in relation to the account.

(3) Interest paid or credited in respect of a relevant dormant account includes interest paid or credited by a person who administers the account on behalf of an authorised reclaim fund after the balance has been transferred.

(4) "The 2008 Act" means the Dormant Bank and Building Society Accounts Act 2008; and terms used in this section and in that Act have the same meaning in this section as in that Act.

(5) Regulations under subsection (1) are to be made by statutory instrument.

(6) A statutory instrument containing regulations under that subsection is subject to annulment in pursuance of a resolution of the House of Commons.

(7) (*inserts* TCGA 1992 s 26A)

(8) Subsection (7) comes into force in accordance with provision made by order made by the Treasury.

Commentary—*Simon's Taxes* **E1.404A**.
HMRC Manuals—Corporate Finance Manual CFM71050 (the dormant accounts scheme).
Orders—Finance Act 2008, Section 39(7) (Commencement) Order, SI 2011/23 (1 February 2011 appointed as the day on which sub-s (7) comes into force).
Regulations—Dormant Bank and Building Society Accounts (Tax) regulations, SI 2011/22.
Amendments—[1]   Sub-s (1)(*a*) repealed by FA 2011 s 86(1), Sch 23 paras 60, 61 with effect from 1 April 2012 in relation to relevant data with a bearing on any period (whether before, on or after 1 April 2012) subject to FA 2011 Sch 23 para 3(2). Sub-s (1)(*a*) will continue to have effect in relation to notices given, or requests made, under any of the provisions repealed by FA 2011 Sch 23 Pt 6 before 1 April 2012 as if the repeal had not been made (FA 2011 Sch 23 para 65(2)).

40 Individual investment plan regulations

(*inserts* ITTOIA 2005 s 701(4), (5))

Commentary—*Simon's Taxes* **E1.530**.

Insurance companies and friendly societies

43 Insurance companies etc

Schedule 17 contains provisions relating to insurance companies etc.

Employment matters

45 Homes outside UK owned through company etc

(1) (*inserts* ITEPA 2003 ss 100A, 100B)

(2) The amendment made by subsection (1) is treated as always having had effect.

(3) Section 145 of ICTA (living accommodation provided for employee) is to be treated as never having applied to living accommodation outside the United Kingdom provided in circumstances in which, had it been provided on or after 6 April 2003, section 100A(1) of ITEPA 2003 would cause Chapter 5 of Part 3 of ITEPA 2003 (taxable benefits: living accommodation) not to apply.

Commentary—*Simon's Taxes* **E4.607**.

HMRC Manuals—Employment Income Manual EIM11372 (living accommodation exemption: homes outside the United Kingdom owned through a company: specific conditions in section 100A ITEPA 2003).

EIM11373 (living accommodation exemption: homes outside the United Kingdom owned through a company: exceptions in section 100B ITEPA 2003).

46 In-work and return to work credits and payments

(1) (*amends* ITEPA 2003 s 677(1) Table)

(2) (*amends* ITEPA 2003 Sch 1 Pt 1 Table)

(3) The amendments made by this section have effect for the tax year 2008–09 and subsequent tax years.

Commentary—*Simon's Taxes* **E4.328**.

HMRC Manuals—Employment Income Manual EIM76100 (list of non-taxable social security benefits).

47 Company cars: lower threshold for CO2 emissions figure

(1) . . . [1]

(2) (*repeals* FA 2003 s 138(3), and FA 2006 s 59(6))

(3) The amendments made by this section have effect for the tax year 2008–09 and subsequent tax years.

Amendments—[1]   Sub-s (1) repealed by FA 2009 s 53, Sch 28 para 10 with effect for the tax year 2011–12 and subsequent tax years.

48 Van fuel benefit

(1) (*amends* ITEPA 2003 s 239(3))

(2) (*amends* ITEPA 2003 s 269(2))

Commentary—*Simon's Taxes* **E4.630, E4.630C**.

HMRC Manuals—Employment Income Manual EIM22710 (van benefit from 2005/06: scope and prohibition of other tax charges).

49 Employment-related securities etc: deductible amounts etc

(1) (*inserts* TCGA 1992 s 149AA(7))

(2) ITEPA 2003 is amended as follows.

(3) In section 428(2)(*b*) as originally enacted (conditional interests in shares: amount of charge), insert at the end "(other than an amount of exempt income)".

(4) (*amends* ITEPA 2003 s 428(7)(*b*))

(5) (*amends* ITEPA 2003 s 446T(3)(*b*))

(6) (*amends* ITEPA 2003 s 480(5)(*a*))

(7) (amends FA 2003 Sch 23 para 21(3))

(8) (amends FA 2003 Sch 23 para 22C(3))

(9) The amendment made by subsection (1) has effect in relation to disposals made on or after 12 March 2008.

(10) The amendment made by subsection (3) has effect in relation to events within section 427(1)(*a*) or (*b*) of ITEPA 2003 (as originally enacted) occurring on or after that date.

(11) The amendments made by subsections (4) and (6) have effect in relation to chargeable events occurring on or after that date.

(12) The amendment made by subsection (5) has effect in relation to employment-related securities acquired (or treated as acquired) on or after that date.

(13) The amendments made by subsections (7) and (8) have effect in relation to awards of shares made on or after that date.

HMRC Manuals—Capital Gains Manual CG56339 (employment income: restricted securities).

Amendments—Sub-ss (7), (8), (13) repealed by CTA 2009 s 1326, Sch 3 Pt 1. CTA 2009 applies for accounting periods ending on or after 1 April 2009 (for corporation tax purposes) and for tax years 2009–10 onwards (for income and capital gains tax purposes).

50 Employment-related securities: repeal of obsolete provisions

(1) (*repeals* TA 1988 ss 138, 139)

(2) (*repeals* ITEPA 2003 s 418(4), Sch 7 para 57)

(3) The amendments made by this section have effect for the tax year 2008–09 and subsequent tax years.

51 Armed forces: the Council Tax Relief

(1) (*inserts* ITEPA 2003 s 297B)

(2) The amendment made by subsection (1) has effect in relation to payments made on or after 1 April 2008.

HMRC Manuals—Tax Credits Technical Manual TCTM04203 (council tax relief for armed forces).

52 Greater London Authority: severance payments

(1)–(3) (*insert* ITEPA 2003 s 291(2)(*g*))

(4) The amendments made by this section have effect in relation to payments made on or after 6 April 2008.

Charities etc

53 Gift aid: payments to charities

Schedule 19 contains provision for the Commissioners for Her Majesty's Revenue and Customs to make payments to charities which receive donations under the gift aid scheme.

Leasing

55 Leases of plant or machinery

Schedule 20 contains provision about leases of plant or machinery.

58 UK residents and foreign partnerships

(1) (inserts TA 1988 s 115(5C))

(2) (inserts TCGA 1992 s 59(4))

(3) (inserts ITTOIA 2005 s 858(4))

(4) The amendments made by subsections (1) to (3) are treated as always having had effect.

(5) For the purposes of the predecessor provisions, the members of a partnership are to be treated as having included, at all times to which those provisions applied, a person entitled to a share of income or capital gains of the partnership.

(6) "The predecessor provisions" means—

　　(*a*) section 153(4) and (5) of the Income and Corporation Taxes Act 1970 (c 10) (as it had effect under section 62(2) of F(No 2)A 1987), and

　　(*b*) sections 112(4) to (6) and 115(5) of ICTA.

HMRC Manuals—Capital Gains Manual CG10731 (partners).

CG11000 (effects of residence/domicile on partnerships).

Partnership Manual PM41400 (mixed member partnerships and international aspects: double taxation).

Amendments—Sub-s (1) repealed by CTA 2009 s 1326, Sch 3 Pt 1. CTA 2009 applies for accounting periods ending on or after 1 April 2009 (for corporation tax purposes) and for tax years 2009–10 onwards (for income and capital gains tax purposes).

Other anti-avoidance provisions

60 Restrictions on trade loss relief for individuals

Schedule 21 contains provision restricting relief for losses made by individuals who, otherwise than in partnership, carry on trades in a non-active capacity.

Commentary—*Simon's Taxes* E1.1007.

HMRC Manuals—Business Income Manual BIM85765 (non-active traders).

BIM85767 (non-active traders - basis period straddling 12 March 2008).

61 Non-active partners

(1) (*amends* ITA 2007 s 103B(2))

(2) The amendment made by subsection (1) has effect in relation to relevant periods ending on or after 12 March 2008.

Commentary—*Simon's Taxes* B7.522.

HMRC Manuals—Business Income Manual BIM85765 (meaning of 'non-active capacity').

62 Financial arrangements avoidance

Schedule 22 contains provision about avoidance involving financial arrangements.

HMRC Manuals—Business Income Manual BIM01035 (anti-avoidance rules: disposal of income streams).

63 Manufactured payments

(1) Schedule 23 contains anti-avoidance provisions about manufactured payments.

(2) The amendments made by that Schedule have effect in relation to manufactured payments (including deemed manufactured payments) made (or treated as made) on or after 31 January 2008.

Commentary—*Simon's Taxes* D9.702 - D9.703A.

HMRC Manuals—Corporate Finance Manual CFM74310 (overview of manufactured payments).

CFM74440 (payments made on or after 1 January 2014: taxation).

64 Controlled foreign companies

(1) Chapter 4 of Part 17 of ICTA (controlled foreign companies) is amended as follows.

(2) (*inserts* TA 1988 s 747(6)(*aa*) and (7)–(9))

(3) (*inserts* TA 1988 s 755D(1A) and *amends* s 755D(2))

(4) (amends TA 1988 Sch 25 para 2A(2) and inserts para 2A(4A)–(4D); repealed by FA 2009 s 36, Sch 16 para 5(j))

(5) (*inserts* TA 1988 Sch 25 para 6(5C)–(5E))

(6) The amendments made by subsections (2) and (5) have effect in relation to income accruing on or after 12 March 2008.

(7) The amendments made by subsection (3) have effect for determining whether, at any time on or after 12 March 2008, a company is controlled by persons resident in the United Kingdom for the purposes of Chapter 4 of Part 17 of ICTA.

(8) The amendments made by subsection (4) have effect in relation to any dividend paid on or after 12 March 2008.

(9) In relation to an accounting period of a company beginning before, and ending on or after, 12 March 2008 ("the straddling period"), the amendments made by this section have effect as if, for the purposes of Chapter 4 of Part 17 of ICTA, so much of the period as falls before that date, and so much of the period as falls on or after that date, were separate accounting periods.

(10) The company's chargeable profits for the straddling period, and its creditable tax (if any) for that period, are to be apportioned to the two separate accounting periods on a just and reasonable basis.

(11) In this section "accounting period", "chargeable profits" and "creditable tax" have the same meaning as in Chapter 4 of Part 17 of ICTA.

66 Repeal of obsolete anti-avoidance provisions

(1) In Part 17 of ICTA (tax avoidance)—

    (a)

        (i)   (*repeals* TA 1988 s 704 para B)

        (ii) (*repeals* TA 1988 s 704 para C(1)(*b*))

    (b) (*repeals* TA 1988 s 709(2A))

    (c) (*repeals* TA 1988 ss 731 to 735)

    (d) (*repeals* TA 1988 s 736)

(2) In Part 13 of ITA 2007 (tax avoidance)—

    (a) (*amends* ITA 2007 s 684(2))

    (b) (*repeals* ITA 2007 s 687)

    (c) (*repeals* ITA 2007 s 688(3)(*b*), (4), (5), (9))

(3) In consequence of the amendments made by subsection (1)(*a*) and (*b*), omit—

    (a) (*repeals* FA 1997 s 73)

    (b) (*repeals* ITA 2007 Sch 1 para 155(4) and (5) and (6)(*b*))

(4) In consequence of the amendments made by subsection (1)(*c*) and (*d*), omit—

    (a) (*repeals* TA 1988 ss 343(5) and 738)

    (b) (*repeals* FA 1990 s 53)

    (c) (*repeals* FA 1991 ss 55 and 56)

    (d) (*repeals* TCGA 1992 Sch 10 para 14(40) and (41))

    (e) (*repeals* FA 1994 Sch 16 para 17)

    (f) (*repeals* FA 1995 s 81)

    (g) (*repeals* FA 1996 Sch 20 para 36, Sch 38 para 9)

    (h) (*repeals* FA 1997 s 77)

    (i) (*repeals* F(No 2)A 1997 s 26, Sch 6 para 14)

    (j) (*repeals* FA 2003 Sch 38 para 6)

    (k) (*repeals* ITTOIA 2005 Sch 1 paras 302 and 303)

    (l) (*repeals* ITA 2007 s 64(8)(f), s 72(5)(f), s 451, s 506, Sch 1 paras 167–170, words in ss 448(3), 449(3), 505(4), (5))

    (m) (*repeals* FA 2007 Sch 14 para 6)

(5) The amendments made by subsections (1)(*a*) and (*b*), (2) and (3) have effect in relation to transactions in securities entered into on or after 1 April 2008.

(6) The amendment made by subsection (1)(*c*) has effect in relation to cases where the purchase by the first buyer (within the meaning of section 731(2) of ICTA) is made on or after that date.

(7) The amendment made by subsection (1)(*d*) has effect in relation to distributions made on or after that date.

(8) The amendments made by subsection (4) have effect in accordance with subsections (6) and (7).

Commentary—*Simon's Taxes* D9.201, E1.802, D9.207.

HMRC Manuals—General Insurance Manual GIM5050 (UK dividends and other distributions exemption).

Miscellaneous

67 Income of beneficiaries under settlor-interested settlements

(1) (*inserts* ITTOIA 2005 s 685(5A), (5B))

(2) (*amends* ITTOIA 2005 s 1012(4))

(3) The amendments made by this section have effect for the tax year 2006–07 and subsequent tax years.

68 Income charged at dividend upper rate

(1) (*inserts* ITA 2007 s 13(2)(*c*))

(2) The amendments made by subsection (1) have effect for the tax year 2008–09 and subsequent tax years.

Commentary—*Simon's Taxes* E1.603.

HMRC Manuals—Savings And Investment Manual SAIM1080 (dividend income: the dividend rates).

69 Payments on account of income tax

(1) (*repeals* ITA 2007 s 964(5))

(2) The repeal made by subsection (1) has effect for the purpose of calculating the amount of any payments to be made under section 59A of TMA 1970 on account of liability to income tax for the tax year 2008–09 and subsequent tax years.

Commentary—*Simon's Taxes* **E1.804**.
HMRC Manuals—Compliance Handbook Manual CH146100 (interest: allocating payments).

70 Allowances etc for non-resident nationals of an EEA state

(1) (*amends TA 1988 s 278(2)(a), repeals s 278(9)*)
(2) (*inserts ITA 2007 s 56(3)*)
(3) (*repeals FA 1996 s 145*)
(4) The amendments made by this section have effect for the tax year 2008–09 and subsequent tax years.

Commentary—*Simon's Taxes* **E1.920, E1.924, E6.125**.

PART 3
CAPITAL ALLOWANCES

Plant and machinery: qualifying expenditure

71 Thermal insulation of buildings

(1) Section 28 of CAA 2001 (thermal insulation of industrial buildings) is amended as follows.
(2) (*amends CAA 2001 s 28(1)*)
(3) (*amends CAA 2001 s 28(2)*)
(4) (*inserts CAA 2001 s 28(2A)–(2C)*)
(5) (*repeals CAA 2001 s 28(3)*)
(6) (*amends CAA 2001 s 28 heading*)
(7) (*amends CAA 2001 s 23(2)*)
(8) The amendments made by this section have effect—
    (a) for corporation tax purposes, in relation to expenditure incurred on or after 1 April 2008, and
    (b) for income tax purposes, in relation to expenditure incurred on or after 6 April 2008.

Commentary—*Simon's Taxes* **B3.310**.
HMRC Manuals—Capital Allowances Manual CA22220 (thermal installation of industrial buildings).

72 Expenditure on required fire precautions

(1) (*repeals CAA 2001 s 29*)
(2) (*amends CAA 2001 s 23(2)*)
(3) In consequence of the amendment made by subsection (1)—
    (a) in the Fire and Rescue Services Act 2004 (c 21), omit paragraph 96 of Schedule 1, and
    (b) in the Fire and Rescue Services (Northern Ireland) Order 2006 (SI 2006/1254 (NI 9)), omit paragraph 24 of Schedule 3 (and the entry relating to CAA 2001 in Schedule 4).
(4) The amendments made by subsections (1) and (2) have effect—
    (a) for corporation tax purposes, in relation to expenditure incurred on or after 1 April 2008, and
    (b) for income tax purposes, in relation to expenditure incurred on or after 6 April 2008.

Commentary—*Simon's Taxes* **B3.310**.
HMRC Manuals—Capital Allowances Manual CA22230 (the assets - more detail).

73 Integral features

(1) In section 23 of CAA 2001 (expenditure unaffected by sections 21 and 22)—
    (a) (*amends CAA 2001 s 23(2)*)
    (b) (*amends CAA 2001 s 23(4) List C*)
(2) (*inserts CAA 2001 ss 33A, 33B*)
(3) (*inserts TA 1988 s 74(1)(da)*)
(4) (*inserts ITTOIA 2005 s 55A*)
(5) (*amends ITTOIA 2005 s 272(2) Table*)
(6) The amendments made by this section have effect—
    (a) for corporation tax purposes, in relation to expenditure incurred on or after 1 April 2008, and
    (b) for income tax purposes, in relation to expenditure incurred on or after 6 April 2008.

Commentary—*Simon's Taxes* **B3.345, B3.308**.
HMRC Manuals—Capital Allowances Manual CA22030 (buildings & structures: expenditure unaffected by legislation).
Amendments—Sub-s (3) repealed by CTA 2009 s 1326, Sch 3 Pt 1. CTA 2009 applies for accounting periods ending on or after 1 April 2009 (for corporation tax purposes) and for tax years 2009–10 onwards (for income and capital gains tax purposes).

Plant and machinery: annual investment allowance

74 Annual investment allowance

Schedule 24 contains provision about an annual investment allowance in respect of certain qualifying expenditure on plant or machinery.

Plant and machinery: first-year allowances

Commentary—*Simon's Taxes* **B3.329**.
HMRC Manuals—Capital Allowances Manual CA23081 (qualifying expenditure: annual investment allowance: outline).

75 First-year allowance for small and medium-sized enterprises discontinued

(1) CAA 2001 is amended as follows.

(2) (*repeals* CAA 2001 s 44)

(3) In consequence of the repeal made by subsection (2)—

    (*a*)   (*amends* CAA 2001 s 39)

    (*b*)   (*amends* CAA 2001 s 46(1))

    (*c*)   (*repeals* CAA 2001 ss 47 to 49)

    (*d*)   (*amends* CAA 2001 s 52(3))

(4) (*repeals* FA 2004 s 142, FA 2006 s 30, FA 2007 s 37)

(5) The repeals made by subsections (2) and (3) have effect in relation to expenditure incurred on or after the relevant date.

(6) But subsection (7) applies in relation to an additional VAT liability incurred on or after the relevant date which under section 235 of CAA 2001 is treated as qualifying expenditure.

(7) If the original expenditure (within the meaning of that section) was first-year qualifying expenditure by virtue of section 44 of CAA 2001, Chapter 18 of Part 2 of that Act (additional VAT liabilities and rebates) applies to the additional VAT liability as if the provisions repealed by this section were not so repealed.

(8) The relevant date is—

    (*a*)   for corporation tax purposes, 1 April 2008, and

    (*b*)   for income tax purposes, 6 April 2008.

Commentary—*Simon's Taxes* B3.320, B3.324, B3.324A.

HMRC Manuals—Capital Allowances Manual CA23110 (expenditure on which available and rates).

76 Repeal of spent first-year allowances

(1) CAA 2001 is amended as follows.

(2) (*repeals* CAA 2001 ss 40 to 43)

(3) (*repeals* CAA 2001 s 45)

(4) (*repeals* CAA 2001 Sch 3 paras 46 to 51)

(5) In consequence of the amendments made by subsections (2) to (4), omit the following provisions—

    (*a*)   (*amends* CAA 2001 s 39)

    (*b*)   (*amends* CAA 2001 s 46)

    (*c*)   (*repeals* CAA 2001 s 51)

    (*d*)   (*amends* CAA 2001 s 52(3))

    (*e*)   (*repeals* CAA 2001 s 237(2))

    (*f*)   (*repeals* CAA 2001 Sch 3)

(6) In consequence of the amendments made by this section, omit—

    (*a*)   (*amends* TMA 1970 s 98)

    (*b*)   (*repeals* FA 2003 ss 165, 166)

    (*c*)   (*repeals* CRCA 2005 Sch 4 para 84)

(7) Subsection (8) applies in relation to an additional VAT liability incurred on or after the day this section comes into force which under section 235 of CAA 2001 is treated as qualifying expenditure.

(8) If the original expenditure (within the meaning of that section) was first-year qualifying expenditure by virtue of a provision repealed by subsections (2) to (4), Chapter 18 of Part 2 of that Act (additional VAT liabilities and rebates) applies to the additional VAT liability as if that provision were not so repealed.

Commentary—*Simon's Taxes* B3.320, B3.375.

HMRC Manuals—Capital Allowances Manual CA29230 (additional VAT).

CA23110 (expenditure on which first-year allowances are available and rates; with examples).

77 Cars with low carbon dioxide emissions

(1) Section 45D of CAA 2001 (expenditure on cars with low carbon dioxide emissions) is amended as follows.

(2) (*amended* CAA 2001 s 45D(1)(*a*); *repealed by* FA 2013 s 68(4)(*a*))

(3) (*amended* CAA 2001 s 45D(4); *repealed by* FA 2013 s 68(4)(*b*))

(4) In consequence of the amendment made by subsection (2)—

    (*a*)   (*amends* FA 2002 s 60(2)(*b*))[2]

    (*b*)   (*amended* ITTOIA 2005 s 50(3); *repealed by* FA 2009 s 30, Sch 11 para 64(*a*))

(5) The amendment made by subsection (3) has effect in relation to expenditure incurred on or after 1 April 2008.

(6) But in relation to expenditure incurred on the hiring of a car—

    (*a*)   for a period of hire which begins on or before 31 March 2008, and

    (*b*)   under a contract entered into on or before 31 March 2008,

[section 50 of ITTOIA 2005 applies][1] on and after 1 April 2008 as if the amendment made by subsection (3) did not have effect.

Commentary—*Simon's Taxes* B2.413, B3.324A.

HMRC Manuals—Capital Allowances Manual CA23153 (expenditure on cars with low carbon dioxide emissions).

Amendments—[1]   In sub-s (6) words after para (*b*) substituted for words "section 578A of ICTA and section 50 of ITTOIA 2005 apply", by CTA 2009 s 1322, Sch 1 paras 728, 731. CTA 2009 applies for accounting periods ending on or after 1 April 2009 (for corporation tax purposes) and for tax years 2009–10 onwards (for income and capital gains tax purposes).

[2]   Sub-s (4)(*a*) repealed by CTA 2009 s 1326, Sch 3 Pt 1. CTA 2009 applies for accounting periods ending on or after 1 April 2009 (for corporation tax purposes) and for tax years 2009–10 onwards (for income and capital gains tax purposes).

78 Gas refuelling stations

(1) Section 45E of CAA 2001 (expenditure on plant or machinery for gas refuelling station) is amended as follows.

(2) (*amends* CAA 2001 s 45E(1)(*a*))

(3), (4) (*amend* CAA 2001 s 45E(2)–(4))

(5) The amendments made by subsections (3) and (4) have effect in relation to expenditure incurred on or after 1 April 2008.

Commentary—*Simon's Taxes* **B3.324B.**

HMRC Manuals—Capital Allowances Manual CA23155 (expenditure on natural gas and hydrogen refuelling equipment).

Plant and machinery: writing-down allowances and pools

80 Main rate of writing down allowance

(1) Section 56 of CAA 2001 (amount of allowances and charges) is amended as follows.

(2) (*amends* CAA 2001 s 56(1))

(3) (*inserts* CAA 2001 s 56(1A))

(4) In subsection (2), for "Subsection (1) is" substitute "Subsections (1) and (1A) are".

(5) (*repealed by* FA 2011 s 57(7))

(6) (*amended* FA 2000 Sch 22 paras 94(3)(*a*) and (4), 95(4), 97(2) and (3), 98(8), 99(2); *repealed by* FA 2011 s 57(7))

(7) (*amended* FA 2000 Sch 22 para 99(4) and *inserted* FA 2000 Sch 22 para 99(5); *repealed by* FA 2011 s 57(7))

(8) The amendments made by this section have effect in relation to chargeable periods—

    (*a*) beginning on or after the relevant date, and

    (*b*) beginning before, and ending on or after, the relevant date.

(9) But in respect of a chargeable period within subsection (8)(*b*), they apply as if in—

    (*a*) section 56(1) of CAA 2001,

    (*b*) the provisions listed in subsection (6), and

    (*c*) paragraph 99(5) of Schedule 22 to FA 2000,

the references to 20% were to x%.

(10) For the purposes of subsection (9)—

$$X = \left(25 \times \frac{BRD}{CP}\right) + \left(20 \times \frac{ARD}{CP}\right)$$

Where X would be a figure with more than 2 decimal places, it is to be rounded up to the nearest second decimal place.

(11) In subsection (10)—

    BRD is the number of days in the chargeable period before the relevant date,

    ARD is the number of days in the chargeable period on and after the relevant date, and

    CP is the number of days in the chargeable period.

(12) The relevant date is—

    (*a*) for corporation tax purposes, 1 April 2008, and

    (*b*) for income tax purposes, 6 April 2008.

Commentary—*Simon's Taxes* **B3.332, D7.1018.**

HMRC Manuals—Capital Allowances Manual CA23220 (pma: wda rate of wda).

81 Small pools

(1) CAA 2001 is amended as follows.

(2) (*inserts* CAA 2001 s 56(2)(*za*))

(3) (*inserts* CAA 2001 s 56A)

(4) (*amends* CAA 2001 s 59(1))

(5) The amendments made by this section have effect—

    (*a*) for corporation tax purposes, in relation to chargeable periods beginning on or after 1 April 2008, and

    (*b*) for income tax purposes, in relation to chargeable periods beginning on or after 6 April 2008.

Commentary—*Simon's Taxes* **B3.333.**

HMRC Manuals—Capital Allowances Manual CA23225 (wdas for small pools).

Employment Income Manual EIM36695 (small pools allowance).

82 Special rate expenditure and the special rate pool

Schedule 26 contains provision about special rate expenditure and the special rate pool.

Commentary—*Simon's Taxes* **B3.331.**

HMRC Manuals—Capital Allowances Manual CA22320 (definition and related provisions).
CA22335 (solar panels).
CA22340 (meaning of 'replacement expenditure').

83 Existing long-life asset expenditure treated as special rate expenditure

(1) This section applies in relation to long-life asset expenditure—

    (a) incurred before the relevant date, and

    (b) allocated to a pool in a chargeable period beginning before the relevant date.

(2) In relation to a transitional chargeable period, section 102 of CAA 2001 applies as if the percentage figure specified in subsection (1) of that section were X%, where—

$$X = \left(6 \times \frac{BRD}{CP}\right) + \left(10 \times \frac{ARD}{CP}\right)$$

Where X would be a figure with more than 2 decimal places, it is to be rounded up to the nearest second decimal place.

(3) In subsection (2)—

    BRD is the number of days in the chargeable period before the relevant date,

    ARD is the number of days in the chargeable period on and after the relevant date, and

    CP is the number of days in the chargeable period.

(4) Any unrelieved qualifying expenditure in a long-life asset pool at the end of—

    (a) a transitional chargeable period, or

    (b) a chargeable period which ends immediately before the relevant date,

is to be carried forward to the special rate pool.

(5) In subsequent chargeable periods, expenditure so carried forward is to be treated for the purposes of CAA 2001 as if it were special rate expenditure carried forward in the special rate pool from the chargeable period mentioned in subsection (4).

(6) Any unrelieved qualifying expenditure in a single asset pool at the end of—

    (a) a transitional chargeable period, or

    (b) a chargeable period which ends immediately before the relevant date,

is in subsequent chargeable periods to be treated for the purposes of CAA 2001 as if it were special rate expenditure carried forward in the single asset pool from that chargeable period.

(7) Where expenditure is treated as special rate expenditure because of this section, for the purposes of section 104E of CAA 2001—

    (a) the reference in subsection (1)(a) of that section to section 104D of CAA 2001 includes a reference to section 102 of that Act (writing-down allowances in respect of long-life asset expenditure), and

    (b) the allowances that could have been made to the taxpayer in respect of the expenditure include allowances that could have been made under section 102 of that Act for chargeable periods before that in which the expenditure was first treated as special rate expenditure.

(8) A "transitional chargeable period" is one which begins before, and ends on or after, the relevant date.

(9) "The relevant date" means—

    (a) for corporation tax purposes, 1 April 2008, and

    (b) for income tax purposes, 6 April 2008.

(10) Expressions used in this section and in CAA 2001 have the same meaning in this section as in that Act.

Commentary—*Simon's Taxes* B3.344.
HMRC Manuals—Capital Allowances Manual CA23720 (plant and long-life assets: meaning and definitions).
CA23770 (plant and long-life assets: anti-avoidance).

Industrial and agricultural buildings allowances

84 Abolition of allowances from 2011

(1) Parts 3 and 4 of CAA 2001 (industrial buildings allowances and agricultural buildings allowances) do not apply in relation to expenditure incurred on or after the relevant date.

(2) Omit those Parts of that Act.

(3) The amendment made by subsection (2) has effect in relation to chargeable periods beginning on or after the relevant date.

(4) The relevant date is—

    (a) for corporation tax purposes, 1 April 2011, and

    (b) for income tax purposes, 6 April 2011.

(5) Schedule 27 contains amendments and savings related to this section.

Commentary—*Simon's Taxes* B3.101, B3.280, B3.280.
HMRC Manuals—Capital Allowances Manual CA14600 (abolition of allowances).

Supplementary provision

88 Power to make consequential and transitional provision

(1) The Treasury may by order make such amendments (including repeals and revocations) of enactments or instruments as may appear appropriate in consequence of, or otherwise in connection with, sections 71 to 87.

(2) The Treasury may by order make such transitional or saving provision as may appear appropriate in consequence of, or otherwise in connection with, those sections.

(3) An order under subsection (1) may make transitional provision and savings.

(4) An order under subsection (1) or (2) may—

    (*a*) make different provision for different cases, and

    (*b*) include provision having effect in relation to times before the order is made if that provision does not increase any person's liability to tax.

(5) An order under subsection (1) or (2) is to be made by statutory instrument.

(6) A statutory instrument containing an order under subsection (1) or (2) is subject to annulment in pursuance of a resolution of the House of Commons.

PART 4

PENSIONS

90 Spreading of relief on indirect contributions

(1) (*inserts* FA 2004 s 199A)

(2) The amendment made by this section has effect in relation to payments within section 199A(2) of FA 2004 made on or after 10 October 2007, except for such payments made pursuant to a contract entered into before 9 October 2007.

Commentary—*Simon's Taxes* **E7.224**.

HMRC Manuals—Pensions Tax Manual PTM043400 (spreading of relief on indirect contributions).

91 Inheritance etc of tax-relieved pension savings

Schedule 28 contains provision about the inheritance etc of tax-relieved pension savings.

HMRC Manuals—Pensions Tax Manual PTM133200 (unauthorised payments: assignment of a member's rights).
PTM133300 (unauthorised payments: surrender of rights or benefits).
PTM133400 (unauthorised payments: increase in rights of a connected person on death).

92 Pension schemes: further provision

Schedule 29 contains further provision about pension schemes.

PART 6

OIL

Petroleum revenue tax

102 Meaning of "participator"

(1)–(4) (*amend* definition of "participator" in OTA 1975 s 12)

(5) The amendments made by this section have effect in relation to expenditure incurred after 30 June 2008.

HMRC Manuals—Oil Taxation Manual OT03100 (participator).

103 Abandonment expenditure: default by participator met by former participator

(1) (*substitutes* OTA 1975 Sch 5 paras 2A–2C)

(2) The amendment made by subsection (1) has effect in relation to expenditure incurred after 30 June 2008.

106 Returns of relevant sales of oil

(1) Section 62 of FA 1987 (returns of relevant sales of oil) is amended as follows.

(2) (*inserts* FA 1987 s 62(3A))

(3), (4) (*amend* FA 1987 s 62(4))

(5) (*amends* FA 1987 s 62(6))

(6) (*inserts* FA 1987 s 62(8A))

(7) The amendments made by this section have effect in relation to chargeable periods ending on or after 30 June 2008.

HMRC Manuals—Oil Taxation Manual OT04095 (returns by participators).

107 Elections for oil fields to become non-taxable

(1) Section 185 of FA 1993 is amended as follows.

(2) (*inserts* FA 1993 s 185(A1))

(3) (*amends* FA 1993 s 185(1))

(4) (*inserts* FA 1993 s 185(1ZA))

(5) (*inserts* FA 1993 s 185(1A)(*za*))

(6) (*inserts* FA 1993 Sch 20A)

(7) Part 2 of Schedule 33 contains other amendments relating to the amendments made by this section.

Commentary—*Simon's Taxes* **D7.906**.
HMRC Manuals—Oil Taxation Manual OT01007 (non-taxable fields).

Corporation tax

108 Capital allowances: plant and machinery for use in ring fence trade

(1) (*amends* CAA 2001 s 52(3))
(2) The amendment made by subsection (1) has effect in relation to expenditure incurred on or after 12 March 2008.
Commentary—*Simon's Taxes* **B3.324C, D7.919**.
HMRC Manuals—Oil Taxation Manual OT21242 (first year allowances for a ring fence trade: plant and machinery).

109 Capital allowances: decommissioning expenditure

(1)–(5) (*amend* CAA 2001 s 163)
(6) Schedule 34 contains amendments consequential on this section.
(7) The amendments made by this section and that Schedule have effect in relation to expenditure incurred on or after 12 March 2008.
Commentary—*Simon's Taxes* **B3.354**.
HMRC Manuals—Oil Taxation Manual OT28040 (meaning of general decommissioning expenditure).

110 Capital allowances: abandonment expenditure after ceasing ring fence trade

(1)–(5) (*amend* CAA 2001 s 165)[1]
(6) Section 393A of ICTA (losses: set off against profits of the same, or an earlier, accounting period) is amended as follows.
(7), (8) (*amend* TA 1988 s 393A(11), and *insert* s 393A(11A))
(9) The amendments made by this section have effect in relation to ring fence trades that cease to be carried on or after 12 March 2008.
Commentary—*Simon's Taxes* **D7.925**.
HMRC Manuals—Oil Taxation Manual OT28220 (relief for expenditure incurred after cessation of ring fence trade and on or before 11 march 2008).
Amendments—[1]   Sub-s (1) repealed by CTA 2010 s 1181, Sch 3 Pt 1. CTA 2010 has effect for corporation tax purposes for accounting periods ending on or after 1 April 2010, and for income and capital gains tax purposes for the tax year 2010–11 and subsequent tax years.

111 Losses: set off against profits of earlier accounting periods

(1) (*inserts* TA 1988 s 393B)
(2) Schedule 35 contains minor and consequential amendments relating to the amendments made by this section.
(3) The amendments made by this section and that Schedule have effect in relation to losses incurred in accounting periods beginning on or after 12 March 2008.
Commentary—*Simon's Taxes* **D7.925**.

PART 7

ADMINISTRATION

CHAPTER 1

INFORMATION ETC

New information etc powers

113 Information and inspection powers

(1) Schedule 36 contains provision about the powers of officers of Revenue and Customs to obtain information and to inspect businesses.
(2) That Schedule comes into force on such day as the Treasury may by order made by statutory instrument appoint.
(3) An order under subsection (2) may contain transitional provision and savings.
Commentary—*Simon's Taxes* **E6.455, E1.262**.
HMRC Manuals—Company Taxation Manual CTM06550 (information powers).
Orders—Finance Act 2008, Schedule 36 (Appointed Day and Savings) Order, SI 2009/404.

114 Computer records etc

(1) This section applies to any enactment that, in connection with an HMRC matter—
    (*a*) requires a person to produce a document or cause a document to be produced,
    (*b*) requires a person to permit the Commissioners or an officer of Revenue and Customs—
        (i) to inspect a document, or
        (ii) to make or take copies of or extracts from or remove a document,
    (*c*) makes provision about penalties or offences in connection with the production or inspection of documents, including in connection with the falsification of or failure to produce or permit the inspection of documents, or
    (*d*) makes any other provision in connection with a requirement mentioned in paragraph (*a*) or (*b*).

(2) An enactment to which this section applies has effect as if—

(a) any reference in the enactment to a document were a reference to anything in which information of any description is recorded, and

(b) any reference in the enactment to a copy of a document were a reference to anything onto which information recorded in the document has been copied, by whatever means and whether directly or indirectly.

(3) An authorised person may, at any reasonable time, obtain access to, and inspect and check the operation of, any computer and any associated apparatus or material which is or has been used in connection with a relevant document.

(4) In subsection (3) "relevant document" means a document that a person has been, or may be, required pursuant to an enactment to which this section applies—

(a) to produce or cause to be produced, or

(b) to permit the Commissioners or an officer of Revenue and Customs to inspect, to make or take copies of or extracts from or to remove.

(5) An authorised person may require—

(a) the person by whom or on whose behalf the computer is or has been so used, or

(b) any person having charge of, or otherwise concerned with the operation of, the computer, apparatus or material,

to provide the authorised person with such reasonable assistance as may be required for the purposes of subsection (3).

(6) Any person who—

(a) obstructs the exercise of a power conferred by this section, or

(b) fails to comply within a reasonable time with a requirement under subsection (5),

is liable to a penalty of £300.

(7) Paragraphs 45 to 49 and 52 of Schedule 36 (assessment of and appeals against penalties) apply in relation to a penalty under this section as they apply in relation to a penalty under paragraph 39 of that Schedule.

(8) Omit the following—

(a) section 10 of FA 1985 (production of computer records etc in connection with assigned matters),

(b) *(repeals* FA 1988 s 127)

(c) paragraphs 11(2) to (4) and 13(2) and (3) of Schedule 1 to the Civil Evidence Act 1995 (c 38).

(9) In this section—

"authorised person" means a person who is, or is a member of a class of persons who are, authorised by the Commissioners to exercise the powers under subsection (3),

"the Commissioners" means the Commissioners for Her Majesty's Revenue and Customs,

"enactment" includes an enactment contained in subordinate legislation (within the meaning of the Interpretation Act 1978 (c 30)),

"HMRC matter" means a matter in relation to which the Commissioners, or officers of Revenue and Customs, have a power or duty, and

"produce", in relation to a document, includes furnish, deliver and any other equivalent expression.

Commentary—*Simon's Taxes* A6.409, A6.632.
HMRC Manuals—Compliance Handbook Manual CH23440 (HMRC inspection powers: serving notices).
CH13100 (general).
CH13400 (computer records).
CH23360 (what is an electronic document or record).
CH218400 (powers to check computer systems).

Other measures

115 Record-keeping

(1) Schedule 37 contains provision about the obligations to keep records for the purposes of income tax, capital gains tax, corporation tax and value added tax.

(2) The amendments made by that Schedule come into force on such day as the Treasury may by order made by statutory instrument appoint.

Commentary—*Simon's Taxes* A4.570, A6.204, A6.630.
HMRC Manuals—Compliance Handbook Manual CH10100 (record keeping: overview).
Orders—Finance Act 2008, Schedule 37 (Appointed Day) Order, SI 2009/402.

116 Disclosure of tax avoidance schemes

(1) Schedule 38 contains amendments relating to the disclosure of tax avoidance schemes.

(2) The amendments made by that Schedule come into force on such day as the Treasury may by order made by statutory instrument appoint; and different days may be appointed for different purposes.

Commentary—*Simon's Taxes* A7.201, A7.202.
HMRC Manuals—Apprenticeship Levy Manual ALM19100 (DOTAS: introduction).

Orders—Finance Act 2008, Schedule 38, (Appointed Day) Order, SI 2008/1935 (the amendments made by Sch 38 come into force with effect from 1 November 2008 (except in relation to stamp duty land tax, for which the effective date is 1 April 2010 by virtue of the Finance Act 2008, Schedule 38, (Appointed Day) Order, SI 2010/28).

CHAPTER 2

TIME LIMITS FOR CLAIMS AND ASSESSMENTS ETC

General

118 Time limits for assessments, claims etc

(1) Schedule 39 contains provision about time limits for assessments, claims etc
(2) The amendments and saving made by that Schedule come into force on such day as the Treasury may by order made by statutory instrument appoint.
(3) An order under subsection (2)—
    (*a*) may make different provision for different purposes, and
    (*b*) may include transitional provision and further savings.

Commentary—*Simon's Taxes* **D8.342, E5.103**.
Orders—Finance Act 2008, Schedule 39 (Appointed Day, Transitional Provision and Savings) Order, SI 2009/403.

Income tax and corporation tax

119 Correction and amendment of tax returns

(1) In section 9ZB(1) of TMA 1970 (correction of personal or trustee return by HMRC)—
    (*a*) after "correct" insert "—
        (*a*) ", and
    (*b*) insert at the end ", and
        (*b*) anything else in the return that the officer has reason to believe is incorrect in the light of information available to the officer."
(2) In section 12ABB(1) of that Act (correction of partnership return by HMRC)—
    (*a*) after "correct" insert "—
        (*a*) ", and
    (*b*) insert at the end ", and
        (*b*) anything else in the return that the officer has reason to believe is incorrect in the light of information available to the officer."
(3) Schedule 18 to FA 1998 (company tax returns) is amended as follows.
(4) In paragraph 16(1) (correction of company tax return by HMRC)—
    (*a*) after "correct" insert "—
        (*a*) ", and
    (*b*) insert at the end ", and
        (*b*) anything else in the return that the officer has reason to believe is incorrect in the light of information available to the officer."
(5) In paragraph 31 (amendment of return by company during enquiry), in sub-paragraph (4), for paragraph (*b*) substitute—
    "(*b*) in any other case, the amendment takes effect as part of the amendments made by the closure notice."
(6) In paragraph 34 (amendment of company tax return after enquiry), for sub-paragraphs (1) and (2) substitute—
    "(1) This paragraph applies where a closure notice is given to a company by an officer.
    (2) The closure notice must—
        (*a*) state that, in the officer's opinion, no amendment is required of the return that was the subject of the enquiry, or
        (*b*) make the amendments of that return that are required—
            (i) to give effect to the conclusions stated in the notice, and
            (ii) in the case of a return for the wrong period, to make it a return appropriate to the designated period.
    (2A) The officer may by further notice to the company make any amendments of other company tax returns delivered by the company that are required to give effect to the conclusions stated in the closure notice."
(7) In sub-paragraph (3) of that paragraph, for "any such amendment of a company's return" substitute "an amendment of a company's return under sub-paragraph (2) or (2A)".
(8) In sub-paragraph (4)(*c*) of that paragraph, for "notice of amendment" substitute "closure notice".
(9) In paragraph 61(1)(*a*) and (3)(*a*) (consequential claims etc), for "34(2)(*b*)" substitute "34(2A)".
(10) In paragraph 88 (conclusiveness of amounts stated in return)—
    (*a*) in sub-paragraph (3)(*b*), omit the words from "and" to the end,
    (*b*) in sub-paragraph (3)(*c*), for "34(2)" substitute "34",

(*c*) in sub-paragraph (4)(*b*), for "the end of the period specified in paragraph 34(1)" substitute "the completion of the enquiry", and

(*d*) in sub-paragraph (4)(*c*), for "34(2)" substitute "34".

(11) In paragraph 93(1)(*b*) (general jurisdiction of Special or General Commissioners), for "34(2)" substitute "34".

(12) In the following provisions, for "34(2)" substitute "34"—

    (*a*) in TMA 1970—

        (i), (ii) . . . [1]

        (iii) section 46D(2)(*aa*) (questions to be determined by Land Tribunal), and

        (iv) section 55(1)(*a*)(ii) (recovery of tax not postponed), and

    (*b*) in ICTA, section 754(2E) (assessment, recovery and postponement of tax).

(13) The amendments made by this section come into force on such day as the Treasury may by order appoint.

Commentary—*Simon's Taxes* **A6.401, D1.1314, E1.223, D1.1315.**

HMRC Manuals—Corporate Finance Manual CFM91710 (amendment of other returns made by the company).

Amendments—[1] Sub-s (12)(*a*)(i), (ii) repealed by the Transfer of Tribunal Functions and Revenue and Customs Appeals Order, SI 2009/56 art 3, Sch 1 para 469 with effect from 1 April 2009.

CHAPTER 3

PENALTIES

122 Penalties for errors

(1) Schedule 40 contains provisions amending Schedule 24 to FA 2007 (penalties for errors in returns etc).

(2) That Schedule comes into force on such day as the Treasury may by order appoint.

(3) An order under subsection (2)—

    (*a*) may commence a provision generally or only for specified purposes, and

    (*b*) may appoint different days for different provisions or for different purposes.

(4) The Treasury may by order make any incidental, supplemental, consequential, transitional, transitory or saving provision which may appear appropriate in consequence of, or otherwise in connection with, Schedule 24 to FA 2007 or Schedule 40.

(5) An order under subsection (4) may include provision amending, repealing or revoking any provision of any Act or subordinate legislation whenever passed or made (including this Act and any Act amended by it).

(6) An order under subsection (4) may make different provision for different purposes.

(7) The power to make an order under this section is exercisable by statutory instrument.

(8) A statutory instrument containing an order under subsection (4) which includes provision amending or repealing any provision of an Act is subject to annulment in pursuance of a resolution of the House of Commons.

Commentary—*Simon's Taxes* **A4.586.**

HMRC Manuals—Compliance Handbook Manual CH401100 (penalties for inaccuracies and under-assessments - FA07/sch 24).

Orders—Finance Act 2008, Schedule 41 (Appointed Day and Transitional Provisions) Order, SI 2009/511.

Finance Act 2008, Schedule 40 (Appointed Day, Transitional Provisions and Consequential Amendments) Order, SI 2009/571.

Finance Act 2008 (Penalties for Errors and Failure to Notify etc) (Consequential Amendments) Order 2010, SI 2010/530.

Pension Schemes (Miscellaneous Amendments) Order, SI 2013/1114.

123 Penalties for failure to notify etc

(1) Schedule 41 contains provisions for imposing penalties on persons in respect of failures to notify HMRC that they are chargeable to tax etc and certain wrongdoings relating to invoices showing VAT and excise duties.

(2) That Schedule comes into force on such day as the Treasury may by order appoint.

(3) An order under subsection (2)—

    (*a*) may commence a provision generally or only for specified purposes, and

    (*b*) may appoint different days for different provisions or for different purposes.

(4) The Treasury may by order make any incidental, supplemental, consequential, transitional, transitory or saving provision which may appear appropriate in consequence of, or otherwise in connection with, Schedule 41.

(5) An order under subsection (4) may include provision amending, repealing or revoking any provision of any Act or subordinate legislation whenever passed or made (including this Act and any Act amended by it).

(6) An order under subsection (4) may make different provision for different purposes.

(7) The power to make an order under this section is exercisable by statutory instrument.

(8) A statutory instrument containing an order under subsection (4) which includes provision amending or repealing any provision of an Act is subject to annulment in pursuance of a resolution of the House of Commons.

HMRC Manuals—Compliance Handbook Manual CH74200 (when you must tell the person of the penalty).
CH93050 (three types of wrongdoing).
Orders—Finance Act 2008, Schedule 41 (Appointed Day and Transitional Provisions) Order, SI 2009/511.
Finance Act 2008 (Penalties for Errors and Failure to Notify etc) (Consequential Amendments) Order 2010, SI 2010/530.

CHAPTER 4

APPEALS ETC

Reviews and appeals etc: general

124 HMRC decisions etc: reviews and appeals

(1) The Treasury may by order made by statutory instrument make provision—

    (*a*) for and in connection with reviews by the Commissioners, or by an officer of Revenue and Customs, of HMRC decisions, and

    (*b*) in connection with appeals against HMRC decisions.

(2) An order under subsection (1) may, in particular, contain provision about—

    (*a*) the circumstances in which, or the time within which—

        (i) a right to a review may be exercised, or

        (ii) an appeal may be made, and

    (*b*) the circumstances in which, or the time at which, an appeal or review is, or may be treated as, concluded.

(3) An order under subsection (1) may, in particular, contain provision about the payment of sums by, or to, the Commissioners in cases where—

    (*a*) a right to a review is exercised, or

    (*b*) an appeal is made or determined.

(4) That includes provision about payment of sums where an appeal has been determined, but a further appeal may be or has been made, including provision—

    (*a*) requiring payments to be made,

    (*b*) enabling payments to be postponed, or

    (*c*) imposing conditions in connection with the making or postponement of payments.

(5) An order under subsection (1) may, in particular, contain provision about interest on any sum that is payable by, or to, the Commissioners in accordance with a decision made on the determination of an appeal.

(6) Provision under subsection (1) may be made by amending, repealing or revoking any provision of any Act or subordinate legislation (whenever passed or made, including this Act and any Act amended by it).

(7) An order under subsection (1) may—

    (*a*) provide that any provision contained in the order comes into force on a day appointed by an order of the Treasury made by statutory instrument (and may provide that different days may be appointed for different purposes),

    (*b*) contain incidental, supplemental, consequential, transitional, transitory and saving provision, and

    (*c*) make different provision for different purposes.

(8) A statutory instrument containing an order under subsection (1) may not be made unless a draft of it has been laid before and approved by resolution of the House of Commons.

(9) But if the order, or any other order under subsection (1) contained in the statutory instrument, is made in connection with a transfer of functions carried out under the Tribunals, Courts and Enforcement Act 2007 (c 15), the statutory instrument may only be made if a draft of it has been laid before and approved by resolution of each House of Parliament.

(10) In this section—

    (*a*) references to appeals against HMRC decisions include any other kind of proceedings relating to an HMRC matter, and

    (*b*) references to the making, determination or conclusion of appeals are to be read accordingly.

(11) In this section—

    "the Commissioners" means the Commissioners for Her Majesty's Revenue and Customs;
    "HMRC decision" means—

        (*a*) any decision of the Commissioners relating to an HMRC matter, or

        (*b*) any decision of an officer of Revenue and Customs relating to an HMRC matter,

    and references to an HMRC decision include references to anything done by such a person in connection with making such a decision or in consequence of such a decision;
    "HMRC matter" means any matter connected with a function of the Commissioners or an officer of Revenue and Customs.

Orders—Revenue and Customs Appeals Order SI 2012/533.
Tax Credits (Late Appeals) Order, SI 2014/885.
Tax Credits, Child Benefit and Guardian's Allowance Reviews and Appeals Order, SI 2014/886
Revenue and Customs (Amendment of Appeal Provisions for Out of Time Reviews) Order, SI 2014/1264.

CHAPTER 5

PAYMENT AND ENFORCEMENT

Taking control of goods etc

127 Enforcement by taking control of goods: England and Wales

(1) This section applies if a person does not pay a sum that is payable by that person to the Commissioners under or by virtue of an enactment or under a contract settlement.

(2) The Commissioners may use the procedure in Schedule 12 to the Tribunals, Courts and Enforcement Act 2007 (c 15) (taking control of goods) to recover that sum.

(3) This section extends to England and Wales only.

Commentary—*Simon's Taxes* **E8.1012.**

HMRC Manuals—Debt Management and Banking Manual DMBM67050 (the notice of enforcement).

Commencement—Finance Act 2008, Section 127 and Part 1 of Schedule 43 (Appointed Day) Order, SI 2014/906 (the appointed day for the coming into force of this section is 6 April 2014).

128 Summary warrant: Scotland

(1) This section applies if a person does not pay a sum that is payable by that person to the Commissioners under or by virtue of any enactment or under a contract settlement.

(2) An officer of Revenue and Customs may apply to the sheriff for a summary warrant.

(3) An application under subsection (2) must be accompanied by a certificate which—

   (a) complies with subsection (4), and

   (b) is signed by the officer.

(4) A certificate complies with this subsection if—

   (a) it states that—

      (i) none of the persons specified in the application has paid the sum payable by that person,

      (ii) the officer has demanded payment from each such person of the sum payable by that person, and

      (iii) the period of 14 days beginning with the day on which the demand is made has expired without payment being made, and

   (b) it specifies the sum payable by each person specified in the application.

(5) Subsection (4)(a)(iii) does not apply to an application under subsection (2) insofar as it relates to—

   (a) sums payable in respect of value added tax,

   (b) sums payable in respect of deductions required to be made under section 61 of FA 2004 (sub-contractors in the construction industry), and

   (c) sums payable by a person in that person's capacity as an employer.

(6) The sheriff must, on an application by an officer of Revenue and Customs under subsection (2), grant a summary warrant in, or as nearly as may be in, the form prescribed by Act of Sederunt.

(7) A summary warrant granted under subsection (6) authorises the recovery of the sum payable by—

   (a) attachment,

   (b) money attachment,

   (c) earnings arrestment,

   (d) arrestment and action of furthcoming or sale.

(8) Subject to subsection (9) and without prejudice to section 39(1) of the Debt Arrangement and Attachment (Scotland) Act 2002 (asp 17) (expenses of attachment)—

   (a) the sheriff officer's fees, and

   (b) any outlays necessarily incurred by that officer,

in connection with the execution of a summary warrant are to be chargeable against the person in relation to whom the warrant was granted.

(9) No fees are to be chargeable by the sheriff officer against the person in relation to whom the summary warrant was granted for collecting, and accounting to the Commissioners for, sums paid to that officer by that person in respect of the sum payable.

(10) This section extends to Scotland only.

Commentary—*Simon's Taxes* **E8.1012.**

HMRC Manuals—Debt Management And Banking Manual DMBM670000 (summary warrant: contents).

Commencement—Finance Act 2008, Section 128 and Part 2 of Schedule 43 (Appointed Day, Transitional Provision and Savings) Order, SI 2009/3024 art 3 (the appointed day for the coming into force of this section is 23 November 2009).

129 Consequential provision and commencement

(1) Part 1 of Schedule 43 contains provision consequential on section 127.

(2) Part 2 of that Schedule contains provision consequential on section 128.

(3) The extent of the amendments and repeals in Schedule 43 is the same as the provision amended or repealed.

(4) Sections 127 and 128 and Schedule 43 come into force on such day as the Commissioners may by order made by statutory instrument appoint.

(5) An order under subsection (4) may—

(a) make different provision for different purposes, and

(b) contain transitional provision and savings.

Order—Finance Act 2008, Section 128 and Part 2 of Schedule 43 (Appointed Day, Transitional Provision and Savings) Order, SI 2009/3024.

Finance Act 2008, Section 127 and Part 1 of Schedule 43 (Appointed Day) Order, SI 2014/906.

Set off

130 Set-off . . . [1]

(1) This section applies where there is both a credit and a debit in relation to a person.

(2) The Commissioners may set the credit against the debit (subject to section 131 and any obligation of the Commissioners to set the credit against another sum).

(3) The obligations of the Commissioners and the person concerned are discharged to the extent of any set-off under subsection (2).

(4) "Credit", in relation to a person, means—

(a) a sum that is payable by the Commissioners to the person under or by virtue of an enactment, or

(b) a relevant sum that may be repaid to the person by the Commissioners.

(5) For the purposes of subsection (4), in relation to a person, "relevant sum" means a sum that was paid in connection with any liability (including any purported or anticipated liability) of that person to make a payment to the Commissioners under or by virtue of an enactment or under a contract settlement.

(6) "Debit", in relation to a person, means a sum that is payable by the person to the Commissioners under or by virtue of an enactment or under a contract settlement.

(7) In this section references to sums paid, repaid or payable by or to a person (however expressed) include sums that have been or are to be credited by or to a person.

(8) This section has effect without prejudice to any other power of the Commissioners to set off amounts.

(9) *(amended* ITA 2007 s 429(5); *repealed by* FA 2012 s 50(3)(a))

(10) . . . [1]

Commentary—*Simon's Taxes* **E8.916.**

HMRC Manuals—Debt Management And Banking Manual DMBM700050 (when we can set-off).

DMBM700030 (definitions of credit and debit).

VAT Refunds Manual VRM7000 (set-off - section 130 of the finance act 2008).

Amendments—[1]   In heading, words ": England and Wales and Northern Ireland" repealed, and sub-s (10) repealed, by FA 2016 s 178(2), (3) with effect from 15 September 2016.

131 No set-off where insolvency procedure has been applied

(1) This section applies where—

(a) an insolvency procedure has been applied to a person, and

(b) there is a post-insolvency credit in relation to that person.

(2) The Commissioners may not use the power under section 130 to set that post-insolvency credit against a pre-insolvency debit in relation to the person.

(3) "Post-insolvency credit" means a credit that—

(a) became due after the insolvency procedure was applied to the person, and

(b) relates to, or to matters occurring at, times after it was so applied.

(4) "Pre-insolvency debit" means a debit that—

(a) arose before the insolvency procedure was applied to the person, or

(b) arose after that procedure was so applied but relates to, or to matters occurring at, times before it was so applied.

(5) Subject to subsection (6), an insolvency procedure is to be taken, for the purposes of this section, to be applied to a person when—

(a) a bankruptcy order or winding up order [or award of sequestration][2] is made or an administrator is appointed in relation to that person,

(b) that person is put into administrative receivership,

(c) if the person is a corporation, that person passes a resolution for voluntary winding up,

(d) a voluntary arrangement comes into force in relation to that person, . . . [2]

(e) a deed of arrangement takes effect in relation to that person[, or

(f) that person's estate becomes vested in any other person as that person's trustee under a trust deed (within the meaning of the Bankruptcy (Scotland) Act 1985).][2]

(6) In this section references to the application of an insolvency procedure to a person do not include—

(a) the application of an insolvency procedure to a person at a time when another insolvency procedure applies to the person, or

(b) the application of an insolvency procedure to a person immediately upon another insolvency procedure ceasing to have effect.

(7) For the purposes of this section—

    (*a*) a person shall be treated as being in administrative receivership throughout any continuous period for which there is an administrative receiver of that person (disregarding any temporary vacancy in the office of receiver), and

    (*b*) the reference in subsection (5) to a person being put into administrative receivership shall be interpreted accordingly.

(8) In this section—

    "administrative receiver" means an administrative receiver within the meaning of section 251 of the Insolvency Act 1986 (c 45) or Article 5(1) of the Insolvency (Northern Ireland) Order 1989 (SI 1989/2405 (NI 19)),

    "administrator" means a person appointed to manage the affairs, business and property of another person under Schedule B1 to that Act or to that Order,

    "credit" and "debit" have the same meaning as in section 130,

    "deed of arrangement" means a deed of arrangement registered in accordance with . . . [1] or Chapter 1 of Part 8 the Insolvency (Northern Ireland) Order 1989 (SI 1989/2405 (NI 19)), and

    "voluntary arrangement" means a voluntary arrangement approved in accordance with Part 1 or Part 8 of the Insolvency Act 1986 (c 45) or Part 2 or Chapter 2 of Part 8 of the Insolvency (Northern Ireland) Order 1989.

(9) . . . [2]

Commentary—*Simon's Taxes* **E8.916**.

HMRC Manuals—Debt Management And Banking Manual DMBM700060 (certain types of insolvency).

Amendments—[1]   In sub-s (8), in definition of "deed of arrangement", words "the Deeds of Arrangement Act 1914 (c 47) or" repealed by the Deregulation Act 2015 s 19, Sch 6 para 2(1), (21) with effect from 1 October 2015 (by virtue of SI 2015/1732 art 2(e)(i)). This repeal has no effect in relation to a deed of arrangement registered under the Deeds of Arrangement Act 1914 s 5 before 1 October 2015 if, immediately before that date, the estate of the debtor who executed the deed of arrangement has not been finally wound up (Deregulation Act Sch 6 para 3).

[2]   In sub-s (5)(*a*), words inserted, in sub-s (5)(*d*), word "or" repealed, sub-s (5)(*f*) and preceding word inserted, and sub-s (9) repealed, by FA 2016 s 178(2), (4) with effect from 15 September 2016.

132 VAT: requirement to set-off

(1) Section 81 of VATA 1994 (set-off of credits etc) is amended as follows.

(2) (*substitutes* VATA 1994 s 81(4C))

(3) (*amends* VATA 1994 s 81(5))

Commentary—*Simon's Taxes* **E8.916, A4.216**.

133 Set-off etc where right to be paid a sum has been transferred

(1) This section applies where there has been a transfer from one person ("the original creditor") to another person ("the current creditor") of a right to be paid a sum ("the transferred sum") by the Commissioners.

(2) The Commissioners—

    (*a*) must set the transferred sum against a sum payable to them by the original creditor if they would have had an obligation to do so under or by virtue of an enactment had the original creditor retained the right, and

    (*b*) may do so if they would have had a power to do so under or by virtue of an enactment or under a rule of law had the original creditor retained the right.

(3) Subsection (2) applies whether the sum payable by the original creditor to the Commissioners first became payable before or after the transfer (but not if it only became payable after the Commissioners discharged their obligation to pay the transferred sum to the current creditor).

(4) The following are discharged to the extent of any set-off under this section—

    (*a*) the obligations of the Commissioners in relation to the current creditor, and

    (*b*) the obligations of the original creditor.

(5) An obligation under or by virtue of an enactment (other than this section) to set the transferred sum against a sum payable to the Commissioners by a person other than the original creditor has effect subject to the obligation under subsection (2)(*a*) and to any exercise of the power under subsection (2)(*b*).

(6) A power under or by virtue of an enactment (other than this section) or under a rule of law to set the transferred sum against a sum payable to the Commissioners by a person other than the original creditor has effect subject to the obligation under subsection (2)(*a*).

(7) In determining the sum (if any) to be paid, the Commissioners may make any reduction that they could have made if the original creditor had retained the right to be paid the transferred sum (in addition to any other reduction that they are entitled to make), including a reduction arising from any defence to a claim for the sum.

(8) In this section—

    (*a*) references to the transfer of a right are to its transfer by assignment, assignation or any other means, . . . [1]

    (*b*) references to a sum that is payable by or to a person are to a sum that is to be paid, repaid or credited by or to that person and references to the payment of the sum (however expressed) are to be interpreted accordingly, and

(c) where a right in relation to a sum has been transferred more than once, references to the original creditor are to the person from whom the right was first transferred (except in subsection (1)).

(9) Where the right to be paid the transferred sum is dependent on the making of a claim—

(a) subsection (2) does not apply unless a claim in respect of the transferred sum has been made, and

(b) the references in subsections (2) and (7) to the obligations or powers that the Commissioners would have had if the original creditor had retained the right are references to those that they would have had if the original creditor had also made the claim in respect of the transferred sum.

(10) This section has effect where the right to be paid the transferred sum was transferred from the original creditor on or after 25 June 2008.

Commentary—*Simon's Taxes* **A4.216.**
HMRC Manuals—VAT Refunds Manual VRM7000 (set-off - section 133 of the finance act 2008).
Amendments—[1] Words in sub-s (8)(a) repealed by FA 2012 s 50(2)(c). This amendment is treated as having come into force on 6 April 2012.

134 Retained funding bonds: tender by Commissioners

(1) Section 939 of ITA 2007 (duty to retain bonds where issue treated as payment of interest) is amended as follows.

(2) (*inserts* ITA 2007 s 939(4A)–(4C))

(3) Omit subsection (5).

(4) (*inserts* ITA 2007 s 940A)

(5) The amendments made by this section have effect in relation to funding bonds issued on or after 12 March 2008.

Commentary—*Simon's Taxes* **A4.216.**
HMRC Manuals—Savings And Investment Manual SAIM2210 (specific exclusions: funding bonds).

Other measures

135 Interest on unpaid tax in case of disaster etc of national significance

(1) This section applies in any case where the Commissioners agree that the payment of a relevant sum may be deferred by reason of circumstances arising as a result of a disaster or emergency specified in an order under this section (an "agreement for deferred payment").

(2) In subsection (1) "relevant sum" means a sum to meet any liability to the Commissioners [that—

(a) arises under or by virtue of an enactment or a contract settlement, and

(b) is of a description (if any) specified in the order.][1]

(3) No interest on the amount deferred is chargeable in respect of the relief period and no liability to a surcharge on the deferred amount arises during that period.

(4) The relief period[, in relation to a deferred amount,][1] is the period—

(a) beginning with a date specified in the order or, if the Commissioners so direct, a later date from which the agreement for deferred payment has effect, and

(b) ending with the date on which the agreement for deferred payment ceases to have effect or, if earlier, the date on which the order is revoked [or amended so that it ceases to have effect in relation to the deferred amount][1].

(5) The agreement for deferred payment ceases to have effect at the end of the period of deferment specified in the agreement or, if the Commissioners agree to extend (or further extend) that period by reason of circumstances arising as a result of the disaster or emergency, with the end of that extended (or further extended) period.

(6) If the agreement for deferred payment is an agreement for payment by instalments, the period of deferment in relation to each instalment ends with the date on or before which that instalment is to be paid; but if an instalment is not paid by the agreed date and the Commissioners do not agree to extend the period of deferment, the whole of the agreement for deferred payment is to be treated as ceasing to have effect on that date.

(7) This section applies whether the agreement for deferred payment was made—

(a) before or after the amount to which it relates becomes due and payable, or

(b) before or after the making of the order concerned.

(8) If in any case the Commissioners are satisfied that, although no agreement for deferred payment was made, one could have been made, this section applies as if one had been made; and the terms of the notional agreement for deferred payment are to be assumed to be such as the Commissioners are satisfied would have been agreed in the circumstances.

(9) An order under this section may be made only in relation to a disaster or emergency which the Treasury consider to be of national significance.

(10) Such an order—

(a) may specify a disaster or emergency which has begun (or both begun and ended) before it is made (including one which has begun, or both begun and ended, before the passing of this Act), . . .[1]

    (*b*) may specify a date before the date on which it is made (including a date before the passing of this Act)[, and

    (*c*) may specify different dates in relation to liabilities of different descriptions.][1]

(11) The power to make an order under this section is exercisable by the Treasury by statutory instrument.

(12) A statutory instrument containing such an order is subject to annulment in pursuance of a resolution of the House of Commons.

(13) (*repeals* FA 2001 s 107)

Commentary—*Simon's Taxes* **A4.535, A4.620, A4.565**.

Order—The Finance Act 2008 Section 135 (Disaster or Emergency) Order, SI 2008/1936 (deferral of interest and surcharge on tax following the floods that occurred in the UK during June and July 2007).

Amendments—[1]   In sub-s (2), words substituted for words "arising under or by virtue of an enactment or a contract settlement.", in sub-s (4) words inserted, and in sub-s (10) word "and" at end of para (*a*) repealed, and para (*c*) and preceding word inserted, by FA 2020 s 105 with effect from 20 March 2020.

136 Fee for payment

(1) The Commissioners may by regulations provide that, where a person makes a payment to the Commissioners or a person authorised by the Commissioners using a method of payment specified in the regulations, the person must also pay a fee specified in, or determined in accordance with, the regulations.

(2) A method of payment may only be specified in regulations made under this section if the Commissioners expect that they, or the person authorised by them, will be required to pay a fee or charge (however described) in connection with amounts paid using that method of payment.

(3) Regulations under this section—

    (*a*) may make provision about the time and manner in which the fee must or may be paid,

    (*b*) may make provision generally or only for specified purposes, and

    (*c*) may make different provision for different purposes.

(4) Regulations under this section are to be made by statutory instrument.

(5) A statutory instrument containing regulations under this section is subject to annulment in pursuance of a resolution of the House of Commons.

Commentary—*Simon's Taxes* **A4.613**.

Regulations—Fees for Payment of Taxes, etc. by Credit Card Regulations, SI 2016/333.

Fees for Payment of Taxes, etc. by Credit Card (Amendment) Regulations, SI 2017/1262.

137 County court proceedings

(1) In section 25 of CRCA 2005 (conduct of civil proceedings)—

    (*a*) (*inserts* CRCA 2005 s 25(1A))

    (*b*) (*inserts* CRCA 2005 s 25(6))

(2) (*amends* TMA 1970 s 66(1), *repeals* sub-s (2))

(3) Accordingly, in FA 1984, omit section 57(2).

(4) (*amends* IHTA 1984 s 244)

(5) (*amends* SSCTFA 1999 Sch 4 para 3)

(6) (*amends* FA 2003 Sch 12 para 5)

(7) Nothing in subsections (2) to (6) affects proceedings commenced or brought in the name of a collector or authorised officer before this Act is passed.

Commentary—*Simon's Taxes* **A1.702, A3.101A**.

HMRC Manuals—Debt Management And Banking Manual DMBM665000 (county court proceedings: contents).

138 Certificates of debt

(1) (*inserts* CRCA 2005 s 25A)

(2) Schedule 44 contains provisions consequential on this section.

Commentary—*Simon's Taxes* **A1.702, A1.705**.

Supplementary

139 Interpretation of Chapter

In this Chapter—

    "the Commissioners" means the Commissioners for Her Majesty's Revenue and Customs, and "contract settlement" means an agreement made in connection with any person's liability to make a payment to the Commissioners under or by virtue of an enactment.

PART 8

MISCELLANEOUS

Alternative finance arrangements

154 Stamp duty and stamp duty reserve tax: alternative finance investment bonds

(1) FA 1986 is amended as follows.

(2) (*inserts* FA 1986 s 78(7)(*d*))

(3) Section 79 (loan capital: instruments not chargeable to stamp duty) is amended as follows.

(4) (*inserts* FA 1986 s 79(8A))

(5) (*inserts* FA 1986 s 99(9A))

(6) The amendments made by subsections (2) to (4) have effect in relation to instruments executed on or after the day on which this Act is passed (and for this purpose it does not matter when the arrangements falling within section 48A of FA 2005 [or section 507 of CTA 2009][1] are made).

(7) The amendment made by subsection (5) has effect in relation to—

(a) agreements to transfer chargeable securities made on or after the day on which this Act is passed, and

(b) the transfer, issue or appropriation of chargeable securities after that day in pursuance of an agreement made after that day;

(and for this purpose it does not matter when the arrangements falling within section 48A of FA 2005 are made).

Amendments—[1] In sub-s (6), words inserted by CTA 2009 s 1322, Sch 1 paras 728, 732. CTA 2009 applies for accounting periods ending on or after 1 April 2009 (for corporation tax purposes) and for tax years 2009–10 onwards (for income and capital gains tax purposes).

155 Alternative property finance: anti-avoidance

(1) FA 2003 is amended as follows.

(2) (*amends* FA 2003 s 73A)

(3) (*inserts* FA 2003 s 73AB)

(4) The amendment made by subsection (3) has effect in relation to alternative finance arrangements entered into on or after 12 March 2008.

157 Government borrowing: alternative finance arrangements

(1) The Treasury may by regulations make provision for raising money through alternative finance arrangements.

(2) Regulations under subsection (1) must specify the purpose or purposes for which money may be raised through each kind of alternative finance arrangements that, under regulations under subsection (1), is available for raising money.

(3) The Treasury may not raise money through a particular kind of alternative finance arrangements unless, in the Treasury's opinion, raising the money would be in accordance with the provision made under subsection (2) in relation to that kind of arrangements.

(4) Regulations under subsection (2) may, in particular, specify a purpose or purposes for which money may be raised under the National Loans Act 1968 (c 13).

(5) Money to be raised under regulations made under this section—

(a) may either be raised within or outside the United Kingdom, and

(b) may be raised either in sterling or in any other currency or medium of exchange, whether national or international.

(6) Subsection (5) is subject to provision made in or under the regulations.

(7) Schedule 46 contains further provision about regulations under this section.

(8) In this section and Schedule 46 "alternative finance arrangements" means arrangements which in the Treasury's opinion—

(a) equate in substance to a loan, deposit or other transaction of a kind that generally involves the payment of interest (including the issuance of government securities), but

(b) achieve a similar effect to such a transaction without including provision for the payment of interest.

Commentary—*Simon's Taxes* A1.305, A1.301.

Regulations—Government Alternative Finance Arrangements Regulations, SI 2014/1327.

Payments from Exchequer accounts

158 Power of Treasury to make payments

(1) This section applies if a person makes a claim which, in the Treasury's opinion, is a financial claim that concerns an Exchequer account.

(2) The Treasury may pay money from any Exchequer account—

(a) to satisfy the claim (in whole or in part), or

(b) to enable the claim to be satisfied (in whole or in part) from another government account.

(3) The reference in this section to a financial claim that concerns an Exchequer account includes, in particular, either of the following cases.

(4) The first case is where a financial claim relates to—

(a) a case where money is paid into a government account, but the money should not have, or need not have, been paid into that account, or

(b) a case where money should have been, or needed to be, paid out of a government account, but the money—

(i) was not paid out of that account, or

(ii) was paid out of that account, but not as it should have been, or needed to be, paid.

(5) The second case is where a financial claim relates to the exercise of functions that relate to an Exchequer account (whether the functions are exercisable by the Treasury or another person).

(6) In this section—

"Exchequer account" means—

    (*a*) the Consolidated Fund,

    (*b*) the Debt Management Account,

    (*c*) the Exchange Equalisation Account, or

    (*d*) the National Loans Fund;

and a reference to an Exchequer account includes a reference to the assets or liabilities of the account;

"financial claim" means a claim (whether or not legally enforceable) for the payment of an amount of money, including a claim in respect of—

    (*a*) money paid or not paid by any person,

    (*b*) interest earned or not earned by any person, or

    (*c*) loss, costs or expenses incurred by any person;

"government account" means—

    (*a*) an Exchequer account, or

    (*b*) any other account in which money is held by or on behalf of Her Majesty's Government in the United Kingdom.

159 Payments from certain Exchequer accounts: mechanism

(1) This section applies to money to be paid under section 158 from—

    (*a*) the Consolidated Fund, or

    (*b*) the National Loans Fund.

(2) In the case of the Consolidated Fund—

    (*a*) the Comptroller and Auditor General shall on receipt of a requisition from the Treasury grant a credit on the Exchequer Account at the Bank of England (or on its growing balance), and

    (*b*) an issue shall be made on orders given to the Bank by the Treasury in accordance with a credit granted under paragraph (*a*).

(3) An issue made under subsection (2) shall be recorded in the daily account under section 15(5) of the Exchequer and Audit Departments Act 1866 (c 39).

(4) In the case of the National Loans Fund—

    (*a*) the Comptroller and Auditor General shall at the request of the Treasury grant a credit on the National Loans Fund, and

    (*b*) a payment out of the Fund shall be made by the Treasury in accordance with a credit granted under paragraph (*a*).

(5) A payment made under subsection (4) shall be recorded in the daily account under section 1(2) of the National Loans Act 1968 (c 13).

Other matters

160 Power to give statutory effect to concessions

(1) The Treasury may by order make provision for and in connection with giving effect to any existing HMRC concession.

(2) "Existing HMRC concession" means a statement made by the Commissioners for Her Majesty's Revenue and Customs before the passing of this Act, and having effect at that time, that they will treat persons as if they were entitled to—

    (*a*) a reduction in a liability to a tax or duty, or

    (*b*) any other concession relating to a tax or duty,

to which they are not, or may not be, entitled in accordance with the law.

(3) For this purpose "statement" means a statement of any sort, whether it was described as an extra-statutory concession, a statement of practice, an interpretation, a decision or a press release or in any other way.

(4) The reference in subsection (2) to the Commissioners for Her Majesty's Revenue and Customs includes the Commissioners of Inland Revenue and the Commissioners of Customs and Excise.

(5) An order under this section—

    (*a*) may give effect to an existing HMRC concession with or without modification,

    (*b*) may include supplementary, incidental, consequential or transitional provision, and

    (*c*) may include provisions amending (or repealing or revoking) any enactment or instrument (whenever passed or made).

(6) The power to make an order under this section is exercisable by statutory instrument.

(7) No order is to be made under this section unless a draft of the order has been laid before, and approved by a resolution of, the House of Commons.

Commentary—*Simon's Taxes* **A5.302, B2.476, D1.321, D2.327.**

Orders—Enactment of Extra-Statutory Concessions Order, SI 2009/730.

Enactment of Extra-Statutory Concessions Order, SI 2010/157.

Enactment of Extra-Statutory Concessions Order, SI 2012/266.

Enactment of Extra-Statutory Concessions Order, SI 2013/234.

Enactment of Extra-Statutory Concessions Order, SI 2017/495.
Enactment of Extra-Statutory Concessions Order, SI 2018/282.

163 National savings

(1) Section 10 of the National Debt Act 1972 (c 65) (national savings stamps and gift tokens) is amended as follows.

(2) In subsection (2), after "tokens; and" insert "(subject to regulations under subsection (2A))".

(3) *(inserts* National Debt Act 1972 s 10(2A))

PART 9
FINAL PROVISIONS

165 Interpretation

(1) In this Act—

"ALDA 1979" means the Alcoholic Liquor Duties Act 1979 (c 4),
"BGDA 1981" means the Betting and Gaming Duties Act 1981 (c 63),
"CAA 2001" means the Capital Allowances Act 2001 (c 2),
"CEMA 1979" means the Customs and Excise Management Act 1979 (c 2),
"CRCA 2005" means the Commissioners for Revenue and Customs Act 2005 (c 11),
["CTA 2009" means the Corporation Tax Act 2009][1]
["CTA 2010" means the Corporation Tax Act 2010][2]
"CTTA 1984" means the Capital Transfer Tax Act 1984 (c 51),
"HODA 1979" means the Hydrocarbon Oil Duties Act 1979 (c 5),
"ICTA" means the Income and Corporation Taxes Act 1988 (c 1),
"IHTA 1984" means the Inheritance Tax Act 1984 (c 51),
"ITA 2007" means the Income Tax Act 2007 (c 3),
"ITEPA 2003" means the Income Tax (Earnings and Pensions) Act 2003 (c 1),
"ITTOIA 2005" means the Income Tax (Trading and Other Income) Act 2005 (c 5),
"OTA 1975" means the Oil Taxation Act 1975 (c 22),
"TCGA 1992" means the Taxation of Chargeable Gains Act 1992 (c 12),
"TMA 1970" means the Taxes Management Act 1970 (c 9),
"TPDA 1979" means the Tobacco Products Duty Act 1979 (c 7),
"VATA 1994" means the Value Added Tax Act 1994 (c 23), and
"VERA 1994" means the Vehicle Excise and Registration Act 1994 (c 22).

(2) In this Act—

"FA", followed by a year, means the Finance Act of that year, and
"F(No 2)A", followed by a year, means the Finance (No 2) Act of that year.

Amendments—[1]   In sub-s (1) definition of "CTA 2009" inserted by CTA 2009 s 1322, Sch 1 paras 728, 733. CTA 2009 applies for accounting periods ending on or after 1 April 2009 (for corporation tax purposes) and for tax years 2009–10 onwards (for income and capital gains tax purposes).

[2]   In sub-s (1) definition of "CTA 2010" inserted by CTA 2010 s 1177, Sch 1 paras 576, 579. CTA 2010 has effect for corporation tax purposes for accounting periods ending on or after 1 April 2010, and for income and capital gains tax purposes for the tax year 2010–11 and subsequent tax years.

166 Short title

This Act may be cited as the Finance Act 2008.

SCHEDULES

SCHEDULE 1

ABOLITION OF STARTING AND SAVINGS RATES AND CREATION OF STARTING RATE
FOR SAVINGS

Section 5

PART 1
AMENDMENTS OF ITA 2007

1   ITA 2007 is amended as follows.

2   *(substitutes* ITA 2007 s 7)

3—(1) Section 10 (income charged at main rates: individuals) is amended as follows.

(2) *(repeals* ITA 2007 s 10(1))

(3) *(substitutes* ITA 2007 s 10(2))

(4) *(amends* ITA 2007 s 10(4))

(5) *(inserts* ITA 2007 s 10(6), (7))

(7) See section 21 for indexation of the basic rate limit."

(6) Accordingly, in the heading, omit "**starting,**".

4   In section 11(2) (income charged at the basic rate: persons other than individuals), omit the reference to section 12.

5   (*substitutes* ITA 2007 s 12)

6   (*amends* ITA 2007 s 13)

7   (*amends* ITA 2007 s 16(1))

8   (*amends* ITA 2007 s 17)

9   (*amends* heading above ITA 2007 s 20)

10   (*repeals* ITA 2007 s 20)

11—(1) Section 21 (indexation of starting and basic rate limits) is amended as follows.
(2) (*repeals* ITA 2007 s 21(2))
(3) (*inserts* ITA 2007 s 21(3A))
(4) (*amends* ITA 2007 s 21(4))
(5) (*amends* ITA 2007 s 21(5))
(6) (*amends* ITA 2007 s 21 heading)

12   In section 31(2), omit "or savings rate".

13—(1) Section 158 (form and amount of EIS relief) is amended as follows.
(2) (*amends* ITA 2007 s 158(2))
(3) (*inserts* ITA 2007 s 158(2A))

14   (*amends* ITA 2007 s 209(3))

15   (*amends* ITA 2007 s 210(1)(*b*))

16   (*amends* ITA 2007 s 213(2))

17   (*amends* ITA 2007 s 220(1)(*b*))

18   (*amends* ITA 2007 s 224(2))

19   (*amends* ITA 2007 s 229(1)(*b*))

20   (*amends* ITA 2007 s 414(2))

21   (*amends* ITA 2007 s 486(1) Step 5)

22   (*amends* ITA 2007 s 498)

24   (*amends* ITA 2007 s 745(1))

26   (*amends* ITA 2007 s 874(2))

27   (*amends* ITA 2007 s 889(4))

28   (*amends* ITA 2007 s 892(2))

29   (*amends* ITA 2007 s 901(4))

30   (*repeals* ITA 2007 s 902)

31   (*amends* ITA 2007 s 919(2))

32   (*amends* ITA 2007 s 939(2))

33   (*amends* ITA 2007 s 989)

34   (*amends* ITA 2007 s 1014(5)(*b*)(i))

35   (*repeals* ITA 2007 Sch 1 paras 85(2), 86, 112, 151, 152, 191, 244, 259, 279, 530, 535(2), 536(3), 537, 538, 564, 565 and 592(47) and (49))

36   (*amends* ITA 2007 Sch 4)

PART 2
OTHER AMENDMENTS

TMA 1970

37   TMA 1970 is amended as follows.

38   (*amends* TMA 1970 s 7(6))

39   (*amends* TMA 1970 s 91(3)(*c*))

ICTA

40   ICTA is amended as follows.

45   (*amends* TA 1988 s 701(3A))

46   (*repeals* TA 1988 s 789(2))

FA 1989

47   (*amends* FA 1989 s 88(1))

FA 1996

49   (*repeals* FA 1996 Sch 6 para 21)

ITTOIA 2005

50   ITTOIA 2005 is amended as follows.

51   (*amends* ITTOIA 2005 s 465A(1)(*b*))

52   (*amends* ITTOIA 2005 s 466(2))

53   (*amends* ITTOIA 2005 s 467(7))

54   (*amends* ITTOIA 2005 s 530(1) and *repeals* s 530(6))

55   (*amends* ITTOIA 2005 s 535(3))

56   (*amends* ITTOIA 2005 s 536(1))

57   (*amends* ITTOIA 2005 s 537)

58   (*amends* ITTOIA 2005 s 539(5))

60   (*repeals* ITTOIA 2005 s 679(3)(*b*))

61   (*amends* ITTOIA 2005 s 680(4))

62—(1) Section 680A (income treated as savings income or dividend income) is amended as follows.
(2) (*amends* ITTOIA 2005 s 680A(1))
(3) (*repeals* ITTOIA 2005 s 680A(2))
(4) (*amends* ITTOIA 2005 s 680A(3))
(5) (*amends* ITTOIA 2005 s 680A(4))
(6) (*repeals* ITTOIA 2005 s 680A(5))
(7) (*amends* ITTOIA 2005 s 680A(6))
(8) Accordingly, in the heading omit "**savings income or**".

63—(1) Schedule 4 (index of defined expressions) is amended as follows.
(2) (*substitutes* entries in ITTOIA 2005 Sch 4)
(3) Omit the entry relating to "savings rate".

F(No 2)A 2005

64   (*amends* F(No 2)A 2005 s 7(5))

PART 3
COMMENCEMENT

65   Apart from the amendments made by paragraph 11, the amendments made by this Schedule have effect for the tax year 2008–09 and subsequent tax years.

SCHEDULE 2
CAPITAL GAINS TAX REFORM

Section 8

Rate: consequentials

1   TCGA 1992 is amended as follows.

2   (*amends* TCGA 1992 s 2(7)(*a*))

3   (*repeals* TCGA 1992 s 6)

4   (*repeals* TCGA 1992 s 13(7A)(*b*)–(*d*))

5   (*repeals* TCGA 1992 ss 77–79)

6   (*repeals* TCGA 1992 s 88(6))

7—(1) Schedule 4A (disposal of interest in settled property: deemed disposal of underlying assets) is amended as follows.
(2) (*amends* TCGA 1992 Sch 4A para 7(4), (5))
(3) (*amends* TCGA 1992 Sch 4A para 12)

8—(1) Schedule 4B (transfers of value by trustees linked with trustee borrowing) is amended as follows.
(2) (*amends* TCGA 1992 Sch 4B para 1(1))
(3) (*amends* TCGA 1992 Sch 4B para 3(1), (2), heading)

9   (*repeals* TCGA 1992 Sch 4C para 6(3))

10   (*amends* TCGA 1992 Sch 5 para 1(1))

11   Chapter 4 of Part 2 of FA 2005 (trusts with vulnerable beneficiary) is amended as follows.

12   (*amends* FA 2005 s 23(4))

13   (*amends* FA 2005 s 26(1))

14—(1) Section 28 (vulnerable person's liability: VQTI) is amended as follows.
(2) (*amends* FA 2005 s 28(1))
(3) (*amends* FA 2005 s 28(2))
(4) (*repeals* FA 2005 s 28(4)(*b*))
(5) (*amends* FA 2005 s 28(7)(*b*))

15   (*repeals* FA 2005 s 30(1A), (3A))

16—(1) Section 31 (UK resident vulnerable persons: section 77 treatment) is amended as follows.
(2) (*substitutes* FA 2005 s 31(2), (3))
(3) In the heading, for "**section 77 treatment**" substitute "**amount of relief**".

17—(1) Section 32 (non-UK resident vulnerable persons: amount of relief) is amended as follows
(2) (*amends* FA 2005 s 32(2))
(3) (*inserts* FA 2005 s 32(3), (4))

18   Omit section 33 (non-UK resident vulnerable person's liability: VQTG).

19   In section 41(3) (interpretation), for "33" substitute "32".

20—(*repeals* FA 2005 Sch 1 paras 1, 2 and 4 and *amends* para 7(1))

21   In consequence of section 8 and paragraphs 1 to 20, omit—
    (*a*) paragraphs 27 to 29 of Schedule 17 to FA 1995,
    (*b*) paragraphs 24 and 25 of Schedule 4 to F(No 2)A 1997,
    (*c*) in FA 1998—
        (i) section 120, and
        (ii) paragraph 6(1) of Schedule 21,
    (*d*) section 26 of FA 1999,
    (*e*) section 37 of FA 2000,
    (*f*) paragraph 3 of Schedule 11 to FA 2002,
    (*g*) paragraph 2 of Schedule 21 to FA 2004,
    (*h*) paragraphs 427 and 428 of Schedule 1 to ITTOIA 2005,
    (*i*) section 44(2) of FA 2005,
    (*j*) paragraphs 3, 13, 29, 31 and 48(1) of Schedule 12 to FA 2006, and
    (*k*) paragraphs 295, 296 and 301 of Schedule 1 to ITA 2007.

22   The amendments made by paragraphs 1 to 21 have effect for the tax year 2008–09 and subsequent tax years.

Abolition of taper relief

23   TCGA 1992 is amended as follows.

24—(1) Section 2 (chargeable gains and allowable losses) is amended as follows.
(2) (*substitutes* TCGA 1992 s 2(4), (5))

(3) (*amends* TCGA 1992 s 2(7))
(4) Omit subsection (8).

25   Omit section 2A (taper relief).

26   (*amends* TCGA 1992 s 3(5), (5C)(*c*))

27   (*amends* TCGA 1992 s 3A(2)(*b*), repeals s 3A(2)(*a*))

28   Omit section 13(10A) (attribution of gains to members of non-resident companies).

29   (*amends* TCGA 1992 s 62(2A), *repeals* s 62(2B))

30   (*amends* TCGA 1992 s 86(1)(*e*))

31—(1) Section 86A (attribution of gains to settlor in section 10A cases) is amended as follows.
(2) (*amends* TCGA 1992 s 86A(2))
(3) Omit subsection (2A).
(4) Omit subsection (2B).
(5) (*amends* TCGA 1992 s 86A(7))
(6) Omit subsection (7A).

32   (*repeals* TCGA 1992 s 150D)

33   (*substitutes* TCGA s 165(8)(*aa*))

34   (*inserts* TCGA 1992 s 165A)

35   (*amends* TCGA 1992 s 214C)

36   (*amends* TCGA 1992 s 228(8))

37   (*amends* TCGA 1992 s 241(3A))

38   (*amends* TCGA 1992 s 253(14)(*b*))

39   (*repeals* TCGA 1992 s 261C(2)(*a*))

40   (*repeals* TCGA 1992 s 279(2)(*a*))

41   (*repeals* TCGA 1992 s 279A(7)(*b*))

42   (*substitutes* TCGA 1992 s 279B(1)(*b*))

43—(1) Section 279C (effect of election under section 279A) is amended as follows.
(2) (*substitutes* TCGA 1992 s 279C(3), (4), (4A))
(3) (*amends* TCGA 1992 s 279C(6)(*c*))
(4) Omit subsection (8).
(5) Omit subsection (10).

44   (*repeals* TCGA 1992 s 284B(1))

45   (*repeals* TCGA 1992 Sch A1)

46   Schedule 4C (transfers of value: attribution of gains to beneficiaries) is amended as follows.

47   (*amends* TCGA 1992 Sch 4C para 6(1), *repeals* para 6(1A))

48   (*repeals* TCGA 1992 Sch 4C para 11)

49   (*repeals* TCGA 1992 Sch 5BA)

50   (*repeals* TCGA 1992 Sch 7D para 15)

52   (*amends* ITEPA 2003 Sch 7 para 86(2))

53   (*repeals* FA 2004 s 185G(3)(*c*))

54   (*repeals* ITA 2007 s 161(5))

55   In consequence of paragraphs 23 to 54, omit—
     (*a*) (*repeals* FA 1998 ss 121(1), (2), 140(5), Sch 20, Sch 21 paras 2, 4, 6(3) and (4), 7 and 9)
     (*b*) (*repeals* FA 1999 s 72, Sch 7)
     (*c*) (*repeals* FA 2000 ss 66, 67)
     (*d*) (*repeals* FA 2001 s 78, Sch 26)
     (*e*) (*repeals* FA 2002 ss 46, 47, Sch 9 para 5(13), Sch 10, Sch 11 paras 2(2), 4–6)
     (*f*) (*repeals* FA 2003 s 160, Sch 29 para 5)
     (*g*) (*repeals* FA 2004 Sch 21 paras 3(4), 8, words in para 10(4), and (6))

(h) (*repeals* FA 2006 Sch 12 paras 13, 27)

(i) (*repeals* ITA 2007 Sch 1 paras 313, 343)

56—(1) The amendments made by paragraph 31(2) and (3) have effect where the intervening year is the tax year 2008–09 or any subsequent tax year.

(2) The amendments made by paragraphs 41 and 43 have effect where the eligible year is the tax year 2008–09 or any subsequent tax year.

(3) The other amendments made by paragraphs 23 to 55 have effect in relation to chargeable gains accruing or treated as accruing in the tax year 2008–09 or any subsequent tax year.

Abolition of "kink" test

57 TCGA 1992 is amended as follows.

58—(1) Section 35 (assets held on 31 March 1982) is amended as follows.

(2) (*amends* TCGA 1992 s 35(2))

(3) (*inserts* TCGA 1992 s 35(2A))

(4) (*amends* TCGA 1992 s 35(3)(*d*))

(5) (*amends* TCGA 1992 s 35(4))

(6) (*amends* TCGA 1992 s 35(5))

(7) (*amends* TCGA 1992 s 35(6))

(8) (*amends* TCGA 1992 s 35(7))

(9) (*amends* TCGA 1992 s 35(9))

(10) (*amends* TCGA 1992 s 35(10))

59 (*inserts* TCGA 1992 s 35A)

60 (*amends* TCGA 1992 s 55(5))

61 (*amends* TCGA 1992 s 73(1))

62 (*amends* TCGA 1992 s 175(2C))

63 (*inserts* TCGA 1992 s 288(3A))

64—(1) Schedule 2 (assets held on 6 April 1965) is amended as follows.

(2) (*repeals* TCGA 1992 Sch 2 para 1(3))

(3) (*amends* TCGA 1992 Sch 2 para 4(8), (9), (10)(*a*), (11); *repeals* para 4(6))

(4) (*amends* TCGA 1992 Sch 2 para 17(3))

(5) Omit paragraph 22.

65—(1) Schedule 3 (assets held on 31 March 1982) is amended as follows.

(2) (*amends* TCGA 1992 Sch 3 para 1(1), (2))

(3) (*amends* TCGA 1992 Sch 3 para 2(1), (3))

66 (*amends* TCGA 1992 Sch 4 para 7)

67 (*amends* TCGA 1992 Sch 4ZA para 7)

68 (*amends* TCGA 1992 Sch 7A para 12(*b*))

69—(1) FA 1997 is amended as follows.

(2) (*amends* FA 1997 s 89(8)(*a*))

(3) (*amends* FA 1997 Sch 12 para 7(1)(*b*))[1], [2]

Amendments—[1]   Sub-para (3) repealed by CTA 2010 s 1181, Sch 3 Pt 2 with effect for corporation tax purposes for accounting periods ending on or after 1 April 2010.

[2]   Sub-para (3) repealed by TIOPA 2010 s 503, Sch 10 Pt 8. TIOPA 2010 has effect for corporation tax purposes for accounting periods ending on or after 1 April 2010, for income and capital gains tax purposes for the tax year 2010–11 and subsequent tax years, and for petroleum revenue tax purposes for chargeable periods beginning on or after 1 July 2010.

70 In consequence of paragraphs 57 to 69, omit—

(a) (*repeals* F(No 2)A 1992 s 46(2), Sch 9 para 21(2), Sch 17 para 5(9))

(b) (*repeals* FA 1994 Sch 24 para 2(2), Sch 25 para 4(3))

(c) paragraph 2(3) of Schedule 4 to the Coal Industry Act 1994 (c 21),

(d) paragraph 3 of Schedule 7 to the Broadcasting Act 1996 (c 55),

(e) (*repeals* Transport Act 2000 Sch 7 para 2(3), Sch 26 para 37)

(f) paragraph 36 of Schedule 9 to the Energy Act 2004 (c 20),

(g) paragraph 33 of Schedule 10 to the Railways Act 2005 (c 14),

(h) (*repeals* F(No 2)A 2005 s 59(2))

(i) (*repeals* FA 2007 Sch 9 para 14(3))

(j) paragraph 11 of Schedule 7 to the Consumers, Estate Agents and Redress Act 2007 (c 17).

71   The amendments made by paragraphs 57 to 70 have effect in relation to disposals on or after 6 April 2008.

Abolition of "halving relief"

72   TCGA 1992 is amended as follows.

73   (*amends* TCGA 1992 s 36)

74—(1) Schedule 4 (deferred charges on pre-31 March 1982 gains) is amended as follows.
(2) (*inserts* TCGA 1992 Sch 4 para A1)
(3) (*amends* TCGA 1992 Sch 4 para 2(5))
(4) (*amends* TCGA 1992 Sch 4 para 4(2))
(5) (*amends* TCGA 1992 Sch 4 para 9(1))

75   (*repeals* FA 1996 Sch 21 para 43)

76   The amendments made by paragraphs 72 to 75 have effect in relation to disposals which occur on or after 6 April 2008 and to which Schedule 4 to TCGA 1992 would otherwise apply.

Abolition of indexation allowance

77   TCGA 1992 is amended as follows.

78   (*inserts* TCGA 1992 s 52A)

79   (*repeals* TCGA 1992 s 53(1A), *amends* s 53(4))

80   (*repeals* TCGA 1992 s 54(1A), *amends* s 54(1))

81   (*repeals* TCGA 1992 s 145(1A), *amends* s 145(1))

82   (*repeals* FA 1998 s 122(1)–(3), (5))

83   The amendments made by paragraphs 77 to 82 have effect in computing gains on disposals made on or after 6 April 2008.

Simplification of pooling etc

84   TCGA 1992 is amended as follows.

85—(1) Section 104 (share pooling: general interpretative provisions) is amended as follows.
(2) (*substitutes* TCGA 1992 s 104(2), (2A))
(3) In subsection (3), omit ", 110A".
(4) (*inserts* TCGA 1992 s 104(3A))
(5) In subsection (5), omit ", 110A".

86   (*inserts* TCGA 1992 s 105(3))

87—(1) Section 106A (identification of securities: general rules for capital gains tax) is amended as follows.
(2) (*inserts* TCGA 1992 s 106A(5ZA))
(3) (*amends* TCGA 1992 s 106A(6))
(4), (5) (*repeal* TCGA 1992 s 106A(7), (8))
(6) (*substitutes* TCGA 1992 s 106A(10))
(7) In the heading, omit "**general rules for**".

88   (*amends* TCGA 1992 s 107 heading)

89   (*amends* TCGA 1992 s 108 heading)

90   (*amends* TCGA 1992 s 109(1) and heading)

91   (*amends* TCGA 1992 s 110 heading)

92   (*repeals* TCGA 1992 s 110A)

93   (*amends* TCGA 1992 s 112 heading)

94   (*inserts* TCGA 1992 s 113(A1) and *amends* s 113 heading)

95   (*inserts* TCGA 1992 s 114(A1) and *amends* s 114 heading)

96   (*repeals* FA 1998 s 123(1), (2), 125(2), (3))

97   Chapter 6 of Part 4 of ITA 2007 (losses on disposals of shares) is amended as follows.

98—(1) Section 147 (limits on share loss relief) is amended as follows.
(2) (*amends* ITA 2007 s 147(1)(*b*))
(3) (*amends* ITA 2007 s 147(7))

99—(*amends* ITA 2007 s 148(3)(*a*)(ii), (5), (9))

100 The amendments made by paragraphs 84 to 99 have effect in relation to disposals on or after 6 April 2008.

Meaning of "tax year"

101—(1) Section 288 of TCGA 1992 (interpretation) is amended as follows.
(2) (*amends* TCGA 1992 s 288(1))
(3) (*inserts* TCGA 1992 s 288(1ZA))

102 (*repeals* FA 2005 s 41(1) and ITA 2007 Sch 1 para 342(2)(*i*))

SCHEDULE 3
ENTREPRENEURS' RELIEF

Section 9

Introduction

1 TCGA 1992 is amended as follows.

Main provisions

2 (*inserts* TCGA 1992 Chapter 3 ss 169H–169S)

Other amendments

3 (*amends* TCGA 1992 s 241(3A))

4 (*amends* TCGA 1992 Sch 5B para 1(1)(*b*))

Commencement

5 The amendments made by this Schedule have effect in relation to disposals, reorganisations (within the meaning of section 169Q of TCGA 1992) and relevant transactions (within the meaning of section 116 of TCGA 1992) taking place on or after 6 April 2008.

Transitionals: section 169P(4)(d)

6 Section 169P of TCGA 1992 has effect in a case where the period for which the assets are in use for the purposes of the business began before 6 April 2008 as if the reference in subsection (4)(*d*) of that section to that period were to so much of it as falls on or after that date.

Transitionals: reorganisations

7—(1) This paragraph applies where, by virtue of section 116(10)(*b*), a chargeable gain is deemed to accrue to an individual on a disposal made on or after 6 April 2008 (a "relevant disposal") by reason of a relevant transaction to which the individual was a party taking place before that date.
(2) Subject as follows, Chapter 3 of Part 5 (as inserted by this Schedule) has effect as if—
    (*a*) (despite section 116(10)) the relevant transaction were a disposal of the old asset made by the individual,
    (*b*) that Chapter applied in relation to that disposal (even though made before 6 April 2008), and
    (*c*) for the purposes of the time limit for making a claim for entrepreneurs' relief, that disposal were made at the time of the first relevant disposal.
(3) In sub-paragraph (2) "the first relevant disposal" means the first disposal made on or after 6 April 2008 on which a chargeable gain is deemed to accrue to the individual by reason of the relevant transaction.
(4) Where entrepreneurs' relief is claimed by virtue of this paragraph—
    (*a*) the amount of the chargeable gain produced by the calculation under section 116(10)(*a*), reduced by
    (*b*) any amount deemed to accrue under section 116(10)(*b*) and (12) before 6 April 2008 by reason of the relevant transaction,
is to be treated as constituting the amount resulting under section 169N(1).
(5) Accordingly (but subject as follows), the amount of the chargeable gain which is deemed to accrue by virtue of section 116(10)(*b*) on the relevant disposal is that arrived at under [section 169N(1) and (2)]¹ (in accordance with sub-paragraph (4)).

(6) The amount of the chargeable gain which is deemed to accrue by virtue of section 116(10)(*b*) on the relevant disposal is the amount specified in sub-paragraph (7)—

    (*a*) except in a case within paragraph (*b*), where the relevant disposal is not a disposal of the whole of the new asset, and

    (*b*) in a case in which part of the new asset was disposed of before 6 April 2008, where the relevant disposal is not a disposal of the whole of the part not so disposed of.

(7) The amount referred to in sub-paragraph (6) is the appropriate proportion of the amount in sub-paragraph (5); and "the appropriate proportion" means the proportion of the new asset, or of so much of the new asset as was not disposed of before 6 April 2008, which is disposed of on the relevant disposal.

[(7A) Section 169N(3) to (4B) is to apply to the deemed chargeable gain found in accordance with sub-paragraphs (5) to (7).][1]

(8) In this paragraph—

    "new asset",

    "old asset", and

    "relevant transaction",

have the meaning given by section 116.

(9) References in this paragraph to any provision are to be read as they would be if this paragraph formed part of TCGA 1992.

Amendments—[1] In sub-para (5), words substituted for words "section 169N(1) to (3)", and sub-para (7A) inserted, by F(No 2)A 2010 s 2, Sch 1 para 10. This amendment has effect if the first relevant disposal occurs on or after 23 June 2010 (F(No 2)A 2010 Sch 1 para 16).

Transitionals: EIS and VCT

8—(1) This paragraph applies where there is a relevant chargeable event in a case in which the original gain would, apart from Schedule 5B (enterprise investment scheme) or Schedule 5C (venture capital trusts), have accrued before 6 April 2008.

(2) "Relevant chargeable event" means a chargeable event under—

    (*a*) paragraph 3(1) of Schedule 5B, or

    (*b*) paragraph 3(1) of Schedule 5C,

which occurs on or after 6 April 2008 in relation to any of the relevant shares held by the investor immediately before the first relevant chargeable event.

(3) In this paragraph "the first relevant chargeable event" means the first relevant chargeable event in the case.

(4) The following provisions apply if—

    (*a*) the relevant disposal would have been a material disposal of business assets had Chapter 3 of Part 5 applied in relation to it (even though made before 6 April 2008), and

    (*b*) a claim is made on or before the first anniversary of the 31 January following the tax year in which the first relevant chargeable event occurs.

(5) In this paragraph "the relevant disposal" means—

    (*a*) where the original gain would have accrued in accordance with section 164F or 164FA, paragraphs 4 and 5 of Schedule 5B or paragraphs 4 and 5 of Schedule 5C (the "original gain event"), the relevant underlying disposal, and

    (*b*) otherwise, the disposal on which the original gain would have accrued ("the original gain disposal").

(6) In sub-paragraph (5)(*a*) "the relevant underlying disposal" means the disposal (not being a disposal within paragraph 3 of Schedule 5B or 5C) by virtue of which Schedule 5B or 5C has effect.

(7) Subject as follows, the amount treated as accruing on the relevant chargeable event in respect of the original gain event or original gain disposal is the amount which would be arrived at under [section 169N(1) and (2)][1] if—

    (*a*) the relevant chargeable event were a qualifying business disposal (within the meaning of Chapter 3 of Part 5), and

    (*b*) the relevant proportion of the postponed gain constituted the amount resulting under section 169N(1);

and "the relevant proportion" means the proportion of the relevant shares which is held by the investor immediately before the first relevant chargeable event.

(8) The amount treated as accruing on the relevant chargeable event in respect of the original gain event or original gain disposal is that specified in sub-paragraph (9) where the relevant chargeable event is not a chargeable event in relation to all the relevant shares held by the investor immediately before the first relevant chargeable event.

(9) The amount referred to in sub-paragraph (8) is the appropriate proportion of the amount in sub-paragraph (7); and "the appropriate proportion" means the proportion of the relevant shares held by the investor immediately before the first relevant chargeable event as respects which the relevant chargeable event is a chargeable event.

[(9A) Section 169N(3) to (4B) is to apply to the amount treated as accruing in accordance with sub-paragraphs (7) to (9).][1]

(10) In this paragraph—

"chargeable event" is to be construed in accordance with paragraph 3 of Schedule 5B or paragraph 3 of Schedule 5C,

"investor" has the same meaning as in paragraph 1 of Schedule 5B or paragraph 1 of Schedule 5C,

"the original gain" has the same meaning as in paragraph 1 of Schedule 5B or paragraph 1 of Schedule 5C,

"the postponed gain" means so much of the original gain as is treated by paragraph 2(2)(*a*) of Schedule 5B or paragraph 2(2)(*a*) of Schedule 5C as not having accrued at the accrual time, and

"relevant shares" has the same meaning as in Schedule 5B or Schedule 5C.

(11) References in this paragraph to any provision are to be read as they would be if this paragraph formed part of TCGA 1992.

Amendments—[1]   In sub-para (7), words substituted for words "section 169N(1) to (3)", and sub-para (9A) inserted, by F(No 2)A 2010 s 2, Sch 1 para 11. This amendment has effect if the first relevant chargeable event occurs on or after 23 June 2010 (F(No 2)A 2010 Sch 1 para 17).

SCHEDULE 7

REMITTANCE BASIS

Section 25

PART 1

MAIN PROVISIONS

Remittance basis—general

1   (*inserts* ITA 2007 Chapter A1, ss 809A–809Z7)

Employment income

2   ITEPA 2003 is amended as follows.

3—(1) Section 6 (nature of charge to tax on employment income) is amended as follows.
(2), (3) (*inserts* ITEPA 2003 s 6(3)(*aa*), (3A))

4—(1) Section 10 (meaning of "taxable earnings" etc) is amended as follows.
(2), (3) (*amend* ITEPA 2003 s 10(2), *insert* 10(4))

5—(1) Section 13 (person liable to tax) is amended as follows.
(2), (3) (*insert* ITEPA 2003 s 13(4A), *amend* s 13(5))

6   (*amends* ITEPA 2003 Pt 2 Ch 4 heading)

7   (*amends* ITEPA 2003 s 14(1))

8   For the heading before section 15 substitute "*UK resident employees*".

9—(1) Section 15 (earnings for year when employee resident, ordinarily resident and domiciled in UK) is amended as follows.
(2), (3) (*amend* ITEPA 2003 s 15(1), *substitute* s 15(3))
(4) Accordingly, in the heading for "**resident, ordinarily resident and domiciled in UK**" substitute "**UK resident**".

10   (*amends* ITEPA 2003 Pt 2 Ch 5 heading)

11—(1) Section 20 (taxable earnings under Chapter 5: introduction) is amended as follows.
(2) (*substitutes* ITEPA 2003 s 20(1))
(3), (4) (*amend* ITEPA 2003 s 20(2), (3))

12, 13   (*repeal* ITEPA 2003 s 21 and *amend* preceding cross heading)

14—(1) Section 22 (chargeable overseas earnings for year when employee resident and ordinarily resident, but not domiciled, in UK) is amended as follows.
(2) (*amends* ITEPA 2003 s 22(1))
(3) (*substitutes* ITEPA 2003 s 22(3))
(4), (5) (*amend* ITEPA 2003 s 22(4), (5)(*b*))

(6) (*inserts* ITEPA 2003 s 22(6), (7))

(7) (*amends* ITEPA 2003 s 22 heading)

15—(1) Section 23 (calculation of chargeable overseas earnings) is amended as follows.

(2) (*amends* ITEPA 2003 s 23(1))

(3) (*substitutes* ITEPA 2003 s 23(2)(*a*), (*aa*))

16   (*amends* ITEPA 2003 s 24(7))

17, 18   (*repeal* ITEPA 2003 s 25 and *amend* preceding cross heading)

19—(1) Section 26 (foreign earnings for year when employee resident, but not ordinarily resident, in UK) is amended as follows.

(2) (*amends* ITEPA 2003 s 26(1))

(3) (*substitutes* ITEPA 2003 s 26(3))

(4) (*inserts* ITEPA 2003 s 26(5), (6))

(5) (*amends* ITEPA 2003 s 26 heading)

20—(1) Section 27 (UK-based earnings for year when employee non-UK resident) is amended as follows.

(2) (*substitutes* ITEPA 2003 s 27(3))

(3) (*inserts* ITEPA 2003 s 27(5))

21   Omit sections 31 to 37 (and the heading before section 31).

22   (*inserts* ITEPA 2003 Chapter 5A, ss 41A–41E)

23   Omit Chapter 6 of Part 2 (disputes as to domicile or ordinary residence).

24   (*substitutes* ITEPA 2003 s 225(6))

25   (*amends* ITEPA 2003 s 271(2))

26   In section 335(4) (application of deductions provisions), omit ", 21, 25".

27—(1) Section 370 (travel costs and expenses where duties performed abroad) is amended as follows.

(2) (*amends* ITEPA 2003 s 370(1))

(3) (*inserts* ITEPA 2003 s 370(6))

28—(1) Section 371 (travel costs and expenses where duties performed abroad: spouse's travel etc) is amended as follows.

(2) (*amends* ITEPA 2003 s 371(1))

(3) (*inserts* ITEPA 2003 s 371(8))

29—(1) Section 378 (deduction from seafarer's earnings: eligibility) is amended as follows.

(2) (*amends* ITEPA 2003 s 378(1)(*a*))

(3) (*inserts* ITEPA 2003 s 378(5))

30—(1) Section 413 (exception in certain cases of foreign service) is amended as follows.

(2) (*substitutes* ITEPA 2003 s 413(3)(*a*))

(3) (*inserts* ITEPA 2003 s 413(3A))

31   (*amends* ITEPA 2003 s 421E(1))

32   (*inserts* ITEPA 2003 s 446N(7), (8))

33   (*amends* ITEPA 2003 s 474(1))

34   (*amends* ITEPA 2003 s 540(2))

35   (*inserts* ITEPA 2003 s 690(2A))

36   (*inserts* ITEPA 2003 s 698(8))

37   (*inserts* ITEPA 2003 s 700(7))

38   (*inserts* ITEPA 2003 s 700A)

39   (*amends* ITEPA 2003 s 721(1))

40   (*amends* ITEPA 2003 Sch 1)

41   (*substitutes* ITEPA 2003 Sch 2 para 8)

42   (*substitutes* ITEPA 2003 Sch 3 para 6(2)(*c*), (*ca*))

43   (*amends* ITEPA 2003 Sch 5 para 27(2))

44   In Schedule 7 (transitionals and savings), omit paragraphs 9 to 12.

Relevant foreign income

45   In section 575 of ITEPA 2003 (foreign pensions: taxable pension income), omit subsection (4).

46   ITTOIA 2005 is amended as follows.

47   (*repeals* ITTOIA 2005 s 260(1)(*f*))

48   In section 269 (territorial scope of charge to tax), omit subsections (3) and (4).

49   Omit Chapter 11 of Part 3 (overseas property income).

50   (*substitutes* ITTOIA 2005 s 829(*a*))

51—(1) Section 830 (meaning of "relevant foreign income") is amended as follows.
(2) (*substitutes* words in ITTOIA 2005 s 830(1))
(3) (*repeals* ITTOIA 2005 s 830(2)(*d*))

52   Omit section 831 (claims for relevant foreign income to be charged on remittance basis).

53   (*substitutes* ITTOIA 2005 ss 832–832B)

54   Omit sections 833 to 837.

Chargeable gains

55   TCGA 1992 is amended as follows.

56—(1) Section 3 (annual exempt amount) is amended as follows.
(2) (*inserts* TCGA 1992 s 3(1A))
(3) (*inserts* TCGA 1992 s 3(5C)(*aa*), *amends* s 3(5C)(*b*))

57   (*inserts* TCGA 1992 s 3A(5A))

58   In section 9 (residence etc), omit subsection (2).

59   (*inserts* TCGA 1992 s 10A(9ZA))

60   (*substitutes* TCGA 1992 s 12)

61   In section 16 (computation of losses), omit subsection (4).

62   (*inserts* TCGA 1992 ss 16ZA–16ZD)

63   (*inserts* TCGA 1992 s 119A(5A))

64   (*inserts* TCGA 1992 s 119B)

Minor and consequential amendments

65   (*inserts* TMA 1970 s 33(2A)(*c*))

66   ITTOIA 2005 is amended as follows.

67   In section 839 (annual payments payable out of relevant foreign income), omit subsection (6).

68   In section 840 (relief for backdated pensions charged on arising basis), omit subsection (4) (application of section 837).

69   (*inserts* ITTOIA 2005 s 840A)

70—(1) Section 857 (partners to whom the remittance basis may apply) is amended as follows.
(2) (*substitutes* ITTOIA 2005 s 857(1)(*c*))
(3), (4) (*amend* ITTOIA 2005 s 857 heading and sub-s (3))

71   In section 878 (definitions), omit subsection (2).

72   In Schedule 2 (transitional provision etc), omit paragraphs 150 and 151.

73   In Part 2 of Schedule 4 (index of defined expressions), omit the entry for "person to whom the remittance basis applies".

74   ITA 2007 is amended as follows.

75   (*inserts* ITA 2007 s 2(14)(*za*))

76   (*inserts* ITA 2007 s 34(3))

77   (*inserts* ITA 2007 s 42(5))

78   (*inserts* ITA 2007 s 460(4))

79   (*repeals* ITEPA 2003 Sch 6 para 208, ITTOIA 2005 Sch 1 para 429, CRCA 2005 Sch 4 paras 102(3)(*b*)–(*d*) and 104)

Commencement

80   The amendments made by paragraphs 3(3), 4(3), 5(2), 22, 31 to 33, 38 and 64 have effect in relation to employment-related securities and employment-related securities options where the date of the acquisition is on or after 6 April 2008 (except employment-related securities acquired pursuant to a securities option acquired before 6 April 2008).

81   The other amendments made by this Part of this Schedule have effect for the tax year 2008–09 and subsequent tax years.

Transitional provision

82—(1) This paragraph applies in relation to an individual's general earnings for the tax year 2007–08 or any earlier tax year ("the relevant tax year") if the individual—

     (*a*) was UK resident in that year, but

     (*b*) was not domiciled in the United Kingdom, or was not ordinarily UK resident, in that year.

(2) Section 22 or 26 of ITEPA 2003 (as amended by this Part of this Schedule) applies in relation to the general earnings as if—

     (*a*) section 809B of ITA 2007 (claim for remittance basis to apply) applied to the individual for the relevant tax year, and

     (*b*) section 22(7) or 26(6) of ITEPA 2003 were omitted.

(3) In relation to the general earnings, the definition of "foreign employer" in section 721(1) of ITEPA 2003 has effect as if at the end there were inserted "and not resident in the Republic of Ireland".

83—(1) This paragraph applies to an individual's relevant foreign income for the tax year 2007–08 or any earlier tax year ("the relevant tax year") if—

     (*a*) the individual made a claim under section 831 of ITTOIA 2005 for the relevant tax year, or

     (*b*) section 65(5) of ICTA (or any earlier superseded enactment corresponding to that provision) applied in relation to the individual for the relevant tax year.

(2) Section 832 of ITTOIA 2005 (as amended by this Part of this Schedule) applies in relation to the relevant foreign income as if section 809B of ITA 2007 (claim for remittance basis to apply) applied to the individual for the relevant tax year.

(3) But nothing in section 832 of ITTOIA 2005 applies in relation to any of the relevant foreign income that arose in the Republic of Ireland.

(4) Nothing in section 832A of that Act applies in relation to anything remitted to the United Kingdom in the tax year 2007–08 or any earlier tax year.

84—(1) This paragraph applies if section 12 of TCGA 1992 (or any corresponding superseded enactment) applied in relation to a gain accruing to an individual in the tax year 2007–08 or any earlier tax year ("the relevant tax year").

(2) Section 12 of TCGA 1992 (as amended by this Part of this Schedule) applies in relation to that gain as if section 809B of ITA 2007 (claim for remittance basis to apply) applied to the individual for the relevant tax year.

(3) Nothing in section 10A of TCGA 1992 applies in relation to any part of the gain remitted to the United Kingdom in the tax year 2007–08 or any earlier tax year.

85—(1) In section 809E(3)(*b*) of ITA 2007, the reference to a tax year for which section 809B, 809D or 809E of that Act applies to an individual includes a tax year (not later than the tax year 2007–08) in which the individual—

     (*a*) was UK resident, but

     (*b*) was not domiciled in the United Kingdom or was not ordinarily UK resident.

(2) In relation to such a tax year, the reference there to the individual's foreign income and gains includes the individual's relevant foreign income if (and only if)—

     (*a*) the individual made a claim under section 831 of ITTOIA 2005 for the year, or

     (*b*) section 65(5) of ICTA (or any earlier superseded enactment corresponding to that provision) applied in relation to the individual for the year.

86—(1) Section 809L of ITA 2007 (meaning of "remitted to the United Kingdom") has effect subject to this paragraph.

(2) If, before 6 April 2008, property (including money) consisting of or deriving from an individual's relevant foreign income was brought to or received or used in the United Kingdom by or for the benefit of a relevant person, treat the relevant foreign income as not remitted to the United Kingdom on or after that date (if it otherwise would be regarded as so remitted).

(3) If, before 12 March 2008, property (other than money) consisting of or deriving from an individual's relevant foreign income was acquired by a relevant person, treat the relevant foreign income as not remitted to the United Kingdom on or after 6 April 2008 (if it otherwise would be regarded as so remitted).

(4) Subject to sub-paragraphs (2) and (3), in relation to an individual's income and chargeable gains for the tax year 2007–08 or any earlier tax year, section 809L has effect as if the references to a relevant person were to the individual.

[(4A) For the purposes of sub-paragraph (4), section 648(2) to (5) of ITTOIA 2005 (and corresponding earlier enactments) do not apply (so that relevant foreign income which arose under a settlement in the tax year 2007–08 or any earlier tax year is to be treated as income for the tax year in which it arose).][1]

(5) "Money" has the same meaning as in section 809Y of ITA 2007.

Amendments—[1]   Sub-s (4A) inserted by FA 2009 s 51, Sch 27 para 14 with effect for the tax year 2008–09 and subsequent tax years.

87   Section 809N of ITA 2007 (section 809L: gift recipients, qualifying property and enjoyment) has effect in relation to an individual's income and chargeable gains for the tax year 2007–08 or any earlier tax year as if—

    (*a*)   the reference in subsection (2) to a relevant person were to the individual,

    (*b*)   subsections (3) and (4) were omitted, and

    (*c*)   the references in subsection (9) to a relevant person, all relevant persons, or relevant persons were to the individual.

88   Section 809O of ITA 2007 (section 809L: dealings where there is a connected operation) has effect in relation to an individual's income and chargeable gains for the tax year 2007–08 or any earlier tax year as if—

    (*a*)   subsection (2) were omitted, and

    (*b*)   the references in subsections (4) and (6) to a relevant person, all relevant persons, or relevant persons were to the individual.

89   Sections 809Q to 809S of ITA 2007 (transfers from mixed funds) do not apply for the purposes of determining whether income or chargeable gains for the tax year 2007–08 or any earlier tax year are remitted to the United Kingdom (or the amount of any such income or chargeable gains so remitted).

90—(1) This paragraph applies if—

    (*a*)   before 12 March 2008, money was lent to an individual outside the United Kingdom,

    (*b*)   the loan was made for the purpose of enabling the individual to acquire an interest in residential property in the United Kingdom (and for no other purpose), and

    (*c*)   before 6 April 2008—

       (i)   the money was received in the United Kingdom,

       (ii)   the individual used the money to acquire an interest in residential property in the United Kingdom ("the interest"), and

       (iii) repayment of the debt for the money ("the debt"), or of payments made under a guarantee of that repayment ("the guarantee"), was secured on the interest.

(2) Relevant foreign income of the individual used outside the United Kingdom before 6 April 2028 to pay interest on the debt is treated as not remitted to the United Kingdom.

(3) If, at any time on or after 12 March 2008—

    (*a*)   any term upon which the loan was made, or any term of the guarantee, is varied or waived,

    (*b*)   repayment of the debt, or of payments made under the guarantee, ceases to be secured on the interest,

    (*c*)   repayment of any other debt is secured on the interest or is guaranteed by the guarantee, or

    (*d*)   the interest ceases to be owned by the individual,

sub-paragraph (2) does not apply in relation to relevant foreign income used as mentioned there after that time.

(4) If—

    (*a*)   before 12 March 2008, money was lent to the individual outside the United Kingdom ("the subsequent loan"),

    (*b*)   the subsequent loan was made for the purpose of enabling the individual to repay—

       (i)   the loan mentioned in sub-paragraph (1), or

      (ii) another loan in relation to which sub-paragraphs (2) and (3) apply (by virtue of this sub-paragraph),

   and for no other purpose, and

  (c) before 6 April 2008—

      (i) the individual used the money to repay the loan referred to in paragraph (b)(i) or (ii), and

      (ii) repayment of the subsequent loan, or of payments made under a guarantee of that repayment, was secured on the interest,

sub-paragraphs (2) and (3) apply in relation to the subsequent loan (and for this purpose references there to the debt or the loan are to be read as references to the subsequent loan).

(5) In this paragraph "residential property" has the same meaning as in Part 4 of FA 2003 (see section 116 of that Act).

(6) In this paragraph "guarantee" includes an indemnity, and "guaranteed" is to be read accordingly.

91—(1) This paragraph applies in relation to employment-related securities if—

  (a) the date of the acquisition is on or after 6 April 2008 and on or before 31 July 2008, and

  (b) Chapter 2 of Part 7 of ITEPA 2003 (restricted securities) applies in relation to the securities by virtue only of amendments made by this Schedule.

(2) Section 431 of ITEPA 2003 (election for full or partial disapplication of Chapter) has effect in relation to the employment-related securities as if in subsection (5)(b) for "more than 14 days after the acquisition" there were substituted "after 14 August 2008".

PART 2

NON-RESIDENT COMPANIES AND TRUSTS ETC

Offshore income gains

97   *(inserts* ITA 2007 s 734(5))

Offshore income gains: commencement etc

98   The amendments made by paragraphs 92 to 97 have effect for the tax year 2008–09 and subsequent tax years.

99   Paragraphs 120 and 121 apply in relation to offshore income gains as if—

  (a) references to section 2(2) amounts were to OIG amounts,

  (b) references to chargeable gains were to offshore income gains, and

  (c) Step 1 of paragraph 120(2) provided that OIG amounts are to be calculated in accordance with—

      (i) section 762(2) of ICTA (the reference in the second sentence of that Step to section 87(4) of TCGA 1992 being read as a reference to section 762(2) of ICTA), or

      (ii) section 87(5) of TCGA 1992 as applied by section 762(3) of ICTA.

100—(1) This paragraph applies if—

  (a) by virtue of section 87 or 89(2) of, or Schedule 4C to, TCGA 1992 as applied by [regulation 20 of the Offshore Funds (Tax) Regulations 2009 (SI 2009/3001)]¹, income is treated under [such regulations (regulation 17 of those Regulations]¹ as arising to an individual in the tax year 2008–09 or any subsequent tax year, and

  (b) the individual is not domiciled in the United Kingdom in that year.

(2) The individual is not charged to income tax on the income if and to the extent that it is treated as arising by reason of—

  (a) a capital payment received (or treated as received) by the individual before 6 April 2008, or

  (b) the matching of any capital payment with the OIG amount for the tax year 2007–08 or any earlier tax year.

Amendments—¹   In sub-para (1)(a), words substituted for words "section 762 of ICTA" and words "section 761 of ICTA", by the Offshore Funds (Tax) Regulations, SI 2009/3001 reg 130(1), (2) with effect for the purposes of income tax for the tax year 2009–10 and subsequent tax years and for distributions made on or after 1 December 2009; for the purposes of corporation tax, on income, for accounting periods ending on or after 1 December 2009 and for distributions made on or after that date and, on chargeable gains, in relation to disposals made on or after 1 December 2009; and for the purposes of capital gains tax, in relation to disposals made on or after 1 December 2009.

101—(1) This paragraph applies if—

  (a) the trustees of a settlement have made an election under paragraph 126(1) (re-basing election),

  (b) income is treated under [regulation 17 of the Offshore Funds (Tax) Regulations 2009 (SI 2009/3001)]¹ as arising to an individual in the tax year 2008–09 or any subsequent tax year ("the relevant tax year") by reason of the matching, under section 87A of TCGA 1992 as applied by [regulation 20 of those Regulations][1], of an OIG amount with a capital payment received by the individual from the trustees, and

    (c) the individual is resident or ordinarily resident, but not domiciled, in the United Kingdom in the relevant tax year.

(2) The individual is not charged to income tax on so much of the income as exceeds the relevant proportion of that income.

(3) Sub-paragraphs (9) to (18) of paragraph 126 (meaning of "the relevant proportion") apply for the purposes of sub-paragraph (2) above as if—

    (a) references to section 2(2) amounts were to OIG amounts,

    (b) references to chargeable gains were to offshore income gains,

    (c) references to allowable losses were omitted, and

    (d) references to anything accruing were to it arising (and similar references were read accordingly).

Amendments—[1]   In sub-para (1)(*b*), words substituted for words "section 761 of ICTA" and "section 762 of ICTA", by the Offshore Funds (Tax) Regulations, SI 2009/3001 reg 130(1), (3) with effect for the purposes of income tax for the tax year 2009–10 and subsequent tax years and for distributions made on or after 1 December 2009; for the purposes of corporation tax, on income, for accounting periods ending on or after 1 December 2009 and for distributions made on or after that date and, on chargeable gains, in relation to disposals made on or after 1 December 2009; and for the purposes of capital gains tax, in relation to disposals made on or after 1 December 2009.

102—(1) This paragraph applies if—

    (a) in the tax year 2008–09 or any subsequent tax year, the trustees of a settlement ("the transferor settlement") transfer all or part of the settled property to the trustees of another settlement ("the transferee settlement"),

    (b) section 90 of TCGA 1992 applies in relation to the transfer,

    (c) the trustees of the transferor settlement have made an election under paragraph 126(1),

    (d) by virtue of the matching (under section 87A of TCGA 1992 as applied by [regulation 20 of the Offshore Funds (Tax) Regulations 2009 (SI 2009/3001)][1]) of a capital payment with an OIG amount of the transferee settlement, income is treated under [such regulations (regulation 17 of those Regulations][1] as arising to an individual in a tax year ("the relevant tax year"), and

    (e) the individual is resident or ordinarily resident, but not domiciled, in the United Kingdom in the relevant tax year.

(2) If paragraph 101 applies in relation to the transferee settlement, paragraph 126(9) as applied by paragraph 101(3) has effect as if the reference there to relevant assets included relevant assets within the meaning of paragraph 127(4) (as modified by sub-paragraph (4)(*b*) below).

(3) If paragraph 101 does not apply in relation to the transferee settlement, the individual is not charged to income tax on so much of the income mentioned in sub-paragraph (1)(*d*) above as exceeds the relevant proportion of that income.

(4) Sub-paragraphs (4) to (7) of paragraph 127 (meaning of "the relevant proportion") apply for the purposes of sub-paragraph (3) above as if—

    (a) references section 2(2) amounts were to OIG amounts,

    (b) references to chargeable gains were to offshore income gains, and

    (c) references to anything accruing were to it arising.

Amendments—[1]   In sub-para (1)(*d*), words substituted for words "section 762 of ICTA" and words "section 761 of ICTA", by the Offshore Funds (Tax) Regulations, SI 2009/3001 reg 130(1), (3) with effect for the purposes of income tax for the tax year 2009–10 and subsequent tax years and for distributions made on or after 1 December 2009; for the purposes of corporation tax, on income, for accounting periods ending on or after 1 December 2009 and for distributions made on or after that date and, on chargeable gains, in relation to disposals made on or after 1 December 2009; and for the purposes of capital gains tax, in relation to disposals made on or after 1 December 2009.

Attribution of gains to members of non-resident companies

103   In section 13(2) of TCGA 1992 (attribution of gains to members of non-resident companies), for the words from ", who, if" to "and who" substitute "and".

104   (*inserts* TCGA 1992 s 14A)

105   The amendments made by paragraphs 103 and 104 have effect in relation to chargeable gains accruing on or after 6 April 2008.

Attribution of gains to beneficiaries

106   TCGA 1992 is amended as follows.

107   (*amends* TCGA 1992 s 85(11))

108   (*substitutes* TCGA 1992 ss 87–87C)

109—(1) Section 88 (gains of dual resident settlements) is amended as follows.
(2) (*substitutes* TCGA 1992 s 88(2))
(3) Omit subsection (7).

110—(1) Section 89 (migrant settlements) is amended as follows.
(2) (*amends* TCGA 1992 s 89(1))
(3) (*substitutes* TCGA 1992 s 89(1A)–(4))

111   (*substitutes* TCGA 1992 ss 90, 90A)

112—(1) Section 91 (increase in tax payable under section 87 or 89(2)) is amended as follows.
(2) (*substitutes* TCGA 1992 s 91(1), (1A))
(3) (*amends* TCGA 1992 s 91(5)(*a*))
(4) Omit subsection (8).

113   Omit sections 92 to 95 (matching).

114   Omit—
  (*a*) in FA 1998, section 130(1) and (4), and paragraph 6(3) and (4) of Schedule 21,
  (*b*) in FA 2002, paragraph 6 of Schedule 11,
  (*c*) in FA 2003, section 163(3), and
  (*d*) in FA 2006, paragraphs 34(2)(*d*) and 36(2)(*a*) of Schedule 12.

Attribution of gains to beneficiaries: commencement etc

115   The amendments made by paragraphs 106 to 114 have effect for the tax year 2008–09 and subsequent tax years.

116   For the purposes of sections 87 and 87A of TCGA 1992, no account is to be taken of—
  (*a*) any capital payment received before 10 March 1981, or
  (*b*) any capital payment received on or after that date but before 6 April 1984, so far as it represents a chargeable gain which accrued to the trustees before 6 April 1981.

117   In the application of section 87 of TCGA 1992 for a tax year by virtue of section 88, no account is to be taken of any capital payment received before 6 April 1991.

118—(1) This paragraph applies if—
  (*a*) section 87 of TCGA 1992 applies to a settlement for the tax year 2008–09 or any subsequent tax year ("the tax year"),
  (*b*) the settlement was made before 17 March 1998,
  (*c*) none of the settlors fulfilled the residence requirements when the settlement was made, and
  (*d*) none of the settlors fulfils the residence requirements in the tax year.
(2) For the purposes of that section as it applies to the settlement for the tax year, no account is to be taken of—
  (*a*) any gains or losses accruing to the trustees of the settlement before 17 March 1998, or
  (*b*) any capital payments received before that date.
(3) A settlor "fulfils the residence requirements" when the settlor is—
  (*a*) resident or ordinarily resident in the United Kingdom, and
  (*b*) domiciled in any part of the United Kingdom.

119   Section 87C of TCGA 1992 does not apply in relation to any capital payment received before 6 April 2008.

120   (1) This paragraph applies to a settlement if section 87 or 89(2) of TCGA 1992 applied to it for the tax year 2007–08 or any earlier tax year.
(2) The following steps are to be taken for the purposes of calculating the section 2(2) amount for the settlement for the tax year 2007–08 and earlier tax years.
Step 1
Calculate (in accordance with section 87 and, where appropriate, section 88) the section 2(2) amount for the settlement for the tax year 2007–08 and earlier tax years.
For this purpose, references in section 87(4) and (5) of TCGA 1992 (as substituted) to section 87 of that Act applying to a settlement for a tax year are to be read as references to section 87 of that Act (as it had effect before that substitution) applying to a settlement for a tax year.
Step 2
Find the total amount of chargeable gains treated under section 87 or 89(2) as accruing to beneficiaries of the settlement in the tax year 2007–08 or any earlier tax year ("the total deemed gains").

Step 3

Find the earliest tax year for which the section 2(2) amount is not nil.

If the section 2(2) amount for that year is less than or equal to the total deemed gains, reduce that section 2(2) amount to nil.

Otherwise, reduce that section 2(2) amount by the amount of the total deemed gains.

Step 4

Reduce the total deemed gains by the amount by which the section 2(2) amount was reduced under Step 3.

Step 5

If the total deemed gains is not nil, start again at Step 3.

For this purpose, read references to the earliest tax year for which the section 2(2) amount is not nil as references to the earliest tax year—

    (a) which is after the last tax year for which Steps 3 and 4 have been undertaken, and

    (b) for which the section 2(2) amount is not nil.

(3) If, before 6 April 2008, the trustees of the settlement made a transfer of value to which Schedule 4B to TCGA 1992 applied, sub-paragraph (2) has effect subject to such modifications as are just and reasonable on account of Schedule 4C to that Act having applied in relation to the settlement.

(4) This paragraph does not apply if section 90 of TCGA 1992 applied to a transfer of settled property by or to the trustees of the settlement that was made before 6 April 2008 (see paragraph 121).

Modification—FA 2008 Sch 7 para 99 (modification of this para in relation to offshore income gains)

121—(1) If section 90 of TCGA 1992 (as originally enacted) applied to a transfer of settled property made before 6 April 2008, this paragraph applies in relation to the transferor settlement and the transferee settlement.

(2) In this paragraph "the year of transfer" means the tax year in which the transfer occurred.

(3) The following steps are to be taken for the purpose of calculating the section 2(2) amount for the transferor and transferee settlements for the tax year 2007–08 and earlier tax years.

Step 1

Take the steps in paragraph 120(2) for the purpose of calculating the section 2(2) amount (at the end of the year of transfer) for the transferor settlement for the year of transfer and earlier tax years.

For this purpose, read references there to the tax year 2007–08 as references to the year of transfer.

Step 2

Take the steps in paragraph 120(2) for the purpose of calculating the section 2(2) amount (before the year of transfer) for the transferee settlement for the tax year before the year of transfer and earlier tax years.

For this purpose, read references there to the tax year 2007–08 as references to the tax year before the year of transfer.

Step 3

Calculate the section 2(2) amount for the transferee settlement for the year of transfer.

Step 4

Treat the section 2(2) amount for the transferee settlement for the year of transfer or any earlier tax year (as calculated under Step 2 or 3) as increased by—

    (a) the section 2(2) amount for the transferor settlement for that year (as calculated under Step 1), or

    (b) if part only of the settled property was transferred, the relevant proportion of the amount mentioned in paragraph (a).

    "The relevant proportion" here has the same meaning as in section 90(4) of TCGA 1992 (as substituted by this Schedule).

Step 5

Treat the section 2(2) amount for the transferor settlement for any tax year as reduced by the amount by which the section 2(2) amount for the transferee settlement for that year is increased under Step 4.

Step 6

Take the steps in paragraph 120(2) for the purpose of calculating the section 2(2) amount for the transferor settlement for the tax year 2007–08 and earlier tax years.

For this purpose—

    (a) treat the section 2(2) amount for the year of transfer or any earlier tax year as the amount calculated by taking Steps 1 and 5 above, and

    (b) reduce the total deemed gains by the amount of the total deemed gains calculated by taking Step 1 above.

Step 7

Take the steps in paragraph 120(2) for the purpose of calculating the section 2(2) amount for the transferee settlement for the tax year 2007–08 and earlier tax years.

For this purpose—

(a) treat the section 2(2) amount for the year of transfer or any earlier tax year as the amount calculated by taking Steps 2 to 4 above, and

(b) reduce the total deemed gains by the amount of the total deemed gains calculated by taking Step 2 above.

(4) This paragraph applies with any necessary modifications in relation to a settlement as respects which more than one relevant transfer was made.

(5) In sub-paragraph (4) "relevant transfer" means a transfer—

(a) made before 6 April 2008, and

(b) to which section 90 of TCGA 1992 applied.

(6) If, before 6 April 2008, the trustees of the transferor or transferee settlement made a transfer of value to which Schedule 4B to TCGA 1992 applied, this paragraph has effect subject to such modifications as are just and reasonable on account of Schedule 4C to that Act having applied in relation to the settlement.

Modification—FA 2008 Sch 7 para 99 (modification of this para in relation to offshore income gains)

122—(1) If all of a capital payment would (in the tax year 2008–09) have been left out of account by virtue of section 87(6) of TCGA 1992 as originally enacted, the amount of that capital payment is reduced to nil.

(2) If part of a capital payment would (in the tax year 2008–09) have been left out of account by virtue of section 87(6) of TCGA 1992 as originally enacted, the amount of that capital payment is reduced by the amount of that part.

(3) If—

(a) chargeable gains were treated under section 87 or 89(2) of, or paragraph 8 of Schedule 4C to, TCGA 1992 as accruing in the tax year 2007–08 or any earlier tax year to a beneficiary,

(b) more than one capital payment that the beneficiary had received was taken into account for the purposes of determining the amount of chargeable gains treated as accruing to the beneficiary, and

(c) the amount of those chargeable gains was less than the total amount of capital payments taken into account,

for the purposes of this paragraph treat section 87(6) of TCGA 1992 as originally enacted as having effect in relation to earlier capital payments before later ones.

(4) References in this paragraph to section 87(6) of TCGA 1992 include that provision as it would (but for the amendments made by this Schedule) have applied by virtue of section 762(3) of ICTA (offshore income gains).

(5) References in this paragraph to chargeable gains include offshore income gains.

123 Section 89(2) of TCGA 1992 as substituted applies to a settlement for the tax year 2008–09 (and subsequent tax years) if section 89(2) of that Act as originally enacted would (but for the amendments made by this Schedule) have applied to the settlement for the tax year 2008–09.

124—(1) This paragraph applies if—

(a) chargeable gains are treated under section 87 or 89(2) of TCGA 1992 as accruing to an individual in the tax year 2008–09 or any subsequent tax year, and

(b) the individual is not domiciled in the United Kingdom in that year.

(2) The individual is not charged to capital gains tax on the chargeable gains if and to the extent that they are treated as accruing by reason of—

(a) a capital payment received (or treated as received) by the individual before 6 April 2008, or

(b) the matching of any capital payment with the section 2(2) amount for the tax year 2007–08 or any earlier tax year.

125—(1) This paragraph applies in relation to a settlement for the tax year 2008–09 or any subsequent tax year ("the relevant tax year") if—

(a) an individual who was resident or ordinarily resident, but not domiciled, in the United Kingdom in the tax year 2007–08 received a capital payment from the trustees of the settlement on or after 12 March 2008 but before 6 April 2008, and

(b) the individual is resident or ordinarily resident, but not domiciled, in the United Kingdom in the relevant tax year.

(2) For the purposes of sections 87 to 89 of TCGA 1992 as they apply in relation to the settlement for the relevant tax year, no account is to be taken of the capital payment.

126—(1) The following provisions apply to a settlement if—

(a) section 87 applies to the settlement for the tax year 2008–09, and (*b*) the trustees of the settlement have made an election under this sub-paragraph.

(2) An election under sub-paragraph (1) may only be made on or before the first 31 January to occur after the end of the first tax year (beginning with the tax year 2008–09) in which an event within either of the following paragraphs occurs—

(*a*) a capital payment is received (or treated as received) by a beneficiary of the settlement, and the beneficiary is resident in the United Kingdom in the tax year in which it is received, and

(*b*) the trustees transfer all or part of the settled property to the trustees of another settlement, and section 90 of TCGA 1992 applies in relation to the transfer.

(3) For a tax year as respects which the settlement has a Schedule 4C pool, the reference in sub-paragraph (2)(*a*) above to a capital payment received (or treated as received) by a beneficiary of the settlement is to be read as a capital payment received (or treated as received) by a beneficiary of a relevant settlement from the trustees of a relevant settlement.

(4) Paragraph 8A of that Schedule (relevant settlements) applies for the purposes of sub-paragraph (3) above.

(5) An election under sub-paragraph (1) is irrevocable.

(6) An election under that sub-paragraph must be made in the way and form specified by the Commissioners for Her Majesty's Revenue and Customs.

(7) Sub-paragraph (8) applies if—

(*a*) by virtue of the matching of a capital payment with the section 2(2) amount for the settlement for the tax year 2008–09 or any subsequent tax year ("the relevant tax year"), chargeable gains are treated under section 87 or 89(2) of, or paragraph 8 of Schedule 4C to, TCGA 1992 as accruing to an individual in a tax year, and

(*b*) the individual is resident, but not domiciled, in the United Kingdom in that year.

(8) The individual is not charged to capital gains tax on so much of the chargeable gains as exceeds the relevant proportion of those gains.

(9) The relevant proportion is—

$$\frac{A}{B}$$

where—

A is what would be the section 2(2) amount for the settlement for the relevant tax year, if immediately before 6 April 2008 every relevant asset had been sold by the trustees (or the company concerned) and immediately re-acquired by them (or it) at the market value at that time, and

B is the section 2(2) amount for the settlement for the relevant tax year.

(10) For the purposes of sub-paragraph (9) an asset is a "relevant asset" if—

(*a*) by reason of the asset, a chargeable gain or allowable loss accrues to the trustees in the relevant tax year, and

(*b*) the asset has been comprised in the settlement from the beginning of 6 April 2008 until the time of the event giving rise to the chargeable gain or allowable loss.

(11) For those purposes, an asset is also a "relevant asset" if—

(*a*) by reason of the asset, chargeable gains are treated under section 13 of TCGA 1992 as accruing to the trustees in the relevant tax year,

(*b*) the company to whom the chargeable gains actually accrue has owned the asset from the beginning of 6 April 2008 until the time of the event giving rise to those chargeable gains, and

(*c*) had the company disposed of the asset at any time in the relevant period, part of the chargeable gains (if any) accruing on the disposal would have been treated under section 13 of TCGA 1992 as accruing to the trustees.

(12) In sub-paragraph (11)(*c*) "the relevant period" means the period beginning at the beginning of 6 April 2008 and ending immediately before the event giving rise to the chargeable gains.

(13) If—

(*a*) by reason of an asset which would not otherwise be a relevant asset ("the new asset"), chargeable gains or allowable losses accrue, or are treated under section 13 as accruing, to the trustees in the relevant tax year,

(*b*) the value of the new asset derives wholly or in part from another asset ("the original asset"), and

(*c*) section 43 of TCGA 1992 applies in relation to the calculation of the chargeable gains or allowable losses,

the new asset (or part of that asset) is a "relevant asset" if the condition in sub-paragraph (10)(b) or the conditions in sub-paragraph (11)(b) and (c) would be met were the references there to the asset to be read as references to the new asset or the original asset.

(14) If—

    (*a*) on or after 6 April 2008, a company ("company A") disposes of an asset to another company ("company B"), and

    (*b*) section 171 of TCGA (transfers within groups) (as applied by section 14(2) of that Act) applies in relation to the disposal,

for the purposes of sub-paragraph (11) (and this sub-paragraph) treat company B as having owned the asset throughout the period when company A owned it.

(15) If an asset is a relevant asset by virtue of sub-paragraph (14), for the purposes of sub-paragraph (9)—

    (*a*) treat the chargeable gains as having accrued to the company which owned the asset at the beginning of 6 April 2008, and

    (*b*) treat the proportion of those chargeable gains attributable under section 13 of TCGA 1992 to the trustees as being the proportion of the chargeable gains actually accruing that are so attributable.

(16) If—

    (*a*) an asset would otherwise be a "relevant asset" within sub-paragraph (11), and

    (*b*) the proportion of chargeable gains treated under section 13 of TCGA 1992 as accruing to the trustees by reason of the asset ("the relevant proportion") is greater than the minimum proportion,

for the purposes of sub-paragraph (9) treat the appropriate proportion of the asset as a relevant asset and the rest of the asset as if it were not a relevant asset.

(17) "The minimum proportion" is the smallest proportion of chargeable gains (if any) that would have been attributable to the trustees on a disposal of the asset at any time in the relevant period (as defined by sub-paragraph (12)).

(18) "The appropriate proportion" is the minimum proportion divided by the relevant proportion.

Modifications—FA 2008 Sch 7 para 101 (Sub-paras (9)–(18) modified for the purposes of FA 2008 Sch 7 para 101(2) (no charge to income tax on income that exceeds the relevant proportion of that income)).

FA 2008 Sch 7 para 102 (modification of sub-para (9) to have effect as if the reference to relevant assets included relevant assets within the meaning of para 127(4) as modified).

127—(1) This paragraph applies if—

    (*a*) in the tax year 2008–09 or any subsequent tax year, the trustees of a settlement ("the transferor settlement") transfer all or part of the settled property to the trustees of another settlement ("the transferee settlement"),

    (*b*) section 90 of TCGA 1992 applies in relation to the transfer,

    (*c*) the trustees of the transferor settlement have made an election under paragraph 126(1),

    (*d*) by virtue of the matching of a capital payment with the section 2(2) amount for the transferee settlement for the tax year 2008–09 or any subsequent tax year ("the relevant tax year"), chargeable gains are treated under section 87 or 89(2) of, or paragraph 8 of Schedule 4C to, TCGA 1992 as accruing to an individual in a tax year, and

    (*e*) the individual is resident, but not domiciled, in the United Kingdom in that year.

(2) If the trustees of the transferee settlement have made an election under paragraph 126(1), paragraph 126(7) to (9) have effect in relation to the transferee settlement for that year as if the reference in paragraph 126(9) to relevant assets included relevant assets within the meaning of this paragraph.

(3) If the trustees of the transferee settlement have not made an election under paragraph 126(1), the individual is not charged to capital gains tax on so much of the chargeable gains mentioned in sub-paragraph (1)(*d*) above as exceeds the relevant proportion of those gains.

(4) The relevant proportion is—

$$\frac{A}{B}$$

where—

    A is what would be the section 2(2) amount for the transferee settlement for the relevant tax year, if immediately before 6 April 2008 every relevant asset had been sold by the company concerned and immediately re-acquired by it at the market value at that time, and

    B is the section 2(2) amount for the transferee settlement for the relevant tax year.

(5) For the purposes of this paragraph an asset is a "relevant asset" if—

    (*a*) by reason of the asset, chargeable gains are treated under section 13 of TCGA 1992 as accruing to the trustees of the transferee settlement in the relevant tax year,

    (*b*) the company to whom the chargeable gains actually accrue has owned the asset from the beginning of 6 April 2008 until the time of the event giving rise to those chargeable gains,

(c) had the company disposed of the asset at any time in the relevant period, part of the chargeable gains (if any) accruing on the disposal would have been treated under section 13 of TCGA 1992 as accruing to—

(i) the trustees of the transferor settlement (if the disposal had been made before the transfer), or

(ii) the trustees of the transferee settlement (if it had not).

(6) In sub-paragraph (5)(c) "the relevant period" means the period beginning at the beginning of 6 April 2008 and ending immediately before the event giving rise to the chargeable gains.

(7) Sub-paragraphs (13) to (18) of paragraph 126 apply for the purposes of this paragraph (with such modifications as are necessary) as they apply for the purposes of that paragraph.

Modification—FA 2008 Sch 7 para 102(4) (modification of sub-paras (4)–(7) in their application to Sch 7 para 101).

Attribution of gains to beneficiaries: cases involving transfers of value

128   TCGA 1992 is amended as follows.

129—(1) Section 85A (transfers of value: attribution of gains to beneficiaries and treatment of losses) is amended as follows.
(2) (*inserts* TCGA 1992 s 85A(2A))
(3) (*substitutes* TCGA 1992 s 85A(3))

130   (*substitutes* TCGA 1992 Sch 4B para 3(4), (5))

131   Schedule 4C (transfers of value: attribution of gains to beneficiaries) is amended as follows.

132   (*substitutes* TCGA 1992 Sch 4C para 1(2)–(3A))

133   (*inserts* TCGA 1992 Sch 4C para1A)

134   (*amends* TCGA 1992 Sch 4C para 4(2))

135   (*amends* TCGA 1992 Sch 4C para 5(2)(a))

136   Omit paragraph 7A (and the heading before it).

137   (*substitutes* TCGA 1992 Sch 4C para 7B)

138   (*substitutes* TCGA 1992 Sch 4C para 8)

139   (*inserts* TCGA 1992 Sch 4C para 8AA)

140   Omit paragraphs 8B and 8C (including the heading before paragraph 8B).

141   (*substitutes* TCGA 1992 Sch 4C para 9)

142   (*amends* TCGA 1992 Sch 4C para 10(1), *repeals* para 10(2), (3))

143—(1) Paragraph 12 (attribution of gains to settlor in section 10A cases) is amended as follows.
(2) (*substitutes* TCGA 1992 Sch 4C para 12(1), (2))

144   In paragraph 12A(3), for "87(4)" substitute "87(2)".

145—(1) Paragraph 13 (increase in tax payable under this Schedule) is amended as follows.
(2) (*substitutes* TCGA 1992 Sch 4C para 13(1), (1A))
(3) (*amends* TCGA 1992 Sch 4C para 13(5)(a))

146   Omit paragraph 3 and 6(2) and (3) of Schedule 29 to FA 2003.

Attribution of gains to beneficiaries in cases involving transfers of value: commencement etc

147   The amendments made by paragraphs 128 to 146 have effect in relation to transfers of value to which Schedule 4B to TCGA 1992 applies that are made on or after 6 April 2008.

148   For the purposes of paragraph 8 of Schedule 4C to TCGA 1992 (and section 87A of that Act as it applies for the purposes of that paragraph), no account is to be taken of any capital payment received before 21 March 2000.

149   A capital payment received before 6 April 2008 is not within paragraph 9(4) of Schedule 4C to TCGA 1992 (if it otherwise would be).

150   Paragraph 124 applies in relation to chargeable gains treated under paragraph 8 of Schedule 4C to TCGA 1992 as accruing as it applies in relation to chargeable gains treated under section 87 as accruing.

151—(1) This paragraph applies for the tax year 2008–09 or any subsequent tax year ("the relevant tax year") if—

(a) an individual who was resident or ordinarily resident, but not domiciled, in the United Kingdom in the tax year 2007–08 received a capital payment from the trustees of a settlement on or after 12 March 2008 but before 6 April 2008, and

(b) the individual is resident or ordinarily resident, but not domiciled, in the United Kingdom in the relevant tax year.

(2) For the purposes of paragraph 8 of Schedule 4C to TCGA 1992 as it applies for the relevant tax year (and section 87A of that Act as it applies for those purposes), no account is to be taken of the capital payment.

Attribution of gains to beneficiaries: existing Schedule 4C pools

152 Schedule 4C to TCGA 1992 (as it has effect without the amendments made by paragraphs 128 to 146) applies for the tax year 2008–09 and subsequent tax years in relation to Schedule 4C pools created before 6 April 2008 ("existing Schedule 4C pools") as if paragraphs 7B and 9(2) were omitted.

153 Any reduction in the amount of a capital payment has effect for the purposes of Schedule 4C to TCGA 1992 as it applies in relation to existing Schedule 4C pools (as well as for other purposes).

154—(1) If all of a capital payment ceases (in the tax year 2008–09 or any subsequent tax year) to be available, the amount of the capital payment is reduced to nil.

(2) If part of a capital payment ceases (in the tax year 2008–09 or any subsequent tax year) to be available, the amount of the capital payment is reduced by the amount of that part.

(3) A capital payment "ceases to be available" in a tax year if and to the extent that, by reason of the capital payment, chargeable gains are treated under paragraph 8 of Schedule 4C to TCGA 1992 (as it has effect in relation to existing Schedule 4C pools) as accruing in that year to the recipient.

(4) If—

(a) chargeable gains are treated under paragraph 8 of Schedule 4C to TCGA 1992 (as it has effect in relation to existing Schedule 4C pools) as accruing in a tax year,

(b) more than one capital payment that the beneficiary has received is taken into account for the purposes of determining the amount of chargeable gains treated as accruing to the beneficiary, and

(c) the amount of the chargeable gains is less than the total amount of capital payments taken into account,

sub-paragraph (3) applies in relation to earlier capital payments before later ones.

155 In any tax year—

(a) Schedule 4C to TCGA 1992 (as amended by paragraphs 128 to 146) applies in relation to a settlement before that Schedule (as it has effect without those amendments) applies in relation to the settlement, and

(b) that Schedule (as it has effect without those amendments) applies in relation to the settlement before section 87 or 89(2) of that Act applies in relation to the settlement.

Transfers of securities: accrued income profits

156 (*inserts* ITTOIA 2005 s 830(4)(*h*))

157 (*inserts* ITA 2007 s 617(7))

158 Omit section 644 of that Act (accrued income profits: individuals to whom remittance basis applies).

159 (*inserts* ITA 2007 s 670A)

160 The amendments made by paragraphs 156 to 159 have effect in relation to transfers of securities where the settlement day is on or after 6 April 2008.

Transfers of assets abroad

161 (*amends* TMA 1970 s 46B(4)(*c*))

162 (*inserts* ITTOIA 2005 s 830(4)(*i*))

163 ITA 2007 is amended as follows.

164 (*amends* ITA 2007 s 720(4))

165 (*substitutes* ITA 2007 s 726)

166 (*inserts* ITA 2007 s 727(3A))

[**167**   (*substituted* ITA 2007 s 730, *repealed by* the Transfer of Tribunal Functions and Revenue and Customs Appeals Order, SI 2009/56 art 3, Sch 1 para 470 with effect from 1 April 2009*)*

168   (*inserts* ITA 2007 s 731(2A))

169   (*substitutes* ITA 2007 ss 735, 735A)

170   The amendments made by paragraphs 161 to 169 have effect for the tax year 2008–09 and subsequent tax years.

General

171   For the purposes of this Part of this Schedule, the market value of any asset is its market value for the purposes of TCGA 1992.

[**172**   (1) Sub-paragraph (2) has effect for the purposes of—
paragraphs 100(1)(*b*), 101(1)(*c*) and 102(1)(*e*),
paragraph (*b*) of paragraph 118(3) so far as having effect for the purposes of paragraph 118(1)(*d*), and
paragraphs 124(1)(*b*), 126(7)(*b*), 127(1)(*e*) and 151(1)(*b*).
(2) An individual not domiciled in the United Kingdom at a time in the tax year 2017-18, or a later tax year, is to be regarded as domiciled in the United Kingdom at that time if—
   (*a*) the individual was born in the United Kingdom,
   (*b*) the individual's domicile of origin was in the United Kingdom, and
   (*c*) the individual is resident in the United Kingdom for the tax year concerned.][1]

Amendments—[1]   Paragraph 172 inserted by F(No 2)A 2017 s 29(2), Sch 8 para 40 with effect from 16 November 2017.

SCHEDULE 11
VENTURE CAPITAL SCHEMES
Section 32
Corporate Venturing Scheme

1   Part 3 of Schedule 15 to FA 2000 (CVS: the issuing company) is amended as follows.

2   In paragraph 26 (excluded activities)—
   (*a*) (*inserts* FA 2000 Sch 15 para 26(1)(*ha*)–(*hc*))
   (*b*) (*inserts* FA 2000 Sch 15 para 26(2) entries)

3   (*inserts* FA 2000 Sch 15 paras 30A–30C)

Enterprise Investment Scheme

4   Chapter 4 of Part 5 of ITA 2007 (EIS: the issuing company) is amended as follows.

5   In section 192 (meaning of "excluded activities")—
   (*a*) (*inserts* ITA 2007 s 192(1)(*ia*)–(*ic*))
   (*b*) (*inserts* ITA 2007 s 192(2)(*da*)–(*dc*))

6   (*inserts* ITA 2007 ss 196A–196C)

Venture capital trusts

7   Chapter 4 of Part 6 of ITA 2007 (VCTs: qualifying holdings) is amended as follows.

8   In section 303 (meaning of "excluded activities")—
   (*a*) (*inserts* ITA 2007 s 303(1)(*ia*)–(*ic*))
   (*b*) (*inserts* ITA 2007 s 303(2)(*da*)–(*dc*))

9   (*inserts* ITA 2007 ss 307A–307C)

Commencement

10   The amendments made by this Schedule are treated as having come into force on 6 April 2008.

11   But the amendments made by paragraphs 2, 3, 5 and 6 do not have effect in relation to shares issued before that date.

12   And the amendments made by paragraphs 8 and 9 do not have effect in relation to—
   (*a*) a relevant holding issued before that date, or

(b) a relevant holding acquired by a company ("the investing company") [before 6 April 2018][1] by means of the investment of protected money.

Amendments—[1] In sub-para (b), words inserted by FA 2018 s 17, Sch 5 para 10 with effect from 6 April 2018 (by virtue of SI 2018/931 reg 4(e)).

13 For the purposes of paragraph 12(b) "protected money" is—

(a) money raised by the issue before that date of shares in or securities of the investing company, or

(b) money derived from the investment of such money.

SCHEDULE 12

TAX CREDIT FOR CERTAIN FOREIGN DISTRIBUTIONS

Section 34

PART 1

THE TAX CREDIT

1 Chapter 3 of Part 4 of ITTOIA 2005 (dividends etc from UK resident companies etc) is amended as follows.

2 (*amends* ITTOIA 2005 Pt 4 Ch 3 heading)

3 (*amended* ITTOIA 2005 s 397 heading; *repealed by* FA 2016 s 5, Sch 1 para 64)

4 (*inserts* ITTOIA 2005 ss 397A–397C)

PART 2

CONSEQUENTIAL PROVISION

TMA 1970

7 TMA 1970 is amended as follows.

ITTOIA 2005

17 ITTOIA 2005 is amended as follows.

18 (*amends* ITTOIA 2005 s 403(1))

21 (*inserts* ITTOIA 2005 s 408(2A))

22 (*amends* ITTOIA 2005 s 688(1))

ITA 2007

23 ITA 2007 is amended as follows.

24 (*inserted* ITA 2007 s 425(5)(c); *repealed by* FA 2016 s 5, Sch 1 para 64)

27—(1) Section 592 (no tax credits for borrower under stock lending arrangement) is amended as follows.
(2) (amends ITA 2007 s 592(1))
(3) (amends ITA 2007 s 592(2))
Amendments—Sub-paras (2)(a), (c), (3) repealed by FA 2013 s 77, Sch 29 para 33(1), (2) with effect from 1 January 2014.

28—(1) Section 593 (no tax credits for interim holder under repo) is amended as follows.
(2) (*amends* ITA 2007 s 593(1))
(3) (amends ITA 2007 s 593(2))
Amendments—Sub-paras (2)(a), (c), (3) repealed by FA 2013 s 77, Sch 29 para 33(1), (2) with effect from 1 January 2014.

29—(1) Section 594 (no tax credits for original owner under repo) is amended as follows.
(2) (*amends* ITA 2007 s 594(1))
(3) (amends ITA 2007 s 594(2))
Amendments—Sub-paras (2)(a), (c)(i), (d), (3) repealed by FA 2013 s 77, Sch 29 para 33(1), (2) with effect from 1 January 2014.

31 (*amended* ITA 2007 s 989; *repealed by* FA 2016 s 5, Sch 1 para 64)

SCHEDULE 14

COMPANY GAINS FROM INVESTMENT LIFE
INSURANCE CONTRACTS: CONSEQUENTIAL AMENDMENTS ETC

Section 36

ICTA

1   ICTA is amended as follows.

3   Omit sections 539 to 551A (corporation tax in respect of gains arising in connection with life policies etc).

4—(1) Section 552 (information: duty of insurers) is amended as follows.
(2) (*amends* TA 1988 s 552(3))
(3) (*amends* TA 1988 s 552(5))
(4) (*amends* TA 1988 s 552(6))
(5) (*amends* TA 1988 s 552(7))
(6) (*amends* TA 1988 s 552(8)(*c*))
(7) (*amends* TA 1988 s 552(9))
(8) (*amends* TA 1988 s 552(10))
(9) (*repeals* TA 1988 s 552(11))
(10) (*amends* TA 1988 s 552(13))

5   (*amends* TA 1988 s 552ZA(3))

6   (*amends* TA 1988 s 552A(12))

7   Omit sections 553 to 553C (further provisions about corporation tax in respect of gains arising in connection with life policies etc).

8   Omit sections 656 to 658 (purchased life annuities).

9   In paragraph 20 of Schedule 15 (qualifying policies)—
(*a*) (*amends* TA 1988 Sch 15 para 20(1)(*a*))
(*b*) (*amends* TA 1988 Sch 15 para 20(3))

ITTOIA 2005

10   ITTOIA 2005 is amended as follows.

11   (*substitutes* ITTOIA 2005 s 467(5)(*c*))

12   (*amends* ITTOIA 2005 s 469(2))

13   (*repeals* ITTOIA 2005 s 486)

14   (*repeals* ITTOIA 2005 s 501(1)(*c*), (4))

15   (*repeals* ITTOIA 2005 s 541B(7)(*b*))

16   (*repeals* ITTOIA 2005 Sch 1 paras 210 to 221, 226 to 228)

Other Acts

17   (*repeals* FA 1989 s 90, Sch 9; FA 1991 s 76(1); F(No 2)A 1992 Sch 9 para 15; FA 1995 s 55(8); FA 1996 s 168(4) to (6), Sch 9 para 1A; FA 1997 s 79; FA 1998 ss 88, 89, Sch 14 paras 1–4; FA 1999 s 80, Sch 4 paras 16, 18(3); FA 2000 s 46(2A) words; FA 2001 s 83(2), Sch 28 Pt 1; FA 2002 s 87, Sch 25 para 21; FA 2003 s 171, Sch 34; FA 2004 Sch 35 paras 25, 27; ITTOIA 2005 s 473(2)(b); Sch 1 paras 268(1), (2), 269, 493, Sch 2 para 86(3); ITA 2007 Sch 1 paras 111, 141; FA 2007 s 29(1), Sch 7 paras 45, 46)

Commencement

18—(1) The amendments made by this Schedule—
(*a*) so far as relating to corporation tax, have effect for accounting periods beginning on or after 1 April 2008, and
(*b*) so far as relating to income tax, have effect for the tax year 2008–09 and subsequent tax years.
(2) The amendments made by paragraphs 4 to 6 also have effect in relation to deemed surrenders under paragraph 6(1) of Schedule 13.

SCHEDULE 15

CHANGES IN TRADING STOCK

Section 37

PART 1

INCOME TAX

1   ITTOIA 2005 is amended as follows.

3   (*amends* ITTOIA 2005 Pt 2 Ch 12 heading)

4   (*amends* ITTOIA 2005 Sch 4 Pt 2 table)

SCHEDULE 16

NON-RESIDENTS: INVESTMENT MANAGERS

Section 38

PART 2

ELIGIBILITY TO BE AGENT OF INDEPENDENT STATUS

ITA 2007

4   ITA 2007 is amended as follows.

5—(1) Section 827 (meaning of "investment transaction") is amended as follows.
(2) (*substitutes* ITA 2007 s 827(2), (3))
6—(*inserts* ITA 2007 s 1014(2)(*g*)(iib))

PART 3

NON-RESIDENTS LIABLE TO TAX: DISREGARDED INVESTMENT INCOME OR PROFITS

ITA 2007

10—(1) Section 818 of ITA 2007 (the independent investment manager conditions) is amended as follows.
(2) (*amends* ITA 2007 s 818(1))
(3) (*repeals* ITA 2007 s 818(7), (8))

PART 4

COMMENCEMENT

11—*(1) The amendments made by paragraph 1 have effect in relation to business that relates to investment transactions occurring on or after the day on which this Act is passed.*[2]
(2) The amendments made by paragraphs 7 to 9 have effect in relation to accounting periods ending on or after the day on which this Act is passed.[1]
(3) The amendments made by paragraph 10 have effect for the tax year 2008–09 and subsequent tax years.
(4) Subject to sub-paragraphs (1) to (3), the amendments made by this Schedule come into force on the day on which this Act is passed.
(5) But, despite the coming into force of paragraph 2, 3 or 5—
    (*a*) the superseded provision, and
    (*b*) any regulations made under the superseded provision,
continue to have effect until such time as the first regulations under the new regulation-making power come into force.
(6) In sub-paragraph (5)—
    "new regulation-making power" means the regulation-making power substituted by paragraph 2, 3 or 5, and
    "superseded provision" means—
      (*a*) in relation to paragraph 2, the existing section 127(12) and (13) of FA 1995,
      (*b*) in relation to paragraph 3, the existing paragraph 3(3) and (4) of Schedule 26 to FA 2003, or
      (*c*) in relation to paragraph 5, the existing section 827(2) and (3) of ITA 2007.

Amendments—[1]   Sub-para (2) repealed by CTA 2010 s 1181, Sch 3 Pt 1. CTA 2010 has effect for corporation tax purposes for accounting periods ending on or after 1 April 2010, and for income and capital gains tax purposes for the tax year 2010–11 and subsequent tax years.

Errors in connection with payment of gift aid supplement

4—(1) This paragraph applies if an officer of Revenue and Customs discovers that payment or set-off of an amount of gift aid supplement—

    (*a*) ought not to have been made, or

    (*b*) is or has become excessive.

(2) The relevant amount of gift aid supplement may be recovered as if it were an amount of income tax wrongly repaid to the charity (and, in particular, section 30 of TMA 1970 and paragraph 52 of Schedule 18 to FA 1998 apply accordingly).

(3) An amount to be recovered in accordance with sub-paragraph (2) is liable to interest as if it were an amount of income tax wrongly repaid to the charity.

(4) In this paragraph "relevant amount of gift aid supplement" means the payment or set-off of the amount of gift aid supplement, to the extent that it—

    (*a*) ought not to have been made, or

    (*b*) is or has become excessive.

(5) For the purposes of this paragraph income tax is "wrongly repaid" to a charity if it is an amount repaid to the charity which ought not to have been repaid.

(6) For the purposes of this paragraph it does not matter if a charity is within the charge to income tax or the charge to corporation tax.

General

5 Gift aid supplement is not—

    (*a*) income for the purposes of income tax, or

    (*b*) profits for the purposes of corporation tax.

6 Any expenditure incurred by the Commissioners under this Schedule is to be paid out of money provided by Parliament.

7 In this Schedule—

    "charity" has the same meaning as in Chapter 2 of Part 8 of ITA 2007 (gift aid);

    "the Commissioners" means the Commissioners for Her Majesty's Revenue and Customs;

    "gift aid donation" means a gift which is a qualifying donation for the purposes of Chapter 2 of Part 8 of ITA 2007;

    "gift aid supplement" has the meaning given in paragraph 1(1);

    "transitional tax year" means each of the tax years 2008–09, 2009–10 and 2010–11.

Amendments

9 (*inserts* ITA 2007 s 521(7))

SCHEDULE 20

LEASES OF PLANT OR MACHINERY

Section 55

Capital received in respect of lease to be treated as income

2—(1) (*inserts* ITA 2007 Chapter 6, ss 809ZA–809ZD)

(2) The amendment made by sub-paragraph (1) has effect in relation to—

    (*a*) cases where there is first an obligation of the kind mentioned in subsection (1)(*a*) of section 809ZA of ITA 2007 on or after 13 December 2007, and

    (*b*) capital payments within subsection (1)(*b*) of that section made on or after that date.

(3) In relation to a case where the condition in paragraph (*a*) or (*b*) of section 809ZA(1) of ITA 2007 was met before 12 March 2008, sections 809ZA [to 809ZF][1] of that Act have effect as if—

    (*a*) for [section 809ZF(3) to (5)][1] there were substituted—

"([3]) "Lease of plant or machinery"—

        (*a*) includes an equipment lease within the meaning of Chapter 14 of Part 2 of CAA 2001, but

        (*b*) subject to that, does not include a lease of plant or machinery and other property.", and

    (*b*) section 809ZC were omitted.

Amendments—[1] In sub-para (3) words "to 809ZD" substituted, in (3)(*a*) words "section 809ZB(4)" substituted and the substituted subsection renumbered by CTA 2010 s 1177, Sch 1 paras 576, 581(1), (2). CTA 2010 has effect for corporation tax purposes for accounting periods ending on or after 1 April 2010, and for income and capital gains tax purposes for the tax year 2010–11 and subsequent tax years.

3 (*inserts* TA 1988 s 785A(5B))

Plant or machinery subject to a sale and finance leaseback or lease and finance leaseback

6—(1) Part 2 of CAA 2001 (plant and machinery allowances) is amended as follows.

(2) (*amends* CAA 2001 s 13(5))

(3) (*amends* CAA 2001 s 52(5))

(4) (*amends* CAA 2001 s 57(3))

(5) (*amends* CAA 2001 s 66)

(6) (*inserts* CAA 2001 s 70I(10)–(12))

(7) (*amends* CAA 2001 s 89(3)(*b*))

(8) (*substitutes* CAA 2001 s 217(3))

(9) (*substitutes* CAA 2001 s 218(4))

(10) (*amends* CAA 2001 s 219(1))

(11) (*amends* CAA 2001 s 221(1))

(12) (*repeals* CAA 2001 ss 222, 223, 224, 226)

(13) (*amends* CAA 2001 s 227(1)(*b*), (2)(*c*), heading)

(14) (*amends* CAA 2001 s 228(1), *repeals* s 228(4))

(15) (*amends* CAA 2001 s 230(2))

(16) (*amends* CAA 2001 s 241(1)(*b*))

(17) (*repeals* CAA 2001 s 243)

(18) (*amends* TA 1988 s 774E(6))

(19) The amendments made by this paragraph have effect in the case of plant or machinery which is the subject of a sale and finance leaseback (as defined in section 221 of CAA 2001) where the date of the transaction (within the meaning of that section) is on or after 9 October 2007.

(20) In the case of plant or machinery which is the subject of a sale and finance leaseback (as defined in section 221 of CAA 2001) where the date of the transaction (within the meaning of that section) is before 12 March 2008, section 70I(10) of CAA 2001 has effect as if for "any finance lease of a kind" there were substituted "the finance lease".

7—(1) (*inserts* CAA 2001 s 70I(9A))

(2) The amendment made by sub-paragraph (1) has effect in the case of plant or machinery which is the subject of a lease and finance leaseback (as defined in section 228A of CAA 2001) where the date of the transaction mentioned in subsection (2)(*a*) of that section is on or after 12 March 2008.

Restriction on lessee's right to elect that rules for non-long funding leases apply

8—(1) (*inserts* CAA 2001 s 70H(1A), (1B))

(2) The amendment made by sub-paragraph (1) has effect in relation to leases entered into on or after 13 December 2007.

Lessors under long funding leases of plant or machinery

10—(1) Chapter 10A of Part 2 of ITTOIA 2005 (corresponding income tax rules) is amended as follows.

(2) (*inserts* ITTOIA 2005 s 148FA)

(3) (*inserts* ITTOIA 2005 s 148FB)

(4) (*inserts* ITTOIA 2005 s 148FC)

(5) The amendment made by sub-paragraph (2) has effect where—

(*a*) expenditure is incurred on or after 9 October 2007, or

(*b*) a person carrying on a trade becomes entitled to a deduction in calculating the profits or losses of the trade as a result of any plant or machinery forming part of the trading stock of the trade on or after that date.

(6) The amendment made by sub-paragraph (3) has effect where the lease mentioned in section 148FB(1)(*b*) of ITTOIA 2005 is entered into on or after 13 December 2007.

(7) The amendment made by sub-paragraph (4) has effect in relation to arrangements entered into on or after 9 October 2007.

11—(1) If, at the beginning of 13 December 2007 ("the relevant date")—

(*a*) a company or a person carrying on a trade is the lessee of any plant or machinery under a lease that is not a long funding lease ("lease A"), and

(*b*) the company or person is the lessor of any of that plant or machinery under a lease that is a long funding finance lease ("lease B"),

sub-paragraphs (2) to (10) apply in respect of lease B.

(2) . . . .[1] section 148A of ITTOIA 2005 (rental earnings) does not apply in relation to a period of account within sub-paragraph (3).

(3) A period of account is within this sub-paragraph if—

(*a*) it begins on or after the relevant date, and

Credit allowable in relation to interest

2—(1) (*repeals* TA 1988 s 807A(3))

(2) (*repeals* TA 1988 s 807A(5), (6), definitions in (7); FA 1997 s 91(4)))

(3) The repeals made by this paragraph have effect in relation to related transactions on or after 12 March 2008.

Restrictions on relief for interest payments

21—(1) Section 384 of ITA 2007 (general restrictions on relief for interest payments) is amended as follows.

(2) (*amends* ITA 2007 s 384(2))

(3) (*inserts* ITA 2007 s 384(3)–(5))

(4) The amendments made by this paragraph have effect in relation to interest paid on or after 9 October 2007; but in relation to interest paid in the period beginning with that date and ending with 5 April 2008, they have effect as if the references in section 384(2) and (3) to a tax year were to that period.

SCHEDULE 23

MANUFACTURED PAYMENTS: ANTI-AVOIDANCE

Section 63

Section 575

5 (*repeals* ITA 2007 s 575)

Section 580

8 (*repeals* ITA 2007 s 580)

12 (*repeals* ITA 2007 Sch 1 para 335(5))

SCHEDULE 24

ANNUAL INVESTMENT ALLOWANCE

Section 74

PART 1

AMENDMENTS OF CAA 2001

1 CAA 2001 is amended as follows.

2 (*inserts* CAA 2001 ss 38A, 38B)

3 (*inserts* CAA 2001 ss 51A–51N)

4 (*inserts* CAA 2001 s 52A)

5 (*inserts* CAA 2001 s 58(4))

6—(1) Section 205 (reduction of first-year allowances) is amended as follows.

(2) (*amends* CAA 2001 s 205(1))

(3) (*amends* CAA 2001 s 205 heading)

7—(1) Section 210 (reduction of first-year allowances) is amended as follows.

(2) (*amends* CAA 2001 s 210(1))

(3) (*amends* CAA 2001 s 210 heading)

8—(1) Section 217 (restrictions on allowances) is amended as follows.

(2) (*amends* CAA 2001 s 217(1))

(3) (*amends* CAA 2001 s 217(2))

(4) (*amends* CAA 2001 s 217 heading)

9 (*inserts* CAA 2001 s 218A)

10—(1) Section 236 (additional VAT liability generates first-year allowance) is amended as follows.

(2) (*inserts* CAA 2001 s 236(3A)–(3C))

(3) (*amends* CAA 2001 s 236 heading)

11 (*amends* CAA 2001 s 237(1))

12—(1) Section 241 (no first-year allowance in respect of additional VAT liability) is amended as follows.

(2) (*amends* CAA 2001 s 241(1)(*b*))
(3) (*amends* CAA 2001 s 241(2))
(4) (*amends* CAA 2001 s 241(3))
(5) (*amends* CAA 2001 s 241 heading)

13   (*amends* CAA 2001 s 263(3))

14   (*amends* CAA 2001 s 265(4))

15   (*amends* CAA 2001 Sch 1 Pt 2)

PART 2
AMENDMENTS OF OTHER ENACTMENTS
ICTA

16   ICTA is amended as follows.

17   (*amends* TA 1988 s 395(1)(*c*))

18   (*amends* TA 1988 Sch 18 para 1(6)(*b*)(i))

FA 2000

19—(1) Schedule 22 to FA 2000 (tonnage tax) is amended as follows.
(2) (*amends* FA 2000 Sch 22 para 87(1)(*a*))
(3) (*amends* FA 2000 Sch 22 para 94(2))

ITA 2007

20   ITA 2007 is amended as follows.

21   (*amends* ITA 2007 s 76)

22   (*amends* ITA 2007 s 78)

PART 3
COMMENCEMENT

23—(1) This Schedule has effect in relation to expenditure incurred on or after the relevant date.
(2) In relation to a chargeable period which—
   (*a*) begins before the relevant date, and
   (*b*) ends on or after the relevant date,
the maximum allowance under section 51A of CAA 2001 is to be calculated as if the period beginning with the relevant date and ending with the end of the chargeable period were the chargeable period.
(3) The relevant date is—
   (*a*) for corporation tax purposes, 1 April 2008, and
   (*b*) for income tax purposes, 6 April 2008.

SCHEDULE 26
SPECIAL RATE EXPENDITURE AND THE SPECIAL RATE POOL
Section 82

PART 1
AMENDMENTS OF CAA 2001
Introductory

1   CAA 2001 is amended in accordance with this Part of this Schedule.

Special rate expenditure and the special rate pool

2   (*inserts* CAA 2001 ss 104A–104E))

Consequential amendments

3   (*amends* CAA 2001 s 54(5))

4   (*substitutes* CAA 2001 s 56(2)(*a*))

5   (*substitutes* CAA 2001 s 65(1)(*b*))

6   (*amends* CAA 2001 s 66)

7   (*amends* CAA 2001 s 84 table, column 1)

8   (*repeals* CAA 2001 s 92)

9   (*substitutes* CAA 2001 s 101)

10   (*substitutes* CAA 2001 s 102)

11   (*repeals* CAA 2001 s 104)

12   (*amends* CAA 2001 s 266(7))

13   (*inserts* definition in CAA 2001 Sch 1 Pt 2)

PART 2
COMMENCEMENT ETC

Commencement

14—(1) This Schedule has effect in relation to—
     (*a*) expenditure incurred on or after the relevant date, and
     (*b*) long-life asset expenditure (within the meaning of Chapter 10 of CAA 2001) incurred before
        the relevant date but allocated to a pool in a chargeable period beginning on or after that date.
(2) Sub-paragraph (1) is subject to—
     (*a*) section 83 (which provides that certain other long-life asset expenditure is to be treated as
        special rate expenditure for the purposes of CAA 2001), and
     (*b*) paragraphs 15 to 17.
(3) The relevant date is—
     (*a*) for corporation tax purposes, 1 April 2008, and
     (*b*) for income tax purposes, 6 April 2008.

Sale between connected persons

15—(1) This paragraph applies where, on or after the relevant date—
     (*a*) there is a sale of a pre-commencement integral feature,
     (*b*) the buyer and seller are connected persons (within the meaning of section 575 of CAA 2001),
        and
     (*c*) the buyer's expenditure on the integral feature would (apart from this paragraph) be special
        rate expenditure.
(2) An integral feature is a pre-commencement integral feature if the seller—
     (*a*) incurred expenditure on it before the relevant date, or
     (*b*) incurred expenditure on it on or after that date which was not qualifying expenditure because
        of a previous application of this paragraph.
(3) The buyer's expenditure on the integral feature is not qualifying expenditure unless—
     (*a*) the original expenditure was qualifying expenditure, or
     (*b*) the buyer's expenditure would have been qualifying expenditure, had it been incurred at the
        time the original expenditure was incurred.
(4) The "original expenditure"—
     (*a*) where the integral feature is a pre-commencement integral feature because of sub-
        paragraph (2)(*a*), is the expenditure mentioned in that sub-paragraph, and
     (*b*) otherwise, is the expenditure incurred on the integral feature before the relevant date, by
        virtue of which this paragraph first applied.
(5) The "relevant date" has the same meaning as in paragraph 14.

Saving for intra-group transfers

16—(1) This paragraph applies where, on or after the relevant date—
     (*a*) there is a sale of a pre-commencement integral feature,
     (*b*) the buyer and seller are companies which are members of the same group, and
     (*c*) the buyer's expenditure on the integral feature would (apart from this paragraph) be special
        rate expenditure.
(2) An integral feature is a pre-commencement integral feature if qualifying expenditure on it—
     (*a*) was incurred by the seller before the relevant date and allocated to the seller's main pool, or
     (*b*) was incurred by the seller on or after that date and allocated to the seller's main pool because
        of a previous election under this paragraph.
(3) The buyer and seller may jointly elect for paragraph 17 to apply.

(4) The election must be made by notice to an officer of Revenue and Customs within 2 years after the date on which the sale takes place.

(5) All such assessments and adjustments of assessments are to be made as are necessary to give effect to the election.

(6) Whether the buyer and seller are members of the same group is to be determined in accordance with section 170(3) to (6) of TCGA 1992.

(7) The "relevant date" has the same meaning as in paragraph 14.

17—(1) Where this paragraph applies, for the purposes of making allowances and charges under Part 2 of CAA 2001—

    (*a*) the integral feature is treated as having been sold by the seller to the buyer at a price which gives rise to neither a balancing allowance nor a balancing charge, and

    (*b*) the buyer's expenditure on the integral feature is treated as qualifying expenditure which is not special rate expenditure (and, if allocated to a pool, is to be allocated to the buyer's main pool).

(2) Allowances and charges are to be made under Part 2 of CAA 2001 to or on the buyer as if everything done to or by the seller had been done to or by the buyer.

Interpretation

18   Expressions used in this Part of this Schedule and in Part 2 of CAA 2001 have the same meaning in this Part of this Schedule as in that Part of that Act.

SCHEDULE 27

ABOLITION OF ALLOWANCES: CONSEQUENTIAL AMENDMENTS AND SAVINGS

Section 84

PART 1
CONSEQUENTIAL AMENDMENTS

CAA 2001

1   ~~CAA 2001~~ is amended as follows.

2   In section 1 (capital allowances), omit—

    (*a*) subsection (2)(*b*) and (*c*) (entitlement to industrial and agricultural buildings allowances), and

    (*b*) in subsection (3) ", industrial buildings or agricultural buildings,".

3   In section 2(3) (general means of giving effect to capital allowances), omit—

    (*a*) "sections 352 to 355 (industrial buildings allowances);", and

    (*b*) "sections 391 and 392 (agricultural buildings allowances);".

4   In section 3 (claims for capital allowances), omit subsections (4)(*b*) and (5)(*b*).

5—(1) Section 186 (fixture on which an industrial buildings allowance has been made) is amended as follows.

(2) In subsection (1)(*a*) and (*b*), for "is" substitute "was".

(3) In subsection (3)—

    (*a*) at the beginning insert "If the total consideration for the transfer by the past owner exceeds R,", and

    (*b*) in the definition of "R"—

        (i) after "expenditure" insert "which would have been", and

        (ii) at the end insert ", had the time immediately after the transfer fallen immediately before the repeal of Part 3 by section 84 of the Finance Act 2008."

(4) (*inserts* CAA 2001 s 186(3A))

(5) In subsection (5), for "in Part 3" substitute "for the purposes of Part 3 immediately before its repeal by section 84 of the Finance Act 2008."

6   In section 443(3) (disposal values and disposal events), omit "or 3" and "and industrial building allowances".

7   In section 448(3) (additional VAT rebate generates disposal value), in subsection (3) omit "or 3" and "and industrial buildings allowances".

8   In section 537 (contribution allowances), omit ", 3, 4" in—

    (*a*) subsection (1),

    (*b*) subsection (2)(*b*)(ii), and

    (*c*) the heading.

9   Omit section 539 (contribution allowances: industrial buildings).

10   Omit section 540 (contribution allowances: agricultural buildings).

11   In section 542(1) (effect of transfers of trade on contribution allowances), for "Parts 3, 4 and 5" substitute "Part 5".

12   In section 546 (introduction to Chapter 2 of Part 12), omit paragraph (*b*).

13   In section 564 (application of procedure in section 563)—
   (*a*)   in subsection (1), for "3" substitute "3A", and
   (*b*)   omit subsection (3).

14   In section 567(1) (sales treated as for alternative amounts), omit "3," and "4,".

15   In section 569 (election to treat sale as being for an alternative amount), omit—
   (*a*)   in subsections (3)(*a*) and (5)(*a*), "3 or", and
   (*b*)   in subsection (5), "319 (building not an industrial building, etc throughout) or".

16   In section 570 (elections: supplementary), omit—
   (*a*)   in subsection (1), ", 4", and
   (*b*)   in subsection (3), "3,".

17   In section 570A(1) (avoidance affecting proceeds of balancing event), omit "3," and "4,".

18   In section 573(1) (transfers treated as sales), omit "3," and "4,".

19—(1) Part 2 of Schedule 1 (index of defined expressions) is amended as follows.
(2) Omit the entries relating to the following defined expressions—
   "adjusted net cost (in Chapter 7 of Part 3)",
   "agricultural building",
   "balancing adjustment (in Part 3)",
   "balancing adjustment (in Part 4)",
   "balancing event (in Part 3)",
   "balancing event (in Part 4)",
   "building (in Part 3 – includes structure)",
   "commercial building (in Part 3, in relation to qualifying enterprise zone expenditure)",
   "developer, carrying on a trade as (in Chapter 4 of Part 3)",
   "enterprise zone (in Part 3)",
   "expenditure on the construction of a building (in Part 3)",
   "expenditure on the construction of a building (in Part 4)",
   "highway concession (in Chapter 9 of Part 3)",
   "husbandry (in Part 4)",
   "industrial building",
   "lease and related expressions (in Part 3)",
   "lease and related expressions (in Part 4)",
   "proceeds from a balancing event (in Part 3)",
   "proceeds from a balancing event (in Part 4)",
   "qualifying enterprise zone expenditure (in Part 3)",
   "qualifying hotel (in Part 3)",
   "qualifying trade (in Part 3)",
   "related agricultural land (in Part 4)",
   "relevant interest (in Part 3)",
   "relevant interest (in Part 4)",
   "residue of qualifying expenditure (in Part 3)",
   "residue of qualifying expenditure (in Part 4)", and
   "writing-down period (in Part 4)".
(3) In the entry relating to "sale, transfers under Parts 3, 3A, 4, 4A and 10 treated as", omit "3," and "4,".

20   In Schedule 3 (transitional provision and savings), omit—
   (*a*)   paragraphs 56 to 83, and
   (*b*)   paragraph 110.

FA 2000

22 In Schedule 22 (tonnage tax), omit paragraphs 84 and 86.

FA 2001

23—(1) FA 2001 is amended as follows.
(2) In Schedule 19 (insertion of Part 4A of CAA 2001: consequential amendments), omit paragraph 4.
(3) In Schedule 21 (capital allowances: minor amendments), omit paragraphs 5 and 6.

Proceeds of Crime Act 2002 (c 29)

24 In Schedule 10 to the Proceeds of Crime Act 2002 (tax consequences of transfers under Part 5 of that Act), omit paragraphs 18 to 21.

Energy Act 2004 (c 20)

25 In Schedule 4 to the Energy Act 2004 (tax exemption for NDA and NDA companies), omit paragraphs 5 and 6.

ITTOIA 2005

26 In Schedule 1 to ITTOIA 2005 (consequential amendments), omit paragraphs 552 to 558.

ITA 2007

27—(1) ITA 2007 is amended as follows.
(2) In section 24(1)(b) (reliefs deductible at Step 2), omit the entry relating to Part 3 of CAA 2001.
(3) In section 25(3) (reliefs deductible at Steps 2 and 3: supplementary), omit the entry relating to section 355 of that Act.
(4) In Schedule 1 (minor and consequential amendments), omit paragraph 406.

FA 2007

28 In FA 2007, omit section 36 (industrial and agricultural buildings allowances: balancing adjustments).

FA 2008

29 In FA 2008, omit—
    (*a*) section 85 (phasing out of allowances before abolition),
    (*b*) section 86 (qualifying enterprise zone expenditure: transitional provision), and
    (*c*) section 87 (which inserts section 313A of CAA 2001).

Commencement

30—(1) Subject to sub-paragraph (2), this Part of this Schedule has effect in relation to chargeable periods (within the meaning of CAA 2001) beginning on or after—
    (*a*) for corporation tax purposes, 1 April 2011, and
    (*b*) for income tax purposes, 6 April 2011.
(2) The amendments made by paragraph 5 have effect in relation to a transfer by the past owner (within the meaning of section 186 of CAA 2001) in such a chargeable period.

PART 2
SAVINGS

Enterprise zone expenditure

31—(1) Sub-paragraph (2) applies if—
    (*a*) an initial allowance or a writing down allowance has been made under Part 3 of CAA 2001 in respect of qualifying enterprise zone expenditure, and
    (*b*) an event occurs in relation to the building on which the expenditure was incurred which, if that Part of that Act remained in force, would be a balancing event in respect of which a balancing charge would be made.
(2) Unless the event occurs more than 7 years after the building was first used, a balancing charge is to be made in respect of the event as if that Part of that Act remained in force.

32—(1) Sub-paragraph (2) applies if—

   (*a*) an initial allowance has been made under Part 3 of CAA 2001 in respect of qualifying enterprise zone expenditure, and

   (*b*) an event occurs in relation to the building on which the expenditure was incurred which, if section 307 of that Act (withdrawal of allowance if building not industrial building when first used etc) remained in force, would result in the allowance being withdrawn.

(2) Unless the event occurs more than 7 years after the end of the chargeable period for which the allowance was made, the allowance is to be withdrawn as if that section remained in force.

Definition of structure

33 Despite the repeal of Part 3 of CAA 2001 by section 84, Chapter 2 of that Part continues to have effect for the purposes of paragraph (*a*) of item 7 in List B in section 22(1) of that Act (structures which are not plant and machinery).

Definition of qualifying trade

34 Despite the repeal of Part 3 of CAA 2001 by section 84, the following provisions continue to have effect for the purposes of section 484 of that Act (dredging allowances: definition of qualifying trade)—

   (*a*) section 274(1) (definition of qualifying trade), and

   (*b*) sections 276(3) and 341(4) of that Act (parts of trades and undertakings; meaning of "highway concession") so far as they relate to the Tables in that section.

Commencement

35 This Part of this Schedule has effect in relation to chargeable periods (within the meaning of CAA 2001) beginning on or after—

   (*a*) for corporation tax purposes, 1 April 2011, and

   (*b*) for income tax purposes, 6 April 2011.

SCHEDULE 28
INHERITANCE OF TAX-RELIEVED PENSION SAVINGS
Section 91

Amendments of Part 4 of FA 2004

1 Part 4 of FA 2004 (pensions schemes etc) is amended as follows.

2—(1) Section 172 (assignment) is amended as follows.

(2) (*amends* FA 2004 s 172(3))

(3) (*inserts* FA 2004 s 172(6A))

3—(1) Section 172A (surrender) is amended as follows.

(2) (*inserts* FA 2004 s 172A(1)(*aa*))

(3) (*amends* FA 2004 s 172A(3)(*a*))

(4) (*inserts* FA 2004 s 172A(5)(*ca*))

(5) (*inserts* FA 2004 s 172A(9A))

4—(1) Section 172B (increase in rights of connected person on death) is amended as follows.

(2) (*inserts* FA 2004 s 172B(2)(*aa*))

(3) (*amends* FA 2004 s 172B(3)(*a*), (7)(*b*))

(4) (*amends* FA 2004 s 172B(7))

(5) (*inserts* FA 2004 s 172B(7A), (7B))

5 (*amends* FA 2004 Sch 28 para 16(2))

Commencement

15 (1) The amendments made by paragraph 2 have effect in relation to assignments or agreements to assign made on or after 10 October 2007.

(2) The amendments made by paragraph 3 have effect in relation to surrenders and agreements to surrender made on or after that date.

(3) The amendments made by paragraphs 4, 7(2), 8, 10 and 11 to 14 have effect in relation to deaths occurring on or after 6 April 2008.

SCHEDULE 29
FURTHER PROVISION ABOUT PENSION SCHEMES
Section 92
Authorised member payments

1—(1) Part 4 of FA 2004 (pension schemes etc) is amended as follows.
(2) (*inserts* FA 2004 s 163(2))
(3) (*amends* FA 2004 s 216 table)

Definition of investment-regulated pension schemes

3—(1) (*repeals* FA 2004 Sch 29A para 2(1)(*b*))
(2) The amendment made by sub-paragraph (1) is treated as having come into force on 6 April 2006.

Benefit crystallisation event 3

4   Part 4 of FA 2004 (pension schemes etc) is amended as follows.

5   (*amends* FA 2004 s 216(1) table)

6   Schedule 32 (benefit crystallisation events: supplementary) is amended as follows.

7—(1) Paragraph 10 (benefit crystallisation event 3: excepted circumstances) is amended as follows.
(2) The existing provision becomes sub-paragraph (1).
(3) (*substitutes* FA 2004 Sch 32 para 10(1)(*b*))
(4) (*inserts* FA 2004 Sch 32 para 10(2)–(4))

8   (*inserts* FA 2004 Sch 32 para 10A)

9—(1) Paragraph 11 (benefit crystallisation event 3: permitted margin) is amended as follows.
(2) (*amends* FA 2004 Sch 32 para 11(6))
(3) (*inserts* FA 2004 Sch 32 para 11(7A), (7B))

10   (*substitutes* FA 2004 Sch 32 para 13(2)–(2G))

11   (*repeals* FA 2005 Sch 10 para 44)

12—(1) The amendments made by paragraphs 9(2) and (3) come into force on 6 April 2008.
(2) The amendment made by paragraph 10 has effect for the purposes of any benefit crystallisation event 3 occurring on or after 10 October 2007 (including the calculation, for the purposes of such an event, of the amount of XP on any benefit crystallisation event occurring before that date).
(3) Subject to that, the amendments made by paragraphs 4 to 11 are treated as having come into force on 6 April 2006.

Transitional protection of lump sums

13—(1) (*amends* FA 2004 Sch 36 para 34(2))
(2) The amendments made by sub-paragraph (1) are treated as having come into force on 6 April 2006.

Miscellaneous provision about registered pension schemes

14—(1) FA 2004 is amended as follows.
(2) In section 197 (spreading of relief)—
   (*a*) (*amends* FA 2004 s 197(2))
   (*b*) (*amends* FA 2004 s 197(4))
   (*c*) (*inserts* FA 2004 s 197(9A))
(3) (*amends* FA 2004 s 199(2))
(4) (*repeals* ITTOIA 2005 Sch 1 para 648)

15   (*amends* FA 2004 s 215(4)(*a*))

Employer contributions under exempt approved schemes

17—(1) This paragraph applies in relation to section 592 of ICTA (which before its repeal made provision about exempt approved pension schemes), where that section had effect as amended by the 2004 Order.
(2) Section 592 is to be treated as having had effect as if after subsection (4) (as substituted by the 2004 Order) there had been inserted—

"(4A)   No sums other than contributions made by the employer to the pension scheme in respect
of an individual—

    (*a*) the agreement of the taxpayer, or

    (*b*) the approval of the [tribunal][1].

(2) An officer of Revenue and Customs may ask for the approval of the [tribunal][1] to the giving of any taxpayer notice or third party notice (and for the effect of obtaining such approval see paragraphs 29, 30 and 53 (appeals against notices and offence)).

[(2A) An application for approval under this paragraph may be made without notice (except as required under sub-paragraph (3)).][2]

(3) The [tribunal][1] may not approve the giving of a taxpayer notice or third party notice unless—

    (*a*) an application for approval is made by, or with the agreement of, an authorised officer of Revenue and Customs,

    (*b*) the [tribunal][1] is satisfied that, in the circumstances, the officer giving the notice is justified in doing so,

    (*c*) the person to whom the notice is [to be][2] addressed has been told that the information or documents referred to in the notice are required and given a reasonable opportunity to make representations to an officer of Revenue and Customs,

    (*d*) the [tribunal][1] has been given a summary of any representations made by that person, and

    (*e*) in the case of a third party notice, the taxpayer has been given a summary of the reasons why an officer of Revenue and Customs requires the information and documents.

(4) Paragraphs (*c*) to (*e*) of sub-paragraph (3) do not apply to the extent that the [tribunal][1] is satisfied that taking the action specified in those paragraphs might prejudice the assessment or collection of tax.

(5) Where the [tribunal][1] approves the giving of a third party notice under this paragraph, it may also disapply the requirement to name the taxpayer in the notice if it is satisfied that the officer has reasonable grounds for believing that naming the taxpayer might seriously prejudice the assessment or collection of tax.

Commentary—*Simon's Taxes* **A6.301A.**

HMRC Manuals—Compliance Handbook Manual, CH23060 and 23080 (HMRC inspection powers: three types of information notice and approval thereof).

CH23520 (HMRC inspection powers: specific rules regarding taxpayer notice).

CH23620 (HMRC inspection powers: specific rules regarding third party notice).

CH24100 (HMRC inspection powers: the Tribunal).

CH24120–24180 (taxpayer and third party notices).

CH25450 (Tribunal approval).

CH225310–225320 (where no approval is required).

CH225410 (where approval is required).

CH225420 (taxpayer agreement).

CH225430–225440 (summary of reasons and reasons not be given).

CH225460 (opportunity letter requirements).

Amendments—[1]   Word substituted for the words "First-tier Tribunal" in each place; in sub-para (4) word substituted for the word "Tribunal" by the Transfer of Tribunal Functions and Revenue and Customs Appeals Order, SI 2009/56 art 3, Sch 1 para 471 with effect from 1 April 2009.

[2]   Sub-para (2A), and words in sub-para (3)(*c*), inserted, by FA 2009 s 95, Sch 47 para 2 with effect from 21 July 2009.

Copying third party notice to taxpayer

4—(1) An officer of Revenue and Customs who gives a third party notice must give a copy of the notice to the taxpayer to whom it relates, unless the [tribunal][1] has disapplied this requirement.

(2) The [tribunal][1] may not disapply that requirement unless—

    (*a*) an application for approval is made by, or with the agreement of, an authorised officer of Revenue and Customs, and

    (*b*) the [tribunal][1] is satisfied that the officer has reasonable grounds for believing that giving a copy of the notice to the taxpayer might prejudice the assessment or collection of tax.

Commentary—*Simon's Taxes* **A6.301A.**

HMRC Manuals—Compliance Handbook Manual, CH23620 (HMRC inspection powers: specific rules regarding third party notice).

CH23640–23660 (HMRC inspection powers: copy of the notice to the named person).

CH225250 (HMRC inspection powers – how to do a compliance check: copying notice to taxpayer).

Amendments—[1]   Word substituted for the words "First-tier Tribunal" in each place; in sub-para (2)(*b*) word substituted for the word "Tribunal" by the Transfer of Tribunal Functions and Revenue and Customs Appeals Order, SI 2009/56 art 3, Sch 1 para 471 with effect from 1 April 2009.

Power to obtain information and documents about persons whose identity is not known

5—(1) An authorised officer of Revenue and Customs may by notice in writing require a person—

    (*a*) to provide information, or

    (*b*) to produce a document,

if the condition in sub-paragraph (2) is met.

(2) That condition is that the information or document is reasonably required by the officer for the purpose of checking the . . . [4] tax position of—

    (*a*) a person whose identity is not known to the officer, or

    (*b*) a class of persons whose individual identities are not known to the officer.

(3) An officer of Revenue and Customs may not give a notice under this paragraph without the approval of the [tribunal][1].

[(3A) An application for approval under this paragraph may be made without notice.][2]

(4) The [tribunal][1] may not [approve the giving of a notice under][2] this paragraph unless it is satisfied that—

    (*a*) the notice would meet the condition in sub-paragraph (2),

    (*b*) there are reasonable grounds for believing that the person or any of the class of persons to whom the notice relates may have failed or may fail to comply with any provision of [the law (including the law of a territory outside the United Kingdom) relating to tax,][4][3],

    (*c*) any such failure is likely to have led or to lead to serious prejudice to the assessment or collection of . . . [4] tax, and

    (*d*) the information or document to which the notice relates is not readily available from another source.

(5) . . . [4]

Commentary—*Simon's Taxes* A6.301A.

HMRC Manuals—Compliance Handbook Manual, CH23900 (HMRC inspection powers: identity unknown notice). CH24200 (HMRC inspection powers: Tribunal approval of identity unknown notice). CH227100–227200 (HMRC inspection powers – how to do a compliance check: identity unknown notice).

Amendments—[1] In sub-paras (3), (4) word substituted for the words "First-tier Tribunal" by the Transfer of Tribunal Functions and Revenue and Customs Appeals Order, SI 2009/56 art 3, Sch 1 para 471 with effect from 1 April 2009.

[2] Sub-para (3A) inserted, in sub-para (4) words substituted for words "give its approval for the purpose of", by FA 2009 s 95, Sch 47 para 3 with effect from 21 July 2009.

[3] In sub-para (4)(*b*) words substituted for words ", VATA 1994 or any other enactment relating to value added tax charged in accordance with that Act", by FA 2009 s 96, Sch 48 para 2 with effect from 1 April 2010 (by virtue of SI 2009/3054 art 2.

[4] In sub-paras (2), (4)(*c*), word repealed, in sub-para (4)(*b*) words substituted, and sub-para (5) repealed, by FA 2011 s 86(2), Sch 24 paras 1, 2 with effect from 1 April 2012 and from then on in relation to tax regardless of when the tax became due (whether before, on or after that date).

[Power to obtain information about persons whose identity can be ascertained

5A—(1) An authorised officer of Revenue and Customs may by notice in writing require a person to provide relevant information about another person ("the taxpayer") if conditions A to D are met.

(2) Condition A is that the information is reasonably required by the officer for the purpose of checking the tax position of the taxpayer.

(3) Condition B is that—

    (*a*) the taxpayer's identity is not known to the officer, but

    (*b*) the officer holds information from which the taxpayer's identity can be ascertained.

(4) Condition C is that the officer has reason to believe that—

    (*a*) the person will be able to ascertain the taxpayer's identity from the information held by the officer, and

    (*b*) the person obtained relevant information about the taxpayer in the course of carrying on a business.

(5) Condition D is that the taxpayer's identity cannot readily be ascertained by other means from the information held by the officer.

(6) "Relevant information" means all or any of the following—

    (*a*) name,

    (*b*) last known address, and

    (*c*) date of birth (in the case of an individual).

(7) This paragraph applies for the purpose of checking the tax position of a class of persons as for the purpose of checking the tax position of a single person (and references to "the taxpayer" are to be read accordingly).][1]

Amendments—[1] This para inserted by FA 2012 s 224(1), (2) with effect for the purpose of checking the tax position of a taxpayer as regards periods or tax liabilities whenever arising (whether before, on or after 17 July 2012).

Notices

6—(1) In this Schedule, "information notice" means a notice under paragraph 1, 2[, 5 or 5A][3].

(2) An information notice may specify or describe the information or documents to be provided or produced.

(3) If an information notice is given with the approval of the [tribunal][1], it must state that it is given with that approval.

[(4) A decision of the tribunal under paragraph 3, 4 or 5 is final (despite the provisions of sections 11 and 13 of the Tribunals, Courts and Enforcement Act 2007).][2]

CH25560 (wording of inspection notices).

Amendments—[1]   In sub-para (1)(*a*), (*b*), (*c*) words inserted; in sub-para (2)(*c*) words substituted for words "such goods"; in sub-para (4) words substituted in the first place for words "sub-paragraph (1)" and in the second place for words "in that sub-paragraph", by FA 2009 s 95, Sch 47 para 6 with effect from 21 July 2009.

Prospective amendments—Sub-para (1)(*b*), but not the "or" at the end, to be repealed, and in sub-para (2)(*c*), words "the acquisition of goods from other member States under taxable acquisitions" to be repealed, by the Taxation (Cross-border Trade) Act 2018 s 43, Sch 8 paras 112, 113(1), (2) with effect from a day to be appointed.

Carrying out inspections [under paragraph 10, 10A or 11]

12—(1) An inspection under [paragraph 10, 10A or 11][3] may be carried out only—

    (*a*) at a time agreed to by the occupier of the premises, or

    (*b*) if sub-paragraph (2) is satisfied, at any reasonable time.

(2) This sub-paragraph is satisfied if—

    (*a*) the occupier of the premises has been given at least 7 days' notice of the time of the inspection (whether in writing or otherwise), or

    (*b*) the inspection is carried out by, or with the agreement of, an authorised officer of Revenue and Customs.

(3) An officer of Revenue and Customs seeking to carry out an inspection under sub-paragraph (2)(*b*) must provide a notice in writing as follows—

    (*a*) if the occupier of the premises is present at the time the inspection is to begin, the notice must be provided to the occupier,

    (*b*) if the occupier of the premises is not present but a person who appears to the officer to be in charge of the premises is present, the notice must be provided to that person, and

    (*c*) in any other case, the notice must be left in a prominent place on the premises.

(4) The notice referred to in sub-paragraph (3) must state the possible consequences of obstructing the officer in the exercise of the power.

(5) If a notice referred to in sub-paragraph (3) is given [in respect of an inspection approved by][2] the [tribunal][1] (see paragraph 13), it must state that [the inspection has been so approved][2].

Amendments—[1]   In sub-para (5) word substituted for the words "First-tier Tribunal" by the Transfer of Tribunal Functions and Revenue and Customs Appeals Order, SI 2009/56 art 3, Sch 1 para 471 with effect from 1 April 2009.

[2]   In sub-para (5) words substituted in the first place for the words "with the approval of" and in the second place for the words "it is given with that approval", by FA 2009 s 95, Sch 47 para 7 with effect from 21 July 2009.

[3]   In heading words inserted, in sub-para (1) words substituted for words "this Part of this Schedule", by FA 2009 s 96, Sch 48 para 4 with effect from 1 April 2010 (by virtue of SI 2009/3054 art 2).

[Powers to inspect property for valuation etc

12A—(1) An officer of Revenue and Customs may enter and inspect premises for the purpose of valuing the premises if the valuation is reasonably required for the purpose of checking any person's position as regards income tax or corporation tax.

(2) An officer of Revenue and Customs may enter premises and inspect—

    (*a*) the premises, and

    (*b*) any other property on the premises,

for the purpose of valuing, measuring or determining the character of the premises or property.

(3) Sub-paragraph (2) only applies if the valuation, measurement or determination is reasonably required for the purpose of checking any person's position as regards—

    (*a*) capital gains tax,

    (*b*) corporation tax in respect of chargeable gains,

    (*c*) inheritance tax,

    (*d*) stamp duty land tax, .

    (*e*) stamp duty reserve tax[, or

    (*f*) annual tax on enveloped dwellings.][2]

(4) A person who the officer considers is needed to assist with the valuation, measurement or determination may enter and inspect the premises or property with the officer.][1]

Amendments—[1]   Paras 12A, 12B inserted by FA 2009 s 96, Sch 48 para 5 with effect from 1 April 2010 (by virtue of SI 2009/3054 art 2).

[2]   In sub-para (3), word "or" in para (*d*) repealed, and para (*f*) and preceding word "or" inserted by FA 2013 s 164, Sch 34 paras 1, 2 with effect from 17 July 2013.

[Carrying out inspections under paragraph 12A

12B—(1) An inspection under paragraph 12A may be carried out only if condition A or B is satisfied.

(2) Condition A is that—

    (*a*) the inspection is carried out at a time agreed to by a relevant person, and

    (*b*) the relevant person has been given notice in writing of the agreed time of the inspection.

(3) "Relevant person" means—

    (*a*) the occupier of the premises, or

    (*b*) if the occupier cannot be identified or the premises are vacant, a person who controls the premises.

(4) Condition B is that—

    (*a*) the inspection has been approved by the tribunal, and

    (*b*) any relevant person specified by the tribunal has been given at least 7 days' notice in writing of the time of the inspection.

(5) A notice under sub-paragraph (4)(*b*) must state the possible consequences of obstructing the officer in the exercise of the power.

(6) If a notice is given under this paragraph in respect of an inspection approved by the tribunal (see paragraph 13), it must state that the inspection has been so approved.

(7) An officer of Revenue and Customs seeking to carry out an inspection under paragraph 12A must produce evidence of authority to carry out the inspection if asked to do so by—

    (*a*) the occupier of the premises, or

    (*b*) any other person who appears to the officer to be in charge of the premises or property.]

Amendments—Paras 12A, 12B inserted by FA 2009 s 96, Sch 48 para 5 with effect from 1 April 2010 (by virtue of SI 2009/3054 art 2).

Approval of [tribunal]

13—(1) An officer of Revenue and Customs may ask the [tribunal][1] to approve an inspection under this Part of this Schedule [(and for the effect of obtaining such approval see paragraph 39 (penalties))][3].

[(1A) An application for approval under this paragraph may be made without notice [(except as required under sub-paragraph (2A))][3].][2]

(2) The [tribunal][1] may not approve an inspection [under paragraph 10, 10A or 11][3] unless—

    (*a*) an application for approval is made by, or with the agreement of, an authorised officer of Revenue and Customs, and

    (*b*) the [tribunal][1] is satisfied that, in the circumstances, the inspection is justified.

[(2A) The tribunal may not approve an inspection under paragraph 12A unless—

    (*a*) an application for approval is made by, or with the agreement of, an authorised officer of Revenue and Customs,

    (*b*) the person whose tax position is the subject of the proposed inspection has been given a reasonable opportunity to make representations to the officer of Revenue and Customs about that inspection,

    (*c*) the occupier of the premises has been given a reasonable opportunity to make such representations,

    (*d*) the tribunal has been given a summary of any representations made, and

    (*e*) the tribunal is satisfied that, in the circumstances, the inspection is justified.

(2B) Paragraph (*c*) of sub-paragraph (2A) does not apply if the tribunal is satisfied that the occupier of the premises cannot be identified.][3]

[(3) A decision of the tribunal under this paragraph is final (despite the provisions of sections 11 and 13 of the Tribunals, Courts and Enforcement Act 2007).][2]

Amendments—[1]   Word substituted for the words "First-tier Tribunal" in the heading and in each place; in sub-para (2)(*b*) word substituted for the word "Tribunal" by the Transfer of Tribunal Functions and Revenue and Customs Appeals Order, SI 2009/56 Sch 1 para 471 with effect from 1 April 2009.

[2]   Sub-paras (1A), (3) inserted by FA 2009 s 95, Sch 47 para 8 with effect from 21 July 2009.

[3]   In sub-paras (1), (1A), (2), words inserted, and whole of sub-paras (2A), (2B) inserted, by FA 2009 s 96, Sch 48 para 6 with effect from 1 April 2010 (by virtue of SI 2009/3054 art 2).

Restrictions and special cases

14   This Part of this Schedule has effect subject to Parts 4 and 6 of this Schedule.

PART 3
FURTHER POWERS

Power to copy documents

15   Where a document (or a copy of a document) is produced to, or inspected by, an officer of Revenue and Customs, such an officer may take copies of, or make extracts from, the document.

Power to remove documents

16—(1) Where a document is produced to, or inspected by, an officer of Revenue and Customs, such an officer may—

(a) remove the document at a reasonable time, and

(b) retain it for a reasonable period,

if it appears to the officer to be necessary to do so.

(2) Where a document is removed in accordance with sub-paragraph (1), the person who produced the document may request—

(a) a receipt for the document, and

(b) if the document is reasonably required for any purpose, a copy of the document,

and an officer of Revenue and Customs must comply with such a request without charge.

(3) The removal of a document under this paragraph is not to be regarded as breaking any lien claimed on the document.

(4) Where a document removed under this paragraph is lost or damaged, the Commissioners are liable to compensate the owner of the document for any expenses reasonably incurred in replacing or repairing the document.

(5) In this paragraph references to a document include a copy of a document.

Power to mark assets and to record information

17   The powers under Part 2 of this Schedule include—

(a) power to mark business assets, and anything containing business assets, for the purpose of indicating that they have been inspected, and

(b) power to obtain and record information (whether electronically or otherwise) relating to the premises, [property, goods,][1] assets and documents that have been inspected.

Amendments—[1]   In para (b) words inserted by FA 2009 s 96, Sch 48 para 7 with effect from 1 April 2010 (by virtue of SI 2009/3054 art 2).

PART 4
RESTRICTIONS ON POWERS

Documents not in person's possession or power

18   An information notice only requires a person to produce a document if it is in the person's possession or power.

Commentary—*Simon's Taxes* **A6.301A.**

HMRC Manuals—Compliance Handbook Manual, CH22120 (HMRC inspection powers: meaning of possession and power).

Modification—See FA 2016 Sch 20 para 19 (application of this para in relation to penalties for enablers of offshore tax evasion or non-compliance).

Types of information

19—(1) An information notice does not require a person to provide or produce—

(a) information that relates to the conduct of a pending appeal relating to tax or any part of a document containing such information, or

[(aa) information that relates to the conduct of a pending appeal under the Savings (Government Contributions) Act 2017 or any part of a document containing such information,][1] or

(b) journalistic material (as defined in section 13 of the Police and Criminal Evidence Act 1984 (c 60)) or information contained in such material.

(2) An information notice does not require a person to provide or produce personal records (as defined in section 12 of the Police and Criminal Evidence Act 1984) or information contained in such records, subject to sub-paragraph (3).

(3) An information notice may require a person—

(a) to produce documents, or copies of documents, that are personal records, omitting any information whose inclusion (whether alone or with other information) makes the original documents personal records ("personal information"), and

(b) to provide any information contained in such records that is not personal information.

Commentary—*Simon's Taxes* **A6.301A.**

HMRC Manuals—Compliance Handbook Manual, CH22160 (HMRC inspection powers: appeal material, with example). CH22180 and 22200 (personal records, with example).

Amendments—[1]   Sub-para (1)(aa) inserted by the Savings (Government Contributions) Act 2017 s 5(3) with effect from 17 January 2017.

Prospective amendments—Sub-paras (4), (5) to be inserted by the Investigatory Powers Act 2016 s 12(1), Sch 2 para 10 with effect from a date to be appointed. Sub-paras (4), (5) as inserted to read as follows—

"(4) An information notice does not require a telecommunications operator or postal operator to provide or produce communications data.

(5) In sub-paragraph (4) "communications data", "postal operator" and "telecommunications operator" have the same meanings as in the Investigatory Powers Act 2016 (see sections 261 and 262 of that Act).".

Old documents

20 An information notice may not require a person to produce a document if the whole of the document originates more than 6 years before the date of the notice, unless the notice is given by, or with the agreement of, an authorised officer.

Commentary—*Simon's Taxes* **A6.301A**.
HMRC Manuals—Compliance Handbook Manual, CH22140 (HMRC inspection powers: old documents).

Taxpayer notices [following tax return]

21—(1) Where a person has made a tax return in respect of a chargeable period under section 8, 8A or 12AA of TMA 1970 (returns for purpose of income tax and capital gains tax), a taxpayer notice may not be given for the purpose of checking that person's income tax position or capital gains tax position in relation to the chargeable period.
(2) Where a person has made a tax return in respect of a chargeable period under paragraph 3 of Schedule 18 to FA 1998 (company tax returns), a taxpayer notice may not be given for the purpose of checking that person's corporation tax position in relation to the chargeable period.
(3) Sub-paragraphs (1) and (2) do not apply where, or to the extent that, any of conditions A to D is met.
(4) Condition A is that a notice of enquiry has been given in respect of—
    (*a*) the return, or
    (*b*) a claim or election (or an amendment of a claim or election) made by the person in relation to the chargeable period in respect of the tax (or one of the taxes) to which the return relates ("relevant tax"),
and the enquiry has not been completed [so far as relating to the matters to which the taxpayer notice relates][3].
(5) In sub-paragraph (4), "notice of enquiry" means a notice under—
    (*a*) section 9A or 12AC of, or paragraph 5 of Schedule 1A to, TMA 1970, or
    (*b*) paragraph 24 of Schedule 18 to FA 1998.
(6) Condition B is that an officer of Revenue and Customs has reason to suspect that[, as regards the person,][1]
    (*a*) an amount that ought to have been assessed to relevant tax for the chargeable period may not have been assessed,
    (*b*) an assessment to relevant tax for the chargeable period may be or have become insufficient, or
    (*c*) relief from relevant tax given for the chargeable period may be or have become excessive.
(7) Condition C is that the notice is given for the purpose of obtaining any information or document that is also required for the purpose of checking [the][1] person's [position as regards any tax other than income tax, capital gains tax or corporation tax][2].
(8) Condition D is that the notice is given for the purpose of obtaining any information or document that is required (or also required) for the purpose of checking the person's position as regards any deductions or repayments [of tax or withholding of income][1] referred to in paragraph 64(2) [or (2A)][1] (PAYE etc).
[(9) In this paragraph, references to the person who made the return are only to that person in the capacity in which the return was made.][1]

Modification—See FA 2010 Sch 1 para 36 (modification of this para in relation to bank payroll tax).
Amendments—[1]   In sub-paras (6), (8) in both places, words inserted; in sub-para (7) word substituted for the word "that"; and sub-para (9) inserted, by FA 2009 s 95, Sch 47 para 9 with effect from 21 July 2009.
[2]   In the cross-heading words inserted, and in sub-para (7) words substituted for words "VAT position", by FA 2009 s 95, Sch 48 para 8 with effect from 1 April 2010 (by virtue of SI 2009/3054 art 2).
[3]   In sub-para (4), words inserted by F(No 2)A 2017 s 63, Sch 15 para 36 with effect in relation to an enquiry under TMA 1970 ss 9A, 12ZM or 12AC or FA 1998 Sch 18 where notice of the enquiry is given on or after 16 November 2017 or the enquiry is in progress immediately before that day.

Prospective amendments—In sub-para (1), words ", or regulations under paragraph 10 of Schedule A1 to," to be inserted after words "12AA of" by F(No 2)A 2017 s 61(1), Sch 14 para 38(1), (2) with effect from a day to be appointed.

[Application of paragraph 21 in case of returns under Schedule 2 to FA 2019

21ZA   (1) For the purposes of paragraph 21 any reference to the making by a person of a return under section 8 or 8A of TMA 1970 includes the making by the person of a return under Schedule 2 to FA 2019.
(2) In the application of paragraph 21 in relation to a return under Schedule 2 to FA 2019, the return is to be treated as if it required a self-assessment of an amount of capital gains tax.
(3) For the purposes of paragraph 21, the definition of "the notice of enquiry" in its application to a return under Schedule 2 to FA 2019 needs to be read in the light of the provision made by paragraph 20 of that Schedule.][1]

Amendments—[1]   Para 21ZA substituted by FA 2019 s 14, Sch 2 para 28 with effect in relation to disposals made on or after 6 April 2019.

[Taxpayer notices following land transaction return

21A—(1) Where a person has delivered a land transaction return under section 76 of FA 2003 (returns for purposes of stamp duty land tax) in respect of a transaction, a taxpayer notice may not be given for the purpose of checking that person's stamp duty land tax position in relation to that transaction.

(2) Sub-paragraph (1) does not apply where, or to the extent that, any of conditions A to C is met.

(3) Condition A is that a notice of enquiry has been given in respect of—

    (*a*) the return, or

    (*b*) a claim (or an amendment of a claim) made by the person in connection with the transaction,

and the enquiry has not been completed.

(4) In sub-paragraph (3) "notice of enquiry" means a notice under paragraph 12 of Schedule 10, or paragraph 7 of Schedule 11A, to FA 2003.

(5) Condition B is that, as regards the person, an officer of Revenue and Customs has reason to suspect that—

    (*a*) an amount that ought to have been assessed to stamp duty land tax in respect of the transaction may not have been assessed,

    (*b*) an assessment to stamp duty land tax in respect of the transaction may be or have become insufficient, or

    (*c*) relief from stamp duty land tax in respect of the transaction may be or have become excessive.

(6) Condition C is that the notice is given for the purpose of obtaining any information or document that is also required for the purpose of checking that person's position as regards a tax other than stamp duty land tax.]

Amendments—Para 21A inserted by FA 2009 s 96, Sch 48 para 9 with effect from 1 April 2010 (by virtue of SI 2009/3054 art 2).

[Annual tax on enveloped dwellings: taxpayer notices following return

21B—(1) Where a person has delivered, for a chargeable period with respect to a single-dwelling interest—

    (*a*) an annual tax on enveloped dwellings return, or

    (*b*) a return of the adjusted chargeable amount,

a taxpayer notice may not be given for the purpose of checking the person's annual tax on enveloped dwellings position as regards the matters dealt with in that return.

(2) Sub-paragraph (1) does not apply where, or to the extent that, any of conditions A to C is met.

(3) Condition A is that notice of enquiry has been given in respect of—

    (*a*) the return, or

    (*b*) a claim (or an amendment of a claim) made by the person in relation to the chargeable period,

and the enquiry has not been completed.

(4) In sub-paragraph (3) "notice of enquiry" means a notice under paragraph 8 of Schedule 33 to FA 2013 or paragraph 7 of Schedule 11A to FA 2003 (as applied by paragraphs 28(2) and 31(3) of Schedule 33 to FA 2013).

(5) Condition B is that, as regards the person, an officer of Revenue and Customs has reason to suspect that—

    (*a*) an amount that ought to have been assessed to annual tax on enveloped dwellings for the chargeable period may not have been assessed,

    (*b*) an assessment to annual tax on enveloped dwellings for the chargeable period may be or have become insufficient, or

    (*c*) relief from annual tax on enveloped dwellings for the chargeable period may be or have become excessive.

(6) Condition C is that the notice is given for the purpose of obtaining any information or document that is also required for the purpose of checking that person's position as regards a tax other than annual tax on enveloped dwellings.

(7) In this Schedule references to a "single-dwelling interest" are to be read in accordance with section 108 of FA 2013.][1]

Amendments—[1]   Para 21B inserted by FA 2013 s 164, Sch 34 paras 1, 3 with effect from 17 July 2013.

Deceased persons

22   An information notice given for the purpose of checking the tax position of a person who has died may not be given more than 4 years after the person's death.

Privileged communications between professional legal advisers and clients

23—(1) An information notice does not require a person—

    (*a*) to provide privileged information, or

    (*b*) to produce any part of a document that is privileged.

(2) For the purpose of this Schedule, information or a document is privileged if it is information or a document in respect of which a claim to legal professional privilege, or (in Scotland) to confidentiality of communications as between client and professional legal adviser, could be maintained in legal proceedings.

(3) The Commissioners may by regulations make provision for the resolution by the [tribunal][1] of disputes as to whether any information or document is privileged.

(4) The regulations may, in particular, make provision as to—

    (*a*) the custody of a document while its status is being decided, . . . [1]

    (*b*) . . . [1]

Commentary—*Simon's Taxes* **A6.301A**.

HMRC Manuals—Compliance Handbook Manual, CH22240 (HMRC restrictions on inspection powers: legal professional privilege).

Regulations—Information Notice: Resolution of Disputes as to Privileged Communications Regulations, SI 2009/1916.

Amendments—[1]   In sub-para (3) word substituted for the words "First-tier Tribunal"; sub-para (4)(*b*) and the word "and" immediately preceding it repealed by the Transfer of Tribunal Functions and Revenue and Customs Appeals Order, SI 2009/56 art 3, Sch 1 para 471 with effect from 1 April 2009.

Auditors

24—(1) An information notice does not require a person who has been appointed as an auditor for the purpose of an enactment—

    (*a*) to provide information held in connection with the performance of the person's functions under that enactment, or

    (*b*) to produce documents which are that person's property and which were created by that person or on that person's behalf for or in connection with the performance of those functions.

(2) Sub-paragraph (1) has effect subject to paragraph 26.

Commentary—*Simon's Taxes* **A6.301A, A6.310**.

Modification—See FA 2016 Sch 20 para 20(*a*) (disapplication of this para in relation to penalties for enablers of offshore tax evasion or non-compliance).

Tax advisers

25—(1) An information notice does not require a tax adviser—

    (*a*) to provide information about relevant communications, or

    (*b*) to produce documents which are the tax adviser's property and consist of relevant communications.

(2) Sub-paragraph (1) has effect subject to paragraph 26.

(3) In this paragraph—

    "relevant communications" means communications between the tax adviser and—

        (*a*) a person in relation to whose tax affairs he has been appointed, or

        (*b*) any other tax adviser of such a person,

    the purpose of which is the giving or obtaining of advice about any of those tax affairs, and "tax adviser" means a person appointed to give advice about the tax affairs of another person (whether appointed directly by that person or by another tax adviser of that person).

Commentary—*Simon's Taxes* **A6.301A, A6.310**.

HMRC Manuals—Compliance Handbook Manual, CH22240 and 22320 (HMRC restrictions on inspection powers: tax advisers' papers).

Modification—See FA 2016 Sch 20 para 20(*b*) (disapplication of this para in relation to penalties for enablers of offshore tax evasion or non-compliance).

Auditors and tax advisers: supplementary

26—(1) Paragraphs 24(1) and 25(1) do not have effect in relation to—

    (*a*) information explaining any information or document which the person to whom the notice is given has, as tax accountant, assisted any client in preparing for, or delivering to, HMRC, or

    (*b*) a document which contains such information.

(2) In the case of a notice given under paragraph 5, paragraphs 24(1) and 25(1) do not have effect in relation to—

    (*a*) any information giving the identity or address of a person to whom the notice relates or of a person who has acted on behalf of such a person, or

    (*b*) a document which contains such information.

(3) Paragraphs 24(1) and 25(1) are not disapplied by sub-paragraph (1) or (2) if the information in question has already been provided, or a document containing the information in question has already been produced, to an officer of Revenue and Customs.

Commentary—*Simon's Taxes* **A6.301A, A6.310**.

HMRC Manuals—Compliance Handbook Manual, CH22340 (HMRC restrictions on inspection powers: exceptions for auditors' and tax advisers' papers).

Modification—See FA 2016 Sch 20 para 20(*c*) (disapplication of this para in relation to penalties for enablers of offshore tax evasion or non-compliance).

27—(1) This paragraph applies where paragraph 24(1) or 25(1) is disapplied in relation to a document by paragraph 26(1) or (2).

(2) An information notice that requires the document to be produced has effect as if it required any part or parts of the document containing the information mentioned in paragraph 26(1) or (2) to be produced.

Modification—See FA 2016 Sch 20 para 20(*c*) (disapplication of this para in relation to penalties for enablers of offshore tax evasion or non-compliance).

Corresponding restrictions on inspection of . . . documents[1]

28   An officer of Revenue and Customs may not inspect a business document under Part 2 of this Schedule if or to the extent that, by virtue of this Part of this Schedule, an information notice given at the time of the inspection to the occupier of the premises could not require the occupier to produce the document.

Amendments—[1]   In the heading, word "business" repealed by FA 2009 s 96, Sch 48 para 10 with effect from 1 April 2010 (by virtue of SI 2009/3054 art 2).

PART 5
APPEALS AGAINST INFORMATION NOTICES

Right to appeal against taxpayer notice

29—(1) Where a taxpayer is given a taxpayer notice, the taxpayer may appeal . . . [1] against the notice or any requirement in the notice.

(2) Sub-paragraph (1) does not apply to a requirement in a taxpayer notice to provide any information, or produce any document, that forms part of the taxpayer's statutory records.

(3) Sub-paragraph (1) does not apply if the [tribunal][1] approved the giving of the notice in accordance with paragraph 3.

Commentary—*Simon's Taxes* **A6.301A**.

HMRC Manuals—Compliance Handbook Manual, CH23520 (HMRC inspection powers: specific rules regarding taxpayer notice).

CH24100 (HMRC inspection powers: appealing against a taxpayer notice).

Amendments—[1]   In sub-para (1) words "to the First-tier Tribunal" repealed; in sub-para (3) word substituted for the words "First-tier Tribunal" by the Transfer of Tribunal Functions and Revenue and Customs Appeals Order, SI 2009/56 art 3, Sch 1 para 471 with effect from 1 April 2009.

Right to appeal against third party notice

30—(1) Where a person is given a third party notice, the person may appeal . . . [1] against the notice or any requirement in the notice on the ground that it would be unduly onerous to comply with the notice or requirement.

(2) Sub-paragraph (1) does not apply to a requirement in a third party notice to provide any information, or produce any document, that forms part of the taxpayer's statutory records.

(3) Sub-paragraph (1) does not apply if the [tribunal][1] approved the giving of the notice in accordance with paragraph 3.

Commentary—*Simon's Taxes* **A6.301A**.

HMRC Manuals—Compliance Handbook Manual, CH23620 (HMRC inspection powers: specific rules regarding third party notice).

CH24100 (HMRC inspection powers: appealing against a third party notice).

CH24420 (meaning of "unduly onerous").

Amendments—[1]   In sub-para (1) words "to the First-tier Tribunal" repealed; in sub-para (3) word substituted for the words "First-tier Tribunal" by the Transfer of Tribunal Functions and Revenue and Customs Appeals Order, SI 2009/56 art 3, Sch 1 para 471 with effect from 1 April 2009.

Right to appeal against notice given under paragraph 5 [or 5A]

31   Where a person is given a notice under paragraph 5 [or 5A][2], the person may appeal . . . [1] against the notice or any requirement in the notice on the ground that it would be unduly onerous to comply with the notice or requirement.

Amendments—[1]   In sub-para (1) words "to the First-tier Tribunal" repealed by the Transfer of Tribunal Functions and Revenue and Customs Appeals Order, SI 2009/56 art 3, Sch 1 para 471 with effect from 1 April 2009.

[2]   Words inserted by FA 2012 s 224(1), (4), (5) with effect for the purpose of checking the tax position of a taxpayer as regards periods or tax liabilities whenever arising (whether before, on or after 17 July 2012).

Procedure

32—(1) Notice of an appeal under this Part of this Schedule must be given—

    (*a*) in writing,

    (*b*) before the end of the period of 30 days beginning with the date on which the information notice is given, and

    (*c*) to the officer of Revenue and Customs by whom the information notice was given.

(2) Notice of an appeal under this Part of this Schedule must state the grounds of appeal.

(3) On an appeal the [that is notified to the tribunal, the tribunal][1] may—

    (*a*) confirm the information notice or a requirement in the information notice,

    (*b*) vary the information notice or such a requirement, or

    (*c*) set aside the information notice or such a requirement.

(4) Where the [tribunal][1] confirms or varies the information notice or a requirement, the person to whom the information notice was given must comply with the notice or requirement—

    (*a*) within such period as is specified by the [tribunal][1], or

    (*b*) if the [tribunal][1] does not specify a period, within such period as is reasonably specified in writing by an officer of Revenue and Customs following the [tribunal's][1] decision.

[(5) Notwithstanding the provisions of sections 11 and 13 of the Tribunals, Courts and Enforcement Act 2007 a decision of the tribunal on an appeal under this Part of this Schedule is final.][1]

(6) Subject to this paragraph, the provisions of Part 5 of TMA 1970 relating to appeals have effect in relation to appeals under this Part of this Schedule as they have effect in relation to an appeal against an assessment to income tax.

Commentary—*Simon's Taxes* **A6.301A**.

HMRC Manuals—Compliance Handbook Manual, CH24340 (HMRC inspection powers: appeal procedures). CH24440 (what the first-tier Tribunal can decide).

Amendments—[1]   In sub-paras (3), (4) word substituted for the words "First-tier Tribunal"; in sub-para (4)(*a*), (*b*) word substituted for word "Tribunal" and "Tribunal's"; sub-para (5) substituted by the Transfer of Tribunal Functions and Revenue and Customs Appeals Order, SI 2009/56 art 3, Sch 1 para 471 with effect from 1 April 2009.

Special cases

33   This Part of this Schedule has effect subject to Part 6 of this Schedule.

PART 6
SPECIAL CASES

Supply of goods or services etc

34—(1) This paragraph applies to a taxpayer notice or third party notice that refers only to information or documents that form part of any person's statutory records and relate to—

    (*a*) the supply of goods or services,

    (*b*) the acquisition of goods from another member State, or

    (*c*) the importation of goods from a place outside the member States in the course of carrying on a business.

(2) Paragraph 3(1) (requirement for consent to, or approval of, third party notice) does not apply to such a notice.

(3) Where a person is given such a notice, the person may not appeal . . . [1] against the notice or any requirement in the notice.

(4) Sections 5, 11 and 15 of, and Schedule 4 to, VATA 1994, and any orders made under those provisions, apply for the purposes of this paragraph as if it were part of that Act.

Amendments—[1]   In sub-para (3) words "to the First-tier Tribunal" repealed by the Transfer of Tribunal Functions and Revenue and Customs Appeals Order, SI 2009/56 art 3, Sch 1 para 471 with effect from 1 April 2009.

Prospective amendments—Sub-para (1)(*b*), but not the "or" at the end, to be repealed, in sub-para (1)(*c*), words "from a place outside the member States" to be repealed, and in sub-para (4) word ", 11" to be repealed, by the Taxation (Cross-border Trade) Act 2018 s 43, Sch 8 paras 112, 113(1), (3) with effect from a day to be appointed.

[Registered pension schemes etc

34B—(1) This paragraph applies to a third party notice or a notice under paragraph 5 if it refers only to information or documents that relate to any pensions matter.

(2) "Pensions matter" means any matter relating to—

    (*a*) a registered pension scheme,

    (*b*) an annuity purchased with sums or assets held for the purposes of a registered pension scheme or a pre-2006 pension scheme, . . . [2]

    (*c*)   an employer-financed retirement benefits scheme,

    [(*d*)   a QROPS or former QROPS, or

    (*e*)   an annuity purchased with sums or assets held for the purposes of a QROPS or former QROPS.][2]

(3) In relation to such a third party notice—

    (*a*)   paragraph 3(1) (approval etc of third party notices) does not apply,

    (*b*)   paragraph 4(1) (copying third party notices to taxpayer) does not apply, and

    (*c*)   paragraph 30(1) (appeal) has effect as if it permitted an appeal on any grounds.

(4) In relation to such a notice under paragraph 5—

    (*a*)   sub-paragraphs (3) and (4) of that paragraph (approval of tribunal) have effect as if they permitted, but did not require, an authorised officer of Revenue and Customs to obtain the approval of the tribunal, and

    (*b*)   paragraph 31 (appeal) has effect as if it permitted an appeal on any grounds.

[(4A) In relation to a notice to which this paragraph applies that refers only to information or documents relating to a matter within sub-paragraph (2)(*d*) or (*e*), paragraph 20 (old documents) has effect as if the reference to 6 years were to 10 years.][2]

(5) A person may not appeal against a requirement in the notice to provide any information, or produce any document, that forms part of any person's statutory records.

(6) Where the notice relates to a matter within sub-paragraph (2)(*a*) or (*b*), the officer of Revenue and Customs who gives the notice must give a copy of the notice to the scheme administrator in relation to the pension scheme.

(7) Where the notice relates to a matter within sub-paragraph (2)(*c*), the officer of Revenue and Customs who gives the notice must give a copy of the notice to the responsible person in relation to the employer-financed retirement benefits scheme.

[(7A) Where the notice relates to a matter within sub-paragraph (2)(*d*) or (*e*), the officer of Revenue and Customs who gives the notice must give a copy of the notice to the scheme manager in relation to the pension scheme.][2]

(8) Sub-paragraphs (6) [to (7A)][2] do not apply if the notice is given to a person who, in relation to the scheme or annuity to which the notice relates, is a prescribed description of person.][1]

Amendments—[1]   Paras 34A–34C inserted by FA 2009 s 96, Sch 48 para 11 with effect from 1 April 2010 (by virtue of SI 2009/3054 art 2).

[2]   In sub-para (2), word "or" at end of para (*b*) repealed, and paras (*d*), (*e*) inserted; sub-paras (4A), (7A) inserted; and in sub-para (8), words substituted for words "and (7)"; by FA 2013 s 54(1), (2) with effect from 17 July 2013.

[Registered pension schemes etc: interpretation

34C   In paragraph 34B—

"employer-financed retirement benefits scheme" has the same meaning as in Chapter 2 of Part 6 of ITEPA 2003 (see sections 393A and 393B of that Act);

"pension scheme" has the same meaning as in Part 4 of FA 2004;

"pre-2006 pension scheme" means a scheme that, at or in respect of any time before 6 April 2006, was—

    (*a*)   a retirement benefits scheme approved for the purposes of Chapter 1 of Part 14 of ICTA,

    (*b*)   a former approved superannuation fund (as defined in paragraph 1(3) of Schedule 36 to FA 2004),

    (*c*)   a relevant statutory scheme (as defined in section 611A of ICTA) or a pension scheme treated as if it were such a scheme, or

    (*d*)   a personal pension scheme approved under Chapter 4 of Part 14 of ICTA;

"prescribed" means prescribed by regulations made by the Commissioners;

["QROPS" and "former QROPS" have the meanings given by section 169(8) of FA 2004;][2]

"registered pension scheme" means a pension scheme that is or has been a registered pension scheme within the meaning of Part 4 of FA 2004 or in relation to which an application for registration under that Part of that Act has been made;

"responsible person", in relation to an employer-financed retirement benefits scheme, has the same meaning as in Chapter 2 of Part 6 of ITEPA 2003 (see section 399A of that Act);

"scheme administrator", in relation to a pension scheme, has the same meaning as in Part 4 of FA 2004 (see section 270 of that Act).

["scheme manager", in relation to a pension scheme, has the meaning given by section 169(3) of FA 2004.][2]][1]

Amendments—[1]   Paras 34A–34C inserted by FA 2009 s 96, Sch 48 para 11 with effect from 1 April 2010 (by virtue of SI 2009/3054 art 2).

[2]   Definitions of "QROPS" and "former QROPS", and "scheme manager", inserted by FA 2013 s 54(1), (3) with effect from 17 July 2013.

Groups of undertakings

35—(1) This paragraph applies where an undertaking is a parent undertaking in relation to another undertaking (a subsidiary undertaking).

(2) Where a third party notice is given to any person for the purpose of checking the tax position of the parent undertaking and any of its subsidiary undertakings, [—

    (a) paragraph 2(2)][1] only requires the notice to state this and name the parent undertaking[, and

    (b) the references in paragraph 3(5) to naming the taxpayer are to making that statement and naming the parent undertaking][1].

(3) In relation to such a notice—

    (a) in paragraphs 3 and 4 (approval etc of notices and copying third party notices to taxpayer), the references to the taxpayer have effect as if they were references to the parent undertaking, but

    (b) in paragraph 30(2) (no appeal in relation to taxpayer's statutory records), the reference to the taxpayer has effect as if it were a reference to the parent undertaking and each of its subsidiary undertakings.

[(4) Where a third party notice is given to the parent undertaking for the purpose of checking the tax position of more than one subsidiary undertaking—

    (a) paragraph 2(2) only requires the notice to state this, and

    (b) the references in paragraph 3(5) to naming the taxpayer are to making that statement.

(4A) In relation to such a notice—

    (a) in paragraph 3 (approval etc of notices), sub-paragraphs (1) and (3)(e) do not apply,

    (b) paragraph 4(1) (copying third party notices to taxpayer) does not apply,

    (c) [paragraphs 21 and 21A][2] (restrictions on giving taxpayer notice where taxpayer has made return) [apply][2] as if the notice was a taxpayer notice or taxpayer notices given to each subsidiary undertaking (or, if the notice names the subsidiary undertakings to which it relates, to each of those undertakings),

    (d) paragraph 30(1) (appeal) has effect as if it permitted an appeal on any grounds, and

    (e) in paragraph 30(2) (no appeal in relation to taxpayer's statutory records), the reference to the taxpayer has effect as if it were a reference to the parent undertaking or any of its subsidiary undertakings.][1]

(5) Where a notice is given under paragraph 5 to the parent undertaking for the purpose of checking the tax position of one or more subsidiary undertakings whose identities are not known to the officer giving the notice[—

    (a) sub-paragraphs (3) and (4) of that paragraph (approval of tribunal) have effect as if they permitted, but did not require, the officer to obtain the approval of the tribunal, and

    (b) paragraph 31 (appeal) has effect as if it permitted an appeal on any grounds, but the parent undertaking may not appeal against a requirement in the notice to produce any document that forms part of the statutory records of the parent undertaking or any of its subsidiary undertakings][1].

(6) Where a third party notice or a notice under paragraph 5 is given to the parent undertaking for the purpose of checking the tax position of one or more subsidiary undertakings, the parent undertaking may not appeal against a requirement in the notice to produce any document that forms part of the statutory records of the parent undertaking or any of its subsidiary undertakings.[1]

(7) In this paragraph "parent undertaking", "subsidiary undertaking" and "undertaking" have the same meaning as in the Companies Acts (see sections 1161 and 1162 of, and Schedule 7 to, the Companies Act 2006 (c 46)).

Amendments—[1]   In sub-para (2), words substituted for the words "paragraph 2" and words at the end inserted; sub-paras (4), (4A) substituted for previous sub-para (4); words in sub-para (5) substituted for the words ", sub-paragraph (3) of that paragraph (approval of tribunal) does not apply"; and sub-para (6) repealed, by FA 2009 s 95, Sch 47 para 10 with effect from 21 July 2009.

[2]   In sub-para (4A)(c), words substituted for words "paragraph 21", and word substituted for word "applies", by FA 2009 s 96, Sch 48 para 12 with effect from 1 April 2010 (by virtue of SI 2009/3054 art 2).

Change of ownership of companies

36—(1) Sub-paragraph (2) applies where it appears to the Commissioners that—

    (a) there has been a change in the ownership of a company, and

    (b) in connection with that change a person ("the seller") may be or become liable to be assessed and charged to corporation tax under [section 710 or 713 of CTA 2010][1].

(2) Paragraph 21 (restrictions on giving taxpayer notice where taxpayer has made tax return) does not apply in relation to a taxpayer notice given to the seller.

(3) [Chapter 7 of Part 14 of CTA 2010][1] applies for the purposes of determining when there has been a change in the ownership of a company.

Amendments—[1] In sub-para (1)(b) word substituted for the words "First-tier Tribunal" by the Transfer of Tribunal Functions and Revenue and Customs Appeals Order, SI 2009/56 art 3, Sch 1 para 471 with effect from 1 April 2009.
[2] In heading, word "Standard" at the start repealed and words at the end inserted, and in sub-para (2) words substituted for the words "A person to whom this paragraph applies", by FA 2009 s 95, Sch 47 para 13 with effect from 21 July 2009.

Daily default penalties [for failure to comply or obstruction]

40—(1) This paragraph applies if the failure or obstruction mentioned in paragraph 39(1) continues after the date on which a penalty is imposed under that paragraph in respect of the failure or obstruction.
(2) The person is liable to a further penalty or penalties not exceeding £60 for each subsequent day on which the failure or obstruction continues.

Commentary—*Simon's Taxes* A6.301A.
HMRC Manuals—Compliance Handbook Manual, CH26660–26680 (HMRC inspection powers: details regarding daily penalties).
CH26760 (HMRC inspection powers: two examples relating to penalties).
Amendments—In heading words at the end inserted by FA 2009 s 95, Sch 47 para 14 with effect from 21 July 2009.

[Penalties for inaccurate information and documents

40A—(1) This paragraph applies if—
   (a) in complying with an information notice, a person provides inaccurate information or produces a document that contains an inaccuracy, and
   (b) condition [A, B or C][2] is met.
(2) Condition A is that the inaccuracy is careless or deliberate.
(3) An inaccuracy is careless if it is due to a failure by the person to take reasonable care.
[(3A) Condition B is that the person knows of the inaccuracy at the time the information is provided or the document produced but does not inform HMRC at that time.][2]
(4) Condition [C][2] is that the person—
   (a) discovers the inaccuracy some time later, and
   (b) fails to take reasonable steps to inform HMRC.
(5) The person is liable to a penalty not exceeding £3,000.
(6) Where the information or document contains more than one inaccuracy, a penalty is payable for each inaccuracy.][1]

Amendments—[1] Para 40A inserted by FA 2009 s 95, Sch 47 para 15 with effect from 21 July 2009.
[2] In sub-para (1)(b), words substituted, sub-para (3A) inserted, and in sub-para (4), letter substituted, by FA 2011 s 86(2), Sch 24 paras 1, 3 with effect in relation to any inaccuracy in information provided, or in documents produced, on or after 1 April 2012.

Power to change amount of . . . penalties

41—(1) If it appears to the Treasury that there has been a change in the value of money since the last relevant date, they may by regulations substitute for the sums for the time being specified in paragraphs 39(2)[, 40(2) and 40A(5)][1] such other sums as appear to them to be justified by the change.
(2) In sub-paragraph (1)[, in relation to a specified sum,][1] "relevant date" means—
   (a) the date on which this Act is passed, and
   (b) each date on which the power conferred by that sub-paragraph has been exercised [in relation to that sum][1].
(3) Regulations under this paragraph do not apply to[—
   (a)] [1]any failure or obstruction which began before the date on which they come into force[, or
   (b) an inaccuracy in any information or document provided to HMRC before that date.][1]

Amendments—[1] In cross-heading words "standard and daily default" repealed; in sub-para (1) words substituted for the words "and 40(2)"; in sub-para (2) words inserted in both places; in sub-para (3) words inserted, and para (b) and the preceding word "or" inserted; by FA 2009 s 95, Sch 47 para 16 with effect from 21 July 2009.

Concealing, destroying etc documents following information notice

42—(1) A person must not conceal, destroy or otherwise dispose of, or arrange for the concealment, destruction or disposal of, a document that is the subject of an information notice addressed to the person (subject to sub-paragraphs (2) and (3)).
(2) Sub-paragraph (1) does not apply if the person acts after the document has been produced to an officer of Revenue and Customs in accordance with the information notice, unless an officer of Revenue and Customs has notified the person in writing that the document must continue to be available for inspection (and has not withdrawn the notification).
(3) Sub-paragraph (1) does not apply, in a case to which paragraph 8(1) applies, if the person acts after the expiry of the period of 6 months beginning with the day on which a copy of the document was produced in accordance with that paragraph unless, before the expiry of that period, an officer of Revenue and Customs made a request for the original document under paragraph 8(2)(b).

Concealing, destroying etc documents following informal notification

43—(1) A person must not conceal, destroy or otherwise dispose of, or arrange for the concealment, destruction or disposal of, a document if an officer of Revenue and Customs has informed the person that the document is, or is likely, to be the subject of an information notice addressed to that person (subject to sub-paragraph (2)).

(2) Sub-paragraph (1) does not apply if the person acts after—

    (*a*) at least 6 months has expired since the person was, or was last, so informed, or

    (*b*) an information notice has been given to the person requiring the document to be produced.

Failure to comply with time limit

44 A failure by a person to do anything required to be done within a limited period of time does not give rise to liability to a penalty under paragraph 39 or 40 if the person did it within such further time, if any, as an officer of Revenue and Customs may have allowed.

Commentary—*Simon's Taxes* **A6.301A**.

Reasonable excuse

45—(1) Liability to a penalty under paragraph 39 or 40 does not arise if the person satisfies HMRC or [(on an appeal notified to the tribunal) the tribunal][1] that there is a reasonable excuse for the failure or the obstruction of an officer of Revenue and Customs.

(2) For the purposes of this paragraph—

    (*a*) an insufficiency of funds is not a reasonable excuse unless attributable to events outside the person's control,

    (*b*) where the person relies on any other person to do anything, that is not a reasonable excuse unless the first person took reasonable care to avoid the failure or obstruction, and

    (*c*) where the person had a reasonable excuse for the failure or obstruction but the excuse has ceased, the person is to be treated as having continued to have the excuse if the failure is remedied, or the obstruction stops, without unreasonable delay after the excuse ceased.

Commentary—*Simon's Taxes* **A6.301A**.

HMRC Manuals—Compliance Handbook Manual, CH26320–26440 (HMRC inspection powers: what is and is not a reasonable excuse, with example at CH26420).

Amendments—[1] In sub-para (1) words substituted for the words "(on appeal) the First-tier Tribunal" by the Transfer of Tribunal Functions and Revenue and Customs Appeals Order, SI 2009/56 art 3, Sch 1 para 471 with effect from 1 April 2009.

Assessment of . . . penalty

46—(1) Where a person becomes liable for a penalty under paragraph 39[, 40 or 40A][1], ... [1]

    (*a*) [HMRC may][1] assess the penalty, and

    (*b*) [if they do so, they must][1] notify the person.

(2) An assessment of a penalty under paragraph 39 or 40 must be made [within the period of 12 months beginning with the date on which the person became liable to the penalty, subject to sub-paragraph (3)][1].

[(3) In a case involving an information notice against which a person may appeal, an assessment of a penalty under paragraph 39 or 40 must be made within the period of 12 months beginning with the latest of the following—

    (*a*) the date on which the person became liable to the penalty,

    (*b*) the end of the period in which notice of an appeal against the information notice could have been given, and

    (*c*) if notice of such an appeal is given, the date on which the appeal is determined or withdrawn.

(4) An assessment of a penalty under paragraph 40A must be made—

    (*a*) within the period of 12 months beginning with the date on which the inaccuracy first came to the attention of an officer of Revenue and Customs, and

    (*b*) within the period of 6 years beginning with the date on which the person became liable to the penalty.][1]

Modifications—Delivery of Tax Information through Software (Ancillary Metadata) Regulations, SI 2019/360 reg 4: this para applies to a penalty under SI 2019/360 reg 4(1) (penalty for non-compliance with relevant ancillary metadata obligation) as it applies to a penalty under para 39(1)(*a*) for failure to comply with an information notice, as if (a) in sub-para (2) the words "subject to sub-paragraph (3)", and (b) the whole of sub-para (3), were revoked.

Amendments—[1] In the cross-heading, words "standard penalty or daily default" repealed; in sub-para (1) words substituted for the words "or 40"; words "HMRC may" repealed and words at the beginning of paras (*a*), (*b*) inserted; in sub-para (2), words substituted for the words "within 12 months of the relevant date"; and sub-paras (3), (4) substituted for previous sub-para (3), by FA 2009 s 95, Sch 47 para 17 with effect from 21 July 2009.

Right to appeal against . . . penalty

47   A person may appeal . . . [1] against any of the following decisions of an officer of Revenue and Customs—

   (*a*) a decision that a penalty is payable by that person under paragraph 39[, 40 or 40A][2], or

   (*b*) a decision as to the amount of such a penalty.

Commentary—*Simon's Taxes* **A6.301A**.

HMRC Manuals—Compliance Handbook Manual, CH26900 (HMRC inspection powers (penalties): types of appeal and procedures).

Modifications—F(No 2)A 2017 Sch 16 para 42(3) (application of this para in relation to penalties for enablers of defeated tax avoidance).

Delivery of Tax Information through Software (Ancillary Metadata) Regulations, SI 2019/360 reg 4: this para applies to a penalty under SI 2019/360 reg 4(1) (penalty for non-compliance with relevant ancillary metadata obligation) as it applies to a penalty under para 39(1)(*a*) for failure to comply with an information notice, as if (a) the word "or" at the end of sub-para (*a*), and (b) the whole of sub-para (*b*), were revoked.

Amendments—[1]   Words "to the First-tier Tribunal" repealed by the Transfer of Tribunal Functions and Revenue and Customs Appeals Order, SI 2009/56 art 3, Sch 1 para 471 with effect from 1 April 2009.

[2]   In the cross-heading, words "standard penalty or daily default" repealed, in sub-para (*a*) words substituted for the words "or 40", by FA 2009 s 95, Sch 47 para 18 with effect from 21 July 2009.

Procedure on appeal against . . . penalty

48—(1) Notice of an appeal under paragraph 47 must be given—

   (*a*) in writing,

   (*b*) before the end of the period of 30 days beginning with the date on which the notification under paragraph 46 was issued, and

   (*c*) to HMRC.

(2) Notice of an appeal under paragraph 47 must state the grounds of appeal.

(3) On an appeal under paragraph 47(*a*), [that is notified to the tribunal, the tribunal][1] may confirm or cancel the decision.

(4) On an appeal under paragraph 47(*b*), [that is notified to the tribunal, the tribunal][1] may—

   (*a*) confirm the decision, or

   (*b*) substitute for the decision another decision that the officer of Revenue and Customs had power to make.

(5) Subject to this paragraph and paragraph 49, the provisions of Part 5 of TMA 1970 relating to appeals have effect in relation to appeals under this Part of this Schedule as they have effect in relation to an appeal against an assessment to income tax.

Modifications—Delivery of Tax Information through Software (Ancillary Metadata) Regulations, SI 2019/360 reg 4: this para applies to a penalty under SI 2019/360 reg 4(1) (penalty for non-compliance with relevant ancillary metadata obligation) as it applies to a penalty under para 39(1)(*a*) for failure to comply with an information notice, as if sub-para (4), were revoked.

Amendments—In the heading, words "standard penalty or daily default" repealed by FA 2009 s 95, Sch 47 para 19 with effect from 21 July 2009.

[1]   In sub-paras (3), 4) words substituted for the words "First-tier Tribunal" by the Transfer of Tribunal Functions and Revenue and Customs Appeals Order, SI 2009/56 art 3, Sch 1 para 471 with effect from 1 April 2009.

Enforcement of . . . penalty

49—(1) A penalty under paragraph 39[, 40 or 40A][1] must be paid—

   (*a*) before the end of the period of 30 days beginning with the date on which the notification under paragraph 46 was issued, or

   (*b*) if a notice of an appeal against the penalty is given, before the end of the period of 30 days beginning with the date on which the appeal is determined or withdrawn.

(2) A penalty under paragraph 39[, 40 or 40A][1] may be enforced as if it were income tax charged in an assessment and due and payable.

Commentary—*Simon's Taxes* **A6.301A**.

HMRC Manuals—Compliance Handbook Manual, CH26880 (HMRC inspection powers: when is the penalty payable).

Amendments—[1]   In the heading, words "standard penalty or daily default" repealed, in sub-paras (1), (2) words substituted for the words "or 40", by FA 2009 s 95, Sch 47 para 20 with effect from 21 July 2009.

[Increased daily default penalty

49A   (1) This paragraph applies if—

   (*a*) a penalty under paragraph 40 is assessed under paragraph 46 in respect of a person's failure to comply with a notice under paragraph 5,

   (*b*) the failure continues for more than 30 days beginning with the date on which notification of that assessment was issued, and

   (*c*) the person has been told that an application may be made under this paragraph for an increased daily penalty to be imposed.

(2) If this paragraph applies, an officer of Revenue and Customs may make an application to the tribunal for an increased daily penalty to be imposed on the person.

(3) If the tribunal decides that an increased daily penalty should be imposed, then for each applicable day (see paragraph 49B) on which the failure continues—

    (a) the person is not liable to a penalty under paragraph 40 in respect of the failure, and

    (b) the person is liable instead to a penalty under this paragraph of an amount determined by the tribunal.

(4) The tribunal may not determine an amount exceeding £1,000 for each applicable day.

(5) But subject to that, in determining the amount the tribunal must have regard to—

    (a) the likely cost to the person of complying with the notice,

    (b) any benefits to the person of not complying with it, and

    (c) any benefits to anyone else resulting from the person's non-compliance.

(6) Paragraph 41 applies in relation to the sum specified in sub-paragraph (4) as it applies in relation to the sums mentioned in paragraph 41(1).][1]

Modification—See F(No 2)A 2017 Sch 16 para 42(4) (application of this para in relation to penalties for enablers of defeated tax avoidance).

Amendments—[1] Paras 49A–49C inserted by FA 2011 s 86(2), Sch 24 paras 1, 4 with effect in relation to failures to comply with a notice under FA 2008 Sch 36 para 5 that begin on or after 1 April 2012.

[49B (1) If a person becomes liable to a penalty under paragraph 49A, HMRC must notify the person.

(2) The notification must specify the day from which the increased penalty is to apply.

(3) That day and any subsequent day is an "applicable day" for the purposes of paragraph 49A(3).][1]

Modification—See F(No 2)A 2017 Sch 16 para 42(5) (application of this para in relation to penalties for enablers of defeated tax avoidance).

Amendments—[1] Paras 49A–49C inserted by FA 2011 s 86(2), Sch 24 paras 1, 4 with effect in relation to failures to comply with a notice under FA 2008 Sch 36 para 5 that begin on or after 1 April 2012.

[49C (1) A penalty under paragraph 49A must be paid before the end of the period of 30 days beginning with the date on which the notification under paragraph 49B is issued.

(2) A penalty under paragraph 49A may be enforced as if it were income tax charged in an assessment and due and payable.][1]

Modification—See F(No 2)A 2017 Sch 16 para 42(6) (disapplication of this para in relation to penalties for enablers of defeated tax avoidance).

Amendments—[1] Paras 49A–49C inserted by FA 2011 s 86(2), Sch 24 paras 1, 4 with effect in relation to failures to comply with a notice under FA 2008 Sch 36 para 5 that begin on or after 1 April 2012.

Tax-related penalty

50—(1) This paragraph applies where—

    (a) a person becomes liable to a penalty under paragraph 39,

    (b) the failure or obstruction continues after a penalty is imposed under that paragraph,

    (c) an officer of Revenue and Customs has reason to believe that, as a result of the failure or obstruction, the amount of tax that the person has paid, or is likely to pay, is significantly less than it would otherwise have been,

    (d) before the end of the period of 12 months beginning with the relevant date . . . [1], an officer of Revenue and Customs makes an application to the Upper Tribunal for an additional penalty to be imposed on the person, and

    (e) the Upper Tribunal decides that it is appropriate for an additional penalty to be imposed.

(2) The person is liable to a penalty of an amount decided by the Upper Tribunal.

(3) In deciding the amount of the penalty, the Upper Tribunal must have regard to the amount of tax which has not been, or is not likely to be, paid by the person.

(4) Where a person becomes liable to a penalty under this paragraph, HMRC must notify the person.

(5) Any penalty under this paragraph is in addition to the penalty or penalties under paragraph 39 or 40.

(6) In the application of the following provisions, no account shall be taken of a penalty under this paragraph—

    (a) section 97A of TMA 1970 (multiple penalties),

    (b) paragraph 12(2) of Schedule 24 to FA 2007 (interaction with other penalties), and

    (c) paragraph 15(1) of Schedule 41 (interaction with other penalties).

[(7) In sub-paragraph (1)(d) "the relevant date" means—

    (a) in a case involving an information notice against which a person may appeal, the latest of—

        (i) the date on which the person became liable to the penalty under paragraph 39,

        (ii) the end of the period in which notice of an appeal against the information notice could have been given, and

     (iii) if notice of such an appeal is given, the date on which the appeal is determined or withdrawn, and

  (b) in any other case, the date on which the person became liable to the penalty under paragraph 39.][1]

Commentary—*Simon's Taxes* **A6.301A**.

HMRC Manuals—Compliance Handbook Manual, CH26720 (HMRC inspection powers: details regarding tax related penalty). CH26760 (HMRC inspection powers: two examples relating to penalties).

Modification—See FA 2016 Sch 20 para 20(d) (disapplication of this para in relation to penalties for enablers of offshore tax evasion or non-compliance).

See F(No 2)A 2017 Sch 16 para 43 (disapplication of this para in relation to penalties for enablers of defeated tax avoidance).

Amendments—[1]   In sub-para (1)(d) words "(within the meaning of paragraph 46)" repealed, and sub-para (7) inserted, by FA 2011 s 86(2), Sch 24 paras 1, 5(1)–(3) with effect where a person becomes liable to a penalty under FA 2008 Sch 36 para 39 on or after 19 July 2011.

Enforcement of tax-related penalty

51—(1) A penalty under paragraph 50 must be paid before the end of the period of 30 days beginning with the date on which the notification of the penalty is issued.

(2) A penalty under paragraph 50 may be enforced as if it were income tax charged in an assessment and due and payable.

Commentary—*Simon's Taxes* **A6.301A**.

Modification—See FA 2016 Sch 20 para 20(d) (disapplication of this para in relation to penalties for enablers of offshore tax evasion or non-compliance).

See F(No 2)A 2017 Sch 16 para 43 (disapplication of this para in relation to penalties for enablers of defeated tax avoidance).

Double jeopardy

52   A person is not liable to a penalty under this Schedule in respect of anything in respect of which the person has been convicted of an offence.

Commentary—*Simon's Taxes* **A6.301A**.

PART 8
OFFENCE

Concealing etc documents following information notice

53—(1) A person is guilty of an offence (subject to sub-paragraphs (2) and (3)) if—

  (a) the person is required to produce a document by an information notice,

  (b) the [tribunal][1] approved the giving of the notice in accordance with paragraph 3 or 5, and

  (c) the person conceals, destroys or otherwise disposes of, or arranges for the concealment, destruction or disposal of, that document.

(2) Sub-paragraph (1) does not apply if the person acts after the document has been produced to an officer of Revenue and Customs in accordance with the information notice, unless an officer of Revenue and Customs has notified the person in writing that the document must continue to be available for inspection (and has not withdrawn the notification).

(3) Sub-paragraph (1) does not apply, in a case to which paragraph 8(1) applies, if the person acts after the expiry of the period of 6 months beginning with the day on which a copy of the document was so produced unless, before the expiry of that period, an officer of Revenue and Customs made a request for the original document under paragraph 8(2)(b).

Amendments—[1]   In sub-para (1)(b) word substituted for the words "First-tier Tribunal" by the Transfer of Tribunal Functions and Revenue and Customs Appeals Order, SI 2009/56 art 3, Sch 1 para 471 with effect from 1 April 2009.

Concealing etc documents following informal notification

54—(1) A person is also guilty of an offence (subject to sub-paragraph (2)) if the person conceals, destroys or otherwise disposes of, or arranges for the concealment, destruction or disposal of a document after the person has been informed by an officer of Revenue and Customs in writing that—

  (a) the document is, or is likely, to be the subject of an information notice addressed to that person, and

  (b) an officer of Revenue and Customs intends to seek the approval of the [tribunal][1] to the giving of the notice under paragraph 3 or 5 in respect of the document.

(2) A person is not guilty of an offence under this paragraph if the person acts after—

  (a) at least 6 months has expired since the person was, or was last, so informed, or

  (b) an information notice has been given to the person requiring the document to be produced.

Amendments—[1]   In sub-para (1)(b) word substituted for the words "First-tier Tribunal" by the Transfer of Tribunal Functions and Revenue and Customs Appeals Order, SI 2009/56 art 3, Sch 1 para 471 with effect from 1 April 2009.

Fine or imprisonment

55 A person who is guilty of an offence under this Part of this Schedule is liable—

(a) on summary conviction, to a fine not exceeding the statutory maximum, and

(b) on conviction on indictment, to imprisonment for a term not exceeding 2 years or to a fine, or both.

PART 9
MISCELLANEOUS PROVISIONS AND INTERPRETATION

Application of provisions of TMA 1970

56 Subject to the provisions of this Schedule, the following provisions of TMA 1970 apply for the purposes of this Schedule as they apply for the purposes of the Taxes Acts—

(a) section 108 (responsibility of company officers),

(b) section 114 (want of form), and

(c) section 115 (delivery and service of documents).

Regulations under this Schedule

57—(1) Regulations made by the Commissioners or the Treasury under this Schedule are to be made by statutory instrument.

(2) A statutory instrument containing regulations under this Schedule is subject to annulment in pursuance of a resolution of the House of Commons.

General interpretation

58 In this Schedule—

"checking" includes carrying out an investigation or enquiry of any kind,

"the Commissioners" means the Commissioners for Her Majesty's Revenue and Customs,

"document" includes a part of a document (except where the context otherwise requires),

"enactment" includes subordinate legislation (within the meaning of the Interpretation Act 1978 (c 30)),

"HMRC" means Her Majesty's Revenue and Customs,

"premises" includes—

(a) any building or structure,

(b) any land, and

(c) any means of transport,

"the Taxes Acts" means—

(a) TMA 1970,

(b) the Tax Acts, and

(c) TCGA 1992 and all other enactments relating to capital gains tax, . . .[1]

"taxpayer", in relation to a taxpayer notice or a third party notice, has the meaning given in paragraph 1(1) or 2(1) (as appropriate) [and][1]

["tribunal" means the First-tier Tribunal or, where determined by or under Tribunal Procedure Rules, the Upper Tribunal.][1]

Amendments—[1] In sub-para (c) in the definition of "the Taxes Acts" word "and" at the end repealed; definition of "tribunal" and the preceding word "and" inserted by the Transfer of Tribunal Functions and Revenue and Customs Appeals Order, SI 2009/56 art 3, Sch 1 para 471 with effect from 1 April 2009.

Authorised officer of Revenue and Customs

59 A reference in a provision of this Schedule to an authorised officer of Revenue and Customs is a reference to an officer of Revenue and Customs who is, or is a member of a class of officers who are, authorised by the Commissioners for the purpose of that provision.

Business

60—(1) In this Schedule (subject to regulations under this paragraph), references to carrying on a business include—

(a) the letting of property,

(b) the activities of a charity, and

(c) the activities of a government department, a local authority, a local authority association and any other public authority.

[(1A) A person who under section 41 of FA 1996 is liable to pay landfill tax charged on a taxable disposal is treated for the purposes of this Schedule (subject to regulations under this paragraph) as carrying on a business.][2]
(2) In sub-paragraph (1)—

. . .[1]

"local authority" has the meaning given in section 999 of ITA 2007, and

"local authority association" has the meaning given in section 1000 of that Act.

(3) The Commissioners may by regulations provide that for the purposes of this Schedule—

(*a*) the carrying on of an activity specified in the regulations, or

(*b*) the carrying on of such an activity (or any activity) by a person specified in the regulations,

is or is not to be treated as the carrying on of a business.

Amendments—[1]   In sub-s (2) definition of "charity" repealed by FA 2010 s 30, Sch 6 para 24 with effect from 1 April 2012 (SI 2012/736 art 19).

[2]   Sub-para (1A) inserted by FA 2018 s 42(1), Sch 12 para 26(1), (2) with effect in relation to disposals made, or treated as made, on or after 1 April 2018, subject to transitional arrangements relating to disposals before April 2018 at places other than landfill sites (FA 2018 Sch 12 paras 31, 32). This amendment has effect in relation to disposals made in England or Northern Ireland only.

Chargeable period

61   In this Schedule "chargeable period" means—

(*a*) in relation to income tax or capital gains tax, a tax year, and

(*b*) in relation to corporation tax, an accounting period.

[Involved third parties

61A—(1) In this Schedule, "involved third party" means a person described in the first column of the Table below.
(2) In this Schedule, in relation to an involved third party, . . .[3] "relevant document" and "relevant tax" have the meaning given in the corresponding entries in that Table.

	Involved third party	Relevant . . .[3] documents	Relevant tax
1	A body approved by an officer of Revenue and Customs for the purpose of paying donations within the meaning of Part 12 of ITEPA 2003 (donations to charity: payroll giving) (see section 714 of that Act)	[Documents][3] relating to the donations	Income tax
2	A plan manager (see section 696 of ITTOIA 2005 (managers of individual investment plans))	[Documents][3] relating to the plan, including investments which are or have been held under the plan	Income tax
3	An account provider in relation to a child trust fund (as defined in section 3 of the Child Trust Funds Act 2004)	[Documents][3] relating to the fund, including investments which are or have been held under the fund	Income tax
4	A person who is or has been registered as a managing agent at Lloyd's in relation to a syndicate of underwriting members of Lloyd's	[Documents][3] relating to, and to the activities of, the syndicate	Income tax Capital gains tax Corporation tax
5	A person involved (in any capacity) in an insurance business (as defined for the purposes of Part 3 of FA 1994)	[Documents][3] relating to contracts of insurance entered into in the course of the business	Insurance premium tax
6	A person who makes arrangements for persons to enter into contracts of insurance	[Documents][3] relating to the contracts	Insurance premium tax
7	A person who— (*a*) is concerned in a business that is not an insurance business (as defined for the purposes of Part 3 of FA 1994), and (*b*) has been involved in the entry into a contract of insurance providing cover for any matter associated with that business	[Documents][3] relating to the contracts	Insurance premium tax

	Involved third party	*Relevant . . .* [3] *documents*	*Relevant tax*
8	A person who, in relation to a charge to stamp duty reserve tax on an agreement, transfer, issue, appropriation or surrender, is an accountable person (as defined in regulation 2 of the Stamp Duty Reserve Tax Regulations SI 1986/1711 (as amended from time to time))	[Documents][3] relating to the agreement, transfer, issue, appropriation or surrender	Stamp duty reserve tax
9	A responsible person in relation to an oil field (as defined for the purposes of Part 1 of OTA 1975)	[Documents][3] relating to the oil field	Petroleum revenue tax
10	A person involved (in any capacity) in subjecting aggregate to exploitation in the United Kingdom (as defined for the purposes of Part 2 of FA 2001) or in connected activities	[Documents][3] relating to matters in which the person is or has been involved	Aggregates levy
11	A person involved (in any capacity) in making or receiving [supplies of][2] taxable commodities (as defined for the purposes of Schedule 6 to FA 2000) or in connected activities	[Documents][3] relating to matters in which the person is or has been involved	Climate change levy
12	A person involved (in any capacity) with any [disposal of material][4] (as defined for the purposes of Part 3 of FA 1996)	[Documents][3] relating to the disposal	Landfill tax[1]

Amendments—[1]   Para 61A inserted by FA 2009 s 96, Sch 48 para 14 with effect from 1 April 2010 (by virtue of SI 2009/3054 art 2).

[2]   In Table, words in item 11 inserted by FA 2011 s 86(2), Sch 24 paras 1, 6 with effect from 19 July 2011.

[3]   In sub-para (2) words ""relevant information"," repealed, in each entry in second column of the Table word substituted for words "Information and documents", and in heading of that column words "information and relevant" repealed, by FA 2011 s 86(1), Sch 23 paras 60, 62(1), (3) with effect from 1 April 2012 in relation to relevant data with a bearing on any period (whether before, on or after 1 April 2012) subject to FA 2011 Sch 23 para 3(2). This para will continue to have effect in relation to notices given, or requests made, under any of the provisions repealed by FA 2011 Sch 23 Pt 6 before 1 April 2012 as if the amendments had not been made (FA 2011 Sch 23 para 65(2)).

[4]   In Table, words in item 12 substituted for words "landfill disposal" by FA 2018 s 42(1), Sch 12 para 26(1), (3) with effect in relation to disposals made, or treated as made, on or after 1 April 2018, subject to transitional arrangements relating to disposals before April 2018 at places other than landfill sites (FA 2018 Sch 12 paras 31, 32). This amendment has effect in relation to disposals made in England or Northern Ireland only.

Statutory records

62— (1) For the purposes of this Schedule, information or a document forms part of a person's statutory records if it is information or a document which the person is required to keep and preserve under or by virtue of—

    (*a*) the Taxes Acts, or

    [(*b*) any other enactment relating to a tax,][1]

subject to the following provisions of this paragraph.

(2) To the extent that any information or document that is required to be kept and preserved under or by virtue of the Taxes Acts—

    (*a*) does not relate to the carrying on of a business, and

    (*b*) is not also required to be kept or preserved under or by virtue of [any other enactment relating to a tax][1],

it only forms part of a person's statutory records to the extent that the chargeable period or periods to which it relates has or have ended.

(3) Information and documents cease to form part of a person's statutory records when the period for which they are required to be preserved by the enactments mentioned in sub-paragraph (1) has expired.

Amendments—[1]   Sub-para (1)(*b*) substituted, and in sub-para (2) words substituted for words "VATA 1994 or any other enactment relating to value added tax", by FA 2009 s 95, Sch 48 para 15 with effect from 1 April 2010 (by virtue of SI 2009/3054 art 2).

Tax

63—(1) In this Schedule, except where the context otherwise requires, "tax" means all or any of the following—

  (*a*) income tax,

  (*b*) capital gains tax,

  (*c*) corporation tax,

  [(*ca*) diverted profits tax,]⁵

  [(*cb*) apprenticeship levy,]⁶

  [(*cc*) digital services tax,]⁸

  (*d*) VAT, and

  [(*e*) insurance premium tax,

  (*f*) inheritance tax,

  (*g*) stamp duty land tax,

  (*h*) stamp duty reserve tax,

  [(*ha*) annual tax on enveloped dwellings,]³

  (*i*) petroleum revenue tax,

  [(*ia* soft drinks industry levy,]⁷

  (*j*) aggregates levy,

  (*k*) climate change levy,

  (*l*) landfill tax, and

  (*m*) relevant foreign tax,]²

and references to "a tax" are to be interpreted accordingly.

(2) In this Schedule "corporation tax" includes any amount assessable or chargeable as if it were corporation tax.

(3) In this Schedule "VAT" means—

  (*a*) value added tax charged in accordance with VATA 1994, ...¹

  (*b*) value added tax charged in accordance with the law of another member State, [and

  (*c*) amounts listed in sub-paragraph (3A).]¹

[(3A) Those amounts are—

  (*a*) any amount that is recoverable under paragraph 5(2) of Schedule 11 to VATA 1994 (amounts shown on invoices as VAT), and

  (*b*) any amount that is treated as VAT by virtue of regulations under section 54 of VATA 1994 (farmers etc).]¹

(4) In this Schedule "relevant foreign tax" means—

  (*a*) a tax of a member State, other than the United Kingdom, which is covered by the provisions for the exchange of information under [Council Directive 2011/16/EU of 15 February 2011 on administrative cooperation in the field of taxation]⁴ (as amended from time to time), and

  (*b*) any tax or duty which is imposed under the law of a territory in relation to which arrangements having effect by virtue of section 173 of FA 2006 (international tax enforcement arrangements) have been made and which is covered by the arrangements.

Modification—See FA 2010 Sch 1 para 36 (modification of this para in relation to bank payroll tax).

Amendments—¹ In sub-para (3)(*a*) word "and" repealed, sub-para (3)(*c*) and the preceding word "and" substituted for the words "and includes any amount that is recoverable under paragraph 5(2) of Schedule 11 to VATA 1994 (amounts shown on invoices as VAT)", and sub-para (3A) inserted, by FA 2009 s 95, Sch 47 para 21 with effect from 21 July 2009.

² In sub-para (1), paras (*e*)–(*m*) substituted for previous para (*e*) and preceding word "and" by FA 2009 s 96(1) with effect from 1 April 2010 (by virtue of SI 2009/3054 art 2).

³ Sub-para (1)(*ha*) inserted by FA 2013 s 164, Sch 34 paras 1, 5 with effect from 17 July 2013.

⁴ In sub-para (4)(*a*), words substituted by the European Administrative Co-operation (Taxation) Regulations, SI 2012/3062 reg 6 with effect from 1 January 2013.

⁵ Sub-para (1)(*ca*) inserted by FA 2015 s 105(2) with effect in relation to accounting periods beginning on or after 1 April 2015. For accounting periods that straddle that date, see FA 2015 s 116(2).

⁶ Sub-para (1)(*cb*) inserted by FA 2016 s 112 with effect from 15 September 2016. The apprenticeship levy applies in relation to 2017–18 and subsequent tax years.

⁷ Sub-para (1)(*ia*) inserted by FA 2017 s 56, Sch 11 para 1(1), (3) with effect from 6 April 2018 (by virtue of SI 2018/464). The charge to soft drinks industry levy arises on chargeable events which occur on or after 6 April 2018 (FA 2017 s 31(1)).

⁸ Sub-para (1)(*cc*) inserted by FA 2020 s 70, Sch 10 paras 4, 5 with effect from 22 July 2020.

Prospective amendments—Sub-para (3)(*b*), but not the "and" at the end, to be repealed by the Taxation (Cross-border Trade) Act 2018 s 43, Sch 8 paras 112, 113(1), (4) with effect from a day to be appointed.

Tax position

64—(1) In this Schedule, except as otherwise provided, "tax position", in relation to a person, means the person's position as regards any tax, including the person's position as regards—

  (*a*) past, present and future liability to pay any tax,

  (*b*) penalties and other amounts that have been paid, or are or may be payable, by or to the person in connection with any tax, and

  (*c*) claims, elections, applications and notices that have been or may be made or given in connection with [the person's liability to pay]¹ any tax, and references to a person's position as regards a particular tax (however expressed) are to be interpreted accordingly.

(2) References in this Schedule to a person's tax position include, where appropriate, a reference to the person's position as regards any deductions or repayments of tax, or of sums representing tax, that the person is required to make—

    (*a*) under PAYE regulations,

    (*b*) under Chapter 3 of Part 3 of FA 2004 or regulations made under that Chapter (construction industry scheme), or

    (*c*) by or under any other provision of the Taxes Acts.

[(2A) References in this Schedule to a person's tax position also include, where appropriate, a reference to the person's position as regards the withholding by the person of another person's PAYE income (as defined in section 683 of ITEPA 2003).]

(3) References in this Schedule to the tax position of a person include the tax position of—

    (*a*) a company that has ceased to exist, and

    (*b*) an individual who has died.

(4) References in this Schedule to a person's tax position are to the person's tax position at any time or in relation to any period, unless otherwise stated.

Amendments—[1] In sub-para (1)(*c*) words inserted, and sub-para (2A) inserted, by FA 2009 s 95, Sch 47 para 22 with effect from 21 July 2009.

PART 10

CONSEQUENTIAL PROVISIONS

TMA 1970

65 TMA 1970 is amended as follows.

66 Omit section 19A (power to call for documents for purposes of enquiries).

67 Omit section 20 (power to call for documents of taxpayer and others).

68—(1) Section 20B (restrictions on powers to call for documents under ss 20 and 20A) is amended as follows.

(2) In the heading, for "**ss 20 and**" substitute "**section**".

(3) In subsection (1)—

    (*a*) omit "under section 20(1), (3) or (8A), or",

    (*b*) omit "(or, in the case of section 20(3), to deliver or make available)",

    (*c*) omit ", or to furnish the particulars in question", and

    (*d*) omit "section 20(7) or (8A) or, as the case may be,".

(4) Omit subsections (1A) and (1B).

(5) In subsection (2), omit from the beginning to "taxpayer; and".

(6) In subsection (3)—

    (*a*) omit "under section 20(1) or (3) or", and

    (*b*) omit "section 20(3) and (4) and".

(7) In subsection (4)—

    (*a*) omit "section 20(1) or", and

    (*b*) omit ", and as an alternative to delivering documents to comply with a notice under section 20(3) or (8A)".

(8) Omit subsections (5), (6) and (7).

(9) In subsection (8), omit "section 20(3) or (8A) or".

(10) Omit subsections (9) to (14).

69—(1) Section 20BB (falsification etc of documents) is amended as follows.

(2) In subsection (1)(*a*), omit "20 or".

(3) In subsection (2)(*b*), omit "or, in a case within section 20(3) or (8A) above, inspected".

70—(1) Section 20D (interpretation) is amended as follows.

(2) In subsection (2), for "sections 20 and" substitute "section".

(3) Omit subsection (3).

71 In section 29(6)(*c*) (assessment where loss of tax discovered), omit ", whether in pursuance of a notice under section 19A of this Act or otherwise".

72 Omit section 97AA (failure to produce documents under section 19A).

73 In section 98 (penalties), in the Table—

    (*a*) in the first column, omit the entry for section 767C of ICTA, and

    (*b*) in the second column, omit the entry for section 28(2) of F(No 2)A 1992.

3 In section 29(4) (assessment where loss of tax discovered), for "is attributable to fraudulent or negligent conduct on the part of" substitute "was brought about carelessly or deliberately by".

4 In section 30B(5) (amendment of partnership statement where loss of tax discovered), for "is attributable to fraudulent or negligent conduct on the part of" substitute "was brought about carelessly or deliberately by".

5 In section 33(1) (claim for error or mistake), for "not later than five years after the 31st January next following" substitute "not more than 4 years after the end of".

Commentary—*Simon's Taxes* A4.207.

6 In section 33A(2) (error or mistake in partnership return), for "not later than 31st January of Year 6" substitute "not more than 4 years after the end of the year of assessment in question, or in which the relevant period ends,".

7—(1) Section 34 (ordinary time limit for assessments) is amended as follows.
(2) In subsection (1), for "not later than five years after the 31st January next following" substitute "not more than 4 years after the end of".
(3) Accordingly, in the heading, for "**six years**" substitute "**4 years**".

8 In section 35 (time limit: income received after year for which it is assessable), for "within six years after" substitute "not more than 4 years after the end of".

9—(1) Section 36 (fraudulent or negligent conduct) is amended as follows.
(2) For subsection (1) substitute—

"(1) An assessment on a person in a case involving a loss of income tax or capital gains tax brought about carelessly by the person may be made at any time not more than 6 years after the end of the year of assessment to which it relates (subject to subsection (1A) and any other provision of the Taxes Acts allowing a longer period).

(1A) An assessment on a person in a case involving a loss of income tax or capital gains tax—

    (*a*)   brought about deliberately by the person,
    (*b*)   attributable to a failure by the person to comply with an obligation under section 7, or
    (*c*)   attributable to arrangements in respect of which the person has failed to comply with an obligation under section 309, 310 or 313 of the Finance Act 2004 (obligation of parties to tax avoidance schemes to provide information to Her Majesty's Revenue and Customs),

may be made at any time not more than 20 years after the end of the year of assessment to which it relates (subject to any provision of the Taxes Acts allowing a longer period).

(1B) In subsections (1) and (1A), references to a loss brought about by the person who is the subject of the assessment include a loss brought about by another person acting on behalf of that person."

(3) In subsection (2)—

    (*a*)   for "Where the person in default" substitute "Where the person mentioned in subsection (1) or (1A) ("the person in default")", and
    (*b*)   for "subsection (1) above" substitute "subsection (1A) or (1B)".
(4) In subsection (3), after "(1)" insert "or (1A)".
(5) In subsection (4), for "subsection (1)" substitute "subsections (1) and (1A)".
(6) Accordingly, for the heading substitute "**Loss of tax brought about carelessly or deliberately etc**".

10 In section 37A (effect of assessment where allowances transferred), for the words from "for the purpose" to "conduct" substitute "in a case falling within section 36(1) or (1A)".

11—(1) Section 40 (assessment on personal representatives) is amended as follows.
(2) In subsection (1) for "beyond the end of the period of three years beginning with the 31st January next following" substitute "more than 4 years after the end of".
(3) In subsection (2)—

    (*a*)   for the words from the beginning to "died" substitute "In a case involving a loss of tax brought about carelessly or deliberately by a person who has died (or another person acting on that person's behalf before that person's death)", and
    (*b*)   for "before the end of the period of three years beginning with the 31st January next following" substitute "not more than 4 years after the end of".

Commentary—*Simon's Taxes* A4.327.

12 In section 43(1) (time limit for making claims), for "five years after the 31st January next following" substitute "4 years after the end of".

Commentary—*Simon's Taxes* **E5.203A**.

13 In section 43A(1)(*b*) (further assessments: claims etc), for the words from "attributable" to the end substitute "brought about carelessly or deliberately by that person or by someone acting on behalf of that person."

14 In section 43C(1)(*b*) (consequential claims etc), for "attributable to fraudulent or negligent conduct on the part of" substitute "brought about carelessly or deliberately by".

15 (*inserts* TMA 1970 s 118(5)–(7))

ICTA

16 ICTA is amended as follows.

TCGA 1992

28 TCGA 1992 is amended as follows.

29 In section 203(2) (claims in respect of certain capital losses), for "6 years" substitute "4 years".

30 In section 253(4A) (claims for relief for loans to traders)—

(*a*) in paragraph (*a*), for "on or before the fifth anniversary of the 31st January next following" substitute "not more than 4 years after the end of", and

(*b*) in paragraph (*b*), for "6 years" substitute "4 years".

31 In section 279(5) (claims in respect of delayed remittance of gain from disposal of foreign assets)—

(*a*) in paragraph (*a*), for "at any time after the fifth anniversary of the 31st January next following" substitute "more than 4 years after the end of", and

(*b*) in paragraph (*b*), for "6 years" substitute "4 years".

VATA 1994

32–36 (See the *Orange Tax Handbook* for amendments made to VATA 1994)

FA 1998

37 Schedule 18 to FA 1998 (company tax returns) is amended as follows.

38 In paragraph 36(5) (determination of tax payable if no return delivered), for "five years" substitute "3 years".

Commentary—*Simon's Taxes* **A4.312**.

39 In paragraph 37(4) (determination of tax payable if notice complied with in part), for "five years" substitute "3 years".

Commentary—*Simon's Taxes* **A4.312**.

40 In paragraph 40(3) (time limit for self-assessment superseding determination), for "five years" substitute "3 years".

41—(1) Paragraph 43 (fraudulent or negligent conduct) is amended as follows.

(2) For "is attributable to fraudulent or negligent conduct on the part of" substitute "was brought about carelessly or deliberately by".

(3) Accordingly, for the heading before the paragraph substitute "*Loss of tax brought about carelessly or deliberately*".

42—(1) Paragraph 46 (general time limits for assessments) is amended as follows.

(2) In sub-paragraph (1), for "six years" substitute "4 years".

(3) For sub-paragraph (2) substitute—

"(2) An assessment in a case involving a loss of tax brought about carelessly by the company (or a related person) may be made at any time not more than 6 years after the end of the accounting period to which it relates (subject to sub-paragraph (2A) and to any other provision of the Taxes Acts allowing a longer period).

(2A) An assessment in a case involving a loss of tax—

(*a*) brought about deliberately by the company (or a related person),

(*b*) attributable to a failure by the company to comply with an obligation under paragraph 2, or (*c*)   attributable to arrangements in respect of which the company has failed to comply with an obligation under section 309, 310 or 313 of the Finance Act 2004 (obligation of parties to tax avoidance schemes to provide information to Her Majesty's Revenue and Customs),

may be made at any time not more than 20 years after the end of the accounting period to which it relates (subject to any provision of the Taxes Acts allowing a longer period).

   (2B)   In this paragraph "related person", in relation to a company, means—

     (*a*)   a person acting on behalf of the company, or

     (*b*)   a person who was a partner of the company at the relevant time."

43   In paragraph 51(1)(*c*) (relief in case of mistake in return), for "six years" substitute "4 years".

44—(1) Paragraph 53 (time limit for recovery of excessive payments etc) is amended as follows.
(2) In sub-paragraph (1), for "six year" substitute "4 year".
(3) In sub-paragraph (2), for "paragraph 46(2) (time limit for assessment in case of fraud or negligence)" substitute "paragraph 46(2) and (2A) (time limit for assessment in case of loss of tax brought about carelessly or deliberately)".

45   In paragraph 55 (general time limit for making claims), for "six years" substitute "4 years".

46   In paragraph 61(2) (consequential claims etc arising out of certain Revenue amendments or assessments), for "fraudulent or negligent conduct on the part of" substitute "a loss of tax brought about carelessly or deliberately by".

47—(1) Paragraph 65 (consequential claims) is amended as follows.
(2) In sub-paragraph (1), for "fraudulent or negligent conduct on the part of" substitute "a loss of tax brought about carelessly or deliberately by".
(3) Accordingly, in the heading before the paragraph, for "*fraud or negligence*" substitute "*loss of tax brought about carelessly or deliberately*".

ITEPA 2003

49   In section 711(2) (notice requiring officer of Revenue and Customs to give notice requiring tax return), for "5 years" substitute "3 years".

ITTOIA 2005

50   ITTOIA 2005 is amended as follows.

51   In section 301(3) (claims for repayment of tax payable in connection with sale with right to reconveyance), for "6 years" substitute "4 years".

52   In section 302(3) (claims for repayment of tax payable in connection with sale and leaseback transactions), for "6 years" substitute "4 years".

53   In section 840A(1) (claims for relief for backdated pensions charged on arising basis) (inserted by Schedule 7 to this Act), for "on or before the fifth anniversary of the normal self-assessment filing date for" substitute "not more than 4 years after the end of".

ITA 2007

54   ITA 2007 is amended as follows.

55   In section 40(1)(*a*) (election for transfer of blind person's allowance), for "on or before the fifth anniversary of the normal self-assessment filing date for" substitute "not more than 4 years after the end of".

56   In section 46(6)(*b*) (marriages and civil partnerships on or after 5 December 2005: election specifying person entitled to relief), for "on or before the fifth anniversary of the normal self-assessment filing date for" substitute "not more than 4 years after the end of".

57   In section 53(4)(*a*) (notice in respect of transfer of unused relief), for "on or before the fifth anniversary of the normal self-assessment filing date for" substitute "not more than 4 years after the end of".

58   In section 155 (claim for loss relief against miscellaneous income), in each of subsections (1) and (2), for "on or before the fifth anniversary of the normal self-assessment filing date for" substitute "not more than 4 years after the end of".

59—(1) Section 237 (EIS relief: time limits for assessments) is amended as follows.
(2) In subsection (1)—

    (*a*) omit "not", and

    (*b*) for "more than" substitute "at any time not more than".

(3) In subsection (3)—

    (*a*) for "36" substitute "36(1A)", and

    (*b*) for "(fraudulent or negligent conduct)" substitute "(loss of tax brought about deliberately etc)".

60   (*inserts* ITA 2007 s 372(4),(5))

61   In section 668(7) (claim for relief for unremittable transfer proceeds), for "on or before the fifth anniversary of the normal self-assessment filing date for" substitute "not more than 4 years after the end of".

62   In section 669(4) (claim for relief for unremittable transfer proceeds: section 630 profits), for "on or before the fifth anniversary of the normal self-assessment filing date for" substitute "not more than 4 years after the end of".

Consequential amendments

63   In section 178(3) of FA 1993 (stop-loss and quota share insurance)—

    (*a*) in paragraph (*a*), for "six years" substitute "4 years", and

    (*b*) in paragraph (*b*), for "fraudulent or negligent conduct" substitute "loss of tax brought about carelessly or deliberately".

64   In section 225(3)(*b*) of FA 1994 (stop-loss and quota share insurance), for "fraudulent or negligent conduct" substitute "loss of tax brought about carelessly or deliberately".

65   In consequence of the preceding provisions of this Schedule, omit—

    (*a*) section 149(4)(*a*)(i) and (ii) of FA 1989,

    (*b*) paragraphs 4 and 6 of Schedule 21 to FA 1996,

    (*c*) section 47(10) of FA 1997,

    (*d*) paragraph 18 of Schedule 19 to FA 1998, and

    (*e*) section 91(6)(*b*) of FA 2007.

SCHEDULE 40

PENALTIES: AMENDMENTS OF SCHEDULE 24 TO FA 2007

Section 122

1   Schedule 24 to FA 2007 (penalties for errors) is amended as follows.

2—(1) Paragraph 1 (error in taxpayer's document) is amended as follows.

(2) (*amends* FA 2007 Sch 24 para 1(2))

(3) (*amends* FA 2007 Sch 24 para 1(3))

(4) (*amends* FA 2007 Sch 24 para 1 Table)

(5) (*inserts* entries in FA 2007 Sch 24 para 1 Table)

(6) (*amends* FA 2007 Sch 24 para 1 Table)

(7) (*inserts* FA 2007 Sch 24 para 1(5))

3   (*inserts* FA 2007 Sch 24 para 1A)

4—(1) Paragraph 2 (under-assessment by HMRC) is amended as follows.

(2) (*amends* FA 2007 Sch 24 para 2(1))

(3) (*substitutes* FA 2007 Sch 24 para 2(3))

5—(1) Paragraph 3 (degrees of culpability) is amended as follows

(2) (*amends* FA 2007 Sch 24 para 3(1))

(3) (*amends* FA 2007 Sch 24 para 3(2))

6   (*inserts* FA 2007 Sch 24 para 4(1A))

7   (*amends* FA 2007 Sch 24 para 5(1))

8—(1) Paragraph 6 (potential lost revenue: multiple errors) is amended as follows.

(2) (*amends* FA 2007 Sch 24 para 6(1), (2))

(3) (*amends* FA 2007 Sch 24 para 6(5))

9—(1) Paragraph 9 (reductions for disclosure) is amended as follows.

(2) (*inserts* FA 2007 Sch 24 para 9(A1))

(3) (*amends* FA 2007 Sch 24 para 9(1))

(4) (*amends* FA 2007 Sch 24 para 9(2)(*a*))

10   (*amends* FA 2007 Sch 24 para 11(1))

11—(1) Paragraph 12 (interaction with other penalties) is amended as follows.
(2) (*amends* FA 2007 Sch 24 para 12(2))
(3) (*inserts* FA 2007 Sch 24 para 12(4))
(4) (*amends* FA 2007 Sch 24 para 12 heading)

12—(1) Paragraph 13 (assessment) is amended as follows.
(2) (*amends* FA 2007 Sch 24 para 13(1))
(3) (*inserts* FA 2007 Sch 24 para 13(1A))
(4) (*amends* FA 2007 Sch 24 para 13(3))
(5) (*amends* FA 2007 Sch 24 para 13(4))

13   (*amends* FA 2007 Sch 24 para 15)

15   (*amends* FA 2007 Sch 24 para 18(3))

16—(1) Paragraph 19 (companies: officers' liability) is amended as follows.
(2) (*amends* FA 2007 Sch 24 para 19(1))
(3) (*substitutes* FA 2007 Sch 24 para 19(5))
Commentary—*Simon's Taxes* **A4.530**.

17   (*amends* FA 2007 Sch 24 para 21)

18   (*amends* FA 2007 Sch 24 para 22)

19   (*inserts* FA 2007 Sch 24 para 23A)

20—(1) Paragraph 28 (interpretation) is amended as follows.
(2) (*inserts* FA 2007 Sch 24 para 28(*c*)(iv))
(3) (*inserted* FA 2007 Sch 24 para 28(*da*); repealed by FA 2009 s 109, Sch 57 para 14(*b*).)
(4) (*amends* FA 2007 Sch 24 para 28(*f*))
(5) (*inserts* FA 2007 Sch 24 para 28(*fa*))

21   In consequence of this Schedule the following provisions are omitted—
  (*a*) paragraphs 8 and 9 of Schedule 2 to OTA 1975,
  (*b*) in section 1(3B) of the Petroleum Revenue Tax Act 1980, ", 8 and 9"
  (*c*) in IHTA 1984—
    (i) section 247(1) and (2),
    (ii) in section 248, in subsection (1), "account," and "delivered," (in both places) and, in subsection (2), "under section 247 above", and
    (iii) section 250(2),
  (*d*) in FA 1994—
    (i) section 8, and
    (ii) paragraphs 12 and 13 of Schedule 7,
  (*e*) paragraphs 18 to 20 of Schedule 5 to FA 1996,
  (*f*) paragraphs 83ZA(4) and (5), 83F, 83L, 83R and 83X of Schedule 18 to FA 1998,
  (*g*) section 108(2)(*a*) of FA 1999,
  (*h*) paragraphs 98 to 100 of Schedule 6 to FA 2000,
  (*i*) in Schedule 6 to FA 2001, paragraphs 7 to 9, and in paragraph 9A(5), paragraph (*b*) and the "or" before it,
  (*j*) section 133(2) to (4) of FA 2002,
  (*k*) in FA 2003—
    (i) section 192(8), and
    (ii) paragraph 8 of Schedule 10 to FA 2003, and
  (*l*) section 295(4)(*a*) of FA 2004.

SCHEDULE 41

PENALTIES: FAILURE TO NOTIFY AND CERTAIN VAT AND EXCISE WRONGDOING

Section 123

Commentary—*Simon's Taxes* **Division A4.5**.

Failure to notify etc

1   A penalty is payable by a person (P) where P fails to comply with an obligation specified in the Table below (a "relevant obligation").

Tax to which obligation relates	Obligation
Income tax and capital gains tax	Obligation under section 7 of TMA 1970 (obligation to give notice of liability to income tax or capital gains tax).
Corporation tax	Obligation under paragraph 2 of Schedule 18 to FA 1998 (obligation to give notice of chargeability to corporation tax).
[Diverted profits tax	Obligation under section 92 of FA 2015 (duty to notify if within scope of diverted profits tax).][7]
[Digital services tax	Obligation under section 54 of FA 2020 (obligation to notify HMRC when threshold conditions for digital services tax are met).][10]
Value added tax	Obligations under paragraphs 5, 6, 7 and 14(2) and (3) of Schedule 1 to VATA 1994 (obligations to notify liability to register and notify material change in nature of supplies made by person exempted from registration).
[Value added tax	Obligations under paragraphs 5, 6 and 13(3) of Schedule 1A to VATA 1994 (obligations to notify liability to register and notify material change in nature of supplies made by person exempted from registration).][1]
Value added tax	Obligation under paragraph 3 of Schedule 2 to VATA 1994 (obligation to notify liability to register).
Value added tax	Obligations under paragraphs 3 and 8(2) of Schedule 3 to VATA 1994 (obligations to notify liability to register and notify acquisition affecting exemption from registration).
Value added tax	Obligations under paragraphs 3, 4 and 7(2) and (3) of Schedule 3A to VATA 1994 (obligations to notify liability to register and notify relevant change in supplies made by person exempted from registration).
Value added tax	Obligation under regulations under paragraph 2(4) of Schedule 11 to VATA 1994 (obligation to give notification of acquisition of goods from another member State).
Insurance premium tax	Obligations under section 53(1) and (2) of FA 1994 (obligations to register in respect of receipt of premiums in course of taxable business and notify intended receipt of premiums in course of taxable business).
Insurance premium tax	Obligations under section 53AA(1) and (3) of FA 1994 (obligations to register as taxable intermediary and notify intention to charge taxable intermediary's fees).
[soft drinks industry levy	Obligation under section 44 of FA 2017 (obligation to give notice of liability to be registered).][9]
Aggregates levy	Obligations under section 24(2) of, and paragraph 1 of Schedule 4 to, FA 2001 (obligations to register in respect of carrying out of taxable activities and notify intention of carrying out such activities).
Climate change levy	Obligations under paragraphs 53 and 55 of Schedule 6 to FA 2000 (obligations to register in respect of taxable supplies and notify intention to make, or have made, taxable supply).
Landfill tax	Obligations under [section 47(2), (3) and (3A)][8] of FA 1996 (obligations to register in respect of carrying out of taxable activities and notify intention of carrying out such activities).
Air passenger duty	Obligation under section 33(4) [or 33A(4)][2] of FA 1994 (obligation to give notice of liability to register to operate chargeable aircraft).
[Alcohol liquor duties	Obligation to be authorised and registered to obtain and use duty stamps under regulations under paragraph 4 of Schedule 2A to ALDA 1979 (duty stamps).
Alcohol liquor duties	Obligations under sections 12(1), 47(1), 54(2), 55(2) and 62(2) of ALDA 1979 (obligations to hold licence to manufacture spirits, register to brew beer, hold licence to produce wine or made-wine and register to make cider).
Alcohol liquor duties	Obligation to have plant and processes approved for the manufacture of spirits under regulations under section 15(6) of ALDA 1979 (distillers' warehouses).
Tobacco products duty	Obligation to manufacture tobacco products only on premises registered under regulations under section 7 of TPDA 1979 (management of tobacco products duty).
Hydrocarbon oil duties	Obligation to make entry of premises intended to be used for production of oil under regulations under section 21 of HODA 1979 (administration and enforcement).
Excise duties	Obligation to receive, deposit or hold duty suspended excise goods only in premises approved under regulations under section 92 of CEMA 1979 (approval of warehouses).

Tax to which obligation relates	Obligation
Excise duties	Obligation to receive duty suspended excise goods only if approved or registered (or approved and registered) as a REDS or an Occasional Importer under regulations under section 100G or 100H of CEMA 1979 (registered excise dealers and shippers etc).
Excise duties	Obligation to receive, deposit or hold duty suspended excise goods only if approved or registered (or approved and registered) as a registered owner, a duty representative, a registered mobile operator or a fiscal representative of a registered mobile operator or an authorised warehousekeeper under regulations under section 100G or 100H of CEMA 1979 (registered excise dealers and shippers etc).
[General betting duty	Obligation to register under section 164(2) of FA 2014 (registration of persons liable etc for general betting duty).[3]
Pool betting duty	Obligation to register under section 164(2) of FA 2014 (registration of persons liable etc for pool betting duty).][6]
Bingo duty	Obligations under paragraph 10(1) and (1A) of Schedule 3 to BGDA 1981 (obligation to notify and register in respect of bingo-promotion).
Lottery duty	Obligation under section 29(1) of FA 1993 (obligation to register in respect of promotion of lotteries).
Gaming duty	Obligations under paragraphs 3 and 6 of Schedule 1 to FA 1997 (obligations to register in respect of gaming and to notify premises).
[Remote gaming duty	Obligation to register under section 164(2) of FA 2014 (registration of persons liable etc for remote gaming duty).][6]
[Machine games duty	Obligation under paragraph 20(3) of Schedule 24 to FA 2012 (obligation to register in respect of premises).][4]
. . .	. . .][5]

Modifications—FA 2018 Sch 12 paras 32, 33(a) (application of Table in para (1) to obligations in connection with a disposal made before 1 April 2018 at a place other than a landfill site).

Amendments—[1]   Entry inserted by FA 2012 s 203, Sch 28 para 18 with effect in relation to supplies made or to be made on or after 1 December 2012.

[2]   In entry for air passenger duty, words in column 2 inserted by FA 2012 s 190, Sch 23 para 15 with effect from 17 July 2012.

[3]   Words in entries for "general betting duty", "pool betting duty" and "remote gaming duty" substituted by FA 2012 s 194, Sch 25 para 11 with effect in relation to accounting periods ending on or after 1 April 2012 (and, accordingly, the first reconciliation period begins with the first accounting period in relation to which the amendments have effect) (FA 2012 Sch 25 para 12).

[4]   Entry inserted by FA 2012 s 191, Sch 24 para 30 with effect in relation to the playing of machine games on or after 1 February 2013.

[5]   Entry relating to amusement machine licence duty repealed by FA 2012 s 191, Sch 24 para 57 with effect in relation to the provision of amusement machines on or after 1 February 2013. That definition to continue to have effect (with necessary modifications) on and after that date in relation to the provision of amusement machines before that date (FA 2012 Sch 24 para 62).

[6]   Entries for general betting duty, pool betting duty and remote gaming duty substituted by FA 2014 s 196, Sch 28 para 27 with effect from 1 December 2014 (FA 2014 s 198(2)), subject to the transitional provisions and savings in FA 2014 Sch 29.

[7]   Entry for diverted profits tax inserted by FA 2015 s 104(4), (5) with effect in relation to accounting periods beginning on or after 1 April 2015. For accounting periods that straddle that date, see FA 2015 s 116(2).

[8]   In entry for "landfill tax", words substituted for words "section 47(2) and (3)" by FA 2018 s 42(1), Sch 12 para 27(1), (2) with effect in relation to disposals made, or treated as made, on or after 1 April 2018, subject to transitional arrangements relating to disposals before April 2018 at places other than landfill sites (FA 2018 Sch 12 paras 31, 32). This amendment has effect in relation to disposals made in England or Northern Ireland only.

[9]   Entry for soft drinks industry levy inserted by FA 2017 s 56, Sch 11 para 2(1), (2) with effect from 6 April 2018 (by virtue of SI 2018/464). The charge to soft drinks industry levy arises on chargeable events which occur on or after 6 April 2018 (FA 2017 s 31(1)).

[10]   Entry for digital services tax inserted by FA 2020 s 70, Sch 10 paras 4, 6(1), (2) with effect from 22 July 2020.

Prospective amendments—In the table, the second, third, and fifth entries relation to Value Added Tax to be repealed by the Taxation (Cross-border Trade) Act 2018 s 43, Sch 8 paras 112, 114(1), (2) with effect from a date to be appointed.

Issue of invoice showing VAT by unauthorised person

2—(1) A penalty is payable by a person (P) where P makes an unauthorised issue of an invoice showing VAT.

(2) P makes an unauthorised issue of an invoice showing VAT if P—

    (a) is an unauthorised person, and

    (b) issues an invoice showing an amount as being value added tax or as including an amount attributable to value added tax.

(3) In sub-paragraph (2)(a) "an unauthorised person" means anyone other than—

    (a) a person registered under VATA 1994,

    (b) a body corporate treated for the purposes of section 43 of that Act as a member of a group, (*c*) a person treated as a taxable person under regulations under section 46(4) of that Act,

    (*d*) a person authorised to issue an invoice under regulations under paragraph 2(12) of Schedule 11 to that Act, or

    (*e*) a person acting on behalf of the Crown.

(4) This paragraph has effect in relation to any invoice which—

    (*a*) for the purposes of any provision made under subsection (3) of section 54 of VATA 1994 shows an amount as included in the consideration for any supply, and

    (*b*) either fails to comply with the requirements of any regulations under that section or is issued by a person who is not for the time being authorised to do so for the purposes of that section,

as if the person issuing the invoice were an unauthorised person and that amount were shown on the invoice as an amount attributable to value added tax.

Putting product to use that attracts higher duty

3—(1) A penalty is payable by a person ("P") where P does an act which enables HMRC to assess an amount as duty due from P under any of the provisions in the Table below (a "relevant excise provision").

Provision under which assessment may be made	Subject-matter of provision
ALDA 1979 section 8(4)	Spirits for use for medical or scientific purposes.
ALDA 1979 section 10(4)	Spirits for use in art or manufacture.
ALDA 1979 section 11(3)	Imported goods not for human consumption containing spirits.
HODA 1979 section 10(3)	Duty-free oil.
HODA 1979 section 13(1A)	Rebated heavy oil.
HODA 1979 section 13AB(1)(a) or (2)(a)	Kerosene.
HODA 1979 section 13AD(2)	Kerosene.
HODA 1979 section 13ZB(1)	Heating oil etc
HODA 1979 section 14(4)	Light oil for use as furnace oil.
HODA 1979 section 14D(1)	Rebated biodiesel or bioblend.
HODA 1979 section 14F(2)	Rebated heavy oil or bioblend.
HODA 1979 section 23(1B)	Road fuel gas on which no duty paid.
HODA 1979 section 24(4A)	Duty-free and rebated oil.

(2) A penalty is payable by a person ("P") where P supplies a product knowing that it will be used in a way which enables HMRC to assess an amount as duty due from another person under a relevant excise provision.

Prospective amendments—Entry relating to section 14F(2) of HODA 1979 to be substituted by FA 2020 s 89, Sch 11, para 16 with effect from a date to be appointed. Substituted entry to read as follows—

"HODA 1979 section 14F(8)	Rebated heavy oil, biodiesel or bio-blend".

[*Involvement in landfill disposal by unregistered person*****

3A A penalty is payable by a person ("P") where P does an act which enables HMRC to assess an amount as landfill tax due from P under section 50A of FA 1996. This is subject to paragraph 6CA(2).]

Amendments—[1] Paragraph 3A inserted by FA 2018 s 42(1), Sch 12 para 27(1), (3) with effect in relation to disposals made, or treated as made, on or after 1 April 2018, subject to transitional arrangements relating to disposals before April 2018 at places other than landfill sites (FA 2018 Sch 12 paras 31, 32). This amendment has effect in relation to disposals made in England or Northern Ireland only.

Handling goods subject to unpaid excise duty [etc]

4—(1) A penalty is payable by a person (P) where—

    (*a*) after the excise duty point for any goods which are chargeable with a duty of excise, P acquires possession of the goods or is concerned in carrying, removing, depositing, keeping or otherwise dealing with the goods, and

    (*b*) at the time when P acquires possession of the goods or is so concerned, a payment of duty on the goods is outstanding and has not been deferred.

　　　–　　all other relevant obligations arising on or before 5 April 2011;

　　　–　　any unauthorised issue of an invoice taking place on or before 5 April 2011;

　　　–　　any act which enables HMRC to assess an amount as duty under a relevant excise provision and which is done on or before 5 April 2011; and

　　　–　　any act giving rise to a penalty under FA 2008 Sch 41 para 4 which is done on or before 5 April 2011.

² In sub-paras (2)(*a*), (3)(*a*), (6)(*a*), (9)(*a*), words inserted, sub-para (4A), inserted, in sub-para (5), words substituted, and sub-para (8) repealed by FA 2015 s 120, Sch 20 paras 9, 11(3)–(9) with effect from 6 April 2016 in relation to an obligation arising under TMA 1970 s 7 in respect of a tax year commencing on or after that date (by virtue of SI 2016/456 art 4).

Prospective amendments—Sub-paras (A1), (1) to be substituted for sub-para (1) by FA 2015 s 120, Sch 20 paras 9, 11(1), (2) with effect from a day to be appointed. Sub-paragraphs (A1), (1) as substituted to read as follows—

　　"(A1) A failure is in category 0 if—

　　　(*a*)　　it involves a domestic matter,

　　　(*b*)　　it involves an offshore matter or an offshore transfer, the territory in question is a category 0 territory and the tax at stake is income tax or capital gains tax, or

　　　(*c*)　　it involves an offshore matter and the tax at stake is a tax other than income tax or capital gains tax.

　　　(1) A failure is in category 1 if—

　　　(*a*)　　it involves an offshore matter or an offshore transfer,

　　　(*b*)　　the territory in question is a category 1 territory, and

　　　(*c*)　　the tax at stake is income tax or capital gains tax.".

[6AA (1) This paragraph makes provision in relation to offshore transfers.

(2) Where the tax at stake is income tax, the applicable condition is satisfied if the income on or by reference to which the tax is charged, or any part of the income—

　　　(*a*)　　is received in a territory outside the UK, or

　　　(*b*)　　is transferred before the calculation date to a territory outside the UK.

(3) Where the tax at stake is capital gains tax, the applicable condition is satisfied if the proceeds of the disposal on or by reference to which the tax is charged, or any part of the proceeds—

　　　(*a*)　　are received in a territory outside the UK, or

　　　(*b*)　　are transferred before the calculation date to a territory outside the UK.

(4) In the case of a transfer falling within sub-paragraph (2)(*b*) or (3)(*b*), references to the income or proceeds transferred are to be read as including references to any assets derived from or representing the income or proceeds.

(5) In relation to an offshore transfer, the territory in question for the purposes of paragraph 6A is the highest category of territory by virtue of which the failure involves an offshore transfer.

(6) In this paragraph "calculation date" means the date by reference to which the potential lost revenue is to be calculated (see paragraph 7).]¹

Amendments—¹　Paragraphs 6AA, 6AB inserted by FA 2015 s 120, Sch 20 paras 9, 12 with effect from 6 April 2016 in relation to an obligation arising under TMA 1970 s 7 in respect of a tax year commencing on or after that date (by virtue of SI 2016/456 art 4).

[6AB　Regulations under paragraph 21B of Schedule 24 to FA 2007 (location of assets etc) apply for the purposes of paragraphs 6A and 6AA of this Schedule as they apply for the purposes of paragraphs 4A and 4AA of that Schedule.]¹

Amendments—¹　Paragraphs 6AA, 6AB inserted by FA 2015 s 120, Sch 20 paras 9, 12 with effect from 6 April 2016 in relation to an obligation arising under TMA 1970 s 7 in respect of a tax year commencing on or after that date (by virtue of SI 2016/456 art 4).

[6B　The penalty payable under any of paragraphs 2, 3(1) and 4 is—

　　　(*a*)　　for a deliberate and concealed act or failure, 100% of the potential lost revenue,

　　　(*b*)　　for a deliberate but not concealed act or failure, 70% of the potential lost revenue, and

　　　(*c*)　　for any other case, 30% of the potential lost revenue.]¹

Amendments—¹　Paras 6–6D substituted for previous para 6 by FA 2010 s 35 Sch 10 paras 7, 8 with effect from 6 April 2011 (by virtue of SI 2011/975 art 2(1)). Note that (by virtue of SI 2011/975 art 4) these changes do not have effect in relation to—

　　　–　　any relevant obligation arising under TMA 1970 s 7, FA 1998 Sch 18 para 2, and VATA 1994 Sch 1 paras 5, 6, 14(2), (3), Sch 3 para 3, Sch 3A paras 4, 7(2), (3), in relation to a tax period commencing on or before 5 April 2011;

　　　–　　all other relevant obligations arising on or before 5 April 2011;

　　　–　　any unauthorised issue of an invoice taking place on or before 5 April 2011;

　　　–　　any act which enables HMRC to assess an amount as duty under a relevant excise provision and which is done on or before 5 April 2011; and

　　　–　　any act giving rise to a penalty under FA 2008 Sch 41 para 4 which is done on or before 5 April 2011.

[6C　The penalty payable under paragraph 3(2) is 100% of the potential lost revenue.]¹

Amendments—¹　Paras 6–6D substituted for previous para 6 by FA 2010 s 35 Sch 10 paras 7, 8 with effect from 6 April 2011 (by virtue of SI 2011/975 art 2(1)). Note that (by virtue of SI 2011/975 art 4) these changes do not have effect in relation to—

　　　–　　any relevant obligation arising under TMA 1970 s 7, FA 1998 Sch 18 para 2, and VATA 1994 Sch 1 paras 5, 6, 14(2), (3), Sch 3 para 3, Sch 3A paras 4, 7(2), (3), in relation to a tax period commencing on or before 5 April 2011;

–   all other relevant obligations arising on or before 5 April 2011;

–   any unauthorised issue of an invoice taking place on or before 5 April 2011;

–   any act which enables HMRC to assess an amount as duty under a relevant excise provision and which is done on or before 5 April 2011; and

–   any act giving rise to a penalty under FA 2008 Sch 41 para 4 which is done on or before 5 April 2011.

[6CA (1) The penalty payable under paragraph 3A is—

(a) for a deliberate and concealed act or failure, 100% of the potential lost revenue, and

(b) for a deliberate but not concealed act or failure, 70% of the potential lost revenue.

(2) No penalty is payable under paragraph 3A in any other case.]¹

Amendments—¹   Paragraph 6CA inserted by FA 2018 s 42(1), Sch 12 para 27(1), (5) with effect in relation to disposals made, or treated as made, on or after 1 April 2018, subject to transitional arrangements relating to disposals before April 2018 at places other than landfill sites (FA 2018 Sch 12 paras 31, 32). This amendment has effect in relation to disposals made in England or Northern Ireland only.

[6D   Paragraphs 7 to 11 define "potential lost revenue".]¹

Amendments—¹   Paras 6–6D substituted for previous para 6 by FA 2010 s 35 Sch 10 paras 7, 8 with effect from 6 April 2011 (by virtue of SI 2011/975 art 2(1)). Note that (by virtue of SI 2011/975 art 4) these changes do not have effect in relation to— any relevant obligation arising under TMA 1970 s 7, FA 1998 Sch 18 para 2, and VATA 1994 Sch 1 paras 5, 6, 14(2), (3), Sch 3 para 3, Sch 3A paras 4, 7(2), (3), in relation to a tax period commencing on or before 5 April 2011; all other relevant obligations arising on or before 5 April 2011; any unauthorised issue of an invoice taking place on or before 5 April 2011; any act which enables HMRC to assess an amount as duty under a relevant excise provision and which is done on or before 5 April 2011; and any act giving rise to a penalty under FA 2008 Sch 41 para 4 which is done on or before 5 April 2011.

Potential lost revenue

7—(1) "The potential lost revenue" in respect of a failure to comply with a relevant obligation is as follows.

[(1A) In the case of an obligation under section 7 of TMA 1970 which arises by virtue of subsection (1B) of that section, the potential lost revenue is so much of any income tax or capital gains tax to which P is liable in respect of the tax year in question as is, by reason of the failure to comply with the obligation—

(a) where the period specified in subsection (1C)(b)(ii) of that section applies and ends after the relevant date, unpaid at the end of that period, or

(b) in any other case, unpaid on the relevant date.

(1B) For the purposes of sub-paragraph (1A) the relevant date is—

(a) 31 January following the tax year, or

(b) if, after that date, HMRC refund a payment on account in respect of the tax year to P, the day after the refund is issued.]²

(2) In the case of a relevant obligation relating to income tax or capital gains tax and a tax year [(not falling within subparagraph (1A))]², the potential lost revenue is so much of any income tax or capital gains tax to which P is liable in respect of the tax year as by reason of the failure is unpaid on 31 January following the tax year.

(3) In the case of a relevant obligation relating to corporation tax and an accounting period, the potential lost revenue is (subject to sub-paragraph (4)) so much of any corporation tax to which P is liable in respect of the accounting period as by reason of the failure is unpaid 12 months after the end of the accounting period.

(4) In computing the amount of that tax no account shall be taken of any relief under [section 458 of CTA 2010]¹ (relief in respect of repayment etc of loan) which is deferred under [subsection (5)]¹ of that section.

[(4A) In the case of a relevant obligation relating to diverted profits tax, the potential lost revenue is the amount of diverted profits tax for which P would be liable at the end of the period of 6 months beginning immediately after the accounting period assuming—

(a) a charge to diverted profits tax had been imposed on P on the taxable diverted profits arising to P for the accounting period, and

(b) that tax was required to be paid before the end of that period of 6 months.]³

[(4B) In the case of a relevant obligation relating to digital services tax and an accounting period, the potential lost revenue is so much of any digital services tax payable by members of the group for the accounting period as by reason of the failure is unpaid 12 months after the end of the accounting period.]⁵

(5) In any case where the failure is a failure to comply with the obligation under paragraph 2(4) of Schedule 11 to VATA 1994, the potential lost revenue is the value added tax on the acquisition to which the failure relates.

(2C) The Treasury must make regulations setting out what is meant by "additional information" for the purposes of sub-paragraph (2B)(*d*).

(2D) Regulations under sub-paragraph (2C) are to be made by statutory instrument.

(2E) An instrument containing regulations under sub-paragraph (2C) is subject to annulment in pursuance of a resolution of the House of Commons.]¹

(3) Disclosure of a relevant act or failure—

    (*a*) is "unprompted" if made at a time when the person making it has no reason to believe that HMRC have discovered or are about to discover the relevant act or failure, and

    (*b*) otherwise, is "prompted".

(4) In relation to disclosure "quality" includes timing, nature and extent.

[(5) Paragraph 6A(4) to (5) applies to determine whether a failure involves an offshore matter, an offshore transfer or a domestic matter for the purposes of this paragraph.

(6) In this paragraph "relevant failure" means a failure to comply with a relevant obligation.]¹

Regulations—Penalties Relating to Offshore Matters and Offshore Transfers (Additional Information) Regulations, SI 2017/345.

Amendments—¹ Sub-paras (1)–(1B) substituted for sub-para (1); in sub-para (2), word substituted; and sub-paras (2A)–(2E), (5), (6) inserted; by FA 2016 s 163, Sch 21 paras 5, 6 with effect, by virtue of SI 2017/259 regs 2, 3—

    –   for inheritance tax purposes, in relation to transfers of value made on or after 1 April 2017;

    –   for income tax and capital gains tax purposes, in relation to any tax year commencing on or after 6 April 2016; and

    –   for the purpose of making regulations, from 8 March 2017.

[13 (1) If a person who would otherwise be liable to a penalty of a percentage shown in column 1 of the Table (a "standard percentage") has made a disclosure, HMRC must reduce the standard percentage to one that reflects the quality of the disclosure.

(2) But the standard percentage may not be reduced to a percentage that is below the minimum shown for it—

    (*a*) for a prompted disclosure, in column 2 of the Table, and

    (*b*) for an unprompted disclosure, in column 3 of the Table.

(3) Where the Table shows a different minimum for case A and case B—

    (*a*) the case A minimum applies if—

        (i) the penalty is one under paragraph 1, and

        (ii) HMRC become aware of the failure less than 12 months after the time when the tax first becomes unpaid by reason of the failure, and

    (*b*) otherwise, the case B minimum applies.

[Standard %	Minimum % for prompted disclosure	Minimum % for unprompted disclosure
30%	Case A: 10% Case B: 20%	Case A: 0% Case B: 10%
70%	35%	20%
100%	50%	30%]²

Amendments—¹ This para substituted by FA 2010 s 35 Sch 10 paras 7, 9 with effect from 6 April 2011 (by virtue of SI 2011/975 art 2(1)). Note that (by virtue of SI 2011/975 art 4) these changes do not have effect in relation to—

    –   any relevant obligation arising under TMA 1970 s 7, FA 1998 Sch 18 para 2, and VATA 1994 Sch 1 paras 5, 6, 14(2), (3), Sch 3 para 3, Sch 3A paras 4, 7(2), (3), in relation to a tax period commencing on or before 5 April 2011;

    –   all other relevant obligations arising on or before 5 April 2011;

    –   any unauthorised issue of an invoice taking place on or before 5 April 2011;

    –   any act which enables HMRC to assess an amount as duty under a relevant excise provision and which is done on or before 5 April 2011; and

    –   any act giving rise to a penalty under FA 2008 Sch 41 para 4 which is done on or before 5 April 2011.

² In sub-para (3), Table substituted by FA 2016 s 163, Sch 21 paras 5, 7 with effect, by virtue of SI 2017/259 regs 2, 3—

    –   for inheritance tax purposes, in relation to transfers of value made on or after 1 April 2017; and

    –   for income tax and capital gains tax purposes, in relation to any tax year commencing on or after 6 April 2016.

Prospective amendments—In sub-para (3), the following Table entries to be inserted at the appropriate places by FA 2015 s 120, Sch 20 paras 9, 13 with effect from a day to be appointed—

"37.5%	case A: 12.5% case B: 25%	case A: 0% case B: 12.5%"
"87.5%	43.75%	25%"

"125% | 62.5% | 40%"

[13A (1) If a person who would otherwise be liable to a penalty of a percentage shown in column 1 of the Table (a "standard percentage") has made a disclosure, HMRC must reduce the standard percentage to one that reflects the quality of the disclosure.

(2) But the standard percentage may not be reduced to a percentage that is below the minimum shown for it—

    (*a*) for a prompted disclosure, in column 2 of the Table, and

    (*b*) for an unprompted disclosure, in column 3 of the Table.

(3) Where the Table shows a different minimum for case A and case B—

    (*a*) the case A minimum applies if HMRC becomes aware of the failure less than 12 months after the time when the tax first becomes unpaid by reason of the failure;

    (*b*) otherwise, the case B minimum applies.

Standard %	Minimum % for prompted disclosure	Minimum % for unprompted disclosure
30%	Case A: 10% Case B: 20%	Case A: 0% Case B: 10%
37.5%	Case A: 12.5% Case B: 25%	Case A: 0% Case B: 12.5%
45%	Case A: 15% Case B: 30%	Case A: 0% Case B: 15%
60%	Case A: 20% Case B: 40%	Case A: 0% Case B: 20%
70%	45%	30%
87.5%	53.75%	35%
100%	60%	40%
105%	62.5%	40%
125%	72.5%	50%
140%	80%	50%
150%	85%	55%
200%	110%	70%]¹

Amendments— ¹ Paragraph 13A inserted by FA 2016 s 163, Sch 21 paras 5, 8 with effect, by virtue of SI 2017/259 regs 2, 3—
  –   for inheritance tax purposes, in relation to transfers of value made on or after 1 April 2017; and
  –   for income tax and capital gains tax purposes, in relation to any tax year commencing on or after 6 April 2016.

Special reduction

14—(1) If HMRC think it right because of special circumstances, they may reduce a penalty under any of paragraphs 1 to 4.

(2) In sub-paragraph (1) "special circumstances" does not include—

    (*a*) ability to pay, or

    (*b*) the fact that a potential loss of revenue from one taxpayer is balanced by a potential overpayment by another.

(3) In sub-paragraph (1) the reference to reducing a penalty includes a reference to—

    (*a*) staying a penalty, and

    (*b*) agreeing a compromise in relation to proceedings for a penalty.

Interaction with other penalties and late payment surcharges

15—(1) The amount of a penalty for which P is liable under any of paragraphs 1 to 4 shall be reduced by the amount of any other penalty incurred by P, or any surcharge for late payment of tax imposed on P, if the amount of the penalty or surcharge is determined by reference to the same tax liability.

[(1A) In sub-paragraph (2) "any other penalty" does not include a penalty under Part 4 of FA 2014 (penalty where corrective action not taken after follower notice etc) [or Schedule 22 to FA 2016 (asset-based penalty)]².]¹

(2) If P is liable to a penalty under section 9 of FA 1994 in respect of a failure to comply with a relevant obligation, the amount of any penalty payable under paragraph 1 in respect of the failure is to be reduced by the amount of the penalty under that section.

(3) Where penalties are imposed under paragraph 3(1) and (2) in respect of the same act or use, the aggregate of the amounts of the penalties must not exceed 100% of the potential lost revenue.

    (*c*) a secretary, and

    (*d*) any other person managing or purporting to manage any of the company's affairs.

(5) Where HMRC have specified a portion of a penalty in a notice given to an officer under sub-paragraph (1)—

    (*a*) paragraph 14 applies to the specified portion as to a penalty,

    (*b*) the officer must pay the specified portion before the end of the period of 30 days beginning with the day on which the notice is given,

    (*c*) paragraph 16(3) to (5) and (7) apply as if the notice were an assessment of a penalty,

    (*d*) a further notice may be given in respect of a portion of any additional amount assessed in a supplementary assessment in respect of the penalty under paragraph 16(6),

    (*e*) paragraphs 17 to 19 apply as if HMRC had decided that a penalty of the amount of the specified portion is payable by the officer, and

    (*f*) paragraph 23 applies as if the officer were liable to a penalty.

[(6) In this paragraph "company" means any body corporate or unincorporated association, but does not include a partnership, a local authority or a local authority association.][1]

Amendments—[1]   In sub-para (3) words inserted, word "or" repealed and para (*aa*) inserted, sub-paras (3A), (6) inserted, by FA 2009 s 109, Sch 57 para 12 with effect from 21 July 2009.

Double jeopardy

23   P is not liable to a penalty under any of paragraphs 1 to 4 in respect of a failure or action in respect of which P has been convicted of an offence.

Commentary—*Simon's Taxes* A4.530.

Interpretation

24—(1) This paragraph applies for the construction of this Schedule

(2) "HMRC" means Her Majesty's Revenue and Customs.

(3) "Tax", without more, includes duty.

(4) An expression used in relation to value added tax has the same meaning as in VATA 1994.

Consequential repeals

25   In consequence of this Schedule the following provisions are omitted—

    (*a*) in TMA 1970—

        (i)   section 7(8), and

        (ii) in the table in section 98, in the second column, the entry relating to section 55 of FA 2004,

    (*b*) section 170A of CEMA 1979,

    (*c*) in ALDA 1979—

        (i)   in section 47(5), "which shall be calculated by reference to the amount of duty charged on the beer produced",

        (ii) in section 54(5), "which shall be calculated by reference to the amount of duty charged on the wine produced",

        (iii) in section 55(6), "which shall be calculated by reference to the amount of duty charged on the made-wine produced", and

        (iv) in section 62(4), "which shall be calculated by reference to the amount of duty charged on the cider made",

    (*d*) in HODA 1979—

        (i)   section 13AD(4)(*a*) and (*b*), and

        (ii) section 14F(4)(*a*) and (*b*),

    (*e*) in FA 1994—

        (i)   section 33(6),

        (ii) paragraph 13 of Schedule 4, and

        (iii) paragraph 14 of Schedule 7,

    (*f*) section 67 of VATA 1994,

    (*g*) section 32 of FA 1995,

    (*h*) in FA 1996—

        (i)   section 37, and

        (ii) paragraph 21(1), (2) and (4) of Schedule 5,

    (*i*) section 27(11) of FA 1997,

    (*j*) paragraph 2(3) and (4) of Schedule 18 to FA 1998,

    (*k*) in FA 2000—

        (i)   section 136(2), and

(ii) paragraph 55(2) to (6) of Schedule 6, and
(*l*) paragraph 1(2) to (6) of Schedule 4 to FA 2001.

SCHEDULE 43

TAKING CONTROL OF GOODS ETC: CONSEQUENTIAL PROVISION

Section 129

PART 1

CONSEQUENTIAL PROVISION: TAKING CONTROL OF GOODS

TMA 1970

1—(*amends* TMA 1970 s 61)

Social Security Administration Act 1992 (c 5)

2 (*repeals* SSAA 1992 s 121A)

FA 1994

3—(*repeals* FA 1994 s 10A, Sch 7 para 18A)

VATA 1994

4 (*repeals* VATA 1994 s 67A)

FA 1996

5 (*repeals* FA 1995 Sch 5 para 23A)

FA 1997

6 (*repeals* FA 1997 s 51(A1))

FA 2000

7 (*repeals* FA 2000 Sch 6 para 89A)

FA 2001

8 (*repeals* FA 2001 Sch 5 para 14A)

FA 2003

9 (*repeals* FA 2003 Sch 12 para 1A)

Tribunals, Courts and Enforcement Act 2007 (c 15)

10—(*repeals* Tribunal, Courts and Enforcement Act 2007 Sch 12 para 14(5) and *amends* para 19(2).

Other repeals

11   In consequence of the preceding provisions of this Schedule, omit—
(*a*) paragraph 8 of Schedule 5 to the Social Security Contributions (Transfer of Functions, etc) Act 1999 (c 2),
(*b*) paragraph 6 of Schedule 11 to the Welfare Reform and Pensions Act 1999 (c 30),
(*c*) section 5(1) of the National Insurance Contributions and Statutory Payments Act 2004 (c 3), and
(*d*) paragraphs 33, 104(2), 114, 116(2), 119, 123, 126(2), 136, 140 and 147(2) of Schedule 13 to the Tribunals, Courts and Enforcement Act 2007 (c 15).)

PART 2

CONSEQUENTIAL PROVISION: SUMMARY WARRANT

TMA 1970

12   In TMA 1970 omit—
(*a*) section 63 (recovery of tax in Scotland), and
(*b*) section 63A (sheriff officer's fees and outlays).

Debtors (Scotland) Act 1987 (c 18)

13—(*amends* Debtors (Scotland) Act 1987 ss 1, 5, 106)

Social Security Administration Act 1992 (c 5)

14   In the Social Security Administration Act 1992, omit section 121B (recovery of contributions etc in Scotland).

FA 1997

15   In FA 1997, omit section 52 (recovery of relevant tax in Scotland).

FA 2003

16   In Schedule 12 to FA 2003 (stamp duty land tax: collection and recovery), omit paragraph 3 (recovery of tax in Scotland).

SCHEDULE 44
CERTIFICATES OF DEBT: CONSEQUENTIAL PROVISION
Section 138

TMA 1970

1   (*repeals* TMA 1970 s 70(1), (2))

OTA 1975

2   (*amends* OTA 1975 Sch 2 para 2(1) table)

IHTA 1984

3   (*repeals* IHTA 1984 s 254(2))

Social Security Administration Act 1992 (c 5)

4   (*repeals* SSAA 1992 s 118(1), (3), (7))

FA 1994

5   (*amends* FA 1994 Sch 7 para 29(1))

VATA 1994

6   (*amends* VATA 1994 Sch 11 para 14(1))

FA 1996

7   (*amends* FA 1996 Sch 5 para 37(1))

FA 2000

8   (*amends* FA 2000 Sch 6 para 135(1))

FA 2001

9   (*amends* FA 2001 Sch 7 para 12(1))

FA 2003

10   (*repeals* FA 2003 Sch 12 para 7)

Other repeals

11   In consequence of the preceding provisions of this Schedule, omit—
   (*a*) paragraph 21 of Schedule 19 to FA 1994,
   (*b*) section 62(1) of the Social Security Act 1998 (c 14),
   (*c*) paragraph 32 of Schedule 19 to FA 1998,
   (*d*) paragraph 7(2) and (6) of Schedule 5 to the Social Security (Transfer of Functions, etc) Act 1999 (c 2),

(*e*) section 89(3) of FA 2001, and

(*f*) paragraph 135(2) of Schedule 6 to ITEPA 2003.

SCHEDULE 46

GOVERNMENT BORROWING: ALTERNATIVE FINANCE ARRANGEMENTS

Section 157

Commentary—*Simon's Taxes* **A1.305**.

Introduction

1 In this Schedule "regulations" means regulations under section 157.

2 Paragraphs 3 to 14 do not limit the generality of the power conferred by section 157.

Commentary—*Simon's Taxes* **A1.305**.

Regulations—Government Alternative Finance Arrangements Regulations, SI 2014/1327.

Alternative finance arrangements that are to be available

3—(1) Regulations may make provision about the kind or kinds of alternative finance arrangements that are to be available for raising money.

(2) That includes provision specifying, or about the specification of, available arrangements (or any aspect of available arrangements).

Terms, conditions and procedures

4—(1) Regulations may make provision about—

    (*a*) the terms on which money is to be raised through alternative finance arrangements,

    (*b*) the conditions subject to which money is to be raised through alternative finance arrangements, and

    (*c*) the procedures for the raising of money through alternative finance arrangements.

(2) That includes provision specifying, or about the specification of, terms, conditions or procedures.

Decisions to raise money through alternative finance arrangements

5—(1) Regulations may make provision about decisions by the Treasury to raise money through alternative finance arrangements.

(2) Regulations under this paragraph may, in particular, make provision about considerations that may be, must be, or must not be, taken into account in—

    (*a*) deciding the terms on which to raise money through alternative finance arrangements,

    (*b*) deciding whether or not to raise money through alternative finance arrangements, or

    (*c*) deciding what amount of money to raise through alternative finance arrangements.

Commentary—*Simon's Taxes* **A1.305**.

Regulations—Government Alternative Finance Arrangements Regulations, SI 2014/1327.

Involvement of persons other than the Treasury

6—(1) Regulations may make provision about the involvement of persons other than the Treasury in the raising of money through alternative finance arrangements.

(2) Regulations under this paragraph may, in particular, make provision for the Treasury to enter into arrangements with other persons.

Commentary—*Simon's Taxes* **A1.305**.

Regulations—Government Alternative Finance Arrangements Regulations, SI 2014/1327.

Ancillary arrangements

7—(1) Regulations may make provision about ancillary arrangements.

(2) Regulations under this paragraph may, in particular, make provision about the terms or conditions of ancillary arrangements (including terms or conditions about payments).

(3) That includes provision specifying, or about the specification of, terms or conditions.

(4) In this paragraph "ancillary arrangements" means arrangements that are connected with the raising of money through alternative finance arrangements (including arrangements to facilitate or enable money to be raised through alternative finance arrangements).

Commentary—*Simon's Taxes* **A1.305**.

Regulations—Government Alternative Finance Arrangements Regulations, SI 2014/1327.

Property

8—(1) Regulations may make provision about property to be employed in raising money through alternative finance arrangements.

(2) That includes provision—

    (*a*) about selection of property,

    (*b*) specifying, or about the specification of, property selected,

    (*c*) about dealings with property, and

    (*d*) about the holding of property.

(3) Regulations under sub-paragraph (2)(*c*) or (*d*) may, in particular, make provision about the terms on which property is to be dealt with or held (including terms about payments).

(4) That includes provision specifying, or about the specification of, terms or conditions.

(5) In this paragraph "property" includes land.

(6) In this paragraph a reference to a dealing with property includes—

    (*a*) a transfer of property, and

    (*b*) the creation or termination of a right, interest or estate in property (including a legal or equitable right, interest or estate).

Powers and duties

9   Regulations may confer powers, or impose duties, on any person (including the Treasury, the Secretary of State or another Minister of the Crown).

Commentary—*Simon's Taxes* **A1.305**.
Regulations—Government Alternative Finance Arrangements Regulations, SI 2014/1327.

Liabilities

10   Regulations may make—

    (*a*) provision for expenditure and other liabilities to be incurred in connection with raising money through alternative finance arrangements, and

    (*b*) provision about how expenditure and other liabilities are to be met.

Commentary—*Simon's Taxes* **A1.305**.
Regulations—Government Alternative Finance Arrangements Regulations, SI 2014/1327.

Money raised

11—(1) Regulations may make provision about the treatment of money raised through alternative finance arrangements.

(2) That includes provision specifying, or about the specification of, the account or fund into which money is to be paid.

Commentary—*Simon's Taxes* **A1.305**.
Regulations—Government Alternative Finance Arrangements Regulations, SI 2014/1327.

Other legislation

12—(1) Regulations may make modifications of any enactment.

(2) Regulations may provide that available alternative finance arrangements are to be treated for the purposes of any enactment—

    (*a*) as an investment or security of a particular description, or

    (*b*) as an investment or security listed on a particular stock exchange.

(3) In this paragraph—

    "available alternative finance arrangements" means alternative finance arrangements of a kind that, under regulations, are available for raising money;

    "enactment" means an enactment contained in an Act or other instrument;

    "modifications" includes amendments, repeals and revocations.

Commentary—*Simon's Taxes* **A1.305**.
Regulations—Government Alternative Finance Arrangements Regulations, SI 2014/1327.

Things to be done otherwise than in regulations

13—(1) The power under paragraph 3(2), 4(2), 7(3), 8(2)(*b*) or (4), or 11(2) to make provision about the specification of the matter mentioned there may, in particular, be exercised so as to provide for the Treasury or any other person to specify that matter otherwise than in regulations.

(2) Regulations may provide for the Treasury or any other person to do anything else otherwise than in regulations.

14—(1) This paragraph applies if regulations provide for a person to do something otherwise than in regulations.

(2) Regulations may make provision about considerations that may be, must be, or must not be, taken into account by a person in connection with the doing of that thing.

Regulations to be made by SI

15   Regulations are to be made by statutory instrument.

Parliamentary scrutiny

16—(1) A statutory instrument containing regulations that amend or repeal an enactment contained in an Act may not be made unless a draft has been laid before, and approved by resolution of, the House of Commons.

(2) Subject to that, a statutory instrument containing regulations is subject to annulment in pursuance of a resolution of the House of Commons (unless a draft of the statutory instrument has been approved by resolution of the House of Commons).

Interpretation

17—(1) In this Schedule a reference to a person other than the Treasury includes a reference to—

    (*a*) a body corporate established by or under regulations, and

    (*b*) a company formed under the Companies Acts.

(2) For the purposes of sub-paragraph (1)(*b*), it does not matter—

    (*a*) whether a company is formed specially in connection with the raising of money through alternative finance arrangements,

    (*b*) whether a company is formed by the Treasury, or

    (*c*) whether a company is independent of the Treasury.

PART 2

TRANSFERS ETC BETWEEN TAXABLE PUBLIC BODIES

Meaning of "relevant transfer" in Part 2 of Schedule

4   In this Part of this Schedule "relevant transfer" means a transfer, in accordance with a transfer scheme, from a taxable public body to another taxable public body.

Computation of profits and losses in respect of transfer of trade

5—(1) This paragraph applies where a taxable public body ("the predecessor") is carrying on a trade or a part of a trade and, as a result of a transfer scheme—

(*a*) the predecessor ceases to carry on that trade or that part of that trade, and

(*b*) another taxable public body ("the successor") begins to carry on that trade or that part of it.

(2) For the purpose of computing, in relation to the time when the scheme comes into force and subsequent times, the relevant trading profits or losses of the predecessor and the successor—

(*a*) the trade or part is to be treated as having been a separate trade at the time of its commencement and as having been carried on by the successor at all times since its commencement as a separate trade, and

(*b*) the trade carried on by the successor after the time when the scheme comes into force is to be treated as the same trade as that which it is treated, by virtue of paragraph (*a*), as having carried on as a separate trade before that time.

(3) Where a trade or a part of a trade falls to be treated under this paragraph as a separate trade, such apportionments of receipts, expenses, assets and liabilities shall be made for the purpose of computing relevant trading profits or losses as may be just and reasonable.

(4) This paragraph is subject to the other provisions of this Part of this Schedule.

(5) In this paragraph "relevant trading profits or losses" means profits or losses under Case I of Schedule D in respect of the trade or part of a trade in question.

Transfers of trading stock

6—(1) This paragraph applies if—

(*a*) under a relevant transfer trading stock of the transferor is transferred to the transferee, and

(*b*) paragraph 5 does not apply in relation to that transfer.

(2) Sub-paragraphs (3) and (4) have effect in computing for any corporation tax purpose both the profits of the trade in relation to which the stock is trading stock immediately before the transfer takes effect ("the transferor's trade") and—

(*a*) if the stock falls immediately after the transfer takes effect to be treated as trading stock of the transferee, the profits of the trade in relation to which it falls to be treated as trading stock ("the transferee's trade");

(*b*) otherwise, the consideration given by the transferee, or the expenditure incurred by the transferee, for the acquisition of the stock.

(3) The stock must be taken to have been—

(*a*) disposed of by the transferor in the course of the transferor's trade,

(*b*) if sub-paragraph (2)(*a*) applies, acquired by the transferee in the course of the transferee's trade, and

(*c*) subject to that, disposed of and acquired when the transfer takes effect.

(4) The stock must be valued as if the disposal and acquisition had been for a consideration which in relation to the transferor would have resulted in neither a profit nor a loss being brought into account in respect of the disposal in the accounting period of the transferor which ends with, or is current at, the time when the transfer takes effect.

(5) In this paragraph "trading stock" has the same meaning as in section 100 of ICTA.

Capital allowances: transfer of whole trade

7—(1) This paragraph applies where a taxable public body ("the predecessor") is carrying on a trade and, as a result of a transfer scheme—

(*a*) the predecessor ceases to carry on that trade, and

(*b*) another taxable public body ("the successor") begins to carry on that trade.

(2) For the purposes of the allowances and charges provided for by CAA 2001, the trade is not to be treated as permanently discontinued, nor a new trade as set up; but sub-paragraphs (3) and (4) are to apply.

(3) There are to be made to or on the successor, in accordance with CAA 2001, all such allowances and charges as would, if the predecessor had continued to carry on the trade, have fallen to be made to or on the predecessor.

(4) The amounts of those allowances and charges are to be computed as if—

(a) the successor had been carrying on the trade since the predecessor began to do so, and

(b) everything done to or by the predecessor had been done to or by the successor,

but so that transfers in accordance with the scheme, so far as they relate to assets in use for the purposes of the trade, shall not be treated as giving rise to an allowance or charge.

Capital allowances: transfer of part of a trade

8—(1) Where a taxable public body ("the predecessor") is carrying on a trade and, as a result of a transfer scheme—

(a) the predecessor ceases to carry on a trade, and

(b) another taxable public body ("the successor") begins to carry on activities of that trade as part of a trade carried on by the successor,

then that part of the trade carried on by the successor shall be treated for the purposes of paragraph 7 as a separate trade.

(2) Where a taxable public body ("the predecessor") is carrying on a trade and, as a result of a transfer scheme—

(a) the predecessor ceases to carry on a part of a trade, and

(b) another taxable public body begins to carry on activities of that part of that trade,

then the predecessor shall be treated for the purposes of paragraph 7 and sub-paragraph (1) as having carried on that part of its trade as a separate trade.

(3) Where activities fall to be treated for the purposes of this paragraph as a separate trade, such apportionments of receipts, expenses, assets and liabilities shall be made for the purposes of CAA 2001 as may be just and reasonable.

Capital allowances: transfer of plant or machinery

9—(1) This paragraph applies where—

(a) there is a relevant transfer of plant or machinery,

(b) paragraph 7 does not apply in relation to that transfer,

(c) the plant or machinery would be treated for the purposes of CAA 2001 as disposed of by the transferor to the transferee on the transfer taking effect, and

(d) the transfer scheme in accordance with which the transfer is made contains provision for the disposal value of the plant or machinery to be treated for the purposes of that Act as an amount specified in or determined in accordance with the scheme.

(2) For the purposes of CAA 2001—

(a) the provision mentioned in sub-paragraph (1)(d) is to have effect for determining an amount as the disposal value of the plant or machinery or the price at which a fixture is to be treated as sold,

(b) the transferee is to be treated as having incurred capital expenditure of that amount on the provision of the plant or machinery for the purposes for which it is used by the transferee on and after the taking effect of the transfer,

(c) the property is to be treated as belonging to the transferee as a result of the transferee having incurred that expenditure, and

(d) in the case of a fixture, the expenditure which falls to be treated as incurred by the transferee is to be treated for the purposes of sections 181(1) and 182(1) of that Act as being incurred by the giving of a consideration consisting in a capital sum of that amount.

(3) The provision mentioned in sub-paragraph (1)(d) for the determination of an amount may include provision for a determination—

(a) to be made by the Secretary of State in a manner described in the scheme,

(b) to be made by reference to factors so described or to the opinion of a person so described, and

(c) to be capable of being modified (on one or more occasions) in a manner and in circumstances so described.

(4) The consent of the Treasury is required for the making or modification of a determination under the provision mentioned in sub-paragraph (1)(d).

(5) The consent of the transferee is required for the modification of a determination under the provision mentioned in sub-paragraph (1)(d).

(6) As to the making of a determination or a modification of a determination under the provision mentioned in sub-paragraph (1)(d), see further paragraph 43.

(7) Expressions used in this paragraph and in Part 2 of CAA 2001 have the same meanings in this paragraph as in that Part.

Capital allowances: transfers not to be sales

10—(1) This paragraph applies for the purposes of Part 3 of CAA 2001, and the other provisions of that Act which are relevant to that Part, to a relevant transfer of the relevant interest in an industrial building or structure.

(2) Neither section 559 nor section 573 of that Act is to have effect in relation to that transfer.

Chargeable gains: assets to be treated as disposed of without a gain or a loss

11—(1) For the purposes of TCGA 1992 a disposal—

    (*a*) constituted by a relevant transfer, or

    (*b*) to which sub-paragraph (2) applies,

is to be taken (in relation to the person to whom the disposal is made as well as the person making the disposal) to be for a consideration such that no gain or loss accrues to the person making the disposal.

(2) This sub-paragraph applies to a disposal if—

    (*a*) it is made in accordance with provision contained in a transfer scheme by virtue of paragraph 4, 6 or 12 of Schedule 12 to this Act,

    (*b*) the person making the disposal and the person to whom the disposal is made are taxable public bodies, and

    (*c*) each of those persons is either the transferor or a transferee under the scheme.

(3) Sub-paragraph (1) is subject to paragraph 12.

Chargeable gains: roll-over relief

12—(1) This paragraph applies if—

    (*a*) but for section 154 of TCGA 1992 (depreciating assets) a held-over gain would have been carried forward to a depreciating asset, and

    (*b*) the asset is the subject of a relevant transfer.

(2) Section 154 is to have effect as if the gain had accrued to, and the claim for it to be held over had been made by, the transferee and as if the transferor's acquisition of the depreciating asset had been the transferee's acquisition of it.

(3) Expressions used in this paragraph and in section 154 have the same meanings in this paragraph as in that section.

Continuity in relation to transfer of intangible assets

13—(1) For the purposes of Schedule 29 to FA 2002—

    (*a*) a relevant transfer of a chargeable intangible asset of the transferor is to be treated as a tax-neutral transfer, and

    (*b*) an intangible fixed asset which is an existing asset of the transferor at the time of a relevant transfer is to be treated, on and after the transfer, as an existing asset in the hands of the transferee.

(2) Expressions used in this paragraph and in that Schedule have the same meanings in this paragraph as in that Schedule.

Continuity in relation to loan relationships

14—(1) For the purposes of the application of Chapter 2 of Part 4 of FA 1996 (loan relationships) in relation to a relevant transfer, the transferee and the transferor are to be treated as if, at the time of the transfer, they were members of the same group.

(2) In sub-paragraph (1) the reference to being members of the same group must be construed in accordance with paragraph 12(8) of Schedule 9 to that Act.

Continuity in relation to derivative contracts

15—(1) For the purposes of the application of Schedule 26 to FA 2002 (derivative contracts) in relation to a relevant transfer, the transferee and the transferor are to be treated as if, at the time of the transfer, they were members of the same group.

(2) In sub-paragraph (1) the reference to being members of the same group must be construed in accordance with paragraph 28(6) of that Schedule.

Leased assets

16—(1) This paragraph applies for the purposes of section 781 of ICTA (assets leased to traders and others) where—

    (*a*) the interest of the lessor or the lessee under a lease, or any other interest in an asset, is transferred under a relevant transfer, or

(b) a lease, or any other interest in a lease, is granted by a taxable public body to another taxable public body in accordance with provision contained by virtue of paragraph 4, 6 or 12 of Schedule 12 to this Act in a transfer scheme.

(2) Section 783(4) of ICTA is to be disregarded and the transfer or grant is to be treated as made without any capital sum having been obtained in respect of the interest or lease by the transferor or grantor.

(3) In the case of the transfer of an interest under a lease, payments made by the transferor under the lease before the transfer takes effect are to be treated as if they had been made under that lease by the transferee.

(4) Expressions used in this paragraph and in sections 781 to 785 of ICTA have the same meanings in this paragraph as in those sections.

PART 3
TRANSFERS ETC FROM TAXABLE PUBLIC BODIES TO EXEMPT PUBLIC BODIES

Meaning of "relevant transfer" in Part 3 of Schedule

17 In this Part of this Schedule "relevant transfer" means a transfer, in accordance with a transfer scheme, from a taxable public body to an exempt public body.

Transfers of trading stock

18—(1) This paragraph applies if under a relevant transfer trading stock of the transferor is transferred to the transferee.

(2) Sub-paragraphs (3) and (4) have effect in computing for any corporation tax purpose the profits of the trade in relation to which the stock is trading stock immediately before the transfer takes effect ("the transferor's trade").

(3) The stock must be taken to have been—
  (a) disposed of by the transferor in the course of the transferor's trade, and
  (b) subject to that, disposed of when the transfer takes effect.

(4) The value of the stock is to be taken to be—
  (a) if consideration is given to the transferor in respect of the transfer, an amount equal to the value of the consideration, or
  (b) if no such consideration is given, nil.

(5) For the purposes of this paragraph consideration given to a person connected with the transferor is to be treated as given to the transferor.

(6) In this paragraph "trading stock" has the same meaning as in section 100 of ICTA.

(7) For the purposes of this paragraph whether a person is connected with another person is determined in accordance with [section 1122 of CTA 2010][1] (connected persons).

Amendments—[1] In sub-para (7) words substitued for words "section 839 of ICTA" by CTA 2010 s 1177 Sch 1 para 584(1), (3). CTA 2010 has effect for corporation tax purposes for accounting periods ending on or after 1 April 2010, and for income and capital gains tax purposes for the tax year 2010–11 and subsequent tax years.

Capital allowances: determination of disposal value of plant or machinery

19—(1) This paragraph applies to a relevant transfer of plant or machinery which is a disposal event for the purposes of Part 2 of CAA 2001 (capital allowances for plant and machinery).

(2) For the purposes of the application of section 61 of that Act in relation to the transferor, the disposal value of the plant or machinery is to be treated—
  (a) if a capital sum is received by the transferor by way of consideration or compensation in respect of the transfer, as an amount equal to that sum, or
  (b) if no such sum is received, as nil.

(3) For the purposes of this paragraph a sum received by a person connected with the transferor is to be treated as received by the transferor.

(4) Section 88 of CAA 2001 (sales at an undervalue) is to be disregarded.

(5) This paragraph is subject to sections 63(5) and 68 of CAA 2001.

Capital allowances: determination of disposal value of fixtures

20—(1) This paragraph applies to a relevant transfer if—
  (a) it is a disposal event for the purposes of Part 2 of CAA 2001, and
  (b) by virtue of the transfer a person is treated by section 188 of that Act as ceasing to own a fixture.

(2) For the purposes of the application of section 196 of that Act in relation to the transferor, the disposal value of the fixture is to be treated—

    (a) if a capital sum is received by the transferor by way of consideration or compensation in respect of the transfer, as an amount equal to that portion of that sum which, if the person to whom the disposal is made were entitled to an allowance, would fall to be treated for the purposes of Part 2 of that Act as expenditure incurred by that person on the provision of the fixture, or

    (b) if no such sum is received, as nil.

(3) For the purposes of this paragraph a sum received by a person connected with the transferor is to be treated as received by the transferor.

(4) This paragraph is subject to section 63(5) of CAA 2001.

Capital allowances: determination of capital value of industrial buildings etc

21—(1) This paragraph applies for the purposes of Part 3 of CAA 2001, and the other provisions of that Act which are relevant to that Part, in relation to a relevant transfer of the relevant interest in an industrial building or structure.

(2) This paragraph is subject to section 36 of FA 2007 (which makes provision about balancing adjustments etc under Part 3 of CAA 2001).

(3) The transfer is to be treated as a sale of that relevant interest.

(4) The net proceeds of that sale are to be treated—

    (a) if a capital sum is received by the transferor by way of consideration or compensation in respect of the transfer, as an amount equal to that sum, or

    (b) if no such sum is received, as nil.

(5) For the purposes of this paragraph a sum received by a person connected with the transferor is to be treated as received by the transferor.

(6) Sections 567 to 570 of CAA 2001 (sales treated as being for alternative amount) are not to have effect in relation to that sale.

Chargeable gains: assets to be treated as disposed of without a gain or a loss

22—(1) For the purposes of TCGA 1992 a disposal—

    (a) constituted by a relevant transfer, or

    (b) to which sub-paragraph (2) applies,

is to be taken to be for a consideration such that no gain or loss accrues to the person making the disposal.

(2) This sub-paragraph applies to a disposal if—

    (a) it is made in accordance with provision contained in a transfer scheme by virtue of paragraph 4, 6 or 12 of Schedule 12 to this Act,

    (b) the person making the disposal is a taxable public body,

    (c) the person to whom the disposal is made is an exempt public body, and

    (d) each of those persons is either the transferor or a transferee under the scheme.

Neutral effect of transfer of intangible assets

23—(1) For the purposes of Schedule 29 to FA 2002, a relevant transfer of a chargeable intangible asset of the transferor is to be treated as not involving any realisation of the asset by the transferor.

(2) Expressions used in this paragraph and in that Schedule have the same meanings in this paragraph as in that Schedule.

Neutral effect of transfer for loan relationships and derivative contracts

24 No credit or debit shall be required or allowed, in respect of a relevant transfer, to be brought into account in the transferor's case—

    (a) for the purposes of Chapter 2 of Part 4 of FA 1996 (loan relationships), or

    (b) for the purposes of Schedule 26 to FA 2002 (derivative contracts).

Leased assets

25—(1) This paragraph applies for the purposes of section 781 of ICTA (assets leased to traders and others) where—

    (a) the interest of the lessor or the lessee under a lease, or any other interest in an asset, is transferred under a relevant transfer, or

    (b) a lease, or any other interest in a lease, is granted by a taxable public body to an exempt public body in accordance with provision contained by virtue of paragraph 4, 6 or 12 of Schedule 12 to this Act in a transfer scheme.

(2) Section 783(4) of ICTA is to be disregarded and the transfer or grant is to be treated as made without any capital sum having been obtained in respect of the interest or lease by the transferor or grantor.

(3) Expressions used in this paragraph and in sections 781 to 785 of ICTA have the same meanings in this paragraph as in those sections.

PART 4
TRANSFERS FROM EXEMPT PUBLIC BODIES TO TAXABLE PUBLIC BODIES

Meaning of "relevant transfer" in Part 4 of Schedule

26   In this Part of this Schedule "relevant transfer" means a transfer, in accordance with a transfer scheme, from an exempt public body to a taxable public body.

Capital allowances: transfer of plant or machinery

27—(1) This paragraph applies where—
  (a) there is a relevant transfer of plant or machinery,
  (b) the plant or machinery would have been treated for the purposes of CAA 2001 (had the transferor incurred expenditure qualifying for allowances under Part 2 of that Act on the provision of the plant or machinery) as disposed of by the transferor to the transferee on the transfer taking effect, and
  (c) the transfer scheme in accordance with which the transfer is made contains provision for the transferee to be treated for the purposes of that Act as having incurred capital expenditure of an amount specified in or determined in accordance with the scheme on the provision of the plant or machinery.
(2) For the purposes of CAA 2001—
  (a) the transferee is to be treated as having incurred capital expenditure of that amount on the provision of the plant or machinery for the purposes for which it is used by the transferee on and after the taking effect of the transfer,
  (b) the property is to be treated as belonging to the transferee as a result of the transferee having incurred that expenditure, and
  (c) in the case of a fixture, the expenditure which falls to be treated as incurred by the transferee is to be treated for the purposes of sections 181(1) and 182(1) of that Act as being incurred by the giving of a consideration consisting in a capital sum of that amount.
(3) The provision mentioned in sub-paragraph (1)(c) for the determination of an amount may include provision for a determination—
  (a) to be made by the Secretary of State in a manner described in the scheme,
  (b) to be made by reference to factors so described or to the opinion of a person so described, and
  (c) to be capable of being modified (on one or more occasions) in a manner and in circumstances so described.
(4) The consent of the Treasury is required for the making or modification of a determination under the provision mentioned in sub-paragraph (1)(c).
(5) The consent of the transferee is required for the modification of a determination under the provision mentioned in sub-paragraph (1)(c).
(6) As to the making of a determination or a modification of a determination under the provision mentioned in sub-paragraph (1)(c), see further paragraph 43.
(7) Expressions used in this paragraph and in Part 2 of CAA 2001 have the same meanings in this paragraph as in that Part.

Capital allowances: determination of capital value of industrial buildings etc

28—(1) This paragraph applies where there is a relevant transfer of the relevant interest in an industrial building or structure and the transfer scheme in accordance with which the transfer is made contains provision specifying for the purposes of section 311 of CAA 2001—
  (a) the amount to be taken as the amount of the residue of qualifying expenditure immediately after the event, and
  (b) the period to be taken as the period from the date of the event to the end of the period of 25 years beginning with the day on which the building or structure was first used.
(2) For the purposes of that section—
  (a) the transfer is to be treated as the occurrence of a relevant event,
  (b) the residue of qualifying expenditure immediately after the event is to be taken to be the amount specified by virtue of sub-paragraph (1)(a), and
  (c) the period from the date of the event to the end of the period of 25 years beginning with the day on which the building or structure was first used is to be taken to be the period specified by virtue of sub-paragraph (1)(b).
(3) Expressions used in this paragraph and in Part 3 of CAA 2001 have the same meanings in this paragraph as in that Part.

PART 5

OTHER PROVISIONS CONCERNING TRANSFERS BETWEEN PUBLIC BODIES

Meaning of "relevant transfer" in Part 5 of Schedule

29   In this Part of this Schedule "relevant transfer" means a transfer, in accordance with a transfer scheme, from a public body to another public body.

Trading losses: change in ownership

30—(1) This paragraph applies to a relevant transfer of all the issued share capital of a company (the "transferred company").

(2) For the purposes of [Chapters 2 to 5 of Part 14 of CTA 2010][1], the transfer is not to be taken to result in a change in the ownership of—

  (*a*) the transferred company, or

  (*b*) a company which is a wholly-owned subsidiary of the transferred company when the transfer takes effect.

Amendments—[1]   In sub-para (2) words substitued for words "sections 768 to 768E of ICTA" by CTA 2010 s 1177 Sch 1 para 584(1),(4). CTA 2010 has effect for corporation tax purposes for accounting periods ending on or after 1 April 2010, and for income and capital gains tax purposes for the tax year 2010–11 and subsequent tax years.

Chargeable gains: degrouping charges

31—(1) This paragraph applies if a company ("the degrouped company")—

  (*a*) acquired an asset from another company at a time when both were members of the same group of companies ("the old group"),

  (*b*) ceases by virtue of a relevant transfer to be a member of the old group, and

  (*c*) becomes by virtue of the transfer a member of the same group of companies as the transferee ("the new group").

(2) Section 179 of TCGA 1992 (company ceasing to be member of group) is not to treat the degrouped company as having by virtue of the transfer sold and immediately reacquired the asset.

(3) Where sub-paragraph (2) has applied to an asset, section 179 of TCGA 1992 is to have effect on and after the first subsequent occasion on which the degrouped company ceases to be a member of the new group otherwise than by virtue of a relevant transfer as if—

  (*a*) the degrouped company, and

  (*b*) the company from which it acquired the asset,

had been members of the new group at the time of acquisition.

(4) If, disregarding any preparatory transactions, a company would be regarded by virtue of a relevant transfer—

  (*a*) as ceasing to be a member of a group of companies for the purposes of section 179 of TCGA 1992 (and, accordingly, of this paragraph), or

  (*b*) as becoming a member of a group of companies for the purposes of this paragraph,

it is to be regarded for those purposes as so doing by virtue of the relevant transfer and not by virtue of any preparatory transactions.

(5) In this paragraph "preparatory transactions" means anything done under or by virtue of this Act for the purpose of initiating, advancing or facilitating the relevant transfer in question.

(6) Expressions used in this paragraph and in section 179 of TCGA 1992 have the same meanings in this paragraph as in that section.

Stamp duty

32—(1) Stamp duty is not to be chargeable—

  (*a*) on a transfer scheme in the case of which the transferor and each transferee is a public body, or

  (*b*) on an instrument certified by the Secretary of State to the Commissioners for Her Majesty's Revenue and Customs as made for the purposes of such a transfer scheme, or as made for purposes connected with such a transfer scheme.

(2) But where, by virtue of sub-paragraph (1), stamp duty is not chargeable on a scheme or instrument, the scheme or instrument is to be treated as duly stamped only if—

  (*a*) in accordance with section 12 of the Stamp Act 1891 (c 39) it has been stamped with a stamp denoting either that it is not chargeable to duty or that it has been duly stamped, or

  (*b*) it is stamped with the duty to which it would be chargeable apart from sub-paragraph (1).

(3) In this paragraph "instrument" has the same meaning as in the Stamp Act 1891.

PART 6

TRANSFERS ETC INVOLVING PRIVATE PERSONS

Meaning of "relevant transfer" in Part 6 of Schedule

33 In this Part of this Schedule "relevant transfer" means a transfer, in accordance with a transfer scheme, from or to a person other than a public body.

Transfers of trading stock

34—(1) This paragraph applies if under a relevant transfer trading stock of the transferor is transferred to the transferee.

(2) Sub-paragraphs (3) and (4) have effect in computing for any corporation tax or income tax purpose both the profits of the trade in relation to which the stock is trading stock immediately before the transfer takes effect ("the transferor's trade") and—

    (a) if the stock falls immediately after the transfer takes effect to be treated as trading stock of the transferee, the profits of the trade in relation to which it falls to be treated as trading stock ("the transferee's trade");

    (b) otherwise, the consideration given by the transferee, or the expenditure incurred by the transferee, for the acquisition of the stock.

(3) The stock must be taken to have been—

    (a) disposed of by the transferor in the course of the transferor's trade,

    (b) if sub-paragraph (2)(a) applies, acquired by the transferee in the course of the transferee's trade, and

    (c) subject to that, disposed of and acquired when the transfer takes effect.

(4) The value of the stock is to be taken to be—

    (a) if consideration is given to the transferor in respect of the transfer, an amount equal to the value of the consideration, or

    (b) if no such consideration is given, nil.

(5) For the purposes of this paragraph consideration given to a person connected with the transferor is to be treated as given to the transferor.

(6) In this paragraph "trading stock" has the same meaning as in section 100 of ICTA (as respects corporation tax) or section 174 of ITTOIA 2005 (as respects income tax).

(7) For the purposes of this paragraph whether a person is connected with another person is determined in accordance with [section 1122 of CTA 2010][1] (as respects corporation tax) or section 993 of ITA 2007 (as respects income tax).

Amendments—[1]   In sub-para (7) words substitued for words "section 839 of ICTA" by CTA 2010 s 1177 Sch 1 para 584(1), (5). CTA 2010 has effect for corporation tax purposes for accounting periods ending on or after 1 April 2010, and for income and capital gains tax purposes for the tax year 2010–11 and subsequent tax years.

Capital allowances: determination of disposal value of plant or machinery

35—(1) This paragraph applies to a relevant transfer of plant or machinery which is a disposal event for the purposes of Part 2 of CAA 2001 (capital allowances for plant and machinery).

(2) For the purposes of the application of section 61 of that Act (disposal events and disposal value) in relation to the transferor, the disposal value of the plant or machinery is to be treated—

    (a) if a capital sum is received by the transferor by way of consideration or compensation in respect of the transfer, as an amount equal to that sum, or

    (b) if no such sum is received, as nil.

(3) For the purposes of this paragraph a sum received by a person connected with the transferor is to be treated as received by the transferor.

(4) Section 88 of CAA 2001 (sales at an undervalue) is to be disregarded.

(5) This paragraph is subject to sections 63(5) and 68 of CAA 2001.

Capital allowances: determination of disposal value of fixtures

36—(1) This paragraph applies to a relevant transfer if—

    (a) it is a disposal event for the purposes of Part 2 of CAA 2001, and

    (b) by virtue of the transfer a person is treated by section 188 of that Act as ceasing to own a fixture.

(2) For the purposes of the application of section 196 of that Act in relation to the transferor, the disposal value of the fixture is to be treated—

    (a) if a capital sum is received by the transferor by way of consideration or compensation in respect of the transfer, as an amount equal to that portion of that sum which falls (or, if the person to whom the disposal is made were entitled to an allowance, would fall) to be treated for the purposes of Part 2 of that Act as expenditure incurred by that person on the provision of the fixture, or (*b*) if no such sum is received, as nil.

(3) For the purposes of this paragraph a sum received by a person connected with the transferor is to be treated as received by the transferor.

(4) This paragraph is subject to section 63(5) of CAA 2001.

Capital allowances: section 265 of CAA 2001 not to apply in relation to transferee

37—(1) This paragraph applies in relation to a relevant transfer.

(2) For the purposes of the application of Part 2 of CAA 2001 in relation to the transferee, section 265 of that Act (successions: general) is to be disregarded.

Capital allowances: determination of capital value of industrial buildings etc

38—(1) This paragraph applies for the purposes of Part 3 of CAA 2001, and the other provisions of that Act which are relevant to that Part, in relation to a relevant transfer of the relevant interest in an industrial building or structure.

(2) This paragraph is subject to section 36 of FA 2007 (which makes provision about balancing adjustments etc under Part 3 of CAA 2001).

(3) The transfer is to be treated as a sale of that relevant interest.

(4) The net proceeds of that sale are to be treated—

(*a*) if a capital sum is received by the transferor by way of consideration or compensation in respect of the transfer, as an amount equal to that sum, or

(*b*) if no such sum is received, as nil.

(5) For the purposes of this paragraph a sum received by a person connected with the transferor is to be treated as received by the transferor.

(6) Sections 567 to 570 of CAA 2001 (sales treated as being for alternative amount) are not to have effect in relation to that sale.

Chargeable gains: disposals not to be treated as made at market value

39—(1) Section 17 of TCGA 1992 (disposals and acquisitions treated as made at market value) is not to have effect in relation to—

(*a*) a disposal constituted by a relevant transfer,

(*b*) a disposal to which sub-paragraph (2) applies, or

(*c*) the acquisition made by the person to whom the disposal is made;

but this sub-paragraph does not apply if the person making the disposal is connected with the person making the acquisition.

(2) This sub-paragraph applies to a disposal if—

(*a*) it is made in accordance with provision contained in a transfer scheme by virtue of paragraph 4, 6 or 12 of Schedule 12 to this Act,

(*b*) the person making the disposal or the person to whom the disposal is made is a person other than a public body, and

(*c*) each of those persons is either the transferor or a transferee under the scheme.

(3) If sub-paragraph (1) applies to the disposal of an asset, the disposal is to be taken (in relation to the person making the acquisition as well as the person making the disposal) to be—

(*a*) in a case where consideration in money or money's worth is given by the person making the acquisition or on his behalf in respect of the vesting of the asset in him, for a consideration equal to the amount or value of that consideration, or

(*b*) in a case where no such consideration is given, for a consideration of nil.

Loan relationships

40—(1) Paragraph 11 of Schedule 9 to FA 1996 (transactions not at arm's length) is not to have effect where, as a result of a relevant transfer, the transferee replaces the transferor as a party to a loan relationship.

(2) Expressions used in this paragraph and in Chapter 2 of Part 4 of FA 1996 have the same meanings in this paragraph as in that Chapter.

PART 7

OTHER PROVISIONS CONCERNING TRANSFERS

Chargeable gains: value shifting

41 No transfer scheme is to be regarded as a scheme or arrangement for the purposes of section 30 of TCGA 1992.

Group relief

42   The power of the Secretary of State to make a transfer scheme is not to be regarded as constituting—

  (*a*) arrangements falling within [section 154(3) or 155(3) of CTA 2010][1] (arrangements for transfer of company to another group or consortium), or

  (*b*) option arrangements for the purposes of [section 173 of CTA 2010][1].

Amendments—[1]   In sub-para (*a*) words substitued for words "section 410(1) or (2) of ICTA", in sub-para (*b*) words substituted for words "paragraph 5B of Schedule 18 to ICTA" by CTA 2010 s 1177 Sch 1 para 584(1), (6). CTA 2010 has effect for corporation tax purposes for accounting periods ending on or after 1 April 2010, and for income and capital gains tax purposes for the tax year 2010–11 and subsequent tax years.

Modification of transfer schemes and determinations under paragraph 9(1)(d) or 27(1)(c): companies

43—(1) This paragraph applies if—

  (*a*) a company delivers a company tax return,

  (*b*) subsequently, an event mentioned in sub-paragraph (2) below occurs, and

  (*c*) as a result of that event, the return is incorrect.

(2) The events are—

  (*a*) the making of an agreement modifying a transfer scheme under paragraph 15 of Schedule 12 to this Act;

  (*b*) a determination or modification of a determination under the provision mentioned in paragraph 9(1)(*d*) or 27(1)(*c*) above.

(3) The return may be amended under paragraph 15 of Schedule 18 to FA 1998 so as to remedy the error, ignoring any time limit which would otherwise prevent that happening.

(4) But an amendment may not be made in reliance on sub-paragraph (3) above more than 12 months after the end of the accounting period of the company during which (as the case may be)—

  (*a*) the agreement is made, or

  (*b*) the determination or modification of a determination is made.

(5) Sub-paragraphs (6) and (7) below apply if the company does not amend the return so as to remedy the error before the end of that 12 month period.

(6) A discovery assessment or a discovery determination may be made in relation to the error, ignoring any time limit which would otherwise prevent that happening.

(7) But such an assessment or determination may not be made in reliance on sub-paragraph (6) above more than 24 months after the end of the accounting period mentioned in sub-paragraph (4) above.

(8) Expressions used in this paragraph and in Schedule 18 to FA 1998 have the same meaning in this paragraph as in that Schedule.

Modification of transfer schemes: other persons and partnerships

44—(1) This paragraph applies if—

  (*a*) a person delivers a return under section 8, 8A or 12AA of TMA 1970,

  (*b*) subsequently, an agreement is made modifying a transfer scheme under paragraph 15 of Schedule 12 to this Act, and

  (*c*) as a result of that, the return is incorrect.

(2) The return may be amended under section 9ZA or 12ABA of TMA 1970 so as to remedy the error, ignoring any time limit which would otherwise prevent that happening.

(3) But an amendment may not be made in reliance on sub-paragraph (2) above more than 12 months after the end of the year of assessment during which the agreement modifying the transfer scheme is made.

(4) If the return is amended under section 12ABA in reliance on sub-paragraph (2) above, subsection (3) of that section applies, ignoring any time limit which would otherwise prevent the officer from proceeding under that subsection.

(5) Sub-paragraphs (6) and (7) below apply if the return is not amended under section 9ZA or 12ABA so as to remedy the error before the end of the 12 month period mentioned in sub-paragraph (3) above.

(6) An officer of Revenue and Customs may proceed under section 29(1) or 30B(1) and (2) of TMA 1970 in relation to the error, ignoring any time limit which would otherwise prevent the officer from so proceeding.

(7) But an assessment or an amendment may not be made in reliance on sub-paragraph (6) above more than 24 months after the end of the year of assessment mentioned in sub-paragraph (3) above.

Prospective amendments—In sub-para (1)(*a*), words ", or regulations under paragraph 10 of Schedule A1 to," to be inserted after words "12AA of" by F(No 2)A 2017 s 61(1), Sch 14 para 37 with effect from a day to be appointed.

Power to make further provision in relation to transfer schemes

45—(1) The Treasury may by regulations make provision for varying the way in which a relevant tax has effect from time to time (including by virtue of this Schedule) in relation to—

 (*a*) any property, rights or liabilities transferred in accordance with a transfer scheme, or

 (*b*) anything done for the purposes of, or in relation to, or in consequence of, the transfer of any property, rights or liabilities in accordance with a transfer scheme.

(2) The provision that may be made under sub-paragraph (1)(*a*) includes, in particular, provision for—

 (*a*) a tax provision not to apply, or to apply with modifications, in relation to any property, rights or liabilities transferred;

 (*b*) any property, rights or liabilities transferred to be treated in a specified way for the purposes of a tax provision;

 (*c*) the Secretary of State to be required or permitted, with the consent of the Treasury, to determine, or to specify the method for determining, anything which needs to be determined for the purposes of any tax provision so far as relating to any property, rights or liabilities transferred.

(3) The provision that may be made under sub-paragraph (1)(*b*) includes, in particular, provision for—

 (*a*) a tax provision not to apply, or to apply with modifications, in relation to anything done for the purposes of, or in relation to, or in consequence of, the transfer;

 (*b*) anything done for the purposes of, or in relation to, or in consequence of, the transfer to have or not to have a specified consequence or to be treated in a specified way;

 (*c*) the Secretary of State to be required or permitted, with the consent of the Treasury, to determine, or to specify the method for determining, anything which needs to be determined for the purposes of any tax provision so far as relating to anything done for the purposes of, or in relation to, or in consequence of, the transfer.

(4) Regulations under sub-paragraph (1) may amend this Schedule (apart from this paragraph).

(5) Regulations under sub-paragraph (1) may—

 (*a*) make such supplementary, incidental or consequential provision as the Treasury think fit, and

 (*b*) make different provision for different cases.

(6) The power to make regulations under sub-paragraph (1) shall be exercisable by statutory instrument which shall be subject to annulment in pursuance of a resolution of the House of Commons.

(7) In this paragraph references to any property, rights or liabilities transferred in accordance with a transfer scheme include references to any property, rights or liabilities transferred, or any interests, rights or liabilities created, by virtue of paragraph 4, 6 or 12 of Schedule 12 to this Act.

(8) In this paragraph references to the transfer of any property, rights or liabilities in accordance with a transfer scheme include references to the transfer of any property, rights or liabilities, or the creation of any interests, rights or liabilities, by virtue of paragraph 4, 6 or 12 of Schedule 12 to this Act.

(9) In this paragraph—

 "relevant tax" means income tax, corporation tax, capital gains tax, stamp duty, stamp duty land tax or stamp duty reserve tax, and

 "tax provision" means a provision of an enactment about a relevant tax.

(10) In sub-paragraph (9) "enactment" includes an enactment contained in an instrument made under an Act.

(11) Paragraph 20(3) of Schedule 12 to this Act applies for the purposes of this paragraph as it applies for the purposes of that Schedule.

Consequential amendment

46 In section 35(3)(*d*) of TCGA 1992 (no gain no loss disposals), after sub-paragraph (xvii) insert—

 "(xviii)paragraph 11 or 22 of Schedule 13 to the Crossrail Act 2008."

COUNTER-TERRORISM ACT 2008

(2008 Chapter 28)

An Act to confer further powers to gather and share information for counter-terrorism and other purposes; to make further provision about the detention and questioning of terrorist suspects and the prosecution and punishment of terrorist offences; to impose notification requirements on persons convicted of such offences; to confer further powers to act against terrorist financing, money laundering and certain other activities; to provide for review of certain Treasury decisions and about evidence in, and other matters connected with, review proceedings; to amend the law relating to inquiries; to amend the definition of "terrorism"; to amend the enactments relating to terrorist offences, control orders and the forfeiture of terrorist cash; to provide for recovering the costs of policing at certain gas facilities; to amend provisions about the appointment of special advocates in Northern Ireland; and for connected purposes.

[26 November 2008]

PART 5
TERRORIST FINANCING AND MONEY LAUNDERING

62 Terrorist financing and money laundering

Schedule 7 makes provision conferring powers on the Treasury to act against terrorist financing, money laundering and certain other activities.

SCHEDULES

SCHEDULE 7

TERRORIST FINANCING AND MONEY LAUNDERING

Section 62

PART 5
ENFORCEMENT: INFORMATION POWERS

Enforcement authorities and officers

18— (1) In this Schedule "enforcement authority" means—
   (a) [the Financial Conduct Authority ("the FCA"),][2]
   (b) the Commissioners for Her Majesty's Revenue and Customs ("HMRC"), [or][1]
   (c) the Office of Fair Trading ("the OFT"), . . . [2]
   (d) . . . [2]

(2) In this Part of this Schedule "enforcement officer" means—
   (a) an officer of the [FCA][2], including a member of the staff or an agent of the [FCA][2],
   (b) an officer of Revenue and Customs,
   (c) an officer of the OFT,
   (d) an officer of DETINI acting for the purposes of its functions under this Schedule in relation to credit unions in Northern Ireland, or
   (e) a local enforcement officer.

(3) A "local enforcement officer" means—
   (a) in Great Britain, an officer of a local weights and measures authority;
   (b) in Northern Ireland, an officer of DETINI acting pursuant to arrangements made with the OFT for the purposes of this Schedule.

Amendments—[1] In sub-para (1)(b) word at the end inserted, and sub-para (1)(d) and immediately preceding word repealed, by the Terrorist Asset-Freezing Act 2010 s 51(1) with effect from 31 March 2012 (by virtue of SI 2011/2835 art 2(a)).

[2] In sub-para (1)(a), words substituted, and in sub-para (2)(a), acronym substituted by FSA 2012 s 114(1), Sch 18 para 127(1), (2)(a), (b) with effect from 1 April 2013 by virtue of SI 2013/423 art 3, Schedule.

Power to require information or documents

19—(1) An enforcement officer may by notice to a relevant person require the person—
   (a) to provide such information as may be specified in the notice, or
   (b) to produce such documents as may be so specified.

(2) An officer may exercise powers under this paragraph only if the information or documents sought to be obtained as a result are reasonably required in connection with the exercise by the enforcement authority for whom the officer acts of its functions under this Schedule.

(3) Where an officer requires information to be provided or documents produced under this paragraph—

(a) the notice must set out the reasons why the officer requires the information to be provided or the documents produced, and

(b) the information must be provided or the documents produced—

(i) before the end of such reasonable period as may be specified in the notice; and

(ii) at such place as may be so specified.

(4) In relation to a document in electronic form the power to require production of it includes a power to require the production of a copy of it in legible form or in a form from which it can readily be produced in visible and legible form.

(5) An enforcement officer may take copies of, or make extracts from, any document produced under this paragraph.

(6) The production of a document does not affect any lien which a person has on the document.

Entry, inspection without a warrant etc

20—(1) Where an enforcement officer has reasonable cause to believe that any premises are being used by a relevant person in connection with the person's business activities, the officer may on producing evidence of authority at any reasonable time—

(a) enter the premises;

(b) inspect the premises;

(c) observe the carrying on of business activities by the relevant person;

(d) inspect any document found on the premises;

(e) require any person on the premises to provide an explanation of any document or to state where it may be found.

(2) An enforcement officer may take copies of, or make extracts from, any document found under sub-paragraph (1).

(3) An officer may exercise powers under this paragraph only if the information or document sought to be obtained as a result is reasonably required in connection with the exercise by the enforcement authority for whom the officer acts of its functions under this Schedule.

(4) In this paragraph "premises" means any premises other than premises used only as a dwelling.

Entry to premises under warrant

21—(1) A justice may issue a warrant under this paragraph if satisfied on information on oath given by an enforcement officer that there are reasonable grounds for believing that the first, second or third set of conditions is satisfied.

(2) The first set of conditions is—

(a) that there is on the premises specified in the warrant a document in relation to which a requirement could be imposed under paragraph 19(1)(b), and

(b) that if such a requirement were to be imposed—

(i) it would not be complied with, or

(ii) the document to which it relates would be removed, tampered with or destroyed.

(3) The second set of conditions is—

(a) that a person on whom a requirement has been imposed under paragraph 19(1)(b) has failed (wholly or in part) to comply with it, and

(b) that there is on the premises specified in the warrant a document that has been required to be produced.

(4) The third set of conditions is—

(a) that an enforcement officer has been obstructed in the exercise of a power under paragraph 20, and

(b) that there is on the premises specified in the warrant a document that could be inspected under paragraph 20(1)(d).

(5) A justice may issue a warrant under this paragraph if satisfied on information on oath given by an officer that there are reasonable grounds for suspecting that—

(a) an offence under this Schedule has been, is being or is about to be committed by a relevant person, and

(b) there is on the premises specified in the warrant a document relevant to whether that offence has been, or is being or is about to be committed.

(6) A warrant issued under this paragraph shall authorise an enforcement officer—

(a) to enter the premises specified in the warrant;

(b) to search the premises and take possession of anything appearing to be a document specified in the warrant or to take, in relation to any such document, any other steps which may appear to be necessary for preserving it or preventing interference with it;

(c) to take copies of, or extracts from, any document specified in the warrant;

(d) to require any person on the premises to provide an explanation of any document appearing to be of the kind specified in the warrant or to state where it may be found;

(*e*) to use such force as may reasonably be necessary.

(7) Where a warrant is issued by a justice under sub-paragraph (1) or (5) on the basis of information on oath given by an officer of the [FCA][1], for "an enforcement officer" in sub-paragraph (6) substitute "a constable".

(8) In sub-paragraphs (1), (5) and (7), "justice" means—

    (*a*) in relation to England and Wales, a justice of the peace;

    (*b*) in relation to Scotland, a justice within the meaning of section 307 of the Criminal Procedure (Scotland) Act 1995 (c 46) (interpretation);

    (*c*) in relation to Northern Ireland, a lay magistrate.

(9) In the application of this paragraph to Scotland, the references in sub-paragraphs (1), (5) and (7) to information on oath are to be read as references to evidence on oath.

Amendments—[1] In sub-para (7), acronym substituted by FSA 2012 s 114(1), Sch 18 para 127(1), (2)(*c*) with effect from 1 April 2013 by virtue of SI 2013/423 art 3, Schedule.

Restrictions on powers

22—(1) This paragraph applies in relation to the powers conferred by—

    (*a*) paragraph 19 (power to require information or documents),

    (*b*) paragraph 20 (entry, inspection without warrant etc), or

    (*c*) paragraph 21 (entry to premises under warrant).

(2) Those powers are not exercisable in relation to information or documents in respect of which a claim to legal professional privilege (in Scotland, to confidentiality of communications) could be maintained in legal proceedings.

(3) The exercise of those powers and the provision of information or production of documents under them is not otherwise subject to any restriction on the disclosure of information, whether imposed by statute or otherwise.

Failure to comply with information requirement

23—(1) If on an application made by—

    (*a*) an enforcement authority, or

    (*b*) a local weights and measures authority or DETINI pursuant to arrangements made with the OFT—

        (i) by or on behalf of the authority; or

        (ii) by DETINI,

it appears to the court that a person (the "information defaulter") has failed to do something that they were required to do under paragraph 19(1), the court may make an order under this paragraph.

(2) An order under this paragraph may require the information defaulter—

    (*a*) to do the thing that they failed to do within such period as may be specified in the order;

    (*b*) otherwise to take such steps to remedy the consequences of the failure as may be so specified.

(3) If the information defaulter is a body corporate, a partnership or an unincorporated body of persons that is not a partnership, the order may require any officer of the body corporate, partnership or body, who is (wholly or partly) responsible for the failure to meet such costs of the application as are specified in the order.

(4) In this paragraph "the court" means—

    (*a*) in England and Wales and Northern Ireland, the High Court or the county court;

    (*b*) in Scotland, the Court of Session or the sheriff court.

Powers of local enforcement officers

24—(1) A local enforcement officer may only exercise powers under this Part of this Schedule pursuant to arrangements made with the OFT—

    (*a*) by or on behalf of the relevant local weights and measures authority, or

    (*b*) by DETINI.

(2) Anything done or omitted to be done by, or in relation to, a local enforcement officer in the exercise or purported exercise of a power in this Part of this Schedule is treated for all purposes as if done or omitted to be done by, or in relation to, an officer of the OFT.

(3) Sub-paragraph (2) does not apply for the purposes of criminal proceedings brought against the local enforcement officer, the relevant local weights and measures authority, DETINI or the OFT, in respect of anything done or omitted to be done by the officer.

(4) A local enforcement officer must not disclose to any person other than the OFT and the relevant local weights and measures authority or, as the case may be, DETINI information obtained by the officer in the exercise of powers under this Part of this Schedule unless—

    (*a*) the officer has the approval of the OFT to do so, or

    (*b*) the officer is under a duty to make the disclosure.

(b) the date on which HMRC decided to undertake the review (in a case falling within paragraph 26D).

(8) Where HMRC are required to undertake a review but do not give notice of the conclusions within the time period specified in sub-paragraph (6), the review is to be treated as having concluded that the decision is upheld.

(9) If sub-paragraph (8) applies, HMRC must notify P of the conclusion which the review is treated as having reached.][1]

Amendments—[1]   Paras 26A–26F inserted by the Revenue and Customs Appeals Order, SI 2009/777 art 4, Sch para 1, 3 with effect from 1 April 2009.

[Bringing of appeals against decisions of HMRC

26F—(1) An appeal under paragraph 26 is to be made to the tribunal before—

    (a) the end of the period of 30 days beginning with the date of the document notifying the decision to which the appeal relates, or

    (b) if later, the end of the relevant period (within the meaning of paragraph 26C).

(2) But that is subject to sub-paragraphs (3) to (5).

(3) In a case where HMRC are required to undertake a review under paragraph 26B—

    (*a*) an appeal may not be made until the conclusion date, and

    (*b*) any appeal is to be made within the period of 30 days beginning with the conclusion date.

(4) In a case where HMRC are requested to undertake a review in accordance with paragraph 26D—

    (*a*) an appeal may not be made—

        (i) unless HMRC have decided whether or not to undertake a review, and

        (ii) if HMRC decide to undertake a review, until the conclusion date; and

    (*b*) any appeal is to be made within the period of 30 days beginning with—

        (i) the conclusion date (if HMRC decide to undertake a review), or

        (ii) the date on which HMRC decide not to undertake a review.

(5) In a case where paragraph 26E(8) applies, an appeal may be made at any time from the end of the period specified in paragraph 26E(6) to the date 30 days after the conclusion date.

(6) An appeal may be made after the end of the period specified in sub-paragraph (1), (3)(*b*), (4)(b) or (5) if the tribunal gives permission to do so.

(7) In this paragraph "conclusion date" means the date of the document notifying the conclusions of the review.][1]

Amendments—[1]   Paras 26A–26F inserted by the Revenue and Customs Appeals Order, SI 2009/777 art 4, Sch para 1, 3 with effect from 1 April 2009.

Imposition of penalty by other enforcement authority: procedure

27—(1) This paragraph applies if the [FCA][1], the OFT or DETINI ("the authority") proposes to impose a penalty under paragraph 25 on a person.

(2) The authority must give the person notice of—

    (*a*) the proposal to impose the penalty and the proposed amount,

    (*b*) the reasons for imposing the penalty, and

    (*c*) the right to make representations to the authority within a specified period (which may not be less than 28 days).

(3) The authority must then decide, within a reasonable period, whether to impose a penalty under paragraph 25 and must give the person notice—

    (*a*) if it decides not to impose a penalty, of that decision;

    (*b*) if it decides to impose a penalty, of the following matters—

        (i) the decision to impose a penalty and the amount,

        (ii) the reasons for the decision, and

        (iii) the right to appeal under paragraph 28.

Amendments—[1]   In sub-para (1), acronym substituted by FSA 2012 s 114(1), Sch 18 para 127(1), (3)(*a*) with effect from 1 April 2013 by virtue of SI 2013/423 art 3, Schedule.

Appeal against imposition of civil penalty [other than by HMRC]

28—(1) A person may appeal to the tribunal against . . . [1] a decision of the [FCA][3] or the OFT under paragraph 27.

(2) A person may appeal to the High Court in Northern Ireland against a decision of DETINI under paragraph 27.

(3) On the appeal the tribunal or court may—

    (*a*) set aside the decision appealed against, and

    (*b*) impose any penalty that could have been imposed by the body whose decision is appealed or remit the matter to that body.

(4) . . . [1]

(5) In this paragraph "the tribunal" means the First-tier Tribunal or, where so provided by or determined under Tribunal Procedure Rules, the Upper Tribunal.

(6) The Treasury may by order provide that, until a time specified in the order, appeals under sub-paragraph (1) are to be made—

     (a) . . . [1]

     (b) in the case of a decision of the FSA, to the Financial Services and Markets Tribunal;

     (c) in the case of a decision of the OFT, to the Consumer Credit Appeals Tribunal;

(rather than to the tribunal).

(7) An order under sub-paragraph (6) may provide that any enactment applies (with or without modifications) in relation to an appeal to a tribunal mentioned in paragraph . . . [1] *(b) or (c) of that sub-paragraph.*

(8) Such an order is subject to negative resolution procedure. [2]

Amendments—[1]   Words in cross-heading inserted, words in sub-para (1), whole of sub-para (4), sub-para (6)(*a*), and word in sub-para (7), repealed, by the Revenue and Customs Appeals Order, SI 2009/777 art 4, Sch para 1, 4 with effect from 1 April 2009.

[2]   Sub-paras (6)–(8) repealed by the Transfer of Tribunal Functions Order, SI 2010/22 art 5(1), Sch 2 para 145 with effect from 6 April 2010.

[3]   In sub-para (1), acronym substituted by FSA 2012 s 114(1), Sch 18 para 127(1), (3)(*b*) with effect from 1 April 2013 by virtue of SI 2013/423 art 3, Schedule.

Payment and recovery of civil penalties

29—(1) A penalty imposed under paragraph 25 is payable to the enforcement authority that imposed it.

(2) Any such penalty is a debt due to the authority and is recoverable accordingly.

PART 7
ENFORCEMENT: OFFENCES

Offences: failure to comply with requirement imposed by direction

30—(1) A person who fails to comply with a requirement imposed by a direction under this Schedule commits an offence, subject to the following provisions.

(2) No offence is committed if the person took all reasonable steps and exercised all due diligence to ensure that the requirement would be complied with.

(3) In deciding whether a person has committed an offence under this paragraph the court must consider whether the person followed any relevant guidance that was at the time—

     (*a*) issued by a supervisory authority or any other appropriate body,

     (*b*) approved by the Treasury, and

     (*c*) published in a manner approved by the Treasury as suitable in their opinion to bring the guidance to the attention of persons likely to be affected by it.

(4) In sub-paragraph (3) "appropriate body" means a body that regulates or is representative of any trade, profession, business or employment carried on by the alleged offender.

(5) A person guilty of an offence under this paragraph is liable—

     (*a*) on summary conviction, to a fine not exceeding the statutory maximum;

     (*b*) on conviction on indictment, to imprisonment for a term not exceeding two years or a fine or both.

(6) A person who is convicted of an offence under this paragraph is not liable to a penalty under paragraph 25 in respect of the same failure.

[Offences: relevant person circumventing requirements

30A—(1) A relevant person who intentionally participates in activities knowing that the object or effect of them is (whether directly or indirectly) to circumvent a requirement imposed by a direction under this Schedule commits an offence.

(2) A person guilty of an offence under this paragraph is liable—

     (*a*) on summary conviction, to a fine not exceeding the statutory maximum;

     (*b*) on conviction on indictment, to imprisonment for a term not exceeding two years or a fine or both.

(3) A person who is convicted of an offence under this paragraph is not liable to a penalty under paragraph 25A in respect of participation in the same activities.]¹

Amendments—[1]   Para 25A inserted by the Terrorist Asset-Freezing Act 2010 s 50(1), (3) with effect from 17 December 2010: see the Terrorist Asset-Freezing Act 2010 s 55.

Offences in connection with licences

31—(1) A person commits an offence who for the purpose of obtaining a licence under paragraph 17—

    (*a*) provides information that is false in a material respect or a document that is not what it purports to be, and

    (*b*) knows that, or is reckless as to whether, the information is false or the document is not what it purports to be.

(2) A person guilty of an offence under this paragraph is liable on conviction on indictment to imprisonment for a term not exceeding two years or a fine or both.

Extra-territorial application of offences

32—(1) An offence under this Schedule may be committed by a United Kingdom person by conduct wholly or partly outside the United Kingdom.

(2) Nothing in this paragraph affects any criminal liability arising otherwise than under this paragraph.

Prosecution of offences

33—(1) Proceedings for an offence under this Schedule may be instituted in England and Wales only by—

    (*a*) the [FCA][1];

    (*b*) . . .[2]

    (*c*) the OFT;

    (*d*) a local weights and measures authority; or

    (*e*) the Director of Public Prosecutions.

(2) Proceedings for an offence under this Schedule may be instituted in Northern Ireland only by—

    (*a*) the [FCA][1];

    (*b*) HMRC;

    (*c*) the OFT;

    (*d*) DETINI; or

    (*e*) the Director of Public Prosecutions for Northern Ireland.

(3) In section 168(4) of the Financial Services and Markets Act 2000 (c 8) (appointment . . .[1] of persons to carry out investigation), after paragraph (*b*) insert—

    "(*ba*)   a person may be guilty of an offence under Schedule 7 to the Counter-Terrorism Act 2008 (terrorist financing or money laundering);".

(4) In section 402(1) of that Act (power of FSA to institute proceedings), omit the "or" before paragraph (*b*) and after that paragraph insert—

    "or

        (*c*)   Schedule 7 to the Counter-Terrorism Act 2008 (terrorist financing or money laundering).".

(5) HMRC may conduct a criminal investigation into any offence under this Schedule.

(6) In sub-paragraph (5) "criminal investigation" has the meaning given by section 35(5)(*b*) of the Commissioners for Revenue and Customs Act 2005 (c 11).

Amendments—[1]   In sub-paras (1)(*a*), (2)(*a*), acronym substituted, and in sub-para (3), words repealed by FSA 2012 s 114(1), Sch 18 para 127(1), (4) with effect from 1 April 2013 by virtue of SI 2013/423 art 3, Schedule.

[2]   Sub-para (1)(*b*) repealed by the Public Bodies (Merger of the Director of Public Prosecutions and the Director of Revenue and Customs Prosecutions) Order, SI 2014/834 art 3(3), Sch 2 para 60 with effect from 27 March 2014.

Jurisdiction to try offences

34   Where an offence under this Schedule is committed outside the United Kingdom—

    (*a*) proceedings for the offence may be taken at any place in the United Kingdom, and

    (*b*) the offence may for all incidental purposes be treated as having been committed at any such place.

Time limit for summary proceedings

35—(1) An information relating to an offence under this Schedule that is triable by a magistrates' court in England and Wales may be so tried if it is laid—

    (*a*) at any time within three years after the commission of the offence, and

    (*b*) within twelve months after the date on which evidence sufficient in the opinion of the prosecutor to justify the proceedings comes to the knowledge of the prosecutor.

(2) Summary proceedings in Scotland for an offence under this Schedule—

    (*a*) must not be commenced after the expiration of three years from the commission of the offence;

    (*b*) subject to that, may be commenced at any time within twelve months after the date on which evidence sufficient in the Lord Advocate's opinion to justify the proceedings came to the knowledge of the Lord Advocate.

Section 136(3) of the Criminal Procedure (Scotland) Act 1995 (c 46) (date when proceedings deemed to be commenced) applies for the purposes of this sub-paragraph as for the purposes of that section.

(3) A magistrates' court in Northern Ireland has jurisdiction to hear and determine a complaint charging the commission of a summary offence under this Schedule provided that the complaint is made—

    (*a*) within three years from the time when the offence was committed, and

    (*b*) within twelve months from the date on which evidence sufficient in the opinion of the prosecutor to justify the proceedings comes to the knowledge of the prosecutor.

(4) For the purposes of this paragraph a certificate of the prosecutor (or, in Scotland, the Lord Advocate) as to the date on which such evidence as is referred to above came to their notice is conclusive evidence.

Liability of officers of bodies corporate etc

36—(1) If an offence under this Schedule committed by a body corporate is shown—

    (*a*) to have been committed with the consent or the connivance of an officer of the body corporate, or

    (*b*) to be attributable to any neglect on the part of any such officer,

the officer as well as the body corporate is guilty of an offence and liable to be proceeded against and punished accordingly.

(2) If an offence under this Schedule committed by a partnership is shown—

    (*a*) to have been committed with the consent or the connivance of a partner, or

    (*b*) to be attributable to any neglect on the part of a partner,

the partner as well as the partnership is guilty of an offence and liable to be proceeded against and punished accordingly.

(3) If an offence under this Schedule committed by an unincorporated association (other than a partnership) is shown—

    (*a*) to have been committed with the consent or the connivance of an officer of the association, or

    (*b*) to be attributable to any neglect on the part of any such officer,

the officer as well as the association is guilty of an offence and liable to be proceeded against and punished accordingly.

(4) If the affairs of a body corporate are managed by its members, sub-paragraph (1) applies in relation to the acts and defaults of a member in connection with the member's functions of management as if the member were a director of the body.

(5) In this paragraph—

    "officer"—

        (*a*) in relation to a body corporate, means a director, manager, secretary, chief executive, member of the committee of management, or a person purporting to act in such a capacity, and

        (*b*) in relation to an unincorporated association, means any officer of the association or any member of its governing body, or a person purporting to act in such capacity;

    "partner" includes a person purporting to act as a partner.

Proceedings against unincorporated bodies

37—(1) Proceedings for an offence under this Schedule alleged to have been committed by a partnership or an unincorporated association must be brought in the name of the partnership or association (and not in that of its members).

(2) In proceedings for such an offence brought against a partnership or unincorporated association—

    (*a*) section 33 of the Criminal Justice Act 1925 (c 86) (procedure on charge of offence against corporation) and Schedule 3 to the Magistrates' Courts Act 1980 (c 43) (corporations) apply as they do in relation to a body corporate;

    (*b*) section 70 of the Criminal Procedure (Scotland) Act 1995 (c 46) (proceedings against bodies corporate) applies as it does in relation to a body corporate;

    (*c*) section 18 of the Criminal Justice (Northern Ireland) Act 1945 (c 15 (NI)) (procedure on charge) and Schedule 4 to the Magistrates' Courts (Northern Ireland) Order 1981 (SI 1981/1675 (NI 26)) (corporations) apply as they do in relation to a body corporate.

(3) Rules of court relating to the service of documents have effect in relation to proceedings for an offence under this Schedule as if the partnership or association were a body corporate.

SMEs: subsidised qualifying expenditure
104F   Subsidised qualifying expenditure
104G   Subsidised qualifying expenditure on in-house direct R&D
104H   Subsidised qualifying expenditure on contracted out R&D
SMEs: capped R&D expenditure
104I   Capped R&D expenditure
Large companies: qualifying R&D expenditure
104J   Qualifying expenditure on in-house direct R&D
104K   Qualifying expenditure on contracted out R&D
104L   Qualifying expenditure on contributions to independent R&D
Amount of credit
104M   Amount of R&D expenditure credit
Payment of credit
104N   Payment of R&D expenditure credit
104O   Amounts deducted by way of tax adjustment
104P   Total expenditure on workers
104Q   Total amount of company's PAYE and NIC liabilities
104R   Surrender of credit to other group companies
104S   Restrictions on payment of R&D expenditure credit
104T   "Going concern"
Insurance companies
104U   Insurance companies treated as large companies
104V   Entitlement to credit: I minus E basis
Group companies
104W   R&D expenditure of group companies
Ineligible companies
104WA   Ineligible companies
Anti-avoidance
104X   Artificially inflated claims for credit
Interpretation
104Y   Interpretation
Chapter 7 Trade Profits: Gifts to Charities etc
Relief for certain gifts
105   Gifts of trading stock to charities etc
106   Meaning of "designated educational establishment"
107   Gifts of medical supplies and equipment
Benefits associated with gifts
108   Receipt of benefits by donor or connected person
Chapter 8 Trade Profits: Herd Basis Rules
Introduction
109   Election for application of herd basis rules
110   Meaning of "animal", "herd", "production herd" etc
111   Other interpretative provisions
The herd basis rules
112   Initial cost of herd and value of herd
113   Addition of animals to herd
114   Replacement of animals in herd
115   Amount of receipt if old animal slaughtered under disease control order
116   Sale of animals from herd
117   Sale of whole or substantial part of herd
118   Acquisition of new herd begun within 5 years of sale
119   Section 118: sale for reasons outside farmer's control
120   Replacement of part sold begun within 5 years of sale
121   Section 120: sale for reasons outside farmer's control
Elections
122   Herd basis elections
123   Five year gap in which no production herd kept
124   Slaughter under disease control order
Preventing abuse of the herd basis rules
125   Preventing abuse of the herd basis rules
Supplementary
127   Further assessment etc if herd basis rules apply
Chapter 8A Compensation for compulsory slaughter of animals
Introduction
127A   Application of Chapter 8A
127B   Right to make claim
127C   Book value
127D   Effect of claim for spreading of profits
127E   Adjustment: cessation of trading

295   General rule: profits arising from loan relationships chargeable as income

296   Profits and deficits to be calculated using credits and debits given by this Part

297   Trading credits and debits to be brought into account under Part 3

298   Meaning of trade and purposes of trade

299   Charge to tax on non-trading profits

300   Method of bringing non-trading deficits into account

301   Calculation of non-trading profits and deficits from loan relationships: non- trading credits and debits

Chapter 2 Basic Definitions

302   "Loan relationship", "creditor relationship", "debtor relationship"

303   "Money debt"

304   "Related transaction"

305   Payments, interest, rights and liabilities under a loan relationship

Chapter 3 The Credits and Debits to Be Brought Into Account: General

Introduction

306   Overview of Chapter

Matters in respect of which amounts are to be brought into account

306A   Matters in respect of which amounts to be brought into account

General principles about the bringing into account of credits and debits

307   General principles about the bringing into account of credits and debits

Amounts recognised in determining a company's profit or loss

308   Amounts recognised in determining a company's profit or loss

309   Companies without GAAP-compliant accounts

310   Power to make regulations about recognised amounts

311   Amounts not fully recognised for accounting purposes: introduction

312   Determination of credits and debits where amounts not fully recognised

Accounting bases

313   Basis of accounting: "amortised cost basis", "fair value accounting" and "fair value"

314   Power to make regulations about changes from amortised cost basis

Adjustments on change of accounting basis

315   Introduction to sections 316 and 318

316   Change of basis of accounting involving change of value

318   Change of accounting basis following cessation of loan relationship

319   General power to make regulations about changes in accounting policy

Rules differing from generally accepted accounting practice

320   Credits and debits treated as relating to capital expenditure

320A   Amounts recognised in other comprehensive income and not transferred to profit or loss

320B   Hybrid capital instruments: amounts recognised in equity

321A   Restriction on debits resulting from release of loans to participators etc

322   Release of debts: cases where credits not required to be brought into account

323   Meaning of expressions relating to insolvency etc

323A   Substantial modification: cases where credits not required to be brought into account

324   Restriction on debits resulting from revaluation

325   Restriction on credits resulting from reversal of disallowed debits

326   Writing off government investments

327   Disallowance of imported losses etc

Exchange gains and losses

328   Exchange gains and losses

Pre-loan relationship, abortive and pre-trading expenses

329   Pre-loan relationship and abortive expenses

330   Debits in respect of pre-trading expenditure

Pre-commencement debits of property businesses etc of non-UK resident companies

330ZA   Debits referable to times before UK property business etc carried on

Company is not, or has ceased to be, party to loan relationship

330A   Company is not, or has ceased to be, party to loan relationship

330B   Exclusion of debit where relief allowed to another

330C   Avoidance of double charge

Company moving abroad

333   Company ceasing to be UK resident

334   Non-UK resident company ceasing to hold loan relationship for UK permanent establishment

Chapter 4 Continuity of Treatment on Transfers Within Groups or on Reorganisations

Application of this Chapter

335   Introduction to Chapter

336   Transfers of loans on group transactions

337   Transfers of loans on insurance business transfers

338   Meaning of company replacing another as party to loan relationship

339   Issues of new securities on certain cross-border reorganisations

Continuity of treatment: transfer of loan at notional carrying value
340　　Group transfers and transfers of insurance business: transfer at notional carrying value
341　　Transferor using fair value accounting
342　　Issues of new securities on reorganisations: disposal at notional carrying value
343　　Receiving company using fair value accounting
Transferee leaving group after replacing transferor as party to loan relationship
344　　Introduction
345　　Transferee leaving group otherwise than because of exempt distribution
346　　Transferee leaving group because of exempt distribution
Chapter 5 Connected Companies Relationships: Introduction and General
348　　Introduction: meaning of "connected companies relationship"
349　　Application of amortised cost basis to connected companies relationships
352　　Disregard of related transactions
352A　　Exclusion of credits on reversal of disregarded loss
352B　　Eliminating tax mismatch for loan relationships with qualifying link
Chapter 6 Connected Companies Relationships: Impairment Losses and Releases of Debts
Introduction
353　　Introduction to Chapter
Exclusion of debits for impaired or released connected companies debts
354　　Exclusion of debits for impaired or released connected companies debts
355　　Cessation of connection
356　　Exception to section 354: swapping debt for equity
357　　Exception to section 354: insolvent creditors
Exclusion of credits for connected companies debts on release or reversal of impairments
358　　Exclusion of credits on release of connected companies debts: general
359　　Exclusion of credits on release of connected companies debts during creditor's insolvency
360　　Exclusion of credits on reversal of impairments of connected companies debts
Deemed debt releases on impaired debts becoming held by connected company
361　　Acquisition of creditor rights by connected company at undervalue
361C　　The equity-for-debt exception
361D　　Corporate rescue: debt released shortly after acquisition
362　　Parties becoming connected where creditor's rights subject to impairment adjustment etc
362A　　Corporate rescue: debt released shortly after connection arises
363　　Companies connected for sections 361 to 362A
363A　　Arrangements for avoiding section 361 or 362
Chapter 7 Group Relief Claims Involving Impaired or Released Consortium Debts
364　　Introduction to Chapter
365　　Reduction of impairment loss debits where group relief claimed
366　　Effect where credit for release brought into account on amortised cost basis
367　　Reduction of credits exceeding impairment losses
368　　Reduction of claims where there are earlier net consortium debits
369　　Carry forward of claims where there are no net consortium debits
370　　Group accounting periods
371　　Interpretation
Chapter 8 Connected Parties Relationships: Late Interest
372　　Introduction to Chapter
373　　Late interest treated as not accruing until paid in some cases
375　　Loans to close companies by participators etc
376　　Interpretation of section 375
378　　Loans by trustees of occupational pension schemes
379　　Persons indirectly standing in the position of creditor
Chapter 9 Partnerships Involving Companies
380　　Partnerships involving companies
381　　Determinations of credits and debits by company partners: general
382　　Company partners using fair value accounting
383　　Lending between partners and the partnership
384　　Treatment of exchange gains and losses
385　　Company partners' shares where firm owns deeply discounted securities
Chapter 10 Insurance Companies
Introduction
386　　Overview of Chapter
Treatment of deficit on basic life assurance and general annuity business
387　　Treatment of deficit on basic life assurance and general annuity business: introduction
388　　Basic rule: deficit set off against income and gains of deficit period
389　　Claim to carry back deficit
390　　Meaning of "available profits"
391　　Carry forward of surplus deficit to next accounting period
Exclusion of loan relationships of members of Lloyd's

392   Exclusion of loan relationships of members of Lloyd's

Chapter 11 Other Special Kinds of Company

Investment trusts' and venture capital trusts' creditor relationships

395   Investment trusts: profits or losses of a capital nature

396   Venture capital trusts: profits or losses of a capital nature

Credit unions

397   Credit unions

Chapter 12 Special Rules for Particular Kinds of Securities

Introduction

398   Overview of Chapter

Index-linked gilt-edged securities

399   Basic rules

400   Adjustments for changes in index

400A   Adjustments for changes in index: relevant hedging schemes

400B   Interpretation of section 400A: economic profits and losses

400C   Meaning of "associated with"

Other gilt-edged securities

401   Gilt strips

402   Market value of securities

403   Meaning of "strip"

404   Restriction on deductions etc relating to FOTRA securities

405   Certain non-UK residents with interest on 3½% War Loan 1952 or After

Deeply discounted securities: connected companies and close companies

406   Introduction

409   Postponement until redemption of debits for close companies' deeply discounted securities

410   Exceptions to section 409

411   Interpretation of section 409

412   Persons indirectly standing in the position of creditor

Funding bonds

413   Issue of funding bonds

414   Redemption of funding bonds

Derivatives

415   Loan relationships with embedded derivatives

416   Election for application of sections 415 and 585

417   Further provisions about elections under section 416

Options etc

420   Assumptions where options etc apply

Hybrid capital instruments

420A   Amounts payable in respect of hybrid capital instruments

Chapter 13 European Cross-border Transfers of Business

Introduction

421   Introduction to Chapter

Transfers of loan relationships at notional carrying value

422   Transfer of loan relationship at notional carrying value

423   Transferor using fair value accounting

424   Reorganisations involving loan relationships

425   Original holder using fair value accounting

Exception for tax avoidance cases

426   Tax avoidance etc

427   Procedure on application for clearance

428   Decision on application for clearance

Transparent entities

429   Disapplication of Chapter where transparent entities involved

Interpretation

430   Interpretation

Chapter 14 European Cross-border Mergers

Introduction

431   Introduction to Chapter

432   Meaning of "the transferee" and "transferor"

Transfers of loan relationships at notional carrying value

433   Transfer of loan relationship at notional carrying value

434   Transferor using fair value accounting

435   Reorganisations involving loan relationships

436   Original holder using fair value accounting

Exception for tax avoidance cases

437   Tax avoidance etc

Transparent entities

438   Disapplication of Chapter where transparent entities involved

Interpretation
439 Interpretation
Chapter 15 Tax Avoidance
Introduction
440 Overview of Chapter
Unallowable purposes and tax relief schemes
441 Loan relationships for unallowable purposes
442 Meaning of "unallowable purpose"
Transactions not at arm's length: general
444 Transactions not at arm's length: general
445 Disapplication of section 444 where Part 4 of TIOPA 2010 applies
446 Bringing into account adjustments made under Part 4 of TIOPA 2010
Non-market loans
446A Non-market loans
Transactions not at arm's length: exchange gains and losses
447 Exchange gains and losses on debtor relationships: loans disregarded under Part 4 of TIOPA 2010
448 Exchange gains and losses on debtor relationships: equity notes where holder associated with issuer
449 Exchange gains and losses on creditor relationships: no corresponding debtor relationship
450 Meaning of "corresponding debtor relationship"
451 Exception to section 449 where loan exceeds arm's length amount
452 Exchange gains and losses where loan not on arm's length terms
Derecognition
455A Debits arising from derecognition of creditor relationships
Counteracting avoidance arrangements
455B Counteracting effect of avoidance arrangements
455C Interpretation of section 455B
455D Examples of results that may indicate exclusion not applicable
Chapter 16 Non-trading Deficits: pre-1 April 2017 deficits and charities
456 Introduction to Chapter
457 Basic rule for deficits: carry forward to accounting periods after deficit period
458 Claim to carry forward deficit to later accounting periods
459 Claim to set off deficit against profits of deficit period or earlier periods
460 Time limits and procedure for claims under section 459(1)
461 Claim to set off deficit against other profits for the deficit period
462 Claim to carry back deficit to earlier accounting periods
463 Profits available for relief under section 462
Chapter 16A Non-trading deficits: post 1 April 2017 deficits
463A Introduction to Chapter
463B Claim to set off deficit against profits of deficit period or earlier periods
463C Time limits for claims under section 463B(1)
463D Claim to set off deficit against profits for the deficit period
463E Claim to carry back deficit to earlier periods
463F Profits available for relief under section 463E
463G Carry forward of unrelieved deficit against total profits
463H Carry forward of unrelieved deficit against non-trading profits
463I Re-application of section 463G if any deficit remains after previous application
Chapter 17 Priority Rules
464 Priority of this Part for corporation tax purposes
465 Exclusion of distributions except in tax avoidance cases
Chapter 18 General and Supplementary Provisions
Changes in accounting standards
465A Power to make regulations where accounting standards change
Tax-adjusted carrying value
465B "Tax-adjusted carrying value"
Connections between persons
466 Companies connected for an accounting period
467 Connections where partnerships are involved
468 Connection between companies to be ignored in some circumstances
469 Creditors who are financial traders
470 Section 469: supplementary provisions
471 Creditors who are insurance companies carrying on BLAGAB
472 Meaning of "control"
473 Meaning of "major interest"
474 Treatment of connected companies and partnerships for section 473
475 Meaning of expressions relating to exchange gains and losses
Meaning of "hedging relationship"

475A   "Hedging relationship"
Meaning of "matched"
475B   Meaning of "matched"
Meaning of "hybrid capital instrument"
475C   Meaning of "hybrid capital instrument"
Other general definitions
476   Other definitions
Part 6: Relationships Treated as Loan Relationships etc
Chapter 1 Introduction
477   Overview of Part
Chapter 2 Relevant Non-lending Relationships
Introduction: meaning of "relevant non-lending relationship" etc
478   Relevant non-lending relationships: introduction
479   Relevant non-lending relationships not involving discounts
480   Relevant non-lending relationships involving discounts
Application of Part 5 to relevant non-lending relationships
481   Application of Part 5 to relevant non-lending relationships
482   Miscellaneous rules about amounts to be brought into account because of this Chapter
Meaning of "money debt" and "interest" in this Chapter
483   Exchange gains and losses: amounts treated as money debts
484   Provision not at arm's length: meaning of "interest" and "money debt"
Exclusions
485   Exclusion of debts where profits or losses within Part 7 or 8
486   Exclusion of exchange gains and losses in respect of tax debts etc
Chapter 2A Disguised interest
486A   Overview
486B   Disguised interest to be regarded as profit from loan relationship
486C   Exclusion where return otherwise taxable
486D   Exclusion where arrangement has no tax avoidance purpose
486E   Excluded shares
Chapter 2B Transferred Income Streams
486F   Introduction to Chapter
486G   Consideration to be treated as loan relationship
Chapter 3 OEICs, Unit Trusts and Offshore Funds
Introduction
487   Overview of Chapter
488   Meaning of "open-ended investment company" etc
489   Meaning of "offshore fund" etc
Holdings in OEICs, unit trusts and offshore funds treated as creditor relationship rights
490   Holdings in OEICs, unit trusts and offshore funds treated as creditor relationship rights
491   Holding coming within section 490: opening valuations
492   Holding coming within section 490: calculation to undo avoidance
The qualifying investments test
493   The qualifying investments test
494   Meaning of "qualifying investments"
495   Qualifying holdings
496   Meaning of "hedging relationship"
Power to change investments that are qualifying investments
497   Power to change investments that are qualifying investments
Chapter 4 Building Societies
498   Building society dividends and interest
Chapter 5 registered societies
499   Registered society payments treated as interest under loan relationship
500   Exclusion of interest where failure to make return
Chapter 6 Alternative Finance Arrangements
Introduction
501   Introduction to Chapter
502   Meaning of "financial institution"
Arrangements that are alternative finance arrangements
503   Purchase and resale arrangements
504   Diminishing shared ownership arrangements
505   Deposit arrangements
506   Profit share agency arrangements
507   Investment bond arrangements
508   Provision not at arm's length: exclusion of arrangements from sections 503 to 507
Treatment as loan relationships
509   Application of Part 5: general
510   Application of Part 5 to particular alternative finance arrangements
Meaning of "alternative finance return"

511   Purchase and resale arrangements
512   Diminishing shared ownership arrangements
513   Other arrangements
Treatment for other tax purposes
514   Exclusion of alternative finance return from consideration for sale of assets
515   Diminishing shared ownership arrangements not partnerships
516   Treatment of principal under profit sharing agency arrangements
517   Treatment of bond-holder under investment bond arrangements
518   Investment bond arrangements: treatment as securities
519   Investment bond arrangements: other provisions
520   Provision not at arm's length: non-deductibility of relevant return
Chapter 6A Shares Accounted for as Liabilities
521A   Introduction to Chapter
521B   Application of Part 5 to certain shares as rights under creditor relationship
521C   Shares accounted for as liabilities
521D   Excepted shares
521E   Unallowable purpose
521F   Shares becoming or ceasing to be shares to which section 521B applies
Chapter 9 Manufactured Interest etc
539   Introduction to Chapter
540   Manufactured interest treated as interest under loan relationship
541   Debits for deemed interest under stock lending arrangements disallowed
Chapter 10 Repos
Introduction
542   Introduction to Chapter
Creditor repos and creditor quasi-repos
543   Meaning of creditor repo
544   Meaning of creditor quasi-repo
545   Ignoring effect on lender etc of sale of securities
546   Charge on lender for finance return in respect of the advance
Debtor repos and debtor quasi-repos
548   Meaning of debtor repo
549   Meaning of debtor quasi-repo
550   Ignoring effect on borrower of sale of securities
551   Relief for borrower for finance charges in respect of the advance
General provisions
552   General provisions about arrangements
553   Persons buying or selling for others
554   Power to modify this Chapter
555   Cases where section 554 applies: non-standard repos
Interpretation
556   Meaning of securities and similar securities
557   Meaning of person receiving an asset
558   Interpretation of accounting expressions
559   Minor definitions
Chapter 11 Investment Life Insurance Contracts
Introduction
560   Introduction to Chapter
561   Meaning of "investment life insurance contract"
Investment life assurance contracts treated as creditor relationships
562   Contract to be loan relationship
563   Increased non-trading credits for BLAGAB and EEA taxed contracts
564   Section 563: interpretation
565   Relevant amount where the relevant company uses fair value accounting
Old accounting period contracts
566   Introduction
567   Gains on deemed surrenders to be brought into account on related transactions
568   Restriction on credits on old contracts: fair value accounting cases
569   Restriction on debits on old contracts: non-fair value accounting cases
Part 7: Derivative Contracts
Chapter 1 Introduction
Introduction
570   Overview of Part
How profits and losses from derivative contracts are dealt with
571   General rule: profits chargeable as income
572   Profits and losses to be calculated using credits and debits given by this Part
573   Trading credits and debits to be brought into account under Part 3
574   Non-trading credits and debits to be brought into account under Part 5
Chapter 2 Contracts to Which This Part Applies

Introduction
575   Overview of Chapter
Meaning of "derivative contract" and other basic definitions
576   "Derivative contract"
577   "Relevant contract"
578   Relevant contracts of a company and being party to such contracts
579   The accounting conditions
580   "Option"
581   "Future"
582   "Contract for differences"
583   "Underlying subject matter"
Cases where companies treated as parties to relevant contracts
584   Hybrid derivatives with embedded derivatives
585   Loan relationships with embedded derivatives
586   Other contracts with embedded derivatives
Other contracts etc treated as derivative contracts
587   Contract relating to holding in OEIC, unit trust or offshore fund
588   Associated transaction treated as derivative contract
Exclusions from derivative contracts
589   Contracts excluded because of underlying subject matter: general
590   Disregard of subordinate or small value underlying subject matter
591   Conditions A to E mentioned in section 589(5)
592   Embedded derivatives treated as meeting condition in section 591 etc
593   Contracts where part of underlying subject matter is excluded property
Chapter 3 Credits and Debits to be Brought Into Account: General
Introduction
594   Overview of Chapter
Matters in respect of which amounts are to be brought into account
594A   Matters in respect of which amounts are to be brought into account
General principles
595   General principles about the bringing into account of credits and debits
596   Meaning of "related transaction"
Amounts recognised in determining a company's profit or loss
597   Amounts recognised in determining a company's profit or loss
598   Regulations about recognised amounts
599   Meaning of "amounts recognised for accounting purposes"
599A   Amounts not fully recognised for accounting purposes: introduction
599B   Determination of credits and debits where amounts not fully recognised
Application of fair value accounting
600   Contract which is or forms part of financial asset or liability
601   Contract relating to holding in OEIC, unit trust or offshore fund
602   Contract becoming one relating to holding in OEIC, unit trust or offshore fund
603   Associated transaction treated as derivative contract
Rules differing from generally accepted accounting practice
604   Credits and debits treated as relating to capital expenditure
604A   Amounts recognised in other comprehensive income and not transferred to profit or loss
Exchange gains and losses
606   Exchange gains and losses
Miscellaneous
607   Pre-contract or abortive expenses
607ZA   Debits referable to times before UK property business etc carried on
607A   Company is not, or has ceased to be, party to derivative contract
607B   Exclusion of debit where relief allowed to another
607C   Avoidance of double charge
609   Company ceasing to be UK resident
610   Non-UK resident company ceasing to hold derivative contract for UK permanent establishment
611   Release under statutory insolvency arrangement of liability under derivative contract
Chapter 4 Further Provision About Credits and Debits to be Brought Into Account
Introduction
612   Overview of Chapter
Adjustments on change of accounting basis
613   Introduction to sections 614 and 615
614   Change of basis of accounting involving change of value
615   Change of accounting policy after ceasing to be party to derivative contract
Certain embedded derivatives
616   Disapplication of fair value accounting
617   Election for section 616 not to apply

618   Elections under section 617: groups of companies
Partnerships involving companies
619   Partnerships involving companies
620   Determination of credits and debits by company partners
621   Company partners using fair value accounting
Miscellaneous
622   Contracts ceasing to be derivative contracts
623   Index-linked gilt-edged securities with embedded contracts for differences
Chapter 5 Continuity of Treatment on Transfers Within Groups
Introductory
624   Introduction to Chapter
Group member replacing another as party to derivative contract
625   Group member replacing another as party to derivative contract
626   Transactions to which section 625 applies
627   Meaning of company replacing another as party to derivative contract
Exceptions to section 625
628   Transferor using fair value accounting
Transferee leaving group after replacing transferor as party to derivative contract
630   Introduction to sections 631 and 632
631   Transferee leaving group otherwise than because of exempt distribution
632   Transferee leaving group because of exempt distribution
Chapter 6 Special Kinds of Company
Mutual trading companies
633   Mutual trading companies
Insurance companies
634   Insurance companies
635   Creditor relationships: embedded derivatives which are options
636   Modifications of Chapter 5
Investment and venture capital trusts
637   Investment trusts: profits or losses of a capital nature
638   Venture capital trusts: profits or losses of a capital nature
Chapter 7 Chargeable Gains Arising in Relation to Derivative Contracts
Introduction
639   Overview of Chapter
Some credits and debits not to be brought into account under Part 5
640   Credits and debits not to be brought into account under Part 5
Some derivative contracts to be taxed on a chargeable gains basis
641   Derivative contracts to be taxed on a chargeable gains basis
642   Exception from section 641
Derivative contracts to which sections 640 and 641 apply
643   Contracts relating to land or certain tangible movable property
644   Income to be left out of account in determining whether section 643 applies
645   Creditor relationships: embedded derivatives which are options
646   Exclusions from section 645
647   Meaning of certain expressions in section 645
648   Creditor relationships: embedded derivatives which are exactly tracking contracts for differences
649   Meaning of certain expressions in section 648
650   Property based total return swaps
Some credits and debits not to be brought into account under Part 3 or 5
651   Credits and debits not to be brought into account under Part 3 or Part 5
Issuers of securities with embedded derivatives: deemed options
652   Introduction to sections 653 to 655
653   Shares issued or transferred as a result of exercise of deemed option
654   Payment instead of disposal on exercise of deemed option
655   Ceasing to be party to debtor relationship when deemed option not exercised
Issuers of securities with embedded derivatives: deemed contracts for differences
656   Introduction to section 658
657   Meaning of "exactly tracking contract" in section 656
658   Chargeable gain or allowable loss treated as accruing
Interpretation
659   Meaning of "relevant credits" and "relevant debits"
Chapter 8 Further Provision About Chargeable Gains and Derivative Contracts
Company ceasing to be party to certain contracts
660   Contract relating to holding in OEIC, unit trust or offshore fund
661   Contract which becomes derivative contract
Contracts ceasing to be derivative contracts
662   Contracts ceasing to be derivative contracts
Carry back of net losses on certain derivative contracts

663   Contracts to which section 641 applies
664   Meaning of certain expressions in section 663
Issuers of securities with embedded derivatives: equity instruments
665   Introduction to section 666
666   Allowable loss treated as accruing
Treatment of shares acquired in certain circumstances
667   Shares acquired on exercise of non-embedded option
668   Shares acquired on running of future to delivery
669   Meaning of G and L in sections 667 and 668
Treatment of net gains and losses on exercise of option
670   Treatment of net gains and losses on exercise of option
671   Meaning of G, L and CV in section 670
Treatment of net gains and losses on disposal of certain embedded derivatives
672   Treatment of net gains and losses on disposal of certain embedded derivatives
673   Meaning of G, L and CV in section 672
Chapter 9 European Cross-border Transfers of Business
Introduction
674   Introduction to Chapter
Transfers of derivative contracts at notional carrying value
675   Transfer of derivative contract at notional carrying value
676   Transferor using fair value accounting
Exception for tax avoidance cases and clearances
677   Tax avoidance etc
678   Procedure on application for clearance
679   Decision on application for clearance
Transparent entities
680   Disapplication of Chapter where transparent entities involved
Interpretation
681   Interpretation
Chapter 10 European Cross-border Mergers
Introduction
682   Introduction to Chapter
683   Meaning of "the transferee" and "transferor"
Transfers of derivative contracts at notional carrying value
684   Transfer of derivative contract at notional carrying value
685   Transferor using fair value accounting
Exception for tax avoidance cases and clearances
686   Tax avoidance etc
Transparent entities
687   Disapplication of Chapter where transparent entities involved
Interpretation
688   Interpretation
Chapter 11 Tax Avoidance
Introduction
689   Overview of Chapter
Unallowable purposes
690   Derivative contracts for unallowable purposes
691   Meaning of "unallowable purpose"
692   Allowance of accumulated net losses
Transactions not at arm's length
693   Bringing into account adjustments under Part 4 of TIOPA 2010
694   Exchange gains and losses
695   Transfers of value to connected companies
695A   Disguised distribution arrangements involving derivative contracts
Transactions with non-UK residents
696   Derivative contracts with non-UK residents
697   Exceptions to section 696
Disposals for consideration not fully recognised by accounting practice
Derecognition
698A   Debits arising from derecognition of derivative contracts
Counteracting avoidance arrangements
698B   Counteracting effect of avoidance arrangements
698C   Interpretation of section 698B
698D   Examples of results that may indicate exclusion not applicable
Chapter 12 Priority Rules
699   Priority of this Part for corporation tax purposes
700   Relationship of this Part to Part 5: loan relationships
Chapter 13 General and Supplementary Provisions
Power to amend certain provisions

701 Power to amend some provisions
Changes to accounting standards
701A Power to make regulations where accounting standards change
Other general definitions
702 "Tax-adjusted carrying value"
703 "Chargeable asset"
704 "Creditor relationship" and "debtor relationship"
705 Expressions relating to exchange gains and losses
706 "Excluded body"
707 "Hedging relationship"
708 "Plain vanilla contract"
709 "Securities house"
710 Other definitions
Part 8: Intangible Fixed Assets
Chapter 1 Introduction
Introductory
711 Overview of Part
Basic definitions
712 "Intangible asset"
713 "Intangible fixed asset"
714 "Royalty"
Goodwill
715 Application of this Part to goodwill
Accounting rules and definitions
716 "Recognised" amounts and "GAAP-compliant accounts"
717 Companies without GAAP-compliant accounts
718 GAAP-compliant accounts: reference to consolidated group accounts
719 Accounting value
Chapter 2 Credits in Respect of Intangible Fixed Assets
720 Introduction
721 Receipts recognised as they accrue
722 Receipts in respect of royalties so far as not dealt with under section 721
723 Revaluation
724 Negative goodwill
725 Reversal of previous accounting loss
Chapter 3 Debits in Respect of Intangible Fixed Assets
726 Introduction
727 References to expenditure on an asset
728 Expenditure written off as it is incurred
729 Writing down on accounting basis
730 Writing down at fixed rate: election for fixed-rate basis
731 Writing down at fixed rate: calculation
732 Reversal of previous accounting gain
Chapter 4 Realisation of Intangible Fixed Assets
733 Overview of Chapter
734 Meaning of "realisation"
735 Asset written down for tax purposes
736 Asset shown in balance sheet and not written down for tax purposes
737 Apportionment in case of part realisation
738 Asset not shown in balance sheet
738A Realisation of assets previously subject to Northern Ireland rate
739 Meaning of "proceeds of realisation"
740 Abortive expenditure on realisation
741 Meaning of "chargeable intangible asset" and "chargeable realisation gain"
Chapter 5 Calculation of Tax Written-down Value
742 Asset written down on accounting basis
743 Asset written down at fixed rate
744 Effect of part realisation of asset
Chapter 6 How Credits and Debits are Given Effect
Introductory
745 Introduction
746 "Non-trading credits" and "non-trading debits"
Trading etc credits and debits
747 Assets held for purposes of trade
748 Assets held for purposes of property business
749 Assets held for purposes of mines, transport undertakings, etc
750 Assets held for purposes falling within more than one section
Non-trading credits and debits
751 Non-trading gains and losses

1124   Staffing costs: attributable expenditure
Software or consumable items
1125   "Software or consumable items"
1126   Software or consumable items: attributable expenditure
1126A   Attributable expenditure: special rules
1126B   Attributable expenditure: further provision
Qualifying expenditure on externally provided workers
1127   "Qualifying expenditure on externally provided workers"
1128   "Externally provided worker"
1129   Qualifying expenditure on externally provided workers: connected persons
1130   Election for connected persons treatment
1131   Qualifying expenditure on externally provided workers: other cases
1132   External workers: attributable expenditure
Sub-contractor payments
1133   "Sub-contractor" and "sub-contractor payment"
1134   Qualifying element of sub-contractor payment: connected persons
1135   Election for connected persons treatment
1136   Qualifying element of sub-contractor payment: other cases
Miscellaneous
1137   Accounting periods: company not within charge to corporation tax
1138   "Subsidised expenditure"
1140   "Relevant payments to the subjects of a clinical trial"
1141   "Payment period"
1142   "Qualifying body"
Part 14: Remediation of Contaminated Land
Chapter 1 Introduction
Introductory
1143   Overview of Part
Basic definitions
1144   "Qualifying land remediation expenditure"
1145   Land "in a contaminated state"
1145A   Land "in a derelict state"
1145B   Exclusion of nuclear sites
1146   "Relevant contaminated land remediation"
1146A   "Relevant derelict land remediation"
Chapter 2 Reliefs for Expenditure on Contaminated or derelict Land
1147   Deduction for capital expenditure
1148   Election under section 1147
1149   Additional deduction for qualifying land remediation expenditure
1150   No relief if company responsible for contamination or dereliction or polluter has interest
Chapter 3 Land Remediation Tax Credit
Entitlement and payment
1151   Entitlement to and payment of tax credit
1152   Meaning of "qualifying land remediation loss"
1153   Amount of a loss which is "unrelieved"
Amount of tax credit
1154   Amount of tax credit
Supplementary
1155   Payment of tax credit
1156   Tax credit payment not income of company
1157   Exclusion for capital gains purposes of certain expenditure
1158   Restriction on losses carried forward where tax credit claimed
Chapter 4 Special Provision for BLAGAB
I minus E basis
1160   Provision in respect of I minus E basis
Relief
1161   Relief in respect of I minus E basis: expenses payable
1162   Additional relief
1163   No relief if company responsible for contamination or dereliction or polluter has interest
Life assurance company tax credits
1164   Entitlement to tax credit
1165   Meaning of "qualifying BLAGAB loss"
1166   Amount of tax credit
1167   Payment of tax credit etc
1168   Restriction on carrying forward expenses payable where tax credit claimed
Chapter 5 Tax Avoidance
1169   Artificially inflated claims for relief or tax credit

Chapter 6 Supplementary
1170   "Staffing costs"
1171   Staffing costs attributable to relevant land remediation
1172   Expenditure on materials
1173   Expenditure incurred because of contamination or dereliction
1175   Connected sub-contractors
1177   "Subsidised expenditure"
1178   Persons having a "relevant connection" to a company
1178A   "Major interest in land"
1179   Other definitions
Part 15: Film Production
Chapter 1 Introduction
Introductory
1180   Overview of Part
Interpretation
1181   "Film" etc
1182   "Film production company"
1183   "Film-making activities" etc
1184   "Production expenditure", "core expenditure"
1185   "UK expenditure" etc
1186   "Qualifying co-production" and "co-producer"
1187   "Company tax return"
Chapter 2 Taxation of Activities of Film Production Company
Separate film trade
1188   Activities of film production company treated as a separate trade
1189   Calculation of profits or losses of separate film trade
Supplementary
1190   Income from the film
1191   Costs of the film
1192   When costs are taken to be incurred
1193   Pre-trading expenditure
1194   Estimates
Chapter 3 Film Tax Relief
Introductory
1195   Availability and overview of film tax relief
Conditions of relief
1196   Intended theatrical release
1197   British film
1198   UK expenditure
Additional deductions
1199   Additional deduction for qualifying expenditure
1200   Amount of additional deduction
Film tax credits
1201   Film tax credit claimable if company has surrenderable loss
1202   Surrendering of loss and amount of film tax credit
1203   Payment in respect of film tax credit
Miscellaneous
1204   No account to be taken of amount if unpaid
1205   Artificially inflated claims for additional deduction or film tax credit
1206   Confidentiality of information
1207   Wrongful disclosure
Chapter 4 Film Losses
1208   Application of sections 1209 and 1210
1209   Restriction on use of losses while film in production
1210   Use of losses in later periods
1211   Terminal losses
Chapter 5 Provisional Entitlement to Relief
1212   Introduction
1213   Certification as a British film
1214   The UK expenditure condition
1216   Time limit for amendments and assessments
Part 15A: Television production
Chapter 1 Introduction
Introductory
1216A   Overview of Part
Meaning of "television programme", "relevant programme" etc
1216AA   "Television programme"
1216AB   "Relevant programme"
1216AC   Types of programme eligible to be relevant programmes

1216AD   Excluded programmes
1216ADA   Certain children's programmes not to be excluded programmes
Other interpretation
1216AE   Television production company
1216AF   "Television production activities" etc
1216AG   "Production expenditure" and "core expenditure"
1216AH   "UK expenditure" etc
1216AI   "Qualifying co-production" and "co-producer"
1216AJ   "Company tax return"
Chapter 2 Taxation of activities of television production company
Separate programme trade
1216B   Activities of television production company treated as a separate trade
1216BA   Calculation of profits or losses of separate programme trade
Supplementary
1216BB   Income from the relevant programme
1216BC   Costs of the relevant programme
1216BD   When costs are taken to be incurred
1216BE   Pre-trading expenditure
1216BF   Estimates
Chapter 3 Television tax relief
Introductory
1216C   Availability and overview of television tax relief
"Intended for broadcast"
1216CA   Intended for broadcast
British programmes
1216CB   British programme
1216CC   Applications for certification
1216CD   Certification and withdrawal of certification
UK expenditure
1216CE   UK expenditure
Additional deductions
1216CF   Additional deduction for qualifying expenditure
1216CG   Amount of additional deduction
Television tax credits
1216CH   Television tax credit claimable if company has surrenderable loss
1216CI   Surrendering of loss and amount of television tax credit
1216CJ   Payment in respect of television tax credit
Miscellaneous
1216CK   No account to be taken of amount if unpaid
1216CL   Artificially inflated claims for additional deduction or tax credit
1216CM   Confidentiality of information
1216CN   Wrongful disclosure
Chapter 4 Programme losses
1216D   Application of sections 1216DA and 1216DB
1216DA   Restriction on use of losses while programme in production
1216DB   Use of losses in later periods
1216DC   Terminal losses
Chapter 5 Provisional entitlement to relief
1216E   Introduction
1216EA   Certification as a British programme
1216EB   The UK expenditure condition
1216EC   Time limit for amendments and assessments
Part 15B: Video games development
Chapter 1 Introduction
Introductory
1217A   Overview of Part
Interpretation
1217AA   "Video game" etc
1217AB   Video games development company
1217AC   "Video game development activities" etc
1217AD   "Core expenditure"
1217AE   "EEA expenditure" etc
1217AF   "Company tax return"
Chapter 2 Taxation of activities of video games development company
Separate video game trade
1217B   Activities of video games development company treated as a separate trade
1217BA   Calculation of profits or losses of separate video game trade
Supplementary
1217BB   Income from the video game

1217BC   Costs of the video game
1217BD   When costs are taken to be incurred
1217BE   Estimates
Chapter 3 Video games tax relief
Introductory
1217C   Availability and overview of video games tax relief
"Intended for supply"
1217CA   Intended for supply
British video games
1217CB   British video game
1217CC   Applications for certification
1217CD   Certification and withdrawal of certification
EEA expenditure
1217CE   EEA expenditure
Additional deductions
1217CF   Additional deduction for qualifying expenditure
1217CG   Amount of additional deduction
Video game tax credits
1217CH   Video game tax credit claimable if company has surrenderable loss
1217CI   Surrendering of loss and amount of video game tax credit
1217CJ   Payment in respect of video game tax credit
Miscellaneous
1217CK   No account to be taken of amount if unpaid
1217CL   Artificially inflated claims for additional deduction or tax credit
1217CM   Confidentiality of information
1217CN   Wrongful disclosure
Chapter 4 Video game losses
1217D   Application of sections 1217DA and 1217DB
1217DA   Restriction on use of losses while video game in development
1217DB   Use of losses in later periods
1217DC   Terminal losses
Chapter 5 Provisional entitlement to relief
1217E   Introduction
1217EA   Certification as a British video game
1217EB   The EEA expenditure condition
1217EC   Time limit for amendments and assessments
Part 15C: Theatrical Productions
Introduction
1217F   Overview
1217FA   "Theatrical production"
1217FB   Productions not regarded as theatrical
1217FC   "Production company"
Companies qualifying for relief
1217G   How a company qualifies for relief
1217GA   The commercial purpose condition
1217GB   The EEA expenditure condition
1217GC   "Core expenditure"
Claim for additional deduction
1217H   Claim for additional deduction
The separate theatrical trade
1217I   Introduction to sections 1217IA to 1217IF
1217IA   Calculation of profits or losses of separate theatrical trade
1217IB   Income from the production
1217IC   Costs of the production
1217ID   When costs are taken to be incurred
1217IE   Pre-trading expenditure
1217IF   Estimates
Amount of additional deduction
1217J   Amount of additional deduction
1217JA   "Qualifying expenditure"
Theatre tax credits
1217K   Theatre tax credit claimable if company has surrenderable loss
1217KA   Amount of surrenderable loss
1217KB   Payment in respect of theatre tax credit
1217KC   Limit on State aid
Anti-avoidance etc
1217LA   Tax avoidance arrangements
1217LB   Transactions not entered into for genuine commercial reasons
Use of losses

1329   Commencement
1330   Short title
SCHEDULES
Schedule 1—Minor and Consequential Amendments
Schedule 2—Transitionals and Savings
Schedule 3—Repeals and Revocations
Schedule 4—Index of Defined Expressions

PART 1
INTRODUCTION

[A1 Overview of the Corporation Tax Acts

(1) The main Acts relating to corporation tax are—

    (*a*)   this Act (which covers the ground described in section 1),

    (*b*)   CTA 2010 (which covers the ground described in section 1 of that Act), and

    (*c*)   TCGA 1992 (so far as relating to chargeable gains accruing to a company in respect of which the company is chargeable to corporation tax).

(2) Enactments relating to corporation tax are also contained in other Acts: see in particular—

    (*a*)   . . .[3]

    (*b*)   . . .[2]

    (*c*)   Schedule 18 to FA 1998 (company tax returns, assessments and related matters),

    (*d*)   Schedule 22 to FA 2000 (tonnage tax),

    (*e*)   CAA 2001 (allowances for capital expenditure),

    (*f*)   Part 2 of TIOPA 2010 (double taxation relief),

    (*g*)   Parts 4 and 5 of that Act (transfer pricing and advance pricing agreements),

    (*h*)   . . .[5]

    [(*ha*)   Part 6A of that Act (hybrid and other mismatches),][5]

    (*i*)   . . .[6]

    (*j*)   Part 8 of that Act (offshore funds),

    [(*ja*)   Part 9A of that Act (controlled foreign companies).][2]

    [(*jb*)   Part 10 of that Act (corporate interest restriction),][6]

    [(*k*)   Part 2 of FA 2012 (insurance companies carrying on long-term business)][3][, and

    (*l*)   Part 3 of that Act (friendly societies carrying on long-term business).][4]

(3) Schedule 1 to the Interpretation Act 1978 defines "the Corporation Tax Acts" as the enactments relating to the taxation of the income and chargeable gains of companies and of company distributions (including provisions relating to income tax).][1]

Amendments—[1]   This section inserted by TIOPA 2010 s 501, Sch 8 paras 308, 309. TIOPA 2010 has effect for corporation tax purposes for accounting periods ending on or after 1 April 2010, for income and capital gains tax purposes for the tax year 2010–11 and subsequent tax years, and for petroleum revenue tax purposes for chargeable periods beginning on or after 1 July 2010.

[2]   In sub-s (2), para (*b*) repealed and para (*ja*) inserted, by FA 2012 s 180, Sch 20 paras 24, 25 with effect in relation to accounting periods of CFCs beginning on or after 1 January 2013. This is subject to savings in FA 2012 Sch 20 para 50(9) which provides, broadly, that the amendments in question will not take effect until an accounting period under the new CFC rules in TIOPA 2010 Part 9A begins.

[3]   In sub-s (2), para (*a*) repealed, and para (*k*) inserted, by FA 2012 s 146, Sch 16 paras 135, 136 with effect in relation to accounting periods of companies beginning on or after 1 January 2013 (subject to transitional provisions in FA 2012 Sch 17). For accounting periods straddling 1 January 2013, see FA 2012 s 149.

[4]   Sub-s (2)(*l*) and preceding word inserted by FA 2012 s 176, Sch 18 paras 19, 20 with effect in relation to accounting periods of companies beginning on or after 1 January 2013, subject to transitional provisions in FA 2012 s 179.

[5]   Sub-s (2)(*h*) repealed by FA 2016 s 66, Sch 10 para 5(*a*) with effect in relation to accounting periods beginning on or after 1 January 2017. For accounting periods straddling that date see FA 2016 Sch 10 para 24. Sub-s (2)(*ha*) inserted by FA 2016 s 66, Sch 10 para 5(*b*) with effect from 15 September 2016.

[6]   In sub-s (2), para (*i*) repealed, and para (*jb*) inserted by F(No 2)A 2017 s 20, Sch 5 para 5 with effect in relation to periods of account of worldwide groups that begin on or after 1 April 2017, subject to commencement and transitional provisions in Sch 5 paras 27–35. In relation to periods of account that straddle 1 April 2017, see Sch 5 para 25(4)–(11).

1 Overview of Act

(1) Part 2 of this Act contains basic provisions about the charge to corporation tax including—

    (*a*)   the imposition of the charge to corporation tax on the income and chargeable gains of companies (referred to collectively as "profits"), (see section 2),

    (*b*)   the exclusion of income and chargeable gains subject to corporation tax from income tax and capital gains tax (see sections 3 and 4),

    (*c*)   provision about the territorial scope of the charge to corporation tax (see section 5 and [Chapters 3A and 4][2]),

    (*d*)   provision about how corporation tax is charged and assessed, in particular its charging and assessment by reference to accounting periods (see section 8),

    (*e*)   provision about accounting periods (see Chapter 2), and

    (*f*)   rules for determining the residence of companies (see Chapter 3).

CTA 2009

(2) Under section 2(4) the charge to corporation tax on income has effect in accordance with the provisions of the Corporation Tax Acts that deal with its application, the main provisions of this Act that do so being—

    (a) Part 3 (trading income),

    (b) Part 4 (property income),

    (c) Parts 5 and 6 (profits arising from loan relationships),

    (d) Part 7 (profits arising from derivative contracts),

    (e) Part 8 (gains in respect of intangible fixed assets),

    (f) Part 9 (profits arising from disposals of know-how and sales of patent rights),

    [(fa) Part 9A (company distributions),][1] and

    (g) Part 10 (miscellaneous income).

(3) Part 7 also applies the charge to corporation tax on chargeable gains to certain profits arising from derivative contracts.

(4) Parts 5 to 8 also deal with how deficits or losses arising from, or in respect of, the matters to which they relate are brought into account for corporation tax purposes.

(5) The following Parts provide relief for particular types of expenditure—

    (a) Part 11 (relief for particular employee share acquisition schemes),

    (b) Part 12 (other relief for employee share acquisitions),

    (c) Part 13 (additional relief for expenditure on research and development),

    (d) Part 14 (remediation of contaminated land), and

    (e) Part 15 (film production).

(6) The following Parts contain special rules for particular cases—

    (a) Part 15 (film production),

    (b) Part 16 (companies with investment business),

    (c) Part 17 (partnerships), and

    (d) Part 18 (unremittable income).

(7) The following Parts contain provisions of general application—

    (a) Part 19 (general exemptions),

    (b) Part 20 (general calculation rules), and

    (c) Part 21 (other general provisions, including definitions for the purposes of the Act).

(8) For abbreviations and defined expressions used in this Act, see section 1312 and Schedule 4.

Commentary—*Simon's Taxes* **A1.131**.

Amendments—[1]   Sub-s (2)(*fa*) inserted by FA 2009 s 34, Sch 14 paras 20, 21 with effect in relation to distributions paid on or after 1 July 2009.

[2]   In sub-s (1)(*c*) words substituted for words "Chapter 4" by FA 2011 s 48, Sch 13 paras 1, 2 with effect from 19 July 2011, subject to transitional provisions in FA 2011 Sch 13 paras 32–37.

PART 2

CHARGE TO CORPORATION TAX: BASIC PROVISIONS

CHAPTER 1

THE CHARGE TO CORPORATION TAX

Charge to tax on profits

2 Charge to corporation tax

(1) Corporation tax is charged on profits of companies for any financial year for which an Act so provides.

(2) In this Part "profits" means income and chargeable gains, except in so far as the context otherwise requires.

(2A) . . . [1]

(3) In this Act "the charge to corporation tax on income" means the charge under subsection (1) so far as relating to income.

(4) The charge to corporation tax on income has effect in accordance with the provisions of the Corporation Tax Acts that deal with its application.

Commentary—*Simon's Taxes* **D1.102, D1.106, D1.302, A1.104, C3.101, D1.108**.

HMRC Manuals—Company Taxation Manual CTM01110 (company profits: definition).

CTM01130 (computation of profits).

CTM01105 (basis of charge to CT).

Amendments—[1]   Sub-s (2A) repealed by FA 2019 s 13, Sch 1 paras 108, 109 with effect for capital gains tax purposes for the tax year 2019–20 and subsequent tax years, and for corporation tax purposes for accounting periods beginning on or after 6 April 2019. These amendments also have effect for corporation tax purposes in relation to disposals made on or after 6 April 2019 (whether in their application to accounting periods beginning on, and ending on or after, that date or to later accounting periods). See also transitional provisions in FA 2019 Sch 1 paras 121–126.

3 Exclusion of charge to income tax

(1) The provisions of the Income Tax Acts relating to the charge to income tax do not apply to income of a company if—

    (a) the company is UK resident, or

[(*b*) the company is not UK resident [and it is chargeable to corporation tax in respect of the income, or would be so chargeable but for an exemption]²]¹

(2) Subsection (1) does not apply to income accruing to a company in a fiduciary or representative capacity.

Commentary—*Simon's Taxes* **B1.601, B6.215, B7.516, D1.102, D4.122**.
HMRC Manuals—Company Taxation Manual CTM15150 (income tax exclusions).
CTM01170 (IT deducted from income received).
Amendments—¹   Sub-s (1)(*b*) substituted by FA 2016 s 76(6) with effect in relation to disposals on or after 5 July 2016 (FA 2016 s 81(1)), subject to transitional provisions relating to disposals to associated persons on or after 16 March 2016 and before 5 July 2016 (FA 2016 s 81(4)–(15)).
    F(No 2)A 2017 s 39 provides that this amendment has effect (so far as it would not otherwise have effect) in relation to amounts that are recognised in GAAP accounts drawn up for any period of account beginning on or after 8 March 2017 or, in the case of a straddling period, amounts that would be recognised in GAAP accounts drawn up for a period of account beginning on 8 March 2017 and ending when the straddling period ends. "Straddling period" means a period of account beginning before 8 March 2017 and ending on or after that date.
²   In sub-s (1)(*b*), words substituted for words by FA 2019 s 17, Sch 5 paras 10, 11 with effect from 6 April 2020, subject to transitional provisions in FA 2019 Sch 5 Pt 3 (paras 36–50).

4 Exclusion of charge to capital gains tax

Capital gains tax is not charged on gains accruing to a company in respect of which the company is chargeable to corporation tax, or would be so chargeable but for an exemption.

Commentary—*Simon's Taxes* **C3.101, D6.436, D1.102, C1.208**.
Derivation—TA 1988 s 6(3).

General scheme of corporation tax

5 Territorial scope of charge

(1) A UK resident company is [chargeable to corporation tax on income]³ on all its profits wherever arising [(but see Chapter 3A for an exemption from charge in respect of profits of foreign permanent establishments)]¹.

[(2) A non-UK resident company is [within the charge to corporation tax on income]³ only if—
    (*a*) it carries on a trade of dealing in or developing UK land (see section 5B), . . . ⁴
    (*b*) it carries on a trade in the United Kingdom (other than a trade of dealing in or developing UK land) through a permanent establishment in the United Kingdom]²[,
    (*c*) it carries on a UK property business, or
    (*d*) it has other UK property income.]⁴

[(2A) A non-UK resident company which carries on a trade of dealing in or developing UK land is [chargeable to corporation tax on income]³ on all its profits wherever arising that are profits of that trade.]²

(3) A non-UK resident company which carries on a trade in the United Kingdom through a permanent establishment in the United Kingdom is [chargeable to corporation tax on income]³ on all its profits wherever arising that are chargeable profits as defined in section 19 (profits attributable to its permanent establishment in the United Kingdom).

[(3A) A non-UK resident company which carries on a UK property business is chargeable to corporation tax on income on all its profits that are—
    (*a*) profits of that business, or
    (*b*) profits arising from loan relationships or derivative contracts that the company is a party to for the purposes of that business.

(3B) A non-UK resident company which has other UK property income is chargeable to corporation tax on income on all its profits that—
    (*a*) consist of that income, or
    (*b*) are profits arising from loan relationships or derivative contracts that the company is a party to for the purposes of enabling it to generate that income.]⁴

(4) Subsections (1) [and (2A) to (3B)]⁴ and (3) are subject to any exceptions provided for by the Corporation Tax Acts.

[(5) The territorial scope of the charge to corporation tax on chargeable gains is given by section 2B of TCGA 1992.]³

[(5) In this Part "other UK property income" means income dealt with by any of the following Chapters of Part 4—
    (*a*) Chapter 7 (rent receivable in connection with a UK section 39(4) concern);
    (*b*) Chapter 8 (rent receivable for UK electric-line wayleaves);
    (*c*) Chapter 9 (post-cessation receipts arising from a UK property business).]⁴

Commentary—*Simon's Taxes* **D4.101, D1.102, D1.104, D1.303, D4.101, D6.714**.
HMRC Manuals—Company Taxation Manual CTM34210 (liability to CT: scope).
Amendments—¹   In sub-s (1) words inserted by FA 2011 s 48, Sch 13 paras 1, 3 with effect from 19 July 2011, subject to transitional provisions in FA 2011 Sch 13 paras 32–37.
²   Sub-s (2) substituted, and sub-s (2A) inserted, by FA 2016 s 76(1)–(4) with effect in relation to disposals on or after 5 July 2016 (FA 2016 s 81(1)), subject to transitional provisions relating to disposals to associated persons on or after 16 March 2016 and before 5 July 2016 (FA 2016 s 81(4)–(15)).

F(No 2)A 2017 s 39 provides that these amendments have effect (so far as they would not otherwise have effect) in relation to amounts that are recognised in GAAP accounts drawn up for any period of account beginning on or after 8 March 2017 or, in the case of a straddling period, amounts that would be recognised in GAAP accounts drawn up for a period of account beginning on 8 March 2017 and ending when the straddling period ends. "Straddling period" means a period of account beginning before 8 March 2017 and ending on or after that date.

[3]   In sub-ss (1), (2A), (3), words substituted for words "chargeable to corporation tax", in sub-s (2), words substituted for words "within the charge to corporation tax", and sub-s (5) inserted, by FA 2019 s 13, Sch 1 paras 108, 110 with effect for capital gains tax purposes for the tax year 2019–20 and subsequent tax years, and for corporation tax purposes for accounting periods beginning on or after 6 April 2019. These amendments also have effect for corporation tax purposes in relation to disposals made on or after 6 April 2019 (whether in their application to accounting periods beginning on, and ending on or after, that date or to later accounting periods). See also transitional provisions in FA 2019 Sch 1 paras 121–126.

[4]   Amendments to be made by FA 2019 s 17, Sch 5 paras 1–5 with effect from 6 April 2020, subject to transitional provisions in FA 2019 Sch 5 Pt 3 (paras 36–50)

[5A Arrangements for avoiding tax

(1) Subsection (3) applies if a company has entered into an arrangement the main purpose or one of the main purposes of which is to obtain a relevant tax advantage for the company.

(2) In subsection (1) the reference to obtaining a relevant tax advantage includes obtaining a relevant tax advantage by virtue of any provisions of double taxation arrangements, but only in a case where the relevant tax advantage is contrary to the object and purpose of the provisions of the double taxation arrangements (and subsection (3) has effect accordingly, regardless of section 6(1) of TIOPA 2010).

(3) The relevant tax advantage is to be counteracted by means of adjustments.

(4) For this purpose adjustments may be made (whether by an officer of Revenue and Customs or by the company) by way of an assessment, the modification of an assessment, amendment or disallowance of a claim, or otherwise.

(5) In this section "relevant tax advantage" means a tax advantage in relation to corporation tax to which the company is chargeable (or would without the tax advantage be chargeable) by virtue of section 5(2A).

(6) In this section—

> "arrangement" (except in the phrase "double taxation arrangements") includes any agreement, understanding, scheme, transaction or series of transactions, whether or not legally enforceable;
> "double taxation arrangements" means arrangements which have effect under section 2(1) of TIOPA 2010 (double taxation relief by agreement with territories outside the United Kingdom);
> "tax advantage" has the meaning given by section 1139 of CTA 2010.][1]

Amendments—[1]   Sections 5A, 5B inserted by FA 2016 s 76(5) with effect in relation to disposals on or after 5 July 2016 (FA 2016 s 81(1)), subject to transitional provisions relating to disposals to associated persons on or after 16 March 2016 and before 5 July 2016 (FA 2016 s 81(4)–(15)).

F(No 2)A 2017 s 39 provides that this amendment has effect (so far as it would not otherwise have effect) in relation to amounts that are recognised in GAAP accounts drawn up for any period of account beginning on or after 8 March 2017 or, in the case of a straddling period, amounts that would be recognised in GAAP accounts drawn up for a period of account beginning on 8 March 2017 and ending when the straddling period ends. "Straddling period" means a period of account beginning before 8 March 2017 and ending on or after that date.

[5B Trade of dealing in or developing UK land

(1) A non-UK resident company's "trade of dealing in or developing UK land" consists of—

> (a) any activities falling within subsection (2) which it carries on, and
> (b) any activities from which profits, gains or losses arise which are treated under Part 8ZB of CTA 2010 as profits or losses of the company's trade of dealing in or developing UK land.

(2) The activities within this subsection are—

> (a) dealing in UK land;
> (b) developing UK land for the purpose of disposing of it.

(3) In this section "land" includes—

> (a) buildings and structures,
> (b) any estate, interest or right in or over land, and
> (c) land under the sea or otherwise covered by water.

(4) In this section—

> "disposal" is to be interpreted in accordance with section 356OQ of CTA 2010;
> "UK land" means land in the United Kingdom.][1]

Amendments—[1]   Sections 5A, 5B inserted by FA 2016 s 76(5) with effect in relation to disposals on or after 5 July 2016 (FA 2016 s 81(1)), subject to transitional provisions relating to disposals to associated persons on or after 16 March 2016 and before 5 July 2016 (FA 2016 s 81(4)–(15)).

F(No 2)A 2017 s 39 provides that this amendment has effect (so far as it would not otherwise have effect) in relation to amounts that are recognised in GAAP accounts drawn up for any period of account beginning on or after 8 March 2017 or, in the case of a straddling period, amounts that would be recognised in GAAP accounts drawn up for a period of account beginning on 8 March 2017 and ending when the straddling period ends. "Straddling period" means a period of account beginning before 8 March 2017 and ending on or after that date.

[18HD Modification of Chapter 7 of Part 9A of TIOPA 2010

Chapter 7 of Part 9A of TIOPA 2010 (the CFC charge gateway: captive insurance business) applies for the purposes of section 18H(2) with the omission of section 371GA(6)(b).][1]

HMRC Manuals—International Manual INTM286420 (foreign permanent establishments of UK companies: anti-diversion rule: chapter 7).
Amendments—[1]　Sections 18G–18ID substituted for previous ss 18G–18I by FA 2012 s 180, Sch 20 paras 2, 6 with effect for relevant accounting periods beginning on or after 1 January 2013 (FA 2012 Sch 20 para 55(2)).

[18HE Modification of Chapter 9 of Part 9A of TIOPA 2010

(1) Chapter 9 of Part 9A of TIOPA 2010 (exemptions for profits from qualifying loan relationships) applies for the purposes of section 18H(2) with the following modifications.

(2) In section 371IA(2) and (11) the reference to a chargeable company is to be read as a reference to company X (as is the reference in section 371CB(8)); and references elsewhere in Chapter 9 to company C are to be read as references to company X.

(3) For section 371IA(5) there is to be substituted—

　　"(5)　75% of the profits of each qualifying loan relationship are "exempt" under this Chapter."

(4) In section 371IA(9)(a) the words "or Chapter 8 (solo consolidation)" are to be omitted.

(5) Sections 371IB to 371IE are to be omitted.

(6) Section 371IH(11)(a) is to be read ignoring the modification in section 18HC(b) above.

(7) In section 371IJ references to the relevant corporation tax accounting period are to be read as references to period X and subsection (6) is to be omitted.][1]

HMRC Manuals—International Manual INTM286400 (foreign permanent establishments of UK companies: anti-diversion rule: chapter 5 and 9).
Amendments—[1]　Sections 18G–18ID substituted for previous ss 18G–18I by FA 2012 s 180, Sch 20 paras 2, 6 with effect for relevant accounting periods beginning on or after 1 January 2013 (FA 2012 Sch 20 para 55(2)).

[18I Exemptions from anti-diversion rule

(1) The exemptions referred to in section 18G(1)(c) are the exemptions set out in Chapters 11 to 14 of Part 9A of TIOPA 2010 (controlled foreign companies: exemptions from the CFC charge).

(2) In applying those Chapters for the purposes of section 18G(1)(c)—

　　(a) references to section 371BA(2)(b) of TIOPA 2010 are to be read as references to section 18G(1)(c),

　　(b) the assumptions set out in subsection (3) are to be made, and

　　(c) section 371VF(3) of TIOPA 2010 (definition of "related" person) is to be read with the omission of paragraphs (b) and (c).

(3) For the purposes of subsection (2)(b), assume—

　　(a) that the permanent establishment which company X has in territory X is a separate company from company X,

　　(b) that the separate company is a CFC resident in territory X,

　　(c) that period X and company X's other accounting periods for corporation tax purposes are accounting periods of the CFC for the purposes of Part 9A of TIOPA 2010,

　　(d) that the CFC's assumed total profits for period X are the adjusted relevant profits amount,

　　(e) that the CFC's assumed taxable total profits for period X are the same as the CFC's assumed total profits for period X,

　　(f) that the CFC is connected with company X and is also connected or associated with any person with whom company X is connected or associated, and

　　(g) that any person who has an interest in company X also has an interest in the CFC.

(4) Chapters 11 to 14 of Part 9A of TIOPA 2010 are also to be applied subject to sections 18IA to 18ID below.][1]

Commentary—*Simon's Taxes* **D4.801A**.
HMRC Manuals—International Manual INTM286060 (foreign permanent establishments of uk companies: antidiversion rule: proportionate reduction where motive test not met).
INTM286110 (foreign permanent establishments of UK companies: antidiversion rule: proportionate reduction where tainted relevant transactions arise).
INTM286310 (foreign permanent establishments of UK companies: antidiversion rule: when does it apply?).
INTM286470 (foreign permanent establishments of UK companies: anti-diversion rule: application of the entity exemption approach).
Amendments—[1]　Sections 18G–18ID substituted for previous ss 18G–18I by FA 2012 s 180, Sch 20 paras 2, 6 with effect for relevant accounting periods beginning on or after 1 January 2013 (FA 2012 Sch 20 para 55(2)).

[18IA The excluded territories exemption

(1) Chapter 11 of Part 9A of TIOPA 2010 (controlled foreign companies: the excluded territories exemption) applies for the purposes of section 18G(1)(c) with the following modifications.

(2) Sections 371KB(1)(b)(iii) and 371KH are to be omitted.

(3) Section 371KC is to be omitted and the assumption set out in section 18I(3)(b) above in relation to the CFC's residence is to be applied instead; and references to "the CFC's territory" are to be read accordingly.

(4) Section 371KD(3) is to be omitted and references to a CFC's accounting profits for an accounting period are to be read as references to the adjusted relevant profits amount.

(5) Section 371KE(2)(b) is to be omitted.

(6) Section 371KF is to be omitted.

(7) In section 371KG(3) the reference to the CFC's equity or debt is to be read as a reference to company X's equity or debt (ignoring the assumption in section 18I(3)(a) above).

(8) Section 371KI(2) and (3) is to be omitted.

(9) In section 371KJ—

    (a) in subsection (2)(a), the reference to intellectual property held by the CFC is to be read as a reference to intellectual property held by company X (ignoring the assumption in section 18I(3)(a) above), and

    (b) in subsections (2)(b) and (c) and (4), references to the CFC are to be read as references to company X (ignoring that assumption).][1]

HMRC Manuals—International Manual INTM286480 (foreign permanent establishments of UK companies: anti-diversion rule: chapter 11 excluded territories exemption).

Amendments—[1] Sections 18G–18ID substituted for previous ss 18G–18I by FA 2012 s 180, Sch 20 paras 2, 6 with effect for relevant accounting periods beginning on or after 1 January 2013 (FA 2012 Sch 20 para 55(2)).

[18IB The low profits exemption

Chapter 12 of Part 9A of TIOPA 2010 (controlled foreign companies: the low profits exemption) applies for the purposes of section 18G(1)(c) with the omission of section 371LB(2) and (4) and section 371LC(5) and (6).][1]

HMRC Manuals—International Manual INTM286490 (foreign permanent establishments of UK companies: anti-diversion rule: chapter 12 low profits exemption).

Amendments—[1] Sections 18G–18ID substituted for previous ss 18G–18I by FA 2012 s 180, Sch 20 paras 2, 6 with effect for relevant accounting periods beginning on or after 1 January 2013 (FA 2012 Sch 20 para 55(2)).

[18IC The low profit margin exemption

(1) Chapter 13 of Part 9A of TIOPA 2010 (controlled foreign companies: the low profit margin exemption) applies for the purposes of section 18G(1)(c) with the following modifications.

(2) In section 371MB—

    (a) subsection (2) is to be omitted, and

    (b) references to the CFC's accounting profits for an accounting period are to be read as references to the adjusted relevant profits amount determined before any deduction for interest.][1]

HMRC Manuals—International Manual INTM286500 (foreign permanent establishments of UK companies: anti-diversion rule: chapter 13 low profit margin exemption).

Amendments—[1] Sections 18G–18ID substituted for previous ss 18G–18I by FA 2012 s 180, Sch 20 paras 2, 6 with effect for relevant accounting periods beginning on or after 1 January 2013 (FA 2012 Sch 20 para 55(2)).

[18ID The tax exemption

(1) Chapter 14 of Part 9A of TIOPA 2010 (controlled foreign companies: the tax exemption) applies for the purposes of section 18G(1)(c) with the following modifications.

(2) At step 1 in section 371NB(1)—

    (a) in the first paragraph, the reference to section 371TB of TIOPA 2010 is to be read as a reference to the assumption in section 18I(3)(b) above relating to the CFC's residence, and

    (b) the second paragraph is to be omitted.

(3) References to the CFC's local chargeable profits arising in the accounting period are to be read as references to the adjusted relevant profits amount and, accordingly, sections 371NB(4) and 371NC(2) to (4) are to be omitted.

(4) For the purposes of step 3 in section 371NB(1) the amount of the corresponding UK tax for the accounting period is to be determined in accordance with subsection (5) below; and section 371NE is to be omitted accordingly.

(5) "The corresponding UK tax" is the amount of corporation tax which would be payable in respect of the adjusted relevant profits amount if it were subject in full to corporation tax, ignoring any credit which would be allowed against it under section 18(3) of TIOPA 2010 and assuming, where there is more than one rate of corporation tax applicable to period X, that it were chargeable at the average rate over period X.][1]

HMRC Manuals—International Manual INTM286510 (foreign permanent establishments of UK companies: anti-diversion rule: chapter 14 tax exemption).

Amendments—[1] Sections 18G–18ID substituted for previous ss 18G–18I by FA 2012 s 180, Sch 20 paras 2, 6 with effect for relevant accounting periods beginning on or after 1 January 2013 (FA 2012 Sch 20 para 55(2)).

[Companies with total opening negative amount

18J Companies with total opening negative amount

(1) The following sections make provision about a company in relation to which an election under section 18A has effect if there is a total opening negative amount in the case of the company at the beginning of the company's first relevant accounting period.

(2) To determine for the purposes of this Chapter whether there is a total opening negative amount at the beginning of the company's first relevant accounting period, take the following steps.

Step 1

Take the adjusted foreign permanent establishments amount in relation to the earliest affected prior accounting period in relation to which that amount is negative.

Step 2

Add to the amount arrived at under step 1 the adjusted foreign permanent establishments amount in relation to the next affected prior accounting period (but not so as to cause the result to exceed nil).

Step 3

Add to the amount arrived at under step 2 the adjusted foreign permanent establishments amount in relation to each remaining affected prior accounting period, starting with the earliest (but not so as to cause the result to exceed nil).

If after the application of the preceding steps there is a negative amount for the last affected prior accounting period there is a total opening negative amount at the beginning of the company's first relevant accounting period of an amount equal to that negative amount.

(3) In subsection (2) "affected prior accounting period" means—

     (a) the accounting period of the company in which the election under section 18A is made, and

     (b) any earlier accounting period of the company ending less than 6 years before the end of that accounting period.

(4) For the purposes of subsection (2) the "adjusted" foreign permanent establishments amount is what the foreign permanent establishments amount would be if it were determined without reference to gains or losses which are chargeable gains or allowable losses for the purposes of corporation tax.][1]

Commentary—*Simon's Taxes* **D4.802A**.

HMRC Manuals—International Manual INTM284010 (foreign permanent establishments of UK companies: transition to exemption provisions: introduction).

INTM284020 (foreign permanent establishments of UK companies: transition to exemption provisions: opening negative amount).

Amendments—[1] Chapter 3A (ss 18A–18S) inserted by FA 2011 s 48, Sch 13 paras 1, 4 with effect from 19 July 2011, subject to transitional provisions in FA 2011 Sch 13 paras 32–37.

[18K Total opening negative amount: "matching"

(1) At the end of each relevant accounting period of the company (starting with the first) the total opening negative amount is to be reduced (or further reduced) by the amount of any aggregate relevant profits amount of the company for the accounting period (but not to below nil).

(2) In any relevant accounting period of the company for which there is a reduction under subsection (1), section 18A(1) does not apply in relation to the aggregate relevant profits amount of the company for the accounting period.

(3) But in the case of the last relevant accounting period of the company for which there is a reduction under subsection (1), section 18A(1) is disapplied by subsection (2) only in relation to so much of the aggregate relevant profits amount of the company for the accounting period as is equal to the total opening negative amount of the company at the beginning of the accounting period.

(4) The company may, in its company tax return for that relevant accounting period, specify to which part of the aggregate relevant profits amount of the company for the accounting period section 18A(1) is to apply by virtue of subsection (3).

(5) In this Chapter "aggregate relevant profits amount", in relation to an accounting period, means the aggregate of the relevant profits amount in the case of each relevant foreign territory in relation to which there is a relevant profits amount for the accounting period.

(6) This section is subject to section 18L.][1]

Commentary—*Simon's Taxes* **D4.802A**.

HMRC Manuals—International Manual INTM284030 (foreign permanent establishments of UK companies: transition to exemption provisions: matching of opening negative amount).

Amendments—[1] Chapter 3A (ss 18A–18S) inserted by FA 2011 s 48, Sch 13 paras 1, 4 with effect from 19 July 2011, subject to transitional provisions in FA 2011 Sch 13 paras 32–37.

[18L Streaming

(1) If a streaming election has effect in relation to the company sections 18M and 18N apply (instead of section 18K).

(2) For the purposes of this section "streaming election" means an election, made at the same time as the company's election under section 18A, which—

     (a) states that sections 18M and 18N are to have effect in relation to the company (instead of section 18K), and

     (b) specifies which of the territories that are relevant foreign territories in relation to the company are to be streamed territories for the purposes of the operation of sections 18M and 18N in relation to the company.

(3) Subject to subsection (4), a streaming election is irrevocable.

(4) A streaming election can be revoked at any time before the first relevant accounting period of the company.

(5) A streaming election does not have effect unless the company, in the company tax return for the first relevant accounting period of the company, specifies how much of the amount eligible to be streamed to each streamed territory is to constitute for the purposes of sections 18M and 18N the streamed opening negative amount at the beginning of that relevant accounting period.

(6) For the purposes of subsection (5) the amount eligible to be streamed to a territory by the company is the amount that would be the total opening negative amount of the company at the beginning of the first relevant accounting period of the company if at all material times the territory were the only relevant foreign territory in relation to the company.][1]

Commentary—*Simon's Taxes* **D4.802A**.

HMRC Manuals—International Manual INTM284040 (foreign permanent establishments of UK companies: streaming of permanent establishment losses).

Amendments—[1]   Chapter 3A (ss 18A–18S) inserted by FA 2011 s 48, Sch 13 paras 1, 4 with effect from 19 July 2011, subject to transitional provisions in FA 2011 Sch 13 paras 32–37.

[18M Streamed opening negative amounts: "matching"

(1) At the end of each relevant accounting period of the company (starting with the first) the streamed opening negative amount in relation to a territory is to be reduced (or further reduced) by the amount of any relevant profits amount of the company for the territory for the accounting period (but not to below nil).

(2) In any relevant accounting period of the company for which there is a reduction under subsection (1) in relation to a territory, section 18A(1) does not apply in relation to the relevant profits amount of the company for the territory for the accounting period.

(3) But in the case of the last relevant accounting period of the company for which there is a reduction under subsection (1) in relation to a territory, section 18A(1) is disapplied by subsection (2) only in relation to so much of the relevant profits amount of the company for the territory for the accounting period as is equal to the streamed opening negative amount in relation to the territory at the beginning of the accounting period.

(4) The company may, in its company tax return for that relevant accounting period, specify to which part of the relevant profits amount of the company for the territory for the accounting period section 18A(1) is to apply by virtue of subsection (3).][1]

Commentary—*Simon's Taxes* **D4.802A**.

HMRC Manuals—International Manual INTM284040 (foreign permanent establishments of UK companies: streaming of permanent establishment losses).

Amendments—[1]   Chapter 3A (ss 18A–18S) inserted by FA 2011 s 48, Sch 13 paras 1, 4 with effect from 19 July 2011, subject to transitional provisions in FA 2011 Sch 13 paras 32–37.

[18N Residual opening negative amount: "matching"

(1) At the end of each relevant accounting period of the company (starting with the first) the residual opening negative amount is to be reduced (or further reduced) by the amount of any residual aggregate relevant profits amount of the company for the accounting period (but not to below nil).

(2) For the purposes of this section the "residual opening negative amount", at the beginning of the company's first relevant accounting period, is—

    (a) the total opening negative amount of the company at that time, less

    (b) the aggregate of the streamed opening negative amounts of the company at that time.

(3) For the purposes of this section the "residual aggregate relevant profits amount", in relation to an accounting period, means the amount (if any) by which—

    (a) the aggregate relevant profits amount of the company for the accounting period, exceeds

    (b) the aggregate of so much of any relevant profits amounts of the company for the accounting period as has effect to bring about a reduction under section 18M(1) for the accounting period.

(4) In any relevant accounting period of the company for which there is a reduction under subsection (1), section 18A(1) does not apply in relation to the residual aggregate relevant profits amount of the company for the accounting period.

(5) But in the case of the last relevant accounting period of the company for which there is a reduction under subsection (1), section 18A(1) is disapplied by subsection (4) only in relation to so much of the residual aggregate relevant profits amount of the company for the accounting period as is equal to the residual opening negative amount of the company at the beginning of the accounting period.

(6) The company may, in its company tax return for that relevant accounting period, specify to which of the amounts forming part of the residual aggregate relevant profits amount of the company for the accounting period section 18A(1) is to apply by virtue of subsection (4).][1]

Commentary—*Simon's Taxes* **D4.802A**.

HMRC Manuals—International Manual INTM284040 (foreign permanent establishments of UK companies: streaming of permanent establishment losses).

Amendments—[1]   Chapter 3A (ss 18A–18S) inserted by FA 2011 s 48, Sch 13 paras 1, 4 with effect from 19 July 2011, subject to transitional provisions in FA 2011 Sch 13 paras 32–37.

[18O Transfers of foreign permanent establishment business

(1) This section applies if—

   (a) business carried on by a company ("the transferor") through a permanent establishment in a territory outside the United Kingdom is transferred to a connected company that is (or later becomes) a UK resident company ("the transferee"), and

   (b) there is a transferred total opening negative amount in relation to the business transferred.

(2) In a case where the transferor had not made an election under section 18A before the transfer took place, or such an election had not had effect before that time, the "transferred total opening negative amount" is the amount that would have been the total opening negative amount in the case of the transferor at the beginning of the transferor's first relevant accounting period if—

   (a) the only business carried on by the transferor was the business transferred,

   (b) the transfer had not taken place,

   (c) the transferor's first relevant accounting period had begun on the day after the transfer day, and

   (d) any reference in section 18J(3) to the accounting period in which the election is made were a reference to the period beginning with the accounting period in which the transfer took place and ending with the transfer day.

(3) In a case where an election made by the transferor under section 18A had effect before the transfer took place, the "transferred total opening negative amount" is—

   (a) the amount that would have been the total opening negative amount in the case of the transferor on the transfer day if the accounting period in which the transfer took place had ended on that day (the "remaining total opening negative amount"), less

   (b) the amount that would have been the remaining total opening negative amount if the transferor had never carried on the business transferred.

But the transferred total opening negative amount cannot be below nil.

(4) In a case where—

   (a) an election made by the transferee under section 18A first has effect after the transfer takes place, and

   (b) the accounting period of the transferee in which the transfer took place is an affected prior accounting period for the purposes of section 18J(2),

there is to be added to the adjusted foreign permanent establishments amount in relation to that accounting period a negative amount equal to so much (if any) of the transferred total opening negative amount as is attributable to profits or losses arising after the beginning of the earliest affected prior accounting period of the transferee.

(5) In a case where an election made by the transferee under section 18A had effect before the transfer took place, sections 18K to 18N have effect in relation to the transferee and the transferred total opening negative amount as if—

   (a) any reference to the total opening negative amount were a reference to the transferred total opening negative amount,

   (b) any reference to the first relevant accounting period were a reference to the period beginning with the day after the transfer day and ending immediately before the start of the next accounting period of the transferee, and

   (c) the requirement in section 18L(2) that a streaming election be made at the same time as the company's election under section 18A did not apply.

(6) Where for the purposes of this section it is necessary to apportion the profits and losses for any accounting period to different parts of that period, that apportionment is to be made on a just and reasonable basis.

(7) Any amount included in a transferred total opening negative amount is to be disregarded in the application of sections 18J to 18N in the case of the transferor after the transfer day.

(8) In this section "the transfer day" means the day on which the transfer of the business takes place.]¹

HMRC Manuals—International Manual INTM284050 (foreign permanent establishments of UK companies: transition to exemption provisions: transfers of permanent establishment business).

Amendments—¹ Chapter 3A (ss 18A–18S) inserted by FA 2011 s 48, Sch 13 paras 1, 4 with effect from 19 July 2011, subject to transitional provisions in FA 2011 Sch 13 paras 32–37.

[Special cases

18P Exclusions

(1) If a company is a small company at any time during a relevant accounting period, there is for that relevant accounting period no relevant profits amount or relevant losses amount for the purposes of this Chapter in relation to any relevant foreign territory that is not a full treaty territory.

(2) If a company is a close company at any time during a relevant accounting period, so much of the profits of the company for the relevant accounting period as derives from gains which are chargeable gains for the purposes of corporation tax is not to be regarded as forming part of a relevant profits amount or relevant losses amount of the company for the purposes of this Chapter.

[(3) Subsection (2) does not apply in relation to—

(*a*) a chargeable gain accruing on the disposal of an asset used, and used only, for the purposes of a trade so far as carried on by the company in the relevant foreign territory through the company's permanent establishment there, or

(*b*) a chargeable gain accruing on the disposal of currency or of a debt within section 252(1) of TCGA 1992 where the currency or debt is or represents money in use for the purposes of a trade so far as carried on by the company in the relevant foreign territory through the company's permanent establishment there.][2][1]

Commentary—*Simon's Taxes* **D4.801A.**
HMRC Manuals—International Manual INTM282070 (foreign permanent establishments of UK companies: chargeable gains: exclusion of gains of close companies).
INTM287010 (foreign permanent establishments of UK companies: exclusions and definitions: particular circumstances).
Amendments—[1]   Chapter 3A (ss 18A–18S) inserted by FA 2011 s 48, Sch 13 paras 1, 4 with effect from 19 July 2011, subject to transitional provisions in FA 2011 Sch 13 paras 32–37.
[2]   Sub-s (3) inserted by FA 2012 s 180, Sch 20 paras 2, 7 with effect for relevant accounting periods beginning on or after 1 January 2013 (FA 2012 Sch 20 para 55(2)).

[18Q Insurance companies

(1) So much of the profits or losses of a company as consists of profits or losses arising from basic life assurance and general annuity business ...[2] is not to be regarded as forming part of a relevant profits amount or relevant losses amount of the company for the purposes of this Chapter.
(2) . . .[2]
(3) . . .[2]
(4) Any election under section 107(4) of FA 2000 (general insurance: adjustment for technical provision) is to be ignored for the purposes of this Chapter.][1]

Commentary—*Simon's Taxes* **D4.801A.**
Amendments—[1]   Chapter 3A (ss 18A–18S) inserted by FA 2011 s 48, Sch 13 paras 1, 4 with effect from 19 July 2011, subject to transitional provisions in FA 2011 Sch 13 paras 32–37.
[2]   In sub-s (1), words "(as defined in section 431(2) of ICTA)" repealed and sub-ss (2), (3) repealed, by FA 2012 s 146, Sch 16 paras 135, 137 with effect in relation to accounting periods of companies beginning on or after 1 January 2013 (subject to transitional provisions in FA 2012 Sch 17). For accounting periods straddling 1 January 2013, see FA 2012 s 149.

[Interpretation

18R Meaning of "full treaty territory"

(1) For the purposes of this Chapter a territory is a "full treaty territory" if—
(*a*) double taxation arrangements have been made in relation to the territory, and
(*b*) the arrangements contain a relevant non-discrimination provision.
(2) "Relevant non-discrimination provision" means a provision to the effect that the taxation on a permanent establishment of an enterprise of a state which is party to the arrangements (a "contracting state") is not to be less favourably levied in any other contracting state than the taxation levied on enterprises of that other contracting state carrying on the same activities.][1]

HMRC Manuals—International Manual INTM287060 (foreign permanent establishments of UK companies: full treaty territory: definition).
Amendments—[1]   Chapter 3A (ss 18A–18S) inserted by FA 2011 s 48, Sch 13 paras 1, 4 with effect from 19 July 2011, subject to transitional provisions in FA 2011 Sch 13 paras 32–37.

[18S Other interpretation

In this Chapter—
"company tax return" has the same meaning as in Schedule 18 to FA 1998 (see paragraph 3(1));
"double taxation arrangements" means arrangements that have effect under section 2(1) of TIOPA 2010;
"the OECD model" means the Model Tax Convention on Income and on Capital published by the Organisation for Economic Co-operation and Development in July 2010 ("the OECD") or such other document published by the OECD in place of it as is designated from time to time by order made by the Treasury;
"small company" means a micro or small enterprise, as defined in the Annex to Commission Recommendation 2003/361/EC of 6 May 2003.][1]

Commentary—*Simon's Taxes* **D4.802.**
HMRC Manuals—International Manual INTM652060 (distribution exemption: exemption for small companies: definitions).
Amendments—[1]   Chapter 3A (ss 18A–18S) inserted by FA 2011 s 48, Sch 13 paras 1, 4 with effect from 19 July 2011, subject to transitional provisions in FA 2011 Sch 13 paras 32–37.

CHAPTER 4

NON-UK RESIDENT COMPANIES: CHARGEABLE PROFITS

Chargeable profits

19 Chargeable profits

(1) This section applies [for the purposes of the charge to corporation tax on income][2] if a non-UK resident company carries on a trade in the United Kingdom through a permanent establishment in the United Kingdom.

(2) The [company's "chargeable profits][1] are its profits that are—

    (*a*) of a type mentioned in subsection (3), and

    (*b*) attributable to the permanent establishment in accordance with sections 20 to 32.

[(2A) But the company's "chargeable profits" do not include—

    (*a*) profits of a trade of dealing in or developing UK land (see section 5B),

    (*b*) profits of a UK property business,

    (*c*) profits consisting of other UK property income, or

    (*d*) profits arising from loan relationships or derivative contracts that the company is a party to for the purposes of its UK property business or for the purposes of enabling it to generate other UK property income.][3]

(3) The types of profits referred to in subsection (2)(*a*) are—

    (*a*) trading income arising directly or indirectly through or from the establishment, [and][2]

    (*b*) income from property or rights used by, or held by or for, the establishment, and

    (*c*) . . .[2]

[(4) For the purposes of the charge to corporation tax on chargeable gains accruing to the company, see section 2B(3) of TCGA 1992.

(5) That subsection provides (among other things) that the gains are chargeable to corporation tax only so far as they are attributable to the permanent establishment in accordance with sections 20 to 32 of this Act.][2]

Commentary—*Simon's Taxes* **D4.117, C1.602, B7.515.**

Derivation—TA 1988 s 11(1), (2), (2A), s 11AA(1).

HMRC Manuals—International Manual INTM262040 (non - resident companies: profits chargeable to corporation tax). INTM267030 (domestic provisions on quantifying chargeable profits - income tax and corporation tax). INTM267110 (interest receivable by PE).

Amendments—[1]   In sub-s (2), words substituted for words "company's chargeable profits" by FA 2016 s 76(8) with effect in relation to disposals on or after 5 July 2016 (FA 2016 s 81(1)), subject to transitional provisions relating to disposals to associated persons on or after 16 March 2016 and before 5 July 2016 (FA 2016 s 81(4)–(15)).

     F(No 2)A 2017 s 39 provides that these amendments have effect (so far as they would not otherwise have effect) in relation to amounts that are recognised in GAAP accounts drawn up for any period of account beginning on or after 8 March 2017 or, in the case of a straddling period, amounts that would be recognised in GAAP accounts drawn up for a period of account beginning on 8 March 2017 and ending when the straddling period ends. "Straddling period" means a period of account beginning before 8 March 2017 and ending on or after that date.

[2]   In sub-s (1), words inserted; in sub-s (3), word "and" at end of para (*a*) inserted and para (*c*) repealed; and sub-ss (4), (5) inserted; by FA 2019 s 13, Sch 1 paras 108, 112 with effect for capital gains tax purposes for the tax year 2019–20 and subsequent tax years, and for corporation tax purposes for accounting periods beginning on or after 6 April 2019. These amendments also have effect for corporation tax purposes in relation to disposals made on or after 6 April 2019 (whether in their application to accounting periods beginning on, and ending on or after, that date or to later accounting periods). See also transitional provisions in FA 2019 Sch 1 paras 121–126.

[3]   Sub-s (2A) substituted by FA 2019 s 17, Sch 5 paras 10, 13 with effect from 6 April 2020, subject to transitional provisions in FA 2019 Sch 5 Pt 3 (paras 36–50).

20 Profits attributable to permanent establishment: introduction

(1) Sections 21 to 32 apply for the purpose of determining the amount of profits of a non-UK resident company that are attributable to a permanent establishment of the company in the United Kingdom.

(2) Sections 21 to 28 contain provision about the separate enterprise principle.

(3) See also [section 1152 of CTA 2010 (investment managers: disregard of certain chargeable profits)][1], which provides for profits of certain investment transactions to be disregarded in determining the amount of profits attributable to a permanent establishment.

HMRC Manuals—International Manual INTM267622 (attribution of profits to a permanent establishment: introduction).

Amendments—[1]   In sub-s (3) words substituted for words "paragraph 5A of Schedule 26 to FA 2003 (non-resident companies: transactions through broker, investment manager or Lloyd's agent)" by CTA 2010 s 1177, Sch 1 para 590. CTA 2010 has effect for corporation tax purposes for accounting periods ending on or after 1 April 2010, and for income and capital gains tax purposes for the tax year 2010–11 and subsequent tax years.

The separate enterprise principle

21 The separate enterprise principle

(1) The profits of the non-UK resident company that are attributable to the permanent establishment are those that the establishment would have made if it were a distinct and separate enterprise which—

    (*a*) engaged in the same or similar activities under the same or similar conditions, and

    (*b*) dealt wholly independently with the non-UK resident company.

(2) In applying subsection (1) assume that—

    (a) the permanent establishment has the same credit rating as the non-UK resident company, and

    (b) the permanent establishment has such equity and loan capital as it could reasonably be expected to have in the circumstances specified in that subsection.

(3) In sections 22 to 28 the principle in subsection (1) (read with subsection (2)) is called "the separate enterprise principle".

Commentary—*Simon's Taxes* **D4.118, D4.119**.
Derivation—TA 1988 s 11AA(2), (3), Sch A1 para 1(2).
HMRC Manuals—International Manual INTM267622 (attribution of profits to a permanent establishment: the separate enterprise principle).
INTM267762 (tiers 1, 2 and 3).
INTM267769 (the arm's length amount).

22 Transactions treated as being on arm's length terms

In accordance with the separate enterprise principle, transactions between the permanent establishment and any other part of the non-UK resident company are treated as taking place on such terms as would have been agreed between parties dealing at arm's length.

Commentary—*Simon's Taxes* **D4.118**.
Derivation—TA 1988 Sch A1 para 2.

23 Provision of goods or services for permanent establishment

(1) This section applies if the non-UK resident company provides the permanent establishment with goods or services.

(2) If the goods or services are of a kind that the company supplies, in the ordinary course of its business, to third parties dealing with it at arm's length, the matter is dealt with as a transaction to which the separate enterprise principle applies.

(3) If not, the matter is dealt with as an expense incurred by the non-UK resident company for the purposes of the permanent establishment (see section 29).

Commentary—*Simon's Taxes* **D4.118**.
Derivation—TA 1988 Sch A1 para 6.

[24 Application to insurance companies

(1) This section makes provision in a case where the non-UK resident company mentioned in subsection (1) of section 21 is an insurance company.

(2) In accordance with the principle in that subsection, the permanent establishment is treated as holding—

    (a) the same or a similar quantity of assets, and

    (b) assets of the same or similar description,

as would have been held by a distinct and separate enterprise acting as mentioned in paragraphs (a) and (b) of that subsection.

(3) The assets which the permanent establishment is treated as holding in accordance with the principle in that subsection may include a proportion of assets held by the company.

(4) Nothing in subsection (2) or (3) is to be read as preventing the application of similar principles to those provided for by that subsection in a case where the non-UK resident company mentioned in section 21(1) is not an insurance company.

(5) The Commissioners for Her Majesty's Revenue and Customs may by regulations make other provision about the application of section 21(1) in a case where the non-UK resident company mentioned there is an insurance company.

(6) The regulations may, in particular, make provision in place of section 21(2)(b) as to the basis on which, in the case of an insurance company, capital is to be attributed to a permanent establishment in the United Kingdom.][1]

Commentary—*Simon's Taxes* **D4.118**.
Amendments—[1]   This section substituted by FA 2012 s 146, Sch 16 paras 135, 137 with effect in relation to accounting periods of companies beginning on or after 1 January 2013 (subject to transitional provisions in FA 2012 Sch 17). For accounting periods straddling 1 January 2013, see FA 2012 s 149.

The separate enterprise principle: application to non-UK resident banks

25 Non-UK resident banks: introduction

(1) Sections 26 to 28 contain provision in relation to the application of the separate enterprise principle if the non-UK resident company is a bank.

(2) Nothing in sections 26 to 28 is to be read as preventing similar principles to those provided for in those sections from applying when the separate enterprise principle is applied to a non-UK resident company that is not a bank.

(3) In this section and those sections "bank" has the meaning given by [section 1120 of CTA 2010][1].

Commentary—*Simon's Taxes* **D4.119**.
Amendments—[1]   In sub-s (3) words substituted for words "section 840A of ICTA" by CTA 2010 s 1177, Sch 1 para 591. CTA 2010 has effect for corporation tax purposes for accounting periods ending on or after 1 April 2010, and for income and capital gains tax purposes for the tax year 2010–11 and subsequent tax years.

    (*b*) by virtue of an agreement with the appointing company, the director is required to account for the payment to that company, and

    (*c*) either subsection (5) or subsection (6) applies to the appointing company.

(5) This subsection applies if the appointing company had the right to appoint the director by virtue of its shareholding in, or an agreement with, the paying company.

(6) This subsection applies if the appointing company is not one over which—

    (*a*) the director has control, or

    (*b*) any person connected with the director has control, or

    (*c*) the director and any persons connected with him together have control.

(7) For the purposes of subsection (6) the following persons are connected with the director: the spouse, civil partner, parent, child, son-in-law or daughter-in-law of the director.][1]

Amendments—[1]   Sections 40A, 40B inserted by the Enactment of Extra-Statutory Concessions Order, SI 2018/282 art 6 with effect from 6 April 2018.

[40B Professionals in practice: incidental income from an office or employment

(1) This section applies where—

    (*a*) a payment is received by an individual who carries on a profession in partnership,

    (*b*) the payment is made to the individual in his or her capacity as an employee or office-holder, but is not made in respect of employment as a director of a company,

    (*c*) the payment would otherwise be employment income of the individual chargeable to tax under Part 2 of ITEPA 2003, and

    (*d*) the conditions in subsection (3) are met.

(2) The payment is to be treated for corporation tax purposes as a receipt of a trade carried on by the firm.

(3) The conditions referred to in subsection (1)(*d*) are that—

    (*a*) the time spent by the individual in performing the duties of the office or employment is insubstantial compared with the time spent by the individual in carrying on the profession,

    (*b*) the office or employment is related to the profession carried on by the individual,

    (*c*) the amount of the payment is insubstantial compared with so much of the total amount brought into account as receipts when calculating the firm's profits as is attributable to the individual, and

    (*d*) the individual is required by the terms of the partnership agreement to account to the firm for the payment and does so.][1]

Amendments—[1]   Sections 40A, 40B inserted by the Enactment of Extra-Statutory Concessions Order, SI 2018/282 art 6 with effect from 6 April 2018.

Starting and ceasing to trade

41 Effect of company starting or ceasing to be within charge to corporation tax

(1) This section applies if a company starts or ceases to be within the charge to corporation tax in respect of a trade.

(2) The company is treated for the purposes of this Part—

    (*a*) as starting to carry on the trade when it starts to be within the charge, or

    (*b*) as ceasing to carry on the trade when it ceases to be within the charge.

Commentary—*Simon's Taxes* **B2.804, B2.805, B3.390, D1.303, D6.310.**
Derivation—TA 1988 s 337(1).
HMRC Manuals—Company Taxation Manual CTM02100 (commencement and cessation of trade: special rule).
CTM34070 (deemed commencement: specific points).
CTM06005 (without change in ownership: general).
Capital Allowance CA29030 (successions general).

Trading income and property income

42 Tied premises

(1) This section applies if—

    (*a*) in the course of carrying on a trade a company ("the trader") supplies, or is concerned in the supply of, goods sold or used on premises occupied by another person,

    (*b*) the trader has an estate or interest in the premises,

    (*c*) the estate or interest is dealt with as property employed for the purposes of the trade, and

    (*d*) receipts and expenses in connection with the premises would otherwise be brought into account in calculating the profits of a property business of the trader.

(2) Both the receipts and the expenses are instead brought into account in calculating the profits of the trade.

(3) Any apportionment of receipts or expenses that is necessary because—

    (*a*) the receipts or expenses do not relate only to the premises, or

    (*b*) the above conditions are met only in relation to part of the premises,

is to be made on a just and reasonable basis.

Commentary—*Simon's Taxes* **B2.216, B5.611.**
Derivation—TA 1988 s 98.

HMRC Manuals—Business Income Manual BIM51430 (tied premises: rent receivable and paid).
BIM46810 (specific deductions: tied premises).

43 Caravan sites where trade carried on

(1) This section applies if—

  (*a*) a company ("the trader") carries on material activities connected with the operation of a caravan site,

  (*b*) the activities are, or are part of, a trade, and

  (*c*) receipts from, and expenses of, lettings of caravans or pitches for caravans on the site would otherwise be brought into account in calculating the profits of a property business of the trader.

(2) The trader may instead bring both the receipts and the expenses into account in calculating the profits of the trade.

(3) But if the conditions in subsection (1)(*a*) and (*b*) are met for only part of an accounting period of the trader, subsection (2) applies only to the receipts and expenses that would otherwise be brought into account in calculating the profits of the property business for that part of the accounting period.

(4) In this section—

  "caravan site" means—

    (*a*) land on which a caravan is stationed for the purposes of human habitation, and

    (*b*) land which is used in conjunction with land on which a caravan is so stationed, and

  "letting" includes a licence to occupy.

Commentary—*Simon's Taxes* **B2.217, B29, C36**.
Change in the law—See CTA 2009 EN Annex 1, Change 4.

44 Surplus business accommodation

(1) This section applies if—

  (*a*) a company ("the trader") carrying on a trade obtains receipts from a letting of business accommodation that is temporarily surplus to requirements (see subsections (3) and (4)),

  (*b*) the accommodation is not held as trading stock,

  (*c*) the receipts are in respect of part of a building of which another part is used to carry on the trade,

  (*d*) the receipts are relatively small, and

  (*e*) the receipts, and the expenses of the letting, would otherwise be brought into account in calculating the profits of a property business of the trader.

(2) The trader may instead bring both the receipts and the expenses into account in calculating the profits of the trade.

(3) Accommodation is temporarily surplus to requirements only if—

  (*a*) it has been used within the last 3 years to carry on the trade or acquired within the last 3 years,

  (*b*) the trader intends to use it to carry on the trade at a later date, and

  (*c*) the letting is for a term of not more than 3 years.

(4) If accommodation is temporarily surplus to requirements at the beginning of an accounting period, it continues to be temporarily surplus to requirements until the end of that period.

(5) If under this section any of the receipts from and expenses of a letting are brought into account in calculating the profits of the trade, all subsequent receipts from and expenses of the letting must be dealt with in the same way (but only so long as this section continues to apply).

(6) In this section "letting" includes a licence to occupy.

Commentary—*Simon's Taxes* **B2.218, B5.220**.
Change in the law—See CTA 2009 EN Annex 1, Change 5.
HMRC Manuals—Business Income Manual BIM41015 (letting surplus business accommodation and rent as a trading receipt).

45 Payments for wayleaves

(1) This section applies if—

  (*a*) a company ("the trader") carries on a trade on some or all of the land to which a wayleave relates,

  (*b*) rent is receivable, or expenses are incurred, by the trader in respect of the wayleave, and

  (*c*) apart from any rent or expenses in respect of a wayleave, no other receipts or expenses in respect of any of the land are brought into account in calculating the profits of any property business of the trader.

(2) If—

  (*a*) the trader would otherwise be liable to tax under Chapter 8 of Part 4 in respect of the rent for the wayleave (rent receivable for UK electric-line wayleaves), or

  (*b*) expenses incurred by the trader in respect of the wayleave would otherwise be brought into account in calculating profits charged under that Chapter,

the trader may instead bring both the rent and the expenses into account in calculating the profits of the trade.

(3) If—

(a) rent for the wayleave would otherwise be brought into account in calculating the profits of a property business of the trader, or

(b) expenses incurred by the trader in respect of the wayleave would otherwise be so brought into account,

the trader may instead bring both the rent and the expenses into account in calculating the profits of the trade.

(4) In this section "rent" includes—

(a) a receipt mentioned in section 207(3), and

(b) any other receipt in the nature of rent.

(5) In this section "wayleave" means an easement, servitude or right in or over land which is enjoyed in connection with—

(a) an electric, telegraph or telephone wire or cable,

(b) a pipe for the conveyance of any thing, or

(c) any apparatus used in connection with such a pipe.

(6) The reference to the enjoyment of an easement, servitude or right in connection with an electric, telegraph or telephone wire or cable includes (in particular) its enjoyment in connection with—

(a) a pole or pylon supporting such a wire or cable, or

(b) apparatus used in connection with such a wire or cable.

Commentary—*Simon's Taxes* **B2.219, B5.102**.
HMRC Manuals—Business Income Manual BIM67600 (guidance on wayleaves).
Property Income Manual PIM1115 (definition of wayleave).

CHAPTER 3

TRADE PROFITS: BASIC RULES

46 Generally accepted accounting practice

(1) The profits of a trade must be calculated in accordance with generally accepted accounting practice, subject to any adjustment required or authorised by law in calculating profits for corporation tax purposes.

(2) This does not—

(a) require a company to comply with the requirements of the Companies Act 2006 (c 46) or subordinate legislation made under that Act except as to the basis of calculation, or

(b) impose any requirements as to audit or disclosure.

(3) This section does not affect any provisions of the Corporation Tax Acts—

(a) relating to the calculation of the profits of—

(i) Lloyd's underwriters, . . . [1]

(ii) . . . [1]

(b) otherwise laying down special rules for the calculation of the profits of a particular description of business.

Commentary—*Simon's Taxes* **A1.205, B2.102, B2.104, B7.401**.
HMRC Manuals—Business Income Manual BIM37020 (wholly and exclusively: guidance on determining tax adjusted profits).

BIM15040 (ascertaining trade profits based on GAAP and cash basis).
BIM30510 (generally accepted accounting practice: basic computational rule).
BIM31005 (tax and accounting principles: introduction).
Amendments—[1] In sub-s (3)(a), sub-para (ii) and preceding word "or" repealed by FA 2012 s 146, Sch 16 paras 135, 142 with effect in relation to accounting periods beginning on or after 1 January 2013 (subject to transitional provisions in FA 2012 Sch 17). For accounting periods straddling 1 January 2013, see FA 2012 s 149.

47 Losses calculated on same basis as profits

(1) The same rules apply for corporation tax purposes in calculating losses of a trade as apply in calculating profits.

(2) This is subject to any express provision to the contrary.

Commentary—*Simon's Taxes* **B2.101, B2.101**.
HMRC Manuals—Business Income Manual BIM60085 (loss making transactions).
BIM30510 (losses calculated on same basis as profits).

48 Receipts and expenses

(1) In the Corporation Tax Acts, in the context of the calculation of the profits of a trade, references to receipts and expenses are to any items brought into account as credits or debits in calculating the profits.

(2) It follows that references in that context to receipts or expenses do not imply that an amount has actually been received or paid.

(3) This section is subject to any express provision to the contrary.

Commentary—*Simon's Taxes* **B2.108**.
HMRC Manuals—Business Income Manual BIM30515 (statutory rules: receipts and expenses).
BIM40050 (trade receipts).

CTA 2009

49 Items treated as receipts and expenses

The rules for calculating the profits of a trade need to be read with—

    (*a*) the provisions of CAA 2001 which treat allowances as expenses of a trade,

    (*b*) the provisions of CAA 2001 which treat charges as receipts of a trade,

    (*c*) section 297 (credits and debits in respect of a loan relationship to which a company is a party for the purposes of a trade it carries on treated as receipts and expenses of the trade),

    (*d*) section 573 (credits and debits in respect of a derivative contract to which a company is a party for the purposes of a trade it carries on treated as receipts and expenses of the trade),

    (*e*) section 747 (credits and debits in respect of an intangible fixed asset held by a company for the purposes of a trade it carries on treated as receipts and expenses of the trade), and

    (*f*) section 749 (credits and debits in respect of an intangible fixed asset held by a company for the purposes of a section 39(4) concern which it carries on treated as receipts and expenses of the concern).

Commentary—*Simon's Taxes* **B2.108**.

HMRC Manuals—Business Income Manual BIM30515 (statutory rules: receipts and expenses).

[49A Money's worth

(1) Subsection (2) applies—

    (*a*) for the purpose of bringing into account an amount arising in respect of a transaction involving money's worth entered into in the course of a trade, and

    (*b*) if an amount at least equal to the amount that would be brought into account under that subsection is not otherwise brought into account as a receipt in calculating the profits of a trade under a provision of this Part other than a provision mentioned in subsection (3).

(2) For the purpose of calculating the profits of the trade, an amount equal to the value of the money's worth is brought into account as a receipt if, had the transaction involved money, an amount would have been brought into account as a receipt in respect of it.

(3) But where another provision of this Part makes express provision for the bringing into account of an amount in respect of money's worth as a receipt in calculating the profits of a trade (however expressed), that other provision applies instead of subsection (2).][1]

Amendments—[1]   Section 49A inserted by FA 2016 s 71(4), (5) with effect in relation to transactions entered into on or after 16 March 2016.

50 Animals kept for trade purposes

(1) Animals or other living creatures kept for the purposes of a trade are treated as trading stock if they are not kept wholly or mainly—

    (*a*) for the work they do in connection with the carrying on of the trade,

    (*b*) for public exhibition, or

    (*c*) for racing or other competitive purposes.

(2) But they are not treated as trading stock if they are part of a herd in relation to which a herd basis election has effect (see Chapter 8).

(3) This section applies to shares in animals or other living creatures as it applies to the creatures themselves.

Commentary—*Simon's Taxes* **B2.101A, B2.609, B5.140**.

Derivation—TA 1988 Sch 5 paras 1(1), (2), 7, 9(1), (2), (4), (5).

HMRC Manuals—Business Income Manual BIM55401 (general principles: valuation of farming stock).

BIM55425 (farm animals treated as trading stock).

BIM55445 (shares in animals).

BIM55500 (herd basis).

BIM55440 (working horses).

51 Relationship between rules prohibiting and allowing deductions

(1) Any relevant permissive rule in this Part—

    (*a*) has priority over any relevant prohibitive rule, but

    (*b*) is subject to—

        (i) section 56 (car . . . [1] hire),

        (ii) section 1288 (unpaid remuneration),

        (iii) section 1290 (employee benefit contributions),

        (iv) section 1304 (crime-related payments).

[(1A) But, if the relevant permissive rule would allow a deduction in calculating the profits of a trade in respect of an amount which arises directly or indirectly in consequence of, or otherwise in connection with, relevant tax avoidance arrangements, that rule—

    (*a*) does not have priority under subsection (1)(*a*), and

    (*b*) is subject to any relevant prohibitive rule (and to the provisions mentioned in subsection (1)(*b*)).][2]

(2) In this section "any relevant permissive rule in this Part" means any provision of—

    (*a*) Chapter 5 (trade profits: rules allowing deductions), apart from sections 62 to 67,

    (*b*) Chapter 7 (trade profits: gifts to charities etc),

    (*c*) Chapter 9 (trade profits: other specific trades), or

   (c) an independent school within the meaning of the Education Act 1996 (c 56) registered under section 161 of the Education Act 2002 (c 32), . . . [2]

   ([ca) an alternative provision Academy that is not an independent school within the meaning of the Education Act 1996,][3]

   (d) an institution within the further education sector, or the higher education sector, within the meaning of the Further and Higher Education Act 1992 (c 13)[or

   (e) a 16 to 19 Academy.[2]

(2) A body in Scotland is an educational establishment for the purposes of section 70 if it is—

   (a) an education authority within the meaning of the Education (Scotland) Act 1980 (c 44),

   (b) an educational establishment within the meaning of the Education (Scotland) Act 1980 managed by an education authority within the meaning of that Act,

   (c) a public or grant-aided school within the meaning of the Education (Scotland) Act 1980,

   (d) an independent school within the meaning of the Education (Scotland) Act 1980,

   (e) a central institution within the meaning of the Education (Scotland) Act 1980 (c 44),

   (f) an institution within the higher education sector within the meaning of section 56(2) of the Further and Higher Education (Scotland) Act 1992 (c 37), or

   (g) a college of further education within the meaning of section 36(1) of the Further and Higher Education (Scotland) Act 1992.

(3) A body in Northern Ireland is an educational establishment for the purposes of section 70 if it is—

   (a) an education and library board within the meaning of the Education and Libraries (Northern Ireland) Order 1986 (SI 1986/594 (NI 3)),

   (b) a college of education, a grant-aided school or an independent school within the meaning of the Education and Libraries (Northern Ireland) Order 1986, or

   (c) an institution of further education within the meaning of the Further Education (Northern Ireland) Order 1997 (SI 1997/1772 (NI 15)).

   [(4) In subsection (1) "local authority" and "education functions" have the same meaning as in the Education Act 1996 (see section 579(1) of that Act).][1]

HMRC Manuals—Business Income Manual BIM47120 (employees seconded to educational establishments).

Amendments—[1] Sub-s (1)(a) substituted, in sub-(1)(b) words substituted and sub-s (4) inserted by the Local Education Authorities and Children's Services Authorities (Integration of Functions) Order, SI 2010/1158, art 5(1), Sch 2, para 66 with effect from 5 May 2010.

[2] In sub-s (1), word at the end of para (c) repealed and para (e) and preceding word inserted by the Education Act 2011 s 54, Sch 13 para 18 with effect from 1 April 2012 (by virtue of SI 2012/924 art 2). Note that these amendments do not extend to Scotland: see the Education Act 2011 s 81(1).

[3] Sub-s (1)(ca) inserted by the Alternative Provision Academies (Consequential Amendments to Acts) (England) Order, SI 2012/976 art 2, Schedule para 23 with effect from 1 April 2012.

Contributions to agents' expenses

72 Payroll deduction schemes: contributions to agents' expenses

(1) This section applies if—

   (a) a company carrying on a trade ("the employer") is liable to make payments to an individual,

   (b) income tax falls to be deducted from those payments as a result of PAYE regulations, and

   (c) the employer withholds sums from those payments in accordance with an approved scheme and pays the sums to an approved agent.

(2) In calculating the profits of the employer's trade, a deduction is allowed for expenses incurred by the employer in making a payment to the agent for expenses which—

   (a) have been incurred, or

   (b) are to be incurred,

by the agent in connection with the agent's functions under the scheme.

(3) In this section "approved agent" and "approved scheme" have the same meaning as in section 714 of ITEPA 2003.

Commentary—*Simon's Taxes* E4.1116.

HMRC Manuals—Business Income Manual BIM45195 (gifts in kind and payroll giving).

Counselling and retraining expenses

73 Counselling and other outplacement services

(1) In calculating the profits of a trade, a deduction is allowed for counselling expenses if—

   (a) the company carrying on the trade ("the employer") incurs the expenses,

   (b) the expenses are incurred in relation to a person ("the employee") who holds or has held an office or employment under the employer for the purposes of the trade, and

   (c) the relevant conditions are met.

(2) In this section "counselling expenses" means expenses incurred—

   (a) in the provision of services to the employee in connection with the cessation of the office or employment,

   (b) in the payment or reimbursement of fees for such provision, or

   (c) in the payment or reimbursement of travelling expenses in connection with such provision.

(3) In this section "the relevant conditions" means—

(*a*) conditions A to D for the purposes of section 310 of ITEPA 2003 (employment income exemptions: counselling and other outplacement services), and

(*b*) in the case of travel expenses, condition E for those purposes.

Commentary—*Simon's Taxes* **B2.428**.
HMRC Manuals—Business Income Manual BIM47217 (staff counselling expenses).

74 Retraining courses

(1) In calculating the profits of a trade, a deduction is allowed for retraining course expenses if—

(*a*) the company carrying on the trade ("the employer") incurs the expenses,

(*b*) they are incurred in relation to a person ("the employee") who holds or has held an office or employment under the employer for the purposes of the trade, and

(*c*) the relevant conditions are met.

(2) In this section—

"retraining course expenses" means expenses incurred in the payment or reimbursement of retraining course expenses within the meaning given by section 311(2) of ITEPA 2003, and "the relevant conditions" means—

(*a*) the conditions in subsections (3) and (4) of section 311 of ITEPA 2003 (employment income exemptions: retraining courses), and

(*b*) in the case of travel expenses, the conditions in subsection (5) of that section.

Commentary—*Simon's Taxes* **B2.428**.
HMRC Manuals—Business Income Manual BIM47080 (staff training and development).
Employment Income Manual EIM05005 (explanation and further references of section 311 ITEPA 2003).

75 Retraining courses: recovery of tax

(1) This section applies if—

(*a*) an employer's liability to corporation tax for an accounting period is determined on the assumption that a deduction for expenditure is allowed under section 74, and

(*b*) the deduction would not otherwise have been allowed.

(2) If, subsequently—

(*a*) the condition in section 311(4)(*a*) of ITEPA 2003 is not met because of the employee's failure to begin the course within the period of one year after ceasing to be employed, or

(*b*) the condition in section 311(4)(*b*) of ITEPA 2003 is not met because of the employee's continued employment or re-employment,

an assessment of an amount or further amount of corporation tax due as a result of the condition not being met may be made under paragraph 41 of Schedule 18 to FA 1998.

(3) Such an assessment must be made before the end of the period of 6 years immediately following the end of the accounting period in which the failure to meet the condition occurred.

(4) If subsection (2) applies, the employer must give an officer of Revenue and Customs a notice containing particulars of—

(*a*) the employee's failure to begin the course,

(*b*) the employee's continued employment, or

(*c*) the employee's re-employment,

within 60 days of coming to know of it.

(5), (6) . . . [1]

Commentary—*Simon's Taxes* **B2.428**.
HMRC Manuals—Employment Income Manual EIM05030 (explanation to withdrawal of exemption for section 312 ITEPA 2003).
Amendments—[1]   Sub-ss (5), (6) repealed by Finance Act 2009 Schedule 47 (Consequential Amendments) Order, SI 2009/2035, Art 2, Schedule paras 54, 55 with effect from 13 August 2009.

Redundancy payments etc

76 Redundancy payments and approved contractual payments

(1) Sections 77 to 79 apply if—

(*a*) a company ("the employer") makes a redundancy payment or an approved contractual payment to another person ("the employee"), and

(*b*) the payment is in respect of the employee's employment wholly in the employer's trade or partly in the employer's trade and partly in one or more other capacities.

(2) For the purposes of this section and sections 77 to 81 "redundancy payment" means a redundancy payment payable under—

(*a*) Part 11 of the Employment Rights Act 1996 (c 18), or

(*b*) Part 12 of the Employment Rights (Northern Ireland) Order 1996 (SI 1996/1919 (NI 16)).

(3) For the purposes of this section and those sections—

"contractual payment" means a payment which, under an agreement, an employer is liable to make to an employee on the termination of the employee's contract of employment, and a contractual payment is "approved" if, in respect of that agreement, an order is in force under—

(*a*) section 157 of the Employment Rights Act 1996, or

    (*b*) Article 192 of the Employment Rights (Northern Ireland) Order 1996.

Commentary—*Simon's Taxes* **B2.426**.
HMRC Manuals—Business Income Manual BIM47200 (redundancy payments: general principles).
BIM47205 (statutory redundancy and contractual payments).

77 Payments in respect of employment wholly in employer's trade

(1) This section applies if—
    (*a*) the payment is in respect of the employee's employment wholly in the employer's trade, and
    (*b*) no deduction would otherwise be allowable for the payment.
(2) In calculating the profits of the trade, a deduction is allowed under this section for the payment.
(3) The deduction under this section for an approved contractual payment must not exceed the amount which would have been due to the employee if a redundancy payment had been payable.
(4) If the payment is made after the employer has permanently ceased to carry on the trade, it is treated as made on the last day on which the employer carried on the trade.
(5) If there is a partnership change, subsection (4) does not apply so long as a company carrying on the trade in partnership immediately before the change continues to carry it on in partnership after the change.
(6) The reference in subsection (5) to a partnership change is to a change in the persons carrying on the trade in circumstances where the trade is carried on by persons in partnership immediately before or immediately after the change (or at both those times).
(7) The deduction under this section is allowed for the accounting period in which the payment is made (or treated under subsection (4) as made).

Commentary—*Simon's Taxes* **B2.426**.
HMRC Manuals—Business Income Manual BIM47215 (redundancy payments: timing of deductions).
BIM47205 (statutory redundancy payments: the deduction).

78 Payments in respect of employment in more than one capacity

(1) This section applies if the payment is in respect of the employee's employment with the employer—
    (*a*) partly in the employer's trade, and
    (*b*) partly in one or more other capacities.
(2) The amount of the redundancy payment, or the amount which would have been due if a redundancy payment had been payable, is to be apportioned on a just and reasonable basis between—
    (*a*) the employment in the trade, and
    (*b*) the employment in the other capacities.
(3) The part of the payment apportioned to the employment in the trade is treated as a payment in respect of the employee's employment wholly in the trade for the purposes of section 77.

Commentary—*Simon's Taxes* **B2.426**.
HMRC Manuals—Business Income Manual BIM47205 (statutory redundancy payments: the deduction).

79 Additional payments

(1) This section applies if the employer permanently ceases to carry on a trade or part of a trade and makes a payment to the employee in addition to—
    (*a*) the redundancy payment, or
    (*b*) if an approved contractual payment is made, the amount that would have been due if a redundancy payment had been payable.
(2) If, in calculating the profits of the trade—
    (*a*) no deduction would otherwise be allowable for the additional payment, but
    (*b*) a deduction would be allowable for it if the employer had not permanently ceased to carry on the trade or the part of the trade,
a deduction is allowed under this section for the additional payment.
(3) The deduction under this section is limited to 3 times the amount of—
    (*a*) the redundancy payment, or
    (*b*) if an approved contractual payment is made, the amount that would have been due if a redundancy payment had been payable.
(4) If the payment is made after the employer has permanently ceased to carry on the trade or the part of the trade, it is treated as made on the last day on which the employer carried on the trade or the part of the trade.
(5) The deduction under this section is allowed for the accounting period in which the payment is made (or treated under subsection (4) as made).

Commentary—*Simon's Taxes* **B2.306, B2.426**.
HMRC Manuals—Business Income Manual BIM47210 (additional payments to redundant employees).
BIM47215 (redundancy payments: timing of deductions).

80 Application of section 79 in cases involving partnerships

(1) This section deals with the application of section 79 in circumstances where—
    (*a*) there is a change in the persons carrying on a trade, and

(b) the trade is carried on by persons in partnership before or after the change (or at both those times).

(2) The employer is treated for the purposes of section 79 as permanently ceasing to carry on the trade unless a company carrying on the trade in partnership immediately before the change continues to carry it on in partnership after the change.

Commentary—*Simon's Taxes* **B2.426**.
Derivation—TA 1988 s 90(3), s 114(1); drafting.
HMRC Manuals—Business Income Manual BIM47210 (additional payments to redundant employees).

81 Payments made by the Government

(1) This section applies if, in respect of a redundancy payment or an approved contractual payment payable by an employer—

(a) the Secretary of State makes a payment under section 167 of the Employment Rights Act 1996 (c 18), or

(b) the Department for Employment and Learning makes a payment under Article 202 of the Employment Rights (Northern Ireland) Order 1996 (SI 1996/1919 (NI 16)).

(2) So far as the employer reimburses the Secretary of State or Department for the payment, sections 77 to 80 apply as if the payment were—

(a) a redundancy payment, or

(b) an approved contractual payment,

made by the employer.

Commentary—*Simon's Taxes* **B2.426**.
HMRC Manuals—BIM47205 (payments direct to employees by a government department).

Contributions to local enterprise organisations or urban regeneration companies

82 Contributions to local enterprise organisations or urban regeneration companies

(1) This section applies if a company carrying on a trade ("the contributor") incurs expenses in making a contribution (whether in cash or in kind)—

(a) to a local enterprise organisation (see section 83), or

(b) to an urban regeneration company (see section 86),

and a deduction would not otherwise be allowable for the expenses in calculating the profits of the trade.

(2) In calculating the profits of the trade, a deduction is allowed under this section for the expenses.

(3) But if, in connection with the making of the contribution, the contributor or a connected person—

(a) receives a disqualifying benefit of any kind, or

(b) is entitled to receive such a benefit,

the amount of the deduction is restricted to the amount of the expenses less the value of the benefit.

(4) For this purpose it does not matter whether a person receives, or is entitled to receive, the benefit—

(a) from the local enterprise organisation or urban regeneration company concerned, or

(b) from anyone else.

(5) Subsection (6) applies if—

(a) a deduction has been made under this section, and

(b) the contributor or a connected person receives a disqualifying benefit that is in any way attributable to the contribution.

(6) An amount equal to the value of the benefit (so far as not brought into account in determining the amount of the deduction)—

(a) is brought into account in calculating the profits of the trade, as a receipt arising in the accounting period in which the benefit is received, or

(b) if the contributor has permanently ceased to carry on the trade before the benefit is received, is treated as a post-cessation receipt (see Chapter 15).

(7) In this section "disqualifying benefit" means a benefit the expenses of obtaining which, if incurred by the contributor directly in a transaction at arm's length, would not be allowable as a deduction in calculating the profits of the trade.

Commentary—*Simon's Taxes* **B2.450, B2.804**.
HMRC Manuals—Company Taxation Manual CTM15340 (LEAs, LECs & TECs).
Business Income Manual BIM47610 (local enterprise organisations or urban regeneration companies contributions).

83 Meaning of "local enterprise organisation"

(1) For the purposes of section 82 "local enterprise organisation" means—

(a) a local enterprise agency,

(b) a training and enterprise council,

(c) a Scottish local enterprise company, or

(d) a business link organisation.

(2) "Local enterprise agency" means a body for the time being approved as a local enterprise agency for the purposes of section 82 by the relevant national authority, that is to say by—

(a) the Secretary of State (in relation to England or Northern Ireland), (*b*) the Scottish Ministers (in relation to Scotland), or

    (*c*) the Welsh Ministers (in relation to Wales).

For further provision about approvals by the relevant national authority, see sections 84 and 85.

(3) "Training and enterprise council" means a body with which the Secretary of State has an agreement under which the body is to carry out the functions of a training and enterprise council.

(4) "Scottish local enterprise company" means a company with which—

    (*a*) Scottish Enterprise, or

    (*b*) Highlands and Islands Enterprise,

has an agreement under which the company is to carry out the functions of a local enterprise company.

(5) "Business link organisation" means a person authorised by or on behalf of the Secretary of State to use a trade mark designated by the Secretary of State for the purposes of this subsection.

Commentary—*Simon's Taxes* **B2.450**.

HMRC Manuals—Company Taxation Manual CTM41150 (trade organisations).

Business Income Manual BIM47610 (explanation for local enterprise organisations).

84 Approval of local enterprise agencies

(1) The relevant national authority may approve a body as a local enterprise agency for the purposes of section 82 only if conditions A and B are met.

(2) But if those conditions are met, the body may be approved—

    (*a*) whatever its status or structure, and

    (*b*) even if it is not described as a local enterprise agency.

(3) Condition A is that the relevant national authority is satisfied—

    (*a*) that the body's sole aim is the promotion or encouragement of local enterprise, or

    (*b*) that one of the body's main aims is the promotion or encouragement of local enterprise and that it has or is about to have a separate fund for the sole purpose of pursuing that aim.

(4) For this purpose "local enterprise" means industrial and commercial activity or enterprise in a particular area in the United Kingdom, with particular reference to encouraging the formation and development of small businesses.

(5) Condition B is that the body is precluded from paying or transferring any of its income or profit directly or indirectly—

    (*a*) to any of its members, or

    (*b*) to any person charged with the control and direction of its affairs.

(6) The payment of—

    (*a*) reasonable remuneration for goods, labour or power supplied or for services provided,

    (*b*) reasonable interest on money lent, or

    (*c*) reasonable rent for premises,

does not count as a payment or transfer of income or profit for the purposes of subsection (5).

Commentary—*Simon's Taxes* **B2.450**.

Derivation—TA 1988 s 79(4)–(7).

HMRC Manuals—Business Income Manual BIM47610 (local enterprise agency (LEA)).

85 Supplementary provisions with respect to approvals

(1) This section applies for the purposes of section 84.

(2) The relevant national authority may give a body approval that is conditional on its compliance with such requirements as to—

    (*a*) accounts,

    (*b*) provision of information, and

    (*c*) other matters,

as the relevant national authority considers appropriate.

(3) If the relevant national authority approves a body on the basis that it has or is about to have a separate fund (see section 84(3)(*b*))—

    (*a*) the approval must specify the fund, and

    (*b*) section 82 applies only to a contribution to the body made wholly to or for the purposes of the fund.

(4) The relevant national authority must withdraw the approval of a body as a local enterprise agency if—

    (*a*) condition A or B in section 84 is no longer met, or

    (*b*) the body is failing to comply with a requirement imposed as a condition of its approval.

(5) The relevant national authority must give notice of withdrawal to the body concerned, specifying the date from which the withdrawal takes effect (which may be earlier than the date on which the notice is given).

Commentary—*Simon's Taxes* **B2.450**.

Derivation—TA 1988 s 79(4), (8).

HMRC Manuals—Business Income Manual BIM47610 (local enterprise agency (LEA)).

CTA 2009

86 Meaning of "urban regeneration company"

(1) For the purposes of section 82 "urban regeneration company" means any body of persons which the Treasury by order designates as an urban regeneration company for the purposes of that section.

(2) A body may be so designated only if—

    (a) its sole or main function is to co-ordinate the regeneration of a specific urban area in the United Kingdom,

    (b) it is expected to seek to perform that function by creating a plan for the development of that area and trying to secure that the plan is carried into effect, and

    (c) in co-ordinating the regeneration of that area, it is expected to work together with some or all local or other public authorities which exercise functions in relation to the whole or part of that area.

(3) An order under this section may be framed so as to take effect on a date earlier than the making of the order, but not earlier than 3 months before the date on which the order is made.

Commentary—*Simon's Taxes* **B2.450**.
Derivation—TA 1988 s 79B(5)–(8).
HMRC Manuals—Company Taxation Manual CTM41150 (urban regeneration companies (URCs)).
Business Income Manual BIM47610 (urban regeneration company (URC)).

[Contributions to flood and coastal erosion risk management projects

86A Contributions to flood and coastal erosion risk management projects

(1) This section applies if—

    (a) a company carrying on a trade ("the contributor") incurs expenses in making a qualifying contribution to a qualifying flood or coastal erosion risk management project, and

    (b) a deduction would not otherwise be allowable for the expenses in calculating the profits of the trade.

(2) In determining whether the condition in subsection (1)(b) is satisfied, a deduction giving effect to a capital allowance is to be disregarded.

(3) In calculating the profits of the trade, a deduction is allowed under this section for the expenses.

(4) But if, in connection with the making of the contribution, the contributor or a connected person—

    (a) receives a disqualifying benefit, or

    (b) is entitled to receive such a benefit,

no deduction is allowed.

(5) For the purposes of subsection (4) it does not matter whether a person receives, or is entitled to receive, the benefit—

    (a) from the carrying out of the project, or

    (b) from any person.

(6) Subsection (7) applies if—

    (a) a deduction has been made under this section in relation to the contribution, and

    (b) the contributor or a connected person receives—

        (i) a refund of any part of the contribution, if the contribution is a sum of money, or

        (ii) compensation for any part of the contribution, if the contribution is the provision of services,

    in money or money's worth.

(7) The amount of, or an amount equal to the value of, the refund or compensation (so far as not otherwise brought into account in calculating the profits of the trade or treated as a post-cessation receipt)—

    (a) is brought into account in calculating the profits of the trade, as a receipt arising in the accounting period in which the refund or compensation is received, or

    (b) if the contributor has permanently ceased to carry on the trade before the refund or compensation is received, is treated as a post-cessation receipt (see Chapter 15).

(8) In this section "disqualifying benefit" means a benefit consisting of money or other property, but it does not include—

    (a) a refund of the contribution, if the contribution is a sum of money;

    (b) compensation for the contribution, if the contribution is the provision of services;

    (c) a structure that—

        (i) is or is to be used for the purposes of flood or coastal erosion risk management, and

        (ii) is put in place in carrying out the project;

    (d) an addition to a structure where—

        (i) the structure is or is to be used for the purposes of flood or coastal erosion risk management, and

        (ii) the addition is made in carrying out the project;

    (e) land, plant or machinery that is or is to be used, in the realization of the project, for the purposes of flood or coastal erosion risk management;

    (f) a right over land that is or is to be used, in the realization of the project, for the purposes of flood or coastal erosion risk management.

(9) In subsection (8) "structure" includes road, path, pipe, earthwork, plant and machinery.][1]

Commentary—*Simon's Taxes* **B2.411**.
Amendments—[1]   Sections 86A, 86B inserted by FA 2015 s 35, Sch 5 para 3 with effect in relation to contributions paid or provided on or after 1 January 2015.

[86B Interpretation of section 86A

(1) This section applies for the purposes of section 86A.

(2) A flood or coastal erosion risk management project is a qualifying project if—

    (*a*) an English risk management authority has applied to the Environment Agency for a grant under section 16 of the Flood and Water Management Act 2010 in order to fund the project, or

    (*b*) the Environment Agency has determined that it will carry out the project,

and the Environment Agency has allocated funding by way of grant-in-aid to the project.

(3) A contribution to a flood or coastal erosion risk management project is a qualifying contribution if the contribution is made—

    (*a*) for the purposes of the project, and

    (*b*) under an agreement between—

        (i)   the company making the contribution, and

        (ii) the applicant authority or (as the case may be) the Environment Agency,

        or between those two bodies and other persons.

(4) References to a flood risk management project or a coastal erosion risk management project are to be interpreted in accordance with sections 1 to 3 of the Flood and Water Management Act 2010.

(5) In section 86A and this section—

    "contribution", in relation to an accounting period, means—

        (*a*) a sum of money paid in that accounting period, or

        (*b*) any services provided in that accounting period;

    "English risk management authority" has the meaning given by section 6(14) of the Flood and Water Management Act 2010.][1]

Commentary—*Simon's Taxes* **B2.411**.
Amendments—[1]   Sections 86A, 86B inserted by FA 2015 s 35, Sch 5 para 3 with effect in relation to contributions paid or provided on or after 1 January 2015.

Scientific research

87 Expenses of research and development

(1) If a company carrying on a trade incurs expenses of a revenue nature on research and development—

    (*a*) related to the trade, and

    (*b*) directly undertaken by or on behalf of the company,

a deduction is allowed for the expenses in calculating the profits of the trade.

(2) For this purpose expenses incurred on research and development—

    (*a*) do not include expenses incurred in the acquisition of rights in, or arising out of, research and development, but

    (*b*) subject to that, include all expenses incurred in carrying out, or providing facilities for carrying out, research and development.

(3) The reference in this section to research and development related to a trade includes—

    (*a*) research and development which may lead to or facilitate an extension of the trade, and

    (*b*) research and development of a medical nature which has a special relation to the welfare of workers employed in the trade.

(4) The same expenses may not be brought into account under this section in relation to more than one trade.

(5) In this section "research and development" has the meaning given by [section 1138 of CTA 2010][1] and includes oil and gas exploration and appraisal.

Commentary—*Simon's Taxes* **D1.401, D1.401, D1.403, B3.708**.
Amendments—[1]   In sub-s (5) words substituted for words "section 837A of ICTA" by CTA 2010 s 1177, Sch 1 para 594. CTA 2010 has effect for corporation tax purposes for accounting periods ending on or after 1 April 2010, and for income and capital gains tax purposes for the tax year 2010–11 and subsequent tax years.

88 Payments to research associations, universities etc

(1) If a company carrying on a trade—

    (*a*) pays any sum to [a body][1] in the case of which exemption may be claimed under [as a result of section 491 of CTA 2010 (scientific research associations)][1] and which has as its object the undertaking of research and development which may lead to or facilitate an extension of the appropriate class of trade, or

    (*b*) pays to an approved university, college, research institute or other similar institution any sum to be used for scientific research related to the appropriate class of trade,

a deduction is allowed for the sum in calculating the profits of the trade.

(2) The deduction is allowed for the accounting period in which the payment is made.

(3) In this section—

    (*a*) "the appropriate class of trade" means the class of trade to which the trade carried on by the company belongs, and

    (*b*) "scientific research" means any activities in the fields of natural or applied science for the extension of knowledge.

(4) For the purposes of this section a university, college research institute or other similar institution is approved if it is for the time being approved for the purposes of this section by the Secretary of State.

(5) The reference in subsection (1)(*b*) to scientific research related to the appropriate class of trade includes—

    (*a*) scientific research which may lead to or facilitate an extension of trades of the appropriate class, and

    (*b*) scientific research of a medical nature which has a special relation to the welfare of workers employed in trades of the appropriate class.

(6) If a question arises as to—

    (*a*) whether, or

    (*b*) to what extent,

any activities constitute or constituted scientific research, an officer of Revenue and Customs must refer the question for decision to the Secretary of State, whose decision is final.

(7) The same expenses may not be brought into account under this section in relation to more than one trade.

Amendments—[1]   In sub-s (1)(*a*) words substituted for words "an Association" and "section 508 of ICTA" by CTA 2010 s 1177, Sch 1 para 595. CTA 2010 has effect for corporation tax purposes for accounting periods ending on or after 1 April 2010, and for income and capital gains tax purposes for the tax year 2010–11 and subsequent tax years.

Expenses connected with patents, designs and trade marks

89 Expenses connected with patents

In calculating the profits of a trade, a deduction is allowed for expenses incurred—

    (*a*) in obtaining for the purposes of the trade the grant of a patent or the extension of a patent's term, or

    (*b*) in connection with a rejected or abandoned application for a patent made for the purposes of the trade.

Commentary—*Simon's Taxes* **B3.609, B5.331**.

HMRC Manuals—Business Income Manual BIM45951 (costs of obtaining or extending patent rights). BIM45955 (expenditure on acquisition of knowhow).

90 Expenses connected with designs or trade marks

In calculating the profits of a trade, a deduction is allowed for expenses incurred in obtaining for the purposes of the trade—

    (*a*) the registration of a design or trade mark,

    (*b*) the extension of a period for which the right in a registered design subsists, or

    (*c*) the renewal of registration of a trade mark.

Commentary—*Simon's Taxes* **B5.324, B5.350, B5.331**.

HMRC Manuals—Business Income Manual BIM45960 (costs of registering or extending the life of, trade marks and designs).

Export Credits Guarantee Department

91 Payments to Export Credits Guarantee Department

In calculating the profits of a trade, a deduction is allowed for a sum payable by the company carrying on the trade to the Export Credits Guarantee Department—

    (*a*) under an agreement entered into as a result of arrangements made under section 2 of the Export and Investment Guarantees Act 1991 (c 67) (insurance in connection with overseas investment), or

    (*b*) with a view to entering into such an agreement.

Commentary—*Simon's Taxes* **B2.435, B2.445**.

HMRC Manuals—Business Income Manual BIM45580 (export credits guarantee scheme).

Levies under FISMA 2000

92 Levies etc under FISMA 2000

(1) In calculating the profits of a trade carried on by a company, a deduction is allowed for any sum—

    (*a*) spent by the company in paying a levy, or

    (*b*) paid by the company as a result of an award of costs under costs rules,

so far as it is not otherwise allowable.

(2) For the purposes of this section "costs rules" means—

    (*a*) rules made under section 230 of FISMA 2000, or

(*b*) provision relating to costs contained in the standard terms fixed under paragraph 18 of Schedule 17 to FISMA 2000.

(3) For the purposes of this section "levy" means—

    (*a*) a payment required under rules made under section 136(2) of FISMA 2000,

    (*b*) a levy imposed under the Financial Services Compensation Scheme,

    (*c*) a payment required under rules made under section 234 of FISMA 2000,

    (*d*) a payment required under the rules referred to in paragraph 14(1) of Schedule 17 to FISMA 2000 in accordance with paragraph 15(1) of that Schedule, or

    (*e*) a payment required in accordance with the standard terms fixed under paragraph 18 of that Schedule (other than a sum paid as a result of an award of costs under costs rules).

Commentary—*Simon's Taxes* **B5.632**.

[Limited liability partnerships: salaried members]

92A Deductions in relation to salaried members

(1) This section applies in relation to a limited liability partnership if section 1273A(2) (limited liability partnerships: salaried members) applies in the case of a member of the partnership ("M").

(2) In calculating for an accounting period under section 1259 (calculation of firm's profits and losses) the profits of a trade carried on by the limited liability partnership, a deduction is allowed for expenses paid by the partnership in respect of M's employment under section 1273A(2) if no deduction would otherwise be allowed for the payment.

(3) This section is subject to—

    (*a*) section 53 (capital expenditure),

    (*b*) section 54 (expenses not wholly and exclusively for trade etc),

    (*c*) section 1298 (business entertainment and gifts), and

    (*d*) section 1302 (social security contributions).][1]

Commentary—*Simon's Taxes* **B7.514, D7.102**.
Amendments—[1]   Section 92A and preceding crosshead inserted by FA 2014 s 74, Sch 17 para 4(1), (2). This amendment is treated as having come into force on 6 April 2014.

CHAPTER 6

TRADE PROFITS: RECEIPTS
Capital receipts

93 Capital receipts

(1) Items of a capital nature must not be brought into account as receipts in calculating the profits of a trade.

(2) But this does not apply to items which, as a result of any provision of the Corporation Tax Acts, are brought into account as receipts in calculating the profits of the trade.

Commentary—*Simon's Taxes* **B2.202**.
HMRC Manuals—Business Income Manual BIM35002 (exclusion of capital items: introduction).
BIM40060 (capital receipts: particular types of transactions).

Debts released

94 Debts incurred and later released

(1) This section applies if—

    (*a*) in calculating the profits of a trade, a deduction is allowed for the expense giving rise to a debt owed by the company carrying on the trade,

    (*b*) all or part of the debt is released, and

    (*c*) the release is not part of a statutory insolvency arrangement.

(2) The amount released—

    (*a*) is brought into account as a receipt in calculating the profits of the trade, and

    (*b*) is treated as arising in the accounting period in which the release is effected.

Commentary—*Simon's Taxes* **B2.206**.
HMRC Manuals—Business Income Manual BIM40265 (trade debts written back to profit and loss account).
BIM42740 (specific deductions: bad and doubtful debts released).

Amounts received following earlier cessation

95 Acquisition of trade: receipts from transferor's trade

(1) This section applies if—

    (*a*) a person ("the transferor") permanently ceased to carry on a trade at any time,

    (*b*) at that time the transferor transferred to another person ("the transferee") the right to receive sums arising from the carrying on of the trade, and

    (*c*) the transferee subsequently carries on the transferor's trade.

(2) Sums—

    (*a*) which the transferee receives as a result of the transfer, and

    (*b*) which are not brought into account in calculating the profits of the transferor's trade for corporation or income tax purposes of any period before the cessation, are brought into account in calculating the profits of the transferee's trade in the accounting period in which they are received.

(3) Any sums mentioned in subsection (1)(*b*) which are received after the transferor has permanently ceased to carry on the trade are not post-cessation receipts (see Chapter 15).

Commentary—*Simon's Taxes* B2.203, B2.207, B2.802, B2.804.

HMRC Manuals—Business Income Manual BIM90070 (transfer of rights if the transferee carries on the trade).

Reverse premiums

96 Reverse premiums

(1) For the purposes of sections 98 and 99 a payment or other benefit is a reverse premium if—
    (*a*) conditions A, B and C are met, and
    (*b*) it is not excluded by section 97.

(2) Condition A is that a company ("the recipient") receives the payment or other benefit by way of inducement in connection with a transaction being entered into by—
    (*a*) the recipient, or
    (*b*) a person connected with the recipient.

(3) Condition B is that the transaction (the "property transaction") is one under which—
    (*a*) the recipient, or
    (*b*) the person connected with the recipient,
becomes entitled to an estate, interest or right in or over land.

(4) Condition C is that the payment or other benefit is paid or provided by—
    (*a*) the person ("the grantor") by whom the estate, interest or right is granted or was granted at an earlier time,
    (*b*) a person connected with the grantor, or
    (*c*) a nominee of, or a person acting on the directions of, the grantor or a person connected with the grantor.

Commentary—*Simon's Taxes* B2.215E, C2.1233.

Derivation—FA 1999 Sch 6 para 1(1), (2).

HMRC Manuals—Business Income Manual BIM41051 (meaning and terms used in connection with reverse premiums).

97 Excluded cases

(1) A payment or other benefit is not a reverse premium so far as it is brought into account under section 532 of CAA 2001 (the general rule excluding contributions) to reduce the recipient's expenditure qualifying for capital allowances.

(2) A payment or other benefit received in connection with a property transaction is not a reverse premium if—
    (*a*) the person entering into the transaction is an individual, and
    (*b*) the transaction relates to premises occupied or to be occupied by the individual as the individual's only or main residence.

(3) A payment or other benefit is not a reverse premium so far as it is consideration for the transfer of an estate or interest in land which constitutes the sale in a sale and leaseback arrangement.

(4) A "sale and leaseback arrangement" means any such arrangement as is described in [section 681AA(1) or (2) or 681AB(1) or (2) of ITA 2007 or]² [section 835(1) or (2), 836(1) or (2) or 850 of CTA 2010]¹.

Commentary—*Simon's Taxes* B2.215E, C2.1233.

HMRC Manuals—Business Income Manual BIM41140 (specific exclusions of reverse premiums).

Amendments—¹   In sub-s (4) words substituted for words "section 779(1) or (2) or 780(1) of ICTA" by CTA 2010 s 1177, Sch 1 para 596. CTA 2010 has effect for corporation tax purposes for accounting periods ending on or after 1 April 2010, and for income and capital gains tax purposes for the tax year 2010–11 and subsequent tax years.

²   In sub-s (4) words inserted by TIOPA 2010 s 501, Sch 8 paras 262, 263. TIOPA 2010 has effect for corporation tax purposes for accounting periods ending on or after 1 April 2010, for income and capital gains tax purposes for the tax year 2010–11 and subsequent tax years, and for petroleum revenue tax purposes for chargeable periods beginning on or after 1 July 2010.

98 Tax treatment of reverse premiums

(1) A reverse premium is treated for corporation tax purposes as a receipt of a revenue nature.

(2) If the recipient enters into the property transaction for the purposes of a trade carried on (or to be carried on) by the recipient, the reverse premium is brought into account in calculating the profits of the trade.

(3) If subsection (2) does not apply, the reverse premium is charged to corporation tax in accordance with section 250 (reverse premium taxed as property business receipt).

Commentary—*Simon's Taxes* B2.215E, B6.205.

HMRC Manuals—Business Income Manual BIM41055 (reverse premiums: the legislation).

99 Arrangements not at arm's length

(1) This section applies if—
    (*a*) two or more of the parties to the property arrangements are connected persons, and
    (*b*) the terms of those arrangements are not such as would reasonably have been expected if those persons had been dealing at arm's length.

(2) The terms of the property arrangements meet the condition in subsection (1)(*b*) if they differ to a significant extent from the terms which, at the time the arrangements were entered into, would be regarded as normal and reasonable—

(*a*) in the market conditions then prevailing, and

(*b*) between persons dealing with each other at arm's length in the open market.

(3) The whole amount or value of the reverse premium brought into account under section 98 is brought into account in the first relevant period of account.

(4) "The first relevant period of account" means the period of account in which the property transaction is entered into.

(5) However if the recipient enters into the property transaction for the purposes of a trade—

(*a*) which is not then carried on by the recipient, but

(*b*) which the recipient subsequently starts to carry on,

"the first relevant period of account" means the first period of account in which the recipient carries on the trade.

Commentary—*Simon's Taxes* **B2.215E**.
HMRC Manuals—Business Income Manual BIM41130 (the avoidance case: connected persons and property arrangements).
BIM41135 (timing in the avoidance case).

100 Connected persons and property arrangements

For the purposes of this section and sections 96 to 99—

(*a*) persons are treated as connected with each other if they are connected at any time during the period when the property arrangements are entered into, and

(*b*) "the property arrangements" means the property transaction and any arrangements entered into in connection with it (whether before it, at the same time as it or after it).

Commentary—*Simon's Taxes* **B2.215E**.
Derivation—FA 1999 Sch 6 para 8(1), (2).
HMRC Manuals—Business Income Manual BIM41130 (the avoidance case: connected persons and property arrangements).

Other receipts

101 Distribution of assets of mutual concerns

(1) This section applies if—

(*a*) a deduction has been made in calculating the profits of a trade for a payment to a mutual concern for the purposes of its mutual business,

(*b*) the concern is being or has been wound up or dissolved,

(*c*) a company ("the recipient") which is carrying on the trade, or was doing so at the time of the payment, receives money or money's worth representing the concern's assets, and

(*d*) the assets in question represent profits of the mutual business conducted by the concern.

(2) If the recipient is carrying on the trade at the time the money or money's worth is received, the amount or value of the money or money's worth is brought into account as a receipt in calculating the profits of the trade.

(3) If the recipient—

(*a*) is not carrying on the trade at the time the money or money's worth is received, but

(*b*) was doing so at the time of the payment to the mutual concern,

the amount or value of the money or money's worth is treated as a post-cessation receipt (see Chapter 15).

(4) For the purposes of this section money or money's worth represents assets of a mutual concern if it—

(*a*) forms part of the assets of the concern,

(*b*) forms part of the consideration for the transfer of the assets of the concern as part of a scheme of amalgamation or reconstruction which involves its winding up, or

(*c*) consists of the consideration for a transfer or surrender of a right to receive anything falling within paragraph (*a*) or (*b*) and does not give rise to a charge to corporation tax on the company receiving it otherwise than as a result of this section.

(5) If a transfer or surrender of a right to receive anything which—

(*a*) forms part of the assets of a mutual concern, or

(*b*) forms part of the consideration for the transfer of the assets of a mutual concern,

is not at arm's length, the company making the transfer or surrender is treated as receiving consideration equal to the value of the right.

(6) In this section references to a mutual concern are to a body corporate which has at any time carried on a trade which consists of or includes the conduct of mutual business (whether or not confined to the members of the body corporate).

(7) For the purposes of this section a trade does not consist of or include the conduct of mutual business if all the profits of the trade are chargeable to corporation or income tax.

Commentary—*Simon's Taxes* **B1.436, B1.439, B2.804, B6.213**.
HMRC Manuals—Business Income Manual BIM24015 (mutual trading: meaning).
BIM24605 (taxable on first principles or statute).

BIM24615 (what is taxed?).

102 Industrial development grants

(1) This section applies if a company carrying on a trade receives a payment by way of a grant under—

    (a) section 7 or 8 of the Industrial Development Act 1982 (c 52), or

    (b) Article 7, 9 or 30 of the Industrial Development (Northern Ireland) Order 1982 (SI 1982/1083 (NI 15)).

(2) The payment is brought into account as a receipt in calculating the profits of the trade unless—

    (a) the grant is designated as made towards the cost of specified capital expenditure,

    (b) the grant is designated as compensation for the loss of capital assets, or

    (c) the grant is for all or part of a corporation tax liability (including one that has already been met).

Commentary—*Simon's Taxes* **B2.210**.
Derivation—TA 1988 s 93.
HMRC Manuals—Business Income Manual BIM40465 (specific receipts : industrial development grant).

103 Sums recovered under insurance policies etc

(1) This section applies if—

    (a) a deduction has been made for a loss or expense in calculating the profits of a trade,

    (b) a company carrying on the trade recovers a sum under an insurance policy or a contract of indemnity in respect of the loss or expense, and

    (c) the sum is not of a revenue nature.

(2) The sum is brought into account as a receipt in calculating the profits of the trade (but only up to the amount of the deduction).

Commentary—*Simon's Taxes* **B2.211, B2.445**.
HMRC Manuals—Business Income Manual BIM40755 (insurance recoveries: capital recoveries).
BIM45525 (insurance: employees and other key persons).

104 Repayments under FISMA 2000

(1) This section applies if—

    (a) a company carries on a trade, and

    (b) a payment is made to the company as a result of a repayment provision.

(2) The payment is brought into account as a receipt in calculating the profits of the trade.

(3) For the purposes of this section "repayment provision" means—

    (a) any provision made by virtue of section 136(7) or 214(1)(e) of FISMA 2000, or

    (b) any provision made by scheme rules for fees to be refunded in specified circumstances.

(4) In this section "scheme rules" means the rules referred to in paragraph 14(1) of Schedule 17 to FISMA 2000.

Commentary—*Simon's Taxes* **B5.632**.

[CHAPTER 6A

TRADE PROFITS: R&D EXPENDITURE CREDITS]

Amendments—This Chapter (ss 104A–104Y) inserted by FA 2013 s 35, Sch 15 para 1 with effect in relation to expenditure incurred on or after 1 April 2013.

[Claims for credits

104A R&D expenditure credits

(1) A company carrying on a trade may make a claim for an amount (an "R&D expenditure credit") to be brought into account as a receipt in calculating the profits of the trade for an accounting period.

(2) The company is entitled to an R&D expenditure credit for the accounting period if the company has qualifying R&D expenditure which is allowable as a deduction in calculating for corporation tax purposes the profits of the trade for the accounting period.

(3) In the case of a company that is a small or medium-sized enterprise in the accounting period, the company's "qualifying R&D expenditure" means—

    (a) its qualifying expenditure on sub-contracted R&D (see section 104C),

    (b) its subsidised qualifying expenditure (see section 104F), and

    (c) its capped R&D expenditure (see section 104I).

(4) In the case of a company that is a large company throughout the accounting period, the company's "qualifying R&D expenditure" means—

    (a) its qualifying expenditure on in-house direct research and development (see section 104J),

    (b) its qualifying expenditure on contracted out research and development (see section 104K), and

    (c) its qualifying expenditure on contributions to independent research and development (see section 104L).

(5) The amount of an R&D expenditure credit to which a company is entitled is determined in accordance with section 104M.

(6) Section 104N contains provision about the effect of a successful claim for an R&D expenditure credit.

(7) Sections 104U to 104W contain provision about insurance companies and group companies.

[(7A) Section 104WA contains provision about ineligible companies.][2]

(8) Section 104X contains anti-avoidance provision.

(9) Section 104Y contains definitions.

(10) For information about the procedure for making claims under this Chapter, see Schedule 18 to FA 1998, in particular Part 9A of that Schedule.][1]

Commentary—*Simon's Taxes* **D1.414, D1.420, D1.401, D1.409**.

HMRC Manuals—Corporate Intangibles Research & Development Manual CIRD89705 (R&D expenditure credit (RDEC) scheme: overview).

Amendments—[1]   This Chapter (ss 104A–104Y) inserted by FA 2013 s 35, Sch 15 para 1 with effect in relation to expenditure incurred on or after 1 April 2013.

[2]   Sub-s (7A) inserted by F(No 2)A 2015 s 31(1), (2) with effect in relation to expenditure incurred on or after 1 August 2015.

[104B Restriction on claiming relief under Part 13 and credit for same expenditure

A company may not make a claim for an R&D expenditure credit and for relief under Part 13 (additional relief for expenditure on research and development) in respect of the same expenditure.][1]

HMRC Manuals—Corporate Intangibles Research & Development Manual CIRD89705 (RDEC scheme: claims process).

Amendments—[1]   This Chapter (ss 104A–104Y) inserted by FA 2013 s 35, Sch 15 para 1 with effect in relation to expenditure incurred on or after 1 April 2013.

[104BA Restriction on claiming other tax reliefs

(1) For provision prohibiting an R&D expenditure credit being given under this Chapter and relief being given under Chapter 3 of Part 15 (film tax relief), see section 1195(3A).

(2) For provision prohibiting an R&D expenditure credit being given under this Chapter and relief being given under Chapter 3 of Part 15A (television tax relief), see section 1216C(4).

(3) For provision prohibiting an R&D expenditure credit being given under this Chapter and relief being given under Chapter 3 of Part 15B (video games tax relief), see section 1217C(4).

[(4) For provision prohibiting an R&D expenditure credit being given under this Chapter and relief being given under section 1217H or 1217K (theatrical productions: additional deduction or theatre tax credit), see section 1217JA(2).][2]

[(5) For provision prohibiting an R&D expenditure credit being given under this Chapter and relief being given under Chapter 3 of Part 15E (museums and galleries exhibition tax relief), see section 1218ZCG(2).][3]][1]

Amendments—[1]   This section inserted by FA 2013 s 36, Sch 18 para 8.

[2]   Sub-s (4) inserted by FA 2014 s 36, Sch 4 para 9 with effect in relation to accounting periods beginning on or after 1 September 2014, subject to transitional provisions for accounting periods straddling that date (FA 2014 Sch 4 para 17). SI 2014/2228 reg 2 provides that the amendments made by FA 2014 Sch 4 come into force on 22 August 2014 (other than the power to make regulations under Sch 4 para 16(1) which came into force on 17 July 2014).

[3]   Sub-s (5) inserted by F(No 2)A 2017 s 21, Sch 6 paras 9, 10 with effect in relation to accounting periods beginning on or after 1 April 2017.

[SMEs: qualifying expenditure on sub-contracted R&D]

104C Qualifying expenditure on sub-contracted R&D

(1) For the purposes of this Chapter a company's "qualifying expenditure on sub-contracted R&D" means expenditure incurred by it that meets conditions A and B.

(2) Condition A is that the expenditure is incurred on research and development contracted out to the company by—

     (a) a large company, or

     (b) any person otherwise than in the course of carrying on a chargeable trade.

(3) A "chargeable trade" is—

     (a) a trade, profession or vocation carried on wholly or partly in the United Kingdom, the profits of which are chargeable to income tax under Chapter 2 of Part 2 of ITTOIA 2005, or

     (b) a trade carried on wholly or partly in the United Kingdom, the profits of which are chargeable to corporation tax under Chapter 2 of this Part.

(4) Condition B is that the expenditure is expenditure to which section 104D or 104E applies.][1]

Commentary—*Simon's Taxes* **D1.415**.

HMRC Manuals—Corporate Intangibles Research & Development Manual CIRD89750 (RDEC scheme: R&D contracted to a SME).

Amendments—[1]   This Chapter (ss 104A–104Y) inserted by FA 2013 s 35, Sch 15 para 1 with effect in relation to expenditure incurred on or after 1 April 2013.

[104D Expenditure on sub-contracted R&D undertaken in-house

(1) This section applies to expenditure on research and development contracted out to a company if conditions A, B and C are met.

(2) Condition A is that the research and development is undertaken by the company itself.

(3) Condition B is that the expenditure is—

     (a) incurred on staffing costs (see section 1123),

(b) incurred on software or consumable items (see section 1125),

(c) qualifying expenditure on externally provided workers (see section 1127), or

(d) incurred on relevant payments to the subjects of a clinical trial (see section 1140).

(4) Condition C is that the expenditure is attributable to relevant research and development in relation to the company.

(5) See sections 1124, 1126 [to 1126B][2] and 1132 for provision about when expenditure within subsection (3)(a), (b) or (c) is attributable to relevant research and development.][1]

Commentary—*Simon's Taxes* **D1.415.**

HMRC Manuals—Corporate Intangibles Research & Development Manual CIRD89750 (RDEC scheme R&D contracted to a SME).

Amendments—[1]   This Chapter (ss 104A–104Y) inserted by FA 2013 s 35, Sch 15 para 1 with effect in relation to expenditure incurred on or after 1 April 2013.

[2]   In sub-s (5), words inserted by FA 2015 s 28(1), (4) with effect in relation to expenditure incurred on or after 1 April 2015.

[104E Expenditure on sub-contracted R&D not undertaken in-house

(1) This section applies to expenditure on research and development contracted out to a company if conditions A, B and C are met.

(2) Condition A is that the expenditure is incurred in making payments to—

(a) a qualifying body,

(b) an individual, or

(c) a firm, each member of which is an individual,

in respect of research and development contracted out by the company to the body, individual or firm.

(3) Condition B is that the research and development is undertaken by the body, individual or firm itself.

(4) Condition C is that the expenditure is attributable to relevant research and development in relation to the company.

(5) See sections 1124, 1126 [to 1126B][2] and 1132 for provision about when particular kinds of expenditure are attributable to relevant research and development.][1]

Commentary—*Simon's Taxes* **D1.414, D1.414.**

HMRC Manuals—Corporate Intangibles Research & Development Manual CIRD89750 (RDEC scheme: R&D contracted to a SME).

Amendments—[1]   This Chapter (ss 104A–104Y) inserted by FA 2013 s 35, Sch 15 para 1 with effect in relation to expenditure incurred on or after 1 April 2013.

[2]   In sub-s (5), words inserted by FA 2015 s 28(1), (4) with effect in relation to expenditure incurred on or after 1 April 2015.

[SMEs: subsidised qualifying expenditure

104F Subsidised qualifying expenditure

For the purposes of this Chapter a company's "subsidised qualifying expenditure" means—

(a) its subsidised qualifying expenditure on in-house direct research and development (see section 104G), and

(b) its subsidised qualifying expenditure on contracted out research and development (see section 104H).][1]

HMRC Manuals—Corporate Intangibles Research & Development Manual CIRD89760 (RDEC scheme: subsidised qualifying expenditure).

Amendments—[1]   This Chapter (ss 104A–104Y) inserted by FA 2013 s 35, Sch 15 para 1 with effect in relation to expenditure incurred on or after 1 April 2013.

[104G Subsidised qualifying expenditure on in-house direct R&D

(1) A company's "subsidised qualifying expenditure on in-house direct research and development" means expenditure incurred by it in relation to which each of conditions A to D is met.

(2) Condition A is that the expenditure is subsidised.

(3) Condition B is that the expenditure is—

(a) incurred on staffing costs (see section 1123),

(b) incurred on software or consumable items (see section 1125),

(c) qualifying expenditure on externally provided workers (see section 1127), or

(d) incurred on relevant payments to the subjects of a clinical trial (see section 1140).

(4) Condition C is that the expenditure is attributable to relevant research and development undertaken by the company itself.

(5) Condition D is that the expenditure is not incurred by the company in carrying on activities which are contracted out to the company by any person.

(6) See sections 1124, 1126 [to 1126B][2] and 1132 for provision about when expenditure within subsection (3)(a), (b) or (c) is attributable to relevant research and development.][1]

Commentary—*Simon's Taxes* **D1.420A.**

HMRC Manuals—Corporate Intangibles Research & Development Manual CIRD89760 (RDEC scheme: subsidised qualifying expenditure).

Amendments—[1]   This Chapter (ss 104A–104Y) inserted by FA 2013 s 35, Sch 15 para 1 with effect in relation to expenditure incurred on or after 1 April 2013.

[2]   In sub-s (6), words inserted by FA 2015 s 28(1), (4) with effect in relation to expenditure incurred on or after 1 April 2015.

[104H Subsidised qualifying expenditure on contracted out R&D

(1) A company's "subsidised qualifying expenditure on contracted out research and development" means expenditure—

(a) which is incurred by it in making the qualifying element of a sub-contractor payment (see sections 1134 to 1136), and

(b) in relation to which each of conditions A to E is met.

(2) Condition A is that the expenditure is subsidised.

(3) Condition B is that the sub-contractor is—

(a) a qualifying body,

(b) an individual, or

(c) a firm, each member of which is an individual.

(4) Condition C is that the body, individual or firm concerned undertakes the contracted out research and development itself.

(5) Condition D is that the expenditure is attributable to relevant research and development in relation to the company.

(6) Condition E is that the expenditure is not incurred by the company in carrying on activities which are contracted out to the company by any person.

(7) See sections 1124, 1126 [to 1126B]² and 1132 for provision about when particular kinds of expenditure are attributable to relevant research and development.]¹

Commentary—*Simon's Taxes* **D1.416.**
HMRC Manuals—Corporate Intangibles Research & Development Manual CIRD89760 (RDEC scheme: subsidised qualifying expenditure).
Amendments—¹ This Chapter (ss 104A–104Y) inserted by FA 2013 s 35, Sch 15 para 1 with effect in relation to expenditure incurred on or after 1 April 2013.
² In sub-s (7), words inserted by FA 2015 s 28(1), (4) with effect in relation to expenditure incurred on or after 1 April 2015.

[SMEs: capped R&D expenditure

104I Capped R&D expenditure

For the purposes of this Chapter a company's "capped R&D expenditure" means any expenditure—

(a) in respect of which the company is not entitled to relief under Chapter 2 of Part 13 merely because of section 1113 (cap on R&D aid),

(b) which is not qualifying expenditure on sub-contracted R&D, and

(c) which would have been qualifying R&D expenditure had the company been a large company throughout the accounting period in question.]¹

Commentary—*Simon's Taxes* **D1.402A.**
Amendments—¹ This Chapter (ss 104A–104Y) inserted by FA 2013 s 35, Sch 15 para 1 with effect in relation to expenditure incurred on or after 1 April 2013.

[Large companies: qualifying R&D expenditure

104J Qualifying expenditure on in-house direct R&D

(1) A company's "qualifying expenditure on in-house direct research and development" means expenditure incurred by it in relation to which conditions A, B and C are met.

(2) Condition A is that the expenditure is—

(a) incurred on staffing costs (see section 1123),

(b) incurred on software or consumable items (see section 1125),

(c) qualifying expenditure on externally provided workers (see section 1127), or

(d) incurred on relevant payments to the subjects of a clinical trial (see section 1140).

(3) Condition B is that the expenditure is attributable to relevant research and development undertaken by the company itself.

(4) Condition C is that, if the expenditure is incurred in carrying on activities contracted out to the company, the activities are contracted out by—

(a) a large company, or

(b) any person otherwise than in the course of carrying on a chargeable trade.

(5) A "chargeable trade" is—

(a) a trade, profession or vocation carried on wholly or partly in the United Kingdom, the profits of which are chargeable to income tax under Chapter 2 of Part 2 of ITTOIA 2005, or

(b) a trade carried on wholly or partly in the United Kingdom, the profits of which are chargeable to corporation tax under Chapter 2 of this Part.

(6) See sections 1124, 1126 [to 1126B]² and 1132 for provision about when expenditure within subsection (2)(a), (b) or (c) is attributable to relevant research and development.]¹

Commentary—*Simon's Taxes* **D1.409-D1.412.**
HMRC Manuals—Corporate Intangibles Research & Development Manual CIRD89770 (RDEC scheme: qualifying R&D expenditure tax reliefs).
Amendments—¹ This Chapter (ss 104A–104Y) inserted by FA 2013 s 35, Sch 15 para 1 with effect in relation to expenditure incurred on or after 1 April 2013.
² In sub-s (6), words inserted by FA 2015 s 28(1), (4) with effect in relation to expenditure incurred on or after 1 April 2015.

[104K Qualifying expenditure on contracted out R&D

(1) A company's "qualifying expenditure on contracted out research and development" means expenditure incurred by it in relation to which each of conditions A to D is met.

(2) Condition A is that the expenditure is incurred in making payments to—

    (a) a qualifying body,

    (b) an individual, or

    (c) a firm, each member of which is an individual,

in respect of research and development contracted out by the company to the body, individual or firm concerned ("the contracted out R&D").

(3) Condition B is that the body, individual or firm concerned undertakes the contracted out R&D itself.

(4) Condition C is that the expenditure is attributable to relevant research and development in relation to the company.

(5) Condition D is that, if the contracted out R&D is itself contracted out to the company, it is contracted out by—

    (a) a large company, or

    (b) any person otherwise than in the course of carrying on a chargeable trade.

(6) A "chargeable trade" is—

    (a) a trade, profession or vocation carried on wholly or partly in the United Kingdom, the profits of which are chargeable to income tax under Chapter 2 of Part 2 of ITTOIA 2005, or

    (b) a trade carried on wholly or partly in the United Kingdom, the profits of which are chargeable to corporation tax under Chapter 2 of this Part.

(7) See sections 1124, 1126 [to 1126B][2] and 1132 for provision about when particular kinds of expenditure are attributable to relevant research and development.][1]

Commentary—*Simon's Taxes* **D1.414**.

HMRC Manuals—Corporate Intangibles Research & Development Manual CIRD89770 (RDEC scheme: qualifying R&D expenditure tax reliefs).

Amendments—[1] This Chapter (ss 104A–104Y) inserted by FA 2013 s 35, Sch 15 para 1 with effect in relation to expenditure incurred on or after 1 April 2013.

[2] In sub-s (7), words inserted by FA 2015 s 28(1), (4) with effect in relation to expenditure incurred on or after 1 April 2015.

[104L Qualifying expenditure on contributions to independent R&D

(1) A company's "qualifying expenditure on contributions to independent research and development" means expenditure incurred by it in relation to which each of conditions A to E is met.

(2) Condition A is that the expenditure is incurred in making payments to—

    (a) a qualifying body,

    (b) an individual, or

    (c) a firm, each member of which is an individual,

for the purpose of funding research and development carried on by the body, individual or firm concerned ("the funded R&D").

(3) Condition B is that the funded R&D is relevant research and development in relation to the company.

(4) Condition C is that the funded R&D is not contracted out to the qualifying body, individual or firm concerned by another person.

(5) Condition D is that, if the payment is made to an individual, the company is not connected with the individual when the payment is made.

(6) Condition E is that, if the payment is made to a firm (other than a qualifying body), the company is not connected with any member of the firm when the payment is made.][1]

Commentary—*Simon's Taxes* **D1.412**.

HMRC Manuals—Corporate Intangibles Research & Development Manual CIRD89770 (RDEC scheme: qualifying R&D expenditure tax reliefs).

Amendments—[1] This Chapter (ss 104A–104Y) inserted by FA 2013 s 35, Sch 15 para 1 with effect in relation to expenditure incurred on or after 1 April 2013.

[Amount of credit

104M Amount of R&D expenditure credit

(1) The amount of the R&D expenditure credit to which a company is entitled for an accounting period is the relevant percentage of the amount of the company's qualifying R&D expenditure for the period.

(2) In the case of a ring fence trade, the relevant percentage is 49%. In this subsection "ring fence trade" has the meaning given by section 277 of CTA 2010.

(3) In any other case, the relevant percentage is [13%][2].

(4) The Treasury may by order replace the percentage for the time being specified in subsection (2) or (3) with a different percentage.

(5) An order under subsection (4) may contain incidental, supplemental, consequential and transitional provision and savings.][1]

Commentary—*Simon's Taxes* **D1.435A**.

HMRC Manuals—Corporate Intangibles Research & Development Manual CIRD89710 (RDEC scheme: calculation of credit).
Amendments—[1]   This Chapter (ss 104A–104Y) inserted by FA 2013 s 35, Sch 15 para 1 with effect in relation to expenditure incurred on or after 1 April 2013.
[2]   Figure in sub-s (3) substituted for figure "12%" by FA 2020 s 28 with effect in relation to expenditure incurred on or after 1 April 2020.

[Payment of credit

[104N Payment of R&D expenditure credit

(1) This section applies if a company is entitled to an R&D expenditure credit for an accounting period under this Chapter.

(2) The amount to which the company is entitled in respect of the R&D expenditure credit ("the set-off amount") is to be treated in the following way—

Step 1

The set-off amount is to be applied in discharging any liability of the company to pay corporation tax for the accounting period.

If any of the set-off amount is remaining, go to step 2.

Step 2

If the amount remaining after step 1 is greater than the net value of the set-off amount (see subsection (3)), that amount is to be reduced to the net value of the set-off amount.

For provision about the treatment of the amount deducted under this step from the amount remaining after step 1, see section 104O.

Step 3

If the amount remaining after step 2 is greater than the company's total expenditure on workers for the accounting period (see section 104P)—

  (a) that amount is to be reduced to the amount of that expenditure (which may be nil), and

  (b) the amount deducted under paragraph (a) from the amount remaining after step 2 is to be treated for the purposes of this section as an amount of R&D expenditure credit to which the company is entitled for its next accounting period.

If any of the set-off amount is remaining, go to step 4.

Step 4

The amount remaining after step 3 is to be applied in discharging any liability of the company to pay corporation tax for any other accounting period.

If any of the set-off amount is remaining, go to step 5.

Step 5

If the company is a member of a group, it may surrender the whole or any part of the amount remaining after step 4 to any other member of the group (see section 104R).

If no such surrender is made, or any of the set-off amount is otherwise remaining, go to step 6.

Step 6

The amount remaining after step 5 is to be applied in discharging any other liability of the company to pay a sum to the Commissioners under or by virtue of an enactment or under a contract settlement.

If any of the set-off amount is remaining, go to step 7.

Step 7

The amount remaining after step 6 is payable to the company by an officer of Revenue and Customs. But this is subject to section 104S (restrictions on payment of R&D expenditure credit).

(3) To determine the net value of the set-off amount for the purposes of step 2 in subsection (2), deduct from the set-off amount amount A and, in the case of a ring fence trade, amount B.

Amount A is the amount equal to the corporation tax that would be chargeable on the set-off amount if—

  (a) it did not include any amount treated as an amount of R&D expenditure credit for the accounting period by virtue of step 3 in subsection (2), and

  (b) it was an amount of profits (or in the case of a ring fence trade, ring fence profits) of the company for the accounting period and corporation tax on such profits was chargeable at the main rate [(or, in the case of ring fence profits, the main ring fence profits rate)][2].

Amount B is the amount equal to the supplementary charge that would be chargeable on the set-off amount if—

  (a) it did not include any amount treated as an amount of R&D expenditure credit for the accounting period by virtue of step 3 in subsection (2), and

  (b) it was an amount of adjusted ring fence profits for the accounting period.

(4) In this section—

  "adjusted ring fence profits" has the meaning given by section 330(2) of CTA 2010,

  "the Commissioners" means the Commissioners for Her Majesty's Revenue and Customs,

  "contract settlement" means an agreement made in connection with any person's liability to make a payment to the Commissioners under or by virtue of an enactment,

  "ring fence profits" has the meaning given by section 276 of CTA 2010, and

  "ring fence trade" has the meaning given by section 277 of CTA 2010.][1]

Commentary—*Simon's Taxes* **D1.435A.**

HMRC Manuals—Corporate Intangibles Research & Development Manual CIRD89710 (RDEC scheme: calculation of credit), CIRD89920, CIRD89930, CIRD89940, CIRD89950 (practical examples of RDEC calculation). CIRD89780 (RDEC scheme: payment of credit).
Amendments—[1]   This Chapter (ss 104A–104Y) inserted by FA 2013 s 35, Sch 15 para 1 with effect in relation to expenditure incurred on or after 1 April 2013.
[2]   In sub-s (3), in the definition of "*Amount A*", in para (*b*), words inserted by FA 2014 s 7, Sch 1 para 10 with effect for the financial year 2015 and subsequent financial years. For accounting periods straddling 1 April 2015, see FA 2014 Sch 1 para 22.

104O Amounts deducted by way of tax adjustment

(1) This section applies if—
  (*a*) a company is entitled to an R&D expenditure credit for an accounting period under this Chapter, and
  (*b*) the amount of the set-off amount remaining after step 1 in section 104N(2) is greater than the net value of the set-off amount.
(2) An amount equal to the difference between—
  (*a*) the amount remaining after step 1 in section 104N(2), and
  (*b*) the net value of the set-off amount,
("the step 2 amount") is to be applied in discharging any liability of the company to pay corporation tax for any subsequent accounting period.
  This is subject to subsection (3).
(3) If the company is a member of a group, it may surrender the whole or any part of the step 2 amount to any other member of the group (the "relevant group member").
  In such a case, section 104R(3) applies to the amount surrendered as it applies to an amount of R&D expenditure credit surrendered under step 5 in section 104N(2).
(4) If any of the amount surrendered under subsection (3) is remaining after the operation of step 3 in section 104R(3), it is to be treated for the purposes of this section as if it had not been surrendered to the relevant group member.
(5) Any amounts to be applied under subsection (2) or (3) in discharging any liability of a company to pay corporation tax for an accounting period are to be so applied before any amounts that may be so applied under step 1, 4 or 5 in section 104N(2).
(6) The surrender by a company of the whole or any part of the step 2 amount to another company under this section—
  (*a*) is not to be taken into account in determining the profits or losses of either company for corporation tax purposes, and
  (*b*) for corporation tax purposes is not to be regarded as the making of a distribution.
(7) Any reference in this section to the set-off amount, or the net value of the set-off amount, is to be read in accordance with section 104N.][1]

Commentary—*Simon's Taxes* D1.435A.
HMRC Manuals—Corporate Intangibles Research & Development Manual CIRD89780 (RDEC scheme: payment of credit).
Amendments—[1]   This Chapter (ss 104A–104Y) inserted by FA 2013 s 35, Sch 15 para 1 with effect in relation to expenditure incurred on or after 1 April 2013.

[104P Total expenditure on workers

(1) For the purposes of section 104N, the amount of a company's total expenditure on workers for an accounting period is the sum of—
  (*a*) the relevant portion of the company's staffing costs for the period (see subsection (2)), and
  (*b*) if the company is a member of a group and has incurred expenditure on any externally provided workers, the relevant portion of any staffing costs for the period incurred by another member of the group (the "relevant group company") in providing any of those workers for the company (see subsection (3)).
(2) The relevant portion of the company's staffing costs for an accounting period is the amount of those costs that—
  (*a*) are paid to, or in respect of, directors or employees who are directly and actively engaged in relevant research and development (whether they are wholly or partly so engaged), and
  (*b*) form part of the total amount of the company's PAYE and NIC liabilities for the accounting period (see section 104Q).
(3) The relevant portion of any staffing costs for an accounting period incurred by a relevant group company in providing externally provided workers for the company is the sum of the amounts to be determined in the case of each of those workers as follows—
Step 1
Calculate the amount of expenditure that—
  (*a*) has been incurred by the relevant group company in providing the externally provided worker for the company,
  (*b*) has been incurred on staffing costs, and
  (*c*) forms part of the total amount of the relevant group company's PAYE and NIC liabilities for the accounting period (see section 104Q).

(2) For the purposes of this Chapter the company is to be treated as if it were not such an enterprise in the period (and accordingly is to be treated as a large company for the purposes of this Chapter).
(3) Section 1119 (meaning of "small or medium-sized enterprise"), as it has effect for the purposes of this Chapter (see section 104Y), is to be read subject to this section.][1]

HMRC Manuals—Corporate Intangibles Research & Development Manual CIRD89830 (RDEC scheme: insurance companies treated as large companies and IE basis).
Amendments—[1] This Chapter (ss 104A–104Y) inserted by FA 2013 s 35, Sch 15 para 1 with effect in relation to expenditure incurred on or after 1 April 2013.

[104V Entitlement to credit: I minus E basis
(1) This section applies if—
   (a) for an accounting period, an insurance company is charged to tax in respect of its basic life assurance and general annuity business in accordance with the I-E rules, and
   (b) the calculation of the company's charge to tax for the period in respect of that business does not involve the calculation of any BLAGAB trade profit or loss of the company.
(2) Section 104A has effect as if—
   (a) the reference in subsection (1) to calculating the profits of a trade were a reference to calculating the I-E profit of the basic life assurance and general annuity business carried on by the company, and
   (b) the reference in subsection (2) to qualifying R&D expenditure allowable as a deduction in calculating the profits of a trade for an accounting period were a reference to any such expenditure that would be allowable as such a deduction if the company were to calculate its BLAGAB trade profit or loss for the period.
(3) Any receipt to be brought into account by virtue of this section is to be treated for the purposes of section 92 of FA 2012 (certain BLAGAB trading receipts to count as deemed I-E receipts) as if it had been taken into account in calculating the company's BLAGAB trade profit or loss for the period.
(4) In this section "BLAGAB trade profit" and "BLAGAB trade loss" have the meaning given by section 136 of FA 2012.][1]

HMRC Manuals—Corporate Intangibles Research & Development Manual CIRD89830 (RDEC scheme: insurance companies treated as large companies and IE basis).
Amendments—[1] This Chapter (ss 104A–104Y) inserted by FA 2013 s 35 , Sch 15 para 1 with effect in relation to expenditure incurred on or after 1 April 2013.

[Group companies

104W R&D expenditure of group companies
(1) This section applies if—
   (a) a company ("A") incurs expenditure on making a payment to another company ("B") in respect of activities contracted out by A to B,
   (b) the activities would, if carried out by A, be research and development of A (taken together with A's other activities), and
   (c) A and B are members of the same group at the time the payment is made.
(2) If the activities are undertaken by B itself, they are to be treated for the purposes of this Chapter (so far as it would not otherwise be the case) as research and development undertaken by B itself.
(3) If B makes a payment to a third party ("C"), any of the activities—
   (a) contracted out by B to C, and
   (b) undertaken by C itself,
are to be treated for the purposes of this Chapter (so far as it would not otherwise be the case) as research and development contracted out by B to C.][1]

Commentary—*Simon's Taxes* D1.414.
HMRC Manuals—Corporate Intangibles Research & Development Manual CIRD89720 (RDEC scheme: groups).
Amendments—[1] This Chapter (ss 104A–104Y) inserted by FA 2013 s 35, Sch 15 para 1 with effect in relation to expenditure incurred on or after 1 April 2013.

[Ineligible companies

104WA Ineligible companies
(1) No claim for an R&D expenditure credit may be made in respect of expenditure incurred by an ineligible company.
(2) In this section, "ineligible company" means a company that is—
   (a) an institution of higher education (as defined by section 1142(1)(b)),
   (b) a charity, or
   (c) a company of a description prescribed by the Treasury by regulations.][1]

Amendments—[1] This section inserted by F(No 2)A 2015 s 31(1), (3) with effect in relation to expenditure incurred on or after 1 August 2015.

[Anti-avoidance

104X Artificially inflated claims for credit

(1) To the extent that a transaction is attributable to arrangements entered into wholly or mainly for a disqualifying purpose, it is to be disregarded for the purpose of determining for an accounting period R&D expenditure credits to which a company is entitled under this Chapter.

(2) Arrangements are entered into wholly or mainly for a "disqualifying purpose" if their main object, or one of their main objects, is to enable a company to obtain—

    (*a*) an R&D expenditure credit under this Chapter to which it would not otherwise be entitled, or

    (*b*) an R&D expenditure credit under this Chapter of a greater amount than that to which it would otherwise be entitled.

(3) In this section "arrangements" includes any scheme, agreement or understanding, whether or not legally enforceable.][1]

Commentary—*Simon's Taxes* **D1.442.**
HMRC Manuals—Corporate Intangibles Research & Development Manual CIRD97100 (R&D tax relief: types of avoidance).
Amendments—[1] This Chapter (ss 104A–104Y) inserted by FA 2013 s 35, Sch 15 para 1 with effect in relation to expenditure incurred on or after 1 April 2013.

[Interpretation

104Y Interpretation

(1) In this Chapter the following terms have the same meaning as they have in Part 13 (additional relief for expenditure on R&D)—

    "large company" (see section 1122),
    "payment period" (see section 1141),
    "qualifying body" (see section 1142),
    "relevant research and development" (see section 1042),
    "research and development" (see section 1041),
    "small or medium-sized enterprise" (see section 1119).

(2) The following sections apply for the purposes of this Chapter as they apply for the purposes of Part 13—

    sections 1123 and 1124 (staffing costs),
    sections 1125 [to 1126B][2] (software or consumable items),
    sections 1127 to 1132 (qualifying expenditure on externally provided workers),
    sections 1133 to 1136 (sub-contractor payments),
    section 1138 ("subsidised expenditure"),
    section 1140 (relevant payments to the subjects of a clinical trial).

(3) For the purposes of this Chapter two companies are members of the same group if they are members of the same group of companies for the purposes of Part 5 of CTA 2010 (group relief).][1]

Commentary—*Simon's Taxes* **D1.414.**
Amendments—[1] This Chapter (ss 104A–104Y) inserted by FA 2013 s 35, Sch 15 para 1 with effect in relation to expenditure incurred on or after 1 April 2013.
[2] In sub-s (2), words substituted by FA 2015 s 28(1), (5) with effect in relation to expenditure incurred on or after 1 April 2015.

CHAPTER 7

TRADE PROFITS: GIFTS TO CHARITIES ETC

Relief for certain gifts

105 Gifts of trading stock to charities etc

(1) This section applies if a company carrying on a trade ("the donor") gives an article for the purposes of—

    (*a*) a charity, a registered club or a body listed in subsection (4), or

    (*b*) a designated educational establishment (see section 106),

and the article is one manufactured, or of a class or description sold, by the donor in the course of the trade.

(2) In calculating the profits of the trade, no amount is required to be brought into account as a receipt in consequence of the disposal of the article.

(3) In this section[1] "registered club" has the meaning given by [section 658(6) of CTA 2010][1] (relief for community amateur sports clubs).

(4) The bodies referred to in subsection (1)(*a*) are—

    (*a*) the Trustees of the National Heritage Memorial Fund, [and][3]

    (*b*) the Historic Buildings and Monuments Commission for England, . . . [3]

    (*c*) . . . [3]

(5) This section needs to be read with section 108 (receipt of benefits by donor or connected person).

[(6) This section is subject to section 203 of CTA 2010 (certain disposals of investments to charity)[1] [and section 939F of that Act (removal of corporation tax relief in respect of tainted charity donations etc)][2].

Commentary—*Simon's Taxes* **B2.442, D1.323**.

HMRC Manuals—Business Income Manual BIM45155 (relief for gifts of trading stock to charities and other bodies).

Amendments—[1]   In sub-s (3) words substituted for words "paragraph 1 of Schedule 18 to FA 2002", sub-s (6) inserted by CTA 2010 s 1177, Sch 1 para 597. CTA 2010 has effect for corporation tax purposes for accounting periods ending on or after 1 April 2010, and for income and capital gains tax purposes for the tax year 2010–11 and subsequent tax years.

[2]   In sub-s (6) words inserted by FA 2011 s 27, Sch 3 para 17 with effect in relation to relievable charity donations made on or after 1 April 2011.

[3]   In sub-s (4)(*a*), word inserted, and sub-s (4)para (*c*) and preceding word repealed by the Public Bodies (Abolition of the National Endowment for Science, Technology and the Arts) Order, SI 2012/964 art 3(1), Schedule with effect from 1 April 2012.

106 Meaning of "designated educational establishment"

(1) For the purposes of section 105 "designated educational establishment" means an educational establishment designated, or within a category designated, in regulations made—

    (*a*) for England and Scotland, by the Secretary of State,

    (*b*) for Wales, by the Welsh Ministers, and

    (*c*) for Northern Ireland, by the Department of Education.

(2) The regulations may make different provision for different areas.

(3) If any question arises as to whether an educational establishment is within a category designated in the regulations, an officer of Revenue and Customs must refer the question for decision—

    (*a*) in the case of an establishment in England or Scotland, to the Secretary of State,

    (*b*) in the case of an establishment in Wales, to the Welsh Ministers, and

    (*c*) in the case of an establishment in Northern Ireland, to the Department of Education.

(4) The power of the Secretary of State or the Welsh Ministers to make regulations under this section is exercisable by statutory instrument.

(5) A statutory instrument containing any regulations made by the Secretary of State under this section is subject to annulment in pursuance of a resolution of the House of Commons.

(6) A statutory instrument containing any regulations made by the Welsh Ministers under this section is subject to annulment in pursuance of a resolution of the National Assembly for Wales.

(7) Regulations made under this section by the Department of Education—

    (*a*) are a statutory rule for the purposes of the Statutory Rules (Northern Ireland) Order 1979 (SI 1979/1573 (NI 12)), and

    (*b*) are subject to negative resolution within the meaning of section 41(6) of the Interpretation Act (Northern Ireland) 1954 (c 33 (NI)).

Commentary—*Simon's Taxes* **B2.442**.

HMRC Manuals—Business Income Manual BIM45170 (designated educational establishments: tax relief).

107 Gifts of medical supplies and equipment

(1) This section applies if—

    (*a*) a company carrying on a trade makes a gift from trading stock of medical supplies or medical equipment,

    (*b*) it makes the gift for humanitarian purposes, and

    (*c*) the supplies or equipment are for human use.

(2) In calculating the profits of the trade, no amount is required to be brought into account as a receipt in consequence of the gift.

(3) In calculating the profits of the trade, a deduction is allowed for any costs of transportation, delivery or distribution incurred by the company in making the gift.

(4) The deduction is allowed for the accounting period in which the costs are incurred.

(5) The Treasury may by order provide that this section is not to have effect in relation to medical supplies or medical equipment of any description specified in the order.

(6) This section needs to be read with section 108 (receipt of benefits by donor or connected person).

Commentary—*Simon's Taxes* **B2.442, D1.353**.

HMRC Manuals—Business Income Manual BIM45175 (relief for gifts of medical supplies and equipment by companies: introduction).

BIM45180 (relief for gifts of medical supplies and equipment by companies: details of the relief).

BIM45185 (relief for gifts of medical supplies and equipment by companies: definitions).

BIM45190 (relief for gifts of medical supplies and equipment by companies: world health organisation guidelines).

Benefits associated with gifts

108 Receipt of benefits by donor or connected person

(1) This section applies if a company carrying on a trade makes a gift in relation to which relief is given under—

    (*a*) section 105,

    (*b*) section 107(2), or

    (*c*) section 63(2) of CAA 2001 (gifts to charities etc of plant or machinery used in the trade),

and the company, or a person connected with the company, receives a benefit which is in any way attributable to the making of the gift.

(2) This section also applies if—

(*a*) relief is given under section 107(3) for costs of transportation, delivery or distribution incurred by a company carrying on a trade, and

(*b*) the company, or a person connected with the company, receives a benefit which is in any way attributable to the company's incurring of those costs.

(3) An amount equal to the value of the benefit—

(*a*) is brought into account in calculating the profits of the trade, as a receipt of the trade arising in the accounting period in which the benefit is received, or

(*b*) if the company has permanently ceased to carry on the trade before the benefit is received, is treated as a post-cessation receipt (see Chapter 15).

Commentary—*Simon's Taxes* **B2.442, B2.804, B6.213, D1.353.**
HMRC Manuals—Business Income Manual BIM45155 (relief for gifts of trading stock to charities and other bodies).
BIM45165 (relief for gifts of plant and machinery to charities and other bodies).
BIM45180 (relief for gifts of medical supplies and equipment by companies: details of the relief).

CHAPTER 8

TRADE PROFITS: HERD BASIS RULES

Introduction

109 Election for application of herd basis rules

(1) A company, or a firm of which a company is a member, which keeps or has kept a production herd for the purposes of a trade may make an election under this Chapter (a "herd basis election").

(2) In calculating the profits of the trade, animals which are part of a production herd in relation to which a herd basis election has effect—

(*a*) are not treated as trading stock (see section 50), but

(*b*) are treated instead in accordance with sections 112 to 121 ("the herd basis rules").

(3) This Chapter is expressed in terms of farmers but applies to any company, or firm of which a company is a member, which keeps or has kept a production herd for the purposes of a trade, whether or not the trade is farming.

(4) References in this Chapter to keeping a production herd are to keeping it for the purposes of the trade.

Commentary—*Simon's Taxes* **A4.131, B5.101, B5.152**
Derivation—TA 1988 Sch 5 paras 1(2), (3), 2(1), 3(1), 9(1).
HMRC Manuals—Business Income Manual BIM55501 (overview of the herd basis).
BIM55505 (operation of herd basis: main rules).
BIM55515 (which rule to apply).
BIM55565 (who can elect).

110 Meaning of "animal", "herd", "production herd" etc

(1) In this Chapter—

(*a*) "animal" means any animal or other living creature,

(*b*) "herd" includes a flock and any other collection of animals (however named), and

(*c*) "production herd" means, in relation to a farmer, a herd of animals of the same species (irrespective of breed) kept by the farmer wholly or mainly for the products obtainable from the living animal which the animals produce for the farmer to sell.

(2) For this purpose "the products obtainable from the living animal" means—

(*a*) the young of the animal, or

(*b*) any other product obtainable from the animal without slaughtering it.

(3) For the purposes of this Chapter the general rule is that immature animals kept in a production herd are not part of the herd.

(4) There is an exception to this rule if—

(*a*) the nature of the land on which the herd is kept means that animals which die or cease to be part of the herd can be replaced only by animals bred and reared on the land,

(*b*) the immature animals in question are bred in the herd and are maintained in the herd for the purpose of replacing other animals, and

(*c*) it is necessary to maintain the immature animals for that purpose.

(5) In that case the immature animals are part of the herd for the purposes of this Chapter, but only so far as they are required to prevent a fall in the numbers of the herd.

(6) References in this Chapter to an animal being added to a herd include references to an immature animal that is not part of the herd reaching maturity.

(7) This Chapter applies—

(*a*) in relation to animals kept singly as it applies in relation to herds, and

(*b*) in relation to shares in animals as it applies in relation to animals themselves.

Commentary—*Simon's Taxes* **B5.151, B5.153.**
Derivation—TA 1988 Sch 5 paras 8(1)–(5), 9(2), (4).
HMRC Manuals—Business Income Manual BIM55570 (what animals are covered).
BIM55575 (immature animals).
BIM55580 (heafted flocks of hill sheep).

BIM55590 (class of herd).
BIM55635 (shares in animals).
BIM55640 (share farming and the herd basis).
BIM55720 (studs farms on the herd basis).

111 Other interpretative provisions

(1) This section applies for the purposes of this Chapter.

(2) A production herd kept by a farmer is of the same class as another production herd only if—

    (*a*) the animals kept in both herds are of the same species (irrespective of breed), and

    (*b*) the products produced for the farmer to sell (for which the herds are wholly or mainly kept) are of the same kinds in both herds.

(3) References to the sale of an animal include references to its death or destruction.

(4) References to the sale proceeds of an animal include references to—

    (*a*) money received from an insurer because of the animal's death or destruction,

    (*b*) compensation money received because of the animal's death or destruction, and

    (*c*) the sale proceeds of the animal's carcass or any part of its carcass.

(5) Female animals become mature—

    (*a*) in the case of laying birds, when they first lay, and

    (*b*) in any other case, when they produce their first young.

(6) 20% or more of a herd is a substantial part of the herd, but a lesser percentage than 20% is capable of being a substantial part of the herd depending on the circumstances of the case concerned.

Commentary—*Simon's Taxes* **B5.142, B5.151, B5.152.**
HMRC Manuals—Business Income Manual BIM55575 (immature animals).
BIM55525 (what constitutes substantial reduction).

The herd basis rules

112 Initial cost of herd and value of herd

(1) In calculating the profits of the trade, no deduction is allowed for the initial cost of the herd.

(2) In calculating the profits of the trade, the value of the herd is not brought into account.

Commentary—*Simon's Taxes* **B5.153**.
Derivation—TA 1988 Sch 5 para 3(2).
HMRC Manuals—Business Income Manual BIM55530 (initial cost of herd and cost of additions).

113 Addition of animals to herd

(1) This section applies for the purpose of calculating the profits of the trade if an animal is added to the herd, unless it replaces another animal in the herd.

(2) No deduction is allowed for the cost of the animal.

(3) If, immediately before it was added to the herd, the animal was part of the farmer's trading stock, the balancing amount is brought into account as a receipt.

(4) "The balancing amount" means—

    (*a*) in the case of an animal bred by the farmer, the cost of breeding the animal and rearing it to maturity, and

    (*b*) in any other case, the sum of the initial cost of acquiring the animal and the cost (if any) incurred by the farmer in rearing the animal to maturity.

Commentary—*Simon's Taxes* **B5.153**.
Derivation—TA 1988 Sch 5 para 3(2), (3).
HMRC Manuals—Business Income Manual BIM55530 (initial cost of herd and cost of additions).

114 Replacement of animals in herd

(1) This section applies for the purpose of calculating the profits of the trade if—

    (*a*) an animal ("the old animal") is sold from the herd or otherwise ceases to be part of the herd, and

    (*b*) it is replaced in the herd by another animal ("the new animal").

(2) The sale proceeds (if any) of the old animal are brought into account as a receipt.

(3) But this needs to be read with—

    (*a*) section 115 (amount of receipt if old animal slaughtered under disease control order),

    (*b*) section 118 (acquisition of new herd begun within 5 years of sale), and

    (*c*) section 120 (replacement of part sold begun within 5 years of sale).

(4) Except so far as otherwise allowable, a deduction is allowed under this section for the cost of the new animal.

(5) But if the new animal is of better quality than the old animal, the amount of the deduction must not exceed the amount that it would have been necessary to spend to replace the old animal with an animal of the same quality.

Commentary—*Simon's Taxes* **B5.153**.
Derivation—TA 1988 Sch 5 para 3(4), (5).
HMRC Manuals—Business Income Manual BIM55520 (what constitutes a replacement).
BIM55535 (replacements).

115 Amount of receipt if old animal slaughtered under disease control order

(1) This section applies for the purposes of section 114.

(2) If—

    (a) the old animal was slaughtered under a disease control order, and

    (b) the new animal is of worse quality than the old animal,

the amount brought into account as a receipt under section 114 must not exceed the equivalent amount for the new animal.

(3) For this purpose "a disease control order" means an order made under the law relating to the diseases of animals by—

    (a) central government,

    (b) a devolved authority,

    (c) a local authority, or

    (d) another public authority.

(4) If, immediately before it was added to the herd, the new animal was part of the farmer's trading stock, "the equivalent amount for the new animal" means—

    (a) in the case of an animal bred by the farmer, the cost of breeding the animal and rearing it to maturity, and

    (b) in any other case, the sum of the initial cost of acquiring the animal and the cost (if any) incurred by the farmer in rearing the animal to maturity.

(5) Otherwise "the equivalent amount for the new animal" means the cost of the new animal.

116 Sale of animals from herd

(1) This section applies for the purpose of calculating the profits of the trade if an animal is sold from the herd unless—

    (a) it is replaced in the herd by another animal (see section 114), or

    (b) it is sold as part of the sale of the whole or a substantial part of the herd that takes place all at once or over a period not longer than 12 months (see section 117).

(2) A profit arising from the sale is brought into account as a receipt.

(3) A deduction is allowed for a loss arising from the sale.

(4) The amount of the profit or loss is the difference between the sale proceeds of the animal and the deductible amount for the animal.

(5) "The deductible amount for the animal" means—

    (a) in the case of an animal bred by the farmer, the cost of breeding the animal and rearing it to maturity,

    (b) in the case of an animal acquired by the farmer for valuable consideration, the sum of the initial cost to the farmer of acquiring the animal and the cost (if any) incurred by the farmer in rearing the animal to maturity, and

    (c) in the case of an animal acquired by the farmer but not for valuable consideration, the sum of the market value of the animal when acquired and the cost (if any) incurred by the farmer in rearing the animal to maturity.

Commentary—*Simon's Taxes* **B5.153**.
Derivation—TA 1988 Sch 5 para 3(10).
HMRC Manuals—Business Income Manual BIM55550 (minor disposals from the herd without replacement). BIM55555 (identification of animals disposed of).

117 Sale of whole or substantial part of herd

(1) This section applies for the purpose of calculating the profits of the trade if, either all at once or over a period not longer than 12 months, the herd or a substantial part of the herd is sold unless—

    (a) section 118 applies (acquisition of new herd begun within 5 years of sale), or

    (b) section 120 applies (replacement of part sold begun within 5 years of sale),

but paragraph (a) is subject to subsection (5) of section 118 (so far as that section provides for a case in which this section is to apply).

(2) A profit arising from the sale is not brought into account as a receipt.

(3) No deduction is allowed for a loss arising from the sale.

Commentary—*Simon's Taxes* **B5.153**.
HMRC Manuals—Business Income Manual BIM55540 (disposal of whole or substantial part of herd without replacement).

118 Acquisition of new herd begun within 5 years of sale

(1) This section applies for the purpose of calculating the profits of the trade if—

    (a) either all at once or over a period not longer than 12 months, the herd ("the old herd") is sold, and

    (b) the farmer acquires or starts to acquire another production herd of the same class ("the new herd") within 5 years of the sale.

(2) Section 114 (replacement of animals in herd) applies as if a number of animals equal to—

    (a) the number of animals in the old herd, or

    (b) if smaller, the number of animals in the new herd,

had been sold from the old herd and replaced in that herd (but see section 119 (sale for reasons outside farmer's control)).

(3) For the purposes of section 114, the sale proceeds of an animal that is treated as a result of subsection (2) above as if it had been—

    (*a*) sold from the old herd, and

    (*b*) replaced in that herd by another animal ("the new animal"),

are not brought into account as a receipt until the new animal is acquired.

(4) If—

    (*a*) the number of animals in the new herd is smaller than the number of animals in the old herd, and

    (*b*) the difference is not substantial,

section 116 (sale of animals from herd) applies as if a number of animals equal to the difference had been sold from the old herd.

(5) If the number of animals in the new herd is smaller than the number of animals in the old herd and the difference is substantial—

    (*a*) section 117 (sale of whole or substantial part of herd where replacement not begun within 5 years), or

    (*b*) section 120 (sale of substantial part of herd where replacement begun within 5 years),

applies as if a number of animals equal to the difference had been sold from the old herd.

(6) If the number of animals in the new herd is larger than the number of animals in the old herd, section 113 (addition of animals to herd) applies as if a number of animals equal to the difference had been added to the old herd.

(7) For the purposes of this section—

    (*a*) if the difference between the number of animals in the new herd and the number of animals in the old herd is equal to 20% or more of the number of animals in the old herd, the difference is substantial, but

    (*b*) a lesser percentage than 20% is capable of being a substantial difference depending on the circumstances of the case concerned.

Commentary—*Simon's Taxes* **B5.153**.

HMRC Manuals—Business Income Manual BIM55545 (acquisition of new animals following a major disposal).

119 Section 118: sale for reasons outside farmer's control

(1) This section applies for the purposes of section 114, as applied by section 118(2).

(2) If—

    (*a*) the farmer was compelled to sell the old herd for reasons wholly outside the farmer's control, and

    (*b*) an animal ("the new animal") that is treated as a result of section 118(2) as if it replaced an animal sold ("the old animal") is of worse quality than the old animal,

the amount brought into account as a receipt under section 114 must not exceed the equivalent amount for the new animal.

(3) If, immediately before it was added to the herd, the new animal was part of the farmer's trading stock, "the equivalent amount for the new animal" means—

    (*a*) in the case of an animal bred by the farmer, the cost of breeding the animal and rearing it to maturity, and

    (*b*) in any other case, the sum of the initial cost of acquiring the animal and the cost (if any) incurred by the farmer in rearing the animal to maturity.

(4) Otherwise "the equivalent amount for the new animal" means the cost of the new animal.

120 Replacement of part sold begun within 5 years of sale

(1) This section applies for the purpose of calculating the profits of the trade if—

    (*a*) either all at once or over a period not longer than 12 months, a substantial part of the herd is sold, and

    (*b*) the farmer acquires or starts to acquire animals to replace the part sold within 5 years of the sale.

(2) Section 114 (replacement of animals in herd) applies so far as the animals included in the part sold are replaced (but see section 121 (sale for reasons outside farmer's control)).

(3) The sale proceeds of an animal included in the part sold are not brought into account as a receipt until the animal that replaces it in the herd is acquired.

(4) If some of the animals included in the part sold are not replaced—

    (*a*) a profit arising from their sale is not brought into account as a receipt, and

    (*b*) no deduction is allowed for a loss arising from their sale.

121 Section 120: sale for reasons outside farmer's control

(1) This section applies for the purposes of section 114, as applied by section 120(2).

(2) If—

(a) the farmer was compelled to sell the part of the herd for reasons wholly outside the farmer's control, and

(b) an animal ("the new animal") that replaces an animal sold ("the old animal") is of worse quality than the old animal,

the amount brought into account as a receipt under section 114 must not exceed the equivalent amount for the new animal.

(3) If, immediately before it was added to the herd, the new animal was part of the farmer's trading stock, "the equivalent amount for the new animal" means—

(a) in the case of an animal bred by the farmer, the cost of breeding the animal and rearing it to maturity, and

(b) in any other case, the sum of the initial cost of acquiring the animal and the cost (if any) incurred by the farmer in rearing the animal to maturity.

(4) Otherwise "the equivalent amount for the new animal" means the cost of the new animal.

Commentary—*Simon's Taxes* **B5.153**.

Elections

122 Herd basis elections

(1) A herd basis election must specify the class of production herd to which it relates.

(2) A herd basis election must be made—

(a) not later than two years after the end of the first relevant accounting period (if the farmer is not a firm), or

(b) on or before the first anniversary of the normal self-assessment filing date for the tax year in which the first relevant period of account ends (if the farmer is a firm).

(3) For this purpose—

(a) "the first relevant accounting period" means the first accounting period in which the farmer making the election keeps a production herd of the class to which the election relates, and

(b) "the first relevant period of account" means the first period of account in which the firm making the election keeps a production herd of the class to which the election relates (but see subsection (8)).

(4) A herd basis election cannot relate to more than one class of production herd, but separate elections may be made for different classes.

(5) A herd basis election is irrevocable.

(6) A herd basis election has effect in relation to all production herds of the class to which it relates, including any which the farmer—

(a) has ceased to keep before making the election, or

(b) first keeps after making the election.

(7) A herd basis election has effect—

(a) for every accounting period in which the farmer carries on the trade and keeps a production herd of the class to which the election relates (if the farmer is not a firm), or

(b) for every period of account in which the farmer carries on the trade and keeps a production herd of the class to which the election relates (if the farmer is a firm).

(8) If the farmer is a firm and there is a change in the persons who are partners in the firm—

(a) any herd basis election made by the old firm ceases to have effect, and

(b) in relation to the new firm, "the first relevant period of account" means the first period of account in which the new firm keeps a production herd of the class to which the election relates.

Commentary—*Simon's Taxes* **B5.152, E1.265**.
Derivation—TA 1988 Sch 5 para 2(1)–(4), (6).
HMRC Manuals—Business Income Manual BIM55585 (elections for the herd basis).
BIM55590 (class of herd).
BIM55600 (time limit for making election).
BIM55630 (continuing effect of an election).

123 Five year gap in which no production herd kept

(1) This section applies if a farmer—

(a) keeps a production herd of a particular class, and

(b) ceases altogether to keep herds of that class for a period of at least 5 years.

(2) If the farmer keeps a production herd of that class after the end of that period—

(a) the accounting period or (as the case may be) period of account in which the farmer starts to keep the herd is treated as the first accounting period or period of account in which the farmer keeps a production herd of that class, and

(b) any herd basis election previously made by the farmer in relation to production herds of that class ceases to have effect.

Commentary—*Simon's Taxes* **B5.152**.

124 Slaughter under disease control order

(1) This section applies if—

(*a*) the whole or a substantial part of a production herd kept by a farmer is slaughtered under a disease control order, and

(*b*) the circumstances of the slaughter are such that compensation is payable in respect of the animals slaughtered.

(2) The farmer may make a herd basis election in respect of the class of production herd involved in the slaughter as if the accounting period or (as the case may be) period of account—

(*a*) in which the compensation falls to be brought into account in calculating the profits of the trade, or

(*b*) in which it would (but for the election) fall to be so brought into account,

were the first accounting period or period of account in which the farmer keeps a production herd of that class.

(3) An election made as a result of this section has effect for that accounting period or period of account and every subsequent accounting period or period of account in which the farmer—

(*a*) carries on the trade, and

(*b*) keeps a production herd of the class to which the election relates.

(4) In this section "disease control order" means an order made under the law relating to the diseases of animals by—

(*a*) central government,

(*b*) a devolved authority,

(*c*) a local authority, or

(*d*) another public authority.

Commentary—*Simon's Taxes* **B5.142, B5.152, E1.265**.
Derivation—TA 1988 Sch 5 para 6.
HMRC Manuals—Business Income Manual BIM55180 (compensation received for compulsory slaughter of animals). BIM55605 (new right of election: compulsory slaughter).

Preventing abuse of the herd basis rules

125 Preventing abuse of the herd basis rules

(1) This section applies if—

(*a*) a person carrying on a trade (the "transferor") transfers the whole or part of a production herd to another person (the "transferee"),

(*b*) the transfer is not by way of sale or is by way of sale but for a price other than that which the animals sold would have fetched if sold in the open market, and

(*c*) the control condition or herd basis benefit condition is met.

(2) The control condition is met if—

(*a*) the transferor is a body of persons over which the transferee has control,

(*b*) the transferee is a body of persons over which the transferor has control, or

(*c*) both the transferor and transferee are bodies of persons and another person has control over both of them.

(3) For this purpose "body of persons" includes a firm.

(4) The herd basis benefit condition is met if—

(*a*) the transferor or transferee (or both) might (but for this section) have been expected to obtain a herd basis benefit as a result of the transfer or the transactions of which the transfer is one, and

(*b*) the herd basis benefit is the sole or main benefit, or one of the main benefits, that the person in question might have been expected to obtain.

(5) For this purpose a "herd basis benefit" is a benefit resulting from—

(*a*) the obtaining of a right to make a herd basis election,

(*b*) the herd basis rules applying or not applying, or

(*c*) the herd basis rules having a greater or lesser effect.

(6) For the purpose of calculating the profits of—

(*a*) the trade carried on by the transferor, and

(*b*) any trade carried on by the transferee,

the animals transferred are treated as having been sold at the price which they would have fetched if sold in the open market.

Commentary—*Simon's Taxes* **B2.617, B5.154**.
Derivation—TA 1988 Sch 5 para 5(1), (2).
HMRC Manuals—Business Income Manual BIM55560 (transfers not at market price).

Supplementary

127 Further assessment etc if herd basis rules apply

(1) If the herd basis rules apply in calculating the profits of an accounting period after an assessment for that period has become final and conclusive, any assessment or repayment of tax that is necessary to give effect to the rules must be made.

(2) But repayment of tax is due only if a claim for it is made.

Commentary—*Simon's Taxes* **B5.152**.

Derivation—TA 1988 Sch 5 para 11.
HMRC Manuals—Business Income Manual BIM55625 (adjustment of assessments).

[CHAPTER 8A

COMPENSATION FOR COMPULSORY SLAUGHTER OF ANIMALS]

[127A Application of Chapter 8A

(1) This Chapter applies if—

   (a) an animal treated as trading stock of a farming trade is slaughtered under a disease control order,

   (b) the animal is not part of a production herd of a class in respect of which a herd basis election may be made under section 124, and

   (c) the farm company receives or will receive compensation for the animal.

(2) Such an animal is referred to in this Chapter as a "relevant animal".

(3) "Disease control order" has the same meaning as in section 124.][1]

HMRC Manuals—Business Income Manual (covers S127A to S127G). BIM55180 (compensation received for compulsory slaughter of animals).
BIM55185 (Covers S127A to S127G) (spreading relief following compulsory slaughter).
BIM55190 (method of allowing spreading relief).
Amendments—[1] Chapter 8A (ss 127A–127G) inserted by the Enactment of Extra-statutory Concessions Order, SI 2012/266 arts 10, 12 with effect for the purposes of making claims in respect of the total compensation profit for accounting periods beginning on or after 1 March 2012.

[127B Right to make claim

(1) The farm company may make a claim under this section.

(2) A claim may only be made in respect of the total compensation profit for an accounting period.

(3) The total compensation profit for an accounting period is the sum of the profits which the farm company makes for all the relevant animals slaughtered in that period.

(4) For the purposes of this Chapter the profit which the farm company makes for a relevant animal is—

   (a) the amount by which the compensation for the animal exceeds its book value, or

   (b) if the trade is carried on in partnership, the farm company's share of that amount, determined in accordance with Part 17.

(5) Nothing in this section prevents a claim being made before the amount of the compensation has been finally determined.][1]

Commentary—Simon's Taxes **B5.111**.
Amendments—[1] Chapter 8A (ss 127A–127G) inserted by the Enactment of Extra-statutory Concessions Order, SI 2012/266 arts 10, 12 with effect for the purposes of making claims in respect of the total compensation profit for accounting periods beginning on or after 1 March 2012.

[127C Book value

(1) For the purposes of this Chapter the book value of an animal is the value shown in the accounts as the value of the animal at the start of the accounting period in which it was slaughtered.

(2) If, for an animal, no value is shown in the accounts as that value, the book value is as follows—

   (a) in the case of an animal which was born in the accounting period in which it was slaughtered and did not become part of the trading stock in any other way, the book value is 75% of the compensation payable for it,

   (b) in the case of an animal in relation to which section 158 (trading stock supplied by trader) or 160 (acquisitions not made in the course of trade) applies, the book value is the cost treated as incurred under section 158(2) or 160(2) as the case may be, and

   (c) in any other case, the book value is the cost of acquiring the animal for the purposes of the trade.][1]

Commentary—Simon's Taxes **B5.111**.
Amendments—[1] Chapter 8A (ss 127A–127G) inserted by the Enactment of Extra-statutory Concessions Order, SI 2012/266 arts 10, 12 with effect for the purposes of making claims in respect of the total compensation profit for accounting periods beginning on or after 1 March 2012.

[127D Effect of claim for spreading of profits

If the farm company makes a claim under section 127B in respect of the total compensation profit for an accounting period ("period X"), the profits of the trade carried on by the farm company are to be adjusted for corporation tax purposes as follows—

Step 1

Treat the compensation payable for all of the relevant animals slaughtered in period X as a receipt of that period (regardless of when the compensation is finally determined or paid).

Step 2

If the farm company makes a profit in the trade in period X, deduct from the profits of that period an amount equal to—

   (a) the total compensation profit for period X, or

(*b*) if the total compensation profit exceeds the profits of period X, such portion of the total compensation profit as will reduce the profits to nil.

Step 3

In calculating the profits for each of the 3 consecutive accounting periods following period X, include an amount equal to one third of the amount deducted by virtue of step 2.][1]

Commentary—*Simon's Taxes* **B5.111**.
HMRC Manuals—Business Income Manual BIM55190 (method of allowing spreading relief).
Amendments—[1]   Chapter 8A (ss 127A–127G) inserted by the Enactment of Extra-statutory Concessions Order, SI 2012/266 arts 10, 12 with effect for the purposes of making claims in respect of the total compensation profit for accounting periods beginning on or after 1 March 2012.

[127E Adjustment: cessation of trading

If the farm company permanently ceases to carry on the farming trade before the end of the second consecutive accounting period following period X, step 3 in section 127D is to be replaced by the following two steps—

Step 3

Divide the amount deducted by virtue of step 2 by the number of accounting periods ("the remaining accounting periods") in which, or in any part of which, the farm company carried on the farming trade, starting with period X.

Step 4

In calculating the profits for each of the remaining accounting periods, include the amount resulting from the division in step 3.][1]

Commentary—*Simon's Taxes* **B5.111**.
Amendments—[1]   Chapter 8A (ss 127A–127G) inserted by the Enactment of Extra-statutory Concessions Order, SI 2012/266 arts 10, 12 with effect for the purposes of making claims in respect of the total compensation profit for accounting periods beginning on or after 1 March 2012.

[127F Time limits etc for spreading claim

(1) A claim under section 127B must be made on or before the first anniversary of the filing date for the company tax return of the farm company for period X (see paragraph 14 of Schedule 18 to FA 1998).

(2) If the profits for an accounting period are to be adjusted or further adjusted in accordance with this Chapter after an assessment for that period has become final and conclusive, any assessment or repayment or discharge of tax that is necessary to give effect to this Chapter must be made.

(3) But repayment or discharge of tax is due only if a claim for it is made.][1]

Commentary—*Simon's Taxes* **B5.111**.
HMRC Manuals—Business Income Manual BIM55190 (method of allowing spreading relief).
Amendments—[1]   Chapter 8A (ss 127A–127G) inserted by the Enactment of Extra-statutory Concessions Order, SI 2012/266 arts 10, 12 with effect for the purposes of making claims in respect of the total compensation profit for accounting periods beginning on or after 1 March 2012.

[127G Interpretation

In this Chapter—

"animal" means any animal or other living creature;

"farming trade" means a trade of farming;

"the farm company", in relation to a farming trade, means the company that (alone or in partnership) carries on that trade;

"the total compensation profit" has the meaning given by section 127B.][1]

Amendments—[1]   Chapter 8A (ss 127A–127G) inserted by the Enactment of Extra-statutory Concessions Order, SI 2012/266 arts 10, 12 with effect for the purposes of making claims in respect of the total compensation profit for accounting periods beginning on or after 1 March 2012.

CHAPTER 9

TRADE PROFITS: OTHER SPECIFIC TRADES

Dealers in securities etc

128 Taxation of amounts taken to reserves

(1) This section applies for the purpose of calculating the profits of a company's trade if—

(*a*) the company carries on a banking business, an insurance business or a business consisting wholly or partly of dealing in securities, and

(*b*) a profit on the sale of securities held by the company would be brought into account in calculating the trading profits of that business.

(2) Profits and losses from the securities that in accordance with generally accepted accounting practice are—

(*a*) calculated by reference to the fair value of the securities, and

(*b*) recognised in the company's statement of recognised gains and losses or statement of changes in equity,

are brought into account in calculating the profits of the trade.

(3) But subsection (2) does not apply—

  (*a*) to an amount so far as deriving from or otherwise relating to an amount brought into account under that subsection in an earlier period of account, or

  (*b*) to an amount recognised for accounting purposes by way of correction of a fundamental error.

(4) In this section "securities" includes—

  (*a*) shares,

  (*b*) rights of unit holders in unit trust schemes to which TCGA 1992 applies as a result of section 99 of TCGA 1992, and

  (*c*) in the case of a company with no share capital, interests in the company possessed by members of the company,

but does not include a loan relationship (within the meaning of Part 5).

Commentary—*Simon's Taxes* **B2.102, B2.607, B5.628, D7.330**.
Derivation—TA 1988 s 472A.

129 Conversion etc of securities held as circulating capital

(1) This section applies for the purpose of calculating the profits of a company's trade if—

  (*a*) the company carries on a banking business, an insurance business or a business consisting wholly or partly of dealing in securities,

  (*b*) a transaction falling within subsection (2) occurs in relation to securities ("the original holding"), and

  (*c*) a profit on the sale of the securities would be brought into account in calculating the trading profits of that business.

(2) A transaction falls within this subsection if—

  (*a*) it results in a new holding being treated as the same as the original holding as a result of sections 126 to 136 of TCGA 1992 (roll-over relief in cases of conversion etc), or

  (*b*) it is treated, as a result of section 134 of TCGA 1992 (compensation stock), as an exchange for a new holding which does not involve a disposal of the original holding.

(3) This section does not apply to securities in respect of which unrealised profits or losses, calculated by reference to the fair value of the securities at the end of the period of account, are taken into account in the period of account in which the transaction occurs.

(4) The transaction is treated as not involving a disposal of the original holding and the new holding is treated as the same asset as the original holding.

(5) But if, under the transaction, the company carrying on the trade—

  (*a*) receives consideration in addition to the new holding, or

  (*b*) becomes entitled to receive such consideration,

subsection (4) applies as if the references to the original holding were to the proportion of the original holding given by the following fraction.

(6) The fraction is—

$$\frac{NH}{NH+C}$$

where—

  NH is the market value of the new holding at the time of the transaction, and

  C is the market value of the consideration at the time of the transaction or (if the consideration is cash) the amount of the consideration.

(7) In determining whether subsection (2)(*a*) applies as a result of section 135 or 136 of TCGA 1992, the reference to capital gains tax in section 137(1) of TCGA 1992 is to be read as a reference to income tax.

(8) In this section "securities" includes—

  (*a*) shares,

  (*b*) rights of unit holders in unit trust schemes to which TCGA 1992 applies as a result of section 99 of TCGA 1992, and

  (*c*) in the case of a company with no share capital, interests in the company possessed by members of the company.

Commentary—*Simon's Taxes* **B2.607, B5.628, D7.331**.

[Insurers

130 Insurers receiving distributions etc

(1) This section applies for the purpose of calculating the trading profits of—

  (*a*) insurance business other than [business in relation to which section 111 of FA 2012 applies][2] or

  (*b*) any category of such business.

(2) A receipt that is exempt for the purposes of Part 9A (company distributions) is not brought into account in calculating the profits of the trade.][1]

Commentary—*Simon's Taxes* **D5.150, D5.406, D6.610, D7.330, D8.104, D9.705**.
Amendments—[1]   This section substituted by FA 2009 s 34, Sch 14 paras 20, 22 with effect in relation to distributions paid on or after 1 July 2009.
[2]   In sub-s (1)(*a*), words substituted for words "life assurance business" by FA 2012 s 146, Sch 16 paras 135, 144 with effect in relation to accounting periods of companies beginning on or after 1 January 2013 (subject to transitional provisions in FA 2012 Sch 17). For accounting periods straddling 1 January 2013 see FA 2012 s 149.

Building societies

131 Incidental costs of issuing qualifying shares

(1) In calculating the profits of a trade carried on by a building society, a deduction is allowed for incidental costs of obtaining finance by means of issuing shares in the society if—
    (*a*) the shares are qualifying shares for the purposes of section 117(4) of TCGA 1992, and
    (*b*) the condition in subsection (2) is met.
(2) The condition is that the amount of any—
    (*a*) dividend or other distribution, or
    (*b*) interest,
payable in respect of the shares is deductible in calculating, for corporation tax purposes, the profits of the society's trade.
(3) But a deduction is not allowed by virtue of subsection (1) so far as the costs fall to be brought into account as debits for the purposes of Part 5 (loan relationships).
(4) "Incidental costs of obtaining finance" means expenses—
    (*a*) which are incurred on fees, commissions, advertising, printing and other incidental matters, and
    (*b*) which are incurred wholly and exclusively for the purpose of obtaining the finance, providing security for it or repaying it.
(5) Expenses incurred wholly and exclusively for the purpose of—
    (*a*) obtaining finance, or
    (*b*) providing security for it,
are incidental costs of obtaining the finance even if it is not in fact obtained.
(6) But the following are not incidental costs of obtaining finance—
    (*a*) sums paid because of losses resulting from movements in the rate of exchange between different currencies,
    (*b*) sums paid for the purpose of protecting against such losses,
    (*c*) the cost of repaying qualifying shares so far as attributable to their being repayable at a premium or having been issued at a discount, and
    (*d*) stamp duty.

Commentary—*Simon's Taxes* **D7.803, D7.820, D7.821**.
Derivation—TA 1988 s 477A(9), s 477B.
HMRC Manuals—Company Taxation Manual CTM49485 (permanent interest bearing shares (PIBS): incidental costs).

[registered societies]

132 Dividends etc granted by [registered societies]

(1) This section applies if a trade is carried on by a [registered society][2] and—
    (*a*) the society does not sell to persons who are not its members, or
    (*b*) the number of shares in the society is not limited by the society's rules or practice.
(2) In calculating the profits of the trade, a deduction is allowed for sums which meet conditions A and B.
(3) Condition A is that—
    (*a*) the sum represents a discount, rebate, dividend or bonus granted by the society to a member or other person ("the recipient"),
    (*b*) the discount, rebate, dividend or bonus is in respect of—
       (i) amounts paid or payable by the recipient, or
       (ii) amounts paid or payable to the recipient,
       on account of the recipient's transactions with the society, and
    (*c*) those transactions are taken into account in calculating the society's profits chargeable under this Part.
(4) Condition B is that the sum mentioned in subsection (2) is calculated by reference to—
    (*a*) the amounts paid or payable by or to the recipient, or
    (*b*) the size of the transactions,
and not by reference to the amount of any share or interest in the capital of the society.
(5) See also [section 1056 of CTA 2010][1] (dividend or bonus to which this section applies is not treated as a distribution).

Commentary—*Simon's Taxes* **B1.438, D7.628**
Derivation—TA 1988 s 486(10).
HMRC Manuals—Business Income Manual BIM24735 (not conducting a mutual trade).

Amendments—[1]　In sub-s (5) words substituted for words "section 230A of ICTA" by CTA 2010 s 1177, Sch 1 para 598. CTA 2010 has effect for corporation tax purposes for accounting periods ending on or after 1 April 2010, and for income and capital gains tax purposes for the tax year 2010–11 and subsequent tax years.

[2]　In each place where they occur in this Act, words substituted for words "registered industrial and provident society", "the Industrial and Provident Societies Act 1965" and "industrial and provident societies", by the Co-operative and Community Benefit Societies Act 2014 s 151, Sch 4 paras 140–143 with effect from 1 August 2014 and subject to transitional provisions and provisions preserving the continuity of the law in Sch 5 of that Act.

Credit unions

133　Annual payments paid by a credit union

In calculating the profits of a credit union's trade, no deduction is allowed for annual payments made by the credit union.

Commentary—*Simon's Taxes* **D7.644**.
Derivation—TA 1988 s 487(3).
HMRC Manuals—Company Taxation Manual CTM40160 (taxation of union).

[*Banking companies*

133A　Compensation payments: restriction of deductions

(1) In calculating the profits of a trade carried on by a company ("company A") no deduction is allowed for expenses incurred by the company if and so far as—

(a) the expenses are in respect of amounts of relevant compensation (see subsection (3)), and

(b) the disclosure condition is met in relation to the expenses (see section 133C).

(2) Subsection (1) does not apply to expenses which are excluded by section 133D.

(3) In relation to company A, "relevant compensation" means compensation which is paid or payable—

(a) to or for the benefit of a customer of company A in respect of relevant conduct (see subsection (6)) of company A, or

(b) to or for the benefit of a customer of a qualifying company in respect of relevant conduct of that qualifying company (but see subsection (4)).

(4) Compensation paid or payable as mentioned in subsection (3)(b) is not relevant compensation so far as it is paid or payable under arrangements entered into between company A and the qualifying company on arm's length terms.

(5) "Qualifying company", in relation to company A, means a company which is associated with company A (see section 133L) at the time when the expenses in question are recognised for accounting purposes.

(6) For the purposes of this section conduct of a company is "relevant conduct" if the conduct occurs—

(a) on or after 29 April 1988, and

(b) at a time when the company is a banking company (see section 133E).

(7) For the purposes of subsection (1) it does not matter whether the compensation is paid, or to be paid, by company A or another person.

(8) In this section—

"compensation", "payment" and references to compensation "paid or payable" in respect of relevant conduct of a company, are to be read in accordance with section 133K;

"conduct" includes any act or omission;

"customer" has the meaning given by section 133J.][1]

Commentary—*Simon's Taxes* **D7.704**.
Amendments—[1]　This section inserted by F(No 2)A 2015 s 18(1) with effect from "the commencement date". "The commencement date" means 8 July 2015 (F(No 2)A 2015 s 18(3). For the treatment of "straddling accounting periods", where a company has an accounting period beginning before the commencement date and ending on or after that date, see F(No 2)A 2015 s 18 (4), (5).

[133B　Companies affected by section 133A: amounts treated as received

(1) This section applies where a company incurs in an accounting period expenses which would, but for section 133A, be deductible in calculating the profits of a trade carried on by that company.

(2) An amount equal to 10% of the relevant sum is to be brought into account as a receipt in calculating the profits of the trade.

(3) The amount is treated as arising at the end of the accounting period.

(4) In this section "the relevant sum" means the total amount of the expenses which as a result of section 133A are not deductible in calculating the profits of the trade for the accounting period.][1]

Commentary—*Simon's Taxes* **D7.704**.
Amendments—[1]　This section inserted by F(No 2)A 2015 s 18(1) with effect from "the commencement date". "The commencement date" means 8 July 2015 (F(No 2)A 2015 s 18(3). For the treatment of "straddling accounting periods", where a company has an accounting period beginning before the commencement date and ending on or after that date, see F(No 2)A 2015 s 18 (4), (5).

[133C　The disclosure condition

(1) In relation to expenses incurred by a company ("company A") in respect of amounts of relevant compensation, the "disclosure condition" is met if—

    (*a*) a relevant document indicates that the company—

      (i) is or has been, or

      (ii) will become,

    liable to pay compensation in respect of a particular matter and the relevant compensation can reasonably be regarded as relating to that matter, or

    (*b*) a relevant document refers to disciplinary action taken or to be taken by a regulator in respect of a particular matter and the relevant compensation can reasonably be regarded as relating to that matter.

(2) A disclosure in a relevant document is to be disregarded for the purposes of paragraph (*a*) of subsection (1) if the disclosure is concerned with liability to pay compensation to or for the benefit of one (and only one) customer of the company concerned in respect of a single error in the conduct of the company concerned.

(3) In subsection (2) "the company concerned" means company A or a company which is associated with company A (see section 133L).

(4) For the purposes of subsection (1)(*a*) it does not matter whether the indication is express or implicit (or how it is expressed or conveyed) provided that it is reasonably clear from the relevant document that the company is or has been, or will become, liable to pay compensation in respect of the matter concerned.

(5) In this section "a relevant document" means—

    (*a*) relevant accounts,

    (*b*) a relevant statutory report, or

    (*c*) a relevant listing disclosure.

(6) For the purposes of this section the following are "relevant accounts" in relation to expenses incurred by company A—

    (*a*) company A's statutory accounts for a relevant period, and

    (*b*) relevant consolidated accounts for a relevant period.

(7) For the purposes of this section, any of the following is a "relevant statutory report" in relation to company A if the report in question is prepared for a relevant period—

    (*a*) any published report prepared by the directors of the company for the purposes of any provision of the legislation under which company A is registered or, as the case may be, established;

    (*b*) any published consolidated report prepared for such purposes, if the company is included in the consolidation.

(8) In this section "relevant listing disclosure" means a disclosure required—

    (*a*) by rules under section 73A of FISMA 2000, or

    (*b*) by virtue of a requirement imposed by or under a corresponding provision of the law of a territory outside the United Kingdom,

if the disclosure is made in the period of 5 years ending at the end of the period of account in which the expenses are recognised for accounting purposes.

(9) In this section "relevant period", in relation to expenses incurred by company A, means—

    (*a*) the period of account in which the expenses are recognised for accounting purposes, or

    (*b*) any period which begins not more than 5 years before, and ends not later than the end of that period.

(10) In this section, in relation to a company—

    "relevant compensation" has the meaning given by section 133A(3);

    "statutory accounts" means accounts prepared for the purposes of any provision of the legislation under which the company is registered or, as the case may be, established;

    "relevant consolidated accounts" means consolidated accounts prepared for any such purposes, if the company is included in the consolidation.][1]

Commentary—*Simon's Taxes* **D7.704**.

Amendments—[1] This section inserted by F(No 2)A 2015 s 18(1) with effect from "the commencement date". "The commencement date" means 8 July 2015 (F(No 2)A 2015 s 18(3). For the treatment of "straddling accounting periods", where a company has an accounting period beginning before the commencement date and ending on or after that date, see F(No 2)A 2015 s 18 (4), (5).

[133D Excluded expenses

(1) Expenses in respect of relevant compensation are excluded by this section if the compensation is in respect of—

    (*a*) an administrative error,

    (*b*) the failure of a computer or electronic system, or

    (*c*) loss or damage which is wholly or mainly attributable to an unconnected third party.

(2) In subsection (1) "third party" means a person who is neither the company mentioned in section 133A(1) nor (if different) the company in respect of whose conduct the compensation is paid or payable (see section 133A(3)(*b*)).

(3) For the purposes of this section a third party ("TP") is an "unconnected third party" unless—

CTA 2009

(*a*) TP was, at the time of the relevant actions, connected with the company mentioned in section 133A(1) or (if different) the company in respect of whose conduct the compensation is paid or payable, or

(*b*) in taking one or more of the relevant actions, TP was acting under arrangements with the company mentioned in paragraph (*a*) or (as the case may be) either of the companies mentioned in paragraph (*a*).

(4) In this section "the relevant actions" means the actions as a result of which the loss or damage is wholly or mainly attributable to TP (and references to actions or the taking of actions include failures to act).

(5) Section 1122 of CTA 2010 (meaning of "connected persons") applies for the purposes of this section, but subject to the following modification.

(6) Section 1122 has effect as if after subsection (8) there were inserted—

"(9)   A person ("A") is connected with any person who is an employee of A or by whom A is employed.

(10)   For the purposes of this section any director or other officer of a company is to be treated as employed by that company."]¹

Commentary—*Simon's Taxes* **D7.704**.
Amendments—¹   This section inserted by F(No 2)A 2015 s 18(1) with effect from "the commencement date". "The commencement date" means 8 July 2015 (F(No 2)A 2015 s 18(3). For the treatment of "straddling accounting periods", where a company has an accounting period beginning before the commencement date and ending on or after that date, see F(No 2)A 2015 s 18 (4), (5).

[133E Meaning of "banking company"

(1) For the purposes of sections 133A, a company is a "banking company"—

(*a*) at a time when it meets conditions A to D,

(*b*) at a time when it meets condition A and is a member of a partnership which meets conditions B to D, or

(*c*) if it is a building society.

In subsections (2) to (6), "the relevant entity" means the company or partnership.

(2) Condition A is that the company is not an excluded company (see section 133F).

(3) Condition B—

(*a*) in relation to any time on or after 1 December 2001, is that the relevant entity is an authorised person for the purposes of FISMA 2000 (see section 31 of that Act);

(*b*) in relation to any time before that date, is that the relevant entity—

(i) was at that time an authorised person under Chapter 3 of Part 1 of the Financial Services Act 1986 (persons authorised to carry on investment business),

(ii) was authorised under the Banking Act 1987, or

(iii) was entitled by virtue of the Banking Co-ordination (Second Council Directive) Regulations 1992 (S.I. 1992/ 3218) to accept deposits (within the meaning of the Banking Act 1987) in the United Kingdom.

(4) Condition C is that—

(*a*) the relevant entity's activities include the relevant regulated activity described in the provision mentioned in section 133G(1)(*a*), or

(*b*) the relevant entity is an investment bank (see section 133H) whose activities consist wholly or mainly of any of the relevant regulated activities described in the provisions mentioned in section 133G(1)(*b*) to (*f*).

(5) Condition D is that the relevant entity carries on that relevant regulated activity, or those relevant regulated activities, wholly or mainly in the course of trade.

(6) Where the relevant entity carries on activities outside the United Kingdom, Condition B is met—

(*a*) in relation to any time on or after 1 December 2001, if the relevant entity would be required to be an authorised person for the purposes of FISMA 2000 (see section 31 of that Act) in order to carry on any of those activities in the United Kingdom at that time;

(*b*) in relation to any time before that date, if in order to carry on those activities in the United Kingdom at that time the relevant entity—

(i) would have been required to be an authorised person under Chapter 3 of Part 1 of the Financial Services Act 1986 (persons authorised to carry on investment business), or

(ii) would have been required either to be authorised under the Banking Act 1987 or to be entitled by virtue of the Banking Co-ordination (Second Council Directive) Regulations 1992 (S.I. 1992/3218) to accept deposits (within the meaning of the Banking Act 1987) in the United Kingdom.

(7) In this section "partnership" includes—

(*a*) a limited liability partnership, and

(*b*) an entity established under the law of a territory outside the United Kingdom of a similar character to a partnership,

and "member", in relation to a partnership, is to be read accordingly.

(8) For the meaning of "relevant regulated activity", see section 133G.]¹

Commentary—*Simon's Taxes* **D7.702**.

Amendments—¹ This section inserted by F(No 2)A 2015 s 18(1) with effect from "the commencement date". "The commencement date" means 8 July 2015 (F(No 2)A 2015 s 18(3). For the treatment of "straddling accounting periods", where a company has an accounting period beginning before the commencement date and ending on or after that date, see F(No 2)A 2015 s 18 (4), (5).

[133F "Excluded company"

(1) This section gives the meaning of "excluded company" for the purposes of section 133E.

(2) A company is an "excluded company" at any time (in an accounting period) when the company is—

(*a*) an insurance company or an insurance special purpose vehicle;

(*b*) a company which is a member of a group and does not carry on any relevant regulated activities otherwise than on behalf of an insurance company or an insurance special purpose vehicle which is a member of the group;

(*c*) a company which does not carry on any relevant regulated activities otherwise than as the manager of a pension scheme;

(*d*) an investment trust;

(*e*) a company which does not carry on any relevant regulated activities other than asset management activities;

(*f*) an exempt commodities firm;

(*g*) a company which does not carry on any relevant regulated activities otherwise than for the purpose of trading in commodities or commodity derivatives;

(*h*) a company which does not carry on any relevant regulated activities otherwise than for the purpose of dealing in contracts for differences—

    (i) as principal with persons all or all but an insignificant proportion of whom are retail clients, or

    (ii) with any other person to enable the company or that other person to deal in contracts for differences as principal with persons all or all but an insignificant proportion of whom are retail clients;

(*i*) a friendly society;

(*j*) a society registered as a credit union under the Co-operative and Community Benefit Societies Act 2014 or the Credit Unions (Northern Ireland) Order 1985 (S.I. 1985/1205 (N.I. 12));

(*k*) a building society.

[(2A) A company is also an "excluded company" at any time (in an accounting period) if—

(*a*) the company would fall within a relevant relieving provision but for one (and only one) line of business which it carries on,

(*b*) that line of business does not involve the relevant regulated activity described in the provision mentioned in section 133G(1)(*a*), and

(*c*) the company's activities in that line of business would not, on their own, result in it being both a 730k firm and a full scope investment firm.

(2B) For the purposes of subsection (2A) the "relevant relieving provisions" are paragraphs (*b*), (*c*), (*e*), (*g*) and (*h*) of subsection (2).]²

(3) In this section "asset management activities" means activities which consist (or, if they were carried on in the United Kingdom, would consist) of any or all of the following—

(*a*) acting as the operator of a collective investment scheme (see subsection (5)),

(*b*) managing investments on a discretionary basis for clients none of which is a linked entity (see subsection (6)), and

(*c*) acting as an authorised corporate director.

(4) In subsection (2)(*f*) "exempt commodities firm" means—

(*a*) in relation to a time on or after 1 January 2014, an exempt IFPRU commodities firm, as defined by the FCA Handbook at that time,

(*b*) in relation to a time on or after 1 April 2013 but before 1 January 2014, an exempt BIPRU commodities firm, as defined by the PRA Handbook at that time,

(*c*) in relation to a time on or after 1 January 2007 but before 1 April 2013, an exempt BIPRU commodities firm, as defined by the Handbook of the Financial Services Authority at that time, and

(*d*) in relation to a time before 1 January 2007, an exempt BIPRU commodities firm as defined by the Handbook of the Financial Services Authority as in force on 1 January 2007.

(5) In subsection (3)(*a*) "operator of a collective investment scheme"—

(*a*) in relation to times on and after 25 February 2001, has the same meaning as in Part 17 of FISMA 2000 (see sections 235 and 237 of that Act);

(*b*) in relation to times before that date, has the same meaning as in the Financial Services Act 1986.

(6) In subsection (3)(*b*) "linked entity", in relation to a company ("C"), means—

    (*a*) a member of the same group as C;

    (*b*) a company in which a company which is a member of the same group as C has a major interest, or

    (*c*) a partnership the members of which include an entity—

        (i) which is a member of the same group as C, and

        (ii) whose share of the profits or losses of a trade carried on by the partnership for an accounting period of the partnership any part of which falls within the accounting period mentioned in the opening words of subsection (2) is at least a 40% share (see Part 17 for provisions about shares of partnership profits and losses).

(7) In this section—

["730k firm"—

    (*a*) in relation to any time on or after 1 January 2014, means an IFPRU 730k firm,

    (*b*) in relation to any time before that date, means a BIPRU 730k firm;]²

    "authorised corporate director"—

        (*a*) in relation to any time on or after 1 April 2013, has the meaning given by the FCA Handbook at that time;

        (*b*) in relation to any time before 1 April 2013, has the meaning given by the FCA Handbook as in force on 1 April 2013;

["BIPRU 730k firm" and "full scope BIPRU investment firm" have the same meaning as in subsections (2) to (4) of section 133H;]²

    "contract for differences" has the meaning given by section 582;

    "the FCA Handbook" means the Handbook made by the Financial Conduct Authority under FISMA 2000;

    "friendly society" means a registered friendly society or an incorporated friendly society;

["full scope investment firm"—

    (*a*) in relation to any time on or after 1 January 2014, means a full scope IFPRU investment firm,

    (*b*) in relation to any time before that date, means a full scope BIPRU investment firm;]²

    "group" has the same meaning as in Part 7A of CTA 2010 (see section 269BD of that Act);

["IFPRU 730k firm" and full scope IFPRU investment firm" have the meaning given by the FCA Handbook at the time in question;]²

    "incorporated friendly society" means a society incorporated under the Friendly Societies Act 1992;

    "insurance company" has the meaning given by section 133I;

    "insurance special purpose vehicle" has the meaning given by section 139 of FA 2012;

    "major interest" has the same meaning as in Part 5 (see section 473);

    "partnership" has the same meaning as in section 133E;

    "the PRA Handbook", means the Handbook made by the Prudential Regulation Authority under FISMA 2000;

    "registered friendly society" has the same meaning as in the Friendly Societies Act 1992 (and includes any society that as a result of section 96(2) of the Friendly Societies Act 1992 is treated as a registered friendly society);

    "relevant regulated activity" has the meaning given by section 133G;

    "retail client"—

        (*a*) in relation to any time on or after 1 April 2013, has the meaning given by the FCA Handbook at that time;

        (*b*) in relation to any time before 1 April 2013, has the meaning given by the FCA Handbook as in force on 1 April 2013.]¹

Commentary—*Simon's Taxes* D7.702.

Amendments—¹ This section inserted by F(No 2)A 2015 s 18(1) with effect from "the commencement date". "The commencement date" means 8 July 2015 (F(No 2)A 2015 s 18(3). For the treatment of "straddling accounting periods", where a company has an accounting period beginning before the commencement date and ending on or after that date, see F(No 2)A 2015 s 18 (4), (5).

² Sub-ss (2A), (2B) and definitions in sub-s (7) inserted by FA 2016 s 56(1)–(4). These amendments are deemed always to have had effect.

[133G Meaning of "relevant regulated activity"]

(1) In sections 133E and 133F "relevant regulated activity" means an activity which is a regulated activity for the purposes of FISMA 2000 by virtue of any of the following provisions of the Financial Services and Markets Act 2000 (Regulated Activities) Order 2001 (S.I. 2001/544)—

    (*a*) article 5 (accepting deposits);

    (*b*) article 14 (dealing in investments as principal);

    (*c*) article 21 (dealing in investments as agent);

    (*d*) article 25 (arranging deals in investments);

    (*e*) article 40 (safeguarding and administering investments);

    (*f*) article 61 (regulated mortgage contracts).

(2) In determining whether an activity carried on at any time before 1 December 2001 was at that time a relevant regulated activity, it is to be assumed that FISMA 2000 and the order mentioned in subsection (1) were in force in the form in which they had effect on 1 December 2001.][1]

Commentary—*Simon's Taxes* **D7.702.**
Amendments—[1] This section inserted by F(No 2)A 2015 s 18(1) with effect from "the commencement date". "The commencement date" means 8 July 2015 (F(No 2)A 2015 s 18(3). For the treatment of "straddling accounting periods", where a company has an accounting period beginning before the commencement date and ending on or after that date, see F(No 2)A 2015 s 18 (4), (5).

[133H Investment bank

(1) This section gives the meaning of "investment bank" for the purposes of section 133E; and in this section "the relevant entity" has the same meaning as in subsections (2) to (6) of that section.
(2) At any time on or after 1 January 2014, the relevant entity is an investment bank if—
    (a) it is both an IFPRU 730k firm and a full scope IFPRU investment firm, or
    (b) it is designated by the Prudential Regulation Authority under article 3 of the Financial Services and Markets Act 2000 (PRA-regulated Activities) Order 2013 (S.I. 2013/556) (dealing in investments as principal: designation by PRA).
(3) At any time on or after 1 January 2007 but before 1 January 2014, the relevant entity was an investment bank if it was both a BIPRU 730k firm and a full scope BIPRU investment firm.
(4) At any time before 1 January 2007, the relevant entity was an investment bank if it would have been both a BIPRU 730k firm and a full scope BIPRU investment firm if the Handbook of the Financial Services Authority in force on 1 January 2007 had been in force at that earlier time.
(5) In subsections (2) to (4)—
    "IFPRU 730k firm" and "full scope IFPRU investment firm" have the meaning given by the FCA Handbook at the time in question;
    "BIPRU 730k firm" and "full scope BIPRU investment firm"—
        (a) in relation to any time on or after 1 April 2013 have the meaning given by the PRA Handbook at that time;
        (b) in relation to any time on or after 1 January 2007 but before 1 April 2013, have the meaning given by the Handbook of the Financial Services Authority at that time;
        (c) in relation to any time before 1 January 2007, have the meaning given by the Handbook of the Financial Services Authority as in force on 1 January 2007.
(6) If the relevant entity would at any time be an investment bank under subsection (2)(a), (3) or (4) by virtue of activities carried on in the United Kingdom but for the fact that its registered office (or, if it does not have a registered office, its head office) is not in the United Kingdom, the relevant entity is to be treated for the purposes of section 133E as being an investment bank.
(7) In this section—
    "the FCA Handbook" means the Handbook made by the Financial Conduct Authority under FISMA 2000;
    "the PRA Handbook" means the Handbook made by the Prudential Regulation Authority under FISMA 2000.][1]

Commentary—*Simon's Taxes* **D7.702.**
Amendments—[1] This section inserted by F(No 2)A 2015 s 18(1) with effect from "the commencement date". "The commencement date" means 8 July 2015 (F(No 2)A 2015 s 18(3). For the treatment of "straddling accounting periods", where a company has an accounting period beginning before the commencement date and ending on or after that date, see F(No 2)A 2015 s 18 (4), (5).

[133I Meaning of "insurance company"

(1) For the purposes of section 133F a person who carries on the activity of effecting or carrying out contracts of insurance is an "insurance company" if—
    (a) the person has permission under Part 4A of FISMA 2000 to carry on that activity,
    (b) the person is of the kind mentioned in paragraph 5(d) or (da) of Schedule 3 to FISMA 2000 (EEA passport rights) and carries on that activity in the United Kingdom through a permanent establishment there, or
    (c) the person qualifies for authorisation under Schedule 4 to FISMA 2000 (Treaty rights) and carries on that activity in the United Kingdom through a permanent establishment there.
(2) In relation to times in the period beginning with 1 December 2001 and ending with 31 March 2013, the reference in subsection (1)(a) to Part 4A of FISMA 2000 is to be read as a reference to Part 4 of that Act
(3) In relation to times before 1 December 2001, this section has effect as if the following were substituted for subsection (1)—
    "(1) For the purposes of section 133F a person who carries on the activity of effecting or carrying out contracts of insurance is an "insurance company" if the person is—
        (a) authorised under section 3 or 4 of the Insurance Companies Act 1982, or

CTA 2009

(b)   an EC company within the meaning of the Insurance Companies Act 1982 which, by virtue of paragraph 1 or 8 of Schedule 2F to that Act, was able to carry on direct insurance business through a branch in the United Kingdom or provide insurance in the United Kingdom."]¹

Commentary—*Simon's Taxes* **D7.702**.

Amendments—¹ This section inserted by F(No 2)A 2015 s 18(1) with effect from "the commencement date". "The commencement date" means 8 July 2015 (F(No 2)A 2015 s 18(3). For the treatment of "straddling accounting periods", where a company has an accounting period beginning before the commencement date and ending on or after that date, see F(No 2)A 2015 s 18 (4), (5).

Prospective amendments—Sub-s (1)(b) and (c) to be repealed by the Taxes (Amendments) (EU Exit) Regulations, SI 2019/689 reg 16(1), (2) with effect from Implementation Period completion day (see EU(WA)A 2020 Sch 5 para 1(1)). These amendments do not apply where a person qualifies for authorisation under FSMA 2000 Sch 3 by virtue of SI 2001/3084 (SI 2019/689 reg 41(g)). These amendments do not apply in relation to times in the period beginning with 1 December 2001 and ending with the time these amendments come into force (SI 2019/689 reg 45).

[133J Meaning of "customer"

(1) For the purposes of sections 133A and 133C, a person ("P") is a "customer" in relation to a company ("company A") if—

(a) P uses, has used or may have contemplated using a financial service provided by company A, or

(b) has relevant rights or interests in relation to a financial service provided by company A.

(2) In subsection (1) "financial service" means a service provided—

(a) in carrying on regulated activities,

(b) in communicating, or approving the communication by others of, invitations or inducements to engage in investment activity, or

(c) in providing relevant ancillary services (if company A is an investment firm or credit institution).

(3) P has a "relevant right or interest" in relation to any service if P has a right or interest—

(a) which is derived from, or is otherwise attributable to, the use of the service by another person, or

(b) which may be adversely affected by the use of the service by persons acting on P's behalf or in a fiduciary capacity in relation to P.

(4) If company A is providing a service as a trustee, the persons who are, have been, or may have been, beneficiaries of the trust are to be treated as persons who use, have used, or may have contemplated using, the service.

(5) A person who deals with company A in the course of company A providing a service is to be treated as using the service.

(6) In this section—

"credit institution" has the meaning given by section 1H(8) of FISMA 2000;

"engage in investment activity" has the meaning given in section 21 of FISMA 2000;

"investment firm" has the same meaning as in FISMA 2000 (see section 424A of that Act);

"regulated activities" has the same meaning as in FISMA 2000 (see section 22 of that Act);

"relevant ancillary services" means has the meaning given by section 1H(8) of FISMA 2000.]¹

Commentary—*Simon's Taxes* **D7.704**.

Amendments—¹ This section inserted by F(No 2)A 2015 s 18(1) with effect from "the commencement date". "The commencement date" means 8 July 2015 (F(No 2)A 2015 s 18(3). For the treatment of "straddling accounting periods", where a company has an accounting period beginning before the commencement date and ending on or after that date, see F(No 2)A 2015 s 18 (4), (5).

[133K "Compensation" and related expressions

(1) In sections 133A to 133D references to compensation which is paid or payable "in respect of" relevant conduct include compensation which is paid (or to be paid)—

(a) in connection with a claim by the customer for compensation in respect of the conduct, or

(b) in circumstances where there is reason to suspect that company A may (or might in the absence of the payment) be or become liable to pay compensation in respect of relevant conduct—

(i) to the customer, or

(ii) in one or more of a class of cases which includes the customer's case.

(2) In sections 133A to 133D and this section "compensation" includes any form of redress, whether monetary or non-monetary, and accordingly includes interest.

References in those sections to "payment" are to be interpreted accordingly.

(3) In subsection (1)—

"claim" includes any claim or request, however made;

"customer" has the meaning given by section 133J;

"relevant conduct" is to be interpreted in accordance with section 133A(6).]¹

Commentary—*Simon's Taxes* **D7.704**.

Amendments—[1] This section inserted by F(No 2)A 2015 s 18(1) with effect from "the commencement date". "The commencement date" means 8 July 2015 (F(No 2)A 2015 s 18(3). For the treatment of "straddling accounting periods", where a company has an accounting period beginning before the commencement date and ending on or after that date, see F(No 2)A 2015 s 18 (4), (5).

[133L Associated companies

(1) For the purposes of sections 133A and 133C a company ("company B") is associated with another company ("company A") at a time ("the relevant time") if any of the following 5 conditions is met.

(2) The first condition is that the financial results of company A and company B, for a period that includes the relevant time, meet the consolidation condition.

(3) The second condition is that there is a connection between company A and company B for the accounting period of company A in which the relevant time falls.

(4) The third condition is that, at the relevant time, company A has a major interest in company B or company B has a major interest in company A.

(5) The fourth condition is that—

    (a) the financial results of company A and a third company, for a period that includes the relevant time, meet the consolidation condition (see subsection (7)), and

    (b) at the relevant time the third company has a major interest in company B.

(6) The fifth condition is that—

    (a) there is a connection (see subsection (9)) between company A and a third company for the accounting period of company A in which the relevant time falls, and

    (b) at the relevant time the third company has a major interest in company B.

(7) In this section, the financial results of any two companies for any period meet the "consolidation condition" if—

    (a) they are required to be comprised in group accounts,

    (b) they would be required to be comprised in group accounts but for the application of an exemption, or

    (c) they are in fact comprised in such accounts.

(8) In subsection (7), "group accounts" means accounts prepared under—

    (a) section 399 of the Companies Act 2006, or

    (b) any corresponding provision of the law of a territory outside the United Kingdom.

(9) Sections 466 to 471 (companies connected for accounting period) apply for the purposes of this section.

(10) In this section "major interest" has the same meaning as in Part 5 (see section 473).][1]

Commentary—*Simon's Taxes* **D7.704.**
Amendments—[1] This section inserted by F(No 2)A 2015 s 18(1) with effect from "the commencement date". "The commencement date" means 8 July 2015 (F(No 2)A 2015 s 18(3). For the treatment of "straddling accounting periods", where a company has an accounting period beginning before the commencement date and ending on or after that date, see F(No 2)A 2015 s 18 (4), (5).

[133M Application of sections 133A and 133B in relation to corporate partner

(1) If a firm carries on a trade and any partner in the firm ("the corporate partner") is within the charge to corporation tax, this section applies in determining the profits of the trade, in relation to the corporate partner, in accordance with section 1259(3) or (4).

(2) No deduction is allowed for expenses incurred by the firm if and so far as section 133A would prevent the expenses from being deductible if the firm were, and at all relevant times had been, a company.

(3) In its application for the purposes of subsection (2), section 133A is to be read subject to subsections (4) to (6).

(4) Section 133A(3)(b) is to be disregarded.

(5) Conduct of the firm is "relevant conduct" if the conduct occurs—

    (a) on or after 29 April 1988, and

    (b) at a time when—

        (i) the corporate partner is for the purposes of section 133A a banking company, and

      [(ii) the firm would not (if references in section 133F(2) and (3) to companies included firms) be an excluded company for the purposes of section 133E.][2]

(6) The disclosure condition in section 133C may be met by a relevant document relating to the liability of the corporate partner (as well as by a relevant document relating to the liability of the firm).

(7) Where in any accounting period of the firm (as defined by section 1261) the firm incurs expenses which but for section 133A (as read with subsections (2) to (6)) would be deductible in calculating the profits of the trade, the profits of the firm's trade are to be determined as if the references in section 133B to a company were a reference to the firm.][1]

Amendments—[1] This section inserted by F(No 2)A 2015 s 18(1) with effect from "the commencement date". "The Commencement date" means 15 July 2015 (F(No 2)A 2015 s 18(3)(b)). For the treatment of "straddling accounting periods", where a company has an accounting period beginning before the commencement date and ending on or after that date, see F(No 2)A 2015 s 18 (4), (5).

[2] Sub-s (5)(*b*)(ii) substituted by FA 2016 s 56(5), (6). This amendment is deemed always to have had effect.

[133N   Powers to amend

(1) The Treasury may by regulations make such amendments of sections 133A to 133L as they consider appropriate in consequence of—

    (*a*) any change made to, or replacement of, the Financial Services and Markets Act 2000 (Regulated Activities) Order 2001 (S.I. 2001/544) or the Financial Services and Markets Act 2000 (PRA-regulated Activities) Order 2013 (S.I. 2013/556) (or any replacement);

    (*b*) any change made to, or replacement of, the FCA Handbook or the PRA Handbook (or any replacement);

    (*c*) any regulatory requirement, or change to any regulatory requirement, imposed by EU legislation, or by or under any Act (whenever adopted, enacted or made).

(2) The Treasury may by regulations—

    (*a*) amend sections 133A(1) and 133C for the purpose of varying the class of expenses to which section 133A(1) applies;

    (*b*) amend section 133D for the purpose of adding cases to those for the time being listed in subsection (1) of that section;

    (*c*) amend section 133D for any other purpose;

    (*d*) amend any of sections 133E to 133I;

    (*e*) amend section 133M.

(3) Regulations under this section may include transitional provision.

(4) A statutory instrument containing only regulations under subsection (1) or (2)(*b*) is subject to annulment in pursuance of a resolution of the House of Commons.

(5) Any other statutory instrument containing regulations under this section may not be made unless a draft of the instrument has been laid before and approved by a resolution of the House of Commons.

(6) In this section—

"the FCA Handbook" means the Handbook made by the Financial Conduct Authority under FISMA 2000 (as that Handbook has effect from time to time);

"the PRA Handbook" means the Handbook made by the Prudential Regulation Authority under FISMA 2000 (as that Handbook has effect from time to time)."][1]

Amendments—[1]   This section inserted by F(No 2)A 2015 s 18(1) with effect from "the commencement date". "The commencement date" means 8 July 2015 (F(No 2)A 2015 s 18(3). For the treatment of "straddling accounting periods", where a company has an accounting period beginning before the commencement date and ending on or after that date, see F(No 2)A 2015 s 18 (4), (5).

Dealers in land etc

134   Purchase or sale of woodlands

(1) This section applies for the purpose of calculating the profits of a trade of dealing in land.

(2) If the company carrying on the trade buys woodlands in the United Kingdom in the course of the trade, the part of the cost of the woodlands which is attributable to trees or saleable underwood growing on the land is ignored.

(3) If—

    (*a*) the woodlands are subsequently sold in the course of the trade, and

    (*b*) any of the trees or underwood are still growing on the land at the time of the sale,

the part of the price that is equal to the amount ignored under subsection (2) for those trees or that underwood is ignored.

Commentary—*Simon's Taxes* B2.606, B5.627.

HMRC Manuals—Business Income Manual BIM51665 (purchase and sale of woodlands).

136   Lease premiums etc: reduction of receipts

(1) This section applies for the purpose of calculating the profits of a trade of dealing in land if a receipt of the trade falls within one of the following categories—

    (*a*) lease premiums within section 217,

    (*b*) sums within section 219 (sums payable instead of rent),

    (*c*) sums within section 220 (sums payable for surrender of a lease),

    (*d*) sums within section 221 (sums payable for variation or waiver of terms of lease),

    (*e*) consideration for the assignment of a lease within section 222 (lease granted at an undervalue), and

    (*f*) amounts received on the sale of an estate or interest in land within section 224 (sales with right to reconveyance) or section 225 (sale and leaseback transactions).

(2) The receipt is reduced by the relevant amount.

(3) The relevant amount is the amount which is treated as a receipt of a property business as a result of any of sections 217 to 225.

(4) But if—

    (*a*) the company carrying on the trade makes a claim under section 238 or 239, and

    (*b*) as a result of the claim a repayment of tax is made to that company, the relevant amount is the amount which, for the purpose of determining the amount of the repayment of tax, is treated as brought into account as a receipt in calculating the profits of the property business.

(5) If subsection (4) applies, any adjustment of liability to tax may be made—

    (a) by assessment or otherwise, and

    (b) at any time at which it could be made if it related only to tax for the accounting period in which the claim under section 238 or 239 is made.

Commentary—*Simon's Taxes* B5.220, B5.627.
Derivation—TA 1988 s 99(2), (3).
HMRC Manuals—Business Income Manual BIM51525 (premiums).

Mineral exploration and access

137 Mineral exploration and access

(1) This section applies for the purpose of calculating the profits of a trade if—

    (a) the company carrying on the trade incurs expenditure on mineral exploration and access in an area or group of sands, and

    (b) the presence of mineral deposits in commercial quantities has already been established in that area or group of sands.

(2) A deduction is allowed for the expenditure only if a deduction would have been allowed for it if the presence of mineral deposits in commercial quantities had not already been established in that area or group of sands.

(3) In this section "mineral exploration and access" has the same meaning as in Part 5 of CAA 2001 (see section 396(1) of that Act).

Commentary—*Simon's Taxes* B5.650, B5.653
Derivation—TA 1988 s 91C.
HMRC Manuals—Business Income Manual BIM62000 (mineral extraction: contents and introduction), BIM62005 (exploration expenditure).

Intermediaries treated as making employment payments

139 Deduction for deemed employment payment

(1) This section applies for the purpose of calculating the profits of a trade carried on by an intermediary which is treated as making a deemed employment payment in connection with the trade.

(2) A deduction is allowed for—

    (a) the amount of the deemed employment payment, and

    (b) the amount of any employer's national insurance contributions paid by the intermediary in respect of it.

(3) The deduction is allowed for the period of account in which the deemed employment payment is treated as made.

(4) No deduction in respect of—

    (a) the deemed employment payment, or

    (b) any employer's national insurance contributions paid by the intermediary in respect of it,

may be made except in accordance with this section.

(5) In this section "deemed employment payment" and "intermediary" have the same meaning as in Chapter 8 of Part 2 of ITEPA 2003 (see sections 49 and 50 of that Act).

Commentary—*Simon's Taxes* B5.645, E4.1021.
HMRC Manuals—Business Income Manual BIM47225 (deemed employment payments).

140 Special rules for partnerships

(1) This section applies for the purpose of calculating the profits of a trade carried on by a firm that is treated as making a deemed employment payment in connection with the trade.

(2) The amount of the deduction allowed under section 139 is limited to the amount that reduces the profits of the firm of the period of account to nil.

(3) The expenses of the firm in connection with the relevant engagements for any period of account are limited to the total of—

    (a) 5% of the amount taken into account at Step 1 of the calculation in section 54(1) of ITEPA 2003 (calculation of deemed employment payment), and

    (b) the amount deductible at Step 3 of that calculation.

(4) In this section "deemed employment payment" and "the relevant engagements" have the same meaning as in Chapter 8 of Part 2 of ITEPA 2003 (see sections 49 and 50 of that Act).

Commentary—*Simon's Taxes* B5.645, E4.1021.
HMRC Manuals—Business Income Manual BIM47225 (deemed employment payments: partnership).

Managed service companies

141 Deduction for deemed employment payments

(1) This section applies for the purpose of calculating the profits of a trade carried on by a managed service company (the "MSC") which is treated as making a deemed employment payment in connection with the trade.

(2) A deduction is allowed for—

    (a) the amount of the deemed employment payment, and

    (b) the amount of any employer's national insurance contributions paid by the MSC in respect of it.

(3) The deduction is allowed for the period of account in which the deemed employment payment is treated as made.

(4) If the MSC is a firm, the amount of the deduction allowed under subsection (2) is limited to the amount that reduces the profits of the firm of the period of account to nil.

(5) No deduction in respect of—

    (a) the deemed employment payment, or

    (b) any employer's national insurance contributions paid by the MSC in respect of it,

may be made except in accordance with this section.

(6) In this section the following expressions have the same meanings as in Chapter 9 of Part 2 of ITEPA 2003—

    "deemed employment payment" (see section 61D(2) of that Act),

    "employer's national insurance contributions" (see section 61J(1) of that Act),

    "managed service company" (see section 61B of that Act).

Commentary—*Simon's Taxes* **E4.914**.

[[Worker's services provided through intermediary to public authority or medium or large client]

141A Intermediaries providing worker's services to [public authority or medium or large client]²

(1) This section applies for the purposes of calculating the trading profits of a person where—

    (a) the person is the intermediary in a chain identified under section 61N of ITEPA 2003 (see section 61N(1)(b)),

    (b) a deemed direct payment is treated as made under subsection (3) of that section, and

    (c) the person receives a payment which can reasonably be taken to be in respect of the same services as those in respect of which the underlying chain payment is made.

(2) The payment mentioned in subsection (1)(c) is not required to be brought into account in calculating the profits of the trade.

(3) In this section "underlying chain payment" means the payment whose amount is used at Step 1 of section 61Q(1) of ITEPA 2003 as the starting point for calculating the amount of the deemed direct payment mentioned in subsection (1)(b).]¹

Commentary—*Simon's Taxes* **B5.645**.

Amendments—¹   Section 141A inserted by FA 2017 s 6, Sch 1 para 14 with effect from 27 April 2017. The payments to which this amendment applies include payments made before 27 April 2017 (the date of Royal Assent to FA 2017).

²   Heading above s 141A substituted, and in heading to s 141A words substituted for words "public sector", by FA 2020 s 7, Sch 1 paras 21, 22 with effect from 22 July 2020.

Waste disposal

142 Deduction for site preparation expenditure

(1) This section applies for the purpose of calculating the profits of a trade of a period of account in which waste materials are deposited on a waste disposal site if—

    (a) the company carrying on the trade ("the trader"), or a predecessor, has incurred site preparation expenditure in relation to the site in the course of carrying on the trade, and

    (b) at the time the trader first deposits waste materials on the site, the trader holds a waste disposal licence which is then in force.

(2) A deduction is allowed for the amount of the site preparation expenditure allocated to the period of account under section 143.

(3) For the purposes of this section "predecessor", in relation to the trader, means a person who—

    (a) has ceased to carry on the trade carried on by the trader or ceased to carry on a trade so far as relating to the site, and

    (b) has transferred the whole of the site to the trader,

and it does not matter for this purpose whether or not the estate or interest in the site transferred to the trader is the same as that held by that person.

(4) For the purposes of this section and section 143, if site preparation expenditure has been incurred by a predecessor—

    (a) the trade carried on by the trader is treated as the same as the trade carried on by the predecessor, and

    (b) deductions are to be allowed to the trader (and not to the predecessor) as if everything done to or by the predecessor were done to or by the trader.

(5) For—

    (a) the meaning of "site preparation expenditure", "waste disposal licence" and "waste disposal site", and

    (b) a rule about pre-trading expenditure,

see section 144.

Commentary—*Simon's Taxes* **B2.478**.
HMRC Manuals—Business Income Manual BIM67400 (waste disposal: contents).
BIM67450 (site preparation: capital expenditure).
BIM67455 (site preparation: qualifying expenditure).
BIM67460 (site preparation: revenue expenditure).
BIM67516 (site preparation: memorandum of understanding).
BIM67520 (entitlement of successor to allowances).
Modification—If the predecessor ceased to carry on the trade carried on by the trader, or ceased to carry on a trade so far as relating to the site, before 21 March 2000, this section applies as if words ", or a predecessor," in sub-s (1), and whole of sub-ss (3), (4) were repealed (CTA 2009 s 1325, Sch 2 para 30).
If the trade carried on by the trader was started before 1 April 1993, s 144(1) below applies for the purposes of ss 142, 143 as if s 144(1)(*d*), (*e*) were repealed (CTA 2009 s 1325, Sch 2 para 31).
Section 144(3) below does not apply for the purposes of ss 142, 143 if the trade was started before 1 April 1993 (CTA 2009 s 1325, Sch 2 para 32).

143 Allocation of site preparation expenditure

(1) The amount of site preparation expenditure allocated to a period of account for the purposes of section 142(2) is the amount given by the formula—

$$RE \times \frac{WD}{SV + WD}$$

where—
    RE means residual expenditure (see subsection (2)),
    WD means the volume of waste materials deposited on the waste disposal site during the period, and
    SV means the volume of the waste disposal site not used up for the deposit of waste materials at the end of the period.
(2) "Residual expenditure" means the total of all site preparation expenditure incurred by the trader in relation to the waste disposal site at any time before the end of the period, less—
    (*a*) any of that expenditure for which an allowance has been, or may be, made for corporation or income tax purposes under the enactments relating to capital allowances,
    (*b*) any of that expenditure for which a deduction has been made in calculating for corporation or income tax purposes the profits of an earlier period of account, and
    (*c*) if the trader started to carry on the trade before 6 April 1989, the excluded amount of any unrelieved old expenditure (see subsections (3) and (4)).
(3) The excluded amount of unrelieved old expenditure is calculated by multiplying the unrelieved old expenditure (see subsection (4)) by the fraction—

$$\frac{WD}{SV + WD}$$

where—
    WD means the volume of waste materials deposited on the site before 6 April 1989, and
    SV means the volume of the site not used up for the deposit of waste materials immediately before that date.
(4) "Unrelieved old expenditure" means site preparation expenditure which—
    (*a*) was incurred by the trader in relation to the waste disposal site before 6 April 1989, and
    (*b*) does not fall within subsection (2)(*a*) or (*b*).

Commentary—*Simon's Taxes* **B2.478**.
HMRC Manuals—Business Income Manual BIM67480 (site preparation expenditure: calculation of relief).
BIM67495 (allocation of site preparation expenditure).

144 Site preparation expenditure: supplementary

(1) For the purposes of this section and sections 142 and 143 "waste disposal licence" means—
    (*a*) a disposal licence under Part 1 of the Control of Pollution Act 1974 (c 40) or Part 2 of the Pollution Control and Local Government (Northern Ireland) Order 1978 (SI 1978/1049 (NI 19)),
    (*b*) a waste management licence under Part 2 of the Environmental Protection Act 1990 (c 43) or any corresponding provision for the time being in force in Northern Ireland,
    (*c*) a permit or authorisation]² under regulations under—
        (i) section 2 of the Pollution Prevention and Control Act 1999 (c 24), . . . ²
        (ii) Article 4 of the Environment (Northern Ireland) Order 2002 (SI 2002/3153 (NI 7)), [or
        (iii) any corresponding provision for the time being in force in Scotland,]²
    (*d*) . . . ⁷ or
    (*e*) a nuclear site licence under the Nuclear Installations Act 1965 (c 57).
(2) For the purposes of this section and sections 142 and 143—

CTA 2009

"site preparation expenditure", in relation to a waste disposal site, means expenditure incurred on preparing the site for the deposit of waste materials, and

"waste disposal site" means a site used, or to be used, for the disposal of waste materials by their deposit on the site.

(3) For the purposes of sections 142 and 143, expenditure incurred for the purposes of a trade by a company about to carry on the trade is treated as if it were incurred—

    (*a*) on the date on which the company starts to carry on the trade, and

    (*b*) in the course of carrying it on.

Commentary—*Simon's Taxes* **B2.478**.

HMRC Manuals—Business Income Manual BIM67450 (site preparation: capital expenditure).

BIM67455 (site preparation: qualifying expenditure).

BIM67460 (site preparation: revenue expenditure).

BIM67465 (site preparation: conditions).

BIM67545 (relevant licence).

Amendments—[1] Sub-s (1)(*d*) repealed, in relation to England and Wales, by the Environmental Permitting (England and Wales) Regulations, SI 2010/675, regs 107, 109, Sch 26, para 20, Sch 28 with effect from 6 April 2010.

[2] In sub-s (1)(*c*), words inserted, word in para (i) repealed, and para (iii) and preceding word inserted, by the Regulatory Reform (Scotland) Act 2014 (Consequential Modifications) Order, SI 2015/374 art 8 with effect from 26 February 2015.

145 Site restoration payments

(1) This section applies for the purpose of calculating the profits of a trade if the company carrying on the trade makes a site restoration payment in the course of carrying it on.

(2) [Subject to subsection (3A),][1] a deduction is allowed for the unrelieved amount of the payment.

[(3) The deduction is allowed—

    (*a*) (if the payment is made, whether directly or indirectly, to a connected person) for the period of account in which that part of the restoration work to which the payment relates is completed, or

    (*b*) (in any other case) for the period of account in which the payment is made.

(3A) But no deduction is allowed if the payment arises from arrangements—

    (*a*) to which the company carrying on the trade is a party, and

    (*b*) the main purpose, or one of the main purposes, of which is to obtain a deduction under this section.][1]

(4) The unrelieved amount of a site restoration payment is the amount of the payment, less—

    (*a*) any amount of the payment that represents expenditure for which an allowance has been, or may be, made under the enactments relating to capital allowances, and

    (*b*) any amount of the payment that represents expenditure for which a deduction has been made in calculating the profits of the trade of an earlier period of account.

(5) A "site restoration payment" means a payment made in connection with the restoration of a site (or part of a site) in order to comply with—

    (*a*) a condition of a waste disposal licence (as defined in section 144(1)),

    (*b*) a condition imposed on the grant of planning permission to use the site for the collection, treatment, conversion and final depositing of waste materials or for the carrying out of any of those activities, or

    (*c*) a relevant planning obligation.

(6) For this purpose "a relevant planning obligation" means—

    (*a*) an obligation arising under an agreement made under section 106 of the Town and Country Planning Act 1990 (c 8) (as originally enacted) or any corresponding provision for the time being in force in Northern Ireland,

    (*b*) an obligation arising under an agreement made under section 75 of the Town and Country Planning (Scotland) Act 1997 (c 8),

    (*c*) a planning obligation entered into under section 106 of the Town and Country Planning Act 1990 (as substituted by section 12 of the Planning and Compensation Act 1991 (c 34)) or any corresponding provision for the time being in force in Northern Ireland, or

    (*d*) a planning obligation entered into under section 299A of the Town and Country Planning Act 1990 or any corresponding provision for the time being in force in Northern Ireland.

[(7) "Arrangements" includes any agreement, understanding, scheme, transaction or series of transactions (whether or not legally enforceable).][1]

Commentary—*Simon's Taxes* **B2.478**.

Derivation—TA 1988 s 91A.

HMRC Manuals—Business Income Manual BIM67415 (site restoration payments: capital/revenue).

BIM67420 (payments made on or after 6 April 1989).

BIM67430 (expenditure not allowable).

BIM67435 (expenditure not allowable: provisions).

BIM67540 (site restoration payment).

Amendments—[1] Words at the beginning of sub-s (2) and the whole of sub-s (7) inserted, and sub-ss (3), (3A) substituted for previous sub-s (3), by FA 2012 s 53(4)–(6) with effect in relation to any site restoration payment made on or after 21 March

2012, other than a payment made pursuant to an unconditional obligation in a contract made before 21 March 2012. An unconditional obligation is an obligation which may not be varied or extinguished by the exercise of a right (whether or not under the contract): FA 2012 s 53(8).

[Cemeteries and crematoria: interests in land]

146 [Cemeteries and crematoria: introduction

(1) This section and sections 147 to 149 apply for the purpose of calculating the profits of a period of account ("the relevant period") of a trade which consists of or includes—

(*a*) the carrying on of a cemetery, or

(*b*) the carrying on of a crematorium and, in connection with doing so, the maintenance of memorial garden plots,

and the following provisions of this section apply for the interpretation of this section and those sections.

(2) References to the sale of land in a cemetery include the sale of a right of interment in land in a cemetery.

(3) References to the sale of land in a memorial garden include the appropriation of part of a memorial garden in return for a dedication fee or similar payment.

(4) "Ancillary capital expenditure" means capital expenditure incurred for the purposes of the trade by the company carrying on the trade ("the trader"), or a predecessor, on—

(*a*) any building or structure (other than a dwelling-house) which is in the cemetery or memorial garden and is likely to have little or no value when the cemetery or memorial garden is full,

(*b*) the purchase of an interest in, or the preparation of, any land taken up by such a building or structure, or

(*c*) the purchase of an interest in, or the preparation of, any other land in the cemetery or memorial garden which is not suitable or adaptable for use for interments or memorial garden plots and which is likely to have little or no value when the cemetery or memorial garden is full.

(5) "Predecessor", in relation to the trader, means a person who carried on the trade at any time before the trader started to do so.

(6) "Preparation", in relation to land, means levelling or draining the land or making it suitable in some other way for use as a cemetery or memorial garden.

Commentary—*Simon's Taxes* **B5.620**.

Derivation—TA 1988 s 91(1), (2), (5), (7), (8).

HMRC Manuals—Business Income Manual BIM52500 (cemeteries and crematoria: contents).

Amendments—Heading substituted for 'previous heading "Cemeteries and crematoria" by the Enactment of Extra-Statutory Concessions Order, SI 2012/266 art 5(1), (2) with effect in relation to niches and memorials sold, and inscriptions made, after 1 March 2012.

147 Deduction for capital expenditure

(1) This section applies if, in the relevant period, an interest in land in the cemetery or memorial garden is sold with a view to the land being used—

(*a*) for the purpose of interments, or

(*b*) for memorial garden plots.

(2) A deduction is allowed for—

(*a*) capital expenditure incurred by the trader, or a predecessor, on the purchase of an interest in the land or on the preparation of the land, and

(*b*) ancillary capital expenditure allocated to the relevant period under section 148 (allocation of ancillary capital expenditure).

(3) But no expenditure is to be brought into account—

(*a*) under both paragraphs (*a*) and (*b*) of subsection (2), . . . [1]

(*b*) under both subsection (2)(*a*) above and section 170(2)(*b*) of ITTOIA 2005 (relief for income tax purposes) or under both subsection (2)(*b*) above and section 170(2)(*a*) of ITTOIA 2005, [or

(*c*) under both subsection (2)(*b*) above and section 149B(4), 149C(4) or 149D(3).][1]

whether for the same or different periods of account.

(4) Any purchase price paid on a sale in connection with a change in the persons carrying on the trade is ignored in calculating the amount of the deduction.

(5) No deduction is allowed for any expenditure which is excluded by section 149 (exclusion of expenditure met by subsidies).

Commentary—*Simon's Taxes* **B5.620, C2.217**.

Derivation—TA 1988 s 91(1), (4)–(7), (9).

HMRC Manuals—Business Income Manual BIM52501 (cemeteries and crematoria: tax treatment of capital receipts and expenditure).

Amendments—[1] In sub-para (3), in para (*a*) word "or" repealed, and para (*c*) and preceding word "or" inserted, by the Enactment of Extra-Statutory Concessions Order, SI 2012/266 art 5(1), (3) with effect in relation to niches and memorials sold, and inscriptions made, after 1 March 2012.

CTA 2009

148 Allocation of ancillary capital expenditure

(1) The amount of ancillary capital expenditure allocated to the relevant period for the purposes of section 147(2)(b) is the amount given by the formula—

$$RE \times \frac{PSR}{PAR + PSR}$$

where—

RE means residual expenditure (see subsection (2)),

PSR means the number of grave-spaces or memorial garden plots in the cemetery or memorial garden sold in the relevant period, and

PAR means the number of grave-spaces or memorial garden plots in the cemetery or memorial garden which are or could be made available for sale at the end of the relevant period.

(2) "Residual expenditure" means the total of all ancillary capital expenditure incurred at any time before the end of the relevant period, less—

    (a) ancillary capital expenditure incurred on buildings or structures which were destroyed before the beginning of the first sale period,

    (b) the excluded amount of any remaining old expenditure (see subsection (3)),

    (c) if, after the beginning of the first sale period and before the end of the relevant period, an asset representing ancillary capital expenditure was sold or destroyed, the net sale proceeds or the compensation, and

    (d) any amount deducted under section 147(2)(b) above, or under section 170(2)(b) of ITTOIA 2005, for a period of account ending before the relevant period.

(3) The excluded amount of remaining old expenditure is calculated by multiplying the remaining old expenditure by the fraction—

$$RE \times \frac{PSB}{PAB + PSB}$$

where—

PSB means the number of grave-spaces or memorial garden plots in the cemetery or memorial garden sold before the beginning of the basis period for the tax year 1954-55, and

PAB means the number of grave-spaces or memorial garden plots in the cemetery or memorial garden which were or could have been made available for sale immediately before the beginning of the basis period for that tax year.

(4) In this section—

"compensation", in relation to the destruction of an asset, means—

        (a) insurance money or other compensation received by the trader, or a predecessor, in respect of the destruction, and

        (b) money received for the remains of the asset by the trader or predecessor,

"the first sale period" means—

        (a) the period of account in which an interest in land in the cemetery or memorial garden was first sold for the purposes of the trade with a view to the land being used for the purpose of interments or for memorial garden plots, or

        (b) if later, the basis period for the tax year 1954-55, and

"remaining old expenditure" means ancillary capital expenditure which—

        (a) was incurred before the beginning of the basis period for the tax year 1954-55, and

        (b) does not fall within subsection (2)(a).

Commentary—*Simon's Taxes* **B5.620**.
Derivation—TA 1988 s 91(1), (3)–(9).
HMRC Manuals—Business Income Manual BIM52501 (cemeteries and crematoria: deduction for ancillary expenditure).

149 Exclusion of expenditure met by subsidies

(1) Expenditure is excluded for the purposes of section 147 so far as it has been, or is to be, met (directly or indirectly) by—

    (a) the Crown,

    (b) a government or local or other public authority (whether in the United Kingdom or elsewhere), or

    (c) any person other than the person incurring the expenditure.

(2) This is subject to the following exceptions.

(3) Expenditure is not excluded for the purposes of section 147 if it is met (directly or indirectly) by a grant—

    (a) made under Northern Ireland legislation, and

    (b) declared by the Treasury by an order under section 534 of CAA 2001 to correspond to a grant under Part 2 of the Industrial Development Act 1982 (c 52).

(4) Expenditure is not excluded for the purposes of section 147 if it is met (directly or indirectly) by—

> (a) insurance money, or
>
> (b) other compensation money,

payable in respect of an asset which has been destroyed, demolished or put out of use.

(5) Expenditure is not excluded for the purposes of section 147 if—

> (a) it has been, or is to be, met (directly or indirectly) by a person other than the Crown or a government or local or other public authority, and
>
> (b) no deduction is allowed for the expenditure in calculating for corporation or income tax purposes the profits of a trade carried on by that person.

Commentary—*Simon's Taxes* **B5.620.**

Derivation—TA 1988 s 91(9); CAA 2001 s 532.

HMRC Manuals—Business Income Manual BIM52501 (cemeteries and crematoria: excluded expenditure).

[Crematoria: niches, memorials and inscription]

[149A Niches, memorials and inscriptions: introduction

(1) Sections 149B to 149E apply in calculating the profits of a trade which consists of or includes—

> (a) the carrying on of a crematorium, and
>
> (b) in connection with carrying on the crematorium—
>
> > (i) the sale of niches or memorials, or
> >
> > (ii) the making of inscriptions.

(2) In those sections—

> (a) "the trade" is the trade mentioned in subsection (1),
>
> (b) "the trader" is the company carrying on the trade, and
>
> (c) a "predecessor" is a person who carried on the trade at any time before the trader started doing so.][1]

HMRC Manuals—Business Income Manual BIM52520 (cemeteries and crematoria: sale of niches).

Amendments—[1] Sections 149A–149E inserted by the Enactment of Extra-Statutory Concessions Order, SI 2012/266 art 5(1), (4) with effect in relation to niches and memorials sold, an inscriptions made, after 1 March 2012.

[149B Allowable deductions: niches

(1) This section sets out the deductions that are allowed in respect of a niche if proceeds from the sale of the niche are brought into account as a receipt in calculating the profits of the trade.

(2) A deduction is allowed for two-thirds of the costs incurred (by the trader or a predecessor) in the formation of the niche.

(3) Formation of the lining and of any tablet associated with the niche is taken to be part of the formation of the niche.

(4) If the niche is in a building that is used wholly or mainly for the purpose of providing niches, a further deduction is allowed for two-thirds of the associated building costs.

(5) In relation to a niche in a building—

> (a) "the associated building costs" is the relevant proportion of the costs of the building, and
>
> (b) "the relevant proportion" is the proportion that the area occupied by the niche bears to the area of the building as a whole or, if the proportion cannot reasonably be calculated on that basis, such proportion as may be calculated on a just and reasonable basis.][1]

Commentary—*Simon's Taxes* **B5.620.**

HMRC Manuals—Business Income Manual BIM52520 (cemeteries and crematoria: sale of niches).

Amendments—[1] Sections 149A–149E inserted by the Enactment of Extra-Statutory Concessions Order, SI 2012/266 art 5(1), (4) with effect in relation to niches and memorials sold, an inscriptions made, after 1 March 2012.

[149C Allowable deductions: memorials

(1) This section sets out the deductions that are allowed in respect of a memorial if proceeds from the sale of the memorial are brought into account as a receipt in calculating the profits of the trade.

(2) A deduction is allowed for the costs incurred (by the trader or a predecessor) in producing the memorial.

(3) If the memorial includes an inscription, making that inscription is taken to be part of producing the memorial.

(4) If the memorial is attached to a building that is used wholly or mainly for the purpose of accommodating memorials or the memorial comprises an entire building, a further deduction is allowed for two-thirds of the associated building costs.

(5) In relation to a memorial attached to or comprising a building, "the associated building costs" means—

> (a) the amount found by dividing the costs of the building by the total number of memorials that the building is capable of accommodating, or
>
> (b) if the memorial comprises an entire building, the costs of that building.][1]

Commentary—*Simon's Taxes* **B5.620.**

HMRC Manuals—Business Income Manual BIM52525 (cemeteries and crematoria: memorials).

"statutory body" means a body established by or under an enactment,

"trading surplus" means a surplus from the body's trading operations or other trade receipts.

Commentary—*Simon's Taxes* **B5.647.**
HMRC Manuals—Business Income Manual BIM24850 (marketing boards).
Company Taxation Manual CTM40900 (marketing boards).

154 Conditions to be met by reserve fund

(1) These are the conditions to be met by the reserve fund (see section 153(2)).

(2) The first condition is that no sum may be withdrawn from the fund without the authority or consent of a Minister or department.

(3) The second condition is that if—

    (*a*) money has been paid to the body by a Minister or department—

        (i) in connection with arrangements for maintaining guaranteed prices, or

        (ii) in connection with the body's trading arrangements, and

    (*b*) the money is repayable to the Minister or department,

sums standing to the credit of the fund are required to be applied (in whole or in part) in repaying the money.

(4) The requirement mentioned in subsection (3) must be imposed by or under the scheme or arrangement mentioned in section 153(2).

(5) The third condition is that—

    (*a*) the fund is reviewed by a Minister at intervals fixed by or under the scheme or arrangement mentioned in section 153(2), and

    (*b*) if the fund appears to the Minister to exceed what is reasonably required by the body, the excess is withdrawn from the fund.

Commentary—*Simon's Taxes* **B5.647.**
Derivation—TA 1988 s 509(2).
HMRC Manuals—Company Taxation Manual CTM40900 (marketing boards).

155 Interpretation of sections 153 and 154

(1) In sections 153 and 154 "Minister" means—

    (*a*) a Minister of the Crown,

    (*b*) the Scottish Ministers,

    (*c*) the Welsh Ministers, or

    (*d*) a Minister within the meaning of the Northern Ireland Act 1998 (c 47).

(2) In sections 153 and 154 "department" means—

    (*a*) a government department,

    (*b*) a part of the Scottish Administration,

    (*c*) a part of the Welsh Assembly Government, or

    (*d*) a Northern Ireland department.

HMRC Manuals—Business Income Manual BIM24850 (marketing boards).

CHAPTER 10

TRADE PROFITS: CHANGES IN TRADING STOCK

Introduction

156 Meaning of "trading stock"

(1) In this Chapter "trading stock", in relation to a trade, means anything (whether land or other property)—

    (*a*) which is sold in the ordinary course of the trade, or

    (*b*) which would be so sold if it were mature or its manufacture, preparation or construction were complete.

(2) It does not include—

    (*a*) materials used in the manufacture, preparation or construction of any such thing,

    (*b*) any services performed in the ordinary course of the trade, or

    (*c*) any article produced, or any material used, in the performance of any such services.

Commentary—*Simon's Taxes* **B2.205.**
Derivation—FA 2008 Sch 15 para 5(2), (3).
HMRC Manuals—Business Income Manual BIM33630 (nontrading transactions in stock: own goods).

Transfers of trading stock between trade and trader

157 Trading stock appropriated by trader

(1) This section applies if trading stock of a company's trade is appropriated by the company for any other purpose.

(2) In calculating the profits of the trade—

    (*a*) the amount which the stock appropriated would have realised if sold in the open market at the time of the appropriation is brought into account as a receipt, and

    (*b*) the value of anything in fact received for it is left out of account.

(3) The receipt is treated as arising on the date of the appropriation.

Commentary—*Simon's Taxes* **B2.205.**
Derivation—FA 2008 Sch 15 para 6.
HMRC Manuals—Business Income Manual BIM33715 (cost of stock acquired as part of the acquisition).
BIM55715 (animals used for racing).

158 Trading stock supplied by trader

(1) This section applies if something that—
    (a) belongs to a company carrying on a trade, but
    (b) is not trading stock of the trade,
becomes trading stock of the trade.
(2) In calculating the profits of the trade—
    (a) the cost of the stock is taken to be the amount which it would have realised if sold in the open market at the time it became trading stock of the trade, and
    (b) the value of anything in fact given for it is left out of account.
(3) The cost is treated as being incurred on the date it became trading stock of the trade.

Commentary—*Simon's Taxes* **B2.205, B5.111.**
Derivation—FA 2008 Sch 15 para 7.
HMRC Manuals—Business Income Manual BIM55715 (animals used for racing).
BIM66655 (owner occupation of woodlands).

Other disposals and acquisitions not made in the course of trade

159 Disposals not made in the course of trade

(1) This section applies if—
    (a) trading stock of a trade is disposed of otherwise than in the course of the trade, and
    (b) section 157 does not apply.
(2) In calculating the profits of the trade—
    (a) the amount which the stock disposed of would have realised if sold in the open market at the time of the disposal is brought into account as a receipt, and
    (b) any consideration obtained for it is left out of account.
(3) The receipt is treated as arising on the date of the disposal.
(4) This section is subject to section 161.

Commentary—*Simon's Taxes* **B2.205.**
Derivation—FA 2008 Sch 15 para 8.

160 Acquisitions not made in the course of trade

(1) This section applies if—
    (a) trading stock of a trade has been acquired otherwise than in the course of the trade, and
    (b) section 158 does not apply.
(2) In calculating the profits of the trade—
    (a) the cost of the stock is taken to be the amount which it would have realised if sold in the open market at the time of the acquisition, and
    (b) the value of anything in fact given for it is left out of account.
(3) The cost is treated as being incurred on the date of the acquisition.
(4) This section is subject to section 161.

Commentary—*Simon's Taxes* **B2.205, B5.111.**
Derivation—FA 2008 Sch 15 para 9.

Relationship with transfer pricing rules

161 Transfer pricing rules to take precedence

(1) Section 159 or 160 does not apply if the relevant consideration—
    (a) falls to be adjusted for tax purposes under [Part 4 of TIOPA 2010][1], or
    (b) falls within [that Part][1] without falling to be so adjusted.
[(1A) Subsection (1B) applies in relation to a disposal or acquisition if—
    (a) by virtue of subsection (1), section 159 or 160 does not apply, and
    (b) the market value amount is greater than the Part 4 TIOPA amount.
(1B) An amount equal to the market value amount less the Part 4 TIOPA amount is to be brought into account in calculating the profits of the trade (in addition to the Part 4 TIOPA amount).
(1C) In subsections (1A) and (1B)—
    "market value amount" means the amount referred to in section 159(2)(a) or 160(2)(a);
    "Part 4 TIOPA amount" means the amount which, following the application of Part 4 of TIOPA 2010 to the relevant consideration, is brought into account in respect of the relevant consideration in calculating the profits of the trade.][2]
[(2) For the purposes of subsection (1)(b), the relevant consideration falls within Part 4 of TIOPA 2010 without falling to be adjusted under that Part if—
    (a) the condition in section 147(1)(a) of TIOPA 2010 is met, and
    (b) the participation condition is met (see subsection (3A)), but
    (c) either—

    (a) it is sold to a person who carries on, or intends to carry on, a trade, profession or vocation in the United Kingdom and is entitled to deduct the cost of the stock as an expense in calculating the profits of that trade, profession or vocation for corporation or income tax purposes,

    (b) the buyer is connected with the seller, and

    (c) an election is made under this section.

(2) The parties to the sale may make an election under this section if the value of the stock determined under section 166 exceeds both—

    (a) its acquisition value, and

    (b) the amount in fact realised on the sale.

(3) If an election is made, the value is taken to be—

    (a) its acquisition value, or

    (b) if greater, the amount in fact realised on the sale.

(4) An election under this section must be made by both parties not later than two years after the end of the accounting period in which the cessation occurred.

(5) The "acquisition value" of trading stock means the amount which would have been deductible as representing its acquisition value, in calculating the profits of the trade, on the following assumptions—

    (a) that the stock had been sold in the course of the trade, immediately before the cessation, for a price equal to the value of the stock determined under section 166, and

    (b) that the period for which those profits were to be calculated began immediately before the sale.

(6) If the stock is sold together with other assets, so much of the amount realised on the sale as, on a just and reasonable apportionment, is properly attributable to each asset is treated as the amount realised on the sale of that asset.

Commentary—*Simon's Taxes* B2.617, B5.141, B9.201-B9.202.
HMRC Manuals—Business Income Manual BIM33480 (stock transferred to a UK trader).
BIM33495 (stock: valuation on discontinuance of business: meanings).
BIM33530 (valuation on discontinuance of business: examples).

168 Connected persons

For the purposes of sections 164 to 167 two persons are connected with each other if any of the following tests is met—

    (a) they are connected with each other within the meaning of [section 1122 of CTA 2010][1],

    (b) one of them is a firm and the other has a right to a share of the assets or income of the firm,

    (c) one of them is a body corporate and the other has control over that body,

    (d) both of them are firms and some other person has a right to a share of the assets or income of both of them, or

    (e) both of them are bodies corporate, or one of them is a firm and the other is a body corporate, and in either case some other person has control over both of them.

Commentary—*Simon's Taxes* B2.617.
Derivation—TA 1988 s 100(1F).
HMRC Manuals—Business Income Manual BIM33480 (stock transferred to a UK trader).
BIM33495 (stock: valuation on discontinuance of business: meanings).
Amendments—[1] In para (a) words substituted for words "section 839 of ICTA" by CTA 2010 s 1177, Sch 1 para 599. CTA 2010 has effect for corporation tax purposes for accounting periods ending on or after 1 April 2010, and for income and capital gains tax purposes for the tax year 2010–11 and subsequent tax years.

169 Cost to buyer of stock valued on sale basis of valuation

(1) This section applies for the purpose of calculating the profits of the trade carried on by the buyer of trading stock.

(2) If the value of the stock is determined in accordance with—

    (a) section 164(3) or sections 165 to 167 (sale basis of valuation), or

    (b) section 175(3) or sections 176 to 178 of ITTOIA 2005 (corresponding income tax rules),

the cost of the stock to the buyer is taken to be the value as so determined.

Commentary—*Simon's Taxes* B2.615, B2.617.
Derivation—TA 1988 s 100(1E).
HMRC Manuals—Business Income Manual BIM33480 (stock transferred to a UK trader).
BIM33515 (purchaser cost value).

170 Meaning of "sale" and related expressions

(1) In sections 164 to 167 (except in section 167(5)) references to a sale include a transfer for valuable consideration.

(2) In relation to a transfer which is not a sale—

    "amount realised on the sale" means the value of the consideration given for the transfer,

    "buyer" means the person to whom the transfer is made, and

    "seller" means the person who makes the transfer.

171 Determination of questions

Any question arising under section 164(3) or sections 165 to 167 (sale basis of valuation of trading stock) must be determined in the same way as an appeal.

Commentary—*Simon's Taxes* **B2.617**.
Derivation—TA 1988 s 102(1).
HMRC Manuals—Business Income Manual BIM33550 (resolving disputes).

CHAPTER 12

DEDUCTIONS FROM PROFITS: UNREMITTABLE AMOUNTS

172 Application of Chapter

(1) This Chapter applies if—

    (*a*) an amount received by, or owed to, a company carrying on a trade ("the trader") is brought into account as a receipt in calculating the profits of the trade,

    (*b*) the amount is paid or owed in a territory outside the United Kingdom, and

    (*c*) some or all of the amount is unremittable.

(2) An amount received is unremittable if it cannot be transferred to the United Kingdom merely because of foreign exchange restrictions.

(3) An amount owed is unremittable if it cannot be paid in the United Kingdom and—

    (*a*) it temporarily cannot be paid in the territory in which it is owed merely because of foreign exchange restrictions, or

    (*b*) it can be paid in that territory but, if it were paid there, the amount paid would not be transferable to the United Kingdom merely because of foreign exchange restrictions.

(4) "Foreign exchange restrictions" are restrictions imposed by any of the following—

    (*a*) the laws of the territory where the amount is paid or owed,

    (*b*) executive action of its government, and

    (*c*) the impossibility of obtaining there currency that could be transferred to the United Kingdom.

(5) Section 464(1) (matters to be brought into account in the case of loan relationships) does not prevent any amount from being brought into account in accordance with section 173 or 175.

Commentary—*Simon's Taxes* **B2.117**.
Change in the law—See CTA 2009 EN Annex 1, Change 40.
HMRC Manuals—Business Income Manual BIM42750 (bad and doubtful debts: currency restrictions).

173 Relief for unremittable amounts

(1) If—

    (*a*) the trader has profits from the trade in a period of account, and

    (*b*) an unremittable amount has been brought into account as a receipt for that period,

a deduction of the amount is allowed from those profits (but see subsection (5)).

(2) If the trader has profits from the trade in a period of account and the total of—

    (*a*) any unremittable amounts brought into account as receipts for that period, and

    (*b*) any amount carried forward under this subsection or subsection (3) from the previous period of account,

exceeds the amount of those profits, the excess may be carried forward to the next period of account.

(3) If the trader does not have profits from the trade in a period of account and an unremittable amount has been brought into account as a receipt for that period, the total of—

    (*a*) any unremittable amounts brought into account as receipts for that period, and

    (*b*) any amount carried forward under this subsection or subsection (2) from the previous period of account,

may be carried forward to the next period of account.

(4) If an amount is carried forward under this section to a period of account in which the trader has profits from the trade, a deduction of the amount is allowed from those profits (but see subsection (5)).

(5) The total amount deducted under this section from the profits from a trade in a period of account must not exceed the amount of the profits.

Commentary—*Simon's Taxes* **B2.118**.
Change in the law—See CTA 2009 EN Annex 1, Change 40.
HMRC Manuals—Business Income Manual BIM42750 (bad and doubtful debts: currency restrictions).

174 Restrictions on relief

(1) No deduction is allowed under section 173 in relation to an amount so far as—

    (*a*) it is used to finance expenditure or investment outside the United Kingdom, or

    (*b*) it is applied outside the United Kingdom in another way.

(2) No deduction is allowed under section 173 in relation to an amount owed so far as a payment under a contract of insurance has been received in relation to it.

(3) No deduction is allowed under section 173 in relation to an amount brought into account in calculating profits if relief under section 1275 (unremittable income) may be claimed in relation to that amount.

Commentary—*Simon's Taxes* **B2.119**.
Change in the law—See CTA 2009 EN Annex 1, Change 40.
HMRC Manuals—Business Income Manual BIM42750 (bad and doubtful debts: currency restrictions).

175 Withdrawal of relief

(1) This section applies if—
  (*a*) some or all of an unremittable amount has been deducted from profits under section 173, and
  (*b*) any of the following events occurs.
(2) The events are that—
  (*a*) the amount or part of it ceases to be unremittable,
  (*b*) an allowable provision for impairment loss is made in respect of the amount or part of it,
  (*c*) the amount or part of it is used to finance expenditure or investment outside the United Kingdom,
  (*d*) the amount or part of it is applied outside the United Kingdom in another way,
  (*e*) the amount or part of it is exchanged for, or discharged by, an amount that is not unremittable, and
  (*f*) if the amount is an amount owed, a payment under a contract of insurance is received in relation to the amount or part of it.
(3) The amount or the part of it in question is brought into account as a receipt in calculating the profits of the trade of the period of account in which the event occurs, but only so far as—
  (*a*) it has been deducted from profits under section 173, and
  (*b*) it has not already been brought into account as a receipt in calculating the profits of the trade as a result of this section.
(4) If the event is the receipt of a payment under a contract of insurance, the amount brought into account as a receipt must not exceed the amount of the payment.
(5) In subsection (2)(*b*) "allowable provision for impairment loss" means either—
  (*a*) a debit in respect of the impairment of a financial asset (see section 476(1)) which is brought into account under Part 5 (loan relationships), or
  (*b*) a provision in respect of which a deduction is allowable under section 55 (bad debts).

Commentary—*Simon's Taxes* **B2.119**.
Change in the law—See CTA 2009 EN Annex 1, Change 40.
HMRC Manuals—Business Income Manual BIM42750 (bad and doubtful debts: currency restrictions).

CHAPTER 13

DISPOSAL AND ACQUISITION OF KNOW-HOW

176 Meaning of "know-how" etc

(1) In this Chapter "know-how" means any industrial information or techniques likely to assist in—
  (*a*) manufacturing or processing goods or materials,
  (*b*) working a source of mineral deposits (including searching for, discovering or testing mineral deposits or obtaining access to them), or
  (*c*) carrying out any agricultural, forestry or fishing operations.
(2) For this purpose—
  "mineral deposits" includes any natural deposits capable of being lifted or extracted from the earth and for this purpose geothermal energy is treated as a natural deposit, and
  "source of mineral deposits" includes a mine, an oil well and a source of geothermal energy.
(3) For the purposes of this Chapter any consideration received for giving, or wholly or partly fulfilling, an undertaking which—
  (*a*) is given in connection with a disposal of know-how, and
  (*b*) restricts, or is designed to restrict, any person's activities in any way,
is treated as consideration received for the disposal of the know-how.
(4) It does not matter whether or not the undertaking is legally enforceable.
(5) For the purposes of this Chapter references to a sale of know-how include an exchange of know-how and any provision of this Chapter referring to a sale has effect with the necessary modifications.
(6) Those modifications include, in particular, reading references to the proceeds of sale and to the price as including the consideration for the exchange.

Commentary—*Simon's Taxes* **B5.343**.
HMRC Manuals—Capital Allowances Manual CA70010 (Definition of know-how).

177 Disposal of know-how if trade continues to be carried on

(1) This section applies if—
  (*a*) a company carrying on a trade receives consideration for the disposal of know-how which has been used in the trade,
  (*b*) the company continues to carry on the trade after the disposal, and

(*c*) neither section 178 (disposal of know-how as part of disposal of all or part of a trade) nor section 179 (seller controlled by buyer etc) applies.

(2) The amount or value of the consideration is treated for corporation tax purposes as a trading receipt, except so far as it is brought into account under section 462 of CAA 2001 (disposal values).

(3) If the know-how is sold together with other property, the net proceeds of the sale of the know-how are treated as being so much of the net proceeds of the sale of all the property as, on a just and reasonable apportionment, is attributable to the know-how.

(4) For this purpose all property sold as a result of one bargain is treated as sold together even though—

     (*a*) separate prices are, or purport to be, agreed for separate items of that property, or

     (*b*) there are, or purport to be, separate sales of separate items of that property.

(5) Any question about the way in which a sum is to be apportioned under this section must be determined in accordance with section 563(2) to (6) of CAA 2001 (procedure for determining certain questions affecting two or more persons) if it materially affects two or more taxpayers.

(6) For this purpose a question materially affects two or more taxpayers if, at the time when the question falls to be determined, it appears that the determination is material to the liability to tax (for whatever period) of two or more persons.

Commentary—*Simon's Taxes* **B5.345, B5.347**.
Derivation—TA 1988 ss 531(1), 532; CAA 2001 s 562(1)–(3).
HMRC Manuals—Capital Allowances Manual CA70050 (treat as property for capital allowances and ITTOIA purposes).
CA72400 (trading receipt treatment).
CA72500 (treatment of receipts).

178 Disposal of know-how as part of disposal of all or part of a trade

(1) This section applies if—

     (*a*) a person carrying on a trade receives consideration for the disposal of know-how which has been used in the trade, and

     (*b*) the know-how is disposed of as part of the disposal of all or part of the trade.

(2) If the person disposing of the know-how is within the charge to corporation tax, the consideration is treated for corporation tax purposes as a capital receipt for goodwill.

(3) If the person acquiring the know-how—

     (*a*) is within the charge to corporation tax, and

     (*b*) provided the consideration,

the consideration is treated for corporation tax purposes as a capital payment for goodwill.

(4) But the consideration is not treated for corporation tax purposes as a capital payment for goodwill if, before the acquisition, the trade was carried on wholly outside the United Kingdom.

(5) If the person disposing of the know-how is within the charge to corporation tax—

     (*a*) that person, and

     (*b*) the person acquiring the know-how (whether or not within the charge to corporation tax),

may jointly elect for this section not to apply (but see section 179).

(6) The election must be made within two years of the disposal.

(7) If—

     (*a*) an election is made under section 194 of ITTOIA 2005 (corresponding income tax provision), and

     (*b*) the person making the acquisition mentioned in that section is within the charge to corporation tax,

the persons making the election under that section are treated as also making an election under this section (even though the person disposing of the know-how is not within the charge to corporation tax).

Commentary—*Simon's Taxes* **B3.615, B5.346, B5.347**.
Derivation—TA 1988 s 531(2), (3).
HMRC Manuals—Capital Allowances Manual CA72300 (goodwill treatment).
CA71300 (disposal values).

179 Seller controlled by buyer etc

(1) This section applies if a disposal of know-how is by way of sale and—

     (*a*) the seller is a body of persons over which the buyer has control,

     (*b*) the buyer is a body of persons over which the seller has control, or

     (*c*) both the seller and the buyer are bodies of persons and another person has control over both of them.

(2) In such a case—

     (*a*) section 177 does not apply, and

     (*b*) no election may be made under section 178.

(3) For the purposes of this section "body of persons" includes a firm.

Commentary—*Simon's Taxes* **B3.615, B5.345, B5.346**.
Derivation—TA 1988 s 531(7); CAA 2001 s 453, s 572(1).

CHAPTER 14
ADJUSTMENT ON CHANGE OF BASIS
Adjustment on change of basis

180 Application of Chapter

(1) This Chapter applies if—

    (*a*) a company carrying on a trade changes, from one period of account to the next, the basis on which profits of the trade are calculated for corporation tax purposes,

    (*b*) the old basis accorded with the law or practice applicable in relation to the period of account before the change, and

    (*c*) the new basis accords with the law and practice applicable in relation to the period of account after the change.

(2) The practice applicable in any case means the accepted practice in cases of that description as to how profits of a trade should be calculated for corporation tax purposes.

(3) A company changes the basis on which profits of a trade are calculated for corporation tax purposes if the company makes—

    (*a*) a [change of accounting policy][1] (see subsection (4)), or

    (*b*) a change in the tax adjustments applied (see subsections (5) and (6)).

[(4) A "change of accounting policy" includes, in particular—

    (*a*) a change from using UK generally accepted accounting practice to using generally accepted accounting practice with respect to accounts prepared in accordance with international accounting standards, and

    (*b*) a change from using generally accepted accounting practice with respect to accounts prepared in accordance with international accounting standards to using UK generally accepted accounting practice.][1]

(5) A "tax adjustment" means any adjustment required or authorised by law in calculating profits of a trade for corporation tax purposes.

(6) A "change in the tax adjustments applied"—

    (*a*) does not include a change made in order to comply with amending legislation not applicable to the previous period of account, but

    (*b*) includes a change resulting from a change of view as to what is required or authorised by law or as to whether any adjustment is so required or authorised.

Commentary—*Simon's Taxes* **B6.212, B2.114**.

HMRC Manuals—Business Income Manual BIM34040 (change of basis of computing taxable profits: from one valid basis to another valid basis).

BIM34050 (change of basis of computing taxable profits: accounting policy changes).

BIM34070 (change of basis of computing taxable profits: changes in tax adjustment).

BIM34135 (change of basis of computing taxable profits: adjustment income and expenses: meanings).

Amendments—[1] Words in sub-s (3)(*a*) and the whole of sub-s (4) substituted by FA 2012 s 54(2) with effect in relation to a change of basis if the new basis is adopted for a period of account which begins: (a) on or after 1 January 2012; or (b) before 1 January 2012 and the adoption is in consequence of the issue, revocation, amendment or recognition of, or withdrawal of recognition from, an accounting standard by an accounting body on or after 1 January 2012.

181 Giving effect to positive and negative adjustments

(1) An amount by way of adjustment must be calculated in accordance with section 182.

(2) If the amount produced by the calculation is positive—

    (*a*) the amount is brought into account as a receipt in calculating the profits of the trade, and

    (*b*) the receipt is treated as arising on the first day of the first period of account for which the new basis is adopted.

(3) If the amount produced by the calculation is negative—

    (*a*) a deduction is allowed for the amount as an expense of the trade in calculating the profits of the trade, and

    (*b*) the expense is treated as arising on the first day of the first period of account for which the new basis is adopted.

(4) This section is subject to—

    (*a*) section 183 (no adjustment for certain expenses previously brought into account),

    (*b*) section 184 (cases where adjustment not required until assets realised or written off), and

    (*c*) section 185 (change from realisation basis to mark to market).

Commentary—*Simon's Taxes* **B7.401, B2.115, B2.115, D1.1203A**.

HMRC Manuals—Business Income Manual BIM34095 (change of basis of computing taxable profits: adjustment income and expenses).

Corporate Intangibles Research and Development Manual CIRD220210 (relevant IP profits: total gross income of a trade).

182 Calculation of the adjustment

The amount of the adjustment is calculated as follows.

Step 1

Add together any amounts representing the extent to which, comparing the two bases, profits were understated (or losses overstated) on the old basis.

The amounts are—

	Amounts
1	Receipts which on the new basis would have been brought into account in calculating the profits of a period of account before the change, so far as they were not so brought into account.
2	Expenses which on the new basis fall to be brought into account in calculating the profits of a period of account after the change, so far as they were brought into account in calculating the profits of a period of account before the change.
3	Deductions in respect of opening trading stock or opening work in progress in the first period of account on the new basis, so far as they—
	(*a*) are not matched by credits in respect of closing trading stock or closing work in progress in the last period of account before the change, or
	(*b*) are calculated on a different basis that if used to calculate those credits would have given a higher figure.
4	Amounts recognised for accounting purposes in respect of depreciation in the last period of account before the change, so far as they were not the subject of an adjustment for corporation tax purposes, where such an adjustment would be required on the new basis.

Step 2
Then deduct any amounts representing the extent to which, comparing the two bases, profits were overstated (or losses understated) on the old basis.
The amounts are—

	Amounts
1	Receipts which were brought into account in a period of account before the change, so far as they would not have been so brought into account if the profits had been calculated on the new basis.
2	Expenses which were not brought into account in calculating the profits of a period of account before the change, so far as they—
	(*a*) would have been brought into account for a period of account before the change if the profits had been calculated on the new basis, and
	(*b*) would have been brought into account for a period of account after the change if the profits had continued to be calculated on the old basis.
3	Credits in respect of closing trading stock or closing work in progress in the last period of account before the change, so far as they—
	(*a*) are not matched by deductions in respect of opening trading stock or opening work in progress in the first period of account on the new basis, or
	(*b*) are calculated on a different basis that if used to calculate those deductions would have given a lower figure.

An amount so deducted may not be deducted again in calculating the profits of a period of account.
Commentary—*Simon's Taxes* **B2.115**.
HMRC Manuals—Business Income Manual BIM34130 (change of basis of computing taxable profits: adjustment income and expenses: calculation of adjustment).

Expenses previously brought into account

183 No adjustment for certain expenses previously brought into account
(1) This section applies if, as a result of a change of basis, expenses brought into account before the change on the old basis would on the new basis be brought into account over more than one period of account after the change.
(2) In such a case—
    (*a*) no adjustment is made under this Chapter, and
    (*b*) in calculating the profits of the trade no deduction is allowed for the expenses for any period of account after the change.
Commentary—*Simon's Taxes* **B2.115**.
Derivation—FA 2002 s 64(1), Sch 22 para 6(1), (2).
HMRC Manuals—Business Income Manual BIM34105 (change of basis of computing taxable profits: adjustment income and expenses: expenses already allowed).
Corporate Intangibles Research and Development Manual CIRD99400 (R&D tax relief: accountancy: adjustment on change of basis).
CIRD99200 (R&D tax credits: accountancy: IAS38).

Realising or writing off assets

184 Cases where adjustment not required until assets realised or written off
(1) This section applies if there is a change of basis resulting from a tax adjustment affecting the calculation of any of the following amounts.

(2) The amounts are—
- (a) any amount brought into account in respect of closing trading stock in the last period of account before the change of basis,
- (b) any amount brought into account in respect of opening trading stock in the first period of account on the new basis, and
- (c) any amount brought into account in respect of depreciation.

(3) The receipt of the trade or (as the case may be) the expense of the trade is treated as arising only when the asset to which it relates is realised or written off.

Commentary—*Simon's Taxes* **B2.115**.

HMRC Manuals—Business Income Manual BIM34110 (change of basis of computing taxable profits: adjustment income and expenses: stock and depreciation).

Mark to market

185 Change from realisation basis to mark to market

(1) This section applies if there is a change of basis from—
- (a) not recognising a profit or loss on an asset until the asset is realised, to
- (b) bringing assets into account in each period of account at a fair value.

(2) So far as—
- (a) a receipt within item 1 of Step 1 in section 182 represents the fair value of an asset that is trading stock, or
- (b) an expense within item 2 of that step relates to such an asset,

the receipt of the trade or (as the case may be) the expense of the trade is treated as not arising until the period of account in which the value of the asset is realised.

(3) In the case of a receipt of the trade, this is subject to any election under section 186 (election for spreading).

(4) In this section "trading stock" has the same meaning as in section 163.

Commentary—*Simon's Taxes* **B2.115**.

Derivation—FA 2002 s 64(1), Sch 22 para 8(1), (2).

HMRC Manuals—Business Income Manual BIM34115 (change of basis of computing taxable profits: change from realisation basis to mark to market (fair value) accounting).

186 Election for spreading if section 185 applies

(1) If section 185 applies, the company carrying on the trade may elect for any receipt treated as arising under this Chapter to be spread over 6 periods of account.

(2) The election must be made within 12 months of the end of the first accounting period to which the new basis applies.

(3) If an election is made, an amount equal to one-sixth of the amount of the receipt—
- (a) is treated as arising, and
- (b) is brought into account in calculating the profits of the trade,

in each of the 6 periods of account beginning with the first period to which the new basis applies.

(4) But if, before the whole of the receipt has been so brought into account, the company permanently ceases to carry on the trade, the whole of the amount so far as not previously brought into account—
- (a) is treated as arising, and
- (b) is brought into account in calculating the profits of the trade,

immediately before the cessation.

Commentary—*Simon's Taxes* **B7.401, B2.115**.

HMRC Manuals—Business Income Manual BIM34120 (change of basis of computing taxable profits: change from realisation basis to mark to market (fair value) accounting: spreading election).

187 Transfer of insurance business

(1) This section applies if—
- (a) an asset to which section 185 or 186 applies is transferred from one insurance company to another,
- (b) the transfer is made under an insurance business transfer scheme, and
- (c) immediately after the transfer, the transferee is UK resident or the asset is held for the purposes of a business carried on by the transferee in the United Kingdom through a permanent establishment.

(2) For the purposes of section 185, the asset is not to be treated as realised by the transferor merely because of its transfer under the scheme.

(3) If the transfer is of the transferor's whole business, the transferee is responsible under section 185 or 186 for bringing into account any amount required to be brought into account after the transfer.

Commentary—*Simon's Taxes* **B2.115**.

Derivation—FA 2002 Sch 22 para 10(1), (2), (3).

CHAPTER 15

POST-CESSATION RECEIPTS

Charge to tax on post-cessation receipts

188 Charge to tax on post-cessation receipts

The charge to corporation tax on income applies to post-cessation receipts arising from a trade.

Commentary—*Simon's Taxes* **B2.801, B2.803, B2.805**.
HMRC Manuals—Business Income Manual BIM80510 (examples of receipts chargeable under CTA 2009 s 188).
BIM90010 (post cessation receipts and expenses: charge to tax).

189 Extent of charge to tax

(1) A post-cessation receipt is chargeable to tax under this Chapter only so far as it is not otherwise chargeable to corporation or income tax.

(2) Accordingly, a post-cessation receipt arising from a trade is not chargeable to tax under this Chapter so far as it is brought into account in calculating the profits of the trade of any period.

(3) A post-cessation receipt is not chargeable to tax under this Chapter if—

    (*a*) it is received by or on behalf of a non-UK resident company which is beneficially entitled to it, and

    (*b*) it represents income arising outside the United Kingdom.

(4) A post-cessation receipt is not chargeable to tax under this Chapter if it arises from a trade carried on wholly outside the United Kingdom [other than a company's trade of dealing in or developing UK land][1].

Commentary—*Simon's Taxes* **B2.803**.
HMRC Manuals—Business Income Manual BIM90010 (post cessation receipts and expenses: charge to tax).
BIM90015 (post cessation receipts and expenses: territorial scope of the provisions).
Amendments—[1]   In sub-s (4), words inserted by FA 2016 s 76(9) with effect in relation to disposals on or after 5 July 2016 (FA 2016 s 81(1)), subject to transitional provisions relating to disposals to associated persons on or after 16 March 2016 and before 5 July 2016 (FA 2016 s 81(4)–(15)).

    F(No 2)A 2017 s 39 provides that this amendment has effect (so far as it would not otherwise have effect) in relation to amounts that are recognised in GAAP accounts drawn up for any period of account beginning on or after 8 March 2017 or, in the case of a straddling period, amounts that would be recognised in GAAP accounts drawn up for a period of account beginning on 8 March 2017 and ending when the straddling period ends. "Straddling period" means a period of account beginning before 8 March 2017 and ending on or after that date.

Meaning of "post-cessation receipts"

190 Basic meaning of "post-cessation receipt"

(1) In this Part "post-cessation receipt" means a sum—

    (*a*) which is received after a person permanently ceases to carry on a trade, and

    (*b*) which arises from the carrying on of the trade before the cessation.

(2) In this Chapter, except in sections 194 and 195, references to a person permanently ceasing to carry on a trade include—

    (*a*) in the case of a company, the occurrence of an event treated under section 18 of ITTOIA 2005 (companies beginning or ceasing to be within charge to income tax) as the company permanently ceasing to carry on the trade, and

    (*b*) in the case of a trade carried on by a person in partnership, the occurrence of an event treated under section 246(4) of ITTOIA 2005 (basic meaning of "post-cessation receipt") as the person permanently ceasing to carry on the trade.

Commentary—*Simon's Taxes* **B2.804, B2.805**.
Derivation—TA 1988 ss 103(1), (2), 104(1), (2), 110(1A), (1B).
HMRC Manuals—Business Income Manual BIM90030 (post cessation receipts and expenses: meaning of post cessation receipts).

191 Other rules about what counts as post-cessation receipts

(1) The following provisions treat certain amounts as post-cessation receipts for the purposes of this Part—

    section 82(6) (contributions to local enterprise organisations or urban regeneration companies),
    section 101(3) (distribution of assets of mutual concerns),
    section 108(3) (receipt of benefits by donor or connected person),
    section 192 (debts paid after cessation),
    section 193 (debts released after cessation), as qualified, where appropriate, by section 56(4) (car . . . [1] hire),
    section 194 (transfer of rights if transferee does not carry on trade), and
    section 1277 (income charged on withdrawal of relief after source ceases: unremittable income).

(2) Section 95 (acquisition of trade: receipts from transferor's trade) and section 194 (transfer of rights if transferee does not carry on trade) treat certain amounts as not being post-cessation receipts for the purposes of this Part.

Commentary—*Simon's Taxes* **B2.804**.

HMRC Manuals—Business Income Manual BIM90030 (post cessation receipts and expenses: meaning of post cessation receipts).

Amendments—[1]   In sub-s (1) words "or motor cycle" repealed by FA 2009 s 30, Sch 11 para 51 with effect as provided for by FA 2009 Sch 11 paras 65, 66 and subject to savings in FA 2009 Sch 11 para 68. The new system of capital allowances for cars has effect generally from 6 April 2009 (for income tax) and 1 April 2009 (for corporation tax), subject to FA 2009 Sch 11 para 67 (election for new regime not to apply in certain cases).

Sums treated as post-cessation receipts

192 Debts paid after cessation

(1) This section applies if, in calculating the profits of a trade for corporation or income tax purposes, a deduction is made in respect of a debt under—

(*a*) section 55 (bad debts), or

(*b*) section 35 of ITTOIA 2005 (bad and doubtful debts),

and a person permanently ceases to carry on the trade.

(2) A sum received after the cessation is treated as a post-cessation receipt so far as the deduction is made.

Commentary—*Simon's Taxes* **B2.804, B2.805, B6.213**.

HMRC Manuals—Business Income Manual BIM42745 (specific deductions: bad and doubtful debts: business ceased).

BIM90035 (post cessation receipts and expenses: meaning of post cessation receipts: debts paid after cessation).

193 Debts released after cessation

(1) This section applies if—

(*a*) in calculating the profits of a trade of any period for corporation or income tax purposes, a deduction is allowed for the expense giving rise to a debt owed by the person who carried on the trade,

(*b*) the person has permanently ceased to carry on the trade at or after the end of that period,

(*c*) after the cessation, all or part of the debt is released, and

(*d*) the release is not part of a statutory insolvency arrangement.

(2) The amount released is treated as a post-cessation receipt.

Commentary—*Simon's Taxes* **B2.805, B2.804, B6.213, B2.206**.

HMRC Manuals—Business Income Manual BIM42740 (bad and doubtful debts: debts released).

BIM90040 (postcessation receipts and expenses: debts released after cessation).

194 Transfer of rights if transferee does not carry on trade

(1) This section applies if—

(*a*) a company ("the transferor") permanently ceases to carry on a trade,

(*b*) the transferor transfers to another person ("the transferee") for value the right to receive sums arising from the carrying on of the trade, and

(*c*) the transferee does not subsequently carry on the trade.

(2) The transferor is treated as receiving a post-cessation receipt.

(3) The amount of the receipt is—

(*a*) the amount or value of the consideration for the transfer, if the transfer is at arm's length, or

(*b*) the value of the rights transferred as between parties at arm's length, if the transfer is not at arm's length.

(4) Any sums mentioned in subsection (1)(*b*) which are received after the cessation of the trade are not post-cessation receipts.

(5) This section is subject to section 195 (transfer of trading stock).

Commentary—*Simon's Taxes* **B2.804, B2.805**.

Derivation—TA 1988 s 106(1), (2).

HMRC Manuals—Business Income Manual BIM42745 (specific deductions: bad and doubtful debts: business ceased).

BIM90050 (post cessation receipts and expenses: transfer of rights if transferee does not carry on the trade).

Sums that are not post-cessation receipts

195 Transfer of trading stock

(1) When a company permanently ceases to carry on a trade, a sum realised by the transfer of trading stock is not a post-cessation receipt if a valuation of the stock is brought into account in accordance with Chapter 11 (valuation of stock).

(2) In this section "trading stock" has the meaning given by section 163.

Commentary—*Simon's Taxes* **B2.805, B2.806**.

HMRC Manuals—Business Income Manual BIM90055 (post cessation receipts and expenses: transfer of trading stock).

Deductions

196 Allowable deductions

(1) In calculating the amount on which tax is charged under this Chapter, deductions are allowed in accordance with—

(*a*) this section, and

(*b*) section 197,

from the amount which would otherwise be chargeable to tax under this Chapter.

(2) A deduction is allowed for a loss, expense or debit which, if the person carrying on the trade had not permanently ceased to do so—

   (a) would have been deducted in calculating the profits of the trade for corporation or income tax purposes, or

   (b) would have been deducted from or set off against the profits of the trade for corporation or income tax purposes,

but no deduction is allowed if the loss, expense or debit arises directly or indirectly from the cessation itself.

(3) No deduction for an amount is allowed under this section if the amount has been allowed under any other provision of the Tax Acts.

Commentary—*Simon's Taxes* **B2.807, B2.808, B3.280.**
HMRC Manuals—Business Income Manual BIM47145 (specific deductions: staffing costs: remuneration paid after cessation).
BIM90080 (post cessation receipts and expenses: meaning of post cessation expenses).
BIM90090 (post cessation receipts and expenses: overview of reliefs for post cessation expenses).
BIM90095 (post cessation receipts and expenses: relief for post cessation expenses against post cessation receipts).

197 Further rules about allowable deductions

(1) An amount may not be deducted more than once under section 196.

(2) A deduction under that section of a loss must be made from post-cessation receipts charged for an earlier accounting period in preference to those charged for a later accounting period.

(3) But this does not authorise the deduction of a loss from post-cessation receipts charged for an accounting period before the accounting period in which the loss is made.

Commentary—*Simon's Taxes* **B2.807.**
Derivation—TA 1988 s 105(3), s 491(7).
HMRC Manuals—Business Income Manual BIM90090 (post cessation receipts and expenses: overview of reliefs for post cessation expenses).
BIM90095 (post cessation receipts and expenses: relief for post cessation expenses against post cessation receipts).

Election to carry back

198 Election to carry back

(1) This section applies if a post-cessation receipt is received by a company in an accounting period beginning not later than 6 years after the company permanently ceased to carry on the trade.

(2) The company may elect that the tax chargeable in respect of the receipt is to be charged as if the receipt had been received on the date of the cessation (but see sections 199 and 200).

(3) The election must be made before the end of the period of two years beginning immediately after the end of the accounting period in which the receipt is received.

Commentary—*Simon's Taxes* **B2.808.**
Change in the law—See CTA 2009 EN Annex 1, Change 42.
HMRC Manuals—Business Income Manual BIM90075 (post cessation receipts and expenses: election to carry back post cessation receipts).

199 Deductions already made are not displaced

(1) This section applies if—

   (a) a company which has permanently ceased to carry on a trade makes an election under section 198 in respect of a post-cessation receipt ("the carried back receipt"), and

   (b) a deduction in respect of a loss has already been made under section 196 for an accounting period later than that in which the cessation occurred.

(2) Nothing in section 196 (read with section 197(2)) requires or permits a deduction in respect of that loss to be allowed, as a result of the election, for the accounting period in which the cessation occurred instead of the accounting period for which the deduction has already been made.

(3) But if the deduction was made for the accounting period in which the carried back receipt was received, subsection (2) applies to the loss only so far as it has been deducted from post-cessation receipts other than the carried back receipt.

Commentary—*Simon's Taxes* **B2.808.**
Change in the law—See CTA 2009 EN Annex 1, Change 42.
HMRC Manuals—Business Income Manual BIM90075 (post cessation receipts and expenses: election to carry back post cessation receipts).

200 Election given effect in accounting period in which receipt is received

(1) If a company makes an election under section 198, the additional tax is payable for the accounting period in which the receipt is received (and not for the accounting period in which the cessation occurred).

(2) In subsection (1) "the additional tax" means an amount of tax equal to the difference between—

   (a) the amount of tax that is chargeable on the company for the accounting period in which the cessation occurred ("amount A"), and

   (b) the amount of tax that would have been chargeable on the company for that period if the election had not been made ("amount B").

(3) If—

CHAPTER 3

PROFITS OF PROPERTY BUSINESSES: BASIC RULES

Charge to tax on profits of a property business

209 Charge to tax on profits of a property business

The charge to corporation tax on income applies to the profits of a property business.

Commentary—*Simon's Taxes* B5.201, B6.202, D7.531.

HMRC Manuals—Property Income Manual PIM4703 (UK property business/ overseas property; charged to tax).

Calculation of profits

210 Profits of a property business; application of trading income rules

(1) The profits of a property business are calculated in the same way as the profits of a trade.

(2) But the provisions of Part 3 (trading income) which apply as a result of subsection (1) are limited to the following—

In Chapter 3 (basic rules)—	
section 46	generally accepted accounting practice
section 47	losses calculated on same basis as profits
section 48	receipts and expenses
[section 49A	money's worth][4]
section 52	apportionment etc of profits and losses to accounting period
In Chapter 4 (rules restricting deductions)—	
section 53	capital expenditure
section 54	expenses not wholly and exclusively for trade and unconnected losses
section 55	bad debts
sections 56 to [58B][1]	car [...][1] hire
section 59	patent royalties
In Chapter 5 (rules allowing deductions)—	
section 61	pre-trading expenses
. . .	. . .
section 69	payments for restrictive undertakings
sections 70 and 71	seconded employees
section 72	payroll deduction schemes: contributions to agents' expenses
sections 73 to 75	counselling and retraining expenses
sections 76 to 81	redundancy payments etc
sections 82 to 86	contributions to local enterprise organisations or urban regeneration companies
[sections 86A and 86B	contributions to flood and coastal erosion risk management projects][3]
sections 87 and 88	scientific research
sections 89 and 90	expenses connected with patents, designs and trade marks
section 91	payments to Export Credits Guarantee Department
section 92	levies under FISMA 2000
[section 92A	deductions in relation to salaried members of limited liability partnerships][2]
In Chapter 6 (receipts)—	
section 93	capital receipts
section 94	debts incurred and later released
section 101	distribution of assets of mutual concerns
section 102	industrial development grants
section 103	sums recovered under insurance policies etc
section 104	repayments under FISMA 2000
In Chapter 7 (gifts to charities etc)—	
section 108	receipt of benefits by donor or connected person
In Chapter 9 (other specific trades)—	
section 131	incidental costs of issuing qualifying shares (building societies)
section 133	annual payments paid by a credit union
In Chapter 12 (deductions from profits)—	
sections 172 to 175	unremittable amounts

Commentary—*Simon's Taxes* **A1.132, B6.104A, B6.202.**
Derivation—TA 1988 s 21A(1), (2), (4), (5), 21B, s 70A(5), (6).
HMRC Manuals—Business Income Manual BIM00570 (computing property income).
Amendments—[1]   In Table entry relating to ss 56–58, reference substituted for "58", words "or motor cycle" repealed, by FA
    2009 s 30, Sch 11 para 52 with effect as provided for by FA 2009 Sch 11 paras 65, 66 and subject to savings in FA 2009
    Sch 11 para 68. The new system of capital allowances for cars has effect generally from 6 April 2009 (for income tax) and
    1 April 2009 (for corporation tax), subject to FA 2009 Sch 11 para 67 (election for new regime not to apply in certain cases).
[2]   In sub-s (2), Table entry relating to s 92A inserted by FA 2014 s 74, Sch 17 para 4(1), (3). This amendment is treated as having
    come into force on 6 April 2014.
[3]   In sub-s (2), Table entry relating to ss 86A and 86B inserted by FA 2015 s 35, Sch 5 para 4 with effect in relation to
    contributions paid or provided on or after 1 January 2015.
[4]   In sub-s (2), Table entry relating to s 49A inserted by FA 2016 s 71(4), (6) with effect in relation to transactions entered into
    on or after 16 March 2016.
[5]   In sub-s (2), Table entry relating to s 68 repealed by FA 2016 s 72(3) with effect in relation to expenditure incurred on or after
    1 April 2016 for corporation tax purposes and 6 April 2016 for income tax purposes.

211 Loan relationships and derivative contracts

(1) The profits of a property business are calculated without regard to items giving rise to—
   (a) credits or debits within Part 5 (loan relationships), or
   (b) credits or debits within Part 7 (derivative contracts).
(2) This section does not affect the width of the provision made by—
   (a) section 464 (priority of Part 5 for corporation tax purposes), or
   (b) section 699 (priority of Part 7 for corporation tax purposes).

Commentary—*Simon's Taxes* **B6.202, D7.1126, D7.533, D7.534.**
Derivation—TA 1988 s 15(1) (Sch A para 2(3)), s 70A(5).

212 Items treated as receipts and expenses

The rules for calculating the profits of a property business need to be read with—
   (a) the provisions of CAA 2001 which treat allowances as expenses of a property business,
   (b) the provisions of CAA 2001 which treat charges as receipts of a property business, and
   (c) section 748 (credits and debits in respect of an intangible fixed asset held by a company for the purposes of a property business carried on by it treated as receipts and expenses of the business).

Commentary—*Simon's Taxes* **B6.202.**

213 Certain amounts brought into account under Part 3

(1) The rules for calculating the profits of a property business need to be read with the following provisions of Part 3 (trading income)—
   (a) section 42 (tied premises),
   (b) section 43 (caravan sites where trade carried on),
   (c) section 44 (surplus business accommodation), and
   (d) section 45(3) (payments for wayleaves).
(2) Those provisions secure that amounts which would otherwise be brought into account in calculating the profits of the business are, or may be, brought into account instead in calculating the profits of a trade.

Commentary—*Simon's Taxes* **B2.216, B2.217, B2.218, B2.219.**
HMRC Manuals—Property Income Manual PIM4300 (rents related to a trade or profession).

214 Relationship between rules prohibiting and allowing deductions

(1) Any relevant permissive rule in this Part—
   (a) has priority over any relevant prohibitive rule, but
   (b) is subject to the following provisions—
      (i) section 56 (car . . . [1] hire), as applied by section 210,
      (ii) section 1288 (unpaid remuneration),
      (iii) section 1290 (employee benefit contributions),
      (iv) section 1304 (crime-related payments).
[(1A) But, if the relevant permissive rule would allow a deduction in calculating the profits of a property business in respect of an amount which arises directly or indirectly in consequence of, or otherwise in connection with, relevant tax avoidance arrangements, that rule—
   (a) does not have priority under subsection (1)(a), and
   (b) is subject to any relevant prohibitive rule (and to the provisions mentioned in subsection (1)(b)).][2]
(2) In this section "any relevant permissive rule in this Part" means any provision of this Part (apart from sections 231 to 234) which allows a deduction in calculating the profits of a property business.
(3) In this section "any relevant prohibitive rule", in relation to any deduction, means any provision of this Part or Chapter 1 of Part 20 (apart from those mentioned in subsection (1)(b)) which might otherwise be read as—
   (a) prohibiting or deferring the deduction, or

$$S \times \left(\frac{50 - Y}{50} \right)$$

where—

S is the sum payable as consideration for the surrender of the lease, and

Y is the number of complete periods of 12 months (other than the first) comprised in the effective duration of the lease.

(5) But, if the rule in section 228 (the additional calculation rule) applies, the amount given by the formula in subsection (4) is reduced by the amount calculated in accordance with section 228.

Commentary—*Simon's Taxes* B6.304.

HMRC Manuals—Property Income Manual PIM1214 (sums payable for surrender of a lease).

221 Sums payable for variation or waiver of terms of lease

(1) This section applies if—

    (a) a sum becomes payable by the tenant (otherwise than by way of rent) as consideration for the variation or waiver of a term of a lease,

    (b) the sum is due to the landlord or a company which is connected with the landlord, and

    (c) the period for which the variation or waiver has effect is 50 years or less.

(2) The company to which the sum is due is treated as—

    (a) entering into a transaction mentioned in section 205 (if the land to which the lease relates is in the United Kingdom) or section 206 (if that land is outside the United Kingdom), and

    (b) receiving the amount calculated under subsections (4) and (5) as a result of that transaction.

(3) That amount is brought into account as a receipt in calculating the profits of the property business which consists of or includes that transaction for the accounting period in which the contract providing for the variation or waiver is entered into.

(4) The amount of the receipt is given by the formula—

$$S \times \left(\frac{50 - Y}{50} \right)$$

where—

S is the sum payable as consideration for the variation or waiver, and

Y is the number of complete periods of 12 months (other than the first) comprised in the period for which the variation or waiver has effect.

(5) But, if the rule in section 228 (the additional calculation rule) applies, the amount given by the formula in subsection (4) is reduced by the amount calculated in accordance with section 228.

(6) In determining for the purposes of this Chapter the duration of the period for which the variation or waiver has effect, any part of the period that falls after the expiry of the effective duration of the lease is excluded.

Commentary—*Simon's Taxes* B6.305, C2.113, C2.1231.

HMRC Manuals—Property Income Manual PIM1216 (sums payable for variation or waiver of terms of a lease).

[221A Sums to which sections 217 to 221 do not apply

(1) This section applies if a grant of a lease constitutes a disposal of an asset for the purposes of section 758(2)(b) or 763(2)(a) of CTA 2010 (disposals under finance arrangements).

(2) Sections 217 to 221 do not apply in relation to a premium paid in respect of the grant.][1]

Amendments—[1]   This section inserted by CTA 2010 s 1177, Sch 1 para 600. CTA 2010 has effect for corporation tax purposes for accounting periods ending on or after 1 April 2010, and for income and capital gains tax purposes for the tax year 2010–11 and subsequent tax years.

222 Assignments for profit of lease granted at undervalue

(1) This section applies to an assignment of a short-term lease if—

    (a) the lease was granted at an undervalue, and

    (b) a profit is made on the assignment.

(2) The company which assigns the lease is treated as—

    (a) entering into a transaction mentioned in section 205 (if the land to which the lease relates is in the United Kingdom) or section 206 (if that land is outside the United Kingdom), and

    (b) receiving the amount calculated under subsections (4) and (5) as a result of that transaction.

(3) That amount is brought into account as a receipt in calculating the profits of the property business which consists of or includes that transaction for the accounting period in which the consideration for the assignment becomes payable.

(4) The amount of the receipt is given by the formula—

$$P \times \left(\frac{50 - Y}{50} \right)$$

where—

P is the premium, and

where—

P is the lesser of—

(*a*) the profit on the assignment, and

(*b*) the amount by which the undervalue exceeds the total of the profits (if any) made on previous assignments of the lease, and

Y is the number of complete periods of 12 months (other than the first) comprised in the effective duration of the lease.

(5) But, if the rule in section 228 (the additional calculation rule) applies, the amount given by the formula in subsection (4) is reduced by the amount calculated in accordance with section 228.

(6) Section 223 explains references in this section to the grant of a lease at an undervalue and the making of a profit on an assignment of a lease.

Commentary—*Simon's Taxes* **B5.220, B5.627, B6.306**.

HMRC Manuals—Property Income Manual PIM1222 (charge on assignment of lease granted at undervalue).

Capital Gain Manual CG71210 (assignment of short lease granted at under value).

223 Provisions supplementary to section 222

(1) This section operates for the purposes of section 222.

(2) A lease is granted at an undervalue if the terms subject to which it was granted are such that the landlord who granted it could have required the payment of an additional sum by way of premium, or additional premium, for its grant.

(3) The additional sum is the undervalue.

(4) The test in subsection (2) must be applied—

(*a*) having regard to values prevailing at the time the lease was granted, and

(*b*) on the assumption that the negotiations for the lease were at arm's length.

(5) A profit is made on an assignment of a lease if the consideration for the assignment exceeds—

(*a*) if the lease has not previously been assigned, any premium for which it was granted, or

(*b*) in any other case, any consideration for which it was last assigned.

(6) The amount of the excess is the profit.

Commentary—*Simon's Taxes* **B6.306**.

Derivation—TA 1988 s 35(1), s 70A(5).

Other amounts treated as receipts

224 Sales with right to reconveyance

(1) This section applies if—

(*a*) an estate or interest in land is sold subject to terms which provide that it is to be, or may be required to be, reconveyed on a future date to the seller or a person connected with the seller,

(*b*) the period beginning with the sale and ending with the earliest date on which under the terms of the sale the estate or interest would fall to be reconveyed is 50 years or less, and

(*c*) the price at which the estate or interest is sold exceeds the price at which it is to be reconveyed.

(2) The seller is treated as—

(*a*) entering into a transaction mentioned in section 205 (if the land is in the United Kingdom) or section 206 (if the land is outside the United Kingdom), and

(*b*) receiving the amount calculated under subsection (4) as a result of that transaction.

(3) That amount is brought into account as a receipt in calculating the profits of the property business which consists of or includes that transaction for the accounting period in which the estate or interest is sold.

(4) The amount of the receipt is given by the formula—

$$E \times \left(\frac{50 - Y}{50} \right)$$

where—

E is the amount by which the price at which the estate or interest is sold exceeds the price at which it is to be reconveyed, and

Y is the number of complete periods of 12 months (other than the first) comprised in the period beginning with the sale and ending with the earliest date on which under the terms of the sale the estate or interest would fall to be reconveyed.

(5) See section 226 for some provisions which are supplementary to this section.

Commentary—*Simon's Taxes* **B5.220, B5.627, B6.307, C2.1108**.

HMRC Manuals—Property Income Manual PIM1224 (charge on sale of property with right to re-conveyance).

225 Sale and leaseback transactions

(1) This section applies if—

(*a*) an estate or interest in land is sold subject to terms which provide for the grant of a lease directly or indirectly out of the estate or interest to the seller or a person connected with the seller,

(b) the period beginning with the sale and ending with the earliest date on which under the terms of the sale the lease would fall to be granted is 50 years or less, and

(c) the price at which the estate or interest is sold exceeds the total of—

    (i) the amount of any premium for the lease, and

    (ii) the value on the date of the sale of the right to receive a conveyance of the reversion immediately after the lease begins to run.

(2) This section does not apply if the lease is granted and begins to run within one month after the sale.

(3) The seller is treated as—

(a) entering into a transaction mentioned in section 205 (if the land is in the United Kingdom) or section 206 (if the land is outside the United Kingdom), and

(b) receiving the amount calculated under subsection (5) as a result of that transaction.

(4) That amount is brought into account as a receipt in calculating the profits of the property business which consists of or includes that transaction for the accounting period in which the estate or interest is sold.

(5) The amount of the receipt is given by the formula—

$$E \times \left(\frac{50 - Y}{50} \right)$$

where—

E is the amount by which the price at which the estate or interest is sold exceeds the total of—

    (a) the amount of any premium for the lease, and

    (b) the value on the date of the sale of the right to receive a conveyance of the reversion immediately after the lease begins to run, and

Y is the number of complete periods of 12 months (other than the first) comprised in the period beginning with the sale and ending with the earliest date on which under the terms of the sale the lease would fall to be granted.

(6) See section 226 for some provisions which are supplementary to this section.

Commentary—*Simon's Taxes* **B6.308**.
HMRC Manuals—Property Income Manual PIM1226 (sale of property with right to lease back).

226 Provisions supplementary to sections 224 and 225

(1) This section operates for the purposes of sections 224 (sales with right to reconveyance) and 225 (sale and leaseback transactions).

(2) Subsection (3) explains how to determine for the purposes of section 224 the price at which an estate or interest is to be reconveyed when—

(a) the date on which the estate or interest would fall to be reconveyed is not fixed under the terms of the sale, and

(b) the price at which it is to be reconveyed varies with the date.

(3) The price is taken to be the lowest possible under the terms of the sale.

(4) Subsection (5) explains how to determine for the purposes of section 225 the total of—

(a) the amount of any premium for the lease, and

(b) the value on the date of the sale of the right to receive a conveyance of the reversion immediately after the lease begins to run,

when the date for the grant of the lease is not fixed under the terms of the sale and the total varies with the date.

(5) The total is taken to be the lowest possible under the terms of the sale.

(6) For the purposes of sections 224(3) and 225(4) (receipts of property business for accounting period in which estate or interest sold) an estate or interest in land is sold when any of the following occurs—

(a) an unconditional contract for its sale is entered into,

(b) a conditional contract for its sale becomes unconditional, or

(c) an option or right of pre-emption is exercised requiring the seller to enter into an unconditional contract for its sale.

Commentary—*Simon's Taxes* **B6.307, B6.308**.
Derivation—TA 1988 ss 36(2), (3), (4B), 70A(5).

Additional calculation rule for reducing certain receipts

227 Circumstances in which additional calculation rule applies

(1) The rule in section 228 (the additional calculation rule) applies in relation to the calculation of receipts under—

    section 217 (lease premiums),

    section 219 (sums payable instead of rent),

    section 220 (sums payable for surrender of lease),

section 221 (sums payable for variation or waiver of terms of lease), or
section 222 (assignments for profit of lease granted at undervalue).

(2) It applies if conditions A and B are met.

(3) Condition A is that—

   (*a*) in the case of a receipt under section 217, 219 or 220, the lease is granted out of a taxed lease,

   (*b*) in the case of a receipt under section 221, the lease was granted out of a taxed lease, and

   (*c*) in the case of a receipt under section 222, the assignment is of a taxed lease.

(4) A lease is a "taxed lease" for the purposes of this Chapter if—

   (*a*) there is a receipt under any of sections 217 to 222 in respect of the lease,

   (*b*) there would be such a receipt, but for the operation of the rule in section 228 (the additional calculation rule) in the calculation of its amount,

   (*c*) there is a receipt under any of sections 277 to 282 of ITTOIA 2005 (receipts in respect of lease premiums, sums payable instead of rent, for surrender of lease and for variation or waiver of terms of lease and assignments) in respect of the lease, or

   (*d*) there would be such a receipt, but for the operation of the rule in section 288 of that Act (the additional calculation rule) in the calculation of its amount.

In this Chapter a receipt falling within paragraph (*a*), (*b*), (*c*) or (*d*) is referred to as a "taxed receipt".

(5) Condition B is that the taxed receipt, or if there is more than one, at least one of them, has an unused amount.

(6) See section 230 for an explanation of when a taxed receipt has an "unused amount".

Commentary—*Simon's Taxes* **B6.309**.

228 The additional calculation rule

(1) The rule in this section applies if the conditions mentioned in section 227(2) are met.

(2) The additional calculation rule is that the amount given by the formula in section 217, 219, 220, 221 or 222 must be reduced by the amount calculated in accordance with this section in order to give the amount of the receipt under calculation.

(3) The amount of the reduction is—

   (*a*) if there is one taxed receipt which has an unused amount, the basic relieving amount by reference to that receipt, and

   (*b*) if there is more than one taxed receipt which has an unused amount, the total of the basic relieving amounts by reference to each receipt,

adjusted, if necessary, in the light of section 229(5) (reduction not to exceed amount being reduced).

(4) The basic relieving amount by reference to a taxed receipt is given by the formula—

$$\frac{A \times LRP}{TRP}$$

where—

   A is the unreduced amount of the taxed receipt (which is, generally, the amount given by the formula in section 217, 219, 220, 221 or 222, or in section 277, 279, 280, 281 or 282 of ITTOIA 2005, but see section 230(2) to (4) of this Act),

   LRP is the receipt period of the receipt under calculation, and

   TRP is the receipt period of the taxed receipt.

(5) But the basic relieving amount is different if section 229(2) or (4) applies (certain special cases).

(6) For the purposes of this Chapter, the "receipt period" of a receipt is—

   (*a*) in the case of a receipt under section 217 or 220, the effective duration of the lease,

   (*b*) in the case of a receipt under section 219, the period in relation to which the sum payable instead of rent is payable,

   (*c*) in the case of a receipt under section 221, the period for which the variation or waiver has effect,

   (*d*) in the case of a receipt under section 222, the effective duration of the lease remaining at the date of the assignment, and

   (*e*) in the case of a receipt under Chapter 4 of Part 3 of ITTOIA 2005 (profits of property businesses: lease premiums etc), its receipt period within the meaning of that Chapter (see section 288(6) of that Act).

Commentary—*Simon's Taxes* **B6.309**.

229 The additional calculation rule: special cases

(1) This section explains how section 228 operates in some special cases.

(2) If—

   (*a*) the receipt under calculation is under any of sections 217 to 221, and

   (*b*) the lease does not extend to the whole of the premises subject to the taxed lease,

the basic relieving amount by reference to a taxed receipt is calculated by multiplying the amount given by the formula in subsection (4) of section 228 by the fraction of those premises which is subject to the lease.

(3) This fraction is calculated on a just and reasonable basis.

(4) If the basic relieving amount given by section 228(4) or subsection (2) above by reference to a taxed receipt would otherwise exceed the unused amount of the taxed receipt, the basic relieving amount is the unused amount.

(5) If the amount of the reduction under section 228 would otherwise exceed the amount given, in respect of the receipt under calculation, by the formula in section 217, 219, 220, 221 or 222, the amount of the reduction is equal to the amount given by the formula.

Commentary—*Simon's Taxes* **B6.309**.

230 Meaning of "unused amount" and "unreduced amount"

(1) For the purposes of this Chapter, a taxed receipt has an "unused amount" if the unreduced amount exceeds the total of the reductions and deductions referred to in subsection (5).

(2) In this Chapter the "unreduced amount" of a taxed receipt is the amount given, in respect of the taxed receipt, by the formula in—

    (*a*) section 217, 219, 220, 221 or 222 above, or

    (*b*) section 277, 279, 280, 281 or 282 of ITTOIA 2005 (income tax provisions corresponding to those listed in paragraph (*a*)).

(3) Subsection (4) applies—

    (*a*) to a taxed receipt under section 217 (lease premiums) as a result of section 218 (amount treated as lease premium where work required), and

    (*b*) to a taxed receipt under section 277 of ITTOIA 2005 (lease premiums) as a result of section 278 of that Act (amount treated as lease premium where work required).

(4) If the obligation to carry out work included the carrying out of work which gives, or will give, rise to qualifying expenditure under CAA 2001, the unreduced amount of the taxed receipt is calculated as if the obligation had not included the carrying out of that work.

(5) The reductions and deductions mentioned in subsection (1) are—

    (*a*) the reductions under section 228 above or section 288 of ITTOIA 2005 (the additional calculation rule) by reference to the taxed receipt,

    (*b*) the deductions made in calculating the profits of a trade, profession or vocation for expenses under section 63 above or section 61 of ITTOIA 2005 (tenant under taxed lease who uses land in connection with trade treated as incurring expenses) by reference to the taxed receipt, and

    (*c*) the deductions made in calculating the profits of a property business for expenses under section 232 below or section 292 of ITTOIA 2005 (tenant under taxed lease who uses premises for purposes of property business treated as incurring expenses) by reference to the taxed receipt.

(6) For the purposes of this Chapter references to a reduction under section 228 above or section 288 of ITTOIA 2005 by reference to a taxed receipt are to a reduction under the section concerned so far as attributable to the taxed receipt.

Commentary—*Simon's Taxes* **B6.309**.

HMRC Manuals—Business Income Manual BIM46280 (specific deductions: premiums: prevention of double allowance).

Deductions in relation to certain receipts

231 Deductions for expenses under section 232

(1) Section 232 (tenants under taxed leases treated as incurring expenses) applies in calculating the profits of a property business carried on by the tenant under a taxed lease for the purpose of making deductions for the expenses of the property business.

(2) A deduction is allowed for an expense under section 232 for a qualifying day on which the whole or part of the premises subject to the taxed lease is—

    (*a*) occupied by the tenant for the purpose of carrying on the property business, or

    (*b*) sublet.

(3) But any deduction for an expense under section 232 is subject to the application of any provision of Chapter 4 of Part 3 (as applied to property businesses by section 210).

(4) The amount of the deduction for an expense under section 232 for a qualifying day by reference to a taxed receipt may be reduced in order to comply with section 235 (limit on reductions and deductions).

(5) For the meaning of expressions used in this section, see in particular—

    section 227(4) ("taxed lease"), and

    section 227(4) ("taxed receipt").

Commentary—*Simon's Taxes* **B6.309, B6.310**.

HMRC Manuals—Business Income Manual BIM4651 (specific deductions: taxed receipt).

232 Tenants under taxed leases treated as incurring expenses

(1) The tenant under a taxed lease is treated as incurring an expense of a revenue nature in respect of the premises subject to the taxed lease for each qualifying day.

(2) If there is more than one taxed receipt, this section applies separately in relation to each of them.

(3) A day is a "qualifying day", in relation to a taxed receipt, if it falls within the receipt period of the taxed receipt.

(4) The amount of the expense for the qualifying day by reference to the taxed receipt is given by the formula—

$$\frac{A}{TRP}$$

where—

A is the unreduced amount of the taxed receipt, and

TRP is the number of days in the receipt period of the taxed receipt.

[(4A) No expense is to be determined under this section by reference to the taxed receipt if subsection (4B) or (4C) applies.

(4B) This subsection applies if there would have been no taxed receipt but for the application of Rule 1 in section 243 in determining the effective duration of the lease.

(4C) This subsection applies if there would have been no taxed receipt but for the application of Rule 1 in section 303 of ITTOIA 2005 in determining the effective duration of the lease for the purposes of Chapter 4 of Part 3 of that Act.][1]

(5) This section is subject to sections 233 and 234 (restrictions on expenses where the additional calculation rule is relevant).

(6) For the meaning of expressions used in this section, see in particular—

section 228(6) ("receipt period"), and

section 230(2) to (4) ("unreduced amount").

Commentary—*Simon's Taxes* **B6.309, B6.310**.

Amendments—[1] Sub-ss (4A)–(4C) inserted by FA 2013 s 75, Sch 28 paras 5, 7 with effect in relation to leases granted on or after 1 April 2013.

233 Restrictions on section 232 expenses: the additional calculation rule

(1) This section applies if—

    (a) in calculating the amount of a receipt under this Chapter there is a reduction under section 228 (the additional calculation rule) by reference to a taxed receipt, or

    (b) in calculating the amount of a receipt under Chapter 4 of Part 3 of ITTOIA 2005 (profits of a property business: lease premiums etc) there is a reduction under section 288 of that Act (the additional calculation rule) by reference to a taxed receipt.

The receipt that is so reduced is referred to in this section as the "lease premium receipt".

(2) Subsections (3) to (5) provide for the application of section 232 for a qualifying day that falls within the receipt period of the lease premium receipt.

(3) The tenant under the taxed lease is treated as incurring an expense under section 232 for the qualifying day by reference to the taxed receipt only if the daily amount of the taxed receipt exceeds the daily reduction of the lease premium receipt.

(4) If the condition in subsection (3) is met, the amount of the expense under section 232 for the qualifying day by reference to the taxed receipt is equal to that excess.

(5) If the qualifying day falls within the receipt periods of more than one lease premium receipt, the reference in subsection (3) to the daily reduction of the lease premium receipt is to be read as a reference to the total of the daily reductions of each of the lease premium receipts whose receipt period includes the qualifying day.

(6) In this section—

the "daily amount" of the taxed receipt is given by the formula—

$$\frac{A}{TRP}$$

where—

A is the unreduced amount of the taxed receipt (see section 230(2) to (4)), and

TRP is the number of days in the receipt period of the taxed receipt, and

the "daily reduction" of a lease premium receipt is given by the formula—

$$\frac{AR}{RRP}$$

where—

AR is the reduction under section 228 above or section 288 of ITTOIA 2005 by reference to the taxed receipt (see section 230(6)), and

RRP is the number of days in the receipt period of the lease premium receipt.

(7) Section 234 explains how this section operates if the lease premium receipt is in respect of a lease that has been granted out of the taxed lease and does not extend to the whole of the premises subject to the taxed lease.

Commentary—*Simon's Taxes* **B6.310**.

234 Restrictions on section 232 expenses: lease of part of premises

(1) This section applies if—

- (*a*) a lease has been granted out of the taxed lease,
- (*b*) the lease does not extend to the whole of the premises subject to the taxed lease, and
- (*c*) the condition in subsection (2) is met.

(2) The condition is that—

- (*a*) in calculating the amount of a receipt under any of sections 217 to 221 (receipts in respect of lease premiums or sums payable instead of rent, for surrender of lease or for variation or waiver of terms of lease) in respect of the lease, there is a reduction under section 228 by reference to a taxed receipt, or
- (*b*) in calculating the amount of a receipt under any of sections 277 to 281 of ITTOIA 2005 (receipts in respect of lease premiums or sums payable instead of rent, for surrender of lease or for variation or waiver of terms of lease) in respect of the lease, there is a reduction under section 288 of that Act (the additional calculation rule) by reference to a taxed receipt.

The receipt that is so reduced is referred to in this section as the "lease premium receipt".

(3) Subsections (4) to (6) apply for a qualifying day that falls within the receipt period of the lease premium receipt.

(4) Sections 232 and 233 apply separately in relation to the part of the premises subject to the lease and to the remainder of the premises.

(5) If—

- (*a*) more than one lease that does not extend to the whole of the premises subject to the taxed lease has been granted out of the taxed lease, and
- (*b*) the qualifying day falls within the receipt period of two or more lease premium receipts that relate to different leases,

sections 232 and 233 apply separately in relation to each part of the premises subject to a lease to which such a receipt relates and to the remainder of the premises.

(6) Where sections 232 and 233 apply in relation to a part of the premises, A becomes the amount calculated by multiplying the unreduced amount of the taxed receipt by the fraction of the premises constituted by the part.

(7) This fraction is calculated on a just and reasonable basis.

Commentary—*Simon's Taxes* **B6.309, B6.310**.

Limit on effect of additional calculation rule and deductions

235 Limit on reductions and deductions

(1) The total of—

- (*a*) the reductions under section 228 by reference to a taxed receipt, and
- (*b*) the deductions allowed in calculating the profits of a property business for expenses under section 232 (tenant under taxed lease which uses premises for purposes of property business treated as incurring expenses) by reference to the taxed receipt,

must not exceed the amount referred to in subsection (2).

(2) The amount mentioned in subsection (1) is the difference between—

- (*a*) the unreduced amount of the taxed receipt, and
- (*b*) the total of the amounts mentioned in subsection (3).

(3) Those amounts are—

- (*a*) the reductions under section 288 of ITTOIA 2005 (the additional calculation rule) by reference to the taxed receipt,
- (*b*) the deductions made in calculating the profits of a property business for expenses under section 292 of ITTOIA 2005 (tenant under taxed lease who uses premises for purposes of property business treated as incurring expenses) by reference to the taxed receipt, and
- (*c*) the deductions made in calculating the profits of a trade, profession or vocation for expenses under section 63 above or section 61 of ITTOIA 2005 (tenant under taxed lease who uses land in connection with trade treated as incurring expenses) by reference to the taxed receipt.

Commentary—*Simon's Taxes* **B6.309, B6.310**.

Certain administrative provisions

236 Payment of tax by instalments

(1) This section applies if—

- (*a*) there is a receipt under section 217 (lease premiums) in respect of a premium which is payable by instalments, or

(b) there is a receipt under any of sections 219 to 221 (sums payable instead of rent, for surrender of lease or for variation or waiver of terms of lease) in respect of a sum which is payable by instalments.

(2) The company which is liable to pay tax by reference to the receipt may choose to pay the tax by such instalments as an officer of Revenue and Customs may allow.

(3) The period over which the instalments of tax must be paid—

    (a) must be 8 years or less, and

    (b) must end before, or at the same time as, the time when the last of the instalments mentioned in subsection (1)(a) or (b) is payable.

Commentary—*Simon's Taxes* **B6.312**.
HMRC Manuals—Property Income Manual PIM1220 (payable by instalments).

237 Statement of accuracy for purposes of section 222

(1) This section applies if any of the persons mentioned in subsection (3) provides an officer of Revenue and Customs with a statement showing—

    (a) whether or not there is, or may be, a receipt under section 222 (assignments for profit of lease granted at undervalue), and

    (b) the amount of any receipt.

(2) The officer must certify the accuracy of the statement, if satisfied as to its accuracy.

(3) The persons referred to in subsection (1) are—

    (a) the landlord who granted the lease,

    (b) a company which assigned it, or

    (c) a person to whom it was assigned.

Commentary—*Simon's Taxes* **B6.306**.
Derivation—TA 1988 s 35(3).

238 Claim for repayment of tax payable by virtue of section 224

(1) This section applies if—

    (a) there is a receipt under section 224 (sales with right to reconveyance), and

    (b) the date on which the estate or interest would fall to be reconveyed was not fixed under the terms of the sale.

(2) If the seller makes a claim, the seller must be repaid the amount by which A exceeds B, where—

    A is the amount of tax paid by the seller which was payable by virtue of section 224, and

    B is the amount of tax that would have been so payable if the date on which the estate or interest was reconveyed had been taken as the date fixed by the terms of the sale.

(3) The claim must be made within 4 years after the day on which the estate or interest was reconveyed.

Commentary—*Simon's Taxes* **B5.627, B6.307, C2.1108**.
HMRC Manuals—Property Income Manual PIM1224 (date of re-conveyance not fixed, price may vary with date).

239 Claim for repayment of tax payable by virtue of section 225

(1) This section applies if—

    (a) there is a receipt under section 225 (sale and leaseback transactions), and

    (b) the date for the grant of the lease was not fixed under the terms of the sale.

(2) If the seller makes a claim, the seller must be repaid the amount by which A exceeds B, where—

    A is the amount of tax paid by the seller which was payable by virtue of section 225, and

    B is the amount of tax that would have been so payable if the date on which the lease was granted had been taken as the date fixed by the terms of the sale.

(3) The claim must be made within 4 years after the day on which the lease was granted.

Commentary—*Simon's Taxes* **B6.308, B5.627**.

Determinations affecting liability of more than one person

240 Appeals against proposed determinations

(1) Subsection (2) applies if it appears to an officer of Revenue and Customs that—

    (a) a determination is needed of an amount that is to be brought into account as a receipt under this Chapter in calculating the liability to tax of a person ("the first taxpayer"), and

    (b) the determination may affect the liability to corporation tax, income tax or capital gains tax of other persons.

(2) The officer may give notice (a "provisional notice of determination") to the first taxpayer and the other persons of—

    (a) the determination the officer proposes to make, and

    (b) their rights under this section and section 242.

(3) A person to whom a provisional notice of determination is given may object to the proposed determination by giving notice ("a notice of objection") to the officer.

(4) The notice of objection must be given within 30 days of the date on which the provisional notice of determination was given.

(5) If an officer gives provisional notices of determination and no person gives a notice of objection—

(*a*) a determination must be made by the officer as proposed in the provisional notices, and

(*b*) the determination is not to be called in question in any proceedings.

Commentary—*Simon's Taxes* **B6.314**.

Derivation—TA 1988 s 42(1)–(3).

241 Section 240: supplementary

(1) A provisional notice of determination under section 240(2) may include a statement of the grounds on which the officer proposes to make the determination.

(2) Subsection (1) applies despite any obligation as to secrecy or other restriction on the disclosure of information.

(3) . . . ¹

(4) . . . ¹

Commentary—*Simon's Taxes* **B6.314, B6.315**.

Amendments—¹　Sub-ss (3), (4) repealed by FA 2011 s 86(1), Sch 23 para 63 with effect from 1 April 2012 in relation to relevant data with a bearing on any period (whether before, on or after 1 April 2012) subject to FA 2011 Sch 23 para 3(2). These subsections will continue to have effect in relation to notices given, or requests made, under any of the provisions repealed by FA 2011 Sch 23 Pt 6 before 1 April 2012 as if the repeals had not been made (FA 2011 Sch 23 para 65(2)).

242 Determination by tribunal

(1) If a notice of objection is given under section 240(3), the amount mentioned in section 240(1) must be determined in the same way as an appeal.

(2) All persons to whom provisional notices of determination have been given under section 240(2) may [be a party to

(*a*) any proceedings under subsection (1), and

(*b*) any appeal arising out of those proceedings.]¹

(3) Those persons are bound by the determination made in the proceedings or on appeal, whether or not they have taken part in the proceedings.

(4) Their successors in title are bound in the same way.

Commentary—*Simon's Taxes* **B6.314**.

Amendments—¹　In sub-s (2), words substituted by TIOPA 2010 s 371, Sch 7 paras 23, 24. TIOPA 2010 has effect for corporation tax purposes for accounting periods ending on or after 1 April 2010, for income and capital gains tax purposes for the tax year 2010–11 and subsequent tax years, and for petroleum revenue tax purposes for chargeable periods beginning on or after 1 July 2010.

Effective duration of lease

243 Rules for determining effective duration of lease

(1) The following rules apply for determining the effective duration of a lease for the purposes of this Chapter.

　　Rule 1: If—

　　　　(*a*) the terms of the lease or any other circumstances make it unlikely that the lease will continue beyond a date before the end of the term for which the lease was granted, and

　　　　(*b*) the premium was not substantially greater than it would have been had the term been one ending on that date,

　　the lease is treated as ending on that date (or the earliest such date).

　　Rule 2: If the terms of the lease include provision for the extension of the lease beyond a given date by notice given by the tenant, account may be taken of any circumstances making it likely that the lease will be so extended.

　　Rule 3: If the tenant or a person connected with the tenant is, or may become, entitled to a further lease or the grant of a further lease (whenever commencing)—

　　　　(*a*) of the same premises, or

　　　　(*b*) of premises including the whole or part of the same premises,

　　the term of the lease may be treated as continuing until the end of the term of the further lease.

(2) The rules are to be applied in accordance with section 244.

(3) In Rule 1, "premium" includes—

　　(*a*) an amount treated as a premium under section 218 (amount treated as lease premium where work required),

　　(*b*) a sum payable by the tenant under the terms subject to which the lease is granted instead of the whole or a part of the rent for a period,

　　(*c*) a sum payable by the tenant under the terms subject to which the lease is granted as consideration for the surrender of the lease, and

　　(*d*) a sum payable by the tenant (otherwise than by way of rent) as consideration for the variation or waiver of a term of the lease.

(4) In this section and section 244, in relation to Scotland, "term", where referring to the duration of a lease, means period.

Commentary—*Simon's Taxes* **B3.280, B6.313, B2.447, C2.1202**.

HMRC Manuals—Business Income Manual BIM46260 (specific deductions: premiums: artificial leasing transactions).
Modifications—In relation to a lease granted after 24 August 1971 and before 1 April 2009, this section modified so that in sub-s (1), Rule 1 substituted and sub-s (3) repealed, by CTA 2009 s 1325, Sch 2 para 43.
In relation to a lease granted after 12 June 1969 and before 25 August 1971, this section substituted (except if the determination is for the purposes of s 221 above) by CTA 2009 s 1325, Sch 2 para 45.
In relation to a lease granted before 13 June 1969, this section substituted (except if the determination is for the purposes of s 221 above) by CTA 2009 s 1325, Sch 2 para 46.

244 Applying the rules in section 243

(1) The rules in section 243 apply by reference to the facts known or ascertainable—

  (a) at the time of the grant of the lease, or

  (b) if the determination is for the purposes of section 221 (sums payable for variation or waiver of terms of lease), at the time when the contract for the variation or waiver is entered into.

(2) In applying those rules, it is assumed that all parties concerned, whatever their relationship, act as if they were at arm's length.

(3) Subsection (5) applies if—

  (a) special benefits were conferred by the lease or in connection with its grant, or

  (b) payments were made which one would not expect to be made by parties acting at arm's length unless such benefits had been conferred.

(4) But subsection (5) does not apply if it can be shown that the special benefits were not conferred nor the payments made for the purpose of securing—

  (a) a corporation tax advantage in the application of this Chapter, or

  (b) an income tax advantage in the application of Chapter 4 of Part 3 of ITTOIA 2005 (profits of property business: lease premiums etc).

(5) In applying paragraph (b) of Rule 1 in section 243, it is assumed that the special benefits would not have been conferred nor the payments made if the lease had been granted for a term ending on the date mentioned in that rule.

(6) In this section "special benefits" means benefits other than—

  (a) vacant possession and beneficial occupation of the premises, or

  (b) the right to receive rent at a reasonable commercial rate in respect of the premises.

Commentary—*Simon's Taxes* **B6.313**.
Modifications—In relation to a lease granted after 12 June 1969 and before 25 August 1971, this section substituted (except if the determination is for the purposes of s 221 above) by CTA 2009 s 1325, Sch 2 para 45.
In relation to a lease granted before 13 June 1969, this section substituted (except if the determination is for the purposes of s 221 above) by CTA 2009 s 1325, Sch 2 para 46.

Other interpretative provisions

246 Provisions about premiums

(1) For the purposes of this Chapter, the presumption is that a sum paid on or in connection with the granting of a tenancy has been paid by way of premium.

(2) This does not apply if the sum is rent.

(3) This also does not apply so far as other sufficient consideration for the payment can be shown to have been given.

(4) In this section "sum" includes the value of any consideration.

(5) Where Rule 3 in section 243 (rules for determining effective duration of lease) applies, the premium, or an appropriate part of it, payable for or in connection with either lease mentioned in that rule may be treated for the purposes of this Chapter as having been required under the other.

Commentary—*Simon's Taxes* **B6.313**.
Modification—In relation to a lease granted after 12 June 1969 and before 25 August 1971, this section modified so that sub-ss (4), (5) are repealed, by CTA 2009 s 1325, Sch 2 para 48(1), (2).

247 Interpretation

(1) In this Chapter "premium" includes any similar sum payable to the immediate or a superior landlord or to a person connected with such a person.

(2) In subsection (1) "sum" includes the value of any consideration.

(3) In the application of this Chapter to Scotland—

  "premium" includes, in particular, a grassum payable to the landlord under the lease in respect of which the grassum is payable or the landlord under any other lease of the property, and

  "reversion" means the interest of the landlord in the property subject to the lease.

(4) In the application of this Chapter to Scotland—

  (a) references to a lease being granted out of a taxed lease are to the grant of a sublease of land subject to the taxed lease, and

  (b) references to the lease so granted are to be read as references to the sublease.

Commentary—*Simon's Taxes* **B6.313**.
Modification—In relation to a lease granted after 12 June 1969 and before 25 August 1971, this section modified so that, in sub-s (1), words "or to a person connected with such a person", and whole of sub-s (2), are repealed, by CTA 2009 s 1325, Sch 2 para 48(1), (3).

Deductions for expenditure on energy-saving items

251 Deduction for expenditure on energy-saving items

(1) This section applies if—

    (*a*) a company carries on a property business in relation to land which consists of or includes a dwelling-house,

    (*b*) the company incurs expenditure in acquiring and installing an energy-saving item in the dwelling-house or in a building containing the dwelling-house (see subsections (5) to (7)),

    (*c*) the expenditure is incurred before 1 April 2015,

    (*d*) a deduction for the expenditure is not prohibited by the wholly and exclusively rule but would otherwise be prohibited by the capital prohibition rule (see subsection (8)), and

    (*e*) no allowance under CAA 2001 may be claimed in respect of the expenditure.

(2) In calculating the profits of the business, a deduction for the expenditure is allowed.

(3) But any deduction is subject to—

    (*a*) section 252 (restrictions on relief), and

    (*b*) any provision made by regulations under section 253.

(4) If, on a just and reasonable apportionment of any expenditure, part of the expenditure would qualify for the relief (but the remainder would not), a deduction is allowed for that part.

(5) "Energy-saving item" means an item of an energy-saving nature of such description as is for the time being specified in regulations made by the Treasury.

(6) The Treasury may by regulations provide for an item to be an energy-saving item only if it satisfies such conditions as may be—

    (*a*) specified in, or

    (*b*) determined in accordance with,

the regulations.

(7) The conditions may include conditions imposed by reference to information or documents issued by any body, person or organisation.

(8) In this section—

"the capital prohibition rule" means the rule in section 53 (capital expenditure), as applied by section 210, and

"the wholly and exclusively rule" means the rule in section 54 (expenses not wholly and exclusively for trade and unconnected losses), as applied by section 210.

Commentary—*Simon's Taxes* B6.207, B6.310, B6.401.

HMRC Manuals—Property Income Manual PIM2072 (landlord's energy savings allowance: background).

252 Restrictions on relief

(1) This section restricts deductions that would otherwise be allowable under section 251.

(2) No deduction is allowed if, when the energy-saving item is installed, the dwelling-house—

    (*a*) is in the course of construction, or

    (*b*) is comprised in land in which the company does not have an interest or is in the course of acquiring an interest or further interest.

(3) No deduction is allowed in respect of expenditure in an accounting period if—

    (*a*) the business consists of or includes the commercial letting of furnished holiday accommodation (see Chapter 6), and

    (*b*) the dwelling-house constitutes some or all of that accommodation for the accounting period.

(4) No deduction is allowed in respect of expenditure treated by section 61 (as applied by section 210) as incurred on the date on which the company starts to carry on the business unless the expenditure was incurred not more than 6 months before that date.

(5) No deduction is allowed in respect of expenditure incurred in acquiring and installing the energy-saving item in a building containing the dwelling-house in so far as the expenditure is not for the benefit of the dwelling-house.

Commentary—*Simon's Taxes* B6.401.

HMRC Manuals—Property Income Manual PIM2072 (landlord's energy savings allowance: restrictions on relief).

253 Regulations

(1) In relation to any deduction under section 251, the Treasury may make regulations for—

    (*a*) restricting or reducing the amount of expenditure for which the deduction is allowable,

    (*b*) excluding entitlement to the deduction in such cases as may be specified in, or determined in accordance with, the regulations,

    (*c*) determining who is (and is not) entitled to the deduction if different persons have different interests in land that consists of or includes the whole or part of a building containing one or more dwelling-houses,

    (*d*) making apportionments if the property business is carried on by persons in partnership or an interest in land is beneficially owned by persons jointly or in common.

(2) The apportionments that may be made include apportionments to persons within the charge to income tax.

(3) Regulations under this section may—

(*a*) make different provision for different cases, and

(*b*) contain incidental, supplemental, consequential and transitional provision and savings (including provision as to appeals in relation to apportionments mentioned in subsection (1)(*d*)).

Commentary—*Simon's Taxes* **B6.207**.
HMRC Manuals—Property Income Manual PIM2072 (landlord's energy savings allowance: appointments).

Deductions for expenditure on sea walls

254 Deduction for expenditure on sea walls

(1) This section applies if in a tax year a person—

(*a*) is the owner or tenant of any premises, and

(*b*) incurs expenditure in making a sea wall or other embankment necessary for the preservation or protection of the premises against the encroachment or overflowing of the sea or any tidal river.

(2) In calculating the profits of any property business (within the charge to tax under Chapter 3) carried on by the person in relation to the premises, a deduction is allowed for the expenditure in each tax year comprised in the deduction period.

(3) The deduction period comprises—

(*a*) the tax year in which the expenditure is incurred, and

(*b*) the next 20 tax years.

(4) The amount of the deduction is ⅟21 of the expenditure.

(5) The deduction is apportioned between the accounting period or periods comprised in the tax year, but—

(*a*) no apportionment is made to an accounting period which ends before the expenditure is incurred, and

(*b*) if the person is entitled to the deduction because of a transfer dealt with by section 255, no apportionment is made to an accounting period which ends before the transfer takes place.

(6) In the case of the transfer of an interest in the premises dealt with by section 255, this section applies as if the reference to the person in subsection (2) above included the transferor and the transferee.

(7) No deduction is allowed for any expenditure in respect of which a capital allowance has been made.

Commentary—*Simon's Taxes* **B6.208, C2.217**.
HMRC Manuals—Property Income Manual PIM2082 (seawalls : meaning).

255 Transfer of interest in premises

(1) This section applies if, during the deduction period, the whole of the person's interest in the premises or in any part of them is transferred, whether by operation of law or otherwise.

(2) For the tax year in which the transfer takes place—

(*a*) the transferor and the transferee are entitled to a part of any deduction under section 254, and

(*b*) the amount of the deduction is determined by what is just and reasonable.

(3) For subsequent tax years in the deduction period, the entitlement to any deduction under section 254 depends on whether the interest transferred is in the whole of the premises or in part of them.

(4) If the interest transferred is in the whole of the premises, the transferee (but not the transferor) is entitled to any deduction under section 254.

(5) If the interest transferred is in part of the premises—

(*a*) the transferor and the transferee are entitled to a part of any deduction under section 254, and

(*b*) the amount of the deduction is determined by reference to what is properly referable to the part of the premises.

(6) This section is supplemented by sections 256 (ending of lease of premises) and 257 (transfer involving person within the charge to income tax).

Commentary—*Simon's Taxes* **B6.208**.

256 Ending of lease of premises

(1) If a person's interest in the premises is a lease that comes to an end before the end of the deduction period, the interest is treated as if transferred to the following persons.

(2) If a new lease of the premises is granted and the new tenant makes a payment in respect of the embankment in question to the old tenant, the transferee is the new tenant.

(3) Otherwise the transferee is the owner of the interest in immediate reversion on the lease (or, in Scotland, the landlord).

Commentary—*Simon's Taxes* **B6.208**.
Derivation—TA 1988 ss 30(3), 70A(5).

257 Transfer involving person within the charge to income tax

(1) This section explains how section 255 works if—

(*a*) the transferor is a company within the charge to corporation tax and the transferee is a person within the charge to income tax, or

(b) the transferor is a person within the charge to income tax and the transferee is a company within the charge to corporation tax.

(2) Section 255 applies only for the purpose of determining—

    (a) whether the company within the charge to corporation tax is entitled to a deduction (or part of a deduction) under section 254, and

    (b) the amount of any such deduction.

(3) Accordingly, any reference to—

    (a) whether a person is entitled to a deduction (or part of a deduction) under section 254, or

    (b) the amount of any such deduction,

is ignored if the person is within the charge to income tax.

(4) For any entitlement of a person within the charge to income tax to a deduction for any of the expenditure, see sections 316 to 318 of ITTOIA 2005 (corresponding income tax provisions).

Commentary—*Simon's Taxes* **B6.208**.
Derivation—TA 1988 ss 30(2A), 70A(5).

Apportionments on sale of land

259 Nature of item apportioned on sale of estate or interest in land

(1) This section applies if—

    (a) a company sells an estate or interest in land,

    (b) on the sale a part of a receipt or outgoing in respect of the estate or interest is apportioned to the seller, and

    (c) the receipt or outgoing is receivable or to be paid by the buyer after the apportionment is made.

(2) In calculating the profits of the seller's property business, the part apportioned is treated as being of the same nature as the receipt or outgoing.

Commentary—*Simon's Taxes* **B6.210**.
Derivation—TA 1988 ss 40(3), 70A(5).
HMRC Manuals—Property Income Manual PIM2235 (apportionment on sale or purchase of let property: effect).

Mutual business

260 Mutual business

(1) Nothing in this Part is to be read as applying the rules relating to mutual business to property businesses.

(2) Accordingly, receipts and expenses are to be brought into account in calculating the profits of a company's property business even if a relationship of mutuality exists between that company and another person.

(3) Nothing in this section affects the operation of [Chapter 7 of Part 13 of CTA 2010][1] (co-operative housing associations).

Commentary—*Simon's Taxes* **B6.211**.
Derivation—TA 1988 ss 21C, 70A(5).
HMRC Manuals—Business Income Manual BIM24782 (mutuality principle to a property business: meaning).
Amendments—[1] In sub-s (3) words substituted for words "section 488 of ICTA" by CTA 2010 s 1177, Sch 1 para 601. CTA 2010 has effect for corporation tax purposes for accounting periods ending on or after 1 April 2010, and for income and capital gains tax purposes for the tax year 2010–11 and subsequent tax years.

Adjustment on change of basis

261 Adjustment on change of basis

(1) Section 262 applies if—

    (a) a company carrying on a UK property business changes, from one period of account to the next, the basis on which profits of the business are calculated for corporation tax purposes,

    (b) the old basis accorded with the law or practice applicable in relation to the period of account before the change, and

    (c) the new basis accords with the law and practice applicable in relation to the period of account after the change.

(2) The practice applicable in any case means the accepted practice in cases of that description as to how profits of a UK property business should be calculated for corporation tax purposes.

(3) Subsections (3) to (6) of section 180 (what is meant by a company changing the basis on which profits are calculated) apply for the purposes of this section as they apply for the purposes of that section (but as if any reference to a trade were to a UK property business).

262 Giving effect to positive and negative adjustments

(1) An amount by way of adjustment must be calculated in accordance with section 182, which applies in relation to a UK property business as it applies in relation to a trade.

(2) If the amount produced by the calculation is positive—

    (a) the amount is brought into account as a receipt in calculating the profits of the UK property business, and

    (b) the receipt is treated as arising on the first day of the first period of account for which the new basis is adopted.

(3) But if there is a change of basis resulting from a tax adjustment affecting the calculation of any amount brought into account in respect of depreciation, the receipt is treated as arising only when the asset to which it relates is realised or written off.

(4) If the amount produced by the calculation is negative—

(*a*) a deduction is allowed for the amount as an expense of the UK property business in calculating the profits of that business, and

(*b*) the expense is treated as arising on the first day of the first period of account for which the new basis is adopted.

(5) But if there is a change of basis resulting from a tax adjustment affecting the calculation of any amount brought into account in respect of depreciation, the expense is treated as arising only when the asset to which it relates is realised or written off.

(6) This section is subject to section 183 (no adjustment for certain expenses previously brought into account) which applies in relation to a UK property business as it applies in relation to a trade.

Commentary—*Simon's Taxes* **B6.212**.

HMRC Manuals—Business Income Manual BIM34105 (change of basis of computing taxable profits: adjustment income and expenses: expenses already allowed).

BIM34130 (change of basis of computing taxable profits: adjustment income and expenses: calculation of adjustment).

Integral features

263 Expenditure on integral features

Section 33A(3) of CAA 2001 provides that no deduction is allowed in respect of certain expenditure on an integral feature of a building or structure (within the meaning of that section).

Commentary—*Simon's Taxes* **B3.345**.

HMRC Manuals—Capital Allowance CA22300 (Expenditure on integral features : content sheet).

CHAPTER 6

COMMERCIAL LETTING OF FURNISHED HOLIDAY ACCOMMODATION

Introduction

264 Overview of Chapter

(1) This Chapter explains for the purposes of this Part what is meant by the commercial letting of furnished holiday accommodation (see sections 265 to 268).

(2) It matters whether a UK property business consists of or includes the commercial letting of furnished holiday accommodation for the purposes of—

[(*za*) section 250A (replacement domestic items relief: see subsection (7)),]³.

[(*a*) Chapter 4 of Part 4 of CTA 2010 (relief for property business losses: see section 65 of that Act),]¹

(*b*) certain provisions of TCGA 1992 (see section 241 of that Act), and

(*c*) CAA 2001 (see, for example, sections 248 and 249 of that Act).

[(2A) It matters whether an overseas property business consists of or includes the commercial letting of furnished holiday accommodation in one or more EEA states for the purposes of—

[(*za*) section 250A (replacement domestic items relief: see subsection (7)),]³

(*a*) Chapter 4 of Part 4 of CTA 2010 (relief for property business losses: see section 67A of that Act),

(*b*) certain provisions of TCGA 1992 (see section 241A of that Act), and

(*c*) CAA 2001 (see, for example, sections 250 and 250A of that Act).]²

(3) This Chapter also supplements [the provisions mentioned in subsection (2)]² by providing in certain circumstances for the profits of the furnished holiday lettings part of a UK property business to be calculated separately (see section 269).

[(4) This Chapter also supplements the provisions mentioned in subsection (2A) by providing in certain circumstances for the profits of the EEA furnished holiday lettings part of an overseas property business to be calculated separately (see sections 250 and 250A).]²

Commentary—*Simon's Taxes* **B6.401**.

HMRC Manuals—Property Income Manual PIM4105 (furnished holiday lettings : introduction).

Amendments—¹ Sub-s (2)(*a*) substituted by CTA 2010 s 1177, Sch 1 para 602. CTA 2010 has effect for corporation tax purposes for accounting periods ending on or after 1 April 2010, and for income and capital gains tax purposes for the tax year 2010–11 and subsequent tax years.

² Sub-ss (2A), (4) inserted, and in sub-s (3) words substituted for words "the above provisions", by FA 2011 s 52 Sch 14 para 7(1), (2) with effect in relation to accounting periods beginning on or after 1 April 2011.

³ Sub-ss (2)(*za*), (2A)(*za*) inserted by FA 2016 s 73(7) with effect in relation to expenditure incurred on or after 1 April 2016 for corporation tax purposes and 6 April 2016 for income tax purposes.

Definition

265 Meaning of "commercial letting of furnished holiday accommodation"

(1) A letting is a lease or other arrangement under which a person is entitled to the use of accommodation.

(2) A letting of accommodation is commercial if the accommodation is let—
 (a) on a commercial basis, and
 (b) with a view to the realisation of profits.
(3) A letting is of furnished holiday accommodation if—
 (a) the person entitled to the use of the accommodation is also entitled, in connection with that use, to the use of furniture, and
 (b) the accommodation is qualifying holiday accommodation (see sections 267 and 268).
(4) This section applies for the purposes of this Chapter.

Commentary—*Simon's Taxes* **B6.402**.
Derivation—TA 1988 s 504(2), (3), (9).
HMRC Manuals—Property Income Manual PIM4105 (commercial letting of furnished holiday accommodation: definition).

266 Meaning of "relevant period" in sections 267 and 268

(1) For the purposes of sections 267 and 268 "the relevant period" for accommodation let by a company in an accounting period is determined as follows.
(2) If the accommodation was not let by the company as furnished accommodation in the 12 months immediately before the accounting period, "the relevant period" is 12 months beginning with the first day in the accounting period on which it is let by the company as furnished accommodation.
(3) If the accommodation—
 (a) was let by the company as furnished accommodation in the 12 months immediately before the accounting period, but
 (b) is not let by the company as furnished accommodation in the 12 months immediately after the accounting period,
"the relevant period" is 12 months ending with the last day in the accounting period on which it is let by the company as furnished accommodation.
(4) Otherwise "the relevant period" is the period of 12 months ending with the last day of the accounting period.

Commentary—*Simon's Taxes* **B6.403**.
Derivation—TA 1988 s 504(5).
HMRC Manuals—Property Income Manual PIM4115 (period to which tests are to be applied for CT).

267 Meaning of "qualifying holiday accommodation"

(1) Accommodation which is let by a company during an accounting period is "qualifying holiday accommodation" for the accounting period if the availability, letting and pattern of occupation conditions are met.
(2) The availability condition is that, during the relevant period, the accommodation is available for commercial letting as holiday accommodation to the public generally for at least [210][1] days.
(3) The letting condition is that, during the relevant period, the accommodation is commercially let as holiday accommodation to members of the public for at least [105][1] days.
(4) For the purposes of the letting condition, a letting of accommodation for a period of longer-term occupation (see subsection (6)) is not a letting of it as holiday accommodation.
(5) The pattern of occupation condition is that, during the relevant period, not more than 155 days fall during periods of longer-term occupation.
(6) For the purposes of this section a "period of longer-term occupation" is a continuous period of more than 31 days during which the accommodation is in the same occupation otherwise than because of circumstances that are not normal.

Commentary—*Simon's Taxes* **B6.403, C3.302**.
Amendments—[1] In sub-s (2) words substituted for words "140 days", and in sub-s (3) words substituted for words "70 days", by FA 2011 s 52, Sch 14 para 7(1), (3) with effect in relation to accounting periods beginning on or after 1 April 2012. These amendments do not have effect in relation to relevant periods which begin before, and end on or after, 1 April 2012: FA 2011 Sch 14 para 10.

268 Under-used holiday accommodation: averaging elections

(1) This section applies if during an accounting period a company lets both—
 (a) qualifying holiday accommodation, and
 (b) accommodation that would be qualifying holiday accommodation if the letting condition (see section 267(3)) were met in relation to it ("under-used accommodation").
(2) The company may make an election for the accounting period specifying—
 (a) the qualifying holiday accommodation, and
 (b) any or all of the under-used accommodation.
(3) The under-used accommodation so specified is treated as qualifying holiday accommodation for the accounting period if the average of the number of let days for the accounting period of all the accommodation specified in the election is at least [105][2].
(4) "The number of let days" for an accounting period of any accommodation is the number of days during the relevant period for which it is commercially let by the company as holiday accommodation to members of the public.
(5) Qualifying holiday accommodation may not be specified in more than one election for an accounting period.

(6) An election for an accounting period must be made within the period of two years beginning at the end of the accounting period.

[(7) This section is to apply separately in relation to accommodation in the United Kingdom and accommodation in EEA states other than the United Kingdom.]¹

Commentary—*Simon's Taxes* B6.404.

HMRC Manuals—Property Income Manual PIM4113 (furnished holiday lettings: changes to the rules 2011-12 and following).

Amendments—¹ Sub-s (7) inserted by FA 2011 s 52, Sch 14 para 7(1), (4)(*b*) with effect in relation to accounting periods beginning on or after 1 April 2011.

² In sub-s (3) figure substituted for figure "70" by FA 2011 s 52, Sch 14 para 7(1), (4)(*a*) with effect in relation to accounting periods beginning on or after 1 April 2012. This amendment does not have effect in relation to relevant periods which begin before, and end on or after, 1 April 2012: FA 2011 Sch 14 para 10.

Prospective amendments—In sub-s (7) words "other than the United Kingdom" to be repealed by the Taxes (Amendments) (EU Exit) Regulations, SI 2019/689 reg 16(1), (3) with effect from Implementation Period completion day (see EU(WA)A 2020 Sch 5 para 1(l)).

[268A Under-used holiday accommodation: letting condition not met

(1) This section applies if—

   (*a*) during an accounting period a company lets qualifying holiday accommodation,

   (*b*) the accommodation is let by the company—

      (i) during the next accounting period, or

      (ii) during the next two accounting periods,

   (*c*) the accommodation would (apart from this section) not be qualifying holiday accommodation—

      (i) during the accounting period mentioned in paragraph (*b*)(i), or

      (ii) during both of the accounting periods mentioned in paragraph (*b*)(ii),

      only because of a failure to meet the letting condition (see section 267(3)), and

   (*d*) there was a genuine intention to meet the letting condition for the period within subsection (1)(*c*)(i) or each of the periods within subsection (1)(*c*)(ii) (as the case may be).

(2) If the company makes an election in respect of that accommodation for any accounting period in respect of which the failure mentioned in subsection (1)(*c*) occurs, the accommodation is to be treated as qualifying holiday accommodation for that accounting period.

(3) Subsection (2) does not apply for the purposes of section 268 or subsection (1)(*a*).

(4) If an election is not made for the first of the accounting periods within subsection (1)(*c*)(ii), an election may not be made for the second.

(5) An election for an accounting period must be made within the period of two years beginning at the end of the accounting period.

(6) References in subsection (1)(*a*) and (*c*) to qualifying holiday accommodation include accommodation treated as such under section 268.]¹

Commentary—*Simon's Taxes* B6.404.

HMRC Manuals—Property Income Manual PIM4113 (furnished holiday lettings: changes to the rules 2011-12 and following).

Amendments—¹ This section inserted by FA 2011 s 52, Sch 14 para 7(1), (5) with effect where the accounting period mentioned in sub-s (1)(*a*) begins on or after 1 April 2010.

Separate profit calculations

269 Capital allowances and loss [relief: UK property business]³

(1) If a UK property business consists of both—

   (*a*) the commercial letting of furnished holiday accommodation ("the furnished holiday lettings part"), and

   (*b*) other businesses or transactions ("the other part"),

this section requires separate calculations to be made of the profits of the furnished holiday lettings part and the other part.

(2) The calculations must be made if—

   (*a*) section 248 or 249 of CAA 2001 (giving effect to allowances and charges) applies to the furnished holiday lettings part or the other part, or

   (*b*) any provision of [Chapter 2, 4 or 6 of Part 4 of CTA 2010]¹ (loss relief) applies in relation to a loss made in either of those parts . . .

   (*c*) . . . ²

(3) If there is a letting of accommodation only part of which is holiday accommodation, such apportionments are to be made for the purposes of this section as are just and reasonable.

Commentary—*Simon's Taxes* B6.401.

Amendments—¹ In sub-s (2)(*b*) words substituted for words "Chapter 2 of Part 10 of ICTA" by CTA 2010 s 1177, Sch 1 para 603. CTA 2010 has effect for corporation tax purposes for accounting periods ending on or after 1 April 2010, and for income and capital gains tax purposes for the tax year 2010–11 and subsequent tax years.

² Sub-s (2)(*c*) and preceding word "or" inserted by the Enactment of Extra-Statutory Concessions Order, SI 2011/1037 art 12(1), (3) with effect for accounting periods beginning on or after 1 April 2011 (SI 2011/1037 art 13(2)) and repealed by FA 2016 s 74(3)(*b*) with effect in relation to accounting periods beginning on or after 1 April 2016, subject to transitional provisions for accounting periods straddling that date (FA 2016 s 74(5)).

(2) In this Chapter, except in section 284, references to a UK property business include one within the charge to income tax and references to a person permanently ceasing to carry on a UK property business include—

    (*a*) in the case of a company, the occurrence of an event treated under section 362 of ITTOIA 2005 (company starting or ceasing to be within charge to income tax) as the company permanently ceasing to carry on the business, and

    (*b*) in the case of a UK property business carried on by a person in partnership, the occurrence of an event treated under section 353(3) of ITTOIA 2005 (basic meaning of "post-cessation receipt") as the person permanently ceasing to carry on the business.

Commentary—*Simon's Taxes* **B6.213**.
Derivation—TA 1988 ss 21B, 103(1), (2), 104(1), (2), 110(1C), (1D).
HMRC Manuals—Business Income Manual BIM90030 (post cessation receipts: meaning).

283 Other rules about what counts as a "post-cessation receipt"

(1) Section 284 (transfer of rights if transferee does not carry on UK property business) treats certain amounts as being, or not being, post-cessation receipts for the purposes of this Chapter.

(2) The following provisions (which treat certain amounts as post-cessation receipts) apply for the purposes of this Chapter as they apply for the purposes of Chapter 15 of Part 3 (but as if any reference to a trade were to a UK property business)—

    section 82(6) (contributions to local enterprise organisations or urban regeneration companies),
    section 101(3) (distribution of assets of mutual concerns),
    section 108(3) (receipt of benefits by donor or connected person),
    section 192 (debts paid after cessation), and
    section 193 (debts released after cessation), as qualified, where appropriate, by section 56(4) (car [1] hire).

(3) This Chapter also needs to be read with—

    (*a*) section 249(3) (which treats certain amounts as not being post-cessation receipts), and
    (*b*) section 1277 (which treats certain income as a post-cessation receipt: unremittable income).

Commentary—*Simon's Taxes* **B6.213**.
Derivation—TA 1988 ss 21B, 79(9), 103(4), (5), 491(3), (6).
HMRC Manuals—Business Income Manual BIM90030 (other receipts which are treated as post-cessation receipts).
Amendments—[1] In sub-s (2) words "or motor cycle" repealed by FA 2009 s 30, Sch 11 para 54 with effect as provided for by FA 2009 Sch 11 paras 65, 66 and subject to savings in FA 2009 Sch 11 para 68. The new system of capital allowances for cars has effect generally from 6 April 2009 (for income tax) and 1 April 2009 (for corporation tax), subject to FA 2009 Sch 11 para 67 (election for new regime not to apply in certain cases).

284 Transfer of rights if transferee does not carry on UK property business

(1) This section applies if—

    (*a*) a company ("the transferor") permanently ceases to carry on a UK property business,
    (*b*) the transferor transfers to another person ("the transferee") for value the right to receive sums arising from the carrying on of any business ("the transferred business") comprised in the transferor's UK property business, and
    (*c*) the transferee does not subsequently carry on the transferred business.

(2) The transferor is treated as receiving a post-cessation receipt.

(3) The amount of the receipt is—

    (*a*) the amount or value of the consideration for the transfer, if the transfer is at arm's length, or
    (*b*) the value of the rights transferred as between parties at arm's length, if the transfer is not at arm's length.

(4) Any sums mentioned in subsection (1)(*b*) which are received after the cessation of the property business are not post-cessation receipts.

Commentary—*Simon's Taxes* **B6.213**.
Derivation—TA 1988 ss 21B, 106(1), (2).
HMRC Manuals—Business Income Manual BIM90050 (transfer of rights if transferee does not carry on the trade).

Deductions

285 Allowable deductions

Sections 196 and 197 apply for the purposes of this Chapter as they apply for the purposes of Chapter 15 of Part 3 (but as if any reference to a trade were to a UK property business).

Derivation—TA 1988 ss 21B, 105(1), (2), (3).
HMRC Manuals—Business Income Manual BIM90090 (overview of reliefs for post cessation expenses).
BIM90095 (relief for post cessation expenses against post cessation receipts).

Election to carry back

286 Election to carry back

Sections 198 to 200 apply for the purposes of this Chapter as they apply for the purposes of Chapter 15 of Part 3 (but as if any reference to a trade were to a UK property business).

CHAPTER 10

SUPPLEMENTARY
Priority rules

287 Provisions which must be given priority over this Part

Any receipt or other credit item, so far as it falls within—

    (a) Chapter 3 of this Part so far as it relates to an overseas property business or Chapter 7 or 8 of this Part (rent receivable in connection with a UK section 39(4) concern or for UK electric-line wayleaves), and

    (b) Chapter 2 of Part 3 (receipts of a trade),

is dealt with under Part 3.

Commentary—*Simon's Taxes* **B6.103B, B6.502, B5.663, B5.662.**

288 Priority between Chapters within this Part

(1) Any receipt, so far as it falls within—

    (a) Chapter 3 so far as it relates to a UK property business, and

    (b) Chapter 7 (rent receivable in connection with a UK section 39(4) concern),

is dealt with under Chapter 7.

(2) Any receipt, so far as it falls within—

    (a) Chapter 3 so far as it relates to a UK property business, and

    (b) Chapter 8 (rent receivable for UK electric-line wayleaves),

is dealt with under Chapter 8.

(3) Any receipt, so far as it falls within Chapter 7 (rent receivable in connection with a UK section 39(4) concern) and Chapter 8 (rent receivable for UK electric- line wayleaves), is dealt with under Chapter 8.

Commentary—*Simon's Taxes* **B6.103B.**

Other supplementary provisions

289 Effect of company starting or ceasing to be within charge to corporation tax

(1) This section applies if a company starts or ceases to be within the charge to corporation tax in respect of [an overseas property business][1].

(2) The company is treated for the purposes of this Part—

    (a) as starting to carry on the business when it starts to be within the charge, or

    (b) as ceasing to carry on the business when it ceases to be within the charge.

Commentary—*Simon's Taxes* **B6.213, B6.215.**

Amendments—[1] In sub-s (1), words substituted for words "a property business" by FA 2019 s 17, Sch 5 paras 10, 14 with effect from 6 April 2020, subject to transitional provisions in FA 2019 Sch 5 Pt 3 (paras 36–50).

290 Overseas property businesses and overseas land: adaptation of rules

(1) This section applies if a provision of this Part—

    (a) applies to an overseas property business or land outside the United Kingdom, but

    (b) is expressed by reference to a domestic concept of law.

(2) In relation to that business or land, the provision is to be read so as to produce the result most closely corresponding with that produced by the provision in relation to a UK property business or land in the United Kingdom.

Commentary—*Simon's Taxes* **B6.215.**

291 Meaning of "lease" and "premises"

(1) In this Part "lease" includes—

    (a) an agreement for a lease (so far as the context permits), and

    (b) any tenancy,

but does not include a mortgage.

(2) In this Part "premises" includes land.

Commentary—*Simon's Taxes* **B6.216.**
Derivation—TA 1988 ss 24(1), 70A(5).
HMRC Manuals—Capital Allowances Manual CA45950 (Meaning of lease).

PART 5
LOAN RELATIONSHIPS

CHAPTER 1

INTRODUCTION
Introduction

292 Overview of Part

(1) This Part sets out how profits and deficits arising to a company from its loan relationships are brought into account for corporation tax purposes.

(2) For the meaning of "loan relationship" see section 302 and Part 6 (relationships treated as loan relationships etc).

(3) For how such profits and deficits are calculated and brought into account, see—
- (a) section 296 (profits and deficits to be calculated using credits and debits given by this Part),
- (b) section 297 (trading credits and debits to be brought into account under Part 3),
- (c) section 299 (charge to tax on non-trading profits),
- (d) section 300 (method of bringing non-trading deficits into account),
- (e) section 301 (calculation of non-trading profits and deficits from loan relationships: non-trading credits and debits), and
- (f) Chapter 16 (non-trading deficits).

(4) For the priority of this Part for corporation tax purposes, see Chapter 17.

(5) This Part also contains the following Chapters (which mainly relate to the amounts to be brought into account for the purposes of this Part)—
- (a) Chapter 3 (the credits and debits to be brought into account: general),
- (b) Chapter 4 (continuity of treatment on transfers within groups or on reorganisations),
- (c) Chapter 5 (connected companies relationships: introduction and general),
- (d) Chapter 6 (connected companies relationships: impairment losses and releases of debts),
- (e) Chapter 7 (group relief claims involving impaired or released consortium debts),
- (f) Chapter 8 (connected parties relationships: late interest),
- (g) Chapter 9 (partnerships involving companies),
- (h) Chapter 10 (insurance companies),
- (i) Chapter 11 (other special kinds of company),
- (j) Chapter 12 (special rules for particular kinds of securities),
- (k) Chapter 13 (European cross-border transfers of business),
- (l) Chapter 14 (European cross-border mergers),
- (m) Chapter 15 (tax avoidance),
- (n) Chapter 18 (general and supplementary provisions).

(6) This Part needs to be read with Part 19 (general exemptions).

293 Construction of references to profits or losses from loan relationships

(1) In this Part references to profits or losses from loan relationships include references to profits or losses from related transactions.

(2) For the meaning of "related transaction" see section 304.

(3) Except where the context indicates otherwise, in this Part references to profits or losses from loan relationships include references to profits or losses of a capital nature.

Commentary—*Simon's Taxes* **D1.715**.
Derivation—FA 1996 s 84(1).
HMRC Manuals—Corporate Finance Manual CFM35340 (connected companies and impairment: basic rules: related transactions).
CFM35350 (related transactions: examples).
CFM30170 (a short guide on how are taxable amounts computed?).
CFM33160 (computational rules: GAAP: capital Expenditure).

294 Matters treated as loan relationships

(1) Part 6 deals with matters treated for some or all purposes as loan relationships or rights, payments or profits under loan relationships.

(2) Except where the context indicates otherwise, references to this Part in this Act and elsewhere in the Tax Acts include references to Part 6.

Commentary—*Simon's Taxes* **D1.715**.
HMRC Manuals—Corporate Finance Manual CFM30200 (a short guide: deemed loan relationship).
CFM40000 (deemed loan relationships: contents).
CFM40110 (deemed loan relationships: overview).
CFM92820 (debt cap: income from EEA group companies: financing income amounts potentially involved).

How profits and deficits from loan relationships are dealt with

295 General rule: profits arising from loan relationships chargeable as income

(1) The general rule for corporation tax purposes is that all profits arising to a company from its loan relationships are chargeable to tax as income in accordance with this Part.

(2) But see section 465 (exclusion of distributions except in tax avoidance cases).

Derivation—FA 1996 s 80(1).
HMRC Manuals—Corporate Finance Manual CFM30170 (general rule: what is taxable under the loan relationships rules?).
CFM30160 (a short guide: who is taxable?).

296 Profits and deficits to be calculated using credits and debits given by this Part

Profits and deficits arising to a company from its loan relationships are to be calculated using the credits and debits given by this Part.

Derivation—FA 1996 s 82(1).
HMRC Manuals—Corporate Finance Manual CFM30160 (company: who is taxable?).

297 Trading credits and debits to be brought into account under Part 3

(1) This section applies so far as in any accounting period a company is a party to a loan relationship for the purposes of a trade it carries on.

(2) The credits in respect of the relationship for the period are treated as receipts of the trade which are to be brought into account in calculating its profits for that period.

(3) The debits in respect of the relationship for the period are treated as expenses of the trade which are deductible in calculating those profits.

(4) So far as subsection (3) provides for any amount to be deductible, it has effect despite anything in—

    (a) section 53 (capital expenditure),

    (b) section 54 (expenses not wholly and exclusively for trade and unconnected losses), or

    (c) section 59 (patent royalties).

(5) This section is subject to—

    (a) section 330 (debits in respect of pre-trading expenditure),

    (b) section 482(1) (under which credits or debits to be brought into account under Chapter 2 of Part 6 (relevant non-lending relationships) are treated as non-trading credits or debits), and

    (c) [sections 286(5) and 287(5) of CTA 2010][1] (under which some credits and debits affecting ring-fence profits from petroleum extraction activities are treated as non-trading credits and debits).

Commentary—*Simon's Taxes* **D1.739, D7.5139.**
HMRC Manuals—Corporate Finance Manual CFM32020 (trading credits and debits: what is a loan relationship held for the purpose of a trade?).
Business Income Manual BIM64245 (interest: trade).
CFM77650 (tax rules on corporate debt: group mismatch schemes: other specific instances).
Amendments—[1] In sub-s (5)(c) words substituted for words "section 494(2A) of ICTA" by CTA 2010 s 1177, Sch 1 para 604. CTA 2010 has effect for corporation tax purposes for accounting periods ending on or after 1 April 2010, and for income and capital gains tax purposes for the tax year 2010–11 and subsequent tax years.

298 Meaning of trade and purposes of trade

(1) For the purposes of this Part a company is taken to be a party to a creditor relationship for the purposes of a trade it carries on only if it is a party to the relationship in the course of activities forming an integral part of the trade.

(2) For the meaning of "creditor relationship", see section 302(5).

(3) For the purposes of this Part activities carried on by a company in the course of—

    (a) any mutual trading, [or][1]

    (b) any mutual insurance or other mutual business which is not life assurance business, . . . [1]

    (c) . . . [1]

are treated as not constituting the whole or any part of a trade.

(4) Subsection (3) applies for the purposes of any other relevant enactment as it applies for the purposes of this Part.

(5) In subsection (4) "relevant enactment" means so much of any enactment as contains provision by reference to which amounts are to be brought into account for the purposes of this Part.

[(6) In the case of activities carried on by a company in the course of any basic life assurance and general annuity business, provision corresponding to that made by subsection (3) is made by section 88 of FA 2012 for the purpose of applying the I-E rules.][1]

Commentary—*Simon's Taxes* **D1.739.**
HMRC Manuals—Corporate Finance Manual CFM32020 (trading credits and debits).
CFM51030 (derivative contracts: trading and non-trading credits and debits).
General Insurance Manual GIM9090 (tax treatment: general insurance business on a mutual basis).
Business Leasing Manual BLM33115 (interest earned in periods ending after 31 March 1996).
Business Income Manual BIM40801 (specific receipts: interest and dividends: introduction).
Amendments—[1] In sub-s (3), word "or" at end of para (a) inserted, para (c) and preceding word "or" repealed, and sub-s (6) inserted, by FA 2012 s 146, Sch 16 paras 135, 147 with effect in relation to accounting periods of companies beginning on or after 1 January 2013 (subject to transitional provisions in FA 2012 Sch 17). For accounting periods straddling 1 January 2013, see FA 2012 s 149.

299 Charge to tax on non-trading profits

(1) The charge to corporation tax on income applies to any non-trading profits which a company has in respect of its loan relationships.

(2) For the meaning of a company having such profits and how they are calculated, see section 301.

Commentary—*Simon's Taxes* **A4.423, A4.424.**
HMRC Manuals—Corporate Finance Manual CFM32030 (charge to tax: non-trading profits and deficits).
CFM51020 (derivative contracts: how amounts are taxed).
CFM32010 (non-trading profits and deficits: taxing and relieving provisions: overview).
Business Income Manual BIM64295 (interest: non-trade: charge to corporation tax).

300 Method of bringing non-trading deficits into account

(1) Any non-trading deficit which a company has from its loan relationships must be brought into account in accordance with Chapter 16 (non-trading deficits).

(2) For the meaning of a company having such a deficit and how it is calculated, see section 301.

(3) This section and Chapter 16 apply even if none of the company's loan relationships is regarded as a source of income as a result of this Part.

Derivation—FA 1996 s 80(4).

HMRC Manuals—Corporate Finance Manual CFM30180 (how are taxable amounts brought into account).
CFM30100 (loan relationships: a brief history and a short guide: contents).
CFM32030 (relieving non-trading deficits).

301 Calculation of non-trading profits and deficits from loan relationships: non-trading credits and debits

(1) Whether a company has non-trading profits or a non-trading deficit from its loan relationships for an accounting period is determined [in accordance with subsections (4) to (7)][1], using the non-trading credits and non-trading debits given by this Part for the accounting period.

[(1A) In the case of a non-UK resident company, subsections (4) to (7) need to be read with section 5(3), (3A)(b) and (3B)(b) (territorial scope of charge to corporation tax).][2]

(2) In this Part—

    (a) "non-trading credits" means credits for any accounting period in respect of a company's loan relationships that are not brought into account under section 297(2), and

    (b) "non-trading debits" means debits for any accounting period in respect of a company's loan relationships that are not brought into account under section 297(3).

(3) But see also—

    (a) section 330 (debits in respect of pre-trading expenditure), and

    (b) section 482(1) (under which credits or debits to be brought into account under Chapter 2 of Part 6 (relevant non-lending relationships) are treated as non-trading credits or debits).

(4) A company has non-trading profits for an accounting period from its loan relationships if the non-trading credits for the period exceed the non-trading debits for the period or there are no such debits.

(5) The non-trading profits are equal to those credits, less any such debits.

(6) A company has a non-trading deficit for an accounting period from its loan relationships if the non-trading debits for the period exceed the non-trading credits for the period or there are no such credits.

(7) The non-trading deficit is equal to those debits, less any such credits.

Amendments—[1]   In sub-s (1), words substituted for words "as follows" by FA 2019 s 17, Sch 5 paras 10, 15, with effect from 6 April 2020, subject to transitional provisions in FA 2019 Sch 5 Pt 3 (paras 36–50).

[2]   Sub-s (1A) substituted by FA 2020 s 32, Sch 6 para 1 with effect from 6 April 2020. This amendment has effect as if it had been incorporated into FA 2019 Sch 5 and so is subject to transitional provisions in FA 2019 Sch 5 Pt 3 (paras 36–50).

CHAPTER 2

BASIC DEFINITIONS

302 "Loan relationship", "creditor relationship", "debtor relationship"

(1) For the purposes of the Corporation Tax Acts a company has a loan relationship if—

    (a) the company stands in the position of a creditor or debtor as respects any money debt (whether by reference to a security or otherwise), and

    (b) the debt arises from a transaction for the lending of money.

(2) References to a loan relationship and to a company being a party to a loan relationship are to be read accordingly.

(3) For cases where this Part applies as if a relationship were a loan relationship despite the money debt not arising from a transaction for the lending of money see Chapter 2 of Part 6 (relevant non-lending relationships).

(4) See also the following provisions of Part 6 (under which other matters are treated as loan relationships or rights, payments or profits under loan relationships)—

    (a) Chapter 3 (OEICs, unit trusts and offshore funds),

    (b) Chapter 4 (building societies),

    (c) Chapter 5 ([registered societies][1]),

    (d) Chapter 6 (alternative finance arrangements),

    (e) Chapter 7 (shares with guaranteed returns etc),

    (f) Chapter 8 (returns from partnerships),

    (g) Chapter 9 (manufactured interest etc),

    (h) Chapter 10 (repos), and

    (i) Chapter 11 (investment life insurance contracts).

(5) In this Part "creditor relationship", in relation to a company, means any loan relationship of the company where it stands in the position of a creditor as respects the debt in question.

(6) In this Part "debtor relationship", in relation to a company, means any loan relationship of the company where it stands in the position of a debtor as respects the debt in question.

Amendments—[1]   In each place where they occur in this Act, words substituted for words "registered industrial and provident society", "the Industrial and Provident Societies Act 1965" and "industrial and provident societies", by the Co-operative and Community Benefit Societies Act 2014 s 151, Sch 4 paras 140–143 with effect from 1 August 2014 and subject to transitional provisions and provisions preserving the continuity of the law in Sch 5 of that Act.

303 "Money debt"

(1) For the purposes of this Part a money debt is a debt which—

   (*a*) falls to be settled—

      (i) by the payment of money,

      (ii) by the transfer of a right to settlement under a debt which is itself a money debt, or

      (iii) by the issue or transfer of any share in any company,

   (*b*) has at any time fallen to be so settled, or

   (*c*) may at the option of the debtor or the creditor fall to be so settled.

(2) For the purposes of subsection (1) any option exercisable by either party to settle the debt in any other way than is mentioned in subsection (1)(*a*) is ignored.

(3) A money debt is a debt arising from a transaction for the lending of money for the purposes of this Part if an instrument is issued by any person for the purpose of representing—

   (*a*) security for the debt, or

   (*b*) the rights of a creditor in respect of the debt.

(4) A debt does not arise from a transaction for the lending of money for the purposes of this Part so far as it arises from rights conferred by shares in a company.

(5) But see the following provisions (as a result of which some such rights are within this Chapter)—

   (*a*) Chapter 3 of Part 6 (OEICs, unit trusts and offshore funds),

   (*b*) Chapter 7 of that Part (shares with guaranteed returns etc).

(6) For the meaning of "share" see section 476(1).

304 "Related transaction"

(1) In this Part "related transaction", in relation to a loan relationship, means any disposal or acquisition (in whole or in part) of rights or liabilities under the relationship.

(2) For this purpose the cases where there is taken to be such a disposal and acquisition include those where rights or liabilities under the loan relationship are transferred or extinguished by any sale, gift, exchange, surrender, redemption or release.

305 Payments, interest, rights and liabilities under a loan relationship

(1) For the purposes of this Part references to payments or interest under a loan relationship are references to payments or interest paid or payable in pursuance of any of the rights or liabilities under that relationship.

(2) For the purposes of this Part references to rights or liabilities under a loan relationship are references to any of the rights or liabilities under the arrangements as a result of which that relationship subsists.

(3) For the purposes of this Part rights or liabilities under a loan relationship are taken to include the rights or liabilities attached to any security that is issued in relation to the money debt in question (and so is a security representing that relationship).

(4) But for the treatment of funding bonds see—

   (*a*) section 413 (issue of funding bonds), and

   (*b*) section 414 (redemption of funding bonds).

CHAPTER 3

THE CREDITS AND DEBITS TO BE BROUGHT INTO ACCOUNT: GENERAL

Introduction

306 Overview of Chapter

(1) This Chapter contains rules of general application about the credits and debits to be brought into account for the purposes of this Part.

(2) In particular, it—

   [(*za*) makes provision about the matters in respect of which amounts are to be brought into account (see section 306A),][1]

   (*a*) provides for the application of generally accepted accounting practice in determining the amounts to be brought into account as credits and debits and makes provision where accounts do not comply with that practice (see sections 307 to 312),

   (*b*) makes provision about bases of accounting (see sections 313 and 314),

   (*c*) provides for adjustments on changes of accounting [basis][1] (see sections 315 to 319),

   (*d*) sets out some general rules that differ from generally accepted accounting practice (see sections 320 to 327),

   (*e*) provides for exchange gains and losses to be included in the profits and losses of a company from loan relationships (see section 328),

   (*f*) makes provision about debits for pre-loan relationship, abortive or pre- trading expenses (see sections 329 and 330),

CTA 2009

Amendments—[1]   In sub-ss (1), (2) words repealed, and whole of sub-s (5) repealed, by F(No 2)A 2015 s 32, Sch 7 paras 1, 6 with effect for accounting periods beginning on or after 1 January 2016, subject to transitional rules in F(No 2)A 2015 Sch 7 paras 115 to 129.

311 Amounts not fully recognised for accounting purposes: introduction

(1) Section 312 applies for the purpose of determining the credits and debits which a company is to bring into account for a period for the purposes of this Part in the following case.

(2) The case is where—

    (*a*) the company is, or is treated as, a party to a creditor relationship in the period, [and][2]

    [(*b*) as a result of tax avoidance arrangements to which the company is at any time a party, an amount is (in accordance with generally accepted accounting practice) not fully recognised for the period in respect of the creditor relationship.][2]

....[2]

(6) For the purposes of this section [and section 312][2] an amount is not fully recognised for a period in respect of a relationship of a company ...[2], [1] if—

    (*a*) no amount in respect of the relationship[...[2]][1] is recognised in determining its profit or loss for the period, or

    (*b*) an amount is so recognised in respect of only part of the relationship[...[2]][1].

[(7) For the purposes of this section arrangements are "tax avoidance arrangements" if the main purpose, or one of the main purposes, of any party to the arrangements, in entering into them, is to obtain a tax advantage.

(8) In subsection (7) "arrangements" includes any arrangements, scheme or understanding of any kind, whether or not legally enforceable, involving a single transaction or two or more transactions.

(9) For the purposes of this section a company is to be treated as a party to a creditor relationship even though it has disposed of its rights under the relationship to another person—

    (*a*) under a repo or stock lending arrangement, or

    (*b*) under a transaction which is treated as not involving any disposal as a result of section 26 of TCGA 1992 (mortgages and charges not to be treated as disposals).][2]

Commentary—*Simon's Taxes* D1.725, D1.847.

Derivation—FA 1996 s 85C(1)–(4).

HMRC Manuals—Corporate Finance Manual CFM33120 (amounts "not fully recognised" for accounting purposes).

CFM39210 (tax avoidance: periods beginning before and on or after 6 December 2010).

CFM39220 (meaning of tax avoidance arrangements).

CFM39230 (tax avoidance: no debits for derecognition).

CFM56110 (amounts not fully recognised for accounting purposes).

Amendments—[1]   Sub-s (2)(*b*), (*c*) substituted; words in sub-ss (3)(*b*), (4)(*b*) inserted; sub-s (4A) inserted and in sub-s (6) words "or a relevant capital contribution to it" and "or contribution" (in both places) substituted, by FA 2009 s 61, Sch 30 para 2 (1)-(6) with effect in relation to periods of account beginning on or after 22 April 2009 subject to transitional provisions relating to periods of account beginning before, and ending on or after, 22 April 2009: FA 2009 Sch 30 para 2(9).

[2]   In sub-s (2), word at end of para (*a*) inserted and para (*b*) substituted for previous paras (*b*), (*c*); sub-ss (3)–(5A) repealed; in sub-s (6), words inserted and words ", a contribution to it or securities issued by it" repealed, and in paras (*a*), (*b*) words ", contribution or securities" repealed; and sub-ss (7), (8), (9) inserted, by FA 2011 s 28, Sch 4 paras 1, 2 with effect in relation to periods of account beginning on or after 6 December 2010, subject to the transitional provision in FA 2011 Sch 4 para 13(2).

312 Determination of credits and debits where amounts not fully recognised

(1) In determining the credits and debits which a company is to bring into account for the period referred to in section 311(1) for the purposes of this Part in respect of—

    (*a*) the creditor relationship mentioned in section 311(2),

    (*b*) *in a case where condition A in section 311(3) is met, the debtor relationship by reference to which that condition is met,*[1]

the assumption in subsection (2) is to be made.

[(1A) Subsection (1B) applies in a case where—

    (*a*) pursuant to the arrangements mentioned in section 311(2)(*b*), the company becomes, or is treated as becoming, a party to a debtor relationship, and

    (*b*) an amount is (in accordance with generally accepted accounting practice) not fully recognised for any period in respect of the debtor relationship.][2]

[(1B) In determining the debits and credits which a company is to bring into account for any period for the purposes of this Part in respect of the debtor relationship ...[2], the assumption in subsection (2) is to be made.][1]

(2) The assumption is that an amount in respect of the whole of the relationship in question is recognised in determining the company's profit or loss for the period.

(3) [But—

    (*a*) no debits are, as a result of this section, to be brought into account by the company in respect of the creditor relationship mentioned in section 311(2), and (b)] [2] the amount of any debits to be brought into account by the company for a period as a result of this section applying in respect of its debtor relationships must not exceed the amount of any credits to be brought into account by it for the period as a result of this section applying in respect of its creditor relationships.

(4) Subsection (5) applies in any case where—

(a) apart from this section any credits or debits are brought into account for a period for the purposes of this Part by the company in respect of a loan relationship, and

(b) the relationship is a creditor relationship within [subsection (1)][1] or a debtor relationship within [subsection (1B)][1].

(5) The credits and debits which are to be so brought into account as a result of this section are to be determined on the same basis of accounting as that on which the credits or debits mentioned in subsection (4)(a) are determined.

(6) In any other case, the credits and debits which are to be so brought into account as a result of this section are to be determined on an amortised cost basis of accounting.

Commentary—*Simon's Taxes* D1.725.

Amendments—[1]   In sub-s (1), para (b) and preceding word "or" repealed, sub-ss (1A), (1B) inserted, and in sub-s (4), in para (b), words substituted for words "subsection (1)(a)" and "subsection (1)(b)", by F(No 2)A 2010 s 8, Sch 5 para 2 with effect in relation to periods of account beginning on or after 22 June 2010. Note that a period of account beginning before, and ending on or after, 22 June 2010 is to be treated as if so much of the period as falls before that fate, and so much of the period as falls on or after that date, were separate periods of account (F(No 2)A 2010 Sch 5 para 4(2)).

[2]   Sub-s (1A) substituted; in sub-s (1B) words "by reference to which that condition is met" repealed, and in sub-s (3) words substituted for word "But", by FA 2011 s 28, Sch 4 paras 1, 3 with effect in relation to periods of account beginning on or after 6 December 2010, subject to the transitional provision in FA 2011 Sch 4 para 13(2). Note that sub-s (3)(a) does not have effect where it applies by reason of tax avoidance arrangements to which the company became a party before 23 March 2011 (FA 2011 Sch 4 para 13(3)(a)).

Accounting bases

313 Basis of accounting: "amortised cost basis", "fair value accounting" and "fair value"

(1) The general rule is that the amounts to be brought into account by a company as credits and debits for any period of account for the purposes of this Part may be determined on any basis of accounting that is in accordance with generally accepted accounting practice . . . [1].

(2) But subsection (1) is subject to . . . [1] the following provisions (which require a particular accounting basis to be used)—

(a) section 312(5) and (6) (determination of credits and debits where amounts not fully recognised for accounting purposes),

(b) section 349(2) (application of amortised cost basis to connected companies relationships),

(c) section 382(2) (company partners using fair value accounting),

(d) section 399(2) (index-linked gilt-edged securities: application of fair value accounting),

(e) . . . [1]

(f) . . . [1]

(g) section 482(2) (application of amortised cost basis of accounting to discounts arising from a money debt under a relevant non-lending relationship), [and][1]

(h) section 490(3) (holdings in OEICs, unit trusts and offshore funds: application of fair value accounting) . . . [1]

(i) . . . [1]

(3) . . . [1]

(4) In this Part "amortised cost basis of accounting", in relation to a company's loan relationship, means a basis of accounting under which an asset or liability representing the loan relationship is [measured in the company's balance sheet at its amortised cost using the effective interest method, but with that amortised cost being adjusted as necessary where the loan relationship is the hedged item under a designated fair value hedge][1].

[(4A) In subsection (4) each of the following expressions has the meaning that it has for accounting purposes—

"amortised cost", in relation to assets or liabilities;

"the effective interest method", in relation to the measurement of assets or liabilities.][1]

[(5) In this Part "fair value accounting" means a basis of accounting under which—

(a) assets and liabilities are measured in the company's balance sheet at their fair value, and

(b) changes in the fair value of assets and liabilities are recognised as items of profit or loss.][1]

[(6) For the meaning of "fair value", see section 476(1).

(7) In this Part each of the following has the meaning that it has for accounting purposes—

"designated fair value hedge";

"hedged item".][1]

Amendments—[1]   In sub-s (1) words "and, in particular, an amortised cost basis of accounting or fair value accounting" repealed, in sub-s (2) words "sections 307(3) and (4) and", paras (e), (f), (i) repealed, in para (g) word inserted, in para (h) word "and" repealed, sub-s (3) repealed, in sub-s (4) words substituted for words "shown in the company's accounts at cost adjusted for cumulative amortisation and any impairment, repayment or release", sub-s (4A) inserted, sub-s (5) substituted, and sub-ss (6), (7) substituted for previous sub-s (6), by F(No 2)A 2015 s 32, Sch 7 paras 1,7 with effect for accounting periods beginning on or after 1 January 2016, subject to transitional rules in F(No 2)A 2015 Sch 7 paras 115 to 129.

314 Power to make regulations about changes from amortised cost basis

(1) This section applies if the credits or debits to be brought into account for the purposes of this Part in respect of assets or liabilities of a company—

    (a) are required in accordance with generally accepted accounting practice to be dealt with for accounting purposes using fair value accounting, and

    (b) were previously dealt with for those purposes on an amortised cost basis.

(2) The Treasury may by regulations provide that the credits or debits must continue to be determined on an amortised cost basis of accounting.

(3) The regulations may—

    (a) make different provision for different cases,

    (b) make incidental, supplemental, consequential and transitional provision and savings, and

    (c) make provision subject to an election or to other specified conditions.

Adjustments on change of accounting [basis]

315 Introduction to sections 316 [and 318][1]

[(1) Sections 316 and 318 (adjustments on change of accounting basis) apply if—

    (a) a company changes, from one period of account or accounting period to the next, the basis of accounting on which credits and debits relating to its loan relationships or any of them are calculated for the purposes of this Part,

    (b) the change of basis—

        (i) is made in order to comply with a provision made by or under this Part requiring those credits and debits to be determined on a particular basis of accounting, or

        (ii) results from a change of the company's accounting policy,

    (c) the change of basis is not made in order to comply with amending legislation not applicable to the previous period,

    (d) the old basis accorded with the law or practice applicable in relation to the period before the change, and

    (e) the new basis accords with the law and practice applicable to the period after the change.][1]

(2) In this section and sections 316 [and 318][1]—

    (a) the first of [the periods mentioned in subsection (1)][1] is referred to as "the earlier period", and

    (b) the next is referred to as "the later period".

(3) . . . . [1]

(4) For a case where this section and sections 316 to 318 apply as if a change of accounting policy had occurred, see section 416(5) (election for application of sections 415 and 585).

Amendments—[1] In italicised heading word substituted for word "policy, in section heading words substituted for words "to 319", sub-s (1) substituted, in sub-s (2) words substituted for words "to 319" and "those periods of account", and sub-s (3) repealed, by F(No 2)A 2015 s 32, Sch 7 paras 1, 8, 9 with effect for accounting periods beginning on or after 1 January 2016, subject to transitional rules in F(No 2)A 2015 Sch 7 paras 115 to 129.

[316 Change of basis of accounting involving change of value

(1) If there is a difference between—

    (a) the tax-adjusted carrying value of an asset or liability at the end of the earlier period, and

    (b) the tax-adjusted carrying value of that asset or liability at the beginning of the later period,

a credit or debit (as the case may be) of an amount equal to the difference must be brought into account for the purposes of this Part for the later period in the same way as a credit or debit which is brought into account in determining the company's profit or loss for that period in accordance with generally accepted accounting practice.

(2) This section does not apply so far as the credit or debit falls to be brought into account apart from this section.][1]

Amendments—[1] This section substituted by F(No 2)A 2015 s 32, Sch 7 paras 1, 10 with effect for accounting periods beginning on or after 1 January 2016, subject to transitional rules in F(No 2)A 2015 Sch 7 paras 115 to 129 (see in particular Sch 7 para 118).

318 Change of accounting [basis][1] following cessation of loan relationship

(1) This section applies if—

    (a) the company has ceased to be a party to a loan relationship in an accounting period ("the cessation period"),

    [(b) section 330A (company is not, or has ceased to be, party to loan relationship) applied to the cessation, and][1]

    (c) there is a difference between the amount outstanding in respect of the loan relationship (see subsection (5))—

        (i) at the end of the earlier period, and

        (ii) at the beginning of the later period.

[(2) A credit or debit (as the case may be) of an amount equal to the difference must be brought into account for the purposes of this Part for the later period in the same way as a credit or debit which is brought into account in determining the company's profit or loss for that period in accordance with generally accepted accounting practice.][1]

(4) [Subsection (2) does][1] not apply so far as the credit or debit falls to be brought into account apart from this section.

[(5) In this section "the amount outstanding in respect of the loan relationship" means—

    (a) so much of the recognised deferred income or recognised deferred loss from the loan relationship as has not been represented by credits or debits brought into account under this Part in respect of the relationship, and

    (b) any amounts relating to the matters mentioned in section 306A(1) in respect of the loan relationship that have in accordance with generally accepted accounting practice been recognised in the company's accounts as items of other comprehensive income and not transferred to become items of profit or loss.][1]

(6) In subsection (5)—

    "recognised deferred income", in relation to a loan relationship, means the amount recognised in the company's balance sheet in accordance with generally accepted accounting practice as deferred income in respect of the profits which arose from the relationship or a related transaction in the cessation period, and

    "recognised deferred loss", in relation to a loan relationship, means the amount so recognised as deferred loss in respect of the losses which so arose.

[(7) In determining what amounts fall within subsection (5)(b) at the beginning or end of a period, it is to be assumed that the accounting policy applied in drawing up the company's accounts for the period was also applied in previous periods.

(8) But if the company's accounts for the period are in accordance with generally accepted accounting practice drawn up on an assumption as to the accounting policy in previous periods which differs from that mentioned in subsection (7), that different assumption applies in determining what amounts fall within subsection (5)(b) at the beginning or end of the period.][1]

Amendments—[1]   Sub-ss (1)(b), (5) substituted, sub-s (2) substituted for previous sub-ss (2), (3), in sub-s (4) words substituted for words "Subsections (2) and (3) do", sub-ss (7), (8) inserted, and in heading word substituted for words "policy", by F(No 2)A 2015 s 32, Sch 7 paras 1, 12 with effect for accounting periods beginning on or after 1 January 2016, subject to transitional rules in F(No 2)A 2015 Sch 7 paras 115 to 129 (see in particular Sch 7 para 118).

319 General power to make regulations about changes in accounting policy

(1) The Treasury may by regulations make provision for cases where there is a change of accounting policy in drawing up a company's accounts from one period of account to the next which affects the amounts to be brought into account for accounting purposes in respect of the company's loan relationships.

(2) The regulations may provide for any credits or debits which would otherwise be brought into account for the purposes of this Part—

    (a) not to be brought into account,

    (b) to be brought into account only to a prescribed extent, or

    (c) to be brought into account over a prescribed period or in prescribed circumstances.

(3) Regulations under this section may, in particular, modify the operation of sections 315 to 318.

(4) The regulations may make—

    (a) different provision for different cases, and

    (b) incidental, supplemental, consequential and transitional provision and savings.

(5) The regulations may apply to periods of account beginning before they are made, but not earlier than the beginning of the calendar year in which they are made.

Regulations—Loan Relationships and Derivative Contracts (Change of Accounting Practice) (Amendment) Regulations, SI 2014/3187.

Loan Relationships and Derivative Contracts (Change of Accounting Practice) (Amendment) Regulations, SI 2015/1541.

Loan Relationships and Derivative Contracts (Change of Accounting Practice) (Amendment No 2) Regulations, SI 2015/1962.

Loan Relationships and Derivative Contracts (Change of Accounting Practice) (Amendment) Regulations, SI 2016/1234.

Rules differing from generally accepted accounting practice

320 Credits and debits treated as relating to capital expenditure

[(1) This section applies if—

    (a) an amount for an accounting period in respect of a company's loan relationship relates to any of the matters in section 306A(1),

    (b) generally accepted accounting practice allows the amount to be treated in the company's accounts as an amount recognised in determining the carrying value of an asset or liability, and

    (c) any profit or loss for corporation tax purposes in relation to that asset or liability will not fall to be calculated in accordance with generally accepted accounting practice.

(2) Despite that treatment, the amount is to be brought into account as a credit or debit for the purposes of this Part, for the accounting period for which it is recognised, in the same way as an amount which is brought into account as a credit or debit in determining the company's profit or loss for that period in accordance with generally accepted accounting practice.

(3) But subsection (2) does not apply to an amount which relates to an intangible fixed asset to which an election under section 730 (writing down at fixed rate: election for fixed-rate basis) applies.][1]

(4) . . . [1]

[(5) If an amount relating to an asset or liability is brought into account as mentioned in subsection (2) as a debit, no debit may be brought into account for the purposes of this Part in respect of—

    (a) the writing down of so much of the value of the asset or liability as is attributable to that debit, or

    (b) so much of any amortisation or depreciation representing a writing-off of that value as is attributable to that debit.][1]

Amendments—[1]   Sub-ss (1)–(3) substituted, sub-s (4) repealed, and sub-s (5) substituted for previous sub-ss (5), (6), by F(No 2)A 2015 s 32, Sch 7 paras 1, 13 with effect for accounting periods beginning on or after 1 January 2016, subject to transitional rules in F(No 2)A 2015 Sch 7 paras 115 to 129.

[320A Amounts recognised in other comprehensive income and not transferred to profit or loss

(1) This section applies if—

    (a) in a period of account an asset or liability representing a loan relationship of a company ceases in accordance with generally accepted accounting practice to be recognised in the company's accounts,

    (b) amounts relating to the matters mentioned in section 306A(1) in respect of that loan relationship have in accordance with generally accepted accounting practice been recognised in the company's accounts as items of other comprehensive income and have not subsequently been transferred to become items of profit or loss, and

    (c) condition A or B is met.

(2) Condition A is that, at the time when the asset or liability ceases to be recognised, it is not expected that the amounts mentioned in subsection (1)(b) will in future be transferred to become items of profit or loss.

(3) Condition B is that, at any later time, it is no longer expected that the amounts mentioned in subsection (1)(b) will in future be transferred to become items of profit or loss.

(4) The amounts mentioned in subsection (1)(b)—

    (a) must be brought into account for the purposes of this Part as credits or debits for the period of account in which the time mentioned in subsection (2) or (3) falls, in the same way as a credit or debit which is brought into account in determining the company's profit or loss for that period in accordance with generally accepted accounting practice, and

    (b) must not be brought into account for a later period of account even if they are subsequently transferred to become items of profit or loss for the later period.

(5) This section applies in a case where part of an asset or liability representing a loan relationship of a company ceases to be recognised in the company's accounts as it applies in a case where the whole of an asset or liability representing a loan relationship ceases to be recognised, but as if the reference in subsection (1)(b) to amounts in respect of the loan relationship were a reference to so much of those amounts as are attributable to that part of the asset or liability.

(6) In determining what amounts fall within subsection (1)(b) at any time in an accounting period, it is to be assumed that the accounting policy applied in drawing up the company's accounts for the period was also applied in previous accounting periods.

(7) But if the company's accounts for the period are in accordance with generally accepted accounting practice drawn up on an assumption as to the accounting policy in previous accounting periods which differs from that mentioned in subsection (6), that different assumption applies in determining what amounts fall within subsection (1)(b) at the time in question.

(8) In this section "item of profit or loss" and "item of other comprehensive income" each has the meaning that it has for accounting purposes.][1]

Amendments—[1]   This section inserted by F(No 2)A 2015 s 32, Sch 7 paras 1, 14 with effect for accounting periods beginning on or after 1 January 2016, subject to transitional rules in F(No 2)A 2015 Sch 7 paras 115 to 129.

[320B Hybrid capital instruments: amounts recognised in equity

(1) This section applies if in accordance with generally accepted accounting practice, an amount in respect of a hybrid capital instrument relating to any of the matters in section 306A(1) of CTA 2009—

    (a) is recognised in equity or shareholders' funds for a period, and

    (b) is not recognised in the company's accounts for the period as an item of profit or loss or as an item of other comprehensive income.

(2) The amount is to be brought into account for the period for the purposes of this Part in the same way as an amount which is brought into account as a credit or debit in determining the company's profit or loss for the period in accordance with generally accepted accounting practice.

(3) But this section does not bring into account for the purposes of this Part any exchange gain or loss of the company which is recognised in the company's statement of total recognised gains and losses, statement of recognised income and expense, statement of changes in equity or statement of income and retained earnings.][1]

Amendments—[1]   Section 320B inserted by FA 2019 s 89, Sch 20 para 5 with effect for accounting periods beginning on or after 1 January 2019 and subject to transitional and savings provisions in FA 2019 Sch 20 paras 11–16.

[321A Restriction on debits resulting from release of loans to participators etc

(1) This section applies if—
    (*a*) a loan gives rise to a charge to tax under section 455 of CTA 2010 (including a charge by virtue of section 459 or 460 of that Act), and
    (*b*) the whole or a part of the debt in respect of the loan is released or written off.
(2) No debit is to be brought into account for the purposes of this Part in respect of the release or writing off.][1]

Amendments—[1]   This section inserted by FA 2010 s 43 with effect in relation to debts (or parts of debts) released or written off on or after 24 March 2010.

322 Release of debts: cases where credits not required to be brought into account

(1) This section applies if—
    (*a*) a liability to pay an amount under a company's debtor relationship is released, and
    (*b*) the release takes place in an accounting period for which an amortised cost basis of accounting is used in respect of that relationship.
(2) The company is not required to bring into account a credit in respect of the release for the purposes of this Part if [any of conditions A to [E][4]][2] is met.
(3) Condition A is that the release is part of a statutory insolvency arrangement.
(4) Condition B is that the release is [not a release of relevant rights and is][1]
    (*a*) in consideration of shares forming part of the ordinary share capital of the debtor company, or
    (*b*) in consideration of any entitlement to such shares.
(4A) . . .[4]
(5) Condition C is that—
    (*a*) the debtor company meets one of the insolvency conditions (see subsection (6)), and
    (*b*) the debtor relationship is not a connected companies relationship (see section 348).
[(5A) Condition D is that the liability is released in consequence of [the making of a mandatory reduction instrument or a third country instrument or][3] the exercise of a stabilisation power under Part 1 of the Banking Act 2009.][2]
[(5B) Condition E is that—
    (*a*) the release is neither a deemed release, as defined by section 358(3), nor a release of relevant rights, and
    (*b*) immediately before the release, it is reasonable to assume that, without the release and any arrangements of which the release forms part, there would be a material risk that at some time within the next 12 months the company would be unable to pay its debts.][4]
(6) For the purposes of this section a company meets the insolvency conditions if—
    (*a*) it is in insolvent liquidation,
    (*b*) it is in insolvent administration,
    (*c*) it is in insolvent administrative receivership,
    (*d*) an appointment of a provisional liquidator is in force in relation to the company under section 135 of the Insolvency Act 1986 (c 45) or Article 115 of the Insolvency (Northern Ireland) Order 1989 (SI 1989/2405 (NI 19)), or
    (*e*) under the law of a country or territory outside the United Kingdom circumstances corresponding to those mentioned in paragraph (*a*), (*b*), (*c*) or (*d*) exist.
[(6A) In subsections (4) and (5B)(*a*), "relevant rights" has the same meaning as in section 358.][4]
(7) Section [323(A1) applies for the interpretation of subsection (5B)(*b*); and the rest of section][4] 323 applies for the interpretation of subsection (6).
(8) For further cases where no credit in respect of the release is to be brought into account, see—
    (*a*) section 358 (exclusion of credits on release of connected companies debts: general), and
    (*b*) section 359 (exclusion of credits on release of connected companies debts during creditor's insolvency).

Amendments—[1]   Words in sub-s (4) inserted by FA 2010 s 44, Sch 15 para 1 with effect in relation to a release of rights that takes place on or after 9 November 2009, subject to transitional provisions: see FA 2010 Sch 15 para 4.
[2]   In sub-s (2), words substituted, and sub-s (5A) inserted, by FA 2014 s 26 with effect in relation to releases of liabilities on or after 26 November 2013.
[3]   In sub-s (5A), words inserted by the Bank Recovery and Resolution Order, SI 2015/3329 art 123 with effect from 1 January 2015.
[4]   In sub-s (2), "E" substituted for "D", sub-s (4A) repealed, sub-ss (5B), (6A) inserted, and in sub-s (7) words inserted, by F(No 2)A 2015 s 32, Sch 7 paras 1, 16 with effect in relation to the release, modification or replacement of a debtor relationship of a company on or after 1 January 2015.

323 Meaning of expressions relating to insolvency etc

[(A1) For the purposes of sections 322(5B) and 323A(1)(*b*) a company is unable to pay its debts if—

    (*a*) it is unable to pay its debts as they fall due, or

    (*b*) the value of the company's assets is less than the amount of its liabilities, taking into account its contingent and prospective liabilities.][1]

(1) For the purposes of section 322(6) a company is in insolvent liquidation during the period—

    (*a*) beginning when it goes into liquidation at a time when its assets are insufficient for the payment of its debts and other liabilities and the expenses of the winding up, and

    (*b*) ending when the winding up is completed or otherwise brought to an end (whether under paragraph 37 or 38 of Schedule B1 to the Insolvency Act 1986 (c 45) or otherwise).

(2) In subsection (1) "liquidation" has the meaning given in—

    (*a*) section 247(2) of the Insolvency Act 1986, or

    (*b*) Article 6(2) of the Insolvency (Northern Ireland) Order 1989 (SI 1989/ 2405 (NI 19)).

(3) For the purposes of section 322(6) a company in administration is in insolvent administration if it entered administration under—

    (*a*) Schedule B1 to the Insolvency Act 1986, or

    (*b*) Schedule B1 to the Insolvency (Northern Ireland) Order 1989 (SI 1989/ 2405 (NI 19)),

at a time when its assets were insufficient for the payment of its debts and other liabilities and the expenses of the administration.

(4) For the purposes of section 322(6) a company is in insolvent administrative receivership if—

    (*a*) an appointment of an administrative receiver is in force in relation to the company, and

    (*b*) the company was put into administrative receivership at a time when its assets were insufficient for the payment of its debts and other liabilities and the expenses of administrative receivership.

(5) In subsection (4) "administrative receiver" has the same meaning as in—

    (*a*) Chapter 1 or 2 of Part 3 of the Insolvency Act 1986 (c 45), or

    (*b*) Part 4 of the Insolvency (Northern Ireland) Order 1989 (SI 1989/2405 (NI 19)),

and "administrative receivership" is to be read accordingly.

Amendments—[1]   Sub-s (A1) inserted by F(No 2)A 2015 s 32, Sch 7 paras 1, 17 with effect in relation to the release, modification or replacement of a debtor relationship of a company on or after 1 January 2015.

[323A Substantial modification: cases where credits not required to be brought into account

(1) Subsection (2) applies if—

    (*a*) a debtor relationship of a company is modified or replaced by another,

    (*b*) immediately before the modification or replacement it is reasonable to assume that, without the modification or replacement and any arrangements of which the modification or replacement forms part, there would be a material risk that at some time within the next 12 months the company would be unable to pay its debts, and

    (*c*) the modification or replacement is treated for accounting purposes as a substantial modification of the terms of a loan relationship of the company.

(2) The company is not required to bring into account for the purposes of this Part a credit in respect of any change in the carrying value of the liability representing the modified or replacement debtor relationship.

(3) If as a result of subsection (2) no credit was brought into account in respect of a change in the carrying value of a liability representing a debtor relationship, the company may not bring into account a debit for the purposes of this Part in respect of a change in the carrying value of that liability, to the extent that the change represents a reversal of the change in carrying value to which subsection (2) applied.

(4) Section 323(A1) applies for the interpretation of subsection (1)(*b*).][1]

Amendments—[1]   This section inserted by F(No 2)A 2015 s 32, Sch 7 paras 1, 18 with effect in relation to the release, modification or replacement of a debtor relationship of a company on or after 1 January 2015.

324 Restriction on debits resulting from revaluation

(1) No debit is to be brought into account for the purposes of this Part as a result of the revaluation of an asset representing a creditor relationship of a company except—

    (*a*) an impairment loss, or

    (*b*) a debit resulting from a release by the company of any liability under the relationship.

(2) For the meaning of "impairment loss" see section 476(1).

(3) The reference in subsection (1) to revaluation of an asset includes any case where a provision or allowance is made by the company reducing the carrying value of the asset or of a group of assets including the asset in question.

[(3A) Where a company has a hedging relationship between a relevant contract ("the hedging instrument") and the asset or liability representing the loan relationship, this section does not prevent credits or debits being brought into account in respect of changes in the fair value of the asset or liability which are attributable to any of the risks in respect of which the hedging instrument was intended to act as a hedge.][1]

(4) This section does not affect the debits to be brought into account in respect of exchange gains or losses.

(5) This section does not apply if fair value accounting is used.

Amendments—[1]   Sub-s (3A) inserted by F(No 2)A 2015 s 32, Sch 7 paras 1, 19 with effect for accounting periods beginning on or after 1 January 2016, subject to transitional rules in F(No 2)A 2015 Sch 7 paras 115 to 129.

325 Restriction on credits resulting from reversal of disallowed debits

(1) No credit is to be brought into account for the purposes of this Part in respect of the reversal of a debit disallowed by section 324(1).

(2) This section does not apply if fair value accounting is used.

(3) See also paragraph 61 of Schedule 2 (restriction on bringing into account credits resulting from reversal of debits disallowed in a period of account beginning before 1 January 2005).

326 Writing off government investments

(1) This section applies if a government investment in a company is written off by the release of a liability to pay any amount under a debtor relationship of the company.

(2) The company is not required to bring into account a credit for the purposes of this Part in respect of the release.

(3) [Section 94 of CTA 2010][1] (write-off of government investment) applies for interpreting the reference in subsection (1) to a government investment in a company being written off as it applies for the purposes of [Chapter 7 of Part 4][1].

Amendments—[1]   In sub-s (3) words substituted for words "Section 400(7) and (8) of ICTA" and "section 400(1) of that Act" by CTA 2010 s 1177, Sch 1 para 605. CTA 2010 has effect for corporation tax purposes for accounting periods ending on or after 1 April 2010, and for income and capital gains tax purposes for the tax year 2010–11 and subsequent tax years.

327 Disallowance of imported losses etc

(1) This section applies for an accounting period of a company ("the loss period") if—

    (*a*) apart from this section, a loss arising in connection with a loan relationship of the company would fall to be brought into account for the purposes of this Part, and

    (*b*) the loss is wholly or partly referable to a time when the relationship was not subject to United Kingdom taxation.

(2) The amounts brought into account for the loss period for the purposes of this Part must be such as to secure that none of the loss referable to a time when the relationship was not so subject is treated for those purposes as arising in the loss period or any other accounting period of the company.

(3) For the purposes of this section a loss is referable to a time when a relationship is not subject to United Kingdom taxation so far as, at the time to which the loss is referable, the company would not have been chargeable to corporation tax in the United Kingdom on any profits arising from the relationship.

(4) If the company was not a party to the relationship at the time to which the loss is referable, subsection (3) applies as if the reference to the company were a reference to the person who at that time was in the same position as respects the relationship as is subsequently held by the company.

(5) An amount which would be brought into account for the purposes of this Part in respect of any matter apart from this section is treated for the purposes of section 464(1) (amounts brought into account under this Part excluded from being otherwise brought into account) as if it were so brought into account.

(6) Accordingly, that amount must not be brought into account for corporation tax purposes as respects that matter either under this Part or otherwise.

(7) This section does not apply if fair value accounting is used.

Exchange gains and losses

328 Exchange gains and losses

(1) The reference in [section 306A(1)][1] to the profits and losses arising to a company from its loan relationships and related transactions includes a reference to exchange gains and losses so arising.

(2) . . .[1]

(2A) . . .[1]

[(3) But subsection (1) does not apply to an exchange gain or loss of a company so far as it—

    (*a*) arises as a result of the translation of the assets, liabilities, income and expenses of all or part of the company's business from the functional currency of the business, or that part of the business, into another currency, and

    (*b*) has been recognised as an item of other comprehensive income.

(3A) In subsection (3)—

    (*a*) the reference to the functional currency of a business or part of a business is a reference to the currency of the primary economic environment in which the business or part operates, and

    (*b*) "assets, liabilities, income and expenses" and "item of other comprehensive income" each has the meaning that it has for accounting purposes.

(3B) No amount is to be brought into account for the purposes of this Part in respect of an exchange gain or loss of an investment company (within the meaning of section 17 of CTA 2010) which would not have arisen but for a change in the company's functional currency (within the meaning of section 17(4) of that Act) as between—

    (*a*) the period of account of the company in which the gain or loss arises, and

    (*b*) a period of account of the company ending in the 12 months immediately preceding that period.

(3C) But subsection (3B) does not apply to an exchange gain or loss arising at a time when an election under section 9A of CTA 2010 (designated currency of UK resident investment company) has effect in relation to the company.][1]

[(4) The Treasury may by regulations make provision—

    (*a*) excluding exchange gains or losses of a specified description from being brought into account for the purposes of this Part,

    (*b*) requiring exchange gains or losses of a specified description which would not otherwise be brought into account for the purposes of this Part to be brought into account in specified circumstances,

    (*c*) as to the way in which, including the currency by reference to which, any exchange gains or losses to be brought into account as a result of provision made under paragraph (*b*) are to be calculated, and

    (*d*) as to the way in which any such exchange gains or losses are to be brought into account.

(4ZA) For the purposes of subsection (4)(*b*), it does not matter whether the exchange gains or losses would otherwise be excluded from being brought into account as a result of regulations under subsection (4)(*a*) or otherwise.][1]

(4A) . . .[1]

(5) . . .[1]

[(6) The reference in subsection (4) to bringing exchange gains or losses into account is a reference to bringing them into account—

    (*a*) for the purposes of this Part as credits or debits arising to a company from its loan relationships, or

    (*b*) for the purposes of corporation tax on chargeable gains.][1]

(7) The regulations may—

    (*a*) make different provision for different cases, and

    (*b*) make provision subject to an election or to other specified conditions.

(8) For the meaning of references to exchange gains or losses from loan relationships, see section 475.

Regulations—Exchange Gains and Losses (Bringing into Account Gains or Losses) (Amendment) Regulations, SI 2013/1843.

Loan Relationships and Derivative Contracts (Disregard and Bringing into Account of Profits and Losses) (Amendment) Regulations, SI 2013/2781.

Loan Relationships and Derivative Contracts (Disregard and Bringing into Account of Profits and Losses) (Amendment) Regulations, SI 2014/3188.

Exchange Gains and Losses (Bringing into Account Gains or Losses) (Amendment) Regulations, SI 2015/1960.

Loan Relationships and Derivative Contracts (Disregard and Bringing into Account of Profits and Losses) (Amendment) Regulations, SI 2015/1961.

Note—This section was to have been repealed, with effect from a date to be appointed, by CTA 2009 ss 1325, 1326, 1329(3), Sch 2 para 71, Sch 3 Part 2. Those provisions were, however, themselves repealed by F(No 2)A 2015 s 32, Sch 7 para 101 with effect from 18 November 2015.

Amendments—[1]   In sub-s (1) words substituted for words "section 307(3)", sub-ss (2), (2A), (4A), (5) repealed, sub-ss (3)–(3C) substituted for previous sub-s (3), sub-s (4), (4ZA) substituted for previous sub-s (4), and sub-s (6) substituted, by F(No 2)A 2015 s 32, Sch 7 paras 1, 20 with effect for accounting periods beginning on or after 1 January 2016, subject to transitional rules in F(No 2)A 2015 Sch 7 paras 115 to 129. Sub-s (4A) repealed by F(No 2)A 2015 s 32, Sch 7 paras 1, 20 with effect in relation to arrangements entered into on or after 18 November 2015: see F(No 2)A 2015 Sch 7 para 111.

Pre-loan relationship, abortive and pre-trading expenses

329 Pre-loan relationship and abortive expenses

(1) This section applies if—

    (*a*) a company may enter into a loan relationship or related transaction but has not yet done so,

    (*b*) it incurs any expenses for purposes connected—

        (i) with entering into it, or

        (ii) with giving effect to any obligation which might arise under it, and

    (*c*) had the company entered into the relationship or transaction, the expenses would be expenses within [section 306A(1)(*c*)][1].

(2) The expenses are treated as expenses in relation to which debits may be brought into account in accordance with [section 307(2)][1] to the same extent as if the company had entered into the relationship or transaction.

Amendments—[1]   In sub-s (1)(*c*) words substituted for words "section 307(3)(*c*)", and in sub-s (2) words substituted for words "section 307(3)", by F(No 2)A 2015 s 32, Sch 7 paras 1, 22 with effect for accounting periods beginning on or after 1 January 2016, subject to transitional rules in F(No 2)A 2015 Sch 7 paras 115 to 129.

330 Debits in respect of pre-trading expenditure

(1) This section applies if—

   (a) a non-trading debit is given for an accounting period of a company for the purposes of this Part, and

   (b) within the period of 2 years beginning with the end of the period the company makes an election for the purposes of this section in respect of the debit.

(2) The debit must not be brought into account for the purposes of this Part as a non-trading debit for that period.

(3) Instead, if conditions A and B are met in respect of a trade, the debit—

   (a) is treated for the purposes of this Part as if it were a debit for the accounting period in which the company begins to carry on the trade, and

   (b) is to be brought into account in accordance with section 297(3) (trading debits).

(4) Condition A is that the company begins to carry on the trade within the period of 7 years after the end of the accounting period for which a non-trading debit is given for the purposes of this Part.

(5) Condition B is that that debit is such that, if it were given for the accounting period in which the company begins to carry on the trade, it would be brought into account by reference to that trade in accordance with section 297(3).

[Pre-commencement debits of property businesses etc of non-UK resident companies

330ZA Debits referable to times before UK property business etc carried on

(1) This section applies if—

   (a) a non-UK resident company has debits in respect of a loan relationship to which it is a party for the purposes of its UK property business,

   (b) the debits are referable to times ("the pre-rental times") before (but not more than 7 years before) the date on which it starts to carry on the business, and

   (c) the debits are not otherwise brought into account for tax purposes.

(2) If, on the assumption that the company had been carrying on the business at the pre-rental times, the debits—

   (a) would have been recognised in determining its profit or loss for a period consisting of or including those times, and

   (b) would have been brought into account for the purposes of this Part,

the debits are (so far as they exceed relevant credits) treated for the purposes of this Part as if they were debits for the accounting period in which it started to carry on the business.

(3) For this purpose "relevant credits" means credits of the company in respect of the loan relationship which, on the assumption that the company had been carrying on the business at the pre-rental times—

   (a) would have been recognised in determining its profit or loss for a period consisting of or including those times,

   (b) would have been brought into account for the purposes of this Part, and

   (c) would not otherwise have been brought into account for tax purposes.

(4) This section is subject to section 327 (disallowance of imported losses etc).

(5) This section also applies in relation to a non-UK resident company which is a party to a loan relationship for the purpose of enabling it to generate other UK property income (within the meaning given by section 5(6)).][1]

Amendments—[1]   Section 330ZA inserted by FA 2020 s 32, Sch 6 para 3 with effect from 6 April 2020. This amendment has effect as if it had been incorporated into FA 2019 Sch 5 and so is subject to transitional provisions in FA 2019 Sch 5 Pt 3 (paras 36–50).

[Company is not, or has ceased to be, party to loan relationship

330A Company is not, or has ceased to be, party to loan relationship

(1) This section applies if—

   (a) amounts in respect of a qualifying relationship are recognised in a company's accounts for an accounting period ("the current period") as an item of profit or loss even though during all or part of the period the company is not a party to the qualifying relationship,

   (b) any of conditions A to D is met, and

   (c) in the absence of this section, the credits and debits brought into account by the company for the purposes of this Part or Part 7 for the current period would not include credits or debits representing the whole of those amounts.

(2) In this section "qualifying relationship" means—

   (a) a loan relationship, or

   (b) a relationship that would be a loan relationship if references in section 302(1) to a company were references to any person.

References in this section to a company being a party to a qualifying relationship are to be read accordingly.

(3) Condition A is that—

   (a) the company was a party to the qualifying relationship,

(6) In this Chapter references to a company being a member of a group of companies are to be read in accordance with section 170 of TCGA 1992 (interpretation of sections 171 to 181 of that Act: groups).

336 Transfers of loans on group transactions

(1) The case referred to in section 335(1)(*a*) is where—

   (*a*) there is a transaction within subsection (2) or a series of transactions within subsection (3), and

   (*b*) as a result one of the companies involved ("the transferee") directly or indirectly replaces the other ("the transferor") as a party to a loan relationship.

(2) A transaction is within this subsection if it is a related transaction between two companies which are—

   (*a*) members of the same group, and

   (*b*) within the charge to corporation tax in respect of that transaction.

(3) A series of transactions is within this subsection if it is a series having the same effect as a related transaction between two companies each of which—

   (*a*) has been a member of the same group at any time in the course of that series, and

   (*b*) would be within the charge to corporation tax in respect of such a related transaction.

(4) This Chapter does not apply as a result of this section in relation to—

   (*a*) a transfer of an asset, or

   (*b*) a transfer of rights under, or an interest in, an asset,

as a result of a transaction within subsection (2) or a series of transactions within subsection (3) if immediately before or after the transfer the asset [is held for the purposes of a company's long-term business][1].

[(4A) For the purposes of subsection (4)—

   (*a*) in the case of an overseas life insurance company, ignore transfers in relation to assets which are not UK assets (within the meaning of section 117 of FA 2012), and

   (*b*) section 122 of that Act applies as it applies for the purposes of Chapter 8 of Part 2 of that Act.][1]

(5) In this Chapter, in relation to a case within subsection (1), "the transferee" and "the transferor" have the same meaning as in that subsection.

Amendments—[1]   In sub-s (4), words substituted for words "is within one of the categories set out in section 440(4)(a), (d) and (e) of ICTA (assets held for certain categories of long-term business)", and sub-s (4A) inserted, by FA 2012 s 146, Sch 16 paras 135, 148 with effect in relation to accounting periods of companies beginning on or after 1 January 2013 (subject to transitional provisions in FA 2012 Sch 17). For accounting periods straddling 1 January 2013 see FA 2012 s 149.

337 Transfers of loans on insurance business transfers

(1) The case referred to in section 335(1)(*b*) is where—

   (*a*) a transfer between two companies occurs to which this section applies, and

   (*b*) as a result one of the companies ("the transferee") directly or indirectly replaces the other ("the transferor") as a party to a loan relationship.

(2) This section applies to the transfers specified in subsection (3), so far as they are not excluded by subsection (4).

(3) They are—

   (*a*) a transfer between two companies of business consisting of the effecting or carrying out of contracts of long-term insurance which has effect under an insurance business transfer scheme, and

   (*b*) any transfer between two companies which is a qualifying overseas transfer.

[(3A) In subsection (3)(*b*) "qualifying overseas transfer" means so much of a transfer of the whole or any part of the business of an overseas life insurance company carried on through a permanent establishment in the United Kingdom as takes place in accordance with an authorisation granted outside the United Kingdom for the purposes of [Article 39 of Directive 2009/138/EC of the European Parliament and of the Council of 25 November 2009 on the taking-up and pursuit of the business of Insurance and Reinsurance (Solvency II)][2].][1]

(4) Subsection (3) does not apply to a transfer of an asset, or of rights under or an interest in an asset, if the asset—

   (*a*) was within one of [the applicable categories][1] immediately before the transfer, and

   (*b*) is not within that category immediately after it.

[(4A) For the purposes of subsection (4)(*a*) "the applicable categories" means—

   (*a*) in the case of a UK life insurance company, the long-term business categories or a category of assets which are not held for the purposes of its long-term business, and

   (*b*) in the case of an overseas life insurance company, the UK long-term business categories, a category of UK assets which are not held for the purposes of its long-term business or a category of assets which are held by it but which are not UK assets.

(4B) For the purposes of subsection (4A)—

   (*a*) "the long-term business categories" has the same meaning as in section 116 of FA 2012,

(b) "the UK long-term business categories" and "UK assets" have the same meanings as in section 117 of that Act, and

(c) section 122 of that Act applies as it applies for the purposes of Chapter 8 of Part 2 of that Act.]¹

(5) Subsection (6) applies for the purposes of subsection (4) if one of the companies mentioned in subsection (3) is an overseas life insurance company.

(6) An asset is taken as being in the same category both immediately before and immediately after a transfer if the asset—

(a) was in one category immediately before the transfer, and

(b) is within the corresponding category immediately after it.

(7) In this Chapter, in relation to a case within subsection (1), "the transferee" and "the transferor" have the same meaning as in that subsection.

Amendments—¹ Sub-ss (3A), (4A), (4B) inserted, and in sub-s (4)(a) words substituted for words "the categories set out in section 440(4) of ICTA", by FA 2012 s 146, Sch 16 paras 135, 149 with effect in relation to accounting periods of companies beginning on or after 1 January 2013 (subject to transitional provisions in FA 2012 Sch 17). For accounting periods straddling 1 January 2013 see FA 2012 s 149.

² In sub-s (3A), words substituted for words "Article 14 of the Council Directive of 5 November 2002 concerning life assurance (2002/83/EC)" by the Solvency 2 Regulations, SI 2015/575 reg 59, Sch 1 para 26(1), (2) with effect from 1 January 2016.

338 Meaning of company replacing another as party to loan relationship

(1) References in this Chapter to one company ("A") replacing another company ("B") as a party to a loan relationship include references to A becoming a party to a loan relationship which—

(a) confers rights within subsection (2),

(b) imposes obligations within subsection (2), or

(c) both confers such rights and imposes such obligations.

(2) Rights or obligations are within this subsection if they are equivalent to those of B under a loan relationship to which B has previously ceased to be a party.

(3) For the purposes of subsection (2), A's rights under a creditor relationship are equivalent to rights under another creditor relationship if each set of rights gives the holder of an asset representing the relationship in question—

(a) the same rights against the same persons as to capital, interest and dividends, and

(b) the same remedies to enforce those rights.

(4) For the purposes of subsection (3), any difference in—

(a) the total nominal amounts of the assets representing each relationship,

(b) the form in which they are held, or

(c) the way in which they can be transferred,

is ignored.

(5) For the purposes of subsection (2), A's obligations under a debtor relationship are equivalent to obligations under another debtor relationship if each set of obligations subjects the holder of the liability representing the relationship in question to—

(a) the same obligations to the same persons as to capital, interest and dividends, and

(b) the same remedies to enforce those obligations.

(6) For the purposes of subsection (5), any difference in—

(a) the total nominal amounts of the assets representing the creditor relationship corresponding to each relationship,

(b) the form in which those assets are held, or

(c) the way in which they can be transferred,

is ignored.

Modification—In determining whether Chapter 4 of Part 5 applies in the case mentioned in ss 336 or 337 where the transferee became party to the loan relationship before 9 April 2003, this section modified to apply with the following amendments—
- sub-s (1)(b), (c) repealed;
- in sub-s (2), words "or obligations" repealed; and
- sub-ss (5), (6) repealed.
(CTA 2009 s 1325, Sch 2 para 58.)

339 Issues of new securities on certain cross-border reorganisations

(1) The case referred to in section 335(1)(c) is where each of conditions A to D is met.

(2) Condition A is that sections 127 to 130 of TCGA 1992 (reorganisations: equation of original shares and new holding)—

(a) apply in relation to an exchange as a result of section 135(3) of that Act (which provides for sections 127 to 130 to apply to an exchange of securities for those in another company as if it were a reorganisation), or

(b) would so apply but for section 116(5) of that Act (which disapplies sections 127 to 130 where the original shares or the new holding consist of or include a qualifying corporate bond).

(3) Condition B is that the original shares consist of or include an asset representing a loan relationship.

(4) In this section and sections 345 and 346—

"the relevant 6 year period" means the period of 6 years following—

    (a) in a case where section 340 applies because of a transaction within section 336(2) ("case A"), that transaction, or

    (b) in a case where section 340 applies because of a series of transactions within section 336(3) ("case B"), the last transaction of that series,

"the relevant group" means—

    (a) in case A, the group mentioned in section 336(2), and

    (b) in case B, the group mentioned in section 336(3), and

"the relevant loan relationship" means the loan relationship mentioned in section 336(1)(b).

345 Transferee leaving group otherwise than because of exempt distribution

(1) This section applies if—

    (a) the transferee ceases to be a member of the relevant group, and

    (b) it does not so cease just because of a distribution which is exempt [as a result of section 1075 of CTA 2010 (exempt distributions),][1]

(2) . . .[2] This Part applies as if—

    (a) the transferee had assigned the asset or liability representing the relevant loan relationship immediately before ceasing to be a member of the relevant group,

    (b) the assignment had been for consideration of an amount equal to the fair value of the asset or liability at that time, and

    (c) the transferee had immediately reacquired the asset or liability for consideration of the same amount.

(3) . . .[2]

(4) . . .[2]

(5) . . .[2]

Amendments—[1] In sub-s (1)(b) words substituted by CTA 2010 s 1177, Sch 1 para 606. CTA 2010 has effect for corporation tax purposes for accounting periods ending on or after 1 April 2010, and for income and capital gains tax purposes for the tax year 2010–11 and subsequent tax years.

[2] In sub-s (2) words "If condition A or B is met,", and sub-ss (3)–(5) repealed, by FA 2014 s 28(1), (2) with effect where the cessation of membership of the relevant group occurs on or after 1 April 2014.

346 Transferee leaving group because of exempt distribution

(1) This section applies if—

    (a) the transferee ceases to be a member of the relevant group just because of a distribution which is exempt [as a result of section 1075 of CTA 2010 (exempt distributions),][1] and

    (b) there is a chargeable payment within the meaning of [section 1088(1) of CTA 2010][1] of that Act (chargeable payments connected with exempt distributions) within 5 years after the making of that distribution.

(2) . . .[2] This Part applies as if—

    (a) the transferee had assigned the asset or liability representing the relevant loan relationship immediately before the chargeable payment was made,

    (b) the assignment had been for consideration of an amount equal to the fair value of the asset or liability immediately before the transferee ceased to be a member of the relevant group, and

    (c) the transferee had immediately reacquired the asset or liability for consideration of the same amount.

(3) . . .[2]

(4) . . .[2]

(5) . . .[2]

Amendments—[1] In sub-s (1)(a) words substituted, in sub-s (1)(b) words substituted for words "section 214(2)" by CTA 2010 s 1177, Sch 1 para 607. CTA 2010 has effect for corporation tax purposes for accounting periods ending on or after 1 April 2010, and for income and capital gains tax purposes for the tax year 2010–11 and subsequent tax years.

[2] In sub-s (2) words "If condition A or B is met,", and sub-ss (3)–(5) repealed, by FA 2014 s 28(1), (2) with effect where the cessation of membership of the relevant group occurs on or after 1 April 2014.

CHAPTER 5

CONNECTED COMPANIES RELATIONSHIPS: INTRODUCTION AND GENERAL

348 Introduction: meaning of "connected companies relationship"

(1) This Chapter contains some general rules relating to connected companies relationships.

(2) For the purposes of this Part a debtor relationship of a company is a connected companies relationship if there is a connection between—

    (a) the company, and

    (b) another company standing in the position of a creditor as respects the debt in question.

(3) For the purposes of subsection (2) a company is treated as standing in the position of a creditor if it indirectly stands in that position by reference to a series of loan relationships or relevant money debts.

(4) For the purposes of this Part a creditor relationship of a company is a connected companies relationship if there is a connection between—

    (*a*) the company, and

    (*b*) another company standing in the position of a debtor as respects the debt in question.

(5) For the purposes of subsection (4) a company is treated as standing in the position of a debtor if it indirectly stands in that position by reference to a series of loan relationships or relevant money debts.

(6) For the purposes of this Part, if a loan relationship is a connected companies relationship at any time in an accounting period, it is treated as being such a relationship for the period.

(7) In this section "relevant money debt" means a money debt which would be a loan relationship if a company directly stood in the position of creditor or debtor.

(8) Section 466 (companies connected for an accounting period) applies for the purposes of this section.

349 Application of amortised cost basis to connected companies relationships

(1) This section applies if a loan relationship is a connected companies relationship for an accounting period.

(2) The credits and debits which are to be brought into account for the purposes of this Part in respect of the relationship for the period are determined on an amortised cost basis of accounting.

[(2A) Where—

    (*a*) a company has a hedging relationship between a relevant contract ("the hedging instrument") and the asset or liability representing the loan relationship, and

    (*b*) the loan relationship is dealt with in the company's accounts on the basis of fair value accounting,

it is to be assumed in applying an amortised cost basis of accounting for the purpose of subsection (2) that the hedging instrument has where possible been designated for accounting purposes as a fair value hedge of the loan relationship.][1]

(3)   . . . [1]

(4)   . . . [1]

Amendments—[1]   Sub-s (2A) inserted, and sub-ss (3), (4) repealed by F(No 2)A 2015 s 32, Sch 7 paras 1, 28 with effect in relation to loan relationships entered into by a company in an accounting period beginning on or after 1 January 2016, subject to the provisions in F(No 2)A 2015 Sch 7 para 106(3)–(6) for loan relationships entered into by a company in an accounting period beginning before 1 January 2016. Sub-s (3) repealed by F(No 2)A 2015 s 32, Sch 7 paras 1, 28 with effect where conditions A and B in CTA 2009 s 454 were first met in relation to the asset on or after 18 November 2015.

352 Disregard of related transactions

(1) This section applies in an accounting period if—

    (*a*) section 349 applies in respect of a creditor relationship of a company for the period, and

    (*b*) a related transaction takes place in relation to the relationship in the period.

(2) The credits brought into account in respect of the relationship for the period for the purposes of this Part must not be less than they would have been if—

    (*a*) the transaction had not taken place, and

    (*b*) no amounts had accrued after the transaction took place.

(3) The debits brought into account in respect of the loan relationship for the period for the purposes of this Part must not be more than they would have been in that case.

[(3A) Subsections (2) and (3) do not affect the credits or debits to be brought into account for the purposes of this Part in respect of changes in the fair value of the asset that are attributable to changes in the corresponding market rate.

(3B) Subsection (3A) is subject to section 354 (exclusion of debits for impaired or released connected companies debts).

(3C) In relation to a debt, "the corresponding market rate" at any time is the lowest rate at which a company of good financial standing might at that time expect to be able to borrow money at arm's length in the currency applicable to the debt, for repayment at the same time as the debt and otherwise on similar terms.][1]

(4) Nothing in this section affects the credits or debits to be brought into account for the purposes of this Part in respect of exchange gains or losses arising from a debt.

Amendments—[1]   Sub-ss (3A)–(3C) inserted by F(No 2)A 2015 s 32, Sch 7 paras 1, 30 with effect for accounting periods beginning on or after 1 January 2016, subject to transitional rules in F(No 2)A 2015 Sch 7 paras 115 to 129.

[352A Exclusion of credits on reversal of disregarded loss

(1) If as a result of section 352 the debits brought into account by a company in respect of a loan relationship are reduced, no credit is to be brought into account for the purposes of this Part to the extent that it represents the reversal of so much of the loss as was not brought into account as a debit.

(2) Nothing in this section affects the credits to be brought into account for the purposes of this Part in respect of exchange gains or losses resulting from a debt.][1]

Amendments—[1]   This section inserted by F(No 2)A 2015 s 32, Sch 7 paras 1, 31 with effect for accounting periods beginning on or after 1 January 2016, subject to transitional rules in F(No 2)A 2015 Sch 7 paras 115 to 129.

[352B Eliminating tax mismatch for loan relationships with qualifying link

(1) This section applies if—

  (a) section 349 applies in respect of a loan relationship of a company for an accounting period (application of amortised cost basis to connected companies relationships),

  (b) the company is a party to another loan relationship ("the external loan relationship") in respect of which that section does not apply for the period,

  (c) the external loan relationship is a debtor relationship dealt with in its accounts on the basis of fair value accounting, and

  (d) the external loan relationship has a qualifying link with one or more other loan relationships of the company.

(2) For this purpose the external loan relationship has "a qualifying link" with one or more other loan relationships of the company if—

  (a) each of those other loan relationships of the company is a loan relationship in respect of which section 349 applies for the accounting period, and

  (b) taking those other loan relationships together, the money received by the company under the external loan relationship is wholly or mainly used to lend money under those other loan relationships.

(3) The credits and debits which are to be brought into account for the purposes of this Part in respect of the external loan relationship for the period are to be determined on an amortised cost basis of accounting.

(4) If a company has a hedging relationship between—

  (a) a relevant contract ("the hedging instrument"), and

  (b) the liability representing the external loan relationship,

it is to be assumed in applying the amortised cost basis of accounting for the purposes of subsection (3) that the hedging instrument has where possible been designated for accounting purposes as a fair value hedge of that loan relationship.][1]

Amendments—[1]   Section 352B inserted by FA 2019 s 29, Sch 12 para 1 with effect for accounting periods beginning on or after 1 January 2019, subject to transitional provisions where an accounting period straddles that date. See also the transitional provisions in FA 2019 Sch 12 para 4.

CHAPTER 6

CONNECTED COMPANIES RELATIONSHIPS: IMPAIRMENT LOSSES AND RELEASES OF DEBTS

Introduction

353 Introduction to Chapter

(1) This Chapter contains rules about impairment losses and releases of debts in the case of companies connected with other companies.

(2) In particular, see—

  (a) sections 354 to 357 (which prevent debits in respect of impairment losses and release debits from being brought into account in the case of connected companies relationships, subject to some exceptions),

  (b) sections 358 to 360 (which exclude credits in respect of the release of debts or the reversal of impairments from being brought into account in that case, [subject to some exceptions][2]), and

  (c) sections 361 to 363 (which treat debt releases as occurring when impaired debts become held by companies which might otherwise benefit from the exclusion under section 358).

(3) . . . . [1]

(4) Section 466 (companies connected for an accounting period) applies for the purposes of sections 354 to 360.

(5) For the circumstances in which companies are connected for sections 361 and 362, see section 363.

(6) For the meaning of "impairment loss" [and "release debit"][1] see section 476(1).

Amendments—[1]   Sub-s (3) repealed and in sub-s (6) words inserted by FA 2009 s 42(2) with effect from 22 April 2009.
[2]   In sub-s (2)(b) words substituted for words "except where the release is a deemed release under section 361 or 362" by FA 2010 s 44, Sch 15 para 2(1), (2) with effect in relation to a relevant acquisition that is made on or after 14 October 2009, subject to transitional provisions: see FA 2010 Sch 15 para 4.

Exclusion of debits for impaired or released connected companies debts

354 Exclusion of debits for impaired or released connected companies debts

(1) The general rule is that no impairment loss or release debit in respect of a company's creditor relationship is to be brought into account for the purposes of this Part for an accounting period if section 349 (application of amortised cost basis to connected companies relationship) applies to the relationship for the period.

(2) That rule is subject to—

    (*a*) section 356 (swapping debt for equity), and

    (*b*) section 357 (insolvent creditors).

[(2A) Where the carrying value of an asset representing the creditor relationship has at any time been adjusted as a result of the asset being the hedged item under a designated fair value hedge, the rule in subsection (1) does not prevent a credit or debit being brought into account for the purposes of this Part in respect of any reversal of that adjustment.][1]

(3) Nothing in this section affects the debits to be brought into account for the purposes of this Part in respect of exchange gains or losses arising from a debt.

Amendments—[1]   Sub-s (2A) inserted by F(No 2)A 2015 s 32, Sch 7 paras 1, 32 with effect for accounting periods beginning on or after 1 January 2016, subject to transitional rules in F(No 2)A 2015 Sch 7 paras 115 to 129.

355 Cessation of connection

(1) This section applies if, in the case of a creditor relationship of a company—

    (*a*) an impairment loss or release debit is excluded by section 354 from being brought into account for any accounting period, and

    (*b*) there is a later accounting period for which the creditor relationship in respect of the debt is not a connected companies relationship.

(2) So far as any amount represents the impairment loss or release debit, no debit may be brought into account in respect of it—

    (*a*) for the first accounting period within subsection (1)(*b*), or

    (*b*) for any subsequent such accounting period.

356 Exception to section 354: swapping debt for equity

(1) An impairment loss or release debit in relation to a liability to pay any amount to a company ("the creditor company") under its creditor relationship is not prevented from being brought into account by section 354 if conditions A, B and C are met.

(2) Condition A is that the creditor company treats the liability as discharged.

(3) Condition B is that it does so in consideration of—

    (*a*) any shares forming part of the ordinary share capital of the company on which the liability would otherwise have fallen, or

    (*b*) any entitlement to such shares.

(4) Condition C is that there would be no connection between the two companies for the accounting period in which the consideration is given if the question whether there is such a connection were determined by reference only to times before the creditor company—

    (*a*) acquired possession of the shares, or

    (*b*) acquired any entitlement to them.

357 Exception to section 354: insolvent creditors

(1) An impairment loss or release debit is not prevented from being brought into account by section 354 in relation to an amount accruing to a company ("the creditor") if—

    (*a*) condition A, B, C, D or E is met in relation to the creditor, and

    (*b*) the amount accrues to the creditor at a time which is the relevant time for the condition in question.

(2) Condition A is that the creditor is in insolvent liquidation, and for this condition the relevant time is any time in the course of the winding up.

(3) Condition B is that the creditor is in insolvent administration, and for this condition the relevant time is any time in the course of the administration.

(4) Condition C is that the creditor is in insolvent administrative receivership, and for this condition the relevant time is any time when the appointment of the administrative receiver is in force.

(5) Condition D is that an appointment of a provisional liquidator is in force in relation to the creditor under section 135 of the Insolvency Act 1986 (c 45) or Article 115 of the Insolvency (Northern Ireland) Order 1989 (SI 1989/2405 (NI 19)), and for this condition the relevant time is any time when the appointment is in force.

(6) Condition E is that under the law of a country or territory outside the United Kingdom, circumstances exist corresponding to those described in condition A, B, C or D, and for this condition the relevant time is any time corresponding to that described in the case of the condition in question.

(7) Section 323 applies for interpreting this section as it applies for interpreting section 322(6).

Exclusion of credits for connected companies debts on release or reversal of impairments

358 Exclusion of credits on release of connected companies debts: general

(1) This section applies if—

    (*a*) a liability to pay an amount under [a debtor relationship of a company ("D") is released, and][1]

    (*b*) the release takes place in an accounting period for which—

        (i) an amortised cost basis of accounting is used in respect of the relationship, and

        (ii) the relationship is a connected companies relationship.

(2) [D][1] is only required to bring a credit into account in respect of the release for the purposes of this Part if[—
  (a) it is a deemed release, or
  (b) it is a release of relevant rights.][1]
(3) In subsection (2) "deemed release" means a release which is deemed to occur because of—
  (a) section 361 (acquisition of creditor rights by connected company at undervalue), or
  (b) section 362 (parties becoming connected where creditor's rights subject to impairment adjustment).
[(4) For the purposes of this section "relevant rights" means rights of a company ("C") that—
  (a) were acquired by C, before the day on which F(No2)A 2015 was passed, in circumstances that, but for the application of the old corporate rescue exception or the old debt-for-debt exception, would have resulted in a deemed release under section 361(3), or
  (b) were acquired by another company before that day in such circumstances and transferred to C by way of an assignment or assignments.
(4A) In subsection (4)(a)—
  (a) "the old corporate rescue exception" means the exception in section 361A (as it had effect before F(No2)A 2015);
  (b) "the old debt-for-debt exception" means the exception in section 361B (as it had effect before that Act).][2]
[(5) The amount of the credit that D is required to bring into account in respect of a release of relevant rights is—
  (a) the amount of the discount received on the acquisition, less
  (b) the sum of any credits brought into account in respect of that amount (whether in the accounting period in which the release takes place or in a previous accounting period) by C or, in a case within subsection (4)(b), by the company that acquired the rights or any company to which the rights were subsequently assigned.
(6) A reference in subsection (5) to the amount of the discount received on the acquisition is to the amount that would have been treated as released under section 361(4) on the acquisition, but for the application of the corporate rescue exception or the debt-for-debt exception.][1]
[(7) Where the carrying value of a liability representing the debtor relationship has at any time been adjusted as a result of the liability being the hedged item under a designated fair value hedge, this section does not prevent a credit or debit being brought into account for the purposes of this Part in respect of any reversal of that adjustment.
(8) Nothing in this section affects the credits or debits to be brought into account for the purposes of this Part in respect of exchange gains or losses arising from a debt.][2]

Amendments—[1] In sub-s (1)(a) words substituted for words "a company's debtor relationship is released,", in sub-s (2) word substituted for words "The company" and "it is a deemed release", and sub-ss (5), (6) inserted, by FA 2010 s 44, Sch 15 paras 2(1), (3) with effect in relation to a release of rights that takes place on or after 14 October 2009.
[2] Sub-ss (4), (4A) substituted for previous sub-s (4) with effect in relation to the release of a debtor relationship of a company on or after 18 November 2015, and sub-ss (7), (8) inserted by F(No 2)A 2015 s 32, Sch 7 paras 1, 33 with effect for accounting periods beginning on or after 1 January 2016, subject to transitional rules in F(No 2)A 2015 Sch 7 paras 115 to 129.

359 Exclusion of credits on release of connected companies debts during creditor's insolvency
(1) This section applies if—
  (a) a liability to pay an amount under a company's debtor relationship is released,
  (b) the release takes place in an accounting period for which an amortised cost basis of accounting is used in respect of that relationship,
  (c) condition A, B, C, D or E in section 357 is met in relation to the company releasing the amount,
  (d) immediately before the time when [any of those conditions][1] was first met the relationship was a connected companies relationship, and
  (e) immediately after that time it was not such a relationship.
(2) The company is not required to bring into account a credit in respect of the release for the purposes of this Part.
[(3) Where the carrying value of a liability representing the debtor relationship has at any time been adjusted as a result of the liability being the hedged item under a designated fair value hedge, this section does not prevent a credit being brought into account for the purposes of this Part in respect of any reversal of that adjustment.][1]

Amendments—[1] In sub-s (1)(d) words substituted for words "the condition in question", and sub-s (3) inserted, by F(No 2)A 2015 s 32, Sch 7 paras 1, 34 with effect for accounting periods beginning on or after 1 January 2016, subject to transitional rules in F(No 2)A 2015 Sch 7 paras 115 to 129.

360 Exclusion of credits on reversal of impairments of connected companies debts
(1) If an impairment loss is prevented from being brought into account by section 354, no credit in respect of any reversal of the impairment may be brought into account for the purposes of this Part.
(2) Nothing in this section affects the credits to be brought into account for the purposes of this Part in respect of exchange gains or losses arising from a debt.

Deemed debt releases on impaired debts becoming held by connected company

361 Acquisition of creditor rights by connected company at undervalue

(1) This section applies if—

(a) a company ("D") is a party to a loan relationship as debtor,

(b) another company ("C") becomes a party to it as creditor,

(c) immediately after it does so C and D are connected,

(d) in a case where the person from whom C acquires its rights under the loan relationship is a company, in the period of account in which C acquires them there is no connection between C and that company,

(e) the amount or value of any consideration given by C for the acquisition is less than the pre-acquisition carrying value (see subsection (5)), and

[(f) the equity-for-debt exception (see section 361C) does not apply.][1]

[(2) . . . [1]

(3) C is treated as releasing its rights under the loan relationship when it acquires them.

(4) The amount treated as released is the amount of the difference referred to in subsection (1)(e).

(5) In subsection (1)(e) "the pre-acquisition carrying value" means the amount which would be the carrying value of the liability under the loan relationship in D's accounts if a period of account had ended immediately before C became a party to it.

(6) For the purposes of subsection (5) the carrying value is determined taking no account of—

(a) accrued amounts, or

(b) amounts paid or received in advance.

[(7) Subsections (3) and (4) are subject to section 361D (corporate rescue: debt released shortly after acquisition).][1]

HMRC Manuals—Corporate Finance Manual CFM35440 (tax treatment of impaired debt).
CFM35450, 35460, 35470 (application of s 361 prior to 14 October 2009).
CFM35510 (deemed releases on or after 14 October 2009: overview).
CFM35530, 35540 (deemed releases on impaired debt on or after 14 October 2009).
Amendments—[1]   Sub-s (1)(f) substituted, sub-s (2) repealed, and sub-s (7) inserted, by F(No 2)A 2015 s 32, Sch 7 paras 1, 35 with effect where the company acquiring the rights under the loan relationship as creditor does so on or after 18 November 2015.

[361C The equity-for-debt exception

(1) For the purposes of section 361 the "equity-for-debt exception" applies if the following two conditions are met.

(2) The first condition is that the acquisition is an arm's length transaction.

(3) The second condition is that the consideration given by C for the acquisition consists only of—

(a) shares forming part of the ordinary share capital of C,

(b) shares forming part of the ordinary share capital of a company connected with C, or

(c) an entitlement to shares within paragraph (a) or (b).][1]

Amendments—[1]   Sections 361A–361C inserted by FA 2010 s 44, Sch 15 paras 2(1), (5) with effect in relation to a relevant acquisition that is made on or after 14 October 2009, subject to transitional provisions: see FA 2010 Sch 15 para 4.

[361D   Corporate rescue: debt released shortly after acquisition

(1) This section applies if—

(a) the case is one in which section 361 would otherwise apply,

(b) within 60 days after C becomes a party to the loan relationship as creditor, C or a company connected with C releases D's liability to pay an amount under the loan relationship, and

(c) the corporate rescue conditions are met.

(2) If the release is of the whole debt, section 361 does not apply to the acquisition of the rights by C.

(3) If the release is of part of the debt, the amount that C is treated by section 361 as having released when it acquired the rights under the loan relationship is reduced (but not below nil) by the amount that is actually released as mentioned in subsection (1)(b).

(4) The corporate rescue conditions are—

(a) that the acquisition by C of its rights under the loan relationship is an arm's length transaction,

(b) that immediately before C became a party to the loan relationship as creditor, it was reasonable to assume that, without the release and any arrangements of which the release forms part, there would be a material risk that at some time within the next 12 months the company would have been unable to pay its debts.

(5) For the purposes of subsection (4)(b), a company is unable to pay its debts if—

(a) it is unable to pay its debts as they fall due, or

(b) the value of the company's assets is less than the amount of its liabilities, taking into account its contingent and prospective liabilities.][1]

Amendments—[1]   Section 361D inserted by F(No 2)A 2015 s 32, Sch 7 paras 1, 37 with effect where the company acquiring the rights under the loan relationship as creditor does so on or after 18 November 2015.

362 Parties becoming connected where creditor's rights subject to impairment adjustment [etc]

(1) This section applies if—

    (*a*) a company ("D") is a party to a loan relationship as debtor, [and][1]

    (*b*) another company ("C") which—

        (i) is a party to the loan relationship as creditor, and

        (ii) is not connected with D,

    becomes connected with D. . . . [1]

    (*c*) . . . [1]

(2) C is treated as releasing its rights under the loan relationship when C and D become connected.

[(3) The amount treated as released is the amount (if any) by which the pre-connection carrying value in D's accounts exceeds the pre-connection carrying value in C's accounts.

(4) In subsection (3)—

    "the pre-connection carrying value in D's accounts" means the amount that would be the carrying value of the liability representing the loan relationship in D's accounts if a period of account had ended immediately before C and D became connected, and

    "the pre-connection carrying value in C's accounts" means—

        (*a*) in any case where C was a party to the loan relationship as creditor on the last day of the period of account ending immediately before the one in which C and D became connected, the cost of the asset representing the loan relationship which would be given on that day on an amortised cost basis of accounting, and

        (*b*) in any other case, the amount or value of any consideration given by C for the acquisition of the asset representing the loan relationship.][1]

(5) For the purposes of subsection (4) [no account is to be taken of—][2]

    (*a*) accrued amounts, [or][2]

    (*b*) amounts paid or received in advance. . . . [2]

    (*c*) . . . [2]

[(6) Subsections (2) and (3) are subject to section 362A (corporate rescue: debt released shortly after connection arises).][3]

Modifications—See FA 2012 s 23(4) (sub-ss (3), (4) modified in relation to companies becoming connected on or after 27 February 2012 but before 1 April 2012).

FA 2012 s 23(12) (this section does not apply if s 361 has effect in accordance with FA 2012 s 23(8)).

Amendments—[1]   Sub-s (1)(*c*) and preceding word "and" repealed; word in heading and word at end of sub-s (1)(*a*) inserted; and sub-ss (3), (4) substituted; by FA 2012 s 23(1), (2)(*a*), (*b*), (*d*), with effect in relation to any case where the companies become connected on or after 27 February 2012.

[2]   Sub-s (5)(*c*) and preceding word "and" repealed; word at the end of sub-s (5)(*a*) inserted; and words in sub-s (5) substituted; by FA 2012 s 23(1), (2)(*c*), with effect in relation to any case where the companies become connected on or after 1 April 2012.

[3]   Sub-s (6) inserted by F(No 2)A 2015 s 32, Sch 7 paras 1, 38 with effect where the companies become connected with each other on or after 18 November 2015.

[362A Corporate rescue: debt released shortly after connection arises]

(1) This section applies if—

    (*a*) the case is one in which section 362 would otherwise apply,

    (*b*) within 60 days after C and D become connected, C releases D's liability to pay an amount under the loan relationship, and

    (*c*) the corporate rescue conditions are met.

(2) If the release is of the whole debt, section 362 does not apply by reason of C and D becoming connected.

(3) If the release is of part of the debt, the amount that C is treated by section 362 as having released when it became connected with D is reduced (but not below nil) by the amount actually released.

(4) The corporate rescue conditions are—

    (*a*) that C and D became connected as a result of an arm's length transaction, and

    (*b*) that immediately before C and D became connected it was reasonable to assume that, without the connection and any arrangements of which the connection forms part, there would be a material risk that at some time within the next 12 months D would have been unable to pay its debts.

(5) For the purposes of subsection (4)(*b*), a company is unable to pay its debts if—

    (*a*) it is unable to pay its debts as they fall due, or

    (*b*) the value of the company's assets is less than the amount of its liabilities, taking into account its contingent and prospective liabilities.][1]

Amendments—[1]   This section inserted by F(No 2)A 2015 s 32, Sch 7 paras 1, 39 with effect where the companies become connected with each other on or after 18 November 2015.

363 Companies connected for sections 361 [to 362A][1]

(1) For the purposes of sections 361 [to 362A][1] there is a connection between two companies at any time if condition A or B is met at that time.

(2) Condition A is that one company has control of the other.

(3) Condition B is that both companies are under the control of the same person (but see subsection (6)).

(4) For the purposes of sections 361 [to 362A][1] there is a connection between two companies in a period of account if there is a connection between them (within subsection (1)) at any time in the period.

(5) Section 472 (meaning of "control") applies for the purposes of this section.

(6) Condition B is not taken to be met just because two companies have been under the control of—
  (a) the Crown,
  (b) a Minister of the Crown,
  (c) a government department,
  (d) a Northern Ireland department,
  (e) a foreign sovereign power, or
  (f) an international organisation.

(7) Section 468 (connection between companies to be ignored in some circumstances) applies for the purposes of this section as it applies for the purposes of the provisions which apply section 466, taking references in sections 468 and 469 to the accounting period as references to the period of account.

(8) For the meaning of "international organisation", see section 476(2) and (3).

Amendments—[1]   In heading and sub-ss (1), (4) words substituted for words "to 362" by F(No 2)A 2015 s 32, Sch 7 paras 1, 40 with effect where the companies become connected with each other on or after 18 November 2015.

[363A Arrangements for avoiding section 361 or 362
(1) This section applies in any case where arrangements are entered into and the main purpose, or one of the main purposes, of any party in entering into them (or any part of them) is—
  (a) to avoid an amount being treated as released under section 361 or 362, or
  (b) to reduce the amount which is treated as released under section 361 or 362.

(2) The arrangements (or part of the arrangements) are not to achieve that effect (so that an amount, or a greater amount, falls to be treated as released under section 361 or 362).

(3) In this section "arrangements" includes any agreement, understanding, scheme, transaction or series of transactions (whether or not legally enforceable).][1]

Amendments—[1]   This section inserted by FA 2012 s 23(1), (3) with effect in relation to arrangements entered into—
  (a)   on or after 27 February 2012; or
  (b)   before that date where the amount is treated as released, or would have been treated as released, on or after that date. This does not apply, however, if the amount is treated as released, or would have been treated as released, pursuant to an unconditional obligation in a contract made before 27 February 2012 (FA 2012 s 23(6)).

CHAPTER 7

GROUP RELIEF CLAIMS INVOLVING IMPAIRED OR RELEASED CONSORTIUM DEBTS

364 Introduction to Chapter
(1) This Chapter applies if—
  (a) there is (or was) a relevant consortium creditor relationship (see subsection (2)), and
  (b) either—
    (i) an impairment loss is or has been brought into account for the purposes of this Part for any group accounting period by the creditor, or
    (ii) a debit in respect of a release of liability under the relationship is or has been so brought into account.

(2) For the purposes of this Chapter a relationship is a relevant consortium creditor relationship if—
  (a) it is a creditor relationship of—
    (i) a company (the "member company"), which is a member of a consortium by which a consortium company is owned, or
    (ii) a company (a "group member") which is a member of the same group of companies as the member company but is not itself a member of the consortium, and
  (b) the consortium company or, if that company is a holding company, a consortium company which is a subsidiary of that company is (or was) the debtor (the "debtor consortium company").

(3) The provisions of this Chapter—
  (a) reduce debits for impairment losses and release debits under relevant consortium creditor relationships where an amount surrendered as group relief by the consortium company is claimed by a member company or group member (see section 365),
  (b) provide for a corresponding reduction in credits in respect of such relationships where a reduction within paragraph (a) has occurred (see section 367),
  (c) reduce claims for group relief where debits within paragraph (a) for earlier group accounting periods exceed reductions within paragraph (b) (see section 368), and
  (d) provide for such claims to be carried forward where they exceed such debits (see section 369).

(4) In this Chapter—

"release debit" means a debit in respect of a release of liability under a relevant consortium creditor relationship, [and

"group relief" means—

    (a) group relief under Part 5 of CTA 2010 (see section 97(2) of that Act), and

    (b) group relief for carried-forward losses under Part 5A of CTA 2010 (see section 188AA(4) of that Act).][2]

(5) If [section 143[, 144 or 188DH][2] of CTA 2010 (which limit the amount of group relief to be given in certain cases involving a consortium)][1] applies, effect must be given to that section before effect is given to this Chapter.

(6) Expressions defined in this section have the same meaning in the other provisions of this Chapter, and sections 370 and 371 also apply for the interpretation of this Chapter.

(7) For the meaning of "impairment loss" see section 476(1).

Amendments—[1] In sub-s (5) words substituted for words "section 403C of ICTA (amount of relief in consortium cases)" by CTA 2010 s 1177, Sch 1 para 608. CTA 2010 has effect for corporation tax purposes for accounting periods ending on or after 1 April 2010, and for income and capital gains tax purposes for the tax year 2010–11 and subsequent tax years.

[2] In sub-s (4) words inserted, and in sub-s (5) words substituted for words "or 144", by F(No 2)A 2017 s 18, Sch 4 paras 128, 130 with effect in relation to accounting periods beginning on or after 1 April 2017, subject to transitional provisions in Sch 4 para 194. For accounting periods beginning before 1 April 2017 and ending on or after that date ("straddling periods") see F(No 2)A 2017 Sch 4 paras 190–192.

365 Reduction of impairment loss debits where group relief claimed

(1) This section applies for any group accounting period for which there is a net consortium debit.

(2) For the purposes of this Chapter there is a net consortium debit for a group accounting period if—

    (a) the total of the impairment losses and release debits brought into account for that period in respect of relevant consortium creditor relationships by—

        (i) the member company, and

        (ii) every group member,

    exceeds

    (b) the total credits so brought into account by them in connection with debts owed by the companies which are the debtor consortium companies in respect of those relationships.

(3) The net consortium debit is equal to that excess.

(4) If there is a claim for that group accounting period by the member company or a group member for group relief in respect of an amount which may be surrendered as group relief by the debtor consortium companies, the debits brought into account in respect of the impairment losses and the release debits mentioned in subsection (2)(a) are reduced.

(5) The amount of reduction in the case of each of the debits referred to in subsection (4) ("the relevant debits") is calculated as follows.

Step 1

Find the total amount which—

    (a) may be surrendered as group relief by the debtor consortium companies, and

    (b) is claimed as group relief for the group accounting period by the member company or any group member.

Step 2

If the amount found at Step 1 does not exceed the net consortium debit, apportion the amount found at Step 1 between the relevant debits in proportion to their respective amounts.

If the amount found at Step 1 exceeds the net consortium debit, apportion so much of the amount found at Step 1 as does not exceed it between the relevant debits in proportion to their respective amounts.

(6) This section is subject to section 366.

366 Effect where credit for release brought into account on amortised cost basis

(1) This section applies if—

    (a) a company releases liability under a relevant consortium creditor relationship of the company ("the release amount"), and

    (b) the debtor consortium company brings into account an amount in respect of the release for any accounting period in accordance with an amortised cost basis of accounting.

(2) An amount equal to the release amount is treated for the purposes of this Chapter as not being a debit brought into account for that period in relation to the relevant consortium creditor relationship.

367 Reduction of credits exceeding impairment losses

(1) This section applies if, apart from this section, for any group accounting period—

    (a) the total of the impairment losses and release debits brought into account for that period in respect of relevant consortium creditor relationships by—

        (i) the member company, and

        (ii) every group member,

is less than

(b) the total credits so brought into account by them in connection with debts owed by the companies which are the debtor consortium companies in respect of those relationships.

(2) Those credits are reduced (but not below nil) in accordance with subsection (3).

(3) The amount of reduction in the case of each credit is calculated as follows.

Step 1

Find the total amount by which the debits in respect of the relationships for previous group accounting periods have been reduced under section 365(4).

Step 2

Deduct the total amount by which credits have previously been reduced under this section from the amount found at Step 1.

Step 3

Apportion the amount found at Step 2 between the credits in proportion to their respective amounts.

368 Reduction of claims where there are earlier net consortium debits

(1) This section applies if—

    (a) for any group accounting period there is a claim by the member company or a group member for group relief in respect of an amount which may be surrendered as group relief by debtor consortium companies, and

    (b) the total amount of the net consortium debits for earlier group accounting periods in respect of the relevant consortium creditor relationships exceeds any reductions in respect of those debits falling to be made under section 365(4).

(2) In this section that excess is referred to as "the unreduced debits amount".

(3) If—

    (a) the claim is the only claim for that period, and

    (b) it exceeds the unreduced debits amount,

the claim is reduced by the unreduced debits amount.

(4) If—

    (a) the claim is not the only claim for that period, and

    (b) the total of the claims exceeds the unreduced debits amount,

the claim is reduced by the same proportion of the unreduced debits amount as the claim bears to that total.

(5) In any other case, the claim is reduced to nil.

369 Carry forward of claims where there are no net consortium debits

(1) This section applies if for any group accounting period there is—

    (a) a claim by the member company or a group member for group relief in respect of an amount which may be surrendered as group relief by debtor consortium companies (as reduced under section 368, if it applies), and

    (b) no net consortium debit in respect of the relevant consortium creditor relationships.

(2) The claim (as so reduced) is carried forward and treated for the purposes of section 365—

    (a) as increasing any such claim for group relief made by the claimant company for its next accounting period, or

    (b) if apart from this subsection there would be no such claim, as being such a claim.

370 Group accounting periods

(1) In this Chapter "group accounting period" means—

    (a) any accounting period of the member company beginning on or after 1 October 2002, or

    (b) any accounting period of a group member which—

        (i) begins on or after that date, and

        (ii) corresponds to such an accounting period of the member company.

(2) Any such accounting period of the member company and any such corresponding accounting periods of group members are treated for the purposes of this Chapter as being the same accounting period.

(3) For the purposes of this Chapter an accounting period of a group member corresponds to an accounting period of the member company if condition A, B or C is met.

(4) Condition A is that the periods coincide.

(5) Condition B is that the accounting period of the member company includes more than half of the accounting period of the group member.

(6) Condition C is that—

    (a) the accounting period of the member company includes part of the accounting period of the group member, and

    (b) the remainder of that period is not within any accounting period of the member company.

"CIS-based close company" means a company which would not be a close company apart from the rights and powers of one or more partners in a CIS limited partnership being attributed to another of the partners under [section 451(4) to (6) of CTA 2010 because of section 448(1)(*a*) of that Act][2],

"CIS limited partnership" means a limited partnership—

(*a*) which is a collective investment scheme, or

(*b*) which would be a collective investment scheme if it were not a body corporate,

"non-qualifying territory" has the meaning given by [section 173 of TIOPA 2010][3],

["resident for tax purposes" means liable, under the law of the non-qualifying territory, to tax there by reason of domicile, residence or place of management, and"][1]

"small or medium-sized enterprise" has the meaning given by [section 172 of TIOPA 2010][3].

[(6) For the purposes of section 375, a non-qualifying territory is "non- taxing" if companies are not under its law liable to tax by reason of domicile, residence or place of management.][1]

Amendments—[1]   In sub-s (5) definition of "resident" substituted and sub-s (6) inserted, by FA 2009 s 41, Sch 20 paras 1, 4 where the actual accrual period (within the meaning of CTA 2009 Pt 5 Ch 8), or the relevant period (within the meaning of CTA 2009 ss 407(1), 409(1)), begins on or after 1 April 2009, subject to transitional provisions: FA 2009 Sch 20 para 9.

[2]   In sub-s (1) words substituted for words "section 414 of ICTA (meaning of "close company" in the Tax Acts) applies with the omission of section 414(1)(a) (exclusion of non-UK resident companies)", in sub-s (3) words substituted for words "for the purposes of Part 11 of ICTA because of section 417 of that Act" and "participator for those purposes", in sub-s (5), in the definition of "CIS-based close company", words substituted for words "section 416(6) of ICTA because of section 417(3)(*a*) of that Act" by CTA 2010 s 1177, Sch 1 para 610. CTA 2010 has effect for corporation tax purposes for accounting periods ending on or after 1 April 2010, and for income and capital gains tax purposes for the tax year 2010–11 and subsequent tax years.

[3]   In sub-s (5) in the definition of "non-qualifying territory" words "paragraph 5E of Schedule 28AA to ICTA" substituted and in the definition of "small or medium-sized enterprise" words "paragraph 5D of that Schedule" substituted by TIOPA 2010 s 501, Sch 8 paras 123, 128. TIOPA 2010 has effect for corporation tax purposes for accounting periods ending on or after 1 April 2010, for income and capital gains tax purposes for the tax year 2010–11 and subsequent tax years, and for petroleum revenue tax purposes for chargeable periods beginning on or after 1 July 2010.

378 Loans by trustees of occupational pension schemes

(1) The case to which this section applies is where—

(*a*) the loan is one made by trustees of an occupational pension scheme, and

(*b*) condition A, B or C is met.

(2) Condition A is that there is a time in the actual accrual period when the company which has the debtor relationship ("D") is the employer of employees to whom the scheme relates.

(3) Condition B is that there is a connection between D and such an employer for the actual accrual period.

(4) Condition C is that a company is such an employer and there is a time in the actual accrual period when—

(*a*) D has a major interest in that company, or

(*b*) that company has a major interest in D.

(5) In this section "occupational pension scheme" has the meaning given in section 150(5) of FA 2004.

(6) Section 466 (companies connected for an accounting period) applies for the purposes of this section.

379 Persons indirectly standing in the position of creditor

(1) For the purposes of this Chapter a person is treated as standing in the position of a creditor as respects a loan relationship if the person indirectly stands in that position by reference to a series of loan relationships or relevant money debts.

(2) If—

(*a*) a person ("C") indirectly stands in the position of creditor as respects a loan relationship by reference to such a series of relationships or debts, and

(*b*) section 373 (late interest treated as not accruing until paid in some cases) applies in relation to the debtor relationship because of subsection (1),

the reference in section 373(3) to the corresponding creditor relationship is a reference to C's creditor relationship.

(3) In subsection (1) "relevant money debt" means a money debt which would be a loan relationship if a company directly stood in the position of creditor or debtor.

CHAPTER 9

PARTNERSHIPS INVOLVING COMPANIES

380 Partnerships involving companies

(1) This section applies if—

(*a*) a trade or business is carried on by a firm,

(*b*) any of the partners in the firm is a company (a "company partner"), and

(*c*) a money debt is owed by or to the firm.

(2) In calculating the profits and losses of the trade or business for corporation tax purposes under section 1259 (calculation of firm's profits or losses), no credits or debits may be brought into account under this Part—

    (*a*) in relation to the money debt, or

    (*b*) in relation to any loan relationship that would fall to be treated for the purposes of the calculation as arising from the money debt,

(3) Instead, each company partner must bring credits and debits into account under this Part in relation to the debt or relationship for each of its accounting periods in which the conditions in subsection (1) are met.

(4) The following provisions of this Chapter contain special rules about the credits and debits to be brought into account under subsection (3)—

    (*a*) section 381 (determinations of credits and debits by company partners: general),

    (*b*) section 382 (company partners using fair value accounting),

    (*c*) section 383 (lending between partners and the partnership),

    (*d*) section 384 (treatment of exchange gains and losses), and

    (*e*) section 385 (company partners' shares where firm owns deeply discounted securities).

(5) In those provisions "company partner" has the same meaning as in this section.

381 Determinations of credits and debits by company partners: general

(1) The credits and debits to be brought into account under section 380(3) are to be determined separately for each company partner as follows.

(2) The money debt owed by or to the firm is treated as if—

    (*a*) it were owed by or, as the case may be, to the company partner, and

    (*b*) it were so owed for the purposes of the trade or business which the company partner carries on.

(3) If the money debt arises from a transaction for the lending of money—

    (*a*) it continues to be treated as so arising, and

    (*b*) accordingly the company partner is treated as having a loan relationship.

(4) Anything done by or in relation to the firm in connection with the money debt is treated as done by or in relation to the company partner.

(5) The credits and debits in the case of each company partner are the partner's appropriate share of the total credits and debits determined in accordance with subsections (2) to (4) (without any reduction for the fact that the debt is treated as owed by or to each company partner).

(6) A company partner's "appropriate share" is the share that would be apportioned to it on the assumption in subsection (7).

(7) The assumption is that the total credits and debits determined in accordance with subsections (2) to (4) are apportioned between the partners in the shares in which any profit or loss would be apportioned between them in accordance with the firm's profit-sharing arrangements.

382 Company partners using fair value accounting

(1) This section applies if a company partner uses fair value accounting in relation to its interest in the firm.

(2) The credits and debits to be brought into account by the company partner under section 380(3) are to be determined on the basis of fair value accounting.

383 Lending between partners and the partnership

(1) This section applies if—

    (*a*) the money debt owed by or to the firm arises from a transaction for the lending of money, and

    (*b*) there is a time in an accounting period of a company partner ("the relevant accounting period") when conditions A, B and C are met.

(2) Condition A is that—

    (*a*) if the debt is owed by the firm, the company partner stands in the position of a creditor and accordingly has a creditor relationship, and

    (*b*) if the debt is owed to the firm, the company partner stands in the position of a debtor and accordingly has a debtor relationship.

(3) Condition B is that the company partner controls the firm either alone or taken together with one or more other company partners connected with the company partner (see subsection (7)).

(4) Condition C is that the company partner or any other company partner is treated under section 381(3) as if—

    (*a*) it had the debtor relationship which corresponds to the creditor relationship mentioned in subsection (2)(*a*), or

    (*b*) it had the creditor relationship which corresponds to the debtor relationship mentioned in subsection (2)(*b*).

(5) If this section applies, for the purposes of this Part for the relevant accounting period there is taken to be a connection between—

    (*a*) the company partner, and

(3) That part is so much as is proportionate to the part of the accounting period in the permitted period.

(4) References in this section to a company's BLAGAB non-trading loan relationships profits for an accounting period are references to the amount (if any) [of the BLAGAB credits in respect of the company's loan relationships that count as income for the purposes of the I-E rules for that period (as determined by section 88(3) and (4)) of FA 2012][2].

(5) The unused part of the relevant deductions for an accounting period is found as follows.

Step 1

Add together—

    (a) [the amount for the purposes of section 73 of FA 2012 of the adjusted BLAGAB management expenses of the company for the period][2], and

    (b) so much of the sum of the deductions made in the case of the company in respect of [qualifying charitable donations][1] for that period as is [referable to BLAGAB][2]

Step 2

Add together—

    (a) so much of the amount for the purposes of section 73 of FA 2012 of the adjusted BLAGAB management expenses of the company for the period as, on the assumption that the company had no BLAGAB non-trading loan relationships profits for the period, could be subtracted at step 6 under that section without producing a negative amount, and[2]

    (b) the total amounts [referable to BLAGAB][2] which could be applied for the period in making deductions in respect of [qualifying charitable donations][1] if those profits were disregarded.

Step 3

Subtract the amount found at Step 2 from the amount found at Step 1.

The result is the unused part of the relevant deductions for the accounting period.

[(6) In the case of any claim under section 389, references in subsection (5) to the amount for the purposes of section 73 of FA 2012 of the adjusted BLAGAB management expenses of the company for the period are references to that amount as determined on the assumptions in subsections (7) and (8).][2]

(7) The first assumption is that no account is taken of—

    (a) that claim, or

    (b) any other claim under section 389 relating to a deficit for an accounting period after the deficit period.

(8) The second assumption is that all such adjustments are made as are required as a result of any sum having been carried back under the Corporation Tax Acts to the accounting period mentioned in subsection (5), otherwise than as a result of—

    (a) the claim mentioned in subsection (6), or

    (b) any such other claim as is mentioned in subsection (7)(b).

Amendments—[1] In sub-s (5),Step 1 para (b), Step 2 para (b) words substituted for words "charges on income" by CTA 2010 s 1177, Sch 1 para 612. CTA 2010 has effect for corporation tax purposes for accounting periods ending on or after 1 April 2010, and for income and capital gains tax purposes for the tax year 2010–11 and subsequent tax years.

[2] In sub-s (4), words substituted for words "which is chargeable to tax for that period under section 299 (charge to tax on non-trading profits) for the company's BLAGAB", in sub-s (5), in step 1(a) words substituted for words "so much of the expenses deduction for the period given by Step 8 in section 76(7) of ICTA (expenses of insurance companies) as is referable to BLAGAB", in step1(b), words substituted for words "so referable", in step 2 para (a) substituted, in step 2(b), words substituted for words "so referable", and sub-s (6) substituted, by FA 2012 s 146, Sch 16 paras 135, 154 with effect in relation to accounting periods of companies beginning on or after 1 January 2013 (subject to transitional provisions in FA 2012 Sch 17). For accounting periods straddling 1 January 2013 see FA 2012 s 149.

391 Carry forward of surplus deficit to next accounting period

(1) This rule applies if any of the deficit is not—

    (a) set off against the income and gains referred to in section 388(1), or

    (b) set off against the profits referred to in section 389(1) as the result of a claim under that section.

(2) That deficit must be carried forward to the accounting period immediately after the deficit period ("the next period").

[(3) Any deficit so carried forward is treated for the purposes of section 76 of FA 2012 as a deemed BLAGAB management expense for the next period.][1]

Commentary—Simon's Taxes **D1.521, D7.533, D7.438.**

Derivation—FA 1996 Sch 11 para 4(4).

HMRC Manuals—Corporate Finance Manual CFM64390 (meaning of carried forward amount).

Cross reference—FA 2012 s 78 (3) (deemed BLAGAB management expense for the accounting period).

Amendments—[1] Sub-s (3) substituted by FA 2012 s 146, Sch 16 paras 135, 155 with effect in relation to accounting periods of companies beginning on or after 1 January 2013 (subject to transitional provisions in FA 2012 Sch 17). For accounting periods straddling 1 January 2013, see FA 2012 s 149.

Exclusion of loan relationships of members of Lloyd's

392 Exclusion of loan relationships of members of Lloyd's

(1) This section applies to any loan relationship of a corporate member of Lloyd's.

(2) This Part does not apply as respects the relationship so far as rights or liabilities under it or securities representing it are—

   (a) assets forming part of the member's premium trust fund, or

   (b) liabilities attached to that fund.

(3) In this section "corporate member" and "premium trust fund" have the same meaning as in Chapter 5 of Part 4 of FA 1994 (Lloyd's underwriters: corporations etc) (see section 230(1) of that Act).

CHAPTER 11
OTHER SPECIAL KINDS OF COMPANY
Investment trusts' and venture capital trusts' creditor relationships

395 Investment trusts: profits or losses of a capital nature

(1) Profits or losses of a capital nature arising to an investment trust from a creditor relationship may not be brought into account as credits or debits for the purposes of this Part.

(2) For the purposes of this section "profits or losses of a capital nature" means profits or losses that—

   (a) are accounted for through the capital column of the income statement in accordance with the Statement of Recommended Practice, or

   (b) would have been so accounted for if that Statement had been applied correctly.

(3) "The Statement of Recommended Practice", in relation to an accounting period for which it is required or permitted to be used, means—

   (a) the Statement of Recommended Practice relating to Investment Trust Companies, issued by the Association of Investment Trust Companies in January 2003, as from time to time modified, amended or revised, or

   (b) any subsequent Statement of Recommended Practice relating to investment trusts, as from time to time modified, amended or revised.

(4) The Treasury may by order amend the definition of "profits or losses of a capital nature" in subsection (2), so far as it applies in relation to an investment trust that prepares accounts in accordance with international accounting standards.

(5) An order under subsection (4) may make—

   (a) different provision for different cases, and

   (b) incidental, supplemental, consequential and transitional provision and savings.

396 Venture capital trusts: profits or losses of a capital nature

(1) Profits or losses of a capital nature arising to a venture capital trust from a creditor relationship may not be brought into account as credits or debits for the purposes of this Part.

(2) For the purposes of this section "profits or losses of a capital nature" means profits or losses that—

   (a) are accounted for through the capital column of the income statement in accordance with the Statement of Recommended Practice, or

   (b) would have been so accounted for if the venture capital trust had been an investment trust and that Statement had been applied correctly.

(3) In this section "the Statement of Recommended Practice" has the meaning given in section 395(3) (investment trusts: profits or losses of a capital nature).

(4) The Treasury may by order amend the definition of "profits or losses of a capital nature" in subsection (2), so far as it applies in relation to a venture capital trust that prepares accounts in accordance with international accounting standards.

(5) An order under subsection (4) may make—

   (a) different provision for different cases, and

   (b) incidental, supplemental, consequential and transitional provision and savings.

Credit unions

397 Credit unions

(1) In calculating the income of a credit union for any accounting period, no credit is to be brought into account for the purposes of this Part in respect of a loan relationship of the union if a member of the union stands in the position of debtor in relation to the debt in question.

(2) But subsection (1) does not apply if the credit union—

   (a) is obliged to make a return under section 887(2) of ITA 2007 for the accounting period, and

   (b) has not done so within—

      (i) 3 months after the end of the period, or

      (ii) such longer period as an officer of Revenue and Customs allows.

(3) No debit is to be brought into account for the purposes of this Part in respect of a loan relationship of a credit union if a member of the union stands in the position of creditor in relation to the debt in question.

(4) A reference in section 400A to a "pre-tax" economic profit or loss is a reference to an economic profit or loss determined disregarding any gain or loss made as a result of the operation of any provision of the Corporation Tax Acts.][1]

Amendments—[1]   Sections 400A–400C inserted by FA 2010 s 41, Sch 14 paras 1, 6 with effect in relation to adjustments made under CTA 2009 s 400(2) in respect of increases in the retail prices index over periods beginning on or after 9 December 2009, subject to transitional provisions; see FA 2010 Sch 14 para 9.

[400C Meaning of "associated with"

(1) For the purposes of section 400A, a company ("company B") is associated with company A at a time ("the relevant time") during an accounting period of company A ("the accounting period") if any of the following five conditions is met.

(2) The first condition is that the financial results of company A and company B, for a period that includes the relevant time, meet the consolidation condition.

(3) The second condition is that there is a connection between company A and company B for the accounting period.

(4) The third condition is that, at the relevant time, company A has a major interest in company B or company B has a major interest in company A.

(5) The fourth condition is that—

   (a) the financial results of company A and a third company, for a period that includes the relevant time, meet the consolidation condition, and

   (b) at the relevant time the third company has a major interest in company B.

(6) The fifth condition is that—

   (a) there is a connection between company A and a third company for the accounting period, and

   (b) at the relevant time the third company has a major interest in company B.

(7) In this paragraph the financial results of any two companies for any period meet "the consolidation condition" if—

   (a) they are required to be comprised in group accounts prepared under section 399 of the Companies Act 2006 (duty of certain parent companies to prepare group accounts), or

   (b) they would be required to be comprised in such accounts but for the application of an exemption mentioned in subsection (3) of that section.

(8) Section 466 (companies connected for an accounting period) applies for the purposes of this section.

(9) In this section "scheme" includes any scheme, arrangements or understanding of any kind whatever, whether or not legally enforceable, involving a single transaction or two or more transactions.][1]

Amendments—[1]   Sections 400A–400C inserted by FA 2010 s 41, Sch 14 paras 1, 6 with effect in relation to adjustments made under CTA 2009 s 400(2) in respect of increases in the retail prices index over periods beginning on or after 9 December 2009, subject to transitional provisions; see FA 2010 Sch 14 para 9.

[Other gilt-edged securities][1]

Amendments—[1]   Heading inserted by FA 2010 s 41, Sch 14 paras 1, 6 with effect in relation to adjustments made under CTA 2009 s 400(2) in respect of increases in the retail prices index over periods beginning on or after 9 December 2009, subject to transitional provisions; see FA 2010 Sch 14 para 9.

401 Gilt strips

(1) This section applies if a loan relationship is represented by—

   (a) a strip of a gilt-edged security, or

   (b) any other gilt-edged security.

(2) Subsections (3) and (4) apply if a person exchanges a gilt-edged security for strips of that security.

(3) The security is treated as having been redeemed at the time of the exchange by the payment to that person of its market value.

(4) The person is treated as having acquired each strip for an amount equal to—

$$A \times \frac{B}{C}$$

where—

   A is the market value of the security at the time of the exchange,

   B is the market value of the strip at that time, and

   C is the total of the market values at that time of all the strips received in the exchange.

(5) Subsections (6) and (7) apply if strips of a gilt-edged security are consolidated into a single gilt-edged security by being exchanged by any person for that security.

(6) Each strip is treated as having been redeemed at the time of the exchange by the payment to that person of the amount equal to its market value.

(7) The person is treated as having acquired the security for the amount equal to the total of the market values of all the strips given in the exchange.

(8) For the meaning of "market value" and "strip" in relation to securities, see section 402 and section 403 respectively.

402 Market value of securities

(1) References in section 401 to the market value of a security given or received in exchange for another are references to its market value at the time of the exchange.

(2) The Treasury may by regulations make provision for the purposes of section 401 and this section as to the way of determining the market value at any time of—

   (*a*) any strip, or

   (*b*) any other gilt-edged security.

(3) The regulations may make—

   (*a*) different provision for different cases, and

   (*b*) incidental, supplemental, consequential and transitional provision and savings.

403 Meaning of "strip"

(1) In sections 401 and 402 "strip", in relation to a gilt-edged security, means a security issued under the National Loans Act 1968 (c 13) which meets conditions A, B and C.

(2) Condition A is that the security is issued for the purpose of representing the right to or of securing—

   (*a*) a payment corresponding to a payment of interest or principal remaining to be made under the gilt-edged security, or

   (*b*) two or more payments each corresponding to a payment to be so made.

(3) Condition B is that the security is issued in conjunction with the issue of one or more other securities which, together with that security—

   (*a*) represent the right to, or

   (*b*) secure,

payments corresponding to every payment remaining to be made under the gilt-edged security.

(4) Condition C is that the security is not itself a security that—

   (*a*) represents the right to, or

   (*b*) secures,

payments corresponding to a part of every payment remaining to be made under the gilt-edged security.

(5) After the balance has been struck for a dividend on a gilt-edged security, a payment to be made in respect of that dividend is treated for the purposes of conditions A, B and C as not being a payment remaining to be made under that security.

404 Restriction on deductions etc relating to FOTRA securities

(1) A company which meets conditions A and B is not to bring into account for the purposes of this Part—

   (*a*) any amount relating to changes in the value of a FOTRA security, or

   (*b*) any debit in respect of the loan relationship represented by the security, including any expenses related to holding the security or any transaction concerning it.

(2) Condition A is that the company is the beneficial owner of the security.

(3) Condition B is that the company is a company which would be exempt from corporation tax on the security under section 1279 (exemption of profits from FOTRA securities).

(4) In this section "FOTRA security" has the same meaning as in that section (see section 1280(1)).

405 Certain non-UK residents with interest on 3½% War Loan 1952 or After

(1) This section applies if—

   (*a*) in any accounting period a non-UK resident company carries on a business in the United Kingdom—

     (i) consisting of banking or insurance, or

     (ii) consisting wholly or partly of dealing in securities, and

   (*b*) in calculating the profits of the business for the period any amount is disregarded as a result of section 1279 (exemption of profits from FOTRA securities) because of a condition subject to which any 3½% War Loan 1952 or After was issued.

(2) Interest on money borrowed for the purposes of the business is to be brought into account as a debit for the purposes of this Part for that period only so far as it exceeds the ineligible amount.

(3) The ineligible amount is found as follows—

Step 1

Add together all sums borrowed for the purposes of the business and still owing in the accounting period.

Step 2

Deduct any sums carrying interest that is not brought into account as a debit under this Part (otherwise than because of subsection (2)).

Step 3

If the amount found at Step 2 exceeds the total cost of the 3½% War Loan 1952 Or After held for the purposes of the business in the accounting period, deduct the excess from that amount.
Step 4
Calculate the average rate of interest in the accounting period on money borrowed for the purposes of the business.
Step 5
Calculate the amount of interest payable on the amount found at Step 3 at the rate found at Step 4 for the accounting period.
The result is the ineligible amount.
(4) If the company's holding of 3½% War Loan 1952 Or After has fluctuated during the accounting period, the total cost for the purposes of Step 3 is taken to be—

$$C \times \frac{AH}{TH}$$

where—
> C is the cost of acquisition of the initial holding (if any) and any holdings acquired during the accounting period,
> AH is the average holding in that period, and
> TH is the total of the initial holding (if any) and any holdings acquired during the accounting period.

(5) In subsection (4) "initial holding" means the holding held by the company at the beginning of the accounting period.

Deeply discounted securities: connected companies and close companies

406 Introduction

(1) The following sections deal with deeply discounted securities—
> (a) sections 407 and 408 (deeply discounted securities where companies have a connection),[1]
> (b) sections 409 to 411 (deeply discounted securities of close companies), and
> (c) section 412 (persons indirectly standing in the position of creditor).

(2) In this section and sections [409][1] to 412 "deeply discounted security" has the same meaning as in Chapter 8 of Part 4 of ITTOIA 2005 (profits from deeply discounted securities) (see section 430 of that Act).
(3) In sections [409][1] to 412 "the discount" means the difference between—
> (a) the issue price of the security, and
> (b) the amount payable on redemption.

(4) The provisions of Chapter 8 of Part 4 of ITTOIA 2005 apply for the purposes of this section and sections [409][1] to 412 for determining the difference between the issue price of a security and the amount payable on redemption as they apply for the purposes of section 430 of that Act.

Amendments—[1]   Sub-s (1)(a) repealed, and in sub-ss (2), (3), (4) reference substituted for reference "407", by FA 2015 s 25(1), (5) with effect in relation to debtor relationships entered into by a company on or after 3 December 2014, and in relation to debtor relationships entered into by a company before 3 December 2014, where the relevant period (within the meaning of CTA 2009 s 407) begins on or after 1 January 2016. For accounting periods straddling 1 January 2016, see FA 2015 s 25(9). For debtor relationships/deeply discounted securities entered into/issued by a company before 3 December 2014 and modified on or after 3 December 2014 and before 1 January 2016, see FA 2015 s 25(10)–(14).

409 Postponement until redemption of debits for close companies' deeply discounted securities

(1) This section applies for any accounting period ("the relevant period") if—
> (a) a debtor relationship of a close company ("the issuing company") is represented by a deeply discounted security it has issued,
> (b) at any time in the period there is a person [("C")][1] who stands in the position of a creditor as respects the security and is—
>> (i) a participator in the issuing company,
>> (ii) an associate of such a participator,
>> (iii) a company of which such a participator has control,
>> (iv) a person who controls a company which is such a participator,
>> (v) an associate of a person within sub-paragraph (iv), or
>> (vi) a company controlled by a person within sub-paragraph (iv),
> (c) the period is not the accounting period in which the security is redeemed, and
> (d) this section is not disapplied by section 410
[and, where it applies, the non-qualifying territory condition is met.][1]
(2) The debits which are to be brought into account for the purposes of this Part by the issuing company in respect of the loan relationship are to be adjusted so that debits relating to the amount of the discount that is referable to the relevant period ("relevant debits")—
> (a) are not brought into account for the relevant period, but
> (b) are brought into account for the accounting period in which the security is redeemed.

(3) If there is a person within subsection (1)(*b*) for only part of the relevant period, subsection (2) applies only to the appropriate proportion of the relevant debits.

(4) In subsection (3) "the appropriate proportion" means the proportion that the part of the relevant period for which there is such a person bears to the whole of that period.

(5) The amount of the discount that is referable to the relevant period is the amount of it which would be brought into account for the purposes of this Part for the relevant period in the case of the issuing company, apart from subsections (2) and (3).

(6) For the meaning of other expressions used in this section, see—

    (*a*) section 411 (interpretation of this section), and

    (*b*) section 412 (persons indirectly standing in the position of creditor).

Modification—Sub-s (2) modified, in relation to securities held before 1 October 2002, so as to apply as if FA 1996 Sch 9 para 18(2), instead of preventing the bringing of amounts into account for any accounting period before that in which the security was redeemed, had provided for the deferred amount to be brought into account for the accounting period in which the security was redeemed rather than for the relevant period, by CTA 2009 s 1325, Sch 2 para 59(3), (4).

Cross-references—See CTA 2009 Sch 2 para 65 (deeply discounted securities of close companies: discounts for periods beginning before 1 April 2007).

Amendments—[1]   In sub-s (1) words inserted by FA 2009 s 41, Sch 20 paras 1, 7 where the actual accrual period (within the meaning of CTA 2009 Pt 5 Ch 8), or the relevant period (within the meaning of CTA 2009 ss 407(1), 409(1)), begins on or after 1 April 2009, subject to transitional provisions: FA 2009 Sch 20 para 9.

410 Exceptions to section 409

(1) Section 409 does not apply for any accounting period ("the relevant period") if any of the following conditions are met—

    (*a*) the corresponding creditor relationship conditions (see subsection (2)),

    (*b*) the CIS-based close company conditions (see subsection (3)), or

    (*c*) the CIS limited partnership conditions (see subsection (4)).

(2) The corresponding creditor relationship conditions are that—

    (*a*) at all times in the relevant period when there is a person within section 409(1)(*b*), that person is a company, and

    (*b*) credits representing the full amount of the discount that is referable to the period are brought into account for the purposes of this Part for any accounting period in respect of the corresponding creditor relationship (see section 412(3)).

(3) The CIS-based close company conditions are that—

    (*a*) the issuing company is a CIS-based close company,

    (*b*) at no time in the relevant period when there is a person within section 409(1)(*b*) is that person resident [for tax purposes][1] in a non-qualifying territory, and

    (*c*) the issuing company is a small or medium-sized enterprise for the relevant period.

(4) The CIS limited partnership conditions are that—

    (*a*) the debt is one which is owed to, or to persons acting for, a CIS limited partnership,

    (*b*) no member of that partnership is resident [for tax purposes][1] in a non-qualifying territory at any time in the relevant period when there is a person within section 409(1)(*b*),

    (*c*) the issuing company has received written notice from the partnership containing information from which it appears that the condition in paragraph (*b*) is met, and

    (*d*) the issuing company is a small or medium-sized enterprise for the relevant period.

[(4A) The non-qualifying territory condition applies if C is a company; and the non-qualifying territory condition is that C is—

    (*a*) resident for tax purposes in a non-qualifying territory at any time in the relevant period, or

    (*b*) effectively managed in a non-taxing non-qualifying territory at any such time.][1]

(5) In this section—

    "CIS-based close company" means a company that would not be a close company apart from the rights and powers of one or more partners in a CIS limited partnership being attributed to another of the partners under [section 451(4) to (6) of CTA 2010 because of section 448(1)(*a*) of that Act][2],

    "CIS limited partnership" means a limited partnership—

        (*a*) which is a collective investment scheme, or

        (*b*) which would be a collective investment scheme if it were not a body corporate,

    "issuing company" has the same meaning as in section 409 (see subsection (1)(*a*) of that section),

    "non-qualifying territory" has the meaning given by [section 173 of TIOPA 2010][3] (provision not at arm's length),

    ["resident for tax purposes" means liable, under the law of the non-qualifying territory, to tax there by reason of domicile, residence or place of management, and][1]

    "small or medium-sized enterprise" has the meaning given by [section 172 of TIOPA 2010][3].

[(5A) For the purposes of this section, a non-qualifying territory is "non-taxing" if companies are not under its law liable to tax by reason of domicile, residence or place of management.][1]

(6) For the meaning of "corresponding creditor relationship", see section 412 (persons indirectly standing in the position of creditor).

Amendments—[1]   In sub-ss (3)(*b*), (4)(*b*) words inserted; sub-s (4A), (5A) inserted; and words in sub-s (5) and definition of "resident" substituted, by FA 2009 s 41, Sch 20 paras 1, 8 where the actual accrual period (within the meaning of CTA 2009 Pt 5 Ch 8), or the relevant period (within the meaning of CTA 2009 ss 407(1), 409(1)), begins on or after 1 April 2009, subject to transitional provisions: FA 2009 Sch 20 para 9.

[2]   In sub-s (5), in the definition of "CIS-based close company", words substituted for words "section 416(6) of ICTA because of section 417(3)(*a*) of that Act" by CTA 2010 s 1177, Sch 1 para 613. CTA 2010 has effect for corporation tax purposes for accounting periods ending on or after 1 April 2010, and for income and capital gains tax purposes for the tax year 2010–11 and subsequent tax years.

[3]   In sub-s (5) in the definition of "non-qualifying territory" words "paragraph 5E of Schedule 28AA to ICTA" substituted and in the definition of "small or medium-sized enterprise" words "paragraph 5D of that Schedule" substituted by TIOPA 2010 s 501, Sch 8 paras 123, 131. TIOPA 2010 has effect for corporation tax purposes for accounting periods ending on or after 1 April 2010, for income and capital gains tax purposes for the tax year 2010–11 and subsequent tax years, and for petroleum revenue tax purposes for chargeable periods beginning on or after 1 July 2010.

411 Interpretation of section 409

(1) Section 472 (meaning of "control") applies for the purposes of section 409 and this section.

(2) A person who is a participator in a company which controls another company is treated for the purposes of section 409 as being a participator in that other company also.

(3) Subject to that, in section 409 and this section "participator", in relation to a company, means a person who is a participator in the company [within the meaning given by section 454 of CTA 2010][1], but not a person who is [such a participator][1] just because of being a loan creditor of the company.

(4) In determining whether a person who carries on the trade of banking is a participator in a company for the purposes of section 409 and this section, securities of the company acquired by the person in the ordinary course of the person's business are ignored.

Amendments—[1]   In sub-s (3) words substituted for words "for the purposes of Part 11 of ICTA because of section 417 of that Act" and "a participator for those purposes" by CTA 2010 s 1177, Sch 1 para 614. CTA 2010 has effect for corporation tax purposes for accounting periods ending on or after 1 April 2010, and for income and capital gains tax purposes for the tax year 2010–11 and subsequent tax years.

412 Persons indirectly standing in the position of creditor

(1) For the purposes of sections 407(1)(*b*) and 409 a person is treated as standing in the position of a creditor if the person indirectly stands in that position by reference to a series of loan relationships or relevant money debts.

(2) If a company ("C") is so treated for the purposes of section 407(1)(*b*), the reference in section 407(1)(*e*) to the corresponding creditor relationship is a reference to C's creditor relationship.

(3) If a person ("P") is so treated for the purposes of section 409, the reference in section 410(2)(*b*) to the corresponding creditor relationship is a reference to P's creditor relationship.

(4) In subsection (1) "relevant money debt" means a money debt which would be a loan relationship if a company directly stood in the position of creditor or debtor.

Funding bonds

413 Issue of funding bonds

(1) This section applies to the issue of funding bonds to a creditor in respect of a liability to pay interest on a debt incurred by a body corporate, a government, a public institution or other public authority.

(2) The issue is treated for the purposes of the Corporation Tax Acts as if it were the payment of so much of that interest as equals the market value of the bonds at their issue.

(3) In this section "funding bonds" includes any bonds, stocks, shares, securities or certificates of indebtedness [(but does not include any instrument providing for payment in the form of goods or services or a voucher)][1].

Amendments—[1]   Words in sub-s (3) inserted by FA 2013 s 27, Sch 11 para 11 with effect in relation to any payment of interest made on or after 17 July 2013.

414 Redemption of funding bonds

(1) The redemption of funding bonds is not treated as the payment of interest on a debt for the purposes of the Corporation Tax Acts if their issue was treated as the payment of interest on the debt under—

(*a*) section 413, or

(*b*) section 380 of ITTOIA 2005 (which makes provision corresponding to section 413 for income tax purposes).

(2) In this section "funding bonds" includes any bonds, stocks, shares, securities or certificates of indebtedness.

Derivatives

415 Loan relationships with embedded derivatives

(1) This section applies if in accordance with generally accepted accounting practice a company treats the rights and liabilities under a loan relationship to which it is a party as divided between—

(*a*) rights and liabilities under a loan relationship ("the host contract"), and

(*b*) rights and liabilities under one or more derivative financial instruments or equity instruments.

(2) The company is treated for the purposes of this Part as a party to a loan relationship whose rights and liabilities consist only of those of the host contract.

(3) For the corresponding treatment of the rights and liabilities within subsection (1)(*b*), see section 585 (loan relationships with embedded derivatives).

416 Election for application of sections 415 and 585

(1) This section applies if—

    (*a*) a company is subject to old UK GAAP for a period of account,

    (*b*) at the beginning of its first relevant period of account the company did not hold any assets ("relevant assets") which it is not permitted under old UK GAAP to treat as mentioned in section 415(1),

    (*c*) the company subsequently acquires one or more relevant assets (to which sections 415 and 585 do not apply because of the company being subject to old UK GAAP), and

    (*d*) the company would have been permitted to treat the relevant assets as mentioned in section 415(1) if it had been subject to—

        (i) international accounting standards, or

        (ii) new UK GAAP.

(2) The company may elect that this Part and Part 7 (derivative contracts) should apply as if sections 415 and 585 did apply.

(3) The election has effect in relation to all relevant assets held by the company including those subsequently acquired, except as provided in subsection (4).

(4) . . .

(5) If an election is made under this section, sections 315 to 318 (adjustments on change of accounting policy) apply as if there were a change of accounting policy consisting of the company treating its relevant assets as mentioned in section 415(1) as from the date the election has effect.

(6) See also section 613(4) (which makes provision corresponding to subsection (5) for the purposes of Part 7).

(7) In this section—

    "first relevant period of account", in relation to a company, means the first period of account of the company beginning on or after 1 January 2005 (the first period in relation to which section 94A of FA 1996 (which is rewritten in section 415) had effect),

    "old UK GAAP" means UK generally accepted accounting practice as it applied for periods of account beginning before 1 January 2005, and

    "new UK GAAP" means UK generally accepted accounting practice as it applies for periods of account beginning on or after that date.

(8) Section 417 makes further provision about elections under this section.

Amendments—[1] Sub-s (4) repealed by FA 2011 s 30, Sch 5 para 7(2)(*c*) with effect in relation to loan relationships to which a company is a party (or to which it is treated as a party under s 418(6A)), on or after 19 July 2011 (but subject to FA 2011 Sch 5 para 7(4)).

    (4) An election made on or after 12 March 2008 does not have effect in relation to any relevant assets in the case of which section 418 (loan relationships treated differently by connected debtor and creditor) applies.

417 Further provisions about elections under section 416

(1) An election under section 416 must be made not later than 90 days after the acquisition of the relevant assets or, if there is more than one acquisition, the first of them.

(2) The election is irrevocable.

(3) The election has effect from the beginning of the period of account in which the first relevant asset is acquired.

(4) In this section "relevant assets" has the same meaning as in section 416.

Options etc

420 Assumptions where options etc apply

(1) This section applies if—

    (*a*) the answer to any question specified in subsection (2)—

        (i) depends on the exercise of an option by a party to a loan relationship ("A") or A's associate, or

        (ii) is otherwise under the control of A or A's associate, and

    (*b*) an amortised cost basis of accounting applies for an accounting period.

(2) The questions are—

    (*a*) whether any amount will become due under the relationship after the period ends,

    (*b*) how much will become due under it after the period ends, and

    (*c*) when after the end of the period an amount will become due under the relationship.

(3) In determining the credits and debits to be brought into account for the accounting period in accordance with an amortised cost basis, the assumption in subsection (4) is to be made.

(4) The assumption is that A or A's associate will exercise the power to determine whether and on what date any amount will become due in the way which appears to be the most advantageous to A.

(ii) condition C in section 421 is met in relation to that transfer.

(2) For the purposes of this Part such debits and credits are to be brought into account as would be brought into account if the reorganisation were a disposal of the asset representing the loan relationship for consideration of an amount equal to its notional carrying value.

(3) For the purposes of this section, the notional carrying value of that asset is the amount which would have been [its tax-adjusted carrying value based on][1] the accounts of the original holder if a period of account had ended immediately before the date when the reorganisation occurred.

(4) In this section—

. . .[1]

"original holder" means a person holding the original shares immediately before the reorganisation,

"original shares" has the meaning given by section 126(1) of TCGA 1992 (application of sections 126 to 131 of that Act), and

"reorganisation" includes anything to which sections 127 to 130 of that Act apply as if it were a reorganisation.

(5) This section is subject to—

(a) section 425 (original holder using fair value accounting), and

(b) section 429 (disapplication of Chapter where transparent entities involved).

Amendments—[1] In sub-s (3) words substituted for words "its carrying value in", and in sub-s (4) definition of "carrying value" repealed, by F(No 2)A 2015 s 32, Sch 7 paras 1, 42 with effect for accounting periods beginning on or after 1 January 2016, subject to transitional rules in F(No 2)A 2015 Sch 7 paras 115 to 129.

425 Original holder using fair value accounting

(1) This section applies instead of section 424 if, in a case where that section would otherwise apply, the original holder is regarded for the purposes of this section as using fair value accounting in respect of the loan relationship constituting or included in the original shares.

(2) The amount which is to be brought into account by the original holder in respect of the reorganisation ("the disposal amount") is the fair value of the asset representing the loan relationship as at the date when the reorganisation occurred, or of the rights under or interest in that relationship as at that date.

(3) For any accounting period in which a successor creditor company is a party to the loan relationship, for the purpose of determining the credits and debits to be brought into account in respect of the relationship for the purposes of this Part, the successor creditor company is treated as if it had acquired the asset representing the loan relationship for consideration of an amount equal to the disposal amount.

(4) Subsections (4) and (5) of section 423 apply for the purposes of this section as they apply for the purposes of that section, but taking the references in that section to the transferor as references to the original holder.

(5) In this section—

"successor creditor company" means a company in relation to which the loan relationship constituting or included in the original shares is a creditor relationship immediately after the reorganisation, and

"original holder" and "original shares" have the same meaning as in section 424.

(6) This section is subject to section 429 (disapplication of Chapter where transparent entities involved).

Exception for tax avoidance cases

426 Tax avoidance etc

(1) This Chapter does not apply in relation to the transfer of business if—

(a) the transfer of business is not effected for genuine commercial reasons, or

(b) the transfer of business forms part of a scheme or arrangements of which the main purpose, or one of the main purposes, is avoiding liability to corporation tax, capital gains tax or income tax.

(2) But subsection (1) does not prevent this Chapter from applying if before the transfer of business—

(a) the companies mentioned in section 421(3)(a), (4)(a) or (5)(a) have applied to the Commissioners for Her Majesty's Revenue and Customs, and

(b) the Commissioners have notified them that they are satisfied that subsection will not have that effect.

427 Procedure on application for clearance

(1) This section applies in relation to an application under section 426(2).

(2) The application must be in writing and must contain particulars of the operations which are to be effected.

(3) The Commissioners for Her Majesty's Revenue and Customs may by notice require the applicant to provide further particulars for the purpose of enabling them to make their decision.

(4) Such a notice may only be given within 30 days of the receipt of the application or of any further particulars previously required under subsection (3).

(5) If such a notice is not complied with within 30 days or such longer period as the Commissioners for Her Majesty's Revenue and Customs may allow, they need not proceed further on the application.

428 Decision on application for clearance

(1) The Commissioners for Her Majesty's Revenue and Customs must notify their decision on an application under section 426(2) to the applicant—

    (*a*) within 30 days of receiving the application, or

    (*b*) if they give a notice under section 427(3), within 30 days of the notice being complied with.

(2) If the Commissioners for Her Majesty's Revenue and Customs—

    (*a*) notify the applicant that they are not satisfied as mentioned in section 426(2)(*b*), or

    (*b*) do not notify their decision to the applicant within the time required by subsection (1),

the applicant may within 30 days of the notification or of that time require them to transmit the application to the tribunal, together with any notice given and further particulars provided under section 427(3).

(3) In that case any notification by the tribunal has effect for the purposes of section 426(2)(*b*) as if it were a notification by the Commissioners for Her Majesty's Revenue and Customs.

(4) If any particulars provided under section 427 do not fully and accurately disclose all facts and considerations material for the decision—

    (*a*) of the Commissioners for Her Majesty's Revenue and Customs, or

    (*b*) of the tribunal,

any resulting notification by the Commissioners for Her Majesty's Revenue and Customs or the tribunal is void.

Transparent entities

429 Disapplication of Chapter where transparent entities involved

(1) This Chapter does not apply in relation to the transfer of business if the transferor is a transparent entity.

(2) If any transferee is a transparent entity, sections 424 and 425 (reorganisations involving loan relationships) do not apply.

(3) In this section "transparent entity" means a company which is resident in a member State other than the United Kingdom and does not have an ordinary share capital.

(4) For the meaning of "resident in a member State", see section 430.

Prospective amendments—In sub-s (3) words "other than the United Kingdom" to be repealed, and in sub-s (4) words "relevant state" to be substituted for words "member State", by the Taxes (Amendments) (EU Exit) Regulations, SI 2019/689 reg 16(1), (5) with effect from Implementation Period completion day (see EU(WA)A 2020 Sch 5 para 1(1)).

Interpretation

430 Interpretation

(1) In this Chapter "company" means any entity listed as a company in [Part A of Annex I][1] to the Mergers Directive.

(2) For the purposes of this Chapter, a company is resident in a member State if—

    (*a*) it is within a charge to tax under the law of the State as being resident for that purpose, and

    (*b*) it is not regarded, for the purpose of any double taxation relief arrangements to which the State is a party, as resident in a territory not within a member State.

Commentary—*Simon's Taxes* **D1.770**.

Amendments—[1]   In sub-s (1) words substituted for "the Annex" by SI 2011/1431 reg 4(2) with effect from 1 July 2011.

Prospective amendments—In sub-s (2) words "relevant state" to be substituted for words "member State" in both places where the expression occurs, and words "relevant state" to be substituted for words "State", in both places where the word occurs other than as part of the expression "member State", by the Taxes (Amendments) (EU Exit) Regulations, SI 2019/689 reg 16(1), (6) with effect from Implementation Period completion day (see EU(WA)A 2020 Sch 5 para 1(1)).

CHAPTER 14

EUROPEAN CROSS-BORDER MERGERS

Introduction

431 Introduction to Chapter

(1) This Chapter applies if the following conditions are met—

    (*a*) conditions A to D,

    (*b*) in the case of a merger within subsection (3)(*a*), (*b*) or (*c*), condition E, and

    (*c*) in the case of a merger within subsection (3)(*c*) or (*d*), condition F,

but see section 437 (tax avoidance etc) and section 438 (disapplication of Chapter where transparent entities involved).

(2) Sections 435 and 436 (reorganisations involving loan relationships) also apply in cases that would be within subsection (1) apart from condition D not being met if, in addition to the conditions in section 435(1)(*a*) and (*b*), condition G is met in relation to a transfer in the course of the merger in which the reorganisation in question occurs.

(3) Condition A is that—

(*a*) an SE is formed by the merger of two or more companies in accordance with Articles 2(1) and 17(2)(*a*) or (*b*) of Council Regulation (EC) No. 2157/2001 on the Statute for a European company (Societas Europaea),

(*b*) an SCE is formed by the merger of two or more co-operative societies, at least one of which is a society registered under the [the Co-operative and Community Benefit Societies Act 2014][1], in accordance with Articles 2(1) and 19 of Council Regulation (EC) No. 1435/2003 on the Statute for a European Co-operative Society (SCE),

(*c*) a merger is effected by the transfer by one or more companies of all their assets and liabilities to a single existing company, or

(*d*) a merger is effected by the transfer by two or more companies of all their assets and liabilities to a single new company (other than an SE or an SCE) in exchange for the issue by the transferee, to each person holding shares in or debentures of a transferor, of shares or debentures.

(4) Condition B is that each merging company is resident in a member State.

(5) Condition C is that the merging companies are not all resident in the same State.

(6) Condition D is that immediately after the merger the transferee is within the charge to corporation tax.

(7) Condition E is that—

(*a*) the transfer of assets and liabilities to the transferee in the course of the merger is made in exchange for the issue of shares or debentures by the transferee to each person holding shares in or debentures of a transferor, or

(*b*) that transfer is not so made only because, and only so far as, the transferee is prevented from so issuing such shares or debentures by section 658 of the Companies Act 2006 (c 46) (general rule against limited company acquiring own shares) or by a corresponding provision of the law of another member State preventing such an issue.

(8) Condition F is that in the course of the merger each transferor ceases to exist without being in liquidation (within the meaning given by section 247 of the Insolvency Act 1986 (c 45)).

(9) Condition G is that—

(*a*) in the course of the merger a company resident in the United Kingdom ("company A") transfers to a company resident in another member State all assets and liabilities relating to a business which company A carried on in a member State other than the United Kingdom through a permanent establishment, and

(*b*) that transfer includes the transfer of an asset or liability representing a loan relationship.

(10) In this Chapter, "the merger" and "the merging companies" have the same meaning as in this section.

(11) See—

(*a*) section 432 for the meaning of "the transferee" and "transferor", and

(*b*) section 439 for the meaning of "company", "co-operative society" and "resident in a member State".

Amendments—[1]   In each place where they occur in this Act, words substituted for words "registered industrial and provident society", "the Industrial and Provident Societies Act 1965" and "industrial and provident societies", by the Co-operative and Community Benefit Societies Act 2014 s 151, Sch 4 paras 140–143 with effect from 1 August 2014 and subject to transitional provisions and provisions preserving the continuity of the law in Sch 5 of that Act.

Prospective amendments—In sub-s (4) words "relevant state" to be substituted for words "member State", in sub-s (5) words "relevant state" to be substituted for word "State", in sub-s (7)(*b*) word "a" to be substituted for word "another", in sub-s (9)(*a*) word "a" to be substituted for word "another" and words "other than the United Kingdom" to be repealed, in sub-s (10) words from ""the merger"" to the end to become para (*a*) and para (*b*) to be inserted, and in sub-s (11)(*b*) words "relevant state" to be substituted for words "member State", by the Taxes (Amendments) (EU Exit) Regulations, SI 2019/689 reg 16(1), (7) with effect from Implementation Period completion day (see EU(WA)A 2020 Sch 5 para 1(1)). Sub-s (10)(*b*) to read as follows—

"(*b*) "relevant state" means the United Kingdom or a member State.".

432 Meaning of "the transferee" and "transferor"

(1) In this Chapter, "the transferee" means—

(*a*) in relation to a merger within section 431(3)(*a*), the SE,

(*b*) in relation to a merger within section 431(3)(*b*), the SCE, and

(*c*) in relation to a merger within section 431(3)(*c*) or (*d*), the company to which assets and liabilities are transferred.

(2) In this Chapter "transferor" means—

(*a*) in relation to a merger within section 431(3)(*a*), a company merging to form the SE,

(*b*) in relation to a merger within section 431(3)(*b*), a co-operative society merging to form the SCE, and

(c) in relation to a merger within section 431(3)(c) or (d), a company transferring all its assets and liabilities.

Transfers of loan relationships at notional carrying value

433 Transfer of loan relationship at notional carrying value

(1) This section applies if in the course of the merger a transferor transfers an asset or liability representing a loan relationship to the transferee.

(2) For the purpose of determining the credits and debits to be brought into account in respect of the loan relationship in accordance with this Part, the transferor and the transferee are treated as having entered into the transfer of that asset or liability for consideration of an amount equal to the notional carrying value of the asset or liability.

(3) For the purposes of this section—

    (a) . . . [1]

    (b) "notional carrying value", in relation to an asset or liability, means the amount which would have been [its tax-adjusted carrying value based on][1] the accounts of the transferor if a period of account had ended immediately before the date when the transferor ceased to be a party to the loan relationship.

(4) This section is subject to section 434.

Amendments—[1]   Sub-s (3)(a) repealed, and in sub-s (3)(b) words substituted for words "its carrying value in" by F(No 2)A 2015 s 32, Sch 7 paras 1, 43 with effect for accounting periods beginning on or after 1 January 2016, subject to transitional rules in F(No 2)A 2015 Sch 7 paras 115 to 129.

434 Transferor using fair value accounting

(1) This section applies instead of section 433 if, in a case where that section would otherwise apply, the transferor is regarded for the purposes of this section as using fair value accounting in respect of the loan relationship (see subsection (4)).

(2) The amount which is to be brought into account by the transferor in respect of the transfer of the asset or liability mentioned in section 433(1) ("the transferor's amount") is—

    (a) if an asset is to be brought into account, its fair value as at the date when the transferee becomes a party to the loan relationship, or the fair value of the rights under or interest in it as at that date, and

    (b) if a liability is to be brought into account, its fair value as at that date.

(3) For any accounting period in which the transferee is a party to the loan relationship, for the purpose of determining the credits and debits to be brought into account in respect of it for the purposes of this Part, the transferee is treated as if it had acquired the asset or liability representing the relationship for consideration of an amount equal to the transferor's amount.

(4) The transferor is regarded for the purposes of this section as using fair value accounting in respect of the loan relationship only if the credits and debits to be brought into account for the purposes of this Part as respects the relationship are determined on that basis.

(5) It does not matter for the purposes of subsection (4) if the transferor does not otherwise use fair value accounting in respect of the loan relationship.

435 Reorganisations involving loan relationships

(1) This section applies if—

    (a) sections 127 to 130 of TCGA 1992 (reorganisations: equation of original shares and new holding)—

        (i) apply in relation to a reorganisation, or

        (ii) would so apply but for section 116(5) of that Act (which disapplies those sections where the original shares or the new holding consists of or includes a qualifying corporate bond),

    (b) the original shares consist of or include an asset representing a loan relationship, and

    (c) section 433 or 434 applies in relation to a transfer in the course of the merger in which the reorganisation occurs or, in a case where those sections would apply apart from condition D in section 431 not being met, condition G in that section is met in relation to such a transfer.

(2) For the purposes of this Part such debits and credits are to be brought into account as would be brought into account if the reorganisation were a disposal of the asset representing the loan relationship for consideration of an amount equal to its notional carrying value.

(3) For the purposes of this section, the notional carrying value of that asset is the amount which would have been [its tax-adjusted carrying value based on][1] the accounts of the original holder if a period of account had ended immediately before the date when the reorganisation occurred.

(4) In this section—

    . . . [1]

    "original holder" means a person holding the original shares immediately before the reorganisation,

    "original shares" has the meaning given by section 126(1) of TCGA 1992 (application of sections 126 to 131 of that Act), and "reorganisation" includes anything to which sections 127 to 130 of that Act apply as if it were a reorganisation.

(5) This section is subject to—

(a) section 436 (original holder using fair value accounting), and

(b) section 438 (disapplication of Chapter where transparent entities involved).

Amendments—[1]   In sub-s (3) words substituted for words "its carrying value in", and in sub-s (4) definition of "carrying value" repealed, by F(No 2)A 2015 s 32, Sch 7 paras 1, 44 with effect for accounting periods beginning on or after 1 January 2016, subject to transitional rules in F(No 2)A 2015 Sch 7 paras 115 to 129.

436 Original holder using fair value accounting

(1) This section applies instead of section 435 if, in a case where that section would otherwise apply, the original holder is regarded for the purposes of this section as using fair value accounting in respect of the loan relationship constituting or included in the original shares.

(2) The amount which is to be brought into account by the original holder in respect of the reorganisation ("the disposal amount") is the fair value of the asset representing the loan relationship as at the date when the reorganisation occurred, or of the rights under or interest in that relationship as at that date.

(3) For any accounting period in which a successor creditor company is a party to the loan relationship, for the purpose of determining the credits and debits to be brought into account in respect of the relationship for the purposes of this Part, the successor creditor company is treated as if it had acquired the asset representing the loan relationship for consideration of an amount equal to the disposal amount.

(4) Subsections (4) and (5) of section 434 apply for the purposes of this section as they apply for the purposes of that section, but taking the references in that section to the transferor as references to the original holder.

(5) In this section—

"successor creditor company" means a company in relation to which the loan relationship constituting or included in the original shares is a creditor relationship immediately after the reorganisation, and

"original holder" and "original shares" have the same meaning as in section 435.

(6) This section is subject to section 438 (disapplication of Chapter where transparent entities involved).

Exception for tax avoidance cases

437 Tax avoidance etc

(1) This Chapter does not apply in relation to the merger if—

(a) the merger is not effected for genuine commercial reasons, or

(b) the merger forms part of a scheme or arrangements of which the main purpose, or one of the main purposes, is avoiding liability to corporation tax, capital gains tax or income tax.

(2) But subsection (1) does not prevent this Chapter from applying if before the merger—

(a) any of the merging companies has applied to the Commissioners for Her Majesty's Revenue and Customs, and

(b) the Commissioners have notified the merging companies that they are satisfied that subsection will not have that effect.

(3) Sections 427 and 428 have effect in relation to subsection (2) as in relation to section 426(2), taking the references in section 428 to section 426(2)(b) as references to subsection (2)(b) of this section.

Transparent entities

438 Disapplication of Chapter where transparent entities involved

(1) This section applies if one or more of the merging companies is a transparent entity.

(2) If as a result of the merger the assets and liabilities of a transparent entity are transferred to another company, this Chapter does not apply in relation to the transfer.

(3) If as a result of the merger the assets and liabilities of one or more other companies are transferred to a transparent entity, sections 435 and 436 do not apply to the new holding.

(4) In this section—

"new holding" has the meaning given by section 126(1) of TCGA 1992 (application of sections 126 to 131 of that Act), and

"transparent entity" means a company which is resident in a member State other than the United Kingdom and does not have an ordinary share capital.

Prospective amendments—In sub-s (4) in the definition of "transparent entity" words "other than the United Kingdom" to be repealed by the Taxes (Amendments) (EU Exit) Regulations, SI 2019/689 reg 16(1), (8) with effect from Implementation Period completion day (see EU(WA)A 2020 Sch 5 para 1(1)).

Interpretation

439 Interpretation

(1) In this Chapter—

"company" means any entity listed as a company in [Part A of Annex I][1] to the Mergers Directive, and

"co-operative society" means a society registered under the [the Co-operative and Community Benefit Societies Act 2014][2] or a similar society governed by the law of a member State other than the United Kingdom.

(2) For the purposes of this Chapter, a company is resident in a member State if—

    (a) it is within a charge to tax under the law of the State as being resident for that purpose, and

    (b) it is not regarded, for the purpose of any double taxation relief arrangements to which the State is a party, as resident in a territory not within a member State.

Amendments—[1]   In sub-s (1) words substituted for "the Annex" by the Corporation Tax (Implementation of the Mergers Directive) Regulations, SI 2011//1431 reg 4(3) with effect from 1 July 2011.

[2]   In each place where they occur in this Act, words substituted for words "registered industrial and provident society", "the Industrial and Provident Societies Act 1965" and "industrial and provident societies", by the Co-operative and Community Benefit Societies Act 2014 s 151, Sch 4 paras 140–143 with effect from 1 August 2014 and subject to transitional provisions and provisions preserving the continuity of the law in Sch 5 of that Act.

Prospective amendments—In sub-s (1) in the definition of "co-operative society" words "other than the United Kingdom" to be repealed, and in sub-s (2) words "relevant state" to be substituted for words "member State", in both places where the expression occurs, and words "relevant state" to be substituted for word "State", in both places where the expression occurs other than as part of the expression "member State", by the Taxes (Amendments) (EU Exit) Regulations, SI 2019/689 reg 16(1), (9) with effect from Implementation Period completion day (see EU(WA)A 2020 Sch 5 para 1(1)).

CHAPTER 15

TAX AVOIDANCE

Introduction

440 Overview of Chapter

(1) This Chapter contains rules connected with tax avoidance.

(2) In particular—

    (a) for rules about unallowable purposes . . . . [2], see sections 441 [and 442][2],

    (b) for rules relating to credits and debits where transactions are not at arm's length (other than credits and debits relating to exchange gains and losses), see sections 444 to 446,

    (c) for rules relating to credits and debits relating to exchange gains and losses where transactions are not at arm's length, see sections 447 to 452,

    (d) for rules about connected parties deriving benefit from creditor relationships, see section 453,

    (e) for rules dealing with tax advantages from resetting interest rates, see section 454, ...[1]

    (f) . . . [1]

    (g) for rules about debits arising as a result of the derecognition of creditor relationships, see section 455A,][1] [and

    (h) for rules dealing with tax avoidance arrangements, see sections 455B to 455D.][2]

Amendments—[1]   In sub-s (2), word ", and" at end of para (e) repealed, and para (g) and preceding word "and" inserted, by FA 2011 s 28, Sch 4 paras 1, 3 with effect in relation to accounting periods beginning on or after 6 December 2010, subject to the transitional provision in FA 2011 Sch 4 para 13(2).

[2]   In sub-s (2)(a) words repealed and substituted, and sub-s (2)(h) and preceding word inserted, by F(No 2)A 2015 s 32, Sch 7 paras 1, 45(a), (c) with effect in relation to arrangements entered into on or after 18 November 2015. Sub-s (2)(f) repealed by F(No 2)A 2015 s 32, Sch 7 paras 1, 45(b) with effect in relation to disposals on or after 18 November 2015.

Unallowable purposes and tax relief schemes

441 Loan relationships for unallowable purposes

(1) This section applies if in any accounting period a loan relationship of a company has an unallowable purpose.

(2) The company may not bring into account for that period for the purposes of this Part so much of any credit in respect of exchange gains from that relationship as on a just and reasonable apportionment is attributable to the unallowable purpose.

(3) The company may not bring into account for that period for the purposes of this Part so much of any debit in respect of that relationship as on a just and reasonable apportionment is attributable to the unallowable purpose.

[(3A) If—

    (a) a credit brought into account for that period for the purposes of this Part by the company would (in the absence of this section) be reduced, and

    (b) the reduction represents an amount which, if it did not reduce a credit, would be brought into account as a debit in respect of that relationship,

subsection (3) applies to the amount of the reduction as if it were an amount that would (in the absence of this section) be brought into account as a debit.][1]

(4) An amount which would be brought into account for the purposes of this Part as respects any matter apart from this section is treated for the purposes of section 464(1) (amounts brought into account under this Part excluded from being otherwise brought into account) as if it were so brought into account.

(5) Accordingly, that amount is not to be brought into account for corporation tax purposes as respects that matter either under this Part or otherwise.

(6) For the meaning of "has an unallowable purpose" and "the unallowable purpose" in this section, see section 442.

Amendments—[1]   Sub-s (3A) inserted by F(No 2)A 2015 s 32, Sch 7 paras 1, 46 with effect for accounting periods beginning on or after 1 January 2016, subject to transitional rules in F(No 2)A 2015 Sch 7 paras 115 to 129.

442 Meaning of "unallowable purpose"

(1) For the purposes of section 441 a loan relationship of a company has an unallowable purpose in an accounting period if, at times during that period, the purposes for which the company—

    (*a*) is a party to the relationship, or

    (*b*) enters into transactions which are related transactions by reference to it,

include a purpose ("the unallowable purpose") which is not amongst the business or other commercial purposes of the company.

[(1A) In subsection (1)(*b*) "related transaction", in relation to a loan relationship, includes anything which equates in substance to a disposal or acquisition of the kind mentioned in section 304(1) (as read with section 304(2)).][1]

(2) If a company is not within the charge to corporation tax in respect of a part of its activities, for the purposes of this section the business and other commercial purposes of the company do not include the purposes of that part.

(3) Subsection (4) applies if a tax avoidance purpose is one of the purposes for which a company—

    (*a*) is a party to a loan relationship at any time, or

    (*b*) enters into a transaction which is a related transaction by reference to a loan relationship of the company.

(4) For the purposes of subsection (1) the tax avoidance purpose is only regarded as a business or other commercial purpose of the company if it is not—

    (*a*) the main purpose for which the company is a party to the loan relationship or, as the case may be, enters into the related transaction, or

    (*b*) one of the main purposes for which it is or does so.

(5) The references in subsections (3) and (4) to a tax avoidance purpose are references to any purpose which consists of securing a tax advantage for the company or any other person.

Amendments—[1]   Sub-s (1A) inserted by F(No 2)A 2015 s 32, Sch 7 paras 1, 47 with effect for accounting periods beginning on or after 1 January 2016, subject to transitional rules in F(No 2)A 2015 Sch 7 paras 115 to 129.

Transactions not at arm's length: general

444 Transactions not at arm's length: general

(1) If—

    (*a*) credits or debits in respect of a loan relationship of a company are to be brought into account for the purposes of this Part in respect of a related transaction, and

    (*b*) that transaction is not a transaction at arm's length,

those credits or debits are to be determined for the purposes of this Part in accordance with the independent terms assumption.

(2) The independent terms assumption is that the transaction was entered into on the terms on which it would have been entered into between knowledgeable and willing parties dealing at arm's length.

(3) This section is subject to section 445 (disapplication of this section where [Part 4 of TIOPA 2010][1] applies).

(4) Subsection (1) does not apply to debits arising from the acquisition of rights under a loan relationship if those rights are acquired for less than market value.

(5) In a case where the related transaction is a transaction within section 336(2) or part of a series of transactions within 336(3) (group transactions), subsection (1) does not apply if—

    (*a*) section 340 (group transfers and transfers of insurance business: transfer at notional carrying value) applies as a result of that transaction or, as the case may be, that series of transactions, or

    (*b*) section 340 would so apply apart from section 341 (transferor using fair value accounting).

(6) Subsection (1) does not apply to exchange gains or losses (but see sections 447 to 452).

Amendments—[1]   In sub-s (3) words "Schedule 28AA to ICTA" substituted by TIOPA 2010 s 501, Sch 8 paras 123, 132. TIOPA 2010 has effect for corporation tax purposes for accounting periods ending on or after 1 April 2010, for income and capital gains tax purposes for the tax year 2010–11 and subsequent tax years, and for petroleum revenue tax purposes for chargeable periods beginning on or after 1 July 2010.

445 Disapplication of section 444 where [Part 4 of TIOPA 2010][1] applies

(1) Section 444 does not apply, and [Part 4 of TIOPA 2010][1] (provision not at arm's length) applies instead, to credits or debits in respect of amounts which—

    (*a*) fall to be adjusted for tax purposes under [that Part][1], or

    (*b*) are within [that Part][1] without falling to be so adjusted (see subsection (3)).

(2) Subsection (1) applies despite section 464 (amounts brought into account under this Part excluded from being otherwise brought into account), but is subject to—

   (*a*) section 340(7) (disapplication of [Part 4 of TIOPA 2010][1] where group member replaces another as party to loan), and

   (*b*) section 447(5) (disapplication of [that Part][1] for exchange gains and losses).

(3) For the purposes of subsection (1), an amount is within [Part 4 of TIOPA 2010][1] without falling to be adjusted under it in a case where—

   [(*a*) the condition in section 147(1)(*a*) of TIOPA 2010 is met,

   (*aa*) the participation condition is met (see subsection (3A)), and][1]

   (*b*) the actual provision does not differ from the arm's length provision.

[(3A) Section 148 of TIOPA 2010 (when the participation condition is met) applies for the purposes of subsection (3)(*aa*) as it applies for the purposes of section 147(1)(*b*) of TIOPA 2010.][1]

(4) For the way in which this Part applies where adjustments are made under [Part 4 of TIOPA 2010][1] see section 446.

(5) In this section "the actual provision" and "the arm's length provision" have the same meaning as in [Part 4 of TIOPA 2010 (see sections 149 and 151 of that Act)][1].

Amendments—[1] In sub–ss (1),(2)(*a*),(3),(4) and the title words "Schedule 28AA to ICTA" substituted, in sub-ss (1)(*a*),(*b*), (2)(*b*) words "that Schedule" substituted, sub-s (3)(*a*) substituted, sub-s (3A) inserted and in sub-s (5) words "Schedule 28AA to ICTA (see paragraph 1 of that Schedule)" substituted by TIOPA 2010 s 501, Sch 8 paras 123, 133. TIOPA 2010 has effect for corporation tax purposes for accounting periods ending on or after 1 April 2010, for income and capital gains tax purposes for the tax year 2010–11 and subsequent tax years, and for petroleum revenue tax purposes for chargeable periods beginning on or after 1 July 2010.

446 Bringing into account adjustments made under [Part 4 of TIOPA 2010][1]

(1) This section deals with the credits and debits which are to be brought into account for the purposes of this Part as a result of [Part 4 of TIOPA 2010][1] (provision not at arm's length) applying in relation to a company's loan relationships or related transactions.

(2) Subsection (3) applies if under [Part 4 of TIOPA 2010][1] an amount ("the imputed amount") is treated as an amount of profits or losses arising to a company from any of its loan relationships or related transactions.

(3) Credits or debits relating to the imputed amount are to be brought into account for the purposes of this Part to the same extent as they would be in the case of an actual amount of such profits or losses.

(4) Subsection (5) applies if under [Part 4 of TIOPA 2010][1] an amount is treated as interest payable under any of a company's loan relationships.

(5) Credits or debits relating to that amount are to be brought into account for the purposes of this Part to the same extent as they would be in the case of an actual amount of such interest.

(6) Subsection (7) applies if under [Part 4 of TIOPA 2010][1] an amount is treated as expenses incurred by a company under or for the purposes of any of its loan relationships or related transactions.

(7) Debits relating to the amount are to be brought into account for the purposes of this Part to the same extent as they would be in the case of an actual amount of such expenses.

[(8) No credit is to be brought into account for the purposes of this Part to the extent that it corresponds to an amount which, as a result of the preceding provisions of this section, has not previously been brought into account as a debit.][2]

Amendments—[1] In sub–ss (1), (2), (4), (6) and the title words "Schedule 28AA to ICTA" substituted by TIOPA 2010 s 501, Sch 8 paras 123, 134. TIOPA 2010 has effect for corporation tax purposes for accounting periods ending on or after 1 April 2010, for income and capital gains tax purposes for the tax year 2010–11 and subsequent tax years, and for petroleum revenue tax purposes for chargeable periods beginning on or after 1 July 2010.

[2] Sub-s (8) inserted by FA 2016 s 49, Sch 7 paras 1, 3 with effect in relation to accounting periods beginning on or after 1 April 2016 (FA 2016 Sch 7 para 12(1)). Where a company has an accounting period beginning before 1 April 2016 and ending on or after that date ("the straddling period") the periods before and after 1 April 2016 are treated as separate accounting periods (FA 2016 Sch 7 para 12(2)).

[Non-market loans

446A Non-market loans

(1) This section applies as respects any accounting period if—

   (*a*) a company has a debtor relationship in the period,

   (*b*) the amount recognised in the company's accounts in respect of the debt at the time the company became party to the debtor relationship was less than the transaction price,

   (*c*) credits in respect of the whole or part of the discount were not brought into account for the purposes of this Part, and

   (*d*) in a case where the creditor is a company, the non-qualifying territory condition is met.

(2) The debits which are to be brought into account for the accounting period for the purposes of this Part by the debtor company in respect of the loan relationship are not to include debits relating to the relevant discount amount, to the extent that that amount is referable to the accounting period.

(3) In this section "relevant discount amount" means—

   (*a*) in a case where credits in respect of the whole of the discount were not brought into account for the purposes of this Part, an amount equal to the whole discount, and

(b) in a case where credits in respect of part of the discount were not brought into account for the purposes of this Part, an amount equal to that part of the discount.

(4) The non-qualifying territory condition referred to in subsection (1)(d) is that the creditor company is—

(a) resident for tax purposes in a non-qualifying territory at any time in the accounting period, or

(b) effectively managed in a non-taxing non-qualifying territory at any such time.

(5) In this section—

"discount" means the difference between the two amounts referred to in subsection (1)(b);

"non-qualifying territory" has the meaning given in section 173 of TIOPA 2010;

"non-taxing non-qualifying territory" means a non-qualifying territory under whose law companies are not liable to tax by reason of domicile, residence or place of management;

"resident for tax purposes" means liable, under the law of the non-qualifying territory, to tax there by reason of domicile, residence or place of management.]¹

Amendments—¹   Section 446A inserted by FA 2016 s 49, Sch 7 paras 1, 2 with effect in relation to accounting periods beginning on or after 1 April 2016 (FA 2016 Sch 7 para 12(1)). Where a company has an accounting period beginning before 1 April 2016 and ending on or after that date ("the straddling period") the periods before and after 1 April 2016 are treated as separate accounting periods (FA 2016 Sch 7 para 12(2)).

Transactions not at arm's length: exchange gains and losses

447 Exchange gains and losses on debtor relationships: loans disregarded under [Part 4 of TIOPA 2010]¹

(1) Subsections (2) and (3) apply if—

(a) a company has a debtor relationship in an accounting period,

(b) an exchange gain or loss arises in the period in respect of a liability representing the relationship, and

(c) as a result of [section 147(3) or (5) of TIOPA 2010]¹ (provision not at arm's length) the profits and losses of the company are calculated for tax purposes for the period as if—

(i) the loan had not been made, or

(ii) part of the loan had not been made.

(2) In a case where subsection (1)(c)(i) applies, the exchange gain or loss must be left out of account in determining the credits or debits to be brought into account for the purposes of this Part.

(3) In a case where subsection (1)(c)(ii) applies, a proportion of the exchange gain or loss must be left out of account in determining those credits or debits.

(4) That proportion is the proportion that the part of the loan that is treated as if it had not been made bears to the whole of the loan.

[(4A) If the debtor relationship is to any extent matched, subsections (2) and (3) apply to leave out of account only the lesser of—

(a) the amount of the exchange gain or loss (in the case of subsection (2)) or the proportion of the exchange gain or loss (in the case of subsection (3)) which would be left out of account apart from this subsection, and

(b) the amount of the exchange gain or loss arising in respect of a liability representing the debtor relationship to the extent that the debtor relationship is unmatched (an amount which may be nil).]²

(5) Nothing in [Part 4 of TIOPA 2010]¹ requires the amounts brought into account under this Part in respect of exchange gains or losses from loan relationships to be calculated on the assumption that the arm's length provision had been made instead of the actual provision.

(6) But subsection (5) does not affect the application of subsections (2) and (3) under subsection (1).

(7) In this section "the arm's length provision" and "the actual provision" have the same meaning as in [Part 4 of TIOPA 2010 (see sections 149 and 151 of that Act)]¹.

Amendments—¹   In sub-s (1)(c) words "paragraph 1 of Schedule 28AA to ICTA" substituted, in sub-s (5) and the title words "Schedule 28AA to ICTA" substituted, in sub-s (7) words "Schedule 28AA to ICTA (see paragraph 1 of that Schedule)" substituted by TIOPA 2010 s 501, Sch 8 paras 123, 135. TIOPA 2010 has effect for corporation tax purposes for accounting periods ending on or after 1 April 2010, for income and capital gains tax purposes for the tax year 2010–11 and subsequent tax years, and for petroleum revenue tax purposes for chargeable periods beginning on or after 1 July 2010.

²   Sub-s (4A) inserted by FA 2016 s 49, Sch 7 paras 1, 5 with effect in relation to accounting periods beginning on or after 1 April 2016 (FA 2016 Sch 7 para 12(1)). Where a company has an accounting period beginning before 1 April 2016 and ending on or after that date ("the straddling period") the periods before and after 1 April 2016 are treated as separate accounting periods (FA 2016 Sch 7 para 12(2)).

448 Exchange gains and losses on debtor relationships: equity notes where holder associated with issuer

(1) This section applies if—

(a) a company has a debtor relationship in an accounting period,

(b) an exchange gain or loss arises in the period in respect of a liability representing the relationship, and

(c) the whole of any interest or other distribution out of the assets of the company in respect of securities of the company which represent the relationship is regarded as a distribution because of [section 1015(6) of CTA 2010][1] (equity notes held by company associated with issuer or by a funded company).

(2) The exchange gain or loss must be left out of account in determining the credits or debits to be brought into account for the purposes of this Part.

[(3) If the debtor relationship is to any extent matched, subsection (2) applies to leave out of account only the amount of the exchange gain or loss arising in respect of a liability representing the debtor relationship to the extent that the debtor relationship is unmatched (an amount which may be nil).][2]

Amendments—[1]   In sub-s (1)(c) words substituted for words "section 209(2)(e)(vii) of ICTA" by CTA 2010 s 1177, Sch 1 para 617. CTA 2010 has effect for corporation tax purposes for accounting periods ending on or after 1 April 2010, and for income and capital gains tax purposes for the tax year 2010–11 and subsequent tax years.

[2]   Sub-s (3) inserted by FA 2016 s 49, Sch 7 paras 1, 6 with effect in relation to accounting periods beginning on or after 1 April 2016 (FA 2016 Sch 7 para 12(1)). Where a company has an accounting period beginning before 1 April 2016 and ending on or after that date ("the straddling period") the periods before and after 1 April 2016 are treated as separate accounting periods (FA 2016 Sch 7 para 12(2)).

449 Exchange gains and losses on creditor relationships: no corresponding debtor relationship

(1) This section applies if—

(a) a company has a creditor relationship in an accounting period, and

(b) an exchange gain or loss arises in the period in respect of an asset representing the relationship.

(2) The exchange gain or loss must be left out of account in determining the credits or debits to be brought into account for the purposes of this Part if conditions A and B are met.

(3) Condition A is that the transaction giving rise to the loan is such that it would not have been entered into at all if the parties had been dealing at arm's length.

(4) Condition B is that there is no corresponding debtor relationship.

[(4A) If the creditor relationship is to any extent matched, subsection (2) applies to leave out of account only the amount of the exchange gain or loss arising in respect of an asset representing the creditor relationship to the extent that the creditor relationship is unmatched (an amount which may be nil).][1]

(5) For the meaning of "corresponding debtor relationship", see section 450.

(6) This section is subject to section 451 (exception to this section where loan exceeds arm's length amount).

Amendments—[1]   Sub-s (4A) inserted by FA 2016 s 49, Sch 7 paras 1, 7 with effect in relation to accounting periods beginning on or after 1 April 2016 (FA 2016 Sch 7 para 12(1)). Where a company has an accounting period beginning before 1 April 2016 and ending on or after that date ("the straddling period") the periods before and after 1 April 2016 are treated as separate accounting periods (FA 2016 Sch 7 para 12(2)).

450 Meaning of "corresponding debtor relationship"

(1) In section 449 "corresponding debtor relationship" means a debtor relationship which—

(a) corresponds to the creditor relationship mentioned in section 449(1), and

(b) is of such a kind that conditions A and B are met.

(2) Condition A is that such credits as are mentioned in subsection (3) would fall to be brought into account for the purposes of this Part in respect of exchange gains from that debtor relationship.

(3) Those credits are credits corresponding to, and of the same amount as, the debits that would fall to be so brought into account in respect of exchange losses from the creditor relationship apart from section 449.

(4) Condition B is that such debits as are mentioned in subsection (5) would fall to be so brought into account in respect of exchange losses from that debtor relationship.

(5) Those debits are debits corresponding to, and of the same amount as, the credits that would fall to be so brought into account in respect of exchange gains from the creditor relationship apart from section 449.

(6) In determining for the purposes of this section whether credits or debits would fall to be so brought into account, section [328(3) to (7)][1] (as a result of which some exchange gains and losses are excluded from this Part) is ignored.

Amendments—[1]   In sub-s (6) words substituted for words "328(2) to (7)" by F(No 2)A 2015 s 32, Sch 7 paras 1, 49 with effect for accounting periods beginning on or after 1 January 2016, subject to transitional rules in F(No 2)A 2015 Sch 7 paras 115 to 129.

Prospective amendment—Sub-s (6) to be repealed with effect from a date to be appointed, by CTA 2009 ss 1325, 1326, 1329(3), Sch 2 para 71, Sch 3 Part 2.

451 Exception to section 449 where loan exceeds arm's length amount

(1) Section 449 does not apply if the circumstances are such that, had the parties to the relevant transaction been dealing at arm's length, the amount of the loan would have been an amount ("the arm's length amount") greater than nil, but less than its actual amount.

(2) Accordingly, an exchange gain or loss which arises in the accounting period in respect of an asset representing the creditor relationship is not required by that section to be left out of account.

(3) But if—

(a) the circumstances are as mentioned in subsection (1), and

(b) there is no corresponding debtor relationship,

only a proportion of the exchange gain or loss may be taken into account in determining the credits or debits to be brought into account for the purposes of this Part.

(4) That proportion is the proportion which the arm's length amount bears to the actual amount of the loan.

[(4A) If the creditor relationship is to any extent matched, subsections (3) and (4) apply to leave out of account only the lesser of—

(a) the proportion of the exchange gain or loss which would be left out of account apart from this subsection, and

(b) the amount of the exchange gain or loss arising in respect of an asset representing the creditor relationship to the extent that the creditor relationship is unmatched (an amount which may be nil).][1]

(5) In this section—

"corresponding debtor relationship" has the same meaning as in section 449 (see section 450), and

"the relevant transaction" means the transaction giving rise to the loan as a result of which the company has the creditor relationship in the accounting period in question.

Amendments—[1]   Sub-s (4A) inserted by FA 2016 s 49, Sch 7 paras 1, 8 with effect in relation to accounting periods beginning on or after 1 April 2016 (FA 2016 Sch 7 para 12(1)). Where a company has an accounting period beginning before 1 April 2016 and ending on or after that date ("the straddling period") the periods before and after 1 April 2016 are treated as separate accounting periods (FA 2016 Sch 7 para 12(2)).

452 Exchange gains and losses where loan not on arm's length terms

(1) This subsection applies if—

(a) a company would be treated as having a debtor relationship in an accounting period if a claim were made under [section 192(1) of TIOPA 2010][1] in relation to that period, and

(b) for that period there is a connection between that company and the company that would have the corresponding creditor relationship.

(2) If subsection (1) applies, it is assumed that such a claim is made for the purpose of determining the debits or credits to be brought into account for the purposes of this Part in respect of any exchange gains or losses arising in that period in respect of the liability representing that debtor relationship.

[(3) Subsections (4) and (5) apply if, because of a claim made under section 192(1) of TIOPA 2010, or because of the claim that is assumed to be made under subsection (2)—

(a) one company is treated for any purpose as having a debtor relationship, or

(b) more than one company is treated for any purpose as having a debtor relationship represented by the same liability.][2]

(4) The total amount of the credits brought into account for the purposes of this Part in respect of exchange gains [from that debtor relationship (in a subsection (3)(a) case) or][2] from those debtor relationships [(in a subsection (3)(b) case)][2] must not exceed the total amount of the [exchange gains or the proportion of the exchange gains to be left out of account under section 447 by the issuing company in respect of the loan relationship][2].

(5) The total amount of the debits brought into account for those purposes in respect of exchange losses [from that debtor relationship (in a subsection (3)(a) case) or][2] from those debtor relationships [(in a subsection (3)(b) case)][2] must not exceed the total amount of the [exchange losses or the proportion of the exchange losses to be left out of account under section 447 by the issuing company in respect of the loan relationship][2].

[(5A) In this section "issuing company" is to be construed in accordance with section 191(1)(a) of TIOPA 2010.][2]

(6) Section 466 (companies connected for an accounting period) applies for the purposes of this section.

Amendments—[1]   In sub-ss (1)(a), (3)(a) words "paragraph 6D(2) of Schedule 28AA to ICTA" substituted by TIOPA 2010 s 501, Sch 8 paras 123, 136. TIOPA 2010 has effect for corporation tax purposes for accounting periods ending on or after 1 April 2010, for income and capital gains tax purposes for the tax year 2010–11 and subsequent tax years, and for petroleum revenue tax purposes for chargeable periods beginning on or after 1 July 2010.

[2]   Sub-s (5A) inserted, sub-s (3) substituted, and words in sub-ss (4), (5) inserted and substituted, by FA 2016 s 49, Sch 7 paras 1, 9 with effect in relation to accounting periods beginning on or after 1 April 2016 (FA 2016 Sch 7 para 12(1)). Where a company has an accounting period beginning before 1 April 2016 and ending on or after that date ("the straddling period") the periods before and after 1 April 2016 are treated as separate accounting periods (FA 2016 Sch 7 para 12(2)).

[Derecognition

455A Debits arising from derecognition of creditor relationships

(1) This section applies where—

(a) a company is at any time a party to tax avoidance arrangements, (*b*) as a result of those arrangements, a creditor relationship to which the company is party, or any part of such a relationship, is (in accordance with generally accepted accounting practice) derecognised by the company, and

(*c*) the company continues to be a party to the creditor relationship immediately after the transaction or other event giving rise to the derecognition.

(2) No debit that would apart from this section be brought into account by the company for the purposes of this Part as a result of the derecognition is to be so brought into account.

(3) An amount that would be brought into account for the purposes of this Part as respects any matter apart from this section—

(*a*) is treated for the purposes of section 464(1) (priority of this Part for corporation tax purposes) as if it were so brought into account, and

(*b*) accordingly, may not be brought into account for any other corporation tax purposes as respects that matter.

(4) For the purposes of this section a company is to be treated as a party to a creditor relationship even though it has disposed of its rights under the relationship to another person—

(*a*) under a repo or stock lending arrangement, or

(*b*) under a transaction which is treated as not involving any disposal as a result of section 26 of TCGA 1992 (mortgages and charges not to be treated as disposals).

(5) For the purposes of this section arrangements are "tax avoidance arrangements" if the main purpose, or one of the main purposes, of any party to the arrangements, in entering into them, is to obtain a tax advantage.

(6) In subsection (5) "arrangements" includes any arrangements, scheme or understanding of any kind, whether or not legally enforceable, involving a single transaction or two or more transactions.][1]

Amendments—[1] This section inserted by FA 2011 s 28, Sch 4 paras 1, 5 with effect in relation to periods of account beginning on or after 6 December 2010, subject to the transitional provision in FA 2011 Sch 4 para 13(2).

[Counteracting avoidance arrangements

455B Counteracting effect of avoidance arrangements

(1) Any loan-related tax advantages that would (in the absence of this section) arise from relevant avoidance arrangements are to be counteracted by the making of such adjustments as are just and reasonable in relation to credits and debits to be brought into account for the purposes of this Part.

(2) Any adjustments required to be made under this section (whether or not by an officer of Revenue and Customs) may be made by way of an assessment, the modification of an assessment, amendment or disallowance of a claim, or otherwise.

(3) For the meaning of "relevant avoidance arrangements" and "loan-related tax advantage", see section 455C.][1]

Amendments—[1] Sections 455B–455D inserted by F(No 2)A 2015 s 32, Sch 7 paras 1, 51 with effect in relation to arrangements entered into on or after 18 November 2015.

[455C Interpretation of section 455B

(1) This section applies for the interpretation of section 455B (and this section).

(2) "Arrangements" include any agreement, understanding, scheme, transaction or series of transactions (whether or not legally enforceable).

(3) Arrangements are "relevant avoidance arrangements" if their main purpose, or one of their main purposes, is to enable a company to obtain a loan-related tax advantage.

(4) But arrangements are not "relevant avoidance arrangements" if the obtaining of any loan-related tax advantages that would (in the absence of section 455B) arise from them can reasonably be regarded as consistent with any principles on which the provisions of this Part that are relevant to the arrangements are based (whether expressed or implied) and the policy objectives of those provisions.

(5) A company obtains a "loan-related tax advantage" if—

(*a*) it brings into account a debit to which it would not otherwise be entitled,

(*b*) it brings into account a debit which exceeds that to which it would otherwise be entitled,

(*c*) it avoids having to bring a credit into account,

(*d*) the amount of any credit brought into account by the company is less than it would otherwise be, or

(*e*) it brings a debit or credit into account earlier or later than it otherwise would.

(6) In subsection (5), references to bringing a debit or credit into account are references to bringing a debit or credit into account for the purposes of this Part.][1]

Amendments—[1] Sections 455B–455D inserted by F(No 2)A 2015 s 32, Sch 7 paras 1, 51 with effect in relation to arrangements entered into on or after 18 November 2015.

[455D Examples of results that may indicate exclusion not applicable

(1) Each of the following is an example of something which might indicate that arrangements whose main purpose, or one of whose main purposes, is to enable a company to obtain a loan-related tax advantage are not excluded by section 455C(4) from being "relevant avoidance arrangements" for the purposes of section 455B—

CTA 2009

(a) the elimination or reduction, for purposes of corporation tax, of profits of a company arising from any of its loan relationships, where for economic purposes profits, or greater profits, arise to the company from that relationship;

(b) the creation or increase, for purposes of corporation tax, of a loss or expense arising from a loan relationship, where for economic purposes no loss or expense, or a smaller loss or expense, arises from that relationship;

(c) preventing or delaying the recognition as an item of profit or loss of an amount that would apart from the arrangements be recognised in the company's accounts as an item of profit or loss or be so recognised earlier;

(d) ensuring that a loan relationship is treated for accounting purposes in a way in which it would not have been treated in the absence of some other transaction forming part of the arrangements;

(e) enabling a company to bring into account for the purposes of this Part a debit in respect of an exchange loss, in circumstances where a corresponding exchange gain would not give rise to a credit or would give rise to a credit of a smaller amount;

(f) enabling a company to bring into account for the purposes of this Part a debit in respect of a fair value loss in circumstances where a corresponding fair value gain would not give rise to a credit or would give rise to a credit of a smaller amount;

(g) ensuring that the effect of the provisions of Chapter 4 is to produce an overall reduction in the credits brought into account for the purposes this Part or an overall increase in the debits brought into account for those purposes;

(h) bringing into account for the purposes of this Part an impairment loss or release debit in a case where the provisions of Chapter 6 would but for the arrangements have prevented this.

(2) But in each case the result concerned is only capable of indicating that section 455C(4) is not available if it is reasonable to assume that such a result was not the anticipated result when the provisions of this Part that are relevant to the arrangements were enacted.

(3) In subsection (1)(*f*) references to a fair value gain or a fair value loss, in relation to a company, are references respectively to—

(a) a profit to be brought into account in relation to an asset or liability representing a loan relationship where fair value accounting is used for the period in question, or

(b) a loss to be brought into account in relation to such an asset or liability where fair value accounting is used for the period in question.

(4) "Arrangements" and "loan-related tax advantage" have the same meaning as in section 455C.][1]

Amendments—[1]   Sections 455B–455D inserted by F(No 2)A 2015 s 32, Sch 7 paras 1, 51 with effect in relation to arrangements entered into on or after 18 November 2015.

CHAPTER 16

NON-TRADING DEFICITS[: PRE-1 APRIL 2017 DEFICITS AND CHARITIES]

456 Introduction to Chapter

(1) This Chapter applies if[—

(a)][1] for any accounting period a company has a non-trading deficit from its loan relationships under section 301(6)[, and

(b) either—

  (i) that accounting period begins before 1 April 2017, or

  (ii) at the end of that accounting period the company is a charity][1].

(2) In this Chapter "the deficit" and "the deficit period" mean that deficit and that period respectively (but see section 458(5)).

(3) Sections 457 and 458 set out the rules about carrying the deficit forward to later accounting periods.

(4) Sections 459 and 460 deal with claims for the deficit to be dealt with differently.

(5) Sections 461 to 463 deal with the consequences of such claims.

Amendments—[1]   Words in heading inserted, and in sub-s (1), para (a) designated as such and para (b) inserted, by F(No 2)A 2017 s 18, Sch 4 paras 1–3 with effect in relation to accounting periods beginning on or after 1 April 2017, subject to transitional provisions in Sch 4 para 194. For accounting periods beginning before 1 April 2017 and ending on or after that date ("straddling periods") see F(No 2)A 2017 Sch 4 paras 190–192.

457 Basic rule for deficits: carry forward to accounting periods after deficit period

(1) The basic rule is that the deficit must be carried forward and set off against non-trading profits of the company for accounting periods after the deficit period in accordance with subsection (3) and section 458.

(2) That rule does not apply to so much of the deficit as—

(a) is surrendered as group relief under [Part 5 of CTA 2010][1], or

(b) is the subject of a claim by the company under section 459 (claim to set off deficit against profits of deficit period or earlier periods).

(3) So much of the amount carried forward from the deficit period as is not the subject of a claim under section 458(1) must be set off against the non-trading profits of the company for the next accounting period after the deficit period.

(4) Those profits are reduced accordingly.

(5) In this Chapter "non-trading profits", in relation to a company, means so much of the company's profits as does not consist of trading income for the purposes of [section 37 of CTA 2010 (deduction of trading losses from total][1] profits of the same or an earlier period).

Amendments—[1] In sub-s (2)(*a*) words substituted for words "section 403 of ICTA", in sub-s (5) words substituted for words "section 393A of ICTA (setting-off of trading losses against" by CTA 2010 s 1177, Sch 1 para 618. CTA 2010 has effect for corporation tax purposes for accounting periods ending on or after 1 April 2010, and for income and capital gains tax purposes for the tax year 2010–11 and subsequent tax years.

458 Claim to carry forward deficit to later accounting periods

(1) The company may make a claim for so much of the amount carried forward from the deficit period as is specified in the claim to be excepted from being set off against non-trading profits of the first accounting period after the deficit period ("the first later period").

(2) Any such claim must be made within the period of 2 years after the end of the first later period.

(3) Subsection (4) applies if any amount is carried forward from the deficit period under section 457(1) which—

    (*a*) cannot be set off under section 457(3) against non-trading profits of the first later period, or

    (*b*) is the subject of a claim under subsection (1).

(4) That amount is treated for the purposes of this Part as if it were—

    (*a*) an amount of non-trading deficit from the company's loan relationships for the first later period, and

    (*b*) an amount which falls to be carried forward and set against non- trading profits of later accounting periods under section 457(1).

(5) Accordingly, section 457 and this section apply as if the first later period were the deficit period.

459 Claim to set off deficit against profits of deficit period or earlier periods

(1) The company may make a claim for the whole or part of the deficit—

    (*a*) to be set off against [any profits of the company (of whatever description)][2] for the deficit period, or

    (*b*) to be carried back to be set off against profits for earlier accounting periods.

(2) No claim may be made under subsection (1) in respect of a deficit which is surrendered as group relief under [Part 5 of CTA 2010][1].

(3) Subsection (1) does not apply if the company is a charity.

(4) For time limits and other provisions applicable to claims under subsection (1), see section 460.

(5) For what happens when a claim is made under subsection (1)(*a*), see section 461.

(6) For what happens when a claim is made under subsection (1)(*b*), and for the profits available for relief where such a claim is made, see sections 462 and 463.

Amendments—[1] In sub-s (2) words substituted for words "section 403 of ICTA" by CTA 2010 s 1177, Sch 1 para 619. CTA 2010 has effect for corporation tax purposes for accounting periods ending on or after 1 April 2010, and for income and capital gains tax purposes for the tax year 2010–11 and subsequent tax years.
[2] In sub-s (1)(*a*) words substituted by the Corporation Tax Act 2009 (Amendment) Order 2010 SI 2010/614 reg 3(1), (3) with effect for accounting periods ending on or after 1 April 2009.

460 Time limits and procedure for claims under section 459(1)

(1) A claim under section 459(1) must be made within—

    (*a*) the period of 2 years after the deficit period ends, or

    (*b*) such further period as an officer of Revenue and Customs allows.

(2) Different claims may be made in respect of different parts of a non-trading deficit for any deficit period.

(3) But no claim may be made in respect of any part of a deficit to which another such claim relates.

461 Claim to set off deficit against other profits for the deficit period

(1) This section applies if a claim is made under section 459(1)(*a*) for the whole or part of the deficit to be set off against profits for the deficit period.

(2) The general rule is that the amount to which the claim relates must be set off against the profits of the company for the deficit period which are identified in the claim.

(3) Those profits are reduced accordingly.

(4) The general rule is subject to subsections (5) and (7).

(5) Relief for any deficit incurred in a trade in an earlier accounting period must be given before relief under this section.

(6) But relief under this section must be given before relief is given against profits for the deficit period—

    (*a*) under [section 37 or 62(1) to (3) of CTA 2010 (deduction of losses from total][1] profits for the same or earlier accounting periods), or

    (*b*) as a result of a claim under section 459(1)(*b*) (carry-back) in respect of a deficit for a later period.

(7) No relief may be given under this section against ring fence profits of the company within the meaning of [Part 8 of CTA 2010 (oil activities)][1].

Amendments—[1]   In sub-s (6)(*a*) words substituted for words "section 392A(1) or 393A(1) of ICTA (losses set against", in sub-s (7) words substituted for words "Chapter 5 of Part 12 of ICTA (petroleum extraction activities)" by CTA 2010 s 1177, Sch 1 para 620. CTA 2010 has effect for corporation tax purposes for accounting periods ending on or after 1 April 2010, and for income and capital gains tax purposes for the tax year 2010–11 and subsequent tax years.

462 Claim to carry back deficit to earlier accounting periods
(1) This section applies if a claim is made under 459(1)(*b*) for the whole or part of the deficit to be carried back to be set off against profits for accounting periods before the deficit period.
(2) The claim has effect only if it relates to an amount equal to the lesser of—
  (*a*) so much of the deficit as is not an amount in relation to which a claim is made under section 459(1)(*a*), and
  (*b*) the total amount of the profits available for relief under this section.
(3) Section 463 explains which profits are so available.
(4) The amount to which the claim relates is set off against those profits by treating them as reduced accordingly.
(5) If those profits are profits for more than one accounting period, the relief is applied by setting off the amount to which the claim relates against profits for a later period before setting off any remainder of that amount against profits for an earlier period.

463 Profits available for relief under section 462
(1) The profits available for relief under section 462 are the amounts which (apart from the relief) would be charged under this Part as profits for accounting periods ending within the permitted period, after giving every prior relief.
(2) In this section—
  "the permitted period" means the period of 12 months immediately before the deficit period, and
  "prior relief" means a relief which subsection (5) provides must be given before relief under section 462.
(3) If an accounting period ending within the permitted period begins before it, only a part of the amount which (apart from the relief) would be chargeable under this Part for that period, after giving every prior relief, is available for relief under section 462.
(4) That part is so much as is proportionate to the part of the accounting period in the permitted period.
(5) The reliefs which must be given before relief under section 462 are—
  (*a*) relief as a result of a claim under section 459(1)(*a*) (claim for deficit to be set off against total profits for the deficit period),
  (*b*) relief in respect of a loss or deficit incurred or treated as incurred in an accounting period before the deficit period,
  (*c*) relief under Part 6 of CTA 2010 (charitable donations relief][1] in respect of payments made wholly and exclusively for the purposes of a trade,
  (*d*) relief under [section 37 of CTA 2010 (losses deducted from total][1] profits of the same, or an earlier, accounting period), and
  (*e*) if the company is a company with investment business for the purposes of Part 16 (companies with investment business)—
    (i) any deduction in respect of management expenses under section 1219 (expenses of management of a company's investment business),
    (ii) relief under [Part 6 of CTA 2010][1] in respect of payments made wholly and exclusively for the purposes of its business, and
    (iii) any allowance under Part 2 of CAA 2001 (plant and machinery allowances).

Amendments—[1]   In sub-s (5)(*c*), words substituted for words "section 338 of ICTA (charges on income deducted from total profits)", in sub-s (5)(*d*) words substituted for words "section 393A of ICTA (losses set off against", in sub-s (5)(*e*)(*ii*) words substituted for words "section 338 of ICTA" by CTA 2010 s 1177, Sch 1 para 621. CTA 2010 has effect for corporation tax purposes for accounting periods ending on or after 1 April 2010, and for income and capital gains tax purposes for the tax year 2010–11 and subsequent tax years.

[CHAPTER 16A

NON-TRADING DEFICITS: POST 1 APRIL 2017 DEFICITS

463A Introduction to Chapter
(1) This Chapter applies if—
  (*a*) for any accounting period beginning on or after 1 April 2017 a company has a non-trading deficit from its loan relationships under section 301(6), and
  (*b*) at the end of that accounting period the company is not a charity.
(2) In this Chapter "the deficit" and "the deficit period" mean that deficit and that period respectively.
(3) Sections 463B and 463C deal with claims to set off the deficit against profits of the deficit period or earlier periods.

(4) Sections 463D to 463F deal with the consequences of such claims.

(5) Sections 463G to 463I provide for so much of the deficit as is not—

    (a) set off against profits under section 463B, or

    (b) surrendered as group relief under Part 5 of CTA 2010,

to be carried forward to later accounting periods.][1]

Amendments—[1]   Chapter 16A (ss 463A–463I) inserted by F(No 2)A 2017 s 18, Sch 4 paras 1, 4 with effect in relation to accounting periods beginning on or after 1 April 2017, subject to transitional provisions in Sch 4 para 194. For accounting periods beginning before 1 April 2017 and ending on or after that date ("straddling periods") see F(No 2)A 2017 Sch 4 paras 190–192.

[463B Claim to set off deficit against profits of deficit period or earlier periods

(1) The company may make a claim for the whole or part of the deficit—

    (a) to be set off against any profits of the company (of whatever description) for the deficit period, or

    (b) to be carried back to be set off against profits for earlier accounting periods.

(2) No claim may be made under subsection (1) in respect of so much of the deficit as is surrendered as group relief under Part 5 of CTA 2010.

(3) For time limits and other provisions applicable to claims under subsection (1), see section 463C.

(4) For what happens when a claim is made under subsection (1)(a), see section 463D.

(5) For what happens when a claim is made under subsection (1)(b), and the profits available for relief when such a claim is made, see sections 463E and 463F.][1]

Amendments—[1]   Chapter 16A (ss 463A–463I) inserted by F(No 2)A 2017 s 18, Sch 4 paras 1, 4 with effect in relation to accounting periods beginning on or after 1 April 2017, subject to transitional provisions in Sch 4 para 194. For accounting periods beginning before 1 April 2017 and ending on or after that date ("straddling periods") see F(No 2)A 2017 Sch 4 paras 190–192.

[463C Time limits for claims under section 463B(1)

(1) A claim under section 463B(1) must be made within—

    (a) the period of 2 years after the deficit period ends, or

    (b) such further period as an officer of Revenue and Customs allows.

(2) Different claims may be made in respect of different parts of a non-trading deficit for any deficit period.

(3) But no claim may be made in respect of any part of a deficit to which another such claim relates.][1]

Amendments—[1]   Chapter 16A (ss 463A–463I) inserted by F(No 2)A 2017 s 18, Sch 4 paras 1, 4 with effect in relation to accounting periods beginning on or after 1 April 2017, subject to transitional provisions in Sch 4 para 194. For accounting periods beginning before 1 April 2017 and ending on or after that date ("straddling periods") see F(No 2)A 2017 Sch 4 paras 190–192.

[463D Claim to set off deficit against profits for the deficit period

(1) This section applies if a claim is made under section 463B(1)(a) for the whole or part of the deficit to be set off against profits for the deficit period.

(2) The amount of the deficit to which the claim relates must be set off against the profits of the company for the deficit period which are identified in the claim.

(3) Those profits are reduced accordingly.

(4) Relief under this section must be given before relief is given against profits for the deficit period—

    (a) under section 37 or 62(1) to (3) of CTA 2010 (deduction of losses from total profits for the same or earlier accounting periods), or

    (b) as a result of a claim under section 463B(1)(b) (carry-back) in respect of a deficit for a later period.

(5) No relief may be given under this section against ring fence profits of the company within the meaning of Part 8 of CTA 2010 (oil activities) or contractor's ring fence profits of the company within the meaning of Part 8ZA of that Act (oil contractors).][1]

Amendments—[1]   Chapter 16A (ss 463A–463I) inserted by F(No 2)A 2017 s 18, Sch 4 paras 1, 4 with effect in relation to accounting periods beginning on or after 1 April 2017, subject to transitional provisions in Sch 4 para 194. For accounting periods beginning before 1 April 2017 and ending on or after that date ("straddling periods") see F(No 2)A 2017 Sch 4 paras 190–192.

[463E Claim to carry back deficit to earlier periods

(1) This section applies if a claim is made under section 463B(1)(b) for the whole or part of the deficit to be carried back to be set off against profits for accounting periods before the deficit period.

(2) The claim has effect only if it relates to an amount no greater than the lesser of—

    (a) so much of the deficit as is not an amount in relation to which a claim is made under section 463B(1)(a), and

    (b) the total amount of the profits available for relief under this section.

(3) Section 463F explains which profits are so available.

(4) The amount to which the claim relates is set off against those profits by treating them as reduced accordingly.

(5) If those profits are profits for more than one accounting period, the relief is applied by setting off the amount to which the claim relates against profits for a later period before setting off any remainder of that amount against profits for an earlier period.]¹

Amendments—¹   Chapter 16A (ss 463A–463I) inserted by F(No 2)A 2017 s 18, Sch 4 paras 1, 4 with effect in relation to accounting periods beginning on or after 1 April 2017, subject to transitional provisions in Sch 4 para 194. For accounting periods beginning before 1 April 2017 and ending on or after that date ("straddling periods") see F(No 2)A 2017 Sch 4 paras 190–192.

[463F Profits available for relief under section 463E

(1) The profits available for relief under section 463E are the amounts which (apart from the relief) would be charged under this Part as profits for accounting periods ending within the permitted period after giving every prior relief.

(2) In this section—

"the permitted period" means the period of 12 months immediately before the deficit period, and "prior relief" means a relief which subsection (5) provides must be given before relief under section 463E.

(3) If an accounting period ending within the permitted period begins before it, only a part of the amount which (apart from the relief) would be chargeable under this Part for the period, after giving every prior relief, is available for relief under section 463E.

(4) That part is so much as is proportionate to the part of the accounting period in the permitted period.

(5) The reliefs which must be given before relief under section 463E are—

(a) relief as a result of a claim under section 459(1)(a) or section 463B(1)(a) (claim for deficit to be set off against total profits for the deficit period),

(b) relief in respect of a loss or deficit incurred or treated as incurred in an accounting period before the deficit period,

(c) relief under Part 6 of CTA 2010 (charitable donations relief in respect of payments made wholly and exclusively for the purposes of a trade),

(d) relief under section 37 of CTA 2010 (losses deducted from total profits of the same or an earlier accounting period), and

(e) if the company is a company with investment business for the purposes of Part 16 (companies with investment business)—

(i) any deduction in respect of management expenses under section 1219 (expenses of management of a company's investment business),

(ii) relief under Part 6 of CTA 2010 in respect of payments made wholly and exclusively for the purposes of its business, and

(iii) any allowance under Part 2 of CAA 2001 (plant and machinery allowances).]¹

Amendments—¹   Chapter 16A (ss 463A–463I) inserted by F(No 2)A 2017 s 18, Sch 4 paras 1, 4 with effect in relation to accounting periods beginning on or after 1 April 2017, subject to transitional provisions in Sch 4 para 194. For accounting periods beginning before 1 April 2017 and ending on or after that date ("straddling periods") see F(No 2)A 2017 Sch 4 paras 190–192.

[463G Carry forward of unrelieved deficit against total profits

(1) This section applies if conditions A to D are met.

(2) Condition A is that—

(a) any amount of the deficit ("the unrelieved amount") is not—

(i) set off against profits on a claim under section 463B(1), or

(ii) surrendered as group relief under Part 5 of CTA 2010.

(3) Condition B is that it is not the case—

(a) that the company ceased to be a company with investment business in the deficit period, or

(b) (if the company was a company with investment business immediately before the beginning of the deficit period) that its investment business became small or negligible in the deficit period.

(4) Condition C is that (if the company is a Solvency 2 insurance company) it is not the case that the whole of the deficit is a shock loss.

(5) Condition D is that (if the company is a general insurance company) the first accounting period after the deficit period is not an excluded accounting period.

(6) The unrelieved amount is carried forward to the first accounting period after the deficit period.

(7) The company may make a claim for the whole or part of the unrelieved amount to be set off against the company's total profits for the first accounting period after the deficit period.

(8) If a claim is made under subsection (7)—

(a) the unrelieved amount, or the part of it to which the claim relates, must be set off against the company's total profits for the first accounting period after the deficit period, and

(b) those profits are reduced accordingly.

(9) No claim may be made under subsection (7) in respect of so much of the unrelieved amount as is surrendered under Part 5A of CTA 2010 (group relief for carried-forward losses).

(10) A claim under subsection (7) must be made within—

(*a*) the period of two years after the end of the first accounting period after the deficit period, or

(*b*) such further period as an officer of Revenue and Customs allows.

(11) No relief may be given under this section against ring fence profits of the company within the meaning of Part 8 of CTA 2010 (oil activities) or contractor's ring fence profits of the company within the meaning of Part 8ZA of that Act (oil contractors).

(12) If —

(*a*) the company is a Solvency 2 insurance company, and

(*b*) the deficit is partly (but not wholly) a shock loss,

subsections (6) to (9) have effect as if references to the unrelieved amount were to the eligible amount (see subsection (13)).

(13) In this section "the eligible amount" means so much of the unrelieved amount as is not a shock loss; and for the purpose of determining how much of the unrelieved amount is, or is not, a shock loss, it is to be assumed that in setting off or surrendering amounts as mentioned in subsection (2)(*a*)(i) and (ii) the company uses shock losses before other amounts.

(14) In this Chapter—

"company with investment business" has the same meaning as in Part 16 (see section 1218B);

"excluded accounting period" has the meaning given by section 269ZG of CTA 2010;

"general insurance company" is to be interpreted in accordance with section 269ZG of CTA 2010;

"shock loss" has the meaning given by section 269ZK of CTA 2010;

"Solvency 2 insurance company" means an insurance company as defined in section 269ZP(2) of CTA 2010.

(15) In this Chapter references to a company's investment business are to be construed in accordance with section 1219(2).]¹

Amendments—¹ Chapter 16A (ss 463A–463I) inserted by F(No 2)A 2017 s 18, Sch 4 paras 1, 4 with effect in relation to accounting periods beginning on or after 1 April 2017, subject to transitional provisions in Sch 4 para 194. For accounting periods beginning before 1 April 2017 and ending on or after that date ("straddling periods") see F(No 2)A 2017 Sch 4 paras 190–192.

[463H Carry forward of unrelieved deficit against non-trading profits

(1) Subsections (4) to (8) apply if—

(*a*) section 463G would apply but for the fact that the company's investment business became small or negligible in the accounting period mentioned in subsection (3)(*b*) of that section,

(*b*) section 463G would apply but for condition D in that section (no carry-forward to an excluded accounting period of a general insurance company), or

(*c*) the company is a Solvency 2 insurance company and any amount of the deficit would be eligible to be carried forward under section 463G(6) were that amount not a shock loss (see section 463G(4), (12) and (13)).

(2) Subsections (4) to (8) also apply if—

(*a*) subsections (6) to (10) of section 463G would apply but for the fact that the company's investment business became small or negligible in the accounting period mentioned in section 463I(1)(*c*)(ii), or

(*b*) subsections (6) to (10) of section 463G would apply but for section 463I(1)(*d*) (no carry-forward under those subsections to an excluded accounting period of a general insurance company).

(3) In this section the "unrelieved amount"—

(*a*) in a case within paragraph (*a*) or (*b*) of subsection (1), is to be interpreted in accordance with section 463G(2);

(*b*) in a case within paragraph (*c*) of subsection (1), means the amount mentioned in that paragraph;

(*c*) in a case within subsection (2), means so much of the deficit mentioned in section 463I(1)(*a*) as is not set off as mentioned in section 463I(1)(*b*)(i) or surrendered as mentioned in section 463I(1)(*b*)(ii).

(4) The unrelieved amount is carried forward to the first accounting period ("period 2") after—

(*a*) (in a case within subsection (1)) the deficit period, or

(*b*) (in a case within subsection (2)) the period mentioned in section 463I(1)(*a*).

(5) So much of the unrelieved amount as is not the subject of a claim under subsection (7) must be set off against the non-trading profits of the company for period 2.

(6) Those profits are reduced accordingly.

(7) The company may make a claim for relief under subsection (5) not to be given in period 2 for the unrelieved amount or so much of it as is specified in the claim.

(8) A claim under subsection (7) is effective if, and only if, it is made—

(*a*) within the period of two years after the end of period 2, or

(*b*) within such further period as an officer of Revenue and Customs may allow.

(9) Subsection (10) applies if any amount is carried forward under subsection (4) to an accounting period ("the carry forward period") and—

(a) are brought into account by the company as credits or debits for any period for the purposes of this Part, or

(b) would be so brought into account but for any provision made by or under this Part.

(4) Regulations under subsection (1) may amend this Part (apart from this section).

(5) Regulations under subsection (1) may—

(a) make different provision for different cases,

(b) make incidental, supplemental, consequential and transitional provision and savings, and

(c) make provision subject to an election or other specified circumstances.

(6) Regulations making consequential provision by virtue of subsection (5)(b) may, in particular, include provision amending a provision of the Corporation Tax Acts.

(7) Regulations under subsection (1) may apply to a pre-commencement period if they make provision in relation to a relevant accounting change which may or must be adopted, for accounting purposes, for a period of account, or part of a period of account, which coincides with that pre-commencement period.

(8) In this section—

"accounting body" means the International Accounting Standards Board or the Accounting Standards Board, or a successor body to either of those Boards;

"accounting standard" includes any statement of practice, guidance or other similar document;

"pre-commencement period", in relation to regulations, means an accounting period, or part of an accounting period, which begins before the regulations are made.]¹

Regulations—Changes in Accounting Standards (Loan Relationships and Derivative Contracts) Regulations, SI 2014/3325.

Amendments—¹ This section and preceding cross-head inserted by FA 2010 s 62, Sch 19 para 1 with effect from 8 April 2010.

[Tax-adjusted carrying value

465B "Tax-adjusted carrying value"

(1) This section applies for the purposes of this Part.

(2) "Tax-adjusted carrying value", in relation to the asset or liability representing a loan relationship, means the carrying value of the asset or liability recognised for accounting purposes, except as provided by subsection (8).

(3) For the purposes of this section the "carrying value" of the asset or liability includes amounts recognised for accounting purposes in relation to the loan relationship in respect of—

(a) accrued amounts,

(b) amounts paid or received in advance, or

(c) impairment losses (including provisions for bad or doubtful debts).

(4) For the meaning of "impairment loss" see section 476(1).

(5) In determining the tax-adjusted carrying value of an asset or liability in a period of account of a company, it is to be assumed that the accounting policy applied in drawing up the company's accounts for the period was also applied in previous periods of account.

(6) But if the company's accounts for the period are in accordance with generally accepted accounting practice drawn up on an assumption as to the accounting policy in previous periods of account which differs from that mentioned in subsection (5), that different assumption applies in determining the tax-adjusted carrying value of the asset or liability in the period.

(7) In determining the tax-adjusted carrying value of an asset or liability at a time other than the end (or beginning) of a period of account of a company, it is to be assumed that a period of account of the company had ended at the time in question.

(8) In determining the tax-adjusted carrying value of the asset or liability, the provisions specified in subsection (9) apply as they apply for the purposes of determining the credits and debits to be brought into account under this Part.

(9) Those provisions are—

(a) section 308(1A) (amounts recognised in other comprehensive income and transferred to profit and loss),

(b) sections 311 and 312 (amounts not fully recognised for accounting purposes),

(c) section 320A (amounts recognised in other comprehensive income and not transferred to profit and loss),

(d) section 323A (substantial modification: cases where credits not required to be brought into account),

(e) section 324 (restriction on debits resulting from revaluation),

(f) section 325 (restriction on credits resulting from reversal of disallowed debits),

(g) sections 333 and 334 (company ceasing to be UK resident and non-UK company ceasing to hold loan relationship for UK permanent establishment),

(h) Chapter 4 (continuity of treatment on transfers within groups or organisations),

(i) section 349(2) (application of amortised cost basis of accounting to connected companies relationships),

(j) section 352 (disregard of related transactions),

(k) section 352A (exclusion of credits on reversal of disregarded loss),

[(ka) section 352B (eliminating tax mismatch for loan relationships with qualifying link),]² (*l*)   section 354 (exclusion of debits for impaired or released connected companies debts),

    (*m*) section 360 (exclusion of credits on reversal of impairments of connected companies debts),

    (*n*)   sections 361 to 363 (deemed debt releases on impaired debts becoming held by connected company),

    (*o*)   Chapter 8 (connected parties relationships: late interest),

    (*p*)   section 382 (company partners using fair value accounting),

    (*q*)   sections 399 to 400C (treatment of index-linked gilt-edged securities),

    (*r*)   section 404 (restriction on deductions etc relating to FOTRA securities),

    (*s*)   sections 406 to 412 (deeply discounted securities and close companies),

    (*t*)   section 415(2) (loan relationships with embedded derivatives),

    (*u*)   Chapter 13 (European cross-border transfers of business), and

    (*v*)   Chapter 14 (European cross-border mergers).]¹

Amendments—¹   This section inserted by F(No 2)A 2015 s 32, Sch 7 paras 1, 52 with effect for accounting periods beginning on or after 1 January 2016, subject to transitional rules in F(No 2)A 2015 Sch 7 paras 115 to 129.

²   Sub-s (9)(*ka*) inserted by FA 2019 s 29, Sch 12 para 2 with effect for accounting periods beginning on or after 1 January 2019, subject to transitional provisions for an accounting period straddling that date. See also the transitional provisions in FA 2019 Sch 12 para 4.

Connections between persons

466 Companies connected for an accounting period

(1) This section and sections 467 to 471 have effect for the purposes of any provisions of this Part which apply this section (but this does not affect the application of section 1316(1) (meaning of "connected" persons) for other purposes of this Part).

(2) There is a connection between a company ("A") and another company ("B") for an accounting period if there is a time in the period when—

    (*a*)   A controls B,

    (*b*)   B controls A, or

    (*c*)   A and B are both controlled by the same person.

(3) But A and B are not taken to be controlled by the same person just because they have been under the control of—

    (*a*)   the Crown,

    (*b*)   a Minister of the Crown,

    (*c*)   a government department,

    (*d*)   a Northern Ireland department,

    (*e*)   a foreign sovereign power, or

    (*f*)   an international organisation.

(4) Subsection (2) is subject to section 468 (connection between companies to be ignored in some circumstances).

(5) For a case where companies are treated as if one controlled the other, see section 383(5) (inter-partnership lending between connected company partners etc).

(6) Section 472 (meaning of "control") applies for the purposes of this section.

467 Connections where partnerships are involved

(1) This section applies for the purposes of the provisions which apply section 466 ("the relevant provisions") if—

    (*a*)   a trade or business is carried on by a firm, and

    (*b*)   the firm stands in the position of a creditor or debtor as respects a money debt.

(2) The questions about connections specified in subsection (3) must be determined as if each of the partners in the firm separately (rather than the firm), stood in that position as respects the debt to the extent of that partner's appropriate share.

(3) The questions are—

    (*a*)   whether for the purposes of this Part there is a connection for the purposes of the relevant provisions between any two companies for an accounting period in the case of a loan relationship, and

    (*b*)   how far any amount is treated under this Part in any particular way as a result of there being, or not being, such a connection.

(4) For the purposes of subsection (2), a partner's "appropriate share" is the same share as the share in which any profit or loss for the accounting period in question would be apportioned to the partner in accordance with the firm's profit-sharing arrangements.

(5) The references in subsections (2) to (4) to partners do not include references to the general partner of a limited partnership which is a collective investment scheme.

468 Connection between companies to be ignored in some circumstances

(1) In the case of a company ("the creditor") which has a creditor relationship, any connection for an accounting period between the creditor and another company which stands in the position of a debtor as respects the debt is ignored for the purposes of the relevant provisions if the creditor is a party to the relationship in circumstances where—

    (*a*)   conditions A to E in section 469 (creditors who are financial traders) are met, or

(4) Subsection (5) applies if—

(*a*) a trade or business is carried on by a firm, and

(*b*) the firm stands in the position of a creditor or debtor as respects a money debt.

(5) The questions in subsection (6) are to be determined as if each of the partners in the firm separately, instead of the firm, stood in the position of a creditor or, as the case may be, a debtor as respects the money debt to the extent of that partner's appropriate share (see subsection (8)).

(6) The questions are—

(*a*) whether a company has a major interest in another company for an accounting period in the case of a loan relationship, or

(*b*) how far any amount is treated under this Part in any particular way as a result of a company having or, as the case may be, not having such a major interest.

(7) The references to partners in subsections (3) and (5) do not include a reference to the general partner of a limited partnership which is a collective investment scheme.

(8) For the purposes of subsection (5), a partner's "appropriate share" is the same share as the partner's share under the firm's profit-sharing arrangements of any profit or loss calculated in accordance with section 1259 for the accounting period in question.

475 Meaning of expressions relating to exchange gains and losses

(1) References in this Part to exchange gains or exchange losses, in relation to a company, are references respectively to—

(*a*) profits or gains which arise as a result of comparing at different times the expression in one currency of the whole or some part of the valuation put by the company in another currency on an asset or liability of the company, or

(*b*) losses which so arise.

(2) If the result of such a comparison is that neither an exchange gain nor an exchange loss arises, for the purposes of this Part an exchange gain of nil is taken to arise in the case of that comparison.

(3) The Treasury may make provision by regulations as to the way in which exchange gains or losses are to be calculated for the purposes of this section .

(4) The regulations may be made so as to apply to periods of account beginning before the regulations are made, but not earlier than the beginning of the calendar year in which they are made.

(5) Any reference in this Part to an exchange gain or loss from a loan relationship of a company is a reference to an exchange gain or loss arising to a company in relation to an asset or liability representing a loan relationship of the company.

Regulations—Loan Relationships and Derivative Contracts (Exchange Gains and Losses using Fair Value Accounting) (Amendment) Regulations, SI 2015/1963.

Amendments—[1]   In sub-s (3) words "in a case where fair value accounting is used by the company" repealed by F(No 2)A 2015 s 32, Sch 7 paras 1, 53 with effect for accounting periods beginning on or after 1 January 2016, subject to transitional rules in F(No 2)A 2015 Sch 7 paras 115 to 129.

[Meaning of "hedging relationship"]

475A "Hedging relationship"

(1) This section applies for the purposes of this Part.

(2) A company has a "hedging relationship" between a relevant contract ("the hedging instrument") and an asset or liability ("the hedged item") so far as condition A or B is met.

(3) Condition A is that the hedging instrument and the hedged item are designated as a hedge by the company.

(4) Condition B is that—

(*a*) the hedging instrument is intended to act as a hedge of the exposure to changes in fair value of the hedged item which is attributable to a particular risk and could affect the profit or loss of the company, and

(*b*) the hedged item is an asset or liability recognised for accounting purposes or is an identified portion of such an asset or liability.

(5) For the purposes of subsections (2) and (4), the liabilities of a company include its own share capital.]¹

Amendments—[1]   This section inserted by F(No 2)A 2015 s 32, Sch 7 paras 1, 54 with effect for accounting periods beginning on or after 1 January 2016, subject to transitional rules in F(No 2)A 2015 Sch 7 paras 115 to 129.

[Meaning of "matched"]

475B Meaning of "matched"

(1) This section applies for the purposes of this Part.

(2) A loan relationship of a company is matched if and to the extent that—

(*a*) it is in a matching relationship with another loan relationship or a derivative contract of the company, or

(*b*) exchange gains or losses arising in relation to an asset or liability representing the loan relationship are excluded from being brought into account under regulations under section 328(4),

and "unmatched" is to be construed accordingly.

(3) A loan relationship is in a matching relationship with another loan relationship or derivative contract if one is intended by the company to act to eliminate or substantially reduce the economic risk of the other.

(4) In this section "economic risk" means a risk which can be attributed to fluctuations in exchange rates between currencies over a period of time.

(5) In this section "derivative contract" has the same meaning as in Part 7 (see section 576).][1]

Amendments—[1]   Section 475B inserted by FA 2016 s 49, Sch 7 paras 1, 10 with effect in relation to accounting periods beginning on or after 1 April 2016 (FA 2016 Sch 7 para 12(1)). Where a company has an accounting period beginning before 1 April 2016 and ending on or after that date ("the straddling period") the periods before and after 1 April 2016 are treated as separate accounting periods (FA 2016 Sch 7 para 12(2)).

[Meaning of "hybrid capital instrument"

475C Meaning of "hybrid capital instrument"

(1) For the purposes of this Part, a loan relationship is a "hybrid capital instrument" for an accounting period of the debtor if—

  (a) the loan relationship makes provision under which the debtor is entitled to defer or cancel a payment of interest under the loan relationship,

  (b) the loan relationship has no other significant equity features, and

  (c) the debtor has made an election in respect of the loan relationship which has effect for the period.

(2) For the purposes of this section a loan relationship "has no other significant equity features" if under the loan relationship—

  (a) there are neither voting rights in the debtor (ignoring insignificant voting rights in the debtor) nor a right to exercise a dominant influence over the debtor,

  (b) any provision for altering the amount of the debt is limited to write-down or conversion events in qualifying cases, and

  (c) any provision for the creditor to receive anything other than interest or repayment of the debt is limited to conversion events in qualifying cases.

(3) For the purposes of subsection (2)(a)—

  (a) the loan relationship makes provision for "insignificant voting rights in the debtor" if (and only if) the voting rights of any creditor under the loan relationship are limited to one vote exercisable in relation to matters generally affecting the debtor without conferring any special advantage or other right on the creditor, and

  (b) "the right to exercise a dominant influence over the debtor" means the right to give directions with respect to the debtor's operating and financial policies with which it is obliged to comply (whether or not they are for the debtor's benefit).

(4) For the purposes of subsection (2)(b) a "write-down event" means—

  (a) a permanent release of some or all of the debt, or

  (b) a reduction in the amount of the debt (including to nil) in a case where provision is made for the reduction to be temporary (whether on the meeting of conditions or the exercise of a right or otherwise).

(5) For the purposes of subsection (2) a "conversion event" means—

  (a) the conversion of the loan relationship into shares forming part of the debtor's ordinary share capital, or

  (b) the conversion of the loan relationship into shares forming part of the ordinary share capital of [a company ("C") which, after the conversion, has control of the debtor or would have control of the debtor if C were taken to have all the rights and interests in the debtor of any company connected with C][2]

. . .[2]

(6) For the purposes of subsection (2), a loan relationship makes provision for a qualifying case if—

  (a) the provision applies only in the event that there is a material risk of the debtor becoming unable to pay its debts as they fall due,

  (b) the provision applies only in the event that the value of the debtor's assets is less than the amount of its liabilities, taking into account contingent and prospective liabilities, or

  (c) the provision is included in the loan relationship solely because of a need to comply with a regulatory or other legal requirement,

and, in each case, the provision in question does not include a right exercisable by the creditor.

(7) Provision is not to be regarded as failing to meet the condition in subsection (2)(b) merely because, in the case of a write-down event mentioned in subsection (4)(b), it provides for a subsequent increase in the amount of the debt (but not above the original amount).

(8) An election under this section—

  (a) is irrevocable,

  [(b) must be made before the end of the period of 6 months beginning with—

    (i) the day on which the company becomes a party to the loan relationship, or

    (*a*) section 485 (exclusion of debts where profits or losses within Part 7 or 8), and

    (*b*) section 486 (exclusion of exchange gains and losses in respect of tax debts etc).

479 Relevant non-lending relationships not involving discounts

(1) A company has a relevant non-lending relationship if—

    (*a*) the company stands, or has stood, in the position of a creditor or debtor in relation to a money debt,

    (*b*) the money debt did not arise from a transaction for the lending of money (and so, because of section 302(1)(*b*), there is no loan relationship), and

    (*c*) the money debt is one of the kinds mentioned in subsection (2).

(2) The kinds of debt are—

    (*a*) a debt on which interest is payable to or by the company,

    (*b*) a debt in relation to which exchange gains or losses arise to the company, . . .[1]

    (*c*) a debt in relation to which an impairment loss (or credit in respect of the reversal of an impairment loss) [or release debit][1] arises to the company in respect of an unpaid (or previously unpaid) business payment[, and

    (*d*) a debt in relation to which a relevant deduction has been allowed to the company and which is released.][1]

(3) In subsection [(2)(*c*)][1] "business payment" means a payment which, if it were paid, would fall to be brought into account for corporation tax purposes as a receipt of a trade, UK property business or overseas property business carried on by the company.

[(3A) In subsection (2)(*d*) "relevant deduction" means a deduction allowed in calculating the profits of a trade, UK property business or overseas property business.][1]

(4) For the meaning of "money debt" and "interest" in this Chapter, see—

    (*a*) section 483 (exchange gains and losses: amounts treated as money debts) and

    (*b*) section 484 (provision not at arm's length: meaning of "interest" and "money debt").

(5) For the meaning of "exchange gains or losses", see section 475.

(6) This section is subject to section 485 (exclusion of debts where profits or losses within Part 7 or 8).

Amendments—[1]   In sub-s (2)(*b*) word "and" repealed; words in sub-s (2)(*c*) and whole of sub-ss (2)(*d*), (3A) inserted; and in sub-s (3) words substituted for the words "(2)", by FA 2009 s 42(4)–(7) with effect from 22 April 2009.

480 Relevant non-lending relationships involving discounts

(1) A company has a relevant non-lending relationship if—

    (*a*) the company stands in the position of creditor in relation to a money debt,

    (*b*) the money debt did not arise from a transaction for the lending of money (and so, because of section 302(1)(*b*), there is no loan relationship),

    (*c*) the money debt is one from which a discount arises to the company,

    (*d*) the discount does not fall to be brought into account under section 509 (treatment of alternative finance arrangements as loan relationships etc) as a result of arrangements to which section 503 (purchase and resale arrangements) applies, and

    (*e*) in a case where the money debt is some or all of the consideration payable for a disposal of property, conditions A and B are met.

(2) Condition A is that the property in question is not—

    (*a*) an asset representing a loan relationship the disposal of which is a disposal to which subsection (3) applies, or

    (*b*) an asset representing a derivative contract the disposal of which is such a disposal.

(3) This subsection applies to a disposal if—

    (*a*) section 340 (group transfers and transfers of insurance business: transfer at notional carrying value) applies to it or would apply apart from section 341 (transferor using fair value accounting),

    (*b*) section 625 (group member replacing another as party to derivative contract) applies to it or would apply apart from section 628 (transferor using fair value accounting), or

    (*c*) the whole of the consideration for the disposal is brought into account for the purposes of Part 5 (loan relationships) or Part 7 (derivative contracts).

(4) Condition B is that, assuming that the money debt will be paid in full, it does not fall to be brought into account for corporation tax purposes as a trading receipt of the company.

(5) For the purposes of this section, a discount is, in particular, taken to arise from a money debt if—

    (*a*) there is a sale of property for consideration some or all of which is money which falls to be paid after the sale,

    (*b*) the amount or value of the whole consideration exceeds what the purchaser would have paid for the property if payment in full had been required at the time of the sale, and

    (*c*) some or all of the excess can reasonably be regarded as representing a return on an investment of money at interest (and so as being a discount arising from the money debt).

(6) It does not matter for the purposes of subsection (1)(*c*) whether the discount is of a revenue or capital nature.

(7) This section is subject to section 485 (exclusion of debts where profits or losses within Part 7 or 8).

Application of Part 5 to relevant non-lending relationships

481 Application of Part 5 to relevant non-lending relationships

(1) If a company has a relevant non-lending relationship—

    (a) Part 5 (loan relationships) applies in relation to the relevant matters (see subsections (3) and (5)) as it applies in relation to such matters arising under or in relation to a loan relationship, but

    (b) the only credits or debits to be brought into account for the purposes of that Part in respect of the relationship are those relating to those matters.

(2) Accordingly, subject to subsection (1)(b), references in the Corporation Tax Acts to a loan relationship include a reference to a relevant non-lending relationship.

(3) The relevant matters in the case of a relevant non-lending relationship within section 479 are—

    (a) interest payable to or by the company in respect of the relevant non- lending relationship,

    (b) exchange gains or losses arising to the company as a result of the relationship,

    (c) in the case of a debt on which interest is payable to the company, profits (but not losses) arising to the company from any related transaction in respect of the right to receive interest,

    (d) in the case of a debt in relation to which an impairment loss [or release debit][1] arises to the company in respect of an unpaid business payment, the [impairment or release,][1]

    (e) in the case of a debt in relation to which a credit in respect of the reversal of an impairment loss arises to the company in respect of a previously unpaid business payment, the reversal[and

    (f) in the case of a debt in relation to which a relevant deduction has been allowed to the company and which is released, the release.][1].

(4) In subsection [(3)(d) and (e)][1] "business payment" has the meaning given in section 479(3).

[(4A) In subsection (3)(f) "relevant deduction" has the meaning given in section 479(3A).][1]

(5) The relevant matters in the case of a relevant non-lending relationship within section 480 are—

    (a) the matters referred to in subsection (3),

    (b) the discount arising to the company from the money debt,

    (c) profits (but not losses) arising to the company from any related transaction,

    (d) any impairment arising to the company in respect of the discount, and

    (e) any reversal of any such impairment.

(6) Subsection (7) applies if a company—

    (a) has a relevant non-lending relationship within section 479 because of a debt on which interest is payable to the company, but

    (b) enters into a related transaction in respect of the right to receive interest as a result of which interest is not payable.

(7) Even though the interest is not payable to the company, for the purpose of bringing credits into account in respect of that or any other related transaction as a result of the application of subsection (3)(c), the company is still treated as having a relevant non-lending relationship within section 479.

(8) Section 480(5) (when discount arises) applies for the purpose of this section as it applies for the purposes of section 480.

Amendments—[1]   In sub-s (3)(d) words inserted and words substituted for the words "impairment, and"; sub-s (3)(f), (4A) inserted; and in sub-s (4) words substituted for the word "(3)", by FA 2009 s 42(8)–(11) with effect from 22 April 2009.

482 Miscellaneous rules about amounts to be brought into account because of this Chapter

(1) Any credits or debits which—

    (a) relate to interest payable under the Tax Acts, and

    (b) fall to be brought into account because of this Chapter,

are treated for the purposes of Part 5 as non-trading credits or debits.

(2) The credits to be brought into account for the purposes of that Part in respect of a discount arising from a money debt under a relevant non-lending relationship are to be determined using an amortised cost basis of accounting.

Meaning of "money debt" and "interest" in this Chapter

483 Exchange gains and losses: amounts treated as money debts

(1) This section applies for the purposes of this Chapter so far as relating to exchange gains and losses.

(2) Any currency held by a company is treated as a money debt owed to the company.

(3) A provision made by a company for the purposes of its statutory accounts in respect of a liability to which the company may become subject is treated as a money debt owed by the company if it meets conditions A and B.

(4) Condition A is that if the company became subject to the liability, the duty to settle it would be owed for the purposes of—

    (a) a trade,

    (b) a UK property business, or

Amendments—[1] Sections 468A–486E inserted by FA 2009 s 48, Sch 24 para 3 with effect in relation to any arrangement which produces for a company a return which is economically equivalent to interest if the company becomes a party to the arrangement on or after 22 April 2009.

[486D Exclusion where arrangement has no tax avoidance purpose

(1) This Chapter does not apply in relation to a return produced by an arrangement to which a company is a party unless it is reasonable to assume that the main purpose, or one of the main purposes, of the company being a party to the arrangement is to obtain a relevant tax advantage.

(2) But a company for which a return is produced by an arrangement to which this Chapter would otherwise be prevented from applying by subsection (1) may elect that this Chapter is to apply in relation to the return.

(3) An election under subsection (2)—

   (a) may not be made by a company if section 486B applies to the company in relation to the return in accordance with subsection (6) of that section,

   (b) must be made no later than the time when the arrangement begins to produce a return for the company, and

   (c) is irrevocable.

(4) In this section "obtain a relevant tax advantage" means secure that the return (or any part of it) is produced in a way which means that its treatment for corporation tax purposes is more advantageous to the company than it would be if it were—

   (a) charged to corporation tax as income of the company, or

   (b) brought into account as income of the company for corporation tax purposes,

at the time when amounts would be brought into account in relation to the return in accordance with section 486B.

(5) . . .[2]

(6) . . .[2]]1

Amendments—[1] Sections 468A–486E inserted by FA 2009 s 48, Sch 24 para 3 with effect in relation to any arrangement which produces for a company a return which is economically equivalent to interest if the company becomes a party to the arrangement on or after 22 April 2009.

[2] Sub-ss (5), (6) repealed by FA 2012 s 180, Sch 20 paras 24, 26 with effect in relation to accounting periods of CFCs beginning on or after 1 January 2013. This is subject to savings in FA 2012 Sch 20 para 50(9) which provides, broadly, that the amendments in question will not take effect until an accounting period under the new CFC rules in TIOPA 2010 Part 9A begins.

[486E Excluded shares

(1) This Chapter does not apply in relation to an accounting period ("the relevant accounting period") of a company ("the holding company") for which an arrangement produces a return for the company if the arrangement involves only relevant shares held by the company throughout the relevant period.

(2) In this section "the relevant period" means the period—

   (a) beginning with the later of—

     (i) the time when the holding company becomes party to the arrangement, and

     (ii) the time when the arrangement begins to produce a return for the company, and

   (b) ending with the earliest of—

     (i) the end of the relevant accounting period,

     (ii) the time when the holding company ceases to be party to the arrangement, and

     (iii) the time when the arrangement ceases to produce a return for the company.

(3) For the purposes of this section an arrangement "involves only" relevant shares if (and only if) the return produced reflects only an increase in the fair value of the shares.

(4) For the purposes of subsection (3)—

   (a) "fair value", in relation to relevant shares held by the holding company, means an amount which the company would obtain from a knowledgeable and willing purchaser of the shares dealing at arm's length, and

   (b) there is an increase in the fair value of shares even if the increase is realised by the payment of a distribution in respect of the shares.

(5) In this section "relevant shares" means shares which, throughout the relevant period, are—

   (a) fully paid-up shares of a relevant company, or

   (b) shares of a company, other than a relevant company, which would be accounted for as a liability by the company in which they are shares in accordance with generally accepted accounting practice and which produce for the holding company a return in relation to any amount which is economically equivalent to interest (as to which see Chapter 6A).

(6) For the purposes of subsection (5)(a) shares are fully paid-up if there are no actual or contingent obligations—

   (a) to meet unpaid calls on the shares, or

   (b) to make a contribution to the capital of the company in which they are shares that could affect the value of the shares.

(7) For the purposes of subsection (5) a company is "a relevant company" if—

   (*a*) it and the holding company are connected companies,

   (*b*) it is a relevant joint venture company, or

   (*c*) it is a [CFC within the meaning of Part 9A of TIOPA 2010][2].

(8) Section 466 (companies connected for an accounting period) applies for the purposes of subsection (7)(*a*).

[(9) For the purposes of subsection (7)(*b*) a company ("C") is a relevant joint venture company if—

   (*a*) the holding company is one of two persons who, taken together, control C,

   (*b*) the holding company has interests, rights and powers representing at least 40% of the holdings, rights and powers in respect of which the holding company and the second person fall to be taken as controlling C, and

   (*c*) the second person has interests, rights and powers representing—

      (i) at least 40%, but

      (ii) no more than 55%,

   of the holdings, rights and powers in respect of which the holding company and the second person fall to be taken as controlling C.

(10) For the purposes of subsection (9)—

   (*a*) section 371RB of TIOPA 2010 (read with section 371RD of that Act) applies for the purpose of determining if two persons, taken together, control a company, and

   (*b*) section 371RD of that Act applies for the purpose of determining if the requirements of paragraphs (*b*) and (*c*) are met in any case.][2]

(11) . . .[2]

(12) Section 550(3) (repos: ignoring effect on borrower of sale of securities) does not apply for the purposes of this section.][1]

[Sections 355 to 363 of TIOPA 2010 (meaning of "offshore fund")]

Amendments—[1]   Sections 468A–486E inserted by FA 2009 s 48, Sch 24 para 3 with effect in relation to any arrangement which produces for a company a return which is economically equivalent to interest if the company becomes a party to the arrangement on or after 22 April 2009.

[2]   In sub-s (7)(*c*), words substituted for words "relevant controlled foreign company", sub-ss (9), (10) substituted, and sub-s (11) repealed by FA 2012 s 180, Sch 20 paras 24, 27 with effect in relation to accounting periods of CFCs beginning on or after 1 January 2013. This is subject to savings in FA 2012 Sch 20 para 50(9) which provides, broadly, that the amendments in question will not take effect until an accounting period under the new CFC rules in TIOPA 2010 Part 9A begins. By virtue of FA 2012 Sch 20 para 51, the substitution of sub-ss (9), (10) has no effect for relevant periods beginning before 1 January 2013 (and the relevant provisions of TA 1988 Part 17 Chapter 4 continue to have effect accordingly notwithstanding the repeal of that Chapter by FA 2012 Sch 20 para 14).

[CHAPTER 2B

TRANSFERRED INCOME STREAMS

[486F Introduction to Chapter

(1) This Chapter provides for Part 5 to apply in relation to a company to which an income stream transfer is made ("the transferee").

(2) An "income stream transfer" is a transfer by a person ("the transferor") to which either of the following provisions applies—

   (*a*) [Chapter 1 of Part 16 of CTA 2010][2] (transfers of income streams by companies), or

   (*b*) Chapter 5A of Part 13 of ITA 2007 (transfers of income streams by individuals).][1]

Amendments—[1]   Sections 468F–486G inserted by FA 2009 s 49, Sch 25 para 8 with effect in relation to transfers on or after 22 April 2009.

[2]   In sub-s (2)(*a*) words substituted for words "Part 1 of Schedule 25 to FA 2009" by CTA 2010 s 1177, Sch 1 para 625. CTA 2010 has effect for corporation tax purposes for accounting periods ending on or after 1 April 2010, and for income and capital gains tax purposes for the tax year 2010–11 and subsequent tax years.

[486G Consideration to be treated as loan relationship

(1) For the purposes of this Part—

   (*a*) the consideration for the transfer of the right to relevant receipts is to be treated as a money debt which is owed to the transferee by the person by whom the relevant receipts fall to be paid, and

   (*b*) the transfer is to be treated as a transaction for the lending of money from which that debt is treated as arising.

(2) For the meaning of "relevant receipts" see [section 752(2) of CTA 2010][2] or section 809AZA(2) of ITA 2007.][1]

Amendments—[1]   Sections 468F–486G inserted by FA 2009 s 49, Sch 25 para 8 with effect in relation to transfers on or after 22 April 2009.

[2]   In sub-s (2) words substituted for words "paragraph 1(2) of Schedule 25 to FA 2009" by CTA 2010 s 1177, Sch 1 para 626. CTA 2010 has effect for corporation tax purposes for accounting periods ending on or after 1 April 2010, and for income and capital gains tax purposes for the tax year 2010–11 and subsequent tax years.

(3) References in this section and sections 494 and 495 to investments of a unit trust scheme are references to investments subject to the trusts of the scheme, other than cash awaiting investment.

(4) References in this section and sections 494 and 495 to investments of an offshore fund are references to assets of the fund, other than cash awaiting investment.

(5) In this section "collective investment scheme" has the meaning given by section 235 of FISMA 2000.

(6) A person with rights in a part of an umbrella company which is regarded under [section 615(3) of CTA 2010][1] as an open-ended investment company is treated for the purposes of this section as not owning shares in the umbrella company.

(7) For the meaning of references to investments subject to the trusts of the scheme in the case of certain authorised unit trusts, see [section 619 of CTA 2010][1] (umbrella schemes).

Amendments—[1] In sub-ss (2)(*b*), (6) words substituted for words "section 468A(3) of ICTA", in sub-s (7) words substituted for words "section 468(9) of ICTA" by CTA 2010 s 1177, Sch 1 para 628. CTA 2010 has effect for corporation tax purposes for accounting periods ending on or after 1 April 2010, and for income and capital gains tax purposes for the tax year 2010–11 and subsequent tax years.

494 Meaning of "qualifying investments"

(1) In section 493 "qualifying investments", in relation to an open-ended investment company, a unit trust scheme or an offshore fund, means investments of the company, scheme or fund of any of the following descriptions—

    (*a*) money placed at interest,

    (*b*) securities,

    (*c*) shares in a building society,

    (*d*) qualifying holdings in an open-ended investment company, a unit trust scheme or an offshore fund,

    (*e*) alternative finance arrangements,

    (*f*) derivative contracts whose underlying subject matter consists wholly of any one or more of—

        (i) the matters referred to in paragraphs (*a*) to (*e*) (other than diminishing shared ownership arrangements), and

        (ii) currency,

    (*g*) contracts for differences whose underlying subject matter consists wholly of any one or more of—

        (i) interest rates,

        (ii) creditworthiness, and

        (iii) currency, and

    (*h*) derivative contracts not within paragraph (*f*) or (*g*) where there is a hedging relationship between the contract and an asset within paragraphs (*a*) to (*d*).

(2) In this section—

"contract for differences" has the same meaning as in Part 7 (derivative contracts) (see section 582),

"diminishing shared ownership arrangements" means arrangements to which section 504 applies,

"hedging relationship" has the meaning given by section 496,

"qualifying holding" has the meaning given by section 495(1),

"security" does not include shares in a company, and

"underlying subject matter" has the same meaning as in Part 7 (derivative contracts) (see section 583).

495 Qualifying holdings

(1) For the purposes of section 494(1)(*d*) a holding in an open-ended investment company, a unit trust scheme or an offshore fund is a qualifying holding at any time if—

    (*a*) at that time, or

    (*b*) at any other time in the relevant accounting period,

the company, scheme or fund [itself fails][2] to meet the qualifying investments test . . . . . [2]

(2) . . . [2]

(3) In this section "holding"—

    (*a*) in relation to an open-ended investment company, means—

        (i) except where sub-paragraph (ii) applies, shares in the company, and

        (ii) in a case where under [section 615(3) of CTA 2010][1] part of an umbrella company is regarded as an open-ended investment company, rights in the separate pool in question,

    (*b*) in relation to a unit trust scheme, means an entitlement to a share in the investments of the scheme, and

    (*c*) in relation to an offshore fund, means—

        (i) shares in any company by which the fund is constituted, or

        (ii) an entitlement to a share in the investments of the fund.

(4) In this section "relevant accounting period" means the accounting period referred to in section 490(1).

Amendments—[1]   In sub-s (3)(*a*), (*ii*) words substituted for words "section 468A(3) of ICTA" by CTA 2010 s 1177, Sch 1 para 629. CTA 2010 has effect for corporation tax purposes for accounting periods ending on or after 1 April 2010, and for income and capital gains tax purposes for the tax year 2010–11 and subsequent tax years.

[2]   In sub-s (1), words substituted for words "would itself fail" and words ", even on the assumption in subsection (2)" repealed, and sub-s (2) repealed, by FA 2014 s 27(1), (6) with effect in relation to accounting periods beginning on or after 1 April 2014. For accounting periods straddling 1 April 2014, see FA 2014 s 27(8), (9).

496 Meaning of "hedging relationship"

(1) For the purposes of section 494, in relation to an open-ended investment company, a unit trust scheme or an offshore fund, there is a hedging relationship between a derivative contract ("the hedging instrument") and an asset ("the hedged item") so far as condition A or B is met.

(2) Condition A is that the hedging instrument and the hedged item are designated as a hedge by the company, scheme or fund.

(3) Condition B is that the hedging instrument is intended to act as a hedge of exposure to changes in fair value of a hedged item which is—

    (*a*) a recognised asset which could affect the total net return of the company, scheme or fund, or

    (*b*) an identified part of such an asset which is attributable to a particular risk.

(4) For the purposes of subsection (3) "the total net return" of a company, scheme or fund means its total net return calculated—

    (*a*) in accordance with generally accepted accounting practice, or

    (*b*) in the case of accounts prepared in a jurisdiction outside the United Kingdom, in accordance with generally accepted accounting practice in that jurisdiction.

Power to change investments that are qualifying investments

497 Power to change investments that are qualifying investments

(1) The Treasury may by order amend sections 493 to 496 so as to extend or restrict the descriptions of investments of an open-ended investment company, a unit trust scheme or an offshore fund that are qualifying investments for the purposes of those provisions.

(2) The order may make—

    (*a*) different provision for different cases, and

    (*b*) incidental, supplemental, consequential and transitional provision and savings.

(3) In particular, the order may make such incidental modifications of section 495(2) as the Treasury consider appropriate.

CHAPTER 4
BUILDING SOCIETIES

498 Building society dividends and interest

(1) This section deals with how building society dividends and interest are dealt with for corporation tax purposes.

(2) Liability to pay building society interest or building society dividends is treated for the purposes of Part 5 as a liability arising under a loan relationship (so far as it would not otherwise be such a liability).

(3) If building society interest or building society dividends are payable to a company, they are treated as so payable as the result of a right arising under a loan relationship of the company (so far as they would not otherwise be so payable).

(4) Subsection (3) applies to interest paid under a certified SAYE savings arrangement with a building society as if it were a dividend on a share in the society.

(5) In this section—

    "building society dividends" means dividends payable in respect of shares in a building society,

    "building society interest" means interest payable in respect of shares in, deposits with, or loans to, a building society,

    "certified SAYE savings arrangement" has the meaning given by section 703 of ITTOIA 2005, and

    "dividend" includes any distribution, however described.

CHAPTER 5
[REGISTERED SOCIETIES]

499 [Registered society] payments treated as interest under loan relationship

(1) Any dividend, bonus or other sum payable to a shareholder in—

    (*a*) a [registered society][1], or

    (*b*) a UK agricultural or fishing co-operative,

(c) the eventual owner is to make payments to the first owner amounting in aggregate to the consideration paid for the acquisition of the first owner's beneficial interest (but subject to any adjustment required for such a reduction as is mentioned in subsection (5)),

(d) the eventual owner is to acquire the first owner's beneficial interest (whether or not in stages) as a result of those payments,

(e) the eventual owner is to make other payments to the first owner (whether under a lease forming part of the arrangements, or otherwise),

(f) the eventual owner has the exclusive right to occupy or otherwise to use the asset, and

(g) the eventual owner is exclusively entitled to any income, profit or gain arising from or attributable to the asset (including, in particular, an increase in its value).

(2) For the purposes of subsection (1)(a) it does not matter if—

(a) the first owner acquires its beneficial interest from the eventual owner,

(b) the eventual owner, or another person who is not the first owner, also has a beneficial interest in the asset, or

(c) the first owner also has a legal interest in it.

(3) Subsection (1)(f) does not prevent the eventual owner from granting an interest or right in relation to the asset if the conditions in subsection (4) are met.

(4) The conditions are that—

(a) the grant is not to—

(i) the first owner,

(ii) a person controlled by the first owner, or

(iii) a person controlled by a person who also controls the first owner, and

(b) the grant is not required by the first owner or arrangements to which the first owner is a party.

(5) Subsection (1)(g) does not prevent the first owner from—

(a) having responsibility for any reduction in the asset's value, or

(b) having a share in a loss arising out of any such reduction.

(6) This section is subject to section 508 (provision not at arm's length: exclusion of arrangements from section 503, this section and sections 505 to 507).

505 Deposit arrangements

(1) This section applies to arrangements if under them—

(a) a person ("the depositor") deposits money with a financial institution,

(b) the money, together with money deposited with the institution by other persons, is used by it with a view to producing a profit,

(c) from time to time the institution makes or credits a payment to the depositor out of profit resulting from the use of the money,

(d) the payment is in proportion to the amount deposited by the depositor, and

(e) the payments so made or credited by the institution equate, in substance, to the return on an investment of money at interest.

(2) This section is subject to section 508 (provision not at arm's length: exclusion of arrangements from sections 503 and 504, this section, and sections 506 and 507).

506 Profit share agency arrangements

(1) This section applies to arrangements if under them—

[(a) a person ("the principal") appoints an agent,

(ab) one or both of the principal and agent is a financial institution,]¹

(b) the agent uses money provided by the principal with a view to producing a profit,

(c) the principal is entitled, to a specified extent, to profits resulting from the use of the money,

(d) the agent is entitled to any additional profits resulting from its use (and may also be entitled to a fee paid by the principal), and

(e) payments made because of the principal's entitlement to profits equate, in substance, to the return on an investment of money at interest.

(2) This section is subject to section 508 (provision not at arm's length: exclusion of arrangements from sections 503 to 505, this section and section 507).

HMRC Manuals—Corporate Finance Manual CFM44100 (profit share agency arrangements classed as an alternative finance arrangement).
CFM44110 (examples of profit share agency arrangements).

¹ In sub-s (1), paras (a), (ab) substituted for previous para (a), by the Alternative Finance Arrangements (Amendment) Order, SI 2009/2568 art 3(1), (3) with effect in relation to arrangements entered into on or after 15 October 2009.

507 Investment bond arrangements

(1) This section applies to arrangements if—

(a) they provide for one person ("the bond-holder") to pay a sum of money ("the capital") to another ("the bond-issuer"),

(b) they identify assets, or a class of assets, which the bond-issuer will acquire for the purpose of generating income or gains directly or indirectly ("the bond assets"),

(c) they specify a period at the end of which they cease to have effect ("the bond term"), (*d*) the bond-issuer undertakes under the arrangements—

        (i) to dispose at the end of the bond term of any bond assets which are still in the bond-issuer's possession,

        (ii) to make a repayment of the capital ("the redemption payment") to the bond-holder during or at the end of the bond-term (whether or not in instalments), and

        (iii) to pay to the bond-holder other payments on one or more occasions during or at the end of the bond term ("additional payments"),

    (*e*) the amount of the additional payments does not exceed an amount which would be a reasonable commercial return on a loan of the capital,

    (*f*) under the arrangements the bond-issuer undertakes to arrange for the management of the bond assets with a view to generating income sufficient to pay the redemption payment and additional payments,

    (*g*) the bond-holder is able to transfer the rights under the arrangements to another person (who becomes the bond-holder because of the transfer),

    (*h*) the arrangements are a listed security on a recognised stock exchange [or admitted to trading on a multilateral trading facility operated by an EEA-regulated recognised stock exchange][1], and

    (i) the arrangements are wholly or partly treated in accordance with international accounting standards as a financial liability of the bond-issuer, or would be if the bond-issuer applied those standards.

(2) For the purposes of subsection (1)—

    (*a*) the bond-issuer may acquire bond assets before or after the arrangements take effect,

    (*b*) the bond assets may be property of any kind, including rights in relation to property owned by someone other than the bond-issuer,

    (*c*) the identification of the bond assets mentioned in subsection (1)(*b*) and the undertakings mentioned in subsection (1)(*d*) and (*f*) may (but need not) be described as, or accompanied by a document described as, a declaration of trust,

    (*d*) a reference to the management of assets includes a reference to disposal,

    (*e*) the bond-holder may (but need not) be entitled under the arrangements to terminate them, or participate in terminating them, before the end of the bond term,

    (*f*) the amount of the additional payments may be—

        (i) fixed at the beginning of the bond term,

        (ii) determined wholly or partly by reference to the value of or income generated by the bond assets, or

        (iii) determined in some other way,

    (*g*) if the amount of the additional payments is not fixed at the beginning of the bond term, the reference in subsection (1)(*e*) to the amount of the additional payments is a reference to the maximum amount of the additional payments,

    (*h*) the amount of the redemption payment may (but need not) be subject to reduction in the event of a fall in the value of the bond assets or in the rate of income generated by them, . . .[1]

    (*i*) entitlement to the redemption payment may (but need not) be capable of being satisfied (whether or not at the option of the bond-issuer or the bond-holder) by the issue or transfer of shares or other securities,

    [(*j*) a recognised stock exchange is an "EEA-regulated recognised stock exchange" if it is regulated in the European Economic Area, and

    (*k*) "multilateral trading facility" has the same meaning as in Article 4.1.22 of Directive 2014/65/EU of the European Parliament and of the Council of 15 May 2014 on markets in financial instruments.][1]

(3) This section is subject to section 508.

Amendments—[1] In sub-s (1)(*h*), words inserted, in sub-s (2)(*h*), word repealed, and sub-s (2)(*j*), (*k*) inserted, by FA 2018 s 34(2) with effect—

    – for corporation tax purposes, in relation to accounting periods beginning on or after 1 April 2018; and

    – for income tax and capital gains tax purposes, for the tax year 2018–19 and subsequent tax years.

Prospective amendments—In sub-s (1)(*h*) words "a regulated" to be substituted for words "an EEA-regulated", in sub-s (2)(*h*) word "and" to be inserted at the end, sub-s (2)(*j*) and (*k*) to be repealed, and sub-s (2A) to be inserted, by the Taxes (Amendments) (EU Exit) Regulations, SI 2019/689 reg 16(1), (10) with effect from Implementation Period completion day (see EU(WA)A 2020 Sch 5 para 1(1)). Sub-s (2A) to read as follows—

    "(2A) For the purposes of subsection (1)—

    "regulated recognised stock exchange" means a recognised stock exchange that is regulated in the United Kingdom, the European Economic Area or Gibraltar;

    "multilateral trading facility" means—

        (*a*) a UK multilateral trading facility within the meaning given by Article 2.1(14A) of Regulation (EU) No 600/2014 of the European Parliament and of the Council of 15 May 2014 on markets in financial instruments,

(3) In the case of investment bond arrangements, the additional payments under the arrangements are alternative finance return for the purposes of this Part.

(4) In subsection (3) "additional payments" has the same meaning as in section 507 (see subsection (1)(d)(iii) of that section).

Treatment for other tax purposes

514 Exclusion of alternative finance return from consideration for sale of assets

(1) If under purchase and resale arrangements an asset is sold by one party to the arrangements to the other party, the alternative finance return is excluded in determining the consideration for the sale and purchase of the asset for the purposes of the Corporation Tax Acts (apart from section 503).

(2) If under diminishing shared ownership arrangements an asset is sold by one party to the arrangements to the other party, the alternative finance return is excluded in determining the consideration for the sale and purchase of the asset for the purposes of the Corporation Tax Acts (apart from section 504).

(3) If under investment bond arrangements an asset is sold by one party to the arrangements to the other party, the alternative finance return is excluded in determining the consideration for the sale and purchase of the asset for the purposes of the Corporation Tax Acts (apart from section 507).

(4) Subsections (1) to (3) do not affect the operation of any provision of the [Tax Acts or TCGA 1992][1] which provides that the consideration for a sale or purchase is taken for any purpose to be an amount other than the actual consideration.

Amendments—[1] In sub-s (4) words substituted for words "Corporation Tax Acts" by the Corporation Tax Act 2009 (Amendment) Order, SI 2009/2860 art 6(1), (3) with effect for corporation tax purposes for accounting periods ending on or after 1 April 2009, and for income tax and capital gains tax purposes for the tax year 2009–10 and subsequent tax years.

515 Diminishing shared ownership arrangements not partnerships

Diminishing shared ownership arrangements are not treated as a partnership for the purposes of the Corporation Tax Acts.

516 Treatment of principal under profit sharing agency arrangements

(1) The principal under profit sharing agency arrangements is not treated for the purposes of the Corporation Tax Acts as entitled to profits to which the agent is entitled in accordance with section 506(1)(d).

(2) And the agent under such arrangements is treated for those purposes as entitled to those profits and the profits specified in section 506(1)(c).

(3) In this section "the principal" and "the agent" are to be read in accordance with section 506.

517 Treatment of bond-holder under investment bond arrangements

(1) This section applies for the purposes of the Corporation Tax Acts and irrespective of the position for other purposes.

(2) The bond-holder under investment bond arrangements is not treated as having a legal or beneficial interest in the bond assets.

(3) The bond-issuer under such arrangements is not treated as a trustee of the bond assets.

(4) Profits accruing to the bond-issuer in connection with the bond assets are profits of the bond-issuer and not of the bond-holder (and do not arise to the bond-issuer in a fiduciary or representative capacity).

(5) Payments made by the bond-issuer by way of redemption payment or additional payment are not made in a fiduciary or representative capacity.

(6) The bond-holder is not entitled to relief for capital expenditure in connection with the bond assets.

(7) Expressions used in this section have the same meaning as in section 507.

518 Investment bond arrangements: treatment as securities

(1) Investment bond arrangements are securities for the purposes of the Corporation Tax Acts.

(2) For those purposes—

  (a) a reference in an enactment to redemption is to be taken as a reference to making the redemption payment, . . .[1]

  (b) a reference in an enactment to interest is to be taken as a reference to alternative finance return[, and

  (c) the bond-issuer is to be treated for the purposes of [Chapter 4 of Part 13 of CTA 2010 (securitisation companies)][2] as being party as debtor to a capital market arrangement][1].

(3) In subsection (2) "the redemption payment" has the same meaning as in section 507 (see subsection (1)(d)(ii) of that section).

Amendments—[1] In sub-s (2), word "and" at end of para (a) repealed, and para (c) and preceding word "and" inserted, by the Corporation Tax Act 2009 (Amendment) Order, SI 2009/2860 art 6(1), (4) with effect for corporation tax purposes for accounting periods ending on or after 1 April 2009, and for income tax and capital gains tax purposes for the tax year 2009–10 and subsequent tax years.

[2] In sub-s (2)(c) words substituted for words "section 84 of FA 2005 (taxation of securitisation companies)" by CTA 2010 s 1177, Sch 1 para 631. CTA 2010 has effect for corporation tax purposes for accounting periods ending on or after 1 April 2010, and for income and capital gains tax purposes for the tax year 2010–11 and subsequent tax years.

519 Investment bond arrangements: other provisions

(1) A bond-issuer is not a securitisation company for the purposes of section 83 of FA 2005 (application of accounting standards to securitisation companies) unless it is one as a result of arrangements which are not investment bond arrangements.

(2) For the purposes of [sections 453 and 454 of CTA 2010 (definitions related to close companies)][1]

    (a) a bond-holder is a loan creditor in respect of the bond-issuer, and

    (b) investment bond arrangements must be ignored in the application of [section 454(2)(e) of CTA 2010][1].

(3) For the purposes of [Chapter 6 of Part 5 of CTA 2010][1] (group relief)—

    (a) a bond-holder is a loan creditor in respect of the bond-issuer, and

    (b) [condition C in section 162(4) of CTA 2010][1] must be ignored in determining whether a person is an equity holder as a result of investment bond arrangements.

[(4) Investment bond arrangements are not—

    (a) a unit trust scheme for the purposes of section 1119 of CTA 2010, or

    (b) an offshore fund for the purposes of section 354 of TIOPA 2010 so far as relating to corporation tax.][1]

Amendments—[1]   The following amendments made by CTA 2010 s 1177, Sch 1 para 632—
-   in sub-s (2) words substituted for words "section 417 of ICTA (close companies)" and "section 417(1)(d) of that Act";
-   in sub-s (3) words substituted for words "Schedule 18 to ICTA" and "paragraph 1(5)(b) of that Schedule";
-   sub-s (4) inserted.

CTA 2010 has effect for corporation tax purposes for accounting periods ending on or after 1 April 2010, and for income and capital gains tax purposes for the tax year 2010–11 and subsequent tax years.

520 Provision not at arm's length: non-deductibility of relevant return

(1) This section applies if arrangements to which section 508 (provision not at arm's length: exclusion of arrangements from sections 503 to 507) applies would, but for that section, be alternative finance arrangements.

(2) A company paying relevant return under the arrangements is not entitled to—

    (a) any deduction in calculating profits or gains for corporation tax purposes, or

    (b) any deduction [from][1] total profits,

in respect of the relevant return.

(3) In this section "relevant return" has the same meaning as in section 508 (see subsection (3) of that section).

Amendments—[1]   In sub-s (2)(b) word substituted for word "against" by CTA 2010 s 1177, Sch 1 para 633. CTA 2010 has effect for corporation tax purposes for accounting periods ending on or after 1 April 2010, and for income and capital gains tax purposes for the tax year 2010–11 and subsequent tax years.

Power to extend this Chapter to other arrangements

[CHAPTER 6A
SHARES ACCOUNTED FOR AS LIABILITIES

521A Introduction to Chapter

(1) This Chapter contains rules for Part 5 (and the other provisions of the Corporation Tax Acts) to apply in some cases as if at some times in the accounting period of a company ("A") which holds shares of a certain kind in another company ("B") the shares were rights under a creditor relationship of A.

(2) See, in particular—

    (a) section 521B (application of Part 5 to some shares as rights under creditor relationship), and

    (b) section 521C (which describes the shares to which the rules apply).

(3) In this Chapter references to the investing company are to A and references to the issuing company are to B.

(4) For the purposes of this Chapter, the definition of "share" in section 476(1) only applies so far as it provides that "share" does not include a share in a building society.

(5) Section 550(3) (repos: ignoring effect on borrower of sale of securities) does not apply for the purposes of this Chapter.

(6) See section 116B of TCGA 1992 for the effect for chargeable gains purposes of shares beginning or ceasing to be shares to which section 521C applies.][1]

Amendments—[1]   Sub-ss 521A–521F inserted by FA 2009 s 48, Sch 24 para 4 with effect from 22 April 2009.

[521B Application of Part 5 to certain shares as rights under creditor relationship

(1) This section applies in relation to the times in a company's accounting period when—

    (a) the company holds a share in another company, and

    (b) section 521C (shares accounted for as liabilities) applies to the share.

(2) Part 5 (and the other provisions of the Corporation Tax Acts) apply as if at those times—

    (a) the share were rights under a creditor relationship of the investing company, and

(5) In this Chapter—

"manufactured interest", in relation to a manufactured interest relationship, means an amount within subsection (3)(*a*), and

"the real interest" means the interest mentioned in subsection (4)(*a*).

(6) References in the Corporation Tax Acts to a company being a party to a manufactured interest relationship are to be read in accordance with this section.

(7) . . . . [1]

Amendments— [1] Sub-s (7) repealed by FA 2013 s 77, Sch 29 paras 34, 35 with effect from 1 January 2014.

540 Manufactured interest treated as interest under loan relationship

(1) If a company has a manufactured interest relationship under which manufactured interest is payable by it, Part 5 applies to the company and the manufactured interest as it would if the manufactured interest were interest payable on a loan to the company (and so were interest under a loan relationship to which the company is a party).

(2) If a company has a manufactured interest relationship under which manufactured interest is payable to it, Part 5 applies to the company and the manufactured interest as it would if—

(*a*) the manufactured interest were interest payable on a loan by the company (and so were interest under a loan relationship to which the company is a party), and

(*b*) the manufactured interest relationship were the loan relationship under which the real interest is payable.

(3) Accordingly, subject to subsection (2)(*b*), references in the Corporation Tax Acts to a loan relationship include a reference to a manufactured interest relationship [and the credits and debits to be brought into account in respect of manufactured interest for any period are those that are recognised in determining the company's profit or loss for the period in accordance with generally accepted accounting practice (but subject to the provisions of Part 5 . . . . [3] . . . . . . [2] .][1]

(4) Subsection (5) applies if a company—

(*a*) has a manufactured interest relationship, but

(*b*) enters into a related transaction in respect of the right to receive manufactured interest as a result of which the manufactured interest is not payable to the company.

(5) Even though the manufactured interest is not payable to the company, for the purpose of bringing credits into account in respect of that or any other related transaction because of the application of subsection (2), the company is still treated as having a manufactured interest relationship.

(6) This section is subject to Chapter 10 (repos).

Amendments— [1] In sub-s (3) words inserted by FA 2009 s 61, Sch 30 para 5(1) with effect in relation to manufactured interest whenever paid, apart from payments treated under TA 1988 s 737A(5) as made before 27 January 2009.

[2] In sub-s (3), words "and to section 799 of CTA 2010" repealed by FA 2013 s 77, Sch 29 paras 34, 36 with effect from 1 January 2014.

[3] In sub-s (3), words ", including, in particular, section 307(3)" repealed by F(No 2)A 2015 s 32, Sch 7 paras 56, 58 with effect for accounting periods beginning on or after 1 January 2016, subject to transitional rules in F(No 2)A 2015 Sch 7 paras 115 to 129.

541 Debits for deemed interest under stock lending arrangements disallowed

(1) This section applies if a company is the borrower under a stock lending arrangement for the purposes of [section 812 of CTA 2010][1] (which treats such a borrower as having made a payment representative of interest for the purposes of this Chapter).

(2) In accordance with [subsection (3) of that section][1] (which prevents deductions or group relief for the borrower in stock lending cases), the company may not bring debits into account for the purposes of Part 5 [of this Act][1] in respect of the representative payment which is treated as having been made under [subsection (2) of that section][1].

Amendments— [1] In sub-s (1) words substituted for words "section 736B(2) of ICTA", in sub-s (2) words substituted for words "section 736B(2A) of that Act" and "section 736B(2) of that Act", words inserted by CTA 2010 s 1177, Sch 1 para 637. CTA 2010 has effect for corporation tax purposes for accounting periods ending on or after 1 April 2010, and for income and capital gains tax purposes for the tax year 2010–11 and subsequent tax years.

CHAPTER 10

REPOS

Introduction

542 Introduction to Chapter

(1) The purpose of this Chapter is to secure that in the case of an arrangement—

(*a*) which involves the sale of securities and the subsequent purchase of those or similar securities, and

(*b*) which equates, in substance, to a transaction for the lending of money at interest from or to a company, with the securities which were sold as collateral for the loan,

the charge to corporation tax reflects the fact that the arrangement equates, in substance, to such a transaction.

(2) Sections 543 to [546][1] make provision about arrangements which are creditor repos or creditor quasi-repos.

(3) Sections 548 to 551 make provision about arrangements which are debtor repos or debtor quasi-repos.

Amendments—[1] In sub-s (2) words substituted for "547" by FA 2009 s 48, Sch 24 para 10 with effect from 22 April 2009.

Creditor repos and creditor quasi-repos

543 Meaning of creditor repo

(1) For the purposes of this Chapter a company ("the lender") has a creditor repo if each of conditions A to E is met.

(2) Condition A is that under an arrangement another person ("the borrower") receives from the lender any money or other asset ("the advance").

(3) Condition B is that, in accordance with generally accepted accounting practice, the accounts of the lender for the period in which the advance is made record a financial asset in respect of the advance.

(4) Condition C is that under the arrangement the borrower sells any securities at any time to the lender.

(5) Condition D is that the arrangement makes provision conferring a right or imposing an obligation on the lender to sell those or similar securities at any subsequent time.

(6) Condition E is that, in accordance with generally accepted accounting practice, the subsequent sale of those or similar securities would extinguish the financial asset in respect of the advance recorded in the accounts of the lender.

(7) For the purposes of conditions A to E references to the lender include a firm of which the lender is a member.

544 Meaning of creditor quasi-repo

(1) For the purposes of this Chapter a company ("the lender") has a creditor quasi-repo in any case if—

(a) the lender does not have a creditor repo in that case, and

(b) each of conditions A to E is met in that case.

(2) Condition A is that under an arrangement a person receives from the lender any money or other asset ("the advance").

(3) Condition B is that, in accordance with generally accepted accounting practice, the accounts of the lender for the period in which the advance is made record a financial asset in respect of the advance.

(4) Condition C is that under that or any other arrangement a person sells any securities at any time to the lender or any other person.

(5) Condition D is that the arrangement or other arrangement—

(a) makes provision conferring a right or imposing an obligation on the lender to sell the securities or any other securities at any subsequent time, or

(b) makes provision conferring such a right or imposing such an obligation on any other person and makes other relevant provision.

(6) For this purpose an arrangement makes other relevant provision if it makes provision—

(a) for the receipt of any money, securities or other asset from the lender under that arrangement for the purpose of enabling the other person to make that subsequent sale, or

(b) for the discharge of any liability to the lender under that arrangement for that purpose (whether by way of set off or otherwise).

(7) Condition E is that, in accordance with generally accepted accounting practice—

(a) the subsequent sale of the securities or the other securities by the lender, or

(b) the receipt of the asset from the lender, or the discharge of the liability to the lender, under the arrangement or other arrangement,

would extinguish the financial asset in respect of the advance recorded in the accounts of the lender.

(8) For the purposes of conditions A to E references to the lender include a firm of which the lender is a member.

545 Ignoring effect on lender etc of sale of securities

(1) This section applies if a company ("the lender") has a creditor repo or a creditor quasi-repo.

(2) For the purposes of the charge to corporation tax in respect of income of the lender arising while the arrangement is in force, the Corporation Tax Acts have effect as if—

(a) the lender did not hold the securities that are initially sold for any period for which the arrangement is in force, and

(b) the lender did not make in that period any payment representative of income payable in respect of the securities.

(3) But subsection (2) is subject to subsections (4) and (5).

(4) An amount is not to be ignored for the purposes of that charge as a result of subsection (2)(a) if—

(a) it is, in accordance with generally accepted accounting practice, recognised in determining the lender's profit or loss for that or any other period, or

(b) is owed to the person to whom the securities are initially sold.

(3) The arrangement is, in the case of the borrower, to be treated for the purposes of Part 5 and this Part as a transaction for the lending of money from which that debt is treated as arising for those purposes.

(4) Any amount which, in accordance with generally accepted accounting practice, is recorded as a finance charge in respect of the advance in—

    (a) the accounts of the borrower, or

    (b) if the borrower is a member of a firm which receives the advance, the accounts of the firm,

is treated for the purposes of Part 5, this Part and Part 15 of ITA 2007 (deduction of income tax at source) as interest payable under that debt.

(5) That interest is treated for those purposes as paid at the earlier of—

    (a) the time when the relevant repurchase takes place, and

    (b) the time when it becomes apparent that that repurchase will not take place.

(6) For this purpose "the relevant repurchase" means—

    (a) if the borrower has a debtor repo, the subsequent buying of the securities or similar securities, and

    (b) if the borrower has a debtor quasi-repo—

        (i) the subsequent buying of the securities or other securities by the borrower,

        (ii) the receipt of the asset from the borrower, or

        (iii) the discharge of the liability to the borrower,

    as the case may be.

General provisions

552 General provisions about arrangements

(1) For the purposes of this Chapter it does not matter whether or not provision of any arrangement conferring a right or imposing an obligation on any person to buy any securities is subject to any conditions.

(2) For the purposes of this Chapter an arrangement is in force from the time when the securities are initially sold until the earlier of—

    (a) the time when the relevant repurchase takes place, and

    (b) the time when it becomes apparent that that repurchase will not take place.

(3) In subsection (2) "the relevant repurchase" has the meaning given by subsections (4) to (7).

(4) In the case of a creditor repo, it means the subsequent sale of the securities or similar securities.

(5) In the case of a creditor quasi-repo, it means—

    (a) the subsequent sale of the securities or other securities by the lender,

    (b) the receipt of the asset from the lender, or

    (c) the discharge of the liability to the lender,

as the case may be.

(6) In the case of a debtor repo, it means the subsequent buying of the securities or similar securities.

(7) In the case of a debtor quasi-repo, it means—

    (a) the subsequent buying of the securities or other securities by the borrower,

    (b) the receipt of the asset from the borrower, or

    (c) the discharge of the liability to the borrower,

as the case may be.

553 Persons buying or selling for others

(1) For the purposes of this Chapter, in any case where—

    (a) a person ("A") buys securities (or has a right or obligation to buy securities), but

    (b) the securities are (or are to be) held for the benefit of another person ("B"),

B (not A) is treated as buying (or having the right or obligation to buy) the securities.

(2) In any case where—

    (a) a person ("C") sells securities, but

    (b) the proceeds of the sale are held for the benefit of another person ("D"),

D (not C) is treated as selling the securities.

554 Power to modify this Chapter

(1) The Treasury may by regulations provide for all or any of the provisions of this Chapter to apply with modifications in relation to—

    (a) cases where section 555 (non-standard repo cases) applies, or

    (b) cases involving redemption arrangements, or

    (c) both of those cases.

(2) A case involves redemption arrangements if—

    (a) arrangements, corresponding to those made in cases where a company has a repo, are made in relation to securities that are to be redeemed in the period after their sale, and (*b*) the arrangements are such that a person (instead of having the right or obligation to buy those securities, or similar or other securities, at any subsequent time) has a right or obligation in respect of the benefits which will result from the redemption.

(3) The regulations may make—

    (*a*) different provision for different cases, and

    (*b*) incidental, supplemental, consequential and transitional provision and savings.

(4) In this section and section 555—

    "modifications" include exceptions and omissions, and

    "repo" means—

        (*a*) a debtor repo or debtor quasi-repo, or

        (*b*) a creditor repo or creditor quasi-repo (including anything treated, as a result of section 547, as a creditor repo for the purposes of section 546).

555 Cases where section 554 applies: non-standard repos

(1) The cases to which this section applies are where—

    (*a*) a company has a repo,

    (*b*) there has been a sale of the securities under the arrangement or arrangements by reference to which the company has the repo, and

    (*c*) any of conditions A to C is met in relation to the repo.

(2) Condition A is that those securities, or similar or other securities, are not subsequently bought under the arrangement or arrangements.

(3) Condition B is that provision is made by or under an arrangement for different or additional securities to be treated as, or as included with, securities which, for the purposes of the subsequent purchase, are to represent those initially sold.

(4) Condition C is that provision is made by or under an arrangement for securities to be treated as not so included.

Interpretation

556 Meaning of securities and similar securities

(1) In this Chapter "securities" (except in the definition of "overseas securities" in section 559) means—

    (*a*) shares, stock or other securities issued by—

        (i) the government of the United Kingdom,

        (ii) any public or local authority in the United Kingdom, or

        (iii) any UK resident company or other UK resident body, or

    (*b*) overseas securities.

(2) For the purposes of this Chapter securities are similar if they entitle their holders to—

    (*a*) the same rights against the same persons as to capital, interest and dividends, and

    (*b*) the same remedies for the enforcement of those rights.

(3) For the purposes of subsection (2) any difference in—

    (*a*) the total nominal amounts of the respective securities,

    (*b*) the form in which they are held, or

    (*c*) the way in which they can be transferred,

is ignored.

557 Meaning of person receiving an asset

For the purposes of this Chapter references to a person receiving any asset include the person—

    (*a*) obtaining the value of any asset directly or indirectly, or

    (*b*) otherwise deriving any benefit from it directly or indirectly.

558 Interpretation of accounting expressions

(1) In determining for the purposes of this Chapter whether an amount is recorded as a financial asset or liability in respect of the advance, it is assumed that the period of account in which the advance is received or made ended immediately after the receipt or making of the advance.

(2) In its application for the purposes of this Chapter, section 309(1) applies as if the reference to a company were a reference to a person.

559 Minor definitions

In this Chapter—

    "advance"—

        (*a*) in the case of a creditor repo, has the same meaning as in section 543,

        (*b*) in the case of a creditor quasi-repo, has the same meaning as in section 544,

        (*c*) in the case of a debtor repo, has the same meaning as in section 548, and

        (*d*) in the case of a debtor quasi-repo, has the same meaning as in section 549,

    "arrangement" includes any agreement or understanding (whether or not it is legally enforceable),

(6) Condition C is that the charge applies at a rate of at least 20% in relation to the amounts subject to tax in the company's hands, other than amounts arising or accruing in respect of investments of a description for which a special relief or exemption is generally available.

(7) Condition D is that the charge is made otherwise than by reference to the company's profits.

Amendments—[1] In sub-(1), words substituted for words "section 460 of ICTA" by FA 2012 s 176, Sch 18 paras 19, 21 with effect in relation to accounting periods of companies beginning on or after 1 January 2013, subject to transitional provisions in FA 2012 s 179.

565 Relevant amount where the relevant company uses fair value accounting

(1) This section applies if the relevant company brings credits and debits in respect of the investment life insurance contract into account on the basis of fair value accounting.

(2) If this section applies, the relevant amount for section 563 is—

$$PC \times \frac{AR}{100 - AR}$$

where—

    PC is the profit from the contract (see subsections (3) and (4)), and

    AR is the appropriate rate for the accounting period (as defined in section 563(6)).

(3) For the purposes of this section, except where subsection (4) applies, the profit from the contract is any amount by which—

    (a) the amount payable as a result of the related transaction, exceeds

    (b) the fair value of the contract at the beginning time (see subsection (6)).

(4) If the related transaction is an assignment or surrender of only part of the rights conferred by the contract, the profit from the contract is any amount by which—

    (a) the amount payable as a result of the related transaction, exceeds

    (b) the relevant fraction of the fair value of the contract at the beginning time.

(5) In subsection (4) "the relevant fraction" means—

$$\frac{C}{FVC}$$

where—

    C is the amount payable as a result of the related transaction, and

    FVC is the fair value of the contract immediately before the related transaction.

(6) In this section "the beginning time" means—

    (a) if the contract was made before the beginning of the first accounting period of the company beginning on or after 1st April 2008, at the beginning of that period, and

    (b) otherwise when the contract was made.

Old accounting period contracts

566 Introduction

(1) This section and sections 567 to 569 apply if the relevant company was a party to an investment life insurance contract immediately before the beginning of the first accounting period of the company beginning on or after 1 April 2008.

(2) In those sections—

    "the deemed surrender" means the surrender of all the rights under that contract that the relevant company was deemed for the purposes of Chapter 2 of Part 13 of ICTA (life policies etc) to have made . . .[1] under paragraph 6(1) of Schedule 13 to FA 2008 . . .[1]

    "the first accounting period" means the first accounting period of the company beginning on or after [1 April 2008][1], and

    "the old contract" means the contract mentioned in subsection (1).

Amendments—[1] In sub-s (2), in definition of "the deemed surrender" words repealed in both places, and in definition of "the first accounting period" words substituted by the Corporation Tax Act 2009 (Amendment) Order 2010 SI 2010/614 reg 3(1), (4) with effect for accounting periods ending on or after 1 April 2009.

567 Gains on deemed surrenders to be brought into account on related transactions

(1) Any gain which arose under Chapter 2 of Part 13 of ICTA (life policies etc) as a result of the deemed surrender ("the deemed gain") is to be brought into account by the relevant company as a non-trading credit for the accounting period in which there is a related transaction (so far as not previously brought into account under this section).

(2) But if the relevant company is still a party to the old contract immediately after the related transaction, only the relevant fraction of the deemed gain which would otherwise be brought into account under subsection (1) is to be so brought into account.

(3) The relevant fraction" is—

$$\frac{P}{SAR}$$

where—

P is the amount payable as a result of the related transaction, and

SAR is the amount which would have been payable on a surrender of all the rights under the old contract immediately before the related transaction.

568 Restriction on credits on old contracts: fair value accounting cases

(1) This section applies if—

    (a) at all times since the old contract was made the rights conferred by it have been in the beneficial ownership of the relevant company,

    (b) the company brings into account credits and debits in respect of the old contract on the basis of fair value accounting, and

    (c) the old contract cost exceeds the fair value of the contract immediately before the beginning of the first accounting period.

(2) In subsection (1)(c) "the old contract cost" means—

    (a) if section 541 of ICTA applied on the deemed surrender, the amount specified in section 541(1)(b)(i) of that Act, less the amount or value of any relevant capital payments (as defined in section 541(5)(a) of that Act), and

    (b) if section 543 of that Act applied on the deemed surrender, the amount specified in section 543(1)(a)(i) of that Act, less the amount or value of any relevant capital payments (as defined in section 543(3) of that Act).

(3) No amount is to be brought into account as a credit in relation to the old contract by the relevant company as a result of section 562 except so far as the total of—

    (a) the amount of the credit, and

    (b) the amount of any other credits which have previously arisen in relation to the old contract as a result of that section,

is greater than the excess mentioned in subsection (1)(c).

569 Restriction on debits on old contracts: non-fair value accounting cases

(1) This section applies where—

    (a) the relevant company brings into account credits and debits in respect of the old contract otherwise than on the basis of fair value accounting, and

    (b) the carrying value of the old contract, as recognised for accounting purposes immediately before the beginning of the first accounting period, exceeds its fair value at that time.

(2) No amount is to be brought into account as a debit in relation to the old contract by the relevant company as a result of section 562 except so far as the total of—

    (a) the amount of the debit, and

    (b) the amount of any other debits which have previously arisen in relation to the contract as a result of that section,

is greater than the excess mentioned in subsection (1)(b).

PART 7
DERIVATIVE CONTRACTS

CHAPTER 1

INTRODUCTION
Introduction

570 Overview of Part

(1) This Part is about how profits and losses arising to a company from its derivative contracts are brought into account for corporation tax purposes.

(2) For the meaning of "derivative contract", see section 576 and the remainder of Chapter 2.

(3) For how such profits and losses are calculated and brought into account, see—

    (a) section 572 (profits and losses to be calculated using credits and debits given by this Part),

    (b) section 573 (trading credits and debits to be brought into account under Part 3),

    (c) section 574 (non-trading credits and debits to be brought into account under Part 5), and

    (d) Chapter 7 (chargeable gains arising in relation to derivative contracts).

(4) For the priority of this Part for corporation tax purposes, see Chapter 12.

(5) This Part also contains the following Chapters (which mainly relate to the amounts to be brought into account in respect of derivative contracts)—

    (a) Chapter 3 (credits and debits to be brought into account: general),

    (b) Chapter 4 (further provision about credits and debits to be brought into account),

    (c) Chapter 5 (continuity of treatment on transfers within groups),

(a) it is or does so for the purposes of the relevant accounting standard used by the company for that period, or

(b) it would be or would do so if the company used the relevant accounting standard for that period in respect of the contract.

(5) In this section "relevant accounting standard" means—

(a) for any accounting period in relation to which it is required or permitted to be used, Financial Reporting Standard 25 issued in December 2004 by the Accounting Standards Board, as from time to time modified, amended or revised, or

(b) for any accounting period in relation to which it is required or permitted to be used, any subsequent accounting standard dealing with transactions which are derivatives, as from time to time modified, amended or revised.

(6) For the meaning of "underlying subject matter", see section 583.

580 "Option"

(1) In this Part "option" includes a warrant.

(2) References in this Part to an option do not include a contract whose terms—

(a) provide—

    (i) that, after setting off their obligations to each other under the contract, a cash payment is to be made by one party to the other in respect of the excess, if any, or

    (ii) that each party is liable to make to the other party a cash payment in respect of all that party's obligations to the other under the contract, and

(b) do not provide for the delivery of any property.

(3) Subsection (2) does not prevent an option whose underlying subject matter is currency from being an option.

(4) But see—

(a) section 652 (introduction to sections 653 to 655),

(b) section 665 (issuers of securities with embedded derivatives: equity instruments), and

(c) section 695 (transfers of value to connected companies),

in which "option" is to be construed as if subsections (2) and (3) were omitted.

581 "Future"

(1) In this Part "future" means a contract for the sale of property under which delivery is to be made—

(a) at a future date agreed when the contract is made, and

(b) at a price so agreed,

but this is subject to subsection (3).

(2) For the purposes of subsection (1)(b), a price is agreed when the contract is made even if—

(a) the price is left to be determined by reference to the price at which a contract is to be entered into on a market or exchange or could be entered into at a time and place specified in the contract, or

(b) in a case where the contract is expressed to be by reference to a standard lot and quality, provision is made for a variation in the price to take account of any variation in quantity or quality on delivery.

(3) References in this Part to a future do not include a contract whose terms—

(a) provide—

    (i) that, after setting off their obligations to each other under the contract, a cash payment is to be made by one party to the other in respect of the excess, if any, or

    (ii) that each party is liable to make to the other party a cash payment in respect of all that party's obligations to the other under the contract, and

(b) do not provide for the delivery of any property.

(4) Subsection (3) does not prevent a future whose underlying subject matter is currency from being a future.

582 "Contract for differences"

(1) In this Part "contract for differences" means a contract the purpose or pretended purpose of which is to make a profit or avoid a loss by reference to fluctuations in—

(a) the value or price of property described in the contract, or

(b) an index or other factor designated in the contract,

[and includes a contract which falls within section 6(2) of, or paragraph 1(1) of Schedule 2 to, the Energy Act 2013][1].

(2) But none of the following is a contract for differences—

(a) an option,

(b) a future,

(c) a contract of insurance,

(d) a capital redemption policy,

(e) a contract of indemnity,

(f) a guarantee,

$$\frac{P}{SAR}$$

where—

P is the amount payable as a result of the related transaction, and
SAR is the amount which would have been payable on a surrender of all the rights under the old contract immediately before the related transaction.

568 Restriction on credits on old contracts: fair value accounting cases

(1) This section applies if—
  (a) at all times since the old contract was made the rights conferred by it have been in the beneficial ownership of the relevant company,
  (b) the company brings into account credits and debits in respect of the old contract on the basis of fair value accounting, and
  (c) the old contract cost exceeds the fair value of the contract immediately before the beginning of the first accounting period.
(2) In subsection (1)(c) "the old contract cost" means—
  (a) if section 541 of ICTA applied on the deemed surrender, the amount specified in section 541(1)(b)(i) of that Act, less the amount or value of any relevant capital payments (as defined in section 541(5)(a) of that Act), and
  (b) if section 543 of that Act applied on the deemed surrender, the amount specified in section 543(1)(a)(i) of that Act, less the amount or value of any relevant capital payments (as defined in section 543(3) of that Act).
(3) No amount is to be brought into account as a credit in relation to the old contract by the relevant company as a result of section 562 except so far as the total of—
  (a) the amount of the credit, and
  (b) the amount of any other credits which have previously arisen in relation to the old contract as a result of that section,
is greater than the excess mentioned in subsection (1)(c).

569 Restriction on debits on old contracts: non-fair value accounting cases

(1) This section applies where—
  (a) the relevant company brings into account credits and debits in respect of the old contract otherwise than on the basis of fair value accounting, and
  (b) the carrying value of the old contract, as recognised for accounting purposes immediately before the beginning of the first accounting period, exceeds its fair value at that time.
(2) No amount is to be brought into account as a debit in relation to the old contract by the relevant company as a result of section 562 except so far as the total of—
  (a) the amount of the debit, and
  (b) the amount of any other debits which have previously arisen in relation to the contract as a result of that section,
is greater than the excess mentioned in subsection (1)(b).

PART 7
DERIVATIVE CONTRACTS

CHAPTER 1

INTRODUCTION
Introduction

570 Overview of Part

(1) This Part is about how profits and losses arising to a company from its derivative contracts are brought into account for corporation tax purposes.
(2) For the meaning of "derivative contract", see section 576 and the remainder of Chapter 2.
(3) For how such profits and losses are calculated and brought into account, see—
  (a) section 572 (profits and losses to be calculated using credits and debits given by this Part),
  (b) section 573 (trading credits and debits to be brought into account under Part 3),
  (c) section 574 (non-trading credits and debits to be brought into account under Part 5), and
  (d) Chapter 7 (chargeable gains arising in relation to derivative contracts).
(4) For the priority of this Part for corporation tax purposes, see Chapter 12.
(5) This Part also contains the following Chapters (which mainly relate to the amounts to be brought into account in respect of derivative contracts)—
  (a) Chapter 3 (credits and debits to be brought into account: general),
  (b) Chapter 4 (further provision about credits and debits to be brought into account),
  (c) Chapter 5 (continuity of treatment on transfers within groups),

   (*d*) Chapter 6 (special kinds of company),
   (*e*) Chapter 8 (further provision about chargeable gains and derivative contracts),
   (*f*) Chapter 9 (European cross-border transfers of business),
   (*g*) Chapter 10 (European cross-border mergers),
   (*h*) Chapter 11 (tax avoidance), and
   (*i*) Chapter 13 (general and supplementary provisions).
(6) See also section 980 of ITA 2007 (payments under derivative contracts excepted from duty to deduct income tax).

How profits and losses from derivative contracts are dealt with

571 General rule: profits chargeable as income
(1) The general rule for corporation tax purposes is that all profits arising to a company from its derivative contracts are chargeable to corporation tax as income in accordance with this Part.
(2) But see Chapter 7, which makes provision for cases in which profits arising to a company from its derivative contracts are chargeable to corporation tax as chargeable gains.

572 Profits and losses to be calculated using credits and debits given by this Part
(1) Profits and losses arising to a company from its derivative contracts are to be calculated using the credits and debits given by this Part.
(2) For exceptions to this section, see sections 652 to 658 (issuers of securities with embedded derivatives: deemed options and contracts for differences).

573 Trading credits and debits to be brought into account under Part 3
(1) This section applies so far as in an accounting period a company is a party to a derivative contract for the purposes of a trade it carries on.
(2) The credits in respect of the contract for the period are treated as receipts of the trade which are to be brought into account in calculating the profits of the trade for that period.
(3) The debits in respect of the contract for the period are treated as expenses of the trade which are deductible in calculating those profits.
(4) So far as subsection (3) provides for any amount to be deductible, it applies despite anything in—
   (*a*) section 53 (capital expenditure),
   (*b*) section 54 (expenses not wholly and exclusively for trade and unconnected losses), or
   (*c*) section 59 (patent royalties).
(5) For cases in which this section does not apply, see—
   (*a*) section 616 (disapplication of fair value accounting for certain embedded derivatives), and
   (*b*) Chapter 7 (chargeable gains arising in relation to derivative contracts).

574 Non-trading credits and debits to be brought into account under Part 5
(1) This section applies if, for an accounting period, there are credits or debits in respect of the derivative contracts of a company which are not brought into account in accordance with section 573.
(2) Those credits or debits—
   (*a*) are to be treated as non-trading credits or non-trading debits (within the meaning of Part 5 (loan relationships)) for the period, and
   (*b*) are accordingly to be brought into account in determining whether the company has non-trading profits or a non-trading deficit from its loan relationships for the period.
[(2A) In the case of a non-UK resident company, subsection (2) needs to be read with section 5(3), (3A)(*b*) and (3B)(*b*) (territorial scope of charge to corporation tax).][1]
(3) For cases in which this section does not apply, see—
   (*a*) section 616 (disapplication of fair value accounting for certain embedded derivatives), and
   (*b*) Chapter 7 (chargeable gains arising in relation to derivative contracts).

Amendments—[2]   Sub-s (2A) inserted by FA 2020 s 32, Sch 6 para 2 with effect from 6 April 2020. This amendment has effect as if it had been incorporated into FA 2019 Sch 5 and so is subject to transitional provisions in FA 2019 Sch 5 Pt 3 (paras 36–50).

CHAPTER 2

CONTRACTS TO WHICH THIS PART APPLIES
Introduction

575 Overview of Chapter
(1) This Chapter makes provision about the contracts to which this Part applies.
(2) In particular, it—
   (*a*) contains a definition of "derivative contract" (see section 576),
   (*b*) contains other definitions (such as "relevant contract", "option", "future" and "contract for differences") which are used in determining whether a contract is a derivative contract (see sections 577 to 583),
   (*c*) makes provision about cases in which companies are treated as parties to relevant contracts (see sections 584 to 586),

(*d*) provides for certain contracts and transactions to be treated as derivative contracts (see sections 587 and 588), and

(*e*) provides for certain contracts to be treated as not being derivative contracts because of their underlying subject matter (see sections 589 to 593).

Meaning of "derivative contract" and other basic definitions

576 "Derivative contract"

(1) For the purposes of this Part, a contract of a company is a derivative contract of the company for an accounting period if it—

(*a*) is a relevant contract (see sections 577 and 578),

(*b*) meets any of the accounting conditions for the accounting period (see section 579), and

(*c*) is not prevented from being a derivative contract by section 589 (contracts excluded because of underlying subject matter: general) or any other provision of the Corporation Tax Acts.

(2) See also sections 587 and 588 (other contracts etc treated as derivative contracts).

(3) But note section 701 which includes power to amend the provisions of this Chapter relating to the meaning of "derivative contract".

577 "Relevant contract"

(1) In this Part "relevant contract" means—

(*a*) an option,

(*b*) a future, or

(*c*) a contract for differences.

(2) For the meaning of "option", "future" and "contract for differences", see sections 580, 581 and 582 respectively.

578 Relevant contracts of a company and being party to such contracts

(1) For the purposes of this Part, references to a relevant contract of a company are references to a relevant contract entered into or acquired by the company (but see subsection (3)).

(2) For the purposes of this Part, a relevant contract is acquired by a company if the company becomes—

(*a*) entitled to the rights under the relevant contract, and

(*b*) subject to the liabilities under it.

(3) For particular cases where companies are treated as parties to relevant contracts, see—

(*a*) section 584 (hybrid derivatives with embedded derivatives),

(*b*) section 585 (loan relationships with embedded derivatives), and

(*c*) section 586 (other contracts with embedded derivatives).

(4) References in this Part to a company being a party to a relevant contract are to be read in accordance with this section.

579 The accounting conditions

(1) The accounting conditions for any accounting period are that—

(*a*) the relevant contract is treated for accounting purposes as a derivative,

(*b*) the relevant contract—

(i) is not so treated just because of not meeting the requirement in paragraph 9(*b*) of Financial Reporting Standard 26 issued in December 2004 by the Accounting Standards Board (requirement for no initial net investment or smaller initial net investment than comparable types of contract), but

(ii) is or forms part of a financial asset or liability for accounting purposes, or

(*c*) the relevant contract is not within paragraph (*a*) or (*b*), but is within subsection (2).

(2) A relevant contract is within this subsection if—

(*a*) its underlying subject matter is commodities, or

(*b*) it is a contract for differences whose underlying subject matter is—

(i) land,

(ii) tangible movable property, other than commodities which are tangible assets,

(iii) intangible fixed assets,

(iv) weather conditions, or

(v) creditworthiness.

(3) For the purposes of subsection (1)(*a*), a relevant contract of a company is treated for accounting purposes as a derivative for an accounting period if for that period—

(*a*) it is so treated for the purposes of the relevant accounting standard used by the company for that period, or

(*b*) it would be so treated if the company used the relevant accounting standard for that period in respect of the contract.

(4) For the purposes of subsection (1)(*b*), a relevant contract of a company is or forms part of a financial asset or liability for accounting purposes for an accounting period if for that period—

(*a*) it is or does so for the purposes of the relevant accounting standard used by the company for that period, or

(*b*) it would be or would do so if the company used the relevant accounting standard for that period in respect of the contract.

(5) In this section "relevant accounting standard" means—

(*a*) for any accounting period in relation to which it is required or permitted to be used, Financial Reporting Standard 25 issued in December 2004 by the Accounting Standards Board, as from time to time modified, amended or revised, or

(*b*) for any accounting period in relation to which it is required or permitted to be used, any subsequent accounting standard dealing with transactions which are derivatives, as from time to time modified, amended or revised.

(6) For the meaning of "underlying subject matter", see section 583.

580 "Option"

(1) In this Part "option" includes a warrant.

(2) References in this Part to an option do not include a contract whose terms—

(*a*) provide—

(i) that, after setting off their obligations to each other under the contract, a cash payment is to be made by one party to the other in respect of the excess, if any, or

(ii) that each party is liable to make to the other party a cash payment in respect of all that party's obligations to the other under the contract, and

(*b*) do not provide for the delivery of any property.

(3) Subsection (2) does not prevent an option whose underlying subject matter is currency from being an option.

(4) But see—

(*a*) section 652 (introduction to sections 653 to 655),

(*b*) section 665 (issuers of securities with embedded derivatives: equity instruments), and

(*c*) section 695 (transfers of value to connected companies),

in which "option" is to be construed as if subsections (2) and (3) were omitted.

581 "Future"

(1) In this Part "future" means a contract for the sale of property under which delivery is to be made—

(*a*) at a future date agreed when the contract is made, and

(*b*) at a price so agreed,

but this is subject to subsection (3).

(2) For the purposes of subsection (1)(*b*), a price is agreed when the contract is made even if—

(*a*) the price is left to be determined by reference to the price at which a contract is to be entered into on a market or exchange or could be entered into at a time and place specified in the contract, or

(*b*) in a case where the contract is expressed to be by reference to a standard lot and quality, provision is made for a variation in the price to take account of any variation in quantity or quality on delivery.

(3) References in this Part to a future do not include a contract whose terms—

(*a*) provide—

(i) that, after setting off their obligations to each other under the contract, a cash payment is to be made by one party to the other in respect of the excess, if any, or

(ii) that each party is liable to make to the other party a cash payment in respect of all that party's obligations to the other under the contract, and

(*b*) do not provide for the delivery of any property.

(4) Subsection (3) does not prevent a future whose underlying subject matter is currency from being a future.

582 "Contract for differences"

(1) In this Part "contract for differences" means a contract the purpose or pretended purpose of which is to make a profit or avoid a loss by reference to fluctuations in—

(*a*) the value or price of property described in the contract, or

(*b*) an index or other factor designated in the contract,

[and includes a contract which falls within section 6(2) of, or paragraph 1(1) of Schedule 2 to, the Energy Act 2013][1].

(2) But none of the following is a contract for differences—

(*a*) an option,

(*b*) a future,

(*c*) a contract of insurance,

(*d*) a capital redemption policy,

(*e*) a contract of indemnity,

(*f*) a guarantee,

(g) a warranty, or

(h) a loan relationship.

(3) For the purposes of subsection (1)(b), an index or factor may be determined by reference to any matter.

Amendments—[1] In sub-s (1), words inserted by the Corporation Tax Act 2009, Section 582 (Contract for Differences) (Amendment) Order, SI 2013/3218 art 2 with effect in relation to accounting periods ending on or after 31 December 2013.

583 "Underlying subject matter"

(1) In this Part references to the underlying subject matter of a relevant contract are to be read as follows.

(2) The underlying subject matter of an option is—

(a) the property which would fall to be delivered if the option were exercised, or

(b) if the property which would so fall is a derivative contract, the underlying subject matter of that contract.

(3) The underlying subject matter of a future is—

(a) the property which, if the future were to run to delivery, would fall to be delivered at the date and price agreed when the contract is made, or

(b) if the property which would so fall is a derivative contract, the underlying subject matter of that contract.

(4) The underlying subject matter of a contract for differences is—

(a) if the contract for differences relates to fluctuations in the value or price of property described in the contract, the property so described, or

(b) if an index or factor is designated in the contract for differences, the matter by reference to which the index or factor is determined.

(5) The things which may be the subject matter of a contract for differences include—

(a) interest rates,

(b) weather conditions, and

(c) creditworthiness.

(6) Interest rates are not the underlying subject matter of a relevant contract if—

(a) under the terms of that contract—

(i) the date on which a party to that contract becomes subject to a duty to make a payment is a variable date, and

(ii) the amount of that payment varies according to the date of payment, and

(b) those terms refer to an interest rate only for the purpose of establishing that amount.

(7) The underlying subject matter of a relevant contract is not treated as being—

(a) land,

(b) shares in a company, or

(c) rights of a unit holder under a unit trust scheme,

just because its underlying subject matter includes income from that kind of property.

Cases where companies treated as parties to relevant contracts

584 Hybrid derivatives with embedded derivatives

(1) This section applies if—

(a) a company is a party to a relevant contract which meets the condition in section 579(1)(b) or (c) (contracts not treated for accounting purposes as derivatives),

(b) in accordance with generally accepted accounting practice, the company treats the rights and liabilities under the contract as divided between—

(i) rights and liabilities under one or more derivatives ("embedded derivatives"), and

(ii) the remaining rights and liabilities, and

(c) a contract consisting of only those remaining rights and liabilities would be a relevant contract.

(2) The company is treated for the purposes of this Part—

(a) as a party to a relevant contract whose rights and liabilities consist only of those of the embedded derivative, or (if there is more than one embedded derivative) as a party to relevant contracts each of whose rights and liabilities consist only of those of one of the embedded derivatives, and

(b) as a party to a relevant contract whose rights and liabilities are those within subsection (1)(b)(ii).

(3) Each relevant contract to which a company is treated as a party under subsection (2) is treated for the purposes of this Part as an option, a future or a contract for differences depending on what the character of a separate contract containing the rights and liabilities of the deemed relevant contract would be.

(4) In this Part "hybrid derivative" means a relevant contract within subsection (1)(a).

(5) See also—

(a) section 592 (embedded derivatives treated as meeting condition in section 591 etc), and (*b*) section 616 (disapplication of fair value accounting for certain embedded derivatives).

585 Loan relationships with embedded derivatives

(1) This section applies if in accordance with generally accepted accounting practice a company treats the rights and liabilities under a loan relationship to which it is a party as divided between—
 (*a*) rights and liabilities under a loan relationship, and
 (*b*) rights and liabilities under one or more derivative financial instruments or equity instruments ("embedded derivatives").
(2) The company is treated for the purposes of this Part—
 (*a*) as a party to a relevant contract whose rights and liabilities consist only of those of the embedded derivative, or
 (*b*) if there is more than one embedded derivative, as a party to relevant contracts each of whose rights and liabilities consist only of those of one of the embedded derivatives.
(3) Each relevant contract to which a company is treated as a party under subsection (2) is treated for the purposes of this Part as an option, a future or a contract for differences depending on what the character of a separate contract containing the rights and liabilities of the embedded derivative would be.
(4) For the corresponding treatment of the rights and liabilities within subsection (1)(*a*), see section 415 (loan relationships with embedded derivatives).
(5) See also—
 (*a*) section 416 (election for section 415 and this section to apply), and
 (*b*) section 635 (some creditor relationships treated as ones in relation to which section 415 and this section have effect).

586 Other contracts with embedded derivatives

(1) This section applies if a company—
 (*a*) is a party to a contract which is neither a hybrid derivative nor a loan relationship, and
 (*b*) in accordance with generally accepted accounting practice, treats the rights and liabilities under the contract as divided between—
  (i)   rights and liabilities under one or more derivatives ("embedded derivatives"), and
  (ii) the remaining rights and liabilities.
(2) The company is treated for the purposes of this Part—
 (*a*) as a party to a relevant contract whose rights and liabilities consist only of those of the embedded derivative, or
 (*b*) if there is more than one embedded derivative, as a party to relevant contracts each of whose rights and liabilities consist only of those of one of the embedded derivatives.
(3) Each relevant contract to which a company is treated as a party under subsection (2) is treated for the purposes of this Part as an option, a future or a contract for differences depending on what the character of a separate contract containing the rights and liabilities of the embedded derivative would be.
(4) See also section 616 (disapplication of fair value accounting for certain embedded derivatives).

Other contracts etc treated as derivative contracts

587 Contract relating to holding in OEIC, unit trust or offshore fund

(1) This section applies in relation to a relevant contract to which a company is a party in an accounting period if—
 (*a*) it is not a derivative contract for the purposes of this Part but for this section, and
 (*b*) its underlying subject matter consists wholly or partly of a relevant holding in that period.
(2) This Part has effect—
 (*a*) for that accounting period, and
 (*b*) for any succeeding accounting period in which the relevant contract is a relevant contract of the company,
as if the relevant contract were a derivative contract.
(3) For the purposes of this section, the underlying subject matter of a contract consists wholly or partly of a relevant holding in an accounting period if—
 (*a*) at any time in that period it consists wholly or partly of—
  (i)   any shares in an open-ended investment company,
  (ii) any rights under a unit trust scheme, or
  (iii) [an interest in an offshore fund (within the meaning of section 355 of TIOPA 2010)][1], and
 (*b*) there is a time in the period when that company, scheme or fund fails to meet the qualifying investments test.
(4) In subsection (3) "meeting the qualifying investments test" has the same meaning as in section 493 (the qualifying investments test).

(5) See section 18(2)(*c*)(ii) of F(No 2)A 2005 (section 17(3): specific powers) for the power to modify the meaning of "relevant holding" for the purposes of this section by regulations under section 17(3) of that Act (regulations about authorised unit trusts and OEICs).

(6) For the way in which credits and debits are to be brought into account where this section applies, see section 601 (application of fair value accounting).

(7) See also—

(*a*) section 602 (contract becoming one relating to holding in OEIC, unit trust or offshore fund), and

(*b*) section 660 (company ceasing to be party to contract relating to holding in OEIC, unit trust or offshore fund).

Amendments—[1]   In sub-s(3)(*a*)(iii), words substituted for "a material interest in an offshore fund within the meaning of Chapter 3 of part 6 (see section 489)" by the Offshore Funds (Tax) (Amendment No 2) Regulations, SI 2013/1411 reg 13(*a*) with effect from 28 June 2013.

588 Associated transaction treated as derivative contract

(1) This section is to be read as if it were in Chapter 7 (shares with guaranteed returns etc) of Part 6 (relationships treated as loan relationships etc).

(2) See, in particular—

section 526(2) (meaning of "non-qualifying share"), and

section 532 (meaning of "associated transaction" and "the associated transactions condition").

(3) Subsection (4) applies in a case which falls within section 523(1)(*b*)(ii) (loan relationships: non-qualifying shares) because the share mentioned in section 523(1)(*a*) is a non-qualifying share as a result of the associated transactions condition being met.

(4) An associated transaction is treated for the purposes of this Part as a derivative contract or a transaction in respect of a derivative contract if it is not in fact such a contract or transaction.

(5) Corporate Finance Manual CFM45260 (associated transactions).

Exclusions from derivative contracts

589 Contracts excluded because of underlying subject matter: general

(1) A relevant contract is not a derivative contract for the purposes of this Part if its underlying subject matter—

(*a*) consists wholly of excluded property (see subsections (2) to (5)), or

(*b*) is treated as consisting wholly of such property.

(2) "Excluded property" means—

(*a*) intangible fixed assets,

(*b*) shares in a company other than shares within subsection (3), or

(*c*) rights of a unit holder under a unit trust scheme other than a scheme in relation to which section 490 (holdings in OEICs, unit trusts and offshore funds treated as creditor relationship rights) has effect.

(3) The shares within this subsection are—

(*a*) shares to which section 524 or 526 (shares subject to outstanding third party obligations and shares which are non-qualifying shares) applies, and

(*b*) shares in an open-ended investment company in relation to which section 490 has effect.

(4) Subsection (2)(*a*) applies only in relation to a relevant contract which is an option or future.

(5) Subsection (2)(*b*) and (*c*) apply only in relation to a relevant contract which—

(*a*) meets any of conditions A to E in section 591, and

(*b*) is not designed to produce a return which equates in substance to the return on an investment of money at a commercial rate of interest.

(6) Section 590 applies for determining whether the underlying subject matter of a relevant contract is to be treated as consisting wholly of excluded property.

590 Disregard of subordinate or small value underlying subject matter

(1) This section applies in relation to a relevant contract if its underlying subject matter consists only of—

(*a*) excluded property, and

(*b*) other underlying subject matter which is—

(i) subordinate in relation to any of the excluded property, or

(ii) of small value in comparison with the value of the underlying subject matter as a whole.

(2) The underlying subject matter of the contract is treated for the purposes of this Part as if it consisted wholly of excluded property.

(3) For the purposes of this section, whether part of the underlying subject matter of a relevant contract of a company is subordinate or of small value is to be determined by reference to the time when the company enters into or acquires the contract.

(4) In this section "excluded property" has the same meaning as in section 589.

591 Conditions A to E mentioned in section 589(5)

(1) The following are the conditions mentioned in section 589(5).

(2) Condition A is that the relevant contract—

(*a*) is a plain vanilla contract entered into or acquired by a company carrying on [long-term business][1],

(*b*) is an approved derivative for the purposes of Rule 3.2.5 of the [Prudential Sourcebook for Insurers][2] [(within the meaning given by section 139(4) of FA 2012)][1], and

(*c*) does not meet the condition in section 579(1)(*b*) (contract which is or forms part of a financial asset or liability for accounting purposes).

(3) Condition B is that—

(*a*) the relevant contract is entered into or acquired by a company otherwise than for the purposes of a trade carried on by it,

(*b*) there is a hedging relationship between the contract and—

(i) an asset of the company which consists of shares or rights of a unit holder under a unit trust scheme, or

(ii) any share capital of the company or any liability related to share capital of the company, and

(*c*) the relevant contract is not one to which the company is treated as a party under section 585(2) (loan relationships with embedded derivatives).

(4) Condition C is that—

(*a*) the relevant contract is entered into or acquired by a company otherwise than for the purposes of a trade carried on by it, and

(*b*) the relevant contract is an option which is listed on a recognised stock exchange to subscribe for shares in a company.

(5) Condition D is that—

(*a*) the relevant contract is entered into or acquired by a company otherwise than in the course of activities forming an integral part of a trade carried on by it,

(*b*) the relevant contract is—

(i) an option to acquire shares in a company, or

(ii) a future requiring delivery of shares in a company,

(*c*) the relevant contract is not one to which the company is treated as a party under section 585(2), and

(*d*) the shares to be acquired or delivered—

(i) constitute a substantial shareholding within the meaning of paragraph 8 of Schedule 7AC to TCGA 1992 (meaning of "substantial shareholding"), or

(ii) would do so if acquired or delivered.

(6) Condition E is that—

(*a*) the company which is a party to the relevant contract has a hedging relationship between—

(i) the relevant contract, and

(ii) an asset or liability representing a loan relationship which is treated as mentioned in section 585(1) (loan relationships with embedded derivatives), and

(*b*) each relevant contract to which the company is treated as a party under section 585(2) in the case of that loan relationship is a derivative contract to which any of the provisions in subsection (7) applies.

(7) The provisions mentioned in subsection (6)(*b*) are—

(*a*) section 645 (creditor relationships: embedded derivatives which are options),

(*b*) section 648 (creditor relationships: embedded derivatives which are exactly tracking contracts for differences),

(*c*) sections 653 to 655 (issuers of securities with embedded derivatives: deemed options), and

(*d*) section 658 (issuers of securities with embedded derivatives: deemed contracts for differences).

(8) For the cases in which sections 653 to 655 and section 658 apply, see sections 652 and 656 respectively.

Amendments—[1] In sub-s (2), in para (*a*), words substituted for words "life assurance business", and in para (*b*) words inserted, by FA 2012 s 146, Sch 16 paras 135, 167 with effect in relation to accounting periods of companies beginning on or after 1 January 2013 (subject to transitional provisions in FA 2012 Sch 17). For accounting periods straddling 1 January 2013, see FA 2012 s 149.

[2] In sub-s (2)(*b*), words substituted by the Financial Services Act 2012 (Consequential Amendments) Order, SI 2013/636 art 2, Schedule para 11 with effect from 1 April 2013.

592 Embedded derivatives treated as meeting condition in section 591 etc

(1) This section applies if for an accounting period—

(*a*) a company is a party to a hybrid derivative which meets the condition in section 579(1)(*b*) (contract which is or forms part of a financial asset or liability for accounting purposes),

(*b*) the embedded derivative is a relevant contract which meets the condition in section 579(1)(*a*) (contract treated for accounting purposes as derivative),

(*c*) the underlying subject matter of that contract consists, or is treated as consisting, wholly of—

(i) shares in a company, or

(ii) rights of a unit holder under a unit trust scheme, and

(d) the host contract is or forms part of a financial asset or liability for accounting purposes.

(2) The embedded derivative is treated—

    (a) for the purposes of section 589 (contracts excluded because of underlying subject matter: general) as meeting one of the conditions in section 591, and

    (b) as a chargeable asset.

(3) The host contract is treated for the purposes of the Corporation Tax Acts as if it were a creditor relationship of the company (see Part 5 (loan relationships)).

(4) Section 590 (disregard of subordinate or small value underlying subject matter) applies for the purpose of determining whether the underlying subject matter is to be treated as consisting wholly of property mentioned in subsection (1)(c) as that section so applies in relation to excluded property.

(5) In this section—

    "the embedded derivative" means the relevant contract to which the company is treated as a party under section 584(2)(a) because of the hybrid derivative mentioned in subsection (1)(a), and

    "the host contract" means the relevant contract to which the company is treated as a party under section 584(2)(b) because of that hybrid derivative.

593 Contracts where part of underlying subject matter is excluded property

(1) This section applies to a relevant contract of a company—

    (a) which is an option or future,

    (b) which meets any of the accounting conditions in section 579(1), and

    (c) whose underlying subject matter consists of—

        (i) excluded property, and

        (ii) other underlying subject matter.

(2) A relevant contract to which this section applies is treated for the purposes of the Corporation Tax Acts as if it were the following two contracts—

    (a) a relevant contract whose underlying subject matter consists of the excluded property, and

    (b) a relevant contract whose underlying subject matter consists of the other underlying subject matter.

(3) For the purposes of giving effect to subsection (2), all such apportionments as are just and reasonable are to be made.

(4) This section does not apply to a relevant contract if it is determined in accordance with section 590 (disregard of subordinate or small value underlying subject matter) that the underlying subject matter of the relevant contract is to be treated as consisting wholly of excluded property.

(5) In this section "excluded property" has the same meaning as in section 589 (contracts excluded because of underlying subject matter: general).

CHAPTER 3
CREDITS AND DEBITS TO BE BROUGHT INTO ACCOUNT: GENERAL

Introduction

594 Overview of Chapter

(1) This Chapter contains rules of general application about the credits and debits to be brought into account for the purposes of this Part.

(2) In particular, it—

    [(za) makes provision about the matters in respect of which amounts are to be brought into account (see section 594A),][1]

    (a) sets out the general principles which are to apply in relation to the bringing into account of credits and debits, including the use of generally accepted accounting practice and the taking into account of related transactions (see sections 595 and 596),

    (b) makes provision about the interpretation of the expression "amounts recognised in determining a company's profit or loss" (see sections 597 to 599),

    (c) makes provision in relation to the application of fair value accounting (see sections 600 to 603),

    (d) sets out some general rules which differ from generally accepted accounting practice (see sections 604 and 605),

    (e) makes provision about exchange gains and losses (see section 606),

    (f) makes provision about pre-contract or abortive expenses (see section 607),

    [(g) makes provision about cases where amounts are recognised even though companies are not, or have ceased to be, parties to derivative contracts (see section 607A),

    (ga) makes provision about companies moving abroad (see sections 609 and 610), and][1]

    (h) makes provision in relation to statutory insolvency arrangements (see section 611).

Amendments—[1] In sub-s (2), para (za) inserted and paras (g), (ga) substituted for previous para (g), by F(No 2)A 2015 s 32, Sch 7 paras 59, 60 with effect for accounting periods beginning on or after 1 January 2016, subject to transitional rules in F(No 2)A 2015 Sch 7 paras 115 to 129.

    (a) no amount in respect of the contract . . . .[2] is recognised in determining its profit or loss for the period, or

    (b) an amount is so recognised in respect of only part of the contract . . .[2].][1]

[(7) For the purposes of this section arrangements are "tax avoidance arrangements" if the main purpose, or one of the main purposes, of any party to the arrangements, in entering into them, is to obtain a tax advantage.

(8) In subsection (7)—

    (a) "arrangements" includes any arrangements, scheme or understanding of any kind, whether or not legally enforceable, involving a single transaction or two or more transactions, and

    (b) "tax advantage" has the meaning given by section 1139 of CTA 2010.

(9) For the purposes of this section a company is to be treated as a party to a derivative contract even though it has disposed of its rights and liabilities under the contract to another person—

    (a) under a repo or stock lending arrangement, or

    (b) under a transaction which is treated as not involving any disposal as a result of section 26 of TCGA 1992 (mortgages and charges not to be treated as disposals).][2]

Commentary—*Simon's Taxes* D1.847.

HMRC Manuals—Corporate Finance Manual CFM56110 (amounts not fully recognised for accounting purposes). CFM56114 (periods beginning on or after 6 December 2010).

Cross-references—See FA 2011 Sch 4 para 13(2) (periods of account straddling 6 December 2010).

Amendments—[1]   Sections 599A, 599B inserted by FA 2009 s 61, Sch 30 para 3 with effect in relation to periods of account beginning on or after 22 April 2009, subject to transitional provisions relating to periods of account beginning before, and ending on or after, 22 April 2009: FA 2009 Sch 30 para 3(4).

[2]   In sub-s (2), word in para (a) inserted and para (b) substituted for previous paras (b), (c); sub-ss (3)–(5B) repealed; in sub-s (6), in opening words, words ", a contribution to it or securities issued by it" repealed, and in paras (a), (b) words ", contribution or securities" repealed; and sub-ss (7), (8), (9) inserted, by FA 2011 s 28, Sch 4 paras 7, 8 with effect in relation to periods of account beginning on or after 6 December 2010, subject to the transitional provision in FA 2011 Sch 4 para 13(2).

[599B Determination of credits and debits where amounts not fully recognised

(1) In determining the credits and debits which a company is to bring into account for the period referred to in section 599A(1) for the purposes of this Part in respect of the derivative contract mentioned in section 599A(2), the assumption in subsection (2) is to be made.

(2) The assumption is that an amount in respect of the whole of the contract in question is recognised in determining the company's profit or loss for the period.

[(2A) But no debits are, as a result of this section, to be brought into account by the company in respect of the derivative contract.][2]

(3) The credits and debits which are to be brought into account for the purposes of this Part by the company in respect of the contract are to be determined on the basis of fair value accounting.][1]

[(4) If—

    (a) the company is, or is treated as, a party to the contract at the beginning of the period referred to in section 599A(1), and

    (b) the fair value of the contract at that time is greater than the [tax-adjusted carrying value][3] of that contract at that time,

a credit of an amount equal to the difference is to be brought into account for that period for the purposes of this Part in respect of the contract.][2]

Amendments—[1]   Sections 599A, 599B inserted by FA 2009 s 61, Sch 30 para 3 with effect in relation to periods of account beginning on or after 22 April 2009, subject to transitional provisions relating to periods of account beginning before, and ending on or after, 22 April 2009: FA 2009 Sch 30 para 3(4).

[2]   Sub-ss (2A), (4) inserted by FA 2011 s 28, Sch 4 paras 7, 9 with effect in relation to periods of account beginning on or after 6 December 2010, subject to the transitional provision in FA 2011 Sch 4 para 13(2). Note that sub-ss (2A), (4) do not have effect where they apply by reason of tax avoidance arrangements to which the company became a party before 23 March 2011 (FA 2011 Sch 4 para 13(3)(b), (c)).

[3]   In sub-s (4)(b) words substituted for words "carrying value" by F(No 2)A 2015 s 32, Sch 7 paras 59, 64 with effect for accounting periods beginning on or after 1 January 2016, subject to transitional rules in F(No 2)A 2015 Sch 7 paras 115 to 129.

Application of fair value accounting

600 Contract which is or forms part of financial asset or liability

(1) This section applies to a derivative contract which meets the condition in section 579(1)(b) (contract which is or forms part of a financial asset or liability for accounting purposes).

(2) The amounts to be brought into account in accordance with this Part in respect of the contract are to be determined on the basis of fair value accounting.

601 Contract relating to holding in OEIC, unit trust or offshore fund

(1) This section applies if a company is a party in an accounting period to a relevant contract which is treated as a derivative contract under section 587 (contract relating to holding in OEIC, unit trust or offshore fund).

(2) The credits and debits which are to be brought into account in accordance with this Part in respect of the relevant contract are to be determined on the basis of fair value accounting.

602 Contract becoming one relating to holding in OEIC, unit trust or offshore fund

(1) This section applies if—

    (a) a company is a party to a relevant contract in two successive accounting periods,

    (b) section 587 (contract relating to holding in OEIC, unit trust or offshore fund) applies in relation to the relevant contract for the second accounting period but not the first accounting period, and

    (c) immediately before the beginning of the second accounting period the relevant contract was a chargeable asset.

(2) For the purposes of section 601(2), the opening valuation of the contract as at the beginning of the second accounting period is taken to be equal to the market value of the contract.

(3) In subsection (2) "the market value of the contract" means the amount which would have been the market value of the contract for the purposes of corporation tax on chargeable gains if it had been disposed of immediately before the end of the first accounting period.

(4) For the rules which apply where the company ceases to be a party to the contract, see section 660 (company ceasing to be party to contract relating to holding in OEIC, unit trust or offshore fund).

603 Associated transaction treated as derivative contract

(1) This section is to be read as if it were in Chapter 7 (shares with guaranteed returns etc) of Part 6 (relationships treated as loan relationships etc).

(2) See, in particular, section 532(3) (meaning of "associated transaction").

(3) Subsection (4) applies if credits and debits are required to be brought into account in accordance with this Part in respect of any associated transaction because of section 588 (which treats such a transaction which is not a derivative contract as if it were).

(4) Those credits and debits are to be determined on the basis of fair value accounting.

Rules differing from generally accepted accounting practice

604 Credits and debits treated as relating to capital expenditure

[(1) This section applies if—

    (a) an amount for an accounting period in respect of a company's derivative contract relates to any of the matters mentioned in section 594A(1),

    (b) generally accepted accounting practice allows the amount to be treated in the company's accounts as an amount recognised in determining the carrying value of an asset or liability, and

    (c) any profit or loss for corporation tax purposes in relation to that asset or liability will not fall to be calculated in accordance with generally accepted accounting practice.

(2) Despite that treatment, the amount must be brought into account as a credit or debit in accordance with this Part, for the accounting period in which it is recognised, in the same way as an amount which is brought into account as a credit or debit in determining the company's profit or loss for that period in accordance with generally accepted accounting practice.

(3) But subsection (2) does not apply to an amount which relates to an intangible fixed asset to which an election under section 730 (writing down at fixed rate: election for fixed-rate basis) applies.][1]

(4) . . .[1]

[(5) If an amount is brought into account as mentioned in subsection (2) as a debit, no debit may be brought into account in accordance with this Part in respect of—

    (a) the writing down of so much of the value of the asset or liability as is attributable to that debit, or

    (b) so much of any amortisation or depreciation representing a writing off of that value as is attributable to that debit.][1]

Commentary—*Simon's Taxes* D1.876.

Derivation—FA 2002 Sch 26 para 25(1)–(4).

Change in the law—See CTA 2009 EN Annex 1, Change 65.

HMRC Manuals—Corporate Finance Manual CFM52040 (treatment of capitalised amounts).

Amendments—[1] Sub-ss (1)–(3), (5) substituted, and sub-s (4) repealed, by F(No 2)A 2015 s 32, Sch 7 paras 59, 65 with effect for accounting periods beginning on or after 1 January 2016, subject to transitional rules in F(No 2)A 2015 Sch 7 paras 115 to 129.

[604A   Amounts recognised in other comprehensive income and not transferred to profit or loss

(1) This section applies if—

    (a) in a period of account a derivative contract of a company ceases in accordance with generally accepted accounting practice to be recognised in the company's accounts,

    (b) amounts relating to the matters mentioned in section 594A(1) in respect of that derivative contract have in accordance with generally accepted accounting practice been recognised in the company's accounts as items of other comprehensive income and have not subsequently been transferred to become items of profit or loss, and

    (c) condition A or B is met.

the debits are (so far as they exceed relevant credits) treated for the purposes of this Part as if they were debits for the accounting period in which it started to carry on the business.

(3) For this purpose "relevant credits" means credits of the company in respect of the derivative contract which, on the assumption that the company had been carrying on the business at the pre-rental times—

    (*a*) would have been recognised in determining its profit or loss for a period consisting of or including those times,

    (*b*) would have been brought into account for the purposes of this Part, and

    (*c*) would not otherwise have been brought into account for tax purposes.

(4) This section also applies in relation to a non-UK resident company which is a party to a derivative contract for the purpose of enabling it to generate other UK property income (within the meaning given by section 5(6)).][1]

Amendments—[1]   Section 607ZA inserted by FA 2020 s 32, Sch 6 para 4 with effect from 6 April 2020. This amendment has effect as if it had been incorporated into FA 2019 Sch 5 and so is subject to transitional provisions in FA 2019 Sch 5 Pt 3 (paras 36–50).

[607A Company is not, or has ceased to be, party to derivative contract

(1) This section applies if—

    (*a*) amounts in respect of a qualifying contract are recognised in a company's accounts for an accounting period ("the current period") as an item of profit or loss even though during all or part of the period the company is not a party to the qualifying contract,

    (*b*) any of conditions A to D is met, and

    (*c*) in the absence of this section, the credits and debits brought into account by the company for the purposes of this Part for the current period would not include credits or debits representing the whole of those amounts.

(2) In this section "qualifying contract" means—

    (*a*) a derivative contract, or

    (*b*) a contract that would be a derivative contract if references in section 576(1) to a company were references to any person.

(3) Condition A is that—

    (*a*) the company was a party to the qualifying contract,

    (*b*) amounts in respect of the qualifying contract were recognised in the company's accounts as an item of profit or loss when it was a party to the contract, and

    (*c*) any amounts in respect of the contract continue to be recognised in those accounts as an item of profit or loss.

(4) Condition B is that the amounts recognised as mentioned in subsection (1)(*a*) are recognised as a result of a transaction which has the effect of transferring to the company all or part of the risk or reward relating to the qualifying contract without a corresponding transfer of rights or obligations under the contract.

(5) Condition C is that the amounts recognised as mentioned in subsection (1)(*a*) are recognised as a result of a related transaction in relation to a qualifying contract to which the company was, but has ceased to be, a party.

(6) Condition D is that—

    (*a*) the amounts recognised as mentioned in subsection (1)(*a*) are recognised because the company may enter into a qualifying contract or related transaction but has not yet done so, and

    (*b*) the amounts are not expenses to which section 607 applies.

(7) The company must bring credits and debits into account for the purposes of this Part for the accounting period as if the company were a party to the qualifying contract for the whole of the accounting period.

(8) The amounts that must be brought into account are those amounts in respect of the qualifying contract that are recognised in the company's accounts for the accounting period as an item of profit or loss (but subject to the provisions of this Part).

(9) This section is subject to sections 607B and 607C.

(10) In this section—

    "item of profit or loss" has the meaning it has for accounting purposes;

    "recognised" means recognised in accordance with generally accepted accounting practice;

    "related transaction", in relation to a qualifying contract, is to be read as if the references in section 596(1) and (2) to a derivative contract were to a qualifying contract.][1]

Amendments—[1]   Sections 607A–607C inserted by F(No 2)A 2015 s 32, Sch 7 paras 59, 71 with effect for accounting periods beginning on or after 1 January 2016, subject to transitional rules in F(No 2)A 2015 Sch 7 paras 115 to 129.

[607B Exclusion of debit where relief allowed to another

(1) A company is not to bring into account as a debit for the purposes of this Part as a result of section 607A any amount which—

    (*a*) is brought into account as a debit for those purposes by another company,

(b) is brought into account so as to reduce the assumed taxable total profits of another company for the purposes of Part 9A of TIOPA 2010 (controlled foreign companies), or

(c) is allowable as a deduction by a person for the purposes of income tax.][1]

Amendments—[1] Sections 607A–607C inserted by F(No 2)A 2015 s 32, Sch 7 paras 59, 71 with effect for accounting periods beginning on or after 1 January 2016, subject to transitional rules in F(No 2)A 2015 Sch 7 paras 115 to 129.

[607C Avoidance of double charge

(1) This section applies if at any time a company ("the relevant company") is required by section 607A to bring into account as a credit for the purposes of this Part an amount—

(a) which is brought into account as a credit for those purposes by another company,

(b) which is brought into account in determining the assumed taxable total profits of another company for the purposes of Part 9A of TIOPA 2010 (controlled foreign companies), or

(c) on which a person is charged to income tax.

(2) In order to avoid a double charge to tax in respect of the amount, the relevant company may make a claim for one or more consequential adjustments to be made in respect of the amount brought into account as a credit.

(3) On a claim under this section an officer of Revenue and Customs must make such of the consequential adjustments claimed (if any) as are just and reasonable.

(4) Consequential adjustments may be made—

(a) in respect of any period,

(b) by way of an assessment, the modification of an assessment, the amendment of a claim, or otherwise, and

(c) despite any time limit imposed by or under any enactment.][1]

Amendments—[1] Sections 607A–607C inserted by F(No 2)A 2015 s 32, Sch 7 paras 59, 71 with effect for accounting periods beginning on or after 1 January 2016, subject to transitional rules in F(No 2)A 2015 Sch 7 paras 115 to 129.

609 Company ceasing to be UK resident

(1) If a company ceases to be UK resident, this Part applies as if—

(a) immediately before so ceasing the company had assigned the rights and liabilities under its derivative contracts for consideration of an amount equal to their fair value at that time, and

(b) it had immediately reacquired them for consideration of the same amount.

(2) Subsection (1) does not apply in relation to a derivative contract so far as immediately after the company ceases to be UK resident its rights and liabilities under the contract are held or owed[—

(a)] for the purposes of a permanent establishment of the company in the United Kingdom[,

(b) for the purposes of the company's trade of dealing in or developing UK land,

(c) for the purposes of the company's UK property business, or

(d) for the purposes of enabling the company to generate other UK property income (within the meaning given by section 5(5)).][1]

(3) Subsection (1) does not apply if—

(a) the conditions in section 630(1)(a) and (b) are met in relation to the company (transferee leaving group after replacing transferor as party to derivative contract), and

(b) it ceases to be UK resident at the same time as it ceases to be a member of the relevant group.

(4) In subsection (3) "the relevant group" has the meaning given by section 630(4).

Commentary—Simon's Taxes **D1.895, D4.132.**
HMRC Manuals—Corporate Finance Manual CFM53100 (deemed assignment when company ceases to be resident).
Amendments—[1] In sub-s (2), para (a) designated as such, and paras (b)–(d) inserted, by FA 2019 s 17, Sch 5 paras 10, 19 with effect from 6 April 2020, subject to transitional provisions in FA 2019 Sch 5 Pt 3 (paras 36–50).

610 Non-UK resident company ceasing to hold derivative contract for [section 609(2) purposes]

(1) This section applies if the rights and liabilities under a derivative contract of a company which is not UK resident cease to any extent to be held or owed for [section 609(2) purposes][1] in circumstances not involving a related transaction.

(2) This Part applies as if—

(a) immediately before the rights and liabilities so cease the company had assigned them, so far as so ceasing, for consideration of an amount equal to their fair value at that time, and

(b) the company had immediately reacquired them for consideration of the same amount.

(3) This section does not apply if—

(a) the conditions in section 630(1)(a) and (b) are met in relation to the company (transferee leaving group after replacing transferor as party to derivative contract), and

(b) the rights and liabilities mentioned in subsection (1) cease to be held or owed for [section 609(2) purposes][1] at the same time as the company ceases to be a member of the relevant group.

(4) In subsection (3) "the relevant group" has the meaning given by section 630(4).

[(5) A right or liability ceases to be held or owed for section 609(2) purposes if and in so far as—

(a) it ceases to be held or owed for any purposes mentioned in section 609(2), and

(b) on doing so, it does not begin or continue to be held or owed for any of the other purposes so mentioned.][1]

Commentary—Simon's Taxes **D1.895, D4.132.**

HMRC Manuals—Corporate Finance Manual CFM53100 (non-resident company; derivative contract held for UK permanent establishment).
Amendments—[1]   The following amendments made by FA 2019 s 17, Sch 5 paras 10, 20 with effect from 6 April 2020, subject to transitional provisions in FA 2019 Sch 5 Pt 3 (paras 36–50)—
- in heading, words substituted for words "UK permanent establishment";
- in sub-s (1), words substituted for words "the purposes of a permanent establishment of the company in the United Kingdom";
- in sub-s (3)(*b*), words substituted for words "the purposes of the permanent establishment"; and
- sub-s (5) inserted.

611 Release under statutory insolvency arrangement of liability under derivative contract

No credit is required to be brought into account by a company in respect of the release of the company's liability to pay an amount under a derivative contract of the company if the release is part of a statutory insolvency arrangement.

Commentary—*Simon's Taxes* D1.850.
Derivation—FA 2002 Sch 26 para 22(5).
HMRC Manuals—Corporate Finance Manual CFM52060 (release of liability in insolvency).

CHAPTER 4

FURTHER PROVISION ABOUT CREDITS AND DEBITS TO BE BROUGHT INTO ACCOUNT

Introduction

612 Overview of Chapter

(1) This Chapter makes further provision about the credits and debits to be brought into account for the purposes of this Part.
(2) In particular, it—
  (*a*) provides for adjustments on a change of accounting [basis][1] (see sections 613 to 615),
  (*b*) makes provision in relation to certain embedded derivatives (see sections 616 to 618),
  (*c*) makes provision about partnerships involving companies (see sections 619 to 621),
  (*d*) makes provision about contracts ceasing to be derivative contracts (see section 622), and
  (*e*) makes provision in relation to some gilt-edged securities (see section 623).

Amendments—[1]   In sub-s (2)(*a*) word substituted for word "policy" by F(No 2)A 2015 s 32, Sch 7 paras 59, 73 with effect for accounting periods beginning on or after 1 January 2016, subject to transitional rules in F(No 2)A 2015 Sch 7 paras 115 to 129.

Adjustments on change of accounting [basis]

613 Introduction to sections 614 and 615

[(1) Sections 614 and 615 (adjustments on change of accounting basis) apply if—
  (*a*) a company changes, from one period of account or accounting period to the next, the basis of accounting on which credits and debits relating to its derivative contracts or any of them are calculated for the purposes of this Part,
  (*b*) the change of basis—
    (i) is made in order to comply with a provision made by or under this Part requiring those credits and debits to be determined on a particular basis of accounting, or
    (ii) results from a change of the company's accounting policy,
  (*c*) the change of basis is not made in order to comply with amending legislation not applicable to the previous period,
  (*d*) the old basis accorded with the law or practice applicable in relation to the period before the change, and
  (*e*) the new basis accords with the law and practice applicable to the period after the change.][1]
(2) In this section and those sections—
  (*a*) the first of [the periods mentioned in subsection (1)][1] is referred to as "the earlier period", and
  (*b*) the next is referred to as "the later period".
(3) . . . [1]
(4) If an election is made under section 416, this section and sections 614 and 615 apply as if there were a change of accounting policy consisting of the company treating the assets referred to in section 416(1)(*c*) as mentioned in section 585(1) as from the date the election has effect.

Commentary—*Simon's Taxes* D1.845.
Amendments—[1]   In cross-heading word substituted for word "policy", sub-s (1) substituted, in sub-s (2) words substituted for words "those periods of account", and sub-s (3) repealed, by F(No 2)A 2015 s 32, Sch 7 paras 59, 74, 75 with effect for accounting periods beginning on or after 1 January 2016, subject to transitional rules in Sch 7 paras 115 to 129.

[614 Change of basis of accounting involving change of value

(1) If there is a difference between—
  (*a*) the tax-adjusted carrying value of a derivative contract at the end of the earlier period, and
  (*b*) the tax-adjusted carrying value of that derivative contract at the beginning of the later period,

a credit or debit (as the case may be) of an amount equal to the difference must be brought into account for the purposes of this Part for the later period in the same way as a credit or debit which is brought into account in determining the company's profit or loss for that period in accordance with generally accepted accounting practice.

(2) This section does not apply so far as the credit or debit falls to be brought into account apart from this section.][1]

Commentary—*Simon's Taxes* **D1.845.**
HMRC Manuals—Corporate Finance Manual CFM52030 (adjustments on change of accounting policy).
Amendments—[1] This section substituted by F(No 2)A 2015 s 32, Sch 7 paras 59, 76 with effect for accounting periods beginning on or after 1 January 2016, subject to transitional rules in F(No 2)A 2015 Sch 7 paras 115 to 129.

615 Change of accounting policy after ceasing to be party to derivative contract
(1) This section applies if—
- (a) the company has ceased to be a party to a derivative contract in an accounting period ("the cessation period"),
- [(b) section 607A (company is not, or has ceased to be, party to derivative contract) applied to the cessation, and][1]
- (c) there is a difference between the amount outstanding in respect of the derivative contract (see subsection (5))—
  - (i) at the end of the earlier period, and
  - (ii) at the beginning of the later period.

[(2) A credit or debit (as the case may be) of an amount equal to the difference must be brought into account for the purposes of this Part for the later period in the same way as a credit or debit which is brought into account in determining the company's profit or loss for that period in accordance with generally accepted accounting practice.][1]

(4) [Subsection (2) does][1] not apply so far as the credit or debit falls to be brought into account apart from this section.

[(5) In this section "the amount outstanding in respect of the derivative contract" means—
- (a) so much of the recognised deferred income or recognised deferred loss from the derivative contract as has not been represented by credits or debits brought into account in accordance with this Part in respect of the contract, and
- (b) any amounts relating to the matters mentioned in section 594A(1) in respect of the derivative contract that have in accordance with generally accepted accounting practice been recognised in the company's accounts as items of other comprehensive income and not transferred to become items of profit or loss.][1]

(6) In subsection (5)—
"recognised deferred income", in relation to a derivative contract, means the amount recognised in the company's balance sheet in accordance with generally accepted accounting practice as deferred income in respect of the profits which arose from the contract or a related transaction in the cessation period, and
"recognised deferred loss", in relation to a derivative contract, means the amount so recognised as deferred loss in respect of the losses which so arose.

[(7) In determining what amounts fall within subsection (5)(b) at the beginning or end of a period, it is to be assumed that the accounting policy applied in drawing up the company's accounts for the period was also applied in previous periods.
(8) But if the company's accounts for the period are in accordance with generally accepted accounting practice drawn up on an assumption as to the accounting policy in previous periods which differs from that mentioned in subsection (7), that different assumption applies in determining what amounts fall within subsection (5)(b) at the beginning or end of the period.][1]

Amendments—[1] Sub-ss (1)(b), (5) substituted, sub-s (2) substituted for previous sub-ss (2), (3), in sub-s (4) words substituted for words "Subsections (2) and (3) do", and sub-ss (7), (8) inserted, by F(No 2)A 2015 s 32, Sch 7 paras 59, 77 with effect for accounting periods beginning on or after 1 January 2016, subject to transitional rules in F(No 2)A 2015 Sch 7 paras 115 to 129 (see in particular Sch 7 para 123).

Certain embedded derivatives

616 Disapplication of fair value accounting
(1) This section applies if—
- (a) a company is treated as a party to a relevant contract under section 584(2)(a) or 586(2) ("the embedded derivative"),
- (b) the embedded derivative is a derivative contract which meets the condition in section 579(1)(a) (contract treated for accounting purposes as derivative),
- (c) section 592 (embedded derivatives treated as meeting condition in section 591 etc) does not apply in relation to the embedded derivative, and
- (d) regulation 9 of the Disregard Regulations (interest rate contracts) does not apply to the embedded derivative.
(2) If this section applies—

CTA 2009

(a) sections 573 and 574 (trading credits and debits to be brought into account under Part 3 and non-trading credits and debits to be brought into account under Part 5) do not apply in relation to the embedded derivative, and

(b) subsection (3) or subsections (4) to (6) apply in relation to the original contract, depending on whether that contract is a hybrid derivative or a contract within section 586(1).

(3) If the original contract is a hybrid derivative, profits and losses are to be calculated for the purposes of this Part as if that contract—

(a) were not one where the rights and liabilities are treated for accounting purposes as divided as mentioned in section 584(1) (hybrid derivatives with embedded derivatives), and

(b) were not one in relation to which a fair value basis of accounting is used.

(4) If the original contract is a contract within section 586(1), profits and losses are to be brought into account for the purposes of the Corporation Tax Acts in relation to that contract as if that contract—

(a) were not one where the rights and liabilities are treated for accounting purposes as divided as mentioned in section 586(1) (other contracts with embedded derivatives), and

(b) were not one in relation to which a fair value basis of accounting is used.

(5) Accordingly, this Part does not apply to the original contract (except for the purposes of this section), but section 46 applies to that contract as if fair value accounting were not generally accepted accounting practice in relation to the company.

(6) Subsections (4) and (5) apply despite section 699(1) (priority of this Part for corporation tax purposes).

(7) In this section—

"the Disregard Regulations" means the Loan Relationships and Derivative Contracts (Disregard and Bringing into Account of Profits and Losses) Regulations 2004 (SI 2004/3256), and

"the original contract" means—

(a) the hybrid derivative as a result of which the company falls to be treated under section 584(2) (hybrid derivatives with embedded derivatives) as a party to the embedded derivative, or

(b) the contract within section 586(1) (other contracts with embedded derivatives) as a result of which the company falls to be treated under section 586(2) as a party to the embedded derivative.

617 Election for section 616 not to apply

(1) A company may elect that section 616 is not to apply in relation to its contracts.

(2) But such an election does not apply to a contract if—

(a) the contract is a contract of long-term insurance, or

(b) the underlying subject matter of the embedded derivative is, or includes, commodities.

(3) An election under this section—

(a) must be made before the end of the first applicable accounting period of the company, and

(b) is irrevocable.

(4) In subsection (3) "the first applicable accounting period" means the first accounting period in which the conditions in section 616(1) are met.

(5) Section 618 makes further provision about elections under this section.

618 Elections under section 617: groups of companies

(1) If—

(a) a company makes an election under section 617 in relation to its contracts, and

(b) another company, which is a member of the same group as the company making the election, is a party to a contract to which the election applies,

the other company is treated, in relation to that contract, as if it had also made such an election.

(2) If—

(a) a company ("the electing company") makes an election under section 617 in relation to its contracts,

(b) another company ("the transferee") becomes a party to a contract to which section 584 (hybrid derivatives with embedded derivatives) or section 586 (other contracts with embedded derivatives) applies, in place of the electing company (whether before or after the election is made), and

(c) the transferee is a member of the same group of companies as the electing company at the time of the transfer,

the transferee is treated, in relation to the contract mentioned in paragraph (b), as if it had also made such an election.

(3) If—

(a) a company ("A") is treated under section 584 or 586 as a party to a relevant contract in relation to which section 616(1) applies,

(b) another company ("B") becomes a party to that contract in place of A,

(c) A and B are members of the same group of companies when B becomes a party to the contract, and

(d) section 616(1) does not apply in relation to B's other relevant contracts because of an election under section 617 (whenever made),

subsection (4) applies, unless A, subsequent to B's becoming a party to the contract, makes such an election.

(4) B is treated, in relation to the contract mentioned in subsection (3)(b), as if section 616(1) applied in relation to it.

(5) In this section, references to a company being a member of the same group of companies are to be read in accordance with section 170 of TCGA 1992 (interpretation of sections 171 to 181 of that Act: groups).

Partnerships involving companies

619 Partnerships involving companies

(1) This section applies if—

    (a) a trade or business is carried on by a firm,

    (b) any of the partners in the firm is a company (a "company partner"), and

    (c) the firm is a party to a contract which is a derivative contract or would be a derivative contract if the firm were a company.

(2) No credits or debits may be brought into account in accordance with this Part in respect of the contract in calculating the profits and losses of the trade or business for corporation tax purposes under section 1259 (calculation of firm's profits and losses).

(3) Instead, each company partner must bring into account in accordance with this Part credits and debits in respect of the contract for each of its accounting periods in which the conditions in subsection (1) are met.

(4) Sections 620 (determination of credits and debits by company partners) and 621 (company partners using fair value accounting) contain special rules about the credits and debits to be brought into account under subsection (3).

(5) In sections 620 and 621 "company partner" has the same meaning as in this section.

620 Determination of credits and debits by company partners

(1) The credits and debits to be brought into account under section 619(3) are to be determined separately for each company partner as follows.

(2) The contract entered into or acquired by the firm is treated as if it were instead entered into or acquired by the company partner for the purposes of the trade or business which the company partner carries on.

(3) Anything done by or in relation to the firm in connection with the contract is treated as done by or in relation to the company partner.

(4) So far as exchange gains or losses arising from the contract are recognised in the firm's—

    (a) statement of total recognised gains and losses,

    (b) statement of recognised income and expense,

    (c) statement of changes in equity, or

    (d) statement of income and retained earnings,

they are treated as if they had been recognised in the corresponding statement of the company partner.

(5) The credits and debits in the case of each company partner are the partner's appropriate share of the total credits and debits determined in accordance with subsections (2) to (4).

(6) A company partner's "appropriate share" is the share which would be apportioned to it on the assumption in subsection (7).

(7) The assumption is that the total credits and debits determined in accordance with subsections (2) to (4) are apportioned between the partners in the shares in which any profit or loss would be apportioned between them in accordance with the firm's profit-sharing arrangements.

621 Company partners using fair value accounting

(1) This section applies if a company partner uses fair value accounting in relation to its interest in the firm.

(2) The credits and debits to be brought into account by the company partner under section 619(3) are to be determined on the basis of fair value accounting.

Miscellaneous

622 Contracts ceasing to be derivative contracts

(1) This section applies if a company is a party to a relevant contract which ceases to be a derivative contract.

(2) The company is treated for the purposes of this Part as if it had disposed of the contract in a related transaction at the relevant time for consideration of an amount equal to the notional carrying value of the contract at that time.

(3) In this section "the relevant time" means the time when the contract ceases to be a derivative contract.

(b) the transferee ceases to be a member of the relevant group in consequence of the transfer or merger.

(3) In a case where subsection (2) applies, if the transferee becomes a member of another group in consequence of the transfer or merger, it is to be treated for the purposes of this section and sections 631 and 632 as if the relevant group and the other group were the same.

(4) In this section and sections 631 and 632—

"the relevant 6 year period" means the period of 6 years following—

(a) in a case where section 625 applies because of a transaction within section 626(2) ("case A"), that transaction, or

(b) in a case where section 625 applies because of a series of transactions within section 626(3) ("case B"), the last transaction of that series,

"the relevant derivative contract" means the derivative contract mentioned in section 625(1),

"the relevant group" means—

(a) in case A, the group mentioned in section 626(2),

(b) in case B, the group mentioned in section 626(3), and

"the transferee" has the same meaning as in section 625.

631 Transferee leaving group otherwise than because of exempt distribution

(1) This section applies if—

(a) the transferee ceases to be a member of the relevant group, and

(b) it does not so cease just because of a distribution which is exempt [as a result of section 1075 of CTA 2010 (exempt distributions),][1]

(2) . . .[2] This Part applies as if—

(a) the transferee had assigned its rights and liabilities under the relevant derivative contract immediately before so ceasing,

(b) the assignment had been for consideration of an amount equal to their fair value at that time, and

(c) the transferee had immediately reacquired them for consideration of the same amount.

(3) . . .[2]

(4) . . .[2]

Amendments—[1] In sub-s (1) words substituted by CTA 2010 s 1177, Sch 1 para 640 with effect for corporation tax purposes for accounting periods ending on or after 1 April 2010, and for income and capital gains tax purposes for the tax year 2010–11 and subsequent tax years.

[2] In sub-s (2) words repealed, and sub-ss (3), (4) repealed, by FA 2014 s 28(1), (3) with effect where the cessation of membership of the relevant group occurs on or after 1 April 2014.

632 Transferee leaving group because of exempt distribution

(1) This section applies if—

(a) the transferee ceases to be a member of the relevant group just because of a distribution which is exempt [as a result of section 1075 of CTA 2010 (exempt distributions),][1]

(b) there is a chargeable payment within the meaning of [section 1088(1) of CTA 2010][1] (chargeable payments connected with exempt distributions) within 5 years after the making of the distribution.

(2) . . .[2] This Part applies as if—

(a) the transferee had assigned its rights and liabilities under the relevant derivative contract immediately before that chargeable payment was made,

(b) the assignment had been for consideration of an amount equal to their fair value immediately before the transferee ceased to be a member of the relevant group, and

(c) the transferee had immediately reacquired them for consideration of the same amount.

(3) . . .[2]

(4) . . .[2]

Amendments—[1] In sub-s (1) words substituted, in sub-s (1)(b) words substituted for words "section 214(2) of that Act" by CTA 2010 s 1177, Sch 1 para 641 with effect for corporation tax purposes for accounting periods ending on or after 1 April 2010, and for income and capital gains tax purposes for the tax year 2010–11 and subsequent tax years.

[2] In sub-s (2) words "If condition A or B is met,", and sub-ss (3), (4) repealed, by FA 2014 s 28(1), (3) with effect where the cessation of membership of the relevant group occurs on or after 1 April 2014.

CHAPTER 6

SPECIAL KINDS OF COMPANY

Mutual trading companies

633 Mutual trading companies

For the purposes of this Part, activities carried on by a company in the course of any mutual trading are treated as not constituting the whole or any part of a trade.

Insurance companies

634 Insurance companies

[(1)] For the purposes of this Part, activities carried on by a company in the course of—

    (a) any mutual insurance or other mutual business which is not life assurance business, . . . [1]

    (b) . . . [1]

are treated as not constituting the whole or any part of a trade.

[(2) In the case of activities carried on by a company in the course of any basic life assurance and general annuity business, provision corresponding to that made by subsection (1) is made by section 88 of FA 2012 for the purpose of applying the I-E rules.][1]

HMRC Manuals—Corporate Finance Manual CFM54020 (insurance companies).

Amendments—[1]   Sub-s (1) numbered as such, para (b) and preceding word "or" repealed, and sub-s (2) inserted, by FA 2012 s 146, Sch 16 paras 135, 168 with effect in relation to accounting periods of companies beginning on or after 1 January 2013 (subject to transitional provisions in FA 2012 Sch 17). For accounting periods straddling 1 January 2013, see FA 2012 s 149.

635 Creditor relationships: embedded derivatives which are options

(1) This section applies if in any accounting period—

    (a) a company is a party to a creditor relationship for the purposes of its [basic life assurance and general annuity business][1], and

    (b) that creditor relationship is one in relation to which sections 415 and 585 (which both apply to loan relationships with embedded derivatives) would have effect but for the fact that the company accounts for the creditor relationship at fair value through profit and loss.

(2) [For the purpose of applying the I-E rules, this Part][1] and Part 5 (loan relationships) have effect for that accounting period as they would if the creditor relationship were one in relation to which those sections have effect.

Amendments—[1]   In sub-s (1)(a), words substituted for words "life assurance business", and in sub-s (2), words substituted for words "This Part", by FA 2012 s 146, Sch 16 paras 135, 169 with effect in relation to accounting periods of companies beginning on or after 1 January 2013 (subject to transitional provisions in FA 2012 Sch 17). For accounting periods straddling 1 January 2013, see FA 2012 s 149.

636 Modifications of Chapter 5

(1) Chapter 5 (continuity of treatment on transfers within groups) has effect in relation to insurance companies with the following modifications.

(2) Section 625(1)(a) (which sets out one of the conditions for that section to apply) has effect as if for "section 626(2)" there were substituted "section 626(2), (2A) or (2B)".

(3) Section 626 (transactions to which section 625 applies) has effect as if after subsection (2) there were inserted—

    "(2A)   A transaction is within this subsection if it is a transfer between two companies of business consisting of the effecting or carrying out of contracts of long-term insurance which has effect under an insurance business transfer scheme.

    (2B)   A transaction is within this subsection if it is a transfer between two companies which is a qualifying overseas transfer.

    [(2C)   In subsection (2B) "qualifying overseas transfer" means so much of a transfer of the whole or any part of the business of an overseas life insurance company carried on through a permanent establishment in the United Kingdom as takes place in accordance with an authorisation granted outside the United Kingdom for the purposes of [Article 39 of Directive 2009/138/EC of the European Parliament and of the Council of 25 November 2009 on the taking-up and pursuit of the business of Insurance and Reinsurance (Solvency II)][2].][1]

(4) Section 625 (group member replacing another as party to derivative contract) does not apply as a result of a transaction or series of transactions within section 626(2) or (3) in relation to a transfer of an asset, or of rights or duties under or an interest in an asset, if[, immediately before or after the transfer, the asset was held for the purposes of a company's long-term business (but, in the case of an overseas life insurance company, ignoring assets which are not UK assets (within the meaning of section 117 of FA 2012))][1]

(5) Section 625 does not apply as a result of a transaction within section 626(2A) or (2B) in relation to a transfer of an asset, or of rights or duties under or an interest in an asset, if the asset—

    (a) was within one of [the applicable categories][1] immediately before the transfer, and

    (b) is not within that category immediately after it.

[(5A) For the purposes of subsection (5)(a) "the applicable categories" means—

    (a) in the case of a UK life insurance company, the long-term business categories or a category of assets which are not held for the purposes of its long-term business, and

    (b) in the case of an overseas life insurance company, the UK long-term business categories, a category of UK assets which are not held for the purposes of its long-term business or a category of assets which are held by it but which are not UK assets.][1]

(6) Subsection (7) applies for the purposes of subsection (5) if one of the companies is an overseas life insurance company.

(7) An asset is taken to be within the same category both immediately before the transfer and immediately after it if the asset—

(*a*) was within one category immediately before the transfer, and

(*b*) is within the corresponding category immediately after it.

[(8) For the purposes of this section—

(*a*) "the long-term business categories" has the same meaning as in section 116 of FA 2012, and "the UK long-term business categories" and "UK assets" have the same meanings as in section 117 of FA 2012, and

(*b*) section 122 of FA 2012 applies as it applies for the purposes of Chapter 8 of Part 2 of that Act.][1]

Commentary—*Simon's Taxes* **D7.519**.

Derivation—FA 2002 Sch 26 paras 28(1), (2), 29(1)–(3).

HMRC Manuals—Corporate Finance Manual CFM54020 (continuity of treatment on transfers within groups).

Amendments—[1]   In sub-s (3), sub-s (2C) inserted, in sub-s (4), words substituted, in sub-s (5)(*a*) words substituted for words "the categories set out in section 440(4) of ICTA (transfers of assets etc)", and sub-ss (5A), (8) inserted, by FA 2012 s 146, Sch 16 paras 135, 170 with effect in relation to accounting periods of companies beginning on or after 1 January 2013 (subject to transitional provisions in FA 2012 Sch 17). For accounting periods straddling 1 January 2013, see FA 2012 s 149.

[2]   In sub-s (3), words substituted for words "Article 14 of the Council Directive of 5 November 2002 concerning life assurance (2002/83/EC)" by the Solvency 2 Regulations, SI 2015/575 reg 59, Sch 1 para 26(1), (3) with effect from 1 January 2016.

Investment and venture capital trusts

637 Investment trusts: profits or losses of a capital nature

(1) Profits or losses of a capital nature arising to an investment trust from a derivative contract may not be brought into account as credits or debits in accordance with this Part.

(2) For the purposes of this section, "profits or losses of a capital nature" means profits or losses which—

(*a*) are accounted for through the capital column of the income statement in accordance with the Statement of Recommended Practice, or

(*b*) would have been so accounted for if that Statement had been applied correctly.

(3) "The Statement of Recommended Practice", in relation to an accounting period for which it is required or permitted to be used, means—

(*a*) the Statement of Recommended Practice relating to Investment Trust Companies, issued by the Association of Investment Trust Companies in January 2003, as from time to time modified, amended or revised, or

(*b*) any subsequent Statement of Recommended Practice relating to investment trusts, as from time to time modified, amended or revised.

(4) The Treasury may by order amend the definition of "profits or losses of a capital nature" in subsection (2), so far as it applies in relation to an investment trust which prepares accounts in accordance with international accounting standards.

638 Venture capital trusts: profits or losses of a capital nature

(1) Profits or losses of a capital nature arising to a venture capital trust from a derivative contract may not be brought into account as credits or debits in accordance with this Part.

(2) For the purposes of this section, "profits or losses of a capital nature" means profits or losses which—

(*a*) are accounted for through the capital column of the income statement in accordance with the Statement of Recommended Practice, or

(*b*) would have been so accounted for if the venture capital trust had been an investment trust and that Statement had been applied correctly.

(3) In this section "the Statement of Recommended Practice" has the meaning given by section 637(3) (investment trusts: profits or losses of a capital nature).

(4) The Treasury may by order amend the definition of "profits or losses of a capital nature" in subsection (2), so far as it applies in relation to a venture capital trust which prepares accounts in accordance with international accounting standards.

CHAPTER 7

CHARGEABLE GAINS ARISING IN RELATION TO DERIVATIVE CONTRACTS

Introduction

639 Overview of Chapter

(1) This Chapter makes provision about cases in which—

(*a*) credits and debits are not to be brought into account in accordance with section 574 (non-trading credits and debits to be brought into account under Part 5: loan relationships) (see sections 640 and 643 to 650), but

(*b*) instead profits arising to a company from its derivative contracts are chargeable to corporation tax as chargeable gains (see sections 641 to 650).

(2) This Chapter also makes provision about cases in which—

(*a*) credits and debits are not to be brought into account in accordance with section 573 (trading credits and debits to be brought into account under Part 3: trading income) or section 574 (non-trading credits and debits to be brought into account under Part 5: loan relationships) (see section 651), but

(*b*) instead provisions relating to corporation tax on chargeable gains apply in relation to derivative contracts (see sections 652 to 658).

Some credits and debits not to be brought into account under Part 5

640 Credits and debits not to be brought into account under Part 5

(1) If any of the provisions in subsection (2) applies to a derivative contract of a company for an accounting period, section 574 (non-trading credits and debits to be brought into account under Part 5: loan relationships) does not apply to the relevant credits and debits.

(2) The provisions are—

(*a*) section 643 (contracts relating to land or certain tangible movable property),

(*b*) section 645 (creditor relationships: embedded derivatives which are options),

(*c*) section 648 (creditor relationships: embedded derivatives which are exactly tracking contracts for differences), and

(*d*) section 650 (property based total return swaps).

(3) For the meaning of "relevant credits" and "relevant debits", see section 659.

(4) For the treatment of the relevant credits and debits in the case of a derivative contract to which section 643, 645, 648 or 650 applies, see section 641 (derivative contracts to be taxed on a chargeable gains basis).

Some derivative contracts to be taxed on a chargeable gains basis

641 Derivative contracts to be taxed on a chargeable gains basis

(1) This section applies to a derivative contract of a company for an accounting period if any of the provisions in subsection (2) applies to the derivative contract for the period.

(2) The provisions are—

(*a*) section 643 (contracts relating to land or certain tangible movable property),

(*b*) section 645 (creditor relationships: embedded derivatives which are options),

(*c*) section 648 (creditor relationships: embedded derivatives which are exactly tracking contracts for differences), and

(*d*) section 650 (property based total return swaps).

(3) For the purposes of corporation tax on chargeable gains—

(*a*) if C exceeds D, a chargeable gain equal to the amount of the excess is treated as accruing to the company in the accounting period,

(*b*) if D exceeds C, an allowable loss equal to the amount of the excess is treated as accruing to the company in the accounting period.

(4) "C" means the sum of the relevant credits for the accounting period in respect of the derivative contract.

(5) "D" means the sum of the relevant debits for the accounting period in respect of the derivative contract.

(6) For a case in which this section does not apply, see section 642.

(7) See also section 663 (carry back of net losses on derivative contracts to which this section applies).

642 Exception from section 641

(1) Section 641 does not apply to a derivative contract to which section 645 applies if, on the assumptions in subsection (2), paragraph 2 of Schedule 7AC to TCGA 1992 (substantial shareholding exemptions: gain on disposal of asset related to shares not a chargeable gain) would apply to the gain mentioned in subsection (2)(*d*).

(2) Those assumptions are that—

(*a*) the rights and liabilities treated as comprised in the derivative contract were contained in a separate contract,

(*b*) that separate contract was an option,

(*c*) that option was disposed of at the end of the accounting period, and

(*d*) a gain accrued to the company on the disposal for the purposes of corporation tax on chargeable gains.

Derivative contracts to which sections 640 and 641 apply

643 Contracts relating to land or certain tangible movable property

(1) This section applies to a derivative contract of a company for an accounting period if conditions A, B [, C and D][1] are met.

(2) Condition A is that the underlying subject matter of the derivative contract consists of either or both of the following—

    (*a*) land,

    (*b*) tangible movable property, other than commodities which are tangible assets.

(3) Condition B is that the company is not a party to the derivative contract at any time in the accounting period for the purposes of a trade carried on by it.

(4) Condition C is that the company is not an excluded body.

[(4A) Condition D is that no two or more of the parties to the derivative contract are connected persons.][1]

(5) For the case where the underlying subject matter of a derivative contract also includes income from property within subsection (2)(*a*) or (*b*), see section 644.

Amendments—[1]   In sub-s (1) words substituted for "and C", and sub-s (4A) inserted, by FA 2013 s 41(1), (2) with effect in relation to accounting periods beginning on or after 5 December 2012. For accounting periods spanning this date, see FA 2013 s 41(6).

644 Income to be left out of account in determining whether section 643 applies

(1) This section applies if the underlying subject matter of a derivative contract includes income from property within section 643(2)(*a*) or (*b*).

(2) If that income is subordinate income, it is left out of account in determining for the purposes of section 643 whether condition A is met.

(3) Income is "subordinate income" if it is—

    (*a*) subordinate in relation to so much of the underlying subject matter of the derivative contract as consists of property within section 643(2)(*a*) or (*b*), or

    (*b*) of small value in comparison with the value of the underlying subject matter as a whole.

(4) For the purposes of this section, whether part of the underlying subject matter of a derivative contract of a company is subordinate or of small value is to be determined by reference to the time when the company enters into or acquires the contract.

645 Creditor relationships: embedded derivatives which are options

(1) This section applies to a derivative contract of a company for an accounting period if each of conditions A to E is met.

(2) Condition A is that the derivative contract is a relevant contract to which the company is treated as a party under section 585(2) (loan relationships with embedded derivatives) because of a creditor relationship of the company.

(3) Condition B is that the derivative contract is treated as an option by section 585(3) (contract treated as option, future or contract for differences).

(4) Condition C is that the underlying subject matter of the derivative contract—

    (*a*) is qualifying ordinary shares, or

    (*b*) is mandatorily convertible preference shares.

(5) Condition D is that the company is not a party to the creditor relationship at any time in the accounting period for the purposes of a trade carried on by it.

(6) Condition E is that the company is not an excluded body.

(7) Where this section applies to a derivative contract, the asset representing the creditor relationship is treated for corporation tax purposes as not being a qualifying corporate bond.

(8) See also—

    (*a*) section 647 (meaning of certain expressions in this section), and

    (*b*) section 670 (treatment of net gains and losses on exercise of option).

646 Exclusions from section 645

(1) Section 645 does not apply to a derivative contract of a company for an accounting period if condition A or B is met in the period.

(2) Condition A is that the rights and liabilities which fall to be treated as comprised in the derivative contract are such that the extent to which shares may be acquired in accordance with them is to be determined using a cash value—

    (*a*) which is specified in the contract for the asset representing the creditor relationship mentioned in section 645(2), or

    (*b*) which is or will be ascertainable by reference to that contract.

(3) Condition B is that the rights and liabilities which fall to be treated as comprised in the derivative contract are such that—

    (*a*) the company is entitled or obliged to receive a payment instead of the shares which are the underlying subject matter of the derivative contract, and

    (*b*) the amount of that payment differs by more than an insignificant amount from the value of the shares which the company would be entitled to acquire in accordance with those rights and liabilities at the time it became entitled or obliged to receive the payment.

647 Meaning of certain expressions in section 645

(1) This section applies for the purposes of section 645.

(2) "Mandatorily convertible preference shares" means shares which—

(a) represent the creditor relationship mentioned in section 645(2),

(b) are not qualifying ordinary shares, and

(c) are issued upon terms which stipulate that they must be converted into, or exchanged for, qualifying ordinary shares by a relevant time.

(3) In subsection (2) "relevant time" means a time no more than 24 hours after the acquisition of the shares by a person who, immediately before that acquisition, had the creditor relationship.

(4) "Qualifying ordinary shares" means shares in a company which satisfy conditions A and B.

(5) Condition A is that the shares are all or part of the issued share capital (however described) of the company, other than—

(a) capital the holders of which have a right to a dividend at a fixed rate but have no other right to share in the profits of the company, or

(b) capital the holders of which have no right to a dividend of any description nor any other right to share in the profits of the company.

(6) Condition B is that the shares—

(a) are listed on a recognised stock exchange, or

(b) are shares in a holding company or a trading company.

(7) In subsection (6) "holding company" and "trading company" have the same meaning as in section 165 of TCGA 1992 (see section 165A of that Act).

648 Creditor relationships: embedded derivatives which are exactly tracking contracts for differences

(1) This section applies to a derivative contract of a company for an accounting period if each of conditions A to F is met.

(2) Condition A is that the derivative contract is a relevant contract to which the company is treated as a party under section 585(2) (loan relationships with embedded derivatives) because of a creditor relationship of the company.

(3) Condition B is that the derivative contract is treated as a contract for differences by section 585(3) (contract treated as option, future or contract for differences).

(4) Condition C is that the derivative contract is an exactly tracking contract.

(5) Condition D is that the underlying subject matter of the derivative contract is qualifying ordinary shares listed on a recognised stock exchange.

(6) Condition E is that the company is not a party to the creditor relationship at any time in the accounting period for the purposes of a trade carried on by it.

(7) Condition F is that the company is not an excluded body.

(8) Where this section applies to a derivative contract, the asset representing the creditor relationship is treated for corporation tax purposes as not being a qualifying corporate bond.

(9) See also section 672 (treatment of net gains and losses on disposal of certain embedded derivatives).

649 Meaning of certain expressions in section 648

(1) This section applies for the purposes of section 648.

(2) "Exactly tracking contract" means a contract where the amount which is to be paid to discharge the rights and liabilities which fall to be treated as comprised in the contract is equal to the amount found by applying R% to C, where—

R% is the percentage change (if any) over the relevant period in—

(a) the value of the assets which are the underlying subject matter of the contract, or

(b) any index of the value of those assets, and

C is the amount falling to be regarded in accordance with generally accepted accounting practice as the cost of the asset representing the creditor relationship mentioned in section 648(2) on the date when that asset came into existence.

(3) In subsection (2) "the relevant period" means—

(a) the period between—

(i) the date when the asset representing that creditor relationship came into existence, and

(ii) the date when the debtor relationship corresponding to that creditor relationship comes to an end, or

(b) any other period in which almost all of that period falls, and which differs from that period only for purposes connected with giving effect to a valuation in relation to rights or liabilities under that asset.

(4) "Qualifying ordinary shares" means shares in a company which are all or part of the issued share capital (however described) of the company, other than—

(a) capital the holders of which have a right to a dividend at a fixed rate but have no other right to share in the profits of the company, or

(b) capital the holders of which have no right to a dividend of any description nor any other right to share in the profits of the company.

650 Property based total return swaps

(1) This section applies to a derivative contract of a company for an accounting period if each of conditions A [to H][1] is met.

(2) Condition A is that the derivative contract is a contract for differences.

(3) Condition B is that one or more indices are specified in the contract.

(4) Condition C is that at least one index so specified ("the capital value index") is an index of changes in the value of land.

(5) Condition D is that the underlying subject matter of the derivative contract also includes interest rates.

(6) Condition E is that the company is not a party to the derivative contract at any time in the accounting period for the purposes of a trade carried on by it.

(7) Condition F is that the company is not an excluded body.

[(8) Condition G is that no two or more of the parties to the derivative contract are connected persons.

(9) Condition H is that the securing of a tax advantage is neither the main purpose, nor one of the main purposes, for which the company is a party to the derivative contract.

"Tax advantage" has the meaning given by section 1139 of CTA 2010.][1]

Amendments—[1]　In sub-s (1) words substituted for words "to F", and sub-ss (8), (9) inserted, by FA 2013 s 41(1), (3) with effect in relation to accounting periods beginning on or after 5 December 2012. For accounting periods spanning that date, see FA 2013 s 41(6).

Some credits and debits not to be brought into account under Part 3 or 5

651 Credits and debits not to be brought into account under Part 3 or Part 5

(1) If the provisions in subsection (2)(*a*) or (*b*) apply to a derivative contract for an accounting period, sections 573 (trading credits and debits to be brought into account under Part 3: trading income) and 574 (non-trading credits and debits to be brought into account under Part 5: loan relationships) do not apply to the relevant credits and debits.

(2) The provisions are—

　　(*a*) sections 653 to 655 (issuers of securities with embedded derivatives: deemed options), and

　　(*b*) section 658 (issuers of securities with embedded derivatives: deemed contracts for differences).

(3) For the cases in which sections 653 to 655 and section 658 apply, see sections 652 and 656 respectively.

(4) For the provision which applies where sections 653 to 655 or 658 apply, see those sections.

Issuers of securities with embedded derivatives: deemed options

652 Introduction to sections 653 to 655

(1) Sections 653 to 655 apply to a derivative contract of a company for an accounting period if each of conditions A to E is met.

(2) Condition A is that the derivative contract is a relevant contract to which the company is treated as a party under section 585(2) (loan relationships with embedded derivatives) because of a debtor relationship of the company.

(3) Condition B is that the derivative contract is treated as an option by section 585(3) (contract treated as option, future or contract for differences).

(4) Condition C is that the underlying subject matter of the derivative contract is shares.

(5) Condition D is that at the time when the company became a party to the debtor relationship—

　　(*a*) it was not carrying on a banking business or a business as a securities house, or

　　(*b*) if it was carrying on such a business, it did not become a party to the debtor relationship in the ordinary course of that business.

(6) Condition E is that the company is not an excluded body.

(7) In this section "option" is to be construed as if section 580(2) and (3) (meaning of "option") were omitted.

653 Shares issued or transferred as a result of exercise of deemed option

(1) Subsections (2) and (3) apply if—

　　(*a*) the option mentioned in section 652(3) is exercised at any time in the accounting period, and

　　(*b*) shares are issued or transferred in fulfilment of the obligations under the option ("the relevant disposal").

(2) Section 144(2) of TCGA 1992 (exercise of options) applies to the relevant disposal as if the [tax-adjusted carrying value][1] of the option at the time the company became a party to the debtor relationship mentioned in section 652(2) were the consideration for the grant of the option.

(3) So far as it would otherwise apply, section 17(1) of TCGA 1992 (deemed market value consideration) does not apply to the relevant disposal.

Amendments—[1]　In sub-s (2) words substituted for words "carrying value", by F(No 2)A 2015 s 32, Sch 7 paras 59, 81 with effect for accounting periods beginning on or after 1 January 2016, subject to transitional rules in F(No 2)A 2015 Sch 7 paras 115 to 129.

654 Payment instead of disposal on exercise of deemed option

(1) Subsection (2) applies if—

  (a) the option mentioned in section 652(3) is exercised at any time in the accounting period,

  (b) no shares are issued or transferred in fulfilment of the obligations under the option, and

  (c) an amount is paid in fulfilment of those obligations.

(2) If—

  (a) CV exceeds X, a chargeable gain equal to the amount of the excess is treated as accruing to the company in the accounting period,

  (b) X exceeds CV, an allowable loss equal to the amount of the excess is treated as accruing to the company in the accounting period.

(3) In this section—

    "CV" means—

      (a) if the company was a party to the debtor relationship mentioned in section 652(2) at the time it was created, the [tax-adjusted carrying value][1] of the option at that time, or

      (b) if the company became a party to that relationship at a later time, the [tax-adjusted carrying value][1] of the option at that time,

    "X" means the amount paid by the debtor in fulfilment of the obligations under the debtor relationship reduced (but not below nil) by the fair value of the host contract at the date on which the option is exercised, and

    "the host contract" means the loan relationship to which the company is treated as a party under section 415(2) (loan relationships with embedded derivatives) because of the debtor relationship.

Amendments—[1]   In sub-s (3) in the definition of "CV", in paras (a), (b), words substituted for words "carrying value", by F(No 2)A 2015 s 32, Sch 7 paras 59, 82 with effect for accounting periods beginning on or after 1 January 2016, subject to transitional rules in F(No 2)A 2015 Sch 7 paras 115 to 129.

655 Ceasing to be party to debtor relationship when deemed option not exercised

(1) Subsection (2) applies if the company ceases to be a party to the debtor relationship mentioned in section 652(2) at a time when the option mentioned in section 652(3) has not been exercised.

(2) The company is treated for the purposes of corporation tax on chargeable gains—

  (a) as having acquired an asset for consideration of an amount equal to Y, and

  (b) as having disposed of that asset for consideration of an amount equal to CV.

(3) In this section—

    "CV" has the same meaning as in section 654,

    "Y" means—

      (a) if the company ceases to be a party to the debtor relationship as a result of the redemption or repayment of the liability representing that relationship, the amount paid by the company, or

      (b) otherwise, the consideration given by the company on its ceasing to be a party to that relationship,

    in either case reduced (but not below nil) by the fair value of the host contract at the date on which it so ceases, and

    "the host contract" has the same meaning as in section 654.

Issuers of securities with embedded derivatives: deemed contracts for differences

656 Introduction to section 658

(1) Section 658 (chargeable gain or allowable loss treated as accruing) applies to a derivative contract of a company for an accounting period if each of conditions A to F is met.

(2) Condition A is that the derivative contract is a relevant contract to which the company is treated as a party under section 585(2) (loan relationships with embedded derivatives) because of a debtor relationship of the company.

(3) Condition B is that the derivative contract—

  (a) is treated as a contract for differences by section 585(3) (contract treated as option, future or contract for differences), and

  (b) is not within section 652.

(4) Condition C is that the derivative contract is an exactly tracking contract.

(5) Condition D is that the underlying subject matter of the derivative contract is shares.

(6) Condition E is that at the time when the company became a party to the debtor relationship—

  (a) it was not carrying on a banking business or a business as a securities house, or

  (b) if it was carrying on such a business, it did not become a party to the debtor relationship in the ordinary course of that business.

(7) Condition F is that the company is not an excluded body.

(8) For the meaning of "exactly tracking contract", see section 657.

657 Meaning of "exactly tracking contract" in section 656

(1) This section applies for the purposes of section 656.

(2) "Exactly tracking contract" means a contract where the amount which is to be paid to discharge the rights and liabilities which fall to be treated as comprised in the contract is equal to the amount found by applying R% to C, where—

R% is the percentage change (if any) over the relevant period in—

    (*a*) the value of the assets which are the underlying subject matter of the contract, or

    (*b*) any index of the value of those assets, and

C is the amount falling to be regarded in accordance with generally accepted accounting practice as the proceeds of issue of the liability which represents the debtor relationship mentioned in section 656(2).

(3) In subsection (2) "the relevant period" means—

  (*a*) the period between—

    (i) the date when the liability representing that debtor relationship came into existence, and

    (ii) the date when the creditor relationship corresponding to that debtor relationship comes to an end, or

  (*b*) any other period in which almost all of that period falls, and which differs from that period only for purposes connected with giving effect to a valuation in relation to rights or liabilities under the liability representing that debtor relationship.

658 Chargeable gain or allowable loss treated as accruing

(1) Subsection (2) applies if—

  (*a*) the debtor relationship mentioned in section 656(2) comes to an end, and

  (*b*) an amount ("the discharge amount") is paid to discharge all the company's obligations under that relationship.

(2) For the purposes of corporation tax on chargeable gains, a chargeable gain or allowable loss equal to the amount mentioned in subsection (3) is treated as accruing to the company.

(3) That amount is the amount of the gain or loss (as the case may be) which would accrue on the assumptions in subsection (4).

(4) Those assumptions are that—

  (*a*) the derivative contract is an asset of the company,

  (*b*) there is a disposal of that asset at the time when the debtor relationship comes to an end,

  (*c*) the consideration for the disposal of that asset is equal to the relevant amount, and

  (*d*) the cost of the asset is equal to the discharge amount.

(5) In subsection (4) "the relevant amount" means—

  (*a*) if the company was a party to the debtor relationship at the time it was created, the amount of the proceeds of issue of the security representing that relationship, or

  (*b*) if the company became a party to the debtor relationship after that time, the amount of the [tax-adjusted carrying value][1] of the host contract at that time.

(6) In this section "the host contract" means the loan relationship to which the company is treated as a party under section 415(2) (loan relationships with embedded derivatives) because of the debtor relationship.

Amendments—[1]   In sub-s (5)(*b*) words substituted for words "carrying value" by F(No 2)A 2015 s 32, Sch 7 paras 59, 83 with effect for accounting periods beginning on or after 1 January 2016, subject to transitional rules in F(No 2)A 2015 Sch 7 paras 115 to 129.

Interpretation

659 Meaning of "relevant credits" and "relevant debits"

(1) This section applies for the purposes of this Chapter.

(2) In the case of a derivative contract which is not one to which section 650 (property based total return swaps) applies for an accounting period, the relevant credits and debits are the credits and debits which are given in relation to the derivative contract for the accounting period by section 595.

(3) In the case of a derivative contract to which section 650 applies for an accounting period, the relevant credits and debits are the credits and debits which—

  (*a*) are given in relation to the derivative contract for the accounting period by section 595, and

  (*b*) are within subsection (4).

(4) The credits and debits are those found for the period by applying R% to N, where—

N is the amount which is the notional principal amount in the case of the derivative contract, and

R% is the percentage change (if any) in the capital value index over the relevant period.

[(4A) But if the derivative contract has effect such that the return arising from the contract, so far as calculated by reference to that index, is calculated by reference to a percentage ("the capped percentage") which is closer to zero than the full percentage change in that index over that period (or which is zero even though there has been a change in that index), for the purposes of subsection (4) R% is the capped percentage.][1]

(5) In subsection (4) "the relevant period" means—

(a) the accounting period, if the company is a party to the derivative contract throughout that period,

(b) in any other case, any part of the accounting period throughout which the company is a party to the derivative contract.

(6) For the meaning of "the capital value index", see section 650(4).

Amendments— Sub-s (4A) inserted by FA 2013 s 41(1), (4) with effect in relation to accounting periods beginning on or after 5 December 2012. For accounting periods spanning this date, see FA 2013 s 41(6).

CHAPTER 8

FURTHER PROVISION ABOUT CHARGEABLE GAINS AND DERIVATIVE CONTRACTS

Company ceasing to be party to certain contracts

660 Contract relating to holding in OEIC, unit trust or offshore fund

(1) This section applies if—

(a) a company is a party to a relevant contract in two successive accounting periods,

(b) section 587 (contract relating to holding in OEIC, unit trust or offshore fund) applies in relation to the relevant contract for the second of those periods but not the first, and

(c) immediately before the beginning of the second period the relevant contract was a chargeable asset.

(2) The company must bring into account for the accounting period in which it ceases to be a party to the contract the amount of any chargeable gain or allowable loss which would have been treated as accruing to it on the assumptions in subsection (3).

(3) Those assumptions are that—

(a) the company disposed of the relevant contract immediately before the beginning of the second period mentioned in subsection (1), and

(b) the disposal was for consideration of an amount equal to the value (if any) given to the relevant contract in the accounts of the company at the end of the first such period.

661 Contract which becomes derivative contract

(1) This section applies if—

(a) a company is a party to a relevant contract which (not having been a derivative contract) becomes a derivative contract, and

(b) immediately before the relevant contract becomes a derivative contract it is a chargeable asset.

(2) The company must bring into account for the accounting period in which it ceases to be a party to the relevant contract the amount of any chargeable gain or allowable loss which would have been treated as accruing to it on the assumptions in subsection (3).

(3) Those assumptions are that—

(a) the company disposed of the relevant contract immediately before the relevant time, and

(b) the disposal was for consideration of an amount equal to the notional carrying value of the relevant contract at that time.

(4) In this section "the relevant time" means the time when the relevant contract becomes a derivative contract.

(5) Section 622(4) (meaning of "notional carrying value") applies for the purposes of this section.

Contracts ceasing to be derivative contracts

662 Contracts ceasing to be derivative contracts

(1) This section applies if a company is a party to a relevant contract which ceases to be a derivative contract.

(2) The company is treated for the purposes of corporation tax on chargeable gains as if it had acquired the contract immediately after the relevant time for consideration of an amount equal to the notional carrying value of the contract at that time.

(3) In this section "the relevant time" means the time when the contract ceases to be a derivative contract.

(4) Section 622(4) (meaning of "notional carrying value") applies for the purposes of this section.

Carry back of net losses on certain derivative contracts

663 Contracts to which section 641 applies

(1) This section applies in the case of a company if—

(a) there are net section 641 losses for an accounting period ("the loss period"),

(b) there are net section 641 gains for a previous accounting period ("the gains period"),

(c) the gains period falls wholly or partly within the period of 24 months immediately preceding the start of the loss period, and

(d) within two years after the end of the loss period the company makes a claim in respect of the whole or a part of the net section 641 losses for the loss period.

(*a*) conditions A to D,

(*b*) in the case of a merger within subsection (2)(*a*), (*b*) or (*c*), condition E, and

(*c*) in the case of a merger within subsection (2)(*c*) or (*d*), condition F,

but see section 686 (tax avoidance etc) and section 687 (disapplication of Chapter where transparent entities involved).

(2) Condition A is that—

(*a*) an SE is formed by the merger of two or more companies in accordance with Articles 2(1) and 17(2)(*a*) or (*b*) of Council Regulation (EC) No 2157/2001 on the Statute for a European company (Societas Europaea),

(*b*) an SCE is formed by the merger of two or more co-operative societies, at least one of which is a society registered under the [the Co-operative and Community Benefit Societies Act 2014][1], in accordance with Articles 2(1) and 19 of Council Regulation (EC) No 1435/2003 on the Statute for a European Co-operative Society (SCE),

(*c*) a merger is effected by the transfer by one or more companies of all their assets and liabilities to a single existing company, or

(*d*) a merger is effected by the transfer by two or more companies of all their assets and liabilities to a single new company (other than an SE or an SCE) in exchange for the issue by the transferee, to each person holding shares in or debentures of a transferor, of shares or debentures.

(3) Condition B is that each merging company is resident in a member State.

(4) Condition C is that the merging companies are not all resident in the same State.

(5) Condition D is that immediately after the merger the transferee is within the charge to corporation tax.

(6) Condition E is that—

(*a*) the transfer of assets and liabilities to the transferee in the course of the merger is made in exchange for the issue of shares or debentures by the transferee to each person holding shares in or debentures of a transferor, or

(*b*) that transfer is not so made only because, and only so far as, the transferee is prevented from so issuing such shares or debentures by section 658 of the Companies Act 2006 (c 46) (general rule against limited company acquiring own shares) or by a corresponding provision of the law of another member State preventing such an issue.

(7) Condition F is that in the course of the merger each transferor ceases to exist without being in liquidation (within the meaning given by section 247 of the Insolvency Act 1986 (c 45)).

(8) In this Chapter, "the merger" and "the merging companies" have the same meaning as in this section.

(9) See—

(*a*) section 683 for the meaning of "the transferee" and "transferor", and

(*b*) section 688 for the meaning of "company", "co-operative society" and "resident in a member State".

Amendments—[1]   In each place where they occur in this Act, words substituted for words "registered industrial and provident society", "the Industrial and Provident Societies Act 1965" and "industrial and provident societies", by the Co-operative and Community Benefit Societies Act 2014 s 151, Sch 4 paras 140–143 with effect from 1 August 2014 and subject to transitional provisions and provisions preserving the continuity of the law in Sch 5 of that Act.

Prospective amendments—In sub-s (3) words "relevant state" to be substituted for words "member State", in sub-s (4) words "relevant state" to be substituted for word "State", in sub-s (6)(*b*) word "a" to be substituted for word "another", in sub-s (8) the words from "'the merger'" to the end become para (*a*), sub-s (8)(*b*) to be inserted, and in sub-s (9)(*b*) words "relevant state" to be substituted for words "member State", by the Taxes (Amendments) (EU Exit) Regulations, SI 2019/689 reg 16(1), (14) with effect from Implementation Period completion day (see EU(WA)A 2020 Sch 5 para 1(1)). Sub-s (8)(*b*) to read as follows—

"(*b*) 'relevant state' means the United Kingdom or a member State.".

683 Meaning of "the transferee" and "transferor"

(1) In this Chapter, "the transferee" means—

(*a*) in relation to a merger within section 682(2)(*a*), the SE,

(*b*) in relation to a merger within section 682(2)(*b*), the SCE, and

(*c*) in relation to a merger within section 682(2)(*c*) or (*d*), the company to which assets and liabilities are transferred.

(2) In this Chapter "transferor" means—

(*a*) in relation to a merger within section 682(2)(*a*), a company merging to form the SE,

(*b*) in relation to a merger within section 682(2)(*b*), a co-operative society merging to form the SCE, and

(*c*) in relation to a merger within section 682(2)(*c*) or (*d*), a company transferring all of its assets and liabilities.

Transfers of derivative contracts at notional carrying value

684 Transfer of derivative contract at notional carrying value

(1) This section applies if in the course of the merger a transferor transfers the rights and liabilities under a derivative contract to the transferee.

(2) For the purpose of determining the credits and debits to be brought into account in respect of the derivative contract in accordance with this Part, the transferor and the transferee are treated as having entered into the transfer of those rights and liabilities for consideration of an amount equal to the notional carrying value of the contract.

(3) For the purposes of this section, the notional carrying value of a contract is the amount which would have been [its tax-adjusted carrying value based on][1] the accounts of the transferor if a period of account had ended immediately before the date when the transferor ceased to be a party to the contract.

(4) This section is subject to section 685 (transferor using fair value accounting).

Amendments—[1]   In sub-s (3) words substituted for words "its carrying value in", by F(No 2)A 2015 s 32, Sch 7 paras 59, 88 with effect for accounting periods beginning on or after 1 January 2016, subject to transitional rules in F(No 2)A 2015 Sch 7 paras 115 to 129.

685 Transferor using fair value accounting

(1) This section applies instead of section 684 if, in a case where that section would otherwise apply, the transferor uses fair value accounting as respects the derivative contract.

(2) The amount which is to be brought into account by the transferor in respect of the transfer of the rights and liabilities mentioned in section 684(1) is the fair value of the derivative contract as at the date of transfer to the transferee.

(3) For any accounting period in which the transferee is a party to the derivative contract, for the purpose of determining the credits and debits to be brought into account in respect of the contract in accordance with this Part, the transferee is treated as if it had acquired the contract for consideration of an amount equal to the fair value of the contract as at the date of transfer to it.

Exception for tax avoidance cases and clearances

686 Tax avoidance etc

(1) This Chapter does not apply in relation to the merger if—

    (*a*) the merger is not effected for genuine commercial reasons, or

    (*b*) the merger forms part of a scheme or arrangements of which the main purpose, or one of the main purposes, is avoiding liability to corporation tax, capital gains tax or income tax.

(2) But subsection (1) does not prevent this Chapter from applying if before the merger—

    (*a*) any of the merging companies has applied to the Commissioners for Her Majesty's Revenue and Customs, and

    (*b*) the Commissioners have notified the merging companies that they are satisfied that subsection will not have that effect.

(3) Sections 678 and 679 have effect in relation to subsection (2) as in relation to section 677(2), taking the references in section 679 to section 677(2)(*b*) as references to subsection (2)(*b*) of this section.

Transparent entities

687 Disapplication of Chapter where transparent entities involved

(1) This section applies if one or more of the merging companies is a transparent entity.

(2) If as a result of the merger the assets and liabilities of a transparent entity are transferred to another company, this Chapter does not apply in relation to the transfer.

(3) In this section "transparent entity" means a company which is resident in a member State other than the United Kingdom and which does not have an ordinary share capital.

Prospective amendments—In sub-s (3) words "other than the United Kingdom" to be repealed by the Taxes (Amendments) (EU Exit) Regulations, SI 2019/689 reg 16(1), (15) with effect from Implementation Period completion day (see EU(WA)A 2020 Sch 5 para 1(1)).

Interpretation

688 Interpretation

(1) In this Chapter—

    "company" means any entity listed as a company in [Part A of Annex I][1] to the Mergers Directive, and

    "co-operative society" means a society registered under the [the Co-operative and Community Benefit Societies Act 2014][2] or a similar society governed by the law of a member State other than the United Kingdom.

(2) For the purposes of this Chapter, a company is resident in a member State if—

    (*a*) it is within a charge to tax under the law of the State as being resident for that purpose, and

    (*b*) it is not regarded, for the purpose of any double taxation relief arrangements to which the State is a party, as resident in a territory not within a member State.

Amendments—[1]   In sub-s (1) words substituted for "the Annex" by the Corporation Tax (Implementation of the Mergers Directive) Regulations, SI 2011/1431 reg 4(5) with effect from 1 July 2011.

[2]   In each place where they occur in this Act, words substituted for words "registered industrial and provident society", "the Industrial and Provident Societies Act 1965" and "industrial and provident societies", by the Co-operative and Community Benefit Societies Act 2014 s 151, Sch 4 paras 140–143 with effect from 1 August 2014 and subject to transitional provisions and provisions preserving the continuity of the law in Sch 5 of that Act.

Prospective amendments—In sub-s (1) in the definition of "co-operative society" words "other than the United Kingdom" to be repealed, and in sub-s (2) words "relevant state" to be substituted for words "member State", in both places where the expression occurs, and words "relevant state" to be substituted for word "State", in both places where the word occurs other than as part of the expression "member State", by the Taxes (Amendments) (EU Exit) Regulations, SI 2019/689 reg 16(1), (16) with effect from Implementation Period completion day (see EU(WA)A 2020 Sch 5 para 1(1)).

CHAPTER 11

TAX AVOIDANCE

Introduction

689 Overview of Chapter

(1) This Chapter contains rules connected with tax avoidance.

(2) In particular—

  (*a*) for rules about unallowable purposes, see sections 690 to 692,

  (*b*) for rules relating to credits and debits where transactions are not at arm's length, see sections 693 to 695,

  (*c*) for rules relating to credits and debits in the case of transactions with non-UK residents, see sections 696 and 697, . . . [1]

  (*d*) . . . [2]

  (*e*) for rules about debits arising as a result of the derecognition of derivative contracts, see section 698A,][1] [and

  (*f*) for rules dealing with tax avoidance arrangements, see sections 698B to 698D.][2]

Amendments—[1]   In sub-s (2), in para (*c*) word "and" repealed, and para (*e*) inserted, by FA 2011 s 28, Sch 4 paras 7, 10 with effect in relation to periods of account beginning on or after 6 December 2010, subject to the transitional provision in FA 2011 Sch 4 para 13(2).

[2]   Sub-s (2)(*d*) repealed in relation to disposals on or after 18 November 2015, and sub-s (2)(*f*), and preceding word "and" inserted in relation to arrangements entered into on or after 18 November 2015 by F(No 2)A 2015 s 32, Sch 7 paras 59, 89. See also the transitional provisions in F(No 2)A 2015 Sch 7 paras 115 to 129.

Unallowable purposes

690 Derivative contracts for unallowable purposes

(1) This section applies if in any accounting period a derivative contract of a company has an unallowable purpose.

(2) The company may not bring into account for that period for the purposes of this Part so much of any exchange credit in respect of that contract as is referable to the unallowable purpose on a just and reasonable apportionment.

(3) The company may not bring into account for that period for the purposes of this Part so much of any debit in respect of that contract as is referable to the unallowable purpose on a just and reasonable apportionment.

[(3A) If—

  (*a*) a credit brought into account for that period for the purposes of this Part by the company would (in the absence of this section) be reduced, and

  (*b*) the reduction represents an amount which, if it did not reduce a credit, would be brought into account as a debit in respect of that contract,

subsection (3) applies to the amount of the reduction as if it were an amount that would (in the absence of this section) be brought into account as a debit.][1]

(4) Subsections (2) and (3) are subject to section 692 (allowance of accumulated net losses).

(5) An amount which would be brought into account in accordance with this Part as respects any matter apart from this section and section 692—

  (*a*) is treated for the purposes of section 699(1) (priority of this Part for corporation tax purposes) as if it were so brought into account, and

  (*b*) accordingly may not be brought into account for any other corporation tax purposes as respects that matter.

(6) For the purposes of this section and section 692, a credit is an exchange credit, in the case of any company, so far as it is attributable to any exchange gains arising to the company . . . [1].

(7) For the meaning of "has an unallowable purpose" and "the unallowable purpose" in this section and section 692, see section 691.

Amendments—[1]   Sub-s (3A) inserted, and in sub-s (6) words "which are included in the reference to profits of the company in section 595(3) (see section 606 (exchange gains and losses from derivative contracts))" repealed, by F(No 2)A 2015 s 32, Sch 7 paras 59, 90 with effect for accounting periods beginning on or after 1 January 2016, subject to transitional rules in F(No 2)A 2015 Sch 7 paras 115 to 129.

691 Meaning of "unallowable purpose"

(1) For the purposes of sections 690 and 692, a derivative contract of a company has an unallowable purpose in an accounting period if the purposes for which, at times during that period, the company—

    (*a*) is a party to the contract, or

    (*b*) enters into transactions which are related transactions by reference to it,

include a purpose ("the unallowable purpose") which is not amongst the business or other commercial purposes of the company.

[(1A) In subsection (1)(*b*) "related transaction", in relation to a derivative contract, includes anything which equates in substance to a disposal or acquisition of the kind mentioned in section 596(1) (as read with section 596(2)).][2]

(2) If a company is not within the charge to corporation tax in respect of a part of its activities, for the purposes of this section the business and other commercial purposes of the company do not include the purposes of that part.

(3) Subsection (4) applies if a tax avoidance purpose is one of the purposes for which a company—

    (*a*) is a party to a derivative contract at any time, or

    (*b*) enters into a transaction which is a related transaction by reference to a derivative contract of the company.

(4) For the purpose of subsection (1), the tax avoidance purpose is only regarded as a business or other commercial purpose of the company if it is not—

    (*a*) the main purpose for which the company is a party to the derivative contract or, as the case may be, enters into the related transaction, or

    (*b*) one of the main purposes for which it is or does so.

(5) The references in subsections (3) and (4) to a tax avoidance purpose are references to any purpose which consists of securing a tax advantage for the company or any other person.

(6) In this section "tax advantage" has the meaning given by [section 1139 of CTA 2010][1] (meaning of "tax advantage").

Amendments—[1]   In sub-s (6) words substituted for words "section 840ZA of ICTA" by CTA 2010 s 1177, Sch 1 para 642. CTA 2010 has effect for corporation tax purposes for accounting periods ending on or after 1 April 2010, and for income and capital gains tax purposes for the tax year 2010–11 and subsequent tax years.

[2]   Sub-s (1A) inserted by F(No 2)A 2015 s 32, Sch 7 paras 59, 91 with effect for accounting periods beginning on or after 1 January 2016, subject to transitional rules in F(No 2)A 2015 Sch 7 paras 115 to 129.

692 Allowance of accumulated net losses

(1) This section applies if—

    (*a*) in any accounting period a derivative contract of a company has an unallowable purpose, and

    (*b*) there is a net loss in respect of that contract for that period.

(2) For the purposes of this section, there is such a net loss if—

    (*a*) the sum of the debits in respect of that contract which are excluded from being brought into account for that period by section 690(3), exceeds

    (*b*) the sum of the exchange credits in respect of that contract which are so excluded by section 690(2).

(3) The amount of that excess is the amount of the net loss in respect of the contract for the period.

(4) The amount of the excess accumulated net losses in respect of the contract for an accounting period is to be brought into account as a debit for that period.

(5) The amount of the excess accumulated net losses in respect of a contract for an accounting period is found as follows.

Step 1

Add together the amount of any net loss arising in respect of the contract for that accounting period and earlier accounting periods.

Step 2

Deduct from the result of Step 1 any amount which was brought into account in accordance with this section in any earlier accounting period.

Step 3

Add together [so much][1] of any credits (other than exchange credits) arising in respect of the contract for that accounting period or any earlier accounting period [as are referable to the unallowable purpose mentioned in subsection (1)(*a*) on a just and reasonable apportionment][1].

Step 4

Deduct from the result of Step 3 (but not so as to reduce it below nil)—

    (*a*) so much of any debits arising in respect of the contract for that accounting period or any earlier accounting period as is not excluded from being brought into account by section 690(3), and

    (*b*) any amount which was brought into account in accordance with this section in any earlier accounting period.

Step 5

Compare the result of Step 2 and the result of Step 4.

The amount of the excess accumulated net losses for the period is the lower of those results.

Amendments—[1]   In sub-s (5) at Step 3, words substituted for words "the amount", and words inserted, by F(No 2)A 2015 s 32, Sch 7 paras 59, 92 with effect for accounting periods beginning on or after 1 January 2016, subject to transitional rules in F(No 2)A 2015 Sch 7 paras 115 to 129.

Transactions not at arm's length

693 Bringing into account adjustments under [Part 4 of TIOPA 2010][1]

(1) This section deals with the credits and debits which are to be brought into account in accordance with this Part as a result of [Part 4 of TIOPA 2010][1] (provision not at arm's length) applying in relation to a company's derivative contracts or related transactions.

(2) Subsection (3) applies if under [Part 4 of TIOPA 2010][1] an amount ("the imputed amount") is treated as an amount of profits or losses arising to a company from any of its derivative contracts or related transactions.

(3) Credits or debits relating to the imputed amount are to be brought into account in accordance with this Part to the same extent as they would be in the case of an actual amount of such profits or losses.

(4) Subsection (5) applies if under [Part 4 of TIOPA 2010][1] an amount is treated as expenses incurred by a company under or for the purposes of any of its derivative contracts or related transactions.

(5) Debits relating to the amount are to be brought into account in accordance with this Part to the same extent as they would be in the case of an actual amount of such expenses.

[(6) No credit is to be brought into account for the purposes of this Part to the extent that it corresponds to an amount which, as a result of the preceding provisions of this section, has not previously been brought into account as a debit.][2]

Amendments—[1]   In sub-ss (1), (2), (4) and the title words "Schedule 28AA to ICTA" substituted by TIOPA 2010 s 501, Sch 8 paras 123, 142. TIOPA 2010 has effect for corporation tax purposes for accounting periods ending on or after 1 April 2010, for income and capital gains tax purposes for the tax year 2010–11 and subsequent tax years, and for petroleum revenue tax purposes for chargeable periods beginning on or after 1 July 2010.

[2]   Sub-s (6) inserted by FA 2016 s 49, Sch 7 paras 1, 4 with effect in relation to accounting periods beginning on or after 1 April 2016 (FA 2016 Sch 7 para 12(1)). Where a company has an accounting period beginning before 1 April 2016 and ending on or after that date ("the straddling period") the periods before and after 1 April 2016 are treated as separate accounting periods (FA 2016 Sch 7 para 12(2)).

694 Exchange gains and losses

(1) Subsections (2) to (7) apply if—

    (*a*) a company is a party to a derivative contract in an accounting period, and

    (*b*) an exchange gain or exchange loss arises to the company for the accounting period from the contract.

(2) Subsection (3) applies if as a result of [Part 4 of TIOPA 2010][1] (provision not at arm's length) the company's profits and losses are calculated for tax purposes as if it were not a party to the contract.

(3) Any exchange gains or losses which arise to the company from the contract for the accounting period are left out of account in determining the credits and debits to be brought into account in accordance with this Part.

    [(3A) If the contract is to any extent matched, subsection (3) applies to leave out of account only the amount of the exchange gains or losses arising to the company in relation to the contract to the extent that the contract is unmatched (an amount which may be nil).][2]

(4) Subsection (5) applies if as a result of [Part 4 of TIOPA 2010][1] the company's profits and losses are calculated for tax purposes as if the terms of the contract were those which would have been agreed by the company and the other party to the contract had they been dealing at arm's length ("the arm's length terms").

(5) The credits and debits which are to be brought into account in accordance with this Part in the case of the company are to be determined on the assumption that the amount of any exchange gain or loss arising to the company from the contract in the accounting period is the adjusted amount.

(6) In subsection (5), the "adjusted amount" means the amount of an exchange gain or loss which would have arisen from the contract if its terms were the arm's length terms.

(7) That amount may be nil.

    [(7A) Subsections (5) to (7) apply only to the extent that the contract is unmatched.][2]

(8) Nothing in [Part 4 of TIOPA 2010][1] requires the amounts brought into account in accordance with this Part in respect of exchange gains and losses from derivative contracts to be calculated on the assumption that the arm's length provision had been made instead of the actual provision.

(9) But subsection (8) does not affect the application of—

    (*a*) subsection (3) under subsection (2), or

    (*b*) subsection (5) under subsection (4).

(10) In subsection (8) "the actual provision" and "the arm's length provision" have the same meaning as in [Part 4 of TIOPA 2010 (see sections 149 and 151 of that Act)][1].

[(11) For the purposes of this section a derivative contract of a company is matched if and to the extent that—

(a) it is in a matching relationship with another derivative contract or loan relationship of the company, or

(b) exchange gains or losses arising in relation to the derivative contract are excluded from being brought into account under regulations under section 606(4)(b),

and "unmatched" is to be construed accordingly.

(12) A derivative contract is in a matching relationship with another derivative contract or loan relationship if one is intended by the company to act to eliminate or substantially reduce the economic risk of the other.

(13) In this section "economic risk" means a risk which can be attributed to fluctuations in exchange rates between currencies over a period of time.

(14) In this section "loan relationship" has the same meaning as in Part 5 (see section 302).][2]

Amendments—[1]   In sub-ss (2), (4) and (8) words "Schedule 28AA to ICTA" substituted and in sub-s (10) words "Schedule 28AA to ICTA (see paragraph 1 of that Schedule)" substituted by TIOPA 2010 s 501, Sch 8 paras 123, 143. TIOPA 2010 has effect for corporation tax purposes for accounting periods ending on or after 1 April 2010, for income and capital gains tax purposes for the tax year 2010–11 and subsequent tax years, and for petroleum revenue tax purposes for chargeable periods beginning on or after 1 July 2010.

[2]   Sub-ss (3A), (7A), (11)–(14) inserted by FA 2016 s 49, Sch 7 paras 1, 11 with effect in relation to accounting periods beginning on or after 1 April 2016 (FA 2016 Sch 7 para 12(1)). Where a company has an accounting period beginning before 1 April 2016 and ending on or after that date ("the straddling period") the periods before and after 1 April 2016 are treated as separate accounting periods (FA 2016 Sch 7 para 12(2)).

695 Transfers of value to connected companies

(1) This section applies if—

    (a) a company ("A") paid an amount ("amount X") to a company ("B") for the grant of an option,

    (b) there is a failure to exercise in full all the rights under the option,

    (c) until the failure the option was a derivative contract of A,

    (d) as a result of the failure there is a transfer of value by A to B,

    (e) B is a connected company in relation to A, and

    (f) B is not chargeable to corporation tax in accordance with this Part in respect of the derivative contract.

(2) A must bring into account a credit of the appropriate amount in respect of the derivative contract for the accounting period in which the option expired or would have expired if none of the rights under it had been exercised.

(3) If the option expired, "the appropriate amount" means amount X.

(4) If any rights under the option were exercised (in whole or in part), "the appropriate amount" means amount X less so much of it as is referable, on a just and reasonable basis, to the rights which have been so exercised.

(5) In determining for the purposes of subsection (1)(d) whether there is a transfer of value, the assumption in subsection (6) is made.

(6) That assumption is that if there had not been a connection between A and B—

    (a) all the rights under the option would have been exercised in full, and

    (b) all of those rights would have been exercised on the latest date on which they were exercisable.

(7) In this section "option" is to be construed as if section 580(2) and (3) (meaning of "option") were omitted.

(8) For the purposes of this section, B is a connected company in relation to A in an accounting period if there is a time in the period when—

    (a) A controls B,

    (b) B controls A, or

    (c) A and B are both controlled by the same person.

(9) But A and B are not taken to be controlled by the same person just because they have been under the control of—

    [(za) the Crown,][1]

    (a) a Minister of the Crown,

    (b) a government department,

    (c) a Northern Ireland department,

    (d) a foreign sovereign power, or

    (e) an international organisation.

(10) Section 472 (meaning of "control") applies for the purposes of this section.

Amendments—[1]   Sub-s (9)(za), inserted by the Corporation Tax Act 2009 (Amendment) Order, SI 2009/2860 art 6(1), (6) with effect for corporation tax purposes for accounting periods ending on or after 1 April 2009, and for income tax and capital gains tax purposes for the tax year 2009–10 and subsequent tax years.

[695A Disguised distribution arrangements involving derivative contracts

(1) This section applies if—

    (a) a company ("A") is a party to arrangements involving one or more derivative contracts (each of which is referred to in this section as a "specified contract"), (*b*) another company ("B") is also a party to the arrangements (whether or not at the same time as A),

(*c*) A and B are members of the same group,

(*d*) the arrangements result in what is, in substance, a payment (directly or indirectly) from A to B of all or a significant part of the profits of the business of A or of a company which is a member of the same group as A or B (or both) ("the profit transfer"), and

(*e*) the arrangements are not arrangements of a kind which companies carrying on the same kind of business as A would enter into in the ordinary course of that business.

(2) No debits in respect of a specified contract, which—

(*a*) relate to the profit transfer, and

(*b*) apart from this section, would be brought into account by A or B for the purposes of this Part,

are to be so brought into account.

(3) Where one or more debits in respect of a specified contract are not brought into account by virtue of subsection (2), credits arising from the same contract which—

(*a*) relate to the same profit transfer, and

(*b*) apart from this section, would be brought into account by A or B for the purposes of this Part,

are not to be so brought into account to the extent that the total of those credits does not exceed the total of those debits.

(4) Subsection (3) does not apply to any credit which arises directly or indirectly in consequence of, or otherwise in connection with, arrangements the main purpose of which, or one of the main purposes of which, is the securing of a tax advantage for any person.

(5) For the purposes of this section a company is a member of the same group as another company if it is (or has been) a member of the same group at a time when the arrangements mentioned in subsection (1) have effect.

(6) In this section—

"arrangements" includes any scheme, arrangement or understanding of any kind, whether or not legally enforceable, involving a single transaction or two or more transactions;

"group" has the meaning given by section 357GD of CTA 2010;

"tax advantage" has the meaning given by section 1139 of CTA 2010.]¹

Amendments—¹   This section inserted by FA 2014 s 29(1) with effect in relation to accounting periods beginning on or after 5 December 2013, subject to the transitional provisions in FA 2014 s 29(3)–(6).

Transactions with non-UK residents

696 Derivative contracts with non-UK residents

(1) This section applies in relation to a company ("A") if, as a result of any transaction—

(*a*) A becomes a party to a derivative contract to which a non-UK resident ("NR") is a party,

(*b*) NR becomes a party to a derivative contract to which A is a party, or

(*c*) A and NR both become a party to a derivative contract.

(2) For each accounting period for any part of which A and NR are both a party to a derivative contract which makes provision for notional interest payments, the credits and debits which fall to be brought into account in accordance with this Part in respect of the contract in the case of A do not include the amount of any excluded debit in relation to that contract.

(3) The amount of an excluded debit is calculated by determining for the accounting period the amount (if any) by which—

(*a*) the sum of any notional interest payments made by A to NR while A and NR are both a party to the contract,

exceeds

(*b*) the sum of any notional interest payments made by NR to A during that time.

(4) For the purposes of this section, a payment is a notional interest payment if—

(*a*) a derivative contract specifies—

(i) a notional principal amount,

(ii) a period, and

(iii) a rate of interest,

(*b*) the amount of the payment is determined (wholly or mainly) by applying a rate to the specified notional principal amount for the specified period, and

(*c*) the value of the rate is the same at all times as that of the specified rate of interest.

(5) This section is subject to section 697.

697 Exceptions to section 696

(1) Section 696 does not apply if A—

(*a*) is a bank, building society, financial trader[, recognised clearing house, [recognised CSD,]³ EEA central counterparty or third country central counterparty]²,

(*b*) is a party to the derivative contract solely for the purposes of a trade or part of a trade it carries on in the United Kingdom, and

(*c*) is a party to it otherwise than as agent or nominee of another person.

[(2) Section 696 does not apply if NR—

    (*a*) is chargeable to corporation tax or income tax in respect of income arising from the derivative contract (or would be if there were any such income), and

    (*b*) is a party to the derivative contract otherwise than as agent or nominee of another person.][4]

(3) Section 696 does not apply if arrangements made in relation to the territory in which NR is resident—

    (*a*) have effect [under section 2(1) of TIOPA 2010][1] (double taxation relief), and

    (*b*) make provision in relation to interest (as defined in the arrangements).

(4) It does not matter whether the provision mentioned in subsection (3)(*b*) is for relief or otherwise.

(5) If NR is a party to the contract as agent or nominee of another person, subsection (3) applies as if the reference to the territory in which NR is resident were a reference to the territory in which that other person is resident.

(6) In this section—

    ["recognised clearing house", ["recognised CSD",][3] "EEA central counterparty" and "third country central counterparty" have the meanings given by section 285 of FISMA 2000 (exemptions for recognised [bodies][3]).][2] . . .[4]

Amendments—[1]   In sub-s (3)(*a*), words substituted for words "because of section 788 of ICTA", by TIOPA 2010 s 501, Sch 8 paras 89, 93. TIOPA 2010 has effect for corporation tax purposes for accounting periods ending on or after 1 April 2010, for income and capital gains tax purposes for the tax year 2010–11 and subsequent tax years, and for petroleum revenue tax purposes for chargeable periods beginning on or after 1 July 2010.

[2]   In sub-s (1)(*a*), words substituted, and in sub-s (6) definition substituted by SI 2013/504 reg 26 with effect from 1 April 2013.

[3]   In sub-ss (1)(*a*) and (6) words inserted, and in sub-s (6) words substituted for words "investment exchanges and clearing houses", by the Central Securities Depositories Regulations, SI 2017/1064 with effect from 28 November 2017.

[4]   Sub-s (2) substituted, and in sub-s (6), definition of "relevant entity" and preceding word ", and" repealed, by FA 2019 s 17, Sch 5 paras 10, 21, with effect from 6 April 2020, subject to transitional provisions in FA 2019 Sch 5 Pt 3 (paras 36–50).

Prospective amendments—In sub-ss (1)(*a*) and (6) words ", EEA central counterparty" to be repealed by the Financial Services (Miscellaneous) (Amendment) (EU Exit) Regulations, SI 2019/710 reg 5 with effect from Implementation Period completion day (see EU(WA)A 2020 Sch 5 para 1(1)).

[Derecognition

698A Debits arising from derecognition of derivative contracts

(1) This section applies where—

    (*a*) a company is at any time a party to tax avoidance arrangements,

    (*b*) as a result of those arrangements, a derivative contract to which the company is party, or any part of such a contract, is (in accordance with generally accepted accounting practice) derecognised by the company, and

    (*c*) the company continues to be a party to the derivative contract immediately after the transaction or other event giving rise to the derecognition.

(2) No debit that would apart from this section be brought into account by the company for the purposes of this Part as a result of the derecognition is to be so brought into account.

(3) An amount that would be brought into account for the purposes of this Part as respects any matter apart from this section—

    (*a*) is treated for the purposes of section 699(1) (priority of this Part for corporation tax purposes) as if it were so brought into account, and

    (*b*) accordingly, may not be brought into account for any other corporation tax purposes as respects that matter.

(4) For the purposes of this section a company is to be treated as a party to a derivative contract even though it has disposed of its rights and liabilities under the contract to another person—

    (*a*) under a repo or stock lending arrangement, or

    (*b*) under a transaction which is treated as not involving any disposal as a result of section 26 of TCGA 1992 (mortgages and charges not to be treated as disposals).

(5) For the purposes of this section arrangements are "tax avoidance arrangements" if the main purpose, or one of the main purposes, of any party to the arrangements, in entering into them, is to obtain a tax advantage.

(6) In subsection (5)—

    (*a*) "arrangements" includes any arrangements, scheme or understanding of any kind, whether or not legally enforceable, involving a single transaction or two or more transactions, and

    (*b*) "tax advantage" has the meaning given by section 1139 of CTA 2010.][1]

Amendments—[1]   This section inserted by FA 2011 s 28, Sch 4 paras 7, 11 with effect in relation to periods of account beginning on or after 6 December 2010, subject to the transitional provision in FA 2011 Sch 4 para 13(2).

[Counteracting avoidance arrangements

698B Counteracting effect of avoidance arrangements

(1) Any derivative-related tax advantages that would (in the absence of this section) arise from relevant avoidance arrangements are to be counteracted by the making of such adjustments as are just and reasonable in relation to credits and debits to be brought into account for the purposes of this Part.

(2) Any adjustments required to be made under this section (whether or not by an officer of Revenue and Customs) may be made by way of an assessment, the modification of an assessment, amendment or disallowance of a claim, or otherwise.

(3) For the meaning of "relevant avoidance arrangements" and "derivative-related tax advantage", see section 698C.][1]

Amendments—[1]   Sections 698B–698D inserted by F(No 2)A 2015 s 32, Sch 7 paras 59, 94 in relation to arrangements entered into on or after 18 November 2015.

[698C Interpretation of section 698B

(1) This section applies for the interpretation of section 698B (and this section).

(2) "Arrangements" include any agreement, understanding, scheme, transaction or series of transactions (whether or not legally enforceable).

(3) Arrangements are "relevant avoidance arrangements" if their main purpose, or one of their main purposes, is to enable a company to obtain a derivative-related tax advantage.

(4) But arrangements are not "relevant avoidance arrangements" if the obtaining of any derivative-related tax advantages that would (in the absence of section 698B) arise from them can reasonably be regarded as consistent with any principles on which the provisions of this Part that are relevant to the arrangements are based (whether expressed or implied) and the policy objectives of those provisions.

(5) A company obtains a "derivative-related tax advantage" if—

    (*a*) it brings into account a debit to which it would not otherwise be entitled,

    (*b*) it brings into account a debit which exceeds that to which it would otherwise be entitled,

    (*c*) it avoids having to bring a credit into account,

    (*d*) the amount of any credit brought into account by the company is less than it would otherwise be, or

    (*e*) it brings a debit or credit into account earlier or later than it otherwise would.

(6) In subsection (5), references to bringing a debit or credit into account are references to bringing a debit or credit into account for the purposes of this Part.][1]

Amendments—[1]   Sections 698B–698D inserted by F(No 2)A 2015 s 32, Sch 7 paras 59, 94 in relation to arrangements entered into on or after 18 November 2015.

[698D Examples of results that may indicate exclusion not applicable

(1) Each of the following is an example of something which might indicate that arrangements whose main purpose, or one of whose main purposes, is to enable a company to obtain a derivative-related tax advantage are not excluded by section 698C(4) from being "relevant avoidance arrangements" for the purposes of section 698B—

    (*a*) the elimination or reduction, for purposes of corporation tax, of profits of a company arising from any of its derivative contracts, where for economic purposes profits, or greater profits, arise to the company from that contract;

    (*b*) the creation or increase, for purposes of corporation tax, of a loss or expense arising from a derivative contract, where for economic purposes no loss or expense, or a smaller loss or expense, arises from that contract;

    (*c*) preventing or delaying the recognition as an item of profit or loss of an amount that would apart from the arrangements be recognised in the company's accounts as an item of profit or loss or be so recognised earlier;

    (*d*) ensuring that a derivative contract is treated for accounting purposes in a way in which it would not have been treated in the absence of some other transaction forming part of the arrangements;

    (*e*) enabling a company to bring into account a debit in respect of an exchange loss, in circumstances where a corresponding exchange gain would not give rise to a credit or would give rise to a credit of a smaller amount;

    (*f*) enabling a company to bring into account a debit in respect of a fair value loss in circumstances where a corresponding fair value gain would not give rise to a credit or would give rise to a credit of a smaller amount.

(2) But in each case the result concerned is only capable of indicating that section 698C(4) is not available if it is reasonable to assume that such a result was not the anticipated result when the provisions of this Part that are relevant to the arrangements were enacted

(3) In subsection (1)(*f*) references to a fair value gain or a fair value loss are references respectively to—

    (*a*) a profit to be brought into account in relation to a derivative contract where fair value accounting is used for the period in question, or

    (*b*) a loss to be brought into account in relation to a derivative contract where fair value accounting is used for the period in question.

(4) "Arrangements" and "derivative-related tax advantage" have the same meaning as in section 698C.][1]

Amendments—[1]   Sections 698B–698D inserted by F(No 2)A 2015 s 32, Sch 7 paras 59, 94 in relation to arrangements entered into on or after 18 November 2015.

CHAPTER 12

PRIORITY RULES

699 Priority of this Part for corporation tax purposes

(1) The amounts which are brought into account in accordance with this Part in respect of any matter are the only amounts which may be brought into account for corporation tax purposes in respect of it.

(2) Subsection (1) is subject to any provision to the contrary.

(3) For such provisions, see in particular—

    (a) section 616 (disapplication of fair value accounting for certain derivative contracts), [and][1]

    (b) paragraph 93 of Schedule 2 (plain vanilla contracts which became derivative contracts before 30 December 2006), . . . [1]

    (c) . . . [1]

Commentary—*Simon's Taxes* D1.811, D1.8121, D7.5100.

HMRC Manuals—Corporate Finance Manual CFM50060 (priority rules).

Amendments—[1] In sub-s (3), word inserted at end of para (a) and para (c) and preceding word "and" repealed, by FA 202 s 146, Sch 16 paras 135, 171 with effect in relation to accounting periods of companies beginning on or after 1 January 2013 (subject to transitional provisions in FA 2012 Sch 17). For accounting periods straddling 1 January 2013, see FA 2012 s 149.

700 Relationship of this Part to Part 5: loan relationships

(1) This section applies if—

    (a) a company is a party to a loan relationship because of a derivative contract, and

    (b) in accordance with this Part, a profit or loss accrues to the company on the contract for an accounting period ("the derivative profit or loss").

(2) The general rule is that this Part does not apply to the derivative profit or loss if—

    (a) an amount representing the derivative profit or loss, or

    (b) an amount representing the profit or loss accruing to that company on the contract,

is brought into account for that period for the purposes of Part 5 otherwise than because of section 574.

(3) But in a case where section 585 (loan relationships with embedded derivatives) applies, the general rule does not apply so far as—

    (a) the derivative profit or loss accrues from the rights and liabilities mentioned in section 585(1)(b) (rights and liabilities under derivative financial instruments or equity instruments), and

    (b) that profit or loss is dealt with in accordance with that section and this Part.

Commentary—*Simon's Taxes* D1.707, D1.811.

HMRC Manuals—Corporate Finance Manual CFM50060 (derivative contracts: priority rules for loan relationship).

CHAPTER 13

GENERAL AND SUPPLEMENTARY PROVISIONS

Power to amend certain provisions

701 Power to amend some provisions

(1) The Treasury may by order amend—

    (a) Chapter 2 (except sections 578(1), (2) and (4), 585, 587 and 588),

    (b) Chapter 4 (except section 613(4)),

    (c) section 635,

    (d) Chapter 7,

    (e) Chapter 8 (except section 660),

    (f) section 702,

    (g) section 706,

    (h) section 707,

    (i) section 708,

    (j) section 709,

    (k) the definitions in section 710 specified in subsection (2), and

    (l) paragraphs 80 to 94 of Schedule 2.

(2) The definitions mentioned in subsection (1)(k) are—

    capital redemption policy,

    depositary receipt (in relation to shares),

    designated,

    intangible fixed assets,

    shares, and

    warrant.

(3) The provision that may be made by an order under this section includes provision—

(a) adding to or varying the descriptions of contract which are derivative contracts within section 576 (meaning of "derivative contract") or removing any such description of contract, or

(b) adding to or varying the descriptions of contract which are excluded under section 589 (contracts excluded because of underlying subject matter: general) or removing any such description of contract.

(4) The provision that may be made under subsection (3)(b), in relation to contracts which are excluded under section 589, includes provision—

(a) adding to the provisions which qualify the exclusion of contracts under that section,

(b) varying any such provision, or

(c) removing any such provision.

(5) An order under this section may provide for any of its provisions to have effect in relation to—

(a) accounting periods ending on or after the day on which the order comes into force (whenever they begin),

(b) periods of account beginning before the order is made, but not earlier than the beginning of the calendar year in which it is made.

(6) An order under this section may—

(a) make different provision for different cases, and

(b) contain incidental, supplemental, consequential and transitional provision and savings (including provision amending any enactment or any instrument made under an enactment).

Orders—Corporation Tax Act 2009, Section 582 (Contract for Differences) (Amendment) Order, SI 2013/3218.

[Changes to accounting standards

701A Power to make regulations where accounting standards change

(1) The Treasury may by regulations make provision for cases where, in consequence of a change in accounting standards, there is a relevant accounting change.

(2) "Change in accounting standards" means the issue, revocation, amendment or recognition of, or withdrawal of recognition from, an accounting standard by an accounting body.

(3) "Relevant accounting change" means a change in the way in which a company is permitted or required, for accounting purposes, to recognise amounts which—

(a) are brought into account by the company as credits or debits for any period for the purposes of this Part, or

(b) would be so brought into account but for any provision made by or under this Part.

(4) Regulations under subsection (1) may amend this Part (apart from this section).

(5) Regulations under subsection (1) may—

(a) make different provision for different cases,

(b) make incidental, supplemental, consequential and transitional provision and savings, and

(c) make provision subject to an election or other specified circumstances.

(6) Regulations making consequential provision by virtue of subsection (5)(b) may, in particular, include provision amending a provision of the Corporation Tax Acts.

(7) Regulations under subsection (1) may apply to a pre-commencement period if they make provision in relation to a relevant accounting change which may or must be adopted, for accounting purposes, for a period of account (or part of a period of account) which coincides with that pre-commencement period.

(8) In this section—

"accounting body" means the International Accounting Standards Board or the Accounting Standards Board, or a successor body to either of those Boards;

"accounting standard" includes any statement of practice, guidance or other similar document;

"pre-commencement period", in relation to regulations, means an accounting period (or part of an accounting period) which begins before the regulations are made.][1]

Amendments—[1]   This section and preceding cross-head inserted by FA 2010 s 62, Sch 19 para 2 with effect from 8 April 2010.

Other general definitions

[702 "Tax-adjusted carrying value"

(1) This section applies for the purposes of this Part.

(2) "Tax-adjusted carrying value", in relation to a contract, means the carrying value of the contract recognised for accounting purposes, except as provided by subsection (7).

(3) For the purposes of this section the "carrying value" of the contract includes amounts recognised for accounting purposes in relation to the contract in respect of—

(a) accrued amounts,

(b) amounts paid or received in advance, or

(c) impairment losses (including provisions for bad or doubtful debts).

(4) In determining the tax-adjusted carrying value of a contract in a period of account of a company, it is to be assumed that the accounting policy applied in drawing up the company's accounts for the period was also applied in previous periods of account.

(5) But if the company's accounts for the period are in accordance with generally accepted accounting practice drawn up on an assumption as to the accounting policy in previous periods of account which differs from that mentioned in subsection (4), that different assumption applies in determining the tax-adjusted carrying value of the contract in the period.

(6) In determining the tax-adjusted carrying value of a contract at a time other than the end (or beginning) of a period of account of a company, it is to be assumed that a period of account of the company had ended at the time in question.

(7) In determining the profits and losses to be recognised in determining the tax-adjusted carrying value of the contract, the provisions specified in subsection (8) apply as they apply for the purposes of determining the credits and debits to be brought into account in accordance with this Part.

(8) Those provisions are—

   (a)   section 584 (hybrid derivatives with embedded derivatives),
   (b)   section 585 (loan relationships with embedded derivatives),
   (c)   section 586 (other contracts with embedded derivatives),
   (d)   section 597 (amounts recognised in determining profit or loss),
   (e)   sections 599A and 599B (amounts not fully recognised for accounting purposes),
   (f)   section 604A (amounts recognised in other comprehensive income and not transferred to profit and loss),
   (g)   Chapter 5 (transactions within groups),
   (h)   Chapter 9 (European cross-border transfers of business), and
   (i)   Chapter 10 (European cross-border mergers).

(9) In this section "impairment loss" means a debit in respect of the impairment of a financial asset and "impairment" includes uncollectability.][1]

HMRC Manuals—Corporate Finance Manual CFM76040 (meaning of "carrying value").
Amendments—[1]   This section substituted by F(No 2)A 2015 s 32, Sch 7 paras 59, 95 with effect for accounting periods beginning on or after 1 January 2016, subject to transitional rules in F(No 2)A 2015 Sch 7 paras 115 to 129.

703 "Chargeable asset"

(1) For the purposes of this Part, an asset is a chargeable asset if any gain accruing on its disposal would be a chargeable gain for corporation tax purposes.

(2) For the purposes of this section, "asset" includes any obligations under futures contracts which are regarded because of section 143 of TCGA 1992 as assets to the disposal of which that Act applies.

704 "Creditor relationship" and "debtor relationship"

(1) In this Part "creditor relationship" has the same meaning as in Part 5 (loan relationships) (see section 302(5) (meaning of "creditor relationship")).

(2) In this Part "debtor relationship" has the same meaning as in Part 5 (see section 302(6) (meaning of "debtor relationship")).

705 Expressions relating to exchange gains and losses

(1) References in this Part to exchange gains or exchange losses, in relation to a company, are references respectively to—

   (a)   profits or gains which arise as a result of comparing at different times the expression in one currency of the whole or some part of the valuation put by the company in another currency on an asset or liability of the company, or
   (b)   losses which so arise.

(2) If the result of such a comparison is that neither an exchange gain nor an exchange loss arises, for the purposes of this Part an exchange gain of nil is taken to arise in the case of that comparison.

(3) The Treasury may make provision by regulations as to the way in which exchange gains or losses are to be calculated for the purposes of this section . . . .[1]

(4) The regulations may be made so as to apply to periods of account beginning before the regulations are made, but not earlier than the beginning of the calendar year in which they are made.

(5) Any reference in this Part to an exchange gain or loss from a derivative contract of a company is a reference to an exchange gain or loss arising to a company in relation to a derivative contract of the company.

Regulations—Loan Relationships and Derivative Contracts (Exchange Gains and Losses using Fair Value Accounting) (Amendment) Regulations, SI 2015/1963.
Amendments—[1]   In sub-s (3) words "in a case where fair value accounting is used by the company" repealed by F(No 2)A 2015 s 32, Sch 7 paras 59, 96 with effect for accounting periods beginning on or after 1 January 2016, subject to transitional rules in F(No 2)A 2015 Sch 7 paras 115 to 129.

706 "Excluded body"

In this Part "excluded body" means—

   an authorised unit trust,
   an investment trust,
   an open-ended investment company, or
   a venture capital trust.

707 "Hedging relationship"

(1) This section applies for the purposes of this Part.

(2) A company has a "hedging relationship" between a relevant contract ("the hedging instrument") and an asset or liability ("the hedged item") so far as condition A or B is met.

(3) Condition A is that the hedging instrument and the hedged item are designated as a hedge by the company.

(4) Condition B is that—

    (*a*) the hedging instrument is intended to act as a hedge of the exposure to changes in fair value of the hedged item which is attributable to a particular risk and could affect the profit or loss of the company, and

    (*b*) the hedged item is an asset or liability recognised for accountancy purposes or is an identified portion of such an asset or liability.

(5) For the purposes of subsections (2) and (4), the liabilities of a company include its own share capital.

708 "Plain vanilla contract"

In this Part "plain vanilla contract" means a relevant contract other than one to which a company is treated as being a party under—

    (*a*) section 584 (hybrid derivatives with embedded derivatives),

    (*b*) section 585 (loan relationships with embedded derivatives), or

    (*c*) section 586 (other contracts with embedded derivatives).

HMRC Manuals—Corporate Finance Manual CFM50750 (plain vanilla contract: meaning).

709 "Securities house"

In this Part "securities house" means a person—

    (*a*) who is authorised for the purposes of FISMA 2000, and

    (*b*) whose business consists wholly or mainly of dealing as a principal in financial instruments within the meaning of section 984 of ITA 2007.

Commentary—*Simon's Taxes* D1.892, D1.893.

710 Other definitions

In this Part—

    ["accounting policy", in relation to a company, means the principles, bases, conventions, rules and practices that the company applies in preparing and presenting its financial statements,][3]

    "bank" means—

        (*a*) the Bank of England,

        (*b*) a person within [section 1120(2)(*b*) of CTA 2010][1], or

        (*c*) a firm within [section 1120(2)(*c*) of CTA 2010][1],

    "capital redemption policy" means a contract made in the course of capital redemption business (as defined in [section 56(3) of FA 2012][2]),

    "contract of insurance" has the meaning given by [section 64 of FA 2012][2],

    "contract of long-term insurance" has the meaning given by [section 64 of FA 2012][2]

    "depositary receipt", in relation to shares (as defined in this section), has the same meaning as it has in Part 4 of FA 1986 in relation to shares (within the meaning of that Part),

    "designated" has the meaning it has for accounting purposes,

    "equity instrument" has the meaning it has for accounting purposes,

    "fair value", in relation to a derivative contract of a company, means the amount which, at the time as at which the value is to be determined, is the amount which the company would obtain from or, as the case may be, would have to pay to an independent person dealing at arm's length for—

        (*a*) the transfer of the company's rights under the contract, and

        (*b*) the release of all the company's liabilities under it,

    ["fair value accounting" means a basis of accounting under which—

        (*a*) assets and liabilities are measured in the company's balance sheet at their fair value, and

        (*b*) changes in the fair value of assets and liabilities are recognised as items of profit or loss,][3]

    "financial trader" means—

        (*a*) a person who—

            (i) is within section 31(1)(*a*), (*b*) or (*c*) of FISMA 2000, and

           (ii) has permission under that Act to carry on one or more of the activities specified in Article 14 and, in so far as it applies to that Article, Article 64 of the Financial Services and Markets Act (Regulated Activities) Order 2001 (SI 2001/544), or

        (*b*) a person not within paragraph (*a*) who is approved by the Commissioners for Her Majesty's Revenue and Customs for the purposes of this section,

    "income statement" has the meaning it has for accounting purposes, "intangible fixed asset" has the same meaning as in Part 8 (intangible fixed assets), and sections 804 to 807 and 809 (assets wholly excluded from that Part) (and sections 800 to 802 so far as they relate to those sections) apply for the purposes of this Part as they apply for the purposes of that Part,

"open-ended investment company" has the meaning given by [section 613 of CTA 2010][1],

"profit-sharing arrangements", in relation to a firm, has the meaning given by section 1262(4) (allocation of firm's profits or losses between partners),

"shares", in relation to a company, means any shares in the company under which an entitlement to receive distributions may arise, including—

> (a) a depository receipt for shares under which such an entitlement may arise, and
>
> (b) in the case of a company which has no share capital, any interests in the company possessed by members of the company,

"statement of changes in equity" has the meaning it has for accounting purposes,

. . . [3]

"statement of income and retained earnings" has the meaning it has for accounting purposes,

"statement of recognised income and expense" has the meaning it has for accounting purposes,

"statement of total recognised gains and losses" has the meaning it has for accounting purposes, and

"warrant" means an instrument which entitles the holder to subscribe for—

> (a) shares in a company, or
>
> (b) assets representing a loan relationship of a company,

whether or not the shares or assets exist or are identifiable.

Commentary—*Simon's Taxes* **D1.809, D1.820, D1.895**.

Derivation—FA 2002 Sch 26 paras 12(1), (2), (9), (11), (12), (13), (17), 54(1), (4).

HMRC Manuals—Corporate Finance Manual CFM50720 (options or futures over intangible fixed assets).

CFM83030 (meaning of shares).

Amendments—[1] The following amendments made by CTA 2010 s 1177, Sch 1 para 643 with effect for corporation tax purposes for accounting periods ending on or after 1 April 2010, and for income and capital gains tax purposes for the tax year 2010–11 and subsequent tax years—

> – in definition of "bank", words in para (b) substituted for words "section 840A(1)(b) of ICTA", words in para (c) substituted for words "section 840A(1)(c) of that Act";
>
> – in definition of "open-ended investment company" words substituted for words "section 468A(2) of ICTA".

[2] In definition of "capital redemption policy", words substituted for words "section 431(2ZF) of ICTA", in definitions of "contract of insurance" and "contract of long-term insurance", words substituted for words "section 431(2) of ICTA", by FA 2012 s 146, Sch 16 paras 135, 172 with effect in relation to accounting periods of companies beginning on or after 1 January 2013 (subject to transitional provisions in FA 2012 Sch 17). For accounting periods straddling 1 January 2013, see FA 2012 s 149.

[3] Definition of "accounting policy" inserted, definition of "fair value accounting" substituted, and definition of "statement of comprehensive income" repealed, by F(No 2)A 2015 s 32, Sch 7 paras 59, 97 with effect for accounting periods beginning on or after 1 January 2016, subject to transitional rules in F(No 2)A 2015 Sch 7 paras 115 to 129.

CHAPTER 1
INTRODUCTION
Introductory

711 Overview of Part

(1) This Part sets out how a company's gains and losses in respect of intangible fixed assets are calculated and brought into account for corporation tax purposes.

(2) For the meaning of "intangible fixed assets" and rules about the assets to which this Part applies, see—

    (*a*) sections 712 to 715,

    (*b*) Chapter 10 (excluded assets), and

    (*c*) Chapter 16 (pre-FA 2002 assets etc).

(3) For how such gains and losses are calculated and brought into account, see, in particular, Chapter 6 which—

    (*a*) deals with the use of credits and debits in respect of some intangible fixed assets in calculating the profits and losses of trades, businesses and other concerns (see sections 747 to 750),

    (*b*) provides for the calculation of gains and losses where there are credits or debits in respect of other intangible fixed assets (see section 751),

    (*c*) makes gains so calculated subject to the charge to corporation tax on income (see section 752), and

    (*d*) gives an allowance for losses so calculated (see section 753).

(4) For the priority of this Part for corporation tax purposes, see Chapter 18 (under which the general rule is that the amounts brought into account in accordance with this Part in respect of any matter are the only amounts that may be brought into account for corporation tax purposes in respect of it).

(5) This Part operates by reference to the accounts of companies and amounts recognised for accounting purposes.

(6) For the meaning of "amounts recognised for accounting purposes" and other expressions related to accounting and for rules about "GAAP-compliant accounts", see sections 716 to 719.

(7) Chapters 2 to 6 contain basic rules about the credits and debits to be brought into account for corporation tax purposes in respect of intangible fixed assets.

(8) For rules about particular situations and cases, see—

    (*a*) Chapter 7 (roll-over relief in case of realisation and reinvestment),

    (*b*) Chapters 8 and 9 (groups of companies),

    (*c*) Chapter 11 (transfer of business or trade),

    (*d*) Chapter 12 and 13 (related parties),

    (*e*) Chapter 14 (further provisions relating to miscellaneous cases),

    (*f*) Chapter 15 (adjustments on change of accounting policies),

    [(*fa*) Chapter 15A (debits in respect of goodwill and certain other assets),][1]

    [(*fb*) Chapter 16A (debits in respect of assets that were pre-FA 2002 assets etc),

    (*fc*) Chapter 16B (fungible assets),][2] and

    (*g*) Chapter 17 (insurance companies).

Commentary—*Simon's Taxes* **D1.602, D1.610, D1.611**.

HMRC Manuals—Corporate Intangibles Research & Development Manual CIRD10000 (intangible assets regime: contents).

Amendments—[1]   Sub-s (8)(*fa*) inserted by FA 2019 s 25, Sch 9 paras 1, 2 with effect in relation to accounting periods beginning on or after 1 April 2019. An accounting period beginning before, and ending on or after, 1 April 2019 is to be treated as if so much of the accounting period as falls before that date, and so much of the accounting period as falls on or after that date, were separate accounting periods (FA 2019 Sch 9 para 7(2)).

[2]   Sub-s (8)(*fb*), (*fc*) inserted by FA 2020 s 31(1), (2) with effect in relation to accounting periods beginning on or after 1 July 2020. An accounting period beginning before, and ending on or after, 1 July 2020 is to be treated as if so much of the accounting period as falls before that date, and so much of the accounting period as falls on or after that date, were separate accounting periods (FA 2020 s 31(15)).

Basic definitions

712 "Intangible asset"

(1) In this Part "intangible asset" has the meaning it has for accounting purposes [(and includes an internally-generated intangible asset)][1].

(2) In particular, "intangible asset" includes intellectual property.

(3) For this purpose "intellectual property" means—

    (*a*) any patent, trade mark, registered design, copyright or design right, plant breeders' rights or rights under section 7 of the Plant Varieties Act 1997 (c 66),

    (*b*) any right under the law of a country or territory outside the United Kingdom corresponding or similar to a right within paragraph (*a*),

(c) any information or technique not protected by a right within paragraph (a) or (b) but having industrial, commercial or other economic value, or

(d) any licence or other right in respect of anything within paragraph (a), (b) or (c).

(4) This section is subject to Chapter 10 (excluded assets).

Commentary—*Simon's Taxes* **D1.602, D4.118, D6.438**.

HMRC Manuals—Corporate Intangibles Research and Development Manual CIRD11120 (meaning of "intangible asset").
CIRD11100 (intangible asset conditions: other than goodwill).
CIRD11150 (meaning of intellectual property).

Amendments—[1]   In sub-s (1) words inserted by FA 2009 s 70(2) with effect in relation to accounting periods beginning on or after 22 April 2009 (and, in relation to those accounting periods, are to be treated as always having had effect). In the case of an accounting period (a "straddling period")—

    (a)   beginning before 22 April 2009; and

    (b)   ending on or after that date,

the amended provisions apply as if the different parts of the straddling period falling in the different financial years were separate accounting periods (FA 2009 s 70(8)).

713 "Intangible fixed asset"

(1) In this Part an "intangible fixed asset", in relation to a company, means an intangible asset acquired or created by the company for use on a continuing basis in the course of the company's activities.

(2) In this Part "intangible fixed asset" includes an option or other right—

    (a) to acquire an intangible asset that would be a fixed asset if it were acquired, or

    (b) to dispose of an intangible fixed asset.

(3) This Part applies to an intangible fixed asset whether or not it is capitalised in the company's accounts.

(4) Subsection (3) is subject to any indication to the contrary.

(5) This section is subject to any such provision of regulations under section 854 (finance leasing etc) as is mentioned in section 855(1) (assets to be treated as intangible fixed assets of finance lessor).

Commentary—*Simon's Taxes* **D1.602**.

HMRC Manuals—Corporate Intangibles Research and Development Manual CIRD11170 (requirement that asset must be fixed).
CIRD11175 (options in respect of intangible fixed assets).

714 "Royalty"

In this Part "royalty" means a royalty in respect of the enjoyment or exercise of rights that constitute an intangible fixed asset.

Commentary—*Simon's Taxes* **D1.626, D1.621, D1.603, D1.602**.

HMRC Manuals—Corporate Intangibles Research and Development Manual CIRD11705 (royalty : outline).
CIRD11710 (meaning of "royalty").

Goodwill

715 Application of this Part to goodwill

(1) This Part applies to goodwill as it applies to an intangible fixed asset.

(2) Subsection (1) is subject to any indication to the contrary [(see, in particular, [Chapter 15A (debits in respect of goodwill and certain other assets)).][3][2].

(3) In this Part "goodwill" has the meaning it has for accounting purposes [(and includes internally-generated goodwill)][1].

[(4) For the purposes of this Part, goodwill is treated as created in the course of carrying on the business in question.][1]

Commentary—*Simon's Taxes* **D1.601A, D1.602**.

HMRC Manuals—Corporate Intangibles Research and Development Manual CIRD11070 (meaning of "goodwill").

Amendments—[1]   In sub-s (3) words inserted, and the whole of sub-s (4) inserted, by FA 2009 s 70(3) with effect in relation to accounting periods beginning on or after 22 April 2009 (and, in relation to those accounting periods, these amendments are to be treated as always having had effect). In the case of an accounting period (a "straddling period")—

    (a)   beginning before 22 April 2009; and

    (b)   ending on or after that date,

the amended provisions apply as if the different parts of the straddling period falling in the different financial years were separate accounting periods (FA 2009 s 70(8)).

[2]   In sub-s (2), words inserted by F(No 2)A 2015 s 33(1), (2) with effect in relation to accounting periods beginning on or after 8 July 2015. But the amendments do not apply in a case in which a company acquires a relevant asset if the company does so before 8 July 2015, or in pursuance of an obligation, under a contract, that was unconditional before that date. An obligation is "unconditional" if it may not be varied or extinguished by the exercise of a right (whether under the contract or otherwise). For accounting periods straddling 8 July 2015 see F(No 2)A 2015 s 33(11), (12).

[3]   In sub-s (2), words substituted for words "section 816A (restrictions on goodwill and certain other assets))" by FA 2019 s 25, Sch 9 paras 1, 3 with effect in relation to accounting periods beginning on or after 1 April 2019. An accounting period beginning before, and ending on or after, 1 April 2019 is to be treated as if so much of the accounting period as falls before that date, and so much of the accounting period as falls on or after that date, were separate accounting periods (FA 2019 Sch 9 para 7(2)).

Accounting rules and definitions

716 "Recognised" amounts and "GAAP-compliant accounts"

(1) References in this Part to an amount "recognised" in determining a company's profit or loss for a period are to—

   (*a*) an amount recognised in—

      (i) the company's profit and loss account, income statement or statement of comprehensive income for that period,

      (ii) the company's statement of total recognised gains and losses, statement of recognised income and expense, statement of changes in equity or statement of income and retained earnings for that period, or

      (iii) any other statement of items brought into account in calculating the company's profits and losses for that period, and

   (*b*) an amount that would have been so recognised if such an account or statement had been drawn up for that period in accordance with generally accepted accounting practice.

(2) An amount that in accordance with generally accepted accounting practice is shown as a prior period adjustment in any such statement as is mentioned in subsection (1) must be brought into account for the purposes of this Part in calculating the company's profits and losses for the period to which the statement relates.

(3) Subsection (2) does not apply to an amount recognised for accounting purposes by way of correction of a fundamental error.

(4) In this Part "GAAP-compliant accounts" means accounts drawn up in accordance with generally accepted accounting practice.

(5) In the case of a company that is a member of a group, see also section 718.

Commentary—*Simon's Taxes* **D1.611**.

Derivation—FA 2002 Sch 29 paras 5(1), 134(1), (2).

HMRC Manuals—Corporate Intangibles Research and Development Manual CIRD12230 (core computational rules: accounting period for which entries taken into account for tax).

717 Companies without GAAP-compliant accounts

(1) If a company—

   (*a*) draws up accounts that are not GAAP-compliant accounts, or

   (*b*) does not draw up accounts at all,

this Part applies as if GAAP-compliant accounts had been drawn up.

(2) References in this Part to amounts recognised for accounting purposes are references to the amounts which would have been recognised if GAAP-compliant accounts had been drawn up for the period of account in question and any relevant earlier period.

(3) For this purpose a period of account is relevant to a later period if the accounts for the later period rely to any extent on amounts derived from the earlier period.

Commentary—*Simon's Taxes* **D1.611**.

718 GAAP-compliant accounts: reference to consolidated group accounts

(1) In determining whether a company's accounts are GAAP-compliant, reference may be made to any view about—

   (*a*) the useful life of an asset, or

   (*b*) the economic value of an asset,

taken for the purposes of consolidated group accounts prepared for any group of companies of which the company is a member.

(2) This section does not apply if the consolidated group accounts—

   (*a*) are drawn up using a different accounting framework from that used for the company's individual accounts, and

   (*b*) as a result are prepared on a basis that, in relation to the matters mentioned in subsection (1), substantially diverges from the basis used in the company's individual accounts.

(3) This section does not apply so far as the consolidated group accounts are prepared—

   (*a*) in accordance with the requirements of the law of a country outside the United Kingdom, and

   (*b*) on a basis that, in relation to the matters mentioned in subsection (1), substantially diverges from generally accepted accounting practice.

Commentary—*Simon's Taxes* **D1.611**.

719 Accounting value

In this Part "accounting value", in relation to an asset, means the net book value (or carrying amount) of the asset recognised for accounting purposes.

Commentary—*Simon's Taxes* **D1.616, D1.626, D1.627, D1.630, D1.629C, D1.632**.

Derivation—FA 2002 Sch 29 para 135.

HMRC Manuals—Corporate Intangibles Research and Development Manual CIRD12770 (accounting value: meaning).

CHAPTER 2

CREDITS IN RESPECT OF INTANGIBLE FIXED ASSETS

720 Introduction

(1) This Chapter provides for credits to be brought into account by a company for tax purposes in respect of—

    (a) receipts in respect of intangible fixed assets that are recognised in determining the company's profit or loss as they accrue (see section 721),

    (b) receipts in respect of royalties, so far as the receipts do not give rise to a credit under section 721 (see section 722),

    (c) revaluation of an intangible fixed asset (see section 723),

    (d) credits recognised for accounting purposes in respect of negative goodwill (see section 724), and

    (e) the reversal of previous accounting debits in respect of an intangible fixed asset (see section 725).

(2) This Chapter does not apply in relation to amounts brought into account in connection with the realisation of an intangible fixed asset within the meaning of Chapter 4 (see section 734).

(3) For the rules about those amounts, see that Chapter.

Commentary—*Simon's Taxes* **D1.626**.

721 Receipts recognised as they accrue

(1) If in a period of account a gain representing a receipt in respect of an intangible fixed asset is recognised in determining the company's profit or loss, a corresponding credit must be brought into account for tax purposes.

(2) The amount of the credit is the same as the amount of the gain recognised by the company for accounting purposes.

(3) Subsection (2) is subject to any adjustments required by this Part or [Part 4 of TIOPA 2010][1] (provision not at arm's length).

Commentary—*Simon's Taxes* **D1.626, D1.621**.
Derivation—FA 2002 Sch 29 paras 14(1), (2), 136.
HMRC Manuals—Corporate Intangibles Research and Development Manual CIRD13020 (receipts recognised as they accrue).
Amendments—[1] In sub–s (3) words "Schedule 28AA to ICTA" substituted by TIOPA 2010 s 501, Sch 8 paras 123, 145. TIOPA 2010 has effect for corporation tax purposes for accounting periods ending on or after 1 April 2010, for income and capital gains tax purposes for the tax year 2010–11 and subsequent tax years, and for petroleum revenue tax purposes for chargeable periods beginning on or after 1 July 2010.

722 Receipts in respect of royalties so far as not dealt with under section 721

(1) So far as a receipt in respect of any royalty does not give rise to a credit under section 721 in the period of account in which it is received or in a subsequent period of account, a credit must be brought into account for tax purposes.

(2) The credit must be brought into account in the accounting period in which the receipt is recognised for accounting purposes.

(3) The amount of the credit is equal to so much of the amount of the receipt as does not give rise to a credit under section 721.

Commentary—*Simon's Taxes* **D1.621**.
Derivation—FA 2002 Sch 29 para 14A(1)–(3).

723 Revaluation

(1) If in a period of account there is an increase in the accounting value of an intangible fixed asset on a revaluation, a credit must be brought into account for tax purposes.

(2) The amount of the credit is the lesser of—

    (a) the amount corresponding for tax purposes to the increase (see subsection (3)), and

    (b) the net total of relevant previous tax debits (see subsection (4)).

(3) The amount corresponding for tax purposes to the increase is—

$$I \times \frac{WDV}{AV}$$

where—

    I is the increase,

    WDV is the tax written-down value of the asset immediately before the revaluation, and

    AV is the accounting value of the asset by reference to which the revaluation is carried out.

(4) The net total of relevant previous tax debits is—

$$D - C$$

where—

D is the total debits previously brought into account for tax purposes in respect of the asset, and

C is the total credits so brought into account.

(5) For the purposes of this section "revaluation" includes—

    (a) the valuation of an asset for which a value is shown in the company's balance sheet, but which has not previously been the subject of a valuation, and

    (b) the restoration of past losses.

(6) This section does not apply to an asset in respect of which an election has been made under section 730 (writing down at fixed rate: election for fixed-rate basis).

Commentary—*Simon's Taxes* **D1.626, D1.622, D1.629D, D1.629E**.

Derivation—FA 2002 Sch 29 para 15(1)–(6).

HMRC Manuals—Corporate Intangibles Research and Development Manual CIRD12790 (accounts-based relief). CIRD13050 (revaluation of intangible assets).

724 Negative goodwill

(1) If in a period of account a gain is recognised in determining the company's profit or loss in respect of negative goodwill arising on an acquisition of a business, a corresponding credit must be brought into account for tax purposes.

(2) The amount of the credit is so much of the gain recognised for accounting purposes as, on a just and reasonable apportionment, is attributable to intangible fixed assets.

Commentary—*Simon's Taxes* **D1.626, D1.624**.

Derivation—FA Sch 29 para 16(1), (2).

HMRC Manuals—Corporate Intangibles Research and Development Manual CIRD13080 (negative goodwill).

725 Reversal of previous accounting loss

(1) This section applies if—

    (a) in a period of account a gain is recognised in determining the company's profit or loss ("the recognised gain"),

    (b) the gain wholly or partly reverses a loss recognised in a previous period of account ("the reversed loss"), and

    (c) a debit was brought into account for tax purposes under Chapter 3 (debits in respect of intangible fixed assets) in respect of that loss ("the tax debit").

(2) A corresponding credit must be brought into account for tax purposes.

(3) The amount of the credit is—

$$RG \times \frac{D}{RL}$$

where—

    RG is the recognised gain,

    D is the tax debit, and

    RL is the reversed loss.

(4) This section does not apply to a gain on a revaluation within the meaning of section 723 (see subsection (5) of that section).

Commentary—*Simon's Taxes* **D1.626, D1.629D, D1.629E, D1.625**.

Derivation—FA 2002 Sch 29 para 17(1)–(3).

HMRC Manuals—Corporate Intangibles Research and Development Manual CIRD13090 (reversing previous accounting losses).

CHAPTER 3

DEBITS IN RESPECT OF INTANGIBLE FIXED ASSETS

726 Introduction

(1) This Chapter provides for debits to be brought into account by a company for tax purposes in respect of—

    (a) expenditure on an intangible fixed asset that is written off for accounting purposes as it is incurred (see section 728),

    (b) writing down the capitalised cost of an intangible fixed asset—

        (i) on an accounting basis (see section 729), or

        (ii) on a fixed-rate basis (see sections 730 and 731), and

    (c) the reversal of a previous accounting gain in respect of an intangible fixed asset (see section 732).

(2) This Chapter does not apply in relation to amounts brought into account in connection with the realisation of an intangible fixed asset within the meaning of Chapter 4 (see section 734).

(3) For the rules about those amounts, see that Chapter.

Commentary—*Simon's Taxes* **D1.626**.

Derivation—FA 2002 Sch 29 para 7(1)–(2).

727 References to expenditure on an asset

(1) References in this Part to expenditure on an asset are to any expenditure (including abortive expenditure)—

    (a) for the purpose of acquiring or creating, or establishing title to, the asset,

    (b) by way of royalty in respect of the use of the asset, or

    (c) for the purpose of maintaining, preserving or enhancing, or defending title to, the asset.

(2) No account may be taken of capital expenditure on tangible assets in determining for the purposes of this Part the amount of expenditure on an intangible asset.

(3) In subsection (2) "capital expenditure" has the same meaning as in CAA 2001.

(4) If expenditure is incurred partly as mentioned in subsection (1) or (2) and partly otherwise, any necessary apportionment must be made on a just and reasonable basis.

Commentary—*Simon's Taxes* **D1.626**.

Derivation—FA 2002 Sch 29 para 133(1)–(3).

HMRC Manuals—Corporate Intangibles Research and Development Manual CIRD12250 (link to deductible debits). CIRD12260 (exclusion of expenditure on intangible assets).

728 Expenditure written off as it is incurred

(1) If in a period of account expenditure on an intangible fixed asset is recognised in determining a company's profit or loss, a corresponding debit must be brought into account for tax purposes.

(2) The amount of the debit recognised for tax purposes is the same as the amount of the loss recognised by the company for accounting purposes.

(3) Subsection (2) is subject to any adjustments required by this Part or [Part 4 of TIOPA 2010][1] (provision not at arm's length).

(4) This section does not apply if the loss represents previously capitalised expenditure.

(5) Nothing in section 59 (patent royalties) prevents a debit from being brought into account in accordance with this section, and so given effect under Chapter 6 of this Part.

Commentary—*Simon's Taxes* **D1.614, D1.626, D1.626**.

Derivation—FA 2002 Sch 29 paras 8(1)–(4), 136.

HMRC Manuals—Corporate Intangibles Research and Development Manual CIRD12530 (expenditure charged to the profit and loss account as it accrues).

Amendments—[1]   In sub–s (3) words "Schedule 28AA to ICTA" substituted by TIOPA 2010 s 501, Sch 8 paras 123, 145. TIOPA 2010 has effect for corporation tax purposes for accounting periods ending on or after 1 April 2010, for income and capital gains tax purposes for the tax year 2010–11 and subsequent tax years, and for petroleum revenue tax purposes for chargeable periods beginning on or after 1 July 2010.

729 Writing down on accounting basis

(1) If in a period of account a loss is recognised in determining a company's profit or loss in respect of capitalised expenditure on an intangible fixed asset—

    (a) by way of amortisation, or

    (b) as a result of an impairment review,

a corresponding debit must be brought into account for tax purposes.

(2) The reference in subsection (1) to an "impairment review" does not include the valuation of an asset for the purpose of determining the amount of expenditure to be capitalised in the first place.

(3) In the period of account in which expenditure on an asset is capitalised the amount of the debit for tax purposes in respect of the expenditure is—

$$L \times \frac{E}{CE}$$

where—

    L is the amount of the loss recognised for accounting purposes,

    E is the amount of expenditure on the asset that is recognised for tax purposes, and

    CE is the amount capitalised in respect of expenditure on the asset.

(4) For the purposes of subsection (3), subject to any adjustments required by this Part or [Part 4 of TIOPA 2010][1] (provision not at arm's length), the amount of expenditure on the asset that is recognised for tax purposes is the same as the amount of expenditure on the asset capitalised by the company.

(5) In a subsequent period of account the amount of the debit for tax purposes in respect of the expenditure on an asset is—

$$L \times \frac{WDV}{AV}$$

where—

    L is the amount of the loss recognised for accounting purposes,

WDV is the tax written-down value of the asset (see section 742) immediately before the amortisation charge is made or, as the case may be, the impairment loss is recognised for accounting purposes, and

AV is the value of the asset recognised for accounting purposes immediately before the amortisation charge or, as the case may be, the impairment review.

(6) In this section "capitalised" means capitalised for accounting purposes.

(7) This section does not apply to an asset in respect of which an election is made under section 730.

Commentary—*Simon's Taxes* **D1.627, D1.628.**

Derivation—FA 2002 Sch 29 paras 9(1)–(6), 10(6), 136.

HMRC Manuals—Corporate Intangibles Research and Development Manual CIRD12755 (accounts-based relief).

CIRD12760 (period expenditure first capitalised).

CIRD12770 (period after expenditure first capitalised).

Amendments—[1]   In sub–s (4) words "Schedule 28AA to ICTA" substituted by TIOPA 2010 s 501, Sch 8 paras 123, 145. TIOPA 2010 has effect for corporation tax purposes for accounting periods ending on or after 1 April 2010, for income and capital gains tax purposes for the tax year 2010–11 and subsequent tax years, and for petroleum revenue tax purposes for chargeable periods beginning on or after 1 July 2010.

730 Writing down at fixed rate: election for fixed-rate basis

(1) A company may elect to write down the cost of an intangible fixed asset for tax purposes at a fixed rate.

(2) The election may be made whether or not the asset is written down for accounting purposes.

(3) The election may only be made—

    (*a*) in writing,

    (*b*) to an officer of Revenue and Customs, and

    (*c*) not later than 2 years after the end of the accounting period in which the asset is created or acquired by the company.

(4) The election applies to all expenditure on the asset that is capitalised for accounting purposes.

(5) The election is irrevocable.

Commentary—*Simon's Taxes* **D1.628, D1.1445, T1.138.**

HMRC Manuals—Corporate Intangibles Research and Development Manual CIRD12905 (fixed rate relief).

731 Writing down at fixed rate: calculation

(1) If an election is made under section 730 for writing down at a fixed rate, a debit equal to the lesser of—

    (*a*) 4% of the cost of the asset, and

    (*b*) the balance of the tax written-down value,

must be brought into account for tax purposes in each accounting period beginning with that in which the relevant expenditure is incurred.

(2) If the accounting period is less than 12 months, the amount mentioned in subsection (1)(*a*) must be proportionately reduced.

(3) In this section "the cost of the asset" means the cost recognised for tax purposes.

(4) The cost of the asset recognised for tax purposes is the same as the amount capitalised for accounting purposes in respect of expenditure on the asset.

(5) Subsection (4) is subject to any adjustments required by this Part or [Part 4 of TIOPA 2010][1] (provision not at arm's length).

(6) If there is a part realisation of the asset (see section 734(4)), the reference in subsection (1)(*a*) to the cost of the asset must be read as a reference to the sum of—

    (*a*) the cost recognised for tax purposes in respect of the value of the asset recognised for accounting purposes immediately after the part realisation, and

    (*b*) the cost recognised for tax purposes of any subsequent expenditure on the asset that is capitalised for accounting purposes.

(7) If there is a further part realisation, subsection (6) applies again.

Commentary—*Simon's Taxes* **D1.628.**

HMRC Manuals—Corporate Intangibles Research and Development Manual CIRD12920 (fixed rate relief – debits following part-realisation).

CIRD12910 (relief for capitalised expenditure on an intangible asset).

Modifications—CTA 2009 s 879B(3) (company acquiring or creating a relevant asset on or after 1 April 2019 treated as having elected to write down cost at fixed rate; modification of sub–s (1)(*a*) to substitute 6.5% (rather than 4%) in relation to the asset).

Amendments—[1]   In sub–s (5) words "Schedule 28AA to ICTA" substituted by TIOPA 2010 s 501, Sch 8 paras 123, 145. TIOPA 2010 has effect for corporation tax purposes for accounting periods ending on or after 1 April 2010, for income and capital gains tax purposes for the tax year 2010–11 and subsequent tax years, and for petroleum revenue tax purposes for chargeable periods beginning on or after 1 July 2010.

732 Reversal of previous accounting gain

(1) This section applies if—

    (*a*) in a period of account a loss is recognised in determining a company's profit or loss ("the recognised loss"), (*b*) the loss wholly or partly reverses a gain recognised in a previous period of account ("the reversed gain"), and

(*c*) a credit was brought into account for tax purposes under Chapter 2 (credits in respect of intangible fixed assets) in respect of that gain ("the previous credit").

(2) A corresponding debit must be brought into account for tax purposes.

(3) The amount of that debit is—

$$RL \times \frac{PC}{RG}$$

where—

RL is the recognised loss,

PC is the previous credit, and

RG is the reversed gain.

(4) References in this section to the recognition of a loss that reverses a gain recognised in a previous period of account do not include a loss recognised—

(*a*) by way of amortisation of an asset that has previously been the subject of a revaluation, or

(*b*) as a result of an impairment review of such an asset.

(5) In subsection (4) "revaluation" has the same meaning as in section 723 (see subsection (5) of that section).

Commentary—*Simon's Taxes* **D1.626, D1.629D, D1.629E, D1.629**.

Derivation—FA 2002 Sch 29 para 12(1)–(3).

HMRC Manuals—Corporate Intangibles Research and Development Manual CIRD12560 (accounting losses in respect of reversal of previous accounting gains).

CHAPTER 4

REALISATION OF INTANGIBLE FIXED ASSETS

733 Overview of Chapter

(1) This Chapter provides for credits or debits to be brought into account for tax purposes on the realisation by a company of an intangible fixed asset.

(2) For the meaning of "realisation", see section 734.

(3) Sections 735 to 738 are subject to Chapter 7 (roll-over relief in case of realisation and reinvestment).

(4) This Chapter is also relevant for determining—

(*a*) whether an asset is a chargeable intangible asset for the purposes of this Part, and

(*b*) whether a gain is a chargeable realisation gain for the purposes of this Part.

(5) For the meaning of "chargeable intangible asset" and "chargeable realisation gain", see section 741.

Commentary—*Simon's Taxes* **D1.626, D1.630, D1.629C**.

Derivation—FA 2002 Sch 29 paras 18, 25.

734 Meaning of "realisation"

(1) References in this Part to the realisation of an intangible fixed asset are to a transaction resulting, in accordance with generally accepted accounting practice—

(*a*) in the asset ceasing to be recognised in the company's balance sheet, or

(*b*) in a reduction in the accounting value of the asset.

(2) In subsection (1) "transaction" includes any event giving rise to a gain recognised for accounting purposes.

(3) In relation to an intangible fixed asset that has no balance sheet value (or no longer has a balance sheet value), subsections (1) and (2) apply as if it did have a balance sheet value.

(4) References in this Part to a "part realisation" are to a realisation falling within subsection (1)(*b*).

Commentary—*Simon's Taxes* **D1.630, D1.629C**.

Derivation—FA 2002 Sch 29 para 19(1)–(3).

HMRC Manuals—Corporate Intangibles Research and Development Manual CIRD13230 (meaning of "realisation").

735 Asset written down for tax purposes

(1) This section applies if there is a realisation of an intangible fixed asset in respect of which debits have been brought into account for tax purposes.

(2) If the proceeds of realisation exceed the tax written-down value of the asset, a credit equal to the excess must be brought into account for tax purposes.

(3) If the proceeds of realisation are less than the tax written-down value of the asset, a debit equal to the shortfall must be brought into account for tax purposes.

(4) If there are no proceeds of realisation, a debit equal to the tax written-down value must be brought into account for tax purposes.

(5) References in this section to the tax written-down value of an asset are to its tax written-down value immediately before the realisation.

Commentary—*Simon's Taxes* **D1.630, D1.629C.**
Derivation—FA 2002 Sch 29 para 20(1)–(3).
HMRC Manuals—Corporate Intangibles Research and Development Manual CIRD13250 (computational rules: realisation of assets).

736 Asset shown in balance sheet and not written down for tax purposes

(1) This section applies if—
    (a) there is a realisation of an intangible fixed asset to which section 735 does not apply, and
    (b) a value is shown for the asset in the company's balance sheet.
(2) If the proceeds of realisation exceed the cost of the asset, a credit equal to the excess must be brought into account for tax purposes.
(3) If the proceeds of realisation are less than the cost of the asset, a debit equal to the shortfall must be brought into account for tax purposes.
(4) If there are no proceeds of realisation, a debit equal to the cost of the asset must be brought into account for tax purposes.
(5) In this section "the cost of the asset" means the cost recognised for tax purposes.
(6) The cost of the asset recognised for tax purposes is the same as the amount of expenditure on the asset capitalised by the company for accounting purposes.
(7) Subsection (6) is subject to any adjustments required by this Part or [Part 4 of TIOPA 2010][1] (provision not at arm's length)).
(8) If this section has applied on a part realisation of an asset and applies again (on the realisation of the unrealised asset) the references in subsections (2) to (4) to the cost of the asset must be read as references to the sum of—
    (a) the cost recognised for tax purposes in respect of the value of the asset recognised for accounting purposes immediately after the part realisation, and
    (b) the cost recognised for tax purposes of any subsequent expenditure on the asset that is capitalised for accounting purposes.
(9) If there is a further part realisation, subsection (8) applies again.

Commentary—*Simon's Taxes* **D1.630, D1.629C.**
Derivation—FA 2002 Sch 29 paras 21(1)–(6), 136.
HMRC Manuals—Corporate Intangibles Research and Development Manual CIRD13250 (asset on balance sheet but not written down).
Amendments—[1]   In sub-s (7) words "Schedule 28AA to ICTA" substituted by TIOPA 2010 s 501, Sch 8 paras 123, 145. TIOPA 2010 has effect for corporation tax purposes for accounting periods ending on or after 1 April 2010, for income and capital gains tax purposes for the tax year 2010–11 and subsequent tax years, and for petroleum revenue tax purposes for chargeable periods beginning on or after 1 July 2010.

737 Apportionment in case of part realisation

(1) In the case of a part realisation—
    (a) the references in section 735 to the tax written-down value of the asset, and
    (b) the references in section 736 to the cost of the asset,
must be read as references to the appropriate proportion of that amount.
(2) That proportion is—

$$\frac{AVB - AVA}{AVB}$$

where—
    AVB is the accounting value immediately before the realisation, and
    AVA is the accounting value immediately after the realisation.

Commentary—*Simon's Taxes* **D1.630, D1.629C.**
Derivation—FA 2002 Sch 29 para 22(1), (2).
HMRC Manuals—Corporate Intangibles Research and Development Manual CIRD13260 (partial realisation).

738 Asset not shown in balance sheet

(1) This section applies if—
    (a) there is a realisation of an intangible fixed asset, and
    (b) neither section 735 (asset written down for tax purposes) nor section 736 (asset shown in balance sheet and not written down for tax purposes) applies.
(2) A credit equal to any proceeds of realisation must be brought into account for tax purposes.

Commentary—*Simon's Taxes* **D1.630, D1.629C.**
Derivation—FA 2002 Sch 29 para 23(1), (2).
HMRC Manuals—Corporate Intangibles Research and Development Manual CIRD13250 (asset not on balance sheet).

[738A Realisation of assets previously subject to Northern Ireland rate

(1) This section applies if—
    (a) a company is required by section 735, 736 or 738 to bring into account for tax purposes a credit or debit on the realisation of an intangible fixed asset in an accounting period ("the relevant period"),

(b) the company is not a Northern Ireland company as defined by section 357KA of CTA 2010 in the relevant period,

(c) the asset is not a pre-commencement asset for the purposes of Chapter 8 of Part 8B of CTA 2010 (trading profits taxable at the Northern Ireland rate: intangible fixed assets),

(d) the credit or debit is treated for the purposes of that Chapter as including a Northern Ireland element, and

(e) at any time during the relevant period, the Northern Ireland rate is lower than the main rate.

(2) The amount of the credit or debit to be brought into account for tax purposes under section 735, 736 or 738 is reduced by an amount determined under this section ("the appropriate reduction").

(3) If the relevant period falls within only one financial year, the appropriate reduction is—

$$E \times \frac{MR - NIR}{MR}$$

where—

E is the Northern Ireland element of the credit or debit (see subsection (5));

MR is the main rate for the financial year;

NIR is the Northern Ireland rate for the financial year.

(4) If the relevant period falls within more than one financial year, take the following steps to find the appropriate reduction—

Step 1

Apportion the Northern Ireland element of the credit or debit (see subsection (5)) between the financial years on a time basis according to the respective lengths of the parts of the relevant period falling within those years.

Step 2

Where an amount is apportioned under step 1 to a financial year in which the Northern Ireland rate is lower than the main rate, multiply that amount by the following fraction—

$$\frac{MR - NIR}{MR}$$

where—

MR is the main rate for the financial year;

NIR is the Northern Ireland rate for the financial year.

Step 3

To find the appropriate reduction, add together each amount determined under step 2.

(5) In subsections (3) and (4), the "Northern Ireland element" of the credit or debit is an amount determined in accordance with sections 357OE to 357OG of CTA 2010.]

Prospective amendments—Section 738A to be inserted by the Corporation Tax (Northern Ireland) Act 2015 s 3, Sch 2 para 1 with effect in relation to accounting periods beginning on or after the first day of the appointed financial year ("the commencement day"). Any power of the Treasury or the Commissioners under the amendments made by Sch 2 to make regulations or an order may be exercised on or after 26 March 2015.

739 Meaning of "proceeds of realisation"

(1) In this Part "proceeds of realisation" of an asset means the amount recognised for accounting purposes as the proceeds of realisation, less the amount so recognised as incidental costs of realisation.

[(1A) But if the realisation involved the receipt of something other than money, subsection (1) has effect as if the reference to the amount recognised for accounting purposes as the proceeds of realisation were a reference to the amount that would have been so recognised had the receipt been a receipt of a sum of money equal to the price the thing concerned might reasonably have been expected to fetch on a sale in the open market.][2]

(2) The amounts referred to in subsection (1) are subject to any adjustments required by this Part or [Part 4 of TIOPA 2010][1] (provision not at arm's length).

Commentary—*Simon's Taxes* D1.630, D1.629C.

Derivation—FA 2002 Sch 29 paras 24(1), (2), 136.

HMRC Manuals—Corporate Intangibles Research and Development Manual CIRD13240 (meaning of realisation proceeds).

Amendments—[1] In sub-s (2) words "Schedule 28AA to ICTA" substituted by TIOPA 2010 s 501, Sch 8 paras 123, 145. TIOPA 2010 has effect for corporation tax purposes for accounting periods ending on or after 1 April 2010, for income and capital gains tax purposes for the tax year 2010–11 and subsequent tax years, and for petroleum revenue tax purposes for chargeable periods beginning on or after 1 July 2010.

[2] Sub-s (1A) inserted by FA 2018 s 20 with effect in relation to a realisation which takes place on or after 22 November 2017, unless it takes place pursuant to an obligation, under a contract, that was unconditional before that date. An obligation is deemed "unconditional" if it may not be varied or extinguished by the exercise of a right (whether under the contract or otherwise) (FA 2018 Sch 5 para 20(3)).

740 Abortive expenditure on realisation

(1) This section applies if—

    (a) in a period of account a loss is recognised in determining the company's profit or loss in respect of expenditure by the company for the purposes of a transaction,

    (b) the transaction does not proceed to completion, but

    (c) were it completed, it would constitute a realisation of an intangible fixed asset.

(2) A corresponding debit must be brought into account for tax purposes.

(3) The amount of the debit is the same as the amount of the loss recognised by the company for accounting purposes.

(4) Subsection (3) is subject to any adjustments required by this Part or [Part 4 of TIOPA 2010][1] (provision not at arm's length).

Commentary—*Simon's Taxes* **D1.630, D1.629C**.
Derivation—FA 2002 Sch 29 paras 26(1), (2), 136.
HMRC Manuals—Corporate Intangibles Research and Development Manual CIRD12550 (abortive expenditure on realisation).
Amendments—[1]   In sub-s (4) words "Schedule 28AA to ICTA" substituted by TIOPA 2010 s 501, Sch 8 paras 123, 145. TIOPA 2010 has effect for corporation tax purposes for accounting periods ending on or after 1 April 2010, for income and capital gains tax purposes for the tax year 2010–11 and subsequent tax years, and for petroleum revenue tax purposes for chargeable periods beginning on or after 1 July 2010.

741 Meaning of "chargeable intangible asset" and "chargeable realisation gain"

(1) For the purposes of this Part, an asset is a "chargeable intangible asset" in relation to a company at any time if any gain on its realisation by the company at that time would be a chargeable realisation gain.

(2) For the purposes of this Part, "chargeable realisation gain", in relation to an asset, means a gain on the realisation of the asset that gives rise to a credit required to be brought into account under this Chapter.

(3) For the purposes of subsections (1) and (2), there is a gain on the realisation of an asset in any case if section 735(2), 736(2) or 738(2) applies.

(4) For the purpose of subsections (1) and (2), ignore any question whether—

    (a) relief under Chapter 7 (roll-over relief in case of realisation and reinvestment) is available, or

    (b) a transfer of an asset is tax-neutral for the purposes of this Part (see section 776).

Commentary—*Simon's Taxes* **D1.635, D1.646, D1.647**.
Derivation—FA 2002 Sch 29 para 137(1), (2).

CHAPTER 5

CALCULATION OF TAX WRITTEN-DOWN VALUE

742 Asset written down on accounting basis

(1) For the purposes of this Part, the tax written-down value of an intangible fixed asset to which section 729 (writing down on accounting basis) applies is the cost of the asset recognised for tax purposes, less the total net debits brought into account for tax purposes previously in respect of the asset.

(2) For the purposes of subsection (1) the cost of the asset recognised for tax purposes is the same as the amount of the expenditure on the asset that is capitalised for accounting purposes.

(3) Subsection (2) is subject to any adjustments required by this Part or [Part 4 of TIOPA 2010][1] (provision not at arm's length).

(4) For the purposes of subsection (1) "the total net debits brought into account for tax purposes previously in respect of the asset", means the total debits so brought into account, less the total credits so brought into account (if any).

(5) In the case of an asset that has been the subject of a part realisation, this section is subject to section 744.

(6) In the case of an asset that has been subject to adjustment on a change of accounting policy, this section is subject to Chapter 15 (adjustments on a change of accounting policy).

Commentary—*Simon's Taxes* **D1.614**.
Derivation—FA 2002 Sch 29 paras 27(1)–(3), 136.
HMRC Manuals—Corporate Intangibles Research and Development Manual CIRD12770 (Period after expenditure first capitalised).
Amendments—[1]   In sub-s (3) words "Schedule 28AA to ICTA" substituted by TIOPA 2010 s 501, Sch 8 paras 123, 145. TIOPA 2010 has effect for corporation tax purposes for accounting periods ending on or after 1 April 2010, for income and capital gains tax purposes for the tax year 2010–11 and subsequent tax years, and for petroleum revenue tax purposes for chargeable periods beginning on or after 1 July 2010.

743 Asset written down at fixed rate

(1) For the purposes of this Part, the tax written-down value of an intangible fixed asset in respect of which an election has been made under section 730 (writing down at fixed rate: election for fixed-rate basis) is the cost of the asset recognised for tax purposes, less any debits brought into account for tax purposes previously in respect of the asset under section 731 (writing down at fixed rate: calculation).

(2) For the purposes of subsection (1), the cost of the asset recognised for tax purposes is the same as the amount of the expenditure on the asset that is capitalised for accounting purposes.

(3) Subsection (2) is subject to any adjustments required by this Part or [Part 4 of TIOPA 2010][1] (provision not at arm's length).

(4) In the case of an asset that has been the subject of a part realisation, this section is subject to section 744.

(5) In the case of an asset that has been subject to adjustment on a change of accounting policy, this section is subject to Chapter 15 (adjustments on change of accounting policy).

Commentary—*Simon's Taxes* **D1.632**.
Derivation—FA 2002 Sch 29 paras 28(1)–(3), 136.
HMRC Manuals—Corporate Intangibles Research and Development Manual CIRD12910 (intangible asset: fixed rate relief: computation).
Amendments—[1] In sub-s (3) words "Schedule 28AA to ICTA" substituted by TIOPA 2010 s 501, Sch 8 paras 123, 145. TIOPA 2010 has effect for corporation tax purposes for accounting periods ending on or after 1 April 2010, for income and capital gains tax purposes for the tax year 2010–11 and subsequent tax years, and for petroleum revenue tax purposes for chargeable periods beginning on or after 1 July 2010.

744 Effect of part realisation of asset

(1) The tax written-down value of an intangible asset that has been the subject of a part realisation is determined as follows.

(2) Immediately after the part realisation the tax written-down value of the asset is—

$$\text{WDVB} \times \frac{\text{AVA}}{\text{AVB}}$$

where—

WDVB is the tax written-down value of the asset immediately before the part realisation,
AVA is the accounting value of the asset immediately after the part realisation, and
AVB is the accounting value immediately before the part realisation.

(3) Subsequently, the tax written-down value of the asset is determined in accordance with section 742 or 743, but subject to subsections (4) and (5).

(4) The cost of the asset recognised for tax purposes is the sum of—
  (a) the tax written-down value in accordance with subsection (2), and
  (b) the cost recognised for tax purposes of subsequent expenditure on the asset that is capitalised for accounting purposes.

(5) Only credits and debits brought into account for tax purposes after the part realisation are taken account of.

(6) If there is a further part realisation, subsections (1) to (5) apply again.

(7) If there is a subsequent change of accounting policy affecting the asset, Chapter 15 (adjustments on change of accounting policy) applies.

Commentary—*Simon's Taxes* **D1.632**.
Derivation—FA 2002 Sch 29 para 29(1)–(5).
HMRC Manuals—Corporate Intangibles Research and Development Manual CIRD12795 (accounts-based relief). CIRD12920 (fixed rate relief).

CHAPTER 6

HOW CREDITS AND DEBITS ARE GIVEN EFFECT

Introductory

745 Introduction

(1) Credits and debits to be brought into account for tax purposes under this Part are given effect in accordance with this Chapter.

(2) Credits and debits in respect of assets held for the purposes mentioned in any of the following sections are given effect in accordance with that section—
  (a) section 747 (assets held for purposes of trade),
  (b) section 748 (assets held for purposes of property business),
  (c) section 749 (assets held for purposes of mines, transport undertakings, etc).

(3) Credits and debits in respect of intangible fixed assets that are not within sections 747 to 749 are dealt with in accordance with sections 751 to 753.

(4) This section is subject to section 901 (effect of application of the I minus E basis: non-trading amounts).

Commentary—*Simon's Taxes* **D1.629E**.
Derivation—FA 2002 Sch 29 para 30(1)–(3), (5).
HMRC Manuals—Corporate Intangibles Research and Development Manual CIRD13510 (CT computation: general).

746 "Non-trading credits" and "non-trading debits"

(1) In this Part credits and debits in respect of intangible fixed assets that are not within sections 747 to 749 are referred to respectively as "non-trading credits" and "non-trading debits".

(2) See also—

    (*a*) section 781(5) (character of credits and debits brought into account as a result of section 780),

    [(*b*) section 793A (effect of election to reallocate charge within group),][4]

    [(*ba*) sections 879C(3), 879I(3), 879K(5) and 879O(3)(*b*) (debits in respect of goodwill and certain other assets treated as nontrading debits),][3] and

    (*c*) [section 901][1] (insurance companies: effect of application of the I minus E basis: non-trading amounts).

Amendments—[1]   In sub-s (2)(*c*), words substituted for words "section 901(3)" by FA 2012 s 146, Sch 16 paras 135, 173 with effect in relation to accounting periods of companies beginning on or after 1 January 2013 (subject to transitional provisions in FA 2012 Sch 17). For accounting periods straddling 1 January 2013, see FA 2012 s 149.

[3]   Sub-s (2)(*ba*) substituted by FA 2019 s 25, Sch 9 paras 1, 4 with effect in relation to accounting periods beginning on or after 1 April 2019. An accounting period beginning before, and ending on or after, 1 April 2019 is to be treated as if so much of the accounting period as falls before that date, and so much of the accounting period as falls on or after that date, were separate accounting periods (FA 2019 Sch 9 para 7(2)).

[4]   Sub-s (2)(*b*) substituted, by FA 2019 s 17, Sch 5 paras 10, 22, with effect from 6 April 2020, subject to transitional provisions in FA 2019 Sch 5 Pt 3 (paras 36–50).

Trading etc credits and debits

[747] Assets held for purposes of trade

(1) This section applies if credits or debits are to be brought into account in an accounting period in respect of an asset held by a company for the purposes of a trade carried on by it in that period.

(2) The credits are given effect by treating them as receipts of the trade in calculating the profits of the trade for tax purposes.

(3) The debits are given effect by treating them as expenses of the trade in calculating the profits of the trade for tax purposes.

Commentary—*Simon's Taxes* **D1.629E.**

Derivation—FA 2002 Sch 29 para 31.

HMRC Manuals—Corporate Intangibles Research and Development Manual CIRD13520 (intangible assets used for a trade).

748 Assets held for purposes of property business

(1) This section applies if credits or debits are to be brought into account in an accounting period in respect of an asset held by a company for the purposes of a property business carried on by it in that period.

(2) The credits are given effect by treating them as receipts of the business in calculating the profits of the business for tax purposes.

(3) The debits are given effect by treating them as expenses of the business in calculating the profits of the business for tax purposes.

(4) In subsection (1) "property business" means—

    [(*a*) an ordinary UK property business,

    (*b*) a UK furnished holiday lettings business,

    (*c*) an ordinary overseas property business, or

    (*d*) an EEA furnished holiday lettings business.][1]

[(5) In this section—

    "commercial letting of furnished holiday accommodation" has the meaning given by section 265,

    "EEA furnished holiday lettings business" means an overseas property business so far as it consists of the commercial letting of furnished holiday accommodation in one or more EEA states,

    "ordinary overseas property business" means an overseas property business except so far as it is an EEA furnished holiday lettings business,

    "ordinary UK property business" means a UK property business except so far as it is a UK furnished holiday lettings business, and

    "UK furnished holiday lettings business" means a UK property business so far as it consists of the commercial letting of furnished holiday accommodation.][1]

Commentary—*Simon's Taxes* **B6.202, D1.629E, D1.860.**

Derivation—FA 2002 Sch 29 para 32(1)–(3).

HMRC Manuals—Corporate Intangibles Research and Development Manual CIRD13520 (intangible assets used for a property business).

Amendments—[1]   Sub-s (4)(*a*)–(*d*) substituted for former sub-s (4)(*a*)–(*c*), and sub-s (5) substituted, by FA 2011 s 52, Sch 14 para 7(1), (8) with effect in relation to accounting periods beginning on or after 1 April 2011.

749 Assets held for purposes of mines, transport undertakings, etc

(1) This section applies if credits or debits are to be brought into account in an accounting period in respect of an asset held by a company for the purposes of a concern listed in section 39(4) (mines, quarries and other concerns) that is carried on by it in that period.

(2) The credits are given effect by treating them as receipts of the concern in calculating the profits of the concern under Part 3 (trading income).

(3) The debits are given effect by treating them as expenses of the concern in calculating the profits of the concern under that Part.

Commentary—*Simon's Taxes* **D1.629E**.

Derivation—FA 2002 Sch 29 para 33.

HMRC Manuals—Corporate Intangibles Research and Development Manual CIRD13520 (intangible assets used for a mines, transport undertakings, etc).

750 Assets held for purposes falling within more than one section

If an asset is held—

    (*a*) for purposes falling within more than one of sections 747 to 749, or

    (*b*) for purposes falling within one or more of those sections and for purposes not so falling,

any necessary apportionment must be made on a just and reasonable basis.

Commentary—*Simon's Taxes* **D1.629E**.

Derivation—FA 2002 Sch 29 para 30(4).

Non-trading credits and debits

751 Non-trading gains and losses

(1) If there are non-trading credits or debits in an accounting period in respect of inculated. fixed assets, the company's non-trading gain or loss on such assets in the period must if subsection (3) or

(2) There is a non-trading gain on intangible fixed assets in an accounting

(4) applies.

(3) If in the accounting period—

    (*a*) there are non-trading credits, but

    (*b*) there are no non-trading debits,

there is a non-trading gain on intangible fixed assets equal to the sum of the credits.

(4) If in the accounting period—

    (*a*) there are both non-trading credits and non-trading debits, and

    (*b*) the total non-trading credits exceed the total non-trading debits,

there is a non-trading gain on intangible fixed assets equal to the excess.

(5) There is a non-trading loss on intangible fixed assets in an accounting period if subsection (6) or (7) applies.

(6) If in the accounting period—

    (*a*) there are non-trading debits, but

    (*b*) there are no non-trading credits,

there is a non-trading loss on intangible fixed assets equal to the sum of the debits.

(7) If in the accounting period—

    (*a*) there are both non-trading credits and non-trading debits, and

    (*b*) the total non-trading debits exceed the total non-trading credits,

there is a non-trading loss on intangible fixed assets equal to the excess.

(8) For the treatment of non-trading gains and losses see—

    (*a*) section 752 (charge to tax on non-trading gains on intangible fixed assets), and

    (*b*) section 753 (treatment of non-trading losses).

Commentary—*Simon's Taxes* **D1.629E**.

HMRC Manuals—Corporate Intangibles Research and Development Manual CIRD13530 (intangible assets not used for trade or property business).

752 Charge to tax on non-trading gains on intangible fixed assets

The charge to corporation tax on income applies to non-trading gains arising to a company on intangible fixed assets.

Commentary—*Simon's Taxes* **D7.436, D1.629E**.

753 Treatment of non-trading losses

(1) A company that has a non-trading loss on intangible fixed assets for an accounting period may claim to have the whole or part of the loss set off against the company's total profits for that period.

(2) Such a claim must be made—

    (*a*) not later than the end of the period of 2 years immediately following the end of the accounting period to which it relates, or

    (*b*) within such further period as an officer of Revenue and Customs may allow.

(3) To the extent that the loss is not[, in any period ("the reference period")]² —

    (*a*) set off against total profits on a claim under subsection (1), or

    (*b*) surrendered by way of group relief [under Part 5 of CTA 2010]¹, it is carried forward to the next accounting period of the company and treated as if it were a non-trading [loss on intangible fixed assets for][2] that period.

[(4) But subsection (3) does not apply if the company ceased to be a company with investment business in the reference period.

(5) In the application of subsection (3) to an amount of a loss previously carried forward under that subsection, the reference in paragraph (b) to group relief under Part 5 of CTA 2010 is to be read as a reference to group relief for carried-forward losses under Part 5A of that Act.

(6) In this section "company with investment business" has the same meaning as in Part 16 (see section 1218B).][2]

Commentary—*Simon's Taxes* **D1.629E, B3.340CA.**

HMRC Manuals—Corporate Intangibles Research and Development Manual CIRD13540 (set-off of non-trading loss against total profits).

Amendments—[1]   In sub-s (3))b) words substituted for words "(see section 403 of ICTA)" by CTA 2010 s 1177, Sch 1 para 644. CTA 2010 has effect for corporation tax purposes for accounting periods ending on or after 1 April 2010, and for income and capital gains tax purposes for the tax year 2010–11 and subsequent tax years.

[2]   In sub-s (3), in words before para (a) words inserted, and in words after para (b) words substituted for words "debit of", and sub-ss (4)–(6) inserted, by F(No 2)A 2017 s 18, Sch 4 paras 1, 5 with effect in relation to accounting periods beginning on or after 1 April 2017, subject to transitional provisions in Sch 4 para 194. For accounting periods beginning before 1 April 2017 and ending on or after that date ("straddling periods") see F(No 2)A 2017 Sch 4 paras 190–192.

CHAPTER 7

ROLL-OVER RELIEF IN CASE OF REALISATION AND REINVESTMENT

When the relief is given

754 The relief: the "old asset" and "other assets"

(1) This Chapter provides for relief if a company realises an intangible fixed asset and incurs expenditure on other intangible fixed assets.

(2) In this Chapter references to the "old asset" are references to the asset that is realised and references to "other assets" are references to the other assets on which expenditure is incurred.

(3) A company is entitled to relief under this Chapter only if—

    (a) the conditions in section 755 are met in relation to the old asset and its realisation,

    (b) the conditions in section 756 are met in relation to the expenditure on other assets, and

    (c) the company claims the relief in accordance with section 757.

(4) See also the following provisions (which extend or restrict the circumstances in which relief is available)—

    (a) sections 777 to 779 (application of roll-over relief where there is reinvestment by group members),

    (b) section 791 (application of roll-over relief in relation to degrouping charge),

    (c) section 794 (application of roll-over relief in relation to reallocated charge),

    (d) section 850 (part realisation involving related party acquisition: exclusion of roll-over relief), and

    (e) sections 898 and 899 (roll-over relief for disposals of pre-FA 2002 assets).

Commentary—*Simon's Taxes* **D1.630, D1.629C, D1.635, D6.436.**

Derivation—FA 2002 Sch 29 para 37(1), (2).

HMRC Manuals—Corporate Intangibles Research and Development Manual CIRD20020 (reinvestment relief : conditions to be satisfied before relief is available).

755 Conditions relating to the old asset and its realisation

(1) The old asset must have been a chargeable intangible asset of the company throughout the period during which it was held by the company (but see subsection (5)).

(2) The proceeds of realisation of the old asset must exceed—

    (a) the cost of the asset,

    (b) in the case of a part realisation, the appropriate proportion of the cost of the asset (see section 759(1) and (2)), or

    (c) in the case of the realisation of an asset that has previously been the subject of a part realisation, the adjusted cost of the asset (see section 759(3)).

(3) In subsection (2) "the cost of the asset" means the total capitalised expenditure on the asset recognised for tax purposes.

(4) The condition in subsection (2) is met if the old asset has no cost as defined in subsection (3).

(5) Subsection (6) applies if the old asset was a chargeable intangible asset of the company—

    (a) at the time of its realisation, and

    (b) for a substantial proportion of the period during which it was held by the company, but not for the whole of that period.

(6) The same proportion of the asset is treated for the purposes of this Chapter as if it were a separate asset in relation to which the condition in subsection (1) was wholly met.

(7) Any apportionment necessary for the purposes of subsections (5) and (6) must be made on a just and reasonable basis.

(2) Reacquisitions that do not actually occur but are treated as occurring are ignored for the purposes of this Chapter.

Commentary—*Simon's Taxes* **D1.635**.

Derivation—FA 2002 Sch 29 para 45(1), (2).

HMRC Manuals—Corporate Intangibles Research and Development Manual CIRD20070 (reinvestment relief: on realisation: exclusion of deemed realisations).

CHAPTER 8
GROUPS OF COMPANIES: INTRODUCTION
Introductory

764 Meaning of "company", "group" and "subsidiary"

(1) This Chapter applies for the purposes of this Part to determine whether companies form a group and, where they do, which is the principal company of the group.

(2) In this Chapter, references to a company apply only to—

   (a) a company within the meaning of the Companies Act 2006 (c 46),

   (b) a company (other than a limited liability partnership) constituted under any other Act or by a Royal Charter or letters patent,

   (c) a company formed under the law of a country or territory outside the United Kingdom,

   (d) a [registered society][1],

   (e) an incorporated friendly society within the meaning of the Friendly Societies Act 1992 (c 40), or

   (f) a building society.

(3) In this Part "group" and "subsidiary" must be read with any necessary modifications if applied to a company formed under the law of a country or territory outside the United Kingdom.

Commentary—*Simon's Taxes* **D1.645**.

Amendments—[1] In each place where they occur in this Act, words substituted for words "registered industrial and provident society", "the Industrial and Provident Societies Act 1965" and "industrial and provident societies", by the Co-operative and Community Benefit Societies Act 2014 s 151, Sch 4 paras 140–143 with effect from 1 August 2014 and subject to transitional provisions and provisions preserving the continuity of the law in Sch 5 of that Act.

Rules

765 General rule: a company and its 75% subsidiaries form a group

(1) The general rule is that—

   (a) a company ("A") and all its 75% subsidiaries form a group, and

   (b) if any of those subsidiaries have 75% subsidiaries, the group includes them and their 75% subsidiaries, and so on.

(2) A is referred to in this Chapter and in Chapter 9 as the principal company of the group.

(3) Subsections (1) and (2) are subject to the following provisions of this Chapter.

Commentary—*Simon's Taxes* **D1.645**.

Derivation—FA 2002 Sch 29 para 47(1), (2).

HMRC Manuals—Corporate Intangibles Research and Development Manual CIRD40030 (intangible assets: groups: definitional rules).

766 Only effective 51% subsidiaries of principal company to be members of group

(1) A group of companies does not include any company (other than the principal company of the group) that is not an effective 51% subsidiary of the principal company of the group.

(2) For the meaning of "effective 51% subsidiary", see section 771.

Commentary—*Simon's Taxes* **D1.645**.

Derivation—FA 2002 Sch 29 para 48.

HMRC Manuals—Corporate Intangibles Research and Development Manual CIRD40030 (intangible assets: effective 51% subsidiary test).

767 Principal company cannot be 75% subsidiary of another company

(1) The general rule is that a company ("A") is not the principal company of a group if it is itself a 75% subsidiary of another company ("B").

(2) That rule is subject to subsection (3).

(3) A is the principal company of a group ("group C") if—

   (a) A and B are prevented from being members of another group by section 766,

   (b) the requirements of sections 765 and 766 are met in relation to group C, and

   (c) A being the principal company of group C does not enable a further company to be the principal company of a group of which A would be a member.

Commentary—*Simon's Taxes* **D1.645**.

Derivation—FA 2002 Sch 29 para 49(1), (2).

HMRC Manuals—Corporate Intangibles Research and Development Manual CIRD40045 (intangible assets: groups: principal company).

768 Company cannot be member of more than one group

(1) A company cannot be a member of more than one group.

(2) If, apart from subsection (1), a company ("A") would be a member of 2 or more groups, the group of which it is a member is determined by applying the rules in subsections (4), (6), (7) and (8) successively in that order until an answer is obtained.

(3) In those subsections the principal company of each group is referred to as its head.

(4) A is a member of the group of which it would be a member if in applying section 766 (only effective 51% subsidiaries of principal company to be members of group) the amounts specified in subsection (5) were ignored.

(5) Those amounts are—

(a) any amount to which a head of a group is beneficially entitled of any profits available for distribution to equity holders of a head of another group (see section 772), and

(b) any amount to which a head of a group would be beneficially entitled of any assets of a head of another group available for distribution to its equity holders on a winding up (see that section).

(6) A is a member of the group the head of which is beneficially entitled to a percentage of the profits available for distribution to A's equity holders that is greater than the percentage of those profits to which any other head of a group is so entitled.

(7) A is a member of the group the head of which would be beneficially entitled to a percentage of any of A's assets available for distribution to its equity holders on a winding up that is greater than the percentage of those assets to which any other head of a group would be so entitled.

(8) A is a member of the group the head of which owns directly or indirectly a percentage of A's ordinary share capital that is greater than the percentage of that capital owned directly or indirectly by any other head of a group.

[(9) For the purposes of subsection (8) share capital is owned directly or indirectly if it would be so owned by a body corporate for the purposes of section 1154(2) of CTA 2010 (meaning of "51% subsidiary").][1]

Commentary—*Simon's Taxes* D1.645.
Derivation—FA 2002 Sch 29 para 50(1)–(7).
HMRC Manuals—Corporate Intangibles Research and Development Manual CIRD40040 (intangible assets: groups: company cannot belong to more than one group).
Amendments—[1]   Sub-s (9) substituted by CTA 2010 s 1177, Sch 1 para 645 with effect for corporation tax purposes for accounting periods ending on or after 1 April 2010, and for income and capital gains tax purposes for the tax year 2010–11 and subsequent tax years.

769 Continuity of identity of group

(1) A group of companies remains the same group of companies for the purposes of this Part so long as the same company is the principal company of the group.

(2) If the principal company of a group becomes a member of another group—

(a) the groups are treated as the same group for the purposes of this Part, and

(b) the question whether a company has ceased to be a member of a group must be determined accordingly.

(3) The passing of a resolution or the making of an order, or any other act, for the winding up of a company is not treated for the purposes of this Part as causing any company to cease to be a member of any group of which it is a member.

Commentary—*Simon's Taxes* D1.645.
Derivation—FA 2002 Sch 29 para 51(1), (2).
HMRC Manuals—Corporate Intangibles Research and Development Manual CIRD40050 (intangible assets: groups: continuity: takeover or winding up).

770 Continuity where group includes an SE

(1) This section applies if the principal company of a group ("Group 1")—

(a) becomes an SE as a result of being the acquiring company in the formation of an SE by merger by acquisition (in accordance with Articles 2(1), 17(2)(a) and 29(1) of Council Regulation (EC) No 2157/ 2001 on the Statute for a European company),

(b) becomes a subsidiary of a holding SE (formed in accordance with Article 2(2) of that Regulation), or

(c) is transformed into an SE (in accordance with Article 2(4) of that Regulation).

(2) For the purposes of this Part—

(a) Group 1 and any group of which the SE is a member on formation is treated as the same, and

(b) the question whether a company has ceased to be a member of a group must be determined accordingly.

Commentary—*Simon's Taxes* D1.650.

771 Meaning of "effective 51% subsidiary"

(1) For the purposes of this Part a company ("the subsidiary") is an effective 51% subsidiary of another company ("the parent") if (and only if) conditions A and B are met.

(2) Condition A is that the parent is beneficially entitled to more than 50% of any profits available for distribution to equity holders of the subsidiary (see section 772).

(3) Condition B is that the parent would be beneficially entitled to more than 50% of any assets of the subsidiary available for distribution to its equity holders on a winding up (see section 772).

Commentary—*Simon's Taxes* **D1.645**.

Derivation—FA 2002 Sch 29 para 52.

HMRC Manuals—Corporate Intangibles Research and Development Manual CIRD40030 (meaning of effective 51% subsidiary).

772 Equity holders and profits or assets available for distribution

[(1) Chapter 6 of Part 5 of CTA 2010 (group relief: equity holders and profits or assets available for distribution) applies for the purposes of sections 768 and 771.][1]

[(2) In that Chapter as it applies for those purposes—

    (*a*) section 158 of CTA 2010 has effect as if after subsection (2) there were inserted—

      "(2A) But for those purposes a person carrying on a business of banking is not treated as a loan creditor of a company in respect of any loan capital or debt issued or incurred by the company for money lent by the person to the company in the ordinary course of that business.", and

    (*b*) sections 171(1)(*b*) and (3), 173, 174 and 176 to 182 of that Act are to be treated as omitted.][2]

Commentary—*Simon's Taxes* **D1.645**.

Derivation—FA 2002 Sch 29 para 53(1), (2).

HMRC Manuals—Corporate Intangibles Research and Development Manual CIRD40030 (intangible assets: groups: definitional rules).

Amendments—[1] Sub-s (1) substituted by CTA 2010 s 1177, Sch 1 para 646 with effect for corporation tax purposes for accounting periods ending on or after 1 April 2010, and for income and capital gains tax purposes for the tax year 2010–11 and subsequent tax years.

[2] Sub-s (2) substituted by the Corporation Tax Act 2010 (Amendment) Order, SI 2010/2902 art 3 with effect for corporation tax purposes for accounting periods ending on or after 1 April 2010, and for income tax and capital gains tax purposes for the tax year 2010–11 and subsequent tax years.

773 Supplementary provisions

(1) In applying the definition of "75% subsidiary" in [section 1154 of CTA 2010][1] for the purposes of this Chapter, any share capital of a [registered society][2] is treated as ordinary share capital.

(2) Section 170(12) to (14) of TCGA 1992 (application to certain statutory bodies of provisions relating to groups of companies) applies for the purposes of this Chapter as it applies for the purposes of sections 171 to 181 of TCGA 1992.

Commentary—*Simon's Taxes* **D1.645**.

Derivation—FA 2002 Sch 29 para 54(1), (2).

HMRC Manuals—Corporate Intangibles Research and Development Manual CIRD40030 (intangible assets: statutory bodies).

Amendments—[1] In sub-s (1) words substituted for words "section 838 of ICTA" by CTA 2010 s 1177, Sch 1 para 647. CTA 2010 has effect for corporation tax purposes for accounting periods ending on or after 1 April 2010, and for income and capital gains tax purposes for the tax year 2010–11 and subsequent tax years.

[2] In each place where they occur in this Act, words substituted for words "registered industrial and provident society", "the Industrial and Provident Societies Act 1965" and "industrial and provident societies", by the Co-operative and Community Benefit Societies Act 2014 s 151, Sch 4 paras 140–143 with effect from 1 August 2014 and subject to transitional provisions and provisions preserving the continuity of the law in Sch 5 of that Act.

CHAPTER 9

APPLICATION OF THIS PART TO GROUPS OF COMPANIES

Introductory

774 Overview of Chapter

(1) This Chapter makes provision about how this Part applies in the case of certain transactions involving groups.

(2) In particular—

    (*a*) for the treatment of transfers within groups as "tax-neutral transfers" and the meaning of that expression, see sections 775 and 776,

    (*b*) for the application of Chapter 7 (roll-over relief in case of realisation and reinvestment) in relation to a company that is a member of a group, see sections 777 to 779,

    (*c*) for the rules that apply where a company ceases to be a member of a group, see—

      (i) sections 780 to 791 (which provide for the deemed realisation of chargeable intangible fixed assets and their deemed reacquisition at market value), and

      (ii) sections 792 to 798 (which provide for elections for a different member of the group to be treated as the company to which any gain on the deemed transfer accrues, how roll-over relief applies in such a case and for the recovery of the charge on any such gain), and

    (*d*) for the disregard of some payments made in connection with claims for relief under Chapter 7 where this Chapter applies and payments made in connection with such elections as are mentioned in paragraph (*c*)(ii), see section 799.

(3) Section 788 contains provisions that supplement sections 780 to 787.

HMRC Manuals—Corporate Intangibles Research and Development Manual CIRD40200 (groups: tax neutral transfers: contents).

Transfers within a group treated as tax-neutral

775 Transfers within a group

(1) A transfer of an intangible fixed asset from one company ("the transferor") to another company ("the transferee") is tax-neutral for the purposes of this Part if—

    (a) at the time of the transfer both companies are members of the same group,

    (b) immediately before the transfer the asset is a chargeable intangible asset in relation to the transferor, and

    (c) immediately after the transfer the asset is a chargeable intangible asset in relation to the transferee.

(2) For the consequences of a transfer being tax-neutral for the purposes of this Part, see section 776.

(3) [Part 4 of TIOPA 2010][2] (provision not at arm's length) does not apply in relation to a transfer to which subsection (1) applies.

(4) Subsection (1) does not apply if—

    (a) the transferor or transferee is a qualifying society within the meaning of section 461A of ICTA (incorporated friendly societies entitled to exemption from tax), . . . [3]

    (b) the transferee is a dual resident investing company within the meaning of [section 949 of CTA 2010 (dual resident investing companies)][1] [; or

    (c) an election under section 18A has effect in relation to the transferor and the asset has at any time been held by the transferor wholly or partly for the purposes of a permanent establishment in a territory outside the United Kingdom through which the transferor carries on business.][3]

Commentary—*Simon's Taxes* D1.646, A2.204.
Derivation—FA 2002 Sch 29 para 55(1), (1A), (2).
HMRC Manuals—Corporate Intangibles Research and Development Manual CIRD40220 (groups: tax-neutral transfers: introduction).
Amendments—[1] In sub-s (4)(*b*) words substituted for words "section 404 of that Act (limitation of group relief)" by CTA 2010 s 1177, Sch 1 para 648. CTA 2010 has effect for corporation tax purposes for accounting periods ending on or after 1 April 2010, and for income and capital gains tax purposes for the tax year 2010–11 and subsequent tax years.
[2] In sub-s (3) words "Schedule 28AA to ICTA" substituted by TIOPA 2010 s 501, Sch 8 paras 123, 146. TIOPA 2010 has effect for corporation tax purposes for accounting periods ending on or after 1 April 2010, for income and capital gains tax purposes for the tax year 2010–11 and subsequent tax years, and for petroleum revenue tax purposes for chargeable periods beginning on or after 1 July 2010.
[3] In sub-s (4)(*a*) word "or" repealed, and sub-(4)(*c*) and preceding word "or" inserted, by FA 2011 s 48, Sch 13 paras 1, 5 with effect from 19 July 2011, subject to transitional provisions in FA 2011 Sch 13 paras 32–37.

776 Meaning of "tax-neutral" transfer

(1) This section sets out the consequences of a transfer of an asset being "tax-neutral" for the purposes of this Part.

(2) The transfer is treated for those purposes as not involving—

    (a) any realisation of the asset by the transferor, or

    (b) any acquisition of the asset by the transferee.

(3) The transferee is treated for those purposes—

    (a) as having held the asset at all times when it was held by the transferor, and

    (b) as having done all such things in relation to the asset as were done by the transferor.

(4) In particular—

    (a) the original cost of the asset in the hands of the transferor is treated as the original cost in the hands of the transferee, and

    (b) all such credits and debits in relation to the asset as have been brought into account for tax purposes by the transferor under this Part are treated as if they had been brought into account by the transferee.

(5) The references in subsection (4)(*a*) to the cost of the asset are to the cost recognised for tax purposes.

Commentary—*Simon's Taxes* D1.646.
Derivation—FA 2002 Sch 29 para 140(1)–(3).
HMRC Manuals—Corporate Intangibles Research and Development Manual CIRD40300 (groups: tax-neutral transfers: effect).

Roll-over relief under Chapter 7 (realisation and reinvestment)

777 Relief on realisation and reinvestment: application to group member

(1) This section deals with the application of Chapter 7 (roll-over relief in case of realisation and reinvestment) in relation to a company that is a member of a group.

(2) Chapter 7 does not apply if the expenditure on other assets is expenditure on the acquisition of assets from another member of the same group by a tax-neutral transfer.

(3) Chapter 7 applies as if two companies ("A" and "B") are the same person if—

    (a) the realisation of the old asset is by A,

    (b) at the time of the realisation A is a member of a group,

(c) the expenditure on other assets is by B,

(d) B is a member of the same group as A at the time the expenditure is incurred ("the expenditure time"),

(e) B is not a dual resident investing company within the meaning of [section 949 of CTA 2010 (dual resident investing companies)][1] at the expenditure time,

(f) immediately after the expenditure time the other assets are chargeable intangible assets in relation to B, and

(g) both A and B make a claim for relief under Chapter 7.

(4) Expressions used in this section that are defined for the purposes of Chapter 7 have the same meaning in this section.

(5) In particular, see section 754 for the meaning of "the old asset" and "the other assets".

Commentary—*Simon's Taxes* **D1.647**.

Derivation—FA 2002 Sch 29 para 56(1)–(4).

HMRC Manuals—Corporate Intangibles Research and Development Manual CIRD20410 (relief: groups of companies: expenditure on new assets by another group member).

Amendments—[1] In sub-s (3)(e) words substituted for words "section 404 of ICTA (limitation of group relief)" by CTA 2010 s 1177, Sch 1 para 649. CTA 2010 has effect for corporation tax purposes for accounting periods ending on or after 1 April 2010, and for income and capital gains tax purposes for the tax year 2010–11 and subsequent tax years.

778 Relief on reinvestment: acquisition of group company: introduction

(1) Chapter 7 (roll-over relief in case of realisation and reinvestment) applies in accordance with section 779 if—

(a) a company ("A") acquires a controlling interest in another company ("B"), and

(b) intangible fixed assets ("underlying assets") are held by B or one or more other companies within subsection (2).

(2) A company is within this subsection if—

(a) it was not in the same group as A before the acquisition, and

(b) as a result of the acquisition it is in the same group as A immediately after it.

(3) For this purpose A acquires a controlling interest in B if—

(a) A and B are not in the same group,

(b) A acquires shares in B, and

(c) as a result of the acquisition A and B are in the same group immediately after the acquisition.

(4) A claim for relief under Chapter 7 made because of section 779 must be made jointly by A and the company or companies holding the underlying assets concerned.

(5) In this section and section 779 expressions that are defined for the purposes of Chapter 7 have the same meaning as in that Chapter.

Commentary—*Simon's Taxes* **D1.647**.

Derivation—FA 2002 Sch 29 para 57(1), (6)–(8).

HMRC Manuals—Corporate Intangibles Research and Development Manual CIRD20420 (expenditure on shares of company which becomes group member).

779 Rules that apply to cases within section 778(1)

(1) The expenditure by A on the acquisition is treated as expenditure on acquiring the underlying assets.

(2) The amount of the expenditure so treated is taken to be the lower of—

(a) the tax written-down value of the underlying assets immediately before the acquisition, and

(b) the amount or value of the consideration for the acquisition.

(3) The requirement in section 756(3) (that immediately after the expenditure on acquiring the assets is incurred the assets must be chargeable intangible assets in relation to A) is treated as met in relation to the underlying assets if the condition in subsection (4) is met.

(4) That condition is that the underlying assets are chargeable intangible assets in relation to the company by which they are held immediately after the acquisition by A.

(5) The tax written-down value of the underlying assets in the hands of the company by which they are held is reduced by the amount available for relief (but see subsections (6) and (7)).

(6) If—

(a) there is more than one underlying asset, and

(b) the amount of expenditure on other assets that is treated as incurred exceeds the amount available for relief,

the company which holds the underlying assets may decide how the amount available for relief is to be allocated in reducing the tax written-down values of the assets.

(7) If there are two or more such companies, they may agree between them how that amount is to be allocated.

(8) In this section references to "A" and "B" and "underlying assets" must be read in accordance with section 778(1).

Commentary—*Simon's Taxes* **D1.647**.

Derivation—FA 2002 Sch 29 para 57(2)–(5).

HMRC Manuals—Corporate Intangibles Research and Development Manual CIRD20430 (expenditure on shares of a company which becomes a group member: further rules).

Company ceasing to be member of group

780 Deemed realisation and reacquisition at market value

(1) This section applies if—

   (a) a company ("the transferor") that is a member of a group ("the group") transfers an intangible fixed asset ("the relevant asset") to another company ("the transferee"),

   (b) immediately before the transfer the relevant asset is a chargeable intangible asset in relation to the transferor,

   (c) immediately after the transfer the relevant asset is a chargeable intangible asset in relation to the transferee,

   (d) the transferee—

      (i) is a member of the group at the time of the transfer, or

      (ii) subsequently becomes a member of the group,

   (e) the transferee ceases to be a member of the group during the period of 6 years after the date of the transfer, and

   (f) when the transferee ceases to be a member of the group, the relevant asset is held by the transferee or an associated company (see section 788(3)) also leaving the group.

(2) This Part applies as if the transferee—

   (a) had realised the relevant asset immediately after its transfer to the transferee for its market value at that time, and

   (b) had immediately reacquired the asset at that value.

(3) The adjustments to be made as a result of subsection (2), by the transferee or a company to which the relevant asset has been subsequently transferred, in relation to the relevant period must be made by bringing the total net credit or debit into account as if it had arisen immediately before the transferee ceased to be a member of the group.

(4) In subsection (3) "the relevant period" means the period between—

   (a) the transfer of the relevant asset to the transferee, and

   (b) the transferee ceasing to be a member of the group.

(5) This section is subject to—

   (a) section 782 (certain transferees of businesses etc not treated as leaving group),

   [(aa) section 782A (company leaving group because of relevant share disposal),][2]

   (b) section 783 ([certain][1] associated companies leaving group at the same time),

   (c) section 785 (principal company becoming member of another group),

   (d) section 787 (company ceasing to be member of group because of exempt distribution), and

   (e) section 789 (merger carried out for genuine commercial reasons).

(6) See section 788 (provisions supplementing this section and sections 781 to 787) for the interpretation of certain expressions used in this section or those sections.

(7) For the way in which Chapter 7 applies if a company is treated as having realised an asset as a result of this section, see section 791 (application of roll- over relief in relation to degrouping charge).

Commentary—*Simon's Taxes* **D1.649, D1.650**.

HMRC Manuals—Corporate Intangibles Research and Development Manual CIRD40520 (groups: de-grouping: general conditions for adjustment).

Amendments—[1] In sub-s (5)(b) word inserted by FA 2011 s 45, Sch 10 para 7(1), (2) with effect in relation to any disposal of an asset by one company ("company B") to another company ("company A") made at a time when company B is a member of a group, if: (a) company A ceases to be a member of the group on or after 19 July 2011; or (b) where company A ceased to be such a member before 19 July 2011 in circumstances where CTA 2009 s 783 applied, company A ceases to be a member of another group on or after 19 July 2011.

[2] Sub-s (5)(aa) inserted by FA 2019 s 26(1), (2) with effect in relation to a company that ceases to be a member of a group or ceases to meet the condition in CTA 2009 s 785(2)(b) (as amended by FA 2019 s 26(4)) on or after 7 November 2018. In its application in relation to a company that ceases to be a member of a group or ceases to meet the condition in CTA 2009 s 785(2)(b) before 21 December 2018, CTA 2009 s 782A has effect as if s 782A(3) was omitted.

781 Character of credits and debits brought into account as a result of section 780

(1) For the purposes of Chapter 6 (how credits and debits are given effect) credits or debits brought into account as a result of section 780 take their character from the purposes for which the relevant asset was held by the transferee immediately after the transfer.

(2) But subsection (1) does not apply if conditions A and B are met.

(3) Condition A is that immediately after the transfer the relevant asset was held by the transferee for the purposes of a trade, business or concern within section 747, 748 or 749.

(4) Condition B is that the transferee ceased to carry on that trade, business or concern before it ceased to be a member of the group.

(5) If conditions A and B are met, a credit or debit brought into account because of section 780 is treated for the purposes of Chapter 6 as a non-trading credit or debit.

(6) References in this section to "the transferee" and the relevant asset" must be read in accordance with section 780.

Commentary—*Simon's Taxes* **D1.649.**

Derivation—FA 2002 Sch 29 para 58(4).

HMRC Manuals—Corporate Intangibles Research and Development Manual CIRD40520 (classification of net credit or debit).

782 Certain transferees of businesses etc not treated as leaving group

(1) This section applies if—

    (*a*) the relevant asset is transferred in the course of a transfer of business to which section 820 applies or which includes such a transfer as is mentioned in [section 116(2)(*b*)(iii) of TIOPA 2010][1] and in respect of which [section 117][1] of that Act applies (European cross-border transfers of business), and

    (*b*) in consequence of the transfer the transferee ceases to be a member of a group ("Group 1").

(2) For the purposes of section 780, the transferee is not treated as having left Group 1.

(3) If as a result of the transfer the transferee becomes a member of another group ("Group 2"), it is treated for the purposes of section 780 as if Group 1 and Group 2 were the same.

(4) References in this section to "the transferee" and "the relevant asset" must be read in accordance with section 780.

Commentary—*Simon's Taxes* D1.650, D2.331.

Amendments—[1] In sub-s (1)(*a*), words substituted for words "section 807B(2)(*b*)(iii) of ICTA" and "section 807C", by TIOPA 2010 s 501, Sch 8 paras 89, 94. TIOPA 2010 has effect for corporation tax purposes for accounting periods ending on or after 1 April 2010, for income and capital gains tax purposes for the tax year 2010–11 and subsequent tax years, and for petroleum revenue tax purposes for chargeable periods beginning on or after 1 July 2010.

[782A Company leaving group because of relevant share disposal

(1) Section 780 does not apply if a company ceases to be a member of a group because of a relevant disposal of shares by another company.

(2) A disposal of shares by a company is "relevant" if—

    (*a*) the company would not be chargeable to corporation tax in respect of any gain accruing on the disposal by reason of the exemption conferred by paragraph 1 of Schedule 7AC to TCGA 1992 (assuming the company was within the charge to corporation tax), and

    (*b*) the disposal is not part of an arrangement under which the recipient of the shares is to dispose of any of them to another person.

(3) For the purposes of subsection (2)(*a*) ignore paragraph 6 of Schedule 7AC to TCGA 1992 (cases in which exemptions do not apply).][1]

Commentary—*Simon's Taxes* D1.650.

Amendments—[1] Section 782A inserted by FA 2019 s 26(1), (3) with effect in relation to a company that ceases to be a member of a group or ceases to meet the condition in CTA 2009 s 785(2)(*b*) (as amended by FA 2019 s 26(4)) on or after 7 November 2018. In its application in relation to a company that ceases to be a member of a group or ceases to meet the condition in CTA 2009 s 785(2)(*b*) before 21 December 2018, CTA 2009 s 782A has effect as if s 782A(3) was omitted.

783 [Certain associated][1] companies leaving group at the same time

[(1) Where two companies cease to be members of a group at the same time, section 780 does not apply in relation to a transfer by one of the companies to the other if condition A or B is met.

(1A) Condition A is that the companies—

    (*a*) are both 75% subsidiaries and effective 51% subsidiaries of another company on the date of the transfer, and

    (*b*) remain both 75% subsidiaries and effective 51% subsidiaries of that other company until immediately after they cease to be members of the group.

(1B) Condition B is that one of the companies—

    (*a*) is both a 75% subsidiary and an effective 51% subsidiary of the other on the date of the transfer, and

    (*b*) remains both a 75% subsidiary and an effective 51% subsidiary of the other until immediately after the companies cease to be members of the group.][1]

(2) This subsection applies if—

    (*a*) a company ("the transferee") that is a member of a group of companies ("the first group") acquires an asset from another company ("the transferor") which is a member of that group at the time of the transfer,

    (*b*) the transferee ceases to be a member of the first group,

    (*c*) subsection (1) applies in relation to the transferee ceasing to be a member of the first group (so that section 780 does not apply),

    (*d*) the transferee subsequently ceases to be a member of another group of companies ("the second group"), and

    (*e*) there is a relevant connection between the two groups (see section 784).

(3) If subsection (2) applies, section 780 applies in relation to the transferee ceasing to be a member of the second group as if both companies had been members of the second group at the time of the transfer.

(4) This section is subject to section 789 (merger carried out for genuine commercial reasons).

Commentary—*Simon's Taxes* D1.650.

Derivation—FA 2002 Sch 29 para 59(1), (2).

HMRC Manuals—Corporate Intangibles Research and Development Manual CIRD40530 (groups: de-grouping: associated companies leaving group together).

CIRD40540 (associated companies leaving group: subsequent charge).
Amendments—[1] In heading words substituted for word "Associated", and sub-ss (1)–(1B) substituted for former sub-s (1), by FA 2011 s 45, Sch 10 para 7(1), (3) with effect in relation to any disposal of an asset by one company ("company B") to another company ("company A") made at a time when company B is a member of a group, if: (a) company A ceases to be a member of the group on or after 19 July 2011; or (b) where company A ceased to be such a member before 19 July 2011 in circumstances where CTA 2009 s 783 applied, company A ceases to be a member of another group on or after 19 July 2011.

784 Groups with a relevant connection

(1) For the purposes of section 783(2) there is a relevant connection between the first group and the second group if, at the time when the transferee ceases to be a member of the second group, the company which is the principal company of that group is under the control of—

    (a) a person within subsection (2),

    (b) a person or persons within subsection (3), or

    (c) a person or persons within subsection (4).

(2) A person is within this subsection if it is the company—

    (a) that is the principal company of the first group, or

    (b) if that group no longer exists, that was its principal company when the transferee ceased to be a member of it.

(3) A person or persons are within this subsection if they—

    (a) control the company within subsection (2), or

    (b) have had it under their control at any time in the period since the transferee ceased to be a member of the first group.

(4) A person or persons are within this subsection if they have, at any time in that period, had under their control either—

    (a) a company that would have fallen within subsection (3) if it had continued to exist, or

    (b) a company to which subsection (5) applies.

(5) This subsection applies to a company if, had the company continued to exist—

    (a) it would have fallen within subsection (4) because of its control of another company that would have fallen within subsection (3) if that other company had continued to exist, or

    (b) it would have fallen within subsection (4) because of its control of a company to which paragraph (a) or this paragraph would have applied.

[(6) For the purposes of this section "control" is to be read in accordance with sections 450 and 451 of CTA 2010 (close companies: meaning of control).][1]

(7) But a person carrying on a business of banking is not treated for those purposes as having control of a company just because of—

    (a) having any rights in respect of loan capital or debt issued or incurred by the company for money lent by that person to the company in the ordinary course of that business, or

    (b) the consequences of having exercised such rights.

(8) References in this section to "the first group", "the second group" and "the transferee" must be read in accordance with section 783.

Commentary—*Simon's Taxes* **D1.650.**
Derivation—FA 2002 Sch 29 para 59(3), (4).
HMRC Manuals—Corporate Intangibles Research and Development Manual CIRD40545 (de-grouping: when is there a relevant connection between groups?).
Amendments—[1] Sub-s (6) substituted by CTA 2010 s 1177, Sch 1 para 650 with effect for corporation tax purposes for accounting periods ending on or after 1 April 2010, and for income and capital gains tax purposes for the tax year 2010–11 and subsequent tax years.

785 Principal company becoming member of another group

(1) Section 780 does not apply if a company ceases to be a member of a group just because the principal company of the group becomes a member of another group ("the second group").

(2) This subsection applies if—

    (a) section 780 would have applied but for subsection (1),

    (b) after the transfer and before the end of the period of 6 years after the date of the transfer, the transferee ceases to meet the condition that it is [a relevant][1] subsidiary of one or more members of the second group ("the qualifying condition"), and

    (c) at the time at which the transferee ceases to do so, the relevant asset is held by the transferee or another company in the same group.

[(2A) For the purposes of subsection (2)(b) the transferee is a "relevant subsidiary" of a member of the second group ("A") if, but for sections 767 to 770, the transferee would be a member of another group of which A would be the principal company.

(2B) Subsection (2) does not apply if the transferee ceases to meet the qualifying condition by reason of a relevant disposal of shares by another company (within the meaning given by section 782A(2)).][1]

(3) If subsection (2) applies, this Part applies as if immediately after the transfer to the transferee of the relevant asset the transferee had—

    (a) realised the asset for its market value at that time, and

    (b) immediately reacquired the asset at that value.

(4) The adjustments to be made as a result of subsection (3), by the transferee or a company to which the relevant asset has been subsequently transferred, in relation to the relevant period must be made by bringing the total net credit or debit into account as if it had arisen immediately before the transferee ceased to meet the qualifying condition.

(5) In subsection (4) "the relevant period" means the period between—

    (a) the transfer of the relevant asset to the transferee, and

    (b) the transferee ceasing to meet the qualifying condition.

(6) This section is subject to section 789 (merger carried out for genuine commercial reasons).

(7) References in this section to "the transferee" and "the relevant asset" must be read in accordance with section 780.

(8) For the way in which Chapter 7 applies if a company is treated as having realised an asset as a result of this section, see section 791 (application of roll-over relief in relation to degrouping charge).

Commentary—*Simon's Taxes* **D1.649, D1.650**.

Derivation—FA 2002 Sch 29 para 60(1)–(3), (5).

HMRC Manuals—Corporate Intangibles Research and Development Manual CIRD40550 (principal company becoming member of another group).

CIRD40560 (principal company becoming member of another group: subsequent restoration of de-grouping adjustment).

Amendments—[1] In sub-s (2)(b) words substituted for words "both a 75% subsidiary and an effective 51%", and sub-ss (2A), (2B) inserted, by FA 2019 s 26(1), (4) with effect in relation to a company that ceases to be a member of a group or ceases to meet the condition in CTA 2009 s 785(2)(b) (as amended by FA 2019 s 26(4)) on or after 7 November 2018. In its application in relation to a company that ceases to be a member of a group or ceases to meet the condition in CTA 2009 s 785(2)(b) before 21 December 2018, CTA 2009 s 782A has effect as if s 782A(3) was omitted.

786 Character of credits and debits brought into account as a result of section 785

(1) For the purposes of Chapter 6 (how credits and debits are given effect) credits or debits brought into account because of section 785 take their character from the purposes for which the relevant asset was held by the transferee immediately after the transfer.

(2) But subsection (1) does not apply if conditions A and B are met.

(3) Condition A is that immediately after the transfer the asset was held by the transferee for the purposes of a trade, business or concern within section 747, 748 or 749.

(4) Condition B is that the transferee ceased to carry on that trade, business or concern before it ceased to meet the qualifying condition.

(5) If conditions A and B are met, a credit or debit brought into account because of section 785 is treated for the purposes of Chapter 6 as a non-trading credit or debit.

(6) References in this section to "the transferee" and the relevant asset" must be read in accordance with section 780.

Derivation—FA 2002 Sch 29 para 60(4).

HMRC Manuals—Corporate Intangibles Research and Development Manual CIRD40560 (computational consequences). CIRD40520 (classification of net credit or debit).

787 Company ceasing to be member of group because of exempt distribution

(1) Sections 780 and 785 do not apply if a company ceases to be a member of a group just because of an exempt distribution, unless subsection (2) applies.

(2) This subsection applies if there is a chargeable payment within 5 years after the making of the exempt distribution.

(3) If subsection (2) applies, all such adjustments as may be required, by way of assessment, amendment of returns or otherwise, may be made within the period of 3 years after the making of the chargeable payment.

(4) Those adjustments may be made despite any time limit on the making of an assessment or the amendment of a return.

(5) In this section—

    "exempt distribution" means a distribution that is exempt because of [section 1076 or 1077 of CTA 2010][1] (distributions involving shares in 75% subsidiaries), and

    "chargeable payment" has the meaning given in [section 1088(1) of CTA 2010][1].

(6) Subsections (7) and (8) apply for determining for the purposes of this section whether one company is a 75% subsidiary of another company.

(7) The other company is treated as not being the owner of any share capital that it owns directly in a body corporate if a profit on a sale of the shares would be treated as a trading receipt of its trade.

(8) The other company is treated as not being the owner of any share capital that—

    (a) it owns indirectly, and

    (b) is owned directly by a body corporate for which a profit on the sale of the shares would be a trading receipt.

Commentary—*Simon's Taxes* **D1.650**.

Derivation—FA 2002 Sch 29 para 61(1)–(4).

HMRC Manuals—Corporate Intangibles Research and Development Manual CIRD40590 (de-grouping: exclusion of exempt distributions).

Amendments—[1] In sub-s (5), in the definition of "exempt distribution", words substituted for words "section 213(2) of ICTA", in the definition of "chargeable payment" words substituted for words "section 214(2) of that Act" by CTA 2010 s 1177, Sch

1 para 651. CTA 2010 has effect for corporation tax purposes for accounting periods ending on or after 1 April 2010, and for income and capital gains tax purposes for the tax year 2010–11 and subsequent tax years.

788 Provisions supplementing sections 780 to 787

(1) References in sections 780 to 787 (degrouping) to a company ceasing to be a member of a group do not include cases where a company ceases to be a member of a group in consequence of another member of the group ceasing to exist.

(2) For the purposes of those sections an asset acquired by a company is treated as the same as an asset owned at a later time by that company or an associated company if the value of the second asset is derived in whole or in part from the first asset.

[(3) For the purposes of those sections and this section two companies are associated with each other if one is a 75% subsidiary of the other or both are 75% subsidiaries of another company.][1]

Commentary—*Simon's Taxes* D1.649, D1.650.

Amendments—[1]   Sub-s (3) substituted by FA 2011 s 45, Sch 10 para 7(1), (4) with effect in relation to any disposal of an asset by one company ("company B") to another company ("company A") made at a time when company B is a member of a group, if: (a) company A ceases to be a member of the group on or after 19 July 2011; or (b) where company A ceased to be such a member before 19 July 2011 in circumstances where CTA 2009 s 783 applied, company A ceases to be a member of another group on or after 19 July 2011.

789 Merger carried out for genuine commercial reasons

(1) Sections 780 to 787 do not apply if—
    (*a*) the transferee ceases to be a member of a group of companies ("the group") as part of a merger,
    (*b*) the merger is carried out for genuine commercial reasons, and
    (*c*) the avoidance of liability to tax is not the main purpose of the merger or one of its main purposes.

(2) For this purpose "merger" means an arrangement in respect of which each of conditions A to D is met.

(3) Condition A is that—
    (*a*) as a result of the arrangement one or more companies ("the acquiring company" or "the acquiring companies") acquire one or more interests in the whole or part of the business which, before the arrangement took effect, was carried on by the transferee,
    (*b*) the acquiring company is not a member of the group or, as the case may be, none of the acquiring companies is such a member,
    (*c*) at least 25% by value of each of the interests acquired consists of a holding of ordinary share capital, and
    (*d*) the acquisition is not with a view to the disposal of the interests.

(4) Condition B is that—
    (*a*) as a result of the arrangement one or more members of the group acquire one or more interests in the whole or part of the business or each of the businesses which, before the arrangement took effect, was carried on—
       (i) by the acquiring company or acquiring companies, or
       (ii) by a company at least 90% of whose ordinary share capital was then beneficially owned by two or more of the acquiring companies,
    (*b*) at least 25% by value of each of the interests acquired consists of a holding of ordinary share capital,
    (*c*) the remainder of the interest, or as the case may be of each of the interests, acquired consists of a holding of share capital (of any description) or debentures or both, and
    (*d*) the acquisition is not with a view to the disposal of the interests.

(5) Condition C is that the value or, as the case may be, the total value of the interest or interests acquired as mentioned in subsection (3) is substantially the same as the value or, as the case may be, the total value of the interest or interests acquired as mentioned in subsection (4).

(6) Condition D is that the consideration for the acquisition of the interest or interests acquired by the acquiring company or acquiring companies as mentioned in subsection (3)—
    (*a*) consists of, or is applied in the acquisition of, the interest or interests acquired by members of the group as mentioned in subsection (4), or
    (*b*) consists partly of, and as to the balance is applied in the acquisition of, that interest or those interests.

(7) Section 790 supplements this section.

Commentary—*Simon's Taxes* D1.650.

Derivation—FA 2002 Sch 29 para 62(1), (2), (4).

HMRC Manuals—Corporate Intangibles Research and Development Manual CIRD40580 (de-grouping: exclusion of commercial mergers).

790 Provisions supplementing section 789

(1) In section 789 "arrangement" includes a series of arrangements.

(2) For the purposes of section 789(3) and (4) a member of a group of companies is treated as carrying on as one business the activities of that group.

(b) an amount of corporation tax has been assessed on A for the relevant accounting period, and

(c) the whole or part of that amount is unpaid at the end of the period of 6 months after the time when it became payable.

(2) An officer of Revenue and Customs may serve a notice on the persons to whom this subsection applies (see subsections (3) and (4)) requiring them to pay the lesser of—

(a) the amount of corporation tax referable to the degrouping charge (see section 796(2)), or

(b) the amount that remains unpaid of the corporation tax payable for the relevant accounting period by A.

(3) If A was a member of a group at the relevant time, subsection (2) applies to—

(a) a company that was at that time the principal company of the group, and

(b) any other company that at any time in the period of 12 months ending with the relevant time—

(i) was a member of that group, and

(ii) owned the relevant asset or any part of it.

(4) If at the relevant time A is not UK resident . . . [1], subsection (2) applies to any person who is a controlling director—

(a) of A,

(b) of a company that has control of A,

(c) of a company that had control of A within the period of 12 months ending with the relevant time,

or was such a controlling director during that period.

(5) Section 796 applies for the interpretation of this section and in that section references to "A" must be read in accordance with this section.

Commentary—*Simon's Taxes* D1.653.

Derivation—FA 2002 Sch 29 paras 68(1), (2), 69(1).

HMRC Manuals—Corporate Intangibles Research and Development Manual CIRD40720 (groups: de-grouping: unpaid degrouping charge: recovery from others: candidates).

Amendments—[1]   In sub-s (4), words "but carries on a trade in the United Kingdom through a permanent establishment" repealed by FA 2019 s 17, Sch 5 paras 10, 26, with effect from 6 April 2020, subject to transitional provisions in FA 2019 Sch 5 Pt 3 (paras 36–50).

796 Interpretation of section 795

(1) For the purposes of section 795 and this section—

"the relevant accounting period" is the accounting period in which the degrouping charge falls to be brought into account by A,

"the relevant time" is—

(a) in a case within section 780, when A ceased to be a member of the group,

(b) in a case within section 785, when A ceased to meet the qualifying condition (within the meaning of that section), and

(c) if there has been an election under section 792, the time that would have been the relevant time under paragraph (a) or (b) had there been no such election, and

"the relevant asset" is the asset in respect of which the degrouping charge arises.

(2) For the purposes of section 795 the amount of corporation tax referable to a degrouping charge is the difference between—

(a) the tax in fact payable for the relevant accounting period, and

(b) the tax that would have been payable for that period in the absence of the degrouping charge.

(3) References in section 795 and this section to a degrouping charge are to—

(a) a credit required to be brought into account under section 780(3) or 785(4), or

(b) if there has been an election under section 792, a credit required to be brought into account as a result of the election.

(4) In section 795 and this section—

"director", in relation to a company—

(a) has the meaning given by section 67(1) of ITEPA 2003 (read with section 67(2) of that Act) and

(b) includes any person falling within [section 452(1) of CTA 2010][1],

"controlling director", in relation to a company, means a director of the company who has control of it, and

"group" and "principal company" have the meaning that would be given by Chapter 8 if in that Chapter for references to 75% subsidiaries there were substituted references to 51% subsidiaries.

(5) In subsection (4) "control" [is to be read in accordance with sections 450 and 451 of CTA 2010][1].

Commentary—*Simon's Taxes* D1.653.

Derivation—FA 2002 Sch 29 para 68(3)–(6).

HMRC Manuals—Corporate Intangibles Research and Development Manual CIRD40730 (unpaid de-grouping charge: recovery from others: definitions).

Amendments—[1]   In sub-s (4), in definition of "director", words substituted for words "section 417(5) of ICTA (read with section 417(6) of that Act)", in sub-s (5) words substituted for "words has the meaning given by section 416(2) to (6) of ICTA" by CTA 2010 s 1177, Sch 1 para 653. CTA 2010 has effect for corporation tax purposes for accounting periods ending on or after 1 April 2010, and for income and capital gains tax purposes for the tax year 2010–11 and subsequent tax years.

797 Recovery under section 795: procedure etc

(1) A notice served under section 795(2) may require the payment of the amount required to be paid by the notice within 30 days of the service of the notice.

(2) The notice must state—

    (*a*) the amount of the tax referable to the degrouping charge (within the meaning given in section 796(2)),

    (*b*) the amount of corporation tax assessed on A for the relevant accounting period that remains unpaid,

    (*c*) the date when it first became payable, and

    (*d*) the amount required to be paid by the person on whom the notice is served.

(3) The notice has effect—

    (*a*) for the purposes of the recovery from that person of the amount required to be paid and of interest on that amount, and

    (*b*) for the purposes of appeals,

as if it were a notice of assessment and that amount were an amount of tax due from that person.

(4) A person who has paid an amount required to be paid by a notice under section 795(2) may recover the amount paid from A.

(5) A payment required to be made by such a notice is not allowed as a deduction in calculating any income, profits or losses for any tax purposes.

(6) In this section "A" and "the relevant accounting period" have the same meaning as in section 795 (see section 795(1) and section 796(1) respectively).

Commentary—*Simon's Taxes* **D1.653**.
Derivation—FA 2002 Sch 29 para 69(1)–(3), (5), (6).
HMRC Manuals—Corporate Intangibles Research and Development Manual CIRD40740 (unpaid de-grouping charge: recovery from others: procedures).

798 Recovery under section 795: time limit

(1) A notice under section 795(2) must be served before the end of the period of 3 years beginning with the date on which A's liability to corporation tax for the relevant accounting period is finally determined.

(2) In subsection (1) "A" and "the relevant accounting period" have the same meaning as in section 795 (see section 795(1) and section 796(1) respectively).

(3) If the unpaid tax is charged because of a determination under paragraph 36 or 37 of Schedule 18 to FA 1998 (determination where no return delivered or return incomplete), the date mentioned in subsection (1) is the date on which the determination was made.

(4) If the unpaid tax is charged in a self-assessment, the date mentioned in subsection (1) is the latest of—

    (*a*) the last date on which notice of enquiry may be given into the return containing the self-assessment,

    (*b*) if notice of enquiry is given, 30 days after the enquiry is completed,

    (*c*) if more than one notice of enquiry is given, 30 days after the last notice of completion,

    (*d*) if after such an enquiry an officer of Revenue and Customs amends the return, 30 days after notice of the amendment is issued, and

    (*e*) if an appeal is brought against such an amendment, 30 days after the appeal is finally determined.

(5) If the unpaid tax is charged in a discovery assessment, the date mentioned in subsection (1) is—

    (*a*) if there is no appeal against the assessment, the date when the tax becomes due and payable, and

    (*b*) if there is such an appeal, the date on which the appeal is finally determined.

(6) In this section—

    "self-assessment" includes a self-assessment that supersedes a determination as a result of paragraph 40 of Schedule 18 to FA 1998, and

    "discovery assessment" means an assessment under paragraph 41(1) of that Schedule.

Commentary—*Simon's Taxes* **D1.653**.
Derivation—FA 2002 Sch 29 para 70(1)–(4).
HMRC Manuals—Corporate Intangibles Research and Development Manual CIRD40740 (unpaid de-grouping charge: recovery from others: time limit).

Disregard of payments between group members for reliefs

799 Disregard of payments between group members for reliefs

(1) If a payment for group roll-over relief or for the reallocation of a degrouping charge does not exceed the amount of the relevant relief—

    (*a*) it is not taken into account in calculating profits or losses of either of the companies involved for corporation tax purposes, and

    (*b*) it is not a distribution for any of the purposes of the Corporation Tax Acts.

(2) A payment for group roll-over relief is a payment made—

    (*a*) in connection with a claim for relief under Chapter 7 (roll-over relief in case of realisation and reinvestment) made because of—

        (i) section 777 (relief on realisation and reinvestment: application to group member), or

        (ii) section 779 (rules that apply to cases within section 778(1)),

    (*b*) by the company whose proceeds of realisation are reduced as a result of the claim,

    (*c*) to a company whose acquisition costs are reduced (in a case within section 777) or the tax written-down value of whose assets is reduced (in a case within section 779) as a result of the claim, and

    (*d*) in accordance with an agreement between those companies in connection with the claim.

(3) A payment for the reallocation of a degrouping charge is a payment made—

    (*a*) in connection with an election under section 792 (reallocation of charge within group),

    (*b*) by the company to which the chargeable realisation gain accrues,

    (*c*) to the company to which as a result of the election the whole or part of that gain is treated as accruing, and

    (*d*) in accordance with an agreement between those companies in connection with the election.

(4) In the case of a payment in connection with such a claim for relief as is mentioned in section 777(3), the amount of the relevant relief is the amount of the reduction, as a result of the claim, in the acquisition costs of the company to which the payment is made.

(5) In the case of a payment in connection with such a claim for relief as is mentioned in section 778(4), the amount of the relevant relief is the amount of the reduction, as a result of the claim, in the tax written-down value of the assets of the company to which the payment is made.

(6) In the case of a payment in connection with an election under section 792, the amount of the relevant relief is the amount treated as a result of the election as accruing to the company to which the payment is made.

Commentary—*Simon's Taxes* **D1.654**.

Derivation—FA 2002 Sch 29 para 71(1)–(5).

HMRC Manuals—Corporate Intangibles Research and Development Manual CIRD40750 (de-grouping: intra-group payments for reinvestment relief and reallocation of taxable credit).

CHAPTER 10

EXCLUDED ASSETS

Introductory

800 Introduction

(1) This Chapter provides for the exclusion from this Part of certain assets.

(2) This Chapter provides for 3 kinds of exclusion—

    (*a*) assets within sections 803 to 809 are wholly excluded from this Part,

    (*b*) assets within sections 810 to 813 are excluded from this Part except as respects royalties, and

    (*c*) assets within [any of sections 814 to 816A][2] are excluded from this Part to the extent specified in [the section concerned][2].

(3) For further rules about the exclusion of assets from this Part, see—

    (*a*) Chapter 16 (pre-FA 2002 assets etc), . . . [1]

    (*b*) . . . [1]

Commentary—*Simon's Taxes* **D1.603**.

Derivation—FA 2002 Sch 29 para 72(1), (2).

HMRC Manuals—Corporate Intangibles Research and Development Manual CIRD25010 (intangible assets excluded from schedule 29: introduction).

Amendments—[1] Sub-s (3)(*b*) and preceding word "and" repealed by FA 2012 s 146, Sch 16 paras 135, 174 with effect in relation to accounting periods of companies beginning on or after 1 January 2013 (subject to transitional provisions in FA 2012 Sch 17). For accounting periods straddling 1 January 2013, see FA 2012 s 149.

[2] In sub-s (2)(*c*), words substituted in the first place for "section 814 or 815", and in the second place for "that section" by F(No 2)A 2015 s 33(1), (4) with effect in relation to accounting periods beginning on or after 8 July 2015. But the amendments do not apply in a case in which a company acquires a relevant asset if the company does so before 8 July 2015, or in pursuance of an obligation, under a contract, that was unconditional before that date. An obligation is "unconditional" if it may not be varied or extinguished by the exercise of a right (whether under the contract or otherwise). For accounting periods straddling 8 July 2015 see F(No 2)A 2015 s 33(11), (12).

801 Right to dispose of or acquire excluded asset also excluded

So far as an asset of any description is excluded from this Part by this Chapter, an option or other right to acquire or dispose of an asset of that description is similarly excluded.

Commentary—*Simon's Taxes* **D1.603**.

Derivation—FA 2002 Sch 29 para 72(1).

HMRC Manuals—Corporate Intangibles Research and Development Manual CIRD25010 (intangible assets excluded from schedule 29: options).

CIRD11175 (options or other rights to acquire or dispose of intangible fixed assets).

802 Effect of partial exclusion

(1) If because of any of sections 803 to 815 an asset is excluded to the extent that—

    (*a*) it represents particular rights,

    (*b*) it is an asset of a particular description,

    (*c*) it is held for particular purposes, or

    (*d*) it represents expenditure of a particular kind,

this Part applies as if there were a separate asset representing so much of the asset as is not so excluded.

(2) The other provisions of the Corporation Tax Acts apply as if there were a separate asset representing so much of the asset as is excluded.

(3) Any apportionment necessary for the purposes of this section must be made on a just and reasonable basis.

Commentary—*Simon's Taxes* **D1.603**.
Derivation—FA 2002 Sch 29 para 72(3)–(5).
HMRC Manuals—Corporate Intangibles Research and Development Manual CIRD25015 (intangible assets excluded from schedule 29: partial exclusion of asset: apportionment).

Assets wholly excluded from this Part

803 Non-commercial purposes etc

This Part does not apply to an intangible fixed asset so far as it is held—

    (*a*) for a purpose that is not a business or other commercial purpose of the company, or

    (*b*) for the purpose of activities in respect of which the company is not within the charge to corporation tax[, otherwise than as a result of Chapter 3A of Part 2.][1]

Commentary—*Simon's Taxes* **D1.603**.
Derivation—FA 2002 Sch 29 para 77.
HMRC Manuals—Corporate Intangibles Research and Development Manual CIRD25070 (intangible assets excluded from schedule 29: assets held for nonqualifying purposes).
Amendments—[1]   In para (*b*) words inserted by FA 2011 s 48, Sch 13 paras 1, 6 with effect from 19 July 2011, subject to transitional provisions in FA 2011 Sch 13 paras 32–37.

804 Assets for which capital allowances previously made

(1) This Part does not apply to an intangible asset of a company if conditions A, B and C are met.

(2) Condition A is that the asset falls to be treated as an intangible asset in accounts of the company.

(3) Condition B is that in a previous period of account the asset fell to be treated as a tangible asset in accounts of the company.

(4) Condition C is that an allowance under Part 2 of CAA 2001 (plant and machinery allowances) was made to the company in respect of the asset on the basis that it was a tangible asset.

Commentary—*Simon's Taxes* **D1.603**.
Derivation—FA 2002 Sch 29 para 73A(1), (2).
HMRC Manuals—Corporate Intangibles Research and Development Manual CIRD25145 (special tax rules: web sites in respect of which capital allowances have been claimed).

805 Rights over tangible assets

This Part does not apply to an intangible fixed asset so far as it represents—

    (*a*) rights enjoyed by virtue of an estate, interest or right in or over land, or

    (*b*) rights in relation to tangible movable property.

Commentary—*Simon's Taxes* **D1.603**.
Derivation—FA 2002 Sch 29 para 73.
HMRC Manuals—Corporate Intangibles Research and Development Manual CIRD25030 (intangible assets excluded from schedule 29: rights over tangible assets).

806 Financial assets

(1) This Part does not apply to financial assets.

(2) In this Part "financial asset" has the same meaning as it has for accounting purposes.

(3) "Financial asset" includes—

    (*a*) loan relationships (see Parts 5 and 6),

    (*b*) derivative contracts (see Part 7),

    (*c*) contracts or policies of insurance or capital redemption policies,

    [(*ca*) assets so far as they are derived from, or are referable to, contracts or policies of insurance or capital redemption policies,][1] and

    (*d*) rights under a collective investment scheme within the meaning of FISMA 2000 (see section 235 of that Act).

Commentary—*Simon's Taxes* **D1.603**.
Derivation—FA 2002 Sch 29 para 75(1)–(3).
HMRC Manuals—Corporate Intangibles Research and Development Manual CIRD25050 (intangible assets excluded from schedule 29: financial assets).
Amendments—[1]   Sub-s (3)(*ca*) inserted by FA 2012 s 146, Sch 16 paras 135, 175 with effect in relation to accounting periods of companies beginning on or after 1 January 2013 (subject to transitional provisions in FA 2012 Sch 17). For accounting periods straddling 1 January 2013, see FA 2012 s 149.

807 Rights in companies, trusts etc

(1) This Part does not apply to an asset so far as it represents—

    (*a*) shares or other rights in relation to the profits, governance or winding up of a company,

    (*b*) rights under a trust, or

    (*c*) the interest of a partner in a firm.

(2) Subsection (1)(*b*) does not apply to rights that for accounting purposes fall to be treated as representing an interest in trust property that is an intangible fixed asset to which this Part applies.

(3) Subsection (1)(*c*) does not apply to an interest that for accounting purposes falls to be treated as representing an interest in partnership property that is an intangible fixed asset to which this Part applies.

Commentary—*Simon's Taxes* **D1.603**.

Derivation—FA 2002 Sch 29 para 76(1)–(3).

HMRC Manuals—Corporate Intangibles Research and Development Manual CIRD25060 (intangible assets excluded from schedule 29: rights in companies, trusts and partnerships).

808 Assets representing production expenditure on films

(1) This Part does not apply to an intangible fixed asset held by a film production company so far as it represents production expenditure on a film to which Chapter 2 of Part 15 (taxation of activities of film production company) applies.

(2) In this section—

    (*a*) "film" has the same meaning as in Part 15 (see section 1181),

    (*b*) "film production company" has the same meaning as in that Part (see section 1182), and

    (*c*) "production expenditure" has the same meaning as in that Part (see section 1184(1)).

Commentary—*Simon's Taxes* **D1.603, D7.1290**.

Derivation—FA 2002 Sch 29 para 80A(1).

HMRC Manuals—Corporate Intangibles Research and Development Manual CIRD25130 (intangible assets excluded from schedule 29: certain films - effective from 1 January 2007).

Film Production Company Manual FPC10100 (meaning of 'film').

FPC10100 (meaning of 'film production company').

FPC10100 (meaning of 'production expenditure').

[808A Assets representing production expenditure on certain TV programmes

(1) This Part does not apply to an intangible fixed asset held by a television production company so far as it represents production expenditure on a television programme to which Chapter 2 of Part 15A (taxation of activities of television production company) applies.

(2) In this section—

    (*a*) "television programme" has the same meaning as in Part 15A (see section 1216AA),

    (*b*) "television production company" has the same meaning as in that Part (see section 1216AE), and

    (*c*) "production expenditure" has the same meaning as in that Part (see section 1216AG(2),][1]

Commentary—*Simon's Taxes* **D7.1290**.

HMRC Manuals—Film Production Company Manual FPC20130 (taxation: separate trade television productions).

Amendments—[1] This section inserted by FA 2013 s 36, Sch 18 para 9.

[808B Assets representing core expenditure on video games

(1) This Part does not apply to an intangible fixed asset held by a video games development company so far as it represents core expenditure on a video game to which Chapter 2 of Part 15B (taxation of activities of video games development company) applies.

(2) In this section—

    (*a*) "video game" has the same meaning as in Part 15B (see section 1217AA),

    (*b*) "video games development company" has the same meaning as in that Part (see section 1217AB), and

    (*c*) "core expenditure" has the same meaning as in that Part (see section 1217AD).][1]

Commentary—*Simon's Taxes* **D7.1290**.

HMRC Manuals—Video Games Development Company Manual VGDC10000 (overview and general definitions: contents).

VGDC10100 (meaning of 'video game').

VGDC10110 (meaning of 'video games development company').

VGDC10130 (meaning of 'core expenditure').

Amendments—[1] This section inserted by FA 2013 s 36, Sch 18 para 9.

[808C Assets representing expenditure incurred in course of separate theatrical trade

(1) This Part does not apply to an intangible fixed asset held by a theatrical production company so far as the asset represents expenditure on a theatrical production that is treated under Part 15C as expenditure of a separate trade (see particularly sections 1217H and 1217IE).

(2) In this section—

    "theatrical production" has the same meaning as in Part 15C (see section 1217FA);

    "theatrical production company" means a company which, for the purposes of that Part, is the production company in relation to a theatrical production (see section 1217FC).][1]

Commentary—*Simon's Taxes* **D7.1290**.

Amendments—[1]   This section inserted by FA 2014 s 36, Sch 4 para 10 with effect in relation to accounting periods beginning on or after 1 September 2014, subject to transitional provisions for accounting periods straddling that date (FA 2014 Sch 4 para 17). SI 2014/2228 reg 2 provides that the amendments made by FA 2014 Sch 4 come into force on 22 August 2014 (other than the power to make regulations under Sch 4 para 16(1) which came into force on 17 July 2014).

[808D Assets representing expenditure incurred in course of separate orchestral trade

(1) This Part does not apply to an intangible fixed asset held by an orchestral concert production company so far as the asset represents expenditure on an orchestral concert or orchestral concert series that is treated under Part 15D as expenditure of a separate trade (see particularly sections 1217Q and 1217QF).

(2) In this section—

"orchestral concert" has the same meaning as in Part 15D (see section 1217PA);

"orchestral concert production company" means a company which, for the purposes of that Part, is the production company in relation to a concert (see section 1217PB).][1]

Commentary—*Simon's Taxes* **D7.1290.**

Amendments—[1]   This section inserted by FA 2016 s 54, Sch 8 para 9 with effect in relation to accounting periods beginning on or after 1 April 2016, subject to transitional provisions for accounting periods straddling that date (FA 2016 Sch 8 para 17). Note that any power conferred on the Treasury by FA 2016 Sch 8 to make regulations came into force on 15 September 2016 (FA 2016 Sch 8 para 16).

[808E Assets representing expenditure incurred in course of separate exhibition trade

(1) This Part does not apply to an intangible fixed asset held by a museums and galleries exhibition production company so far as the asset represents expenditure on an exhibition that is treated under Part 15E as expenditure of a separate trade (see particularly sections 1218ZB and 1218ZBE).

(2) In this section—

"exhibition" has the same meaning as in Part 15E (see section 1218ZAA);

"museums and galleries exhibition production company" means a company which, for the purposes of that Part, is the primary production company or a secondary production company for an exhibition (see sections 1218ZAC and 1218ZAD).][1]

Amendments—[1]   Section 808E inserted by F(No 2)A 2017 s 21, Sch 6 paras 9, 11 with effect in relation to accounting periods beginning on or after 1 April 2017.

809 Oil licences

(1) This Part does not apply to an oil licence or an interest in an oil licence.

[(1A) The reference in subsection (1) to an oil licence or an interest in an oil licence includes all goodwill, and any intangible asset, which relates to, derives from or is connected with an oil licence or an interest in an oil licence.][1]

(2) In [this section][1] "oil licence" means a UK oil licence or a foreign oil concession.

(3) In this section—

"UK oil licence" means a licence under—

(a) Part 1 of the Petroleum Act 1998 (c 17) ("the 1998 Act"), or

(b) the Petroleum Production (Northern Ireland) Act 1964 (c 28 (NI)) ("the 1964 Act"),

authorising the winning of oil, and

"foreign oil concession" means any right that—

(a) is a right to search for or win oil that exists in its natural condition in a place to which neither the 1998 Act nor the 1964 Act applies, and

(b) is conferred or exercisable (whether or not under a licence) in relation to a particular area.

(4) In [this section][1] "interest in an oil licence" includes any entitlement under an agreement to, or to a share of, oil or the proceeds of its sale if the agreement—

(a) relates to oil from the whole or a part of the licensed area, and

(b) was made before the extraction of the oil to which it relates.

(5) In subsection (4)(a) "licensed area" means—

(a) in relation to a UK oil licence, the area to which the licence applies, and

(b) in relation to a foreign oil concession, the area in relation to which the right to search for or win oil is conferred or exercisable under the concession.

(6) In this section "oil"—

(a) in relation to a UK oil licence, means any substance won or capable of being won under the authority of a licence granted under Part 1 of the 1998 Act or the 1964 Act, other than methane gas won in the course of making and keeping mines safe, and

(b) in relation to a foreign oil concession, means any petroleum (as defined in section 1 of the 1998 Act).

Commentary—*Simon's Taxes* **D1.603.**

Derivation—FA 2002 Sch 29 para 74(1)–(6).

HMRC Manuals—Corporate Intangibles Research and Development Manual CIRD25040 (oil licences: definitions). CIRD48300 (goodwill and intangible assets relating to an oil and gas licence excluded). Oil Taxation Manual OT20315 (intangible fixed assets: oil exclusion from the scheme).

    (*a*) two or more societies to which this section applies amalgamate or there is a transfer of engagements from one such society to another,

    (*b*) in the course of the amalgamation or transfer of engagements or as part of it intangible fixed assets are transferred from one society ("the transferor") to another ("the transferee"),

    (*c*) those assets are chargeable intangible assets in relation to the transferor immediately before the transfer, and

    (*d*) those assets are chargeable intangible assets in relation to the transferee immediately after the transfer.

(2) The transfer of those assets is tax-neutral for the purposes of this Part.

(3) This section applies to—

    (*a*) a building society,

    (*b*) a [registered society][2], and

    (*c*) a co-operative association in relation to which [section 1057 of CTA 2010 (UK agricultural or fishing co-operatives) applies.][1]

Commentary—*Simon's Taxes* **D1.660, D7.828**.

Derivation—FA 2002 Sch 29 para 91(1), (2).

HMRC Manuals—Corporate Intangibles Research and Development Manual CIRD42140 (company reorganisation: amalgamation of business of building societies, industrial and provident societies and cooperative associations).

Amendments—[1]   In sub-s (3)(*c*), words substituted for words "section 486(1) and (8) of ICTA has effect as it has effect in relation to a registered industrial and provident society." by CTA 2010 s 1177, Sch 1 para 656. CTA 2010 has effect for corporation tax purposes for accounting periods ending on or after 1 April 2010, and for income and capital gains tax purposes for the tax year 2010–11 and subsequent tax years.

[2]   In each place where they occur in this Act, words substituted for words "registered industrial and provident society", "the Industrial and Provident Societies Act 1965" and "industrial and provident societies", by the Co-operative and Community Benefit Societies Act 2014 s 151, Sch 4 paras 140–143 with effect from 1 August 2014 and subject to transitional provisions and provisions preserving the continuity of the law in Sch 5 of that Act.

Transfer of assets to non-UK resident company

827 Claims to postpone charge on transfer

(1) This section applies if—

    (*a*) a UK resident company carrying on a trade outside the United Kingdom through a permanent establishment ("the transferor") transfers that trade or part of it to a non-UK resident company ("the transferee"),

    (*b*) the transfer meets conditions A, B and C,

    (*c*) the transfer includes intangible fixed assets that are chargeable intangible assets in relation to the transferor immediately before the transfer ("relevant assets"), and

    (*d*) the transferor makes a claim under this section.

(2) If this section applies, this Part applies in accordance with sections 828 to 830.

(3) Condition A is that the transfer includes—

    (*a*) the whole assets of the transferor used for the purposes of the trade or part, or

    (*b*) the whole of those assets other than cash.

(4) Condition B is that the transfer is wholly or partly in exchange for securities consisting of—

    (*a*) shares within subsection (5) that are issued by the transferee to the transferor, or

    (*b*) shares within paragraph (*a*) and loan stock that is so issued.

(5) Shares are within this subsection if they—

    (*a*) amount in all to at least one quarter of the ordinary share capital of the transferee, or

    (*b*) do so if taken together with any other shares in the transferee already held by the transferor.

(6) Condition C is that the transfer meets the genuine commercial transaction requirement (see section 831).

(7) No claim may be made under this section if a claim is made in relation to the transfer under [section 116(6) of TIOPA 2010][1] (European cross-border transfers of business: application for [section 117][1] of that Act to apply).

(8) In sections 828 to 830 "transferor", "transferee" and "relevant assets" have the same meaning as in this section.

Commentary—*Simon's Taxes* **D1.662, D1.663, D1.664, D1.660**.

Derivation—FA 2002 Sch 29 para 86(1), (2), (8), (10).

HMRC Manuals—Corporate Intangibles Research and Development Manual CIRD42040 (company reorganisation: transfer of foreign permanent establishment from UK to a non resident company: deferral of charge).

CIRD42045 (company reorganisation: transfer of foreign permanent establishment from UK to a non resident company: amount of charge deferred).

Amendments—[1]   In sub-s (7), words substituted for words "section 807B(6) of ICTA" and "section 807C", by TIOPA 2010 s 501, Sch 8 paras 89, 96. TIOPA 2010 has effect for corporation tax purposes for accounting periods ending on or after 1 April 2010, for income and capital gains tax purposes for the tax year 2010–11 and subsequent tax years, and for petroleum revenue tax purposes for chargeable periods beginning on or after 1 July 2010.

828 Relief on transfer

(1) If the proceeds of realisation of a relevant asset exceed the cost of the asset recognised for tax purposes, the proceeds are treated as reduced.

(2) If the securities are the whole consideration for the transfer, the reduction is by the amount of the excess.

(3) If the securities are not the whole of that consideration, the reduction is by the appropriate proportion of the excess.

(4) In subsection (3) "the appropriate proportion" means the proportion that the market value of the securities at the time of the transfer bears to the market value of the whole of the consideration at that time.

Commentary—*Simon's Taxes* **D1.662**.
Derivation—FA 2002 Sch 29 para 86(3).
HMRC Manuals—Corporate Intangibles Research and Development Manual CIRD42045 (company reorganisation: transfer of foreign permanent establishment from UK to a non resident company: amount of charge deferred).

829 Charge on subsequent realisations

(1) If at any time after the transfer the transferor realises the whole or part of the securities held by it immediately before that time, the transferor must bring into account for tax purposes a credit equal to the whole or the appropriate proportion of the total deferred gain.

(2) In subsection (1)—

"the total deferred gain" means the sum of the amounts by which the proceeds of realisation of relevant assets were reduced under section 828(2) or (3), so far as not already taken into account under subsection (1) or (3) of this section, and

"the appropriate proportion" means the proportion that the market value of the part of the securities realised bears to the market value of the securities held immediately before the realisation.

(3) If at any time within 6 years after the transfer the transferee realises all or some of the relevant assets held by it immediately before that time, the transferor must bring into account for tax purposes a credit equal to the whole or the appropriate proportion of the total deferred gain.

(4) In subsection (3)—

"the total deferred gain" has the meaning given in subsection (2), and

"the appropriate proportion" means the proportion that the deferred gain attributable to the relevant assets realised bears to the deferred gain attributable to the relevant assets held immediately before the realisation.

(5) For the purposes of subsection (4) the deferred gain attributable to relevant assets means the sum of the amounts by which the proceeds of realisation of those assets were reduced under section 828(2) or (3).

(6) For cases where transfers are ignored for the purposes of subsection (1) or (3), see section 830.

Commentary—*Simon's Taxes* **D1.662**.
Derivation—FA 2002 Sch 29 para 86(4), (5).
HMRC Manuals—Corporate Intangibles Research and Development Manual CIRD42050 (when does deferral under FA02/SCH29/PARA86 cease?

830 Exclusion from section 829 of group transfers

(1) For the purposes of section 829(1), any disposal within section 171 of TCGA 1992 (transfers within a group) is ignored.

(2) For the purposes of section 829(3), any transfer by one member of a group to another is ignored.

(3) This subsection applies if—

(a) a person ("A") acquires securities on a transfer that is ignored under subsection (1), and

(b) any previous transfer that has occurred was ignored under subsection (1) or (2).

(4) If subsection (3) applies, a subsequent realisation of the securities by A is treated as a realisation by the transferor.

(5) This subsection applies if—

(a) a person ("B") acquires an asset on a transfer that is ignored under subsection (2), and

(b) no previous transfer has occurred that was not ignored under subsection (1) or (2).

(6) If subsection (5) applies, a subsequent realisation of the asset by B is treated as a realisation by the transferee.

Commentary—*Simon's Taxes* **D1.662**.
Derivation—FA 2002 Sch 29 para 86(6), (7).
HMRC Manuals—Corporate Intangibles Research and Development Manual CIRD42055 (intangible assets: company reorganisation: transfer of foreign permanent establishment from UK to a non resident company: further deferral).

The genuine commercial transaction requirement and clearance

831 The genuine commercial transaction requirement and clearance

(1) For the purposes of this Chapter, a reconstruction, transfer or merger meets the genuine commercial transaction requirement if it—

(a) is effected for genuine commercial reasons, and

(b) does not form part of a scheme or arrangements of which the main purpose, or one of the main purposes, is avoidance of liability to corporation tax, capital gains tax or income tax.

(2) The conditions in subsection (1) are treated as met if before the reconstruction, transfer or merger—

(2) Sections 838 to 840 (rights and powers to be taken into account) apply in relation to the determination for the purposes of this Chapter whether a person has control of a company.

Commentary—*Simon's Taxes* **D1.601B, A1.156**.

Derivation—FA 2002 Sch 29 para 96(1), (3).

HMRC Manuals—Corporate Intangibles Research and Development Manual CIRD45150 (related party rules: definition of control).

837 "Major interest"

(1) For the purposes of this Chapter, a person has a "major interest" in a company if—

- (a) the person and one other person together have control of that company, and
- (b) the rights and powers by means of which they have such control represent, in the case of each of them, at least 40% of the total.

(2) The reference in subsection (1)(a) to two persons together having control of a company is to two persons who, taken together, have the power mentioned in section 836.

(3) Sections 838 to 840 (rights and powers to be taken into account) apply in relation to the determination for the purposes of this Chapter whether a person has a major interest in a company.

Commentary—*Simon's Taxes* **D1.601B**.

Derivation—FA 2002 Sch 29 para 96(2), (3).

HMRC Manuals—Corporate Intangibles Research and Development Manual CIRD45160 (related party rules: definition of control: major interest).

Rights and powers to be taken into account

838 General rule

(1) This section provides for a person ("A") to be treated as having rights and powers where A's rights or powers are relevant in determining if a person—

- (a) has control of a company, or
- (b) has a major interest in a company.

(2) A is treated as having rights and powers that A—

- (a) is entitled to acquire at a future date, or
- (b) will, at a future date, become entitled to acquire.

(3) A is treated as having rights and powers of other persons, so far as they are required or may be required to be exercised in any one or more of the following ways—

- (a) on A's behalf,
- (b) under A's direction, or
- (c) for A's benefit.

(4) A is treated as having rights and powers of a person connected with A (see section 842).

(5) A is treated as having rights and powers that a person connected with A would be treated as having if that person were a person whose rights or powers are relevant in determining if a person has control of or a major interest in a company.

(6) For the purposes of subsections (3) to (5), a person is treated as having rights or powers that the person—

- (a) is entitled to acquire at a future date, or
- (b) will, at a future date, become entitled to acquire.

(7) Subsection (3) does not apply to rights and powers conferred in relation to property of a borrower by the terms of any security relating to the borrower's loan.

Commentary—*Simon's Taxes* **D1.601B**.

Derivation—FA 2002 Sch 29 para 97(1)–(4).

HMRC Manuals—Corporate Intangibles Research and Development Manual CIRD45195 (attribution of rights and powers).

839 Rights and powers held jointly

(1) References in this Chapter—

- (a) to rights and powers of a person, or
- (b) to rights and powers that a person is or will become entitled to acquire,

include rights or powers that are exercisable by that person, or when acquired will be exercisable by that person, only jointly with one or more other persons.

(2) Subsection (1) is subject to section 840 (partnerships).

Commentary—*Simon's Taxes* **D1.601B**.

Derivation—FA 2002 Sch 29 para 98(1), (2).

HMRC Manuals—Corporate Intangibles Research and Development Manual CIRD45200 (jointly held interests).

840 Partnerships

(1) The rights and powers of a person as a member of a firm are ignored unless the person has control of or a major interest in the firm.

(2) Whether a person has control of or a major interest in a firm is determined in accordance with sections 836 to 839 as in relation to a company.

(3) For the purposes of subsection (2), references in those sections to any other company must be read as including any other firm.

Commentary—*Simon's Taxes* **D1.601B**.

Derivation—FA 2002 Sch 29 para 99(1), (2).

HMRC Manuals—Corporate Intangibles Research and Development Manual CIRD45200 (jointly held interests).

Meaning of "participator" and "associate"

841 "Participator" and "associate"

(1) In this Chapter "participator", in relation to a close company, has the meaning [given by section 454 of CTA 2010][1], except as provided in subsection (2).

(2) "Participator" does not include a person just because the person is a loan creditor of the company within the meaning [given by section 453 of CTA 2010][1].

(3) In this Chapter "associate", in relation to a participator in a close company, has the meaning given by [section 448 of CTA 2010][1].

Commentary—*Simon's Taxes* **D1.601B**.

Derivation—FA 2002 Sch 29 para 100(1), (2).

HMRC Manuals—Company Taxation Manual CTM60107 (tests: participator).

CTM60130 (loan creditor: meaning).

CTM60150 (associates: meaning).

Amendments—[1] In sub-s (1), words substituted for words "it has for the purposes of Part 11 of ICTA (close companies) (see section 417(1) of that Act)", in sub-s (2), words substituted for words "of that Part (see section 417(7) to (9) of ICTA)", sub-s (3), words substituted for words "section 417(3) of ICTA" by CTA 2010 s 1177, Sch 1 para 657. CTA 2010 has effect for corporation tax purposes for accounting periods ending on or after 1 April 2010, and for income and capital gains tax purposes for the tax year 2010–11 and subsequent tax years.

Connected persons

842 Introduction

(1) Section 843 explains what is meant in this Chapter when a person is referred to as being connected with another person.

(2) If that section provides that one person ("A") is connected with another person ("B"), B is connected with A too.

(3) In that section—

"relative" means brother, sister, ancestor or lineal descendant, and

"settlement" and "settlor" have the same meaning as in Chapter 5 of Part 5 of ITTOIA (see section 620 of that Act).

Commentary—*Simon's Taxes* **D1.601B**.

Derivation—FA 2002 Sch 29 para 101(1)–(3).

HMRC Manuals—Corporate Intangibles Research and Development Manual CIRD45190 (power to attribute interests of one person to another: connected persons).

843 Who are connected persons

(1) An individual ("A") is connected with another individual ("B") if—

    (a) A is B's spouse or civil partner,

    (b) A is a relative of B,

    (c) A is the spouse or civil partner of a relative of B,

    (d) A is a relative of B's spouse or civil partner, or

    (e) A is the spouse or civil partner of a relative of B's spouse or civil partner.

(2) A person in the capacity of a trustee of a settlement is connected with—

    (a) any individual who is a settlor in relation to the settlement,

    (b) any person connected with such an individual, and

    (c) any body corporate that is connected with the settlement.

(3) For the purposes of subsection (2) a body corporate is connected with a settlement if—

    (a) it is a close company (or not a close company only because it is not UK resident) and the participators include the trustees of the settlement, or

    (b) it is controlled by a company within paragraph (a).

(4) A person is connected with a company if they are related parties because of section 835(2) or (3).

(5) For the purposes of subsection (4) and for the purposes of section 835 as it applies for the purposes of subsection (4)—

    (a) "company" includes any body corporate or unincorporated association, but does not include a firm, and

    (b) a unit trust scheme is treated as if it were a company and as if the rights of the unit holders were shares in the company.

Commentary—*Simon's Taxes* **D1.601B**.

Derivation—FA 2002 Sch 29 para 101(2)–(6).

HMRC Manuals—Corporate Intangibles Research and Development Manual CIRD45190 (power to attribute interests of one person to another: definition: connected persons).

(b) in a case where that section applies and the asset is transferred to the company from the related party, the transfer is at more than its market value, and

(c) conditions A and B apply.

(2) Condition A is that the related party—

(a) is not a company, or

(b) is a company in relation to which the asset is not a chargeable intangible asset immediately after the transfer to it or, as the case may be, immediately before the transfer from it.

(3) Condition B is that the transfer—

(a) gives rise to an amount to be taken into account in calculating any person's income, profits or losses for tax purposes because of a relevant provision, or

(b) would do so apart from section 845(1).

(4) If this section applies, section 845(1) does not apply in relation to the calculation referred to in subsection (3) for the purposes of any relevant provision.

(5) In this section "relevant provision" means—

(a) [Chapter 2 of Part 23 of CTA 2010 (matters which are distributions), except section 1000(2),][1] and

(b) Part 3 of ITEPA 2003 (employment income: earnings and benefits etc treated as earnings).

Commentary—*Simon's Taxes* D1.611A, D1.601B.

HMRC Manuals—Corporate Intangibles Research and Development Manual CIRD45033 (transfers giving rise to a distribution or employment income charge).

Amendments—[1] In sub-s (5)(a), words substituted for words "section 209 of ICTA (meaning of "distribution")," by CTA 2010 s 1177, Sch 1 para 658. CTA 2010 has effect for corporation tax purposes for accounting periods ending on or after 1 April 2010, and for income and capital gains tax purposes for the tax year 2010–11 and subsequent tax years.

848 Tax-neutral transfers

(1) Section 845 does not apply if the transfer is tax-neutral for the purposes of this Part as a result of any provision in this Part.

(2) For such provisions, see, in particular—

(a) section 775 (transfers within a group), and

(b) sections 818 to 826 (transfer of business or trade).

Commentary—*Simon's Taxes* D1.611A, D1.601B.
Derivation—FA 2002 Sch 29 para 92(4).

[848A Assets held for purposes of exempt foreign permanent establishments

(1) This section applies if—

(a) subsection (1) of section 775 (transfers within a group) would apply in relation to the transfer but for paragraph (c) of subsection (4) of that section, and

(b) the asset has not at all times when the election under section 18A had effect been held by the transferor wholly for the purposes of a permanent establishment such as is mentioned in that paragraph.

(2) The transfer is treated for the purposes of this Part as being at the following value—

WDV + FPEA

where—

WDV is the tax written-down value of the asset, and

FPEA is the amount which, for the purposes of Chapter 3A of Part 2, would in the case of the transferor be the foreign permanent establishments amount attributable to the transfer for the accounting period in which it took place if the transfer were at market value.][1]

Commentary—*Simon's Taxes* D1.646, D1.611A, D1.601B.

HMRC Manuals—International Manual INTM283020 (foreign permanent establishments of UK companies: intangible fixed assets: partial use).

Amendments—[1] This section inserted by FA 2011 s 48, Sch 13 paras 1, 8 with effect from 19 July 2011, subject to transitional provisions in FA 2011 Sch 13 paras 32–37.

849 Transfers involving gifts of business assets

(1) This section applies if—

(a) the asset is transferred to the company mentioned in section 845(1), and

(b) on a claim for relief under section 165 of TCGA 1992 (relief for gifts of business assets) in respect of the transfer, a reduction is made under section 165(4)(a).

(2) The transfer is treated for the purposes of this Part as being at market value, less the amount of the reduction.

(3) Any necessary adjustments may be made, by way of assessment, amendment of returns or otherwise, regardless of any relevant time limits.

Commentary—*Simon's Taxes* D1.611A, D1.601B.

HMRC Manuals—Corporate Intangibles Research and Development Manual CIRD45035 (transfers where CGT gift hold-over relief claimed).

[849A Disincorporation relief: transfer values for post-FA 2002 goodwill

(1) This section applies where—

(a) a company transfers its business to some or all of the shareholders of the company, and

(b) a claim for disincorporation relief in respect of the transfer has been made under section 58 of the Finance Act 2013.

(2) If section 735 applies to the transfer of the goodwill of the business, the transfer is treated for the purposes of this Part as being at the lower of—

    (a) the tax written-down value of the goodwill, and

    (b) its market value.

(3) If section 736 applies to the transfer of the goodwill of the business, the transfer is treated for the purposes of this Part as being at the lower of—

    (a) the cost of the goodwill, and

    (b) its market value.

(4) If section 738 applies to the transfer of the goodwill of the business, the proceeds of realisation of the goodwill are treated for the purposes of this Part as being nil.

(5) In subsection (2)(a) the reference to the tax written-down value of the goodwill is to its tax written-down value immediately before the transfer.

(6) In subsection (3)(a) "the cost of the goodwill" means the cost recognised for tax purposes (determined in accordance with section 736(6) and (7)).

(7) In this section market value has the meaning given in section 845(5).]¹

Commentary—*Simon's Taxes* **B9.202, D1.611A, D1.601B, C1.414.**

HMRC Manuals—Corporate Intangibles Research and Development Manual CIRD43150 (post FA 2002 goodwill: effect of disincorporation relief: computation: overview).
CIRD43200 (post FA 2002 goodwill: effect of disincorporation relief on company: goodwill written-down for tax).
CIRD43250 (post FA 2002 goodwill: effect of disincorporation relief on company: goodwill on balance sheet but not written-down).
CIRD43300 (post FA 2002 goodwill: effect of disincorporation relief on company: goodwill not on balance sheet).

Amendments—¹ Section 849A inserted by FA 2013 s 61(2), (5) with effect in relation to a transfer of a business with a business transfer date of 1 April 2013 or a later date.

[Grants treated as being at market value

849AB Grant of licence or other right treated as at market value

(1) This section applies if—

    (a) a company which holds an intangible asset grants a licence or other right in respect of the asset to a related party, or

    (b) a company is granted a licence or other right in respect of an intangible asset by a related party that holds the asset.

(2) The grant of the licence or other right is treated for all purposes of the Taxes Acts as being at market value as respects the grantor if—

    (a) the licence or other right was actually granted at less than market value, and

    (b) condition A or B is met.

(3) The grant of the licence or other right is treated for all purposes of the Taxes Acts as being at market value as respects the grantee if—

    (a) the licence or other right was actually granted at more than market value, and

    (b) condition A or B is met.

(4) Condition A is that the asset is a chargeable intangible asset in relation to the grantor immediately before the licence or right in respect of it is granted.

(5) Condition B is that the licence or right is a chargeable intangible asset in relation to the grantee immediately after it is granted.

(6) This section is subject to—

    (a) section 849AC (grants not at arm's length),²

    (b) section 849AD (grants involving other taxes)[, and

    (c) section 900F (special rules in respect of assets that were pre-FA 2002 assets etc).]²

(7) References in subsection (1) to a related party in relation to a company are to be read as including references to a person in circumstances where the participation condition is met as between that person and the company.

(8) References in subsection (7) to a company include a firm in a case where, for the purposes of section 1259, references in subsection (1) to a company are read as references to the firm.

(9) Section 148 of TIOPA 2010 (when the participation condition is met) applies for the purposes of subsection (7) as it applies for the purposes of section 147(1)(b) of TIOPA 2010.

(10) Subsection (11) applies where—

    (a) a gain on the grant by a firm of a licence or other right in respect of an intangible fixed asset is a gain to be taken into account for the purposes of section 1259, and

    (b) for those purposes, references in subsection (1) to a company are read as references to the firm.

(11) Where this subsection applies, the gain referred to in subsection (10)(a) is to be treated for the purposes of this section as if it were a chargeable realisation gain for the purposes of section 741(1) (meaning of "chargeable intangible asset").

(12) In this section—

855 Further provision about regulations under section 854

(1) Regulations under section 854 may provide that this Part applies as if the asset were an intangible fixed asset of the finance lessor and not a financial asset, even though the asset is accounted for by the finance lessor as a financial asset.

(2) The regulations may provide that this Part applies as if the amount at which the asset is recognised in the finance lessor's balance sheet were capitalised expenditure on an intangible fixed asset, but that—

    (a) no election may be made under section 730 (writing down at fixed rate: election for fixed-rate basis) in respect of that amount, and

    (b) that amount is not to be treated as capitalised expenditure for the purposes of section 756(2) (roll-over relief in case of realisation and reinvestment: conditions to be met in relation to expenditure on other assets).

(3) The regulations may provide that if an asset formerly recognised by the finance lessor for accounting purposes as an intangible fixed asset becomes subject to a finance lease (and so comes to be accounted for as a financial asset), the value of the asset so created is recognised as realisation proceeds of the intangible fixed asset on the change of accounting treatment.

(4) The regulations may provide that assets partially excluded from this Part by sections 810 to 813 . . . [1] (assets excluded except as respects royalties) are entirely excluded from this Part as respects the finance lessor if they—

    (a) are subject to a finance lease, and

    (b) are accounted for by the finance lessor as financial assets.

(5) The regulations may provide for excluding from the regulations assets used by the finance lessee for the purposes of a trade or business in respect of which the finance lessee is liable to income tax.

(6) The regulations may provide that an intangible asset counts as a pre-FA 2002 asset in the hands of the finance lessor if the finance lessee is—

    (a) a company for which the asset was the whole or part of a pre-FA 2002 asset, or

    (b) a person who is a related party in relation to such a company.

(7) The regulations may make incidental, supplemental, consequential and transitional provision and savings.

(8) That provision may include modifications of the operation of other provisions of the Corporation Tax Acts.

Commentary—*Simon's Taxes* **D1.603.**

Derivation—FA 2002 Sch 29 para 104(2), (3).

HMRC Manuals—Corporate Intangibles Research and Development Manual CIRD27050 (finance leasing of intangible assets: lessors: general).

CIRD27090 (finance leasing of intangible assets: text of financial instrument SI2002/1967).

Amendments—[1] In sub-s (4), words "or section 902 " repealed by FA 2012 s 146, Sch 16 paras 135, 178 with effect in relation to accounting periods of companies beginning on or after 1 January 2013 (subject to transitional provisions in FA 2012 Sch 17). For accounting periods straddling 1 January 2013, see FA 2012 s 149.

Values to be used in special cases

856 Assets acquired or realised together

(1) Any reference in this Part to the acquisition or realisation of an asset includes a reference to the acquisition or realisation of that asset together with other assets.

(2) For the purposes of this Part assets acquired or realised as a result of one bargain are treated as acquired or realised together even though—

    (a) separate prices are, or purport to be, agreed for separate assets, or

    (b) there are, or purport to be, separate acquisitions or realisations of separate assets.

(3) If assets are acquired together, any values allocated to particular assets by the company in accordance with generally accepted accounting practice must be accepted for the purposes of this Part.

(4) If no such values are so allocated, so much of the expenditure as on a just and reasonable apportionment is properly attributable to each asset is treated for the purposes of this Part as referable to that asset.

(5) If assets are realised together, so much of the proceeds of realisation as on a just and reasonable apportionment is properly attributable to each asset is treated for the purposes of this Part as proceeds of the realisation of that asset.

Commentary—*Simon's Taxes* **D1.602, D1.614, D6.438.**

Derivation—FA 2002 Sch 29 para 105(1)–(4).

HMRC Manuals—Corporate Intangibles Research and Development Manual CIRD12730 (attribution of costs where intangible asset acquired as part of a larger bargain).

CIRD12740 (just and reasonable apportionment).

CIRD12735 (GAAP acquisition accounting).

CIRD13245 (realisation proceeds: assets disposed of together).

857 Deemed market value acquisition: adjustment where nil accounting value

(1) This section applies if—

    (a) a company is treated for the purposes of this Part as acquiring an asset at market value, but

(b) the accounting value of the asset transferred is nil in the hands of the transferee.
(2) In such a case any reference in this Part to—
    (a) the cost of the asset recognised for accounting purposes,
    (b) the accounting value of the asset, or
    (c) any loss recognised for accounting purposes in respect of capitalised expenditure on the asset,
is a reference to the cost, value or loss that would have been recognised if the asset had been acquired at market value.
(3) If the asset is revalued, the revaluation is ignored.
(4) In this section "revaluation" has the same meaning as in section 723 (see subsection (5) of that section) and "revalued" must be read accordingly.
Commentary—*Simon's Taxes* **D1.649, D1.611A, D1.601B.**
Derivation—FA 2002 Sch 29 para 106(1), (2).
HMRC Manuals—Corporate Intangibles Research and Development Manual CIRD12780 (accounts-based relief).

Fungible assets

858 Fungible assets
(1) For the purposes of this Part—
    (a) fungible assets of the same kind that are held by the same person in the same capacity are
        treated as indistinguishable parts of a single asset,
    (b) that asset is treated as growing as additional assets of the same kind are created or acquired,
        and
    (c) that asset is treated as diminishing as some of the assets are realised.
(2) In this Part "fungible assets" means assets of a nature to be dealt in without identifying the particular assets involved.[1]
Commentary—*Simon's Taxes* **D1.602.**
Derivation—FA 2002 Sch 29 para 107(1), (2).
HMRC Manuals—Corporate Intangibles Research and Development Manual CIRD11760 (general treatment of fungible assets).
Amendments—[1] Section 858 repealed by FA 2020 s 31(1), (5) with effect in relation to accounting periods beginning on or after 1 July 2020. An accounting period beginning before, and ending on or after, 1 July 2020 is to be treated as if so much of the accounting period as falls before that date, and so much of the accounting period as falls on or after that date, were separate accounting periods (FA 2020 s 31(15)).

Assets ceasing to be or becoming chargeable intangible assets

859 Asset ceasing to be chargeable intangible asset: deemed realisation at market value
(1) If an asset ceases to be a chargeable intangible asset in relation to a company in any of the circumstances specified in subsection (2), this Part applies as if—
    (a) immediately before the asset ceased to be a chargeable intangible asset in relation to the company, the company had realised the asset for its market value at that time, and
    (b) the company had immediately reacquired it at that value.
(2) The circumstances are—
    (a) that the company ceases to be UK resident,
    (b) in the case of a company that is not UK resident, any circumstances not involving the realisation of the asset by the company, and
    (c) that the asset begins to be held for the purposes of a mutual trade or business.
(3) Subsection (1) is subject to section 860.[1]
Commentary—*Simon's Taxes* **D1.629H.**
Derivation—FA 2002 Sch 29 para 108(1), (2).
HMRC Manuals—Corporate Intangibles Research and Development Manual CIRD13270 (asset deemed to be realised while remaining in hands of company).
Amendments—[1] Sub-s (3) repealed by FA 2019 s 23, Sch 8 para 10(2), (3) with effect in relation to a company in a case where this section applies to the company by reason of its ceasing to be resident in the United Kingdom on or after 1 January 2020.

863 Asset becoming chargeable intangible asset
(1) This section applies if an asset becomes a chargeable intangible asset in relation to a company—
    (a) on the company becoming UK resident,
    (b) in the case of a company that is not UK resident, on the asset beginning to be held[—
        (i)]for the purposes of a trade carried on by the company in the United Kingdom through a permanent establishment,
        [(ii) for the purposes of a trade carried on by the company of dealing in or developing UK land,
        (iii) for the purposes of a UK property business carried on by the company, or
        (iv) for the purposes of enabling the company to generate other UK property income (within the meaning given by section 5(5)),][2]
    (c) on the asset ceasing to be held for the purposes of a mutual trade or business.
(2) This Part applies as if—
    (a) the company had acquired the asset immediately after it became a chargeable intangible asset in relation to the company, and

HMRC Manuals—Corporate Intangibles Research and Development Manual CIRD12640 (deferral of tax relief for delayed pension contributions).

869 Bad debts etc

(1) No debit may be brought into account for the purposes of this Part in respect of a debt owed to the company, except—

    (a) by way of impairment loss, or

    (b) so far as the debt is released as part of a statutory insolvency arrangement.

(2) If a debt is so released, any gain in respect of the release that is brought into account for accounting purposes by the debtor is disregarded for the purposes of this Part.

(3) Any other gain in respect of an unpaid debt in respect of an intangible fixed asset that is brought into account by the debtor for accounting purposes is treated for the purposes of section 721 (receipts recognised as they accrue) as a gain in respect of an intangible fixed asset.

(4) Any adjustment required by this section of an accounting gain or loss that is partly referable to an amount affected by this section and partly to other matters must be made on a just and reasonable basis.

(5) In this section "debt" includes an obligation or liability that falls to be discharged otherwise than by the payment of money.

Commentary—*Simon's Taxes* D1.614.

Derivation—FA 2002 Sch 29 para 115(1), (3)–(6).

HMRC Manuals—Corporate Intangibles Research and Development Manual CIRD12670 (debt impairment losses and bad debts).

[Roll-over relief under TCGA 1992]

870A Claims for relief made under sections 152 and 153 of TCGA 1992

(1) Subsection (2) applies where—

    (a) a company has made a claim for relief under section 152 or 153 of TCGA 1992 (roll-over relief) during the period beginning with 1 April 2009 and ending with 19 March 2014, and

    (b) the relief claimed relates to disposal proceeds that are applied in acquiring an intangible fixed asset within the meaning of this Part.

(2) The company is treated for the purposes of this Part as if the cost of the asset recognised for tax purposes were reduced on 19 March 2014 by the amount in respect of which the relief under section 152 or 153 of TCGA 1992 is given.

(3) But the effect of subsection (2) must not be to reduce the tax written-down value of the asset to below nil.

(4) The references to adjustments in sections 742(3) and 743(3) (assets written down) include any adjustment required by subsection (2).][1]

Commentary—*Simon's Taxes* D1.641.

Amendments—[1] Section 870A inserted by FA 2014 s 62(2) with effect in relation to accounting periods beginning on or after 19 March 2014. An accounting period beginning before, and ending on or after, 19 March 2014 is to be treated as if so much of the period as falls before that date, and so much of the period as falls on or after that date, were separate accounting periods.

CHAPTER 15

ADJUSTMENTS ON CHANGE OF ACCOUNTING POLICY

Introductory

871 Introduction to Chapter

(1) This Chapter applies if—

    (a) there is a change of accounting policy in drawing up a company's accounts from one period of account to the next, and

    (b) the approach in each of those periods accords with the law and practice applicable in relation to that period.

(2) In this Chapter—

    (a) the first of those periods of account is referred to as "the earlier period", and

    (b) the next is referred to as "the later period".

(3) This Chapter applies, in particular, if—

    (a) the company prepares accounts for the earlier period in accordance with UK generally accepted accounting practice and for the later period in accordance with international accounting standards, or

    (b) the company prepares accounts for the earlier period in accordance with international accounting standards and for the later period in accordance with UK generally accepted accounting practice.

Commentary—*Simon's Taxes* D1.629D, D1.629E.

Derivation—FA 2002 Sch 29 para 116A(1), (2).

HMRC Manuals—Corporate Intangibles Research and Development Manual CIRD12300 ((change in accounting value).

Change of policy involving change of value

872 Adjustments in respect of change

(1) This section and section 873 apply if—

   (a) as a result of the change of accounting policy there is a difference ("the accounting difference") between—

      (i) the accounting value of an intangible fixed asset of the company at the end of the earlier period, and

      (ii) the accounting value of that asset at the beginning of the later period, and

   (b) no election has been made in respect of the asset under section 730 (writing down at fixed rate: election for fixed-rate basis).

(2) If there is an increase in that value, a corresponding credit must be brought into account for tax purposes in the later period.

(3) If there is a decrease in that value, a corresponding debit must be brought into account for tax purposes in the later period.

(4) The amount of the credit or debit is—

$$D \times \frac{\text{WDVE}}{\text{AVE}}$$

where—

    D is the accounting difference,

    WDVE is the tax written-down value of the asset at the end of the earlier period, and

    AVE is the accounting value of the asset at the end of the earlier period.

(5) But if subsection (2) applies, the credit must not exceed—

   (a) the sum of debits brought into account for tax purposes in respect of the asset before the later period, less

   (b) the sum of the credits so brought into account.

(6) This section is subject to section 878 (exclusion of credits or debits brought into account under other provisions).

Commentary—*Simon's Taxes* **D1.629D, D1.629E.**

Derivation—FA 2002 Sch 29 paras 116B(1), (3), (6), (7), 116F(1), (2).

HMRC Manuals—Corporate Intangibles Research and Development Manual CIRD12300 (change in accounting value).

873 Effect of application of section 872 in later period and subsequently

(1) A credit or debit that is required to be brought into account under section 872 is treated as arising at the beginning of the later period ("the relevant time").

(2) If a credit is to be brought into account, the tax written-down value of the asset at the relevant time is the sum of—

   (a) the tax written-down value of the asset at the end of the earlier period, and

   (b) the credit.

(3) If a debit is to be brought into account, the tax written-down value of the asset at the relevant time is—

   (a) the tax written-down value of the asset at the end of the earlier period, less

   (b) the debit.

(4) After the relevant time the cost recognised for tax purposes is the sum of—

   (a) the tax written-down value given by subsection (2) or (3), and

   (b) the cost recognised for tax purposes of any subsequent expenditure on the asset that is capitalised for accounting purposes.

(5) After the relevant time the tax written-down value is determined taking account only of subsequent credits and debits.

Change of policy involving disaggregation

874 Original asset not subject to fixed-rate writing down

(1) This section and section 875 apply if—

   (a) the change of accounting policy results in an intangible fixed asset of the company that was treated as one asset ("the original asset") in the earlier period being treated as two or more assets ("the resulting assets") in the later period,

   (b) there is a difference ("the accounting difference") between—

      (i) the accounting value of the original asset at the end of the earlier period, and

      (ii) the sum of the accounting values of the resulting assets at the beginning of the later period,

   (c) no election under section 730 (writing down at fixed rate: election for fixed-rate basis) has been or is subsequently made in respect of the original asset, and

   (d) no such election is subsequently made in respect of any of the resulting assets.

(2) If the accounting difference is an increase, a corresponding credit must be brought into account for tax purposes in the later period.

(3) If the accounting difference is a decrease, a corresponding debit must be brought into account for tax purposes in the later period.

(4) The credit or debit is—

$$D \times \frac{\text{WDVE}}{\text{AVE}}$$

where—

    D is the accounting difference,

    WDVE is the tax written-down value of the original asset at the end of the earlier period, and

    AVE is the accounting value of that asset at the end of that period.

(5) But if subsection (2) applies the credit must not exceed—

    (a) the sum of the debits brought into account for tax purposes in respect of the original asset before the later period, less

    (b) the sum of the credits so brought into account.

(6) This section is subject to section 878 (exclusion of credits or debits brought into account under other provisions).

Commentary—*Simon's Taxes* **D1.629D, D1.629E**.

Derivation—FA 2002 Sch 29 paras 116C(1), (2), (4), (7), (8), 116F(1), (3).

HMRC Manuals—Corporate Intangibles Research and Development Manual CIRD12310 (treatment of accounting difference on disaggregated asset).

875 Effect of application of section 874 in later period and subsequently

(1) A credit or debit that is required to be brought into account under section 874 is treated as arising at the beginning of the later period ("the relevant time").

(2) If section 874(2) applies, the tax written-down value of each resulting asset at the relevant time is—

$$(\text{WDVE} + \text{C}) \times \frac{\text{AV}}{\text{TAV}}$$

where—

    WDVE is the tax written-down value of the original asset at the end of the earlier period,

    C is the credit,

    AV is the accounting value of the resulting asset in question at the relevant time, and

    TAV is the sum of the accounting values of all the resulting assets at the relevant time.

(3) If section 874(3) applies, the tax written-down value of each resulting asset at the relevant time is—

$$(\text{WDVE} + \text{D}) \times \frac{\text{AV}}{\text{TAV}}$$

where—

    WDVE, AV and TAV have the same meaning as in subsection (2), and

    D is the debit.

(4) After the relevant time the cost recognised for tax purposes for each resulting asset is taken to be the sum of—

    (a) the tax written-down value given by subsection (2) or, as the case may be, subsection (3), and

    (b) the cost recognised for tax purposes of any subsequent expenditure on the asset that is capitalised for accounting purposes.

(5) After the relevant time the tax written-down value for each resulting asset is determined taking account only of subsequent credits and debits.

876 Original asset subject to fixed-rate writing down

(1) This section applies if—

    (a) the change of accounting policy results in an intangible fixed asset of the company that was treated as one asset ("the original asset") in the earlier period being treated as two or more assets ("the resulting assets") in the later period, and

    (b) an election under section 730 (writing down at fixed rate: election for fixed-rate basis) has been or is subsequently made in respect of the original asset.

(2) That election has effect—

    (a) in relation to the original asset, for periods up to and including the earlier period, and

    (b) in relation to each of the resulting assets, for the later period and subsequent periods.

(3) The tax written-down value of each resulting asset at the beginning of the later period ("the relevant time") is—

$$\text{WDVE} \times \frac{\text{AVL}}{\text{TAVL}}$$

where—

WDVE is the tax written-down value of the original asset at the end of the earlier period,

AVL is the accounting value of the asset in question at the beginning of the later period, and

TAVL is the sum of the accounting values of all the resulting assets at the beginning of that period.

(4) After the relevant time the cost recognised for tax purposes for each resulting asset is the sum of—

　　(a) the tax written-down value given by subsection (3), and

　　(b) the cost recognised for tax purposes of any subsequent expenditure on the asset that is capitalised for accounting purposes.

(5) After the relevant time the tax written-down value for each resulting asset is determined taking account only of subsequent credits and debits.

Commentary—*Simon's Taxes* **D1.629D, D1.629E.**
Derivation—FA 2002 Sch 29 para 116D(1)–(4).
HMRC Manuals—Corporate Intangibles Research and Development Manual CIRD12905 (relief for capitalised expenditure on an intangible asset: fixed rate relief: general).

877 Election for fixed-rate writing down in relation to resulting asset

(1) This section applies if—

　　(a) the change of accounting policy results in an intangible fixed asset of the company that was treated as one asset ("the original undivided asset") in the earlier period being treated as two or more assets ("the resulting assets") in the later period, and

　　(b) no election under section 730 (writing down at fixed rate: election for fixed-rate basis) has been or is subsequently made in respect of the original undivided asset.

(2) An election under that section may be made in respect of any of the resulting assets.

(3) But such an election may be made only within the period during which such an election could have been made in relation to the original undivided asset.

(4) The effect of the election is that—

　　(a) the original undivided asset is treated as if it had at all material times consisted of as many assets ("notional original assets") as there are resulting assets,

　　(b) each notional original asset is taken to be the same asset as one of the resulting assets (its "corresponding resulting asset"),

　　(c) the appropriate proportion of every amount falling to be taken into account in relation to the original undivided asset is attributed to each of the notional original assets, and

　　(d) this Part applies in relation to each of the notional original assets and its corresponding resulting asset accordingly.

(5) For the purposes of subsection (4)(c) the appropriate proportion of every amount falling to be taken into account in relation to the original undivided asset that is to be attributed to each notional original asset is found by reference to the notional original asset's corresponding resulting asset.

(6) The appropriate proportion in relation to each resulting asset is—

$$\frac{\text{AVL}}{\text{TAVL}}$$

where—

AVL is the accounting value of that resulting asset at the beginning of the later period, and

TAVL is the sum of the accounting values of all the resulting assets at the beginning of that period.

Commentary—*Simon's Taxes* **D1.629D, D1.629E.**
Derivation—FA 2002 Sch 29 para 116E(1)–(4).
HMRC Manuals—Corporate Intangibles Research and Development Manual CIRD12905 (relief for capitalised expenditure on an intangible asset: fixed rate relief: general).

Supplementary

878 Exclusion of credits or debits brought into account under other provisions

(1) A credit or debit is not required to be brought into account under this Chapter so far as a credit or debit representing the accounting difference in question is brought into account for tax purposes under a provision specified in subsection (2).

(2) Those provisions are—

　　(a) section 723 (revaluation),

(*b*) section 725 (reversal of previous accounting loss), or

(*c*) section 732 (reversal of previous accounting gain).

Commentary—*Simon's Taxes* **D1.629D, D1.629E**.

Derivation—FA 2002 Sch 29 para 116G.

HMRC Manuals—Corporate Intangibles Research and Development Manual CIRD12300 (primacy of other parts of part 8).

879 Subsequent events affecting asset subject to adjustment under this Chapter

(1) On a further change of accounting policy affecting an intangible fixed asset in relation to which this Chapter has applied, the previous provisions of this Chapter apply again.

(2) On a subsequent part realisation affecting the asset in question, section 744 (effect of part realisation of asset) applies.

[CHAPTER 15A

DEBITS IN RESPECT OF GOODWILL AND CERTAIN OTHER ASSETS

Introduction

879A Introduction

(1) This Chapter contains special rules about the debits to be brought into account by a company for tax purposes in respect of relevant assets.

(2) In this Chapter "relevant asset" means—

(*a*) goodwill in a business or part of a business,

(*b*) an intangible fixed asset that consists of information which relates to customers or potential customers of a business or part of a business,

(*c*) an intangible fixed asset that consists of a relationship (whether contractual or not) between a person carrying on a business and one or more customers of that business or part of that business,

(*d*) an unregistered trade mark or other sign used in the course of a business or part of a business, or

(*e*) a licence or other right in respect of an asset within any of paragraphs (*a*) to (*d*).][1]

Amendments—[1] Sections 879A–879P inserted by FA 2019 s 25, Sch 9 paras 1, 6 with effect in relation to accounting periods beginning on or after 1 April 2019. An accounting period beginning before, and ending on or after, 1 April 2019 is to be treated as if so much of the accounting period as falls before that date, and so much of the accounting period as falls on or after that date, were separate accounting periods (FA 2019 Sch 9 para 7(2)).

[Requirement to write down at a fixed rate

879B Requirement to write down at a fixed rate

(1) This section applies if a company acquires or creates a relevant asset on or after 1 April 2019.

(2) The company is to be treated as having made an election under section 730 to write down the cost of the asset for tax purposes at a fixed rate.

(3) In its application in relation to the asset, section 731 (writing down at fixed rate: calculation) has effect as if in subsection (1)(*a*) for "4%" there was substituted "6.5%".

(4) The Treasury may by regulations amend subsection (3) so as to alter the percentage substituted for 4%.][1]

Amendments—[1] Sections 879A–879P inserted by FA 2019 s 25, Sch 9 paras 1, 6 with effect in relation to accounting periods beginning on or after 1 April 2019. An accounting period beginning before, and ending on or after, 1 April 2019 is to be treated as if so much of the accounting period as falls before that date, and so much of the accounting period as falls on or after that date, were separate accounting periods (FA 2019 Sch 9 para 7(2)).

[Restrictions on debits: pre-FA 2019 relevant assets

879C Restrictions on debits: pre-FA 2019 relevant assets

(1) This section applies in respect of a relevant asset of a company if it is a pre-FA 2019 relevant asset.

(2) No debits in respect of the asset are to be brought into account by the company for tax purposes under Chapter 3 (debits in respect of intangible fixed assets) or Chapter 15 (adjustments on change of accounting policy).

(3) Any debit in respect of the asset that is brought into account by the company for tax purposes under Chapter 4 (realisation of intangible fixed assets) is treated for the purposes of Chapter 6 as a non-trading debit.

(4) Sections 879D to 879H set out the cases in which a relevant asset of a company is a pre-FA 2019 relevant asset for the purposes of this Chapter.][1]

Amendments—[1] Sections 879A–879P inserted by FA 2019 s 25, Sch 9 paras 1, 6 with effect in relation to accounting periods beginning on or after 1 April 2019. An accounting period beginning before, and ending on or after, 1 April 2019 is to be treated as if so much of the accounting period as falls before that date, and so much of the accounting period as falls on or after that date, were separate accounting periods (FA 2019 Sch 9 para 7(2)).

[879D Pre-FA 2019 relevant asset: the first case

For the purposes of this Chapter a relevant asset of a company is a pre-FA 2019 relevant asset if—

(*a*) the company acquired or created the asset during the period beginning with 8 July 2015 and ending with 31 March 2019, and

(*b*) the asset was a chargeable intangible asset in relation to the company at any time during the period beginning with 29 October 2018 and ending with 31 March 2019.][1]

Amendments—[1] Sections 879A–879P inserted by FA 2019 s 25, Sch 9 paras 1, 6 with effect in relation to accounting periods beginning on or after 1 April 2019. An accounting period beginning before, and ending on or after, 1 April 2019 is to be treated as if so much of the accounting period as falls before that date, and so much of the accounting period as falls on or after that date, were separate accounting periods (FA 2019 Sch 9 para 7(2)).

[879E Pre-FA 2019 relevant asset: the second case

(1) For the purposes of this Chapter a relevant asset of a company ("C") is a pre-FA 2019 relevant asset if—

(*a*) another company acquired or created the asset during the period beginning with 8 July 2015 and ending with 31 March 2019,

(*b*) it was a chargeable intangible asset in relation to that other company at any time during the period beginning with 29 October 2018 and ending with 31 March 2019, and

(*c*) C acquired the asset on or after 1 April 2019 otherwise than in case A or case B from a person who was a related party in relation to C.

(2) Case A is where—

(*a*) C acquired the asset from a company that was within the charge to corporation tax at the time of the acquisition, and

(*b*) the asset was not a pre-FA 2019 relevant asset in the hands of that company immediately before the acquisition.

(3) Case B is where C acquired the asset from a person ("the intermediary") who acquired the asset on or after 1 April 2019 from a third person—

(*a*) who was not at the time of the intermediary's acquisition a related party in relation—

(i) to the intermediary, or

(ii) if the intermediary was not a company, to a company in relation to which the intermediary was a related party, and

(*b*) who is not, at the time of the acquisition by C, a related party in relation to C.

(4) References in this section to one person being (or not being) a related party in relation to another person are to be read as including references to the participation condition being met (or, as the case may be not being met) as between those persons.

(5) References in subsection (4) to a person include a firm in a case where, for section 1259 purposes, references in this section to a company are read as references to the firm.

(6) In subsection (5) "section 1259 purposes" means the purposes of determining under section 1259 the amount of profits or losses to be allocated to a partner in a firm.

(7) Section 148 of TIOPA 2010 (when the participation condition is met) applies for the purposes of subsection (4) as it applies for the purpose of section 147(1)(*b*) of TIOPA 2010.][1]

Amendments—[1] Sections 879A–879P inserted by FA 2019 s 25, Sch 9 paras 1, 6 with effect in relation to accounting periods beginning on or after 1 April 2019. An accounting period beginning before, and ending on or after, 1 April 2019 is to be treated as if so much of the accounting period as falls before that date, and so much of the accounting period as falls on or after that date, were separate accounting periods (FA 2019 Sch 9 para 7(2)).

[879F Pre-FA 2019 relevant asset: the third case

(1) For the purposes of this Chapter a relevant asset of a company ("C") is a pre-FA 2019 relevant asset if—

(*a*) the relevant asset was created on or after 29 October 2018,

(*b*) C acquired the relevant asset on or after 1 April 2019 from a person ("the transferor") who was a related party in relation to C at the time of the acquisition,

(*c*) the value of the relevant asset derives in whole or in part from another asset ("the other asset"), and

(*d*) the other asset meets the preserved status condition (see section 879G).

(2) But if only part of the value of the relevant asset derives from the other asset—

(*a*) the relevant asset is to be treated for the purposes of this Chapter as if it were two separate assets—

(i) one representing the part of the value of the relevant asset that does so derive, and

(ii) the other representing the part of the value of the relevant asset that does not so derive, and

(*b*) subsection (1) applies only in relation to the separate asset representing the part of the value of the relevant asset that does so derive.

(3) For the purposes of this section the cases in which the value of a relevant asset may be derived from another asset include any case where—

(*a*) assets have been merged or divided,

(*b*) assets have changed their nature, or

(*c*) rights or interests in or over assets have been created or extinguished.

(4) Section 879G supplements this section.][1]

Amendments—[1]   Sections 879A–879P inserted by FA 2019 s 25, Sch 9 paras 1, 6 with effect in relation to accounting periods beginning on or after 1 April 2019. An accounting period beginning before, and ending on or after, 1 April 2019 is to be treated as if so much of the accounting period as falls before that date, and so much of the accounting period as falls on or after that date, were separate accounting periods (FA 2019 Sch 9 para 7(2)).

[879G The preserved status condition etc

(1) For the purposes of section 879F the other asset meets the preserved status condition if subsection (2) or (3) applies.

(2) This subsection applies if the other asset—

    (*a*) was acquired or created by a company during the period beginning with 8 July 2015 and ending with 31 March 2019, and

    (*b*) was a chargeable intangible asset in the hands of that company at any time during the period beginning with 29 October 2018 and ending with 31 March 2019 when—

        (i) that company and C were related parties, or

        (ii) that company and the transferor were related parties.

(3) This subsection applies if the other asset was a pre-FA 2019 relevant asset in the hands of a company at any time during the period beginning with 1 April 2019 and ending with the acquisition mentioned in section 879F(1)(*b*) when—

    (*a*) that company and C were related parties, or

    (*b*) that company and the transferor were related parties.

(4) It does not matter for the purposes of section 879F(1)(*a*) who created the relevant asset.

(5) Any apportionment necessary for the purposes of section 879F(2) must be made on a just and reasonable basis.

(6) Section 879E(4) to (7) applies for the purposes of section 879F and this section.

(7) Expressions used in this section have the same meaning as in section 879F.][1]

Amendments—[1]   Sections 879A–879P inserted by FA 2019 s 25, Sch 9 paras 1, 6 with effect in relation to accounting periods beginning on or after 1 April 2019. An accounting period beginning before, and ending on or after, 1 April 2019 is to be treated as if so much of the accounting period as falls before that date, and so much of the accounting period as falls on or after that date, were separate accounting periods (FA 2019 Sch 9 para 7(2)).

[879H Pre-FA 2019 relevant asset: the fourth case

(1) For the purposes of this Chapter a relevant asset of a company is a pre-FA 2019 relevant asset if—

    (*a*) the company acquired the asset on or after 1 April 2019 directly or indirectly in consequence of, or otherwise in connection with, a disposal of a relevant asset by another person, and

    (*b*) the asset disposed of would have been a pre-FA 2019 relevant asset in the hands of the company had the person transferred it to the company at the time of the disposal.

(2) For the purposes of this section it does not matter whether—

    (*a*) the asset disposed of is the same asset as the acquired asset,

    (*b*) the acquired asset is acquired at the time of the disposal, or

    (*c*) the acquired asset is acquired by merging assets or otherwise.][1]

Amendments—[1]   Sections 879A–879P inserted by FA 2019 s 25, Sch 9 paras 1, 6 with effect in relation to accounting periods beginning on or after 1 April 2019. An accounting period beginning before, and ending on or after, 1 April 2019 is to be treated as if so much of the accounting period as falls before that date, and so much of the accounting period as falls on or after that date, were separate accounting periods (FA 2019 Sch 9 para 7(2)).

[Restrictions on debits: no business or no qualifying IP assets acquired

879I Restrictions on debits: no business or no qualifying IP assets acquired

(1) This section applies in respect of a relevant asset of a company if the company acquires the asset on or after 1 April 2019 otherwise than as part of the acquisition of a business.

(2) This section also applies in respect of a relevant asset of a company if—

    (*a*) the company acquires the asset on or after 1 April 2019 as part of the acquisition of a business, and

    (*b*) the company does not acquire any qualifying IP assets as part of the acquisition of the business for use on a continuing basis in the course of the business.

(3) No debits in respect of the asset are to be brought into account by the company for tax purposes under Chapter 3 (debits in respect of intangible fixed assets) or Chapter 15 (adjustments on change of accounting policy).

(4) Any debit in respect of the asset that is brought into account by the company for tax purposes under Chapter 4 (realisation of intangible fixed assets) is treated for the purposes of Chapter 6 as a non-trading debit.][1]

Amendments—[1]   Sections 879A–879P inserted by FA 2019 s 25, Sch 9 paras 1, 6 with effect in relation to accounting periods beginning on or after 1 April 2019. An accounting period beginning before, and ending on or after, 1 April 2019 is to be treated as if so much of the accounting period as falls before that date, and so much of the accounting period as falls on or after that date, were separate accounting periods (FA 2019 Sch 9 para 7(2)).

[879J Meaning of qualifying IP asset

(1) In section 879I "qualifying IP asset", in relation to a company, means an intangible fixed asset that meets the following two conditions.

(2) The first condition is that the asset is—

    (*a*) a patent, registered design, copyright or design right, plant breeders' right, or right under section 7 of the Plant Varieties Act 1997,

    (*b*) a right under the law of a country or territory outside the United Kingdom corresponding or similar to a right within paragraph (*a*), or

    (*c*) a licence or other right in respect of anything within paragraph (*a*) or (*b*).

(3) The second condition is that in the hands of the company the asset—

    (*a*) is not to any extent excluded from this Part by Chapter 10, and

    (*b*) is not a pre-FA 2002 asset (see section 881).

(4) The reference in subsection (2)(*c*) to a licence or other right does not include a licence or other right that permits the use of computer software but does not permit its manufacture, adaptation or supply.

(5) The Treasury may by regulations amend the meaning of qualifying IP asset for the purposes of this Chapter.][1]

Amendments—[1]   Sections 879A–879P inserted by FA 2019 s 25, Sch 9 paras 1, 6 with effect in relation to accounting periods beginning on or after 1 April 2019. An accounting period beginning before, and ending on or after, 1 April 2019 is to be treated as if so much of the accounting period as falls before that date, and so much of the accounting period as falls on or after that date, were separate accounting periods (FA 2019 Sch 9 para 7(2)).

[Restrictions on debits: acquisition from individual or firm

879K Restrictions on debits: acquisition from individual or firm

(1) This section applies in respect of a relevant asset of a company if—

    (*a*) the company acquires the asset on or after 1 April 2019 directly or indirectly from an individual or firm ("the transferor"),

    (*b*) the related party condition is met, and

    (*c*) the third party acquisition condition is not met.

(2) The related party condition is met if—

    (*a*) in a case where the transferor is an individual, the transferor is a related party in relation to the company at the time of the acquisition;

    (*b*) in a case where the transferor is a firm, any individual who is a member of the transferor is a related party in relation to the company at that time.

(3) The third party acquisition condition is met if—

    (*a*) in a case where the relevant asset is goodwill—

        (i) the transferor acquired all or part of the relevant business in one or more third party acquisitions as part of which the transferor acquired goodwill, and

        (ii) the relevant asset is acquired by the company as part of an acquisition of all the relevant business;

    (*b*) in a case where the relevant asset is not goodwill—

        (i) the transferor acquired the relevant asset in a third party acquisition, and

        (ii) the relevant asset is acquired by the company as part of an acquisition of all the relevant business.

(4) No debits in respect of the asset are to be brought into account by the company for tax purposes under Chapter 3 (debits in respect of intangible fixed assets) or Chapter 15 (adjustments on change of accounting policy).

(5) Any debit in respect of the asset that is brought into account by the company for tax purposes under Chapter 4 (realisation of intangible fixed assets) is treated for the purposes of Chapter 6 as a non-trading debit.][1]

Commentary—*Simon's Taxes* **B9.120**.

Amendments—[1]   Sections 879A–879P inserted by FA 2019 s 25, Sch 9 paras 1, 6 with effect in relation to accounting periods beginning on or after 1 April 2019. An accounting period beginning before, and ending on or after, 1 April 2019 is to be treated as if so much of the accounting period as falls before that date, and so much of the accounting period as falls on or after that date, were separate accounting periods (FA 2019 Sch 9 para 7(2)).

[879L Meaning of relevant business and third party acquisition

(1) This section applies for the purposes of section 879K(3).

(2) "Relevant business" means—

    (*a*) in a case where the relevant asset is within paragraph (*e*) of subsection (2) of section 879A, the business or (as the case may be) the part of the business mentioned in the paragraph of that subsection within which the licensed asset falls, and

    (*b*) in any other case, the business or (as the case may be) the part of the business mentioned in the paragraph of that subsection within which the relevant asset falls.

(3) The transferor acquires something in a "third party acquisition" if—

    (*a*) the transferor acquires it from a company ("C") and, at the time of that acquisition—

        (i) if the transferor is an individual, the transferor is not a related party in relation to C, or

        (ii) if the transferor is a firm, no individual who is a member of the transferor is a related party in relation to C, or

(b) the transferor acquires it from a person ("P") who is not a company and, at the time of that acquisition—

    (i) if the transferor is an individual, P is not connected with the transferor, or

    (ii) if the transferor is a firm, no individual who is a member of the transferor is connected with P.

(4) But an acquisition is not a "third party acquisition" if—

    (a) its main purpose, or one of its main purposes, is for any person to obtain a tax advantage (within the meaning of section 1139 of CTA 2010), or

    (b) it occurs during the period beginning with 8 July 2015 and ending with 31 March 2019.

(5) In this section "connected" has the same meaning as in Chapter 12 (see section 842).]¹

Amendments—¹ Sections 879A–879P inserted by FA 2019 s 25, Sch 9 paras 1, 6 with effect in relation to accounting periods beginning on or after 1 April 2019. An accounting period beginning before, and ending on or after, 1 April 2019 is to be treated as if so much of the accounting period as falls before that date, and so much of the accounting period as falls on or after that date, were separate accounting periods (FA 2019 Sch 9 para 7(2)).

[Partial restrictions on debits]

879M When the partial restrictions apply: qualifying IP assets

(1) Section 879O (the partial restrictions on debits) applies in respect of a relevant asset ("the asset concerned") of a company if—

    (a) the company acquires the asset concerned on or after 1 April 2019 as part of the acquisition of a business,

    (b) the company also acquires qualifying IP assets as part of the acquisition of the business for use on a continuing basis in the course of the business, and

    (c) the amount in subsection (3) is less than 1.

(2) But section 879O does not apply in respect of the asset concerned if either of the following sections applies in respect of it—

    (a) section 879C (restrictions on debits: pre-FA 2019 relevant assets);

    (b) section 879K (restrictions on debits: acquisition from individual or firm).

(3) The amount is—

(A x N) / B

where—

    A is the expenditure incurred by the company for or in connection with the acquisition of the qualifying IP assets mentioned in subsection (1)(b),

    B is the expenditure incurred by the company for or in connection with the acquisition of the asset concerned and any other relevant assets acquired with the business, and

    N is 6.

(4) The Treasury may by regulations amend the meaning of N.

(5) In this section—

    "expenditure" means expenditure that is—

        (a) capitalised for accounting purposes, or

        (b) recognised in determining the profit or loss of the company concerned without being capitalised for accounting purposes,

    subject to any adjustments under this Part or Part 4 of TIOPA 2010;

    "qualifying IP asset" has the same meaning as in section 879I (see section 879J).]¹

Amendments—¹ Sections 879A–879P inserted by FA 2019 s 25, Sch 9 paras 1, 6 with effect in relation to accounting periods beginning on or after 1 April 2019. An accounting period beginning before, and ending on or after, 1 April 2019 is to be treated as if so much of the accounting period as falls before that date, and so much of the accounting period as falls on or after that date, were separate accounting periods (FA 2019 Sch 9 para 7(2)).

[879N When the partial restrictions apply: acquisition from individual or firm

(1) Section 879O (the partial restrictions on debits) also applies in respect of a relevant asset of a company if—

    (a) the company acquires the asset on or after 1 April 2019 directly or indirectly from an individual or firm ("the transferor"),

    (b) the related party condition is met,

    (c) the third party acquisition condition is met, and

    (d) the amount in subsection (6) is less than 1.

(2) But section 879O does not apply in respect of the relevant asset if either of the following sections applies in respect of it—

    (a) section 879C (restrictions on debits: pre-FA 2019 relevant assets);

    (b) section 879I (restrictions on debits: no business or no qualifying IP assets acquired).

(3) The related party condition is met if—

    (a) in a case where the transferor is an individual, the transferor is a related party in relation to the company at the time of the acquisition;

    (b) in a case where the transferor is a firm, any individual who is a member of the transferor is a related party in relation to the company at that time.

(4) The third party acquisition condition is met if—

    (*a*) in a case where the relevant asset is goodwill—

        (i) the transferor acquired all or part of the relevant business in one or more third party acquisitions as part of which the transferor acquired goodwill, and

        (ii) the relevant asset is acquired by the company as part of an acquisition of all the relevant business;

    (*b*) in a case where the relevant asset is not goodwill—

        (i) the transferor acquired the relevant asset in a third party acquisition, and

        (ii) the relevant asset is acquired by the company as part of an acquisition of all the relevant business.

(5) Section 879L (meaning of relevant business and third party acquisition) applies for the purposes of this section.

(6) The amount is—

$$A / B$$

where—

    A is the relevant accounting value of third party acquisitions (see subsections (7) to (9)), and

    B is the expenditure incurred by the company for or in connection with the acquisition of the relevant asset that is—

        (*a*) capitalised by the company for accounting purposes, or

        (*b*) recognised in determining the company's profit or loss without being capitalised for accounting purposes,

    subject to any adjustments under this Part or Part 4 of TIOPA 2010.

(7) In a case in which the relevant asset is goodwill, the relevant accounting value of third party acquisitions is the notional accounting value of the goodwill mentioned in subsection (4)(*a*)(i) ("the previously acquired goodwill").

(8) In a case in which the relevant asset is not goodwill, the relevant accounting value of third party acquisitions is the notional accounting value of the relevant asset.

(9) The "notional accounting value" of the previously acquired goodwill, or the relevant asset, is what its accounting value would have been in GAAP-compliant accounts drawn up by the transferor—

    (*a*) immediately before the relevant asset was acquired by the company, and

    (*b*) on the basis that the relevant business was a going concern.][1]

Amendments—[1]   Sections 879A–879P inserted by FA 2019 s 25, Sch 9 paras 1, 6 with effect in relation to accounting periods beginning on or after 1 April 2019. An accounting period beginning before, and ending on or after, 1 April 2019 is to be treated as if so much of the accounting period as falls before that date, and so much of the accounting period as falls on or after that date, were separate accounting periods (FA 2019 Sch 9 para 7(2)).

[879O The partial restrictions on debits

(1) Where this section applies in respect of a relevant asset of a company, the following restrictions have effect.

(2) If a debit in respect of the relevant asset is to be brought into account by the company for tax purposes under a provision of Chapter 3 (debits in respect of intangible fixed assets) or Chapter 15 (adjustments on change of accounting policy), the amount of that debit is—

$$D \times RA$$

where—

    D is the amount of the debit that would be brought into account disregarding this section (and, accordingly, for the purposes of any calculation of the tax written-down value of the relevant asset needed to determine D, this section's effect in relation to any debits previously brought into account is to be disregarded), and

    RA is the relevant amount (see subsection (6)).

(3) If, but for this section, a debit in respect of any of the relevant assets would be brought into account by the company for tax purposes under a provision of Chapter 4 (realisation of intangible fixed assets), the following two debits are to be brought into account under that provision instead—

    (*a*) a debit determined in accordance with subsection (4), and

    (*b*) a debit determined in accordance with subsection (5), which is to be treated for the purposes of Chapter 6 as a non-trading debit ("the non-trading debit").

(4) The amount of the debit determined in accordance with this subsection is—

$$D \times RA$$

where—

    D is the amount of the debit that would be brought into account under Chapter 4 disregarding this section (and, accordingly, for the purposes of any calculation of the tax written down value of the relevant asset needed to determine D, this section's effect in relation to any debits previously brought into account is to be disregarded), and

    RA is the relevant amount (see subsection (6)).

(5) The amount of the non-trading debit is—

When assets are treated as created or acquired

883 Assets treated as created or acquired when expenditure incurred

(1) This section—

    (*a*) applies for the purposes of section 882 (application of this Part to assets created or acquired on or after 1 April 2002), and

    [(*b*) has effect subject to the provisions specified in subsection (2).][1]

(2) The provisions referred to in subsection (1)(*b*) are—

    (*a*) section 884 (. . . [1] goodwill: time of creation),

    (*b*) section 885 ([assets representing non-qualifying expenditure][1]: time of creation), and

    (*c*) section 886 (assets representing production expenditure on films: time of creation).

(3) An intangible asset . . . [1] is treated as created or acquired on or after 1 April 2002 so far as expenditure on its creation or acquisition is incurred on or after that date.

[(3A) An intangible asset is treated as acquired on or after 1 July 2020 so far as expenditure on its acquisition is incurred on or after that date.

(3B) An intangible asset is treated as acquired during the period beginning with 1 April 2002 and ending with 30 June 2020 so far as expenditure on its acquisition is incurred during that period.

(3C) An intangible asset is treated as acquired during the period beginning with 19 March 2020 and ending with 30 June 2020 so far as expenditure on its acquisition is incurred during that period.][2]

(4) As to [when][2] expenditure on the creation or acquisition of the asset is incurred . . . [2], see sections 887 to 889.

[(5) If by reason of any of subsections (3) to (3C) of this section this Part would apply to an intangible fixed asset of a company to a limited extent only, the asset is to be treated as if it consisted of two separate assets—

    (*a*) one asset being an asset to which this Part applies, and

    (*b*) one asset being an asset to which the alternative enactments apply.][2]

(6) In subsection (5) "the alternative enactments" means the enactments that apply where this Part does not apply.

(7) Any apportionment necessary for the purposes of subsection (5) must be made on a just and reasonable basis.

Commentary—*Simon's Taxes* **D1.608**.

HMRC Manuals—Corporate Intangibles Research and Development Manual CIRD11670 (time when asset treated as created or acquired).

Amendments—[1]   Sub-s (1)(*b*) substituted; in sub (2)(*b*) words substituted; in sub-ss (2)(*a*), (3) words repealed by FA 2009 s 70(4) with effect in relation to accounting periods beginning on or after 22 April 2009 (and, in relation to those accounting periods, are to be treated as always having had effect). In the case of an accounting period (a "straddling period"): (a) beginning before 22 April 2009; and (b) ending on or after that date, the amended provisions apply as if the different parts of the straddling period falling in the different financial years were separate accounting periods (FA 2009 s 70(8)).

[2]   Sub-ss (3A)–(3C) inserted, in sub-s (4) word substituted for word "whether" and words "on or after 1 April 2002" repealed, and sub-s (5) substituted, by FA 2020 s 31(1), (7) with effect in relation to accounting periods beginning on or after 1 July 2020. An accounting period beginning before, and ending on or after, 1 July 2020 is to be treated as if so much of the accounting period as falls before that date, and so much of the accounting period as falls on or after that date, were separate accounting periods (FA 2020 s 31(15)).

884 . . . [1] goodwill: time of creation

For the purposes of section 882 (application of this Part to assets created or acquired on or after 1 April 2002) . . . [1] goodwill is treated as created [—

    (*a*) before (and not on or after) 1 April 2002 in a case in which the business in question was carried on at any time before that date by the company or a related party, and

    (*b*) on or after 1 April 2002 in any other case.][1]

Commentary—*Simon's Taxes* **D1.608**.

HMRC Manuals—Corporate Intangibles Research and Development Manual CIRD11675 (time when asset created). CIRD11680 (exceptions to the expenditure rule).

CIRD45265 (technical arguments in relation to partnership incorporation of pre-FA 2002 business).

Amendments—[1]   Words repealed in section and in the heading, and words substituted by FA 2009 s 70(5) with effect in relation to accounting periods beginning on or after 22 April 2009 (and, in relation to those accounting periods, are to be treated as always having had effect). In the case of an accounting period (a "straddling period"): (a) beginning before 22 April 2009; and (b) ending on or after that date, the amended provisions apply as if the different parts of the straddling period falling in the different financial years were separate accounting periods (FA 2009 s 70(8)).

885 [Assets representing non-qualifying expenditure][1]: time of creation

(1) This section—

    (*a*) applies for the purposes of section 882 (application of this Part to assets created or acquired on or after 1 April 2002), and

    (*b*) applies to an . . . [1] asset representing non-qualifying expenditure.

(2) In this section "non-qualifying expenditure" means expenditure that under the law as it was before 1 April 2002 is not qualifying expenditure for the purposes of any allowance under CAA 2001.

(3) If only part of the expenditure on the creation or acquisition of the asset is non- qualifying expenditure, this Part applies as if there were separate assets representing the non-qualifying expenditure and the other expenditure.

(4) If this Part does not apply to the asset representing the non-qualifying expenditure, the alternative enactments also apply as if there were a separate asset representing that expenditure.

(5) In subsection (4) "the alternative enactments" means the enactments that apply where this Part does not apply.

(6) Any apportionment necessary for the purposes of subsection (3) or (4) must be made on a just and reasonable basis.

(7) An asset to which this section applies is treated for the purposes of section 882 as created [—

    (*a*) before (and not on or after) 1 April 2002 in a case in which the asset in question was held at any time before that date by the company or a related party, and

    (*b*) on or after 1 April 2002 in any other case.][1]

Commentary—*Simon's Taxes* **D1.608**.
HMRC Manuals—Corporate Intangibles Research and Development Manual CIRD11685 (exceptions to the expenditure rule).
Amendments—[1]   In sub-s (1)(*b*) words repealed; in sub-s (7) words substituted; and in section heading words substituted, by FA 2009 s 70(6) with effect in relation to accounting periods beginning on or after 22 April 2009 (and, in relation to those accounting periods, are to be treated as always having had effect). In the case of an accounting period (a "straddling period"): (a) beginning before 22 April 2009; and (b) ending on or after that date, the amended provisions apply as if the different parts of the straddling period falling in the different financial years were separate accounting periods (FA 2009 s 70(8)).

886 Assets representing production expenditure on films: time of creation

(1) In determining for the purposes of this Part whether an asset representing production expenditure on a film was created before 1 April 2002 or on or after that date, the asset is treated as created when the film is completed.

(2) In this section—

    (*a*) "completed" has the same meaning as in Part 15 (see section 1181(5)),

    (*b*) "film" has the same meaning as in that Part (see section 1181), and

    (*c*) "production expenditure" has the same meaning as in that Part (see section 1184).

Commentary—*Simon's Taxes* **D1.603**.
Derivation—FA 2006 s 51(2).
HMRC Manuals—Film Prodcution Company Manual FPC20130 (taxation: separate trade television productions).
FPC50010 (film tax relief: eligible expenditure: core expenditure).
Business Income Manual BIM56010 (films and sound recordings: old regime for films).

When expenditure treated as incurred

887 General rule

(1) For the purposes of section 883 (assets treated as created or acquired when expenditure incurred) the general rule is that expenditure on the acquisition of an asset is treated as incurred when it is recognised for accounting purposes.

(2) This is subject to—

    section 888 (cases where chargeable gains rule applies), and

    section 889 (cases where capital allowances general rule applies).

Commentary—*Simon's Taxes* **D1.608**.
Derivation—FA 2002 Sch 29 para 123(1), (2).
HMRC Manuals—Corporate Intangibles Research and Development Manual CIRD11690 (expenditure incurred rule).

888 Cases where chargeable gains rule applies

(1) This section applies if—

    (*a*) expenditure on the acquisition of an asset does not qualify for any form of tax relief against income under the law as it was before 1 April 2002,

    (*b*) that expenditure would be treated as incurred on or after that date under the general rule in section 887, and

    (*c*) the relevant disposal of the asset is treated as occurring before that date for the purposes of TCGA 1992 or would be so treated under the law as it was before 1 April 2002.

(2) For the purposes of section 883 (assets treated as created or acquired when expenditure incurred), the expenditure is treated as incurred before 1 April 2002.

(3) In subsection (1) "the relevant disposal" means the disposal on which the acquisition mentioned in subsection (1)(*a*) occurred.

Commentary—*Simon's Taxes* **D1.608**.
Derivation—FA 2002 Sch 29 paras 117(2), 124.
HMRC Manuals—Corporate Intangibles Research and Development Manual CIRD11690 (cases where chargeable gains rule applies).

889 Cases where capital allowances general rule applies

(1) This section applies if under the law as it was before 1 April 2002 expenditure on the creation or acquisition of an asset is qualifying expenditure for the purposes of any allowance under CAA 2001.

(2) For the purposes of section 883 (assets treated as created or acquired when expenditure incurred) the expenditure is treated as incurred when an unconditional obligation to pay it arises.

(3) For this purpose the fact that the whole or part of the expenditure is not required to be paid until a later date does not prevent there being an unconditional obligation to pay it.

Commentary—*Simon's Taxes* **D1.608**.

Derivation—FA 2002 Sch 29 paras 117(1), 125(1), (2).

HMRC Manuals—Corporate Intangibles Research and Development Manual CIRD11670 (FA02 rule: general conditions: time when asset treated as created or acquired: scope of rules).

Capital Allowances Manual CA11800 (when capital expenditure is incurred).

Fungible assets

890 Fungible assets: application of section 858

(1) This section and section 891 apply for the purposes of this Chapter in relation to assets to which section 858 (treatment of fungible assets) applies.

(2) Section 858 applies as if—

> *(a) pre-FA 2002 assets, and*
>
> *(b) intangible fixed assets that are not pre-FA 2002 assets,*

were assets of different kinds.

(3) If section 858 applies (whether or not it is a case where subsection (2) has effect)—

> *(a) a single asset comprising pre-FA 2002 assets is treated as itself being a pre-FA 2002 asset, and*
>
> *(b) a single asset comprising intangible fixed assets that are not pre-FA 2002 assets is treated as itself being an asset to which this Part applies.[1]*

Commentary—*Simon's Taxes* **D1.608**.

Derivation—FA 2002 Sch 29 para 126(1)–(3).

HMRC Manuals—Corporate Intangibles Research and Development Manual CIRD11770 (additions to existing holdings outside Pt 8).

Amendments—[1] Section 890 repealed by FA 2020 s 31(1), (8) with effect in relation to accounting periods beginning on or after 1 July 2020. An accounting period beginning before, and ending on or after, 1 July 2020 is to be treated as if so much of the accounting period as falls before that date, and so much of the accounting period as falls on or after that date, were separate accounting periods (FA 2020 s 31(15)).

891 Realisation and acquisition of fungible assets

(1) Subsection (2) applies if—

> *(a) a company realises a fungible asset, and*
>
> *(b) apart from section 890(2), the asset would be treated as part of a single asset comprising both pre-FA 2002 assets and assets that are not pre-FA 2002 assets.*

(2) The realisation is treated as diminishing the single asset of the company comprising pre-FA 2002 assets in priority to diminishing the single asset of the company comprising assets that are not pre-FA 2002 assets.

(3) Fungible assets acquired by a company that would not otherwise be treated as pre-FA 2002 assets are so treated so far as they are identified, in accordance with the following rules, with pre-FA 2002 assets realised by the company.

(4) Rule 1 is that assets acquired are identified with pre-FA 2002 assets of the same kind realised by the company within the period beginning 30 days before and ending 30 days after the date of the acquisition.

(5) The reference in subsection (4) to assets "of the same kind" is to assets that are, or but for section 890(2) would be, treated as part of a single asset because of section 858.

(6) Rule 2 is that assets realised earlier are identified before assets realised later.

(7) Rule 3 is that assets acquired earlier are identified before assets acquired later.

(8) In this section "fungible asset" means an intangible fixed asset to which section 858 applies.[1]

Commentary—*Simon's Taxes* **D1.608**.

Derivation—FA 2002 Sch 29 para 126(1), (4)–(6).

HMRC Manuals—Corporate Intangibles Research and Development Manual CIRD11770 (additions to existing holding outside Pt 8).

CIRD11780 (anti-avoidance rule).

Amendments—[1] Section 891 repealed by FA 2020 s 31(1), (9) with effect in relation to accounting periods beginning on or after 1 July 2020. An accounting period beginning before, and ending on or after, 1 July 2020 is to be treated as if so much of the accounting period as falls before that date, and so much of the accounting period as falls on or after that date, were separate accounting periods (FA 2020 s 31(15)).

Assets treated as pre-FA 2002 assets

892 Certain assets acquired on transfer of business [or transfer within a group][1]

(1) This section applies if—

> *(a) a company ("the transferor") transfers to another company ("the transferee") an asset that is a pre-FA 2002 asset in the hands of the transferor company,*
>
> *(b) the transfer is one in relation to which the transferor is treated for the purposes of TCGA 1992 as disposing of the asset for a consideration that secures that neither a gain nor a loss accrues to it, and*
>
> *(c) it is so treated because of a provision specified in subsection (2).*

(2) The provisions are—
- (a) section 139 of TCGA 1992 (reconstruction involving transfer of business),
- (b) section 140A of that Act (transfer or division of UK business),[1]
- (c) section 140E of that Act (merger leaving assets within UK tax charge)[, and
- (d) section 171 of that Act (transfers within a group).][1]

(3) In the hands of the transferee the asset is treated for the purposes of this Part as a pre-FA 2002 asset.

(4) This section does not apply if the transfer mentioned in subsection (1) occurred before 28 June 2002.

[(5) If the transfer mentioned in subsection (1) occurred before 1 July 2020, this section applies as if paragraph (d) of subsection (2) were omitted.][1]

Commentary—*Simon's Taxes* **D1.608**.

Derivation—FA 2002 Sch 29 para 127(1)–(3).

HMRC Manuals—Corporate Intangibles Research and Development Manual CIRD11660 (exception for asset transfers within TCGA92/S139 or S140A).

AMENDMENTS—

[1]   Words in heading inserted, in sub-s (2)(b) word "and" repealed, and sub-ss (2)(c), (5) inserted, by FA 2020 s 31(1), (10) with effect in relation to accounting periods beginning on or after 1 July 2020. An accounting period beginning before, and ending on or after, 1 July 2020 is to be treated as if so much of the accounting period as falls before that date, and so much of the accounting period as falls on or after that date, were separate accounting periods (FA 2020 s 31(15)).

893 Assets whose value derives from pre-FA 2002 assets

(1) This section applies if—
- (a) [during the period beginning with 1 April 2002 and ending with 30 June 2020][1] a company ("the acquiring company") acquires an intangible fixed asset ("the acquired asset") from a person ("the transferor"),
- (b) the acquired asset is created on or after 1 April 2002,
- (c) at the time of the acquisition the transferor and the acquiring company are related parties,
- (d) the value of the acquired asset derives in whole or in part from any other asset ("the other asset"), and
- (e) the other asset meets the preserved status conditions (see section 894).

(2) In the hands of the acquiring company the acquired asset is treated for the purposes of this Part as a pre-FA 2002 asset so far as its value derives from the other asset.

(3) If only part of the value of the acquired asset derives from the other asset—
- (a) this Part applies as if there were a separate asset representing the part of the value that does not so derive, and
- (b) the alternative enactments apply as if there were a separate asset representing the part of the value that does so derive.

(4) In subsection (3) "the alternative enactments" means the enactments that apply where this Part does not apply.

(5) For the purposes of this section the cases in which the value of an asset may be derived from any other asset include any case where—
- (a) assets have been merged or divided,
- (b) assets have changed their nature, or
- (c) rights or interests in or over assets have been created or extinguished.

(6) Section 894 supplements this section.

Commentary—*Simon's Taxes* **D1.608**.

Derivation—FA 2002 Sch 29 paras 122(2), 127A(1), (3)–(5).

HMRC Manuals—Corporate Intangibles Research and Development Manual CIRD48280 (change to rules: new assets derived from companies' existing assets).

AMENDMENTS—

[1]   In sub-s (1)(a) words substituted for words "on or after 1 April 2002" by FA 2020 s 31(1), (11) with effect in relation to accounting periods beginning on or after 1 July 2020. An accounting period beginning before, and ending on or after, 1 July 2020 is to be treated as if so much of the accounting period as falls before that date, and so much of the accounting period as falls on or after that date, were separate accounting periods (FA 2020 s 31(15)).

894 The preserved status conditions etc

(1) For the purposes of section 893(1) the other asset meets the preserved status conditions if subsections (2) and (3) apply.

(2) This subsection applies if on or after 1 April 2002 the other asset—
- (a) has been a pre-FA 2002 asset in the hands of the transferor at a time when the transferor and the acquiring company were related parties, or
- (b) has been a pre-FA 2002 asset in the hands of any other person at a time when—
  - (i) the other person and the acquiring company were related parties, or
  - (ii) the other person and the transferor were related parties.

(4) For the purposes of subsection (2) it does not matter whether—

    (a) the other asset is the same as the asset concerned,

    (b) the asset concerned is acquired at the time of the realisation of the other asset, or

    (c) the asset concerned is acquired by merging assets or otherwise.]¹

Amendments—¹ Chapter 16A (ss 900A–900I) inserted by FA 2020 s 31(1), (13) with effect in relation to accounting periods beginning on or after 1 July 2020. An accounting period beginning before, and ending on or after, 1 July 2020 is to be treated as if so much of the accounting period as falls before that date, and so much of the accounting period as falls on or after that date, were separate accounting periods (FA 2020 s 31(15)).

[The special rules]

900E Special rule: section 900B case

(1) This section applies in respect of a restricted asset of a company if it is a restricted asset by reason of section 900B.

(2) If the company was the first company to acquire the asset on or after 1 July 2020, the relevant Chapters of this Part have effect as if the company acquired the asset at no cost.

(3) If the company was not the first company to acquire the asset on or after 1 July 2020, the relevant Chapters of this Part have effect as if the company acquired the asset for the adjusted amount.

(4) The adjusted amount is—

$$A - B$$

where—

A is the amount of consideration—

    (a) for which the company actually acquired the asset, or

    (b) if different, for which it would (ignoring this section) be treated for the purposes of the Taxes Acts as having acquired the asset, and

B is the market value of the asset on the date it was first acquired by a company on or after 1 July 2020.

(5) Where B is greater than A the adjusted amount is nil.

(6) In this section—

    "market value", in relation to an asset, means the price the asset might reasonably be expected to fetch on a sale in the open market, and

    "the relevant Chapters of this Part" means—

        (a) Chapter 3 (debits in respect of intangible fixed assets),

        (b) Chapter 15 (adjustments on change of accounting policy), and

        (c) Chapter 5 (calculation of tax written-down value) in so far as it has effect for the purposes of Chapters 3 and 15.]¹

Amendments—¹ Chapter 16A (ss 900A–900I) inserted by FA 2020 s 31(1), (13) with effect in relation to accounting periods beginning on or after 1 July 2020. An accounting period beginning before, and ending on or after, 1 July 2020 is to be treated as if so much of the accounting period as falls before that date, and so much of the accounting period as falls on or after that date, were separate accounting periods (FA 2020 s 31(15)).

[900F Special rule: section 900C or 900D case

(1) This section applies in respect of a restricted asset of a company if it is a restricted asset by reason of section 900C or 900D.

(2) The relevant Chapters of this Part have effect as if the company acquired the asset for the adjusted amount.

(3) The adjusted amount is calculated as follows—

Step 1

Find the amount—

    (a) for which the company actually acquired the asset, or

    (b) if different, for which it would (ignoring this section) be treated for the purposes of the Taxes Acts as having acquired the asset.

Step 2

Deduct from the amount found at Step 1 such proportion of the notional deduction amount for the relevant other asset or each relevant other asset as is just and reasonable in the circumstances.

(4) Where the deduction at Step 2 results in a negative value the adjusted amount is nil.

(5) In subsection (3)—

    "relevant other asset" means an asset by reference to which the conditions in paragraphs (c) and (d) of section 900C(2) or (as the case may be) the conditions in section 900D(2) were met, and

    "the notional deduction amount", in relation to a relevant other asset, means—

        (a) in a case where section 900E(2) would have applied had the company acquired the relevant other asset instead of the restricted asset, an amount equal to the market value of the relevant other asset at the time the restricted asset was acquired, and

(b) in a case where section 900E(3) would have applied had the company acquired the relevant other asset instead of the restricted asset, an amount equal to the market value of the relevant other asset at the time it was first acquired by a company on or after 1 July 2020, and

(c) in a case where subsection (2) of this section would have applied had the company acquired the relevant other asset instead of the restricted asset, the amount that would have been deducted at step 2 of subsection (3) of this section if the company had acquired the relevant other asset instead of the restricted asset.

(6) In this section "market value" and "the relevant Chapters of this Part" have the same meaning as in section 900E.][1]

Amendments—[1] Chapter 16A (ss 900A–900I) inserted by FA 2020 s 31(1), (13) with effect in relation to accounting periods beginning on or after 1 July 2020. An accounting period beginning before, and ending on or after, 1 July 2020 is to be treated as if so much of the accounting period as falls before that date, and so much of the accounting period as falls on or after that date, were separate accounting periods (FA 2020 s 31(15)).

[Supplementary provisions

900G Meaning of "relieving acquisition"
For the purposes of this Chapter, an asset is the subject of a relieving acquisition if it is acquired by a company from a person who at the time of the acquisition is not a related party in relation to the company.][1]

Amendments—[1] Chapter 16A (ss 900A–900I) inserted by FA 2020 s 31(1), (13) with effect in relation to accounting periods beginning on or after 1 July 2020. An accounting period beginning before, and ending on or after, 1 July 2020 is to be treated as if so much of the accounting period as falls before that date, and so much of the accounting period as falls on or after that date, were separate accounting periods (FA 2020 s 31(15)).

[900H Supplementary provision about when two persons are related
(1) References in this Chapter to one person being a related party in relation to another person are to be read as including references to the participation condition being met as between those persons.
(2) References in subsection (1) to a person include a firm in a case where, for section 1259 purposes, references in this Chapter to a company are read as references to the firm.
(3) In subsection (2) "section 1259 purposes" means the purposes of determining under section 1259 the amount of profits or losses to be allocated to a partner in a firm.
(4) Section 148 of TIOPA 2010 (when the participation condition is met) applies for the purposes of subsection (1) as it applies for the purposes of section 147(1)(b) of TIOPA 2010.][1]

Amendments—[1] Chapter 16A (ss 900A–900I) inserted by FA 2020 s 31(1), (13) with effect in relation to accounting periods beginning on or after 1 July 2020. An accounting period beginning before, and ending on or after, 1 July 2020 is to be treated as if so much of the accounting period as falls before that date, and so much of the accounting period as falls on or after that date, were separate accounting periods (FA 2020 s 31(15)).

[900I Acquisition of asset in pursuance of an unconditional obligation
(1) A company that acquires an intangible fixed asset in pursuance of an unconditional obligation under a contract is to be treated for the purposes of this Chapter as having acquired the asset on the date on which the company became subject to that obligation or (if later) the date on which that obligation became unconditional.
(2) An obligation is unconditional if it may not be varied or extinguished by the exercise of a right (whether under contract or otherwise).][1]

Amendments—[1] Chapter 16A (ss 900A–900I) inserted by FA 2020 s 31(1), (13) with effect in relation to accounting periods beginning on or after 1 July 2020. An accounting period beginning before, and ending on or after, 1 July 2020 is to be treated as if so much of the accounting period as falls before that date, and so much of the accounting period as falls on or after that date, were separate accounting periods (FA 2020 s 31(15)).

[CHAPTER 16B

FUNGIBLE ASSETS

900J Fungible assets: general
(1) For the purposes of this Part—
  (a) fungible assets of the same kind that are held by the same person in the same capacity are treated as indistinguishable parts of a single asset,
  (b) that asset is treated as growing as additional assets of the same kind are created or acquired, and
  (c) that asset is treated as diminishing as some of the assets are realised.
(2) In this Part "fungible assets" means assets of a nature to be dealt in without identifying the particular assets involved.][1]

Amendments—[1] Chapter 16B (ss 900J–900O) inserted by FA 2020 s 31(1), (13) with effect in relation to accounting periods beginning on or after 1 July 2020. An accounting period beginning before, and ending on or after, 1 July 2020 is to be treated as if so much of the accounting period as falls before that date, and so much of the accounting period as falls on or after that date, were separate accounting periods (FA 2020 s 31(15)).

[2] In sub-s (3), para b) repealed by FA 2012 s 146, Sch 16 paras 135, 182 with effect in relation to accounting periods of companies beginning on or after 1 January 2013 (subject to transitional provisions in FA 2012 Sch 17). For accounting periods straddling 1 January 2013, see FA 2012 s 149.

PART 9

INTELLECTUAL PROPERTY: KNOW-HOW AND PATENTS

CHAPTER 1

INTRODUCTION

907 Overview of Part

(1) This Part applies the charge to corporation tax on income to—

(a) profits from disposals of know-how (see Chapter 2), and

(b) profits from sales of patent rights (see Chapter 3).

(2) This Part also provides for relief from corporation tax on patent income (see Chapter 4).

(3) Chapter 5 contains supplementary provision relevant to Chapters 2 to 4.

(4) This Part needs to be read in the light of Part 8 (intangible fixed assets).

(5) See in particular the following provisions of Part 8, which are relevant to the application of that Part—

(a) section 713 (meaning of "intangible fixed asset"),

(b) Chapter 16 (which limits the application of Part 8 to assets which are not pre-FA 2002 assets within the meaning of section 881), and

(c) section 906 (which contains a rule about the priority of Part 8 for corporation tax purposes).

CHAPTER 2

DISPOSALS OF KNOW-HOW

908 Charge to tax on profits from disposals of know-how

(1) The charge to corporation tax on income applies to profits arising where consideration is received by a company—

(a) for the disposal of know-how, or

(b) for giving, or wholly or partly fulfilling, an undertaking which—

(i) is given in connection with a disposal of know-how, and

(ii) restricts or is designed to restrict any person's activities in any way.

(2) For the purposes of subsection (1)(b), it does not matter whether or not the undertaking is legally enforceable.

(3) Subsection (1) is subject to the exceptions in section 909.

(4) In this Chapter "know-how" means any industrial information or techniques likely to assist in—

(a) manufacturing or processing goods or materials,

(b) working a source of mineral deposits (including searching for, discovering or testing mineral deposits or obtaining access to them), or

(c) carrying out any agricultural, forestry or fishing operations.

(5) In subsection (4)—

(a) "mineral deposits" includes any natural deposits capable of being lifted or extracted from the earth and for this purpose geothermal energy is treated as a natural deposit, and

(b) "source of mineral deposits" includes a mine, an oil well and a source of geothermal energy.

Commentary—*Simon's Taxes* B5.347, B5.343.

HMRC Manuals—Capital Allowances Manual CA70010 (meaning of know-how).
CA72000 (normally revenue).

909 Exceptions to charge under section 908

(1) Section 908 does not apply in the following cases.

(2) Case A is if the consideration is brought into account under section 462 of CAA 2001 (disposal values).

(3) Case B is if the consideration is dealt with in relation to the company receiving it as a trading receipt under section 177(2) (disposal of know-how if trade continues to be carried on).

(4) Case C is if the consideration is dealt with in relation to the person receiving it as a capital receipt for goodwill under section 178(2) (disposal of know-how as part of disposal of all or part of a trade).

(5) Case D is if the disposal of the know-how is by way of a sale and—

(a) the buyer is a body of persons over which the seller has control,

(b) the seller is a body of persons over which the buyer has control, or

(c) the buyer and the seller are both bodies of persons and another person has control over both of them.

(6) In subsection (5) "body of persons" includes a firm.

Commentary—*Simon's Taxes* B5.347.
Derivation—TA 1988 s 531(4), (7).

HMRC Manuals—Capital Allowance Manual CA71300 (disposal value).
CA72500 (treatment of receipts).

910 Profits charged under section 908

(1) The profits charged under section 908 are—
  (a) the amount of the consideration, less
  (b) any expenditure incurred by the company wholly and exclusively in the acquisition or disposal of the know-how.

(2) Such expenditure may not be taken into account more than once, whether under this section or otherwise.

(3) This section needs to be read with section 926 (contributions to expenditure).

Commentary—*Simon's Taxes* B5.347.
Derivation—TA 1988 s 531(5).

CHAPTER 3

SALES OF PATENT RIGHTS
Introductory

911 Overview of Chapter

(1) This Chapter—
  (a) applies the charge to corporation tax on income to profits from sales of patent rights (see sections 912 and 913),
  (b) contains provision about how the amount chargeable is taxed (see sections 914 to 918), and
  (c) contains related provision, including provision relevant to the application of the Chapter (see sections 919 to 923).

(2) Section 848 of ITA 2007, under which a sum representing income tax deducted under section 910 of that Act (deduction from payment to non-UK residents in respect of sale of patent rights) is treated as income tax paid by the recipient, is also relevant to the tax treatment of payments made to non-UK resident companies in respect of sales of patent rights.

HMRC Manuals—Capital Allowances Manual CA75200 (sale of patent rights).

Charge to tax

912 Charge to tax on profits from sales of patent rights

(1) The charge to corporation tax on income applies to profits from sales by a company of the whole or part of any patent rights.

(2) Subsection (1) applies in the case of a non-UK resident company if the patent is granted under the laws of the United Kingdom.

(3) In this Chapter "patent rights" means the right to do or authorise the doing of anything which, but for the right, would be an infringement of a patent.

Commentary—*Simon's Taxes* B1.431, B5.333, B5.336, B5.334.
Derivation—TA 1988 ss 524(1), (3), 533(1).
HMRC Manuals—Capital Allowances Manual CA75210 (taxation: patent rights).

913 Profits charged under section 912

(1) A company's profits from the sale of the whole or part of patent rights are—
  (a) any capital sum comprised in the proceeds of sale, less
  (b) the deductible costs.

(2) The deductible costs are—
  (a) the capital cost (if any) of the rights sold, and
  (b) any incidental expenses incurred by the company in connection with the sale.

(3) If—
  (a) the company acquired the rights sold, or the rights out of which they were granted, by purchase,
  (b) the company has previously sold part of the purchased rights, and
  (c) the proceeds of that sale, after deducting any incidental expenses, consisted wholly or partly of a capital sum,
the capital cost is reduced by that sum.

(4) References in this Chapter to the capital cost of patent rights are to any capital sum included in any price paid by the company to purchase—
  (a) the rights, or
  (b) the rights out of which they were granted.

(5) This section needs to be read with sections 924 (relief for expenses: patent income) and 926 (contributions to expenditure).

Commentary—*Simon's Taxes* B5.333.
Derivation—TA 1988 s 524(1), (3), (7), (8).

Spreading of charge to tax

914 UK resident companies: proceeds of sale not received in instalments

(1) This section applies if a company liable for tax under section 912—

    (*a*) is UK resident, and

    (*b*) does not receive the proceeds of sale in instalments.

(2) The appropriate fraction of the amount chargeable is taxed—

    (*a*) in the accounting period in which the company receives the proceeds of sale ("the period of receipt"), and

    (*b*) in successive accounting periods, until the expiry of the 6-year period beginning at the start of the period of receipt.

(3) The appropriate fraction is the same fraction of the amount chargeable as the accounting period in question is of 6 years (or, in the last period, such smaller fraction of that amount as has not already been taxed).

(4) The company may elect that the whole of the amount chargeable is to be taxed instead in the period of receipt.

(5) An election under subsection (4) must be made within the two-year period beginning at the end of the period of receipt.

Commentary—*Simon's Taxes* **B5.333**.
Derivation—TA 1988 s 524(1), (2), (2A).
HMRC Manuals—Capital Allowances Manual CA75210 (taxation of lump sum).

915 UK resident companies: proceeds of sale received in instalments

(1) This section applies if a company liable for tax under section 912—

    (*a*) is UK resident, and

    (*b*) receives the proceeds of sale in instalments.

(2) The appropriate fraction of the amount chargeable in respect of each instalment is taxed—

    (*a*) in the accounting period in which the company receives the instalment ("the period of receipt"), and

    (*b*) in successive accounting periods, until the expiry of the 6-year period beginning at the start of the period of receipt.

(3) The appropriate fraction of the amount chargeable in respect of an instalment is the same fraction of that amount as the accounting period in question is of 6 years (or, in the last period, such smaller fraction of the amount as has not already been taxed).

(4) The company may elect that the whole of any instalment is to be taxed instead in the period of receipt.

(5) An election under subsection (4) must be made within the two-year period beginning at the end of the period of receipt.

Commentary—*Simon's Taxes* **B5.333**.
Derivation—TA 1988 s 524(1), (2), (2A).
HMRC Manuals—Capital Allowances Manual CA75210 (taxation of lump sum).

916 Non-UK resident companies: proceeds of sale not received in instalments

(1) This section applies if a company liable for tax under section 912—

    (*a*) is not UK resident, and

    (*b*) does not receive the proceeds of sale in instalments.

(2) The whole of the amount chargeable is taxed in the accounting period in which the company receives the proceeds ("the period of receipt").

(3) The company may elect instead that the amount chargeable—

    (*a*) is to be treated as arising rateably in the accounting periods ending 6 years from the start of the period of receipt, and

    (*b*) is taxed accordingly.

(4) An election under subsection (3) must be made within the two-year period beginning at the end of the period of receipt.

(5) The election has effect in relation to accounting periods of the company during which the company is within the charge to corporation tax in respect of any proceeds of the sale not consisting of a capital sum.

(6) Such repayments and assessments are to be made for each of the accounting periods affected as are necessary to give effect to the election.

(7) Subsection (6) is subject to the qualifications in section 920 (adjustments where tax has been deducted).

Commentary—*Simon's Taxes* **B5.336**.
HMRC Manuals—Capital Allowances Manual CA75210 (taxation of lump sum).

917 Non-UK resident companies: proceeds of sale received in instalments

(1) This section applies if a company liable for tax under section 912—

    (*a*) is not UK resident, and

    (*b*) receives the proceeds of sale in instalments.

(2) The amount chargeable in respect of each instalment is taxed in the accounting period in which the company receives the instalment ("the period of receipt").

(3) The company may, for any instalment, elect instead that the amount chargeable in respect of the instalment—

    (*a*) is to be treated as arising rateably in the accounting periods ending 6 years from the start of the period of receipt, and

    (*b*) is taxed accordingly.

(4) An election under subsection (3) must be made within the two-year period beginning at the end of the period of receipt.

(5) The election has effect in relation to accounting periods of the company during which the company is within the charge to corporation tax in respect of any proceeds of the sale not consisting of a capital sum.

(6) Such repayments and assessments are to be made for each of the accounting periods affected as are necessary to give effect to the election.

(7) Subsection (6) is subject to the qualifications in section 920 (adjustments where tax has been deducted).

Commentary—*Simon's Taxes* **B5.336**.
HMRC Manuals—Capital Allowances Manual CA75210 (taxation of lump sum).

918 Winding up of a body corporate

(1) If a body corporate which is liable for tax under section 912 commences to be wound up, any amounts falling within subsection (2) are taxed in the accounting period in which the winding up commences.

(2) The amounts are—

    (*a*) any amounts which would have been chargeable in later accounting periods under section 914(2) or 915(2) (UK resident companies: spreading of charge to tax), and

    (*b*) any amounts which would have been chargeable in later accounting periods under section 916(3) or 917(3) (non-UK resident companies: election to spread charge to tax).

Commentary—*Simon's Taxes* **B5.339**.
Derivation—TA 1988 s 525(1).
HMRC Manuals—Capital Allowances Manual CA75220 (death of a seller).

Miscellaneous

919 Deduction of tax from payments to non-UK resident companies

(1) This section applies if a non-UK resident company is liable for tax under section 912 on profits from the sale of the whole or part of any patent rights.

(2) The rules in section 913 allowing the capital cost (if any) of the rights sold to be deducted in calculating the profits from the sale do not affect the amount of income tax which is to be deducted under section 910 of ITA 2007.

(3) No election made by the company under section 916(3) or 917(3) (election to spread charge to tax) in relation to the proceeds of sale or any instalment affects the amount of income tax which is to be deducted under section 910 of ITA 2007.

Commentary—*Simon's Taxes* **B5.330**.
Derivation—TA 1988 s 524(3), (9).

920 Adjustments where tax has been deducted

Where any sum has been deducted from a payment under section 910 of ITA 2007, any adjustment necessary—

    (*a*) because of section 919(2), or

    (*b*) because of an election under section 916(3) or 917(3),

must be made by way of repayment of tax.

921 Licences connected with patents

(1) The acquisition of a licence in respect of a patent is treated for the purposes of this Chapter as a purchase of patent rights.

(2) The grant of a licence in respect of a patent is treated for the purposes of this Chapter as a sale of part of patent rights.

(3) But the grant by a person entitled to patent rights of an exclusive licence is treated for the purposes of this Chapter as a sale of the whole of those rights.

(4) In subsection (3) "exclusive licence" means a licence to exercise the rights to the exclusion of the grantor and all other persons for the period remaining until the rights come to an end.

Commentary—*Simon's Taxes* **B5.333**.
Derivation—TA 1988 s 533(2), (3).
HMRC Manuals—Capital Allowances Manual CA75030 (patents: licences).

922 Rights to acquire future patent rights

(1) If a sum is paid to obtain a right to acquire future patent rights, then for the purposes of this Chapter—

    (*a*) the payer is treated as purchasing patent rights for that sum, and

    (*b*) the recipient is treated as selling patent rights for that sum.
(2) If a person—
    (*a*) pays a sum to obtain a right to acquire future patent rights, and
    (*b*) subsequently acquires those rights,
the expenditure is to be treated for the purposes of this Chapter as having been expenditure on the purchase of those rights.
(3) In this section "a right to acquire future patent rights" means a right to acquire in the future patent rights relating to an invention in respect of which the patent has not yet been granted.

Commentary—*Simon's Taxes* **B5.333**.
Derivation—TA 1988 s 533(5), (6).
HMRC Manuals—Capital Allowances Manual CA75410 (patent rights for future).

923 Sums paid for Crown use etc treated as paid under licence

(1) This section applies if an invention which is the subject of a patent is used by or for the service of—
    (*a*) the Crown under sections 55 to 59 of the Patents Act 1977 (c 37), or
    (*b*) the government of a country outside the United Kingdom under corresponding provisions of
        the law of that country.
(2) The use is treated for the purposes of this Chapter as having taken place under licence.
(3) Sums paid in respect of the use are treated for the purposes of this Chapter as having been paid under a licence.

Commentary—*Simon's Taxes* **B5.333**.
Derivation—TA 1988 s 533(4).
HMRC Manuals—Capital Allowances Manual CA75410 (crown use).

CHAPTER 4

RELIEF FROM CORPORATION TAX ON PATENT INCOME

924 Relief for expenses: patent income

(1) Relief may be claimed under this section for patent application and maintenance expenses.
(2) In this section "patent application and maintenance expenses" means expenses incurred by a company in connection with—
    (*a*) the grant or maintenance of a patent,
    (*b*) the extension of the term of a patent, or
    (*c*) a rejected or abandoned application for a patent,
but not incurred for the purposes of any trade carried on by the company.
(3) Relief may not be claimed under this section for patent application and maintenance expenses unless they are expenses which would, if incurred for the purposes of a trade, have been allowable as a deduction in calculating the profits of the trade.
(4) This section needs to be read with section 926 (contributions to expenditure).

Commentary—*Simon's Taxes* **B5.331**.
Derivation—TA 1988 ss 526(1), 528(2), (3).
HMRC Manuals—Capital Allowances Manual CA75300 (fees).

925 How relief is given under section 924

(1) This section sets out how relief for expenses is given where a company makes a claim under section 924.
(2) The amount of the expenses must be deducted from or set off against the company's income from patents for the accounting period in which the expenses were incurred.
(3) If the amount to be allowed is greater than the amount of the company's income from patents for that accounting period, then (so long as the company remains within the charge to corporation tax) the excess must be deducted from or set off against the company's income from patents for the next accounting period, and so on for subsequent accounting periods, without the need for a further claim.
(4) In this section "income from patents" means—
    (*a*) royalties or other sums paid in respect of the use of a patent,
    (*b*) amounts on which tax is payable under section 912, 918 or 1272, and
    (*c*) amounts on which tax is payable under—
        (i) section 472(5) of CAA 2001 (patent allowances: balancing charges), or
        (ii) paragraph 100 of Schedule 3 to that Act (balancing charges in respect of pre-1st April
           1986 expenditure on purchase of patent rights),
but does not include any amount chargeable to income tax.
(5) In this section references to a company's income from patents are to the income after any allowance has been deducted from or set off against it under section 480 of CAA 2001 (certain allowances against income from patents).

Commentary—*Simon's Taxes* **B5.331**.
Derivation—TA 1988 ss 526(1), 528(3), (3A), 533(1).

HMRC Manuals—Capital Allowances Manual CA75300 (fees).

926 Contributions to expenditure

(1) For the purposes of sections 910, 913 and 924, the general rule is that a company is to be regarded as not having incurred expenditure so far as it has been, or is to be, met (directly or indirectly) by—

   (*a*) a public body, or

   (*b*) a person other than the company.

(2) In this Chapter "public body" means the Crown or any government, local authority or other public authority (whether in the United Kingdom or elsewhere).

(3) The general rule does not apply to the expenses mentioned in section 913(2)(*b*) (incidental expenses incurred by a seller of patent rights).

(4) The general rule is subject to the exception in section 927.

Commentary—*Simon's Taxes* B5.333, B5.347.

Derivation—TA 1988 s 532; CAA 2001 s 532(1), (2).

HMRC Manuals—Capital Allowances Manual CA14100 (contributions by public body).

927 Contributions not made by public bodies nor eligible for tax relief

(1) A company is to be regarded as having incurred expenditure (despite section 926(1)) so far as the requirements in subsections (2) and (3) are met in relation to the expenditure.

(2) The first requirement is that the person meeting the company's expenditure ("X") is not a public body.

(3) The second requirement is that—

   (*a*) no allowance can be made under Chapter 2 of Part 11 of CAA 2001 (contribution allowances) in respect of X's expenditure, and

   (*b*) the expenditure is not allowed to be deducted in calculating the profits of a trade, profession or vocation carried on by X.

(4) When determining for the purposes of subsection (3)(*a*) whether such an allowance can be made, assume that X is within the charge to tax.

928 Exchanges

(1) In this Part references to the sale of property include the exchange of property.

(2) In this section—

   references to property include know-how, and

   references to the sale of property include the disposal of know-how.

(3) For the purposes of subsection (1), any provision of this Part referring to a sale has effect with the necessary modifications, including, in particular, those in subsections (4) and (5).

(4) References to the proceeds of sale and to the price include the consideration for the exchange.

(5) References to capital sums included in the proceeds of sale include references to so much of the consideration for the exchange as would have been a capital sum if it had been a money payment.

Commentary—*Simon's Taxes* B5.333, B5.343.

Derivation—TA 1988 s 532; CAA 2001 ss 453(1), (2), 572(1)–(3).

HMRC Manuals—Capital Allowances Manual CA70050 (treat as property for capital allowances).

929 Apportionment where property sold together

(1) Any reference in this Part to the sale of property includes the sale of that property together with other property.

(2) In this section—

   references to property include know-how, and

   references to the sale of property include the disposal of know-how.

(3) For the purposes of subsection (1), all property sold as a result of one bargain is to be treated as sold together even though—

   (*a*) separate prices are, or purport to be, agreed for separate items of that property, or

   (*b*) there are, or purport to be, separate sales of separate items of that property.

(4) If an item of property is sold together with other property, then, for the purposes of the charges under sections 908 and 912—

   (*a*) the net proceeds of the sale of that item are treated as being so much of the net proceeds of the sale of all the property as, on a just and reasonable apportionment, is attributable to that item, and

   (*b*) the expenditure incurred on the provision or purchase of that item is treated as being so much of the consideration given for all the property as, on a just and reasonable apportionment, is attributable to that item.

Commentary—*Simon's Taxes* B5.333, B3.110.

Derivation—TA 1988 s 532; CAA 2001 ss 453(1), (2), 562(1)–(3).

HMRC Manuals—Capital Allowances Manual CA12100 (property sold with other property).

HMRC Manuals—International Manual INTM653010 (exemption for all other companies).
Amendments—[1] Part 9A (ss 931A–931W) inserted by FA 2009 s 34, Sch 14 para 1 with effect in relation to distributions paid on or after 1 July 2009 ("the commencement date").

[2] In (*b*), words substituted for words "paragraph (*d*) or (*e*) of section 209(2) of ICTA" by CTA 2010 s 1177, Sch 1 para 660. CTA 2010 has effect for corporation tax purposes for accounting periods ending on or after 1 April 2010, and for income and capital gains tax purposes for the tax year 2010–11 and subsequent tax years.

Exempt classes

[931E Distributions from controlled companies

(1) A dividend or other distribution falls into an exempt class if condition A or B is met.

(2) Condition A is that the recipient controls the payer.

[(3) Condition B is that—

  (a) the recipient is one of two persons who, taken together, control the payer,

  (b) the recipient has interests, rights and powers representing at least 40% of the holdings, rights and powers in respect of which the recipient and the second person fall to be taken as controlling the payer, and

  (c) the second person has interests, rights and powers representing—

    (i) at least 40%, but

    (ii) no more than 55%,

  of the holdings, rights and powers in respect of which the recipient and the second person fall to be taken as controlling the payer.

(4) Section 371RB of TIOPA 2010 (read with section 371RD of that Act) applies for the purposes of this section.

(5) Section 371RD of TIOPA 2010 applies for the purpose of determining if the requirements of subsection (3)(b) and (c) are met in any case.

(6) In subsections (4) and (5) references to section 371RD of TIOPA 2010 are to that section omitting subsection (3)(c) and (d).][2]][1]

Commentary—*Simon's Taxes* D5.153-D5.157.
HMRC Manuals—International Manual INTM653030 (controlled companies: exemption).
Amendments—[1] Part 9A (ss 931A–931W) inserted by FA 2009 s 34, Sch 14 para 1 with effect in relation to distributions paid on or after 1 July 2009 ("the commencement date").

[2] Sub-ss (3)– (6) substituted for previous sub-ss (3)–(5) by FA 2012 s 180, Sch 20 paras 24, 31 with effect in relation to dividends or other distributions received on or after 1 January 2013 (see FA 2012 Sch 20 para 53).

[931F Distributions in respect of non-redeemable ordinary shares

A dividend or other distribution falls into an exempt class if it is made in respect of a share that—

  (*a*) is an ordinary share, and

  (*b*) is not redeemable.][1]

Commentary—*Simon's Taxes* D5.153-D5.157.
HMRC Manuals—International Manual INTM653040 (non redeemable ordinary shares).
Amendments—[1] Part 9A (ss 931A–931W) inserted by FA 2009 s 34, Sch 14 para 1 with effect in relation to distributions paid on or after 1 July 2009 ("the commencement date").

[931G Distributions in respect of portfolio holdings

(1) A dividend or other distribution falls into an exempt class if the recipient—

  (*a*) holds less than 10% of the issued share capital of the payer,

  (*b*) is entitled to less than 10% of the profits available for distribution to holders of the issued share capital of the payer, and

  (*c*) would be entitled on a winding up to less than 10% of the assets of the company available for distribution to holders of the issued share capital of the payer.

(2) Where the payer has more than one class of share, references in subsection (1) to the issued share capital of the payer are to issued share capital of the same class as the share in respect of which the distribution is made.

(3) For the purposes of this section shares are not of the same class if the amounts paid up on them (otherwise than by way of premium) are different.][1]

Commentary—*Simon's Taxes* D5.153-D5.157.
HMRC Manuals—International Manual INTM653080 (exemption for all other companies: portfolio holdings).
Amendments—[1] Part 9A (ss 931A–931W) inserted by FA 2009 s 34, Sch 14 para 1 with effect in relation to distributions paid on or after 1 July 2009 ("the commencement date").

[931H [Distributions][3] derived from transactions not designed to reduce tax

(1) A dividend [or other distribution][3] falls into an exempt class if it is [made][3] in respect of relevant profits.

(2) In this section "relevant profits" means any profits available for distribution at the time that the [distribution is made][3], other than profits that reflect the results of a transaction, or of one or more of a series of transactions, where—

  (*a*) the transaction or series of transactions achieve a reduction (other than a negligible reduction) in United Kingdom tax, and (*b*) the purpose or one of the main purposes of that transaction or series of transactions is to achieve that reduction.

(3) A [distribution][3] that falls into an exempt class otherwise than by virtue of this section is for the purposes of this section treated, so far as possible, as [made][3] in respect of relevant profits.

(4) Any other [distribution][3] is for the purposes of this section treated, so far as possible, as [made][3] in respect of profits other than relevant profits.

(5) Where by virtue of subsection (4) part of a [distribution][3] is treated as [made][3] in respect of relevant profits and part is treated as [made][3] in respect of profits other than relevant profits, the two parts are treated for the purposes of this Part and [Part 2 of TIOPA 2010][2] (double taxation relief) as separate [distributions][3].][1]

Commentary—*Simon's Taxes* **D5.156.**

HMRC Manuals—International Manual INTM653090 (transactions not designed to reduce tax).
INTM653100 (exemption for all other companies: relevant profits).

Amendments—[1]   Part 9A (ss 931A–931W) inserted by FA 2009 s 34, Sch 14 para 1 with effect in relation to distributions paid on or after 1 July 2009 ("the commencement date"), subject to transitional arrangements (FA 2009 Sch 14 para 32).

[2]   In sub-s (5), words substituted for words "Part 18 of ICTA" by TIOPA 2010 s 501, Sch 8 paras 89, 99. TIOPA 2010 has effect for corporation tax purposes for accounting periods ending on or after 1 April 2010, for income and capital gains tax purposes for the tax year 2010–11 and subsequent tax years, and for petroleum revenue tax purposes for chargeable periods beginning on or after 1 July 2010.

[3]   In heading, word substituted for word "Dividends", in sub-s (1), words inserted and word substituted for word "paid", in sub-s (2), words substituted for words "dividend is paid", in sub-ss (3), (4), words substituted for words "dividend" and "paid" respectively, and in sub-s (5), words substituted for words "dividend", "paid" (in both places) and "dividends" respectively, by F(No 3)A 2010 s 9, Sch 3 para 3(1), (3) with effect in relation to distributions made on or after 1 July 2009. Note that if a company so elects, F(No 3)A 2010 Sch 3 has effect in relation to a relevant distribution (a distribution made before 22 June 2010) received by the company as if the amendments made by para 1 to 4 were of no effect, and paras 5(2) and 6 were of no effect. Such an election has effect only in relation to such distributions as are specified in the election (F(No 2)A 2010 Sch 3 para 7).

[931I Dividends in respect of shares accounted for as liabilities]

A dividend falls into an exempt class if the dividend is paid in respect of a share to which, at the time of the payment, section 521C (shares accounted for as liabilities treated as loan relationships) does not apply only because the condition in subsection (1)(*f*) of that section is not met.][1]

Commentary—*Simon's Taxes* **D5.153–D5.157.**

HMRC Manuals—International Manual INTM653120 (shares accounted for as liabilities).

Amendments—[1]   Part 9A (ss 931A–931W) inserted by FA 2009 s 34, Sch 14 para 1 with effect in relation to distributions paid on or after 1 July 2009 ("the commencement date").

Exempt classes: anti-avoidance

[931J Schemes involving manipulation of controlled company rules]

(1) This section applies to a dividend that would, apart from this section, fall into an exempt class by virtue of section 931E.

(2) The dividend does not fall into an exempt class by virtue of that section if—

    (*a*) the dividend is paid as part of a scheme the main purpose, or one of the main purposes, of which is to secure that dividends of the payer received by the recipient fall into an exempt class by virtue of that section, and

    (*b*) the following condition is met.

(3) The condition is that the dividend is paid in respect of pre-control profits.

(4) A dividend that falls into an exempt class otherwise than by virtue of section 931E is for the purposes of this section treated, so far as possible, as paid in respect of profits other than pre-control profits.

(5) Any other dividend is for the purposes of this section treated, so far as possible, as paid in respect of pre-control profits.

(6) In this section "pre-control profits" means any profits available for distribution at the time the dividend is paid that arose at a time when neither condition A nor condition B in section 931E was met.

(7) Where—

    (*a*) the condition in subsection (2)(*a*) is met, and

    (*b*) by virtue of subsection (5) part of a dividend is treated as paid in respect of pre-control profits and part is treated as paid in respect of profits other than pre-control profits,

the two parts are treated for the purposes of this Part and [Part 2 of TIOPA 2010][2] (double taxation relief) as separate dividends.][1]

Commentary—*Simon's Taxes* **D5.153–D5.157.**

HMRC Manuals—International Manual INTM654020 (manipulation of controlled company rules).
INTM654030 (manipulation of controlled company rules: purpose test).
INTM654010 (distribution exemption: antiavoidance legislation: outline).

Amendments—[1]   This section inserted by FA 2009 s 34, Sch 14 para 1 with effect in relation to distributions paid on or after 1 July 2009 ("the commencement date"),subject to transitional arrangements (FA 2009 Sch 14 para 32).

HMRC Manuals—International Manual INTM654100 (diversion of trade income).
Amendments—[1] Part 9A (ss 931A–931W) inserted by FA 2009 s 34, Sch 14 para 1 with effect in relation to distributions paid on or after 1 July 2009 ("the commencement date").

CHAPTER 4

SUPPLEMENTARY

Election that distribution should not be exempt

[931R Election that distribution should not be exempt

(1) This section applies where, apart from this section, a distribution ("the distribution") would be exempt.

(2) If the recipient so elects, the distribution is not exempt.

(3) An election under this section must be made on or before the second anniversary of the end of the accounting period in which the distribution is received.

(4) Subsection (5) applies where the distribution is a dividend that is treated for certain purposes of Part 18 of ICTA (double taxation relief) as two separate dividends by virtue of section 801C of that Act (separate streaming of dividend so far as representing an ADP dividend of a CFC).

(5) If the recipient so elects—

(a) the distribution is to be treated for the purposes of this Part as if it were an ADP dividend and a separate residual dividend as provided for in that section of that Act, and

(b) the ADP dividend is not exempt.

(6) The reference in subsection (4) to section 801C of ICTA is to that section as it continues to have effect in accordance with paragraph 8(1) of Schedule 16 to FA 2009 in relation to dividends paid on or after 1 July 2009 for accounting periods beginning before that day.][1]

Commentary—*Simon's Taxes* D5.150, D8.141.

HMRC Manuals—International Manual INTM655010 (election that a distribution should not be exempt).
Amendments—[1] Part 9A (ss 931A–931W) inserted by FA 2009 s 34, Sch 14 para 1 with effect in relation to distributions paid on or after 1 July 2009 ("the commencement date").

[Chargeable gains

931RA Chargeable gains

The fact that a dividend or other distribution is exempt does not prevent it from being taken into account in the calculation of chargeable gains.][1]

Commentary—*Simon's Taxes* D5.150.

Amendments—[1] Section 931RA and preceding heading inserted by F(No 3)A 2010 s 9, Sch 3 para 3(1), (4) with effect in relation to distributions made on or after 1 July 2009. Note that if a company so elects, F(No 3)A 2010 Sch 3 has effect in relation to a relevant distribution (a distribution made before 22 June 2010) received by the company as if the amendments made by para 1 to 4 were of no effect, and paras 5(2) and 6 were of no effect. Such an election has effect only in relation to such distributions as are specified in the election (F(No 3)A 2010 Sch 3 para 7).

Interpretation

[931S Meaning of "small company"

(1) For the purposes of this Part a company is a "small company" in an accounting period if it is in that period a micro or small enterprise, as defined in the Annex to Commission Recommendation 2003/361/ EC of 6 May 2003.

(2) But a company is not a "small company" in an accounting period if it is at any time in that period—

(a) an open-ended investment company,

(b) an authorised unit trust scheme,

(c) an insurance company, or

(d) a friendly society.

(3) In subsection (2)—

"open-ended investment company" has the meaning given by section 236 of FISMA 2000;

"authorised unit trust scheme" means a unit trust scheme (within the meaning given by section 237 of FISMA 2000) in relation to which a order under section 243 of that Act (authorisation orders) is in force;

"insurance company" has the meaning given by [section 65 of FA 2012][2];

"friendly society" has the meaning given by [section 172 of FA 2012][3].][1]

Commentary—*Simon's Taxes* D5.151.

HMRC Manuals—International Manual INTM652060 (small companies: definition). INTM652080 (exclusions from definition).
Amendments—[1] Part 9A (ss 931A–931W) inserted by FA 2009 s 34, Sch 14 para 1 with effect in relation to distributions paid on or after 1 July 2009 ("the commencement date").
[2] In sub-s (3), in definition of "insurance company", words substituted for words "section 431 of ICTA" by FA 2012 s 146, Sch 16 paras 135, 183 with effect in relation to accounting periods of companies beginning on or after 1 January 2013 (subject to transitional provisions in FA 2012 Sch 17). For accounting periods straddling 1 January 2013, see FA 2012 s 149.

³ In sub-(3), in definition of "friendly society", words substituted for words "section 466(2) of ICTA" by FA 2012 s 176, Sch 18 paras 19, 22 with effect in relation to accounting periods of companies beginning on or after 1 January 2013, subject to transitional provisions in FA 2012 s 179.

[931T Meaning of "payer", "recipient" and "relevant person"

In this Part—

"the payer", in relation to a distribution, means the company that makes the distribution;

"the recipient", in relation to a distribution, means the company that receives the distribution;

"a relevant person", in relation to a distribution, means—

(a) the company that receives the distribution, or

(b) any person connected with that company.]¹

Commentary—*Simon's Taxes* D5.153-D5.157, D9.703A.

HMRC Manuals—International Manual INTM651040 (definitions).

Amendments—¹ Part 9A (ss 931A–931W) inserted by FA 2009 s 34, Sch 14 para 1 with effect in relation to distributions paid on or after 1 July 2009 ("the commencement date").

[931U Meaning of "ordinary share" and "redeemable"

(1) In this Part "ordinary share" means a share that does not carry any present or future preferential right to dividends or to a company's assets on its winding up.

(2) A share is regarded as "redeemable" for the purposes of this Part only if it is redeemable as a result of its terms of issue (or any collateral arrangements)—

(a) requiring redemption,

(b) entitling the holder to require redemption, or

(c) entitling the issuing company to redeem.]¹

Commentary—*Simon's Taxes* D5.153-D5.157, D5.153-D5.157.

HMRC Manuals—International Manual INTM653050 (ordinary shares: meaning). INTM653070 (redeemable: meaning).

Amendments—¹ Part 9A (ss 931A–931W) inserted by FA 2009 s 34, Sch 14 para 1 with effect in relation to distributions paid on or after 1 July 2009 ("the commencement date").

[931V Meaning of "scheme" and "tax advantage scheme"

(1) For the purposes of this Part—

"scheme" includes any scheme, arrangements or understanding of any kind whatever, whether or not legally enforceable, involving a single transaction or two or more transactions;

"tax advantage scheme" means a scheme the main purpose, or one of the main purposes, of which is to obtain a tax advantage (other than a negligible tax advantage).

(2) In this section "tax advantage" has the meaning given by [section 1139 of CTA 2010]².]¹

Commentary—*Simon's Taxes* D5.151, D5.153-D5.157.

HMRC Manuals—International Manual INTM651040 (scheme and tax advantage scheme: definitions). INTM652050 (tax advantage scheme : meaning).

Amendments—¹ Part 9A (ss 931A–931W) inserted by FA 2009 s 34, Sch 14 para 1 with effect in relation to distributions paid on or after 1 July 2009 ("the commencement date").

² In sub-para (2) words substituted for words "section 840ZA of ICTA" by CTA 2010 s 1177, Sch 1 para 661. CTA 2010 has effect for corporation tax purposes for accounting periods ending on or after 1 April 2010, and for income and capital gains tax purposes for the tax year 2010–11 and subsequent tax years.

Boundary provisions

[931W Provisions which must be given priority over this Part

(1) Any income so far as it falls within—

(a) this Part, and

(b) Chapter 2 of Part 3 (income taxed as trade profits), is dealt with under Part 3.

(2) Any income so far as it falls within—

(a) this Part, and

(b) Chapter 3 of Part 4 (profits of property businesses) so far as the Chapter relates to a UK property business, is dealt with under Part 4.

(3) . . .²]¹

Commentary—*Simon's Taxes* D5.150.

Amendments—¹ Part 9A (ss 931A–931W) inserted by FA 2009 s 34, Sch 14 para 1 with effect in relation to distributions paid on or after 1 July 2009 ("the commencement date").

² Sub-s (3) repealed by FA 2012 s 146, Sch 16 paras 135, 184 with effect in relation to accounting periods of companies beginning on or after 1 January 2013 (subject to transitional provisions in FA 2012 Sch 17). For accounting periods straddling 1 January 2013, see FA 2012 s 149.

PART 10

MISCELLANEOUS INCOME

CHAPTER 1

INTRODUCTION

932 Overview of Part

(1) This Part applies the charge to corporation tax on income to—

   (a) . . .¹

   (b) beneficiaries' income from estates in administration (see Chapter 3),

   (c) income from the holding of an office (see Chapter 4),

   (d) *income treated as received from unauthorised unit trusts (see Chapter 5),*²

   (e) income treated as arising from the sale or other realisation of dividend coupons in respect of foreign holdings (see Chapter 6),

   (f) annual payments not otherwise charged to corporation tax (see Chapter 7), and

   (g) other income not otherwise charged to corporation tax (see Chapter 8).

(2) Chapter 9 contains rules that give priority to provisions outside this Part in relation to matters that fall within Chapter 2, 5 or 6.

(3) This Part needs to be read with Part 19 (general exemptions).

Amendments—¹ Sub-s (1)(a) repealed by FA 2009 s 34, Sch 14 paras 20, 23 with effect in relation to distributions paid on or after 1 July 2009.

² Sub-s (1)(d) repealed by the Unauthorised Unit Trusts (Tax) Regulations, SI 2013/2819 reg 38(1), (2) with effect from 6 April 2014. Note that an unauthorised unit trust is not a non-exempt unauthorised unit trust, and this amendment does not apply in relation to the trust, if at all times in the period beginning with 24 May 2012 and ending with 5 April 2014 it had at least one unit holder which was, and at least one unit holder which was not, an eligible investor (ie a mixed unauthorised unit trust); this ceases to apply in relation to the trust if subsequently it no longer has any unit holders which are eligible investors (SI 2013/2819 reg 32).

CHAPTER 3

BENEFICIARIES' INCOME FROM ESTATES IN ADMINISTRATION

Introduction

934 Charge to tax on estate income

(1) The charge to corporation tax on income applies to estate income.

(2) In this Chapter—

   "estate" means the estate of a deceased person (whether a UK estate or a foreign estate), and

   "estate income" means the income treated under this Chapter as arising from an absolute, limited or discretionary interest in the whole or part of the residue of an estate.

(3) If different parts of an estate are subject to different residuary dispositions, those parts are treated for the purposes of this Chapter as if they were separate estates.

Commentary—*Simon's Taxes* **C4.115**.

Derivation—TA 1988 ss 695(2)–(4), 696(3), (6), 698(3), 701(11).

HMRC Manuals—Trusts, Settlements and Estates Manual TSEM7676 (interests in residue: practical and computational aspects: introduction).

935 Absolute, limited and discretionary interests

(1) A person has an absolute interest in the whole or part of the residue of an estate for the purposes of this Chapter if—

   (a) the capital of the residue or that part is properly payable to the person, or

   (b) it would be so payable if the residue had been ascertained.

(2) A person has a limited interest in the whole or part of the residue of an estate during any period for the purposes of this Chapter if—

   (a) the person does not have an absolute interest in it, and

   (b) the income from it would be properly payable to the person if the residue had been ascertained at the beginning of that period.

(3) A person has a discretionary interest in the whole or part of the residue of an estate for the purposes of this Chapter if—

   (a) a discretion may be exercised in the person's favour, and

   (b) on its exercise in the person's favour any of the income of the residue during the whole or part of the administration period (see section 938) would be properly payable to the person if the residue had been ascertained at the beginning of that period.

(4) For the purposes of this section, an amount is only treated as properly payable to a person ("A") if—

   (a) it is properly payable to A, or to another person in A's right, for A's benefit, or

   (b) A is a personal representative and subsection (5) applies.

(5) The personal representatives of a deceased person ("B") are to be treated as having an absolute or limited interest in the whole or part of the residue of the estate of another deceased person ("C") if—

(*a*) they have a right in their capacity as B's personal representatives, and

(*b*) were the right vested in them for their own benefit, they would have that interest in C's estate.

(6) For the purposes of subsection (4), it does not matter whether the amount is payable directly by the personal representatives or through a trustee or other person.

Commentary—*Simon's Taxes* **C4.117**.
Derivation—TA 1988 ss 698(1), (3), 701(2), (3).
HMRC Manuals—Trusts, Settlements and Estates Manual TSEM7452 (absolute, limited and discretionary interests: meaning). TSEM7652 (deceased persons: limited interests in residue description). TSEM7602 (absolute interests in residue: definition).

936 Meaning of "UK estate" and "foreign estate"

(1) In this Chapter—

"UK estate", in relation to a tax year, means an estate which meets conditions A and B, or condition C, for that year, and

"foreign estate", in relation to a tax year, means an estate which is not a UK estate in relation to that year.

(2) Condition A is that all the income of the estate either—

(*a*) has borne United Kingdom income tax by deduction, or

(*b*) is income in respect of which the personal representatives are directly assessable to United Kingdom income tax for the tax year.

(3) Condition B is that none of the income of the estate is income for which the personal representatives are not liable to United Kingdom income tax for the tax year because they are not UK resident . . . [1].

(4) For the purposes of conditions A and B, sums within section 963(3) or (4) (sums treated as bearing income tax) are ignored.

(5) Condition C is that the aggregate income of the estate for the tax year consists only of sums within section 963(3) or (4).

Commentary—*Simon's Taxes* **C4.104**.
Derivation—TA 1988 ss 699A(1B), 701(9), (10), (10A).
HMRC Manuals—Trusts, Settlements and Estates Manual TSEM7680 (UK estate: meaning).
Amendments—[1]   Words in sub-s (3) repealed by FA 2013 s 219, Sch 46 paras 137, 139 with effect if the tax year in question begins on or after 6 April 2013.

Types of estate income

937 Absolute interests in residue

(1) Income is treated as arising in an accounting period from a company's absolute interest in the whole or part of the residue of an estate if—

(*a*) the company has an assumed income entitlement for the accounting period in respect of the interest (see sections 948 to 952), and

(*b*) condition A or B is met.

(2) Condition A is that a payment is made in respect of the interest in the accounting period and before the end of the administration period (see section 938).

(3) Condition B is that the accounting period is the final accounting period (see section 938).

(4) Income treated as arising as a result of this section is estate income for the purposes of this Chapter.

Commentary—*Simon's Taxes* **C4.121**.
Derivation—TA 1988 ss 696(3), (5).
HMRC Manuals—Trusts, Settlements and Estates Manual TSEM7604 (absolute interests in residue tax rules). TSEM7608 (absolute interests in residue payments made during the administration period).

938 Meaning of "the administration period", "the final accounting period" and "the final tax year"

(1) In this Chapter "the administration period", in relation to the estate of a deceased person, means the period beginning with the deceased's death and ending with the completion of the administration of the estate.

(2) In the application of subsection (1) to Scotland, the reference to the completion of the administration is to be taken as a reference to the date at which, after discharge of, or provision for, liabilities falling to be met out of the deceased's estate, the free balance held in trust for the residuary legatees or for the persons with the right to the intestate estate has been ascertained.

(3) In this Chapter "the final accounting period" means the accounting period in which the administration period ends.

(4) In this Chapter "the final tax year" means the tax year in which the administration period ends.

Commentary—*Simon's Taxes* **C4.103**.
Derivation—TA 1988 ss 695(1), 701(13), 702.
HMRC Manuals—Trusts, Settlements and Estates Manual TSEM7360 (definition of period of administration).

939 Limited interests in residue

(1) Income is treated as arising in an accounting period from a company's limited interest in the whole or part of the residue of an estate in cases A, B and C.

(2) Case A is where—

   (a) the interest has not ceased before the beginning of the accounting period, and

   (b) a sum is paid in respect of the interest in that period and before the end of the administration period.

(3) Case B is where—

   (a) the accounting period is the final accounting period,

   (b) the interest has not ceased before the beginning of that period, and

   (c) a sum remains payable in respect of the interest at the end of the administration period.

(4) Case C is where—

   (a) the accounting period is a period before the final accounting period,

   (b) the interest ceases in the accounting period, and

   (c) a sum is paid in respect of the interest in a later accounting period but before the end of the administration period, or remains payable in respect of it at the end of the administration period.

(5) This section does not apply to limited interests to which section 957 (successive interests: holders of limited interests) applies.

(6) Income treated as arising as a result of this section or section 957 is estate income for the purposes of this Chapter.

Commentary—*Simon's Taxes* **C4.122**.

Derivation—TA 1988 s 695(2), (3).

HMRC Manuals—Trusts, Settlements and Estates Manual TSEM7652 (limited interests in residue description). TSEM7655 (limited interests in residue: statutory conventional basis of taxation).

940 Discretionary interests in residue

(1) Income is treated as arising in an accounting period from a company's discretionary interest in the whole or part of the residue of an estate if a payment is made in the accounting period in exercise of the discretion in the company's favour.

(2) Income treated as arising as a result of this section is estate income for the purposes of this Chapter.

Commentary—*Simon's Taxes* **C4.123**.

Derivation—TA 1988 s 698(3).

HMRC Manuals—Trusts, Settlements and Estates Manual TSEM7660 (limited interests in residue discretionary interests in residue: definition).

Income charged

941 UK estates

(1) In the case of a UK estate, tax is charged under section 934 on the amount of estate income treated as arising in the accounting period.

(2) That amount is the basic amount of that income for the accounting period (see subsection (4)), grossed up by reference to the applicable rate for the relevant tax year (see section 946).

(3) The gross amount is treated as having borne income tax by deduction at that rate.

(4) In this Chapter "the basic amount", in relation to estate income, has the meaning given by—

   (a) section 943 (basic amount of estate income: absolute interests),

   (b) section 944 (basic amount of estate income: limited interests),

   (c) section 945 (basic amount of estate income: discretionary interests), and

   (d) section 958 (basic amount of estate income: successive limited interests).

Commentary—*Simon's Taxes* **C4.118, C4.123**.

Derivation—TA 1988 ss 695(2)–(4), 696(3), (4), 698(3).

HMRC Manuals—Trusts, Settlements and Estates Manual TSEM7684 (interests in residue: practical and computational aspects tax rules for UK estates). TSEM7655 (limited interests in residue: statutory conventional basis of taxation).

942 Foreign estates

(1) In the case of a foreign estate, tax is charged under section 934 on the amount of estate income treated as arising in the accounting period.

(2) That amount depends on whether the estate income arising in the accounting period is paid from sums within section 963(3) or (4) (sums treated as bearing income tax).

(3) So far as the estate income is paid from such sums, that amount is the basic amount of that income for the accounting period grossed up by reference to the applicable rate for the relevant tax year (see section 946).

(4) That gross amount is treated as having borne income tax by deduction at that rate.

(5) So far as the estate income is not paid from sums within section 963(3) or (4), the amount of estate income treated as arising in the accounting period is the basic amount of that income for that period.

Commentary—*Simon's Taxes* **C4.119**.

Derivation—TA 1988 ss 12(1), 695(4), 696(6), 698(3), 699A(3).

HMRC Manuals—Trusts, Settlements and Estates Manual TSEM7682 (interests in residue: practical and computational aspects foreign estates).

Company Taxation Manual CTM02130 (special rules: trades abroad charged under case V).

Basic amount of estate income: general calculations rules

943 Absolute interests

(1) The basic amount of estate income relating to a company's absolute interest in the whole or part of the residue of an estate for an accounting period before the final accounting period is the lower of—

    (*a*) the total of all sums paid in the accounting period in respect of that interest, and

    (*b*) the amount of the company's assumed income entitlement for the accounting period in respect of it.

(2) The basic amount for the final accounting period is equal to the amount of the company's assumed income entitlement for that accounting period in respect of that interest.

(3) But if the residuary income of the estate for the final tax year is nil because the allowable estate deductions exceed the aggregate income of the estate, the basic amount for the final accounting period is reduced—

    (*a*) where the company has an absolute interest in the whole of the residue of the estate, by an amount equal to the excess, and

    (*b*) in any other case, by an amount equal to such part of the excess as is just and reasonable.

(4) See sections 948 to 952 for the meaning of references to assumed income entitlement and residuary income of an estate.

(5) See sections 947 and 949(2) for the meaning of aggregate income of an estate and allowable estate deductions respectively.

(6) This section is subject to sections 953 to 956 (successive interests).

Commentary—*Simon's Taxes* **C4.121**.

944 Limited interests

(1) The basic amount of estate income relating to a company's limited interest in the whole or part of the residue of an estate for an accounting period is the total of the sums within section 939(2)(*b*), (3)(*c*) and (4)(*c*) for that period.

(2) This does not apply, and section 958 applies instead, if the limited interest is one to which section 957 (successive interests: holders of limited interests) applies.

Commentary—*Simon's Taxes* **C4.122**.

Derivation—TA 1988 s 695(2)–(4).

HMRC Manuals—Trusts, Settlements and Estates Manual TSEM7655 (limited interests in residue: statutory conventional basis of taxation).

945 Discretionary interests

The basic amount of estate income relating to a company's discretionary interest in the whole or part of the residue of an estate for an accounting period is the total of the payments made in the accounting period in exercise of the discretion in favour of the company.

Commentary—*Simon's Taxes* **C4.123**.

Derivation—TA 1988 ss 695(4), 698(3).

HMRC Manuals—Trusts, Settlements and Estates Manual TSEM7660 (limited interests in residue discretionary interests in residue: definition).

946 Applicable rate for grossing up basic amounts of estate income

(1) The applicable rate by reference to which a basic amount of estate income is grossed up for the purposes of sections 941 and 942 depends on the rate at which income tax is borne by the aggregate income of the estate for the relevant tax year (see subsection (5)).

(2) If the aggregate income of the estate all bears income tax at the same rate, the applicable rate is that rate.

(3) If—

    (*a*) different parts of the aggregate income of the estate bear income tax at different rates, and

    (*b*) the same rate applies to all the income from which section 962 treats the basic amount as having been paid,

the applicable rate is that rate.

(4) If—

    (*a*) different parts of the aggregate income of the estate bear income tax at different rates, and

    (*b*) different rates apply to different parts of the income from which section 962 treats the basic amount as having been paid,

each of those rates is the applicable rate by reference to which the corresponding part of the basic amount is grossed up.

(5) In this Chapter "the relevant tax year" in relation to an amount of estate income, means the tax year in which the amount of estate income would be treated as arising if—

    (*a*) the references in this Chapter to accounting periods were references to tax years, and

(5) For the purposes of calculating the total mentioned in subsection (1)(*b*)—

   (*a*) if the estate is a UK estate in relation to a tax year in which a sum is paid, the sum is to be grossed up by reference to the basic rate for that year, and

   (*b*) if the estate is a UK estate in relation to the final tax year, a sum payable at the end of the administration period is to be grossed up by reference to the basic rate for that year.

(6) For the application of this section where two or more absolute interests in the whole or the same part of the residue are held successively by different persons, see section 954(5) and (6).

Commentary—*Simon's Taxes* **C4.121.**

952 Applicable rate for determining assumed income entitlement (UK estates)

(1) The applicable rate by reference to which income tax on a company's share of the residuary income of the estate is calculated for the purposes of step 2 of the calculation in section 948(1) depends on the rate at which income tax is borne by the aggregate income of the estate for the tax year in question.

(2) If the aggregate income of the estate all bears income tax at the same rate, the applicable rate is that rate.

(3) If different parts of the aggregate income of the estate bear income tax at different rates, the applicable rate is the rate that applies to the income to which the company's share of the residuary income of the estate relates.

(4) If different rates apply to different parts of that income, each of those rates is the applicable rate that applies to the corresponding part of the income to which the company's share of the residuary income of the estate relates.

(5) For the purposes of this section, if there is more than one person with an absolute interest in the residue of the estate, such apportionments of parts of the aggregate income of the estate bearing income tax at different rates are to be made as are just and reasonable for their different interests.

(6) Section 650(1) of ITTOIA 2005 (absolute interests) applies for the purposes of subsection (5) in the case of any person who is not a company chargeable to corporation tax.

Commentary—*Simon's Taxes* **C4.121.**
Derivation—TA 1988 s 701(3A).

Successive interests

953 Introduction

(1) Sections 954 to 959 relate to cases where two or more interests in the whole or part of the residue of an estate are held successively during the administration period by different persons.

(2) For the purposes of this section and those sections, two interests are held successively even where one is not held immediately before or after the other.

(3) It is assumed for the purposes of those sections—

   (*a*) that each of the persons holding the interests in question is a company within the charge to corporation tax (but without prejudice to the references to interests ceasing otherwise than by death), and

   (*b*) that in the case of a person who is not a company the person's accounting periods correspond with tax years.

954 Successive absolute interests

(1) This section applies if two or more absolute interests in the whole or part of the residue of an estate are held successively during the administration period by different persons.

(2) In determining whether a company with a later such interest ("the later holder") has an assumed income entitlement in respect of that interest and, if so, its amount—

   (*a*) the later holder's share of the residuary income of the estate in respect of that interest for any accounting period is to be treated as including the share of any person with a previous such interest ("a previous holder"), and

   (*b*) the basic amounts relating to the later holder's interest are to be treated as including the basic amounts relating to any previous such interest.

(3) In applying subsection (2), all determinations under that subsection or section 955(2) that fall to be made in relation to a person with an earlier interest are to be made before determinations under those provisions relating to a person with a later interest.

(4) A company which is a previous holder in the final accounting period is to be taxed for that period, in relation to the interest as to which that company is a previous holder, as if that period were not the final accounting period, and the later holder's assumed income entitlement is to be calculated accordingly (or, where the previous holder is not a company, having regard to the application of section 671(4) of ITTOIA 2005 to the previous holder).

(5) The calculation under section 951(1)(*a*) and (*b*) (amount of reduction in the share of the residuary income of the company with an absolute interest at the end of the administration period) is to be made by reference to all the absolute interests taken together.

(6) If the amount resulting from that calculation is greater than the total amount of the reductions which can be made under section 951(2) and (3), the share of the residuary income of the estate of the last previous holder of the interest for the last accounting period in which that last holder had that interest is to be reduced, and so on.

(7) But if subsection (6) applies in a case where the last previous holder or any earlier previous holder is not a company, in applying that subsection regard must be had to the application of section 671(6) of ITTOIA 2005 to the previous holder.

Commentary—*Simon's Taxes* **C4.124**.

955 Assumed income entitlement of holder of absolute interest following limited interest

(1) This section applies if—

    (*a*) two or more interests in the whole or part of the residue of an estate are held successively during the administration period by different persons,

    (*b*) each later interest arises or is created on the cessation of the previous interest otherwise than by death,

    (*c*) at least one of the interests is an absolute interest, and

    (*d*) at least one of the interests preceding that interest is a limited interest.

(2) Rules A and B apply to determine in relation to such an absolute interest—

    (*a*) whether the company with the interest has an assumed income entitlement in respect of the interest, and

    (*b*) if so, its amount.

(3) Rule A is that the company's share of the residuary income of the estate in respect of the absolute interest for any accounting period is treated as including any amount which would be included in it if—

    (*a*) the interest had subsisted throughout the period when any such limited interest subsisted, and

    (*b*) no such limited interest had ever subsisted.

(4) Rule B is that the basic amounts relating to the absolute interest are treated as including the basic amounts relating to any such limited interest.

Commentary—*Simon's Taxes* **C4.124**.

956 Payments in respect of limited interests followed by absolute interests

(1) This section applies if—

    (*a*) two or more interests in the whole or part of the residue of an estate are held successively during the administration period by different persons,

    (*b*) each later interest arises or is created on the cessation of the previous interest otherwise than by death,

    (*c*) at least one of the interests is an absolute interest, and

    (*d*) at least one of the interests preceding that interest is a limited interest.

(2) A sum to which a company ("C") with such an absolute interest is entitled in respect of any such limited interest which is paid while C has the absolute interest is treated as paid in respect of the absolute interest (and not the limited interest).

(3) Subsection (4) applies if—

    (*a*) C's absolute interest ceases during the administration period, and

    (*b*) a sum to which C is entitled in respect of any such limited interest—

        (i) is paid after the absolute interest ceases but before the end of the administration period, or

        (ii) remains payable at the end of it.

(4) This Chapter applies as respects any such sum as if the limited interest had continued to subsist while that absolute interest subsisted and had been held by C.

(5) Subsection (4) is subject to subsection (6).

(6) For the purposes only of section 951 (reduction in share of residuary income of estate), any such sum is treated as paid or payable in respect of the absolute interest.

Commentary—*Simon's Taxes* **C4.124**.

Derivation—TA 1988 s 698(1A), (1B).

957 Holders of limited interests

(1) This section applies if—

    (*a*) two or more interests in the whole or part of the residue of an estate are held successively during the administration period by different persons,

    (*b*) the earlier or, if there are more than two, the earliest of the interests is a limited interest, and

    (*c*) each later interest arises or is created on the cessation of the previous interest otherwise than by death.

(2) Income is treated as arising from a limited interest in the whole or part of the residue of the estate in an accounting period in cases A, B and C.

(3) Case A is where—

(i) section 947(2)(*c*) (stock dividends), or

(ii) section 947(2)(*d*) (release of loan to participator in close company where debt due from personal representatives).

(4) A sum that is part of the aggregate income of the estate because of falling within section 947(2)(*e*) (gains from life insurance contracts etc) is treated as bearing income tax at the basic rate.

(5) Income tax treated as borne under section 941(3) or 942(4) (gross amount of estate income treated as bearing tax at the applicable rate) is not repayable so far as the basic amount of the estate income in question is paid from sums within this section.

Commentary—*Simon's Taxes* **C4.104, C4.106.**

HMRC Manuals—Trusts, Settlements and Estates Manual TSEM7686 (practical and computational aspects underlying source of income).

964 Transfers of assets etc treated as payments

(1) For the purposes of this Chapter—

(*a*) a transfer of assets, or

(*b*) the appropriation of assets by personal representatives to themselves,

is treated as the payment of an amount equal to the assets' value at the date of transfer or appropriation.

(2) The set off or release of a debt is treated for the purposes of this Chapter as the payment of an amount equal to it.

(3) If at the end of the administration period—

(*a*) there is an obligation to transfer assets to any person, or

(*b*) personal representatives are entitled to appropriate assets to themselves,

an amount equal to the assets' value at that time is treated as payable then for the purposes of this Chapter.

(4) If at the end of the administration period—

(*a*) there is an obligation to release or set off a debt owed by any person, or

(*b*) personal representatives are entitled to release or set off a debt in their own favour,

a sum equal to the debt is treated as payable then for the purposes of this Chapter.

Commentary—*Simon's Taxes* **C4.116.**

Derivation—TA 1988 s 701(12).

HMRC Manuals—Trusts, Settlements and Estates Manual TSEM6078 (value of assets transferred from an estate).

965 Assessments, adjustments and claims after the administration period

(1) This subsection applies if after the administration period ends it is apparent that a company is liable for corporation tax on estate income for any accounting period for which it previously appeared not to be so liable or to be liable for tax on a lesser amount.

(2) If subsection (1) applies—

(*a*) the company may be assessed and taxed for the accounting period, and

(*b*) any relief or additional relief to which the company may be entitled for the accounting period is to be allowed if a claim is made.

(3) This subsection applies if after the administration period ends it is apparent that a company which previously appeared to be liable for corporation tax on estate income for any accounting period is not so liable or is liable for tax on a lesser amount.

(4) If subsection (3) applies—

(*a*) all necessary adjustments and repayments of corporation tax for the accounting period are to be made, and

(*b*) if the company has been allowed relief which exceeds the relief that could have been given by reference to the amount actually charged for the accounting period, the excess is to be treated as chargeable for that accounting period under the charge to corporation tax on income.

(5) An assessment or adjustment made for the purposes of this Chapter or a claim made as a result of this Chapter may be made after the end of the period otherwise allowed if it is made on or before the third anniversary of the 31 January following the accounting period in which the administration period ends.

Commentary—*Simon's Taxes* **C4.127.**

Derivation—TA 1988 s 700(1)–(3).

HMRC Manuals—Trusts, Settlements and Estates Manual TSEM7692 (interests in residue: practical and computational aspects time limit).

967 Statements relating to estate income

(1) If a company within subsection (2) requests it in writing, a personal representative of a deceased person must provide the company with a statement showing—

(*a*) the amount treated as estate income arising from the company's interest in the whole or part of the deceased person's estate for which the company is liable to corporation tax for an accounting period, and

(b) the amount of any tax at the applicable rate which any such amount is treated as having borne.

(2) A company is within this subsection if—

    (a) it has or has had an absolute or limited interest in the whole or part of the residue of the estate, or

    (b) estate income has arisen to it from a discretionary interest it has or has had in the whole or part of the residue of the estate.

(3) A statement under subsection (1) must be in writing.

(4) The duty to comply with a request under this section is enforceable by the company which made it.

Commentary—*Simon's Taxes* **C4.128.**
Derivation—TA 1988 s 700(5), (6).
HMRC Manuals—Trusts, Settlements and Estates Manual TSEM6071 (the end of an administration period).
TSEM6054 (statements relating to estate income).

CHAPTER 4

INCOME FROM HOLDING AN OFFICE

969 Charge to tax on income from holding an office

(1) The charge to corporation tax on income applies to income from the holding of an office.

(2) The amount of any income charged to tax under this section is to be calculated in accordance with income tax principles and all questions as to any of the following matters are to be determined in accordance with income tax law and practice as if accounting periods were years of assessment—

    (a) the amounts which are or are not to be taken into account as a person's income from the holding of an office,

    (b) the amounts which are or are not to be taken into account in calculating a person's income from the holding of an office,

    (c) the amounts which are or are not to be charged to tax as a person's income from the holding of an office, and

    (d) the time when any such amount is to be treated as arising.

(3) Subsection (2) is subject to the provisions of the Corporation Tax Acts.

(4) Accordingly—

    (a) for corporation tax purposes income from the holding of an office is to be calculated under Part 2 of ITEPA 2003 (employment income) and the provisions applicable to that Part, and

    (b) any provision of the Income Tax Acts (other than ITTOIA 2005 or ITA 2007) which has the effect of conferring an exemption from income tax in relation to income from the holding of an office has the corresponding effect for corporation tax purposes, unless otherwise provided.

(5) For the purposes of this section "income tax law" means, in relation to an accounting period of a company, the law applying to the charge on individuals of income tax for the tax year in which the period ends, but does not include—

    (a) such of the enactments of the Income Tax Acts as make special provision for individuals in relation to matters referred to in subsection (2), or

    (b) ITA 2007.

(6) In this section "office" includes in particular any position which has an existence independent of the person who holds it and may be filled by successive holders.

Commentary—*Simon's Taxes* **B2.410, C1.222.**
Derivation—TA 1988 s 9(1), (2), (3), (4); ITEPA 2003 s 5(3).
HMRC Manuals—Company Taxation Manual CTM01150 (application of IT exemptions).

970 Rule restricting deductions for bad debts

(1) This section applies only to debts to which Part 5 (loan relationships) does not apply.

(2) In calculating the income of an office held by a company, no deduction is allowed in respect of a debt owed to the company, except—

    (a) by way of impairment loss, or

    (b) so far as the debt is released wholly and exclusively for the purposes of the office as part of a statutory insolvency arrangement.

(3) In this section "debt" includes an obligation or liability that falls to be discharged otherwise than by the payment of money.

Commentary—*Simon's Taxes* **B2.410.**
Derivation—TA 1988 s 88D(1)–(4).
HMRC Manuals—Business Income Manual BIM42701 (bad and doubtful debts: overview).

CHAPTER 6

SALE OF FOREIGN DIVIDEND COUPONS

974 Charge to tax under this Chapter

(1) The charge to corporation tax on income applies to income treated under subsection (2) as arising from foreign holdings.

(2) Income is treated as arising from such holdings in the following cases.

(3) The first case is where a bank's office in the United Kingdom—

   (a) pays over the proceeds of a sale or other realisation of [taxable]¹ dividend coupons in respect of the holdings which has been effected by the bank, or

   (b) carries such proceeds into an account.

(4) The second case is where proceeds of sale arise from a sale of [taxable]¹ dividend coupons in respect of the holdings by a person who is not a bank or a dealer to a person dealing in coupons in the United Kingdom.

[(4A) For the purposes of subsections (3) and (4) a dividend coupon is "taxable" if the associated dividend would not have been exempt for the purposes of Part 9A (company distributions) had it been paid to the holder of the shares.]¹

(5) The amount of the income that is treated as arising is equal to the proceeds of the sale or realisation.

(6) In this section "bank" has the meaning given by [section 1120 of CTA 2010]².

Commentary—*Simon's Taxes* D7.726, D7.625.

HMRC Manuals—IHTM Inheritance Tax Manual IHTM04380 (bank : meaning).

Amendments—¹   In sub-ss (3)(a), (4) words inserted and sub-s (4A) inserted by FA 2009 s 34, Sch 14 paras 20, 25 with effect in relation to distributions paid on or after 1 July 2009.

²   In sub-s (6) words substituted for words "section 840A of ICTA" by CTA 2010 s 1177, Sch 1 para 664. CTA 2010 has effect for corporation tax purposes for accounting periods ending on or after 1 April 2010, and for income and capital gains tax purposes for the tax year 2010–11 and subsequent tax years.

975 Meaning of "foreign holdings" etc

(1) In this Chapter "foreign holdings" means shares outside the United Kingdom that are issued by or on behalf of a non-UK resident body of persons.

(2) In section 974 "dividend coupons" means coupons for dividends payable in respect of foreign holdings.

(3) In this Chapter "coupons" includes—

   (a) warrants, and

   (b) bills of exchange that purport to be drawn or made in payment of dividends payable in respect of foreign holdings.

Commentary—*Simon's Taxes* D7.726.

Derivation—TA 1988 s 18(3B)–(3E).

HMRC Manuals—Trusts, Settlements and Estates Manual TSEM3240 (foreign dividend coupons: meaning). Saving And Investment Manual SAIM5220 (foreign holdings : meaning).

CHAPTER 7

ANNUAL PAYMENTS NOT OTHERWISE CHARGED

976 Overview of Chapter

(1) This Chapter—

   (a) applies the charge to corporation tax on income to annual payments not otherwise charged to corporation tax (see section 977), . . . ¹

   (b) . . . ¹

(2) The following are also relevant to the tax treatment of annual payments within this Chapter—

   (a) section 687A(3) of ICTA (discretionary payments by trustees to companies),

   (b) section 494 of ITA 2007 (grossing up of discretionary payment and payment of income tax),

   (c) section 848 of ITA 2007 (under which a sum representing income tax deducted under Chapter 6 or 7 of Part 15 of that Act (deduction from annual payments, patent royalties and other payments connected with intellectual property) from an annual payment within this Chapter is treated as income tax paid by the recipient), and

   (d) Chapter 8 of Part 15 of ITA 2007 (special provision in relation to royalties).

Commentary—*Simon's Taxes* A1.138.

Amendments—¹   Sub-s (1)(b) and preceding word repealed by FA 2012 s 227, Sch 39 para 22(2) with effect in relation to payments made on or after 1 April 2013.

977 Charge to tax on annual payments not otherwise charged

(1) The charge to corporation tax on income applies to annual payments that are not otherwise within the application of that charge under the Corporation Tax Acts.

(2) Subsection (1) does not apply to annual payments in respect of which no liability to corporation tax arises because of an exemption.

(3) The frequency with which payments are made is ignored in determining whether they are annual payments for the purposes of this Chapter.

Commentary—*Simon's Taxes* **B5.316, A1.138**.
Derivation—TA 1988 ss 9(1), (2), (2B), (2C), (3), 18(1), (2), (3) ("Case III"), (3) ("Case V"), (3A).

CHAPTER 8

INCOME NOT OTHERWISE CHARGED

979 Charge to tax on income not otherwise charged
(1) The charge to corporation tax on income applies to income that is not otherwise within the application of that charge under the Corporation Tax Acts.
(2) Subsection (1) does not apply to—
    (*a*) annual payments,
    (*b*) income in respect of which no liability to corporation tax arises because of an exemption, or
    (*c*) deemed income.

Commentary—*Simon's Taxes* **A1.138, B2.620, B5.102, D4.805, E3.522, B5.113, B5.127**.
Derivation—TA 1988 ss 9(1), (2), (2B), (2C), (3), (4), 18(1), (3) ("Case V"), (3) ("Case VI").
HMRC Manuals—Business Income Manual BIM100101 (scope of the provisions: overview).

980 Exemption for commercial occupation of woodlands in UK
(1) No liability to corporation tax arises under this Chapter in respect of income arising from the commercial occupation of woodlands in the United Kingdom.
(2) For this purpose the occupation of woodlands is commercial if the woodlands are managed—
    (*a*) on a commercial basis, and
    (*b*) with a view to the realisation of profits.

Commentary—*Simon's Taxes* **B5.130, B5.130**.
Derivation—FA 1988 Sch 6 paras 2(1), 3(2).
HMRC Manuals—Business Income Manual BIM67701 (woodlands).

981 Exemption for gains on financial futures
(1) No liability to corporation tax arises under this Chapter in respect of a gain arising to a company in the course of dealing in—
    (*a*) financial futures,
    (*b*) traded options, or
    (*c*) financial options.
(2) The reference in subsection (1) to a gain arising in the course of dealing in financial futures includes a gain regarded as so arising under section 143(3) of TCGA 1992 (gains arising from transactions otherwise than in the course of dealing on a recognised futures exchange, involving authorised persons).
(3) In this section—
    "financial futures" means financial futures which are for the time being dealt in on a recognised futures exchange,
    "financial option" has the meaning given by section 144(8)(*c*) of TCGA 1992,
    "recognised futures exchange" means the London International Financial Futures Exchange and any other futures exchange which is for the time being designated for the purposes of that Act by order made by the Commissioners for Her Majesty's Revenue and Customs under section 288(6) of that Act, and
    "traded option" has the meaning given by section 144(8)(*b*) of that Act.

Commentary—*Simon's Taxes* **C2.1011, C2.1010**.
Derivation—TA 1988 s 128(2), (3).
HMRC Manuals—Corporate Finance Manual CFM50070 (gains on financial futures: exemption).
Capital Gain Tax Manual CG56004 (futures income : treatment).

CHAPTER 9

PRIORITY RULES

982 Provisions which must be given priority over this Part
(1) Any income, so far as it falls within—
    (*a*) Chapter . . . ¹ . . . ² 6, and
    (*b*) Chapter 2 of Part 3,
is dealt with under Part 3.
(2) Any income, so far as it falls within—
    (*a*) Chapter . . . ¹ . . . ² 6, and
    (*b*) Chapter 3 of Part 4 so far as the Chapter relates to a UK property business,
is dealt with under Part 4.

Amendments—¹   In sub-ss (1)(*a*), (2)(*a*) "2," repealed by FA 2009 s 34, Sch 14 paras 20, 26 with effect in relation to distributions paid on or after 1 July 2009.

[2] In sub-ss (1)(*a*), (2)(*a*) words "5 or" repealed by the Unauthorised Unit Trusts (Tax) Regulations, SI 2013/2819 reg 38(1), (4) with effect from 6 April 2014. Note that an unauthorised unit trust is not a non-exempt unauthorised unit trust, and these amendments do not apply in relation to the trust, if at all times in the period beginning with 24 May 2012 and ending with 5 April 2014 it had at least one unit holder which was, and at least one unit holder which was not, an eligible investor (ie a mixed unauthorised unit trust); this ceases to apply in relation to the trust if subsequently it no longer has any unit holders which are eligible investors (SI 2013/2819 reg 32).

PART 11
RELIEF FOR PARTICULAR EMPLOYEE SHARE ACQUISITION SCHEMES

CHAPTER 1
SHARE INCENTIVE PLANS

Introductory

983 Overview of Chapter

(1) This Chapter is about deductions relating to [Schedule 2][1] share incentive plans.

(2) Section 984 relates to the interpretation of this Chapter.

(3) Sections 985 and 986 set out—

    (*a*) how effect is given to deductions allowed under this Chapter, and

    (*b*) how amounts treated as received under this Chapter are dealt with.

(4) Sections 987 and 988 deal with deductions allowed for the costs of setting up plans and their running expenses.

(5) Sections 989 to 993 deal with deductions allowed for payments used to acquire shares for plan trusts.

(6) Sections 994 to 997 deal with other deductions relating to free shares, matching shares, partnership shares and dividend shares.

(7) Section 998 deals with the withdrawal of deductions if [a plan ceases to be a Schedule 2 share incentive plan][1].

Amendments—[1] In sub-s (1) words substituted for word "approved" and in sub-s (7) words substituted for words "approval for a plan is withdrawn" by FA 2014 s 51, Sch 8 paras 74, 75 with effect from 6 April 2014. The effect of the FA 2014 changes on SIPs established before 6 April 2014 is set out in FA 2014 Sch 8 paras 91 to 96.

984 Chapter to form part of SIP code etc

(1) This Chapter forms part of the SIP code (see section 488 of ITEPA 2003).

(2) Therefore expressions used in this Chapter and contained in the index at the end of Schedule 2 to ITEPA 2003 have the meaning indicated by that index.

(3) Subsection (4) applies if any of a participant's plan shares are forfeited.

(4) For the purposes of this Chapter the shares are treated as acquired by the trustees—

    (*a*) when the forfeiture occurs, and

    (*b*) for no consideration.

Commentary—*Simon's Taxes* D1.333.
Derivation—TA 1988 Sch 4AA paras 1(1), (2), 6(1), (2).
HMRC Manuals—Business Income Manual BIM44010 (share incentive plans : meaning).

Deductions and receipts: general

985 References to a deduction being allowed to a company

(1) References in this Chapter to a deduction being allowed to a company are to be read in accordance with this section (and references to a deduction being made are to be read in that light).

(2) If a deduction is allowed to a company, the deduction is made in calculating for corporation tax purposes the profits of a trade or property business carried on by the company.
This is subject to subsections (3) and (4).

(3) If the company is a company with investment business (as defined in section [1218B][2]), the amount of the deduction is treated as expenses of management of the company.

But this subsection does not apply if the company's business is a property business (in which case subsection (2) applies instead).

[(4) If—

    (*a*) the company is a company in relation to which the I-E rules apply, and

    (*b*) the expenses are referable, in accordance with Chapter 4 of Part 2 of FA 2012, to the company's basic life assurance and general annuity business,

the expenses are treated for the purposes of section 76 of that Act as ordinary BLAGAB management expenses of the company.][1]

(5) So far as this Chapter provides for a deduction to be allowed, it has effect despite section 53 (no deduction for items of a capital nature in calculating trading profits), including that section as applied by section 210 to the calculation of profits of a property business.

Commentary—*Simon's Taxes* D1.333.
Derivation—TA 1988 ss 21A(2), 75(2), Sch 4AA paras 1(3), (4), 13(1), (2).

HMRC Manuals—Business Income Manual BIM44253 (providing shares to employees: share incentive plans: general rules). BIM44275 (qualifying shares : how the relief is given).

Amendments—[1]   Sub-s (4) substituted by FA 2012 s 146, Sch 16 paras 135, 185 with effect in relation to accounting periods of companies beginning on or after 1 January 2013 (subject to transitional provisions in FA 2012 Sch 17). For accounting periods straddling 1 January 2013, see FA 2012 s 149.

[2]   In sub-s (3), "section 1218B" substituted for "section 1218" by FA 2013 s 36, Sch 18 para 21(2).

986 Treatment of receipts under Chapter

(1) This section applies if a company is treated under this Chapter as receiving an amount.

(2) If the company is carrying on a trade or property business in respect of which it is within the charge to corporation tax, the amount is treated as a receipt of that trade or business.

(3) If the company has permanently ceased to carry on a trade or property business in respect of which it was within the charge to corporation tax, the amount is treated as a post-cessation receipt of that trade or business (see Chapter 15 of Part 3).

(4) Otherwise, the amount is treated as a receipt chargeable under the charge to corporation tax on income.

Deductions relating to setting up and running costs

987 Deduction for costs of setting up [a Schedule 2] share incentive plan

(1) This section applies if a company incurs expenses in setting up a share incentive plan that is [a Schedule 2 share incentive plan][1].

(2) A deduction for the expenses is allowed to the company.

(3) ...

(4) If the [relevant date falls][1] more than 9 months after the end of the period of account in which the expenses are incurred, the deduction is allowed for the period of account in which the [relevant date falls][1].

[(4A) In subsection (4) "the relevant date", in relation to a share incentive plan, has the meaning given in paragraph 81A(6) of Schedule 2 to ITEPA 2003.][1]

(5) No other deduction is allowed in respect of expenses for which a deduction is allowed under this section.

Commentary—*Simon's Taxes* D1.333, D7.309.

Derivation—TA 1988 Sch 4AA para 7(1)–(4).

HMRC Manuals—Business Income Manual BIM44020 (employee share schemes: costs of setting up schemes).

Amendments—[1]   In heading words substituted for words "an approved", in subs-s (1) words substituted for words "approved by an officer of Revenue and Customs", sub-s (3) repealed, in sub-s(4) words substituted for words "approval is given" in both places, and sub-s (4A) inserted, by FA 2014 s 51, Sch 8 paras 74, 76 with effect from 6 April 2014. The effect of the FA 2014 changes on SIPs established before 6 April 2014 is set out in FA 2014 Sch 8 paras 91 to 96. Note that, in relation to a SIP established before 6 April 2014, if the SIP was an approved SIP before that date the amendments made by FA 2014 Sch 8 Part 1 do not affect the deductions which may be made in relation to the SIP under this section if they otherwise would do so (FA 2014 Sch 8 para 95).

988 Deductions for running expenses of [a Schedule 2] share incentive plan

(1) This section applies if a company incurs expenses in contributing to the expenses of the trustees in running [a Schedule 2][1] share incentive plan.

(2) This Chapter does not affect the deductions that, apart from this Chapter, are allowed to the company in relation to those expenses incurred by it.

(3) For the purposes of this section expenses of the trustees in running [a Schedule 2][1] share incentive plan do not include expenses incurred in acquiring shares for the purposes of the plan other than expenses within subsection (4).

(4) The expenses within this subsection are—

  (*a*) interest paid on money borrowed by the trustees for the purpose of acquiring the shares, and

  (*b*) any of the following—

    (i) fees,

    (ii) commission,

    (iii) stamp duty,

    (iv) stamp duty reserve tax, and

    (v) other incidental costs similar to any mentioned in sub-paragraphs (i) to (iv).

Commentary—*Simon's Taxes* D1.333.

Derivation—TA 1988 Sch 4AA para 8(1)–(3).

HMRC Manuals—Business Income Manual BIM44253 (share incentive plan : interaction with other deductions).

Amendments—[1]   In heading and in sub-ss (1), (3) words substituted for words "an approved" by FA 2014 s 51, Sch 8 paras 74, 77 with effect from 6 April 2014. The effect of the FA 2014 changes on SIPs established before 6 April 2014 is set out in FA 2014 Sch 8 paras 91 to 96.

Deductions relating to payments used to acquire shares

989 Deduction for contribution to plan trust

(1) A deduction is allowed to a company ("the paying company") if—

  (*a*) the paying company makes a payment to the trustees of [a Schedule 2][2] share incentive plan to enable them to acquire shares in the paying company or a company that controls it,

995 Deduction for additional expense in providing partnership shares

(1) This section applies if—

   (a) under [a Schedule 2][1] share incentive plan, partnership shares are awarded to employees because of their employment with a company ("the employing company"), and

   (b) the market value of the shares when they were acquired by the trustees of the plan trust exceeds the partnership share money paid by the participants to acquire those shares.

(2) A deduction is allowed to the employing company for the period of account in which the shares are awarded.

(3) The amount of the deduction is an amount equal to the excess mentioned in subsection (1)(b).

(4) No deduction, other than one under this section, is allowed to the employing company or any associated company in relation to the provision of the shares.

(5) But subsection (4)—

   (a) does not prevent a deduction being allowed under section 987 in relation to expenses incurred by a company in setting up a share incentive plan, and

   (b) is subject to section 988.

(6) If the shares are awarded to the employees because of their employment with two or more companies, only one of those companies may make a deduction under this section in relation to the award.

(7) This section is subject to section 996.

Commentary—*Simon's Taxes* D1.333.

Derivation—TA 1988 Sch 4AA para 3(1)–(5).

HMRC Manuals—Business Income Manual BIM44253 (the amount of the deduction: partnership shares).

Amendments—[1] In sub-s (1)(a) words substituted for words "an approved" by FA 2014 s 51, Sch 8 paras 74, 80 with effect from 6 April 2014. The effect of the FA 2014 changes on SIPs established before 6 April 2014 is set out in FA 2014 Sch 8 paras 91 to 96.

996 Shares excluded from sections 994 and 995

(1) No deduction is allowed under section 994 or 995 in relation to shares to which any of exclusions 1 to 5 applies.

(2) Exclusion 1 applies to shares awarded to an excluded employee.

(3) For the purposes of subsection (2) an employee is excluded if, at the time the shares are awarded to the employee, the earnings from the employee's employment with the employing company are not (or would not be if there were any) chargeable earnings—

   (a) to which section 15 of ITEPA 2003 applies, or

   (b) to which a section listed in section 20(1) of ITEPA 2003 applies.

(4) Exclusion 2 applies to shares in a company that are liable to depreciate substantially in value for reasons that do not apply generally to shares in that company.

(5) Exclusion 3 applies to shares in relation to which a deduction has been made by the employing company or an associated company in relation to the provision of the shares for the plan trust or for another trust.

(6) For the purposes of subsection (5)—

   (a) it does not matter upon what basis that deduction was made or what the nature or purpose of the other trust is, and

   (b) if the trustees of the plan trust acquire shares on different days, in determining whether the same shares have been provided to more than one trust, assume that shares acquired on an earlier day are awarded under the plan trust before those acquired on a later day.

(7) Exclusion 4 applies to shares acquired by the trustees of the plan trust as a result of a payment in relation to which a deduction is made under section 989 or 991.

(8) Exclusion 5 applies to shares awarded after having been forfeited by a participant.

Commentary—*Simon's Taxes* D1.333.

Derivation—TA 1988 Sch 4AA paras 4(1)–(9), 6(1), (3), 9(5).

HMRC Manuals—Business Income Manual BIM44253 (SIP : exclusions).

997 No deduction for expenses in providing dividend shares

(1) No deduction is allowed to a company for expenses in providing shares that are acquired on behalf of employees under [a Schedule 2][1] share incentive plan as dividend shares.

(2) This is subject to section 988.

Commentary—*Simon's Taxes* D1.333.

Derivation—TA 1988 Sch 4AA para 5(1)–(2).

HMRC Manuals—Business Income Manual BIM44253 (employee share schemes: share incentive plans: general rule on dividend shares).

Amendments—[1] In sub-s (1) words substituted for words "an approved" by FA 2014 s 51, Sch 8 paras 74, 81 with effect from 6 April 2014. The effect of the FA 2014 changes on SIPs established before 6 April 2014 is set out in FA 2014 Sch 8 paras 91 to 96.

[Plan ceasing to be a Schedule 2 SIP]

998 Withdrawal of deductions if [share incentive plan ceases to be a Schedule 2 share incentive plan][1]

(1) This section applies if—

    (a) a deduction is made by a company under section [987,][1] 989, 991, 994 or 995 in relation to [a Schedule 2][1] share incentive plan, and

    [(b) by virtue of paragraph 81H or 81I of Schedule 2 to ITEPA 2003 the plan is not to be a Schedule 2 share incentive plan.][1]

(2) An officer of Revenue and Customs may by notice direct that the deduction is withdrawn.

(3) If a direction is made, the company is treated as receiving an amount equal to the deduction.

(4) The amount is treated as received when the direction is made.

Commentary—*Simon's Taxes* D1.333, E4.542, E4.542D.

HMRC Manuals—Business Income Manual BIM44253 (withdrawal of deduction).

BIM44255 (SIP conditions for withdrawal of full amount of deduction).

Amendments—[1] Cross-heading substituted, in heading to this section words substituted for words "approval for share incentive plan withdrawn", in sub-s (1)(a) reference to s 987 inserted and words substituted for words "an approved", and sub-s (1)(b) substituted, by FA 2014 s 51, Sch 8 paras 74, 82, 83 with effect from 6 April 2014. The effect of the FA 2014 changes on SIPs established before 6 April 2014 is set out in FA 2014 Sch 8 paras 91 to 96. Note that, in relation to a SIP established before 6 April 2014, if the SIP was an approved SIP before that date the insertion of the reference to s 987 in sub-s (1)(a) has no effect in relation to deductions made in relation to the SIP under that section (FA 2014 Sch 8 para 95).

CHAPTER 2

SAYE OPTION SCHEMES, COMPANY SHARE OPTION SCHEMES AND EMPLOYEE SHARE OPTIONS TRUSTS

999 Deduction for costs of setting up SAYE option scheme or CSOP scheme

(1) This section applies if—

    (a) a company incurs expenses in setting up a scheme within subsection (2) . . . [3]

    (b) . . . [3]

(2) The schemes within this subsection are—

    (a) [Schedule 3][3] SAYE option schemes within the meaning of the SAYE code (see section 516(4) of ITEPA 2003), and

    (b) [Schedule 4][3] CSOP schemes within the meaning of the CSOP code (see section 521(4) of ITEPA 2003).

. . . [3]

(3) A deduction for the expenses is to be made in calculating for corporation tax purposes the profits of a trade or property business carried on by the company.

This is subject to subsections (4) and (5).

(4) If the company is a company with investment business (as defined in section [1218B][2]), the expenses are treated as expenses of management of the company.

But this subsection does not apply if the company's business is a property business (in which case subsection (3) applies instead).

[(5) If—

    (a) the company is a company in relation to which the I-E rules apply, and

    (b) the expenses are referable, in accordance with Chapter 4 of Part 2 of FA 2012, to the company's basic life assurance and general annuity business,

the expenses are treated for the purposes of section 76 of that Act as ordinary BLAGAB management expenses of the company.][1]

(6) If the [relevant date falls][3] more than 9 months after the end of the period of account in which the expenses are incurred—

    (a) for the purposes of subsection (3) the deduction is to be made for the period of account in which the [relevant date falls][3], or

    (b) for the purposes of subsection (4) or (5) the expenses are treated as referable to the accounting period in which the [relevant date falls][3].

[(6A) In subsection (6) "the relevant date"—

    (a) in relation to a Schedule 3 SAYE option scheme, has the meaning given in paragraph 40A(6) of Schedule 3 to ITEPA 2003, and

    (b) in relation to a Schedule 4 CSOP scheme, has the meaning given in paragraph 28A(6) of Schedule 4 to ITEPA 2003.][3]

(7) So far as this section provides for a deduction to be allowed, it has effect despite section 53 (no deduction for items of a capital nature in calculating trading profits), including that section as applied by section 210 to the calculation of profits of a property business.

Commentary—*Simon's Taxes* D1.330, D7.307, D7.309, E4.572, E4.583.

HMRC Manuals—Business Income Manual BIM44020 (costs deduction of setting up schemes: SAYE and CSOP schemes).

"the relevant employment" has the meaning given by section 1007(1)(*b*) or 1015(1)(*b*) (as the case may be), and

"restricted shares" means shares that are—

    (*a*) restricted securities, or

    (*b*) a restricted interest in securities,

for the purposes of Chapter 2 of Part 7 of ITEPA 2003 (see sections 423 and 424 of that Act).

Commentary—*Simon's Taxes* **D1.337, D1.338.**

Derivation—FA 2003 Sch 23 paras 4(3), 19, 22B(1), (3), 30.

Amendments—[2]   At the end of definition of "the employee" words inserted, and in definition of "the qualifying business" words substituted for words "or 1015(1)(*b*)", by FA 2014 s 52, Sch 9 paras 39, 41 with effect from 6 April 2015, subject to any transitional provision or savings that the Treasury may make by regulations under FA 2014 Sch 9 para 49.

[3]   Entry for "employee shareholder share" repealed by FA 2017 s 12(4)(*a*) with effect in relation to shares acquired in consideration of an employee shareholder agreement entered into on or after the relevant day. The relevant day is 1 December 2016 (FA 2017 s 12(6)), but for circumstances in which the relevant day is 2 December 2016, see FA 2017 s 12(7)).

CHAPTER 2

RELIEF IF SHARES ACQUIRED BY EMPLOYEE OR OTHER PERSON

Introductory

1006 Overview of Chapter

(1) This Chapter provides for relief if shares are acquired by an employee or another person because of the employee's employment by a company.

(2) Sections 1007 to 1009 set out the requirements that must be met for relief to be available.

(3) Sections 1010 to 1012 set out how the amount of relief is calculated.

(4) Section 1013 sets out how the relief is given.

Requirements to be met for relief to be available

1007 Basic requirements for relief under Chapter 2

(1) Relief under this Chapter is available to a company ("the employing company") if—

    (*a*) a person ("the employee") has employment with the employing company,

    (*b*) that employment ("the relevant employment") is in relation to a business within subsection (2) ("the qualifying business"),

    (*c*) the employee or another person acquires shares because of the relevant employment,

    (*d*) the conditions set out in sections 1008 and 1009 are met as mentioned in those sections, and

    (*e*) relief under Chapter 3 is not available to the employing company in relation to the acquisition of the shares.

The person who acquires the shares is, in that capacity, called "the recipient".

(2) A business is within this subsection so far as—

    (*a*) the business is carried on by the employing company, and

    (*b*) the employing company is within the charge to corporation tax in relation to the profits of the business [or would be but for section 18A][1].

Commentary—*Simon's Taxes* **D1.335.**

Derivation—FA 2003 Sch 23 paras 1(1), (3), 2, 3(1), (2), 21(2), 22C(2).

HMRC Manuals—Business Income Manual BIM44270 (qualifying shares : requirements for relief).

BIM44300 (employing company: meaning).

BIM44305 (providing shares to employees: qualifying shares: the relevant business requirements).

Amendments—[1]   In sub-s (2)(*b*) words inserted by FA 2011 s 48, Sch 13 paras 1, 9 with effect from 19 July 2011, subject to transitional provisions in FA 2011 Sch 13 paras 32–37.

[1007A Application of Chapter in relation to employees of overseas companies who work for companies in the UK

(1) This section applies if—

    (*a*) a person has an employment ("the actual employment") with a non-UK resident company not within the charge to corporation tax ("the overseas employer"),

    (*b*) in performing any of the duties of the actual employment, the person works in the United Kingdom for, but is not employed by, another company ("the host employer"), and

    (*c*) the host employer is—

        (i) a UK resident company, or

        (ii) a non-UK resident company within the charge to corporation tax.

(2) For the purposes of this Chapter, the person is to be treated as having an employment with the host employer ("the deemed employment"), the duties of which consist of the work the person does for the host employer.

(3) Subsection (4) applies if—

    (*a*) shares ("relevant shares") are acquired because of the actual employment, and (*b*) because of the work the person does for the host employer, an amount of employment income of the person is charged to tax under ITEPA 2003 in relation to the acquisition of the relevant shares.

(4) For the purposes of section 1007(1)(*c*) (requirement that shares are acquired because of employment) the relevant shares are (regardless of when the acquisition takes place) to be treated, so far as would not otherwise be the case, as if they are acquired because of the deemed employment.

(5) In section 1008 (conditions relating to the shares acquired) references to the employing company are to be read as including references to the overseas employer.

(6) If, in relation to an acquisition of shares, the amount of relief would otherwise be more than the total amount of employment income of the person charged to tax under ITEPA 2003, the amount of relief is (notwithstanding any other provision of this Chapter) limited to the total amount of that income so charged.

(7) If relief is available to more than one company in respect of the same acquisition of shares, relief may only be given to one of them in respect of that acquisition.

(8) For the purposes of this section a person works for another person if the person provides, and is obliged to provide, personal service to the other person.]¹

Commentary—*Simon's Taxes* **D1.336A, D1.337, D1.338**.

Amendments—¹ Section 1007A inserted by FA 2014 s 52, Sch 9 paras 39, 42 with effect from 6 April 2015, subject to any transitional provision or savings that the Treasury may make by regulations under FA 2014 Sch 9 para 49.

1008 Conditions relating to shares acquired

(1) Each of the following conditions must be met in relation to the shares acquired.

Condition 1

The shares are ordinary shares that are fully paid-up and not redeemable.

Condition 2

The shares are—

(*a*) shares of a class listed on a recognised stock exchange,

(*b*) shares in a company that is not under the control of another company, or

(*c*) shares in a company that is under the control of a listed company.

Condition 3

The shares are shares in—

(*a*) the employing company,

(*b*) a company that, when the shares are acquired, is a parent company of the employing company,

(*c*) a company that, when the shares are acquired, is a member of a consortium that owns the employing company,

(*d*) a company that, when the shares are acquired, is a member of a consortium that owns a parent company of the employing company, or

(*e*) a company within subsection (2).

(2) A company ("company A") is—

(2) A company ("company A") is— ... owns another company ("company B"), and ... the employing company is ... ber of a ... consortium and ... pany B.

(i) a member of that consortium or a parent company ... acquired).

(ii) a member of the same commercial associ... conditions must be met in relation ...

Commentary—*Simon's Taxes* **D1.335**.
Derivation—FA 2003 Sch 23 paras 4(1), (2), (3), 6 ... 2003 in relation to the acquisition of the ...
HMRC Manuals—Business Income Manual B... ply in relation to the shares.
BIM44295 (qualifying shares: company ... the following condition must be met in relation to the ...

1009 Conditions relating ...

(1) If the shares acqui... acquisition of the shares, [relevant earnings]² from the relevant to the income ...
*Condi... subject to the charge under Part 2 of that Act, or

(b) is not within paragraph (a) but will be subject to a charge under ITEPA 2003 as a result of section 426 of that Act if an event occurs in relation to the shares that is a chargeable event for the purposes of that section.

[(2A) "Relevant earnings" means—

(a) earnings within Chapter 1 of Part 3 of ITEPA 2003, and

(b) any amount that is treated as earnings by virtue of section 226A of that Act (employee shareholder shares).][2]

(3) Subsection (4) applies if—

(a) the conditions are, or the condition is, not met, but

(b) the conditions or the condition would be met if at all material times the employee had been a UK employee.

(4) This Chapter applies as if the employee had been a UK employee as mentioned in subsection (3)(b).

(5) The employee is a UK employee if—

(a) the employee is UK resident . . . [1], and

(b) the duties of the relevant employment are performed in the United Kingdom.

(6) . . . [3]

Commentary—*Simon's Taxes* **D1.335, D1.337**.

Derivation—FA 2003 Sch 23 paras 7(1)–(3), 20(1), (2), (4), 21(11), 22C(10).

HMRC Manuals—Business Income Manual BIM44320 (qualifying shares: income tax position of employee).

Amendments—[1]   Words in sub-s (5)(a) repealed by FA 2013 s 219, Sch 46 paras 137, 141 with effect in relation to shares acquired on or after 6 April 2013.

[2]   In sub-s (2)(a), words substituted, and sub-s (2A) inserted, by FA 2013 s 55, Sch 23 paras 21, 23 with effect from 1 September 2013 (by virtue of SI 2013/1755 art 2).

[3]   Sub-s (6) repealed by FA 2017 s 12(4)(b) with effect in relation to shares acquired in consideration of an employee shareholder agreement entered into on or after the relevant day. The relevant day is 1 December 2016 (FA 2017 s 12(6)), but for circumstances in which the relevant day is 2 December 2016, see FA 2017 s 12(7)).

Calculation of amount of relief

1010 Calculation of relief if shares are neither restricted nor convertible

(1) If the shares acquired are neither restricted shares nor convertible shares, the amount of relief to be given is an amount equal to—

(a) the market value of the shares when they are acquired, less

(b) the total amount or value of any consideration given by any person in relation to the acquisition of the shares.

This is subject to section 1012 . . . [1].

(2) The consideration mentioned in subsection (1)(b) does not include the performance of any duties of, or in connection with, the relevant employment.

(3) A just and reasonable apportionment is to be made of any consideration given partly in relation to the acquisition of the shares and partly in relation to other matters.

Commentary—*Simon's Taxes* **D1.336A**.

Derivation—FA 2003 Sch 23 paras 8(1)–(3), 19.

HMRC Manuals—Business Income Manual BIM44315 (unrestricted and non-convertible shares).

Amendments—[1]   In sub-s (1), words repealed by FA 2017 s 12(4)(c) with effect in relation to shares acquired in consideration of an employee shareholder agreement entered into on or after the relevant day. The relevant day is 2 December 2016 (FA

1011 Calculation of relief if shares are restricted or convertible

(1) If the shares are restricted shares or convertible shares (or both), the amount of relief to be given is calculated under this section.

This is subject to section 1012.

(2) If the shares are restricted shares or convertible shares (or both), in calculating the amount of relief the acquisition of the shares is to be the acquisition of the shares are—

(3) If the shares are—

In calculating the employ the amount of relief is equal to the amount that, as a result of the acquisition of the shares, counts as earnings of the employee][1] from the relevant employment.

determined as if they were the amount of relief is equal to the amount that, as a result of the acquisition of the shares, counts as earnings of the employee][1] from the relevant employment.

[(4) For the purposes within Chapt of the employee][1] for the purpose the market value of the shares is to be

(a) earnings within Chapter 1 of Part 3 of ITEPA 2003, and

(b) any amount that is treated as earnings by virtue of section 226A of that Act (employee shareholder shares).][1]

except that it does not include any amount that . . .

ITEPA 2003.][1]

(5) If the shares are both restricted and convertible shares, the meaning of section 8 of greater of the amounts of relief given by . . . "earnings" means— is whichever is the case, that amount). the same in each

Commentary—*Simon's Taxes* **D1.337, D1.338**.

Derivation—FA 2003 Sch 23 paras 21(3), (5), 22C(3),

(*b*) is not within paragraph (*a*) but will be subject to a charge under ITEPA 2003 as a result of section 426 of that Act if an event occurs in relation to the shares that is a chargeable event for the purposes of that section.

[(2A) "Relevant earnings" means—
    (*a*) earnings within Chapter 1 of Part 3 of ITEPA 2003, and
    (*b*) any amount that is treated as earnings by virtue of section 226A of that Act (employee shareholder shares).][2]

(3) Subsection (4) applies if—
    (*a*) the conditions are, or the condition is, not met, but
    (*b*) the conditions or the condition would be met if at all material times the employee had been a UK employee.

(4) This Chapter applies as if the employee had been a UK employee as mentioned in subsection (3)(*b*).

(5) The employee is a UK employee if—
    (*a*) the employee is UK resident . . . [1], and
    (*b*) the duties of the relevant employment are performed in the United Kingdom.

(6) . . . [3]

Commentary—*Simon's Taxes* **D1.335, D1.337.**
Derivation—FA 2003 Sch 23 paras 7(1)–(3), 20(1), (2), (4), 21(11), 22C(10).
HMRC Manuals—Business Income Manual BIM44320 (qualifying shares: income tax position of employee).
Amendments—[1]   Words in sub-s (5)(*a*) repealed by FA 2013 s 219, Sch 46 paras 137, 141 with effect in relation to shares acquired on or after 6 April 2013.
[2]   In sub-s (2)(*a*), words substituted, and sub-s (2A) inserted, by FA 2013 s 55, Sch 23 paras 21, 23 with effect from 1 September 2013 (by virtue of SI 2013/1755 art 2).
[3]   Sub-s (6) repealed by FA 2017 s 12(4)(*b*) with effect in relation to shares acquired in consideration of an employee shareholder agreement entered into on or after the relevant day. The relevant day is 1 December 2016 (FA 2017 s 12(6)), but for circumstances in which the relevant day is 2 December 2016, see FA 2017 s 12(7)).

Calculation of amount of relief

1010 Calculation of relief if shares are neither restricted nor convertible

(1) If the shares acquired are neither restricted shares nor convertible shares, the amount of relief to be given is an amount equal to—
    (*a*) the market value of the shares when they are acquired, less
    (*b*) the total amount or value of any consideration given by any person in relation to the acquisition of the shares.
This is subject to section 1012 . . . [1].

(2) The consideration mentioned in subsection (1)(*b*) does not include the performance of any duties of, or in connection with, the relevant employment.

(3) A just and reasonable apportionment is to be made of any consideration given partly in relation to the acquisition of the shares and partly in relation to other matters.

Commentary—*Simon's Taxes* **D1.336A.**
Derivation—FA 2003 Sch 23 paras 8(1)–(3), 18.
HMRC Manuals—Business Income Manual BIM44315 (unrestricted and non-convertible shares).
Amendments—[1]   In sub-s (1), words repealed by FA 2017 s 12(4)(*c*) with effect in relation to shares acquired in consideration of an employee shareholder agreement entered into on or after the relevant day. The relevant day is 1 December 2016 (FA 2017 s 12(6)), but for circumstances in which the relevant day is 2 December 2016, see FA 2017 s 12(7)).

1011 Calculation of relief if shares are restricted or convertible

(1) If the shares acquired are restricted shares or convertible shares (or both), the amount of relief to be given is calculated as follows.
This is subject to section 1012.

(2) If the shares are restricted shares, the amount of relief is equal to the amount that, as a result of the acquisition of the shares, is [relevant earnings of the employee][1] from the relevant employment.

(3) If the shares are convertible shares, the amount of relief is equal to the amount that, as a result of the acquisition of the shares, is [relevant earnings of the employee][1] from the relevant employment. In calculating the employee's earnings for this purpose the market value of the shares is to be determined as if they were not convertible shares.

[(4) For the purposes of subsections (2) and (3) "relevant earnings" means—
    (*a*) earnings within Chapter 1 of Part 3 of ITEPA 2003, and
    (*b*) any amount that is treated as earnings by virtue of section 226A of that Act (employee shareholder shares) . . . [2],
except that it does not include any amount of exempt income (within the meaning of section 8 of ITEPA 2003).][1]

(5) If the shares are both restricted and convertible, the total amount of relief is whichever is the greater of the amounts of relief given by subsections (2) and (3) (or, if the amount is the same in each case, that amount).

Commentary—*Simon's Taxes* **D1.337, D1.338.**
Derivation—FA 2003 Sch 23 paras 21(3), (5), 22C(3), (4A), (5).

(b) because of the work the person does for the host employer, an amount of employment income of the person is charged to tax under ITEPA 2003 in relation to the acquisition of the relevant shares.

(4) For the purposes of section 1007(1)(c) (requirement that shares are acquired because of employment) the relevant shares are (regardless of when the acquisition takes place) to be treated, so far as would not otherwise be the case, as if they are acquired because of the deemed employment.

(5) In section 1008 (conditions relating to the shares acquired) references to the employing company are to be read as including references to the overseas employer.

(6) If, in relation to an acquisition of shares, the amount of relief would otherwise be more than the total amount of employment income of the person charged to tax under ITEPA 2003, the amount of relief is (notwithstanding any other provision of this Chapter) limited to the total amount of that income so charged.

(7) If relief is available to more than one company in respect of the same acquisition of shares, relief may only be given to one of them in respect of that acquisition.

(8) For the purposes of this section a person works for another person if the person provides, and is obliged to provide, personal service to the other person.][1]

Commentary—*Simon's Taxes* **D1.336A, D1.337, D1.338.**
Amendments—[1]   Section 1007A inserted by FA 2014 s 52, Sch 9 paras 39, 42 with effect from 6 April 2015, subject to any transitional provision or savings that the Treasury may make by regulations under FA 2014 Sch 9 para 49.

1008 Conditions relating to shares acquired

(1) Each of the following conditions must be met in relation to the shares acquired.

> *Condition 1*
> The shares are ordinary shares that are fully paid-up and not redeemable.
> *Condition 2*
> The shares are—
>> (a) shares of a class listed on a recognised stock exchange,
>> (b) shares in a company that is not under the control of another company, or
>> (c) shares in a company that is under the control of a listed company.
> *Condition 3*
> The shares are shares in—
>> (a) the employing company,
>> (b) a company that, when the shares are acquired, is a parent company of the employing company,
>> (c) a company that, when the shares are acquired, is a member of a consortium that owns the employing company,
>> (d) a company that, when the shares are acquired, is a member of a consortium that owns a parent company of the employing company, or
>> (e) a company within subsection (2).

(2) A company ("company A") is within this subsection if when the shares are acquired—
> (a) the employing company or a parent company of the employing company is a member of a consortium that owns another company ("company B"), and
> (b) company A is—
>> (i) a member of that consortium or a parent company of a member of that consortium, and
>> (ii) a member of the same commercial association of companies as company B.

Commentary—*Simon's Taxes* **D1.335.**
Derivation—FA 2003 Sch 23 paras 4(1), (2), (3), 6.
HMRC Manuals—Business Income Manual BIM44290 (qualifying shares: kind of shares acquired).
BIM44295 (qualifying shares: company whose shares are acquired).

1009 Conditions relating to employee's income tax position

(1) If the shares acquired are not restricted shares, the following conditions must be met in relation to the income tax position of the employee.

> *Condition 1*
> The employee is subject to a charge under ITEPA 2003 in relation to the acquisition of the shares.
> *Condition 2*
> Section 446UA of ITEPA 2003 does not apply in relation to the shares.

(2) If the shares acquired are restricted shares, the following condition must be met in relation to the income tax position of the employee.

> The Condition
> The employee—
>> (a) has, as a result of the acquisition of the shares, [relevant earnings][2] from the relevant employment that are subject to the charge under Part 2 of that Act, or

HMRC Manuals—Business Income Manual BIM44315 (restricted and/or convertible shares).
Amendments—[1]   In sub-ss (2), (3), words substituted, and sub-s (4) substituted, by FA 2013 s 55, Sch 23 paras 21, 25 with effect from 1 September 2013 (by virtue of SI 2013/1755 art 2).
[2]   In sub-s (4)(*b*), words repealed by FA 2017 s 12(4)(*d*) with effect in relation to shares acquired in consideration of an employee shareholder agreement entered into on or after the relevant day. The relevant day is 1 December 2016 (FA 2017 s 12(6)), but for circumstances in which the relevant day is 2 December 2016, see FA 2017 s 12(7)).

1012 Reduction in amount of relief
(1) This section applies if the relevant employment is in relation to both the qualifying business and a business (or part of a business) that is not within section 1007(2).
(2) The amount of relief is to be reduced by a just and reasonable amount.

Giving of relief

1013 How the relief is given
(1) The relief is given for the accounting period in which the shares are acquired.
(2) The amount of relief is allowed as a deduction in calculating the profits of the qualifying business for corporation tax purposes (subject to subsections (3) and (4)).
(3) If the employing company is a company with investment business (as defined in section [1218B][2]), the amount of relief is treated as expenses of management of the company.
But this subsection does not apply if the qualifying business is a property business (in which case subsection (2) applies instead).
[(4) If—
   (*a*) the employing company is a company in relation to which the I-E rules apply, and
   (*b*) the relief is referable, in accordance with Chapter 4 of Part 2 of FA 2012, to the employing company's basic life assurance and general annuity business,
the amount of relief is treated for the purposes of section 76 of that Act as ordinary BLAGAB management expenses of the company referable to the accounting period.][1]
(5) If the relevant employment is in relation to more than one business (or part of a business) within section 1007(2), the relief is to be apportioned on a just and reasonable basis.

HMRC Manuals—Business Income Manual BIM44275 (qualifying shares: how the relief is given).
BIM44310 (qualifying shares: when the deduction is given).
Amendments—[1]   Sub-s (4) substituted by FA 2012 s 146, Sch 16 paras 135, 188 with effect in relation to accounting periods of companies beginning on or after 1 January 2013 (subject to transitional provisions in FA 2012 Sch 17). For accounting period straddling 1 January 2013, see FA 2102 s 149.
[2]   In sub-s (3), "section 1218B" substituted for "section 1218" by FA 2013 s 36, Sch 18 para 21(2).

CHAPTER 3

RELIEF IF EMPLOYEE OR OTHER PERSON OBTAINS OPTION TO ACQUIRE SHARES
Introductory

1014 Overview of Chapter
(1) This Chapter provides for relief if—
   (*a*) an employee or another person obtains an option to acquire shares because of the employee's employment by a company, and
   (*b*) shares are acquired pursuant to the option.
(2) Sections 1015 to 1017 set out the requirements that must be met for relief to be available.
(3) Sections 1018 to 1020 set out how the amount of relief is calculated.
(4) Section 1021 sets out how the relief is given.
(5) Sections 1022 and 1023 deal with cases in which a person obtains an option to acquire shares in a company and that company is subsequently taken over.
(6) Section 1024 provides for relief to be given to a successor company if the qualifying business is transferred by group transfers.

Requirements to be met for relief to be available

1015 Basic requirements for relief under Chapter 3
(1) Relief under this Chapter is available to a company ("the employing company") if—
   (*a*) a person ("the employee") has employment with the employing company,
   (*b*) that employment ("the relevant employment") is in relation to a business within subsection (2) ("the qualifying business"),
   (*c*) the employee or another person obtains an option to acquire shares because of the relevant employment,
   (*d*) the person who obtains the option acquires shares pursuant to the option, and
   (*e*) the conditions set out in sections 1016 and 1017 are met as mentioned in those sections.
The person who obtains the option is, in that capacity, called "the recipient".
(2) A business is within this subsection so far as—
   (*a*) the business is carried on by the employing company, and
   (*b*) the employing company is within the charge to corporation tax in relation to the profits of the business [or would be but for section 18A][1].

(3) If—
   (a) the recipient dies, and
   (b) subsequently another person acquires shares pursuant to the option,
this Chapter applies as if the recipient were alive and the shares were acquired by the recipient.

Commentary—*Simon's Taxes* **D1.335**.
Derivation—FA 2003 Sch 23 paras 1(1), (3), 2, 3(1), (2), 21(2), 22C(2), 27(2).
HMRC Manuals—Business Income Manual BIM44270 (business for purposes of which options or awards granted).
BIM44305 (qualifying shares: the relevant business requirements).
BIM44300 (qualifying shares: which company gets the deduction).
Amendments—[1]   In sub-s (2)(b) words inserted by FA 2011 s 48, Sch 13 paras 1, 10 with effect from 19 July 2011, subject to transitional provisions in FA 2011 Sch 13 paras 32–37.

[1015A Application of Chapter: employees of overseas companies who take up employment with a UK company

(1) This section applies if—
   (a) a person ("E") has, or had, an employment with a non-UK resident company not within the charge to corporation tax ("the overseas employment"),
   (b) E or another person obtains an option to acquire shares because of the overseas employment,
   (c) E has an employment ("the UK employment") with a company that is a UK resident company or a non-UK resident company within the charge to corporation tax,
   (d) the person who obtained the option acquires shares pursuant to it, and
   (e) subsection (2) applies.
(2) This subsection applies if—
   (a) an amount of employment income of E is charged to tax under ITEPA 2003 in relation to the acquisition because of the UK employment, or
   (b) it is because of the UK employment that E or another person is able to acquire the shares pursuant to the option.
(3) For the purposes of section 1015(1)(c) (requirement that option is obtained because of employment), the option is (regardless of when it is obtained) to be treated as if it is obtained because of the UK employment.
(4) In section 1016 (conditions relating to the shares acquired) references to the employing company are to be read as including references to the company mentioned in subsection (1)(a).
(5) If, in relation to the acquisition, an amount of relief would otherwise be available that is more than the total amount of employment income of E charged to tax under ITEPA 2003, the amount of relief is (notwithstanding any other provision of this Chapter) limited to the total amount of that income so charged.
(6) If relief is available to more than one company in respect of the same acquisition of shares pursuant to an option, relief may only be given to one of them in respect of that acquisition.][1]

Commentary—*Simon's Taxes* **D1.335, D1.338, D1.336A, D1.337**.
Amendments—[1]   Sections 1015A, 1015B inserted by FA 2014 s 52, Sch 9 paras 39, 43 with effect from 6 April 2015, subject to any transitional provision or savings that the Treasury may make by regulations under FA 2014 Sch 9 para 49.

[1015B Application of Chapter in relation to employees of overseas companies who work for companies in the UK

(1) This section applies if—
   (a) a person has an employment ("the actual employment") with a non-UK resident company not within the charge to corporation tax ("the overseas employer"),
   (b) in performing any of the duties of the actual employment, the person works in the United Kingdom for, but is not employed by, another company ("the host employer"), and
   (c) the host employer is—
      (i) a UK resident company, or
      (ii) a non-UK resident company within the charge to corporation tax.
(2) For the purposes of this Chapter, the person is to be treated as having an employment ("the deemed employment") with the host employer, the duties of which consist of the work the person does for the host employer.
(3) Subsection (4) applies if—
   (a) an option to acquire shares ("the relevant option") is obtained because of the actual employment,
   (b) shares are acquired pursuant to the relevant option, and
   (c) because of the work the person does for the host employer, an amount of employment income of the person is charged to tax under ITEPA 2003 in relation to the acquisition of the shares.
(4) For the purposes of section 1015(1)(c) (requirement that option is obtained because of employment), the relevant option is (regardless of when it is obtained) to be treated, so far as would not otherwise be the case, as if it is obtained because of the deemed employment.
(5) In section 1016 (conditions relating to the shares acquired) references to the employing company are to be read as including references to the overseas employer.

(6) If, in relation to an acquisition of shares pursuant to an option, the amount of relief would otherwise be more than the total amount of employment income of the person charged to tax under ITEPA 2003, the amount of relief is (notwithstanding any other provision of this Chapter) limited to the total amount of that income so charged.

(7) If relief is available to more than one company in respect of the same acquisition of shares pursuant to an option, relief may only be given to one of them in respect of that acquisition.

(8) For the purposes of this section a person works for another person if the person provides, and is obliged to provide, personal service to the other person.][1]

Commentary—*Simon's Taxes* D1.335, D1.338, D1.336A, D1.337.

Derivation—FA 2003 Sch 23 paras 14(1), (2), (3)(a), 21(1).

Amendments—[1] Sections 1015A, 1015B inserted by FA 2014 s 52, Sch 9 paras 39, 43 with effect from 6 April 2015, subject to any transitional provision or savings that the Treasury may make by regulations under FA 2014 Sch 9 para 49.

1016 Conditions relating to shares acquired

(1) Each of the following conditions must be met in relation to the shares acquired.

Condition 1

The shares are ordinary shares that are fully paid-up and not redeemable.

Condition 2

The shares are—

    (a) shares of a class listed on a recognised stock exchange,

    (b) shares in a company that is not under the control of another company, . . .[1]

    (c) shares in a company that is under the control of a listed company[, or

    (d) shares within subsection (1A)][1]

Condition 3

The shares are shares in—

    (a) the employing company,

    (b) a company that, when the option is obtained, is a parent company of the employing company,

    (c) a company that, when the option is obtained, is a member of a consortium that owns the employing company,

    (d) a company that, when the option is obtained, is a member of a consortium that owns a parent company of the employing company,

    (e) a company within subsection (2), or

    (f) a qualifying successor company (see section 1022).

[(1A) Shares are within this subsection if—

    (a) after the option is obtained, the company in which the shares are to be acquired ("the relevant company") comes to be controlled by another company ("the takeover"),

    (b) immediately before the takeover, the shares were within any of paragraphs (a) to (c) of Condition 2,

    (c) as a result of the takeover, the shares cease to be within any of those paragraphs,

    (d) the shares are acquired pursuant to the option within the period of 90 days beginning with the day of the takeover, and

    (e) the avoidance of tax is not the main purpose (or one of the main purposes) of the takeover.][1]

(2) A company ("company A") is within this subsection if when the option is obtained—

    (a) the employing company or a parent company of the employing company is a member of a consortium that owns another company ("company B"), and

    (b) company A is—

        (i) a member of that consortium or a parent company of a member of that consortium, and

        (ii) a member of the same commercial association of companies as company B.

Commentary—*Simon's Taxes* D1.335.

Derivation—FA 2003 Sch 23 paras 4(1)–(3), 12.

HMRC Manuals—Business Income Manual BIM44290 (qualifying shares: kind of shares acquired).

BIM44285 (conditions must be satisfied when employees acquire the shares).

BIM44295 (qualifying shares: company whose shares are acquired).

Amendments—[1] In sub-s (1), in Condition 2, word "or" at end of para (b) repealed, and para (d) and preceding word "or" inserted, and sub-s (1A) inserted, by FA 2014 s 52, Sch 9 paras 39, 44 with effect from 17 July 2014.

1017 Condition relating to employee's income tax position

(1) The following condition must be met in relation to the income tax position of the employee.

The Condition

The acquisition of the shares is a chargeable event in relation to the employee for the purposes of section 476 of ITEPA 2003 (whether or not an amount counts as employment income of the employee because of that event).

(2) Subsection (3) applies if the condition—

    (a) is not met, but

    (b) would be met if at all material times the employee had been a UK employee.

Amendments—[1]   Sub-s (5) repealed by FA 2017 s 12(4)(*f*) with effect in relation to shares acquired in consideration of an employee shareholder agreement entered into on or after the relevant day. The relevant day is 1 December 2016 (FA 2017 s 12(6)), but for circumstances in which the relevant day is 2 December 2016, see FA 2017 s 12(7)).

1023 Supplementary provision for purposes of section 1022

(1) This section applies for the purposes of section 1022.

(2) An option is a qualifying option if condition 3 in section 1016 would be met in relation to shares acquired pursuant to the option.

(3) There is a takeover of a company when another company ("the acquiring company") acquires control of it.

(4) The following companies are qualifying companies—

(*a*) the acquiring company,

(*b*) a company that, when the takeover occurs, is a parent company of the acquiring company,

(*c*) a company that, when the takeover occurs, is a member of a consortium that owns the acquiring company,

(*d*) a company that, when the takeover occurs, is a member of a consortium that owns a parent company of the acquiring company, and

(*e*) a company within subsection (5).

(5) A company ("company A") is within this subsection if when the takeover occurs—

(*a*) the acquiring company or a parent company of the acquiring company is a member of a consortium that owns another company ("company B"), and

(*b*) company A is—

(i) a member of that consortium or a parent company of a member of that consortium, and

(ii) a member of the same commercial association of companies as company B.

Commentary—*Simon's Taxes* D1.335.

Derivation—FA 2003 Sch 23 para 13(3), (4).

HMRC Manuals—Business Income Manual BIM44300 (qualifying shares: which company gets the deduction).

1024 Transfer of qualifying business by group transfers

(1) This section applies in relation to relief to be given under this Chapter if—

(*a*) during the option period, the whole, or substantially the whole, of the qualifying business is transferred, and

(*b*) conditions A and B are met.

(2) Condition A is that—

(*a*) the transfer is a group transfer, or

(*b*) if there is more than one transfer, all the transfers are group transfers.

(3) Condition B is that, as a result of the transfer or transfers, at the end of the option period—

(*a*) the whole, or substantially the whole, of the qualifying business is carried on by one company ("the successor company") only and that company is not the employing company, or

(*b*) the whole, or substantially the whole, of the qualifying business is carried on by companies ("the successor companies") none of which is the employing company.

(4) The relief is to be given to—

(*a*) the successor company, or

(*b*) whichever one of the successor companies is nominated by them,

instead of the employing company (and references to the employing company in section 1021(3) and (4) are to be read as references to the company to which the relief is to be given).

(5) In this section "the option period" means the period—

(*a*) beginning when the option is obtained, and

(*b*) ending when the shares are acquired.

Derivation—FA 2003 Sch 23 para 23(1)–(3).

HMRC Manuals—Business Income Manual BIM44300 (a successor company).

CHAPTER 4

ADDITIONAL RELIEF IN CASES INVOLVING RESTRICTED SHARES

1025 Additional relief available if shares acquired are restricted shares

(1) This Chapter applies if—

(*a*) relief ("the original relief") is available under Chapter 2 or 3 in relation to an acquisition of restricted shares, and

(*b*) after the acquisition—

(i) an event that is a chargeable event in relation to the restricted shares for the purposes of section 426 of ITEPA 2003 occurs, or

(ii) Chapter 2 of Part 7 of ITEPA 2003 ceases to apply to the restricted shares because the employee dies (see section 421B(4) and (6) of that Act).

For the purposes of paragraph (*a*) it does not matter if the amount of relief is calculated as nil.

(2) Relief under this Chapter is available to the employing company.

(3) Subsection (4) applies if section 426 of ITEPA 2003—
- *(a)* does not apply in relation to the restricted shares, but
- *(b)* would apply if at all material times the employee had been a UK employee.

(4) This Chapter applies as if the employee had been a UK employee as mentioned in subsection (3)(b).

(5) The employee is a UK employee if—
- *(a)* the employee is UK resident . . . .[1], and
- *(b)* the duties of the relevant employment are performed in the United Kingdom.[2]

(6) If—
- *(a)* the original relief is available as a result of section 1015(3) (death of recipient), and
- *(b)* the recipient is not the employee,

this Chapter applies as if the recipient were alive and the restricted shares were acquired by the recipient.

(7) If the original relief is available as a result of section 1022 (takeover of company whose shares are subject to an option), this Chapter applies as if the restricted shares were acquired pursuant to the qualifying option mentioned in that section.

(8) To find out what accounting period the relief is given for and how to calculate the amount of relief, see—
- *(a)* section 1026 for relief available as a result of the occurrence of a chargeable event, and
- *(b)* section 1027 for relief available as a result of the employee's death.

Those sections are supplemented by section 1028.

(9) Section 1029 provides for the relief to be given to a successor company if the qualifying business is transferred by group transfers.

Commentary—*Simon's Taxes* **D1.337.**
Derivation—FA 2003 Sch 23 paras 13(2), 21(1), (2), (7), (11), 27(2).
HMRC Manuals—Business Income Manual BIM44385 (providing shares to employees: restricted shares).
Amendments—[1]   Words in sub-s (5)(*a*) repealed by FA 2013 s 219, Sch 46 paras 137, 143 with effect in relation to restricted shares acquired on or after 6 April 2013.
[2]   Sub-ss (3)–(5) repealed by FA 2014 s 52, Sch 9 paras 30, 32 with effect from 6 April 2015 in relation to employment-related securities and employment-related securities options irrespective of the date of acquisition, subject to any transitional provision or savings that the Treasury may make by regulations under FA 2014 Sch 9 para 49.

[1025A Application of Chapter: employees of overseas companies who take up employment with, or work for, a UK company
(1) This section applies if—
- *(a)* a person ("E") has, or had, an employment ("the overseas employment") with a non-UK resident company not within the charge to corporation tax ("the overseas company"),
- *(b)* E or another person acquired restricted shares because of the overseas employment (whether or not pursuant to an option),
- *(c)* the case is not within section 1025(1)(*a*),
- *(d)* relief under Chapter 2 or 3 would have been available to the overseas company in relation to the acquisition if, at all material times—
  - (i) the overseas company had carried on a business within subsection (2) ("a qualifying business"), and
  - (ii) the overseas employment had related to that business,
- *(e)* E has a UK employment with a UK company (see subsections (3) and (4)),
- *(f)* the UK employment is in relation to a qualifying business carried on by the UK company,
- *(g)* an event occurs that is a chargeable event in relation to the restricted shares for the purposes of section 426 of ITEPA 2003, and
- *(h)* because of the UK employment, an amount of employment income of E is charged to tax under ITEPA 2003 in relation to the chargeable event.

For the purposes of paragraph (*d*) it does not matter if the amount of the relief would have been calculated as nil.

(2) A business is within this subsection so far as—
- *(a)* it is carried on by a company, and
- *(b)* the company is within the charge to corporation tax in relation to the profits of the business or would be but for section 18A.

(3) A company is a "UK company" if it is a UK resident company or a non-UK resident company within the charge to corporation tax.

(4) E has a "UK employment" with a UK company if—
- *(a)* E is employed by the UK company, or
- *(b)* E is not employed by the UK company but provides, and is obliged to provide, personal service to the UK company, in the course of performing the duties of the overseas employment (in which case, references to the UK employment are to the personal service E provides).

(5) Relief under this Chapter is available to the UK company as a result of the chargeable event.

CTA 2009

(6) References in this Chapter to the original relief (other than in section 1025B) are to be treated as references to the relief that would have been available as mentioned in subsection (1)(d).

(7) In section 1026(3) (amount of relief on occurrence of chargeable event), the reference to the employee is to be read as a reference to E.

(8) For the purposes of section 1028(2) (giving relief), as that provision has effect by virtue of subsection (6), in section 1013(2) to (5) or (as the case may be) 1021(2) to (5)—

    (*a*) references to the employing company are to be treated as references to the UK company,

    (*b*) the reference to the relevant employment is to be treated as a reference to the UK employment, and

    (*c*) references to a business within section 1007(2) or (as the case may be) 1015(2) are to be treated as references to a business within subsection (2).

(9) If, in relation to the chargeable event, the amount of relief available would otherwise be more than the total amount of employment income of E charged to tax under ITEPA 2003, the amount of relief is (notwithstanding any other provision of this Chapter) limited to the total amount of that income so charged.

(10) If relief is available to more than one company as a result of the same chargeable event, relief may only be given to one of them in respect of that event.]¹

Commentary—*Simon's Taxes* D1.337, D1.335.

Amendments—¹ Sections 1025A, 1025B inserted by FA 2014 s 52, Sch 9 paras 39, 45 with effect from 6 April 2015, subject to any transitional provision or savings that the Treasury may make by regulations under FA 2014 Sch 9 para 49.

[1025B Application of Chapter where original relief a consequence of section 1007A, 1015A or 1015B

(1) This section applies if the original relief is available under—

    (*a*) Chapter 2 as a consequence of section 1007A, or

    (*b*) Chapter 3 as a consequence of section 1015A or 1015B.

(2) If the original relief is available as a consequence of section 1007A or 1015B, subsection (2) of the section concerned applies for the purposes of this Chapter.

(3) If, in relation to a chargeable event, the amount of relief available would otherwise be more than the total amount of employment income of the employee charged to tax under ITEPA 2003, the amount of relief is (notwithstanding any other provision of this Chapter) limited to the total amount of that income so charged.

(4) If relief is available to more than one company as a result of the same chargeable event, relief may only be given to one of them in respect of that event.

(5) No relief is available as a result of the employee's death.]¹

Commentary—*Simon's Taxes* D1.337.

Amendments—¹ Sections 1025A, 1025B inserted by FA 2014 s 52, Sch 9 paras 39, 45 with effect from 6 April 2015, subject to any transitional provision or savings that the Treasury may make by regulations under FA 2014 Sch 9 para 49.

1026 Relief available on occurrence of chargeable event

(1) This section applies in relation to relief available as a result of the occurrence of a chargeable event.

(2) The relief is given for the accounting period in which the chargeable event occurs.

(3) The amount of relief is equal to the amount that counts as employment income of the employee under section 426 of ITEPA 2003 in relation to the chargeable event.

(4) For the purposes of subsection (3) the following are to be ignored—

    (*a*) any relief under section 428A of ITEPA 2003,

    (*b*) section 446E(6) of ITEPA 2003, and

    (*c*) the amount of any non-commercial increase (as defined in section 446K(4) of ITEPA 2003) in the market value of the restricted shares after their acquisition.

(5) . . .¹

Commentary—*Simon's Taxes* D1.337.

Derivation—FA 2003 Sch 23 paras 21(6), (8), (9), 22(5).

HMRC Manuals—Business Income Manual BIM44385 (qualifying shares: restricted shares).
Employment Related Securities Manual ERSM60100 (charge on non-commercial increases).

Amendments—¹ Sub-s (5) repealed by FA 2017 s 12(4)(*f*) with effect in relation to shares acquired in consideration of an employee shareholder agreement entered into on or after the relevant day. The relevant day is 1 December 2016 (FA 2017 s 12(6)), but for circumstances in which the relevant day is 2 December 2016, see FA 2017 s 12(7)).

1027 Relief available on death of employee

(1) This section applies in relation to relief available as a result of the employee's death.

(2) The relief is given for the accounting period in which the employee dies.

(3) The amount of relief is equal to the amount that would have counted as employment income of the employee under section 426 of ITEPA 2003 had a chargeable event within section 427(3)(*c*) of that Act occurred immediately before Chapter 2 of Part 7 of that Act ceased to apply to the restricted shares because of the employee's death.

(4) For the purposes of subsection (3)—

   (*a*) the amount of expenses resulting from section 428(6) of ITEPA 2003 is to be treated as nil, and

   (*b*) the following are to be ignored—

      (i) sections 428(9) and 446E(6) of ITEPA 2003, and

      (ii) the amount of any non-commercial increase (as defined in section 446K(4) of ITEPA 2003) in the market value of the restricted shares after their acquisition.

(5) . . . [1]

Commentary—*Simon's Taxes* **D1.337**.
Derivation—FA 2003 Sch 23 paras 21(7)–(9), 22(6).
HMRC Manuals—Business Income Manual BIM44385 (death of employee: relief).
Employment Related Securities Manual ERSM20270 (exclusions: death).
Amendments—[1]   Sub-s (5) repealed by FA 2017 s 12(4)(*f*) with effect in relation to shares acquired in consideration of an employee shareholder agreement entered into on or after the relevant day. The relevant day is 1 December 2016 (FA 2017 s 12(6)), but for circumstances in which the relevant day is 2 December 2016, see FA 2017 s 12(7)).

1028 Supplementary provision for purposes of sections 1026 and 1027

(1) If section 1012 or 1020 (reduction in amount of relief) applies in relation to the original relief, that section applies in relation to the relief under this Chapter as it applies in relation to the original relief.

(2) For the purposes of the giving of the relief under this Chapter—

   (*a*) if the original relief is available under Chapter 2, apply section 1013(2) to (5), and

   (*b*) if the original relief is available under Chapter 3, apply section 1021(2) to (5).

Commentary—*Simon's Taxes* **D1.338**.
Derivation—FA 2003 Sch 23 paras 9(1)–(4), 16(1)–(4), 21(10).

1029 Transfer of qualifying business by group transfers

(1) This section applies in relation to relief to be given under this Chapter if—

   (*a*) during the interim period (see subsections (5) to (7)), the whole, or substantially the whole, of the qualifying business is transferred, and

   (*b*) conditions A and B are met.

(2) Condition A is that—

   (*a*) the transfer is a group transfer, or

   (*b*) if there is more than one transfer, all the transfers are group transfers.

(3) Condition B is that, as a result of the transfer or transfers, at the end of the interim period—

   (*a*) the whole, or substantially the whole, of the qualifying business is carried on by one company ("the successor company") only and that company is not the employing company, or

   (*b*) the whole, or substantially the whole, of the qualifying business is carried on by companies ("the successor companies") none of which is the employing company.

(4) The relief is to be given to—

   (*a*) the successor company, or

   (*b*) whichever one of the successor companies is nominated by them,

instead of the employing company (and references to the employing company in section 1013(3) and (4) or 1021(3) and (4) (as applied by section 1028(2)) are to be read as references to the company to which the relief is to be given).

(5) "The interim period" is to be read in accordance with subsections (6) and (7).

(6) The interim period begins—

   (*a*) if the original relief is available under Chapter 2, when the restricted shares are acquired, and

   (*b*) if the original relief is available under Chapter 3, when the option is obtained.

(7) The interim period ends—

   (*a*) if the relief under this Chapter is available as a result of the occurrence of a chargeable event, when the chargeable event occurs, and

   (*b*) if the relief under this Chapter is available as a result of the employee's death, when the employee dies.

CHAPTER 5

ADDITIONAL RELIEF IN CASES INVOLVING CONVERTIBLE SECURITIES

1030 Application of Chapter

(1) This Chapter applies if relief under Chapter 2 or 3 is available in relation to an acquisition of convertible shares.

(2) This Chapter also applies if—

   (*a*) there is an acquisition of convertible securities that are not shares, and

   (*b*) relief under Chapter 2 or 3 would have been available in relation to the acquisition but for the fact that the securities were not shares in relation to which all the conditions set out in section 1008 or 1016 were met.

(3) For the purposes of subsections (1) and (2)(*b*) it does not matter if the amount of relief is calculated or would have been calculated as nil.

(4) In this Chapter—

"the acquired securities" means the convertible shares mentioned in subsection (1) or the convertible securities mentioned in subsection (2),

"convertible securities" includes an interest in convertible securities, and

"the original relief" means the relief mentioned in subsection (1) or (2)(*b*).

(5) If the original relief is or would have been available as a result of section 1015(3) (death of recipient), this Chapter applies as if the recipient were alive and the acquired securities were acquired by the recipient.

(6) If the original relief is or would have been available as a result of section 1022 (takeover of company whose shares are subject to an option), this Chapter applies as if the acquired securities were acquired pursuant to the qualifying option mentioned in that section.

Commentary—*Simon's Taxes* **D1.338**.
Derivation—FA 2003 Sch 23 paras 13(2), 22B(2), 22C(1), 27(2).
HMRC Manuals—Business Income Manual BIM44400 (qualifying shares: convertible shares: overview).

[1030A Application of Chapter: employees of overseas companies who take up employment with, or work for, a UK company

(1) This section applies if—

(*a*) a person ("E") has, or had, an employment ("the overseas employment") with a non-UK resident company not within the charge to corporation tax ("the overseas company"),

(*b*) E or another person acquired convertible securities because of the overseas employment (whether or not pursuant to an option),

(*c*) the case is not within section 1030(1) or (2),

(*d*) relief under Chapter 2 or 3 would have been available to the overseas company in relation to the acquisition if—

(i) in a case in which the convertible securities were not shares, they had been shares in relation to which the conditions set out in section 1008 or (as the case may be) 1016 were met, and

(ii) at all material times, the overseas company had carried on a business within subsection (2) ("a qualifying business") and the overseas employment had related to that business,

(*e*) E has a UK employment with a UK company (see subsections (3) and (4)),

(*f*) the UK employment is in relation to a qualifying business carried on by the UK company,

(*g*) an event occurs that is a chargeable event (within the meaning given by section 1032 modified in accordance with subsections (6) and (7)) in relation to the convertible securities, and

(*h*) because of the UK employment, an amount of employment income of E is charged to tax under ITEPA 2003 in relation to the chargeable event.

For the purposes of paragraph (*d*) it does not matter if the amount of the relief would have been calculated as nil.

(2) A business is within this subsection so far as—

(*a*) it is carried on by a company, and

(*b*) the company is within the charge to corporation tax in relation to the profits of the business or would be but for section 18A.

(3) A company is a "UK company" if it is a UK resident company or a non-UK resident company within the charge to corporation tax.

(4) E has a "UK employment" with a UK company if—

(*a*) E is employed by the UK company, or

(*b*) E is not employed by the UK company but provides, and is obliged to provide, personal service to the UK company, in the course of performing the duties of the overseas employment (in which case, references to the UK employment are to the personal service E provides).

(5) Relief under this Chapter is available to the UK company as a result of the chargeable event.

(6) References in this Chapter to the original relief (other than in section 1030B) are to be treated as references to the relief that would have been available as mentioned in subsection (1)(d).

(7) For the purposes of section 1032(2), references to the employing company in the conditions set out in section 1008 or (as the case may be) 1016 are to be read as references to the overseas company or the UK company.

(8) In section 1033(3) (amount of relief available on occurrence of chargeable event), the reference to the employee is to be read as a reference to E.

(9) For the purposes of section 1035(2) (giving relief), as that provision has effect by virtue of subsection (6), in section 1013(2) to (5) or (as the case may be) 1021(2) to (5)—

(*a*) references to the employing company are to be treated as references to the UK company,

(*b*) the reference to the relevant employment is to be treated as a reference to the UK employment, and

(c) references to a business within section 1007(2) or (as the case may be) 1015(2) are to be treated as references to a business within subsection (2).

(10) If, in relation to the chargeable event, the amount of relief available would otherwise be more than the total amount of employment income of E charged to tax under ITEPA 2003, the amount of relief is (notwithstanding any other provision of this Chapter) limited to the total amount of that income so charged.

(11) If relief is available to more than one company as a result of the same chargeable event, relief may only be given to one of them in respect of that event.][1]

Commentary—*Simon's Taxes* **D1.338**.
Amendments—[1]   Sections 1030A, 1030B inserted by FA 2014 s 52, Sch 9 paras 39, 46 with effect from 6 April 2015, subject to any transitional provision or savings that the Treasury may make by regulations under FA 2014 Sch 9 para 49.

[1030B Application of Chapter where original relief a consequence of section 1007A, 1015A or 1015B

(1) This section applies if the original relief is, or would have been, available under—
  (a) Chapter 2 as a consequence of section 1007A, or
  (b) Chapter 3 as a consequence of section 1015A or 1015B.

(2) If the original relief is, or would have been, available as a consequence of section 1007A or 1015B, subsection (2) of the section concerned applies for the purposes of this Chapter.

(3) Section 1007A(5), 1015A(4) or (as the case may be) 1015B(5) applies for the purposes of section 1032(2).

(4) If, in relation to a chargeable event, the amount of relief available would otherwise be more than the total amount of employment income of the employee charged to tax under ITEPA 2003, the amount of relief is (notwithstanding any other provision of this Chapter) limited to the total amount of that income so charged.

(5) If relief is available to more than one company as a result of the same chargeable event, relief ~~may only be given to one of them in respect of that event.~~ ...death.][1]

Commentary—*Simon's Taxes* **D1.338**.
Amendments—[1]   Sections 1030A, 1030B inserted by FA 2014 s 52, Sch 9 paras 39, 46 with effect from 6 April 2015, subject to any transitional provision or savings that the Treasury may make by regulations under FA 2014 Sch 9 para 49.

1031 Additional relief available if shares acquired are convertible shares etc

(1) Relief under this Chapter is available to the employing company if, after the acquisition of the acquired securities, a chargeable event (see section 1032) occurs in relation to those securities.

(2) Relief under this Chapter is also available to the employing company if the employee—
  (a) is dead when that acquisition occurs, or
  (b) dies after that acquisition.

(3) But relief resulting from subsection (2) does not become available until the occurrence of the first event (referred to in this Chapter as "the relief event") occurring after the employee's death that would have been a chargeable event in relation to the acquired securities had the employee been alive.

(4) To find out what accounting period the relief is given for and how to calculate the amount of relief, see—
  (a) section 1033 for relief available as a result of the occurrence of a chargeable event, and
  (b) section 1034 for relief available as a result of the employee's death.

Those sections are supplemented by section 1035.

(5) Section 1036 provides for the relief to be given to a successor company if the qualifying business is transferred by group transfers.

Commentary—*Simon's Taxes* **D1.338**.
Derivation—FA 2003 Sch 23 paras 22C(1), (2), (7), 22D(6).
HMRC Manuals—Business Income Manual BIM44400 (providing shares to employees: convertible shares).

1032 Meaning of "chargeable event"

(1) In this Chapter "chargeable event" means an event that—
  (a) is a chargeable event for the purposes of section 438 of ITEPA 2003,
  (b) is within section 439(3)(a) of ITEPA 2003, and
  (c) is within subsection (2).

(2) An event is within this subsection if it is the conversion of convertible securities into shares in relation to which—
  (a) if the original relief is or would have been available under Chapter 2, all the conditions set out in section 1008 are met, or
  (b) if the original relief is or would have been available under Chapter 3, all the conditions set out in section 1016 are met (ignoring paragraph (f) of condition 3).

(3) Subsection (4) applies if section 438 of ITEPA 2003—
  (a) does not apply in relation to the acquired securities, but
  (b) would apply if at all material times the employee had been a UK employee.

(4) This Chapter applies as if the employee had been a UK employee as mentioned in subsection *(3)(b)*.

(5) The employee is a UK employee if—

    (a) the employee is UK resident . . . [1], and

    (b) the duties of the relevant employment are performed in the United Kingdom.[2]

Commentary—*Simon's Taxes* **D1.338.**

Derivation—FA 2003 Sch 23 para 22C(10), (11).

HMRC Manuals—Employment Related Securities Manual ERSM40060 (chargeable events in connection with convertible securities).

Amendments—[1] Words in sub-s (5)(a) repealed by FA 2013 s 219, Sch 46 paras 137, 144 with effect in relation to convertible shares acquired on or after 6 April 2013.

[2] Sub-ss (3)–(5) repealed by FA 2014 s 52, Sch 9 paras 30, 33 with effect from 6 April 2015 in relation to employment-related securities and employment-related securities options irrespective of the date of acquisition, subject to any transitional provision or savings that the Treasury may make by regulations under FA 2014 Sch 9 para 49.

1033 Relief available on occurrence of chargeable event

(1) This section applies in relation to relief available as a result of the occurrence of a chargeable event.

(2) The relief is given for the accounting period in which the chargeable event occurs.

(3) The amount of relief is equal to the amount that counts as employment income of the employee under section 438 of ITEPA 2003 in relation to the chargeable event.

(4) For the purposes of subsection (3) the following are to be ignored—

    (a) any relief under section 442A of ITEPA 2003, and

    (b) sections 446G and 446H of ITEPA 2003.

(5) . . . [1]

Commentary—*Simon's Taxes* **D1.338.**

Amendments—[1] Sub-s (5) repealed by FA 2017 s 12(4)(f) with effect in relation to shares acquired in consideration of an employee shareholder agreement entered into on or after the relevant day. The relevant day is 1 December 2016 (FA 2017 s 12(6)), but for circumstances in which the relevant day is 2 December 2016, see FA 2017 s 12(7)).

1034 Relief available following death of employee

(1) This section applies in relation to relief available as a result of the employee's death.

(2) The relief is given for the accounting period in which the relief event occurs.

(3) The amount of relief is equal to the amount that would have counted as employment income of the employee under section 438 of ITEPA 2003 in relation to the relief event had the employee been alive.

(4) For the purposes of subsection (3) sections 446G and 446H of ITEPA 2003 are to be ignored.

(5) . . . [1]

Commentary—*Simon's Taxes* **D1.338.**

Amendments—[1] Sub-s (5) repealed by FA 2017 s 12(4)(f) with effect in relation to shares acquired in consideration of an employee shareholder agreement entered into on or after the relevant day. The relevant day is 1 December 2016 (FA 2017 s 12(6)), but for circumstances in which the relevant day is 2 December 2016, see FA 2017 s 12(7)).

1035 Supplementary provision for purposes of sections 1033 and 1034

(1) If section 1012 or 1020 (reduction in amount of relief) applies or would have applied in relation to the original relief, that section applies in relation to the relief under this Chapter as it applies or would have applied in relation to the original relief.

(2) For the purposes of the giving of the relief under this Chapter—

    (a) if the original relief is or would have been available under Chapter 2, apply section 1013(2) to (5), and

    (b) if the original relief is or would have been available under Chapter 3, apply section 1021(2) to (5).

1036 Transfer of qualifying business by group transfers

(1) This section applies in relation to relief to be given under this Chapter if—

    (a) during the interim period (see subsections (5) to (7)), the whole, or substantially the whole, of the qualifying business is transferred, and

    (b) conditions A and B are met.

(2) Condition A is that—

    (a) the transfer is a group transfer, or

    (b) if there is more than one transfer, all the transfers are group transfers.

(3) Condition B is that, as a result of the transfer or transfers, at the end of the interim period—

    (a) the whole, or substantially the whole, of the qualifying business is carried on by one company ("the successor company") only and that company is not the employing company, or

    (b) the whole, or substantially the whole, of the qualifying business is carried on by companies ("the successor companies") none of which is the employing company.

(4) The relief is to be given to—

    (a) the successor company, or

(8) Chapter 8 contains provision limiting the amount of relief available under Chapter 2 . . . ³ in relation to expenditure on a particular research and development project.

(9) Chapter 9 contains supplementary provision, including definitions.

(10) For information about the procedure for making claims under this Part see Schedule 18 to FA 1998, in particular Part 9A of that Schedule (claims for R&D tax reliefs).

Commentary—*Simon's Taxes* **D1.401, D1.440, D1.460**.

HMRC Manuals—Corporate Intangibles Research and Development Manual CIRD81200 (claimant must be a company subject to corporation tax).

Amendments—¹ In sub-s (6), words substituted for words "companies (whether they are small or medium-sized enterprises or large companies)", in sub-s (7), words substituted for words "Chapters 2 and 7 also provide", and in sub-s 7(*a*), words "or 7" repealed, by FA 2012 s 20, Sch 3 paras 1, 16 with effect in relation to expenditure incurred on or after 1 April 2012.

² In sub-s (3), words substituted for words "Chapters 2 to 4", and paras (*b*), (*c*) repealed; sub-s (4) repealed; and in sub-s (5), words substituted for words "Chapters 2 to 5", and paras (*b*), (*c*) repealed; by FA 2013 s 35, Sch 15 paras 12, 13 with effect in relation to expenditure incurred on or after 1 April 2016, subject to the transitional provisions in FA 2013 Sch 15 para 29 (cases where a company claims an R&D expenditure credit under s 104A for an accounting period beginning before 1 April 2016).

³ Sub-s (6) repealed, and in sub-s (8) words repealed, by FA 2016 s 47(1), (3) with effect in relation to expenditure incurred on or after 1 April 2017.

1040 Relief may be available under more than one Chapter of Part

Expenditure may be eligible for relief under more than one Chapter of this Part.

[1040ZA Restriction on claiming other tax reliefs

(1) For provision prohibiting relief being given under this Part and under Chapter 3 of Part 15 (film tax relief), see section 1195(3A).

(2) For provision prohibiting relief being given under this Part and under Chapter 3 of Part 15A (television tax relief), see section 1216C(4).

(3) For provision prohibiting relief being given under this Part and under Chapter 3 of Part 15B (video games tax relief), see section 1217C(4).

[(4) For provision prohibiting relief being given under this Part and under section 1217H or 1217K (theatrical productions: additional deduction or theatre tax credit), see section 1217JA(2).]²

[(5) For provision prohibiting relief being given under this Part and under Chapter 3 of Part 15E (museums and galleries exhibition tax relief), see section 1218ZCG(2).]³]¹

Amendments—¹ This section inserted by FA 2013 s 36, Sch 18 para 10.

² Sub-s (4) inserted by FA 2014 s 36, Sch 4 para 11 with effect in relation to accounting periods beginning on or after 1 September 2014, subject to transitional provisions for accounting periods straddling that date (FA 2014 Sch 4 para 17). SI 2014/2228 reg 2 provides that the amendments made by FA 2014 Sch 4 come into force on 22 August 2014 (other than the power to make regulations under Sch 4 para 16(1) which came into force on 17 July 2014).

³ Sub-s (5) inserted by F(No 2)A 2017 s 21, Sch 6 paras 9, 12 with effect in relation to accounting periods beginning on or after 1 April 2017.

[1040A R&D expenditure credits

(1) For provision enabling a company carrying on a trade to make a claim for an amount in respect of expenditure on research and development (an "R&D expenditure credit") to be brought into account as a receipt in calculating the profits of the trade for an accounting period, see Chapter 6A of Part 3.

(2) For provision prohibiting a company from making a claim for an R&D expenditure credit and for relief under this Part in respect of the same expenditure, see section 104B.]¹

HMRC Manuals—Corporate Intangibles Research and Development Manual CIRD89705 (R&D expenditure credit RDEC).

Amendments—¹ This section inserted by FA 2013 s 35, Sch 15 para 2(1), (2) with effect in relation to expenditure incurred on or after 1 April 2013.

Interpretation

1041 "Research and development"

In this Part "research and development" has the meaning given by [section 1138 of CTA 2010]¹.

Commentary—*Simon's Taxes* **D1.401**.

Derivation—FA 2000 Sch 20 para 25(1); FA 2002 Sch 12 para 19(1), Sch 13 para 27(1).

HMRC Manuals—Corporate Intangibles Research and Development Manual CIRD81300 (definition of R&D).

Amendments—¹ Words substituted for words "section 837A of ICTA" by CTA 2010 s 1177, Sch 1 para 666. CTA 2010 has effect for corporation tax purposes for accounting periods ending on or after 1 April 2010, and for income and capital gains tax purposes for the tax year 2010–11 and subsequent tax years.

1042 "Relevant research and development"

(1) In this Part "relevant research and development", in relation to a company, means research and development—

    (*a*) related to a trade carried on by the company, or

    (*b*) from which it is intended that a trade to be carried on by the company will be derived.

(2) Research and development related to a trade carried on by a company includes—

    (*a*) research and development which may lead to or facilitate an extension of the trade, and

    (*b*) research and development of a medical nature which has a special relation to the welfare of workers employed in the trade.

(3) . . . [1]

Commentary—*Simon's Taxes* **D1.409, D1.453**.

Derivation—FA 2000 Sch 20 para 4(1), (2); FA 2002 Sch 12 para 17, Sch 13 para 5(1), (2).

HMRC Manuals—Corporate Intangibles Research and Development Manual CIRD81400 (meaning of relevant research and development).

Amendments—[1]   Sub-s (3) repealed by FA 2016 s 47(1), (4) with effect in relation to expenditure incurred on or after 1 April 2017.

CHAPTER 2

RELIEF FOR SMES: COST OF R&D INCURRED BY SME

Introductory

1043 Overview of Chapter

(1) This Chapter provides for relief for companies which are small or medium-sized enterprises for expenditure on—

    (*a*) in-house direct research and development, or

    (*b*) contracted out research and development,

where the cost of the research and development is incurred by the company.

(2) The reliefs available are—

    (*a*) an additional deduction under section 1044, or

    (*b*) a deemed trading loss under section 1045.

(3) Sections 1046 to 1053 contain provision relevant to the reliefs available under this Chapter, namely—

    (*a*) provision preventing a company from making a claim or election for relief if it is not a going concern (see section 1046),

    (*b*) information about elections under section 1045 for a deemed trading loss (see section 1047),

    (*c*) information about the treatment of a deemed trading loss (see section 1048),

    (*d*) a restriction on consortium relief where relief is obtained (see section 1049),

    (*e*) . . . [1] and

    (*f*) provision about when a company's expenditure is "qualifying Chapter 2 expenditure" for those purposes (see sections 1051 to 1053).

(4) Sections 1054 to 1062 deal with R&D tax credits which can be claimed if a company—

    (*a*) obtains relief under this Chapter, and

    (*b*) makes, or is treated as making, a trading loss.

Commentary—*Simon's Taxes* **D1.401, D1.403**.

Cross-references—See FA 2016 s 180, Sch 24 Pt 1 (power to obtain information about tax advantages claimed under this Chapter which constitute the grant of State aid).

Amendments[1]   Sub-s (3)(*e*) repealed by FA 2012 s 20, Sch 3 paras 1, 3(1), (2) with effect in relation to accounting periods ending on or after 1 April 2012.

Reliefs

1044 Additional deduction in calculating profits of trade

(1) A company is entitled to corporation tax relief for an accounting period if it meets each of conditions A to D.

(2) Condition A is that the company is a small or medium-sized enterprise in the period.

(3) . . . [2]

(4) Condition C is that the company carries on a trade in the period.

(5) Condition D is that the company has qualifying Chapter 2 expenditure which is allowable as a deduction in calculating for corporation tax purposes the profits of the trade for the period.

(6) For the company to obtain the relief it must make a claim.

See section 1046 (which prevents a company from making a claim if it is not a going concern).

(7) The relief is an additional deduction in calculating the profits of the trade for the period.

(8) The amount of the additional deduction is [130%][1] of the qualifying Chapter 2 expenditure.

(9) This section is subject to section 1113 (cap on R&D aid in relation to a particular research and development project).

(10) For the meaning of "qualifying Chapter 2 expenditure" see section 1051.

Commentary—*Simon's Taxes* **D1.420, D1.420, D1.405, B3.708, D1.401, D1.403**.

HMRC Manuals—Corporate Intangibles Research and Development Manual CIRD81450 (allowable as deduction in computing profits).

CIRD81700 (exclusion for capital expenditure).

CIRD81800 (HMRC approach to late claims).

Modification—In relation to expenditure incurred before 1 August 2008, this section is modified so that, in sub-s (8), figure "50%" substituted for figure "75%", by CTA 2009 s 1325, Sch 2 para 112(1), (2)(*a*).

Amendments[1]   Figure in sub-s (8) substituted for figure "125%" by FA 2015 s 27(1), (3)(*a*) with effect in relation to expenditure incurred on or after 1 April 2015.

[2]   Sub-s (3) repealed by FA 2012 s 20, Sch 3 paras 1, 3(1), (3) with effect in relation to accounting periods ending on or after 1 April 2012.

1045 Alternative treatment for pre-trading expenditure: deemed trading loss

(1) A company is entitled to corporation tax relief for an accounting period if it meets conditions A . . . [2] and C.

(2) Condition A is that the company is a small or medium-sized enterprise in the period.

(3) . . . [2]

(4) Condition C is that the company has incurred qualifying Chapter 2 expenditure in the period which—

    (*a*) is not allowable as a deduction in calculating for corporation tax purposes the profits of a trade carried on by it at the time the expenditure was incurred, but

    (*b*) would have been so allowable had it, at that time, been carrying on a trade consisting of the activities in respect of which the expenditure was incurred.

(5) For the company to obtain the relief it must make an election.

See section 1046 (which prevents a company from making an election if it is not a going concern).

(6) The relief is that the company is treated as if it had made a trading loss in the period.

(7) The trading loss is equal to [230%][1] of the qualifying Chapter 2 expenditure.

(8) If a company makes an election under this section in respect of qualifying Chapter 2 expenditure, section 61 (pre-trading expenses) does not apply to the expenditure.

(9) This section is subject to section 1113 (cap on R&D aid in relation to a particular research and development project).

(10) For the meaning of "qualifying Chapter 2 expenditure" see section 1051.

(11) See also section 1137, which makes provision about the accounting periods of a company which is not within the charge to corporation tax.

Commentary—*Simon's Taxes* **D1.422**.

HMRC Manuals—Corporate Intangibles Research and Development Manual CIRD90200 (treatment of pre-trading expenditure under SME scheme).

Modification—In relation to expenditure incurred before 1 August 2008, this section is modified so that, in sub-s (7), figure "150%" substituted for figure "175%", by CTA 2009 s 1325, Sch 2 para 112(1), (2)(*b*).

Amendments—[1]   Figure in sub-s (7) substituted for figure "225%" by FA 2015 s 27(1), (3)(*b*) with effect in relation to expenditure incurred on or after 1 April 2015.

[2]   Word ", B" in sub-s (1), and the whole of sub-s (3), repealed, by FA 2012 s 20, Sch 3 paras 1, 3(1), (4) with effect in relation to accounting periods ending on or after 1 April 2012.

Reliefs: further provision

1046 Relief only available where company is going concern

(1) A company may only make—

    (*a*) a claim under section 1044, or

    (*b*) an election under section 1045,

at a time when it is a going concern.

(2) For the purposes of this section a company is a going concern if—

    (*a*) its latest published accounts were prepared on a going concern basis, and

    (*b*) nothing in those accounts indicates that they were only prepared on that basis because of an expectation that the company would receive relief or R&D tax credits under this Chapter[2]

    [This is subject to subsection (2A).][1]

[(2A) A company is not a going concern at any time if it is in administration or liquidation at that time.

(2B) For the purposes of this section a company is in administration if—

    (*a*) it is in administration under Part 2 of the Insolvency Act 1986 or Part 3 of the Insolvency (Northern Ireland) Order 1989 (S.I. 1989/2405 (N.I. 19)), or

    (*b*) a corresponding situation under the law of a country or territory outside the United Kingdom exists in relation to the company.

(2C) For the purposes of this section a company is in liquidation if—

    (*a*) it is in liquidation within the meaning of section 247 of that Act or Article 6 of that Order, or

    (*b*) a corresponding situation under the law of a country or territory outside the United Kingdom exists in relation to the company.][1]

(3) Section 436(2) of the Companies Act 2006 (meaning of "publication" of documents) has effect for the purposes of this section.

Commentary—*Simon's Taxes* **D1.422, D1.409**.

HMRC Manuals—Corporate Intangibles Research and Development Manual CIRD90200 (treatment of pre-trading expenditure under SME scheme).

CIRD81130 (company a going concern).

Amendments—[1]   Sub-ss (2A)–(2C), and the words at the end of sub-s (2), inserted, by FA 2012 s 20, Sch 3 paras 1, 9, 10 with effect in relation to claims or elections made on or after 1 April 2012.

[2]   In sub-s (2)(*b*) words "or Chapter 7" repealed by FA 2012 s 20, Sch 3 paras 1, 18 with effect in relation to expenditure incurred on or after 1 April 2012.

1047 Elections under section 1045

(1) An election under section 1045 must specify the accounting period in respect of which it is made.

(2) The election must be made by notice in writing to an officer of Revenue and Customs.

(3) The notice must be given before the end of the period of two years beginning immediately after the end of the accounting period to which the election relates.

Commentary—*Simon's Taxes* **D1.422**.

HMRC Manuals—Corporate Intangibles Research and Development Manual CIRD90200 (treatment of pre-trading expenditure under SME scheme).

1048 Treatment of deemed trading loss under section 1045

(1) This section applies if under section 1045 a company is treated as making a trading loss in an accounting period [("the deemed loss-making period")][2].

(2) The trading loss may not be [deducted from][1] profits of a preceding accounting period under [section 37(3)(b) or 42 of CTA 2010][1] unless the company is entitled to relief under section 1045 for the earlier period.

(3) Subsection (4) applies if—

[(*za*) the deemed loss-making period begins before 1 April 2017][2]

(*a*) the company begins, in [the deemed loss-making period][2] or a later period, to carry on a trade, and

(*b*) the trade is derived from the research and development in relation to which the relief mentioned in subsection (1) was obtained.

(4) In that case, so far as—

(*a*) the company has not obtained relief in respect of the trading loss under any other provision, and

(*b*) the loss has not been surrendered under [Part 5 of CTA 2010 (group relief)][1] (surrender of relief to group or consortium members),

the trading loss is to be treated as if it were a loss of that trade brought forward under [section 45 of CTA 2010][1].

[(4A) Subsection (4B) applies if—

(*a*) the deemed loss-making period begins on or after 1 April 2017,

(*b*) the company—

   (i) begins to carry on a trade in the deemed loss-making period which it continues to carry on in the following accounting period, or

   (ii) begins to carry on a trade in an accounting period after the deemed-loss making period, and

(*c*) the trade is derived from the research and development in relation to which the relief mentioned in subsection (1) was obtained.

(4B) In that case, so far as—

(*a*) the company has not obtained relief in respect of the trading loss under any other provision, and

(*b*) the loss has not been surrendered under Part 5 of CTA 2010 (group relief) (surrender of relief to group or consortium members),

the trading loss is to be treated as if it were a loss of that trade brought forward under the relevant provision (see subsection (4C)) to the relevant period (see subsection (4D).

(4C) In subsection (4B) "the relevant provision" is—

(*a*) section 45A(4) of CTA 2010 if—

   (i) the trade is not a ring fence trade within the meaning of Part 8 of CTA 2010 (see section 277 of that Act), and

   (ii) relief under section 37 of CTA 2010 would not be unavailable by reason of section 44 of that Act for a loss (assuming there was one) made in the trade in the relevant period (see subsection (4D), and

(*b*) section 45B(2) of CTA 2010 if either of the conditions in paragraph (*a*) is not met.

(4D) In subsection (4B) and (4C) "the relevant period" means—

(*a*) in a case where the company began the trade in the deemed loss-making period and continued to carry on the trade in the following accounting period, that following accounting period, and

(*b*) in a case where the company began the trade in an accounting period after the deemed loss-making period, the accounting period in which the company began the trade.][2]

(5) [Subsections (4) and (4B) are][2] subject to section 1062 (restriction on losses carried forward where tax credit claimed).

Commentary—*Simon's Taxes* **D1.422**.

HMRC Manuals—Corporate Intangibles Research and Development Manual CIRD90200 (deemed trading loss).

Amendments—[1] In sub-s (2) words substituted for words "set off against" and "section 393A(1)(*b*) or 393B(3) of ICTA", in sub-s (4) words substituted for words "section 403(1) of ICTA" and "section 393 of ICTA (relief of trading losses against future trading profits)" by CTA 2010 s 1177, Sch 1 para 667. CTA 2010 has effect for corporation tax purposes for accounting periods ending on or after 1 April 2010, and for income and capital gains tax purposes for the tax year 2010–11 and subsequent tax years.

2   In sub-s (1), words inserted, sub-ss (3)(*za*), (4A)–(4D) inserted, in sub-s (3)(*a*) words substituted for words "the accounting period", and in sub-s (5) words substituted for words "Subsection (4) is", by F(No 2)A 2017 s 18, Sch 4 paras 128, 133 with effect in relation to accounting periods beginning on or after 1 April 2017, subject to transitional provisions in Sch 4 para 194. For accounting periods beginning before 1 April 2017 and ending on or after that date ("straddling periods") see F(No 2)A 2017 Sch 4 paras 190–192.

1049 Restriction on consortium relief

(1) This section applies if—

    (*a*) a company claims relief under section 1044 or elects to obtain relief under section 1045 in respect of an accounting period,

    (*b*) at any time during the period the company is owned by a consortium, and

    (*c*) at least one of the members of the consortium is a large company.

(2) The amount of the relief obtained in respect of the accounting period may not be surrendered by the company to another company, for the purposes of a consortium group relief claim, unless the other company is a small or medium-sized enterprise.

(3) A "consortium group relief claim" means a claim to group relief [based on consortium condition 1, 2 or 3 in sections 132 and 133 of CTA 2010][1] (group relief available between members of consortia).

Commentary—*Simon's Taxes* **D1.420**.

HMRC Manuals—Corporate Intangibles Research and Development Manual CIRD90400 (consortium relief: restriction).

Amendments—[1]   In sub-s (3) words substituted for words set off against" and "section 393A(1)(*b*) or 393B(3) of ICTA", in sub-s (4) words substituted for words "under section 402(3) of ICTA" by CTA 2010 s 1177, Sch 1 para 668. CTA 2010 has effect for corporation tax purposes for accounting periods ending on or after 1 April 2010, and for income and capital gains tax purposes for the tax year 2010–11 and subsequent tax years.

Qualifying expenditure

1051 Qualifying Chapter 2 expenditure

For the purposes of this Part a company's "qualifying Chapter 2 expenditure" means—

    (*a*) its qualifying expenditure on in-house direct research and development (see section 1052), and

    (*b*) its qualifying expenditure on contracted out research and development (see section 1053).

Commentary—*Simon's Taxes* **D1.403**.

Cross-references—See FA 2016 s 180, Sch 24 Pt 1 (power to obtain information about tax advantages claimed under this Chapter which constitute the grant of State aid).

1052 Qualifying expenditure on in-house direct R&D

(1) A company's "qualifying expenditure on in-house direct research and development" means expenditure incurred by it in relation to which each of [conditions A, B, D and E][1] is met.

(2) Condition A is that the expenditure is—

    (*a*) incurred on staffing costs (see section 1123),

    (*b*) incurred on software or consumable items (see section 1125),

    (*c*) qualifying expenditure on externally provided workers (see section 1127), or

    (*d*) incurred on relevant payments to the subjects of a clinical trial (see section 1140).

(3) Condition B is that the expenditure is attributable to relevant research and development undertaken by the company itself.

(4) . . .[1]

(5) Condition D is that the expenditure is not incurred by the company in carrying on activities which are contracted out to the company by any person.

(6) Condition E is that the expenditure is not subsidised (see section 1138).

(7) See sections 1124, 1126 [to 1126B][2] and 1132 for provision about when expenditure within subsection (2)(*a*), (*b*) or (*c*) is attributable to relevant research and development.

Commentary—*Simon's Taxes* **D1.409, D1.420A**.

HMRC Manuals—Corporate Intangibles Research and Development Manual CIRD81470 (sub-contracted R & D).

CIRD81500 (categories of qualifying expenditure).

CIRD81650 (subsidies under SME scheme).

Modifications—In relation to expenditure incurred before 1 April 2004, this Part modified so as to substitute words "consumable stores" for words "software or consumable items", in each place where they occur, by CTA 2009 Sch 2 para 122(1), (2).

In relation to expenditure incurred before 27 September 2003, Chapters 2, 4 apply with the omission of sub-s (2)(*c*) (CTA 2009 Sch 2 para 123(1)(*a*)).

In relation to expenditure incurred before 1 August 2008, Chapter 2 of this Part applies with the omission of sub-s (2)(*d*) (CTA 2009 Sch 2 para 124(1)(*a*)).

Amendments—[1]   In sub-s (1), words substituted for words "conditions A to E", and sub-s (4) repealed, by F(No 3)A 2010 s 13(1), (2) with effect in relation to expenditure incurred by a company in an accounting period ending on or after 9 December 2009.

[2]   In sub-s (7), words inserted by FA 2015 s 28(1), (4) with effect in relation to expenditure incurred on or after 1 April 2015.

1053 Qualifying expenditure on contracted out R&D

(1) A company's "qualifying expenditure on contracted out research and development" means expenditure—

　　(*a*) which is incurred by it in making the qualifying element of a sub-contractor payment (see sections 1134 to 1136), and

　　(*b*) in relation to which each of [conditions A, C and D][1] is met.

(2) Condition A is that the expenditure is attributable to relevant research and development undertaken on behalf of the company.

(3) . . .[1]

(4) Condition C is that the expenditure is not incurred by the company in carrying on activities which are contracted out to the company by any person.

(5) Condition D is that the expenditure is not subsidised (see section 1138).

(6) See sections 1124, 1126 [to 1126B][2] and 1132 for provision about when particular kinds of expenditure are attributable to relevant research and development.

Commentary—*Simon's Taxes* **D1.414**.

HMRC Manuals—Corporate Intangibles Research and Development Manual CIRD81470 (sub-contracted R & D).

CIRD81500 (categories of qualifying expenditure).

CIRD81650 (subsidies under SME scheme).

Amendments—[1]　In sub-s (1)(*b*), words substituted for words "conditions A to D", and sub-s (3) repealed, by F(No 3)A 2010 s 13(1), (3) with effect in relation to expenditure incurred by a company in an accounting period ending on or after 9 December 2009.

[2]　In sub-s (6), words inserted by FA 2015 s 28(1), (4) with effect in relation to expenditure incurred on or after 1 April 2015.

Tax credit: entitlement and payment

1054 Entitlement to and payment of tax credit

(1) A company is entitled to an R&D tax credit for an accounting period if it has a Chapter 2 surrenderable loss in the period (see section 1055).

(2) For the company to obtain an R&D tax credit in respect of all or part of the Chapter 2 surrenderable loss it must make a claim.

See section 1057 (which prevents a company from making a claim if it is not a going concern).

(3) The amount of an R&D tax credit to which the company is entitled is determined in accordance with section 1058.

(4) If a company makes a claim for an R&D tax credit to which it is entitled for an accounting period, an officer of Revenue and Customs must pay to the company the amount of the credit.

　This is subject to section 1060.

(5) This section is subject to section 1113 (cap on R&D aid in relation to a particular research and development project).

(6) See also section 1062, which restricts the carry forward of losses where a company claims an R&D tax credit.

Commentary—*Simon's Taxes* **D1.420**.

HMRC Manuals—Corporate Intangibles Research and Development Manual CIRD90500 (payable tax credit for surrenderable loss).

CIRD81130 (company a going concern).

1055 Meaning of "Chapter 2 surrenderable loss"

(1) For the purposes of this Chapter a company has a "Chapter 2 surrenderable loss" if in an accounting period—

　　(*a*) it obtains an additional deduction under section 1044 in calculating the profits of a trade and it makes a trading loss in that period in the trade, or

　　(*b*) it is treated as making a trading loss under section 1045.

(2) If relief is obtained under section 1044 the amount of the Chapter 2 surrenderable loss is—

　　(*a*) so much of the trading loss as is unrelieved, or

　　(*b*) if less, [230%][1] of the qualifying Chapter 2 expenditure in respect of which the relief was obtained.

(3) If relief is obtained under section 1045 the amount of the Chapter 2 surrenderable loss is so much of the trading loss as is unrelieved.

Commentary—*Simon's Taxes* **D1.420, D1.401, D1.403, D1.420**.

HMRC Manuals—Corporate Intangibles Research and Development Manual CIRD90500 (surrenderable loss: meaning).

Modification—In relation to expenditure incurred before 1 August 2008, this section is modified so that, in sub-s (2)(*b*), figure "150%" substituted for figure "175%", by CTA 2009 s 1325, Sch 2 para 112(1), (2)(*c*).

Amendments—[1]　Figure in sub-s (2)(*b*) substituted for figure "225%" by FA 2015 s 27(1), (3)(*c*) with effect in relation to expenditure incurred on or after 1 April 2015.

1056 Amount of trading loss which is "unrelieved"

(1) This section applies for the purposes of section 1055.

(2) The amount of a trading loss that is "unrelieved" is the amount of the loss reduced by—

(a) any relief that was or could have been obtained by the company making a claim under [section 37(3)(a) of CTA 2010 to deduct the loss from total]¹ profits of the same accounting period,

(b) any other relief obtained by the company in respect of the loss, including relief [section 37(3)(b) or 42 of CTA 2010 (losses deducted from]¹ profits of an earlier accounting period), and

(c) any loss surrendered under [Part 5 [or Part 5A]² of CTA 2010]¹ (surrender of relief to group or consortium members).

(3) No account is to be taken for this purpose of any losses—

(a) brought forward from an earlier accounting period under [section 45[, 45A or 45B]² of CTA 2010], or

(b) carried back from a later accounting period under [section 37(3)(b) or 42]¹.

Commentary—*Simon's Taxes* **D1.420**.

HMRC Manuals—Corporate Intangibles Research and Development Manual CIRD90500 (unrelieved trading loss).

Amendments—¹   Amendments made by CTA 2010 s 1177, Sch 1 para 669

CTA 2010 has effect for corporation tax purposes for accounting periods ending on or after 1 April 2010, and for income and capital gains tax purposes for the tax year 2010–11 and subsequent tax years.

² In sub-ss (2)(c), (3)(a), words inserted, by F(No 2)A 2017 s 18, Sch 4 paras 128, 134 with effect in relation to accounting periods beginning on or after 1 April 2017, subject to transitional provisions in Sch 4 para 194. For accounting periods beginning before 1 April 2017 and ending on or after that date ("straddling periods") see F(No 2)A 2017 Sch 4 paras 190–192.

1057 Tax credit only available where company is going concern

(1) A company may only make a claim under section 1054 at a time when it is a going concern.

(2) If a company ceases to be a going concern after making a claim under section 1054, it is treated as if it had not made the claim (and accordingly there is treated as having been no payment of R&D tax credit to carry interest under section 826 of ICTA).

(3) Subsection (2) does not apply so far as the claim relates to an amount that was paid or applied before the company ceased to be a going concern.

(4) For the purposes of this section a company is a going concern if—

(a) its latest published accounts were prepared on a going concern basis, and

(b) nothing in those accounts indicates that they were only prepared on that basis because of an expectation that the company would receive relief or R&D tax credits under this Chapter . . . ².

[This is subject to subsection (4A).]¹

[(4A) A company is not a going concern at any time if it is in administration or liquidation at that time.

(4B) For the purposes of this section a company is in administration if—

(a) it is in administration under Part 2 of the Insolvency Act 1986 or Part 3 of the Insolvency (Northern Ireland) Order 1989 (S.I. 1989/2405 (N.I. 19)), or

(b) a corresponding situation under the law of a country or territory outside the United Kingdom exists in relation to the company.

(4C) For the purposes of this section a company is in liquidation if—

(a) it is in liquidation within the meaning of section 247 of that Act or Article 6 of that Order, or

(b) a corresponding situation under the law of a country or territory outside the United Kingdom exists in relation to the company.]¹

(5) Section 436(2) of the Companies Act 2006 (meaning of "publication" of documents) has effect for the purposes of this section.

Commentary—*Simon's Taxes* **D1.420**.

HMRC Manuals—Corporate Intangibles Research and Development Manual CIRD90500 (going concern).

Amendments—¹   Sub-ss (4A)–(4C), and the words at the end of sub-s (4), inserted, by FA 2012 s 20, Sch 3 paras 1, 9, 11, with effect in relation to claims or elections made on or after 1 April 2012.

² In sub-s (4)(b) words "or Chapter 7" repealed by FA 2012 s 20, Sch 3 paras 1, 19 with effect in relation to expenditure incurred on or after 1 April 2012.

Amount of tax credit

1058 Amount of tax credit

(1) The amount of the R&D tax credit to which a company is entitled for an accounting period is—

(a) [14.5%]¹ of the amount of the Chapter 2 surrenderable loss for the period, . . . ²

(b) . . . ²

(2) The Treasury may by order replace the percentage for the time being specified in subsection (1)(a) with a different percentage.

(3) An order under subsection (2) may contain incidental, supplemental, consequential and transitional provision and savings.

Commentary—*Simon's Taxes* **D1.420, D1.401, D1.403, D1.420**.

HMRC Manuals—Corporate Intangibles Research and Development Manual CIRD90500 (amount to tax credit).

Modification—In relation to expenditure incurred before 1 August 2008, this section is modified so that, in sub-s (1)(a), figure "16%" substituted for figure "14%", by CTA 2009 s 1325, Sch 2 para 112(1), (2)(d).

Amendments—[1]   Figure in sub-s (1)(*a*) substituted for figure of 11% by FA 2014 s 31 with effect in relation to expenditure incurred on or after 1 April 2014.

[2]   Sub-s (1)(*b*) and preceding word "or" repealed by FA 2012 s 20, Sch 3 paras 1, 15(1), (2) with effect in relation to accounting periods ending on or after 1 April 2012.

Supplementary

1060 Payment of tax credit

(1) This section applies if an R&D tax credit for an accounting period is payable to a company under this Chapter.

(2) The amount payable in respect of—

    (*a*) the R&D tax credit, or

    (*b*) interest on the credit payable under section 826 of ICTA,

may be applied in discharging any liability of the company to pay corporation tax.

(3) So far as the amount is so applied, the duty of the officer of Revenue and Customs to pay the credit under section 1054(4) is discharged.

(4) Subsection (5) applies if the company's tax return for the accounting period is enquired into by an officer of Revenue and Customs.

(5) In that case—

    (*a*) no payment in respect of the R&D tax credit for the period need be made before the officer's enquiries are completed (see paragraph 32 of Schedule 18 to FA 1998), but

    (*b*) the officer may make a payment on a provisional basis of such amount as the officer thinks fit.

(6) No payment need be made in respect of the R&D tax credit if the company has outstanding PAYE and NIC liabilities for the period.

(7) A company has outstanding PAYE and NIC liabilities for an accounting period if it has not paid to an officer of Revenue and Customs any amount that it is required to pay—

    (*a*) under PAYE regulations, or

    (*b*) in respect of Class 1 national insurance contributions,

for payment periods ending in the accounting period.

Commentary—*Simon's Taxes* **D1.420**.
HMRC Manuals—Corporate Intangibles Research and Development Manual CIRD90600 (restriction of the credit).

1061 Tax credit payment not income of company

A payment in respect of an R&D tax credit under this Chapter is not income of the company for any tax purposes.

Commentary—*Simon's Taxes* **D1.420**.

1062 Restriction on losses carried forward where tax credit claimed

(1) This section applies if a company claims an R&D tax credit to which it is entitled for an accounting period.

(2) For the purposes of [[sections 45, 45A and 45B][2] of CTA 2010][1] (relief of trading losses against future . . . [2] profits) the company's trading loss for the period is treated as reduced by the amount of the surrendered loss for the period.

(3) The "amount of the surrendered loss" for the period means the amount of the Chapter 2 surrenderable loss in respect of which the company claims an R&D tax credit for the period.

Commentary—*Simon's Taxes* **D1.422, D1.420**.
Amendments—[1]   In sub-s (2) words substituted for words "section 393 of ICTA" by CTA 2010 s 1177, Sch 1 para 670. CTA 2010 has effect for corporation tax purposes for accounting periods ending on or after 1 April 2010, and for income and capital gains tax purposes for the tax year 2010–11 and subsequent tax years.

[2]   In sub-s (2), words substituted for words "section 45", and word "trading" repealed, by F(No 2)A 2017 s 18, Sch 4 paras 128, 135 with effect in relation to accounting periods beginning on or after 1 April 2017, subject to transitional provisions in Sch 4 para 194. For accounting periods beginning before 1 April 2017 and ending on or after that date ("straddling periods") see F(No 2)A 2017 Sch 4 paras 190–192.

[2]   This Chapter repealed by FA 2013 s 35, Sch 15 paras 12, 15 with effect in relation to expenditure incurred on or after 1 April 2016, subject to the transitional provisions in FA 2013 Sch 15 para 29 (cases where a company claims an R&D expenditure credit under s 104A for an accounting period beginning before 1 April 2016).

CHAPTER 6

CHAPTERS 2 TO 5: FURTHER PROVISION

1081 Insurance companies treated as large companies

(1) This section applies if an insurance company—

    (*a*) carries on life assurance business in an accounting period, and

    (*b*) is a small or medium-sized enterprise in the period.

(2) For the purposes of [Chapter 2][1] the company is to be treated as if it were not such an enterprise in the period.

(3) . . . [1]

Commentary—*Simon's Taxes* **D1.404B**.

Amendments—[1]   In sub-s (2), words substituted for words "Chapters 2 to 5" and sub-s (3) repealed by FA 2013 s 35, Sch 15 paras 12, 17 with effect in relation to expenditure incurred on or after 1 April 2016, subject to the transitional provisions in FA 2013 Sch 15 para 29 (cases where a company claims an R&D expenditure credit under s 104A for an accounting period beginning before 1 April 2016).

[2]   This section repealed by FA 2013 s 35, Sch 15 paras 12, 18 with effect in relation to expenditure incurred on or after 1 April 2016, subject to the transitional provisions in FA 2013 Sch 15 para 29 (cases where a company claims an R&D expenditure credit under s 104A for an accounting period beginning before 1 April 2016).

1084 Artificially inflated claims for relief or tax credit

(1) To the extent that a transaction is attributable to arrangements entered into wholly or mainly for a disqualifying purpose, it is to be disregarded for the purposes mentioned in subsection (2).

(2) Those purposes are—

    (a) determining for an accounting period relief to which a company is entitled under [Chapter 2][1], and

    (b) determining for an accounting period R&D tax credits to which a company is entitled under Chapter 2.

(3) Arrangements are entered into wholly or mainly for a "disqualifying purpose" if their main object, or one of their main objects, is to enable a company to obtain—

    (a) relief under [Chapter 2][1] to which it would not otherwise be entitled,

    (b) relief under [Chapter 2][1] of a greater amount than that to which it would otherwise be entitled,

    (c) an R&D tax credit under Chapter 2 to which it would not otherwise be entitled, or

    (d) an R&D tax credit under Chapter 2 of a greater amount than that to which it would otherwise be entitled.

(4) In this section "arrangements" includes any scheme, agreement or understanding, whether or not legally enforceable.

Commentary—*Simon's Taxes* **D1.440.**
Derivation—FA 2000 Sch 20 para 21(1)–(3); FA 2002 Sch 12 para 16(1)–(3).
HMRC Manuals—Corporate Intangibles Research and Development Manual CIRD97150 (specific statutory defences).
Amendments—[1]   In sub-ss (2)(a), (3)(a), (b), words substituted for "Chapters 2 to 5" by FA 2013 s 35, Sch 15 paras 12, 20 with effect in relation to expenditure incurred on or after 1 April 2016, subject to the transitional provisions in FA 2013 Sch 15 para 29 (cases where a company claims an R&D expenditure credit under s 104A for an accounting period beginning before 1 April 2016).

CHAPTER 8

CAP ON AID FOR R&D

1113 Cap on R&D aid under Chapter 2 . . . . [2]

(1) A company is only entitled to qualifying R&D relief in respect of expenditure attributable to a research and development project if, or so far as, the condition in subsection (2) is met at that time.

(2) The condition is that the total R&D aid in respect of expenditure by the company attributable to the project would not exceed 7.5 million euros.

(3) In subsection (2) "total R&D aid" means the total R&D aid calculated—

    (a) in accordance with section 1114, and

    (b) as if a claim or election had been made for the R&D relief mentioned in subsection (1).

(4) In this Chapter "qualifying R&D relief" means any relief or R&D tax credit under—

    (a) Chapter 2 (relief for SMEs: cost of R&D incurred by SME), . . . [2]

    (b) . . . . [2]

(5) The Treasury may by regulations—

    (a) increase the amount specified in subsection (2), and

    (b) amend this Chapter (apart from this section).

Commentary—*Simon's Taxes* **D1.402A, D1.450.**
Derivation—FA 2008 s 29(1)–(3), Sch 10 para 6.
HMRC Manuals—Corporate Intangibles Research and Development Manual CIRD81160 (total aid).
Amendments—[1]   In sub-s (4)(b) words repealed by FA 2012 s 20, Sch 3 paras 1, 31(1), (2) with effect in relation to expenditure incurred on or after 1 April 2012.

[2]   In heading, words repealed, in sub-s (4)(a), word repealed, and sub-s (4)(b), repealed, by FA 2016 s 47(1), (5) with effect in relation to expenditure incurred on or after 1 April 2017.

1114 Total R&D aid

For the purposes of section 1113 the total R&D aid, in respect of expenditure by a company ("the claimant") attributable to a research and development project, is calculated as follows—

$$A = (TC + R + (P \times CT)) - N$$

where—

    A is the total R&D aid,

    TC is the tax credits (see section 1115),

    R is the actual reduction in tax liability (see section 1116),

1122 "Large company"

In this Part "large company" means a company that is not a small or medium-sized enterprise.

Commentary—*Simon's Taxes* **D1.404**.
Derivation—FA 2002 Sch 12 para 2(1); FA 2008 Sch 10 para 5(2).

Staffing costs

1123 "Staffing costs"

(1) For the purposes of this Part the staffing costs of a company are amounts to which subsection (2), (3), (4), (5) or (7) applies.

(2) This subsection applies to an amount paid by the company to a director or an employee of the company which—

    (*a*) is earnings consisting of money, and

    (*b*) is paid because of the director's or employee's employment.

(3) This subsection applies to an amount paid by the company to a director or an employee of the company, other than an amount paid in respect of benefits in kind, if—

    (*a*) the amount is paid in respect of expenses paid by the director or employee, and

    (*b*) the amount is paid because of the director's or employee's employment.

(4) This subsection applies to secondary Class 1 national insurance contributions paid by the company.

(5) This subsection applies to compulsory contributions paid by the company in respect of benefits for directors or employees of the company under the social security legislation of an EEA State (other than the United Kingdom) or Switzerland.

(6) In subsection (5) "social security legislation" means legislation relating to any of the branches of social security listed in Article 3(1) of Regulation (EC) No. 883/2004 of the European Parliament and of the Council on the co-ordination of social security systems (as amended from time to time).

(7) This subsection applies to contributions paid by the company to a pension fund operated for the benefit of directors or employees of the company.

(8) In subsection (7) "pension fund" means a scheme, fund or other arrangement established and maintained (whether in the United Kingdom or elsewhere) for the purpose of providing pension benefits.

For this purpose "scheme" includes a deed, agreement or series of agreements.

(9) In subsection (8) "pension benefits" means pensions, retirement annuities, allowances, lump sums, gratuities or other superannuation benefits (with or without subsidiary benefits).

Commentary—*Simon's Taxes* **D1.409, E8.259**.
HMRC Manuals—Corporate Intangibles Research and Development Manual CIRD83000 (treatment of staffing costs). CIRD83200 (measuring staffing costs).
Modification—In its application to expenditure incurred before 1 April 2004 and in an accounting period ending on or after 6 April 2003, this section is modified, by CTA 2009 Sch 2 para 119, so as to substitute sub-ss (2), (3) as follows—

    "(2) This subsection applies to earnings paid by the company to directors or employees of the company.

    For this purpose "earnings" means earnings or amounts treated as earnings which constitute employment income (see section 7(2)(*a*) or (*b*) of ITEPA 2003).".

In its application to expenditure incurred before 1 August 2008, this section has effect with the omission of sub-s (5), (6) (CTA 2009 Sch 2 para 120).

Prospective amendments—In sub-s (5) words "(other than the United Kingdom)" to be repealed by the Taxes (Amendments) (EU Exit) Regulations, SI 2019/689 reg 16(1), (21) with effect from Implementation Period completion day (see EU(WA)A 2020 Sch 5 para 1(1)).

1124 Staffing costs: attributable expenditure

(1) This section applies for the purposes of this Part to identify when staffing costs are attributable to relevant research and development.

(2) The costs which are so attributable are those paid to, or in respect of, directors or employees who are directly and actively engaged in relevant research and development.

(3) Subsection (4) applies if a director or employee is partly engaged directly and actively in relevant research and development.

(4) The appropriate proportion of the staffing costs relating to the director or employee is treated as attributable to relevant research and development.

(5) Subsection (6) applies if persons provide services, such as secretarial or administrative services, in support of activities carried on by others.

(6) Those persons are not, as a result of providing those services, to be treated as themselves directly and actively engaged in those activities.

Commentary—*Simon's Taxes* **D1.409**.
Derivation—FA 2000 Sch 20 para 5(2)–(4); FA 2002 Sch 12 para 17, Sch 13 para 5(3).
HMRC Manuals—Corporate Intangibles Research and Development Manual CIRD83000 (treatment of staffing costs). CIRD83800 (employee partly engaged on R&D).
Modification—In relation to expenditure incurred before 27 September 2003, this section applies, for the purposes of Part 13 Chapters 2, 7, with the modification below.

In relation to expenditure incurred before 9 April 2003, this section applies, for the purposes of Part 13 Chapters 3–5, with the modification below.

In both cases, the modification is the substitution of sub-ss (3), (4) by the following—

"(3) In the case of a director ("D") or employee ("E") partly engaged directly and actively in relevant research and development the following rules apply—

    (a)   if the time D or E spends so engaged is less than 20% of D's or E's total working time, none of the staffing costs relating to D or E is treated as attributable to relevant research and development,

    (b)   if the time D or E spends so engaged is more than 80% of D's or E's total working time, the whole of the staffing costs relating to D or E is treated as attributable to relevant research and development,

    (c)   in any other case, an appropriate proportion of the staffing costs relating to D or E is treated as attributable to relevant research and development.".

Software or consumable items

1125 "Software or consumable items"

(1) For the purposes of this Part expenditure on software or consumable items means expenditure on—

    (a) computer software, or

    (b) consumable or transformable materials.

(2) For the purposes of subsection (1)(b) consumable or transformable materials include water, fuel and power.

Commentary—*Simon's Taxes* **D1.410**.
Derivation—FA 2000 Sch 20 para 6(1), (2); FA 2002 Sch 12 para 17, Sch 13 para 5(3).
HMRC Manuals—Corporate Intangibles Research and Development Manual CIRD82300 (relief for expenditure on consumable items).
CIRD82500 (expenditure on software).
CIRD82400 (meaning: consumable or transformable materials).
Modification—In relation to expenditure incurred before 1 April 2004, this section modified by CTA 2009 Sch 2 para 122(1), (3) so as to substitute new s 1125 for ss 1125, 1126 as follows—

    "1125 Consumable stores—

    (1)   For the purposes of this Part expenditure on consumable stores means expenditure that would be treated as expenditure on consumable stores in accordance with normal accounting practice.

    (2)   For the purposes of this Part expenditure on consumable stores is attributable to relevant research and development if the stores are employed directly in such research and development.".

1126 Software or consumable items: attributable expenditure

(1) This section applies for the purposes of this Part to identify when expenditure on software or consumable items is attributable to relevant research and development.

(2) Expenditure on software or consumable items is so attributable if the software or consumable items are employed directly in relevant research and development.

(3) Subsection (4) applies if software or consumable items are partly employed directly in relevant research and development.

(4) The appropriate proportion of the expenditure on the software or consumable items is treated as attributable to relevant research and development.

(5) Subsection (6) applies if software or consumable items are employed in the provision of services, such as secretarial or administrative services, in support of other activities.

(6) The software or consumable items are not, as a result of their employment in the provision of those services, to be treated as themselves directly employed in those activities.

[(7) This section is subject to sections 1126A and 1126B.][1]

Commentary—*Simon's Taxes* **D1.410**.
Derivation—FA 2000 Sch 20 para 6(3)–(5); FA 2002 Sch 12 para 17, Sch 13 para 5(3).
HMRC Manuals—Corporate Intangibles Research and Development Manual CIRD82300 (relief for expenditure on consumable items).
CIRD82500 (expenditure on software).
Modification—In relation to expenditure incurred before 1 April 2004, this section modified by CTA 2009 Sch 2 para 122(1), (3) so as to substitute new s 1125 for ss 1125, 1126 as follows—

    "1125 Consumable stores—

    (1)   For the purposes of this Part expenditure on consumable stores means expenditure that would be treated as expenditure on consumable stores in accordance with normal accounting practice.

    (2)   For the purposes of this Part expenditure on consumable stores is attributable to relevant research and development if the stores are employed directly in such research and development.".

Amendments—[1]   Sub-s (7) inserted by FA 2015 s 28(1), (2) with effect in relation to expenditure incurred on or after 1 April 2015.

[1126A Attributable expenditure: special rules

(1) Expenditure on consumable items is not to be treated as attributable to relevant research and development if—

In relation to expenditure incurred before 9 April 2003, Chapters 3, 5 of this Part apply with the omission of this section as it applies for the purposes of those Chapters (CTA 2009 Sch 2 para 123(2)(*b*), (3)(*b*)).

In relation to expenditure incurred by a large company before 27 September 2003, Chapter 7 of this Part applies in the case of such a company with the omission of this section as it applies for the purposes of that Chapter (CTA 2009 Sch 2 para 123(4)(*b*)).

Amendments—[1]   Words in sub-s (7) substituted for words " the staff provider", and sub-s (9) inserted, by FA 2012 s 20, Sch 3 paras 33, 34 with effect in relation to expenditure incurred on or after 1 April 2012.

1129 Qualifying expenditure on externally provided workers: connected persons

(1) This section applies if—

    (*a*) a company makes a staff provision payment,

    [(*b*) the company, the staff provider and (if different) the staff controller (or staff controllers) are all connected, and

    (*c*) in accordance with generally accepted accounting practice—

        (i)   the whole of the staff provision payment has been brought into account in determining the staff provider's profit or loss for a relevant period, and

        (ii) all of the relevant expenditure of each staff controller has been brought into account in determining the staff controller's profit or loss for a relevant period.][1]

(2) The company's qualifying expenditure on externally provided workers is—

    (*a*) the entire staff provision payment, or

    (*b*) if less, an amount equal to [the aggregate of the relevant expenditure of each staff controller][1].

(3) "Relevant expenditure"[, in relation to a staff controller,][1] means expenditure that—

    (*a*) is incurred by the [staff controller][1] in providing for the company the externally provided workers to whom the staff provision payment relates,

    (*b*) is not of a capital nature, and

    (*c*) is incurred on staffing costs or agency workers' remuneration.

(4) "Relevant period"[, in relation to a person,][1] means a period—

    (*a*) for which accounts are drawn up for the [person][1], and

    (*b*) that ends not more than 12 months after the end of the company's period of account in which the staff provision payment is, in accordance with generally accepted accounting practice, brought into account in determining the company's profit or loss.

(5) In section 1123 (meaning of "staffing costs"), which applies for the purpose of determining whether [the expenditure of a staff controller][1] meets the requirements of subsection (3)(*c*), references to a company are to be read as references to [a staff controller][1].

(6) "Agency workers' remuneration", in the case of any person who is an externally provided worker in relation to the company, means remuneration that—

    (*a*) is receivable by the worker under or in consequence of the contract mentioned in section 1128(7), but

    (*b*) does not constitute employment income of the worker apart from Chapter 7 of Part 2 of ITEPA 2003 (application of provisions to agency workers).

(7) Any apportionment of expenditure of the company or [a staff controller][1] necessary for the purposes of this section is to be made on a just and reasonable basis.

Commentary—*Simon's Taxes* D1.409A.

Derivation—FA 2000 Sch 20 para 8C(1)–(5); FA 2002 Sch 12 para 17, Sch 13 para 5(3).

HMRC Manuals—Corporate Intangibles Research and Development Manual CIRD84000 (expenditure on externally-provided workers).

CIRD84050 (connected staff supplier).

Modifications—In relation to expenditure incurred before 27 September 2003, Chapters 2, 4 of this Part apply with the omission of ss 1127–1132 as they apply for the purposes of those Chapters (CTA 2009 Sch 2 para 123(1)(*e*)).

In relation to expenditure incurred before 9 April 2003, Chapters 3, 5 of this Part apply with the omission of this section as it applies for the purposes of those Chapters (CTA 2009 Sch 2 para 123(2)(*b*), (3)(*b*)).

In relation to expenditure incurred by a large company before 27 September 2003, Chapter 7 of this Part applies in the case of such a company with the omission of this section as it applies for the purposes of that Chapter (CTA 2009 Sch 2 para 123(4)(*b*)).

Amendments—[1]   Amendments made by FA 2012 s 20, Sch 3 paras 33, 35 with effect in relation to expenditure incurred on or after 1 April 2012

Prospective amendments—Sub-s (4A) to be inserted by FA 2020 s 7, Sch 1 para 23(1), (2) with effect in relation to expenditure incurred on or after 6 April 2021 (subject to transitional provisions in FA 2020 Sch 1 paras 30–34). Sub-s (4A) to read as follows—

"(4A) In subsection (2) the reference to the staff provision payment is to that payment before any deduction is made from the payment under—

    (*a*) section 61S of ITEPA 2003,

    (*b*) regulation 19 of the Social Security Contributions (Intermediaries) Regulations 2000, or

    (*c*) regulation 19 of the Social Security Contributions (Intermediaries) (Northern Ireland) Regulations 2000.".

1130 Election for connected persons treatment

[(1) If—

    (*a*) a company makes a staff provision payment, and

   (*b*) the company, the staff provider and (if different) the staff controller (or staff controllers) are not all connected,

they may jointly elect that section 1129 is to apply to them as if they were all connected.][1]

(2) Any such election [has effect][1] in relation to all staff provision payments paid under the same contract or other arrangement.

(3) The election must be made by notice in writing to an officer of Revenue and Customs.

(4) The notice must be given before the end of the period of two years beginning immediately after the end of the company's accounting period in which the contract or other arrangement is entered into.

(5) An election under this section is irrevocable.

Commentary—*Simon's Taxes* **D1.409A**.

Derivation—FA 2000 Sch 20 para 8D(1)–(5); FA 2002 Sch 12 para 17, Sch 13 para 5(3).

HMRC Manuals—Corporate Intangibles Research and Development Manual CIRD84000 (expenditure on externally-provided workers).

Modifications—In relation to expenditure incurred before 27 September 2003, Chapters 2, 4 of this Part apply with the omission of ss 1127–1132 as they apply for the purposes of those Chapters (CTA 2009 Sch 2 para 123(1)(*e*)).

In relation to expenditure incurred before 9 April 2003, Chapters 3, 5 of this Part apply with the omission of this section as it applies for the purposes of those Chapters (CTA 2009 Sch 2 para 123(2)(*b*), (3)(*b*)).

In relation to expenditure incurred by a large company before 27 September 2003, Chapter 7 of this Part applies in the case of such a company with the omission of this section as it applies for the purposes of that Chapter (CTA 2009 Sch 2 para 123(4)(*b*)).

Amendments—[1]   Sub-s (1) substituted and in sub-s (2), words substituted for words "must be made", by FA 2012 s 20, Sch 3 paras 33, 36 with effect in relation to expenditure incurred on or after 1 April 2012.

1131 Qualifying expenditure on externally provided workers: other cases

(1) This section applies if—

   (*a*) a company makes a staff provision payment,

   [(*b*) the company, the staff provider and (if different) the staff controller (or staff controllers) are not all connected,][1] and

   (*c*) no election is made under section 1130.

(2) The company's qualifying expenditure on externally provided workers is 65% of the staff provision payment.

Commentary—*Simon's Taxes* **D1.409A**.

Derivation—FA 2000 Sch 20 para 8E; FA 2002 Sch 12 para 17, Sch 13 para 5(3).

HMRC Manuals—Corporate Intangibles Research and Development Manual CIRD84000 (expenditure on externally-provided workers).

Modifications—In relation to expenditure incurred before 27 September 2003, Chapters 2, 4 of this Part apply with the omission of ss 1127–1132 as they apply for the purposes of those Chapters (CTA 2009 Sch 2 para 123(1)(*e*)).

In relation to expenditure incurred before 9 April 2003, Chapters 3, 5 of this Part apply with the omission of this section as it applies for the purposes of those Chapters (CTA 2009 Sch 2 para 123(2)(*b*), (3)(*b*)).

In relation to expenditure incurred by a large company before 27 September 2003, Chapter 7 of this Part applies in the case of such a company with the omission of this section as it applies for the purposes of that Chapter (CTA 2009 Sch 2 para 123(4)(*b*)).

Amendments—[1]   Sub-s (1)(*b*) substituted by FA 2012 s 20, Sch 3 paras 33, 37 with effect in relation to expenditure incurred on or after 1 April 2012.

Prospective amendments—Sub-s (3) to be inserted by FA 2020 s 7, Sch 1 para 23(1), (3) with effect in relation to expenditure incurred on or after 6 April 2021 (subject to transitional provisions in FA 2020 Sch 1 paras 30–34). Sub-s (3) to read as follows—

"(3) In subsection (2) the reference to the staff provision payment is to that payment before any deduction is made from the payment under—

   (*a*) section 61S of ITEPA 2003,

   (*b*) regulation 19 of the Social Security Contributions (Intermediaries) Regulations 2000, or

   (*c*) regulation 19 of the Social Security Contributions (Intermediaries) (Northern Ireland) Regulations 2000.".

[1131A Sections 1129 and 1131: secondary Class 1 NICS paid by company

(1) This section applies if—

   (*a*) a company makes a staff provision payment,

   (*b*) the company is treated as making a payment of deemed direct earnings the amount of which is calculated by reference to the amount of the staff provision payment, and

   (*c*) the company pays a secondary Class 1 national insurance contribution in respect of the payment of deemed direct earnings.

(2) In determining the company's qualifying expenditure on externally provided workers in accordance with section 1129(2) or section 1131(2) the amount of the staff payment provision is to be treated as increased by the amount of the contribution.

(3) In determining the company's qualifying expenditure on externally provided workers in accordance with section 1129(2) the aggregate of the relevant expenditure of each staff controller is to be treated as increased by the amount of the contribution.

(4) But subsection (2) does not apply to the extent that the expenditure incurred by the company in paying the contribution is met directly or indirectly by a staff controller.

(5) "A payment of deemed direct earning" means a payment the company is treated as making by reason of regulation 14 of the Social Security Contributions (Intermediaries) Regulations 2000 or regulation 14 of the Social Security Contributions (Intermediaries) (Northern Ireland) Regulations 2000.]

Prospective amendments—Section 1131A to be inserted by FA 2020 s 7, Sch 1 para 23(1), (4) with effect in relation to expenditure incurred on or after 6 April 2021 (subject to transitional provisions in FA 2020 Sch 1 paras 30–34).

1132 External workers: attributable expenditure

(1) This section applies for the purposes of this Part to identify when qualifying expenditure on externally provided workers is attributable to relevant research and development.

(2) Qualifying expenditure on externally provided workers is so attributable if the workers are directly and actively engaged in relevant research and development.

(3) Subsection (4) applies if an externally provided worker is partly engaged directly and actively in relevant research and development.

(4) The appropriate proportion of the qualifying expenditure relating to the worker is treated as attributable to relevant research and development.

(5) Subsection (6) applies if persons provide services (such as secretarial or administrative services) in support of activities carried on by others.

(6) Those persons are not, as a result of providing those services, to be treated as themselves directly and actively engaged in those activities.

Commentary—*Simon's Taxes* D1.409A.

Modifications—In relation to expenditure incurred before 27 September 2003, Chapters 2, 4 of this Part apply with the omission of ss 1127–1132 as they apply for the purposes of those Chapters (CTA 2009 Sch 2 para 123(1)(*e*)).

In relation to expenditure incurred before 9 April 2003, Chapters 3, 5 of this Part apply with the omission of this section as it applies for the purposes of those Chapters (CTA 2009 Sch 2 para 123(2)(*b*), (3)(*b*)).

In relation to expenditure incurred by a large company before 27 September 2003, Chapter 7 of this Part applies in the case of such a company with the omission of this section as it applies for the purposes of that Chapter (CTA 2009 Sch 2 para 123(4)(*b*)).

Sub-contractor payments

1133 "Sub-contractor" and "sub-contractor payment"

(1) In this Part a "sub-contractor payment" means a payment made by a company to another person ("the sub-contractor") in respect of research and development contracted out by the company to that person.

(2) Sections 1134 to 1136 apply if a company makes a sub-contractor payment.

(3) They apply for the purpose of determining the qualifying element of the payment for the purposes of—

> section 1053(1)(*a*),
> . . . [1] , . . . [2]
> . . . [2]

HMRC Manuals—Corporate Intangibles Research and Development Manual CIRD84200 (subcontracted activities).

Amendments—[1] In sub-s (3), words "section 1072(1)(*a*)" repealed by FA 2013 s 35, Sch 15 paras 12, 22 with effect in relation to expenditure incurred on or after 1 April 2016, subject to the transitional provisions in FA 2013 Sch 15 para 29 (cases where a company claims an R&D expenditure credit under s 104A for an accounting period beginning before 1 April 2016).

[2] In sub-s (3), words repealed by FA 2016 s 47(1), (7) with effect in relation to expenditure incurred on or after 1 April 2017.

1134 Qualifying element of sub-contractor payment: connected persons

(1) This section applies if—

  (*a*) a company makes a sub-contractor payment,

  (*b*) the company and the sub-contractor are connected, and

  (*c*) in accordance with generally accepted accounting practice, the whole of the sub-contractor payment and all of the sub-contractor's relevant expenditure have been brought into account in determining the sub-contractor's profit or loss for a relevant period.

(2) The qualifying element of the sub-contractor payment is—

  (*a*) the entire payment, or

  (*b*) if less, an amount equal to the sub-contractor's relevant expenditure.

(3) "Relevant expenditure" of the sub-contractor means expenditure that—

  (*a*) is incurred by the sub-contractor in carrying on, on behalf of the company, the activities to which the sub-contractor payment relates,

  (*b*) is not of a capital nature,

  (*c*) is incurred on staffing costs, software or consumable items or relevant payments to the subjects of a clinical trial or is qualifying expenditure on externally provided workers, and

  (*d*) is not subsidised.

(4) "Relevant period" means a period—

  (*a*) for which accounts are drawn up for the sub-contractor, and

  (*b*) that ends not more than 12 months after the end of the company's period of account in which the sub-contractor payment is, in accordance with generally accepted accounting practice, brought into account in determining the company's profit or loss.

(5) In the following sections, which apply for the purpose of determining whether a sub-contractor's expenditure meets the requirements of subsection (3)(*c*) and (*d*)—

    (*a*)   section 1123 (staffing costs),

    (*b*)   sections 1127 to 1131 (qualifying expenditure on externally provided workers), and

    (*c*)   section 1138 (subsidised expenditure),

references to a company are to be read as references to the sub-contractor.

(6) Any apportionment of expenditure of the company or the sub-contractor necessary for the purposes of this section is to be made on a just and reasonable basis.

Commentary—*Simon's Taxes* **D1.414**.

Derivation—FA 2000 Sch 20 para 10(1)–(4); FA 2002 Sch 12 para 10B, Sch 13 paras 8(1)–(3), 9(1)–(4).

HMRC Manuals—Corporate Intangibles Research and Development Manual CIRD84200 (subcontracted activities).

Modifications—In relation to expenditure incurred before 1 April 2004, this Part modified so as to substitute words "consumable stores" for words "software or consumable items", in each place where they occur, by CTA 2009 Sch 2 para 122(1), (2).

In relation to expenditure incurred before 27 September 2003, this section modified by CTA 2009 Sch 2 para 123(1)(*c*), (*d*) so that Part 13 Chapters 2, 4 apply with the omission of the following—

   –   in sub-s (3)(*c*), words "or is qualifying expenditure on externally provided workers"; and

   –   sub-s (5)(*b*).

In relation to expenditure incurred before 1 August 2008, Chapter 2 of this Part applies with the omission in sub-s (3)(*c*) of words "or relevant payments to the subjects of a clinical trial" (CTA 2009 Sch 2 para 124(1)(*c*)).

In relation to expenditure incurred before 1 April 2006, Chapter 4 of this Part applies with the omission, in sub-s (3)(*c*) of words "or relevant payments to the subjects of a clinical trial" (CTA 2009 Sch 2 para 124(3)(*b*)).

1135 Election for connected persons treatment

(1) A company and a sub-contractor who are not connected may jointly elect that section 1134 is to apply to them as if they were connected.

(2) Any such election must be made in relation to all sub-contractor payments paid under the same contract or other arrangement.

(3) The election must be made by notice in writing to an officer of Revenue and Customs.

(4) The notice must be given before the end of the period of two years beginning immediately after the end of the company's accounting period in which the contract or other arrangement is entered into.

(5) An election under this section is irrevocable.

Commentary—*Simon's Taxes* **D1.414**.

HMRC Manuals—Corporate Intangibles Research and Development Manual CIRD84200 (subcontracted activities).

1136 Qualifying element of sub-contractor payment: other cases

(1) This section applies if—

    (*a*)   a company makes a sub-contractor payment,

    (*b*)   the company and the sub-contractor are not connected persons, and

    (*c*)   no election is made under section 1135.

(2) The qualifying element of the sub-contractor payment is 65% of the sub-contractor payment.

Commentary—*Simon's Taxes* **D1.414**.

Derivation—FA 2000 Sch 20 para 12; FA 2002 Sch 12 para 10B, Sch 13 para 11.

HMRC Manuals—Corporate Intangibles Research and Development Manual CIRD84200 (subcontracted activities).

Miscellaneous

1137 Accounting periods: company not within charge to corporation tax

(1) This section applies to a company if—

    (*a*)   it is not within the charge to corporation tax, and

    (*b*)   it incurs qualifying Chapter 2 expenditure . . . [1].

(2) For the purposes of this Part the company is treated as having the accounting periods it would have if—

    (*a*)   it carried on a trade consisting of the activities in respect of which the expenditure is incurred, and

    (*b*)   it had started to carry on that trade when it started to carry on relevant research and development.

Commentary—*Simon's Taxes* **D1.402A, D1.467**.

Amendments—[1]   In sub-s (1)(*b*), words repealed by FA 2016 s 47(1), (8) with effect in relation to expenditure incurred on or after 1 April 2017.

1138 "Subsidised expenditure"

(1) For the purposes of this Part a company's expenditure is treated as subsidised—

    (*a*)   if a notified State aid is, or has been, obtained in respect of—

        (i)   the whole or part of the expenditure, or

        (ii)   any other expenditure (whenever incurred) attributable to the same research and development project,

    (*b*)   to the extent that a grant or subsidy (other than a notified State aid) is obtained in respect of the expenditure,

    (*c*)   to the extent that it is otherwise met directly or indirectly by a person other than the company.

(2) In this section "notified State aid" means a State aid notified to and approved by the European Commission.

(3) For this purpose the following are not State aids—

　(a) relief under this Part, . . .[1]

　(b) R&D tax credits under this Part,

　[(c) R&D expenditure credits under Chapter 6A of Part 3.][1]

(4) For the purposes of this Part a notified State aid, grant, subsidy or payment that is not allocated to particular expenditure is to be allocated to expenditure of the recipient on a just and reasonable basis.

Commentary—*Simon's Taxes* **D1.420A**.

Derivation—FA 2000 Sch 20 para 8(1)–(3); FA 2002 Sch 12 para 17, Sch 13 para 5(3).

HMRC Manuals—Corporate Intangibles Research and Development Manual CIRD81650 (subsidies under SME scheme).

Amendments—[1]　In sub-s (3), word "and" at end of para (a) repealed, and para (c) inserted, by FA 2013 s 35, Sch 15 para 2(1), (3) with effect in relation to expenditure incurred on or after 1 April 2013.

1140 "Relevant payments to the subjects of a clinical trial"

(1) For the purposes of this Part "relevant payment", in relation to a subject of a clinical trial, means a payment made to the subject for participating in the trial.

(2) For the purposes of this Part "clinical trial" means an investigation in human subjects undertaken in connection with the development of a health care treatment or procedure.

Commentary—*Simon's Taxes* **D1.412**.

Derivation—FA 2000 Sch 20 para 6A(1), (2); FA 2002 Sch 12 para 17, Sch 13 para 5(3).

HMRC Manuals—Corporate Intangibles Research and Development Manual CIRD84400 (application to clinical trial volunteers).

Modifications—In relation to expenditure incurred before 1 August 2008, Chapters 2, 3, 7 of this Part apply with the omission of this section, as it applies for the purposes of those Chapters (CTA 2009 Sch 2 para 124(1)(d), (2)(b), (5)(b)).

In relation to expenditure incurred before 1 April 2006, Chapters 4, 5 of this Part apply with the omission of this section as it applies for the purposes of those Chapters (CTA 2009 Sch 2 para 124(3)(c), (4)(b)).

1141 "Payment period"

In this Part a "payment period" means a period—

　(a) which ends on the fifth day of a month, and

　(b) for which the company is liable to account for income tax and national insurance contributions to an officer of Revenue and Customs.

Commentary—*Simon's Taxes* **D1.420**.

Derivation—FA 2000 Sch 20 para 17(2); FA 2002 Sch 13 para 27(1).

1142 "Qualifying body"

(1) For the purposes of this Part "qualifying body" means—

　(a) a charity,

　(b) an institution of higher education,

　[(c) an association (in the sense that word has in section 469(1)(a) of CTA 2010) which meets conditions A and B in that section (conditions for qualifying as a scientific research association),][1] and

　(d) a health service body within the meaning of [section 986][1] of that Act, or

　(e) any other body prescribed, or of a description prescribed, by the Treasury, by order, for the purposes of this Part.

(2) In subsection (1)(b) "institution of higher education" means—

　(a) an institution within the higher education sector within the meaning of the Further and Higher Education Act 1992 (c 13),

　(b) an institution within the higher education sector within the meaning of Part 2 of the Further and Higher Education (Scotland) Act 1992 (c 37) or a central institution within the meaning of the Education (Scotland) Act 1980 (c 44), or

　(c) a higher education institution within the meaning of Article 30(3) of the Education and Libraries (Northern Ireland) Order 1993 (SI 1993/2810 (NI 12)).

(3) An order under this section is to have effect in relation to the accounting periods or expenditure specified in the order.

(4) The order may specify accounting periods beginning, or expenditure incurred, before the time the order is made.

Commentary—*Simon's Taxes* **D1.412**.

Derivation—FA 2002 Sch 12 para 18(1)–(3).

HMRC Manuals—Corporate Intangibles Research and Development Manual CIRD82250 (meaning of "qualifying body").

Orders—Research and Development (Qualifying Bodies) (Tax) Order, SI 2012/286.

Research and Development (Qualifying Bodies) (Tax) Order, SI 2018/217.

Amendments—[1]　Sub-s (1)(c) substituted, in sub-s (1)(d) words substituted for words "section 519A(2) " by CTA 2010 s 1177, Sch 1 para 676 with effect for corporation tax purposes for accounting periods ending on or after 1 April 2010, and for income and capital gains tax purposes for the tax year 2010–11 and subsequent tax years.

PART 14

REMEDIATION OF CONTAMINATED [OR DERELICT][1] LAND

Amendments—[1]   Words in heading inserted by FA 2009 s 26, Sch 7 paras 1, 2 with effect in relation to expenditure incurred on or after 1 April 2009. For this purposes no account is to be taken of CTA 2009 s 61 (FA 2009 Sch 7 para 28).

CHAPTER 1

INTRODUCTION

Introductory

1143 Overview of Part

(1) This Part provides for corporation tax relief for expenditure on land in the United Kingdom, where the expenditure is incurred for the purpose of remedying contamination [or dereliction][1] of the land.

(2) The reliefs available under Chapter 2 are—

    (*a*) a deduction in calculating the profits of a UK property business or a trade carried on by a company for expenditure which is capital expenditure, and

    (*b*) an additional deduction for expenditure which is allowed as a deduction in calculating the profits of such a business or trade.

(3) Chapter 3 provides for the payment of tax credits ("land remediation tax credits") where a company—

    (*a*) obtains relief under Chapter 2, and

    (*b*) makes a loss in a UK property business or a trade.

(4) Chapter 4 contains provision about—

    (*a*) the relief available to a company which carries on [basic life assurance and general annuity business][2], and

    (*b*) the payment of tax credits (["BLAGAB tax credits"][2]) to such a company.

(5) Chapter 5 contains an anti-avoidance provision dealing with artificially inflated claims for relief under this Part or tax credits.

(6) Chapter 6 contains supplementary provision, including definitions.

(7) For information about the procedure for making claims under this Part see Schedule 18 to FA 1998, in particular Part 9B (claims relating to remediation of contaminated [or derelict][1] land) of that Schedule.

HMRC Manuals—Corporate Intangibles Research and Development Manual CIRD60005 (land remediation relief: outline).

Amendments—[1]   Words in sub-ss (1), (7) inserted by FA 2009 s 26, Sch 7 paras 1, 3 with effect in relation to expenditure incurred on or after 1 April 2009. For this purposes no account is to be taken of CTA 2009 s 61 (FA 2009 Sch 7 para 28),
[2]   In sub-s (4), in para (*a*), words substituted for words "life assurance business", and in para (*b*) words substituted for words " "basic life assurance and general annuity business" " by FA 2012 s 146, Sch 16 paras 135, 192 with effect in relation to accounting periods of companies beginning on or after 1 January 2013 (subject to transitional provisions in FA 2012 Sch 17). For accounting periods straddling 1 January 2013, see FA 2012 s 149.

Basic definitions

1144 "Qualifying land remediation expenditure"

(1) For the purposes of this Part a company's "qualifying land remediation expenditure" means expenditure incurred by it in relation to which each of conditions A to [F][1] is met.

(2) Condition A is that it is expenditure on land all or part of which is in a contaminated state (see section 1145) [or a derelict state (see section 1145A)][1].

(3) Condition B is that the expenditure would not have been incurred if the land had not been in a contaminated [or derelict][1] state.

[(4) Condition C is that it is—

    (*a*) in the case of land in a contaminated state, expenditure on relevant contaminated land remediation undertaken by the company (see section 1146), or

    (*b*) in the case of land in a derelict state, expenditure on relevant derelict land remediation so undertaken (see section 1146A).][1]

(5) Condition D is that the expenditure is—

    (*a*) incurred on staffing costs (see section 1170),

    (*b*) incurred on materials (see section 1172), . . . [1]

    [(*c*) incurred in respect of relevant land remediation contracted out by the company to another person with whom the company is not connected, or

    (*d*) qualifying expenditure on connected sub-contracted land remediation (see section 1175).][1]

(6) Condition E is that the expenditure is not subsidised (see section 1177).

[(6A) Condition F is that the expenditure is not incurred on landfill tax.][1]

(7) See also section 1173 for provision about some cases in which condition B is treated as met.

Commentary—*Simon's Taxes* D1.503.

Derivation—FA 2001 Sch 22 para 2(1)–(6).

HMRC Manuals—Corporate Intangibles Research and Development Manual CIRD63050 (meaning of "qualifying land remediation expenditure").

(4) An order under subsection (3) may contain incidental, supplemental, consequential and transitional provision and savings.

(5) For the purposes of subsection (1)(*b*) "relevant preparatory activity" has the same meaning as for the purposes of subsection (1)(*b*) of section 1146 (see subsection (4) of that section, but reading the reference to subsection (1)(*a*) of that section as a reference to subsection (1)(*a*) of this section).][1]

Commentary—*Simon's Taxes* **D1.503B**.

HMRC Manuals—Corporate Intangibles Research and Development Manual CIRD60051 (acquiring land). CIRD62035 (qualifying works). CIRD63215 (derelict land).

Order—The Corporation Tax (Land Remediation Relief) Order, SI 2009/2037 art 6 (for the purposes of Condition B in sub-s (3), the specified purposes are the removal of post-tensioned concrete heavyweight construction, building foundations and machinery bases, reinforced concrete pilecaps, reinforced concrete basements, or redundant services which are located below the ground).

Amendments—[1] This section inserted by FA 2009 s 26, Sch 7 paras 1, 7 with effect in relation to expenditure incurred on or after 1 April 2009. For this purpose no account is to be taken of CTA 2009 s 61. The power to make orders, conferred on the Treasury by virtue of this amendment, may be exercised at any time after 21 July 2009, and any order made by virtue of this amendment before 6 April 2010 may make provision having effect in relation to expenditure incurred on or after 1 April 2009 (FA 2009 Sch 7 para 27).

CHAPTER 2

RELIEFS FOR EXPENDITURE ON CONTAMINATED [OR DERELICT] LAND

Amendments—In heading to Chapter 2 words inserted by FA 2009 s 26, Sch 7 paras 1, 8, 9 with effect in relation to expenditure incurred on or after 1 April 2009. For this purpose no account is to be taken of CTA 2009 s 61. The power to make orders, conferred on the Treasury by virtue of this amendment, may be exercised at any time after 21 July 2009, and any order made by virtue of this amendment before 6 April 2010 may make provision having effect in relation to expenditure incurred on or after 1 April 2009 (FA 2009 Sch 7 para 27).

1147 Deduction for capital expenditure

(1) A company is entitled to relief for an accounting period if conditions A, B and C are met.

(2) Condition A is that [a major interest in][1] land in the United Kingdom is, or has been, acquired by the company for the purposes of a UK property business or a trade carried on by it.

[(3) Condition B is that—

    (*a*) in the case of land in a contaminated state, the land was in a contaminated state at the time of the acquisition, and

    (*b*) in the case of land in a derelict state, the land was in a derelict state throughout the period beginning with the earlier of—

        (i) 1 April 1998, and

        (ii) the date on which a major interest in the land was first acquired by the company or a person who was connected with the company.

(3A) The Treasury may by order—

    (*a*) specify circumstances in which the condition in paragraph (*a*) of subsection (3) need not be met, or

    (*b*) replace the date for the time being specified in paragraph (*b*)(i) of that subsection with a later date.

(3B) An order under subsection (3A) may contain incidental, supplemental, consequential and transitional provision and savings.][1]

(4) Condition C is that the company incurs capital expenditure which is qualifying land remediation expenditure in respect of the land.

(5) For the company to obtain the relief it must make an election.

(6) The relief is that for corporation tax purposes the capital expenditure is allowed as a deduction in calculating the profits of the UK property business or the trade for the period in which the expenditure is incurred.

(7) For the purposes of this section capital expenditure incurred for the purposes of a UK property business or a trade by a company about to carry on the business or trade is to be treated as incurred by the company—

    (*a*) on the first day on which it does carry it on, and

    (*b*) in the course of doing so.

(8) Relief is not available under this section in relation to so much of the qualifying land remediation expenditure as represents capital expenditure in respect of which an allowance[, other than an allowance under Part 2A of CAA 2001 (structures and buildings allowances),][2] has been, or may be, made under the enactments relating to capital allowances.

Commentary—*Simon's Taxes* **D1.502, D1.503A**.

HMRC Manuals—Corporate Intangibles Research and Development Manual CIRD60080 (pre-commencement expenditure). CIRD60085 (land remediation relief denied if capital allowances could be claimed). CIRD60070 (land remediation relief: capital expenditure: contents).

Modification—The Corporation Tax (Land Remediation Relief) Order, SI 2009/2037 art 7(*a*) (the condition in sub-s (3)(*a*) need not be met where land is in a contaminated state by virtue of the presence in, on or under it of Japanese Knotweed).

Amendments—[1]   In sub-s (2), words inserted, and sub-ss (3)–(3B) substituted for previous sub-s (3), by FA 2009 s 26, Sch 7 paras 1, 8, 9 with effect in relation to expenditure incurred on or after 1 April 2009. For this purpose no account is to be taken of CTA 2009 s 61. The power to make orders, conferred on the Treasury by virtue of this amendment, may be exercised at any time after 21 July 2009, and any order made by virtue of this amendment before 6 April 2010 may make provision having effect in relation to expenditure incurred on or after 1 April 2009 (FA 2009 Sch 7 para 27).

[2]   In sub-s (8), words inserted by the Capital Allowances (Structures and Buildings Allowances) Regulations, SI 2019/1087 reg 7(1),(2) with effect from 5 July 2019. Note that the structures and buildings allowance in CAA 2001 Part 2A applies from 29 October 2018 (see CAA 2001 s 270AA).

1148 Election under section 1147

(1) An election under section 1147 must specify the accounting period in respect of which it is made.

(2) The election must be made by notice in writing to an officer of Revenue and Customs.

(3) The notice must be given before the end of the period of two years beginning immediately after the end of the accounting period to which the election relates.

Commentary—*Simon's Taxes* **D1.1445**.

Derivation—FA 2001 Sch 22 para 1(6)–(8).

HMRC Manuals—Corporate Intangibles Research and Development Manual CIRD60075 (election to treat capital expenditure as a deduction).

1149 Additional deduction for qualifying land remediation expenditure

(1) A company is entitled to corporation tax relief for an accounting period if each of conditions A to D is met.

(2) Condition A is that [a major interest in][1] land in the United Kingdom is, or has been, acquired by the company for the purposes of a UK property business or a trade carried on by it.

[(3) Condition B is that—

    (*a*) in the case of land in a contaminated state, the land was in a contaminated state at the time of the acquisition, and

    (*b*) in the case of land in a derelict state, the land was in a derelict state throughout the period beginning with the earlier of—

        (i) 1 April 1998, and

        (ii) the date on which a major interest in the land was first acquired by the company or a person who was connected with the company.

(3A) The Treasury may by order—

    (*a*) specify circumstances in which the condition in paragraph (*a*) of subsection (3) need not be met, or

    (*b*) replace the date for the time being specified in paragraph (*b*)(i) of that subsection with a later date.

(3B) An order under subsection (3A) may contain incidental, supplemental, consequential and transitional provision and savings.][1]

(4) Condition C is that the company carries on a UK property business or a trade in the accounting period.

(5) Condition D is that the company incurs qualifying land remediation expenditure in respect of the land which is allowable as a deduction in calculating for corporation tax purposes the profits of the business or the trade for the period.

(6) For the company to obtain the relief it must make a claim.

(7) The relief is an additional deduction in calculating the profits of the business or the trade for the period.

(8) The amount of the additional deduction is 50% of the qualifying land remediation expenditure.

Commentary—*Simon's Taxes* **D1.501, D1.510, D1.511**.

HMRC Manuals—Corporate Intangibles Research and Development Manual CIRD60051 (acquiring land). CIRD62010 (meaning of "long-term derelict land"). CIRD62015 (requirement that land must be derelict at acquisition). CIRD60055 (land remediation relief: timing of relief).

Modification—The Corporation Tax (Land Remediation Relief) Order, SI 2009/2037 art 7(*b*) (the condition in sub-s (3)(*a*) need not be met where land is in a contaminated state by virtue of the presence in, on or under it of Japanese Knotweed).

Amendments—[1]   Words in sub-s (2) inserted, and sub-ss (3)–(3B) substituted for previous sub-s (3), by FA 2009 s 26, Sch 7 paras 1, 10 with effect in relation to expenditure incurred on or after 1 April 2009. For this purpose no account is to be taken of CTA 2009 s 61. The power to make orders, conferred on the Treasury by virtue of this amendment, may be exercised at any time after 21 July 2009, and any order made by virtue of this amendment before 6 April 2010 may make provision having effect in relation to expenditure incurred on or after 1 April 2009 (FA 2009 Sch 7 para 27).

1150 No relief if company responsible for contamination [or dereliction or polluter has interest][1]

[(1)] [1] A company is not entitled to relief under this Chapter in respect of expenditure on land all or part of which is in a contaminated [or derelict state if the land is in a contaminated or derelict][1] state wholly or partly as a result of any thing done, or omitted to be done, at any time by—

    (*a*) the company, or

    (*b*) a person with a relevant connection to the company (see section 1178).

[(2) A company is not entitled to relief under this Chapter in respect of expenditure on land all or part of which is in a contaminated or derelict state if—

    (*a*) the land is in that state wholly or partly as a result of any thing done, or omitted to be done, by a person not within subsection (1), and

    (*b*) that person, or a person connected with that person, has a relevant interest in the land.

(3) For the purposes of subsection (2) a person has a relevant interest in land if the person—

    (*a*) holds any interest in, right over or licence to occupy the land (including an option to acquire any such interest, right or licence in any circumstances), or

    (*b*) has disposed of any estate or interest in the land for a consideration that to any extent reflects the impact, or likely impact, on the value of the land of the remediation of its contamination or dereliction.][1]

Commentary—*Simon's Taxes* **D1.502, D1.510, D1.520.**

Derivation—FA 2001 Sch 22 paras 1(5), 12(4).

HMRC Manuals—Corporate Intangibles Research and Development Manual CIRD60125 (no apportionment of responsibility where more than one polluter).

CIRD60135 (identifying polluter where land acquired in a contaminated state).

CIRD60150 (polluter retains interest in land).

CIRD60155 (slice of action contracts).

CIRD60160 (polluter obtains benefit of relief).

CIRD60170 (exclusions: polluter pays: derelict land).

CIRD60190 (landlords denied relief for cleaning up contamination by tenant).

CIRD60120 ((land remediation relief: exclusions: polluter pays: contents).

Amendments—[1] Sub-s (1) numbered as such; words in sub-s (1) substituted for words "state if the land is in that"; and sub-ss (2), (3), and words in heading, inserted, by FA 2009 s 26, Sch 7 paras 1, 11 with effect in relation to expenditure incurred on or after 1 April 2009. For this purpose no account is to be taken of CTA 2009 s 61. The power to make orders, conferred on the Treasury by virtue of this amendment, may be exercised at any time after 21 July 2009, and any order made by virtue of this amendment before 6 April 2010 may make provision having effect in relation to expenditure incurred on or after 1 April 2009 (FA 2009 Sch 7 para 27).

CHAPTER 3

LAND REMEDIATION TAX CREDIT

Entitlement and payment

1151 Entitlement to and payment of tax credit

(1) A company is entitled to a land remediation tax credit for an accounting period if it has a qualifying land remediation loss in the period (see section 1152).

(2) For the company to obtain a land remediation tax credit in respect of all or part of the qualifying land remediation loss it must make a claim.

(3) The amount of a land remediation tax credit to which the company is entitled is determined in accordance with section 1154.

(4) If a company claims a land remediation tax credit to which it is entitled for an accounting period, an officer of Revenue and Customs must pay to the company the amount of the credit.

This is subject to section 1155.

(5) See also section 1158, which restricts the carry forward of losses where a company claims a land remediation tax credit.

Commentary—*Simon's Taxes* **D1.513.**

Derivation—FA 2001 Sch 22 paras 14(1), 16(1).

HMRC Manuals—Corporate Intangibles Research and Development Manual CIRD6800 (tax credit: contents).

1152 Meaning of "qualifying land remediation loss"

(1) For the purposes of this Chapter a company has a "qualifying land remediation loss" in an accounting period if in the period—

    (*a*) it obtains an additional deduction under section 1149 in calculating the profits of a UK property business or a trade, and

    (*b*) it makes a UK property business loss in the business or a trading loss in the trade.

(2) The amount of the qualifying land remediation loss is—

    (*a*) so much of the UK property business loss or trading loss as is unrelieved (see section 1153), or

    (*b*) if less, 150% of the qualifying land remediation expenditure in respect of which the relief was obtained.

Commentary—*Simon's Taxes* **D1.512.**

Derivation—FA 2001 Sch 22 para 14(2), (3).

HMRC Manuals—Corporate Intangibles Research and Development Manual CIRD68015 (tax credit: qualifying land remediation loss example).

CIRD68010 (tax credit: qualifying land remediation loss unrelieved losses).

1153 Amount of a loss which is "unrelieved"

(1) The amount of a UK property business loss or trading loss that is "unrelieved" is the amount of the loss reduced by—

(*a*) any relief obtained by the company under [section 62(1) to (3) of CTA 2010][1], or that was or could have been obtained by it making a claim under [section 37(3)(*a*) of CTA 2010, to deduct the loss from total][1] profits of the same accounting period,

(*b*) any other relief obtained by the company in respect of the loss, including relief under [section 37(3)(*a*) of CTA 2010, to deduct the loss from total][1] profits of an earlier accounting period), and

(*c*) any loss surrendered under [Part 5 [or Part 5A][3] of CTA 2010][1] (surrender of relief to group or consortium members).

(2) No account is to be taken for this purpose of—

(*a*) any UK property business losses or trading losses brought forward from an earlier accounting period under [section 45[, 45A, 45B][3] or 62(5) of CTA 2010][1], or

(*b*) any trading losses carried back from a later accounting period under [section 37(3)(*b*) of CTA 2010][1].

(3) Subsections (4) to (7) apply (instead of subsection (1)) to determine the amount of a UK property business loss that is "unrelieved" in an accounting period ("the relevant accounting period") in a case where[, as a result of section 87(3) of FA 2012, the loss is treated for the purposes of section 76 of that Act as a deemed BLAGAB management expense for the relevant accounting period.][2]

(4) If in the relevant accounting period no amount falls to be carried forward to a subsequent accounting period under [section 73 of FA 2012][2] (unrelieved expenses carried forward), no amount of the UK property business loss is unrelieved.

(5) If in the relevant accounting period there is an amount which falls to be carried forward to a subsequent accounting period under [section 73 of FA 2012][2], the amount of the UK property business loss that is unrelieved is—

(*a*) the amount which so falls to be carried forward, or

(*b*) if less, the amount of the UK property business loss.

(6) In determining for the purposes of subsection (4) or (5) whether there is an amount which falls to be carried forward to a subsequent accounting period under [section 73 of FA 2012][2], no account is to be taken of the amounts specified in subsection (7).

(7) Those amounts are amounts—

(*a*) brought forward from an earlier accounting period, and

[(*b*) taken into account in calculating for the purposes of section 73 of FA 2012 the amount of adjusted BLAGAB management expenses of the company for the relevant accounting period as a result of—

(i) the previous application of section 73 or 93 of FA 2012, or

(ii) the carry forward to the relevant accounting period of an amount under section 391 of this Act (surplus deficit).][2]

(8) If—

(*a*) the company is an insurance company, and

(*b*) it is treated under [section 86 of FA 2012][2] as carrying on more than one UK property business,

references in this section to a UK property business loss are to be read in accordance with [section 87(4) of FA 2012][2] (aggregation of losses).

Commentary—*Simon's Taxes* **D1.512**.
Derivation—FA 2001 Sch 22 para 14(4)–(10).
HMRC Manuals—Corporate Intangibles Research and Development Manual CIRD68010 (unrelieved loss).
Amendments—[1] Amendments made by CTA 2010 s 1177, Sch 1 para 677
[2] In sub-s (3), words substituted for words ", as a result of section 432AB(3) of ICTA, the loss is treated for the purposes of section 76 of that Act as expenses payable which fall to be brought into account at Step 3 in subsection (7) of that section.", in sub-ss (4)–(6), words substituted for words "section 76(12) of ICTA", in sub-s (7), para (*b*) substituted, and in sub-s (8), in para (*b*) words substituted for words "section 432AA of ICTA" and in words after that para, words substituted for words "section 432AB(4) of ICTA", by FA 2012 s 146, Sch 16 paras 135, 193 with effect in relation to accounting periods of companies beginning on or after 1 January 2013 (subject to transitional provisions in FA 2012 Sch 17). For accounting periods straddling 1 January 2013, see FA 2012 s 149.
[3] Words in sub-ss (1)(*c*), (2)(*a*) inserted by F(No 2)A 2017 s 18, Sch 4 paras 128, 137 with effect in relation to accounting periods beginning on or after 1 April 2017, subject to transitional provisions in Sch 4 para 194. For accounting periods beginning before 1 April 2017 and ending on or after that date ("straddling periods") see F(No 2)A 2017 Sch 4 paras 190–192.

Amount of tax credit

1154 Amount of tax credit

(1) The amount of the land remediation tax credit to which a company is entitled for an accounting period is 16% of the amount of the qualifying land remediation loss for the period.

(2) The Treasury may by order replace the percentage for the time being specified in subsection (1) with a different percentage.

(3) An order under subsection (2) may contain incidental, supplemental, consequential and transitional provision and savings.

Commentary—*Simon's Taxes* **D1.512**.

Derivation—FA 2001 Sch 22 para 15(1)–(3).

HMRC Manuals—Corporate Intangibles Research and Development Manual CIRD68025 (tax credit: amount of tax credit).

Supplementary

1155 Payment of tax credit

(1) This section applies if a land remediation tax credit for an accounting period is payable to a company.

(2) The amount payable in respect of—

(*a*) the land remediation tax credit, or

(*b*) interest on the credit payable under section 826 of ICTA,

may be applied in discharging any liability of the company to pay corporation tax.

(3) So far as the amount is so applied, the duty of the officer of Revenue and Customs to pay the credit under section 1151(4) is discharged.

(4) Subsection (5) applies if the company's tax return for the accounting period is enquired into by an officer of Revenue and Customs.

(5) In that case—

(*a*) no payment in respect of the land remediation tax credit for the period need be made before the officer's enquiries are completed (see paragraph 32 of Schedule 18 to FA 1998), but

(*b*) an officer may make a payment on a provisional basis of such amount as the officer thinks fit.

(6) No payment need be made in respect of the land remediation tax credit if the company has outstanding PAYE and NIC liabilities for the period.

(7) A company has outstanding PAYE and NIC liabilities for an accounting period if it has not paid to an officer of Revenue and Customs any amount that it is required to pay—

(*a*) under PAYE regulations, or

(*b*) in respect of Class 1 national insurance contributions,

for payment periods ending in the accounting period.

(8) "Payment period" means a period—

(*a*) which ends on the 5th day of a month, and

(*b*) for which the company is liable to account for income tax and national insurance contributions to an officer of Revenue and Customs.

Commentary—*Simon's Taxes* **D1.513**.

Derivation—FA 2001 Sch 22 para 16(2)–(5).

HMRC Manuals—Corporate Intangibles Research and Development Manual CIRD68045 (tax credit not paid until arrears of PAYE or NIC cleared).

CIRD68040 (tax credit: set off against corporation tax).

CIRD68055 (tax credit not paid while enquiry into return open but HMRC may make provisional payment).

1156 Tax credit payment not income of company

A payment in respect of a land remediation tax credit is not income of the company for any tax purposes.

Commentary—*Simon's Taxes* **D1.513**.

Derivation—FA 2001 Sch 22 para 18.

HMRC Manuals—Corporate Intangibles Research and Development Manual CIRD68000 (tax credit: not income of company).

1157 Exclusion for capital gains purposes of certain expenditure

(1) This section applies if in an accounting period a payment is made to a company in respect of a land remediation tax credit.

(2) The qualifying land remediation expenditure in respect of which the payment is made is to be treated as if it were excluded by section 39 of TCGA 1992 from the sums allowable under section 38 of that Act.

Commentary—*Simon's Taxes* **D1.513**.

Derivation—FA 2001 Sch 22 para 19.

HMRC Manuals—Corporate Intangibles Research and Development Manual CIRD68070 (tax credit: chargeable gains).

1158 Restriction on losses carried forward where tax credit claimed

(1) For the purposes of [section 62 of CTA 2010 (relief for losses made in UK property business)][1] a company's UK property business loss for an accounting period in which it claims a land remediation tax credit to which it is entitled is treated as reduced by the amount of the surrendered loss for the period.

(2) For the purposes of [[sections 45, 45A and 45B][3] of CTA 2010][1] (relief of trading losses against future . . . [3] profits) a company's trading loss for an accounting period in which it claims a land remediation tax credit to which it is entitled is treated as reduced by the amount of the surrendered loss for the period.

(3) Subsection (4) applies (instead of subsection (1)) if in an accounting period—

(*a*) as a result of section 87(3) of FA 2012, a company's UK property business loss is treated for the purposes of section 76 of that Act as a deemed BLAGAB management expense for the accounting period,][2]

(b) an amount falls to be carried forward to a subsequent accounting period under [section 73 of FA 2012][2] (unrelieved expenses carried forward), and

(c) the company claims a land remediation tax credit for the period.

(4) The amount which falls to be carried forward to a subsequent accounting period under [section 73 of FA 2012][2] is treated as reduced by the amount of the surrendered loss for the period.

(5) References in this section to "the amount of the surrendered loss" for an accounting period are to the amount of any qualifying land remediation loss in respect of which a land remediation tax credit is claimed for the period.

Commentary—*Simon's Taxes* **D1.513.**

Derivation—FA 2001 Sch 22 para 17(1)–(5).

HMRC Manuals—Corporate Intangibles Research and Development Manual CIRD68020 (restriction on losses carried forward).

Amendments—[1]   In sub-s (1) words substituted for words "section 392A of ICTA (UK property business losses carried forward)", in sub-s (2) words substituted for words "section 393 of ICTA" by CTA 2010 s 1177, Sch 1 para 678. CTA 2010 has effect for corporation tax purposes for accounting periods ending on or after 1 April 2010, and for income and capital gains tax purposes for the tax year 2010–11 and subsequent tax years.

[2]   In sub-s (3), para (a) substituted and in para (b) words substituted for words "section 76(12) of ICTA" and in sub-s (4), words substituted for words "section 76(12) of ICTA", by FA 2012 s 146, Sch 16 paras 135, 194 with effect in relation to accounting periods of companies beginning on or after 1 January 2013 (subject to transitional provisions in FA 2012 Sch 17). For accounting periods straddling 1 January 2013, see FA 2012 s 149.

[3]   In sub-s (2), words substituted for words "section 45", and word "trading" repealed, by F(No 2)A 2017 s 18, Sch 4 paras 128, 138 with effect in relation to accounting periods beginning on or after 1 April 2017, subject to transitional provisions in Sch 4 para 194. For accounting periods beginning before 1 April 2017 and ending on or after that date ("straddling periods") see F(No 2)A 2017 Sch 4 paras 190–192.

CHAPTER 4

SPECIAL PROVISION FOR [BLAGAB]

Amendment—In heading, words substituted for words "Life Assurance Business" by FA 2012 s 146, Sch 16 paras 135, 195 with effect in relation to accounting periods of companies beginning on or after 1 January 2013 (subject to transitional provisions in FA 2012 Sch 17). For accounting periods straddling 1 January 2013, see FA 2012 s 149.

I minus E basis

1160 Provision in respect of I minus E basis

[This Chapter applies][1] if, for an accounting period, an insurance company is charged to tax [in respect of its basic life assurance and general annuity business in accordance with the I-E rules].[2]

Commentary—*Simon's Taxes* **D1.520.**

Amendments—[1]   Words substituted for words "The remaining provisions of this Chapter apply" and "under the I minus E basis in respect of its life assurance business" by FA 2012 s 146, Sch 16 paras 135, 197 with effect in relation to accounting periods of companies beginning on or after 1 January 2013 (subject to transitional provisions in FA 2012 Sch 17). For accounting periods straddling 1 January 2013, see FA 2012 s 149.

Relief . . .

1161 Relief in respect of I minus E basis: . . . [1] **expenses payable**

(1) A company is entitled to relief for an accounting period if conditions A, B and C are met.

(2) Condition A is that [a major interest in][1] land in the United Kingdom is a management asset of the company.

[(3) Condition B is that—

  (a) in the case of land in a contaminated state, the land was in a contaminated state at the time of the acquisition by the company of a major interest in the land, and

  (b) in the case of land in a derelict state, the land was in a derelict state throughout the period beginning with the earlier of—

    (i) 1 April 1998, and

    (ii) the date on which a major interest in the land was first acquired by the company or a person who was connected with the company.

(3A) The Treasury may by order—

  (a) specify circumstances in which the condition in paragraph (a) of subsection (3) need not be met, or

  (b) replace the date for the time being specified in paragraph (b)(i) of that subsection with a later date.

(3B) An order under subsection (3A) may contain incidental, supplemental, consequential and transitional provision and savings.][1]

(4) Condition C is that the company incurs qualifying [land remediation][1] expenditure in the accounting period in respect of the land . . . .[1]

(5) . . . [1]

(6) The relief is that the company may treat . . . [1] the qualifying Chapter 4 expenditure as expenses payable which fall to be brought into account for the accounting period at Step 1 in [section 76 of FA 2012][2] (deduction for expenses payable).

(7) For the purposes of this section land is a management asset of a company if it is—

(a) for any reference to a land remediation tax credit substitute a reference to [a BLAGAB tax credit][1], and

(b) in section 1157(2) for the reference to qualifying land remediation expenditure substitute a reference to qualifying Chapter 4 expenditure.

Commentary—*Simon's Taxes* **D1.521**.

Amendments—[1] In sub-s (1), (3)(a), words substituted for words "a life assurance company tax credit", by FA 2012 s 146, Sch 16 paras 135, 204 with effect in relation to accounting periods of companies beginning on or after 1 January 2013 (subject to transitional provisions in FA 2012 Sch 17). For accounting periods straddling 1 January 2013, see FA 2012 s 149.

1168 Restriction on carrying forward expenses payable where tax credit claimed

(1) This section applies if a company claims [a BLAGAB tax credit][1] to which it is entitled for an accounting period.

(2) For the purposes of [section 73 of FA 2012][1] the amount which may be—

(a) carried forward from the accounting period under [that section as excess BLAGAB expenses][1], and

(b) brought into account in accordance with [step 5 in section 76 of FA 2012][1],

is treated as reduced by the amount of the surrendered loss for the period.

(3) The "amount of the surrendered loss" for the period means the amount of the [qualifying BLAGAB loss][1] in respect of which the land remediation tax credit is claimed for the period.

Commentary—*Simon's Taxes* **D1.521**.

Amendments—[1] In sub-s (1), words substituted for words "a life assurance company tax credit", in sub-s (2), words substituted for words "section 76 of ICTA", "subsection (12) of that section" and "Step 7 in subsection (7) of that section", and in sub-s (3), words substituted for words "qualifying life assurance business loss", by FA 2012 s 146, Sch 16 paras 135, 205 with effect in relation to accounting periods of companies beginning on or after 1 January 2013 (subject to transitional provisions in FA 2012 Sch 17). For accounting periods straddling 1 January 2013, see FA 2012 s 149.

CHAPTER 5

TAX AVOIDANCE

1169 Artificially inflated claims for relief or tax credit

(1) To the extent that a transaction is attributable to arrangements entered into wholly or mainly for a disqualifying purpose, it is to be disregarded for the purposes mentioned in subsection (2).

(2) Those purposes are determining for an accounting period the amount of—

(a) any relief to which a company is entitled under Chapter 2,

(b) any land remediation tax credits to which a company is entitled under section 1151,

(c) any relief to which a company carrying on [basic life assurance and general annuity business][2] is entitled under section 1161 [or 1162][1], and

(d) any [BLAGAB tax credits][2] to which such a company is entitled under section 1164.

(3) Arrangements are entered into wholly or mainly for a "disqualifying purpose" if their main object, or one of their main objects, is to enable a company to obtain—

(a) relief under Chapter 2 to which the company would not otherwise be entitled or of a greater amount than that to which it would otherwise be entitled,

(b) a land remediation tax credit to which it would not otherwise be entitled or of a greater amount than that to which it would otherwise be entitled,

(c) relief under section 1161 [or 1162][1] to which it would not otherwise be entitled or of a greater amount than that to which it would otherwise be entitled, or

(d) a life assurance company tax credit to which it would not otherwise be entitled or of a greater amount than that to which it would otherwise be entitled.

(4) In this section "arrangements" includes any scheme, agreement or understanding, whether or not legally enforceable.

Commentary—*Simon's Taxes* **D1.515**.

Derivation—FA 2001 Sch 22 para 29(1)–(3).

HMRC Manuals—Corporate Intangibles Research and Development Manual CIRD60105 (arrangements to create or enhance a claim).

Amendments—[1] In sub-ss (2)(c), (3)(c), words inserted by FA 2009 s 26, Sch 7 paras 1, 16 with effect in relation to expenditure incurred on or after 1 April 2009. For this purpose no account is to be taken of CTA 2009 s 61.

[2] In sub-s (2), in para (c), words substituted for words "life assurance business", and in para (d), words substituted for words "life assurance company tax credits", by FA 2012 s 146, Sch 16 paras 135, 206 with effect in relation to accounting periods of companies beginning on or after 1 January 2013 (subject to transitional provisions in FA 2012 Sch 17). For accounting periods straddling 1 January 2013, see FA 2012 s 149.

CHAPTER 6

SUPPLEMENTARY

1170 "Staffing costs"

(1) For the purposes of this Part the staffing costs of a company are amounts to which any of subsections (2) to (5) applies.

(2) This subsection applies to an amount paid by the company to a director or an employee of the company which—

    (*a*) is earnings consisting of money, and

    (*b*) is paid because of the director's or employee's employment.

(3) This subsection applies to an amount paid by the company to a director or an employee of the company, other than an amount paid in respect of benefits in kind, if—

    (*a*) the amount is paid in respect of expenses paid by the director or employee, and

    (*b*) the amount is paid because of the director's or employee's employment.

(4) This subsection applies to secondary Class 1 national insurance contributions paid by the company.

(5) This subsection applies to contributions paid by the company to a pension fund operated for the benefit of directors or employees of the company.

(6) In subsection (5) "pension fund" means a scheme, fund or other arrangement established and maintained (whether in the United Kingdom or elsewhere) for the purpose of providing pension benefits.

For this purpose "scheme" includes a deed, agreement or series of agreements.

(7) In subsection (6) "pension benefits" means pensions, retirement annuities, allowances, lump sums, gratuities or other superannuation benefits (with or without subsidiary benefits).

Commentary—*Simon's Taxes* **D1.503C**.

HMRC Manuals—Corporate Intangibles Research and Development Manual CIRD69030 (meaning of relevant staffing costs).

Modification—In its application to expenditure incurred before 1 April 2004 and in an accounting period ending on or after 6 April 2003, this section has effect with the following modification. For sub-ss (2), (3) substitute—

    "(2) This subsection applies to earnings paid by the company to directors or employees of the company.

    For this purpose "earnings" means earnings or amounts treated as earnings which constitute employment income (see section 7(2)(*a*) or (*b*) of ITEPA 2003).".

1171 Staffing costs attributable to relevant land remediation

(1) This section applies for the purposes of this Part to identify the staffing costs of a company which are attributable to relevant land remediation.

(2) The costs which are so attributable are those paid to, or in respect of, directors or employees who are directly and actively engaged in relevant land remediation.

(3) Subsection (4) applies if a director ("D") or employee ("E") is partly engaged directly and actively in relevant land remediation.

(4) In that case—

    (*a*) if the time D or E spends so engaged is less than 20% of D's or E's total working time, none of the staffing costs relating to D or E is treated as attributable to relevant land remediation,

    (*b*) if the time D or E spends so engaged is more than 80% of D's or E's total working time, the whole of the staffing costs relating to D or E is treated as attributable to relevant land remediation, and

    (*c*) in any other case, the appropriate proportion of the staffing costs relating to D or E is treated as attributable to relevant land remediation.

(5) Subsection (6) applies if persons provide services (such as secretarial or administrative services) in support of activities carried on by others.

(6) Those persons are not, as a result of providing those services, to be treated as themselves directly and actively engaged in those activities.

Commentary—*Simon's Taxes* **D1.503C**.

Derivation—FA 2001 Sch 22 para 5(2)–(4).

HMRC Manuals—Corporate Intangibles Research and Development Manual CIRD69030 (exclusion for costs of secretarial and administrative staff).

1172 Expenditure on materials

For the purposes of this Part expenditure on materials is attributable to relevant land remediation if the materials are employed directly in the relevant land remediation.

Commentary—*Simon's Taxes* **D1.503**.

Derivation—FA 2001 Sch 22 para 6.

HMRC Manuals—Corporate Intangibles Research and Development Manual CIRD69020 (definitions: materials).

1173 Expenditure incurred because of contamination [or dereliction][1]

(1) This section applies to identify cases in which the condition in section 1144(3) is to be treated as met (expenditure incurred because of land in contaminated [or derelict][1] state).

(2) If the only reason that expenditure on the land is increased is that the land is in a contaminated [or derelict][1] state, the amount by which the expenditure is increased is to be treated as expenditure meeting the condition in section 1144(3).

[(3) Subsection (4) applies—

    (*a*) in the case of land in a contaminated state, if the main purpose of any activities is any of those specified in section 1146(3), or

CTA 2009

(b) in the case of land in a derelict state, if the main purpose of any activities is any of those specified in section 1146A(3).][1]

(4) Expenditure on such works, operations or steps is to be treated as meeting the condition in section 1144(3).

(5) This section does not affect the width of the provision made by section 1144(3).

Commentary—*Simon's Taxes* **D1.503**.

Derivation—FA 2001 Sch 22 para 7(1)–(3).

HMRC Manuals—Corporate Intangibles Research and Development Manual CIRD63100 (expenditure incurred because of contamination or dereliction).

CIRD63210 (qualifying land remediation expenditure: landfill additional costs).

Amendments—[1] In sub-ss (1), (2), words inserted; sub-s (3) substituted; and words in heading inserted, by FA 2009 s 26, Sch 7 paras 1, 17 with effect in relation to expenditure incurred on or after 1 April 2009. For this purpose no account is to be taken of CTA 2009 s 61.

1175 [Connected sub-contractors][1]

(1) This section applies if—

(a) a company makes a sub-contractor payment,

(b) the company and the sub-contractor are connected, and

(c) in accordance with generally accepted accounting practice, the whole of the sub-contractor payment and all of the sub-contractor's relevant expenditure have been brought into account in determining the sub-contractor's profit or loss for a relevant period.

[(1A) In this section, a "sub-contractor payment" means a payment made by the company to the sub-contractor in respect of relevant land remediation contracted out by the company to the sub-contractor.][1]

(2) The amount of the sub-contractor payment which is "qualifying expenditure on [connected sub-contracted land remediation" for the purposes of section 1144(5)] is—

(a) the entire payment, or

(b) if less, an amount equal to the sub-contractor's relevant expenditure.

(3) "Relevant expenditure" of the sub-contractor means expenditure that—

(a) is incurred by the sub-contractor in carrying on [or arranging for carrying on][1], on behalf of the company, the activities to which the sub-contractor payment relates,

(b) is not of a capital nature,

(c) is [in respect of][1] staffing costs or materials, and

(d) is not subsidised.

(4) "Relevant period" means a period—

(a) for which accounts are drawn up for the sub-contractor, and

(b) that ends not more than 12 months after the end of the company's period of account in which the sub-contractor payment is, in accordance with generally accepted accounting practice, brought into account in determining the company's profit or loss.

(5) In the following sections, which apply for the purpose of determining whether a sub-contractor's expenditure meets the requirements of subsection (3)(c) and (d)—

(a) section 1170 (staffing costs), and

(b) section 1177 (subsidised expenditure),

references to a company are to be read as references to the sub-contractor.

(6) Any apportionment of expenditure of the company or the sub-contractor necessary for the purposes of this section is to be made on a just and reasonable basis.

Commentary—*Simon's Taxes* **D1.504**.

Derivation—FA 2001 Sch 22 para 10(1)–(4).

HMRC Manuals—Corporate Intangibles Research and Development Manual CIRD63240 (payments to a connected sub-contractor).

Amendments—[1] Sub-s (1A) inserted; in sub-s (2), words substituted for words "sub-contracted land remediation"; in sub-s (3)(a), words inserted; in sub-s (3)(c) words substituted for words "incurred on"; and heading substituted, by FA 2009 s 26, Sch 7 paras 1, 19 with effect in relation to expenditure incurred on or after 1 April 2009. For this purpose no account is to be taken of CTA 2009 s 61.

1177 "Subsidised expenditure"

(1) For the purposes of this Part a company's expenditure is treated as subsidised to the extent that—

(a) a grant or subsidy is obtained in respect of the expenditure, or

(b) it is otherwise met directly or indirectly by a person other than the company.

(2) For the purposes of this a grant, subsidy or payment that is not allocated to particular expenditure is to be allocated to expenditure of the recipient on a just and reasonable basis.

Commentary—*Simon's Taxes* **D1.503**.

Derivation—FA 2001 Sch 22 para 8(1), (2).

HMRC Manuals—Corporate Intangibles Research and Development Manual CIRD63130 (relief denied for expenditure covered by a grant or subsidy).

CIRD63135 (relief denied where costs covered by compensation).

1178 Persons having a "relevant connection" to a company

For the purposes of this Part a person has a "relevant connection" to a company in a case where the company's land is in a contaminated [or derelict][1] state wholly or partly as a result of any thing done, or omitted to be done, by the person if—

    (a)   the person is or was connected to the company when any such thing is or was done, or omitted to be done, by the person,

    (b)   the person is or was connected to the company at the time when [a major interest in][1] the land in question is or was acquired by the company, or

    (c)   the person is or was connected to the company at any time when relevant land remediation is or was undertaken (whether by the company itself or on its behalf).

Commentary—*Simon's Taxes* **D1.502, D1.510, D1.520**.

Derivation—FA 2001 Sch 22 para 31(3).

HMRC Manuals—Corporate Intangibles Research and Development Manual CIRD60145 (identifying the "relevant connection" to the polluter).

CIRD69025 (person with a relevant connection to a company).

Amendments—[1]   Words inserted by FA 2009 s 26, Sch 7 paras 1, 21 with effect in relation to expenditure incurred on or after 1 April 2009. For this purpose no account is to be taken of CTA 2009 s 61.

[1178A "Major interest in land"

(1) References in this Part to the acquisition of a major interest in land are to the acquisition of a freehold interest in the land or of a relevant leasehold interest in the land.

(2) The reference in subsection (1) to the acquisition of a freehold interest in land is—

    (a)   in relation to land in England and Wales, to the acquisition of an estate in fee simple absolute (whether subsisting at law or in equity),

    (b)   in relation to land in Scotland, to the acquisition of the interest of an owner of land, and

    (c)   in relation to land in Northern Ireland, to the acquisition of any freehold estate (whether subsisting at law or in equity).

(3) The reference in subsection (1) to the acquisition of a relevant leasehold interest in land is to the acquisition by grant or assignment (or assignation) of—

    (a)   in relation to land in England and Wales, a term of years absolute (whether subsisting at law or in equity),

    (b)   in relation to land in Scotland, the tenant's right over or interest in a property subject to a lease, or

    (c)   in relation to land in Northern Ireland, any leasehold estate (whether subsisting at law or in equity),

in relation to which the condition in subsection (4) is met.

(4) That condition is that—

    (a)   in the case of a grant, the term of years or period of the lease is at least 7 years, and

    (b)   in the case of an assignment (or assignation) the unexpired portion of the term or period is at least 7 years.][1]

Commentary—*Simon's Taxes* **D1.510, D1.520, D1.502, D1.503B**.

HMRC Manuals—Corporate Intangibles Research and Development Manual CIRD69015 (definitions: major interest in land).

Amendments—[1]   This section inserted by FA 2009 s 26, Sch 7 paras 1, 22 with effect in relation to expenditure incurred on or after 1 April 2009. For this purpose no account is to be taken of CTA 2009 s 61.

1179 Other definitions

In this Part—

    "controlled waters"—

        (a)   in relation to England and Wales, has the same meaning as in Part 3 of the Water Resources Act 1991 (c 57),

        (b)   in relation to Scotland, has the same meaning as in section 30A of the Control of Pollution Act 1974 (c 40), and

        (c)   in relation to Northern Ireland, means water in waterways and underground strata (as defined in Article 2(2) of the Water (Northern Ireland) Order 1999 (SI 1999/662 (NI 6)),

    . . . [1]

    . . . [1]

    "pollution of controlled waters" means the entry into controlled waters of—

        (a)   any poisonous, noxious or polluting matter, or

        (b)   any solid waste matter,

    . . . [1] and

    ["UK property business loss", in relation to a company, means a loss incurred by the company in carrying on a UK property business.][2]

Commentary—*Simon's Taxes* **D1.503A**.

Derivation—FA 2001 Sch 22 para 31(1), (2).

HMRC Manuals—Corporate Intangibles Research and Development Manual CIRD69001 (controlled waters: definition).

BIM60450 (definitions: land).

Amendments—[1] Definitions of "harm", "land" and "substance" repealed by FA 2009 s 26, Sch 7 paras 1, 23 with effect in relation to expenditure incurred on or after 1 April 2009. For this purpose no account is to be taken of CTA 2009 s 61.
[2] Definition of "UK property business loss" substituted by CTA 2010 s 1177, Sch 1 para 679 with effect for corporation tax purposes for accounting periods ending on or after 1 April 2010, and for income and capital gains tax purposes for the tax year 2010–11 and subsequent tax years.

PART 15
FILM PRODUCTION

CHAPTER 1

INTRODUCTION
Introductory

1180 Overview of Part

(1) This Part is about film production.

(2) Sections 1181 to 1187 contain definitions and other provisions about interpretation that apply for the purposes of this Part.

See, in particular, section 1182 which explains how a company comes to be treated as the film production company in relation to a film.

(3) Chapter 2 is about the taxation of the activities of a film production company and includes—

    (*a*) provision for the company's activities in relation to its film to be treated as a separate trade, and

    (*b*) provision about the calculation of the profits and losses of that trade.

(4) Chapter 3 is about relief (called "film tax relief") which can be given to a film production company—

    (*a*) by way of additional deductions to be made in calculating the profits or losses of the company's separate trade, or

    (*b*) by way of a payment (a "film tax credit") to be made on the company's surrender of losses from that trade.

(5) Chapter 4 is about the relief which can be given for losses made by a film production company in its separate trade including provision for certain such losses to be transferred to other separate trades.

(6) Chapter 5 provides—

    (*a*) for relief under Chapters 3 and 4 to be given on a provisional basis, and

    (*b*) for such relief to be withdrawn if it turns out that conditions that must be met for such relief to be given are not actually met.

Cross-references—See FA 2016 s 180, Sch 24 Pt 1 (power to obtain information about tax advantages claimed under Parts 15, 15A, 15C, 15D which constitute the grant of State aid).

Interpretation

1181 "Film" etc

(1) This section applies for the purposes of this Part.

(2) "Film" includes any record, however made, of a sequence of visual images that is capable of being used as a means of showing that sequence as a moving picture.

(3) Each part of a series of films is treated as a separate film, unless—

    (*a*) the films form a series with not more than 26 parts,

    (*b*) the combined playing time is not more than 26 hours, and

    (*c*) the series constitutes a self-contained work or is a series of documentaries with a common theme,

in which case the films are treated as a single film.

(4) References to a film include the film soundtrack.

(5) A film is completed when it is first in a form in which it can reasonably be regarded as ready for copies of it to be made and distributed for presentation to the general public.

Commentary—*Simon's Taxes* **D7.1203, D7.1205.**
HMRC Manuals—Film Production Company Manual FPC10100 (meaning of film).

1182 "Film production company"

(1) For the purposes of this Part "film production company" is to be read in accordance with this section.

(2) There cannot be more than one film production company in relation to a film.

(3) A company that (otherwise than in partnership)—

    (*a*) is responsible—

        (i) for pre-production, principal photography and post-production of the film, and

        (ii) for delivery of the completed film,

    (*b*) is actively engaged in production planning and decision-making during pre-production, principal photography and post-production, and

    (*c*) directly negotiates, contracts and pays for rights, goods and services in relation to the film, is the film production company in relation to the film.

(4) In relation to a qualifying co-production, a company that (otherwise than in partnership)—

(a) is a co-producer, and

(b) makes an effective creative, technical and artistic contribution to the film,

is the film production company in relation to the film.

(5) If there is more than one company meeting the description in subsection (3) or (4), the company that is most directly engaged in the activities referred to in that subsection is the film production company in relation to the film.

(6) If there is no company meeting the description in subsection (3) or (4), there is no film production company in relation to the film.

(7) A company may elect to be regarded as a company which does not meet the description in subsection (3) or (4).

(8) The election—

(a) must be made by the company by being included in its company tax return for an accounting period (and may be included in the return originally made or by amendment), and

(b) may be withdrawn by the company only by amending its company tax return for that accounting period.

(9) The election has effect in relation to films which commence principal photography in that or any subsequent accounting period.

Commentary—*Simon's Taxes* D7.1201, D7.1203.

HMRC Manuals—Film Production Company Manual FPC10110 (meaning of film production company).

1183 "Film-making activities" etc

(1) In this Part "film-making activities", in relation to a film, means the activities involved in development, pre-production, principal photography and post-production of the film.

(2) If all or any of the images in a film are generated by computer, references in this Part to principal photography are to be read as references to, or as including, the generation of those images.

(3) The Treasury may by regulations—

(a) amend subsections (1) and (2),

(b) provide that specified activities are or are not to be regarded as film-making activities or as film-making activities of a particular description, and

(c) provide that, in relation to a specified description of film, references to film-making activities of a particular description are to be read as references to such activities as may be specified.

"Specified" means specified in the regulations.

Commentary—*Simon's Taxes* D7.1205.

HMRC Manuals—Film Production Company Manual FPC10130 (film making activities: meaning).

1184 "Production expenditure", "core expenditure" . . .

(1) In this Part, in relation to a film—

"production expenditure" means expenditure on film-making activities in connection with the film, and

"core expenditure" means production expenditure on pre-production, principal photography and post-production.

(2), (3) . . . [1]

Commentary—*Simon's Taxes* D.1217, D7.1220, D7.1221, D7.1222.

HMRC Manuals—Film Production Company Manual FPC10130 (production expenditure and core expenditure: meaning). FPC10160 (limited budget film: meaning).

Amendments—[1] Sub-ss (2), (3) repealed, and in heading, words repealed, by FA 2015 s 29(1), (2) with effect in relation to films the principal photography of which is not completed before 1 April 2015 (by virtue of SI 2015/1741).

1185 "UK expenditure" etc

(1) In this Part "UK expenditure", in relation to a film, means expenditure on goods or services that are used or consumed in the United Kingdom.

(2) Any apportionment of expenditure as between UK expenditure and non-UK expenditure for the purposes of this Part is to be made on a just and reasonable basis.

(3) The Treasury may by regulations amend subsection (1).

Commentary—*Simon's Taxes* D7.1217.

HMRC Manuals—Film Production Company Manual FPC10140 (UK expenditure: meaning).

1186 "Qualifying co-production" and "co-producer"

In this Part—

(a) "qualifying co-production" means a film that falls to be treated as a national film in the United Kingdom as a result of an agreement between Her Majesty's Government in the United Kingdom and any other government, international organisation or authority, and

(b) "co-producer" means a person who is a co-producer for the purposes of the agreement mentioned in paragraph (a).

Commentary—*Simon's Taxes* D7.1203.

HMRC Manuals—Film Production Company Manual FPC10120 (co-producer and qualifying co-production: meanings).

HMRC Manuals—Film Production Company Manual FPC40010 (qualifying films: introduction).
Amendments—[1] Sub-s (3A) inserted by FA 2013 s 36, Sch 18 para 12.

Conditions of relief

1196 Intended theatrical release

(1) The film must be intended for theatrical release.

(2) For this purpose—

    (a) "theatrical release" means exhibition to the paying public at the commercial cinema, and

    (b) a film is not regarded as intended for theatrical release unless it is intended that a significant proportion of the earnings from the film should be obtained by such exhibition.

(3) Whether this condition is met is determined for each accounting period of the company during which film-making activities are carried on in relation to the film, in accordance with the following rules.

(4) If at the end of an accounting period the film is intended for theatrical release, the condition is treated as having been met throughout that period (subject to subsection (5)(b)).

(5) If at the end of an accounting period the film is not intended for theatrical release, the condition—

    (a) is treated as having been not met throughout that period, and

    (b) cannot be met in any subsequent accounting period.

This does not affect any entitlement of the company to relief in an earlier accounting period for which the condition was met.

Commentary—*Simon's Taxes* D7.1218.
HMRC Manuals—Film Production Company Manual FPC40020 (qualifying films: intended theatrical release).

1197 British film

The film must be certified by the Secretary of State as a British film under Schedule 1 to the Films Act 1985 (c 21).

Commentary—*Simon's Taxes* D7.1219.
HMRC Manuals—Film Production Company Manual FPC40030 (qualifying films: British film).

1198 UK expenditure

(1) At least [10%][1] of the core expenditure on the film incurred—

    (a) in the case of a British film other than a qualifying co-production, by the company, and

    (b) in the case of a qualifying co-production, by the co-producers,

must be UK expenditure.

(2) The Treasury may by regulations amend the percentage specified in subsection (1).

Commentary—*Simon's Taxes* D7.1217, D7.1222.
HMRC Manuals—Film Production Company Manual FPC70050 (co-productions: minimum UK expenditure).
Amendments—[1] In sub-s (1), figure substituted for figure "25%" by FA 2014 s 32(1), (2) with effect in relation to films the principal photography of which is not completed before 1 April 2014 (by virtue of SI 2014/2880 art 2). The Treasury may by order make further amendments to sub-s (1) (as amended) in connection with an application for State aid approval (FA 2014 s 32(7)–(9)).

Additional deductions

1199 Additional deduction for qualifying expenditure

(1) If film tax relief is available to the company, it may (on making a claim) make an additional deduction in respect of qualifying expenditure on the film.

(2) The deduction is made in calculating the profit or loss of the separate film trade.

(3) In this Chapter "qualifying expenditure" means core expenditure on the film that falls to be taken into account under Chapter 2 in calculating the profit or loss of the separate film trade for tax purposes.

(4) The Treasury may by regulations—

    (a) amend subsection (3), and

    (b) provide that expenditure of a specified description is or is not to be regarded as qualifying expenditure.

Commentary—*Simon's Taxes* D7.1220.
HMRC Manuals—Film Production Company Manual FPC50005 (eligible expenditure: introduction).

1200 Amount of additional deduction

(1) For the first period of account during which the separate film trade is carried on, the amount of the additional deduction is given by—

$$E \times R$$

where—

    E is—

        (a) so much of the qualifying expenditure as is UK expenditure, or

        (b) if less, 80% of the total amount of qualifying expenditure, and

R is the rate of enhancement (see subsection (3)).
(2) For any period of account after the first, the amount of the additional deduction is given by—

$$(E \times R) - P$$

where—

E is—

(a) so much of the qualifying expenditure incurred to date as is UK expenditure, or

(b) if less, 80% of the total amount of qualifying expenditure incurred to date,

R is the rate of enhancement (see subsection (3)), and

P is the total amount of the additional deductions given for previous periods.

[(3) The rate of enhancement is 100%.][1]

(4) The Treasury may by regulations amend the percentage specified in subsection (1) or (2).

Commentary—*Simon's Taxes* D7.1220.
HMRC Manuals—Film Production Company Manual FPC55020 (calculation: maximum amount of core expenditure subject to claim).
FPC55030 (calculation: rates of relief).
Amendments—[1]   Sub-s (3) substituted by FA 2015 s 29(1), (3) with effect in relation to films the principal photography of which is not completed before 1 April 2015 (by virtue of SI 2015/1741).

Film tax credits

1201 Film tax credit claimable if company has surrenderable loss
(1) If film tax relief is available to the company, it may claim a film tax credit for an accounting period in which it has a surrenderable loss.
(2) The company's surrenderable loss in [an accounting period][1] is—

(a) [the company's available loss][1] for the period in the separate film trade, or

(b) if less, the available qualifying expenditure for the period.

[(2A) The company's available loss for an accounting period is given by—
L + RUL
where—

L is the amount of the company's loss for the period in the separate film trade, and

RUL is the amount of any relevant unused loss of the company.

(2B) The "relevant unused loss" of a company is so much of any available loss of the company for the previous accounting period as has not been—

(a) surrendered under section 1202(1), or

(b) carried forward under section 45 [or 45B][2] of CTA 2010 and set against profits of the separate film trade.][1]

(3) For the first period of account during which the separate film trade is carried on, the available qualifying expenditure is the amount that is E for that period for the purposes of section 1200(1).
(4) For any period of account after the first, the available qualifying expenditure is given by—

$$E - S$$

where—

E is the amount that is E for that period for the purposes of section 1200(2), and

S is the total amount [previously surrendered][1] under section 1202(1).

[(5) If a period of account of the separate film trade does not coincide with an accounting period, any necessary apportionments are to be made by reference to the number of days in the periods concerned.][1]

Commentary—*Simon's Taxes* D7.1221.
HMRC Manuals—Film Production Company Manual FPC55100 (calculation: surrenderable losses and film tax credit).
Amendments—[1]   In sub-s (2) words substituted for words "any period", and in para (a) words substituted for words "the company's loss", sub-ss (2A), (2B), (5) inserted, and in sub-s (4) in definition of "S" words substituted for words "surrendered in previous periods", by F(No 3)A 2010 s 14(1)–(5) with effect in relation to accounting periods ending on or after 9 December 2009. In relation to those accounting periods these amendments, and corresponding amendments of FA 2006 Sch 5 paras 6, 11 are to be treated as always having had effect (F(No 3)A 2010 s 14(8)).
[2]   In sub-s (2B)(b), words inserted by F(No 2)A 2017 s 18, Sch 4 paras 128, 139 with effect in relation to accounting periods beginning on or after 1 April 2017, subject to transitional provisions in Sch 4 para 194. For accounting periods beginning before 1 April 2017 and ending on or after that date ("straddling periods") see F(No 2)A 2017 Sch 4 paras 190–192.

1202 Surrendering of loss and amount of film tax credit
(1) The company may surrender the whole or part of its surrenderable loss in an accounting period.
(2) If the company surrenders the whole or part of that loss, the amount of the film tax credit to which it is entitled for the accounting period is given by—

$$L \times R$$

where—

[Meaning of "television programme", "relevant programme" etc

1216AA "Television programme"

(1) This section applies for the purposes of this Part.

(2) "Television programme" means any programme (with or without sounds) which—

 (*a*) is produced to be seen on television, and

 (*b*) consists of moving or still images or of legible text or of a combination of those things.

(3) In subsection (2) "television" includes the internet.

(4) Any television programmes that are commissioned together under the same agreement are treated as a single television programme.

(5) A television programme is completed when it is first in a form in which it can reasonably be regarded as ready for broadcast to the general public.][1]

Commentary—*Simon's Taxes* **D7.1230.**

HMRC Manuals—Television Production Company Manual TPC10100 (television programme: meaning).

Amendments—[1] This Part (ss 1216A–1216EC) inserted by FA 2013 s 36, Sch 16 para 1. The amendments made by Sch 16 come into force on 19 July 2013 (by virtue of SI 2013/1817 art 2(1)). Those amendments have effect in relation to accounting periods beginning on or after 1 April 2013, subject to transitional provisions. Note that any power conferred on the Secretary of State or the Treasury, by virtue of Sch 16, to make regulations or an order came into force on 17 July 2013. See FA 2013 Sch 16 paras 2, 3 for commencement provisions.

[1216AB "Relevant programme"

(1) This section applies for the purposes of this Part.

(2) A television programme is a "relevant programme" if—

 (*a*) conditions A and B are met, and

 (*b*) in the case of a television programme that is [neither animation nor a children's programme][2], conditions C and D are met.

(3) Condition A is that the programme is—

 (*a*) a drama,

 (*b*) a documentary,

 (*c*) animation [, or

 (*d*) a children's programme.][2]

 For further provision about these terms, see section 1216AC.

(4) Condition B is that the programme is not an excluded programme (see section 1216AD).

(5) Condition C is that the slot length in relation to the programme is greater than 30 minutes.

(6) Condition D is that the average core expenditure per hour of slot length in relation to the programme is not less than £1 million.

 For the meaning of "core expenditure", see section 1216AG.

(7) "Slot length", in relation to a television programme, means the period of time which the programme is commissioned to fill.][1]

Commentary—*Simon's Taxes* **D7.1230.**

HMRC Manuals—Television Production Company Manual TPC10100 (relevant programme: meaning).

Amendments—[1] This Part (ss 1216A–1216EC) inserted by FA 2013 s 36, Sch 16 para 1. The amendments made by Sch 16 come into force on 19 July 2013 (by virtue of SI 2013/1817 art 2(1)). Those amendments have effect in relation to accounting periods beginning on or after 1 April 2013, subject to transitional provisions. Note that any power conferred on the Secretary of State or the Treasury, by virtue of Sch 16, to make regulations or an order came into force on 17 July 2013. See FA 2013 Sch 16 paras 2, 3 for commencement provisions.

[2] In sub-s (2)(*b*), words substituted, in sub-s (3)(*b*) word "or" repealed, and sub-s (3)(*d*) inserted, by FA 2015 s 30(1)–(3) with effect in relation to accounting periods beginning on or after 1 April 2015. Where a company has an accounting period beginning before and ending on or after 1 April 2015, see FA 2015 s 30(8)–(10).

[1216AC Types of programme eligible to be relevant programmes

(1) This section applies for the purposes of this Part.

(2) A programme is a "drama" if—

 (*a*) it consists wholly or mainly of a depiction of events,

 (*b*) the events are depicted (wholly or mainly) by one or more persons performing, and

 (*c*) the whole or a major proportion of what is done by the person or persons performing, whether by way of speech, acting, singing or dancing, involves the playing of a role,

and for these purposes "drama" includes comedy.

[(2A) A programme is a children's programme if, when television production activities begin, it is reasonable to expect that the persons who will make up the programme's primary audience will be under the age of 15.][2]

(3) A drama or documentary that includes animation is to be treated as animation if the core expenditure on the completed animation constitutes at least 51% of the total core expenditure on the completed programme.][1]

HMRC Manuals—Television Production Company Manual TPC10100 (programmes eligible to be relevant programmes).

Amendments—[1] This Part (ss 1216A–1216EC) inserted by FA 2013 s 36, Sch 16 para 1. The amendments made by Sch 16 come into force on 19 July 2013 (by virtue of SI 2013/1817 art 2(1)). Those amendments have effect in relation to accounting

periods beginning on or after 1 April 2013, subject to transitional provisions. Note that any power conferred on the Secretary of State or the Treasury, by virtue of Sch 16, to make regulations or an order came into force on 17 July 2013. See FA 2013 Sch 16 paras 2, 3 for commencement provisions.

² Sub-s (2A) inserted by FA 2015 s 30(1), (4) with effect in relation to accounting periods beginning on or after 1 April 2015. Where a company has an accounting period beginning before and ending on or after 1 April 2015, see FA 2015 s 30(8)–(10).

[1216AD Excluded programmes

(1) For the purposes of this Part[, but subject to section 1216ADA,]² a television programme is an excluded programme if it falls within any of the Heads set out in the following subsections—

    (*a*) subsection (2) (advertisements etc),

    (*b*) subsection (3) (current affairs etc),

    (*c*) subsection (4) (entertainment shows),

    (*d*) subsection (5) (competitions),

    (*e*) subsection (6) (live performances),

    (*f*) subsection (7) (training programmes).

(2) Head 1 is any advertisement or other promotional programme.

(3) Head 2 is any news or current affairs programme or discussion programme.

(4) Head 3 is any quiz show, game show, panel show, variety show, chat show or similar entertainment.

(5) Head 4 is any programme consisting of or including—

    (*a*) a competition or contest, or

    (*b*) the results of a competition or contest.

(6) Head 5 is any broadcast of a live event or of a theatrical or artistic performance given otherwise than for the purpose of being filmed.

(7) Head 6 is any programme produced for training purposes.]¹

HMRC Manuals—Television Production Company Manual TPC10100 (excluded programmes).

Amendments—¹ This Part (ss 1216A–1216EC) inserted by FA 2013 s 36, Sch 16 para 1. The amendments made by Sch 16 come into force on 19 July 2013 (by virtue of SI 2013/1817 art 2(1)). Those amendments have effect in relation to accounting periods beginning on or after 1 April 2013, subject to transitional provisions. Note that any power conferred on the Secretary of State or the Treasury, by virtue of Sch 16, to make regulations or an order came into force on 17 July 2013. See FA 2013 Sch 16 paras 2, 3 for commencement provisions.

² In sub-s (1), words inserted by FA 2015 s 30(1), (5) with effect in relation to accounting periods beginning on or after 1 April 2015. Where a company has an accounting period beginning before and ending on or after 1 April 2015, see FA 2015 s 30(8)–(10).

[1216ADA Certain children's programmes not to be excluded programmes

(1) A children's programme is not an excluded programme for the purposes of this Part if—

    (*a*) the programme falls within—

        (i) sub-head 3A set out in subsection (2), or

        (ii) Head 4 set out in section 1216AD(5), and

    (*b*) the prize total (see subsection (3)) does not exceed £1,000.

(2) Sub-head 3A is any quiz show or game show.

(3) "The prize total" for a programme is the total of—

    (*a*) the amount of each relevant prize that is a money prize, and

    (*b*) the amount spent on each other relevant prize by, or on behalf of, its provider,

and here "relevant prize" means a prize offered in connection with participation in a quiz, game, competition or contest in, or promoted by, the programme.

(4) The Treasury may by regulations amend subsection (1)(*b*) for the purpose of increasing the amount of the money limit for the time being specified in subsection (1)(*b*).]¹

Commentary—*Simon's Taxes* **D7.1230**.

Amendments—¹ Section 1216ADA inserted by FA 2015 s 30(1), (6) with effect in relation to accounting periods beginning on or after 1 April 2015. Where a company has an accounting period beginning before and ending on or after 1 April 2015, see FA 2015 s 30(8)–(10).

[Other interpretation

1216AE Television production company

(1) For the purposes of this Part "television production company" is to be read in accordance with this section.

(2) There cannot be more than one television production company in relation to a relevant programme.

(3) A company is the television production company in relation to a relevant programme if the company (otherwise than in partnership)—

    (*a*) is responsible—

        (i) for pre-production, principal photography and post-production of the programme, and

        (ii) for delivery of the programme,

    (*b*) is actively engaged in production planning and decision-making during pre-production, principal photography and post-production, and

(c) directly negotiates, contracts and pays for rights, goods and services in relation to the programme.

(4) A company is the television production company in relation to a relevant programme that is a qualifying co-production if the company (otherwise than in partnership)—

(a) is a co-producer, and

(b) makes an effective creative, technical and artistic contribution to the programme.

(5) If there is more than one company meeting the description in subsection (3) or (4), the company that is most directly engaged in the activities referred to in that subsection is the television production company in relation to the relevant programme.

(6) If there is no company meeting the description in subsection (3) or (4), there is no television production company in relation to the relevant programme.

(7) A company may elect to be regarded as a company which does not meet the description in subsection (3) or (4).

(8) The election—

(a) must be made by the company by being included in its company tax return for an accounting period (and may be included in the return originally made or by amendment), and

(b) may be withdrawn by the company only by amending its company tax return for that accounting period.

(9) The election has effect in relation to relevant programmes which commence principal photography in that or any subsequent accounting period.][1]

Commentary—Simon's Taxes **D7.1232**.

HMRC Manuals—Television Production Company Manual TPC10110 (television production company: meaning).

Amendments—[1] This Part (ss 1216A–1216EC) inserted by FA 2013 s 36, Sch 16 para 1. The amendments made by Sch 16 come into force on 19 July 2013 (by virtue of SI 2013/1817 art 2(1)). Those amendments have effect in relation to accounting periods beginning on or after 1 April 2013, subject to transitional provisions. Note that any power conferred on the Secretary of State or the Treasury, by virtue of Sch 16, to make regulations or an order came into force on 17 July 2013. See FA 2013 Sch 16 paras 2, 3 for commencement provisions.

[1216AF "Television production activities" etc

(1) In this Part "television production activities", in relation to a relevant programme, means the activities involved in development, pre-production, principal photography and post-production of the programme.

(2) If all or any of the images in a relevant programme are generated by computer, references in this Part to principal photography are to be read as references to, or as including, the generation of those images.

(3) The Treasury may by regulations—

(a) amend subsections (1) and (2),

(b) provide that specified activities are or are not to be regarded as television production activities or as television production activities of a particular description, and

(c) provide that, in relation to a specified description of relevant programme, references to television production activities of a particular description are to be read as references to such activities as may be specified.

"Specified" means specified in the regulations.][1]

Commentary—Simon's Taxes **D7.1232**.

HMRC Manuals—Television Production Company Manual TPC10130 (television production activities: meaning).

Amendments—[1] This Part (ss 1216A–1216EC) inserted by FA 2013 s 36, Sch 16 para 1. The amendments made by Sch 16 come into force on 19 July 2013 (by virtue of SI 2013/1817 art 2(1)). Those amendments have effect in relation to accounting periods beginning on or after 1 April 2013, subject to transitional provisions. Note that any power conferred on the Secretary of State or the Treasury, by virtue of Sch 16, to make regulations or an order came into force on 17 July 2013. See FA 2013 Sch 16 paras 2, 3 for commencement provisions.

[1216AG "Production expenditure" and "core expenditure"

(1) This section applies for the purposes of this Part.

(2) "Production expenditure", in relation to a relevant programme, means expenditure on television production activities in connection with the programme.

(3) "Core expenditure", in relation to a relevant programme, means production expenditure on pre-production, principal photography and post-production of the programme.][1]

Commentary—Simon's Taxes **D7.1239, D7.1244**.

HMRC Manuals—Television Production Company Manual TPC10130 (production expenditure and core expenditure: meanings).

Amendments—[1] This Part (ss 1216A–1216EC) inserted by FA 2013 s 36, Sch 16 para 1. The amendments made by Sch 16 come into force on 19 July 2013 (by virtue of SI 2013/1817 art 2(1)). Those amendments have effect in relation to accounting periods beginning on or after 1 April 2013, subject to transitional provisions. Note that any power conferred on the Secretary of State or the Treasury, by virtue of Sch 16, to make regulations or an order came into force on 17 July 2013. See FA 2013 Sch 16 paras 2, 3 for commencement provisions.

[1216AH "UK expenditure" etc

(1) In this Part "UK expenditure", in relation to a relevant programme, means expenditure on goods or services that are used or consumed in the United Kingdom.

(2) Any apportionment of expenditure as between UK expenditure and non-UK expenditure for the purposes of this Part is to be made on a just and reasonable basis.
(3) The Treasury may by regulations amend subsection (1).][1]

Commentary—*Simon's Taxes* **D7.1239**.
HMRC Manuals—Television Production Company Manual TPC10140 (meaning of UK expenditure).
TPC50050 (eligible UK expenditure).
Amendments—[1] This Part (ss 1216A–1216EC) inserted by FA 2013 s 36, Sch 16 para 1. The amendments made by Sch 16 come into force on 19 July 2013 (by virtue of SI 2013/1817 art 2(1)). Those amendments have effect in relation to accounting periods beginning on or after 1 April 2013, subject to transitional provisions. Note that any power conferred on the Secretary of State or the Treasury, by virtue of Sch 16, to make regulations or an order came into force on 17 July 2013. See FA 2013 Sch 16 paras 2, 3 for commencement provisions.

[1216AI "Qualifying co-production" and "co-producer"

In this Part—
  (a) "qualifying co-production" means a relevant programme that is eligible to be certified as a British programme under section 1216CB as a result of an agreement between Her Majesty's Government in the United Kingdom and any other government, international organisation or authority, and
  (b) "co-producer" means a person who is a co-producer for the purposes of the agreement mentioned in paragraph (a).][1]

Commentary—*Simon's Taxes* **D7.1232**.
HMRC Manuals—Television Production Company Manual TPC10120 (co-producer and qualifying co-production: meaning).
Amendments—[1] This Part (ss 1216A–1216EC) inserted by FA 2013 s 36, Sch 16 para 1. The amendments made by Sch 16 come into force on 19 July 2013 (by virtue of SI 2013/1817 art 2(1)). Those amendments have effect in relation to accounting periods beginning on or after 1 April 2013, subject to transitional provisions. Note that any power conferred on the Secretary of State or the Treasury, by virtue of Sch 16, to make regulations or an order came into force on 17 July 2013. See FA 2013 Sch 16 paras 2, 3 for commencement provisions.

[1216AJ "Company tax return"

In this Part "company tax return" has the same meaning as in Schedule 18 to FA 1998 (see paragraph 3(1)).][1]

Commentary—*Simon's Taxes* **D1.1309**.
Amendments—[1] This Part (ss 1216A–1216EC) inserted by FA 2013 s 36, Sch 16 para 1. The amendments made by Sch 16 come into force on 19 July 2013 (by virtue of SI 2013/1817 art 2(1)). Those amendments have effect in relation to accounting periods beginning on or after 1 April 2013, subject to transitional provisions. Note that any power conferred on the Secretary of State or the Treasury, by virtue of Sch 16, to make regulations or an order came into force on 17 July 2013. See FA 2013 Sch 16 paras 2, 3 for commencement provisions.

[CHAPTER 2

TAXATION OF ACTIVITIES OF TELEVISION PRODUCTION COMPANY]

Amendments—This Part (ss 1216A–1216EC) inserted by FA 2013 s 36, Sch 16 para 1. The amendments made by Sch 16 come into force on 19 July 2013 (by virtue of SI 2013/1817 art 2(1)). Those amendments have effect in relation to accounting periods beginning on or after 1 April 2013, subject to transitional provisions. Note that any power conferred on the Secretary of State or the Treasury, by virtue of Sch 16, to make regulations or an order came into force on 17 July 2013. See FA 2013 Sch 16 paras 2, 3 for commencement provisions.

[Separate programme trade

1216B Activities of television production company treated as a separate trade

(1) This Chapter applies for corporation tax purposes to a company that is the television production company in relation to a [qualifying][2] relevant programme.
(2) The company's activities in relation to the programme are treated as a trade separate from any other activities of the company (including any activities in relation to any other [qualifying relevant][2] programme).
(3) In this Chapter the separate trade is called "the separate programme trade".
(4) The company is treated as beginning to carry on the separate programme trade—
  (a) when pre-production begins, or
  (b) if earlier, when any income from the relevant programme is received by the company.][1]
[(5) In this section "qualifying relevant programme" means a relevant programme in relation to which the conditions for television tax relief are met (see section 1216C(2)).][2]

Commentary—*Simon's Taxes* **D7.1233**.
HMRC Manuals—Television Production Company Manual TPC20100 (taxation: separate trade commencement).
Amendments—[1] This Part (ss 1216A–1216EC) inserted by FA 2013 s 36, Sch 16 para 1. The amendments made by Sch 16 come into force on 19 July 2013 (by virtue of SI 2013/1817 art 2(1)). Those amendments have effect in relation to accounting periods beginning on or after 1 April 2013, subject to transitional provisions. Note that any power conferred on the Secretary of State or the Treasury, by virtue of Sch 16, to make regulations or an order came into force on 17 July 2013. See FA 2013 Sch 16 paras 2, 3 for commencement provisions.
[2] In sub-s (1), word inserted, in sub-s (2), words substituted for word "television", and sub-s (5) inserted, by FA 2014 s 33(1), (3) with effect from 17 July 2014..

[1216BA Calculation of profits or losses of separate programme trade
(1) This section applies for the purpose of calculating the profits or losses of the separate programme trade.
(2) For the first period of account the following are brought into account—
  (*a*) as a debit, the costs of the relevant programme incurred (and represented in work done) to date, and
  (*b*) as a credit, the proportion of the estimated total income from the relevant programme treated as earned at the end of that period.
(3) For subsequent periods of account the following are brought into account—
  (*a*) as a debit, the difference between the amount of the costs of the relevant programme incurred (and represented in work done) to date and the corresponding amount for the previous period, and
  (*b*) as a credit, the difference between the proportion of the estimated total income from the relevant programme treated as earned at the end of that period and the corresponding amount for the previous period.
(4) The proportion of the estimated total income treated as earned at the end of a period of account is given by—
(C / T) x I
where—
  C is the total to date of costs incurred (and represented in work done),
  T is the estimated total cost of the relevant programme, and
  I is the estimated total income from the relevant programme.][1]

Commentary—*Simon's Taxes* **D7.1233**.
HMRC Manuals—Television Production Company Manual TPC20250 (estimating total income earned at the end of an accounting period).
TPC20255 (taxation: profit/loss calculation: matching income to expenditure in different periods of account).
Amendments—[1] This Part (ss 1216A–1216EC) inserted by FA 2013 s 36, Sch 16 para 1. The amendments made by Sch 16 come into force on 19 July 2013 (by virtue of SI 2013/1817 art 2(1)). Those amendments have effect in relation to accounting periods beginning on or after 1 April 2013, subject to transitional provisions. Note that any power conferred on the Secretary of State or the Treasury, by virtue of Sch 16, to make regulations or an order came into force on 17 July 2013. See FA 2013 Sch 16 paras 2, 3 for commencement provisions.

[Supplementary

1216BB Income from the relevant programme
(1) References in this Chapter to income from the relevant programme are to any receipts by the company in connection with the making or exploitation of the programme.
(2) This includes—
  (*a*) receipts from the sale of the programme or rights in it,
  (*b*) royalties or other payments for use of the programme or aspects of it (for example, characters or music),
  (*c*) payments for rights to produce games or other merchandise, and
  (*d*) receipts by the company by way of a profit share agreement..
(3) Receipts that (apart from this subsection) would be regarded as of a capital nature are treated as being of a revenue nature.][1]

Commentary—*Simon's Taxes* **D7.1233**.
HMRC Manuals—Television Production Company Manual TPC20210 (taxation: profit/loss calculation: income nature).
Amendments—[1] This Part (ss 1216A–1216EC) inserted by FA 2013 s 36, Sch 16 para 1. The amendments made by Sch 16 come into force on 19 July 2013 (by virtue of SI 2013/1817 art 2(1)). Those amendments have effect in relation to accounting periods beginning on or after 1 April 2013, subject to transitional provisions. Note that any power conferred on the Secretary of State or the Treasury, by virtue of Sch 16, to make regulations or an order came into force on 17 July 2013. See FA 2013 Sch 16 paras 2, 3 for commencement provisions.

[1216BC Costs of the relevant programme
(1) References in this Chapter to the costs of the relevant programme are to expenditure incurred by the company on—
  (*a*) television production activities in connection with the programme, or
  (*b*) activities with a view to exploiting the programme.
(2) This is subject to any provision of the Corporation Tax Acts prohibiting the making of a deduction, or restricting the extent to which a deduction is allowed, in calculating the profits of a trade.
(3) Expenditure that (apart from this subsection) would be regarded as of a capital nature by reason only of being incurred on the creation of an asset (the relevant programme) is treated as being of a revenue nature.][1]

Commentary—*Simon's Taxes* **D7.1233**.
HMRC Manuals—Television Production Company Manual TPC20230 (taxation: profit/loss calculation: expenditure nature).
Amendments—[1] This Part (ss 1216A–1216EC) inserted by FA 2013 s 36, Sch 16 para 1. The amendments made by Sch 16 come into force on 19 July 2013 (by virtue of SI 2013/1817 art 2(1)). Those amendments have effect in relation to accounting

periods beginning on or after 1 April 2013, subject to transitional provisions. Note that any power conferred on the Secretary of State or the Treasury, by virtue of Sch 16, to make regulations or an order came into force on 17 July 2013. See FA 2013 Sch 16 paras 2, 3 for commencement provisions.

[1216BD When costs are taken to be incurred

(1) For the purposes of this Chapter costs are incurred when they are represented in the state of completion of the work in progress.

(2) Accordingly—

    (*a*) payments in advance for work to be done are ignored until the work has been carried out, and

    (*b*) deferred payments are recognised to the extent that the work is represented in the state of completion.

(3) The costs incurred on the relevant programme are taken to include an amount that has not been paid only if it is the subject of an unconditional obligation to pay.

(4) If an obligation is linked to income being earned from the relevant programme, no amount is to be brought into account in respect of the costs of the obligation unless an appropriate amount of income is or has been brought into account.][1]

Commentary—*Simon's Taxes* **D7.1233, D7.1244, D7.1246**.

HMRC Manuals—Television Production Company Manual TPC20240 (taxation: profit/loss calculation: expenditure timing).

Amendments—[1] This Part (ss 1216A–1216EC) inserted by FA 2013 s 36, Sch 16 para 1. The amendments made by Sch 16 come into force on 19 July 2013 (by virtue of SI 2013/1817 art 2(1)). Those amendments have effect in relation to accounting periods beginning on or after 1 April 2013, subject to transitional provisions. Note that any power conferred on the Secretary of State or the Treasury, by virtue of Sch 16, to make regulations or an order came into force on 17 July 2013. See FA 2013 Sch 16 paras 2, 3 for commencement provisions.

[1216BE Pre-trading expenditure

(1) This section applies if, before the company began to carry on the separate programme trade, it incurred expenditure on development of the relevant programme.

(2) The expenditure may be treated as expenditure of the separate programme trade and as if incurred immediately after the company began to carry on that trade.

(3) If expenditure so treated has previously been taken into account for other tax purposes, the company must amend any relevant company tax return accordingly.

(4) Any amendment or assessment necessary to give effect to subsection (3) may be made despite any limitation on the time within which an amendment or assessment may normally be made.][1]

Commentary—*Simon's Taxes* **D7.1233**.

HMRC Manuals—Television Production Company Manual TPC20120 (taxation: separate trade pre-trading expenditure).

Amendments—[1] This Part (ss 1216A–1216EC) inserted by FA 2013 s 36, Sch 16 para 1. The amendments made by Sch 16 come into force on 19 July 2013 (by virtue of SI 2013/1817 art 2(1)). Those amendments have effect in relation to accounting periods beginning on or after 1 April 2013, subject to transitional provisions. Note that any power conferred on the Secretary of State or the Treasury, by virtue of Sch 16, to make regulations or an order came into force on 17 July 2013. See FA 2013 Sch 16 paras 2, 3 for commencement provisions.

[1216BF Estimates

Estimates for the purposes of this Chapter must be made as at the balance sheet date for each period of account, on a just and reasonable basis taking into consideration all relevant circumstances.][1]

Commentary—*Simon's Taxes* **D7.1233**.

HMRC Manuals—Television Production Company Manual TPC20260 (taxation: profit/loss calculation: estimating amounts).

Amendments—[1] This Part (ss 1216A–1216EC) inserted by FA 2013 s 36, Sch 16 para 1. The amendments made by Sch 16 come into force on 19 July 2013 (by virtue of SI 2013/1817 art 2(1)). Those amendments have effect in relation to accounting periods beginning on or after 1 April 2013, subject to transitional provisions. Note that any power conferred on the Secretary of State or the Treasury, by virtue of Sch 16, to make regulations or an order came into force on 17 July 2013. See FA 2013 Sch 16 paras 2, 3 for commencement provisions.

[CHAPTER 3

TELEVISION TAX RELIEF]

Amendments—This Part (ss 1216A–1216EC) inserted by FA 2013 s 36, Sch 16 para 1. The amendments made by Sch 16 come into force on 19 July 2013 (by virtue of SI 2013/1817 art 2(1)). Those amendments have effect in relation to accounting periods beginning on or after 1 April 2013, subject to transitional provisions. Note that any power conferred on the Secretary of State or the Treasury, by virtue of Sch 16, to make regulations or an order came into force on 17 July 2013. See FA 2013 Sch 16 paras 2, 3 for commencement provisions.

[Introductory

1216C Availability and overview of television tax relief

(1) This Chapter applies for corporation tax purposes to a company that is the television production company in relation to a relevant programme.

(2) Relief under this Chapter ("television tax relief") is available to the company if the conditions specified in the following sections are met in relation to the programme—

    (*a*) section 1216CA (intended for broadcast),

    (*b*) section 1216CB (British programme), and

    (*c*) section 1216CE (UK expenditure).

(3) Television tax relief is given by way of—

(*a*) additional deductions (see sections 1216CF and 1216CG), and

(*b*) television tax credits (see sections 1216CH to 1216CJ).

(4) But television tax relief is not available in respect of any expenditure if—

(*a*) the company is entitled to an R&D expenditure credit under Chapter 6A of Part 3 in respect of the expenditure, or

(*b*) the company has obtained relief under Part 13 (additional relief for expenditure on research and development) in respect of the expenditure.

(5) Sections 1216CK to 1216CN contain provision about unpaid costs, artificially inflated claims and confidentiality of information.

(6) In this Chapter "the separate programme trade" means the company's separate trade in relation to the relevant programme (see section 1216B).

(7) See Schedule 18 to FA 1998 (in particular, Part 9D) for information about the procedure for making claims for television tax relief.][1]

Commentary—*Simon's Taxes* **D7.1235, D7.1238**.

HMRC Manuals—Television Production Company Manual TPC40010 (qualifying television programmes: introduction).

Amendments—[1]   This Part (ss 1216A–1216EC) inserted by FA 2013 s 36, Sch 16 para 1. The amendments made by Sch 16 come into force on 19 July 2013 (by virtue of SI 2013/1817 art 2(1)). Those amendments have effect in relation to accounting periods beginning on or after 1 April 2013, subject to transitional provisions. Note that any power conferred on the Secretary of State or the Treasury, by virtue of Sch 16, to make regulations or an order came into force on 17 July 2013. See FA 2013 Sch 16 paras 2, 3 for commencement provisions.

["Intended for broadcast"

1216CA Intended for broadcast

(1) The relevant programme must be intended for broadcast to the general public.

(2) Whether this condition is met is determined when television production activities begin, so that—

(*a*) where a relevant programme is originally intended for broadcast, this condition continues to be met even if that ceases to be the intention, and

(*b*) where a relevant programme is not originally intended for broadcast, this condition is not met even if that becomes the intention.][1]

Commentary—*Simon's Taxes* **D7.1240**.

HMRC Manuals—Television Production Company Manual TPC40020 (qualifying television programmes: intended for broadcast).

Amendments—[1]   This Part (ss 1216A–1216EC) inserted by FA 2013 s 36, Sch 16 para 1. The amendments made by Sch 16 come into force on 19 July 2013 (by virtue of SI 2013/1817 art 2(1)). Those amendments have effect in relation to accounting periods beginning on or after 1 April 2013, subject to transitional provisions. Note that any power conferred on the Secretary of State or the Treasury, by virtue of Sch 16, to make regulations or an order came into force on 17 July 2013. See FA 2013 Sch 16 paras 2, 3 for commencement provisions.

[British programmes

1216CB British programme

(1) The relevant programme must be certified by the Secretary of State as a British programme.

(2) The Secretary of State, with the approval of the Treasury, may by regulations specify conditions which must be met by a relevant programme before it may be certified as a British programme.

These conditions are known as the "cultural test".

(3) Regulations under subsection (2) may—

(*a*) specify different conditions in relation to different descriptions of relevant programme,

(*b*) provide that specified descriptions of programme may not be certified as a British programme, and

(*c*) enable the Secretary of State to direct that any provision made by virtue of paragraph (*b*) does not apply to a programme that meets specified conditions.

"Specified" means specified in the regulations.

(4) Regulations under subsection (2) are to be made by statutory instrument.

(5) A statutory instrument containing regulations under subsection (2) is subject to annulment in pursuance of a resolution of the House of Commons.

(6) Sections 1216CC and 1216CD contain further provision about certification of programmes as British programmes, including provision about applications for, and withdrawal of, certification.][1]

Commentary—*Simon's Taxes* **D7.1241**.

HMRC Manuals—Television Production Company Manual TPC40030 (qualifying television programmes: British programme).

Regulations—Cultural Test (Television Programmes) Regulations, SI 2013/1831.

Cultural Test (Television Programmes) (Amendment) Regulations, SI 2015/1449.

Cultural Test (Television Programmes) (Amendment) (No 2) Regulations, SI 2015/1941.

Cultural Test (Television Programmes) (Amendment) Regulations, SI 2017/1138.

Amendments—[1]   This Part (ss 1216A–1216EC) inserted by FA 2013 s 36, Sch 16 para 1. The amendments made by Sch 16 come into force on 19 July 2013 (by virtue of SI 2013/1817 art 2(1)). Those amendments have effect in relation to accounting periods beginning on or after 1 April 2013, subject to transitional provisions. Note that any power conferred on the Secretary of State or the Treasury, by virtue of Sch 16, to make regulations or an order came into force on 17 July 2013. See FA 2013 Sch 16 paras 2, 3 for commencement provisions.

[1216CC Applications for certification

(1) An application for certification of a relevant programme as a British programme is to be made to the Secretary of State by the television production company.

(2) The application may be for an interim or final certificate.

(3) An interim certificate is a certificate that—

(a) is granted before the programme is completed, and

(b) states that the programme, if completed in accordance with the proposals set out in the application, will be a British programme.

(4) A final certificate is a certificate that—

(a) is granted after the programme is completed, and

(b) states that the programme is a British programme.

(5) The applicant must provide the Secretary of State with any documents or information which the Secretary of State requires in order to determine the application.

(6) The Secretary of State may require information provided for the purposes of the application to be accompanied by a statutory declaration, made by the person providing it, as to the truth of the information.

(7) The Secretary of State may by regulations make provision supplementing this section, including—

(a) provision about the form of applications,

(b) provision about the particulars and evidence necessary for satisfying the Secretary of State that a programme meets the cultural test, and

(c) provision that any statutory declaration which is required by subsection (6) to be made by any person may be made on the person's behalf by such person as is specified in the regulations.

(8) Regulations under subsection (7) are to be made by statutory instrument.

(9) A statutory instrument containing regulations under subsection (7) is subject to annulment in pursuance of a resolution of the House of Commons.][1]

Commentary—*Simon's Taxes* **D7.1241**.

HMRC Manuals—Television Production Company Manual TPC40030 (interim and final certificates).

Regulations—Cultural Test (Television Programmes) Regulations, SI 2013/1831.

Cultural Test (Television Programmes) (Amendment) Regulations, SI 2015/1449.

Amendments—[1] This Part (ss 1216A–1216EC) inserted by FA 2013 s 36, Sch 16 para 1. The amendments made by Sch 16 come into force on 19 July 2013 (by virtue of SI 2013/1817 art 2(1)). Those amendments have effect in relation to accounting periods beginning on or after 1 April 2013, subject to transitional provisions. Note that any power conferred on the Secretary of State or the Treasury, by virtue of Sch 16, to make regulations or an order came into force on 17 July 2013. See FA 2013 Sch 16 paras 2, 3 for commencement provisions.

[1216CD Certification and withdrawal of certification

(1) If the Secretary of State is satisfied that the requirements are met for interim or final certification of a relevant programme as a British programme, the Secretary of State must certify the programme accordingly.

(2) If the Secretary of State is not satisfied that those requirements are met, the Secretary of State must refuse the application.

(3) An interim certificate—

(a) may be given subject to conditions, and (unless the Secretary of State directs otherwise) is of no effect if the conditions are not met, and

(b) may be expressed to expire after a specified period, and (unless the Secretary of State directs otherwise) ceases to have effect at the end of that period.

(4) An interim certificate ceases to have effect when a final certificate is issued.

(5) If it appears to the Secretary of State that a relevant programme certified under this Part ought not to have been certified, the Secretary of State may revoke its certification.

(6) Unless the Secretary of State directs otherwise, a certificate that is revoked is treated as never having had effect.][1]

Commentary—*Simon's Taxes* **D7.1241**.

Cross-references—See FA 2016 s 180, Sch 24 Pt 1 (power to obtain information about tax advantages claimed under Parts 15, 15A, 15C, 15D which constitute the grant of State aid).

HMRC Manuals—Television Production Company Manual TPC80010 (media and sport (DCMS)/British Film Institute (BFI) certification).

Amendments—[1] This Part (ss 1216A–1216EC) inserted by FA 2013 s 36, Sch 16 para 1. The amendments made by Sch 16 come into force on 19 July 2013 (by virtue of SI 2013/1817 art 2(1)). Those amendments have effect in relation to accounting periods beginning on or after 1 April 2013, subject to transitional provisions. Note that any power conferred on the Secretary of State or the Treasury, by virtue of Sch 16, to make regulations or an order came into force on 17 July 2013. See FA 2013 Sch 16 paras 2, 3 for commencement provisions.

[UK expenditure

1216CE UK expenditure

(1) At least [10%][2] of the core expenditure on the relevant programme incurred—

(a) in the case of a British programme that is not a qualifying coproduction, by the company, and

(b) in the case of a qualifying co-production, by the co-producers, must be UK expenditure.

(2) The Treasury may by regulations amend the percentage specified in subsection (1).][1]

Commentary—*Simon's Taxes* **D7.1239**.

Cross-references—See FA 2016 s 180, Sch 24 Pt 1 (power to obtain information about tax advantages claimed under Parts 15, 15A, 15C, 15D which constitute the grant of State aid).

HMRC Manuals—Television Production Company Manual TPC40040 (qualifying television programmes: minimum UK expenditure).

Amendments—[1] This Part (ss 1216A–1216EC) inserted by FA 2013 s 36, Sch 16 para 1. The amendments made by Sch 16 come into force on 19 July 2013 (by virtue of SI 2013/1817 art 2(1)). Those amendments have effect in relation to accounting periods beginning on or after 1 April 2013, subject to transitional provisions. Note that any power conferred on the Secretary of State or the Treasury, by virtue of Sch 16, to make regulations or an order came into force on 17 July 2013. See FA 2013 Sch 16 paras 2, 3 for commencement provisions.

[2] In sub-s (1), figure substituted for "25%" by FA 2015 s 31 with effect in relation to relevant programmes the principal photography of which is not completed before 1 April 2015.

[Additional deductions

1216CF Additional deduction for qualifying expenditure

(1) If television tax relief is available to the company, it may (on making a claim) make an additional deduction in respect of qualifying expenditure on the relevant programme.

(2) The deduction is made in calculating the profit or loss of the separate programme trade.

(3) In this Chapter "qualifying expenditure" means core expenditure on the relevant programme that falls to be taken into account under Chapter 2 in calculating the profit or loss of the separate programme trade for tax purposes.

(4) The Treasury may by regulations—

    (*a*) amend subsection (3), and

    (*b*) provide that expenditure of a specified description is or is not to be regarded as qualifying expenditure.][1]

Commentary—*Simon's Taxes* **D7.1244**.

Cross-references—See FA 2016 s 180, Sch 24 Pt 1 (power to obtain information about tax advantages claimed under Parts 15, 15A, 15C, 15D which constitute the grant of State aid).

HMRC Manuals—Television Production Company Manual TPC55020 (additional deduction on qualifying expenditure).

Amendments—[1] This Part (ss 1216A–1216EC) inserted by FA 2013 s 36, Sch 16 para 1. The amendments made by Sch 16 come into force on 19 July 2013 (by virtue of SI 2013/1817 art 2(1)). Those amendments have effect in relation to accounting periods beginning on or after 1 April 2013, subject to transitional provisions. Note that any power conferred on the Secretary of State or the Treasury, by virtue of Sch 16, to make regulations or an order came into force on 17 July 2013. See FA 2013 Sch 16 paras 2, 3 for commencement provisions.

[1216CG Amount of additional deduction

(1) For the first period of account during which the separate programme trade is carried on, the amount of the additional deduction is—

E

where E is—

    (*a*) so much of the qualifying expenditure as is UK expenditure, or

    (*b*) if less, 80% of the total amount of qualifying expenditure.

(2) For any period of account after the first, the amount of the additional deduction is given by—

E – P

where—

    E is—

        (*a*) so much of the qualifying expenditure incurred to date as is UK expenditure, or

        (*b*) if less, 80% of the total amount of qualifying expenditure incurred to date, and

    P is the total amount of the additional deductions given for previous periods.

(3) The Treasury may by regulations amend this section.][1]

Commentary—*Simon's Taxes* **D7.1244**.

Cross-references—See FA 2016 s 180, Sch 24 Pt 1 (power to obtain information about tax advantages claimed under Parts 15, 15A, 15C, 15D which constitute the grant of State aid).

HMRC Manuals—Television Production Company Manual TPC55020 (calculation: maximum amount of core expenditure subject to claim).

Amendments—[1] This Part (ss 1216A–1216EC) inserted by FA 2013 s 36, Sch 16 para 1. The amendments made by Sch 16 come into force on 19 July 2013 (by virtue of SI 2013/1817 art 2(1)). Those amendments have effect in relation to accounting periods beginning on or after 1 April 2013, subject to transitional provisions. Note that any power conferred on the Secretary of State or the Treasury, by virtue of Sch 16, to make regulations or an order came into force on 17 July 2013. See FA 2013 Sch 16 paras 2, 3 for commencement provisions.

[Television tax credits

1216CH Television tax credit claimable if company has surrenderable loss

(1) If television tax relief is available to the company, it may claim a television tax credit for an accounting period in which it has a surrenderable loss.

(2) The company's surrenderable loss in an accounting period is—

(a) the company's available loss for the period in the separate programme trade (see subsection (3)), or

(b) if less, the available qualifying expenditure for the period (see subsections (5) and (6)).

(3) The company's available loss for an accounting period is given by—

L + RUL

where—

L is the amount of the company's loss for the period in the separate programme trade, and

RUL is the amount of any relevant unused loss of the company (see subsection (4)).

(4) The "relevant unused loss" of a company is so much of any available loss of the company for the previous accounting period as has not been—

(a) surrendered under section 1216CI(1), or

(b) carried forward under section 45 [or 45B][2] of CTA 2010 and set against profits of the separate programme trade.

(5) For the first period of account during which the separate programme trade is carried on, the available qualifying expenditure is the amount that is E for that period for the purposes of section 1216CG(1).

(6) For any period of account after the first, the available qualifying expenditure is given by—

E − S

where—

E is the amount that is E for that period for the purposes of section 1216CG(2), and

S is the total amount previously surrendered under section 1216CI(1).

(7) If a period of account of the separate programme trade does not coincide with an accounting period, any necessary apportionments are to be made by reference to the number of days in the periods concerned.][1]

Commentary—*Simon's Taxes* D7.1246.

Cross-references—See FA 2016 s 180, Sch 24 Pt 1 (power to obtain information about tax advantages claimed under Parts 15, 15A, 15C, 15D which constitute the grant of State aid).

HMRC Manuals—Television Production Company Manual TPC55100 (calculation: surrenderable losses and television tax credit).

Amendments—[1] This Part (ss 1216A–1216EC) inserted by FA 2013 s 36, Sch 16 para 1. The amendments made by Sch 16 come into force on 19 July 2013 (by virtue of SI 2013/1817 art 2(1)). Those amendments have effect in relation to accounting periods beginning on or after 1 April 2013, subject to transitional provisions. Note that any power conferred on the Secretary of State or the Treasury, by virtue of Sch 16, to make regulations or an order came into force on 17 July 2013. See FA 2013 Sch 16 paras 2, 3 for commencement provisions.

[2] In sub-s (4)(b), words inserted by F(No 2)A 2017 s 18, Sch 4 paras 128, 140 with effect in relation to accounting periods beginning on or after 1 April 2017, subject to transitional provisions in Sch 4 para 194. For accounting periods beginning before 1 April 2017 and ending on or after that date ("straddling periods") see F(No 2)A 2017 Sch 4 paras 190–192.

[1216CI Surrendering of loss and amount of television tax credit

(1) The company may surrender the whole or part of its surrenderable loss in an accounting period.

(2) If the company surrenders the whole or part of that loss, the amount of the television tax credit to which it is entitled for the accounting period is 25% of the amount of the loss surrendered.

(3) The company's available loss for the accounting period is reduced by the amount surrendered.][1]

Commentary—*Simon's Taxes* D7.1246.

Cross-references—See FA 2016 s 180, Sch 24 Pt 1 (power to obtain information about tax advantages claimed under Parts 15, 15A, 15C, 15D which constitute the grant of State aid).

HMRC Manuals—Television Production Company Manual TPC55100 (the amount of the surrenderable loss).

Amendments—[1] This Part (ss 1216A–1216EC) inserted by FA 2013 s 36, Sch 16 para 1. The amendments made by Sch 16 come into force on 19 July 2013 (by virtue of SI 2013/1817 art 2(1)). Those amendments have effect in relation to accounting periods beginning on or after 1 April 2013, subject to transitional provisions. Note that any power conferred on the Secretary of State or the Treasury, by virtue of Sch 16, to make regulations or an order came into force on 17 July 2013. See FA 2013 Sch 16 paras 2, 3 for commencement provisions.

[1216CJ Payment in respect of television tax credit

(1) If the company—

(a) is entitled to a television tax credit for a period, and

(b) makes a claim,

the Commissioners for Her Majesty's Revenue and Customs ("the Commissioners") must pay to the company the amount of the credit.

(2) An amount payable in respect of—

(a) a television tax credit, or

(b) interest on a television tax credit under section 826 of ICTA,

may be applied in discharging any liability of the company to pay corporation tax.

To the extent that it is so applied the Commissioners' liability under subsection (1) is discharged.

(3) If the company's company tax return for the accounting period is enquired into by the Commissioners, no payment in respect of a television tax credit for that period need be made before the Commissioners' enquiries are completed (see paragraph 32 of Schedule 18 to FA 1998).

[1216D Application of sections 1216DA and 1216DB

(1) Sections 1216DA and 1216DB apply to a company that is the television production company in relation to a relevant programme.

(2) In those sections—

"the completion period" means the accounting period of the company—

(*a*) in which the relevant programme is completed, or

(*b*) if the company does not complete the relevant programme, in which it abandons television production activities in relation to the programme,

"loss relief" includes any means by which a loss might be used to reduce the amount in respect of which the company, or any other person, is chargeable to tax,

"pre-completion period" means an accounting period of the company before the completion period, and

"the separate programme trade" means the company's separate trade in relation to the relevant programme (see section 1216B).]¹

Amendments—¹ This Part (ss 1216A–1216EC) inserted by FA 2013 s 36, Sch 16 para 1. The amendments made by Sch 16 come into force on 19 July 2013 (by virtue of SI 2013/1817 art 2(1)). Those amendments have effect in relation to accounting periods beginning on or after 1 April 2013, subject to transitional provisions. Note that any power conferred on the Secretary of State or the Treasury, by virtue of Sch 16, to make regulations or an order came into force on 17 July 2013. See FA 2013 Sch 16 paras 2, 3 for commencement provisions.

[1216DA Restriction on use of losses while programme in production

(1) This section applies if in a pre-completion period a loss is made in the separate programme trade.

(2) The loss is not available for loss relief except to the extent that it may be carried forward under section 45 [or 45B]² of CTA 2010 to be [deducted from]² profits of the separate programme trade in a subsequent period.

[(3) If the loss is carried forward under section 45 or 45B of CTA 2010 and deducted from profits of the separate programme trade in a subsequent period, the deduction is to be ignored for the purposes of section 269ZB of CTA 2010 (restriction on deductions from trading profits).]²]¹

HMRC Manuals—Television Production Company Manual TPC30020 (losses: pre-completion periods: relief limited to carry forward).

Amendments—¹ This Part (ss 1216A–1216EC) inserted by FA 2013 s 36, Sch 16 para 1. The amendments made by Sch 16 come into force on 19 July 2013 (by virtue of SI 2013/1817 art 2(1)). Those amendments have effect in relation to accounting periods beginning on or after 1 April 2013, subject to transitional provisions. Note that any power conferred on the Secretary of State or the Treasury, by virtue of Sch 16, to make regulations or an order came into force on 17 July 2013. See FA 2013 Sch 16 paras 2, 3 for commencement provisions.

² In sub-s (2), words inserted and words substituted for words "set against", and sub-s (3) inserted, by F(No 2)A 2017 s 18, Sch 4 paras 31, 32 with effect in relation to accounting periods beginning on or after 1 April 2017, subject to transitional provisions in Sch 4 para 194. For accounting periods beginning before 1 April 2017 and ending on or after that date ("straddling periods") see F(No 2)A 2017 Sch 4 paras 190–192.

[1216DB Use of losses in later periods

(1) This section applies to the following accounting periods of the company ("relevant later periods")—

(*a*) the completion period, and

(*b*) any subsequent accounting period during which the separate programme trade continues.

(2) Subsection (3) applies if a loss made in the separate programme trade is carried forward under section 45 [or 45B]² of CTA 2010 from a pre-completion period to a relevant later period.

(3) So much (if any) of the loss as is not attributable to television tax relief (see subsection (6)) may be treated for the purposes of [section 37 and Part 5 of CTA 2010]² as if it were a loss made in the period to which it is carried forward.

(4) [Subsections (5) and (5A) apply]² if in a relevant later period a loss is made in the separate programme trade.

(5) The amount of the loss that may be—

(*a*) deducted from total profits of the same or an earlier period under section 37 of CTA 2010,

[(*ab*) carried forward under section 45A of that Act to be deducted from the total profits of a later period,]²

(*b*) surrendered as group relief under Part 5 of that Act,

is restricted to the amount (if any) that is not attributable to television tax relief (see subsection (6)).

[(5A) A deduction under section 45 or 45B of CTA 2010 which is made in respect of so much of the loss as is attributable to television tax relief is to be ignored for the purposes of section 269ZB of that Act (restriction on deductions from trading profits).]²

(6) The amount of a loss in any period that is attributable to television tax relief is calculated by deducting from the total amount of the loss the amount there would have been if there had been no additional deduction under Chapter 3 in that or any earlier period.

(7) This section does not apply to a loss to the extent that it is carried forward or surrendered under section 1216DC.]¹

Commentary—*Simon's Taxes* D7.1235.

Cross-references—See FA 2016 s 180, Sch 24 Pt 1 (power to obtain information about tax advantages claimed under Parts 15, 15A, 15C, 15D which constitute the grant of State aid).

HMRC Manuals—Television Production Company Manual TPC30030 (losses: completion and later periods).

Amendments—[1]　This Part (ss 1216A–1216EC) inserted by FA 2013 s 36, Sch 16 para 1. The amendments made by Sch 16 come into force on 19 July 2013 (by virtue of SI 2013/1817 art 2(1)). Those amendments have effect in relation to accounting periods beginning on or after 1 April 2013, subject to transitional provisions. Note that any power conferred on the Secretary of State or the Treasury, by virtue of Sch 16, to make regulations or an order came into force on 17 July 2013. See FA 2013 Sch 16 paras 2, 3 for commencement provisions.

[2]　In sub-s (2) words inserted, in sub-s (3) words substituted for words "loss relief", in sub-s (4) words substituted for words "Subsection (5) applies", and sub-ss (5)(*ab*), (5A) inserted, by F(No 2)A 2017 s 18, Sch 4 paras 31, 33 with effect in relation to accounting periods beginning on or after 1 April 2017, subject to transitional provisions in Sch 4 para 194. For accounting periods beginning before 1 April 2017 and ending on or after that date ("straddling periods") see F(No 2)A 2017 Sch 4 paras 190–192.

[1216DC　Terminal losses

(1) This section applies if—

   (*a*)　a company ("company A") is the television production company in relation to a qualifying programme,

   (*b*)　company A ceases to carry on its separate trade in relation to that programme ("trade X") (see section 1216B), and

   (*c*)　if company A had not ceased to carry on trade X, it could have carried forward an amount under section 45[, 45A or 45B][2] of CTA 2010 to be set against profits of　. . . [2] a later period ("the terminal loss").

(2) If on cessation of trade X company A—

   (*a*)　is the television production company in relation to another qualifying programme, and

   (*b*)　is carrying on its separate trade in relation to that programme ("trade Y"),

it may (on making a claim) make an election under subsection (3).

(3) The election is to have the terminal loss (or a part of it) treated[—

   (*a*)　in a case where the loss could have been carried forward under section 45 of CTA 2010 had trade X not ceased, as if it were a loss carried forward under that section to be set against the profits of trade Y of the first accounting period beginning after the cessation and so on, and

   (*b*)　in a case where the loss could have been carried forward under section 45A or 45B of CTA 2010 had trade X not ceased, as if it were a loss made in trade Y which has been carried forward under section 45B of that Act to the first accounting period beginning after the cessation.][2]

(4) Subsection (5) applies if on cessation of trade X—

   (*a*)　there is another company ("company B") that is the television production company in relation to a qualifying programme,

   (*b*)　company B is carrying on its separate trade in relation to that programme ("trade Z"), and

   (*c*)　company B is in the same group as company A for the purposes of Part 5 of CTA 2010 (group relief).

(5) Company A may surrender the terminal loss (or a part of it) to company B.

(6) On the making of a claim by company B the amount surrendered is treated—

   (*a*)　in a case where the amount could have been carried forward under section 45 of CTA 2010 had trade X not ceased, as if it were a loss carried forward under that section to be set against the profits of trade Z of the first accounting period beginning after the cessation and so on, and

   (*b*)　in a case where the amount could have been carried forward under section 45A or 45B of CTA 2010 had trade X not ceased, as if it were a loss made in trade Z which has been carried forward under section 45B of that Act to the first accounting period beginning after the cessation.][2]

(7) The Treasury may, in relation to the surrender of a loss under subsection (5) and the resulting claim under subsection (6), make provision by regulations corresponding, subject to such adaptations or other modifications as appear to them to be appropriate, to that made by Part 8 of Schedule 18 to FA 1998 (company tax returns: claims for group relief).

[(7A) A deduction under section 45 or 45B of CTA 2010 which is made in reliance on this section is to be ignored for the purposes of section 269ZB of that Act (restriction on deductions from trading profits).][2]

(8) "Qualifying programme" means a relevant programme in relation to which the conditions for television tax relief are met (see 1216C(2)).][1]

Commentary—*Simon's Taxes* **D7.1235, D7.1248**.

Cross-references—See FA 2016 s 180, Sch 24 Pt 1 (power to obtain information about tax advantages claimed under Parts 15, 15A, 15C, 15D which constitute the grant of State aid).

HMRC Manuals—Television Production Company Manual TPC30040 (losses: terminal losses).

Amendments—[1]　This Part (ss 1216A–1216EC) inserted by FA 2013 s 36, Sch 16 para 1. The amendments made by Sch 16 come into force on 19 July 2013 (by virtue of SI 2013/1817 art 2(1)). Those amendments have effect in relation to accounting

periods beginning on or after 1 April 2013, subject to transitional provisions. Note that any power conferred on the Secretary of State or the Treasury, by virtue of Sch 16, to make regulations or an order came into force on 17 July 2013. See FA 2013 Sch 16 paras 2, 3 for commencement provisions.

[2]   In sub-s (1)(c) words inserted and words "trade X in" repealed, in sub-ss (3), (6) words substituted, and sub-s (7A) inserted, by F(No 2)A 2017 s 18, Sch 4 paras 31, 34 with effect in relation to accounting periods beginning on or after 1 April 2017, subject to transitional provisions in Sch 4 para 194. For accounting periods beginning before 1 April 2017 and ending on or after that date ("straddling periods") see F(No 2)A 2017 Sch 4 paras 190–192.

[CHAPTER 5

PROVISIONAL ENTITLEMENT TO RELIEF]

Amendments—This Part (ss 1216A–1216EC) inserted by FA 2013 s 36, Sch 16 para 1. The amendments made by Sch 16 come into force on 19 July 2013 (by virtue of SI 2013/1817 art 2(1)). Those amendments have effect in relation to accounting periods beginning on or after 1 April 2013, subject to transitional provisions. Note that any power conferred on the Secretary of State or the Treasury, by virtue of Sch 16, to make regulations or an order came into force on 17 July 2013. See FA 2013 Sch 16 paras 2, 3 for commencement provisions.

[1216E Introduction

(1) In this Chapter—

"the company" means the television production company in relation to a relevant programme,

"the completion period" means the accounting period of the company—

    (*a*) in which the relevant programme is completed, or

    (*b*) if the company does not complete the relevant programme, in which it abandons television production activities in relation to it,

"interim accounting period" means any earlier accounting period of the company during which television production activities are carried on in relation to the relevant programme,

"interim certificate" and "final certificate" have the meaning given by section 1216CC,

"the separate programme trade" means the company's separate trade in relation to the relevant programme (see section 1216B), and

"special television relief" means—

    (*a*) television tax relief, or

    (*b*) relief under section 1216DC (transfer of terminal losses from one relevant programme to another).

(2) The company's company tax return for the completion period must state that the relevant programme has been completed or that the company has abandoned television production activities in relation to it (as the case may be).][1]

Commentary—*Simon's Taxes* **D7.1248**.

Amendments—[1]   This Part (ss 1216A–1216EC) inserted by FA 2013 s 36, Sch 16 para 1. The amendments made by Sch 16 come into force on 19 July 2013 (by virtue of SI 2013/1817 art 2(1)). Those amendments have effect in relation to accounting periods beginning on or after 1 April 2013, subject to transitional provisions. Note that any power conferred on the Secretary of State or the Treasury, by virtue of Sch 16, to make regulations or an order came into force on 17 July 2013. See FA 2013 Sch 16 paras 2, 3 for commencement provisions.

[1216EA Certification as a British programme

(1) The company is not entitled to special television relief for an interim accounting period unless its company tax return for the period is accompanied by an interim certificate.

(2) If an interim certificate ceases to be in force (otherwise than on being superseded by a final certificate) or is revoked, the company—

    (*a*) is not entitled to special television relief for any period for which its entitlement depended on the certificate, and

    (*b*) must amend accordingly its company tax return for any such period.

(3) If the relevant programme is completed by the company—

    (*a*) its company tax return for the completion period must be accompanied by a final certificate,

    (*b*) if that requirement is met, the final certificate has effect for the completion period and for any interim accounting period, and

    (*c*) if that requirement is not met, the company—

        (i) is not entitled to special television relief for any period, and

        (ii) must amend accordingly its company tax return for any period for which such relief was claimed.

(4) If the company abandons television production activities in relation to the relevant programme—

    (*a*) its company tax return for the completion period may be accompanied by an interim certificate, and

    (*b*) the abandonment of television production activities does not affect any entitlement to special television relief in that or any previous accounting period.

(5) If a final certificate is revoked, the company—

    (*a*) is not entitled to special television relief for any period, and

    (*b*) must amend accordingly its company tax return for any period for which such relief was claimed.][1]

Commentary—*Simon's Taxes* **D7.1248**.

Cross-references—See FA 2016 s 180, Sch 24 Pt 1 (power to obtain information about tax advantages claimed under Parts 15, 15A, 15C, 15D which constitute the grant of State aid).

HMRC Manuals—Television Production Company Manual TPC60040 (claims: abandonment).

Amendments—[1]　This Part (ss 1216A–1216EC) inserted by FA 2013 s 36, Sch 16 para 1. The amendments made by Sch 16 come into force on 19 July 2013 (by virtue of SI 2013/1817 art 2(1)). Those amendments have effect in relation to accounting periods beginning on or after 1 April 2013, subject to transitional provisions. Note that any power conferred on the Secretary of State or the Treasury, by virtue of Sch 16, to make regulations or an order came into force on 17 July 2013. See FA 2013 Sch 16 paras 2, 3 for commencement provisions.

[1216EB The UK expenditure condition

(1) The company is not entitled to special television relief for an interim accounting period unless—

(*a*) its company tax return for the period states the amount of planned core expenditure on the relevant programme that is UK expenditure, and

(*b*) that amount is such as to indicate that the condition in section 1216CE (the UK expenditure condition) will be met on completion of the programme.

If those requirements are met, the company is provisionally treated in relation to that period as if that condition was met.

(2) If such a statement is made but it subsequently appears that the condition will not be met on completion of the programme, the company—

(*a*) is not entitled to special television relief for any period for which its entitlement depended on such a statement, and

(*b*) must amend accordingly its company tax return for any such period.

(3) When the relevant programme is completed or the company abandons television production activities in relation to it (as the case may be), the company's company tax return for the completion period must be accompanied by a final statement of the amount of core expenditure on the programme that is UK expenditure.

(4) If that statement shows that the condition in section 1216CE is not met, the company—

(*a*) is not entitled to special television relief for any period, and

(*b*) must amend accordingly its company tax return for any period for which such relief was claimed.][1]

Commentary—*Simon's Taxes* **D7.1248**.

Cross-references—See FA 2016 s 180, Sch 24 Pt 1 (power to obtain information about tax advantages claimed under Parts 15, 15A, 15C, 15D which constitute the grant of State aid).

HMRC Manuals—Television Production Company Manual TPC40040 (minimum UK expenditure: interim accounting periods).

Amendments—[1]　This Part (ss 1216A–1216EC) inserted by FA 2013 s 36, Sch 16 para 1. The amendments made by Sch 16 come into force on 19 July 2013 (by virtue of SI 2013/1817 art 2(1)). Those amendments have effect in relation to accounting periods beginning on or after 1 April 2013, subject to transitional provisions. Note that any power conferred on the Secretary of State or the Treasury, by virtue of Sch 16, to make regulations or an order came into force on 17 July 2013. See FA 2013 Sch 16 paras 2, 3 for commencement provisions.

[1216EC Time limit for amendments and assessments

Any amendment or assessment necessary to give effect to the provisions of this Chapter may be made despite any limitation on the time within which an amendment or assessment may normally be made.][1]

Commentary—*Simon's Taxes* **D7.1248**.

Cross-references—See FA 2016 s 180, Sch 24 Pt 1 (power to obtain information about tax advantages claimed under Parts 15, 15A, 15C, 15D which constitute the grant of State aid).

HMRC Manuals—Television Production Company Manual TPC60060 (claims: amending returns).

Amendments—[1]　This Part (ss 1216A–1216EC) inserted by FA 2013 s 36, Sch 16 para 1. The amendments made by Sch 16 come into force on 19 July 2013 (by virtue of SI 2013/1817 art 2(1)). Those amendments have effect in relation to accounting periods beginning on or after 1 April 2013, subject to transitional provisions. Note that any power conferred on the Secretary of State or the Treasury, by virtue of Sch 16, to make regulations or an order came into force on 17 July 2013. See FA 2013 Sch 16 paras 2, 3 for commencement provisions.

[PART 15B
VIDEO GAMES DEVELOPMENT]

Commentary—*Simon's Taxes* **D7.1250**.

Amendments—This Part (ss 1217A–1217EC) inserted by FA 2013 s 36, Sch 17 para 1 with effect in relation to accounting periods beginning on or after 1 April 2014 (by virtue of SI 2014/1962). Powers conferred on the Secretary of State or the Treasury, by virtue of Sch 17, to make regulations or an order came into force on 17 July 2013. See FA 2013 Sch 17 paras 2–4 for commencement provisions.

[CHAPTER 1

INTRODUCTION]

[Introductory

1217A Overview of Part

(1) This Part is about video games development.

(2) Sections 1217AA to 1217AF contain definitions and other provisions about interpretation that apply for the purposes of this Part.

See, in particular—

(*a*) section 1217AA, which contains provision about the meaning of "video game", and

(*b*) section 1217AB, which explains how a company comes to be treated as the video games development company in relation to a video game.

(3) Chapter 2 is about the taxation of the activities of a video games development company and includes—

(*a*) provision for the company's activities in relation to [each qualifying]² video game to be treated as a separate trade, and

(*b*) provision about the calculation of the profits and losses of that trade.

(4) Chapter 3 is about relief (called "video games tax relief") which can be given to a video games development company—

(*a*) by way of additional deductions to be made in calculating the profits or losses of the company's separate trade, or

(*b*) by way of a payment (a "video game tax credit") to be made on the company's surrender of losses from that trade.

(5) Chapter 4 is about the relief which can be given for losses made by a video games development company in its separate trade, including provision for certain such losses to be transferred to other separate trades.

(6) Chapter 5 provides—

(*a*) for relief under Chapters 3 and 4 to be given on a provisional basis, and

(*b*) for such relief to be withdrawn if it turns out that conditions that must be met for such relief to be given are not actually met.]¹

HMRC Manuals—Video Games Development Company Manual VGDC10010 (overview and general definitions: introduction).
Amendments—¹ This Part (ss 1217A–1217EC) inserted by FA 2013 s 36, Sch 17 para 1 with effect in relation to accounting periods beginning on or after 1 April 2014 (by virtue of SI 2014/1962). Powers conferred on the Secretary of State or the Treasury, by virtue of Sch 17, to make regulations or an order came into force on 17 July 2013. See FA 2013 Sch 17 paras 2–4 for commencement provisions.
²   In sub-s (3)(*a*) words substituted for word "its" by FA 2014 s 34(1), (2) with effect in relation to accounting periods beginning on or after 1 April 2014 (the day specified by Treasury Order made under FA 2013 Sch 17 para 3). (See FA 2014 s 34(8) for commencement provision.)

[Interpretation

1217AA "Video game" etc

(1) This section applies for the purposes of this Part.

(2) "Video game" does not include—

(*a*) anything produced for advertising or promotional purposes, or

(*b*) anything produced for the purposes of gambling (within the meaning of the Gambling Act 2005).

(3) References to a video game include the game's soundtrack.

(4) A video game is completed when it is first in a form in which it can reasonably be regarded as ready for copies of it to be made and made available to the general public.]¹

Commentary—*Simon's Taxes* D7.1252.
HMRC Manuals—Video Games Development Company Manual VGDC10150 (when a video game is 'completed').
VGDC40050 (qualifying video games: video games).
Amendments—¹ This Part (ss 1217A–1217EC) inserted by FA 2013 s 36, Sch 17 para 1 with effect in relation to accounting periods beginning on or after 1 April 2014 (by virtue of SI 2014/1962). Powers conferred on the Secretary of State or the Treasury, by virtue of Sch 17, to make regulations or an order came into force on 17 July 2013. See FA 2013 Sch 17 paras 2–4 for commencement provisions.

[1217AB Video games development company

(1) For the purposes of this Part "video games development company" is to be read in accordance with this section.

(2) There cannot be more than one video games development company in relation to a video game.

(3) A company is the video games development company in relation to a video game if the company (otherwise than in partnership)—

(*a*) is responsible for designing, producing and testing the video game,

(*b*) is actively engaged in planning and decision-making during the design, production and testing of the video game, and

(*c*) directly negotiates, contracts and pays for rights, goods and services in relation to the video game.

(4) If there is more than one company meeting the description in subsection (3), the company that is most directly engaged in the activities referred to in that subsection is the video games development company in relation to the video game.

(5) If there is no company meeting the description in subsection (3), there is no video games development company in relation to the video game.

(6) A company may elect to be regarded as a company which does not meet the description in subsection (3).

(7) The election—

> (a) must be made by the company by being included in its company tax return for an accounting period (and may be included in the return originally made or by amendment), and
>
> (b) may be withdrawn by the company only by amending its company tax return for that accounting period.

(8) The election has effect in relation to video games which begin to be produced in that or any subsequent accounting period.]¹

Commentary—*Simon's Taxes* D7.1252.

HMRC Manuals—Video Games Development Company Manual VGDC10110 (video games development company).

Amendments—¹ This Part (ss 1217A–1217EC) inserted by FA 2013 s 36, Sch 17 para 1 with effect in relation to accounting periods beginning on or after 1 April 2014 (by virtue of SI 2014/1962). Powers conferred on the Secretary of State or the Treasury, by virtue of Sch 17, to make regulations or an order came into force on 17 July 2013. See FA 2013 Sch 17 paras 2–4 for commencement provisions.

[1217AC "Video game development activities" etc

(1) In this Part "video game development activities", in relation to a video game, means the activities involved in designing, producing and testing the video game.

(2) The Treasury may by regulations—

> (a) amend subsection (1),
>
> (b) provide that specified activities are or are not to be regarded as video game development activities or as video game development activities of a particular description, and
>
> (c) provide that, in relation to a specified description of video game, references to video game development activities of a particular description are to be read as references to such activities as may be specified.

"Specified" means specified in the regulations.]¹

Commentary—*Simon's Taxes* D7.1252.

HMRC Manuals—Video Games Development Company Manual VGDC10130 (video game development activities and development expenditure).

Amendments—¹ This Part (ss 1217A–1217EC) inserted by FA 2013 s 36, Sch 17 para 1 with effect in relation to accounting periods beginning on or after 1 April 2014 (by virtue of SI 2014/1962). Powers conferred on the Secretary of State or the Treasury, by virtue of Sch 17, to make regulations or an order came into force on 17 July 2013. See FA 2013 Sch 17 paras 2–4 for commencement provisions.

[1217AD "Core expenditure"

(1) In this Part "core expenditure", in relation to a video game, means expenditure on designing, producing and testing the video game.

(2) But the following descriptions of expenditure are not to be regarded as core expenditure for the purposes of this Part—

> (a) any expenditure incurred in designing the initial concept for a video game;
>
> (b) any expenditure incurred in debugging a completed video game or carrying out any maintenance in connection with such a video game.]¹

Commentary—*Simon's Taxes* D7.1259, D7.1264.

HMRC Manuals—Video Games Development Company Manual VGDC10130 (core expenditure and stages of video game development).

VGDC50010 (eligible expenditure: core expenditure).

Amendments—¹ This Part (ss 1217A–1217EC) inserted by FA 2013 s 36, Sch 17 para 1 with effect in relation to accounting periods beginning on or after 1 April 2014 (by virtue of SI 2014/1962). Powers conferred on the Secretary of State or the Treasury, by virtue of Sch 17, to make regulations or an order came into force on 17 July 2013. See FA 2013 Sch 17 paras 2–4 for commencement provisions.

[1217AE "[EEA] expenditure" etc

[(1) In this Part, "EEA expenditure", in relation to a video game, means expenditure on goods or services that are provided from within the European Economic Area.]²

(2) Any apportionment of expenditure as between [EEA expenditure and non-EEA expenditure]² for the purposes of this Part is to be made on a just and reasonable basis.

(3) The Treasury may by regulations amend subsection (1).]¹

Commentary—*Simon's Taxes* D7.1259.

HMRC Manuals—Video Games Development Company Manual VGDC10140 (meaning of 'EEA expenditure').

VGDC50050 (eligible expenditure: European economic area (EEA) expenditure).

VGDC50110 (eligible expenditure: apportionments 'fair and reasonable').

Amendments—¹ This Part (ss 1217A–1217EC) inserted by FA 2013 s 36, Sch 17 para 1 with effect in relation to accounting periods beginning on or after 1 April 2014 (by virtue of SI 2014/1962). Powers conferred on the Secretary of State or the Treasury, by virtue of Sch 17, to make regulations or an order came into force on 17 July 2013. See FA 2013 Sch 17 paras 2–4 for commencement provisions.

² In the heading, word substituted, sub-s (1) substituted, and in sub-s (2) words substituted, by FA 2014 s 34(1), (3) with effect in relation to accounting periods beginning on or after 1 April 2014 (the day specified by Treasury order made under FA 2013 Sch 17 para 3). (See FA 2014 s 34(8) for commencement provision.)

Amendments—[1] This Part (ss 1217A–1217EC) inserted by FA 2013 s 36, Sch 17 para 1 with effect in relation to accounting periods beginning on or after 1 April 2014 (by virtue of SI 2014/1962). Powers conferred on the Secretary of State or the Treasury, by virtue of Sch 17, to make regulations or an order came into force on 17 July 2013. See FA 2013 Sch 17 paras 2–4 for commencement provisions.

[CHAPTER 3

VIDEO GAMES TAX RELIEF]

Commentary—*Simon's Taxes* D7.1258, D7.1255.
Amendments—This Part (ss 1217A–1217EC) inserted by FA 2013 s 36, Sch 17 para 1 with effect in relation to accounting periods beginning on or after 1 April 2014 (by virtue of SI 2014/1962). Powers conferred on the Secretary of State or the Treasury, by virtue of Sch 17, to make regulations or an order came into force on 17 July 2013. See FA 2013 Sch 17 paras 2–4 for commencement provisions.

[Introductory

1217C Availability and overview of video games tax relief
(1) This Chapter applies for corporation tax purposes to a company that is the video games development company in relation to a video game.
(2) Relief under this Chapter ("video games tax relief") is available to the company if the conditions specified in the following sections are met in relation to the video game—
   (*a*) section 1217CA (intended for supply),
   (*b*) section 1217CB (British video game), and
   (*c*) section 1217CE ([EEA expenditure]²).
(3) Video games tax relief is given by way of—
   (*a*) additional deductions (see sections 1217CF and 1217CG), and
   (*b*) video game tax credits (see sections 1217CH to 1217CJ).
(4) But video games tax relief is not available in respect of any expenditure if—
   (*a*) the company is entitled to an R&D expenditure credit under Chapter 6A of Part 3 in respect of the expenditure, or
   (*b*) the company has obtained relief under Part 13 (additional relief for expenditure on research and development) in respect of the expenditure.
(5) Sections 1217CK to 1217CN contain provision about unpaid costs, artificially inflated claims and confidentiality of information.
(6) In this Chapter "the separate video game trade" means the company's separate trade in relation to the video game (see section 1217B).
(7) See Schedule 18 to FA 1998 (in particular, Part 9D) for information about the procedure for making claims for video games tax relief.]¹

Commentary—*Simon's Taxes* D7.1258, D7.1255.
HMRC Manuals—Video Games Development Company Manual VGDC40010 (qualifying video games: introduction). VGDC80070 (avoidance and disclosure: interaction with research and development credits and state aid).
Amendments—[1] This Part (ss 1217A–1217EC) inserted by FA 2013 s 36, Sch 17 para 1 with effect in relation to accounting periods beginning on or after 1 April 2014 (by virtue of SI 2014/1962). Powers conferred on the Secretary of State or the Treasury, by virtue of Sch 17, to make regulations or an order came into force on 17 July 2013. See FA 2013 Sch 17 paras 2–4 for commencement provisions.
² In sub-s (2), words substituted for words "UK expenditure" by FA 2014 s 34(1), (6)(*a*) with effect in relation to accounting periods beginning on or after 1 April 2014 (the day specified by Treasury order made under FA 2013 Sch 17 para 3). (See FA 2014 s 34(8) for commencement provision.)
Prospective amendments—In sub-s (2)(*c*) word "European" to be substituted for word "EEA" by the Taxes (Amendments) (EU Exit) Regulations, SI 2019/689 reg 16(1), (23) with effect from Implementation Period completion day (see EU(WA)A 2020 Sch 5 para 1(1)).

["Intended for supply"

1217CA Intended for supply
(1) The video game must be intended for supply to the general public.
(2) Whether this condition is met is determined when video game production activities begin, so that—
   (*a*) where a video game is originally intended for supply, this condition continues to be met even if that ceases to be the intention, and
   (*b*) where a video game is not originally intended for supply, this condition is not met even if that becomes the intention.]¹

Commentary—*Simon's Taxes* D7.1260.
HMRC Manuals—Video Games Development Company Manual VGDC40020 (qualifying video games: intended for supply).
Amendments—[1] This Part (ss 1217A–1217EC) inserted by FA 2013 s 36, Sch 17 para 1 with effect in relation to accounting periods beginning on or after 1 April 2014 (by virtue of SI 2014/1962). Powers conferred on the Secretary of State or the Treasury, by virtue of Sch 17, to make regulations or an order came into force on 17 July 2013. See FA 2013 Sch 17 paras 2–4 for commencement provisions.

[British video games

1217CB British video game

(1) The video game must be certified by the Secretary of State as a British video game.

(2) The Secretary of State, with the approval of the Treasury, may by regulations specify conditions which must be met by a video game before it may be certified as a British video game.

These conditions are known as the "cultural test".

(3) Regulations under subsection (2) may—

    (*a*) specify different conditions in relation to different descriptions of video game,

    (*b*) provide that specified descriptions of video game may not be certified as a British video game, and

    (*c*) enable the Secretary of State to direct that any provision made by virtue of paragraph (*b*) does not apply to a video game that meets specified conditions.

"Specified" means specified in the regulations.

(4) Regulations under subsection (2) are to be made by statutory instrument.

(5) A statutory instrument containing regulations under subsection (2) is subject to annulment in pursuance of a resolution of the House of Commons.

(6) Sections 1217CC and 1217CD contain further provision about certification of video games as British video games, including provision about applications for, and withdrawal of, certification.][1]

Commentary—*Simon's Taxes* **D7.1261**.

HMRC Manuals—Video Games Development Company Manual VGDC40030 (qualifying video games: British video game). VGDC80010 (avoidance and disclosure: exchange of information between HMRC and DCMS/BFI certification unit).

Regulations—Cultural Test (Video Games) Regulations, SI 2014/1958.

Amendments—[1] This Part (ss 1217A–1217EC) inserted by FA 2013 s 36, Sch 17 para 1 with effect in relation to accounting periods beginning on or after 1 April 2014 (by virtue of SI 2014/1962). Powers conferred on the Secretary of State or the Treasury, by virtue of Sch 17, to make regulations or an order came into force on 17 July 2013. See FA 2013 Sch 17 paras 2–4 for commencement provisions.

[1217CC Applications for certification

(1) An application for certification of a video game as a British video game is to be made to the Secretary of State by the video games development company.

(2) The application may be for an interim or final certificate.

(3) An interim certificate is a certificate that—

    (*a*) is granted before the video game is completed, and

    (*b*) states that the video game, if completed in accordance with the proposals set out in the application, will be a British video game.

(4) A final certificate is a certificate that—

    (*a*) is granted after the video game is completed, and

    (*b*) states that the video game is a British video game.

(5) The applicant must provide the Secretary of State with any documents or information which the Secretary of State requires in order to determine the application.

(6) The Secretary of State may require information provided for the purposes of the application to be accompanied by a statutory declaration, made by the person providing it, as to the truth of the information.

(7) The Secretary of State may by regulations make provision supplementing this section, including—

    (*a*) provision about the form of applications,

    (*b*) provision about the particulars and evidence necessary for satisfying the Secretary of State that a video game meets the cultural test, and

    (*c*) provision that any statutory declaration which is required by subsection (6) to be made by any person may be made on the person's behalf by such person as is specified in the regulations.

(8) Regulations under subsection (7) are to be made by statutory instrument.

(9) A statutory instrument containing regulations under subsection (7) is subject to annulment in pursuance of a resolution of the House of Commons.][1]

Commentary—*Simon's Taxes* **D7.1261**.

HMRC Manuals—Video Games Development Company Manual VGDC40030 (qualifying video games: certification).

Regulations—Cultural Test (Video Games) Regulations, SI 2014/1958.

Amendments—[1] This Part (ss 1217A–1217EC) inserted by FA 2013 s 36, Sch 17 para 1 with effect in relation to accounting periods beginning on or after 1 April 2014 (by virtue of SI 2014/1962). Powers conferred on the Secretary of State or the Treasury, by virtue of Sch 17, to make regulations or an order came into force on 17 July 2013. See FA 2013 Sch 17 paras 2–4 for commencement provisions.

[1217CD Certification and withdrawal of certification

(1) If the Secretary of State is satisfied that the requirements are met for interim or final certification of a video game as a British video game, the Secretary of State must certify the video game accordingly.

(2) If the Secretary of State is not satisfied that those requirements are met, the Secretary of State must refuse the application.

CTA 2009

(3) An interim certificate—

   (a) may be given subject to conditions, and (unless the Secretary of State directs otherwise) is of no effect if the conditions are not met, and

   (b) may be expressed to expire after a specified period, and (unless the Secretary of State directs otherwise) ceases to have effect at the end of that period.

(4) An interim certificate ceases to have effect when a final certificate is issued.

(5) If it appears to the Secretary of State that a video game certified under this Part ought not to have been certified, the Secretary of State may revoke its certification.

(6) Unless the Secretary of State directs otherwise, a certificate that is revoked is treated as never having had effect.][1]

Commentary—*Simon's Taxes* **D7.1261**.

HMRC Manuals—Video Games Development Company Manual VGDC80010 (authority to revoke a certificate).

Amendments—[1]   This Part (ss 1217A–1217EC) inserted by FA 2013 s 36, Sch 17 para 1 with effect in relation to accounting periods beginning on or after 1 April 2014 (by virtue of SI 2014/1962). Powers conferred on the Secretary of State or the Treasury, by virtue of Sch 17, to make regulations or an order came into force on 17 July 2013. See FA 2013 Sch 17 paras 2–4 for commencement provisions.

[[EEA expenditure]

1217CE [EEA expenditure]

(1) At least 25% of the core expenditure on the video game incurred by the company must be [EEA expenditure][2].

(2) The Treasury may by regulations amend the percentage specified in subsection (1).][1]

Commentary—*Simon's Taxes* **D7.1259**.

HMRC Manuals—Video Games Development Company Manual VGDC40040 (minimum European economic area (EEA) expenditure).

Amendments—[1]   This Part (ss 1217A–1217EC) inserted by FA 2013 s 36, Sch 17 para 1 with effect in relation to accounting periods beginning on or after 1 April 2014 (by virtue of SI 2014/1962). Powers conferred on the Secretary of State or the Treasury, by virtue of Sch 17, to make regulations or an order came into force on 17 July 2013. See FA 2013 Sch 17 paras 2–4 for commencement provisions.

[2]   In section heading and italic heading preceding it, and in sub-s (1), words substituted for words "UK expenditure" by FA 2014 s 34(1), (6)(b)–(d) with effect in relation to accounting periods beginning on or after 1 April 2014 (the day specified by Treasury order made under FA 2013 Sch 17 para 3). (See FA 2014 s 34(8) for commencement provision.)

Prospective amendments—In sub-s (1), and in the heading, words "European expenditure" to be substituted for words "EEA expenditure" by the Taxes (Amendments) (EU Exit) Regulations, SI 2019/689 reg 16(1), (24) with effect from Implementation Period completion day (see EU(WA)A 2020 Sch 5 para 1(1)).

[Additional deductions

1217CF Additional deduction for qualifying expenditure

(1) If video games tax relief is available to the company, it may (on making a claim) make an additional deduction in respect of qualifying expenditure on the video game.

(2) The deduction is made in calculating the profit or loss of the separate video game trade.

(3) In this Chapter "qualifying expenditure" means core expenditure on the video game that falls to be taken into account under Chapter 2 in calculating the profit or loss of the separate video game trade for tax purposes.

[(3A) But if the core expenditure on the video game includes subcontractor payments which (in total) exceed £1 million, the excess is not "qualifying expenditure".][2]

(4) The Treasury may by regulations—

   (a) amend [subsections (3) and (3A)][2], and

   (b) provide that expenditure of a specified description is or is not to be regarded as qualifying expenditure.

[(5) In this section, "sub-contractor payment" means a payment made by the company to another person in respect of work on design, production or testing of the video game that is contracted out by the company to the person.][2]][1]

Commentary—*Simon's Taxes* **D7.1264**.

HMRC Manuals—Video Games Development Company Manual VGDC50060 (subcontractor costs).

Amendments—[1]   This Part (ss 1217A–1217EC) inserted by FA 2013 s 36, Sch 17 para 1 with effect in relation to accounting periods beginning on or after 1 April 2014 (by virtue of SI 2014/1962). Powers conferred on the Secretary of State or the Treasury, by virtue of Sch 17, to make regulations or an order came into force on 17 July 2013. See FA 2013 Sch 17 paras 2–4 for commencement provisions.

[2]   Sub-ss (3A), (5) inserted, and in sub-s (4)(a) words substituted for words "subsection (3)", by FA 2014 s 34(1), (5) with effect in relation to accounting periods beginning on or after 1 April 2014 (the day specified by Treasury order made under FA 2013 Sch 17 para 3). (See FA 2014 s 34(8) for commencement provision.)

[1217CG Amount of additional deduction

(1) For the first period of account during which the separate video game trade is carried on, the amount of the additional deduction is—

E

where E is—

   (a) so much of the qualifying expenditure as is [EEA expenditure][2], or (*b*) if less, 80% of the total amount of qualifying expenditure.

(2) For any period of account after the first, the amount of the additional deduction is given by—

E − P

where—

     E is—

         (*a*) so much of the qualifying expenditure incurred to date as is [EEA expenditure][2], or

         (*b*) if less, 80% of the total amount of qualifying expenditure incurred to date, and

     P is the total amount of the additional deductions given for previous periods.

(3) The Treasury may by regulations amend this section.][1]

Commentary—*Simon's Taxes* **D7.1264.**

HMRC Manuals—Video Games Development Company Manual VGDC55040 (additional deduction). VGDC55050 (additional deduction multi- period developments). VGDC55030 (rates of relief).

Amendments—[1]   This Part (ss 1217A–1217EC) inserted by FA 2013 s 36, Sch 17 para 1 with effect in relation to accounting periods beginning on or after 1 April 2014 (by virtue of SI 2014/1962). Powers conferred on the Secretary of State or the Treasury, by virtue of Sch 17, to make regulations or an order came into force on 17 July 2013. See FA 2013 Sch 17 paras 2–4 for commencement provisions.

[2]   In sub-ss (1)(*a*), (2)(*a*), words substituted for words "UK expenditure" by FA 2014 s 34(1), (6)(*e*) with effect in relation to accounting periods beginning on or after 1 April 2014 (the day specified by Treasury order made under FA 2013 Sch 17 para 3). (See FA 2014 s 34(8) for commencement provision.)

Prospective amendments—Words "European expenditure" to be substituted for words "EEA expenditure", in both places where the expression occurs, by the Taxes (Amendments) (EU Exit) Regulations, SI 2019/689 reg 16(1), (25) with effect from Implementation Period completion day (see EU(WA)A 2020 Sch 5 para 1(1)).

[Video game tax credits

1217CH Video game tax credit claimable if company has surrenderable loss

(1) If video games tax relief is available to the company, it may claim a video game tax credit for an accounting period in which it has a surrenderable loss.

(2) The company's surrenderable loss in an accounting period is—

         (*a*) the company's available loss for the period in the separate video game trade (see subsection (3)), or

         (*b*) if less, the available qualifying expenditure for the period (see subsections (5) and (6)).

(3) The company's available loss for an accounting period is given by—

L + RUL

where—

     L is the amount of the company's loss for the period in the separate video game trade, and

     RUL is the amount of any relevant unused loss of the company (see subsection (4)).

(4) The "relevant unused loss" of a company is so much of any available loss of the company for the previous accounting period as has not been—

         (*a*) surrendered under section 1217CI(1), or

         (*b*) carried forward under section 45 [or 45B][2] of CTA 2010 and set against profits of the separate video game trade.

(5) For the first period of account during which the separate video game trade is carried on, the available qualifying expenditure is the amount that is E for that period for the purposes of section 1217CG(1).

(6) For any period of account after the first, the available qualifying expenditure is given by—

E − S

where—

     E is the amount that is E for that period for the purposes of section 1217CG(2), and

     S is the total amount previously surrendered under section 1217CI(1).

(7) If a period of account of the separate video game trade does not coincide with an accounting period, any necessary apportionments are to be made by reference to the number of days in the periods concerned.][1]

Commentary—*Simon's Taxes* **D7.1266.**

HMRC Manuals—Video Games Development Company Manual VGDC55100 (surrenderable losses and video games tax credit).

Amendments—[1]   This Part (ss 1217A–1217EC) inserted by FA 2013 s 36, Sch 17 para 1 with effect in relation to accounting periods beginning on or after 1 April 2014 (by virtue of SI 2014/1962). Powers conferred on the Secretary of State or the Treasury, by virtue of Sch 17, to make regulations or an order came into force on 17 July 2013. See FA 2013 Sch 17 paras 2–4 for commencement provisions.

[2]   In sub-s (4)(*b*), words inserted by F(No 2)A 2017 s 18, Sch 4 paras 128, 141 with effect in relation to accounting periods beginning on or after 1 April 2017, subject to transitional provisions in Sch 4 para 194. For accounting periods beginning before 1 April 2017 and ending on or after that date ("straddling periods") see F(No 2)A 2017 Sch 4 paras 190–192.

[1217CI Surrendering of loss and amount of video game tax credit

(1) The company may surrender the whole or part of its surrenderable loss in an accounting period.

(2) If the company surrenders the whole or part of that loss, the amount of the video game tax credit to which it is entitled for the accounting period is 25% of the amount of the loss surrendered.

(3) The company's available loss for the accounting period is reduced by the amount surrendered.][1]

Commentary—*Simon's Taxes* **D7.1266**.

HMRC Manuals—Video Games Development Company Manual VGDC55100 (surrenderable losses and video games tax credit).

Amendments—[1] This Part (ss 1217A–1217EC) inserted by FA 2013 s 36, Sch 17 para 1 with effect in relation to accounting periods beginning on or after 1 April 2014 (by virtue of SI 2014/1962). Powers conferred on the Secretary of State or the Treasury, by virtue of Sch 17, to make regulations or an order came into force on 17 July 2013. See FA 2013 Sch 17 paras 2–4 for commencement provisions.

[1217CJ Payment in respect of video game tax credit

(1) If the company—

    (*a*) is entitled to a video game tax credit for a period, and

    (*b*) makes a claim,

the Commissioners for Her Majesty's Revenue and Customs ("the Commissioners") must pay to the company the amount of the credit.

(2) An amount payable in respect of—

    (*a*) a video game tax credit, or

    (*b*) interest on a video game tax credit under section 826 of ICTA,

may be applied in discharging any liability of the company to pay corporation tax.

To the extent that it is so applied the Commissioners' liability under subsection (1) is discharged. (3) If the company's company tax return for the accounting period is enquired into by the Commissioners, no payment in respect of a video game tax credit for that period need be made before the Commissioners' enquiries are completed (see paragraph 32 of Schedule 18 to FA 1998). In those circumstances the Commissioners may make a payment on a provisional basis of such amount as they consider appropriate.

(4) No payment need be made in respect of a video game tax credit for an accounting period before the company has paid to the Commissioners any amount that it is required to pay for payment periods ending in that accounting period—

    (*a*) under PAYE regulations,

    (*b*) under section 966 of ITA 2007 (visiting performers), or

    (*c*) in respect of Class 1 national insurance contributions under Part 1 of the Social Security Contributions and Benefits Act 1992 or Part 1 of the Social Security Contributions and Benefits (Northern Ireland) Act 1992.

(5) A payment in respect of a video game tax credit is not income of the company for any tax purpose.][1]

Commentary—*Simon's Taxes* **D7.1266**.

HMRC Manuals—Video Games Development Company Manual VGDC60070 (payment of credit).

Amendments—[1] This Part (ss 1217A–1217EC) inserted by FA 2013 s 36, Sch 17 para 1 with effect in relation to accounting periods beginning on or after 1 April 2014 (by virtue of SI 2014/1962). Powers conferred on the Secretary of State or the Treasury, by virtue of Sch 17, to make regulations or an order came into force on 17 July 2013. See FA 2013 Sch 17 paras 2–4 for commencement provisions.

[Miscellaneous]

1217CK No account to be taken of amount if unpaid

(1) In determining for the purposes of this Chapter the amount of costs incurred on a video game at the end of a period of account, ignore any amount that has not been paid 4 months after the end of that period.

(2) This is without prejudice to the operation of section 1217BD (when costs are taken to be incurred).][1]

Commentary—*Simon's Taxes* **D7.1264, D7.1266**.

HMRC Manuals—Video Games Development Company Manual VGDC80040 (unpaid amounts).

Amendments—[1] This Part (ss 1217A–1217EC) inserted by FA 2013 s 36, Sch 17 para 1 with effect in relation to accounting periods beginning on or after 1 April 2014 (by virtue of SI 2014/1962). Powers conferred on the Secretary of State or the Treasury, by virtue of Sch 17, to make regulations or an order came into force on 17 July 2013. See FA 2013 Sch 17 paras 2–4 for commencement provisions.

[1217CL Artificially inflated claims for additional deduction or tax credit

(1) So far as a transaction is attributable to arrangements entered into wholly or mainly for a disqualifying purpose, it is to be ignored in determining for any period—

    (*a*) any additional deduction which a company may make under this Chapter, and

    (*b*) any video game tax credit to be given to a company.

(2) Arrangements are entered into wholly or mainly for a disqualifying purpose if their main object, or one of their main objects, is to enable a company to obtain—

    (*a*) an additional deduction under this Chapter to which it would not otherwise be entitled or of a greater amount than that to which it would otherwise be entitled, or

    (*b*) a video game tax credit to which it would not otherwise be entitled or of a greater amount than that to which it would otherwise be entitled.

(3) "Arrangements" includes any scheme, agreement or understanding, whether or not legally enforceable.][1]

Commentary—*Simon's Taxes* **D7.1258**.

HMRC Manuals—Video Games Development Company Manual VGDC80050 (inflation of claims). VGDC80030 (avoidance valuation of core expenditure).

Amendments—[1] This Part (ss 1217A–1217EC) inserted by FA 2013 s 36, Sch 17 para 1 with effect in relation to accounting periods beginning on or after 1 April 2014 (by virtue of SI 2014/1962). Powers conferred on the Secretary of State or the Treasury, by virtue of Sch 17, to make regulations or an order came into force on 17 July 2013. See FA 2013 Sch 17 paras 2–4 for commencement provisions.

[1217CM Confidentiality of information

(1) Section 18(1) of the Commissioners for Revenue and Customs Act 2005 (restriction on disclosure by Revenue and Customs officials) does not prevent disclosure to the Secretary of State for the purposes of the Secretary of State's functions under any of the provisions listed in subsection (2).

(2) The provisions referred to in subsection (1) are—

    (a) sections 1216CB to 1216CD (certification of relevant programmes as British),

    (b) sections 1217CB to 1217CD (certification of video games as British), and

    (c) Schedule 1 to the Films Act 1985 (certification of films as British).

(3) Information so disclosed may be disclosed to the British Film Institute.

(4) The Treasury may by order amend subsection (3)—

    (a) so as to substitute for the person or body specified in that subsection a different person or body, or

    (b) in consequence of a change in the name of the person or body so specified.

(5) A person to whom information is disclosed under subsection (1) or (3) may not otherwise disclose it except—

    (a) for the purposes of the Secretary of State's functions under any of the provisions listed in subsection (2),

    (b) if the disclosure is authorised by an enactment,

    (c) in pursuance of an order of a court,

    (d) for the purposes of a criminal investigation or legal proceedings (whether civil or criminal) connected with the operation of any of Parts 15 to 15B of this Act or Schedule 1 to the Films Act 1985,

    (e) with the consent of the Commissioners for Her Majesty's Revenue and Customs, or

    (f) with the consent of each person to whom the information relates.][1]

HMRC Manuals—Video Games Development Company Manual VGDC80010 (avoidance and disclosure: confidentiality).

Amendments—[1] This Part (ss 1217A–1217EC) inserted by FA 2013 s 36, Sch 17 para 1 with effect in relation to accounting periods beginning on or after 1 April 2014 (by virtue of SI 2014/1962). Powers conferred on the Secretary of State or the Treasury, by virtue of Sch 17, to make regulations or an order came into force on 17 July 2013. See FA 2013 Sch 17 paras 2–4 for commencement provisions.

[1217CN Wrongful disclosure

(1) A person ("X") commits an offence if—

    (a) X discloses revenue and customs information relating to a person (as defined in section 19(2) of the Commissioners for Revenue and Customs Act 2005),

    (b) the identity of the person to whom the information relates is specified in the disclosure or can be deduced from it, and

    (c) the disclosure contravenes section 1217CM(5).

(2) If a person ("Y") is charged with an offence under subsection (1), it is a defence for Y to prove that Y reasonably believed—

    (a) that the disclosure was lawful, or

    (b) that the information had already and lawfully been made available to the public.

(3) A person guilty of an offence under subsection (1) is liable—

    (a) on conviction on indictment, to imprisonment for a term not exceeding two years or a fine or both, or

    (b) on summary conviction, to imprisonment for a term not exceeding 12 months or a fine not exceeding the statutory maximum or both.

(4) A prosecution for an offence under subsection (1) may be brought in England and Wales [only by or with the consent of the Director of Public Prosecutions.][2]

(5) A prosecution for an offence under subsection (1) may be brought in Northern Ireland only—

    (a) by the Commissioners for Her Majesty's Revenue and Customs, or

    (b) with the consent of the Director of Public Prosecutions for Northern Ireland.

(6) In the application of this section—

    (a) in England and Wales, in relation to an offence committed before the commencement of section 282 of the Criminal Justice Act 2003, or

    (b) in Northern Ireland,

the reference in subsection (3)(b) to 12 months is to be read as a reference to 6 months.][1]

HMRC Manuals—Video Games Development Company Manual VGDC80010 (wrongful disclosure).

[(7A) A deduction under section 45 or 45B of CTA 2010 which is made in reliance on this section is to be ignored for the purposes of section 269ZB of that Act (restriction on deductions from trading profits).][2]

(8) "Qualifying video game" means a video game in relation to which the conditions for video games tax relief are met (see 1217C(2)).][1]

Commentary—*Simon's Taxes* D7.1255, D7.1268.

HMRC Manuals—Video Games Development Company Manual VGDC30040 (losses: terminal losses).

Amendments—[1]   This Part (ss 1217A–1217EC) inserted by FA 2013 s 36, Sch 17 para 1 with effect in relation to accounting periods beginning on or after 1 April 2014 (by virtue of SI 2014/1962). Powers conferred on the Secretary of State or the Treasury, by virtue of Sch 17, to make regulations or an order came into force on 17 July 2013. See FA 2013 Sch 17 paras 2–4 for commencement provisions.

[2]   In sub-s (1)(c) words inserted and words "trade X in" repealed, in sub-ss (3), (6) words substituted, sub-s (7A) inserted, by F(No 2)A 2017 s 18, Sch 4 paras 35, 38 with effect in relation to accounting periods beginning on or after 1 April 2017, subject to transitional provisions in Sch 4 para 194. For accounting periods beginning before 1 April 2017 and ending on or after that date ("straddling periods") see F(No 2)A 2017 Sch 4 paras 190–192.

[CHAPTER 5

PROVISIONAL ENTITLEMENT TO RELIEF]

Commentary—*Simon's Taxes* D7.1268.

Amendments—This Part (ss 1217A–1217EC) inserted by FA 2013 s 36, Sch 17 para 1 with effect in relation to accounting periods beginning on or after 1 April 2014 (by virtue of SI 2014/1962). Powers conferred on the Secretary of State or the Treasury, by virtue of Sch 17, to make regulations or an order came into force on 17 July 2013. See FA 2013 Sch 17 paras 2–4 for commencement provisions.

[1217E Introduction

(1) In this Chapter—

"the company" means the video games development company in relation to a video game,

"the completion period" means the accounting period of the company—

   (a) in which the video game is completed, or

   (b) if the company does not complete the video game, in which it abandons video game development activities in relation to it,

"interim accounting period" means any earlier accounting period of the company during which video game development activities are carried on in relation to the video game,

"interim certificate" and "final certificate" have the meaning given by section 1217CC,

"the separate video game trade" means the company's separate trade in relation to the video game (see section 1217B), and

"special video games relief" means—

   (a) video games tax relief, or

   (b) relief under section 1217DC (transfer of terminal losses from one video game to another).

(2) The company's company tax return for the completion period must state that the video game has been completed or that the company has abandoned video game development activities in relation to it (as the case may be).][1]

Commentary—*Simon's Taxes* D7.1268.

Amendments—[1]   This Part (ss 1217A–1217EC) inserted by FA 2013 s 36, Sch 17 para 1 with effect in relation to accounting periods beginning on or after 1 April 2014 (by virtue of SI 2014/1962). Powers conferred on the Secretary of State or the Treasury, by virtue of Sch 17, to make regulations or an order came into force on 17 July 2013. See FA 2013 Sch 17 paras 2–4 for commencement provisions.

[1217EA Certification as a British video game

(1) The company is not entitled to special video games relief for an interim accounting period unless its company tax return for the period is accompanied by an interim certificate.

(2) If an interim certificate ceases to be in force (otherwise than on being superseded by a final certificate) or is revoked, the company—

   (a) is not entitled to special video games relief for any period for which its entitlement depended on the certificate, and

   (b) must amend accordingly its company tax return for any such period.

(3) If the video game is completed by the company—

   (a) its company tax return for the completion period must be accompanied by a final certificate,

   (b) if that requirement is met, the final certificate has effect for the completion period and for any interim accounting period, and

   (c) if that requirement is not met, the company—

      (i) is not entitled to special video games relief for any period, and

      (ii) must amend accordingly its company tax return for any period for which such relief was claimed.

(4) If the company abandons video game development activities in relation to the video game—

(*a*) its company tax return for the completion period may be accompanied by an interim certificate, and

(*b*) the abandonment of video game development activities does not affect any entitlement to special video games relief in that or any previous accounting period.

(5) If a final certificate is revoked, the company—

(*a*) is not entitled to special video games relief for any period, and

(*b*) must amend accordingly its company tax return for any period for which such relief was claimed.][1]

Commentary—*Simon's Taxes* **D7.1268**.

HMRC Manuals—Video Games Development Company Manual VGDC40050 (interim and final certificates).

Amendments—[1] This Part (ss 1217A–1217EC) inserted by FA 2013 s 36, Sch 17 para 1 with effect in relation to accounting periods beginning on or after 1 April 2014 (by virtue of SI 2014/1962). Powers conferred on the Secretary of State or the Treasury, by virtue of Sch 17, to make regulations or an order came into force on 17 July 2013. See FA 2013 Sch 17 paras 2–4 for commencement provisions.

[1217EB The [EEA expenditure] condition

(1) The company is not entitled to special video games relief for an interim accounting period unless—

(*a*) its company tax return for the period states the amount of planned core expenditure on the video game that is [EEA expenditure][2], and

(*b*) that amount is such as to indicate that the condition in section 1217CE (the [EEA expenditure][2] condition) will be met on completion of the video game.

If those requirements are met, the company is provisionally treated in relation to that period as if that condition was met.

(2) If such a statement is made but it subsequently appears that the condition will not be met on completion of the video game, the company—

(*a*) is not entitled to special video games relief for any period for which its entitlement depended on such a statement, and

(*b*) must amend accordingly its company tax return for any such period.

(3) When the video game is completed or the company abandons video game development activities in relation to it (as the case may be), the company's company tax return for the completion period must be accompanied by a final statement of the amount of core expenditure on the video game that is [EEA expenditure][2].

(4) If that statement shows that the condition in section 1217CE is not met, the company—

(*a*) is not entitled to special video games relief for any period, and

(*b*) must amend accordingly its company tax return for any period for which such relief was claimed.][1]

Commentary—*Simon's Taxes* **D7.1268**.

Amendments—[1] This Part (ss 1217A–1217EC) inserted by FA 2013 s 36, Sch 17 para 1 with effect in relation to accounting periods beginning on or after 1 April 2014 (by virtue of SI 2014/1962). Powers conferred on the Secretary of State or the Treasury, by virtue of Sch 17, to make regulations or an order came into force on 17 July 2013. See FA 2013 Sch 17 paras 2–4 for commencement provisions.

[2] In section heading and in sub-ss (1)(*a*), (*b*), (3), words substituted for words "UK expenditure" by FA 2014 s 34(1), (6)(*f*), (*g*) with effect in relation to accounting periods beginning on or after 1 April 2014 (the day specified by Treasury order made under FA 2013 Sch 17 para 3). (See FA 2014 s 34(8) for commencement provision.)

Prospective amendments—Words "European expenditure" to be substituted for words "EEA expenditure", in each place where the expression occurs (including the heading), by the Taxes (Amendments) (EU Exit) Regulations, SI 2019/689 reg 16(1), (26) with effect from Implementation Period completion day (see EU(WA)A 2020 Sch 5 para 1(1)).

[1217EC Time limit for amendments and assessments

Any amendment or assessment necessary to give effect to the provisions of this Chapter may be made despite any limitation on the time within which an amendment or assessment may normally be made.][1]

Commentary—*Simon's Taxes* **D7.1268**.

HMRC Manuals—Video Games Development Company Manual VGDC60060 (amending returns).

Amendments—[1] This Part (ss 1217A–1217EC) inserted by FA 2013 s 36, Sch 17 para 1 with effect in relation to accounting periods beginning on or after 1 April 2014 (by virtue of SI 2014/1962). Powers conferred on the Secretary of State or the Treasury, by virtue of Sch 17, to make regulations or an order came into force on 17 July 2013. See FA 2013 Sch 17 paras 2–4 for commencement provisions.

[PART 15C
THEATRICAL PRODUCTIONS]

Amendments—This Part (ss 1217F–1217OB) inserted by FA 2014 s 36, Sch 4 para 1 with effect in relation to accounting periods beginning on or after 1 September 2014, subject to transitional provisions for accounting periods straddling that date (FA 2014 Sch 4 para 17). Note that any power conferred on the Treasury, by virtue of Sch 4, to make regulations comes into force on 17 July 2014 (FA 2014 Sch 4 para 16(1)). SI 2014/2228 reg 2 provides that the amendments made by FA 2014 Sch 4 (other than the power to make regulations under para 16(1)) come into force on 22 August 2014.

[Introduction

1217F Overview

(1) This Part contains provision about tax relief for production companies in respect of their theatrical productions.

(2) Sections 1217FA to 1217FC define "production company" and "theatrical production".

(3) Section 1217G sets out the conditions a production company must meet to qualify for relief in relation to its theatrical production.

(4) Section 1217H provides for relief by way of additional deductions in respect of certain expenditure (and section 1217J is about the amount of the additional deduction).

(5) This Part also contains provision—

    (*a*) for a company that claims relief to be treated as carrying on a separate trade relating to the theatrical production (see section 1217H(3)), and

    (*b*) about the calculation of the profits and losses of that trade (see sections 1217I to 1217IF).

(6) Sections 1217K to 1217KC—

    (*a*) provide for relief by way of payments (called "theatre tax credits") to be made on the company's surrender of certain losses of that trade, and

    (*b*) set out an upper limit on relief, in connection with State aid legislation.

(7) Sections 1217LA and 1217LB are about certain cases involving tax avoidance arrangements or arrangements entered into otherwise than for genuine commercial reasons.

(8) Sections 1217M to 1217MC contain provision about the use of losses of the separate trade (including provision about relief for terminal losses).

(9) Sections 1217N and 1217NA are concerned with the provisional nature of relief given for periods preceding the period in which the company ceases to carry on the separate theatrical trade.]¹

Commentary—*Simon's Taxes* **D7.1272, D7.1275.**

Amendments—¹ This Part (ss 1217F–1217OB) inserted by FA 2014 s 36, Sch 4 para 1 with effect in relation to accounting periods beginning on or after 1 September 2014, subject to transitional provisions for accounting periods straddling that date (FA 2014 Sch 4 para 17). Note that any power conferred on the Treasury, by virtue of Sch 4, to make regulations comes into force on 17 July 2014 (FA 2014 Sch 4 para 16(1)). SI 2014/2228 reg 2 provides that the amendments made by FA 2014 Sch 4 (other than the power to make regulations under para 16(1)) come into force on 22 August 2014.

[1217FA "Theatrical production"

(1) In this Part "theatrical production" means a dramatic production or a ballet (and any ballet is therefore a theatrical production, whether or not it is also a dramatic production).
But see section 1217FB.

(2) "Dramatic production" means a production of a play, opera, musical, or other dramatic piece (whether or not involving improvisation) in relation to which the following conditions are met—

    (*a*) the actors, singers, dancers or other performers are to give their performances wholly or mainly through the playing of roles,

    (*b*) each performance in the proposed run of performances is to be live, and

    (*c*) the presentation of live performances is the main object, or one of the main objects, of the company's activities in relation to the production.

(3) "Dramatic piece" may also include, for example, a show that is to be performed by a circus.

(4) For the purposes of this section a performance is "live" if it is to an audience before whom the performers are actually present.]¹

Commentary—*Simon's Taxes* **D7.1271.**

Amendments—¹ This Part (ss 1217F–1217OB) inserted by FA 2014 s 36, Sch 4 para 1 with effect in relation to accounting periods beginning on or after 1 September 2014, subject to transitional provisions for accounting periods straddling that date (FA 2014 Sch 4 para 17). Note that any power conferred on the Treasury, by virtue of Sch 4, to make regulations comes into force on 17 July 2014 (FA 2014 Sch 4 para 16(1)). SI 2014/2228 reg 2 provides that the amendments made by FA 2014 Sch 4 (other than the power to make regulations under para 16(1)) come into force on 22 August 2014.

1217FB Productions not regarded as theatrical

(1) A dramatic production or ballet is not regarded as a theatrical production if—

    (*a*) the main purpose, or one of the main purposes, for which it is made is to advertise or promote any goods or services,

    (*b*) the performances are to consist of or include a competition or contest,

    (*c*) a wild animal is to be used in any performance,

    (*d*) the production is of a sexual nature (see subsection (3)), or

    (*e*) the making of a relevant recording is the main object, or one of the main objects, of the company's activities in relation to the production.

(2) For the purposes of subsection (1)(*c*) an animal is used in a performance if the animal performs, or is shown, in the course of the performance.

(3) A production is of a sexual nature for the purposes of subsection (1)(*d*) if the performances are to include any content the nature of which is such that, ignoring financial gain, it would be reasonable to assume the content to be included solely or principally for the purpose of sexually stimulating any member of the audience (whether by verbal or other means).

(4) "Relevant recording" means a recording of a performance—

(a) as a film (or part of a film) for exhibition to the paying general public at the commercial cinema, or

(b) for broadcast to the general public.

(5) In this section—

"broadcast" means broadcast by any means (including television, radio or the internet);

"film" has the same meaning as in Part 15 (see section 1181);

"wild animal" means an animal of a kind which is not commonly domesticated in the British Islands (and in this definition "animal" has the meaning given by section 1(1) of the Animal Welfare Act 2006).][1]

Commentary—*Simon's Taxes* **D7.1271**.

Amendments—[1] This Part (ss 1217F–1217OB) inserted by FA 2014 s 36, Sch 4 para 1 with effect in relation to accounting periods beginning on or after 1 September 2014, subject to transitional provisions for accounting periods straddling that date (FA 2014 Sch 4 para 17). Note that any power conferred on the Treasury, by virtue of Sch 4, to make regulations comes into force on 17 July 2014 (FA 2014 Sch 4 para 16(1)). SI 2014/2228 reg 2 provides that the amendments made by FA 2014 Sch 4 (other than the power to make regulations under para 16(1)) come into force on 22 August 2014.

[1217FC "Production company"

(1) A company is the production company in relation to a theatrical production if the company (acting otherwise than in partnership)—

(a) is responsible for producing, running and closing the theatrical production,

(b) is actively engaged in decision-making during the production, running and closing phases,

(c) makes an effective creative, technical and artistic contribution to the production, and

(d) directly negotiates for, contracts for and pays for rights, goods and services in relation to the production.

(2) No more than one company can be the production company in relation to a theatrical production.

(3) If more than one company meets the conditions in subsection (1) in relation to a theatrical production, the company that is most directly engaged in the activities mentioned in subsection (1) is the production company.

(4) If there is no company meeting the conditions in subsection (1), there is no production company in relation to the production.][1]

Commentary—*Simon's Taxes* **D7.1271**.

Cross-references—See FA 2016 s 180, Sch 24 Pt 1 (power to obtain information about tax advantages claimed under Parts 15, 15A, 15C, 15D which constitute the grant of State aid).

HMRC Manuals—Animation Production Company Manual APC10110 (production company: meaning).

Amendments—[1] This Part (ss 1217F–1217OB) inserted by FA 2014 s 36, Sch 4 para 1 with effect in relation to accounting periods beginning on or after 1 September 2014, subject to transitional provisions for accounting periods straddling that date (FA 2014 Sch 4 para 17). Note that any power conferred on the Treasury, by virtue of Sch 4, to make regulations comes into force on 17 July 2014 (FA 2014 Sch 4 para 16(1)). SI 2014/2228 reg 2 provides that the amendments made by FA 2014 Sch 4 (other than the power to make regulations under para 16(1)) come into force on 22 August 2014.

[*Companies qualifying for relief*

1217G How a company qualifies for relief

(1) A company qualifies for relief in relation to a theatrical production if—

(a) it is the production company in relation to the production, and

(b) the commercial purpose condition (see section 1217GA) and the EEA expenditure condition (see section 1217GB) are met.

(2) There is further provision relating to subsection (1) in section 1217LA (tax avoidance arrangements).][1]

Commentary—*Simon's Taxes* **D7.1275**.

Amendments—[1] This Part (ss 1217F–1217OB) inserted by FA 2014 s 36, Sch 4 para 1 with effect in relation to accounting periods beginning on or after 1 September 2014, subject to transitional provisions for accounting periods straddling that date (FA 2014 Sch 4 para 17). Note that any power conferred on the Treasury, by virtue of Sch 4, to make regulations comes into force on 17 July 2014 (FA 2014 Sch 4 para 16(1)). SI 2014/2228 reg 2 provides that the amendments made by FA 2014 Sch 4 (other than the power to make regulations under para 16(1)) come into force on 22 August 2014.

Prospective amendments—In sub-s (1)(b) word "European" to be substituted for word "EEA" by the Taxes (Amendments) (EU Exit) Regulations, SI 2019/689 reg 16(1), (27) with effect from Implementation Period completion day (see EU(WA)A 2020 Sch 5 para 1(1)).

[1217GA The commercial purpose condition

(1) The "commercial purpose condition" is that at the beginning of the production phase the company intends that all, or a high proportion of, the live performances that it proposes to run will be—

(a) to paying members of the general public, or

(b) provided for educational purposes.

(2) The reference in subsection (1) to "live performances" is to be read in accordance with section 1217FA(4).

(3) A performance is not regarded as provided for educational purposes if the production company is, or is associated with, a person who—

(a) has responsibility for the beneficiaries, or

(*b*) is otherwise connected with the beneficiaries (for instance, by being their employer).

(4) For the purposes of subsection (3), a production company is associated with a person ("P") if—

    (*a*) P controls the production company, or

    (*b*) P is a company which is controlled by the production company or by a person who also controls the production company.

(5) In this section—

    "the beneficiaries" means persons for whose benefit the performance will or may be provided;

    "control" has the same meaning as in Part 10 of CTA 2010 (see section 450 of that Act).][1]

Commentary—*Simon's Taxes* D7.1277.

Amendments—[1] This Part (ss 1217F–1217OB) inserted by FA 2014 s 36, Sch 4 para 1 with effect in relation to accounting periods beginning on or after 1 September 2014, subject to transitional provisions for accounting periods straddling that date (FA 2014 Sch 4 para 17). Note that any power conferred on the Treasury, by virtue of Sch 4, to make regulations comes into force on 17 July 2014 (FA 2014 Sch 4 para 16(1)). SI 2014/2228 reg 2 provides that the amendments made by FA 2014 Sch 4 (other than the power to make regulations under para 16(1)) come into force on 22 August 2014.

[1217GB The EEA expenditure condition

(1) The "EEA expenditure condition" is that at least 25% of the core expenditure on the theatrical production incurred by the company is EEA expenditure.

(2) In this Part "EEA expenditure" means expenditure on goods or services that are provided from within the European Economic Area.

(3) Any apportionment of expenditure as between EEA and non-EEA expenditure for the purposes of this Part is to be made on a just and reasonable basis.

(4) The Treasury may by regulations—

    (*a*) amend the percentage specified in subsection (1);

    (*b*) amend subsection (2).

(5) See also sections 1217N and 1217NA (which are about the giving of relief provisionally on the basis that the EEA expenditure condition will be met).][1]

Commentary—*Simon's Taxes* D7.1276.

Amendments—[1] This Part (ss 1217F–1217OB) inserted by FA 2014 s 36, Sch 4 para 1 with effect in relation to accounting periods beginning on or after 1 September 2014, subject to transitional provisions for accounting periods straddling that date (FA 2014 Sch 4 para 17). Note that any power conferred on the Treasury, by virtue of Sch 4, to make regulations comes into force on 17 July 2014 (FA 2014 Sch 4 para 16(1)). SI 2014/2228 reg 2 provides that the amendments made by FA 2014 Sch 4 (other than the power to make regulations under para 16(1)) come into force on 22 August 2014.

Prospective amendments—Word "European" to be substituted for word "EEA", in each place where this occurs (including the heading), in sub-s (2) after "within" words "the United Kingdom or" to be inserted, and in sub-s (3) words "non-European" to be substituted for words "non-EEA", by the Taxes (Amendments) (EU Exit) Regulations, SI 2019/689 reg 16(1), (28) with effect from Implementation Period completion day (see EU(WA)A 2020 Sch 5 para 1(1)).

[1217GC "Core expenditure"

(1) In this Part "core expenditure", in relation to a theatrical production, means expenditure on the activities involved in—

    (*a*) producing the production, and

    (*b*) closing the production.

(2) The reference in subsection (1)(*a*) to "expenditure on the activities involved in producing the production"—

    (*a*) does not include expenditure on any matters not directly involved in producing the production (for instance, financing, marketing, legal services or storage);

    (*b*) does not include expenditure on the ordinary running of the production; but expenditure incurred on or after the date of the first performance of the production to the paying general public may fall within subsection (1)(*a*) (for instance, if it is incurred in connection with a substantial recasting or a substantial redesign of the set).][1]

Commentary—*Simon's Taxes* D7.1276.

Cross-references—See FA 2016 s 180, Sch 24 Pt 1 (power to obtain information about tax advantages claimed under Parts 15, 15A, 15C, 15D which constitute the grant of State aid).

HMRC Manuals—Animation production Company Manual APC50010 (core expenditure: meaning).

Amendments—[1] This Part (ss 1217F–1217OB) inserted by FA 2014 s 36, Sch 4 para 1 with effect in relation to accounting periods beginning on or after 1 September 2014, subject to transitional provisions for accounting periods straddling that date (FA 2014 Sch 4 para 17). Note that any power conferred on the Treasury, by virtue of Sch 4, to make regulations comes into force on 17 July 2014 (FA 2014 Sch 4 para 16(1)). SI 2014/2228 reg 2 provides that the amendments made by FA 2014 Sch 4 (other than the power to make regulations under para 16(1)) come into force on 22 August 2014.

[Claim for additional deduction

1217H Claim for additional deduction

(1) A company which qualifies for relief in relation to a theatrical production may claim an additional deduction in relation to the production.

(2) A claim under subsection (1) is made with respect to an accounting period.

(See Schedule 18 to FA 1998, and in particular, Part 9D, for provision about the procedure for making claims.)

(3) Where a company has made a claim under subsection (1)—

   (a) the company's activities in relation to the theatrical production are treated for corporation tax purposes as a trade separate from any other activities of the company (including activities in relation to any other theatrical production), and

   (b) the company is entitled to make an additional deduction, in accordance with section 1217J, in calculating the profit or loss of the separate trade for the accounting period concerned.

(4) The company is treated as beginning to carry on the separate trade—

   (a) when the production phase begins, or

   (b) if earlier, at the time of the first receipt by the company of any income from the theatrical production.

(5) Where the company tax return in which a claim under subsection (1) is made is for an accounting period later than that in which the company begins to carry on the separate trade, the company must make any amendments of company tax returns for earlier periods that may be necessary.

(6) Any amendment or assessment necessary to give effect to subsection (5) may be made despite any limitation on the time within which an amendment or assessment may normally be made.

(7) If the company ceases at any time to meet the conditions in section 1217FC(1) (meaning of "production company") in relation to the production, it is treated as ceasing to carry on the separate trade at that time.]¹

Commentary—*Simon's Taxes* D7.1278, D7.1272, D7.1273.

Amendments—¹ This Part (ss 1217F–1217OB) inserted by FA 2014 s 36, Sch 4 para 1 with effect in relation to accounting periods beginning on or after 1 September 2014, subject to transitional provisions for accounting periods straddling that date (FA 2014 Sch 4 para 17). Note that any power conferred on the Treasury, by virtue of Sch 4, to make regulations comes into force on 17 July 2014 (FA 2014 Sch 4 para 16(1)). SI 2014/2228 reg 2 provides that the amendments made by FA 2014 Sch 4 (other than the power to make regulations under para 16(1)) come into force on 22 August 2014.

[The separate theatrical trade

1217I Introduction to sections 1217IA to 1217IF

Where a company is treated under section 1217H(3)(a) as carrying on a separate trade ("the separate theatrical trade"), the profits or losses of the trade are calculated for corporation tax purposes in accordance with sections 1217IA to 1217IF.]¹

Amendments—¹ This Part (ss 1217F–1217OB) inserted by FA 2014 s 36, Sch 4 para 1 with effect in relation to accounting periods beginning on or after 1 September 2014, subject to transitional provisions for accounting periods straddling that date (FA 2014 Sch 4 para 17). Note that any power conferred on the Treasury, by virtue of Sch 4, to make regulations comes into force on 17 July 2014 (FA 2014 Sch 4 para 16(1)). SI 2014/2228 reg 2 provides that the amendments made by FA 2014 Sch 4 (other than the power to make regulations under para 16(1)) come into force on 22 August 2014.

[1217IA Calculation of profits or losses of separate theatrical trade

(1) For the first period of account during which the separate theatrical trade is carried on, the following are brought into account—

   (a) as a debit, the costs of the theatrical production incurred (and represented in work done) to date;

   (b) as a credit, the proportion of the estimated total income from the production treated as earned at the end of that period.

(2) For subsequent periods of account the following are brought into account—

   (a) as a debit, the difference between the amount ("C") of the costs of the theatrical production incurred (and represented in work done) to date and the amount corresponding to C for the previous period, and

   (b) as a credit, the difference between the proportion ("PI") of the estimated total income from the production treated as earned at the end of that period and the amount corresponding to PI for the previous period.

(3) The proportion of the estimated total income treated as earned at the end of a period of account is—

$$\frac{C}{T} \times I$$

where—

C is the total to date of costs incurred (and represented in work done);

T is the estimated total cost of the theatrical production;

I is the estimated total income from the theatrical production.]¹

Commentary—*Simon's Taxes* D7.1272, D7.1278, D7.1280.

Cross-references—See FA 2016 s 180, Sch 24 Pt 1 (power to obtain information about tax advantages claimed under Parts 15, 15A, 15C, 15D which constitute the grant of State aid).

HMRC Manuals—Animation production Company Manual APC20250 (profit/ loss calculation).

Amendments—¹ This Part (ss 1217F–1217OB) inserted by FA 2014 s 36, Sch 4 para 1 with effect in relation to accounting periods beginning on or after 1 September 2014, subject to transitional provisions for accounting periods straddling that date (FA 2014 Sch 4 para 17). Note that any power conferred on the Treasury, by virtue of Sch 4, to make regulations comes into

Commentary—*Simon's Taxes* **D7.1278**.

Amendments—[1] This Part (ss 1217F–1217OB) inserted by FA 2014 s 36, Sch 4 para 1 with effect in relation to accounting periods beginning on or after 1 September 2014, subject to transitional provisions for accounting periods straddling that date (FA 2014 Sch 4 para 17). Note that any power conferred on the Treasury, by virtue of Sch 4, to make regulations comes into force on 17 July 2014 (FA 2014 Sch 4 para 16(1)). SI 2014/2228 reg 2 provides that the amendments made by FA 2014 Sch 4 (other than the power to make regulations under para 16(1)) come into force on 22 August 2014.

[Theatre tax credits

1217K Theatre tax credit claimable if company has surrenderable loss

(1) A company which—

    (*a*) is treated under section 1217H(3) as carrying on a separate trade during the whole or part of an accounting period, and

    (*b*) has a surrenderable loss in that period,

may claim a theatre tax credit for that accounting period.

(2) Section 1217KA sets out how to calculate the amount of any surrenderable loss that the company has in the accounting period.

(3) A company making a claim may surrender the whole or part of its surrenderable loss in the accounting period.

(4) The amount of the theatre tax credit to which a company making a claim is entitled for the accounting period is—

    (*a*) 25% of the amount of the loss surrendered if the theatrical production is a touring production, or

    (*b*) 20% of the amount of the loss surrendered if the theatrical production is not a touring production.

(5) The company's available loss for the accounting period (see section 1217KA(2)) is reduced by the amount surrendered.

(6) A theatrical production is a "touring production" only if the company intends at the beginning of the production phase—

    (*a*) that it will present performances of the production in 6 or more separate premises, or

    (*b*) that it will present performances of the production in at least two separate premises and that the number of performances will be at least 14.

(7) See Schedule 18 to FA 1998 (in particular, Part 9D) for provision about the procedure for making claims under subsection (1).][1]

Commentary—*Simon's Taxes* **D7.1275, D7.1280**.

Cross-references—See FA 2016 s 180, Sch 24 Pt 1 (power to obtain information about tax advantages claimed under Parts 15, 15A, 15C, 15D which constitute the grant of State aid).

HMRC Manuals—Animation production Company Manual APC30100 (losses surrendered for payable tax credit).

Amendments—[1] This Part (ss 1217F–1217OB) inserted by FA 2014 s 36, Sch 4 para 1 with effect in relation to accounting periods beginning on or after 1 September 2014, subject to transitional provisions for accounting periods straddling that date (FA 2014 Sch 4 para 17). Note that any power conferred on the Treasury, by virtue of Sch 4, to make regulations comes into force on 17 July 2014 (FA 2014 Sch 4 para 16(1)). SI 2014/2228 reg 2 provides that the amendments made by FA 2014 Sch 4 (other than the power to make regulations under para 16(1)) come into force on 22 August 2014.

[1217KA Amount of surrenderable loss

(1) The company's surrenderable loss in the accounting period is—

    (a) the company's available loss for the period in the separate theatrical trade (see subsections (2) and (3)), or

    (b) if less, the available qualifying expenditure for the period (see subsections (4) and (5)).

(2) The company's available loss for an accounting period is—

L + RUL

where—

L is the amount of the company's loss for the period in the separate theatrical trade, and

RUL is the amount of any relevant unused loss of the company (see subsection (3)).

(3) The "relevant unused loss" of a company is so much of any available loss of the company for the previous accounting period as has not been—

    (*a*) surrendered under section 1217K, or

    (*b*) carried forward under section 45 [or 45B][2] of CTA 2010 and set against profits of the separate theatrical trade.

(4) For the first period of account during which the separate theatrical trade is carried on, the available qualifying expenditure is the amount that is E for that period for the purposes of section 1217J(2).

(5) For any period of account after the first, the available qualifying expenditure is—

E − S

where—

E is the amount that is E for that period for the purposes of section 1217J(3), and

S is the total amount previously surrendered under section 1217K.

(6) If a period of account of the separate theatrical trade does not coincide with an accounting period, any necessary apportionments are to be made by reference to the number of days in the periods concerned.][1]

Commentary—*Simon's Taxes* **D7.1280**.

Amendments—[1]   This Part (ss 1217F–1217OB) inserted by FA 2014 s 36, Sch 4 para 1 with effect in relation to accounting periods beginning on or after 1 September 2014, subject to transitional provisions for accounting periods straddling that date (FA 2014 Sch 4 para 17). Note that any power conferred on the Treasury, by virtue of Sch 4, to make regulations comes into force on 17 July 2014 (FA 2014 Sch 4 para 16(1)). SI 2014/2228 reg 2 provides that the amendments made by FA 2014 Sch 4 (other than the power to make regulations under para 16(1)) come into force on 22 August 2014.

[2]   In sub-s (3)(b), words inserted by F(No 2)A 2017 s 18, Sch 4 paras 128, 142 with effect in relation to accounting periods beginning on or after 1 April 2017, subject to transitional provisions in Sch 4 para 194. For accounting periods beginning before 1 April 2017 and ending on or after that date ("straddling periods") see F(No 2)A 2017 Sch 4 paras 190–192.

[1217KB Payment in respect of theatre tax credit

(1) If a company—

    (a) is entitled to a theatre tax credit for an accounting period, and

    (b) makes a claim,

the Commissioners for Her Majesty's Revenue and Customs ("the Commissioners") must pay the amount of the credit to the company.

(2) An amount payable in respect of—

    (a) a theatre tax credit, or

    (b) interest on a theatre tax credit under section 826 of ICTA,

may be applied in discharging any liability of the company to pay corporation tax.

To the extent that it is so applied the Commissioners' liability under subsection (1) is discharged.

(3) If the company's company tax return for the accounting period is enquired into by the Commissioners, no payment in respect of a theatre tax credit for that period need be made before the Commissioners' enquiries are completed (see paragraph 32 of Schedule 18 to FA 1998).

In those circumstances the Commissioners may make a payment on a provisional basis of such amount as they consider appropriate.

(4) No payment need be made in respect of a theatre tax credit for an accounting period before the company has paid to the Commissioners any amount that it is required to pay for payment periods ending in that accounting period—

    (a) under PAYE regulations,

    (b) under section 966 of ITA 2007 (visiting performers), or

    (c) in respect of Class 1 national insurance contributions under Part 1 of the Social Security Contributions and Benefits Act 1992 or Part 1 of the Social Security Contributions and Benefits (Northern Ireland) Act 1992.

(5) A payment in respect of a theatre tax credit is not income of the company for any tax purpose.][1]

Commentary—*Simon's Taxes* **D7.1280**.

Amendments—[1]   This Part (ss 1217F–1217OB) inserted by FA 2014 s 36, Sch 4 para 1 with effect in relation to accounting periods beginning on or after 1 September 2014, subject to transitional provisions for accounting periods straddling that date (FA 2014 Sch 4 para 17). Note that any power conferred on the Treasury, by virtue of Sch 4, to make regulations comes into force on 17 July 2014 (FA 2014 Sch 4 para 16(1)). SI 2014/2228 reg 2 provides that the amendments made by FA 2014 Sch 4 (other than the power to make regulations under para 16(1)) come into force on 22 August 2014.

[1217KC Limit on State aid

(1) The total amount of any theatre tax credits payable under section 1217KB in the case of any undertaking is not to exceed 50 million euros per year.

(2) In this section "undertaking" has the same meaning as in the General Block Exemption Regulation.

(3) In this section "the General Block Exemption Regulation" means any regulation that—

    (a) is for the time being in force under Article 1 of Council Regulation (EC) No 994/98, and

    (b) makes, in relation to aid in favour of culture and heritage conservation, the declaration provided for by that Article.][1]

Commentary—*Simon's Taxes* **D7.1280**.

Amendments—[1]   This Part (ss 1217F–1217OB) inserted by FA 2014 s 36, Sch 4 para 1 with effect in relation to accounting periods beginning on or after 1 September 2014, subject to transitional provisions for accounting periods straddling that date (FA 2014 Sch 4 para 17). Note that any power conferred on the Treasury, by virtue of Sch 4, to make regulations comes into force on 17 July 2014 (FA 2014 Sch 4 para 16(1)). SI 2014/2228 reg 2 provides that the amendments made by FA 2014 Sch 4 (other than the power to make regulations under para 16(1)) come into force on 22 August 2014.

[Anti-avoidance etc

[1217LA Tax avoidance arrangements

(1) A company does not qualify for relief in relation to a theatrical production if there are any tax avoidance arrangements relating to the production.

(2) Arrangements are "tax avoidance arrangements" if their main purpose, or one of their main purposes, is the obtaining of a tax advantage.

(3) In this section—

"arrangements" includes any scheme, agreement or understanding, whether or not legally enforceable;

"tax advantage" has the meaning given by section 1139 of CTA 2010.][1]

Commentary—*Simon's Taxes* **D7.1275**.

Amendments—[1]   This Part (ss 1217F–1217OB) inserted by FA 2014 s 36, Sch 4 para 1 with effect in relation to accounting periods beginning on or after 1 September 2014, subject to transitional provisions for accounting periods straddling that date (FA 2014 Sch 4 para 17). Note that any power conferred on the Treasury, by virtue of Sch 4, to make regulations comes into force on 17 July 2014 (FA 2014 Sch 4 para 16(1)). SI 2014/2228 reg 2 provides that the amendments made by FA 2014 Sch 4 (other than the power to make regulations under para 16(1)) come into force on 22 August 2014.

[1217LB Transactions not entered into for genuine commercial reasons

(1) A transaction is to be ignored for the purpose of determining a relief mentioned in subsection (2) so far as the transaction is attributable to arrangements (other than tax avoidance arrangements) entered into otherwise than for genuine commercial reasons.

(2) The reliefs mentioned in subsection (1) are—

(*a*) any additional deduction which a company may make under this Part, and

(*b*) any theatre tax credit to be given to a company.

(3) In this section "arrangements" and "tax avoidance arrangements" have the same meaning as in section 1217LA.][1]

Commentary—*Simon's Taxes* **D7.1275**.

Amendments—[1]   This Part (ss 1217F–1217OB) inserted by FA 2014 s 36, Sch 4 para 1 with effect in relation to accounting periods beginning on or after 1 September 2014, subject to transitional provisions for accounting periods straddling that date (FA 2014 Sch 4 para 17). Note that any power conferred on the Treasury, by virtue of Sch 4, to make regulations comes into force on 17 July 2014 (FA 2014 Sch 4 para 16(1)). SI 2014/2228 reg 2 provides that the amendments made by FA 2014 Sch 4 (other than the power to make regulations under para 16(1)) come into force on 22 August 2014.

[Use of losses]

1217M Application of sections 1217MA to 1217MC

(1) Sections 1217MA to 1217MC apply to a company that is treated under section 1217H(3) as carrying on a separate trade in relation to a theatrical production.

(2) In those sections—

"the completion period" means the accounting period in which the company ceases to carry on the separate theatrical trade;

"loss relief" includes any means by which a loss might be used to reduce the amount in respect of which a company, or any other person, is chargeable to tax.][1]

Commentary—*Simon's Taxes* **D7.1273**.

Amendments—[1]   This Part (ss 1217F–1217OB) inserted by FA 2014 s 36, Sch 4 para 1 with effect in relation to accounting periods beginning on or after 1 September 2014, subject to transitional provisions for accounting periods straddling that date (FA 2014 Sch 4 para 17). Note that any power conferred on the Treasury, by virtue of Sch 4, to make regulations comes into force on 17 July 2014 (FA 2014 Sch 4 para 16(1)). SI 2014/2228 reg 2 provides that the amendments made by FA 2014 Sch 4 (other than the power to make regulations under para 16(1)) come into force on 22 August 2014.

[1217MA Restriction on use of losses before completion period

(1) [This section][2] applies if a loss is made by the company in the separate theatrical trade in an accounting period preceding the completion period.

(2) The loss is not available for loss relief, except to the extent that the loss may be carried forward under section 45 [or 45B][2] of CTA 2010 to be [deducted from][2] profits of the separate theatrical trade in a subsequent period.

[(3) If the loss is carried forward under section 45 or 45B of CTA 2010 and deducted from profits of the separate theatrical trade in a subsequent period, the deduction is to be ignored for the purposes of section 269ZB of CTA 2010 (restriction on deductions from trading profits).][2]][1]

Commentary—*Simon's Taxes* **D7.1273**.

Cross-references—See FA 2016 s 180, Sch 24 Pt 1 (power to obtain information about tax advantages claimed under Parts 15, 15A, 15C, 15D which constitute the grant of State aid).

HMRC Manuals—Animation production Company Manual APC30020 (losses: pre-completion periods).

Amendments—[1]   This Part (ss 1217F–1217OB) inserted by FA 2014 s 36, Sch 4 para 1 with effect in relation to accounting periods beginning on or after 1 September 2014, subject to transitional provisions for accounting periods straddling that date (FA 2014 Sch 4 para 17). Note that any power conferred on the Treasury, by virtue of Sch 4, to make regulations comes into force on 17 July 2014 (FA 2014 Sch 4 para 16(1)). SI 2014/2228 reg 2 provides that the amendments made by FA 2014 Sch 4 (other than the power to make regulations under para 16(1)) come into force on 22 August 2014.

[2]   In sub-s (1) words substituted for words "Subsection (2)", in sub-s (2) words inserted and words substituted for words "set against", and sub-s (3) inserted, by F(No 2)A 2017 s 18, Sch 4 paras 39, 40 with effect in relation to accounting periods beginning on or after 1 April 2017, subject to transitional provisions in Sch 4 para 194. For accounting periods beginning before 1 April 2017 and ending on or after that date ("straddling periods") see F(No 2)A 2017 Sch 4 paras 190–192.

[1217MB Use of losses in the completion period

(1) Subsection (2) applies if a loss made in the separate theatrical trade is carried forward under section 45 [or 45B][2] of CTA 2010 to the completion period.

(2) So much (if any) of the loss as is not attributable to relief under section 1217H (see subsection (4)) may be treated for the purposes of [section 37 and Part 5 of CTA 2010]² as if it were a loss made in the completion period.

(3) If a loss is made in the separate theatrical trade in the completion period, the amount of the loss that may be—

    (*a*) deducted from total profits of the same or an earlier period under section 37 of CTA 2010, or

    (*b*) surrendered as group relief under Part 5 of that Act,

is restricted to the amount (if any) that is not attributable to relief under section 1217H.

(4) The amount of a loss in any period that is attributable to relief under section 1217H is found by—

    (*a*) calculating what the amount of the loss would have been if there had been no additional deduction under that section in that or any earlier period, and

    (*b*) deducting that amount from the total amount of the loss.

(5) This section does not apply to loss surrendered, or treated as carried forward, under section 1217MC (terminal losses).]¹

Commentary—*Simon's Taxes* **D7.1273**.

Cross-references—See FA 2016 s 180, Sch 24 Pt 1 (power to obtain information about tax advantages claimed under Parts 15, 15A, 15C, 15D which constitute the grant of State aid).

HMRC Manuals—Animation production Company Manual APC30030 (losses: completion and later periods).

Amendments—¹   This Part (ss 1217F–1217OB) inserted by FA 2014 s 36, Sch 4 para 1 with effect in relation to accounting periods beginning on or after 1 September 2014, subject to transitional provisions for accounting periods straddling that date (FA 2014 Sch 4 para 17). Note that any power conferred on the Treasury, by virtue of Sch 4, to make regulations comes into force on 17 July 2014 (FA 2014 Sch 4 para 16(1)). SI 2014/2228 reg 2 provides that the amendments made by FA 2014 Sch 4 (other than the power to make regulations under para 16(1)) come into force on 22 August 2014.

²   In sub-s (1) words inserted, and in sub-s (2) words substituted for words "loss relief", by F(No 2)A 2017 s 18, Sch 4 paras 39, 41 with effect in relation to accounting periods beginning on or after 1 April 2017, subject to transitional provisions in Sch 4 para 194. For accounting periods beginning before 1 April 2017 and ending on or after that date ("straddling periods") see F(No 2)A 2017 Sch 4 paras 190–192.

[1217MC   Terminal losses

(1) This section applies if—

    (*a*) the company ceases to carry on the separate theatrical trade, and

    (*b*) if the company had not ceased to carry on the separate theatrical trade, it could have carried forward an amount under section 45 [or 45B]² of CTA 2010 to be set against profits of that trade in a later period ("the terminal loss").

Below in this section the company is referred to as "company A" and the separate theatrical trade is referred to as "trade 1".

(2) If company A—

    (*a*) is treated under section 1217H(3) as carrying on a separate theatrical trade in relation to another theatrical production ("trade 2"), and

    (*b*) is carrying on trade 2 when it ceases to carry on trade 1,

company A may (on making a claim) elect to transfer the terminal loss (or a part of it) to trade 2.

(3) If company A makes an election under subsection (2), the terminal loss (or part of the loss) is treated[—

    (*a*) in a case where the loss could have been carried forward under section 45 of CTA 2010 had trade 1 not ceased, as if it were a loss carried forward under that section to be set against the profits of trade 2 of the first accounting period beginning after the cessation and so on, and

    (*b*) in a case where the loss could have been carried forward under section 45B of CTA 2010 had trade 1 not ceased, as if it were a loss made in trade 2 which has been carried forward under that section to the first accounting period beginning after the cessation.]²

(4) Subsection (5) applies if—

    (*a*) another company ("company B") is treated under section 1217H(3) as carrying on a separate theatrical trade ("company B's trade") in relation to another theatrical production,

    (*b*) company B is carrying on that trade when company A ceases to carry on trade 1, and

    (*c*) company B is in the same group as company A for the purposes of Part 5 of CTA 2010 (group relief).

(5) Company A may surrender the loss (or part of it) to company B.

(6) On the making of a claim by company B the amount surrendered is treated[—

    (*a*) in a case where the amount could have been carried forward under section 45 of CTA 2010 had trade 1 not ceased, as if it were a loss carried forward by company B under that section to be set against the profits of company B's trade of the first accounting period beginning after the cessation and so on, and

    (*b*) in a case where the amount could have been carried forward under section 45B of CTA 2010 had trade 1 not ceased, as if it were a loss made in company B's trade which has been carried forward under that section to the first accounting period beginning after the cessation.]²

(7) The Treasury may by regulations make administrative provision in relation to the surrender of a loss under subsection (5) and the resulting claim under subsection (6).

(8) "Administrative provision" means provision corresponding, subject to such adaptations or other modifications as appear to the Treasury to be appropriate, to that made by Part 8 of Schedule 18 to FA 1998 (company tax returns: claims for group relief).][1]

[(9) A deduction under section 45 or 45B of CTA 2010 which is made in reliance on this section is to be ignored for the purposes of section 269ZB of that Act (restriction on deductions from trading profits).][2]

Commentary—*Simon's Taxes* **D7.1273**.

Cross-references—See FA 2016 s 180, Sch 24 Pt 1 (power to obtain information about tax advantages claimed under Parts 15, 15A, 15C, 15D which constitute the grant of State aid).

HMRC Manuals—Animation production Company Manual APC30040 (losses: terminal losses).

Amendments—[1]   This Part (ss 1217F–1217OB) inserted by FA 2014 s 36, Sch 4 para 1 with effect in relation to accounting periods beginning on or after 1 September 2014, subject to transitional provisions for accounting periods straddling that date (FA 2014 Sch 4 para 17). Note that any power conferred on the Treasury, by virtue of Sch 4, to make regulations comes into force on 17 July 2014 (FA 2014 Sch 4 para 16(1)). SI 2014/2228 reg 2 provides that the amendments made by FA 2014 Sch 4 (other than the power to make regulations under para 16(1)) come into force on 22 August 2014.

[2]   In sub-s (1)(*b*) words inserted, in sub-ss (3), (6) words substituted, and sub-s (9) inserted, by F(No 2)A 2017 s 18, Sch 4 paras 39, 42 with effect in relation to accounting periods beginning on or after 1 April 2017, subject to transitional provisions in Sch 4 para 194. For accounting periods beginning before 1 April 2017 and ending on or after that date ("straddling periods") see F(No 2)A 2017 Sch 4 paras 190–192.

[Provisional entitlement to relief

1217N Provisional entitlement to relief

(1) In relation to a company that has made a claim under section 1217H in relation to a theatrical production, "interim accounting period" means any accounting period that—

(*a*) is one in which the company carries on the separate theatrical trade, and

(*b*) precedes the accounting period in which it ceases to do so.

(2) A company is not entitled to relief under any of the relieving provisions for an interim accounting period unless—

(*a*) its company tax return for the period states the amount of planned core expenditure on the theatrical production that is EEA expenditure, and

(*b*) that amount is such as to indicate that the EEA expenditure condition (see section 1217GB) will be met in relation to the production.

If those requirements are met, the company is provisionally treated in relation to that period as if the EEA expenditure condition were met.

(3) In this section "the relieving provisions" means—

(*a*) section 1217H (additional deduction),

(*b*) section 1217K (theatre tax credits), and

(*c*) section 1217MC (terminal losses).][1]

Commentary—*Simon's Taxes* **D7.1281**.

Amendments—[1]   This Part (ss 1217F–1217OB) inserted by FA 2014 s 36, Sch 4 para 1 with effect in relation to accounting periods beginning on or after 1 September 2014, subject to transitional provisions for accounting periods straddling that date (FA 2014 Sch 4 para 17). Note that any power conferred on the Treasury, by virtue of Sch 4, to make regulations comes into force on 17 July 2014 (FA 2014 Sch 4 para 16(1)). SI 2014/2228 reg 2 provides that the amendments made by FA 2014 Sch 4 (other than the power to make regulations under para 16(1)) come into force on 22 August 2014.

Prospective amendments—Word "European" to be substituted for word "EEA", in each place where this occurs, by the Taxes (Amendments) (EU Exit) Regulations, SI 2019/689 reg 16(1), (30) with effect from Implementation Period completion day (see EU(WA)A 2020 Sch 5 para 1(1)).

[1217NA Clawback of provisional relief

(1) If a statement is made under section 1217N(2) but it subsequently appears that the EEA expenditure condition will not be met on the company's ceasing to carry on the separate theatrical trade, the company—

(*a*) is not entitled to relief under any of the relieving provisions for any period for which its entitlement depended on such a statement, and

(*b*) must amend its company tax return for any such period accordingly.

(2) When a company which has made a claim under section 1217H ceases to carry on the separate theatrical trade, the company's company tax return for the period in which that cessation occurs must—

(*a*) state that the company has ceased to carry on the separate theatrical trade, and

(*b*) be accompanied by a final statement of the amount of the core expenditure on the theatrical production that is EEA expenditure.

(3) If that statement shows that the EEA expenditure condition is not met—

(*a*) the company is not entitled to relief under any of the relieving provisions for any period,

(*b*) the company is treated for corporation tax purposes as if section 1217H(3)(a) (treatment as a separate trade) did not apply in relation to the theatrical production for any period, and

(*c*) accordingly, sections 1217MA and 1217MB (provisions about use of losses) do not apply in relation to the theatrical production for any period.

THE WEST HIGHLAND WHITE TERRIER

Jill Arnel

Interpet Publishing

The West Highland White Terrier
An Interpet Book

Project Team
Editor: Heather Russell-Revesz
Copy Editor: Carrie Hornbeck
Design: Tilly Grassa
Series Design: Mada Design
Series Originator: Dominique De Vito

First published in UK by
Interpet Publishing
Vincent Lane
Dorking
Surrey
RH4 3YX

ISBN 13 978-1-84286-144-8

This book has been published with the intent to provide accurate and authoritative information in regard to the subject matter within. While every precaution has been taken in preparation of this book, the author and publisher expressly disclaim responsibility for any errors, omissions, or adverse effects arising from the use or application of the information contained herein. The techniques and suggestions are used at the reader's discretion and are not to be considered a substitute for veterinary care. If you suspect a medical problem consult your vet.

Interpet Publishing

TABLE OF CONTENTS

Chapter 1
HISTORY OF THE WEST HIGHLAND WHITE TERRIER 5
Earth Dogs • Westie Origins • Breed History in Scotland and England •
Breed History in the United States

Chapter 2
CHARACTERISTICS OF THE WEST HIGHLAND WHITE TERRIER . . .15
The Westie Mystique: Looks, Brains, and Makeup • Is the Westie Your Dream Dog? •
Are You a Westie's Dream Mate?

Chapter 3
PREPARING FOR YOUR WEST HIGHLAND WHITE TERRIER 33
Puppy or Adult? • Westie Laddie or Westie Lassie? • Where to Find the Westie of
Your Dreams • Westie Comes Home • Supplies! • Identifying Your Dog •
Travelling with Your Westie • If You Can't Take Your Westie With You

Chapter 4
FEEDING YOUR WEST HIGHLAND WHITE TERRIER 59
Commercial Dog Foods • Noncommercial Diets • Age-Appropriate Feeding •
Supplements and Special Diets • Obesity • Treats • Bones

Chapter 5
GROOMING YOUR WEST HIGHLAND WHITE TERRIER 79
The Great Debate: Stripper or Clipper? • Brushing • Bathing • Nail Care •
Ear Care • Eye Care • Staining • Dental Care • Professional Grooming

Chapter 6
TRAINING AND BEHAVIOUR OF
YOUR WEST HIGHLAND WHITE TERRIER 95
Training Starts Early • The Importance of Socialisation • Crate Training •
Hold That Thought: Housetraining Your Westie • Training Your Westie •
Basic Commands • Problem Behaviours • How to Find a Canine Behaviourist

Chapter 7
ADVANCED TRAINING & ACTIVITIES
WITH YOUR WEST HIGHLAND WHITE TERRIER 127
Competitive Events • Noncompetitive Activities

Chapter 8
HEALTH OF YOUR WEST HIGHLAND WHITE TERRIER 147
Finding a Vet • Partners in Heath • Puppy's First Visit • Spaying and Neutering •
Vaccinations • Diseases that May Affect Your Westie • Other Common Canine
Diseases • Parasites • Holistic Medicine • First Aid and Other Emergencies • Your
Venerable Westie • Saying Good-bye

Appendix 200

Resources 202

Index 204

of the West Highland White Terrier

The Latin name for dog is *Canis familiaris*. The generic *Canis* stands for the dentition it shares with its cousins: wolves, coyotes, and jackals; the species, *familiaris,* stands for the characteristic eye structure that lacks the slit pupils of its feral cousins. The domestic dog, like the wolf *(Canis lupus)* and the coyote *(Canis latrans),* has a total of 78 chromosomes, explaining why domestic dogs are biologically able to breed with wolves and coyotes. The dog's 78 chromosomes account for the amazing physical diversity throughout dogdom. Only the minutest genetic difference separates the statuesque Afghan Hound from the diminutive West Highland White Terrier.

Appearances range from that of the plush-coated, heavy-shedding Norwegian Elkhound to the hairless Chinese Crested and everything in between. Shaving each down to the skin (not recommended) would reveal a basic similar structure; however, the differences in size, coat type, eye colour, ear style, and carriage vary greatly. Add evolution and adaptation to this cauldron of diversification, and you get dogs in all their numerous forms. The world's many terrains and climates, along with human selection, influenced which dogs would become the first symbiotic companion animals.

EARTH DOGS

Terriers originate from the British Isles. The word *terrier* derives from the Latin *terra,* which means "earth." So these are "earth dogs," dogs selectively bred to go to ground to bolt or capture prey, typically foxes and badgers. Keenly intelligent and truculent—sometimes to a fault—they have the nerve to fight to the end rather than retreat unvictorious.

Terriers, as a rule, bark a lot, but this is an asset to performing their job. Stentorian barks, belying their relatively small size, often force their quarry from its hole, for easy elimination.

Although the origin of the word *dog* is murky, etymologists have the following theories:

Dogca, the Old English word for *dog,* emerged in the thirteenth century. It replaced the commonly used *hund*—a word rooted in the Indo-European word *kuntos*—supporting the theory that dogs were part of human daily life during the earliest days of spoken language.

Kuntos became the Greek word kyon, the root of the word *cynic.* A group of ancient Greek philosophers was so-named for their "dog-like" sneering at convention.

From *canis,* the Latin word for dog, derives *canine*—but also *kennel* and *canary.* Apparently those musically gifted yellow birds were named for the large breed of brown or brindled dogs indigenous to the Canary Islands.

WESTIE ORIGINS

The Westie appears to be native to Argyllshire, Scotland. As for its origins, some contend that the modern Westie is simply a Cairn Terrier that took a detour. Cairns and Westies appear to be closest in type to the original Scotch Terrier, and some believe that the Westie descends from the white, sandy, and cream-coloured Cairn Terriers. Still, the Westie's shorter back, heavier bone, and more refined grooming distinguishes it from the "tidied dishevelment" of its Cairn cousins. A gay, "noon" tail carriage contrasts with its cousin's "one or two o'clock" set.

Another hypothesis establishes the Westie's birthright as an original ancient terrier—not as descended from the Cairn Terrier, per se, but in fact on equal footing—one and the same. Only later did a "colour war" cause them to follow divergent paths.

BREED HISTORY IN SCOTLAND AND ENGLAND

The first known mention of the West Highland White Terrier appears in records that date back to King James I in the late 1500s and the 1600s, when the monarch shipped six little white "earthdogges" from Argyllshire, Scotland to the French king. Many believe that these were ancestors to today's Westie. However, the colour of these "earthdogges" is debatable. Mrs. May Pacey, one of the great pioneering Westie breeders, refers to these dogs in her 1963 book, but Bryan Cummins, in *Terriers of Scotland and Ireland,* suggests that Mrs. Pacey might have woven into the story a bit of wishful thinking. Logical evidence suggests that these "earthdogges" were early Scotch Terriers, but since coloured ones were then favoured, it's unlikely that these voyagers were white. In fact, the original records contain no colour description whatsoever. However, these émigrés were close in type to the original Scotch Highland Terrier—the progenitors of both the Cairn Terrier and the West Highland White Terrier.

THREE VARIETIES OF WESTIES

Along the way in the history and breeding of the Westie, several different varieties were developed.

The Poltalloch Variety

Clearer documentation of the Westie's history began in the early 1800s with the Malcolm family of Poltalloch in Argyllshire. Colonel Edward Donald Malcolm of Poltalloch, generally credited as the breed's originator, took great pains to establish a hardy type of small white-coated terriers who would be well suited to the difficult terrain of the Western Highlands, breeding for exceptional working and hunting ability. For a century before, the Malcolm clan had been among the few who bred both white and coloured terriers. They recognised the value of the white terriers: They were less likely than their darker kennel mates to blend in with their surroundings.

Like other lairds of the time, Colonel Malcolm kept only the best working dogs—and his were both white and coloured. It was an unfortunate hunting

On the northern shore of Loch Crinan in the Argyllshire rests the estate where the modern Westie was born, and Duntrune Castle, where the current chief of Clan MacCallum/Malcolm— Robin Neill Malcolm—a direct descendent of Colonel Malcolm, resides.

7

accident that initially led Malcolm to start breeding white terriers exclusively. During a hunt, Colonel Malcolm mistook a favourite reddish brown dog for a fox, and shot it. Devastated by his mistake, he vowed never to allow this to happen again, thereafter keeping only the cream-coloured or white terriers. This put him at odds with the then-popular superstitious belief (to which the Malcolm family never quite subscribed) that white dogs were inherently inferior to their darker littermates. White dogs were often destroyed at birth because of this superstition, but luckily, the attempt to drive them into oblivion was unsuccessful. Otherwise, when, if ever, would they have had the opportunity to prove their mettle?

The Roseneath Variety

Another breeder of white terriers who figures prominently into the contemporary Westie development was the Duke of Argyll of Roseneath, whose gamekeeper, George Clark, was breeding a strain of terriers similar to the Poltalloch. These were reputed to have whiter coats of softer texture than Colonel Malcolm's terriers. However, the names Roseneath and Poltalloch were often used interchangeably until the turn of the twentieth century.

Colonel Malcolm did not breed to the Roseneath stock, as he was not fond of the longer "Skye heads." But some crossing between the two types occurred nonetheless.

The Pittenweem Variety

Dr. Americ Flaxman, of Fife on the coastal area of the Firth of Forth, began breeding white dogs primarily out of a Scottish Terrier bitch who, when bred to other white Highland Terriers, consistently threw white puppies. Possessing "linty" white coats and exceptional black pigmentation on noses, pads, and eye rims, they

For generations Cairn Terriers and West Highland White Terriers were interbred and often littermates. And in the early 1900s, Cairn Terriers and Westies continued to be interbred and sorted according to colour. Finally, in 1917, the AKC began refusing to register any Cairn Terrier with a Westie within the first three generations of its pedigree—and vice versa. The two breeds parted ways for good and became more distinct from each other. England's Kennel Club (KC) followed suit in 1924—seven years after the AKC decreed the terriers of "mixed heritage" ineligible.

essentially resembled white Scotties. Other strains produced cream-coloured dogs with hard coats.

Flaxman's dogs were known as Pittenweem Terriers. Flaxman and Colonel Malcolm were at odds regarding their visions as to what comprised a proper head, but this disagreement over "type" did not completely curtail interbreeding among these dogs (providing a plausible argument for the slightly closer ear set of the Westie compared to that of the Cairn).

Eventually, the Pittenweem Terrier faded into oblivion. No Scottish Terrier breeders wanted white dogs, nor did admirers of Poltalloch's more moderate type want the exaggerated appearance of a Scottie.

- In 1860 a "white scotch terrier" was a winner at a dog show in Birmingham, England.
- Shown in October 1905 as a West Highland White Terrier, Morvan, at a mere seven and a half months old, won a Challenge Certificate (CC); Morvan later become a champion.
- By 1907 there were three West Highland White Terrier champions.

The Poltalloch Prevails

All three varieties were entered at dog shows in England in the nineteenth century. Judges, however, came to favour the shorter head and muzzle of Colonel Malcolm's Poltalloch dogs. The Duke of Argyll's Roseneaths fared somewhere in the middle, but Flaxman's Pittenweem Terriers' exaggerated heads were quickly deemed serious faults. So Malcolm's type—the Poltalloch—prevailed and remains closest to what survives today.

In fact, Colonel Malcolm came up with the descriptive name for the breed: West Highland White Terrier, and he remained a force in unifying the various factions to contribute significantly to the breed's standardisation. Through his diplomacy, the West Highland White Terrier Club of Scotland—of which he was the first president—was formed. A club in England followed, and by 1907 there were classes for Westies at Crufts, England's premier dog show.

Modern Westie Breeders In England

Mrs. Cyril (May) Pacey and her famous "Wolveys" figure prominently into the breed's lore. Starting early in the Westie's official history, Mrs. Pacey exerted worldwide influence for about fifty years before her death in 1963. Through her unparalleled dedication, she became an authority on the breed.

Ch. Wolvey Piper was her first official Champion of Record, in 1911. The period between 1920 and 1939 yielded 125 Westie champions: A full quarter of them were of Mrs. Pacey's breeding, including one of the most admired show bitches, Ch. Wolvey Pintail. With an eye to the integrity and perpetuation of the breed,

Crufts winner "Paddy" made his mark in the dog world as a sire and as a champion show dog to boot.

Mrs. Pacey shared her finest stock worldwide to ensure the welfare of the terriers she loved. Sixty-plus Wolvey Westies became champions, and there is Wolvey blood behind many top winners. Mrs. Pacey survived the cessation of showing (1916) and breeding (1917) that accompanied World War I, and slogged through the lean years of World War II, when rations and the dangers of far-reaching hostilities continued to threaten the hobby of keeping purebred dogs. During the WWI food shortages, she reluctantly put down fifteen of her dogs. By 1939, showing was officially restricted, but breeding remained legal. So Mrs. Pacey cannily sent some of her best stock abroad, which greatly contributed to the breed's survival. She kept a few dogs for herself, kenneled separately to ensure the survival in case her kennel was bombed. All survived, except for one—tragically run over by an army truck. Without Mrs. Pacey's selfless vision, the breed would not thrive as it does today.

Starting around 1946, shows resumed and the breed flourished. A show on July 11, 1946 ushered in a new era, with an astonishing entry of 225 Westies. And in 1950, a Westie named Shiningcliff Simon won Best Terrier honours at the prestigious Crufts show. The resumption of all-breed shows sparked a renaissance in purebred dogs in general and—with these favourably timed wins—in the West Highland White Terrier specifically.

The modern-day Westie star was Eng. Ch. Olac Moonpilot—owned, bred, and handled by Derek Tattersall. In 1990 "Paddy" won Best in Show at Crufts.

BREED HISTORY IN THE UNITED STATES

In 1906 the Westie debuted in the United States as the Roseneath Terrier, but soon that name would be supplanted by the current name, West Highland White Terrier. By 1908 the breed received official listing in the American Kennel Club (AKC) Stud Book. The West Highland White Terrier Club of America formed and was admitted to the AKC in 1909. On September 21, 1909, the West Highland White Terrier Club of America was founded on the East Coast with a charter membership of fourteen. Three months later, the club submitted a breed standard to the AKC, which essentially cloned the British standard. Since then, little has changed.

"I CAME BACK"

CH. ELFINBROOK SIMON
BEST IN SHOW
WEST HIGHLAND WHITE TERRIER CLUB
OF SOUTHERN CALIFORNIA
1968

"And we're glad you did!"
WISHING WELL KENNELS

Ch. Elfinbrook Simon, shown here in a 1968 ad from Terrier Type, had a huge impact on the breed in the United States.

Champions in America

At first, most of the Westie champions were combinations of both imports and American-bred dogs. Popularity came gradually, but things would change in 1942 when Ch. Wolvey Pattern of Edgerstone (of Mrs. Pacey's previously mentioned Wolvey Westies, exported to the States during World War II) took Best of Show at Westminster, the first of two Westies ever to have earned the honour. This high-status win signaled the beginning of the breed's popularity. In the early 1960s, registrations of the breed reached upwards of a thousand.

In 1962, Ch. Elfinbrook Simon smashed records by winning 12 Best in Shows in America and 3 in Canada. In 1962, Simon won the National Specialty. When he won Westminster in 1963, the advent

of TV broadcasting further boosted the breed's popularity, and Westie registrations tripled in the decade that followed. Regional clubs mushroomed throughout the United States. With an astonishing 27 Best in Shows, Simon set a new record for the breed, which still remains.

Eng. Ch. Cruben Dexter, owned by Barbara Worcester Keenan of Wishing Well Kennels, became a champion in Canada, and won the breed's first back-to-back Westie Best in Shows in the United States in 1954. Mrs. Keenan later became a respected AKC all-breed judge. In 1960, Wishing Well import Ch. Symmetra Snip was the first Westie to win a Best in Show at the National Terrier Show at Montgomery County. Among the wins of Wishing Well Kennel's Am. Can. Ch. Whitebriar Journeyman was one under Mr. Alva Rosenberg, the legendary "dean of judges"—a gentleman of unparalleled integrity and reputation.

Furthering the Westie cause in America, Bea and John T. Marvin were among the greatest stewards, promoters, and educators ever to grace the breed. Bea oversaw the breeding programme while John concentrated on observing, studying, and writing. Both were esteemed AKC judges as well.

Breeding Trends

Breeder trends in the United States have changed over the years. While individual breeders may have strong lines, the general decline of the larger kennels makes it difficult to follow any particular line in the United States. By the turn of the twenty-first century, many breeders were beginning to keep fewer than ten dogs. Furthermore, possibly due to the size of the United States, breeding has evolved to become more regional, rather than national, in character. Washington breeder Sandy Davis cites as a possible rationale the longer distances people have to travel in the West. "Or maybe we are just too independent," she quips (terrierlike).

Breed numbers have swollen in recent years. The proliferation of Westies in television and print ads continues to augment their popularity. However, without the Westie's delightful personality, no amount of advertising could sustain the breed's place in human hearts.

A few long-lived influential kennels continue to produce many show, companion, and performance dogs. Two examples are Donnybrook Kennels in Baltimore, Maryland, and Dawn's

Highland Scots Kennels in Pennsylvania. Billye and Tom Ward's Donnybrook Kennels has produced more than 100 champions and one known and admired for their longevity. Dawn Martin has bred more than 70 conformation champions, and her kennels are distinguished for breeding for both conformation and performance.

Can. Ch. Celtic Legacy with owner David Gignac.

Breed Clubs

Westie breed clubs help maintain the standard and the integrity of their breed. They foster dialogue and study and gather information and history in pursuit of "the perfect Westie." They provide and sponsor recreational activities and share important knowledge. Furthermore, Westie enthusiasts are very willing to help newcomers to the breed. Not to be overlooked, Westie clubs offer many opportunities for friendship, based on mutual love for a very special breed.

The West Highland White Terrier Club (www.thewesthighlandwhite terrierclub.co.uk) is the national club for Westie owners, breeders and exhibitors. In addition, there is the Southern West Highland White Terrier Club (www.southernwesthighlandwhiteterrier club.co.uk), the West Highland White Terrier Club of England (www.thewesthighlandwhiteterrier clubofengland.co.uk) the North of Ireland White Terrier Club (www. northofirelandwesthighlandwhite terrierclub.co.uk) and the West Highland White Terrier Club of Wales (www.welshclub.dog-lovers.org.uk).

In America, the West Highland White Terrier Club of America (WHWTCA) is the central and only official AKC national club for Westies. The WHWTCA is dedicated to Westie health, welfare, preservation, enhancement, and stewardship and unites all Westie-lovers, from serious breeders and fanciers to pet owners.

CHARACTERISTICS
of the West Highland White Terrier

The West Highland White Terrier's fashionable tidy white coat and chic appearance belies his strong, fearless character and his independence. For these free-spirited and iconoclastic terriers, certain rules were made to be broken. They may look pure and angelic, but they are far from trivial froufrou dogs willing to sit around and drink tea from bone china. The Westie is a terrier, not a toy dog.

Colonel Edward Malcolm (arguably the "father" of the modern West Highland White Terrier) wrote for Rawdon Lee's Modern Dog in 1894, "They are gameness itself, and terrible poachers. They love above all things to get away with a young retriever, and ruin him forever, teaching him everything he ought not to know." These feisty white terriers were bred to hunt vermin and small predators; in fact, Edward Malcolm's Westies virtually wiped out the fox population around his estate in the 1890s.

Today, for the most part, the West Highland White Terrier remains in the hands of capable stewards. The changes to the original breed have been minor: The shortening of the back is perhaps a small compromise that doesn't seem to have affected the Westie's natural talents and prowess for hunting.

THE WESTIE MYSTIQUE: LOOKS, BRAINS, AND MAKEUP

Alert-looking, adorable, and stylish, Westies are functional little dogs with an attractive balance of soundness and athleticism, making them ready for just about anything. They're 110 percent terrier, crammed full of Scottish hardiness, nerve, and a large measure of temerity, tenacity, and loyalty. It's truly incredible that so much can be distilled into such a small package. Westies love the outdoors; they are excellent hunters with efficient little bodies and a canniness that amuses and amazes. They also love their homes, and are happy to curl up contentedly by the hearth, safely out of the blustery cold.

The "package" of the West Highland White Terrier is small but potent. One of the relatively short-legged terriers indigenous to the rocky, rough contour of the Scottish terrain, he has the substance and strength needed to deal with those challenging lands.

According to the Kennel Club, "the basis of breed shows is the judging of dogs against the Breed Standard, which is the prescribed blueprint of the particular breed of dog."

The Westie has strong front legs, thick nails and pads, with an ever-so-slight turnout to the front feet—which are larger that the rear ones. This trait is essential so that he can move the earth sideways in search of his quarry without the risk of digging himself into his hole.

The Westie possesses strong jaws, large teeth, and keen intelligence, as well as the high predatory drive appropriate to his life's work. This is a dog that's changed little since his beginnings and, at best, whose "form follows his function." The changes effected by selective breeding have been few—the most notable being a slight increase in substance and a slight shortening of the back, which does not appear to alter function. The bigger changes have been more superficial (grooming styles among them). Westies have been tidied up for exhibition in dog shows, something exhibitors have found necessary for competing in the cutthroat Terrier Group ring—with its highly stylised and meticulously groomed competitors, with their tighter-plucked jackets and manicured look—as well as in the Best in Show ring.

Composed for the benefit of dog show exhibitors, the breed standard describes the quintessential Westie—a written vision of the ideal. While perfection does not exist in the dog world (or anywhere on earth, for that matter), for a Westie to become a show dog, he should fit the standard's specifications as closely as possible. Breeders strive to produce dogs that "conform" to the official breed standard, hence the word *conformation*—meaning a dog show.

General Appearance

Small but confident, plucky and hardy, the West Highland White Terrier is a beautifully balanced, stellar showman of a dog possessing a deep chest and well-sprung ribs. His back is straight and level and his hindquarters strong. He's an agile, active, and efficient mover with a seemingly endless reserve of endurance. His double coat is composed of a topcoat of hard guard hairs—which should ideally be about 2 inches (5 cm) long—and a downy thermal protective undercoat. When groomed for show, the coat is neatened up—leaving more hair on the back and sides but blended into a shorter neck and shoulder coat. Longer hair is left to frame the face to reveal the typical smart Westie.

Size, Proportion, and Substance

The breed standard for the Westie states that 11 inches (27.9 cm) at the withers. The Kennel Club does not differentiate between males and females. More important than size is the overall impression of a compact dog with good balance and substance—and moderation.

Head

The Westie's head should be groomed to a round appearance and should be in good proportion to the body. The broad, substantial, slightly domed skull underneath the hair ought to be a bit longer than his muzzle, gradually tapering to the eyes. A blunt muzzle with powerful jaws tapers to the nose, which should be large and black as licorice; so should the lips.

A Westie's teeth are his stock-in-trade, and the bigger the teeth,

During times of limited sunshine, winter nose or "snow nose" may occur, in which the Westie's nose loses some of its black pigment. Calcium and vitamin D (and, of course, sunshine) can correct this temporary and harmless condition, which generally rights itself as the days grow longer.

The Westie's head should be groomed to a round appearance and should be in good proportion to the body.

Pigmentation in the ears, around the eyes, on the pads and nails is always desirable, and Westies develop this after they are born as quickly as any other breed.

the better. Six incisors must be present on both the upper and lower jaws between the canines. A snug scissors bite or a level bite is acceptable, but an overshot or undershot mouth or one with misaligned, missing incisors or several missing premolars is undesirable.

Expression

"Sharp and intelligent, looking out from under heavy eyebrows, which impart a piercing look" describes the Westie's expression. Wide set, slightly sunken eyes edged by black kohl-like pigmentation present a striking appearance. Eyes should be of almond shape and dark brown.

Ears

Ears should be small, pricked, and carried erect, widely set, and ending in a sharp tip. Short trimming leaves ears smooth and velvety with no errant hairs at the tips. Dark pigmentation on the skin at the ears' tips is desirable.

Neck, Topline, and Body

The Westie should be well muscled, well set on sloping shoulders, and his length should be in good proportion to the rest of his body. Medium is key here—the neck ought not be either too long or too short. A Westie's body should be compact—but again, not too short—and substantial without being coarse. Ribs should be deep, well sprung, and heart shaped. The chest should be deep and should extend to the elbows in good proportion.

His carrot-shaped tail should be carried as straight as possible and not curled over the back; its length should not exceed the top of the skull. Undocked and covered with hard hair, it should be set straight on at back level.

The Westie's expression should be inquisitive and alert; intelligent-looking dark brown eyes are also desired.

Angulation and Shoulders

Shoulder blades should be well laid back and connected at the spine, attaching to a moderately long upper arm, which allows the body to overhang. A faulty shoulder is one that is too straight, too steep, or one with too short an upper arm. This type of assembly impedes the Westie's movement.

Legs

Front legs should be straight, muscular, covered with short, hard hair, and set directly under the shoulders. The lengths from the withers to the elbow and the elbow to the ground should be nearly equal.

Feet

For a Westie, large, round forefeet—larger than the hind feet— are correct and desirable. Ideally, feet should have thick black pads

and nails, and there should be a slight turnout at the foot—on otherwise nice, straight legs.

Hindquarters

Muscular, well-angulated thighs should not be set wide apart. Hocks should be well bent and should look parallel from the rear. Hind legs should be fairly short, with strong hocks. Hind feet should be smaller than forefeet, and thick black pads are most desirable.

A "loaded shoulder," considered a fault in the Westie, occurs when the shoulder blades are shoved out from the body by overdeveloped muscles. Westies should not have a Superman physique.

Gait

A Westie should move freely, easily, and straight—with a definite reach and drive. This is a double-tracking terrier. Double tracking refers to the movement of a dog when he reaches forward; in Westies the front-paw movement is fairly parallel, so that each paw makes a separate track, in contrast to most breeds, whose front feet converge toward a single point, or track. Still, double-tracking terriers such as Westies tend to move toward the centre of gravity.

Rear movement is ideally free and strong, with the hocks freely flexing and drawing close under the body, so the dog can propel itself with adequate force. This is an efficient-moving dog, built for stamina. Flexibility and agility is essential for manoevering the terrain of its country of origin.

This tough little terrier needs hindquarters that can propel him with adequate force and efficiency.

Yes and no. Westies are actually "off-white" or yellow dogs with modifying factors in their genetic makeup that make them appear white. This explains the dark pigment on their pads, noses, lips, and eye rims. The whiteness is nuanced—almost like the different interior "white" wall paints you are likely to find at your local DIY store. Westies can have coat colours that contain variations of white, blue white, cream white, and so on. "There have got to be about twenty-five shades of white in the Westie," longtime breeder and professional handler, Dee Hanna (D and D Kennels) comments. Check an interior wall-paint chart, or swatches of bridal-gown fabrics in eggshell or ivory to see the enormous range of whites. Or imagine descriptions of Westie colours like "glacier," "snowdrop," "lily of the valley," "vanilla ice," "silver lined," "cloudburst," "meringue," and you should get the picture.

Coat

The Westie's coat is one of his most important assets. A double coat is a must. The outer coat should consist of hard, straight, white hair, of approximately 2 inches (5 cm) in length. The coat is best stripped shorter on the neck and shoulders, and blended smoothly into the longer furnishings of the head, jacket, and skirt—which remain long.

The harder, the straighter, the whiter the outer coat is, the more desirable. A bit of wheaten tipping on a hard, straight coat is considered more correct than a fluffy pure white coat. (In dogs, "wheaten" is a pale, yellowish to ruddy fawn colour.) Furnishings can be softer than the main jacket, but they should never appear fluffy. Soft coats, single coats, dead coats, and short coats are undesirable.

Colour

The Westie's coat is white! It's actually a part of the breed's name: West Highland *White* Terrier. There is a range of whiteness here, but any coat colour other than white, such as a heavy wheaten colour, is penalised in competition.

Some breeders think that the colour and

The Westie's Functional Coat

The Westie's double coat is fully functional. The topcoat of hard guard hairs repels water, and his downy, soft undercoat insulates him from the frequently inclement weather of his place of origin—the Scottish moors and highlands. It also provides natural defense against the nasty adversaries that challenge him—particularly in his indigenous terrain—like fierce animals and unforgiving prickly bramble. The undercoat naturally grows thicker around the neck area to protect against injury and attacks.

Show grooming used to require at least two inches of healthy coat. Now, tighter, tidier grooming with a much more manicured look is favoured over the more casual, natural style that used to be favoured. This change came about in an effort to make Westies more competitive against the more stylised terriers in the group.

This Westie sports a more casual appearance.

harshness of the coat are related. Sandy Davis of Lanarkstone Kennels has observed over her many years of breeding that soft coats are often whiter, but there are always exceptions to this.

Although a harsher coat often accompanies a darker shade, these traits are determined by two separate genes. A darker coat shade seems related to a genetically occurring "dorsal streak," which can be exacerbated by the dryness of a particularly coarse coat. This is why you tend to see this streak in harsh-coated dogs most often. Dorsal streaks run along the top of the back and upper sides of the body, but are absent from the head, legs, lower body, front, and sides of the neck. This trait, though not universal, is not uncommon.

Naturally, most breeders and judges do not want to see a dorsal streak. In the UK, the breed standard gives the colour as "white", with no room for compromise.

The AKC standard states: "The colour is white as defined by the breed's name."

The skin of the Westie should ideally have a grey tinge. A grey-pink colour on the skin and dark grey ear points are desired, accompanied by black eye and lip rims, although many Westies have pink skin.

White Dog Problems

Westie breeders have strived toward the whitest coats possible, but taking this too far has the potential to encourage problems such as those seen in some of the "true" white dogs—Bull Terriers, white Boxers, and other such breeds. These breeds commonly show a tendency toward deafness and blindness. Though these problems are uncommon in Westies, John T. Marvin, long considered an authority on the breed, admonishes breeders to be aware of the link between the depth of pigmentation and its effect on Westie well-being. It is equally important for the buyer to be wary. When choosing a puppy, look for dark pigmentation on the pads. That decreases your risk of "white dog problems." (Thick, dark pads also indicate that the dog has the toughness that developed in the breed as a necessity of navigating their rough, indigenous terrain.)

Most important, though, is the foundation of the West Highland White Terrier as a functional, healthy, strong terrier. Structure is too often sacrificed for that pure white coat. Breeder Dee Hanna asks—rhetorically, one hopes, "Would you eat a strychnine cake if it were frosted with the whitest, most beautiful and tasty frosting in the world?"

The Westie has a double coat that is fully functional—it repels water and keeps him warm.

Temperament

This little terrier is ready for anything. He's bold but not belligerent; if confronted, he's not about to turn tail and run away. He's feisty, intelligent, extremely adept at problem solving, and moderately obedient. He's more responsive to obedience training than many other breeds. Terriers are not known for being "pleaser" dogs, but Westies can be the exception. Bargains between Westies

Neither timid nor pugnacious, the Westie is a people-person dog who aims to please.

and their handlers have been struck many times, and they can be trained and have wowed more than one judge or show spectator.

Despite their independence, there are Westies that have excelled in the obedience ring, particularly in the United States. Most Westie owners who compete in obedience competitions acquire their dogs because they love the breed's personality—obedience is merely an afterthought. Westies are among the most people oriented of the terrier group, and they generally do not hold grudges. Inquisitive, upbeat, and persistent, they do like to please—and it's a double bonus for them to please themselves as well as their owners. Although the self-reliance and independent hunting ability they were bred for can sometimes be an obstacle, those traits are not certain deterrents to obedience. The standard is quite clear in stating that Westies must be neither timid nor pugnacious.

IS THE WESTIE YOUR DREAM DOG?

Before deciding to bring home a Westie, the first question you need to ask yourself is, "Why do I want a dog?" Owning a dog will not save a relationship; it will not help an uncooperative child learn responsibility. The dog may be great "date bait," but the success of your relationship will not ultimately rest on your Westie's lily-white shoulders. If you are thinking of adopting a Westie for your child (and Westies aren't the best choice for children under the age of six), realise that you will end up as his prime carer. If your child becomes involved, that's great, but you can't expect it. A responsible breeder will look for signs that the adult is at least as excited—or more excited—by the prospect of inviting a Westie to join the family.

If you choose well, you'll get a wonderful, intelligent companion with a good sense of humour, and a pal who is game for almost anything this side of bungee jumping. The West Highland White Terrier Club of America has a questionnaire called "The Westie Profiler" on its website, www.westieclubamerica.com, which offers some insight on the question, "Is a West Highland White Terrier the right dog for you?" It's a great tool for deciding if the Westie is your dream dog.

ARE YOU A WESTIE'S DREAM MATE?

The key is adaptability. A West Highland White Terrier can thrive almost anywhere there's someone to love him and keep him secure. But how adaptable are you?

Time Needs

Do you have enough time to spend with your Westie? It's necessary to be available for the dog for frequent companionship; a bored and lonely Westie can act out destructively— even if he doesn't see it that way. Even the best-cared-for West Highland White Terrier may act out because of his instinctive desire to hunt rodents. Balance between work and love works best for a happy Westie, so he should not be kept in solitary confinement. He likes his space, but he also loves his owner—not in an obnoxious or obsequious

Your Westie will depend on you to take care of him for his entire life.

Westie Tale: The City

Laurie Cochin's family, which includes her Westie, Sally, lives in an apartment on the Upper East Side of Manhattan. Sally loves to sit outside and watch the world go by while Laurie chats with all her doggy friends on their busy New York City street. Laurie reports, "One night, on her last walk of the day, she just rolled on her side and fell fast asleep on the sidewalk! People actually pointed to her and said, 'By the way, do you know your dog is asleep?' I had no idea. . ."

way—and he's loyal to the end. When he wants to be with you, you will know it.

Independence

It has been said that he "won't take no for an answer." No, he figures, is a mere consideration—a temporary barrier to yes. Although a good alpha human is necessary so that your Westie doesn't abscond with your credit cards and tell you how to use them, control freaks and Westies don't mesh well. As much as they like to please their loved ones, they also cherish their independence and practice a degree of free will. A puppy socialisation class that teaches general manners will enhance your relationship. The curriculum may not specifically address this aspect of the Westie persona, but a competent and observant instructor should help you establish who's boss.

As long as you provide him with plenty of exercise, your Westie can get by happily in an apartment setting.

City Slicker, Suburban Sentinel, or Thank-God-I'm-a-Country-Dog?

West Highland White Terriers are an adaptable breed. Some living situations may seem more desirable than others, but if a Westie's owners have the sufficient dedication and commitment, the dog can thrive in practically every environment. Some situations may, however, require adjustments—and plenty of tender loving care. Breeder Sandy Davis of Lanarkstone Kennels feels that a Westie deserves a home where he is loved and considered a member of the family, and where there is a lifetime commitment to him. Davis has visions of an "ideal home" (i.e., someone home all day, fenced garden, and so on) but has successfully placed Westies in homes where the physical reality was different from that ideal. Flexibility is never a bad thing.

In the City

As long as you exercise him frequently and allow him to explore the world—on lead, of course—Westies can be very amenable to life in the city. Obviously you must obey local laws and pick up all waste. From the Westie's point of view, the city is a feast for the nose. "Pee-mail" from other dogs will alert him to a tremendous underground canine community. Take advantage of parks and green spots. This is a great opportunity to meet other dog owners, and your Westie will enjoy spending time in canine company. Keep an eye open for large dogs who appear aggressive with other dogs.

In the Suburbs

Westies make perfect suburban watchdogs; they're living, breathing security systems. Their formidable bark belies their size. In fact, your doorbell could become obsolete. First-class deterrents for would-be burglars, Westies will alert residents and neighbours of any suspicious behaviour. They are your "neighbourhood-watch" dogs. However, most are pretty sorry excuses for guard dogs.

A fenced garden on the order of a stockade is necessary, as these terriers are master diggers—in some cases, veritable miniature backhoes wearing white uniforms. Remember that these are clever, problem-solving dogs with Houdini-like escape abilities.

Keep your Westie on a lead when you are out and about. Even the best-trained terriers may only be 99 percent reliable: That one

Westie Tale: The Suburbs

Sherron Corner lives in a California town house, which would be an obstacle to her obtaining a Westie from most responsible hobby breeders. But when she looked into moving, Sherron kept her Westies in mind: a big patio and a nice grassy area for daily exercising and training. Soon after moving in—along with an exceptionally well-trained and accomplished Westie—she purchased a second Westie, Clarence, who has not only earned his championship, but also obedience and agility titles. Sherron proves that there is an exception to (almost) every rule.

The two dogs used on the bottle of Black and White Scotch were the Scottish Terrier and the West Highland White. The dogs on the bottle were named "Blackie" and "Whitey." Many people have erroneously assumed that "Whitey" was a "melanin-challenged" Scottie. False!

squirrel darting across a busy street can claim that 1 percent and cause more grief than you can bear. Westies have a prey drive that rivals the best.

In the Country

In the country, you'll want to keep an eye on your Westie as it is easier for him to stray from home. If a Westie picks up an enticing scent, he may well forget everything else, including where he lives.

However, your Westie can also be useful, as Westies have always been, at keeping the rodent population in check. A pet Westie will turn hunter at the drop of a hat, and will suddenly transform into a fierce ratter.

Some Westies will roll around in really odiferous substances. Others enjoy their fruits and vegetables, and are adept at picking blackberries and other toothsome treats.

Age and Longevity

In general, Westies are a long-lived breed, but that, of course, is never long enough. You can generally expect to have your Westie companion with you for at least 12 to 16 years—and some will remain with you for even longer—sometimes up to 18 or 20 years.

Exercise Needs

A West Highlander will gratefully take whatever exercise he can. He loves to run, play, and tussle. Many are ball players, retrievers, flyballers, and some are

making quite a name for themselves in competitive obedience and agility.

Certain Westies and their "partners" enjoy canine freestyle, sometimes referred to as "dancing with your dog." But it's far more than that—although the result can look like something out of an old Fred Astaire and Ginger Rogers movie (except that neither you nor your dog are required to do it in high heels, backwards).

Most Westies adore the thrill of the chase. And since their conformation has changed so little, they remain among the truly functional terriers. They love to go on hikes—especially to places where the terrain is rough and challenging. They move across and around obstacles with confidence and stamina.

Exercise is essential to keep your West Highland White Terrier in good physical condition. Westies are capable of creating their own games and exercise regimes along with the ones they play with you, so a fenced garden and/or an owner who is willing to take reasonably long walks is beneficial. Suffice it to say that the marvellous things you can do with your Westie are numerous.

Other Pets

Some believe that Westies are more placid than other terriers—milder. But Westies will react if they perceive that they're put upon. An adaptable breed, Westies can be happy as "only dogs" or can enjoy living with other dogs. But they do like attention.

Westies—especially ones that have been spayed or neutered—can be highly compatible with other animals. If you have two, your optimal couple would be one of each sex. Two neutered males can work well, although two intact males can be trouble (and triple trouble if there's a fertile female in the equation). Keeping two females, spayed or intact, can be tricky. They may decide they like each other, but heaven help you if they don't. Two bitches hell-bent on eliminating each other can be very unpleasant and costly in terms of vet bills if you do not separate them.

Competing in agility is a great way to exercise your Westie.

As for feline friendships, variables exist. Westies and cats can be the best of friends: This is especially true if you bring a young puppy into a household where the cat already resides. But if your Westie chases the cat, you might find the cat poring over the classifieds in search of new digs . . .

In general, Westies don't tend to form deep friendships with rats, guinea pigs, or ferrets. These creatures risk losing not only their turf but also their lives!

Westies and Children

This can be a beautiful combination—like strawberries and cream—but the best relationships are forged with care and respect for both the Westie and the child. Sadly, puppies are at great risk when in contact with unthinking or overly exuberant children. On

Teaching Table Manners

Make it very clear to your children—and it is often necessary to repeat this to yourself and to any other adults in the family—that no one is to feed the Westie from the table. It's tempting for little Ashley to pawn off her generous portion of unwanted haggis to the dog, who considers it as good as—well—haggis (he is Scottish, after all). If you don't enforce this rule, you'll end up with a pudgy little dog with an annoying habit of disrupting meals on a regular basis.

the other hand, some recent studies have shown that early childhood exposure to pets reduces the chances of children developing allergies—and not just to pets.

Many breeders are careful to find a situation where children are older—at least six or seven—well supervised, and where they will be taught how to treat their potential playmate with respect. Success depends upon the degree of supervision of both dog and child—again, it is essential for the adult to teach the child proper respect for the puppy's rights. Although complete responsibility for a Westie's care and feeding should never rest on the shoulders of a child, adults can do much to teach children basic care and to set reasonable limits that will take into account both the dog's and the child's rights.

Older, well-socialised children can have a blast with their Westies. Many Westies are quite athletic; they may love to retrieve tennis balls, to play catch, or to act like canine Pelés when it comes to soccer. Certain Westies have demonstrated sophisticated footwork; since they never have to worry about getting their hands on the ball, Westies have a great advantage over their human opponents. Some

Westies can get along well with children as long as proper respect is taught.

31

Learn how to keep your Westie focused and able to settle down if he gets overexcited by playing with others.

will even execute "headers" that rival those observed in World Cup tournaments!

However, rough children of any age are a liability to Westies; parents should exercise great vigilance to make sure a child never gets too aggressive—and if the child does, supervision must be increased to prevent injury to either the dog or the child. In general, a Westie is not the best choice for a neighbourhood where gangs of kids congregate to play. All the excitement and activity are almost irresistible to your Westie's prey drive. The stimulation may be just too much for him and could result in nonmalicious—but nevertheless dangerous—nipping. These are tough little dogs, and with excessive action and motion they have the potential to act like athletes on steroids.

If a Baby Arrives

Though breeders don't recommend Westies to families with newborn babies or toddlers, sometimes the pair is inevitable—especially if the Westie was there first. The arrival of a new baby is cause for stepped-up care and security. It can be a bit easier to teach your dog the new rules before the baby is crawling or walking. You can introduce the dog to the baby and its smells from a distance, but you certainly don't want to place the two in the same playpen just because it would make a cute photo. And please *don't leave them alone together for one moment.*

As the baby grows, the various stages of development offer opportunities to teach the baby how to treat the dog properly. Toys can become veritable "bones of contention," so it's best not to allow the baby and the dog to sit among the baby's toys—or the baby to sit among the dog's playthings. In such situations, your Westie may consider the baby equivalent to a littermate and vie for dominance. (There are also sanitary reasons.)

Eventually, you can teach the child to pet the dog gently—without squeezing— to leave him alone while he's in his crate, and to never disturb the dog while he's eating (disturbing him is asking for trouble). It is also important to teach the child never to hit the dog, hassle him, scream at him, or drag him around. Training a child to treat a pet well offers an opportunity to establish the importance of boundaries and respect— relevant in any relationship. So what might not appear to be an optimum situation can be turned into an opportunity if handled with watchfulness and understanding. Westie and baby will grow up together, and with a foundation of mutual respect, the growing child may naturally wish to take on some of the responsibilities of caring for the dog. Picking up the dog's toys (assuming that you haven't already taught your Westie to pick up his own toys—as well as your child's), accompanying you and the dog to the vet, and helping you prepare the dog's meal can help cement a bond between your two cherished ones.

Westies love attention, and their desire for it can be channeled into teaching them tricks to earn rewards.

C h a p t e r

3

PREPARING

for Your West Highland White Terrier

Sure, he may appear white as the driven snow, but he's 100 percent terrier—attractive and stylish on the outside, but tough on the inside. Capable of convincing lenient owners to let him get away with mischief, he's a giant dog compressed into a small body. He may sometimes even act like the angel he resembles, but there's a bit of the devil in him too. Nevertheless, this sweet, lovable terrier is ever ready for work or play, and his individual personality is every bit as unique as the human with whom he shares his home.

PUPPY OR ADULT?

Some people have never considered that they may have a choice between a young puppy and an older Westie. To avoid the difficulty of and the necessary vigilance that comes with adding a puppy to your family, getting an older puppy or even a mature dog may be just the ticket. In some cases, an older Westie may already be house-trained and crate trained, or simply better suited to your living situation.

A Westie Puppy

Many people prefer a puppy because they think he will be like "putty in their hands," able to be moulded to fit their needs. This thinking is only partly correct. There are personality traits, characteristics, and genetic propensities hardwired into the breed. Once you've determined that you're up to the demands of a tenacious terrier—sometimes with his own agenda—then you can work within those parameters and try to educate or "lead out" your puppy to adapt to your requirements. But it is hard work to socialise a creature with such great temerity, strong instincts—and hypodermic needle-sharp teeth. You will have the opportunity to set the boundaries, and with the feisty Westie, it will be an adventure and an exercise in patience—guaranteed!

Remember that although a Westie puppy is irresistible beyond belief, taking on your young charge is no small commitment. Housetraining, bite inhibition (which one hopes the breeder has at least initiated), and keeping tabs on the puppy when he's not confined to a crate can be a 24/7 job. Some Westies are veritable rubbish disposals and will chew or ingest anything not nailed down.

A Westie Adult

Many breeders will place a retired champion, stud dog, or brood bitch to make room in their breeding programmes for newer stock. Or, a breeder will keep a show prospect, only later to decide to place the dog in a pet home. These dogs are in good health (or any health issues will be identified) and deserve good homes. Also, breeders generally charge less for them. You can also find Westie adults through rescue centres.

A well-socialised Westie with a stable temperament will adapt beautifully to a new, loving home. He will probably be thrilled to become the centre of attention in his new home. He may be house-trained and have had some basic training, and as long as he's loved and cherished and treated with patience and consistency, you'll win his heart. Find out all you can about his past—history, habits, likes, pet peeves, and diet. If well treated and loved, he will never look back; he'll only look forward to his life with his new family.

One of your first decisions will be whether a Westie puppy or adult is right for you.

Many breeders suggest a trial period to ensure a good match. If your dog's primary caretaker can initially take some time off to help him adjust to his new environment, it's a boon. After about a month, consider an obedience class. Not only will it teach him skills or reinforce ones he already has, it will cement the bond between the two of you.

WESTIE LADDIE OR WESTIE LASSIE?

Which make better pets, males or females? Both are great—but if you're adding a puppy, and your preexisting dog is a male, the best choice for a second dog is a female (especially if one or both are or will be spayed or neutered). Two neutered males are the next best option, but adding a second bitch can be dicey. Two females can get along, but for some, it's "hate at first sight," and they will make each other—and you—miserable. There are many exceptions, but why tempt fate?

Males are perfect for people who want a "giving" pet. If you prefer to "care for" a pet, choose a female. If you ask most breeders, they'll agree that the males are generally more affectionate than the females, who tend toward independence. But both make great pets, and you should choose the individual dog with whom you relate best. Many breeders excel at matching puppy to potential owner. But regardless of gender, most dogs grow up to be a combination of their genetic makeup and exactly what their owners train them to be.

Responsible Westie owners check out the legal obligations of owning a dog.

Do not get a Westie—or any other dog—if you are in rented accommodation that has restrictions about having dogs.

Always pick up after your dog. This is not one of the fun aspects of dog ownership, but you face hefty fines for neglecting this obligation.

WHERE TO FIND THE WESTIE OF YOUR DREAMS

Once you've made the decision that the Westie is the breed for you, it's time to explore your options on where to buy, rescue, or adopt your new best friend.

Breeder

By far, the best choice of breeder is the person who breeds for sheer love of the breed. If a breeder's first priority is profit, they may not be as scrupulous as you would wish. A dedicated breeder probably spends more money breeding, showing, testing and caring for her Westies than she earns from selling the occasional pet. In her quest for improving the breed and producing the best Westies she can, she exhibits her dogs at shows to gauge how close she can come to breeding the "ideal Westie." This kind of breeder enjoys the respect she has earned among other breeders and will be as careful and honest in selling you a pet as she is in placing her show dogs. Membership of a Westie breed club indicates that a breeder networks with others currently in the breed and presumably breeds according to a prescribed code of ethics.

When visiting a breeder, look over the puppies to see if they are healthy.

Locating a Good Breeder

Many responsible breeders do not advertise. So how do you find one? If you're online, the Kennel Club website can direct you to Westie breeders in your area. Log on to www.the-kennel-club.org.uk. You can also contact Westie breed clubs for information on the litters being produced in your area.

Dog shows are among the best places to locate a good breeder. Shows are where you'll see what a Westie should look like, and you may get a chance to speak to breeders. If you see a Westie that particularly strikes your fancy, ask the handler if he knows of anyone who is expecting a litter related to this dog. Some people are a little tense before exhibiting their dogs, so wait until breed judging has ended before approaching the handler.

Most breeders love educating those curious about their breed, but should you encounter someone who is rude, don't take it personally. Perhaps she just lost in the ring, so she takes it out on the nearest target—you. Keep trying, and talk to someone else.

Show Quality Versus Pet Quality

Some breeders will offer both "show quality" and "pet quality" Westies. Of course when it comes to quality, it's impossible for anyone to ascertain whether a young puppy will work out as a show dog. The breeder simply hedges her bets. Many "keepers" have had their bite reverse or a testicle stay lodged in the abdomen, while a "less-than-perfect prospect" morphs into a knockout, causing at least one breeder to kick herself for letting him go. But no one really loses in the end. Both "show quality" and "pet quality" dogs should be healthy and of wonderful temperament.

Visiting the Breeder

When you visit the breeder, you can see the whole litter with their dam. If the sire isn't present, ask to see a photo. Caring breeders are very particular about the homes their puppies go to, so expect an interrogation. They may want to know what kinds of dogs you've had in the past and how long the dog will be left alone each day; some ask to check out your house and garden. This may seem intrusive, but all you have to gain is a happy, healthy, well-socialised Westie puppy from a breeder who cares—and an ally!

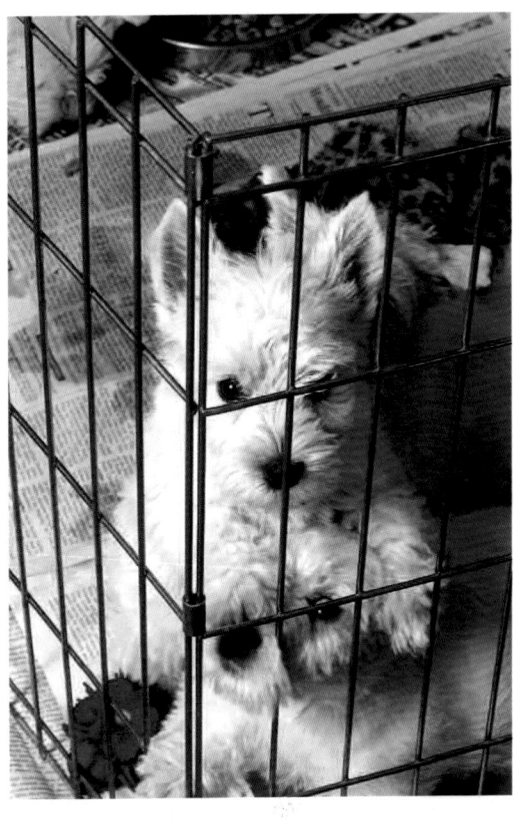

Puppies you visit at a breeder's facility should be in clean, safe environments and eager to visit with you.

At the breeder's, the puppies' environment should be kept clean, and the puppies should appear bright-eyed, healthy, and playful with their littermates. Observe how they interact with

Co-ownership

The breeder may offer to "co-own" a show-quality dog with you, so that the dog may obtain his KC Championship. If the Westie is a female, the breeder may want to whelp a litter. In most cases, this means the breeder makes the arrangements to show her, while you can still keep her as a pet most of the time. All this should be clearly indicated in the contract. If you want to learn to show and groom your Westie, some breeders make outstanding mentors. However, co-ownerships have their risks, and the concept attracts its share of control freaks, so proceed cautiously.

Kennel Club registration papers do not guarantee that you have a quality Westie. The Kennel Club is merely a registry that does its best to ensure that your dog is the offspring of known and registered purebred KC-registered parents of the same breed. The KC does not protect against fraud and mix-ups by disreputable breeders. The fate of your Westie's quality rests upon your support of breeders who breed ethically.

humans as well. Young Westie puppies should not live exclusively in outdoor kennels, nor should they be confined to a shed or flimsy outbuilding. Home-reared puppies stand the best chance of becoming ideal pets.

Questions to Ask the Breeder

Don't be afraid to ask the breeder questions, either. If anything, the breeder will be impressed that you have done your research. Ask her how she got started breeding and showing. Willingness to share enthusiasm is a hallmark of a good breeder. How long has she been breeding Westies? (More than three years is good if this is your first Westie.) What can the breeder tell you about your puppy's ancestors? Trust your intuition and don't be impulsive. Take your time and ask away!

An ethical breeder will be honest about the pros and cons of owning a Westie. She should be familiar with the breed's most common health issues. If she denies ever having had any health problems, she is either being dishonest or she hasn't been in the breed very long. Also, be very suspicious of breeders who whelp one litter after another.

Request references from previous customers, follow up, and ask them questions about the Westie they bought from this breeder. A breeder who baulks at this or tries to minimise the opinions of their other clients may not be your best bet. Also, most devoted Westie breeders will ask that the pup be returned to them if for any reason you decide you need to give it up.

Temperament Tests

Some good breeders use temperament tests to assist them in evaluating the behavioural tendencies of a pup. Breeders use them for the following reasons:

- to help select puppies for show or obedience.
- to place puppies in the most appropriate homes.
- to determine how to encourage the puppies to grow into mentally sound adults.

This test is fairly reliable and points to character tendencies. Remember that environment also plays a great role in shaping temperament; nevertheless, temperament testing can be a valuable tool for placing a puppy in his best environment.

Backyard Breeder

You need to be wary of certain breeders, often called "backyard breeders." This type of breeder is not always malevolent, but they can often be unaware of important genetic and health issues that good breeders watch out for. If you choose to buy from one of these breeders, you should subject him to the same degree of questioning that you should any breeder. However, run like the wind if any of the following are true of the breeder:

- He makes his living from selling dogs. He typically has a number of breeds, sometimes as many as ten to twenty—and offers puppies of each.
- She doesn't ask many questions and doesn't want to answer many either.
- He doesn't test the dogs for genetic problems.
- Price comes up early in the conversation (usually first).
- She will sell to anyone—no questions asked.
- He refuses to show you the facility where the dogs are housed.
- She arranges to meet you in a car park or a service area to sell you your puppy.

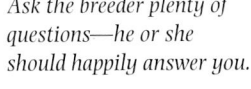

Ask the breeder plenty of questions—he or she should happily answer you.

Rescue Me!

West Highland White Terrier Rescue can be an excellent source for acquiring an older dog (rescues rarely have puppies). Not only can you find a wonderful companion, you can help a dog in need. A grateful Westie is a wellspring of affection to the human who gives him the love and attention he deserves. Please note that some rescued dogs come with health and behavioural issues that need to be addressed, although often these issues ease or disappear with the work of dedicated foster homes, generous advice from experts, and consistent follow-up in the adoptive home.

Registering Your Dog

The Kennel Club

At the time of the sale, the breeder will sign and date the Breeder Registration Certificate, which the new owner will receive with the puppy and all other documentation. The new owner completes a Change of Ownership form by supplying the required information on the back and returns it to the Kennel Club within ten days for the Kennel Club to validate.

The new owner receives Kennel Club Registration Documents, a full colour Registration Certificate, and a booklet that provides general information about the Kennel Club and the fascinating world of purebred dogs in England.

American Kennel Club (AKC)

When you buy a dog represented as AKC eligible, the seller should give you a properly filled out AKC Dog Registration Application form. Submitting the completed form with the fee enables you to register the dog with AKC. After processing is complete, you receive an AKC Registration Certificate. Sometimes a breeder will sell you a dog on a Limited Registration. This is to encourage you to sterilise the dog. Offspring of dogs registered on a Limited Registration will not be AKC eligible. A Limited Registration entitles your dog to participate in all AKC activities except conformation.

Where do these rescued Westies come from? Some may have been picked up as strays, but most are surrendered because of extenuating circumstances, such as the death of an owner, difficulties with young children, or residential restrictions. Others come from households that were just not prepared to care for a dog.

The key is finding a rescue organisation that understands the crucial importance of balancing these dogs' needs with those of the people who adopt them. You can contact breed specific rescue organisations, which are often run on a local, volunteer basis. A Westie breed club will put you in touch with reputable Westie rescue oganisations.

Westie rescue organisations affiliated with the breed clubs have strict codes of conduct and require that rescue applicants undergo thorough screening. These groups never knowingly place dogs with biting issues or major aggression issues. Sadly, the people who surrender them sometimes consider rescue organisations as "dumping grounds" for a maladjusted, aggressive dog (often that way through the family's own fault) that they were ill equipped to nurture in the first place. For this reason, assuming they have resources, most rescues try to foster their dogs before placement to get a true reading of the dog's characters.

Rescue Westies, some of unknown background and others who

carry more emotional baggage than those with happier beginnings, can potentially bring with them handsome rewards. Plus, with their devotion, they remind you that you can make a difference in an innocent animal's life. But more than likely, you'll end up feeling gratitude toward them for letting *you* into their lives. You can find a Westie rescue through www.westierescuescheme.org.uk.

Gimme Shelter

Occasionally a Westie will come into an all-breed rescue centre, but they are hard to come by—and the paucity of smaller dogs means that, if they're adoptable, they're likely to be snatched up quickly. But its worth taking time to find out if any Westies are available for rescue. The best plan is to contact the major charities that specialise in rehoming.

Not only can rescuing a Westie provide you with an excellent companion, it can mean helping a dog in need.

These include the RSPCA www.rspca.org.uk, Blue Cross (www.bluecross.org.uk). Dogs Trust (www.dogstrust.org.uk) and Battersea Dogs Home (www.dogshome.org). These organisations have branches nationwide, so you can be directed to a rescue centre near you.

Dog Match

At most rescue centres, you will be asked to fill in a questionnaire so that staff have some idea of the type of dog you are looking for, and your home circumstances. Obviously if you are looking for a Westie, you will be quite specific when you fill in the questionnaire.

The questions that you will be asked will probably include the following:

- Have you owned dogs before?

Rescue dog Maggie Mae.

Maggie Mae, adopted from Westie Rescue of Missouri became WHWTCA's Versatile Dog Maggie Mae Beason, CGC, TDI, CG, CD, ME. She came to rescue unspayed and with a large hernia. After her convalescence, volunteers transported her to Illinois, where she lives with her Westie "brother," Winston, and her human, Pam Groves. She is the first rescue Westie ever to have earned a prestigious Versatility Award.

Glendennin's Pride, CGC, NAP, NJP, was abandoned at seven months of age and adopted by his foster "mother." Glennie's issues included fear of men and separation anxiety. Helped by many, including a male truck driver/rescue volunteer and then a dedicated male instructor, he overcame his fears. Now more confident than ever, Glennie earned his Canine Good Citizen and began agility training (and has earned his novice titles), earthdog, and obedience. He lives with his Westie sister, Molly, and has become a happy little boy.

Portraits of rescue dog Glennie and his "sister," Molly.

- Who lives at home?
- Do you want a male or a female?
- Do you have a garden?
- Is your garden enclosed?
- Will your dog be left alone at home?
- Do you own other dogs?
- Do you own other pets?

Rehoming staff at the rescue centre work hard at finding the best possible homes for the dogs in their care. There is no point rehoming a Westie in a family with children if that dog has a history of being fearful or even aggressive with children, regardless of how much you want the only Westie currently available at the centre. You must be prepared to accept the decisions that are made in the knowledge that they are in the best interests of the dog concerned.

Adopting a Westie

If you find a Westie that looks as if he could be a good match for you and your family, you will need to get to know the dog to see if everyone gets on with each other. Rehoming staff recommend that you visit the centre on a number of occasions, so you can take the dog for walks, and spend some time with it. In some rehoming centres there are 'real life' rooms, which are like a family rooms where the dog to be adopted and family can spend time together at close quarters. This is particularly important if you have children in the family.

The aim of this 'getting to know you' period is to see how a Westie will react in a variety of situations to check out that he can cope with his new family. If you already have a dog at home, you will be encouraged to arrange a meeting at the centre so the two dogs can be supervised and their reactions monitored. If a Westie has behavioural problems, a professional behaviourist will work with the dog, and will help you with a training programme if you decide to go ahead and adopt.

Show breeders often keep only one or two puppies for show and sell the rest as "pets." Often the differences are subtle. These pets have been bred with the same health, temperament, and looks as the future champions.

Home Check

If you find a Westie that is likely to fit in with your lifestyle, the rehoming centre will organise a home check to ensure you can provide a safe, comfortable and secure home for your new Westie. Staff will pay particular attention to the garden, and will insist that fencing is in good repair.

Do not be resentful of this intrusion. Remember, the staff have only one objective—ensuring a dog is rehomed permanently and can look forward to a long, happy and fulfilling life with his new family.

WESTIE COMES HOME

After considering how adding a pup or adult dog will affect your family, you come to an enthusiastic consensus about purchasing or rescuing your Westie. Now it's time to bring your little white bundle of joy home. If possible, schedule your newcomer's arrival on a weekend or during a holiday in order to spend time with the new puppy.

Puppy Proof Like it's Going Out of Style

Your house is a cornucopia of both dangerous and valuable items. Within your adorable, innocent Westie rests the potential to destroy anything "by any means necessary." I have verifiable reports of Westies having swallowed 9-volt batteries, disposable razors, air conditioner plugs, and bubbler-head sprinklers—sometimes to the tune of hundred of pounds in veterinary bills. And as for the years whittled off owners' lives—priceless!

Working Dogs Register

A purebred dog may be ineligible for conventional KC registration for many reasons. Her litter may be unregistered, she may have unregistered parents, or her papers may be lost. Surrendered or abandoned dogs adopted by new owners from rescue centres may come without papers. However, the Kennel Club has a Working Dogs register that allows dog and owner the opportunity to participate in all approved KC performance and companion activities—except for conformation. Check out the details at the Kennel Club website (www.the-kennel-club.org.uk).

Electrical wires, poisonous plants, antifreeze, cosmetics, and cleaning supplies, which can be extremely hazardous, are attractive to dogs—especially puppies. Keep holiday decorations out of your Westie's reach. Never burn candles where he can get to them. Keep cellar doors and upper-story windows closed. Rubbish should be inaccessible to your dog. Be extremely cautious if you use insecticides, pesticides, or chemical fertilisers. (Better yet, avoid them altogether.) Keep printed literature out of reach. Westies are intelligent, but their idea of "devouring books" is more literal than ours.

Although the breed is small, the fencing that contains a Westie needs to be able to stand up to his persistence.

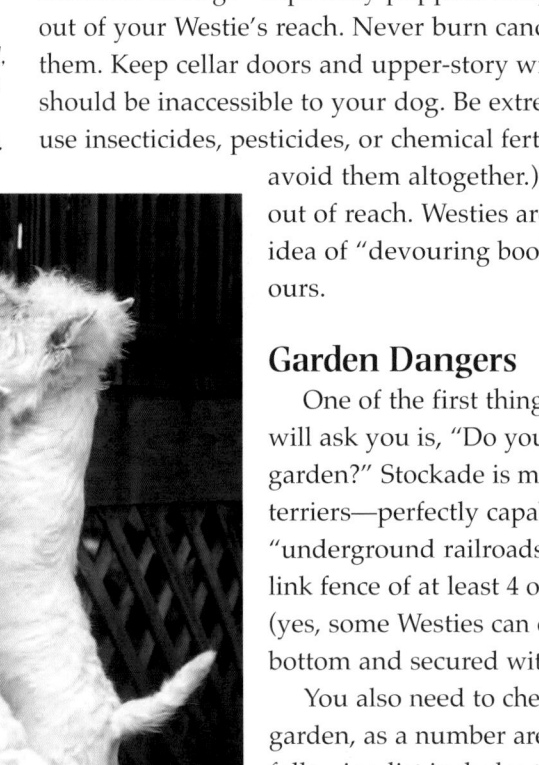

Garden Dangers

One of the first things a good Westie breeder will ask you is, "Do you have a securely fenced garden?" Stockade is more like it. Westies are terriers—perfectly capable of digging their own "underground railroads" to freedom. A chain-link fence of at least 4 or 5 feet (1.2 or 1.5m) (yes, some Westies can climb) reinforced at the bottom and secured with a padlock works well.

You also need to check the plants in your garden, as a number are poisonous to dogs. The following list includes the common plants that are toxic to dogs. For further information, contact your local garden centre.

- Azalea
- Daffodil
- Dumb cane
- Elderberry
- Foxglove
- Holly
- Hyacinth
- Iris
- Laurel
- Lily of the valley
- Milkweed
- Mistletoe

- Nightshade
- Primrose
- Stinging nettle
- Oleander
- Ragwort
- Wisteria
- Philodendron
- Rhododendron
- Yew

Timing

As a rule, "Christmas puppies" are a bad idea. With all the holiday activity and the visitors, one would be hard-pressed to find a more stressful time for new dogs and new owners. The exception is a quiet household that doesn't make much of the holidays. Spring and summer can be optimal for housetraining, but puppies are born in their own time—and if you're committed, you can make any time work.

Leaving his mother, home, and littermates is one of the great stresses in a puppy's young life. The stimulus flooding of a new home, new people, and even new pets can be intense. But given your patience and compassion, your puppy will quickly bond with his new family. Remember also that puppies need lots of sleep, so resist the temptation to overload your Westie with too much excitement; you'll both be happier. Keeping him on his former routine can soften the transition. Continue to feed him at the same time and place every day, and all will be well. Set up your Westie's

A securely fenced garden is a necessity with a Westie.

No-Tie-Out

Chaining your Westie outside to a stake in the ground (called a tie-out) not only deprives him of love, training, and attention, but it is cruel and can be dangerous. Westies are social creatures—they want to be with you, not alone in a garden.

crate in a special place in the house—this will be his refuge. Never use this spot to punish the dog.

The First Night

Your Westie puppy's first night may be traumatic for him. It is strange for him to be away from his family and littermates, so why not let him spend the night with you (in his crate) in your bedroom? By doing this, you will stay attuned to any stirring that could indicate he needs to relieve himself. As you head out in your nightshirt and nightcap into the starry, starry night, know that this can help expedite the house-training process.

He may cry a lot. Just talk to him in a soothing voice as he drifts off again. At the beginning, you may miss a few z's before he sleeps through the night, but there is light at the end of the tunnel. Try putting a few of your T-shirts in his crate. This will comfort, pacify, and make his initial night's sleep less stressful.

Introducing Your Westie to Other Pets

If you already have another dog, Deb Duncan—trainer, behaviourist, and Westie owner—recommends setting up the new dog's "personal effects" about a week before introducing the little interloper to your first dog. This helps your first dog get used to the physical changes in his environment. "Prior to bringing home the new pup or dog, try, if possible, to bring home a towel or a T-shirt with the 'new' dog's scent on it. Place it where your current dog can investigate it. Arrange to expose your new dog to an item with your present dog's smell," suggests Duncan.

Allow the two future roomies to meet on neutral territory. Don't be shocked if your current dog regresses in his housetraining or manners. Duncan stresses that ignoring this behaviour is the best way to reduce the anxiety that causes it. Create situations where you can reward or pay attention to both dogs simultaneously. This helps diminish any latent "sibling rivalry" and reinforces the idea that good things happen when the two are together. Treat and praise in tandem.

If you have a cat, you'll want to prevent cat-o-mania. Separate the new pup from your cat until the pup is tired. Make the initial, supervised introduction or get-acquainted visit when the pup's energy is depleted. If your cat is extremely testy, consult with your vet about mild sedation for the feline. Observation: It is definitely easier when the cat is there first.

Here are a few tips for picking the perfect name for your new Westie. If you have multiple pets, make sure that their names sound distinct enough as to not cause confusion. If your first one is named "Sharon," don't name your next one "Darrin." Some owners recommend that you select a name that ends with either an a (as in the name "Cara") or an o (as in the name "Elmo") The long e sound also works well. Names ending with long vowel sounds are easier for your dog to hear, since they carry well over longer distances. Some people like to name a Westie to match his heritage. Books on naming a baby or websites that list Scottish names abound.

Some people name their dogs according to their physical traits or personality. There aren't many Westies named "Spot" or "Ebony." But some names arise spontaneously. When an adorable Westie puppy urinated on the lap of Oregon Westie breeder Mary Lou Ludlow, little "Peony" unwittingly chose her own name.

Names that mean "fair" or "white" are plentiful for these beautiful white terriers: Alban, Blanche, Bianca, Guinevere, Jennifer, Berrin, Gandolf, Bevin, Banya, Muriel, Leigan, Kennan, Keevin, and Finola are all possibilities. Scottish names with associations to the words white or clouds or brightness include Alpin, Ceana, Fiona, Sorcha, Fingal, Findlay, Lilias, and Kenna.

It's important to only invoke your Westie's name in association with something positive. You don't want to yell, "Here, Cloudy! Come here and let's express your anal glands!" or your Westie will simply stop coming to you.

SUPPLIES!

Here are a few essentials you'll need for your new addition.

Food and Water

Your Westie requires a high-quality, nutritionally balanced diet, and fresh, clean water at all times. Common wisdom suggests that you obtain—from the breeder or rescue centre—a transitional supply of the food the dog has been eating and continue feeding the same food. Abruptly changing your Westie's food can result in diarrhoea and general gastric upset. If you opt to change foods, do it on a half-and-half basis for the first week—and keep him on a high quality food. (High quality does not mean "performance" food, unless you're planning to add your Westie to an Iditarod team.) A cheap dog food is lower in essential nutrients than the pricier brands, so you may end up at the vet's spending any money you save. Feed only the best quality food with whole ingredients and natural preservatives.

What to serve your Westie's food in? Inexpensive, durable, and easy to clean stainless steel food and water dishes work best. Avoid plastic bowls; they're incubators for bacteria. Ceramic bowls, though breakable, work well too.

Westie Gift Certificate

If you must give a puppy as a Christmas gift, and the breeder insists (rightly) on delaying his homecoming, try this: Make a "Westie gift certificate." Incorporate a picture of the puppy you'll be purchasing into a card. Buy a crate and fill it with a baby (temporary) collar, a few squeaky toys, stainless steel food and water bowls, and perhaps a tiny chew like a Nylabone. Be creative, and don't forget to include a book on West Highland White Terriers— like this one!

Collar and Lead

An adjustable, lightweight collar made of either leather or nylon, with a secure clasp or a buckle is the best choice. A "choke" or a "slip" collar is inappropriate and dangerous for everyday wear. These types of collars tighten around your dog's neck, and if caught on something can seriously injure or strangle the dog. Collars of this type are used in some training methods, and should only be used by professionals.

The best leads are 4 to 6 feet / 1.2 m long and made of leather or nylon. Quality leather leads are comfortable, last a long time, and break in like a good pair of loafers. Cheap ones can chafe your hands. Do not allow your Westie to mouth or chew on the lead or he'll quickly acquire a taste for it.

Bed

A bed can be made of any soft, washable material. Many dogs find the faux sheepskin type very comfortable. If you'd like something more basic, plain towels or T-shirts that carry your scent work fine. Avoid wicker—a Westie puppy can easily transform it into a dangerous chew-fest.

Crate

An important housetraining tool and general all-purpose den for your Westie, a crate is arguably the mother of all dog supplies: a refuge, a safe travel container, a convalescent haven, a time-out place—and at ten o'clock you will know where your Westie is! Whether to select a plastic, wire mesh, or solid oak crate is up to you.

Exercise Pen (Ex-pen)

An ex-pen is a portable wire playpen for your dog. Perfect for travelling or for confining him to a small area of the house, an ex-pen allows you to keep tabs on each other.

Dog Door

A dog door that opens into a securely fenced garden makes life (and often housetraining) a breeze. Your Westie won't need your permission to go outside. Easy to install, the most common type has a clear plastic panel that opens easily and closes with magnets. Like most gadgets, they come in different grades and qualities.

Toys

Safe toys have parts that won't detach. Rubber toys provide the best jaw and mouth exercise—they're ideal for chewers and dogs that spend a lot of time alone. Hard, hollow, rubber beehive-shaped toys are popular with most dogs. Stuff the hollow middle with treats such as peanut butter, or biscuits. Vinyl squeaky toys also work well for the more tentative chewers. Plush toys pick up different smells, so dogs are fond of these, but some dogs seem determined to disembowel stuffed toys. Watch out for squeakers, which can be dangerous. Flavoured floss toys can keep teeth and gums in shape. Nylon bones like Nylabones are sturdy and beneficial and come infused with appealing flavours. Discard any toy that gets reduced to a size your Westie can swallow.

Don't overdo it. Too many toys can lead to a jaded, bored Westie, but a few well-chosen ones can keep him from destroying your pricey footwear or handbags. It's amazing how quickly Jimmy Choos can be transformed, much to your horror, into "Jimmy Chews," or your beloved black Prada bag to "nada."

Baby Gates

When you don't want your Westie playing unsupervised in your house, a baby gate can provide the necessary barrier. It may also prevent your puppy from stumbling down (or ascending) steep stairs.

Cleaning Supplies

Rags, paper towels, and enzymatic cleaners made for cleaning up pet "mistakes" are good to have on hand. White vinegar works well for cleaning out plastic crates.

A baby gate can provide necessary safety for your Westie.

Locket-style tags allow you to insert a piece of paper where you can write down your dog's home information, final travel desination, or your emergency contact person. It's convenient because you can update or change the information as needed.

IDENTIFYING YOUR DOG

Provide your Westie with a flat collar and tag that carries your name, address, and phone number. Some collars allow you to write information with a laundry marker, so that even if the tags fall off, he can still be identified.

Microchipping

Microchips provide positive and reliable identification for your pet. A chip about the size of a grain of rice is painlessly inserted into your pet. Modern rescue centres and vets can scan animals for this ID device. Find out which brand of chip is most used in your area and go with that one. Usually, there is a central database that houses the chip's ID number, so you can notify the company if you or your Westie relocates. However, the microchip should not replace a traditional ID tag.

Tattooing

Tattoos also provide positive identification when done correctly. The best place to apply a tattoo is on the inner thigh, where it will be visible.

What to Do If Your Westie Is Lost

Hopefully, you will never have to go through the trauma of a lost dog. But in case it does happen, do should do the following:

- Keep on file current photographs of your Westie for identification purposes. Including yourself in some of the photos helps establish your ownership.
- Always have a current identification tag attached to your pet's collar. You can be found by the number on the tag. Animals without identification may be euthanised after a relatively short time. Identification buys time.
- Small dogs can get into some weird and tiny places, so search your property thoroughly. Look everywhere—inside appliances, inside pipes, and under anything! A frightened or injured dog will hide in dark spaces, so bring a torch. Check under houses, in storage sheds, garages, rubbish bins and under cars.
- Gather your whole family to call your Westie's name. Use a dog whistle to get your pet's attention. The high-pitched sound from these whistles can carry up to a mile or more.

Stop, be quiet, and listen for your pet to "reply."

- Stroll the neighbourhood: Talk to the residents of each house in the area where your pet was lost. Leave with them a written description of your pet and your phone number. Because of scam artists, never leave your full name or address.

- Contact the dog warden in your area, and also visit all of the rescue centres in the vicinity. Many have computerised lost and found information, but it's up to you to go to the centre to check out any leads in person. Walk through the kennels; don't assume that telephoning is sufficient.

- Check listings of animals left at local veterinary surgeries; leave behind a flyer and a picture.

- Vist pet stores in your neighbourhood. Talk to the staff who have contact with many doggy people who may have news. You may also be allowed to post a flyer on the noticeboard.

- Post flyers within a mile radius of the place the dog was lost. Posting flyers results in more found pets than any other method. Be sure to include a colour photo of your Westie. List the date and place you last saw him, his breed, sex, age, and weight, along with your telephone number. But do withhold

If you lose your Westie, do not despair. Get to work and try all possible methods to find him.
A larger number of all missing dogs are reunited with their owners, and lost dogs have been known to turn up even after several months have passed by!

It's important to have a clear photo of your dog that will show any distinguishing marks or features in case he gets lost.

Never allow your Westie to dangle his head out the window. Perils include close-moving vehicles that can graze your dog, airborne particles that can harm eyes, and automatic windows carelessly kept unlocked (so that the dog can inadvertently operate them).

several distinguishing characteristics of your dog. If the person who claims to have found your pet cannot describe these features to you, they do not have your pet.

- Check the "found" ads in newspapers and place a "lost" ad.
- Ask schools in your area to post flyers. Kids are everywhere and may see your dog.
- Talk to everybody you run across and give them your Westie's description and your phone number. Neighbourhood kids are a great resource.
- Talk to local businesses, your postman, refuse workers, and your neighbours.
- Call radio stations that offer lost-pet notices as a public service.
- Notify the Westie breed club that covers your area.
- In all instances, offer a reward, but avoid revealing the amount.
- Don't ever give up. Lost dogs have been known to return home after months!

TRAVELLING WITH YOUR WESTIE

The Westie's size makes him very easy to take along with you wherever you go.

By Car

Leaving your Westie loose in the car is dangerous. The safest way to travel in a car with your precious cargo is to place him in his crate with a blanket, pad, or towel in the backseat. To prevent the crate from shifting, use either the seatbelt or bungee cords.

There are also special harness-style seatbelts that you can use in combination with the car seatbelts. This gives your dog a safe alternative to roaming, posing on the dashboard as an ornament, sitting on your lap in order to influence your driving, working the automatic windows (which can be dangerous and distracting), or wending his way on the floor toward the accelerator pedal under your feet—the perfect den in his mind. However, Westies are problem solvers, and some escape artists have found ways to extricate themselves from seat belts. (Most, however, are incapable of unlatching their crates.) When buying the harness, get your dog's measurements and weight. If you take the dog with you, you can try the harness out on him in the store. A Westie will usually wear a small or medium, depending on the brand. Practice putting your dog in his harness. Once you've purchased it, allow him to wear it around the house until he no longer notices it.

Getting Your Westie Adjusted to Car Travel

Some techniques might help your Westie adjust to car travel. The younger he starts, the better. Either harness or crate your puppy in the backseat, and take a short ride. When he's quiet, reinforce that behaviour with a treat. Extend the duration of your trips, making sure they're frequently associated with positive places—the pet-supply store, the park, a play date with another dog—so as to overshadow the trips to those places not on his wish list. If you're using a harness and he tangles it, simply readjust it—and continue on. Be as tenacious as he is, and all will work out. Use the same methods with an adult dog as you would with a puppy. For particularly tough cases, just proceed more gradually and with more patience.

Make sure your Westie's ID tags are up to date before you travel.

- On long trips, provide your Westie with a stretch and a toilet break (on a lead) at least every four hours.
- Some owners have found that feeding their carsick puppy a gingersnap or two can settle his stomach. (And you, too, can enjoy a snack.)

Car Sickness

Most Westies love car travel, but you may have one prone to car sickness. This can arise either from insecurity or from some physical tendency. Short car rides can help puppies adjust to this aspect of car travel. Take your puppy on an empty stomach, and provide lots of fresh air by opening a window. Start short and work toward longer trips. Many pups will fall asleep in their crates. Also, natural and homeopathic remedies for car sickness are available online or at health food stores; these are effective for some dogs. You may obtain prescription pills or give a car sickness medicine as per vet instructions, but if the sickness is so severe that your Westie needs sedation, you're better off leaving him home.

By Air

In the UK, it was formerly a rare occurence to travel abroad with your dog. But with the introduction of the Pets Passport Scheme, foreign travel—including air travel—is becoming increasingly popular. When you make arrangements for your flight, inform the agent that you are travelling with your dog. Check back to ensure that both reservations are confirmed; airlines usually only allow one or two pets in the cabin. Your carry-on dog-carrier bag must be airline approved. Weight requirements vary with each airline, but the dog must always fit comfortably into his carrier. He needs enough room to stand up and turn around, and the bag must fit under the seat. Westies generally travel quite well; many are lulled to sleep by the whirring of the plane's engine.

Before your flight, your Westie will require some prior exposure to the carrier bag. Start by opening the bag and placing some treats in it so that he'll enter it of his own volition. Leave it out, and let him get accustomed to the pleasant associations. Eventually, let him go inside with the treat, and zip up the bag. If he's sedate enough, start carrying it around the room while praising him constantly. Then carry the bag to the car and take him for a short ride. Continue the praise and up the ante—taking him into a store or a building in the bag. As he adjusts, add more distractions and situations—such as lifts and noisy places.

Consider tranquilisers only as a last resort for a super-anxious dog, since they can interfere with breathing. If tranquilising is inevitable, confer with your vet about trying the medication once before the flight to ensure your Westie doesn't react adversely. You don't want a surprise like that when you're in the air where your dog cannot get medical attention.

Also, consider the following tips for before and during the cabin flight:

- Bathe and groom him to reduce dandruff, smells, and allergens.
- Toilet and exercise him before you get to the airport, and arrive there no earlier than necessary.
- Trim his nails so that they do not catch on the mesh of the carrier or—if he's in cargo—on any wire of the kennel.
- Withhold food and water for a few hours before boarding.
- At the airport, keep your dog in his bag—except in designated areas.
- Double check that all paperwork, including proof of rabies vaccination, is correct.
- Once you've boarded, place the carrier under the seat. Don't unzip the bag—Westies are quick, and your little jack-in-the-box will pop out in a split second. If you need to slip him a morsel of food or water while in flight, wait until after the onboard food service has ended.
- If your layover requires leaving the plane, ask a flight attendant or other airline employee if there is an area where your Westie may relieve himself.

Airline flight regulations in regard to pets change almost constantly. For more specific information about travelling abroad, go to www.defra.gov.uk.

Staying at a Hotel or Motel

Many hotels and motels offer accommodations to people travelling with small pets. Online, you can check www.dogsinvited.co.uk and www.petfriendly.co.uk, which will provide up-to-date information.

In the hotel room, be courteous and practice etiquette. When you go out and leave your dog in the room, turn on the TV. (so that your dog does not feel deserted.) Set up his food and water in the bathroom—or some other noncarpeted area. Ask the hotel if they use any antipest products, and if they do,

A kennel or pet sitter may be good options when you can't take your Westie with you.

Don't Leave Your Westie Alone in the Car

You should not leave your dog alone in the car, especially on hot, sunny days, and *never* in extremely hot or cold temperatures. If you absolutely must leave him (in moderate temperatures), it's essential to at least minimise risks: Always park close to your destination, so that he is never out of your field of vision. Do not park in the middle of large car parks. When stopping for food, try to use a drive-through, or select a restaurant that has glass windows to allow you to see your dog.

find them and remove them. Always clean up after your dog—inside and outside. If you've got a male Westie who enjoys leaving "liquid mail," consider buying and bringing a bellyband or cummerbund. There are many venues, including dog shows and websites, that sell these ingenious items.

IF YOU CAN'T TAKE YOUR WESTIE WITH YOU

If you're going to explore the Galapagos Islands, attend the Academy Awards, or bicycle across the United States, your Westie may be unable to accompany you, so you'll have to figure out how to provide for his care. Some breeders willingly board any dog they've bred, or a friend or relative might offer to take care of your Westie during your absence. But not everyone is that fortunate.

Boarding Kennels

If you do not have an instant solution to your holiday problem, you will need to find one. For a normal, healthy Westie, consider a boarding kennel. But before committing, request a tour. And during holidays and summers, many kennels are booked up for months in advance, so plan ahead.

Ask your vet or other dog owners for boarding recommendations. Any facility you consider for your Westie should meet the following criteria:
- It should be clean.
- It should have both indoor and outdoor runs.
- It should allow dogs opportunities for exercise and play.
- It should offer grooming and bathing facilities.
- It should require proof of health and vaccination.
- It should have easy and dependable access to veterinary services.

A good kennel will allow you to bring your Westie's food, toys, and bedding, if you choose. They'll provide climate control as needed. If you have any doubts about the boarding kennel, keep on looking until you find an establishment that you are happy with.

Pet Sitter

Some pet sitting services will house-sit as well as pet-sit; others will make arrangements to come in and walk, feed, and play with your dog. If you are considering this option, meet the caretaker first and observe how he or she interacts with your Westie. Ask for references and inquire about experience. Ask how the caretaker might handle certain emergencies and how many clients he or she cares for at once. Set up a specific schedule together for caring for your dog. Provide instructions on how to get in touch with you and your vet and any other pertinent information.

Home Boarding

If your Westie gets on well with other dogs, you might consider home boarding. In this situation dogs are cared for in a home environment rather than being confined to kennels. Obviously, you need to check out the people running home boarding and ensure that the number of 'boarders' are kept at a reasonable level.

If you choose this option, make sure the provider realises that the rough-and-tumble, growly playing typical of Westies and other terriers is perfectly appropriate and not a sign of abnormal aggression.

A regular pet sitter will come to love your Westie as her own, making the experience of outside care a positive one.

Your West Highland White Terrier

You may have noticed that your Westie likes to eat pretty much anything. Although he's technically classified as a carnivore, or meat eater, he'll even eat (what you'll see as) rubbish if you allow him. So it's up to you to feed him a good, nutritious diet, and provide him with fresh, clean water at all times. When it comes to food, the choice is practically unlimited: dry food, canned food, semimoist, home-cooked human food, species-appropriate raw food (ARF), or any mixture thereof. Factors that influence your choice are convenience, expense, nutritional value, taste, availability, allergies, and whether you like the human resources and animal practices of the company that manufactures a food. What's appropriate for one dog and owner may not be appropriate for another.

Avoid feeding your Westie anything he hates. How would you like to be offered deep-fried lard burgers for every meal? Sure, he'll eat almost anything (even the lard burgers) rather than starve. But mealtimes should be fun and festive for everyone, so why not go the extra mile and find something nutritious that your dog really enjoys? If he likes something for a while and then tires of it, just change it. (Gradually, of course.)

COMMERCIAL DOG FOODS

Financially, there is little that separates the best and worst commercial foods, but the disparity in quality is priceless. Feeding a top-of-the-line food can make all the difference in the world when it comes to your Westie's well-being.

Dogs have been eating ready-to-eat foods only since World War II, when the army needed a convenient, easy-to-store food for its dogs of war, so it developed K-9 rations to accompany its K rations. Today, a vast majority of dog owners feed their dog primarily or solely a commercial diet—usually dry food. (There has, however, been a growing trend toward alternative diets.) Many of these cheaper products contain barely enough nutrients to be considered "nutritionally complete," so many of them are not particularly ideal nourishment for your dog. Their greatest advantage is their convenience.

Digestive problems are typical of a dog fed a poor-quality dry food, canned, or soft,

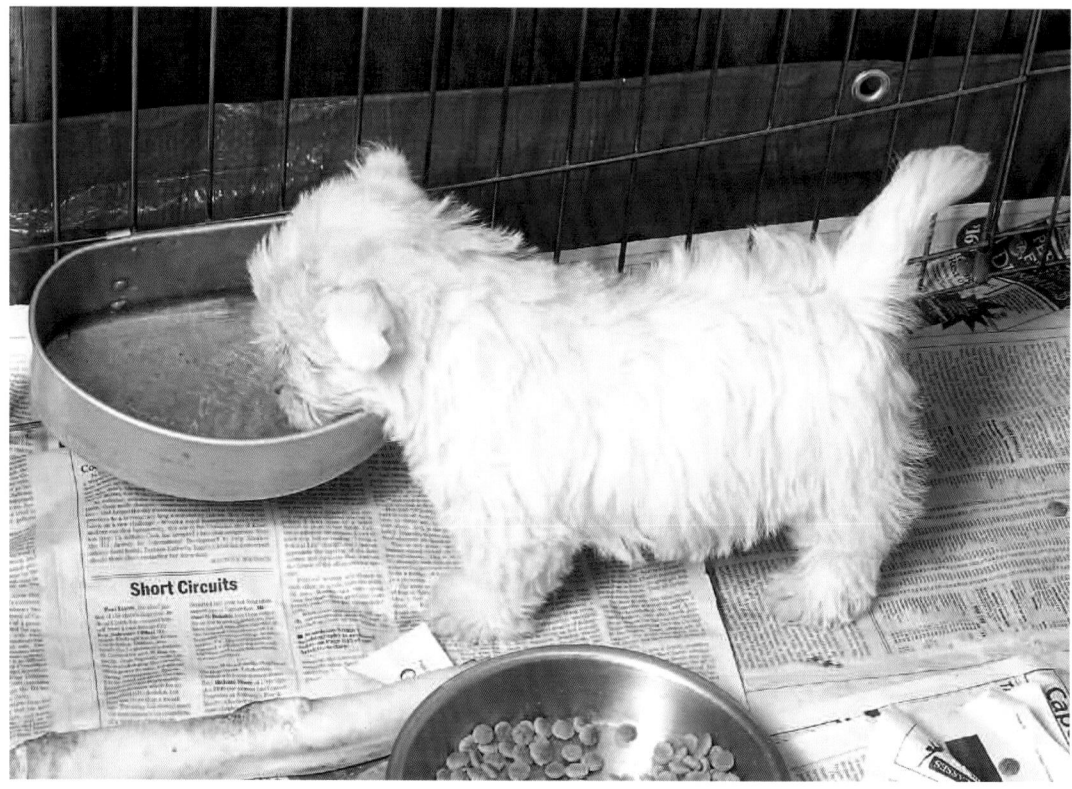

Remember to provide your Westie with plenty of fresh water.

moist processed dog food. Symptoms of digestive upset include flatulence, copious and odiferous stools, diarrhoea, several bowel movements per day, halitosis, and frequent vomiting.

Some newer premium products come close to top nutrition, but you probably won't find them in supermarkets. More and more pet stores are offering them, or you can get them online. Some companies will deliver food right to your door. Also, there's been some growth in the holistic pet movement, and there are stores that specialise in high-quality, organic, and all-natural pet food.

Fortunately, the highly competitive dog food market is driving up the overall quality of commercial foods. More decent choices exist than ever before, but it's up to consumers to educate themselves about what they're buying. So how do you know what food is best for your Westie? Start with the label.

Reading the Label

In the UK, pet food is controlled by the Food Standards Agency (FSA), which has to adhere to EC guidelines. Manufacturers also belong to the Pet Food Manufacturer's Association (PFMA), which, in turn, follows guidelines laid down by the European Pet Food Industry Federation (FEDIAF). Every label contains the following information:

- Typical Analysis. The percentage of the following must be listed: proteins, oils and fats, fibre, moisture (when it exceeds 14 per cent), ash (this represents the mineral content of the food and is determined by the burning of the product).
- Ingredients List. The ingredients must be listed in descending order by weight. They can be indicated using category names laid down by the Regulations (e.g. 'meat and animal derivatives') or by individual names. If particular attention is drawn to a specific ingredient (e.g. With Chicken), the percentage of that ingredient component must also be listed.
- Additives. If preservatives, antioxidants or colourants have been added to the product their presence has to be declared.
- Vitamins. If Vitamins A, D and E are added to the product, their presence has to be declared.
- Best Before Date.
- Bar Code.
- Batch Number. A batch number or the date of manufacture must be given to facilitate traceability of the product.
- Net Weight. The net weight must be given in accordance with the Feeding Stuffs Regulations 2002.
- Name and Address. This is the name and address of the company responsible for the products. It may be a manufacturer, packer, importer, seller or distributor.

Processed foods, even high-quality ones, are still cooked. Since heat destroys essential enzymes, adding an enzyme food supplement to your dog's diet may help. In many cases, replacing the enzymes can make a big difference, but feeding a higher-quality food is necessary, too.

Dry Food

Dry food can be a convenient, nutritionally adequate dog food. Dry food can help reduce tartar buildup on teeth, although it's no substitute for proper dental hygiene. However, it doesn't clean the canine teeth, since dogs chew it with their molars (that is, if they don't simply bolt it down). Compared to other feeding options, basic dry food is the least expensive, primarily due to its high grain content. Dry food tends to be low in fat, an advantage if your dog is overweight or a couch potato. Fancy colours and shapes may appeal to humans, but your Westie couldn't care less. Have you ever heard any dog rejoice, "Would you check this out? A purple rainbow!"

Many, but not all, dry food companies use BHA or BHT as preservatives. Until recently, ethoxyquin (originally a rubber hardener developed in the 1950s) was commonly used in both human and dog foods, but due to increasing consumer pressure, ethoxyquin was proclaimed unsafe for human food. It cannot legally be used to preserve human food, since some fairly

Puppies have different nutritional needs than older dogs.

compelling evidence links it to cancer, liver disease, and immune disorders. However, it is still being used in a few pet products. Fortunately, an increasing number of companies are switching to vitamin E as a natural and effective preservative. Play it safe by opting for those foods.

Other things to consider if feeding a conventional dry food-based diet: Westies, unlike other larger working breeds, thrive on a diet that is lower in protein. Dry food varies in its percentage of protein and fat and fat-to-protein ratios, so check the label. If you feed a product with 21 percent protein, the fat content should be at least a 10.5 percent or greater. The higher fat content helps lubricate a drier coat, a common problem in Westies.

Canned Food

Although canned dog food smells, well, like dog food to us, given a choice, most dogs would choose it over dry. However, canned food is considerably pricier than dry food. To find the best canned food for your dog, look for one containing whole meat, fish, or poultry as the first ingredient. Most inferior canned foods list water as the first ingredient. You rarely find premium canned foods at your supermarket. You can find better-quality food via the manufacturer, pet stores, dog shows, or at some veterinary surgeries.

Canned food contains a very high percentage of water—generally about 75 percent. However, if the food is labeled as "gravy," "sauce," or "stew," the water content may exceed that. Some canned dog food contains grain products; some contains only meat. Whether or not grain products benefit dogs is controversial. The best canned foods use whole veggies instead of "grain fractions" such as rice bran, rice flour, or brewer's rice. Since dogs, though primarily carnivorous, are on the cusp of omnivorous, fresh vegetables add necessary nutrients to their regime.

High in fat, canned food is best used by mixing it with dry food, especially if your dog needs a taste enhancer. Due to the increased water content of the food, dogs with urinary tract infections frequently do better on canned dog foods than on dry food.

Semimoist Food

Semimoist food contains about 25 percent water and just as much sugar, in its many guises: corn syrup, beet pulp, sucrose, and/or caramel. Sugar promotes obesity and tooth decay. The shelf

- Some people feed their dogs a basic dry food diet and enhance it by adding different foods every day: green beans, carrots, gravy, or canned meat for extra nutrition and variety.
- Often, dog food bags carry the recommendation that you feed your Westie enough food to sustain Bigfoot. Talk to your vet about how much food your Westie really needs for each stage of life.
- Serve food at room temperature if possible. Very cold food eaten rapidly can make a dog vomit. Some dogs prefer food if it's slightly warmed.

life of these products is lower than either canned or dry food. Semimost food is not usually recommended for Westies.

Picking the Best Commercial Food

Almost any kind of meat can end up in dog food. In many places, pet food manufacturers are free to use road kill, diseased cattle, or any other source of protein that tickles their fancy. Fortunately, some companies use only human-grade meat. Companies were not formerly permitted to state this valuable fact on their labels. However, this regulation has now been changed, so you can easily choose human-grade meats for your dog.

For the best nutritional options, stick to the following simple guidelines:

- Avoid dog foods containing "by-products." Meat by-products are the part of the animal not deemed fit for human consumption.
- Avoid food overloaded with grain or cereal by-products. These ingredients are the part of the plant left over after the milling process. Technically called "fragments," they appear on labels in many aliases. Carbohydrates in food should be whole grains.
- Stay away from soy, which many dogs are allergic to.

If you are feeding your dog a commercial diet, make sure it is high quality.

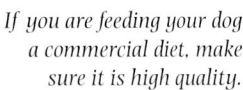

Storing Food

Improperly stored food can become breeding grounds for moulds and toxins, some deadly. Buy only the freshest foods available. If you use a commercial food, check the manufacturing date. With a small breed like a Westie, you're best off buying in small bags. Buying in bulk may save you some money, but in the long run the money you save on food may end up going to your vet. Smaller bags get used more quickly, which means the food stays fresher.

Store the food in a dry, cool place away from sunlight. Keep the food in the house or in another place with a stable temperature. Temperature fluctuations can produce moisture in the food storage container and encourage the development of mould or toxins. Store the food in its original packaging or in a special airtight container. Don't use a plastic rubbish bin—even clean plastics can produce dangerous vapours.

If the food smells bad, or if your dog suddenly refuses to eat it—even though he appears hungry enough to chew his own feet off, discard the food, or return it for a refund.

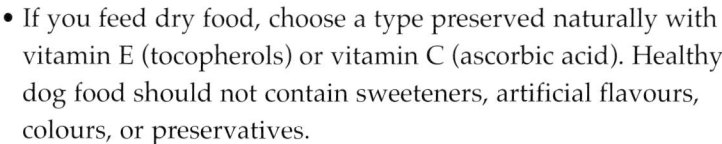

- If you feed dry food, choose a type preserved naturally with vitamin E (tocopherols) or vitamin C (ascorbic acid). Healthy dog food should not contain sweeteners, artificial flavours, colours, or preservatives.
- Select food with the specific name of a meat ("beef," "chicken," "turkey") as the first ingredient. Avoid foods whose label lists a generic "meat" or "poultry." Also be aware that just because a product has "beef" listed as the first ingredient doesn't mean the product is mostly beef. Some companies engage in a deceptive practice called "splitting." If they can possibly do so, they will divide the cereal products up into separate categories, like "rice" and then "brown rice." Added together, there will be more grain fragment than beef. But because the companies are allowed to list them as separate ingredients, beef is listed first.

Be sure that any foods you feed your dog do not have any of the following on the label:

- Meat by-products.
- Chicken by-products.
- Fats or proteins named generically such as "animal fat" or "poultry fat." Instead look for "beef fat" or "chicken fat" or "lamb meal."
- Food fragments such as brewer's rice, corn gluten, etc.
- Artificial colours.
- Sweeteners including corn syrup, sucrose, and ammoniated glycyrrhizin, added to attract dogs to otherwise unappealing food.

- Propylene glycol. This toxin is added to some "chewy" foods to keep them moist.
- Artificial preservatives such as BHA, BHT, and ethoxyquin.

Any one of the above can cause dogs to vomit, or worse, to develop health problems over a period of time.

NONCOMMERCIAL DIETS

Appropriate Raw Food (ARF)

Raw, natural diets have steadily gained popularity (and spurred much controversy) over the last several years. Some vets are adamantly opposed; others support them or maintain a wait-and-see attitude. Many holistic practitioners wholeheartedly endorse the diets.

Raw feeding/natural rearing advocate Christine Swingle, a Westie breeder and exhibitor for over forty years, points out that dogs have short digestive systems, designed to digest food quickly. This means they are well suited to digesting raw meat and bones and will stay healthy on a species-appropriate raw-food diet (ARF).

Swingle and others correlate the general decline in canine health to improper diets. For example, cancer is now the leading medical cause of death in all dogs, but forty years ago, cancer was uncommon. Additionally, autoimmune disease is on the rise, and more than 85 percent of all dogs will, by the age of three, manifest some level of periodontal disease. A healthy immune system and digestive system start with the foods we feed. They're the foundation for good health.

Much, though not all, processed commercial dog food is a concoction of grains, cereals, chemicals, and dyes. A great way to recycle society's waste and very convenient for the increasingly busy and overworked consumer, these products mainly benefit the burgeoning pet food industry, which profits handsomely. Raw food, full of live enzymes, is digested quickly, and the

If your Westie eats grass, he will not suddenly turn into a sheep. Although they can't digest it, most dogs will occasionally graze. It's just one of the mysteries of the universe. They probably just think it tastes good.

A home-cooked diet can be tailored to your dog's specific needs.

nutrients are utilised with greater efficiency.

Swingle stresses that learning to feed raw food correctly is absolutely crucial to anyone planning to attempt such a diet. Feeding a raw-food diet, although easy to master, requires extra thought, understanding, research, and knowledge. Without this understanding, converting to an ARF diet can be tricky and even dangerous, especially if the appropriate foods are not fed over a week's time. Before starting your Westie on ARF, make sure you read up on the subject. The resources section at the end of this book contains some titles for suggested reading. Swingle also recommends, if possible, joining an online support group and continuing to learn as much as possible.

If you feed your dog raw meat, obtain the freshest cuts available. For example, chicken necks and wings have a perfect calcium/phosphorus ratio. But common bacterial components of raw meat may include campylobacterosis, E. coli, listeriosis, salmonellosis, trichinosis, and tapeworm. Protozoan infections are also possible. Still, it's rare for a dog to contract these diseases, since a healthy dog's system is essentially equipped to handle them.

The most dangerous consequence of bone consumption is a perforated intestine, which allows toxins to escape into the dog's system. Even some raw bones can splinter when dogs chew them and can puncture the oesophagus or stomach. One way to reduce this risk is to grind the bones thoroughly or feed a commercially prepared raw diet.

What you include in a raw diet over a week's time is important.

With the right guidance and information, it is not that difficult. It is important to feed a properly rounded raw diet. Excessive dairy, too many vegetables (a few will suffice), or extra grains and cereals (there is some debate here) are not recommended. Misuse of supplements can also thwart correct nutritional balance.

A raw diet isn't a cure-all. A switch to raw repast is no guarantee that all health issues will disappear. Diet merely supports and promotes good health. Although digestive and some other problems often clear up with ARF, diet alone cannot restore health.

Yet there are many positive results of feeding ARF, as follows:
- reduction or absence of tartar on teeth and healthy gums
- small, odourless stools
- absence of flatulence
- anal glands that generally "self-express"
- easier weight control and better muscular condition
- elimination of bad breath

Very young puppies need to eat several times a day.

Switching from processed dog food to raw food should be gradual, as should any diet change. Also, some dogs simply cannot regain sufficient digestive health to tolerate ARF. In those cases, a high-quality dry food, supplemented by digestive enzymes and raw grated veggies, is a good choice.

Home-Cooked Meals

Many people opt to prepare their dog's diet at home. You can tailor the diet to his particular needs, and you'll be using quality ingredients that exclude artificial preservatives and by-products. Home-cooked diets are more expensive than commercial ones, but you can offset the cost by including healthy leftovers from your own meals with your Westie's.

Preparing a diet at home does require vigilance and training. The main perils of such diets are calcium/ phosphorus imbalance and inadequate levels of calcium, copper, iodine, and certain vitamins—especially the fat-soluble ones and some of the B vitamins. People who feed their dogs a diet of fresh meat without the bone and vegetables must supplement the food with a calcium source like bone meal. The correct amount is difficult to gauge, and some bone meal supplements contain dangerously high levels of lead. In this regard, you are probably safer using a commercially prepared food or feeding raw meaty bones. Many excellent books contain nourishing homemade diets that you can adapt to your own purposes.

People Food

It's not a crime to feed your dog most foods that are healthy for human beings. "Don't feed your dog table scraps" was part of a slick propaganda campaign perpetuated by dog food manufacturers. Dogs thrive on fresh vegetables, chicken, beef, and fish. Many dogs also like fruits, including apple slices, melons, bananas, and berries. (Mine adore the seedless mandarins they receive in their Christmas stockings every year.) Low-fat plain yogurt and small amounts of cottage cheese are also delightful treats and add a bit of calcium. However, most dogs don't have the necessary enzymes to process large quantities of dairy.

Neither you nor your Westie needs biscuits, crisps, doughnuts, or pork rinds. Many of these cause gastrointestinal upset, not to mention obesity. Hopefully your dog is unaccustomed to high-fat foods; several organs in a dog's body can be stressed from eating these, and pancreatitis, which is potentially fatal, can also result.

Food can be a tool—a reward for good behaviour—that helps your Westie associate pleasing you with pleasing himself. But there is a subtle difference between using food as a bribe and as a reward. A Westie who is not food-motivated is a rare find, but if yours is more motivated by a favourite toy or a tennis ball, use whatever works.

The single best thing you can do to ensure your dog is well nourished is to feed him a variety of different foods. This will not only make eating more pleasurable for him, but if you start early enough, it may help protect him from developing allergies. Provide your Westie with something besides a steady diet of commercial foods. Well-chosen, lower-fat table food can boost the quality of a meal by providing high-quality human-grade nutrients. (Rotation and variety are also important components of the ARF diet.)

AGE-APPROPRIATE FEEDING

Puppies

Very young puppies (two to four months) need to eat three or four times a day—their rapid development of mind and body require extra fortification. Usually a high-quality growth formula kibble softened with some warm water is best. You can add some yogurt, rape-seed oil or corn oil, or cottage cheese for palatability. Follow the instructions of your breeder and/or vet.

Let your baby Westie eat as little or as much of his portion as he chooses. Pick up unfinished food after about ten minutes. Coaxing, cajoling, or adding *pâté de fois gras* will only make him finicky, and he'll be wondering why any dog would eat dog food unless stranded on a desert island.

Around six months, start feeding two meals—breakfast and dinner. At a year, you may want to reduce it to once a day, although some owners choose to stick with two meals.

Feed your baby Westie in a quiet place away from people and other pets. You can also feed him in his crate, which will reinforce the crate as a safe place. In any case, your puppy should get accustomed to your close presence while he eats. He should learn that you control his food. If he growls, remove his food until he stops the inappropriate behaviour. This is the best way to discourage food-guarding. However, tempting fate by allowing children or others to hassle the dog while he's eating is unfair.

Adults

The right time to make the switch from puppy chow to adult formula can easily vary from Westie to Westie. Generally, by the time he is nine months to a year old, it's time for the transition.

Things to Avoid Feeding Your Westie

Chocolate
Chocolate, especially baker's chocolate, can cause a range of problems, including cardiovascular difficulties and even seizures.

Hoofin' It?
Cow hooves as dog treats are dangerous. They are the number one cause of tooth breakage in dogs (and they smell disgusting, to boot).

Grapes and Raisins
Reports have recently implicated large amounts of grapes and raisins (between 9 ounces and 2 pounds) in acute canine kidney failure (although no one knows exactly why). The kidney shutdown is so dramatic that aggressive treatment may be necessary to save a dog's life.

Hold the Onions
Do not feed your dog raw onions. They are potentially toxic and can cause a serious condition called Heinz-body haemolytic anaemia. Ingestion of large amounts of raw or cooked onions in dogs can cause toxicity, leading to the destruction of red blood cells. This causes anaemia, weakness, jaundice, bloody urine, and eventually death, one to six days after the ingestion. Don't freak out, though, if your dog eats a single onion ring. Large amounts cause the disorder, but to be prudent, shun them altogether.

Rawhide
Many Westies like rawhide chews, sometimes so much that they'll practically inhale the stuff—and the rawhide can stick in their throats. Even if your Westie gets it down, it's bleached, treated, and preserved with who-knows-what. Some are basted with flavours that can cause diarrhoea. If you notice this, switch to plain rawhide treats, or—better yet—eliminate them altogether.

However, if your Westie is looking rotund at five or six months, he may be ready for adult food—that is, if you are not overfeeding him. (Package recommendations tend to be "generous"—both to your puppy's girth and to the manufacturer.) Your Westie's feeding requirements will vary with his individual metabolism and level of activity. Ask your vet if you have any questions about how much to feed your Westie.

Free Feeding Versus Scheduled Feeding

You have the choice of feeding your adult Westie on a schedule, or "free feeding," which means leaving food out all day. In most cases, dogs should be fed on a schedule—once or twice a day, if they are being fed a high-quality commercial adult food. Although feeding on a schedule is slightly more time-consuming than free feeding, it gives you much more control over what your Westie is eating.

Free feeding is strongly linked to obesity. It's hard to monitor how much a free-fed dog is actually consuming, and if you own more than one dog, someone may be hogging all the food. Dogs don't make very good decisions about these things. Their genetic heritage has programmed them to gorge whenever food is available, and even though your Westie hasn't been living off the fat of the land for eons, his genes don't know that. Where food is concerned, he thinks he's still a wolf.

Make sure you feed your Westie age-appropriate food.

Treats and Bones

Most people enjoy giving their dogs treats, and as long as you don't overfeed, go for it. Read the label on any box of dog treats. There are a growing variety of nutritious dog biscuits on the market, made with health-supporting organically grown ingredients. Avoid treats that contain artificial colours, flavours, and dyes.

If your Westie is getting a bit round in the middle, replace high-calorie treats with fresh vegetables like broccoli. (My dogs go nuts for bell peppers and even artichoke leaves!) Offer your Westie raw carrots or any vegetable or fruit that he will eat.

Bones are naturally balanced sources of calcium and phosphorous that dogs practically worship. Avoid feeding cooked bones, since they easily splinter and can damage your dog's throat and digestive system. Also, forgo the sterilised bones available in stores. Their unnatural hardness can break teeth. Whole fresh bones are safer, but some people prefer to have the bones thoroughly ground.

Raw bones may carry bacterial dangers, but after personally feeding fresh raw chicken wings and necks to my dogs for years—without incident—I feel that the nutritional and dental benefits are hard to deny. It's important that the bones be both fresh and meaty. Start your dog off gradually, and watch him carefully. Supervision is important—dogs need to learn to eat bones properly.

Seniors

As your Westie ages, he will becomes less active and require fewer calories. Westies are considered "seniors" at about age seven, but ten is probably more accurate. At this age, if your Westie is eating a high-quality dog food, you can safely reduce his portion. Lower-grade dog foods, however, contain just enough vitamins and minerals to keep your dog going at the amount indicated, so you will have to supplement with vitamins and minerals. Fish oil, glucosamine, chondroitin, and MSM (methylsufonylmethan) can benefit many older animals. Just check with your vet before supplementing your senior Westie.

Geriatric dogs do develop special dietary needs. Unless they have kidney trouble, they need more protein than young adults, which the better commercial food manufacturers take into account. They also benefit from arginine, an essential immune-system-booster amino acid, and from omega-3 fatty acids to keep their brains and nervous system in good repair.

If your older dog continues to do well on his regular diet and is not losing weight or condition, there's no reason at all to switch him. So-called senior dog foods are not required to meet any predetermined standards, so there's a fair amount of variation in formulas—read the label and select carefully if you do decide to switch.

SUPPLEMENTS AND SPECIAL DIETS

Supplements are less necessary for your dog if you're feeding a higher-quality diet. Puppies are particularly vulnerable to the dangers of oversupplementation, so don't add minerals or vitamins to your puppy's diet without a recommendation from your veterinary surgeon.

Sometimes a medical condition can necessitate a special veterinary diet. Conventional allopathic vets will prescribe a special diet to address a dog's particular medical issue. Many people who have chosen holistic care for their Westies have found alternative supplements, herbs, homeopathic, and other alternatives helpful in preventing problems, maintaining balance, or treating special medical conditions. But even these alternatives emphasise sound nutrition as a starting point in treatment.

OBESITY

Obesity is the number one nutritional disorder in dogs (and people). A growing proportion of adult dogs in the United Kingdom are overweight. This exacerbates problems such as diabetes and arthritis, and shortens a dog's life.

Obesity is defined as being 10 to 25 percent above ideal weight. How can you tell if your Westie is overweight? Look at him from above. You should be able to see an actual waist. By running your thumbs along your dog's spine, you should be able feel each rib without putting pressure on the rib cage. When viewed from the side, his waist should be well defined—like Scarlett O'Hara's.

Don't give in to overfeeding your puppy just because he's cute.

Most cases of obesity arise from overfeeding and underexercising. (In a few instances, a medical condition like hypothyroidism or insulin imbalance can cause the problem. Check with your vet to rule out any medical issues before attempting to slim him down to "Speedo" weight.) Unless your Westie can drive to the store, fill a shopping cart with junk food, and escape without paying or setting off an alarm, you cannot blame him for being hefty. You're the one with the loot and the wheels. You decide what goes into his bowl and what treats to give him.

Like the rest of us, Westies enjoy tasty treats. Watch his weight by giving him small pieces of carrot or apple instead of high-calorie goodies.

To make sure your Westie's weight stays normal, feed him a proper amount of food for his ideal weight, and exercise him—it's that easy. Your vet can advise. Try to stay away from treats, but if you do like to treat your dog, try baby carrots. If your Westie is overweight, a commercial "lite" food may help him shed unwanted blubber. Pick a high-quality formula that includes specific weight loss directions.

Most dogs don't seem to mind exercise nearly as much as most people do. A long power walk will benefit both of you. Some people take turns with their dogs on the treadmill. However, before starting any exercise or weight-loss programme for your dog, consult your vet.

GROOMING

Your West Highland White Terrier

The Westie is often classified as a "nonshedding breed." Westies have a double coat: an outer coat that consists of straight, hard white hair, and an undercoat that is short and downy with insulating properties. In its natural state, the Westie's hair needs help to "shed," usually with the help of a groomer. Otherwise it will mat and you will end up with a tangled and unhappy Westie. In the breed's indigenous Scottish Highlands, the double coat provided protection against the elements, but there were enough natural bramble and bush to "groom" him naturally.

Most Westie owners find that working with a professional groomer is the best way to keep their Westie looking good. The Westie coat does need some special attention, and many find that it's best to leave it to the professionals. Even with professional grooming, though, you'll still need to spend time brushing your Westie.

Some owners do learn to do their own grooming. They may be dissatisfied with professionals, wish to learn the skill themselves, or want to save some money. In any case, grooming your own Westie can contribute to the bonding between the two of you. Count on making mistakes while learning, but have faith that the hair will grow out.

THE GREAT DEBATE: STRIPPER OR CLIPPER?

There are two ways to care for your Westie's coat: stripping and clipping. If you have a show Westie, the breed standard requires hand stripping, but if you are not showing your dog, it's more than likely that you will end up clipping him.

Stripping

With a stripped coat, loose, dead hairs are plucked out to leave a vibrant, healthy, and functional coat. Using a stripping knife, you hold a small amount of hair on the blade and pull dead hairs out of the coat. Finger and thumb can also be used for hand stripping. If you are not showing your dog, whether or not you strip (or "pluck") your pet is strictly optional.

Some advantages of stripping are that it makes your Westie's coat harsher and coarser,

helps maintain its double-coated protection, and cuts down on doggy odour. On the other hand, stripping can irritate your dog (many Westie's don't like it), it's harder to find a groomer willing to strip your dog, and it's more expensive and time-consuming than clipping.

Few "garden variety" groomers are willing to strip a Westie: It takes too long, and it requires a great degree of skill to master the art (and it is an art). However, some breeder/exhibitors may be willing to teach you the process. Others may "moonlight" and will strip your Westie for you if you're willing to pay. You may occasionally run into a professional groomer who'll strip your Westie, but it can be expensive. There are also books and pamphlets that provide instruction on how to do it yourself.

Clipping

If you are not showing your dog, clipping your Westie will probably be your best option. Clipping, which you will probably want a professional groomer to handle, requires special dog clippers with various blade attachments. It can also involve the use of scissors. Clipping is a lot easier on the dog and far less time-consuming than stripping.

Clipping the coat discourages the growth of hard hair, and eventually the dog's coat becomes just soft undercoat. A clipped coat tends to lose pigment, but that is hardly a problem in this breed, where whiter coats are desirable. The soft coat that results

Not only will grooming get your Westie ready for his "glamour shots," it will give you the opportunity to check for any growths, sores, external parasites, or bruises. You will notice if there's anything you need to bring to your vet's attention. Grooming is actually a good habit to get into, and good preventative medicine.

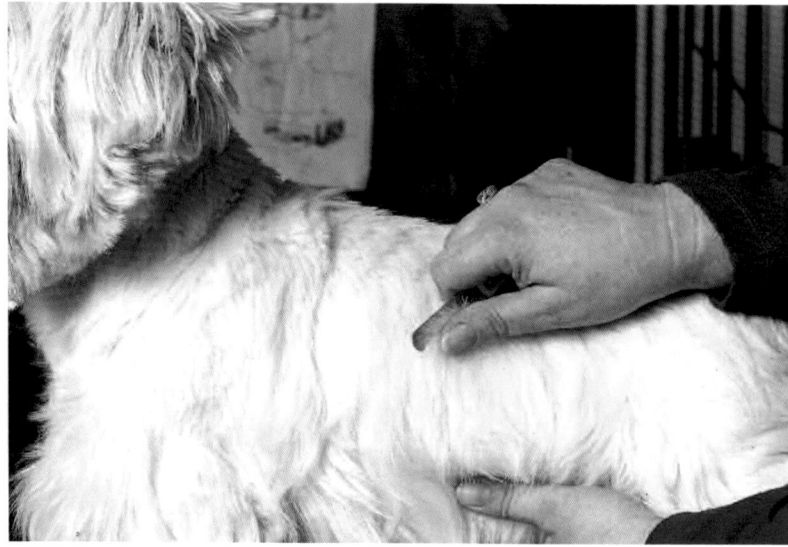

above: Stripping the coat involves plucking out dead hairs with a stripping knife.

from clipping will not be as dirt-repellant or water-resistant as a hard, stripped coat. However, with regular brushing, most dogs, either clipped or stripped, should remain fairly clean and odour-free.

A well-clipped Westie can look quite winsome—if you and the groomer know the look you're after. Many competent all-breed groomers can do a decent job of clipping. Most pet Westie owners are quite comfortable with a clipped dog, who—if groomed by a professional—generally requires trips to the groomer every four to eight weeks for bathing, clipping, and nail trimming.

Keeping your Westie neat doesn't have to take a lot of time, especially if you do it regularly. If you do strip him, pulling out a little hair a couple of times a week can keep things from getting out of hand. And if your dog is clipped, keep him brushed between grooming sessions.

Westies with certain skin conditions may benefit from stripping, as it toughens the skin and removes any dead coat. (A good brushing will also remove some dead hair.)

BRUSHING

Brushing not only makes your dog look beautiful, it keeps him clean and healthy. And as for your Westie, well, he gets to be the centre of attention. Brushing your Westie stimulates his skin and spreads the skin's natural oils throughout his coat. It encourages good circulation and reduces shedding. Westies are considered a low-shedding breed (there is no such thing as a nonshedding breed that has hair), and brushing helps shed the hair and prevents any mats from forming, which can be a real drag. If mats form and are allowed to remain too long they will tighten against your Westie's

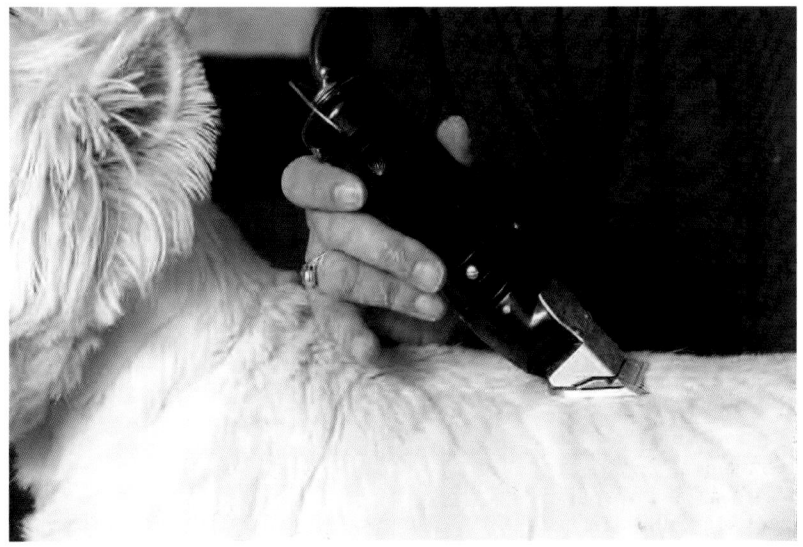

Clipping the coat requires special dog clippers.

A new generation of "hybrid" grooming tools allow the Westie owner to do a little of both stripping and clipping. These ingenious tools remove or strip out a fair amount of loose hair, and cut some hair as well. Easy to use with very acceptable results, these tools offer a nice compromise between stripping and clipping.

skin and cause irritation. (Note: Mats often hide in armpits.) Pet-supply outlets do offer special tools to detangle and break the mats.

Whether you are stripping or clipping your Westie's coat, you still need to accustom your dog to the idea of brushing between formal sessions. Initially, brushing is a strange feeling for him. Begin slowly, especially if he appears stressed or nervous. A conscientious breeder has probably done a bit of "priming" in this area—perhaps by pulling out the puppy coat before placing him with his new family.

Brushing Tools

It's important to use the proper grooming tools for the job, as follows:

- A high-quality slicker brush works well.
- A waist-high table or bench with a rubber mat for your dog to stand or lie on will make brushing more comfortable.
- A professional grooming table with an arm and a noose can be a good investment.
- Finer-coated Westies require a comb with teeth that are close together, such as a flea comb, which will help reduce dead undercoat (and fleas, of course). Removing dead coat allows the skin to breathe.
- Heavy-coated Westies require hairbrushes. A brush with round balls on the end of each bristle gets through with less resistance. Or—and this especially applies to hand-stripped terriers—a wider-toothed comb or an undercoat rake will do the trick.
- Another option for grooming/brushing is a "hybrid tool" that both pulls out the loosest dead hair and cuts some as well. These can produce very attractive and satisfactory results.

How to Brush Your Westie

Before you start, pay heed to the condition of the coat. Is it dry, or greasy? Hot spots, thickening of the skin, and other deviations from normal could indicate a problem.

To brush, place your Westie on a stable surface such as a grooming table or the floor. In nice weather, you can do it on a patio or on a deck. (You'll be providing nice building supplies for nest-building birds!) Work through the coat with a slicker brush, brushing the leg hair up and then down into place. Brush the hair of the head up to make the typical Westie "chrysanthemum" look. Follow all grooming and brushing time with a treat or a toy or some one-on-one playtime. Many dogs find the end of the session a relief—even cathartic. Don't forget to praise your dog to the skies.

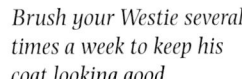

Brush your Westie several times a week to keep his coat looking good.

How Frequently?

How often should you brush? According to longtime Westie owner Beth Widdows, brushing several times a week will help keep the coat looking good.

BATHING

A full grooming may include a bath. A bath or a utility sink works well. Use a nonskid mat in the tub to prevent slipping and potential injury. You might also want to buy a handheld spray nozzle. It's worth the modest investment because it makes it easier to thoroughly rinse off your Westie, which is important for preventing skin irritation.

Supplies

First gather all your supplies: shampoo, towels, skin conditioner, and a handheld dryer (if you are using one). You don't want to forget something and have to leave your soaking wet Westie in the bath. Some owners place cotton-wool balls in the ears to keep water from getting in, but because the Westie's ears are naturally pricked, they drain properly, so cotton-wool isn't necessary.

Choose a shampoo that is specially formulated for your Westie's needs. Do not use anything else unless your vet recommends it. Because the pH levels required for dogs are different from those required for people, human shampoos are not appropriate. There are several good shampoos especially formulated for hard-coated terriers (if you're stripping), and ones that will enhance a vibrant white coat.

If you have a lighter-skinned dog, leave more hair to protect the skin from burning. Your Westie lacks the melanin of a darker-skinned dog, and the skin is more prone to burn. If you have your Westie professionally groomed, tell the groomer to "leave a little extra on the top."

How to Bathe Your Westie

A Westie's bath water should be tepid. Lather the shampoo in your hands and work from the neck toward the back. Wash the feet, between the toes, under the tail, under the skirt. Gently wash the face with a washcloth and a bit of shampoo, carefully avoiding the eyes. Most important of all, after you lather, rinse thoroughly. Then rinse again. When you are sure you have rinsed off every molecule of shampoo, rinse once more! Shampoo residue is a major cause of itching.

There are special nongreasy skin conditioners that penetrate the coat and moisturise the skin without leaving any residue. These can prevent your Westie's skin from drying out—especially if you bathe him frequently. Follow the instructions carefully. For dogs with dry, flaky skin, these conditioners can be sprayed on in between baths. However, if the flaky condition persists, seek veterinary advice: This condition may result from a thyroid function disorder that is easily treated.

After you've rinsed, towel dry. You may choose to air dry, but make sure the dog stays warm. Handheld dryers designed for dogs work well, but some human ones set on low temperature are fine to use, as long as you are extremely careful to avoid getting close to his skin. When drying, be especially cautious around the head.

How Frequently?

There is much to consider when answering this question for your particular dog. Many exhibitors and owners bathe their dogs only about three or four times a year because they believe that too many baths will dry out a Westie's skin and cause itching problems. This is especially true for hand-stripped dogs, whose coats tend to retain a particularly self-cleaning quality. If you are doing your own clipping and you keep up the work and brushing between "formal" grooming, this could work for you as well. Many Westie owners who take their dogs to a professional groomer simply follow the groomer's recommendations (often every four to six weeks) and bring him in for the bathing and grooming in one fell swoop.

More often than every four weeks may be too frequent for the typical Westie; however, some people cannot tolerate the "bouquet" of a clipped dog and—for their own threshold of comfort—choose to bathe him more often. And a Westie with overactive oil glands may require more baths to keep the problem in check. For those dogs who get truly dirty, a bath is acceptable, as long as they are thoroughly dried afterward. In some cases, such as for dogs with skin problems frequent bathing with a medicated shampoo can help alleviate itching. Some contact allergies require that you bathe a dog (often with a prescribed shampoo) as many as two or three times a week during the worst of the contact allergy season.

NAIL CARE

Nail care is very important for any dog. If nails are neglected and allowed to grow too long, it can affect the conformation of the foot and cause deformity. When it comes to nail trimming, start young. If you have a puppy, handle his paws and feet gently to make him comfortable with it.

Tools

Use quality canine (not human) nail clippers, either scissor or guillotine type. Both kinds of clipper work fine, as long as you keep them sharp. Dull blades don't work, and they hurt the dog, and human nail clippers do not work well. Most groomers prefer guillotine-type clippers for their ease of use. Good scissor-type clippers are often stronger and sharper, and a little more accurate (for avoiding the quick of the nail). Some breeders simply use a metal file to keep nail growth under control.

Get your Westie used to nail trimming at an early age.

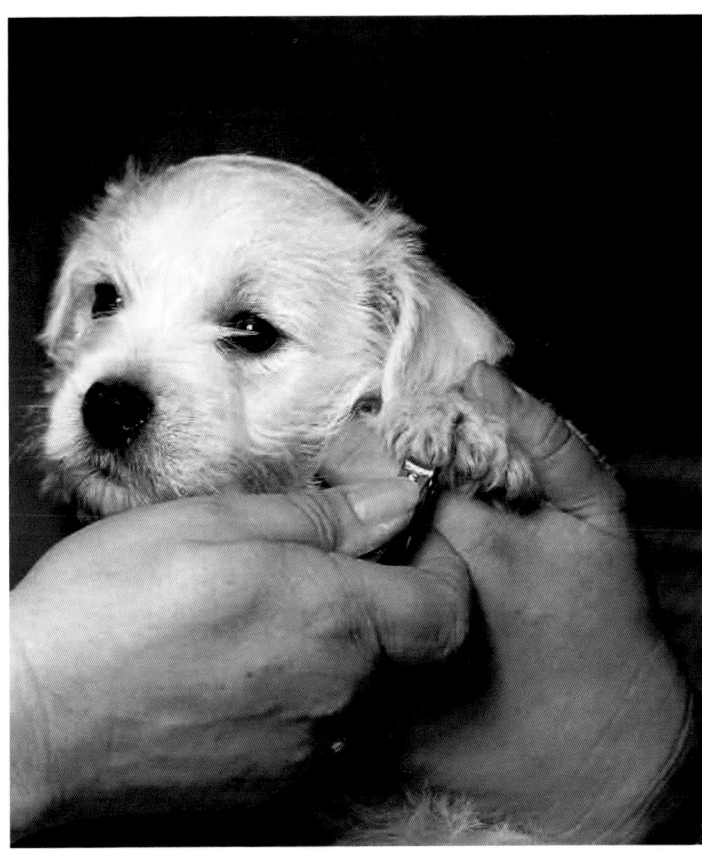

A cordless grinding tool is wonderful, and some dogs prefer it once they get used to the noise. You get a nicely rounded result—free of sharp edges. One drawback is that this tool can overheat the nails. But by not spending too much time on each nail and by alternating, you can prevent it from getting too hot. I recently discovered that after a walk in the rain, my dogs' wet nails tend to reduce the friction that causes overheating and also softens the nails. Some people put a nylon stocking over the paw and let the nails peek through so that the grinder won't get caught in the hair of the paw.

How To Trim Your Westie's Nails

Nail clipping probably won't be your Westie's favourite part of grooming, but he can learn to tolerate it if you work patiently and kindly with him.

Nail clipping can be stressful, and I have known some dogs to hide even if they suspect or anticipate its prospect. Owners worry about hurting the dog, and their fear is translated to him. Try to make this experience as pleasant as possible for the dog. You'll need to control him, something that's best accomplished with a grooming table, although some people sit right on the floor or couch with their dog. You may need an assistant, especially at first, since many Westies, especially those without desensitisation, abhor having their nails done and will resort to hiding or trying to distract you. Plying him with a tasty morsel may entice him, but not always. The trick is not to blow the process up in your own mind so that your Westie picks up on it and freaks out. (Of course, this can be prevented by getting your new puppy very used to letting you handle his feet.)

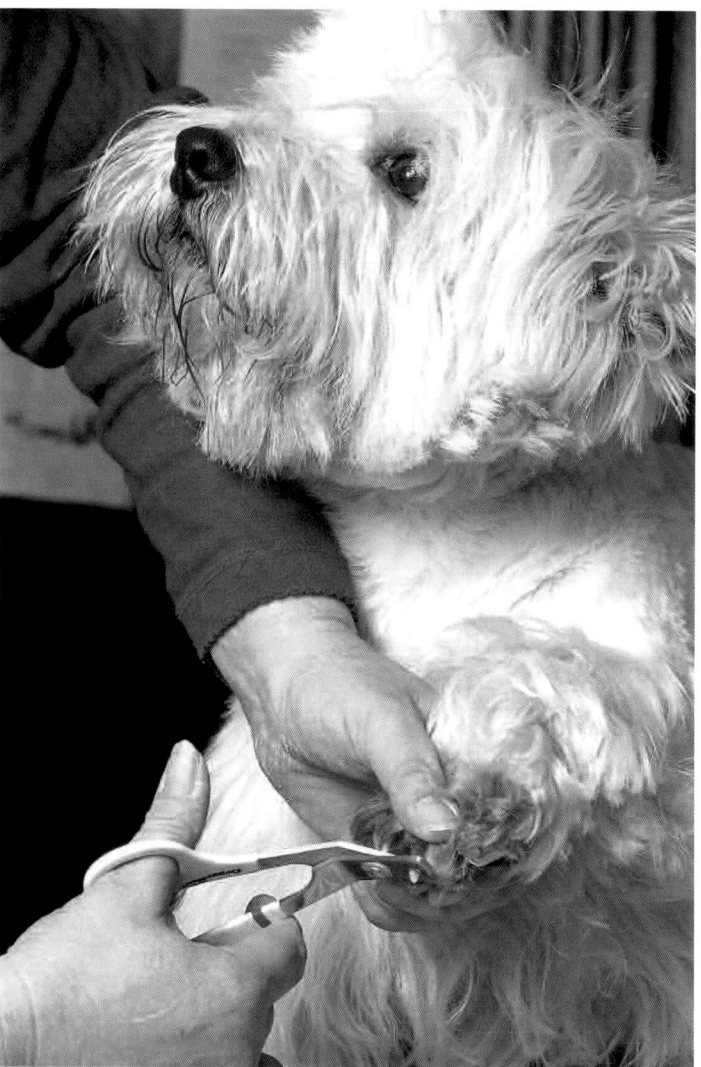

When clipping, try to avoid the quick, which is the vein that runs through the

Dealing With Dirt

Most adventurous Westies will get dirty no matter how often they are bathed. Following are some ideas to keep your Westie clean between baths:

- When the dog comes in from a dig-a-thon, train him to wait at the door while you towel him dry. Keep a towel by the door handy for this purpose. Cover the furniture and put down a towel, sheet, or some other protection at the door.
- Crate him with a towel; within a half-hour to an hour, he'll shed most of the dirt! (You'll want to clean the crate later.) Westies naturally shed dirt once it has had a chance to dry. This tends to be especially true of hard-coated Westies. It never hurts to brush through to remove the rest of the dirt.

More adventurous Westies need to be bathed more often.

- Wash off your Westie's paws and skirt with a little lukewarm water. Try to make this a pleasurable experience; offer liberal treats and praise.
- To freshen him up for special occasions, use a little baking soda or even grooming chalk. Rub it in and brush it out—and presto, he's dazzling white and fresh as a lily.
- Waterless shampoos do a good job in a pinch. All you need is the shampoo—usually a foam—and a clean towel.
- Avoid perfumes. People may have resorted to the practice in medieval times to mask odours due to the scarcity of bathing opportunities, but this is the twenty-first century. Besides, many dogs (and people) may be allergic to them.

nail. If you accidentally clip the quick, it will hurt your Westie, and will bleed. You can easily see the quick on lighter nails, but if your dog has black nails, don't cut past the natural curve of the nail. If you haven't kept up the process, you must do this with extra caution, because if you don't cut often enough, the quick will tend to grow past the curve. Keep styptic powder around just in case you draw blood.

Hold one rear paw in one hand, firmly, but without squeezing. Most dogs are less fussy about their rear paws, so it's often easier to begin there. Separate the toes and clip (or grind) each nail right below the quick. If you leave any ragged edges, a touch-up with a nail file will polish the nails off nicely. If you use a grinder, you can round the edges with that. If you go down too far and reach the quick, apply some styptic powder to the nail to stem bleeding. A small pinch pressed against the cut nail will stop the bleeding. If you don't have styptic powder, a little cornstarch will do the trick. Try not to make a big deal of it, or your Westie may begin to fear getting his nails trimmed.

You'll also want to check the pads of your Westie's paws for foreign substances, tar, dirt, mats, or thorns. Trim the hair between

Some Westies love to roll in any smelly substance they find — and there is nothing you can do about it except take a deep breath and start running the bath...

the pads and tidy up the feet. Such maintenance can prevent infections.

How Frequently?

Trim his nails every other week or so. You may be able to get away with less often if your Westie walks a lot on hard pavement, which helps wear down the nail. But even then, it's a matter of luck. Some nails tend to grow more out than curled under—and it's the ones with the curve that benefit most from the pavement.

EAR CARE

The Westie's prick ears make him less prone to ear problems than most breeds, and often they are virtually self-cleaning. But problems can arise, such as ear infections. Many owners don't even realise their dog has an ear infection until they have to clean out the ears. So it is important that whenever you groom your Westie you check and clean his ears.

Your breeder, vet, or groomer can recommend a good ear-cleaning product. Do not use cotton buds. Cotton-wool balls are safe, but a bud can easily damage his ear if he doesn't remain stationary—and most Westies don't.

EYE CARE

Your Westie's eyes should be bright and shiny, reflecting his keen intelligence. Although eye problems are not pervasive in the breed, problems can occur in all dogs. So it's a good idea to keep tabs and seek veterinary advice if you detect any problems, such as any persistent discharge from your dog's eyes. If he squints or rubs his eyes, this could indicate a serious problem. If the white of the eye has a cloudy or bluish cast, it could be symptomatic of such inflammatory conditions such as iritis, a corneal ulcer, or glaucoma. Corneal abrasions can occur—one possible source being the scratch of a cat not thrilled by your Westie's attentions. Plants can also be the culprit. If your Westie acts confused and collides with people or objects, his vision could be impaired.

More common problems include plugged tear ducts, eye injuries, and dry eye. Diet, overall heath, and genetics can factor into these problems. They are not that common, and your vet can help eliminate them if they do occur.

STAINING

Tear Staining

Tear staining—brownish streaks under the eyes—occasionally occurs in dogs, and can be particularly noticeable in light-coloured dogs. To get rid of the staining, try the commercial products that are available through pet-supply stores and catalogues, or you can try a do-it-yourself formula: a tablespoon of hydrogen peroxide (make sure it's not old), a dash of milk of magnesia, and sufficient cornstarch to form a paste. Apply the mixture to the stain—careful to avoid getting any into your Westie's eyes. After it has a little time to set and dry, rinse thoroughly. Soon the stains will disappear or at least diminish.

Tear-stain removers are just a temporary solution; they don't fix the problem. However, a change in diet to a higher-quality commercial food, home-prepared, or appropriate raw diet can correct the problem. Low-quality food that contains beet pulp may cause your Westie's eyes to run. Also, tear staining may indicate a problem that should be investigated by a vet.

Petroleum jelly works well for removing tar on the pads. Follow with a mild soap and warm water. Avoid using paint thinners or turpentine on your Westie's feet—they are far too harsh.

Muzzle, Beard, and Paw Staining

Muzzle, beard, and paw stains may be reddish brown to burgundy in hue. Several factors are suspected of causing this condition, but saliva is the most common cause. If your dog licks a lot, staining is likely. It can happen wherever he licks his own coat, usually on the paws and muzzle. Soft coats are more prone to staining than harder ones.

So what causes the licking? Suspects include the following:
- fungi and yeast infections
- allergies with food and inhalant origins
- long hair on pads that causes objects (some as tiny as a mustard seed) to lodge in paws
- cuts and abrasions

Hair that's white at the base and that becomes stained at the top indicates that licking is the issue. Hair stained down to the base indicates that the hair is growing in stained and more likely to be of a fungal origin. If this is the case, your vet can provide fungicides or treatments.

If the problem is not an infection, there are some things you might try to tackle the problem yourself. Trim the pad-hair as short

Often, professional grooming includes nail care. An experienced groomer may accomplish nail trimming more easily than you, because it's routine, and he or she may not communicate the same level of anxiety that you do. Vets can provide the same service, but it may be more expensive.

as possible. This may reveal hidden objects. You might also try dipping paws in either hydrogen peroxide or a half-and-half solution of bleach and water. Rinse either off after a minute or so. The peroxide and bleach should be used sparingly since they are quite drying to the skin. You can also mix Epsom salts and strong salt water. You needn't rinse these off and you can use these more frequently. Westie breeder/handler Dee Hanna uses a formula of one-third chalk, one-third milk of magnesia, and one-third 20-percent-strength hydrogen peroxide.

If your dog's muzzle is stained, you can dip a cotton-wool ball in fresh hydrogen peroxide and wipe the beard daily. At first the stain may turn pink, but eventually it should begin to whiten until new growth replaces the old. When the new hair grows in unstained, continue to use this as part of your maintenance grooming. If the muzzle stains are directly related to the licking problem, they too will probably disappear. Often the staining on the muzzle is directly related to the issue in the paws that has caused the licking, and will begin to grow out when the issue is resolved.

If the muzzle, but not the paws, is stained, look for other causes and remedies. Is red dye or beets contained in your Westie's commercial dog food? This can cause staining. Check treats also. Tomato-based spaghetti sauce will stain both human and Westie beards. (You might select an Alfredo or a white clam sauce instead of a marinara if you're planning to share an Italian dinner with him.) Water with high iron concentrations may be the culprit and might warrant a switch to bottled—or at least filtered—water. Some Westie people swear by Ester C as a preventative and antidote to staining.

DENTAL CARE

Like people, dogs are susceptible to plaque, tartar, and gum disease, which arise from the combination of food, saliva, bacteria, and cells in the mouth lining. When tartar forms on the teeth, it provides a base for more plaque to accumulate. Unless controlled, it progresses to the point of dental problems and gum disease. Since canine periodontal problems can cause myriads of other problems, prevention is key. Infections that start in the gums can migrate to other parts of the body and cause disease.

The good news is that much of this is preventable. Fortunately Westies are less likely to develop dental caries (cavities) than people are. Although it's not common for dogs to get cavities, don't tempt fate by feeding sweets, because when cavities do appear in dogs, the culprit is usually a diet high in sugar content along with poor preventative dental care. Regular brushing, a good, balanced diet, and appropriate chews can all help your Westie's teeth to stay strong and in good condition.

Supplies

Toothbrushes specifically made for dogs are available at pet-supply stores. Finger brushes are another option, but the toothbrush's stronger bristles are more effective at getting below the gum line, where plaque causes problems. Some dogs will tolerate electric toothbrushes, but don't count on it—the noise can be disconcerting.

Many owners brush their Westies' teeth regularly with specially formulated toothpastes flavoured with beef and chicken. From their reactions, you'd think the dogs had found ambrosia (or "the food of the dogs," at least). Keep in mind that human toothpaste is inappropriate for dogs.

Dental care is essential for your Westie's health.

Brushing Your Westie's Teeth

Brushing is a good way to take inventory for broken teeth, tartar control, or any unusual changes. It also removes plaque both above and below the gum line, so concentrate the effort on those areas that dental chews and other aids do not reach. Another benefit of brushing the teeth is that it can minimise "doggie breath." If you start the brushing routine while your Westie is young, he may even look forward to it.

Start at a time when both you and your Westie are relaxed, and ease yourselves into the process. At first, don't even use a toothbrush. Hold him as if you're

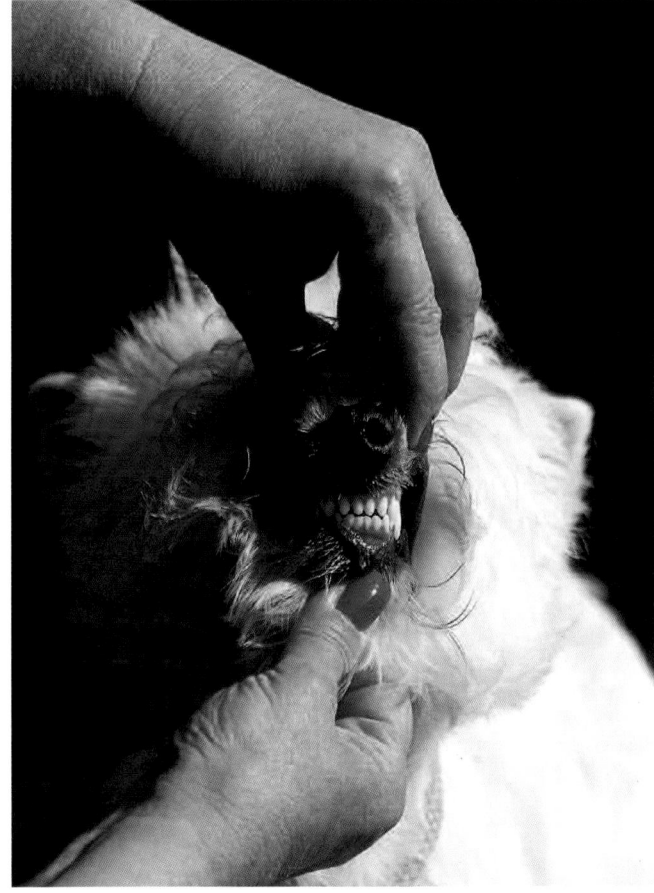

- Rawhide chews help to clean the teeth; however, great care should be exercised when using rawhide products. Westies can choke on large pieces of rawhide, and they can become lodged in the throat, causing choking.
- Dental chew toys made of nylon and hard knobbly rubber satisfy a Westie's desire for chewing and help support dental health. Another benefit is that they are virtually indestructible.

cuddling him and gently stroke the outside of his cheek with your finger. As he mellows out, place a dab of dog-appropriate toothpaste on your finger and allow him to sample it. (Most dogs are crazy about it.) With a tiny bit of toothpaste on the brush, gently use it on one or two teeth and on the gum line. This step accustoms your Westie to the feel of the brush. Over the next several days, gradually increase the number of teeth. Eventually brush the rear teeth; this is where plaque tends to accumulate most. Be slow and gentle, and stop before he begins to get restless. This technique establishes that it is *you* who determines when you stop, not *him*. Increase to about 30 seconds per side, concentrating on the outer tooth surfaces, since little tartar accumulates on the inner ones. Conclude each session while it is still fun, and praise your dog profusely so that your Westie will look forward to toothbrushing as an incredibly *fun* activity.

Some human plaque-attacking mouthwashes, applied with a gauze pad and wiped across the teeth, are considered safe. Your vet may stock special canine oral rinses that can be helpful. Some owners say that the tartar just slides off. Additionally, you can now buy little pop-up cloths that contain baking soda. The slight abrasiveness of the baking soda can help remove plaque. Other over-the-counter dental wipes found in pet-supply stores are infused with antiplaque ingredients. New products, including a gel that you can rub on your dog's teeth and gum line, kill plaque-causing bacteria and have even proven to reverse gingivitis. There is also a safe water additive that can aid in dental hygiene.

How Frequently?

In a perfect world, you would brush your Westie's teeth as frequently as you do your own. But if a daily routine just isn't possible, try for at least three times a week. Your Westie's mouth will benefit enormously from it.

Diet and Dental Health

Many vets and breeders have found that feeding a hard dry food diet can slightly reduce your dog's chances of developing dental problems. Some vets recommend special diets formulated for tartar control. Certain veterinary rawhide chews infused with enzymes may prevent plaque accumulation and are popular with many dog owners.

Some Appropriate Raw Food (ARF) adherents testify that their dogs' teeth and gums are so healthy that they've never required professional dental cleanings, since some of the diet's staples, which include raw chicken wings and necks, do double-duty as nutrition and dentifrice. The natural enzymes in these foods have proven effective in maintaining excellent tooth and gum health.

For those who choose to follow a more conventional feeding regime, offering your Westie a human-quality raw bone periodically can do wonders to help stave off the dental and periodontal disease that can compromise his health. Some Westie owners offer their dogs a raw beef bone every couple of weeks to naturally maintain their dogs' dental health. The head of the femur bones are primo because the gristle functions much like the bristles of a toothbrush.

Professional Cleaning

Many dogs need to have regular dental cleanings under anaesthesia. But regular preventative dental care can save you money in the long run and keep dental cleanings and extractions over the years to a minimum.

A professional cleaning entails anaesthesia, a thorough flushing of the mouth, and the use of ultrasonic scalers and other instruments to remove all tartar. The vet will also polish the teeth to help eliminate the little pits or scratches that plaque likes to call home. It sure beats deterioration, which would make your Westie a candidate for dental

If you are showing your Westie, you will probably end up seeking out a professional groomer.

Good preventative dental care will do much to minimise canine halitosis. But there are other ways to address this problem. Christine Swingle, a breeder for more than forty years, offers her Westies fresh mint leaves, which they seem to enjoy. And I have been known to slip my dogs the occasional peppermint breath mint every now and again.

Although it's most likely to be caused by a dental problem, bad breath can arise from other organic problems such as diabetes, kidney disease, gastrointestinal issues, respiratory problems—and even tonsillitis. Of course, a temporary dalliance with this problem may have to do with his "choice of cuisine." If you're the proud owner of a Westie who enjoys "recycling" poop, this could explain a lot. There is no accounting for taste.

implants and da Vinci porcelain veneers à la *Extreme Makeover* (Terrier Version).

PROFESSIONAL GROOMING

Some Westie owners handle all of their dogs' grooming needs at home, but some prefer to go the route of the professional groomer. If do you choose to use a professional groomer, start getting your Westie used to it at a young age. After the puppy has had all his vaccinations—at about 14 weeks—make an appointment for a "puppy cut" (a modified, less-time-consuming version of the adult cut) to expose him to the grooming experience while he's still in a spongelike learning stage. If the groomer has the right touch, the puppy will discover that it's a pleasant experience, and he will come to accept grooming as "just another trip to the beauty salon." After a few appointments, ask the groomer to give him a "Westie cut." The groomer may know exactly what you mean, but just in case bring along a photo of how you would like your Westie to look (presumably, like a Westie). Politely and clearly insist that you do not want your Westie to resemble a Schnauzer or a Scottie. The modern Westie looks quite tailored. The groomer needs to know that the Westie has a round head, a carrot tail, and a skirt blended without obvious lines. This takes more time, but by that point, your Westie should be perfectly OK with it.

Finding a Groomer

Interview the groomer before the first appointment. Ask about the process. Does he or she use a drying cage? If so, is it an open crate? The open crate is safer than the enclosed ones some groomers use. Will your dog be attended to when he's noosed and on the grooming table? Does the groomer express anal glands as part of the routine? If so, you may wish to opt out, since this is rarely necessary in Westies; so let the groomer know and remind him or her each time until he or she gets the idea. If the groomer baulks at any of your questions or requests, or acts rude, find another groomer. If you cannot find a good groomer in your area, contact a Westie breed club to see if any members have their dogs groomed in your neighbourhood.

If you choose to use a groomer, you might have to leave your dog for several hours. Some days tend to be busier than others, so arrange an appointment according to your preferences. If you want your dog back sooner, you might ask which days are slowest. Perhaps, if you have some free time, you can hang out in the waiting area and read the newspaper or a novel. Sometimes the extra time is just what you need to regroup, get a cup of coffee, or accomplish an errand or two. If you have to work or require more time, your Westie should be able to remain at the shop a bit longer.

You want your Westie to come home from the groomer having had a pleasant experience and looking his best.

TRAINING AND BEHAVIOUR
of Your West Highland White Terrier

I n the continuum of purebred dogs, Westies are considered moderately obedient. Generally a person will not say, "Gee, I want an obedience dog—I'm getting a Westie." A Westie can be compliant, but in the pool of multiple intelligences, he will rate higher in areas of independent problem solving than he will in rote learning or obsequiousness. He wants to please, but he was bred to be a working dog—and part of that incorporates his naturally high prey drive and his desire to rid the universe of all vermin.

Even so, it's a myth that you cannot train a Westie. (There are even some obedience judges who believe that using the words *terrier* and *obedience* in the same sentence is oxymoronic!) With your patience, consistency, and positive training, your Westie can be well trained, as long as you keep things interesting and mentally stimulating for him. What fun it is to attend an obedience competition and watch the only Westie in the ring blow away his competition, including Border Collies, Golden Retrievers, and other so-called obedience breeds!

TRAINING STARTS EARLY

Whether your ultimate goal is competitive obedience or simple puppy socialisation and household manners, training really does begin in the whelping box very soon after birth. Each puppy, through social interaction, learns from the very beginning about positive and negative experiences. First, their mother provides them with warmth, food, and physical stimulation. She washes them with her tongue and her licking helps them relieve themselves, after which she cleans up. If all goes well, they begin to see life as something enjoyable.

In the litter, puppies socialise with each other. They react to the force of each other's mouthing and biting, and if it's too severe, the perpetrator will get an unequivocal message (a yelp). They begin to work out their hierarchy; though theoretically much of it is imprinted and only needs to emerge and be sorted out in these tiny beings' growing world.

The earlier you start training, the better. When starting with a younger dog, you have

Be sure to socialise your Westie with other friendly dogs.

fewer reinforced bad habits to overcome.

THE IMPORTANCE OF SOCIALISATION

A responsible and canny breeder, as well as a puppy's dam and his littermates, will initiate and supervise a puppy's early socialisation. You can continue to socialise your Westie when you bring him into his new home.

If your Westie puppy is between 4 and 12 months, he's in his main socialisation period. It's his opportunity to learn how to interact appropriately with others and respond positively to training. Take advantage of this period to ensure his development into a happy and confident member of your family.

Around the middle of this period is the so-called "fear period." This corresponds to a similar time for pups or wolf cubs in the wild, who would first leave their dens to meet the world—a world full of dangers, so that the puppies were programmed to act with caution for survival. Today, those same instincts remain intact, so it's essential that during this period your puppy have as few fearful experiences as possible to prevent them from becoming instilled in his psyche.

Gradually introduce him to new things; let him meet other dogs and people a few at a time. Avoid immersing him into a large group of strangers. You know your puppy best, so try to gauge his readiness to expand his world. Puppy parties, playgroups, friends' houses, and pet-supply stores are appropriate initiations, as long as the experiences are kept positive.

As his confidence grows, introduce him—in a positive way—to nail clippers, the vacuum cleaner, and other noisy appliances. He will learn that raucous sounds don't necessarily mean pain, and his self-assurance will grow.

Take him on walks to meet people of all ages, races, dress, and size. Expose him slowly to people in wheelchairs, people with sticks, and people using walkers. Have him make friends with babies, children, people in uniform, men with beards, people with purple hair, tattoos, and funny hats. Getting used to many different types of people and things in a positive way will prevent him from becoming a fearful dog.

CRATE TRAINING

Few things you will acquire for your Westie will be more useful than a crate. To the novice dog owner, the crate is often misunderstood. It's not a prison; it's an essential basic item for any new puppy or dog. In reality, this multipurpose, inexpensive item combines security, a hangout, travel safety, a time-out room, a housetraining tool, and a shelter. It will protect your puppy and your house when you cannot be home with him. No dog owner should be without one.

The safest mode of transportation for your Westie is your crate or carrier. Secured in a vehicle (bungee cords and seatbelts work well together), crates have saved thousands of dogs' lives. Furthermore, your dog will associate it with adventure, travel, and being with you—his very favourite person.

Used judiciously, a crate is an "inanimate babysitter." When you go out for a while, it keeps your dog safe and out of mischief. After a dog's surgery or injury, vets often recommend crate rest, and with a terrier—who's curious and doesn't like to be kept down—you will ooze with gratitude that you have such a versatile and wonderful tool. And of course, housetraining becomes a snap.

Size and Type

Your Wonderful Westie

A Westie is the perfect size to take everywhere with you—small enough to travel easily and sturdy enough to join you on hikes and other outings. It is critical to socialise him in puppyhood so that he grows into a confident, adaptable dog who can get along with the many others you meet in your travels. This means lots of positive interactions with different people, places, and things.

Crates come in a variety of styles and are made from an assortment of materials—from straight wire to plastic and metal. You can even buy a furniture-grade solid-oak version, sure to become a cherished antique and heirloom in years to come.

Making a den is a natural urge for a dog, harking back to his wolfish roots for safety and refuge. It should not be palatial, but the crate needs to be wide enough for your Westie pup to stand up, turn around, and lie down in comfortably. Some Westie owners start with a smaller crate, graduating to a larger one as the puppy reaches full size. The advantage to that is that a dog will rarely, if ever, soil his own living quarters. Another option is to purchase a larger crate and partition off a section of it, so that the actual space the dog uses is reduced. As your Westie grows, you can adjust the size of the crate by increasing its usable space.

A crate can be a haven that reinforces your Westie's feeling of security.

Location

Place the crate in a central location—where there is some activity, but not so busy that it's like Paddington Station. You want him to be relatively calm, but you also want him to become used to being a part of his human family. You might choose to place the crate in your bedroom, so the puppy feels more secure. Avoid placing it near draughts or heaters, and make it comfy and fun with a soft blanket or a crate pad and a soft toy or safe chew toy.

How to Crate Train

Here's how to accustom your dog to a crate:
- Choose a location for the crate.
- Tell your puppy to get into his crate—you can throw a treat in the back to make him more interested. Shut the door, treat him, and praise him highly. Repeat this process again and again, leaving him in for just a few minutes at a time.

- Increase your puppy's time in the crate to five minutes, but do not leave the room—quietly remain within sight. Gradually increase this time.
- Next, leave the room while your dog is in the crate (filled with his assortment of goodies). Start with a few minutes and gradually work your way up to longer times.
- Always have the crate out and available for your Westie. When he is out and about, leave the door open, and you will notice that he will begin to retreat to it by his own volition.
- Give him a toy or snack to occupy him and help him associate the crate with marvelous things. Try filling a toy with peanut butter or cheese.

A crate can be a haven that, when filled with his cherished objects, reinforces your Westie's security. Feeding a dog in the crate and giving him special treats will make it all the more enticing. Eventually your Westie *will* go to his crate of his own volition. And every time he does, effusively praise and treat!

How Long?

Forcing a dog to stay in a crate too long defeats the very purpose of crate training. After all, he can only hold it so long, and if left in a crate for an extended period of time, your poor Westie will be forced to urinate in it. This in turn breaks down the natural inhibitions he has about converting his boudoir into a bathroom. And it just goes downhill from there.

The common lore is that a puppy up to eight months old can control his bladder for as many hours as his age in months, plus one. Ergo, a two-month-old puppy should be continent for three hours. However, puppies need plenty of exercise and opportunity to explore their environment, so crating an eight-month-old dog all day is cruel. Even if he manages to develop the bladder of a camel,

If used properly, a crate is a fine place for a dog; if not, your dog will associate it with unpleasant experiences.

Installing a dog door can work well with Westies, as they learn quickly how to use it for housetraining.

overcrating could predispose him to bladder stones.

Four hours is a good maximum, because it's important to heed your Westie's psychological and exercise needs. He will not appreciate the sensory deprivation that comes with long periods of solitary confinement. (Of course, at night—if you're lucky—he'll eventually sleep for longer than four hours!)

If crating your Westie for longer periods is inevitable, exercise him liberally before and after—even if this means getting up at the crack of dawn. If your schedule forces you to leave him much longer, hire a dog walker to attend to his needs.

HOLD THAT THOUGHT: HOUSETRAINING YOUR WESTIE

Westies are very intelligent, and most are easily housetrained. However, well-bred and socialised pups raised by an attentive mother and given clean living quarters have a leg up when it comes to housetraining.

Getting Started

Set up a schedule for taking your Westie out for toilet breaks. After all, preventing mistakes is much easier than correcting them. Take your Westie puppy out before he has a chance to have an accident. Natural times include immediately after a nap, in the morning, after a vigorous play session, and after meals. Also, keep a close eye on him—he will cue you that he has to go out whenever he begins to sniff the ground or walk in circles. You may want to have a simultaneous command like "go" or "hurry up" that he associates with relieving himself. After he relieves himself, praise him profusely! You want him to think he has done something incredibly important, like won the Nobel Prize or the lottery jackpot.

Using the Crate for Housetraining

Restrict your dog from having full run of the house until he is reliable. If he's having accidents, he is not ready for unrestricted freedom. This is where the crate comes in handy. If you're too busy or preoccupied to watch him like a hawk, place him in his crate—remember, it should be no larger than he needs in order to stand up, turn around, and lie down. If you use a larger crate, you can insert a barrier to make the usable area smaller. When you remove

Cleaning Up Accidents

Dogs are olfactory wonders; they can smell a million things that you cannot. If your dog smells remnants of urine or faeces, it's as if he's received an invitation from a best friend to join the party and add more "fun." So it's important to immediately clean up any area where he's just had an accident. Special enzymatic cleaners, available at pet-supply stores, neutralise the odour. These really do work.

Vinegar may work for linoleum and other hard, nonabsorbent floorings. But it only really works on carpets if you don't mind the aroma of dog "piss and vinegar." It does not remove dog-urine odours from carpet. Avoid using ammonia-based cleaners to remove a dog urine stain. Since ammonia smells like urine to a dog, you'll only succeed in "indicating the restroom."

your puppy from the crate for a toilet break and he doesn't go, replace him in the crate for another 15 minutes or so before trying again—you may need to repeat this several times, but eventually, nature will prevail, your Westie will relieve himself, and then you can praise him like there's no tomorrow!

Accidents Will Happen

You can turn an almost-miss into a hit. It is merely opportunity knocking if you catch your Westie pup starting to toilet in the house. You have just been awarded a bonus occasion to enforce desired behaviour. This requires good reflexes and absolute vigilance. You can startle him with a sharp "No," quickly scoop him up, change your tone to a cheerful, jovial, "Let's go outside," and hightail it out the door to puppy's toilet area. Then place the puppy there, and give him his command to go. Be consistent and always use the same command. Let him finish, and once again lavish him with praise for his stellar accomplishment. If he doesn't oblige, it's back to the crate again. Repeat as necessary.

Patience and consistency are essential for housetraining.

Punishment Doesn't Work

A missed opportunity is just that—a missed opportunity. This is true even if you scold your puppy five seconds after he's relieved himself on your expensive Persian rug. (Wait! What were you thinking, taking an unreliable puppy into that room with a priceless rug?) Young puppies live in the "here and now" and really do have the retention ability of only about five seconds. Moreover, you should blame yourself for not supervising closely. (But don't forget to forgive yourself soon.) Just vow to be more alert next time.

Scolding a dog by rubbing his nose in his faeces may allow you to vent your own frustration, but it will do nothing to help your pup get the message. (One dog owner believes that this sort of punishment might actually cause the puppy to start "eating the evidence" himself. Then you'll have two nasty habits with which to wrestle.) If you yell and punish for housetraining accidents, your Westie will have no idea why you are upset with him.

The process of housetraining your Westie can be frustrating and tiring at times, but it's worth it. Hang in there, be patient, and don't give up. With consistency and patience you will prevail over his "spontaneous nature." Remember that most dogs eventually become housetrained—just like kids.

You can start at home with positive, reward-based training.

TRAINING YOUR WESTIE

Whether you're just aiming for a well-mannered Westie or preparing for formal obedience competition, it's a

Training Goals

Trainer Marsha Tracy emphasises that whatever your ultimate goals—agility, formal obedience competition, or just having a good canine citizen—basic household manners are the foundation on which to build. It's essential that your Westie puppy eventually shed his juvenile and adolescent "wild child" ways. She offers the following common sense tips:

- Be clear about your goals. How much time do you have to train? What are your limits—and your Westie's?
- Find a good trainer. Good sources include recommendations from other Westie owners, breed clubs, and websites. Your vet may also have some good suggestions.

good idea to enroll your Westie in a beginning obedience class. Dog obedience clubs are organised in most towns and villages. Contact the Kennel Club (www.the-kennel-club.org.uk) for more information.

Puppy classes offer opportunities for socialisation (for both dogs and owners), basic canine etiquette, and further bonding between you and your Westie. You'll get the most out of these classes if you not only attend them regularly but also practice what you've learned and encourage other family members to do so, too. Puppies assimilate information quickly; "you can't teach an old dog new tricks" is a myth. Dogs are lifelong learners.

Finding a Trainer

Ask your vet, other Westie owners, your breeder, or a Westie breed club for recommendations. You can also check out the Association of Pet Behaviour Counsellors (APBC), which carries details of registered trainers. Visit their website at www.apbc.org.uk.

Interview prospective obedience instructors and observe their methods. If possible, observe a class and talk to the instructor and students. If the dogs and handlers seem happy and working well together, it's a good sign. An instructor who understands and appreciates that special, plucky, confident, and often vocal terrier personality—and knows what motivates terriers—will recognise that they can do very well in obedience.

Opinions on training methods vary according to instructor and by degrees; to choose correctly for your dog or your situation, carefully evaluate all the variables. Trust your heart and cue into your Westie for clues. With the help of a competent instructor with whom both you and the dog have a rapport, you'll figure out the

Repetition bores a Westie, so mix your training up a bit. A Westie who knows he's loved is not lacking in self-confidence. Sure, they like praise, but Westies are not considered a needy or clingy breed. Training that remains fun will motivate your Westie.

most suitable approach for your dog. And if you're not getting the results you want, try another trainer.

At-Home Training

Your Westie will respond well to the mutual trust that comes with positive, reward-based training. Positive training may not be the fastest way to get the results you want, but because it builds rather than damages your relationship, it is the most satisfying method. Establishing trust and creating a safe environment pay off in spades. Praise is always preferable to punishment, and training is essentially teaching.

These days the prevailing philosophy on dog training focuses on positive, reward-based training, but this has not always been the case. In the past, the aim was to get your dog to behave through commands and correction. The "reward" was that your dog would not have to suffer the constant yank on the collar. Though these practices often resulted in a compliant dog, they often came at the expense of a happy attitude and a dog/owner bond that mutual respect fosters.

Like a child, a puppy thrives in an environment with generous measures of both consistency and love. Such an environment works miracles. Your Westie probably wants to please you, so if you communicate your limits clearly, he will gladly cooperate. Terriers, in particular, do not suffer with grace nagging and punishment that they don't understand. A rebellious Westie is like the teenager from Hades!

Decide what you really want your Westie to learn, and advance step-by-step, building new skills upon older ones. What motivates him most? Food is usually a good bet. But there are some Westies who will go wild for a toy or would sell their own mothers for a ratty tennis ball. Praise will reinforce him, but few terriers live for praise alone. They're negotiators by nature. However, each Westie is an individual, and you need to discover whatever it is that "floats his boat."

While dogs (and especially Westies) can develop pretty extensive passive vocabularies, they are more attuned to your tone of voice than to your words. Tone should match meaning. Praising your dog in a gruff or lacklustre tone of voice won't convey the message, just as scolding him in a voice and tone radiating sweetness and light is apt to bewilder him.

Just like in stand-up comedy, in training, timing is everything. Reward desirable behaviour the instant it occurs—not one minute later. Westies are better than we are at living in the moment.

Though some Westies will do anything for a favourite toy, many are food-crazy. Good edible rewards include string cheese, natural meat jerky, and raw vegetable morsels—all cut into very small pieces. You might want to try visiting an Asian grocery store and buying a bag of dried anchovies. This healthy snack is inexpensive, neat, and great for a Westie's skin and coat.

If weight control is an issue and you are feeding a dry food, reserve a small amount of the day's quota for training. Or if you're as lucky as I am, your terrier will work for lettuce (romaine, naturally—no iceberg, if you please).

BASIC COMMANDS

All training commands make use of treats, bait, incentives—all different names for the same thing. When you are first teaching a new skill, use a treat every time. As your Westie learns to respond to your commands, start doling out treats intermittently. Once animals understand what you require of them, they actually learn better this way.

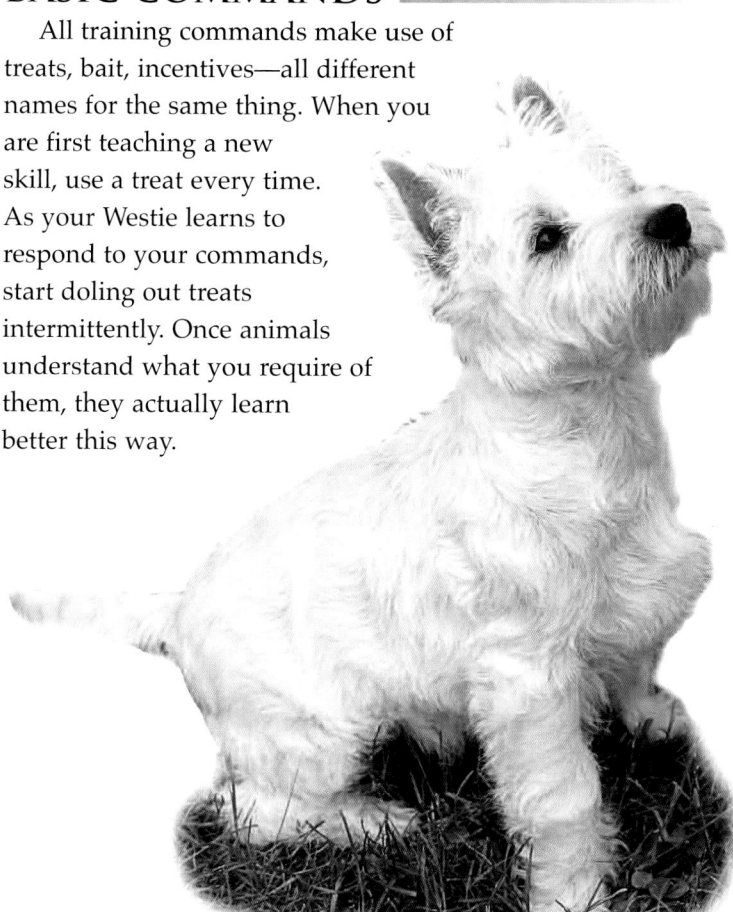

Hold a small treat at your Westie's nose, then move it above his head to get him to sit.

Clicker Training

One popular training technique is "clicker training," which is a form of operant conditioning incorporating a clicker to help a dog identify behaviour that produces a reward (usually a small bit of food). You treat the dog only after he reliably repeats a desired command. The clicker indicates to the dog that he's exercising the correct behaviour. This mode of training had its beginnings in the successful training of dolphins and was then found to be applicable to terrestrial quadrupeds—like dogs.

Training should be gentle and noncoercive. If your Westie breaks any of the commands too quickly, simply refrain from rewarding him. He needs to learn that he receives a treat only when he has completed and held the command.

Sit

This is probably the easiest command to teach your puppy. Grab a few treats. Then, holding a treat at your puppy's nose level, move your hand slowly over toward the top of his head and say, "Sit." Most puppies will automatically move into a sit in order to retrieve the treat. Reward him the instant he sits, and lay the praise on thickly. Practice this several times, but don't overdo it. Do not force him into the sit; encouragement and rewards alone will work.

Teach your puppy to sit before he eats, before he goes out the door, or before any exciting activity. This will give him an opportunity to chill out, and give you the chance to maintain control over his behaviour.

Down

Most dogs would rather lie down on their own volition than be told to do so. This is because the "down" position puts them in a physically and psychologically vulnerable place. Just the same, you'll want to teach your Westie this command.

Start with a treat in your hand. While the dog is sitting, lower the treat slowly, moving it between his front legs, toward the floor, and using the command "down." Most dogs will lie down naturally. If after a few tries, your Westie refuses, gently extend his front legs and ease him to the floor, praising him all the time. Practice a few times; he should soon oblige. Avoid forcing him down, so that he doesn't associate this command with fear or discomfort.

Stay

This command can literally save your dog's life. It can prevent him from bolting out the front door into a busy, dangerous street. It can also calm him down in a potentially stressful situation such as a visit to the vet's surgery. An extension of the sit command—if you teach him to hold his sit until you release him—the stay command is a natural outgrowth. Ask your dog to sit, then intermittently reinforce his position with praise and treats and repeat, "Stay." Over time, you can slowly extend the time. You can use the same method to solidify the down command into a down-stay command.

Come

Teaching your Westie to come on command is one of the most important lessons of all. Like the stay command, the come command can save your dog's life. It reinforces the behaviour that causes your dog to check in with you. Through this you gain enough control that he looks to you for security. If he's keyed in to

Training Tip

Some people will use the command "down" when a dog jumps up on a person. Instead, substitute the command "off" so that your Westie can make a distinction between the two.

Ask your pup to sit in all kinds of different places so that he learns what the command really means.

you, he'll be more attracted to coming when called—to the one he loves and trusts most—than he will to potentially perilous situations.

While this command is extremely important, it can be the most difficult to teach. Your Westie's independent nature runs contrary to coming when called, but with your patience, he will learn. If you provide him with a good incentive to come, he will be more likely to happily oblige. It helps that he is learning that you are the source of treats, praise, and many worthwhile things. The cardinal rule is to avoid ever calling your Westie when you plan to do something he might not want to do—like taking a bath or getting a nail trim.

Start in your fenced garden and start as young as possible, when your dog is more dependent on you. First, move away from him, then encourage him to follow by calling softly to him. Dogs, especially terriers, can see a moving target more clearly than a stationary one. He will probably follow you, but keep a lead on him for all the early lessons. If he starts to run away, don't chase him; he'll see this reaction as an invitation to a game of "keep away."

You can also start inside, in a small room. Call him gently, proffering a treat. As he toddles over to you, give him the treat and shower him with praise. If he doesn't come, gently and encouragingly draw his lead toward you, taking care not to jerk on it. This is important—the lead is there to help him focus. As soon as he heads toward you, pour on the praise, and when he reaches you, treat him. Kneeling to his level will give

Reward your Westie with a small treat when he performs the proper command.

a reluctant dog confidence. Lean back with open arms as you call him. This inviting gesture usually elicits the desired response.

Practice this three or four times a day, but only when the environment is calm and free from distractions. If your Westie is unable to concentrate, failure is guaranteed. In essence, in order to get him to come to you in the beginning, you need to be the most interesting thing in his world.

Leave It

Dogs are forever getting into rubbish, pantries, and underwear drawers. In order to get yours to stop chewing something valuable, or to put down something dangerous he's picked up, teach him the "leave it" command.

Wait until he begins halfheartedly chewing on an object (preferably not a family heirloom). As he's chewing, approach him, and say, "Leave it!" Trade him the object for something more toothsome, and praise him when he accepts the exchange.

This command is especially useful in real-life situations. A normal Westie will not voluntarily trade a filet mignon for a dried-out old dog biscuit, but he can—with persistence and reinforcement—learn to do so (albeit reluctantly). When he does, reward him with a jar of caviar.

Stand

"Stand" is an especially useful command. Dogs stand while they are being bathed, groomed, and examined by the vet; show dogs stand in the show ring. To teach this command, get some treats. Slowly raise one to the point where his nose would be if he were standing and say, "Stand." Before you know it, with your firm command, your Westie will stand. Reinforce this with food or a favourite game or toy.

Lead Training

Westies can be pullers, so it's important for your dog to learn to walk calmly and pleasantly on a lead. Think of this as a way to stay close to your dog. After all, your Westie will anticipate fresh air and sunshine, because a lead means that it is time for a walk! If you don't master this very early, get used to everyone in the street asking you, "Who's walking whom?"

To get your Westie used to his lead, attach it to his collar and let him drag it around the house. Make sure you supervise him the

Watch Me

"Watch me!" is an essential command that can help with other obedience exercises. Without your Westie's attention, you won't be able to teach him anything— except to ignore you. You can teach this command by using the command and rewarding him when he looks at you for direction. Intermittent reinforcement, treats, and praise will keep him checking back at you. Refrain from treating him every time; keep him guessing.

Boredom Barking

If your Westie barks out of boredom, the blame is yours. It's a symptom that he is deprived of socially acceptable outlets for his mental and physical energies. Take more time for walks or play. If you're not available, an interactive toy, such as a plastic cube that gradually dispenses treats as your Westie manipulates it, can help. Chew items and hard, hollow, rubber toys stuffed with cheese or peanut butter may provide long-lasting amusement as your Westie works to "liberate" the treat.

entire time, so he doesn't accidentally get the lead caught on something and end up hurting himself. He may baulk a bit at first, but soon he will forget the lead is there. After a few minutes, gently pick up the end of the lead and follow your dog. Hold the lead end, call him toward you, then praise and treat him. Continue enticing him with treats. If he resists, don't tug; just remain stationary and call him again, tasty morsel in hand. Keeping the sessions short and fun will allow him to catch on quickly. Westies are quick studies, especially if there's something in it for them.

PROBLEM BEHAVIOURS

Dogs will exhibit problem behaviours for a variety of reasons. Boredom, loneliness, and pent-up energy can result in destructive chewing, nuisance barking, and ignoring limits or guidance from their owners. So-called aggressive behaviours can result from a lack of bite-inhibition training or even from fear. Though domesticated, dogs are predators. Without appropriate outlets, they may chase, stalk, bite, and destroy. They're also—and this is especially true of terriers—pack animals, so isolation can result in scratching, digging, chewing, or melancholy (and often annoying) vocalisation. Essentially, they misbehave because they have no idea who's the boss! Our tendency to anthropomorphise dogs only widens the communication gap between our two species.

Just because a Westie is a small dog doesn't mean he isn't equipped with large teeth and a powerful jaw, so it is important to address any issues that might put him, yourself, or anyone else at risk. Do not hesitate to seek professional help for any problem that you cannot handle yourself.

Much of the information in the following sections is based on the philosophies, advice, and writings of Westie owner, trainer, author, and canine behaviourist, Deb Duncan (www.thedogspeaks.com).

Barking

"Barking is a major aspect of a dog's communication system," says Duncan. "They bark to alert their pack of possible danger and to warn off perceived interlopers or predators." They also bark during play, to initiate play, in response to another dog's barking, to communicate a need, to get your attention ("feed me!"), or just to let off steam. An instinctual trigger, such as a squirrel in the garden can cause barking. Many dogs bark out of unmitigated boredom.

Duncan notes that when dogs bark, most people yell to stop the barking. Not only will this not work, it will exacerbate the situation. A dog's hearing is extremely acute, so when we yell, our voices sound distorted to his ultra-acute hearing—distorted to the point that any speech is incomprehensible. When loud sounds disturb us—for instance, when a commercial comes on during a television show—we rush to turn down the volume. He cannot do that. So if we shout at the dog, we actually produce what he perceives as cacophony! To him, we might as well be another barking dog. Consider the chain reaction among dogs when one dog begins to bark. When we yell, we perpetuate a barking frenzy between ourselves and our dogs, which escalates the very behaviour we wish to eradicate.

The curious Westie will bark to let others know he's interested in them and that they should be interested in him.

Your overexcitement and extreme physical body language will fuel your dog's already heightened emotional state and reinforce his barking. If your dog's barks are reactions to the doorbell, your desperate efforts to quiet him (or even incarcerate him) will only exacerbate the problem—especially if you, too, are freaking out. Your dog is probably thinking of the situation as a version of *Let's Make a Deal.* What's behind the door—a side of corn-fed organic beef or a dognapper hired by Cruella de Ville?

Modify your dog's barking by remaining unruffled. Duncan advises getting the dog's attention by calmly approaching him, raising his head so he looks at you, and telling him, "No bark" in a firm but controlled tone of voice. Verbally reinforce his behaviour the second he stops barking ("Good 'no bark'!"). Then redirect his attention away from whatever set off his barking by using a toy, a treat, a command like sit, or whatever else works.

Be consistent, patient, and understanding. Dogs learn desirable

Terriers are very vocal and can sound ferocious and even vicious to the untrained ear. They are also extremely communicative. Many first-time terrier owners unprepared for these vocalisations misread them as aggression.

behaviours through "patterning." "This is especially true if the behaviour contradicts the dog's basic nature," Duncan emphasises. Find a way to reinforce the new positive behaviour even when you're not around. Since barking is "self-reinforcing," the last thing you want is for your dog to engage in unchecked barking. Successfully deter this by restricting him from a particular area—blocking his view of, for instance, the neighbourhood cat, whose sole purpose in life is to sun herself in your driveway while teasing your Westie. During the time you are "patterning" new behaviours to those triggers, Duncan suggests masking outside sounds that may provoke your dog to react, by using alternate sounds. Mozart played in a continuous loop will not only camouflage a reaction-provoking auditory catalyst, it might add a few points to your Westie's already high IQ. If you're using the television for this purpose, a TV show featuring rodents may not be the best choice, but an all-news channel may be sufficiently nontriggering (unless your Westie has a manic interest in all political and world events).

Duncan stresses that your efforts require consistency, patience, and understanding—especially since you are asking your dog to behave in a manner that contradicts his instincts. How you handle his behaviours will either support or thwart your desired results as well as your relationship. So it is essential to remain positive. Take the time to understand and realise the whys and wherefores of your Westie's behaviour; your reactions do impact his emotional state.

Chewing

Deb Duncan affirms that puppies will chew, and so will older dogs never taught not to. They chew because it is natural, and when they are teething, chewing gives them physical relief. Like a teething infant, a puppy needs teething toys, too—or he will, out of sheer desperation, chew on practically everything not nailed down—just to alleviate the pain of new teeth breaking through the gums.

Provide your Westie with plenty of chew toys. Keep all "enticing" forbidden items out of his reach until he learns the difference between what's acceptable to chew and what's not. (It's not his fault if he destroys, beyond recognition, the favourite pair of sandals that you left on the floor.)

Products made of bitter apple, available in both spray and cream formulas, may help deter your Westie puppy from destroying your possessions. The spray is safe to use on most items. Use the cream on the antique furniture, cabinets, mouldings, and on metal items. Reapply it regularly, as it loses its potency quickly. Also hope that your dog doesn't acquire a taste for the stuff (as one of mine did).

To correct puppies and older dogs not previously taught "chewing etiquette," Duncan recommends catching them in the act. Scolding them after the fact merely perplexes them. So if your dog appears penitent or looks guilty, it's in reaction to your current disapproval. A shake can is an effective distraction for inappropriate chewing. Shake the can and say, "No chew; good no chew," and immediately shift his attention to a permissible chew toy. Then play with him for a few minutes. With your consistency, he will soon learn the impetus for the unpleasant shake-can noise, and curb his enthusiasm. He'll simultaneously learn that "legal" chew toys are not only lots of fun, they'll also garner him extra attention from you.

Puppies love to chew, so be sure to provide your Westie with appropriate chew toys.

Duncan warns that the first several times you correct for chewing, the dog will not associate the "punishment with the crime." Only numerous repetitions, near-perfect consistency, and a saint's patience will accomplish the task and reinforce the desired behaviour. Understand that deprogramming the chewing mechanism is an actual remodeling of his inborn nature, so it's unrealistic to expect such radical change in so few exposures.

Following are a few antichewing hints that support Deb Duncan's methods and give credence to the old adage that "an ounce of

Fresh earth, moist earth, mulches, topsoil, and soft dirt or sand are especially enticing to dogs. If you don't barricade off your country garden, you will set the scene for a "digging war." Even if he does not tend to dig—and in Westies, this is pretty much a long shot—your garden will tempt him toward undesirable behaviour. If his favourite digging place is in your magnificent flower bed, you may have to securely fence it off to make a lovely cottage garden that your Westie may admire but not decimate.

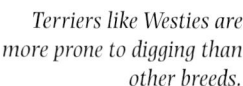

Terriers like Westies are more prone to digging than other breeds.

prevention is worth a pound of cure":

- Chew-proof your house. Pick up all items that could tempt your Westie to chew.
- Keep all socks and shoes out of his reach. If he chews them, it's you who deserves the blame. Do not give him his "own" shoe or sock. It is unrealistic to expect him to distinguish your designer pumps from your old sneakers.
- Carpet edges, couch skirts, and pillows are exceedingly tantalising to pups' and untrained dogs' mouths. Block their access to these items.
- Don't ever let a pup or untrained dog out of your sight. If he's out of sight and quiet, he's probably contentedly chewing on your trendy new handbag.
- For teething pups, keep nylon bones in your freezer. These are

very comforting during teething. A frozen wet rag works well, too.

The secret is to set your Westie up for success. He really does want to please you—even if it means adapting to your rules. And the results will be more than worth your dedicated time and effort.

Digging

Although digging is natural to all dogs, some dogs are more prone to this "industry" than others, and Westies number among this elite group. Other breeds may find alternate impetuses that activate their digging response. Duncan notes that wild dogs dig to bury food, to find food, to hunt quarry, to "make their beds," to create a cool place when it's hot, and to whelp litters. Even a dog who does not dig in the garden will "dig" to adjust his bedding until his place is just right. Then he'll lie down to rest.

"Almost all puppies will have some initial digging behaviours," says Duncan. Sudden onset of digging can result from boredom, an incentive (like a rabbit) on the other side of a fence, a neighbourhood bitch in season, or grasses starting into growing season—whose roots smell like ambrosia to many dogs. (I am still hopeful that my own terriers will learn to unearth some Oregon white truffles!)

Deterring digging behaviour may take a combination of approaches. Duncan recommends the "shake can" method. Sprays or dry treatments can be sprinkled over an area, but since the deterrent odour is short-lived, the inconvenience of having to refresh the treatment constantly makes it less practical.

When your dog has dug a hole, Duncan suggests, place chicken wire, gravel, or rocks in it and cover it over with dirt. A dog often returns to the same areas he has dug in before, so when he encounters these substances—not exactly his textures of choice—he'll abandon the idea. Putting the dog's faeces in the hole and covering it also works with some dogs.

If your dog tries to excavate under your fence, dig a trench around the fence, place chicken wire in it, and cover it. This is a major project but well worth it when you consider the alternative. Stone borders, reinforced cherry-tone logs, and even concrete can keep your Westie from making the great escape. Avoid using any material in a way that could injure your dog.

Try creating an acceptable digging area for your dog. This way,

Digging is such a major part of terriers' instincts that through adaptation, their nails had to grow faster than most other breeds.

If they were left to their own devices, their constant digging would be enough to wear down their nails very quickly—and the nails grow back faster than, say, a sight hound. Therefore, in most domestic environments, Westies need their nails trimmed more frequently than most dogs.

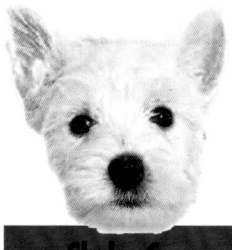

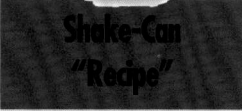

your Westie can dig until the cows come home and you won't have to worry. Select an area and bury toys or treats in it. Demonstrate to him that buried treasures await him underground in this special spot. When you catch him digging where it is forbidden, Duncan advises scolding him by saying, "No dig," and replacing him in his designated area. Choose whatever method suits your preference, but remember, no method is a guarantee.

Growling

A dog's growling sounds are quite diverse, and there are many communication elements and nuances to the sounds he generates. And a Westie's vocal range truly makes him the Julie Andrews of the dog world. But not all growls are negative or aggressive. It's important to assess your dog's growl sounds within a broader

Shake-Can "Recipe"

Take an (empty) can and put ten small metal articles in it. Seal with duct tape. To use: When your dog engages in undesirable behaviour, shake once. This will startle him and interrupt his behaviour. With 100 percent consistency and several repetitions, it can work like a charm. It's important that you give it just a single shake. Any more and he'll desensitise.

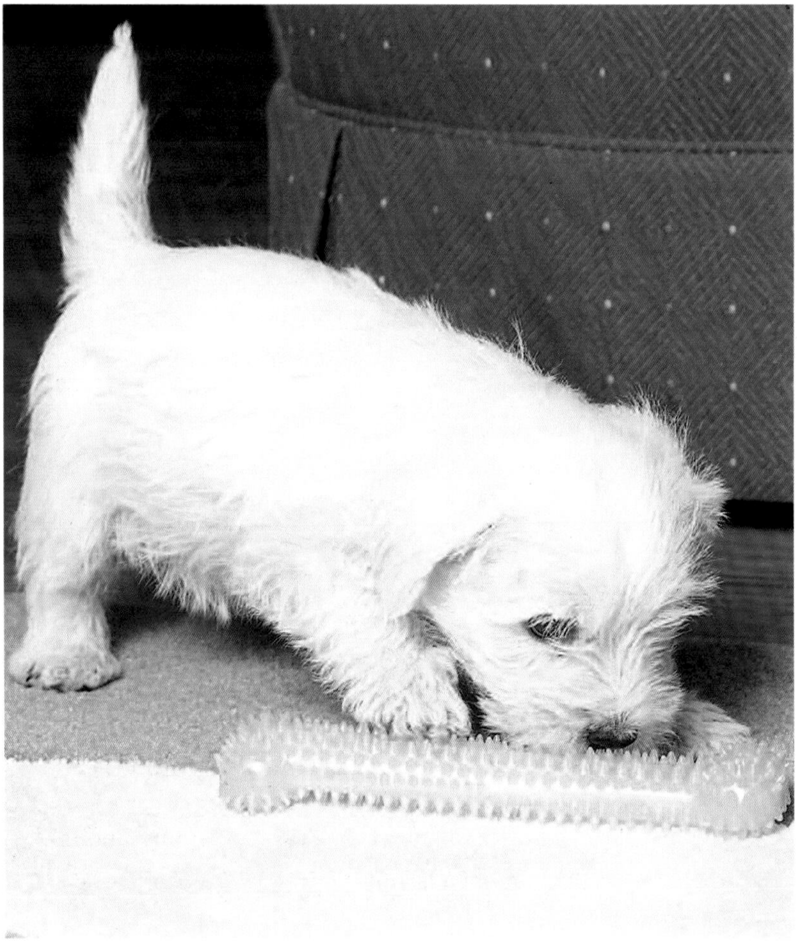

Puppies use their mouths to explore their world. Direct your pup to an appropriate chew item when he gets mouthy with you

context. What (the actual noise) he expresses may differ from how (type of growl) he emits. Certainly there are times when a growl is an unacceptable growl, so becoming a "student of growl-ology" gives you more understanding of your Westie's linguistic capabilities.

Mouthing

Dogs appear to enjoy having mouths. They naturally use their mouths for play and communication. Duncan notes that this is central to their relationships with their mother and littermates. However, in order to harmoniously coexist with humans, puppies must learn new rules. It's our responsibility to show them that we, as caretakers and companions, will not condone mouthing.

You may notice that when your hands are out of reach, your puppy will jump up to try to grab one, hoping to snag it with his puppy teeth. Duncan stresses that this is not aggression: He's really just asking you for interaction and using his mouth to communicate, just as he has seen you use your hands for the same purpose. Again, this presents an opportunity to guide him toward appropriate behaviour.

Dog Phobias

Dog phobias are similar to human ones (although ailurophobia—fear of cats—probably doesn't show up too frequently in Westies). Phobias can occur in any breed, at any age, although they commonly first arise in dogs between the ages of six months and a year. Untreated they tend to increase in severity over time.

- Any time the puppy's mouth so much as grazes you, "yelp" in pain to startle him.
- With the behaviour interrupted, calmly say to him, "No mouth! Good 'no mouth'!"
- Numerous repetitions and several sessions will elapse before he connects your yelp with his own mouth; the key is 100 percent consistency.
- Minimise situations that require you to react.
- Be more careful during playtime; use a toy as a buffer so he will go for that instead of your hand.
- Stay vigilant and decrease opportunities for him grab your hand. You will end up yelping less, and this will help clarify the process for him.

A dog will make mouth contact almost anytime, but during the heightened stimulation and excitement of human/canine play, the "toy" that he'll go for just happens to be your hand, foot, or ankle. People often mistake this for intentional biting: It's not, insists Duncan. Often, it's just a matter of poor timing and inexact aim. Westies are terriers, and terriers are especially attracted to moving targets.

About 19 percent of dogs fear thunder. Dogs may be cued into approaching thunder by the change in barometric pressure. They are very sensitive to natural phenomena, which many appear to find disturbing.

Noise Phobia

Dogs with noise phobias may react by salivating, hiding, pacing, whining, or panting. Some will even injure themselves in their desperate attempt to escape the stimulus. Hiding in a cool, dark room is a common reaction.

Some phobias will develop gradually; others may surface after a single terrifying experience. Without intervention, a dog may become more afraid with each exposure to the source of his fear. One phobia often leads to others. A dog with a thunder phobia may, by association, become afraid of rain, too. Eventually the rain alone will scare him—even in the absence of thunder. (Then the dog may develop a fear of towns or traffic.) Whatever the trigger, there is evidence that there is a genetic component to phobias.

The dog that fears thunder and fireworks may be unable to avoid either of them. In mild cases, simply mask the sound by turning on the radio or TV or one of those white noise machines you can get from holistic health outlets. Serious cases may require more radical measures.

Current research suggests that the best approach to curing neutralising phobias is a two-pronged approach of audio recording desensitisation (some kits include strobe lights) and dog-appeasing pheromones (DAPs). Another solution is melatonin, a natural hormone produced by the pineal gland. This is not available over the counter in the UK, but can be prescribed by vets or purchased on the internet. It has been proven to have a remarkable effect on the "thunderstruck." Some vets will prescribe antianxiety drugs.

Possession Aggression: Yours, Mine, or Ours?

Possessiveness is an unacceptable behaviour pattern that probably arises from deficient puppy socialisation. If your dog stands over his toy or food bowl and stares hard at anyone who deigns to approach him, it is a behaviour you need to eliminate immediately. Other signs can include growling, snapping, biting, or not eating.

This type of behaviour is actually quite natural. Dogs are programmed to hang on to their sustenance. In the wild, if they give up their bone to another animal, they won't get to eat. However, feral dogs and wolves will surrender a meal to the dominant member of the pack. That's you! Ideally, every other human being in your house should precede your dog in the hierarchy. It's doesn't feel natural to every dog, but it's something you must teach him.

With a possessive dog, avoid suddenly snatching his food or toys. This only validates his suspicion that you might be an adversary. Dogs need reassurance that their livelihood is unthreatened. When approaching a dog that seems to be guarding a treat, dog bowl, or toy, try barter. If he's eating dry food, he'll probably trade you for a piece of cheese. (A Westie will be quick to see that you are offering a superior treat.) In the case of a more stubborn dog, avoid giving him long-lasting chewing treats altogether—at least until he budges. Give him only small biscuits he can eat at once without having to "possess" them.

Teach your Westie to sit and wait before you put his food bowl in front of him. Reward him for his compliance by feeding him a bit of something better than what is in the bowl. (Clue him in, though—or he'll inhale what's in his bowl before you dig the fresh Dungeness crab out of your pocket.)

Keep his food bowl in a large, empty space instead of in a corner. Giving him a "special corner" just reinforces the overprotective behaviour you want to eliminate. Move the bowl

Seek help if your dog exhibits possessiveness over certain items or toys.

around; remove it immediately after he's eaten. By staying in the room while he's eating, he'll comprehend that you hold all control over his food.

In established cases of food aggression, take away the dog's food bowl completely and feed him by hand until he realises that all food comes from you. If he seems suspicious when you approach, drop a tasty piece of food in the bowl every time he eats from your hand.

Always seek professional help with any type of problem behaviour that makes you uncomfortable.

Another Dog?

If your dog is alone longer than is good for him, you may wish to get him a companion. Although auxiliary pets are no substitute for people, sometimes having a companion will help. Westie owners who start with one will often later add another.

Separation Anxiety

One of the most serious psychological problems plaguing the modern domestic dog is separation anxiety. Mostly it's just a dog's flawed attempt to solve what he perceives as a terrible dilemma—being alone, scared, or bored.

Dogs have been selectively bred and conditioned for thousands of years to thrive on human companionship, so when that disappears, some dogs find separation intolerable. They did not evolve to spend hours by themselves. Dogs who have suffered abandonment in the past are especially vulnerable to separation anxiety. They haven't a clue when—or if—you'll return after you leave. For all they know, this time could be the "final good-bye."

When they return, owners may find that their freaked-out Westie has taken up some mutant form of interior design. He has "redecorated" the house in grunge style—by adding fringes to your sofa, removing the stuffing from your overstuffed chair, and manifesting

Some problem behaviours are a result of lack of attention or boredom.

other destructive behaviours. He's either cavorting about manically, or he's crouched somewhere in a corner. Once the cycle begins, things tend to worsen because the owner is now drawn into "fearing the unknown." What's next? Aunt Stella's antique rolltop desk with the mother-of-pearl inlay? So the dog picks up the owner's growing tension, and it crescendos as he starts adding more innovative destruction to his repertoire.

If your dog has separation anxiety, he is not alone. He is joined by 7 million other dogs with the same problem. Too bad they can't get together and form a support group.

Some vets use the generic drug clomimpramine to treat separation anxiety. Though it's no magic bullet and has some undesirable side effects, it's one of several options that might give your anxious Westie some palliative relief, in combination with behavioural measures. (The behaviour modification aspect of the therapy is most intensive.) If the owner is committed to working with his dog to conquer the problem, the prognosis for its resolution is good.

To keep both your home and your anxious Westie safe, you may need to confine your dog in your absence. If you'll be gone long, don't crate him. Instead, put him in a large room with a variety of chew toys, a comfortable bed, and access to water. Many dogs with separation anxiety get more agitated when confined, and some will destroy their crates or even self-mutilate in their desperation.

To desensitise your dog to your absences, practice taking "momentary" trips. Practice getting ready to leave (include all your predeparture rituals), but don't actually leave. This helps defuse the energy around the situation by showing him that just because you're going through these activities, it doesn't necessarily mean that it's time for you to go for the day.

When you leave, just go. Don't hang around the house or attempt to placate the dog by cascading him with kisses. He'll just feel worse when you finally withdraw. The more you can ignore him just prior to your departure, the easier the separation will be for him. Provide him with an extra-special toy that he gets only when you leave. Again, treat-stuffed toys work well. Anything that displaces his anxiety will make him feel much better all day. Leave the TV or radio on, but make sure that *Casablanca* isn't playing—the farewell scene between Ingrid Bergman and Humphrey Bogart may be more than he can bear.

Get up a little earlier and take longer walks than usual. Not only will it benefit both of your cardiovascular systems and help

You can help relieve mild cases of separation anxiety by not overdramatising homecomings and partings, by hiding food-stuffed chew treats around the house, and by ignoring the dog for about 20 minutes prior to leaving and after getting home.

Outside activities and exercise are physically and mentally good for your Westie.

produce endorphins, but you may tire him out a tad. A tired dog is a good dog.

Establishing yourself as a trusted leader helps dogs with separation anxiety. As the bond between you strengthens, the dog begins to trust that your decisions are for his own well-being. With that knowledge, your dog can relax.

Separation anxiety doesn't go away on its own, so enlist the help of an experienced behaviourist to deal with this problem.

"True" Aggression

Some truly dangerous aggressive behaviour has genetic links, but other causes can include illness or mishandling. If you feel the situation is out of hand, consult a trained behaviourist. Most pet-dog trainers do not have the specialised training needed to deal with aggressive, dangerous dogs, so talk to your vet about finding certified help. A small percentage of dogs are beyond cure, but most are not.

In most cases, owners let aggression happen. Some people allow their dogs to lord over their household. They allow their dog to stake claim to a favourite chair or (in extreme cases) all the furniture. The dog will snatch food, nip children, or defend his

- Never provoke a situation where the dog may bite. Chasing him or trying to pull him out of a hiding place is probably a manifestation of a death wish!
- Get your dog vet checked for any possible physical problems. Request a thyroid test.
- Find special training opportunities for aggressive dogs. Regular obedience classes are neither appropriate nor fair to him or to the other dogs and handlers.
- For at least two weeks, restrict your interactions with your dog to a bare minimum; make him beg for your attention.
- Keep the dog completely off the bed, furniture, or other high places.
- Make the dog sit or lie down before feeding him.
- Give your dog twice the exercise he's getting now—outside the garden. Busy dogs have more opportunity to work off stress and are less apt to bite.
- If necessary, keep a soft muzzle on the dog while working with him.
- Keep small children away from the aggressive dog at all times.
- Consult a competent canine behaviourist.
- Avoid any competitive games like tug-of-war. If you do play them, make sure you always win.
- Don't give the dog any toys or possessions at all.

food bowls from his owners—who not only put up with it, but also add to the problem.

A well-behaved Westie should do the following:

- Move when told.
- Give up his toys when told.
- Allow any human to approach his food bowl and pet him while he eats. (It's best to allow a dog to eat in peace, but approaching him prepares him for that stray curious child who breaks that rule.)
- Avoid disturbing people while they are eating.
- Avoid nipping unless provoked beyond reason.
- Allow a human to pick him up and carry him.
- Allow his nails to be clipped and his ears cleaned without striking out with his mouth.

Establish early on that you are the boss. In fact, decisiveness is a quality that dogs admire. Your Westie actually wants a good and benevolent leader. To become that leader you must prove yourself worthy with firm, consistent training methods, an even temper, and a no-nonsense attitude. You get to decide when and where the dog eats, plays, and sleeps.

Some dogs battle for dominion over furniture. To a bossy Westie, furniture can be a fortress, a high place that allows him more status than does the lowly floor. Some dogs equate being elevated with being exalted. So, if he shows any propensities for being bossy, deny him couch privileges until he is ready to surrender them to any human being, including a child, without an altercation. And Westies can certainly be vociferous.

If your dog growls, snarls, or snaps at a person who attempts to "dethrone" him, take firm measures. Strongly prompt him to leave with an unyielding "off!" If he doesn't obey, use a shake can to catch him off guard.

Whenever dealing with an overly assertive dog, stand erect and speak in a firm, no-nonsense voice. Use food to lure your dog off the couch only if he has *not* growled or snapped. A growler will think you're rewarding him for his poor manners. Use the shake can. If you do not achieve success, consult an expert.

HOW TO FIND A CANINE BEHAVIOURIST

Never hesitate to seek professional help with your Westie if you need it. Your happiness and his well-being could depend on it. If your dog becomes aggressive toward people or toward other animals or manifests any traits that make you uneasy, immediately seek assistance. Without intervention, it's unlikely that his undesirable behaviour will vanish or improve. Your dog needs to learn how to live harmoniously in society. In the first instance, ask your vet to recommend a behaviourist. In many cases, the behaviourist will seek a vet referral before examining a dog. You can also talk to Westie rescue groups and all-breed rescue centres, who will regularly use the services of a professional behaviourist. The Association of Pet Behaviour Counsellors (APBC) has details of APBC-approved counsellors and trainers nationwide. Log on to www.apbc.org.uk.

An animal behaviourist is often an academically trained specialist who's typically completed graduate work in psychology in such specific areas as learning processes, psychoneurology, psychobiology, and zoology. He or she will also have additional experience in dog training and

canine behaviour on a practical 'hands on' level.

Among the various behaviours an animal behaviourist treats are phobias, anxiety, aggression (in its many forms and degrees), and obsessive-compulsive disorders. In most cases, a conventional dog trainer lacks the qualifications to treat these cases.

When choosing a canine behaviourist, check out his or her educational credentials; but even more important, ask about the depth of his or her experience and about the kinds of problems he or she has helped solve. The behaviourist should be more than willing to offer you several references from satisfied clients. Behaviourists charge by the hour, but they may also offer treatment programmes with set rates based on the individual programme. Many will offer phone consultations as well as one-on-one sessions.

Canine behaviourists who also have veterinary degrees sometimes use medications that physicians use on people to treat phobias, aggression, anxiety, and other symptoms. These medications have been proven to be helpful in some cases, but their efficacy is far from perfect. Side effects can, in some instances, add to your problem rather than improve it. The best veterinary canine behaviourists do not use drugs alone, but if they do use them, they combine (and monitor) the medicine with sound behavioural training.

A canine behaviourist can evaluate all aspects of your dog's behaviour to help you solve problems.

ADVANCED TRAINING AND ACTIVITIES

With Your West Highland White Terrier

Your Westie has the basics down and her manners would put Emily Post to shame. But you want more, right? Many fun activities await both of you. However, before leaping into any new activity, it is important to do the following:

- Check out the activity. Do you have the time, money, energy, and interest?
- Assess your Westie's general well-being with a vet before embarking on any new activity.
  - Immerse yourselves gradually, especially in the more intense activities such as agility and flyball.
    - Attend to your Westie's natural limits and take cues from him when he's had enough. Westies are hardy but not invincible.
    - Adjust feeding to sustain your Westie's increased level of activity, if necessary.
    - Stop when either of you has had enough, is tired, injured, or overly frustrated. Never work a sick dog.

COMPETITIVE EVENTS

There are many events you and your Westie can compete in. A number of them are held through the Kennel Club (KC). You can find out more about each of these events at www.the-kennel-club.org.uk, and then go to websites for each individual activity.

Agility

Agility is an exciting canine sport for both participants and spectators. In this event, a dog demonstrates his athleticism and attentiveness by taking cues from the handler while following a timed obstacle course. The course consists of jumps, tunnels, weave poles, and other obstacles. The activity cements bonds between dog and handler and provides fun and vigorous exercise for both.

Agility was launched in England and is currently the fastest-growing dog sport on both sides of the Atlantic. All breeds can take part in Agility, and if your dog is the on the Working Dogs Register, dogs without papers, and cross-breeds, can also take part. A standard Agility course contains about 20 obstacles. The hurdles are at different heights depending on the size of the dog. The Westie competes in 'small dog' classes. Most Westies jump somewhere around 12 inches (30 cm). The tyre is lowered, and the long jump is shortened, but all other obstacles remain the same for all sizes. Agility offers two classes: Jumping classes that have no contact equipment, and Agility Classes, which have a full set of equipment.

Good Citizen Scheme

The Good Citizen Scheme was launched by the Kennel Club to reward dogs and their owners who have socialised their dogs to behave well at home and in their communities. This programme promotes responsible pet ownership.

Any dog—purebred or mixed—is eligible to take the puppy foundation, bronze, silver and gold awards. In addition to

Agility consists of obstacles like weave poles, dog walks, and jumps.

The Good Citizen Scheme

Many other countries (including the USA, Australia, Japan, Hungary, Denmark, Sweden, Canada, and Finland) have developed Good Citizen programmes. The schemes promote responsible ownership and help dogs to be more widely accepted and tolerated in the community.

nurturing the dog/owner relationship, Good Citizen training is excellent preparation for formal obedience work. Obedient dogs are not only wonderful companions, they also adjust well to household routines and demonstrate good etiquette toward people and other dogs—enough to impress Miss Manners. Your Westie will be grateful that you considered him important enough to invest the time to train, stimulate, and care for him, and you will have certificates to prove it.

A Westie who is a Canine Good Citizen will allow friendly strangers to pet and groom him.

Earthdog Tests

The AKC runs Earthdog tests, which provide opportunities to measure your dog's working abilities, and many West Highland White Terriers have excelled at this. The AKC currently offers four levels: a "nontitling" class, Introduction to Quarry (a basic exposure to earthwork), Junior Earthdog (JE), Senior Earthdog (SE), and Master Earthdog (ME). The first two are essentially instinct tests, the last two are ostensibly designed to replicate actual hunting situations.

All tests include a den with tunnels and turns, which become progressively more complex at each ascending level. Each 9-inch (22.9 cm) diameter wood-lined tunnel ends with a cage of (often terminally bored) rats. The judge sprays the path to the quarry with "rat tea," a delightful concoction derived from urine-soaked rat-cage shavings.

Flyball

Flyball is a team sport for dogs that started in California almost 30 years ago. This fast, fun sport is open to all dogs, pedigree and non-pedigree alike. It wasn't long before flyball captured the imagination of dog trainers and dog clubs everywhere throughout North America. From then on, it spread to the United Kingdom and the rest of the world in a very short space of time.

With four dogs on each team, flyball is a relay race. The 51-foot-long (15.5 m) course consists of a starting line, 4 hurdles spaced 10 feet (3 m) apart, and a spring-loaded box that ejects a tennis ball. Each dog jumps the hurdles and steps on the box to trigger release of the ball. After catching the ejected ball, he clears the hurdles to cross the starting line, prompting the next dog to go. The first team to have all four dogs run without errors wins the heat.

The type of flyball competition may vary from country to country, but basically tournaments are either a double elimination or round robin. In both cases, each member of the first team to win three heats out of five receives 1 point towards his standing.

The shortest dog's stature determines the hurdle heights—4 inches (10 cm) below the shoulder height of the shortest dog for an 8-inch (20 cm) minimum height and a 16-inch (40.6 cm) maximum. Shorter dogs, such as speedy, ball-crazy Westies are coveted by teams of Border Collies, for instance, since lower hurdles can shave seconds off the team's total time. For more information on flyball in the UK, visit the British Flyball Association website by logging on to www.flyball.org.uk.

This Westie has entered a tunnel in an earthdog competition.

Flyball is a fast-paced relay race in which dogs catch tennis balls and race over hurdles.

Obedience

Obedience competition tests a dog's ability to work with his handler and perform prescribed scored exercises. These trials emphasise the usefulness of the purebred dog as an animal companion. Pre-beginner and beginner competitive obedience exercises include heeling on lead and off lead, coming when called, and remaining in both a sit and a down position until the handler is instructed by the judge to release the dog. For the levels after novice (classes A, B and C) the exercises get increasingly complicated.

A dog trained for obedience trials is responsive to his handler's requests.

In the UK obedience competitions tend to be dominated by breeds such as the Border Collie. However, although the West Highland White Terrier may not be considered a "conventional" obedience breed, these small terriers are nevertheless trainable and they can make quite an impression in the obedience ring.

The feisty attitude and keen intelligence that is typical of the average Westie can result in very good obedience competitors. Though originally selectively bred for their independent problem-solving abilities, Westies are loyal to their humans, and the opportunity to work together can result—and has resulted—in top-notch obedience dogs.

Rally Obedience

Rally obedience is a relatively new sport that officially became an AKC titling event in 2005. It is not yet recognised in the UK, but if its increasing popularity in the US is anything to go by, it is highly likely that the sport will soon find its way to the United Kingdom.

Unlike conventional obedience, your dog doesn't have to work at perfect heel position. You are encouraged to praise and communicate with your dog. Precision, attitude, and enthusiasm rate high in this event. In rally, you and your Westie work as real partners.

Numbered signs that provide specific instructions mark each of 10 to 20 stations on a rally course. The number of signs and the complexity of the instructions increase at each level. At the novice level, as in the corresponding level in conventional AKC Obedience, dogs work on the lead, and exercises are basic. As dog-handler duo progresses, the sport becomes more challenging and includes some jumping and work off lead. Speed is not critical and is only used as a tiebreaker. With a score of 70 percent out of a possible 100 percent, you and your dog qualify for one of three legs required for a title.

You can practice at home: All you need are the cones and rally signs and—later—an 8-inch (20 cm) jump, which you can order from AKC. Rosenblatt finds this time relaxing and rewarding for herself and her Westies. Not bad for a competitive event!

A Westie completing a station at a rally course.

Showing (Conformation)

Dog shows (conformation events) are intended to evaluate breeding stock. Therefore, only sexually intact dogs qualify for conventional Kennel Club conformation events. The size of these events ranges from large all-breed shows, with huge entries to small club shows featuring a specific breed. The dog's overall appearance and structure, or conformation—often an indication of the dog's ability to produce quality puppies—is judged.

There are three types of conformation dog shows, as follows:

- All-breed shows offer competitions for over 150 breeds and varieties of dogs recognised by the Kennel Club. Crufts is the premier all-breed show in the UK, and it is often shown on television.
- Shows restricted to dogs of a specific breed or to varieties of one breed.
- Group shows are limited to dogs belonging to one of the seven KC groups. Westies compete in the Terrier Group.

Conformation shows are where you expect to see Westies that look like Westies and Shar-Peis that look unmistakably Shar-Pei-ish. Numerous opportunities to show your Westie to his championship title abound. Like flea markets and horse shows, you can find one nearly every weekend of the year—holidays included. There are lots of rosettes on offer at every show, and winning Best of Breed is a great honour. If you're not careful, dog showing can become an addiction!

If your dog is show quality, your Westie's breeder or knowledgeable members of a Westie club will honestly help you assess his chances of attaining his Championship. Showing a dog, however, is hardly as easy as it appears. That's the paradox: It requires a lot of skill to make it look easy. Training your dog to "stack" (pose properly), to stand still while being examined, and to "show his heart out" requires practice. It takes more than good conformation and flashy movement to make a winner. It's that hypnotic je ne sais quoi that tells the judge, "You will pick me!" Many gorgeous dogs simply lack the necessary attitude to achieve the top levels or even finish a championship. A beautiful dog with the personality of tapioca pudding is unlikely to win shows.

For most people, that top level is a Kennel Club Championship. To become a Champion, a dog must win three

Breed Standard & Type

The breed standard describes the characteristics that allow the breed to perform the function for which it was bred. These standards include specifications for structure, temperament, and movement. Breed type clearly distinguishes one breed from another. My own definition of type includes the word quintessence—as in Westie-ness. A so-called typey dog's physical appearance and bearing fairly yells out the breed standard.

Challenge Certificates (CCs) under three different judges. Judges examine the dogs and then give awards according to how closely each dog compares to their mental image of the "perfect" dog as described in the breed's official standard.

A dog show is really an elimination contest. Male dogs compete against males (called "dogs") and females against females (called "bitches"—their proper appellation) in each breed, with the best of each sex being awarded a Challenge Certificate.

Do It Yourself or Bring in the Pros?

Many Westie breeders and owners enjoy showing their dogs themselves. For various reasons, other owners cannot show or don't enjoy it, and they hire a professional handler.

So what do you look for in a professional handler? Breeder and handler Linda Wells stresses that a handler should be honest with you. If she does not believe that your dog is of show quality, she should tell you so—even at the risk of losing a potential client. This is a hallmark of a responsible handler.

Another successful professional terrier handler, Sally George, elaborates, "Watch your potential handler at shows before you consider contracting her services." Do the handler's "charges" appear happy and in good physical condition? How does she interact with the dogs? George brings up several additional important questions and criteria, as follows:

- How does the handler care for her dogs? Does she have the facility, equipment, ability, and experience to properly care for yours?

Showing Tip

Caution: Excessive repetition may result in boredom or "creative improvisation" in the show ring. But if you keep things interesting and challenging, your Westie should rise to the occasion.

Crufts and Westminster

The United Kingdom has Crufts, a somewhat more informal show than Westminster, the US equivalent. Run by the Kennel Club, it features 197 different breeds (more than the 150 currently recognised in the United States). The original Cruft, named Charles, made his living selling dog cakes all across Europe. Inspired by the multiplicity of breeds, he organised the first show in 1891.

The most famous dog show in the United States is Westminster, where only AKC Champions are eligible to compete. It used to be a mad race to get entries in. As a result, many top-ranked dogs did not make the entry. Now the five top-ranked dogs of each breed receive an invitation which, if accepted, guarantees entry.

What Makes a Good Show Dog?

Longtime Westie breeder and professional handler Linda Wells shares what she looks for in a potential show dog. The best indicators are conformation, health, attitude, and good breed type. She looks for a Westie that matches the AKC standard as closely as possible "with more plusses than minuses." Obviously, the dog should manifest no disqualifying faults. Wells likes to see a happy dog who is neither timid nor pugnacious—with the endurance and energy typical of the breed. If he's a show-off (even bordering on obnoxious), that can be an asset in the ring. She notes that judges often consider Westies a "head breed," so a good headpiece will receive a lot of credit.

- Does the handler have the skill to groom and condition a Westie so that he will be competitive? Look for other Westies she's shown. Get some show pictures of the handler's top-winning dogs. At a glance, do the dogs she handles look like winners?
- Do the handler's dogs make a good first impression? George stresses that Westies are a highly trimmed breed, so the show-ring judging—for better or for worse—is generally based 50 percent on dog and 50 percent on presentation. Judges have only two and a half minutes to totally evaluate each dog, so first impressions are crucial.

Seek a handler with whom you can communicate. You need to understand why the handler will not show your dog on a particular weekend and where she wants to take him. Communication fosters

Show handlers know how to bring out the best in the dogs they work with

Westies competing in the show ring.

trust, which is essential to any relationship.

You're entrusting your precious Westie to this person. It's imperative that you feel assured that your dog will receive the best treatment possible. Do not tolerate any handler who lies to you or mistreats your dog. Once your trust is violated, find another handler.

What Not to Wear!

- Do not dress to upstage your dog.
- Do not buy clothing that is two sizes too snug, no matter how ambitious you are about shedding those extra pounds; it distracts from your dog.
- White clunky running shoes with a suit look tacky.
- Heels look inappropriate and make it difficult to move around the ring. Moreover, they guarantee sore feet after a day on concrete or grass.
- You may believe that dressing tackily makes your dog appear better by comparison — and he very well may look better. But that's not what wins shows.
- Wearing gold and purple will not "subliminally" influence the judge to award your dog a Best of Breed rosette. Resist that temptation with all you've got.

What to Wear

Breeder Sandy Davis follows the following sensible rules when exhibiting her Westies:

- Dress to complement the colour of the dog and to subtly enhance his appearance. This means that you dress conservatively: no jeans, shorts, miniskirts, or low necklines—and nothing too tight.
- Blue, grey, black, red, green, and even purple complement a white dog. Brown, tan, and yellow do not, as they tend to shed their colour onto the dog. Turquoise works well with any breed or colour of dog. Plaids or prints, unless very muted, are too busy and detract from the dog. Neat casual clothing is all right at the class level.
- If you are competing at the group level or beyond, consider something more formal like a suit.
- Wear sensible shoes with low heels in neutral browns, tans, greys, or black. Rubber-cushioned soles work well for comfort and function.

This American champion Westie, "Sprite," has the distinction of being the only Champion Tracker terrier to date.

Tracking

Are you seeking a pleasurable outdoor activity for your Westie? Why not tracking? Consider this: A German Shepherd has 220 million olfactory cells, compared to a human's measly 5 million. This number varies according to breed: Longer-muzzled dogs have an advantage over brachiocephalic (flat-faced) dogs. Though relatively short muzzled, your Westie has a bumper crop of these cells and proves it as you watch him track naturally, identifying scents of various animals and people who have passed his way on your walks. He'll try to follow the interesting ones—even if you have other ideas.

How to Earn an English Championship

In the United Kingdom, a dog must win Best Bitch or Best Dog at a championship show three times to earn Championship Certificates (or CCs). The dogs first compete in classes according to age or place of origin. In UK competitions, four-month-old puppies may compete, whereas in the United States, entrants must be at least six months of age. The judge selects the winner from among the winners of each class (again divided by gender).

There is no age limit, but if a puppy gets three CCs before he turns a year old (and this is highly unlikely), he has to wait until after he's turned a year old to become a champion.

In the United Kingdom, exhibitors usually wait until a dog is fully mature before showing him in earnest. In contrast, in the States, many dogs have attained their championships before their first birthday.

In the UK, tracking is included in Working Trials rather than being an event in its own right. Unfortunately, small breeds do not have the scope to compete in all the disciplines demanded in Working Trials.

In the US, the American Kennel Club runs tracking events and Westies have had a fair degree of success. In a tracking competition, a judge will choose the scent for your Westie to follow. A properly trained dog can follow a path someone has taken five hours earlier.

Individuals differ in aptitude, but AKC Tracking Judge Allison Platt suggests that tracking may be an appropriate "prelude" to formal obedience or agility training. For example, a younger dog that has not yet been taught to totally rely on you for guidance may have an advantage. A younger dog often has no qualms about pulling you—this is actually desirable in tracking—and loves working so much that he couldn't care less whether you're

A Versatile Dog has won points by competing in events like agility and obedience.

behind him or not. Older, more self-reliant dogs may also do well in this sport. But for any Westie, tracking is a great confidence builder; and it also gives the two of you a great opportunity to embark on adventures both rewarding and healthful, and that will help you to form an even closer bond.

A minimum of equipment, as follows, will get you started tracking:

- a nonrestrictive harness for your Westie, and a 40-foot line
- some personal articles with your scent on them (gloves or socks, for instance)
- surveyors' flags or brightly spray-painted clothespins to mark your training tracks
- weather-resistant clothes—just the rationalisation you need for buying more clothing!

The Nose Knows

What if your nose were as sensitive as your Westie's? With his nose, he "sees" a whole network of paths as acutely as if they were strewn with distinct multicoloured lines. Tracking theory suggests that a dog can pick up one of these scent paths and follow it to its conclusions, as easily as a person can connect the dots to form a picture.

Top Dog

The West Highland White Terrier Club of America's Versatile Dog programme was the brainchild of William (Sil) Sanders. The Versatile Dog Award programme awards Westies who achieve certain high levels of accomplishment in their lifetimes. Awards are based on a point system in which each level of achievement in an area earns a point. The areas Westies compete in are conformation, obedience, tracking, agility, and earthdog.

In 1980, Ch. Skaket's Chunkies, UD, CG became the first Versatile Dog. The programme flourished to become one of the most impressive AKC Versatility programmes in the United States.

NONCOMPETITIVE ACTIVITIES

You may decide that organised events just aren't for you and your Westie. Never fear—there are plenty of exercises and games you can play together at home that will keep your dog's mind and body occupied and increase the bond between the two of you.

Fun and Games

The following are some favourite games Westie owners play with their dogs:

- Nancy's Westie Andy loves playing with a giant kick ball. He likes when it is thrown, so he can chase it and try to bite it.
- Westie Sophie enjoys being chased around the house in order

Non-Westie Events

Kennel Club rules do not permit Westies to compete in lure coursing, herding, or hunting trials, although I recently met a Westie with the most perfect point! Come to think about it, it's not that they would be unable to do some of these events. Many fun days with terriers include an informal kind of lure coursing—they certainly don't lack the prey drive. Herding is a little trickier. Some Westies might do quite well at it, and I have heard of terriers imbued with this instinct, but others might see the ducks more as an all-you-can-eat buffet rather than as something to herd and care for.

While Westies don't officially participate in hunting trials, some still know how to point.

to capture her favourite toy. The exercise benefits both Sophie and her owner, Vicki. But her absolute favourite thing is to bat and chase empty plastic milk jugs.

- Evy's Westie, Thurston, likes to catch her. It's a game of mutual keep-away. Also, like many other Westies, he loves to compete with 65-pound (29.5-kg) dog (and housemate) Archie and knock the tennis ball thrown for Archie out of the dog's mouth.

You and your playful Westie can enjoy all kinds of games together.

- Riley inherited a collection of stuffed ladybugs, which he enjoys chasing when Karen goads him on. Another tennis ball chaser, he soon learned that linoleum can be slippery, so he works fast to intercept it before the carpet ends and the bare floor begins.

- Charlie is a soccer goalie. When owner Wilma tosses the tennis ball, he blocks it. She also hides and challenges him to find her just by calling his name. "Tracking" with dry food or cereal is another favourite.

- Nancy's Westie, Fergus, herds his blue basketball all over the house and garden while barking with great enthusiasm.

- Hampton is another compulsive ball retriever. Peggy says he enjoys barking at squirrels, as do many Westies. He and Westie sibling Abby play tug-o-war with Hampton's chew bunny.

- Joan and her Westie push a ball back and forth between them and play catch. They conclude with a high five, and for his finale he rolls over and "chills out."

End a game by teaching your Westie to roll over and "chill out."

Sally and the Nursing Home

Westie owner Laurie Cochin reports, "My Westie Sally visits my mother-in-law at her nursing home every day—sometimes twice!" Without fail, she jumps onto Fannie Cochin's bed and provides her with unlimited kisses and cuddles. Sensing her need for security, Sally nestles against her body. A dog person all her life, Fannie looks forward to her "grand-dog's" visits; they are the highlight of her day.

Laurie continues, "One day, we realised Sally had wandered out of the room. We discovered her right next door, on the bed of my mother-in-law's neighbour Marie, happily eating mashed potatoes off her lunch tray. My husband actually remoulded the potatoes, and no one ever found out! But after that, Sally always made a beeline for Marie's room." But it was destiny! Marie never talks—she usually sits silently in her wheelchair—with only one exception. Whenever she sees Sally, she stuns everyone by demanding, "Bring him to me." When she lifts Sally to bestow a good-night kiss, she always giggles and exclaims, "He loves me!" "Yes *she* does," replies Laurie, good-naturedly.

- Matt's Westie, Brodie, loves empty 2-litre soda bottles, proving that the best toys are often the cheapest. Brodie picks one up by the cap and watches it roll and make strange noises. He tries to stalk it (carefully, of course, so as not to alert it). However, his favourite tug toy is an inch-wide 6-foot nylon lead. By cutting off the buckle, Matt allowed the end to fray, and Brodie is entertained for hours while Matt grips the loop grip. The bonus is that it helped him learn to walk much better on lead because he no longer chews his real lead—he knows that playtime is coming with the "fake" one. Brodie also enjoys finding hidden toys.

- Dawn Martin reports, "My dogs enjoy a good game of 'bobbing for hotdogs.'" She uses a big basin of water, and her dogs literally go to great depths for each morsel. This well-known breeder of conformation and performance star Westies adds that this game trains them to use their noses.

- Kathy's Westie Nicky plays "whatever game he chooses." He trolls Kathy and her husband for kisses. He also has a penchant (checked) for shredding toilet paper, so Kathy removes that temptation from the roller in her bathroom.

(Thanks to the Westie aficionados at Westie-l, an e-mail list dedicated to all things Westie, for sharing their fun and games.)

Walking and Jogging

Walking or jogging with your Westie will benefit both of you. Remember that your Westie is a terrier, and, as such, he is vulnerable to the lure of the occasional errant squirrel as it scurries

across the street. That should be enough to persuade you to keep him on a lead at all times. Westie endurance is amazing. Barring disability or old age, Westies are little canine bundles of energy. Just be sure to check with your vet before starting any strenuous activity with your dog.

If you don't want to participate in organised sports, there's still plenty of fun to be had with your Westie.

Robust, hardy terriers that they are, Westies are often eager, able, and willing to walk for miles without showing signs of fatigue—even if you do! Be sure to bring along some extra water for him *and* yourself. However, in hot weather, take it easy—consider abbreviating your outing to avoid dangerous heatstroke.

Westies inspire love, making them excellent therapy dogs.

THERAPY WORK

Therapy dogs comfort the sick, cheer the elderly, and enhance the lives of those with whom their paths cross. That they provide benefits for heart patients, AIDS patients, people with disabilities, children with autism, and people with other disorders has been well documented. They also can visit nursing homes, homeless shelters, and hospitals. Therapy dogs have even played key roles in the rehabilitation of convicted criminals in prisons.

In the UK, the governing body for therapy dogs is Pets as Therapy (PAT). For detailed information on registering your Westie as a PAT dog, visit their website (www.petsastherapy.org).

A dog must be a minimum of 9 months of age before applying to be a therapy dog. A registered evaluator will check on the dog's general health and temperament. The dog will then be tested to see if he will walk on a loose lead, remain under control despite distractions, and not react to loud or sudden noises. The evaluator will also check to see if the dog is happy to be groomed, as this shows whether a dog will accept all over handling and touching.

Once your dog is accepted to work as a PAT dog, you can approach local hospitals and care homes and make arrangements

Getting Involved in Pet Therapy

Those who participate say there is often no more satisfying experience than working with a dog in pet therapy. Seeing how your dog will instinctively know how to be with people of different ages experiencing different kinds of problems is a special gift for both yourself and your dog. If it's something in which you are seriously interested, research the requirements of organisations with certified programmes, or contact your local physical and mental health care facilities and ask about whether they participate in pet therapy visits and who coordinates them. Any of these sources can direct you to the kind of training or special instruction you and your dog need to do this special work.

Find out more about therapy dogs and the Pets as Therapy scheme by visiting the PAT Dog website at www.petsastherapy.org.

so that you and your Westie can start visiting.

A well-behaved Westie can make a terrific therapy dog—and a bit of a novelty too, since larger dogs make up the majority of those doing this type of work. The portable, stable Westie may gladly play the role of "love sponge" on a patient's lap, lie on someone's bed, perform a few selections from a repertoire of remarkable tricks, or dispense kisses—if that's what's wanted and needed. Westies have provided solace to hospitalised people of all ages, listened—without judgment—to stories read by children with learning disabilities, and brightened many days at nursing homes.

Who can resist a face like this one? Your Westie has love to share with all who meet him.

C h a p t e r

HEALTH

of Your West Highland White Terrier

In general, among purebred dogs, Westies are considered a hardy and sturdy breed. Remember that no dog—purebred or mixed breed—is immune to health problems. Environmental as well as genetic predispositions can factor into any dog's well-being.

Since you want your Westie to live a long, joyful, and comfortable life, proper home care and plenty of TLC are important. Also essential for his optimum health is regular veterinary care—for preventative, prompt, and competent treatment for any problems that arise. If you are concerned about any aspect of your Westie's well-being, it's always better to seek veterinary advice than to worry yourself to shreds. Err on the side of caution.

HOW TO FIND A VET

After you, your vet is your dog's best friend. To find the right vet, ask people who share your own approach to pet care. Seek recommendations from your Westie's breeder, friends, dog trainers, or your pet sitter. Telephone directories provide important information about hours, services, and staff. And don't wait until you really need one to find a vet—start looking as soon as you know you are getting a dog.

When looking for a vet, make sure to check out the practice, and request a tour. You're looking for someone to meet both your needs and your Westie's—a vet who has people skills as well "crate-side manners." Try to assess the entire veterinary team's competence and their people skills. If you like the vet but dislike the staff, keep looking. If the fees are a bargain yet you're uncomfortable about some other aspect of the practice, move on. The longer drive or slightly higher fees could pay "healthy" dividends.

Veterinary surgeons undergo a tough training course before they can be registered with the British Veterinary Association and set up in practice. In most cases, a vet with a small animal practice is rather like a doctor in general practice. The vet or doctor is a highly skilled practitioner. But if your Westie needs specialist treatment, you will be referred to a vet who has taken further qualifications and is an expert in his field—opthalmology or cardiology, for example.

The optimal health of your West Highland White Terrier starts with YOU! As his parent, you need to find the person you think will be the best vet for your dog. As his constant caregiver, you will be the first to notice when something seems to be bothering him. You are responsible for his need for a good diet, exercise, grooming, and a loving environment. That's why his good health starts with you first!

After narrowing your search, schedule a visit to meet the staff, and discuss the hospital's philosophy and policies. Following are some questions to ask and points to observe:

- Are appointments required?
- How many vets are in the practice?
- Are there veterinary nurses or other professional staff members?
- Is the practice clean, comfortable, and well organised?
- Is the staff caring, calm, competent, and courteous, and do they communicate effectively?
- Do the vets have special interests such as geriatrics or behaviour?
- Do the fees fit your budget, and are discounts for senior citizens or multi-pet households available?
- Are X-rays, ultrasound, blood work, EKG, endoscopies, and other diagnostics done in-house or referred to a specialist?
- What emergency services are available?
- Is the vet familiar with Westies and their special needs?
- What services does the clinic provide? Grooming? Home visits?
- Are any of the staff specialists?
- What hours is the clinic open?
- How close is the vet to your home? (I have discovered that having more than one vet can work well. One is close to home, and another, though farther away, I'll visit for particular issues.)
- Does the clinic accept pet insurance?

PARTNERS IN HEALTH

As our animals' guardians, caregivers, and advocates, we must educate ourselves. If we don't take the responsibility and make informed choices regarding our pets' well-being, no one else will. Learn to recognise the first signs of illness, and see your vet regularly for preventive visits. If your pet is not well, don't wait until he is really sick before calling your vet. Remember that Westies are notorious for their stoicism, so your dog may not appear as ill as he really is.

However, we're the ones who make the ultimate decisions regarding our pets. The vet's extra training and medical knowledge merit respect, but that does not preclude our own research and our responsibility for asking the right questions. A

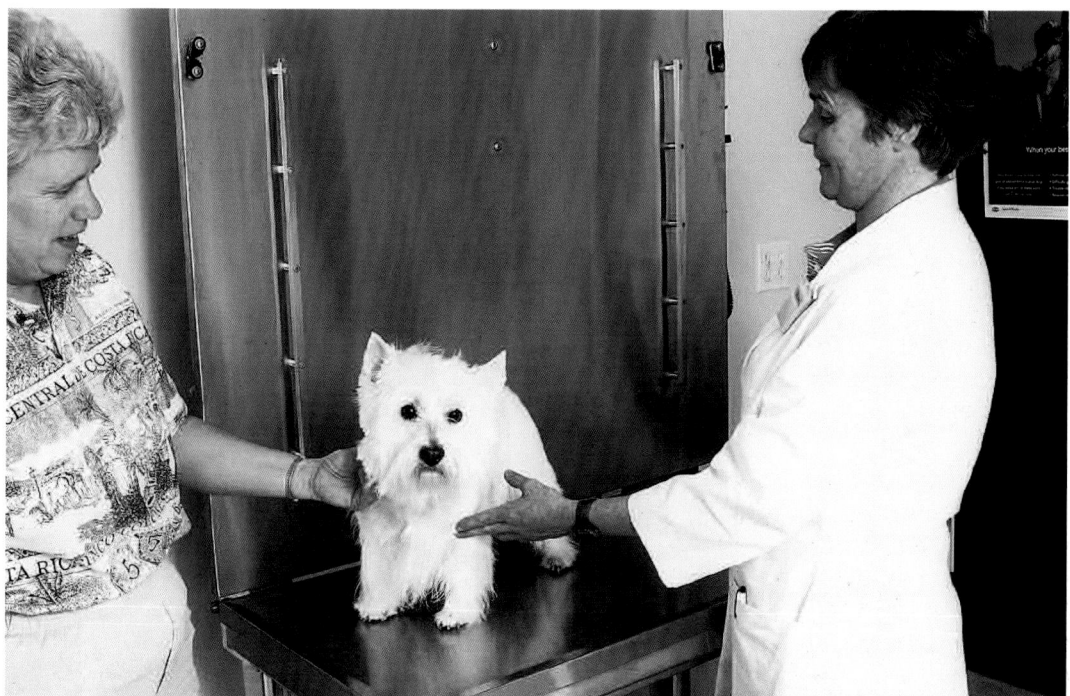

You and your vet should work together for your Westie's health.

caring vet shares our concern for our dog's well-being. Ideally, it's a partnership, and you and the vet should share some similar philosophies and hold each other in mutual respect. If you feel your needs as a client or those of your pet are unsatisfactorily met, find a new vet. This applies to both allopathic and holistic—or alternative—vets.

If your dog has been diagnosed with a serious ailment, do ask the following tough questions:

- "What is wrong with my Westie?" Get both the official medical name for the disorder and a layperson's explanation of its meaning.
- "What's his prognosis?" Is the disease curable? Manageable? If not, is it fatal?
- "What's the best course of action?" Your vet may want to do surgery, radiation, herbal therapy, or acupuncture, so you need to find out what he or she wants to do and its potential benefits. (I often ask my vet, "If he were your dog, what would you do?")
- "How will this disease and its treatment affect my dog?" Will he lose his appetite, become incontinent, and so on? Is the disease contagious?

Unless you're a responsible breeder, you'll want to avoid having entire Westies of opposite sexes under one roof. Otherwise, about twice a year, your life will be a living hell. Your Westie girl will turn into a strumpet, and your Westie boy will turn into an alien version of an oversexed teenage boy.

- "What's my role?" You may need to medicate him regularly or take him to a special clinic.
- "How much will this cost?" This important query can prevent disputes.
- "Should my Westie see a specialist?" Asking your general practitioner vet for a recommendation for a specialist is neither inappropriate nor insulting. Your vet may get to this question before you do.

Get everything in writing, and stay until you understand completely. If you later realise that you forgot to ask about something, call back for clarification. If you are dissatisfied with anything about your Westie's treatment, consider switching vets. Furthermore, it is perfectly OK to seek a second opinion or an alternative treatment.

You also want to make sure you do your part to make your vet's job easier. Schedule appointments, be punctual, and for everyone's safety, bring your dog to the clinic on a lead or in a carrier. If you have an emergency, call ahead to ensure that the vet is available as soon as possible. Post your vet's number near your telephone. Unless you have a special arrangement with her, do not disturb your vet during nonworking hours for nonemergencies.

PUPPY'S FIRST VISIT

The check-up actually begins before the vet even touches your dog. You'll fill out forms, answer questions, and provide information. Everything you know about your puppy and convey to the vet can ensure your dog's health.

The examination usually starts with a weigh-in and a check of the nose and mouth, which includes a dental check. For puppies, the vet will look at the deciduous teeth and then examine the face and head to check the neurological function of the cranial nerves. Then the vet will examine the ears.

A check for fleas and signs of allergy and infection will follow. The vet will palpate the neck to rule out abnormalities in the lymph nodes or thyroid area.

The vet will also palpate the dog's muscles and extend and bend the dog's legs to test for reflexes or pain on motion. Let your vet check the puppy's patellas; do not manipulate them yourself, as this may actually cause damage—this is a specific skill. The examination proceeds with a listen to the dog's heart and lungs through a stethoscope and an external check of the kidneys, liver, and intestines. An experienced examiner can spot abnormalities by touch or by a painful reaction from the puppy. The vet will take your puppy's temperature and perform a simple rectal check.

If your Westie puppy is due for immunisations, your vet will make sure that he is following the prescribed schedule and administer them as needed.

Seek Advice

Dogs at low risk of disease exposure may not need annual boosters for most diseases. Consult with your vet to determine the appropriate vaccination schedule for your dog.

SPAYING AND NEUTERING

If you're not planning on entering the wild, woolly world of exhibiting and breeding your Westie, seriously consider spaying or neutering your dog. This not only cuts down on the unwanted dog population, but it can have health benefits as well.

When you spay your bitch, you're removing the entire reproductive system, thus eliminating any possibility of future uterine infections and cancers, and ovarian tumours. Spaying before her first heat cycle (six months is a good time) essentially ensures that she will never develop mammary tumours. There is still a probability reduction if you spay after one or two oestrus cycles, but after three or four, that benefit ends.

Spaying and neutering can have health benefits for your dog.

However, she will not attract unwanted suitors once she is spayed.

Neutering your male early has advantages as well. Male-to-male aggression rarely develops into an issue with neutered dogs. Furthermore, neutering eliminates the wanderlust associated with his finding his "dream bitch." (Canine standards are generally low.) The risks associated with prostate and testicular cancers disappear. This benefit remains even if the procedure is done later in life. In older males, indoor marking either vanishes or reduces significantly. Generally, the earlier you neuter, the better the chance that the behaviour will disappear, but this varies with each individual.

Advances in anaesthesia, and vets who routinely perform these sterilisations minimise the risks. Recovery is speedy, but keeping your Westie from overdoing it the day after surgery may take diligence. Given the Westie's determination, enforced crate rest works best.

Don't worry—there is little risk associated with neutering your dog, while the benefits abound.

Before surgery, follow your vet's pre-op instructions. And make sure you follow any instructions for a speedy recovery—some vets will require you to return, to remove stitches. Others use self-dissolving sutures.

VACCINATIONS

The purpose of a vaccine is to prompt an animal's immune response against a specific disease. The vaccine stimulates the immune system with a virus or bacteria that has been killed or modified in such a way that it no longer poses a danger to the pet. The dog then develops "memory cells" that help it fight off the dangerous disease-causing form of the virus he is exposed to.

In order to obtain the best response, puppies and unvaccinated older dogs receive repeated doses. The first shot primes the immune system, and subsequent inoculations boost the immune response. Usually the second vaccine is given two to four weeks after the first. If too long a period elapses, the immune system loses its "jump start" and will not produce a sufficient immune response. (This doesn't apply to rabies vaccines, however.)

Newborn puppies receive some protection (antibodies) from their mothers' bodies and then from their milk. Only when the maternal antibodies drop, after weaning, will a commercial vaccine be effective. However, there is a period when the maternal antibodies are too low to protect but still high enough to block the vaccine. Unfortunately, this period coincides with the time when the puppy is most at risk for many viral diseases. The length and timing of this window is variable among different litters and even among different puppies.

Vaccination Protocols

Proper vaccinations can save lives. Before the days of effective veterinary vaccines, dogs often succumbed to canine distemper, hepatitis, and rabies. Now these diseases are rare. When parvo first emerged in the late 1970s, countless dogs died until a vaccine was developed. However, vaccination protocols have changed over the years, and it's important to discuss this issue with your vet. There is ongoing discussion about how often and against what illnesses dogs need to be vaccinated. Consult with your vet to ask about his or her vaccine protocol. Opinions on commercial vaccinations, schedules, and even on whether to vaccinate at all vary greatly and are subjects of much debate.

The most recent research supports a new protocol for vaccinating your Westie, recommending minimal vaccine use. On recommendations from Dr. Jean Dodds, one of the leading authorities on canine immune systems, all 27 veterinary schools in North America are in the process of changing their protocols for vaccinating dogs and cats.

Diseases to Vaccinate Against

Following are the diseases a Westie will most commonly be vaccinated against:

Bordetella

Bordetellosis, or "kennel cough," is like a bad cold in older dogs but can be serious in puppies. Many organisms can cause this condition, which is highly contagious. Infected dogs cough, wheeze, and sneeze. The common vaccine does not protect against all its forms because there are so many. The disease is often self-limiting, but can threaten a dog whose health is otherwise compromised.

Kennel Cough

Kennel cough can be treated with a combination of cough suppressants and antibiotics, but there's no cure. It usually runs its course, like a common cold. However, a cough doesn't necessarily indicate kennel cough. It could be something more serious, so be sure to check with your vet.

Coronavirus

Coronavirus is related to the human cold. Vaccination is recommended solely in areas where the illness is rampant. Most serious in puppies, corona passes through food contaminated by an infected dog's faeces. This virus produces symptoms similar to those of parvovirus, but less severe. There is no real cure for this disease, only management.

Distemper

Distemper destroys the nervous system, attacking every tissue in the body. Caused by an airborne, measles-like virus, incubation period is 7 to 21 days. Initial symptoms of lethargy, fever, runny nose, yellow discharge from the eyes, laboured breathing, and appetite loss progress to a nervous twitch and thickening of the pads and nose. By this stage, recovery is unlikely.

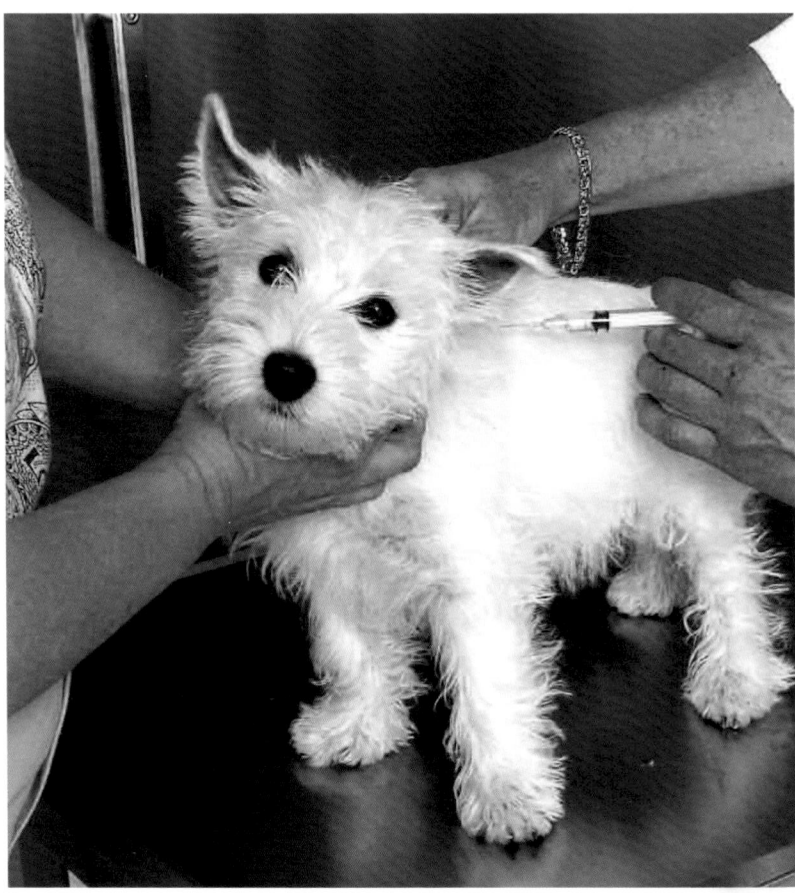

Proper vaccination can save your Westie's life.

Puppies are susceptible to several potentially fatal diseases for which they should receive vaccinations. Discuss your options with your vet.

Hepatitis

Hepatitis, caused by an adenovirus, is most dangerous in puppies. Contact with an infected dog or with his urine or faeces spreads hepatitis, causing white-blood-cell-count drops and sometimes clotting problems. It also affects the kidneys and liver. Symptoms include high fever, red mucous membranes, depression, and appetite loss. Even dogs who recover can experience subsequent chronic illnesses; they may also shed the virus for months, which makes this highly contagious. Due largely to the effectiveness of the vaccination, this disease is rare nowadays.

Leptospirosis

The bacterially caused leptospirosis can transmit to human beings. Dogs contract this disease through exposure to the urine of infected animals. Affecting the liver and kidney, in its most dangerous form it can cause renal failure. Even if the dog survives the disease, he can sustain permanent kidney damage. Treatment

Check your pet carefully for the presence of fleas or other pests after your outings.

includes antibiotics and, in severe cases, dialysis. A vaccine is available for some forms of leptospirosis, but many vets do not recommend it, especially for young puppies. The "older" strains of lepto are rare, and the vaccine can cause adverse reactions in some dogs. A new, virulent strain, one previously seen only in horses and cows, is on the rise. A vaccine against this form is being tested.

Lyme Disease

Lyme disease is carried by the deer tick and it was first identified in the 1970s in Old Lyme, Connecticut, USA. It has spread more widely in the US, but it is still rare in the UK. The incubation period is from 2 to 5 months. Lyme disease causes acute, intermittent lameness, fever, and heart and kidney disease. If untreated, your dog can develop arthritis. A vaccine is available for dogs in high risk areas.

Parvo

The virulent, deadly parvovirus first appeared in 1978. Transmitted through the faeces of infected dogs, it invades and destroys fast-growing cells in multiple vital organs. Nausea, depression, vomiting, and severe bloody diarrhoea result. The disease can be mild to fatal; puppies are especially vulnerable. Unfortunately, parvo is cold resistant, surviving in infected faeces at temperatures as low as 20°F (-6°C). Incubation period is from two to seven days.

Rabies

Rabies is a deadly neurological viral disease transmitted through the bite of an infected animal. Rabies vaccinations are only required in the UK if you plan to take your dog overseas. In the US and in many other countries, vaccination is mandatory.

DISEASES THAT MAY AFFECT YOUR WESTIE

The following are some problems that may affect Westies. The breed is fairly sound with fewer problems than many other breeds, but every breed is susceptible to specific problems while practically "immune" to others. It's useful to be aware of these diseases' existence, but there is no need to anticipate any of them.

Addison's Disease

Addison's disease is characterised by a complete loss of function of both adrenal glands, which help maintain the normal levels of sodium, potassium, and glucose in the dog's blood. Most cases result from an autoimmune process—the dog's immune system attacks its own adrenal glands.

If you suspect a problem with your Westie's skin or coat, have your vet give him a careful examination.

Addison's disease is most common among young to middle-aged dogs and is more common in females. Typical symptoms are lethargy, lack of appetite, vomiting, and weight loss—often severe. Other symptoms can include a slower-than-normal heart rate, and dehydration. The clinical signs are vague and in no way conclusively diagnostic of Addison's disease.

Abnormally high blood potassium levels and lower-than-normal blood sodium levels are key indicators. Blood count and chemistry profile determinations help with the diagnosis. Replacement steroid therapy comprises Addison's main treatment. With the appropriate treatment, stress reduction, and follow-up care, the prognosis is good, and the affected dog should have a normal life expectancy.

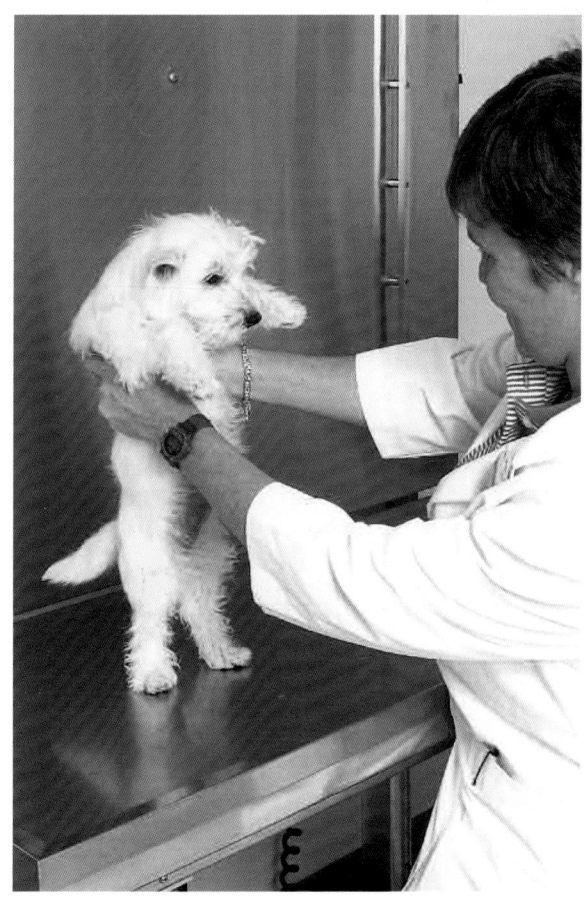

Atopic Dermatitis

Atopic dermatitis (AD) is a common skin condition in dogs typically caused by airborne allergens such as dandruff, pollens of grasses, weeds, or trees, and

CMO Facts

A simple recessive gene causes CMO: Both parents must carry at least one gene for it (i.e., they are "carriers" or, in the case of a recovered affected dog bred, "affected carriers"). Although studies on Westies, Scotties, and Cairns are in full swing in an attempt to isolate the rogue gene, the birth of an affected puppy provides the only method of confirming both parents as carriers. Dr. Patrick Venta is working diligently to complete a map of the canine genome and isolate the genetic marker to help to develop a test for CMO.

house dust or moulds. Some Westies seem to be able to tolerate these; others do not.

The airborne allergens are inhaled, make initial contact with the upper respiratory system, then enter the body and interact with cells—resulting in the release of histamine and other chemicals that typically result in itchy skin (or paws, ears, face, armpits, and so on). These areas become reddened after the dog scratches or licks.

Signs of AD typically appear in dogs between ages six months and three years—with 75 percent of cases arising in dogs between the ages one and three. The disease occurs in both sexes, but some studies have reported higher incidence in females. AD often worsens during the summer, when pollen and mould levels increase. In about 75 percent of cases, the disease eventually becomes year-round.

Check with your vet, who will first rule out other skin disorders such as mange, ringworm, hookworm, and food allergies by performing skin scrapings, bacterial and fungal cultures, faecal analysis, and dietary trials. Subsequent tests may confirm AD. Approximately 90 percent of affected dogs give a positive immediate skin reaction, depending on the allergen. Intradermal skin tests are AD's only accurate diagnostic tool.

There's no real cure for allergies, but several treatment options ranging from avoidance to special shampoos and oils to medications may help. The most desirable treatment—and least practical—is to avoid the allergen. (Westies do not do well in "plastic bubbles.") Steroids such as prednisone are often effective in the short term. Antihistamines work well in some cases. The disease is clearly genetic, but its exact mode of inheritance has not been discovered.

Copper Toxicosis (CT)

Copper toxicosis (CT), a disease that can affect Westies, is caused by an inborn glitch in copper metabolism that allows copper to accumulate in the liver, resulting in cirrhosis. Untreated, it is fatal.

The disease is usually well advanced before the first clinical signs appear. As copper continues to accumulate, widespread liver deterioration occurs, from which the dog can sometimes recover. He may lose weight and exhibit listlessness, anorexia, vomiting, abdominal pain, and jaundice. Eventually, cirrhosis occurs after continued loss of liver cells, and he may develop fluid in the abdominal cavity, causing death. Onset of clinical signs varies greatly but usually occurs in dogs four years of age or older.

The goal is to reduce the amount of copper deposited in the liver by using one of two medications. Both have effected positive results. Already approved for human use, another, zinc acetate, is also cheaper and being evaluated for approval for canine application. Any treatment for CT should be administered only under veterinary supervision. The mode of inheritance remains undetermined for Westies. CT has been reported in at least 21 other breeds.

Craniomandibular Osteopathy (CMO)

Craniomandibular osteopathy (CMO—or "lion jaw") is a noncancerous growth of bone on the lower jaw. It usually affects both sides, but not always. Inflammation is the earliest symptom. You may notice the condition when a puppy shows discomfort while chewing or when you attempt to examine his mouth. So-called silent cases (where the pup appears unfazed) exist. Casual examination may not reveal an enlarged or abnormal jaw.

Most often recognised between the ages of four and seven months, it can occur as early as three to four weeks and, rarely, as late as nine to ten months. Experienced breeders and vets usually recognise it before four months either by clinical signs or by palpation. X-rays of the skull and jaw will confirm CMO.

CMO is treatable. Depending on its severity, the amount of medication and length of treatment vary. (Four to ten months is the average length of treatment.) Many affected puppies will require some dose of cortisone until they are ten months old or older.

A dog's immune system is complex and confusing, and it operates at many levels. When all systems are working properly, a dog will resist infections, develop good immunity from vaccinations, and destroy tumour cells. When attacked by disease bacteria or tetanus toxin, the immune system will produce antibodies or antitoxins to fight them off or neutralise them, protecting the dog in the process.

Autoimmune diseases occur as a result of tissue injury caused by a specific immune reaction of the host to its own tissues. Since the immune system carries a diverse set of components, the clinical signs are complex as well. When it falls out of kilter, disease and allergies emerge. In autoimmune diseases the body can attack its own tissues, kidney, liver, and joints. Recent years have brought a large increase in liver disease to the canine population. Allergies are also on the increase. Blood work and a complete chemistry profile is the first step when immunity problems are suspected.

Progress and research in the treatment of several autoimmune diseases show promise. Allergies are not usually life threatening, but other autoimmune diseases can be quite serious. However, the potential for discomfort and severe debility is significant. Gaining control of allergies through diet is becoming popular: New innovative treatments are on the horizon.

Although many believe that autoimmune diseases have environmental origins, a genetic component is being researched. The Westie is susceptible to allergies and to other autoimmune diseases. Feeding and vaccine reactions in your Westie may also be triggers.

Most anti-inflammatory drugs work well, but since CMO may necessitate long-term therapy, veterinary advice is essential. Mild cases require little more than baby aspirin. Puppies nearly always recover. After therapy, the jaw remodels, and by the time the dog is two or three years old, it may be impossible to detect that he ever had the disease.

Ear Infections

Ear infections can be serious. Clean your Westie's ears with a canine ear cleaner on a regular basis. Check ears weekly to ensure the absence of infection or dark discharge. Keep hair out of the ear canals; trim hair from the ear tips about an inch down. Less hair weight puts less pressure on the ear cartilage. If infections occur, your vet may recommend a multipurpose antibacterial ointment. Chronic infections of the ear canal require prolonged treatment.

Yeast or fungal infections, common in Westies, indicate the need for an "ear culture." These conditions require treatment different from those for bacterial infections. Monitor ear infections closely and report hearing changes to your vet immediately.

Epidermal Dysplasia

Epidermal dysplasia (Westie Armadillo Syndrome) begins with reddening and itching of the skin, especially on the feet, legs, and the ventral parts of the body. The disease will intensify, with widespread redness developing. Hair loss and chronic inflammatory changes enter the picture. Eventually the dog's skin becomes thick and turns black, greasy, and foul smelling, which gave rise to the nickname Westie armadillo syndrome. Generalised severe itching worsens.

Armadillo Syndrome can appear in pups as young as a few weeks to a few months of age. Both sexes are affected. This condition does not respond well to treatment, although there are two forms of the disease. In one, all treatment fails; in the other, high doses of systemic corticosteroids for a short period of time often bring a favourable response. Allow reasonable treatment time for possible recovery before euthanasia becomes necessary. How it's passed on remains undetermined. Although this condition does occur in this breed, cases are relatively uncommon.

Ear infections can be serious, so it's important to check your Westie's ears weekly.

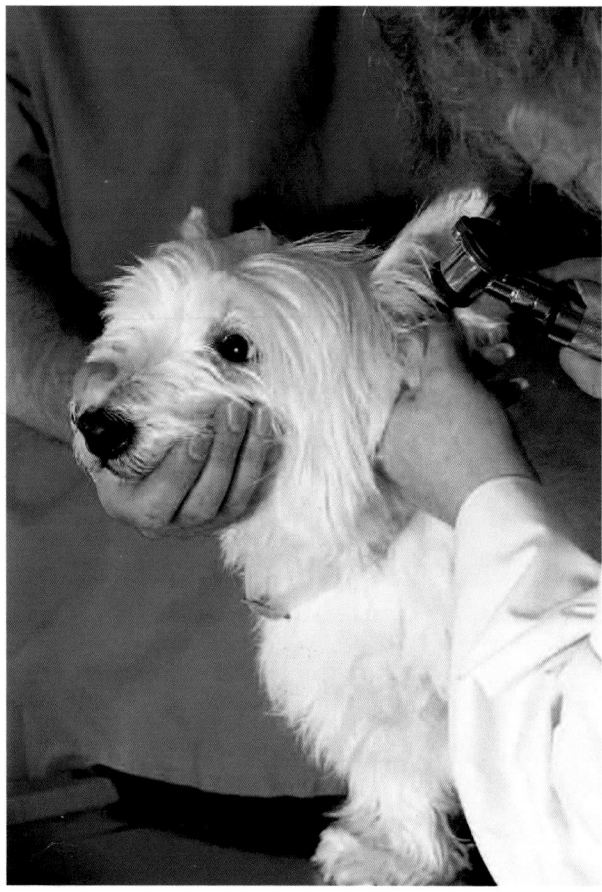

Globoid Cell Leukodystrophy (GCL)

Globoid cell leukodystrophy (GCL, or Krabbe's disease in humans) is a degenerative disease of the brain and spinal cord. It occurs from a lack of myelin, a necessary lipid that coats the spinal cord and other nerves. It's the result of a genetic deficiency of an enzyme (galactocerebroside b-galactosidase) involved in the breakdown of certain fats in the brain and spinal cord.

Symptoms begin early in life and progress rapidly and include weakness, stumbling, loss of control of the hindquarters, and tail tremors. Then the dog will develop a wide stance, lack of coordination, and

Westies are generally considered a healthy, hardy breed.

posterior or total limb paralysis. He may become blind or fail to recognise familiar individuals. GCL may occur as early as four weeks of age and nearly always occurs before five or six months of age. The typical clinical signs and measurement of the mean activity of galactocerebroside b-galactosidase in white blood cells will confirm a positive diagnosis.

No treatment exists; GCL is fatal. Most common in Westies and Cairns, the disease is known to be a simple (autosomal) recessive.

Fortunately, an accurate blood test (using DNA technology) is now available to concerned breeders. It can accurately identify a dog as a carrier, as affected, or as clear of the disease. Testing a small blood sample identifies "carriers," whose offspring have a 50 percent chance of carrying the gene, but who will themselves be clear.

Breeders should test any dog in their breeding programme to determine whether or not he's a carrier. This important tool is an opportunity to minimise the number of carriers in the Westie population and eventually eliminate GCL altogether. Dr. David Wenger, who developed the test for GCL in dogs, is currently working on developing a gene "fix" for affected children.

Inflammatory Bowel Disease (IBD)

Inflammatory bowel disease (IBD) is a condition of the dog's digestive system that involves the stomach, small intestine, and/or large intestine. According to Dr. Kay McGuire, a breeder/exhibitor for 30 years (18 of which were with Westies) and veterinary consultant to the WHWTCA Health Committee, this condition's cause remains unknown.

Dogs can see colour, although differently than people do. They can see various shades of blue and even distinguish different shades of grey that humans see as one. However red, yellow, orange, and green look pretty much the same to them.

In IBD, the dog's digestive tract is hypersensitive to foreign agents present in the bowel and its mucous membranes. Parasites, bacteria, dietary constituents, and drugs have all been suspects as possible causes of the condition. Chronic small bowel diarrhoea, weight loss, flatulence, and foul-smelling stools characterise this syndrome. Vomiting is another sign seen in IBD. If symptoms remain chronic, large bowel diarrhoea, halitosis, and anorexia may develop.

The most common initial tests a vet runs on a dog who is vomiting and having diarrhoea are faecal flotation and stained faecal smears, which the vet evaluates for parasites. To be prudent, the vet commonly deworms the dog regardless of whether evidence of parasites exists. (Whipworms are notoriously hard to detect, so if they are the problem the dewormer will handle them.)

If your puppy seems upset when you take him out, try to find out what may be bothering him, and let your vet know about your concerns.

Food antigens can trigger IBD, especially in Westies. The vet may suggest you switch your dog to a food whose protein and carbohydrates come from a different source than his current food. There is also support for immune stimulation using a raw natural diet—efficacious in some cases, though questionable in others. After four to eight weeks, depending upon whether this effects any positive change, further diagnostic tests may be appropriate.

The British Veterinary Association (BVA) works in conjunction with the Kennel Club to operate a hip scoring scheme in order to evaluate predisposition to hip dysplasia.

Kidney Disease

Renal (kidney) disease and renal failure are two distinct problems. Renal disease represents any degree of structural or functional kidney abnormality. It may be mild or extensive and progressive, resulting in kidney failure. Renal failure is the condition characterised by the inability of the kidneys to excrete wastes and to help maintain the balance of electrolytes. This usually occurs when about 75 percent of normal renal function is lost, and will eventually have a deleterious effect on many other organs in the body.

Renal failure, whether associated with hereditary disease or with other causes, manifests identical symptoms. Rapid onset of symptoms is typical, even when the disease has been latent for quite some time. Owners report loss of appetite, excessive thirst and urination, depression, vomiting, and diarrhoea. Bad breath, gum and tongue ulcers, anaemia, dehydration, stunted growth, and loose teeth characterise kidney disease in immature dogs.

In addition to a complete blood count and chemistry profile, urinalysis provides valuable diagnostic information. X-rays reveal the size and shape of the kidneys, and a needle biopsy of the kidney will determine the extent of renal disease, to monitor its progression.

Treatment is directed toward delaying ultimate renal failure.

Hereditary kidney diseases are significant causes of kidney failure in young dogs of many breeds. Varieties of structural and/or functional defects may account for this disorder. How it's inherited remains vague, but research is in full swing. Recognising the disease and removing Westies who manifest or produce pups with the disorder from breeding programmes are the only ways of eliminating this type of genetic trait.

Legg-Calve-Perthes Disease

Legg-Calve-Perthes disease, also known as Legg-Perthes, refers to the "death" of the femoral head in one or both legs. An interruption of the blood supply to the femoral head results in the death and fracturing of bone cells. New bone growth and the remodeling of the femoral head and neck follow and lead to stiffness and pain in the rear leg or legs. Painful arthritis of the joint may occur.

In some cases, trauma, such as a fracture, can initiate the

disorder. Sudden onset may also occur after the dog jumps off furniture. Other speculative predisposing causes are inflammation, nutritional factors, hip dysplasia, circulatory problems, and—possibly—excessive hormone production. Although specific causes of the disease are unknown, its mode of inheritance appears to be genetic, with trauma's only role being that of a trigger. Legg-Perthes can occur from three to eleven months of age.

Irritability and intermittent lameness that progresses to chronic hind-end lameness characterise its onset. As the disease progresses, the dog may exhibit pain when the leg is flexed. In severe cases, the dog becomes totally lame and avoids using the affected leg. The leg muscles begin to atrophy after extended periods of nonuse. Mild cases can be asymptomatic. X-rays provide the only certain method of diagnosis.

There's no specific treatment, although many vets prefer nonsurgical therapy: limiting activity, and treatment with nonsteroidal anti-inflammatory drugs for one month. If ineffective, surgical removal of the femur head eases pain and helps restore some function. Some dogs recover reasonable function without treatment.

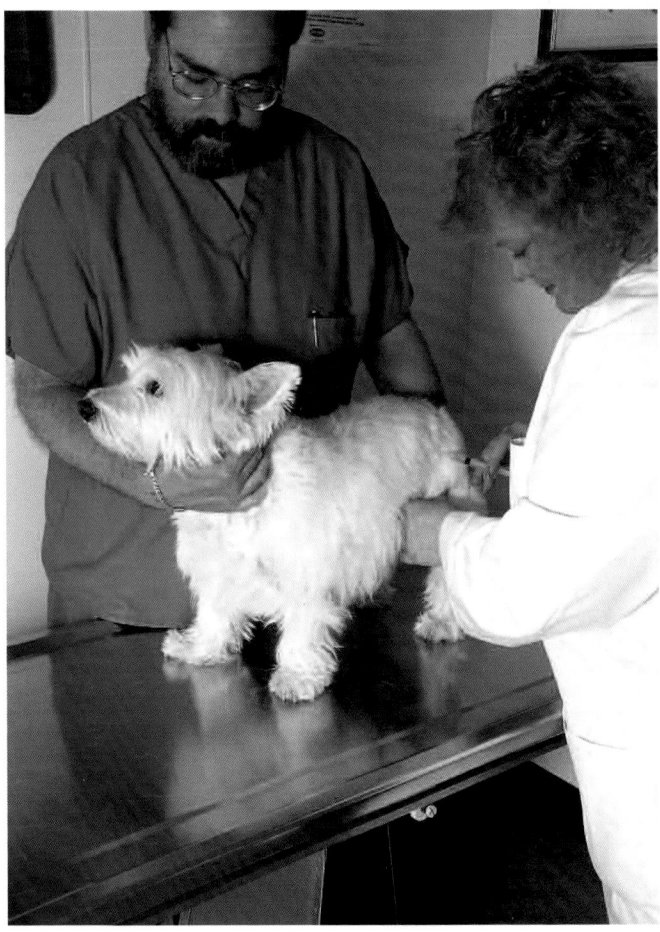

Yearly checkups are essential for keeping your Westie in tip-top shape.

The prognosis is generally excellent, and within several months the dog can again walk and run. In some cases, the affected leg may remain slightly shorter and the muscles may atrophy somewhat. Increased risk of arthritis, as the dog ages, is likely. Responsible breeders exclude Westies with Legg-Perthes—and those who have produced it—from their breeding programmes. This polygenic trait arises in several small breed of dogs.

Luxating Patella

The patella is the kneecap; *luxation* means "dislocation." Therefore, luxating patella is a dislocation of the kneecap. Other terms are "slipped kneecap," "slipped patella," or "slipped stifle." The kneecap protects the front of the stifle joint, which corresponds to the human knee joint. Anchored by ligaments, the patella fits in a groove in the femur.

Predisposing conditions to dislocation include shallow trochlear grooves, weak ligaments, and/or misalignment of the tendons and muscles that straighten the joint, so the patella slips inward or outward. It can occur in either one or both knees and may cause severe pain. It is inherited or acquired through trauma. With some small dogs, an isolated incident such as jumping off the couch can cause dislocation. No one has yet determined its exact mode of inheritance.

In severe cases, pain or lameness may lead to limping. Sometimes the slipped kneecap slips back into place. Manipulating the stifle joint and pushing the kneecap in and out of position can confirm diagnosis. X-rays to examine the trochlear ridges may help

Exercise can do wonders for the health of your dog.

determine prognosis. Treatment consists of slipping the patella back into place, but relapses can occur. Surgery can repair the problem and may be the best option in the most severe cases.

Portosystemic Shunt

The liver filters blood from the digestive tract and stores energy. Portosystemic shunt (PSS) is an abnormal blood flow between the portal vein and a systemic vein that diverts blood from the liver into the general circulatory system. This allows blood from the intestine to bypass the liver. Toxins are not removed or metabolised from the circulation, resulting in neurological symptoms that appear gradually and may include episodic weakness, head pressing, disorientation, circling, pacing, behavioural changes, blindness, seizures, and coma. These often develop within minutes of a dog eating.

Most portosystemic shunts are congenital; they are most common in terriers. Affected animals may have a history of stunted growth or failure to gain weight. Definitive diagnosis of PSS is usually made by one year of age, and many puppies develop symptoms by four weeks of age. PSS tends to run in families but is believed to be polygenetic in nature, so research poses many challenges.

An ammonia tolerance test is the most reliable diagnostic tool to determine this hepatic abnormality. X-ray imaging studies where contrast dyes are injected into the liver will further confirm diagnosis. However, blood chemistry profile results can be normal. Many cases can be treated by partial surgical closure of the shunt. Dietary management may benefit dogs not treated surgically, but management is only palliative.

Researching Health Issues

The Animal Health Trust is a British charity that has been helping dogs for more than half a century. A team of scientists and vets work together to treat dogs and to research health conditions.

Successes include breakthroughs in surgical and anaesthesia techniques, and development of vaccines.

Pulmonary Fibrosis

We know very little about pulmonary fibrosis. Idiopathic pulmonary fibrosis (Westie Lung Disease) is a scarring and fibrosing of the lungs' air sacs and connective tissue. The scarring may result from chronic inflammation of the air sacs and can replace much of the normal structure of the lungs. (A similar disorder exists in humans.)

Its cause is unknown, as research has barely begun. However, some veterinary researchers suspect links between pulmonary fibrosis, the immune system, and allergies. Westies are more prone to pulmonary fibrosis than other breeds.

Other diseases can mimic its symptoms, so vets need to be cautious when diagnosing pulmonary fibrosis. Following are some signs to look for when diagnosing pulmonary fibrosis; a Westie may not exhibit all of them:

- rapid shallow breathing or laboured breathing
- loss of exercise tolerance
- scar tissue build-up in the lungs
- crackles in the lungs
- dry cough
- pulmonary hypertension or enlargement of the heart (due to breathing patterns)

Ask your pup's breeder about what diseases your Westie might develop and when you may need to start testing for them.

Correct diagnosis requires a lung biopsy. A tricky procedure in normal patients, lung biopsy may be quite risky in affected dogs. Furthermore, since many lung diseases exist, differentiation is difficult. Since so few samples have been taken, pathologist competence varies in interpreting these samples.

Responsible breeding helps cut down on many diseases that can affect Westies.

X-rays may reveal changes in the lungs, and abnormal blood gas levels may show lack of oxygen delivery to the tissues. A specialised machine can effectively screen people for a similar disease; the machine is presently being tested on a control group of Westies.

Few treatment options exist. Once scarring occurs, little can be done. Preventing respiratory tract infections, limiting exercise, and incorporating planned weight loss for overweight Westies are all important. Bronchial dilating drugs may strengthen respiratory muscles, but Westies tend to develop tolerance, and the medicine loses its efficacy. Some dogs may benefit from controlled use of steroids, such as Prednisone and Interferon. Experimental usage of inhaled steroids has been tried in some cases, and cough suppressants can alleviate some discomfort.

The prognosis is very poor. Lung disease appears to affect older Westies, with the average age of onset about nine years. After diagnosis, most patients survive an average of 17 to 24 months. Recently, veterinary respiratory specialists formed an international study group, which should help speed research.

A healthy Westie will have energy to burn when you take him outside.

Pyruvate Kinase Deficiency (PK)

Pyruvate kinase (PK) deficiency (erythrocyte pyruvate kinase deficiency) in red blood cells (erythrocytes) causes a severe haemolytic (red cell rupture) anaemia as a result of the premature destruction of PK-deficient red blood cells.

PK is an enzyme in glycolysis, which is essential for the metabolism of glucose into an energy source utilised by cells such as red blood cells. Without this source of energy, red blood cells are unable to function properly and are consequently destroyed.

The clinical signs of anaemia are very pale mucous membranes (gums), increased heart rate and pounding pulses, weakness, and exercise intolerance. The liver and spleen may be enlarged, and after one year of age, the density of all bones, particularly long bones and the skull, appear increased. Well-confined affected dogs may not show any obvious signs but may acutely decompensate and die when severely exercised or stressed.

After excluding the more common causes of haemolytic anaemia—autoimmune, toxic, and infectious haemolytic anemia, PK deficiency should be considered. A chronic, severe, highly regenerative haemolytic anaemia associated with increased radiographic bone density in older animals suggests of PK deficiency, which is diagnosed through DNA analysis. A simple determination of PK activity will not diagnose an affected dog, but it does allow the detection of carriers.

There is no simple treatment. When large iron deposition occurs in tissues, treatment may include chelation. At least in research, bone marrow transplant shows potential for curing the disease. Affected dogs usually die young (one to four years) due to progressive anaemia or liver failure.

Seborrhea

Seborrhea is a skin disorder that can appear in either primary or secondary forms. Therapy depends largely upon which of the two forms the dog manifests; so it is necessary to distinguish between them. Primary seborrhea is idiopathic—it exists by itself. This form, which occurs in Westies and some other breeds, most often appears in young animals and is generally thought to have a genetic component.

Primary seborrhea is characterised by symptoms of this disease alone. A trained dermatologist should rule out all other causes. Symptoms include scaly, oily patches adhering to the skin. Since the oil collects dirt, it's sometimes called dirty puppy disease. Abrasions tend to be more severe on elbows, hocks, and ears. Typically, lesions are hairless, dark centred, scaly patches surrounded by a reddened area and flaking; they typically occur on the trunk and chest.

Secondary seborrhea, which arises primarily in adults, occurs if the signs are associated with an underlying disease indirectly related

Any unusual coat or skin conditions should be reported to your vet for closer examination.

to the seborrhea itself. Endocrine disorders like hypothyroidism or hypoadrenocorticism can trigger the secondary form. Nutritional disorders, especially those involving fat, can be a root cause. Parasites, drug hypersensitivity, local trauma, tumours, and any chronic catabolic state may also cause secondary seborrhea. Although secondary seborrhea resembles primary seborrhea, treatment of secondary seborrhea heavily depends on the cause of the problem.

Primary seborrhea is a chronic condition: It must be managed since it cannot be cured. Medicated shampoos and some ointments containing tar, salicylic acid, and sulphur can relieve symptoms. Systemic and topical corticosteroids may help. Systemic antibiotics, vitamin A, and retinoids have netted good results.

Skin Allergy Problems

Skin problems are usually caused by an allergic reaction to something in the environment—whether it's fleas, mould, dust, pollen, grass, food, or chemicals—that causes a dog to itch and

It is not uncommon for older Westie puppies to retain their baby canines. If they are not loose or have not been shed by the time the adult canines are two-thirds of the way in, it may be necessary for the vet to extract them.

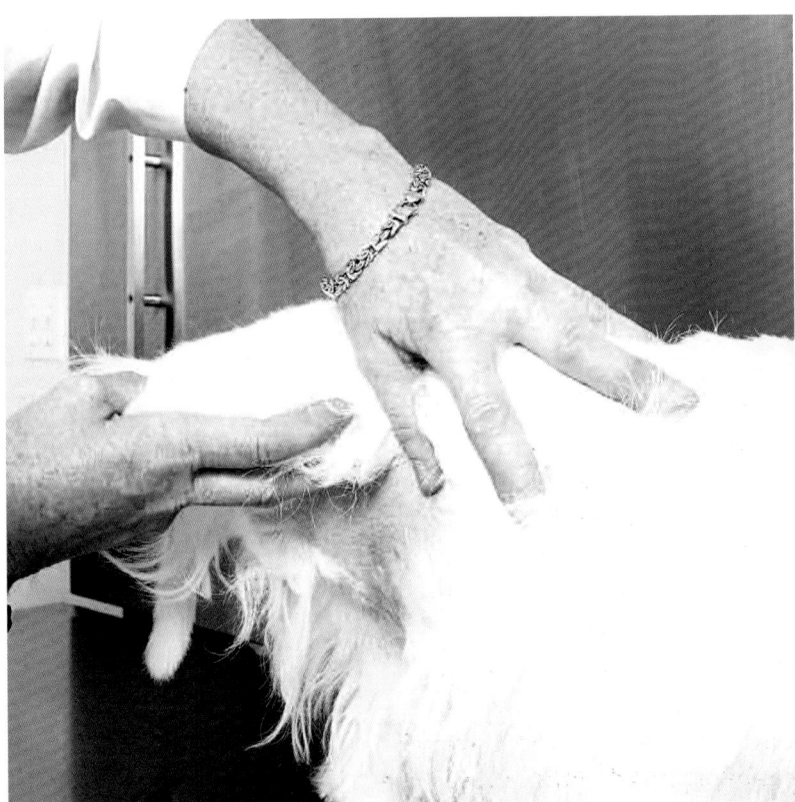

A vet is trained to look for abnormalities in the skin that may not be able to be detected by a dog's owner.

leads to scratching. Constant scratching may cause a breakdown in the skin that leads to bacterial infection—and the problem.

We cannot rid all allergens from a dog's environment, but we can control some—we can eliminate fleas, adjust diet, and boost the immune system. One flea can wreak havoc on a dog with a flea allergy.

The next very important issue is dealing with infection. If your dog has one or more of the following symptoms, you may have to treat for secondary bacterial infection:

- hair loss
- scaling, flaky skin
- open sores
- greasy skin and coat
- thick black skin
- pimples
- moist, puffy skin
- chronic ear infection
- odour
- red swollen feet and pads

Antibiotics may actually cure the infection; treatment length is dependant upon how long your Westie has had symptoms. Chronic cases require oral antibiotic treatment anywhere from two to six weeks, in addition to topical treatment. The type of antibiotic used is extremely important. Keep the skin clean whenever treating skin infections. The type of shampoo prescribed and the frequency of bathing depend upon the symptoms. Medicated cornstarch and zinc both heal and soothe the skin.

The use of prednisone to treat skin conditions remains controversial. Considered for years the only way to treat the chronic allergy/skin condition, this has been proved untrue. Prednisone may

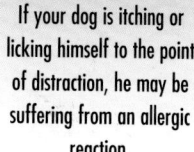

If your dog is itching or licking himself to the point of distraction, he may be suffering from an allergic reaction.

You can get your Westie back on the path to great health by following your vet's advice and possibly supplementing his diet with vitamins and fatty acids.

be used in combination with other therapies for skin problems—with caution. Steroids suppress the immune system. Furthermore, prednisone does not cure the skin infection; it merely provides temporary relief. Antihistamines relieve the itching associated with allergic reactions and present fewer risks than steroids.

Improper diet can cause some allergies. Many vets recommend a change—perhaps to a high-quality lamb and rice diet formula exclusive of soya, wheat, corn, beet pulp, fillers, beef products, animal by-products, and preservatives. Fish and potato foods are another option, or you may choose to prepare your Westie's food or feed a raw natural diet. The best plan is to contact experienced Westie breeders through a breed club, and gather information on alternative dietary options that have worked for many other West Highland White Terrier owners.

Supplementing with vitamins C, E, zinc, and omega-3 and -6 fatty acids may help restore the body to a healthy state. These supplements come in all-in-one gel capsules. Owners have found that adding digestive enzymes to the diet of dogs with compromised immune systems can be beneficial.

Not all skin problems are allergy generated. It is easy to assume that the Westie's problem is allergies. Underlying thyroid condition, dog lice, and sarcoptic or demodetic mange mites can cause similar symptoms. For proper diagnosis, your vet may recommend blood tests, skin scrapings, or biopsies.

White Shaker Dog Syndrome

This syndrome is a unique generalised tremor that occurs in young, predominately small dogs. Because this syndrome was initially seen in larger numbers of dogs with white coats, it is called white shaker dog syndrome (WSS).

Dogs with WSS have a fine tremor of the entire body. Young dogs (nine months to three years old) are most frequently affected. The tremor usually persists throughout the day and worsens with handling, excitement, or stress. Without therapy, the magnitude of the tremor may increase or remain constant. Other occasional clinical signs include head tilts, limb weakness, and seizures.

The disease is most often associated with a mild central nervous system inflammation, which commonly affects the brain's cerebellum; its dysfunction may initiate the tremor. Some vets believe that its cause is an underlying virus, but no research supports this theory, nor has any infectious basis been found. Whether the inflammation is really the source of the tremor or whether some other associated neurotransmitter abnormality results in this abnormal firing of nerves is unknown.

WSS diagnosis is based on clinical symptoms alone. Lab tests and physical examinations are usually normal. The disease, though rarely fatal, can be very disturbing.

WSS is characterised by a sudden onset of constant tremors all over the body, including the head and eyeballs, with chaotic

If you notice your dog shaking or trembling for no apparent reason, suspect White Shaker Dog Syndrome and consult your vet.

random eye movement and rapid, involuntary, rhythmic eye movement of a type that often indicates central nervous system dysfunction. The tremors are exacerbated by handling, forced locomotion, excitement, and high levels of stress, and decrease but may not completely disappear with total relaxation. Putting the dog in a crate in a minimally darkened, quiet room may help reduce the tremors, which may be severe enough to cause an uncoordinated gait during stressful periods. Occasionally a dog convulses. Usually for a short time at the onset, he refuses to eat. If you can't gently coax your Westie to eat or drink, you will have to hand-feed him. Eventually, he'll return to eating and drinking on his own. Elevating his food and water bowls may be helpful so that he does not have to lower his head to eat.

Supportive therapy includes reducing the tremors with diazepam and anti-inflammatory drugs (corticosteroids), but neither alone is rapidly or consistently effective. According to veterinary neurologist, Dr. Alan Parker, using both drugs simultaneously has been the most effective and reliable. Early diagnosis is beneficial, as many dogs will respond in a few days to immunosuppressive levels of corticosteroids. Some dogs need maintenance on low levels of these drugs for several months, but others never require them. Do not decrease the corticosteroid dose too quickly.

The duration of therapy is critical; ending therapy prematurely usually leads to a relapse. This simultaneous dual-drug treatment can cause symptoms to decrease as quickly as the second day. By the fifth day, dogs are usually 80 percent normal.

OTHER COMMON CANINE DISEASES

Arthritis

Arthritis is an inflammation of the joint. It may be associated with any combination of swelling, pain, fluid accumulation, cartilage degeneration, or bone proliferation. While mild arthritis is uncomfortable, severe arthritis is very painful. Symptoms of osteoarthritis in your Westie might include stiffness in the joints, limb favouring, difficulty in sitting or standing, hesitancy to jump, decreased activity level, irritability, aggression, and lethargy.

Several treatments exist for pain management for canine arthritis, but there is no cure. Your vet may also prescribe medication to reduce inflammation and discomfort. But if using these in the long term, make sure you monitor your Westie for side effects—especially liver damage.

Newer treatment appears in the nutraceuticals glucosamine and chondroitin. These can help relieve inflammation and even delay the degenerative process in some dogs. By attracting fluid to the joint's remaining cartilage system, the body may repair damaged joints while keeping the cartilage-destroying enzymes in check. They show promise as a preventative measure for dogs with high risk factors for arthritis.

Other alternative therapies, such as acupuncture, Chinese medicine, and herbs have provided many dogs with relief. Personal experience treating one of my dogs with these has yielded amazing results.

Cancer

Cancer is a general term for more than 200 different types of malignancies that can affect the body. What they have in common is "modus operandi": they result from accelerated cell growth; the cells are all "undifferentiated," meaning that they can no longer be recognised as a cell from a particular organ. In a cruel irony, unlike normal cells that are born and die, cancer cells reproduce indefinitely.

Many factors may initiate cancers, but scientists believe that

Older dogs are prone to the same kinds of ailments as older people, arthritis among them. A number of remedies exist to help ease the pain.

Dogs with diabetes can continue to lead normal lives if properly cared for.

hormones may play a prominent role, especially in cancers of the reproductive system and thyroid. Hormones can stimulate abnormal cells to divide and develop into tumours.

Age, type of cancer, cure rate, and even personality type can help determine the best treatment. Be sure to discuss all options with your vet. Costs can also vary widely, ranging from little more than an average surgery to your life's savings.

Diabetes Mellitus

Diabetes mellitus, often called sugar diabetes, strikes dogs as well as humans. This endocrine disease results from a deficiency in the pancreas's production of the hormone insulin.

This disease occurs most frequently in overweight dogs six to nine years of age and is more common among intact females. There may be a genetic propensity for diabetes. It is noncurable and ultimately affects all organs. Its cause remains unknown, and many dogs develop it in conjunction with other disorders.

Symptoms include increased appetite and water consumption, increased frequency and volume of urination, and weight loss. In more advanced cases, lethargy, loss of appetite, vomiting, dehydration, weakness, and coma may occur. Veterinary surgeons diagnose based on history, physical examination, and laboratory test results: urinalysis and blood sugar levels and other diagnostic tests.

With daily treatment, prognosis is good. Diet and exercise alone can control some mild cases. Others need more comprehensive management: daily insulin injections, urine testing, dietary management, regular exercise, and avoidance or control of concurrent illnesses. Most dogs require insulin injections twice a day to control blood glucose levels. Insulin requirements cannot be predicted solely on the basis of the dog's weight because the degree of pancreatic failure is different in each dog, so treatment must be individualised.

Obesity reduces the responsiveness to insulin, making diabetes more difficult to control. A specialised, gradual weight reduction plan will help your diabetic dog reach his ideal body weight. His weight and activity level determines his calorie intake. Feeding multiple small meals throughout the day minimises risk of hypoglycaemia; daily calorie consumption must remain consistent.

A diabetic Westie requires a strict insulin-injection schedule. Your vet may fine-tune treatment based on monitored test results. Oh, and cancel that stop at the doughnut shop you had planned. You'll both live longer and look better in a swimsuit.

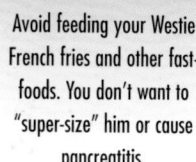

Avoid feeding your Westie French fries and other fast-foods. You don't want to "super-size" him or cause pancreatitis.

Heart Disease

A congenital heart defect is present at birth. Acquired heart disease is that which develops after birth. Many dogs show no outward signs of heart disease; others exhibit weakness, exercise intolerance, coughing, laboured breathing, poor growth, collapse, or have a blue tinge to the mouth's mucous membranes.

Heart disease can remain undetected until a veterinary check is performed. Coordinate puppy examinations with their vaccine schedule and periodically check thereafter. The vet may discover congenital heart defects by listening for a heart murmur, which is classified according to loudness, location, and timing in the cardiac cycle. Innocent or flow murmurs, not uncommon in puppies, are not loud and generally disappear by four to six months of age. However, if physical examination suggests a cardiac anomaly, your vet will perform tests such as an electrocardiogram and

Check your Westie for fleas and ticks after he's been outside.

radiographs to assess severity. A yearly checkup is good preventative care for all dogs. Carefully monitor your older Westie.

Treatment varies according to each case. Some dogs need medication; others require surgical intervention or a pacemaker. Congenital heart defects may be inherited or may develop during gestation for unknown reasons or after exposure to toxins.

Pancreatitis

The pancreas produces enzymes (needed to digest food) and hormones, including insulin. Pancreatitis occurs when the organ starts leaking those enzymes and actually starts digesting itself. Some types are sudden and acute; others develop over time. Both kinds are life threatening.

Pancreatitis is notoriously difficult to diagnose. Risk factors can include abnormally high fat content in the blood, obesity, infection, or contaminated food. Other diseases such as diabetes and even some drugs have been known to trigger it. A high-fat meal just before the onset of the disease is also common.

Symptoms may include vomiting, appetite loss, changes in body temperature (either way) and a painful abdomen. Diarrhoea and depression are also common; so is dehydration. Your vet will run tests including a check on the pancreatic enzymes for more clues. Sometimes X-rays are required.

The only treatment is supportive therapy, usually feeding through IVs for a few days in order to rest the digestive system. A low-fat diet is a likely prescription for your recovering Westie.

PARASITES

Parasites cause problems running the gamut from mild itching to death. External parasites include various mites, fleas, and ticks. Internal ones are usually worms like roundworm, hookworm, whipworm, and heartworm. Many of these can be prevented or controlled.

Fleas can jump 150 times their own length, accelerate faster than a cheetah, and survive without food for up to a year! All this without anabolic steroids!

External Parasites

These are parasites that live on—but not inside—a dog's body. With the exception of some mites, they are visible.

Fleas

A female flea can lay 2,000 eggs in her lifetime. Despite this astonishing skill and the species' reputation for putting on circuses rivaling the Cirque de Soleil, many people aren't too keen on them.

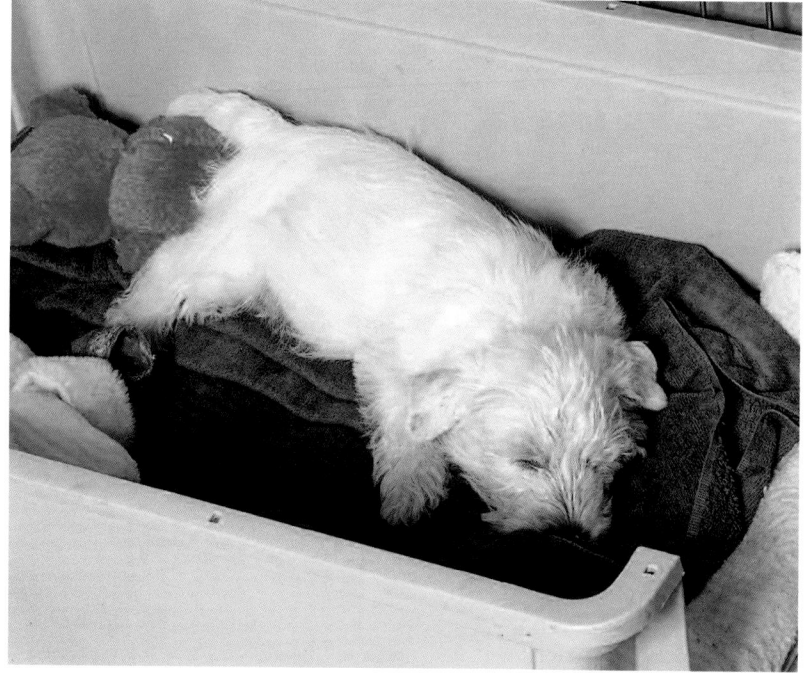

Puppies are often born with roundworms, an internal parasite that gets passed from their mother.

Worming

Modern worming treatment is highly effective if given routinely, according to the manufacturer's instructions.

Perhaps this is because they are bloodsucking and nasty, cause your beloved Westie allergic reactions, and transmit tapeworm as an added bonus. Fleas bite people, too, although dogs are their eating establishments of choice.

Besides constant scratching, a sure of sign of fleas on your dog is the presence of blackish/reddish granules. These are flea faeces, largely composed of your dog's blood.

Flea and tick preventatives come in two basic kinds: adulticides that kill adult fleas on contact, and insect growth regulators (IGR), which function like flea birth control: They interrupt their life cycle. They don't kill adult fleas, so it's more of a "community service" than a flea-bite preventative.

Mange, Demodectic (Demodex)

Demodectic mange, also called red mange or *Demodex*, is a fairly common skin disease. While the mite that is the catalyst, *Demodex canis*, is found on most dogs, only some seem to suffer adverse effects—likely due to a subpar or immature immune system. (Puppies are most commonly affected.) Demodectic mites crowd out the hair follicles, causing them to fall out. In addition, follicles

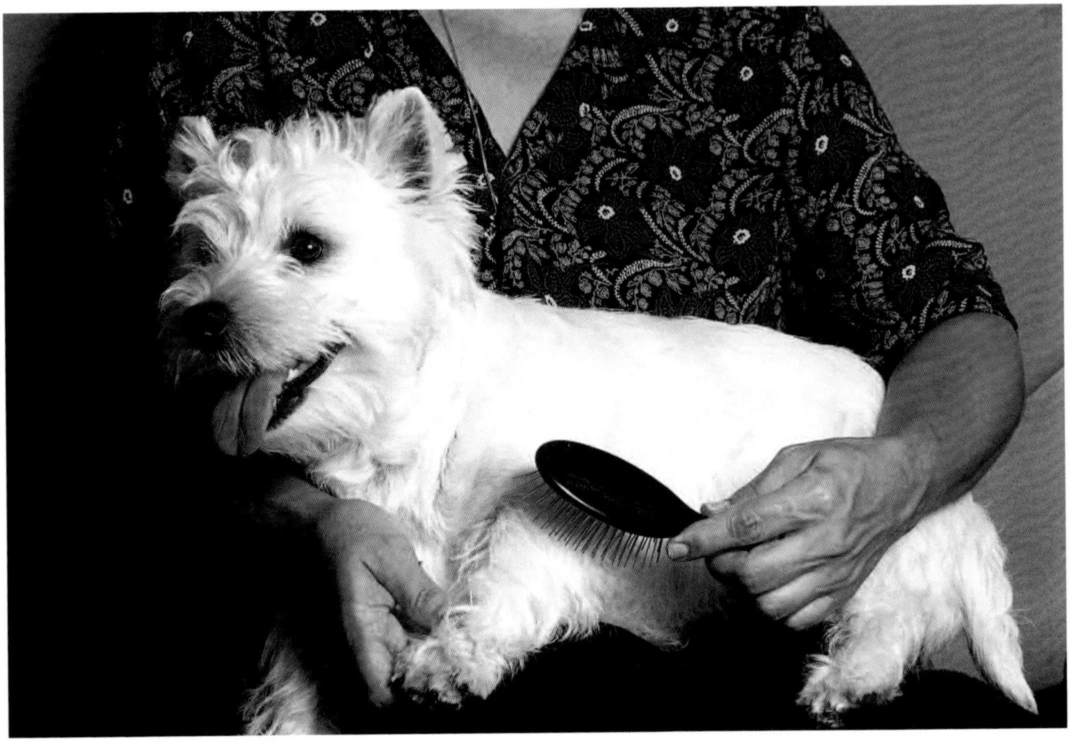

Use grooming time as an opportunity to inspect your dog for skin diseases.

often become infected and the skin red and inflamed. A skin scraping will confirm the diagnosis. Mange in puppies usually resolves itself but is often treated with insecticides.

Demodectic mange in an adult dog may indicate a weakened immune system. It is very serious and requires competent veterinary attention.

Mange, Sarcoptic (Scabies)

Sarcoptic mange, or scabies, a highly contagious parasitic disease, affects susceptible humans and dogs—and livestock. The "perpetrator" is a tiny mite called *Sarcoptes scabiei* that burrows in the skin to cause itchiness, redness, and hair loss in both people and dogs. Treatment for scabies includes an arsenal of special shampoos, dips, pills, and injections.

Ticks

Although a tick or two doesn't seem to cause any discomfort to the affected dog the way a flea infestation does, all 850 species can be dangerous. They carry quite an array of diseases, including the most notorious: Lyme disease and tick paralysis.

If you discover a tick on your dog, pull it off with a pair of fine-tipped tweezers. Wear gloves if possible. Grip it as close to the head as possible to avoid crushing it. Once removed, toss it into some alcohol to kill it. Disinfect the site of the bite and wash your hands. Bite wounds may develop into welts from the tick's saliva but should heal in about a week.

If you see something that looks like white rice in your Westie's faeces, it's probably tapeworm. Dogs become infested by eating a flea with a tapeworm larvae. Tapeworm isn't as serious in dogs as it is in people, and a weight-appropriate dose of wormer will eliminate it.

Internal Parasites

Worms are disturbing parasites that affect both puppies and adult dogs. There are dozens of varieties. Different species can infect different parts of the dog's body. Some kinds attack the oesophagus and stomach; others go for the small intestine (roundworms, hookworms, threadworms, trichina worms, tapeworms, and flukes). Still others, like whipworm, target the colon. Almost every organ can be prey to some kind of worm: liver, nasal cavity, trachea, lungs, heart, kidney, nervous system, arteries, and veins. Some worms are transmitted though food. Freezing meat to minus 40°F (4°C) for two days or heating it to 140°F (60°C) kills them. Unless you live in a meat locker or have a few tanks of liquid nitrogen handy, this could prove impractical. Some worms can transmit diseases to people.

Hookworms, in particular, are a real public-health concern.

You can keep your dog worm-free by using a regular dewormer (many heartworm preventives work). Also keep your Westie's quarters and your garden clean.

Heartworm

Heartworms are found in the right side of the heart, obstructing its large blood vessels. They are rarely seen in the UK. Badly infected dogs can have hundreds of these in their hearts for years. Heartworms lay tiny larvae in the bloodstream (microfilaria) that live for three years. Their offspring circulate in the bloodstream. Transmitted to other animals via mosquitoes, they enter a new host.

It takes six to seven months from the time an animal is bitten until the symptoms appear. These include coughing, fluid accumulation, decreased appetite, and heart failure. Reliable tests can detect infection. The disease, left untreated, is nearly always fatal. Furthermore, the treatment is risky, long, and difficult.

Heartworm is a potentially fatal parasite that can be guarded against by giving a monthly preventive medication.

Monthly preventative tablets, available by prescription, will keep your Westie free of heartworm. A single mosquito bite can transmit heartworm, so play it safe (especially where mosquitoes fly rampant) and keep your dog on the preventative tablets. They work by immediately killing larvae acquired within the previous 30 days—but they won't kill adult worms. Heartworm medication also safeguards your Westie from hookworms, roundworms, and whipworms.

Hookworm

This unsavory creature latches on to the intestinal wall with its tiny teeth. Hookworms cause intestinal bleeding, pain, and anaemia; just a few dozen of them can kill a puppy. They deposit their larvae where they can be easily picked up again—either through the skin or by mouth. They like shady, sandy areas best, so barefoot children are also at risk. Larvae can actually penetrate the skin and cause lesions. They leech out nutrients, causing malnutrition as well.

Ringworm

"Worm" is a misnomer for this disease. Ringworm is actually a highly contagious fungus dogs catch from each other—or from kids. More common in puppies than in adult dogs, classic signs include scabs, irregular-shaped skin infections, or hair loss at the site. Ringworm is very similar to many other skin problems, and the only definitive diagnosis is by culture. Since ringworm is contagious to people, you'll want to treat it with your vet's guidance. Your vet will clip the hair from around the affected areas and bathe the skin with a special shampoo; for more serious cases, a prescription may be required.

Roundworm

Nearly every puppy born comes with roundworms; it's one of their mother's first gifts. Roundworms penetrate the small intestine and travel through the bloodstream to the liver and lungs, and even up the trachea, where they are swallowed. This cycle perpetuates as they continue to produce eggs that are excreted with the faeces. The worms can relocate to muscle tissue, form cysts, and go dormant. Though less likely to be infected, older dogs can pick up roundworms from contaminated soil.

Children playing in areas where dogs have defecated can get roundworm from placing dirty fingers in their mouths. Children with roundworms may be misdiagnosed as having contracted flu.

Whipworm

This is the most difficult of all worms to vanquish; whipworms' eggs seem impervious to time and cold weather, and a whipworm can lay 2,000 eggs a day. Severe infestations can give dogs horrendous cases of colitis.

HOLISTIC MEDICINE

The holistic approach to addressing disease and health refers to treating the patient as a whole organism rather than merely eliminating the symptoms of an isolated problem or part of the anatomy. It is, in the general sense, the least intrusive way to assist

The "father" of homeopathy was Samuel Hahnemann, a German doctor who found that quinine, the medicine used at the time to cure malaria, actually caused malarial symptoms when given to a healthy person.

your dog to heal himself and regain his maximum level of health. Many alternative modalities address appropriate treatment for each individual animal. Holistic medicine can also dovetail with allopathic (conventional) medicine beautifully.

Illness indicates an imbalance within the body: A runny eye might indicate problems with the liver, or allergies might lead to chronic ear problems. Within the body, everything is connected. Strict allopathic (or Western) vets, when treating an ear infection, will help eliminate symptoms, but may not address the underlying cause. The holistic approach seeks to address the animal as a whole. Some proponents of holistic care believe that when only a symptom is relieved, the underlying problem simply burrows itself deeper within the body. However, these two approaches are not mutually exclusive. Obviously, allopathic medication and surgery will save lives when holistic remedies fall short.

You might want to explore holistic medicine for your Westie.

Holistic medicine includes homeopathy, Chinese medicine, herbal supplementation, essential oils, acupuncture, and chiropractic, as well as other therapies.

Acupuncture

Acupuncture is an ancient Chinese art ideal for dogs with arthritis, hip dysplasia, and other muscular-skeletal issues. Dogs with cancer, allergies, and nervous and circulatory system issues have also reaped its benefits.

Acupuncture involves the gentle insertion of fine needles. Many dogs hardly seem to notice it or only experience slight discomfort. Electroacupuncture, where traditional needle acupuncture is combined with a microcurrent of electricity, has further refined the therapy. Why acupuncture works—especially to Westerners—is somewhat mysterious. Eastern acupuncturists believe it channels the flow of Chi, a Chinese word for "energy," through certain "body paths" known as meridians.

Western practitioners have noted that the sites of acupuncture usually have thinner skin than surrounding tissues and that each one contains a lymph vessel, arteriole, and vein, plus a bundle of nerve fibres. So the needles stimulate the central and automatic nervous systems, which release endorphins, diminishing the perception of pain. Other acupoints may release cortisol, a natural steroid. Whatever the explanation, personal experience with my own dog, who sustained injury-induced arthritis, has convinced me that it really does work.

Never substitute homeopathic home care for qualified veterinary practice, and never attempt homeopathic remedies for an emergency condition, unless you are also en route to the vet!

Chiropractic Care

Dogs who develop bone and joint problems may benefit from veterinary chiropractic care.

As a supplement to conventional care, it may enhance its efficacy. Some vets provide chiropractic; some vets are specialists themselves. However, you must always check that a practitioner is fully qualified.

The benefits of chiropractic care are many, but it's not a cure-all. It cannot cure hip or elbow dysplasia. However, by carefully manipulating vertebrae, it can help delay deterioration. Chiropractors examine for irregularities between vertebrae, and adjust them in order to restore spinal alignment. Chiropractic can benefit disk problems, may help prevent surgery, or can offer valuable aftercare. Even conformation dogs, obedience dogs, and canine athletes, like agility dogs, can benefit from a chiropractic "tune-up" to enhance performance.

Flower Essences

Edward Bach developed this branch of alternative medicine in England early in the 1900s. Today there are about 50,000 active practitioners worldwide. Although there are 38 different combinations of flower essences in Bach's pharmacopeias (and more than 200 other blends developed since), the most famous is Bach's special blend of five flower essences, produced and most commonly sold under the name Rescue Remedy, widely touted for

its calming effect on nervous and stressed dogs.

The theory behind flower-essence therapy is called resonance, and healers caution that it works best when the essence you select matches the core emotional challenges the dog faces—if you can figure out what they are. The therapy is not designed to cure physical ailments but rather to aid in psychological and emotional problems than can develop into physical distress. Flower essences are usually preserved in brandy, but you can also use cider vinegar. (Mightn't a good single-malt scotch whisky be more suited to Westies?)

Flower essences are usually administered in doses of four drops four times a day. These essences can be rubbed into the gums or added to some bread and fed to the dog. Flower-essence therapy requires frequent application, as its effects are transient. Holistic vets usually combine these with other kinds of therapy—particularly with herbs and essential oils.

Flower-essence therapy does nothing to worsen the condition, and many consider its effects just short of miraculous.

Herbal Therapy

Dog owners looking for alternatives to Western medications might consider herbal medicine. Traditional Chinese medicine, Western herbalism, and Ayurvedic medicine, which originated in India and the Middle East, are all examples of herbal therapy. Each branch of herbal medicine has a slightly different emphasis, but all aim to encourage the body to maintain its own health. The focus is on wellness, whereas conventional Western medicine concentrates on the treatment of disease.

Since herbal medicine is complex, you increase your chances of getting good results by consulting a qualified herbalist that

Safety Tip

If you're not an expert, refrain from collecting herbal remedies in the wild. Also, some native plants are becoming extremely rare due to overcollection, so buy your herbs commercially and on the advice of an experienced practitioner.

Herbal Safety

Herbal overdoses can be as toxic as overdoses from conventional medication. Simply because herbs are "natural" doesn't necessarily ensure their safety. Comfrey, for example, contains a significant amount of an alkaloid that can cause liver damage in some individuals. Red clover is rich in the anticoagulant compound coumarin, which is contraindicated in dogs with clotting disorders. Other herbs contain such potentially dangerous substances as sterols, tannins, and volatile oils. Signs of overdose include vomiting, diarrhoea, and itching. Follow the recommendations of an expert and treat herbal medicines with the same caution you would prescription drugs.

specialises in the treatment of animals. Your vet may be able to give you a recommendation.

Herbs are not a quick fix. In fact, most herbs act more slowly than potent drugs (many of which derive from them). Neither are herbs panaceas that will eliminate all your dog's health issues. Moreover, not every herb will work on every disease, and some diseases are simply incurable. Many herbs may lack the purity of laboratory-tested medications, so dosing may be trickier to get right.

These shortcomings, however, do not invalidate their value in veterinary medicine. They often alleviate pain and relieve symptoms. In fact, many have the same properties (not necessarily holistic, either) as conventional medications. Treating a symptom and treating the underlying condition won't necessarily call for the same herbal or drug regimen, and confused pet owners who mix the two modalities may get disappointing results.

Although herbal dosages vary from case to case, they are much more forgiving than are Western-style drugs. In most cases, you can administer doses to your pet roughly in proportion to the recommended human dose—that is, according to weight. However, since dogs' metabolic rates are higher than people's, dogs may require proportionately higher initial dosages to reach therapeutic levels. To be safe, work this out with your animal herbalist.

Herbs act in a variety of ways, just as conventional medications do. Some help kill bacteria and fungi in the body. Others act as astringents and promote skin and bowel health. Some have sedative properties; others are diuretics. Herbs can support cardiovascular health, reduce inflammation, and promote optimal digestive system function. Others benefit the entire immune system and promote healing.

Herbal medications come in many forms. The dried, bulk form is useful because you can add some directly to your dog's food. Shelf life varies and depends on how it's preserved. Read labels carefully, and don't buy more than you will use.

Homeopathy

Homeopathy has become an important part of legitimate veterinary practice. Its use is about 200 years old, but it has been a part of folk medicine for centuries. Today there are 1,350 recognised homeopathic remedies. Many people dispute their efficacy, but others swear by them.

Don't Give Up!

Westie breeder Christine Swingle had a Westie diagnosed with WSS at age three. Drugs worsened the situation to the point where she was forced to consider euthanising him. After discontinuing the drugs, he began to eat and drink on his own. Today, when things get stressful, she isolates him in a quiet room for 15 minutes to half an hour. She has discovered, also, that Rescue Remedy helps him immensely during times of strain.

Homeopathy works on the simple principle that "like cures like." To cure an illness, you give the patient a very small diluted (attenuated) amount of a substance which, in large amounts, would produce symptoms similar to the target disease. In theory, the body responds by resetting its systems to heal itself. The major difference in philosophy between homeopathy and conventional Western medicine is that traditional medicine usually works by introducing a foreign substance into the body to treat the illness. Homeopaths believe that this can cause harm by overloading the body with two problems instead of one.

Remember to stay calm during emergencies—your Westie is counting on you.

The most curious thing about homeopathic remedies concerns the "potency" of the substance (not to be confused with the "strength" of a conventional drug). In homeopathy, the more dilute the substance is, the greater its potency. Very potent remedies have none of the original substance left in them, but they theoretically retain the "energy" from it. Pellets commonly come with numbers like 6C, 12C, or 30C. The higher the number, the more attenuated the substance, and the higher the potency. Without professional advice, *do not use anything above 30C, and always check with a homeopathic vet* before administering remedies designed for humans to dogs. An "almost" right dose can be very wrong in homeopathy.

Homeopathy remedies are usually given one at time and should not be combined with conventional medicine, acupuncture, or herbal treatments. However, homeopathic remedies may be combined with flower-essence therapy. Massage, nutritional therapy, and chiropractic care also do not interfere. Opinions differ regarding acupressure.

A growing number of vets are turning to

homeopathic veterinary medicine as a safe and effective alternative to conventional veterinary practice. For more information, contact the Alternative Veterinary Medicine Centre at www.bahvs.com.

As your puppy grows and you get to know him better, you may want to explore alternative health care options.

Physical Therapy

Many dogs benefit from physical therapy after surgery or when plagued with a chronic condition. A canine physical therapist may be a vet, licensed veterinary technician, or licensed human physiotherapist with special training in canine therapy. Make sure a regular physical therapist certified to practice on animals will work in partnership with your vet for the best results.

Types and advantages of physical therapy include the following:

- *Hydrotherapy* improves range of motion and muscle strength, usually by means of the underwater treadmill. Some vets recommend swimming.
- *Therapeutic ultrasound* uses high-frequency sound waves to reduce pain and muscle spasms, enhance collagen production, increase blood flow, and speed healing.

Many plants are poisonous, so keep an eye on your Westie while he is outside.

- *Neuromuscular stimulation* uses electrical stimulation to help dogs regain muscle function and improve range of motion.
- *Passive range-of-motion* therapies involve manipulating the dog's limbs and joints to stimulate blood flow and increase range of motion in weakness or paralysis.
- *Therapeutic exercises* build muscle, recover balance, and strengthen the cardiovascular system.

FIRST AID AND OTHER EMERGENCIES

In any emergency, first take a deep, cleansing breath and try to stay calm. This will enable you to act rationally, and your Westie's life may depend on it. For instance, you just noticed that your Westie has eaten the entire population of your daughter's ant farm, and you are uncertain whether ants are toxic. (Most are not.) Call your vet and never act out of panic.

First Aid Supplies for Dogs

Obviously you hope your Westie is never going to get hurt, or suffer a medical emergency—but it is much better to be prepared. A first aid kit is a must for all responsible dog owners. It can be as basic or as complete as you want to make it.

The following are all useful and would cover just about any emergency:

- gauze sponges
- self-adhering bandages
- petroleum jelly
- hydrogen peroxide
- rubbing alcohol (a good cleaning agent)
- antacids that combine with stomach acid to neutralize it
- Benadryl (use the children's liquid)
- triple antibiotic ointment
- hydrocortisone acetate 1% (ointment or cream)
- buffered aspirin
- Kaopectate tablets
- cold pack
- stainless steel hemostat or kelly forceps (wonderful multipurpose tools)
- digital thermometer dedicated to dog use
- adhesive tape (I prefer the cotton athletic tape.)
- pair of EMT (utility) scissors
- blanket
- tweezers
- muzzle
- zip-type plastic bags
- paperwork, including your Westie's health records (vaccination, worming and parasitic programmes), medications, regular veterinary clinic hours and telephone numbers.

CPR (cardiopulmonary resuscitation) means you are giving your dog artificial respiration and chest compressions simultaneously to get his heart going. It's best to have two people working on your dog—one for the breathing and one for the heart. Check your home veterinary manual or go to www.dogpatch.org/doginfo /cpr.html, one of many good websites for CPR instructions.

Heatstroke

Heatstroke can occur any time the temperature rises above 70°F (21°C). Dogs perspire through the pads of their feet, which is not all that efficient. Their only other method of heat exchange, panting, allows them to move large volumes of warm air outside their bodies. Westies are hardly tropical animals, so heat and humidity can be perilous.

Access to cool, fresh water and a well-shaded haven, especially outdoors, help prevent heatstroke. Never leave your Westie outside in the hot sun, and confine exercise periods to the cooler parts of the day or to evenings. Some Westies really enjoy a small

Medicating Your Westie

Here's how to give your Westie medications:

Liquids

Get a syringe from your vet. Tuck the syringe neatly down the "cheek pocket" of the dog's mouth, and hold the jaws closed. Squirt the medication into the back of the dog's mouth. Avoid cramming it down his throat; this could force the medication into his lungs by mistake.

Pills

If the medication can be given with food, wrap it in a piece of cheese and he'll probably not notice it. For pills taken on an empty stomach, open the mouth and shove the pill as far down as possible and clamp his muzzle shut briefly. Works like a charm. (A little reassurance and praise for him afterward is a nice gesture.)

Also, keep the following in mind with your medications:

- Throw out any old medicine.
- Use all the antibiotics your vet prescribes for your dog, even if you think the dog doesn't need them any more.
- Follow label directions carefully.
- Don't mix medications without first checking with your vet.
- Store medication in its original container.
- Carefully observe your Westie for adverse reactions to any medication.

children's paddling pool. Others love hose play and leap in ecstasy after the water plumes.

Signs of heatstroke include panting, weakness, and loss of coordination. Gums may appear grey or dark red instead of healthy pink. Vomiting, diarrhoea, seizures, and death may follow. If you suspect heatstroke, drench your Westie with cool (not cold) water. If his body temperature rises above 105°F (40°C), he will need hospitalisation and intravenous fluids. Such elevated temperatures prevent sufficient oxygen from reaching tissues and can cause brain damage.

Insect Stings

Unless your Westie has a serious allergic reaction, treat bee stings with liquid or capsule Benadryl. If his breathing becomes laboured, however, he may be having an allergic reaction; promptly get him to the vet. (One of my dogs eats bees like candy—I am fortunate that he is not allergic to them.)

Moving an Injured Dog

The best way to move your injured dog depends upon the nature of the injury. If possible, muzzle him beforehand. Even the gentlest dog can bite when injured and frightened. With a suspected back or neck injury, gently slide him onto a board. This reduces the possibility of further injury. In case of other types of injuries, carry him, cradle his body, and wrap him in a blanket. Hold the injured side against your body. You might also carry him in a box or pet carrier.

Poisoning

So many plants, drugs, and cleaning products are poisonous to dogs that it's impossible to list them all. However, you can find a comprehensive listing of toxic plants and other vital information at www.takingthelead.co.uk

If you suspect your Westie has been poisoned, immediately call your veterinary practice and ask to speak to a vet. You may be given first aid advice before taking the dog to the surgery. It is also important to bring any packaging with you, as this will help the vet

Give your dog appropriate chew toys to help him from ingesting things that he shouldn't.

to work out what has poisoned your dog and the quantity ingested. Never delay in seeking expert advice as poisoning can often be fatal if left untreated.

Wounds and Bleeding

If the wound is comparatively minor (no major bleeding), first remove debris and any foreign objects stuck in the wound. If you have clippers, cut the hair away from the wound site, and clean the area with a cleansing solution. Soap works, too. Avoid hydrogen peroxide, which can damage the tissue. If bleeding is profuse, you may be looking at a life-threatening situation that requires veterinary attention. To control bleeding, apply direct pressure with a clean bandage and, if possible, raise the bleeding portion above the rest of the body.

You can expect to find your Westie welcoming you home for many happy years if you care for him properly

YOUR VENERABLE WESTIE

For Westies, the onset of old age is somewhat variable: the ageing process begins somewhere between ages seven and ten. Proper health measures can help stave off the ageing process. Older dogs should have an annual check-up to evaluate all systems. This examination might include a baseline blood work panel, urinalysis, and faecal check, with other tests as needed.

Vision and hearing are primary concerns as your Westie ages. Older Westies may develop a greyish haze or opacity in the eyes due to the ageing of the lens—an early sign of geriatric cataracts. Even if opaque cataracts occur, surgical removal is possible. However, real treatment for gradual hearing loss does not exist. A preventative is to teach your puppy verbal commands in tandem with hand signals so that he can understand you, even when his hearing goes. Routinely check ear canals to ensure that they are clean and clear.

Incidence of tooth and gum disease increases with age, so good dental care is essential. Hard biscuits and bones can help to remove tartar, but a vet may recommend extracting loose teeth during a dental cleaning.

Due to decreased activity, older dogs require fewer calories.

The older your Westie gets, the more he may be prone to certain conditions. The following is a short list of health issues that your dog may experience as he ages:

- canine cognitive dysfunction
- fatty tumours or cysts
- hearing problems
- osteoarthritis
- tooth and gum disease
- urinary tract problems
- vision problems
- weight gain

Excess weight gain puts additional strain on ageing organs. Too much protein can harm dogs with kidney or liver disease. Discuss special diets for dogs with heart, kidney, or liver disease with your vet. You may need to restrict salt intake. Any diet change should be gradual. Add small amounts of cooked lean chopped meat or cottage cheese to a veteran complete diet if your dog appears to be losing weight. For an essentially toothless Westie, soak dry food in water or switch to canned or home-cooked food.

If your older Westie seems to be having an "off" day, pamper him a little bit and stay alert to any other symptoms of a greater problem.

Urinary tract difficulties commonly arise in older dogs. Often the kidneys lose the ability to concentrate waste. The dog may drink more water. Bladder-control loss could signal failing kidneys, so take him out more frequently.

Osteoarthritis may occur in the geriatric dog. Indulge your Westie with a soft warm bed away from draughts. Moderate exercise and baby aspirin may help relieve the pain. Consult your vet for additional treatments and dosages. Some vets now prescribe glucosamine, which some commercial dog food companies have added to their senior formulas. Alternative therapies including acupuncture can relieve arthritic discomfort.

Small fatty tumours or cysts often appear on the skin. These are usually benign, but do keep your vet informed, especially if they increase in size.

Older dogs often adjust poorly to stress. Environment changes can be unsettling. If you travel, choose having someone care for him at home over kenneling. With the proper exercise, diet, and medical care, your geriatric Westie should live comfortably.

General Appearance: Strongly built; deep in chest and back ribs; level back and powerful quarters on muscular legs and exhibiting in a marked degree a great combination of strength and activity.

Characteristics: Small, active, game, hardy, possessed of no small amount of self-esteem with a varminty appearance.

Temperament: Alert, gay, courageous, self-reliant but friendly.

Size, Proportion, Substance: The ideal size is eleven inches at the withers for dogs and ten inches for bitches. A slight deviation is acceptable. The Westie is a compact dog, with good balance and substance. The body between the withers and the root of the tail is slightly shorter than the height at the withers. Short-coupled and well boned. *Faults – Over or under height limits. Fine boned.*

Head and Skull: Skull slightly domed; when handled across forehead presents a smooth contour. Tapering very slightly from skull at level of ears to eyes. Distance from occiput to eyes slightly greater than length of foreface. Head thickly coated with hair, and carried at right angle or less, to axis of neck. Head not to be carried in extended position. Foreface gradually tapering from eye to muzzle. Distinct stop formed by heavy, bony ridges immediately above and slightly overhanging eye, and slight indentation between eyes. Foreface not dished nor falling away quickly below eyes, where it is well made up. Jaws strong and level. Nose black and fairly large, forming smooth contour with rest of muzzle. Nose not projecting forward.

Eyes: Set wide apart, medium in size, not full, as dark as possible. Slightly sunk in head, sharp and intelligent, which, looking from under heavy eyebrows, impart a piercing look. Light coloured eyes highly undesirable.

Ears: Small, erect and carried firmly, terminating in sharp point, set neither too wide nor too close. Hair short and smooth (velvety), should not be cut. Free from any fringe at top. Round-pointed, broad, large or thick ears or too heavily coated with hair most undesirable.

Mouth: As broad between canine teeth as is consistent with varminty expression required. Teeth large for large size of dog, with regular scissor bite, i.e. upper teeth closely overlapping lower teeth and set square to the jaws.

Neck: Sufficiently long to allow proper set on of head required, muscular and gradually thickening towards base allowing neck to merge into nicely sloping shoulders.

Forequarters: Shoulders sloping backwards. Shoulder blades broad and lying close to chest wall. Shoulder joint placed forward, elbows well in, allowing foreleg to move freely, parallel to axis of body. Forelegs short and muscular, straight and thickly covered with short, hard hair.

Body: Compact. Back level, loins broad and strong. Chest deep and ribs well arched in upper half presenting a flattish side appearance. Back ribs of considerable depth and distance from last rib of quarters as short as compatible with free movement of body.

Hindquarters: Strong, muscular and wide across top. Legs short, muscular and sinewy. Thighs very muscular and not too wide apart. Hocks bent and well set in under body so as to be fairly close to each other when standing or moving. Straight or weak hocks most undesirable.

Feet: Forefeet larger than hind, round, proportionate in size, strong, thickly padded and covered with short harsh hair. Hindfeet are smaller and thickly padded. Under surface of pads and all nails preferably black.

Tail: 13-15 cms (5-6 ins) long, covered with harsh hair, no feathering, as straight as possible, carried jauntily, not gay or carried over back. A long tail undesirable, and on no account should tails be docked.

Gait/Movement: Free, straight and easy all round. In front, legs freely extended forward from shoulder. Hind movement free, strong and close. Stifle and hocks well flexed and hocks drawn under body giving drive. Stiff, stilted movement behind and cowhocks highly undesirable.

Coat: Double coated. Outer coat consists of harsh hair, about 5 cms (2 ins) long, free from any curl. Undercoat, which resembles fur, short, soft and close. Open coats most undesirable.

Colour: White.

Size: Height at withers approximately 28 cms (11 ins).

Faults: Any departure from the foregoing points should be considered a fault and the seriousness with which the fault should be regarded should be in exact proportion to its degree and its effect upon the health and welfare of the dog.

Note: Male animals should have two apparently normal testicles fully descended into the scrotum.

Last Updated—September 2000

BREED CLUBS AND KENNEL CLUBS

American Kennel Club (AKC)
5580 Centerview Drive,
Raleigh, NC 27606
Telephone: 919 233 9767
Fax: 919 233 3627
E-mail: info@akc.org
www.akc.org

Canadian Kennel Club (CKC)
89 Skyway Avenue, Suite 100
Etobicoke, Ontario M9W 6R4
Telephone: 416 675 5511
Fax: 416 675 6506
E-mail: information@ckc.ca
www.ckc.ca

Federation Cynologique Internationale (FCI)
Secretariat General de la FCI
Place Albert 1er, 13B – 6530 Thuin
Belqique
www.fci.be

The Kennel Club
1 Clarges Street
LondonW1J 8AB
Telephone: 0870 606 6750
Fax: 0207 518 1058
www.the-kennel-club.org.uk

United Kennel Club (UKC)
100 E. Kilgore Road
Kalamazoo, MI 49002-5584
Telephone: 269 343 9020
Fax: 269 343 7037
E-mail: pbickell@ukcdogs.com
www.ukcdogs.com

West Highland White Terrier Club
Secretary: Mr McLean
Telephone: 01875 813909

West Highland White Terrier Club of England
Secretary: Mrs S Hooper
Telephone: 01963 440493
E-mail: YORSARWESTIES@aol.com
www.thewesthighlandwhiteterrierclubo
fengland.co.uk/

West Highland White Terrier Club of Wales
Secretary: Sola Hurst
Dilkhuish Bungalow, Church Lane
Nantgarw, CF15 7TQ
Telephone: 01443 841743
E-mail: secretary@whwtclubofwales.co.uk
http://www.welshclub.dog-
lovers.org.uk/Welcome.htm

North of Ireland West Highland White Terrier Club
Secretary: Mrs M Johnston
Telephone: 01662 841618
E-mail GlenveaghWesties@aol.com
http://www.northofirelandwesthighlan
dwhiteterrierclub.co.uk/

PET SITTERS

National Association of Registered Petsitters
www.dogsit.com

UK Petsitters
Telephone: 01902 41789
www.ukpetsitter.com

Dog Services UK
www.dogservices.co.uk

RESCUE ORGANISATIONS AND ANIMAL WELFARE GROUPS

British Veterinary Association Animal Welfare Foundation (BVA AWF)
7 Mansfield Street
London W1G 9NQ
Telephone: 0207 636 6541
Fax: 0207 436 2970
Email: bva-awf@bva.co.uk www.bva-
awf.org.uk/about

Royal Society for the Prevention of Cruelty to Animals (RSPCA)
Telephone: 0870 3335 999
Fax: 0870 7530 284
www.rspca.org.uk

Scottish Society for the Prevention of Cruelty to Animals (SSPCA)
Braehead Mains, 603 Queensferry Road
Edinburgh EH4 6EA
Telephone: 0131 339 0222
Fax: 0131 339 4777
Email: enquiries@scottishspca.org
www.scottishspca.org/about

Westie Rescue Scheme
http://www.westierescuescheme.org.uk/

SPORTS

Agility Club UK
www.agilityclub.co.uk

British Flyball Association
PO Box 109
Petersfield GU32 1XZ
Telephone: 01753 620110
Fax: 01726 861079
Email: bfa@flyball.org.uk
www.flyball.org.uk

Canine Freestyle Federation, Inc.
Secretary: Brandy Clymire
E-Mail: secretary@canine-freestyle.org
www.canine-freestyle.org

International Agility Link (IAL)
Global Administrator: Steve Drinkwater
E-mail: yunde@powerup.au
www.agilityclick.com/~ial

World Canine Freestyle Organisation
P.O. Box 350122Brooklyn, NY 11235-2525
Telephone: (718) 332-8336
www.worldcannefreestyle.org

THERAPY

Pets As Therapy
3 Grange Farm Cottages
Wycombe Road, Saunderton
Princes Risborough
Bucks HP27 9NS
Telephone: 0870 977 0003
Fax: 0870 706 2562
www.petsastherapy.org

Therapy Dogs International (TDI)
88 Bartley Road
Flanders, NJ 07836
Telephone: (973) 252-9800
Fax: (973) 252-7171
E-mail: tdi@gti.netwww.tdi-dog.org

TRAINING AND BEHAVIOUR

Association of Pet Dog Trainers (APDT)
PO Box 17
Kempsford GL7 4W7
Telephone: 01285 810811

Association of Pet Behaviour Counsellors
PO Box 46
Worcester WR8 9YS
Telephone: 01386 751151
Fax: 01386 750743
Email: info@apbc.org.uk
www.apbc.org.uk

VETERINARY AND HEALTH RESOURCES

Association of British Veterinary Acupuncturists (ABVA)
66A Easthorpe, Southwell
Nottinghamshire NG25 0HZ
Email: jonnyboyvet@hotmail.com
www.abva.co.uk

Association of Chartered Physiotherapists Specialising in Animal Therapy (ACPAT)
52 Littleham Road
Exmoouth, Devon EX8 2QJ
Telephone/Fax: 01395 270648
Email: bexsharples@hotmail.com
www.acpat.org.uk

British Association of Homoeopathic Veterinary Surgeons
Alternative Veterinary Medicine Centre
Chinham House
Stanford in the Vale
Oxfordshire SN7 8NQ
Email: enquiries@bahvs.com
www.bahvs.com

British Association of Veterinary Opthalmologists (BAVO)
Email: hjf@vetspecialists.co.uk
Email: secretary@bravo.org.uk
www.bravo.oprg.uk

British Small Animal Veterinary Association (BSAVA)
Woodrow House
1 Telford Way
Waterwells Business Park
Quedgley
Gloucester GL2 2AB
Telephone: 01452 726700
Fax: 01452 726701
Email: customerservices@bsava.com
www.bsava.com

British Veterinary Association (BVA)
7 Mansfield Street
LondonW1G 9NQ
Telephone: 020 7636 6541
Fax: 020 7436 2970
E-mail: bvahq@bva.co.uk
www.bva.co.uk

British Veterinary Hospitals Association (BHVA)
Station Bungalow
Main Road, Stockfield
Northumberland NE43 7HJ
Telephone: 07966 901619
Fax: 07813 915954
Email: office@bvha.org.uk
www.BVHA.org.uk

Royal College of Veterinary Surgeons (RCVS)
Belgravia House
62-64 Horseferry Road
London SW1P 2AF
Telephone: 0207 222 2001
Fax: 0207 222 2004
Email: admin@rcvs.org.uk
www.rcvs.org.uk

NEWSPAPERS AND MAGAZINES

Dog World **Ltd**
Somerfield House
Wotton Road, Ashford
Kent TN23 6LW
Telephone: 01233 621877
Fax: 01233 645669

Dogs Monthly
Ascot House, High Street,
Ascot, Berkshire SL5 7JG
Telephone: 0870 730 8433
Fax: 0870 730 8431
E-mail: admin@rtc-associates.freeserve.co.uk
www.corsini.co.uk/dogsmonthly

Dogs Today
Town Mill, Bagshot Road
Chobham, Surrey GU24 8BZ
Telephone: 01276 858880
Fax: 01276 858860
Email: enquiries@dogstodaymagazine.co.uk
www.dogstodaymagazine.co.uk

Kennel Gazette
Kennel Club
1 Clarges Street
London W1J 8AB

Telephone: 0870 606 6750
Fax: 0207 518 1058
www.the-kennel-club.co.uk

K9 Magazine
21 High Street
Warsop
Nottinghamshire NG20 0AA
Telephone: 0870 011 4114
Fax: 0870 706 4564
Email: mail@k9magazine.com
www.k9magazine.com

Our Dogs
Our Dogs Publishing
5 Oxford Road
Station Approach
Manchester M60 1SX
www.ourdogs.co.uk

Your Dog
Roebuck House
33 Broad Street
Stamford
Lincolnshire PE9 1RB
Telephone: 01780 766199
Fax: 01780 766416

BOOKS
Book of The Bitch.
Evans, J M,
Dorking: Ringpress, 1998

Doglopaedia
Evans, J M & White, Kay, Dorking:
Ringpress, 1998

Give Your Dog a Bone
Billinghurst, Dr. Ian,
Self, 1993.

Grow Your Pups with Bones
Billinghurst, Dr. Ian,
Self, 1998.

Living With a Rescued Dog
Barnes, Julia,
Dorking: Interpet Publishing, 2004

Mini Encyclopedia of Dog Training & Behaviour.
Tennant, Colin, Dorking: Interpet
Publishing, **2005**

Natural Nutrition for Dogs and Cats: The Ultimate Diet
Schultze, Kymythy,
Carlsbad, CA: Hay House, 1999.

Tracking from the Ground Up
Ganz, Sandy,
Ballwin, MO: Show-me Publications, 1992.

What If my Dog?
Evans, J M, Dorking: Interpet
Publishing, **2005**

WEBSITES

Responsible Dog Breeding

www.britishdogbreeders.co.uk
A cornucopia of information and
pertinent links on responsible dog
breeding for British breeders.

Dog Behaviour
www.dogbehaviour.com
Canine Behaviourist Gwen Bailey's site,
filled with useful advice on canine
behaviour, communication, and relevant
links.
Petfinder
http://www.pet-locator.co.uk/
Search shelters and rescue groups for
adoptable pets.

BIBLIOGRAPHY

- Ackerman, Lowell, DVM, *Dr. Ackerman's Book of West Highland White Terriers*, Neptune City, NJ: TFH Publications, 1997.
- Carlson, Delbert G., DVM and James M. Griffin, MD, *Dog Owner's Home Veterinary Handbook*, New York: Howell Book House, 1992.
- Cummins, Brian, PhD, *Terriers of Scotland and Ireland: Their History and Development*, Phoenix, AZ: Doral Publishing, 2003.
- Faherty, Ruth, *Westies from Head to Tail*, Loveland, CO: Alpine Publications, Inc., 1981
- Fogel, Bruce, DVM, *The Encyclopedia of the Dog*, New York: Dorling Kindersly Publishing, Inc., 1995.
- Hanks, Lisa, ed., *West Highland White Terrier* (Popular Dog Series, Volume 36), Viejo, CA: Bowtie, Inc., 2004.
- Hubbard, Clifford L.B., *The Observer's Book of Dogs*, London: Frederick Warne and Co., Ltd., 1962.
- Kern, Kerry, *The New Terrier Handbook,* New York: Barron's Educational Series, Inc., 1988.
- Kilcommons, Brian and Sarah Wilson, *Paws to Consider,* New York: Warner Books, 1999.
- Martin, Dawn, *A New Owner's Guide to West Highland White Terriers*, Neptune City, NJ: TFH Publications, 2001.
- Marvin, John T., *The Book of All Terriers*, New York Howell Book House, Inc., 1976 (revised).
- Nicholas, Anna Katherine, *The Book of the West Highland White Terrier*, Neptune City, NJ: TFH Publications, 1993.
- Rugaas, Turid, *On Talking Terms With Dogs*, Carlsborg, WA: Legacy By Mail, Inc., 1997.
- Ruggles-Smythe, Penelope, *West Highland White Terrier*, Allenhurst, NJ: Kennel Club Books, 2003 (revised American edition).
- Sanders, William R. (Sil), *Enthusiastic Tracking: The Step-By-Step Training Manual,* Stanwood, WA, Rime.

Note: Boldface numbers indicate illustrations.

A

accidents in housetraining, cleaning up, 103
accidents, moving injured dogs and, 197
acupuncture, 188–189
Addison's disease, 159
adopting adult dogs vs. puppies, 35–36
adult dogs
    adoption of, 35–36
    feeding of, 73–74
aggression, 120–122, 124–126
agility competition, **30**, 129–131, **130**, **140**
air travel, 56–57
allergies, 85, 159–160, 162, 174–176
    atopic dermatitis (AD) in, 159–160
    fleas and flea control in, 175, 183–184
    immune system function and, 162
    insect bites and stings in, 196
    seborrhea and, 173–174
American Kennel Club (AKC), 8, 11, 42
    conform,ation showing and, 135
    registering your Westie with the, 40, 42, 45
angulation and shoulders, 19
appearance, 16–19
ARF/BARF diets, 68–71
Argyll, Duke of, 8, 9
Armadillo syndrome. *See* epidermal dysplasia
arthritis, 178–179, 199
artificial substance, preservatives in food, 64, 66, 67
Association of Pet Behaviour Counsellors (APBC), 105
atopic dermatitis (AD) in, 159–160

B

baby gates, 51, **51**
baby teeth, retained, 174
Bach, Edward, 189
backyard breeders, 41
bad breath, 94
barking, 5, 112–114
bathing, 83–85
beds, 50
behaviourists, canine, 126–127
BHA/BHT, 64, 68
Black and White Scotch whisky and the Westie, 28
bleeding, 198
boarding your Westie, 58–59
bones and joints

arthritis in, 178–179, 199
craniomandibular osteopathy (CMO) in, 160, 161–162
Legg-Calve-Perthes disease in, 166–167
patellar luxation in, 168–169
bones in diet, 68–71, 75
bordetella (kennel cough) in, 155
bowls for food and water, 49
Boxers, 23
breed standard, 16, 135
breeder screening, 12–13, 37–41
breeding trends, 12–13
British Flyball Association, 132
British Veterinary Association (BVA), 166
brushes and brushing, 81–83, **83**
brushing your Westie's teeth, 91–92, **91**
Bull Terriers, 23

C

Cairn Terriers, 6, 7, 8
Canada and the Westie, 12
cancer, 178, 179–180
canine behaviourists, 126–127
canned dog foods, 65
car sickness, 55
car travel, 54–56
cats and Westie, 30, 48
Celtic Legacy, **13**
champion Westies, 9, 11–12
chew toys and dental health, 92
chewing, 51, 114–117
children and Westies, 30–33, **31**, 42
chiropractic, 189
city life and the Westie, 26, 27
Clarence, 27
Clark, George, 8
cleaning supplies, 51
clicker training, 108
clipping the coat, 80–81, **81**
clubs and organisations, 9, 11, 13
co-ownership, 39
coat and skin, 16, 21–23. *See also* grooming
    allergies and, 174–176
    atopic dermatitis (AD) in, 159–160
    epidermal dysplasia (Armadillo syndrome) in, 163
    fleas and flea control in, 175, 183–184
    ringworm and, 187
    seborrhea in, 173–174
    shedding and, 79, 81
    stain removal, 89–90
    ticks and tick control in, 185
Cochin, Laurie, 26, 143
collars, 50
colouration, 18, 21–23
    white shaker dog syndrome

(WSS) and, 177–178, 191
come command, 109–111
commercial dog food, 61–64
conformation showing, 16, 135–139, **138**
    breed standard and, 135
    co-ownership of champions and, 39
    do it yourself vs. handlers for, 136–139
    dress for, 138–139
    good sportsmanship and, 144
    Kennel Club (AKC) and, 135, 140
copper toxicosis (CT), 160–161
Corner, Sherron, 27
coronavirus, 156
craniomandibular osteopathy (CMO), 160, 161–162
crate training, 99–102, **100**
crates, 50, 99–102, **100**
Cream of the Skies, 12
Cruben Dexter, 12
Crufts, 9, 11
Cummins, Bryan, 6

D

Davis, Sandy, 12, 21–22, 27, 139
Dawn's Highland Scots Kennels, 12
Delta Society, 147
demodectic mange, 184–185
dental care, 90–94, **91**
    bad breath and, 94
    chew toys and, 92
    craniomandibular osteopathy (CMO) in, 160, 161–162
    food selection and, 92–93
    retained baby teeth and, 174
    veteran dogs and, 198
diabetes mellitus, 180–181
digging, 117–118
dirt removal from coat, 87
distemper, 156
dog appeasing pheromones (DAPs), 120
dog doors, 50, 102
dog food, 61–64
doggy daycare, 59
domestication of the dog, 5, 6
Donnybrook Kennels, 12, 13
down command, 108
dressing for show, 138–139
dry food or kibble, 63–65
Duncan, Deb, 48, 112, 113–117, 119

E

ears and ear care, 18, 88
    ear infections and, 162
earthdog, 5–6
earthdog trials, 131–132
Elfinbrook Simon, 11, **11**
emergency medical care,194–196
England and the Westie, 6–7, 9–11
epidermal dysplasia (Armadillo
    syndrome), 163
ethoxyquin, 64, 68
exercise pens (ex-pens), 50
exercise requirements, 29
expression, 18, **19**
eyes and eye care, 18, 88
    tear stain removal and, 89

F

fatty tumours and cysts, 199
feeding, 49, 61–77
    adult dogs, 73–74
    age-appropriate, 72–74
    allergies and, 174–176
    artificial substance, preserva-
        tives in, 64, 66, 67
    bones in, 68–71, 75
    bowls for, 49
    canned foods in, 65
    choosing foods for, 66–68
    commercial dog food in, 61–64
    dental health and, 92–93
    dry food or kibble in, 63–65
    grass eating and, 68
    home-cooked meals in, 71
    inflammatory bowel disease
        (IBD) and, 165
    label contents of dog foods in,
        62–63
    obesity and, 74, 76–77
    people food in, 71
    puppies and, 72–73
    quality of, 66–68
    raw food or ARF/BARF diets
        in, 68–71
    scheduled vs. free, 74
    semimoist foods in, 65–66
    storing foods for, 67
    supplements and special diets
        in, 76, 176
    toxic or dangerous items in, 73
    treats and, 71, 75
    variety in, 72
    veteran dogs and, 75, 198–199
feet, 19–20
fencing, 46–47
first aid, 194–196
Flaxman, Americ, 8–9
fleas and flea control, 175, 183–184
flower essence therapy, 189–190
flyball competition, 132–133, **133**
free feeding, 74

fun and games with your Westie,
    141–144
Furzfield Piper, 12

G

gait, 20
George, Sally, 136–137
gifting a Westie, 50
Gignac, David, 13
giving medicine, 196
Glendennin's Pride, 44, **44**
globoid cell leukodystrophy (GCL)
    or Krabbe's disease in, 163–164
Good Citizen Scheme, 131, 146
grass eating, 68
grooming, 16, 21, 79–95
    bad breath and, 94
    bathing in, 83–85
    brushes and brushing in, 81–83,
        83
    clipping in, 80–81, **81**
    dental care and, 90–94, **91**
    dirt removal from coat and, 87
    ear care in, 88
    eye care in, 88
    health check during, 80
    nail care and, 85–88, **85**, **86**
    professionals for, 94–95
    shampoos and conditioners in,
        83
    shedding and, 79, 81
    skunks and, 88
    stripping in, 79–81, **80**
    tar removal in, 89
    tear stain removal in, 89–90
    tools for, 82
Groves, Pam, 44
growling, 118–119

H

handlers, for conformation show-
    ing, 136–139
Hanna, Dee, 23, 90
head, 17
health issues, 149–199
    acupuncture in, 188–189
    Addison's disease and, 159
    allergies and, 85, 159–160, 162,
        174–176
    arthritis in, 178–179, 199
    atopic dermatitis (AD) in,
        159–160
    bad breath and, 94
    Bordetella (kennel cough) in,
        155
    cancer in, 178, 179–180
    canine behaviourists and,
        126–127
    car sickness and, 55
    chiropractic in, 189
    colour of coat and, 23
    copper toxicosis (CT) in,

160–161
    coronavirus in, 156
    craniomandibular osteopathy
        (CMO) in, 160, 161–162
    dental care and, 90–94, **91**, 198
    diabetes mellitus in, 180–181
    distemper in, 156
    ears and ear infections in, 88,
        162
    emergency care in,194–196
    epidermal dysplasia (Armadillo
        syndrome) in, 163
    eyes and, 88
    fatty tumours and cysts in, 199
    first aid, 194–196
    fleas and flea control in, 175,
        183–184
    flower essences in, 189–190
    giving medicine in, 196
    globoid cell leukodystrophy
        (GCL) or Krabbe's disease
        in, 163–164
    grass eating and, 68
    grooming and, as health check,
        80
    hearing problems and, 198
    heart disease in, 181–182
    heartworm and, 184, 186
    heatstroke in, 195–196
    hepatitis in, 157
    herbal therapy in, 190–191
    holistic medicine and, 187–194
    homeopathy in, 191–193
    hookworm and, 186–187
    immune system function and,
        162
    inflammatory bowel disease
        (IBD) in, 165
    insect bites and stings in, 196
    kidney disease in, 166
    Legg-Calve-Perthes disease in,
        166–167
    leptospirosis in, 157–158
    longevity and, 28–29
    Lyme disease in, 158, 185
    mange and mites in, 184–185
    moving injured dogs and, 197
    obesity and, 74, 76–77
    pancreatitis in, 182
    parasite control and, 183–187
    parvovirus in, 158
    patellar luxation in, 168–169
    phobias and, 120
    physical therapy in, 193–194
    poisoning in, 197–198
    portosystemic liver shunt in,
        169
    pulmonary fibrosis in, 170–171
    puppy checkups and, 152–153
    pyruvate kinase (PK) deficiency
        in, 172–173

rabies in, 156, 158
research on, 169
retained baby teeth and, 174
ringworm and, 187
roundworm and, 187
seborrhea in, 173–174
separation anxiety and,
    122–124
spaying and neutering, 30, 152,
    153–154
supplements and special diets
    in, 76, 176
tapeworm and, 185
ticks and tick control in, 158,
    185
toxic or dangerous food items
    in, 73
urinary tract disorders in, 199
vaccination and, 153, 154–158
vet selection in, 149–152
veteran dogs and, 198–199
vision problems and, 198
whipworm and, 187
white shaker dog syndrome
    (WSS) in, 177–178, 191
worms and worming in,
    185–187
wounds and bleeding in, 198
hearing problems, 198
heart disease, 181–182
heartworm, 184, 186
heatstroke, 195–196
hepatitis, 157
herbal therapy, 190–191
herding competition, 142
hindquarters, 20
history of the Westie, 5–13
hobby breeders, 37
holistic medicine, 187–194
home-cooked meals, 71
homeopathy, 191–193
hookworm, 186–187
hotels, motels and your Westie,
    57–58
housetraining, 101, 102–104
hunting trials, 142

I
identification, 52
immune system function, 162
independent nature of Westie, 26
inflammatory bowel disease (IBD),
    165
injuries, moving injured dogs and,
    197, 198
insect bites and stings, 196
Internet and Westie information, 38

J
jogging with your Westie, 144–145

K
Keenan, Barbara Worcester, 12
Kennel Club (KC), 8
    registering your Westie with
        the, 42, 45
kennel cough (Bordetella), 155
kidney disease, 166
Krabbe's disease (globoid cell
    leukodystrophy), 163–164

L
label contents of dog foods, 62–63
Lanarkstone Kennels, 21, 27
laws and regulations concerning
    dogs, 37
lead training, 111–112
leads, 50
leave it command, 111
Lee, Rawdon, 15
Legg-Calve-Perthes disease,
    166–167
legs, 19
leptospirosis, 157–158
liver, portosystemic shunt in, 169
longevity, 28–29
lost dogs, 52–54
Ludlow, Mary Lou, 49
lure coursing competition, 142
luxating patella, 168–169
Lyme disease, 158, 185

M
Maggie Mae, 44, **44**
Malcolm, Edward Donald, 7–8, 9,
    15
males vs. females, 37
mange and mites, 184–185
Marvin, Bea and John T., 12, 23
McGuire, Kay, 165
medications, administering, 196
microchipping, 52
mites and mange, 184–185
Modern Dog, 15
modern Westie breeders in
    England, 9–11
Molly, 44, **44**
mouthing in, 119
moving injured dogs, 197

N
nail care, 85–88, **85**, **86**
naming your Westie, 49
neck, topline, body, 18–19
noise phobias, 120
nose, winter or snow, 17
Nylabones, 51

O
obedience competition, 133–134
obesity, 74, 76–77
Olac Moonpilot, 11

other pets and the Westie, 30, 48,
    122

P
Pacey, May, 6, 9–11
Paddy, **10**
pancreatitis, 182
parasite control, 183–187
Parker, Alan, 178
parvovirus, 158
patellar luxation, 168–169
people food for dogs, 71
personality and temperament, 15,
    23–24, 40
pet sitters, 59
pet vs. show quality dogs, 39
Pets as Therapy.com, 147
phobias, 120
physiotherapy, 193–194
Pittenweem variety of Westie, 8–9
poisoning, 197–198
Poltalloch variety of Westie, 7, 9–10
portosystemic liver shunt, 169
positive reinforcement training,
    106–107
possession aggression, 120–122
preservatives in food, 64, 66, 67
problem behaviours, 112–127
    aggression as, 124–126
    barking as, 112–114
    canine behaviourists for,
        126–127
    chewing as, 114–115
    digging as, 117–118
    growling as, 118–119
    mouthing in, 119
    noise phobias as, 120
    possession aggression, 120–122
    separation anxiety and,
        122–124
    shake cans and, 118
professional groomers, 94–95
professional trainers, 105–106
pulmonary fibrosis, 170–171
puppies
    adoption of, 35–36
    breeder screening for, 37–41
    chewing and, 114–117
    feeding, 49, 72–73
    fencing and, 46–47
    first night, 48
    first vet visit for, 152–153
    housetraining and, 101,
        102–104
    male vs. female, 37
    naming, 49
    pet store, 43–45
    pet vs. show quality, 39
    puppy parties in, 105
    puppy proofing your home for,
        45–46
    registering your Westie with

the KC, 40, 42, 45
socialisation and, 26, 98–99, 105
spaying and neutering in, 152, 153–154
timing arrival of, 47–48
training and, 97
puppy parties, 105
puppy proofing your home, 45–46
pyruvate kinase (PK) deficiency, 172–173

Q
questionnaire, is the Westie right for you?, 25

R
rabies, 156, 158
rally obedience competition, 134–135, **134**
raw food or ARF/BARF diets, 68–71
registering your Westie with the Kennel Club, 40, 42, 45
Working dogs Register and, 46
renal failure, 166
rescue organisations, 41–43, 44
research into dog health, 169
responsible dog ownership, 37
ringworm, 187
Rosenberg, Alva, 12
Roseneath Terrier, 11
Roseneath variety of Westie, 8, 9
roundworm, 187
rural life and the Westie, 27, 28

S
Sally, 26
Sanders, William (Sil), 141
sarcoptic mange, 185
scabies. *See* sarcoptic mange, 185
scheduled vs. free feeding, 74
Scotch Terrier, 6, 7, 9
Scotland and the Westie, 6–7
seborrhea, 173–174
semimoist foods, 65–66
separation anxiety, 122–124
service dogs, 143
shaker cans and training, 118
shampoos and conditioners, 83
shedding, 79, 81
shelters as source of Westie, 43
Shiningcliff Simon, 11
shoulders, 19, 20
show vs. pet quality dogs, 39
sit command, **107**, 108, **109**
size, proportion, substance, 12, 16, 17
Skatet's Chunkies, 141
skin. *See* coat and skin
snow nose, 17
socialisation, 26, 98–99, 105
spaying and neutering, 30, 152, 153–154

special diets, 76, 176
stain removal, in coat, 89–90
stand command, 111
stay command, 109
storing foods, 67
stripping the coat, 79–81, **80**
supplements, 76, 176
suburban life and the Westie, 27–28
Swingle, Christine, 68–69, 191
Symmetra Snip, 12

T
tail, 19
Talloch, 12
tapeworm, 185
tar removal from coat, 89
Tattersall, Derek, 11
tattooing, 52
tear stain removal, 89–90
teeth, 17–18
temperament. *See* personality and temperament
terriers, 5–6, 16, 97
Terriers of Scotland and Ireland, 6
therapy dogs, 146–147
thunder, 120. *See also* noise phobia
ticks and tick control, 158, 185
tie-outs, 48
time requirements, 25–26
timing the arrival of a new puppy, 47–48
tools for grooming, 82
toxic or dangerous food items, 73
toys, 51
tracking competition, 139–141
Tracy, Marsha, 105
training, 97–127
clicker in, 108
come command in, 109–111
crate training in, 99–102, **100**
down command in, 108
goals of, 105
housetraining and, 101, 102–104
lead in, 111–112
leave it command in, 111
positive reinforcement in, 106–107
problem behaviours and. *See* problem behaviours
professional trainers for, 105–106
puppies and, 97, 105
shake cans and, 118
sit command in, **107**, 108, **109**
socialisation and, 98–99, 105
stand command in, 111
stay command in, 109
treats and, 71, 106–107, **107**
voice and body language in, 106
watch me command in, 111
travelling with your Westie, 54–58
treats, 71, 75, 106–107, **107**

U
United States and the Westie, 11–12
urinary tract disorders, 199

V
vaccination, 153, 154–158
varieties of Westie, 7–9
variety in feeding, 72
Versatile Dog programme, 141
vet selection, 149–152
veteran dogs, 28–29
arthritis in, 199
dental care and, 198
fatty tumours and cysts in, 199
feeding of, 75, 198–199
health issues and health care for, 198–199
hearing problems and, 198
urinary tract disorders in, 199
vision problems and, 198
vision problems, 198
vitamin/mineral supplements, 76, 176
voice and body language in training, 106

W
walking with your Westie, 111–112, 144–145
Ward, Billye and Tom, 13
watch me command, 111
Wells, Linda, 137
Westie Profiler questionnaire, 25
Westminster, 11
whipworm, 187
white shaker dog syndrome (WSS), 177–178, 191
Whitebriar Journeyman, 12
Widdows, Beth, 42, 83
winter nose, 17
Wishing Well Kennels, 12
Wolvey Pattern of Edgestone, 11
Wolvey Westie, 9–11
Working Dogs Register, 46
World Wars and the Westie, 10
worms and worming, 185–187
wounds, 198

ACKNOWLEDGEMENTS

Sandy Davis, your quick answers to my frequent (and possibly annoying) email requests were more important than you'll ever know. Deb Duncan, you kept me honest in a way that made me grow; you taught me so much—including that there are people way more opinionated than I am. Beth Widdows, your tireless work for Westie Rescue is beyond inspiring. All purebred rescue groups should clone you. Donna Hegstrom, I would not have known to contact others committed to Westie health concerns—especially Kay McGuire, DVM, who was a tremendous help. What would I have done without Sil Sanders and his great versatility information or without Allison Platt, Tracking Goddess Extraordinaire—and very cool person? Roz Rosenblatt—Rally Ho! Dee Hanna, you always have a smile and kind words for everyone and you made time to talk to me. Mary Lou Ludlow—it's been fun. Thanks to Christine Swingle, Jane Fink, and Wendell Marumoto for your ideas on ARF and natural rearing. Nancy Staab: you made me laugh, you informed me, you've been my "directory assistance," and you've introduced me to Trapper, "the Will Rogers of Westies." Linda Wells and Sally George: your information on handling and conformation was exactly what I needed. David Gignac, merci for the benefit of your experience and some Canadian breed history. Thanks, Derek Tattersall for sharing Paddy's and your triumph at Crufts. Lorayne Tennet in New Zealand, Networker Supreme; you hooked me up with numerous people worldwide including Derek, Marcella Lee, Doreen Lancaster and gave me some good information and became my friend. Suzanne Renaud, thanks for allowing me to use your beautiful artwork. Also thank you, Lisa Brown (and Suebeth Jordan), Beth Bowling, and Sherron Corner for sharing your stories and pictures. Thank you, Janice Beck, who's ever ready to lend a helping hand when it comes to things terrier. Dawn Martin and Billye and Tom Ward—I'm glad we finally connected. Thanks also to Clan Chief Mr. Robin Malcolm (direct descendant of Colonel Malcolm) for answering my letter, and to Westie-l Yahoo! List—and to the many others to whom I am grateful. Oh, and thanks, Diane Morgan, for showing me the ropes. To Maggie and Geordie (my two "Westies of Colour" AKA Cairn terriers) and my husband, Larry Holtz: I'm back!

ABOUT THE AUTHOR

Jill Arnel is a freelance writer who lives in Oregon. Some of her articles have appeared in *Off-Lead Magazine* and Portland's *Dog Nose News*. She also writes fiction, literary analysis, and essays; designs websites; and does freelance editing and copywriting. A member of The Dog Writers' Association of America and Willamette Writers, she lives with her husband, Larry Holtz, and her two Cairn terriers, Maggie and Geordie, with whom she has participated (and titled) in obedience, earthdog, therapy work, conformation, and more. She has two grown sons.

PHOTO CREDITS